Terme	Abréviation	Traduction
écologie	ÉCOL / ECOL	ecology
économie	ÉCON / ECON	economy
éducation	ÉDUC	education
électricité	ÉLECTR / ELEC	electricity
électronique	ÉLECTRON / ELECTRON	electronics
enseignement	ENS	teaching
entomologie	ENTOM	entomology
équitation	ÉQUIT / EQUIT	horse riding
ethnologie	ETHN	ethnology
euphémisme	euphém / euph	euphemism
exclamation	excl	exclamation
féminin	f	feminine
familier	fam	informal
figuré	fig	figurative
finance	FIN	finance
soutenu	fml	formal
football	FOOT	football
féminin pluriel	fpl	plural feminine noun
football	FTBL	football
généralement	gén / gen	generally
géographie	GÉOGR / GEOG	geography
géologie	GÉOL / GEOL	geology
géométrie	GÉOM / GEOM	geometry
grammaire	GRAM	grammar
héraldique	HÉRALD / HERALD	heraldry
histoire	HIST	history
horticulture	HORT	horticulture
humoristique	hum	humorous
chasse	HUNT	hunting
verbe impersonnel	impers vb	impersonal verb
imprimerie	IMPR	printing
dans des composés	in comp	in compounds
article indéfini	indef art	indefinite article
indicatif	indic	indicative
industrie	INDUST	industry
familier	inf	informal
infinitif	infin	infinitive
informatique	INFORM	computing
injurieux	injur	offensive
inséparable	insép / insep	inseparable
interjection	interj	interjection
invariable	inv	invariable
ironique	iron / iro	ironic
joaillerie	JOAILL	jewellery
linguistique	LING	linguistics
sens propre	lit	literal
littéraire	litt / liter	literary
littérature	LITTÉR / LITER	literature
locution	loc	locution
locution adjectivale	loc adj	adjectival phrase
locution adverbiale	loc adv	adverbial phrase
locution conjonctive	loc conj	conjunctive phrase
locution ayant valeur de déterminant	loc dét	phrase functioning as determiner
locution impersonnelle	loc impers	impersonal phrase
locution interjective	loc interj	exclamatory phrase
locution prépositionnelle	loc prép	prepositional phrase
locution pronominale	loc pron	pronominal phrase
masculin	m	masculine
mathématiques	MATH	mathematics
mécanique	MÉCAN / MECH	mechanics
médecine	MÉD / MED	medicine
menuiserie	MENUIS	carpentry
métallurgie	MÉTALL / METALL	metallurgy
météorologie	MÉTÉOR / METEOR	meteorology
masculin et féminin	mf	masculine and feminine
militaire	MIL	military
argot militaire	mil sl	military slang
mines	MIN	mining
minéralogie	MINÉR / MINER	mineralogy

DICTIONNAIRE

français-anglais
anglais-français

French-English
English-French

DICTIONARY

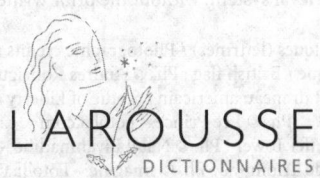

LAROUSSE
DICTIONNAIRES

© Larousse, 2012
21, rue du Montparnasse
75283 Paris Cedex 06
France
www.larousse.fr

ISBN 978- 2-03-584230-5

Publié aux États-Unis et au Canada par :
Published in the United States of America and Canada by:
Éditions LAROUSSE
21, rue du Montparnasse
75283 Paris Cedex 06
France

ISBN 978-2-03-570004-9

Diffusion/Sales: Houghton Mifflin Harcourt, Boston
Library of Congress CIP Data has been applied for

Crédits photographiques (lettrines) / Photographic credits (running initials) :
Drapeau britannique / British flag : Ph. © Andres Rodriguez – Fotolia.com
Statue de la Liberté et drapeau américain / Statue of Liberty and American flag :
Ph. © Lee Prince – Fotolia.com
Tour Eiffel / Eiffel Tower : Ph. © Nabil Biyahmadine – Fotolia.com
Arc de Triomphe : Ph. © Imagine – Fotolia.com

Direction de la publication – Publishing director
Carine Girac-Marinier

Direction éditoriale – Editorial management
Claude Nimmo

Suivi éditorial – Editorial coordination
Beata Assaf

Édition – Editors
Luca Basili, Marc Chabrier, Valérie Katzaros, Marie Ollivier, Giovanni Picci,
David Tarradas, Marie-Noëlle Tilliette, Donald Watt, Garret White

Informatique éditoriale et composition – Data management and Typesetting
Dalila Abdelkader, Monika Al Mourabit, Philippe Cazabet, Ivo Kulev

Mise en page – Layout
Sophie Rivoire

Fabrication – Production
Marlène Delbeken

Remerciements
Nous tenons à remercier tout spécialement
Joanne Hornsby et Emily Pickett.

Acknowledgments
Special thanks to Joanne Hornsby and Emily Pickett.

Texte établi à partir du Grand Dictionnaire Larousse français-anglais / anglais-français.
Based on the Larousse Unabridged French-English / English-French Dictionary.

Sommaire
Contents

Préface

Ce nouveau dictionnaire est l'ouvrage de référence français-anglais / anglais-français le plus actuel.

Conçu de manière à répondre au mieux aux besoins des lycéens, il allie à une présentation conviviale un contenu riche reflétant l'évolution de l'anglais et du français et couvrant aussi bien la langue courante que les domaines de spécialité qui connaissent une forte progression, tels que les nouvelles technologies, l'environnement et l'Internet. L'anglais américain a fait l'objet d'un traitement spécifique et les variantes britanniques et américaines sont clairement indiquées. Le fond et la forme étant intimement liés, nous avons apporté un soin particulier à la structure des articles, de façon à identifier précisément les différents sens des mots et à mettre en relief les mots composés, les expressions figées et les locutions.

Outre le lexique, ce nouveau dictionnaire offre à ses utilisateurs des aides, sous forme de notes et d'encadrés, pour déjouer les pièges de la langue et comprendre des points de grammaire là où la syntaxe diffère entre le français et l'anglais. Ces informations complémentaires sont insérées dans les articles afin de faciliter l'expression dans l'autre langue.

Enfin, fidèles à la tradition encyclopédique de Larousse, nous avons donné à ce dictionnaire une ouverture encyclopédique qui, au-delà des noms propres et des termes géographiques figurant dans sa nomenclature, s'étend aux développements complétant certains articles. Ainsi, les réalités historiques, culturelles ou institutionnelles dont les connotations ne peuvent être rendues par la seule traduction sont expliquées dans des notes.

L'Éditeur

Foreword

This new dictionary, aimed at students, is the most up-to-date reference book on modern French available today.

Designed with the specific needs of its readers in mind, its user-friendly layout provides access to a wealth of words, meanings and expressions that reflect how both French and English have evolved. It covers everyday language as well as a wide range of specialist fields, with particular emphasis on those where new coinages often appear such as new technologies, environment and the Internet. Regional varieties of French are well represented, with many words and expressions specific to Belgium, Switzerland and Quebec. The layout of the dictionary has been carefully designed to make different meanings easy to identify, and to make compounds, set structures and idioms stand out.

However, this dictionary is much more than just an inventory of words. It offers a wealth of extra information in the form of notes and boxes to help the reader avoid common pitfalls and to explain tricky grammar points. This extra information appears where it is most useful, in (or close to) the relevant entries.

Larousse is well known as the leading French publisher of encyclopaedias, and this dictionary has a uniquely rich encyclopaedic dimension, providing translations or explanations for proper names and place names. Historical or cultural events and names of institutions whose connotations cannot be rendered by a simple translation are explained in helpful boxes.

The Publisher

mot d'entrée
headword

acuponcture, acupuncture [akupɔ̃ktyʀ] nf
acupuncture.

variante graphique
variant spelling

homographes
homographs

clocher¹ [klɔʃe] nm [tour] bell-tower, church tower.
❖ **de clocher** loc adj ▸ **querelles de clocher** petty bickering.
clocher² [3] [klɔʃe] vi *fam* to be wrong / *qu'est-ce qui cloche ?* what's wrong ou up?

exemple
le mot d'entrée est
montré en contexte
example
headword is shown in context

forme féminine
feminine form

créatif, ive [kʀeatif, iv] ◆ adj [esprit] creative, imaginative, inventive. ◆ nm, f [gén] creative person ; [de publicité] designer.

graphie de la Réforme de
l'orthographe
French reformed spelling

prononciation
voir pages 10 et 11 pour la liste
des symboles phonétiques
pronunciation
see pages 10 and 11 for a list
of the phonetic symbols

fair-play (*pl* fair-play), **fairplay*** [fɛʀplɛ] ◆ nm
fair play, fair-mindedness. ◆ adj fair-minded ▸ **il est fair-play** a) [joueur] he plays fair b) *fig* he has a sense of fair play.

lave-linge [lavlɛ̃ʒ] (*pl* lave-linge ou lave-linges*)
nm washing machine, washer ▸ **lave-linge séchant** washer-dryer.

numéros introduisant
les différents sens
numbered meanings

renvoi aux tableaux de
conjugaison
reference to verb tables

cultiver [3] [kyltive] vt **1.** AGR [champ, terres] to cultivate, to farm ; [plantes] to grow **2.** [conserver obstinément - accent] to cultivate / *elle cultive le paradoxe* she cultivates a paradoxical way of thinking **3.** [entretenir - relations, savoir] to keep up. ❖ **se cultiver** vpt : *se cultiver l'esprit* to cultivate the mind.

indication du sens
ou du contexte
indication of meaning
or context

sous-entrée
verbes pronominaux
sub-entry
French reflexive /
pronominal verbs

adresse [adʀɛs] nf **1.** [domicile] address ▸ **parti sans laisser d'adresse** gone without leaving a forwarding address ▸ **une bonne adresse** a) [magasin] a good shop UK ou store US b) [restaurant] a good restaurant c) [hôtel] a good hotel **2.** [dextérité] skill, dexterity, deftness ▸ **jeu d'adresse** game of skill **3.** INFORM address **4.** ▸ **adresse électronique** e-mail address ▸ **adresse IP** IP address ▸ **adresse URL** URL address. ❖ **à l'adresse de** loc prép intended for, aimed at.

catégorie grammaticale
part of speech

sous-entrée
structures figées
sub-entry
set structures

nom composé,
locution
compound,
idiom

indicateur de
domaine
field label

indication du registre
register label

tangent, e [tɑ̃ʒɑ̃, ɑ̃t] adj **1.** GÉOM & MATH tangent, tangential **2.** *fam* [limite - cas, candidat] borderline / *ses notes sont tangentes* her grades put her on the borderline / *je ne l'ai pas renvoyé, mais c'était tangent* I didn't fire him but I was very close to doing so. ❖ **tangente** nf **1.** GÉOM & MATH tangent **2.** EXPR **prendre la tangente** a) *fam* [se sauver] to make off b) [esquiver une question] to dodge the issue.

les différents sens des
expressions sont indiqués
different meanings of an
expression

expressions figées
set phrases

proliférer [18] [pʀɔlifeʀe] vi to proliferate.
🖋 In reformed spelling (see p. 16), this verb is conjugated like
semer : *il proliférera, elle proliférerait.*

pluriel
plural

note sur les mots
concernés par la
Réforme de l'orthographe
note on French
reformed spelling

fuseau, x [fyzo] nm **1.** [bobine] spindle ▸ **dentelle / ouvrage aux fuseaux** bobbin lace / needlework **2.** VÊT stirrup pants. ❖ **fuseau horaire** nm time zone.

traduction
translation

genre
French gender

forme développée des abréviations
full form of abbreviations

variétés de l'anglais
regional varieties of English

renvoi des pluriels irréguliers aux entrées au singulier
cross-reference from irregular plurals

renvoi des formes irrégulières des verbes à l'infinitif
cross-reference from irregular verb forms to main verb

entrées complexes
of complex entries

pluriels irréguliers avec leur transcription phonétique
irregular plurals with pronunciation

précisions grammaticales
extra grammatical information

verbes à particules et verbes prépositionnels
phrasal verbs and prepositional verbs

précisions sur la traduction
extra information that clarifies the translation

explication lorsqu'il n'y a pas d'équivalent exact
explanatory gloss provided where there is no direct equivalent

équivalent culturel
cultural equivalent

variétés du français
regional varieties of French

renvoi des variantes orthographiques aux entrées principales
cross-reference from alternative spelling

formes irrégulières des verbes avec leur transcription phonétique
irregular verb forms with pronunciation

comparatifs et superlatifs irréguliers
irregular comparatives and superlatives

expressions figées
set phrases

indication de l'usage
usage label

Alice band n bandeau m (pour les cheveux).

adventure holiday n voyages organisés avec des activités sportives et de découverte.

A-level (abbr of **advanced level**) n UK SCH ▶ **A-levels** or **A-level exams** ≃ baccalauréat m / he teaches A-level physics ≃ il est professeur de physique en terminale / to take one's A-levels ≃ passer son bac.

adviser UK, **advisor** US [əd'vaɪzər] n conseiller m, -ère f ; SCH & UNIV conseiller m, -ère f pédagogique.

bonzer ['bɒnzər] adj AUSTR & NZ v inf vachement bien.

char [ʃɑːr] nm **1.** MIL tank ▶ **char d'assaut** ou **de combat** tank **2.** LOISIRS float ▶ **char à voile** sand yacht / faire du char à voile to go sand yachting **3.** ANTIQ chariot **4.** QUÉBEC fam [voiture] car.

selves [selvz] pl → **self**.

acclimate ['æklɪmeɪt] vt & vi US = **acclimatize**.

had (weak form [həd], strong form [hæd]) pt & pp → **have**.

go² [ɡəʊ] (pres (3rd pers sg) **goes** [ɡəʊz], pt **went** [went], pp **gone** [ɡɒn], pl **goes** [ɡəʊz]) ◆ vi
A. TRAVEL OR PROCEED **1.** [move, travel -person] aller ; [-vehicle] aller, rouler / I want to go home je veux rentrer / the truck was going at 150 kilometres an hour le camion roulait à or faisait 150 kilomètres à l'heure / to go to the

foggy ['fɒɡɪ] (compar **foggier**, superl **foggiest**) adj **1.** [misty] brumeux / it's foggy il y a du brouillard or de la brume **2.** PHOT [film] voilé **3.** PHR **I haven't the foggiest idea** or **notion** je n'ai aucune idée, je n'en ai pas la moindre idée.

loaf [ləʊf] (pl **loaves** [ləʊvz]) ◆ n **1.** [of bread] pain m ; [large round loaf] miche f **2.** PHR **use your loaf!** UK inf fais travailler tes méninges ! ◆ vi inf fainéanter, traîner.

aged ◆ adj **1.** [eɪdʒd] [of the age of] : a man aged 50 un homme (âgé) de 50 ans **2.** ['eɪdʒɪd] [old] âgé, vieux (before vowel or silent 'h' **vieil**, f **vieille**). ◆ pl n ▶ **the aged** les personnes fpl âgées.

fend [fend] vi ▶ **to fend for o.s.** a) se débrouiller tout seul b) [financially] s'assumer, subvenir à ses besoins. ❖ **fend off** vt sep [blow] parer ; [attack, attacker] repousser ; fig [question] éluder, se dérober à ; [person at door, on telephone] éconduire.

faux amis / false friends

 Le mot anglais **adept** signifie « expert » et non adepte.

 In modern French, **affluence** refers to crowds of people arriving somewhere, never to wealth.

notes signalant des difficultés de traduction / notes on nuances of translation

politics ou **policy** ?
Politics se réfère à la politique au sens de l'art de gouverner, tandis que **a policy** est une politique au sens d'une stratégie ou d'un ensemble de mesures.

cerveau or **cervelle**?
The anatomical term is **cerveau**; **cervelle** is used when brains are being referred to as a food item (**cervelle d'agneau**), or metaphorically to refer to the human mind (**se creuser la cervelle**; **il n'a rien dans la cervelle**).

notes pour déjouer les pièges grammaticaux / useful grammar tips

Attention ! Le mot **accommodation** est indénombrable en anglais britannique. Il ne s'emploie jamais ni au pluriel ni avec l'article indéfini an :
Je cherche un logement provisoire. *I'm looking for (some) temporary accommodation.*

Note that **avoir honte que** is followed by a verb in the subjunctive:
I was ashamed that my brother had found out my secret. *J'avais honte que mon frère ait découvert mon secret.*

événements historiques clés / key historical events

 Mai 1968
The events of May 1968 came about when student protests, coupled with widespread industrial unrest, culminated in a general strike and rioting. De Gaulle's government survived the crisis, but the issues raised made the events a turning point in French social history.

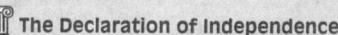 **The Declaration of Independence**
Document rédigé par Thomas Jefferson et proclamant, le 4 juillet 1776, l'indépendance des 13 colonies de la Nouvelle-Angleterre. Cette déclaration est considérée comme l'acte de naissance des États-Unis d'Amérique.

zooms sur les grandes institutions / insight into important institutions

 Quai
The names **Quai d'Orsay** and **Quai des Orfèvres** are often used to refer to the government departments situated on the streets of the same name (the foreign office and the police department respectively). **Le Quai de Conti** is sometimes used to refer to the **Académie française**.

 Downing Street
C'est à **Downing Street**, à Londres, que se trouvent les résidences officielles du Premier ministre (au n° 10) et du chancelier de l'Échiquier (au n° 11). Tony Blair a été le premier chef de gouvernement à avoir choisi de résider au n° 11 pour des raisons de confort familial. Par extension, le nom de la rue est employé pour désigner le Premier ministre et ses fonctions.

culture et société	culture and society

 RTT

Initially planned as a measure to reduce unemployment, the law on a 35-hour working week known as **les trente-cinq heures** has not entirely succeeded but it has generated more leisure time for people in paid employment in the form of days off known as **journées (de) RTT**.

Flag day

En Grande-Bretagne, les **flag days** ont lieu en général le samedi. On fait appel à la générosité des particuliers qui, en contrepartie de leurs dons pour des œuvres de bienfaisance, reçoivent un insigne ou un badge. Aux États-Unis, **Flag Day** commémore l'adoption le 14 juin 1777 de **Stars and Stripes**, l'actuel drapeau américain.

système éducatif	education system

 Bizutage

In some French schools and colleges, students take to the streets in fancy-dress and play practical jokes on each other and on passers-by at the beginning of the school year. This is part of the traditional initiation ceremony known as **bizutage**.

 GCSE

Examen sanctionnant la fin de la première partie de l'enseignement secondaire. Chaque élève présente les matières de son choix (généralement entre 5 et 10) selon un système d'unités de valeur. Le nombre d'unités et les notes obtenues déterminent le passage dans la classe supérieure. Après cet examen, les élèves peuvent choisir d'arrêter leurs études ou de préparer les **A-levels**.

symboles culturels expliqués	symbols explained

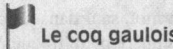 **Le coq gaulois**

The cockerel is the symbol of France. Its cry, **cocorico!**, is sometimes used to express national pride: **trois médailles d'or pour la France, cocorico!**

 Bald eagle

Cet oiseau est l'emblème des États-Unis. Il figure sur le sceau officiel.

noms géographiques	lists of geographical names

 **Caps**

le cap de Bonne-Espérance	the Cape of Good Hope
cap Canaveral	Cape Canaveral
le cap Gris-Nez	Gris-Nez Cape
le cap Horn	Cape Horn

 **Capes**

Cape Canaveral	cap Canaveral
Cape Cod	cap Cod
the Cape of Good Hope	le cap de Bonne-Espérance
Cape Horn	le cap Horn

Voyelles

[ɪ]	pit, big, rid
[e]	pet, tend
[æ]	pat, bag, mad
[ʌ]	putt, cut
[ɒ]	pot, log
[ʊ]	put, full
[ə]	mother, suppose
[iː]	bean, weed
[ɑː]	barn, car, laugh
[ɔː]	born, lawn
[uː]	loop, loose
[ɜː]	burn, learn, bird

Diphtongues

[eɪ]	bay, late, great
[aɪ]	buy, light, aisle
[ɔɪ]	boy, foil
[əʊ]	no, road, blow
[aʊ]	now, shout, town
[ɪə]	peer, fierce, idea
[eə]	pair, bear, share
[ʊə]	poor, sure, tour

Semi-voyelles

[j]	you, spaniel
[w]	wet, why, twin

Consonnes

[p]	pop, people
[b]	bottle, bib
[t]	train, tip
[d]	dog, did
[k]	come, kitchen
[g]	gag, great
[ʧ]	chain, wretched
[ʤ]	jig, fridge
[f]	fib, physical
[v]	vine, livid
[θ]	think, fifth
[ð]	this, with
[s]	seal, peace
[z]	zip, his
[ʃ]	sheep, machine
[ʒ]	usual, measure
[h]	how, perhaps
[m]	metal, comb
[n]	night, dinner
[ŋ]	sung, parking
[l]	little, help
[r]	right, carry
[x]	loch

Notes sur la transcription phonétique

ANGLAIS - FRANÇAIS

1. Accents primaire et secondaire
Les symboles ['] et [ˌ] indiquent respectivement un accent primaire et un accent secondaire sur la syllabe suivante.

2. Prononciation du « r » final
Le symbole [ʳ] indique que le « r » final d'un mot anglais ne se prononce que lorsqu'il forme une liaison avec la voyelle du mot suivant ; le « r » final est presque toujours prononcé en anglais américain.

3. Anglais britannique et américain
Les différences de prononciation entre l'anglais britannique et l'anglais américain ne sont signalées que lorsqu'elles sortent du cadre de règles générales préétablies. Le « o » de dog, par exemple, est généralement plus allongé en anglais américain, et ne bénéficie pas d'une seconde transcription phonétique. En revanche, des mots comme schedule, clerk, cliché, etc., dont la prononciation est moins évidente, font l'objet de deux transcriptions phonétiques.

4. Mots ayant deux prononciations
Nous avons choisi de ne donner que la prononciation la plus courante du mot, sauf dans les cas où une variante est particulièrement fréquente, comme par exemple le mot kilometre ['kɪləˌmiːtəʳ or kɪ'lɒmɪtəʳ].

5. Les formes accentuées et atones
La prononciation de certains mots monosyllabiques anglais varie selon le degré d'emphase qu'ils ont dans la phrase ; the, par exemple, se prononce [ðiː] en position accentuée, [ðə] en position atone, et [ðɪ] devant une voyelle. Ces informations sont présentées de la manière suivante dans le dictionnaire: the (weak form [ðə], before vowel [ðɪ], strong form [ðiː]).

FRANÇAIS - ANGLAIS

1. Le symbole ['] représente le « h aspiré » français, par exemple hachis ['aʃi].

2. Comme le veut la tendance actuelle, nous ne faisons pas de distinction entre le « a » de pâte et celui de patte, tous deux transcrits [a].

3. Prononciation du « e » muet
Lorsque le « e » peut ne pas être prononcé dans le discours continu, il a été mis entre parenthèses, comme par exemple pour le mot cheval [ʃ(ə)val].

Oral vowels

[i]	fille, île
[e]	pays, année, aider, ferai
[ɛ]	bec, aime, lait, ferais
[a]	lac, papillon
[y]	usage, lune
[u]	outil, goût
[ə]	le, je
[œ]	peuple, bœuf
[ø]	aveu, jeu
[o]	drôle, aube
[ɔ]	hotte, automne

Nasal vowels

[ɛ̃]	limbe, main
[œ̃]	parfum, brun
[ã]	champ, ennui
[ɔ̃]	ongle, mon

Semi-vowels

[j]	yeux, lieu
[ɥ]	lui, nuit
[w]	ouest, oui

Oral Consonants

[p]	prendre, grippe
[t]	théâtre, temps
[k]	coq, quatre, orchestre
[b]	bateau, rosbif
[d]	dalle, ronde
[g]	garder, épilogue, zinc
[f]	physique, fort
[s]	cela, savant, inertie, dix
[ʃ]	charrue, schéma, shérif
[v]	voir, rive
[l]	halle, lit
[z]	fraise, zéro
[ʒ]	rouge, jabot
[ʀ]	arracher, sabre

Nasal consonants

[m]	mât, drame
[n]	nager, trône
[ɲ]	agneau, peigner
[ŋ]	parking

Notes on phonetic transcription

FRENCH - ENGLISH

1. The symbol ['] has been used to represent the French 'h aspiré', e.g. hachis ['aʃi].

2. We have followed the modern tendency not to distinguish between the 'a' in pâte and the 'a' in patte. Both are represented in the text by the phonetic symbol [a].

3. Internal schwa
In cases where the schwa [ə] is likely to be ignored in connected speech but retained in the citation form, the [ə] has been shown in brackets, e.g. cheval [ʃ(ə)val].

ENGLISH - FRENCH

1. Primary and secondary stress
The symbol ['] indicates that the following syllable carries primary stress and the symbol [ˌ] that the following syllable carries secondary stress.

2. Pronunciation of final 'r'
The symbol [ʳ] in English phonetics indicates that the final 'r' is pronounced only when followed by a word beginning with a vowel. Note that it is nearly always pronounced in American English.

3. British and American English
Differences between British and American pronunciation have not been shown where the pronunciation can be predicted by a standard set of rules, for example where the 'o' in dog is lengthened in American English. However, phonetics have been shown for the more unpredictable cases of schedule, clerk, cliché, etc.

4. Alternative pronunciations
Our approach being primarily functional rather than descriptive, we have avoided giving variant pronunciations unless both variants are met with equal frequency, e.g. kilometre ['kɪləˌmiːtəʳ or kɪ'lɒmɪtəʳ].

5. Strong and weak forms
The pronunciation of certain monosyllabic words varies according to their prominence in a sentence, e.g. the when stressed is pronounced [ðiː]; when unstressed, [ðə] and before a vowel [ðɪ]. This information is presented in the text as follows: the (weak form [ðə], before vowel [ðɪ], strong form [ðiː]).

Notes on culture
French - English section

🚩 **culture and society   culture et société**

📚 **education system   système éducatif**

🏛 **key historical events   événements historiques clés**

Notes on culture
French - English section

 insight into important institutions   zooms sur les grandes institutions

Notes sur la culture
Partie anglais - français

🚩 **culture et société** culture and society

📚 **système éducatif** education system

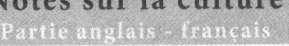

Notes sur la culture
Partie anglais - français

événements historiques clés   key historical events

zooms sur les grandes institutions   insight into important institutions

Réforme de l'orthographe française

Des recommandations pour une orthographe française revue et modernisée ont été faites en 1990 par le groupe de travail du *Conseil supérieur de la langue française*. Elles avaient pour but de supprimer des exceptions, d'établir des régularités, de mettre en adéquation la graphie avec la prononciation actuelle et ainsi de faciliter l'apprentissage de la langue. L'Académie française s'est prononcée pour souligner que ces règles n'avaient aucun caractère obligatoire et qu'aucune des graphies, la traditionnelle ou la nouvelle, n'était tenue pour fautive. Récemment, par son *Bulletin officiel* du 12 avril 2007, le ministère français de l'Éducation nationale a demandé aux enseignants de l'école primaire de prendre en compte ces nouvelles graphies.

Ce dictionnaire ne montre pas la nouvelle graphie. Voici néanmoins les 5 grands principes qui sous-tendent cette réforme et donnent à chacun les règles pour écrire en nouvelle orthographe.

Une graphie plus phonétique...

- **plus intuitive** : *exéma* au lieu de *eczéma*, *ognon* au lieu de *oignon*.

- **plus simple** : certaines lettres superflues peuvent être omises : le « e » de *asseoir*, *rasseoir* et *surseoir* (infinitif et formes conjuguées) ; le « h » de *saccharine*, etc.

Des familles réassorties

Par exemple le fameux *charriot*, seul sans double « r » *(chariot)* de la série des *charrue*, *charretier*, etc., *boursouffler* (avec deux « f ») comme *souffler*, *prud'hommal* (avec deux « m ») comme *prud'homme*, *quincailler* (sans « i » après le double « l ») comme *poulailler*, etc.

Un trait d'union...

- **plus systématique** : tous les adjectifs numéraux composés peuvent prendre un trait d'union. On peut donc écrire maintenant : *vingt-et-un* (21) et *vingt-et-unième* (21e), ainsi que *cent-deux* (102), *deux-mille* (2 000), etc.

- **ou supprimé**. Peuvent s'écrire sans trait d'union, donc « soudés » :
  - les mots composés commençant par « contre », « entre », « extra », « infra », « intra », « ultra » ;
  - les mots composés formés d'un verbe et d'un nom : *croquemonsieur*, *portemonnaie* ;
  - des mots, formés d'un adverbe et d'un nom (*bienpensant*) ou commençant par un préfixe d'origine latine ou grecque (*néocalédonien*) ;
  - des mots formés d'onomatopées ou d'origine étrangère moderne : *cahincaha*, *weekend*.

Des changements d'accentuation

- **L'accent circonflexe**. Selon la Réforme de l'orthographe, cet accent peut être supprimé. Ainsi, par exemple, pour les verbes (infinitif et formes conjuguées) : *connaitre*, il/elle connait, il/elle connaitra, il/elle connaitrait et non plus forcément *connaître*, il/elle connaît, il/elle connaîtra, il/elle connaîtrait.

Cela vaut pour le « i » de *apparaitre* (*apparaître*), *naitre* (*naître*), *paraitre* (*paraître*), et tous les verbes de même modèle, mais aussi pour le « u » de *bruler* (*brûler*), ainsi que sur des noms tels que *buche* (*bûche*), *bucheron* (*bûcheron*), *flute* (*flûte*), *ile* (*île*), etc.

Exceptions : l'accent circonflexe est conservé...
  - pour distinguer deux homophones : *il croit* vs. *il croît*, *jeune* vs. *jeûne* ;
  - aux formes du passé simple de l'indicatif et au subjonctif : *nous partîmes*, *qu'il partît*.

- **L'accent grave** sur le « e » est admis à la place du « é » (prononcé comme un « e » ouvert à l'oral) :
  - dans certains mots tels que *évènement*, au lieu de *événement*, *règlement* au lieu de *réglement* ;
  - dans les conjugaisons de certains verbes. Il s'agit surtout des verbes ayant pour modèle *céder* et des verbes en *-eler*, *-érer*, *-eter* :

j'amoncèle	au lieu de	*j'amoncelle*
je cèderais	au lieu de	*je céderais*

- **Le tréma** peut être placé au-dessus du « u », lettre dont il signale la prononciation : *ambigüité* et non plus seulement *ambiguïté*, *aigüe* et non plus seulement *aiguë*, etc.

Les accords / Des accords plus réguliers

• Singulier et pluriel des mots composés. On écrit *un sèche-cheveux* et *des amuse-gueule*. En nouvelle orthographe, le mot composé est vu comme un mot simple dont seul le dernier composant varie en nombre : *un sèche-cheveu* → *des sèche-cheveux*.

• Les emprunts aux langues étrangères peuvent être accentués selon leur prononciation et suivent le pluriel du français : *un flash* → *des flashs* ; *un jazzman* → *des jazzmans* ; *un référendum* → *des référendums*.

• Le participe passé de « *laisser* ». L'accord du participe passé est une difficulté du français à l'écrit. Les semi-auxiliaires *faire* et *laisser* sont considérés comme deux cas particuliers ; or l'orthographe traditionnelle ne les traite pas de la même façon :
  - *Faire* devant un infinitif reste invariable en genre et en nombre :

    Elle s'est fait faire une mise en plis.
  - *Laisser* devant un infinitif est variable ou non, selon la fonction du sujet par rapport à l'infinitif.

    Elle s'est laissé prendre [invariable : ce n'est pas elle qui prend]

    mais

    Elle s'est laissée tomber [variable : c'est elle qui tombe]

Le cas est simplifié en nouvelle orthographe : *laisser* est lui aussi admis comme étant invariable en genre et en nombre.

French spelling reform

In 1990 the *Conseil supérieur de la langue française* issued a series of recommendations for revised and modernized spelling of French. They were intended to make the language easier to learn by removing exceptions, bringing spelling into line with current pronunciation, and generally making things more regular. The *Académie française* responded by declaring that the new spellings were in no way compulsory and that neither traditional nor reformed spelling was to be considered incorrect. More recently, in the *Bulletin officiel* dated 12 April 2007, the French Education Minister asked primary school teachers to "take the new spellings into account".

Below we present the five main principles of the reform. For consistency and clarity, the main body of this dictionary does not show the new written form of the French language.

Spelling that more closely reflects pronunciation

• More intuitive: exéma instead of eczéma, ognon instead of oignon.

• Some superfluous letters can be omitted: the "e" in asseoir, rasseoir and surseoir; the "h" in saccharine, etc.

Harmonization of word families

Sets of words seen as making up "families" have been harmonized. The word *chariot*, the only word without a double "r" in the series *charrue, charretier*, etc., can now be spelt *charriot*. Similarly, *boursoufler* can be written *boursouffler* (in line with *souffler*), the new double "m" in *prud'hommal* echoes that in *prud'homme*, and *quincaillier* can become *quincailler*, modelled on *poulailler*.

More systematic hyphenation rules

• Adding a hyphen. All compound numerals can now be written with a hyphen: *vingt-et-un* (21) and *vingt-et-unième* (21ᵉ) as well as *cent-deux* (102), *deux-mille* (2 000), and so on.

• Removing a hyphen. Many compounds can now be spelt as one word:
  - words that begin with "contre", "entre", "extra", "infra", "intra" and "ultra";
  - words that are made up of a verb and a noun (*croquemonsieur, portemonnaie*);
  - other compound forms such as *bienpensant* or words that begin with a prefix of Latin or Greek origin (such as *néocalédonien*);
  - words that are onomatopoeic (*cahincaha*) or of modern foreign origin (*weekend*).

Use of accents

• The circumflex accent can in some cases be omitted: *connaître* can now be written *connaitre*, and its conjugated forms can also lose their circumflex (*il/elle connait, connaitra, connaitrait*).

This is also the case for *apparaître, naître* and *paraître* as well as *brûler*, and for some nouns, such as *buche* (*bûche*), *bucheron* (*bûcheron*), *flute* (*flûte*), *ile* (*île*), etc.

Exceptions. The circumflex is still required in the following cases:

- to distinguish between homophones: *il croit* (= he believes) vs. *il croît* (= it grows), *jeune* (= young) vs. *jeûne* (= fasting);
- in conjugated forms (past simple indicative, subjunctive): *nous partîmes, qu'il partît*.

• The grave accent on the "e" can replace the acute accent where the open "e" sound has been used for a long time:

- *évènement* instead of *événement*, *règlement* instead of *réglement*;
- in certain verb conjugations, mainly those following the same pattern as *céder*, and verbs that end in -*eler*, -*érer* or -*eter*:

j'amoncèle	instead of	*j'amoncelle*
je cèderais	instead of	*je céderais*

• The diaeresis (*tréma*) can now be placed on the "u", since it indicates that the "u" is pronounced: *ambiguïté* instead of *ambiguïté*, *aigüe* instead of *aiguë*, etc.

Agreement/More regular agreement

• **Singular and plural of compounds.** Traditionally, one writes *un sèche-cheveux* (hairdryer), *des amuse-gueule* (appetizers). In reformed spelling, the compound is considered as a single word and only its second component varies in number: *un sèche-cheveu → des sèche-cheveux*.

• **Loan words** can now be accentuated according to their modern pronunciation and pluralized according to the standard rules of French: *un flash → des flashs; un jazzman → des jazzmans; un référendum → des référendums*.

• **Past participle of "*laisser*".** Agreement of the past participle is a thorny problem in French. The semi-auxiliaries *faire* and *laisser* are usually considered special cases, and traditional spelling confusingly treats them in different ways:

- *Faire* followed by an infinitive always remains invariable in gender and number:

    Elle s'est fait faire une mise en plis.

- *Laisser* followed by an infinitive is variable or not according to the function of the subject in relation to the infinitive:

    Elle s'est laissé prendre en photo
    (invariable: she wasn't the one taking the photograph) but

    Elle s'est laissée tomber (variable: she was the one who fell).

Spelling reform has simplified all this, and the past participle of *laisser* can now be considered invariable in gender and number.

Français - Anglais
French - English

a, A [a] nm EXPR de **A à Z** from A to Z. Voir aussi **g**.

a (abr écrite de **are**) a.

A 1. (abr écrite de **ampère**) A, Amp 2. abr écrite de **autoroute**.

à [a] *(contraction de à avec le devant consonne ou «h» aspiré au, contraction de à avec les aux* [o]*)* prép

A. DANS L'ESPACE 1. [indiquant la position] at ; [à l'intérieur de] in ; [sur] on / *elle habite au Canada* she lives in Canada / *elle travaille à l'hôpital* she works at the hospital / *il fait 45 °C au soleil* it's 45°C in the sun ▸ **au mur / plafond** on the wall / ceiling / *c'est au rez-de-chaussée* it's on the ground floor ▸ **à ma droite** on ou to my right / *la gare est à 500 m d'ici* the station is 500 m from here 2. [indiquant la direction] to / *aller à Paris / aux États-Unis / à la Jamaïque* to go to Paris / to the United States / to Jamaica / *aller au cinéma* to go to the cinema 3. [indiquant la provenance, l'origine] : *puiser de l'eau à la fontaine* to get water from the fountain / *retenir l'impôt à la source* to deduct tax at source.

B. DANS LE TEMPS 1. [indiquant un moment précis] at ; [devant une date, un jour] on ; [indiquant une époque, une période] in ▸ **à 6 h** at 6 o'clock ▸ **à Noël** at Christmas ▸ **le 12 au soir** on the evening of the 12th ▸ **à mon arrivée** on my arrival ▸ **à ma naissance** when I was born ▸ **au XVIIᵉ siècle** in the 17th century 2. [indiquant un délai] : *nous sommes à deux semaines de Noël* there are only two weeks to go before Christmas, Christmas is only two weeks away ▸ **à demain / la semaine prochaine / mardi** see you tomorrow / next week / (on) Tuesday.

C. DE QUELLE FAÇON 1. [indiquant le moyen, l'instrument, l'accompagnement] ▸ **cousu à la main** hand-sewn ▸ **jouer qqch à la guitare** to play sthg on the guitar ▸ **cuisiner au beurre** to cook with butter ▸ **aller à pied / à cheval** to go on foot / on horseback 2. [indiquant la manière] ▸ **à voix haute** out loud ▸ **je l'aime à la folie** I love her to distraction ▸ **à toute vitesse** at full speed ▸ **à jeun** on ou with an empty stomach ▸ **faire qqch à la russe / turque** to do sthg the Russian / Turkish way.

D. DE QUI : *encore une idée à Papa !* fam another of Dad's ideas ! / *c'est un ami à moi qui m'a parlé de vous* fam it was a friend of mine who told me about you.

E. À QUI : *je suis à vous dans une minute* I'll be with you in a minute ▸ **c'est à moi de jouer / parler** it's my turn to play / to speak.

F. ÉVALUANT, RÉPARTISSANT 1. [introduisant un prix] : *un livre à 49 euros* a book which costs 49 euros, a book worth 49 euros 2. [indiquant un rapport, une mesure] ▸ **vendus à la douzaine / au poids / au détail** sold by the dozen / by weight / individually 3. [introduisant un nombre de per-

sonnes] : *ils ont soulevé le piano à quatre* it took four of them to lift the piano / *ils sont venus à plusieurs* several of them came 4. [indiquant une approximation] : *je m'entraîne de trois à cinq heures par jour* I practise three to five hours a day / *j'en ai vu de 15 à 20* I saw 15 or 20 of them.

G. DE PAR 1. [indiquant la cause] : *on l'a distribué à sa demande* it was given out at his request 2. [indiquant la conséquence] : *il lui a tout dit, à ma grande surprise* he told her everything, much to my surprise 3. [d'après] ▸ **je l'ai reconnu à sa voix / démarche** I recognized (him by) his voice / walk ▸ **à ce que je vois / comprends** from what I see / understand.

H. SUIVI DE L'INFINITIF 1. [indiquant l'hypothèse, la cause] : *à t'entendre, on dirait que tu t'en moques* listening to you, I get the feeling that you don't care 2. [exprimant l'obligation] : *la somme est à régler avant le 10* the full amount has to ou must be paid by the 10th / *c'est une pièce à voir absolument* this play is really worth seeing 3. [en train de] : *il était assis là à bâiller* he was sitting there yawning 4. [au point de] : *ils en sont à se demander si ça en vaut la peine* they've got to the stage of wondering whether or not it's worth the effort.

I. QUI A, QUI SERT À : *l'homme au pardessus* the man in ou with the overcoat / *une chemise à manches courtes* a short-sleeved shirt, a shirt with short sleeves ▸ **glace à la framboise** raspberry ice cream ▸ **tasse à thé** teacup.

J. COMME LIEN SYNTAXIQUE 1. [introduisant le complément du verbe] ▸ **parler à qqn** to talk to sb ▸ **dire à qqn de faire qqch** to tell sb to do sthg 2. [introduisant le complément d'un nom] ▸ **l'appartenance à un parti** membership of a party 3. [introduisant le complément de l'adjectif] : *c'est difficile à dessiner* it's difficult to draw.

A+ (abr écrite de **à plus tard**) SMS CUL.

a2m1 SMS abr écrite de **à demain**.

AB 1. (abr écrite de **assez bien**) *fair grade (as assessment of schoolwork)* ; ≃ C+ ; ≃ B- 2. (abr écrite de **agriculture biologique**) *food label guaranteeing that a product is made from at least 95% organic ingredients (100% in the case of a single ingredient)*.

ab1to (abr écrite de **à bientôt**) SMS CU.

abaissable [abɛsabl] adj [dossier, plateau] lowerable.

abaisser [4] [abese] vt [faire descendre - vitre] to lower ; [- store] to pull down *(sép)* ; [- siège] to put down ; [- voilette] to let down *(sép)* ; [- pont-levis] to lower, to let down *(sép)* ; [- température] to lower ▸ **abaisser la manette a)** [en tirant] to pull the lever down **b)** [en poussant] to push the lever down. ◆ **s'abaisser à** vp + prép ▸ **s'abaisser à des compromissions** to stoop to compromise.

abandon [abɑ̃dɔ̃] nm 1. [fait de rejeter] abandonment, rejection ▸ **abandon de domicile** ou **du domicile**

conjugal DR desertion of the marital home **2.** SPORT withdrawal **3.** INFORM abort. ✦ **à l'abandon** ✦ loc adj ▶ **un potager à l'abandon** a neglected kitchen garden. ✦ loc adv ▶ **laisser son affaire / ses enfants à l'abandon** to neglect one's business / one's children.

abandonné, e [abɑ̃dɔne] adj **1.** [parc] neglected ; [mine, exploitation] disused ; [village] deserted ; [maison, voiture] abandoned ; [vêtement, chaussure] discarded **2.** [enfant, animal] abandoned / *tout colis abandonné sera détruit* any package left unattended will be destroyed.

abandonner [3] [abɑ̃dɔne] vt **1.** [quitter - enfant, chien] to abandon ; [-épouse] to leave, to desert ; [-lieu] to abandon, to leave ; [-poste] to desert, to abandon ▶ **abandonné de tous** forsaken by all **2.** [renoncer à - projet, principe] to discard, to abandon ; [-hypothèse] to abandon ; [-espoir] to give up ; [-course] to drop out of ; [-études] to give up ; [-carrière] to give up, to leave ; [-droit, privilège] to relinquish, to renounce / *abandonner le pouvoir* to leave ou to retire from ou to give up office ▶ **abandonner la partie a)** *pr* to give up **b)** *fig* to throw in the sponge ou towel **3.** [livrer] ▶ **abandonner qqn à** to leave ou to abandon sb to **4.** *(en usage absolu)* [dans une lutte, une discussion] to give up / *il ne comprendra jamais, j'abandonne* he'll never understand, I give up. ✦ **s'abandonner** vpi [se laisser aller] to let (o.s.) go / *elle s'abandonna dans ses bras* she surrendered herself to him. ✦ **s'abandonner à** vp + prép [désespoir] to give way to ; [rêverie] to drift off into ; [plaisirs] to give o.s. up to.

abasourdi, e [abazurdi] adj stunned.

abasourdir [32] [abazurdir] vt **1.** [stupéfier] to stun / *la nouvelle nous avait abasourdis* we were stunned by the news **2.** [suj : bruit, clameur] to stun, to deafen.

abat-jour [abaʒur] *(pl abat-jour ou abat-jours)* nm lampshade, shade.

abats [aba] nmpl [de porc, de bœuf] offal *(U)* ; [de volaille] giblets.

abattage [abataʒ] nm **1.** [d'arbres] felling **2.** [d'animaux] slaughter, slaughtering.

abattement [abatmɑ̃] nm **1.** [épuisement - physique] exhaustion ; [-moral] despondency, dejection **2.** [rabais] reduction ▶ **abattement (fiscal)** tax allowance.

abattis [abati] nmpl [de volaille] giblets.

abattoir [abatwar] nm slaughterhouse, abattoir.

abattre [83] [abatr] vt **1.** [faire tomber - arbre] to cut down *(sép)*, to fell ; [-mur] to pull ou to knock down *(sép)* ; [-quille] to knock down *(sép)* ▶ **abattre de la besogne** ou **du travail** *fam & fig* to get through a lot of work **2.** [mettre à plat - main, battant] to bring down *(sép)* ▶ **abattre ses cartes** ou **son jeu a)** *pr* to lay down one's cards **b)** *fig* to lay one's cards on the table, to show one's hand **3.** [faire retomber - blé, poussière] to settle ; [-vent] to bring down *(sép)* **4.** [tuer - personne] to shoot (down) ; [-avion] to shoot ou to bring down *(sép)* ; [-lièvre] to shoot ; [-perdrix] to shoot, to bring down *(sép)* ; [-animal domestique] to put down *(sép)* ; [-animal de boucherie] to slaughter **5.** [démoraliser] to shatter ; [épuiser] to drain, to wear out *(sép)* / *la défaite l'a complètement abattu* [moralement] the defeat completely crushed him / *ne nous laissons pas abattre* let's not let things get us down. ✦ **s'abattre** vpi [s'écrouler - maison] to fall down ; [-personne] to fall (down), to collapse. ✦ **s'abattre sur** vp + prép **1.** [pluie] to come pouring down on ; [grêle] to come pelting ou beating down on ; [coups] to rain down on **2.** [se jeter sur] to swoop down on.

abattu, e [abaty] adj **1.** [démoralisé] despondent, dejected, downcast **2.** [épuisé] exhausted, worn-out.

abbaye [abei] nf abbey.

abbé [abe] nm **1.** [d'une abbaye] abbot **2.** [ecclésiastique] *title formerly used in France for members of the secular clergy.*

abc [abese] nm inv **1.** [base] basics, fundamentals **2.** [livre] primer, alphabet book.

abcès [apsɛ] nm abscess ▶ **crever** ou **ouvrir** ou **vider l'abcès** *fig* to make a clean breast of things.

abdication [abdikasjɔ̃] nf abdication.

abdiquer [3] [abdike] ✦ vt [pouvoir] to abdicate, to surrender ; [responsabilité, opinion] to abdicate, to renounce. ✦ vi to abdicate, to give in.

abdomen [abdɔmɛn] nm abdomen.

abdominal, e, aux [abdɔminal, o] adj abdominal. ✦ **abdominaux** nmpl **1.** [muscles] stomach ou abdominal muscles **2.** [exercices] ▶ **faire des abdominaux** to do exercises for the stomach muscles.

abdos [abdo] nmpl **1.** [muscles] abs, stomach muscles **2.** [exercices] stomach exercises, abs (exercises) ▶ **faire des abdos** to do abs ou stomach exercises.

abécédaire [abesedɛr] nm primer, alphabet book.

abeille [abɛj] nf bee.

aberrant, e [abɛrɑ̃, ɑ̃t] adj [comportement] deviant, aberrant ; [prix] ridiculous ; [idée] preposterous, absurd.

aberration [abɛrasjɔ̃] nf [absurdité] aberration.

abime, abime* [abim] nm **1.** *litt* [gouffre] abyss, chasm, gulf **2.** *litt* [infini] depths.

abimer, abimer* [3] [abime] vt [gâter - aliment, vêtement] to spoil ; [-meuble] to damage ; [-yeux] to ruin. ✦ **s'abimer, s'abimer*** ✦ vpt ▶ **s'abimer la santé** *pr* to ruin one's health. ✦ vpi [aliment] to spoil, to go off 🇬🇧 ou bad ; [meuble] to get damaged.

abject, e [abʒɛkt] adj despicable, contemptible / *il a été abject avec elle* he behaved despicably towards her.

ablation [ablasjɔ̃] nf MÉD removal, ablation *spéc.*

ablution [ablysjɔ̃] nf *hum* [toilette] ▶ **faire ses ablutions** to perform one's ablutions.

abnégation [abnegasjɔ̃] nf abnegation, self-denial ▶ **avec abnégation** selflessly.

aboiement [abwamɑ̃] nm [d'un chien] bark ▶ **des aboiements** barking.

abois [abwa] ✦ **aux abois** loc adj *fig* ▶ **être aux abois** to have one's back against ou to the wall.

abolir [32] [abɔlir] vt to do away *(insép)* with, to abolish.

abolition [abɔlisjɔ̃] nf abolition.

abominable [abɔminabl] adj **1.** [désagréable - temps, odeur] appalling, abominable **2.** [abject - crime] heinous, abominable, vile.

abominablement [abɔminabləmɑ̃] adv [laid, cher, habillé] horribly, frightfully ▶ **abominablement (mal) organisé** appallingly ou abominably badly organized.

abomination [abɔminasjɔ̃] nf [acte, propos] abomination.

abondamment [abɔ̃damɑ̃] adv [servir, saler] copiously ; [rincer] thoroughly / *elle a abondamment traité la question* she has amply ou fully dealt with the question.

abondance [abɔ̃dɑ̃s] nf [prospérité] affluence ▶ **vivre dans l'abondance** to live in affluence.

abondant, e [abɔ̃dɑ̃, ɑ̃t] adj **1.** [en quantité - nourriture] abundant, copious ; [-récolte] bountiful ; [-vivres] plentiful ; [-végétation] luxuriant, lush ; [-larmes] copious ; [-chevelure] luxuriant, thick / *elle reçoit un abondant courrier* she receives a large quantity of mail ▶ **d'abondantes illustrations / recommandations** a wealth of illustrations / recommendations **2.** MÉD [règles] heavy.

abonder [3] [abɔ̃de] vi **1.** [foisonner] to be plentiful ▶ **abonder en** to abound in, to be full of **2.** *fig & sout* : *abonder dans le sens de* to be in complete agreement with, to go along with.

abonné, e [abɔne] nm, f **1.** PRESSE & TÉLÉC subscriber **2.** [au théâtre, au concert, au stade] season ticket-holder **3.** [au gaz, à l'électricité] consumer **4.** *fam & hum* [habitué] : *c'est un abonné aux gaffes* he's always putting his foot in it.

abonnement [abɔnmɑ̃] nm **1.** PRESSE subscription ▶ **prendre un abonnement à** to take out a subscription to **2.** [pour un trajet, au théâtre, au stade] season ticket **3.** [au téléphone] rental ; [au gaz, à l'électricité] standing charge.

abonner [3] [abɔne] vt **1.** ▶ **abonner qqn à qqch a)** [journal] to take out a subscription for sb to sthg **b)** [théâtre, concert, stade] to buy sb a season ticket for sthg / *être abonné à un journal* to subscribe to a paper **2.** [pour un service] : *être abonné au gaz* to have gas / *être abonné au téléphone* to have a phone, to be on the phone █. ◆ **s'abonner** vp *(emploi réfléchi)* ▶ **s'abonner à a)** [un journal] to take out a subscription to **b)** [au théâtre, au concert, au stade] to buy a season ticket for.

abord [abɔʀ] nm **1.** [contact] manner / *elle est d'un abord déconcertant* / *chaleureux* she puts you off your stride / makes you feel very welcome when you first meet her ▶ **être d'un abord facile** / **difficile** to be approachable / unapproachable **2.** [accès -à une côte] approach ; [-à une maison] access ▶ **d'un abord facile a)** [demeure] easy to get to **b)** [texte] easy to understand ou to get to grips with. ◆ **abords** nmpl [alentours] surroundings. ◆ **aux abords** loc adv all around. ◆ **aux abords de** loc prép : *aux abords de la ville* on the outskirts of the town / *aux abords du château* / *de la maison* in the area around the castle / the house. ◆ **d'abord** loc adv **1.** [en premier lieu] first / *nous irons d'abord à Rome* we'll go to Rome first ▶ **tout d'abord** first of all **2.** [au début] at first, initially, to begin with **3.** [introduisant une restriction] to start with, for a start / *d'abord, tu n'es même pas prêt !* to start with ou for a start, you're not even ready ! **4.** [de toute façon] anyway / *et puis d'abord, qu'est-ce que tu veux ?* and anyway, what do you want ?

abordable [abɔʀdabl] adj **1.** [peu cher -prix] reasonable ; [-produit] reasonably priced, affordable **2.** [ouvert -patron, célébrité] approachable **3.** [facile -texte] accessible ; [-problème] that can be discussed.

aborder [3] [abɔʀde] ◆ vt **1.** [accoster -passant] to accost, to walk up to *(insép)*, to approach **2.** [arriver à -entrée de] to enter **3.** [faire face à -profession] to take up *(sép)* ; [-nouvelle vie] to embark on *(insép)* ; [-tâche] to tackle, to get to grips with ; [-retraite] to approach / *à 18 ans, on est prêt à aborder la vie* when you're 18, you're ready to start out in life **4.** [se mettre à examiner -texte, problème] to approach / *il n'a pas eu le temps d'aborder le sujet* he didn't have time to get onto ou to broach the subject **5.** NAUT [attaquer] to board ; [percuter] to collide with *(insép)*, to ram into *(insép)*. ◆ vi to (touch) ou reach land.

aborigène [abɔʀiʒɛn] ◆ adj [autochtone] aboriginal ; [d'Australie] Aboriginal, native Australian. ◆ nmf [autochtone] aborigine ; [autochtone d'Australie] Aborigine, Aboriginal, native Australian.

abortif, ive [abɔʀtif, iv] adj abortive.

abouti, e [abuti] adj [projet, démarche] successful.

aboutir [32] [abutiʀ] vi **1.** [réussir -projet, personne] to succeed / *l'entreprise n'a pas abouti* the venture fell through ou never came to anything ▶ **faire aboutir des négociations** to bring talks to a satisfactory conclusion **2.** [finir] : *aboutir en prison* to end up in prison. ◆ **aboutir à** v + prép **1.** [voie, rue] to end at ou in, to

lead to ; [fleuve] to end in **2.** [avoir pour résultat] to lead to, to result in / *de bonnes intentions qui n'aboutissent à rien* good intentions which come to nothing / *tu aboutiras au même résultat* you'll arrive at ou get the same result ▶ **aboutir à un compromis** to come to a compromise.

aboutissement [abutismɑ̃] nm [conclusion] (final) outcome, result ; [résultat positif] success.

aboyer [13] [abwaje] vi **1.** [animal] to bark **2.** *péj* [personne] to bark ▶ **aboyer après** ou **contre qqn** to yell at sb.

abracadabrant, e [abʀakadabʀɑ̃, ɑ̃t] adj bewildering.

abrasif, ive [abʀazif, iv] adj abrasive. ◆ **abrasif** nm abrasive.

abrégé [abʀeʒe] nm **1.** [d'un texte] summary **2.** [livre] abstract, epitome *sout* ▶ **faire un abrégé de qqch** to make a précis of sthg.

abréger [22] [abʀeʒe] vt **1.** [interrompre -vacances] to curtail, to cut short, to shorten ; [-vie] to cut short, to put an (early) end to ▶ **abréger les souffrances de qqn** *euphém* to put an end to sb's suffering **2.** [tronquer -discours] to cut ; [-texte] to cut, to abridge ; [-conversation] to cut short ; [-mot] to abbreviate, to truncate *sout* ; *(en usage absolu)* ▶ **abrège !** [ton agressif] get to the point !

🖋 In reformed spelling (see p. 16-18), this verb is conjugated like *semer* : *elle abrègera, il abrègerait*.

abreuver [5] [abʀœve] vt **1.** [faire boire -animaux] to water **2.** *fig* : *nous sommes abreuvés d'images de violence* we get swamped with violent images. ◆ **s'abreuver** vpi [animal] to drink.

abreuvoir [abʀœvwaʀ] nm [bac] (drinking) trough ; [plan d'eau] watering place.

abréviation [abʀevjasjɔ̃] nf abbreviation.

abri [abʀi] nm [cabane] shelter, refuge ; [toit] shelter ; [sous terre] shelter ; [improvisé] shelter ▶ **abri antiatomique** ou **antinucléaire** (nuclear) fallout shelter ▶ **abri antiaérien** air-raid shelter ▶ **abri à vélos** bicycle shed. ◆ **à l'abri** loc adv **1.** [des intempéries] ▶ **être à l'abri** to be sheltered ▶ **mettre qqn à l'abri** to find shelter for sb ▶ **se mettre à l'abri** to take cover, to shelter **2.** [en lieu sûr] in a safe place / *mettre sa fortune à l'abri dans le pétrole* to invest one's money safely in oil. ◆ **à l'abri de** loc prép **1.** [pluie] sheltered from ; [chaleur, obus] shielded from ; [regards] hidden from / *conserver à l'abri de la lumière* / *de l'humidité* store in a dark / dry place **2.** *fig* : *nos économies nous mettront à l'abri de la misère* our savings will shield us against poverty ou will protect us from hardship / *à l'abri des contrôles* safe from checks ▶ **personne n'est à l'abri d'une erreur** / **d'un maître-chanteur** anyone can make a mistake / fall victim to a blackmailer.

Abribus® [abʀibys] nm bus shelter.

abricot [abʀiko] nm BOT apricot.

abricotier [abʀikɔtje] nm apricot tree.

abrier [10] [abʀije] QUÉBEC ◆ **s'abrier** vp **1.** [pour se protéger] : *s'abrier sous une couverture* to hide under a blanket **2.** *fig* [cacher, dissimuler] to hide.

abriter [3] [abʀite] vt **1.** [protéger] ▶ **abriter qqn** / **qqch de la pluie** to shelter sb / sthg from the rain ▶ **abriter qqn** / **qqch du soleil** to shade sb / sthg **2.** [loger -personnes] to house, to accommodate ; [-société, machine] to house. ◆ **s'abriter** vp *(emploi réfléchi)* ▶ **s'abriter de la pluie** / **du vent** to shelter from the rain / from the wind ▶ **s'abriter derrière la loi** / **ses parents** *fig* to hide behind the law / one's parents.

abroger [17] [abʀɔʒe] vt to repeal, to rescind, to abrogate *sout*.

abrupt, e [abʀypt] adj **1.** [raide -côte] steep, abrupt ; [-versant] sheer **2.** [brusque -manières] abrupt, brusque ; [-refus] blunt, abrupt, curt ; [-personne] short, sharp, abrupt ; [-changement] abrupt, sudden, sharp.

abruptement [abʀyptəmɑ̃] adv [descendre] steeply, abruptly ; [répondre] abruptly, brusquely, curtly ; [changer] abruptly, suddenly.

abruti, e [abʀyti] nm, f *fam* idiot.

abrutir [32] [abʀytiʀ] vt **1.** [abêtir] to turn into an idiot **2.** [étourdir] to stupefy ▸ **abruti de fatigue** numb ou dazed with tiredness ∕ *abruti par l'alcool* stupefied with drink **3.** [accabler] ▸ **abrutir qqn de conseils** to pester sb with endless advice. ❖ **s'abrutir** ◆ vp *(emploi réfléchi)* ▸ **s'abrutir de travail** to overwork o.s., to work o.s. into the ground. ◆ vpi [s'abêtir] to turn into an idiot.

abrutissant, e [abʀytisɑ̃, ɑ̃t] adj **1.** [qui rend bête] mind-numbing **2.** [qui fatigue] wearing, exhausting.

abrutissement [abʀytismɑ̃] nm mindless state.

abscisse [apsis] nf abscissa.

absence [apsɑ̃s] nf **1.** [fait de n'être pas là] absence ▸ **sa troisième absence a)** [à l'école] the third time he's been away from ou missed school **b)** [au travail] the third time he's been off work **c)** [à une réunion] the third time he's stayed away from ou not attended the meeting **2.** [de goût, d'imagination] lack, absence **3.** [défaillance] ▸ **absence (de mémoire)** mental blank ∕ *elle a des absences par moments* her mind wanders at times, at times she can be absent-minded. ❖ **en l'absence de** loc prép in the absence of ▸ **en mon absence** during ou in my absence ∕ *en l'absence de son fils* in her son's absence, while her son is ∕ was away.

absent, e [apsɑ̃, ɑ̃t] ◆ adj **1.** [personne -de l'école] absent ; [-du travail] off work, absent ; [-de son domicile] away **2.** [inattentif] absent ▸ **regard absent** vacant look ▸ **d'un air absent** absent-mindedly. ◆ nm, f [du travail, de l'école] absentee ; [dans une famille] absent person ▸ **les absents ont toujours tort** *prov* the absent are always in the wrong.

absentéisme [apsɑ̃teism] nm absenteeism ▸ **absentéisme scolaire** truancy.

absentéiste [apsɑ̃teist] nmf absentee ▸ **les absentéistes** [au travail] persistent absentees.

absenter [3] [apsɑ̃te] ❖ **s'absenter** vpi to be absent ▸ **s'absenter de son travail** to be off ou to stay away from work ∕ *je ne m'étais absentée que quelques minutes* I'd only gone out for a few minutes ∕ *elle a dû s'absenter une semaine* she had to go away for a week.

absolu, e [apsɔly] adj [total -liberté] absolute, complete ; [-repos] complete ; [-silence] total ▸ **un dénuement absolu** abject poverty ▸ **en cas d'absolue nécessité** when absolutely necessary. ◆ nm PHILOS ▸ **l'absolu** the Absolute. ❖ **dans l'absolu** loc adv in absolute terms.

absolument [apsɔlymɑ̃] adv [entièrement -croire, avoir raison] absolutely, entirely ; [-ravi, faux] absolutely, completely ; [-défendu] strictly ▸ **absolument pas** not at all ▸ **absolument rien** absolutely nothing, nothing whatsoever.

absolution [apsɔlysjɔ̃] nf RELIG absolution ▸ **donner l'absolution à qqn** to give sb absolution.

absolutisme [apsɔlytism] nm absolutism.

absorbant, e [apsɔʀbɑ̃, ɑ̃t] adj **1.** [tissu] absorbent **2.** [lecture] absorbing, gripping.

absorber [3] [apsɔʀbe] vt **1.** [éponger -gén] to absorb, to soak up *(sép)* ; [-avec un buvard] to blot ; [-avec une éponge] to sponge off *(sép)* **2.** [consommer -aliment] to take, to consume ; [-bénéfices, capitaux] to absorb ; ÉCON [entreprise] to take over *(sép)*, to absorb **3.** [préoccuper -suj : travail] to absorb, to engross, to occupy ; [-suj : pensée] to absorb, to grip ∕ *très absorbée par son activité politique* very much

engrossed in her political activities ▸ **être absorbé dans ses pensées** to be lost ou deep in thought.

absorption [apsɔʀpsjɔ̃] nf **1.** [ingestion] swallowing, taking ∕ *l'absorption d'alcool est fortement déconseillée* you are strongly advised not to drink alcohol **2.** [pénétration] absorption ∕ *masser jusqu'à absorption complète par la peau* massage well into the skin.

abstenir [40] [apstəniʀ] ❖ **s'abstenir de** vp + prép [éviter de] to refrain ou to abstain from ; *(en usage absolu)* ▸ **dans ce cas, mieux vaut s'abstenir** in that case, it's better not to do anything.

abstention [apstɑ̃sjɔ̃] nf **1.** POL abstention **2.** [renoncement] abstention.

abstentionnisme [apstɑ̃sjɔnism] nm abstention.

abstentionniste [apstɑ̃sjɔnist] adj & nmf abstentionist.

abstinence [apstinɑ̃s] nf [chasteté] abstinence.

abstraction [apstʀaksjɔ̃] nf **1.** [notion] abstraction, abstract idea **2.** [fait d'isoler] abstraction ▸ **faire abstraction de** [ignorer] to take no account of, to ignore, to disregard.

abstrait, e [apstʀɛ, ɛt] [conçu par l'esprit] abstract.

absurde [apsyʀd] ◆ adj [remarque, idée] absurd, preposterous ; [personne] ridiculous, absurd ∕ *ne soyez pas absurde !* don't be absurd ou talk nonsense ▸ **d'une manière absurde** absurdly. ◆ nm **1.** [absurdité] absurd **2.** LITTÉR, PHILOS & THÉÂTRE ▸ **l'absurde** the absurd.

absurdité [apsyʀdite] nf [parole, action] absurdity ∕ *ne dis pas d'absurdités !* don't be absurd ou talk nonsense!

abus [aby] nm **1.** [excès -de stupéfiants, de médicament] abuse ▸ **abus d'alcool** excessive drinking, alcohol abuse ▸ **faire des abus** to overindulge ▸ **il y a de l'abus** *fam* that's a bit much **2.** DR & POL misuse ▸ **abus de biens sociaux** misappropriation of funds ▸ **abus de confiance** breach of trust ▸ **abus de pouvoir** abuse of power.

abuser [3] [abyze] vt *litt* to deceive, to mislead. ❖ **abuser de** v + prép **1.** [consommer excessivement] to overuse ▸ **abuser de la boisson** to drink too much ▸ **il ne faut pas abuser des bonnes choses** good things should be enjoyed in moderation, enough is as good as a feast ▸ **abuser de ses forces** to overtax o.s. **2.** [mal utiliser -autorité, privilège] to abuse, to misuse **3.** [exploiter -ami, bonté, patience] to take advantage of, to exploit ▸ **je ne voudrais pas abuser de votre gentillesse** I don't want to impose ▸ **je ne veux pas abuser de votre temps** I don't want to take up your time ▸ **abuser de la situation** to take unfair advantage of the situation ; *(en usage absolu)* : *je veux bien t'aider mais là, tu abuses !* I don't mind helping you but there is a limit! **4.** *euphém* [violer] to sexually abuse.

abusif, ive [abyzif, iv] adj **1.** [immodéré] excessive **2.** [outrepassant ses droits -père, mère] domineering **3.** [incorrect] misused.

acabit [akabi] nm *péj* ▸ **de cet acabit** of that type ∕ *son amie est du même acabit* she and her friend are two of a kind.

acacia [akasja] nm acacia.

académicien, enne [akademisjɛ̃, ɛn] nm, f [membre -d'une académie] academician ; [-de l'Académie française] member of the French Academy ou Académie française.

académie [akademi] nf **1.** [société savante] learned society, academy ▸ **l'Académie des sciences** the Academy of Science ▸ **l'Académie française** the French Academy, the Académie française *(learned society of leading men and women of letters)* **2.** [école] academy ▸ **académie de danse** ∕ **musique** academy of dance ∕ music **3.** ADMIN & ENS ≃ local education authority 🇬🇧 ; ≃ school district 🇺🇸.

▶ **L'Académie française**

Originally a group of men of letters who were encouraged by Cardinal Richelieu in 1635 to become an official body. **L'Académie française** consists of forty distinguished writers known as **les Quarante** or **les Immortels**. Its chief task is to produce a definitive dictionary and to be the ultimate authority in matters concerning the French language.

académique [akademik] adj **1.** [d'une société savante] academic ; [de l'Académie française] of the French Academy ou Académie française **2.** ÉDUC ▶ **l'année académique** Suisse & Québec the academic year.

acadien, enne [akadjɛ̃, ɛn] adj Acadian. ❖ **Acadien, enne** nm, f Acadian. ❖ **acadien** nm LING Acadian.

acajou [akaʒu] nm **1.** BOT mahogany (tree) ; [anacardier] cashew **2.** MENUIS mahogany.

acalorique [akalɔrik] adj calorie-free.

acariâtre [akarjatr] adj [caractère] sour ; [personne] bad-tempered.

acarien [akarjɛ̃] nm acarid.

accablant, e [akablɑ̃, ɑ̃t] adj [chaleur] oppressive ; [preuve, témoignage, vérité] damning ; [travail] exhausting ; [douleur] excruciating ; [chagrin] overwhelming.

accabler [3] [akable] vt **1.** [abattre - suj : fatigue, chaleur] to overcome, to overwhelm ; [- suj : soucis] to overcome ; [- suj : chagrin, deuil, travail] to overwhelm ▶ **accablé de chagrin** grief-stricken ▶ **accablé de dettes** burdened with debts ▶ **accablé d'impôts** overburdened with taxes **2.** [accuser - suj : témoignage] to condemn / *je ne veux pas l'accabler mais il faut reconnaître qu'elle a commis des erreurs* I don't want to be too hard on her but it has to be said that she made some mistakes **3.** [couvrir] ▶ **accabler qqn de** : *accabler qqn d'injures* to heap abuse upon ou to hurl insults at sb ▶ **accabler qqn de critiques** to be highly critical of sb ▶ **accabler qqn de conseils** to pester sb with advice.

accalmie [akalmi] nf [du bruit, du vent, de la pluie, d'un combat, d'une crise politique] lull ; [d'une maladie] temporary improvement ; [de souffrances] temporary relief ou respite ; [du commerce] slack period ; [dans le travail, l'agitation] break.

accaparer [3] [akapare] vt **1.** [monopoliser - conversation, personne] to monopolize ; [- victoires, récompenses] to carry off *(insép)* ; [- places] to grab / *ne laisse pas les enfants t'accaparer* don't let the children monopolize you ou take you over **2.** [absorber - suj : travail, soucis] to absorb ▶ **son travail l'accapare** her work takes up all her time.

accédant, e [aksedɑ̃, ɑ̃t] nm, f ▶ **un accédant à la propriété** a new home-owner, a first-time buyer.

accéder [18] [aksede] ❖ **accéder à** v + prép **1.** [atteindre - trône] to accede to ; [- poste, rang] to rise to ; [- indépendance, gloire] to gain, to attain ; [- lieu] to reach / *on accède à la maison par un petit chemin* you get to the house via a narrow path, access to the house is by a narrow path ▶ **accéder à la propriété** to become a home-owner ▶ **faire accéder qqn au pouvoir** to bring sb to power **2.** [accepter - demande, requête] to grant ; [- désir] to meet, to give in to.

✍ In reformed spelling (see p. 16-18), this verb is conjugated like *semer* : *elle accédera, il accéderait.*

accélérateur [akseleratœr] nm accelerator ▶ **donner un coup d'accélérateur a)** *pr* to accelerate **b)** *fig* to speed things up.

accélération [akselerasjɔ̃] nf **1.** AUTO, MÉCAN & PHYS acceleration **2.** [accroissement du rythme - du cœur, du pouls] acceleration ; [- d'un processus] speeding up.

accéléré [akselere] ❖ **en accéléré** ◆ loc adj speeded-up, accelerated. ◆ loc adv speeded-up.

accélérer [18] [akselere] ◆ vt [allure] to accelerate ; [rythme cardiaque] to raise, to increase ; [pouls] to quicken ; [démarches, travaux] to speed up ▶ **accélérer le pas** to quicken one's pace ▶ **accélérer le mouvement** *fam* to get things moving. ◆ vi AUTO to accelerate ▶ **allez, accélère !** come on, step on it! ❖ **s'accélérer** vpi [pouls, cœur] to beat faster ▶ **son débit s'accélère** he's talking faster and faster.

✍ In reformed spelling (see p. 16-18), this verb is conjugated like *semer* : *il accélèrera, elle accélèrerait.*

accent [aksɑ̃] nm **1.** [prononciation] accent ▶ **avoir un accent** to speak with ou to have an accent / *il n'a pas d'accent* he doesn't have an accent ▶ **l'accent du midi** a southern (French) accent **2.** PHON stress ▶ **accent de hauteur** pitch ▶ **accent d'intensité** tonic stress, main stress ▶ **accent tonique a)** tonic accent **b)** [signe] stress mark ▶ **mettre l'accent sur a)** *pr* to stress **b)** *fig* to stress, to emphasize **3.** [signe graphique] accent ▶ **accent grave / circonflexe / aigu** grave / circumflex / acute (accent) ▶ **e accent grave / aigu** e grave / acute.

accentuation [aksɑ̃tɥasjɔ̃] nf **1.** PHON stressing, accentuation / *l'accentuation, en anglais, se définit ainsi* the stress pattern of English is defined as follows **2.** [exagération - d'une ressemblance, d'une différence, des traits] emphasizing ; [- d'un effort] intensification, increase ; [- du chômage, d'une crise] increase, rise.

accentuer [7] [aksɑ̃tɥe] vt **1.** PHON [son, syllabe] to accent, to accentuate, to bring out *(insép)* **2.** [dans l'écriture] to put an accent on **3.** [rendre plus visible - ressemblance, différence] to accentuate, to bring out *(insép)*, to emphasize ; [- forme, traits] to emphasize, to accentuate, to highlight. ❖ **s'accentuer** vpi [contraste, ressemblance] to become more marked ou apparent ou pronounced ; [tendance] to become more noticeable ; [chômage] to rise, to increase ; [crise] to increase in intensity.

acceptable [akseptabl] adj [offre, condition] acceptable ; [attitude] decent, acceptable ; [travail] fair, acceptable ; [repas] decent ; [réponse] satisfactory ; [prix] fair, reasonable.

acceptation [akseptasjɔ̃] nf [accord] acceptance.

accepter [4] [aksepte] vt **1.** [recevoir volontiers - cadeau, invitation] to accept ; [s'engager volontiers dans - défi, lutte] to take up *(sép)* **2.** [admettre - hypothèse, situation, excuse] to accept ; [- condition] to agree to, to accept ; [- mort, échec, sort] to accept, to come to terms with ; [- requête] to grant ▶ **accepter que** : *j'accepte que cela soit difficile* I agree that it is ou might be difficult ▶ **accepter de faire qqch** to agree to do sthg **3.** [tolérer - critique, hypocrisie] to take, to stand for, to put up with *(insép)* / *il accepte tout de sa femme* he'd put up with anything from his wife / *je n'accepte pas qu'on se moque de moi* I will not be made fun of ▶ **accepter de** to be prepared to **4.** [accueillir] to accept / *elle a tout de suite été acceptée dans la famille* she was readily accepted ou made welcome by the family / *acceptez-vous les cartes de crédit ?* do you take credit cards?

acception [aksepsjɔ̃] nf meaning, sense ▶ **dans toutes les acceptions du mot** ou **du terme** in every sense of the word.

accès [aksɛ] nm **1.** [entrée] access ▶ **d'accès facile, facile d'accès a)** [lieu] accessible **b)** [île] easy to get to **c)** [personne] approachable **d)** [œuvre] accessible ▶ **d'accès difficile, difficile d'accès a)** [lieu] hard to get to **b)** [personne] not very approachable, unapproachable **c)** [œuvre] difficult **2.** [chemin, voie] way in, access, entrance **3.** [crise de folie, de jalousie] fit ▸ **un accès de colère** a fit of anger, an angry outburst ▸ **un accès de fièvre a)** MÉD a bout of fever **b)** *fig* a sudden burst of activity **4.** INFORM access ▸ **accès à distance** remote access ▸ **accès à Internet** Web access.

accessible [aksesibl] adj [livre, œuvre] accessible ; [personne] approachable ; [lieu] accessible ; [auteur] easily understood ; [prix] affordable ▸ **accessible au public** open to the public ▸ **accessible à tous** [financièrement] within everyone's pocket.

accession [aksesjɔ̃] nf [arrivée] ▸ **accession au trône** accession ou acceding to the throne ▸ **depuis son accession au poste / rang de…** since he rose to the post / rank of… ▸ **faciliter l'accession à la propriété** to make it easier for people to become home-owners.

accessit [aksesit] nm ≃ certificate of merit 🇬🇧 ; ≃ Honourable Mention 🇺🇸.

accessoire [akseswaʀ] ◆ adj [avantage] incidental ▸ **des considérations accessoires** considerations of secondary importance. ◆ nm **1.** [dispositif, objet] accessory **2.** CINÉ, THÉÂTRE & TV prop.

accessoirement [akseswaʀmɑ̃] adv **1.** [secondairement] secondarily **2.** [éventuellement] if necessary, if need be.

accident [aksidɑ̃] nm **1.** [chute, coup] accident ; [entre véhicules] crash, accident, collision ▸ **accident d'avion / de voiture** plane / car crash ▸ **accident de la circulation** ou **de la route** road accident ▸ **accident de montagne** mountaineering accident ▸ **accident du travail** industrial accident ▸ **accidents domestiques** accidents in the home **2.** [fait imprévu] mishap, accident ▸ **accident (de parcours)** hitch **3.** MÉD ▸ **accident de santé** (sudden) health problem ▸ **accident vasculaire cérébral** stroke. ◆ **par accident** loc adv accidentally, by accident ou chance, as chance would have it.

accidenté, e [aksidɑ̃te] ◆ adj **1.** [endommagé - voiture, avion] damaged **2.** [inégal - terrain] uneven, broken, irregular. ◆ nm, f injured person, casualty ▸ **accidenté de la route** road casualty.

accidentel, elle [aksidɑ̃tɛl] adj [dû à un accident] accidental ; [dû au hasard] fortuitous *sout*, incidental, accidental.

accidentellement [aksidɑ̃tɛlma] adv [dans un accident] in an accident ; [par hasard] accidentally.

accidentogène [aksidɑ̃tɔʒɛn] adj **1.** [zone, route] hazardous **2.** [facteur] accident-causing.

acclamation [aklamasjɔ̃] nf acclamation *litt*, applause / **être accueilli par les acclamations de la foule** to be cheered by the crowd.

acclamer [3] [aklame] vt to acclaim, to applaud, to cheer.

acclimatation [aklimatasjɔ̃] nf acclimatization, acclimation 🇺🇸.

acclimater [3] [aklimate] vt BOT & ZOOL to acclimatize, to acclimate 🇺🇸. ◆ **s'acclimater** vpi [personne] to adapt.

accointances [akwɛ̃tɑ̃s] nfpl *péj* contacts, links.

accolade [akɔlad] nf **1.** [embrassade] embrace ▸ **donner l'accolade à qqn** to embrace sb **2.** [signe] brace, bracket.

accoler [3] [akɔle] vt [disposer ensemble] to place ou to put side by side.

accommodant, e [akɔmɔdɑ̃, ɑ̃t] adj accommodating, obliging.

accommodement [akɔmɔdma] nm **1.** [accord] arrangement / **trouver des accommodements avec sa conscience** to come to terms with one's conscience **2.** POL compromise.

accommoder [3] [akɔmɔde] ◆ vt **1.** [adapter] to adapt, to adjust, to fit **2.** CULIN to prepare / *accommo-*

der les restes to use up the leftovers. ◆ vi OPT to focus. ◆ **s'accommoder de** vp + prép to put up with.

accompagnateur, trice [akɔ̃paɲatœʀ, tʀis] nm, f **1.** [de touristes] guide, courier ; [d'enfants] group leader, accompanying adult ; [de malades] nurse **2.** MUS accompanist.

accompagnement [akɔ̃paɲma] nm **1.** CULIN [d'un rôti] trimmings ; [d'un mets] garnish / *servi avec un accompagnement de petits légumes* served with mixed vegetables **2.** MUS accompaniment **3.** [soutien] support ▸ **accompagnement thérapeutique** supportive therapy.

accompagner [3] [akɔ̃paɲe] vt **1.** [aller avec] to go with ; [venir avec] to come with ▸ **accompagner qqn à l'aéroport a)** [gén] to go to the airport with sb **b)** [en voiture] to take sb to the airport / *elle vient toujours accompagnée* she never comes alone, she always brings somebody with her **2.** [compléter] to go with **3.** [malade] to give support to. ◆ **s'accompagner** vp *(emploi réfléchi)* MUS : *s'accompagner à un instrument* to accompany o.s. on an instrument. ◆ **s'accompagner de** vp + prép to come with.

⚠ Lorsque accompagner signifie « aller quelque part avec qqn », il ne peut être traduit systématiquement par **to accompany** qui est d'un registre plus soutenu dans ce contexte.

accompli, e [akɔ̃pli] adj **1.** [parfait] accomplished **2.** [révolu] : *elle a vingt ans accomplis* she's turned ou over 20.

accomplir [32] [akɔ̃pliʀ] vt **1.** [achever - mandat, obligation] to fulfil ; [- mission, travail] to carry out, to accomplish / *accomplir son devoir* to perform one's duty / *accomplir de bonnes actions* to do good (deeds) / *accomplir de mauvaises actions* to commit evil (deeds) / *il n'a rien accompli à ce jour* up to now he hasn't achieved ou accomplished anything **2.** [réaliser - miracle] to perform / *accomplir un exploit technique* to perform a feat of engineering ▸ **accomplir les dernières volontés de qqn** to carry out sb's last wishes. ◆ **s'accomplir** vpi [être exécuté - vœu] to come true, to be fulfilled ; [- prophétie] to come true / *la volonté de Dieu s'accomplira* God's will shall be done.

⚠ D'un registre plus soutenu, **to accomplish** ne doit pas être employé systématiquement pour traduire accomplir.

accomplissement [akɔ̃plismɑ̃] nm [exécution] accomplishment, fulfilment 🇬🇧, fulfillment 🇺🇸.

accord [akɔʀ] nm **1.** [approbation] consent, agreement ▸ **demander l'accord de qqn** to ask for sb's consent ▸ **donner son accord à** to consent to ▸ **d'un commun accord** by mutual agreement, by common consent **2.** [entente] agreement ; [harmonie] harmony / *il faut un bon accord entre les participants* the participants must all get on well with each other / *accord de l'expression et de la pensée* harmony between expression and thought ▸ **vivre en parfait accord** to live in perfect harmony **3.** [convention] agreement ▸ **conclure un accord avec** to come to an agreement with ▸ **accord à l'amiable** amicable agreement ▸ **accord de principe** agreement in principle ▸ **accord salarial** wage settlement **4.** LING agreement ▸ **accord en genre / nombre** gender / number agreement **5.** MUS [son] chord ; [réglage] tuning. ◆ **d'accord** loc adv ▸ **être d'accord (avec qqn)** to agree (with sb) ▸ **(je ne suis) pas d'accord !** **a)** [je refuse] no (way)! **b)** [c'est faux] I disagree! / *tu viens ? — d'accord* are you coming? — OK /

(c'est) d'accord pour ce soir it's OK for tonight ▶ **se mettre d'accord (sur qqch)** to agree (on sthg) ▶ **tomber d'accord** to come to an agreement ▶ **tomber d'accord sur qqch** to agree on sthg. ❖ **en accord avec** loc prép ▶ **en accord avec qqn** : *en accord avec le chef de service, nous avons décidé que...* together with the head of department, we have decided that / *en accord avec les directives* according to the guidelines.

accordéon [akɔʀdeɔ̃] nm MUS accordion. ❖ **en accordéon** loc adj [chaussettes] wrinkled ; [voiture] crumpled.

accorder [3] [akɔʀde] vt **1.** [octroyer - congé, permission] to give, to grant ; [- faveur] to grant ; [- subvention] to grant, to award ; [- interview] to give ▶ **accorder le droit de vote à qqn** to give sb the right to vote, to enfranchise sb ▶ **accorder la grâce d'un** ou **sa grâce à un condamné** to grant a condemned man a pardon, to extend a pardon to a condemned man ▶ **accorder la main de sa fille à qqn** to give sb one's daughter's hand in marriage ▶ **accorder toute sa confiance à qqn** to give sb one's complete trust ▶ **accorder de l'importance à qqch** to attach importance to sthg / *pouvez-vous m'accorder quelques minutes ?* can you spare me a few minutes? / *je vous accorde une heure, pas plus* I'll allow you one hour, no more **2.** [concéder] ▶ **accorder à qqn que** to admit to ou to grant sb that / *vous m'accorderez que, là, j'avais raison* you must admit that on this point I was right **3.** GRAM to make agree / *accorder le verbe avec le sujet* to make the verb agree with the subject **4.** MUS [piano, guitare] to tune / *les musiciens accordent leurs instruments* [avant un concert] the players are tuning up / *il faudrait accorder vos violons !* make your minds up!, get your stories straight! ❖ **s'accorder** ◆ vpi **1.** [être du même avis] ▶ **s'accorder à** : *tous s'accordent à dire que...* they all agree ou concur that... ▶ **s'accorder pour** : *ils se sont accordés pour baisser leurs prix* they agreed among themselves that they would drop their prices **2.** [s'entendre] : *on ne s'est jamais accordé (tous les deux)* we two never saw eye to eye ou got along **3.** [être en harmonie - caractères] to blend ; [- opinions] to match, to tally, to converge / *ce qu'il dit ne s'accorde pas avec sa personnalité* he's saying things which are out of character **4.** GRAM to agree ▶ **s'accorder en genre avec** to agree in gender with. ◆ vpt : *s'accorder quelques jours de repos* to take a few days off.

accordeur [akɔʀdœʀ] nm (piano) tuner.

accoster [3] [akɔste] vt **1.** [personne] to go up to *(insép)*, to accost **2.** NAUT to come ou to draw alongside.

accotement [akɔtmɑ̃] nm **1.** [d'une route] shoulder, verge ⬚ / **'accotements non stabilisés'** 'soft shoulders ⬚ ', 'soft verges ⬚ ' **2.** RAIL shoulder.

accouchement [akuʃmɑ̃] nm [travail] childbirth, labour ; [expulsion] delivery ▶ **accouchement sans douleur** painless delivery ou childbirth.

accoucher [3] [akuʃe] ◆ vi **1.** [avoir un bébé] to have a baby, to give birth **2.** tfam [parler] ▶ **accouche !** spit it out!, let's have it! ◆ vt : *c'est lui qui l'a accouchée* he delivered her baby. ❖ **accoucher de** v + prép **1.** [enfant] to give birth to, to have **2.** fam [produire] to come up with, to produce.

accouder [3] [akude] ❖ **s'accouder** vpi : *s'accouder à la fenêtre* to lean out of the window ▶ **être accoudé à qqch** to lean on sthg.

accoudoir [akudwaʀ] nm armrest.

accouplement [akupləmɑ̃] nm ZOOL mating.

accoupler [3] [akuple] vt [raccorder - mots] to link ou to join (together) ; MÉCAN to couple, to connect ; ÉLECTR to connect. ❖ **s'accoupler** vpi [animaux] to mate.

accourir [45] [akuʀiʀ] vi to run, to rush.

accoutré, e [akutʀe] adj péj : *être bizarrement accoutré* to be strangely got up.

accoutrement [akutʀəmɑ̃] nm outfit.

accoutrer [3] [akutʀe] ❖ **s'accoutrer** vp *(emploi réfléchi)* péj to get dressed up.

accoutumance [akutymɑ̃s] nf **1.** [adaptation] habituation **2.** [d'un toxicomane] addiction, dependency.

accoutumé, e [akutyme] adj usual, customary. ❖ **comme à l'accoutumée** loc adv *sout* as usual, as always.

accoutumer [3] [akutyme] vt ▶ **accoutumer qqn à (faire) qqch** to accustom sb to (doing) sthg, to get sb used to (doing) sthg. ❖ **s'accoutumer à** vp + prép to get used to.

accréditation [akʀeditajɔ̃] nf FIN accreditation.

accréditer [3] [akʀedite] vt [rumeur, nouvelle] to substantiate, to give credence to ; [personne] to accredit ▶ **accréditer qqn auprès de** to accredit sb to.

accro [akʀo] fam ◆ adj hooked ▶ **être accro à qqch a)** [drogue] to be hooked on sthg **b)** fig to be hooked on ou really into sthg. ◆ nmf fanatic.

Accrobranche® [akʀobʀɑ̃ʃ] nf treetop walking.

accroc [akʀo] nm **1.** [déchirure] tear, rip / *faire un accroc à sa chemise* to tear ou to rip one's shirt **2.** [incident] snag, hitch ▶ **un voyage sans accroc** ou **accrocs** an uneventful trip.

accrochage [akʀoʃaʒ] nm **1.** [collision - entre véhicules] collision / *ce n'est qu'un tout petit accrochage* it's only a scratch **2.** [querelle] quarrel, squabble ▶ **avoir un accrochage avec qqn** to clash with sb **3.** [combat] skirmish.

accroche [akʀoʃ] nf attention-getter, attention-catcher *(in advertising)*.

accrocher [3] [akʀoʃe] ◆ vt **1.** [suspendre - tableau] to hang ; [- manteau, rideau] to hang up *(sép)* **2.** [saisir] to hook **3.** [relier] ▶ **accrocher qqch à** to tie sthg (on) to / *accrocher un wagon à un train* to couple ou to hitch a wagon to a train **4.** [retenir l'intérêt de] to grab the attention of ; [attirer - regard] to catch **5.** [déchirer - collant, vêtement] to snag, to catch **6.** [heurter - piéton] to hit. ◆ vi fam [bien fonctionner] : *ça n'a pas accroché entre eux* they didn't hit it off / *je n'ai jamais accroché en physique* I never really got into physics / *en musique, il a tout de suite accroché* he took to music straight away. ❖ **s'accrocher** ◆ vp *(emploi passif)* to hang, to hook on. ◆ vp *(emploi réciproque)* **1.** [entrer en collision - voitures] to crash (into each other), to collide ; [- boxeurs] to clinch **2.** [se disputer] to clash / *ils ne peuvent pas se supporter, ils vont s'accrocher tout de suite* they can't stand each other so they're bound to start arguing straight away. ◆ vpi fam [persévérer - athlète, concurrent] to apply o.s. / *avec lui, il faut s'accrocher !* he's hard work! ◆ vpt EXPR ▶ **tu peux te l'accrocher ! a)** tfam [tu ne l'auras jamais] you can whistle for it! **b)** [tu ne l'auras plus] you can kiss it goodbye! ❖ **s'accrocher à** vp + prép ▶ **s'accrocher au pouvoir / à la vie / à qqn** fig to cling to power / to life / to sb. ❖ **s'accrocher avec** vp + prép to clash with.

accrocheur, euse [akʀoʃœʀ, øz] fam adj **1.** [tenace - vendeur] pushy **2.** [attirant - titre] eye-catching ; [- slogan, tube] catchy ; [- sourire] beguiling.

accroissement [akʀwasmɑ̃] nm [augmentation] : *l'accroissement de la population* population growth ▶ **accroissement naturel** natural growth.

accroître, accroitre* [94] [akʀwatʀ] vt [fortune, sentiment] to increase ; [désordre] to spread ; [domaine] to add (on) to ; [popularité] to enhance. ❖ **s'accroître, s'accroitre*** vpi [tension] to rise ; [sentiment] to grow ; [population] to rise, to increase, to grow.

---

* In reformed spelling (see p. 16-18).

accroupir [32] [akʀupiʀ] ❖ **s'accroupir** vpi to squat ou to crouch (down) / *il était accroupi* he was squatting ou crouching.

accu (abr de accumulateur) [aky] nm *fam* battery.

accueil [akœj] nm **1.** [réception - d'invités] welcome, greeting ▸ **faire bon accueil à qqn** to give sb a warm welcome ▸ **faire mauvais accueil à qqn** to give sb a cool reception ▸ **faire bon / mauvais accueil à une proposition** *fig* to receive a proposal warmly / coldly **2.** [bureau, comptoir] desk, reception.

accueillant, e [akœjɑ̃, ɑ̃t] adj [peuple, individu] welcoming, friendly ; [sourire] warm, welcoming ; [maison] hospitable.

accueillir [41] [akœjiʀ] vt **1.** [aller chercher] to meet **2.** [recevoir] ▸ **accueillir qqn froidement** to give sb a cool reception ▸ **être très bien / mal accueilli** to get a very pleasant / poor welcome ▸ **accueillir une idée avec scepticisme / enthousiasme** to greet an idea with scepticism / enthusiasm **3.** [héberger] to house, to accommodate / *j'étais sans abri et ils m'ont accueilli* I was homeless and they took me in ou gave me a home.

acculer [3] [akyle] vt **1.** [bloquer] ▸ **acculer qqn contre qqch** to drive sb back against sthg **2.** [contraindre] ▸ **acculer qqn au désespoir** to drive sb to despair.

accumulateur [akymylatœʀ] nm ÉLECTR (storage) battery, storage cell.

accumulation [akymylasjɔ̃] nf **1.** [action] accumulation, amassing, building up **2.** [collection] mass ; [d'erreurs] series **3.** ÉLECTR storage ▸ **chauffage par accumulation** storage heating ▸ **radiateur à accumulation** storage heater.

accumuler [3] [akymyle] vt **1.** [conserver - boîtes, boutons] to keep ou to hoard (in large quantities), to accumulate ; [- denrées] to stockpile, to hoard ; [- papiers] to keep **2.** [réunir - preuves] to pile on (sép), to accumulate ; [- fortune, argent] to amass ▸ **accumuler les erreurs** to make a series of mistakes. ❖ **s'accumuler** vpi to accumulate, to mount (up), to pile up.

accusateur, trice [akyzatœʀ, tʀis] adj [silence, regard] accusing ; [bilan] incriminating ; [preuve] accusatory, incriminating.

accusation [akyzasjɔ̃] nf **1.** DR charge, indictment ▸ **mettre qqn en accusation** to indict ou to charge sb **2.** [reproche] accusation, charge ▸ **lancer une accusation contre qqn / un parti** to make an accusation against sb / a party.

accusé, e [akyze] nm, f defendant ▸ **l'accusé** the accused. ❖ **accusé de réception** nm acknowledgment of receipt.

accuser [3] [akyze] vt **1.** [désigner comme coupable] to accuse / *je ne t'accuse pas !* I'm not saying you did it! ▸ **tout l'accuse** everything points to his guilt ▸ **accuser qqn de qqch** to accuse sb of sthg ; DR ▸ **accuser qqn de meurtre / viol** to charge sb with murder / rape **2.** [rejeter la responsabilité sur] to blame, to put the blame on **3.** [indiquer] : *son visage accuse une grande fatigue* her face shows how tired she is / *le compteur accuse 130 km/h* the meter's registering ou reading 130 km/h **4.** EXPR ▸ **accuser réception de** to acknowledge receipt of ▸ **accuser le coup a)** BOXE to reel with the punch **b)** [fatigue] to show the strain **c)** [moralement] to take it badly. ❖ **s'accuser** vp *(emploi réfléchi)* to accuse o.s.

acerbe [asɛʀb] adj [parole, critique] cutting, acerbic.

acéré, e [aseʀe] adj [lame, pointe] sharp.

acériculture [aseʀikyltyʀ] nf maple sugar production.

acétate [asetat] nm CHIM acetate.

acétone [asetɔn] nf acetone.

achalandage [aʃalɑ̃daʒ] nm ᴼᵁᴱᴮᴱᶜ [fréquentation en grand nombre] popularity.

achalandé, e [aʃalɑ̃de] adj **1.** ▸ **bien achalandé** well-stocked **2.** ᴼᵁᴱᴮᴱᶜ [très fréquenté] busy.

achalant, e [aʃalɑ̃, ɑ̃t] ᴼᵁᴱᴮᴱᶜ ◆ adj annoying. ◆ nm, f [personne] pest, nuisance.

achaler [3] [aʃale] vt ᴼᵁᴱᴮᴱᶜ *fam* to annoy.

acharné, e [aʃaʀne] adj [combat, lutte, concurrence] fierce ; [travail] relentless ; [travailleur] hard ; [joueur] hardened ; [défenseur, partisan] staunch.

acharnement [aʃaʀnəmɑ̃] nm [dans un combat] fury ; [dans le travail] relentlessness, perseverance / *acharnement au travail* dedication to work ▸ **acharnement thérapeutique** use of intensive medication. ❖ **avec acharnement** loc adv [combattre] tooth and nail, furiously ; [travailler] relentlessly ; [résister] fiercely.

acharner [3] [aʃaʀne] ❖ **s'acharner** vpi **1.** ▸ **s'acharner sur** ou **contre** ou **après qqn** [le tourmenter] to persecute ou to hound sb / *le sort s'acharne sur lui* he's dogged by bad luck **2.** ▸ **s'acharner sur qqch** [persévérer] to work (away) at sthg ▸ **s'acharner à faire qqch** to strive to do sthg ; *(en usage absolu)* : *il s'acharne inutilement* he's wasting his efforts.

achat [aʃa] nm **1.** [fait d'acheter] purchasing, buying ▸ **faire un achat** to purchase ou to buy something ▸ **achat groupé** combined purchase ▸ **achats en ligne** online shopping, cybershopping **2.** [article acheté] purchase, buy ▸ **c'est un bon / mauvais achat** it's a good / bad buy.

acheminer [3] [aʃmine] vt **1.** [marchandises] to convey, to forward **2.** RAIL to route ▸ **acheminer un train vers** ou **sur** to route a train to ou towards. ❖ **s'acheminer vers** vp + prép [endroit] to head for ; [accord, solution] to move towards.

acheter [28] [aʃte] vt **1.** [cadeau, objet d'art, denrée] to buy, to purchase ▸ **acheter qqch à qqn a)** [pour soi] to buy sthg from sb **b)** [pour le lui offrir] to buy sb sthg, to buy sthg for sb **2.** [soudoyer - témoin, juge] to bribe, to buy (off) ; [- électeurs] to buy. ❖ **s'acheter** vpt ▸ **s'acheter qqch** to buy o.s. sthg.

> 📋 Notez la construction à double complément qui en anglais peut prendre deux formes sans différence de sens :
>
> • une structure identique à celle du français :
> verbe + COD + préposition + COI
> buy sthg for sb
>
> • une structure qui diffère de celle du français, sans préposition, et dans laquelle l'ordre des compléments est inversé :
> verbe + COI + COD
> buy sb sthg

acheteur, euse [aʃtœʀ, øz] nm, f [client] buyer, purchaser ▸ **acheteur impulsif** impulse buyer.

achevé, e [aʃve] adj [sportif, artiste] accomplished ; [œuvre] perfect ; [style] polished ▸ **d'un ridicule achevé** *sout* utterly ridiculous.

achèvement [aʃɛvmɑ̃] nm completion.

> ⚠ **Achievement** signifie « exploit », « accomplissement » et non achèvement.

achever [19] [aʃve] vt **1.** [finir - repas, discours, lettre] to finish, to end, to bring to a close ou an end ; [- journal, livre] to reach the end of, to finish ▶ **achever de faire qqch** to finish doing sthg ; *(en usage absolu)* [finir de parler] to finish (talking) **2.** [tuer -animal] to destroy ; [-personne] to finish off *(sép).* ❖ **s'achever** vpi [vie, journée, vacances] to come to an end, to draw to a close ou an end ; [dîner, film] to end, to finish ▶ **ainsi s'achève notre journal** RADIO & TV (and) that's the end of the news.

> ⚠ To achieve signifie « accomplir », « réaliser » et non achever.

achoppement [aʃɔpmã] nm ⟶ **pierre**.

achopper [3] [aʃɔpe] vi ▶ **achopper sur a)** *pr & vieilli* to stumble on ou over **b)** *fig* to come up against, to meet with.

acide [asid] ◆ adj [goût] acidic, acid, sour ; [propos] cutting, caustic. ◆ nm CHIM acid ▶ **acide aminé** amino acid ▶ **acide gras saturé / insaturé** saturated / unsaturated fatty acid.

acidité [asidite] nf [d'un goût, d'un fruit] acidity, sourness ; [d'un propos] tartness, sharpness.

acid jazz [asiddʒaz] nm acid jazz.

acidulé, e [asidyle] adj acidulous.

acier [asje] nm steel ▶ **acier inoxydable / trempé** stainless / tempered steel. ❖ **d'acier** loc adj MÉTALL steel *(modif)* ; *fig* [regard] steely.

aciérie [asjeʀi] nf steelworks, steel plant.

acné [akne] nf acne ▶ **acné juvénile** teenage acne.

acolyte [akɔlit] nm **1.** RELIG acolyte **2.** [complice] sidekick.

acompte [akɔ̃t] nm [avance sur -une commande, des travaux] down payment ; [-un salaire] advance ; [-un loyer] deposit.

> ⚠ Account signifie « compte » et non acompte.

acoquiner [3] [akɔkine] ❖ **s'acoquiner** vpi *péj* ▶ **s'acoquiner à** ou **avec qqn** to take ou to team up with sb.

Açores [asɔʀ] npr fpl ▶ **les Açores** the Azores.

à-côté [akote] *(pl* à-côtés*)* nm **1.** [aspect -d'une question] side issue ; [-d'une histoire, d'un événement] side ou secondary aspect **2.** [gain] bit of extra money ; [frais] incidental expense.

à-coup [aku] *(pl* à-coups*)* nm [secousse -d'un moteur, d'un véhicule] cough, judder ; [-d'une machine] jerk, jolt. ❖ **par à-coups** loc adv [travailler] in spurts ; [avancer] in fits and starts. ❖ **sans à-coups** loc adv [se dérouler] smoothly.

acouphène [akufɛn] nm tinnitus.

acoustique [akustik] ◆ adj acoustic. ◆ nf [science] acoustics *(sg)* ; [qualité sonore] acoustics *(pl).*

acquéreur [akeʀœʀ] nm purchaser, buyer ▶ **se porter acquéreur de qqch** to announce one's intention to buy ou purchase sthg.

acquérir [39] [akeʀiʀ] vt **1.** [biens] to buy, to purchase, to acquire ; [fortune] to acquire **2.** *fig* [habitude] to develop ; [célébrité] to attain, to achieve ; [droit] to obtain ; [expérience] to gain ; [savoir-faire] to acquire ; [information, preuve] to obtain, to get hold of. ❖ **s'acquérir** vpt ▶ **s'acquérir la confiance de qqn** to gain ou to win sb's trust.

acquiescement [akjɛsmã] nm [accord] agreement ; [consentement] assent, agreement.

acquiescer [21] [akjese] vi to agree, to approve / *acquiescer d'un signe de tête* to nod (one's) approval.

acquis, e [aki, iz] ◆ pp ⟶ **acquérir**. ◆ adj **1.** [avantage, droit, fait] established ; [fortune, titre] acquired ▶ **tenir qqch pour acquis** : *je tiens votre soutien pour acquis* I take it for granted that you'll support me **2.** [personne] ▶ **être acquis à une cause** to be a committed supporter of a cause. ❖ **acquis** nm **1.** [savoir] knowledge **2.** [expérience] experience **3.** [avantages, droits] established privileges, rights to which one is entitled ▶ **les acquis sociaux** social benefits.

acquisition [akizisjɔ̃] nf **1.** [apprentissage] acquisition **2.** [achat] purchase ▶ **faire l'acquisition d'une maison** to buy ou to purchase a house ▶ **nouvelle acquisition a)** [achat] new purchase **b)** [dans un musée] new acquisition.

acquit [aki] nm COMM receipt / **'pour acquit'** 'paid', 'received (with thanks)'. ❖ **par acquit de conscience** loc adv in order to set my / his, etc. mind at rest.

acquittement [akitmã] nm **1.** [règlement -d'une facture, d'une dette] payment ; [-d'une obligation] discharge ; [-d'une promesse] fulfilment ; [-d'une dette] paying off ; [-d'une fonction, d'un travail] performance ; [-d'un engagement] fulfilment **2.** DR acquittal.

acquitter [3] [akite] vt [payer -facture, note] to pay, to settle ; [-droits] to pay. ❖ **s'acquitter de** vp + prép [obligation] to discharge ; [promesse] to carry out ; [dette] to pay off ; [fonction, travail] to perform ; [engagement] to fulfil.

âcre [akʀ] adj [saveur, odeur] acrid.

acrimonie [akʀimɔni] nf acrimony, acrimoniousness.

acrobate [akʀɔbat] nmf [gén] acrobat ; [au trapèze] trapeze artist.

acrobatie [akʀɔbasi] nf **1.** SPORT acrobatics *(pl)* **2.** *fig* : *il a réussi à remonter son affaire par quelques acrobaties* he managed to save his business by doing some skilful manœuvring **3.** AÉRON ▶ **acrobaties aériennes** ou **en vol** aerobatics *(pl).*

acrobatique [akʀɔbatik] adj acrobatic.

acrosport [akʀɔspɔʀ] nm acrosport.

acrylique [akʀilik] adj & nm acrylic.

acte [akt]
nm

A. SÉQUENCE D'UNE ŒUVRE MUS & THÉÂTRE act.

B. ACTION 1. [gén] action, act ▶ **juger qqn sur ses actes** to judge sb by his / her actions ▶ **acte de bravoure** act of bravery, brave deed, courageous act ▶ **acte gratuit** PHILOS gratuitous act, acte gratuit *spéc* ▶ **acte sexuel** sex act ▶ **acte de terrorisme** terrorist action, act of terrorism ▶ **faire acte de candidature a)** [chercheur d'emploi] to submit one's application, to apply **b)** [maire] to stand 🇬🇧, to run 🇺🇸 ▶ **faire acte d'autorité** to show one's authority ▶ **faire acte de bonne volonté** to show willing ▶ **faire acte de présence** to put in an appearance **2.** MÉD ▶ **acte (médical) a)** [consultation] (medical) consultation **b)** [traitement] (medical) treatment **3.** PSYCHOL ▶ **passer à l'acte a)** [gén] to act **b)** [névrosé, psychopathe] to act out ▶ **acte manqué** acte manqué / *c'était peut-être un acte manqué* maybe subconsciously I / he did it deliberately.

C. DOCUMENT, ACTION LÉGALE 1. DR act, action **2.** POL [en Grande-Bretagne] ▶ **l'Acte unique européen** the Single European Act **3.** ADMIN certificate ▶ **acte de décès** death certificate ▶ **acte de naissance** birth certificate ▶ **dont acte** duly noted ou acknowledged ▶ **prendre acte de qqch a)** [faire constater légalement] to record sthg **b)** [noter] to take a note of ou to note sthg **4.** [en droit pénal] ▶ **acte d'accusation** (bill of) indictment **5.** [en droit civil] ▶ **acte authentique** ou

notarié notarial act **6.** [en droit commercial] ▶ **acte de vente** bill of sale. ❖ **actes** nmpl [procès-verbaux] proceedings ; [annales] annals.

acter [akte] vt to formally record / **acter une décision** to formally record a decision.

acteur, trice [aktœʀ, tʀis] nm, f CINÉ & THÉÂTRE actor (actress) ▶ **acteur comique** comic actor ▶ **actrice comique** comedienne, comic actress.

actif, ive [aktif, iv] adj **1.** [qui participe - membre, militaire, supporter] active ▶ **participer de façon** ou **prendre une part active à** to take part fully ou an active part in **2.** [dynamique - vie] busy, active ; [-personne] active, lively, energetic **3.** [qui travaille - population] working, active. ❖ **actif** nm **1.** LING active voice **2.** [travailleur] member of the active ou working population ▶ **les actifs** the active ou working population **3.** FIN & DR [patrimoine] credit, credits, asset, assets ▶ **avoir qqch à son actif** to have sthg to one's credit.

action [aksjɔ̃] nf **1.** [acte] action, act / **responsable de ses actions** responsible for his actions ▶ **l'action humanitaire** humanitarian aid ▶ **faire une bonne action** to do a good deed ▶ **faire une mauvaise action** to commit an evil deed **2.** [activité] action (U) ▶ **passer à l'action** to take action / **dans le feu de l'action, en pleine action** right in the middle ou at the heart of the action / **l'action se passe en Europe** ou **l'an 2000** the action takes place in Europe / the year 2000 **3.** [intervention] action ▶ **une action syndicale est à prévoir** some industrial action is expected **4.** [effet] action, effect / **un médicament à l'action lente** a slow-acting medicine **5.** FIN share ▶ **action différée / nominative** deferred / registered stock ▶ **action au porteur** transferable ou bearer share **6.** DR action, lawsuit ▶ **intenter une action contre** ou **à qqn** to bring an action against sb, to take legal action against sb, to take sb to court ▶ **action civile / en diffamation** civil / libel action **7.** GRAM action **8.** Suisse [vente promotionnelle] sale, special offer. ❖ **d'action** loc adj **1.** [mouvementé - roman] action-packed ▶ **film d'action** action film **2.** [qui aime agir] ▶ **homme / femme d'action** man / woman of action **3.** POL & SOCIOL ▶ **journée / semaine d'action** day / week of action. ❖ **en action** loc adv & loc adj in action ▶ **entrer en action a)** [pompiers, police] to go into action **b)** [loi, règlement] to become effective, to take effect ▶ **mettre qqch en action** to set sthg in motion / **la sirène s'est / a été mise en action** the alarm went off / was set off. ❖ **sous l'action de** loc prép due to, because of.

actionnaire [aksjɔnɛʀ] nmf shareholder UK, stockholder US ▶ **actionnaire majoritaire / minoritaire** majority / minority shareholder, majority / minority stockholder.

actionner [3] [aksjɔne] vt [mettre en mouvement - appareil] to start up *(sép)* ; [-sirène] to set off *(sép)* ; [-sonnette] to ring.

activement [aktivmɑ̃] adv actively ▶ **participer activement à qqch** to take an active part ou to be actively engaged in sthg.

activer [3] [aktive] vt **1.** [feu] to stoke (up) ; [travaux, processus] to speed up **2.** fam [presser] ▶ **active le pas !** get a move on! ❖ **s'activer** vpi **1.** [s'affairer] to bustle about **2.** fam [se dépêcher] : **il est tard, dis-leur de s'activer !** it's late, tell them to get a move on.

activisme [aktivism] nm activism.

activiste [aktivist] adj & nmf activist, militant.

activité [aktivite] nf **1.** [animation] activity (U) / **le restaurant / l'aéroport débordait d'activité** the restaurant / airport was very busy **2.** ADMIN & ÉCON ▶ **avoir une activité professionnelle** to be actively employed ▶ **être sans activité** to be unemployed ▶ **cesser ses activités** [entreprise] to cease trading **3.** [occupation] activity ▶ **pratiquer**

une activité physique régulière to take regular exercise ▶ **mes activités professionnelles** my professional activities. ❖ **en activité** loc adj [fonctionnaire, militaire] (currently) in post ; [médecin] practising. ❖ **en pleine activité** loc adj [industrie, usine] fully operational ; [bureau, restaurant] bustling ; [marché boursier, secteur] very busy ▶ **être en pleine activité a)** [très affairé] to be very busy **b)** [non retraité] to be in the middle of one's working life.

actu [akty] **(abr de actualité)** nf : **l'actu** the (latest) news.

actualisation [aktɥalizasjɔ̃] nf [mise à jour - d'un texte] updating.

actualiser [3] [aktɥalize] vt [manuel] to update, to bring up to date.

actualité [aktɥalite] nf **1.** [caractère actuel] topicality **2.** [événements récents] current developments / **se tenir au courant de l'actualité politique / théâtrale** to keep abreast of political / theatrical events. ❖ **actualités** nfpl ▶ **les actualités** [les informations] current affairs, the news. ❖ **d'actualité** loc adj [film, débat, roman] topical ▶ **c'est un sujet d'actualité** it's very topical (at the moment).

⚠️ **Actuality** signifie « réalité » et non actualité.

actuel, elle [aktɥɛl] adj **1.** [présent] present, current ▶ **à l'époque actuelle** nowadays, in this day and age **2.** [d'actualité] topical.

⚠️ **Actual** signifie « réel » et non actuel.

actuellement [aktɥɛlmɑ̃] adv [à présent] at present, at the moment ; [de nos jours] nowadays, currently.

⚠️ **Actually** signifie « en fait », « vraiment » et non actuellement.

acuité [akɥite] nf **1.** [intensité - de l'intelligence] sharpness ; [-d'une crise] severity ; [-du regard] penetration ; [-d'un chagrin] keenness ; [-d'une douleur] intensity, acuteness **2.** MÉD acuity, acuteness ▶ **acuité visuelle** acuteness of vision.

acuponcteur, trice, acupuncteur, trice [akypɔ̃ktœʀ, tʀis] nm, f acupuncturist.

acuponcture, acupuncture [akypɔ̃ktyʀ] nf acupuncture.

adage [adaʒ] nm [maxime] adage, saying.

adaptateur, trice [adaptatœʀ, tʀis] nm, f [personne] adapter, adaptor. ❖ **adaptateur** nm [objet] adapter, adaptor.

adaptation [adaptasjɔ̃] nf [flexibilité] adaptation ▶ **faculté d'adaptation** adaptability / **ils n'ont fait aucun effort d'adaptation** they didn't try to adapt.

adapter [3] [adapte] vt **1.** ▶ **adapter qqch à** [harmoniser qqch avec] : **adapter son discours à son public** to fit one's language to one's audience **2.** CINÉ, THÉÂTRE & TV to adapt. ❖ **s'adapter** vpi **1.** [s'ajuster] ▶ **s'adapter à** to fit ▶ **s'adapter sur** to fit on **2.** [s'habituer] to adapt (o.s.) ▶ **savoir s'adapter** to be adaptable.

addictif, ive [adiktif, iv] adj addictive.

addictologie [adiktɔlɔʒi] nf addictology ▶ **centre d'addictologie** centre for addictology.

additif [aditif] nm **1.** [à un texte] additional clause **2.** [ingrédient] additive.

addition [adisjɔ̃] nf **1.** MATH sum ▸ **faire une addition** to add (figures) up, to do a sum **2.** [facture] bill 🇬🇧, check 🇺🇸.

additionnel, elle [adisjɔnɛl] adj additional.

additionner [3] [adisjɔne] vt **1.** MATH [nombres] to add (up) / *additionner 15 et 57* to add 15 and 57, to add 15 to 57, to add together 15 and 57 **2.** [altérer] ▸ **additionner qqch de** : *du vin / lait additionné d'eau* watered-down wine / milk. ❖ **s'additionner** vpi to build up.

adduction [adyksjɔ̃] nf TRAV PUB ▸ **adduction d'eau** water conveyance.

adepte [adɛpt] nmf **1.** RELIG & POL follower **2.** fig ▸ **faire des adeptes** to become popular.

⚠ Le mot anglais **adept** signifie « expert » et non **adepte**.

adéquat, e [adekwa, at] adj suitable, appropriate.

adéquation [adekwasjɔ̃] nf appropriateness ▸ **être en adéquation avec qqch** to match sthg.

adhérence [aderɑ̃s] nf **1.** [par la colle, le ciment] adhesion **2.** [au sol] adhesion, grip / *le manque d'adhérence d'une voiture* a car's lack of ou poor road-holding.

adhérent, e [aderɑ̃, ɑ̃t] ◆ adj [gén] adherent. ◆ nm, f member.

adhérer [18] [adere] ❖ **adhérer à** v + prép **1.** [coller sur] to adhere to ▸ **adhérer à la route** to hold the road **2.** [se rallier à - opinion] to adhere to, to support ; [- cause] to support ; [- idéal] to adhere to ; [- association] to join, to become a member of.

📝 In reformed spelling (see p. 16-18), this verb is conjugated like *semer* : *elle adhèrera, il adhèrerait.*

adhésif, ive [adezif, iv] adj adhesive, sticky. ❖ **adhésif** nm [ruban] sticky tape, Sellotape® 🇬🇧, Scotch tape® 🇺🇸.

adhésion [adezjɔ̃] nf **1.** [accord] support, adherence **2.** [inscription] membership.

⚠ Le mot anglais **adhesion** a des emplois particuliers et ne peut être employé systématiquement pour traduire **adhésion**.

adieu, x [adjø] nm farewell *litt*, good-bye ▸ **dire adieu à qqn** to say good-bye ou farewell to sb ▸ **tu peux dire adieu à ta voiture / tes ambitions** you can say good-bye to your car / ambitions ▸ **faire ses adieux à qqn** to say good-bye ou one's farewells to sb ▸ **faire ses adieux à la scène / au music-hall** to make one's final appearance on stage / on a music-hall stage.

adjectif [adʒɛktif] nm adjective ▸ **adjectif possessif** possessive adjective.

adjoindre [82] [adjwɛ̃dʀ] vt [ajouter] ▸ **adjoindre à** to add to. ❖ **s'adjoindre** vpt ▸ **s'adjoindre qqn** to take sb on.

adjoint, e [adʒwɛ̃, ɛ̃t] ◆ adj assistant *(modif.)*. ◆ nm, f [assistant] assistant ▸ **adjoint au maire** deputy mayor.

adjonction [adʒɔ̃ksjɔ̃] nf **1.** [fait d'ajouter] adding / **'sans adjonction de sucre / sel'** 'with no added sugar / salt' **2.** [chose ajoutée] addition.

adjudant, e [adʒydɑ̃, ɑ̃t] nm, f MIL [dans l'armée de terre] ≃ warrant officer 2nd class 🇬🇧 ; ≃ warrant officer 🇺🇸 ; [dans l'armée de l'air] ≃ warrant officer 🇬🇧 ; ≃ chief master sergeant 🇺🇸.

adjudication [adʒydikasjɔ̃] nf **1.** [enchères] auction sale ; [attribution] auctioning (off) **2.** COMM [appel d'offres] invitation to tender 🇬🇧 ou bid 🇺🇸 ; [attribution] awarding, allocation.

adjuger [17] [adʒyʒe] vt [aux enchères] ▸ **adjuger qqch à qqn** to knock sthg down to sb / *adjuger un objet au plus offrant* to sell an item to the highest bidder / *une fois, deux fois, trois fois, adjugé, vendu !* going, going, gone! ❖ **s'adjuger** vpt to take / *elle s'est adjugé la plus jolie chambre* she took ou commandeered the prettiest room.

adjuvant [adʒyvɑ̃] nm [produit] additive.

ADM [adɛm] (abr de **arme de destruction massive**) nf WMD.

admettre [84] [admɛtʀ] vt **1.** [laisser entrer - client, spectateur] to allow ou to let in *(sép)* / **'on n'admet pas les animaux'** 'pets are not allowed', 'no pets' **2.** [recevoir] ▸ **admettre qqn dans un groupe** to let ou to allow sb into a group ▸ **admettre qqn dans un club** to admit sb to (membership of) a club / *elle a été admise à l'Académie / à l'hôpital* she was elected to the Académie / admitted to hospital **3.** ENS to pass ▸ **être admis** to pass **4.** [reconnaître] to admit to / *j'admets m'être trompé* I admit ou accept that I made a mistake / *il faut admettre que c'est un résultat inattendu* you've got to admit that the result is unexpected ; [accepter] : *il n'a pas reçu ta lettre, admettons* OK, so he didn't get your letter **5.** [permettre - suj : personne] to tolerate, to stand for *(insép)* ; [- suj : chose] to allow, to admit ou to be susceptible of *sout* / *tout texte admet de multiples interprétations* any text can lend itself to many different readings ▸ **un ton qui n'admet pas la discussion** ou **réplique** a tone brooking no argument / *le règlement n'admet aucune dérogation* there shall be no breach of the regulations / *je n'admets pas d'être accusé sans preuve* I refuse to let myself be accused without proof / *je n'admets pas qu'on me parle sur ce ton !* I won't tolerate ou stand for this kind of talk! **6.** [supposer] to assume. ❖ **admettons que** loc conj let's suppose ou assume, supposing, assuming.

administrateur, trice [administʀatœʀ, tʀis] nm, f **1.** [dans une société] director / *il est l'administrateur / elle est l'administratrice de l'entreprise* he's / she's the director of the firm ▸ **administrateur de biens** property manager ▸ **administrateur judiciaire** receiver **2.** [dans une institution, une fondation] trustee.

administratif, ive [administʀatif, iv] adj administrative.

administration [administʀasjɔ̃] nf **1.** [fait de donner] ▸ **l'administration d'un remède / sédatif** administering a remedy / sedative **2.** [gestion - d'une entreprise] management ; [- d'une institution] administration ; [- de biens] management, administration ; [- d'un pays] government, running ; [- d'une commune] running ▸ **administration judiciaire** : *être placé sous administration judiciaire* to go into administration **3.** [fonction publique] ▸ **l'Administration** the Civil Service ▸ **entrer dans l'Administration** to become a civil servant, to enter the Civil Service **4.** [service public] ▸ **administration communale** local government ▸ **l'administration des Impôts** the Inland Revenue 🇬🇧, the Internal Revenue Service 🇺🇸 **5.** [équipe présidentielle] ▸ **l'Administration Obama** the Obama administration.

administrer [3] [administʀe] vt **1.** [diriger - entreprise] to manage ; [- institution, fondation, département, bien] to administer, to run ; [- succession] to be a trustee of ; [- pays] to govern, to run ; [- commune] to run **2.** [donner - remède, sacrement] to administer ; [- gifle, fessée] to give.

admirable [admiʀabl] adj admirable.

admirablement [admiʀabləmɑ̃] adv wonderfully.

admirateur, trice [admiʀatœʀ, tʀis] nm, f admirer.

admiratif, ive [admiʀatif, iv] adj admiring.

admiration [admiʀasjɔ̃] nf admiration, wonder ▸ **être en admiration devant qqn / qqch** to be filled with admiration for sb / sthg.

admirer [3] [admiʀe] vt to admire.

admissible [admisibl] adj **1.** [procédé, excuse] acceptable / *il n'est pas admissible que...* it is unacceptable that... **2.** ENS [après la première partie] *eligible to take the second part of an exam* ; [après l'écrit] *eligible to take the oral exam.*

admission [admisjɔ̃] nf [accueil] admission, admittance, entry ▸ **demande d'admission a)** [à l'hôpital] admission form **b)** [dans un club] membership application.

admonester [3] [admɔnɛste] vt *litt* to admonish.

ADN (abr de **acide désoxyribonucléique**) nm DNA ▸ **test ADN** DNA test.

ado [ado] (abr de **adolescent**) nmf *fam* teenager.

adolescence [adɔlesɑ̃s] nf adolescence.

adolescent, e [adɔlesɑ̃, ɑ̃t] nm, f adolescent, teenager.

adonner [3] [adɔne] ◈ **s'adonner à** vp + prép [lecture, sport, loisirs] to devote o.s. to, to go in for ; [travail, études] to devote o.s. to, to immerse o.s. in ▸ **s'adonner à la boisson / au jeu** to take to drink / to gambling ▸ **être adonné à qqch** to be addicted to sthg.

adopter [3] [adɔpte] vt **1.** [enfant] to adopt **2.** [suivre - cause] to take up *(sép)* ; [-point de vue] to adopt, to approve ; [-politique] to adopt, to take up ; [-loi, projet] to adopt, to pass ; [-mode] to follow, to adopt **3.** [se mettre dans - position, posture] to adopt, to assume **4.** [emprunter - nom] to assume ; [-accent] to put on *(sép)* ▸ **adopter un profil bas** to adopt a low profile.

adoptif, ive [adɔptif, iv] adj [enfant] adopted ; [parent] adoptive ; [patrie] adopted.

adoption [adɔpsjɔ̃] nf **1.** [d'un enfant] adoption **2.** [d'une loi, d'un projet] adoption, passing. ◈ **d'adoption** loc adj [pays] adopted ▸ **c'est un Parisien d'adoption** he's Parisian by adoption, he's adopted Paris as his home town.

adorable [adɔrabl] adj [charmant - personne] adorable ; [-endroit] beautiful ; [-vêtement] lovely ; [-sourire] charming.

adorateur, trice [adɔratœr, tris] nm, f RELIG worshipper [UK], worshiper [US].

adoration [adɔrasjɔ̃] nf [admiration] adoration ▸ **être en adoration devant qqn** to dote on ou to worship sb.

adorer [3] [adɔre] vt [aimer - personne] to adore, to love ; [-maison, robe, livre] to love, to adore.

adosser [3] [adose] vt ▸ **adosser qqch à ou contre qqch** to put sthg (up) against sthg. ◈ **s'adosser** vpi ▸ **s'adosser à ou contre qqch** to lean against sthg.

adoucir [32] [adusir] vt **1.** [rendre plus doux - peau, regard, voix, eau] to soften ; [-amertume, caractère, acidité] to take the edge off ▸ **l'âge l'a beaucoup adouci** he's mellowed a lot with age **2.** [atténuer - couleur, propos, dureté] to tone down *(sép)* ; [-difficulté, antagonisme] to ease **3.** [rendre supportable - peine, punition] to reduce, to lessen the severity of ; [-chagrin] to ease. ◈ **s'adoucir** vpi **1.** [devenir plus doux - peau, voix, lumière] to soften ; [-regard] to soften ; [-personne, caractère] to mellow **2.** MÉTÉO [temps, température] to become milder.

adoucissant, e [adusisɑ̃, ɑ̃t] adj emollient. ◈ **adoucissant** nm [pour le linge] fabric conditioner.

adoucisseur [adusisœr] nm ▸ **adoucisseur (d'eau)** water softener.

adrénaline [adrenalin] nf adrenalin.

adresse [adrɛs] nf **1.** [domicile] address ▸ **parti sans laisser d'adresse** gone without leaving a forwarding address ▸ **une bonne adresse a)** [magasin] a good shop [UK] ou store [US] **b)** [restaurant] a good restaurant **c)** [hôtel] a good hotel **2.** [dextérité] skill, dexterity, deftness ▸ **jeu d'adresse** game of skill **3.** INFORM address **4.** ▸ **adresse électronique** e-mail address ▸ **adresse IP** IP address

▸ **adresse URL** URL address. ◈ **à l'adresse de** loc prép intended for, aimed at.

adresser [4] [adrese] vt **1.** [envoyer] ▸ **adresser qqch à qqn a)** [gén] to address ou to direct sthg to sb **b)** [par courrier] to send ou to forward sthg to sb **2.** [libeller] to address ▸ **adresser qqch à qqn** to address sthg to sb **3.** [destiner] ▸ **adresser qqch à qqn** [une remarque] to address sthg to ou to direct sthg at sb ▸ **adresser la parole à qqn** to speak to sb ▸ **adresser un compliment à qqn** to pay sb a compliment ▸ **adresser un reproche à qqn** to level a reproach at sb ▸ **adresser un signe à qqn** to wave at sb ▸ **adresser un sourire à qqn** to smile at sb **4.** [diriger - personne] : *adresser un malade à un spécialiste* to refer a patient to a specialist / *on m'a adressé à vous* I've been referred to you **5.** INFORM to address. ◈ **s'adresser à** vp + prép **1.** [parler à] to speak to, to address / *c'est à vous que je m'adresse* I'm talking to you ▸ **s'adresser à la conscience / générosité de qqn** *fig* to appeal to sb's conscience / generosity **2.** [être destiné à] to be meant for ou aimed at / *à qui s'adresse cette remarque ?* who's this remark aimed at? **3.** [pour se renseigner] ▸ **adressez-vous à la concierge** you'd better see the porter.

Adriatique [adrijatik] ◆ adj Adriatic ▸ **la mer Adriatique** the Adriatic Sea. ◆ npr f ▸ **l'Adriatique** the Adriatic (Sea).

adroit, e [adrwa, at] adj **1.** [habile - gén] deft, dexterous ; [-apprenti, sportif, artisan] skilful [UK], skillful [US] ▸ **être adroit de ses mains** to be clever with one's hands **2.** [astucieux - manœuvre] clever ; [-diplomate] skilful ; [-politique] clever.

adroitement [adrwatmɑ̃] adv **1.** [avec des gestes habiles] skilfully [UK], skillfully [US] **2.** [astucieusement] cleverly.

ADSL (abr de **asymmetric digital subscriber line**) nm ADSL ▸ **liaison** ou **connexion ADSL** ADSL connection.

aduler [3] [adyle] vt *litt* to adulate, to fawn upon *(insép)*.

adulte [adylt] ◆ adj **1.** [individu] adult ; [attitude] mature **2.** ZOOL full-grown, adult ; BOT full-grown. ◆ nmf adult.

adultère [adyltɛr] ◆ adj [relation] adulterous. ◆ nm [infidélité] adultery.

advenir [40] [advənir] vi to happen. ◈ **il advient** v impers : *qu'est-il advenu de lui ?* what ou whatever became of him? ▸ **il advient que...** it (so) happens that... / *quoi qu'il advienne, quoi qu'il puisse advenir* come what may, whatever may happen ▸ **advienne que pourra** come what may.

adverbe [advɛrb] nm adverb.

adversaire [advɛrsɛr] nmf adversary, opponent.

> ⚠ D'un registre plus soutenu, **adversary** ne peut être employé systématiquement pour traduire adversaire.

adverse [advɛrs] adj [bloc, opinion] opposing.

adversité [advɛrsite] nf adversity.

AELE (abr de **Association européenne de libre-échange**) npr f EFTA.

aération [aerasjɔ̃] nf TECHNOL [d'une pièce] airing, ventilation.

aéré, e [aere] adj **1.** [chambre] well-ventilated, airy **2.** [présentation, texte] well-spaced.

aérer [18] [aere] vt **1.** [ventiler - chambre, maison] to air, to ventilate **2.** [alléger] : *aère un peu ton texte avant de le rendre* improve the presentation of your text before handing it in. ◈ **s'aérer** vp *(emploi réfléchi)* to get some fresh air.

📝 In reformed spelling (see p. 16-18), this verb is conjugated like *semer* : *il aèrera, elle aèrerait.*

aérien, enne [aeʁjɛ̃, ɛn] adj **1.** AÉRON [tarif, base, raid, catastrophe] air *(modif)* ; [combat, photographie] aerial **2.** [à l'air libre - câble] overhead.

aérobic [aeʁɔbik] nm aerobics *(U).*

aéro-club *(pl* aéro-clubs), **aéroclub*** [aeʁɔklœb] nm flying club.

aérodrome [aeʁɔdʁom] nm airfield.

aérodynamique [aeʁɔdinamik] ◆ adj [étude, soufflerie] aerodynamic ; [ligne, profil, voiture] streamlined. ◆ nf aerodynamics *(U).*

aérogare [aeʁɔgaʁ] nf [pour les marchandises] airport building ; [pour les voyageurs] air terminal.

aéroglisseur [aeʁɔglisœʁ] nm hovercraft.

aéronautique [aeʁɔnotik] ◆ adj aeronautic, aeronautical ▸ **l'industrie aéronautique** the aviation industry. ◆ nf aeronautics *(U).*

aéronaval, e, als [aeʁɔnaval] adj [bataille] air and sea *(modif).* ❖ **aéronavale** nf ▸ **l'aéronavale** ≃ Fleet Air Arm [UK] ; ≃ Naval Air Command [US].

aérophagie [aeʁɔfaʒi] nf wind, aerophagia *spéc* ▸ **avoir ou faire de l'aérophagie** to have wind.

aéroport [aeʁɔpɔʁ] nm airport.

aéroporté, e [aeʁɔpɔʁte] adj MIL airborne.

aéroportuaire [aeʁɔpɔʁtɥeʁ] adj airport *(modif).*

aérosol [aeʁɔsɔl] nm COMM aerosol. ❖ **en aérosol** *loc adj* spray *(modif)* / **nous l'avons aussi en aérosol** we also have it in spray form.

aérospatial, e, aux [aeʁɔspasjal, o] adj aerospace *(modif).* ❖ **aérospatiale** nf INDUST aerospace industry.

affable [afabl] adj *sout* affable, friendly.

affabulateur, trice [afabylatœʁ, tʁis] nmf inveterate liar.

affaiblir [32] [afebliʁ] vt [personne] to weaken. ❖ **s'affaiblir** vpi **1.** [dépérir] to weaken, to become weaker / **s'affaiblir de jour en jour** to get weaker and weaker every day, to get weaker by the day **2.** [s'atténuer - signification, impact] to weaken, to grow weaker ; [-lumière] to fade.

affaiblissement [afeblismɑ̃] nm [d'une personne, d'une idée, d'un sentiment] weakening ; [d'une lumière, d'un bruit] fading.

affaire [afɛʁ] nf **1.** [société] business, firm, company ▸ **monter une affaire** to set up a business ▸ **gérer** ou **diriger une affaire** to run a business **2.** [marché] business deal ou transaction ▸ **faire affaire avec qqn** to have dealings with sb ▸ **faire une (bonne) affaire** to get a (good) bargain **3.** [problème, situation délicate] business / **ce n'est pas une mince affaire, c'est tout une affaire** it's quite a business ▸ **sortir** ou **tirer qqn d'affaire** a) [par amitié] to get sb out of trouble b) [médicalement] to pull sb through ▸ **être sorti** ou **tiré d'affaire** a) [après une aventure, une faillite] to be out of trouble ou in the clear b) [après une maladie] to be off the danger list [UK] ou critical list [US] **4.** [scandale] ▸ **affaire d'État** affair of state ▸ **n'en fais pas une affaire d'État !** *fig* don't blow the thing out of all proportion! ▸ **l'affaire Dreyfus** the Dreyfus affair **5.** [ce qui convient] ▸ **la mécanique c'est pas / c'est son affaire** *fam* car engines aren't exactly / are just his cup of tea ▸ **faire son affaire à qqn** *fam*: **je vais lui faire son affaire** I'll sort ou straighten him out! **6.** [responsabilité] ▸ **fais ce que tu veux, c'est ton affaire** do what you like, it's your business ou problem **7.** [question] ▸ **c'est l'affaire d'une seconde** it can be done in a trice / **c'est l'affaire d'un coup de fil** *fam* all it takes is a phone call / **c'est une affaire de vie ou de mort** it's a matter of life and death ▸ **affaire de principe** matter of principle ▸ **affaire de goût** question of taste **8.** [EXPR] **avoir affaire à** to (have to) deal with /

il vaut mieux n'avoir pas affaire à lui it's better to avoid having anything to do with him / **tu vas avoir affaire à moi si tu tires la sonnette !** if you ring the bell, you'll have me to deal with! ▸ **avoir affaire à plus fort / plus malin que soi** to be dealing with someone stronger / more cunning than o.s. ▸ **être à son affaire**: *à la cuisine, il est à son affaire* in the kitchen ou when he's cooking he's in his element. ❖ **affaires** nfpl **1.** COMM & ÉCON business *(U)* ▸ **parler affaires** to talk business ▸ **les affaires vont bien / mal** business is good / bad ▸ **être dans les affaires** to be a businessman (businesswoman) / *les affaires sont les affaires !* business is business! ▸ **pour affaires** [voyager, rencontrer] for business purposes, on business ▸ **voyage / repas d'affaires** business trip / lunch **2.** ADMIN & POL affairs ▸ **être aux affaires** to run the country, to be the head of state ▸ **les affaires courantes** everyday matters ▸ **les affaires de l'État** the affairs of state ▸ **les Affaires étrangères** ≃ the Foreign Office *(sg)* [UK] ; ≃ the State Department *(sg)* [US] ▸ **affaires intérieures** internal ou domestic affairs ▸ **affaires internationales** international affairs ▸ **les affaires** POL *financial scandals involving members of government* **3.** [situation matérielle] : *mettre de l'ordre dans ses affaires (avant de mourir)* to put one's affairs in order (before dying) ; [situation personnelle] : *s'il revient, elle voudra le revoir et ça n'arrangera pas tes affaires* if he comes back, she'll want to see him and that won't help the situation / *mêle-toi de tes affaires !* mind your own business!, keep your nose out of this! / *c'est mes affaires, ça te regarde pas !* *fam* that's MY business! ▸ **affaires de cœur** love life **4.** [objets personnels] things, belongings, (personal) possessions ▸ **ses petites affaires** a) *hum* his little things b) *péj* his precious belongings. ❖ **en affaires** *loc adv* when (you're) doing business, in business ▸ **être dur en affaires** [gén] to drive a hard bargain, to be a tough businessman (businesswoman).

⚠ **Affair** n'est pas toujours la traduction adéquate pour affaire. Voir article.

affairé, e [afeʁe] adj busy.

affairer [4] [afeʁe] ❖ **s'affairer** vpi to bustle.

affairisme [afeʁism] nm *péj* wheeling and dealing.

affairiste [afeʁist] nmf *péj* wheeler-dealer.

affaissement [afɛsmɑ̃] nm **1.** [effondrement] subsidence ▸ **affaissement de sol, affaissement de terrain** subsidence **2.** [relâchement - d'un muscle, des traits] sagging.

affaisser [4] [afese] ❖ **s'affaisser** vpi **1.** [se tasser - gén] to subside, to collapse, to sink ; [-bâtiment] to collapse **2.** [s'affaler] to collapse, to slump.

affaler [3] [afale] vt NAUT [voile] to haul down *(sép).* ❖ **s'affaler** vpi ▸ **s'affaler dans un fauteuil** to flop into an armchair ▸ **s'affaler sur le sol** to collapse on the ground.

affamé, e [afame] adj famished, starving.

affectation [afɛktasjɔ̃] nf **1.** [manière] affectation ▸ **avec affectation** affectedly **2.** [attribution] allocation **3.** [assignation] appointment, nomination ; MIL posting.

affecté, e [afɛkte] adj [personne] affected, mannered.

affecter [4] [afɛkte] vt **1.** [feindre] to affect, to feign / *affecter une grande joie* to pretend to be overjoyed **2.** [assigner] to allocate, to assign / *affecter des crédits à la recherche* to allocate funds to research **3.** [nommer - à une fonction] to appoint, to nominate ; [-à une ville, un pays] to post **4.** [atteindre] to affect **5.** [émouvoir] to affect, to move ▸ **très affecté par cette lettre** / **l'accident de ses parents** greatly affected by this letter / his parents' accident.

affectif, ive [afɛktif, iv] adj **1.** [problème, réaction] emotional **2.** PSYCHOL affective.

affection [afɛksjɔ̃] nf **1.** [attachement] affection, fondness, liking ▸ **avoir de l'affection pour** to be fond of, to have a fondness for, to have a liking for ▸ **prendre qqn en affection** to become fond of sb **2.** MÉD disease, disorder.

affectionner [3] [afɛksjɔne] vt [objet, situation] to be fond of.

affectivité [afɛktivite] nf [réactions] ▸ **l'affectivité** emotionality *spéc*, emotional life.

affectueusement [afɛktɥøzmɑ̃] adv **1.** [tendrement] affectionately, fondly **2.** [dans une lettre] ▸ **bien affectueusement** kindest regards.

affectueux, euse [afɛktɥø, øz] adj loving, affectionate.

affermir [32] [afɛRmiR] vt [consolider - mur] to reinforce, to strengthen. ❖ **s'affermir** vpi [muscle, chair] to firm ou to tone up, to get firmer.

affichage [afiʃaʒ] nm **1.** [sur une surface] posting / **'affichage interdit'** 'stick no bills' **2.** INFORM display ▸ **affichage du numéro** caller display ▸ **affichage numérique** digital display.

affiche [afiʃ] nf **1.** [annonce officielle] public notice ; [image publicitaire] advertisement, poster ; [d'un film, d'une pièce, d'un concert] poster **2.** ▸ **tenir l'affiche** to run ▸ **quitter l'affiche** to close. ❖ **à l'affiche** loc adv ▸ **rester à l'affiche** to run.

afficher [3] [afiʃe] vt **1.** [placarder] to post ou to stick up _(sép)_ **2.** [annoncer] to bill, to have on the bill / *on affiche complet pour ce soir* the house is full tonight. ❖ **s'afficher** vpi **1.** [apparaître] to be displayed **2.** *péj* [se montrer] ▸ **elle s'affiche avec lui** she makes a point of being seen with him.

affichette [afiʃɛt] nf small poster.

afficheur [afiʃœR] nm billposter, billsticker.

affilé, e [afile] adj [aiguisé] sharp. ❖ **d'affilée** loc adv : *il a pris plusieurs semaines de congé d'affilée* he took several weeks' leave in a row ▸ **deux / trois heures d'affilée** for two / three hours at a stretch.

affiler [3] [afile] vt [couteau, lame] to sharpen.

affilié, e [afilje] nm, f affiliate, affiliated member.

affilier [9] [afilje] ❖ **s'affilier** vp *(emploi réfléchi)* ▸ **s'affilier à** to affiliate o.s. ou to become affiliated to.

affiner [3] [afine] vt **1.** [purifier - verre, métal] to refine **2.** [adoucir - traits] to fine down **3.** [raffiner - goût, sens] to refine **4.** [mûrir] ▸ **affiner du fromage** to allow cheese to mature. ❖ **s'affiner** vpi **1.** [se raffiner] to become more refined **2.** [mincir] to become thinner.

affinité [afinite] nf [sympathie] affinity ▸ **avoir des affinités avec qqn** to have an affinity with sb.

affirmatif, ive [afiRmatif, iv] adj [catégorique] affirmative. ❖ **affirmative** nf ▸ **répondre par l'affirmative** to answer yes ou in the affirmative / *nous aimerions savoir si vous serez libre mercredi ; dans l'affirmative, nous vous prions de...* we'd like to know if you are free on Wednesday ; if you are ou if so, please...

affirmation [afiRmasjɔ̃] nf [gén] affirmation.

affirmativement [afiRmativmɑ̃] adv affirmatively.

affirmer [3] [afiRme] vt **1.** [assurer] to assert, to affirm *sout* / *elle affirme ne pas l'avoir vu de la soirée* she maintains she didn't see him all evening **2.** [exprimer - volonté, indépendance] to assert. ❖ **s'affirmer** vpi [personne] to assert o.s. ; [qualité, désir, volonté] to assert ou to express itself.

> ⚠ D'un registre plus soutenu, **to affirm** ne doit pas être employé systématiquement pour traduire affirmer.

affleurer [5] [aflœRe] vi [écueil] to show on the surface ; GÉOL [filon] to outcrop ; *fig* to show through.

affligé, e [afliʒe] adj afflicted.

affligeant, e [afliʒɑ̃, ɑ̃t] adj **1.** *litt* [attristant] distressing **2.** [lamentable] appalling, pathetic.

affliger [17] [afliʒe] vt [atteindre] to afflict, to affect ▸ **être affligé d'un handicap** to be afflicted with a handicap.

affluence [aflyɑ̃s] nf [foule] crowd ▸ **il y a affluence** it's crowded.

affluent [aflyɑ̃] nm tributary, affluent.

affluer [3] [aflye] vi **1.** [couler] to rush ▸ **les capitaux affluent** *fig* money's flowing ou rolling in **2.** [arriver] to surge / *les manifestants affluaient vers la cathédrale* the demonstrators were flocking to the cathedral.

afflux [afly] nm **1.** [de sang] rush, afflux *sout* **2.** [de voyageurs] influx, flood.

affolant, e [afɔlɑ̃, ɑ̃t] adj [inquiétant] frightening, terrifying.

affolé, e [afɔle] adj [bouleversé] panic-stricken.

affolement [afɔlmɑ̃] nm **1.** [panique] panic ▸ **pas d'affolement !** don't panic! **2.** [d'une boussole] spinning.

affoler [3] [afɔle] vt [terrifier] to throw into a panic ; [bouleverser] to throw into turmoil. ❖ **s'affoler** vpi [s'effrayer] to panic.

affranchi, e [afRɑ̃ʃi] adj **1.** HIST [esclave] freed **2.** [émancipé] emancipated, liberated.

affranchir [32] [afRɑ̃ʃiR] vt **1.** HIST [esclave] to (set) free **2.** [colis, lettre] to stamp, to put a stamp ou stamps on ▸ **paquet insuffisamment affranchi** parcel with insufficient postage on it **3.** *arg crime* [renseigner] ▸ **affranchir qqn** to give sb the lowdown, to tip sb off *(sép)*. ❖ **s'affranchir** vpi [colonie] to gain one's freedom ; [adolescent] to gain one's independence ; [opprimé] to become emancipated ou liberated.

affranchissement [afRɑ̃ʃismɑ̃] nm **1.** [d'une lettre - avec des timbres] stamping ; [- à l'aide d'une machine] franking ; [- prix] postage **2.** [libération] freeing.

affres [afR] nfpl *litt* pangs / *les affres de la création* the throes of creativity.

affréter [18] [afRete] vt [avion, navire] to charter.

> ✍ In reformed spelling (see p. 16-18), this verb is conjugated like *semer* : **elle affrètera, il affrèterait.**

affreusement [afRøzmɑ̃] adv **1.** [en intensif] dreadfully, horribly, terribly / *elle a été affreusement mutilée* she was horribly mutilated **2.** [laidement] : *affreusement habillé / décoré* hideously dressed / decorated.

affreux, euse [afRø, øz] adj **1.** [répugnant] horrible, ghastly **2.** [très désagréable] dreadful, awful.

affriolant, e [afRijɔlɑ̃, ɑ̃t] adj alluring, appealing ▸ **des dessous affriolants** sexy underwear.

affront [afRɔ̃] nm affront.

affrontement [afRɔ̃tmɑ̃] nm confrontation.

affronter [3] [afRɔ̃te] vt [ennemi, mort] to face ; [problème] to face (up to), to square up to *(insép)*. ❖ **s'affronter** vp *(emploi réciproque)* to confront one another.

affubler [3] [afyble] vt *péj* [habiller] to rig out *(sép)* ▸ **on l'avait affublé d'un surnom idiot** *fig* the poor boy had been given an absurd nickname.

affût, affut* [afy] ❖ **à l'affût de**, **à l'affut de*** loc prép **1.** CHASSE ▸ **être à l'affût de** to be lying in wait for **2.** [à la recherche de] ▸ **il est toujours à l'affût des ragots / des articles les plus récents** he's always on the look-out for juicy bits of gossip / the latest articles.

affûter, affuter* [3] [afyte] vt to grind, to sharpen.

---

afghan, e [afgɑ̃, an] adj Afghan. **Afghan, e** nm, f Afghan, Afghani.

Afghanistan [afganistɑ̃] npr m ▸ **(l')Afghanistan** Afghanistan.

afin [afɛ̃] **afin de** loc prép in order to, so as to. **afin que** loc conj *(suivi du subjonctif)* in order ou so that / *préviens-moi si tu viens afin que je puisse préparer ta chambre* tell me if you are coming so that I can prepare your bedroom.

AFNOR, Afnor [afnɔʀ] (abr de **Association française de normalisation**) npr f *French industrial standards authority* ; ≃ BSI 🇬🇧 ; ≃ ASA 🇺🇸.

a fortiori, à fortiori* [afɔʀsjɔʀi] loc adv a fortiori, even more so, with all the more reason.

africain, e [afʀikɛ̃, ɛn] adj African. **Africain, e** nm, f African.

afrikaner [afʀikanɛʀ], **afrikaander** [afʀikɑ̃dɛʀ] adj Afrikaner. **Afrikaner, Afrikaander** nmf Afrikaner.

Afrique [afʀik] npr f ▸ **(l')Afrique** Africa ▸ **(l')Afrique australe** Southern Africa ▸ **(l')Afrique noire** Black Africa ▸ **(l')Afrique du Nord** North Africa ▸ **(l')Afrique du Sud** South Africa.

afro [afʀo] adj inv afro.

after-shave [aftœʀʃɛv] *(pl* after-shave) ◆ adj after-shave / *une lotion after-shave* aftershave (lotion). ◆ nm aftershave (lotion).

AG (abr de **assemblée générale**) nf GM.

agaçant, e [agasɑ̃, ɑ̃t] adj [irritant] irritating, annoying.

agacement [agasmɑ̃] nm irritation, annoyance.

agacer [16] [agase] vt [irriter] to irritate, to annoy / *ses plaisanteries m'agacent* his jokes get on my nerves.

agate [agat] nf agate.

âge [aʒ] nm **1.** [nombre d'années] age / *quel âge as-tu ?* how old are you? / *être du même âge que* to be the same age ou as old as / *à ton âge, on ne pleure plus* you're old enough not to cry now ▸ **avoir l'âge légal (pour voter)** to be old enough to vote, to be of age ▸ **l'âge scolaire** compulsory school age ▸ **à cause de son jeune / grand âge** because he's so young / old ▸ **avoir l'âge (de faire qqch)** : *il veut se marier, c'est normal, il a l'âge* he wants to get married, it's normal at his age ▸ **j'ai passé l'âge !** I'm too old (for this kind of thing)! ▸ **c'est de mon / son âge** : *les boums, c'est de son âge* they all want to have parties at that age ▸ **ce n'est pas de ton âge !** a) [tu es trop jeune] you're not old enough! b) [tu es trop vieux] you're too old (for it)! ▸ **prendre de l'âge** to get older / *on ne lui donne vraiment pas son âge* he doesn't look his age at all / *elle ne fait ou ne paraît pas son âge* she doesn't look her age, she looks younger than she actually is / *un whisky vingt ans d'âge* a twenty-year-old whisky **2.** [période] age, time (of life) ▸ **l'âge adulte a)** [gén] adulthood b) [d'un homme] manhood c) [d'une femme] womanhood ▸ **l'âge bête** *fam* ou **ingrat** the awkward ou difficult age ▸ **l'âge mûr** maturity ▸ **l'âge de raison** the age of reason **3.** ARCHÉOL age ▸ **l'âge de bronze** the Bronze Age ▸ **l'âge de fer** the Iron Age **4.** PSYCHOL **âge mental** mental age. **à l'âge de** loc prép ▸ **je l'ai connu à l'âge de 17 ans a)** [j'avais 17 ans] I met him when I was 17 **b)** [il avait 17 ans] I met him when he was 17. **en bas âge** loc adj [enfant] very young ou small.

âgé, e [aʒe] adj **1.** [vieux] old / *elle est plus âgée que moi* she's older than I am ▸ **dame âgée** elderly lady ▸ **les personnes âgées** the elderly **2.** ▸ **âgé de** [de tel âge] : *être âgé de 20 ans* to be 20 years old / *une jeune fille âgée de 15 ans* a 15-year-old girl.

agence [aʒɑ̃s] nf **1.** [bureau] agency ▸ **agence commerciale** sales office ▸ **agence immobilière** estate agent's 🇬🇧, real-estate office 🇺🇸 ▸ **agence d'intérim** temping agency ▸ **agence matrimoniale** marriage bureau ▸ **agence de placement** employment agency ▸ **agence de presse** press ou news agency ▸ **agence de publicité** advertising agency ▸ **agence de tourisme** tourist agency ▸ **agence de voyages** travel agency, travel agent's 🇬🇧 ▸ **Agence nationale pour l'emploi** *former national employment agency* **2.** [succursale] branch.

agencement [aʒɑ̃smɑ̃] nm [d'un lieu] layout, design ; [d'un texte] layout ; [d'éléments] order, ordering.

agencer [16] [aʒɑ̃se] vt **1.** [aménager] to lay out **2.** [organiser] to put together *(sép)*, to construct.

agenda [aʒɛ̃da] nm diary ▸ **agenda de bureau** desk diary 🇬🇧 ou calendar 🇺🇸 ▸ **agenda électronique** electronic organizer.

⚠ Le mot anglais **agenda** signifie « ordre du jour », « programme » et non « carnet », « calendrier ».

agenouiller [3] [aʒnuje] **s'agenouiller** vpi to kneel (down).

agent, e [aʒɑ̃, ɑ̃t] nm, f **1.** COMM & POL agent ; ADMIN official, officer ▸ **agent artistique** agent ▸ **agent d'assurances** insurance agent ▸ **agent commercial** sales representative ▸ **agent double** double agent ▸ **agent de l' État** ou **public sector employee** ▸ **agent du fisc** tax officer ▸ **agent immobilier** estate agent 🇬🇧, real estate agent 🇺🇸, realtor 🇺🇸 ▸ **agent de liaison** MIL liaison officer ▸ **agent littéraire** literary agent ▸ **agent secret** secret agent **2.** [policier] ▸ **agent (de police) a)** [homme] policeman, constable 🇬🇧, patrolman 🇺🇸 **b)** [femme] policewoman, woman police constable 🇬🇧, woman police officer 🇺🇸 / *s'il vous plaît, monsieur l'agent* excuse me, officer. **agent** nm **1.** [cause -humaine] agent ; [-non humaine] factor **2.** GRAM agent.

agglomération [aglɔmeʀasjɔ̃] nf **1.** [ville et sa banlieue] town ▸ **l'agglomération parisienne** Paris and its suburbs, greater Paris **2.** TRANSP built-up area **3.** [assemblage] conglomeration.

aggloméré [aglɔmeʀe] nm CONSTR chipboard ; GÉOL conglomerate ; [de liège] agglomerated cork.

agglutiner [3] [aglytine] **s'agglutiner** vpi to congregate / *ils s'agglutinaient à la fenêtre* they were all pressing up against the window.

aggravation [agʀavasjɔ̃] nf [d'une maladie, d'un problème] aggravation, worsening ; [de l'inflation] increase.

aggraver [3] [agʀave] vt [mal, problème] to aggravate, to make worse, to exacerbate ; [mécontentement, colère] to increase ▸ **n'aggrave pas ton cas** don't make your position worse than it is. **s'aggraver** vpi to get worse, to worsen / *la situation s'aggrave* the situation is getting worse.

⚠ D'un registre plus soutenu, **to aggravate** ne peut être employé systématiquement pour traduire aggraver.

agile [aʒil] adj nimble, agile.

agilement [aʒilmɑ̃] adv [grimper, se mouvoir] nimbly, agilely.

agilité [aʒilite] nf agility.

agio [aʒjo] nm (bank) charge ▸ **payer 15 euros d'agios** to pay 15 euros in bank charges.

agir [32] [aʒiʀ]
vi

A. ENTRER EN ACTION **1.** [intervenir] to act, to take action / *en cas d'incendie, il faut agir vite* in the event of a fire, it is important to act quickly ▸ **agir auprès de qqn** [essayer de l'influencer] to try to influence sb **2.** [passer à l'action] to do something / *assez parlé, maintenant il faut agir !* enough talk, let's have some action! **3.** [se comporter] to act, to behave ▸ **bien / mal agir envers qqn** to behave well / badly towards sb / *il a agi en bon citoyen* he did what any honest citizen would have done.

B. AVOIR UN EFFET **1.** [fonctionner - poison, remède] to act, to take effect, to work ; [- élément nutritif] to act, to have an effect ; [- détergent] to work / *pour faire agir le médicament plus efficacement* to increase the efficiency of the drug **2.** [avoir une influence] ▸ **agir sur** to work ou to have an effect on. ❖ **s'agir de** v impers **1.** [être question de] ▸ **il s'agit de** : *je voudrais te parler — de quoi s'agit-il ?* I'd like to talk to you — what about? ▸ **de qui s'agit-il ?** who is it? / *je voudrais vous parler d'une affaire importante, voici ce dont il s'agit* I'd like to talk to you about an important matter, namely this / *mais enfin, il s'agit de sa santé !* but her health is at stake (here)! ▸ **je peux te prêter de l'argent — il ne s'agit pas de ça** ou **ce n'est pas de ça qu'il s'agit** I can lend you some money — that's not the point ou the question / *quand il s'agit de râler, tu es toujours là !* you can always be relied upon to moan! / *une voiture a explosé, il s'agirait d'un accident* a car has exploded, apparently by accident **2.** [falloir] ▸ **il s'agit de** : *maintenant, il s'agit de lui parler* now we must talk to her / *il s'agit de savoir si...* the question is whether... ❖ **s'agissant de** loc prép [en ce qui concerne] as regards, with regard to.

agissements [aʒismɑ̃] nmpl machinations, schemes.

agitateur, trice [aʒitatœr, tris] nm, f POL agitator.

agitation [aʒitasjɔ̃] nf **1.** [mouvement - de l'air] turbulence ; [- de l'eau] roughness ; [- de la rue] bustle **2.** [fébrilité] agitation, restlessness **3.** POL unrest.

agité, e [aʒite] adj **1.** [mer] rough, stormy **2.** [personne - remuante] restless ; [- angoissée] agitated, worried **3.** [troublé - vie] hectic ; [- nuit, sommeil] restless.

agiter [3] [aʒite] vt **1.** [remuer - liquide] to shake ; [- queue] to wag ; [- mouchoir, journal] to wave about (inség) / *agiter les bras* to flap ou to wave one's arms **2.** [brandir] to brandish ▸ **agiter le spectre de qqch devant qqn** to threaten sb with the spectre of sthg **3.** [troubler] to trouble, to upset **4.** [débattre] to debate, to discuss. ❖ **s'agiter** vpi [bouger] to move about ▸ **s'agiter dans son sommeil** to toss and turn in one's sleep / *cesse de t'agiter sur ta chaise !* stop fidgeting about on your chair!

⚠ **To agitate** signifie avant tout «troubler» et ne doit pas être employé systématiquement pour traduire agiter.

agneau, x [aɲo] nm **1.** ZOOL lamb **2.** CULIN lamb *(U).*

agnostique [agnɔstik] adj & nmf agnostic.

agonie [agɔni] nf death throes, pangs of death, death agony / *il a eu une longue agonie* he died a slow and painful death ▸ **être à l'agonie a)** *pr* to be at the point of death **b)** *fig* to suffer agonies.

⚠ **Agony** signifie « grande souffrance » et non agonie.

agoniser [3] [agɔnize] vi to be dying.

⚠ **To agonise** signifie « se tourmenter » et non agoniser.

agoraphobie [agɔʀafɔbi] nf agoraphobia.

agrafe [agraf] nf [pour papier] staple ; [pour vêtement] hook, fastener ; [pour bois ou métal] clamp ; MÉD clamp.

agrafer [3] [agrafe] vt [papiers] to staple (together) ; [bords d'un tissu] to hook ou to fasten (up).

agrafeuse [agraføz] nf stapler.

agrandir [32] [agrɑ̃dir] vt **1.** [élargir - trou] to enlarge, to make bigger ; [- maison, jardin] to extend ; [- couloir, passage] to widen ▸ **la Communauté agrandie** the enlarged Community **2.** IMPR & PHOT [cliché, copie] to enlarge, to blow up (sép) ; [sur écran] to magnify. ❖ **s'agrandir** vpi **1.** [s'élargir] to grow, to get bigger / *le cercle de famille s'agrandit* the family circle is widening **2.** ÉCON to expand **3.** [avoir plus de place] ▸ **nous voudrions nous agrandir** we want more space for ourselves.

agrandissement [agrɑ̃dismɑ̃] nm **1.** PHOT enlargement **2.** [d'un appartement, d'une affaire] extension.

agréable [agreabl] adj pleasant, nice, agreeable / *je la trouve plutôt agréable physiquement* I think she's quite nice-looking / *il me serait bien agréable de le revoir* I would love to see him again ▸ **agréable à** : *une couleur agréable à l'œil* ou *à voir* a colour pleasing to the eye / *voilà quelqu'un qui est agréable à vivre* he's / she's really easy to get on with.

⚠ L'adjectif anglais **agreeable** signifie « plaisant » dans un registre soutenu et ne peut être employé systématiquement pour traduire agréable.

agréablement [agreabləmɑ̃] adv pleasantly, agreeably.

agréé, e [agree] adj **1.** DR registered **2.** [organisme, agent] recognized, authorized **3.** [produit] approved.

agréer [15] [agree] vt [dans la correspondance] : *veuillez agréer mes sentiments distingués* yours faithfully 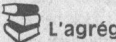, sincerely yours 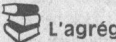.

agrég [agreg] nf *fam* **abr de** agrégation.

agrégat [agrega] nm [de roches, de substances] aggregate ; *fig & péj* conglomeration, mish-mash *péj* ; *fig & péj* [amas] hotchpotch 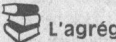, hodgepodge 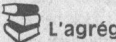.

agrégation [agregasjɔ̃] nf ENS & UNIV high-level competitive examination for teachers.

📖 **L'agrégation**

This is a prestigious professional qualification for teachers in France. Those who pass the challenging competitive exam for the **agrég** become **professeurs titulaires**, and as such are entitled to higher pay and a less onerous timetable.

agrégé, e [agreʒe] ◆ adj UNIV *who has passed the agrégation.* ◆ nm, f UNIV *person who has passed the agrégation (examination which commands certain salary and timetable privileges within the teaching profession).*

agrément [agremɑ̃] nm *sout* **1.** [attrait] charm, appeal, attractiveness ; [plaisir] pleasure ▸ **les agréments de la vie** the pleasures of life **2.** [accord] approval, consent. ❖ **d'agrément** loc adj [jardin, voyage] pleasure *(modif).*

agrémenter [3] [agʀemɑ̃te] vt ▸ **agrémenter qqch avec** ou **de** to decorate sthg with / *une lettre agrémentée de quelques expressions à l'ancienne* a letter graced ou adorned with a few quaint old phrases.

agrès [agʀɛ] nmpl SPORT piece of apparatus.

agresser [4] [agʀese] vt **1.** [physiquement] to attack, to assault ▸ **se faire agresser** to be assaulted **2.** [verbalement] to attack.

agresseur [agʀesœʀ] nm [d'une personne] attacker, assailant, aggressor ; [d'un pays] aggressor.

agressif, ive [agʀesif, iv] adj [hostile - personne, pays] aggressive, hostile, belligerent *litt*.

agression [agʀesjɔ̃] nf [attaque - contre une personne] attack, assault ; [- contre un pays] aggression ▸ **être victime d'une** ou **subir une agression** to be assaulted / *les agressions de la vie moderne fig* the stresses and strains of modern life.

agressivement [agʀesivmɑ̃] adv aggressively.

agressivité [agʀesivite] nf aggressivity, aggressiveness.

agricole [agʀikɔl] adj agricultural, farming *(modif)*.

agriculteur, trice [agʀikyltœʀ, tʀis] nm, f farmer.

agriculture [agʀikyltyʀ] nf agriculture, farming ▸ **agriculture biologique** organic farming ou agriculture ▸ **agriculture raisonnée** sustainable agriculture ou farming.

agripper [3] [agʀipe] vt [prendre] to grab, to snatch. ❖ **s'agripper** vpi to hold on ▸ **s'agripper à qqch** to cling to ou to hold on (tight) to sthg.

agritourisme [agʀituʀism] nf agritourism.

agroalimentaire [agʀoalimɑ̃tɛʀ] ◆ adj food-processing *(modif)*. ◆ nm ▸ **l'agroalimentaire** the food-processing industry, agribusiness.

agrocarburant [agʀokaʀbyʀɑ̃] nm agrofuel.

agrochimique [agʀoʃimik] adj agrochemical.

agroenvironnemental, e, aux [agʀoɑ̃viʀɔnmɑ̃tal] adj agro-environmental.

agro-industrie [agʀoɛ̃dystʀi] *(pl* **agro-industries)** nf ▸ **l'agro-industrie a)** [en amont de l'agriculture] the farm machines, implements and fertilizers industry **b)** [en aval de l'agriculture] the food-processing industry, agribusiness.

agro-industriel, elle [agʀoɛ̃dystʀijɛl] adj agro-industrial.

agronome [agʀɔnɔm] nmf agronomist.

agronomie [agʀɔnɔmi] nf agronomics *(sg)*.

agro-terrorisme [agʀoteʀɔʀism] nm agroterrorism.

agrotourisme [agʀotuʀism] nm agrotourism.

agrume [agʀym] nm citrus fruit.

aguerrir [32] [ageʀiʀ] vt to harden, to toughen (up). ❖ **s'aguerrir** vpi to become tougher.

aguets [agɛ] ❖ **aux aguets** loc adv ▸ **être aux aguets** to be on watch ou the lookout.

aguicher [3] [agiʃe] vt to seduce, to entice, to allure.

aguicheur, euse [agiʃœʀ, øz] ◆ adj seductive, enticing, alluring. ◆ nm, f tease.

ah [a] interj **1.** [renforce l'expression d'un sentiment] ah, oh **2.** [dans une réponse] : *il est venu — ah bon !* he came — did he (really)? / *ils n'en ont plus en magasin — ah bon !* [ton résigné] they haven't got any more in stock — oh well! ▸ **ah non alors !** certainly not! ▸ **ah oui ?** really?

ahuri, e [ayʀi] adj **1.** [surpris] dumbfounded, amazed, stunned **2.** [hébété] stupefied, dazed / *il avait l'air complètement ahuri* he looked as if he was in a daze.

ahurissant, e [ayʀisɑ̃, ɑ̃t] adj stunning, stupefying.

aidant [edɑ̃] nm ▸ **aidant familial** family caregiver.

aide[1] [ɛd] ◆ nm [assistant - payé] assistant ; [- bénévole] helper / *les aides du président* the presidential aides. ◆ nf ▸ **aide familiale** home help 🇬🇧, home helper 🇺🇸 ▸ **aide ménagère** home help 🇬🇧, home helper 🇺🇸.

aide[2] [ɛd] nf **1.** [appui] help, assistance, aid ▸ **à l'aide !** help! ▸ **appeler à l'aide** to call for help ▸ **offrir son aide à qqn** to give sb help, to go to sb's assistance ▸ **venir en aide à qqn** to come to sb's aid **2.** [don d'argent] aid ▸ **aide au développement économique (des pays du tiers-monde)** economic aid (to third world countries) ▸ **aide à l'emploi** employment support ▸ **aide fiscale** tax credit ▸ **aide humanitaire** humanitarian aid ▸ **aide judiciaire** ≃ legal aid ▸ **aide à la mobilité** relocation allowance *(paid to job seekers)* ▸ **aide personnalisée au logement** ≃ housing benefit (U) ▸ **aide sociale** social security 🇬🇧, welfare 🇺🇸 **3.** INFORM ▸ **aide en ligne** online help. ❖ **à l'aide de** loc prép **1.** [avec] with the help of / *marcher à l'aide de béquilles* to walk with crutches **2.** [au secours de] ▸ **aller / venir à l'aide de qqn** to go / to come to sb's aid.

aide-éducateur, trice [ɛdedykatœʀ, tʀis] *(mpl* **aides-éducateurs**, *fpl* **aides-éducatrices)** nm, f ÉDUC teaching assistant.

aide-mémoire [ɛdmemwaʀ] *(pl* **aide-mémoire** ou **aide-mémoires)** nm notes.

aider [4] [ede] vt **1.** [apporter son concours à] to help ▸ **aider qqn à faire qqch** to help sb (to) do sthg ; *(en usage absolu)* to help (out) **2.** [financièrement] to help out, to aid, to assist ▸ **subventions pour aider l'industrie** subsidies to industry **3.** *(en usage absolu)* [favoriser] ▸ **ça aide** *fam* it's a help ▸ **des diplômes, ça aide** qualifications come in handy / *la fatigue aidant, je me suis endormi tout de suite* helped by exhaustion, I fell asleep right away / *elle l'oubliera, le temps aidant* she'll forget him in time ▸ **ne pas être aidé** *fam*: *il n'est pas aidé !* he hasn't got much going for him! ❖ **aider à** v + prép to help / *aider à la digestion* to help digestion / *ça aide à passer le temps* it helps to pass the time. ❖ **s'aider de** vp + prép to use / *marcher en s'aidant d'une canne* to walk with a stick.

aide-soignant, e [ɛdswaɲɑ̃, ɑ̃t] *(mpl* **aides-soignants**, *fpl* **aides-soignantes)** nm, f nursing auxiliary 🇬🇧, nurse's aid 🇺🇸.

aïe [aj] interj [cri - de douleur] ouch ; [- de surprise] ▸ **aïe, la voilà !** oh dear ou oh no, here she comes!

aïeul, e [ajœl] nm, f grandparent, grandfather (grandmother).

aïeux [ajø] nmpl *litt* forefathers, ancestors.

aigle [ɛgl] nm ORNITH eagle.

aiglefin [ɛglǝfɛ̃] = **églefin**.

aigre [ɛgʀ] ◆ adj **1.** [acide - vin] acid, sharp ; [- goût, lait] sour **2.** [méchant] cutting, harsh, acid. ◆ nm ▸ **tourner à l'aigre a)** [lait] to turn sour **b)** [discussion] to turn sour ou nasty.

aigre-doux, aigre-douce [ɛgʀǝdu, ɛgʀǝdus] *(mpl* **aigres-doux**, *fpl* **aigres-douces)** adj CULIN sweet-and-sour / *ses lettres étaient aigres-douces fig* his letters were tinged with bitterness.

aigrelet, ette [ɛgʀǝlɛ, ɛt] adj [odeur, saveur] sourish ; [son, voix] shrillish ; [propos] tart, sour, acid.

aigrette [ɛgʀɛt] nf ORNITH egret.

aigreur [ɛgʀœʀ] nf **1.** [acidité] sourness **2.** [animosité] sharpness, bitterness. ❖ **aigreurs** nfpl ▸ **avoir des aigreurs (d'estomac)** to have heartburn.

aigri, e [egʀi] adj bitter, embittered.

aigrir [32] [egʀiʀ] vt [lait, vin] to make sour ; [personne] to embitter, to make bitter. ❖ **s'aigrir** vpi [lait] to turn (sour), to go off ; [caractère] to sour ; [personne] to become embittered.

aigu, aiguë *ou* **aigüe*** [egy] adj **1.** [perçant -voix] high-pitched, shrill *péj*; piercing *péj*; [-glapissement, hurlement] piercing, shrill; ACOUST & MUS high-pitched **2.** [pénétrant -esprit, intelligence] sharp, keen ▸ **avoir un sens aigu de l'observation** *ou* **un regard aigu** to be an acute observer **3.** [grave -crise, douleur] severe, acute, extreme; MÉD [phase, appendicite] acute. ◆ **aigu** nm high pitch ▸ **l'aigu, les aigus** treble range.

aiguillage [eguijaʒ] nm RAIL [manœuvre] shunting, switching US; [dispositif] points *(pl)* UK, shunt, switch US.

aiguille [eguij] nf **1.** COUT needle ▸ **aiguille à coudre / tricoter / repriser** sawing / knitting / darning needle **2.** MÉD needle **3.** [d'une montre, d'une pendule] hand; [d'un électrophone] arm; [d'une balance] pointer; [d'une boussole] needle ▸ **la petite aiguille** *ou* **l'aiguille des heures** the hour hand / **la grande aiguille, l'aiguille des minutes** the minute hand **4.** BOT needle ▸ **aiguille de pin / de sapin** pine / fir tree needle.

aiguiller [3] [eguije] vt [orienter -recherche] to steer.

aiguilleur [eguijœr] nm AÉRON ▸ **aiguilleur (du ciel)** air traffic controller.

aiguillon [eguijɔ̃] nm ENTOM sting.

aiguillonner [3] [eguijɔne] vt **1.** [piquer -bœuf] to goad **2.** [stimuler -curiosité] to arouse; [-personne] to spur on, to goad on.

aiguise-crayon [egizkrɛjɔ̃] *(pl* **aiguise-crayons)** nm QUÉBEC pencil sharpener.

aiguiser [3] [eg(ч)ize] vt **1.** [rendre coupant -couteau, lame] to sharpen **2.** [stimuler -curiosité] to stimulate, to rouse; [-faculté, sens] to sharpen; [-appétit] to whet, to stimulate.

aïkido [ajkido] nm aikido.

ail [aj] *(pl* **ails** *ou* **aulx** [o]) nm garlic.

aile [ɛl] nf **1.** ZOOL wing; *fig* ▸ **avoir des ailes** to run like the wind ▸ **couper** *ou* **rogner les ailes à qqn** to clip sb's wings ▸ **prendre qqn sous son aile** to take sb under one's wing **2.** [d'un moulin] sail; [d'un avion] wing **3.** AUTO wing UK, fender US **4.** ANAT ▸ **les ailes du nez** the nostrils **5.** ARCHIT wing **6.** SPORT ▸ **aile delta** *ou* **aile libre**: *faire de l'aile delta* ou *de l'aile libre* to go hang-gliding **7.** MIL wing, flank.

aileron [ɛlrɔ̃] nm **1.** ZOOL [d'un poisson] fin; [d'un oiseau] pinion **2.** AÉRON aileron.

ailier, ère [elje, ɛr] nm, f SPORT [au football] winger; [au rugby] wing.

ailleurs [ajœr] adv elsewhere, somewhere *ou* someplace US else ▸ **nulle part ailleurs** nowhere *ou* noplace US else ▸ **partout ailleurs** everywhere *ou* everyplace US else ▸ **il est ailleurs !** he's miles away! ◆ **d'ailleurs** loc adv **1.** [de toute façon] besides, anyway **2.** [de plus] what's more **3.** [du reste] for that matter. ◆ **par ailleurs** loc adv **1.** [d'un autre côté] otherwise **2.** [de plus] besides, moreover.

aïlloli [ajɔli] = **aïoli**.

aimable [ɛmabl] adj [gentil] kind, pleasant, amiable / *vous êtes trop aimable, merci beaucoup* you're most kind, thank you very much / *c'est très aimable à vous* it's very kind of you.

aimablement [ɛmabləmɑ̃] adv kindly, pleasantly, amiably.

aimant¹ [ɛmɑ̃] nm [instrument] magnet.

aimant², e [ɛmɑ̃, ɑ̃t] adj loving, caring.

aimanter [3] [ɛmɑ̃te] vt to magnetize.

aimer [4] [eme] vt **1.** [d'amour] to love ▸ **je l'aime beaucoup** I'm very fond of him ▸ **je l'aime bien** I like him ▸ **qui m'aime me suive** *(allusion à Philippe VI de Valois)* anyone want to join me? **2.** [apprécier -vin, musique, sport]

to like, to love, to be fond of / *je n'aime plus tellement le jazz* I'm not so keen on jazz now ▸ **j'aime à croire** *ou* **à penser que tu m'as dit la vérité cette fois** *sout* I'd like to think that you told me the truth this time ▸ **aimer mieux** [préférer] to prefer ▸ **aimer autant** *ou* **mieux** to prefer / *pas de dessert, merci, j'aime autant* ou *mieux le fromage* no dessert, thanks, I'd much rather have cheese ▸ **j'aime autant** *ou* **mieux ça** it's just as well ▸ **elle aime autant** *ou* **mieux que tu y ailles** she'd rather you *ou* she'd prefer it if you went ▸ **aimer que**: *il aime que ses enfants l'embrassent avant d'aller au lit* he loves his children to kiss him good night **3.** *(au conditionnel)* [souhaiter]: *j'aimerais un café s'il vous plaît* I'd like a coffee please. ◆ **s'aimer** ◆ vp *(emploi réfléchi)* to like o.s. / *je ne m'aime pas* I don't like myself ▸ **je m'aime bien en bleu / avec les cheveux courts** I think I look good in blue / with short hair. ◆ vp *(emploi réciproque)* to love each other ▸ **un couple qui s'aime** a loving *ou* devoted couple; *litt* [faire l'amour] to make love.

aine [ɛn] nf groin.

aîné, e, aîné, e [ene] ◆ adj ▸ **l'enfant aîné** a) [de deux] the elder *ou* older child b) [de plusieurs] the eldest *ou* oldest child. ◆ nm, f [entre frères et sœurs] ▸ **l'aîné a)** [de deux] the elder *ou* older boy b) [de plusieurs] the eldest *ou* oldest boy ▸ **l'aînée a)** [de deux] the elder *ou* older girl b) [de plusieurs] the eldest *ou* oldest girl. ◆ **aînés** nmpl *sout* [d'une famille, d'une tribu] ▸ **les aînés** the elders.

aînesse, aînesse* [ɛnɛs] nf ⟶ **droit**.

ainsi [ɛ̃si] adv **1.** [de cette manière] in this way so that way ▸ **je suis ainsi faite** that's the way I am / *s'il en était vraiment ainsi* if this were really so *ou* the case ▸ **c'est toujours ainsi** it's always like that / *tout s'est passé ainsi* this is how it happened ▸ **on voit ainsi que...** in this way *ou* thus we can see that... **2.** [par conséquent] so, thus. ◆ **ainsi que** loc conj **1.** [comme] as **2.** [et] as well as. ◆ **et ainsi de suite** loc adv and so on, and so forth. ◆ **pour ainsi dire** loc adv **1.** [presque] virtually **2.** [si l'on peut dire] so to speak, as it were.

aïoli [ajɔli] nm [sauce] aïoli, garlic mayonnaise.

air [ɛr] nm **1.** [apparence] air, look / *ne te laisse pas prendre à son faux air de gentillesse* don't be taken in by his apparent kindness ▸ **avoir l'air**: *Maria, tu as l'air heureux* ou *heureuse* Maria, you look happy ▸ **elle n'a pas l'air satisfait** *ou* **satisfaite** she doesn't look as if she's pleased / *tu avais l'air fin !* *fam* you looked a real fool! ▸ **avoir l'air de**: *il a l'air de t'aimer beaucoup* he seems to be very fond of you / *je ne voudrais pas avoir l'air de lui donner des ordres* I wouldn't like (it) to look as though I were ordering him about ▸ **ça a l'air d'un** *ou* **d'être un scarabée** it looks like a beetle ▸ **avec son air de ne pas y toucher** *ou* **sans avoir l'air d'y toucher, il arrive toujours à ses fins** though you wouldn't think it to look at him, he always manages to get his way ▸ **ne pas avoir l'air (comme ça)** *fam*: *elle n'a pas l'air comme ça, mais elle sait ce qu'elle veut !* you wouldn't think it to look at her, but she knows what she wants! ▸ **prendre de grands airs** to put on airs (and graces) UK **2.** [ressemblance] likeness, resemblance ▸ **un air de famille** *ou* **parenté** a family resemblance *ou* likeness ▸ **il a un faux air de James Dean** he looks a bit like James Dean **3.** MUS [mélodie] tune; [à l'opéra] aria **4.** [qu'on respire] air ▸ **air conditionné** [système] air-conditioning ▸ **ils ont l'air conditionné** their building is air-conditioned ▸ **prendre l'air** to get some fresh air, to take the air *vieilli* **5.** [ciel] air ▸ **dans l'air** *ou* **les airs** (up) in the air *ou* sky *ou* skies *litt* **6.** [ambiance] atmosphere / *la ville tout entière s'était emplie d'un petit air de fête* there was a party atmosphere in the whole town ▸ **vivre de l'air du temps** to live on (thin) air. ◆ **à l'air libre** loc adv out in the open.

---

* In reformed spelling (see p. 16-18).

❖ **au grand air** loc adv [dehors] (out) in the fresh air. ❖ **dans l'air** loc adv in the air / *il y a de l'orage dans l'air* pr & fig there's a storm brewing / *la révolution est dans l'air* revolution is in the air. ❖ **de l'air** loc adj [hôtesse, mal, musée] air *(modif)*. ❖ **en l'air** loc adj **1.** [levé] in the air, up / *les pattes en l'air* with its feet in the air / *les mains en l'air !* hands up! **2.** [non fondé - promesse] empty / *encore des paroles en l'air !* more empty words! ◆ loc adv **1.** [vers le haut] (up) in the air ▶ **jeter** ou **lancer qqch en l'air** to throw sthg (up) in the air ▶ **tirer en l'air** to fire in the air ▶ **regarde en l'air** look up **2.** fig rashly ▶ **parler en l'air** to say things without meaning them ▶ **flanquer** fam ou **foutre** tfam **qqch en l'air a)** [jeter] to chuck sthg out, to bin sthg **b)** [gâcher] to screw sthg up.

Airbag® [ɛʀbag] nm Airbag®.

aire [ɛʀ] nf **1.** [terrain] area ▶ **aire de jeux** playground ▶ **aire de repos** [sur autoroute] rest area ▶ **aire de service** service station, rest and service plaza US ▶ **aire de stationnement** parking area **2.** AÉRON & ASTRON ▶ **aire d'atterrissage** landing area ▶ **aire d'embarquement** boarding area ▶ **aire de lancement** launching site.

airelle [ɛʀɛl] nf [myrtille] blueberry, bilberry ; [rouge] cranberry.

aisance [ɛzɑ̃s] nf **1.** [naturel] ease ▶ **parler une langue avec aisance** to speak a language fluently **2.** [prospérité] affluence ▶ **vivre dans l'aisance** to live a life of ease.

aise [ɛz] litt ◆ adj delighted / *je suis bien aise de vous revoir* I'm delighted to see you again. ◆ nf [plaisir] pleasure, joy. ❖ **à l'aise, à son aise** loc adj & loc adv : *on est mal à l'aise dans ce fauteuil* this armchair isn't very comfortable ▶ **être à l'aise** [riche] to be well-to-do ou well-off / *il s'est senti mal à l'aise pendant toute la réunion* fig he felt ill-at-ease during the entire meeting ▶ **il nous a mis tout de suite à l'aise** ou **à notre aise** he put us at (our) ease right away ▶ **mettez-vous donc à l'aise** ou **à votre aise** make yourself comfortable ▶ **à l'aise** fam: *on y sera ce soir, à l'aise !* we'll be there tonight, no hassle ou sweat! ▶ **être à l'aise dans ses baskets** fam to be together ▶ **à mon / ton, etc. aise**: *à ton aise !* please yourself! ▶ **à votre aise** as you please ▶ **tu en parles à ton aise** it's easy for you to talk.

aisé, e [eze] adj **1.** [facile] easy **2.** [prospère] well-to-do, well-off.

aisément [ezemɑ̃] adv easily.

aisselle [ɛsɛl] nf ANAT armpit.

ajiste [aʒist] nmf member of the Fédération des auberges de jeunesse ; ≃ youth-hosteller.

ajonc [aʒɔ̃] nm gorse *(U)*, furze *(U)*.

ajournement [aʒuʀnəmɑ̃] nm **1.** [renvoi] postponement, deferment, adjournment **2.** [d'un candidat] referral ; [d'un soldat] deferment.

ajourner [3] [aʒuʀne] vt **1.** [différer] to postpone, to defer sout, to put off *(sép)* **2.** [étudiant] to refer ; [soldat] to defer.

ajout [aʒu] nm addition.

ajouter [3] [aʒute] vt **1.** [mettre] to add / *ajoute donc une assiette pour ton frère* lay an extra place ou add a plate for your brother **2.** MATH to add / *ils ont ajouté 15 % de service* they added on 15% for the service **3.** [dire] to add / *il est parti sans rien ajouter* he left without saying another word **4.** sout ▶ **ajouter foi à** [croire] to believe, to give credence to sout. ❖ **ajouter à** v + prép to add to. ❖ **s'ajouter** vpi to be added / *vient s'ajouter là-dessus le loyer* the rent is added ou comes on top.

ajusté, e [aʒyste] adj close-fitting.

ajuster [3] [aʒyste] vt **1.** [adapter] to fit ▶ **ajuster un vêtement** COUT to alter a garment ▶ **ajuster qqch à** ou **sur** to fit sthg to ou on **2.** [mécanisme, réglage] to adjust

3. ▶ **ajuster son coup** ou **tir** pr to aim one's shot / *tu as bien ajusté ton coup* ou **tir** fig your aim was pretty accurate, you had it figured out pretty well **4.** [arranger - robe, coiffure] to rearrange ; [- cravate] to straighten.

ajusteur [aʒystœʀ] nm fitter.

alaise [alɛz] nf drawsheet.

alambiqué, e [alɑ̃bike] adj convoluted, involved, tortuous.

alarmant, e [alaʀmɑ̃, ɑ̃t] adj alarming.

alarme [alaʀm] nf **1.** [dispositif] ▶ **alarme antivol** burglar alarm **2.** [alerte] alarm ▶ **donner l'alarme a)** to give ou to raise the alarm **b)** fig to raise the alarm **3.** [inquiétude] alarm, anxiety ▶ **à la première alarme** at the first sign of danger.

alarmer [3] [alaʀme] vt **1.** [inquiéter - suj : personne, remarque] to alarm ; [- suj : bruit] to startle **2.** [alerter - opinion, presse] to alert. ❖ **s'alarmer** vpi to become alarmed / *il n'y a pas de quoi s'alarmer* there's no cause for alarm.

alarmiste [alaʀmist] adj & nmf alarmist.

Alaska [alaska] npr m ▶ **(l')Alaska** Alaska.

albanais, e [albanɛ, ɛz] adj Albanian. ❖ **Albanais, e** nm, f Albanian.

Albanie [albani] npr f ▶ **(l')Albanie** Albania.

albâtre [albɑtʀ] nm MINÉR alabaster.

albatros [albatʀos] nm ORNITH & SPORT albatross.

albinos [albinos] adj & nmf albino.

album [albɔm] nm **1.** [livre] album ▶ **album à colorier** colouring ou painting book ▶ **album (de) photos** photograph album **2.** [disque] album, LP.

albumine [albymin] nf albumin.

alcalin, e [alkalɛ̃, in] adj CHIM alkaline.

alchimie [alʃimi] nf alchemy.

alchimiste [alʃimist] nmf alchemist.

alcool [alkɔl] nm **1.** [boissons alcoolisées] ▶ **l'alcool** alcohol ▶ **boisson sans alcool** non-alcoholic drink ▶ **bière sans alcool** alcohol-free beer ; [spiritueux] ▶ **alcool de prune** plum brandy ▶ **il ne tient pas l'alcool** he can't take his drink **2.** CHIM & PHARM alcohol, spirit ▶ **alcool à brûler** methylated spirits, meths UK ▶ **alcool de menthe** medicinal mint spirit ▶ **alcool à 90 °** surgical spirit. ❖ **à alcool** loc adj [réchaud, lampe] spirit *(modif)*.

alcoolémie [alkɔlemi] nf alcohol level *(in the blood)*.

alcoolique [alkɔlik] ◆ adj alcoholic. ◆ nmf alcoholic.

alcoolisé, e [alkɔlize] adj [qui contient de l'alcool] ▶ **boissons alcoolisées** alcoholic drinks ou beverages sout, intoxicating liquors sout ▶ **non alcoolisé** nonalcoholic.

alcoolisme [alkɔlism] nm alcoholism.

alcoologue [alkɔlɔg] nmf alcohologist.

Alco(o)test® [alkɔtest] nm **1.** [appareil] ≃ Breathalyser® UK ; ≃ Breathalyzer® US **2.** [vérification] breath test.

alcôve [alkov] nf alcove, recess.

aléa [alea] nm unforeseen turn of events / *tenir compte des aléas* to take the unforeseen ou unexpected into account ▶ **les aléas de l'existence** the ups and downs of life.

aléatoire [aleatwaʀ] adj **1.** [entreprise, démarche] risky, hazardous, chancy ▶ **c'est aléatoire** it's uncertain, there's nothing definite about it **2.** MATH random.

alentour [alɑ̃tuʀ] adv ▶ **dans la campagne alentour** in the surrounding countryside. ❖ **alentours** nmpl neighbourhood, vicinity, (surrounding) area ▶ **aux alentours de** [dans l'espace, le temps] around.

alerte¹ [alɛʀt] adj [démarche] quick, alert ; [esprit] lively, alert ; [style] lively, brisk ; [personne] spry.

alerte² [alɛʀt] nf **1.** [signal] alert ▸ **donner l'alerte** to give the alert ▸ **alerte !** a) [aux armes] to arms! b) [attention] watch out! ▸ **fausse alerte** false alarm ▸ **alerte aérienne** air raid ou air strike warning ▸ **alerte à la bombe** bomb scare ▸ **alerte orange** MÉTÉOR amber alert ▸ **alerte rouge** red alert ▸ **fin d'alerte** all clear **2.** [signe avant-coureur] alarm, warning sign ▸ **à la première alerte** at the first warning ▸ **l'alerte a été chaude** that was a close call. ❖ **en alerte, en état d'alerte** loc adv on the alert ▸ **être en état d'alerte** to be in a state of alert.

alerter [3] [alɛʀte] vt **1.** [alarmer] to alert **2.** [informer - autorités] to notify, to inform ; [-presse] to alert.

alèse [alɛz] = **alaise.**

alevin [alvɛ̃] nm alevin, young fish.

alexandrin [alɛksɑ̃dʀɛ̃] nm LITTÉR Alexandrine.

alezan, e [alzɑ̃, an] adj & nm, f chestnut.

algarade [algaʀad] nf quarrel.

algèbre [alʒɛbʀ] nf algebra.

Alger [alʒe] npr Algiers.

Algérie [alʒeʀi] npr f ▸ **(l')Algérie** Algeria ▸ **la guerre d'Algérie** the Algerian War.

🏛 **La guerre d'Algérie**

The most bitter of France's post-colonial struggles, 1954-1962. In a country dominated by a million white settlers, the **pieds-noirs**, the government's failure to crush the revolt of the **Front de libération nationale (FLN)**, despite massive military intervention, led settlers and army officers to attempt a takeover of the colony. The recall to power of General de Gaulle (1958) and the **accords d'Évian (1962)** led to Algeria's independence and to the resettlement of the **pieds-noirs** in France.

---

algérien, enne [alʒeʀjɛ̃, ɛn] adj Algerian. ❖ **Algérien, enne** nm, f Algerian.

algoculture [algɔkyltyʀ] nf seaweed cultivation.

algorithme [algɔʀitm] nm algorithm.

algue [alg] nf (piece of) seaweed, alga *spéc.*

alias [aljas] adv alias, a.k.a.

aliassage [aljasaʒ] nm INFORM aliasing.

alibi [alibi] nm **1.** DR alibi **2.** [prétexte] alibi, excuse.

alicament [alikamɑ̃] nm [avec additifs] nutraceutical, dietary supplement ; [biologique] organic food *(consumed for its health benefits)*.

alien [aljen] nm alien.

aliénation [aljenasjɔ̃] nf **1.** PHILOS & POL alienation **2.** PSYCHOL ▸ **aliénation mentale** insanity, mental illness.

aliéné, e [aljene] nm, f PSYCHOL mental patient.

aliéner [18] [aljene] vt [abandonner -indépendance, liberté, droit] to give up *(sép)* ; DR to alienate. ❖ **s'aliéner** vpt ▸ **s'aliéner qqn** to alienate sb.

🖉 In reformed spelling (see p. 16-18), this verb is conjugated like *semer : il aliènera, elle aliènerait.*

alignement [aliɲmɑ̃] nm *fig* aligning, bringing into alignment / *leur alignement sur la politique des socialistes* their coming into line with the socialists' policy.

aligner [3] [aliɲe] vt **1.** [mettre en rang] to line up *(sép)*, to align **2.** [présenter -preuves] to produce one by one ; [-en écrivant] to string together ; [-en récitant] to string together, to reel off *(sép)* **3.** [mettre en conformité] ▸ **aligner qqch sur** to line sth up with, to bring sth into line with.

❖ **s'aligner** vpi *fam* EXPR ▸ **pouvoir (toujours) s'aligner** : *il peut toujours s'aligner !* he's got no chance (of getting anywhere)! ❖ **s'aligner sur** vp + prép [imiter - nation, gouvernement] to fall into line ou to align o.s. with.

aliment [alimɑ̃] nm [nourriture] (type ou kind of) food ; [portion] (piece of) food ▸ **des aliments** food, foodstuffs ▸ **aliments pour bébé / chien** baby / dog food ▸ **aliments biologiques** organic food ▸ **aliments complets** whole food.

alimentaire [alimɑ̃tɛʀ] adj **1.** COMM & MÉD food *(modif)* **2.** [pour gagner de l'argent] ▸ **œuvre alimentaire** potboiler / *je fais des enquêtes mais c'est purement alimentaire* I do surveys, but it's just to make ends meet.

alimentation [alimɑ̃tasjɔ̃] nf **1.** [fait de manger] (consumption of) food ; [fait de faire manger] feeding **2.** [régime] diet / *une alimentation carnée* a meat-based diet **3.** COMM [magasin] grocer's UK, food store US ; [rayon] groceries ; [activité] ▸ **l'alimentation** food distribution, the food (distribution) trade **4.** INFORM ▸ **alimentation en papier** paper feed **5.** TECHNOL supply / *ils ont l'alimentation en eau* they have running water.

alimenter [3] [alimɑ̃te] vt **1.** [nourrir -malade, bébé] to feed **2.** TECHNOL [moteur, pompe] to feed ; [ville] to supply ▸ **alimenter qqn en eau** to supply sb with water **3.** [approvisionner -compte] to put money into **4.** [entretenir -conversation] to sustain ; [-curiosité, intérêt] to feed, to sustain ; [-doute, désaccord] to fuel. ❖ **s'alimenter** vp *(emploi réfléchi)* [gén] to eat / *elle ne s'alimente plus depuis une semaine* she hasn't had any solid food for a week ▸ **s'alimenter bien / mal** to have a good / poor diet ; [bébé] to feed o.s.

alinéa [alinea] nm [espace] indent ; [paragraphe] paragraph.

aliter [3] [alite] ❖ **s'aliter** vpi to take to one's bed ▸ **rester alité** to be confined to one's bed, to be bedridden.

Allah [ala] npr Allah.

allaitement [alɛtmɑ̃] nm [processus] feeding, suckling UK, nursing US ; [période] breast-feeding period ▸ **allaitement maternel** ou **au sein** breast-feeding.

allaiter [4] [alete] vt to breastfeed.

allant [alɑ̃] nm *sout* energy, drive ▸ **être plein d'allant** to have plenty of drive.

alléchant, e [aleʃɑ̃, ɑ̃t] adj [proposition, projet, offre] enticing, tempting.

allécher [18] [aleʃe] vt [suj : offre, proposition, projet - gén] to tempt, to seduce, to entice ; [-dans le but de tromper] to lure.

🖉 In reformed spelling (see p. 16-18), this verb is conjugated like *semer : il allèchera, elle allècherait.*

allée [ale] nf [à la campagne] footpath, lane ; [dans un jardin] alley ; [dans un parc] walk, path ; [en ville] avenue ; [devant une maison, une villa] drive, driveway ; [dans un cinéma, un train] aisle ▸ **les allées du pouvoir** the corridors of power. ❖ **allées et venues** nfpl comings and goings.

allégation [alegasjɔ̃] nf allegation, (unsubstantiated) claim.

allégé, e [aleʒe] adj low-fat.

allègement [alɛʒmɑ̃] nm **1.** [diminution -d'un fardeau] lightening ; [-d'une douleur] relief, alleviation, soothing **2.** ÉCON & FIN reduction ▸ **allègement fiscal** tax reduction.

alléger [22] [aleʒe] vt **1.** [rendre moins lourd -malle, meuble] to make lighter, to lighten / *il va falloir alléger le paquet de 10 grammes* we'll have to take 10 grammes off the parcel **2.** ÉCON & FIN [cotisation, contribution] to reduce **3.** [soulager -douleur] to relieve, to soothe **4.** [faciliter -procédure, texte] to simplify, to trim (down) **5.** ENS ▸ **alléger le programme** to trim the curriculum.

🖉 In reformed spelling (see p. 16-18), this verb is conjugated like *semer : il allègera, elle allègerait.*

allégorie [alegɔʀi] nf allegory.

allègre [alɛgʀ] adj cheerful, light-hearted.

allègrement [alɛgʀəmɑ̃] adv [joyeusement] cheerfully, light-heartedly.

allégresse [alegʀɛs] nf cheerfulness, liveliness ▶ **l'allégresse était générale** there was general rejoicing.

alléguer [18] [alege] vt [prétexter] to argue ▶ **alléguer comme excuse / prétexte que** to put forward as an excuse / a pretext that.

✎ In reformed spelling (see p. 16-18), this verb is conjugated like *semer : il allèguera, elle allèguerait.*

Allemagne [almaɲ] npr f ▶ **(l')Allemagne** Germany ▶ **(l')Allemagne de l'Est** East Germany ▶ **(l')Allemagne de l'Ouest** West Germany.

allemand, e [almɑ̃, ɑ̃d] adj German. ❖ **Allemand, e** nm, f German. ❖ **allemand** nm LING German.

aller¹ [ale] nm **1.** [voyage] outward journey / *je suis passé les voir à l'aller* I dropped in to see them on the way (there) / *l'avion était en retard à l'aller et au retour* the flight was delayed both ways ▶ **un aller (et) retour** a round trip / **faire des allers et retours** [personne, document] to go back and forth, to shuttle back and forth **2.** [billet] ▶ **aller (simple)** single (ticket) 🇬🇧, one-way ticket 🇺🇸 ▶ **aller (et) retour** return 🇬🇧 ou round-trip 🇺🇸 (ticket) **3.** *fam* ▶ **aller et retour** [gifle] slap.

aller² [31] [ale]
❖ v aux **1.** *(suivi de l'infinitif)* [exprime le futur proche] to be going ou about to / *tu vas tomber !* you're going to fall!, you'll fall! ▶ **attendez-le, il va arriver** wait for him, he'll be here any minute now / *il va être 5 h* it's going on 5 **2.** *(suivi de l'infinitif)* [en intensif] to go ▶ **ne va pas croire / penser que…** don't go and believe / think that… / *tu ne vas pas me faire croire que tu ne savais rien !* you can't fool me into thinking that you didn't know anything! **3.** *(suivi du gérondif)* [exprime la continuité] ▶ **aller en**: *aller en s'améliorant* to get better and better, to improve.
❖ vi
A. EXPRIME LE MOUVEMENT 1. [se déplacer] to go ▶ **va vite !** a) hurry up! b) [à un enfant] run along (now)! ▶ **aller (et) venir** a) [de long en large] to pace up and down b) [entre deux destinations] to come and go, to go to and fro **2.** [se rendre - personne] ▶ **aller à** to go to / *aller à la mer / à la montagne* to go to the seaside / mountains ▶ **où vas-tu ?** where are you going? ▶ **comment y va-t-on ?** how do you get there? ▶ **j'irai en avion / voiture** I'll fly / drive, I'll go by plane / car ▶ **aller chez**: *aller chez un ami* to go to see a friend, to go to a friend's ▶ **aller dans**: *il a peur d'aller dans l'eau* he's afraid to go into the water / *je vais dans les Pyrénées* I'm going to the Pyrenees ▶ **aller en**: *aller en Autriche* to go ou to travel to Austria ▶ **aller vers**: *j'allais vers le nord* I was heading ou going north **3.** *(suivi de l'infinitif)* [pour se livrer à une activité] ▶ **aller faire qqch** to go and do sthg, to go do sthg 🇺🇸 / *je vais faire mes courses tous les matins* I go shopping every morning **4.** [mener - véhicule, chemin] to go / *cette rue va vers le centre* this street leads towards the city centre ▶ **aller droit au cœur de qqn** to go straight to sb's heart **5.** [se ranger - dans un contenant] to go, to belong ; [- dans un ensemble] to fit.
B. S'ÉTENDRE 1. [dans l'espace] ▶ **aller de… à…**: *le passage qui va de la page 35 à la page 43* the passage which goes from page 35 to page 43 ▶ **aller jusqu'à** a) [vers le haut] to go ou to reach up to b) [vers le bas] to go ou to reach down to c) [en largeur, en longueur] to go to, to stretch as far as **2.** [dans le temps] : *aller de… à…* to go from… to… ▶ **aller jusqu'à** [bail, contrat] to run till.
C. PROGRESSER 1. [se dérouler] ▶ **aller vite / lentement** to go fast / slow ▶ **plus ça va…**: *plus ça va, moins je comprends la politique* the more I see of politics, the less I understand it **2.** [personne] : *j'irais même jusqu'à dire que…* I would even go so far as to say that… ▶ **sans aller jusque-là**

without going that far ▶ **aller sur** ou **vers** [approcher de]: *il va sur* ou *vers la cinquantaine* he's getting on for ou going on 50 ▶ **allons (droit) au fait** let's get (straight) to the point ▶ **aller au plus pressé** to do the most urgent thing first.
D. ÊTRE DANS TELLE SITUATION 1. [en parlant de l'état de santé : *bonjour, comment ça va ?* — *ça va* hello, how are you? — all right ▶ **ça va ?** [après un choc] are you all right? / *ça ne va pas du tout* I'm not at all well ▶ **aller bien**: *je vais bien* I'm fine ou well ▶ **ça va bien ?** are you OK? ▶ **ça va pas (bien)** ou **la tête !, ça va pas, non ?** *fam* you're off your head!, you must be mad! **2.** [se passer] : *comment vont les affaires ?* — *elles vont bien* how's business? — (it's doing) OK ou fine ▶ **les choses vont** ou **ça va mal** things aren't too good ou aren't going too well / *obéis-moi ou ça va mal aller (pour toi) !* do as I say or you'll be in trouble! / *ça a l'air d'aller* you seem to be coping.
E. EXPRIME L'ADÉQUATION 1. [être seyant] ▶ **aller (bien) à qqn** a) [taille d'un vêtement] to fit sb b) [style d'un vêtement] to suit sb / *ça te va bien de me donner des conseils ! iron* you're a fine one to give advice! ▶ **cela te va à ravir** ou **à merveille** that looks wonderful on you, you look wonderful in that **2.** [être en harmonie] : *j'ai acheté un chapeau pour aller avec ma veste* I bought a hat to go with ou to match my jacket ▶ **aller ensemble** a) [couleurs, styles] to go well together, to match b) [éléments d'une paire] to belong together **3.** [convenir] : *nos plats vont au four* our dishes are oven-proof / *tu veux de l'aide ?* — *non, ça ira !* do you want a hand? — no, I'll manage ou it's OK! ▶ **ça ira pour aujourd'hui** that'll be all for today, let's call it a day.
F. LOCUTIONS ▶ **allez, un petit effort** come on, put some effort into it ▶ **allez, je m'en vais !** right, I'm going now! ▶ **allez-y !** go on!, off you go! ▶ **allons-y !** let's go! ▶ **c'est mieux comme ça, va !** it's better that way, you know! / *(espèce de) frimeur, va !* *fam* you show-off! ▶ **ça va bien**, *fam*, **ça va comme ça** *fam* OK ▶ *je t'aurai prévenu !* — *ça va, ça va !* don't say I didn't warn you! — OK, OK! ▶ **y aller** *fam*: *quand faut y aller, faut y aller* when you've got to go, you've got to go ▶ **vas-y mollo avec le vin !** *fam* go easy on the wine! ▶ **ça y va** *fam*: *ça y va, les billets de 50 € !* 50-euro notes are going as if there was no tomorrow! ▶ **y aller de**: *elle y est allée de sa petite larme* she had a little cry ▶ **il** ou **cela** ou **ça va de soi (que)** it goes without saying (that) / *va pour le Saint-Émilion !* *fam* all right ou OK then, we'll have the Saint-Emilion! ❖ **s'en aller** vpi **1.** [partir - personne] to go ▶ **va-t'en !** go away! / *tous les jeunes s'en vont du village* all the young people are leaving the village **2.** [se défaire, se détacher] to come undone **3.** *sout* [mourir - personne] to die, to pass away **4.** [disparaître - tache] to come off, to go (away) ; [- son] to fade away ; [- forces] to fail ; [- jeunesse] to pass ; [- lumière, soleil, couleur] to fade (away) ; [- peinture, vernis] to come off ▶ **ça s'en ira au lavage / avec du savon** it'll come off in the wash / with soap.

📋 **Aller faire qqch**

Notez l'emploi de *go and do sthg* qui sert à insister sur l'accomplissement de l'action (avec *go to do sthg*, on n'est pas certain que l'action soit accomplie). En anglais américain, *and* est souvent omis :
J'irai le voir demain. *I'll go and see him tomorrow* ou *I'll go see him tomorrow* 🇺🇸.
Va chercher du pain. *Go and get some bread* ou *Go get some bread* 🇺🇸.

Au passé, les deux verbes sont au prétérit. Dans ce cas, *and* ne peut pas être omis :
Il est allé chercher de la peinture. *He went and got some paint.*

Notez que la construction *go and do sthg* relève d'un registre plutôt oral.

allergénique [alɛrʒenik] adj allergenic.

allergie [alɛrʒi] nf MÉD allergy ▸ **avoir** ou **faire une allergie à** to be allergic to.

allergique [alɛrʒik] adj MÉD [réaction] allergic ▸ **être allergique à qqch** to be allergic to sthg.

aller-retour [alɛrətur] (pl **allers-retours**) nm [billet] return 🇬🇧 ou round-trip 🇺🇸 (ticket) / *je voudrais deux allers-retours pour Paris, s'il vous plaît* two returns to Paris, please.

alliage [aljaʒ] nm MÉTALL & TECHNOL alloy.

alliance [aljɑ̃s] nf **1.** [pacte] alliance, pact, union ▸ **conclure une alliance avec qqn** to ally o.s. with sb **2.** [bague] wedding ring. ⬧ **par alliance** loc adj by marriage.

allié, e [alje] ◆ adj allied. ◆ nm, f **1.** [pays, gouvernement] ally **2.** [ami] ally, supporter.

allier [9] [alje] vt **1.** [unir - pays, gouvernements, chefs] to unite, to ally (together) ; [-familles] to relate ou to unite by marriage **2.** [combiner - efforts, moyens, qualités] to combine (together) ; [-sons, couleurs, parfums] to match, to blend (together) / *elle allie l'intelligence à l'humour* she combines intelligence and humour. ⬧ **s'allier** vpi [pays] to become allied ▸ **s'allier avec un pays** to ally o.s. to a country, to form an alliance with a country ; *sout* [par le mariage - personnes] to marry ; [-familles] to become allied ou related by marriage.

alligator [aligatɔr] nm alligator.

allô [alo] interj hello, hullo / *allô, qui est à l'appareil ?* hello, who's speaking?

allocataire [alɔkatɛr] nmf beneficiary.

allocation [alɔkasjɔ̃] nf **1.** [attribution] allocation ; FIN [de parts] allotment, allotting **2.** SOCIOL [prestation] allowance, benefit 🇬🇧, welfare 🇺🇸 ▸ **avoir** ou **toucher des allocations** to be on benefit 🇬🇧 ou welfare 🇺🇸 ▸ **allocation (de) chômage** unemployment benefit *(U)* 🇬🇧 ou compensation *(U)* 🇺🇸 ▸ **allocations familiales** family allowance ▸ **allocation (de) logement, allocation-logement** housing benefit 🇬🇧, rent subsidy ou allowance 🇺🇸. ⬧ **allocations** nfpl *fam* ▸ **les allocations** a) [service] social security 🇬🇧, welfare 🇺🇸 b) [bureau] the social security office.

allocution [alɔkysjɔ̃] nf [discours] (formal) speech.

allongé, e [alɔ̃ʒe] adj **1.** [long] long **2.** [couché] : *il était allongé sur le canapé* he was lying on the sofa / *il est resté allongé pendant trois mois* he was bedridden for three months.

allongement [alɔ̃ʒmɑ̃] nm [extension - d'une route, d'un canal] extension ; [-d'une distance] increasing, lengthening ; [-d'une durée, de la vie] lengthening, extension ; [-des jours] lengthening / *l'allongement du temps de loisir* the increased time available for leisure pursuits.

allonger [17] [alɔ̃ʒe] ◆ vt **1.** [rendre plus long - robe, route, texte] to lengthen, to make longer ▸ **allonger le pas** to take longer strides **2.** [étirer - bras, jambe] to stretch out *(sép)* **3.** [coucher - blessé, malade] to lay down *(sép)* **4.** *tfam* [donner - argent] to produce, to come up with ▸ **allonger un coup à qqn** to fetch sb a blow **2.** CULIN ▸ **allonger la sauce** a) *pr* to make the sauce thinner b) *fig* to spin things out. ◆ vi ▸ **les jours allongent** the days are drawing out ou getting longer. ⬧ **s'allonger** vpi **1.** [se coucher] to stretch out ▸ **allongez-vous !** lie down! **2.** [se prolonger - visite, récit] to drag on ; [-vie, période] to become longer **3.** [se renfrogner] ▸ **son visage s'allongea** her face fell, she pulled 🇬🇧 ou made 🇺🇸 a long face.

allouer [6] [alwe] vt **1.** [argent] to allocate ; [indemnité] to grant ; FIN [actions] to allot **2.** [temps] to allot, to allow.

allumage [alymaʒ] nm **1.** [d'un feu, d'une chaudière] lighting ; [du gaz] lighting, turning on **2.** [d'une ampoule, d'un appareil électrique] turning ou switching on **3.** AUTO & MÉCAN ignition.

allumé, e [alyme] *fam* adj crazy.

allume-cigare(s) [alymsigar] (pl **allume-cigares**) nm cigarette lighter.

allume-feu [alymfø] (pl **allume-feu** ou **allume-feux**) nm [à alcool] fire-lighter.

allume-gaz [alymgaz] nm inv gas lighter.

allumer [3] [alyme] vt **1.** [enflammer - bougie, réchaud, cigarette, torche, gaz] to light ; [-bois, brindille] to light, to kindle ; [-feu, incendie] to light, to start **2.** [mettre en marche - lampe, appareil] to turn ou to switch ou to put on *(sép)* ; [-phare] to put on, to turn on *(sép)* / *j'ai laissé la radio allumée !* I forgot to turn off the radio! ▸ **le bureau est allumé** there's a light on in the office, the lights are on in the office ; *(en usage absolu)* ▸ **allume !** turn the light on! / *comment est-ce qu'on allume ?* how do you switch 🇬🇧 ou turn it on? / *où est-ce qu'on allume ?* where's the switch? ⬧ **s'allumer** vpi [se mettre en marche - appareil, radio] to switch ou to turn on ; [-lumière] to come on.

allumette [alymɛt] nf **1.** [pour allumer] match, matchstick ▸ **allumette suédoise** ou **de sûreté** safety match **2.** CULIN [gâteau - salé] allumette, straw ; [-sucré] allumette.

allumeuse [alymøz] nf *fam & péj* tease.

allure [alyr] nf **1.** [vitesse d'un véhicule] speed **2.** [vitesse d'un marcheur] pace ▸ **courir à toute allure** to run as fast as one can **3.** [apparence - d'une personne] look, appearance ▸ **avoir de l'allure** ou **grande allure** to have style / *il a une drôle d'allure* he looks odd ou weird ▸ **un personnage à l'allure** ou **d'allure suspecte** a suspicious-looking character.

allusion [alyzjɔ̃] nf **1.** [référence] allusion, reference ▸ **faire allusion à qqch** to allude to sthg, to refer to sthg **2.** [sous-entendu] hint.

alluvions [alyvjɔ̃] nmpl alluvion *(U)*, alluvium *(U)*.

alma mater [almamatɛr] nf sg 🇶🇨 ÉDUC & UNIV alma mater.

aloès [alɔɛs] nm aloe.

aloe vera [alɔevera] nm inv [plante, produit] aloe vera.

aloi [alwa] nm ▸ **de bon aloi** a) [marchandise, individu] of sterling ou genuine worth b) [plaisanterie] in good taste ▸ **de mauvais aloi** a) [marchandise] worthless b) [individu] worthless, no-good c) [plaisanterie] in bad taste d) [succès] cheap.

alors [alɔr] adv **1.** [à ce moment-là] then / *le Premier ministre d'alors refusa de signer les accords* the then Prime Minister refused to sign the agreement ▸ **jusqu'alors** until then **2.** [en conséquence] so / *il s'est mis à pleuvoir, alors nous sommes rentrés* it started to rain, so we came back in **3.** [dans ce cas] then, so, in that case / *je préfère renoncer tout de suite, alors !* in that case I'd just as soon give up straight away! **4.** [emploi expressif] : *il va se mettre en colère, et alors ?* so what if he gets angry? / *et alors, qu'est-ce qui s'est passé ?* so what happened then? / *alors, tu viens oui ou non ?* so are you coming or not?, are you coming or not, then? / *dites-le-lui, ou alors je ne viens pas* tell him, otherwise ou or else I'm not coming / *alors là, il exagère !* he's going a bit far there! / *ça alors, je ne l'aurais jamais cru !* my goodness, I would never have believed it! ⬧ **alors que** loc conj **1.** [au moment où] while, when / *l'orage éclata alors que nous étions encore loin de la maison* the storm broke while ou when we were still a long way from the house **2.** [bien que, même si] even though / *elle est sortie alors que c'était interdit* she went out, even though she wasn't supposed to **3.** [tandis que] while / *il part en vacances alors que je reste ici tout l'été* he's going on holiday while I stay here all summer.

alouette [alwɛt] nf ORNITH lark.

alourdir [32] [aluʀdiʀ] vt **1.** [ajouter du poids à] to weigh down *(sép)*, to make heavy ou heavier **2.** [style, allure, traits] to make heavier ou coarser ; [impôts] to increase. ❖ **s'alourdir** vpi **1.** [grossir - personne] to put on weight ; [- taille] to thicken, to get thicker **2.** [devenir lourd] to become heavy ou heavier **3.** [devenir plus grossier] to get coarser / *ses traits s'alourdissent* his features are getting coarser.

aloyau [alwajo] nm sirloin.

ALP SMS abr écrite de **à la prochaine.**

alpaga [alpaga] nm alpaca.

alpage [alpaʒ] nm [pâturage] high (mountain) pasture.

alpaguer [3] [alpage] vt *tfam* [arrêter] to nab, to bust US ▶ **se faire alpaguer** to get nabbed ou busted US.

Alpes [alp] npr fpl ▶ **les Alpes** the Alps.

alpha [alfa] nm alpha ▶ **l'alpha et l'oméga de** *fig* the beginning and the end of.

alphabet [alfabɛ] nm **1.** [d'une langue] alphabet ▶ **alphabet arabe / cyrillique / grec / romain** Arabic / Cyrillic / Greek / Roman alphabet **2.** [abécédaire] spelling ou ABC book, alphabet **3.** [code] ▶ **alphabet phonétique** phonetic alphabet.

alphabétique [alfabetik] adj alphabetic, alphabetical.

alphabétisation [alfabetizasjɔ̃] nf elimination of illiteracy ▶ **campagne / taux d'alphabétisation** literacy campaign / rate.

alphabétiser [3] [alfabetize] vt to teach to read and write.

alpin, e [alpɛ̃, in] adj **1.** BOT & GÉOL alpine **2.** SPORT [club] mountaineering *(modif)*, mountain-climbing *(modif)* ; [ski] downhill.

alpinisme [alpinism] nm mountaineering, mountain-climbing.

alpiniste [alpinist] nmf mountaineer, climber.

alsacien, enne [alzasjɛ̃, ɛn] adj Alsatian. ❖ **Alsacien, enne** nm, f Alsatian ▶ **les Alsaciens** the people of Alsace.

altération [alteʀasjɔ̃] nf [dégradation] alteration.

altercation [alteʀkasjɔ̃] nf *sout* quarrel, altercation *sout*.

alter ego [alteʀego] nm inv *hum* [ami] alter ego.

altérer [18] [alteʀe] vt **1.** [dégrader - couleur] to spoil ; [- denrée] to affect the quality of **2.** *sout* [falsifier - fait, histoire] to distort ; [- vérité] to distort, to twist **3.** [changer - composition, équilibre] to change, to alter, to modify. ❖ **s'altérer** vpi [se dégrader - denrée] to spoil ; [- sentiment, amitié] to deteriorate ; [- couleurs] to fade ; [- voix] to be distorted ▶ **sa santé s'est altérée** her health has deteriorated.

✍ In reformed spelling (see p. 16-18), this verb is conjugated like *semer* : *il altèrera, elle altèrerait.*

altermondialisation [alteʀmɔ̃djalizasjɔ̃] nf alterglobalisation.

altermondialisme [alteʀmɔ̃djalism] nm alterglobalism.

altermondialiste [alteʀmɔ̃djalist] ❖ adj alterglobalist. ❖ nmf alterglobalist.

alternance [alteʀnɑ̃s] nf **1.** [succession] alternation ; AGR crop rotation **2.** POL ▶ **alternance (du pouvoir)** changeover of power between parties. ❖ **en alternance** loc adv ▶ **jouer en alternance avec qqn** to alternate with another actor ▶ **faire qqch en alternance avec qqn** to take turns to do sthg.

alternatif, ive [alteʀnatif, iv] adj **1.** [périodique] alternate, alternating ; [mouvement, musique] alternative **2.** [à option] alternative ; SOCIOL alternative. ❖ **alternative** nf [solution de remplacement] alternative.

alternativement [alteʀnativmɑ̃] adv (each) in turn, alternately.

⚠ **Alternatively** signifie « autrement » et non alternativement.

alterner [3] [alteʀne] ❖ vt [faire succéder] to alternate. ❖ vi [se succéder - phases] to alternate ; [- personnes] to alternate, to take turns.

altesse [altɛs] nf Highness ▶ **Son Altesse Royale a)** [prince] His Royal Highness **b)** [princesse] Her Royal Highness.

altier, ère [altje, ɛʀ] adj haughty, arrogant.

altimètre [altimɛtʀ] nm altimeter.

altitude [altityd] nf altitude / *à haute / basse altitude* at high / low altitude ▶ **prendre de l'altitude** to gain altitude, to climb ▶ **perdre de l'altitude** to lose altitude. ❖ **en altitude** loc adv high up, at high altitude.

alto [alto] nm **1.** [instrument] viola **2.** [voix] contralto ou alto (voice) ; [chanteuse] contralto, alto.

altruisme [altʀɥism] nm altruism.

altruiste [altʀɥist] ❖ adj altruistic. ❖ nmf altruist.

alu [aly] (abr de aluminium) adj ▶ **papier alu** aluminium UK ou aluminum US foil, tinfoil.

aluminium [alyminjɔm] nm aluminium UK, aluminum US.

alunir [32] [alyniʀ] vi to land (on the moon).

alvéole [alveɔl] nf **1.** [d'une ruche] cell, alveolus *spéc* **2.** GÉOL cavity, pit.

Alzheimer [alzajmɛʀ] npr ▶ **la maladie d'Alzheimer** Alzheimer's disease.

amabilité [amabilite] nf [qualité] kindness, friendliness, amiability / *veuillez avoir l'amabilité de...* please be so kind as to... ❖ **amabilités** nfpl [politesses] polite remarks ▶ **faire des amabilités à qqn** to be polite to sb.

amadouer [6] [amadwe] vt **1.** [enjôler] to cajole **2.** [adoucir] to mollify, to soften (up).

amaigri, e [amegʀi] adj [visage] gaunt ; [trait] (more) pinched / *je le trouve très amaigri* he looks a lot thinner ou as if he's lost a lot of weight.

amaigrissant, e [amegʀisɑ̃, ɑ̃t] adj slimming UK, reducing US.

amaigrissement [amegʀismɑ̃] nm [perte de poids - du corps] weight loss ; [- des cuisses, de la silhouette] weight reduction.

amalgame [amalgam] nm [mélange] mixture, amalgam / *il ne faut pas faire l'amalgame entre ces deux questions* the two issues must not be confused.

amalgamer [3] [amalgame] vt **1.** [mélanger - ingrédients] to combine, to mix up *(sép)* **2.** [réunir - services, sociétés] to amalgamate.

amancher [3] [amɑ̃ʃe] QUÉBEC vt *fam* [tromper, duper] to fool. ❖ **s'amancher** vp *fam* to make sure.

amande [amɑ̃d] nf **1.** [fruit] almond **2.** [noyau] kernel.

amandier [amɑ̃dje] nm almond tree.

amant [amɑ̃] nm (male) lover.

AMAP [amap] (abr de Association pour le maintien d'une agriculture paysanne) French association promoting community-supported agriculture.

amarre [amaʀ] nf mooring line ou rope ▶ **rompre les amarres** *pr & fig* to break one's moorings.

amarrer [3] [amaʀe] vt NAUT [cordages] to fasten, to make fast ; [navire] to hitch, to moor. ❖ **s'amarrer** vpi ASTRONAUT to dock.

amas [ama] nm [tas] heap, mass, jumble.

amasser [3] [amase] vt [entasser - vivres, richesses] to amass, to hoard. ❖ **s'amasser** vpi [foule, troupeau] to gather ou to mass (in large numbers) ; [preuves] to accumulate, to pile up.

amateur, trice [amatœr, tris] ◆ adj **1.** *(avec ou sans trait d'union)* [non professionnel] amateur *(modif)* ▶ **théâtre amateur** amateur theatre ; SPORT amateur, non-professional **2.** [friand, adepte] ▶ **amateur de** : être amateur de qqch to be very interested in sthg / *il est amateur de bonne chère* he's very fond of good food. ◆ nmf **1.** SPORT [non professionnel] amateur **2.** [connaisseur] ▶ **amateur de** connoisseur of ▶ **amateur d'art** art lover ou enthusiast **3.** *fam* [preneur] taker / *je ne suis pas amateur* I'm not interested, I don't go in for that sort of thing. ❖ **d'amateur** loc adj *péj* amateurish ▶ **c'est du travail d'amateur** it's a shoddy piece of work. ❖ **en amateur** loc adv non-professionally ▶ **s'intéresser à qqch en amateur** to have an amateur interest in sthg.

amateurisme [amatœrism] nm LOISIRS & SPORT amateurism, amateur sport.

amazone [amazon] ❖ **en amazone** loc adv ▶ **monter en amazone** to ride side-saddle.

Amazone [amazon] npr f GÉOGR ▶ **l'Amazone** the Amazon (river).

Amazonie [amazoni] npr f ▶ **(l')Amazonie** the Amazon (Basin).

amazonien, enne [amazɔnjɛ̃, ɛn] adj Amazonian. ❖ **Amazonien, enne** nm, f Amazonian.

ambages [ɑ̃baʒ] ❖ **sans ambages** loc adv *sout* without beating about the bush.

ambassade [ɑ̃basad] nf **1.** [bâtiment] embassy / *l'ambassade du Canada* the Canadian embassy **2.** [mission] mission.

ambassadeur, drice [ɑ̃basadœr, dris] nm, f **1.** [diplomate] ambassador ▶ **ambassadeur auprès de** ambassador to **2.** *fig* [représentant] representative, ambassador.

ambiance [ɑ̃bjɑ̃s] nf **1.** [atmosphère] mood, atmosphere **2.** [cadre] surroundings, ambiance *sout* ; [éclairage] lighting effects **3.** *fam* [animation] : *il y a de l'ambiance !* it's pretty lively in here!

ambiant, e [ɑ̃bjɑ̃, ɑ̃t] adj [température] ambient.

ambidextre [ɑ̃bidɛkstr] adj ambidextrous.

ambigu, ambiguë ou **ambigüe*** [ɑ̃bigy] adj [à deux sens] ambiguous, equivocal.

ambiguïté, ambigüité* [ɑ̃bigɥite] nf [équivoque] ambiguity ▶ **répondre sans ambiguïté** to answer unequivocally ou unambiguously.

ambitieux, euse [ɑ̃bisjø, øz] ◆ adj ambitious. ◆ nm, f ambitious man (woman).

ambition [ɑ̃bisjɔ̃] nf **1.** [désir] ambition, aspiration ▶ **j'ai l'ambition** ou **mon ambition est de...** it's my ambition to... **2.** [désir de réussite] ambition ▶ **avoir de l'ambition** to be ambitious.

ambitionner [3] [ɑ̃bisjɔne] vt [poste] to have one's heart set on ▶ **ambitionner de faire qqch** : *elle ambitionne de monter sur les planches* her ambition is to go on the stage.

ambivalent, e [ɑ̃bivalɑ̃, ɑ̃t] adj ambivalent.

amblyope [ɑ̃blijɔp] adj amblyopic / *il est amblyope* he has a lazy eye.

ambre [ɑ̃br] ◆ adj inv amber. ◆ nm ▶ **ambre gris** ambergris.

ambulance [ɑ̃bylɑ̃s] nf ambulance.

ambulancier, ère [ɑ̃bylɑ̃sje, ɛr] nm, f **1.** [chauffeur] ambulance driver **2.** [infirmier] ambulance man (woman).

ambulant, e [ɑ̃bylɑ̃, ɑ̃t] adj itinerant, travelling UK, traveling US ▶ **c'est un dictionnaire ambulant** *fam* he's a walking dictionary.

âme [am] nf **1.** [vie] soul ▶ **rendre l'âme** to pass away **2.** [personnalité] soul, spirit ▶ **avoir une âme de chef** to be a born leader **3.** [principe moral] ▶ **en mon âme et conscience** in all conscience **4.** [cœur] soul, heart ▶ **faire qqch avec / sans âme** to do sthg with / without feeling ▶ **de toute mon âme** with all my heart ou soul / *c'est un artiste dans l'âme* he's a born artist **5.** [personne] soul / *un village de 500 âmes* a village of 500 souls ▶ **âme charitable** ou **bonne âme** kind soul ▶ **âme sensible** sensitive person ▶ **âmes sensibles, s'abstenir** not for the squeamish ▶ **chercher / trouver l'âme sœur** to seek / to find a soulmate.

amélioration [ameljɔrasjɔ̃] nf **1.** [action] improving, bettering **2.** [résultat] improvement ▶ **apporter des améliorations à** qqch to improve on sthg, to carry out improvements to sthg / *on observe une nette amélioration de son état de santé* her condition has improved considerably **3.** MÉTÉOR ▶ **amélioration (du temps)** better weather.

améliorer [3] [ameljɔre] vt [changer en mieux - sol] to improve ; [- relations] to improve, to make better ; [- productivité] to increase, to improve. ❖ **s'améliorer** vpi to improve.

amen [amɛn] nm inv amen.

aménagement [amenaʒmɑ̃] nm **1.** [d'une pièce, d'un local] fitting (out) ; [d'un parc] laying out, designing ; [d'un terrain] landscaping **2.** ADMIN ▶ **aménagement du territoire** town and country planning, regional development ▶ **aménagement urbain** urban planning **3.** [assouplissement] : *il a obtenu des aménagements d'horaire* he managed to get his timetable rearranged.

aménager [17] [amenaʒe] vt **1.** [parc] to design, to lay out *(sép)* ; [terrain] to landscape **2.** [équiper] to fit out, to equip **3.** [transformer] ▶ **aménager qqch en** : *aménager une pièce en atelier* to convert a room into a workshop **4.** [installer] to install, to fit / *aménager un placard sous un escalier* to fit ou to install a cupboard under a staircase **5.** [assouplir - horaire] to plan, to work out *(insép)*.

amende [amɑ̃d] nf fine / *avoir une amende de 100 euros* to be fined 100 euros.

amendement [amɑ̃dmɑ̃] nm DR & POL amendment.

amender [3] [amɑ̃de] vt **1.** DR & POL to amend **2.** AGR to fertilize.

amener [19] [amne] vt **1.** [faire venir - personne] to bring (along) ▶ **amener qqn chez soi** to bring sb round to one's place, to bring sb home ▶ **qu'est-ce qui vous amène ?** what brings you here? **2.** [acheminer] to bring, to convey ; [conduire - suj : véhicule, chemin] to take **3.** [provoquer - perte, ruine] to bring about *(sép)*, to cause ; [- guerre, maladie, crise] to bring (on) ou about, to cause ; [- paix] to bring about **4.** [introduire - sujet] to introduce. ❖ **s'amener** vpi *fam* to come along, to turn ou to show up / *alors, tu t'amènes ?* are you coming or aren't you? / *elle s'est amenée avec deux types* she showed up with two blokes.

✎ **Amener** qqn / qqch à qqn *Bring sb* / sthg to sb ou *bring sb sb* / sthg.

Notez la construction à double complément qui en anglais peut prendre deux formes dont le sens est le même :

• une structure identique à celle du français :
verbe + COD + préposition + COI
bring sb / sthg to sb

• une structure qui diffère de celle du français, sans préposition, et dans laquelle l'ordre des compléments est inversé :

verbe + COI + COD

bring sb sb / sthg

Ils ont amené plusieurs enfants blessés aux médecins de l'association. *They brought several injured children to the charity's doctors* ou *They brought the charity's doctors several injured children.*

Amenez-moi votre fille, je souhaite lui parler. *Bring your daughter to me, I want to talk to her* ou *Bring me your daughter, I want to talk to her.*

Dans un registre plus familier, amener est employé pour signifier «apporter, porter vers un lieu / une personne» et se traduira alors par take.

Amène-lui ses lunettes. *Take his glasses to him* ou *Take him his glasses.*

aménorrhée [amenɔʀe] nf amenorrhoea, amenorrhea US.

amenuiser [3] [amənɥize] ❖ **s'amenuiser** vpi [provisions, espoir] to dwindle, to run low ; [chances] to grow ou to get slimmer ; [distance] to grow smaller.

amer, ère [amɛʀ] adj [fruit] bitter ; *fig* [déception] bitter.

amèrement [amɛʀmɑ̃] adv bitterly.

américain, e [ameʀikɛ̃, ɛn] adj American. ❖ **Américain, e** nm, f American. ❖ **américain** nm LING American English. ❖ **américaine** nf *fam* [voiture] American car. ❖ **à l'américaine** loc adj ARCHIT American style.

américaniser [3] [ameʀikanize] vt to americanize.

américanisme [ameʀikanism] nm **1.** [science] American studies **2.** [tournure] americanism.

amérindien, enne [ameʀɛ̃djɛ̃, ɛn] adj Amerindian, American Indian. ❖ **Amérindien, enne** nm, f Amerindian, American Indian.

Amérique [ameʀik] npr f ❖ **(l')Amérique** America ❱ **l'Amérique centrale / latine / du Nord / du Sud** Central / Latin / North / South America.

amerrir [32] [ameʀiʀ] vi AÉRON to land (on the sea), to make a sea landing ; ASTRONAUT to splash down.

amertume [amɛʀtym] nf bitterness ❱ **avec amertume** bitterly.

améthyste [ametist] nf amethyst.

ameublement [amœblɔmɑ̃] nm **1.** [meubles] furniture ❱ **articles d'ameublement** furnishings **2.** [activité] furniture trade.

ameublir [32] [amœbliʀ] vt AGR to loosen, to break down (sép).

ameuter [3] [amœte] vt [attirer l'attention de] : *le bruit a ameuté les passants* the noise drew a crowd of passersby / *il a ameuté toute la rue* he got the whole street out ❱ **ameuter l'opinion sur qqch** to awaken public opinion to sthg.

ami, e [ami] ◆ adj [voix, peuple, rivage] friendly / *dans une maison amie* in the house of friends ❱ **être très ami avec qqn** to be great friends with sb. ◆ nm, f **1.** [camarade] friend ❱ *c'est un de mes amis* / *une de mes amies* he's / she's a friend of mine / *des amis à nous fam* friends of ours / *Tom et moi sommes restés amis* I stayed friends with Tom / *un médecin de mes amis sout* a doctor friend of mine ❱ **un ami de la famille** ou **de la maison** a friend of the family / *je m'en suis fait une amie* she became my friend / a friend (of mine) ❱ **devenir l'ami de qqn** to

become friends ou friendly with sb / *ne pas avoir d'amis* to have no friends / *nous sommes entre amis (ici)* we're among ou we're all friends (here) ❱ **ami d'enfance** childhood friend ❱ **les amis de mes amis sont mes amis** any friend of yours is a friend of mine **2.** [amoureux] ❱ **petit** ou *vieilli* **bon ami** boyfriend ❱ **petite** ou *vieilli* **bonne amie** girlfriend **3.** [bienfaiteur] ❱ **un ami des arts** a patron of the arts.

amiable [amjabl] ❖ **à l'amiable** loc adv privately, amicably ❱ **régler qqch à l'amiable a)** [gén] to reach an amicable agreement about sthg **b)** [sans procès] to settle sthg out of court.

amiante [amjɑ̃t] nm asbestos.

amical, e, aux [amikal, o] adj friendly. ❖ **amicale** nf association, club.

amicalement [amikalmɑ̃] adv in a friendly manner ❱ **bien amicalement** [en fin de lettre] (ever) yours.

amidon [amidɔ̃] nm starch.

amidonner [3] [amidɔne] vt to starch.

amincir [32] [amɛ̃siʀ] vt [amaigrir] to thin down (sép) ; [rendre svelte] to slim down (sép) ❱ **cette veste t'amincit** this jacket makes you look slimmer.

amincissant, e [amɛ̃sisɑ̃, ɑ̃t] adj slimming, reducing US.

amiral, e, aux [amiʀal, o] adj ❱ **vaisseau** ou **navire amiral** flagship. ❖ **amiral, aux** nm admiral.

amitié [amitje] nf **1.** [sentiment] friendship ❱ **se lier d'amitié avec qqn** to make friends ou to strike up a friendship with sb ❱ **prendre qqn en amitié, se prendre d'amitié pour qqn** to befriend sb, to make friends with sb **2.** [relation] friendship. ❖ **amitiés** nfpl [salutations, compliments] ❱ **faites-lui** ou **présentez-lui mes amitiés** give him my compliments ou best regards ❱ **amitiés, Marie** love ou yours, Marie.

ammoniac, aque [amɔnjak] adj ammoniac. ❖ **ammoniac** nm ammonia. ❖ **ammoniaque** nf ammonia (water), aqueous ammonia.

amnésie [amnezi] nf amnesia.

amnésique [amnezik] adj amnesic.

amniocentèse [amnjɔsɛ̃tez] nf amniocentesis.

amniotique [amnjɔtik] adj amniotic.

amnistie [amnisti] nf amnesty.

amnistier [9] [amnistje] vt to amnesty.

amocher [3] [amɔʃe] vt *fam* [meubles, vêtements] to ruin, to mess up (sép) ; [voiture] to bash up (sép) ; [adversaire, boxeur] to smash up (sép) ; [visage, jambe] to mess up (sép).

amoindrir [32] [amwɛ̃dʀiʀ] vt **1.** [faire diminuer - valeur, importance] to diminish, to reduce ; [- forces] to weaken ; [- autorité, faculté] to weaken, to lessen, to diminish ; [- réserves] to diminish **2.** [rendre moins capable] to weaken, to diminish.

amollir [32] [amɔliʀ] vt [beurre, pâte] to soften, to make soft ; [volonté, forces] to weaken, to diminish.

amonceler [24] [amɔ̃sle] vt [entasser - boîtes, livres, chaussures] to heap ou to pile up (sép) ; [- neige, sable, feuilles] to bank up (sép) ; [- vivres, richesses] to amass, to hoard / *amonceler une fortune* to build up ou to amass a fortune. ❖ **s'amonceler** vpi [papiers, boîtes, feuilles] to heap ou to pile up ; [preuves] to accumulate, to pile up ; [dettes] to mount, to pile up ; [neige, sable, nuages] to bank up.

✎ In reformed spelling (see p. 16-18), this verb is conjugated like *peler : il amoncèle, elle amoncèlera.*

amoncellement, amoncèlement* [amɔ̃sɛlmɑ̃] nm [d'objets divers, d'ordures] heap, pile ; [de neige, de sable, de feuilles, de nuages] heap ; [de richesses] hoard.

amont [amɔ̃] nm [d'une rivière] upstream water ; [d'une montagne] uphill slope. ❖ **en amont de** loc prép [rivière] upstream from ; [montagne] uphill from ou above / *les étapes en amont de la production* fig the stages upstream of production, the pre-production stages.

amoral, e, aux [amɔral, o] adj amoral.

amorce [amɔʀs] nf **1.** ARM [détonateur] primer, detonator ; [d'un obus] percussion cap ; [d'une balle] cap, primer ; [pétard] cap **2.** PÊCHE bait **3.** [début] beginning.

amorcer [16] [amɔʀse] vt **1.** [commencer - travaux] to start, to begin ; [- réforme] to initiate, to begin ; [- discussion, réconciliation] to start, to begin, to initiate ; [- virage] to go into (*insép*) ; [- descente] to start, to begin / *les travaux sont bien amorcés* the work is well under way **2.** ARM & TECHNOL to prime ; ÉLECTR to energize **3.** PÊCHE to bait.

amorphe [amɔʀf] adj fam [indolent] lifeless, passive.

amortir [32] [amɔʀtiʀ] vt **1.** [absorber - choc] to cushion, to absorb ; [- son] to deaden, to muffle ; [- douleur] to deaden ; SPORT to trap the ball / *l'herbe a amorti sa chute* the grass broke his fall ▶ **amortir le coup a)** pr to cushion ou to soften the blow **b)** fig to soften the blow **2.** FIN [dette] to pay off, to amortize ; [équipement] to depreciate ; BOURSE to redeem.

amortissement [amɔʀtismã] nm FIN [d'une dette] paying ou writing off ; [d'un titre] redemption ; [d'un emprunt] paying off, amortization ▶ **amortissement annuel** annual depreciation ▶ **amortissement du capital** depreciation of capital.

amortisseur [amɔʀtisœʀ] nm shock absorber.

amour [amuʀ] nm **1.** [sentiment] love ▶ **éprouver de l'amour pour qqn** to feel love for sb ▶ **faire qqch par amour** to do sthg out of ou for love ▶ **faire qqch par amour pour qqn** to do sthg for the love of ou out of love for sb **2.** [amant] lover, love **3.** [liaison] (love) affair, romance **4.** [acte sexuel] love-making ▶ **faire l'amour à** ou **avec qqn** to make love to ou with sb **5.** [vif intérêt] love ▶ **faire qqch avec amour** to do sthg with loving care ou love **6.** [terme affectueux] ▶ **mon amour** my love ou darling / *apporte les glaçons, tu seras un amour* be a dear ou darling and bring the ice cubes **7.** ART cupid. ❖ **amours** nfpl hum [relations amoureuses] love life ▶ **à vos amours !** **a)** [pour trinquer] cheers!, here's to you! **b)** [après un éternuement] bless you! ❖ **pour l'amour de** loc prép for the love ou sake of ▶ **pour l'amour de Dieu !** **a)** [ton suppliant] for the love of God! **b)** [ton irrité] for God's sake!

amouracher [3] [amuʀaʃe] ❖ **s'amouracher de** vp + prép ▶ **s'amouracher de qqn** to become infatuated with sb.

amourette [amuʀɛt] nf [liaison] casual love affair, passing romance ou fancy.

amoureusement [amuʀøzmã] adv lovingly.

amoureux, euse [amuʀø, øz] ◆ adj [tendre - regard, geste] loving, tender ; [- vie, exploit] love (*modif*) ; [épris] ▶ **être amoureux de qqn** to be in love with sb ▶ **tomber amoureux de qqn** to fall in love with sb / *être fou amoureux* to be madly in love. ◆ nm, f **1.** [amant] love, lover **2.** [adepte] lover. ❖ **en amoureux** loc adv : *si nous sortions en amoureux ce soir ?* how about going out tonight, just the two of us?

amour-propre [amuʀpʀɔpʀ] (*pl* **amours-propres**) nm pride.

amovible [amɔvibl] adj removable.

ampère [ãpɛʀ] nm ampere.

amphétamine [ãfetamin] nf amphetamine.

amphi [ãfi] (**abr de amphithéâtre**) nm fam lecture hall ou theatre.

amphibie [ãfibi] adj AÉRON & MIL amphibious.

amphithéâtre [ãfiteatʀ] nm ANTIQ amphitheatre 🇬🇧, amphitheater 🇺🇸 ; ENS lecture theatre 🇬🇧 ou hall ; [d'un théâtre] amphitheatre, (upper) gallery ; [salle de dissection] dissection room.

ample [ãpl] adj **1.** VÊT [large - pull] loose, baggy ; [- cape, jupe] flowing, full **2.** [mouvement, geste] wide, sweeping **3.** [abondant - stock, provisions] extensive, ample ▶ **de plus amples renseignements** further details ou information.

amplement [ãpləmã] adv fully, amply ▶ **ça suffit amplement, c'est amplement suffisant** that's more than enough.

ampleur [ãplœʀ] nf **1.** VÊT [largeur - d'un pull] looseness ; [- d'une cape, d'une jupe] fullness **2.** [importance - d'un projet] scope ; [- d'un stock, de ressources] abundance ▶ **l'ampleur des dégâts** the extent of the damages ▶ **prendre de l'ampleur** to gain in importance.

ampli [ãpli] (**abr de amplificateur**) nm fam amp.

amplificateur, trice [ãplifikatœʀ, tʀis] adj ÉLECTR & PHYS amplifying ; OPT magnifying ; PHOT enlarging. ❖ **amplificateur** nm ÉLECTR & RADIO amplifier.

amplifier [9] [ãplifje] vt **1.** ÉLECTR & PHYS to amplify ; OPT to magnify ; PHOT to enlarge **2.** [développer - courant, tendance] to develop, to increase ; [- conflit] to deepen ; [- hausse, baisse] to increase ; [- différence] to widen ; [- relations] to develop ; péj [exagérer] to exaggerate, to magnify. ❖ **s'amplifier** vpi [augmenter - courant, tendance] to develop, to increase ; [- conflit] to deepen ; [- hausse, baisse] to increase ; [- différence] to widen.

amplitude [ãplityd] nf **1.** ASTRON, MATH & PHYS amplitude **2.** MÉTÉOR range.

ampoule [ãpul] nf **1.** ÉLECTR bulb ▶ **ampoule à baïonnette** bayonet bulb ▶ **ampoule à économie d'énergie** energy-saving bulb ▶ **ampoule à vis** screw-fitting bulb ▶ **ampoule basse consommation** low-energy light bulb **2.** [récipient] phial **3.** MÉD blister.

ampoulé, e [ãpule] adj péj pompous, bombastic.

amputation [ãpytasjɔ̃] nf **1.** MÉD amputation **2.** fig [suppression] removal, cutting out.

amputer [3] [ãpyte] vt **1.** MÉD [membre] to amputate, to remove **2.** [ôter une partie de - texte] to cut (down), to reduce ; [- budget] to cut back (sép).

Amsterdam [amstɛʀdam] npr Amsterdam.

amusant, e [amyzã, ãt] adj **1.** [drôle] funny, amusing **2.** [divertissant] entertaining.

amuse-bouche [amyzbuʃ] (*pl* amuse-bouche ou amuse-bouches) nm appetizer, nibble.

amuse-gueule [amyzgœl] (*pl* amuse-gueule ou amuse-gueules) nm appetizer, nibble 🇬🇧.

amusement [amyzmã] nm **1.** [sentiment] amusement **2.** [chose divertissante] entertainment ; [jeu] recreational activity, pastime.

amuser [3] [amyze] vt **1.** [faire rire] to make laugh, to amuse ▶ **elle m'amuse** she makes me laugh ▶ **amuser la galerie** fam to play to the gallery **2.** [plaire à] to appeal to / *ça ne l'amuse pas de travailler chez eux* he doesn't enjoy ou like working there / *tu crois que ça m'amuse d'être pris pour un imbécile ?* do you think I enjoy being taken for a fool? / *si ça t'amuse, fais-le* do it if that's what you want, if it makes you happy, do it **3.** [divertir] to entertain. ❖ **s'amuser** vpi [jouer - enfant] to play / *à cet âge-là, on s'amuse avec presque rien* at that age, they amuse themselves very easily.

amygdale [amidal] nf tonsil / *se faire opérer des amygdales* to have one's tonsils removed ou out.

an [ɑ̃] nm **1.** [durée de douze mois] year ▶ **dans un an** one year from now / *j'ai cinq ans de métier* I have five years' experience in this field / *une amitié de vingt ans* a friendship of twenty years' standing ▶ **deux fois par an** twice a year ▶ **tous les ans a)** [gén] every ou each year **b)** [publier, réviser] yearly, on a yearly basis **2.** *(avec l'article défini)* [division du calendrier] (calendar) year ▶ **l'an dernier** ou **passé** last year / *en l'an 10 après Jésus-Christ* in (the year) 10 AD / *en l'an 200 avant notre ère* in (the year) 200 BC ▶ **le jour** ou **le premier de l'An** New Year's day ▶ **le Nouvel An** : *que fais-tu pour le Nouvel An ?* what are you doing for New Year? **3.** [pour exprimer l'âge] ▶ **à trois ans** at three (years of age) ▶ **elle a cinq ans** she's five (years old) / *un enfant de cinq ans* a five-year-old (child).

anabolisant [anabɔlizɑ̃] nm anabolic steroid.

anachronique [anakʀɔnik] adj anachronistic, anachronic.

anachronisme [anakʀɔnism] nm anachronism.

anagramme [anagʀam] nf anagram.

anal, e, aux [anal, o] adj anal.

analgésique [analʒezik] adj & nm analgesic.

analogie [analɔʒi] nf analogy. ❖ **par analogie** loc adv by analogy ▶ **par analogie avec** by analogy with.

analogique [analɔʒik] adj [présentant un rapport] analogic, analogical.

analogue [analɔg] adj analogous, similar.

analphabète [analfabɛt] adj & nmf illiterate.

analphabétisme [analfabetism] nm illiteracy.

analyse [analiz] nf **1.** [étude] analysis ▶ **analyse de faisabilité** feasibility study ▶ **analyse financière** financial analysis ▶ **analyse de marché** market survey ou research **2.** ENS analysis ▶ **analyse logique / grammaticale** GRAM sentence / grammatical analysis **3.** BIOL analysis ▶ **analyse de sang** blood analysis ou test **4.** PSYCHOL analysis, psychoanalysis.

analyser [3] [analize] vt **1.** [étudier] to analyse UK, to analyze US **2.** BIOL & CHIM to analyse UK, to analyze US, to test **3.** PSYCHOL to analyse UK, to analyze US / *se faire analyser* to undergo analysis.

analyste [analist] nmf **1.** [gén] analyst **2.** PSYCHOL analyst, psychoanalyst.

analyste-programmeur, euse [analistpʀɔgʀamœʀ, øz] (*mpl* **analystes-programmeurs**, *fpl* **analystes-programmeuses**) nm, f systems analyst.

analytique [analitik] adj analytic, analytical.

ananas [anana(s)] nm pineapple.

anarchie [anaʀʃi] nf **1.** POL anarchy **2.** [désordre] anarchy, lawlessness.

anarchique [anaʀʃik] adj anarchic, anarchical.

anarchiste [anaʀʃist] ◆ adj anarchist, anarchistic. ◆ nmf anarchist.

anathème [anatɛm] nm **1.** [condamnation] anathema ▶ **jeter l'anathème sur** to pronounce an anathema upon, to anathematize **2.** RELIG anathema.

anatomie [anatɔmi] nf SCI [étude, structure] anatomy.

anatomique [anatɔmik] adj anatomical.

ANC (abr de **African National Congress**) ANC.

ancestral, e, aux [ɑ̃sɛstʀal, o] adj [venant des ancêtres] ancestral.

ancêtre [ɑ̃sɛtʀ] nmf [ascendant] ancestor, forefather.

anchoïade [ɑ̃ʃɔjad] nf anchovy paste.

anchois [ɑ̃ʃwa] nm anchovy.

ancien, enne [ɑ̃sjɛ̃, ɛn] ◆ adj **1.** [vieux - coutume, tradition, famille] old, ancient, time-honoured ; [-amitié, relation] old, long-standing ; [-bague, châle] old, antique ▶ **un meuble ancien** an antique **2.** ANTIQ [langue, histoire, civilisation] ancient **3.** *(avant nom)* [ex - président, époux, employé] former, ex ; [-stade, église] former / *ses anciens camarades* his old ou former comrades / *mon ancienne école* my old school / *une ancienne colonie française* a former French colony ▶ **un ancien combattant** a (war) veteran, an ex-serviceman. ◆ nm, f **1.** [qui a de l'expérience] old hand **2.** [qui est plus vieux] elder **3.** [qui a participé] ▶ **un ancien de l'ENA** a former student of the ENA / *un ancien du parti communiste* an ex-member of the Communist Party / *un ancien de la guerre de Corée* a Korean war veteran, a veteran of the Korean war. ❖ **ancien** nm **1.** [objets] ▶ **l'ancien** antiques **2.** [construction] ▶ **l'ancien** old ou older buildings. ❖ **à l'ancienne** loc adj old-fashioned ▶ **bœuf à l'ancienne** beef in traditional style.

> ⚠ Attention, **ancient** signifie « très ancien », « antique ». Il ne doit pas être employé pour traduire les autres sens du mot ancien.

anciennement [ɑ̃sjɛnmɑ̃] adv previously, formerly.

ancienneté [ɑ̃sjɛnte] nf **1.** [d'une chose] oldness **2.** [d'une personne] length of service ; [avantages acquis] seniority / *avancer* ou *être promu à l'ancienneté* to be promoted by seniority.

ancrage [ɑ̃kʀaʒ] nm **1.** NAUT [arrêt] moorage, anchorage ; [droits] anchorage ou moorage ou berthing (dues) **2.** [enracinement] : *l'ancrage d'un parti dans l'électorat* a party's electoral base.

ancre [ɑ̃kʀ] nf NAUT ▶ **ancre (de marine)** anchor ▶ **jeter l'ancre a)** *pr* to cast ou to drop anchor **b)** *fig* to put down roots.

ancrer [3] [ɑ̃kʀe] vt **1.** NAUT to anchor **2.** *fig* to root / *la propagande a ancré le parti dans la région* propaganda has established the party firmly in this area / *c'est une idée bien ancrée* it's a firmly-rooted idea.

Andes [ɑ̃d] npr fpl ▶ **les Andes** the Andes.

Andorre [ɑ̃dɔʀ] npr f ▶ **(la principauté d')Andorre** (the principality of) Andorra.

andouille [ɑ̃duj] nf **1.** CULIN chitterlings sausage *(eaten cold)* **2.** *fam* [imbécile] dummy ▶ **faire l'andouille** to fool around.

andouillette [ɑ̃dujɛt] nf chitterlings sausage *(for grilling)*.

androgyne [ɑ̃dʀɔʒin] adj androgynous.

âne [an] nm **1.** ZOOL donkey, ass **2.** [imbécile] idiot, fool.

anéantir [32] [aneɑ̃tiʀ] vt **1.** [détruire - armée, ville] to annihilate, to destroy, to wipe out *(sép)* ; [-rébellion, révolte] to quell, to crush ; [-espoir] to dash, to destroy ; [-succès, effort] to ruin, to wreck ; [-amour, confiance] to destroy **2.** [accabler - suj : nouvelle, événement] to overwhelm, to crush / *être anéanti par le chagrin* to be overcome by grief / *elle est anéantie* she's devastated ; [épuiser] to exhaust ▶ **elle est anéantie par la chaleur / fatigue** she's overwhelmed by the heat / utterly exhausted.

anéantissement [aneɑ̃tismɑ̃] nm [destruction] ruin, annihilation, destruction.

anecdote [anɛkdɔt] nf anecdote / *tout cela, c'est de l'anecdote péj* this is all trivial detail, this is just so much trivia.

anecdotique [anɛkdɔtik] adj **1.** [qui contient des anecdotes] anecdotal **2.** [sans intérêt] trivial péj.

anémie [anemi] nf MÉD anaemia UK, anemia US.

anémié, e [anemje] adj MÉD anaemic UK, anemic US.

anémier [9] [anemje] vt **1.** MÉD to make anaemic UK ou anemic US **2.** [affaiblir] to weaken, to enfeeble *litt*.

s'anémier vp MÉD to become anaemic 🇬🇧 ou anemic 🇺🇸 ; *fig* to weaken.

anémone [anemɔn] nf BOT anemone.

ânerie [anʀi] nf [parole] stupid ou silly remark ▶ **dire des âneries** to make stupid ou silly remarks, to talk rubbish.

ânesse [anɛs] nf she-ass, jenny.

anesthésie [anɛstezi] nf anaesthesia, anesthesia 🇺🇸 ▶ **être sous anesthésie** to be anaesthetized ou under an anaesthetic ▶ **anesthésie locale / générale** local / general anaesthesia.

anesthésier [9] [anɛstezje] vt MÉD to anaesthetize, to anesthetize 🇺🇸.

anesthésique [anɛstezik] adj & nm anaesthetic, anesthetic 🇺🇸.

anesthésiste [anɛstezist] nmf anaesthetist, anesthetist 🇺🇸, anesthesiologist 🇺🇸.

aneth [anɛt] nm dill.

anévrysme, anévrisme [anevʀism] nm MÉD aneurism ▶ **rupture d'anévrysme** aneurysmal rupture.

anfractuosité [ɑ̃fʀaktɥozite] nf [cavité] crevice, crack.

ange [ɑ̃ʒ] nm **1.** RELIG angel ▶ **c'est mon bon ange** he's my guardian angel ▶ **c'est mon mauvais ange** he's a bad influence on me ▶ **être aux anges** to be beside o.s. with joy **2.** [personne parfaite] angel / *passe-moi le pain, tu seras un ange* be an angel ou a dear and pass me the bread.

angélique [ɑ̃ʒelik] adj RELIG & *fig* angelic.

angelot [ɑ̃ʒlo] nm cherub.

angélus [ɑ̃ʒelys] nm Angelus.

angine [ɑ̃ʒin] nf **1.** [infection - des amygdales] tonsillitis ; [- du pharynx] pharyngitis **2.** [douleur cardiaque] angina ▶ **angine de poitrine** angina (pectoris).

> ⚠ Attention, lorsqu'il s'agit de problèmes de gorge, il ne faut pas traduire angine par angina.

anglais, e [ɑ̃glɛ, ɛz] adj [d'Angleterre] English ; [de Grande-Bretagne] British ▶ **l'équipe anglaise** SPORT the England team. ❖ **Anglais, e** nm, f [d'Angleterre] Englishman (Englishwoman) ; [de Grande-Bretagne] Briton ▶ **les Anglais a)** [d'Angleterre] English people, the English **b)** [de Grande-Bretagne] British people, the British. ❖ **anglais** nm LING English ▶ **anglais américain / britannique** American / British English. ❖ **anglaises** nfpl ringlets. ❖ **à l'anglaise** ◆ *loc adj* HORT ▶ **jardin / parc à l'anglaise** landscaped garden / park. ◆ *loc adv* ▶ **se sauver** ou **filer à l'anglaise** to take French leave.

angle [ɑ̃gl] nm **1.** [coin - d'un meuble, d'une rue] corner ▶ **la maison qui est à** ou **qui fait l'angle** the house on the corner / *la statue est à l'angle de deux rues* the statue stands at a crossroads ▶ **meuble d'angle** corner unit ▶ **arrondir les angles** to smooth things over **2.** GÉOM angle ▶ **angle aigu / droit / obtus** acute / right / obtuse angle **3.** [aspect] angle, point of view / *présenter les choses sous un certain angle* to present things from a certain point of view. ❖ **angle mort** nm [en voiture] blind spot.

Angleterre [ɑ̃glətɛʀ] npr f ▶ **(l')Angleterre a)** England **b)** [Grande-Bretagne] (Great) Britain.

anglican, e [ɑ̃glikɑ̃, an] adj & nm, f Anglican.

anglicisme [ɑ̃glisism] nm anglicism.

angliciste [ɑ̃glisist] nmf **1.** [étudiant] student of English **2.** [spécialiste] Anglicist, expert in English language and culture.

anglo-normand, e [ɑ̃glonɔʀmɑ̃, ɑ̃d] (*mpl* **anglo-normands,** *fpl* **anglo-normandes**) adj **1.** HIST Anglo-

Norman **2.** GÉOGR of the Channel islands ▶ **les îles Anglo-Normandes** the Channel Islands.

anglophone [ɑ̃glɔfɔn] adj & nmf Anglophone.

anglo-saxon, onne [ɑ̃glɔsaksɔ̃, ɔn] (*mpl* **anglo-saxons,** *fpl* **anglo-saxonnes**) adj [culture, civilisation] Anglo-American, Anglo-Saxon. ❖ **Anglo-Saxon, onne** nm, f Anglo-Saxon ▶ **les Anglo-Saxons a)** [peuples] British and American people **b)** HIST the Anglo-Saxons. ❖ **anglo-saxon** nm LING Old English, Anglo-Saxon.

Anglo-Saxon

The adjective **anglo-saxon** and the noun **Anglo-Saxon** are often used in French to refer to British and American people, culture, customs, etc.: **la musique anglo-saxonne, la littérature anglo-saxonne.**

angoissant, e [ɑ̃gwasɑ̃, ɑ̃t] adj [expérience] distressing, harrowing, agonizing ; [nouvelle, livre, film] distressing, harrowing.

angoisse [ɑ̃gwas] nf [inquiétude] anxiety ; [tourment] anguish ▶ **être** ou **vivre dans l'angoisse** to live in (a constant state of) anxiety ▶ **l'angoisse de** : *l'angoisse de la mort* the fear of death ▶ **c'est l'angoisse !** *fam* I dread the very idea !

angoissé, e [ɑ̃gwase] ◆ adj [personne] anxious ; [regard] haunted, anguished, agonized ; [voix, cri] agonized, anguished / *être angoissé avant un examen* to feel anxious before an exam. ◆ nm, f anxious person.

angoisser [3] [ɑ̃gwase] vt ▶ **angoisser qqn a)** [inquiéter] to cause sb anxiety, to cause anxiety to sb **b)** [tourmenter] to cause sb anguish.

Angola [ɑ̃gɔla] npr m ▶ **(l')Angola** Angola.

angolais, e [ɑ̃gɔlɛ, ɛz] adj Angolan. ❖ **Angolais, e** nm, f Angolan.

angora [ɑ̃gɔʀa] ◆ adj angora. ◆ nm [laine] angora.

anguille [ɑ̃gij] nf ZOOL eel ▶ **il y a anguille sous roche** there's something fishy going on.

anguleux, euse [ɑ̃gylø, øz] adj [objet] angular ; [visage] bony, sharp-featured, angular ; [personne] skinny, bony ; [esprit, caractère] stiff, angular.

anicroche [anikʀɔʃ] nf hitch, snag ▶ **sans anicroche** smoothly, without a hitch.

animal, e, aux [animal, o] adj animal. ❖ **animal, aux** nm **1.** ZOOL animal ▶ **animal familier** ou **domestique** pet ▶ **animal virtuel** cyberpet **2.** *fam* [personne] dope, oaf / *c'est qu'il a encore raison, cet animal-là* ou *l'animal !* the beggar's right again !

animalerie [animalʀi] nf [magasin] pet shop.

animalier, ère [animalje, ɛʀ] adj [peintre, sculpteur] animal (*modif*) ▶ **parc animalier** wildlife park.

animateur, trice [animatœʀ, tʀis] nm, f **1.** [responsable - de maison de jeunes, de centre sportif] youth leader, coordinator ; [- de groupe] leader ; [- d'entreprise, de service] coordinator **2.** [gén & RADIO & TV] presenter ; [de jeux, de variétés] host.

> ⚠ Le mot anglais **animator** signifie « auteur de films d'animation ».

animation [animasjɔ̃] nf **1.** [entrain] life, liveliness, excitement ▶ **mettre un peu d'animation dans une réunion** to liven up a meeting **2.** [vivacité] liveliness, vivacity, animation **3.** [d'un quartier, d'une ville] life **4.** [coordination - d'un groupe] running ; [- d'un débat] chairing **5.** CINÉ animation.

anime [anim], **animé** [anime] nm [série d'animations japonaises] anime.

animé, e [anime] adj **1.** [doué de vie] animate ▶ **les êtres animés** animate beings **2.** [doté de mouvement] moving, animated **3.** [plein de vivacité - personne, discussion] lively, animated ; [- marché, ville, quartier] lively ▶ **des rues animées** bustling ou lively streets.

animer [3] [anime] vt **1.** [doter de mouvement - mécanisme, robot] to move, to actuate, to motivate **2.** [inspirer] to prompt, to motivate **3.** [égayer - soirée, repas] to bring life to, to liven up *(sép)* ; [- regard] to light up *(sép)* / *animer un personnage* to make a character come to life **4.** [présenter - débat] to chair ; [- émission d'actualité] to present ; [- émission de variétés] to host ; [faire fonctionner - atelier] to run. ❖ **s'animer** vpi [personne, conversation] to become animated ; [quartier, rue, visage, yeux] to come alive ; [pantin, poupée] to come to life.

animosité [animozite] nf animosity, hostility, resentment ▶ **ressentir de l'animosité contre qqn** to feel resentment ou hostility towards sb.

anis [ani(s)] nm **1.** BOT anise ▶ **anis étoilé** star anise **2.** CULIN aniseed ▶ **à l'anis** aniseed *(modif)*, aniseed-flavoured.

ankyloser [3] [ãkiloze] vt to ankylose ▶ **être tout ankylosé** to be stiff all over. ❖ **s'ankyloser** vpi [devenir raide - bras, jambe] to become numb ; [- personne] to go stiff.

annales [anal] nfpl annals ▶ **rester dans les annales** to go down in history.

anneau, x [ano] nm **1.** JOAILL ring **2.** [pour rideaux] ring ; [maillon] link ; [boucle - de ficelle] loop **3.** MATH ring. ❖ **anneaux** nmpl SPORT rings ; JEUX hoopla.

année [ane] nf **1.** [division du calendrier] year ▶ **année bissextile** leap year ▶ **année civile** calendar ou civil year **2.** [date] year ▶ **année de fabrication** date ou year of construction **3.** [durée] year ▶ **d'année en année** from year to year ▶ **d'une année à l'autre** from one year to the next / *entrer dans sa trentième année* to enter one's thirtieth year / *les plus belles années de ma vie* the best years of my life ▶ **première année** UNIV first year US, freshman year US ▶ **dernière année** UNIV final year ▶ **l'année scolaire / universitaire / judiciaire** the school / academic / judicial year ▶ **l'année fiscale** the tax year, the fiscal year US **4.** [nouvel an] ▶ **bonne année !** happy New Year! ▶ **souhaiter la bonne année à qqn** to wish sb a happy New Year. ❖ **années** nfpl ▶ **les années 60 / 70** the sixties / seventies.

année-lumière [anelymjɛr] *(pl* **années-lumière)** nf light year ▶ **à des années-lumière de** *fig* light years away from.

annexe [anɛks] ◆ adj **1.** [accessoire - tâche, détail, fait] subsidiary, related ; [sans importance] minor ▶ **des considérations annexes** side issues **2.** [dossier] additional ▶ **les documents ou pièces annexes** the attached documents. ◆ nf **1.** [bâtiment] annexe US, annex US **2.** [supplément] annexe ▶ **mettre qqch en annexe à** to append sthg to ; [d'un bilan] schedule ; [d'un dossier] appendix, annexe US, annex US ; DR [d'une loi] rider.

annexer [4] [anɛkse] vt **1.** [joindre] to annex, to append **2.** HIST & POL to annex. ❖ **s'annexer** vpt *fam* ▶ **s'annexer qqch a)** [le monopoliser] to hog sthg **b)** *euphém* [le voler] to filch sthg, to purloin sthg *hum*.

annexion [anɛksjɔ̃] nf annexation.

annihiler [3] [aniile] vt [efforts, révolte] to annihilate, to destroy ; [personne] to crush, to destroy *fig*.

anniversaire [anivɛrsɛr] ◆ adj anniversary *(modif)* / *le jour anniversaire de leur rencontre* the anniversary of the day they first met. ◆ nm **1.** [d'une naissance] birthday ; [d'un mariage, d'une mort, d'un événement] anniversary

▶ **anniversaire de mariage** (wedding) anniversary ▶ **joyeux anniversaire !** happy birthday! **2.** [fête] birthday party.

⚠ Attention à ne pas confondre **anniversary**, qui signifie l'**anniversaire** d'un événement ou d'un mariage, et **birthday**, qui désigne l'anniversaire d'une naissance.

annonce [anɔ̃s] nf **1.** [nouvelle] notice, notification ; [fait de dire] announcement ▶ **faire une annonce** [gén] to make an announcement **2.** [texte publicitaire] advertisement ▶ **mettre** ou **insérer une annonce dans un journal** to put ou to place an advert US ou advertisement in a paper ▶ **annonce judiciaire** legal notice ▶ **annonce publicitaire** advertisement ▶ **les petites annonces a)** [location, vente] classified advertisements, small ad US, want ad US **b)** [courrier du cœur] personal column **3.** JEUX declaration ▶ **faire une annonce** to declare.

annoncer [16] [anɔ̃se] vt **1.** [communiquer - décision, événement] to announce ; [- mauvaise nouvelle] to break, to announce / *je n'ose pas le lui annoncer* I daren't break it to her / *on m'a annoncé sa mort* I was told ou informed of his death / *je vous annonce que je me marie* I'd like to inform you that I'm getting married / *je leur ai annoncé que je m'en allais* I told them I was leaving **2.** [prédire] to forecast / *ils annoncent du soleil pour demain* sunshine is forecast for tomorrow, the forecast for tomorrow is sunny **3.** COMM [proposer] to quote ▶ **annoncer un prix** to quote a price **4.** [présenter - visiteur] to announce ; [- projet, changement] to introduce, to usher in *(sép)* ▶ **qui dois-je annoncer ?** what name shall I say? ▶ **se faire annoncer** to give one's name **5.** [présager] to announce, to foreshadow, to herald *litt* / *ça n'annonce rien de bon* it doesn't bode well, it isn't a very good sign ; [être signe de] to be a sign ou an indication of **6.** JEUX to declare ▶ **annoncer la couleur** *fam : j'ai annoncé la couleur, ils savent que je démissionnerai s'il le faut* I've laid my cards on the table ou made no secret of it, they know I'll resign if I have to. ❖ **s'annoncer** ◆ vp *(emploi réfléchi)* [prévenir de sa visite] to notify ou to warn (that one will visit). ◆ vpi **1.** [se profiler] to be looming ou on the horizon / *une grave crise s'annonce* a serious crisis is looming **2.** [dans des constructions attributives] : *la journée s'annonce très belle* it looks like it's going to be a beautiful day ▶ **s'annoncer bien** : *cela s'annonce très bien* things are looking very promising ou good ▶ **s'annoncer mal** : *cela s'annonce plutôt mal* it doesn't look very promising, the picture doesn't look ou isn't too good.

annonceur [anɔ̃scœr] nm ▶ **annonceur (publicitaire)** advertiser.

annonciateur, trice [anɔ̃sjatœr, tris] adj announcing, heralding, foreshadowing / *les secousses annonciatrices d'un tremblement de terre* the tremors that are the warning signs of an earthquake.

Annonciation [anɔ̃sjasjɔ̃] nf **1.** BIBLE ▶ **l'Annonciation** the Annunciation **2.** [fête] Annunciation ou Lady Day.

annotation [anɔtasjɔ̃] nf [note explicative] annotation.

annoter [3] [anɔte] vt [commenter] to annotate.

annuaire [anɥɛr] nm [recueil - d'une association, d'une société] yearbook, annual ▶ **annuaire électronique** electronic directory.

annualisation [anɥalizasjɔ̃] nf annualization / *l'annualisation du temps de travail* the calculation of working hours on a yearly basis.

annualiser [3] [anɥalize] vt to annualize, to calculate on a yearly basis / *annualiser la durée du temps de travail* to annualize the work time.

annuel, elle [anɥɛl] adj [qui revient chaque année] yearly, annual.

annuellement [anɥɛlmã] adv annually, yearly, on a yearly basis.

annuité [anɥite] nf **1.** FIN annuity **2.** [année de service] year.

annulaire [anylɛʀ] nm [doigt] third ou ring finger.

annulation [anylasjɔ̃] nf **1.** [d'un ordre, d'un rendez-vous] cancellation, calling off ; [d'une réservation] cancellation ; [d'une commande] cancellation, withdrawal ; [d'une proposition] withdrawal **2.** DR [d'un décret, d'un acte judiciaire] cancellation, annulment ; [d'un contrat] voidance, annulment ; [d'un jugement] quashing, nullification ; [d'un droit] defeasance ; [d'une loi] revocation, rescindment.

annuler [3] [anyle] vt **1.** [ordre, rendez-vous, projet] to cancel, to call off *(sép)* ; [réservation] to cancel ; [commande] to cancel, to withdraw **2.** DR [contrat] to annul, to render null and void, to invalidate ; [loi] to rescind, to revoke ; [mariage] to annul ; [testament] to set aside *(sép)*, to nullify ; [jugement, verdict] to quash. ❖ **s'annuler** vp *(emploi réciproque)* to cancel each other out.

anoblir [32] [anɔbliʀ] vt to ennoble, to confer a title on.

anodin, e [anɔdɛ̃, in] adj **1.** [inoffensif] harmless **2.** [insignifiant - personne, propos] ordinary, commonplace ; [- détail] trifling, insignificant ; [- événement] meaningless, insignificant.

anomalie [anɔmali] nf **1.** [bizarrerie - d'une expérience, d'une attitude] anomaly ; [- d'une procédure, d'une nomination] irregularity **2.** BIOL abnormality.

ânonner [3] [anɔne] vt to stumble through ❱ **ânonner sa leçon** to recite one's lesson falteringly.

anonymat [anɔnima] nm anonymity ❱ **conserver** ou **garder l'anonymat** to remain anonymous / *l'anonymat le plus total est garanti* confidentiality is guaranteed.

anonyme [anɔnim] adj **1.** [sans nom - manuscrit, geste] anonymous **2.** [inconnu - auteur, attaquant] anonymous, unknown.

anonymement [anɔnimmã] adv anonymously.

anorak [anɔrak] nm anorak.

anorexie [anɔʀɛksi] nf anorexia.

anorexique [anɔʀɛksik] adj & nmf anorexic.

anormal, e, aux [anɔʀmal, o] adj **1.** [inhabituel - événement] abnormal, unusual ; [- comportement] abnormal, aberrant *sout* **2.** [injuste] unfair, unjustified.

anormalement [anɔʀmalmã] adv [inhabituellement] unusually, abnormally.

anse [ãs] nf **1.** [poignée] handle **2.** GÉOGR cove, bight.

antagonisme [ãtagɔnism] nm antagonism.

antagoniste [ãtagɔnist] nmf antagonist.

antalgique [ãtalʒik] adj & nm analgesic.

antarctique [ãtaʀktik] adj Antarctic. ❖ **Antarctique** ❖ npr m [océan] ❱ **l'Antarctique** the Antarctic (Ocean). ❖ npr f [continent] ❱ **(l')Antarctique** Antarctica.

antécédent [ãtesedã] nm GRAM, LOGIQUE & MATH antecedent. ❖ **antécédents** nmpl **1.** [faits passés] antecedents, past ou previous history **2.** MÉD case history.

antenne [ãten] nf **1.** ENTOM antenna, feeler ❱ **avoir des antennes** a) *fam* [avoir de l'intuition] to be very intuitive b) [avoir des contacts] to know all the right people **2.** ÉLECTRON aerial 🇬🇧, antenna 🇺🇸 ❱ **antenne parabolique** dish aerial ou antenna, satellite dish **3.** RADIO & TV ❱ **être à l'antenne** to be on (the air) ❱ **passer à l'antenne** to go on the air ❱ **garder l'antenne** to stay on the air ❱ **rendre l'antenne** to hand back to the studio ❱ **sur notre antenne** a) RADIO on this frequency ou station b) TV on this chan-

nel ❱ **temps d'antenne** air time **4.** [agence, service] office ❱ **antenne chirurgicale** surgical unit.

antenne(-)relais [ãtɛnʀəle] (*pl* antennes-relais ou antennes relais) nf TÉLÉC mobile phone mast.

antépénultième [ãtepenyltjɛm] *sout* ❖ adj antepenultimate *sout*. ❖ nf antepenult.

antérieur, e [ãteʀjœʀ] adj **1.** [précédent] anterior, prior ❱ **la situation antérieure** the previous ou former situation ❱ **une vie antérieure** a former life ❱ **antérieur à** prior to, before **2.** [de devant] anterior.

antérieurement [ãteʀjœʀmã] adv previously. ❖ **antérieurement à** loc prép prior to, previous to, before.

anthologie [ãtɔlɔʒi] nf anthology.

anthracite [ãtʀasit] ❖ adj inv charcoal grey 🇬🇧 ou gray 🇺🇸. ❖ nm anthracite, hard coal.

anthropologie [ãtʀɔpɔlɔʒi] nf anthropology.

anthropologue [ãtʀɔpɔlɔg], **anthropologiste** [ãtʀɔpɔlɔʒist] nmf anthropologist.

anthropophage [ãtʀɔpɔfaʒ] ❖ adj cannibal *(modif)*, cannibalistic, anthropophagous *spéc*. ❖ nmf cannibal, anthropophagite *spéc*.

antiacarien, enne [ãtiakaʀjɛ̃, ɛn] adj anti-mite / *traitement* ou *shampooing antiacarien* anti-mite treatment ou shampoo. ❖ **antiacarien** nm anti-mite treatment.

antiadhésif, ive [ãtiadezif, iv] adj [gén] antiadhesive *(avant nom)* ; [poêle] nonstick. ❖ **antiadhésif** nm antiadhesive.

antiaérien, enne [ãtiaeʀjɛ̃, ɛn] adj antiaircraft.

anti-âge, antiâge* [ãtiaʒ] adj ❱ **crème anti-âge** antiageing 🇬🇧 ou antiaging 🇺🇸 cream.

anti-aliassage [ãtialjasaʒ] nm INFORM anti-aliasing.

antiaméricanisme [ãtiamerikanism] nm anti-Americanism.

antiatomique [ãtiatɔmik] adj antiatomic, antiradiation.

antiavortement [ãtiavɔʀtəmã] adj inv antiabortion, pro-life.

antibactérien, enne [ãtibakteʀjɛ̃, ɛn] adj antibacterial.

antibiothérapie [ãtibjoteʀapi] nf antibiotherapy.

antibiotique [ãtibiɔtik] adj & nm antibiotic.

antibrouillard [ãtibʀujaʀ] adj inv fog *(modif)* ❱ **phare** ou **dispositif antibrouillard** fog lamp 🇬🇧 ou light 🇺🇸.

antibruit [ãtibʀɥi] adj inv **1.** [matériau] soundproof **2.** ACOUST ❱ **mur antibruit** antinoise barrier.

anticalcaire [ãtikalkɛʀ] adj antiliming, antiscale *(avant nom)*.

anticancéreux, euse [ãtikɑ̃seʀø, øz] adj **1.** [centre, laboratoire] cancer *(modif)* **2.** [médicament] anticancer *(avant nom)*, carcinostatic *spéc*.

anticapitaliste [ãtikapitalist] adj anticapitalist.

anticerne [ãtisɛʀn] nm concealer.

antichambre [ãtiʃɑ̃bʀ] nf anteroom, antechamber.

antichoc [ãtiʃɔk] adj shockproof.

anticipation [ãtisipasjɔ̃] nf [prévision] anticipation. ❖ **d'anticipation** loc adj [roman, film] science-fiction *(modif)*, futuristic. ❖ **par anticipation** loc adj FIN advance *(modif)* ❱ **paiement par anticipation** advance payment.

anticipé, e [ãtisipe] adj **1.** [avant la date prévue - retraite, départ] early / *faire le règlement anticipé d'une facture* to pay a bill in advance **2.** [fait à l'avance] ❱ **avec nos remerciements anticipés** thanking you in advance ou anticipation.

anticiper [3] [ãtisipe] vt [prévoir] to anticipate. ❖ **anticiper sur** v + prép ❱ **anticiper sur ce qui va se passer** a) [deviner] to guess what's going to happen

b) [raconter] to explain what's going to happen ; *(en usage absolu)* : *mais j'anticipe !* but I'm getting ahead of myself! ◗ **n'anticipons pas !** let's just wait and see!, all in good time!

anticlérical, e, aux [ɑ̃tikleʀikal, o] adj & nm, f anti-clerical.

anticoagulant, e [ɑ̃tikoagylɑ̃, ɑ̃t] adj MÉD anticoagulating. ❖ **anticoagulant** nm MÉD anticoagulant.

anticonformiste [ɑ̃tikɔ̃fɔʀmist] adj & nmf nonconformist.

anticonstitutionnel, elle [ɑ̃tikɔ̃stitysjɔnɛl] adj unconstitutional.

anticorps [ɑ̃tikɔʀ] nm antibody.

anticyclone [ɑ̃tisiklon] nm anticyclone.

antidater [3] [ɑ̃tidate] vt to antedate, to predate.

antidémarrage [ɑ̃tidemaʀaʒ] adj inv ◗ **système anti-démarrage** immobilizer.

antidémocratique [ɑ̃tidemɔkratik] adj antidemocratic.

antidépresseur [ɑ̃tidepʀɛsœʀ] adj m & nm antidepressant.

antidiarrhéique [ɑ̃tidjaʀeik] nm MÉD diarrhoea treatment.

antidopage [ɑ̃tidɔpaʒ], **antidoping** [ɑ̃tidɔpiŋ] adj inv ◗ **contrôle / mesure antidopage** drug detection test / measure.

antidote [ɑ̃tidɔt] nm antidote.

antidouleur [ɑ̃tidulœʀ] adj inv [médicament] painkilling / *centre antidouleur* pain control unit.

antidrogue [ɑ̃tidʀɔg] adj inv drug-prevention *(modif)*.

antidumping [ɑ̃tidœmpiŋ] adj antidumping.

antieffraction [ɑ̃tiefʀaksjɔ̃] adj inv [dispositif] burglarproof.

antiémeutes [ɑ̃tiemœt] adj [brigade] riot *(modif)*.

antieuropéen, enne [ɑ̃tiøʀopeɛ̃, ɛn] adj & nm, f anti-European.

antifumée [ɑ̃tifyme] adj inv anti-smoke.

antigang [ɑ̃tigɑ̃g] adj ⟶ **brigade**.

antigel [ɑ̃tiʒɛl] nm AUTO antifreeze.

antiglobalisation [ɑ̃tiglɔbalizasjɔ̃] nf antiglobalization.

antigrippe [ɑ̃tigʀip] adj inv ◗ **vaccin antigrippe** flu vaccine.

antihistaminique [ɑ̃tiistaminik] nm antihistamine.

anti-inflammatoire [ɑ̃tiɛ̃flamatwaʀ] *(pl* **anti-inflammatoires)** ◆ adj anti-inflammatory. ◆ nm anti-inflammatory agent.

antijeu [ɑ̃tiʒø] nm SPORT unsportsmanlike conduct.

antillais, e [ɑ̃tijɛ, ɛz] adj West Indian. ❖ **Antillais, e** nm, f West Indian.

Antilles [ɑ̃tij] npr fpl ◗ **les Antilles** the Antilles, the West Indies ◗ **les Antilles françaises / néerlandaises** the French / Dutch West Indies ◗ **la mer des Antilles** the Caribbean Sea.

🏛 Les Antilles

The French West Indies include the overseas **départements** of Martinique and Guadeloupe, the latter including the islands of la Désirade, Marie-Galante, Saint-Barthélemy (Saint-Barth), les Saintes and Saint-Martin.

---

antilope [ɑ̃tilɔp] nf antelope.

antimigraineux, euse [ɑ̃timigʀɛnø, øz] adj anti-migraine. ❖ **antimigraineux** nm migraine treatment.

antimilitariste [ɑ̃timilitaʀist] adj & nmf antimilitarist.

antimite [ɑ̃timit] ◆ adj inv ◗ **boules antimite** mothballs. ◆ nm mothproofing agent, moth repellent.

antimondialisation [ɑ̃timɔ̃djalizasjɔ̃] nf anti-globalization.

antimondialiste [ɑ̃timɔ̃djalist] ◆ adj anti-globalization. ◆ nmf antiglobalist.

antimoustique [ɑ̃timustik] adj ◗ **répulsif antimoustique** mosquito repellent.

antinucléaire [ɑ̃tinykleɛʀ] adj antinuclear.

antipanique [ɑ̃tipanik] adj inv anti-panic.

antiparasite [ɑ̃tipaʀazit] adj inv anti-interference *(avant nom)*.

antipathie [ɑ̃tipati] nf antipathy ◗ **éprouver de l'anti-pathie pour qqn** to dislike sb.

antipathique [ɑ̃tipatik] adj unpleasant / *je le trouve assez antipathique, il m'est plutôt antipathique* I don't like him much.

antipelliculaire [ɑ̃tipelikylɛʀ] adj dandruff *(modif)*.

antiperspirant nm antiperspirant.

antiphrase [ɑ̃tifʀaz] ❖ **par antiphrase** loc adv paradoxically.

antipode [ɑ̃tipɔd] nm antipode ; fig : *c'est aux anti-podes de ce que je pensais* it's light-years away from what I imagined.

antipoison [ɑ̃tipwazɔ̃] adj inv ◗ **centre antipoison** emergency poisons unit.

antiquaire [ɑ̃tikɛʀ] nmf antique dealer.

antique [ɑ̃tik] adj **1.** [d'époque - meuble, bijou, châle] antique, old **2.** *(avant nom)* [démodé] antiquated, ancient.

antiquité [ɑ̃tikite] nf **1.** [objet] antique ◗ **des antiqui-tés** antiques ◗ **magasin d'antiquités** antique shop / *sa voiture, c'est une antiquité !* fig & hum his car is an old wreck ou ancient! **2.** [période] ◗ **l'Antiquité (grecque et romaine)** Ancient Greece and Rome.

antirabique [ɑ̃tiʀabik] adj anti-rabies *(avant nom)*.

antiradiation [ɑ̃tiʀadjasjɔ̃] adj ◗ **bouclier antiradia-tion** radiation shield ◗ **étui antiradiation** [pour téléphone portable] anti-radiation case.

antireflet [ɑ̃tiʀəflɛ] adj inv coated, bloomed *spéc*.

antirides [ɑ̃tiʀid] adj inv anti-wrinkle *(avant nom)*.

antirouille [ɑ̃tiʀuj] ◆ adj inv antirust *(avant nom)*, rust-resistant. ◆ nm rust preventive, rust inhibitor.

antisèche [ɑ̃tisɛʃ] nf arg scol crib (sheet), cheat sheet , pony .

antisémite [ɑ̃tisemit] ◆ adj anti-Semitic. ◆ nmf anti-Semite.

antisémitisme [ɑ̃tisemitism] nm anti-Semitism.

antiseptique [ɑ̃tisɛptik] adj & nm antiseptic.

antisismique [ɑ̃tisismik] adj antiseismic.

antislash [ɑ̃tislaʃ] nm INFORM backslash.

antistress [ɑ̃tistʀɛs] adj stress-reducing.

antisyndicalisme [ɑ̃tisɛ̃dikalism] nm union bashing fam ⊞.

antitabac [ɑ̃titaba] adj inv ◗ **campagne antitabac** anti-smoking campaign ◗ **loi antitabac** law prohibiting smoking in public places.

antitache [ɑ̃titaʃ] adj inv stain-repellent.

antiterrorisme [ɑ̃titeʀɔrism] nm antiterrorism.

antithèse [ɑ̃titɛz] nf antithesis.

antitranspirant, e [ɑ̃titʀɑ̃spiʀɑ̃, ɑ̃t] adj anti-perspirant.

antitrust [ātitʀœst] adj inv antimonopoly 🇬🇧, antitrust 🇺🇸.

antiviral, e, aux [ātiviʀal, o] adj MÉD & INFORM antiviral. ❖ **antiviral, aux** nm MÉD antiviral.

antivirus [ātiviʀys] nm INFORM anti-virus software.

antivol [ātivɔl] ◆ adj inv antitheft. ◆ nm **1.** AUTO theft protection ; [sur la direction] steering (wheel) lock **2.** [de vélo] (bicycle) lock.

antonyme [ātɔnim] nm antonym.

antre [ātʀ] nm [repaire - d'un fauve, d'un ogre] lair, den ; [- d'un brigand] hideout.

anus [anys] nm anus.

Anvers [āvɛʀ(s)] npr Antwerp.

anxiété [āksjete] nf anxiety, worry ▸ *attendre qqch avec anxiété* to wait anxiously for sthg.

anxieusement [āksjøzmā] adv anxiously, worriedly.

anxieux, euse [āksjø, øz] ◆ adj [inquiet - attente] anxious ; [- regard, voix, personne] anxious, worried ▸ **anxieux de** anxious ou impatient to. ◆ nm, f worrier.

anxiogène [āksjɔʒɛn] adj anxiety-provoking.

anxiolytique [āksjɔlitik] ◆ adj anxiolitic. ◆ nm tranquillizer 🇬🇧, tranquilizer 🇺🇸.

AOC abr écrite de appellation d'origine contrôlée.

aorte [aɔʀt] nf aorta.

août, aout* [u(t)] nm August. **Voir aussi mars.**

aoûtat, aoutat* [auta] nm harvest mite, chigger 🇺🇸, redbug 🇺🇸.

aoûtien, enne, aoutien*, enne [ausjɛ̃, ɛn] nm, f August holidaymaker 🇬🇧 ou vacationer 🇺🇸.

apache [apaʃ] adj Apache. ❖ **Apache** npr Apache.

apaisement [apɛzmā] nm [fait de calmer - soif, désir] quenching ; [- faim] assuaging ; [- chagrin] soothing, easing ; [fait de se calmer] quietening down.

apaiser [4] [apeze] vt [calmer - opposants, mécontents] to calm down (sép), to pacify, to appease ; [- douleur, chagrin] to soothe, to alleviate, to lessen ; [- faim] to assuage ▸ **apaiser les esprits** to calm things down. ❖ **s'apaiser** vpi [se calmer - personne] to calm down ; [- bruit, dispute, tempête, vent] to die down, to subside ; [- colère, chagrin, douleur] to subside ; [- faim] to be assuaged.

apanage [apanaʒ] nm prerogative, privilege ▸ **avoir l'apanage de qqch** to have a monopoly on sthg ▸ **être l'apanage de qqn** to be sb's privilege.

aparté [apaʀte] nm **1.** [discussion] private conversation **2.** THÉÂTRE aside. ❖ **en aparté** loc adv as an aside.

apartheid [apaʀtɛd] nm apartheid.

apathie [apati] nf apathy, listlessness.

apathique [apatik] adj apathetic, listless.

apatride [apatʀid] ◆ adj stateless. ◆ nmf stateless person.

APEC [apɛk] (abr de **Association pour l'emploi des cadres**) nf employment agency for professionals and managers.

apercevoir [52] [apɛʀsəvwaʀ] vt **1.** [voir brièvement] to glimpse, to catch sight of **2.** [distinguer] to make out (sép) **3.** [remarquer] to see, to notice. ❖ **s'apercevoir** ◆ vp (emploi réfléchi) to catch sight of o.s. ◆ vp (emploi réciproque) to catch a glimpse of one another. ❖ **s'apercevoir de** vp + prép **1.** [remarquer] to notice, to see **2.** [comprendre] to become aware of, to realize ▸ **sans s'en apercevoir** inadvertently, without realizing it ▸ **s'apercevoir que** to realize ou to understand that.

aperçu [apɛʀsy] nm **1.** outline, idea / un aperçu du sujet en deux mots a quick survey ou a brief outline of the

subject **2.** INFORM ▸ **aperçu avant impression** print preview.

apéritif [apeʀitif] nm drink, aperitif / venez à 19 h pour l'apéritif come round for drinks at 7 p.m.

apesanteur [apəzātœʀ] nf weightlessness.

à-peu-près [apøpʀɛ] nm inv [approximation] approximation / dans votre devoir, on ne vous demande pas d'à-peu-près your homework answers should be very specific.

apeuré, e [apœʀe] adj frightened.

aphone [afɔn] adj [sans voix] hoarse / il est devenu aphone tellement il a crié he's shouted himself hoarse.

aphorisme [afɔʀism] nm aphorism.

aphrodisiaque [afʀɔdizjak] adj & nm aphrodisiac.

aphte [aft] nm mouth ulcer, aphtha spéc.

apiculteur, trice [apikyltœʀ, tʀis] nm, f beekeeper, apiculturist spéc, apiarist spéc.

apiculture [apikyltyʀ] nf beekeeping, apiculture spéc.

apitoyer [13] [apitwaje] vt to arouse the pity of ▸ **il veut m'apitoyer** he's trying to make me feel sorry for him. ❖ **s'apitoyer sur** vp + prép ▸ **s'apitoyer sur qqn** to feel sorry for ou to pity sb ▸ **s'apitoyer sur son sort** to wallow in self-pity.

aplanir [32] [aplaniʀ] vt **1.** [niveler - terrain] to level (off), to grade ; [- surface] to smooth, to level off (sép) **2.** fig [difficulté] to smooth out ou over (sép), to iron out (sép) ; [obstacle] to remove.

aplati, e [aplati] adj flattened.

aplatir [32] [aplatiʀ] vt **1.** [rendre plat - tôle, verre, surface] to flatten (out) ; [- métal] to beat flat ; [- terre, sol] to roll, to crush ; [- rivet] to clench, to close ; [- couture, pli] to press (flat), to smooth (out) ; [- cheveux] to smooth ou to plaster down (sép) **2.** [écraser] to flatten, to squash, to crush. ❖ **s'aplatir** vpi **1.** [se coller] ▸ **s'aplatir contre le mur** to flatten o.s. against the wall **2.** fam [s'humilier] to grovel, to fawn ▸ **s'aplatir devant qqn** to go crawling to sb.

aplomb [aplɔ̃] nm **1.** [verticalité] perpendicularity ▸ **à l'aplomb de** a) [au-dessus de] directly above b) [au-dessous de] directly below **2.** [confiance en soi] aplomb ; péj [insolence] nerve / il ne manque pas d'aplomb he really has a nerve. ❖ **d'aplomb** loc adj **1.** [vertical] perpendicular ▸ **être d'aplomb** to be vertical ▸ **mettre qqch d'aplomb** a) CONSTR to plumb sthg (up) b) [redresser] to straighten sthg up ▸ **ne pas être d'aplomb** a) CONSTR to be out of plumb ou off plumb b) [en déséquilibre] to be askew / être bien d'aplomb sur ses jambes to be steady on one's feet **2.** [en bonne santé] well ▸ **remettre qqn d'aplomb** to put sb back on his / her feet, to make sb better.

APN nm abr de appareil photo numérique.

apnée [apne] nf apnoea ▸ **descendre** ou **plonger en apnée** to dive without breathing apparatus.

apocalypse [apɔkalips] nf [catastrophe] apocalypse. ❖ **d'apocalypse** loc adj [vision] apocalyptic ; [récit] doom-laden ▸ **un paysage d'apocalypse** a scene of devastation.

apogée [apɔʒe] nm [sommet] peak, summit, apogee / à l'apogée de sa carrière at the height ou at the peak of his career.

apologie [apɔlɔʒi] nf apologia ▸ **faire l'apologie de qqch** to (seek to) justify sthg.

⚠ En anglais moderne, **apology** signifie « excuses ».

apoplexie [apɔplɛksi] nf apoplexy.

a posteriori, à postériori* [aposterjɔri] loc adv afterwards / *il est facile de juger a posteriori* it's easy to be wise after the event.

apostrophe [apɔstrɔf] nf **1.** [interpellation] invective **2.** [signe] apostrophe.

apostropher [3] [apɔstrɔfe] vt to shout at.

apothéose [apoteoz] nf **1.** [apogée] summit **2.** THÉÂTRE (grand) finale / *cela s'est terminé en apothéose* it ended in fine ou grand style **3.** [consécration] great honour UK ou honor US.

apôtre [apotr] nm **1.** RELIG apostle, disciple **2.** [avocat] advocate / *se faire l'apôtre d'une idée* to champion ou to speak for an idea.

Appalaches [apalaʃ] npr mpl ▸ **les Appalaches** the Appalachian Mountains, the Appalachians.

apparaître, apparaître* [91] [aparɛtr] vi **1.** [à la vue] to appear ▸ **apparaître à qqn en songe** ou **rêve** to appear ou to come to sb in a dream ; [à l'esprit] to appear, to transpire, to emerge **2.** [se manifester - symptôme, bouton] to appear ; [-maladie] to develop ; [-préjugé, habitude] to develop, to surface ▸ **faire apparaître** to reveal **3.** [sembler] to seem, to appear ; *(tournure impersonnelle)* ▸ **il apparaît que...** it appears ou emerges that...

apparat [apara] nm [cérémonie] pomp ▸ **costume / discours d'apparat** ceremonial dress / speech.

appareil [aparɛj] nm **1.** [dispositif] apparatus, device ▸ **appareil dentaire a)** [prothèse] dentures, (dental) plate **b)** [pour corriger] brace UK ou braces US, plate ▸ **appareil électroménager** household appliance ▸ **appareil photo** (still) camera ▸ **appareil photo numérique** digital camera ▸ **appareil (téléphonique)** telephone / *qui est à l'appareil ?* who's speaking? ▸ **Berlot à l'appareil !** Berlot speaking! **2.** AÉRON craft, aircraft **3.** ANAT apparatus, system ▸ **appareil digestif** digestive apparatus ou system ▸ **appareil respiratoire** respiratory apparatus **4.** CONSTR bond **5.** [système] apparatus / *l'appareil du parti* the party apparatus ou machinery ▸ **l'appareil d'État** POL the state apparatus.

appareillage [aparɛjaʒ] nm **1.** TECHNOL equipment **2.** MÉD prosthesis **3.** NAUT casting off.

appareiller [4] [aparɛje] ◆ vt **1.** MÉD to fit with a prosthesis **2.** [assortir] to match, to pair **3.** ZOOL to mate. ◆ vi NAUT to cast off, to get under way.

apparemment [aparamɑ̃] adv apparently.

apparence [aparɑ̃s] nf [aspect - d'une personne] appearance ; [-d'un objet, d'une situation] appearance, look ▸ **juger sur** ou **d'après les apparences** to judge ou to go by appearances ▸ **faire qqch pour sauver les apparences** to do sthg for appearances' sake. ◆ **en apparence** loc adv apparently, by ou to all appearances / *en apparence il travaille, mais comment le savoir vraiment ?* to all appearances he works ou it would seem that he works, but how can one be sure?

apparent, e [aparɑ̃, ɑ̃t] adj **1.** [visible] visible ▸ **avec poutres apparentes** with exposed beams ▸ **couture apparente** topstitched seam **2.** [évident] obvious, apparent, evident ▸ **sans cause apparente** for no obvious ou apparent reason **3.** [superficiel] apparent ▸ **une tranquillité apparente** outward ou surface calm.

apparenté, e [aparɑ̃te] adj **1.** [parent] related **2.** [ressemblant] similar.

apparenter [3] [aparɑ̃te] ◆ **s'apparenter à** vp + prép [ressembler à] to be like / *cette histoire s'apparente à une aventure que j'ai vécue* this story is similar to ou is like an experience I once had.

appariteur [aparitœr] nm UNIV porter UK, campus policeman US.

apparition [aparisjɔ̃] nf **1.** [arrivée - d'une personne, d'une saison] arrival, appearance ▸ **faire une apparition** to put in ou to make an appearance ▸ **faire son apparition a)** [maladie] to develop **b)** [soleil] to come out **2.** [première manifestation] (first) appearance **3.** [vision] apparition, vision.

appart [apar] nm fam flat UK, apartment US.

appartement [apartəmɑ̃] nm flat UK, apartment US.

appartenance [apartənɑ̃s] nf [statut de membre] ▸ **appartenance à** membership of UK ou in US ▸ **appartenance à un parti** membership of UK ou in US a party.

appartenir [40] [apartənir] ◆ **appartenir à** v + prép **1.** [être la propriété de] to belong to **2.** [faire partie de - groupe] to belong to, to be part of ; [- professorat, syndicat] to belong to **3.** [dépendre de] ▸ **la décision t'appartient** it's up to you, it's for you to decide ; *(tournure impersonnelle)* : *il appartient à chacun de faire attention* it's everyone's responsibility to be careful.

appart hôtel [apartotɛl] nm apartment hotel.

appât [apa] nm **1.** CHASSE & PÊCHE bait *(U)* **2.** [attrait] ▸ **l'appât du gain** the lure ou attraction of money.

appâter [3] [apate] vt [attirer - poisson, animal] to lure ; [-personne] to lure, to entice.

appauvrir [32] [apovrir] vt [rendre pauvre - personne] to impoverish, to make poor ; [-pays] to impoverish, to drain ; [-terre] to impoverish, to drain, to exhaust ; [-sang] to make thin, to weaken ; [-langue] to impoverish. ◆ **s'appauvrir** vpi [personne, famille, pays] to get ou to grow poorer ; [sol] to become exhausted ; [sang] to become thin ; [langue] to become impoverished, to lose its vitality.

appel [apɛl] nm **1.** [cri] call ▸ **un appel au secours** ou à **l'aide a)** pr a call for help **b)** fig a cry for help ▸ **appel au rassemblement** call for unity ▸ **appel de détresse a)** NAUT distress call **b)** [d'une personne] call for help ▸ **appel de phares** : *faire un appel de phares (à qqn)* to flash ou blink US one's headlights ou lights (at sb) ▸ **faire un appel du pied à qqn** to make covert advances to sb ▸ **appel radio** radio message **2.** [coup de téléphone] ▸ **appel (téléphonique)** (telephone ou phone) call **3.** [sollicitation] appeal ▸ **faire appel à a)** [clémence, générosité] to appeal to **b)** [courage, intelligence, qualité, souvenirs] to summon (up) / *cela fait appel à des notions complexes* it involves complex notions **4.** ÉCON call ▸ **appel de fonds** call for funds ▸ **appel d'offres** invitation to tender / *répondre à un appel d'offres* to make a bid **5.** DR appeal ▸ **en appel** on appeal ▸ **faire appel** to appeal ▸ **appel à témoins** appeal for witnesses (to come forward) **6.** [liste de présence] roll call ; MIL [mobilisation] call-up ▸ **faire l'appel a)** ÉDUC to take the register UK, to call (the) roll US **b)** MIL to call the roll ▸ **répondre à l'appel** to be present **7.** INFORM call ▸ **programme / séquence d'appel** call routine / sequence **8.** JEUX ▸ **faire un appel à cœur / carreau** to signal for a heart / diamond **9.** SPORT take-off ▸ **prendre son appel** to take off **10.** TECHNOL ▸ **appel d'air** draught. ◆ **sans appel** loc adj **1.** DR without (the possibility of an) appeal **2.** [irrévocable] irrevocable / *sa décision est sans appel* his decision is final.

appelé, e [aple] nm, f ▸ **il y a beaucoup d'appelés et peu d'élus** many are called but few are chosen.

appeler [24] [aple] vt **1.** [interpeller] to call (out) to, to shout to / *attendez que je vous appelle* wait till I call you ▸ **appeler au secours a)** pr to shout "help", to call for help **b)** fig to call for help **2.** [au téléphone] to call (up) / *appelez ce numéro en cas d'urgence* dial this number in an emergency **3.** [faire venir - médecin] to call, to send for *(insép)* ; [-police] to call ; [-renforts] to call up ou out *(sép)* ; [-ascenseur] to call / *appeler du secours* to go for help ▸ **appeler qqn à l'aide** to call ou to sb for help ▸ **appeler un taxi a)** [dans la rue] to hail a taxi **b)** [par téléphone] to phone

for ou to call a taxi ▶ **le devoir m'appelle !** *hum* duty calls!
4. DR to summon ▶ **être appelé à comparaître** to be summoned ou issued with a summons **5.** [inciter] : *appeler aux armes* to call to arms ▶ **il faut appeler les gens à voter** ou **aux urnes** people must be urged to vote **6.** [destiner] ▶ **être appelé à** to be bound to / *ce quartier est appelé à disparaître* this part of town is due to be demolished (eventually) **7.** [nommer] to call / *appeler les choses par leur nom* to be blunt / *comment on appelle ça en chinois ?* what's (the word for) this in Chinese? ▶ **appelez-moi Jo** call me Jo **8.** INFORM [programme] to call (up) ; [réseau] to dial. ❖ **en appeler à** v + prép to appeal to / *j'en appelle à vous en dernier recours* I'm coming to you as a last resort. ❖ **s'appeler** ◆ vp *(emploi passif)* to be called ▶ **comment s'appelle-t-il ?** what's his name?, what's he called? / *voilà ce qui s'appelle une gaffe !* that's what's called ou that's what I call putting your foot in it! ▶ **ça s'appelle revient** *fam* make sure you give it back. ◆ vp *(emploi réciproque)* to call one another.

appelette [aplɛt] nf INFORM applet.

appellation [apelasjɔ̃] nf appellation, designation ▶ **appellation (d'origine) contrôlée** *government certification guaranteeing the quality of a French wine or cheese.*

appendice [apɛ̃dis] nm **1.** [note] appendix **2.** ANAT appendix.

appendicite [apɛ̃disit] nf appendicitis.

appentis [apɑ̃ti] nm **1.** [bâtiment] lean-to **2.** [toit] lean-to, sloping roof.

appesantir [32] [apəzɑ̃tiʀ] ❖ **s'appesantir** vpi [insister] ▶ **s'appesantir sur un sujet** to concentrate on ou to dwell at length on a subject.

appétissant, e [apetisɑ̃, ɑ̃t] adj **1.** [odeur, mets] appetizing, mouthwatering ▶ **peu appétissant** unappetizing **2.** *fam* [attirant] attractive.

appétit [apeti] nm [envie de manger] appetite / *avoir de l'appétit* ou *grand appétit* ou *bon appétit* to have a good ou hearty appetite ▶ **manger avec appétit** ou **de bon appétit** to eat heartily / *ça va te couper l'appétit* it'll spoil your appetite, it'll take your appetite away ▶ **perdre l'appétit** to lose one's appetite ▶ **bon appétit !** enjoy your meal!, have a nice meal!

applaudir [32] [aplodiʀ] ◆ vt [personne] to applaud, to clap ; [discours, pièce] to applaud / *et on l'applaudit encore une fois !* let's give him another big hand!, let's hear it for him one more time! ◆ vi to clap, to applaud ▶ **applaudir à tout rompre** : *les gens applaudissaient à tout rompre* there was thunderous applause.

applaudissements [aplodismɑ̃] nmpl applause *(U)*, clapping *(U)* ▶ **un tonnerre** ou **une tempête d'applaudissements** thunderous applause.

appli [apli] **(abr de application)** nf INFORM app.

applicable [aplikabl] adj applicable / *loi applicable à partir du 1ᵉʳ mars* law to be applied as of March 1st.

application [aplikasjɔ̃] nf **1.** [pose] application / *laisser sécher après l'application de la première couche* allow to dry after applying the first coat of paint **2.** [mise en pratique -d'une loi] application, enforcement ; [-d'une sentence] enforcement ▶ **mettre qqch en application** to put sthg into practice, to apply sthg **3.** [soin] application ▶ **travailler avec application** to work diligently, to apply o.s. (to one's work).

applique [aplik] nf [lampe] wall lamp.

appliqué, e [aplike] adj **1.** [studieux] assiduous, industrious **2.** SCI & UNIV applied.

appliquer [3] [aplike] vt **1.** [poser -masque, crème, ventouse] to apply ; [-enduit] to apply, to lay on *(sép)* / *appliquer son oreille contre la porte* to put one's ear to the door **2.** [mettre en pratique -décret] to enforce, to apply ;

[-peine] to enforce ; [-idée, réforme] to put into practice, to implement ; [-recette, méthode] to use ; [-théorie, invention] to apply, to put into practice. ❖ **s'appliquer** ◆ vp *(emploi passif)* [être utilisé] to apply / *cela ne s'applique pas dans notre cas* it doesn't apply in ou it's not applicable to our case. ◆ vpi **1.** [être attentif -élève, apprenti] to take care (over one's work), to apply o.s. (to one's work) **2.** [s'acharner] ▶ **s'appliquer à faire** to try to do.

appliquette [aplikɛt] nf INFORM applet.

appoint [apwɛ̃] nm [argent] ▶ **faire l'appoint** to give the exact money ou change. ❖ **d'appoint** loc adj ▶ **radiateur d'appoint** extra radiator ▶ **salaire d'appoint** extra income.

appointements [apwɛ̃tmɑ̃] nmpl salary.

⚠ Le mot anglais **appointment** signifie « rendez-vous » et n'a jamais le sens de rémunération.

apport [apɔʀ] nm [action d'apporter] contribution / *un apport d'argent frais* an injection of new money / *l'apport journalier en fer et en calcium* **a)** [fourni] the daily supply of iron and calcium **b)** [reçu] the daily intake of iron and calcium.

apporter [3] [apɔʀte] vt **1.** [objet] to bring / *apporte-le à papa dans la cuisine* take it to Dad in the kitchen **2.** [fournir -message, nouvelle] to give ; [-preuve] to give, to provide, to supply ; [-résultat] to produce ; [-soulagement, satisfaction] to bring ; [-modification] to introduce ▶ **apporter de l'attention** ou **du soin à (faire) qqch** to exercise care in (doing) sthg ▶ **apporter de l'aide à qqn** to help sb.

📋 **Apporter qqch à qqn** *Bring / take sthg to sb* ou *bring / take sb sthg.*

Bring si le COI est me ou us et **take** si le COI est you, her/him, them, etc.

Notez la construction à double complément qui en anglais peut prendre deux formes dont le sens est le même :

• une structure identique à celle du français :
  verbe + COD + préposition + COI
  bring / take sthg to sb

• une structure qui diffère de celle du français, sans préposition, et dans laquelle l'ordre des compléments est inversé :
  verbe + COI + COD
  bring / take sb sthg

J'ai apporté les journaux de ce matin à mon père. *I took the morning papers to my father* ou *I took my father the morning papers.*
Il m'a apporté des dessins. *He brought some drawings to me* ou *He brought me some drawings.*
Attention
Apporte-le-nous / moi *Bring it to us / me* **(et non** *bring us / me it*).

apposer [3] [apoze] vt **1.** [ajouter -cachet, signature] to affix, to append ; DR [insérer -clause] to insert **2.** [poser -affiche, plaque] to put up *(sép)*.

apposition [apozisjɔ̃] nf **1.** [ajout] affixing, appending **2.** GRAM apposition.

appréciable [apʀesjabl] adj **1.** [perceptible -changement] appreciable, noticeable **2.** [considérable -somme, effort] appreciable **3.** [agréable -qualité, situation] pleasant /

c'est appréciable de pouvoir se lever une heure plus tard it's nice to be able to get up an hour later.

appréciation [apresjasjɔ̃] nf **1.** [estimation - d'un poids, d'une valeur] appreciation, estimate, assessment; [- d'une situation] assessment, appreciation, grasp / *je laisse cela à votre appréciation* I leave it to your judgment **2.** [observation] remark, comment / *il a obtenu d'excellentes appréciations* ÉDUC he got very good comments from his teachers *(in his report)* **3.** [augmentation - d'une devise] appreciation.

apprécier [9] [apresje] vt **1.** [évaluer - valeur] to estimate, to assess; [- distance] to estimate, to judge **2.** [discerner - ironie, subtilités] to appreciate **3.** [aimer] to appreciate / *je n'apprécie pas du tout ce genre de blagues* I don't care for ou like that sort of joke at all / *le sel dans son café, il n'a pas apprécié !* fam he was not amused when he found his coffee had salt in it! **s'apprécier** vpi [monnaie] to appreciate (in value).

⚠ **Appreciate** n'est pas toujours la traduction adéquate pour **apprécier**. Voir article.

appréhender [3] [apreɑ̃de] vt **1.** [craindre - examen, réaction] to feel apprehensive about **2.** [comprendre] to comprehend *sout*, to grasp **3.** DR [arrêter] to arrest, to apprehend *sout*.

appréhension [apreɑ̃sjɔ̃] nf **1.** [crainte] fear, apprehension **avoir** ou **éprouver de l'appréhension** to feel apprehensive, to have misgivings **avec appréhension** apprehensively **2.** PHILOS [compréhension] apprehension.

apprendre [79] [aprɑ̃dʀ] vt **1.** [s'initier à] to learn **apprendre qqch de qqn** to learn sthg from sb, to be taught sthg by sb **apprendre qqch par cœur** to learn sthg (off) by heart ou rote **apprendre à connaître qqn / une ville** to get to know sb / a town **2.** [enseigner] **apprendre qqch à qqn** to teach sb sthg ou sthg to sb **il / ça va lui apprendre à vivre !** he'll / it'll teach him a thing or two! **3.** [donner connaissance de] to tell **apprendre qqch à qqn** to tell sb sthg **4.** [être informé de - départ, mariage] to learn ou to hear of *(insép)*; [- nouvelle] to hear / *tiens, tiens, on en apprend des choses !* fam well, well, who'd have thought such a thing? / *on en apprend tous les jours !* hum you learn something new every day!

📋 **Apprendre qqch à qqn** *Teach sthg to sb* ou *teach sb sthg.*

Notez la construction à double complément qui en anglais peut prendre deux formes dont le sens est le même :

• une structure identique à celle du français :
verbe + COD + préposition + COI
teach sthg to sb

• une structure qui diffère de celle du français, sans préposition et dans laquelle l'ordre des compléments est inversé :
verbe + COI + COD
teach sb sthg

Lara a appris des chansons algériennes à ses amies. *Lara taught some Algerian songs to her friends* ou *Lara taught her friends some Algerian songs.*

apprenti, e [aprɑ̃ti] nm, f apprentice **jouer les apprentis sorciers** ou **à l'apprenti sorcier** fig to play at being God.

apprentissage [aprɑ̃tisaʒ] nm **1.** [fait d'apprendre] **l'apprentissage des langues** language learning, learning languages **apprentissage en ligne** e-learning **2.** [durée] (period of) apprenticeship. **d'apprentissage** loc adj [centre, école] training; [contrat] of apprenticeship. **en apprentissage** loc adv **être en apprentissage chez qqn** to be apprenticed to ou to be serving one's apprenticeship with sb.

apprêter [4] [aprete] vt *litt* [préparer - repas] to get ready, to prepare; [habiller] to get ready, to dress. **s'apprêter à** vp + prép : *je m'apprêtais à te rendre visite* I was getting ready to call on you.

apprivoiser [3] [aprivwaze] vt [animal] to tame, to domesticate; [enfant, peur] to tame. **s'apprivoiser** vpi [animal] to become tame; [personne] to become more sociable.

approbateur, trice [aprɔbatœr, tris] adj [regard, sourire] approving; [commentaire] supportive.

approbation [aprɔbasjɔ̃] nf **1.** [assentiment] approval, approbation *sout* / *donner son approbation à un projet* to approve a plan **2.** [autorisation] approval.

approchant, e [aprɔʃɑ̃, ɑ̃t] adj similar / *il a dû le traiter d'escroc ou quelque chose d'approchant* he must have called him a crook or something like that ou something of the sort.

approche [aprɔʃ] nf **1.** [venue] approach **l'approche des examens** the coming of the exams, the approaching exams **2.** [accès] approachability **il est d'approche facile / difficile** he is approachable / unapproachable **3.** [conception] approach / *une approche écologique du problème* an ecological approach to the problem. **à l'approche de** loc prép **1.** [dans le temps] : *tous les ans, à l'approche de l'été* every year, as summer draws near / *à l'approche de la trentaine* as one nears ou approaches (the age of) thirty **2.** [dans l'espace] : *à l'approche de son père, il s'est enfui* he ran away as his father approached.

approcher [3] [aprɔʃe] ◆ vt **1.** [mettre plus près - lampe, chaise] to move ou to draw nearer, to move ou to draw closer **2.** [se mettre près de] to go ou to come near / *ne l'approchez / m'approchez surtout pas !* please don't go near him / come near me! ◆ vi **1.** [dans l'espace] to come ou to get nearer, to approach / *toi, approche !* you, come over here! / *on approche de Paris* we're getting near to ou we're nearing Paris; *fig* to be close **2.** [dans le temps - nuit, aube] to draw near; [- événement, saison] to approach, to draw near. **s'approcher** vpi **approche-toi** come here ou closer. **s'approcher de** vp + prép [se mettre plus près de] **s'approcher de qqn** to come close to sb, to come up to sb **s'approcher de qqch** to go near sthg.

approfondi, e [aprɔfɔ̃di] adj thorough, detailed, extensive.

approfondir [32] [aprɔfɔ̃diʀ] vt **1.** [détailler - sujet, étude] to go deeper ou more thoroughly into / *il faut approfondir la question* the question needs to be examined in more detail **sans approfondir** superficially **2.** [parfaire - connaissances] to improve, to deepen.

approprié, e [aprɔprije] adj [solution, technique] appropriate, apposite *sout*, suitable; [tenue] proper, right.

approprier [10] [aprɔprije] **s'approprier** vpt [biens, invention] to appropriate; [pouvoir] to seize.

approuver [3] [apruve] vt **1.** [être d'accord avec - méthode, conduite] to approve of *(insép)* **je vous approuve entièrement** I think you're entirely right **2.** [autoriser - alliance, fusion] to approve, to agree to *(insép)*; [- médicament, traitement] to approve; [- contrat] to ratify; [- projet de loi] to approve, to pass.

approvisionnement [apʀɔvizjɔnmɑ̃] nm **1.** [action] supplying **2.** [provisions] supply, provision, stock ▸ **approvisionnement en eau** water supply.

approvisionner [3] [apʀɔvizjɔne] vt **1.** [village, armée] to supply ▸ **être approvisionné en électricité** to be supplied with electricity **2.** BANQUE [compte] to pay (funds) into. ❖ **s'approvisionner** vpi [personne] to shop ; [commerce, entreprise] to stock up ▸ **s'approvisionner en** [stocker] to stock up on.

approximatif, ive [apʀɔksimatif, iv] adj [coût, évaluation] approximate, rough ; [traduction] rough ; [réponse] vague.

approximation [apʀɔksimasjɔ̃] nf **1.** [estimation] approximation **2.** MATH approximation ▸ **calcul par approximations successives** calculus by continual approach.

approximativement [apʀɔksimativmɑ̃] adv [environ] approximately, roughly ; [vaguement] vaguely.

appui [apɥi] nm **1.** CONSTR [d'un balcon, d'un garde-fou] support **2.** [dans les positions du corps] ▸ **prendre appui sur** to lean (heavily) on ; [d'un alpiniste] press hold **3.** [soutien] support, backing ▸ **avoir l'appui de qqn** to have sb's support ou backing ; MIL support. ❖ **à l'appui** loc adv : *il a lu, à l'appui, une lettre datée du 24 mai* in support of this ou to back this up, he read out a letter dated 24th May ▸ **preuves à l'appui** with supporting evidence.

appui-tête (*pl* appuis-tête), **appuie-tête** (*pl* appuie-tête ou appuie-têtes*) [apɥitɛt] nm headrest.

appuyé, e [apɥije] adj [allusion] heavy, laboured ; [regard] insistent.

appuyer [14] [apɥije] ❖ vt **1.** [faire reposer] to lean, to rest / *le vélo était appuyé contre la grille* the bicycle was resting ou leaning against the railings **2.** [donner son soutien à - candidat, réforme] to back, to support / *la police, appuyée par l'armée* the police, backed up ou supported by the army. ❖ vi **1.** [exercer une pression] to press, to push down ▸ **appuyer sur a)** [avec le doigt] to press, to push **b)** [avec le pied] to press down on **2.** [insister] ▸ **appuyer sur a)** [mot] to stress, to emphasize **b)** [note] to sustain **3.** AUTO ▸ **appuyer sur la droite / la gauche** to bear right / left / *appuyer sur la pédale de frein* to brake / *appuyer sur la pédale* fam to put one's foot down , to step on the gas . ❖ **s'appuyer contre** vp + prép to lean against / *s'appuyer contre la rampe* to lean against the banister. ❖ **s'appuyer sur** vp + prép **1.** [s'en remettre à - ami] to lean ou to depend ou to rely on ; [-amitié, aide] to count ou to rely on ; [-témoignage] to rely on **2.** [se fonder sur] : *ce récit s'appuie sur une expérience vécue* this story is based on a real-life experience.

âpre [apʀ] adj **1.** [âcre - goût] sour ; [- vin] rough **2.** [rude - voix, froid] harsh ; [féroce - concurrence, lutte] bitter, fierce ▸ **âpre au gain** péj greedy, money-grabbing.

âprement [apʀəmɑ̃] adv [sévèrement] bitterly, harshly.

après [apʀe] ❖ prép **1.** [dans le temps] after / *après le départ de Paul* after Paul left / **après (le) dîner** after dinner ▸ **530 après Jésus-Christ** 530 AD / *après ça, il ne te reste plus qu'à aller t'excuser* the only thing you can do now is apologize / *après avoir dîné, ils bavardèrent* after dining ou after dinner they chatted ▸ **jour après jour** day after day **2.** [dans l'espace] after / *la gare est après le parc* the station is past ou after the park **3.** [dans un rang, un ordre, une hiérarchie] after / *après vous, je vous en prie* after you / *vous êtes après moi* [dans une file d'attente] you're after me / *il était juste après moi dans la file* he was just behind me in the queue **4.** [indiquant un mouvement de poursuite, l'attachement, l'hostilité] ▸ **courir après qqn** to run after sb ▸ **il est constamment après moi a)** [me surveille] he's always breathing down my neck **b)** [me harcèle] he's always nagging (at) ou going on at me. ❖ adv

1. [dans le temps] afterwards , afterward ▸ **un mois après** a month later ▸ **bien après** a long ou good while after, much later ▸ **peu après** shortly after ou afterwards / *nous sommes allés au cinéma et après au restaurant* we went to the cinema and then to a restaurant / *après, tu ne viendras pas te plaindre !* don't come moaning to me afterwards! / *et après ? qu'est-ce que ça peut faire ?* fam so what? who cares? **2.** [dans l'espace] after **3.** [dans un rang, un ordre, une hiérarchie] next ▸ **qui est après ?** [dans une file d'attente] who's next? ❖ **après** loc adv afterwards , afterward , later / *il n'a réagi qu'après coup* it wasn't until afterwards ou later that he reacted. ❖ **après que** loc conj after / *je me suis couché après que tu aies téléphoné* I went to bed after you phoned. ❖ **après tout** loc adv **1.** [introduisant une justification] after all / *après tout, ça n'a pas beaucoup d'importance* after all, it's not particularly important **2.** [emploi expressif] then / *débrouille-toi tout seul, après tout !* sort it out yourself then! ❖ **d'après** loc prép **1.** [introduisant un jugement] according to ▸ **d'après moi** in my opinion / *alors, d'après vous, qui va gagner ?* so who do you think is going to win? ▸ **d'après ce qu'elle dit** from what she says **2.** [introduisant un modèle, une citation] ▸ **d'après Tolstoï** [adaptation] adapted from Tolstoy / *d'après une idée originale de...* based on ou from an original idea by... ❖ loc adj **1.** [dans le temps] following, next **2.** [dans l'espace] next / *je descends à la station d'après* I'm getting off at the next station.

après-demain [apʀedmɛ̃] adv the day after tomorrow ▸ **après-demain matin / soir** the day after tomorrow in the morning / evening.

après-guerre [apʀegɛʀ] (*pl* après-guerres) nm ou nf post-war era ou period / *le théâtre d'après-guerre* post-war drama.

après-midi [apʀemidi] (*pl* après-midi ou après-midis*) nm ou nf afternoon / *je le ferai dans l'après-midi* I'll do it this afternoon.

après-rasage [apʀeʀazaʒ] (*pl* après-rasages) ❖ adj inv aftershave (*modif*). ❖ nm aftershave (lotion).

après-shampooing [apʀeʃɑ̃pwɛ̃] (*pl* après-shampooings), **après-shampoing** [apʀeʃɑ̃pwɛ̃] (*pl* après-shampoings) nm (hair) conditioner.

après-ski [apʀeski] (*pl* après-skis) nm [botte] snow boot.

après-soleil [apʀesɔlɛj] (*pl* après-soleils) nm after-sun cream.

après-vente (*pl* après-vente ou après-ventes*) [apʀevɑ̃t] adj after-sales.

âpreté [apʀəte] nf **1.** [âcreté] sourness **2.** [dureté - d'un ton, d'une voix] harshness, roughness ; [- d'une saison] harshness, rawness ; [- d'un reproche] bitterness, harshness.

a priori, à priori* [apʀijɔʀi] ❖ loc adv on the face of it / *a priori, je ne vois pas d'inconvénient* in principle I can't see any reason why not. ❖ nm inv [préjugé] preconception, preconceived idea ▸ **juger sans a priori** to judge impartially, to be an unbiased judge.

apr. J.-C. (abr écrite de après Jésus-Christ) AD.

à-propos [apʀopo] nm inv aptness, relevance ▸ **votre remarque manque d'à-propos** your remark is not relevant ou to the point.

apte [apt] adj ▸ **apte à qqch a)** [par sa nature] fit for ou suited to sthg **b)** [par ses qualifications] qualified for sthg **c)** [par ses capacités] capable of sthg ▸ **apte à faire qqch a)** [par sa nature] suited to doing sthg **b)** [par ses qualifications] qualified to do sthg.

aptitude [aptityd] nf [capacité] ability, aptitude. ❖ **aptitudes** nfpl ▸ **avoir / montrer des aptitudes en langues** to have / to show a gift for languages.

Aquagym® [akwaʒim] nf SPORT aquaerobics.

aquarelle [akwaʀɛl] nf [tableau] watercolour US, watercolor US.

aquarium [akwaʀjɔm] nm **1.** [décoratif] fish tank, aquarium **2.** [au zoo] aquarium.

aquatique [akwatik] adj aquatic, water (modif).

aqueduc [akdyk] nm [conduit] aqueduct.

aquilin [akilɛ̃] adj m aquiline.

AR¹ **1.** abr écrite de accusé de réception **2.** abr écrite de arrière.

AR², **A-R** (abr écrite de aller-retour) R.

arabe [aʀab] adj [cheval, pays] Arab, Arabian. ❖ **Arabe** nmf Arab. ❖ **arabe** nm LING Arabic.

Arabie [aʀabi] npr f ▶ (l')**Arabie** Arabia ▶ (l')**Arabie Saoudite** Saudi Arabia.

arable [aʀabl] adj arable.

arabophone [aʀabɔfɔn] ❖ adj Arabic-speaking. ❖ nmf Arabic speaker.

arachide [aʀaʃid] nf peanut, groundnut spéc.

araignée [aʀeɲe] nf ZOOL spider ▶ **araignée (de mer)** spider crab.

araser [3] [aʀaze] vt **1.** [égaliser - mur] to level, to make level ou flush ; [- planche] to plane down (sép) **2.** GÉOL to erode.

arbalète [aʀbalɛt] nf crossbow.

arbitrage [aʀbitʀaʒ] nm **1.** DR arbitration **2.** [gén & SPORT] refereeing ; [au volley-ball, tennis, cricket] umpiring.

arbitraire [aʀbitʀɛʀ] adj [choix, arrestation] arbitrary.

arbitrairement [aʀbitʀɛʀmɑ̃] adv arbitrarily.

arbitre [aʀbitʀ] nmf **1.** DR arbiter, arbitrator **2.** [gén & SPORT] referee ; [au volley-ball, tennis, cricket] umpire.

arbitrer [3] [aʀbitʀe] vt [gén & SPORT] to referee ; [au volley-ball, tennis, cricket] to umpire.

arboré, e [aʀbɔʀe] adj planted with trees, wooded, arboreous spéc.

arborer [3] [aʀbɔʀe] vt **1.** [porter - veste, insigne] to sport, to wear ; [- drapeau] to bear, to display **2.** [afficher - sourire] to wear ; [- manchette, titre] to carry.

arborescence [aʀbɔʀesɑ̃s] nf arborescence ; INFORM tree (structure) ; [diagramme] tree diagram.

arboriculteur, trice [aʀbɔʀikyltœʀ, tʀis] nm, f tree grower, arboriculturist spéc.

arboriculture [aʀbɔʀikyltyʀ] nf arboriculture.

arbouse [aʀbuz] nf arbutus berry.

arbre [aʀbʀ] nm **1.** BOT tree ▶ **arbre fruitier** fruit tree ▶ **arbre généalogique** family tree ▶ **arbre de Noël** Christmas tree **2.** MÉCAN shaft ▶ **arbre de transmission** drive ou propeller shaft.

arbrisseau, x [aʀbʀiso] nm shrub.

arbuste [aʀbyst] nm shrub, bush.

arc [aʀk] nm **1.** ARM bow **2.** MATH arc ▶ **arc de cercle** arc of a circle **3.** ARCHIT arch ▶ **arc brisé** pointed arch ▶ **l'arc de triomphe (de l'Étoile)** the Arc de Triomphe.

arcade [aʀkad] nf **1.** ARCHIT archway ▶ **des arcades** arches, an arcade **2.** ANAT arch ▶ **arcade sourcilière** arch of the eyebrows.

arc-bouter, arcbouter* [3] [aʀkbute] ❖ **s'arc-bouter, s'arcbouter*** vpi to brace o.s. ▶ **s'arc-bouter contre un mur** to brace one's back against a wall.

arceau, x [aʀso] nm ARCHIT arch (of vault).

arc-en-ciel [aʀkɑ̃sjɛl] (pl **arcs-en-ciel**) nm rainbow.

archaïque [aʀkaik] adj [vieux] archaic, outmoded, antiquated.

arche [aʀʃ] nf **1.** ARCHIT arch **2.** RELIG ark ▶ **l'arche de Noé** Noah's Ark.

archéologie [aʀkeɔlɔʒi] nf archeology, archaeology.

archéologique [aʀkeɔlɔʒik] adj archeological, archaeological.

archéologue [aʀkeɔlɔg] nmf archeologist, archaeologist.

archet [aʀʃɛ] nm MUS bow.

archétype [aʀketip] nm [symbole] archetype.

archevêché [aʀʃəveʃe] nm [palais] archbishop's palace.

archevêque [aʀʃəvɛk] nm archbishop.

archi [aʀʃi] fam [extrêmement] incredibly.

archipel [aʀʃipɛl] nm archipelago.

architecte [aʀʃitɛkt] nmf ARCHIT architect ▶ **architecte d'intérieur** interior designer.

architectural, e, aux [aʀʃitɛktyʀal, o] adj architectural.

architecture [aʀʃitɛktyʀ] nf **1.** [art, style] architecture ▶ **architecture durable** sustainable architecture **2.** [structure - d'une œuvre d'art] structure, architecture.

archiver [3] [aʀʃive] vt **1.** [document, revue] to file ou to store (away) **2.** INFORM archive.

archives [aʀʃiv] nfpl [documents] archives, records ; INFORM archive.

archiviste [aʀʃivist] nmf archivist.

arctique [aʀktik] adj Arctic. ❖ **Arctique** npr m ▶ **l'Arctique** the Arctic (Ocean).

ardemment [aʀdamɑ̃] adv ardently, fervently, passionately ▶ **désirer qqch ardemment** to yearn for ou to crave sthg.

ardent, e [aʀdɑ̃, ɑ̃t] adj **1.** [brûlant - chaleur] burning, scorching ; [- soleil] blazing, scorching ; [- fièvre] burning, raging **2.** [vif - température] fiery, passionate ; [- désir] ardent, eager, fervent ; [- imagination] vivid, fiery **3.** [passionné - amant] ardent, eager, hot-blooded ; [- révolutionnaire, admirateur] ardent, fervent.

ardeur [aʀdœʀ] nf [fougue] passion, ardour US, ardor US, fervour US, fervor US / **il n'a jamais montré une grande ardeur au travail** he's never shown much enthusiasm for work.

ardoise [aʀdwaz] nf **1.** [matière] slate ▶ **toit d'ardoises** ou **en ardoises** slate roof **2.** [objet] slate **3.** fam [compte] bill, slate.

ardu, e [aʀdy] adj [difficile - problème, question] tough, difficult ; [- tâche] arduous, hard.

are [aʀ] nm are, hundred square metres.

aréna [aʀena] nm QUÉBEC sports centre with skating rink ; arena US.

arène [aʀɛn] nf [pour la corrida] bullring ▶ **descendre** ou **entrer dans l'arène** fig to enter the fray ou the arena. ❖ **arènes** nfpl ANTIQ amphitheatre (sg) US, amphitheater (sg) US.

arête [aʀɛt] nf **1.** [de poisson] (fish) bone / **enlever les arêtes d'un poisson** to bone a fish **2.** [angle - d'un toit] arris ; [- d'un cube] edge ; [- d'une voûte] groin.

argan [aʀgã] nm argan ▶ **huile d'argan** argan oil.

argent [aʀʒã] ❖ nm **1.** [métal] silver **2.** [monnaie] money ▶ **avoir de l'argent** to have money, to be wealthy / **(se) faire de l'argent** to make money ▶ **argent comptant: payer** ou **régler en argent comptant** to pay cash ▶ **accepter** ou **prendre qqch pour argent comptant** to take sthg at face value ▶ **argent liquide** ready cash ou money ▶ **argent de poche** pocket money US, allowance US ▶ **argent sale** dirty money ▶ **en avoir pour son argent** : **tu en auras pour ton argent** you'll get your money's worth, you'll get value for money ▶ **jeter l'argent par les fenêtres** to throw money down the drain, to squander money **3.** [couleur] silver colour. ◆ adj inv silver, silver-coloured. ❖ **d'argent** loc adj **1.** [en métal] silver *(modif)* **2.** [couleur] silver, silvery, silver-coloured. ❖ **en argent** loc adj silver *(modif)*.

argenté, e [aʀʒɑ̃te] adj **1.** [renard] silver *(modif)* ; [tempes] silver, silvery **2.** [plaqué] silver-plated, silver *(modif)* ▶ **métal argenté** silver plate.

argenterie [aʀʒɑ̃tʀi] nf silver, silverware.

argentin, e [aʀʒɑ̃tɛ̃, in] adj GÉOGR Argentinian, Argentine. ❖ **Argentin, e** nm, f Argentinian, Argentine.

Argentine [aʀʒɑ̃tin] npr f ▶ **(l')Argentine** Argentina, the Argentine.

argentique [aʀʒɑ̃tik] adj [photographie] traditional, nondigital.

argile [aʀʒil] nf clay.

argot [aʀɡo] nm slang, argot ▶ **argot de métier** jargon.

argotique [aʀɡɔtik] adj slang *(modif)*, slangy.

arguer [aʀɡe ou aʀɡɥe], **argüer*** [aʀɡɥe] [8] vt [prétexter] ▶ **arguer que...** to put forward the fact that... / *arguant qu'il avait une mauvaise vue* pleading his poor eyesight. ❖ **arguer de**, **argüer de*** v + prép to use as an excuse, to plead / *elle argua d'une migraine pour se retirer* she pleaded a headache in order to withdraw.

> ⚠ Le verbe anglais **to argue** est beaucoup plus courant que **arguer** en français et signifie « se disputer » ou « argumenter ». Voir article.

argument [aʀɡymɑ̃] nm [raison] argument ▶ **ses arguments** his reasoning ▶ **des arguments pour et contre** pros and cons.

argumentaire [aʀɡymɑ̃tɛʀ] nm COMM promotion leaflet.

argumentation [aʀɡymɑ̃tasjɔ̃] nf **1.** [raisonnement] argumentation, rationale **2.** [fait d'argumenter] reasoning.

argumenter [3] [aʀɡymɑ̃te] vi [débattre] to argue.

argus [aʀɡys] nm PRESSE ▶ **l'argus de l'automobile** the price guide for used cars.

aride [aʀid] adj [sec - terre] arid, barren ; [- vent] dry ; [- cœur] unfeeling.

aridité [aʀidite] nf [du sol] aridity, barrenness ; [du vent] dryness.

aristocrate [aʀistɔkʀat] nmf aristocrat.

aristocratie [aʀistɔkʀasi] nf aristocracy.

aristocratique [aʀistɔkʀatik] adj aristocratic.

arithmétique [aʀitmetik] ◆ adj MATH [moyenne, progression] arithmetical. ◆ nf [matière] arithmetic.

armagnac [aʀmaɲak] nm Armagnac (brandy).

armateur [aʀmatœʀ] nm [propriétaire - d'un navire] ship owner ; [- d'une flotte] fleet owner ; [locataire] shipper.

armature [aʀmatyʀ] nf **1.** [cadre - d'une tente, d'un abat-jour] frame ; [structure - d'un exposé, d'une théorie] basis, framework **2.** CONSTR framework **3.** COUT underwiring ▶ **soutien-gorge à armature** underwired bra **4.** MUS key signature.

arme [aʀm] nf **1.** [objet] weapon ▶ **arme biologique** bioweapon ▶ **l'arme chimique / nucléaire** chemical / nuclear weapons ▶ **arme blanche** knife ▶ **arme à feu** firearm ▶ **arme de poing** handgun ▶ **arme de service** [d'un policier] service gun **2.** [armée] force, service **3.** [instrument] weapon ▶ **arme à double tranchant** fig double-edged sword. ❖ **armes** nfpl **1.** [matériel de guerre] arms, weapons, weaponry ▶ **aux armes !** to arms! ▶ **prendre les armes** to take up arms ▶ **passer qqn par les armes** to send sb to the firing squad ▶ **faire ses premières armes** to

start out, begin one's career ▶ **mettre bas** ou **déposer** ou **rendre les armes** to lay down one's arms ▶ **armes de destruction massive** weapons of mass destruction **2.** HÉRALD coat of arms. ❖ **à armes égales** loc adv on equal terms.

> ⚠ Attention, **des armes** = **arms** ou **weapons**, MAIS **une arme** = **a weapon**, jamais **an arm**.

armé, e [aʀme] adj [personne] armed ▶ **armé de...** armed with... ▶ **bien / mal armé contre le froid** well-protected / defenceless against the cold. ❖ **armée** nf **1.** MIL army ▶ **être à l'armée** to be doing one's military service ▶ **l'armée de l'air** the Air Force ▶ **armée de métier** professional army ▶ **armée d'occupation** army of occupation ▶ **l'Armée rouge** the Red Army ▶ **l'Armée du Salut** the Salvation Army ▶ **l'armée de terre** the Army **2.** fig army, host.

armement [aʀməmɑ̃] nm **1.** [militarisation - d'un pays, d'un groupe] arming **2.** NAUT commissioning, fitting-out **3.** [d'un appareil photo] winding (on) ; [d'un pistolet] cocking **4.** [armes] arms, weapons, weaponry ▶ **limitation** ou **réduction des armements stratégiques** strategic arms limitation.

Arménie [aʀmeni] npr f ▶ **(l')Arménie** Armenia.

arménien, enne [aʀmenjɛ̃, ɛn] adj Armenian. ❖ **Arménien, enne** nm, f Armenian. ❖ **arménien** nm LING Armenian.

armer [3] [aʀme] vt **1.** MIL [guérilla, nation] to arm, to supply with weapons ou arms **2.** fig [préparer] to arm **3.** ARM to cock **4.** PHOT to wind (on) *(sép)* **5.** NAUT to commission, to fit out *(sép)*. ❖ **s'armer** vp *(emploi réfléchi)* [prendre une arme - policier, détective] to arm o.s. ; [- nation] to arm. ❖ **s'armer de** vp + prép **1.** [s'équiper - arme] to arm o.s. with ; [- instrument] to equip o.s. with **2.** fig [prendre] ▶ **s'armer de courage / patience** to muster ou summon up one's courage / patience.

armistice [aʀmistis] nm armistice ▶ **(l'anniversaire de) l'Armistice** Armistice ou Remembrance Day 🇬🇧, Veteran's Day 🇺🇸.

armoire [aʀmwaʀ] nf wardrobe, cupboard 🇬🇧, closet 🇺🇸 ▶ **armoire frigorifique** cold room ou store ▶ **armoire à glace** pr mirrored wardrobe ▶ **c'est une véritable armoire à glace** fig & hum he's built like the side of a house ▶ **armoire à linge** linen cupboard ou closet ▶ **armoire à pharmacie** medicine cabinet ou chest.

armoiries [aʀmwaʀi] nfpl coat of arms, armorial bearings.

armure [aʀmyʀ] nf HIST armour 🇬🇧, armor 🇺🇸 ▶ **vêtu de son armure** armour-clad.

armurerie [aʀmyʀʀi] nf [magasin] armourer's, gunsmith's.

armurier [aʀmyʀje] nm [fabricant] gunsmith, armourer.

ARN (abr de **acide ribonucléique**) nm RNA.

arnaque [aʀnak] nf fam swindle, rip-off.

arnaquer [3] [aʀnake] vt fam [duper] to rip off *(sép)* ▶ **arnaquer qqn de 200 euros** to do sb out of 200 euros.

arnica [aʀnika] nm ou nf arnica.

arobase [aʀɔbaz] nm INFORM "at", @ ▶ **l'arobase** the "at" symbol ou sign.

aromate [aʀɔmat] nm [herbe] herb ; [condiment] spice ▶ **aromates** seasoning.

aromathérapie [aʀɔmateʀapi] nf MÉD aromatherapy.

aromatique [aʀɔmatik] adj aromatic, fragrant.

aromatisant, e [aʀɔmatizɑ̃, ɑ̃t] adj ▶ **substance aromatisante** flavouring.

aromatiser [3] [aʀɔmatize] vt to flavour `UK`, to flavor `US` / *chocolat aromatisé au rhum* chocolate flavoured with rum, rum-flavoured chocolate.

arôme [aʀom] nm [parfum] aroma, fragrance ; [goût] flavour `UK`, flavor `US` ▸ **arôme artificiel / naturel** artificial / natural flavouring.

arpège [aʀpɛʒ] nm arpeggio.

arpenter [3] [aʀpɑ̃te] vt [parcourir - couloir] to pace up and down.

arpenteur [aʀpɑ̃tœʀ] nm ▸ **arpenteur-géomètre** surveyor, land-surveyor.

arqué, e [aʀke] adj [sourcils] arched ; [nez] hooked ; [jambes] bandy, bow *(modif)* ▸ **aux jambes arquées** bandy-legged, bow-legged.

arr. abr écrite de **arrondissement**.

arraché [aʀaʃe] nm SPORT snatch ▸ **gagner à l'arraché** *fig* to snatch a victory ▸ **une victoire à l'arraché** a hard-won victory.

arrachement [aʀaʃmɑ̃] nm **1.** [fait d'enlever - plante] uprooting, pulling out ; [-feuille, papier peint] ripping ou tearing out **2.** *fig* [déchirement] wrench.

arrache-pied [aʀaʃpje]
❖ **d'arrache-pied, d'arrachepied*** loc adv [travailler] relentlessly.

arracher [3] [aʀaʃe] vt **1.** [extraire - clou, cheville] to pull ou to draw out *(sép)* ; [-arbuste] to pull ou to root up *(sép)* ; [-betterave, laitue] to lift ; [-mauvaises herbes, liseron] to pull ou to root out *(sép)* ; [-poil, cheveu] to pull out *(sép)* ; [-dent] to pull out *(sép)*, to draw, to extract / *se faire arracher une dent* to have a tooth out / *il a eu un bras arraché dans l'explosion* he had an arm blown off in the explosion **2.** [déchirer - papier peint, affiche] to tear ou to rip off *(sép)* ; [-page] to tear out *(sép)*, to pull out *(sép)* **3.** [prendre - sac, billet] to snatch, to grab ; [obtenir - victoire] to snatch ▸ **arracher des aveux / une signature à qqn** to wring a confession / signature out of sb ▸ **arracher des larmes à qqn** to bring tears to sb's eyes **4.** [enlever - personne] ▸ **arracher qqn à son lit** to drag sb out of ou from his bed / *comment l'arracher à son ordinateur ?* how can we get ou drag him away from his computer? / *arracher un bébé à sa mère* to take a child from its mother ▸ **arracher qqn au sommeil** to force sb to wake up **5.** ▸ **arracher qqn à** [le sauver de] to snatch ou to rescue sb from. ❖ **s'arracher** vpt **1.** ▸ **c'est à s'arracher les cheveux** *fam* it's enough to drive you crazy **2.** [se disputer - personne, héritage] to fight over *(insép)*. ❖ **s'arracher à, s'arracher de** vp + prép to tear o.s. away from.

arraisonner [3] [aʀɛzɔne] vt NAUT [navire] to board (for inspection).

arrangeant, e [aʀɑ̃ʒɑ̃, ɑ̃t] adj accommodating, obliging.

arrangement [aʀɑ̃ʒmɑ̃] nm **1.** [fait de disposer] arrangement, laying out ; [résultat] arrangement, layout **2.** [accord] arrangement, settlement ▸ **parvenir à un arrangement** to reach an agreement, to come to an arrangement ▸ **nous avons un arrangement** we have an understanding **3.** MUS arrangement.

arranger [17] [aʀɑ̃ʒe] vt **1.** [mettre en ordre - chignon] to tidy up *(sép)* ; [-tenue] to straighten ; [-bouquet] to arrange ; [-chambre] to lay out *(sép)*, to arrange / *il a bien arrangé son appartement* his appartment is nicely laid out **2.** [organiser - rencontre, entrevue] to arrange, to fix ; [-emploi du temps] to organize / *c'est Paul qui a arrangé la cérémonie / l'exposition* Paul organized the ceremony / put the exhibition together ▸ **arranger qqch à l'avance** to prearrange sthg **3.** [résoudre - dispute, conflit] to settle, to sort out *(sép)* / *c'est arrangé, tu peux partir* it's all settled, you're free to leave now ▸ **et mes rhumatismes n'arrangent pas**

les choses ou **n'arrangent rien à l'affaire** my rheumatism doesn't help matters either / *voilà qui n'arrange pas mes affaires !* that's all I needed ! **4.** MUS to arrange **5.** [convenir à] to suit / *ce soir ou demain, comme ça t'arrange* tonight or tomorrow, as it suits you ou as is convenient for you / *mardi ? non, ça ne m'arrange pas* Tuesday? no, that's no good for me **6.** *fam* [réparer - radio, réveil, voiture] to fix ; [-chaussures] to fix, to mend ; [-robe] to alter **7.** [modifier - histoire, récit] to alter, to modify / *je ne t'ai jamais rien promis, tu arranges l'histoire (à ta façon)* I never promised you anything, you're just twisting things. ❖ **s'arranger** ❖ vp *(emploi réfléchi)* **1.** [s'habiller, se maquiller] : *elle sait s'arranger* she knows how to make the best of herself **2.** [se faire mal] : *tu t'es encore bien arrangé / bien arrangé la figure !* *fam & iron* you've made a fine mess of yourself / your face again ! ❖ vp *(emploi réciproque)* [se mettre d'accord] to come to an agreement. ❖ vpi **1.** [se débrouiller] to manage ▸ **s'arranger pour** : *arrangez-vous pour avoir l'argent, sinon...* make sure ou see that you have the money, or else... / *je me suis arrangé pour vous faire tous inviter* I've managed to get an invitation for all of you / *il s'arrange toujours pour partir plus tôt* he always manages to leave early **2.** [s'améliorer - santé, temps] to improve, to get better / *tout a fini par s'arranger* everything worked out fine in the end. ❖ **s'arranger avec** vp + prép to come to an agreement with / *on s'est arrangé avec les voisins* we sorted something out with the neighbours / *il s'est arrangé à l'amiable avec ses créanciers* he came to an amicable agreement with his creditors ▸ **arrange-toi avec lui** you'll have to sort it out with him / *je m'arrangerai avec ce que j'ai* I'll make do with what I've got.

⚠ Attention, **to arrange** ne peut être employé pour traduire arranger qu'au sens de « mettre en ordre ».

arrdt abr écrite de **arrondissement**.

arrestation [aʀɛstasjɔ̃] nf arrest ▸ **procéder à une arrestation** to make an arrest ▸ **être en état d'arrestation** to be under arrest.

arrêt [aʀɛ] nm **1.** [interruption] stopping ▸ **l'arrêt se fait automatiquement** it stops automatically / *appuyer sur le bouton « arrêt »* press the "stop" ou "halt" button ▸ **marquer un temps d'arrêt** to stop ou to pause for a moment ▸ **arrêt des hostilités** cessation of hostilities ▸ **arrêt de travail a)** [grève] stoppage **b)** [congé] sick leave **c)** [certificat] doctor's ou medical certificate **2.** TRANSP [pause] stop, halt / *avant l'arrêt complet de l'appareil* before the aircraft has come to a complete stop ou standstill / *ce train est sans arrêt jusqu'à Arcueil* this train is non-stop ou goes straight through to Arcueil / **'arrêts fréquents'** 'slow deliveries' / **'arrêt demandé'** 'stop requested' ▸ **arrêt facultatif** request stop *UK*, flag stop *US* ; [lieu] ▸ **arrêt (d'autobus)** bus stop / *je descends au prochain arrêt* I'm getting off at the next stop **3.** ▸ **arrêt de jeu** stoppage / *jouer les arrêts de jeu* to play injury time **4.** CINÉ & TV ▸ **arrêt sur image** freeze frame / *faire un arrêt sur image* to freeze a frame **5.** MÉD ▸ **arrêt cardiaque** ou **du cœur** cardiac arrest, cardiac failure **6.** DR [décision] judgment, ruling ▸ **arrêt de mort** death sentence. ❖ **arrêts** nmpl MIL arrest ▸ **mettre qqn aux arrêts** to place sb under arrest. ❖ **à l'arrêt** loc adj [véhicule] stationary / *l'appareil est à l'arrêt sur la piste* the aircraft is at a standstill on the runway. ❖ **en arrêt** loc adv ▸ **tomber en arrêt** [chien] to point / *je suis tombé en arrêt devant un magnifique vaisselier* I stopped short in front of a splendid dresser. ❖ **sans arrêt** loc adv [sans interruption] non-stop ; [à maintes reprises] constantly.

arrêté¹ [aʀete] nm [décret] order, decree ▸ **arrêté ministériel** ministerial order ▸ **arrêté municipal** ≃ by-law.

arrêté², e [aʀete] adj [opinion] fixed, set ; [intention] firm.

arrêter [4] [aʀete] ◆ vt **1.** [empêcher d'avancer - passant, taxi] to stop / *la circulation est arrêtée sur la N7* traffic is held up ou has come to a standstill on the N7 (road) ▸ **arrêter un ballon** SPORT to make a save, to save a goal **2.** [retenir - personne] to stop ; [- regard] to catch, to fix ; [interrompre] to interrupt **3.** [mettre fin à - élan] to stop, to check ; [- écoulement, saignement] to stem, to stop ; [- croissance, chute] to stop, to arrest, to bring to a halt / *on n'arrête pas le progrès !* *fam & hum* what will they think of next! **4.** [abandonner - construction, publication, traitement] to stop ; [- sport, chant] to give up *(sép)* ; [cesser de fabriquer] to discontinue (the manufacture of) **5.** [suj : police] to arrest ▸ **se faire arrêter** to get ou be arrested **6.** [déterminer - date, lieu] to appoint, to decide on *(insép)*, to fix ; [- plan, procédure] to decide on *(insép)*, to settle on *(insép)*, to settle upon *(insép)* ▸ **arrêter son choix** to make one's choice **7.** [suj : médecin] ▸ **arrêter qqn** to put sb on sick leave **8.** FIN ▸ **arrêter un compte a)** [le fermer] to close ou to settle an account **b)** [en faire un relevé] to draw up ou to make up a statement of account. ◆ vi : *arrête, tu me fais mal !* stop it, you're hurting me! / *quatre albums en un an ! mais vous n'arrêtez pas !* four albums in a year! you never stop ou you don't ever take a break, do you? / *il a arrêté de travailler l'an dernier* he retired last year ▸ **j'ai arrêté de fumer** I've given up ou stopped smoking ; *(tournure impersonnelle)* : *il n'a pas arrêté de neiger* it hasn't stopped snowing, it's been snowing non-stop. ◆ **s'arrêter** vpi **1.** [cesser - bruit, pluie, saignement] to stop ▸ **s'arrêter de a)** [cesser de] to stop **b)** [renoncer à] to give up, to stop / *elle s'est arrêtée de jouer en me voyant* she stopped playing when she saw me **2.** [s'immobiliser - montre] to stop ; [- ascenseur, véhicule] to stop, to come to a stop ou halt / *une voiture vint s'arrêter à ma hauteur* a car pulled up alongside me ▸ **s'arrêter net** to stop dead ou short **3.** [faire une halte, une pause] to stop ▸ **passer sans s'arrêter devant qqn** to pass by sb without stopping / *on s'est arrêtés plusieurs fois en route* we made several stops on the way ▸ **s'arrêter chez qqn** to call at sb's / *tu peux t'arrêter chez l'épicier en venant ?* could you stop off at the grocer's on your way here? / *nous nous étions arrêtés à la page 56* we'd left off at page 56 **4.** [se fixer] ▸ **s'arrêter sur** : *son regard s'arrêta sur leur ami* his gaze fell on their friend / *notre choix s'est arrêté sur le canapé en cuir* we decided ou settled on the leather couch. ◆ **s'arrêter à** vp + prép [faire attention à] to pay attention to.

📋 Attention à ne pas confondre stop doing sthg et stop to do sthg :

• Arrêter de + infinitif se traduit par stop + -ing.
Arrête d'embêter ton frère ! *Stop bothering your brother!*
Emma n'arrête pas de penser à Paul. *Emma can't stop thinking about Paul.*

• S'arrêter pour + infinitif se traduit par stop to + base verbale :
Ils se sont arrêtés pour déjeuner dans un village / prendre une photo. *They stopped to have lunch in a village / to take a photo.*

---

arrhes [aʀ] nfpl deposit, earnest money ▸ **verser des arrhes** to pay a deposit.

arrière [aʀjɛʀ] ◆ adj inv **1.** AUTO [roue, feu] rear ; [siège] back **2.** SPORT backward. ◆ nm **1.** [d'une maison] back, rear ; [d'un véhicule] rear (end), back (end) ▸ **à l'arrière a)** [dans une voiture] in the back 🇬🇧, in back 🇺🇸 **b)** [dans un avion, un bus] at the back ou rear / *asseyez-vous à l'arrière* sit in the back **2.** SPORT [au basket-ball] guard ; [au football, au rugby] back ; [au volley-ball] rearline player ▸ **arrière central** centre-back. ◆ **arrières** nmpl MIL rear ▸ **assurer** ou **protéger ses arrières a)** to protect one's rear **b)** *fig* to leave o.s. a way out ou an escape route. ◆ **en arrière** *loc adv* **1.** [regarder] back ; [se pencher, tomber] backward, backwards ▸ **revenir en arrière** to retrace one's steps ▸ **rester en arrière** [d'un convoi, d'un défilé] to stay at the back ou rear **2.** [dans le temps] back ▸ **revenir en arrière** to go back in time. ◆ **en arrière de** *loc prép* behind.

arriéré, e [aʀjeʀe] adj **1.** [impayé - loyer, intérêt] overdue, in arrears ; [- dette] outstanding **2.** *vieilli* PSYCHOL backward, (mentally) retarded **3.** [archaïque - idée, technologie] backward. ◆ **arriéré** nm **1.** [dette] arrears *(pl)* **2.** [retard] backlog.

arrière-boutique [aʀjɛʀbutik] *(pl* arrière-boutiques) nf ▸ **dans mon arrière-boutique** at the back of my shop 🇬🇧 ou store 🇺🇸.

arrière-garde [aʀjɛʀgaʀd] *(pl* arrière-gardes) nf rearguard.

arrière-goût *(pl* arrière-goûts), **arrière-gout*** *(pl* arrière-gouts*) [aʀjɛʀgu] nm aftertaste.

arrière-grand-mère [aʀjɛʀgʀɑ̃mɛʀ] *(pl* arrière-grands-mères) nf great-grandmother.

arrière-grand-père [aʀjɛʀgʀɑ̃pɛʀ] *(pl* arrière-grands-pères) nm great-grandfather.

arrière-grands-parents [aʀjɛʀgʀɑ̃paʀɑ̃] nmpl great-grandparents.

arrière-pays [aʀjɛʀpei] nm inv hinterland ▸ **dans l'arrière-pays** in the hinterland.

arrière-pensée [aʀjɛʀpɑ̃se] *(pl* arrière-pensées) nf thought at the back of one's mind, ulterior motive ▸ **sans arrière-pensées** without any ulterior motives.

arrière-petite-fille [aʀjɛʀpətitfij] *(pl* arrière-petites-filles) nf great-granddaughter.

arrière-petit-fils [aʀjɛʀpətifis] *(pl* arrière-petits-fils) nm great-grandson.

arrière-petits-enfants [aʀjɛʀpətizɑ̃fɑ̃] nmpl great-grandchildren.

arrière-plan [aʀjɛʀplɑ̃] *(pl* arrière-plans) nm background / *être à l'arrière-plan* *fig* to remain in the background.

arrière-saison [aʀjɛʀsɛzɔ̃] *(pl* arrière-saisons) nf end of the autumn 🇬🇧 ou fall 🇺🇸.

arrière-train [aʀjɛʀtʀɛ̃] *(pl* arrière-trains) nm ZOOL hindquarters.

arrimer [3] [aʀime] vt NAUT [ranger] to stow ; [attacher] to secure.

arrivage [aʀivaʒ] nm delivery, consignment.

arrivant, e [aʀivɑ̃, ɑ̃t] nm, f newcomer, new arrival / *il y a dix nouveaux arrivants* there are ten newcomers ou new arrivals.

arrivé, e [aʀive] adj [qui a réussi] successful. ◆ **arrivée** nf **1.** [venue - d'une saison, du froid] arrival, coming ; [- d'un avion, d'un ami] arrival / *on attend son arrivée pour le mois prochain* we're expecting him to arrive ou he's expected to arrive next month / *à mon arrivée à la gare* on ou upon my arrival at the station, when I arrived at the station / *quelques mois après son arrivée au pouvoir* a few months after he came to power ▸ **heure d'arrivée a)** [d'un train] time of arrival **b)** [du courrier] time of delivery **2.** SPORT finish **3.** TECHNOL ▶ **arrivée d'air / de gaz a)** [robinet] air / gas inlet **b)** [passage] inflow of air / gas.

arriver [3] [aʀive]
◆ vi *(aux être)*

A. DANS L'ESPACE 1. [parvenir à destination - voyageur, véhicule, courrier] to arrive ▶ **arriver chez qqn** to arrive at sb's place ▶ **arriver chez soi** to get ou to arrive home / *arriver au sommet* to reach the summit / *on arrive à quelle heure ?* what time do we get there? ▶ **nous sommes bientôt ou presque arrivés** we're almost there / *les invités vont bientôt arriver* the guests will be arriving soon ▶ **être bien arrivé** [personne, colis] to have arrived safely / *ils arrivent de Tokyo* they've just arrived ou come from Tokyo / *j'arrive tout juste de vacances* I'm just back from my holidays **2.** [finir - dans un classement] to come (in) ▶ **arriver le premier / dernier a)** [coureur] to come in first / last, to take first / last place **b)** [invité] to arrive first / last, to be the first / last to arrive **3.** [venir] to come, to approach ▶ **tu es prêt ? — j'arrive tout de suite / dans une minute** are you ready? — I'm coming / I'll be with you in a minute.

B. DANS LE TEMPS 1. [événement, jour, moment] to come ▶ **Noël arrive bientôt** Christmas will soon be here ou with us / *le grand jour est arrivé !* the big day's here at last! **2.** [se produire] to happen / *comment est-ce arrivé ?* how did it happen? / *un accident est si vite arrivé !* accidents will happen! / *ce sont des choses qui arrivent* these things happen / *ça peut arriver à tout le monde de se tromper !* everybody makes mistakes! / *ça ne t'arrive jamais d'être de mauvaise humeur ?* aren't you ever in a bad mood?
◆ v impers **1.** [venir] : *il arrive un train toutes les heures* there's a train every hour **2.** [aventure, événement] : *il est arrivé un accident* there's been an accident / *il m'est arrivé une histoire incroyable !* something incredible happened to me! / *s'il m'arrivait quelque chose, prévenez mon père* if anything happens ou should anything happen to me, let my father know **3.** [se produire parfois] ▶ **il arrive que** : *ne peut-il pas arriver que l'ordinateur se trompe ?* couldn't the computer ever make a mistake? ◆ **arriver à** + prép **1.** [niveau, taille, lieu] : *le bas du rideau arrive à 20 cm du sol* the bottom of the curtain is 20 cm above the ground / *des bruits de conversation arrivaient jusqu'à nous* the sound of chatter reached us / *ses cheveux lui arrivent à la taille* her hair comes down to her waist / *ma nièce m'arrive à l'épaule* my niece comes up to my shoulder **2.** [étape, moment, conclusion] to come to, to reach / *où (en) étions-nous arrivés la semaine dernière ?* [dans une leçon] where did we get up to ou had we got to last week? / *j'arrive à un âge où...* I've reached an age when... **3.** [rang, résultat] to get ; [succès] to achieve / *tu as refait l'addition ? — oui, j'arrive au même total que toi* did you redo the calculations? — yes, I get the same result as you **4.** [pouvoir, réussir à] ▶ **arriver à faire qqch** to manage to do sthg, to succeed in doing sthg / *tu n'arriveras jamais à la convaincre* you'll never manage to convince her, you'll never succeed in convincing her / *je n'arrive pas à m'y habituer* I just can't get used to it / *tu m'aides ? je n'y arrive pas !* can you help me? I can't do ou manage it! **5.** [EXPR] **(en) arriver à qqch** [en venir à] : *j'en arrive à penser que...* I'm beginning to think that... / *j'en arrive parfois à me demander si...* sometimes I (even) wonder if... ▶ **en arriver là** : *depuis, je ne lui parle plus — c'est malheureux d'en arriver là* since then, I haven't spoken to him — it's a shame it has come to that.

arriviste [aʀivist] nmf careerist.

arrogance [aʀɔgɑ̃s] nf arrogance ▶ **parler avec arrogance** to speak arrogantly.

arrogant, e [aʀɔgɑ̃, ɑ̃t] adj arrogant.

arroger [17] [aʀɔʒe] ◆ **s'arroger** vpt *sout* to assume, to arrogate (to o.s.) *sout* ▶ **s'arroger le droit de faire qqch** to assume the right to do sthg.

arrondi, e [aʀɔ̃di] adj round.

arrondir [32] [aʀɔ̃diʀ] vt **1.** [rendre rond] to make into a round shape, to round (off) (sép) ; [incurver] to round off (sép) **2.** [augmenter - capital, pécule] to increase ; [-patrimoine, domaine] to extend ▶ **arrondir ses fins de mois** fam to make a little extra on the side **3.** MATH to round off (sép) ▶ **arrondir un total à l'euro supérieur / inférieur** to round a sum up / down to the nearest euro. ◆ **s'arrondir** vpi [grossir - femme enceinte, ventre] to get bigger ou rounder ; [-somme] to mount up.

arrondissement [aʀɔ̃dismɑ̃] nm **1.** [dans une ville] administrative subdivision of major French cities such as Paris, Lyon or Marseille **2.** [au niveau départemental] administrative subdivision of a département, governed by a "sous-préfet".

arrosage [aʀozaʒ] nm [d'un jardin] watering ; [de la chaussée] spraying.

arroser [3] [aʀoze] vt **1.** [asperger - jardin, pelouse] to water / *arroser une voiture au jet* to hose down ou to spray a car ▶ **se faire arroser** fam [par la pluie] to get drenched ou soaked **2.** [inonder] to soak ▶ **arroser qqn de qqch** to pour sthg over sb, to drench sb in sthg **3.** CULIN [gigot, rôti] to baste **4.** [repas] ▶ **(bien) arroser son déjeuner** fam to drink (heavily) with one's lunch **5.** fam [fêter] to drink to ▶ **arroser une naissance** to wet a baby's head [UK], to drink to a new baby **6.** GÉOGR ▶ **la Seine arrose Paris** the river Seine flows through Paris **7.** fam [corrompre] to grease the palm of. ◆ **s'arroser** vp *(emploi passif)* fam : *la naissance de ta fille, ça s'arrose !* let's drink to your new baby daughter!

arrosoir [aʀozwaʀ] nm watering can [UK] ou pot [US].

arsenal, aux [aʀsənal, o] nm MIL & NAUT arsenal ▶ **arsenal maritime** naval dockyard.

arsenic [aʀsənik] nm arsenic.

art [aʀ] nm **1.** ART art ▶ **l'art pour l'art** art for art's sake ▶ **art déco** art deco ▶ **Art nouveau** Art nouveau **2.** [technique] art / *découper un poulet, c'est tout un art !* carving a chicken is quite an art! ▶ **l'art dramatique** dramatic art, dramatics **3.** [don] art, talent / *il a l'art de m'énerver* he has a knack of getting on my nerves / *je voulais juste le prévenir ! — oui, mais il y a l'art et la manière* I didn't want to offend him, just to warn him! — yes, but there are ways of going about it. ◆ **arts** nmpl arts ▶ **arts appliqués** ≃ art and design ▶ **arts décoratifs** decorative arts ▶ **arts graphiques** graphic arts ▶ **arts martiaux** martial arts ▶ **Salon des arts ménagers** ≃ Ideal Home Exhibition [UK] home crafts exhibition ou show [US] ▶ **les Arts et Métiers** ENS college for the advanced education of those working in commerce, manufacturing, construction and design ▶ **les arts plastiques** the visual arts.

Arte [aʀte] npr Franco-German cultural television channel created in 1992.

artère [aʀtɛʀ] nf **1.** ANAT artery **2.** [avenue] arterial road [UK], (main) road ou street ou thoroughfare ▶ **les grandes artères** the main roads.

artériel, elle [aʀteʀjɛl] adj arterial.

arthrite [aʀtʀit] nf arthritis.

arthrose [aʀtʀoz] nf osteoarthritis, degenerative joint disease.

artichaut [aʀtiʃo] nm (globe) artichoke.

article [aʀtikl] nm **1.** COMM article, item ▶ **articles de toilette** toiletries ▶ **articles de mode** fashion accessories ▶ **articles de voyage** travel goods ▶ **faire l'article pour a)** pr to do a sales pitch for **b)** fig to praise **2.** PRESSE article

article de fond feature article ; [d'un dictionnaire, d'un guide] entry **3.** [sujet] point **4.** [paragraphe] article, clause ▸ **l'article 10 du contrat** point ou paragraph ou clause 10 of the contract **5.** LING article ▸ **article défini / indéfini** definite / indefinite article **6.** ⟨EXPR⟩ **à l'article de la mort** at death's door, on the point of death.

articulation [aʀtikylasjɔ̃] nf **1.** ANAT & ZOOL joint **2.** [prononciation] articulation **3.** [liaison] link, link-up **4.** MÉCAN connection, joint.

articulé, e [aʀtikyle] adj **1.** [mobile] articulated **2.** ANAT articulated, jointed **3.** MÉCAN hinged, jointed ▸ **poupée articulée** jointed doll.

articuler [3] [aʀtikyle] vt **1.** [prononcer] to articulate ; *(en usage absolu) : il articule mal* he doesn't speak clearly **2.** [dire] to utter **3.** [enchaîner - démonstration, thèse] to link up ou together *(sép)* ; [-faits] to connect. ❖ **s'articuler autour de** vp + prép to hinge ou to turn on.

artifice [aʀtifis] nm [stratagème] (clever) device ou trick.

artificiel, elle [aʀtifisjɛl] adj **1.** [colorant, fleur, lumière, intelligence, insémination] artificial ; [lac, soie] artificial, man-made ; [perle] artificial, imitation *(modif)* ; [dent] false ; [bras, hanche] replacement *(modif)* ; [mouche] artificial **2.** [factice - besoin, plaisir] artificial **3.** [affecté] artificial, false, insincere **4.** [arbitraire] artificial.

artificiellement [aʀtifisjɛlmã] adv artificially.

artificier [aʀtifisje] nm **1.** [en pyrotechnie] fireworks expert **2.** MIL [soldat] blaster ; [spécialiste] bomb disposal expert.

artillerie [aʀtijʀi] nf artillery.

artisan, e [aʀtizã, an] nm, f **1.** [travailleur] craftsman (craftswoman), artisan **2.** [responsable] architect, author ▸ **l'artisan de la paix** the peacemaker.

artisanal, e, aux [aʀtizanal, o] adj **1.** [des artisans - classe, tradition] artisan *(modif)* **2.** [traditionnel - méthode, travail] traditional / *un fauteuil fabriqué de façon artisanale* a hand-made armchair / *une bombe de fabrication artisanale* a home-made bomb **3.** [rudimentaire] basic, crude.

artisanat [aʀtizana] nm **1.** [profession] ▸ **l'artisanat** the craft industry, the crafts **2.** [produits] arts and crafts / *le travail du cuir fait partie de l'artisanat local* leatherwork is part of local industry.

artiste [aʀtist] nmf **1.** ART [créateur] artist ▸ **artiste peintre** painter **2.** CINÉ, LOISIRS & THÉÂTRE [interprète] performer ; [comédien] actor ; [chanteur] singer ; [de music-hall] artiste, entertainer.

artistique [aʀtistik] adj [enseignement, richesses] artistic.

ARVA [aʀva] **(abr de appareil de recherche de victimes en avalanches)** nm *equipment for searching for avalanche victims.*

as [as] nm **1.** JEUX [carte, dé, domino] ace ; [aux courses] number one **2.** *fam* [champion] ace, champ, wizard ▸ **un as de la route** ou **du volant** a crack driver.

a/s (abr écrite de aux soins de) c/o.

ASA, Asa [aza] ASA, Asa.

ASAP (abr de as soon as possible) SMS ASAP.

asbestose [asbɛstoz] nf asbestosis.

ascendant, e [asɑ̃dã, ɑ̃t] adj [mouvement] rising, ascending. ❖ **ascendant** nm **1.** [emprise] influence, ascendancy ▸ **subir l'ascendant de qqn** to be under the influence of sb **2.** ASTROL ascendant. ❖ **ascendants** nmpl DR [parents] ascendants, ancestors.

ascenseur [asɑ̃sœʀ] nm **1.** lift ⟨UK⟩, elevator ⟨US⟩ **2.** INFORM scroll bar.

ascension [asɑ̃sjɔ̃] nf **1.** [montée - d'un ballon] ascent **2.** [escalade - d'un alpiniste] ascent, climb ▸ **faire l'ascension d'un pic** to climb a peak **3.** RELIG ▸ **l'Ascension** the Ascension ▸ **le jour de l'Ascension** Ascension Day.

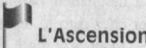

L'Ascension

In France many people take an extended weekend break after Ascension Day, **le jeudi de l'Ascension.**

ascensionnel, elle [asɑ̃sjɔnɛl] adj upward.

ascensoriste [asɑ̃sɔʀist] nmf elevator engineer.

ascèse [asɛz] nf asceticism, ascetic lifestyle.

ascète [asɛt] nmf ascetic.

ASCII [aski] **(abr de American Standard Code for Information Interchange)** adj ASCII *(modif)*.

aseptisé, e [asɛptize] adj MÉD sterilized ; *fig* [ambiance] impersonal ; [discours, roman, univers] sanitized.

aseptiser [3] [asɛptize] vt to asepticize.

ashkénaze [aʃkenaz] adj & nmf ▸ **(juif) ashkénaze** Ashkenazi ▸ **les Ashkénazes** the Ashkenazim.

asiatique [azjatik] adj **1.** [de l'Asie en général] Asian **2.** [d'Extrême-Orient] Oriental ▸ **un restaurant asiatique** a *restaurant serving Oriental cuisine.* ❖ **Asiatique** nmf Asian.

Asie [azi] npr f Asia ▸ **l'Asie centrale** Central Asia ▸ **l'Asie Mineure** HIST Asia Minor ▸ **l'Asie du Sud-Est** Southeast Asia.

asile [azil] nm **1.** [abri] refuge **2.** HIST & POL asylum ▸ **demander l'asile diplomatique / politique** to seek diplomatic protection / political asylum **3.** [établissement - gén] home ▸ **asile de nuit** night shelter.

asocial, e, aux [asɔsjal, o] ◆ adj asocial *sout*, antisocial. ◆ nm, f dropout, social outcast.

aspartam(e) [aspaʀtam] nm aspartame ▸ **yaourt à l'aspartame** artificially sweetened yoghurt.

aspect [aspɛ] nm **1.** [apparence] appearance, look **2.** [point de vue] aspect, facet ▸ **envisager** ou **examiner une question sous tous ses aspects** to consider a question from all angles ▸ **vu sous cet aspect** seen from this angle ou point of view ▸ **sous un aspect nouveau** in a new light **3.** ASTROL & LING aspect.

asperge [aspɛʀʒ] nf **1.** BOT asparagus **2.** *fam* [personne] ▸ **une (grande) asperge** a beanpole.

asperger [17] [aspɛʀʒe] vt **1.** [légèrement] to sprinkle ▸ **asperger qqn d'eau** ou **avec de l'eau** to spray sb with water **2.** [tremper] to splash, to splatter ▸ **se faire asperger** to get splashed. ❖ **s'asperger** vp *(emploi réfléchi)* ▸ **s'asperger de qqch** to splash o.s. with sthg, to splash sthg on o.s.

aspérité [aspeʀite] nf [proéminence] rough bit.

asphalte [asfalt] nm [bitume] asphalt.

asphyxie [asfiksi] nf **1.** MÉD asphyxia **2.** *fig* paralysis / *la guerre conduit le pays à l'asphyxie* war is paralysing the country.

asphyxier [9] [asfiksje] vt **1.** [priver d'air] to suffocate ; [faire respirer du gaz à] to asphyxiate ▸ **mourir asphyxié** to die of asphyxiation **2.** *fig* [personne] to oppress ; [pays, économie] to paralyse ⟨UK⟩, to paralyze ⟨US⟩. ❖ **s'asphyxier** vpi [accidentellement] to suffocate.

aspic [aspik] nm **1.** ZOOL asp **2.** BOT & CULIN aspic.

aspirant, e [aspiʀã, ãt] nm, f candidate. ❖ **aspirant** nm officer cadet.

aspirateur [aspiʀatœʀ] nm **1.** [domestique] Hoover®, vacuum cleaner ▸ **passer l'aspirateur** to do the hoovering UK ou vacuuming **2.** TECHNOL aspirator.

aspiration [aspiʀasjɔ̃] nf **1.** [ambition] aspiration, ambition **2.** [souhait] yearning, longing, craving **3.** [absorption - d'air] inhaling ; [- d'un gaz, d'un fluide] sucking up.

aspirer [3] [aspiʀe] vt **1.** [inspirer] to inhale, to breathe in *(sép)* **2.** [pomper] to suck up *(sép)* ; [avec un aspirateur] to vacuum, to hoover UK. ❖ **aspirer à** v + prép [paix, repos] to crave, to long for *(insép)*, to yearn for *(insép)* ; [rang, dignité] to aspire to *(insép)*.

aspirine [aspiʀin] nf aspirin / **un comprimé d'aspirine** an aspirin.

assagir [32] [asaʒiʀ] vt *litt* [apaiser - personne] to quieten down *(sép)* ; [- passion, violence] to soothe, to allay ; [faire se ranger] to cause to settle down. ❖ **s'assagir** vpi [personne] to settle down.

assaillant [asajɑ̃] nm assailant, attacker.

assaillir [47] [asajiʀ] vt MIL to attack, to assail *litt* ; [esprit, imagination] to beset / *le bureau est assailli de demandes* the office is swamped ou besieged with inquiries.

assainir [32] [aseniʀ] vt **1.** [nettoyer - quartier, logement] to clean up *(sép)* ; [- air] to purify **2.** [assécher - plaine, région] to improve the drainage of **3.** [épurer - situation] to clear up ; [- marché, monnaie] to stabilize. ❖ **s'assainir** vpi to improve, to become healthier.

assainissement [asenismɑ̃] nm **1.** [nettoyage - d'une ville] improvement ; [- d'un appartement] cleaning up **2.** [assèchement] draining **3.** [d'une monnaie, d'un marché] stabilization, stabilizing.

assaisonnement [asezɔnmɑ̃] nm **1.** [processus] dressing, seasoning **2.** [condiments] seasoning ; [sauce] dressing.

assaisonner [3] [asezɔne] vt CULIN [plat, sauce] to season ; [salade] to dress.

assassin [asasɛ̃] nm [gén] murderer, killer ; [d'une personnalité connue] assassin / *à l'aide, à l'assassin !* help, murder!

assassinat [asasina] nm murder ; [d'une personnalité connue] assassination.

assassiner [3] [asasine] vt **1.** [tuer - gén] to murder ; [- vedette, homme politique] to assassinate ▸ **se faire assassiner** to be murdered **2.** *fam & péj* [malmener - musique, symphonie] to murder, to slaughter.

assaut [aso] nm MIL assault, attack, onslaught ▸ **aller** ou **monter à l'assaut a)** *pr* to attack, to storm **b)** *fig* to attack ▸ **à l'assaut !** charge! ▸ **donner l'assaut** to launch ou to mount an attack ▸ **prendre d'assaut un palais** to storm a palace / *le bar était pris d'assaut* the bar was mobbed.

assécher [18] [aseʃe] vt [drainer - terre, sol] to drain (the water off) ; [vider - étang, réservoir] to empty. ❖ **s'assécher** vpi to become dry, to dry up.

✍ In reformed spelling (see p. 16-18), this verb is conjugated like *semer* : *elle assèchera, il assècherait.*

ASSEDIC, Assedic [asedik] (abr de **Association pour l'emploi dans l'industrie et le commerce**) npr French unemployment insurance scheme, now part of the *Pôle emploi* ; ≃ Unemployment Benefit Office UK ; ≃ Unemployment Office US ▸ **toucher les ASSEDIC** to get unemployment benefit UK ou welfare US.

assemblage [asɑ̃blaʒ] nm **1.** [fait de mettre ensemble] assembling, constructing, fitting together **2.** [ensemble] assembly ; CONSTR framework, structure ; MENUIS joint **3.** *péj* [amalgame] collection, concoction *péj*.

assemblée [asɑ̃ble] nf **1.** [auditoire] gathering, audience ▸ **l'assemblée des fidèles** RELIG the congregation **2.** [réunion] meeting ▸ **assemblée générale / annuelle** general /

annual meeting **3.** POL [élus] ▸ **l'Assemblée (nationale)** the (French) National Assembly.

assembler [3] [asɑ̃ble] vt **1.** [monter] to assemble, to put ou to fit together *(sép)* ; MENUIS to joint / *assemblez le dos et le devant du tricot* sew the back and the front of the sweater together **2.** [combiner - pensées] to gather (together) *(sép)* ; [- documents] to collate. ❖ **s'assembler** vpi to gather (together).

asséner [19] [asene] vt [coup] to deliver, to strike / *je lui ai asséné quelques vérités bien senties* *fig* I threw a few home truths at him.

✍ In reformed spelling (see p. 16-18), this verb is conjugated like *semer* : *il assènera, elle assènerait.*

assentiment [asɑ̃timɑ̃] nm assent, agreement ▸ **donner son assentiment à** to give one's assent to.

asseoir, assoir* [65] [aswaʀ] ❖ vt **1.** [mettre en position assise] ▸ **asseoir qqn a)** [le mettre sur un siège] to sit sb down **b)** [le redresser dans son lit] to sit sb up ▸ **être assis** : *j'étais assise sur un tabouret* I was sitting on a stool / *nous étions assis au premier rang* we were seated in the first row ▸ **êtes-vous bien assis ?** are you sitting comfortably? / *je préfère être assise pour repasser* I prefer doing the ironing sitting down **2.** *sout* [consolider] to establish ▸ **asseoir sa réputation sur qqch** to base one's reputation on sthg **3.** *fam* [étonner] to stun, to astound. ❖ vi ▸ **faire asseoir qqn** to ask sb to sit down. ❖ **s'asseoir, s'assoir*** vpi **1.** [s'installer] to sit down ▸ **asseyez-vous donc** please, do sit down / *asseyons-nous par terre* let's sit on the floor / *venez vous asseoir à table avec nous* come and sit at the table with us **2.** EXPR **s'asseoir dessus** *tfam*: *ton opinion, je m'assois dessus* I couldn't give a damn about your opinion.

assermenté, e [asɛʀmɑ̃te] adj [policier] sworn, sworn in.

assertion [asɛʀsjɔ̃] nf assertion.

asservir [32] [asɛʀviʀ] vt [assujettir] to enslave.

asservissement [asɛʀvismɑ̃] nm [sujétion] enslavement.

assesseur [asesœʀ] nm assessor.

assez [ase] adv **1.** [suffisamment] enough / *la maison est assez grande pour nous tous* the house is big enough for all of us / *j'ai assez travaillé pour aujourd'hui* I've done enough work for today ▸ **c'est plus qu'assez** that's more than enough / *assez parlé, agissons !* that's enough talk ou talking, let's DO something! ; *(en corrélation avec « pour »)* : *elle est assez grande pour s'habiller toute seule* she's old enough to dress herself **2.** [plutôt, passablement] quite, rather ▸ **j'aime assez sa maison** I quite like his house / *je suis assez contente de moi* I'm quite pleased with myself. ❖ **assez de** loc dét enough / *il y en a assez* there is / are enough ; *(en corrélation avec « pour »)* : *j'ai assez d'argent pour vivre* I have enough money to live on / *j'en ai (plus qu')assez de toutes ces histoires !* *fam* I've had (more than) enough of all this fuss!

assidu, e [asidy] adj **1.** [zélé] assiduous *sout*, diligent *sout*, hard-working ▸ **élève assidu** hard-working pupil **2.** [constant] unflagging, unremitting, untiring **3.** [fréquent] regular, constant.

assiduité [asidɥite] nf [régularité] assiduousness *sout* / *l'assiduité aux répétitions est essentielle* regular attendance at rehearsals is vital.

assidûment, assidument* [asidymã] adv **1.** [avec zèle] assiduously *sout* **2.** [régulièrement] assiduously *sout*, unremittingly, untiringly.

assiéger [22] [asjeʒe] vt **1.** MIL [ville, forteresse] to lay siege to *(insép)*, to besiege **2.** [se présenter en foule à] to besiege, to mob / *les guichets ont été assiégés* the ticket office was stormed by the public.

In reformed spelling (see p. 16-18), this verb is conjugated like **semer** : *elle assiègera, il assiègerait.*

assiette [asjɛt] nf **1.** [récipient] plate ▸ **assiette à dessert** dessert plate ▸ **assiette creuse** ou **à soupe** soup dish ▸ **assiette plate** (dinner) plate ; [contenu] plate, plateful ▸ **assiette anglaise** assorted cold meats *(pl)* 🇬🇧, cold cuts *(pl)* 🇺🇸 **2.** [assise] foundation, basis ; [d'une voie ferrée, d'une route] bed ; FIN [d'une hypothèque] basis ▸ **l'assiette fiscale** ou **de l'impôt** the base (taxation) rate, taxable income **3.** ÉQUIT seat **4.** EXPR **ne pas être dans son assiette** to feel off colour 🇬🇧 ou color 🇺🇸.

assignation [asiɲasjɔ̃] nf [de témoin] subpoena ; [d'un accusé] summons ▸ **assignation à résidence** house arrest.

assigner [3] [asiɲe] vt **1.** [attribuer - poste] to assign ; [-tâche] to allot, to allocate, to assign / *assigner un même objectif à deux projets* to set the same goal for two projects **2.** DR : *assigner un témoin (à comparaître)* to subpoena a witness ▸ **assigner qqn à résidence** to put sb under house arrest ▸ **assigner qqn (en justice) pour diffamation** to issue a writ for libel against sb.

assimilation [asimilasjɔ̃] nf **1.** PHYSIOL assimilation **2.** [intégration] assimilation, integration.

assimiler [3] [asimile] vt **1.** PHYSIOL to assimilate, to absorb, to metabolize ; [digérer] to digest **2.** [comprendre] to assimilate, to take in *(sép)* **3.** [intégrer] to assimilate, to integrate. ⟐ **assimiler à** v + prép to compare to / *être assimilé à un cadre supérieur* to be given equivalent status to an executive. ⟐ **s'assimiler** vp *(emploi passif)* PHYSIOL to become absorbed ou metabolized ; [être digéré] to be assimilated ou digested.

assis, e [asi, iz] ◆ pp ⟶ **asseoir**. ◆ adj [non debout] sitting (down) ▸ **rester assis** : *je vous en prie, restez assis* please don't get up / *tout le monde est resté assis* everyone remained seated ▸ **assis !** [à un chien] sit! ⟐ **assises** nfpl **1.** DR ▸ **(cour d')assises** ≃ crown court 🇬🇧 ; ≃ circuit court 🇺🇸 **2.** [réunion] meeting, conference.

assistanat [asistana] nm **1.** ÉDUC (foreign) assistant exchange scheme **2.** UNIV assistantship **3.** [secours - privé] aid ; [-public] state aid.

assistance [asistɑ̃s] nf **1.** [aide] assistance ▸ **prêter assistance à qqn** to lend ou give assistance to sb, to assist sb ▸ **assistance judiciaire** legal aid ▸ **l'Assistance (publique)** [à Paris et Marseille] *authority which used to manage the social services and is now in charge of state-owned hospitals* **2.** MÉD ▸ **assistance respiratoire** artificial respiration **3.** [spectateurs - d'une pièce, d'un cours] audience ; [-d'une messe] congregation **4.** [présence] : *l'assistance aux conférences n'est pas obligatoire* attendance at lectures is not compulsory.

assistant, e [asistɑ̃, ɑ̃t] nm, f **1.** [second] assistant **2.** ÉDUC (foreign language) assistant **3.** UNIV lecturer 🇬🇧, assistant teacher 🇺🇸 **4.** SOCIOL ▸ **assistant maternel, assistante maternelle a)** [à son domicile] childminder 🇬🇧, babysitter **b)** [en collectivité] crèche 🇬🇧 ou daycare center 🇺🇸 worker ▸ **assistant social, assistante sociale** social worker.

assister [3] [asiste] vt [aider] to assist, to aid. ⟐ **assister à** v + prép **1.** [être présent à - messe, gala] to attend ; [-concert de rock, enregistrement de télévision] to be at **2.** [être témoin

de] to witness, to be a witness to **3.** [remarquer] to note, to witness.

⚠️ **To assist ne peut pas être employé pour traduire** assister **qu'au sens d'« aider ».**

associatif, ive [asɔsjatif, iv] adj associative ▸ **la vie associative** community life.

association [asɔsjasjɔ̃] nf **1.** [groupement] society, association ▸ **association de consommateurs** consumer group ▸ **association de malfaiteurs** criminal conspiracy ▸ **association de parents d'élèves** ≃ Parent-Teacher Association 🇬🇧 ; ≃ Parent-Teacher Organization 🇺🇸 **2.** [collaboration] partnership, association **3.** [combinaison - d'images] association ; [- de couleurs] combination ▸ **associations (d'idées)** associations.

associé, e [asɔsje] ◆ adj associate. ◆ nm, f associate, partner.

associer [9] [asɔsje] vt **1.** [idées, images, mots] to associate **2.** [faire participer] ▸ **associer qqn à** : *il m'a associé à son projet* he included me in his project **3.** [saveurs, couleurs] ▸ **associer qqch à** to combine sthg with. ⟐ **s'associer** ◆ vpi [s'allier] to join forces ; COMM to enter ou to go into partnership, to become partners ou associates. ◆ vpt ▸ **s'associer qqn** to take sb on as a partner. ⟐ **s'associer à** vp + prép to share (in) / *s'associer à une entreprise criminelle* to be an accomplice to ou to take part in a crime.

assoiffé, e [aswafe] adj thirsty.

assombrir [32] [asɔ̃bʀiʀ] vt **1.** [rendre sombre] to darken, to make dark ou darker **2.** [rendre triste] to cast a shadow ou cloud over, to mar. ⟐ **s'assombrir** vpi **1.** [s'obscurcir] to darken, to grow dark **2.** [s'attrister - visage] to become gloomy, to cloud over ; [- personne, humeur] to become gloomy.

assommant, e [asɔmɑ̃, ɑ̃t] adj *fam* **1.** [ennuyeux] boring, tedious **2.** [fatigant] : *tu es assommant, à la fin, avec tes questions !* all these questions are getting really annoying!

assommer [3] [asɔme] vt **1.** [frapper] to knock out *(sép)*, to stun **2.** *fam* [ennuyer] ▸ **assommer qqn** to bore sb stiff ; [importuner] to harass, to wear down *(sép)* **3.** [abrutir] to stun.

Assomption [asɔ̃psjɔ̃] nf ▸ **l'Assomption** the Assumption.

L'Assomption

Assumption, on the 15th of August, is a Catholic feast. It is a public holiday in France.

assorti, e [asɔʀti] adj **1.** [en harmonie] ▸ **un couple bien assorti** a well-matched couple ▸ **un couple mal assorti** an ill-matched ou ill-assorted couple / *les deux couleurs sont très bien assorties* the two colours match (up) ou blend (in) perfectly ▸ **pantalon avec veste assortie** trousers 🇬🇧 ou pants 🇺🇸 with matching jacket **2.** [chocolats] assorted.

assortiment [asɔʀtimã] nm **1.** [ensemble] assortment, selection **2.** COMM [choix] selection, range, stock.

assortir [32] [asɔʀtiʀ] vt **1.** [teintes, vêtements] to match / *assortir ses chaussures à sa ceinture* to match one's shoes with ou to one's belt **2.** COMM [approvisionner] to supply **3.** [accompagner] ▸ **assortir de** : *il a assorti son discours d'un paragraphe sur le racisme* he added a paragraph on racism to his speech.

assoupi, e [asupi] adj [endormi - personne] asleep, sleeping, dozing.

assoupir [32] [asupiʀ] ❖ **s'assoupir** vpi [s'endormir] to doze off, to fall asleep.

assouplir [32] [asupliʀ] vt **1.** [rendre moins dur - corps] to make supple, to loosen up (sép) ; [-linge, cuir] to soften **2.** [rendre moins strict] to ease / le règlement de l'école a été considérablement assoupli the school rules have been considerably relaxed.

assouplissant [asuplisɑ̃] nm (fabric) softener.

assouplissement [asuplismɑ̃] nm **1.** LOISIRS & SPORT ｜ imbering up, loosening up ▶ **des exercices** ou **une séance d'assouplissement** limbering-up exercises **2.** ÉCON ▶ **assouplissement du crédit** easing of credit.

assourdir [32] [asuʀdiʀ] vt [personne] to deafen ; [bruit, son] to dull, to deaden, to muffle.

assourdissant, e [asuʀdisɑ̃, ɑ̃t] adj deafening, earsplitting.

assouvir [32] [asuviʀ] vt sout [désir, faim] to appease, to assuage sout ; [soif] to quench.

assujetti, e [asyʒeti] adj litt [population, prisonnier] subjugated.

assujettir [32] [asyʒetiʀ] vt **1.** [astreindre] to compel / être assujetti à un contrôle médical très strict to be subjected to very strict medical checks **2.** [arrimer] to fasten, to secure. ❖ **s'assujettir à** vp + prép to submit (o.s.) to.

assumer [3] [asyme] vt **1.** [endosser] to take on (sép), to take upon o.s., to assume ▶ **j'en assume l'entière responsabilité** I take ou I accept full responsibility for it / nous assumerons toutes les dépenses we'll meet all the expenses **2.** [accepter] to accept ; (en usage absolu) ▶ **j'assume !** I don't care what other people think! ❖ **s'assumer** vpi : il a du mal à s'assumer en tant que père he's finding it hard to come to terms with his role as father.

> ⚠ **To assume** n'est pas toujours la traduction adéquate pour **assumer**. Voir article.

assurance [asyʀɑ̃s] nf **1.** COMM [contrat] insurance (policy) / assurance contre le vol insurance against theft ▶ **assurance auto** ou **automobile** car ou automobile 🇺🇸 insurance ▶ **assurance chômage** unemployment insurance ▶ **assurance maladie** health insurance ▶ **assurance tous risques** comprehensive insurance ▶ **les assurances sociales** ≃ National Insurance 🇬🇧 ; ≃ Welfare 🇺🇸 ▶ **assurance vieillesse** retirement pension **2.** sout [promesse] assurance / j'ai reçu l'assurance formelle que l'on m'aiderait financièrement I was assured I would receive financial help **3.** [garantie] ▶ **une assurance de** a guarantee of **4.** [aisance] self-confidence, assurance ▶ **manquer d'assurance** to be insecure, to have no self-confidence ▶ **s'exprimer avec assurance** to speak with assurance ou confidently / elle a de l'assurance dans la voix she sounds confident **5.** [certitude] ▶ **avoir l'assurance que** to feel certain ou assured that **6.** [dans la correspondance] : veuillez croire à l'assurance de ma considération distinguée yours faithfully ou sincerely, sincerely yours 🇺🇸.

assuré, e [asyʀe] ❖ adj **1.** [incontestable] certain, sure / succès assuré pour son nouvel album ! her new album is sure to be a hit! **2.** [résolu] assured, self-confident ▶ **marcher d'un pas assuré** to walk confidently ▶ **d'une voix mal assurée** quaveringly, in an unsteady voice / avoir un air assuré to look self-confident. ❖ nm, f **1.** [qui a un contrat d'assurance] insured person, policyholder **2.** ADMIN ▶ **assuré social** ≃ National Insurance contributor 🇬🇧 ; ≃ contributor to Social Security 🇺🇸.

assurément [asyʀemɑ̃] adv sout assuredly, undoubtedly, most certainly.

assurer [3] [asyʀe] ❖ vt **1.** [certifier] to assure / il m'a assuré qu'il viendrait he assured me he'd come / mais si, je t'assure ! yes, I swear! **2.** [rendre sûr] to assure / laissez-moi vous assurer de ma reconnaissance let me assure you of my gratitude **3.** [procurer] to maintain, to provide / pour mieux assurer la sécurité de tous to ensure greater safety for all ▶ **assurer une liaison aérienne / ferroviaire** to operate an air / a rail link ▶ **assurer qqch à qqn** : assurer à qqn un bon salaire to secure a good salary for sb **4.** [mettre à l'abri] to ensure, to secure ▶ **assurer l'avenir** to make provision ou provide for the future **5.** COMM to insure / j'ai fait assurer mes bijoux I had my jewels insured **6.** SPORT to belay. ❖ vi fam ▶ **il assure en physique / anglais** he's good at physics / English / il va falloir assurer ! we'll have to show that we're up to it! ❖ **s'assurer** ❖ vp (emploi réfléchi) COMM to insure o.s. ▶ **s'assurer contre le vol / l'incendie** to insure o.s. against theft / fire. ❖ vpt [se fournir -revenu] to secure, to ensure. ❖ **s'assurer de** vp + prép [contrôler] : assurez-vous de la validité de votre passeport make sure your passport is valid ▶ **s'assurer que** to make sure (that), to check (that).

assureur [asyʀœʀ] nm insurer, underwriter.

astérisque [asteʀisk] nm asterisk.

astéroïde [asteʀɔid] nm asteroid.

asthmatique [asmatik] adj & nmf asthmatic.

asthme [asm] nm asthma ▶ **avoir de l'asthme** to suffer from asthma.

asticot [astiko] nm [ver] maggot ; PÊCHE gentle.

asticoter [3] [astikɔte] vt fam to bug.

astigmate [astigmat] adj & nmf astigmatic.

astiquer [3] [astike] vt to polish, to shine.

astrakan [astʀakɑ̃] nm astrakhan (fur) ▶ **un manteau en astrakan** an astrakhan coat.

astral, e, aux [astʀal, o] adj astral.

astre [astʀ] nm ASTROL & ASTRON star.

astreignant, e [astʀɛɲɑ̃, ɑ̃t] adj demanding, exacting.

astreindre [81] [astʀɛ̃dʀ] vt ▶ **astreindre qqn à qqch** to tie sb down to sthg / il est astreint à un régime sévère he's on a very strict diet ▶ **astreindre qqn à faire qqch** to compel ou to force ou to oblige sb to do sthg. ❖ **s'astreindre à** vp + prép ▶ **s'astreindre à (faire) qqch** to compel ou to force o.s. to do sthg.

astringent, e [astʀɛ̃ʒɑ̃, ɑ̃t] adj PHARM astringent ; [vin] sharp. ❖ **astringent** nm astringent.

astrologie [astʀɔlɔʒi] nf astrology.

astrologique [astʀɔlɔʒik] adj astrological.

astrologue [astʀɔlɔg] nmf astrologer.

astronaute [astʀɔnot] nmf astronaut.

astronautique [astʀɔnotik] nf astronautics (U).

astronome [astʀɔnɔm] nmf astronomer.

astronomie [astʀɔnɔmi] nf astronomy.

astronomique [astʀɔnɔmik] adj **1.** SCI astronomic, astronomical **2.** fam [somme] astronomic, astronomical.

astrophysicien, enne [astʀofizisjɛ̃, ɛn] nm, f astrophysicist.

astrophysique [astʀofizik] nf astrophysics (U).

astuce [astys] nf **1.** fam [plaisanterie] joke, gag / je n'ai pas compris l'astuce ! I didn't get it! **2.** fam [procédé ingénieux] trick / en page 23, notre rubrique « astuces » our tips are on page 23.

astucieux, euse [astysjø, øz] adj shrewd, clever.

asymétrique [asimetʀik] adj asymmetric, asymmetrical.

atelier [atəlje] nm **1.** [d'un bricoleur, d'un artisan] workshop ; [d'un peintre, d'un photographe] studio ; COUT workroom. **2.** [d'une usine] shop / *l'atelier s'est mis en grève* the shopfloor has gone on strike. **3.** [cours] workshop ; ART class / *participer à un atelier de peinture sur soie* to take part in a silk painting workshop ou a workshop on silk painting.

atermoyer [13] [atɛrmwaje] vi to procrastinate *sout*, to delay.

athée [ate] ◆ adj atheistic, atheist *(modif)*. ◆ nmf atheist.

athénée [atene] nm 〈Belg〉 high ou secondary school.

Athènes [atɛn] npr Athens.

athlète [atlɛt] nmf athlete ▶ **un corps / une carrure d'athlète** an athletic body / build.

athlétique [atletik] adj athletic.

athlétisme [atletism] nm athletics *(sg)* 〈UK〉, track and fields 〈US〉.

atlantique [atlɑ̃tik] adj Atlantic ▶ **la côte atlantique** the Atlantic coast.

Atlantique [atlɑ̃tik] npr m ▶ **l'Atlantique** the Atlantic (Ocean).

atlas [atlas] nm [livre] atlas.

Atlas [atlas] npr m GÉOGR ▶ **l'Atlas** the Atlas Mountains.

atmosphère [atmɔsfɛr] nf **1.** GÉOGR atmosphere **2.** [ambiance] atmosphere, ambiance **3.** [air que l'on respire] air **4.** PHYS atmosphere.

atmosphérique [atmɔsferik] adj [condition, couche, pression] atmospheric.

atoca [atɔka] nm 〈Québec〉 cranberry.

atoll [atɔl] nm atoll.

atome [atom] nm atom ▶ **avoir des atomes crochus avec qqn** *fam* to have things in common with sb.

atomique [atomik] adj [masse] atomic ; [énergie] atomic, nuclear ; [explosion] nuclear.

atomiseur [atomizœr] nm spray ▶ **parfum en atomiseur** spray perfume.

atout [atu] nm **1.** JEUX trump / *il a joué atout carreau* diamonds were trumps **2.** [avantage] asset, trump *fig* ▶ **il a tous les atouts dans son jeu** ou **en main** he has all the trumps ou all the winning cards.

âtre [atr] nm *litt* hearth.

atroce [atrɔs] adj **1.** [cruel] atrocious, foul **2.** [insupportable] excruciating, dreadful, atrocious.

atrocement [atrɔsmɑ̃] adv **1.** [cruellement] atrociously, horribly **2.** [en intensif] atrociously, dreadfully, horribly ▶ **j'ai atrocement soif** I'm parched.

atrocité [atrɔsite] nf **1.** [caractère cruel] atrociousness **2.** [crime] atrocity.

atrophie [atrɔfi] nf atrophy.

atrophier [9] [atrɔfje] ❖ **s'atrophier** vpi to atrophy.

attabler [3] [atable] ❖ **s'attabler** vpi to sit down (at the table).

attachant, e [ataʃɑ̃, ɑ̃t] adj [personnalité] engaging, lovable ; [livre, spectacle] captivating / *c'est un enfant très attachant* he's such a lovable child.

attache [ataʃ] nf **1.** [lien - gén] tie ; [- en cuir, en toile] strap ; [- en ficelle] string ; [- d'un vêtement] clip, fastener ; [- d'un rideau] tie-back **2.** [ami] tie, friend ; [parent] relative, family tie.

attaché, e [ataʃe] ◆ adj attached ▶ **bien attaché** firmly attached ▶ **mal attaché** poorly attached, loose. ◆ nm, f attaché ▶ **attaché militaire / d'ambassade** military / embassy attaché ▶ **attaché de presse** press attaché.

attaché-case [ataʃekɛz] *(pl* **attachés-cases)** nm attaché case.

attachement [ataʃmɑ̃] nm [affection] affection, attachment.

attacher [3] [ataʃe] ◆ vt **1.** [accrocher] to tie, to tie up *(sép)* ▶ **attacher son chien** to tie up one's dog ▶ *attacher les mains d'un prisonnier* to tie a prisoner's hands together ▶ **attacher qqn / qqch à** to tie sb / sthg to **2.** [pour fermer] to tie / *attacher un colis avec une ficelle* to tie up a parcel **3.** [vêtement] to fasten ▶ **attacher ses lacets** to tie one's shoelaces ▶ **attachez votre ceinture** fasten your seatbelt **4.** [accorder] to attach. ◆ vi CULIN to stick ▶ **poêle / casserole qui n'attache pas** nonstick pan / saucepan. ❖ **s'attacher** vp *(emploi passif)* to fasten, to do up ▶ **s'attacher avec une fermeture Éclair® / des boutons** to zip / to button up. ❖ **s'attacher à** vp + prép **1.** [se lier avec] to become fond of ou attached to **2.** [s'efforcer de] to devote o.s. to.

attaquant, e [atakɑ̃, ɑ̃t] nm, f attacker, assailant. ❖ **attaquant** nm SPORT striker.

attaque [atak] nf **1.** [agression] attack, assault ▶ **passer à l'attaque a)** *pr* to attack **b)** *fig* to attack, to go on the offensive ▶ **attaque aérienne** air attack ou raid ▶ **attaque à main armée** [contre une banque] armed robbery **2.** [diatribe] attack, onslaught / *il a été victime d'odieuses attaques dans les journaux* he was subjected to scurrilous attacks in the newspapers **3.** MÉD stroke, seizure ; [crise] fit, attack. ❖ **d'attaque** loc adj *fam* ▶ **être d'attaque** to be on 〈UK〉 ou in 〈US〉 form ▶ **se sentir d'attaque** : *je ne me sens pas d'attaque pour aller à la piscine* I don't feel up to going to the swimming pool.

attaquer [3] [atake] vt **1.** [assaillir - ennemi, pays, forteresse] to attack, to launch an attack upon ; [- passant, touriste] to mug / *il s'est fait attaquer par deux hommes* he was attacked ou assaulted by two men **2.** [critiquer] to attack, to condemn ; DR ▶ **attaquer qqn en justice** to bring an action against sb, to take sb to court ▶ **attaquer un testament** to contest a will **3.** [entreprendre - tâche] to tackle, to attack, to get started on *(insép)* / *prêt à attaquer le travail ?* ready to get ou to settle down to work? **4.** *fam* [commencer - repas, bouteille] ▶ **attaquer le petit déjeuner** to dig into breakfast **5.** MUS to attack ; *(en usage absolu)* ▶ **quand l'orchestre attaque** when the orchestra strikes up. ❖ **s'attaquer à** vp + prép **1.** [combattre] to take on, to attack / *il s'est tout de suite attaqué au problème* he tackled the problem right away **2.** [agir sur] to attack.

attarder [3] [atarde] ❖ **s'attarder** vpi **1.** [rester tard - dans la rue] to linger ; [- chez quelqu'un] to stay late ; [- au bureau, à l'atelier] to stay on ou late / *ne nous attardons pas, la nuit va tomber* let's not stay, it's almost nightfall / *je me suis attardée près de la rivière* I lingered by the river **2.** ▶ **s'attarder sur** [s'intéresser à] to linger over, to dwell on.

atteindre [81] [atɛ̃dr] vt **1.** [lieu] to reach, to get to *(insép)* ; RADIO & TV to reach **2.** [situation, objectif] to reach, to attain *sout* / *il a atteint son but* but he's reached his goal ou achieved his aim **3.** [âge, valeur, prix] to reach ▶ **atteindre 70 ans** to reach the age of 70 / *le sommet atteint plus de 4 000 mètres* the summit is over 4,000 metres high / *les dégâts atteignent cent mille euros* one hundred thousand euros' worth of damage has been done **4.** [communiquer avec] to contact, to reach **5.** [toucher] to reach, to get at, to stretch up to *(insép)* / *je n'arrive pas à atteindre le dictionnaire qui est là-haut* I can't reach the dictionary up there **6.** ARM to hit ▶ **atteint à l'épaule** wounded in the shoulder ; [blesser moralement] to affect, to move, to stir ▶ **rien ne l'atteint** nothing affects ou can reach him **7.** [affecter - suj : maladie, fléau] to affect.

atteint, e [atɛ̃, ɛ̃t] adj **1.** [d'une maladie, d'un fléau] affected / *quand le moral est atteint* when depression sets in **2.** *fam* [fou] touched. ❖ **atteinte** nf [attaque] attack ▸ **atteinte à la sûreté de l'État** high treason ▸ **atteinte à la vie privée** violation of privacy ▸ **porter atteinte au pouvoir de qqn** to undermine sb's power ▸ **porter atteinte à l'ordre public** to commit a breach of ou to disturb the peace ▸ **hors d'atteinte** out of reach.

attelage [atlaʒ] nm **1.** [fait d'attacher - un cheval] harnessing ; [-un bœuf] yoking ; [-une charrette] hitching up **2.** [plusieurs animaux] team ; [paire d'animaux] yoke **3.** RAIL [processus] coupling ; [dispositif] coupling.

atteler [24] [atle] vt [cheval] to harness ; [bœuf] to yoke ; [carriole] to hitch up *(sép)*. ❖ **s'atteler à** vp + prép to get down to, to tackle.

✐ In reformed spelling (see p. 16-18), this verb is conjugated like *peler : il attèle, il attèlera.*

attelle [atɛl] nf MÉD splint.

attenant, e [atnɑ̃, ɑ̃t] adj adjoining, adjacent / *cour attenante à la maison* back yard adjoining the house.

attendre [73] [atɑ̃dʀ]

❖ vt

A. **ÊTRE EN ATTENTE DE, PRÊT POUR** **1.** [rester jusqu'à la venue de - retardataire, voyageur] to wait for *(insép)* ▸ **je l'attends pour partir** I'm waiting till he gets here before I leave, I'll leave as soon as he gets here ▸ **(aller) attendre qqn à l'aéroport /la gare** to (go and) meet sb at the airport / the station ▸ **attendre qqn au passage** ou **au tournant** *fig* to wait for a chance to pounce on sb **2.** [escompter l'arrivée de - facteur, invité] to wait for *(insép)*, to expect ; [-colis, livraison] to expect, to await *sout* ; [-réponse, événement] to wait for *(insép)*, to await / *je ne t'attendais plus !* I'd given up waiting for you!, I'd given up on you ▸ **attendre qqn à** ou **pour dîner** to expect sb for dinner / *vous êtes attendu, le docteur va vous recevoir immédiatement* the doctor's expecting you, he'll see you straightaway / *qu'est-ce qu'il attend pour les renvoyer ?* why doesn't he just fire them? ▸ **attendre son tour** to wait one's turn / *cela peut attendre demain* that can wait till ou until tomorrow / *je lui ai prêté 500 euros et je les attends toujours* I lent him 500 euros and I still haven't got it back ▸ **se faire attendre** to keep others waiting / *désolé de m'être fait attendre* sorry to have kept you waiting ▸ **les résultats ne se sont pas fait attendre a)** [après une élection] the results didn't take long to come in **b)** [conséquences d'une action] there were immediate consequences ▸ **attendre qqn comme le Messie** to wait eagerly for sb **3.** [suj : femme enceinte] ▸ **attendre un bébé** ou **enfant, attendre famille** Belg to be expecting (a child), to be pregnant ▸ **attendre des jumeaux** to be pregnant with ou expecting twins / *elle attend son bébé pour le 15 avril* her baby's due on 15 April ▸ **attendre un heureux événement** *euphém* to be expecting **4.** [être prêt pour] to be ready for, to await *sout* / *la voiture vous attend* the car's ready for you, your car awaits *sout* ou *hum* **5.** [suj : destin, sort, aventure] to await *sout*, to be ou to lie in store for / *une mauvaise surprise l'attendait* there was a nasty surprise in store for her ▸ **si tu savais** ou **tu ne sais pas ce qui t'attend !** you haven't a clue what you're in for, have you? **6.** [espérer] ▸ **attendre qqch de** to expect sthg from ▸ **qu'attendez-vous de moi ?** what do you expect of me? / *nous attendons beaucoup de la réunion* we expect a lot (to come out) of the meeting.

B. **AVEC « QUE »** ▸ **attendre que** : *nous attendrons qu'elle soit ici* we'll wait till ou until she gets here ou for her to get here / *elle attendait toujours qu'il rentre avant d'aller se coucher* she would always wait up for him.

C. **AVEC « DE »** : *nous attendions de sortir* we were waiting to go out ▸ **j'attends avec impatience de la revoir** I can't wait to see her again, I'm really looking forward to seeing her again.

❖ vi **1.** [patienter] to wait / *je passe mon temps à attendre* I spend all my time waiting around ▸ **faites-les attendre** ask them to wait / *mais enfin attends, je ne suis pas prêt !* wait a minute, will you, I'm not ready! / *et attends, tu ne sais pas le plus beau !* wait (for it) ou hold on, the best part's yet to come! / *attendez voir, je crois me souvenir...* let's see ou let me see ou think, I seem to remember / *attends voir, toi !* *fam* [menace] just you wait! **2.** [être reporté] to wait / *votre projet attendra* your plan'll have to wait. ❖ **attendre après** v + prép *fam* **1.** [avoir besoin de] ▸ **attendre après qqch** to be in great need of sthg **2.** [compter sur] ▸ **attendre après qqn** to rely ou to count on sb / *si tu attends après lui, tu n'auras jamais tes renseignements* if you're counting on him ou if you leave it up to him, you'll never get the information you want. ❖ **s'attendre** vp *(emploi réciproque)* to wait for each other / *on s'attend à l'entrée du cinéma* we'll wait for each other ou we'll meet outside the cinema. ❖ **s'attendre à** vp + prép to expect / *il faut s'attendre à des embouteillages* traffic jams are expected / *s'attendre au pire* to expect the worst ▸ **savoir à quoi s'attendre** to know what to expect / *je ne m'attendais pas à cela de votre part* I didn't expect that from you ▸ **s'y attendre** : *il fallait s'y attendre* that was to be expected ▸ **je m'y attendais** I expected as much. ❖ **en attendant** loc adv **1.** [pendant ce temps] : *finis ton dessert, en attendant je vais faire le café* finish your dessert, and in the meantime I'll make the coffee **2.** *fam* [malgré cela] : *oui mais, en attendant, je n'ai toujours pas mon argent* that's as may be but I'm still missing my money. ❖ **en attendant que** loc conj until (such time as) / *en attendant qu'il s'explique, on ne sait rien* until (such time as) he's explained himself ou as long as he hasn't provided any explanations, we don't know anything.

attendrir [32] [atɑ̃dʀiʀ] vt **1.** [émouvoir] to move to tears ou pity **2.** [apitoyer] ▸ **se laisser attendrir** to give in to pity **3.** [viande] to tenderize. ❖ **s'attendrir** vpi **1.** [être ému] to be moved ou touched ▸ **s'attendrir sur qqn / qqch** to be moved by sb / sthg, to be touched by sb / sthg **2.** [être apitoyé] to feel compassion ▸ **s'attendrir sur le sort de qqn** to feel pity ou sorry for sb.

attendrissant, e [atɑ̃dʀisɑ̃, ɑ̃t] adj moving, touching.

attendrissement [atɑ̃dʀismɑ̃] nm **1.** [tendresse] emotion *(U)* ▸ **pas d'attendrissement !** let's not get emotional! **2.** [pitié] pity, compassion.

attendrisseur [atɑ̃dʀisœʀ] nm tenderizer.

attendu[1] [atɑ̃dy] prép considering, given. ❖ **attendu que** loc conj since, considering ou given that ; DR whereas.

attendu[2]**, e** [atɑ̃dy] ❖ pp ⟶ **attendre.** ❖ adj ▸ **très attendu** eagerly-awaited.

attentat [atɑ̃ta] nm **1.** [assassinat] assassination attempt **2.** [explosion] attack ▸ **attentat à la bombe** bomb attack, bombing ▸ **attentat à la voiture piégée** car bomb explosion ▸ **attentat terroriste** terror attack **3.** ▸ **attentat à la pudeur** act outraging public decency.

attentat-suicide [atɑ̃tasɥisid] *(pl* **attentats-suicides)** nm suicide attack ; [à la bombe] suicide bombing.

attente [atɑ̃t] nf **1.** [fait d'attendre, moment] wait ▸ **l'attente est longue** it's a long time to wait / *le plus dur, c'est l'attente* the toughest part is the waiting ▸ **pendant l'attente du verdict / des résultats** while awaiting the sentence / results ▸ **deux heures d'attente** a two-hour wait **2.** [espérance] expectation ▸ **répondre à l'attente de qqn** to come up to sb's expectations / *si la marchandise ne répond pas à votre attente* should the goods not meet your requirements. ❖ **dans l'attente de** loc prép **1.** [dans le temps] ▸ **être dans l'attente de qqch** to be waiting for ou awaiting *sout* sthg / *il vit dans l'attente de ton retour* he lives for the moment when you return **2.** [dans la correspondance] ▶ **dans l'attente de vous lire / de votre réponse / de vous rencontrer** looking forward to hearing from you / to your reply / to meeting you. ✤ **en attente** ◆ loc adv ▶ **laisser qqch en attente** to leave sthg pending. ◆ loc adj : *les plans sont en attente* the plans have been shelved.

attenter [3] [atɑ̃te] ✤ **attenter à** v + prép **1.** [commettre un attentat contre] ▶ **attenter à la vie de qqn** to make an attempt on sb's life ▶ **attenter à ses jours** ou **à sa vie** to attempt suicide **2.** [porter atteinte à] ▶ **attenter à l'honneur / à la réputation de qqn** to undermine sb's honour / reputation.

attentif, ive [atɑ̃tif, iv] adj **1.** [concentré - spectateur, public, élève] attentive ▶ **soyez attentifs !** pay attention! ▶ **écouter qqn d'une oreille attentive** to listen to sb attentively, to listen to every word sb says **2.** [prévenant - présence] watchful ; [- gestes, comportement, parole] solicitous *sout*, thoughtful **3.** [scrupuleux] ▶ **un examen attentif** a close ou careful examination **4.** ▶ **attentif à** [prêtant attention à] : *il était attentif au moindre bruit / mouvement* he was alert to the slightest sound / movement / *être attentif à ce qui se dit* to pay attention to ou to listen carefully to what is being said ▶ **être attentif aux besoins de qqn** to be attentive to sb's needs.

attention [atɑ̃sjɔ̃] ◆ nf **1.** [concentration] attention ▶ **appeler** ou **attirer l'attention de qqn sur qqch** to call sb's attention to sthg, to point sthg out to sb ▶ **écouter qqn avec attention** to listen to sb attentively, to listen hard to what sb's saying **a)** [écoutez] **faites bien attention a)** [écoutez] listen carefully, pay attention **b)** [regardez] look carefully ▶ **faire attention à** to pay attention to, to heed *sout* / *faire attention (à ce) que...* to make sure ou to ensure (that)... **2.** [égard] attention *(U)*, attentiveness *(U)*, thoughtfulness *(U)* ▶ **entourer qqn d'attentions, être plein d'attentions pour qqn** to lavish attention on sb **3.** [capacité à remarquer] attention ▶ **attirer l'attention** to attract attention ▶ **attirer l'attention de qqn** to catch ou to attract sb's attention ▶ **faire attention à:** *tu as fait attention au numéro de téléphone ?* did you make a (mental) note of the phone number ? / *quand il est entré, je n'ai d'abord pas fait attention à lui* when he came in I didn't notice him at first / *ne fais pas attention à lui, il dit n'importe quoi* don't mind him ou pay no attention to him, he's talking nonsense **4.** EXPR faire attention à [surveiller, s'occuper de] : *faire attention à soi / à sa santé* to take care of ou to look after o.s. / one's health / *faire attention à sa ligne* to watch one's weight / *il ne fait pas assez attention à sa femme* he doesn't pay enough attention to his wife ▶ **faire attention** [être prudent] to be careful ou cautious / *fais attention aux voitures* watch out for the cars ▶ **attention à la marche / porte** mind the step / door ▶ **attention au départ !** stand clear of the doors! ◆ interj [pour signaler un danger] watch ou look out / *attention, attention, tu vas le casser !* gently ou easy (now), you'll break it! ▶ **'attention peinture fraîche'** 'wet paint' / **'attention travaux'** 'men at work'. ✤ **à l'attention de** loc prép [sur une enveloppe] : *à l'attention de Madame Chaux* for the attention of Mme Chaux.

attentionné, e [atɑ̃sjɔne] adj thoughtful, solicitous *sout*.

attentisme [atɑ̃tism] nm wait-and-see policy.

attentiste [atɑ̃tist] ◆ adj ▶ **attitude attentiste** wait-and-see attitude ▶ **politique attentiste** waiting game. ◆ nmf ▶ **les attentistes** those who play a waiting game.

attentivement [atɑ̃tivmɑ̃] adv [en se concentrant] attentively, carefully, closely.

atténuant, e [atenɥɑ̃, ɑ̃t] adj [excuse, circonstance] mitigating.

atténuation [atenɥasjɔ̃] nf [d'une responsabilité] reduction, lightening *(U)* ; [d'une faute] mitigation ; [de propos] toning down *(U)* ; [d'une douleur] easing *(U)* ; [d'un coup] cushioning *(U)*, softening *(U)*.

atténuer [7] [atenɥe] vt **1.** [rendre moins perceptible - douleur] to relieve, to soothe ; [- couleur] to tone down *(sép)*, to soften ; [- bruit] to muffle **2.** [rendre moins important, moins grave - responsabilité] to reduce, to lighten, to lessen ; [- accusation] to tone down *(sép)*. ✤ **s'atténuer** vpi [chagrin, cris, douleur] to subside, to die down ; [effet] to subside, to fade, to wane ; [lumière] to fade, to dim ; [bruit] to diminish, to tone down ; [couleur] to dim.

atterrer [4] [atere] vt to dismay, to appal / *sa réponse m'a atterré* I was appalled at his answer ▶ **il les regarda d'un air atterré** he looked at them aghast ou in total dismay.

atterrir [32] [aterir] vi **1.** AÉRON to land, to touch down **2.** *fam* [retomber] to land, to fetch UK ou to wind up **3.** *fam* [se retrouver] to end ou to wind ou to land up ▶ **atterrir en prison** to end up ou to land up in jail.

atterrissage [aterisaʒ] nm landing ▶ **atterrissage en douceur** soft landing.

attestation [atɛstasjɔ̃] nf [document] certificate ▶ **attestation d'assurance** insurance certificate.

attester [3] [atɛste] vt **1.** [certifier] to attest / *ce document atteste que...* this is to certify that... **2.** [témoigner] to attest ou to testify to, to vouch for / *cette version des faits est attestée par la presse* this version of the facts is borne out by the press.

attifer [3] [atife] vt *fam & péj* to get up *(sép)*, to rig out *(sép)*. ✤ **s'attifer** vp *(emploi réfléchi) fam* to get o.s. up, to rig o.s. out.

attirail [atiraj] nm equipment ▶ **attirail de pêche** fishing tackle.

attirance [atirɑ̃s] nf attraction ▶ **éprouver de l'attirance pour qqn / qqch** to feel attracted to sb / sthg.

attirant, e [atirɑ̃, ɑ̃t] adj attractive.

attirer [3] [atire] vt **1.** [tirer vers soi] to draw **2.** [inciter à venir - badaud] to attract ; [- proie] to lure ▶ **attirer qqn dans un coin / piège** to lure sb into a corner / trap **3.** [capter - attention, regard] to attract, to catch ▶ **attirer l'attention de qqn sur qqch** to call sb's attention to sthg, to point sthg out to sb **4.** [plaire à] to attract, to seduce ▶ **se sentir attiré par qqn** to feel attracted to sb / *le jazz ne m'attire pas beaucoup* jazz doesn't appeal to me much **5.** [avoir comme conséquence] to bring, to cause ▶ **attirer des ennuis à qqn** to cause trouble for sb, to get sb into trouble. ✤ **s'attirer** vpt ▶ **s'attirer des ennuis** to get o.s. into trouble, to bring trouble upon o.s. ▶ **s'attirer la colère de qqn** to incur sb's anger.

attiser [3] [atize] vt **1.** [flammes, feu] to poke ; [incendie] to fuel **2.** [colère, haine, désir] to stir up *(sép)*, to rouse.

attitré, e [atitre] adj **1.** [accrédité] accredited, appointed **2.** [habituel - fournisseur, marchand] usual, regular **3.** [favori - fauteuil, place] favourite.

attitude [atityd] nf **1.** [comportement] attitude ; *péj* [affectation] attitude **2.** [maintien] bearing, demeanour ; [position] position, posture.

attouchement [atuʃmɑ̃] nm touching *(U)* ▶ **se livrer à des attouchements sur qqn** DR to fondle sb, to interfere with sb.

attractif, ive [atraktif, iv] adj **1.** PHYS attractive **2.** *sout* [plaisant] attractive, appealing.

attraction [atraksjɔ̃] nf **1.** ASTRON & PHYS attraction ▶ **attraction universelle** gravity **2.** [attirance] attraction **3.** [centre d'intérêt] attraction / *les attractions touristiques* *de la région* the area's tourist attractions **4.** LOISIRS attraction / *il y aura des attractions pour les enfants* entertainment will be provided for children.

attractivité [atʀaktivite] nf [d'un pays, d'un métier] attractiveness.

attrait [atʀɛ] nm **1.** [beauté - d'un visage, d'une ville, d'une idéologie] attraction, attractiveness **2.** [fascination] appeal, fascination. ❖ **attraits** nmpl *euphém & litt* charms.

attrape-nigaud [atʀapnigo] (*pl* **attrape-nigauds**) nm confidence trick.

attraper [3] [atʀape] vt **1.** [prendre] to pick up (*sép*) **2.** [saisir au passage - bras, main, ballon] to grab ▸ **attraper qqn par le bras** to grab sb by the arm ▸ **attraper qqn par la taille** to grab sb round the waist **3.** [saisir par force, par ruse] to capture, to catch **4.** [surprendre - voleur, tricheur] to catch ; [- bribe de conversation, mot] to catch **5.** [réprimander] to tell off (*sép*) ▸ **se faire attraper** to get a telling-off **6.** [prendre de justesse - train] to catch **7.** *fam* [avoir] to get / *attraper un coup de soleil* to get sunburnt ▸ **attraper froid** ou **un rhume** ou **du mal** *vieilli* to catch ou to get a cold.

attrape-touristes [atʀapturist] nm inv tourist trap.

attrayant, e [atʀejã, ãt] adj [homme, femme] good-looking, attractive ; [suggestion] attractive, appealing ▸ **peu attrayant** unattractive, unappealing.

attribuer [7] [atʀibɥe] vt **1.** [distribuer - somme, bien] to allocate ; [- titre, privilège] to grant ; [- fonction, place] to allocate, to assign ; [- prix, récompense] to award **2.** [imputer] ▸ **attribuer qqch à qqn** to ascribe ou to attribute sthg to sb / *j'attribue sa réussite à son environnement* I put her success down ou I attribute her success to her environment **3.** [accorder] ▸ **attribuer de l'importance / de la valeur à qqch** to attach importance to / to find value in sthg.

attribut [atʀiby] nm **1.** [caractéristique] attribute, (characteristic) trait **2.** GRAM predicate ▸ **adjectif attribut** predicative adjective.

attribution [atʀibysjõ] nf **1.** [distribution - d'une somme] allocation ; [- d'une place, d'une part] allocation, attribution ; [- d'un prix] awarding ; ÉCON [d'actions] allotment **2.** [reconnaissance - d'une œuvre, d'une responsabilité, d'une découverte] attribution. ❖ **attributions** nfpl ▸ **cela n'est pas** ou **n'entre pas dans mes attributions** this doesn't come within my remit ⓤ⒦.

attrister [3] [atʀiste] vt to sadden, to depress / *cela m'attriste de voir que…* it makes me sad ou I find it such a pity to see that…

attroupement [atʀupmã] nm crowd.

attrouper [3] [atʀupe] ❖ **s'attrouper** vpi [gén] to gather together ; [en grand nombre] to flock together.

au [o] ⟶ **à**.

aubaine [obɛn] nf [argent] windfall ; [affaire] bargain ; [occasion] godsend, golden opportunity ▸ **quelle aubaine !** what a godsend! ▸ **profiter de l'aubaine** to take advantage ou to make the most of a golden opportunity.

aube [ob] nf **1.** [aurore] dawn ▸ **à l'aube** at dawn, at daybreak ▸ **l'aube d'une ère nouvelle** *fig* the dawn ou dawning of a new era **2.** NAUT paddle, blade **3.** [d'un moulin] vane ; [pale] blade.

aubépine [obepin] nf hawthorn.

auberge [obɛʀʒ] nf inn ▸ **auberge de jeunesse** youth hostel ▸ **il n'est pas sorti / on n'est pas sortis de l'auberge** *fam* he's / we're not out of the woods yet.

aubergine [obɛʀʒin] ❖ nf BOT aubergine ⓤ⒦, eggplant ⓤⓢ. ❖ adj inv [couleur] aubergine.

aubergiste [obɛʀʒist] nmf inn-keeper.

auburn [obœʀn] adj inv auburn.

aucun, e [okœ̃, yn] ❖ adj indéf **1.** [avec une valeur négative] : *il ne fait aucun effort* he doesn't make any effort / *aucune décision n'a encore été prise* no decision has been reached yet / *il n'y a aucun souci à se faire* there is nothing to worry about / *je ne vois aucun inconvénient à ce que vous restiez* I don't mind your staying at all ▸ **sans aucun doute** undoubtedly, without any doubt ▸ **aucune idée !** no idea! **2.** [avec une valeur positive] any / *il est plus rapide qu'aucun autre coureur* he's faster than any other runner. ❖ pron indéf **1.** [avec une valeur négative] none / *je n'ai lu aucun de ses livres* I haven't read any of her books ▸ **aucun (des deux)** neither (of them) **2.** [servant de réponse négative] none **3.** [avec une valeur positive] any / *il est plus fort qu'aucun de vos hommes* he's stronger than any of your men ▸ **d'aucuns** *sout* some.

aucunement [okynmã] adv [dans des énoncés négatifs avec «ne» ou «sans»] in no way, not in the least ou slightest.

audace [odas] nf **1.** [courage] daring, boldness, audaciousness **2.** [impudence] audacity / *il a eu l'audace de dire non* he dared (to) ou he had the audacity to say no.

audacieux, euse [odasjø, øz] adj **1.** [courageux] daring, bold, audacious **2.** [impudent] bold, audacious, impudent **3.** [innovateur] bold, audacious, innovative.

au-dehors [odəɔʀ] adv **1.** [à l'extérieur] outside **2.** [en apparence] outwardly / *elle est généreuse même si au-dehors elle paraît dure* she's generous even if she looks cold ou if she's outwardly cold.

au-delà [odəla] ❖ nm ▸ **l'au-delà** the hereafter, the next world. ❖ loc adv beyond / *2 000 €, et je n'irai pas au-delà* 2,000 euros, and that's my final offer / *il a obtenu tout ce qu'il voulait et bien au-delà* he got everything he wanted and more. ❖ **au-delà de** loc prép [dans l'espace] beyond ; [dans le temps] after ▸ **au-delà de la frontière** on the other side of ou beyond the border / *réussir au-delà de ses espérances* to succeed beyond one's expectations ▸ **au-delà de ses forces / moyens** beyond one's strength / means.

au-dessous [odsu] adv **1.** [dans l'espace] below, under, underneath / *il n'y a personne (à l'étage) au-dessous* there's no one on the floor below **2.** [dans une hiérarchie] under, below / *enfants âgés de 10 ans et au-dessous* children aged 10 and below ▸ **taille au-dessous** next size down. ❖ **au-dessous de** loc prép **1.** [dans l'espace] below, under, underneath / *elle habite au-dessous de chez moi* she lives downstairs from me **2.** [dans une hiérarchie] below ▸ **au-dessous de zéro** below zero ▸ **au-dessous d'un certain prix** under ou below a certain price.

au-dessus [odsy] adv **1.** [dans l'espace] above ▸ **il habite au-dessus** he lives upstairs **2.** [dans une hiérarchie] above / *les enfants de 10 ans et au-dessus* children aged 10 and above ▸ **la taille au-dessus** the next size up. ❖ **au-dessus de** loc prép **1.** [dans l'espace] above / *il habite au-dessus de chez moi* he lives upstairs from me **2.** [dans une hiérarchie] above / *10 degrés au-dessus de zéro* 10 degrees above zero / *vivre au-dessus de ses moyens* to live beyond one's means ▸ **au-dessus de tout soupçon** above all ou beyond suspicion / *c'était au-dessus de mes forces* it was too much for ou beyond me.

au-devant [odvã] ❖ **au-devant de** loc prép ▸ **aller au-devant des désirs de qqn** to anticipate sb's wishes / *aller au-devant du danger* to court danger.

audible [odibl] adj audible / *règle ton micro, tu es à peine audible* adjust your microphone, we can barely hear you.

audience [odjɑ̃s] nf **1.** [entretien] audience ▸ **donner audience** ou **accorder une audience à qqn** to grant sb an audience **2.** DR hearing **3.** [public touché - par un livre] readership ; [- par un film, une pièce, un concert] public ▸ **faire de l'audience** to attract a large audience ▸ **battre tous les records d'audience** to break all viewing ou listening records.

Audimat® [odimat] nm audience rating ; ≃ Nielsen® ratings 🇺🇸 ▸ **course à l'Audimat®** ratings war.

audio [odjo] adj inv [matériel, fichier, livre] audio.

audioblog [odjoblog] nm audioblog.

audioconférence [odjokɔ̃feRɑ̃s] nf audio conference.

audiodescription [odjodɛskRipsjɔ̃] nf audio description / *ce film vous est proposé en audiodescription* this film is available with audio description.

audioguide [odjɔgid] nm audio guide, headset.

audiophone [odjɔfɔn] nm hearing aid.

audiovisuel, elle [odjovizɥɛl] adj audiovisual. ❖ **audiovisuel** nm **1.** [matériel] ▸ **l'audiovisuel a)** [des médias] radio and television equipment **b)** [dans l'enseignement] audiovisual aids **2.** [médias] ▸ **l'audiovisuel** broadcasting **3.** [techniques] ▸ **l'audiovisuel** media techniques.

audit [odit] nm audit.

auditeur, trice [oditœR, tRis] nm, f **1.** [d'une radio, d'un disque] listener ▸ **les auditeurs** the audience **2.** ENS ▸ **auditeur libre** unregistered student, auditor 🇺🇸.

auditif, ive [oditif, iv] adj hearing, auditory *spéc* ▸ **troubles auditifs** hearing disorder.

audition [odisjɔ̃] nf **1.** DANSE, MUS & THÉÂTRE audition ▸ **passer une audition** to audition **2.** DR ▸ **pendant l'audition des témoins** while the witnesses were being heard **3.** PHYSIOL hearing.

auditionner [3] [odisjɔne] ❖ vt ▸ **auditionner qqn** to audition sb, to give sb an audition. ❖ vi to audition.

auditoire [oditwaR] nm [public] audience.

auditorium [oditɔRjɔm] nm auditorium.

augmentation [ogmɑ̃tasjɔ̃] nf **1.** [fait d'augmenter] increase ▸ **une augmentation de 3 %** a 3% increase ▸ **en augmentation** rising, increasing **2.** [majoration de salaire] (pay) rise 🇬🇧, raise 🇺🇸 ▸ **demander une augmentation** to ask for a rise.

augmenter [3] [ogmɑ̃te] ❖ vt **1.** [porter à un niveau plus élevé - impôt, prix, nombre] to put up (*sép*), to increase, to raise ; [- durée] to increase ; [- tarif] to step up (*sép*) ; [- salaire] to increase, to raise, to give a rise 🇬🇧 ou raise 🇺🇸 ; [- dépenses] to increase ▸ **augmenter le pain** ou **le prix du pain** to put up bread prices / *la crise a fait augmenter le prix du pétrole* the crisis has pushed up the price of oil ▸ **elle a été augmentée** *fam* she got a (pay) rise 🇬🇧 ou a raise 🇺🇸 ▸ **augmenter qqch de**: *augmenter les impôts de 5 %* to put up ou to raise ou to increase taxes by 5% / *nous voulons augmenter les ventes de 10 %* we want to boost sales by 10% / *ils ont augmenté les employés de 10 euros* *fam* they put up the employees' pay by 10 euros **2.** [intensifier - tension, difficulté] to increase, to step up (*sép*), to make worse. ❖ vi **1.** [dette, population] to grow, to increase, to get bigger ; [quantité, poids] to increase ; [prix, impôt, salaire] to increase, to go up, to rise ▸ **tout** ou **la vie augmente !** everything's going up! **2.** [difficulté, tension] to increase, to grow / *la violence augmente dans les villes* urban violence is on the increase.

augure [ogyR] nm [présage] omen ; ANTIQ augury. ❖ **de bon augure** loc adj auspicious ▸ **c'est de bon augure** it's auspicious, it augurs well, it bodes well. ❖ **de mauvais augure** loc adj ominous, inauspicious ▸ **c'est de mauvais augure** it's ominous, it doesn't augur well, it bodes ill.

augurer [3] [ogyRe] vt to foresee / *sa visite ne laisse pas augurer de progrès significatif* no significant progress can be expected as a result of his visit ▸ **sa réponse augure mal / bien de notre prochaine réunion** his answer doesn't augur well / augurs well for our next meeting.

aujourd'hui [oʒuRdɥi] adv **1.** [ce jour] today ▸ **le journal d'aujourd'hui** today's paper / *nous sommes le trois aujourd'hui* today's the third / *il y a huit jours aujourd'hui* a week ago today **2.** [à notre époque] today, nowadays ▸ **la France d'aujourd'hui** modern ou present-day France, the France of today.

aulne [on] nm alder.

aumône [omon] nf charity, alms ▸ **demander l'aumône** to beg for alms.

aumônier [omonje] nm chaplain.

auparavant [opaRavɑ̃] adv [tout d'abord] beforehand, first.

auprès [opRɛ] adv nearby. ❖ **auprès de** loc prép **1.** [à côté de] close to, near, by ▸ **rester auprès de qqn** to stay with ou close to sb **2.** [dans l'opinion de] : *il passe pour un fin connaisseur auprès de ses amis* he's considered a connoisseur by his friends **3.** [en s'adressant à] : *chercher du réconfort auprès d'un ami* to seek comfort from a friend / *faire une demande auprès d'un organisme* to make an application ou to apply to an organization.

auquel [okɛl] m ⟶ **lequel**.

aura [oRa] nf aura.

auréole [oReɔl] nf **1.** ART halo **2.** [tache] ring **3.** ASTRON halo.

auréoler [3] [oReɔle] vt **1.** [parer] : *tout auréolée de ses victoires américaines, elle vient se mesurer aux basketteuses européennes* basking in the glory of her American victories, she's come to challenge the European basketball teams **2.** ART to paint a halo around the head of / *tête auréolée de cheveux roux* *fig* head with a halo of red hair.

auriculaire [oRikylɛR] nm little finger.

aurore [oRɔR] nf **1.** [matin] daybreak, dawn **2.** ASTRON aurora ▸ **aurore boréale** aurora borealis. ❖ **aux aurores** loc adv *hum* at the crack of dawn.

ausculter [3] [oskylte] vt to listen to ou to sound the chest of, to auscultate *spéc* / *il t'a ausculté ?* did he listen to your chest?

aussi [osi] ❖ adv **1.** [également] too, also / *il a faim, moi aussi* he's hungry, and so am I ou me too ▸ **elle parle russe, moi aussi** SHE speaks Russian and so do I / *c'est aussi leur avis* they think so too **2.** [en plus] too, also / *elle travaille aussi à Rome* she also works in Rome, she works in Rome too ou as well **3.** (*devant adj*) [terme de comparaison] : *il est aussi grand que son père* he's as tall as his father ▸ **elle est aussi belle qu'intelligente** ou **qu'elle est intelligente** she is as beautiful as she is intelligent / *ils sont aussi bons l'un que l'autre* they're both equally good ; (*devant adv*) ▸ **aussi doucement que possible** as quietly as possible / *il ne s'est jamais senti aussi bien que depuis qu'il a arrêté de fumer* he's never felt so well since he stopped smoking ▸ **aussi bien**: *il peut aussi bien rentrer chez lui* he might just as well go home **4.** [tellement] so ; [avec un adjectif épithète] such / *je n'ai jamais rien vu d'aussi beau* I've never seen anything so beautiful ; (*antéposé au verbe*) : *aussi curieux que cela puisse paraître strange* ou *though it may seem.* ❖ conj [indiquant la conséquence] therefore, and so / *il était très timide, aussi n'osa-t-il rien répondre* he was very shy, and so he didn't dare reply.

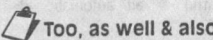
Too, as well & also

Aussi au sens d'«également» peut être rendu par too, as well et also, mais il convient de faire attention à leur place dans la phrase.

• **As well** (fréquent en anglais parlé) se place toujours en fin de phrase, tandis que **also** se place le plus souvent entre le sujet et le verbe (à l'exception de be) :
Il parle russe aussi. *He speaks Russian as well* ou *He also speaks Russian.*
Je suis pilote aussi. *I am a pilot as well* ou *I am also a pilot.*

En anglais américain, **also** se place parfois en fin de phrase :
Il parle chinois aussi. *He speaks Chinese also.*
Elle est traductrice aussi. *She's a translator also.*

• **Also** se place après le modal :
Ses parents peuvent venir aussi. *His parents can also come.*
Il te faudra aussi un gros pull. *You will also need a thick sweater.*

• **Too** se place soit en fin de phrase, soit directement après le sujet. Lorsque **too** est employé en fin de phrase, celle-ci peut être ambiguë ; il en va de même lorsqu'on emploie **as well** :
C'est aussi un bon cuisinier. *He's a good cook too* ou *as well.*

En plaçant **too** directement après le sujet, on évite cette ambiguïté (surtout à l'écrit) :
Lui aussi est bon cuisinier *He too is a good cook.*

À l'oral, c'est l'intonation qui enlève cette ambiguïté (les mots en bleu sont accentués) :
C'est aussi un bon cuisinier. *He's a good cook, too* ou *He's a good cook as well.*
Lui aussi est bon cuisinier. *He's a good cook, too* ou *He's a good cook as well.*

aussitôt [osito] adv immediately ▶ **aussitôt après son départ** immediately ou right after he left / *aussitôt rentré chez lui, il se coucha* as soon as he got home, he went to bed ▶ **aussitôt dit, aussitôt fait** no sooner said than done. ❖ **aussitôt que** loc conj as soon as ▶ **aussitôt que possible** as soon as possible.

austère [ostɛʀ] adj [architecture, mode de vie] austere, stark ; [style] dry ; [personnalité] stern, austere.

austérité [osteʀite] nf **1.** [dépouillement - d'une architecture, d'un mode de vie] austerity, starkness ; [- d'un style] dryness **2.** ÉCON ▶ **mesures d'austérité** austerity measures.

austral, e, als ou **aux** [ostʀal, o] adj [hémisphère] southern ; [pôle] south ; [constellation] austral. ⟶ **île**

Australie [ostʀali] npr f ▶ **l'Australie** Australia.

australien, enne [ostʀaljɛ̃, ɛn] adj Australian. ❖ **Australien, enne** nm, f Australian.

autant [otɑ̃] adv **1.** [marquant l'intensité] : *j'ignorais que tu l'aimais autant* I didn't know that you loved him so much ; (en corrélation avec «que») as much as ▶ **je l'aime autant que toi a)** [que tu l'aimes] I like him as much as you do **b)** [que je l'aime] I like him as much as you **2.** [indiquant la quantité] : *je ne pensais pas qu'ils seraient autant* I didn't think there would be so many of them ; (en corrélation avec «que») : *ils sont autant que nous* there are as many of them as (there are of) us **3.** (avec «en») [la même chose] : *tu devrais en faire autant* you should do the same **4.** (avec l'infinitif) [mieux vaut] ▶ **autant reve-**

nir demain I / you, etc. might as well come back tomorrow. ❖ **autant... autant** loc corrélative : *autant j'aime le vin, autant je déteste la bière* I hate beer as much as I love wine. ❖ **autant de** loc dét [avec un nom non comptable] as much ; [avec un nom comptable] as many ▶ **il y a autant d'eau / de sièges ici** there's as much water / there are as many seats here / *ces livres sont autant de chefs-d'œuvre* every last one of these books is a masterpiece ; (en corrélation avec «que») : *il y a autant de femmes que d'hommes* there are as many women as (there are) men / *(c'est) autant de gagné* ou *de pris* at least that's something. ❖ **autant dire** loc adv in other words / *j'ai été payé 500 euros, autant dire rien* I was paid 500 euros, in other words a pittance. ❖ **autant dire que** loc conj : *trois heures dans le four, autant dire que le poulet était carbonisé !* after three hours in the oven, needless to say the chicken was burnt to a cinder! ❖ **autant que** loc conj **1.** [dans la mesure où] as far as ▶ **autant que possible** as far as (is) possible **2.** [il est préférable que] : *autant que je vous le dise tout de suite...* I may as well tell you straightaway... ❖ **d'autant** loc adv : *si le coût de la vie augmente de 2 %, les salaires seront augmentés d'autant* if the cost of living goes up by 2%, salaries will be raised accordingly. ❖ **d'autant mieux** loc adv all the better, much better. ❖ **d'autant mieux que** loc conj : *il a travaillé d'autant mieux qu'il se sentait encouragé* he worked all the better for feeling encouraged. ❖ **d'autant moins que** loc conj : *je le vois d'autant moins qu'il est très occupé en ce moment* I see even less of him now that he's very busy. ❖ **d'autant moins... que** loc corrélative : *elle est d'autant moins excusable qu'on l'avait prévenue* what she did is all the less forgivable as she'd been warned. ❖ **d'autant plus** loc adv all the more reason. ❖ **d'autant plus que** loc conj especially as. ❖ **d'autant plus... que** loc corrélative : *c'est d'autant plus stupide qu'il ne sait pas nager* it's particularly ou all the more stupid given (the fact) that he can't swim. ❖ **d'autant que** loc conj [vu que, attendu que] especially as, particularly as / *c'est une bonne affaire, d'autant que le crédit est très avantageux* it's a good deal, especially as the terms of credit are very advantageous. ❖ **pour autant** loc adv : *la situation n'est pas perdue pour autant* the situation isn't hopeless for all that, it doesn't necessarily mean all is lost / *fais-le-lui remarquer sans pour autant le culpabiliser* point it out to him, but don't make him feel guilty about it. ❖ **pour autant que** loc conj as far as / *pour autant que je (le) sache* as far as I know.

autarcie [otaʀsi] nf self-sufficiency, autarky *spéc* ▶ **vivre en autarcie** to be self-sufficient.

autel [otɛl] nm RELIG altar.

auteur, e [otœʀ] nm, f **1.** [qui a écrit - un livre, un article, une chanson] writer, author ▶ **auteur de a)** [d'une toile] painter of **b)** [d'un décor, d'un meuble, d'un vêtement] designer of **c)** [d'un morceau de musique] composer of **d)** [d'une statue] sculptor of **e)** [d'un film, d'un clip] director of / *quelle jolie chanson, qui en est l'auteur ?* what a lovely song, who wrote it? **2.** [responsable] ▶ **l'auteur de** : *l'auteur d'un accident* the person who caused an accident / *les auteurs présumés de l'attentat* those suspected of having planted the bomb.

auteur-compositeur [otœʀkɔ̃pozitœʀ] (pl **auteurs-compositeurs**) nm composer and lyricist ▶ **auteur-compositeur interprète** singer-songwriter ▶ **je suis auteur-compositeur interprète** I write and sing my own material.

authenticité [otɑ̃tisite] nf **1.** [d'un document, d'un tableau, d'un tapis] authenticity ; [d'un sentiment] genuineness **2.** DR authenticity.

authentifier [9] [otɑ̃tifje] vt to authenticate.

authentique [otɑ̃tik] adj **1.** [document, tableau, tapis, objet d'art] genuine, authentic ; [sentiment] genuine, heartfelt **2.** DR authentic ; [copie] certified.

autisme [otism] nm autism.

autiste [otist] ◆ adj autistic. ◆ nmf autistic person.

autistique [otistik] adj autistic.

auto [oto] nf car, automobile US ▶ **autos tamponneuses** bumper cars, dodgems.

autoadhésif, ive [otoadezif, iv] adj self-adhesive.

autobiographie [otobjɔgʀafi] nf autobiography.

autobiographique [otobjɔgʀafik] adj autobiographical.

autobronzant, e [otobʀɔ̃zɑ̃, ɑ̃t] adj tanning. ❖ **autobronzant** nm [crème] tanning cream.

autobus [otobys] nm bus ▶ **autobus à impériale** double-decker (bus) UK.

autocar [otokaʀ] nm coach UK, bus US ▶ **autocar pullman** luxury coach.

autocariste [otokaʀist] nmf **1.** [propriétaire d'autocars] coach operator UK, bus company owner US **2.** [chauffeur] coach driver UK, bus driver US.

autocassable [otokasabl] adj ⟶ ampoule.

autocensure [otosɑ̃syʀ] nf self-censorship, self-regulation.

autocensurer [3] [otosɑ̃syʀe] ❖ **s'autocensurer** vp (emploi réfléchi) to censor o.s.

autochtone [otɔktɔn] ◆ adj native. ◆ nmf native.

autocollant, e [otokɔlɑ̃, ɑ̃t] adj self-adhesive. ❖ **autocollant** nm sticker.

autocrate [otokʀat] nm autocrat.

autocritique [otokʀitik] nf self-criticism ▶ **faire son autocritique** to make a thorough criticism of o.s.

autocuiseur [otokɥizœʀ] nm pressure cooker.

autodéfense [otodefɑ̃s] nf self-defence UK, self-defense US. ❖ **d'autodéfense** loc adj [arme] defensive ▶ **groupe d'autodéfense** vigilante group.

autodérision [otodeʀizjɔ̃] nf self-mockery.

autodestructeur, trice [otodɛstʀyktœʀ, tʀis] adj self-destroying.

autodétermination [otodetɛʀminasjɔ̃] nf self-determination.

autodétruire [98] [otodetʀɥiʀ] ❖ **s'autodétruire** vp (emploi réfléchi) to self-destruct.

autodidacte [otodidakt] ◆ adj self-taught, self-educated. ◆ nmf autodidact.

autodiscipline [otodisiplin] nf self-discipline.

auto-école (pl auto-écoles), **autoécole*** [otoekɔl] nf driving-school ; (comme adj) ▶ **voiture auto-école** driving-school car.

autoentrepreneur, euse [otoɑ̃tʀəpʀənœʀ, øz] n self-employed businessman (businesswoman).

autoévaluation [otoevalyasjɔ̃] nf self-assessment.

autoévaluer [3] [otoevalye] ❖ **s'autoévaluer** vp to assess oneself.

autofocus [otofokys] ◆ adj autofocus. ◆ nm **1.** [système] autofocus system **2.** [appareil] autofocus camera.

autogéré, e [otoʒeʀe] adj self-managed, self-run.

autographe [otogʀaf] nm autograph.

autoguidé, e [otogide] adj [avion] remotely-piloted ; [missile] guided.

automate [otomat] nm **1.** [robot] automaton, robot **2.** SUISSE [machine] vending machine ; [à billets] cash dispenser.

automatique [otomatik] ◆ adj automatic. ◆ nm ARM automatic. ◆ nf AUTO automatic (car).

automatiquement [otomatikmɑ̃] adv automatically.

automatisation [otomatizasjɔ̃] nf automation.

automatiser [3] [otomatize] vt to automate.

automatisme [otomatism] nm automatism / j'éteins toutes les lampes, c'est un automatisme I always switch lamps off, I do it without thinking ou it's automatic with me.

automédication [otomedikasjɔ̃] nf self-prescription (of drugs), self-medication.

automitrailleuse [otomitʀajøz] nf armoured UK ou armored US car.

automnal, e, aux [otɔnal, o] adj autumnal litt, autumn (modif), fall US (modif).

automne [otɔn] nm autumn, fall US.

automobile [otomobil] ◆ nf **1.** [véhicule] motor car UK, automobile US **2.** SPORT driving, motoring UK **3.** [industrie] car industry. ◆ adj **1.** MÉCAN [des voitures] car (modif) ; [bateau, engin] automotive, self-propelled **2.** ADMIN [vignette] car (modif) ; [assurance] car, automobile.

automobiliste [otomobilist] nmf driver, motorist UK.

autoneige [otonɛʒ] nf QUÉBEC snowmobile.

autonettoyant, e [otonɛtwajɑ̃, ɑ̃t] adj self-cleaning.

autonome [otonɔm] adj **1.** [autogéré - territoire, gouvernement, organisme] autonomous, self-governing **2.** [non affilié - syndicat] independent **3.** [libre - caractère, personnalité] autonomous, independent ▶ **elle est très autonome** she likes to make her own decisions.

autonomie [otonɔmi] nf **1.** [d'une personne] autonomy, independence ; [d'un État, d'un pays] autonomy, self-government **2.** [d'un véhicule, d'un avion] range ; [d'un appareil rechargeable] : ce rasoir a une autonomie de 30 minutes the razor will run for 30 minutes before it needs recharging.

autonomiste [otonɔmist] adj & nmf separatist.

autopartage [otopaʀtaʒ] nm an urban rent-a-car service which allows short-term car hire.

autoportrait [otopɔʀtʀɛ] nm self-portrait ▶ **faire son autoportrait** to paint a self-portrait.

autoproclamer [otopʀɔklame] ❖ **s'autoproclamer** vp to proclaim o.s. / il s'est autoproclamé expert he has proclaimed himself (to be) an expert.

autopropulsé, e [otopʀopylse] adj self-propelled.

autopsie [otopsi] nf MÉD autopsy ▶ **pratiquer une autopsie** to carry out an autopsy.

autoradio [otoʀadjo] nm car radio.

autorail [otoʀaj] nm railcar.

autorisation [otoʀizasjɔ̃] nf **1.** [consentement - d'un parent] permission, consent ; [- d'un supérieur] permission, authorization ; [- d'un groupe] authorization ▶ **donner à qqn l'autorisation de faire qqch** to give sb permission to do sthg ▶ **autorisation parentale** parental consent **2.** ADMIN [acte officiel] authorization, permit **3.** BANQUE ▶ **autorisation de découvert** overdraft facility.

autorisé, e [otoʀize] adj **1.** PRESSE official / de source autorisée, le président aurait déjà signé l'accord sources close to the President say that he's already signed the agreement **2.** [agréé - aliment, colorant] permitted **3.** [qui a la permission] ▶ **personnes autorisées** authorized persons.

autoriser [3] [otoʀize] vt **1.** [permettre - manifestation, réunion, publication] to authorize, to allow ; [- emprunt] to authorize, to approve **2.** [donner l'autorisation à] ▶ **autoriser qqn à** to allow sb ou to give sb permission to do ▶ **autoriser qqn à faire** [lui en donner le droit] to entitle sb ou to give sb the right to do / sa réponse nous autorise à penser que... from his reply we may deduce ou his reply leads us to conclude that... **3.** [justifier] to permit of *sout*, to justify. ❖ **s'autoriser** vpt : *je m'autorise un petit verre de vin le soir* I allow myself a small glass of wine in the evening.

autoritaire [ɔtɔʀitɛʀ] adj authoritarian ▸ **il est très autoritaire** he's very overbearing.

autoritarisme [ɔtɔʀitaʀism] nm authoritarianism.

autorité [ɔtɔʀite] nf **1.** [pouvoir] authority, power ▸ **avoir de l'autorité sur qqn** to be in ou to have authority over sb ▸ **l'autorité parentale a)** [droits] parental rights **b)** [devoirs] parental responsibilities **2.** [fermeté] authority / *faire preuve d'autorité envers un enfant* to show some authority towards a child / *il a besoin d'un peu d'autorité* he needs to be taken in hand **3.** [compétence] authority ▸ **faire autorité**: *édition qui fait autorité* authoritative edition ; [expert] authority, expert / *c'est une autorité en matière de...* he's an authority ou expert on... **4.** ADMIN ▸ **l'autorité** ou **les autorités** those in authority ou the authorities ; [police] ▸ **les autorités** the police force.

autoroute [ɔtɔʀut] nf **1.** TRANSP motorway 🇬🇧, freeway 🇺🇸 ▸ **autoroute à péage** toll motorway 🇬🇧, turnpike 🇺🇸 ▸ **l'autoroute du Soleil** *the motorway linking Paris, Lyon and Marseille, famously congested during the "grands départs" of July and August* **2.** INFORM ▸ **autoroute électronique** information superhighway.

 Autoroute

In France, motorways are indicated with the letter **A** followed by a number. Many motorways are privately run and operate a toll system (**péage**).

autoroutier, ère [ɔtɔʀutje, ɛʀ] adj motorway 🇬🇧 (modif), freeway 🇺🇸 (modif). ❖ **autoroutière** nf car particularly suited to motorway driving conditions / *c'est une bonne autoroutière* it's ideal for motorway driving.

auto-stop, autostop* [ɔtɔstɔp] nm sg hitch-hiking, hitching ▸ **faire de l'auto-stop** to hitch-hike, to hitch ▸ **prendre qqn en auto-stop** to give sb a lift ou ride.

auto-stoppeur, euse (mpl **auto-stoppeurs**, fpl **auto-stoppeuses**), **autostoppeur*, euse** [ɔtɔstɔpœʀ, øz] nm, f hitch-hiker ▸ **prendre un auto-stoppeur** to pick up a hitch-hiker.

autosuggestion [ɔtɔsygʒɛstjɔ̃] nf autosuggestion.

autour [otuʀ] adv around, round / *il y avait un arbre et les enfants couraient (tout) autour* there was a tree and the children were running round it. ❖ **autour de** loc prép **1.** [dans l'espace] around / *il observait les gens autour de lui* he looked at the people around him **2.** [indiquant une approximation] around / *ils sont arrivés autour de 20 h* they arrived (at) around 8 p.m.

autre [otʀ] ❖ dét (adj indéf) **1.** [distinct, différent] ▸ **un autre homme** another ou a different man ▸ **dans d'autres circonstances...** in other circumstances .., had the circumstances been different... / *tu veux autre chose ?* do you want anything else ? / *je me faisais une tout autre idée de la question* I had quite a different concept of the matter ▸ **ça c'est une autre histoire** ou **affaire** ou **paire de manches** fam that's something else altogether, that's another story ou kettle of fish (altogether) **2.** [supplémentaire] : *voulez-vous un autre café ?* would you like another coffee ? / *il nous faut une autre chaise* we need one more ou an extra ou another chair **3.** [devenu différent] different / *je me sens un autre homme* I feel a different ou new man **4.** [marquant la supériorité] : *le Japon, ah c'est autre chose !* Japan, now that's really something else ! **5.** [avec les pronoms 'nous' et 'vous'] ▸ **nous autres consommateurs...**

we consumers... **6.** [dans le temps] other / *on y est allés l'autre jour* we went there the other day ▸ **un autre jour** some other day ▸ **dans une autre vie** in another life **7.** [en corrélation avec 'l'un'] : *l'une et l'autre hypothèses sont valables* both hypotheses are valid. ❖ pron **1.** [désignant des personnes] ▸ **un autre** someone else, somebody else / *on n'attend pas les autres ?* aren't we going to wait for the others? ▸ **tout** ou **un autre que lui aurait refusé** anyone else but him would have refused ▸ **quelqu'un d'autre** someone else ▸ **personne d'autre** no one else, nobody else ; [désignant des choses] ▸ **un autre** another one ▸ **d'autres** other ones, others / *une maison semblable à une autre* a house like any other / *je n'en ai pas besoin d'autres* I don't need any more ▸ **rien d'autre** nothing else ▸ **à d'autres !** fam go on with you!, come off it! **2.** [en corrélation avec 'l'un'] ▸ **l'un et l'autre** both of them ▸ **l'un ou l'autre** (either) one or the other, either one / *ni l'un ni l'autre n'est venu* neither (of them) came / *on les prend souvent l'un pour l'autre* people often mistake one for the other ▸ **présente-les l'un à l'autre** introduce them to each other ▸ **l'un dans l'autre** all in all, at the end of the day.

autrefois [otʀəfwa] adv in the past, in former times ou days / *les maisons d'autrefois n'avaient aucun confort* in the past ou in the old days, houses were very basic.

autrement [otʀəmɑ̃] adv **1.** [différemment] another ou some other way / *la banque est fermée, je vais me débrouiller autrement* the bank's closed, I'll find some other way (of getting money) / *il est habillé autrement que d'habitude* he hasn't got his usual clothes on ▸ **en être autrement**: *comment pourrait-il en être autrement* how could things be different? ▸ **faire autrement**: *il n'y a pas moyen de faire autrement* there's no other way ou no alternative ▸ **faire autrement que**: *je n'ai pu faire autrement que de les entendre* I couldn't help but overhear them **2.** [sinon] otherwise, or else / *payez car autrement vous aurez des ennuis* pay up or else you'll get into trouble **3.** (suivi d'un comparatif) [beaucoup] far / *c'est autrement plus grave cette fois-ci* it's far more serious this time. ❖ **autrement dit** loc adv in other words.

Autriche [otʀiʃ] npr f ▸ **(l')Autriche** Austria.

autrichien, enne [otʀiʃjɛ̃, ɛn] adj Austrian. ❖ **Autrichien, enne** nm, f Austrian.

autruche [otʀyʃ] nf ostrich ▸ **faire l'autruche** to bury one's head in the sand.

autrui [otʀɥi] pron indéf inv sout others, other people / *peu m'importe l'opinion d'autrui* other people's opinion ou the opinion of others means little to me.

auvent [ovɑ̃] nm **1.** [en dur] porch roof **2.** [en toile] awning, canopy.

aux [o] ⟶ **à**.

auxiliaire [oksiljɛʀ] ❖ adj **1.** LING auxiliary **2.** [annexe] assistant (modif), auxiliary **3.** TECHNOL auxiliary, standby. ❖ nmf **1.** MÉD ▸ **auxiliaire médical** paramedic ▸ **les auxiliaires médicaux** the paramedical profession **2.** [travailleur social] ▸ **auxiliaire de vie (sociale)** carer, homecare assistant **3.** [aide] helper, assistant. ❖ nm LING auxiliary.

auxquelles, auxquels [okɛl] fpl & mpl ⟶ **lequel**.

av. abr écrite de **avenue**.

AV abr écrite de **avant**.

avachi, e [avaʃi] adj **1.** [sans tenue - vêtement] crumpled, shapeless ; [- chapeau] crumpled ; [- cuir] limp ; [- sommier, banquette] sagging ; [- chaussure] shapeless, down-at-heel ; [- gâteau] soggy ; [- soufflé] collapsed **2.** [fatigué] drained ; [indolent] flabby, spineless / *avachi dans un fauteuil* slumped in an armchair.

aval [aval] ❖ nm **1.** [autorisation] authorization ▸ **avoir l'aval des autorités** to have (an) official authorization

2. [d'une rivière] downstream water. ◆ adj ▶ **ski / skieur aval** downhill ski / skier. ◆ **en aval de** loc prép **1.** [en suivant une rivière] downstream ou down-river from **2.** [en montagne] downhill from **3.** [après] following on from / *les étapes qui se situent en aval de la production* the post-production stages.

avalanche [avalɑ̃ʃ] nf **1.** GÉOGR avalanche **2.** fig [quantité - de courrier, de protestations, de compliments, de lumière] flood ; [- de coups, d'insultes] shower / *il y eut une avalanche de réponses* the answers came pouring in.

avaler [3] [avale] vt **1.** [consommer - nourriture] to swallow ; [- boisson] to swallow, to drink ▶ **avaler qqch de travers**: *j'ai dû avaler quelque chose de travers* something went down the wrong way / *je n'ai rien avalé depuis deux jours* I haven't had a thing to eat for two days / *avaler du lait à petites gorgées* to sip milk ▶ **avaler sa salive** to swallow ; *(en usage absolu)* [manger, boire] to swallow **2.** [inhaler - fumée, vapeurs] to inhale, to breathe in *(sép)* **3.** [lire - roman, article] to devour **4.** fam [croire - mensonge] to swallow, to buy / *elle lui ferait avaler n'importe quoi* he believes anything she says **5.** fam [accepter - insulte] to swallow ▶ **pilule difficile à avaler** fig hard ou bitter pill to swallow ▶ **avaler la pilule** to swallow the bitter pill.

avance [avɑ̃s] nf **1.** [par rapport au temps prévu] ▶ **j'ai pris de l'avance sur le** ou **par rapport au planning** I'm ahead of schedule ▶ **avoir de l'avance sur** ou **par rapport à ses concurrents** to be ahead of the competition ou of one's competitors ▶ **arriver avec 10 minutes / jours d'avance** to arrive 10 minutes / days early / *le maillot jaune a pris 37 secondes d'avance* the yellow jersey's 37 seconds ahead of time **2.** [d'une montre, d'un réveil] : *ta montre prend de l'avance* your watch is fast ▶ **ma montre a une minute d'avance / prend une seconde d'avance toutes les heures** my watch is one minute fast / gains a second every hour **3.** [avantage - d'une entreprise] lead ; [- d'une armée] progress ▶ **avoir 10 points d'avance sur qqn** to have a 10 point lead over sb ▶ **avoir une demi-longueur d'avance** to lead by half a length **4.** [acompte] advance ▶ **faire une avance de 500 euros à qqn** to advance 500 euros to sb ▶ **avance sur salaire** advance (on one's salary). ◆ **avances** nfpl [propositions - d'amitié, d'association] overtures, advances ; [- sexuelles] advances ▶ **faire des avances à qqn a)** [suj : séducteur] to make advances to sb **b)** [suj : entreprise] to make overtures to sb. ◆ **à l'avance** loc adv [payer] in advance, beforehand / *je n'ai été averti que deux minutes à l'avance* I was only warned two minutes beforehand, I only got two minutes' notice ▶ **réservez longtemps à l'avance** book early. ◆ **d'avance, par avance** loc adv [payer, remercier] in advance ▶ **savourant d'avance sa revanche** already savouring his revenge / *d'avance je peux te dire qu'il n'est pas fiable* I can tell you right away ou now that he's not reliable. ◆ **en avance** loc adj : *elle est en avance sur le reste de la classe* she's ahead of the rest of the class ▶ **être en avance sur son temps** ou **époque** to be ahead of one's time. ◆ loc adv [avant l'heure prévue] early / *être en avance de 10 minutes / jours* to be 10 minutes / days early / *je me dépêche, je ne suis pas en avance !* I must rush, I'm (rather) late!

avancé, e [avɑ̃se] adj **1.** [dans le temps - heure] late ▶ **à une heure avancée** late at night ▶ **la saison est avancée** it's very late in the season / *arriver à un âge avancé* to be getting on in years **2.** [pourri - poisson, viande] off [UK], bad ; [- fruit] overripe **3.** [développé - intelligence, économie] advanced / *un garçon avancé pour son âge* a boy who's mature for ou ahead of his years / *à un stade peu avancé* at an early stage ▶ **te voilà bien avancé !** iron a (fat) lot of good that's done you! ◆ **avancée** nf **1.** [progression] progress **2.** [d'un toit] overhang.

avancement [avɑ̃smɑ̃] nm **1.** [promotion] promotion, advancement ▶ **avoir** ou **obtenir de l'avancement** to get (a) promotion ou promoted **2.** [progression] progress.

avancer [16] [avɑ̃se] ◆ vt **1.** [pousser vers l'avant] to push ou to move forward *(sép)* ; [amener vers l'avant] to bring forward *(sép)* / *tu es trop loin, avance ta chaise* you're too far away, move ou bring your chair forward ▶ **avancer un siège à qqn** to pull ou draw up a seat for sb **2.** [allonger] ▶ **avancer la tête** to stick one's head out **3.** [dans le temps] to bring ou to put forward *(sép)*, to move up [US] / *l'heure du départ a été avancée de 10 minutes* the starting time was put forward 10 minutes ▶ **la réunion a été avancée à demain / lundi** the meeting has been brought forward to tomorrow / Monday **4.** [proposer - explication, raison, opinion] to put forward *(sép)*, to suggest, to advance ; [- argument, théorie, plan] to put forward / *être sûr de ce que l'on avance* to be certain of what one is saying **5.** [faire progresser] : *trêve de bavardage, tout cela ne m'avance pas* that's enough chatting, all this isn't getting my work done / *ça t'avance à quoi de mentir ?* fam what do you gain by lying? ◆ vi **1.** [se déplacer - argent, somme, loyer] to lend, to advance. ◆ vi **1.** [se déplacer dans l'espace] to move forward, to proceed sout, to advance ; MIL to advance ▶ **avancer à grands pas** to stride along ▶ **avancer avec difficulté** to plod along / *avoir du mal à avancer* to make slow progress / *ne restez pas là, avancez !* don't just stand there, move on! **2.** [progresser - temps, action] to be getting on, to progress ▶ **l'heure avance** time's ou it's getting on, it's getting late ▶ **ça avance ?** how's it going? ▶ **le projet n'avance plus** the project's come to a halt ou standstill ▶ **faire avancer les choses a)** [accélérer une action] to speed things up **b)** [améliorer la situation] to improve matters **3.** [faire des progrès] to make progress, to get further forward / *j'ai l'impression de ne pas avancer* I don't feel I'm getting anywhere ou I'm making any headway ▶ **avancer dans une enquête / son travail** to make progress in an investigation / one's work ▶ **avancer en âge a)** [enfant] to grow up, to get older **b)** [personne mûre] to be getting on (in years) **4.** [montre, réveil] ▶ **votre montre avance** ou **vous avancez de 10 minutes** your watch is ou you are 10 minutes fast. ◆ **s'avancer** vpi **1.** [approcher] to move forward ou closer ▶ **il s'avança vers moi** he came towards me **2.** [prendre de l'avance] ▶ **s'avancer dans son travail** to make progress ou some headway in one's work **3.** [prendre position] to commit o.s. / *je ne voudrais pas m'avancer mais il est possible que…* I can't be positive but it might be that… / *je m'avance peut-être un peu trop en affirmant cela* it might be a bit rash of me to say this.

avant [avɑ̃] ◆ prép **1.** [dans le temps] before / *il est arrivé avant la nuit / le dîner* he arrived before nightfall / dinner ▶ **avant son élection** prior to his election, before being elected ▶ **200 ans avant Jésus-Christ** 200 (years) BC / *nous n'ouvrons pas avant 10 h* we don't open until 10 / *il faut que je termine avant ce soir* I've got to finish by this evening **2.** [dans l'espace] before / *vous tournez à droite juste avant le feu* you turn right just before the lights **3.** [dans un rang, un ordre, une hiérarchie] before / *il était juste avant moi dans la file* he was just in front of me in the queue / *ta santé passe avant ta carrière* your health is more important than ou comes before your career. ◆ adv **1.** [dans le temps] before / *avant, j'avais plus de patience avec les enfants* I used to be more patient with children / *la maison est comme avant* the house has remained the same ou is the same as it was (before) / *bien* ou *longtemps avant* well ou long before / *il est parti quelques minutes avant* he left a few minutes before ou earlier **2.** [dans l'espace] : *vous voyez le parc ? il y a un restaurant juste avant* see the park? there's a restaurant just before ou this side of it **3.** [dans un rang, un ordre, une hiérarchie] : *est-ce que je peux passer avant ?* can I go first? ◆ adj inv [saut périlleux, roulade] forward ; [roue, siège, partie] front. ◆ nm **1.** [d'un véhicule] front ▸ **aller de l'avant** pr & fig to forge ahead **2.** SPORT forward ; [au volley] frontline player / **jouer avant droit / gauche** to play right / left forward **3.** Québec ▸ **mettre qqch de l'avant** [mettre en avant] to put sthg forward. ❖ **avant de** loc prép before / **avant de partir, il faudra...** before leaving, it'll be necessary to... ❖ **avant que** loc conj : **je viendrai la voir avant qu'elle (ne) parte** I'll come and see her before she leaves / **avant qu'il comprenne, celui-là !** by the time he's understood! ❖ **avant tout** loc adv **1.** [surtout] : **c'est une question de dignité avant tout** it's a question of dignity above all (else) **2.** [tout d'abord] first / **avant tout, je voudrais vous dire ceci** first (and foremost), I'd like to tell you this. ❖ **d'avant** loc adj ▸ **le jour / le mois d'avant** the previous day / month, the day / month before / **les locataires d'avant étaient plus sympathiques** the previous tenants were much nicer. ❖ **en avant** loc adv [marcher] in front ; [partir] ahead ; [se pencher, tomber, bondir] forward ▸ **en avant !** forward! ▸ **en avant, marche !** MIL forward march! ; fig ▸ **mettre qqn en avant** a) [pour se protéger] to use sb as a shield b) [pour le faire valoir] to push sb forward ou to the front ▸ **mettre qqch en avant** to put sthg forward.

avantage [avɑ̃taʒ] nm **1.** [supériorité] advantage ▸ **avoir un avantage sur qqn / qqch** to have an advantage over sb / sthg / **cela vous donne un avantage sur eux** this gives you an advantage over them ▸ **avoir l'avantage sur qqn** to have the advantage over sb **2.** [intérêt] advantage / **cette idée présente l'avantage d'être simple** the idea has the advantage of being simple / **exploiter une idée à son avantage** to exploit an idea to one's own advantage / **tu as tout avantage à l'acheter ici** you'd be much better off buying it here / **tirer avantage de la situation** to turn the situation to (one's) advantage **3.** FIN [bénéfice] benefit ▸ **avantage fiscal** tax benefit, tax incentive ▸ **avantages en nature** payment in kind ▸ **avantages sociaux** benefits **4.** EXPR être à son avantage** a) [avoir belle allure] to look one's best b) [dans une situation] to be at one's best.

avantager [17] [avɑ̃taʒe] vt **1.** [favoriser] to advantage, to give an advantage to, to favour UK, to favor US / **ils ont été avantagés par rapport aux étudiants étrangers** they were given an advantage over the foreign students ▸ **être avantagé dès le départ par rapport à qqn** to have a head start on ou over sb **2.** [mettre en valeur] to show off (sép), to show to advantage / **cette coupe ne t'avantage pas** this hairstyle isn't very flattering.

avantageusement [avɑ̃taʒøzmɑ̃] adv **1.** [peu cher] at ou for a good price **2.** [favorablement] favourably UK, favorably US / **l'opération se solde avantageusement pour elle** the transaction has worked to her advantage.

avantageux, euse [avɑ̃taʒø, øz] adj **1.** [contrat, affaire] profitable ; [prix] attractive ; [condition, situation] favourable / **c'est une offre très avantageuse** it's an excellent bargain **2.** [flatteur - pose, décolleté, uniforme] flattering ▸ **prendre des airs avantageux** to look self-satisfied.

avant-bras [avɑ̃bʀa] nm inv forearm.

avant-centre [avɑ̃sɑ̃tʀ] (pl **avants-centres**) nm centre UK ou center US forward.

avant-coureur [avɑ̃kuʀœʀ] (pl **avant-coureurs**) adj m precursory.

avant-dernier, ère [avɑ̃dɛʀnje, ɛʀ] (mpl **avant-derniers**, fpl **avant-dernières**) ◆ adj next to last ▸ **l'avant-dernière fois** the time before last. ◆ nm, f last but one ▸ **arriver avant-dernier** to be last but one.

avant-garde [avɑ̃gaʀd] (pl **avant-gardes**) nf **1.** MIL vanguard **2.** [élite] avant-garde / **peinture / architecture d'avant-garde** avant-garde painting / architecture.

avant-gardiste [avɑ̃gaʀdist] (pl **avant-gardistes**) adj avant-garde.

avant-goût (pl **avant-goûts**), **avant-gout*** (pl **avant-gouts***) [avɑ̃gu] nm foretaste.

avant-hier [avɑ̃tjɛʀ] adv the day before yesterday.

avant-midi [avɑ̃midi] (pl **avant-midi** ou **avant-midis***) nm ou nf Belg & Québec morning.

avant-première [avɑ̃pʀəmjɛʀ] (pl **avant-premières**) nf **1.** THÉÂTRE dress rehearsal **2.** CINÉ preview ▸ **présenter qqch en avant-première** to preview sthg.

avant-projet [avɑ̃pʀɔʒe] (pl **avant-projets**) nm pilot study.

avant-propos [avɑ̃pʀopo] nm inv foreword.

avant-veille [avɑ̃vɛj] (pl **avant-veilles**) nf two days before ou earlier / **l'avant-veille de son mariage** two days before he got married.

avare [avaʀ] ◆ adj **1.** [pingre] mean, miserly, tight-fisted **2.** fig : **il n'a pas été avare de compliments / de conseils** he was generous with his compliments / advice. ◆ nmf miser.

avarice [avaʀis] nf miserliness, avarice.

avarie [avaʀi] nf damage (sustained by a ship).

avarié, e [avaʀje] adj **1.** [aliment, marchandise] spoilt, damaged ▸ **cette viande est avariée** this meat has gone off **2.** NAUT ▸ **navire avarié** damaged ship.

avatar [avataʀ] nm **1.** [mésaventure] misadventure, mishap / **les avatars de la vie politique** the vicissitudes of political life **2.** INTERNET avatar.

AVC (abr de **accident vasculaire cérébral**) nm CVA.

avec [avɛk] ◆ prép **1.** [indiquant la complémentarité, l'accompagnement, l'accord] with / **je ne prends jamais de sucre avec mon café** I never take sugar in my coffee ▸ **une maison avec jardin** a house with a garden / **un homme avec une blouse blanche** a man in a white coat ou with a white coat on ▸ **avec dans le rôle principal / dans son premier rôle, X** starring / introducing X ▸ **un film avec Gabin** a film featuring Gabin ; [envers] to, towards UK, toward US ▸ **être patient / honnête avec qqn** to be patient / honest with sb ▸ **être gentil avec qqn** to be kind ou nice to sb ▸ **se comporter bien / mal avec qqn** to behave well / badly towards sb ; [en ce qui concerne] : **avec lui c'est toujours la même chose** it's always the same with him ▸ **et avec ceci ?** anything else? **2.** [indiquant la simultanéité] : **se lever avec le jour** to get up at the crack of dawn / **le paysage change avec les saisons** the countryside changes with the seasons **3.** [indiquant une relation d'opposition] with / **être en guerre avec un pays** to be at war with a country **4.** [indiquant une relation de cause] with / **ils ne pourront pas venir, avec cette pluie** they won't be able to come with (all) this rain **5.** [indiquant la manière] with ▸ **faire qqch avec plaisir** to do sthg with pleasure, to take pleasure in doing sthg ▸ **regarder qqn avec passion / mépris** to look at sb passionately / contemptuously **6.** [indiquant le moyen, l'instrument] with ▸ **fonctionner avec des piles** to run on batteries, to be battery-operated. ◆ adv fam : **ôtez vos chaussures, vous ne pouvez pas entrer avec** take off your shoes, you can't come in with them (on). ❖ **d'avec** loc prép ▸ **divorcer d'avec qqn** to divorce sb.

avenant¹ [avnɑ̃] nm **1.** [gén] amendment ▸ **avenant à un contrat** amendment to a contract **2.** [dans les assurances] endorsement, additional clause. ❖ **à l'avenant** loc adv : **un exposé sans intérêt et des questions à l'avenant** a boring lecture with equally boring questions.

avenant², e [avnɑ̃, ɑ̃t] adj pleasant.

avènement [avɛnmɑ̃] nm **1.** [d'un souverain] accession ; [du Messie] advent sout, coming **2.** [d'une époque, d'une mode] advent.

avenir [avniʀ] nm **1.** [période future] future ▸ **dans un avenir proche / lointain** in the near / distant future / *l'avenir dira si j'ai raison* time will tell if I'm right / *les moyens de transport de l'avenir* the transport systems of the future ; [générations futures] future generations **2.** [situation future] future ; [chances de succès] future, (future) prospects ▸ **une invention sans avenir** an invention with no future / *les nouveaux procédés techniques ont de l'avenir* the new technical processes are promising ou have a good future ▸ **découverte d'un matériau d'avenir** discovery of a promising new material ▸ **les professions d'avenir** up-and-coming professions. ❖ **à l'avenir** loc adv in future.

avent [avɑ̃] nm ▸ **l'Avent** Advent.

aventure [avɑ̃tyʀ] nf **1.** [incident - gén] experience, incident ; [- extraordinaire] adventure ; [risque] adventure, venture ▸ **dire la bonne aventure à qqn** to tell sb's fortune **2.** [liaison] (love) affair. ❖ **à l'aventure** loc adv at random, haphazardly / *partir à l'aventure* to go off in search of adventure. ❖ **d'aventure** loc adj [roman, film] adventure *(modif)*.

aventurer [3] [avɑ̃tyʀe] ❖ **s'aventurer** vpi [aller] to venture. ❖ **s'aventurer à** vp + prép : *je ne m'aventure plus à faire des pronostics* I no longer venture ou dare to make any forecasts / *téléphone-lui si tu veux, moi je m'y aventurerais pas* ring her up if you like, I wouldn't chance it myself.

aventureux, euse [avɑ̃tyʀø, øz] adj **1.** [hardi - héros] adventurous **2.** [dangereux - projet] risky, chancy.

aventurier [avɑ̃tyʀje] nm [explorateur] adventurer ; [aimant le risque] risk-taker.

aventurière [avɑ̃tyʀjɛʀ] nf *péj* adventuress.

avenue [avny] nf avenue.

avéré, e [aveʀe] adj [fait, information] known, established.

avérer [18] [aveʀe] ❖ **s'avérer** vpi **1.** *(suivi d'un adj ou d'une loc adj)* [se révéler] to prove **2.** *(tournure impersonnelle)* : *il s'avère difficile d'améliorer les résultats* it's proving difficult to improve on the results / *il s'avère que mon cas n'est pas prévu par le règlement* it turns out ou it so happens that my situation isn't covered by the regulations.

✐ In reformed spelling (see p. 16-18), this verb is conjugated like *semer : il s'avèrera, elle s'avèrerait.*

averse [avɛʀs] nf shower.

aversion [avɛʀsjɔ̃] nf aversion, loathing / *il les a pris en aversion* he took a violent dislike to them.

averti, e [avɛʀti] adj [informé] informed, mature ; [connaisseur] well-informed / *le consommateur est de plus en plus averti* consumers are better and better informed.

avertir [32] [avɛʀtiʀ] vt **1.** [informer] to inform, to tell / *avertis-moi dès que tu (le) sais* tell me ou let me know as soon as you know **2.** [mettre en garde] to warn.

avertissement [avɛʀtismɑ̃] nm **1.** [signe] warning, warning sign **2.** [appel à l'attention] notice, warning **3.** [blâme] warning, reprimand ; ADMIN [lettre] admonitory letter *sout* **4.** [en début de livre] ▸ **avertissement (au lecteur)** foreword.

⚠ **Advertisement** signifie « publicité » et non avertissement.

avertisseur [avɛʀtisœʀ] nm alarm, warning signal ▸ **avertisseur sonore** a) [gén] alarm b) AUTO horn.

aveu, x [avø] nm [confession] ▸ **faire un aveu** to acknowledge ou to confess ou to admit something ▸ **faire des aveux complets** a) [à la police] to make a full confession b) *fig & hum* to confess all ▸ **passer aux aveux** pr & *fig* to confess. ❖ **de l'aveu de** loc prép according to / *la tour ne tiendra pas, de l'aveu même de l'architecte* the tower will collapse, even the architect says so.

aveuglant, e [avœɡlɑ̃, ɑ̃t] adj [éclat, lueur] blinding, dazzling ; [évidence, preuve] overwhelming ; [vérité] self-evident, glaring.

aveugle [avœɡl] ❖ adj **1.** [privé de la vue] blind, sightless ▸ **devenir aveugle** to go blind **2.** [extrême - fureur, passion] blind, reckless **3.** [absolu - attachement, foi, soumission] blind, unquestioning. ❖ nmf blind man (woman) ▸ **les aveugles** the blind ou sightless.

aveuglement [avœɡləmɑ̃] nm blindness, blinkered state.

aveuglément [avœɡlemɑ̃] adv [inconsidérément] blindly.

aveugler [5] [avœɡle] vt [priver de la vue] to blind ; [éblouir] to blind. ❖ **s'aveugler sur** vp + prép to close one's eyes to / *ne vous aveuglez pas sur vos chances de réussite* don't overestimate your chances of success.

aveuglette [avœɡlɛt] ❖ **à l'aveuglette** loc adv **1.** [sans voir - conduire] blindly / *il m'a fallu marcher à l'aveuglette le long d'un tunnel* I had to grope my way through a tunnel **2.** *fig* : *je ne veux pas agir à l'aveuglette* I don't want to act without first weighing the consequences.

aviateur, trice [avjatœʀ, tʀis] nm, f pilot, aviator *vieilli.*

aviation [avjasjɔ̃] nf **1.** TRANSP aviation ▸ **aviation civile / marchande** civil / commercial aviation **2.** [activité] flying **3.** MIL [armée de l'air] air force ; [avions] aircraft, air force.

aviculture [avikyltyʀ] nf [élevage - de volailles] poultry farming ou breeding ; [- d'oiseaux] aviculture *spéc*, bird breeding.

avide [avid] adj **1.** [cupide] greedy, grasping **2.** [enthousiaste] eager, avid ▸ **avide de louanges** hungry for praise ▸ **avide de nouveauté** eager ou avid for novelty ▸ **avide de savoir** eager to learn, thirsty for knowledge / *avide de connaître le monde* eager ou anxious ou impatient to discover the world.

avidement [avidmɑ̃] adv **1.** [gloutonnement] greedily, ravenously ▸ **boire avidement** to drink thirstily ▸ **manger avidement** to eat hungrily **2.** [avec enthousiasme] eagerly, avidly, keenly **3.** [par cupidité] greedily, covetously.

avidité [avidite] nf **1.** [voracité] voracity, greed, gluttony *péj* **2.** [enthousiasme] eagerness, impatience **3.** [cupidité] greed, cupidity, covetousness.

Avignon [aviɲɔ̃] npr Avignon ▸ **à** ou **en Avignon** in Avignon ▸ **le Festival d'Avignon** the Avignon festival.

🚩 **Le Festival d'Avignon**

Founded by Jean Vilar in 1947 and held every summer in and around Avignon in the south of France, this arts festival is a showcase for new theatre and dance performances: *sa nouvelle pièce sera d'abord donnée à / en Avignon.*

avilir [32] [aviliʀ] vt [personne] to debase, to shame. ❖ **s'avilir** vp *(emploi réfléchi)* to demean ou to debase ou to disgrace o.s.

avilissant, e [avilisɑ̃, ɑ̃t] adj degrading, demeaning.

avion [avjɔ̃] nm **1.** [véhicule] plane, aeroplane 🇬🇧, airplane 🇺🇸 ▸ **avion militaire / de chasse** military / fighter plane ▸ **avion de ligne** airliner ▸ **avion à réaction** jet (plane) ▸ **avion de tourisme** private aircraft ou plane **2.** [mode de transport] : *irez-vous en avion ou en train ?* are you flying or going by train? ▶ **je déteste (prendre) l'avion** I hate flying / **'par avion'** 'air mail'.

aviron [aviʁɔ̃] nm **1.** [rame] oar **2.** [activité] rowing.

avis [avi] nm **1.** [point de vue] opinion, viewpoint ▶ **avoir son** ou **un avis sur qqch** to have views on sthg ▶ **j'aimerais avoir votre avis** I'd like to hear your views ou to know what you think (about it) / **toi, je ne te demande pas ton avis !** I didn't ask for your opinion! ▶ **donner son avis** to give ou to contribute one's opinion ▶ **donner** ou **émettre un avis favorable a)** [à une demande] to give the go-ahead **b)** [à une proposition] to give a positive response, to come out in favour ▶ **émettre un avis défavorable** to give a negative response / **à mon avis, c'est un mensonge** in my opinion, it's a lie, I think it's a lie ▶ **à mon humble avis** hum in my humble opinion / **elle est d'avis qu'il est trop tard** she's of the opinion that it's too late ▶ **de l'avis de** [selon] according to ▶ **je suis de votre avis** I agree with you ▶ **sur l'avis de** on the advice ou at the suggestion of **2.** [information] announcement ; [sommation - légale] notice ; [- fiscale] notice, demand ▶ **jusqu'à nouvel avis** until further notice ▶ **nous irons sauf avis contraire a)** [de votre part] unless we hear otherwise ou to the contrary, we'll go **b)** [de notre part] unless you hear otherwise ou to the contrary, we'll go ▶ **avis aux amateurs**: *il reste encore quelques parts de gâteau, avis aux amateurs* there's still some cake left if anyone's interested ▶ **avis de décès** death notice ▶ **avis d'imposition** tax notice ▶ **avis de réception** acknowledgement of receipt ▶ **avis de recherche** [d'un criminel] wanted (person) poster ▶ [d'un disparu] missing person poster.

avisé, e [avize] adj shrewd, prudent ▶ **bien avisé** well-advised ▶ **mal avisé** ill-advised.

aviser [3] [avize] ◆ vt **1.** [informer] to inform, to notify **2.** [voir] to notice, to glimpse, to catch sight of. ◆ vi to decide, to see (what one can do) / **maintenant nous allons devoir aviser** we'll have to see what we can do now. ◆ **s'aviser de** vp + prép **1.** [remarquer] to become aware of / **je me suis avisé de sa présence quand elle a ri** I suddenly noticed her presence when she laughed **2.** [oser] to dare to / **et ne t'avise pas de recommencer !** and don't you dare do that again!

aviver [3] [avive] vt [intensifier - flammes] to fan, to stir up (sép) ; [- feu] to revive, to rekindle ; [- couleur] to brighten, to revive ; [- sentiment] to stir up ; [- désir] to excite, to arouse ; [- blessure] to irritate ; [- querelle] to stir up, to exacerbate ; [- crainte] to heighten.

av. J.-C. (abr écrite de avant Jésus-Christ) BC.

avocat¹ [avɔka] nm BOT avocado (pear).

avocat², e [avɔka, at] nm, f **1.** DR lawyer, barrister UK, attorney-at-law US ▶ **mon avocat** my counsel ▶ **avocat d'affaires** business lawyer ▶ **avocat de la défense** counsel for the defence UK ; ≃ defending counsel UK ; ≃ defense counsel US ▶ **avocat général** ≃ counsel for the prosecution UK ; ≃ prosecuting attorney US ▶ **avocat de la partie civile** counsel for the plaintiff **2.** [porte-parole] advocate, champion / **se faire l'avocat d'une mauvaise cause** to advocate ou to champion a lost cause ▶ **se faire l'avocat du diable** to be devil's advocate.

avoine [avwan] nf [plante] oat ; [grains] oats.

avoir¹ [avwaʁ] nm **1.** COMM credit note ; [en comptabilité] credit side / **la fleuriste m'a fait un avoir** the florist gave me a credit note / **j'ai un avoir de 30 euros à la boucherie** I've got 30 euros' credit at the butcher's ▶ **avoir fiscal** FIN tax credit **2.** ÉCON & FIN ▶ **avoirs** assets, holdings ▶ **avoirs numéraires** ou **en caisse** cash holdings **3.** litt

[possessions] assets, worldly goods / **vivre d'un petit avoir personnel** to live off a small personal income.

avoir² [1] [avwaʁ]

◆ v aux

A. TEMPS COMPOSÉS 1. [avec des verbes transitifs] : **as-tu lu sa lettre ?** did you read ou have you read his letter? ▶ **j'aurais voulu vous aider** I'd have liked to help you **2.** [avec des verbes intransitifs] ▶ **j'ai maigri** I've lost weight ▶ **as-tu bien dormi ?** did you sleep well? **3.** [avec le verbe 'être'] ▶ **j'ai été surpris** I was surprised ▶ **il aurait été enchanté** he would've ou would have been delighted.

B. AVOIR À, N' AVOIR QUE 1. [exprime la possibilité] ▶ **avoir à**: *tu as à manger dans le réfrigérateur* there's something to eat in the fridge for you ▶ **n'avoir qu'à**: *s'il vous manque quelque chose, vous n'avez qu'à me le faire savoir* if you're missing anything, just let me know **2.** [exprime l'obligation] ▶ **avoir à** to have to / **je n'ai pas à me justifier auprès de vous** I don't have to justify myself to you **3.** [exprime le besoin] ▶ **avoir à** to have to / **tu n'as pas à t'inquiéter** you shouldn't worry, you have nothing to worry about.

◆ vt

A. DÉTENIR, ATTRAPER 1. [être propriétaire de - action, bien, domaine, etc.] to have, to own, to possess ; [- chien, hôtel, voiture] to have, to own ▶ **avoir de l'argent** to have money / **tu n'aurais pas un stylo en plus ?** have you got ou do you happen to have a spare pen? ; COMM to have **2.** [ami, collègue, famille, etc.] to have ▶ **elle a trois enfants** she has three children **3.** [détenir - permis de conduire, titre] to have, to hold ; [- droits, privilège] to have, to enjoy ; [- emploi, expérience, devoirs, obligations] to have ; [- documents, preuves] to have, to possess / **quand nous aurons le pouvoir** when we're in power ; SPORT to have ▶ **avoir le ballon** to be in possession of ou to have the ball **4.** [obtenir - amende, article] to get ; [- information, rabais, récompense] to get, to obtain / **je pourrais vous avoir des places gratuites** I could get you free tickets ; [au téléphone] to get through to / **je l'ai eu au téléphone** I got him on the phone **5.** [jouir de - beau temps, bonne santé, liberté, bonne réputation] to have, to enjoy ; [- choix, temps, mauvaise réputation] to have ▶ **avoir la confiance de qqn** to be trusted by sb / **vous avez toute ma sympathie** you have all my sympathy / **il a tout pour lui et il n'est pas heureux !** he's got everything you could wish for and he's still not happy! **6.** [recevoir chez soi] ▶ **avoir de la famille / des amis à dîner** to have relatives / friends over for dinner **7.** [attraper - otage, prisonnier] to have / **les flics ne l'auront jamais** fam the cops'll never catch him **8.** [atteindre - cible] to get, to hit **9.** [monter à bord de - avion, bus, train] to catch.

B. ARBORER, MESURER 1. [présenter - tel aspect] to have (got) / **elle a un joli sourire** she's got ou has a nice smile / **elle a une jolie couleur de cheveux** her hair's a nice colour ▶ **avoir tout de**: *il a tout de l'aristocrate* he's the aristocratic type / **la méthode a l'avantage d'être bon marché** this method has the advantage of being cheap ; [avec pour complément une partie du corps] to have ▶ **avoir l'estomac vide** to have an empty stomach **2.** [porter sur soi - accessoire, vêtement, parfum] to have on (sép), to wear / **tu vois la dame qui a le foulard ?** do you see the lady with the scarf? **3.** [faire preuve de] ▶ **avoir de l'audace** to be bold ▶ **avoir du culot** fam to be cheeky, to have a nerve ▶ **avoir du talent** to have talent, to be talented ▶ **ayez la gentillesse de...** would you ou please be kind enough to... **4.** [exprime la mesure] ▶ **le voilier a 4 m de large** ou **largeur** the yacht is 4 m wide ▶ **en avoir pour**: *tu en as pour 12 jours / deux heures* it'll take you 12 days / two hours **5.** [exprime l'âge] to be ▶ **j'ai 35 ans** I'm 35 (years old) / **nous avons le même âge** we're the same age / *il a deux ans de plus que moi* he's two years older than me / *il vient d'avoir 74 ans* he's just turned 74.

C. SOUFFRIR DE, ÉPROUVER 1. [subir - symptôme] to have, to show, to display ; [- maladie, hoquet, mal de tête, etc.] to have ; [- accident, souci, ennuis] to have ; [- difficultés] to have, to experience ; [- opération] to undergo, to have ; [- crise] to have, to go through *(insép)* ▸ **avoir de la fièvre** to have ou to be running a temperature ▸ **avoir un cancer** to have cancer 2. [émettre, produire - mouvement] to make ; [- ricanement, regard, soupir] to give ▸ **avoir un sursaut** to (give a) start / *il eut une moue de dédain* he pouted disdainfully 3. [ressentir] ▸ **avoir faim** to be ou to feel hungry ▸ **avoir peur** to be ou to feel afraid ▸ **avoir des remords** to feel remorse ▸ **avoir du chagrin** to feel ou to be sad ▸ **avoir de l'amitié pour qqn** to regard ou to consider sb as a friend ▸ **avoir du respect pour qqn** to have respect for ou to respect sb ▸ **en avoir après** ou **contre qqn** *fam* to be angry with sb ▸ **en avoir après** ou **contre qqch** to be angry about sthg 4. [élaborer par l'esprit - avis, idée, suggestion] to have ▸ **j'ai mes raisons** I have my reasons / *elle a toujours réponse à tout* she's got an answer for everything *fam*.

D. VAINCRE, DUPER 1. [battre, surpasser] to get, to beat / *il va se faire avoir dans la dernière ligne droite* he's going to get beaten in the final straight 2. [escroquer] to have, to do, to con / *900 euros pour ce buffet ? tu t'es fait avoir !* 900 euros for that dresser? you were conned ou had ou done! 3. [duper] to take in *(sép)*, to take for a ride, to have.

E. SUR SON AGENDA [devoir participer à - débat, élection, réunion] to have, to hold ; [- rendez-vous] to have / *j'ai (un) cours de chimie ce matin* I've got a chemistry lesson this morning. ❖ **il y a** *v impers* 1. [dans une description, une énumération - suivi d'un singulier] there is ; [- suivi d'un pluriel] there are / *il y a du soleil* the sun is shining / *il n'y a qu'ici qu'on en trouve* this is the only place (where) you can find it / them ▸ **avoue qu'il y a de quoi être énervé !** you must admit it's pretty irritating! ▸ **il n'y a pas de quoi ! : merci — il n'y a pas de quoi !** thank you — don't mention it ou you're welcome! ▸ **il n'y a rien à faire** : *il n'y a rien à faire, la voiture ne démarre pas* it's no good, the car won't start ▸ **il n'y a pas à dire** : *il n'y a pas à dire, il sait ce qu'il veut* there's no denying he knows what he wants ▸ **il n'y a que lui / moi, etc. pour…** : *il n'y a que lui pour dire une chose pareille !* trust him to say something like that! 2. [exprimant la possibilité, l'obligation, etc.] : *il n'y a qu'à lui dire* you / we, etc. just have to tell him 3. [indiquant la durée] : *il y a 20 ans de ça* 20 years ago / *il y a une heure que j'attends* I've been waiting for an hour 4. [indiquant la distance] : *il y a bien 3 km d'ici au village* it's at least 3 km to the village 5. (à l'infinitif) : *il doit y avoir une raison* there must be a ou some reason.

📋 Le verbe avoir se traduit généralement par have. En anglais britannique, on emploie très fréquemment have + got, notamment à l'oral :

Il a une voiture. *He has a car* ou *He's got a car.*

Elle a les cheveux bruns. *She has brown hair* ou *She's got brown hair.*

Have + got s'emploie généralement au présent, mais peut également s'employer au passé :

Il avait une voiture. *He had a car* **(had got est impossible ici).**

Il a dit qu'il avait une voiture. *He said he had a car* ou *He said he'd got a car.*

Elle avait les yeux bleus. *She had blue eyes* **(had got est impossible ici).**

Il a pensé qu'elle avait la grippe. He thought she had flu ou He thought she'd got flu.

Notez l'emploi de be avec certains adjectifs lorsque avoir introduit une caractéristique, un état :

J'ai sommeil / faim / soif / peur / raison / tort. *I'm sleepy / hungry / thirsty / afraid / right / wrong.*

Notez également l'emploi de be avec le mot shape :

Ces pièces peuvent avoir différentes formes. *These parts can be different shapes.*

Celle-ci a une forme différente. *This one is a different shape.*

avoisinant, e [avwazinɑ̃, ɑ̃t] adj neighbouring 🇬🇧, neighboring 🇺🇸, nearby *(adj)* / *les quartiers avoisinants ont été évacués* the surrounding streets were evacuated.

avoisiner [3] [avwazine] vt 1. [dans l'espace] to be near ou close to, to border on *(insép)* 2. [en valeur] to be close on, to come close to.

avortement [avɔrtəmɑ̃] nm MÉD & ZOOL abortion ▸ **campagne contre l'avortement** anti-abortion campaign ▸ **avortement thérapeutique** termination of pregnancy *(for medical reasons)*.

avorter [3] [avɔrte] ◆ vi 1. MÉD to abort, to have an abortion ; ZOOL to abort 2. [plan] to fall through, to miscarry ; [réforme] to fall through ; [révolution] to fail, to come to nothing. ◆ vt to abort, to carry out an abortion on ▸ **se faire avorter** to have an abortion.

avorton [avɔrtɔ̃] nm [chétif] runt ; [monstrueux] freak, monster.

avoué [avwe] nm ≃ solicitor 🇬🇧 ; ≃ attorney 🇺🇸.

avouer [6] [avwe] vt 1. [erreur, forfait] to admit, to confess (to), to own up to *(insép)* / *elle a avoué voyager sans billet / tricher aux cartes* she owned up to travelling without a ticket / to cheating at cards ; *(en usage absolu)* ▸ **il a avoué** [à la police] he owned up, he made a full confession 2. [doute, sentiment] to admit ou to confess to / *je t'avoue que j'en ai assez* I must admit that I've had all I can take / *il lui a fallu du courage, j'avoue, mais…* what he did required courage, I grant you, but… ❖ **s'avouer** vpi : *elle ne s'avoue pas encore battue* she won't admit defeat yet / *je m'avoue complètement découragé* I confess ou admit to feeling utterly discouraged.

avril [avril] nm April. **Voir aussi mars.**

AVS (abr de **assurance vieillesse et survivants**) nf Swiss pension scheme.

axe [aks] nm 1. GÉOM axis ▸ **axe des abscisses / des ordonnées** x- / y-axis 2. [direction] direction, line 3. [voie] ▸ **l'axe Lyon-Genève** RAIL the Lyon-Geneva line / *tous les (grands) axes routiers sont bloqués par la neige* all major roads are snowed up.

axer [3] [akse] vt ▸ **axer qqch sur qqch** to centre 🇬🇧 ou center 🇺🇸 sthg on sthg / *il est très axé sur le spiritisme* he is very keen on spiritualism / *axer une campagne publicitaire sur les enfants* to build an advertising campaign around children / *une modernisation axée sur l'importation des meilleures techniques étrangères* modernization based on importing the best foreign techniques.

axiome [aksjom] nm axiom.

ayant p prés ⟶ avoir.

ayant droit [ɛjɑ̃drwa] (pl **ayants droit**) nm [gén] beneficiary ; [à une propriété] rightful owner ; [à un droit] eligible party.

ayatollah [ajatɔla] nm ayatollah.

ayé SMS abr écrite de ça y est.

ayurvédique [ajyʀvedik] adj Ayurvedic ▶ **massage ayurvédique** Ayurvedic massage.

azalée [azale] nf azalea.

azimut [azimyt] nm azimuth. ❖ **tous azimuts** fam ◆ loc adj all out, full scale. ◆ loc adv all over (the place) / *prospecter tous azimuts* to canvass all over ▶ **la jeune société se développe tous azimuts** the new firm is really taking off.

azimuté, e [azimyte] adj fam [fou] crazy.

azote [azɔt] nm nitrogen.

azur [azyʀ] nm **1.** [couleur] azure litt, sky-blue ▶ **la Côte d'Azur** the French Riviera, the Côte d'Azur **2.** litt [ciel] skies.

azyme [azim] adj ⟶ **pain**.

B (abr écrite de **bien**) *good grade (as assessment of school-work)* ; ≃ B.

b1sur SMS abr écrite de **bien sûr.**

B2i [bedøzi] nm abr de **brevet informatique et Internet.**

BA (abr de **bonne action**) nf *fam good deed* ▶ **faire une BA** to do a good deed.

baba [baba] ◆ adj *fam* ▶ **être** ou **rester baba** to be flabbergasted. ◆ nm CULIN ▶ **baba (au rhum)** (rum) baba.

b.a.-ba [beaba] nm ABCs, rudiments / *apprendre le b.a.-ba du métier* to learn the ABCs ou basics of the trade.

babiller [3] [babije] vi [oiseau] to twitter ; [ruisseau] to murmur, to babble ; [enfant] to prattle, to babble, to chatter ; [bavard] to prattle (on), to chatter (away).

babines [babin] nfpl ZOOL chops.

babiole [babjɔl] nf knick-knack, trinket / *je voudrais lui acheter une babiole pour marquer son anniversaire* I would like to buy her a little something for her birthday.

bâbord [babɔʀ] nm port ▶ **à bâbord** on the port side.

babouche [babuʃ] nf (oriental) slipper.

babouin [babwɛ̃] nm baboon.

baby boom, babyboum* [bebibum] nm baby boom.

baby-boomer [babibumœʀ ou bebibumœʀ] (*pl* **baby-boomers**) nmf baby boomer.

baby-boomeur, euse [babibumœʀ, øz ou bebibumœʀ, øz] (*mpl* **baby-boomeurs**, *fpl* **euses**) nm, f baby boomer.

baby-foot (*pl* **baby-foot**), **babyfoot*** [babifut] nm table football 🇬🇧, foosball 🇺🇸.

baby-sitter (*pl* **baby-sitters**), **babysitteur*** [bebisitœr] nmf baby-sitter.

baby-sitting (*pl* **baby-sittings**), **babysitting*** [bebisitiŋ] nm baby-sitting ▶ **faire du baby-sitting** to baby-sit.

bac [bak] nm **1.** NAUT (small) ferry ou ferryboat **2.** [dans un réfrigérateur] compartment, tray ▶ **bac à glace** ice-cube tray ▶ **bac à légumes** vegetable compartment ; [pour plantes] ▶ **bac (à fleurs)** plant holder **3.** COMM [présentoir] dump bin **4.** [fosse, réserve - pour liquides] tank, vat ; [- pour stockage de pièces] container ▶ **bac à sable a)** [d'enfant] sandpit 🇬🇧, sandbox 🇺🇸 **b)** [pour routes] grit bin **5.** *fam* [diplôme] ▶ **bac plus trois / quatre / cinq** *expression indicating the number of years of formal study completed after the baccalauréat* ▶ **niveau bac + 3** 3 years of higher education.

BAC [bak] (abr de **brigade anticriminalité**) nf *police squad specializing in patrols to combat crime.*

baccalauréat [bakalɔʀea] nm *final secondary school examination, qualifying for university entrance* ; ≃ A-levels 🇬🇧 ; ≃ high school diploma 🇺🇸.

 Baccalauréat

The **baccalauréat** or **bac** is taken by students who have completed their final year at the **lycée**; successful candidates may go to university. There are three main types (**filières**) of **bac**, each corresponding to a specific field: **bac L (littéraire)** being arts-oriented, **bac S (scientifique)** science-based and **bac ES (économique et social)** economics and social studies. Within each domain various obligatory and optional subjects can be combined to give up to eleven different types of diploma. There is also the **bac professionnel** which offers seventy-five different specialist or vocational subjects, and the **bac technologique**, with seven specialist subjects. Grades **mentions** at the baccalauréat are as follows: **assez bien** (**AB**, 12-14/20); **bien** (**B**, 14-16/20); **très bien** (**TB**, over 16/20).

The different levels of studies in France are referred to in terms of **bac +** (**bac + 2** for the BTS and DUT, **bac + 3** for the **licence**, **bac + 4** for the **master**, **bac + 5** for a **doctorat**) and are used in job advertisements, CVs and day-to-day life in order to indicate one's level or years of studies.

bâche [baʃ] nf transport cover, canvas sheet, tarpaulin ▶ **bâches imperméables** waterproof tarpaulin.

bachelier, ère [baʃəlje, ɛʀ] nm, f *student who has passed the baccalauréat.*

⚠ Attention à ne pas traduire **bachelier** par **bachelor**, qui n'a jamais ce sens.

bachotage [baʃɔtaʒ] nm *fam* cramming ▶ **faire du bachotage** to cram, to swot up 🇬🇧, to bone up 🇺🇸.

bacille [basil] nm bacillus ▶ **bacille de Koch** tubercle bacillus.

bâcler [3] [bakle] vt to skimp on (*insép*), to botch ▶ **c'est du travail bâclé a)** [réparation] it's a botched job **b)** [devoir] it's slapdash work.

bacon [bekɔn] nm [petit lard] bacon ; [porc fumé] smoked loin of pork, Canadian bacon.

bactérie [bakteʀi] nf bacterium.

bactérien, enne [bakteʀjɛ̃, ɛn] adj bacterial.

bactériologique [bakteʀjɔlɔʒik] adj bacteriological.

badaud, e [bado, od] nm, f [curieux] curious onlooker ; [promeneur] stroller.

badge [badʒ] nm **1.** [insigne] badge ; [carte] swipe card **2.** [autocollant] sticker.

badger [17] [badʒe] vi [à l'entrée] to swipe in ; [à la sortie] to swipe out.

badgeuse [badʒøz] nf swipe card reader.

badiane [badjan] nf [fruit] star anise.

badigeonner [3] [badiʒɔne] vt **1.** CONSTR [intérieur] to distemper ; [extérieur] to whitewash ; [en couleur] to paint with coloured distemper, to colourwash UK **2.** CULIN & MÉD to paint, to brush.

badin, e [badɛ̃, in] adj [gai] light-hearted ; [plaisant] playful.

badiner [3] [badine] vi to jest, to banter, to tease ▶ **badiner avec** : *ne badine pas avec ta santé* don't trifle with your health.

badminton [badmintɔn] nm badminton.

BAFA, bafa [bafa] (abr de **brevet d'aptitude aux fonctions d'animation**) nm *diploma for youth leaders and workers.*

baffe [baf] nf *fam* slap, clout, smack.

baffle [bafl] nm AUDIO speaker ; TECHNOL baffle.

bafouer [6] [bafwe] vt [autorité, loi] to flout, to defy ; [sentiment] to ridicule, to scoff at *(insép).*

bafouille [bafuj] nf *tfam* letter, missive *hum.*

bafouiller [3] [bafuje] vi [bégayer] to stutter, to stammer.

bâfrer [3] [bafʀe] *tfam* ◆ vt to gobble, to wolf (down) *(sép).* ◆ vi to stuff one's face, to pig o.s.

bagage [bagaʒ] nm **1.** [pour voyager] baggage, luggage ▶ **mes bagages** my luggage ▶ **faire ses bagages** to pack one's bags ▶ **un seul bagage de cabine est autorisé** only one piece of hand baggage is allowed ▶ **un bagage à main** a piece of hand-luggage ▶ **soute à bagages** hold **2.** *(toujours au sg)* [formation] background (knowledge).

> Attention ! Les mots luggage et baggage sont indénombrables. Ils ne s'emploient jamais ni au pluriel ni avec l'article indéfini a :
> **J'ai perdu tous mes bagages.** *I've lost all my luggage.*
> **Plusieurs bagages furent endommagés.** *Several pieces / items of luggage were damaged.*
> **Avez-vous des bagages à main ?** *Do you have any hand baggage?*

bagagiste [bagaʒist] nmf [dans un hôtel] porter ; [dans un aéroport] baggage handler.

bagarre [bagaʀ] nf **1.** [échange de coups] fight, brawl / *des bagarres ont éclaté dans la rue* scuffles ou fighting broke out in the street **2.** *fig* battle, fight.

bagarrer [3] [bagaʀe] ◆ **se bagarrer** ◆ vp *(emploi réciproque)* **1.** [se combattre] to fight, to scrap **2.** [se quereller] to quarrel, to have a scene. ◆ vpi [combattre] to fight, to scrap.

bagarreur, euse [bagaʀœʀ, øz] adj *fam* aggressive / *elle a des enfants bagarreurs* her kids are always ready for a scrap.

bagatelle [bagatɛl] nf **1.** [chose - sans valeur] trinket, bauble ; [- sans importance] trifle, bagatelle / *ça m'a coûté la bagatelle de 10 000 €* iron it cost me a mere 10,000 € **2.** *fam* [sexe] ▶ **il est porté / elle est portée sur la bagatelle** he / she likes to play around.

Bagdad [bagdad] npr Baghdad.

bagel [bagɛl] nm bagel.

baggy [bagi] nm baggy pants.

bagnard [baɲaʀ] nm convict.

bagne [baɲ] nm **1.** [prison] prison, labour UK ou labor US camp ; HIST penal colony / *c'est le bagne, ici !* *fig* they work you to death in this place! **2.** [sentence] hard labour UK ou labor US.

bagnole [baɲɔl] nf *fam* car ▶ **une vieille bagnole** an old banger UK ou car.

bagou(t) [bagu] nm *fam* glibness ▶ **il a du bagout** he has the gift of the gab, he can talk the hind legs off a donkey.

bague [bag] nf **1.** JOAILL ring ▶ **bague de fiançailles** engagement ring **2.** MÉCAN collar, ring.

baguer [3] [bage] vt [oiseau] to ring ; [doigt] to put a ring on.

baguette [bagɛt] nf **1.** [petit bâton] switch, stick ▶ **baguette magique** magic wand / *d'un coup de baguette magique* as if by magic **2.** CULIN [pain] French stick UK ou loaf, baguette ; [pour manger] chopstick **3.** MUS [pour diriger] baton ▶ **baguette de tambour** drumstick ▶ **mener ou faire marcher qqn à la baguette** to rule sb with an iron hand ou a rod of iron.

Bahamas [baamas] npr fpl ▶ **les Bahamas** the Bahamas ▶ **aux Bahamas** in the Bahamas.

bahut [bay] nm **1.** [buffet] sideboard **2.** [coffre] trunk **3.** *fam* [collège, lycée] school.

bai, e [bɛ] adj bay.

baie [bɛ] nf **1.** BOT berry **2.** ARCHIT opening ▶ **baie vitrée** picture ou bay window **3.** GÉOGR bay.

 **Baies**

la baie de Baffin	Baffin Bay
la baie des Cochons	the Bay of Pigs
la baie d'Hudson	Hudson Bay
la baie de San Francisco	San Francisco Bay

baignade [bɛɲad] nf [activité] swimming, bathing UK / **'baignade interdite'** 'no swimming' ; [lieu] bathing ou swimming place.

baigner [4] [bɛɲe] ◆ vt **1.** [pour laver] to bath UK, to bathe US ; [pour soigner] to bathe **2.** *litt* [suj : fleuve, mer] to wash, to bathe **3.** [mouiller] to soak, to wet. ◆ vi **1.** [être immergé - dans l'eau, le lait] to soak ; [- dans l'alcool, le vinaigre] to steep ; *litt* [être environné - de brouillard, de brume] to be shrouded ou swathed **2.** *fig* : *elle baigne dans la musique depuis sa jeunesse* she's been immersed in music since she was young **3.** EXPR **ça** ou **tout baigne (dans l'huile) !** *fam* everything's great ou fine! ◆ **se baigner** vpi [dans une baignoire] to have UK ou to take US a bath ; [dans un lac, dans la mer] to go swimming ou bathing UK.

baigneur, euse [bɛɲœʀ, øz] nm, f swimmer, bather UK. ◆ **baigneur** nm baby doll.

baignoire [bɛɲwaʀ] nf **1.** [dans une salle de bains] bath UK, bathtub US ▶ **baignoire sabot** hip bath **2.** THÉÂTRE ground floor box.

bail, baux [baj, bo] nm **1.** [de location] lease ▶ **prendre qqch à bail** to take out a lease on sthg **2.** EXPR **il y a** ou **ça fait un bail que...** *fam* it's been ages since...

 Bail

In France, the usual duration of the **bail** or lease for private rented accommodation is three years. The expression **bail à céder**, often seen on signs in shop windows, means that the lease on the shop or office is for sale.

bâillement [bajmɑ̃] nm [action] yawn.

bâiller [3] [baje] vi **1.** [de sommeil, d'ennui] to yawn **2.** [être entrouvert - porte, volet] to be ajar ou half-open ; [-col] to gape.

bailleur, eresse [bajœʀ, ʀɛs] nm, f lessor ▸ **bailleur de fonds** backer, sponsor.

bâillon [bajɔ̃] nm [sur une personne] gag.

bâillonner [3] [bajɔne] vt [otage, victime] to gag ; [adversaire, opposant] to gag, to muzzle.

bain [bɛ̃] nm **1.** [pour la toilette] bath, bathing ▸ **donner un bain à qqn** to bath sb, to give sb a bath ▸ **prendre un bain** to have ou to take a bath ▸ **vider / faire couler un bain** to empty / to run a bath ▸ **bain moussant / parfumé** bubble / scented bath ▸ **bain de bouche** mouthwash, mouth rinse ▸ **bain de pieds** footbath ▸ **bain à remous** whirlpool spa bath ▸ **être dans le bain a)** [s'y connaître] to be in the swing of things **b)** [être compromis] to be in it up to one's neck ▸ **se mettre** ou **se remettre dans le bain** to get (back) into the swing of things ou the routine **2.** [baignoire] bath 🇬🇧, bathtub 🇺🇸 ▸ **bain à remous** Jacuzzi® **3.** LOISIRS & SPORT [activité] bathing, swimming **4.** [bassin] ▸ **grand bain a)** [bassin] big pool **b)** [côté] deep end ▸ **petit bain a)** [bassin] children's pool **b)** [côté] shallow end **5.** fig [immersion] ▸ **bain de foule** walkabout / prendre un bain de foule to go on a walkabout ▸ **bain linguistique** ou **de langue** immersion in a language / prendre un bain de soleil to sunbathe **6.** [substance pour trempage] bath ; [cuve] vat. ❖ **bains** nmpl [établissement] baths.

bain-marie [bɛ̃maʀi] (pl **bains-marie**) nm [casserole] bain-marie. ❖ **au bain-marie** loc adv in a bain-marie.

baïonnette [bajɔnɛt] nf bayonet.

baise [bɛz] nf vulg [sexe] ▸ **la baise** sex.

baisemain [bɛzmɛ̃] nm ▸ **faire le baisemain** to kiss a woman's hand.

baiser¹ [beze] nm kiss ▸ **donner / envoyer un baiser à qqn** to give / to blow sb a kiss.

baiser² [4] [beze] ❖ vt **1.** litt [embrasser] to kiss **2.** vulg [coucher avec] to screw, to fuck **3.** vulg [tromper] to shaft, to con ; [vaincre] to outdo ; [prendre] : ils se sont fait baiser par le contrôleur they were had ou caught by the ticket inspector. ❖ vi vulg to fuck ▸ **baiser avec qqn** to screw sb.

baisse [bɛs] nf **1.** [perte de valeur] fall, drop **2.** [perte d'intensité] decline, drop ▸ **baisse de prix** fall in prices ▸ **baisse de température** drop in temperature **3.** [perte de quantité] drop ▸ **baisse de la production** drop in production. ❖ **à la baisse** loc adv on the downswing ou downturn ou decline ▸ **revoir à la baisse** to revise downwards. ❖ **en baisse** loc adj [crédit, fonds] declining, sinking, decreasing.

baisser [4] [bese] ❖ vt **1.** [vitre de voiture] to lower, to wind ou to let down (sép) ; [store] to lower, to take ou to let down (sép) ; [tableau] to lower ▸ **le rideau est baissé a)** THÉÂTRE the curtain's down **b)** [boutique] the iron curtain's down **2.** [main, bras] to lower ▸ **baisser les yeux** ou **paupières** to lower one's eyes, to look down, to cast one's eyes down ▸ **marcher les yeux baissés a)** [de tristesse] to walk with downcast eyes **b)** [en cherchant] to walk with one's eyes to the ground ▸ **en baissant la tête a)** [posture] with one's head down ou bent **b)** [de tristesse] head bowed (with sorrow) ▸ **baisser la tête** ou **le nez (de honte)** fig to hang one's head (in shame) ▸ **baisser les bras** to throw in the sponge ou towel fig **3.** [en intensité, en valeur] to lower, to turn down (sép) ▸ **baisser la voix** to lower one's voice ▸ **baisser le feu** CULIN to turn down the heat ▸ **baisser un prix** to bring down ou to lower a price ▸ **faire baisser la tension** ou **le chômage** to reduce tension / unemployment. ❖ vi [espoir, lumière] to fade ; [marée] to go out ; [soleil] to go down, to sink ; [température] to go down, to

drop, to fall ; [prix, action boursière] to drop, to fall ; [santé, faculté] to decline ; [pouvoir] to wane, to dwindle, to decline ▸ **le jour baisse** the daylight's fading / nos réserves de sucre ont baissé our sugar reserves have run low, we're low on sugar ▸ **sa vue baisse** his eyesight's fading ou getting weaker ou failing ▸ **sa mémoire baisse** her memory's failing. ❖ **se baisser** vpi [personne] to bend down / se baisser pour éviter un coup to duck in order to avoid a blow ▸ **il n'y a qu'à se baisser pour les prendre** ou **les ramasser** they're two a penny 🇬🇧 ou a dime a dozen 🇺🇸.

bajoue [baʒu] nf ZOOL chop, chap.

bakchich [bakʃiʃ] nm fam [pourboire] tip ; [pot-de-vin] bribe, backhander 🇬🇧.

bal, bals [bal] nm [réunion - populaire] dance ; [- solennelle] ball, dance ▸ **bal en plein air** open-air dance ▸ **aller au bal** to go dancing ou to a dance ▸ **bal costumé** fancy-dress ball ▸ **bal masqué** masked ball ▸ **bal populaire** (local) dance open to the public ▸ **mener le bal a)** pr to lead off (at a dance) **b)** fig to have the upper hand.

BAL [bal] (abr de **boîte aux lettres (électronique)**) nf E-mail, email.

balade [balad] nf **1.** [promenade - à pied] walk, stroll, ramble ; [- en voiture] drive, spin ; [- à cheval] ride ▸ **faire une balade a)** [à pied] to go for a walk **b)** [en voiture] to go for a drive **c)** [à cheval] to go for a ride **2.** [voyage] jaunt, trip.

balader [3] [balade] vt fam **1.** [promener - enfant, chien] to take (out) for a walk ; [- touriste, visiteur] to take ou to show around (sép) / je les ai baladés en voiture I took them (out) for a drive **2.** [tromper] ▸ **balader qqn** to string sb along fam. ❖ **se balader** vpi fam **1.** [se promener - à pied] to stroll ou to amble along / aller se balader dans les rues to go for a walk ou stroll through the streets ▸ **aller se balader a)** [en voiture] to go for a drive **b)** [à cheval] to go for a ride **2.** [voyager] to go for a trip ou jaunt **3.** [traîner] to lie around.

baladeur, euse [baladœʀ, øz] adj fam ▸ **avoir la main baladeuse** to have wandering hands. ❖ **baladeur** nm AUDIO Walkman®, personal stereo. ❖ **baladeuse** nf [lampe] inspection ou portable lamp.

baladodiffusion [baladodifyzjɔ̃] nf 🇶🇧 podcasting.

balafre [balafʀ] nf **1.** [entaille] slash, gash, cut **2.** [cicatrice] scar.

balafré, e [balafʀe] adj scarred.

balai [balɛ] nm **1.** [de ménage] broom ▸ **du balai !** fam scram ! **2.** AUTO ▸ **balai d'essuie-glace** windscreen 🇬🇧 ou windshield 🇺🇸 wiper blade **3.** tfam [année] year / il a cinquante balais he's fifty.

balai-brosse [balɛbʀɔs] (pl **balais-brosses**) nm (long-handled) scrubbing 🇬🇧 ou scrub 🇺🇸 brush.

balance [balɑ̃s] nf **1.** [instrument de mesure] scales ▸ **mettre tout son poids** ou **tout mettre dans la balance** fig to use (all of) one's influence to tip the scales **2.** [équilibre] balance ; ÉCON balance ▸ **balance commerciale** balance of trade ▸ **balance des paiements** balance of payments **3.** arg crime [dénonciateur] squealer, grass 🇬🇧, rat 🇺🇸. ❖ **en balance** loc adv : mettre en balance les avantages et les inconvénients to weigh (up) the pros and cons.

⚠ Le mot anglais **balance** n'est pas toujours la traduction adéquate pour balance. Voir article.

Balance [balɑ̃s] npr f **1.** ASTRON Libra **2.** ASTROL Libra ▸ **être Balance** to be Libra ou a Libran.

balancement [balɑ̃smɑ̃] nm [mouvement - d'un train] sway, swaying ; [- d'un navire] pitching, roll, rolling ; [- de la tête] swinging ; [- des hanches] swaying ; [- d'une jupe] swinging.

balancer [16] [balɑ̃se] vt **1.** [bras, hanches] to swing ; [bébé] to rock ; [personne - dans un hamac] to push **2.** *fam* [se débarrasser de - objet] to throw away *(sép)*, to chuck out *(sép)* ▸ **tout balancer** to chuck it all in **3.** *fam* [donner - coup] to give ; [lancer - livre, clefs] to chuck *ou* to toss (over) **4.** *fam* [dire - insulte] to hurl ▸ *elle n'arrête pas de me balancer des trucs vraiment durs* she's always making digs at me **5.** *arg crime* [dénoncer - bandit] to shop 🇬🇧, to squeal on *(insép)* ; [- complice] to rat on *(insép)* **6.** FIN [budget, compte] to balance. ◆ **se balancer** vpi **1.** [osciller - personne] to rock, to sway ; [- train] to roll, to sway ; [- navire] to roll, to pitch ; [- branche] to sway / *se balancer sur sa chaise* to tip back one's chair **2.** [sur une balançoire] to swing ; [sur une bascule] to seesaw ; [pendu au bout d'une corde] to swing, to dangle **3.** *fam* EXPR ▸ **s'en balancer** [s'en moquer] : *je m'en balance* I don't give a damn.

⚠ Le verbe anglais **to balance** signifie rarement balancer.

balancier [balɑ̃sje] nm [de funambule] pole.

balançoire [balɑ̃swaʀ] nf **1.** [suspendue] swing ▸ **faire de la balançoire** to have a (go on the) swing, to play on the swing **2.** [bascule] seesaw.

balayage [balɛjaʒ] nm **1.** [d'un sol, d'une pièce] sweeping ; [d'épluchures, de copeaux] sweeping up **2.** [avec un projecteur, un radar] scanning, sweeping **3.** [de la chevelure] highlighting ▸ **se faire faire un balayage** to have highlights put in one's hair **4.** ÉLECTRON scanning, sweep, sweeping.

balayer [11] [baleje] vt **1.** [nettoyer - plancher] to sweep ; [- pièce] to sweep (out) ; [- tapis] to brush, to sweep **2.** [pousser - feuilles, nuages] to sweep along *ou* away *ou* up ; [- poussière, copeaux, épluchures] to sweep up *(sép)* **3.** [parcourir - suj : vent, tir] to sweep (across *ou* over) ; [- suj : faisceau, regard] to sweep, to scan ; [- suj : caméra] to pan across *(insép)* **4.** [détruire - obstacles, préjugés] to sweep away *ou* aside *(sép)* **5.** ÉLECTRON to scan.

balayette [balɛjɛt] nf brush.

balayeur, euse [balɛjœʀ, øz] nm, f street *ou* road sweeper. ◆ **balayeuse** nf street cleaner.

balbutiement [balbysimɑ̃] nm [d'un bègue] stammering, stuttering ; [d'un ivrogne] slurred speech ; [d'un bébé] babbling. ◆ **balbutiements** nmpl [d'une technique, d'un art] early stages, beginnings, infancy.

balbutier [9] [balbysje] vi [bègue] to stammer, to stutter ; [ivrogne] to slur (one's speech) ; [bébé] to babble.

balcon [balkɔ̃] nm **1.** [plate-forme] balcony **2.** THÉÂTRE balcony ▸ **premier balcon** dress circle ▸ **deuxième balcon** upper circle.

balconnet [balkɔnɛ] nm [soutien-gorge] half-cup bra.

baldaquin [baldakɛ̃] nm [sur un lit] canopy, tester.

Bâle [bal] npr Basel, Basle.

Baléares [baleaʀ] npr fpl Baleares ▸ **les (îles) Baléares** the Balearic Islands. ⟶ **île**

baleine [balɛn] nf **1.** ZOOL whale ▸ **baleine blanche / bleue / à bosse** white / blue / humpback whale ▸ **rire** *ou* **rigoler** *ou* **se tordre comme une baleine** *fam* to split one's sides laughing **2.** [fanon] whalebone, baleen **3.** [de parapluie] rib.

baleineau, x [balɛno] nm whale calf.

baleinier, ère [balenje, ɛʀ] adj whaling. ◆ **baleinier** nm **1.** [navire] whaling ship, whaler

2. [chasseur] whaler. ◆ **baleinière** nf PÊCHE whaleboat, whaler, whale catcher.

balèze [balɛz] *tfam* adj **1.** [grand] hefty, huge **2.** [doué] great, brilliant.

balise [baliz] nf **1.** NAUT beacon, (marker) buoy ; AÉRON marker, beacon ; [sur route] road marker cone, police cone ; [sur sentier] waymark ▸ **balise de détresse** distress beacon.

baliser [3] [balize] ◆ vt **1.** NAUT to mark out *(sép)*, to buoy **2.** AÉRON ▸ **baliser une piste** to mark out a runway with lights **3.** [trajet] to mark out *ou* off *(sép)* ▸ **baliser le terrain** *fig* to prepare the ground ▸ **sentier balisé** waymarked path. ◆ vi *tfam* to be scared stiff.

balistique [balistik] ◆ adj ballistic. ◆ nf ballistics (U).

balivernes [balivɛʀn] nfpl [propos] nonsense ▸ **dire des balivernes** to talk nonsense.

Balkans [balkɑ̃] npr mpl ▸ **les Balkans** the Balkans.

ballade [balad] nf **1.** [poème lyrique, chanson] ballad **2.** [en prosodie, pièce musicale] ballade.

ballant, e [balɑ̃, ɑ̃t] adj [jambes] dangling ; [poitrine] wobbling / *il était debout, les bras ballants* he stood with his arms dangling at his sides.

ballast [balast] nm **1.** NAUT ballast tank *ou* container **2.** CONSTR & RAIL ballast.

balle [bal] nf **1.** ARM bullet ▸ **tué par balles** shot dead ▸ **balle à blanc** blank ▸ **balle en caoutchouc** rubber bullet **2.** [pour jouer] ball ▸ **jouer à la balle** to play with a ball ▸ **balle de caoutchouc** rubber ball ▸ **balle de golf** golfball ▸ **balle de tennis** tennis ball ▸ **la balle est dans son camp** *fig* the ball's in his court ▸ **c'est de la balle !** *fam* it's absolutely wicked! 🇬🇧, it's totally awesome! 🇺🇸 **3.** [point, coup] stroke, shot ▸ **faire des balles** TENNIS to practice, to knock up 🇬🇧 ▸ **balle de jeu / match** TENNIS game / match point ▸ **balle de service** service ball **4.** *vieilli franc* ▸ **à deux balles** [médiocre] pathetic, lame / *de la philosophie / psychologie à deux balles* pop philosophy / psychology.

balle(-)molle [balmɔl] (pl **balles(-)molles**) nf 🇶🇧 SPORT softball.

ballerine [balʀin] nf **1.** [danseuse] ballerina, ballet dancer **2.** [chaussure - de danse] ballet *ou* dancing shoe ; [- de ville] pump.

ballet [balɛ] nm **1.** [genre] ballet (dancing) **2.** [œuvre] ballet (music) ; [spectacle] ballet **3.** [troupe] ballet company **4.** SPORT ▸ **ballet aquatique** aquashow, aquacade 🇺🇸.

ballon [balɔ̃] nm **1.** JEUX & SPORT ball ▸ **jouer au ballon** to play with a ball ▸ **ballon de foot** *ou* **football** football 🇬🇧, soccer ball 🇺🇸 ▸ **ballon de basket** basketball ▸ **ballon de rugby** rugby ball ▸ **le ballon ovale** [le rugby] rugby ▸ **le ballon rond** [le foot] football 🇬🇧, soccer 🇺🇸 **2.** [sphère] ▸ **ballon (de baudruche)** (party) balloon ▸ **ballon d'oxygène a)** MÉD oxygen tank **b)** *fig* life-saver **3.** AÉRON (hot-air) balloon ▸ **ballon d'essai a)** *pr* pilot balloon **b)** *fig* test **4.** CHIM round-bottomed flask, balloon ; [pour l'Alcootest] (breathalyser) bag ▸ **souffler dans le ballon** to be breathalysed 🇬🇧 *ou* breathalyzed 🇺🇸 **5.** [verre] (round) wine glass, balloon glass ▸ **ballon de rouge** glass of red wine ; [contenu] glassful **6.** [réservoir] ▸ **ballon (d'eau chaude)** hot water tank.

ballonné, e [balɔne] adj bloated ▸ **être ballonné** to feel bloated.

ballon-sonde [balɔ̃sɔ̃d] (pl **ballons-sondes**) nm pilot balloon.

ballot [balo] nm **1.** [paquet] bundle, package **2.** *fam* [sot] nitwit, blockhead.

ballottage, ballotage* [balɔtaʒ] nm second ballot *ou* round ▸ **être en ballottage** to have to stand 🇬🇧 *ou* to run 🇺🇸 again in a second round.

ballotter, balloter* [3] [balɔte] ◆ vt [navire] to toss (about) ; [passager, sac] to roll around ; *fig* : *être ballotté*

---

* In reformed spelling (see p. 16-18).

entre deux endroits to be shifted ou shunted around constantly from one place to the other. ◆ vi [tête] to loll, to sway ; [valise] to bang ou to shake about, to rattle around.

ballottine [balɔtin] nf stuffed and boned meat roll, ballottine.

ball(l)oune nf QUÉBEC *fam* balloon.

ball-trap (*pl* **ball-traps**), **balltrap*** [baltʀap] nm [tir - à une cible] trapshooting, clay-pigeon shooting ; [- à deux cibles] skeet, skeet shooting.

balluchon [balyʃɔ̃] nm bundle ▶ **faire son balluchon** *pr & fig* to pack one's bags.

balnéaire [balneɛʀ] adj seaside (*modif*).

balnéothérapie [balneɔteʀapi] nf balneotherapy.

balourd, e [baluʀ, uʀd] nm, f awkward person.

balsamique [balzamik] adj BOT & MÉD balsamic.

balte [balt] adj Baltic ▶ **les pays Baltes** the Baltic states.

baltique [baltik] adj Baltic. ◆ **Baltique** npr f ▶ **la (mer) Baltique** the Baltic (Sea).

baluchon [balyʃɔ̃] = **balluchon**.

balustrade [balystʀad] nf [d'un balcon] balustrade ; [d'un pont] railing.

bambin [bɑ̃bɛ̃] nm toddler.

bambou [bɑ̃bu] nm bamboo ▶ **avoir le coup de bambou a)** *fam* [devenir fou] to go crazy **b)** [être fatigué] to feel very tired / *c'est le coup de bambou dans ce restaurant !* *fam* [très cher] this restaurant's a real rip-off!

ban [bɑ̃] nm **1.** [applaudissements] : *un ban pour...* three cheers ou a big hand for... **2.** HIST [condamnation] banishment, banning ; [convocation] ban ; [vassaux] vassals ▶ **le ban et l'arrière-ban** *fig* the world and his wife. ◆ **bans** nmpl banns. ◆ **au ban de** loc prép : *être au ban de la société* to be an outcast ou a pariah.

banal, e, als [banal] adj **1.** [courant] commonplace, ordinary, everyday (*avant nom*) / *ce n'est vraiment pas banal* it's most unusual, it's really strange **2.** [sans originalité - idée, histoire] trite, banal ; [- chose] commonplace ; [- argument] standard, well-worn ; [- vie] humdrum ; [- événement] everyday.

banalisé, e [banalize] adj [véhicule] unmarked.

banaliser [3] [banalize] vt **1.** [rendre courant - pratique] to trivialize, to make commonplace **2.** [véhicule] to remove the markings from ; [marque déposée] to turn into a household name. ◆ **se banaliser** vpi to become commonplace ou a part of (everyday) life ; [violence] to become routine.

banalité [banalite] nf **1.** [d'une situation, d'un propos] triteness, banality, triviality ; [d'une tenue] mundaneness **2.** [propos, écrit] platitude, commonplace, cliché.

banane [banan] nf **1.** BOT banana **2.** *fam* [coiffure] quiff UK **3.** [sac] bum-bag UK, fanny pack US, waist-bag US **4.** *tfam* [idiot] nitwit, twit UK, dumbbell US **5.** *fam* EXPR **avoir la banane** to have a great beam on one's face ▶ **20 € et des bananes** just over 20 €.

bananier [bananje] nm BOT banana, banana tree.

banc [bɑ̃] nm **1.** [meuble] bench, seat ▶ **banc (d'église)** pew UK ▶ **(au) banc des accusés** (in the) dock ▶ **(au) banc des témoins** (in the) witness box UK ou stand US ▶ **sur les bancs de l'école** in one's schooldays ▶ **banc public** park bench **2.** [de poissons] shoal, school **3.** [amas] bank ▶ **banc de neige** QUÉBEC snowdrift ▶ **banc de sable** sandbank, sandbar. ◆ **banc d'essai** nm INDUST test rig, test bed ; INFORM benchmark ; *fig* test.

bancaire [bɑ̃kɛʀ] adj banking, bank (*modif*) ▶ **chèque bancaire** cheque UK, check US.

bancal, e, als [bɑ̃kal] adj **1.** [meuble] rickety, wobbly ; [personne] lame **2.** [peu cohérent - idée, projet] unsound ; [- raisonnement] weak, unsound.

bancassurance [bɑ̃kasyʀɑ̃s] nf bancassurance.

bandage [bɑ̃daʒ] nm [pansement] bandage, dressing.

bandant, e [bɑ̃dɑ̃, ɑ̃t] adj *vulg* exciting / *elle est bandante* she's a real turn-on ; [sens affaibli] : *pas très bandant comme boulot !* *hum* this job's hardly the most exciting thing going!

bande [bɑ̃d]
nf
A. GROUPE 1. [groupe - de malfaiteurs] gang ; [- d'amis] group ; [- d'enfants] troop, band ; [- d'animaux] herd ; [- de chiens, de loups] pack / *faire partie de la bande* to be one of the group ▶ **bande armée** armed gang ou band **2.** EXPR **faire bande à part** : *il fait toujours bande à part* he keeps (himself) to himself ▶ **bande de** *péj* pack ou bunch of ▶ **une bande de menteurs / voleurs** a bunch of liars / crooks.
B. RUBAN 1. [d'étoffe, de papier, etc.] strip, band **2.** [de territoire] strip / *bande de sable* strip ou spit ou tongue of sand ▶ **bande d'arrêt d'urgence** TRANSP emergency lane, hard shoulder UK, shoulder US **3.** [sur une route] band, stripe **4.** CINÉ reel ▶ **bande (magnétique)** AUDIO (magnetic) tape **5.** ÉLECTRON & RADIO band ▶ **bande passante** bandwidth **6.** INFORM ▶ **bande perforée** punched paper tape UK, perforated tape **7.** MÉD bandage ▶ **bande Velpeau** crepe bandage **8.** LITTÉR & LOISIRS ▶ **bande dessinée a)** [dans un magazine] comic strip **b)** [livre] comic book ▶ **la bande dessinée** [genre] comic strips. ◆ **en bande** loc adv as ou in a group, all together / *ils ne se déplacent qu'en bande* they always move around in a gang.

bande-annonce [bɑ̃danɔ̃s] (*pl* **bandes-annonces**) nf trailer.

bandeau, x [bɑ̃do] nm **1.** [serre-tête] headband **2.** [sur les yeux] blindfold ▶ **avoir un bandeau sur les yeux a)** *pr* to be blindfolded **b)** *fig* to be blind to reality ; [sur un œil] eye patch **3.** [espace publicitaire] advertising space (*in the shape of a band around a vehicle*).

bandelette [bɑ̃dlɛt] nf [bande] strip ▶ **les bandelettes d'une momie** the wrappings of a mummy.

bander [3] [bɑ̃de] ◆ vt **1.** [panser - main, cheville] to bandage (up) ▶ **bander les yeux à qqn** [pour qu'il ne voie pas] to blindfold sb ▶ **avoir les yeux bandés a)** MÉD to have one's eyes bandaged **b)** [avec un bandeau] to be blindfolded **2.** [tendre - arc] to draw, to bend ; [- ressort, câble] to stretch, to tense ; *litt* [muscle] to tense, to tauten. ◆ vi *vulg* to have a hard-on.

banderole [bɑ̃dʀɔl] nf [bannière - sur un mât, une lance] banderole ; [- en décoration] streamer ; [- dans une manifestation] banner.

bande-son [bɑ̃dsɔ̃] nf (*pl* **bandes-son**) nf soundtrack.

bandit [bɑ̃di] nm **1.** [brigand] bandit ; [gangster] gangster **2.** [escroc] crook, conman.

banditisme [bɑ̃ditism] nm crime ▶ **grand banditisme** organized crime.

bandoulière [bɑ̃duljɛʀ] nf [d'un sac] shoulder strap. ◆ **en bandoulière** loc adv : *porter un sac en bandoulière* to carry a shoulder bag.

bangladais, e [bɑ̃glade, ɛz], **bangladeshi, e** [bɑ̃gladeʃi] adj Bangladeshi. ◆ **Bangladais, e, Bangladeshi, e** nm, f Bangladeshi.

Bangladesh [bɑ̃gladeʃ] npr m ▶ **le Bangladesh** Bangladesh.

banjo [bɑ̃(d)ʒo] nm banjo.

banlieue [bɑ̃ljø] nf suburb ▶ **la banlieue** suburbia, the suburbs / *la maison est en banlieue* the house is on the outskirts of the town ou in the suburbs ▸ **grande banlieue** outer suburbs, commuter belt ▸ **proche banlieue** inner suburbs.

Banlieue

Although the word **banlieue** simply means suburb, its connotations in French society are much more complex. The post-war development of areas on the fringes of major cities led to the creation of huge housing projects which have, in many cases, effectively become ghettos occupied by increasingly disenfranchised populations. These troubled **cités de banlieue**, officially referred to as **quartiers sensibles**, have become a major symbol of social malaise in France.

banlieusard, e [bɑ̃ljøzaʀ, aʀd] nm, f [gén] suburbanite ; TRANSP commuter.

bannette [banɛt] nf **1.** [pour courrier] letter tray **2.** [store] awning.

bannière [banjɛʀ] nf **1.** [étendard] banner ▸ **la bannière étoilée** the star-spangled banner **2.** INFORM ▸ **bannière publicitaire** banner (ad ou advertisement).

bannir [32] [baniʀ] vt [supprimer - idée, pensée] to banish ; [- aliment] to cut out *(sép)*.

banque [bɑ̃k] nf **1.** [établissement] bank ▸ **avoir / mettre une somme à la banque** to have / put some money in the bank **2.** INFORM & MÉD bank ▸ **banque du sang / du sperme / de données** blood / sperm / data bank ▸ **banque d'images** picture library.

banqueroute [bɑ̃kʀut] nf [faillite] bankruptcy ▸ **faire banqueroute** to go bankrupt.

banquet [bɑ̃kɛ] nm banquet.

banquette [bɑ̃kɛt] nf [siège - de salon] seat, banquette US ; [- de piano] (duet) stool ; [- de restaurant] wall seat ; [- de voiture, de métro] seat.

banquier, ère [bɑ̃kje, ɛʀ] nm, f banker.

banquise [bɑ̃kiz] nf [côtière] ice, ice shelf ; [dérivante] pack ice, ice field ou floe.

baobab [baɔbab] nm baobab.

baptême [batɛm] nm **1.** RELIG baptism ; [cérémonie] christening, baptism / *recevoir le baptême* to be baptized ou christened **2.** [d'un bateau] christening, naming ; [d'une cloche] christening, dedication **3.** [première expérience] ▸ **baptême de l'air** first ou maiden flight ▸ **baptême de plongée** first scuba dive.

baptiser [3] [batize] vt **1.** RELIG to christen, to baptize **2.** [nommer - personne, animal] to name, to call ; [surnommer] to nickname, to christen, to dub **3.** [bateau] to christen, to name ; [cloche] to christen, to dedicate.

baquet [bakɛ] nm [récipient] tub.

bar [baʀ] nm **1.** [café] bar ▸ **bar à vin** wine bar **2.** [comptoir] bar.

baragouiner [3] [baʀagwine] *fam* ◆ vt [langue] to speak badly ; [discours] to gabble. ◆ vi [de façon incompréhensible] to jabber, to gibber, to talk gibberish ; [dans une langue étrangère] to jabber away.

baraka [baʀaka] nf *fam* [chance] luck ▸ **avoir la baraka** to be lucky.

baraque [baʀak] nf **1.** [cabane - à outils] shed ; [- d'ouvriers, de pêcheurs] shelter, hut ; [- de forains] stall ; [- de vente] stall, stand, booth **2.** *fam* [maison] shack, shanty.

baraqué, e [baʀake] adj *fam* muscular, hefty, beefy *péj*.

baraquement [baʀakmɑ̃] nm MIL camp.

baratin [baʀatɛ̃] nm *fam* [boniment] flannel ▸ **faire du baratin à qqn** to spin sb a yarn, to flannel sb.

baratiner [3] [baʀatine] *fam* vt ▸ **baratiner qqn a)** [en vue d'un gain] to flannel sb **b)** [pour le séduire] to chat sb up UK, to give sb a line US **c)** [pour l'impressionner] to shoot one's mouth off to sb.

Barbade [baʀbad] npr f ▸ **la Barbade** Barbados.

barbant, e [baʀbɑ̃, ɑ̃t] adj *fam* boring ▸ **il est barbant** he's a drag ou bore.

barbare [baʀbaʀ] ◆ adj **1.** HIST [primitif] barbarian, barbaric **2.** [cruel] barbaric. ◆ nmf barbarian.

barbarisme [baʀbaʀism] nm barbarism.

barbe [baʀb] nf [d'homme - drue] (full) beard ; [- clairsemée] stubble ; [- en pointe] goatee ▸ **porter la barbe** to have a beard ▸ **barbe à papa** candy floss UK, cotton candy US ▸ **c'est la barbe !, quelle barbe !** *fam* what a drag ou bore! ▸ **la barbe ! a)** *fam* [pour faire taire] shut up!, shut your mouth! *tfam*, shut your trap! *tfam* **b)** [pour protester] damn!, hell!, blast! ◆ **barbes** nfpl [de papier] ragged edge ; [d'encre] smudge.

barbecue [baʀbəkju] nm **1.** [appareil] barbecue (set) / *faire cuire de la viande au barbecue* to barbecue meat **2.** [repas] barbecue.

barbelé, e [baʀbəle] adj barbed. ◆ **barbelé** nm barbed wire, barbwire US.

barber [3] [baʀbe] vt *fam* [lasser] to bore / *je vais lui écrire, mais ça me barbe !* I'll write to him, but what a drag! ◆ **se barber** vpi to be bored stiff ou to tears ou to death.

barbiche [baʀbiʃ] nf goatee.

barbiturique [baʀbityʀik] nm barbiturate.

barboter [3] [baʀbɔte] ◆ vi **1.** [s'ébattre] to paddle, to splash around ou about **2.** [patauger] to wade. ◆ vt *fam* [dérober] to pinch, to swipe.

barboteuse [baʀbɔtøz] nf **1.** (pair of) rompers ou crawlers, playsuit **2.** QUÉBEC [pataugeuse] wading pool.

barbouiller [3] [baʀbuje] vt **1.** [salir] : *son menton était barbouillé de confiture* his chin was smeared with jam **2.** [peindre] to daub ▸ **barbouiller qqch de peinture** to slap paint on sthg, to daub sthg with paint **3.** [gribouiller] to scrawl, to scribble ▸ **il barbouille du papier a)** *péj* he's scribbling away **b)** *fig & péj* he's just a scribbler **4.** *fam* [donner la nausée à] to nauseate ▸ **avoir l'estomac ou se sentir barbouillé** to feel queasy ou nauseated, to feel sick UK ou nauseous US.

barbu, e [baʀby] adj bearded. ◆ **barbu** nm [homme] bearded man, man with a beard.

Barcelone [baʀsəlɔn] npr Barcelona.

barda [baʀda] nm *fam* **1.** MIL gear, kit UK **2.** [chargement] stuff, gear, paraphernalia.

barde [baʀd] ◆ nm [poète] bard. ◆ nf CULIN bard.

barder [3] [baʀde] ◆ vt **1.** CULIN to bard **2.** *fig* ▸ **être bardé de diplômes** to have a string of academic titles. ◆ v impers *fam* : *quand il a dit ça, ça a bardé !* things really turned nasty when he said that! / *si tu ne te dépêches pas, ça va barder !* you'll get it ou be for it if you don't hurry up!

barème [baʀɛm] nm [tarification] scale ▸ **barème des prix** price list, schedule of prices ▸ **barème des salaires** wage scale, variable sliding scale.

barge[1] [baʀʒ] nf NAUT barge, lighter.

barge[2] [baʀʒ] adj *fam* [fou] nuts, bananas, off one's head UK.

baril [baʀil] nm [de vin] barrel, cask ; [de pétrole] barrel ; [de lessive] pack ▸ **baril de poudre** powder keg.

barillet [baʀijɛ] nm ARM & TECHNOL cylinder.

bariolé, e [baʀjɔle] adj [tissu] motley, multicoloured 🇬🇧, multicolored 🇺🇸, parti-coloured 🇬🇧, parti-colored 🇺🇸 ; [foule] colourful 🇬🇧, colorful 🇺🇸.

barjo(t) [baʀʒo] adj *tfam* nuts, bananas.

barmaid [baʀmɛd] nf barmaid.

barman [baʀman] (*pl* **barmans** *ou* **barmen** [-mɛn]) nm barman 🇬🇧, bartender 🇺🇸.

baromètre [baʀɔmɛtʀ] nm barometer, glass.

baron, onne [baʀɔ̃, ɔn] nm, f **1.** [noble] baron (baroness) **2.** [magnat] ▶ **baron de la finance** tycoon.

baroque [baʀɔk] ◆ adj **1.** ARCHIT, ART & LITTÉR baroque **2.** [étrange - idée] weird. ◆ nm Baroque.

barque [baʀk] nf small boat ▶ **barque de pêcheur** small fishing boat ▶ **mener sa barque** *fig* to look after o.s. ▶ **il a bien / mal mené sa barque** he managed / didn't manage his affairs well.

barquette [baʀkɛt] nf **1.** CULIN *boat-shaped tartlet* **2.** [emballage] carton, punnet.

barrage [baʀaʒ] nm **1.** [réservoir] dam ; [régulateur] weir, barrage ▶ **barrage (de retenue)** dam ▶ **faire barrage à** to stand in the way of, to obstruct, to hinder **2.** [dispositif policier] ▶ **barrage (de police)** police cordon ▶ **barrage routier** roadblock.

barre [baʀ] nf **1.** [tige - de bois] bar ; [- de métal] bar, rod ▶ **barre de fer** iron bar ▶ **avoir un coup de barre** *fig* to be shattered 🇬🇧 ou pooped 🇺🇸 ▶ **barre de céréales** muesli bar ▶ **barre de chocolat** chocolate bar ▶ **barre tendre** Québec CULIN chewy bar **2.** SPORT ▶ **barres asymétriques / parallèles** asymmetric / parallel bars ▶ **barre fixe** high ou horizontal bar ; DANSE barre ▶ **exercices à la barre** barre work ou exercises **3.** NAUT ▶ **barre (de gouvernail) a)** [gén] helm **b)** [sur un voilier] tiller **c)** [sur un navire] wheel ▶ **prendre la barre a)** *pr* to take the helm **b)** *fig* to take charge **4.** [trait] line ▶ **barre oblique** slash ▶ **double barre** double bar **5.** [niveau] level / *le dollar pourrait descendre au-dessous de la barre des 2 euros* the dollar could fall below the level of 2 euros ▶ **mettre** ou **placer la barre trop haut** to set too high a standard **6.** DR ▶ **barre des témoins** witness box 🇬🇧 ou stand 🇺🇸 ▶ **appeler qqn à la barre** to call sb to the witness box 🇬🇧 ou stand 🇺🇸 **7.** INFORM ▶ **barre d'espacement** space bar ▶ **barre d'état** status bar ▶ **barre de menu** menu bar ▶ **barre d'outils** toolbar.

barré, e [baʀe] adj *fam* EXPR ▶ **être bien / mal barré**: *on est mal barré(s) pour y être à 8 h* we haven't got a hope in hell ou we don't stand a chance of being there at 8 ▶ **c'est mal barré** it's got off to a bad start.

barreau, x [baʀo] nm **1.** [de fenêtre] bar ; [d'échelle] rung ▶ **être derrière les barreaux** [prisonnier] to be behind bars **2.** DR ▶ **le barreau** the Bar ▶ **être admis** ou **reçu au barreau** to be called to the Bar.

barrer [3] [baʀe] ◆ vt **1.** [bloquer - porte, issue] to bar ; [- voie, route] to block, to obstruct / *la rue est temporairement barrée* the street has been temporarily closed ▶ **barrer le passage à qqn** to block sb's way ▶ **barrer la route à qqn** *pr & fig* to stand in sb's way **2.** [rayer - chèque] to cross ; [- erreur, phrase] to cross ou to score out (*sép*), to strike out **3.** NAUT to steer. ◆ vi NAUT to steer, to be at the helm. ◆ **se barrer** vpi *fam* **1.** [partir] to beat it, to split, to clear off / *barre-toi de là, tu me gênes !* shift, you're in my way! **2.** [se détacher] to come off.

barrette [baʀɛt] nf **1.** [pince] ▶ **barrette (à cheveux)** (hair) slide 🇬🇧, barrette 🇺🇸 **2.** INFORM ▶ **barrette de mémoire** memory module **3.** *arg* ▶ **barrette de haschisch** bar of hashish.

barreur, euse [baʀœʀ, øz] nm, f **1.** [gén] helmsman **2.** [en aviron] coxswain.

barricade [baʀikad] nf barricade.

barricader [3] [baʀikade] vt [porte, rue] to barricade. ◆ **se barricader** vp (*emploi réfléchi*) **1.** [se retrancher] to barricade o.s. **2.** [s'enfermer] to lock ou to shut o.s.

barrière [baʀjɛʀ] nf **1.** [clôture] fence ; [porte] gate ▶ **barrière de passage à niveau** level 🇬🇧 ou grade 🇺🇸 crossing gate ▶ **barrière de sécurité** guardrail **2.** [obstacle] barrier / *la barrière de la langue* the language barrier **3.** GÉOGR ▶ **la Grande Barrière** the Great Barrier Reef.

barrir [32] [baʀiʀ] vi [éléphant] to trumpet.

bar-tabac [baʀtaba] (*pl* **bars-tabacs**) nm *bar also selling cigarettes and tobacco*.

baryton [baʀitɔ̃] nm [voix] baritone (voice) ; [chanteur] baritone.

bas¹ [ba] nm [de femme] stocking ▶ **des bas avec / sans couture** seamed / seamless stockings ▶ **bas de soie** silk stockings ▶ **bas de laine a)** *pr* woollen 🇬🇧 ou woolen 🇺🇸 stocking **b)** *fig* savings, nest egg ▶ **bas (de) Nylon®** nylon stockings ▶ **bas résille** fishnet stockings ▶ **bas à varices** support stockings.

bas², basse [bɑ, bas] (*devant nm commençant par voyelle ou «h» muet* [bɑz]) adj

A. DANS L'ESPACE 1. [de peu de hauteur - bâtiment, mur] low ; [- herbes] low, short ; [- nuages] low **2.** [peu profond] low ▶ **aux basses eaux a)** [de la mer] at low tide **b)** [d'une rivière] when the water level is low **3.** [incliné vers le sol] ▶ **marcher la tête basse** to hang one's head as one walks **4.** GÉOGR ▶ **les basses terres** the lowlands.

B. DANS UNE HIÉRARCHIE 1. [en grandeur - prix, fréquence, pression, etc.] low ▶ **à bas prix** cheap, for a low price ▶ **bas de gamme** [produit] low-end, bottom-of-the-range ▶ **à basse température** [laver] at low temperatures / *son moral est très bas* he's down, he's in very low spirits **2.** [médiocre - intérêt, rendement] low, poor ; [- dans les arts] inferior, minor, crude / *le niveau de la classe est très bas* the (achievement) level of the class is very low ▶ **les bas morceaux** [en boucherie] the cheap cuts **3.** [inférieur dans la société] low, lowly *litt*, humble ▶ **le bas clergé** the minor clergy **4.** MUS [grave - note] low, bottom (*modif*) ; [- guitare, flûte] bass (*modif*) **5.** [peu fort] low, quiet ▶ **parler à voix basse** to speak in a low ou quiet voice **6.** *péj* [abject, vil - âme] low, mean, villainous ; [- acte] low, base, mean ; [- sentiment] low, base, abject / *à moi toutes les basses besognes* I get stuck with all the dirty work **7.** [le plus récent] ▶ **le bas Moyen Âge** the late Middle Ages. ◆ **bas** ◆ adv **1.** [à faible hauteur, à faible niveau] low / *je mettrais l'étagère plus bas* I'd put the shelf lower down / *les prix ne descendront pas plus bas* prices won't come down any further / *il est tombé bien bas dans mon estime* he's gone down a lot in my estimation / *plus bas, vous trouverez la boulangerie* [plus loin] you'll find the baker's a little further on ; [dans un document] ▶ **voir plus bas** see below ▶ **bas les pattes !** *fam* hands off! **2.** ACOUST [d'une voix douce] in a low voice ; [d'une voix grave] in a deep voice / *mets le son plus bas* turn the sound down ▶ **il dit tout haut ce que les autres pensent tout bas** he voices the thoughts which others keep to themselves **3.** MUS low **4.** VÉTÉR ▶ **mettre bas** to give birth. ◆ nm [partie inférieure - d'un pantalon, d'un escalier, d'une hiérarchie, etc.] bottom ; [- d'un visage] lower part ▶ **le bas du dos** the small of the back. ◆ **basse** nf **1.** MUS [partie] bass (part) ou score **2.** [voix d'homme] bass (voice) ; [chanteur] bass **3.** [instrument - gén] bass (instrument) ; [- violoncelle] (double) bass. ◆ **à bas** loc adv ▶ **à bas la dictature !** down with dictatorship! ◆ **au bas de** loc prép ▶ **au bas des escaliers** at the foot ou bottom of the stairs. ◆ **de bas en haut** loc adv from bottom to top, from the bottom up.

d'en bas ◆ loc adj [du niveau inférieur] downstairs / *les voisins d'en bas* the people downstairs. ◆ loc adv [dans une maison] from downstairs / *le bruit vient d'en bas* the noise is coming from downstairs ; [d'une hauteur] from the bottom / *vu d'en bas on dirait un château* seen from below it looks like a castle. ◆ **du bas** loc adj **1.** [de l'étage inférieur] ▶ **l'appartement du bas** the flat underneath ou below ou downstairs **2.** [du rez-de-chaussée] downstairs *(modif)* **3.** [de l'endroit le moins élevé] lower. ◆ **en bas** loc adv **1.** [à un niveau inférieur - dans un bâtiment] downstairs, down / *la maison a deux pièces en bas et deux en haut* the house has two rooms downstairs and two upstairs **2.** [vers le sol] : *je ne peux pas regarder en bas, j'ai le vertige* I can't look down, I feel dizzy. ◆ **en bas de** loc prép : *en bas de la côte* at the bottom ou foot of the hill.

basalte [bazalt] nm basalt.

basané, e [bazane] adj [bronzé - touriste] suntanned ; [- navigateur] tanned, tan, weather-beaten.

bas-côté [bakote] *(pl* **bas-côtés)** nm [de route] side, verge, shoulder ; [d'église] aisle.

bascule [baskyl] nf **1.** [balance] weighing machine ; [pèse-personne] scales **2.** [balançoire] seesaw.

basculer [3] [baskyle] ◆ vi **1.** [personne] to topple, to fall over ; [vase] to tip over ; [benne] to tip up / *un peu plus et il faisait basculer la voiture dans le vide* it would only have taken a little push to send the car over the edge **2.** *fig* ▶ **son univers a basculé** his world collapsed. ◆ vt [renverser - chariot] to tip up *(sép)* ; [- chargement] to tip out *(sép)*.

base [baz] nf **1.** [fondement] basis, groundwork *(U)*, foundations ▶ **établir qqch / reposer sur une base solide** to set sthg up / to rest on a sound basis **2.** MIL ▶ **base (aérienne / militaire / navale)** (air / army / naval) base **3.** ASTRONAUT ▶ **base de lancement** launching site **4.** POL ▶ **la base** the grass roots, the rank and file **5.** FIN ▶ **base d'imposition** taxable amount **6.** GÉOM, INFORM & MATH base ▶ **base de données** database **7.** SPORT [détente] ▶ **base de loisirs** (outdoor) leisure ou sports complex. ◆ **bases** nfpl [fondations] foundations, basis ; [acquis] basic knowledge ▶ **avoir de bonnes bases en arabe / musique** to have a good grounding in Arabic / in music. ◆ **à base de** loc prép ▶ **à base de café** coffee-based. ◆ **à la base** loc adv **1.** [en son fondement] : *le raisonnement est faux à la base* the basis of the argument is false **2.** [au début] at the beginning, to begin ou to start off with. ◆ **à la base de** loc prép ▶ **être à la base de qqch** to be at the root of sthg. ◆ **de base** loc adj **1.** [fondamental - vocabulaire, industrie] basic ; [- principe] basic, fundamental ▶ **militant de base** grassroots militant **2.** [de référence - salaire, traitement] basic.

base-ball *(pl* **base-balls)**, **baseball*** [bezbol] nm baseball.

base line [bezlain] nf strapline.

baser [3] [baze] vt **1.** [fonder] ▶ **baser qqch sur (qqch)** to base sthg on (sthg) **2.** MIL & COMM [installer] to base ▶ **être basé à** to be based at ou in. ◆ **se baser sur** vp + prép to base one's judgment on / *je me base sur les chiffres de l'année dernière* I've taken last year's figures as the basis for my calculations.

bas-fond *(pl* **bas-fonds)**, **basfond*** [baf̃ɔ] nm GÉOGR & NAUT shallow, shoal. ◆ **bas-fonds, basfonds*** nmpl *litt* : *les bas-fonds de New York* the slums of New York.

basilic [bazilik] nm BOT basil.

basilique [bazilik] nf basilica.

basique [bazik] adj CHIM basic.

basket [baskɛt] ◆ nm ou nf [chaussure] ▶ **baskets** trainers, sneakers ▶ **être bien dans ses baskets** *fam* to be comfortable with o.s. ◆ nm *fam* = **basket-ball**.

basket-ball *(pl* **basket-balls)**, **basketball*** [basketbol] nm basketball.

basketteur, euse [basketœr, øz] nm, f basketball player.

basmati [basmati] nm basmati (rice).

basque¹ [bask] nf COUT basque ▶ **s'accrocher** ou **se pendre aux basques de qqn** to dog sb's footsteps, to stick to sb like glue.

basque² [bask] adj Basque ▶ **le Pays basque** the Basque Country / *au Pays basque* in the Basque Country. ◆ **Basque** nmf Basque. ◆ **basque** nm LING Basque.

bas-relief [baRəljɛf] *(pl* **bas-reliefs)** nm bas ou low relief.

basse [bas] f ⟶ **bas**.

basse-cour *(pl* **basses-cours)**, **bassecour*** [baskuR] nf [lieu] farmyard.

bassement [basmɑ̃] adv [agir] basely, meanly / *parlons de choses bassement matérielles* let's talk money.

bassesse [bases] nf [action - mesquine] base ou despicable act ; [- servile] servile act.

basset [base] nm basset (hound).

bassin [basɛ̃] nm **1.** ANAT pelvis **2.** [piscine] pool ; [plan d'eau] pond, ornamental lake **3.** [récipient] basin, bowl ▶ **bassin hygiénique** ou **de lit** bedpan **4.** GÉOGR basin ▶ **le Bassin parisien** the Paris Basin **5.** [région] ▶ **bassin d'emploi(s)** labour market area **6.** NAUT dock.

bassine [basin] nf basin, bowl.

bassiner [3] [basine] vt *fam* [ennuyer] to bore / *tu nous bassines avec ça !* stop going on and on about it!

bassiste [basist] nmf **1.** [guitariste] bass guitarist **2.** [contrebassiste] double bass player.

basson [basɔ̃] nm **1.** [instrument] bassoon **2.** [musicien] bassoonist.

bastide [bastid] nf [maison] Provençal cottage ; [ferme] Provençal farmhouse.

bastion [bastjɔ̃] nm **1.** CONSTR bastion **2.** [d'une doctrine, d'un mouvement] bastion.

baston [bastɔ̃] nm *tfam* : *il y a eu de la baston* there was a bit of trouble.

bastonner [bastɔne] ◆ **se bastonner** vp *(emploi réciproque)* *fam* to fight.

bas-ventre [bavɑ̃tR] *(pl* **bas-ventres)** nm (lower) abdomen, pelvic area.

bât [ba] nm packsaddle ▶ *c'est là que* ou *où le bât blesse* that's where the shoe pinches.

bataille [bataj] nf **1.** [combat] battle, fight ▶ **bataille aéronavale** sea-air battle ▶ **bataille de boules de neige** snowball fight ▶ **bataille de rue** street fight ou brawl ▶ **bataille juridique** legal battle **2.** JEUX ≃ beggar-my-neighbour ▶ **bataille navale** battleships.

batailler [3] [bataje] vi **1.** [physiquement] to fight, to scuffle **2.** *fig* to struggle, to fight.

bataillon [batajɔ̃] nm **1.** MIL battalion **2.** [foule] ▶ **un bataillon de** scores of, an army of.

bâtard, e [batar, ard] adj **1.** [enfant] illegitimate ; [animal] crossbred ▶ **chien bâtard** mongrel **2.** [genre, œuvre] hybrid ; [solution] half-baked, ill thought-out. ◆ **bâtard** nm [pain] short thick loaf.

batavia [batavja] nf batavia lettuce.

bateau, x [bato] nm [navire, embarcation] boat, ship ▶ **je prends le bateau à Anvers / à 10 h** I'm sailing from Antwerp / at 10 ▶ **faire du bateau** a) [en barque, en vedette] to go boating **b)** [en voilier] to go sailing ▸ **bateau à moteur / rames** motor / rowing boat ▸ **bateau de pêche** fishing boat ▸ **bateau de plaisance** pleasure boat ou craft ▸ **bateau pneumatique** rubber boat, dinghy ▸ **mener** ou **conduire qqn en bateau** *fam* to lead sb up the garden path, to take sb for a ride. ⬦ **bateau** adj inv [banal] hackneyed ▸ **un sujet bateau** an old chestnut.

bateau-bus [batobys] (*pl* bateaux-bus) nm riverbus.

bateau-mouche [batomuʃ] (*pl* bateaux-mouches) nm river boat (*on the Seine*).

bâti, e [bati] adj **1.** [personne] ▸ **être bien bâti** to be well-built **2.** [terrain] built-up, developed. ⬦ **bâti** nm COUT [technique] basting, tacking ; [fil] tacking.

batifoler [3] [batifɔle] vi **1.** [s'amuser] to frolic **2.** [flirter] to flirt.

bâtiment [batimã] nm **1.** [édifice] building **2.** [profession] ▸ **le bâtiment** the building trade, the construction industry **3.** NAUT ship, (sea-going) vessel.

bâtir [32] [batir] vt **1.** CONSTR to build / **se faire bâtir une maison** to have a house built **2.** [créer - fortune] to build up (*sép*) ; [- foyer] to build **3.** COUT to baste, to tack.

bâtisse [batis] nf *péj* building ▸ **une grande bâtisse** a big barn of a place.

bâton [batɔ̃] nm **1.** [baguette - gén] stick ; [- d'agent de police] truncheon 🇬🇧, billy (club) 🇺🇸 ; [- de berger] staff, crook ; [- de skieur] pole ▸ **mettre des bâtons dans les roues à qqn a)** [continuellement] to impede sb's progress **b)** [en une occasion] to throw a spanner 🇬🇧 ou wrench 🇺🇸 in the works for sb **2.** [de craie, de dynamite, etc.] stick ▸ **bâton de rouge à lèvres** lipstick **3.** ÉDUC [trait] (vertical) line **4.** *tfam & vieilli* [dix mille francs] ten thousand francs. ⬦ **à bâtons rompus** *loc adv* ▸ **parler à bâtons rompus** to make casual conversation.

bâtonnet [batɔnɛ] nm [petit bâton] stick ▸ **bâtonnet glacé** ice pop ▸ **bâtonnets de poisson pané** fish fingers 🇬🇧, fish sticks 🇺🇸.

bâtonnier, ère [batɔnje, ɛʀ] nm, f ≃ President of the Bar.

batracien [batʀasjɛ̃] nm batrachian.

battage [bataʒ] nm *fam* ▸ **battage (publicitaire)** hype, ballyhoo 🇺🇸 / **faire du battage autour d'un livre** to hype ou 🇺🇸 to ballyhoo a book ▸ **battage médiatique** media hype.

battant, e [batã, ãt] nm, f fighter *fig* ▸ **c'est une battante !** she's a real fighter ! ⬦ **battant** nm [vantail, volet] flap / **le battant droit était ouvert** the right half (of the double door) was open.

batte [bat] nf SPORT bat ▸ **batte de base-ball / cricket** baseball / cricket bat.

battement [batmã] nm **1.** [mouvement - des ailes] flapping ; [- des paupières] flutter **2.** SPORT ▸ **battement des jambes** leg movement **3.** [rythme du cœur, du pouls] beating, throbbing, beat **4.** [pause] break / **un battement de 10 minutes** a 10-minute break ; [attente] wait / **j'ai une heure de battement entre la réunion et le déjeuner** I have an hour between the meeting and lunch.

batterie [batʀi] nf **1.** AUTO, ÉLECTR & PHYS battery **2.** MUS [en jazz, rock, pop] drums, drum kit ; [en musique classique] percussion instruments ; [roulement] drum roll / **Harvey Barton à la batterie** Harvey Barton on drums **3.** [série] battery ▸ **batterie de tests / mesures** battery of tests / of measures ▸ **batterie de cuisine** *pr* set of kitchen utensils **4.** AGR ▸ **poulet de batterie** battery hen.

batteur [batœʀ] nm **1.** MUS drummer **2.** [appareil] ▸ **batteur (à œufs)** egg beater ou whisk.

battre [83] [batʀ] ⬦ vt **1.** [brutaliser - animal] to beat ; [- personne] to batter ▸ **battre qqn à mort** to batter sb to

death **2.** [vaincre - adversaire] to beat, to defeat ▸ **battre qqn aux échecs** to defeat ou to beat sb at chess ▸ **se tenir pour** ou **s'avouer battu** to admit defeat ▸ **battre qqn à plate couture** ou **plates coutures** to beat sb hollow **3.** [surpasser - record] to beat ▸ **battre tous les records** *pr & fig* to set a new record / **j'ai battu tous les records de vitesse pour venir ici** I must have broken the record getting here **4.** [frapper - tapis, or] to beat (out) ; [- blé, grain] to thresh ▸ **battre qqch à froid** to cold-hammer sthg ▸ **il faut battre le fer quand il est chaud** *prov* strike while the iron is hot *prov* **5.** [remuer - beurre] to churn ; [- blanc d'œuf] to beat ou to whip (up), to whisk **6.** JEUX ▸ **battre les cartes** to shuffle the cards ou pack **7.** MUS [mesure] to beat (out) ; MIL & MUS [tambour] to beat (out) ▸ **battre le rappel** to drum up troops ▸ **mon cœur bat la chamade** my heart's racing **8.** EXPR ▸ **battre son plein** [fête] to be in full swing. ⬦ vi **1.** [cœur, pouls] to beat, to throb ; [pluie] to lash, to beat down ; [porte] to rattle, to bang ; [store] to flap / **l'émotion faisait battre mon cœur** my heart was beating ou racing with emotion **2.** EXPR ▸ **battre en retraite a)** *pr* to retreat **b)** *fig* to beat a retreat. ⬦ **battre de** v + prép ▸ **l'oiseau bat des ailes a)** *pr* [lentement] the bird flaps its wings **b)** [rapidement] the bird flutters its wings ▸ **battre de l'aile** to be in a bad way. ⬦ **se battre** ⬥ vp (*emploi réciproque*) to fight, to fight (with) one another ▸ **se battre en duel** to fight (each other in) a duel / **ne vous battez pas, il y en a pour tout le monde** don't get excited, there's enough for everyone / **surtout ne vous battez pas pour m'aider !** *iron* don't all rush to help me ! ⬥ vpi **1.** [lutter] to fight ▸ **se battre avec / contre qqn** to fight with / against sb ▸ **se battre contre des moulins à vent** to tilt at windmills **2.** *fig* to fight, to struggle ▸ **nous nous battons pour la paix / contre l'injustice** we're fighting for peace / against injustice. ⬥ vpt [frapper] ▸ **se battre les flancs** to struggle pointlessly.

battu¹, e [baty] adj [maltraité] battered.

battue² [baty] nf **1.** CHASSE battue, beat **2.** [recherche] search (*through an area*).

baudruche [bodʀyʃ] nf [peau] goldbeater's skin.

baume [bom] nm balsam, balm ▸ **baume pour les lèvres** lip balm ▸ **mettre un peu de baume au cœur de qqn** *fig* to soothe sb's aching heart.

baux [bo] pl COMM ⟶ **bail**.

bavard, e [bavaʀ, aʀd] ⬦ adj [personne] talkative ; [roman, émission] wordy, long-winded ▸ **il est bavard comme une pie** he's a real chatterbox. ⬦ nm, f ▸ **quelle bavarde celle-là !** she's a real chatterbox!

bavardage [bavaʀdaʒ] nm chatting, chattering. ⬦ **bavardages** nmpl [conversation] chatter (*U*) ; *péj* [racontars] gossip (*U*).

bavarder [3] [bavaʀde] vi **1.** [parler] to chat, to talk ▸ **bavarder avec qqn** to (have a) chat with sb **2.** *péj* [médire] to gossip.

bavarois, e [bavaʀwa, az] adj Bavarian. ⬦ **Bavarois, e** nm, f Bavarian. ⬦ **bavaroise** nf CULIN Bavarian cream.

bave [bav] nf [d'un bébé] dribble ; [d'un chien] slobber, slaver ; [d'un malade] foam, froth ; [d'un escargot] slime.

baver [3] [bave] vi **1.** [bébé] to dribble, to drool, to slobber ; [chien] to slaver, to slobber ; [malade] to foam ou to froth at the mouth **2.** [encre, stylo] to leak **3.** *fam* EXPR ▸ **en baver** [souffrir] to have a rough ou hard time of it / **on va t'en faire baver à l'armée** they'll make you sweat blood ou they'll put you through it in the army.

bavette [bavɛt] nf **1.** [bavoir] bib **2.** [viande] ▸ **bavette (d'aloyau)** top of sirloin.

Bavière [bavjɛʀ] npr f ▸ **(la) Bavière** Bavaria.

bavoir [bavwaʀ] nm bib.

bavure [bavyʀ] nf **1.** IMPR smudge, ink stain **2.** [erreur] flaw, mistake ▸ **un spectacle sans bavure** a faultless ou flawless show ▸ **bavure (policière)** police error.

bayer [3] [baje] vi ▸ **bayer aux corneilles a)** *pr* to stand gaping **b)** [être inactif] to stargaze.

bazar [bazaʀ] nm **1.** [souk] bazaar, bazar ; [magasin] general store, dime store **2.** *fam* [désordre] clutter, shambles *(sg)* / *quel bazar, cette chambre !* what a shambles ou mess this room is! / *il a mis un sacré bazar dans mes papiers* he made a hell of a mess of my papers **3.** *fam* [attirail] stuff, junk, clobber UK / *et tout le bazar !* and (all that) stuff!

bazarder [3] [bazaʀde] vt *fam* [jeter] to dump, to chuck (out).

BCBG (abr de **bon chic bon genre**) adj inv *term used to describe an upper-class lifestyle reflected especially in expensive but conservative clothes* / *elle est très BCBG* ≃ she's really Sloany UK *fam* / *il est très BCBG* ≃ he's a real preppie type US *fam*.

BCG® (abr de **(vaccin) bacille Calmette-Guérin**) nm BCG.

bcp abr écrite de **beaucoup**.

BD (abr de **bande dessinée**) nf = **bédé**.

🚩 **BD**

A common abbreviation for **bande dessinée** or comic book. Considered a serious and important art form in France, the comic book has become popular among teenagers and intellectuals alike. An annual festival of comic book art is held in Angoulême.

---

beach-volley [bitʃvɔlɛ] *(pl* **beach-volleys)** nm beach volleyball / *jouer au beach-volley* to play beach volleyball.

béant, e [beɑ̃, ɑ̃t] adj [gouffre] gaping, yawning ; [plaie] gaping, open.

béarnaise [beaʀnɛz] nf CULIN ▸ **(sauce à la) béarnaise** béarnaise sauce.

béat, e [bea, at] adj [heureux] blissfully happy ; *péj* [niais -air, sourire] vacuous ; [-optimisme] smug ; [-admiration] blind ▸ **être béat d'admiration** to be open-mouthed ou agape *litt* with admiration.

béatitude [beatityd] nf [bonheur] bliss, beatitude *litt*.

beau, belle [bo, bɛl] *(mpl* **beaux** [bo]*, fpl* **belles** [bɛl]*) (devant nm commençant par voyelle ou « h » muet* **bel** [bɛl]*)* adj

A. ESTHÉTIQUEMENT 1. [bien fait, joli -femme] beautiful, good-looking ; [-homme] good-looking, handsome ; [-enfant, physique, objet, décor] beautiful, lovely / *il est beau garçon* ou *fam gosse* he's good-looking, he's a good-looking guy / *ils forment un beau couple* they make a lovely couple ▸ **se faire beau /belle** to get dressed up, to do o.s. up ▸ **être beau comme un dieu** : *il est beau comme un dieu* he's extremely handsome ▸ **sois belle et tais-toi !** *fam* just concentrate on looking pretty! **2.** [attrayant pour l'oreille -chant, mélodie, voix] beautiful, lovely **3.** [remarquable, réussi -poème, texte] fine, beautiful ; [-chanson, film] beautiful, lovely ▸ **de beaux vêtements** fine clothes / *il y a eu quelques beaux échanges* there were a few good ou fine rallies / *nous avons fait un beau voyage* we had a wonderful trip **4.** MÉTÉOR fine, beautiful / *temps froid mais beau sur tout le pays* the whole

country will enjoy cold but sunny weather ▸ **du beau temps** nice ou good weather ▸ **les derniers beaux jours** the last days of summer.

B. MORALEMENT, SOCIALEMENT 1. [digne] noble, fine ; [convenable] nice / *ce n'est pas beau de mentir !* it's very naughty ou it's not nice to lie! **2.** [brillant intellectuellement] wonderful, fine / *c'est un beau sujet de thèse* it's a fine topic for a thesis.

C. NON NÉGLIGEABLE 1. [gros, important -gains, prime, somme] nice, handsome, tidy ▸ **donnez-moi un beau melon / poulet** give me a nice big melon / chicken / *il a un bel appétit* he has a good ou hearty appetite **2.** [en intensif] : *je me suis fait une belle bosse* I got a great big bump **3.** [agréable] good ▸ **présenter qqch sous un beau jour** to show sthg in a good light / *c'est trop beau pour être vrai* it's too good to be true ▸ **c'est beau l'amour !** love's a wonderful thing! **4.** [prospère] good / *tu as encore de belles années devant toi* you still have quite a few good years ahead of you ▸ **avoir une belle situation a)** [argent] to have a very well-paid job **b)** [prestige] to have a high-flying job **5.** [dans des appellations] : *mon beau monsieur, personne ne vous a rien demandé !* my friend, this is none of your business! **6.** [certain] ▸ **un beau jour / matin** one fine day / morning.

D. EMPLOIS IRONIQUES iron : *c'est du beau travail !* a fine mess this is! ▸ **en apprendre** ou **en entendre de belles sur qqn** : *j'en ai appris* ou *entendu de belles sur toi !* I heard some fine ou right things about you! ❖ **beau** ◆ adv **1.** MÉTÉOR ▸ **il fait beau** the weather's ou it's fine / *il n'a pas fait très beau l'été dernier* the weather wasn't very nice ou good last summer **2.** EXPR ▸ **avoir beau faire (qqch)** : *j'avais beau tirer, la porte ne s'ouvrait pas* however hard I pulled, the door wouldn't open / *j'ai eu beau le lui répéter plusieurs fois, il n'a toujours pas compris* I have told him and told him but he still hasn't understood. ◆ nm EXPR ▸ *nos relations sont au beau fixe* fam things between us are looking rosy / *il a le moral au beau fixe* fam he's in high spirits ▸ **faire le beau** [chien] to sit up and beg. ❖ **belle** nf **1.** fam [en appellatif] : *tu te trompes, ma belle !* you're quite wrong my dear! **2.** SPORT decider, deciding match ; JEUX decider, deciding game **3.** EXPR ▸ **(se) faire la belle** fam to do a runner UK, to cut and run US. ❖ **bel et bien** loc adv well and truly / *elle s'est bel et bien échappée* she got away and no mistake. ❖ **de plus belle** loc adv [aboyer, crier] louder than ever, even louder ; [frapper] harder than ever, even harder ; [taquiner, manger] more than ever, even more / *il s'est mis à travailler de plus belle* he went back to work with renewed energy.

beaucoup [boku] adv **1.** [modifiant un verbe] a lot, a great deal ; [dans des phrases interrogatives ou négatives] much, a lot, a great deal ▸ **il travaille beaucoup** he works a lot ou a great deal / *je ne l'ai pas beaucoup vu* I didn't see much of him ▸ **je vous remercie beaucoup** thank you very much (indeed) **2.** [modifiant un adverbe] much, a lot / *beaucoup trop fort* much ou far too loud ▸ **il parle beaucoup trop** he talks far too much ▸ **en faire beaucoup trop** to overdo it **3.** [de nombreuses personnes] many, a lot ; [de nombreuses choses] a lot / *il n'y en a pas beaucoup qui réussissent* not a lot of people ou not many succeed ▸ **être pour beaucoup dans qqch** : *il est pour beaucoup dans son succès* he played a large part in ou he had a great deal to do with her success ❖ *c'est beaucoup dire* that's a bit of an overstatement. ❖ **beaucoup de** loc dét [suivi d'un nom comptable] many, a lot of ; [suivi d'un nom non comptable] much, a lot of, a great deal of ▸ **beaucoup de monde** a lot of people ▸ **beaucoup d'entre nous** many ou a lot of us / *elle a beaucoup de goût* she has a lot of ou a great deal of taste / *il ne nous reste plus beaucoup de temps* we've not got much time left. ❖ **de beaucoup** loc adv

1. [avec un comparatif ou un superlatif] by far / *elle est de beaucoup la plus douée* she's the most talented by far, she is by far the most talented **2.** [avec un verbe] : *il te dépasse de beaucoup* he's far ou much taller than you.

 A lot, very much & a great deal

Pour modifier un verbe, beaucoup peut être rendu par a lot, very much ou a great deal. Attention toutefois à leur place dans la phrase.

•A lot et, en anglais britannique, a great deal, sont employés lorsqu'il s'agit de rendre le sens quantitatif, ou de fréquence, de beaucoup et se placent toujours en fin de proposition :
Il parle beaucoup de sa femme. *He talks about his wife a lot* ou *He talks about his wife a great deal.*
Ils se voient beaucoup. *They see each other a lot.*

Pas beaucoup peut se traduire par not... (very) much.
Elle ne sort pas beaucoup. *She doesn't go out (very) much* ou *a lot.*

•Very much est employé pour signifier l'idée qualitative contenue dans beaucoup et se place lui aussi toujours en fin de proposition :
Elle aime beaucoup voyager. *She likes travelling very much.*

D'autres traductions de beaucoup + verbe s'imposent dans certains cas :
Son livre m'a beaucoup intéressée. *I found his book very interesting.*
J'ai beaucoup apprécié son honnêteté. *I really appreciated his honesty.*

beauf [bof] nm *tfam* **1.** [beau-frère] brother-in-law **2.** *péj & fig* archetypal lower-middle-class Frenchman.

beau-fils [bofis] (*pl* **beaux-fils**) nm **1.** [gendre] son-in-law **2.** [fils du conjoint] stepson.

beau-frère [bofʀɛʀ] (*pl* **beaux-frères**) nm brother-in-law.

beau-père [bopɛʀ] (*pl* **beaux-pères**) nm **1.** [père du conjoint] father-in-law **2.** [époux de la mère] stepfather.

beauté [bote] nf [d'une femme, d'une statue] beauty, loveliness ; [d'un homme] handsomeness. **⬩ de toute beauté** loc adj magnificent, stunningly beautiful. **⬩ en beauté** loc adv **▸ finir en beauté** to end with a flourish ou on a high note.

beaux-arts [bozaʀ] nmpl **1.** [genre] fine arts **2.** [école] **▸ les Beaux-Arts** French national art school.

beaux-parents [bopaʀɑ̃] nmpl father-in-law and mother-in-law, in-laws.

bébé [bebe] nm **1.** [nourrisson] baby / *attendre un bébé* to be expecting a baby **▸ faire le bébé** *péj* to act like ou to be being a baby **2.** ZOOL baby / *la lionne s'occupe de ses bébés* the lioness looks after her babies ou young ou cubs.

bébé-éprouvette [bebepʀuvɛt] (*pl* **bébés-éprouvette**) nm test-tube baby.

bébelle [bebɛl] nf ᴏᵁᴇʙᴇᴄ *fam* **1.** [jouet] toy **2.** [objet quelconque, gadget] thing.

bec [bɛk] nm **1.** ZOOL beak, bill / *donner des coups de bec à* to peck (at) **▸ avoir bec et ongles** to be well-equipped and ready to fight **2.** *fam* [bouche] mouth **▸ ça lui a bouclé** ou **cloué** ou **clos le bec** it shut him up, it reduced him to silence **▸ être** ou **rester le bec dans l'eau** to be left high

and dry **3.** [de casserole] lip ; [de bouilloire, de théière] spout **4.** MUS [de saxophone, de clarinette] mouthpiece **5.** ʙᴇʟɢ, ꜱᴜɪꜱꜱᴇ & ᴏᵁᴇʙᴇᴄ *fam* [baiser] kiss.

bécane [bekan] nf *fam* **1.** [moto, vélo] bike **2.** *hum* [machine] **▸ ma bécane a)** [ordinateur] my machine, my computer **b)** [machine à écrire] my old typewriter.

bécarre [bekaʀ] **◆** adj **▸ la bécarre** A natural. **◆** nm natural sign.

bécasse [bekas] nf **1.** [oiseau] woodcock **2.** *fam* [sotte] twit ᴜᴋ, silly goose.

bec-de-lièvre [bɛkdəljɛvʀ] (*pl* **becs-de-lièvre**) nm harelip.

béchamel [beʃamɛl] nf **▸ (sauce) béchamel** white sauce, béchamel.

bêche [bɛʃ] nf spade.

bêcher [4] [beʃe] vt [sol] to dig (over) ; [pommes de terre] to dig (up ou out).

bêcheur, euse [beʃœʀ, øz] nm, f *fam péj* [prétentieux] stuck-up person, snooty person.

bécoter [3] [bekɔte] vt *fam* to kiss. **⬩ se bécoter** vp *(emploi réciproque) fam* to smooch, to kiss (and cuddle).

becquée [beke] nf beakful **▸ donner la becquée** [oiseau] to feed.

becqueter [27] [bɛkte] vt *tfam* [manger] to eat.

✐ In reformed spelling (see p. 16-18), this verb is conjugated like *acheter* : *elle becquètera, il becquèterait.*

bedaine [bədɛn] nf paunch.

bédé [bede] nf *fam* **▸ la bédé** comic strips **▸ une bédé** a comic strip.

bedonnant, e [bədɔnɑ̃, ɑ̃t] adj *fam* paunchy.

bée [be] adj f **▸ être bouche bée devant qqn** to gape at sb / *j'en suis restée bouche bée* I was flabbergasted.

bégaiement [begɛmɑ̃] nm [trouble de la parole] stammer, stutter **▸ bégaiements a)** [d'un bègue] stammering **b)** [d'embarras, d'émotion] faltering.

bégayer [11] [begeje] vi [hésiter - bègue] to stammer, to stutter ; [- ivrogne] to slur (one's speech).

bégonia [begɔnja] nm begonia.

bègue [bɛg] adj stammering, stuttering **▸ être bègue** to (have a) stammer.

bégueule [begœl] *fam* adj prudish, squeamish.

béguin [begɛ̃] nm *fam* [attirance] **▸ avoir le béguin pour qqn** to have a crush on sb.

beige [bɛʒ] adj & nm beige.

beigne [bɛɲ] **◆** nf *tfam* [gifle] slap, clout **▸ filer une beigne à qqn** to slap sb, to give sb a smack. **◆** nm ᴏᵁᴇʙᴇᴄ [beignet] doughnut ᴜᴋ, donut ᴜꜱ.

beignet [bɛɲɛ] nm [gén] fritter ; [au sucre, à la confiture] doughnut **▸ beignet aux pommes** apple doughnut **▸ beignet de crevettes a)** [chips] prawn cracker **b)** [avec de la pâte] prawn fritter.

bel [bɛl] adj ⟶ beau.

Bélarus [belaʀys] npr **▸ la république de Bélarus** the Republic of Belarus.

bêler [4] [bele] vi to bleat.

belette [bəlɛt] nf weasel.

belge [bɛlʒ] adj Belgian. **⬩ Belge** nmf Belgian.

belgicisme [bɛlʒisism] nm [mot] Belgian-French word ; [tournure] Belgian-French expression.

Belgique [bɛlʒik] npr f **▸ la Belgique** Belgium.

Belgrade [bɛlgʀad] npr Belgrade.

bélier [belje] nm ZOOL ram.

Bélier [belje] npr m ASTROL Aries **▸ je suis Bélier** I'm Aries ou an Arian.

Belize [beliz] npr m ▶ **le Belize** Belize ▶ **au Belize** in Belize.

belle [bɛl] f ⟶ **beau**.

belle-famille [bɛlfamij] (pl **belles-familles**) nf ▶ **sa belle-famille a)** [de l'époux] her husband's family, her in-laws **b)** [de l'épouse] his wife's family, her in-laws.

belle-fille [bɛlfij] (pl **belles-filles**) nf **1.** [bru] daughter-in-law **2.** [fille du conjoint] stepdaughter.

belle-mère [bɛlmɛʀ] (pl **belles-mères**) nf **1.** [mère du conjoint] mother-in-law **2.** [épouse du père] stepmother.

belle-sœur [bɛlsœʀ] (pl **belles-sœurs**) nf sister-in-law.

belligérant, e [beliʒeʀɑ̃, ɑ̃t] ◆ adj belligerent, warring. ◆ nm, f belligerent.

belliqueux, euse [belikø, øz] adj [peuple] warlike ; [ton, discours] aggressive, belligerent ; [enfant, humeur] bellicose sout, quarrelsome.

belote [bəlɔt] nf belote.

béluga, bélouga [beluga] nm **1.** ZOOL white ou beluga whale **2.** [caviar] beluga (caviar).

belvédère [bɛlvedɛʀ] nm [pavillon] belvedere, gazebo ; [terrasse] panoramic viewpoint.

bémol [bemɔl] ◆ adj ▶ **mi bémol** E flat. ◆ nm flat ▶ **mettre un bémol a)** [parler moins fort] to pipe down **b)** [modérer ses propos] to climb down.

ben [bɛ̃] adv fam [pour renforcer] : ben quoi ? so what? ▶ **ben non** well, no ▶ **ben voyons (donc)** ! what next!

bénédictin, e [benediktɛ̃, in] adj & nm, f Benedictine.

bénédiction [benediksjɔ̃] nf **1.** RELIG benediction, blessing / la bénédiction nuptiale leur sera donnée à... the marriage ceremony will take place ou the marriage will be solemnized sout at... **2.** [accord] blessing **3.** [aubaine] blessing, godsend.

bénef [benɛf] nm tfam profit ▶ **c'est tout bénef pour elle** she gets quite a deal out of this.

bénéfice [benefis] nm **1.** FIN profit ▶ **c'est tout bénéfice** fam : à ce prix-là, c'est tout bénéfice at that price, you make a 100% profit on it **2.** [avantage] benefit, advantage ▶ **le bénéfice du doute** : laisser à qqn le bénéfice du doute to give sb the benefit of the doubt. ◆ **au bénéfice de** loc prép [en faveur de] for (the benefit of).

bénéficiaire [benefisjɛʀ] ◆ adj [opération] profitable, profit-making ; [marge] profit (modif). ◆ nmf [d'une mesure] beneficiary ; [d'un mandat, d'un chèque] payee, recipient / qui en seront les principaux bénéficiaires ? who will benefit by it most?

bénéficier [9] [benefisje] ◆ **bénéficier de** v + prép **1.** [avoir] to have, to enjoy / bénéficier de conditions idéales / d'avantages sociaux to enjoy ideal conditions / welfare benefits ; DR ▶ **bénéficier de circonstances atténuantes** to have the benefit of ou to be granted extenuating circumstances **2.** [profiter de] to benefit by ou from ▶ **bénéficier d'une forte remise** to get a big reduction ▶ **faire bénéficier qqn de ses connaissances** to allow sb to benefit by ou to give sb the benefit of one's knowledge. ◆ **bénéficier à** v + prép to benefit / à qui vont bénéficier ces mesures ? who are these measures going to benefit?, who is going to benefit from these measures?

bénéfique [benefik] adj [avantageux] beneficial, advantageous.

Benelux [benelyks] npr m ▶ **le Benelux** Benelux.

benêt [bənɛ] péj nm simpleton / son grand benêt de fils his great fool of a son.

bénévolat [benevɔla] nm [travail] voluntary help ou work ; [système] system of voluntary work ▶ **faire du bénévolat** to do voluntary work.

bénévole [benevɔl] ◆ adj [aide, conseil] voluntary, free ; [association] voluntary ; [médecin] volunteer (modif). ◆ nmf volunteer, voluntary worker.

bénévolement [benevɔlmɑ̃] adv voluntarily ▶ **travailler bénévolement pour qqn** to do voluntary work for sb.

Bengale [bɛ̃gal] npr m ▶ **le Bengale** Bengal ▶ **au Bengale** in Bengal.

bénin, igne [benɛ̃, iɲ] adj **1.** MÉD [maladie] mild ; [tumeur] non-malignant, benign **2.** [accident] slight, minor.

Bénin [benɛ̃] npr m ▶ **le Bénin** Benin ▶ **au Bénin** in Benin.

béninois, e [beninwa, az] adj Beninese. **Béninois, e** nm, f Beninese.

bénir [32] [beniʀ] vt **1.** RELIG [fidèles] to bless, to give one's blessing to ; [eau, pain] to consecrate ; [union] to solemnize **2.** [remercier] : je bénis le passant qui m'a sauvé la vie I'll be eternally thankful to the passer-by who saved my life / elle bénit le ciel de lui avoir donné un fils she thanked God for giving her a son.

bénit, e [beni, it] adj consecrated, blessed.

bénitier [benitje] nm stoup, font.

benjamin, e [bɛ̃ʒamɛ̃, in] nm, f **1.** [de famille] youngest child ; [de groupe] youngest member **2.** SPORT junior.

benne [bɛn] nf **1.** MIN tub, tram ▶ **benne basculante** tipper (truck) **2.** [à ordures] skip 🇬🇧, Dumpster® 🇺🇸.

béotien, enne [beɔsjɛ̃, ɛn] nm, f péj [rustre] philistine.

BEP (abr de brevet d'études professionnelles) nm vocational diploma (taken after two years of study at a "lycée professionnel").

BEPC (abr de brevet d'études du premier cycle) nm former name of French school certificate taken after four years of secondary education; now called **diplôme national du brevet**.

béquille [bekij] nf **1.** [canne] crutch ▶ **marcher avec des béquilles** to walk on ou with crutches **2.** [de moto] stand.

berbère [bɛʀbɛʀ] adj Berber. **Berbère** nmf Berber. **berbère** nm LING Berber.

bercail [bɛʀkaj] nm sheepfold ▶ **rentrer** ou **revenir au bercail a)** [à la maison] to get back home **b)** RELIG to return to the fold.

berceau, x [bɛʀso] nm [lit] cradle.

bercer [16] [bɛʀse] vt [bébé] to rock, to cradle / les chansons qui ont bercé mon enfance the songs I was brought up on. **se bercer de** vp + prép ▶ **se bercer d'illusions** to delude o.s. with ou to nurse ou to entertain illusions.

berceuse [bɛʀsøz] nf [chanson d'enfant] lullaby ; MUS berceuse.

béret [beʀɛ] nm beret.

Berezina [beʀezina] npr f ▶ **c'était la Berezina** fig it was an absolute disaster.

bergamote [bɛʀgamɔt] nf bergamot orange. **à la bergamote** loc adj [savon] bergamot-scented ; [thé] with bergamot, bergamot-flavoured.

berge [bɛʀʒ] nf **1.** GÉOGR [rive] bank ▶ **route** ou **voie sur berge** [dans une grande ville] embankment road **2.** tfam [an] year / à 25 berges, elle a monté sa boîte when she was 25, she set up her own business.

berger, ère [bɛʀʒe, ɛʀ] nm, f [pâtre] shepherd (shepherdess). **berger** nm ZOOL sheepdog ▶ **berger (allemand)** Alsatian, German shepherd.

bergerie [bɛʀʒəʀi] nf AGR sheepfold.

bergeronnette [bɛʀʒəʀɔnɛt] nf wagtail.

berk [bɛʀk] interj fam ugh, yuk.

Berlin [bɛʀlɛ̃] npr Berlin.

berline [bɛʀlin] nf AUTO saloon car 🇬🇧, sedan 🇺🇸.

berlingot [bɛʀlɛ̃go] nm **1.** [bonbon] ≃ boiled sweet 🇬🇧 ; ≃ hard candy 🇺🇸 **2.** [emballage] carton.

berlue [bɛʀly] nf ▶ **avoir la berlue** to be seeing things.

bermuda [bɛʀmyda] nm ▶ **un bermuda** (a pair of) Bermuda shorts, Bermudas.

Bermudes [bɛʀmyd] npr fpl ▶ **les Bermudes** Bermuda ▶ **aux Bermudes** in Bermuda.

berne [bɛʀn] ❖ **en berne** loc adv at half-mast.

Berne [bɛʀn] npr Bern.

berner [3] [bɛʀne] vt [tromper] to fool, to dupe, to hoax.

berzingue [bɛʀzɛ̃g] ❖ **à tout(e) berzingue** loc adv fam at full speed, double quick.

besace [bəzas] nf [sac] beggar's bag.

besogne [bəzɔɲ] nf [travail] task, job, work / *se mettre à la besogne* to get down to work.

besoin [bəzwɛ̃] nm **1.** [nécessité] need ▶ **nos besoins en pétrole / ingénieurs** our oil / engineering requirements ▶ **avoir** ou **sentir** ou **ressentir le besoin de faire qqch** to feel the need to do sthg ▶ **si besoin est** if necessary, if needs be **2.** [pauvreté] need ▶ **dans le besoin** in need **3.** EXPR avoir besoin de qqch to need sthg ▶ **avoir besoin de faire qqch** to need to do sthg / *je n'ai pas besoin de vous rappeler que...* I don't need to ou I needn't remind you that... ▶ **avoir bien** ou **grand besoin de qqch** to be in dire need of sthg, to need sthg badly / *un pneu crevé ! on en avait bien besoin* ou *on avait bien besoin de ça !* iron a flat tyre, that's all we needed! ❖ **au besoin** loc adv if necessary, if needs ou need be. ❖ **pour les besoins de** loc prép : *pour les besoins de la cause* for the purpose in hand.

bestial, e, aux [bɛstjal, o] adj [instinct, acte] bestial, brutish.

bestiaux [bɛstjo] nmpl [d'une exploitation] livestock ; [bovidés] cattle.

bestiole [bɛstjɔl] nf [insecte] creature hum.

best of [bɛstɔf] nm inv : *un best of de Serge Gainsbourg* a selection of Serge Gainsbourg's most popular songs / *le best of du championnat* selected highlights from the championship.

best-seller (*pl* best-sellers), **bestseller*** [bɛst-selœʀ] nm best-seller.

bétail [betaj] nm ▶ **le bétail** a) [gén] livestock b) [bovins] cattle ▶ **gros bétail** (big) cattle.

bête [bɛt] ❖ adj **1.** [peu intelligent] stupid, idiotic / *il est plus bête que méchant* he's not wicked, just (plain) stupid / *mais non, cela ne me dérange pas, ce que tu peux être bête !* of course you're not putting me out, how silly (can you be ou of you)! / *mais oui, je me souviens maintenant, suis-je bête !* ah, now I remember, how stupid of me! / *pas si bête, j'ai pris mes précautions* I took some precautions, since I'm not a complete idiot ▶ **être bête comme ses pieds** ou **comme une cruche** ou **comme une oie** ou **à manger du foin** to be as thick as two short planks 🇬🇧, to be as dumb as the day is long 🇺🇸 **2.** [regrettable] : *c'est bête de ne pas y avoir pensé* it's silly ou stupid not to have thought of it / *ce serait trop bête de laisser passer l'occasion* it would be a pity not to take advantage of the occasion **3.** [simple] : *c'est tout bête, il suffisait d'y penser !* it's so simple, we should have thought of it before! / *ce n'est pas bête, ton idée !* that's quite a good idea you've got there! ▶ **c'est bête comme tout** ou **chou** fam it's simplicity itself ou easy as pie ou easy as falling off a log. ❖ nf **1.** [animal - gén] animal ; [- effrayant] beast ▶ **bête féroce** ou **sauvage** wild animal ou beast ▶ **bête de charge** beast of burden ▶ **bête à bon Dieu** ladybird 🇬🇧, ladybug 🇺🇸 **2.** [personne] ▶ **c'est une bonne** ou **brave bête a)** fam [généreux] he's a good sort **b)** [dupe] he's a

bit of a sucker ▶ **bête à concours** fam swot 🇬🇧 ou grind 🇺🇸 (who does well at competitive exams) / *ils nous regardaient comme des bêtes curieuses* they were staring at us as if we'd come from Mars ▶ **sa / ma bête noire** his / my bugbear / *le latin, c'était ma bête noire* Latin was my pet hate ▶ **bête de scène / télévision** great live / television performer ▶ **travailler comme une bête** to work like a slave ou dog / *s'éclater comme une bête* fam to have a great time.

bêtement [bɛtmã] adv **1.** [stupidement] foolishly, stupidly, idiotically **2.** [simplement] ▶ **tout bêtement** purely and simply, quite simply.

bêtise [betiz] nf **1.** [stupidité] idiocy, foolishness, stupidity / *j'ai eu la bêtise de ne pas vérifier* I was foolish enough not to check **2.** [remarque] silly ou stupid remark ▶ **dire une bêtise** to say something stupid ▶ **dire des bêtises** to talk nonsense **3.** [action] stupid thing, piece of foolishness ou idiocy / *ne recommencez pas vos bêtises* don't start your stupid tricks again ▶ **faire une bêtise** to do something silly ou stupid **4.** [vétille] trifle / *on se dispute toujours pour des bêtises* we're always arguing over trifles ou having petty squabbles **5.** CULIN ▶ **bêtises de Cambrai** humbug 🇬🇧, (hard) mint candy 🇺🇸.

bêtisier [betizje] nm collection of howlers.

béton [betɔ̃] nm **1.** CONSTR concrete ▶ **béton armé / précontraint** reinforced / prestressed concrete **2.** EXPR laisse béton ! fam forget it!, let it drop! ❖ **en béton** loc adj **1.** CONSTR concrete (*modif*) **2.** fam [résistant - estomac] cast-iron ; [- défense, garantie] watertight, surefire.

bétonner [3] [betɔne] ❖ vt **1.** CONSTR to concrete **2.** [surcharger de bâtiments] to overdevelop / *la côte est complètement bétonnée* the coast is overdeveloped. ❖ vi FOOT to pack the defence, to play defensively.

bétonnière [betɔnjɛʀ] nf cement mixer.

bette [bɛt] nf (Swiss) chard.

betterave [bɛtʀav] nf ▶ **betterave fourragère** mangelwurzel ▶ **betterave rouge** beetroot 🇬🇧, red beet 🇺🇸.

beugler [5] [bøgle] vi **1.** [crier - vache] to moo, to low ; [- taureau] to bellow ; [- chanteur, ivrogne] to bellow, to bawl **2.** [être bruyant - radio] to blare.

beur [bœʀ] adj born in France of North African parents. ❖ **Beur** nmf person born in France of North African immigrant parents.

beurre [bœʀ] nm **1.** [de laiterie] butter ▶ **au beurre** (all) butter (*modif*) ▶ **beurre demi-sel** slightly salted butter ▶ **beurre doux** unsalted butter ▶ **beurre d'érable** 🇶🇧 maple butter ▶ **faire son beurre** fam to make money hand over fist ▶ **ça met du beurre dans les épinards** fam it's a nice little earner ▶ **vouloir le beurre et l'argent du beurre** to want to have one's cake and eat it (too) **2.** [pâte] ▶ **beurre d'arachide** ou **de cacahuètes** peanut butter ▶ **beurre de cacao** ou **de muscade** cocoa / nutmeg butter ▶ **beurre d'anchois** anchovy paste.

beurré, e [bœʀe] adj **1.** CULIN ▶ **tartine beurrée** piece of bread and butter **2.** tfam [ivre] plastered, pissed 🇬🇧. ❖ **beurrée** nf 🇶🇧 [tartine] buttered bread ; [substance] bread and butter (and jam) spread ; ▶ **une beurrée** fam [fortune] a fortune.

beurrer [5] [bœʀe] vt [tartine, moule] to butter. ❖ **se beurrer** vpi tfam to get plastered, to get pissed 🇬🇧, to get sloshed.

beurrier [bœʀje] nm [récipient] butter dish.

beuverie [bœvʀi] nf fam drinking binge, bender.

bévue [bevy] nf [gaffe] blunder, gaffe ▶ **commettre une bévue** to blunder.

Beyrouth [beʀut] npr Beirut, Beyrouth.

bi [bi] adj inv [bisexuel] bi.

biais [bjɛ] nm **1.** COUT [bande] piece (of material) cut on the bias ; [sens] bias / *travailler dans le biais* to cut on the bias ou cross **2.** [moyen] way ▶ **par le biais de** through, via, by means of **3.** [aspect] angle / *je ne sais pas par quel biais le prendre* I don't know how ou from what angle to approach him. ❖ **de biais** loc adv [aborder] indirectly, tangentially *sout.* ❖ **en biais** loc adv sideways, slantwise, at an angle / *traverser la rue en biais* to cross the street diagonally.

biaisé, e [bjeze] adj [statistiques, raisonnement] distorted.

biaiser [4] [bjeze] vi to prevaricate, to equivocate / *il va falloir biaiser pour avoir des places pour l'opéra* we'll have to be a bit clever to get seats for the opera.

biathlon [biatlɔ̃] nm biathlon.

bibande [bibɑ̃d] adj bi-band, dual-band.

bibelot [biblo] nm [précieux] curio, bibelot ; [sans valeur] trinket, knick-knack.

biberon [bibʀɔ̃] nm feeding UK ou baby US bottle ▶ **donner le biberon à un bébé / agneau** to bottle-feed a baby / lamb.

bibit(t)e [bibit] nf Québec *fam* insect, bug.

bible [bibl] nf **1.** RELIG ▶ **la Bible** the Bible **2.** [référence] bible.

bibliobus [biblijɔbys] nm mobile library UK, bookmobile US.

bibliographie [biblijɔgʀafi] nf bibliography.

bibliophile [biblijɔfil] nmf book-lover, bibliophile.

bibliothécaire [biblijɔtekeʀ] nmf librarian.

bibliothèque [biblijɔtɛk] nf [lieu] library ; [meuble] book-case ; [collection] collection ▶ **la Bibliothèque nationale de France (BNF)** *the French national library.*

▶ **La Bibliothèque nationale de France**

The **BNF** is a large copyright deposit library comparable to the British Library and the Library of Congress. The original building on the rue de Richelieu in central Paris houses the library's collection of manuscripts, engravings, coins, medals and maps; the main bulk of the book collection is housed in the Bibliothèque François-Mitterrand, a modern complex on the banks of the Seine whose four towers are designed to look like open books.

biblique [biblik] adj biblical.

Bic® [bik] nm ball (point) pen ; ≃ Biro® UK ; ≃ Bic® US.

bicarbonate [bikaʀbɔnat] nm bicarbonate ▶ **bicarbonate de soude** bicarbonate of soda.

bicentenaire [bisɑ̃tnɛʀ] adj & nm bicentenary UK, bicentennial US.

biceps [bisɛps] nm biceps.

biche [biʃ] nf **1.** ZOOL doe, hind **2.** [en appellatif] ▶ **ma biche** *fam* my darling.

bichonner [3] [biʃɔne] vt [choyer] to pamper, to pet, to mollycoddle *péj.* ❖ **se bichonner** vp *(emploi réfléchi)* [se pomponner] to spruce o.s. up.

bicoque [bikɔk] nf shack.

bicorne [bikɔʀn] nm cocked ou two-pointed hat.

bicross [bikʀɔs] nm [vélo] mountain bike ; [sport] mountain biking.

bicyclette [bisiklɛt] nf **1.** [engin] bicycle ▶ **faire de la bicyclette** to ride a bicycle **2.** LOISIRS & SPORT ▶ **la bicyclette** cycling.

bidasse [bidas] nm *fam* [soldat] private, squaddie UK, grunt US.

bide [bid] nm *fam* **1.** [ventre] belly, gut **2.** [échec] flop, washout.

bidet [bidɛ] nm bidet.

bidoche [bidɔʃ] nf *tfam* meat.

bidon [bidɔ̃] ◆ adj inv *fam* [histoire, excuse] phoney ; [élections] rigged. ◆ nm **1.** [récipient] can, tin ; MIL water bottle, canteen **2.** *fam* [ventre] belly, gut **3.** *tfam* [mensonge] : *c'est du bidon tout ça* that's all baloney.

bidonner [3] [bidɔne] ❖ **se bidonner** vpi *fam* to split one's sides laughing, to laugh one's head off.

bidonville [bidɔ̃vil] nm shantytown.

bidouiller [3] [biduje] vt *fam* [serrure, logiciel] to fiddle (about) with, to tamper with.

bidule [bidyl] nm *fam* [objet] thingamajig, thingummy UK, contraption.

biélorusse [bjelɔʀys] adj Belorussian, Byelorussian. ❖ **Biélorusse** nmf Belorussian, Byelorussian.

Biélorussie [bjelɔʀysi] npr f ▶ **la Biélorussie** Belarussia, Byelorussia.

bien [bjɛ̃] ◆ adv **1.** [de façon satisfaisante] well ▶ **tout allait bien** everything was going well ou fine ▶ **il cuisine bien** he's a good cook ▶ **la pièce finit bien** the play has a happy ending ▶ **faire bien** to look good ▶ **bien prendre qqch** to take sthg well ▶ **bien s'y prendre** : *il s'y est bien pris* he tackled it well ▶ **vivre bien qqch** to have a positive experience of sthg ▶ **tiens-toi bien !** a) [à la rambarde] hold on tight! b) [sur la chaise] sit properly! c) [à table] behave yourself! ▶ **tu tombes bien !** you've come at (just) the right time! **2.** [du point de vue de la santé] ▶ **aller** ou **se porter bien** to feel well ou fine **3.** [conformément à la raison, à la loi, à la morale] well, decently ▶ **tu as bien fait** you did the right thing, you did right / *tu fais bien de me le rappeler* thank you for reminding me, it's a good thing you reminded me (of it) / *pour bien faire, nous devrions partir avant 9 h* ideally, we should leave before 9 **4.** [sans malentendu] rightly, correctly / *ai-je bien entendu ce que tu viens de dire* ? did I hear you right? **5.** [avec soin] ▶ **écoute-moi bien** listen (to me) carefully ▶ **as-tu bien vérifié ?** did you check properly? ▶ **soigne-toi bien** take good care of yourself **6.** *(suivi d'un adjectif)* [très] really, very / *c'est bien agréable* it's really ou very nice ▶ *bois un thé bien chaud* have a nice hot cup of tea ; *(suivi d'un adverbe)* : *c'était il y a bien longtemps* that was a very long time ago ▶ **embrasse-le bien fort** give him a big hug ▶ **bien souvent** (very) often ▶ **bien avant / après** well before / after **7.** *(suivi d'un verbe)* [beaucoup] ▶ **on a bien ri** we had a good laugh, we laughed a lot **8.** [véritablement] ▶ **j'ai bien cru que...** I really thought that... / *il a bien failli se noyer* he very nearly drowned **9.** [pour renforcer, insister] *où peut-il être ?* where on earth is he? / *je sais bien que tu dis la vérité* I know very well that you're telling the truth ▶ **c'est bien ça** that's it ou right ▶ **c'est bien ce que je disais / pensais** that's just what I was saying / thinking ▶ **tu penses bien !** : *il ne m'aidera pas, tu penses bien !* he won't help me, you can be sure of that! ▶ **être bien de qqn** : *c'est bien de lui, ça !* that's typical of him!, that's just like him! **10.** [volontiers] ▶ **j'irais bien avec toi** I'd really like to go with you / *je boirais bien quelque chose* I could do with ou I wouldn't mind a drink **11.** [exprimant la supposition, l'éventualité] ▶ **tu verras bien** you'll see ▶ **ça se pourrait bien** it's perfectly possible **12.** [pourtant] : *mais il fallait bien le lui dire !* but he had to be told (all the same)! **13.** [beaucoup] ▶ **bien de, bien des** [suivi d'un nom] quite a lot of / *elle a bien du courage !* isn't she brave!, she's got a great deal of courage! ▶ **bien des fois…** more than once… **14.** [dans la correspondance] ▶ **bien à vous** yours. ◆ adj inv **1.** [qui donne satisfaction] good / *c'est bien de s'amuser mais il faut aussi travailler* it's all right to have fun but you have to work too / *qu'est-ce qu'il est bien dans son dernier film !* fam he's great ou really good in his new film! ; ÉDUC [sur un devoir] good **2.** [esthétique - personne] good-looking, attractive ; [-chose] nice, lovely ▶ **tu es très bien en jupe a)** [cela te sied] you look very nice in a skirt **b)** [c'est acceptable pour l'occasion] a skirt is perfectly all right **3.** [convenable - personne] decent, nice / *ce n'est pas bien de tirer la langue* it's naughty ou it's not nice to stick out your tongue / *ce n'est pas bien de tricher* you shouldn't cheat **4.** [en forme] well ▶ **vous ne vous sentez pas bien ?** aren't you feeling well? / *il n'est pas bien, celui-là !* fam he's got a problem, he has! ▶ **me / te / nous voilà bien !** NOW I'm / you're / we're in a fine mess! **5.** [à l'aise] ▶ **on est bien ici** it's nice here / *je suis bien avec toi* I like being with you **6.** [en bons termes] ▶ **être bien avec qqn** to be well in with sb. ◆ nm **1.** PHILOS & RELIG ▶ **le bien** good ▶ **faire le bien** to do good **2.** [ce qui est agréable, avantageux] : *c'est pour ton bien que je dis ça* I'm saying this for your own good ou benefit ▶ **vouloir du bien à qqn** to wish sb well ▶ **dire / penser du bien de** to speak / to think well of / *on ne m'a dit que du bien de votre cuisine* I've heard the most flattering things about your cooking ▶ **faire du bien** : *cela fait du bien de se dégourdir les jambes* it's nice to be able to stretch your legs ▶ **faire du bien** ou **le plus grand bien à qqn** [médicament, repos] to do sb good, to benefit sb ▶ **grand bien te / lui fasse !** iron much good may it do you / him! **3.** [propriété personnelle] possession, (piece) ou item of property ; [argent] fortune / *mon bien t'appartient* what's mine is yours ▶ **tous mes biens** all my worldly goods, all I'm worth **4.** DR & ÉCON ▶ **bien de consommation courante** consumer good ▶ **biens d'équipement** capital equipment ou goods ▶ **biens sociaux** corporate assets. ◆ interj **1.** [indiquant une transition] OK, right (then) **2.** [marquant l'approbation] : *je n'irai pas ! — bien, n'en parlons plus !* I won't go! — very well ou all right (then), let's drop the subject! / *bien, bien, on y va* all right, all right ou OK, OK, let's go. ◆▶ **bien entendu** loc adv of course. ◆▶ **bien que** loc conj despite the fact that, although, though. ◆▶ **bien sûr** loc adv of course. ◆▶ **bien sûr que** loc conj of course / *c'est vrai ? — bien sûr que oui !* is it true? — of course it is!

📋 Notez que, à la différence de **bien**, **well** ne précède jamais le complément d'objet :
Il a bien traité ses enfants. *He treated his children well.*
J'ai essayé de bien décrire le paysage. *I tried to describe the landscape well.*

---

bien-aimé, e (*mpl* **bien-aimés**, *fpl* **bien-aimées**), **bienaimé*, e** [bjɛ̃neme] adj & nm, f beloved.

biénergie [bienɛʀʒi] nf [chauffage, chaudière] dual-energy.

bien-être, bienêtre* [bjɛ̃nɛtʀ] nm sg **1.** [aise] well-being **2.** [confort matériel] (material) well-being.

bienfaisance [bjɛ̃fəzɑ̃s] nf [charité] charity.
◆▶ **de bienfaisance** loc adj [bal] charity *(modif)* ; [association, œuvre] charity *(modif)*, charitable / *travailler pour les œuvres de bienfaisance* to do charity work.

bienfaisant, e [bjɛ̃fəzɑ̃, ɑ̃t] adj [bénéfique - effet, climat] beneficial, salutary sout.

bienfait [bjɛ̃fɛ] nm **1.** litt [acte de bonté] kindness **2.** [effet salutaire] benefit / *les bienfaits d'un séjour à la montagne* the benefits ou beneficial effects of a stay in the mountains.

bienfaiteur, trice [bjɛ̃fɛtœʀ, tʀis] nm, f benefactor (benefactress).

bien-fondé (*pl* **bien-fondés**), **bienfondé*** [bjɛ̃fɔ̃de] nm [d'une revendication] rightfulness ; [d'un argument] validity.

bienheureux, euse [bjɛ̃nøʀø, øz] adj **1.** RELIG blessed **2.** [heureux - personne, vie] happy, blissful ; [-hasard] fortunate, lucky.

biennale [bjenal] nf biennial arts festival.

bien-pensant, e (*mpl* **bien-pensants**, *fpl* **bien-pensantes**), **bienpensant*, e** [bjɛ̃pɑ̃sɑ̃, ɑ̃t] péj nm, f right-thinking ou right-minded person.

bienséance [bjɛ̃seɑ̃s] nf decorum, propriety.

bienséant, e [bjɛ̃seɑ̃, ɑ̃t] adj decorous, proper, becoming.

bientôt [bjɛ̃to] adv [prochainement] soon, before long ▶ **à (très) bientôt !** see you soon! / *il sera bientôt de retour* he'll soon be back, he'll be back before long ▶ **j'ai bientôt fini** I've almost finished ▶ **il est bientôt midi** it's nearly midday ▶ **c'est pour bientôt ? a)** will it be long? **b)** [naissance] is it ou is the baby due soon?

bienveillance [bjɛ̃vejɑ̃s] nf [qualité] benevolence, kindliness ▶ **parler de qqn avec bienveillance** to speak favourably of sb.

bienveillant, e [bjɛ̃vejɑ̃, ɑ̃t] adj [personne] benevolent, kindly ; [regard, sourire] kind, kindly, gentle.

bienvenu, e [bjɛ̃vny] ◆ adj opportune, apposite. ◆ nm, f : *être le bienvenu* to be welcome / *cet argent était vraiment le bienvenu* that money was most welcome. ◆▶ **bienvenue** ◆ nf welcome ▶ **souhaiter la bienvenue à qqn** to welcome sb / *bienvenue à toi, ami !* welcome to you, my friend! ◆ interj QUÉBEC you're welcome. ◆▶ **de bienvenue** loc adj [discours] welcoming ; [cadeau] welcome *(modif)*.

bière [bjɛʀ] nf **1.** [boisson] beer ▶ **bière blonde** lager ▶ **bière brune** brown ale UK, dark beer US **2.** [cercueil] coffin, casket US ▶ **mettre qqn en bière** to place sb in his / her coffin.

biffer [3] [bife] vt to cross ou to score ou to strike out (sép).

bifteck [biftɛk] nm **1.** [tranche] (piece of) steak ▶ **un bifteck haché** a beefburger **2.** [catégorie de viande] steak / *du bifteck haché* (best) mince UK, lean ground beef US.

bifurcation [bifyʀkasjɔ̃] nf [intersection] fork, junction, turn-off.

bifurquer [3] [bifyʀke] vi **1.** TRANSP [route] to fork, to branch off, to bifurcate sout ; [conducteur] to turn off / *on a alors bifurqué sur Lyon* we then turned off towards Lyon / *bifurquer à gauche* to take the left fork, to fork left, to turn left **2.** [changer] to branch off (into), to switch to.

bigarré, e [bigaʀe] adj [vêtement, fleur] variegated, multicoloured UK, multicolored US, parti-coloured UK, parti-colored US ; [foule] colourful UK, colorful US.

bigleux, euse [biglø, øz] fam adj short-sighted.

bigorneau, x [bigɔʀno] nm periwinkle, winkle.

bigot, e [bigo, ɔt] nm, f (religious) bigot.

bigoudi [bigudi] nm curler, roller / *(se) mettre des bigoudis* to put one's hair into curlers ou rollers.

bijou, x [biʒu] nm **1.** [parure] jewel ▶ **bijoux fantaisie** costume jewellery **2.** [fleuron] gem.

bijouterie [biʒutʀi] nf [magasin] jeweller's UK ou jeweler's US (shop), jeweler's (store) US.

bijoutier, ère [biʒutje, ɛʀ] nm, f jeweller UK, jeweler US.

Bikini® [bikini] nm bikini.

bilan [bilɑ̃] nm **1.** FIN balance sheet, statement of accounts **2.** [appréciation] appraisal, assessment / *le bilan du gouvernement* the government's track record / *quand on fait le bilan de sa vie* when one takes stock of ou when one assesses one's (lifetime) achievements / *quel est le bilan de ces discussions ?* what is the end result of these talks?, what have these talks amounted to? / *le bilan définitif fait état de 20 morts* the final death toll stands at 20 **3.** MÉD ▸ **bilan (de santé)** (medical) check-up / *se faire faire un bilan (de santé)* to have a check-up.

bile [bil] nf **1.** ANAT bile **2.** *fam* EXPR se faire de la bile to fret.

biler [3] [bile] ⬩ **se biler** vpi *fam* [s'inquiéter] to fret, to worry o.s. sick ▸ **te bile pas !** no problem!

bilingue [bilɛ̃g] adj bilingual.

bilinguisme [bilɛ̃gɥism] nm bilingualism.

billard [bijaʀ] nm **1.** [jeu] billiards *(sg)* / *faire un billard* to play a game of billiards ▸ **billard américain** pool **2.** [meuble] billiard 🇬🇧 ou pool 🇺🇸 table ▸ **billard électrique a)** [jeu] pinball **b)** [machine] pinball machine.

bille [bij] nf JEUX [de verre] marble ▸ **jouer aux billes** to play marbles ▸ **reprendre ses billes** to pull out *(of a deal)* ▸ **toucher sa bille en** *fam* to be bloody 🇬🇧 *tfam* ou darned 🇺🇸 good at ; [de billard] ball. ⬩ **à bille** loc adj [crayon, stylo] ball-point *(modif)* ; [déodorant] roll-on *(avant nom)*. ⬩ **bille en tête** loc adv straight, straightaway / *il est allé bille en tête se plaindre à la direction* he went straight to the management with a complaint.

billet [bije] nm **1.** LOISIRS & TRANSP ticket **2.** FIN ▸ **billet (de banque)** note 🇬🇧, banknote 🇬🇧, bill 🇺🇸, bankbill 🇺🇸 ▸ **le billet vert** the dollar, the US currency.

billetterie [bijetʀi] nf **1.** TRANSP & LOISIRS [opérations] ticket distribution ; [guichet] ticket office **2.** BANQUE [distributeur] cash dispenser.

bimensuel, elle [bimɑ̃sɥel] adj twice monthly, fortnightly 🇬🇧, semimonthly 🇺🇸.

bimestre [bimɛstʀ] nm two-month period.

bimode [bimɔd] adj dual-use.

bi-monétaire [bimɔnetɛʀ] adj [système] dual-currency.

bimoteur [bimɔtœʀ] ◆ adj m twin-engined. ◆ nm twin-engined plane ou aircraft.

binaire [binɛʀ] adj INFORM & MATH binary.

biner [3] [bine] vt to harrow, to hoe.

biniou [binju] nm (Breton) bagpipes *(pl)*.

binôme [binom] nm binomial ▸ **travailler en binôme** to work in pairs.

bin's [bins], **binz** [binz] nm *fam* **1.** [désordre] mess / *quel binz sur ton bureau !* your desk is a complete mess! **2.** [situation compliquée] hassle / *c'est tout un binz pour aller chez elle* it's such a hassle getting to her place.

bio [bjo] adj inv [nourriture, style de vie] organic.

biocarburant [bjokaʀbyʀɑ̃] nm biomass fuel.

biochimie [bjoʃimi] nf biochemistry.

bioclimatique [bjoklimatik] adj bioclimatic.

biocombustible [bjokɔ̃bystibl] nm biofuel.

biocompatible [bjokɔ̃patibl] adj biocompatible.

biodégradable [bjodegʀadabl] adj biodegradable.

biodiesel, biodiésel* [bjodjezɛl] nm biodiesel.

biodiversité [bjodivɛʀsite] nf biodiversity.

bioéthique [bjoetik] nf bioethics.

biographie [bjɔgʀafi] nf biography.

biographique [bjɔgʀafik] adj biographical.

bio-industrie [bjoɛ̃dystʀi] *(pl* **bio-industries)** nf bioindustry.

bio-informatique [bjoɛ̃fɔʀmatik] *(pl* **bio-informatiques)** nf biocomputing.

biologie [bjɔlɔʒi] nf biology.

biologique [bjɔlɔʒik] adj **1.** BIOL biological **2.** [naturel - produit, aliment] natural, organic.

biologiste [bjɔlɔʒist] nmf biologist.

biomédecine [bjomedsin] nf biomedicine.

biométrique [bjometʀik] adj biometric.

biopesticide [bjopɛstisid] nm biopesticide.

biopic [bjopik] nm biopic.

biopiratage [bjopiʀataʒ] nm = biopiraterie.

biopiraterie [bjopiʀatʀi] nf biopiracy.

biopsie [bjɔpsi] nf biopsy.

biorythme [bjɔʀitm] nm biorhythm.

biosciences [bjosjɑ̃s] nfpl bioscience.

biosphère [bjosfɛʀ] nf biosphere.

biotechnologie [bjotɛknɔlɔʒi], **biotechnique** [bjotɛknik] nf biotechnology.

biotechnologique [bjotɛknɔlɔʒik], **biotechnique** [bjotɛknik] adj biotechnological.

bioterrorisme [bjotɛʀɔʀism] nm bioterrorism.

bioterroriste [bjotɛʀɔʀist] adj & nmf bioterrorist.

bip [bip] nm **1.** [signal sonore] beep / *« parlez après le bip (sonore) »* "please speak after the beep ou tone" ▸ **émettre un bip** to bleep **2.** [appareil] pager, beeper.

bipède [biped] adj & nm biped.

biper [3] [bipe] vt to page.

bipeur [bipœʀ] nm beeper.

bipolaire [bipolɛʀ] adj bipolar.

bique [bik] nf **1.** ZOOL nanny-goat **2.** *fam & péj* [femme] ▸ **vieille bique** old bag ou cow.

biréacteur [biʀeaktœʀ] nm twin-engined jet.

birman, e [biʀmɑ̃, an] adj Burmese. ⬩ **Birman, e** nm, f Burmese ▸ **les Birmans** the Burmese. ⬩ **birman** nm LING Burmese.

Birmanie [biʀmani] npr f ▸ **(la) Birmanie** Burma.

bis, e [bi, biz] adj [couleur] greyish-brown 🇬🇧, grayish-brown 🇺🇸 ▸ **pain bis** brown bread.

bisannuel, elle [bizanɥel] adj [tous les deux ans] biennial.

biscornu, e [biskɔʀny] adj **1.** [irrégulier - forme] irregular, misshapen **2.** [étrange - idée] cranky, queer, weird ; [- esprit, raisonnement] twisted, tortuous.

biscotte [biskɔt] nf ▸ **des biscottes** *toasted bread sold in packets and often eaten for breakfast*.

biscuit [biskɥi] nm **1.** [gâteau sec] biscuit 🇬🇧, cookie 🇺🇸 ▸ **biscuit à la cuiller** ladyfinger, sponge finger ▸ **biscuit salé** savoury biscuit 🇬🇧, cracker 🇺🇸 **2.** [gâteau] ▸ **biscuit de Savoie** sponge cake.

bise [biz] nf **1.** GÉOGR North ou northerly wind **2.** [baiser] kiss / *donne-moi* ou *fais-moi une bise* give me a kiss ▸ **grosses bises** [dans une lettre] love and kisses.

biseau, x [bizo] nm bevel ▸ **en biseau** bevelled 🇬🇧, beveled 🇺🇸.

bisexuel, elle [biseksɥel] adj bisexual.

bison [bizɔ̃] nm **1.** [d'Amérique] American buffalo ou bison **2.** [d'Europe] European bison, wisent.

bisou [bizu] nm *fam* kiss / *donne-moi* ou *fais-moi un bisou* give me a kiss.

bisque [bisk] nf bisque ▸ **bisque de homard** lobster bisque.

bissextile [bisɛkstil] adj f ⟶ année.

bistouri [bistuʀi] nm lancet.

bistro(t) [bistʀo] nm ≃ café ; ≃ pub 🇬🇧 ; ≃ bar 🇺🇸.

Bistrot

This word can refer either to a small café or to a cosy restaurant, especially one frequented by regulars. The **style bistrot** refers to a style of furnishing inspired by the chairs, tables and zinc countertops typical of the traditional **bistrot**.

bit [bit] nm INFORM bit.

bite [bit] nf vulg prick, cock.

bitoniau [bitɔnjo] nm fam thingy.

bitte [bit] nf **1.** NAUT bitt **2.** vulg [pénis] = **bite**.

bitturer [3] [bityʀe] ❖ **se bitturer** vpi tfam to get plastered.

bitume [bitym] nm **1.** MIN bitumen **2.** TRAV PUB asphalt, bitumen.

bivouac [bivwak] nm bivouac.

bivouaquer [3] [bivwake] vi to bivouac, to set up camp overnight.

biz (abr écrite de bises) SMS KOTC, HAK.

bizarre [bizaʀ] adj [comportement, personne, idée, ambiance] odd, peculiar, strange / se sentir bizarre to feel (a bit) funny.

bizarrement [bizaʀmɑ̃] adv oddly, strangely, peculiarly / bizarrement, ce matin-là, il ne s'était pas rasé for some strange reason, he hadn't shaved that morning.

bizarrerie [bizaʀʀi] nf **1.** [caractère bizarre] strangeness **2.** [action bizarre] eccentricity.

bizutage [bizytaʒ] nm arg scol practical jokes played on new arrivals in a school or college ; ≃ ragging 🇬🇧 ; ≃ hazing 🇺🇸.

Bizutage

In some French schools and colleges, students take to the streets in fancy-dress and play practical jokes on each other and on passers-by at the beginning of the school year. This is part of the traditional initiation ceremony known as **bizutage**.

bjr SMS abr écrite de bonjour.

black [blak] adj fam black. ❖ **Black** nmf fam Black.

blackbouler [3] [blakbule] vt [candidat] to blackball / il s'est fait blackbouler à son examen they failed him at his exam.

blacklister, black-lister [blakliste] vt to blacklist.

black-out (pl black-out), **blackout*** [blakaut] nm blackout.

blafard, e [blafaʀ, aʀd] adj pallid, wan litt.

blague [blag] nf **1.** [histoire] joke **2.** [duperie] hoax, wind-up 🇬🇧 ▸ **c'est une blague ?** are you kidding?, you can't be serious! / vous allez arrêter, non mais, sans blague ! fam will you PLEASE give it a rest! **3.** [farce] (practical) joke, trick ▸ **faire une blague à qqn** to play a joke on sb **4.** [maladresse] blunder, boob 🇬🇧, blooper 🇺🇸 ; [sottise] silly ou stupid thing (to do).

blaguer [3] [blage] fam ❖ vi to joke / j'aime bien blaguer I like a joke. ❖ vt to tease.

blagueur, euse [blagœʀ, øz] fam ❖ adj [enfant, expression] joking, teasing. ❖ nm, f joker, prankster.

blaireau, x [blεʀo] nm **1.** ZOOL badger **2.** [pour se raser] shaving brush **3.** fam & péj [homme conformiste] ≃ Essex man 🇬🇧 ; ≃ Joe Sixpack 🇺🇸.

blairer [4] [blεʀe] vt tfam : personne ne peut le blairer no one can stand ou stick 🇬🇧 him.

blâme [blam] nm **1.** [condamnation] disapproval (U) **2.** ADMIN & ÉDUC reprimand ▸ **donner un blâme à qqn** to reprimand sb.

blâmer [3] [blame] vt **1.** [condamner] to blame / je ne le blâme pas d'avoir agi ainsi I don't blame him for having acted that way **2.** ADMIN & ÉDUC [élève, fonctionnaire] to reprimand.

blanc, blanche [blɑ̃, blɑ̃ʃ] adj **1.** [couleur] white ▸ **être blanc comme un cachet d'aspirine** fam & hum [non bronzé] to be completely white ▸ **blanc comme neige a)** pr snow-white, (as) white as snow, (as) white as the driven snow **b)** fig (as) pure as the driven snow **2.** [race] white, Caucasian ; [personne] white, white-skinned, Caucasian **3.** [vierge] blank ▸ **elle a remis (une) copie blanche** she handed in a blank sheet of paper ▸ **écrire sur du papier blanc** to write on plain ou unlined paper ▸ **vote blanc** blank vote **4.** [examen] mock. ❖ **blanc** nm **1.** [couleur] white ▸ **blanc cassé** off-white **2.** [cornée] ▸ **blanc de l'œil** white of the eye **3.** CULIN ▸ **blanc d'œuf** egg white, white of an egg ▸ **blanc de poulet** chicken breast **4.** [linge] ▸ **le blanc** (household) linen / faire une machine de blanc to do a machine-load of whites **5.** [vin] white wine **6.** [espace libre] blank space, blank, space ; [dans une conversation] blank. ❖ **Blanc, Blanche** nm, f ANTHR white ou Caucasian man (woman) ▸ **les Blancs** white people. ❖ **blanche** nf **1.** MUS minim 🇬🇧, half note 🇺🇸 **2.** arg crime [héroïne] ▸ **la blanche** smack. ❖ **à blanc** loc adv ARM ▸ **tirer à blanc** to fire blanks. ❖ **en blanc** loc adv [peindre, colorer] white ; [s'habiller, sortir] in white ▸ **laisser une ligne / page en blanc** to leave a line / page blank.

blanchâtre [blɑ̃ʃatʀ] adj [mur] offwhite, whitish ; [nuage] whitish ; [teint] pallid.

blanche [blɑ̃ʃ] f ⟶ **blanc**.

Blanche-Neige [blɑ̃ʃnεʒ] npr Snow White.

blancheur [blɑ̃ʃœʀ] nf [couleur] whiteness.

blanchiment [blɑ̃ʃimɑ̃] nm [de l'argent] laundering.

blanchir [32] [blɑ̃ʃiʀ] ❖ vt **1.** [couvrir de blanc] to whiten, to turn white ▸ **blanchir à la chaux** to whitewash ; [décolorer] to turn white, to bleach **2.** [nettoyer -linge] to launder **3.** [innocenter] to exonerate, to clear ; [argent] : blanchir l'argent de la drogue to launder money made from drug trafficking **4.** CULIN to blanch ; HORT [légumes, salade] to blanch (industrially). ❖ vi [barbe, cheveux] to turn white. ❖ **se blanchir** vp (emploi réfléchi) to exonerate o.s., to clear one's name.

blanchissant, e [blɑ̃ʃisɑ̃, ɑ̃t] adj **1.** [produit] whitening **2.** [cheveux, barbe] greying 🇬🇧, graying 🇺🇸.

blanchisserie [blɑ̃ʃisʀi] nf laundry.

blanquette [blɑ̃kεt] nf **1.** [vin] ▸ **blanquette de Limoux** sparkling white wine **2.** CULIN blanquette ▸ **blanquette de veau** blanquette of veal.

blasé, e [blaze] ❖ adj blasé. ❖ nm, f blasé person ▸ **jouer les blasés** to act as if one's seen it all.

blason [blazɔ̃] nm [écu] arms, blazon.

blasphématoire [blasfematwaʀ] adj blasphemous.

blasphème [blasfεm] nm blasphemy.

blasphémer [18] [blasfeme] vi to blaspheme.

✎ In reformed spelling (see p. 16-18), this verb is conjugated like semer : il blasphèmera, elle blasphèmerait.

---

blatte [blat] nf cockroach.

blazer [blazɛʀ] nm blazer.

blé [ble] nm **1.** BOT wheat ▶ **blé noir** buckwheat **2.** tfam [argent] dosh 🇬🇧, dough 🇺🇸.

bled [blɛd] nm fam [petit village] small village ; péj dump, hole ▶ **un petit bled paumé** a little place out in the sticks ou the middle of nowhere.

blême [blɛm] adj pale, wan litt, ashen-faced ▶ **blême de peur / rage** ashen-faced with fear / rage.

blêmir [32] [blemiʀ] vi to blanch, to (turn) pale ▶ **blêmir de peur / rage** to go ashen-faced with fear / rage.

blennorragie [blenɔʀaʒi] nf blennorrhagia, gonorrhoea 🇬🇧, gonorrhea 🇺🇸.

blessant, e [blɛsɑ̃, ɑ̃t] adj wounding, hurtful.

blessé, e [blese] ◆ adj **1.** [soldat] wounded ; [accidenté] injured / **blessé au genou** hurt in the knee **2.** [vexé - amour-propre, orgueil, personne] hurt. ◆ nm, f [victime - d'un accident] injured person ; [- d'une agression] wounded person ▶ **les blessés de la route** road casualties ▶ **blessé léger / grave** slightly / severely injured person ▶ **blessé de guerre a)** [en service] wounded soldier **b)** [après la guerre] wounded veteran.

blesser [4] [blese] vt **1.** [au cours d'un accident] to injure, to hurt ; [au cours d'une agression] to injure, to wound / **il a été blessé par balle** he was hit by a bullet, he sustained a bullet-wound ▶ **blesser qqn avec un couteau** to inflict a knife-wound on sb / **elle est blessée à la jambe** she has a leg injury, her leg's hurt **2.** [offenser] to offend, to upset / **tes paroles m'ont blessé** I felt hurt by what you said. ◆ **se blesser** vpi to injure ou to hurt o.s. / **elle s'est blessée au bras** she injured ou hurt her arm.

blessure [blesyʀ] nf **1.** [lésion] wound, injury **2.** [offense] wound.

blet, ette [blɛ, blɛt] adj mushy, overripe. ◆ **blette** = **bette.**

bleu, e [blø] ◆ adj **1.** [coloré] blue / **avoir les yeux bleus** to have blue eyes, to be blue-eyed **2.** [meurtri, altéré] blue, bruised ▶ **bleu de froid** blue with cold **3.** CULIN very rare **4.** EXPR **avoir une peur bleue** to have the fright of one's life, to be terrified ▶ **avoir une peur bleue de qqch / qqn** to be terrified ou scared stiff of sthg / sb. ◆ nm, f fam [gén] newcomer, greenhorn ; MIL rookie, raw recruit ; [à l'université] fresher 🇬🇧 freshman 🇺🇸. ◆ **bleu** nm **1.** [couleur] blue ▶ **bleu clair** light blue ▶ **bleu foncé** dark blue ▶ **bleu acier** steel blue ▶ **bleu ciel** sky blue ▶ **bleu marine** navy blue ▶ **bleu pétrole** petrol blue ▶ **bleu vert** blue green ▶ **le grand bleu** the blue depths of the sea **2.** [ecchymose] bruise / **se faire un bleu à la cuisse** to bruise one's thigh ▶ **être couvert de bleus** to be black and blue, to be covered in bruises **3.** VÊT ▶ **bleu (de travail)** (worker's denim) overalls 🇬🇧, coveralls 🇺🇸 **4.** [fromage] blue cheese.

bleuâtre [bløatʀ] adj bluish, bluey.

bleuet [bløɛ] nm **1.** [fleur] cornflower **2.** 🇶🇨 [fruit] blueberry, huckleberry.

bleuetier [bløɛtje] nm 🇶🇨 [petit arbrisseau] blueberry plant.

bleuetière [bløɛtjɛʀ] nf 🇶🇨 blueberry field.

bleuir [32] [bløiʀ] ◆ vi to turn ou to go blue. ◆ vt to turn blue.

bleuté, e [bløte] adj [pétale, aile] blue-tinged ; [lentille, verre] blue-tinted.

blindé, e [blɛ̃de] adj **1.** [voiture, tank, train] armoured, armour-clad, armour-plated ; [brigade, division] armoured **2.** [renforcé - porte, paroi] reinforced **3.** fam [insensible] hardened **4.** tfam [ivre] plastered, sloshed 🇬🇧. ◆ **blindé**

nm MIL [véhicule] armoured 🇬🇧 ou armored 🇺🇸 vehicle ; [soldat] member of a tank regiment.

blinder [3] [blɛ̃de] vt **1.** [renforcer - porte] to reinforce, to armour-plate 🇬🇧, to armor-plate 🇺🇸 **2.** fam [endurcir] to toughen (up), to harden. ◆ **se blinder** vpi fam [s'endurcir] to toughen o.s. up.

bling-bling [blingbling] adj fam bling-bling, bling.

blini [blini] nm blini.

blizzard [blizaʀ] nm blizzard.

bloc [blɔk] nm **1.** [masse - de pierre] block ; [- de bois, de béton] block, lump ▶ **être tout d'un bloc a)** [en un seul morceau] to be made of a single block **b)** [trapu] to be stockily built **c)** [direct] to be simple and straightforward **d)** [inflexible] to be unyielding **2.** [de papier] pad ▶ **bloc de bureau / papier** desk / writing pad **3.** [installation] ▶ **bloc frigorifique** refrigeration unit ▶ **bloc opératoire a)** [salle] operating theatre 🇬🇧 ou room 🇺🇸 **b)** [locaux] surgical unit **4.** [maisons] block **5.** [ensemble] block ▶ **former un bloc a)** [sociétés] to form a grouping **b)** [amis, alliés] to stand together **c)** [composants] to form a single whole ▶ **faire bloc** to form a block ▶ **faire bloc avec / contre qqn** to stand together) with / against sb **6.** arg crime [prison] nick 🇬🇧, slammer. ◆ **à bloc** loc adv : **visser une vis à bloc** to screw a screw down hard / **gonfler un pneu à bloc** to blow a tyre right up 🇬🇧, to blow a tire all the way up 🇺🇸. ◆ **en bloc** loc adv as a whole / **j'ai tout rejeté en bloc** I rejected it lock, stock and barrel, I rejected the whole thing.

blocage [blɔkaʒ] nm **1.** ÉCON [des loyers, des tarifs] freeze / **blocage des prix et des salaires** freeze on wages and prices **2.** PSYCHOL block, blockage ▶ **faire un blocage sur qqch** to block sthg off.

bloc-cuisine [blɔkkɥizin] (pl **blocs-cuisines**) nm kitchen unit.

blockbuster [blɔkbœstœʀ] nf [film] blockbuster.

blockhaus [blɔkos] nm blockhouse ; [de petite taille] pill-box.

bloc-notes [blɔknɔt] (pl **blocs-notes**) nm notepad, scratchpad 🇺🇸.

blocus [blɔkys] nm blockade / **faire le blocus d'une ville** to blockade a city.

blog [blɔg] nm INFORM blog.

blogosphère [blɔgɔsfɛʀ] nf blogosphere.

blogroll [blɔgʀɔl] nf INTERNET blogroll.

blogueur, euse [blɔgœʀ, øz] nm, f INFORM blogger.

blond, e [blɔ̃, blɔ̃d] ◆ adj **1.** [chevelure] blond, fair ; [personne] blond, fair-haired ▶ **blond ardent** ou **roux** ou **vénitien** light auburn ▶ **blond cendré** ash blond **2.** [jaune pâle] pale yellow, golden, honey-coloured. ◆ nm, f blonde, fair-haired man (woman). ◆ **blonde** nf **1.** [cigarette] Virginia cigarette **2.** [bière] lager **3.** 🇶🇨 [amie] girlfriend.

blondir [32] [blɔ̃diʀ] ◆ vi **1.** [personne, cheveux] to go fairer **2.** CULIN ▶ **faire blondir des oignons** to fry onions gently until transparent. ◆ vt ▶ **blondir ses cheveux a)** [à l'eau oxygénée] to bleach one's hair **b)** [par mèches] to put highlights in one's hair.

bloquer [3] [blɔke] vt **1.** [caler - table] to wedge, to stop wobbling ▶ **bloque la porte a)** [ouverte] wedge the door open **b)** [fermée] wedge the door shut / **c'est le tapis qui bloque la porte** the carpet's jamming the door ▶ **bloquer une roue a)** [avec une cale] to put a block under ou to chock a wheel **b)** [avec un sabot de Denver] to clamp a wheel / **la roue est bloquée** the wheel is locked ou jammed ▶ **la porte est bloquée** the door is stuck ou jammed **2.** [serrer fort - vis] to screw down hard, to overtighten ; [- frein] to jam on, to lock **3.** [entraver] ▶ **bloquer le passage** ou **la route** to block ou to obstruct sout the way **4.** [empêcher l'accès à - ville, point stratégique] to block,

to seal off *(sép)* ▸ **bloqué par la neige** snowbound **5.** *fam* [retenir - une personne] to hold up *(sép)* **6.** ÉCON [loyers, prix, salaires] to freeze ; FIN [compte] to freeze ; [chèque] to stop ; POL [mesure, vote] to block **7.** [réunir] to group together / *on va bloquer les activités sportives le matin* we'll have all sports events in the morning **8.** PSYCHOL to cause ou to produce a (mental) block in / *ça la bloque* she has a mental block about it **9.** SPORT ▸ **bloquer la balle a)** [au basket] to block the ball **b)** [au football] to trap the ball **10.** ꞯᴜᴇʙᴇᴄ [échouer à - examen] to fail, to flunk. ❖ **se bloquer** vpi **1.** [clef] to jam, to stick, to get stuck ; [roue] to jam ; [machine, mécanisme] to jam, to get stuck ; [frein, roue] to jam, to lock **2.** [personne - ne pas communiquer] to close in on o.s. ; [-se troubler] to have a mental block / *je me bloque quand on me parle sur ce ton* my mind goes blank ou I freeze when somebody speaks to me like that.

blottir [32] [blɔtiʀ] ❖ **se blottir** vpi to curl ou to cuddle ou to snuggle up ▸ **blotti sous mes couvertures** snug in my blankets.

blouse [bluz] nf **1.** [à l'école] smock formerly worn by French schoolchildren ; [pour travailler] overalls ; [à l'ancienne, de paysan] smock ; [corsage] blouse **2.** [d'un médecin] white coat ; [d'un chimiste, d'un laborantin] lab coat.

blouser [3] [bluze] ❖ vt fam [tromper] to con, to trick. ❖ vi to be loose-fitting, to fit loosely.

blouson [bluzɔ̃] nm (short) jacket ▸ **blouson d'aviateur** bomber jacket.

blues [bluz] nm **1.** blues *(sg)* / *chanter le blues* to sing the blues **2.** *fam* [mélancolie] blues ▸ **avoir le blues** to have the blues.

bluff [blœf] nm bluff / *ne le crois pas, c'est du bluff !* don't believe him, he's just bluffing!

bluffant, e [blœfɑ̃, ɑ̃t] adj fam amazing.

bluffer [3] [blœfe] ❖ vi to bluff. ❖ vt **1.** [tromper] to fool **2.** CARTES to bluff **3.** fam [impressionner] to impress.

blush [blœʃ] nm blusher.

BNF npr f abr de **Bibliothèque nationale de France**.

BO (abr de **bande originale**) nf soundtrack.

boa [bɔa] nm **1.** ZOOL boa **2.** VÊT boa.

bob [bɔb] nm **1.** [chapeau] sun hat **2.** = **bobsleigh**.

bobard [bɔbaʀ] nm fam fib / *raconter des bobards* to fib tfam, to tell fibs.

bobettes [bɔbɛt] nfpl ꞯᴜᴇʙᴇᴄ fam underwear.

bobine [bɔbin] nf **1.** TEXT bobbin, reel, spool / *une bobine de fil* a reel of thread **2.** ÉLECTR coil **3.** fam [visage] face, mug.

bobo [bobo] nm langage enfantin [égratignure] scratch ; [bosse] bump ▸ **faire bobo (à qqn)** to hurt (sb) / *se faire bobo* to hurt o.s.

bobsleigh [bɔbslɛg] nm bobsleigh, bobsled ᴜꜱ.

bocal, aux [bɔkal, o] nm **1.** [pour les conserves] jar, bottle / *mettre des haricots verts en bocaux* to preserve ou to bottle green beans **2.** [aquarium] fishbowl, bowl.

body [bɔdi] *(pl* bodys ou bodies*)* nm body(suit).

bodyboard [bɔdibɔʀd] nm SPORT bodyboarding.

bodybuilding, body-building [bɔdibildiŋ] *(pl* bodybuildings ou body-buildings*)* nm ▸ **le bodybuilding** body building.

bœuf [bœf] *(pl* bœufs [bø]*)* nm **1.** ZOOL [de trait] ox ; [de boucherie] bullock, steer **2.** CULIN beef ▸ **bœuf (à la) mode** boiled beef and carrots **3.** fam MUS jam session.

bof [bɔf] interj fam term expressing lack of interest or enthusiasm / *tu as aimé le film ? — bof !* did you like the film? — it was all right I suppose.

bogue [bɔg], **bug** [bœg] nm INFORM bug.

bohème [bɔɛm] ❖ adj bohemian / *lui, c'est le genre bohème* he's the artistic type. ❖ nmf bohemian. ❖ nf ▸ **la bohème** the bohemian ou artistic way of life.

bohémien, enne [bɔemjɛ̃, ɛn] adj Bohemian. ❖ **Bohémien, enne** nm, f [de Bohême] Bohemian.

boire [108] [bwaʀ] ❖ vt **1.** [avaler] to drink / *elle a tout bu d'un coup* she gulped it all down ▸ **boire la tasse a)** fam [en nageant] to swallow water **b)** [perdre de l'argent] to lose a lot of money **c)** [faire faillite] to go under **2.** [absorber] to absorb, to soak up *(sép)*. ❖ vi **1.** [s'hydrater] to drink, to take in a liquid **2.** [pour fêter un événement] : *nous buvons à ta santé* we're drinking to ou toasting your health **3.** [pour s'enivrer] to drink ▸ **il boit trop** he has a drink problem.

bois [bwa] nm **1.** [de grands arbres] wood, wooded area ; [de jeunes ou petits arbres] thicket, copse, coppice ; [d'arbres plantés] grove **2.** [matière] wood *(U)* ▸ **en bois** wooden ▸ **bois à brûler** ou **de chauffage** firewood ▸ **bois blanc** whitewood ▸ **bois de charpente** timber ▸ **bois de rose** rosewood ▸ **bois mort** dead wood ᴜᴋ, deadwood ᴜꜱ ▸ **touchons** ou **je touche du bois** touch wood ᴜᴋ, knock on wood ᴜꜱ. ❖ **bois** nmpl ZOOL antlers ; FOOT goalposts ; MUS woodwind section ou instruments.

boisé, e [bwaze] adj [région, terrain] wooded, woody.

boiserie [bwazʀi] nf piece of decorative woodwork ▸ **des boiseries** panelling ᴜᴋ, paneling ᴜꜱ.

boisson [bwasɔ̃] nf **1.** [liquide à boire] drink ▸ **boisson gazeuse** fizzy drink / *La consommation de boissons alcoolisées est interdite dans l'enceinte du stade* drinking alcohol is forbidden inside the stadium **2.** [alcool] ▸ **la boisson** drink, drinking.

boîte, boite* [bwat] nf **1.** [récipient - à couvercle, à fente] box ▸ **boîte d'allumettes a)** [pleine] box of matches **b)** [vide] matchbox ▸ **boîte à chaussures** shoebox ▸ **boîte à outils** tool box, toolkit ▸ **boîte à ouvrage** sewing box **2.** [pour aliments] ▸ **boîte (de conserve)** tin ᴜᴋ, can **3.** [pour le courrier] ▸ **boîte à** ou **aux lettres** [dans la rue] pillar box ᴜᴋ, postbox ᴜᴋ, mailbox ᴜꜱ **b)** [chez soi] letterbox ᴜᴋ, mailbox ᴜꜱ ▸ **boîte postale** post box ▸ **boîte aux lettres (électronique)** INFORM electronic mailbox **4.** AÉRON & AUTO ▸ **boîte noire** black box **5.** fam [discothèque] ▸ **boîte (de nuit)** (night) club **6.** fam [lieu de travail] office ▸ **boîte d'intérim** temping agency ; [lycée] school ▸ **boîte à bac** ou **bachot** péj crammer ᴜᴋ **7.** ANAT ▸ **boîte crânienne** cranium **8.** AUTO ▸ **boîte à gants** glove compartment ▸ **boîte de vitesses** gearbox ᴜᴋ, transmission ᴜꜱ **9.** INFORM ▸ **boîte d'alerte a)** [avec 'OK'] warning box, alert box **b)** [avec 'oui' et 'non'] confirm box ▸ **boîte de dialogue** dialogue box ▸ **boîte de réception** [pour mails] inbox **10.** TÉLÉC ▸ **boîte vocale** voicemail, message box / *elle est sur boîte vocale* she's on voice mail. ❖ **en boîte, en boite*** ❖ loc adj tinned ᴜᴋ, canned. ❖ loc adv ᴇxᴘʀ mettre qqn en boîte fam to wind sb up ᴜᴋ, to pull sb's leg.

boiter [3] [bwate] vi [en marchant] to limp, to be lame.

boiteux, euse [bwatø, øz] adj **1.** [cheval, personne] lame ; [meuble, table] rickety **2.** [imparfait - paix, alliance] fragile, brittle, shaky ; [-comparaison, raisonnement] unsound, shaky.

boîtier, boitier* [bwatje] nm **1.** [gén] case, casing ; [d'une lampe de poche] battery compartment ▸ **boîtier de montre** watchcase **2.** PHOT camera body.

boitiller [3] [bwatije] vi to limp slightly, to be slightly lame, to hobble.

bol [bɔl] nm **1.** [récipient] bowl **2.** [contenu] bowl, bowlful ▸ **prendre un bol d'air a)** [se promener] to (go and) get some fresh air **b)** [changer d'environnement] to get a change of air **3.** *fam* [chance] luck ▶ **avoir du bol** to be a lucky devil. ❖ **au bol** *loc adj* [coupe de cheveux] pudding-bowl *(modif)* 🇬🇧, bowl *(modif)* 🇺🇸. ❖ **bol alimentaire** *nm* bolus.

bolée [bɔle] *nf* ▶ **bolée de cidre** bowl ou bowlful of cider (*in N.W. France, cider is often served in bowls*).

bolide [bɔlid] *nm* fast car, racing 🇬🇧 ou race 🇺🇸 car ▶ **entrer dans une / sortir d'une pièce comme un bolide** to hurtle into a / out of a room.

Bolivie [bɔlivi] *npr f* ▶ **(la) Bolivie** Bolivia.

bolivien, enne [bɔlivjɛ̃, ɛn] *adj* Bolivian. ❖ **Bolivien, enne** *nm, f* Bolivian.

bombardement [bɔ̃baʀdəmɑ̃] *nm* MIL [avec des obus] shelling ; [avec des bombes] bombing (U).

bombarder [3] [bɔ̃baʀde] *vt* **1.** MIL [avec des obus] to shell ; [avec des bombes] to bomb **2.** [avec des projectiles] to shower, to pelt ; PHYS to bombard ▶ **bombarder qqn de questions** *fig* to bombard sb with questions **3.** *(suivi d'un nom) fam* [promouvoir] : *il a été bombardé responsable du projet* he found himself catapulted into the position of project leader.

bombardier [bɔ̃baʀdje] *nm* AÉRON & MIL [avion] bomber ; [pilote] bombardier.

bombe [bɔ̃b] *nf* **1.** MIL & NUCL bomb ▶ **bombe A** ou **atomique** atom ou atomic bomb ▶ **bombe H** H bomb ▶ **bombe incendiaire** firebomb ▶ **bombe à retardement** *pr & fig* time bomb **2.** [aérosol] spray ▶ **bombe anticrevaison** instant puncture sealant ▶ **bombe insecticide** fly 🇬🇧 ou bug 🇺🇸 spray ▶ **bombe lacrymogène** teargas grenade ▶ **peinture en bombe** spray paint **3.** ÉQUIT riding hat ou cap **4.** *tfam* [personne] ▶ **bombe sexuelle** sex kitten, sex bomb **5.** *fam* [fête] feast, spree ▶ **faire la bombe** to whoop it up, to have a riotous old time.

bombé, e [bɔ̃be] *adj* [renflé - paroi] bulging ; [- front] bulging, domed ; [- poitrine, torse] thrown out, stuck out ; [- forme] rounded.

bomber [bɔ̃bœʀ] *nm* bomber jacket.

bon, bonne [bɔ̃, bɔn] *(devant nm commençant par voyelle ou « h » muet* [bɔn]*)*
◆ *adj*

A. QUI CONVIENT **1.** [en qualité - film, récolte, résultat, connaissance] good / *elle parle un bon espagnol* she speaks good Spanish, her Spanish is good ▶ **de bonnes notes** ÉDUC good ou high marks 🇬🇧 ou grades 🇺🇸 **2.** [qui remplit bien sa fonction - matelas, siège, chaussures, éclairage, freins] good ; [- cœur, veines, charpente, gestion, investissement] good, sound / *une bonne vue, de bons yeux* good eyesight ; SPORT [au tennis] good ▶ **la balle est bonne** the ball's in ▶ **les bonnes vieilles méthodes** the good old methods **3.** [qui n'est pas périmé - nourriture] all right ; [- document, titre de transport] valid **4.** [compétent] good / *bon père et bon époux* a good father and husband / *être / ne pas être bon en musique* to be good / bad at music ▶ **nos bons clients** our good ou regular customers ▶ **à quoi bon ?** what for? / *je pourrais lui écrire, mais à quoi bon ?* I could write to her but what would be the point? ▶ **bon à** [digne de] : *les piles sont bonnes à jeter* the batteries can go straight in the bin 🇬🇧 ou trash can 🇺🇸 ▶ **c'est bon à savoir** that's good to know.

B. PLAISANT **1.** [agréable - repas, odeur] good, nice ; [- soirée, vacances] good, nice, pleasant / *ton gâteau était très bon* your cake was very good ou nice / *l'eau du robinet n'est pas bonne* the tap water isn't very nice ou doesn't taste very nice / *viens te baigner, l'eau est bonne !* come for a swim, the water's lovely and warm! / *avoir une bonne tête* ou *bouille* to have a nice ou a friendly face / *c'est si bon de ne rien faire !* it feels so good to be doing nothing! ▶ **bon anniversaire !** happy birthday! / *bonne (et heureuse) année !*

happy new year! ▶ **bonne chance !** good luck! ▶ **bonne journée !** have a nice day! ▶ **bonnes vacances !** have a nice holiday 🇬🇧 ou vacation 🇺🇸! ▶ **bon voyage !** have a nice ou good trip! ; *(en intensif)* : *un bon grog bien chaud* a nice hot toddy ▶ **elle est bien bonne celle-là ! a)** *iron* that's a good one! **b)** that's a bit much! ▶ **le bon vieux temps** the good old days **2.** [favorable, optimiste - prévisions, présage, nouvelle] good ▶ **c'est (un) bon signe** it's a good sign.

C. JUSTE, ADÉQUAT **1.** [correct - numéro de téléphone] right ; [- réponse, solution] correct, right / *c'est la bonne rue* it's the right street **2.** [opportun] right, convenient, appropriate / *l'héritage est arrivé au bon moment pour elle* the inheritance arrived at the right time ou at a convenient time for her ▶ **juger** ou **trouver bon de / que** to think it appropriate ou fitting to / that / *elle n'a pas jugé bon de s'excuser* she didn't find that she needed to ou she didn't see fit to apologize ▶ **comme / où / quand / si bon vous semble** as / wherever / whenever / if you see fit **3.** [bénéfique, salutaire] good, beneficial / *c'est bon pour la santé* it's good for you, good for your health / *le bon air de la campagne* the good ou fresh country air **4.** *fam* EXPR) **c'est bon ! a)** [c'est juste] that's right! **b)** [ça suffit] that'll do! **c)** [c'est d'accord] OK! / *c'est bon ?* OK?

D. MORALEMENT **1.** [décent, honnête - conduite] good, proper ; [- influence, mœurs] good / *ils n'ont pas bonne réputation* they don't have much of a reputation **2.** [bienveillant - personne] good, kind, kindly / *je suis déjà bien bon de te prêter ma voiture !* it's kind ou decent enough of me to lend you my car as it is! ; [rire, manger] heartily ▶ **bon cœur** : *avoir bon cœur* to be kind-hearted ▶ **de bon cœur** willingly / *tenez, prenez, c'est de bon cœur* please have it, I'd love you to ▶ **le bon Dieu** the (good) Lord **3.** [amical - relation] ▶ **avoir de bons rapports avec qqn** to be on good terms with sb **4.** [brave] good.

E. EN INTENSIF **1.** [grand, gros] good ▶ **une bonne averse** a heavy shower (of rain) / *ça a duré une bonne minute* it lasted a good minute or so **2.** [fort, violent] ▶ **une bonne fessée** a good ou sound spanking ▶ **pleurer un bon coup** *fam* to have a good cry **3.** [complet, exemplaire] good / *le mur a besoin d'un bon lessivage* the wall needs a good scrub ▶ **une bonne fois pour toutes** once and for all.

◆ *nm, f* **1.** [personne vertueuse] good person **2.** [personne idéale, chose souhaitée] right one ▶ **je crois que c'est enfin le bon a)** *fam* [lors d'un recrutement] I think we've got our man at last **b)** [lors d'une rencontre amoureuse] I think it's Mister Right at last. ❖ **bon** ◆ *nm* **1.** [dans les films] goody, goodie / *les bons et les méchants* the goodies and the baddies, the good guys and the bad guys **2.** [coupon] coupon, voucher ▶ **bon d'achat** ou **de caisse** cash voucher ▶ **bon de commande** order form ▶ **bon de livraison** delivery slip ▶ **bon de réduction** discount coupon **3.** FIN ▶ **bon du Trésor** treasury bill. ◆ *adv* **1.** MÉTÉOR ▶ **faire bon** : *il fait bon ici* it's nice and warm here **2.** *(suivi d'un infinitif)* : *il ne faisait pas bon être communiste alors* it wasn't advisable to be a communist in those days. ◆ *interj* **1.** [marque une transition] right, so, well now / *bon, où en étais-je ?* well now ou right ou so, where was I? **2.** [en réponse] right, OK, fine ▶ **bon d'accord, allons-y** OK then, let's go. ❖ **bon à rien, bonne à rien** ◆ *loc adj* **1.** [inutile] : *je suis trop vieux, je ne suis plus bon à rien* I'm too old, I'm useless ou no good now **2.** [incompétent] useless, hopeless. ◆ *nm, f* [personne sans valeur] good-for-nothing ; [personne incompétente] useless individual. ❖ **bonne femme** *nf fam* [femme] woman.

Bon [bɔ̃] *npr* ⟶ **cap.**

bonbon [bɔ̃bɔ̃] *nm* sweet 🇬🇧, (piece of) candy 🇺🇸 ▶ **bonbon acidulé** acid drop ▶ **bonbon à la menthe** mint.

bonbonne [bɔ̃bɔn] nf [pour le vin] demijohn ; [pour des produits chimiques] carboy ▸ **bonbonne de gaz** gas bottle.

bonbonnière [bɔ̃bɔnjɛʀ] nf [boîte] sweet [UK] ou candy [US] box.

bond [bɔ̃] nm **1.** [d'une balle] bounce ▸ **prendre** ou **saisir une remarque au bond** to pounce on a remark **2.** [saut] jump, leap ▸ **faire des bonds a)** pr to jump up and down **b)** fig to go up and down ▸ **faire un bond en avant a)** [économie] to boom **b)** [prix, loyer] to soar **c)** [recherche] to leap forward ▸ **se lever d'un bond** to leap up **3.** EXPR **faire faux bond à qqn**: *elle nous a fait faux bond* **a)** [elle n'est pas venue] she didn't turn up **b)** [elle nous a déçus] she let us down.

bonde [bɔ̃d] nf [bouchon - d'un tonneau] bung, stopper ; [- d'un lavabo] plug.

bondé, e [bɔ̃de] adj packed, jam-packed.

bondir [32] [bɔ̃diʀ] vi **1.** [sauter] to bounce, to bound, to leap (up) ▸ **bondir de**: *bondir de joie* to leap for joy ▸ **bondir sur** [pour importuner, semoncer] to pounce on ▸ **faire bondir**: *pareille inconscience me fait bondir* such recklessness makes my blood boil **2.** [sursauter] to start **3.** [courir] to dash, to rush.

bon enfant [bɔnɑ̃fɑ̃] adj inv [caractère] good-natured, easy-going ; [atmosphère] relaxed, informal.

bonheur [bɔnœʀ] nm **1.** [chance] luck ▸ **par bonheur** fortunately, luckily ▸ **connaître son bonheur**: *tu ne connais pas ton bonheur !* you don't know when you're lucky ou how lucky you are! ▸ **porter bonheur à qqn** to bring sb luck **2.** [contentement] happiness ▸ **faire le bonheur de qqn** [le contenter] to make sb happy, to bring sb happiness ▸ **trouver son bonheur**: *as-tu trouvé ton bonheur ?* did you find what you were looking for? ❖ **au petit bonheur (la chance)** loc adv haphazardly.

bonhomie, bonhommie* [bɔnɔmi] nf geniality, bonhomie.

bonhomme [bɔnɔm] (pl **bonshommes** [bɔ̃zɔm]) fam nm **1.** [homme] chap **2.** [partenaire] old man, fellow vieilli ; [garçon] little chap ou lad / *allez viens, mon petit bonhomme* come along, little man **3.** [figure] man ▸ **bonhomme de neige** snowman **4.** EXPR **aller** ou **continuer son petit bonhomme de chemin** to go ou to carry on at one's own pace.

boniche [bɔniʃ] fam & péj = **bonniche**.

bonification [bɔnifikasjɔ̃] nf **1.** AGR improvement **2.** SPORT [avantage] advantage, extra points **3.** [rabais] discount, reduction.

bonifier [9] [bɔnifje] ❖ **se bonifier** vpi [caractère] to mellow, to improve.

boniment [bɔnimɑ̃] nm **1.** COMM sales talk ou patter **2.** fam [mensonge] tall story ▸ **arrête tes boniments** stop fibbing.

bonjour [bɔ̃ʒuʀ] nm **1.** [salutation - gén] hello ; [- le matin] good morning ; [- l'après-midi] good afternoon ▸ **vous lui donnerez le bonjour** ou **vous lui direz bonjour de ma part** say hello for me **2.** fam [exprime la difficulté] : *pour le faire aller à l'école, bonjour !* no way can you get him to go to school! / *je n'ai pas fait de gym depuis un mois, bonjour les courbatures !* I haven't done any exercise for a month, I'm going to ache, let me tell you!

bonne [bɔn] ❖ f ⟶ **bon.** ❖ nf **1.** [domestique] maid **2.** EXPR **avoir qqn à la bonne** to like sb, to be in (solid) with sb [US].

bonne-maman [bɔnmamɑ̃] (pl **bonnes-mamans**) nf vieilli grand-mama.

bonnement [bɔnmɑ̃] adv : *je lui ai dit tout bonnement ce que je pensais* I quite simply told him what I thought.

bonnet [bɔnɛ] nm **1.** [coiffe - en laine] (woolly) hat [UK], (wooly) hat [US] ; [- de femme, d'enfant] hat, bonnet ; [- de soldat, de marin] hat ▸ **bonnet d'âne** dunce's cap ▸ **bonnet de bain** swimming cap ▸ **bonnet de douche** shower cap ▸ **bonnet à poils** busby, bearskin ▸ **c'est bonnet blanc et blanc bonnet** it's six of one and half a dozen of the other, it's all much of a muchness [UK] **2.** [d'un soutien-gorge] cup.

bonniche [bɔniʃ] nf fam & péj maid, skivvy [UK] / **faire la bonniche** to skivvy [UK], to do all the dirty work.

bonsoir [bɔ̃swaʀ] nm **1.** [en arrivant] good evening ; [en partant] good night **2.** fam [emploi expressif] : *ils paient les heures, mais pour les frais, bonsoir !* they pay for your time, but when it comes to expenses, you might as well forget it!

bonté [bɔ̃te] nf [bienveillance] kindness, goodness / *ayez la bonté de...* please be so kind as to... ▸ **bonté divine !, bonté du ciel !** good gracious!

bonus [bɔnys] nm **1.** [dans les assurances] no-claim ou no-claims bonus **2.** [prime] bonus **3.** [sur un DVD] special feature **4.** [avantage] plus.

boom, boum* [bum] nm [développement] boom, expansion / *le boom de la natalité* the baby boom.

boomerang [bumʀɑ̃g] nm boomerang.

booster¹ [3] [buste] vt to boost.

booster² [bustœʀ] nm ASTRONAUT booster.

bord [bɔʀ] nm **1.** [côté - d'une forêt, d'un domaine] edge ; [- d'une route] side ▸ **sur le bord de** on the edge of / *sur le bord de la route* by the roadside ▸ **sur les bords de** : *sur les bords du fleuve* **a)** [gén] on the river bank **b)** [en ville] on the waterfront ▸ **le bord du trottoir** the kerb [UK] ou curb [US] ▸ **le bord** ou **les bords de mer** the seaside **2.** [pourtour - d'une plaie] edge ; [- d'une assiette, d'une baignoire] rim, edge ; [- d'un verre] rim / *remplir un verre jusqu'au bord* to fill a glass to the brim ou to the top **3.** COUT [non travaillé] edge ; [replié et cousu] hem ; [décoratif] border **4.** NAUT [côté, bastingage] side ▸ **jeter** ou **balancer** fam **qqch par-dessus bord** to throw ou to chuck sthg overboard ▸ **tirer des bords** to tack **5.** [opinion] side / *nous sommes du même bord* we're on the same side. ❖ **à bord** loc adv AUTO on board ; AÉRON & NAUT aboard, on board / *avant de monter à bord* before boarding ou going aboard. ❖ **à bord de** loc prép on board ▸ **à bord d'un navire / d'une voiture** on board a ship / car ▸ **monter à bord d'un bateau / avion** to board a boat / plane. ❖ **au bord de** loc prép **1.** [en bordure de] ▸ **se promener au bord de l'eau / la mer** to walk at the water's edge / the seaside / *s'arrêter au bord de la route* to stop by the roadside **2.** [à la limite de] on the brink ou verge of, very close to ▸ **au bord des larmes / de la dépression** on the verge of tears / a nervous breakdown. ❖ **bord à bord** loc adv edge to edge. ❖ **de bord** loc adj [journal, livre, commandant] ship's. ❖ **sur les bords** loc adv fam slightly, a touch ▸ *il est un peu radin sur les bords* he's a bit tight-fisted.

bordeaux [bɔʀdo] ❖ adj inv [grenat] burgundy (modif), claret (modif). ❖ nm Bordeaux (wine) ▸ **un bordeaux rouge** a red Bordeaux, a claret ▸ **un bordeaux blanc** a white Bordeaux.

bordée [bɔʀde] nf **1.** NAUT [canons, salve] broadside ; [distance] tack ; [partie de l'équipage] watch **2.** fig [série] ▸ **une bordée d'insultes** fig a torrent ou stream of abuse **3.** [Québec] ▸ **bordée de neige** heavy snowfall.

bordel [bɔʀdɛl] tfam ❖ nm **1.** [hôtel de passe] brothel, whorehouse **2.** [désordre] shambles (sg), mess / *mettre le bordel dans une pièce / réunion* to turn a room into a pigsty / a meeting into a shambles. ❖ interj dammit, hell.

border [3] [bɔʁde] vt **1.** [en se couchant] : *va te coucher, je viendrai te border* go to bed, I'll come and tuck you in **2.** [délimiter] to line / *la route est bordée de haies* the road is lined with hedges.

bordereau, x [bɔʁdəʁo] nm FIN & COMM note, slip ▶ **bordereau de versement** paying-in slip UK, deposit slip US.

bordure [bɔʁdyʁ] nf **1.** [bord - d'un évier] edge ; [- d'un verre] edge, brim ; [- d'une plate-bande] border, edge ; [- d'une cheminée] surround UK, border US ▶ **la bordure du trottoir** the kerb ; [bande décorative] border **2.** VÊT border, edge ; [d'un chapeau] brim. ◆ **en bordure de** loc prép : *habiter une maison en bordure de mer* to live in a house by the sea.

borgne [bɔʁɲ] adj **1.** [personne] one-eyed **2.** [mal fréquenté - hôtel] shady.

borne [bɔʁn] nf **1.** [limite] boundary stone, landmark ▶ **borne kilométrique** milepost **2.** [point] ▶ **borne d'appel d'urgence** emergency call box **3.** fam [kilomètre] kilometre UK, kilometer US **4.** INFORM ▶ **borne d'accès** [à Internet] access point ▶ **borne interactive** ou **multimédia** interactive terminal ▶ **borne Wi-Fi** wireless hotspot. ◆ **bornes** nfpl fig bounds, limits ▶ **sans bornes** [patience, ambition] boundless ▶ **dépasser** ou **passer les bornes** to go too far.

borné, e [bɔʁne] adj [individu] narrow-minded ; [esprit] narrow.

Bornéo [bɔʁneo] npr Borneo ▶ **à Bornéo** in Borneo.

borner [3] [bɔʁne] vt [délimiter - champ, terrain] to mark off ou out (sép), to mark the boundary of. ◆ **se borner à** vp + prép [se contenter de] to limit ou to restrict o.s. to.

bosniaque [bɔsnjak] adj Bosnian. ◆ **Bosniaque** nmf Bosnian.

Bosnie-Herzégovine [bɔsniɛʁzegɔvin] npr f ▶ **(la) Bosnie-Herzégovine** Bosnia-Herzegovina.

bosquet [bɔskɛ] nm coppice, copse.

bosse [bɔs] nf **1.** [à la suite d'un coup] bump, lump **2.** ANAT & ZOOL [protubérance] hump **3.** [du sol] bump ; [en ski] mogul.

bosselé, e [bɔsle] adj [carrosserie] dented ; [métal ouvragé] embossed.

bosseler [24] [bɔsle] vt **1.** ART to emboss **2.** [faire des bosses à] to dent.
✏ In reformed spelling (see p. 16-18), this verb is conjugated like **peler** : *il bossèlera, elle bossèlerait.*

bosser [3] [bɔse] fam ◆ vi to work / *j'ai bossé toute la nuit pour cet examen* I stayed up all night working for that exam. ◆ vt to swot up (sép) UK, to grind away at US.

bosseur, euse [bɔsœʁ, øz] fam ◆ adj ▶ **être bosseur** to work hard, to be hardworking. ◆ nm, f hard worker.

bossu, e [bɔsy] ◆ adj humpbacked, hunchbacked. ◆ nm, f humpback, hunchback.

bot [bo] adj m ▶ **pied bot** club foot.

botanique [bɔtanik] ◆ adj botanical. ◆ nf botany.

botaniste [bɔtanist] nmf botanist.

botnet [bɔtnɛt] nm INTERNET botnet.

botte [bɔt] nf **1.** [chaussure] (high) boot ▶ **bottes de cheval** riding boots ▶ **bottes en caoutchouc** gumboots UK, wellington boots UK, rubber boots US ▶ **avoir qqn à sa botte** to have sb under one's thumb ▶ **cirer** ou **lécher les bottes de qqn** fam to lick sb's boots **2.** [de fleurs, de radis] bunch ; [de paille] sheaf, bundle **3.** ESCRIME thrust ▶ **botte secrète** secret weapon.

botter [3] [bɔte] vt **1.** SPORT to kick **2.** EXPR ça me **botte** ! fam it's great! ▶ **botter le train** ou **les fesses** ou **le derrière** fam ou **le cul** tfam **à qqn** to kick sb in the pants.

bottier [bɔtje] nm [fabricant - de bottes] bootmaker ; [- de chaussures] shoemaker.

bottillon [bɔtijɔ̃] nm ankle boot.

Bottin® [bɔtɛ̃] nm telephone directory, phone book ▶ **le Bottin mondain** directory of famous people ; ≃ Who's Who?

bottine [bɔtin] nf ankle boot.

bouc [buk] nm **1.** ZOOL goat, he-goat, billy goat ▶ **bouc émissaire** scapegoat **2.** [barbe] goatee.

boucan [bukɑ̃] nm fam din, racket ▶ **faire du boucan** to kick up a din, to make a racket.

boucane [bukan] nf QUEBEC fam smoke.

bouche [buʃ] nf **1.** ANAT & ZOOL mouth / *ne parle pas la bouche pleine* don't talk with your mouth full / *par le bouche à oreille* through the grapevine, by word of mouth ▶ **il n'a que ce mot** / **nom à la bouche** he only ever talks about one thing / person ▶ **son nom est sur toutes les bouches** her name is on everyone's lips, she's the talk of the town **2.** [orifice - d'un cratère] mouth ; [- d'un canon] muzzle ▶ **bouche d'eau** ou **d'incendie** fire hydrant ▶ **bouche d'aération** air vent ▶ **bouche d'égout** manhole, inspection chamber ▶ **bouche de métro** metro entrance, underground entrance.

bouché, e [buʃe] adj **1.** [nez] blocked ; [oreilles] blocked up ▶ **j'ai le nez bouché** my nose is blocked **2.** MÉTÉOR [ciel, horizon, temps] cloudy, overcast **3.** fam [idiot] stupid, thick UK **4.** [sans espoir - avenir] hopeless ; [- filière, secteur] oversubscribed.

bouche-à-bouche [buʃabuʃ] nm inv mouth-to-mouth resuscitation ▶ **faire du bouche-à-bouche à qqn** to give sb mouth-to-mouth resuscitation ou the kiss of life.

bouche-à-oreille [buʃaɔʁɛj] nm inv word of mouth / *on a trouvé notre maison par le* ou *grâce au bouche-à-oreille* we found our house by word of mouth.

bouchée [buʃe] nf **1.** [contenu] mouthful ▶ **ne faire qu'une bouchée de** : *elle n'a fait qu'une bouchée de ses rivales* she made short work of her rivals ▶ **mettre les bouchées doubles** to work twice as hard, to put on a spurt / *il a acheté ce tableau pour une bouchée de pain* he bought this painting for next to nothing **2.** CULIN (vol-au-vent) case ▶ **bouchée à la reine** chicken vol-au-vent.

boucher¹ [3] [buʃe] vt **1.** [fermer - trou] to fill up (sép) ; [- fuite] to plug, to stop ; [- bouteille] to cork ▶ **en boucher un coin à qqn** fam : *je parie que ça t'en bouche un coin !* I bet you're impressed! **2.** [entraver] to obstruct, to block / *tu me bouches le passage* you're in ou blocking my way / *la tour nous bouche complètement la vue* the tower cuts off ou obstructs our view totally. ◆ **se boucher** ◆ vpi **1.** [s'obstruer - tuyau, narine] to get blocked **2.** MÉTÉOR [temps] to become overcast. ◆ vpt ▶ **se boucher le nez** to hold one's nose ▶ **se boucher les oreilles** a) pr to put one's fingers in ou to plug one's ears b) fig to refuse to listen.

boucher², ère [buʃe, ɛʁ] nm, f butcher.

boucherie [buʃʁi] nf [boutique] butcher's shop UK ou store US.

bouche-trou [buʃtʁu] (pl **bouche-trous**) nm [personne] stand-in, stopgap ; [objet] makeshift replacement.

bouchon [buʃɔ̃] nm **1.** [en liège] cork ; [d'un bidon, d'une bouteille en plastique] cap ; [d'une bouteille en verre, d'une carafe] stopper ▶ **bouchon (du réservoir) d'essence** petrol cap ▶ **bouchons d'oreilles** earplugs **2.** fam [embouteillage] traffic jam ; [à une intersection] gridlock / *un bouchon de 5 km* a 5 km tailback **3.** PÊCHE float.

bouchonner [3] [buʃɔne] ◆ vt [cheval] to rub down (sép). ◆ vi : *ça bouchonne à partir de 5 h* traffic is heavy from 5 p.m. onwards.

boucle [bukl] nf **1.** [de cheveux] curl **2.** [de ceinture] buckle ; [de lacet] loop ; [d'un cours d'eau] loop, meander. ◆ **boucle d'oreille** nf earring.

bouclé, e [bukle] adj [cheveux, barbe] curly ; [personne] curly-haired.

boucler [3] [bukle] ◆ vt **1.** [fermer - ceinture] to buckle, to fasten ▸ **boucler sa valise a)** *pr* to shut one's suitcase **b)** *fig* to pack one's bags ▸ **la boucler** *fam* : *toi, tu la boucles !* not a word out of you! **2.** [dans une opération policière] ▸ **boucler une avenue / un quartier** to seal off an avenue / area **3.** *fam* [enfermer] to shut away *(sép)*, to lock up *(sép)* **4.** [mettre un terme à - affaire] to finish off *(sép)*, to settle ; [- programme de révisions] to finish (off) ▸ **boucler un journal / une édition** PRESSE to put a paper / an edition to bed **5.** [équilibrer] ▸ **boucler son budget** to make ends meet ▸ *il a du mal à boucler ses fins de mois* he's always in the red at the end of the month **6.** AÉRON ▸ **boucler la boucle** to loop the loop ▸ **la boucle est bouclée** ou **on a bouclé la boucle** we're back to square one **7.** [cheveux, mèches] to curl. ◆ vi [cheveux] to curl, to be curly.

bouclier [buklije] nm **1.** [protection de soldat] shield ; [de policier] riot shield **2.** [protection] shield **3.** ÉCON ▸ **bouclier fiscal** tax shield.

bouddhisme [budism] nm Buddhism.

bouddhiste [budist] adj Buddhist.

bouder [3] [bude] ◆ vi to sulk. ◆ vt [ami] to refuse to talk to ; [dessert, cadeau] to refuse to accept ; [élection] to refuse to vote ; [fournisseur] to stay away from / *le public a boudé son film* hardly anyone went to see her film.

boudeur, euse [budœr, øz] adj sulky, sullen.

boudin [budɛ̃] nm **1.** CULIN ▸ **boudin (noir)** blood ou black pudding UK, blood sausage US ▸ **boudin blanc** white pudding UK, white sausage US **2.** *fam & péj* [femme] : *sa sœur est un vrai boudin !* his sister looks like the back of a bus UK ou a Mack truck US!

boudiné, e [budine] adj [doigt, main] podgy UK, pudgy US / *je me sens boudinée dans cette robe* this dress is too tight for me.

boudoir [budwar] nm **1.** [pièce] boudoir **2.** [biscuit] sponge finger UK, ladyfinger US.

boue [bu] nf **1.** [terre détrempée] mud **2.** [dépôt] sludge.

bouée [bwe] nf **1.** [en mer] buoy **2.** [pour nager] rubber ring ▸ **bouée de sauvetage** lifebelt, lifebuoy.

boueux, euse [buø, øz] adj [sale - trottoir] muddy ; [- tapis] mud-stained. ◆ **boueux** nm *fam* bin man UK, dustman UK, garbage collector US.

bouffant, e [bufɑ̃, ɑ̃t] adj [cheveux] bouffant ; [manche] puffed out.

bouffe [buf] nf *fam* food, grub, nosh / *on se fait une bouffe ?* do you fancy getting together for a meal?

bouffée [bufe] nf **1.** [exhalaison] puff ▸ **une bouffée d'air frais** *pr & fig* a breath of fresh air **2.** [accès] fit, outburst ▸ **avoir des bouffées de chaleur** MÉD to have hot flushes UK ou flashes US.

bouffer [3] [bufe] vt *fam* **1.** [manger] to eat ; [manger voracement] to guzzle ▸ **je l'aurais bouffé !** *fig* I could have killed him! ; *(en usage absolu)* : *on a bien / mal bouffé* the food was great / terrible **2.** [accaparer] : *les enfants me bouffent tout mon temps* the kids take up every minute of my time / *tu te laisses bouffer par ta mère* you're letting your mother walk all over you. ◆ **se bouffer** vp *(emploi réciproque) fam* ▸ **se bouffer le nez a)** [une fois] to have a go at one another **b)** [constamment] to be at daggers drawn.

bouffi, e [bufi] adj [yeux] puffed-up, puffy ; [visage] puffed-up, puffy, bloated.

bouffon [bufɔ̃] nm buffoon ▸ **le bouffon du roi** HIST the king's jester.

bouge [buʒ] nm [logement] hovel.

bougeoir [buʒwar] nm candleholder, candlestick.

bougeotte [buʒɔt] nf *fam* fidgets ▸ **avoir la bougeotte a)** [remuer] to have the fidgets **b)** [voyager] to have itchy feet.

bouger [17] [buʒe] ◆ vi **1.** [remuer] to move ▸ **rien ne bouge** nothing's stirring ▸ **rester sans bouger** to stay still **2.** [se déplacer] to move **3.** [se modifier - couleur d'un tissu] to fade / *les prix n'ont pas bougé* prices haven't changed ou altered **4.** [s'activer] to move, to stir / *ce projet a fait bouger les habitants du quartier* the project has spurred the local inhabitants into action. ◆ vt to move, to shift. ◆ **se bouger** vpi *fam* : *si on se bougeait un peu ?* come on, let's get moving ou let's get a move on! / *tu ne t'es pas beaucoup bougé pour trouver un nouveau boulot* you didn't try very hard to find a new job.

bougie [buʒi] nf **1.** [en cire] candle **2.** AUTO ▸ **bougie (d'allumage)** sparking UK ou spark US plug.

bougon, onne [bugɔ̃, ɔn] adj grouchy, grumpy.

bougonner [3] [bugɔne] vi to grouch, to grumble.

bougre [bugr] *fam & vieilli* nm [homme] chap, fellow ▸ **un pauvre bougre** a poor bloke UK ou guy US.

boui-boui *(pl* bouis-bouis*)*, **bouiboui*** [bwibwi] nm *fam* [restaurant] caff UK, greasy spoon.

bouillabaisse [bujabɛs] nf bouillabaisse.

bouillant, e [bujɑ̃, ɑ̃t] adj **1.** [qui bout] boiling ; [très chaud] boiling hot **2.** [ardent] fiery, passionate.

bouille [buj] nf *fam* [figure] face, mug.

bouillie [buji] nf baby food ou cereal ▸ **c'est de la bouillie pour les chats** it's a dog's breakfast. ◆ **en bouillie** loc adj & adv crushed.

bouillir [48] [bujir] vi **1.** [arriver à ébullition] to boil **2.** [s'irriter] to boil ▸ **bouillir d'impatience / de colère** to seethe with impatience / anger.

bouilloire [bujwar] nf kettle.

bouillon [bujɔ̃] nm **1.** CULIN broth, stock ▸ **bouillon cube** stock cube ▸ **bouillon de légumes** vegetable stock **2.** BIOL ▸ **bouillon de culture** *pr* culture medium **3.** [remous] : *éteindre le feu dès le premier bouillon* turn off the heat as soon as it boils / *bouillir à gros bouillons* to boil fast ou hard.

bouillonner [3] [bujɔne] vi [liquide] to bubble ; [source] to foam, to froth ▸ **ils bouillonnent d'idées** *fig* they're full of ideas.

bouillotte [bujɔt] nf hot-water bottle.

boulanger, ère [bulɑ̃ʒe, ɛr] nm, f baker.

boulangerie [bulɑ̃ʒri] nf [boutique] bakery, baker's (shop UK ou store US) ▸ **boulangerie pâtisserie** baker's and confectioner's, bread and cake shop.

boule [bul] nf **1.** [sphère] ball ▸ **boule de billard** billiard ball ▸ **boule de cristal** crystal ball ▸ **boule de loto** billiard ball ▸ **boule de neige** snowball ▸ **boule puante** stinkbomb ▸ **boules Quiès®** earplugs ▸ **avoir une boule dans la gorge** to have a lump in one's throat **2.** *fam* [tête] ▸ **coup de boule** headbutt **3.** JEUX ▸ **boule (de pétanque)** (steel) bowl ▸ **jouer aux boules** to play boules (popular French game played on bare ground with steel bowls). ◆ **boules** nfpl *tfam* ▸ **avoir les boules a)** [être effrayé] to be scared stiff **b)** [être furieux] to be pissed off **c)** [être déprimé] to be feeling down. ◆ **en boule** loc adj & loc adv [en rond - animal] ▸ **se mettre en boule** to curl up into a ball ;

---

* In reformed spelling (see p. 16-18).

fam [en colère] ▸ **être en boule** to be hopping mad, to be furious / *ça me met en boule* it makes me mad, it really gets my goat.

bouleau, x [bulo] nm BOT birch.

bouledogue [buldɔg] nm bulldog.

boulet [bulɛ] nm **1.** ARM ▸ **boulet de canon** cannonball ; [de prisonnier] ball (and chain) **2.** MIN (coal) nut **3.** *fam* [personne] : *quel boulet celui-là !* he's such a drag!

boulette [bulɛt] nf **1.** CULIN ▸ **boulette (de viande)** meatball **2.** [de papier] pellet **3.** *fam* [erreur] blunder, blooper 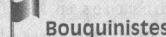.

boulevard [bulvaʀ] nm [avenue] boulevard ; [à Paris] ▸ **le boulevard périphérique** the (Paris) ring road 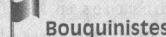 ou beltway 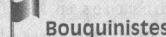. ◆ **de boulevard** loc adj THÉÂTRE ▸ **pièce de boulevard** light comedy.

bouleversant, e [bulvɛʀsã, ãt] adj upsetting, distressing.

bouleversement [bulvɛʀsəmã] nm upheaval, upset / *le bouleversement de toutes mes habitudes* the disruption of my entire routine.

bouleverser [3] [bulvɛʀse] vt [émouvoir] to move deeply ; [affliger] to upset, to distress.

boulgour [bulguʀ] nm bulgar ou bulgur wheat.

boulier [bulje] nm abacus.

boulimie [bulimi] nf compulsive eating, bulimia *spéc* / *être atteint de boulimie* ou *faire de la boulimie* to be a compulsive eater.

bouliste [bulist] nmf boules player.

boulon [bulɔ̃] nm bolt ▸ **boulon avec écrou** nut and bolt ▸ **serrer les boulons** *fam & fig* to tighten the screws.

boulot¹ [bulo] nm *fam* **1.** [fait de travailler] ▸ **le boulot** work **2.** [ouvrage réalisé] piece of work, job / *il s'est coupé les cheveux tout seul, t'aurais vu le boulot !* he cut his own hair, you should have seen the mess! **3.** [travail à faire] : *il y a encore du boulot dessus !* it needs loads more work on it! **4.** [emploi, poste] job ▸ **faire des petits boulots** to do casual work **5.** [lieu] work.

boulot², otte [bulo, ɔt] adj *fam* plump, tubby.

boum [bum] ◆ interj bang ▸ **faire boum** to go bang. ◆ nm [bruit] bang. ◆ nf *fam* party (for teenagers).

bouquet [bukɛ] nm **1.** [fleurs - gén] bunch ; [- grand, décoratif] bouquet ; [- petit] sprig, spray **2.** [groupe - d'arbres] clump, cluster **3.** [dans un feu d'artifice] crowning ou final piece, the (grand) finale ▸ **alors ça, c'est le bouquet !** *fam* that's the limit!, that takes the biscuit 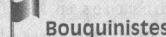 ou cake 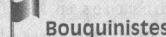! **4.** CULIN ▸ **bouquet garni** bouquet garni **5.** ŒNOL bouquet, nose **6.** TV ▸ **bouquet numérique** digital channel package.

bouquetin [buktɛ̃] nm ibex.

bouquin [bukɛ̃] nm *fam* [livre] book.

bouquiner [3] [bukine] vt & vi *fam* to read.

bouquiniste [bukinist] nmf secondhand bookseller.

🚩 **Bouquinistes**

In Paris, this term can refer specifically to the people who sell books, prints, cards, etc., from small stalls along the banks of the Seine.

---

bourde [buʀd] nf [bêtise] blunder, bloomer 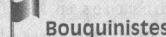, blooper 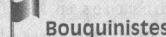 ▸ **faire une bourde a)** [gaffer] to blunder, to put one's foot in it **b)** [faire une erreur] to make a mistake, to mess things up, to goof (up) 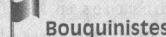.

bourdon [buʀdɔ̃] nm **1.** ZOOL bumblebee, humblebee **2.** [cloche] great bell **3.** EXPR avoir le bourdon *fam* to feel down, to be down in the dumps.

bourdonnement [buʀdɔnmã] nm [vrombissement - d'un insecte, d'une voix] hum, buzz, drone ; [- d'un ventilateur, d'un moteur] hum, drone / *avoir un bourdonnement dans les oreilles* to have a ringing in one's ears.

bourdonner [3] [buʀdɔne] vi [insecte, voix] to hum, to buzz, to drone ; [moteur] to hum ; [oreille] to ring ; [lieu] to buzz.

bourg [buʀ] nm (market) town.

bourgade [buʀgad] nf (large) village, small town.

bourge [buʀʒ] *fam & péj* ◆ adj upper-class. ◆ nmf upper-class person / *chez les bourges* in upper-class circles.

bourgeois, e [buʀʒwa, az] ◆ adj **1.** [dans un sens marxiste] of the bourgeoisie, bourgeois **2.** [dans un sens non marxiste] middle-class **3.** [aisé, confortable] ▸ **quartier bourgeois** comfortable residential area. ◆ nm, f [dans un sens non marxiste] member of the middle class ▸ **grand bourgeois** member of the upper-middle class.

bourgeoisie [buʀʒwazi] nf [classe aisée, professions libérales] middle class ▸ **la petite / moyenne bourgeoisie** the lower middle / the middle class ▸ **la grande** ou **haute bourgeoisie** the upper-middle class.

bourgeon [buʀʒɔ̃] nm BOT & MÉD bud.

bourgeonner [3] [buʀʒɔne] vi BOT to bud.

bourgogne [buʀgɔɲ] ◆ nm Burgundy (wine). ◆ adj inv QUÉBEC [couleur] burgundy.

bourguignon, onne [buʀgiɲɔ̃, ɔn] adj CULIN [sauce] bourguignonne ▸ **bœuf bourguignon** beef stewed in red wine.

bourlinguer [3] [buʀlɛ̃ge] vi [voyager par mer] to sail (around).

bourrage [buʀaʒ] nm **1.** [remplissage - d'un coussin] stuffing ; [- d'une chaise] filling, padding ; [- d'une pipe, d'un poêle] filling ▸ **bourrage de crâne a)** *fam* [propagande] brainwashing **b)** ÉDUC cramming **2.** [d'imprimante, de photocopieur] paper jam.

bourrasque [buʀask] nf [coup de vent] squall, gust ou blast (of wind) ▸ **souffler en bourrasque** to blow in gusts, to gust.

bourrasser [3] [buʀase] vt QUÉBEC to push around, to bully.

bourratif, ive [buʀatif, iv] adj *fam* filling, stodgy *péj*.

bourre [buʀ] ◆ **à la bourre** loc adv *fam* ▸ **être à la bourre a)** to be in a rush **b)** [dans son travail] to be behind.

bourré, e [buʀe] adj *tfam* pissed 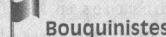, bombed 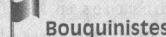.

bourreau, x [buʀo] nm **1.** [exécuteur - gén] executioner ; [- qui pend] hangman **2.** [tortionnaire] torturer ▸ **bourreau d'enfant** child beater ▸ **bourreau des cœurs** heartbreaker ▸ **bourreau de travail** workaholic.

bourrelet [buʀlɛ] nm [de graisse] fold ▸ **bourrelet de chair** roll of flesh.

bourrer [3] [buʀe] vt **1.** [rembourrer] to fill, to stuff **2.** [remplir - pipe] to fill ; [- poche] to fill, to cram, to stuff ; [- valise, tiroir] to cram (full), to pack tightly ▸ **bourrer le crâne** ou **le mou à qqn** *fam* to have 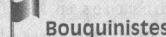 ou to put 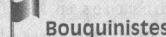 sb on **3.** [gaver - suj : aliment] to fill up **4.** [frapper] ▸ **bourrer qqn de coups** to beat sb (up). ◆ **se bourrer** vp (emploi réfléchi) EXPR **se bourrer la gueule** *tfam* to get pissed 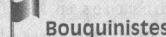 ou bombed 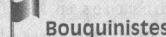.

bourrique [buʀik] nf **1.** ZOOL donkey **2.** *fam* [personne obstinée] pig-headed individual **3.** EXPR **faire tourner qqn en bourrique** to drive sb crazy ou up the wall.

bourru, e [buʀy] adj [rude - personne, manières] gruff, rough.

bourse [buʀs] nf **1.** [porte-monnaie] purse **2.** ÉDUC & UNIV ▶ **bourse (d'études) a)** [gén] grant **b)** [obtenue au mérite] scholarship.

Bourse [buʀs] nf [marché] stock exchange, stock market.

boursicoter [3] [buʀsikɔte] vi to dabble (on the stock exchange).

boursier, ère [buʀsje, ɛʀ] ◆ adj **1.** UNIV & ÉDUC ▶ **un étudiant boursier** a grant ou scholarship holder **2.** [de la Bourse] stock exchange (modif), (stock) market (modif). ◆ nm, f **1.** UNIV & ÉDUC grant ou scholarship holder **2.** BOURSE operator.

boursouflé, e, boursoufflé*, e [buʀsufle] adj [gonflé - visage] swollen, puffy ; [- peinture] blistered ; [- plaie] swollen.

boursoufler, boursouffler* [3] [buʀsufle] ◆ **se boursoufler, se boursouffler*** vpi [visage] to become swollen ou puffy ; [peinture] to blister ; [surface] to swell (up).

bousculade [buskylad] nf **1.** [agitation] crush, pushing and shoving **2.** fam [précipitation] rush.

bousculer [3] [buskyle] vt **1.** [pousser - voyageur, passant] to jostle, to push, to shove ; [- chaise, table] to bump ou to knock into **2.** fig [changer brutalement] to upset, to turn on its head, to turn upside down **3.** [presser] to rush, to hurry ▶ **j'ai été très bousculé** I've had a lot to do ou a very busy time. ◆ **se bousculer** vpi **1.** [dans une cohue] to jostle, to push and shove **2.** [affluer] to rush / **les idées se bousculaient dans sa tête** his head was a jumble of ideas.

bouse [buz] nf ▶ **bouse (de vache) a)** [matière] cow dung **b)** [motte] cowpat.

bousiller [3] [buzije] vt fam **1.** [casser] to bust, to wreck ; [gâcher] to spoil, to ruin **2.** tfam [tuer] to bump off (sép), to do in (sép), to waste. ◆ **se bousiller** vpt fam ▶ **se bousiller les yeux / la santé** to ruin one's eyes / health.

boussole [busɔl] nf **1.** [instrument] compass **2.** fam EXPR **perdre la boussole** : **il a complètement perdu la boussole a)** [vieillard] he's lost his marbles, he's gone gaga **b)** [fou] he's off his head ou rocker.

bout [bu] nm **1.** [extrémité - d'un couteau, d'un crayon] tip ; [- d'une table, d'une ficelle] end ▶ **à bouts ronds** round-tipped ▶ **bout du doigt** fingertip, tip of the finger ▶ **bout du nez** tip of the nose ▶ **bout de sein** nipple ▶ **à bout filtre** filter-tipped ▶ **le bon bout** : **prendre qqch par le bon bout** to get hold of sthg the right way round ▶ **je ne sais pas par quel bout le prendre a)** [personne] I don't know how to handle ou to approach him **b)** [article, travail] I don't know how to tackle ou to approach it ▶ **aborder** ou **considérer** ou **voir les choses par le petit bout de la lorgnette** to take a narrow view of things ▶ **il a accepté du bout des lèvres** he accepted reluctantly ou half-heartedly ▶ **je l'ai sur le bout de la langue** it's on the tip of my tongue ▶ **sur le bout des doigts** perfectly, by heart ▶ **s'asseoir du bout des fesses** to sit down gingerly ▶ **en voir le bout** : **enfin, on en voit le bout** at last, we're beginning to see the light at the end of the tunnel **2.** [extrémité - d'un espace] end ▶ **le bout du monde** the back of beyond ▶ **ce n'est pas le bout du monde!** it won't kill you! **3.** [portion de temps] : **ça fait un bon bout de temps de ça** fam it was quite a long time ago ou a while back **4.** [morceau] ▶ **bout de a)** [pain, bois, terrain] piece of **b)** [papier] scrap of / **un bout de ciel bleu** a patch of blue sky ▶ **bout de chou** ou **zan a)** fam [enfant] toddler **b)** [en appellatif] sweetie, poppet UK ▶ **ça fait un bon bout de chemin** it's quite some ou a way ▶ **faire un bout de chemin avec qqn** to go part of the way with sb ▶ **mettre les bouts** tfam to make o.s. scarce. ◆ **à bout** loc adv ▶ **être à bout** to be at the end of one's tether / **ma patience est à bout !** I've run out of patience! ▶ **mettre** ou **pousser qqn à bout** to push sb to

the limit. ◆ **à bout de** loc prép **1.** ▶ **être à bout de** [ne plus avoir de] : **être à bout d'arguments** to have run out of arguments ▶ **être à bout de forces** : **il est à bout de forces a)** [physiquement] he's got no strength left in him **b)** [psychologiquement] he can't cope any more / **être à bout de nerfs** to be on the verge of a breakdown ▶ EXPR **venir à bout de a)** [adversaire, obstacle] to overcome **b)** [travail] to see the end of. ◆ **à bout portant** loc adv point-blank ▶ **tirer (sur qqn / qqch) à bout portant** to shoot (sb / sthg) at point-blank range. ◆ **à tout bout de champ** loc adv all the time, non-stop. ◆ **au bout de** loc prép **1.** [après] after ▶ **au bout d'un moment** after a while **2.** [à la fin de] : **pas encore au bout de ses peines** not out of the woods yet **3.** [dans l'espace] : **au bout de la rue** at the bottom ou end of the road ▶ **être au bout du rouleau a)** [épuisé] to be completely washed out **b)** [presque mort] to be at death's door. ◆ **au bout du compte** loc adv at the end of the day, in the end. ◆ **bout à bout** loc adv end to end. ◆ **de bout en bout** loc adv [lire] from cover to cover / **elle a mené la course de bout en bout** she led the race from start to finish. ◆ **d'un bout à l'autre** loc adv : **la pièce est drôle d'un bout à l'autre** the play's hilarious from beginning to end ou from start to finish. ◆ **d'un bout de... à l'autre** loc corrélative : **d'un bout à l'autre du pays, les militants s'organisent** (right) throughout the country, the militants are organizing themselves. ◆ **en bout de** loc prép at the end of ▶ **en bout de course** at the end of the race. ◆ **jusqu'au bout** loc adv to the very end.

boutade [butad] nf [plaisanterie] joke, sally sout.

boute-en-train (pl **boute-en-train**), **bouten-train*** [butɑ̃tʀɛ̃] nm [amuseur] funny man, joker / **le boute-en-train de la bande** the life and soul of the group.

bouteille [butej] nf [récipient - pour un liquide] bottle ; [- pour un gaz] bottle, cylinder ▶ **une bouteille de vin** [récipient] a wine bottle ▶ **avoir de la bouteille** to be an old hand ▶ **prendre de la bouteille** fam to be getting on UK knocking on a bit.

boutique [butik] nf [magasin] shop UK, store US ▶ **boutique de mode** boutique.

bouton [butɔ̃] nm **1.** BOT bud **2.** COUT button ▶ **bouton de manchette** cuff link **3.** [poignée de porte, de tiroir] knob **4.** [de mise en marche] button **5.** MÉD pimple, spot ▶ **bouton de fièvre** fever blister, cold sore ▶ **donner des boutons à qqn** to get on sb's nerves / **cette série me donne des boutons !** this series really get on my nerves / **c'est le rapport qui donne des boutons à la majorité** the report that brought the majority out in a cold sweat. ◆ **en bouton** loc adj BOT in bud.

bouton-d'or [butɔ̃dɔʀ] (pl **boutons-d'or**) nm buttercup.

boutonner [3] [butɔne] ◆ vt [vêtement] to button (up), to do up (sép). ◆ vi BOT to bud (up). ◆ **se boutonner** vp [emploi passif] to be fermer] to button (up). ◆ vp [emploi réfléchi] fam [s'habiller] to button o.s. up.

boutonneux, euse [butɔnø, øz] adj [peau, visage, adolescent] spotty, pimply.

boutonnière [butɔnjɛʀ] nf COUT buttonhole. ◆ **à la boutonnière** loc adv on one's lapel.

bouton-pression [butɔ̃pʀesjɔ̃] (pl **boutons-pression**) nm snap (fastener) US, press stud UK, popper UK.

bouture [butyʀ] nf cutting ▶ **faire des boutures** to take cuttings.

bouvreuil [buvʀœj] nm bullfinch.

bovidé [bɔvide] nm bovid.

bovin, e [bɔvɛ̃, in] adj ZOOL [espèce] bovine ; [élevage] cattle *(modif)*. ❖ **bovin** nm bovine ▸ **les bovins a)** ZOOL the Bovini **b)** AGR cattle.

bowling [buliŋ] nm **1.** JEUX (tenpin) bowling ▸ **aller faire un bowling** to go bowling **2.** [salle] bowling alley.

box [bɔks] *(pl* box *ou* boxes*)* nm **1.** [enclos - pour cheval] stall, loose box 🇬🇧 **2.** [garage] lock-up garage **3.** DR ▸ **box des accusés** dock ▸ **dans le box des accusés** *pr & fig* in the dock.

boxe [bɔks] nf boxing ▸ **faire de la boxe** to box ▸ **boxe anglaise** boxing ▸ **boxe française** kick ou French boxing.

boxer[1] [bɔksɛʀ] nm ZOOL boxer.

boxer[2] [3] [bɔkse] ❖ vi to box, to fight ▸ **boxer contre qqn** to box with sb. ❖ vt *fam* to punch, to thump.

boxeur, euse [bɔksœʀ, øz] nm, f boxer.

boyau, x [bwajo] nm **1.** MUS ▸ **boyau (de chat)** catgut, gut **2.** 🇨🇦 [d'arrosage] garden hose ; [d'incendie] fire hose. ❖ **boyaux** nmpl ZOOL guts, entrails ; *fam* [d'une personne] innards, guts.

boycott [bɔjkɔt], **boycottage** [bɔjkɔtaʒ] nm boycott.

boycotter [3] [bɔjkɔte] vt to boycott.

boy-scout *(pl* boy-scouts*)*, **boyscout*** [bɔjskut] nm **1.** *fam* [naïf] idealist **2.** *vieilli* [scout] boyscout, scout.

BP *(abr de* boîte postale*)* nf P.O. Box.

bracelet [brasle] nm **1.** [souple] bracelet ; [rigide] bangle ▸ **bracelet (de cheville)** anklet ▸ **bracelet (de montre)** watchstrap, watchband 🇺🇸 **2.** [pour un condamné] ▸ **bracelet électronique** electronic tag.

bracelet-montre [braslɛmɔ̃tʀ] *(pl* bracelets-montres*)* nm wristwatch.

braconnage [brakɔnaʒ] nm CHASSE poaching.

braconner [3] [brakɔne] vi CHASSE to poach.

braconnier, ère [brakɔnje, ɛʀ] nm, f CHASSE poacher.

brader [3] [brade] vt to sell off *(sép)* cheaply.

braderie [bradʀi] nf [vente - en plein air, dans une salle] ≃ jumble sale 🇬🇧 ; ≃ rummage sale 🇺🇸.

braguette [bragɛt] nf flies 🇬🇧, fly 🇺🇸 *(on trousers)*.

braille [bʀaj] nm Braille.

braillement [bʀajmɑ̃] nm bawl, howl.

brailler [3] [bʀaje] ❖ vi [crier - mégère, ivrogne] to yell, to bawl ; [- radio] to blare (out). ❖ vt to bawl (out), to holler (out) 🇺🇸.

braire [112] [bʀɛʀ] vi ZOOL to bray.

braise [bʀɛz] nf [charbons] (glowing) embers ▸ **un regard de braise** *fig* a smouldering look.

braiser [4] [bʀɛze] vt to braise.

bramer [3] [bʀame] vi ZOOL to bell.

brancard [bʀɑ̃kaʀ] nm [civière] stretcher.

brancardier [bʀɑ̃kaʀdje] nm stretcher-bearer.

branchages [bʀɑ̃ʃaʒ] nmpl (cut) branches.

branche [bʀɑ̃ʃ] nf **1.** BOT [d'arbre] branch, bough ; [de céleri] stick **2.** [secteur] ▸ **branche (d'activité)** field **3.** [d'une famille] side **4.** [tige - de lunettes] sidepiece 🇬🇧, bow 🇺🇸 ; [- d'un compas, d'un aimant] arm, leg ; [- de ciseaux] blade ; [- de tenailles] handle ; [- d'un chandelier] branch.

branché, e [bʀɑ̃ʃe] *fam* ❖ adj fashionable, trendy *péj.* ❖ nm, f : *tous les branchés viennent dans ce café* you get all the fashionable people ou *péj* trendies in this café.

branchement [bʀɑ̃ʃmɑ̃] nm CONSTR, ÉLECTR, TÉLÉC & TRAV PUB connection ▸ **branchement d'appareil a)** [tuyau] connecting branch **b)** [liaison] connection, installation.

brancher [3] [bʀɑ̃ʃe] ❖ vt **1.** CONSTR, ÉLECTR, TÉLÉC & TRAV PUB to connect ▸ **brancher qqch sur une prise** to plug sthg in ▸ **être branché a)** [appareil] to be plugged in **b)** [canalisation] to be connected to the system **2.** *fam* [faire parler] ▸ **brancher qqn sur** to start sb off ou to get sb going on **3.** *fam* [intéresser] : *ça me branche bien !* that's great ! / *ça vous brancherait d'y aller ?* how do you fancy going there ? ❖ vi to roost, to sit. ❖ **se brancher** vp *(emploi passif)* ▸ **se brancher dans** to plug into.

branchies [bʀɑ̃ʃi] nfpl gills, branchiae *spéc.*

brandade [bʀɑ̃dad] nf ▸ **brandade de morue** brandade, salt cod puree.

brandir [32] [bʀɑ̃diʀ] vt to brandish, to wave (about), to flourish.

branlant, e [bʀɑ̃lɑ̃, ɑ̃t] adj **1.** [vieux - bâtiment, véhicule] ramshackle, rickety **2.** [instable - pile d'objets] unsteady, wobbly, shaky ; [- échelle, chaise] rickety, shaky ; [- démarche] tottering ; [- dent] loose ; [- résolution, réputation] shaky.

branle [bʀɑ̃l] nm [mouvement] pendulum motion ; [impulsion] impulsion, propulsion ▸ **mettre en branle a)** [cloche] to set going **b)** [mécanisme, procédure] to set going ou in motion ▸ **se mettre en branle a)** [voyageur] to set off, to start out **b)** [mécanisme] to start moving, to start going **c)** [voiture] to start (moving).

branle-bas *(pl* branle-bas*)*, **branlebas*** [bʀɑ̃lba] nm [agitation] pandemonium, commotion ▸ **branle-bas de combat !** NAUT & *fig* action stations !

branler [3] [bʀɑ̃le] ❖ vi [échelle, pile d'objets] to be shaky ou unsteady ; [fauteuil] to be rickety ; [dent] to be loose. ❖ vt *tfam* [faire] ▸ **mais qu'est-ce qu'il branle ? a)** [il est en retard] where the fuck is he ? **b)** [il fait une bêtise] what the fuck's he up to ? ❖ **se branler** vpi *tfam* to (have a) wank 🇬🇧, to jerk off 🇺🇸 ▸ **je m'en branle** *fig* I don't give a shit ou fuck.

branleur, euse [bʀɑ̃lœʀ, øz] nm, f *tfam* wanker 🇬🇧, little shit.

braquage [bʀakaʒ] nm **1.** AUTO (steering) lock **2.** *fam* [vol] holdup, stickup.

braquer [3] [bʀake] ❖ vt **1.** [pointer - fusil] to point, to aim, to level ; [- projecteur, télescope] to train ▸ **braquer son revolver sur qqn** to level ou to point one's gun at sb **2.** [concentrer] : *son regard était braqué sur moi* she was staring straight at me, her gaze was fixed on me **3.** AUTO & AÉRON to lock **4.** [rendre hostile] to antagonize ▸ **braquer qqn contre** to set sb against **5.** *fam* [attaquer - banque] to hold up *(insép)* ; [- caissier] to hold up at gunpoint. ❖ vi [voiture] to lock ▸ **braquer à droite / gauche** to lock hard to the right / left ▸ **braque à fond !** wheel hard down ! ❖ **se braquer** vpi to dig one's heels in.

braqueur, euse [bʀakœʀ, øz] nm, f holdup man (holdup woman) *(in bank, etc.)*.

bras [bʀa] ❖ nm **1.** [membre] arm ; ANAT upper arm ▸ **tomber dans les bras de qqn** to fall into sb's arms ▸ **serrer qqn dans ses bras** to hold sb in one's arms, to hug sb ▸ **tendre** ou **allonger le bras** to stretch one's arm out ▸ **bras droit** right hand man (woman) ▸ **faire un bras de fer avec qqn a)** *pr* to arm-wrestle with sb **b)** *fig* to have a tussle with sb ▸ **faire un bras d'honneur à qqn** ≃ to give sb a V-sign 🇬🇧 ou the finger & 🇺🇸 ▸ **avoir le bras long** to be influential ▸ **les bras croisés** with one's arms folded ▸ **rester les bras croisés** *fig* to stand idly by ▸ **les bras lui en sont tombés** his jaw dropped ou fell ▸ **les bras vous en tombent** : *quand on entend ça, les bras vous en tombent* the mind boggles when you hear that ▸ **lever les bras au ciel** to throw up one's arms in indignation **2.** [partie - d'une ancre, d'un électrophone, d'un moulin] arm ; [- d'une charrette] arm, shaft ; [- d'une grue] arm, jib ; [- d'un fauteuil] arm, armrest ; [- d'une brouette] handle ; [- d'une manivelle] web, arm ; [- d'un brancard] pole ; [- d'une croix] arm **3.** GÉOGR [d'un delta] arm. ❖ nmpl [main-d'œuvre] workers

▸ **manquer de bras** to be short-handed, to be short of manpower ou labour. ❖ **à bras ouverts** loc adv [accueillir] with open arms. ❖ **au bras de** loc prép on the arm of, arm in arm with. ❖ **bras dessus, bras dessous** loc adv arm in arm. ❖ **sur les bras** loc adv ▸ **avoir qqn / qqch sur les bras** to be stuck with sb / sthg.

brasier [bʀazje] nm [incendie] blaze, fire.

bras-le-corps [bʀalkɔʀ] ❖ **à bras-le-corps** loc adv ▸ **prendre qqn à bras-le-corps** to catch hold of ou to seize sb around the waist.

brassage [bʀasaʒ] nm **1.** [de la bière] brewing ; [du malt] mashing **2.** [de liquides] mixing, swirling together ; [des cultures, des peuples] intermixing, intermingling.

brassard [bʀasaʀ] nm armband.

brasse [bʀas] nf SPORT breaststroke ▸ **brasse papillon** butterfly (stroke).

brassée [bʀase] nf **1.** armful **2.** ⓆUÉBEC [de linge] load.

brasser [3] [bʀase] vt **1.** [bière] to brew ; [malt] to mash **2.** [manier - argent, sommes] to handle ▸ **brasser des affaires** to handle a lot of business ▸ **brasser du vent** péj to blow hot air fam.

brasserie [bʀasʀi] nf **1.** [fabrique de bière] brewery **2.** [café] large café serving light meals.

brasseur, euse [bʀasœʀ, øz] nm, f [fabricant de bière] brewer. ❖ **brasseur d'affaires** nm big businessman.

brassière [bʀasjeʀ] nf **1.** VÊT (baby's) vest ⓊⓀ ou undershirt ⓊS **2.** NAUT ▸ **brassière de sauvetage** life jacket **3.** ⓆUÉBEC bra.

bravade [bʀavad] nf [ostentation] bravado ; [défi] defiance ▸ **faire qqch par bravade a)** [ostentation] to do sthg out of bravado **b)** [défi] to do sthg in a spirit of defiance.

brave [bʀav] ❖ adj **1.** [courageux] brave, bold ▸ **faire le brave** to act brave **2.** (avant nom) [bon] good, decent ▸ **de braves gens** good ou decent people ▸ **un brave type** fam a nice bloke ⓊⓀ ou guy. ❖ nmf [héros] brave man (woman).

⚠ L'adjectif anglais **brave** ne signifie brave qu'au sens de « courageux ».

bravement [bʀavmɑ̃] adv [courageusement] bravely, courageously.

braver [3] [bʀave] vt **1.** [affronter - danger, mort] to defy, to brave ; [- conventions] to go against, to challenge **2.** [défier - autorité] to defy, to stand up to (insép).

bravo [bʀavo] ❖ interj **1.** [applaudissement] bravo **2.** [félicitations] well done, bravo. ❖ nm bravo / **un grand bravo pour nos candidats** let's have a big hand for our contestants.

bravoure [bʀavuʀ] nf bravery, courage.

break [bʀɛk] nm **1.** AUTO estate car ⓊⓀ, station wagon ⓊS **2.** SPORT ▸ **faire le break** to break away ; [à la boxe] break.

breakdance [bʀɛkdɑ̃s] nm breakdancing.

brebis [bʀəbi] nf ZOOL ewe ▸ **brebis galeuse** black sheep.

brèche [bʀɛʃ] nf **1.** [ouverture] breach, gap, break **2.** MIL breach ▸ **être toujours sur la brèche** to be always on the go.

bredouille [bʀəduj] adj empty-handed.

bredouiller [3] [bʀəduje] vi & vt to mumble, to mutter.

bref, brève [bʀɛf, bʀɛv] adj **1.** [court - moment, vision] brief, fleeting ; [concis - lettre, discours] brief, short ▸ **soyez bref** be brief **2.** PHON [syllabe, voyelle] short. ❖ **bref** ❖ adv in short, in a word / **enfin bref, je n'ai pas envie d'y aller** well, basically, I don't want to go / **bref, ce n'est pas possible** anyway, it's not possible. ❖ nm RELIG (papal) brief. ❖ **brève** nf PRESSE, RADIO & TV brief ▸ **brèves de**

comptoir bar talk. ❖ **en bref** loc adv [en résumé] in short, in brief.

brelan [bʀəlɑ̃] nm three of a kind ▸ **brelan de rois** three kings.

breloque [bʀəlɔk] nf [bijou] charm.

Brésil [bʀezil] npr m ▸ **le Brésil** Brazil.

brésilien, enne [bʀeziljɛ̃, ɛn] adj Brazilian. ❖ **Brésilien, enne** nm, f Brazilian. ❖ **brésilien** nm LING Brazilian Portuguese.

Bretagne [bʀətaɲ] npr f ▸ **(la) Bretagne** Brittany.

bretelle [bʀətɛl] nf **1.** [bandoulière] (shoulder) strap **2.** [de robe] shoulder strap ; [de soutien-gorge] (bra) strap ▸ **sans bretelles** [robe, soutien-gorge] strapless **3.** TRANSP slip road ⓊⓀ, access road ▸ **bretelle d'autoroute** motorway slip road ⓊⓀ, highway access road ⓊS ▸ **bretelle de raccordement** motorway ⓊⓀ ou highway ⓊS junction. ❖ **bretelles** nfpl braces ⓊⓀ, suspenders ⓊS.

breton, onne [bʀətɔ̃, ɔn] adj Breton. ❖ **Breton, onne** nm, f Breton. ❖ **breton** nm LING Breton.

breuvage [bʀœvaʒ] nm **1.** [boisson] beverage, drink **2.** [potion] potion, beverage.

brevet [bʀəvɛ] nm **1.** DR ▸ **brevet (d'invention)** patent **2.** ÉDUC diploma ▸ **le brevet** exam taken at 14 years of age at the end of the "collège" ▸ **brevet d'apprentissage** ≃ certificate of apprenticeship ▸ **brevet d'études professionnelles** = BEP ▸ **brevet informatique et Internet** computing proficiency certificate taken at various stages in a child's education ▸ **brevet de technicien** exam taken at 17 after 3 years' technical training ▸ **brevet de technicien supérieur** = BTS **3.** AÉRON ▸ **brevet de pilote** pilot's licence **4.** [certificat] certificate ▸ **brevet de secourisme** first-aid certificate.

breveter [27] [bʀəvte] vt to patent ▸ **faire breveter qqch** to take out a patent for sthg.

📝 In reformed spelling (see p. 16-18), this verb is conjugated like **acheter** : **il brevète, elle brevètera.**

bribes [bʀib] nfpl **1.** [restes - d'un gâteau, d'un repas] scraps, crumbs **2.** [fragments - de discours] snatches, scraps ; [- d'information, de connaissance] scraps.

bric-à-brac [bʀikabʀak] nm inv [tas d'objets] clutter, jumble, bric-à-brac.

bricolage [bʀikɔlaʒ] nm **1.** [travail manuel] do-it-yourself, DIY ⓊⓀ **2.** [réparation] makeshift repair **3.** [mauvais travail] ▸ **c'est du bricolage** it's just been thrown together.

bricole [bʀikɔl] nf **1.** [petit objet] ▸ **des bricoles** things, bits and pieces **2.** [article de peu de valeur] trifle / **je vais lui offrir une bricole** I'm going to give her a little something / **30 euros et des bricoles** 30-odd euros **3.** fam [ennui] trouble.

bricoler [3] [bʀikɔle] ❖ vi **1.** [faire des aménagements] to do DIY **2.** [avoir de petits emplois] to do odd jobs. ❖ vt **1.** [réparer] to fix (up), to mend, to carry out makeshift repairs to **2.** [manipuler] to tinker ou to tamper with.

bricoleur, euse [bʀikɔlœʀ, øz] ❖ nm, f [qui construit ou répare soi-même] handyman (handywoman), DIY enthusiast. ❖ adj ▸ **il est très bricoleur** he's good with his hands ▸ **il n'est pas bricoleur** he's no handyman.

bride [bʀid] nf **1.** ÉQUIT bridle ▸ **tenir son cheval en bride** to curb ou to rein in a horse ▸ **laisser la bride sur le cou à qqn** to give sb a free rein ▸ **serrer** ou **tenir la bride à qqn** to keep sb on a tight rein **2.** COUT bar ; [en dentelle] bride, bar.

bridé, e [bʀide] adj : **avoir les yeux bridés** to have slanting eyes.

brider [3] [bʀide] vt **1.** ÉQUIT to bridle **2.** [émotion] to curb, to restrain ; [personne] to keep in check.

bridge [bʀidʒ] nm **1.** DENT bridge, bridgework **2.** JEUX bridge.

briefer [3] [bʀife] vt to brief.

brièvement [bʀijɛvmɑ̃] adv [pendant peu de temps] briefly, fleetingly, for a short time.

brièveté [bʀijɛvte] nf brevity, briefness.

brigade [bʀigad] nf **1.** MIL [détachement] brigade ▸ **brigade de gendarmerie** squad of gendarmes ▸ **brigade des sapeurs-pompiers** fire brigade ; [régiments] brigade **2.** [corps de police] squad ▸ **brigade antigang** ou **de répression du (grand) banditisme** organized crime division ▸ **brigade financière** Fraud Squad ▸ **brigade des mœurs** vice squad.

brigadier, ère [bʀigadje, ɛʀ] nm, f [de police] sergeant.

brigand [bʀigɑ̃] nm **1.** [bandit] bandit, brigand *litt* **2.** [escroc] crook, thief.

briguer [3] [bʀige] vt [emploi] to angle for *(insép)* ; [honneur] to seek, to pursue, to aspire to *(insép)* ; [suffrage] to seek.

brillamment [bʀijamɑ̃] adv brilliantly, magnificently ▸ **réussir brillamment un examen** to pass an exam with flying colours 🇬🇧 ou colors 🇺🇸.

brillant, e [bʀijɑ̃, ɑ̃t] adj **1.** [luisant - parquet] shiny, polished ; [- peinture] gloss *(modif)* ; [- cheveux, lèvres] shiny, glossy ; [- soie] lustrous ; [- toile, cristal] sparkling, glittering ; [- feuille, chaussure] glossy, shiny ; [- yeux] bright, shining **2.** [remarquable - esprit, intelligence] brilliant, outstanding ; [- personne] outstanding ; [- succès, carrière, talent] brilliant, dazzling, outstanding ; [- conversation] brilliant, sparkling ; [- hommage] superb, magnificent ; [- représentation, numéro] brilliant, superb ▸ **pas brillant** : *ce n'est pas brillant* it's not brilliant / *sa santé n'est pas brillante* he's not well, his health is not too good. ⬦ **brillant** nm JOAILL brilliant.

briller [3] [bʀije] vi **1.** [luire - chaussure, soleil, lumière, regard] to shine ; [- chandelle] to glimmer ; [- étoile] to twinkle, to shine ; [- diamant] to shine, to glitter, to sparkle ; [- dents] to sparkle ; [- eau] to shimmer, to sparkle ; [- feuille] to shine, to glisten ▸ **faire briller** : *faire briller ses chaussures* to shine one's shoes / *des yeux qui brillent de plaisir / d'envie* eyes sparkling with pleasure / glowing with envy **2.** [exceller] to shine, to excel, to be outstanding ; [se distinguer] to stand out ▸ **briller par son absence** to be conspicuous by one's absence.

brimade [bʀimad] nf *arg scol* ragging (U) 🇬🇧, hazing (U) 🇺🇸, initiation ceremony.

brimer [3] [bʀime] vt [tracasser] to victimize / *il se sent brimé* he feels victimized.

brin [bʀɛ̃] nm **1.** [tige - d'herbe] blade ; [- d'osier] twig ; [- de muguet, de persil] sprig ; [- de bruyère, d'aubépine] sprig **2.** [morceau - de laine, de fil] piece, length ▸ **brin de paille** (piece of) straw **3.** [parcelle] ▸ **un brin de** a (tiny) bit of ▸ **faire un brin de** *fam* : *faire un brin de causette (à)* ou *avec qqn* to have a quick chat (with sb) / *faire un brin de toilette* to have a quick wash **4.** EXPR **un beau brin de fille** a good-looking girl.

brindille [bʀɛ̃dij] nf twig.

bringue [bʀɛ̃g] nf *fam* **1.** *péj* [personne] ▸ **une grande bringue** a beanpole **2.** [noce] ▸ **faire la bringue** to live it up, to party.

brinquebaler [3] [bʀɛ̃kbale] ⬦ vt to joggle, to jiggle, to shake. ⬦ vi to rattle.

brinquebaler [bʀɛ̃kbale] = **bringuebaler**.

brio [bʀijo] nm brio, verve. ⬦ **avec brio** loc adv ▸ **s'en tirer avec brio** to carry sthg off with style.

brioche [bʀijɔʃ] nf **1.** CULIN brioche **2.** *fam* [ventre] paunch ▸ **prendre de la brioche** to be getting a paunch ou potbelly.

brioché, e [bʀijɔʃe] adj brioche-like.

brique [bʀik] ⬦ nf **1.** CONSTR brick ▸ **un mur de brique** ou **briques** a brick wall **2.** [emballage - de lait, de jus de fruits] carton **3.** *fam & vieilli* : *une brique* [dix mille francs] ten thousand francs. ⬦ adj inv brick-red. ⬥ **en brique** loc adj brick *(modif)*, made of brick.

briquer [3] [bʀike] vt [pont de navire] to scrub ; *fam* [maison] to clean from top to bottom.

briquet [bʀikɛ] nm [appareil] lighter.

briqueterie, briquèterie* [bʀiketʀi] nf brickworks *(sg)*, brickyard.

bris [bʀi] nm **1.** [fragment] piece, fragment ▸ **des bris de glace** shards, fragments of glass **2.** DR ▸ **bris de scellés** breaking of seals.

brisant [bʀizɑ̃] nm [haut-fond] reef, shoal. ⬥ **brisants** nmpl [vagues] breakers.

brise [bʀiz] nf breeze.

brisé, e [bʀize] adj [détruit] broken ▸ **un homme brisé a)** [par la fatigue] a run-down ou worn-out man **b)** [par les ennuis, le chagrin] a broken man.

brise-glaces *(pl* brise-glaces*)*, **brise-glace*** *(pl* brise-glaces**)* [bʀizglas] nm NAUT icebreaker.

brise-lames *(pl* brise-lames*)*, **brise-lame*** *(pl* brise-lames**)* [bʀizlam] nm breakwater, groyne, mole.

briser [3] [bʀize] vt **1.** [mettre en pièces - verre, assiette] to break, to smash ; [- vitre] to break, to shatter, to smash ; [- motte de terre] to break up *(sép)* ▸ **briser qqch en mille morceaux** to smash sthg to pieces **2.** [séparer en deux - canne, branche] to break, to snap ; [- liens, chaînes] to break ▸ **briser la glace** to break the ice **3.** [défaire - réputation, carrière] to wreck, to ruin ; [- résistance, rébellion] to crush, to quell ; [- contrat] to break ; [- grève] to break (up) **4.** [épuiser - suj : soucis, chagrin] to break, to crush ; [- suj : exercice, voyage] to exhaust, to tire out *(sép)* / *la voix brisée par l'émotion* his voice breaking with emotion. ⬥ **se briser** vpi [se casser - verre] to shatter, to break ▸ **son cœur s'est brisé** he was broken-hearted.

briseur, euse [bʀizœʀ, øz] nm, f *fig* ▸ **briseur de grève** strikebreaker, scab.

bristol [bʀistɔl] nm **1.** [carton] Bristol board, bristol **2.** [carte de visite] visiting 🇬🇧 ou calling 🇺🇸 card.

britannique [bʀitanik] adj British. ⬥ **Britannique** ⬦ adj ▸ **les îles Britanniques** the British Isles. ⬦ nmf Briton, Britisher 🇺🇸 ▸ **les Britanniques** the British.

broc [bʀo] nm [gén] pitcher ; [pour la toilette] ewer.

brocante [bʀokɑ̃t] nf **1.** [objets] ▸ **la brocante** secondhand articles **2.** [commerce] secondhand ou junk shop 🇬🇧, used goods store 🇺🇸.

brocanteur, euse [bʀokɑ̃tœʀ, øz] nm, f dealer in secondhand goods, secondhand ou junk shop owner 🇬🇧, secondhand store keeper 🇺🇸.

brocart [bʀokaʀ] nm brocade.

broche [bʀoʃ] nf **1.** CULIN spit, skewer, broach **2.** [bijou] broach **3.** ÉLECTRON & MÉD pin **4.** QUÉBEC [fil de fer] wire. ⬥ **à la broche** loc adv on a spit ▸ **cuit à la broche** roasted on a spit, spit-roasted.

broché, e [bʀoʃe] adj IMPR paperback *(modif)*.

brochet [bʀoʃɛ] nm ZOOL pike.

brochette [bʀoʃɛt] nf **1.** CULIN [broche] skewer ; [mets] brochette, kebab **2.** [assemblée] lot ▸ **une jolie brochette d'hypocrites** a fine lot of hypocrites.

brochure [bʀoʃyʀ] nf IMPR stitched book, unbound book ; [livret] pamphlet, booklet, brochure.

* In reformed spelling (see p. 16-18).

brocoli [bʀɔkɔli] nm broccoli (U).

brodequin [bʀɔdkɛ̃] nm [chaussure] (laced) boot.

broder [3] [bʀɔde] vt COUT to embroider ▶ **brodé d'or** embroidered in gold thread.

broderie [bʀɔdʀi] nf **1.** COUT [technique] embroidery ▶ **faire de la broderie** to do embroidery ou needlework **2.** [ouvrage] (piece of) embroidery, embroidery work.

bromure [bʀɔmyʀ] nm bromide ▶ **bromure de potassium** potassium bromide.

bronche [bʀɔ̃ʃ] nf bronchus ▶ **les bronches** the bronchial tubes.

broncher [3] [bʀɔ̃ʃe] vi [réagir] to react, to respond / **le premier qui bronche…** the first one to move a muscle ou to budge… ▶ **sans broncher** loc adv without batting an eye ou eyelid, without turning a hair ou flinching.

bronchiolite [bʀɔ̃kjɔlit ou bʀɔ̃ʃjɔlit] nf MÉD bronchiolitis.

bronchite [bʀɔ̃ʃit] nf bronchitis.

broncho-pneumonie (pl broncho-pneumonies), **bronchopneumonie*** [bʀɔ̃kɔpnømɔni] nf bronchopneumonia.

bronzage [bʀɔ̃zaʒ] nm [hâle] suntan, tan.

bronze [bʀɔ̃z] nm ART & MÉTALL bronze.

bronzé, e [bʀɔ̃ze] adj [hâlé] suntanned, tanned 🇬🇧, tan 🇺🇸.

bronzer [3] [bʀɔ̃ze] ◆ vt [hâler] to tan. ◆ vi to tan, to go brown ▶ **se faire bronzer** to sunbathe.

brosse [bʀɔs] nf **1.** [ustensile] brush ▶ **brosse à chaussures** shoe brush ▶ **brosse à cheveux** hairbrush ▶ **brosse à dents** toothbrush ▶ **brosse à habits** clothes brush ▶ **passer la brosse à reluire à qqn** fam to butter sb up, to soft-soap sb **2.** [coiffure] crew cut.

brosser [3] [bʀɔse] vt **1.** [épousseter - miettes] to brush (off) ; [-pantalon, jupe] to brush down **2.** [frictionner] to brush, to scrub **3.** ART [paysage, portrait] to paint ▶ **brosser le portrait de qqn** pr to paint sb's portrait, fig to describe sb. ◆ **se brosser** vp (emploi réfléchi) **1.** [se nettoyer] to brush o.s. (down) ▶ **se brosser les dents / les cheveux** to brush one's teeth / hair **2.** EXPR **il peut toujours se brosser, il n'aura jamais mon livre** fam he can whistle for my book.

brou de noix [bʀudənwa] nm walnut stain.

brouette [bʀuɛt] nf barrow, wheelbarrow.

brouhaha [bʀuaa] nm hubbub, (confused) noise.

brouillard [bʀujaʀ] nm MÉTÉOR [léger] mist ; [épais] fog / **il y a du brouillard** it's misty, there's a mist ▶ **brouillard givrant** freezing fog.

brouille [bʀuj] nf tiff, quarrel.

brouillé, e [bʀuje] adj **1.** [fâché] ▶ **être brouillé avec qqn** to be on bad terms with sb, to have fallen out with sb **2.** CULIN scrambled.

brouiller [3] [bʀuje] vt **1.** [mélanger - cartes] to shuffle / **ça m'a brouillé les idées** it confused ou befuddled me ▶ **brouiller les cartes** fig to confuse the issue ▶ **brouiller les pistes** a) [dans un roman] to confuse the reader b) [dans une poursuite] to cover one's tracks, to put sb off one's scent c) [dans un débat] to put up a smokescreen **2.** [troubler - liquide] to cloud ▶ **brouiller la vue** to cloud ou to blur one's eyesight **3.** RADIO [signal] to garble ; [transmission, circuit] to jam **4.** [fâcher] to turn against, to alienate from. ◆ **se brouiller** vpi [se mélanger - idées] to get confused ou muddled ou jumbled ; [se troubler - vue] to blur, to become blurred. ◆ **se brouiller avec** vp + prép to fall out with.

brouilleur [bʀujœʀ] nm INFORM scrambler.

brouillon, onne [bʀujɔ̃, ɔn] adj **1.** [travail] untidy, messy **2.** [personne] muddleheaded, unmethodical ▶ **avoir l'esprit brouillon** to be muddleheaded. ◆ **brouillon** nm (rough) draft.

broussailles [bʀusaj] nfpl [sous-bois] undergrowth ; [dans un champ] scrub. ◆ **en broussaille** loc adj [cheveux] tousled, dishevelled ; [sourcils, barbe] bushy, shaggy.

broussailleux, euse [bʀusajø, øz] adj **1.** [terrain] brushy, scrubby, covered with brushwood **2.** [sourcils, barbe] shaggy, bushy ; [cheveux] tousled, dishevelled.

brousse [bʀus] nf **1.** GÉOGR [type de végétation] ▶ **la brousse** the bush **2.** [étendue] : **vivre en pleine brousse** fam & fig to live in the backwoods ou out in the sticks ou in the boondocks 🇺🇸.

brouter [3] [bʀute] ◆ vt [suj : bétail] to graze, to feed on (insép) ; [suj : animal sauvage] to browse, to feed on (insép). ◆ vi **1.** [bétail] to graze, to feed ; [animal sauvage] to browse, to feed **2.** [machine-outil] to chatter, to judder 🇬🇧, to jerk ; [embrayage] to slip.

broutille [bʀutij] nf [chose futile] trifle, trifling matter / **il s'inquiète pour des broutilles** he's worrying over nothing.

broyer [13] [bʀwaje] vt **1.** [écraser - couleur, matériau friable, nourriture] to grind ; [-pierre, sucre, ail] to crush ; [-grain] to mill, to grind ; [-fibre] to break, to crush ; [-main, pied] to crush **2.** EXPR **broyer du noir** to be in the doldrums, to think gloomy thoughts.

broyeur [bʀwajœʀ] nm [pulvérisateur - à minerai, à sable] grinder, crusher, mill ; [-à paille] bruiser ; [-à fibre] brake ; [-à déchets] disintegrator, grinder.

bru [bʀy] nf daughter-in-law.

brucelles [bʀysɛl] nfpl 🇨🇭 (pair of) tweezers.

brugnon [bʀyɲɔ̃] nm (white) nectarine.

bruine [bʀɥin] nf drizzle.

bruire [105] [bʀɥiʀ] vi litt [feuilles, vent] to rustle, to whisper ; [eau] to murmur ; [insecte] to hum, to buzz, to drone.

bruissement [bʀɥismɑ̃] nm [des feuilles, du vent, d'une étoffe] rustle, rustling ; [de l'eau] murmuring ; [d'un insecte] hum, humming, buzzing ; [des ailes, d'une voile] flapping.

bruit [bʀɥi] nm **1.** [son] sound, noise ▶ **des bruits de pas** the sound of footsteps ▶ **des bruits de voix** the hum of conversation ▶ **un bruit sec** a snap ▶ **un bruit sourd** a thud ▶ **bruit de fond** background noise **2.** [vacarme] : **j'ai horreur d'expliquer quelque chose dans le bruit** I hate explaining something against a background of noise ▶ **faire du bruit** to be noisy / **ne fais pas de bruit** be quiet / **beaucoup de bruit pour rien** much ado about nothing **3.** [retentissement] sensation, commotion, furore 🇬🇧, furor 🇺🇸 / **on a fait beaucoup de bruit autour de cet enlèvement** the kidnapping caused a furore **4.** [rumeur] rumour 🇬🇧, piece of gossip 🇺🇸 / **le bruit court que…** rumour has it ou it is rumoured that… ▶ **c'est un bruit de couloir** it's a rumour ▶ **faux bruit** false rumour. ◆ **sans bruit** loc adv noiselessly, without a sound.

bruitage [bʀɥitaʒ] nm sound effects.

brûlant, e, brulant*, e [bʀylɑ̃, ɑ̃t] adj **1.** [chaud - lampe, assiette] burning (hot) ; [-liquide] burning ou boiling (hot), scalding ; [-nourriture] burning (hot), piping hot ; [-soleil, température] blazing (hot), scorching, blistering ; [-personne, front] feverish **2.** [actuel, dont on parle] ▶ **sujet ou dossier brûlant** burning issue / **c'est dire l'actualité brûlante de ce livre** this shows how very topical this book is.

brûlé, e, brulé*, e [bʀyle] nm, f badly burnt person ▶ **un grand brûlé** a patient suffering from third-degree burns. ◆ **brûlé, brulé*** nm burnt part ▶ **ça sent le brûlé** a) [odeur] there's a smell of burning b) fam & fig there's trouble brewing.

---

* In reformed spelling (see p. 16-18).

brûlement [bʀylmɑ̃] nm *(surtout pl)* QUÉBEC [d'estomac] heartburn.

brûle-pourpoint [bʀylpuʀpwɛ̃] ❖ **à brûle-pourpoint**, **à brule-pourpoint*** loc adv **1.** [sans détour] point-blank, without beating about the bush **2.** [inopinément] out of the blue.

brûler, bruler* [3] [bʀyle] ◆ vt **1.** [détruire - feuilles, corps, objet] to burn, to incinerate ▸ **brûler qqn vif / sur le bûcher** to burn sb alive / at the stake ▸ **brûler les planches** to give an outstanding performance ▸ **brûler ses dernières cartouches** to shoot one's bolt **2.** [consommer - électricité, fioul] to burn (up), to use, to consume ▸ **brûler la chandelle par les deux bouts** to burn the candle at both ends **3.** [trop cuire] to burn **4.** [trop chauffer - tissu] to burn, to scorch, to singe ; [- cheveux, poils] to singe ; [- acier] to spoil / *un paysage brûlé par le soleil* a landscape scorched by the sun **5.** [irriter - partie du corps] to burn / *la fumée me brûle les yeux* smoke is making my eyes smart ou sting / *le piment me brûle la langue* the chili is burning my tongue ▸ **brûler la cervelle à qqn** *pr* to blow sb's brains out **6.** [endommager - suj : gel] to nip, to burn ; [- suj : acide] to burn ▸ **brûlé par le gel** frost-damaged **7.** *fam* [dépasser] ▸ **brûler un feu** to go through a red light ▸ **brûler un stop** to fail to stop at a stop sign ▸ **brûler les étapes a)** [progresser rapidement] to advance by leaps and bounds **b)** *péj* [cut corners, to take short cuts. ◆ vi **1.** [flamber] to burn (up), to be on fire ; [lentement] to smoulder ▸ **brûler vif** to be burnt alive ou to death ▸ **la forêt a brûlé** the forest was burnt down ou to the ground **2.** [se consumer - charbon, essence] to burn ▸ **faire brûler le rôti** to burn the roast **3.** [être chaud] to be burning ▸ **avoir le front / la gorge qui brûle** to have a burning forehead / a burning sensation in the throat ▸ **ça brûle a)** [plat, sol] it's boiling hot ou burning **b)** [eau] it's scalding **c)** [feu] it's burning ▸ **les yeux me brûlent** my eyes are stinging ou smarting. ◆ **brûler de, bruler de*** v + prép [être animé de] ▸ **brûler d'impatience / de désir** to be burning with impatience / desire. ❖ **se brûler, se bruler*** vp *(emploi réfléchi)* to burn o.s. ▸ **se brûler la main** to burn one's hand ▸ **se brûler les ailes** to get one's fingers burnt.

brûlis, brulis* [bʀyli] nm [mode de culture] slash-and-burn farming.

brûlot, brulot* [bʀylo] nm QUÉBEC ENTOM midge.

brûlure, brulure* [bʀylyʀ] nf **1.** [lésion] burn ▸ **brûlure de cigarette** cigarette burn **2.** [sensation] burning sensation ▸ **brûlures d'estomac** heartburn.

brume [bʀym] nf **1.** [brouillard - de chaleur] haze ; [- de mauvais temps] mist **2.** NAUT fog.

brumeux, euse [bʀymø, øz] adj **1.** MÉTÉOR misty, foggy, hazy **2.** [vague] hazy, vague.

brun, brune [bʀœ̃, bʀyn] ◆ adj [au pigment foncé - cheveux] brown, dark ; [- peau] brown, dark. ◆ nm, f brown-haired ou dark-haired man (woman), brunette. ❖ **brun** nm brown (colour). ❖ **brune** nf **1.** [cigarette] brown tobacco cigarette **2.** [bière] dark beer ; ≃ brown ale UK.

brunâtre [bʀynɑtʀ] adj brownish.

bruncher [bʀœ̃ʃe] vi to have brunch.

brunir [32] [bʀyniʀ] vi [foncer - cheveux, couleur] to get darker, to darken ; [- peau] to get brown ou browner ▸ **brunir au soleil** to tan.

Brushing® [bʀœʃiŋ] nm blow-dry ▸ **faire un Brushing à qqn** to blow-dry sb's hair.

brusque [bʀysk] adj **1.** [bourru - ton] curt, abrupt ; [- personne] abrupt, brusque, blunt ; [- geste] abrupt, rough **2.** [imprévu] abrupt, sudden / *un virage brusque* a sharp bend.

brusquement [bʀyskəmɑ̃] adv [soudainement] suddenly, abruptly ; [sèchement] brusquely.

brusquer [3] [bʀyske] vt [hâter - dénouement] to rush ; [- adieux] to cut short ▸ **brusquer les choses** to rush things.

brusquerie [bʀyskəʀi] nf [brutalité] abruptness, brusqueness, sharpness.

brut, e [bʀyt] adj **1.** [non traité - pétrole, métal] crude, untreated ; [- laine, soie, charbon, brique] untreated, raw ; [- sucre] raw, coarse ; [- pierre précieuse] rough, uncut ; [- minerai] raw ; [- or] unrefined **2.** [émotion, qualité] naked, pure, raw ; [donnée] raw ; [fait] simple, plain ▸ **brut de décoffrage** rough and ready ▸ **à l'état brut** in the rough **3.** [sauvage] brute ▸ **la force brute** brute force **4.** ÉCON gross **5.** [poids] gross **6.** ŒNOL brut, dry. ❖ **brut** ◆ adv gross / *gagner 5 000 euros brut* to earn 5,000 euros gross. ◆ nm [pétrole] crude oil.

brutal, e, aux [bʀytal, o] adj **1.** [violent - personne] brutal, vicious ; [- enfant] rough ; [- choc] strong, violent ; [- force] brute ; [- jeu] rough ▸ **être brutal avec qqn** to treat sb brutally, to be violent with sb **2.** [franc] brutal, blunt **3.** [soudain - changement] sudden, abrupt ; [- transition] abrupt.

brutalement [bʀytalmɑ̃] adv **1.** [violemment] brutally, violently, savagely **2.** [sèchement] brusquely, sharply, bluntly **3.** [tout d'un coup] suddenly.

brutaliser [3] [bʀytalize] vt **1.** [maltraiter] to ill-treat ▸ **brutaliser qqn** to batter sb **2.** [brusquer] to bully.

brutalité [bʀytalite] nf [violence] brutality, violence ▸ **des brutalités** brutalities, violent acts ▸ **brutalités policières** police brutality.

brute [bʀyt] nf **1.** [personne violente] bully ▸ **comme une brute** with all one's might, like mad ▸ **une grande** ou **grosse brute** a big brute (of a man) **2.** [personne fruste] boor, lout.

Bruxelles [bʀysɛl] npr Brussels.

bruxellois, e [bʀysɛlwa, az] adj from Brussels. ❖ **Bruxellois, e** nm, f *inhabitant of or person from Brussels.*

bruyamment [bʀɥijamɑ̃] adv [parler, rire, protester] loudly ; [manger, jouer] noisily.

bruyant, e [bʀɥijɑ̃, ɑ̃t] adj [enfant, rue] noisy ▸ **un rire bruyant** a loud laugh.

bruyère [bʀɥijɛʀ] nf BOT heather / *(racine de) bruyère* briar.

bsr SMS abr écrite de **bonsoir.**

BSR (abr de **brevet de sécurité routière**) nm *proficiency test for riding a moped.*

BTP (abr de **bâtiment et travaux publics**) nmpl *building and public works sector.*

BTS (abr de **brevet de technicien supérieur**) nm *advanced vocational training certificate (taken at the end of a 2-year higher education course).*

bu, e [by] pp ⟶ **boire.**

buanderie [byɑ̃dʀi] nf **1.** [pièce, local - à l'intérieur] laundry, utility room ; [- à l'extérieur] washhouse **2.** QUÉBEC [laverie] laundry.

Bucarest [bykaʀɛst] npr Bucharest.

buccal, e, aux [bykal, o] adj mouth *(modif)*, buccal *spéc.*

bûche, buche* [byʃ] nf **1.** [morceau de bois] log **2.** CULIN & HIST ▸ **bûche glacée** Yule log *(with an ice-cream filling)* ▸ **bûche de Noël** Yule log.

bûcher¹, bucher* [3] [byʃe] vt *fam* [travailler] to swot up UK, to grind US ▸ **bûcher un examen** to cram for an exam.

bûcher², bucher* [byʃe] nm **1.** [supplice] ▸ **le bûcher** the stake **2.** [funéraire] pyre.

bûcheron, onne, bucheron*, onne [byʃʁɔ̃, ɔn]
nm, f woodcutter, lumberjack.

bûcheur, euse, bucheur*, euse [byʃœʁ, øz] *fam*
nm, f hardworking student, swot UK *péj*, grind US *péj*.

bucolique [bykɔlik] adj bucolic, pastoral.

Budapest [bydapɛst] npr Budapest.

budget [bydʒɛ] nm **1.** [d'une personne, d'une entreprise]
budget ▸ **avoir un petit budget** to be on a (tight) budget /
des prix pour les petits budgets budget prices **2.** ▸ **budget
d'exploitation** ou **de fonctionnement** operating budget
▸ **budget prévisionnel** provisional budget.

budgétaire [bydʒetɛʁ] adj budgetary.

budgéter [bydʒete] vt = **budgétiser**.

budgétiser [3] [bydʒetize], **budgéter** [bydʒete] vt
to budget for.

buée [bɥe] nf condensation ▸ **plein** ou **couvert de buée**
misted ou steamed up.

Buenos Aires [bɥenozɛʁ] npr Buenos Aires.

buffet [byfɛ] nm **1.** [de salle à manger] sideboard ▸ **buffet
(de cuisine)** kitchen cabinet ou dresser **2.** [nourriture] :
il y aura un buffet pour le déjeuner there will be a buffet
lunch ▸ **buffet campagnard** buffet *(mainly with country-style
cold meats)* **3.** [salle] ▸ **buffet (de gare)** (station) café ou
buffet ou cafeteria ; [comptoir roulant] refreshment trolley
UK ou cart US.

buffle [byfl] nm ZOOL buffalo.

bug [bœg] nm = **bogue**.

buis [bɥi] nm BOT box, boxtree.

buisson [bɥisɔ̃] nm BOT bush.

buissonnière [bɥisɔnjɛʁ] adj f ⟶ **école**.

bulbe [bylb] nm BOT bulb, corm.

bulgare [bylgaʁ] adj Bulgarian. ❖ **Bulgare** nmf Bulgarian. ❖ **bulgare** nm LING Bulgarian.

Bulgarie [bylgaʁi] npr f ▸ **(la) Bulgarie** Bulgaria.

bulldozer [byldozɛʁ], **bulldozeur*** [byldozœʁ] nm
1. [machine] bulldozer **2.** *fam* [fonceur] bulldozer.

bulle [byl] nf **1.** [d'air, de gaz, de bain moussant] bubble ▸ **bulle d'air** [dans un tuyau] airlock ▸ **faire des bulles
a)** [de savon] to blow bubbles **b)** [bébé] to dribble **2.** [de
bande dessinée] balloon, speech bubble **3.** ÉCON bubble ▸ **la
bulle Internet** the Internet bubble.

bulletin [byltɛ̃] nm **1.** RADIO & TV bulletin ▸ **bulletin
d'informations** news bulletin ▸ **bulletin météorologique**
weather forecast ou report **2.** ADMIN ▸ **bulletin de naissance** birth certificate **3.** ÉDUC ▸ **bulletin (scolaire** ou **de
notes)** (school) report UK, report card US ▸ **bulletin mensuel / trimestriel** monthly / end-of-term report **4.** POL
▸ **bulletin de vote** ballot paper ▸ **bulletin blanc** blank ballot paper **5.** [ticket] ▸ **bulletin de commande** order form
▸ **bulletin de paie** ou **salaire** pay slip, salary advice.

buraliste [byʁalist] nmf tobacconist *(licensed to sell
stamps)*.

bureau, x [byʁo] nm **1.** [meuble - gén] desk ; [- à rabat]
bureau **2.** [pièce d'une maison] study **3.** [lieu de travail] office ▸ **bureau d'accueil** reception ▸ **bureau paysager** open-
plan office *(with plants)* **4.** [agence] ▸ **bureau d'aide sociale**
social security UK ou welfare US office ▸ **bureau de change
a)** [banque] bureau de change, foreign exchange office
b) [comptoir] bureau de change, foreign exchange counter ▸ **bureau d'études a)** [entreprise] research consultancy
b) [service] research department ou unit ▸ **bureau des objets
trouvés** lost property UK ou lost-and-found US office
▸ **bureau de poste** post office ▸ **bureau de tabac** tobacconist's UK, tobacco dealer's US ▸ **bureau de vote** polling

station **5.** [commission] committee ▸ **Bureau international
du travail** International Labour Organization.

bureaucrate [byʁokʁat] nmf bureaucrat.

bureaucratie [byʁokʁasi] nf **1.** [système] bureaucracy
2. [tracasseries] red tape, bureaucracy.

bureaucratique [byʁokʁatik] adj bureaucratic, administrative.

Bureautique® [byʁotik] nf **1.** [système] office automation **2.** [matériel] office equipment.

burette [byʁɛt] nf [bidon] ▸ **burette (d'huile)** oilcan.

burin [byʁɛ̃] nm [outil de graveur] burin, graver.

buriné, e [byʁine] adj [traits] strongly marked ; [visage]
craggy, furrowed.

burka [buʁka] = **burqa**.

Burkina [byʁkina] npr m ▸ **le Burkina** Burkina-Faso ▸ **au
Burkina** in Burkina-Faso.

burkinabé [byʁkinabe] adj from Burkina-Faso.
❖ **Burkinabé** nmf *inhabitant of or person from Burkina-Faso.*

burlesque [byʁlɛsk] adj *péj* [stupide - idée] ludicrous,
ridiculous.

burnous [byʁnu] nm burnous, burnouse.

burqa, burka [buʁka] nm ou nf burqa.

burundais, e [buʁundɛ, ɛz] adj Burundian.
❖ **Burundais, e** nm, f Burundian.

Burundi [buʁundi] npr m ▸ **le Burundi** Burundi ▸ **au
Burundi** in Burundi.

bus [bys] nm bus.

buse [byz] nf **1.** ZOOL buzzard **2.** [conduit] duct.

busqué, e [byske] adj [nez] hook *(modif)*, hooked.

buste [byst] nm **1.** ANAT [haut du corps] chest ; [seins]
bust **2.** [sculpture] bust.

bustier [bystje] nm **1.** [soutien-gorge] strapless bra
2. [corsage] bustier.

but [byt] nm **1.** [dessein] aim, purpose, point ▸ **quel est le
but de la manœuvre** ou **de l'opération ?** what's the point
of such a move? / *dans le but de faire...* for the purpose of
doing..., with the aim of doing... ▸ **aller** ou **frapper droit
au but** to go straight to the point ▸ **à but non lucratif** non
profit-making **2.** [ambition] aim, ambition, objective ▸ **toucher au** ou **le but** to be on the point of achieving one's aim
3. FOOT [limite, point] goal / *gagner / perdre par 5 buts à 2*
to win / to lose by 5 goals to 2 ▸ **marquer** ou **rentrer** *fam*
un but to score a goal ; [cible] target, mark **4.** GRAM purpose. ❖ **de but en blanc** *loc adv* [demander] point-
blank, suddenly ; [rétorquer] bluntly.

butane [bytan] nm ▸ **(gaz) butane a)** CHIM butane
b) [dans la maison] Calor gas.

buté, e [byte] adj mulish, stubborn.

buter [3] [byte] ◆ vi **1.** [trébucher] to stumble, to trip
▸ **buter contre une pierre** to trip over a stone **2.** [co-
gner] ▸ **buter contre qqch** to walk ou to bump into sthg
3. [achopper] ▸ **buter sur** : *buter sur une difficulté* to come
ou to stumble across a problem ▸ **buter sur un mot a)** [en
parlant] to trip over a word **b)** [en lisant pour soi] to have
trouble understanding a word. ◆ vt *arg crime* [tuer] to
bump off *(sép)*, to waste. ❖ **se buter** vpi [se braquer] to
dig one's heels in, to get obstinate.

butin [bytɛ̃] nm **1.** [choses volées - par des troupes] spoils,
booty ; [- par un cambrioleur] loot **2.** [trouvailles] booty.

butiner [3] [bytine] ◆ vi [insectes] to gather nectar
and pollen. ◆ vt **1.** [pollen, nectar] to gather ; [fleurs] to
gather pollen and nectar on **2.** [rassembler - idées] to glean,
to gather.

butte [byt] nf **1.** [monticule] hillock, knoll **2.** HORT mound. ❖ **en butte à** loc prép ▶ **être en butte à** to be exposed to, to be faced with.

buvable [byvabl] adj **1.** [qui n'est pas mauvais à boire] drinkable **2.** PHARM [ampoule] to be taken orally.

buvard [byvaʀ] nm [morceau de papier] piece of blotting-paper ; [substance] blotting-paper.

buvette [byvɛt] nf [dans une foire, une gare] refreshment stall.

buveur, euse [byvœʀ, øz] nm, f **1.** [alcoolique] drinker, drunkard **2.** [consommateur] ▶ **buveur de** : *nous sommes de grands buveurs de café* we are great coffee drinkers.

buzz [bœz] nm : *le film a fait un énorme buzz* the film created a huge buzz.

buzzer [bœze] vi to be all the rage / *un clip qui fait buzzer la Toile* a clip which is all the rage on the Internet.

Byzance [bizɑ̃s] npr **1.** GÉOGR Byzantium **2.** EXPR c'est **Byzance !** *fam* it's fantastic!

C **1.** (abr écrite de **Celsius, centigrade**) C **2.** (abr écrite de **coulomb**) C **3.** SMS abr écrite de **c'est**.

c' [s] ⟶ **ce** (pron dém).

ça [sa] pron dém **1.** [désignant un objet - proche] this, it ; [- éloigné] that, it ▸ *qu'est-ce que tu veux ? — ça, là-bas* what do you want? — that, over there ▸ **regarde-moi ça !** just look at that! **2.** [désignant - ce dont on vient de parler] this, that ; [- ce dont on va parler] this ▸ *la liberté, c'est ça qui est important* freedom, that's what matters ▸ *il y a un peu de ça, c'est vrai* it's true, there's an element of ou a bit of that ▸ *écoutez, ça va vous étonner...* this will surprise you, listen... **3.** [servant de sujet indéterminé] : *et ton boulot, comment ça se passe ?* fam how's your job going? ▸ **ça fait 2 kg / 3 m** that's 2 kg / 3 m ▸ *ça fait deux heures que j'attends* I've been waiting for two hours ▸ *qu'est-ce que ça peut faire ?* what does it matter? ▸ **ça y est** : *ça y est, j'ai fini !* that's it, I'm finished! ▸ *ça y est, ça devait arriver !* now look what's happened! ▸ **c'est ça !** a) that's right b) iron right! ▸ *c'est ça, moquez-vous de moi !* that's right, have a good laugh at my expense! **4.** [emploi expressif] ▸ **qui ça** who?, who's that? ▸ *comment ça, c'est fini ?* what do you mean it's over? ▸ **ah ça oui !** you bet!

çà [sa] adv ▸ **çà et là** here and there.

cabale [kabal] nf [personnes] cabal ; [intrigue] cabal, intrigue.

caban [kabã] nm [longue veste] car coat ; [de marin] reefer jacket , reefer  ; [d'officier] pea jacket.

cabane [kaban] nf [hutte] hut, cabin ; [pour animaux, objets] shed ▸ **cabane à outils** toolshed.

cabaret [kabaʀɛ] nm [établissement] nightclub, cabaret.

cabas [kaba] nm [pour provisions] shopping bag.

cabillaud [kabijo] nm cod.

cabine [kabin] nf **1.** NAUT cabin **2.** AÉRON [des passagers] cabin ▸ **cabine (de pilotage)** cockpit **3.** [de laboratoire de langues] booth ; [de piscine, d'hôpital] cubicle ▸ **cabine de douche** shower cubicle ▸ **cabine d'essayage** changing ou fitting room , dressing room  **4.** TÉLÉC ▸ **cabine téléphonique** phone box  ou booth **5.** TRANSP [de camion, de tracteur, de train] cab ; [de grue] cabin.

cabinet [kabinɛ] nm **1.** [de dentiste] surgery , office  ; [de magistrat] chambers ; [d'avoué, de notaire] office ▸ **cabinet (médical ou de consultation)** (doctor's) surgery  ou office  **2.** [petite salle] ▸ **cabinet de toilette** bathroom **3.** [agence] ▸ **cabinet d'affaires** business consultancy ▸ **cabinet d'avocats** law firm ▸ **cabinet d'architectes** firm of architects ▸ **cabinet conseil** ou **de consultants** consulting firm, consultancy firm **4.** POL [gouvernement] cabinet ▸ **cabinet ministériel** minister's advisers, departmental staff **5.** [meuble] cabinet. ✦ **cabinets** nmpl fam toilet, loo , bathroom .

 **Cabinet**

In a French context this term refers to the team of civil servants who carry out advisory and administrative duties for a minister or a **préfet**. The Prime Minister's **cabinet** is made up of senior civil servants and not of ministers. It includes the **directeur de cabinet**, who has a political role as the Prime Minister's principal private secretary (and can deputize for him or her), and the **chef de cabinet**, whose function is largely administrative.

---

câble [kabl] nm **1.** [cordage - en acier] cable, wire rope ; [- en fibres végétales] line, rope, cable ▸ **câble de démarreur** ou **de démarrage** AUTO jump lead ▸ **câble de halage** ou **remorquage** NAUT towrope, towline ▸ **câble de frein** AUTO brake cable **2.** ÉLECTR cable ▸ **câble électrique** electric cable **3.** TV ▸ **avoir le câble** to have cable TV.

câblé, e [kable] adj TV [ville, région] with cable television ▸ **réseau câblé** cable television network.

cabosser [3] [kabɔse] vt [carrosserie, couvercle] to dent ▸ **voiture cabossée** battered car.

cabot [kabo] nm fam [chien] dog, mutt péj.

cabotage [kabɔtaʒ] nm coastal navigation.

cabotin, e [kabɔtɛ̃, in] ◆ adj [manières, personne] theatrical. ◆ nm, f [personne affectée] show-off, poseur.

cabrer [3] [kabʀe] ✦ **se cabrer** vpi **1.** [cheval] to rear up **2.** [se rebiffer] to balk, to jib.

cabriole [kabʀijɔl] nf [bond - d'un enfant] leap ; [- d'un animal] prancing (U), cavorting (U) ; [acrobatie] somersault ▸ **faire des cabrioles** a) [clown] to do somersaults b) [chèvre] to prance ou to cavort (about) c) [enfant] to dance ou to jump about.

cabriolet [kabʀijɔlɛ] nm [véhicule - automobile] convertible ; [- hippomobile] cabriolet.

CAC, Cac [kak ou sease] (abr de **cotation assistée en continu**) ▸ **l'indice CAC 40** the French Stock Exchange shares index.

caca [kaka] nm fam [poo , poop  ▸ **faire caca** to do a poo  ou poop . ✦ **caca d'oie** nm & adj inv greenish-yellow, greeny-yellow.

cacahouète, cacahuète [kakawɛt] nf peanut.

cacao [kakao] nm CULIN ▸ **(poudre de) cacao** cocoa (powder) ▸ **au cacao** cocoa-flavoured ; [boisson] cocoa.

cachalot [kaʃalo] nm sperm whale.

cache [kaʃ] ◆ nf [d'armes, de drogue] cache. ◆ nm CINÉ & PHOT mask.

cache-cache (pl cache-cache), **cachecache*** [kaʃkaʃ] nm ▶ **jouer à cache-cache (avec qqn)** pr & fig to play hide and seek (with sb).

cachemire [kaʃmiʀ] nm **1.** [tissu, poil] cashmere ▶ **en cachemire** cashmere (modif) **2.** (comme adj) [motif, dessin] paisley (modif).

cache-pot [kaʃpo] (pl **cache-pots**) nm (flower ou plant) pot holder.

cacher [3] [kaʃe] vt **1.** [prisonnier, réfugié] to hide ; [trésor, jouet] to hide, to conceal **2.** [accroc, ride] to hide, to conceal (from view) ▶ **il cache son jeu a)** pr he's not showing his hand **b)** fig he's keeping his plans to himself, he's playing his cards close to his chest **3.** [faire écran devant] to hide, to obscure ▶ **cacher la lumière** ou **le jour à qqn** to be in sb's light **4.** [ne pas révéler - sentiment, vérité] to hide, to conceal, to cover up (sép) ▶ **cacher qqch à qqn** to conceal ou to hide sthg from sb / je ne cache pas que... I must say ou admit that... / je ne (te) cacherai pas que je me suis ennuyé to be frank with you, (I must say that) I was bored. ◆ **se cacher** ◆ vp (emploi réfléchi) **1.** [suivi d'une partie du corps] : je me cachais la tête sous les draps I hid my head under the sheets **2.** [au négatif] ▶ **ne pas se cacher qqch** to make no secret of sthg, to be quite open about sthg / il me plaît, je ne m'en cache pas ! I like him, it's no secret! ◆ vpi **1.** [aller se dissimuler - enfant, soleil] to hide ▶ **se cacher de qqn** : se cacher de ses parents pour fumer, fumer en se cachant de ses parents to smoke behind one's parents' back **2.** [être dissimulé - fugitif] to be hiding ; [- objet] to be hidden.

cache-sexe [kaʃsɛks] (pl **cache-sexes**) nm G-string.

cachet [kaʃɛ] nm **1.** PHARM tablet ▶ **un cachet d'aspirine** an aspirin (tablet) **2.** [sceau] seal ; [empreinte] stamp ▶ **cachet de la poste** postmark / le cachet de la poste faisant foi date of postmark will be taken as proof of postage **3.** [salaire] fee **4.** [charme - d'un édifice, d'une ville] character ; [- d'un vêtement] style ▶ **avoir du cachet a)** [édifice, village] to be full of character **b)** [vêtements] to be stylish.

cacheter [27] [kaʃte] vt [enveloppe, vin] to seal.

✍ In reformed spelling (see p. 16-18), this verb is conjugated like acheter : il cachètera, elle cachèterait.

cachette [kaʃɛt] nf [d'un enfant] hiding place ; [d'un malfaiteur, d'un réfugié] hideout ; [d'un objet] hiding place. ◆ **en cachette** loc adv [fumer, lire, partir] secretly, in secret ; [rire] to o.s., up one's sleeve ▶ **en cachette de qqn a)** [boire, fumer] behind sb's back, while sb's back's turned **b)** [préparer, décider] without sb knowing, unbeknownst to sb.

cachot [kaʃo] nm [de prisonnier] dungeon / 3 ans de cachot 3 years (locked away) in a dungeon.

cachotterie, cachoterie* [kaʃɔtʀi] nf (little) secret ▶ **faire des cachotteries à qqn** to keep secrets from sb.

cachottier, ère, cachotier*, ère [kaʃɔtje, ɛʀ] fam adj secretive.

cacophonie [kakɔfɔni] nf cacophony.

cactus [kaktys] nm cactus.

c.-à-d. (abr écrite de **c'est-à-dire**) i.e.

cadastre [kadastʀ] nm [plans] cadastral register ; ≃ land register.

cadavérique [kadaveʀik] adj [blancheur] deathly, cadaverous ; [teint] deathly pale ; [fixité] corpse-like.

cadavre [kadavʀ] nm [d'une personne - gén] corpse, body ; [- à disséquer] cadaver ; [d'un animal] body, carcass ▶ **c'est un cadavre ambulant** he's a walking corpse.

Caddie® [kadi] nm [chariot] (supermarket ou shopping) trolley UK, (grocery ou shopping) cart US.

caddie, caddy [kadi] nm [au golf] caddie, caddy.

cadeau, x [kado] nm [don] present, gift ▶ **faire un cadeau à qqn** to give sb a present ou a gift ▶ **faire cadeau de qqch à qqn** [le lui offrir] to make sb a present of sthg, to give sb sthg as a present ▶ **il ne m'a pas fait de cadeau a)** [dans une transaction, un match] he didn't do me any favours **b)** [critique] he didn't spare me ▶ **cadeau d'anniversaire / de Noël** birthday / Christmas present ▶ **cadeau de mariage** wedding present ▶ **ce n'est pas un cadeau ! a)** fam [personne insupportable] he's a real pain! **b)** [personne bête] he's no bright spark!

cadenas [kadna] nm padlock ▶ **fermer au cadenas** to padlock.

cadenasser [3] [kadnase] vt [fermer] to padlock.

cadence [kadɑ̃s] nf **1.** DANSE & MUS [rythme] rhythm ▶ **marquer la cadence** to beat out the rhythm ; [accords] cadence ; [passage de soliste] cadenza **2.** [d'un marcheur, d'un rameur] pace ▶ **à une bonne cadence** at quite a pace **3.** INDUST rate. ◆ **à la cadence de** loc prép at the rate of. ◆ **en cadence** loc adv : taper des mains en cadence to clap in time.

cadet, ette [kadɛ, ɛt] ◆ adj [plus jeune] younger ; [dernier-né] youngest. ◆ nm, f **1.** [dans une famille - dernier-né] ▶ **la cadette** the youngest child ou one ▶ **son cadet a)** [fils] his youngest son ou boy **b)** [frère] his youngest brother ; [frère, sœur plus jeune] ▶ **mon cadet** my younger brother ▶ **ma cadette** my younger sister **2.** [entre personnes non apparentées] : je suis son cadet de 4 ans I'm 4 years his junior ou 4 years younger than he is. ◆ **cadet** nm EXPR **c'est le cadet de mes soucis** it's the least of my worries.

cador [kadɔʀ] nm arg **1.** [chien] mutt **2.** [champion] heavyweight / dans sa branche, c'est un cador he's a heavyweight in his field.

cadran [kadʀɑ̃] nm [d'une montre, d'une pendule] face, dial ; [d'un instrument de mesure, d'une boussole] face ; [d'un téléphone] dial ▶ **cadran solaire** sun dial.

cadre¹ [kadʀ] nmf [responsable - dans une entreprise] executive ; [- dans un parti, un syndicat] cadre ▶ **un poste de cadre** an executive ou a managerial post ▶ **cadre supérieur** ou **dirigeant** senior executive, member of (the) senior management ▶ **cadre moyen** middle manager.

Cadre

In French companies, employees are divided into two categories, **employés** and **cadres**. **Cadres**, who usually have a higher level of education and greater responsibilities, enjoy better salaries, more benefits and more prestige. They are also expected to work longer hours.

cadre² nm **1.** [encadrement - d'un tableau, d'une porte, d'une ruche, etc.] frame ▶ **cadre de bicyclette** bicycle frame **2.** [environnement] setting, surroundings ▶ **cadre de vie** (living) environment **3.** [portée, limites - d'accords, de réformes] scope, framework. ◆ **dans le cadre de** loc prép within the framework ou scope of / dans le cadre de mes fonctions as part of my job / cela n'entre pas dans le cadre de mes fonctions it falls outside the scope of my responsibilities.

cadrer [3] [kadʀe] ◆ vi [correspondre - témoignages] to tally, to correspond. ◆ vt CINÉ & PHOT to centre.

cadreur, euse [kadʀœʀ, øz] nm, f cameraman (camerawoman).

caduc, caduque [kadyk] adj **1.** BOT ▸ **à feuilles caduques** deciduous **2.** DR [accord, loi] null and void ; [police d'assurances] lapsed.

cafard [kafaʀ] nm **1.** ENTOM cockroach **2.** fam EXPR **avoir le cafard** to feel low, to feel down ▸ **donner le cafard à qqn** to get sb down.

cafarder [3] [kafaʀde] fam vi **1.** [rapporter] to sneak, to snitch **2.** [être déprimé] to feel depressed ou down.

café [kafe] nm **1.** [boisson, graine] coffee ▸ **café crème** coffee with cream ▸ **café filtre** filter coffee ▸ **café instantané** ou **soluble** instant coffee ▸ **café au lait** white coffee UK, coffee with milk US **2.** [établissement] ▸ **café (bar)** (licensed) café. ⬦ **au café** loc adj [glace, entremets] coffee-, coffee-flavoured. ⬦ **café liégeois** nm coffee ice cream with whipped cream and coffee.

Café

In French cafés, a small cup of strong black coffee is called **un (petit) café**, **un express** or, colloquially, **un petit noir**. This may be served **serré** (extra-strong), **léger** (weak) or **allongé** (diluted with hot water). An **express** with a tiny amount of milk added is called **une noisette**. A large cup of black coffee is **un grand café**, **un double express** or, colloquially, **un grand noir**. Coffee with frothy, steam-heated milk is called **un (grand / petit) crème**. The term **café au lait** is almost never used in cafés.

Parisian cafés have traditionally played an important part in the intellectual and artistic life of the city. For example, the **café de Flore** was a favourite meeting place for the existentialists.

caféine [kafein] nf caffeine.

cafétéria [kafeteʀja] nf cafeteria.

café-théâtre [kafeteatʀ] (pl **cafés-théâtres**) nm [petit théâtre] alternative theatre.

cafetière [kaftjɛʀ] nf [machine] coffee maker ; [récipient] coffeepot.

cafouiller [3] [kafuje] vi fam [projet, service] to get into a muddle ; [décideur, dirigeant] to faff around ou about ; [présentateur, orateur] to get mixed up ou into a muddle.

cafter [3] [kafte] fam vi to sneak, to snitch.

cage [kaʒ] nf **1.** [pour animaux] cage ▸ **cage à lapins** pr rabbit hutch ▸ **cage à oiseau** ou **oiseaux** cage, birdcage **2.** ANAT ▸ **cage thoracique** rib cage **3.** CONSTR ▸ **cage d'ascenseur** lift UK ou elevator US shaft ▸ **cage d'escalier** stairwell.

cageot [kaʒo] nm [contenant] crate ; [contenu] crate, crateful.

cagette [kaʒɛt] nf crate.

cagibi [kaʒibi] nm boxroom UK, storage room US.

cagnard [kaɲaʀ] nm [soleil ardent] hot sun / il nous a attendus en plein cagnard he waited for us in the burning sun.

cagneux, euse [kaɲø, øz] adj [jambes] crooked ; [cheval, personne] knock-kneed ▸ **genoux cagneux** knock knees.

cagnotte [kaɲɔt] nf **1.** [caisse, somme] jackpot **2.** fam [fonds commun] kitty.

cagoulard [kagulaʀ] nm QUÉBEC hooded criminal.

cagoule [kagul] nf [capuchon - d'enfant] balaclava ; [- de voleur] hood ; [- de moine] cowl ; [- de pénitent] hood, cowl.

cahier [kaje] nm **1.** ÉDUC notebook US, exercise book UK ▸ **cahier de brouillon** roughbook UK, notebook (for drafts) ▸ **cahier d'exercices** exercise book ▸ **cahier de textes** a) [d'élève] homework notebook b) [de professeur] (work) record book **2.** [recueil] ▸ **cahier des charges** a) [de matériel] specifications b) [dans un contrat] remit.

cahin-caha, cahincaha* [kaɛ̃kaa] loc adv ▸ **aller cahin-caha** a) [marcheur] to hobble along b) [entreprise, projet] to struggle along / comment va-t-il ? — cahin-caha how is he? — struggling along.

cahot [kao] nm jolt, judder.

cahoter [3] [kaɔte] vi [véhicule] to jolt (along).

caïd [kaid] nm **1.** fam [dans une matière] wizard ; [en sport] ace ; [d'une équipe] star **2.** fam [chef - de bande] gang leader ; [- d'une entreprise, d'un parti] big shot, bigwig / jouer au caïd, faire son caïd to act tough.

caillasse [kajas] nf [éboulis] loose stones, scree.

caillasser [kajase] vt fam to throw stones at.

caille [kaj] nf ZOOL quail.

cailler [3] [kaje] vi **1.** [lait] to curdle ; [sang] to coagulate, to clot **2.** tfam [avoir froid] ▸ **ça caille ici !** it's bloody UK ou goddam US freezing here! ⬦ **se cailler** tfam ◆ vpi to be cold. ◆ vpt : on se les caille dehors ! it's bloody UK ou goddam US freezing outside!

caillot [kajo] nm [de lait] (milk) curd ▸ **caillot (de sang)** bloodclot.

caillou, x [kaju] nm [gén] stone.

Caire [kɛʀ] npr ▸ **Le Caire** Cairo ▸ **au Caire** in Cairo.

caisse [kɛs] nf

🔳 **A. EMBALLAGE, CONTENANT 1.** [gén] box, case, chest ; [à claire-voie] crate ▸ **caisse d'emballage** packing crate ▸ **caisse à outils** toolbox **2.** [boîte de 12 bouteilles] case **3.** HORT box, tub.

🔳 **B. MUSIQUE** [fût de tambour] cylinder ▸ **caisse claire** side ou snare drum ▸ **caisse de résonance** resonance chamber, resonating body ▸ **grosse caisse** a) [tambour] bass drum b) [musicien] bass drummer.

🔳 **C. AUTOMOBILE** [carrosserie] body ; fam [voiture] car.

🔳 **D. BANQUE & COMMERCE 1.** [tiroir] till ; [petit coffre] cashbox ▸ **caisse (enregistreuse)** till ou cash register ▸ **les caisses de l'État** the coffers of the State **2.** [lieu de paiement - d'un supermarché] check-out, till ; [- d'un cinéma, d'un casino, d'un magasin] cash desk ; [- d'une banque] cashier's desk ▸ **passer à la caisse** a) [magasin] to go to the cash desk b) [supermarché] to go through the check-out c) [banque] to go to the cashier's desk ▸ **caisse éclair** [distributeur] cashpoint ▸ **caisse rapide** [dans un supermarché] quick-service till, express checkout **3.** [argent - d'un commerce] cash (in the till), takings ▸ **faire la** ou **sa caisse** to balance the till **4.** [fonds] fund, funds ▸ **caisse noire** slush fund **5.** BANQUE ▸ **caisse d'épargne** ≃ savings bank.

🔳 **E. ADMINISTRATION** [organisme] office ▸ **caisse de prévoyance** contingency fund ▸ **caisse primaire d'assurance maladie** French Social Security office in charge of health insurance ▸ **caisse de retraite** pension ou superannuation fund.

caissier, ère [kesje, ɛʀ] nm, f [d'une boutique, d'un casino, d'une banque] cashier ; [d'un supermarché] check-out assistant UK ou clerk US ; [de cinéma] cashier, box-office assistant UK.

caisson [kesɔ̃] nm NAUT caisson, cofferdam.

cajoler [3] [kaʒɔle] vt [enfant] to cuddle.

cajou [kaʒu] nm ⟶ **noix**.

* In reformed spelling (see p. 16-18).

cake [kɛk] nm fruit cake.

cal [kal] nm **1.** [durillon - à la main] callus ; [- au pied] corn **2.** BOT & MÉD callus.

calamar [kalamaʀ] = **calmar**.

calaminé, e [kalamine] adj coked up.

calamité [kalamite] nf **1.** [événement] calamity, catastrophe, disaster **2.** fam & hum [personne] walking disaster.

calandre [kalɑ̃dʀ] nf AUTO radiator grill.

calanque [kalɑ̃k] nf (Mediterranean) creek.

calcaire [kalkɛʀ] ◆ adj [roche, relief] limestone (modif) ; [sol] chalky, calcareous spéc ; [eau] hard. ◆ nm **1.** GÉOL limestone **2.** [dans une casserole] fur 🇬🇧, sediment 🇺🇸.

calciné, e [kalsine] adj [bois, corps, viande] charred, burned to a cinder ; [mur, maison] charred.

calcium [kalsjɔm] nm calcium.

calcul [kalkyl] nm **1.** [suite d'opérations] calculation ▶ faire un calcul to do a calculation / ça reviendra moins cher, fais le calcul ! it'll be cheaper, just work it out! ▶ calcul différentiel / intégral / vectoriel differential / integral / vector calculus ▶ calcul algébrique calculus **2.** ÉDUC ▶ le calcul sums, arithmetic ▶ calcul mental a) [matière] mental arithmetic b) [opération] mental calculation **3.** [estimation] calculation, computation ▶ d'après mes calculs according to my calculations ▶ un bon calcul a good move ▶ un mauvais ou faux calcul a bad move **4.** péj [manœuvre] scheme ▶ par calcul out of (calculated) self-interest **5.** MÉD stone, calculus spéc ▶ calcul biliaire gall stone.

calculateur, trice [kalkylatœʀ, tʀis] adj péj calculating, scheming. ◆ calculatrice nf [machine] calculator ▶ calculatrice de poche pocket calculator.

calculer [3] [kalkyle] ◆ vt **1.** [dépenses, dimension, quantité, etc.] to calculate, to work out (sép) ▶ calculer qqch de tête ou mentalement to work sthg out in one's head **2.** [avec parcimonie - pourboire, dépenses] to work out to the last penny, to budget carefully **3.** [évaluer - avantages, inconvénients, chances, risque] to calculate, to weigh up (sép) ▶ mal calculer qqch to miscalculate sthg ▶ calculer que to work out ou to calculate that **4.** [préparer - gestes, effets, efforts] to calculate, to work out (sép) ▶ j'ai tout calculé I have it all worked out ▶ calculer son coup fam to plan one's moves carefully / tu as mal calculé ton coup ! you got it all wrong! ◆ vi to calculate / il calcule vite et bien he's quick at arithmetic.

calculette [kalkylɛt] nf pocket calculator.

cale [kal] nf **1.** [pour bloquer - un meuble] wedge ; [- une roue] wedge, chock **2.** NAUT [partie d'un navire] hold **3.** [partie d'un quai] slipway ▶ cale sèche dry dock.

calé, e [kale] adj fam [instruit] : il est calé en histoire he's brilliant at history.

calèche [kalɛʃ] nf barouche, calash ▶ une promenade en calèche a ride in a horse-drawn carriage.

caleçon [kalsɔ̃] nm **1.** [sous-vêtement] ▶ caleçon long, caleçons longs pair of long johns **2.** [pour nager] ▶ caleçon de bain swimming trunks **3.** [pantalon] leggings.

calembour [kalɑ̃buʀ] nm play on words, pun.

calendrier [kalɑ̃dʀije] nm **1.** [tableau, livret] calendar **2.** [emploi du temps] timetable 🇬🇧, schedule 🇺🇸 ; [plan - de réunions] schedule, calendar ; [- d'un festival] calendar ; [- d'un voyage] schedule ▶ calendrier des rencontres FOOT fixture list 🇬🇧, match schedule 🇺🇸.

cale-pied [kalpje] (pl cale-pieds) nm toe-clip.

calepin [kalpɛ̃] nm [carnet] notebook.

caler [3] [kale] ◆ vt **1.** [avec une cale - armoire, pied de chaise] to wedge, to steady with a wedge ; [- roue] to chock, to wedge ▶ caler une porte a) [pour la fermer] to wedge

a door shut b) [pour qu'elle reste ouverte] to wedge a door open **2.** [installer] to prop up (sép) / bien calé dans son fauteuil comfortably settled in his armchair. ◆ vi **1.** AUTO [moteur, voiture] to stall **2.** [s'arrêter - devant un problème] to give up ; [- dans un repas] / prends mon gâteau, je cale have my cake, I can't eat anymore **3.** Québec [s'enfoncer, s'enliser] to sink. ◆ se caler vpi [s'installer] : se caler dans un fauteuil to settle o.s. comfortably in an armchair.

calfeutrer [3] [kalføtʀe] vt [ouverture] to stop up (sép), to fill ; [fenêtre, porte - gén] to make draught-proof ; [- avec un bourrelet] to weatherstrip. ◆ se calfeutrer vp (emploi réfléchi) **1.** [s'isoler du froid] to make o.s. snug **2.** fig [s'isoler] to shut o.s. up ou away.

calibre [kalibʀ] nm **1.** INDUST & MÉCAN gauge **2.** CONSTR & TRAV PUB template **3.** ARM & TECHNOL bore, calibre 🇬🇧, caliber 🇺🇸 ▶ de gros calibre large-bore **4.** COMM grade, (standardized ou standard) size **5.** arg crime [revolver] shooter 🇬🇧, rod 🇺🇸 **6.** fig [type] class, calibre 🇬🇧, caliber 🇺🇸 / il est d'un autre calibre he's not in the same league.

calibrer [3] [kalibʀe] vt **1.** [usiner - obus, revolver, tube] to calibrate **2.** COMM to grade.

calice [kalis] nm **1.** BOT & PHYSIOL calyx **2.** RELIG chalice.

calicot [kaliko] nm **1.** TEXT calico **2.** [bande] banner.

Californie [kalifɔʀni] npr f ▶ (la) Californie California.

califourchon [kalifuʀʃɔ̃] ◆ à califourchon loc adv astride ▶ être à califourchon sur qqch to bestride ou to be astride sthg ▶ monter ou s'asseoir ou se mettre à califourchon sur qqch to sit astride ou to straddle sthg.

câlin, e [kalɛ̃, in] adj [personne] affectionate. ◆ câlin nm cuddle ▶ faire un câlin à qqn to give sb a cuddle.

câliner [3] [kaline] vt to (kiss and) cuddle, to pet.

calligraphie [kaligʀafi] nf calligraphy.

calmant [kalmɑ̃] nm **1.** PHARM [contre l'anxiété] tranquillizer 🇬🇧, tranquilizer 🇺🇸, sedative **2.** [contre la douleur] painkiller.

calmar [kalmaʀ] nm squid.

calme [kalm] ◆ adj **1.** [sans agitation - quartier, rue, moment] quiet, peaceful ; [- journée, ambiance] calm **2.** [sans mouvement - eau, étang, mer] still, calm ; [- air] still **3.** [maître de soi] calm, self-possessed ; [tranquille] quiet ▶ rester calme to stay calm **4.** [peu productif - marché] quiet, dull, slack. ◆ nm **1.** [absence d'agitation] peace, quiet, calm ; [de l'air, de l'eau] stillness ▶ du calme ! a) [nous vous agitez pas] keep quiet! b) [ne paniquez pas] keep cool! ▶ le calme peace and quiet **2.** [sang-froid] composure, calm ▶ du calme ! calm down! ▶ garder son calme to keep calm **3.** [vent] calm ▶ c'est le calme plat a) [en mer] there's no wind b) [il ne se passe rien] there's nothing happening c) [à la Bourse] the Stock Exchange is in the doldrums.

calmement [kalmǝmɑ̃] adv calmly, quietly.

calmer [3] [kalme] vt **1.** [rendre serein - enfant, opposant, foule] to calm down (sép) ▶ nous devons calmer les esprits a) [dans un groupe] we must put everybody's mind at rest b) [dans la nation] we must put the people's minds at rest ▶ calmer le jeu a) SPORT to calm the game down b) fig to calm things down **2.** [dépassionner - mécontentement] to soothe, to calm ; [- colère] to cool, to appease ; [- querelle] to pacify, to defuse ; [- débat] to restore order to **3.** [diminuer - fièvre, inflammation] to bring down (sép) ; [- douleur] to soothe, to ease ; [- faim] to satisfy, to appease ; [- soif] to quench ; [- exaspération, crainte] to ease, to allay ; [- désir, passion, enthousiasme] to dampen ; [- impatience] to relieve / ça devrait leur calmer les nerfs that should soothe their (frayed) nerves. ◆ se calmer vpi **1.** [devenir serein] to calm down **2.** [s'affaiblir - dispute, douleur] to die down ou away, to ease off ou up ; [- fièvre] to die ou to go down ; [- anxiété] to fade ; [- passion] to fade away, to cool ; [- faim, soif] to die down, to be appeased **3.** MÉTÉOR [averse] to ease off ; [mer] to become calm ; [vent] to die down, to drop.

calomnie [kalɔmni] nf slander, calumny / *ce sont de pures calomnies* it's all lies.

calomnier [9] [kalɔmnje] vt [dénigrer - personne] to slander, to calumniate *sout* ; [- par écrit] to libel.

calomnieux, euse [kalɔmnjø, øz] adj [propos] slanderous ; [écrit] libellous UK, libelous US.

calorie [kalɔʀi] nf calorie.

calorifique [kalɔʀifik] adj [perte] heat *(modif)* ; [valeur] calorific.

calorique [kalɔʀik] adj PHYS & PHYSIOL calorific, caloric.

calotte [kalɔt] nf **1.** *fam* [tape] box on the ear **2.** GÉOGR ▸ **calotte glaciaire** icecap.

calque [kalk] nm **1.** [feuille] piece of tracing paper ; [substance] tracing paper **2.** [dessin] tracing, traced design ▸ **prendre** ou **faire un calque de** to trace **3.** LING calque, loan translation.

calquer [3] [kalke] vt [imiter - manières, personne] to copy exactly.

calvaire [kalvɛʀ] nm **1.** [monument - à plusieurs croix] calvary ; [- à une croix] wayside cross ou calvary **2.** [souffrance] ordeal.

calviniste [kalvinist] ◆ adj Calvinist, Calvinistic. ◆ nmf Calvinist.

calvitie [kalvisi] nf [absence de cheveux] baldness ▸ **calvitie précoce** premature baldness.

camaïeu, x [kamajø] nm **1.** [tableau] monochrome painting **2.** [technique] ▸ **un camaïeu de bleus** a monochrome in blue.

camarade [kamaʀad] nmf **1.** [ami] friend ▸ **camarade de classe** classmate ▸ **camarade d'école** schoolmate ▸ **camarade de jeu** playmate ▸ **camarade de régiment** comrade (in arms) **2.** POL comrade.

camaraderie [kamaʀadʀi] nf [entre deux personnes] good fellowship, friendship ; [dans un club, un groupe] companionship, camaraderie.

Cambodge [kɑ̃bɔdʒ] npr m ▸ **le Cambodge** Cambodia.

cambodgien, enne [kɑ̃bɔdʒjɛ̃, ɛn] adj Cambodian. ◆ **Cambodgien, enne** nm, f Cambodian.

cambouis [kɑ̃bwi] nm dirty oil ou grease.

cambré, e [kɑ̃bʀe] adj [dos] arched ; [pied] with a high instep ; [personne] arched-back ; [cheval] bow-legged.

cambrer [3] [kɑ̃bʀe] ◆ **se cambrer** vpi to arch one's back.

cambriolage [kɑ̃bʀijɔlaʒ] nm [coup] burglary, break-in.

cambrioler [3] [kɑ̃bʀijɔle] vt [propriété] to burgle UK, to burglarize US ; [personne] to burgle.

cambrioleur, euse [kɑ̃bʀijɔlœʀ, øz] nm, f burglar, housebreaker.

cambrousse [kɑ̃bʀus], **cambrouse** [kɑ̃bʀuz] nf *fam & péj* country, countryside ▸ **en pleine cambrousse** in the middle of nowhere.

cambrure [kɑ̃bʀyʀ] nf **1.** [posture - du dos] curve ; [- du pied, d'une semelle] arch **2.** TECHNOL [d'une chaussée, d'une pièce de bois] camber **3.** [partie - du pied] instep ; [- du dos] small.

came [kam] nf **1.** MÉCAN cam **2.** *tfam* [drogue] junk.

camé, e [kame] ◆ adj *tfam* high. ◆ nm, f *tfam* junkie.

camée [kame] nm JOAILL cameo.

caméléon [kamelẽ5] nm ZOOL chameleon.

camélia [kamelja] nm camellia.

camelot [kamlo] ◆ nm [dans la rue] street peddler, hawker. ◆ nmf QUÉBEC paper boy (paper girl).

camelote [kamlɔt] nf *fam péj* [mauvaise qualité] ▸ **c'est de la camelote** it's junk ou trash.

camembert [kamɑ̃bɛʀ] nm **1.** [fromage] Camembert (cheese) **2.** [graphique] pie chart.

camer [3] [kame] ◆ **se camer** vpi *tfam* to be a junkie.

caméra [kameʀa] nf AUDIO, CINÉ & TV film UK ou movie US camera / *il s'est expliqué devant les caméras* he gave an explanation in front of the television cameras ▸ **caméra numérique** digicam ▸ **caméra vidéo** video camera.

> ⚠ Le mot anglais **camera** désigne un appareil photo et non une caméra.

cameraman (*pl* **cameramans** ou **cameramen** [kameʀamɛn]), **caméraman*** [kameʀaman] nm cameraman *(nm)*, camera operator.

Cameroun [kamʀun] npr m ▸ **le Cameroun** Cameroon.

camerounais, e [kamʀunɛ, ɛz] adj Cameroonian. ◆ **Camerounais, e** nm, f Cameroonian.

Caméscope® [kameskɔp] nm camcorder ▸ **Caméscope numérique®** digital camcorder.

camion [kamjɔ̃] nm AUTO lorry UK, truck US ▸ **camion de déménagement** removal van UK, moving van US ▸ **camion frigorifique** refrigerated lorry.

camion-citerne [kamjɔ̃sitɛʀn] (*pl* **camions-citernes**) nm tanker (lorry) UK, tank(er) truck US.

camionnette [kamjɔnɛt] nf van.

camionneur, euse [kamjɔnœʀ, øz] nm, f [conducteur] lorry UK ou truck US driver. ◆ **camionneur** nm [entrepreneur] (road) haulage contractor, (road) haulier UK ou hauler US, trucker US.

camion-poubelle [kamjɔ̃pubɛl] (*pl* **camions-poubelles**) nm dustcart, (dust) bin lorry UK, garbage truck US.

camisole [kamizɔl] nf PSYCHOL ▸ **camisole de force** strait jacket.

camomille [kamɔmij] nf **1.** BOT camomile **2.** [infusion] camomile tea.

camouflage [kamuflaʒ] nm MIL [procédé] camouflaging ; [matériel] camouflage ▸ **tenue de camouflage** camouflage fatigues.

camoufler [3] [kamufle] vt **1.** MIL to camouflage **2.** [cacher - passage, gêne] to conceal ; [- bavure] to cover up *(sép)* ; [- vérité] to hide, to conceal **3.** [déguiser] : *de nombreux crimes sont camouflés en suicides* murders are often made to look like suicide. ◆ **se camoufler** vp *(emploi réfléchi)* MIL to camouflage o.s.

camp [kɑ̃] nm **1.** MIL (army) camp **2.** HIST & POL camp ▸ **camp (de concentration)** concentration camp ▸ **camp d'extermination** ou **de la mort** death camp ▸ **camp de réfugiés** refugee camp ▸ **camp de travail (forcé)** forced labour UK ou labor US camp **3.** LOISIRS campsite, camping site / *j'envoie les enfants en camp cet été* I'm sending the children off to summer camp this year ▸ **camp de vacances** holiday UK ou vacation US camp **4.** [campement] ▸ **camp de nomades a)** [dans le désert] nomad camp **b)** [de gens du voyage] travellers' camp **5.** JEUX & SPORT team, side **6.** [faction] camp, side.

campagnard, e [kɑ̃paɲaʀ, aʀd] ◆ adj [accent, charme, style, vie] country *(modif)*, rustic. ◆ nm, f countryman (countrywoman).

campagne [kɑ̃paɲ] nf **1.** GÉOGR [habitat] country ; [paysage] countryside ▸ **à la campagne** in the country ou countryside ▸ **en pleine campagne** out in the country

2. [activité] campaign ▶ **faire campagne pour / contre** to campaign for / against ▶ **campagne électorale** election campaign ▶ **campagne publicitaire** ou **de publicité** COMM advertising campaign **3.** MIL campaign ▶ **faire campagne** to campaign, to fight. ❖ **de campagne** loc adj **1.** [rural - chemin, médecin, curé] country *(modif)* **2.** COMM [pain, saucisson] country *(modif)*. ❖ **en campagne** loc adv in the field, on campaign ▶ **entrer** ou **se mettre en campagne** *pr & fig* to go into action.

campanule [kãpanyl] nf bellflower, campanula *spéc.*

campé, e [kãpe] adj ▶ **bien campé** [robuste] well-built ▶ **des personnages bien campés a)** [bien décrits] well-drawn characters **b)** [bien interprétés] well-played characters.

campement [kãpmã] nm [installation] camp, encampment ; [terrain] camping place ou ground ; [de bohémiens] caravan site.

camper [3] [kãpe] ❖ vi **1.** LOISIRS to camp **2.** MIL to camp (out) ▶ **camper sur ses positions a)** MIL to stand one's ground **b)** *fig* to stand one's ground, to stick to one's guns. ❖ vt **1.** THÉÂTRE [personnage] to play the part of **2.** [par un dessin - silhouette] to draw, to sketch out *(sép)* **3.** [par un écrit - personnage] to portray. ❖ **se camper** vpi ▶ **se camper devant qqn** to plant o.s. in front of sb.

campeur, euse [kãpœr, øz] nm, f camper.

camphre [kãfr] nm camphor.

camping [kãpiŋ] nm **1.** [activité] camping / *on a fait du camping l'été dernier* we went camping last summer / *j'aime faire du camping* I like camping ▶ **camping sauvage a)** [non autorisé] camping on non-authorized sites **b)** [en pleine nature] camping in the open ou in the wild, wilderness camping **2.** [terrain] camp ou camping site 🇬🇧, campground 🇺🇸 ; [pour caravanes] caravan 🇬🇧 ou trailer 🇺🇸 site.

camping-car [kãpiŋkar] *(pl* **camping-cars)** nm camper-van 🇬🇧, camper 🇺🇸.

Camping-Gaz® [kãpiŋgaz] nm inv butane gas-stove.

campus [kãpys] nm campus.

camus, e [kamy, yz] adj [nez] pug ; [personne] pug-nosed.

Canada [kanada] npr m ▶ **le Canada** Canada ▶ **au Canada** in Canada.

Canadair® [kanadɛr] nm fire-fighting plane, tanker plane 🇺🇸.

canadien, enne [kanadjɛ̃, ɛn] adj Canadian. ❖ **Canadien, enne** nm, f Canadian. ❖ **canadienne** nf **1.** [tente] (ridge) tent **2.** VÊT fur-lined jacket.

canaille [kanaj] nf [crapule] scoundrel, crook.

canal, aux [kanal, o] nm **1.** NAUT canal ▶ **canal maritime** ou **de navigation** ship canal **2.** TRAV PUB duct, channel **3.** AGR canal **4.** TV & INFORM channel ▶ **Canal+** ou **Plus** French pay TV channel ; 🇶 [chaîne] (TV) channel **5.** ANAT & BOT duct, canal ▶ **canal lacrymal** tear duct, lacrymal canal *spéc.* ❖ **par le canal de** loc prép through, via.

 **Canaux**

le canal du Midi	*canal linking the Garonne estuary to the Mediterranean*
le canal de Mozambique	*the Mozambique Channel*
le canal de Panamá	*the Panama Canal*
le canal de Suez	*the Suez Canal*

canalisation [kanalizasjɔ̃] nf TRAV PUB [conduit] pipe.

canaliser [3] [kanalize] vt **1.** TRAV PUB [cours d'eau] to channel ; [région] to provide with a canal system **2.** [énergies, foule, pensées, ressources] to channel.

canapé [kanape] nm **1.** [siège] settee, sofa ▶ **canapé clic-clac** *sofa bed operated by a spring mechanism* ▶ **canapé convertible** bed settee, sofa bed **2.** CULIN [pour cocktail] canapé ; [pain frit] canapé, croûton *(spread with forcemeat, served with certain meats)*.

canapé-lit [kanapeli] *(pl* canapés-lits**)** nm bed settee, sofa bed.

canaque [kanak] adj Kanak. ❖ **Canaque** nmf Kanak.

canard [kanar] nm **1.** ZOOL duck ▶ **canard boiteux** *fig* lame duck **2.** CULIN duck ▶ **canard laqué** Peking duck **3.** *fam* [journal] paper, rag.

canari [kanari] ❖ nm canary. ❖ adj inv canary-yellow.

Canaries [kanari] npr fpl ▶ **les (îles) Canaries** the Canary Islands, the Canaries ▶ **aux Canaries** in the Canaries. ⟶ **île**

cancan [kãkã] nm **1.** [danse] (French) cancan **2.** [bavardage] piece of gossip ▶ **des cancans** gossip.

cancaner [3] [kãkane] vi **1.** ZOOL to quack **2.** [médire] to gossip.

cancer [kãsɛr] nm MÉD cancer ▶ **avoir un cancer** to have cancer ▶ **cancer du foie / de la peau** liver / skin cancer ▶ **cancer du col de l'utérus** cervical cancer.

Cancer [kãsɛr] npr m ASTROL Cancer ▶ **être Cancer** to be Cancer ou a Cancerian.

cancéreux, euse [kãserø, øz] ❖ adj [cellule, tumeur] malignant, cancerous ; [malade] cancer *(modif)*. ❖ nm, f cancer victim ou sufferer.

cancérigène [kãseriʒɛn] adj carcinogenic.

cancérogène [kãserɔʒɛn] = cancérigène.

cancérologue [kãserɔlɔg] nmf cancerologist.

cancre [kãkr] nm dunce.

cancrelat [kãkrəla] nm cockroach.

candélabre [kãdelabr] nm [flambeau] candelabra.

candeur [kãdœr] nf ingenuousness, naivety.

candi [kãdi] adj m ▶ **sucre candi** rock sugar, rock candy.

candidat, e [kãdida, at] nm, f **1.** POL candidate ▶ **être candidat aux élections** to be a candidate in the elections, to stand 🇬🇧 ou to run in the elections ▶ **candidat sortant** present incumbent **2.** [à un examen, à une activité] candidate ; [à un emploi] applicant, candidate / *les candidats à l'examen d'entrée* entrance examination candidates / *être candidat à un poste* to be a candidate for a post / *se porter candidat à un poste* to apply for a post.

candidature [kãdidatyr] nf **1.** POL candidature, candidacy **2.** [pour un emploi] application ▶ **poser sa candidature (à)** to apply (for) ▶ **candidature spontanée** prospective application.

candide [kãdid] adj ingenuous, naive.

⚠ **Candid** signifie « franc », « sincère » et non candide.

cane [kan] nf (female) duck.

caneton [kantɔ̃] nm duckling.

canette [kanɛt] nf **1.** [bouteille] (fliptop) bottle **2.** [boîte] can ▶ **canette (de bière)** bottle (of beer) **3.** [bobine] spool.

canevas [kanva] nm **1.** [d'un roman, d'un exposé] framework **2.** TEXT canvas.

caniche [kaniʃ] nm ZOOL poodle.

canicule [kanikyl] nf [grande chaleur] scorching heat / *quelle canicule !* what a scorcher!

canif [kanif] nm penknife, pocketknife.

canin¹, e [kanɛ̃, in] adj canine ▶ **exposition canine** dog show.

canine² [kanin] nf canine tooth.

caniveau, x [kanivo] nm [le long du trottoir] gutter.

cannabis [kanabis] nm [drogue, chanvre] cannabis.

canne [kan] nf **1.** [d'un élégant] cane ; [d'un vieillard] walking-stick ▸ **marcher avec des cannes** to be on crutches ▸ **canne blanche** white stick 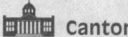 ou cane 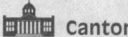 **2.** PÊCHE ▸ **canne à pêche** fishing-rod **3.** BOT ▸ **canne à sucre** sugar cane.

canné, e [kane] adj [en rotin] cane *(modif)*.

canneberge [kanbɛʀʒ] nf cranberry.

cannelle [kanɛl] nf CULIN cinnamon. ❖ **à la cannelle** loc adj cinnamon-flavoured.

cannibale [kanibal] adj & nmf cannibal *aussi fig.*

cannibalisme [kanibalism] nm [anthropophagie] cannibalism.

canoë [kanɔe] nm canoe ▸ **faire du canoë** to go canoeing.

canoë-kayak [kanɔekajak] (*pl* **canoës-kayaks**) nm ▸ **faire du canoë-kayak** to go canoeing.

canon [kanɔ̃] nm **1.** ARM [pièce - moderne] gun ; [- ancienne] cannon ; [tube d'une arme à feu] barrel **2.** AGR ▸ **canon arroseur** irrigation cannon **3.** LOISIRS & SPORT ▸ **canon à neige** snow-making machine **4.** MUS canon ▸ **chanter en canon** to sing a ou in canon.

cañon [kanɔ̃] nm canyon.

canonique [kanɔnik] adj **1.** [conforme aux règles] classic, canonic, canonical **2.** RELIG canonic, canonical **3.** MATH canonical.

canoniser [3] [kanɔnize] vt to canonize.

canot [kano] nm dinghy ▸ **canot pneumatique** pneumatic ou inflatable dinghy ▸ **canot de sauvetage** lifeboat.

canotage [kanɔtaʒ] nm boating.

canot-camping [kanokɑ̃piŋ] nm sg QUÉBEC canoe-camping.

canotier [kanɔtje] nm [chapeau] (straw) boater.

cantal [kɑ̃tal] nm Cantal cheese.

cantate [kɑ̃tat] nf cantata.

cantatrice [kɑ̃tatʀis] nf [d'opéra] (opera) singer ; [de concert] (concert) singer.

cantine [kɑ̃tin] nf **1.** [dans une école] dining hall, canteen ; [dans une entreprise] canteen / *les élèves qui mangent à la cantine* pupils who have school meals ou school dinners **2.** [malle] (tin) trunk.

cantique [kɑ̃tik] nm canticle.

canton [kɑ̃tɔ̃] nm [en France] division of an arrondissement, canton ; [en Suisse] canton ; [au Luxembourg] administrative unit, canton ; [au Canada] township.

▥ Canton

This administrative unit in the French system of local government is administered by the local members of the **conseil général**. There are between 11 and 70 **cantons** in each **département**. Each **canton** is made up of several **communes**.

Switzerland is a confederation of 23 districts known as **cantons**, three of which are themselves divided into **demi-cantons**. Although they are to a large extent self-governing, the federal government reserves control over certain areas such as foreign policy, the treasury, customs and the postal service.

---

cantonade [kɑ̃tɔnad] ❖ **à la cantonade** loc adv [sans interlocuteur précis] to all present, to the company at large ▸ **crier qqch à la cantonade** to call ou to shout sthg (out).

cantonais, e [kɑ̃tɔnɛ, ɛz] adj CULIN [cuisine] Cantonese ▸ **riz cantonais** (special) fried rice.

cantonal, e, aux [kɑ̃tɔnal, o] adj local. ❖ **cantonales** nfpl *election held every six years for the "conseil général"* ; ≃ local elections.

cantonnement [kɑ̃tɔnmɑ̃] nm MIL [lieu - gén] quarters ; [- chez l'habitant] billet.

cantonner [3] [kɑ̃tɔne] vt **1.** [isoler] ▸ **cantonner qqn dans un lieu** to confine sb to a place **2.** *fig* ▸ **cantonner qqch à** ou **dans** [activité, explication] to limit ou to confine sthg to **3.** MIL to billet ▸ **cantonner un soldat chez qqn** to billet a soldier on sb. ❖ **se cantonner à, se cantonner dans** vp + prép [se restreindre] ▸ **se cantonner à** ou **dans** [activité, explication] to confine ou to limit o.s. to.

cantonnier [kɑ̃tɔnje] nm [sur une route] roadman, road mender.

canular [kanylaʀ] nm [action] practical joke, hoax.

canyon [kaɲɔ̃] = **cañon**.

canyoning [kaɲɔniŋ], **canyonisme** [kaɲɔnism] nm canyoning.

CAO (abr de **conception assistée par ordinateur**) nf CAD.

caoutchouc [kautʃu] nm **1.** CHIM (synthetic) rubber ▸ **caoutchouc Mousse** foam rubber **2.** *fam* [élastique] rubber ou elastic band **3.** [ficus] rubber plant. ❖ **de caoutchouc, en caoutchouc** loc adj rubber *(modif)*.

caoutchouteux, euse [kautʃutø, øz] adj [viande] rubbery, chewy ; [fromage] rubbery.

cap [kap] nm **1.** GÉOGR cape, headland, promontory ▸ **doubler** ou **passer un cap** to round a cape **2.** AÉRON, AUTO & NAUT course ▸ **changer de** ou **le cap** to alter one's ou to change course ▸ **mettre le cap sur a)** NAUT to steer ou to head for **b)** AUTO to head for ▸ **suivre un cap** to steer a course **3.** [étape] milestone, hurdle ▸ **passer** ou **franchir le cap de a)** [dans une situation difficile] to get over, to come through **b)** [dans une gradation, des statistiques] to pass the mark of / *l'adolescence est un cap difficile à passer* adolescence is a difficult time to live through / *la revue a dépassé le cap des deux mille lecteurs* the readership of the magazine has passed the two thousand mark.

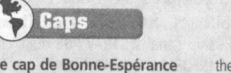

le cap de Bonne-Espérance	the Cape of Good Hope
cap Canaveral	Cape Canaveral
le cap Gris-Nez	Gris-Nez Cape
le cap Horn	Cape Horn

CAP nm (abr de **certificat d'aptitude professionnelle**) *vocational training certificate (taken at secondary school)* ; ≃ City and Guilds examination 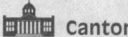.

Cap [kap] npr ▸ **Le Cap a)** [ville] Cape Town **b)** [province] Cape Province ▸ **au Cap** in Cape Town.

capable [kapabl] adj **1.** [compétent] capable, competent, able **2.** ▸ **être capable de a)** [physiquement] to be able to, to be capable of **b)** [psychologiquement] to be capable of ▸ **capable de tout** capable of (doing) anything.

capacité [kapasite] nf **1.** [aptitude] ability, capability / *avoir une grande capacité de travail* to be capable of ou to have a capacity for hard work **2.** [d'un récipient, d'une salle, d'un véhicule] capacity ▸ **sac d'une grande capacité**

roomy bag ▸ **capacité d'accueil a)** [de restaurant] seating capacity **b)** [d'hôtel] accommodation capacity / *la station de ski a une capacité d'accueil de plus de 5 000 lits* the ski resort has a capacity of over 5,000 beds ▸ **capacité hôtelière** hotel capacity **3.** INFORM & TÉLÉC capacity **4.** [diplôme] ▸ **capacité en droit** *law diploma leading to a law degree course.* ❖ **capacités** nfpl ability ▸ **capacités intellectuelles** intellectual capacity.

cape [kap] nf [pèlerine] cloak, cape.
❖ **de cape et d'épée** loc adj cloak-and-dagger *(avant nom).*

CAPES, Capes [kapɛs] **(abr de certificat d'aptitude au professorat de l'enseignement du second degré)** nm *secondary school teaching certificate ;* ≃ PGCE US.

CAPES

Candidates who pass the competitive exam for the **CAPES** become **professeurs certifiés** and are entitled to teach in secondary schools.

CAPET, Capet [kapɛ] **(abr de certificat d'aptitude au professorat de l'enseignement technique)** nm *specialized teaching certificate.*

capharnaüm [kafaʀnaɔm] nm [chaos] shambles.

capillaire [kapilɛʀ] adj [relatif aux cheveux] hair *(modif).*

capitaine [kapitɛn] nmf **1.** NAUT [dans la marine marchande] captain, master ; [dans la navigation de plaisance] captain, skipper **2.** MIL [dans l'armée de terre] captain ; [- de l'air] flight lieutenant US, captain US ; *litt* leader of men, military commander ▸ **les capitaines d'industrie** the captains of industry **3.** SPORT captain **4.** [des pompiers] chief fire officer US, fire chief US.

capitainerie [kapitɛnʀi] nf harbour US ou harbor US master's office.

capital¹, aux [kapital, o] nm **1.** FIN [avoir - personnel] capital *(U)* ; [- d'une société] capital *(U),* assets / *une société au capital de 50 000 euros* a firm with assets of 50,000 euros ▸ **capital social** nominal capital **2.** [accumulation] stock / *un capital de connaissances* a fund of knowledge / *le capital culturel du pays* the nation's cultural wealth / *n'entamez pas votre capital santé* don't overtax your health. ❖ **capitaux** nmpl [valeurs disponibles] capital ▸ **fuite des capitaux** flight of capital.

capital², e, aux [kapital, o] adj **1.** [détail] vital ; [question, aide] fundamental, crucial, vital ; [argument, point] fundamental ▸ *c'est d'une importance capitale* it's of the utmost importance **2.** [œuvre, projet] major **3.** DR capital ▸ **la peine capitale** capital punishment, the death penalty. ❖ **capitale** nf **1.** POL & ADMIN capital (city) ▸ **la capitale** [Paris] the capital, Paris **2.** IMPR capital (letter). ❖ **en capitales** loc adv IMPR in capitals, in block letters / *écrivez votre nom en capitales (d'imprimerie)* write your name in block capitals, print your name.

capitaliser [3] [kapitalize] vt **1.** FIN [capital] to capitalize ; [intérêts] to add ; [revenu] to turn into capital **2.** [accumuler] to accumulate.

capitalisme [kapitalism] nm capitalism.

capitaliste [kapitalist] ◆ adj capitalist, capitalistic. ◆ nmf capitalist.

capiteux, euse [kapitø, øz] adj [fort - alcool, senteur] heady.

capitonné, e [kapitɔne] adj padded ▸ **capitonné de cuir** with leather upholstery.

capituler [3] [kapityle] vi **1.** MIL to surrender, to capitulate **2.** [céder] to surrender, to give in.

capoeira [kapwɛʀa] nf capoeira.

caporal, e, aux [kapɔʀal, o] nmf **1.** [dans l'armée de terre] lance corporal US, private first class US **2.** [dans l'armée de l'air] senior aircraftman US, airman first class US.

capot [kapo] nm AUTO bonnet US, hood US.

capote [kapɔt] nf **1.** *fam* [préservatif] condom **2.** [d'une voiture] hood US, top US.

capoter [3] [kapɔte] vi *fam* [projet] to fall through, to collapse ; [tractation] to fall through.

câpre [kɑpʀ] nf caper.

caprice [kapʀis] nm **1.** [fantaisie] whim, passing fancy **2.** [colère] tantrum ▸ **faire des caprices** to throw tantrums **3.** [irrégularité] : *c'est un véritable caprice de la nature* it's a real freak of nature.

capricieux, euse [kapʀisjø, øz] adj **1.** [coléreux] temperamental ▸ **un enfant capricieux** an awkward child **2.** [fantaisiste] capricious, fickle **3.** [peu fiable - machine, véhicule] unreliable, temperamental ; [- saison, temps] unpredictable.

Capricorne [kapʀikɔʀn] npr m ASTROL Capricorn ▸ **être Capricorne** to be (a) Capricorn.

capsule [kapsyl] nf **1.** [d'un flacon] top, cap **2.** ASTRON ▸ **capsule (spatiale)** (space) capsule **3.** PHARM capsule.

capter [3] [kapte] vt **1.** [attention, intérêt] to capture **2.** PHYS to harness **3.** AUDIO & TÉLÉC to pick up *(insép)*, to receive.

capteur [kaptœʀ] nm **1.** ÉCOL ▸ **capteur (solaire)** solar panel **2.** [pour mesurer] sensor ; [pour commander] probe.

captif, ive [kaptif, iv] adj **1.** COMM [marché] captive **2.** [emprisonné] captive.

captivant, e [kaptivɑ̃, ɑ̃t] adj captivating, riveting, enthralling.

captiver [3] [kaptive] vt to captivate, to rivet.

captivité [kaptivite] nf captivity.

capture [kaptyʀ] nf **1.** [de biens] seizure, seizing, confiscation ; [d'un navire, d'un tank] capture **2.** [arrestation] capture / *après sa capture, il a déclaré... after he was captured ou caught, he said...*

capturer [3] [kaptyʀe] vt **1.** [faire prisonnier] to capture, to catch **2.** CHASSE & PÊCHE to catch **3.** [navire, tank] to capture.

capuche [kapyʃ] nf hood.

capuchon [kapyʃɔ̃] nm **1.** VÊT [bonnet] hood ; [manteau] hooded coat **2.** [d'un stylo] cap, top ; [d'un dentifrice] top.

capucin [kapysɛ̃] nm RELIG Capuchin (Friar).

capucine [kapysin] nf BOT nasturtium.

Cap-Vert [kapvɛʀ] npr m ▸ **le Cap-Vert** Cape Verde.
⟶ **île**

caquelon [kaklɔ̃] nm fondue pot.

caquet [kakɛ] nm *fam* [bavardage] yakking ▸ **rabattre** ou **rabaisser le caquet à qqn** to take sb down a peg or two, to put sb in his / her place.

caqueter [27] [kakte] vi [poule] to cackle.
🖉 In reformed spelling (see p. 16-18), this verb is conjugated like *acheter* : *il caquète, elle caquètera.*

car¹ [kaʀ] nm bus, coach ▸ **car de police** police van ▸ **car de ramassage (scolaire)** school bus.

car² [kaʀ] conj because, for *sout* / *il est efficace, car très bien secondé* he is efficient because he has very good back-up.

carabine [kaʀabin] nf rifle.

carabiné, e [kaʀabine] adj *fam* [note à payer, addition] stiff, steep ; [rhume] filthy, stinking ; [migraine] blinding.

caracoler [3] [kaʀakɔle] vi [sautiller] to skip about, to gambol ▶ **caracoler en tête des sondages** to be riding high in the opinion polls.

caractère [kaʀaktɛʀ] nm **1.** [nature] nature ▶ **à caractère officiel** of an official nature **2.** [tempérament] character, nature / *ce n'est pas dans son caractère d'être agressif* it's not in character for him to be ou it's not in his nature to be aggressive ▶ **avoir bon caractère** to be good-natured ▶ **avoir mauvais caractère** to be bad-tempered ▶ **avoir un caractère de chien** *fam* ou **de cochon** *fam* to have a foul temper **3.** [volonté, courage] character ▶ **avoir du caractère** to have character **4.** [trait] characteristic, feature, trait **5.** [originalité] character ▶ **appartement / maison de caractère** flat / house with character **6.** BIOL characteristic ▶ **caractère acquis / héréditaire** acquired / hereditary characteristic ou trait **7.** IMPR & INFORM character ▶ **en gros / petits caractères** in large / small print.

⚠ Attention, ce mot ne se traduit pas toujours par **character** en anglais. Voir article.

caractériel, elle [kaʀakteʀjel] ◆ adj **1.** PSYCHOL [adolescent] maladjusted, (emotionally) disturbed **2.** [d'humeur changeante] moody **3.** [du caractère] character *(modif)*. ◆ nm, f [enfant] problem child ; [adulte] maladjusted person.

caractérisé, e [kaʀakteʀize] adj [méchanceté] blatant ; [indifférence] pointed.

caractériser [3] [kaʀakteʀize] vt **1.** [constituer le caractère de] to characterize / *avec la générosité qui le caractérise* with characteristic generosity **2.** [définir] to characterize, to define.

caractéristique [kaʀakteʀistik] ◆ adj characteristic, typical. ◆ nf **1.** [trait] characteristic, (distinguishing) feature ou trait **2.** MATH characteristic.

carafe [kaʀaf] nf **1.** [récipient - ordinaire] carafe ; [- travaillé] decanter **2.** [contenu] jugful ; [de vin] carafe.

carafon [kaʀafɔ̃] nm [récipient - ordinaire] small jug ou carafe ; [- travaillé] small decanter.

caraïbe [kaʀaib] adj Caribbean.

Caraïbes [kaʀaib] npr fpl ▶ **les (îles) Caraïbes** the Caribbean, the West Indies ▶ **la mer des Caraïbes** the Caribbean (Sea). ⟶ **île**, ⟶ **mer**

carambolage [kaʀɑ̃bɔlaʒ] nm [de voitures] pileup, multiple crash.

caramel [kaʀamɛl] nm **1.** [pour napper] caramel **2.** [bonbon - dur] toffee, taffy US, caramel ; [- mou] toffee, fudge.

caraméliser [3] [kaʀamelize] vt **1.** [mets] to coat with caramel ; [boisson, glace] to flavour with caramel **2.** [sucre] to caramelize.

carapace [kaʀapas] nf ZOOL shell, carapace *spéc.*

carapater [3] [kaʀapate] ❖ **se carapater** vpi *fam* to skedaddle, to scram, to make o.s. scarce.

carat [kaʀa] nm [d'un métal, d'une pierre] carat, karat US.

caravane [kaʀavan] nf **1.** [véhicule - de vacancier] caravan UK, trailer US ; [- de nomade] caravan **2.** [convoi] caravan.

caravaning [kaʀavaniŋ] nm caravanning.

carbone [kaʀbɔn] nm **1.** [papier] (sheet of) carbon paper **2.** CHIM carbon ▶ **dater au carbone 14** to carbon-date, to date with carbon-14 ▶ **bilan carbone** carbon balance.

carbonique [kaʀbɔnik] adj carbonic.

carboniser [3] [kaʀbɔnize] vt **1.** [brûler - viande] to burn to a cinder ; [- édifice] to burn to the ground / *il est mort carbonisé* he was burned to death **2.** [transformer en charbon] to carbonize, to turn into charcoal.

carburant [kaʀbyʀɑ̃] nm fuel.

carburateur [kaʀbyʀatœʀ] nm carburettor UK, carburetor US.

carbure [kaʀbyʀ] nm carbide.

carburer [3] [kaʀbyʀe] vi *fam* **1.** [travailler dur] to work flat out ; [réfléchir] : *ça carbure, ici !* brains are working overtime in here ! **2.** [fonctionner] : *moi, je carbure au café* I can't do anything unless I have a coffee inside me.

carcajou [kaʀkaʒu] nm Québec wolverine.

carcan [kaʀkɑ̃] nm HIST [collier] collar shackle / *pris dans les règlements comme dans un carcan* fig hemmed in by regulations.

carcasse [kaʀkas] nf **1.** [d'un animal] carcass **2.** [armature - d'un édifice] shell ; [- d'un meuble] carcass ; [- d'un véhicule] shell, body ; [- d'un parapluie] frame **3.** [d'un pneu] carcass ▶ **carcasse radiale** radial-ply tyre.

carcéral, e, aux [kaʀseʀal, o] adj prison *(modif)*.

cardiaque [kaʀdjak] ◆ adj heart *(modif)*, cardiac ▶ **elle est cardiaque** she has a heart condition. ◆ nmf cardiac ou heart patient.

cardigan [kaʀdigɑ̃] nm cardigan.

cardinal, e, aux [kaʀdinal, o] adj **1.** ASTROL & MATH cardinal **2.** GÉOGR ▶ **points cardinaux** points of the compass. ❖ **cardinal, aux** nm RELIG cardinal.

cardiologue [kaʀdjɔlɔg] nmf heart specialist, cardiologist *spéc.*

cardio-vasculaire (*pl* cardio-vasculaires), **cardiovasculaire*** [kaʀdjovaskylɛʀ] adj cardiovascular.

carême [kaʀɛm] nm RELIG ▶ **le carême a)** [abstinence] fasting **b)** [époque] Lent.

carence [kaʀɑ̃s] nf **1.** MÉD deficiency ▶ **avoir une carence alimentaire** to suffer from a nutritional deficiency **2.** [d'une administration, d'une œuvre, d'une méthode] shortcoming, failing **3.** PSYCHOL ▶ **carence affective** emotional deprivation.

carène [kaʀɛn] nf NAUT hull.

caréner [18] [kaʀene] vt AUTO & AÉRON to streamline.

📝 In reformed spelling (see p. 16-18), this verb is conjugated like *semer : elle carènera, il carènerait.*

caresse [kaʀɛs] nf [attouchement] caress, stroke ▶ **faire des caresses à a)** [chat] to stroke **b)** [personne] to caress.

caresser [4] [kaʀese] vt **1.** [toucher - affectueusement] to stroke ; [- sensuellement] to caress / *caresser un enfant* to pet a child / *le chat aime se faire caresser derrière les oreilles* the cat likes being stroked behind the ears ▶ **caresser qqn dans le sens du poil** to stroke sb's ego / *il faut le caresser dans le sens du poil* don't rub him (up) the wrong way **2.** [avoir, former] ▶ **caresser le rêve de faire qqch** to dream of doing sthg.

cargaison [kaʀgɛzɔ̃] nf **1.** [marchandises] cargo, freight **2.** *fam* [quantité] ▶ **une cargaison de** a load of.

cargo [kaʀgo] nm freighter.

cari [kaʀi] nm **1.** [épice] curry powder **2.** [plat] curry.

caribéen, enne [kaʀibeɛ̃, ɛn] adj Caribbean. ❖ **Caribéen, enne** nm, f West Indian.

caribou [kaʀibu] nm Québec caribou, reindeer.

caricatural, e, aux [kaʀikatyʀal, o] adj **1.** [récit, explication] distorted **2.** [dessin, art] caricatural.

caricature [kaʀikatyʀ] nf **1.** [dessin] caricature ▶ **caricature politique** (political) cartoon **2.** [déformation] caricature.

---

* In reformed spelling (see p. 16-18).

carie [kaʁi] nf MÉD caries *spéc* ▶ **carie dentaire** tooth decay, dental caries *spéc* ▶ *elle n'a pas de caries* she doesn't have any bad teeth.

carié, e [kaʁje] adj MÉD [dent] decayed, bad ; [os] carious.

carillon [kaʁijɔ̃] nm **1.** [cloches] carillon **2.** [sonnerie - d'une horloge] chime ; [- d'entrée] chime.

carillonner [3] [kaʁijɔne] ◆ vi [cloches] to ring, to chime. ◆ vt *péj* [rumeur] to broadcast, to shout from the roof tops.

caritatif, ive [kaʁitatif, iv] adj charity *(modif)* ▶ **association caritative** charity.

carlingue [kaʁlɛ̃g] nf AÉRON cabin.

carmélite [kaʁmelit] nf Carmelite.

carnage [kaʁnaʒ] nm slaughter, carnage.

carnassier, ère [kaʁnasje, ɛʁ] adj [animal] carnivorous ; [dent] carnassial. ◆ **carnassier** nm carnivore.

carnaval [kaʁnaval] nm [fête] carnival.

carnet [kaʁnɛ] nm **1.** [cahier] note-book **2.** [registre] ▶ **carnet d'adresses** address book ▶ **carnet de bord** log book ▶ **carnet de notes** school report 🇬🇧, report card 🇺🇸 ▶ **carnet de santé** child's health record **3.** [à feuilles détachables] ▶ **carnet de chèques** chequebook 🇬🇧, checkbook 🇺🇸 ▶ **carnet à souches** counterfoil book ▶ **carnet de tickets (de métro)** ten metro tickets ▶ **carnet de timbres** book of stamps **4.** ÉCON ▶ **carnet de commandes** order book.

carnivore [kaʁnivɔʁ] ◆ adj carnivorous. ◆ nm carnivore, meat-eater.

carotide [kaʁɔtid] nf carotid.

carotte [kaʁɔt] nf **1.** BOT carrot **2.** *fam* [récompense] carrot ▶ **la carotte et le bâton** the carrot and the stick.

carpe [kaʁp] nf carp.

carpette [kaʁpɛt] nf **1.** [tapis] rug **2.** *fam & péj* [personne] doormat, spineless individual.

carré, e [kaʁe] adj **1.** [forme, planche] square **2.** GÉOM & MATH square **3.** [sans détours] straight, straightforward. ◆ **carré** nm **1.** [gén & GÉOM] square **2.** MATH square ▶ **le carré de six** six squared, the square of six ▶ *élever un nombre au carré* to square a number **3.** [coiffure] bob **4.** [viande] ▶ **carré d'agneau / de mouton / de porc / de veau** loin of lamb / mutton / pork / veal **5.** JEUX [au poker] ▶ **carré d'as** four aces.

carreau, x [kaʁo] nm **1.** [sur du papier] square ▶ **papier à carreaux** squared paper, graph paper ; [motif sur du tissu] check ▶ **veste à carreaux** check ou checked jacket / *draps à petits carreaux* sheets with a small check design ou pattern **2.** [plaque de grès, de marbre] tile ▶ **carreau de faïence** ceramic tile **3.** [sol] tiled floor ▶ **rester sur le carreau a)** *fam* [être assommé] to be laid out **b)** [être tué] to be bumped off **c)** [échouer] to come a cropper 🇬🇧, to take a spill 🇺🇸 **4.** [vitre] window-pane ; [fenêtre] window **5.** CARTES diamond **6.** *fam* EXPR se tenir à carreau : *tiens-toi à carreau !* watch your step!

carreauté, e [kaʁote] adj 🇶🇧🇨 = à carreaux.

carrefour [kaʁfuʁ] nm **1.** [de rues] crossroads *(sg)*, junction **2.** [point de rencontre] crossroads.

carrelage [kaʁlaʒ] nm **1.** [carreaux] tiles, tiling ▶ **poser un carrelage** to lay tiles ou a tiled floor **2.** [sol] tiled floor.

carreler [24] [kaʁle] vt [mur, salle de bains] to tile.

   In reformed spelling (see p. 16-18), this verb is conjugated like ***peler : il carrèle, elle carrèlera.***

carrelet [kaʁlɛ] nm ZOOL plaice.

carrément [kaʁemɑ̃] adv **1.** [dire] straight out, bluntly ; [agir] straight **2.** *fam* [en intensif] pretty *(adv)*, downright ▶ *c'est carrément du vol / de la corruption* it's daylight robbery / blatant corruption.

carrer [3] [kaʁe] ◆ **se carrer** vpi to settle, to ensconce o.s. *sout* ou *hum*.

carrière [kaʁjɛʁ] nf **1.** [d'extraction] quarry **2.** [parcours professionnel] career ▶ **faire carrière dans** to pursue a career in. ◆ **de carrière** loc adj [officier] regular ; [diplomate] career *(modif)*.

carriériste [kaʁjeʁist] nmf careerist, career-minded person.

carriole [kaʁjɔl] nf **1.** [à deux roues] cart **2.** 🇶🇧🇨 car sleigh, carriole.

carrossable [kaʁɔsabl] adj suitable for motor vehicles.

carrosse [kaʁɔs] nm [véhicule] coach.

carrosserie [kaʁɔsʁi] nf **1.** AUTO [structure] body ; [habillage] bodywork ▶ **atelier de carrosserie** body shop **2.** [métier] coachwork, coach-building.

carrossier [kaʁɔsje] nm coachbuilder.

carrousel [kaʁuzɛl] nm ÉQUIT carousel.

carrure [kaʁyʁ] nf **1.** [corps] build ▶ **avoir une carrure d'athlète** to be built like an athlete **2.** [qualité] stature, calibre.

cartable [kaʁtabl] nm [à bretelles] satchel ; [à poignée] schoolbag.

carte [kaʁt]
nf

A. PAPIER, PLASTIQUE, DOCUMENT **1.** [courrier] card ▶ **carte postale** postcard ▶ **carte de visite a)** [personnelle] visiting 🇬🇧 ou calling 🇺🇸 card **b)** [professionnelle] business card ▶ **carte de vœux** New Year greetings card **2.** [de restaurant] menu ▶ **la carte des vins** the wine list ; [menu à prix non fixe] à la carte menu **3.** [document officiel] ▶ **carte d'abonnement a)** TRANSP season ticket ou pass **b)** MUS & THÉÂTRE season ticket ▶ **carte d'adhérent** ou **de membre** membership card ▶ **carte d'électeur** polling card 🇬🇧, voter registration card 🇺🇸 ▶ **carte d'embarquement** boarding card ou pass ▶ **carte d'étudiant** student card ▶ **carte de fidélité** loyalty card ▶ **carte grise** ≃ logbook 🇬🇧 ; ≃ car registration papers 🇺🇸 ▶ **carte (nationale) d'identité** (national) identity card ou ID card ▶ **carte de séjour (temporaire)** (temporary) residence permit ▶ **carte verte** green card 🇬🇧, certificate of insurance 🇺🇸 ▶ **donner** ou **laisser carte blanche à qqn** to give sb carte blanche ou a free hand **4.** [moyen de paiement] ▶ **carte bancaire** bank card, cash card 🇬🇧 ▶ **Carte Bleue®** Visa Card® *(with which purchases are debited directly from the holder's current account)* ▶ **carte de crédit** credit card *(to back up signatures on bills and to obtain cash from machines)* ▶ **carte de paiement** credit card *(to effect automatic payment for goods and services)* ▶ **carte de téléphone** ou **téléphonique** Phonecard® **5.** INFORM [circuit] card ou board ▶ **carte magnétique** swipe card ▶ **carte mémoire** memory card ▶ **carte à puce** smart card ▶ **carte son** sound card **6.** TÉLÉC ▶ **carte SIM®** SIM® card.

B. POUR SE REPÉRER GÉOGR & GÉOL map ; ASTRON, MÉTÉOR & NAUT chart ▶ **carte routière** road map.

C. POUR JOUER JEUX ▶ **carte (à jouer)** (playing) card ▶ **jeu de cartes a)** [activité] card game **b)** [paquet] pack of cards ▶ **jouer cartes sur table** to lay one's cards on the table. ◆ **à la carte** ◆ loc adj **1.** [repas] à la carte **2.** [programme, investissement] customized ; [horaire] flexible ; [télévision] pay-per-view. ◆ loc adv ▶ **manger à la carte** to eat à la carte.

Carte de séjour

Foreign nationals from outside the Schengen area living in France are required to carry this document. It is issued by their local **préfecture** as a certificate of residency.

cartel [kaʀtɛl] nm **1.** ÉCON cartel **2.** POL coalition, cartel.

carter [kaʀtɛʀ] nm AUTO ▸ **carter du moteur** crankcase ; [de vélo] chain guard.

carte-réponse [kaʀtʀepɔ̃s] (pl **cartes-réponse** ou **cartes-réponses**) nf reply card.

Carterie® [kaʀtəʀi] nf card shop.

cartésien, enne [kaʀtezjɛ̃, ɛn] adj & nm, f Cartesian.

cartilage [kaʀtilaʒ] nm **1.** ANAT [substance] cartilage (U) **2.** [du poulet] piece of gristle.

cartographie [kaʀtɔgʀafi] nf cartography.

cartographier [kaʀtɔgʀafje] vt [pays, région] to map, to draw a map of ; [génome humain] to map.

cartomancien, enne [kaʀtɔmɑ̃sjɛ̃, ɛn] nm, f fortune-teller (with cards).

carton [kaʀtɔ̃] nm **1.** [matière] cardboard **2.** [boîte - grande] cardboard box ; [- petite] carton **3.** [rangement - pour dossiers] (box) file ; [- pour dessins] portfolio ▸ *le projet est resté dans les cartons* fig the project never saw the light of day, the project was shelved **4.** FOOT ▸ **carton jaune** yellow card ▸ **carton rouge** red card. ❖ **en carton** loc adj cardboard *(modif)*.

cartonné, e [kaʀtɔne] adj [livre] hardback.

cartonner [3] [kaʀtɔne] ❖ vt [film, disque] to be a hit ; [livre] to be a best-seller. ❖ vi fam [réussir] to hit the jackpot.

carton-pâte [kaʀtɔ̃pat] (pl **cartons-pâtes**) nm pasteboard. ❖ **de carton-pâte, en carton-pâte** loc adj péj [décor] cardboard *(modif)* ; [personnage, intrigue] cardboard cut-out *(modif)*.

cartouche [kaʀtuʃ] nf **1.** ARM [projectile, charge] cartridge **2.** COMM [recharge] cartridge ; [emballage groupant plusieurs paquets] carton **3.** PHOT cartridge, cassette, magazine.

cas [ka] nm **1.** [hypothèse] : *dans le meilleur des cas* at best / *dans le pire des cas* at worst ▸ **en aucun cas** under no circumstances, on no account / *envisageons ce cas de figure* let us consider that possibility ▸ **le cas échéant** should this happen **2.** [situation particulière] case, situation ▸ **cas de conscience** matter of conscience ▸ **cas de force majeure** a) pr case of force majeure b) fig case of absolute necessity ▸ **c'est le cas de le dire !** you've said it! **3.** MÉD & SOCIOL case / *ce garçon est un cas !* fam & hum that boy is something else ou a real case! **4.** EXPR faire grand cas de a) [événement] to attach great importance to b) [argument, raison] to set great store by c) [invité, ami] to make a great fuss ou much of ▸ **le faire peu de cas de a)** [argument, raison] to pay scant attention to b) [invité, ami] to ignore. ❖ **au cas où** loc conj in case / *au cas où il ne viendrait pas* in case he doesn't come ; *(comme adv)* ▸ **prends un parapluie au cas où** fam take an umbrella just in case. ❖ **dans tous les cas** = **en tout cas**. ❖ **en cas de** loc prép in case of ▸ **en cas de besoin** in case of need / *en cas de perte de la carte* should the card be lost. ❖ **en tout cas** loc adv in any case ou event, anyway. ❖ **cas social** nm *person needing social worker's assistance*.

> 📋 Notez que in case n'est pas suivi de would :
> **Au cas où ils auraient envie de rester dîner, j'ai prévu large.** *I've made extra in case they want to stay for dinner.*
> **Il avait une canne à la main pour le cas où il aurait à se défendre.** *He carried a stick in case he had to defend himself.*

casanier, ère [kazanje, ɛʀ] ❖ adj stay-at-home. ❖ nm, f stay-at-home type, homebody.

cascade [kaskad] nf [chute d'eau] waterfall, cascade litt.

cascadeur, euse [kaskadœʀ, øz] nm, f stunt man (woman).

case [kaz] nf **1.** [d'un damier] square ; [d'une grille de mots croisés] square ; [d'un formulaire] box ▸ **case départ** : *retournez* ou *retour à la case départ* return to go / *retour à la case départ !* fig back to square one! **2.** [d'un meuble, d'une boîte] compartment ▸ **il a une case (de) vide** fam ou **en moins** fam he's not all there, he's got a screw loose **3.** [hutte] hut.

caser [3] [kaze] vt fam **1.** [faire entrer] ▸ **caser qqch dans qqch** to fit sthg in sthg **2.** [dans un emploi] to fix up (sép) **3.** [marier] to marry off (sép) ▸ **il est enfin casé** he's settled down at last. ❖ **se caser** vpi fam [se marier] to settle down.

caserne [kazɛʀn] nf MIL barracks (sg ou pl) ▸ **caserne de pompiers** fire station.

cash [kaʃ] adv cash ▸ **payer cash** to pay cash.

casier [kazje] nm **1.** [case - ouverte] pigeonhole ; [- fermée] compartment ; [- dans une consigne, un gymnase] locker ▸ **casier de consigne automatique** luggage locker **2.** [meuble - à cases ouvertes] pigeonholes ; [- à tiroirs] filing cabinet ; [- à cases fermées] compartment ; [- à cases fermant à clef] locker ▸ **casier à bouteilles** bottle rack **3.** [pour ranger - des livres] unit ; [- des bouteilles] rack ; [- dans un réfrigérateur] compartment **4.** ADMIN & DR record ▸ **casier judiciaire** police ou criminal record ▸ **un casier judiciaire vierge** a clean (police) record **5.** PÊCHE pot.

casino [kazino] nm casino.

Caspienne [kaspjɛn] npr f ▸ **la (mer) Caspienne** the Caspian Sea. ➞ **mer**

casque [kask] nm **1.** [pour protéger] helmet ; [d'ouvrier] hard hat ▸ **casque de moto** crash helmet ▸ **les casques bleus** the UN peace-keeping force, the blue berets **2.** AUDIO headphones, headset, earphones **3.** [de coiffeur] hood hairdrier.

casquer [3] [kaske] vi tfam to cough up, to come up with the cash.

casquette [kaskɛt] nf cap ▸ **casquette d'officier** officer's peaked cap.

cassant, e [kasɑ̃, ɑ̃t] adj **1.** [cheveux, ongle] brittle ; [métal] short **2.** [réponse] curt.

casse [kas] ❖ nm fam [d'une banque] bank robbery ; [d'une maison] break-in. ❖ nf **1.** IMPR case ▸ **bas / haut de casse** lower / upper case **2.** [de voitures] scrapyard ▸ **mettre** ou **envoyer à la casse** to scrap / *une idéologie bonne pour la casse* fig an ideology fit for the scrapheap **3.** BOT cassia.

cassé, e [kase] adj **1.** ➞ **blanc 2.** ➞ **col.**

casseau [kaso] nm QUÉBEC berry basket ▸ **maigre comme un casseau** fam thin as a rake.

casse-cou [kasku] (pl **casse-cou** ou **casse-cous***) nmf daredevil.

casse-croûte (pl **casse-croûte**), **casse-croute*** (pl **casse-croutes***) [kaskʀut] nm fam [repas léger] snack ; [sandwich] sandwich.

casse-gueule [kasɡœl] (pl **casse-gueule** ou **casse-gueules***) fam adj [chemin] treacherous ; [projet] risky.

casse-noisettes [kasnwazɛt] nm inv nutcracker.

casse-noix [kasnwa] nm inv [instrument] nutcracker.

casse-pieds (pl **casse-pieds**), **casse-pied*** (pl **casse-pieds***) [kaspje] adj fam [ennuyeux] boring ; [agaçant] annoying / *un peu casse-pieds à préparer* a bit of a hassle to prepare.

---

* In reformed spelling (see p. 16-18).

casser [3] [kase] ◆ vt **1.** [mettre en pièces - table] to break (up); [- porte] to break down *(sép)*; [- poignée] to break off *(sép)*; [- noix] to crack (open) ▸ **casser qqch en mille morceaux** to smash sthg to bits ou smithereens ▸ **casser qqch en deux** to break ou to snap sthg in two ▸ **casser du sucre sur le dos de qqn** *fam* to knock sb when his / her back's turned ▸ **casser la baraque a)** *fam* THÉÂTRE to bring the house down **b)** [faire échouer un plan] to ruin it all ▸ **casser la croûte** *fam* ou **graine** *fam* to have a bite to eat ▸ **casser sa pipe** *fam* to kick the bucket ▸ **ça ne casse pas des briques** *fam* it's no great shakes ou no big deal **2.** [interrompre - fonctionnement, déroulement, grève] to break **3.** [démolir] to demolish **4.** [en parlant de parties du corps] to break ▸ **casser la figure** *fam* ou **gueule** *tfam* **à qqn** to smash sb's face in ▸ **casser les oreilles à qqn a)** *fam* [avec de la musique] to deafen sb **b)** [en le harcelant] to give sb a lot of hassle ▸ **casser les pieds à qqn** *fam* to get on sb's nerves ou wick **5.** [abîmer - voix] to damage, to ruin **6.** [annihiler - espoir] to dash, to destroy; [- moral] to crush **7.** DR [jugement] to quash; [arrêt] to nullify, to annul **8.** [rétrograder - officier] to break, to reduce to the ranks; [- fonctionnaire] to demote **9.** COMM ▸ **casser les prix** to slash prices **10.** *tfam* [cambrioler] to do a job on **11.** *fam* [voiture] to take to bits *(for spare parts)*, to cannibalize. ◆ vi [verre, chaise] to break; [fil] to snap; [poignée] to break off. ◈ **se casser** ◆ vpi **1.** [être mis en pièces - assiette] to break; [- poignée] to break off **2.** *tfam* [partir] to push ou to buzz off ▸ **casse-toi!** get lost!, push off! **3.** [cesser de fonctionner - appareil, véhicule] to break down **4.** [être altéré - voix] to crack, to falter **5.** VÊT [tissu] to break (off). ◆ vpt to break ▸ **se casser le cou a)** *pr* to break one's neck **b)** *fig* to come a cropper [UK], to take a tumble ▸ **se casser la figure** *fam* ou **gueule** *tfam* **a)** [personne] to come a cropper [UK], to take a tumble **b)** [livre, carafe] to crash to the ground **c)** [projet] to bite the dust, to take a dive ▸ **se casser le nez a)** *fam* [ne trouver personne] to find no-one in **b)** [échouer] to come a cropper [UK], to bomb [US]. ◈ **à tout casser** *fam* ◆ loc adj [endiablé - fête] fantastic; [- succès] runaway. ◆ loc adv [tout au plus] at the (very) most.

casserole [kasʁɔl] nf [ustensile, contenu] pan, saucepan.

⚠ Le mot anglais **casserole** signifie «ragoût» et non casserole.

casse-tête [kastɛt] *(pl* casse-tête ou casse-têtes*)* nm JEUX puzzle, brainteaser / *organiser cette réception, c'était un vrai casse-tête !* what a headache it was organizing that party!

cassette [kasɛt] nf **1.** AUDIO & INFORM cassette **2.** [coffret] casket.

casseur, euse [kasœʁ, øz] nm, f **1.** [dans une manifestation] rioting demonstrator **2.** *fam* [cambrioleur] burglar.

cassis [kasis] nm **1.** [baie] blackcurrant **2.** [liqueur] blackcurrant liqueur, cassis.

cassonade [kasɔnad] nf light brown sugar.

cassoulet [kasulɛ] nm cassoulet, haricot bean stew *(with pork, goose or duck)*.

cassure [kasyʁ] nf **1.** [fissure] crack **2.** [rupture dans la vie, le rythme] break.

castagne [kastaɲ] nf *fam* fighting.

castagnettes [kastaɲɛt] nfpl castanets.

caste [kast] nf ENTOM & SOCIOL caste.

casting [kastiŋ] nm CINÉ & THÉÂTRE casting ▸ **erreur de casting a)** *pr* casting error **b)** *fig ce n'est pas qu'il soit incompétent, c'est juste une erreur de casting* it's not that he's incompetent, he's just not cut out for this job.

castor [kastɔʁ] nm ZOOL beaver.

castrer [3] [kastʁe] vt [homme, femme] to castrate; [cheval] to castrate, to geld; [chat] to castrate, to neuter, to spay.

cata [kata] nf *fam* : *c'est la cata* it's a disaster.

cataclysme [kataklism] nm GÉOGR natural disaster, cataclysm.

catacombes [katakɔ̃b] nfpl catacombs.

catadioptre [katadjɔptʁ] nm **1.** AUTO reflector **2.** [sur une route] Catseye® [UK], highway reflector [US].

catalan, e [katalɑ̃, an] adj Catalan. ◈ **Catalan, e** nm, f Catalan. ◈ **catalan** nm LING Catalan.

catalogne [katalɔɲ] nf [QUÉBEC] *material woven from strips of coloured fabric*.

Catalogne [katalɔɲ] npr f ▸ **(la) Catalogne** Catalonia.

catalogue [katalɔg] nm [liste - de bibliothèque, d'exposition] catalogue, catalog [US].

cataloguer [3] [katalɔge] vt **1.** [livre] to list, to catalogue, to catalog [US]; [bibliothèque] to catalogue, to catalog [US]; [œuvre, marchandise] to catalogue, to catalog [US], to put into a catalogue **2.** *fam* [juger] to label, to categorize, to pigeonhole.

catalyseur [katalizœʁ] nm **1.** [personne, journal] catalyst **2.** CHIM catalyst.

catalytique [katalitik] adj catalytic.

catamaran [katamaʁɑ̃] nm [voilier] catamaran.

catapulter [3] [katapylte] vt ARM & AÉRON to catapult.

cataracte [kataʁakt] nf MÉD cataract.

catastrophe [katastʁɔf] nf [désastre - en avion, en voiture] disaster; [- dans une vie, un gouvernement] catastrophe, disaster ▸ **catastrophe naturelle** natural disaster. ◈ **en catastrophe** loc adv ▸ **partir en catastrophe** to rush off ▸ **atterrir en catastrophe** to make a forced ou an emergency landing.

catastrophé, e [katastʁɔfe] adj shocked, upset.

catastrophique [katastʁɔfik] adj catastrophic, disastrous.

catastrophisme [katastʁɔfism] nm catastrophism / *ne fais pas de catastrophisme !* don't be so pessimistic!

catastrophiste [katastʁɔfist] adj very pessimistic / *il a prononcé un discours catastrophiste sur l'évolution du climat* he made a very gloomy speech about climate change.

catch [katʃ] nm (all-in) wrestling.

catéchisme [kateʃism] nm RELIG [enseignement, livre] catechism ▸ **aller au catéchisme** to go to catechism; ≃ to go to Sunday school.

catégorie [kategɔʁi] nf **1.** [pour classifier - des objets, des concepts] category, class, type; [- des employés] grade ▸ **catégorie socioprofessionnelle** socioprofessional group **2.** [qualité - dans les transports, les hôtels] class **3.** SPORT class ▸ **toutes catégories** for all comers.

catégorique [kategɔʁik] adj [non ambigu - refus] flat, categorical, point-blank.

catégoriquement [kategɔʁikmɑ̃] adv [nettement - affirmer] categorically; [- refuser] categorically, flatly, point-blank.

caténaire [katenɛʁ] ◆ adj catenary *(modif)*. ◆ nf catenary.

cathédrale [katedʁal] nf [édifice] cathedral.

cathodique [katɔdik] adj cathodic.

catholicisme [katɔlisism] nm (Roman) Catholicism.

catholique [katɔlik] ◆ adj **1.** RELIG (Roman) Catholic **2.** *fam* [EXPR] ▸ **pas très catholique comme façon de faire a)** [peu conventionnel] not a very orthodox way of doing things **b)** [malhonnête] not a very kosher way of doing things. ◆ nmf (Roman) Catholic.

catimini [katimini] ❖ **en catimini** loc adv on the sly ou quiet ▶ **arriver / partir en catimini** to sneak in / out.

catogan [katɔgɑ̃] nm *large bow holding the hair at the back of neck.*

cauchemar [koʃmaʀ] nm [mauvais rêve] nightmare ▶ **faire un cauchemar** to have a nightmare.

cauchemarder [3] [koʃmaʀde] vi to have nightmares.

causant, e [kozɑ̃, ɑ̃t] adj *fam* chatty / *il n'est pas très causant* [coopératif] he's not exactly forthcoming.

cause [koz] nf **1.** [origine, motif] cause, reason, origin ▶ **être (la) cause de qqch** to cause sthg **2.** DR [affaire] case, brief ▶ **plaider la cause de qqn** *pr & fig* to plead sb's case **3.** [parti que l'on prend] cause / *une cause perdue* a lost cause ▶ **pour la bonne cause a)** [pour un bon motif] for a good cause **b)** *hum* [en vue du mariage] with honourable intentions. ❖ **à cause de** loc prép [par la faute de] because ou on account of, due ou owing to. ❖ **en cause** ◆ loc adj **1.** [concerné] in question ▶ **la somme / l'enjeu en cause** the amount / the thing at stake **2.** [que l'on suspecte] ▶ **les financiers en cause** the financiers involved **3.** [contesté] ▶ **être en cause** [talent] to be in question ; DR ▶ **affaire en cause** case before the court. ◆ loc adv **1.** [en accusation] ▶ **mettre qqn en cause** to implicate sb ▶ **mettre qqch en cause** to call sthg into question **2.** [en doute] ▶ **remettre en cause** [principe] to question, to challenge. ❖ **pour cause de** loc prép owing to, because of / *'fermé pour cause de décès'* 'closed owing to bereavement'.

causer [3] [koze] ◆ vt [provoquer - peine, problème] to cause / *cela m'a causé de graves ennuis* it got me into a lot of trouble. ◆ vi fam [bavarder] ▶ **causer (à qqn)** to chat (to sb) ▶ **cause toujours(, tu m'intéresses) !** a) [je fais ce que je veux] yeah, yeah (I'll do what I like anyway)! b) [tu pourrais m'écouter] don't mind me!

causerie [kozʀi] nf informal talk (in front of an audience).

causette [kozɛt] nf fam ▶ **faire la causette à qqn** to chat with sb.

caustique [kostik] adj [mordant] caustic, biting, sarcastic.

cautériser [3] [koteʀize] vt to cauterize.

caution [kosjɔ̃] nf **1.** [somme] bail ▶ **payer la caution de qqn** to post bail for sb, to bail sb out **2.** [garant] ▶ **se porter caution pour qqn** to stand security ou surety ou guarantee for sb **3.** [garantie morale] guarantee ; [soutien] support, backing ▶ **donner** ou **apporter sa caution à** to support, to back ▶ **caution juratoire** guarantee given on oath **4.** COMM security, guarantee / *verser une caution de 100 euros* to put down a 100 euro deposit (as security). ❖ **sous caution** loc adv [libérer] on bail.

cautionner [3] [kosjone] vt [soutenir] to support, to back.

cavalcade [kavalkad] nf [course] stampede.

cavale [kaval] nf *arg crime* jailbreak ▶ **être en cavale** to be on the run.

cavaler [3] [kavale] vi fam [courir] to run ou to rush (around).

cavalerie [kavalʀi] nf MIL cavalry.

cavalier, ère [kavalje, ɛʀ] ◆ adj **1.** ÉQUIT ▶ **allée** ou **piste cavalière** bridle path, bridleway **2.** péj [désinvolte - attitude] offhand, cavalier ; [- réponse] curt, offhand. ◆ nm, f **1.** ÉQUIT rider **2.** [danseur] partner. ❖ **cavalier** nm **1.** [pour aller au bal] escort ▶ **faire cavalier seul a)** [dans une entreprise] to go it alone **b)** POL to be a maverick **2.** JEUX [aux échecs] knight.

cave [kav] nf **1.** [pièce] cellar / *de la cave au grenier* fig [ranger, nettoyer] from top to bottom ▶ **cave à vin** wine cellar **2.** [vins] (wine) cellar ▶ **avoir une bonne cave** to keep a good cellar **3.** [cabaret] cellar 🇬🇧 ou basement 🇺🇸 nightclub **4.** [coffret] ▶ **cave à cigares** cigar box ▶ **cave à liqueurs** cellaret.

⚠ Le mot anglais **cave** signifie «grotte» et non cave.

caveau, x [kavo] nm [sépulture] vault, tomb, burial chamber.

caverne [kavɛʀn] nf [grotte] cave, cavern ▶ **une caverne de brigands** fam a den of thieves.

caverneux, euse [kavɛʀnø, øz] adj [voix] sepulchral.

caviar [kavjaʀ] nm CULIN caviar, caviare ▶ **caviar d'aubergines** aubergine 🇬🇧 ou eggplant 🇺🇸 puree.

caviste [kavist] nmf [responsable de cave] cellarman (cellarwoman) ; [marchand de vin] wine merchant.

cavité [kavite] nf [trou] cavity.

CB [sibi] (abr de **citizen's band, canaux banalisés**) nf CB.

Cb1 SMS abr écrite de **c'est bien**.

CCI (abr de **chambre de commerce et d'industrie**) nf CCI.

CCP (abr de **compte chèque postal, compte courant postal**) nm *post office account* ; ≈ giro account 🇬🇧 ; ≃ Post Office checking account 🇺🇸.

CD ◆ nm (abr de **Compact Disc**) CD ▶ **CD audio** audio CD ▶ **CD vidéo** CD video, CDV. ◆ (abr écrite de **corps diplomatique**) CD.

CDD (abr de **contrat à durée déterminée**) nm fixed term contract ▶ **elle est en CDD** she's on a fixed term contract.

CDI nm **1.** (abr de **centre de documentation et d'information**) *school library* **2.** (abr de **contrat à durée indéterminée**) permanent employment contract.

CD-ROM, CD-Rom [sedeʀɔm] (abr de **compact disk read only memory**) nm inv CD-Rom.

ce¹, cette [sə, sɛt] (pl **ces** [sɛ]) (devant nm commençant par voyelle ou «h» muet **cet** [sɛt]) dét (adj dém) **1.** [dans l'espace - proche] this, these (pl) ; [- éloigné] that, those (pl) ▶ **regarde de ce côté-ci** look over here **2.** [dans le temps - à venir] this, these (pl) ; [- passé] last / *cette nuit nous mettrons le chauffage* tonight we'll turn the heating on / *cette nuit j'ai fait un rêve étrange* last night I had a strange dream ▶ **cette année-là** that year ▶ **ces jours-ci** these days **3.** [désignant - ce dont on a parlé] this, these (pl), that, those (pl) ; [- ce dont on va parler] this, these (pl) **4.** [suivi d'une proposition relative] : *voici ce pont dont je t'ai parlé* here's the ou that bridge I told you about **5.** [emploi expressif] : *cette douleur dans son regard !* such grief in his eyes ! / *cet enfant est un modèle de sagesse !* this ou that child is so well behaved ! / *et pour ces messieurs, ce sera ?* now what will the ou you gentlemen have?

ce² [sə] (devant «e» **c'** [s], devant «a» **ç'** [s]) pron dém **1.** [sujet du verbe 'être'] ▶ **c'était hier** it was yesterday ▶ **c'est un escroc** he's a crook ▶ **ce sont mes frères** they are my brothers / *c'est rare qu'il pleuve en juin* it doesn't often rain in June / *qui est-ce ?* fam who is it? / *c'est à toi ?* is this ou is it yours? **2.** [pour insister] : *c'est la robe que j'ai achetée* this is the dress (that) I bought / *c'est l'auteur que je préfère* he's / she's my favourite writer / *c'est à lui / à toi de décider* it's up to him / up to you to decide **3.** [c'est que] introduisant une explication] : *s'il ne parle pas beaucoup, c'est qu'il est timide* if he doesn't say much, it's because he's shy **4.** [comme antécédent du pronom relatif] ▶ **ce qui, ce que** what / *ce qui m'étonne, c'est que...* what surprises me is that... ; [reprenant la proposition] which / *il dit en avoir les moyens, ce que je crois volontiers* he says he can afford it, which I'm quite prepared to believe ▶ **ce dont**: *ce dont je ne me souviens pas, c'est l'adresse* what I can't remember is the address ; [introduisant une complétive] ▶ **à ce que**: *veille à ce que tout soit prêt* make sure everything's ready ▶ **sur ce que**: *il insiste sur ce que le travail doit être fait en temps voulu* he insists that the work must be done in the specified time **5.** [emploi exclamatif] : *ce que tu es naïf !* you're so naive!, how naive you are! **6.** EXPR **ce me semble** *sout* ou *hum* it seems to me, I think, methinks *litt* ou *hum* ▶ **ce faisant** in so doing ▶ **et ce** : *il n'a rien dit, et ce malgré toutes les menaces* he said nothing, (and this) in spite of all the threats ▶ **sur ce** : *j'arrive et sur ce, le téléphone sonne* I arrive and just then the phone rings / *sur ce, elle se leva* with that, she got up ▶ **pour ce faire** *sout* to this end.

CE ◆ *nm* **1.** abr de **comité d'entreprise 2.** (abr de **cours élémentaire**) ▶ **CE1** *second year of primary school* ▶ **CE2** *third year of primary school.* ◆ *npr f* (abr de **Communauté européenne**) EC.

ceci [səsi] *pron dém this* / *ceci (étant) dit* having said this ou that ▶ **à ceci près que** except ou with the exception that ▶ **retenez bien ceci…** now, remember this…

cécité [sesite] *nf* blindness, cecity *sout.*

céder [18] [sede] ◆ *vt* **1.** [donner] to give (up) / *nous cédons maintenant l'antenne à Mélanie* we're now going to hand over to Mélanie / **'cédez le passage'** 'give way UK', 'yield US' ▶ **céder le passage à qqn** to let sb through, to make way for sb ▶ **céder le pas à qqn a)** *pr* to give way to sb **b)** *fig* to let sb have precedence ▶ **ne le céder à personne en qqch** *sout*: *il ne le cède à personne en ambition* as far as ambition is concerned, he's second to none **2.** [vendre] to sell / **'à céder'** 'for sale' ; [faire cadeau de] to give away *(sép)*, to donate. ◆ *vi* **1.** [à la volonté d'autrui] to give in **2.** [casser - étagère, plancher] to give way ; [- câble, poignée] to break off ; [- couture] to come unstitched.

✍ In reformed spelling (see p. 16-18), this verb is conjugated like *semer* : *il cèdera, elle cèderait.*

cédérom [sedeʀɔm] *nm* INFORM CD-ROM.

CEDEX, Cedex [sedɛks] (abr de **courrier d'entreprise à distribution exceptionnelle**) *nm accelerated postal service for bulk users.*

cédille [sedij] *nf* cedilla.

cèdre [sɛdʀ] *nm* [arbre] cedar (tree), arborvitae Québec.

CEGEP [seʒɛp] (abr de **collège d'enseignement général et professionnel**) *nm* Québec ≃ technical college.

CEI (abr de **Communauté des États indépendants**) *npr f* CIS.

ceinture [sɛ̃tyʀ] *nf* **1.** VÊT [en cuir, métal] belt ; [fine et tressée] cord ; [large et nouée] sash ; [gaine, corset] girdle ▶ **ceinture fléchée** Québec arrow sash ▶ **ceinture de sauvetage** life belt ▶ **ceinture de sécurité** seat ou safety belt ▶ **attachez votre ceinture** fasten your seat belt ▶ **faire ceinture**, **se serrer la ceinture** [se priver] to tighten one's belt **2.** SPORT [à la lutte] waistlock ; [au judo et au karaté] belt **3.** COUT [taille] waistband ; ANAT waist / *de l'eau jusqu'à la ceinture* with water up to his waist **4.** TRANSP ▶ **petite / grande ceinture** inner / outer circle.

ceinturer [3] [sɛ̃tyʀe] *vt* **1.** [saisir par la taille] to grab round the waist ; SPORT to tackle **2.** [lieu] to surround, to encircle.

ceinturon [sɛ̃tyʀɔ̃] *nm* VÊT (broad) belt.

cela [səla] *pron dém* **1.** [désignant un objet éloigné] that **2.** [désignant - ce dont on vient de parler] this, that ; [-ce dont on va parler] that ▶ **cela (étant) dit…** having said this ou that… ▶ **il est parti il y a un mois / une semaine de cela**

he left a month / a week ago / *c'est cela, moquez-vous de moi !* that's right, have a good laugh (at my expense)! **3.** [dans des tournures impersonnelles] it ▶ **cela ne fait rien** it doesn't matter / *cela fait une heure que j'attends* I've been waiting for an hour **4.** [emploi expressif] ▶ **pourquoi cela ?** why?, what for? ▶ **qui cela ?** who?, who's that?

célébration [selebʀasjɔ̃] *nf* celebration.

célèbre [selɛbʀ] *adj* famous, famed.

célébrer [18] [selebʀe] *vt* [fête] to observe ; [anniversaire, messe, mariage] to celebrate.

✍ In reformed spelling (see p. 16-18), this verb is conjugated like *semer* : *elle célébrera, il célébrerait.*

célébrité [selebʀite] *nf* **1.** [gloire] fame, celebrity **2.** [personne] celebrity, well-known personality.

céleri [sɛlʀi] *nm* celery ▶ **céleri en branches** celery.

céleri-rave [sɛlʀiʀav] (*pl* **céleris-raves**) *nm* celeriac.

céleste [selɛst] *adj* **1.** [du ciel] celestial **2.** [du paradis] celestial, heavenly **3.** [surnaturel - beauté, voix, mélodie] heavenly, sublime.

célibat [seliba] *nm* [d'un prêtre] celibacy ; [d'un homme] celibacy, bachelorhood ; [d'une femme] spinsterhood, celibacy.

célibataire [selibatɛʀ] ◆ *adj* **1.** [homme, femme] single, unmarried ; [prêtre] celibate **2.** ADMIN single. ◆ *nm* [homme] single man, bachelor ; ADMIN single man. ◆ *nf* single woman, unmarried woman ; ADMIN single woman.

celle [sɛl] *f* ⟶ **celui.**

celle-ci [sɛlsi], **celle-là** [sɛlla] *f* ⟶ **celui.**

cellier [selje] *nm* storeroom *(for wine or food)*, pantry.

Cellophane® [selɔfan] *nf* Cellophane® ▶ **sous Cellophane** cellophane-wrapped.

cellulaire [selylɛʀ] *adj* **1.** BIOL [de la cellule] cell *(modif)* ; [formé de cellules] cellular **2.** TÉLÉC ⟶ **téléphone 3.** MIN porous, poriferous **4.** TECHNOL [béton] cellular ; [matériau, mousse] expanded **5.** [carcéral] ▶ **emprisonnement** ou **régime cellulaire** solitary confinement ▶ **voiture cellulaire** prison ou police van UK, police wagon US.

cellule [selyl] *nf* **1.** BIOL cell ▶ **cellule nerveuse / sanguine** nerve / blood cell ▶ **cellule souche** stem cell **2.** [élément constitutif] basic element ou unit ▶ **cellule familiale** family unit ou group **3.** [d'une ruche] cell **4.** [d'un prisonnier, d'un religieux] cell **5.** [groupe de travail] ▶ **cellule de crise** crisis centre ▶ **cellule de réflexion** think tank **6.** PHOT ▶ **cellule (photoélectrique)** photoelectric cell.

cellulite [selylit] *nf* cellulitis.

celluloïd [selylɔid] *nm* celluloid.

cellulose [selyloz] *nf* cellulose.

celte [sɛlt] *adj* Celtic. ◆ **Celte** *nmf* Celt.

celtique [sɛltik] *adj* Celtic.

celui, celle [səlɥi, sɛl] (*mpl* **ceux** [sø], *fpl* **celles** [sɛl]) *pron dém* **1.** [suivi de la préposition 'de'] : *le train de 5 h est parti, prenons celui de 6 h* we've missed the 5 o'clock train, let's get the 6 o'clock / *ceux d'entre vous qui veulent s'inscrire* those of you who wish to register **2.** [suivi d'un pronom relatif] ▶ **celui, celle** the one ▶ **ceux, celles** those, the ones / *c'est celle que j'ai achetée* that's the one I bought **3.** [suivi d'un adjectif, d'un participe] : *tous ceux désirant participer à l'émission* all those wishing ou who wish to take part in the show. ◆ **celui-ci, celle-ci** (*mpl* **ceux-ci**, *fpl* **celles-ci**) *pron dém* **1.** [désignant une personne ou un objet proches] ▶ **celui-ci, celle-ci** this one (here) ▶ **ceux-ci, celles-ci** these ones, these (here) / *c'est celui-ci que je veux* this is the one I want, I want this one **2.** [désignant ce dont on va parler ou ce dont on vient de parler] : *elle voulait voir Anne, mais celle-ci était absente* she wanted to see Anne, but she was out / *ah celui-ci,*

il me fera toujours rire ! now he always makes me laugh!
❖ **celui-là, celle-là** (*mpl* ceux-là, *fpl* celles-là) pron dém **1.** [désignant une personne ou un objet éloignés] ▶ **celui-là, celle-là** that one (there) ▶ **ceux-là, celles-là** those ones, those (over there) / *c'est celui-là que je veux* that's the one I want, I want that one **2.** [emploi expressif] : *il a toujours une bonne excuse, celui-là !* he's always got a good excuse, that one!

cendre [sɑ̃dʀ] nf **1.** [résidu - gén] ash, ashes ; [- de charbon] cinders ▶ **mettre** ou **réduire en cendres** [maison] to burn to the ground **2.** GÉOL (volcanic) ash **3.** litt ▶ **les cendres** [dépouille] the ashes, the remains **4.** RELIG ▶ **les Cendres** ou **le mercredi des Cendres** Ash Wednesday.

cendré, e [sɑ̃dʀe] adj **1.** [gris] ashen, ash (*modif*), ash-coloured **2.** [couvert de cendres] ash covered ▶ **fromage cendré** cheese matured in wood ash. ❖ **cendrée** nf [revêtement] cinder ; [piste] cinder track.

cendrier [sɑ̃dʀije] nm [de fumeur] ashtray ; [de fourneau] ash pit ; [de poêle] ashpan ; [de locomotive] ash box.

Cendrillon [sɑ̃dʀijɔ̃] npr Cinderella.

cène [sɛn] nf **1.** [dernier repas] ▶ **la Cène** the Last Supper **2.** [communion] Holy Communion, Lord's Supper.

censé, e [sɑ̃se] adj supposed to ▶ **vous êtes censé arriver à 9 h a)** [indication] you're supposed to arrive at 9 **b)** [rappel à l'ordre] we expect you to arrive at 9.

censément [sɑ̃semɑ̃] adv apparently, seemingly.

censeur [sɑ̃sœʀ] nm [responsable de la censure] censor.

censure [sɑ̃syʀ] nf [interdiction] censorship ; [commission] ▶ **la censure a)** [les censeurs b)** [examen] censorship.

censurer [3] [sɑ̃syʀe] vt [film, livre] to censor.

cent [sɑ̃] ➤ dét **1.** a ou one hundred ▶ **cent mille** a hundred thousand ▶ **deux cents filles** two hundred girls ▶ **trois cent quatre rangs** three hundred and four rows ▶ **elle est aux cent coups** [affolée] she's frantic / *je préfère cent fois celle-ci* I prefer this one a hundred times over ▶ **faire les cent pas** to pace up and down / *je ne vais pas attendre cent sept ans* fam I'm not going to wait forever (and a day) [rappel à l'ordre] ▶ **s'ennuyer à cent sous de l'heure** to be bored stiff ou to death **2.** [dans des séries] ▶ **page deux cent (six)** page two hundred (and six) ▶ **l'an neuf cent** the year nine hundred **3.** SPORT ▶ **le cent mètres** the hundred metres ▶ **le quatre cents mètres haies** the four hundred metres hurdle ou hurdles ▶ **le cent mètres nage libre** the hundred metres free-style. ➤ nm **1.** [chiffre] ▶ **j'habite au cent** I live at number one hundred **2.** [centaine] hundred **3.** BANQUE [centime] cent **4.** EXPR ▶ **pour cent** per cent / *20 pour cent* 20 per cent / *cent pour cent coton* a ou one hundred per cent pure cotton / *il est cent pour cent anglais* he's a hundred per cent English / *je suis cent pour cent contre* I'm whole-heartedly against it ▶ **je te le donne en cent** guess, I'll give you three guesses. Voir aussi **cinq.**

centaine [sɑ̃tɛn] nf **1.** [cent unités] hundred ▶ **la colonne des centaines** the hundreds column **2.** ▶ **une centaine de** [environ cent] about a hundred, a hundred or so ▶ **plusieurs centaines de dollars** several hundred dollars / *elle a traité des centaines de personnes* she treated hundreds of people.

centenaire [sɑ̃tnɛʀ] ➤ adj hundred-year old. ➤ nmf [vieillard] centenarian. ➤ nm [anniversaire] centenary UK, centennial US Can.

centième [sɑ̃tjɛm] ➤ adj num hundredth. ➤ nm [fraction] hundredth part / *ce n'est pas le centième de ce qu'il m'a fait* it doesn't even come close to what he did to me. Voir aussi **cinquième.**

centigrade [sɑ̃tigʀad] adj centigrade.

centigramme [sɑ̃tigʀam] nm centigram.

centilitre [sɑ̃tilitʀ] nm centilitre UK, centiliter US.

centime [sɑ̃tim] nm [de monnaie] centime / *ça ne m'a pas coûté un centime* it didn't cost me a penny UK ou one cent US.

centimètre [sɑ̃timɛtʀ] nm **1.** [unité de mesure] centimetre UK, centimeter US **2.** [ruban] tape measure, tape line US.

centrafricain, e [sɑ̃tʀafʀikɛ̃, ɛn] adj Central African ▶ **la République centrafricaine** the Central African Republic. ❖ **Centrafricain, e** nm, f Central African.

central, e, aux [sɑ̃tʀal, o] adj **1.** [du milieu d'un objet] middle (*avant nom*), central **2.** [du centre d'une ville] central **3.** ADMIN & POL central, national **4.** [principal] main, crucial. ❖ **central** nm TÉLÉC ▶ **central (téléphonique)** (telephone) exchange. ❖ **centrale** nf **1.** [usine] power plant ou station UK ▶ **centrale nucléaire / thermique** nuclear / thermal power station **2.** [prison] county jail, penitentiary US. ❖ **centrale d'achats** nf [groupement] central purchasing department ; [magasin] discount store.

centraliser [3] [sɑ̃tʀalize] vt to centralize.

centre [sɑ̃tʀ] nm **1.** [milieu - gén] centre UK, center US ▶ **le centre** [d'une ville] the centre / *elle était le centre de tous les regards* all eyes were fixed on her ▶ **se prendre pour le centre du monde** ou **de l'univers**: *il se prend pour le centre du monde* ou *de l'univers* he thinks the world revolves around him **2.** [concentration] ▶ **centre industriel** industrial area ▶ **centre urbain** town **3.** [organisme] centre UK, center US ▶ **centre aéré** former name of holiday activity centre for school children, now called **centre de loisirs** ▶ **centre d'appels** call centre UK ou center US ▶ **centre commercial** shopping centre ou UK precinct, (shopping) mall US ▶ **centre culturel** art ou arts centre ▶ **centre de documentation** information centre ▶ **centre hospitalier** hospital (complex) ▶ **centre hospitalo-universitaire** teaching hospital ▶ **centre médical** clinic ▶ **centre de tri** sorting office **4.** [point essentiel] main ou key point, heart, centre UK, center US ▶ **être au centre de** to be the key point of, to be at the heart ou centre of **5.** SCI centre UK, center US ▶ **centre de gravité** pr & fig centre of gravity ▶ **centre nerveux** nerve centre **6.** POL middle ground, centre UK, center US ▶ **centre droit / gauche** moderate right / left **7.** ÉCON ▶ **centre de coûts** cost center **8.** SPORT [au basketball] post, pivot ; FOOT centre pass.

centrer [3] [sɑ̃tʀe] vt **1.** [gén & PHOT] [SPORT] to centre UK, to center US **2.** [orienter] ▶ **être centré sur** to be centred ou focussed around.

centre-ville [sɑ̃tʀavil] (*pl* centres-villes) nm city centre UK ou center US, town centre UK ou downtown US ▶ **aller au centre-ville** to go into the centre (of town).

centrifuge [sɑ̃tʀify3] adj centrifugal.

centrifugeuse [sɑ̃tʀify3øz] nf CULIN juice extractor, juicer US.

centriste [sɑ̃tʀist] adj & nmf centrist.

centuple [sɑ̃typl] ❖ **au centuple** loc adv a hundred-fold.

cep [sɛp] nm BOT ▶ **cep (de vigne)** vine stock.

cépage [sepa3] nm vine.

cèpe [sɛp] nm CULIN cep.

cependant [səpɑ̃dɑ̃] conj however, nevertheless, yet / *je suis d'accord avec vous, j'ai cependant une petite remarque à faire* I agree with you, however I have one small comment to make.

céramique [seramik] ➤ adj ceramic. ➤ nf **1.** [art] ceramics (U), pottery **2.** [objet] piece of ceramic **3.** [matière] ceramic ▶ **des carreaux de céramique** ceramic tiles.

cerceau, x [sɛʀso] nm [d'enfant, d'acrobate, de tonneau, de jupon] hoop ; [de tonnelle] half-hoop.

cercle [sɛrkl] nm **1.** GÉOM circle ; [forme] circle, ring / *décrire des cercles dans le ciel* [avion, oiseau] to fly around in circles, to wheel round, to circle ▸ **faire cercle autour de qqn** to stand ou to gather round sb in a circle ▸ **en cercle** in a circle ▸ **cercle vicieux** vicious circle **2.** [gamme, étendue - d'activités, de connaissances] range, scope **3.** [groupe] circle, group / *le cercle de mes amis* my circle ou group of friends ▸ **cercle de famille** family (circle) ▸ **cercle littéraire** literary circle **4.** [club] club ▸ **un cercle militaire** an officer's club **5.** [objet circulaire] hoop **6.** ASTRON & MATH circle **7.** GÉOGR ▸ **cercle polaire** polar circle ▸ **cercle polaire Arctique / Antarctique** Arctic / Antarctic Circle.

cerclé, e [sɛrkle] adj ringed ▸ **des lunettes cerclées d'écaille** horn-rimmed glasses.

cercueil [sɛrkœj] nm coffin 🇬🇧, casket 🇺🇸.

céréale [sereal] nf CULIN ▸ **des céréales** (breakfast) cereal.

céréalier, ère [serealje, ɛr] adj cereal *(modif).*
❖ **céréalier** nm **1.** [producteur] cereal farmer ou grower **2.** [navire] grain ship.

cérébral, e, aux [serebral, o] adj **1.** ANAT cerebral **2.** [intellectuel - activité, travail] intellectual, mental ; [- film, livre] cerebral, intellectual.

cérémonial, als [seremɔnjal] nm [règles, livre] ceremonial.

cérémonie [seremɔni] nf [fête] ceremony, solemn ou formal occasion ▸ **cérémonie d'ouverture / de clôture** opening / closing ceremony. ❖ **cérémonies** nfpl péj [manières] fuss, palaver / *ne fais pas tant de cérémonies* don't make such a fuss. ❖ **sans cérémonie** loc adv **1.** [simplement] casually, informally **2.** péj [abruptement] unceremoniously, without so much as a by-your-leave.

cérémonieux, euse [seremɔnjø, øz] adj ceremonious, formal.

cerf [sɛr] nm stag.

cerfeuil [sɛrfœj] nm chervil.

cerf-volant [sɛrvɔlɑ̃] *(pl* **cerfs-volants)** nm JEUX kite ▸ **jouer au cerf-volant** to fly a kite.

cerise [sɔriz] ❖ nf [fruit] cherry / *la cerise sur le gâteau* fig the icing on the cake. ❖ adj inv cherry, cherry-red, cerise.

cerisier [sɔrizje] nm **1.** [arbre] cherry (tree) **2.** [bois] cherry (wood).

cerne [sɛrn] nm [sous les yeux] shadow, (dark) ring / *elle a des cernes* she's got dark rings under her eyes.

cerné, e [sɛrne] adj ▸ **avoir les yeux cernés** to have (dark) rings under one's eyes.

cerner [3] [sɛrne] vt **1.** [entourer] to surround, to lie around / *les lacs qui cernent la ville* the lakes dotted around the ou surrounding the town **2.** [assiéger - ville] to surround, to seal off *(sép)* ; [- armée, population] to surround / *vous êtes cernés !* you are surrounded! **3.** [définir - question, problème] to define, to determine / *ceci nous a permis de cerner le problème de près* this has enabled us to home in on the problem / *il est difficile à cerner* I can't make him out **4.** [ouvrir - noix] to crack open, to shell.

certain¹, e [sɛrtɛ̃, sɛrtɛn] *(devant nm commençant par voyelle ou «h» muet* [sɛrtɛn]) adj **1.** [incontestable - amélioration] definite ; [- preuve] definite, positive ; [- avantage, rapport] definite, clear ; [- décision, invitation, prix] definite / *avec un enthousiasme certain* with real ou obvious enthusiasm ▸ **tenir qqch pour certain** to have no doubt about sthg / *le projet a beaucoup de retard — c'est certain, mais...* the project is a long way behind schedule — that's certainly true but... / *j'aurais préféré attendre, c'est certain* I'd have preferred to wait, of course ▸ **une chose est certaine** one thing's for certain ou sure **2.** [inéluctable - échec, victoire] certain / *on nous avait présenté son départ comme certain* we'd been told he was certain to go

3. [persuadé] ▸ **être certain de**: *être certain de ce qu'on avance* to be sure ou certain about what one is saying / *il n'est pas très certain de sa décision* he's not sure he's made the right decision / *si tu pars battu, tu es certain de perdre !* if you think you're going to lose, (then) you're bound ou sure ou certain to lose! / *êtes-vous sûr que c'était lui ? — j'en suis certain !* are you sure it was him? — I'm positive! / *ils céderont — n'en sois pas si certain* they'll give in — don't be so sure / *si j'étais certain qu'il vienne* if I knew (for sure) ou if I was certain that he was coming **4.** MATH & PHILOS certain. ❖ **certain** nm BOURSE fixed ou direct rate of exchange.

certain², e [sɛrtɛ̃, sɛrtɛn] *(devant nm commençant par voyelle ou «h» muet* [sɛrtɛn]) dét *(adj indéf)* **1.** [exprimant l'indétermination] ▸ **à un certain moment** at one point / *un certain nombre d'entre eux* some of them ▸ **d'une certaine façon** ou **manière** in a way ▸ **dans** ou **en un certain sens** in a sense **2.** [exprimant une quantité non négligeable] : *il faut un certain courage !* you certainly need some pluck! **3.** [devant un nom de personne] : *les dialogues sont l'œuvre d'un certain...* the dialogue is by someone called... ou by one... ❖ **certains, certaines** ◆ dét *(adj indéf pl)* [quelques] some, certain ▸ **certains jours** sometimes, on some days / *je connais certaines personnes qui n'auraient pas hésité* I can think of some ou a few people who wouldn't have thought twice about it. ◆ pron indéf pl [personnes] some (people) ; [choses] some ; [d'un groupe] some (of them) / *certains d'entre vous semblent ne pas avoir compris* some of you seem not to have understood.

certainement [sɛrtɛnmɑ̃] adv **1.** [sans aucun doute] certainly, surely, no doubt **2.** [probablement] surely, certainly **3.** [dans une réponse] certainly.

certes [sɛrt] adv sout **1.** [assurément] certainly, indeed **2.** [servant de réponse] certainly **3.** [indiquant la concession] of course, certainly.

certificat [sɛrtifika] nm **1.** [attestation] certificate ▸ **certificat de mariage** marriage certificate ▸ **certificat médical** doctor's certificate ▸ **certificat de naissance** birth certificate ▸ **certificat de travail** ≃ P 45 🇬🇧, attestation of employment **2.** [diplôme] diploma, certificate ▸ **certificat d'aptitude professionnelle** = CAP ▸ **certificat d'études (primaires)** basic school-leaving qualification *(abolished in Metropolitan France in 1989).*

certifié, e [sɛrtifje] ◆ adj holding the CAPES. ◆ nm, f CAPES holder.

certifier [9] [sɛrtifje] vt **1.** [assurer] to assure **2.** DR [garantir - caution] to guarantee, to counter-secure ; [- signature] to witness, to authenticate ; [- document] to authenticate, to certify ▸ **certifié conforme**: *une copie certifiée conforme (à l'original)* a certified copy of the original document.

certitude [sɛrtityd] nf certainty, certitude sout ▸ **avoir la certitude de qqch** to be convinced of sthg.

cérumen [serymɛn] nm earwax, cerumen spéc.

cerveau, x [sɛrvo] nm **1.** ANAT brain **2.** fam [génie] brainy person ▸ **c'est un cerveau** he's got brains **3.** [instigateur] brains ▸ **être le cerveau de qqch** to be the brains behind sthg.

cervelas [sɛrvəla] nm ≃ saveloy *(sausage).*

cervelle [sɛrvɛl] nf **1.** ANAT brain **2.** fam [intelligence] brain / *il n'a ou il n'y a rien dans sa petite cervelle* he's got nothing between his ears **3.** CULIN brains.

cervical, e, aux [sɛrvikal, o] adj cervical.

ces [sɛ] pl ⟶ **ce.**

CES nm abr de **contrat emploi-solidarité.**

césar [sezar] nm CINÉ French cinema award.

César [sezar] npr Caesar.

césarienne [sezaʀjɛn] nf caesarean UK ou cesarean US (section).

césariser [sezaʀize] vt to award a césar to / *l'acteur a été césarisé en 2011* the actor won a césar in 2011.

cessation [sɛsasjɔ̃] nf **1.** [d'une activité] cessation, stopping ▶ **cessation du travail** stoppage **2.** COMM ▶ **cessation de paiement** suspension of payments.

cesse [sɛs] ❖ **sans cesse** loc adv continually, constantly.

cesser [4] [sese] ❖ vi [pluie] to stop, to cease *sout* ; [vent] to die down, to abate *sout* ; [combat] to (come to a) stop ; [bruit, mouvement] to stop, to cease *sout / cesse de pleurer* stop crying / *il n'a pas cessé de pleuvoir* it rained non-stop / *je ne cesse d'y penser* I cannot stop myself thinking about it. ❖ vt [arrêter] to stop, to halt ▶ **cesser le travail** to down tools, to walk out ▶ **faire cesser qqch** to put a stop to sthg.

cessez-le-feu [seselfø] nm inv cease-fire.

cession [sɛsjɔ̃] nf DR transfer, assignment.

c'est-à-dire [setadiʀ] loc adv **1.** [introduisant une explication] that is (to say), i.e., in other words ; [pour demander une explication] ▶ **c'est-à-dire ?** what do you mean? **2.** [introduisant une rectification] or rather **3.** [introduisant une hésitation] : *tu penses y aller ? — eh bien, c'est-à-dire...* are you thinking of going? — well, you know ou I mean... ❖ **c'est-à-dire que** loc conj **1.** [introduisant un refus, une hésitation] actually, as a matter of fact **2.** [introduisant une explication] which means **3.** [introduisant une rectification] or rather.

cet [sɛt] m ⟶ **ce** *(adj dém).*

cétacé [setase] nm cetacean.

cette [sɛt] f ⟶ **ce** *(adj dém).*

ceux [sø] pl ⟶ **celui.**

ceux-ci [søsi], **ceux-là** [søla] mpl ⟶ **celui.**

Ceylan [selɑ̃] npr Ceylon.

cf. (abr de confer) cf.

CFDT (abr de **Confédération française démocratique du travail**) npr f French trade union.

CFF (abr de **Chemins de fer fédéraux**) npr mpl Swiss railways.

CFTC (abr de **Confédération française des travailleurs chrétiens**) npr f French trade union.

CGC (abr de **Confédération générale des cadres**) npr f French management union.

CGT (abr de **Confédération générale du travail**) npr f major French trade union (with links to the Communist Party).

CH (abr écrite de **Confédération helvétique**) Swiss nationality sticker on a car.

chacal, als [ʃakal] nm ZOOL jackal.

chacun, e [ʃakœ̃, yn] pron indéf **1.** [chaque personne, chaque chose] each ▶ **chacun de** each (one) of / *chacun des employés a une tâche à remplir* each employee has a job to do ▶ **chacun son tour** : *Madame, chacun son tour* please wait your turn, Madam / *nous y sommes allés chacun à notre tour* we each went in turn **2.** [tout le monde] everyone, everybody ▶ **à chacun ses goûts** to each his own ▶ **tout un chacun** everybody, each and every person ▶ **chacun pour soi** every man for himself.

chagrin [ʃagʀɛ̃] nm [peine] sorrow, grief ▶ **causer du chagrin à qqn** to cause distress to ou to distress sb ▶ **avoir un chagrin d'amour** to be disappointed in love.

chagriner [3] [ʃagʀine] vt [contrarier] to worry, to bother, to upset.

chahut [ʃay] nm fam rumpus, hullabaloo, uproar ▶ **faire du chahut** [élèves] to make a racket, to kick up a rumpus.

chahuter [3] [ʃayte] fam ❖ vi [être indiscipliné] to kick up a rumpus, to make a racket. ❖ vt [houspiller - professeur] to rag, to bait ; [- orateur] to heckle / *un professeur chahuté* a teacher who can't control his pupils / *le Premier ministre s'est fait chahuter à l'Assemblée* the Prime Minister was heckled in parliament.

chahuteur, euse [ʃaytœʀ, øz] fam ❖ adj rowdy, boisterous. ❖ nm, f rowdy.

chaîne, chaine* [ʃɛn] nf **1.** [attache, bijou] chain ▶ **chaîne de vélo** bicycle chain / *le peuple a brisé ses chaînes* the people shook off their chains **2.** [suite] chain, series ▶ **la chaîne alimentaire** ÉCOL the food chain **3.** TV channel ▶ **chaîne câblée** cable channel ▶ **chaîne cryptée** pay channel *(for which one needs a special decoding unit)* ▶ **chaîne payante** ou **à péage** subscription TV channel **4.** AUDIO ▶ **chaîne hi-fi** hi-fi ▶ **chaîne stéréo** stereo ▶ **chaîne compacte** compact system **5.** INDUST ▶ **chaîne de montage / fabrication** assembly / production line **6.** INFORM string ▶ **chaîne vide / de caractères** nul / character string. ❖ **à la chaîne, à la chaine*** loc adv [travailler, produire] on the production line ▶ **faire qqch à la chaîne** to mass-produce sthg. ❖ **en chaîne, en chaine*** loc adj ▶ **des catastrophes en chaîne** a whole catalogue of disasters.

chaînette, chainette* [ʃɛnɛt] nf JOAILL small chain.

chaînon, chainon* [ʃɛnɔ̃] nm [élément - d'une chaîne, d'un raisonnement] link.

chair [ʃɛʀ] nf flesh ▶ **avoir la chair de poule** to have goose pimples ou gooseflesh, to have goosebumps US.

chaire [ʃɛʀ] nf **1.** [estrade] rostrum ▶ **monter en chaire a)** *pr* to go up on the rostrum **b)** *fig* to start one's speech **2.** UNIV chair.

chaise [ʃɛz] nf [siège] chair ▶ **chaise haute** ou **d'enfant** ou **de bébé** highchair ▶ **chaise électrique** electric chair ▶ **chaise longue a)** [d'extérieur] deck ou canvas chair **b)** [d'intérieur] chaise longue ▶ **chaise pliante** folding chair ▶ **chaise à porteurs** sedan (chair) ▶ **chaise roulante** wheelchair.

chaland [ʃalɑ̃] nm NAUT barge.

chaland, e [ʃalɑ̃, ɑ̃d] nm, f arch [client] regular customer.

châle [ʃal] nm shawl.

chalet [ʃalɛ] nm [maison - alpine] chalet ; [- de plaisance] (wooden) cottage.

chaleur [ʃalœʀ] nf **1.** MÉTÉOR heat ▶ **quelle chaleur !** what a scorcher! / **'craint** ou **ne pas exposer à la chaleur'** 'store in a cool place' **2.** [sentiment] warmth / *il y avait une certaine chaleur dans sa voix* his voice was warm (and welcoming) ▶ **chaleur humaine** human warmth. ❖ **chaleurs** nfpl MÉTÉOR ▶ **les grandes chaleurs** the hottest days of the summer. ❖ **en chaleur** loc adj ZOOL on heat UK, in heat US.

chaleureusement [ʃalœʀøzmɑ̃] adv warmly.

chaleureux, euse [ʃalœʀø, øz] adj [remerciement] warm, sincere ; [accueil] warm, cordial, hearty ; [approbation] hearty, sincere ; [voix] warm ; [ami] warm-hearted.

challenge [tʃalɛndʒ] , **chalenge*** [ʃalɑ̃ʒ] nm **1.** [défi] challenge **2.** SPORT [épreuve] sporting contest ; [trophée] trophy.

challenger [tʃalɛndʒœʀ], **chalengeur*, euse** [ʃalɑ̃ʒœʀ, øz] nm challenger.

chaloupe [ʃalup] nf [à moteur] launch ; [à rames] rowing boat UK, rowboat US.

chalumeau, x [ʃalymo] nm **1.** TECHNOL blowlamp UK, blowtorch US **2.** MUS pipe.

chalut [ʃaly] nm trawl ▶ **pêcher au chalut** to trawl.

chalutier [ʃalytje] nm **1.** [pêcheur] trawlerman **2.** [bateau] trawler.

chamailler [3] [ʃamaje] ◆ **se chamailler** vp *(emploi réciproque)* fam to bicker, to squabble.

chaman, e [ʃaman] nm, f shaman.

chamanisme [ʃamanism] nm shamanism.

chamarré, e [ʃamare] adj richly coloured 🇬🇧 ou colored 🇺🇸, brightly coloured 🇬🇧 ou colored 🇺🇸 ▶ **chamarré d'or** with gold brocade.

chambardement [ʃãbardəmã] nm fam upheaval.

chambarder [3] [ʃãbarde] vt fam [endroit, objets] to mess up *(sép)*, to turn upside down *(sép)* ; [projets] to upset, to overturn, to turn upside down.

chamboulement [ʃãbulmã] nm fam **1.** [désordre] mess, shambles **2.** [changement] total change, upheaval.

chambouler [3] [ʃãbule] vt fam [endroit, objets] to mess up *(sép)*, to turn upside down *(sép)* ; [projets] to ruin, to upset, to mess up *(sép)* / *cette réunion imprévue a chamboulé mon emploi du temps* this last-minute meeting has messed up my schedule.

chambranle [ʃãbrãl] nm [de cheminée] mantelpiece ; [de porte] (door) frame ou casing ; [de fenêtre] (window) frame ou casing.

chambre [ʃãbr] nf **1.** [pièce] ▶ **chambre (à coucher)** (bed) room ▶ **faire chambre à part** to sleep in separate rooms ▶ **chambre individuelle** ou **pour une personne** single (room) ▶ **chambre double** ou **pour deux personnes** double room ▶ **chambre d'hôte** ≃ room in a guest house ▶ **chambre d'amis** guest ou spare room ▶ **chambre de bonne a)** *pr* maid's room **b)** [louée à un particulier] attic room *(often rented to a student)* ▶ **chambre d'enfant a)** child's room **b)** [pour tout-petits] nursery ▶ **chambres d'hôtes** ≃ bed and breakfasts **2.** [local] ▶ **chambre froide** cold room ▶ **chambre à gaz** gas chamber **3.** POL House, Chamber ▶ **la Chambre des communes** the House of Commons 🇬🇧 ▶ **la Chambre des députés** the (French) Chamber of Deputies ; ≃ House of Commons 🇬🇧 ; ≃ House of Representatives 🇺🇸 ▶ **la Chambre haute / basse** the Upper / Lower Chamber ▶ **la Chambre des lords** ou **des pairs** the House of Lords ▶ **la Chambre des représentants** the House of Representatives 🇺🇸 **4.** [organisme] ▶ **Chambre de commerce** Chamber of Commerce **5.** PHOT ▶ **chambre noire** darkroom.

> **La Chambre des députés**
>
> This was the official name for the French parliamentary assembly until 1946, when the name l'**Assemblée nationale** was adopted.

chambrer [3] [ʃãbre] vt **1.** ŒNOL to allow to breathe, to bring to room temperature **2.** fam [se moquer de] to pull sb's leg.

chameau, x [ʃamo] nm **1.** ZOOL camel **2.** fam & péj ▶ **quel chameau !** a) [homme] he's a real swine! b) [femme] she's a real cow!

chamois [ʃamwa] nm ZOOL chamois.

chamoisine [ʃamwazin] nf shammy leather.

champ [ʃã] nm **1.** AGR field / *champ de blé* field of wheat **2.** [périmètre réservé] ▶ **champ de courses** racecourse ▶ **champ de foire** fairground ▶ **champ de tir a)** ARM [terrain] rifle range **b)** [portée d'une arme] field of fire **3.** [domaine, étendue] field, range ▶ **laisser le champ libre à qqn** to leave the field open for sb **4.** CINÉ & PHOT ▶ **sortir du champ** to go out of shot **5.** ÉLECTR & PHYS field ▶ **champ électrique / magnétique** electric / magnetic field **6.** INFORM ▶ **champ d'action** sensitivity **7.** MÉD field ▶ **champ opératoire / visuel** field of operation / view **8.** ▶ **champ de bataille a)** *pr* battlefield, battleground **b)** *fig* mess / *il est mort au champ d'honneur* he died for his country ▶ **champ de mines** minefield. ◆ **champs** nmpl [campagne] country, countryside.

champagne [ʃãpaɲ] nm Champagne ▶ **champagne brut / rosé** extra dry / pink Champagne.

champenois, e [ʃãpənwa, az] adj from Champagne.

champêtre [ʃãpɛtr] adj litt [vie, plaisirs, travaux] country *(modif)*, rustic.

champignon [ʃãpiɲɔ̃] nm **1.** BOT & SCI fungus ; CULIN mushroom ▶ **champignon de Paris** ou **de couche** button mushroom ▶ **champignon hallucinogène** magic mushroom ▶ **grandir** ou **pousser comme un champignon a)** [enfant] to grow (up) fast **b)** [ville, installations] to mushroom **2.** MÉD ▶ **des champignons** a fungus, a fungal infection **3.** [nuage] ▶ **champignon (atomique)** mushroom cloud **4.** fam AUTO accelerator (pedal) ▶ **mettre le pied** ou **appuyer sur le champignon** to put one's foot down 🇬🇧, to step on the gas 🇺🇸, to step on it.

champion, onne [ʃãpjɔ̃, ɔn] nm, f **1.** SPORT champion / *le champion du monde d'aviron* the world rowing champion **2.** [défenseur] champion ▶ **se faire le champion de qqch** to champion sthg.

championnat [ʃãpjɔna] nm championship.

chance [ʃãs] nf **1.** [aléa, hasard] luck **2.** [hasard favorable] (good) luck / *c'est une chance que je sois arrivée à ce moment-là !* it's a stroke of luck that I arrived then! / *quelle chance j'ai eue !* lucky me! ▶ **avoir de la** / **ne pas avoir de chance** to be lucky / unlucky ▶ **tenter sa chance** to try one's luck ▶ **donner** ou **laisser sa chance à qqn** to give sb his chance ▶ **pas de chance !** bad ou hard luck! **3.** *(toujours au sg)* [sort favorable] luck, (good) fortune ▶ **la chance lui sourit** luck favours him ▶ **c'est ta dernière chance** it's your last chance ▶ **jour de chance** lucky day **4.** [éventualité, probabilité] chance / *tu n'as pas une chance sur dix de réussir* you haven't got a one-in-ten chance of succeeding / *il y a peu de chances qu'on te croie* there's little chance (that) you'll be believed / *n'hésite pas, tu as tes chances* don't hesitate, you've got ou you stand a chance / *tu assisteras au débat ? — il y a des chances* fam will you be present at the debate? — maybe. ◆ **par chance** loc adv luckily, fortunately.

> ⚠ Attention, ce mot ne se traduit pas toujours par **chance** en anglais. Voir article.

chanceler [24] [ʃãsle] vi **1.** [vaciller - personne] to totter, to wobble, to stagger ; [- pile d'objets] to be unsteady **2.** [faiblir - pouvoir, institution, autorité] to wobble, to totter ; [- santé] to be failing.

✐ In reformed spelling (see p. 16-18), this verb is conjugated like *peler* : *il chancèlera, elle chancèlerait.*

chancelier, ère [ʃãsəlje, ɛr] nm, f **1.** [d'ambassade] (embassy) chief secretary, chancellor 🇬🇧 ; [de consulat] first secretary **2.** POL [en Allemagne, en Autriche] chancellor.

chancellerie [ʃãsɛlri] nf POL Ministry of Justice 🇬🇧, Department of Justice 🇺🇸.

chanceux, euse [ʃãsø, øz] adj lucky, fortunate, happy litt.

chandail [ʃãdaj] nm pullover, sweater.

Chandeleur [ʃãdlœr] nf ▶ **la Chandeleur** Candlemas.

chandelier [ʃɑ̃dəlje] nm [à une branche] candlestick ; [à plusieurs branches] candelabrum, candelabra.

⚠ Le mot anglais **chandelier** signifie « lustre » et non chandelier.

chandelle [ʃɑ̃dɛl] nf **1.** [bougie] (tallow) candle ▸ **le jeu n'en vaut pas la chandelle** the game's not worth the candle ▸ **brûler la chandelle par les deux bouts** to burn the candle at both ends ▸ **devoir une fière chandelle à qqn** to be deeply indebted to sb, to owe sb a big favour 🇬🇧 ou favor 🇺🇸 **2.** [position de gymnastique] ▸ **faire la chandelle** to perform a shoulder stand. ❖ **aux chandelles** loc adj [dîner, repas] candlelit.

change [ʃɑ̃ʒ] nm FIN [transaction] exchange ; [taux] exchange rate ▸ **faire le change** to deal in foreign exchange ▸ **donner le change à qqn** [le duper] to hoodwink sb, to put sb off the track ▸ **gagner / perdre au change a)** pr to be better / worse off because of the exchange rate **b)** fig to come out a winner / loser on the deal.

changeant, e [ʃɑ̃ʒɑ̃, ɑ̃t] adj **1.** [inconstant - fortune] fickle, unpredictable ; [- humeur] fickle, volatile, shifting **2.** MÉTÉOR [temps] unsettled, changeable ▸ **un ciel changeant** changing skies.

changement [ʃɑ̃ʒmɑ̃] nm **1.** [substitution] change ▸ **changement de** change of / 'changement de propriétaire' 'under new ownership' **2.** [modification] change ▸ **changement de**: *changement de température / temps* change in temperature / (the) weather ▸ **changement de cap** ou **de direction** change of course ▸ **changement de programme a)** TV change in the (published) schedule **b)** fig change of plan ou in the plans **3.** [évolution] ▸ **le changement** change / *je voudrais bien un peu de changement* I'd like things to change a little **4.** TRANSP change / *j'ai trois changements / je n'ai pas de changement pour aller chez elle* I have to change three times / I don't have to change to get to her place **5.** THÉÂTRE ▸ **changement de décor** pr scene change ou shift **6.** AUTO ▸ **changement de vitesse a)** [levier] gear lever 🇬🇧, gear stick 🇬🇧, gear shift 🇺🇸 **b)** [en voiture] gear change ou shift **c)** [en vélo] gear change.

changer [17] [ʃɑ̃ʒe] ❖ vt *(aux avoir)* **1.** [modifier - apparence, règlement, caractère] to change, to alter ; [- testament] to alter / *on ne le changera pas* he'll never change / *cette coupe la change vraiment* that haircut makes her look really different / *mais ça change tout !* ah, that makes a big difference! **2.** [remplacer - installation, personnel] to change, to replace ; [- roue, ampoule, drap, etc.] to change **3.** FIN [en devises, en petite monnaie] to change / *changer des dollars en euros* to change dollars into euros **4.** [transformer] ▸ **changer qqch en qqch** to turn sthg into sthg **5.** [transférer] ▸ **changer qqch de place** to move sthg ▸ **changer son fusil d'épaule** to have a change of heart **6.** fam [désaccoutumer] : *viens, ça te changera les idées* come along, it'll take your mind off things **7.** [bébé] to change ▸ **changer un malade** to put fresh clothes on a sick person. ❖ vi *(aux avoir)* **1.** [se modifier - personne, temps, tarif, etc.] to change ▸ **changer en bien / mal** to change for the better / worse **2.** TRANSP [de métro, de train] to change. ❖ vi *(aux être)* [malade, personnalité] to change. ❖ **changer de** v + prép ▸ **changer d'adresse a)** [personne] to move to a new address **b)** [commerce] to move to new premises ▸ **changer de coiffure** to get a new hairstyle / *je dois changer d'avion à Athènes* I have to get a connecting flight in Athens ▸ **changer de vie** to embark on a new life ▸ **changer d'avis** ou **d'idée** to change one's mind ▸ **changer de place** to move ▸ **changer d'air** to have a break ▸ **changer d'avis comme de chemise** to keep changing one's mind.

❖ **se changer** vp *(emploi réfléchi)* [s'habiller] to get changed. ❖ **se changer en** vp + prép to change ou turn into.

changeur [ʃɑ̃ʒœr] nm [dispositif] ▸ **changeur de monnaie** money changer.

chanoine [ʃanwan] nm canon.

chanson [ʃɑ̃sɔ̃] nf MUS song ; fig ▸ **c'est toujours même chanson** it's always the same old story ▸ **ça va, on connaît la chanson** enough of that, we've heard it all before ▸ **ça, c'est une autre chanson** that's another story ▸ **chanson d'amour / populaire** love / popular song.

chansonnier, ère [ʃɑ̃sɔnje, ɛʀ] nm, f satirical cabaret singer or entertainer.

chant [ʃɑ̃] nm **1.** [chanson] song ; [mélodie] melody ▸ **chant grégorien** Gregorian chant ▸ **chant de Noël** Christmas carol ▸ **son chant du cygne** his swan song **2.** [action de chanter] singing **3.** [art de chanter] singing / *prendre des leçons de chant* to take singing lessons **4.** [sons - d'un oiseau] singing, chirping ; [- d'une cigale] chirping ; [- d'un coq] crowing.

chantage [ʃɑ̃taʒ] nm blackmail ▸ **faire du chantage à qqn** to blackmail sb.

chantant, e [ʃɑ̃tɑ̃, ɑ̃t] adj [langue] musical ; [voix, accent] lilting.

chanter [3] [ʃɑ̃te] ❖ vi **1.** [personne] to sing ▸ **chanter juste / faux** to sing in tune / out of tune **2.** [oiseau] to sing, to chirp ; [cigale] to chirp ; [coq] to crow ; [rivière, mer] to murmur ; [bouilloire] to whistle **3.** EXPR **faire chanter qqn** to blackmail sb ▸ **si ça te chante** if you fancy it. ❖ vt **1.** MUS [chanson, messe] to sing / *qu'est-ce que tu me chantes là* fig what are you talking about? **2.** [célébrer] to sing (of) ▸ **chanter les louanges de qqn** to sing sb's praises.

chanterelle [ʃɑ̃tʀɛl] nf BOT chanterelle.

chanteur, euse [ʃɑ̃tœʀ, øz] nm, f singer ▸ **chanteur de charme** crooner ▸ **chanteur de rock** rock singer.

chantier [ʃɑ̃tje] nm **1.** [entrepôt] yard, depot **2.** [terrain] (working) site / *sur le chantier* on the site **3.** CONSTR ▸ **chantier (de construction)** building site **4.** NAUT ▸ **chantier naval** shipyard. ❖ **en chantier** ❖ loc adj : *la maison est en chantier* they're still doing ou fixing 🇺🇸 up the house. ❖ loc adv : *il a plusieurs livres en chantier* he has several books on the stocks in the pipeline / *mettre un ouvrage en chantier* to get a project started.

chantilly [ʃɑ̃tiji] nf inv whipped cream Chantilly.

chantonner [3] [ʃɑ̃tɔne] vt & vi to hum, to croon, to sing softly.

chanvre [ʃɑ̃vʀ] nm BOT & TEXT hemp.

chaos [kao] nm [confusion] chaos.

chaotique [kaɔtik] adj chaotic.

chaparder [3] [ʃapaʀde] vt fam to pinch, to swipe.

chape [ʃap] nf CONSTR screed ▸ **comme une chape de plomb** like a lead weight.

chapeau, x [ʃapo] nm [couvre-chef] hat ▸ **chapeau haut-de-forme** top hat ▸ **chapeau melon** bowler ou bowler 🇺🇸 (hat) ▸ **chapeau de paille** straw hat ▸ **chapeau de soleil** sunhat ▸ **saluer qqn chapeau bas** to doff one's hat to sb / *je te dis chapeau !* I'll take my hat off to you!, well done!, bravo! ▸ **tirer qqch de son chapeau** to pull sthg out of a hat. ❖ **sur les chapeaux de roue** loc adv ▸ **démarrer sur les chapeaux de roue a)** pr to shoot off **b)** [film, réception, relation] to get off to a great start.

chapeauter [3] [ʃapote] vt fam [superviser] to oversee, to supervise.

chapelain [ʃaplɛ̃] nm chaplain.

chapelet [ʃaplɛ] nm **1.** RELIG [collier] rosary, beads ; [prières] rosary ▸ **réciter** ou **dire son chapelet** to tell one's beads **2.** [d'îles, de saucisses] string ; [d'insultes] string, stream.

chapelle [ʃapɛl] nf RELIG chapel ▸ **chapelle ardente** chapel of rest.

chapelure [ʃaplyʀ] nf breadcrumbs.

chaperon [ʃapʀɔ̃] nm [surveillant] chaperon, chaperone.

chapiteau, x [ʃapito] nm **1.** ARCHIT capital, chapiter **2.** [cirque] big top.

chapitre [ʃapitʀ] nm **1.** [d'un livre] chapter **2.** [question] matter, subject / *tu as raison, au moins sur un chapitre* you're right, at least on one score **3.** RELIG [assemblée] chapter ; [lieu] chapterhouse.

chapitrer [3] [ʃapitʀe] vt [sermonner] to lecture ; [tancer] to admonish.

chapon [ʃapɔ̃] nm capon.

chaque [ʃak] dét *(adj indéf)* **1.** [dans un groupe, une série] each, every / *je pense à elle à chaque instant* I think about her all the time / *chaque chose en son temps !* all in good time! **2.** [chacun] each / *les CD sont vendus 15 euros chaque* CDs are sold at 15 euros each ou a piece.

char [ʃaʀ] nm **1.** MIL tank ▸ **char d'assaut** ou **de combat** tank **2.** LOISIRS float ▸ **char à voile** sand yacht / *faire du char à voile* to go sand yachting **3.** ANTIQ chariot **4.** Québec *fam* [voiture] car.

charabia [ʃaʀabja] nm gobbledegook, gibberish.

charade [ʃaʀad] nf **1.** [devinette] riddle **2.** [mime] (game of) charades.

charbon [ʃaʀbɔ̃] nm **1.** MIN coal ▸ **charbon de bois** charcoal ▸ **aller au charbon** *fam* to do one's bit ▸ **être** ou **marcher sur des charbons ardents** to be on tenterhooks, to be like a cat on hot bricks UK ou a hot tin roof US **2.** [maladie - chez l'animal, chez l'homme] anthrax ; [- des céréales] smut, black rust **3.** PHARM charcoal.

charcuter [3] [ʃaʀkyte] vt *fam & péj* [opérer] to butcher, to hack about.

charcuterie [ʃaʀkytʀi] nf **1.** [magasin] delicatessen **2.** [produits] cooked meats.

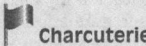
Charcuterie
A **charcuterie** sells mainly food prepared with pork: sausages, pâtés, ham, etc., also known collectively as **charcuterie**. Ready-prepared dishes to take away are usually also sold.

charcutier, ère [ʃaʀkytje,ɛʀ] nm, f [commerçant] pork butcher.

chardon [ʃaʀdɔ̃] nm **1.** BOT thistle **2.** [sur un mur] spike.

chardonneret [ʃaʀdɔnʀɛ] nm goldfinch.

charentaises [ʃaʀɑ̃tez] nfpl [pantoufles] slippers *(traditionally symbolising old-fashioned and home-loving attitudes in France)*.

charge [ʃaʀʒ] nf **1.** [cargaison - d'un animal] burden ; [- d'un camion] load ; [- d'un navire] cargo, freight **2.** [gêne] burden, weight *fig* **3.** [responsabilité] responsibility / *toutes les réparations sont à sa charge* all the repair work will be done at his cost ▸ **prendre en charge**: *nous prenons tous les frais médicaux en charge* we pay for ou take care of all medical expenses ▸ **avoir qqn à (sa) charge** a) [gén] to be responsible for supporting sb b) ADMIN to have sb as a dependant ▸ **enfants à charge** dependent children **4.** ADMIN [fonction] office **5.** ARM charge **6.** ▸ **charge électrique** electric charge **7.** DR [présomption] charge, accusation / *de très lourdes charges pèsent sur lui* there are very serious charges hanging over him. ⬥ **charges** nfpl [frais] costs ▸ **charges de famille** dependants ▸ **charges financières**

financial costs ou expenses ▸ **charges (locatives)** maintenance charges ▸ **charges patronales** employers' contributions ▸ **charges salariales** wage costs ▸ **charges sociales** social security contributions. ⬥ **à charge de** loc prép : *j'accepte, à charge de revanche* I accept, provided you'll let me do the same for you.

Charges
Householders and tenants in blocks of flats are required to pay **charges**, a monthly sum for the general upkeep of the building. In estate agencies, rent is expressed either including this sum (**charges comprises** or **cc**) or excluding it (**hors charges**, **charges en sus**, or **plus charges**). Sometimes, the **charges** include heating costs.

chargé, e [ʃaʀʒe] adj **1.** [occupé - journée] busy, full **2.** *fig* : *avoir la conscience chargée* to have a guilty conscience / *il a un casier judiciaire chargé* he has a long (criminal) record **3.** MÉD ▸ **avoir la langue chargée** to have a furred tongue. ⬥ **chargé** nm [responsable] ▸ **chargé d'affaires** chargé d'affaires ▸ **chargé de cours** ≃ part-time lecturer ▸ **chargé de mission** ≃ (official) representative.

chargement [ʃaʀʒəmɑ̃] nm **1.** [marchandises - gén] load ; [- d'un navire] cargo, freight **2.** [fait de charger - un navire, un camion] loading ; [- une chaudière] stoking ; [- une arme] loading.

charger [17] [ʃaʀʒe] vt **1.** [mettre un poids sur] to load ▸ **être chargé** to be loaded **2.** [prendre en charge - suj : taxi] to pick up *(sép)* **3.** [alourdir, encombrer] to overload ▸ **charger qqn de** to overload sb with **4.** [arme, caméra, magnétoscope] to load (up) ; ÉLECTR to charge (up) **5.** [d'une responsabilité] ▸ **charger qqn de qqch** to put sb in charge of sthg / *il m'a chargé de vous transmettre un message* he asked me to give you a message **6.** [exagérer - portrait] to overdo. ⬥ **se charger de** vp + prép **1.** [obj : responsabilité] to take on, to take care of / *je me charge de lui remettre votre lettre* I'll see to it personally that he gets your letter **2.** [obj : élève, invité] to take care of, to look after / *quant à lui, je m'en charge personnellement* I'll personally take good care of him.

chargeur [ʃaʀʒœʀ] nm **1.** PHOT magazine **2.** ARM cartridge clip **3.** ÉLECTR charger.

charia [ʃaʀja] nf RELIG sharia, sheria.

chariot, charriot* [ʃaʀjo] nm [véhicule - gén] wagon, waggon UK ; [- à bagages] trolley UK, cart US ; [- dans un supermarché] trolley UK, cart US ▸ **chariot élévateur** fork-lift truck.

charismatique [kaʀismatik] adj [séduisant] charismatic.

charisme [kaʀism] nm **1.** RELIG charisma, charism **2.** [influence] charisma.

charitable [ʃaʀitabl] adj **1.** [généreux] charitable **2.** [association, mouvement] charitable, charity *(modif)*.

charité [ʃaʀite] nf **1.** [altruisme] charity, love **2.** [aumône] charity ▸ **faire la charité (à)** to give alms *vieilli* ou a handout (to). ⬥ **de charité** loc adj ▸ **fête de charité** benefit event.

charivari [ʃaʀivaʀi] nm hurly-burly, hullabaloo.

charlatan [ʃaʀlatɑ̃] nm *péj* charlatan.

charlot [ʃaʀlo] nm *fam* clown, joker ▸ **jouer les charlots** to fool around.

charlotte [ʃaʀlɔt] nf CULIN charlotte.

* In reformed spelling (see p. 16-18).

charmant, e [ʃaʀmɑ̃, ɑ̃t] adj charming, engaging, delightful.

charme [ʃaʀm] nm **1.** [attrait] charm **2.** [d'une femme, d'un homme] charm, attractiveness **▸ faire du charme à qqn** to try to charm sb **3.** [enchantement] spell / **être sous le charme de** to be under the spell of **4.** BOT hornbeam **5.** EXPR **se porter comme un charme** to be in excellent health ou as fit as a fiddle. **◆ de charme** loc adj **1.** [plaisant] **▸ hôtel de charme** hotel **2.** euphém [érotique - presse] soft-porn **▸ hôtesse de charme** escort.

charmer [3] [ʃaʀme] vt [plaire à] to delight, to enchant.

charmeur, euse [ʃaʀmœʀ, øz] **◆** adj [air, sourire] charming, engaging, delightful. **◆** nm, f [séducteur] charmer **▸ charmeur de serpents** snake charmer.

charnel, elle [ʃaʀnɛl] adj [sexuel] carnal.

charnier [ʃaʀnje] nm [fosse] mass grave.

charnière [ʃaʀnjɛʀ] nf **1.** ANAT & MENUIS hinge **2.** (comme adjectif, avec ou sans trait d'union) **▸ moment / siècle charnière** moment / century of transition.

charnu, e [ʃaʀny] adj [corps] plump, fleshy ; [lèvres] full, fleshy ; [fruits] pulpy.

charognard [ʃaʀɔɲaʀ] nm **1.** ZOOL carrion feeder **2.** fam [exploiteur] vulture fig.

charogne [ʃaʀɔɲ] nf [carcasse] **▸ une charogne** a decaying carcass.

charpente [ʃaʀpɑ̃t] nf CONSTR skeleton, framework **▸ charpente métallique** steel frame.

charpenté, e [ʃaʀpɑ̃te] adj **▸ bien** ou **solidement charpenté** a) [personne] well-built b) [film, argument] well-structured.

charpentier, ère [ʃaʀpɑ̃tje, ɛʀ] nm, f [ouvrier] carpenter ; [entrepreneur] (master) carpenter.

charpie [ʃaʀpi] **◆ en charpie** loc adv **▸ mettre** ou **réduire qqch en charpie** to tear sthg to shreds.

charretier, ère [ʃaʀtje, ɛʀ] **◆** adj [chemin, voie] cart (modif). **◆** nm, f carter.

charrette [ʃaʀɛt] nf **1.** AGR cart **2.** fam [personnes licenciées] : **faire partie de la première / dernière charrette (de licenciements)** to be among the first / last group of people to be dismissed.

charrier [9] [ʃaʀje] **◆** vt **1.** [suj : personne] to cart ou to carry (along) **2.** tfam [railler] **▸ charrier qqn** to take the mickey out of sb UK, to put sb on US. **◆** vi tfam [exagérer] to go too far ou (way) over the top.

charrue [ʃaʀy] nf plough UK, plow US **▸ mettre la charrue avant les bœufs** to put the cart before the horse.

charte [ʃaʀt] nf [document] charter.

charter [ʃaʀtɛʀ] nm [avion] chartered plane ; [vol] charter flight.

chas [ʃa] nm eye (of a needle).

chasse [ʃas] nf **1.** [activité] hunting ; [occasion] hunt **▸ aller à la chasse** a) [à courre] to go hunting b) [au fusil] to go shooting **▸ chasse à courre** a) [activité] hunting b) [occasion] hunt **▸ qui va à la chasse perd sa place** prov if somebody takes your place it serves you right for leaving it empty **2.** [domaine - de chasse à courre] hunting grounds ; [- de chasse au fusil] shooting ground / **'chasse gardée'** 'private, poachers will be prosecuted' **3.** [butin] game / **la chasse a été bonne** we got a good bag **4.** [période] hunting season, shooting season **5.** [poursuite] chase, hunt / **prendre en chasse une voiture** to chase a car **6.** [recherche] **▸ chasse à l'homme** manhunt **▸ chasse au trésor** treasure hunt **▸ chasse aux sorcières** witch hunt **▸ faire la chasse à** to search for, to (try to) track down **7.** [d'eau] flush **▸ tirer la chasse (d'eau)** to flush the toilet.

chassé-croisé [ʃasekʀwaze] (pl **chassés-croisés**) nm [confusion] **▸ le chassé-croisé ministériel / de limousines** the comings and goings of ministers / of limousines.

chasse-neige (pl **chasse-neige** ou **chasse-neiges***) [ʃasnɛʒ] nm **1.** [véhicule] snowplough UK, snowplow US **2.** [position du skieur] snowplough UK, snowplow US **▸ descendre / tourner en chasse-neige** to snowplough down / round.

chasser [3] [ʃase] **◆** vt **1.** CHASSE to hunt **2.** [expulser] to drive out (sép), to expel **3.** [faire partir] to dispel, to drive away (sép), to get rid of / **le mauvais temps a chassé les touristes** the bad weather drove away the tourists / **sortez pour chasser les idées noires** go out and forget your worries **▸ chassez le naturel, il revient au galop** prov the leopard can't change its spots. **◆** vi **1.** [aller à la chasse - à courre] to go hunting ; [- au fusil] to go shooting / **chasser sur les terres d'autrui** fig to poach on somebody's preserve ou territory **2.** [déraper] to skid.

chasseur, euse [ʃasœʀ, øz] nm, f **1.** CHASSE hunter, huntsman (huntress) **2.** [chercheur] **▸ chasseur d'images** (freelance) photographer **▸ chasseur de têtes** pr & fig headhunter **3.** AÉRON & MIL fighter (plane) **4.** MIL chasseur **▸ chasseur alpin** Alpine chasseur **5.** [dans un hôtel] messenger (boy), bellboy US.

châssis [ʃasi] nm **1.** CONSTR frame **2.** ART stretcher ; PHOT (printing) frame **3.** AUTO chassis, steel frame **4.** tfam [corps féminin] chassis, figure.

chaste [ʃast] adj chaste, innocent.

chasteté [ʃastəte] nf chastity.

chasuble [ʃazybl] nf **1.** RELIG chasuble **2.** VÊT **▸ robe chasuble** pinafore dress.

chat¹ [tʃat] nm INTERNET chat.

chat², chatte [ʃa, ʃat] nm, f **1.** [gén & ZOOL] cat ; [mâle] tomcat ; [femelle] she-cat **▸ chat sauvage** a) [félin] wildcat b) Québec [raton laveur] raccoon **▸ avoir un chat dans la gorge** to have a frog in one's throat **▸ il n'y a pas de quoi fouetter un chat** it's nothing to make a fuss about **▸ j'ai d'autres chats à fouetter** I've got better things to do **▸ il n'y avait pas un chat** fam there wasn't a soul about **▸ quand le chat n'est pas là, les souris dansent** prov when the cat's away, the mice will play prov **▸ chat échaudé craint l'eau froide** once bitten, twice shy prov **2.** LITTÉR / **'le Chat botté'** Perrault 'Puss in Boots' **3.** JEUX **▸ jouer à chat** to play tag **▸ jouer à chat perché** to play off-ground tag **▸ jouer au chat et à la souris avec qqn** fig to play cat-and-mouse with sb.

châtaigne [ʃatɛɲ] nf **1.** BOT chestnut **2.** tfam [coup] biff, clout **▸ il s'est pris une de ces châtaignes !** a) [il a été frappé] he got such a smack! b) [il s'est cogné] he gave himself a nasty knock!

châtaignier [ʃatɛɲe] nm **1.** BOT chestnut tree **2.** [bois] chestnut.

châtain [ʃatɛ̃] adj m [cheveux] chestnut (brown) **▸ châtain clair** light brown / **châtain doré** ou **roux** auburn **▸ être châtain** to have brown hair.

château, x [ʃato] nm **1.** HIST castle **▸ château fort** fortified castle **2.** [palais] castle, palace ; [manoir] mansion, manor (house) **▸ ses illusions se sont écroulées comme un château de cartes** his illusions collapsed like a house of cards **▸ bâtir** ou **faire des châteaux en Espagne** to build castles in the air **3.** ŒNOL chateau. **◆ château d'eau** nm water tower.

châtelain, e [ʃatlɛ̃, ɛn] nm, f [propriétaire - gén] owner of a manor ; [- homme] lord of the manor ; [- femme] lady of the manor.

châtier [9] [ʃatje] vt *litt* **1.** [punir] to chastise, to castigate *litt* **2.** [affiner] to polish, to refine / *parler dans une langue châtiée* to use refined language.

chatière [ʃatjɛʀ] nf **1.** [pour un chat] cat door ou flap **2.** [dans un toit] ventilation hole.

châtiment [ʃatimã] nm *sout* chastisement *sout*, punishment.

chaton [ʃatɔ̃] nm **1.** ZOOL kitten **2.** BOT catkin, ament *spéc*, amentum *spéc*.

chatouiller [3] [ʃatuje] vt **1.** [pour faire rire] to tickle **2.** [irriter] to tickle.

chatouilleux, euse [ʃatujø, øz] adj **1.** [physiquement] ticklish **2.** [pointilleux] sensitive, touchy ▸ **chatouilleux sur** overparticular about.

chatoyer [13] [ʃatwaje] vi **1.** [briller] to gleam, to glisten, to shimmer **2.** [luire] to glimmer.

châtrer [3] [ʃatʀe] vt **1.** [étalon, homme, taureau] to castrate ; [cochon] to geld ; [chat] to castrate, to fix ⓤⓢ **2.** [texte] to make innocuous.

chatte [ʃat] f ⟶ **chat**.

chatter, tchatter [tʃate] vi INFORM to chat.

chatteur, euse, tchatteur, euse [tʃatœʀ,øz] nm, f INFORM chatter.

chaud, e [ʃo, ʃod] adj **1.** [dont la température est - douce] warm ; [- élevée] hot ▸ **une boisson chaude** a hot drink ▸ **chaud devant !** [au restaurant] excuse me! *(said by waiters carrying plates to clear the way)* **2.** [veste, couverture] warm **3.** [qui n'a pas refroidi] warm / *la place du directeur est encore chaude* fig the manager's shoes are still warm **4.** [enthousiaste] ardent, warm, keen / *je ne suis pas très chaud pour le faire* fam I'm not really eager to do it **5.** [ardent - ambiance] warm ▸ **avoir une chaude discussion sur qqch** to debate sthg heatedly **6.** [agité, dangereux] hot / *les points chauds du monde* the danger spots in the world **7.** *tfam* [sexuellement] hot, randy ⓤⓚ, horny ▸ **chaud lapin** randy devil. ◆ **chaud** ◆ adv hot ▸ **servir chaud** serve hot ▸ **avoir chaud** a) [douce chaleur] to feel warm b) [forte chaleur] to feel hot ▸ **il fait chaud** a) [douce chaleur] it's warm b) [forte chaleur] it's hot ▸ **on a eu chaud !** *fam* that was a close ou near thing! ▸ **ça ne me fait ni chaud ni froid** I couldn't care less. ◆ nm [chaleur] ▸ **le chaud** the heat ou hot weather. ◆ **à chaud** *loc adv* [en urgence] : *l'opération s'est faite à chaud* it was emergency surgery / *ne lui pose pas la question à chaud* don't just spring the question on him in the midst of it all. ◆ **au chaud** *loc adv* ▸ **restez bien au chaud** a) [au lit] stay nice and cosy ou warm in your bed b) [sans sortir] don't go out in the cold ▸ **mettre** ou **garder des assiettes au chaud** to keep plates warm.

chaudement [ʃodmã] adv **1.** [contre le froid] warmly ▸ **se vêtir chaudement** to put on warm clothes **2.** [chaleureusement - gén] warmly, warmheartedly ; [- recommander] heartily ; [- féliciter] with all one's heart.

chaudière [ʃodjɛʀ] nf boiler.

chaudron [ʃodʀɔ̃] nm [en fonte] cauldron ; [en cuivre] copper kettle ou boiler.

chauffage [ʃofaʒ] nm **1.** [d'un lieu] heating ▸ **système de chauffage** heating system **2.** [installation, système] heating (system) ▸ **chauffage central / urbain** central / district heating ▸ **chauffage électrique / solaire** electric / solar heating ▸ **chauffage au gaz / au mazout** gas-fired / oil-fired heating ▸ **chauffage par le sol** underfloor heating.

chauffagiste [ʃofaʒist] nm heating specialist.

chauffant, e [ʃofã, ãt] adj [surface] heating.

chauffard [ʃofaʀ] nm reckless driver ; [qui s'enfuit] hit-and-run driver.

chauffe-biberon [ʃofbibʀɔ̃] (*pl* chauffe-biberons) nm bottle warmer.

chauffe-eau [ʃofo] (*pl* chauffe-eau ou chauffe-eaux*) nm water heater.

chauffe-moteur [ʃofmɔtœʀ] (*pl* chauffe-moteurs) nm ⓆⓊⒺⒷⒺⒸ AUTO block heater.

chauffe-pieds (*pl* chauffe-pieds), **chauffe-pied*** (*pl* chauffe-pieds*) [ʃofpje] nm foot-warmer.

chauffe-plats (*pl* chauffe-plats), **chauffe-plat*** (*pl* chauffe-plats*) [ʃofpla] nm chafing dish.

chauffer [3] [ʃofe] ◆ vi **1.** [eau, plat, préparation] to heat up ▸ **mettre qqch à chauffer, faire chauffer qqch** to heat sthg up / *ça chauffe trop, baisse le gaz* it's overheating, turn the gas down **2.** [dégager de la chaleur - radiateur] to give out heat / *en avril, le soleil commence à chauffer* in April, the sun gets hotter **3.** [surchauffer - moteur] to overheat **4.** *fam* [être agité] : *ça commence à chauffer* things are getting hot ▸ **ça va chauffer !** there's trouble brewing! ◆ vt **1.** [chambre, plat] to warm ou to heat up *(sép)* **2.** *fam* [exciter] ▸ **chauffer la salle** to warm up the audience. ◆ **se chauffer** vpi **1.** [se réchauffer] to warm o.s. (up) **2.** [dans un local] ▸ **se chauffer à l'électricité** to have electric heating.

chauffeur [ʃofœʀ] nm **1.** [conducteur] driver ▸ **chauffeur (routier), chauffeur de camion** lorry ⓤⓚ ou truck ⓤⓢ driver ▸ **chauffeur de taxi** taxi ou cab driver **2.** [employé] : *location de voiture avec chauffeur* chauffeur-driven hire-cars.

chaume [ʃom] nm [sur un toit] thatch.

chaumière [ʃomjɛʀ] nf ≃ cottage ; [avec un toit de chaume] thatched cottage ▸ **faire causer** ou **jaser dans les chaumières** to give the neighbours something to talk about.

chaussée [ʃose] nf [d'une route] roadway, pavement ⓤⓢ / '**chaussée déformée**' 'uneven road surface' / '**chaussée glissante**' 'slippery road', 'slippery when wet'.

chausse-pied (*pl* chausse-pieds), **chaussepied*** [ʃospje] nm shoehorn.

chausser [3] [ʃose] ◆ vt **1.** [escarpins, skis, palmes] to put on *(sép)* **2.** [enfant, personne] ▸ **viens chausser les enfants** come and put the children's shoes on for them **3.** [fournir en chaussures] to provide shoes for, to supply with shoes / *je suis difficile à chausser* it's hard for me to find shoes that fit. ◆ vi : *voici un modèle qui devrait mieux chausser* this style of shoe should fit better ▸ **je chausse du 38** I take a size 38 shoe, I take size 38 in shoes. ◆ **se chausser** vp *(emploi réfléchi)* : *chausse-toi, il fait froid* put something on your feet, it's cold. ◆ vpi [se fournir] : *je me chausse chez Lebel* I buy my shoes at ou I get my shoes from Lebel's.

chaussette [ʃosɛt] nf VÊT sock ▸ **en chaussettes** in one's stockinged feet ▸ **laisser tomber qqn comme une vieille chaussette** *fam* to ditch sb.

chausseur [ʃosœʀ] nm **1.** [fabricant] shoemaker **2.** [vendeur] shoemaker, footwear specialist.

chausson [ʃosɔ̃] nm **1.** VÊT [d'intérieur] slipper ; [de bébé] bootee **2.** [de danseuse] ballet shoe, pump ; [de gymnastique] soft shoe ; [dans la chaussure de ski] inner shoe **3.** CULIN turnover ▸ **chausson aux pommes** ≃ apple turnover.

chaussure [ʃosyʀ] nf **1.** VÊT shoe ▸ **chaussures plates** flat shoes, flats ▸ **chaussures à talon** (shoes with) heels ▸ **chaussures de ville** smart shoes ▸ **trouver chaussure à son pied** fig to find a suitable match **2.** LOISIRS & SPORT ▸ **chaussures de ski** ski boots ▸ **chaussures de sport** sports shoes, trainers ⓤⓚ.

chauve [ʃov] adj [crâne, tête] bald ; [personne] bald, bald-headed ; *litt* [montagne] bare ▸ **chauve comme un œuf** *fam* as bald as a coot 🇬🇧 ou as an egg 🇺🇸.

chauve-souris (*pl* chauves-souris), **chauvesouris*** [ʃovsuʀi] nf bat.

chauvin, e [ʃovɛ̃, in] ◆ adj chauvinistic, jingoist, jingoistic. ◆ nm, f chauvinist, jingoist.

chauvinisme [ʃovinism] nm chauvinism, jingoism.

chaux [ʃo] nf lime ▸ **mur passé** ou **blanchi à la chaux** whitewashed wall.

chavirer [3] [ʃaviʀe] ◆ vi **1.** NAUT to capsize, to keel over, to turn turtle **2.** [se renverser] to keel over, to overturn. ◆ vt [émouvoir] to overwhelm, to shatter / *il a l'air tout chaviré* he looks devastated.

check-up (*pl* check-up), **checkup*** [tʃɛkœp] nm checkup.

chef [ʃɛf] ◆ nm **1.** [responsable -gén] head ; [-d'une entreprise] manager, boss ▸ **chef d'atelier** shop foreman ▸ **chef de bureau** head clerk ▸ **chef de cabinet** principal private secretary 🇬🇧 ▸ **chef de chantier** site foreman ▸ **chef d'établissement** ÉDUC headteacher 🇬🇧, headmaster (head-mistress) 🇺🇸, principal 🇺🇸 ▸ **chef de famille** head of the family ▸ **chef de l'État** Head of the State ▸ **chef d'entreprise** company manager ▸ **chef d'équipe** foreman ▸ **chef de projet** project manager ▸ **chef de rayon** department manager ▸ **chef de service** section head **2.** MIL ▸ **chef d'état-major** chief of staff **3.** RAIL ▸ **chef de gare** station master **4.** CULIN ▸ **chef (cuisinier)** chef **5.** [leader] leader ▸ **chef de bande** gang leader ▸ **chef de file** leader ▸ **petit chef a)** *péj* [dans une famille] domestic tyrant **b)** [au bureau, à l'usine] slave driver ▸ **elle s'est débrouillée comme un chef !** *fam* she did really well! **6.** (comme adj) head (modif), chief (modif) ▸ **médecin-chef** head doctor **7.** DR ▸ **chef d'accusation** charge ou count (of indictment). ◆ nf [res-ponsable] ▸ **la chef** the boss. ❖ **de mon propre chef, de son propre chef** loc adv on my / his, etc. own author-ity ou initiative. ❖ **en chef** loc adj ▸ **commandant en chef** commander-in-chief ▸ **ingénieur en chef** chief engi-neer. ▸ **chef d'orchestre** nm MUS conductor.

chef-d'œuvre [ʃedœvʀ] (*pl* chefs-d'œuvre) nm masterpiece.

chef-lieu [ʃefljø] (*pl* chefs-lieux) nm ADMIN in France, administrative centre of a "département", "arrondissement" or "canton" ; ≃ county town 🇬🇧 ; ≃ county seat 🇺🇸.

cheftaine [ʃɛftɛn] nf [de louveteaux] cubmistress 🇬🇧, den mother 🇺🇸 ; [chez les jeannettes] Brown Owl 🇬🇧, den mother 🇺🇸 ; [chez les éclaireuses] captain.

cheik, cheikh [ʃɛk] nm sheik, sheikh.

chelem [ʃlɛm] nm JEUX & SPORT slam ▸ **grand chelem** grand slam.

chemin [ʃəmɛ̃] nm **1.** [allée] path, lane ▸ **chemin de terre** dirt track ▸ **chemin de traverse a)** *pr* path across the fields **b)** *fig* short cut ▸ **tous les chemins mènent à Rome** *prov* all roads lead to Rome *prov* **2.** [parcours, trajet] way ▸ **faire** ou **abattre du chemin** to go a long way / *pas de problème, c'est sur mon chemin* no problem, it's on my way / *nous avons fait tout le chemin à pied* / *en voiture* we walked / drove all the way ▸ **prendre le chemin des écoliers** to go the long way around ▸ **ne pas en prendre le chemin** : *il voudrait devenir avocat, mais il n'en prend pas le chemin* he'd like to be a lawyer, but he's not going about it the right way **3.** *fig* [destinée, progression] way ▸ **ouvrir** / **montrer le chemin** to open / to lead the way / *nos chemins se sont croisés autrefois* we met a long time ago ▸ **faire son chemin a)** [personne] to make one's way in life **b)** [idée] to catch on ▸ **trouver qqn sur son che-min** [ennemi] to find sb standing in one's way / *ne t'ar-rête pas en si bon chemin* don't give up now that you're

doing so well **4.** RELIG ▸ **chemin de croix** Way of the Cross. ❖ **en chemin** loc adv on the way ou one's way / *nous en avons parlé en chemin* we talked about it on the way ou on our way.

chemin de fer [ʃəmɛ̃dfɛʀ] (*pl* chemins de fer) nm **1.** RAIL railway 🇬🇧, railroad 🇺🇸 / *voyager en chemin de fer* to travel by train / *employé des chemins de fer* rail worker 🇬🇧, railman **2.** JEUX chemin de fer.

cheminée [ʃəmine] nf **1.** [gén] shaft ; [de maison] chim-ney (stack) ; [dans un mur] chimney ; [d'usine] chimney (stack), smokestack ; [de paquebot] funnel **2.** [âtre] fireplace ; [chambranle] mantelpiece **3.** GÉOL [d'un volcan] vent ; [d'un massif] chimney.

cheminement [ʃəminmɑ̃] nm **1.** [parcours] movement **2.** *fig* [développement] development, unfolding / *le chemi-nement de sa pensée* the development of her thought.

cheminer [3] [ʃəmine] vi **1.** *litt* [avancer -marcheur] to walk along ; [-fleuve] to flow **2.** *fig* [progresser -régulière-ment] to progress, to develop ; [-lentement] to make slow progress ou headway.

cheminot [ʃəmino] nm RAIL railwayman 🇬🇧, railroad man 🇺🇸.

chemise [ʃəmiz] nf **1.** VÊT shirt ▸ **chemise de nuit a)** [de femme] nightgown, nightdress **b)** [d'homme] night-shirt ▸ **en (bras ou manches de) chemise** in shirt-sleeves ▸ **je m'en fiche** *fam* ou **soucie** ou **moque comme de ma première chemise** I couldn't care less about it **2.** [de car-ton] folder.

chemiserie [ʃəmizʀi] nf **1.** [fabrique] shirt factory **2.** [boutique] gents' outfitter's 🇬🇧, haberdasher's 🇺🇸.

chemisette [ʃəmizɛt] nf [pour femme] short-sleeved blouse ; [pour homme, pour enfant] short-sleeved shirt.

chemisier [ʃəmizje] nm blouse.

chenal, aux [ʃənal, o] nm [canal -dans les terres] chan-nel ; [-dans un port] fairway, channel.

chenapan [ʃənapɑ̃] nm *hum* rascal, rogue, scoundrel.

chêne [ʃɛn] nm BOT oak ▸ **chêne vert** holm oak, ilex.

chenet [ʃənɛ] nm andiron, firedog.

chenil [ʃənil] nm **1.** [établissement -pour la reproduction] breeding kennels ; [-pour la garde] boarding kennels ; [-pour le dressage] training kennels **2.** 🇨🇭 [bric-à-brac] (load of) junk.

chenille [ʃənij] nf **1.** ENTOM caterpillar **2.** MÉCAN cater-pillar ▸ **véhicule à chenilles** tracked vehicle **3.** TEXT chenille.

cheptel [ʃɛptɛl] nm [bétail] livestock.

chèque [ʃɛk] nm **1.** FIN cheque 🇬🇧, check 🇺🇸 ▸ **tirer** / **toucher un chèque** to draw / to cash a cheque ▸ **faire un chèque de 50 euros à qqn** to write sb a cheque for 50 euros ▸ **chèque bancaire** cheque ▸ **chèque de banque** cashier's cheque ▸ **chèque barré** crossed cheque ▸ **chèque en blanc** blank cheque ▸ **chèque en bois** *fam* ou **sans provision** dud cheque 🇬🇧, rubber cheque, bad check 🇺🇸 / *il a fait un chèque sans provision* his cheque bounced ▸ **chèque de caisse** credit voucher ▸ **chèque de caution** cheque given as deposit ▸ **chèque à ordre** cheque to order ▸ **chèque au porteur** bearer cheque ▸ **chèque postal** cheque drawn on the postal banking system ; ≃ giro (cheque) 🇬🇧 ▸ **chèque de voyage** traveller's cheque 🇬🇧, traveler's check 🇺🇸 **2.** [cou-pon] ▸ **chèque-cadeau** gift token ▸ **chèque emploi-service universel** special cheque used to pay casual workers such as part-time cleaners, babysitters, etc. ▸ **chèque-repas** luncheon voucher.

Chèque-Restaurant® [ʃɛkʀɛstɔʀɑ̃] (*pl* Chèques-Restaurants) nm ≃ luncheon voucher.

chèque-vacances [ʃɛkvakɑ̃s] (*pl* chèques-vacances) nm *voucher that can be used to pay for holiday accommoda-tion, activities, meals, etc.*

* In reformed spelling (see p. 16-18).

chéquier [ʃekje] nm chequebook 🇬🇧, checkbook 🇺🇸.

cher, chère [ʃɛʁ] adj **1.** [aimé] dear ▸ **un être cher** a loved one **2.** [dans des formules de politesse] dear ▸ **mes bien** ou **très chers amis** dearest friends **3.** [précieux] dear, beloved / **mon souhait le plus cher** my dearest ou most devout wish **4.** [onéreux] expensive, dear 🇬🇧 ▸ **c'est plus cher** it's dearer 🇬🇧 ou more expensive ▸ **c'est moins cher** it's cheaper ou less expensive ▸ **peu cher** inexpensive. ⬥ **cher** adv **1.** COMM ▸ **coûter cher** to cost a lot, to be expensive ▸ **prendre cher** fam to charge a lot ▸ **il vaut cher a)** [bijou de famille] it's worth a lot ou valuable **b)** [article en magasin] it's expensive / **je l'ai eu pour pas cher** fam I didn't pay much for it **2.** ᴇxᴘʀ ▸ **donner cher**: *je donnerais cher pour le savoir* I'd give anything to know / *je ne donne pas cher de sa vie* I wouldn't give much for his chances of survival.

chercher [3] [ʃɛʁʃe] vt **1.** [dans l'espace] to look ou to search for *(insép)* ▸ **chercher qqn / qqch à tâtons** to fumble ou to grope for sb / sthg ▸ **chercher la petite bête** fam to split hairs ▸ **chercher des poux dans la tête à qqn** fam to try and pick a fight with sb **2.** [mentalement] to try to find, to search for *(insép)* ; *(en usage absolu)* : *tu donnes ta langue au chat ? — attends, je cherche* give up? — wait, I'm still thinking ou trying to think ▸ **chercher chicane** ou **querelle à qqn** to try and pick a quarrel with sb ▸ **chercher midi à quatorze heures** fam to look for complications (where there are none) **3.** [essayer de se procurer] to look ou to hunt for *(insép)* ▸ **chercher du travail** to look for work, to be job-hunting **4.** [aspirer à - tranquillité, inspiration] to look ou to search for *(insép)*, to seek (after) / *il ne cherche que son intérêt* he thinks only of his own interests ▸ [provoquer] to look for *(insép)* / *tu l'as bien cherché !* you asked for it! / *toujours à chercher la bagarre !* always looking ou spoiling for a fight! **6.** [avec des verbes de mouvement] ▸ **aller chercher qqn / qqch** to fetch sb / sthg / *aller chercher les enfants à l'école* to pick the children up from school ▸ **aller chercher** fig: *que vas-tu chercher là ?* what on earth are you going on about? / *ça peut aller chercher jusqu'à dix ans de prison* it could get you up to ten years in prison. ⬥ **chercher à** v + prép to try ou to attempt ou to seek to / *cherche pas à comprendre* fam don't bother to try to ou understand. ⬥ **se chercher** vpi : *il se cherche* he's trying to sort himself out.

chercheur, euse [ʃɛʁʃœʁ, øz] nm, f **1.** UNIV researcher, research worker **2.** ▸ **chercheur d'or** gold digger.

chère [ʃɛʁ] nf litt & hum food, fare ▸ **faire bonne chère** to eat well.

chèrement [ʃɛʁmɑ̃] adv **1.** [à un prix élevé] dearly, at great cost / *la victoire fut chèrement payée* the victory was won at great cost **2.** litt [tendrement] dearly, fondly.

chéri, e [ʃeʁi] ⬥ adj darling, dear, beloved sout. ⬥ nm, f **1.** *(en appellatif)* darling, dear, honey 🇺🇸 / *mon chéri, je te l'ai dit cent fois* darling, I've already told you a hundred times **2.** [personne préférée] : *il a toujours été le chéri de ses parents* he was always the darling of the family.

chérir [32] [ʃeʁiʁ] vt litt [aimer - personne] to cherish, to love (dearly) ; [- démocratie, liberté] to cherish ; [- mémoire, souvenir] to cherish, to treasure.

cherté [ʃɛʁte] nf : *la cherté de la vie* the high cost of living.

chétif, ive [ʃetif, iv] adj [peu robuste] sickly, puny.

cheval, aux [ʃ(ə)val, o] nm **1.** ZOOL horse ▸ **cheval de bataille** fig hobbyhorse, pet subject ▸ **cheval de course** racehorse ▸ **cheval de selle** saddle horse ▸ **cheval de trait** draught 🇬🇧 ou draft 🇺🇸 horse ▸ **monter sur ses grands chevaux** to get on one's high horse **2.** ÉQUIT (horseback) riding ▸ **faire du cheval** to ride, to go riding **3.** AUTO & FIN

▸ **cheval fiscal** horsepower *(for tax purposes)* **4.** [viande] horsemeat. ⬥ **à cheval** loc adv **1.** ÉQUIT on horseback **2.** [à califourchon] : *être à cheval sur une chaise* to be sitting astride a chair / *mon congé est à cheval sur février et mars* my period of leave starts in February and ends in March **3.** fam [pointilleux] ▸ **être à cheval sur** to be particular about / *il est très à cheval sur les principes* he is a stickler for principles. ⬥ **de cheval** loc adj fam ▸ **fièvre de cheval** raging fever ▸ **remède de cheval** drastic remedy.

chevaleresque [ʃ(ə)valʁɛsk] adj [généreux] chivalrous.

chevalerie [ʃəvalʁi] nf **1.** [ordre] knighthood **2.** [institution] chivalry.

chevalet [ʃəvalɛ] nm **1.** [d'un peintre] easel **2.** MUS bridge.

chevalier [ʃəvalje] nm **1.** HIST knight **2.** ADMIN ▸ **chevalier de la Légion d'honneur** chevalier of the Legion of Honour.

chevalière [ʃəvaljɛʁ] nf signet ring.

chevalin, e [ʃəvalɛ̃, in] adj **1.** [race] equine **2.** [air, allure, visage] horsey, horselike.

chevauchée [ʃəvoʃe] nf ride.

chevaucher [3] [ʃəvoʃe] vt [monter sur - moto, cheval, balai, vague] to ride ; [- âne, chaise] to sit astride ou astraddle. ⬥ **se chevaucher** vp *(emploi réciproque)* [être superposé - dents] to grow into each other ; [- tuiles] to overlap.

chevelu, e [ʃəvly] adj [ayant des cheveux] hairy.

chevelure [ʃəvlyʁ] nf **1.** [cheveux] hair / *son abondante chevelure* her thick hair **2.** ASTRON tail.

chevet [ʃ(ə)vɛ] nm [d'un lit] bedhead. ⬥ **au chevet de** loc prép at the bedside of.

cheveu, x [ʃ(ə)vø] nm [poil] hair ▸ **aux cheveux blonds / noirs / frisés** blond- / black- / curly-haired / *une fille aux cheveux courts* a girl with short hair, a short-haired girl / *(les) cheveux au vent* with his / her, etc. hair blowing freely in the wind / *il s'en est fallu d'un cheveu qu'on y reste* we missed death by a hair's breadth ▸ **avoir un cheveu sur la langue** to (have a) lisp ▸ **se faire des cheveux (blancs)** to worry o.s. sick ▸ **venir** ou **arriver** ou **tomber comme un cheveu sur la soupe** to come at the wrong time ▸ **c'est un peu tiré par les cheveux** it's a bit far-fetched.

cheville [ʃ(ə)vij] nf **1.** ANAT ankle ▸ **ne pas arriver à la cheville de qqn** : *son fils ne lui arrive pas à la cheville* his son's hardly in the same league as him **2.** MENUIS [pour visser] (wall) plug, Rawlplug® 🇬🇧, (wall) anchor 🇺🇸 ; [pour boucher] dowel ▸ **il est la cheville ouvrière du mouvement** fig he's the mainspring ou kingpin of the movement. ⬥ **en cheville** loc adv ▸ **être en cheville avec qqn** to be in cahoots with sb.

chèvre [ʃɛvʁ] ⬥ nf ZOOL [mâle] goat, billy-goat ; [femelle] goat, she-goat, nanny-goat ▸ **rendre qqn chèvre** fam to drive sb crazy. ⬥ nm goat's cheese.

chevreau, x [ʃəvʁo] nm ZOOL kid.

chèvrefeuille [ʃɛvʁəfœj] nm honeysuckle.

chevreuil [ʃəvʁœj] nm **1.** ZOOL roe deer **2.** CULIN venison.

chevron [ʃəvʁɔ̃] nm **1.** CONSTR rafter **2.** [motif] chevron ▸ **veste à chevrons a)** [petits] herringbone jacket **b)** [grands] chevron-patterned jacket.

chevronné, e [ʃəvʁone] adj seasoned, experienced, practised.

chevrotant, e [ʃəvʁotɑ̃, ɑ̃t] adj quavering.

chevrotine [ʃəvʁotin] nf piece of buckshot.

chewing-gum [ʃwiŋɡɔm] *(pl* **chewing-gums)** nm gum, chewing-gum.

chez [ʃe] prép **1.** [dans la demeure de] ▸ **rentrer chez soi** to go home ▸ **rester chez soi** to stay at home ou in / *il habite chez moi en ce moment* he's living with me ou he's staying at my place at the moment ▶ **elle l'a raccompagné chez lui a)** [à pied] she walked him home **b)** [en voiture] she gave him a lift home / **les amis chez qui j'étais ce week-end** the friends I stayed with this weekend / **ça s'est passé pas loin de / devant chez nous** it happened not far from / right outside where we live ▶ **chez nous a)** [dans ma famille] in my ou our family **b)** [dans mon pays] in my ou our country ▶ **c'est une coutume / un accent bien de chez nous** it's a typical local custom / accent **2.** [dans un magasin, une société, etc.] ▶ **aller chez le coiffeur / le médecin** to go to the hairdresser's / the doctor's / **je l'ai acheté chez Denver & Smith** I bought it from Denver & Smith / **une robe de chez Dior** a Dior dress, a dress designed by Dior / **il a travaillé chez IBM** he worked at ou for IBM **3.** [dans un pays, un groupe] ▶ **chez les Russes** in Russia / **cette expression est courante chez les jeunes** this expression is widely used among young people ▶ **chez l'homme / la femme** in men / women **4.** [dans une personne] : **il y a quelque chose que j'apprécie particulièrement chez eux, c'est leur générosité** something I particularly like about them is their generosity **5.** [dans l'œuvre de] in **6.** EXPR **de chez** fam: **il est bronzé de chez bronzé** he's as tanned as you can get / **j'ai un téléphone basique de chez basique** my phone is as basic as they come.

📋 La préposition **chez** est rendue de différentes manières en anglais selon le contexte :

• Si **chez** signifie « (dans) la demeure de » et est suivi du nom de la personne ou d'un pronom personnel, on emploie **at + possessif + place**. Place peut être remplacé par **house, flat**, etc.
On va se retrouver chez Marie. *We're going to meet at Marie's place / house / flat.*

Notez que dans un registre familier on peut omettre **place**.
On a dîné chez Anne. *We had dinner at Anne's.*

• **Chez soi** est rendu par **at my / his / their**, etc., **place, at home**, ou (surtout en anglais américain) simplement **home** :
Je suis resté chez moi toute la journée. *I stayed at my place all day* ou *I stayed at home all day* ou *I stayed home all day* US.

• Lorsqu'on parle de se rendre **chez qqn**, on emploie **to + possessif + place / house / flat**, etc. :
C'est la première fois que je viens chez toi. *It's the first time I've been to your place.*

• Lorsque **chez soi** est associé à un verbe de mouvement, on emploie **verbe + home** :
Je vais rentrer chez moi à pied / en voiture. *I'll walk / drive home.*

• Si l'on veut dire que l'on se trouve **chez un commerçant, chez le médecin, chez le dentiste**, etc., on emploie **at + possessif** :
Thomas est chez le coiffeur. *Thomas is at the hairdresser's.*

• Lorsqu'on se rend **chez un commerçant, le médecin**, etc., on emploie **verbe + to + possessif** :
Elle va chez le boucher une fois par semaine. *She goes to the butcher's once a week.*

• Si **chez** signifie parmi, on emploie **in** ou **among** :
C'est assez répandu chez les adolescents. *It's quite common among teenagers.*

Une maladie courante chez le chien. *A common illness in dogs.*

Si c'est d'une seule personne que l'on parle, on emploie **about** :
Ce que j'apprécie le plus chez elle, c'est son humour. *What I like about her the most is her sense of humour.*

chez-soi [ʃeswa] nm inv home.

chiader [3] [ʃjade] vt tfam **1.** [perfectionner] to polish up (sép) / **c'est vachement chiadé comme bagnole !** this car's got the works! **2.** ÉDUC & UNIV to cram for, to swot (up) UK.

chialer [3] [ʃjale] vi tfam to blubber, to bawl.

chiant, e [ʃjɑ̃, ɑ̃t] adj tfam **1.** [assommant - personne, chose à faire, livre] boring **2.** [contrariant - personne, événement] annoying / **t'es chiante de pas répondre quand on te parle !** why can't you answer me when I speak to you, it really pisses me off UK ou ticks me off! US.

chiasse [ʃjas] nf vulg [diarrhée] : **avoir la chiasse** to have the trots ou runs.

chic [ʃik] ◆ adj inv **1.** [élégant] stylish, smart, classy / **pour faire chic** in order to look smart ou classy **2.** [distingué] smart / **il paraît que ça fait chic de...** it's considered smart (these days) to... **3.** [sympathique] nice / **c'est une chic fille !** she's really nice! ◆ nm **1.** [élégance - d'une allure, d'un vêtement] style, stylishness, chic **2.** fam EXPR **avoir le chic pour** : **il a le chic pour dire ce qu'il ne faut pas** he has a gift for ou a knack of saying the wrong thing. ◆ interj fam & vieilli ▶ **chic (alors) !** great!, smashing!

chicane [ʃikan] nf **1.** [querelle] squabble **2.** SPORT [de circuit] chicane ; [de gymkhana] zigzag.

chicaner [3] [ʃikane] ◆ vt ▶ **chicaner qqn sur** to quibble with sb about. ◆ vi to quibble.

chicha, shisha [ʃiʃa] nf hookah.

chiche [ʃiʃ] adj **1.** [avare] mean **2.** fam [capable] ▶ **être chiche de** : **tu n'es pas chiche de le faire !** I'll bet you couldn't do it! ▶ **chiche !** want to bet?

chichement [ʃiʃmɑ̃] adv **1.** [de façon mesquine] meanly, stingily **2.** [pauvrement] scantily, meagrely UK, meagerly US.

chichi [ʃiʃi] nm fam [simagrée] airs (and graces) ▶ **faire des chichis** to put on airs ▶ **un dîner sans chichis** an informal dinner.

chicorée [ʃikɔʀe] nf [salade] endive UK, chicory US.

chicot [ʃiko] nm [d'une dent] stump ; [d'un arbre] tree stump.

chien, chienne [ʃjɛ̃, ʃjɛn] nm, f ZOOL dog (bitch) ▶ **chien d'arrêt** ou **couchant** pointer ▶ **chien d'aveugle** guide dog ▶ **chien de berger** sheepdog ▶ **chien de chasse** retriever ▶ **chien de garde a)** pr guard dog **b)** fig watchdog ▶ **chien policier** police dog ▶ **chien de race** pedigree dog ▶ **chien de traîneau** husky / **'chien méchant'** 'beware of the dog' ▶ **(rubrique des) chiens écrasés** minor news items ▶ **se regarder en chiens de faïence** to stare at one another ▶ **ils sont comme chien et chat** they fight like cat and dog ▶ **comme un chien savant** péj like a trained monkey ▶ **arriver comme un chien dans un jeu de quilles** to turn up at just the wrong moment ▶ **ce n'est pas fait pour les chiens** péj it is there for a good reason ▶ **une vie de chien !** fam life's a bitch! ◆ **chien** nm EXPR **avoir du chien** fam: **elle a du chien** she's got sex-appeal. ◆ **en chien de fusil** loc adv curled up.

chien-assis [ʃjɛ̃asi] (pl chiens-assis) nm dormer window UK, dormer US.

chiendent [ʃjɛ̃dɑ̃] nm couch grass / **ça pousse comme du chiendent** it grows at a phenomenal rate.

chien-guide [ʃjɛ̃gid] (*pl* **chiens-guides**) nm guide dog.

chien-loup [ʃjɛlu] (*pl* **chiens-loups**) nm Alsatian (dog), German shepherd.

chienne [ʃjɛn] f ⟶ **chien**.

chier [9] [ʃje] vi **1.** *vulg* [déféquer] to shit, to have 🇬🇧 ou take 🇺🇸 a shit **2.** *tfam* ⟨EXPR⟩ **envoyer chier qqn** to tell sb to get stuffed ▶ **faire chier qqn a)** [l'importuner, le contrarier] to bug sb **b)** [l'ennuyer] to bore the pants off sb / *(ça) fait chier, ce truc !* this thing's a real pain in the arse 🇬🇧 ou ass 🇺🇸! ❖ **à chier** loc adj *tfam* **1.** [très laid] : *son costard est à chier* his suit looks bloody awful 🇬🇧 ou godawful 🇺🇸 **2.** [insupportable] : *il est à chier, ce prof !* that teacher is a pain in the arse 🇬🇧 ou ass 🇺🇸!

chierie [ʃiʀi] nf *tfam* pain *fam* / *quelle chierie cette machine à laver !* this washing machine's a bloody pain!

chiffe [ʃif] nf ▶ *c'est une vraie chiffe molle* he's got no guts, he's totally spineless / *je suis une vraie chiffe molle aujourd'hui* [fatigué] I feel like a wet rag today.

chiffon [ʃifɔ̃] nm **1.** [torchon] cloth ▶ **chiffon à poussière** duster 🇬🇧, dust cloth 🇺🇸 **2.** [vieux tissu] rag ▶ **parler chiffons** to talk clothes ou fashion.

chiffonné, e [ʃifɔne] adj [fatigué - visage] tired, worn.

chiffonner [3] [ʃifɔne] vt **1.** [vêtement] to rumple, to crumple ; [papier] to crumple **2.** *fam* [préoccuper] to bother, to worry / *ça n'a pas eu l'air de la chiffonner* it didn't seem to bother her.

chiffonnier, ère [ʃifɔnje, ɛʀ] nm, f rag dealer, rag-and-bone man *m*.

chiffre [ʃifʀ] nm **1.** MATH figure, number ▶ **nombre à deux / trois chiffres** two / three digit number ▶ *jusqu'à deux chiffres après la virgule* up to two decimal points ▶ **en chiffres ronds** in round figures ▶ **chiffre arabe / romain** Arabic / Roman numeral **2.** [montant] amount, sum / *le chiffre des dépenses s'élève à 600 euros* total expenditure amounts to 600 euros **3.** [taux] figures, rate ▶ **les chiffres du chômage** the unemployment figures **4.** COMM ▶ **chiffre d'affaires** turnover, sales.

chiffrer [3] [ʃifʀe] ❖ vt [évaluer] to assess, to estimate. ❖ vi *fam* to cost a packet ▶ **ça chiffre !** it mounts up! ❖ **se chiffrer** vp *(emploi passif)* ▶ **se chiffrer à** [se monter à] to add up ou to amount to.

chignon [ʃiɲɔ̃] nm bun, chignon ▶ **faire son chignon** to coil up one's hair.

chiite [ʃiit] adj Shiah, Shiite. ❖ **Chiite** nmf Shiite.

Chili [ʃili] npr m ▶ **le Chili** Chile.

chilien, enne [ʃiljɛ̃, ɛn] adj Chilean. ❖ **Chilien, enne** nm, f Chilean.

chimère [ʃimɛʀ] nf **1.** MYTH chimera **2.** [utopie] dream, fantasy / *je vous laisse à vos chimères* I'll leave you alone with your pipe dreams.

chimérique [ʃimeʀik] adj **1.** [illusoire] fanciful **2.** *litt* [utopiste] chimeric.

chimie [ʃimi] nf chemistry.

chimio [ʃimjo] (*abr de* **chimiothérapie**) nf *fam* chemo.

chimiothérapie [ʃimjoteʀapi] nf chemotherapy.

chimique [ʃimik] adj **1.** [de la chimie] chemical **2.** *fam* [artificiel] chemical, artificial.

chimiquier [ʃimikje] nm chemical tanker.

chimiste [ʃimist] nmf chemist.

chimpanzé [ʃɛ̃pɑ̃ze] nm chimpanzee.

chinchilla [ʃɛ̃ʃila] nm [rongeur, fourrure] chinchilla.

Chine [ʃin] npr f ▶ **(la) Chine** China ▶ **Chine communiste** Red ou Communist China ▶ **Chine populaire, République populaire de Chine** People's Republic of China.

chiné, e [ʃine] adj [tissu] chiné, mottled ; [laine] bicoloured wool.

chiner [3] [ʃine] vi [faire les boutiques] to go round the second-hand shops.

chinois, e [ʃinwa, az] adj [de Chine] Chinese. ❖ **Chinois, e** nm, f Chinese ▶ **les Chinois** the Chinese. ❖ **chinois** nm LING Chinese ▶ **pour moi, c'est du chinois** it's all Greek to me.

chinoiserie [ʃinwazʀi] nf **1.** *fam* [complication] complication **2.** ART chinoiserie.

chiot [ʃjo] nm pup, puppy.

chiotte [ʃjɔt] nf *tfam* [désagrément] drag, hassle / *quel temps de chiotte !* what godawful weather! ❖ **chiottes** nfpl *tfam* bog 🇬🇧, john 🇺🇸.

chiper [3] [ʃipe] vt *fam* to pinch, to swipe.

chipie [ʃipi] nf minx.

chipoter [3] [ʃipɔte] vi *fam* **1.** [discuter] to argue, to quibble / *chipoter sur les prix* to haggle over prices **2.** [sur la nourriture] to pick at one's food.

chips [ʃips] nfpl (potato) crisps 🇬🇧 ou chips 🇺🇸.

⚠ Ce mot ne se traduit par **chips** ou **potato chips** qu'en anglais américain.

chiqué [ʃike] nm *fam* & *péj* ▶ **chiqué** ! [dans un match] that's cheating! ▶ **il n'a pas mal, c'est du** ou **il fait du chiqué** he's not in pain at all, he's putting it on ou just pretending.

chiquenaude [ʃiknod] nf [pichenette] flick.

chiquer [3] [ʃike] ❖ vt to chew. ❖ vi to chew tobacco.

chiromancien, enne [kiʀɔmɑ̃sjɛ̃, ɛn] nm, f chiromancer.

chiropraticien, enne [kiʀɔpratisjɛ̃, ɛn] nm, f chiropractor.

chirurgical, e, aux [ʃiʀyʀʒikal, o] adj **1.** MÉD surgical **2.** [précis] accurate.

chirurgie [ʃiʀyʀʒi] nf surgery ▶ **chirurgie esthétique** cosmetic surgery ▶ **chirurgie d'un jour** ⟨QUÉBEC⟩ outpatient surgery ▶ **chirurgie plastique** plastic surgery ▶ **chirurgie reconstructrice** reconstructive surgery.

chirurgien, enne [ʃiʀyʀʒjɛ̃, ɛn] nm, f surgeon.

chirurgien-dentiste [ʃiʀyʀʒjɛ̃dɑ̃tist] (*pl* **chirurgiens-dentistes**) nm dental surgeon.

chlinguer [3] [ʃlɛ̃ge] vi *tfam* to stink, to pong 🇬🇧 / *ça chlingue, par ici !* it's a bit whiffy 🇬🇧 ou it sure stinks 🇺🇸 around here!

chlore [klɔʀ] nm **1.** CHIM chlorine **2.** [Javel] bleach, bleaching agent.

chlorer [klɔʀe] vt CHIM to chlorinate.

chloroforme [klɔʀɔfɔʀm] nm chloroform.

chlorophylle [klɔʀɔfil] nf BOT chlorophyll.

chlorure [klɔʀyʀ] nm chloride.

chnoque [ʃnɔk] = **schnock**.

choc [ʃɔk] nm **1.** [collision - entre véhicules] crash ; [- entre personnes] collision ; [heurt] impact, shock ▶ **résistant aux chocs** shock-proof, shock-resistant ▶ **la porte s'est cassée sous le choc** the door broke under the impact **2.** MIL [affrontement] clash **3.** [incompatibilité] clash, conflict ▶ **choc culturel** culture shock **4.** [émotion] shock / *ça fait un choc !* it's a bit of a shock! **5.** MÉD shock ▶ **choc opératoire** post-operative trauma ou shock **6.** ÉCON ▶ **choc pétrolier**

oil crisis **7.** *(comme adjectif, avec ou sans trait d'union)*
▸ **argument / discours choc** hard-hitting argument / speech.
✧ **sous le choc** *loc adj* ▸ **être sous le choc a)** MÉD to be in shock **b)** [bouleversé] to be in a daze *ou* in shock.

chocolat [ʃɔkɔla] ← *nm* **1.** CULIN chocolate ▸ **chocolat blanc** white chocolate ▸ **chocolat à croquer** *ou* **noir** dark *ou* plain chocolate ▸ **chocolat au lait** milk chocolate ▸ **chocolat en poudre** drinking chocolate **2.** [friandise] chocolate **3.** [boisson] hot chocolate, cocoa ▸ **un chocolat chaud** a cup of hot chocolate. ← *adj inv* EXPR on est **chocolat !** **a)** [dupés] we've been had! **b)** [coincés] we've blown it! ✧ **au chocolat** *loc adj* chocolate *(modif)*.

chocolaté, e [ʃɔkɔlate] *adj* chocolate *(modif)*, chocolate (flavoured) UK, chocolate (flavored) US.

chocolatier, ère [ʃɔkɔlatje,ɛʀ] *nm, f* **1.** [fabricant] chocolate-maker **2.** [marchand] confectioner.

chocolatine [ʃɔkɔlatin] *nf* QUÉBEC [pain au chocolat] chocolate roll.

chœur [kœʀ] *nm* MUS [chorale] choir, chorus ; [morceau] chorus. ✧ **en chœur** *loc adv* **1.** MUS ▸ **chanter en chœur** to sing in chorus **2.** [ensemble] (all) together / *parler en chœur* to speak in unison.

choisi, e [ʃwazi] *adj* **1.** [raffiné] ▸ **une assemblée choisie** a select audience **2.** [sélectionné] selected, picked ▸ **bien choisi** well-chosen, appropriate.

choisir [32] [ʃwaziʀ] *vt* **1.** [sélectionner] to choose, to pick / *choisis ce que tu veux* take your choice *ou* pick / *tu as choisi ton moment !* *iron* you picked a good time! / *il a choisi la liberté* he chose freedom ; *(en usage absolu)* ▸ **bien choisir** to choose carefully, to be careful in one's choice **2.** [décider] to decide, to choose, to elect *sout* / *ils ont choisi de rester* they decided *ou* chose to stay.

choix [ʃwa] *nm* **1.** [liberté de choisir] choice ▸ **donner le choix à qqn** to give sb a *ou* the choice ▸ **avoir un** *ou* **le choix** to have a choice / *ils ne nous ont pas laissé le choix* they left us no alternative *ou* other option **2.** [sélection] choice ▸ **faire un choix** to make a choice ▸ **mon choix est fait** I've made up my mind **3.** [gamme] ▸ **un choix de** a choice *ou* range *ou* selection of **4.** COMM ▸ **de premier choix** top-quality ▸ **viande** *ou* **morceaux de premier choix** prime cuts ▸ **de second choix a)** [fruits, légumes] standard, grade 2 **b)** [viande] standard ▸ **articles de second choix** seconds. ✧ **au choix** *loc adv* : *vous avez fromage ou dessert au choix* you have a choice of either cheeses or a dessert / *répondre au choix à l'une des trois questions* answer any one of the three questions. ✧ **de choix** *loc adj* [de qualité] choice *(avant nom)*, selected. ✧ **par choix** *loc adv* out of choice.

choléra [kɔleʀa] *nm* MÉD & VÉTÉR cholera.

cholestérol [kɔlɛsteʀɔl] *nm* cholesterol.

chômage [ʃomaʒ] *nm* **1.** [inactivité] unemployment ▸ **chômage de longue durée** long-term unemployment ▸ **chômage partiel** short-time working ▸ **chômage saisonnier** seasonal unemployment ▸ **chômage technique** : *être mis au chômage technique* to be laid off **2.** *fam* [allocation] unemployment benefit, dole (money) UK ▸ **toucher le chômage** to be on the dole. ✧ **au chômage** *loc adj* [sans emploi] unemployed, out of work ▸ **être au chômage** to be unemployed *ou* out of work. ← *loc adv* ▸ **s'inscrire au chômage** to sign on UK, to register as unemployed.

chômé, e [ʃome] *adj* ▸ **jour chômé** public holiday.

chômer [3] [ʃome] *vi* **1.** [être sans emploi] to be unemployed *ou* out of work **2.** [avoir du loisir] to be idle, to have time on one's hands ▸ **il ne chôme pas** he's never short of something to do.

chômeur, euse [ʃomœʀ, øz] *nm, f* [sans emploi] unemployed person ▸ **les chômeurs de longue durée** the long-term unemployed.

chope [ʃɔp] *nf* mug.

choper [3] [ʃɔpe] *fam vt* **1.** [contracter - maladie] to catch **2.** [intercepter] to catch, to get, to grab ▸ **se faire choper a)** [gén] to get caught **b)** [par la police] to be nicked UK *ou* nabbed.

choquant, e [ʃɔkɑ̃, ɑ̃t] *adj* **1.** [déplaisant - attitude] outrageous, shocking **2.** [déplacé - tenue] offensive, shocking / *ça n'a rien de choquant* it's not at all shocking.

choquer [3] [ʃɔke] *vt* **1.** [heurter] to hit, to knock, to bump / *choquer des verres* to clink glasses **2.** [scandaliser] to shock, to offend ▸ **être choqué (de qqch)** to be shocked (at sthg) ; *(en usage absolu)* : *leur album a beaucoup choqué* their album caused great offence **3.** [aller contre] to go against, to be contrary to **4.** [traumatiser] : *ils ont été profondément choqués par sa mort* they were devastated by his death.

choral, als [kɔʀal] *nm* MUS & RELIG choral, chorale. ✧ **chorale** *nf* choir, choral society.

chorégraphe [kɔʀegʀaf] *nmf* choreographer.

chorégraphie [kɔʀegʀafi] *nf* choreography.

choriste [kɔʀist] *nmf* **1.** RELIG chorister **2.** THÉÂTRE chorus singer ▸ **les choristes** [au cabaret] the chorus line.

chose [ʃoz]
← *nf*
A. SENS CONCRET **1.** [bien matériel, nourriture, vêtement] thing / *j'ai encore des choses à lui chez moi* I still have a few of his things *ou* some of his belongings at home **2.** [objet ou produit indéterminé] thing.
B. SENS ABSTRAIT **1.** [acte, fait] ▸ **une chose** a thing, something / *j'ai encore beaucoup de choses à faire* I've still got lots (of things) to do / *une chose est sûre, il perdra* one thing's (for) sure, he'll lose / *ce n'est pas la même chose* [cela change tout] it's a different matter / *ce sont des choses qui arrivent* it's just one of those things / *s'occuper de choses et d'autres* to potter about ▸ **il ne fait pas les choses à demi** *ou* **moitié** he doesn't do things by halves ▸ **chose promise chose due** a promise is a promise **2.** [parole] thing / *il dit une chose et il en fait une autre* he says one thing and does something else ▸ **bavarder** *ou* **parler de choses et d'autres** to chat about this and that ▸ **dites-lui bien des choses** give him my best regards **3.** [écrit] thing / *comment peut-on écrire des choses pareilles !* how can anyone write such things!
← *adj fam* funny, peculiar / *ton fils a l'air tout chose aujourd'hui* your son looks a bit peculiar today. ✧ **choses** *nfpl* [situation] things / *les choses de la vie* the things that go to make up life / *prendre les choses comme elles viennent* to take life as it comes. ✧ **de deux choses l'une** *loc adv* : *de deux choses l'une, ou tu m'obéis ou tu vas te coucher* either you do as I tell you or you go to bed, it's up to you!

chou¹, x [ʃu] *nm* **1.** BOT ▸ **chou de Bruxelles** Brussels sprout ▸ **chou chinois** Chinese cabbage *ou* leaves ▸ **chou frisé** (curly) kale **2.** CULIN ▸ **chou à la crème** cream puff **3.** *fam* EXPR **être dans les choux** to be in a mess ▸ **faire chou blanc** to draw a blank, to be out of luck ▸ **faire ses choux gras de qqch** to put sthg to good use ▸ **rentrer dans le chou à qqn a)** [en voiture] to slam into sb **b)** [agresser] to go for sb.

chou², choute [ʃu, ʃut] *nm, f fam (en appellatif)* honey, sugar, sweetheart.

choucas [ʃuka] *nm* jackdaw.

chouchou, oute [ʃuʃu, ut] nm, f *fam & péj* favourite 🇬🇧, favorite 🇺🇸 / *c'est le chouchou du prof* she's the teacher's pet. ❖ **chouchou** nm [pour les cheveux] scrunchy.

chouchouter [3] [ʃuʃute] vt *fam* [élève] to give preferential treatment to ; [enfant, ami] to mollycoddle, to pamper.

choucroute [ʃukʀut] nf CULIN [chou] pickled cabbage ; [plat] sauerkraut.

chouette¹ [ʃwɛt] nf ZOOL owl.

chouette² [ʃwɛt] *fam* ◆ adj **1.** [agréable - soirée] fantastic, lovely, terrific **2.** [gentil] kind ; [coopératif] helpful. ◆ interj great.

chou-fleur [ʃuflœʀ] (*pl* choux-fleurs) nm cauliflower.

chouia [ʃuja] nm *fam* ▶ **un chouia** a little ou wee ou tiny bit.

choyer [13] [ʃwaje] vt to pamper, to make a fuss of.

CHR (abr de centre hospitalier régional) nm *regional hospital.*

chrétien, enne [kʀetjɛ̃, ɛn] adj & nm, f Christian.

chrétien-démocrate, chrétienne-démocrate [kʀetjẽdemɔkʀat, kʀetjẽndemɔkʀat] (*mpl* chrétiens-démocrates, *fpl* chrétiennes-démocrates) adj & nm, f Christian Democrat.

chrétienté [kʀetjẽte] nf Christendom.

Christ [kʀist] npr m ▶ **le Christ** Christ. ❖ **christ** nm [crucifix] (Christ on the) cross, crucifix.

christianiser [3] [kʀistjanize] vt to evangelize, to convert to Christianity.

christianisme [kʀistjanism] nm Christianity.

chromatique [kʀɔmatik] adj **1.** MUS & OPT chromatic **2.** BIOL chromosomal.

chrome [kʀom] nm CHIM chromium. ❖ **chromes** nmpl [d'un véhicule] chrome (U), chromium-plated parts.

chromé, e [kʀome] adj chrome, chromium-plated.

chromosome [kʀomozom] nm chromosome.

chromosomique [kʀomozomik] adj chromosomal, chromosome *(modif).*

chronique [kʀɔnik] ◆ adj [constant] chronic. ◆ nf **1.** PRESSE [rubrique] column **2.** LITTÉR chronicle.

chrono [kʀɔno] *fam* ◆ nm stopwatch. ◆ adv by the clock ▶ **250 chrono** recorded speed 250 kph.

chronobiologie [kʀɔnɔbjɔlɔʒi] nf chronobiology.

chronologie [kʀɔnɔlɔʒi] nf chronology, time sequence.

chronologique [kʀɔnɔlɔʒik] adj chronological.

chronomètre [kʀɔnɔmɛtʀ] nm stopwatch.

chronométrer [18] [kʀɔnɔmetʀe] vt to time *(with a stopwatch).*

✏ In reformed spelling (see p. 16-18), this verb is conjugated like *semer* : *elle chronomètrera, il chronomètrerait.*

chronophage [kʀɔnɔfaʒ] adj [activité, processus] time-consuming.

chronothérapie [kʀɔnɔteʀapi] nf chronotherapy.

chrysalide [kʀizalid] nf chrysalis.

chrysanthème [kʀizɑ̃tɛm] nm chrysanthemum.

CHU nm abr de centre hospitalo-universitaire.

chuchotement [ʃyʃɔtmɑ̃] nm whisper.

chuchoter [3] [ʃyʃɔte] ◆ vi to whisper. ◆ vt [mot d'amour, secret] to whisper ▶ **chuchoter qqch à qqn** to whisper sthg to sb.

chut [ʃyt] interj hush, sh, shhh.

chute [ʃyt] nf **1.** [perte d'équilibre] fall ▶ **faire une chute** to fall, to take a tumble / *faire une chute de cheval* to come off a horse / *il a fait une chute de neuf mètres* he fell nine metres / *'attention, chute de pierres'* 'dan-

ger! falling rocks' ▶ **chute libre** free fall / *faire du saut en chute libre* to skydive / *la livre est en chute libre fig* the pound's plummetting **2.** [perte] fall ▶ **la chute des cheveux** hair loss / *au moment de la chute des feuilles* when the leaves fall **3.** [baisse - des prix] drop, fall **4.** [effondrement - d'un gouvernement, d'une institution] collapse, fall **5.** MÉTÉOR ▶ **chutes de neige** snowfall ▶ **chutes de pluie** rainfall **6.** ANAT ▶ **chute des reins** small of the back **7.** [déchet - de tissu] scrap ; [- de bois, de métal] offcut, trimming. ❖ **chute d'eau** nf waterfall.

Chutes	
les chutes du Niagara	(the) Niagara Falls
les chutes Victoria	(the) Victoria Falls

chuter [3] [ʃyte] vi **1.** *fam* [tomber] to fall **2.** [baisser] to fall, to tumble ▶ **faire chuter les ventes** to bring sales (figures) tumbling down.

Chypre [ʃipʀ] npr Cyprus ▶ **à Chypre** in Cyprus. ⟶ île

chypriote [ʃipʀijɔt] = cypriote.

ci [si] pron dém inv ▶ **ci et ça** this and that.

-ci [si] adv **1.** [dans l'espace] : *celui-ci ou celui-là ?* this one or that one? **2.** [dans le temps - présent] : *à cette heure-ci il n'y a plus personne* there's nobody there at this time of day ▶ **ce mois-ci** this month ▶ **cette semaine-ci** this week ; [dans le temps - futur] : *ils viennent dîner ce mercredi-ci* they're coming for dinner next Wednesday ; [dans le temps - passé] : *il n'a pas fait très beau ces jours-ci* the weather hasn't been too good just lately / *je ne l'ai pas beaucoup vu ces temps-ci* I haven't seen much of him lately **3.** [pour insister] : *je ne t'ai pas demandé ce livre-ci* THAT's not the book I asked for / *cette fois-ci j'ai compris !* NOW I've got it! / *c'est à cette heure-ci que tu rentres ?* what time do you call this?

CIA (abr de Central Intelligence Agency) npr f CIA.

ciao [tʃao] interj *fam* ciao.

ci-après [siapʀɛ] adv hereafter, hereinafter, following ▶ **les dispositions ci-après** the provisions set out below.

cible [sibl] nf **1.** ARM & PHYS target **2.** *fig* [victime] target ▶ **prendre qqn pour cible** to make sb the target of one's attacks.

cibler [3] [sible] vt [produit] to define a target group for ; [public] to target.

ciboulette [sibulɛt] nf chives *(pl).*

cicatrice [sikatʀis] nf **1.** MÉD scar **2.** *fig* [marque] mark, scar.

cicatriser [3] [sikatʀize] vt **1.** MÉD to heal, to cicatrize *spéc* **2.** [adoucir] to heal. ❖ **se cicatriser** vpi [coupure] to heal ou to close up ; [tissus] to form a scar ; *fig* to heal.

ci-contre [sikɔ̃tʀ] adv opposite ▶ **illustré ci-contre** as shown (in the picture) opposite.

CICR (abr de Comité international de la Croix-Rouge) npr m IRCC.

ci-dessous [sidəsu] adv below.

ci-dessus [sidəsy] adv above ▶ **l'adresse ci-dessus** the above address.

CIDJ (abr de centre d'information et de documentation de la jeunesse) nm *careers advisory service.*

cidre [sidʀ] nm cider 🇬🇧, hard cider 🇺🇸 ▶ **cidre bouché** bottled cider *(with a seal).*

Cie (abr écrite de compagnie) Co.

ciel [sjɛl] (pl **cieux** [sjø]) ◆ nm **1.** [espace] sky ▶ **entre ciel et terre** in the air, in midair ▶ **tomber du ciel** a) [arriver opportunément] to be heaven-sent ou a godsend b) [être stupéfait] to be stunned **2.** (pl **ciels** [sjɛl]) MÉTÉOR : *ciel clair / nuageux* clear / cloudy sky **3.** RELIG Heaven **4.** litt [fatalité] fate ; [providence] : *c'est le ciel qui t'envoie* you're a godsend. ◆ interj vieilli ▶ **(juste) ciel !** heavens above!, (good) heavens! ❖ **ciels** nmpl litt [temps] : *les ciels changeants de Bretagne* the changing skies of Brittany. ❖ **cieux** nmpl litt [région] climes, climate ▶ **partir vers d'autres cieux** to be off to distant parts. ❖ **à ciel ouvert** loc adj **1.** MIN open-cast UK, open-cut US **2.** [piscine, stade] open-air.

cierge [sjɛʀʒ] nm [bougie] altar candle.

cieux [sjø] pl ⟶ ciel.

cigale [sigal] nf cicada.

cigare [sigaʀ] nm [à fumer] cigar.

cigarette [sigaʀɛt] nf **1.** [à fumer] cigarette ▶ **fumer une cigarette** to smoke a cigarette, to have a smoke ▶ **cigarette filtre** filter-tipped cigarette **2.** CULIN ▶ **cigarette (russe)** shortcrust biscuit shaped like a brandy snap.

cigarettier [sigaʀɛtje] nm cigarette manufacturer.

ci-gît, ci-git* [siʒi] adv here lies.

cigogne [sigɔɲ] nf stork.

ci-inclus, e [siɛ̃kly, yz] (mpl ci-inclus, fpl ci-incluses) adj (après le nom) enclosed. ❖ **ci-inclus** adv (invariable avant le nom, variable après le nom) : *ci-inclus vos quittances* please find bill enclosed / *veuillez trouver la copie du testament ci-incluse* please find enclosed the copy of the will.

ci-joint, e [siʒwɛ̃, ɛ̃t] (mpl ci-joints, fpl ci-jointes) adj (invariable avant le nom, variable après le nom) attached, enclosed / *(veuillez trouver) ci-joint la facture correspondante* please find enclosed ou attached the invoice relating to your order.

cil [sil] nm ANAT eyelash, lash, cilium spéc.

ciller [sije] vi **1.** [battre des cils] to blink **2.** [réagir] ▶ **il n'a pas cillé** he didn't bat an eyelid ou turn a hair.

cimaise [simɛz] nf ART picture rail.

cime [sim] nf **1.** GÉOGR peak, summit, top **2.** [haut d'un arbre] crown, top.

ciment [simã] nm **1.** CONSTR cement ▶ **ciment à prise lente / rapide** slow-setting / quick-setting cement **2.** sout [lien] bond.

cimenter [simãte] vt **1.** CONSTR to cement **2.** [renforcer] to consolidate.

cimetière [simtjɛʀ] nm cemetery, graveyard ; [autour d'une église] churchyard ▶ **cimetière de voitures** scrapyard (for cars).

ciné [sine] nm fam **1.** [spectacle] ▶ **le ciné** the pictures / *se faire un ciné* to go and see a film UK ou a movie US **2.** [édifice] cinema UK, movie theater US.

cinéaste [sineast] nmf film-director UK, movie director US.

ciné-club (pl ciné-clubs), **cinéclub*** [sineklœb] nm film society UK, movie club US.

cinéma [sinema] nm **1.** [édifice] cinema UK, movie theater US ▶ **aller au cinéma** to go to the cinema UK ou the movies US **2.** [spectacle, genre] ▶ **le cinéma** the cinema UK, the movies US ▶ **le cinéma d'animation** cartoons, animation ▶ **le cinéma d'art et d'essai** art films UK ou movies US **3.** [métier] ▶ **le cinéma** film-making UK, movie-making US ▶ **faire du cinéma** a) [technicien] to work in films UK ou the movies US b) [acteur] to act in films UK, to be a screen actor **4.** [industrie] ▶ **le cinéma** the film UK ou movie US industry **5.** fam EXPR *c'est du cinéma* it's (all) playacting ▶ **faire du** ou **tout un cinéma (pour)** to kick up a huge fuss (about) ▶ **arrête (de faire) ton cinéma !** a) [de mentir] stop putting us on! b) [de bluffer] stop shooting your mouth off! ▶ **se faire du cinéma** to fantasize. ❖ **de cinéma** loc adj [festival, revue, vedette] film UK (modif), movie US (modif) ; [école] film-making UK, movie-making US.

cinémathèque [sinematɛk] nf film UK ou movie US library.

🚩 **La Cinémathèque française**

Founded in Paris in 1936, the **Cinémathèque** specializes in the conservation and restoration of films; it also screens films for public viewing.

cinématographique [sinematɔgʀafik] adj cinematographic, film UK (modif), movie US (modif).

cinéphile [sinefil] ◆ nmf film UK ou movie US buff. ◆ adj : *être (très) cinéphile* to be a film UK ou movie US buff.

cinglant, e [sɛ̃glã, ãt] adj **1.** [violent] bitter, biting / *une gifle cinglante* a stinging slap **2.** [blessant] biting, cutting, stinging.

cinglé, e [sɛ̃gle] fam ◆ adj crazy, screwy, nuts. ◆ nm, f loony UK, screwball US / *les cinglés du volant / jazz / cinéma* car / jazz / film fanatics.

cingler [3] [sɛ̃gle] vt **1.** [fouetter] to lash **2.** [blesser] to sting.

cinoche [sinɔʃ] nm fam cinema UK, movies US (pl).

cinq [sɛ̃k] dét five.

cinquantaine [sɛ̃kɑ̃tɛn] nf **1.** [nombre] ▶ **une cinquantaine de voitures** fifty or so cars, about fifty cars **2.** [d'objets] (lot of) fifty **3.** [âge] fifty ▶ **il frise la cinquantaine** he's nearly fifty.

cinquante [sɛ̃kɑ̃t] dét fifty.

cinquantenaire [sɛ̃kɑ̃tnɛʀ] ◆ adj fifty-year old. ◆ nm fiftieth anniversary, golden jubilee.

cinquantième [sɛ̃kɑ̃tjɛm] adj num fiftieth. **Voir aussi** cinquième.

cinquième [sɛ̃kjɛm] adj num fifth.

cinquièmement [sɛ̃kjɛmmã] adv fifthly, in the fifth place.

cintre [sɛ̃tʀ] nm [portemanteau] coat-hanger.

cintré, e [sɛ̃tʀe] adj COUT close-fitting (at the waist), waisted.

CIO npr m **1.** (abr de Comité international olympique) IOC **2.** (abr de Centre d'information et d'orientation) information and orientation centre run by the French Education Ministry for schoolgoers, students and young people.

cirage [siʀaʒ] nm [cire] shoe polish ; [polissage] polishing ▶ **être dans le cirage** a) fam AÉRON to be flying blind b) fig to be groggy.

circoncis [siʀkɔ̃si] adj circumcised.

circoncision [siʀkɔ̃sizjɔ̃] nf circumcision.

circonférence [siʀkɔ̃feʀɑ̃s] nf **1.** GÉOM circumference **2.** [tour] periphery.

circonflexe [siʀkɔ̃flɛks] adj circumflex.

circonscription [siʀkɔ̃skʀipsjɔ̃] nf **1.** ADMIN & POL area, district ▶ **circonscription électorale** a) [nationale] constituency UK, district US b) [locale] ward UK **2.** GÉOM circumscription, circumscribing.

circonscrire [99] [siʀkɔ̃skʀiʀ] vt **1.** [limiter - extension, dégâts] to limit, to control ▶ **circonscrire un incendie** to bring a fire under control, to contain a fire **2.** [préciser] to define the limits ou scope of.

circonspect, e [siʀkɔ̃spɛ,ɛkt] adj [observateur, commentateur] cautious, wary ; [approche] cautious, circumspect *sout.*

circonstance [siʀkɔ̃stɑ̃s] nf **1.** [situation] ▸ **étant donné les circonstances** given the circumstances ou situation **2.** [conjoncture] circumstance, occasion ▸ **profiter de la circonstance** to seize the opportunity **3.** DR ▸ **circonstances aggravantes / atténuantes** aggravating / extenuating circumstances. ◈ **de circonstance** loc adj [approprié] appropriate, fitting.

circonstancié, e [siʀkɔ̃stɑ̃sje] adj detailed.

circonstanciel, elle [siʀkɔ̃stɑ̃sjɛl] adj GRAM adverbial.

circuit [siʀkɥi] nm **1.** AUTO & SPORT circuit ▸ **circuit automobile** racing circuit **2.** [randonnée] tour, trip ▸ **faire le circuit des châteaux / vins** to do a tour of the chateaux / vineyards **3.** ÉLECTR & ÉLECTRON circuit ▸ **circuit imprimé** printed circuit ▸ **circuit intégré** integrated circuit **4.** ÉCON channels ▸ **circuit de distribution** distribution channel **5.** [tuyaux] (pipe) system ▸ **circuit de refroidissement** cooling system **6.** EXPR **dans le circuit** : *elle est encore dans le circuit* she's still around. ◈ **en circuit fermé** loc adv **1.** ÉLECTRON in closed circuit **2.** [discuter, vivre] without any outside contact.

circulaire [siʀkylɛʀ] ◆ adj [rond] circular, round. ◆ nf circular.

circulation [siʀkylasjɔ̃] nf **1.** TRANSP : *la circulation des camions est interdite le dimanche* lorries are not allowed to run on Sundays ▸ **circulation aérienne / ferroviaire / routière** air / rail / road traffic **2.** [du sang, de l'air, d'un fluide] circulation / *avoir une bonne / mauvaise circulation* to have good / bad circulation **3.** [déplacement] spread, movement ▸ **la libre circulation des capitaux** free circulation of capital **4.** [circuit] ▸ **enlever** ou **retirer de la circulation a)** COMM to take off the market **b)** *fig* to take out of circulation ▸ **mettre en circulation a)** [argent] to put into circulation **b)** COMM to bring out, to put on the market.

circulatoire [siʀkylatwaʀ] adj [appareil] circulatory.

circuler [siʀkyle] vi **1.** [se déplacer - personne] to move / *circulez, il n'y a rien à voir* move along now, there's nothing to see ; TRANSP [conducteur] to drive ; [flux de voitures] to move ; [train] to run **2.** [air, fluide] to circulate **3.** [passer de main en main] to be passed around ou round / *le rapport circule* the report's being circulated / *faire circuler des faux billets* to put forged banknotes into circulation **4.** [se propager] to circulate ▸ **faire circuler des bruits** to spread rumours.

cire [siʀ] nf **1.** [encaustique] (wax) polish **2.** [dans une ruche] wax ▸ **cire d'abeille** beeswax.

ciré [siʀe] nm VÊT [gén] oilskin ; [de marin] sou'wester.

cirer [siʀe] vt **1.** [faire briller - meuble, parquet] to wax, to polish ; [-chaussure] to polish ▸ **cirer les bottes à qqn** *fam & fig* to lick sb's boots **2.** EXPR **n'en avoir rien à cirer** *tfam* : *il en a rien à cirer* he doesn't give a damn.

cirque [siʀk] nm **1.** LOISIRS [chapiteau] circus, big top ; [représentation] circus **2.** [lieu] : *c'est un vrai cirque ici !* it's chaos ou pandemonium in here ! **3.** *fam* [scène] ▸ **faire son cirque** to make a fuss **4.** GÉOGR cirque, corrie ; [sur la Lune] crater.

cirrhose [siʀoz] nf cirrhosis.

cisaille [sizaj] nf [outil] ▸ **cisaille, cisailles** (pair of) shears.

cisailler [3] [sizaje] vt **1.** [barbelés, tôle] to cut **2.** [couper grossièrement] to hack (at).

ciseaux [sizo] nmpl **1.** [outil] ▸ **(une paire de) ciseaux** (a pair of) scissors ▸ **ciseaux à ongles** nail scissors **2.** SPORT ▸ **saut en ciseaux** scissor jump.

ciseler [25] [sizle] vt MÉTALL [en défonçant] to engrave ; [en repoussant] to emboss / *son nez délicatement ciselé* fig her finely chiselled nose.

Cisjordanie [sisʒɔʀdani] npr f ▸ **la Cisjordanie** the West Bank.

citadelle [sitadɛl] nf **1.** CONSTR citadel **2.** [centre] stronghold.

citadin, e [sitadɛ̃,in] ◆ adj [habitude, paysage] city *(modif)*, town *(modif)*, urban ; [population] town-dwelling, city-dwelling, urban. ◆ nm, f city-dweller, town-dweller.

citation [sitasjɔ̃] nf **1.** [extrait] quotation **2.** DR summons ▸ **citation à comparaître a)** [pour un témoin] subpoena **b)** [pour un accusé] summons.

cité [site] nf **1.** [ville] city ; [plus petite] town **2.** [résidence] (housing) estate ou development 🇺🇸, council estate 🇬🇧 ▸ **les cités de banlieue** suburban housing estates *(in France, often evocative of poverty and delinquency)* ▸ **cité ouvrière** ≃ council estate 🇬🇧 ; ≃ housing project 🇺🇸 ▸ **cité de transit** transit camp ▸ **cité universitaire** hall(s) of residence 🇬🇧, dormitory 🇺🇸.

cité-dortoir [sitedɔʀtwaʀ] *(pl* cités-dortoirs*)* nf dormitory town, bedroom community 🇺🇸.

citer [3] [site] vt **1.** [donner un extrait de] to cite, to quote (from) **2.** [mentionner] to mention ▸ **citer qqn en exemple** to cite sb as an example **3.** [énumérer] to name, to quote, to list **4.** DR [témoin] to subpoena ; [accusé] to summons.

citerne [sitɛʀn] nf [cuve] tank ; [pour l'eau] water tank, cistern.

cité U [sitey] nf *fam* **abr de cité universitaire**.

citoyen, enne [sitwajɛ̃,ɛn] ◆ nm, f HIST & POL citizen. ◆ adj [personne, entreprise] socially responsible, civic-minded.

citoyenneté [sitwajɛnte] nf citizenship.

citron [sitʀɔ̃] nm BOT lemon ▸ **citron pressé** freshly squeezed lemon juice ▸ **citron vert** lime.

citronnade [sitʀɔnad] nf lemonade.

citronné, e [sitʀɔne] adj [gâteau] lemon-flavoured ; [pochette] lemon-scented ; [eau de toilette] lemon *(épithète)*.

citronnelle [sitʀɔnɛl] nf **1.** [aromate tropical] lemongrass **2.** [baume] citronella oil.

citronnier [sitʀɔnje] nm lemon tree.

citrouille [sitʀuj] nf **1.** [fruit] pumpkin **2.** *fam* [tête] nut.

civet [sivɛ] nm civet, stew / *civet de lièvre,* lièvre en civet civet of hare ; ≃ jugged hare.

civière [sivjɛʀ] nf stretcher.

civil, e [sivil] adj **1.** [non religieux] civil **2.** [non militaire] civilian. ◈ **civil** nm DR civil action / *porter une affaire au civil* to bring a case before the civil courts. ◈ **dans le civil** loc adv in civilian life. ◈ **en civil** loc adj ▸ **être en civil** [soldat] to be wearing civilian clothes ▸ **policier en civil** plain clothes policeman.

 civil ou **civilian ?**

Le mot anglais **civil** désigne tout ce qui concerne le citoyen. **Civilian** signifie « non militaire ».

civilement [sivilmɑ̃] adv DR ▸ **se marier civilement** to have a civil wedding, to get married at a registry office 🇬🇧 ou at city hall 🇺🇸 ▸ **être civilement responsable** to be legally responsible.

civilisation [sivilizasjɔ̃] nf **1.** SOCIOL civilization **2.** [action de civiliser] civilization, civilizing **3.** [fait d'être civilisé] civilization.

civilisé, e [sivilize] ◆ adj [nation, peuple] civilized / *on est chez des gens civilisés, ici ! fam* we're not savages! ◆ nm, f civilized person, member of a civilized society.

civiliser [3] [sivilize] vt to civilize, to bring civilization to.

civilité [sivilite] nf *litt* [qualité] politeness, polite behaviour, civility *sout.* ❖ **civilités** nfpl *litt* [paroles] polite greetings.

civique [sivik] adj civic ▸ **avoir l'esprit civique** to be public-spirited ▸ **éducation** ou **instruction civique** civics *(U).*

civisme [sivism] nm sense of citizenship, public-spiritedness.

cl (abr écrite de **centilitre**) cl.

clac [klak] interj [bruit - de fouet] crack ; [- d'une fenêtre] slam.

clafoutis [klafuti] nm *sweet dish made from cherries or other fruit and batter.*

clair, e [klɛʁ] adj **1.** [lumineux - pièce, appartement] light, bright ; [ciel] clear ▸ **par temps clair** in clear weather **2.** [limpide - eau, son] clear ▸ **d'une voix claire** in a clear voice **3.** [peu épais - sauce] thin ▸ **une soupe claire** a clear soup ; [rare] sparse **4.** [couleur - tissu, cheveux] light-coloured 🇬🇧, light-colored 🇺🇸, light / **vert** / **rose clair** light green / pink **5.** [précis - compte-rendu] clear / **se faire une idée claire de** to form a clear ou precise picture of **6.** [évident] clear, obvious ▸ **c'est clair et net** it's perfectly clear / *il n'a rien compris, c'est clair et net* he clearly hasn't understood a thing ▸ **c'est clair comme le jour** ou **comme de l'eau de roche** ou **comme deux et deux font quatre** it's crystal clear. ❖ **au clair** loc adv ▸ **mettre** ou **tirer qqch au clair** to clear sthg up, to clarify sthg / *il faut tirer cette affaire au clair* this matter must be cleared up, we must get to the bottom of this. ❖ **en clair** loc adv **1.** [sans code] ▸ **diffuser en clair** TV to broadcast unscrambled programmes **2.** [en d'autres termes] to put it plainly.

clairement [klɛʁmɑ̃] adv clearly.

claire-voie (pl claires-voies), **clairevoie*** [klɛʁvwa] nf [barrière] lattice, open-worked fence.

clairière [klɛʁjɛʁ] nf [dans une forêt] clearing, glade.

clairon [klɛʁɔ̃] nm MUS [instrument] bugle ; [joueur] bugler ; [orgue] clarion stop.

claironner [3] [klɛʁɔne] ◆ vi to shout. ◆ vt to proclaim far and wide, to broadcast (to all and sundry).

clairsemé, e [klɛʁsəme] adj [barbe, cheveux] sparse, thin ; [arbres] scattered ; [public] sparse.

clairvoyant, e [klɛʁvwajɑ̃, ɑ̃t] adj [lucide] clearsighted, perceptive.

clamer [3] [klame] vt **1.** [proclamer] ▸ **clamer son innocence** to protest one's innocence **2.** [crier] to clamour, to shout.

clameur [klamœʁ] nf clamour *(U)* 🇬🇧, clamor 🇺🇸 / *la clameur du marché montait* ou *les clameurs du marché montaient jusqu'à nos fenêtres* the hubbub of the market could be heard from our windows.

clamser [3] [klamse] vi *tfam* to kick the bucket.

clan [klɑ̃] nm **1.** SOCIOL clan **2.** *péj* [coterie] clan, coterie, clique.

clandestin, e [klɑ̃dɛstɛ̃, in] ◆ adj **1.** [secret] secret, underground, clandestine **2.** [illégal] illegal, illicit *sout.* ◆ nm, f [passager] stowaway ; [immigré] illegal immigrant.

clandestinement [klɑ̃dɛstinmɑ̃] adv **1.** [secrètement] secretly, in secret, clandestinely **2.** [illégalement] illegally, illicitly *sout* ▸ **faire entrer qqn clandestinement dans un pays** to smuggle sb into a country.

clandestinité [klɑ̃dɛstinite] nf secrecy, clandestine nature. ❖ **dans la clandestinité** loc adv underground ▸ **entrer dans la clandestinité** to go underground.

clapet [klapɛ] nm **1.** TECHNOL [soupape] valve **2.** *fam* [bouche] : *ferme ton clapet !* shut your mouth!

clapier [klapje] nm [à lapins] hutch.

clapotement [klapɔtmɑ̃] nm lapping.

clapoter [3] [klapɔte] vi [eau, vague] to lap.

clapotis [klapɔti] = clapotement.

claquage [klaka3] nm MÉD [muscle] strained muscle ; [ligament] strained ligament ▸ **se faire** ou **avoir un claquage** [muscle] to strain a muscle.

claque [klak] nf **1.** [coup] smack, slap **2.** THÉÂTRE claque **3.** 🇶🇧 [chaussure] rubber overshoe **4.** EXPR **j'en ai ma claque** *fam* a) [saturé] I've had it up to here b) [épuisé] I'm shattered 🇬🇧 ou bushed 🇺🇸.

claqué, e [klake] adj **1.** *fam* [éreinté] worn out, shattered 🇬🇧, bushed 🇺🇸 **2.** MÉD strained.

claquement [klakmɑ̃] nm [bruit violent] banging, slamming.

claquemurer [3] [klakmyʁe] ❖ **se claquemurer** vp *(emploi réfléchi)* to shut o.s. in ou away.

claquer [3] [klake] ◆ vt **1.** [fermer] to bang ou slam (shut) ▸ **claquer la porte** a) *pr* to slam the door b) *fig* to storm out ▸ **claquer la porte au nez de qqn** a) *pr* to slam the door in sb's face b) *fig* to send sb packing **2.** [faire résonner] : *claquer sa langue* to click one's tongue **3.** *fam* [dépenser] to spend **4.** *fam* [fatiguer] to wear out *(sép)* **5.** *fam* [gifler] to slap. ◆ vi **1.** [résonner - porte] to bang ; [- drapeau, linge] to flap ▸ **faire claquer ses doigts** to snap one's fingers / *faire claquer sa langue* to click one's tongue **2.** *fam* [mourir] to peg out ; [tomber en panne] to conk out **3.** [céder avec bruit - sangle] to snap ; [- baudruche, chewing-gum] to pop. ❖ **claquer de** v + prép ▸ **il claque des dents** his teeth are chattering ▸ **claquer des doigts** to snap one's fingers. ❖ **se claquer** vpt ▸ **se claquer un muscle** to strain ou to pull a muscle.

claquettes [klakɛt] nfpl **1.** DANSE tap-dancing ▸ **faire des claquettes** to tap-dance **2.** [tongs] flipflops.

clarification [klaʁifikasjɔ̃] nf [explication] clarification.

clarifier [9] [klaʁifje] vt **1.** [rendre limpide - suspension, beurre, sauce] to clarify ; [- vin] to settle **2.** [expliquer] to clarify, to make clear. ❖ **se clarifier** vpi [situation] to become clearer.

clarinette [klaʁinɛt] nf clarinet.

clarté [klaʁte] nf **1.** [lumière] light ▸ **la clarté du jour** daylight ; [luminosité] brightness **2.** [transparence] clarity, limpidness, clearness **3.** [intelligibilité] clarity, clearness / *son raisonnement n'est pas d'une grande clarté* his reasoning is not particularly clear.

classe [klas] nf
◆ nf
A. ENSEIGNEMENT 1. [salle] classroom **2.** [groupe] class ▸ **camarade de classe** classmate ▸ **classe de neige** *residential classes in the mountains for schoolchildren* ▸ **classe verte** *residential classes in the countryside for urban schoolchildren* **3.** [cours] class, lesson ▸ **faire la classe** a) [être enseignant] to teach b) [donner un cours] to teach ou to take a class **4.** [niveau] class, form 🇬🇧, grade 🇺🇸 ▸ **dans les grandes / petites classes** in the upper / lower forms 🇬🇧 ▸ **refaire** ou **redoubler une classe** to repeat a year ▸ **classes préparatoires** *schools specializing in preparing pupils to take grandes écoles entrance exams.*
B. DANS UNE HIÉRARCHIE 1. [espèce] class, kind ; MATH & SCI class ; [dans des statistiques] bracket, class, group ▸ **classe d'âge** age group / *classe de revenus* income bracket

2. [rang] class, rank **3.** POL & SOCIOL class ▶ **classe sociale** social class ▶ **l'ensemble de la classe politique** the whole of the political establishment ou class **4.** TRANSP class ▶ **billet de première / deuxième classe** first- / second-class ticket ▶ **classe affaires / économique** AÉRON business / economy class **5.** [niveau] quality, class ▶ **de première classe** first-class **6.** [distinction] class, style ▶ **avec classe** smartly, with elegance **7.** LING class ▶ **classe grammaticale** part of speech. **C. LANGAGE MILITAIRE** annual contingent / **la classe 70** the 1970 levy.
◆ adj fam ▶ **être classe** to be classy. ◆ **en classe** loc adv ▶ **aller en classe** to go to school / **il a l'âge d'aller en classe** he's of school age.

Classes préparatoires

After the **baccalauréat**, very successful students may choose to attend the **classes préparatoires**, intensive courses organized in **lycées**. Students are completely immersed in their subject and do little else than prepare for the competitive **grandes écoles** entrance exams. If a student fails to gain a place in a grande école, two years of **prépa** are considered equivalent to a certain amount of credits at a university. Classes préparatoires are divided into subject areas or **filières**: economics and commerce (known as prépa ECS), literature (the first year nicknamed "hypokhâgne" and the second "khâgne"), and mathematics (the first year commonly called "math sup" and the second "math spé").

classé, e [klase] adj **1.** [terminé] closed, dismissed **2.** [protégé] listed ▶ **monument / château classé** listed ou scheduled building / castle **3.** SPORT ▶ **joueur classé** [au tennis] ranked player.

classement [klasmã] nm **1.** [tri - de documents] classifying, ordering, sorting ; [- d'objets] sorting, grading / **faire un classement de livres** to sort out ou to classify books ; [rangement] filing **2.** CHIM grading **3.** [palmarès] ranking, placing ▶ **avoir un mauvais / bon classement** to do badly / well ▶ **premier au classement général** first overall **4.** ADMIN listing.

classer [3] [klase] vt **1.** [archiver - vieux papiers] to file (away) ; [- affaire] to close **2.** [agencer] to arrange, to classify, to sort **3.** INFORM to sequence **4.** ADMIN [site] to list, to schedule **5.** [définir] : **à sa réaction, je l'ai tout de suite classé** I could tell straight away what sort of person he was from his reaction. ◆ **se classer** vpi **1.** [dans une compétition] to finish, to rank / **se classer troisième** to rank third **2.** [prendre son rang] ▶ **se classer parmi** to rank among.

classeur [klasœʀ] nm **1.** [chemise] binder, folder, jacket US ▶ **classeur à anneaux** ring binder ▶ **classeur à feuilles mobiles** loose-leaf binder **2.** [tiroir] filing drawer ; [meuble] filing cabinet.

classification [klasifikasjõ] nf **1.** [répartition] classification **2.** [système] classification system.

classique [klasik] ◆ adj **1.** ENS classical ▶ **faire des études classiques** to study classics **2.** LING & LITTÉR classical ; DANSE & MUS [traditionnel] classical ; [dix-huitième siècle] classical, eighteenth-century ; ANTIQ classical **3.** [connu - sketch, plaisanterie, recette] classic ▶ **c'est le coup classique a)** [ça arrive souvent] that's typical! **b)** [une ruse connue] that's a well-known trick! ◆ nm **1.** LITTÉR [auteur] classical

author ; [œuvre] classic **2.** MUS [genre] ▶ **le classique** classical music ; [œuvre - gén] classic ; [- de jazz] (jazz) standard **3.** [style - d'habillement, de décoration] classic style.

classic ou classical ?

L'adjectif **classical** se réfère soit au classicisme gréco-romain, soit à la musique classique. Lorsque classique désigne ce qui relève d'une tradition, d'une norme, il faut le traduire par **classic**.

clause [kloz] nf DR clause, stipulation.

claustrer [3] [klostʀe] vt to confine ▶ **vivre claustré** to lead the life of a recluse. ◆ **se claustrer** vp (emploi réfléchi) to shut o.s. away / **elle s'est claustrée** she has become a recluse.

claustrophobe [klostʀɔfɔb] ◆ adj claustrophobic. ◆ nmf claustrophobe, claustrophobic.

claustrophobie [klostʀɔfɔbi] nf claustrophobia.

clavecin [klavsɛ̃] nm harpsichord.

clavicule [klavikyl] nf collarbone, clavicle spéc.

clavier [klavje] nm **1.** [d'une machine] keyboard ; [d'un téléphone] keypad **2.** MUS [d'un piano] keyboard ; [d'un orgue] manual.

clé [kle] nf **1.** [de porte, d'horloge, de boîte de conserve] key ; [d'un tuyau de poêle] damper ▶ **mettre la clé sous la porte** ou **le paillasson a)** pr to shut up shop **b)** fig to disappear overnight **2.** [outil] spanner US, wrench US ▶ **clé anglaise** ou **à molette** adjustable spanner US ou wrench US, monkey wrench ▶ **clé universelle** adjustable spanner US ou wrench US **3.** AUTO ▶ **clé de contact** ignition key **4.** INFORM ▶ **clé USB** USB key, USB stick **5.** MUS clef, key ; [touche] key ; [d'un instrument - à vent] finger-plate ; [- à corde] peg **6.** [moyen] : **la clé de la réussite** the key to success **7.** [explication] clue, key / **la clé du mystère** the key to the mystery **8.** ARCHIT ▶ **clé de voûte a)** pr keystone, quoin **b)** fig linchpin, cornerstone. ◆ **à clé** loc adv : **fermer une porte à clé** to lock a door. ◆ **à la clé** loc adv [au bout du compte] ▶ **avec... à la clé a)** [récompense] with... as a bonus **b)** [punition] with... into the bargain. ◆ **clé(s) en main** loc adv **1.** COMM ▶ **prix clé** ou **clés en main a)** [d'un véhicule] on-the-road price **b)** [d'une maison] all-inclusive price **2.** INDUST turnkey (modif). ◆ **sous clé** loc adv [à l'abri] ▶ **garder qqch sous clé** to lock sthg away, to put sthg under lock and key.

clean [klin] adj fam [personne] wholesome-looking, clean-cut.

clef^1 [kle] = **clé**.

clef^2 [kle] nm Suisse garden gate.

clématite [klematit] nf clematis.

clémence [klemãs] nf [pardon] leniency, mercy, clemency.

clément, e [klemã, ãt] adj **1.** MÉTÉOR mild **2.** [favorable] : **à une époque moins clémente** in less happy times.

clémentine [klematin] nf clementine.

clerc [klɛʀ] nm **1.** RELIG cleric **2.** [employé] ▶ **clerc de notaire** clerk.

clergé [klɛʀʒe] nm clergy, priesthood.

clérical, e, aux [klerikal, o] adj [du clergé] clerical.

clic [klik] interj & nm click.

cliché [kliʃe] nm **1.** PHOT [pellicule] negative ; [photo] photograph, shot **2.** péj [banalité] cliché.

client, e [klijã, ãt] nm, f [d'un magasin, d'un restaurant] customer ; [d'une banque, d'un salon de coiffure, d'un institut

de beauté] customer, client ; [d'un avocat] client ; [d'un hôtel] guest ; [d'un taxi] passenger / *je suis client chez eux* I'm one of their regular customers ▸ **à la tête du client**: *chez eux, c'est à la tête du client* they charge you what they feel like ▸ **gros client**: *le Mexique est un gros client des États-Unis* the United States does a lot of trade with Mexico.
clientèle [klijɑ̃tɛl] nf [clients] clientele, customers.
cligner [3] [kliɲe] vt [fermer] ▸ **cligner les yeux** to blink. ❖ **cligner de** v + prép [faire signe avec] ▸ **cligner de l'œil (en direction de qqn)** to wink (at sb).
clignotant, e [kliɲɔtɑ̃, ɑ̃t] adj [signal] flashing ; [lampe défectueuse] flickering ; [guirlande] twinkling, flashing. ❖ **clignotant** nm AUTO [lampe] indicator UK, turn signal US ▸ **mettre son clignotant** to indicate UK, to put on one's turn signal US.
clignoter [3] [kliɲɔte] vi **1.** [éclairer - étoile, guirlande] to twinkle ; [- signal] to flash (on and off) ; [- lampe défectueuse] to flicker **2.** [automobiliste] to indicate UK, to put on one's turn signal US.
clim [klim] (abr de **climatisation**) nf fam air conditioning, AC.
climat [klima] nm **1.** GÉOGR climate **2.** [ambiance] climate, atmosphere.
climatique [klimatik] adj **1.** MÉTÉOR weather (modif), climatic **2.** LOISIRS ▸ **centre / station climatique** health centre / resort.
climatisation [klimatizasjɔ̃] nf [dans un immeuble] air conditioning.
climatisé, e [klimatize] adj air-conditioned.
climatiseur [klimatizœr] nm air-conditioner, air-conditioning unit.
clin d'œil [klɛ̃dœj] (pl **clins d'œil**) nm **1.** [clignement] wink ▸ **faire un clin d'œil à qqn** to wink at sb **2.** [allusion] allusion, implied reference / *un clin d'œil à...* an allusion or an implied reference to... ❖ **en un clin d'œil** loc adv in the twinkling of an eye, in less than no time, in a flash.
clinique [klinik] ❖ adj clinical. ❖ nf **1.** [établissement] (private) clinic **2.** [service] teaching department (of a hospital).
clinquant, e [klɛ̃kɑ̃, ɑ̃t] adj **1.** [brillant] glittering, tinselly péj **2.** [superficiel - style] flashy.
clip [klip] nm **1.** [broche] clip, brooch **2.** [boucle d'oreille] clip-on earring **3.** [film] video.
clipart [klipart] nm INFORM clipart.
cliquable [klikabl] adj clickable.
clique [klik] nf [coterie] clique, gang, coterie. ❖ **cliques** nfpl ▸ **prendre ses cliques et ses claques a)** fam [partir] to up and leave **b)** [emporter ses affaires] to pack one's bags (and go).
cliquer [3] [klike] vi : *cliquer deux fois* to double-click.
cliqueter [27] [klikte] vi [clefs] to jangle ; [petite serrure] to click ; [grosse serrure] to clang, to clank ; [épées] to click ; [machine à écrire] to clack ; [assiettes] to clatter ; [verres] to clink ; [moteur] to pink.
In reformed spelling (see p. 16-18), this verb is conjugated like acheter : *il cliquètera, elle cliquèterait.*
cliquetis [klikti] nm [de clefs, de bijoux, de chaînes] jangling (U) ; [d'épées] rattling (U) ; [d'une machine à écrire] clacking (U) ; [d'assiettes] clatter, clattering (U) ; [de verres] clinking (U).
clitoris [klitɔris] nm clitoris.
clivage [klivaʒ] nm [séparation] divide, division ▸ **clivage social** social divide.
cloaque [klɔak] nm **1.** [égout] cesspool, open sewer **2.** litt [lieu sale] cesspool, cloaca litt **3.** ZOOL cloaca.

clochard, e [klɔʃar, ard] nm, f tramp.
cloche [klɔʃ] ❖ adj fam [idiot] stupid. ❖ nf **1.** [instrument, signal] bell **2.** CULIN dome, dish-cover ▸ **cloche à fromage** cheese dish (with cover), cheese-bell **3.** fam [personne] idiot.
cloche-pied [klɔʃpje] ❖ **à cloche-pied, à cloche-pied*** loc adv ▸ **sauter à cloche-pied** to hop.
clocher¹ [klɔʃe] nm [tour] bell-tower, church tower. ❖ **de clocher** loc adj ▸ **querelles de clocher** petty bickering.
clocher² [3] [klɔʃe] vi fam to be wrong / *qu'est-ce qui cloche ?* what's wrong ou up?
clochette [klɔʃɛt] nf [petite cloche] small bell / *clochette à vache* cow-bell.
cloison [klwazɔ̃] nf **1.** CONSTR partition **2.** AÉRON & NAUT bulkhead ▸ **cloison étanche** watertight bulkhead.
cloisonner [3] [klwazɔne] vt **1.** CONSTR to partition off (sép) **2.** [séparer] to compartmentalise.
cloître, cloitre* [klwatr] nm ARCHIT [d'un couvent] cloister ; [d'une cathédrale] close.
cloîtrer, cloitrer* [3] [klwatre] vt **1.** RELIG ▸ **cloîtrer qqn** to shut sb up in a convent **2.** [enfermer] to shut up ou away / *nous sommes cloîtrés toute la journée / dans notre atelier* we're shut up all day / in our workshop. ❖ **se cloîtrer, se cloitrer*** vp (emploi réfléchi) to shut o.s. away.
clonage [klɔnaʒ] nm cloning.
clone [klon] nm clone.
cloner [3] [klone] vt to clone.
clope [klɔp] nm ou nf fam fag UK, smoke US.
clopin-clopant, clopinclopant* [klɔpɛ̃klɔpɑ̃] adv [en boitant] ▸ **avancer clopin-clopant** to hobble along.
clopinettes [klɔpinɛt] nfpl fam ▸ **des clopinettes** (next to) nothing / *gagner des clopinettes* to earn peanuts.
cloporte [klɔpɔrt] nm ZOOL wood-louse.
cloque [klɔk] nf **1.** BOT & MÉD blister **2.** tfam EXPR ▸ **être en cloque** to have a bun in the oven.
clore [113] [klɔr] vt **1.** sout [fermer - porte, volet] to close, to shut ; [entourer - parc] to shut off (sép) **2.** [conclure] to conclude, to end, to finish / *les inscriptions seront closes le lundi 15* UNIV the closing date for enrolment is Monday 15th ▸ **l'incident est clos** the matter is closed.
clos, e [klo, kloz] adj [fermé] closed, shut ▸ **les yeux clos** with one's eyes shut.
clôture [klotyr] nf **1.** [barrière - en bois] fence ; [- en fil de fer] railings **2.** [fermeture] closing / **'clôture annuelle'** 'annual closure' ; [fin] end **3.** BOURSE close ▸ **à la clôture** at the close. ❖ **de clôture** loc adj [séance, date] closing ▸ **cours de clôture** BOURSE closing price. ❖ **en clôture** loc adv BOURSE at closing / *combien valait l'euro en clôture ?* what was the closing price of the euro?, what did the euro close at?
clôturer [3] [klotyre] vt **1.** [fermer] to enclose, to fence (in) (sép) **2.** [terminer] to close, to end **3.** BANQUE [compte] to close.
clou [klu] nm **1.** [pointe] nail **2.** [summum] ▸ **le clou de** the climax ou highlight of **3.** CULIN ▸ **clou de girofle** clove **4.** fam & péj [machine] ▸ **vieux clou a)** [voiture] old banger UK ou crate US **b)** [vélo] old boneshaker UK ou bike **5.** fam EXPR ▸ **pas un clou**: *ça ne vaut pas un clou* it's not worth a bean ▸ **des clous !** no way!, nothing doing! ❖ **clous** nmpl pedestrian ou zebra crossing UK, crosswalk US. ❖ **au clou** loc adv fam in the pawnshop ▸ **mettre qqch au clou** to pawn sthg, to hock sthg.
cloud computing [klaudkɔmpjutiŋ] nm cloud computing.

clouer [3] [klue] vt **1.** [fixer] to nail (down) **2.** [immobiliser - au sol] to pin down *(sép)* / *il est resté cloué au lit pendant trois jours* he was laid up in bed for three days.

clouté, e [klute] adj **1.** [décoré] studded **2.** [renforcé - chaussure, semelle] hobnailed ; [- pneu] studded.

clown [klun] nm clown ▸ **faire le clown** to clown, to fool around.

club [klœb] nm **1.** [groupe - de personnes] club ; [- de nations] group **2.** [centre] ▸ **club de gym** fitness centre, gym ▸ **club de rencontre(s)** singles club ▸ **club de vacances** holiday 🇬🇧 ou vacation 🇺🇸 village ▸ **club nautique** water sports centre.

club-sandwich [klœbsɑ̃dwitʃ] nm club sandwich.

cm (abr écrite de **centimètre**) cm.

CM nm (abr de **cours moyen**) ▸ **CM1** fourth year of primary school ▸ **CM2** fifth year of primary school.

CMU [seemy] (abr de **couverture maladie universelle**) nf health insurance system for the underprivileged ; ≃ Medicaid 🇺🇸.

CNDP (abr de **Centre national de documentation pédagogique**) npr m national organization for educational resources.

CNED [kned] (abr de **Centre national d'enseignement à distance**) npr French national distance learning centre.

CNIL [knil] (abr de **Commission nationale de l'informatique et des libertés**) npr f board which enforces data protection legislation.

CNPF (abr de **Conseil national du patronat français**) npr m former national council of French employers ; ≃ CBI 🇬🇧.

CNRS (abr de **Centre national de la recherche scientifique**) npr m national organization for scientific research ; ≃ SRC 🇺🇸.

coach [kotʃ] (pl coachs ou coaches) nm SPORT coach, trainer ; [conseiller professionnel] coach.

coacher [kotʃe] vt **1.** [entraîner] to coach **2.** [conseiller] to advise.

coaching [kotʃiŋ] nm coaching.

coaguler [3] [kɔagyle] ❖ **se coaguler** vpi [sang] to coagulate ; [lait] to curdle.

coaliser [3] [kɔalize] ❖ **se coaliser** vpi to form a coalition.

coalition [kɔalisjɔ̃] nf POL coalition ; péj conspiracy ▸ **gouvernement de coalition** coalition government.

coaltar [kɔltar] nm coaltar / *être dans le coaltar* fam & fig to be in a daze.

coasser [3] [kɔase] vi [grenouille] to croak.

COB, Cob [kɔb] (abr de **Commission des opérations de Bourse**) nf commission for supervision of stock exchange operations ; ≃ SIB 🇬🇧 ; ≃ SEC 🇺🇸.

cobalt [kɔbalt] nm cobalt.

cobaye [kɔbaj] nm guinea pig.

cobra [kɔbʀa] nm cobra.

coca [kɔka] nf **1.** BOT coca. ❖ **Coca®** nm inv fam [boisson] Coke®.

cocaïne [kɔkain] nf cocaine.

cocarde [kɔkaʀd] nf [en tissu] rosette ; HIST cockade.

cocasse [kɔkas] adj comical.

coccinelle [kɔksinɛl] nf ZOOL ladybird 🇬🇧, ladybug 🇺🇸.

coccyx [kɔksis] nm coccyx.

coche [kɔʃ] nm [voiture] stage coach ▸ **manquer** ou **rater** ou **louper le coche** to miss the boat.

cocher [3] [kɔʃe] vt to tick (off) 🇬🇧, to check (off) 🇺🇸.

cochère [kɔʃɛʀ] adj f ▸ **porte cochère** carriage entrance, porte cochère.

cocheur [kɔʃœʀ] nm 🇶 [golf] : *cocheur d'allée* pitching wedge / *cocheur de sable* sand wedge.

cochon, onne [kɔʃɔ̃, ɔn] fam ◆ adj **1.** [sale] dirty, filthy, disgusting **2.** [obscène] smutty, dirty, filthy. ◆ nm, f **1.** [vicieux] lecher **2.** [personne sale] (filthy) pig / *oh, le petit cochon !* [à un enfant] you mucky pup! ❖ **cochon** nm **1.** ZOOL pig ▸ **cochon de lait** suckling pig ▸ **sale comme un cochon** filthy dirty ▸ **manger comme un cochon** to eat like a pig **2.** [homme méprisable] dirty dog ▸ **cochon qui s'en dédit !** you've got a deal! ❖ **cochon d'Inde** nm guinea pig.

cochonnaille [kɔʃɔnaj] nf pork products.

cochonner [3] [kɔʃɔne] vt fam [dessin, chambre] to make a mess of.

cochonnerie [kɔʃɔnʀi] nf fam **1.** [chose médiocre] rubbish (U) 🇬🇧, trash (U) 🇺🇸 ; [nourriture - mal préparée] pigswill (U) ; [- de mauvaise qualité] junk food (U) **2.** [saleté] mess (U) ▸ **faire des cochonneries** to make a mess **3.** [obscénité] smut (U) ▸ **dire des cochonneries** to say filthy things.

cochonnet [kɔʃɔnɛ] nm **1.** [aux boules] jack **2.** [porcelet] piglet.

cocker [kɔkɛʀ] nm cocker spaniel.

cockpit [kɔkpit] nm cockpit.

cocktail [kɔktɛl] nm **1.** [boisson] cocktail ; [réception] cocktail party **2.** ARM ▸ **cocktail Molotov** Molotov cocktail.

coco [kɔko] nm **1.** fam [tête] nut / *il a rien dans le coco !* he's got nothing between the ears! **2.** fam [individu] ▸ **un drôle de coco** péj a shady customer **3.** fam [en appellatif - à un adulte] love 🇬🇧, honey 🇺🇸 ; [- à un enfant] sweetie **4.** langage enfantin [œuf] egg.

cocon [kɔkɔ̃] nm cocoon.

cocooning [kokuniŋ] nm cocooning 🇺🇸 / *on a fait du cocooning ce week-end* we had a quiet time at home this weekend.

cocorico [kɔkɔʀiko] nm **1.** pr cock-a-doodle-doo ▸ **faire cocorico** to crow **2.** fig expression of French national pride ▸ **cocorico !** three cheers for France!

cocotier [kɔkɔtje] nm coconut palm.

cocotte [kɔkɔt] nf **1.** [casserole] casserole dish ▸ **cuire à la cocotte** to casserole **2.** langage enfantin [poule] hen ▸ **cocotte en papier** paper bird **3.** [en appellatif] darling, love 🇬🇧, honey 🇺🇸 **4.** péj [femme] tart / *sentir* ou *puer la cocotte* to stink of cheap perfume. ❖ **en cocotte** loc adj [œuf] coddled.

Cocotte-Minute® [kɔkɔtminyt] nf pressure cooker.

cocu, e [kɔky] fam ◆ adj : *il est cocu* his wife's been unfaithful to him. ◆ nm, f [conjoint trompé] deceived husband (wife) / *elle l'a fait cocu* she was unfaithful to him.

code [kɔd] nm **1.** [ensemble de lois] code ▸ **le code (civil)** the civil code ▸ **code maritime** navigation laws ▸ **code pénal** penal code ▸ **code de la route** Highway Code 🇬🇧, rules of the road 🇺🇸 ▸ **code du travail** labour 🇬🇧 ou labor 🇺🇸 legislation **2.** [normes] code ▸ **code de la politesse** code of good manners **3.** [groupe de symboles] code ▸ **code (à) barres** bar code ▸ **code confidentiel** ou **personnel** [d'une carte de crédit] personal identification number, PIN ▸ **code couleur** colour 🇬🇧 ou color 🇺🇸 code ▸ **code postal** post 🇬🇧 ou zip 🇺🇸 code **4.** SCI ▸ **code génétique** genetic code. ❖ **codes** nmpl AUTO dipped headlights 🇬🇧, dimmed headlights 🇺🇸, low beams 🇺🇸. ❖ **en code** loc adv AUTO

▶ **se mettre en code** to dip one's headlights , to dim one's headlights , to put on the low beams .

 **Code postal**

A sequence of five numbers used for the automatic sorting of mail. The first two digits of a French postcode correspond to the code number of the **département**.

codé, e [kɔde] adj encoded, coded ▶ **message codé** cryptogram.

code-barres [kɔdbaʀ] (*pl* **codes-barres**) nm bar code.

coder [3] [kɔde] vt [chiffrer] to code, to encipher.

codétenu, e [kɔdetny] nm, f fellow-prisoner.

codirection [kɔdiʀɛksjɔ̃] nf joint management.

coefficient [kɔefisjɑ̃] nm **1.** MATH & PHYS coefficient **2.** [valeur] weight, weighting / *l'anglais est affecté du coefficient 3* English will be weighted at a rate equal to 300%.

 Coefficient

In **baccalauréat** examinations, the grade for each subject is multiplied by a **coefficient** which is determined by the type of **baccalauréat** chosen. For a **bac S**, which has a scientific bias, the **coefficient** for maths will be higher than the **coefficient** for philosophy, for example.

coéquipier, ère [kɔekipje, ɛʀ] nm, f teammate.

coercitif, ive [kɔɛʀsitif, iv] adj coercive.

cœur [kœʀ] nm

A. ORGANE 1. ANAT heart / *il est malade du cœur* he's got a heart condition **2.** [estomac] ▶ **avoir mal au cœur** to feel sick ▶ **ça me fait mal au cœur** it breaks my heart ▶ **lever** ou **soulever le cœur à qqn** to sicken sb, to turn sb's stomach.

B. SYMBOLE DE L'AFFECTIVITÉ 1. [pensées, for intérieur] heart ▶ **en avoir le cœur net**: *je veux en avoir le cœur net* I want to know ou to find out the truth **2.** [énergie, courage] courage / *tu n'aurais pas le cœur de la renvoyer !* you wouldn't have the heart to fire her! ▶ **allez, haut les cœurs !** come on, chin up! **3.** [humeur] ▶ **il est parti le cœur joyeux** ou **gai** he left in a cheerful mood **4.** [charité, bonté] ▶ **avoir du** ou **bon cœur** to be kind ou kind-hearted / *c'était un homme au grand cœur* ou *de cœur* he was a good man ▶ **avoir le cœur sur la main** to be very generous ▶ **avoir le cœur dur** ou **sec, avoir un cœur de pierre** to have a heart of stone **5.** [siège des émotions, de l'amour] heart / *des mots venus du (fond du) cœur* heartfelt words ▶ **aller droit au cœur**: *vos paroles me sont allées droit au cœur* your words went straight to my heart ▶ **briser le cœur à qqn** to break sb's heart ▶ **cela chauffe** ou **réchauffe le cœur** it warms the cockles of your heart, it's heartwarming ▶ **ses problèmes de cœur** the problems he has with his love life ▶ **avoir le cœur gros** to feel sad, to have a heavy heart.

C. PERSONNE 1. [personne ayant telle qualité] ▶ **c'est un cœur d'or** he has a heart of gold **2.** [terme d'affection] darling, sweetheart.

D. CENTRE 1. [d'un chou, d'une salade, d'un fromage] heart ; [d'un fruit, d'un réacteur nucléaire] core ; [d'une ville] heart, centre ▶ **cœur de palmier** palm heart ▶ **cœur d'artichaut** pr artichoke heart **2.** [d'un débat] central point.

E. OBJET EN FORME DE CŒUR JEUX : *dame / dix de cœur* queen / ten of hearts / *jouer à* ou *du cœur* to play hearts. ❖ **à cœur** loc adv **1.** [avec sérieux] ▶ **prendre les choses à cœur** to take things to heart ▶ **tenir à cœur à qqn**: *ce rôle me tient beaucoup à cœur* this part means a lot to me **2.** CULIN ▶ **fromage fait à cœur** fully ripe cheese. ❖ **à cœur joie** loc adv to one's heart's content / *s'en donner à cœur joie* to have tremendous fun ou a tremendous time. ❖ **à cœur ouvert** loc adj [opération] open-heart (*modif*). ❖ **au cœur de** loc prép ▶ **au cœur de l'été** at the height of summer / *au cœur de la nuit* in the ou at dead of night / *au cœur de la ville* in the centre of town, in the town centre. ❖ **de bon cœur** loc adv [volontiers - donner] willingly ; [- rire, manger] heartily ; [- parler] readily ▶ *c'est de bon cœur: ne me remerciez pas, c'est de bon cœur (que je vous ai aidé)* no need to thank me, it was a pleasure (helping you). ❖ **de tout cœur** loc adv wholeheartedly ▶ **être de tout cœur avec qqn** [condoléances] to sympathize wholeheartedly with sb. ❖ **de tout mon cœur, de tout son cœur** loc adv [sincèrement - aimer, remercier] with all my / his, etc. heart ; [- féliciter] warmly, wholeheartedly. ❖ **par cœur** loc adv [apprendre, connaître] by heart ▶ **connaître qqn par cœur** to know sb inside out. ❖ **sur le cœur** loc adv ▶ **la mousse au chocolat m'est restée sur le cœur** pr the chocolate mousse made me feel sick ▶ **avoir qqch sur le cœur** to have sthg on one's mind.

coexister [3] [kɔɛgziste] vi ▶ **coexister (avec)** to coexist (with).

coffre [kɔfʀ] nm **1.** [caisse] box, chest ▶ **coffre à jouets** toybox **2.** AUTO boot , trunk  **3.** [coffre-fort] safe, strongbox ▶ **les coffres de l'État** the coffers of the State ; BANQUE safe-deposit box **4.** fam [poitrine] chest ; [voix] (big) voice ▶ **avoir du coffre** [du souffle] to have a good pair of lungs.

coffre-fort [kɔfʀəfɔʀ] (*pl* **coffres-forts**) nm safe, strongbox.

coffrer [3] [kɔfʀe] vt fam [emprisonner] to put behind bars.

coffret [kɔfʀɛ] nm [petit coffre] box, case ▶ **coffret à bijoux** jewellery  ou jewelry  box.

cogestion [kɔʒɛstjɔ̃] nf joint management ou administration.

cogiter [3] [kɔʒite] hum vi to cogitate / *il faut que je cogite !* I must put my thinking cap on!

cognac [kɔɲak] nm [gén] brandy ; [de Cognac] Cognac.

cogner [3] [kɔɲe] ◆ vi **1.** [heurter] to bang, to knock ▶ **cogner à la fenêtre a)** [fort] to knock on the window **b)** [légèrement] to tap on the window **2.** fam [user de violence] ▶ **cogner sur qqn** to beat sb up / *ça va cogner* things are going to get rough. ◆ vt **1.** [entrer en collision avec] to bang ou to knock ou to smash into **2.** fam [battre] to whack, to wallop. ◆ **se cogner** vpi **1.** [se faire mal] ▶ **je me suis cogné** I banged into something **2.** [se faire mal] ▶ **je m'en suis cogné** tfam: *il s'en cogne* he doesn't give a damn ou monkey's .

cognitif, ive [kɔgnitif, iv] adj cognitive.

cohabitation [kɔabitasjɔ̃] nf **1.** [vie commune] cohabitation, cohabiting, living together **2.** POL coexistence of an elected head of state and an opposition parliamentary majority.

cohabiter [3] [kɔabite] vi **1.** [partenaires] to cohabit, to live together ; [amis] to live together **2.** [coexister] to coexist.

cohérence [kɔeʀɑ̃s] nf [gén & OPT] coherence / *manque de cohérence* inconsistency.

cohérent, e [kɔeʀɑ̃, ɑ̃t] adj **1.** [logique] coherent **2.** [fidèle à soi-même] consistent ▸ **être cohérent** to be true to o.s.

cohésion [kɔezjɔ̃] nf [solidarité] cohesion, cohesiveness.

cohue [kɔy] nf **1.** [foule] crowd, throng **2.** [bousculade] ▸ **dans la cohue** amidst the general pushing and shoving, in the (general) melee.

coi, coite [kwa, kwat] adj speechless ▸ **en rester coi** to be speechless ▸ **se tenir coi** to keep quiet.

coiffage [kwafaʒ] nm ▸ **mousse / gel de coiffage** styling mousse / gel.

coiffant, e [kwafɑ̃, ɑ̃t] adj ▸ **gel coiffant** styling gel.

coiffer [3] [kwafe] vt **1.** [cheveux - avec un peigne] to comb ; [- avec une brosse] to brush ▸ **cheveux faciles / difficiles à coiffer** manageable / unmanageable hair **2.** [réaliser la coiffure de] : *elle s'est fait coiffer par Paolo, c'est Paolo qui l'a coiffée* she had her hair done by Paolo **3.** [diriger] to control ▸ **elle coiffe plusieurs services** she's in charge of several departments **4.** EXPR coiffer qqn au ou sur le poteau to pip sb at the post UK, to pass sb up US ▸ **se faire coiffer au poteau** to be pipped at the post UK, to be nosed out. ❖ **se coiffer** vp *(emploi réfléchi)* [se peigner] to comb one's hair ; [arranger ses cheveux] to do one's hair.

coiffeur, euse [kwafœʀ, øz] nm, f hairdresser, hair stylist ▸ **aller chez le coiffeur** to go to the hairdresser's. ❖ **coiffeuse** nf dressing-table.

coiffure [kwafyʀ] nf **1.** [coupe] hairdo, hairstyle **2.** [technique] ▸ **la coiffure** hairdressing.

coin [kwɛ̃] nm **1.** [angle] corner / *le coin de la rue* the corner of the street **2.** [endroit quelconque] place, spot / *dans un coin de la maison* somewhere in the house ▸ **bon coin**: *il connaît les bons coins* he knows all the right places ; [espace réservé] ▸ **le coin des bricoleurs** COMM the do-it-yourself department ; *(suivi d'un nom, avec ou sans trait d'union)* ▸ **coin cuisine** kitchen recess ; [à la campagne] corner, place, spot ▸ **connaître qqch dans les coins** to know sthg like the back of one's hand ▸ **le petit coin** fam & euphém the smallest room **3.** [parcelle] patch, plot / *il reste un coin de ciel bleu* there's still a patch of blue sky. ❖ **au coin** loc adv [de la rue] on ou at the corner / *mettre un enfant au coin* to make a child stand in the corner (as punishment). ❖ **dans le coin** loc adv [dans le quartier - ici] locally, around here ; [- là-bas] locally, around there / *et Victor ? — il est dans le coin* where's Victor? — somewhere around. ❖ **dans son coin** loc adv ▸ **laisser qqn dans son coin** to leave sb alone ▸ **rester dans son coin** to keep oneself to oneself. ❖ **du coin** loc adj [commerce] local ▸ **les gens du coin a)** [ici] people who live round here, the locals **b)** [là-bas] people who live there, the locals / *désolé, je ne suis pas du coin* sorry, I'm not from around here.

coincé, e [kwɛ̃se] adj fam **1.** péj [inhibé] repressed, hung-up **2.** [mal à l'aise] tense, uneasy.

coincer [16] [kwɛ̃se] ❖ vt **1.** [immobiliser - volontairement] to wedge ; [- accidentellement] to catch, to stick, to jam / *j'ai coincé la fermeture de ma robe* I got the zip of my dress stuck **2.** fam [attraper] to corner, to nab, to collar / *je me suis fait coincer dans le couloir par Darival* I got cornered by Darival in the corridor **3.** fam [retenir] : *plus de trains ? je suis coincé, maintenant !* the last train's gone? I'm in a real fix now! / *elle est coincée entre ses convictions et les exigences de la situation* she's torn between her convictions and the demands of the situation **4.** [mettre en difficulté - par une question] to catch out *(sép)* UK, to put on the spot / *là, ils t'ont coincé !* they've got you there! ❖ vi [être entravé] to stick / *les négociations*

coincent the discussions have come to a sticking point ▸ **ça coince (quelque part)** fam there's a hitch somewhere. ❖ **se coincer** ◆ vpi [se bloquer - clef, fermeture] to jam, to stick. ◆ vpt ▸ **se coincer la main / le pied** to have one's hand / foot caught.

coïncidence [kɔɛ̃sidɑ̃s] nf [hasard] chance ▸ **c'est (une) pure coïncidence** it's purely coincidental. ❖ **par coïncidence** loc adv coincidentally, by coincidence.

coïncider [3] [kɔɛ̃side] vi **1.** [se produire ensemble] to coincide / *nos anniversaires coïncident* our birthdays fall on the same day **2.** [concorder] to concord ▸ **les deux témoignages coïncident** the two statements are consistent.

coing [kwɛ̃] nm quince.

coït [kɔit] nm coitus.

coite [kwat] f ⟶ **coi**.

coke [kɔk] nf fam coke.

col [kɔl] nm **1.** COUT collar ▸ **col blanc / bleu** white-collar / blue-collar worker ▸ **col châle** shawl collar ▸ **col cheminée** turtleneck ▸ **col chemisier** shirt collar ▸ **col Claudine** Peter Pan collar ▸ **col Mao** Mao collar ▸ **col marin** sailor's collar ▸ **col roulé** polo neck UK, turtleneck US ▸ **col V** [d'une bouteille] neck **3.** ANAT cervix, neck ▸ **col du fémur** neck of the thighbone ▸ **col de l'utérus** neck of the womb **4.** GÉOGR pass, col.

colchique [kɔlʃik] nm colchicum ▸ **colchique d'automne** autumn crocus.

coléoptère [kɔleɔptɛʀ] nm member of the Coleoptera.

colère [kɔlɛʀ] nf **1.** [mauvaise humeur] anger, rage ▸ **passer sa colère sur qqn** to take out one's bad temper on sb ▸ **avec colère** angrily, in anger ▸ **colère bleue** ou **noire** towering rage **2.** [crise] fit of anger ou rage ; [d'un enfant] tantrum ▸ **piquer** fam ou **faire une colère** [adulte] to fly into a temper **b)** [enfant] to have ou to throw a tantrum **3.** litt [des éléments, des dieux] wrath. ❖ **en colère** loc adj angry, livid, mad ▸ **être en colère contre qqn** to be angry with sb ▸ **ou at sb** US ▸ **mettre qqn en colère** to make sb angry ▸ **se mettre en colère** to flare up, to lose one's temper.

coléreux, euse [kɔleʀø, øz], **colérique** [kɔleʀik] adj [personne] irritable, quick-tempered.

colibri [kɔlibʀi] nm hummingbird, colibri.

colin [kɔlɛ̃] nm [lieu noir] coley UK, pollock US ; [lieu jaune] pollack ; [merlan] whiting ; [merlu] hake.

colin-maillard [kɔlɛ̃majaʀ] (*pl* **colin-maillards**) nm blind man's buff.

colique [kɔlik] nf **1.** fam [diarrhée] diarrhoea UK, diarrhea US ▸ **avoir la colique** to have diarrhoea **2.** MÉD [douleur] colic, stomach ache.

colis [kɔli] nm package US, packet, parcel UK ▸ **colis piégé** parcel UK ou package US bomb.

colite [kɔlit] nf colitis.

collabo [kɔlabo] nmf péj HIST collaborationist.

collaborateur, trice [kɔlabɔʀatœʀ, tʀis] nm, f **1.** [aide] associate **2.** [membre du personnel] member of staff.

collaboratif, ive [kɔlabɔʀatif, iv] adj : *c'est un travail collaboratif* it's a collaborative effort ▸ **encyclopédie collaborative** collaborative encyclopedia ▸ **espace collaboratif** INFORM collaborative space.

collaboration [kɔlabɔʀasjɔ̃] nf **1.** [aide] collaboration, cooperation, help ▸ **en collaboration étroite avec** in close cooperation with **2.** HIST [politique] collaborationist policy ; [période] collaboration.

collaborer [3] [kɔlabɔʀe] vi **1.** [participer] to participate ▸ **collaborer à** a) to take part ou to participate in **b)** PRESSE to write for, to contribute to, to be a contributor to **2.** péj HIST to collaborate.

collage [kɔlaʒ] nm ART collage.

collant, e [kɔlɑ̃, ɑ̃t] adj **1.** [adhésif] adhesive, sticking ; [poisseux] sticky **2.** [moulant] tightfitting **3.** *fam & péj* [importun] limpet-like ❯ **qu'il est collant ! a)** [importun] he just won't leave you alone! **b)** [enfant] he's so clinging!, he won't give you a minute's peace! ❖ **collant** nm **1.** [bas] (pair of) tights ⓤ, panty hose ⓤ *(U)* **2.** [de danse] leotard. ❖ **collante** nf *arg scol* [convocation] *letter asking a student to present himself for an exam.*

collatéral, e, aux [kɔlateʁal, o] adj **1.** [de chaque côté] collateral *sout* **2.** *fig* [dégâts, dommages] collateral / *effets collatéraux* collateral effects.

collation [kɔlasjɔ̃] nf [repas] light meal, snack.

colle [kɔl] nf **1.** [glu] glue, adhesive **2.** *fam* [énigme] trick question, poser, teaser / *là, vous me posez une colle !* you've got me there! **3.** *arg scol* [examen] oral test ; [retenue] detention ❯ **mettre une colle à qqn** to keep sb behind (in detention).

collecte [kɔlɛkt] nf **1.** [ramassage] collection **2.** INFORM ❯ **collecte des données** data collection ou gathering **3.** [quête] collection ❯ **faire une collecte** to collect money, to make a collection.

collecteur, trice [kɔlɛktœʁ, tʁis] nm, f ADMIN ❯ **collecteur d'impôts** tax collector.

collectif, ive [kɔlɛktif, iv] adj **1.** [en commun] collective, common **2.** [de masse] general, mass *(modif)*, public ❯ **suicide collectif** mass suicide ❯ **licenciements collectifs** mass redundancies **3.** TRANSP group *(modif)* **4.** GRAM collective. ❖ **collectif** nm **1.** GRAM collective noun **2.** FIN ❯ **collectif budgétaire** interim budget, extra credits.

collection [kɔlɛksjɔ̃] nf **1.** [collecte] collecting / *il fait collection de timbres* he collects stamps **2.** [ensemble de pièces] collection **3.** COMM [série - gén] line, collection ; [- de livres] collection, series ❯ **dans la collection jeunesse** in the range of books for young readers / *la collection complète des œuvres de Victor Hugo* the collected works of Victor Hugo **4.** VÊT collection ❯ **les collections** [présentations] fashion shows ❯ **les collections d'été / d'hiver** the summer / winter collections.

collectionner [3] [kɔlɛksjɔne] vt [tableaux, timbres] to collect.

collectionneur, euse [kɔlɛksjɔnœʁ, øz] nm, f collector.

collectivité [kɔlɛktivite] nf **1.** [société] community **2.** ADMIN ❯ **les collectivités locales a)** [dans un État] the local authorities **b)** [dans une fédération] the federal authorities.

collector [kɔlɛktɔʁ] nm collector's edition / *coffret collector* boxed collector's set.

collège [kɔlɛʒ] nm **1.** ÉDUC school ❯ **collège privé / technique** private / technical school ❯ **collège d'enseignement secondaire** = CES ; RELIG private school *(run by a religious organization)* **2.** [corps constitué] college **3.** ADMIN body ❯ **collège électoral** body of electors, constituency.

> ⚠ Évitez d'employer le mot anglais **college** pour désigner un établissement secondaire en France, car dans le monde anglo-saxon ce mot désigne le plus souvent une université.

collégial, e, aux [kɔleʒjal, o] adj collegial, collegiate.

collégialement [kɔleʒjalmɑ̃] adv [délibérer, statuer] collegially.

collégien, enne [kɔleʒjɛ̃, ɛn] nm, f schoolkid, schoolboy (schoolgirl).

collègue [kɔlɛg] nmf [employé] colleague, fellow-worker ❯ **collègue de bureau** : *je l'ai prêté à un collègue de bureau* I lent it to somebody at the office.

coller [3] [kɔle] ❖ vt **1.** [fixer - étiquette, timbre] to stick (down) ; [- tissu, bois] to glue (on) ; [- papier peint] to paste (up) ; [- affiche] to post, to stick up *(sép)*, to put up *(sép)* **2.** [fermer - enveloppe] to close up *(sép)*, to stick down *(sép)* **3.** [appuyer] to press / *coller son nez à la vitre* to press one's face to the window ❯ **coller qqn au mur** to put sb against a wall **4.** *fam* ÉDUC [punir] to keep in *(sép)* ❯ **se faire coller** to get a detention **5.** *fam* [mettre - chose] to dump, to stick ; [- personne] to put, to stick / *ils l'ont collée en pension / en prison* they stuck her in a boarding school / put her in jail / *je vais lui coller mon poing sur la figure !* I'm going to thump him on the nose! **6.** *fam* [imposer] to foist on, to saddle with ❯ **coller qqch / qqn à qqn** : *ils m'ont collé le bébé pour la semaine* they've lumbered ⓤ ou saddled me with the baby for a week. ❖ vi **1.** [adhérer - timbre] to stick ; [être poisseux] to be sticky ❯ **coller aux basques** ou **aux semelles de qqn** *fam* to stick to sb like glue ❯ **coller au derrière** *fam* ou **aux fesses**, *tfam* de qqn *fig* to stick to sb like a limpet **2.** [vêtement] to cling ❯ **coller à la peau de qqn a)** *pr* to cling to sb **b)** *fig* to be inherent to ou innate in sb **3.** *fam* [aller bien] ❯ **ça colle !** it's OK!, right-ho! ⓤ ❯ **ça ne colle pas** it doesn't work, something's wrong / *ça ne colle pas entre eux* they're not hitting it off very well. ❖ **se coller** vpi **1.** *fam* [s'installer] : *les enfants se sont collés devant la télé* the children plonked themselves down in front of the TV **2.** ⟨EXPR⟩ **se coller ensemble** *tfam* [vivre ensemble] to shack up together ❯ **s'y coller** *fam* [s'atteler à un problème, une tâche] to make an effort to do sthg, to set about doing sthg.

collet [kɔlɛ] nm **1.** [col] collar ❯ **mettre la main au collet de qqn** to get hold of sb, to collar sb *fam* ❯ **être collet monté** to be straight-laced **2.** [piège] noose, snare.

collier [kɔlje] nm **1.** JOAILL necklace, necklet ❯ **collier de perles** string of pearls ❯ [parure] collar ❯ **collier de fleurs** garland of flowers **3.** [courroie - pour chien, chat] collar ❯ **collier antipuces** flea collar ; *fig* ❯ **donner un coup de collier** to make a special effort ❯ **reprendre le collier** to get back into harness ou to the treadmill *péj* **4.** [de plumes, de poils] collar, frill, ring ❯ **collier (de barbe)** short ou clipped beard.

collimateur [kɔlimatœʁ] nm ASTRON & OPT collimator ; ARM sight ❯ **avoir qqn dans le collimateur** ou **son collimateur** to have one's eye on sb.

colline [kɔlin] nf hill ❯ **les collines** [au pied d'un massif] the foothills.

collision [kɔlizjɔ̃] nf [choc] collision, impact ❯ **entrer en collision avec** to collide with ; AUTO crash ❯ **collision en chaîne** ou **série** (multiple) pile-up.

colloque [kɔlɔk] nm conference, colloquium, seminar.

collyre [kɔliʁ] nm eyewash, antiseptic eye lotion.

colmater [3] [kɔlmate] vt [boucher] to fill in *(sép)*, to plug, to repair ❯ **colmater les brèches** *pr & fig* to close the gaps.

colo [kɔlo] nf *fam* (children's) holiday camp ⓤ summer camp ⓤ.

coloc [kɔlɔk] *fam* ❖ nmf [colocataire - dans une maison] housemate ⓤ, roommate ⓤ ; [- dans un appartement] flatmate ⓤ, roommate ⓤ. ❖ nf [colocation] shared accommodation ❯ **habiter en coloc** to live in shared accommodation.

colocataire [kɔlɔkatɛʁ] nmf ADMIN cotenant ; [gén] flatmate ⓤ, roommate ⓤ.

colocation [kɔlɔkasjɔ̃] nf joint tenancy, joint occupancy.

colombage [kɔlɔ̃baʒ] ❖ **à colombages** loc adj half-timbered.

colombe [kɔlɔ̃b] nf dove.

Colombie [kɔlɔ̃bi] npr f ▸ **(la) Colombie** Colombia.

colombien, enne [kɔlɔ̃bjɛ̃, ɛn] adj Columbian. ❖ **Colombien, enne** nm, f Columbian.

colon [kɔlɔ̃] nm [pionnier] colonist, settler.

côlon [kolɔ̃] nm colon.

colonel, elle [kɔlɔnɛl] nm, f [de l'armée - de terre] colonel ; [- de l'air] group captain 🇬🇧, colonel 🇺🇸.

colonial, e, aux [kɔlɔnjal, o] adj colonial.

colonialisme [kɔlɔnjalism] nm colonialism.

colonialiste [kɔlɔnjalist] ❖ adj colonialistic. ❖ nmf colonialist.

colonie [kɔlɔni] nf **1.** [population] settlement **2.** POL [pays] colony ; [fondation] ▸ **colonie pénitentiaire** penal colony **3.** [communauté] community, (little) group **4.** LOISIRS ▸ **colonie (de vacances)** organized holidays for children ▸ **l'été dernier, j'ai fait une** ou **je suis allé en colonie** [enfant] I went to summer camp last year 🇺🇸.

Colonie de vacances
The **colonie de vacances**, or **colo**, is an integral part of childhood for many French people. The **colonie** is a sort of summer camp; the children are supervised by **moniteurs** (group leaders), who organize games and activities.

colonisation [kɔlɔnizasjɔ̃] nf [conquête] colonization.

coloniser [3] [kɔlɔnize] vt POL to colonize.

colonne [kɔlɔn] nf **1.** ARCHIT column, pillar **2.** ANAT ▸ **colonne (vertébrale)** backbone, spinal column spéc. ❖ **en colonne** loc adv ▸ **en colonne par trois / quatre** in threes / fours.

colorant [kɔlɔrɑ̃] nm colouring 🇬🇧, coloring 🇺🇸, dye, pigment / **'sans colorants'** 'no artificial colouring'.

coloration [kɔlɔrasjɔ̃] nf **1.** [couleur] pigmentation, colouring 🇬🇧, coloring 🇺🇸 **2.** [chez le coiffeur] hair tinting / **se faire faire une coloration** to have one's hair tinted **3.** [tendance] ▸ **coloration politique** political colour ou tendency.

coloré, e [kɔlɔre] adj **1.** [teinté] brightly coloured 🇬🇧 ou colored 🇺🇸 ; [bariolé] multicoloured 🇬🇧, multicolored 🇺🇸 **2.** [expressif] colourful 🇬🇧, colorful 🇺🇸, vivid, picturesque.

colorer [3] [kɔlɔre] vt [teinter - dessin, objet] to colour 🇬🇧, to color 🇺🇸 ; [- ciel, visage] to tinge, to colour 🇬🇧, to color 🇺🇸 ▸ **colorer qqch en rouge / jaune** to colour sthg red / yellow.

coloriage [kɔlɔrjaʒ] nm **1.** [technique] colouring 🇬🇧, coloring 🇺🇸 ▸ **faire du coloriage** ou **des coloriages** to colour (a drawing) **2.** [dessin] coloured drawing.

colorier [9] [kɔlɔrje] vt to colour in 🇬🇧, to color in 🇺🇸.

coloris [kɔlɔri] nm [couleur] colour 🇬🇧, color 🇺🇸 ; [nuance] shade.

colorisation [kɔlɔrizasjɔ̃] nf colourization 🇬🇧, colorization 🇺🇸.

coloscopie [kɔlɔskɔpi], **colonoscopie** [kɔlɔnɔskɔpi] nf colonoscopy.

colossal, e, aux [kɔlɔsal, o] adj huge, colossal.

colosse [kɔlɔs] nm [statue] colossus ▸ **un colosse aux pieds d'argile** an idol with feet of clay.

colporter [3] [kɔlpɔrte] vt **1.** [vendre] to hawk, to peddle **2.** [répandre] to hawk about (sép).

coltiner [3] [kɔltine] ❖ **se coltiner** vpt fam **1.** [porter] : **se coltiner une valise / boîte** to lug a suitcase / box

around **2.** [supporter - corvée] to take on (sép), to put up with (insép) ; [- personne indésirable] to put up with.

colza [kɔlza] nm colza, rape.

coma [kɔma] nm ▸ **être / tomber dans le coma** to be in / to go ou to fall into a coma ▸ **être dans un coma dépassé** to be brain dead.

comateux, euse [kɔmatø, øz] adj comatose.

combat [kɔ̃ba] ❖ v ⟶ **combattre.** ❖ nm **1.** MIL battle, fight ▸ **combat aérien / naval** air / sea battle ▸ **combat d'arrière-garde** pr & fig rearguard action ▸ **des combats de rue** street fighting ▸ **aller au combat** : **les tanks ne sont jamais allés au combat** the tanks never went into battle **2.** [lutte physique] fight ▸ **combat corps à corps** hand-to-hand combat ; SPORT contest, fight ▸ **combat de boxe** boxing match **3.** [lutte morale, politique] struggle, fight ▸ **mener le bon combat** to fight for a just cause.

combatif, ive, combattif*, ive [kɔ̃batif, iv] adj [animal] aggressive ; [personne] combative, aggressive, pugnacious litt / **être d'humeur combative** to be full of fight.

combativité, combattivité* [kɔ̃bativite] nf combativeness, aggressiveness, pugnacity litt.

combattant, e [kɔ̃batɑ̃, ɑ̃t] nm, f MIL combatant, fighter, soldier ; [adversaire] fighter.

combattre [83] [kɔ̃batʁ] vt **1.** MIL to fight (against) ▸ **combattre l'ennemi** to give battle to the enemy **2.** [s'opposer à - inflation, racisme] to combat, to fight, to struggle against ; [- politique] to oppose, to fight / **il a longtemps combattu la maladie** he fought ou struggled against the disease for a long time **3.** [agir contre - incendie] to fight ; [- effets] to combat.

combien [kɔ̃bjɛ̃] ❖ adv **1.** [pour interroger sur une somme] how much / **c'est combien ?, ça fait combien ?** how much is it? / **combien coûte ce livre ?** how much is this book?, how much does this book cost? / **l'indice a augmenté de combien ?** how much has the rate gone up by? **2.** [pour interroger sur le nombre] how many ▸ **combien sont-ils ?** how many of them are there? **3.** [pour interroger sur la distance, la durée, la mesure, etc.] ▸ **combien tu pèses ?** how much do you weigh? ▸ **combien tu mesures ?** how tall are you? / **combien y a-t-il de Londres à Paris ?** how far is it from London to Paris? / **de combien votre frère est-il votre aîné ?** how much older than you is your brother? **4.** [en emploi exclamatif] how / **vous ne pouvez pas savoir combien il est distrait !** you wouldn't believe how absent-minded he is! ▸ **ô combien !** litt & hum : **elle a souffert, ô combien !** she suffered, oh how she suffered! ❖ nm inv ▸ **le combien sommes-nous ?** what's the date (today)? ❖ **combien de** loc dét [pour interroger - suivi d'un nom non comptable] how much ; [- suivi d'un nom comptable] how many ▸ **combien de fois** how many times, how often / **combien de temps resterez-vous ?** how long will you be staying?

combientième [kɔ̃bjɛ̃tjɛm] adj interr : **c'est la combientième fois que je te le dis ?** how many times have I told you?, I must have told you umpteen times!, if I've told you once I've told you a hundred times!

combinaison [kɔ̃binɛzɔ̃] nf **1.** [d'un cadenas] combination **2.** INFORM ▸ **combinaison de code** password **3.** MATH combination **4.** VÊT [sous-vêtement] slip ; [vêtement] ▸ **combinaison de plongée** diving suit, wetsuit ▸ **combinaison de ski** ski suit ▸ **combinaison spatiale** space suit **5.** [assemblage] : **la combinaison des deux éléments est nécessaire** the two elements must be combined.

combine [kɔ̃bin] nf fam [astuce, truc] scheme, trick / **j'ai une combine pour entrer sans payer** I know a way of getting in for free / **c'est simple, il suffit de connaître la combine** it's easy when you know how ▸ **être dans la combine** to be in on it.

*In reformed spelling (see p. 16-18).

combiné [kɔ̃bine] nm **1.** VÊT corselet, corselette **2.** TÉLÉC receiver, handset **3.** SPORT [gén] athletics event ; [en ski] combined competition ▶ **combiné alpin** alpine combined competition.

combiner [3] [kɔ̃bine] vt **1.** [harmoniser - styles] to combine, to match ; [- couleurs] to match, to harmonize, to mix ; [- sons] to harmonize, to mix / *combiner son travail et ses loisirs* to combine business with pleasure **2.** [comprendre] to combine **3.** [planifier] to plan, to work out *(sép)* **4.** *fam & péj* [manigancer] to think up *(sép)*. ❖ **se combiner** vpi [exister ensemble - éléments] to be combined.

comble [kɔ̃bl] ❖ adj packed, crammed. ❖ nm **1.** [summum] ▶ **le comble de** the height ou epitome of ▶ **le comble du chic** the ultimate in chic ▶ *(c'est)* **un** ou **le comble !** that beats everything!, that takes the biscuit! 🆄🅺 ou takes the cake! 🆄🆂 ▶ **le comble, c'est que...** to crown ou to cap it all... **2.** [charpente] roof timbers ou gable ▶ **les combles** the attic. ❖ **à son comble** loc adv at its height / *la panique était à son comble* the panic was at its height. ❖ **au comble de** loc prép at the height of, in a paroxysm of ▶ **au comble du bonheur** deliriously happy. ❖ **pour comble de** loc prép : *et pour comble de malchance, la voiture est tombée en panne* and then, to cap it all, the car broke down / *pour comble d'hypocrisie, ils envoient leur fille chez les sœurs* then, to compound the hypocrisy, they send their daughter to a convent.

combler [3] [kɔ̃ble] vt **1.** [boucher - cavité, creux] to fill in *(sép)* **2.** [supprimer - lacune, vide] to fill ; [- silence] to break ; [- perte, déficit] to make up for **3.** [satisfaire - personne] to satisfy ; [- désir, vœu] to satisfy, to fulfil / *je suis vraiment comblée !* I have everything I could wish for!, I couldn't ask for anything more! / *voilà un père comblé !* there's a contented father! **4.** *fig* [couvrir, emplir] ▶ **combler qqn de :** *combler un enfant de cadeaux* to shower a child with gifts ▶ **combler qqn de joie** to fill sb with joy.

combustible [kɔ̃bystibl] ❖ adj combustible. ❖ nm fuel.

combustion [kɔ̃bystjɔ̃] nf combustion.

comédie [kɔmedi] nf **1.** [art dramatique] theatre **2.** [pièce comique] comedy ▶ **comédie de mœurs** comedy of manners ▶ **comédie musicale** musical **3.** *péj* [hypocrisie] act / *cette réception, quelle comédie !* what a farce that party was! ▶ **il n'est pas vraiment malade, c'est de la comédie** ou **il nous joue la comédie** he's only play-acting ou it's only an act, he's not really ill **4.** *fam* [caprice, colère] tantrum ▶ **faire** ou **jouer la comédie** to throw a tantrum, to make a fuss **5.** *fam* [histoire] : *pour avoir un rendez-vous, quelle comédie !* what a palaver to get an appointment!

comédien, enne [kɔmedjɛ̃, ɛn] nm, f **1.** [acteur - gén] actor (actress) ; [- comique] comedian (comedienne) **2.** [hypocrite] phoney ▶ **quel comédien !** he's putting it on!

⚠ Le mot anglais **comedian** désigne exclusivement un acteur comique.

comestible [kɔmɛstibl] adj edible. ❖ **comestibles** nmpl food, foodstuffs.

comète [kɔmɛt] nf comet.

coming out [kɔmiŋawt] nm inv ▶ **faire son coming out** to come out.

comique [kɔmik] ❖ adj **1.** LITTÉR comic, comedy *(modif)* **2.** [amusant] comical, funny. ❖ nmf [artiste] comic, comedian (comedienne). ❖ nm **1.** [genre] comedy ▶ **le comique de caractères / situation** character / situation comedy **2.** [ce qui fait rire] : *le comique de l'histoire, c'est que...* the funny part of it is that...

comic ou **comical ?**

Comic désigne ce qui se réfère à la comédie (a **comic film** ; **comic writing**). **Comical** signifie plus largement « amusant » (**his comical behaviour** ; **it was quite comical to watch**).

comité [kɔmite] nm committee, board ▶ **comité d'entreprise** works council ▶ **comité exécutif** POL executive committee ou board ▶ **comité de gestion** board of managers. ❖ **en petit comité, en comité restreint** loc adv as a select group / *on a dîné en petit comité* the dinner was just for a select group.

Comité d'entreprise

In a company with more than 50 employees, the **CE** looks after the general welfare of company employees and organizes subsidized leisure activities, outings, holidays, etc. It also helps deal with industrial disputes.

commandant, e [kɔmɑ̃dɑ̃, ɑ̃t] nm, f **1.** MIL [de l'armée de terre] major ▶ **commandant d'armes** garrison commander ; [de l'armée de l'air] wing commander 🆄🅺, lieutenant colonel 🆄🆂 ; [de la marine] commander ; [de la marine marchande] captain **2.** NAUT captain **3.** AÉRON ▶ **commandant (de bord)** captain.

commande [kɔmɑ̃d] nf **1.** COMM order ▶ **passer / annuler une commande** to put in / to cancel an order / *le garçon a pris la commande* the waiter took the order ; [marchandises] order, goods ordered **2.** TECHNOL control mechanism ▶ **la commande des essuie-glaces** the wiper mechanism ▶ **commande à distance** remote control ▶ **à commande vocale** voice-activated. ❖ **commandes** nfpl [dispositif de guidage] controls ▶ **être aux commandes a)** *pr* to be at the controls **b)** *fig* to be in charge ▶ **prendre les** ou **se mettre aux commandes a)** *pr* to take over at the controls **b)** *fig* to take charge. ❖ **à la commande** loc adv ▶ **payer à la commande** to pay while ordering. ❖ **sur commande** loc adv COMM & *fig* to order.

commandement [kɔmɑ̃dmɑ̃] nm **1.** [ordre] command, order **2.** [fait de diriger] command / *prendre le commandement d'une section* to take over command of a platoon **3.** [état-major] command **4.** BIBLE commandment.

commander [3] [kɔmɑ̃de] vt **1.** [diriger - armée, expédition, soldats, équipe] to command ; [- navire] to be in command of ; *(en usage absolu)* : *c'est moi qui commande ici !* I'm the one who gives the orders around here! **2.** [ordonner] ▶ **commander à qqn de faire** ou **qu'il fasse** *sout* **qqch** to order sb to do sthg **3.** TECHNOL to control / *la télévision est commandée à distance* the television is remote-controlled **4.** COMM [tableau, ouvrage] to commission ; [objet manufacturé, repas] to order ; *(en usage absolu)* : *c'est fait, j'ai déjà commandé* I've already ordered ▶ **vous avez commandé ?** has somebody taken your order? ❖ **se commander** vp *(emploi passif)* *fam* [être imposé] : *l'amour ne se commande pas* you can't make love happen.

commanditaire [kɔmɑ̃ditɛʁ] nm [d'une entreprise commerciale] sleeping 🆄🅺 ou silent 🆄🆂 partner ; [d'un tournoi, d'un spectacle] backer, sponsor.

commanditer [3] [kɔmɑ̃dite] vt [entreprise commerciale] to finance ; [tournoi, spectacle] to sponsor.

commando [kɔmɑ̃do] nm commando.

comme [kɔm] ◆ conj **1.** [introduisant une comparaison] as, like / *c'est un jour comme les autres* it's a day like any other / *ce fut comme une révélation* it was like a revelation / *il fait beau comme en plein été* it's as hot as if it was the middle of summer / *il a fait un signe, comme pour appeler* he made a sign, as if to call out / *je suis comme toi, j'ai horreur de ça* I'm like you, I hate that kind of thing / *fais comme moi, ne lui réponds pas* do as I do, don't answer him ▶ **blanc comme neige** white as snow ▶ **j'ai comme l'impression qu'on s'est perdus !** I've got a feeling we're lost! ▶ **il y a comme un défaut !** *fam* something seems to be wrong! / *il ne m'a pas injurié, mais c'était tout comme* he didn't actually insult me, but it was close ou as good as **2.** [exprimant la manière] as / *fais comme il te plaira* do as you like ou please / *comme on pouvait s'y attendre, nos actions ont baissé* as could be expected, our shares have gone down / *ça s'écrit comme ça se prononce* it's written as it's pronounced ▶ **comme convenu**: *je passerai vous prendre à 9 h comme convenu* I'll pick you up at 9 as (we) agreed ou planned ▶ **comme on dit** as they say / *comme il se doit en pareilles circonstances* as befits the circumstances, as is fitting in such circumstances / *fais comme bon te semble* do whatever you wish ou like ▶ **comme ci comme ça** *fam*: *comment ça va ? — comme ci comme ça* how are you? — so-so **3.** [tel que] like, such as / *mince comme elle est, elle peut porter n'importe quoi* being as slim as she is everything suits her, she is so slim that everything suits her ▶ **D comme Denise** D for Denise **4.** [en tant que] as / *je l'ai eu comme élève* he was one of my students / *qu'est-ce que vous avez comme vin ?* what (kind of) wine do you have? / *c'est plutôt faible comme excuse !* it's a pretty feeble excuse! **5.** [pour ainsi dire] : *il restait sur le seuil, comme paralysé* he was standing on the doorstep, (as if he was) rooted to the spot / *ta robe est comme neuve !* your dress is as good as new! **6.** [et] : *l'un comme l'autre aiment beaucoup voyager* they both love travelling / *le règlement s'applique à tous, à vous comme aux autres* the rules apply to everybody, you included / *à la ville comme à la scène* in real life as well as on stage **7.** [indiquant la cause] since, as **8.** [au moment où] as, when ; [pendant que] while. ◆ adv **1.** [emploi exclamatif] how ▶ **comme c'est triste !** how sad (it is)!, it's so sad! / *comme je te comprends !* I know exactly how you feel! **2.** [indiquant la manière] : *tu sais comme il est* you know what he's like ou how he is. ❖ **comme ça** ◆ loc adj **1.** [ainsi] like that / *il est comme ça, on ne le changera pas !* that's the way he is, you won't change him! **2.** [admirable] great. ◆ loc adv **1.** [de cette manière] like this ou that / *qu'as-tu à me regarder comme ça ?* why are you staring at me like that? / *c'est comme ça, que ça te plaise ou non !* that's how ou the way it is, whether you like it or not! **2.** [en intensif] : *alors comme ça, tu te maries ?* (oh) so you're getting married? / *où vas-tu comme ça ?* where are you off to? **3.** [de telle manière que] that way, so that. ❖ **comme il faut** ◆ loc adj respectable, proper. ◆ loc adv [correctement] properly. ❖ **comme quoi** loc conj [ce qui prouve que] which shows ou (just) goes to show that. ❖ **comme si** loc conj **1.** [exprimant la comparaison] as if / *il se conduit comme s'il était encore étudiant* he behaves as if he was still a student / *elle faisait comme si de rien n'était* she pretended (that) there was nothing wrong, she pretended (that) nothing had happened **2.** [emploi exclamatif] as if, as though / *c'est comme si c'était fait !* it's as good as done! ❖ **comme tout** loc adv really, extremely, terribly / *j'ai été malade comme tout sur le bateau* I was (as) sick as a dog on the boat.

commémoration [kɔmemɔrasjɔ̃] nf commemoration.

commémorer [3] [kɔmemɔre] vt to commemorate, to celebrate the memory of.

commencement [kɔmɑ̃smɑ̃] nm **1.** [première partie - de la vie, d'un processus] beginning, start, early stages ▶ **il y a un commencement à tout** everybody has to learn to walk before they can run **2.** [essai] beginning, start, attempt / *il y a eu un commencement d'émeute, vite réprimé* a riot started, but was soon brought under control. ❖ **au commencement** loc adv in ou at the beginning.

commencer [16] [kɔmɑ̃se] ◆ vt **1.** [entreprendre - ouvrage, jeu, apprentissage] to start, to begin / *il a commencé le repas* he's started eating / *vous commencez le travail demain* you start (work) tomorrow ; (en usage absolu) ▶ **à quelle heure tu commences ? a)** [au lycée] what time do you start school? **b)** [au travail] what time do you start work? **2.** [passer au début de - journée, soirée] to start, to begin ▶ **j'ai bien / mal commencé l'année** I've made a good / bad start to the year **3.** [être au début de] to begin / *c'est son numéro qui commence le spectacle* her routine begins the show, the show begins with her routine. ◆ vi **1.** [débuter] to start ▶ **ne commence pas !** don't start! ▶ **ça commence bien !** *aussi iron* things are off to a good start! ▶ **commencer à faire qqch** to start ou to begin doing sthg / *je commence à en avoir assez !* I'm getting fed up with all this! / *ça commence à bien faire !* *fam* enough is enough!, things have gone quite far enough! ▶ **commencer par**: *la pièce commence par un dialogue* the play starts ou opens with a dialogue ▶ **commençons par le commencement** let's begin at the beginning, first things first ; (tournure impersonnelle) ▶ **il commence à pleuvoir / neiger** it's started to rain ou to snow **2.** [avoir tel moment comme point de départ] to start, to begin / *la séance commence à 20 h* the session starts ou begins at 8 p.m. / *le spectacle est commencé depuis un quart d'heure* the show started a quarter of an hour ago **3.** [se mettre à travailler] ▶ **commencer dans la vie** to start off in life / *j'ai commencé en 78 avec deux ouvrières* I set up ou started (up) in '78 with two workers. ❖ **à commencer par** loc prép starting with / *que tout le monde contribue, à commencer par toi !* let everyone give something, starting with you! ❖ **pour commencer** loc adv **1.** [dans un programme, un repas] first, to start with ▶ **pour commencer, du saumon** to start the meal ou as a first course, salmon **2.** [comment premier argument] for a start, in the first place.

comment [kɔmɑ̃] adv **1.** [de quelle manière] how ▶ **comment t'appelles-tu ?** what's your name? / *comment se fait-il qu'il n'ait pas appelé ?* how come he hasn't called? ▶ **comment faire ?** what shall we do? ▶ **comment allez-vous ?** how are you? **2.** [pour faire répéter] ▶ **comment ?** sorry?, what (was that)? **3.** [exprimant l'indignation, l'étonnement] : *comment, c'est tout ce que tu trouves à dire ?* what! is that all you can say? / *comment ça, tu pars ?* *fam* what do you mean, you're leaving? ▶ **et comment !**: *tu as aimé le concert ? — et comment !* did you like the concert? — I certainly did!

commentaire [kɔmɑ̃tɛr] nm **1.** [remarque] comment, remark, observation / *faire un commentaire* to make a remark ou a comment / *je te dispense ou je me passe de tes commentaires* I can do without your remarks ▶ **sans commentaire !** no comment! **2.** *péj* [critique] comment ▶ **avoir des commentaires (à faire) sur**: *j'aurais des commentaires à faire sur ton soir* I'd like to say something about your attitude last night **3.** RADIO & TV commentary **4.** ENS ▶ **commentaire de texte**: *faire un commentaire de texte* to comment on a text.

commentateur, trice [kɔmɑ̃tatœr, tris] nm, f [d'une cérémonie, d'un match] commentator ; [d'un documentaire] presenter ▶ **commentateur du journal télévisé** broadcaster, anchorman US ; [observateur] observer, critic.

commenter [3] [kɔmɑ̃te] vt **1.** [expliquer - œuvre] to explain, to interpret / *veuillez commenter ce dernier vers du poème* please write a commentary on the last line of the poem / *on leur fait commenter Dante dès la troisième année d'italien* they start doing literary criticism of Dante in the third year of Italian studies / *le directeur va maintenant commenter notre programme de fabrication* the manager will now explain our manufacturing schedule **2.** [donner son avis sur] to comment on (*insép*), to respond to, to give one's response to **3.** RADIO & TV [cérémonie, match] to cover, to do the commentary of ou for.

commérage [kɔmeʀaʒ] nm piece of gossip ▸ **commérages** gossip.

commerçant, e [kɔmeʀsɑ̃, ɑ̃t] ◆ adj **1.** [peuple, port, pays] trading (*modif*) ; [rue, quartier] shopping (*modif*) **2.** [qui a le sens du commerce] : *ils en offrent deux pour le prix d'un, c'est très commerçant* they sell two for the price of one, that's good business sense / *il a l'esprit commerçant* he's a born salesman, he could sell you anything. ◆ nm, f shopkeeper ⓊⓀ, storekeeper ⓊⓈ / *tous les commerçants étaient fermés* all the shops ⓊⓀ ou stores ⓊⓈ were closed ▸ **commerçant de détail** retail trader ▸ **commerçant en gros** wholesale dealer ▸ **les petits commerçants** small ou retail traders.

commerce [kɔmeʀs] nm **1.** [activité] ▸ **le commerce** trade ▸ **faire du commerce avec qqn / un pays** to trade with sb / a country ▸ **le commerce extérieur / intérieur** foreign / domestic trade ▸ **commerce de détail** retail trade ▸ **commerce électronique** electronic trade, e-trade ▸ **commerce équitable** fair ou equitable trade ▸ **le commerce en gros** wholesale trade **2.** [affaires] business ▸ **le commerce marche mal** business is slow ▸ **le petit commerce** (small) business **3.** [circuit de distribution] : *cela ne se trouve plus dans le commerce* this item has gone off the market **4.** [magasin] shop ⓊⓀ, store ⓊⓈ ▸ **tenir un commerce** to run a business.

commercial, e, aux [kɔmeʀsjal, o] ◆ adj [activité] commercial ; [relation] trade (*modif*) ▸ **adressez-vous à notre service** ou **secteur commercial** please apply to our sales department ▸ **l'anglais commercial** business English. ◆ nmf sales representative ou executive. ❖ **commerciale** nf fam AUTO commercial vehicle.

commercialisation [kɔmeʀsjalizasjɔ̃] nf marketing.

commercialiser [3] [kɔmeʀsjalize] vt COMM to market, to commercialize.

commère [kɔmeʀ] nf [médisante] gossip.

commettre [84] [kɔmetʀ] vt **1.** [perpétrer - erreur] to make ; [- injustice] to perpetrate ; [- meurtre] to commit **2.** hum & péj [produire - livre, émission] to perpetrate.

commis [kɔmi] nm **1.** DR agent **2.** [employé - de magasin] helper, assistant ; [- de banque] runner, junior clerk ; [- de ferme] lad, boy, farm hand.

commissaire [kɔmiseʀ] nmf **1.** [membre d'une commission] commissioner **2.** SPORT steward **3.** ADMIN ▸ **commissaire de police** (police) superintendent ⓊⓀ, (police) captain ⓊⓈ, precinct captain ⓊⓈ ▸ **commissaire divisionnaire** chief superintendent ⓊⓀ, police chief ⓊⓈ ▸ **commissaire principal** chief superintendent ⓊⓀ, chief of police ⓊⓈ **4.** FIN ▸ **commissaire aux comptes** auditor.

commissaire-priseur [kɔmiseʀprizœʀ] (*pl* **commissaires-priseurs**) nm auctioneer.

commissariat [kɔmisaʀja] nm [local] ▸ **commissariat (de police)** police station ou precinct ⓊⓈ.

commission [kɔmisjɔ̃] nf **1.** [groupe] commission, committee ▸ **commission d'enquête** board ou commission of inquiry ⓊⓀ, fact-finding committee ⓊⓈ ▸ **la Commission européenne** the European Commission **2.** [pourcentage] commission, percentage / *toucher une commission sur une vente* to get a commission ou percentage on a sale ▸ **travailler à la commission** to work on a commission basis ou for a percentage **3.** [course] errand / *j'ai envoyé mon fils faire des commissions* I've sent my son off on some errands **4.** : *n'oublie pas de lui faire la commission* [de lui donner le message] don't forget to give him the message. ❖ **commissions** nfpl [achats] shopping ▸ **faire les commissions** to do some shopping.

commissure [kɔmisyʀ] nf [de la bouche] corner.

commode¹ [kɔmɔd] adj **1.** [pratique - moyen de transport] useful, convenient ; [- outil] useful, handy **2.** [facile] easy / *ce n'est pas commode à analyser* it's not easy to analyse **3.** [aimable] : *elle n'est pas commode (à vivre)* she's not easy to live with / *il est peu commode* he's awkward ou difficult.

commode² [kɔmɔd] nf chest of drawers.

commodité [kɔmɔdite] nf **1.** [facilité] convenience **2.** [aspect pratique] : *la commodité d'une maison* the comfort ou convenience of a house. ❖ **commodités** nfpl [agréments] conveniences ; vieilli [toilettes] toilet, toilets.

commotion [kɔmɔsjɔ̃] nf **1.** [choc] shock **2.** MÉD ▸ **commotion cérébrale** concussion.

commuer [7] [kɔmɥe] vt to commute / *commuer une peine de prison en amende* to commute a prison sentence to a fine.

commun, e [kɔmœ̃, yn] adj **1.** [partagé - jardin, local] shared, communal ; [- ami] mutual / *hôtel avec salle de télévision commune* hotel with public TV lounge ▸ **commun à** : *une langue commune à cinq millions de personnes* a language shared by five million people **2.** [fait en collaboration - travail, politique] shared, common ; [- décision] joint ; [en communauté] ▸ **la vie commune** [conjugale] conjugal life, the life of a couple **3.** [identique - caractère, passion] similar ; [- habitude] common, shared / *nous avons des problèmes communs* we share the same problems, we have similar problems **4.** [courant - espèce, usage, faute] common, ordinary, run-of-the-mill ▸ **un nom peu commun** a very unusual name **5.** péj [banal] common, coarse. ❖ **commun** nm : *l'homme du commun* vieilli the common man / *un homme hors du commun* an exceptional ou unusual man ▸ **cela sort du commun** this is very unusual ▸ **le commun de** : *le commun des mortels* the common run of people ▸ **le commun des lecteurs** the average reader. ❖ **d'un commun accord** loc adv by mutual agreement, by common consent / *tous d'un commun accord ont décidé que...* they decided unanimously that... ❖ **en commun** loc adv ▸ **avoir qqch en commun (avec)** to have sthg in common (with) ▸ **mettre qqch en commun** to pool sthg.

communal, e, aux [kɔmynal, o] adj **1.** ADMIN [en ville] ≃ of the urban district ; [à la campagne] ≃ of the rural district **2.** [du village - fête] local, village (*modif*). ❖ **communale** nf fam primary ⓊⓀ ou grade ⓊⓈ school.

communautaire [kɔmynotɛʀ] adj POL [de l'Union européenne] EU (*modif*) ; [de la Communauté européenne] Community (*modif*) ; HIST [du Marché commun] Common Market (*modif*).

communauté [kɔmynote] nf [groupe] community ▸ **la Communauté économique européenne** the European Economic Community ▸ **la Communauté des États indépendants** the Commonwealth of Independent States ▸ **la Communauté européenne** the European Community. ❖ **en communauté** loc adv [vivre] communally, as a community.

> ⚠ Attention, ce mot ne se traduit pas toujours par **community**. Voir article.

commune [kɔmyn] nf **1.** ADMIN [agglomération] commune / *une jolie petite commune rurale* a nice little country village ▶ **la commune et ses alentours a)** [en ville] ≃ the urban district **b)** [à la campagne] ≃ the rural district **2.** [habitants] ▶ **la commune a)** [en ville] people who live within the urban district **b)** [à la campagne] people who live within the rural district **3.** [administrateurs] : *c'est la commune qui paie* the local authority ou the council 🇬🇧 is paying **4.** [en Grande-Bretagne] ▶ **les Communes** the House of Commons.

 Commune

A **commune** is an administrative district in France. There are 37,000 **communes**, some with less than 25 inhabitants. Each **commune** has an elected mayor and a town council.

communément [kɔmynemɑ̃] adv commonly, usually.
communiant, e [kɔmynjɑ̃, ɑ̃t] nm, f communicant.
communicant, e [kɔmynikɑ̃, ɑ̃t] adj communicating ▶ **deux chambres communicantes** two connecting 🇬🇧 ou adjoining 🇺🇸 rooms. ❖ **communicant** nm communicator.
communicateur, trice [kɔmynikatœʀ, tʀis] nm, f communicator.
communicatif, ive [kɔmynikatif, iv] adj **1.** [qui se répand - rire, bonne humeur] infectious **2.** [bavard] communicative, talkative.
communication [kɔmynikasjɔ̃] nf **1.** [annonce] announcement, communication ▶ **donner communication de qqch** to communicate sthg **2.** [exposé - fait à la presse] statement ; [- fait à des universitaires, des scientifiques] paper / *faire une communication sur l'atome* to deliver a lecture on the atom **3.** [transmission] communicating, passing on, transmission ▶ **avoir communication d'un dossier** to get hold of a file, to have had a file passed on to one **4.** [contact] communication, contact ▶ **être en communication avec qqn** to be in contact ou touch with sb / *vous devriez vous mettre en communication avec elle* you should get in touch with her **5.** [échange entre personnes] communication / *il a des problèmes de communication (avec les autres)* he has problems communicating with ou relating to people / *il n'y a pas de communication possible avec elle* it's impossible to relate to her ; [diffusion d'informations] ▶ **communication interne** [dans une entreprise] interdepartmental communication **6.** TÉLÉC ▶ **communication téléphonique** (phone) call ▶ **je prends la communication** I'll take the call / *il est en communication avec...* he's speaking to..., he's on the phone to... ▶ **avoir la communication** : *vous avez la communication* you're through ▶ **communication interurbaine** inter-city ou city-to-city call ▶ **communication en PCV** reverse-charge call 🇬🇧, collect call 🇺🇸. ❖ **de communication** loc adj **1.** [réseau, satellite] communications *(modif)* ▶ **moyens de communication** means of communication **2.** [agence] publicity *(modif)*.
communier [9] [kɔmynje] vi RELIG to communicate, to receive Communion.
communion [kɔmynjɔ̃] nf RELIG [communauté de foi] communion ; [cérémonie] ▶ **première communion** first communion.
communiqué [kɔmynike] nm communiqué ▶ **un communiqué de presse** a press release.
communiquer [3] [kɔmynike] ◆ vt **1.** [transmettre - information] to communicate, to give ; [- demande] to transmit ; [- dossier, message] to pass on *(sép)* ; [- savoir, savoir-faire] to pass on, to hand down *(sép)* **2.** [donner

par contamination] to transmit / *il leur a communiqué son fou rire / enthousiasme* he passed on his giggles / enthusiasm to them **3.** [annoncer] to announce, to impart, to communicate. ◆ vi [être relié] to interconnect / *la chambre communique avec la salle de bains* there's a connecting door between the bathroom and the bedroom. ❖ **se communiquer** vpi [se propager - incendie] to spread ; [- maladie] to spread, to be passed on ▶ **se communiquer à** to spread to.
communisme [kɔmynism] nm Communism.
communiste [kɔmynist] ◆ adj Communist. ◆ nmf Communist.
commutateur [kɔmytatœʀ] nm ÉLECTR & ÉLECTRON [de circuits] changeover switch, commutator ; [interrupteur] switch.
Comores [kɔmɔʀ] npr fpl ▶ **les Comores** the Comoro. Islands, the Comoros. ⟶ **île**
comorien, enne [kɔmɔʀjɛ̃, ɛn] adj Comoran, Comorian. ❖ **Comorien, enne** nm, f Comoran, Comorian.
compact, e [kɔ̃pakt] adj **1.** [dense - matière] solid, dense ; [- foule] dense, packed ; [- poudre] pressed, compacted **2.** AUDIO, AUTO & PHOT compact. ❖ **compact** nm **1.** [disque] compact disc, CD **2.** [appareil photo] compact (camera).
compacte [kɔ̃pakt] nf compact car.
compagne [kɔ̃paɲ] nf **1.** [camarade] (female) companion / *compagne de classe / jeux* (female) classmate / playmate **2.** [épouse] wife ; [concubine] girlfriend **3.** [animal domestique] companion.
compagnie [kɔ̃paɲi] nf **1.** [présence] company ▶ **être d'une compagnie agréable / sinistre** to be a pleasant / gloomy companion ▶ **être de bonne / mauvaise compagnie** to be good / bad company ▶ **être en bonne / mauvaise compagnie** to be in good / bad company ▶ **tenir compagnie à qqn** to keep sb company **2.** [groupe] party, company, gang **3.** COMM & INDUST company ▶ **compagnie aérienne** airline (company) ▶ **compagnie d'assurances** insurance company **4.** THÉÂTRE ▶ **compagnie (théâtrale)** (theatre) group ou company ou troupe. ❖ **en compagnie de** loc prép accompanied by, (in company) with.
compagnon [kɔ̃paɲɔ̃] nm **1.** [camarade] companion ▶ **compagnon de jeux** playmate ▶ **compagnon de route** ou **voyage** travelling companion **2.** [époux] husband, companion ; [ami, concubin] boyfriend.
comparable [kɔ̃paʀabl] adj comparable, similar ▶ **ce n'est pas comparable** there's no comparison / *une fonction comparable à celle de comptable* a function comparable with ou similar to that of an accountant.
comparaison [kɔ̃paʀɛzɔ̃] nf **1.** [gén] comparison ▶ **faire la** ou **une comparaison entre deux ordinateurs** to compare two computers ▶ **aucune comparaison !** there's no comparison ! **2.** [figure de style] comparison, simile ▶ **adverbe de comparaison** comparative adverb. ❖ **en comparaison de, en comparaison avec** loc prép in comparison ou as compared with, compared to.
comparaître, comparaître* [91] [kɔ̃paʀɛtʀ] vi to appear ▶ **comparaître en justice** to appear before a court ▶ **faire comparaître qqn devant un tribunal** to bring sb before a court.
comparatif, ive [kɔ̃paʀatif, iv] adj comparative. ❖ **comparatif** nm comparative ▶ **comparatif de supériorité / d'infériorité** comparative of greater / lesser degree.
comparativement [kɔ̃paʀativmɑ̃] adv comparatively, by ou in comparison.
comparé, e [kɔ̃paʀe] adj [littérature] comparative.

comparer [3] [kɔ̃paʀe] vt **1.** [confronter] to compare ▸ **comparer un livre à** ou **avec un autre** to compare a book to ou with another **2.** [assimiler] ▸ **comparer qqch / qqn à** to compare sthg / sb to. ◈ **comparé à** loc prép compared to ou with, in comparison to ou with.

comparse [kɔ̃paʀs] nmf **1.** THÉÂTRE extra, walk-on **2.** péj [d'un brigand, d'un camelot] stooge.

compartiment [kɔ̃paʀtimɑ̃] nm **1.** RAIL compartment **2.** [case - d'une boîte] compartment ; [- d'un sac] pocket. ◈ **à compartiments** loc adj [tiroir, classeur] divided into compartments.

compartimenter [3] [kɔ̃paʀtimɑ̃te] vt [caisse, armoire] to partition, to divide into compartments ; [administration, connaissances] to compartmentalize, to split into small units.

comparution [kɔ̃paʀysjɔ̃] nf appearance.

compas [kɔ̃pa] nm **1.** AÉRON & NAUT compass **2.** GÉOM (pair of) compasses ▸ **compas à pointes sèches** dividers.

compassé, e [kɔ̃pase] adj stiff, strait-laced.

compassion [kɔ̃pasjɔ̃] nf compassion, sympathy.

compatibilité [kɔ̃patibilite] nf compatibility.

compatible [kɔ̃patibl] ◆ adj [gén & TECHNOL & INFORM] compatible ▸ **compatible PC** PC-compatible. ◆ nm INFORM compatible.

compatir [32] [kɔ̃patiʀ] ◈ **compatir à** v + prép (en usage absolu) ▸ **je compatis !** a) I sympathize! b) iron my heart bleeds!

compatriote [kɔ̃patʀijɔt] nmf compatriot, fellow countryman (countrywoman).

compensation [kɔ̃pɑ̃sasjɔ̃] nf [dédommagement] compensation. ◈ **en compensation de** loc prép by way of compensation ou as compensation ou to compensate for.

compensé, e [kɔ̃pɑ̃se] adj [semelle] ▸ **chaussures à semelles compensées** platform shoes.

compenser [3] [kɔ̃pɑ̃se] vt [perte] to make up for (insép), to offset ; (en usage absolu) : pour compenser, je l'ai emmenée au cinéma to make up for it, I took her to the cinema. ◈ **se compenser** vp (emploi réciproque) to make up for one another.

⚠ **To compensate** ne peut être employé systématiquement pour traduire compenser.

compète [kɔ̃pet] nf fam competition.

compétence [kɔ̃petɑ̃s] nf **1.** [qualification, capacité] competence / j'ai des compétences en informatique I have computer skills ▸ **cela n'entre pas dans mes compétences** ou **ce n'est pas de ma compétence** a) [cela n'est pas dans mes attributions] this doesn't come within my remit b) [cela me dépasse] that's beyond my competence **2.** DR competence.

compétent, e [kɔ̃petɑ̃, ɑ̃t] adj **1.** [qualifié] competent, skilful, skilled / en cuisine, je suis assez compétente I'm quite a good cook ▸ **compétent en la matière** : les gens compétents en la matière (qui savent) people who know about ou are conversant with sout this topic **2.** [approprié - service] relevant.

compétitif, ive [kɔ̃petitif, iv] adj competitive.

compétition [kɔ̃petisjɔ̃] nf **1.** [rivalité] competition, competing **2.** [niveau d'activité sportive] competition ▸ **faire de la compétition** a) [athlétisme] to take part in competitive events b) AUTO & NAUT to race. ◈ **de compétition** loc adj ▸ **des skis de compétition** a) [de descente] racing skis b) [de fond] eventing skis ▸ **sport de compétition** competitive sport. ◈ **en compétition** loc adv SPORT at competition level. ◈ **en compétition avec** loc prép competing ou in competition with.

compétitionner [3] [kɔ̃petisjɔne] vi Québec to compete.

compétitivité [kɔ̃petitivite] nf competitiveness.

compil [kɔ̃pil] (abr de **compilation**) nf fam compilation.

compilation [kɔ̃pilasjɔ̃] nf **1.** [fait de réunir des textes] compiling ; [ensemble de textes, de morceaux de musique] compilation **2.** péj [plagiat] plagiarizing, synthesizing ; [ouvrage] (mere) compilation ou synthesis péj.

complainte [kɔ̃plɛ̃t] nf litt LITTÉR & MUS lament, plaint.

complaire [110] [kɔ̃plɛʀ] ◈ **se complaire** vpi ▸ **se complaire dans qqch** to revel ou to delight ou to take pleasure in sthg ▸ **se complaire à dire / faire qqch** to take great pleasure in saying / doing sthg.

complaisance [kɔ̃plɛzɑ̃s] nf **1.** [amabilité] kindness, obligingness **2.** [vanité] complacency, smugness, self-satisfaction **3.** [indulgence - des parents] laxity, indulgence ; [- d'un tribunal, d'un juge] leniency, indulgence ; [- d'un mari] connivance. ◈ **de complaisance** loc adj ▸ **certificat** ou **attestation de complaisance** phoney certificate (given to please the person concerned).

complaisant, e [kɔ̃plɛzɑ̃, ɑ̃t] adj **1.** [aimable] kind ; [serviable] obliging, complaisant **2.** [vaniteux] smug, self-satisfied, complacent / prêter une oreille complaisante aux éloges to lap up praise **3.** [indulgent - parents] lax, indulgent ; [- juge, tribunal] indulgent, lenient / elle a un mari complaisant her husband turns a blind eye to her infidelities.

complément [kɔ̃plemɑ̃] nm **1.** [supplément] : un complément d'information est nécessaire further ou additional information is required **2.** LING complement ▸ **complément (d'objet) direct / indirect** direct / indirect object ▸ **complément d'agent** agent ▸ **complément circonstanciel** adverbial phrase.

complémentaire [kɔ̃plemɑ̃tɛʀ] adj **1.** [supplémentaire - information] additional, further **2.** [industries, couleurs] complementary.

complémentarité [kɔ̃plemɑ̃taʀite] nf [fait de se compléter] complementarity.

complet, ète [kɔ̃plɛ, ɛt] adj **1.** [qui a tous ses éléments - série, collection, parure] complete, full ; [- œuvre] complete ▸ **change complet** disposable nappy UK ou diaper US **2.** [approfondi - compte-rendu, description] full, comprehensive ; [- analyse, examen] thorough, full **3.** [entier] full / nous resterons un mois complet we'll stay a full month **4.** [bondé - bus, métro, stade] full ▸ **'complet'** a) [hôtel] 'no vacancies' b) [parking] 'full' ▸ **nous sommes complets** [salle de concert, théâtre, restaurant] we're (fully) booked **5.** [parfait - homme, artiste] all-round (avant nom), complete **6.** [total, absolu - silence] total, absolute ; [- repos] complete ; [- échec] total / ils vivent dans la pauvreté la plus complète they live in utter ou absolute ou abject poverty ▸ **un fiasco complet** a complete (and utter) disaster **7.** [fournissant tout le nécessaire] : la natation est un sport complet swimming is an all-round sport **8.** CULIN [pain, farine, spaghetti] wholemeal ; [riz] brown. ◈ **complet** nm VÊT ▸ **complet, complet-veston** (man's) suit. ◈ **au (grand) complet** loc adj ▸ **(toute) l'équipe au complet** the whole team.

complètement [kɔ̃plɛtmɑ̃] adv **1.** [totalement] completely, totally ▸ **complètement nu** stark naked **2.** [vraiment] absolutely ▸ **je suis complètement d'accord** I absolutely ou totally agree.

compléter [18] [kɔ̃plete] vt **1.** [ajouter ce qui manque à - collection, dossier] to complete ; [- somme, remboursement] to make up (sép) **2.** [approfondir - analyse, notes, formation] to finish, to complete.

❖ **se compléter** vp *(emploi réciproque)* to complement (one another) / *le vin et le fromage se complètent parfaitement* wine complements cheese perfectly.

✍ In reformed spelling (see p. 16-18), this verb is conjugated like *semer* : *elle complétera, il complèterait.*

complexe [kɔ̃plɛks] ◆ adj [compliqué - processus, trajet] complicated ; [- caractère, personne] complex, complicated. ◆ nm **1.** PSYCHOL complex ▸ **avoir des complexes** *fam* to be hung up ▸ **complexe d'infériorité / de supériorité / d'Œdipe** inferiority / superiority / Oedipus complex **2.** CONSTR & ÉCON complex ▸ **complexe hospitalier / industriel** medical / industrial complex. ❖ **sans complexe(s)** loc adj *péj* [sans honte] uninhibited / *elle est sans complexe, celle-là !* she's so brazen!

complexé, e [kɔ̃plɛkse] adj neurotic / *elle est complexée par son poids* she has a complex about her weight.

complexifier [9] [kɔ̃plɛksifje] vt to complicate, to make more complex.

complexité [kɔ̃plɛksite] nf complexity.

complication [kɔ̃plikasjɔ̃] nf **1.** [problème] complication / *pourquoi faire des complications ?* why make things more difficult than they need be? **2.** [complexité] complicatedness, complexity ▸ **elle aime les complications** she likes things to be complicated. ❖ **complications** nfpl MÉD complications.

complice [kɔ̃plis] ◆ adj [regard, sourire, silence] knowing ▸ **être complice de qqch** to be (a) party to sthg. ◆ nmf **1.** [malfrat] accomplice **2.** [ami, confident] partner, friend / *sa femme et complice de tous les instants* his wife and constant companion.

complicité [kɔ̃plisite] nf **1.** DR complicity ▸ **avec la complicité de qqn** with the complicity of sb, with sb as an accomplice **2.** [entente, amitié] : *elle lui adressa un sourire de complicité* she smiled at him knowingly, she gave him a knowing smile. ❖ **en complicité avec** loc prép in collusion with.

compliment [kɔ̃plimɑ̃] nm **1.** [éloge] compliment ▸ **faire un compliment à qqn** to pay sb a compliment, to pay a compliment to sb **2.** [félicitations] congratulations / *adresser des compliments au vainqueur* to congratulate the winner **3.** [dans des formules de politesse] compliment / *mes compliments à votre épouse* my regards to your wife.

complimenter [3] [kɔ̃plimɑ̃te] vt **1.** [féliciter] to congratulate ▸ **complimenter qqn sur son succès** to congratulate sb on ou for having succeeded **2.** [faire des éloges à] to compliment.

compliqué, e [kɔ̃plike] adj [difficile à comprendre - affaire, exercice, phrase] complicated ; [- jeu, langue, livre, problème] difficult ; [- plan] intricate / *elle avait un nom compliqué* she had a real tongue-twister of a name / *c'est trop compliqué à expliquer* it's too hard to explain / *regarde, ce n'est pourtant pas compliqué !* look, it's not so difficult to understand!

compliquer [3] [kɔ̃plike] vt to complicate, to make (more) difficult ou complicated / *il me complique la vie* he makes things ou life difficult for me. ❖ **se compliquer** ◆ vpi **1.** [devenir embrouillé] to become (more) complicated / *ça se complique !* things are getting complicated!, the plot thickens! *hum* **2.** MÉD to be followed by complications. ◆ vpt ▸ **se compliquer la vie** ou **l'existence** make life difficult for o.s.

complot [kɔ̃plo] nm POL plot.

comploter [3] [kɔ̃plɔte] ◆ vt to plot. ◆ vi to be part of a plot ▸ **comploter de tuer qqn** to conspire to kill sb, to plot sb's murder.

comportement [kɔ̃pɔʀtəmɑ̃] nm **1.** [attitude] behaviour 🇬🇧, behavior 🇺🇸 ▸ **trouble du comportement alimen-**taire eating disorder **2.** AUTO & SCI [d'un véhicule] performance, behaviour 🇬🇧, behavior 🇺🇸 ; [de pneus] performance ; [d'une molécule] behaviour 🇬🇧, behavior 🇺🇸.

comporter [3] [kɔ̃pɔʀte] vt **1.** [être muni de] to have, to include **2.** [être constitué de] to be made up ou to consist of / *la maison comporte trois étages* it's a three-storey house **3.** [contenir] to contain **4.** [entraîner] to entail, to imply **5.** [permettre, admettre] to allow, to admit / *la règle comporte quelques exceptions* there are one or two exceptions to this rule. ❖ **se comporter** vpi [réagir - personne] to act, to behave / *tâche de bien te comporter* try to behave (yourself ou well) ▸ **se comporter en enfant / en adulte** to act childishly / like an adult.

composant [kɔ̃pozɑ̃] nm **1.** [élément] component, constituent **2.** CONSTR, INDUST & LING component.

composé, e [kɔ̃poze] adj **1.** [formé d'un mélange - bouquet, salade] mixed, composite **2.** BOT [feuille] compound ; [inflorescence] composite ▸ **fleur composée** composite (flower) **3.** CHIM, ÉCON & MATH compound *(modif)*. ❖ **composé** nm **1.** [ensemble] ▸ **composé de** mixture ou blend ou combination of **2.** LING compound (word).

composer [3] [kɔ̃poze] ◆ vt **1.** [rassembler - équipe, cabinet] to form, to select (the members of) ; [- menu] to prepare, to put together *(sép)* ; [- bouquet] to make up *(sép)* **2.** [écrire - roman, discours] to write ; [- poème, symphonie] to compose ; [- programme] to draw up *(sép)*, to prepare **3.** [faire partie de] to (go to) make up *(insép)* ▸ **être composé de** to be made up of, to consist of **4.** TÉLÉC [numéro de téléphone] to dial ; [code] to key (in). ◆ vi **1.** [transiger] to compromise ▸ **composer avec qqn / sa conscience** to come to a compromise with sb / one's conscience **2.** ÉDUC to take an exam ▸ **composer en histoire** to take a history test ou exam. ❖ **se composer de** vp + prép to be made up ou composed of / *l'équipe se compose de onze joueurs* the team is made up of ou comprises eleven players.

composite [kɔ̃pozit] ◆ adj **1.** [mobilier, population] heterogeneous, mixed, composite ; [foule, assemblée] mixed **2.** ARCHIT & TECHNOL composite. ◆ nm ARCHIT composite order.

compositeur, trice [kɔ̃pozitœʀ, tʀis] nm, f MUS composer.

composition [kɔ̃pozisjɔ̃] nf **1.** [fabrication, assemblage - d'un produit, d'un plat, d'un menu] making up, putting together ; [- d'un bouquet] making up, arranging ; [- d'une équipe, d'une assemblée, d'un gouvernement] forming, formation, setting up ▸ **composition florale** flower arrangement **2.** [écriture - d'une symphonie] composition ; [- d'un poème, d'une lettre] writing ; [- d'un programme] drawing up **3.** [éléments - d'une assemblée, d'un gouvernement, d'un menu] composition ; [- d'un programme] elements / *quelle sera la composition du jury ?* who will the members of the jury be?, who will make up the jury? ; CULIN, PHARM & CHIM composition / *des conservateurs entrent dans la composition du produit* this product contains preservatives **4.** ÉDUC [dissertation] essay, composition ; [examen] test, exam, paper ▸ **composition française** French paper. ❖ **de ma composition, de sa composition** loc adj : *il a chanté une petite chanson de sa composition* he sang a little song he'd written.

compost [kɔ̃pɔst] nm compost.

composter [3] [kɔ̃pɔste] vt **1.** [pour dater] to date stamp **2.** [pour valider] to punch.

compote [kɔ̃pɔt] nf CULIN : *compote de pommes* stewed apples, apple compote. ❖ **en compote** loc adj **1.** [fruits] stewed **2.** *fam* [meurtri, détruit] smashed up / *j'ai les pieds en compote* my feet are killing me.

compréhensible [kɔ̃pʀeɑ̃sibl] adj [intelligible] comprehensible, intelligible ; [excusable, concevable] understandable.

compréhensif, ive [kɔ̃preãsif, iv] adj [disposé à comprendre] understanding.

⚠ **Comprehensive** signifie « exhaustif », « complet » et non compréhensif.

compréhension [kɔ̃preãsjɔ̃] nf **1.** [fait de comprendre] comprehension, understanding / *des notes nécessaires à la compréhension du texte* notes that are necessary to understand ou for a proper understanding of the text **2.** [bienveillance] sympathy, understanding / *être plein de compréhension* to be very understanding **3.** LING & MATH comprehension.

comprendre [79] [kɔ̃prɑ̃dʀ] vt

A. SAISIR, APPRÉCIER 1. [saisir par un raisonnement] to understand, to comprehend *sout* ▸ *c'est à n'y rien comprendre* it's just baffling ▸ **(c'est) compris ?** a) [vous avez suivi] is it clear?, do you understand? b) [c'est un ordre] do you hear me! ▸ **(c'est) compris !** all right!, OK! ▸ **se faire comprendre** a) [mon exposé est-il clair ?] *est-ce que je me fais bien comprendre ?* is my explanation clear enough? b) [ton menaçant] do I make myself clear? ; *(en usage absolu)* : *elle a fini par comprendre* [se résigner] she finally got the message **2.** [saisir grâce à ses connaissances - théorie, langue] to understand / *se faire comprendre* to make o.s. understood **3.** [saisir par une intuition] to understand, to realize / *comprends-tu l'importance d'une telle décision ?* do you realize how important a decision it is? **4.** [admettre] to understand / *je comprends qu'on s'énerve dans les bouchons* it's quite understandable that people get irritable when caught in traffic jams ; *(en usage absolu)* : *elle n'a pas osé, il faut comprendre (aussi) !* she didn't dare, you have to put yourself in her shoes! **5.** [concevoir] to understand, to see **6.** [avoir les mêmes sentiments que] to understand, to sympathize with / *je vous comprends, cela a dû être terrible* I know how you feel, it must have been awful.

B. INCLURE 1. [être composé entièrement de] to contain, to be made up ou to be comprised ou to consist of **2.** [être composé en partie de] to include, to contain **3.** [englober - frais, taxe] to include **4.** *(au passif)* [se situer] : *l'inflation sera comprise entre 5 % et 8 %* inflation will be (somewhere) between 5% and 8%. ❖ **se comprendre** ◆ vp *(emploi passif)* to be understandable / *cela se comprend, ça se comprend* that's quite understandable. ◆ vp *(emploi réciproque)* to understand one another.

compresse [kɔ̃prɛs] nf compress, pack.

compresser [4] [kɔ̃prese] vt **1.** [gén] to pack (tightly) in, to pack in tight **2.** INFORM [données] to compress ; [fichier] to zip.

compresseur [kɔ̃presœʀ] nm TRAV PUB ▸ **(rouleau) compresseur** steamroller.

compression [kɔ̃presjɔ̃] nf [des dépenses, du personnel] reduction, cutting down / *des compressions budgétaires* cuts ou reductions in the budget.

comprimé [kɔ̃pʀime] nm tablet.

comprimer [3] [kɔ̃pʀime] vt **1.** [serrer - air, vapeur, gaz] to compress ; [-objets] to pack (in) tightly ; [-foin, paille] to compact, to press tight / *cette robe me comprime la taille* this dress is much too tight for me around the waist **2.** [diminuer - dépenses] to curtail, to trim, to cut down *(sép)* ; [-effectifs] to trim ou to cut down *(sép)* **3.** INFORM to pack.

compris, e [kɔ̃pʀi, iz] ◆ adj **1.** [inclus - service, boisson] included / *service non compris* service not included, not inclusive of the service charge ▸ **y compris** included, including ; [dans les dates] inclusive **2.** [pensé] ▸ **bien compris** well

thought-out. ◆ interj *fam* AÉRON & TÉLÉC ▸ **compris !** OK! ❖ **tout compris** loc adv net, all inclusive, all in 🇬🇧.

compromettant, e [kɔ̃pʀɔmetɑ̃, ɑ̃t] adj [document, action] incriminating ; [situation] compromising.

compromettre [84] [kɔ̃pʀɔmetʀ] ◆ vt [nuire à la réputation de] to compromise / *il est compromis dans l'affaire* he's implicated ou involved in the affair. ◆ vi DR to compromise. ❖ **se compromettre** vp *(emploi réfléchi)* to risk ou to jeopardize one's reputation, to be compromised.

compromis [kɔ̃pʀɔmi] nm [concession] compromise ; [moyen terme] compromise (solution) / *faire des compromis* to make compromises / *trouver un compromis* to reach ou to come to a compromise.

comptabiliser [3] [kɔ̃tabilize] vt [compter] to count.

comptabilité [kɔ̃tabilite] nf **1.** [profession] accountancy, accounting **2.** [comptes] accounts, books **3.** [technique] accounting, book-keeping **4.** [service, bureau] accounts (department).

comptable [kɔ̃tabl] ◆ adj **1.** FIN accounting *(modif)*, book-keeping *(modif)* **2.** LING count *(modif)*, countable. ◆ nmf accountant.

comptant [kɔ̃tɑ̃] ◆ adj m : *je lui ai versé 200 € comptants* I paid him 200 € in cash. ◆ adv cash ▸ **payer comptant** to pay cash. ❖ **au comptant** loc adv cash (adv) ▸ **acheter / vendre au comptant** to buy / to sell for cash.

compte [kɔ̃t] nm

A. CALCUL, SOMME CALCULÉE 1. [opération] counting ▸ **faire le compte (de)** a) [personnes] to count (up) b) [dépenses] to add up ▸ **compte à rebours** *pr & fig* countdown **2.** [résultat] (sum) total ▸ **il n'y a pas le compte** a) [personnes] they're not all here ou there, some are missing b) [dépenses] it doesn't add up ▸ **compte rond** : *cela fait un compte rond* that makes it a (nice) round sum ou figure **3.** [avantage] ▸ **il n'y trouvait pas son compte, alors il est parti** a) [il ne gagnait pas assez d'argent] he wasn't doing well enough out of it, so he left b) [dans une relation] he wasn't getting what he wanted out of it, so he left **4.** ▸ **régler son compte à qqn** a) [le payer] to pay sb off b) *fam & fig* to give sb a piece of one's mind ▸ **régler ses comptes** [mettre en ordre ses affaires] to put one's affairs in order ▸ **régler ses comptes avec qqn** a) [le payer] to settle up with sb b) [se venger] to settle a score with sb ▸ **son compte est bon** *fam* he's had it, he's done for.

B. BANQUE & INFORMATIQUE 1. [de dépôt, de crédit] account ▸ **compte bancaire** bank account ▸ **compte courant** current 🇬🇧 ou checking 🇺🇸 account ▸ **compte épargne** savings account **2.** [facture] bill, check 🇺🇸 **3.** [bilan] ▸ **compte de profits et pertes** profit and loss account ▸ **compte de résultat** profit and loss account **4.** INFORM & INTERNET account ▸ **compte utilisateur** user account ▸ **compte de courrier électronique** e-mail account.

C. LOCUTIONS ▸ **être** ou **travailler à son compte** to be self-employed / *il est à son compte* he's his own boss, he's set up on his own ▸ **demander des comptes à qqn** to ask sb for an explanation of sthg, to ask sb to account for sthg ▸ **rendre des comptes (à qqn)** to give ou to offer (sb) an explanation ▸ **rendre compte de qqch à qqn** a) [s'en expliquer] to justify sthg to sb b) [faire un rapport] to give an account of sthg to sb ▸ **prendre qqch en compte** [prendre en considération] to take sthg into account ou consideration ▸ **se rendre compte de qqch** to realize sthg / *non mais, tu te rends compte !* *fam* [indignation] can you believe it? ▸ **tenir compte de qqch** to take account of sthg, to take sthg into consideration ▸ **compte tenu de** in view ou in the light of. ❖ **comptes** nmpl accounts, accounting ▸ **faire / tenir les comptes** to do / to keep the accounts. ❖ **pour compte** loc adv ▸ **laisser qqn pour compte** to neglect sb. ❖ **pour le compte de** loc prép for / *elle travaille pour le compte d'une grande société* she works for a large firm, she freelances for a large firm. ❖ **sur le compte de** loc prép **1.** [à propos de] on, about, concerning **2.** EXPR **mettre qqch sur le compte de qqn** pr to put sth on sb's bill ▸ **mettre qqch sur le compte de qqch** to put sth down to sth. ❖ **tout compte fait, tous comptes faits** loc adv [après tout] thinking about it, on second thoughts.

compte(-)chèques [kɔ̃tʃɛk] (pl **comptes chèques** ou **comptes-chèques**) nm current UK ou checking US account ▸ **compte-chèques postal** *account held at the Post Office* ; ≃ giro account UK.

compte-gouttes (pl **compte-gouttes**), **compte-goutte*** (pl **compte-gouttes***) [kɔ̃tgut] nm dropper. ❖ **au compte-gouttes, au compte-goutte*** loc adv fam very sparingly ▸ **payer qqn au compte-gouttes** to pay sb off in dribs and drabs.

compter [3] [kɔ̃te] ◆ vt **1.** [dénombrer - objets, argent, personnes] to count / *j'ai compté qu'il restait 100 euros dans la caisse* according to my reckoning there are 100 euros left in the till / *compter les heures / jours* [d'impatience] to be counting the hours / days / *il m'a compté absent / présent* he marked me (down as) absent / present ▸ **compter les points** pr & fig to keep score ▸ **compter qqch sur les doigts de la main** : *on peut les compter sur les doigts de la main* you can count them of the fingers of one hand **2.** [limiter] to count (out) ▸ **le temps lui est compté** **a)** [il va mourir] his days are numbered **b)** [pour accomplir quelque chose] he's running out of time ▸ **ses jours sont comptés** his days are numbered **3.** [faire payer] to charge for / *le serveur nous a compté 5 euros de trop* the waiter has overcharged us by 5 euros, the waiter has charged us 5 euros too much **4.** [payer, verser] to pay / *il m'a compté deux jours à 40 euros* he paid me (for) two days at 40 euros **5.** [inclure] to count (in), to include / *dans le total nous n'avons pas compté le vin* wine has not been included in the overall figure **6.** [classer - dans une catégorie] ▸ **compter qqch / qqn parmi** to count sth / sb among, to number sth / sb among **7.** [prendre en considération] to take into account, to take account of / *et je ne compte pas la fatigue !* and that's without mentioning the effort! ▸ **compter qqn / qqch pour** : *nous devons compter sa contribution pour quelque chose* we must take some account of her contribution **8.** [avoir - membres, habitants] to have / *nous sommes heureux de vous compter parmi nous ce soir* we're happy to have ou to welcome you among us tonight / *il compte beaucoup d'artistes au nombre de* ou *parmi ses amis* he numbers many artists among his friends **9.** [s'attendre à] to expect / *je compte recevoir les résultats cette semaine* I'm expecting the results this week **10.** [avoir l'intention de] to intend ▸ **compter faire qqch** to intend to do sth, to mean to do sth, to plan to do sth **11.** [prévoir] to allow ; *(en usage absolu)* ▸ **compter juste** to skimp ▸ **compter large** to be generous / *il faudra deux heures pour y aller, en comptant large* it will take two hours to get there, at the most. ◆ vi **1.** [calculer] to count, to add up ▸ **compter jusqu'à 10** to count (up) to 10 / *compter sur ses doigts* to count on one's fingers / *tu as dû mal compter* you must have got your calculations wrong, you must have miscalculated **2.** [limiter ses dépenses] to be careful (with money) **3.** [importer] to count, to matter ▸ **ce qui compte, c'est ta santé / le résultat** the important thing is your health / the end result / *tu comptes beaucoup pour moi* you mean a lot to me / *à l'examen, la philosophie ne compte presque pas* philosophy is a very minor subject in the exam / *compter double / triple* to count double / triple / *compter pour quelque chose / rien* to count for something / nothing **4.** [figurer] ▸ **compter parmi** to rank with, to be numbered among / *elle compte parmi les plus grands pianistes de sa génération* she is one of the greatest pianists of her generation. ❖ **compter avec** v + prép to reckon with / *désormais, il faudra compter avec l'opposition* from now on, the opposition will have to be reckoned with. ❖ **compter sans** v + prép to fail to take into account, to fail to allow for / *il avait compté sans la rapidité de Jones* he had failed to take Jones' speed into account. ❖ **compter sur** v + prép [faire confiance à] to count ou to rely ou to depend on *(insép)* ; [espérer - venue, collaboration, événement] to count on *(insép)* / *c'est quelqu'un sur qui tu peux compter* he's / she's a reliable person ▸ **il ne faut pas trop y compter** don't count on it, I wouldn't count on it ▸ **compter sur qqn / qqch pour** : *compte sur lui pour aller tout répéter au patron !* you can rely on him to go and tell the boss everything! / *si c'est pour lui jouer un mauvais tour, ne comptez pas sur moi !* if you want to play a dirty trick on him, you can count me out! ❖ **à compter de** loc prép as from ou of / *à compter de ce jour, nous ne nous sommes plus revus* from that day on, we never saw each other again. ❖ **sans compter** loc adv [généreusement] ▸ **donner sans compter** to give generously ou without counting the cost.

compte(-)rendu [kɔ̃tʁɑ̃dy] (pl **comptes rendus** ou **comptes-rendus**) nm [d'une conversation] account, report ; [d'une séance, d'un match, d'une visite professionnelle] report ; [d'un livre, d'un spectacle] review ▸ **compte-rendu d'audience** court session record.

compte-tours (pl **compte-tours**), **compte-tour*** (pl **compte-tours***) [kɔ̃ttuʁ] nm rev counter, tachometer spéc.

compteur [kɔ̃tœʁ] nm [appareil] meter ; [affichage] counter ▸ **compteur à gaz / d'eau / d'électricité** gas / water / electricity meter ▸ **compteur kilométrique** milometer UK, mileometer UK, odometer US ▸ **compteur de vitesse** speedometer.

comptine [kɔ̃tin] nf [chanson] nursery rhyme ; [formule] counting-out rhyme.

comptoir [kɔ̃twaʁ] nm **1.** [bar] bar **2.** [de magasin] counter.

compulsif, ive [kɔ̃pylsif, iv] adj PSYCHOL compulsive.

comte [kɔ̃t] nm count, earl.

comté [kɔ̃te] nm **1.** [territoire d'un comte] earldom **2.** [division géographique] county **3.** [fromage] comté (cheese).

comtesse [kɔ̃tɛs] nf countess.

con, conne [kɔ̃, kɔn] tfam ◆ adj **1.** [stupide] bloody UK ou damn stupid ; [irritant] bloody UK ou damn irritating / *il n'est pas con !* he's no fool! **2.** [regrettable] silly, stupid. ◆ nm, f [personne stupide] bloody UK ou goddam US fool / *pauvre con !* you prat UK ou schmuck US! / *pauvre conne !* silly bitch! / *faire le con* to arse around UK, to screw around US.

concassé, e [kɔ̃kase] adj [poivre] coarse-ground ▸ **blé concassé** cracked wheat.

concasser [3] [kɔ̃kase] vt [pierre, sucre] to crush, to pound ; [poivre] to grind.

concaténer [3] [kɔ̃katene] vt to concatenate / *concaténer des fichiers* to concatenate files.

concave [kɔ̃kav] adj concave.

concéder [18] [kɔ̃sede] vt **1.** [donner - droit, territoire] to concede, to grant **2.** [admettre] to admit, to grant / *elle parle bien, ça je te le concède* I must admit that she's a good speaker, she's a good speaker, I grant you **3.** SPORT [point, corner] to concede, to give away *(sép)*.

🖉 In reformed spelling (see p. 16-18), this verb is conjugated like *semer* : *il concédera, elle concéderait*.

concentration [kɔ̃sɑ̃tʁasjɔ̃] nf **1.** [attention] : *faire un effort de concentration* to try to concentrate **2.** [rassemblement] concentration ▸ **concentration urbaine** conurbation.

concentré, e [kɔ̃sɑ̃tʀe] adj **1.** [attentif] : *je n'étais pas assez concentré* I wasn't concentrating hard enough **2.** CHIM, CULIN & PHARM concentrated. ❖ **concentré** nm CULIN & PHARM [de jus de fruits] concentrate ; [de parfum] extract ▸ **concentré de tomate** tomato purée.

concentrer [3] [kɔ̃sɑ̃tʀe] vt [intérêt, efforts] to concentrate, to focus / *concentrer (toute) son attention sur* to concentrate (all) one's attention on. ❖ **se concentrer** vpi [être attentif] to concentrate ▸ **se concentrer sur qqch** to concentrate ou to focus on sthg.

concept [kɔ̃sɛpt] nm concept, notion.

concepteur, trice [kɔ̃sɛptœr, tʀis] nm, f designer.

conception [kɔ̃sɛpsjɔ̃] nf **1.** [notion] idea, concept, notion **2.** litt [compréhension] understanding **3.** BIOL conception **4.** [élaboration - gén] design ; [- par une entreprise] product design **5.** INFORM ▸ **conception assistée par ordinateur** computer-aided design.

concernant [kɔ̃sɛʀnɑ̃] prép **1.** [relatif à] concerning, regarding **2.** [à propos de] regarding, with regard to.

concerner [3] [kɔ̃sɛʀne] vt to concern / *cette histoire ne nous concerne pas* this business doesn't concern us ou is of no concern to us ou is no concern of ours ▸ **se sentir concerné** to feel involved. ❖ **en ce qui concerne** loc prép concerning, as regards ▸ **en ce qui me / le concerne** as far as I'm / he's concerned, from my / his point of view, as for me / him.

concert [kɔ̃sɛʀ] nm MUS concert ▸ **aller au concert** to go to a concert.

concertation [kɔ̃sɛʀtasjɔ̃] nf [dialogue] dialogue.

concerter [3] [kɔ̃sɛʀte] vt to plan ou to devise jointly. ❖ **se concerter** vp (emploi réciproque) to consult together, to confer.

concession [kɔ̃sesjɔ̃] nf **1.** [compromis] concession ▸ **faire des concessions** to make concessions **2.** [terrain] concession.

concessionnaire [kɔ̃sesjɔnɛʀ] nmf COMM dealer, franchise holder / *renseignez-vous auprès de votre concessionnaire (automobile)* see your (car) dealer.

concevable [kɔ̃svabl] adj conceivable / *il n'est pas concevable que...* it's inconceivable that...

concevoir [52] [kɔ̃s(ə)vwaʀ] vt **1.** [avoir une notion de] to conceive of (insép), to form a notion of **2.** [imaginer] to imagine, to conceive of (insép) / *je ne conçois pas de repas sans vin* I can't imagine a meal without wine **3.** [comprendre] to understand, to see / *c'est ainsi que je conçois l'amour* this is my idea of love ou how I see love **4.** [rédiger - message, réponse] to compose, to couch / *une lettre conçue en ces termes* a letter written as follows ou couched in the following terms **5.** BIOL to conceive. ❖ **se concevoir** vp (emploi passif) to be imagined / *une telle politique se conçoit en temps de guerre* such a policy is understandable in wartime.

concierge [kɔ̃sjɛʀʒ] nmf [gardien - d'immeuble] caretaker 🇬🇧, janitor 🇺🇸, superintendent 🇺🇸 ; [- d'hôtel] porter 🇬🇧, receptionist, concierge.

🚩 **Concierge**

In French apartment buildings, the **concierge** does general cleaning jobs, makes sure no unwelcome visitors enter the building, and often also delivers mail to the occupants of the building. The concierge usually lives in a small flat (**la loge**) just inside the front entrance. The politically correct term for concierge is **gardien/gardienne**.

---

conciliabule [kɔ̃siljabyl] nm consultation.

conciliant, e [kɔ̃siljɑ̃, ɑ̃t] adj [personne] conciliatory, accommodating ; [paroles, ton] conciliatory, placatory.

conciliation [kɔ̃siljasjɔ̃] nf **1.** [médiation] conciliation **2.** litt [entre deux personnes, deux partis] reconciliation.

concilier [9] [kɔ̃silje] vt [accorder - opinions, exigences] to reconcile. ❖ **se concilier** vpt ▸ **se concilier l'amitié de qqn** to gain ou to win sb's friendship.

concis, e [kɔ̃si, iz] adj [style] concise, tight ; [écrivain] concise ▸ **de manière concise** concisely.

concision [kɔ̃sizjɔ̃] nf concision, conciseness, tightness.

concitoyen, enne [kɔ̃sitwajɛ̃, ɛn] nm, f fellow citizen.

concluant, e [kɔ̃klyɑ̃, ɑ̃t] adj [essai, démonstration] conclusive.

conclure [96] [kɔ̃klyʀ] vt **1.** [terminer - discussion, travail] to end, to conclude, to bring to a close ou conclusion ; [- repas] to finish ou to round off (sép) **2.** [déduire] to conclude / *que peut-on conclure de cette expérience ?* what conclusion can be drawn from this experience? **3.** [accord] to conclude ; [traité] to sign ; [cessez-le-feu] to agree to (insép) ▸ **marché conclu !** it's a deal! ❖ **pour conclure** loc adv as a ou in conclusion, to conclude.

conclusion [kɔ̃klyzjɔ̃] nf **1.** [fin] conclusion **2.** [déduction] conclusion / *gardons-nous des conclusions hâtives* let's not jump to conclusions / *conclusion, la voiture est fichue* fam the result is that the car is a write-off 🇬🇧 ou is totaled 🇺🇸 ▸ **tirer une conclusion de qqch** to draw a conclusion from sthg. ❖ **conclusions** nfpl [d'un rapport] conclusions, findings ; DR submissions. ❖ **en conclusion** loc adv as a ou in conclusion, to conclude.

concocter [3] [kɔ̃kɔkte] vt to concoct.

concombre [kɔ̃kɔ̃bʀ] nm BOT cucumber.

concomitant, e [kɔ̃kɔmitɑ̃, ɑ̃t] adj concomitant, attendant.

concordance [kɔ̃kɔʀdɑ̃s] nf [conformité] agreement, similarity.

concorder [3] [kɔ̃kɔʀde] vi [versions, chiffres] to agree, to tally ; [groupes sanguins, empreintes] to match ▸ **faire concorder qqch et** ou **avec qqch** to make sthg and sthg agree.

concourir [45] [kɔ̃kuʀiʀ] vi [être en compétition] to compete. ❖ **concourir à** v + prép to contribute to, to work towards 🇬🇧 ou toward 🇺🇸 / *tout concourt à me faire croire qu'il ment* everything leads me to believe that he's lying.

concours [kɔ̃kuʀ] nm **1.** [aide] aid, help, support ▸ **prêter son concours à** to lend one's support to **2.** [combinaison] ▸ **un heureux / un fâcheux concours de circonstances** a lucky / an unfortunate coincidence **3.** [épreuve] competition, contest ▸ **concours de beauté / de chant** beauty / singing contest ▸ **concours agricole / hippique** agricultural / horse show **4.** ENS competitive (entrance) exam. ❖ **avec le concours de** loc prép with the participation of, in association with.

concret, ète [kɔ̃kʀe, ɛt] adj **1.** [palpable] concrete **2.** [non théorique] concrete, practical / *faire des propositions concrètes* to make concrete ou practical proposals. ❖ **concret** nm : *ce qu'il nous faut, c'est du concret* we need something we can get our teeth into.

concrètement [kɔ̃kʀetmɑ̃] adv concretely, in concrete terms.

concrétiser [3] [kɔ̃kʀetize] vt [rêve] to realize ; [idée, proposition] to make concrete. ❖ **se concrétiser** vpi [rêve] to come true, to materialize ; [proposition, idée] to be realized, to take concrete form ou shape.

concubin, e [kɔ̃kybɛ̃, in] nm, f [amant] concubine, partner.

concubinage [kɔ̃kybinaʒ] nm **1.** [vie de couple] ▸ **vivre en concubinage** to live as man and wife, to cohabit **2.** DR cohabitation, cohabiting.

concurrence [kɔ̃kyRɑ̃s] nf [rivalité] competition / *faire (de la) concurrence à* to be in competition ou to compete with ▸ **concurrence déloyale** unfair competition ou trading. ❖ **en concurrence** loc adv in competition / *il est en concurrence avec son frère* he's competing with his brother. ❖ **jusqu'à concurrence de** loc prép up to, to the limit of.

concurrencer [16] [kɔ̃kyRɑ̃se] vt to compete ou to be in competition with / *ils nous concurrencent dangereusement* they're very dangerous ou serious competitors for us.

concurrent, e [kɔ̃kyRɑ̃, ɑ̃t] ◆ adj competing, rival *(avant nom)*. ◆ nm, f **1.** COMM & SPORT competitor **2.** ÉDUC candidate.

concurrentiel, elle [kɔ̃kyRɑ̃sjɛl] adj competitive.

condamnable [kɔ̃danabl] adj blameworthy, reprehensible.

condamnation [kɔ̃danasjɔ̃] nf **1.** [action] sentencing, convicting / *il a fait l'objet de trois condamnations pour vol* he's already had three convictions for theft, he's been convicted three times for theft ; [peine] sentence ▸ **condamnation à mort** death sentence ▸ **condamnation à la réclusion à perpétuité** life sentence, sentence of life imprisonment **2.** [fin - d'un projet, d'une tentative] end **3.** AUTO [blocage] locking ; [système] locking device.

condamné, e [kɔ̃dane] nm, f DR sentenced ou convicted person ▸ **condamné à mort** prisoner under sentence of death.

condamner [3] [kɔ̃dane] vt **1.** DR [accusé] to sentence ▸ **condamner qqn à mort / aux travaux forcés** to sentence sb to death / to hard labour / *condamné à trois mois de prison pour...* sentenced to three months' imprisonment for... ▸ **condamné à une amende** fined ▸ **condamné pour meurtre** convicted of murder **2.** [interdire - magazine] to forbid publication of ; [- pratique] to forbid, to condemn / *la loi condamne l'usage de stupéfiants* the use of narcotics is forbidden by law **3.** [désapprouver - attentat, propos] to express disapproval of **4.** [suj : maladie incurable] to condemn, to doom / *les médecins disent qu'il est condamné* the doctors say that there is no hope for him **5.** [murer - porte, fenêtre] to block up (sép), to seal off (sép) ; [- pièce] to close up (sép) **6.** [obliger] : *il était condamné à vivre dans la misère* he was condemned to live in poverty.

condensation [kɔ̃dɑ̃sasjɔ̃] nf CHIM & PHYS condensation.

condensé [kɔ̃dɑ̃se] nm digest, summary, abstract.

condenser [3] [kɔ̃dɑ̃se] vt CHIM & PHYS to condense.

condescendance [kɔ̃desɑ̃dɑ̃s] nf condescension ▸ **avec condescendance** condescendingly.

condescendant, e [kɔ̃desɑ̃dɑ̃, ɑ̃t] adj [hautain - regard, parole] condescending, patronizing.

condescendre [73] [kɔ̃desɑ̃dR] ❖ **condescendre à** v + prép to condescend to / *elle a condescendu à me recevoir* aussi hum she condescended ou deigned to see me.

condiment [kɔ̃dimɑ̃] nm [épices] condiment ; [moutarde] (mild) mustard.

condisciple [kɔ̃disipl] nmf ÉDUC classmate, schoolmate ; UNIV fellow student.

condition [kɔ̃disjɔ̃] nf **1.** [préalable] condition ▸ **mettre une condition à qqch** to set a condition before sthg can be done / *j'accepte mais à une condition* I accept but on one condition ▸ **condition nécessaire / suffisante** necessary / sufficient condition ▸ **condition préalable** prerequi-

site **2.** [état] condition, shape / *être en bonne condition physique* to be in condition, to be fit / *être en mauvaise condition physique* to be in poor physical shape, to be unfit. ❖ **conditions** nfpl **1.** [environnement] conditions ▸ **conditions de vie / travail** living / working conditions **2.** [termes] terms / *quelles sont ses conditions ?* what terms is he offering? ▸ **conditions de vente / d'achat** terms of sale / purchase ▸ **conditions de paiement de remboursement** payment / repayment terms. ❖ **à condition de** loc prép on condition that, providing ou provided (that). ❖ **à (la) condition que** loc conj on condition that, provided ou providing (that). ❖ **dans ces conditions** loc adv under these conditions / *dans ces conditions, pourquoi se donner tant de mal ?* if that's the case, why go to so much trouble? ❖ **en condition** loc adv [en bonne forme] in shape ▸ **mettre en condition** [athlète, candidat] to get into condition ou form.

conditionnel, elle [kɔ̃disjɔnɛl] adj **1.** [soumis à condition] conditional, tentative **2.** GRAM conditional. ❖ **conditionnel** nm GRAM conditional (mood). ❖ **au conditionnel** loc adv GRAM in the conditional.

conditionnement [kɔ̃disjɔnmɑ̃] nm **1.** [fait d'emballer, emballage] packaging **2.** PSYCHOL conditioning.

conditionner [3] [kɔ̃disjɔne] vt **1.** [emballer - marchandise, aliments] to package **2.** [influencer] to condition, to influence.

condo [kɔ̃dɔ] nm Québec condominium.

condoléances [kɔ̃dɔleɑ̃s] nfpl condolences / *lettre de condoléances* letter of condolence ▸ **toutes mes condoléances, Paul** with deepest sympathy ou heartfelt condolences, Paul.

conducteur, trice [kɔ̃dyktœR, tRis] nm, f **1.** TRANSP driver **2.** INDUST operator.

⚠ **Conductor**, lorsqu'il s'agit d'une personne, signifie « chef d'orchestre » ou « contrôleur » et non conducteur.

conduire [80] [kɔ̃dɥiR] vt **1.** [emmener - gén] to take ; [- en voiture] to drive, to take / *conduire les enfants à l'école* to take ou to drive the children to school ▸ **conduire qqn jusqu'à la porte** to see sb to the door, to show sb the way out **2.** [guider] to lead / *les empreintes m'ont conduit jusqu'au hangar* the footprints led me to the shed **3.** [donner accès] ▸ **conduire à** to lead to (insép), to open out onto (insép) **4.** [mener] ▸ **conduire qqn à** : *conduire qqn au désespoir* to drive sb to desperation **5.** TRANSP [véhicule] to drive ; [hors-bord] to steer ; *(en usage absolu)* ▸ **conduire à droite / gauche** to drive on the right- / left-hand side of the road ▸ **conduire bien / mal / vite** to be a good / bad / fast driver **6.** [diriger - État] to run, to lead ; [- affaires, opérations] to run, to conduct, to manage ; [- travaux] to supervise ; [- recherches, enquête] to conduct, to lead ; [- délégation, révolte] to head, to lead **7.** PHYS [chaleur, électricité] to conduct, to be a conductor of. ❖ **se conduire** vpi [se comporter] to behave, to conduct o.s. / *se conduire mal* to behave badly, to misbehave.

conduit, e [kɔ̃dɥi, it] pp ⟶ conduire. ❖ **conduit** nm **1.** TECHNOL conduit, pipe ▸ **conduit d'aération** air duct **2.** ANAT canal, duct ▸ **conduit auditif** auditory canal. ❖ **conduite** nf **1.** [pilotage - d'un véhicule] driving ; [- d'un hors-bord] steering ▸ **la conduite à droite / gauche** driving on the right- / left-hand side of the road ▸ **conduite accompagnée** driving practice when accompanied by a qualified driver (authorized for learner drivers over 16 having passed their theoretical exam at a driving school) ▸ **conduite en état d'ivresse** drink-driving 🇬🇧, drunk-driving 🇺🇸, drinking and driving **2.** [comportement] conduct, behaviour ⓊⓀ, behavior ⓊⓈ ▸ **pour bonne conduite** [libéré, gracié] for good behaviour ▸ **mauvaise conduite** misbehaviour ⓊⓀ, misbehavior ⓊⓈ, misconduct **3**. [direction - des affaires] management, conduct ; [- de la guerre] conduct ; [- d'un pays] running ; [- des travaux] supervision **4**. TECHNOL pipe ; [canalisation principale] main ▸ **conduite d'eau / de gaz** water / gas pipe.

cône [kon] nm GÉOM cone.

confection [kɔ̃fɛksjɔ̃] nf **1**. CULIN preparation, making **2**. COUT [d'une robe] making ; [d'un veston] tailoring ▸ **la confection** INDUST the clothing industry ou business. ✧ **de confection** loc adj ready-to-wear, ready-made, off-the-peg ⓊⓀ.

confectionner [3] [kɔ̃fɛksjɔne] vt **1**. [préparer - plat, sauce] to prepare, to make **2**. COUT [robe] to make, to sew ; [veston] to tailor.

confédération [kɔ̃federasjɔ̃] nf [nation] confederation, confederacy ▸ **la Confédération helvétique** the Swiss Confederation.

conférence [kɔ̃feʀɑ̃s] nf **1**. [réunion] conference ▸ **conférence de presse** press conference ▸ **conférence au sommet** summit conference **2**. [cours] lecture / *il a fait une conférence sur Milton* he gave ou he delivered a lecture on Milton, he lectured on Milton.

conférencier, ère [kɔ̃feʀɑ̃sje, ɛʀ] nm, f speaker.

conférer [18] [kɔ̃feʀe] vt **1**. [décerner - titre, droit] to confer, to bestow **2**. fig [donner - importance, prestance] to impart.

✎ In reformed spelling (see p. 16-18), this verb is conjugated like *semer* : *il conférera, elle conférerait*.

confesser [4] [kɔ̃fese] vt **1**. RELIG [péché] to confess (to) ; [personne] to hear the confession of, to be the confessor of **2**. [reconnaître, admettre] to admit, to confess. ✧ **se confesser** vpi to confess, to make one's confession / *se confesser à un prêtre* to confess to a priest.

confession [kɔ̃fesjɔ̃] nf **1**. RELIG [aveu, rite] confession ▸ **faire une confession** pr & fig to make a confession, to confess **2**. [appartenance] faith, denomination ▸ **être de confession luthérienne / anglicane** to belong to the Lutheran / Anglican faith **3**. litt [proclamation] proclaiming **4**. LITTÉR / '**Confessions**' *Rousseau* 'Confessions'.

confessionnel, elle [kɔ̃fesjɔnɛl] adj denominational.

confetti [kɔ̃feti] nm [piece of] confetti ▸ **des confettis** confetti.

confiance [kɔ̃fjɑ̃s] nf **1**. [foi - en quelqu'un, quelque chose] trust, confidence ▸ **avoir confiance en qqn / qqch** to trust sb / sthg, to have confidence in sb / sthg ▸ **faire confiance à qqn** to trust sb / *j'ai confiance en l'avenir de mon pays* I have faith in the future of my country **2**. POL : *voter la confiance au gouvernement* to pass a vote of confidence in the government **3**. [aplomb] ▸ **confiance en soi** confidence, self-confidence, self-assurance. ✧ **de confiance** loc adj : *les hommes de confiance du président* the President's advisers. ✧ **en confiance** loc adv ▸ **se sentir** ou **être en confiance (avec qqn)** to feel safe (with sb). ✧ **en toute confiance** loc adv with complete confidence.

confiant, e [kɔ̃fjɑ̃, ɑ̃t] adj **1**. [qui fait confiance] trusting, trustful **2**. [qui exprime la confiance] trusting, confident **3**. [qui a confiance] : *être confiant dans* ou *en* to have confidence in.

confidence [kɔ̃fidɑ̃s] nf confidence ▸ **faire une confidence à qqn** to confide something to sb, to trust sb with a secret ▸ **faire des confidences à qqn** to confide in sb ▸ **confidences sur l'oreiller** hum pillow talk.

confident, e [kɔ̃fidɑ̃, ɑ̃t] nm, f confidant (confidante).

confidentialité [kɔ̃fidɑ̃sjalite] nf confidentiality.

confidentiel, elle [kɔ̃fidɑ̃sjɛl] adj [secret - information] confidential ; [- entretien] private.

confier [9] [kɔ̃fje] vt **1**. [dire - craintes, intentions] to confide, to entrust ▸ **confier un secret à qqn** to confide ou to entrust a secret to sb, to share a secret with sb / *il m'a confié qu'il voulait divorcer* he confided to me that he wanted a divorce **2**. [donner] to entrust ▸ **confier une mission à qqn** to entrust a mission to sb, to entrust sb with a mission / *la garde de Marie a été confiée à sa mère* Marie has been put in her mother's care **3**. litt [livrer] to consign. ✧ **se confier** vpi [s'épancher] to confide ▸ **se confier à qqn** to confide in sb / *elle ne se confie pas facilement* she doesn't confide in people easily.

configuration [kɔ̃figyrasjɔ̃] nf **1**. [aspect général] configuration, general shape ▸ **la configuration des lieux** the layout of the place **2**. CHIM & INFORM configuration.

configurer [kɔ̃figyre] vt INFORM to configure.

confiné, e [kɔ̃fine] adj [air] stale ; [atmosphère] stuffy ▸ **vivre confiné chez soi** to live shut up indoors.

confins [kɔ̃fɛ̃] ✧ **aux confins de** loc prép on the borders of.

confirmation [kɔ̃firmasjɔ̃] nf **1**. [attestation] confirmation **2**. RELIG confirmation.

confirmer [3] [kɔ̃firme] vt **1**. [rendre définitif - réservation, nouvelle] to confirm / *cela reste à confirmer* it remains to be confirmed, it is as yet unconfirmed **2**. [renforcer - témoignage, diagnostic, impression] to confirm, to bear out *(insép)* / *ceci confirme mes* ou *me confirme dans mes soupçons* this bears out ou confirms my suspicions **3**. [affermir - position, supériorité] to reinforce.

confiscation [kɔ̃fiskasjɔ̃] nf [saisie] confiscation, seizure, seizing.

confiserie [kɔ̃fizri] nf **1**. [produit] sweet ⓊⓀ, candy ⓊⓈ ▸ **acheter des confiseries** to buy confectionery, to buy sweets ⓊⓀ, to buy candy ⓊⓈ **2**. [industrie] confectionery (business ou trade) **3**. [magasin] confectioner's, sweet shop ⓊⓀ, candy store ⓊⓈ **4**. [des olives, des sardines] pickling.

confiseur, euse [kɔ̃fizœr, øz] nm, f confectioner.

confisquer [3] [kɔ̃fiske] vt [retirer - marchandises, drogue] to confiscate, to seize ; [- sifflet, livre] to take away *(sép)*, to confiscate.

confit, e [kɔ̃fi, it] adj **1**. [fruits] candied, crystallized ; [cornichons] pickled **2**. fig : *être confit en dévotion* to be steeped in piety. ✧ **confit** nm conserve ▸ **confit d'oie** goose conserve *(goose cooked in it's own fat to preserve it)*.

confiture [kɔ̃fityr] nf jam, preserve.

conflictuel, elle [kɔ̃fliktɥɛl] adj [pulsions, désirs] conflicting, clashing ▸ **situation / relation conflictuelle** antagonistic situation / relationship.

conflit [kɔ̃fli] nm **1**. [heurt] ▸ **entrer en conflit avec** to conflict with, to come into conflict with ▸ **le conflit des générations** the generation gap, the clash between generations **2**. DR conflict ▸ **conflit d'intérêts** conflict of interests ▸ **conflit social** ou **du travail** labour ou industrial dispute.

confondre [75] [kɔ̃fɔ̃dr] vt **1**. [mêler - films, auteurs, dates] to confuse, to mix up *(sép)* ▸ **confondre qqn / qqch avec** to mistake sb / sthg for ▸ **tous âges confondus** irrespective of age **2**. sout [étonner] to astound, to astonish.

conforme [kɔ̃fɔrm] adj **1**. [qui répond à une règle] standard / *ce n'est pas conforme à la loi* this is not in accordance with the law **2**. [conventionnel] conventional, standard **3**. [semblable] identical ▸ **conforme à l'original** true to the original.

conformément [kɔ̃fɔrmemɑ̃] ✧ **conformément à** loc prép in accordance with, according to.

conformer [3] [kɔ̃fɔrme] vt [adapter] ▸ **conformer qqch à** to adapt ou to match sthg to / *ils ont conformé* *leur tactique à la nôtre* they modelled their tactics on ours. ❖ **se conformer à** vp + prép [se plier à - *usage*] to conform to ; [- *ordre*] to comply with, to abide by / *se conformer à une décision* to abide by ou to comply with a decision.

conformiste [kɔ̃fɔʀmist] ◆ adj [traditionnel] conformist, conventional. ◆ nmf conformist, conventionalist.

conformité [kɔ̃fɔʀmite] nf **1.** [ressemblance] similarity **2.** [obéissance] : *la conformité aux usages sociaux* conformity to social customs **3.** [conventionnalisme] conventionality. ❖ **en conformité avec** loc prép in accordance with, according to ▶ **être en conformité avec** to conform to.

confort [kɔ̃fɔʀ] nm **1.** [commodités] ▶ **le confort** [d'un appartement, d'un hôtel] modern conveniences **2.** [aise physique] ▶ **le confort** comfort **3.** [tranquillité] ▶ **le confort intellectuel** self-assurance.

confortable [kɔ̃fɔʀtabl] adj **1.** [douillet - *lit, maison*] comfortable, cosy, snug **2.** [tranquillisant - *situation, routine*] comfortable.

confortablement [kɔ̃fɔʀtabləmɑ̃] adv comfortably.

conforter [3] [kɔ̃fɔʀte] vt [renforcer - *position, avance*] to reinforce, to strengthen.

confrère [kɔ̃fʀɛʀ] nm colleague.

confrérie [kɔ̃fʀeʀi] nf RELIG confraternity, brotherhood.

confrontation [kɔ̃fʀɔ̃tasjɔ̃] nf **1.** [face-à-face] confrontation **2.** DR confrontation **3.** [comparaison] comparison **4.** [conflit] confrontation ▶ **confrontation armée** armed confrontation ou conflict / *il cherche toujours à éviter les confrontations* ou *la confrontation* he always tries to avoid confrontation.

confronter [3] [kɔ̃fʀɔ̃te] vt **1.** [mettre face à face - *accusés, témoins*] to confront ▶ **être confronté à** ou **avec qqn** to be confronted with sb **2.** [comparer - *textes, points de vue*] to compare.

confus, e [kɔ̃fy, yz] adj **1.** [imprécis - *souvenir, impression*] unclear, confused, vague ; [- *idées*] muddled ; [- *situation, histoire*] confused, involved ; [- *explication*] muddled, confused **2.** [embarrassé] : *je suis confus de t'avoir fait attendre* I'm awfully ou dreadfully sorry to have kept you waiting.

> ⚠ Attention, **confused** ne peut être employé pour traduire confus au sens d'«embarrassé».

confusément [kɔ̃fyzemɑ̃] adv [vaguement] confusedly, vaguely.

confusion [kɔ̃fyzjɔ̃] nf **1.** [méprise] mix-up, confusion **2.** [désordre] confusion, disarray, chaos ▶ **jeter la confusion dans l'esprit de qqn** to sow confusion in sb's mind, to throw sb into confusion **3.** [honte] embarrassment, confusion ▶ **à ma grande confusion** to my great embarrassment **4.** DR ▶ **confusion de dette** confusion.

congé [kɔ̃ʒe] nm **1.** [vacances] holiday 🇬🇧, vacation 🇺🇸 ; ADMIN & MIL leave ▶ **trois semaines de congé** three weeks off, three weeks' leave / *j'ai congé le lundi* I have Mondays off, I'm off on Mondays, Monday is my day off ▶ **congé d'adoption** *leave for an adopting parent* ▶ **congé pour convenance personnelle** compassionate leave ▶ **congé d'enseignement et de recherche** *leave enabling an employee to study or carry out research* ▶ **congé-formation** training leave ▶ **congé de maladie** sick leave ▶ **congé (de) maternité** maternity leave ▶ **congé de naissance** paternity leave ▶ **congé parental (d'éducation)** *parent's right to take time off without pay (after a birth or an adoption)* ▶ **congé de paternité** paternity leave ▶ **congés payés** paid holiday ou holidays ou leave 🇬🇧, paid vacation 🇺🇸 ▶ **congé sabbatique**

sabbatical (leave) ▶ **congés scolaires** school holidays 🇬🇧 ou vacation 🇺🇸 ▶ **congé sans solde** time off without pay, unpaid leave ▶ **jour de congé** day off **2.** [avis de départ] notice / *donner son congé à son patron* to hand in one's notice to the boss / *donner son congé à son propriétaire* to give notice to one's landlord / *donner (son) congé à un employé* to give notice to ou to dismiss an employee **3.** [adieu] ▶ **donner congé à qqn** to dismiss sb ▶ **prendre congé** (take one's) leave, to depart ▶ **prendre congé de** to take one's leave of. ❖ **en congé** loc adv ▶ **être en congé** a) [soldat] to be on leave b) [écolier, salarié] to be on holiday 🇬🇧 ou vacation 🇺🇸 / *je suis en congé demain jusqu'à lundi* I'm off (from) tomorrow till Monday.

congédier [9] [kɔ̃ʒedje] vt [employé] to dismiss, to discharge ; [locataire] to give notice to ; sout [importun] to send away (sép).

congélateur [kɔ̃ʒelatœʀ] nm deep freeze, freezer.

congélation [kɔ̃ʒelasjɔ̃] nf [technique] freezing ; [durée] freezing time ▶ **sac de congélation** freezer bag.

congeler [25] [kɔ̃ʒle] vt to freeze / *tarte / viande congelée* frozen pie / meat.

congélo [kɔ̃ʒelo] nm fam freezer.

congénital, e, aux [kɔ̃ʒenital, o] adj congenital.

congère [kɔ̃ʒɛʀ] nf snowdrift.

congestion [kɔ̃ʒɛstjɔ̃] nf congestion ▶ **congestion cérébrale** stroke ▶ **congestion pulmonaire** congestion of the lungs.

conglomérat [kɔ̃glɔmeʀa] nm ÉCON & GÉOL conglomerate.

Congo [kɔ̃go] npr m ▶ **le Congo** a) [pays] the Congo b) [fleuve] the Congo River, the River Congo.

congolais, e [kɔ̃gɔlɛ, ɛz] adj Congolese. ❖ **Congolais, e** nm, f Congolese ▶ **les Congolais** the Congolese. ❖ **congolais** nm CULIN coconut cake.

congre [kɔ̃gʀ] nm conger (eel).

congrégation [kɔ̃gʀegasjɔ̃] nf [ordre] congregation, order.

congrès [kɔ̃gʀɛ] nm [conférence, colloque] congress ▶ **le Congrès (américain)** Congress.

congressiste [kɔ̃gʀesist] nmf participant at a congress.

conifère [kɔnifɛʀ] nm conifer.

conique [kɔnik] adj [pointu] conical, cone-shaped.

conjecture [kɔ̃ʒɛktyʀ] nf conjecture, surmise ▶ **se perdre en conjectures** to be perplexed / *nous en sommes réduits aux conjectures* we can only guess.

conjecturer [3] [kɔ̃ʒɛktyʀe] vt sout to conjecture sout ou to speculate about (insép) ▶ **conjecturer que** to surmise that.

conjoint, e [kɔ̃ʒwɛ̃, ɛ̃t] nm, f ADMIN spouse / *il faut l'accord des deux conjoints* the agreement of both husband and wife is necessary.

conjointement [kɔ̃ʒwɛ̃tmɑ̃] adv jointly / *conjointement avec mon associé* together with my associate.

conjonctif, ive [kɔ̃ʒɔ̃ktif, iv] adj **1.** GRAM conjunctive **2.** ANAT connective. ❖ **conjonctive** nf **1.** GRAM conjunctive clause **2.** ANAT conjunctiva.

conjonction [kɔ̃ʒɔ̃ksjɔ̃] nf **1.** [union] union, conjunction **2.** GRAM conjunction ▶ **conjonction de coordination / de subordination** coordinating / subordinating conjunction.

conjonctivite [kɔ̃ʒɔ̃ktivit] nf conjunctivitis.

conjoncture [kɔ̃ʒɔ̃ktyʀ] nf **1.** [contexte] situation, conditions ▶ **dans la conjoncture actuelle** under the present circumstances, at this juncture **2.** ÉCON economic situation ou trends.

conjoncturel, elle [kɔ̃ʒɔ̃ktyʀɛl] adj [chômage] cyclical.

conjugaison [kɔ̃ʒygɛzɔ̃] nf BIOL, CHIM & GRAM conjugation.

conjugal, e, aux [kɔ̃ʒygal, o] adj conjugal ▸ **vie conjugale** married life.

conjuguer [3] [kɔ̃ʒyge] vt **1.** [verbe] to conjugate / *conjuguer au futur* to conjugate in the future tense **2.** [unir -efforts, volontés] to join, to combine. ❖ **se conjuguer** ◆ vp *(emploi passif)* GRAM to conjugate, to be conjugated. ◆ vpi [s'unir] to work together, to combine.

conjurer [3] [kɔ̃ʒyʀe] vt **1.** *litt* [supplier] to beg, to beseech *litt* / *il la conjura de ne pas le dénoncer* he begged ou besought *litt* her not to give him away **2.** [écarter -mauvais sort, danger, crise] to ward off *(sép)*, to keep at bay **3.** *litt* [manigancer] to plot. ❖ **se conjurer** vpi *litt* to conspire ▸ **se conjurer contre** to plot ou to conspire against.

connaissance [kɔnɛsɑ̃s] nf **1.** [maîtrise dans un domaine] knowledge ▸ **la connaissance de soi** self-knowledge **2.** PHILOS ▸ **la connaissance** knowledge **3.** [fait d'être informé] : *il n'en a jamais eu connaissance* he never learnt about it, he was never notified of it / *prendre connaissance des faits* to learn about ou to hear of the facts / *il est venu à notre connaissance que...* it has come to our attention that... **4.** [conscience] consciousness / *il gisait là / il est tombé, sans connaissance* he was lying there / he fell unconscious ▸ **perdre connaissance** to lose consciousness ▸ **reprendre connaissance** to come to, to regain consciousness **5.** ▸ **faire la connaissance de qqn, faire connaissance avec qqn** [rencontrer qqn] to make sb's acquaintance, to meet sb ▸ **faire connaissance avec qqch** [aborder qqch] to discover, to get to know **6.** [ami] acquaintance. ❖ **connaissances** nfpl knowledge / *avoir de solides connaissances en* to have a thorough knowledge of ou a good grounding in / *avoir des connaissances sommaires en* to have a basic knowledge of, to know the rudiments of. ❖ **à ma connaissance** loc adv to (the best of) my / his, etc. knowledge, as far as I know / he knows, etc. ▸ **pas à ma connaissance** not to my knowledge, not as far as I know, not that I know of. ❖ **en connaissance de cause** loc adv ▸ **faire qqch en connaissance de cause** to do sthg with full knowledge of the facts.

> 🖊 Attention ! Le mot knowledge est indénombrable. Il ne s'emploie jamais au pluriel :

connaisseur, euse [kɔnɛsœr, øz] nm, f connoisseur / *être connaisseur en pierres précieuses* to be a connoisseur of ou knowledgeable about gems.

connaître, connaitre* [91] [kɔnɛtʀ] vt

A. QUELQUE CHOSE 1. [avoir mémorisé -code postal, itinéraire, mot de passe] to know ▸ **connaître qqch comme sa poche** to know sthg inside out ou like the back of one's hand **2.** [être informé de -information, nouvelle] to know / *je suis impatient de connaître les résultats* I'm anxious to know ou to hear the results ▸ **faire connaître a)** [avis, sentiment] to make known **b)** [décision, jugement] to make known, to announce / *je ne lui connais aucun défaut* I'm not aware of her having any faults **3.** [avoir des connaissances sur -langue, ville, appareil, œuvre] to know, to be familiar with ; [-technique] to know, to be acquainted with ; [-sujet] to know (about) / *je ne connais pas l'italien* I don't know ou can't speak Italian / *il connaît bien les Alpes* he knows the Alps well ▸ **faire connaître** : *faire connaître un produit* to publicize a product / *son dernier film l'a fait connaître dans*

le monde entier his latest film has brought him worldwide fame / *y connaître quelque chose en* to have some idea ou to know something about ▸ **ne rien y connaître** : *je n'y connais rien en biologie* I don't know a thing about biology ▸ **en connaître un bout** ou **rayon sur** *fam* to know a thing or two about.

B. QUELQU'UN 1. [par l'identité] to know ▸ **connaître qqn de vue / nom / réputation** to know sb by sight / name / reputation ▸ **se faire connaître a)** [révéler son identité] to make o.s. known **b)** [devenir une personne publique] to make o.s. ou to become known / *la connaissant, ça ne me surprend pas* knowing her, I'm not surprised / *tu me connais mal !* you don't know me! / *si tu fais ça, je ne te connais plus !* if you do that, I'll have nothing more to do with you! **2.** [rencontrer] to meet / *je l'ai connu au cours du tournage* I got to know him while we were shooting the picture.

C. ÉPROUVER 1. [peur, amour] to feel, to know, to experience **2.** [faire l'expérience de] to experience / *la tour avait connu des jours meilleurs* the tower had seen better days / *ses promesses, je connais !* *fam* don't talk to me about his promises! ▸ **faire connaître qqch à qqn** to introduce sb to sthg ; [obtenir -succès, gloire] to have, to experience **3.** [subir -crise] to go ou to live through *(insép)*, to experience ; [-épreuve, humiliation, guerre] to live through *(insép)*, to suffer, to undergo / *il a connu bien des déboires* he has had ou suffered plenty of setbacks. ❖ **se connaître, se connaître*** ◆ vp *(emploi réfléchi)* to know o.s., to be self-aware / *je n'oserai jamais, je me connais* I'd never dare, I know what I'm like. ◆ vp *(emploi réciproque)* to be acquainted, to have met (before) / *ils se connaissent bien* they know each other well. ◆ vpi ▸ **s'y connaître** [être expert] : *s'y connaître en architecture* to know a lot about architecture / *je m'y connais peu en informatique* I don't know much about computers.

connard [kɔnar] nm *vulg* wanker 🇬🇧, arsehole 🇬🇧, asshole 🇺🇸.

connasse [kɔnas] nf *vulg* stupid cow ou bitch.

connecter [4] [kɔnɛkte] vt to connect. ❖ **se connecter à** vp + prép INFORM to connect o.s. to.

connecteur [kɔnɛktœr] nm connector.

connerie [kɔnri] nf *tfam* **1.** [stupidité] stupidity **2.** [acte, remarque] stupid thing / *arrête de me raconter des conneries* don't talk rubbish.

connexe [kɔnɛks] adj [idées, problèmes] closely related.

connexion [kɔnɛksjɔ̃] nf connection ▸ **connexion (à) Internet** Internet connection.

connivence [kɔnivɑ̃s] nf *sout* connivance, complicity / *ils sont de connivence* they're in league with each other ▸ **un regard de connivence** a conniving look.

connotation [kɔnɔtasjɔ̃] nf LING connotation.

connu, e [kɔny] adj **1.** [découvert -univers] known **2.** [célèbre -personnalité, chanteur] famous, well-known ▸ **peu connu a)** [personne, œuvre] little-known **b)** [lieu] out-of-the-way.

conquérant, e [kɔ̃keʀɑ̃, ɑ̃t] ◆ adj [hautain -sourire] domineering ; [-démarche] swaggering. ◆ nm, f conqueror.

conquérir [39] [kɔ̃keʀiʀ] vt **1.** MIL & POL to conquer **2.** [acquérir -espace, pouvoir] to gain control over, to capture, to conquer **3.** [séduire -cœur, public] to win (over) *(sép)*, to conquer / *conquérir un homme / une femme* to win a man's / a woman's heart.

conquête [kɔ̃kɛt] nf **1.** [action] conquest / *partir à la conquête de l'Amérique* to set out to conquer America **2.** *fam* [personne] conquest.

consacré, e [kɔ̃sakʀe] adj **1.** RELIG [hostie] consecrated ; [terre] hallowed **2.** [accepté -rite, terme] accepted, established ▸ **c'est l'expression consacrée** it's the accepted way of saying it.

consacrer [3] [kɔ̃sakʀe] vt **1.** ▸ **consacrer qqch à** [réserver qqch à] to devote ou to dedicate sthg to / *as-tu dix minutes à me consacrer ?* can you spare me ten minutes? **2.** RELIG [pain, autel, église, évêque] to consecrate / *consacrer un temple à Jupiter* to consecrate ou to dedicate a temple to Jupiter **3.** [entériner - pratique, injustice] to sanction, to hallow ▸ **expression consacrée par l'usage** expression that has become established by usage.

consanguin, e [kɔ̃sɑ̃gɛ̃, in] adj ▸ **mariage consanguin** intermarriage, marriage between blood relatives.

consciemment [kɔ̃sjamɑ̃] adv consciously, knowingly.

conscience [kɔ̃sjɑ̃s] nf **1.** [connaissance] consciousness, awareness ▸ **avoir conscience de** to be conscious ou aware of ▸ **prendre conscience de qqch** to become aware of ou to realize sthg ▸ **conscience collective / politique** collective / political consciousness ▸ **conscience de soi** self-awareness ▸ **conscience de soi** self-awareness **2.** [sens de la morale] conscience ▸ **avoir qqch sur la conscience** to have sthg on one's conscience ▸ **avoir la conscience tranquille** to have an easy conscience / *tu dis ça pour te donner bonne conscience* you're saying this to appease your conscience **3.** [lucidité] consciousness ▸ **perdre conscience** to lose consciousness ▸ **reprendre conscience** to regain consciousness, to come to **4.** [application] ▸ **conscience professionnelle** conscientiousness.

consciencieusement [kɔ̃sjɑ̃sjøzmɑ̃] adv conscientiously.

consciencieux, euse [kɔ̃sjɑ̃sjø, øz] adj [élève] conscientious, meticulous ; [travail] meticulous.

conscient, e [kɔ̃sjɑ̃, ɑ̃t] adj **1.** [délibéré - geste, désir, haine] conscious **2.** [averti] aware ▸ **être conscient du danger** to be aware ou conscious of the danger **3.** [lucide - blessé] conscious. ❖ **conscient** nm ▸ **le conscient** the conscious (mind).

conscription [kɔ̃skʀipsjɔ̃] nf conscription, draft 🇺🇸.

conscrit [kɔ̃skʀi] nm conscript, draftee 🇺🇸.

consécration [kɔ̃sekʀasjɔ̃] nf **1.** RELIG consecration **2.** [confirmation - d'une coutume] establishment, sanctioning ; [- d'une injustice] sanctioning ; [- d'un artiste, d'une carrière] consecration, apotheosis, crowning point.

consécutif, ive [kɔ̃sekytif, iv] adj [successif] consecutive / *c'est la cinquième fois consécutive qu'il remet le rendez-vous* this is the fifth time running ou in a row that he's postponed the meeting.

conseil [kɔ̃sɛj] nm **1.** [avis] piece of advice, counsel *sout* ▸ **un conseil d'ami** a friendly piece of advice ▸ **demander conseil à qqn** to ask sb's advice, to ask sb for advice ▸ **prendre conseil auprès de qqn** to take advice from sb **2.** [activité] consulting ▸ **conseil en stratégie** strategy consulting **3.** [conseiller] adviser, consultant ; *(comme adjectif, avec ou sans trait d'union)* ▸ **ingénieur conseil** consultant engineer ▸ **conseil en organisation** organizational consultant ▸ **conseil juridique** legal adviser **4.** [assemblée] board ; [réunion] meeting ▸ **conseil d'administration a)** [d'une société] board of directors **b)** [d'une organisation internationale] governing body ▸ **le Conseil constitutionnel** *French government body ensuring that laws, elections and referenda are constitutional* ▸ **le Conseil économique et social** *consultative body advising the government on economic and social matters* ▸ **le Conseil d'État** the (French) Council of State ▸ **le Conseil de l'Europe** the Council of Europe ▸ **le Conseil européen** the European Council ▸ **conseil général** ≃ county council ▸ **le Conseil des ministres** ≃ the Cabinet ▸ **conseil municipal a)** [en ville] ≃ town council 🇺🇸 ; ≃ city council 🇺🇸 ▸ **conseil local** [urban] council **b)** [à la campagne] ≃ parish council 🇬🇧 ; ≃ local (rural) council ▸ **conseil régional** regional council ▸ **le**

Conseil de sécurité the Security Council **5.** ENS ▸ **conseil de classe** staff meeting *(concerning a class)* ▸ **conseil de discipline** disciplinary committee ▸ **conseil d'établissement** ≃ board of governors 🇬🇧 ; ≃ board of education 🇺🇸. ❖ **de bon conseil** loc adj : *un homme de bon conseil* a man of sound advice, a wise counsellor.

 Attention ! Le mot **advice** est indénombrable. Il ne s'emploie jamais ni au pluriel ni avec l'article indéfini **an**.

Conseil des ministres

The President himself presides over the **Conseil des ministres**, which traditionally meets every Wednesday morning; strictly speaking, when ministers assemble in the sole presence of the Prime Minister, this is known as le **Conseil de cabinet**.

Le Conseil constitutionnel

The **Conseil constitutionnel**, which ensures that new laws do not contravene the constitution, has nine members appointed for a nine-year period; it also includes the surviving former presidents of France. The president of the Republic, the Prime Minister or any member of Parliament can refer laws to the **Conseil constitutionnel** for scrutiny.

Le Conseil d'État

The French Council of State acts both as the highest court to which the legal affairs of the state can be referred, and as a consultative body to which bills and rulings are submitted by the government prior to examination by the **Conseil des ministres**. It has 200 members.

Conseil municipal

The town council is elected for six years during the **municipales** (local elections). Elected members, or **conseillers municipaux**, oversee the administration of a **commune** in conjunction with the mayor.

Conseil général

The body responsible for the administration of a **département**. Members are elected for a six-year term, with one councillor per **canton**, and are headed by the **président du conseil général**.

Conseil régional

The committee body for the administration of a **Région**. Members are elected for a six-year term and are headed by the **président du conseil régional**. They decide on matters of planning, construction, regional development and education.

conseiller¹ [4] [kɔ̃seje] vt **1.** [recommander - livre, dentiste] to recommend ▸ **conseiller qqch / qqn à qqn** to recommend sthg / sb to sb **2.** [donner son avis à - ami, enfant] to advise, to give advice to ▸ **on m'a bien / mal conseillé** I was given good / bad advice ▸ **conseiller à qqn de faire qqch** to advise sb to do sthg.

conseiller², ère [kɔ̃seje, ɛʀ] nm, f **1.** [guide] adviser, counsellor UK, counselor US ; [spécialiste] adviser, advisor **2.** ENS ▸ **conseiller d'orientation** careers adviser UK, guidance counselor US ▸ **conseiller pédagogique** educational adviser ▸ **conseiller principal d'éducation** non-teaching staff member in charge of general discipline **3.** [membre d'un conseil] councillor UK, councilor US, council member ; ADMIN ▸ **conseiller d'État** member of the Conseil d'État ▸ **conseiller municipal a)** [en ville] ≃ local ou town councillor UK ; ≃ city councilman (councilwoman) US **b)** [à la campagne] ≃ local councillor ▸ **conseiller régional** regional councillor.

 Conseiller municipal

This term refers to any member of the **conseil municipal** or the mayor himself. The number of councillors depends on the size of the town, although there must be a minimum of nine. Paris has 163 councillors, known as the **conseillers de Paris**.

consensuel, elle [kɔ̃sɑ̃sɥɛl] adj [contrat] consensus (modif), consensual.

consensus [kɔ̃sɛ̃sys] nm consensus (of opinion).

consentement [kɔ̃sɑ̃tmɑ̃] nm consent ▸ **donner son consentement à** to give one's consent to.

consentir [37] [kɔ̃sɑ̃tiʀ] vt [délai, réduction] to grant. ◈ **consentir à** v + prép to consent ou to agree to ▸ **elle n'a pas consenti à m'accompagner a)** [n'a pas été d'accord pour le faire] she didn't agree to come with me **b)** [n'a pas daigné le faire] she didn't deign to ou stoop so low as to accompany me.

conséquence [kɔ̃sekɑ̃s] nf consequence, repercussion ▸ **lourd de conséquences** with serious consequences / cela ne tirera pas à conséquence this won't have any repercussions ou will be of no consequence ▸ **une déclaration sans conséquence a)** [sans importance] a statement of no ou little consequence **b)** [sans suite] an inconsequential statement. ◈ **en conséquence** loc adv **1.** [par conséquent] consequently, therefore **2.** [comme il convient] accordingly. ◈ **en conséquence de** loc prép as a consequence ou result of.

conséquent, e [kɔ̃sekɑ̃, ɑ̃t] adj fam [important - moyens, magasin] sizeable ; [- somme] tidy. ◈ **par conséquent** loc adv consequently, as a result.

conservateur, trice [kɔ̃sɛʀvatœʀ, tʀis] ◈ adj **1.** [prudent - placement, gestion] conservative **2.** POL [gén] conservative. ◈ nm, f POL [gén] conservative ; [en Grande-Bretagne] Conservative, Tory. ◈ **conservateur** nm [additif] preservative.

conservation [kɔ̃sɛʀvasjɔ̃] nf **1.** [dans l'agroalimentaire] preserving **2.** [maintien en bon état] keeping, preserving, safeguarding.

conservatoire [kɔ̃sɛʀvatwaʀ] nm [école] school, academy ▸ **conservatoire de musique** conservatoire.

conserve [kɔ̃sɛʀv] nf item of tinned UK ou canned food ▸ **les conserves** tinned UK ou canned food / aliments en conserve tinned UK ou canned food ▸ **mettre en conserve** to tin UK, to can.

conserver [3] [kɔ̃sɛʀve] vt **1.** [aliment - dans le vinaigre] to pickle ; [- dans le sel, par séchage, en congelant] to preserve ; [- dans le sucre] to preserve, to conserve ; [- dans des boîtes] to preserve, to tin UK, to can ; [- en bocal] to bottle **2.** [stocker] to keep, to store, to stock **3.** [avoir en sa possession - photos, relations] to keep, to hang on to (insép) **4.** [garder - charme, force, illusion, calme] to keep, to retain ▸ **conserver (toute) sa tête a)** [rester calme] to keep one's head ou self-control **b)** [être lucide] to have all one's wits about one / le sport, ça conserve fam sport keeps you young ▸ **conserver son amitié à qqn** to stay friendly with sb. ◈ **se conserver** vpi [durer - aliment] to keep ; [- poterie, parchemin] to survive.

considérable [kɔ̃sideʀabl] adj [important - somme, travail] considerable.

considérablement [kɔ̃sideʀabləmɑ̃] adv considerably.

considération [kɔ̃sideʀasjɔ̃] nf **1.** [examen] consideration, scrutiny ▸ **la question mérite considération** the question is worth considering **2.** [préoccupation] consideration, factor / si l'on s'arrête à ce genre de considérations if we pay too much attention to this kind of detail **3.** [respect] regard, esteem ▸ **manque de considération** disregard ▸ **veuillez agréer l'assurance de ma considération distinguée** yours faithfully UK, yours sincerely US. ◈ **en considération** loc adv ▸ **prendre qqch en considération** to take sthg into account ou consideration. ◈ **en considération de** loc prép : en considération de vos services in (full) recognition of your services.

considérer [18] [kɔ̃sideʀe] vt **1.** [regarder] to gaze ou to stare at (insép) ▸ **considérer qqn avec hostilité** to stare at sb in a hostile manner **2.** [prendre en compte - offre, problème] to consider, to take into consideration, to weigh up (sép) / considérer le pour et le contre to weigh up the pros and cons **3.** [croire] to consider, to deem sout / je la considère qualifiée pour ce travail I consider her (to be) qualified for this job **4.** [juger] : considérer bien / mal to hold in high / low esteem / elle me considère comme sa meilleure amie she regards me as ou looks upon me as ou considers me to be her best friend **5.** [respecter] to respect, to hold in high esteem ou regard / un spécialiste hautement considéré a highly-regarded ou highly-respected expert. ◈ **à tout bien considérer, tout bien considéré** loc adv [tout compte fait] on second thoughts ou further consideration.

✐ In reformed spelling (see p. 16-18), this verb is conjugated like semer : il considèrera, elle considèrerait.

consigne [kɔ̃siɲ] nf **1.** [instruction] orders, instructions / ils ont reçu pour consigne de ne pas tirer they've been given orders not to shoot / je n'ai pas (reçu) de consignes I have received no instructions / elle avait pour consigne de surveiller sa sœur she'd been told to keep an eye on her sister **2.** MIL [punition] confinement to barracks ; ÉDUC detention **3.** RAIL left-luggage office UK, checkroom US, baggage room US ▸ **consigne automatique** (left-luggage) lockers UK, lockers US ▸ **mettre qqch à la consigne a)** [automatique] to put sthg in a left-luggage locker **b)** [manuelle] to check sthg in at the left-luggage office **4.** COMM deposit.

consigné, e [kɔ̃siɲe] adj returnable ▸ **non consigné** non returnable.

consigner [3] [kɔ̃siɲe] vt **1.** [emballage] to put ou to charge a deposit on / la bouteille est consignée 50 centimes there's a 50-centime deposit on the bottle **2.** [noter] to record, to put down (sép) ▸ **consigner qqch par écrit** to put down sthg in writing ou on paper **3.** MIL to confine to barracks ; ÉDUC to keep in (detention).

consistance [kɔ̃sistɑ̃s] nf [état] consistency ▸ **prendre consistance** [sauce] to thicken / le projet prend consistance fig the project is taking shape.

consistant, e [kɔ̃sistɑ̃, ɑ̃t] adj **1.** [épais - sauce, pein- ture] thick **2.** [substantiel - plat, repas] substantial.

> ⚠ **Consistent** signifie « constant », « cohé- rent » et non consistant.

consister [3] [kɔ̃siste] ❖ **consister à** v + prép to consist in. ❖ **consister dans, consister en** v + prép to consist of.

conso [kɔso] **(abr de** consommation) nf *fam* drink.

consœur [kɔ̃sœr] nf [collègue] (female) colleague.

consolation [kɔ̃sɔlasjɔ̃] nf [soulagement] consolation, comfort, solace *litt.* ❖ **de consolation** loc adj [épreuve, tournoi] runners-up *(modif)* ; [lot, prix] consolation *(modif)*.

console [kɔ̃sɔl] nf **1.** [table] console table **2.** INFORM console ▶ **console de jeux** video game.

consoler [3] [kɔ̃sɔle] vt to console, to comfort / *si cela peut te consoler* if it's any consolation. ❖ **se consoler** vpi to console o.s., to be consoled / *il ne s'est jamais consolé de la mort de sa femme* he never got over losing his wife.

consolider [3] [kɔ̃sɔlide] vt **1.** [renforcer - édifice, meuble] to strengthen ; [- mur] to brace, to buttress **2.** [affermir - position, majorité, amitié] to consolidate, to strengthen **3.** MÉD to set, to reduce **4.** FIN to consolidate. ❖ **se consolider** vp [parti, régime] to strengthen, to consolidate its position ; [fracture] to knit.

consommateur, trice [kɔ̃sɔmatœr, tris] nm, f **1.** [par opposition à producteur] consumer **2.** [client - d'un service] customer, user.

consommation [kɔ̃sɔmasjɔ̃] nf **1.** [absorption - de nourriture] consumption **2.** [utilisation - de gaz, d'électri- cité] consumption / *elle fait une grande consommation de parfum / papier* she goes through a lot of perfume / paper ▶ **article** ou **produit de consommation courante** staple **3.** ÉCON ▶ **la consommation des ménages** household con- sumption ▶ **biens / société de consommation** consumer goods / society **4.** AUTO : *une consommation de 4 litres aux 100 (km)* a consumption of 4 litres per 100 km **5.** [au café] drink ▶ **prendre une consommation** [boire] to have a drink.

consommé, e [kɔ̃sɔme] adj *sout* consummate. ❖ **consommé** nm clear soup, consommé.

consommer [3] [kɔ̃sɔme] vt **1.** [absorber - nourriture] to eat, to consume *sout* ; [- boisson] to drink, to consume *sout* ; *(en usage absolu)* / *'à consommer avant (fin)…'* 'best before (end)…' **2.** [utiliser - combustible] to use (up), to con- sume, to go through *(sép)* ▶ **une voiture qui consomme beaucoup / peu (d'essence)** a car that uses a lot of / that doesn't use much petrol **3.** DR [mariage] to consummate.

consonance [kɔ̃sɔnɑ̃s] nf **1.** LITTÉR & MUS consonance **2.** [sonorité] sound / *de consonance anglaise, aux conso- nances anglaises* English-sounding.

consonne [kɔ̃sɔn] nf consonant.

consortium [kɔ̃sɔrsjɔm] nm consortium, syndicate.

conspirateur, trice [kɔ̃spiratœr, tris] nmf conspir- ator, plotter, conspirer.

conspiration [kɔ̃spirasjɔ̃] nf conspiracy, plotting.

conspirer [3] [kɔ̃spire] vi to conspire, to plot, to scheme.

conspuer [7] [kɔ̃spɥe] vt *sout* to shout down *(sép)* ▶ **se faire conspuer a)** [orateur] to be shouted down **b)** [comé- dien] to be booed off the stage.

constamment [kɔ̃stamɑ̃] adv [très fréquemment] con- stantly.

constance [kɔ̃stɑ̃s] nf [persévérance] constancy, stead- fastness / *vous avez de la constance !* you don't give up easily !

constant, e [kɔ̃stɑ̃, ɑ̃t] adj **1.** [invariable] unchanging, constant / *être constant dans ses goûts* to be unchan- ging in one's tastes **2.** [ininterrompu] continual, continuous, unceasing. ❖ **constante** nf **1.** MATH & PHYS constant **2.** [caractéristique] stable ou permanent trait.

constat [kɔ̃sta] nm **1.** [acte] certified statement ou re- port ▶ **constat d'accident** accident statement ▶ **constat à l'amiable** mutually-agreed accident report ▶ **constat d'huissier** process-server's affidavit **2.** [bilan] review ▶ **faire un constat d'échec** to acknowledge ou to admit a failure.

 Constat

When there is a car crash in France, the drivers have to produce a report that ex- plains the causes of the accident. It must be signed by both parties and is then used by the insurance companies to determine responsibilities. Insurance companies supply drivers with prepared **constats** which need to be filled out and sent within 5 days of the accident.

constatation [kɔ̃statasjɔ̃] nf **1.** [observation] not- ing, noticing **2.** [remarque] remark, comment, observation. ❖ **constatations** nfpl [d'une enquête] findings ▶ **procé- der aux constatations** to establish the facts.

constater [3] [kɔ̃state] vt **1.** [remarquer] to note, to observe, to notice / *je suis forcée de constater que je ne peux te faire confiance* I am forced to the conclusion that I can't trust you ; *(en usage absolu)* ▶ **constatez par vous- même !** just see for yourself! **2.** [enregistrer - décès] to cer- tify ; [- faits] to record, to list.

constellation [kɔ̃stelasjɔ̃] nf ASTRON constellation.

consternation [kɔ̃sternasjɔ̃] nf consternation, dismay.

consterner [3] [kɔ̃sterne] vt to appall, to fill with con- sternation ▶ **regarder qqch d'un air consterné** to look with consternation upon sthg.

constipation [kɔ̃stipasjɔ̃] nf constipation.

constipé, e [kɔ̃stipe] adj **1.** MÉD constipated **2.** *fam* [guindé] : *être* ou *avoir l'air constipé* to look ill-at-ease ou uncomfortable.

constituant, e [kɔ̃stitɥɑ̃, ɑ̃t] adj [élément] constituent. ❖ **constituant** nm LING constituent.

constituer [7] [kɔ̃stitɥe] vt **1.** [créer - collection] to build up *(sép)*, to put together *(sép)* ; [- bibliothèque] to build ou to set up *(sép)* ; [- société anonyme, association, gouverne- ment] to form, to set up *(sép)* ; [- équipe, cabinet] to form, to select (the members of) ; [- dossier] to prepare **2.** [faire partie de] to form, to constitute, to (go to) make up **3.** [être] to be, to represent / *le vol constitue un délit* theft is ou consti- tutes an offence. ❖ **se constituer** ◆ vpi **1.** [se mettre en position de] ▶ **se constituer prisonnier** to give o.s. up **2.** [se former] to form, to be formed / *ils se sont constitués en association* they formed a society. ◆ vpt ▶ **se consti- tuer un patrimoine** to amass an estate.

constitution [kɔ̃stitysjɔ̃] nf **1.** [création - d'une collec- tion] building up, putting together ; [- d'une bibliothèque] building up, setting up ; [- d'une association, une société, d'un gouvernement] forming, formation, setting up ; [- d'un dossier] preparation, putting together ; [- d'une équipe]

selection 2. [composition -d'un groupe] composition ; [-d'une substance] makeup, composition **3.** POL [lois] constitution **4.** [santé] constitution, physique.

constitutionnel, elle [kɔ̃stitysjɔnɛl] adj constitutional.

constructeur [kɔ̃stryktœr] nm **1.** [d'édifices] builder **2.** [d'appareils, d'engins] manufacturer ▶ **constructeur automobile** car manufacturer.

constructif, ive [kɔ̃stryktif, iv] adj [qui fait progresser] constructive, positive.

construction [kɔ̃stryksjɔ̃] nf **1.** [édifice] building, construction **2.** [fabrication] building, manufacturing ▶ **la construction automobile** car manufacturing / *appareil de construction française* French-built machine ; [entreprise] ▶ **constructions navales** shipbuilding (industry) **3.** [structure -d'une œuvre] structure ; [-d'une phrase] construction, structure. ❖ **de construction** loc adj [matériau] building *(modif)*, construction *(modif)*. ❖ **en construction** loc adv under construction / *la maison est encore en construction* the house is still being built ou still under construction.

construire [98] [kɔ̃strɥir] vt **1.** [route, barrage] to build, to construct ; [maison] to build / *se faire construire une maison* to have a house built / *tous ensemble pour construire l'Europe* / fig all united to build a new Europe! **2.** [structurer -pièce, roman] to structure, to construct ; [-théorie, raisonnement] to build, to develop ; [-figure de géométrie] to draw, to construct. ❖ **se construire** vp *(emploi passif)* **1.** [être édifié] to be built / *ça se construit par ici !* fam a lot of stuff's going up ou a lot of building's going on around here! **2.** GRAM ▶ **se construire avec** to be construed with, to take.

consul, e [kɔ̃syl] nm, f [diplomate] consul.

consulat [kɔ̃syla] nm [résidence, bureaux] consulate.

consultant, e [kɔ̃syltɑ̃, ɑ̃t] ◆ adj **1.** ⟶ **avocat 2.** ⟶ **médecin.** ◆ nm, f consultant ▶ **consultant en stratégie** strategy consultant.

consultatif, ive [kɔ̃syltatif, iv] adj advisory.

consultation [kɔ̃syltasjɔ̃] nf **1.** [d'un plan, d'un règlement] consulting, checking **2.** POL ▶ **consultation électorale** election **3.** [chez un professionnel] consultation ▶ **il est en consultation** [médecin] he's with a patient ▶ **horaires de consultation** [chez un médecin] surgery 🇬🇧 ou office 🇺🇸 hours.

consulter [3] [kɔ̃sylte] ◆ vt [médecin] to visit, to consult ; [avocat, professeur] to consult, to seek advice from ; [voyante] to visit. ◆ vi [docteur] to hold surgery, to see patients. ❖ **se consulter** vp *(emploi réciproque)* [discuter] to confer.

consumer [3] [kɔ̃syme] vt [brûler] to burn, to consume. ❖ **se consumer** vpi **1.** [brûler] to burn **2.** [être tourmenté] : *il se consume de désespoir* he's wasting away in ou with despair.

consumérisme [kɔ̃symerism] nm ▶ **le consumérisme** consumerism.

contact [kɔ̃takt] nm **1.** [toucher] touch, contact **2.** AUTO, ÉLECTR & RADIO contact, switch / *il y a un mauvais contact* there's a loose connection somewhere ▶ **mettre / couper le contact a)** ÉLECTR to switch on / off **b)** AUTO to turn the ignition on / off **3.** [lien] contact ▶ **avoir des contacts avec** to have contact with ▶ **prendre des contacts** to establish some contacts ▶ **prendre contact avec qqn** to contact sb, to get in touch with sb **4.** [personne -dans les affaires, l'espionnage] contact, connection. ❖ **au contact de** loc prép ▶ **au contact de l'air** in contact with ou when exposed to the air. ❖ **en contact** loc adv ▶ **rester en contact avec qqn** to keep ou to stay ou to remain in touch with sb ▶ **entrer en contact avec qqn a)** to contact sb, to get in touch with sb **b)** AÉRON & MIL to make contact with sb ▶ **mettre en contact a)** [personnes] to put in touch (with each other) **b)** [objets, substances] to bring into contact **c)** AÉRON to establish contact between.

contacter [3] [kɔ̃takte] vt to contact, to get in touch with.

contagieux, euse [kɔ̃taʒjø, øz] adj [personne] contagious ; [maladie, rire] infectious, contagious.

container [kɔ̃tɛnɛr] = **conteneur.**

contamination [kɔ̃taminasjɔ̃] nf **1.** MÉD contamination **2.** [de l'environnement, des aliments] contamination.

contaminer [3] [kɔ̃tamine] vt ÉCOL to contaminate.

conte [kɔ̃t] nm story, tale ▶ **conte de fées** pr & fig fairy tale.

contemplation [kɔ̃tɑ̃plasjɔ̃] nf [méditation] contemplation, reflection ▶ **en contemplation devant** lost in admiration of.

contempler [3] [kɔ̃tɑ̃ple] vt to look at ▶ **contempler qqn avec amour** to gaze lovingly at sb.

contemporain, e [kɔ̃tɑ̃pɔrɛ̃, ɛn] ◆ adj **1.** [de la même époque] contemporary **2.** [moderne] contemporary, modern, present-day. ◆ nm, f contemporary.

contemporanéité [kɔ̃tɑ̃pɔraneite] nf [simultanéité] contemporaneousness ; [caractère actuel] contemporary nature.

contenance [kɔ̃tnɑ̃s] nf **1.** [attitude] attitude, bearing ▶ **il essayait de prendre** ou **se donner une contenance** he was trying to put on a brave face ▶ **faire bonne contenance** to put up a bold ou good front ▶ **perdre contenance** to lose one's composure **2.** [capacité -d'un tonneau, d'un réservoir] capacity ; [-d'un navire] (carrying ou holding) capacity.

conteneur [kɔ̃tənœr] nm INDUST container.

contenir [40] [kɔ̃tnir] vt **1.** [renfermer] to contain, to hold **2.** [être constitué de] to contain **3.** [avoir telle capacité] to hold **4.** [réprimer -foule, larmes, sanglots] to hold back *(sép)* ; [-poussée, invasion] to contain ; [-rire, colère] to suppress. ❖ **se contenir** vpi to control o.s.

content, e [kɔ̃tɑ̃, ɑ̃t] adj **1.** [heureux] happy, glad, pleased **2.** [satisfait] ▶ **être content de qqch** to be satisfied with sthg / *non content d'être riche, il veut aussi être célèbre* not content with being rich ou not satisfied with being rich, he wants to be famous as well.

contentement [kɔ̃tɑ̃tmɑ̃] nm satisfaction, contentment.

contenter [3] [kɔ̃tɑ̃te] vt **1.** [faire plaisir à] to please, to satisfy **2.** [satisfaire] to satisfy. ❖ **se contenter de** vp + prép **1.** [s'accommoder de] to be content ou to content o.s. with, to make do with / *il se contente de peu* he's easily satisfied **2.** [se borner à] : *en guise de réponse, elle s'est contentée de sourire* she merely smiled in reply.

contentieux, euse [kɔ̃tɑ̃sjø] nm **1.** [conflit] dispute, disagreement **2.** [service] legal department ou bureau **3.** [affaire] litigation.

contenu [kɔ̃tny] nm **1.** [d'un récipient, d'un paquet] content, contents **2.** [teneur -d'un document, d'une œuvre] content, text.

conter [3] [kɔ̃te] vt litt to relate, to tell.

contestable [kɔ̃tɛstabl] adj debatable, questionable.

contestataire [kɔ̃tɛstatɛr] ◆ adj protesting ou revolting *(against established values)*. ◆ nmf anti-establishment protester.

contestation [kɔ̃tɛstasjɔ̃] nf **1.** [d'une loi, d'un testament, d'un document] contesting, opposing ; [d'un récit, d'un droit] contesting, questioning ; [d'une compétence] questioning, challenging, doubting **2.** [litige] dispute, controversy, debate **3.** POL ▶ **la contestation** protests, protesting, the protest movement.

conteste [kɔ̃tɛst] ❖ **sans conteste** loc adv indisputably, unquestionably.

contester [3] [kɔ̃tɛste] ◆ vt [testament] to contest, to object to ; [récit, document] to dispute, to question ; [compétence] to question, to dispute, to throw into doubt ▶ **une personnalité très contestée** a very controversial personality. ◆ vi **1.** [discuter] : **obéir aux ordres sans contester** to obey orders blindly ou without raising any objections **2.** POL to protest.

conteur, euse [kɔ̃tœʀ, øz] nm, f **1.** [narrateur] narrator, storyteller **2.** [écrivain] storyteller.

contexte [kɔ̃tɛkst] nm [situation] context.

contigu, contiguë ou **contigüe*** [kɔ̃tigy] adj [bâtiments, terrains, objets] contiguous *sout*, adjacent, adjoining.

continent [kɔ̃tinɑ̃] nm **1.** GÉOGR continent **2.** [par opposition à une île] ▶ **le continent** the mainland.

continental, e, aux [kɔ̃tinɑ̃tal, o] adj **1.** [par opposition à insulaire] mainland *(modif)* **2.** GÉOGR [climat, température] continental.

contingences nfpl contingencies, eventualities / **les contingences de la vie quotidienne** everyday happenings ou events.

contingent¹ [kɔ̃tɛ̃ʒɑ̃] nm **1.** [quota] quota **2.** [troupe] contingent ; [ensemble des recrues] national service conscripts UK, call-up UK, draft US.

contingent², e [kɔ̃tɛ̃ʒɑ̃, ɑ̃t] adj PHILOS contingent.

contingenter [3] [kɔ̃tɛ̃ʒɑ̃te] vt COMM to distribute ou to allocate according to a quota.

continu, e [kɔ̃tiny] adj [ininterrompu - effort, douleur, bruit] continuous, unremitting, relentless ; [- soins] constant ; [- ligne, trait] continuous, unbroken ; [- sommeil] unbroken. ❖ **en continu** loc adv continuously, uninterruptedly.

continuation [kɔ̃tinɥasjɔ̃] nf **1.** [suite] continuation, extension **2.** EXPR **bonne continuation !** *fam* all the best!

continuel, elle [kɔ̃tinɥɛl] adj **1.** [ininterrompu] continual **2.** [qui se répète] constant, perpetual.

continuellement [kɔ̃tinɥɛlmɑ̃] adv **1.** [de façon ininterrompue] continually **2.** [de façon répétitive] constantly, perpetually.

continuer [7] [kɔ̃tinɥe] ◆ vt **1.** [faire durer - exposé] to carry on *(insép)* ; [- conversation] to carry on *(insép)*, to maintain, to keep up *(sép)* ; [- études] to continue, to keep up *(sép)*, to go on with *(insép)* / **continuez le repas sans moi** go on with the meal without me **2.** [dans l'espace] to continue, to extend ▶ **continuer son chemin** a) [voyageur] to keep going b) [idée] to keep gaining momentum. ◆ vi **1.** [dans le temps] to go ou to carry on *(insép)* / **si tu continues, ça va mal aller !** if you keep this up, you'll be sorry! / **tu vois, continua-t-elle** you see, she went on / **une telle situation ne peut continuer** this situation cannot be allowed to continue / **il continue de** ou **à pleuvoir** it keeps on raining / **ma plante continue de grandir** my plant keeps getting bigger **2.** [dans l'espace] to continue, to carry on *(insép)*, to go on *(insép)* / **la route continue jusqu'au village** the road runs straight on to the village / **arrête-toi ici, moi je continue** you can stop right here, I'm going on ▶ **continue !** [à avancer] keep going! / **continue tout droit jusqu'au carrefour** keep straight on to the crossroads.

continuité [kɔ̃tinɥite] nf [d'un effort, d'une tradition] continuity ; [d'une douleur] persistence.

contondant, e [kɔ̃tɔ̃dɑ̃, ɑ̃t] adj blunt.

contorsionner [3] [kɔ̃tɔʀsjɔne] ❖ **se contorsionner** vpi to twist one's body, to contort o.s.

contour [kɔ̃tuʀ] nm **1.** [d'un objet, d'une silhouette] contour, outline, shape **2.** [arrondi - d'un visage] curve ; [- d'une rivière, d'un chemin] winding part ou section.

contourner [3] [kɔ̃tuʀne] vt **1.** [faire le tour de - souche, flaque] to walk around *(insép)* ; [- ville] to bypass, to skirt ; MIL [position] to skirt **2.** [éluder - loi, difficulté] to circumvent, to get round *(insép)*.

contraceptif, ive [kɔ̃tʀasɛptif, iv] adj contraceptive. ❖ **contraceptif** nm contraceptive, method of contraception.

contraception [kɔ̃tʀasɛpsjɔ̃] nf contraception / **moyen de contraception** means *(sg)* of contraception.

contracter [3] [kɔ̃tʀakte] vt **1.** [se charger de - dette] to incur, to run up *(sép)* ; [- assurance] to take out *(sép)* ; [- obligation, engagement] to take on *(sép)* ▶ **contracter un emprunt** to take out a loan **2.** [acquérir - manie, habitude] to develop, to acquire ; [- maladie] to contract *sout*, to catch **3.** [raidir - muscle] to contract, to tighten, to tauten ; [- visage, traits] to tense (up), to tighten (up) **4.** [rendre anxieux] to make tense. ❖ **se contracter** vpi **1.** [être réduit - liquide, corps] to contract, to reduce ; [- fibre] to shrink **2.** [se raidir - visage, traits] to tense (up), to become taut.

contraction [kɔ̃tʀaksjɔ̃] nf **1.** [raidissement - d'un muscle] contracting, tensing ; [- du visage, des traits, de l'estomac] tensing, tightening (up) ; [- des mâchoires] clamping ; [raideur - d'un muscle] tenseness, tautness ; [- de l'estomac] tightness ; [- des mâchoires] stiffness **2.** MÉD ▶ **contraction (utérine)** contraction **3.** ÉDUC ▶ **contraction de texte** summary.

contractuel, elle [kɔ̃tʀaktɥɛl] adj contractual, contract *(modif)*. ❖ **contractuel** nm ADMIN contract public servant ; [policier] (male) traffic warden UK ou policeman US. ❖ **contractuelle** nf (female) traffic warden UK, traffic policewoman US.

contradiction [kɔ̃tʀadiksjɔ̃] nf **1.** [contestation] contradiction **2.** [incompatibilité] contradiction, inconsistency. ❖ **en contradiction avec** loc prép in contradiction with / **c'est en contradiction avec sa façon de vivre** it goes against his style of life / **être en contradiction avec soi-même** to be inconsistent.

contradictoire [kɔ̃tʀadiktwaʀ] adj [opposé - théories, idées] contradictory, clashing ; [- témoignage] conflicting ▶ **débat / réunion contradictoire** open debate / meeting.

contragestion [kɔ̃tʀaʒɛstjɔ̃] nf emergency contraception.

contraignant, e [kɔ̃tʀɛɲɑ̃, ɑ̃t] adj [occupation] restricting ; [contrat] restrictive ; [horaire] restricting, limiting.

contraindre [80] [kɔ̃tʀɛ̃dʀ] vt [obliger] ▶ **contraindre qqn à** : **la situation nous contraint à la prudence** the situation forces us to be careful.

contraint, e [kɔ̃tʀɛ̃, ɛ̃t] adj [obligé] ▶ **contraint et forcé** under duress. ❖ **contrainte** nf **1.** [obligation] constraint, imposition **2.** [force] constraint.

contraire [kɔ̃tʀɛʀ] ◆ adj **1.** [point de vue, attitude] opposite ▶ **sauf avis contraire** unless otherwise informed **2.** [inverse - direction, sens] : **dans le sens contraire à celui des aiguilles d'une montre** anticlockwise UK, counterclockwise US **3.** *sout* [défavorable, nuisible] contrary *sout*, unfavourable. ◆ nm [inverse] ▶ **le contraire** the opposite / **elle timide ? c'est tout le contraire !** her, shy? quite the opposite ou contrary! ❖ **au contraire, bien au contraire, tout au contraire** loc adv quite the reverse ou opposite. ❖ **au contraire de** loc prép unlike. ❖ **contraire à** loc prép : **c'est contraire à mes principes** it's against my principles.

contrairement [kɔ̃tʀɛʀmɑ̃] ❖ **contrairement à** loc prép ▶ **contrairement à son frère** unlike his brother.

contrariant, e [kɔ̃tʀaʀjɑ̃, ɑ̃t] adj [personne] annoying ; [nouvelle] annoying.

contrarier [9] [kɔ̃tʀaʀje] vt **1.** [ennuyer - personne] to annoy **2.** [contrecarrer - ambitions, amour] to thwart ; [- mouvement, action] to impede, to bar ▸ **contrarier un gaucher** to force a left-handed person to use his right hand.

contrariété [kɔ̃tʀaʀjete] nf [mécontentement] annoyance, vexation ▸ **éprouver une contrariété** to be annoyed ou upset.

contraste [kɔ̃tʀast] nm contrast. ⬦ **par contraste** loc adv in contrast.

contraster [3] [kɔ̃tʀaste] ⬥ vt [caractères, situations, couleurs] to contrast ; [photo] to show up the contrast in. ⬥ vi to contrast.

contrat [kɔ̃tʀa] nm **1.** [acte, convention] contract ▸ **passer un contrat avec qqn** to enter into a contract with sb ▸ **contrat d'assurance** insurance policy ▸ **contrat à durée déterminée / indéterminée** fixed-term / permanent contract ▸ **contrat de location a)** [de local] tenancy agreement 🆄🅺, rental agreement 🆄🆂 **b)** [de voiture] rental agreement ▸ **contrat de travail** contract of employment ▸ **remplir son contrat a)** DR to fulfil the terms of one's contract **b)** fig [s'exécuter] to keep one's promise **2.** [entente] agreement, deal.

contravention [kɔ̃tʀavɑ̃sjɔ̃] nf **1.** [amende] (parking) fine ; [avis] (parking) ticket **2.** [infraction] contravention, infraction, infringement.

contre [kɔ̃tʀ] ⬥ prép **1.** [indiquant la proximité] against, on ▸ **se frotter contre qqch** to rub (o.s.) against ou on sthg ▸ **se blottir contre qqn** to cuddle up to sb ▸ **tenir qqn tout contre soi** to hold sb close / *un coup contre la vitre* a knock on ou at the window / *je me suis cogné la tête contre le radiateur* I hit my head on the radiator / *lancer une balle contre le mur* to throw a ball against ou at the wall **2.** [indiquant l'opposition] against ▸ **nager contre le courant** to swim upstream ou against the current ▸ **être en colère contre qqn** to be angry at ou with sb / *je suis contre l'intervention* I'm opposed to ou against (the idea of) intervention / *le match contre le Brésil* the Brazil match, the match against ou with Brazil ▸ **avoir qqch contre qqn** to have sthg against sb / *vous allez contre l'usage / le règlement* you're going against accepted custom / the regulations **3.** [pour protéger de] against ▸ **pastilles contre la toux** cough lozenges ▸ **lutter contre l'alcoolisme** to fight (against) alcoholism ▸ **s'assurer contre le vol** to take out insurance against theft **4.** [en échange de] for, in exchange ou return for / *j'ai échangé mon livre contre le sien* I swapped my book for hers **5.** [indiquant une proportion, un rapport] against, to / *10 contre 1 qu'ils vont gagner !* ten to one they'll win! ▸ **156 voix contre 34** 156 votes to 34 **6.** [contrairement à] ▸ **contre toute attente** contrary to ou against all expectations. ⬥ adv **1.** [indiquant la proximité] : *il n'a pas vu le poteau, et sa tête a heurté contre* he didn't see the post, and he banged his head against ou on it **2.** [indiquant l'opposition] against / *on partage ? — je n'ai rien contre* shall we share? — I've nothing against it ou it's OK by me. ⬥ nm **1.** [argument opposé] : *le pour et le contre* the pros and cons **2.** SPORT & JEUX [au volley, au basket] block ; [en escrime] counter ; [au billard] kiss ; [au bridge] double. ⬦ **par contre** loc adv on the other hand / *il est très compétent, par contre il n'est pas toujours très aimable* he's very competent, but on the other hand he's not always very pleasant.

contre-allée (pl **contre-allées**), **contrallée*** [kɔ̃tʀale] nf [d'une avenue] service ou frontage 🆄🆂 road ; [d'une promenade] side track ou path.

contre-argument [kɔ̃tʀaʀgymɑ̃] (pl **contre-arguments**) nm counterargument.

contre-attaque (pl **contre-attaques**), **contrattaque*** [kɔ̃tʀatak] nf **1.** MIL [gén] counterattack ; [à l'explosif] counter-blast **2.** [dans une polémique] counterattack, counter-blast.

contre-attaquer, contrattaquer* [3] [kɔ̃tʀatake] vt to counterattack, to strike back *(sép)*.

contrebalancer [16] [kɔ̃tʀəbalɑ̃se] vt **1.** [poids] to counterbalance **2.** [compenser - inconvénients, efforts] to offset, to make up for *(insép)*, to compensate.

contrebande [kɔ̃tʀəbɑ̃d] nf **1.** [trafic] smuggling, contraband **2.** [marchandises] contraband, smuggled goods ; [alcool] bootleg.

contrebandier, ère [kɔ̃tʀəbɑ̃dje, ɛʀ] nm, f smuggler.

contrebas [kɔ̃tʀəba] ⬦ **en contrebas** loc adv lower down, below *(adv)*.

contrebasse [kɔ̃tʀəbas] nf [instrument] (double) bass, contrabass.

contrecarrer [3] [kɔ̃tʀəkaʀe] vt [personne] to thwart ; [projet, initiative] to thwart, to block.

contrecœur [kɔ̃tʀəkœʀ] ⬦ **à contrecœur** loc adv reluctantly, unwillingly, grudgingly.

contrecoup [kɔ̃tʀəku] nm [répercussion] repercussion, aftereffect.

contre-courant (pl **contre-courants**), **contrecourant*** [kɔ̃tʀəkuʀɑ̃] nm countercurrent. ⬦ **à contre-courant de, à contrecourant de*** loc prép : *aller à contre-courant de la mode* to go against the trend.

contredire [103] [kɔ̃tʀədiʀ] vt [personne, propos] to contradict. ⬦ **se contredire** vp *(emploi réciproque)* **1.** [personnes] : *ils se contredisent (l'un l'autre)* they contradict each other **2.** [témoignages, faits] to be in contradiction (with each other), to contradict each other.

contrée [kɔ̃tʀe] nf *litt* [pays] country, land *litt* ; [région] region, area.

contre-exemple (pl **contre-exemples**), **contrexemple*** [kɔ̃tʀegzɑ̃pl] nm [illustration] counterexample.

contre-expertise (pl **contre-expertises**), **contrexpertise*** [kɔ̃tʀekspɛʀtiz] nf second expert evaluation ou opinion.

contrefaçon [kɔ̃tʀəfasɔ̃] nf **1.** [action d'imiter - une signature, une écriture, une monnaie] counterfeiting, forging ; [- un brevet] infringement **2.** [copie - d'un produit, d'un vêtement] imitation, fake ; [- d'une signature, d'une écriture, monnaie] counterfeit, forgery.

contrefaire [109] [kɔ̃tʀəfɛʀ] vt **1.** [parodier] to mimic, to take off *(sép)* **2.** [signature, écriture, argent] to counterfeit, to forge ; [brevet] to infringe **3.** [déformer - visage] to distort ; [- voix] to alter, to change, to distort.

contreficher [3] [kɔ̃tʀəfiʃe] ⬦ **se contreficher de** vp + prép *fam* to be indifferent to / *je m'en contrefiche* I couldn't care less, who gives a damn?

contrefort [kɔ̃tʀəfɔʀ] nm ARCHIT buttress, abutment. ⬦ **contreforts** nmpl GÉOGR foothills.

contre-indication (pl **contre-indications**), **contrindication*** [kɔ̃tʀɛ̃dikasjɔ̃] nf MÉD contraindication.

contre-indiqué, e (mpl **contre-indiqués**, fpl **contre-indiquées**), **contrindiqué*, e** [kɔ̃tʀɛ̃dike] adj MÉD contraindicated.

contre-interrogatoire (pl **contre-interrogatoires**), **contrinterrogatoire*** [kɔ̃tʀɛ̃teʀɔgatwaʀ] nm cross-examination.

contre-jour (pl **contre-jours**), **contrejour*** [kɔ̃tʀəʒuʀ] nm [éclairage] back light. ⬦ **à contre-jour, à contrejour*** loc adv [être placé - personne] with one's back to the light ; [- objet] against the light ou sunlight / *une photo prise à contre-jour* a contre-jour shot.

contremaître, contremaitre* [kɔ̃tʀəmɛtʀ] nm [dans un atelier] foreman, supervisor.

contremarque [kɔ̃tʀəmaʀk] nf [billet - au spectacle] voucher *(exchanged for ticket at the entrance)* ; [- de transport] extra portion (of ticket).

contre-offensive (*pl* contre-offensives), **controffensive*** [kɔ̃tʀɔfɑ̃siv] nf MIL counteroffensive.

contrepartie [kɔ̃tʀəpaʀti] nf [compensation] compensation ; [financière] compensation, consideration. **en contrepartie** loc adv **1.** [en compensation] in ou by way of compensation **2.** [en retour] in return.

contre-performance (*pl* contre-performances), **contreperformance*** [kɔ̃tʀəpɛʀfɔʀmɑ̃s] nf bad result, performance below expectation.

contre-pied (*pl* contre-pieds), **contrepied*** [kɔ̃tʀəpje] nm **1.** [d'une opinion] opposite (view) ; [d'un argument] converse, obverse / *prenons le contre-pied de sa position* let's take the (exact) opposite position to hers **2.** SPORT : *prendre un adversaire à contre-pied* to catch an opponent off balance, to wrong-foot an opponent.

contreplaqué [kɔ̃tʀəplake] nm plywood.

contrepoids [kɔ̃tʀəpwa] nm [gén] counterbalance, counterweight ; [d'une horloge] balance weight ; [d'un funambule] balancing pole **faire contrepoids (à qqch)** pr & fig to provide a counterweight (to sthg).

contrepoint [kɔ̃tʀəpwɛ̃] nm LITTÉR & MUS counterpoint. **en contrepoint** loc adv **1.** LITTÉR & MUS contrapuntally **2.** litt [en même temps] at the same time, concurrently.

contre-pouvoir (*pl* contre-pouvoirs), **contre-pouvoir*** [kɔ̃tʀəpuvwaʀ] nm *challenge to established authority.*

contre-productif, ive (*mpl* contre-productifs, *fpl* contre-productives), **contreproductif*, ive** [kɔ̃tʀəpʀɔdyktif, iv] adj counterproductive.

contrer [3] [kɔ̃tʀe] vt **1.** [s'opposer à] to block, to counter **2.** JEUX to double **3.** SPORT [au volley] to block *(a smash)* ; [au rugby] to block *(a kick)* ; [à la boxe] to counter *(a punch)*.

contresens [kɔ̃tʀəsɑ̃s] nm **1.** [mauvaise interprétation] misinterpretation ; [mauvaise traduction] mistranslation **2.** [aberration] sheer nonsense. **à contresens** loc adv [traduire, comprendre, marcher] the wrong way.

contretemps [kɔ̃tʀətɑ̃] nm **1.** [empêchement] hitch, mishap, setback **2.** MUS offbeat. **à contretemps** loc adv **1.** [inopportunément] at the wrong time ou moment **2.** MUS off the beat.

contrevenant, e [kɔ̃tʀəvnɑ̃, ɑ̃t] nm, f offender.

contrevenir [40] [kɔ̃tʀəvniʀ] **contrevenir à** v + prép to contravene, to infringe.

contrevérité [kɔ̃tʀəveʀite] nf falsehood, untruth.

contribuable [kɔ̃tʀibɥabl] nmf taxpayer.

contribuer [7] [kɔ̃tʀibɥe] vi [financièrement] to contribute (money), to pay a share. **contribuer à** v + prép : *contribuer à l'achat d'un cadeau* to contribute to (buying) a present **contribuer au succès de** to contribute to ou to have a part in the success of **contribuer à faire qqch** to go towards doing sthg.

contributif, ive [kɔ̃tʀibytif, iv] adj INFORM & INTERNET **logiciel contributif** shareware **encyclopédie contributive** collaborative encyclopedia.

contribution [kɔ̃tʀibysjɔ̃] nf **1.** [argent apporté] contribution, sum contributed **2.** [aide] contribution, help **3.** [impôt] tax **contribution directe / indirecte** direct / indirect taxation **contribution sociale généralisée** supple-

mentary social security contribution to help the underprivileged. **à contribution** loc adv **mettre qqn à contribution** to call upon sb's services / *toute l'équipe a été mise à contribution pour finir le projet* the entire team was called on to finish the project / *mets-le à contribution* ask him to help.

contrit, e [kɔ̃tʀi, it] adj contrite, chastened.

contrôle [kɔ̃tʀol] nm **1.** [maîtrise] control / *garder / perdre le contrôle de sa voiture* to keep / to lose control of one's car **avoir le contrôle de** a) [d'un secteur, de compagnies] to have (owning) control of b) [d'un pays, d'un territoire, d'un match] to be in control of **contrôle de soi-même** self-control **contrôle des naissances** birth control **sous contrôle** under control **2.** [surveillance - de personnes, de travail] supervision, control **contrôle antidopage** dope test **contrôle des changes** exchange control **contrôle de gestion** management control **placé sous contrôle judiciaire** ≃ put on probation **contrôle de qualité** quality control **contrôle radar** radar speed check **contrôle sanitaire** health check **3.** [inspection - d'actes, de documents] control, check, checking **contrôle des bagages** [à l'aéroport] baggage control **contrôle des comptes** ou **fiscal** audit **contrôle d'identité** ou **de police** identification check **contrôle des passeports** passport control **contrôle de sécurité** [à l'aéroport, etc.] security checkpoint **contrôle technique** AUTO test of roadworthiness, MOT (test) UK, inspection US **4.** ÉDUC test / *avoir un contrôle en chimie* to have a chemistry test **contrôle continu (des connaissances)** continuous assessment.

> ⚠ Attention, ce mot ne se traduit pas toujours par **control** en anglais, de même que contrôler ne se traduit pas toujours par to control. Voir aussi l'article **contrôler**.

contrôler [3] [kɔ̃tʀole] vt **1.** [maîtriser - émotions, sentiments] to control, to master, to curb ; [- respiration] to control ; [- discussion, match] to control, to master ; [- véhicule] to control, to be in control of **2.** [surveiller - personnes, travail] to supervise **3.** [vérifier - renseignement, exactitude] to check, to verify ; [- billet, papiers] to check, to inspect ; [- qualité] to control ; [- bon fonctionnement] to check, to monitor ; [- traduction] to check **4.** [avoir sous son autorité - affaires, secteur] to be in control of, to control ; [- territoire, zone] to control, to be in command of. **se contrôler** vp *(emploi réfléchi)* to control o.s., to be in control of o.s.

contrôleur, euse [kɔ̃tʀolœʀ, øz] nm, f **1.** RAIL ticket inspector **2.** AÉRON **contrôleur aérien** air traffic controller **3.** ADMIN & FIN **contrôleur (de gestion)** financial controller **contrôleur (des impôts)** (tax) inspector ou assessor.

contrordre [kɔ̃tʀɔʀdʀ] nm countermand, counterorder / *il y a contrordre, vous ne partez plus* orders have been countermanded ou changed, you're not leaving **à moins d'un** ou **sauf contrordre** unless otherwise informed.

controverse [kɔ̃tʀɔvɛʀs] nf [débat] controversy **donner lieu à controverse** to be controversial.

controversé, e [kɔ̃tʀɔvɛʀse] adj (much) debated ou disputed.

contumace [kɔ̃tymas] **par contumace** loc adv in absentia.

contusion [kɔ̃tyzjɔ̃] nf contusion *spéc*, bruise.

convaincant, e [kɔ̃vɛ̃kɑ̃, ɑ̃t] adj convincing, persuasive.

convaincre [114] [kɔ̃vɛ̃kʀ] vt **1.** [persuader] to convince, to persuade **convaincre qqn de faire qqch** to persuade sb to do sthg, to talk sb into doing sthg **2.** [prouver]

coupable] ▸ **convaincre qqn de vol** to convict sb of theft, to find sb guilty of theft. ❖ **se convaincre** vp *(emploi réfléchi)* to realize, to accept.

convaincu, e [kɔ̃vɛ̃ky] adj convinced ▸ **être convaincu de qqch** to be convinced of sthg / **parler d'un ton convaincu** to talk with conviction.

convalescence [kɔ̃valesɑ̃s] nf MÉD convalescence ▸ **être en convalescence** to be convalescing.

convalescent, e [kɔ̃valesɑ̃, ɑ̃t] adj & nm, f convalescent.

convenable [kɔ̃vnabl] adj **1.** [moment, lieu] suitable, appropriate **2.** [tenue] decent, respectable ; [comportement] seemly, correct ▸ **peu convenable** improper **3.** [devoir] passable, adequate ; [logement, rémunération] decent, adequate.

convenablement [kɔ̃vnabləmɑ̃] adv **1.** [de façon appropriée] suitably, appropriately **2.** [décemment] decently, properly **3.** [de façon acceptable] ▸ **gagner convenablement sa vie** to earn a decent wage.

convenance [kɔ̃vnɑ̃s] nf *litt* [adéquation] appropriateness, suitability. ❖ **convenances** nfpl propriety, decorum, accepted (standards of) behaviour. ❖ **à ma convenance, à sa convenance** loc adv as suits me / him, etc. (best). ❖ **pour convenance(s) personnelle(s)** loc adv for personal reasons.

convenir [40] [kɔ̃vniR] vt : **comme (cela a été) convenu** as agreed ▸ **convenir que** to agree ou to accept ou to admit that. ❖ **convenir à** v + prép [plaire à] to suit / **10 h, cela vous convient-il ?** does 10 o'clock suit you? / **ce travail ne lui convient pas du tout** this job's not right for him at all. ❖ **convenir de** v + prép **1.** [se mettre d'accord sur] to agree upon ▸ **convenir d'un endroit** to agree upon a place ▸ **comme convenu** as agreed **2.** [reconnaître] ▸ **convenir de qqch** to admit sthg. ❖ **il convient de** v impers [il est souhaitable de] it is advisable ou a good idea to / **il voudrait savoir ce qu'il convient de faire** he would like to know the right thing to do.

convention [kɔ̃vɑ̃sjɔ̃] nf **1.** [norme] convention **2.** [règle de bienséance] (social) convention ▸ **respecter les conventions** to conform to accepted social behaviour ou established conventions **3.** [accord - tacite] agreement, understanding ; [- officiel] agreement ; [- diplomatique] convention ▸ **convention collective (du travail)** collective agreement.

conventionné, e [kɔ̃vɑ̃sjɔne] adj **1.** [médecin, clinique] subsidized, designated by the health system ; ≃ National Health 🇬🇧 **2.** [honoraires, prix] set.

conventionnel, elle [kɔ̃vɑ̃sjɔnɛl] adj [conformiste] conventional, conformist ▸ **formules conventionnelles** clichés, platitudes.

convenu, e [kɔ̃vny] adj ▸ **style convenu** conventional style / **l'intrigue est très convenue** the plot is very obvious.

convergent, e [kɔ̃vɛRʒɑ̃, ɑ̃t] adj convergent.

converger [17] [kɔ̃vɛRʒe] vi [confluer] to converge, to meet at a point.

conversation [kɔ̃vɛRsasjɔ̃] nf [discussion] discussion, conversation, talk / **elle est en grande conversation avec son mari** she's deep in conversation with her husband ▸ **engager la conversation (avec qqn)** to start up a conversation (with sb) ▸ **avoir de la conversation** to be a good conversationalist.

converser [3] [kɔ̃vɛRse] vi to converse, to talk.

conversion [kɔ̃vɛRsjɔ̃] nf **1.** [de chiffres, de mesures, de devises] conversion, converting **2.** RELIG conversion.

converti, e [kɔ̃vɛRti] ◆ adj converted. ◆ nm, f convert.

convertible [kɔ̃vɛRtibl] ◆ adj [transformable] convertible ▸ **convertible en qqch** convertible into sthg. ◆ nm [canapé] sofa bed, bedsettee 🇬🇧, convertible sofa 🇺🇸.

convertir [32] [kɔ̃vɛRtiR] vt **1.** [convaincre] to convert ▸ **convertir qqn à a)** [religion] to convert to sb to **b)** [opinion, mouvement] to win sb over ou to convert sb to **2.** [transformer] : **ils ont converti la vieille gare en musée** they converted ou transformed the old railway station into a museum. ❖ **se convertir** vpi [athée] to become a believer ; [croyant] to change religion ▸ **se convertir à** [religion, mouvement] to be converted to, to convert to.

convertisseur nm **1.** TV converter ▸ **convertisseur d'images** image converter **2.** INFORM ▸ **convertisseur numérique** digitizer.

convexe [kɔ̃vɛks] adj convex.

conviction [kɔ̃viksjɔ̃] nf [certitude] conviction, belief / **j'ai la conviction que...** it's my belief that..., I'm convinced that... / **avec** / **sans conviction** with / without conviction. ❖ **convictions** nfpl [credo] fundamental beliefs / **avoir des convictions politiques** to have political convictions.

convier [9] [kɔ̃vje] vt *litt* [faire venir] to invite ▸ **convier qqn à une soirée / un repas** to invite sb to a party / a meal.

convive [kɔ̃viv] nmf guest *(at a meal)*.

convivial, e, aux [kɔ̃vivjal, o] adj **1.** [ambiance, fête] convivial **2.** INFORM user-friendly.

convocation [kɔ̃vɔkasjɔ̃] nf **1.** [d'une assemblée, de ministres] calling together, convening ; [de témoins, d'un employé] summoning **2.** [avis écrit] notification / **vous recevrez bientôt votre convocation** you'll be notified shortly ; DR summons *(sg)*.

convoi [kɔ̃vwa] nm **1.** AUTO & NAUT convoy / **'convoi exceptionnel'** 'wide ou dangerous load' **2.** [cortège] convoy ▸ **convoi funèbre** funeral procession.

convoiter [3] [kɔ̃vwate] vt [vouloir - argent, héritage, poste] to covet, to be after *(insép)*.

convoitise [kɔ̃vwatiz] nf [désir - d'un objet] desire, covetousness ; [- d'argent] greed, cupidity *sout* ▸ **regarder qqch avec convoitise** to stare at sthg greedily.

convoler [3] [kɔ̃vɔle] vi ▸ **convoler en justes noces** to be wed.

convoquer [3] [kɔ̃vɔke] vt [assemblée, concile, ministres] to call together *(sép)*, to convene ; [témoin] to summon to a hearing ; [employé, postulant] to call in *(sép)* ; [journalistes, presse] to invite / **ils m'ont convoqué pour passer un entretien** they've called ou asked me in for an interview / **elle est convoquée chez le proviseur** she's been summoned to the principal's office / **je suis convoqué à 9 h au centre d'examens** I have to be at the examination centre at 9.

convoyer [13] [kɔ̃vwaje] vt [accompagner] to escort ; MIL to convoy.

convoyeur nm **1.** [transporteur] ▸ **convoyeur de fonds a)** [entreprise] security firm *(transporting money)* **b)** [homme] security guard ; ≃ Securicor guard 🇬🇧 **2.** [tapis roulant] conveyor belt.

convulsion [kɔ̃vylsjɔ̃] nf MÉD convulsion ▸ **avoir des convulsions** to have convulsions / **il fut soudain pris de convulsions** he suddenly went into convulsion ou convulsions.

cookie [kuki] nm **1.** [petit gâteau] cookie 🇺🇸, biscuit 🇬🇧 **2.** INFORM cookie.

cool [kul] *fam* ◆ adj inv cool, laid-back, relaxed / **ils sont cool, ses parents** his parents are easy going. ◆ nm inv MUS cool jazz.

coopérant, e [kɔɔpeRɑ̃, ɑ̃t] ◆ adj cooperative. ◆ nm, f aid worker.

coopératif, ive [kɔɔperatif, iv] adj cooperative, helpful. ❖ **coopérative** nf ÉCON cooperative, co-op.

coopération [kɔɔpeRasjɔ̃] nf **1.** [collaboration] cooperation **2.** ÉCON & POL economic cooperation.

coopérer [18] [kɔɔpeʀe] vi to cooperate.

📎 In reformed spelling (see p. 16-18), this verb is conjugated like *semer : il coopèrera, elle coopèrerait.*

coordinateur, trice [kɔɔʀdinatœʀ, tʀis] ◆ adj coordinating. ◆ nm, f coordinator.

coordination [kɔɔʀdinasjɔ̃] nf **1.** [d'une opération] coordination **2.** [des mouvements] coordination / *il n'a aucune coordination* he is totally uncoordinated.

coordonnateur, trice [kɔɔʀdɔnatœʀ, tʀis] = **coordinateur**.

coordonné, e [kɔɔʀdɔne] adj [harmonieux] coordinated. ◆ **coordonnés** nmpl [vêtements] coordinates, (matching) separates. ◆ **coordonnées** nfpl **1.** GÉOGR & MATH coordinates **2.** *fam* [adresse] ▶ **laissez-moi vos coordonnées** leave me your name, address and phone number ▶ **coordonnées bancaires** bank account details.

coordonner [3] [kɔɔʀdɔne] vt [organiser] to coordinate, to integrate.

copain, copine [kɔpɛ̃, kɔpin] *fam* ◆ nm, f [ami] mate 🇬🇧, buddy 🇺🇸, friend / *un copain d'école / de bureau* a school / an office chum / *être / rester bons copains* to be / to remain good friends ▶ **petit copain** boyfriend ▶ **petite copine** girlfriend. ◆ adj ▶ **être très copain** ou **être copain-copain avec** to be very pally with ▶ **copains comme cochons** thick as thieves.

coparentalité [kopaʀɑ̃talite] nf parenting as a couple ; [après séparation] shared ou joint parenting.

copeau, x [kɔpo] nm [de métal] (metal) chip ; [de bois] (wood) chip ▶ **des copeaux a)** [de métal] chips, filings **b)** [pour l'emballage] woodwool.

Copenhague [kɔpənag] npr Copenhagen.

copie [kɔpi] nf **1.** [reproduction légitime - d'un document] copy, duplicate ; [- d'une lettre] copy ▶ **copie certifiée conforme (à l'original)** certified copy ▶ **copie électronique** soft copy **2.** [reproduction frauduleuse - d'une œuvre, d'un produit] copy, imitation, reproduction **3.** ÉDUC [devoir] paper ▶ **rendre copie blanche a)** *pr* to hand in a blank paper **b)** *fig* to fail to come up with the solution *(for a problem)* ▶ **revoir sa copie** : *le ministre va devoir revoir sa copie* the minister will need to have a rethink **4.** INFORM ▶ **copie d'écran** screen dump. ◆ **pour copie conforme** loc adv certified accurate.

copier [9] [kɔpje] vt **1.** [modèle] to reproduce, to copy **2.** [transcrire - document, texte] to copy (out), to make a copy of ; [punition] to copy out *(sép)* ; INFORM to copy **3.** ÉDUC [pour tricher] to copy / *il a copié (l'exercice) sur moi / son livre* he copied (the exercise) from me / his book.

copier-coller [3] [kɔpjekɔle] vt INFORM copy and paste.

copieur, euse [kɔpjœʀ, øz] nm, f [plagiaire] plagiarist ; ÉDUC & UNIV cribber. ◆ **copieur** nm [de documents] copier.

copieusement [kɔpjøzmɑ̃] adv [manger] heartily ; [annoter] copiously ; [servir] generously / *après un repas copieusement arrosé* after a meal washed down with generous amounts of wine.

copieux, euse [kɔpjø, øz] adj [repas] copious, hearty, lavish ; [ration] lavish, big, giant 🇬🇧 ; [notes] copious.

copilote [kɔpilɔt] nmf co-pilot.

copinage [kɔpinaʒ] nm *fam & péj* (mutually profitable) chumminess ▶ **par copinage** through the old boy network 🇬🇧 ou one's connections.

copine [kɔpin] f ⟶ **copain**.

coproduction [kɔpʀɔdyksjɔ̃] nf coproduction.

copropriétaire [kɔpʀɔpʀijetɛʀ] nmf co-owner, joint owner, coproprietor.

copropriété [kɔpʀɔpʀijete] nf **1.** [gén - fait d'être copropriétaire] co-ownership, joint ownership **2.** [immeuble] (jointly owned) apartment building. ◆ **en copropriété** loc adj jointly owned.

copuler [3] [kɔpyle] vi to copulate.

copyright [kɔpiʀajt] nm copyright.

coq [kɔk] ◆ nm **1.** [mâle - de la poule] cock 🇬🇧, rooster 🇺🇸 ; [- des gallinacés] cock, cockbird ▶ **coq de bruyère** capercaillie, capercaillie ▶ **être comme un coq en pâte** to be in clover ▶ **passer** ou **sauter du coq à l'âne** to jump from one subject to another **2.** [figure, symbole] ▶ **coq gaulois** French national symbol *(a cockerel)* **3.** CULIN chicken ▶ **coq au vin** coq au vin. ◆ adj SPORT [catégorie, poids] bantam *(modif)*.

Le coq gaulois
The cockerel is the symbol of France. Its cry, **cocorico!**, is sometimes used to express national pride: **trois médailles d'or pour la France, cocorico!**

coque [kɔk] nf **1.** [mollusque] cockle **2.** [de noix, de noisette, d'amande] shell **3.** *fam* [embarcation] ▶ **coque (de noix)** skiff. ◆ **à la coque** loc adj [œuf] soft-boiled.

coquelet [kɔklɛ] nm young cockerel.

coquelicot [kɔkliko] nm poppy.

coqueluche [kɔklyʃ] nf **1.** MÉD whooping-cough, pertussis *spéc* **2.** *fam & fig* : *il est la coqueluche de l'école* he's the darling ou heartthrob of the school.

coquet, ette [kɔkɛ, ɛt] adj **1.** [qui s'habille bien] smartly dressed ; [soucieux de son apparence] concerned about one's appearance **2.** [élégant - maison, mobilier] fashionable, stylish **3.** *fam* [important - somme, indemnité] tidy, nice (little).

coquetier [kɔktje] nm [godet] eggcup.

coquetterie [kɔketʀi] nf [goût de la toilette] interest in one's looks, desire to look elegant.

coquillage [kɔkijaʒ] nm **1.** [mollusque] shellfish **2.** [coquille] shell.

coquille [kɔkij] nf **1.** [de mollusque, d'œuf, de noix] shell ▶ **sortir de sa coquille** *fig* to come out of one's shell, to open up ▶ **coquille Saint-Jacques a)** [mollusque] scallop **b)** [enveloppe] scallop shell ▶ **coquille vide** *fig* empty shell **2.** SPORT box **3.** IMPR [en composition] misprint ; [d'une seule lettre] literal ; [en dactylographie] typo. ◆ **coquille d'œuf** adj inv eggshell.

coquillette [kɔkijɛt] nf ▶ **des coquillettes** pasta shells.

coquin, e [kɔkɛ̃, in] ◆ adj [espiègle] mischievous / *comme elle est coquine, cette petite !* what a little rascal ou devil she is! ◆ nm, f [enfant] (little) rascal ou devil.

cor [kɔʀ] nm **1.** MUS horn ▶ **cor (de chasse)** hunting horn ▶ **cor anglais** cor anglais, English horn **2.** [au pied] corn. ◆ **à cor et à cri** loc adv ▶ **réclamer qqch / qqn à cor et à cri** to clamour 🇬🇧 ou clamor 🇺🇸 for sthg / sb.

corail, aux [kɔʀaj, o] nm JOAILL, ZOOL & GÉOGR coral. ◆ **corail** adj inv coral(-pink). ◆ **de corail** loc adj [rouge] coral(-pink).

Coran [kɔʀɑ̃] nm ▶ **le Coran** the Koran.

coranique [kɔʀanik] adj [texte, école] Koranic.

corbeau, x [kɔʀbo] nm ORNITH crow.

corbeille [kɔʀbɛj] nf **1.** [contenant, contenu] basket ▶ **corbeille à courrier** desk tray ▶ **corbeille à ouvrage** workbasket ▶ **corbeille à pain** breadbasket ▶ **corbeille à papier** wastepaper basket ou bin, waste basket 🇺🇸 **2.** THÉÂTRE dress circle.

corbillard [kɔʀbijaʀ] nm hearse.

cordage [kɔʀdaʒ] nm **1.** [lien] rope **2.** [d'une raquette] strings ; [action de corder] stringing. ❖ **cordages** nmpl NAUT rigging.

corde [kɔʀd] nf **1.** [lien] rope / *attaché au poteau par une corde* roped to the post ▸ **tirer (un peu trop) sur la corde a)** *fam* [profiter d'autrui] to push one's luck, to go a bit too far **b)** [abuser de sa santé, ses forces] to push o.s. to the limits, to overdo it ▸ **tomber** ou **pleuvoir des cordes** *fam* : *il tombe* ou *pleut des cordes* it's raining cats and dogs, it's bucketing down **2.** [câble tendu] ▸ **corde à linge** clothesline, washing line 🇬🇧 ▸ **être sur la corde raide a)** *pr* to be on ou to walk the tightrope **b)** *fig* to walk a tightrope, to do a (difficult) balancing act **3.** ACOUST & MUS string ▸ **instruments à cordes** string instruments ▸ **toucher** ou **faire vibrer** ou **faire jouer la corde sensible** to touch an emotional chord, to tug at the heartstrings **4.** JEUX, LOISIRS & SPORT rope ; ÉQUIT rail ▸ **corde à nœuds** knotted climbing rope ▸ **corde à sauter** skipping rope 🇬🇧, jump rope 🇺🇸 ▸ **corde lisse** climbing rope **5.** [d'une arbalète, d'une raquette] string ▸ **avoir plus d'une corde** ou **plusieurs cordes à son arc** to have more than one string to one's bow **6.** ANAT cord ▸ **cordes vocales** vocal cords ▸ **c'est dans ses cordes** she's good at that kind of thing / *le bricolage, ce n'est pas dans mes cordes* I'm no good at DIY. ❖ **cordes** nfpl [instruments] strings, stringed instruments. ❖ **à la corde** *loc adv* AUTO & ÉQUIT ▸ **être à la corde** to be on the inside / *prendre un virage à la corde* to hug a bend. ❖ **dans les cordes** *loc adv* [d'un ring] on the ropes.

cordeau, x [kɔʀdo] nm **1.** [fil] string, line ▸ **tiré au cordeau a)** [allée] perfectly straight **b)** *fig* straight as a die **2.** [mèche] fuse.

cordée [kɔʀde] nf roped party.

cordial, e, aux [kɔʀdjal, o] adj warm, cordial, friendly / *une haine / aversion cordiale pour...* a heartfelt hatred of / disgust for...

cordialement [kɔʀdjalmɑ̃] adv **1.** [saluer] warmly, cordially / *ils se détestent cordialement* they heartily detest each other **2.** [dans la correspondance] ▸ **cordialement (vôtre)** kind regards ▸ **bien cordialement** kindest regards.

cordialité [kɔʀdjalite] nf warmth, cordiality.

cordillère [kɔʀdijɛʀ] nf mountain range, cordillera *spéc* ▸ **la cordillère des Andes** the Andes (cordillera).

cordon [kɔʀdɔ̃] nm **1.** [de rideaux] cord ; [d'un bonnet, d'un sac] string ; [de soulier] lace / *cordon de sonnette* bellpull **2.** [ligne - de policiers] row, cordon ; [- d'arbres] row, line ▸ **cordon sanitaire a)** MÉD cordon sanitaire **b)** MIL cordon sanitaire, buffer zone **3.** ANAT ▸ **cordon ombilical** umbilical cord **4.** GÉOL ▸ **cordon littoral** offshore bar **5.** [insigne] sash.

cordonnerie [kɔʀdɔnʀi] nf **1.** [boutique - moderne] heel bar, shoe repair shop 🇬🇧 ou store 🇺🇸 ; [- artisanale] cobbler's **2.** [activité] shoe repairing, cobbling.

cordonnier, ère [kɔʀdɔnje, ɛʀ] nm, f [qui répare] shoe repairer, cobbler ; [qui fabrique] shoemaker.

Corée [kɔʀe] npr f Korea ▸ **(la) Corée du Nord / Sud** North / South Korea.

coréen, enne [kɔʀeɛ̃, ɛn] adj Korean. ❖ **Coréen, enne** nm, f Korean. ❖ **coréen** nm LING Korean.

coriace [kɔʀjas] adj **1.** [dur - viande] tough, chewy **2.** [problème, personne] tough.

coriandre [kɔʀjɑ̃dʀ] nf [plante] (fresh) coriander ; [graines] coriander seeds.

cormoran [kɔʀmɔʀɑ̃] nm cormorant.

corne [kɔʀn] nf **1.** [d'un animal, d'un diable] horn ▸ **faire porter des cornes à qqn** *fam* to cuckold sb **2.** MUS horn

▸ **corne de brume** fog horn **3.** [récipient] horn ▸ **corne d'abondance a)** [ornement] horn of plenty, cornucopia **b)** BOT horn of plenty **4.** [callosité] : *avoir de la corne* to have calluses **5.** [coin de page] dog-ear. ❖ **à cornes** *loc adj* [bête] horned.

cornée [kɔʀne] nf ANAT cornea.

corneille [kɔʀnɛj] nf crow.

cornélien, enne [kɔʀneljɛ̃, ɛn] adj [héros, vers] Cornelian, of Corneille ▸ **choix** ou **dilemme cornélien** conflict of love and duty.

cornemuse [kɔʀnəmyz] nf (set of) bagpipes.

corner¹ [kɔʀnɛʀ] nm FOOT corner kick.

corner² [3] [kɔʀne] vt [plier - par négligence] to dog-ear ; [- volontairement] to turn down the corner ou corners of.

cornet [kɔʀnɛ] nm **1.** [papier] cornet ; [contenu] cornet, cornetful ▸ **un cornet de frites** a bag of chips 🇬🇧 ou French fries 🇺🇸 **2.** 🇨🇭 [sac en papier] paper bag ; [sac en plastique] plastic bag **3.** CULIN ▸ **cornet de glace a)** [gaufrette] cone **b)** [gaufrette en verre] ice cream cone, cornet 🇬🇧.

corniche [kɔʀniʃ] nf **1.** GÉOGR [roche] ledge ; [neige] cornice **2.** [route] corniche (road).

cornichon [kɔʀniʃɔ̃] nm **1.** [légume] gherkin ; [condiment] (pickled) gherkin, pickle 🇺🇸 **2.** *fam* [imbécile] nitwit, nincompoop.

Cornouailles [kɔʀnwaj] npr f ▸ **(la) Cornouailles** Cornwall.

corollaire, corolaire* [kɔʀɔlɛʀ] nm [conséquence] consequence ; LOGIQUE corollary.

corolle, corole* [kɔʀɔl] nf corolla.

coronaire [kɔʀɔnɛʀ] adj coronary.

corporation [kɔʀpɔʀasjɔ̃] nf [groupe professionnel] corporate body ▸ **dans notre corporation** in our profession.

corporel, elle [kɔʀpɔʀɛl] adj [douleur] physical ; [fonction] bodily ; [châtiment] corporal ; [hygiène] personal ▸ **soins corporels** care of ou caring for one's body.

corps [kɔʀ] nm **1.** PHYSIOL body / *vendre ? il faudra me passer sur le corps !* *fig & hum* sell? (it'll be) over my dead body! ▸ **faire corps avec** to be at ou as one with ▸ **près du corps** [vêtement] close-fitting, figure-hugging **2.** [cadavre] body **3.** [élément, substance] body ▸ **corps étranger** foreign body ▸ **corps gras** fatty substance **4.** [groupe, communauté] ▸ **le corps diplomatique** the diplomatic corps ▸ **le corps médical** the medical profession ▸ **le corps électoral** the electorate, the body of voters ▸ **le corps enseignant** the teaching profession ▸ **corps politique** body politic ▸ **un corps de métier** a building trade ▸ **le corps de ballet** DANSE the corps de ballet ▸ **grand corps de l'État** senior civil servants recruited through the École nationale d'administration **5.** MIL ▸ **corps d'armée** army corps ▸ **corps expéditionnaire** task force **6.** [partie principale - d'un texte] body ; [- d'une machine] main part ; [- d'un cylindre] barrel ; [majorité] bulk, greater part **7.** [ensemble - de lois, de textes] body, corpus ; [- de preuves] body **8.** [consistance - d'un tissu, d'un arôme] body ▸ **donner corps à une idée / un plan** to give substance to an idea / a scheme ▸ **prendre corps a)** [sauce] to thicken **b)** [projet] to take shape. ❖ **à corps perdu** *loc adv* with all one's might ▸ **se jeter** ou **se lancer à corps perdu dans une aventure / entreprise** to throw o.s. headlong into an affair / a task. ❖ **corps et biens** *loc adv* NAUT : *il s'est perdu corps et biens* *fig* he's disappeared without trace.

corpulence [kɔʀpylɑ̃s] nf **1.** [volume corporel] build **2.** [obésité] stoutness, corpulence.

corpulent, e [kɔʀpylɑ̃, ɑ̃t] adj stout, corpulent, portly.

corpuscule [kɔʀpyskyl] nm ANAT & PHYS corpuscle.

correct, e [kɔʀɛkt] adj **1.** [sans fautes - calcul, description] correct, accurate ; [- déroulement] correct, proper **2.** [tenue] proper, correct, decent **3.** [courtois] courteous, polite **4.** [honnête - somme, offre] acceptable, fair **5.** [peu remarquable - repas, soirée] decent, OK.

correctement [kɔʀɛktəmɑ̃] adv **1.** [sans fautes] correctly, accurately **2.** [selon la décence, la courtoisie] properly, decently **3.** [de façon peu remarquable] reasonably well.

correcteur, trice [kɔʀɛktœʀ, tʀis] nm, f ÉDUC & UNIV examiner, marker 🇬🇧, grader 🇺🇸. ❖ **correcteur** nm **1.** [dispositif] corrector ▸ **correcteur orthographique** ou **d'orthographe** spell checker ; [produit] ▸ **correcteur liquide** correction fluid **2.** [pour aliments] ▸ **correcteur d'acidité** acidity corrector.

correctif [kɔʀɛktif] nm **1.** [rectification] qualifying statement, corrective / *je voudrais apporter un correctif à ce qu'a dit mon collègue* I'd like to qualify what my colleague said **2.** [atténuation] toning down / *apporter un correctif à des mesures* to soften measures.

correction [kɔʀɛksjɔ̃] nf **1.** [rectificatif] correction / *apporter une correction à une déclaration* a) [mise au point] to qualify a statement b) [atténuation] to tone down a statement ; [action de rectifier] correction, correcting **2.** ÉDUC marking 🇬🇧, grading 🇺🇸 **3.** IMPR ▸ **la correction** a) [lieu] the proofreading department b) [personnel] proofreaders, the proofreading department **4.** [punition] beating **5.** [comportement] correctness, propriety / *il a agi avec correction* he showed good manners.

correctionnel, elle [kɔʀɛksjɔnɛl] adj ▸ **tribunal correctionnel** ≃ magistrate's 🇬🇧 ou criminal & 🇺🇸 court. ❖ **correctionnelle** nf ▸ **passer en correctionnelle** to go ou appear before a magistrate 🇬🇧 ou judge 🇺🇸.

corrélation [kɔʀelasjɔ̃] nf [rapport] correlation / *il y a une (une) corrélation entre A et B* A and B are correlated ▸ **mettre en corrélation** to correlate.

correspondance [kɔʀɛspɔ̃dɑ̃s] nf **1.** [lettres] post 🇬🇧, mail 🇺🇸, correspondence *sout* ; [échange de lettres] correspondence **2.** TRANSP connection ; [train, bus] connection ; [vol] connecting flight / *la correspondance est assurée entre les aérogares* a shuttle service is provided between the air terminals ▸ **assurer la correspondance avec** [train, bateau] to connect with.

correspondant, e [kɔʀɛspɔ̃dɑ̃, ɑ̃t] ❖ adj [qui s'y rapporte] corresponding, relevant. ❖ nm, f **1.** TÉLÉC *person one is calling* / *votre correspondant est en ligne* we are unable to put you through ▸ **nous recherchons votre correspondant** we're trying to connect you ou put you through **2.** [épistolaire] correspondent ; ÉDUC penfriend 🇬🇧, pen pal **3.** [avec qui l'on traite] correspondent / *mon correspondant était Butier* Butier was the person I was dealing with **4.** PRESSE ▸ **correspondant permanent** / **à l'étranger** permanent / foreign correspondent ▸ **correspondant de guerre** war correspondent.

correspondre [75] [kɔʀɛspɔ̃dʀ] vi [par lettre] to correspond *sout*, to write (letters to one another) ; [par téléphone] to be in touch by telephone ▸ **correspondre avec qqn** a) [par lettre] to correspond with sb *sout*, to write to sb b) [par téléphone] to stay in touch with sb. ❖ **correspondre à** v + prép **1.** [équivaloir à] to be equivalent to **2.** [être conforme à - désir] to correspond to ; [- vérité] to correspond to, to tally with ; [- besoin] to meet **3.** [être lié à] to correspond to.

corrida [kɔʀida] nf [de taureaux] bullfight.

corridor [kɔʀidɔʀ] nm [d'un bâtiment] corridor, passage.

corrigé [kɔʀiʒe] nm correct version / *un corrigé du problème de physique* a model answer to the physics problem.

corriger [17] [kɔʀiʒe] vt **1.** ÉDUC [copie] to mark 🇬🇧, to grade 🇺🇸 ; [en cours] to correct, to give the correct version

2. [rectifier - texte] to correct, to amend ; [- faute] to correct ; IMPR to proofread **3.** [punir] to punish **4.** [modifier - vice] to cure ; [- mauvaise habitude] to break ; [- posture] to correct ; [- comportement] to improve **5.** [débarrasser] ▸ **corriger qqn de** a) [vice, mauvaise posture] to cure sb of b) [mauvaise habitude] to rid sb of.

corroborer [3] [kɔʀɔbɔʀe] vt to corroborate, to confirm.

corroder [3] [kɔʀɔde] ❖ **se corroder** vpi to corrode.

corrompre [78] [kɔʀɔ̃pʀ] vt **1.** [pervertir - innocent, enfant] to corrupt **2.** [soudoyer - fonctionnaire] to bribe.

corrompu, e [kɔʀɔ̃py] adj [vil] corrupted.

corrosif, ive [kɔʀozif, iv] adj **1.** [satire, auteur] corrosive, biting, caustic **2.** [acide] corrosive.

corrosion [kɔʀozjɔ̃] nf CHIM, GÉOL & MÉTALL corrosion.

corruption [kɔʀypsjɔ̃] nf [vénalité] corruption ; [fait de soudoyer] corruption, bribing ▸ **corruption de fonctionnaire** bribery and corruption.

corsage [kɔʀsaʒ] nm [blouse] blouse ; [d'une robe] bodice.

corsaire [kɔʀsɛʀ] ❖ nm pirate, corsair. ❖ adj ▸ **pantalon corsaire** breeches.

corse [kɔʀs] adj Corsican. ❖ **Corse** nmf Corsican. ❖ **corse** nm LING Corsican.

Corse [kɔʀs] npr f ▸ **(la) Corse** Corsica.

corsé, e [kɔʀse] adj **1.** [café] full-flavoured ; [vin] full-bodied ; [mets] spicy / *l'addition était plutôt corsée !* the bill was a bit steep! **2.** [scabreux] racy, spicy **3.** [difficile] : *il était corsé, cet examen !* that exam was a real stinker!

corser [3] [kɔʀse] vt [compliquer - problème] to aggravate, to make harder to solve ; [- exercice] to complicate. ❖ **se corser** vpi [se compliquer] to get complicated ▸ **l'affaire se corse** the plot thickens.

corset [kɔʀsɛ] nm [sous-vêtement] corset.

cortège [kɔʀtɛʒ] nm **1.** [accompagnateurs] cortege ; [d'un roi] retinue **2.** [série] series, succession / *la guerre et son cortège de malheurs* the war and its attendant tragedies **3.** [défilé] procession ▸ **cortège funèbre** funeral cortege ou procession ▸ **cortège nuptial** bridal procession.

cortisone [kɔʀtizɔn] nf cortisone.

corvée [kɔʀve] nf **1.** [activité pénible] chore / *repasser, quelle corvée !* ironing's such a chore ou a drag! **2.** [service] duty ; MIL fatigue ▸ **être de corvée** [soldat] to be on fatigue duty / *on est de corvée de vaisselle* we're on dishwashing duty.

cosinus [kɔsinys] nm cosine.

cosmétique [kɔsmetik] adj & nm cosmetic.

cosmique [kɔsmik] adj ASTRON cosmic.

cosmonaute [kɔsmɔnot] nmf cosmonaut.

cosmopolite [kɔsmɔpɔlit] adj **1.** [ville, foule] cosmopolitan, multi-ethnic **2.** [personne] cosmopolitan, international.

cosmos [kɔsmos] nm [univers] cosmos ; [espace] space, outer-space.

cosse [kɔs] nf BOT pod, husk.

cossu, e [kɔsy] adj [famille] affluent, well-off, wealthy ; [quartier] affluent, moneyed ; [maison, pièce] luxurious.

costard [kɔstaʀ] nm *fam* suit.

Costa Rica [kɔstaʀika] npr m ▸ **le Costa Rica** Costa Rica.

costaricain, e [kɔstaʀikɛ̃, ɛn], **costaricien, enne** [kɔstaʀisjɛ̃, ɛn] adj Costa Rican. ❖ **Costaricain, e, Costaricien, enne** nm, f Costa Rican.

costaud, e [kɔsto, od] *fam* adj **1.** [personne] hefty, beefy / *elle est costaud* ou *costaude* she's pretty hefty **2.** [meuble, arbre, tissu] strong, tough, resilient **3.** [problème] tough.

costume [kɔstym] nm **1.** [complet] suit **2.** [tenue] costume ▸ **costume régional / national** regional / national dress.

costumé, e [kɔstyme] adj ▸ **des enfants costumés** children in fancy dress ▸ **bal costumé** fancy-dress ball.

cotation [kɔtasjɔ̃] nf BOURSE quotation ▸ **cotation en Bourse / au second marché** listing ou quotation on the stock exchange / on the second market.

cote [kɔt] nf **1.** BOURSE [valeur] quotation ; [liste] share (price) index **2.** COMM quoted value **3.** [estime] ▸ **cote d'amour** ou **de popularité a)** [d'un homme politique] standing with the electorate ou (popular) rating ou popularity **b)** [d'un film, d'une idée] (popular) rating ▸ **avoir la cote** *fam* to be popular **4.** GÉOGR height ▸ **cote d'alerte a)** *pr* flood ou danger level **b)** *fig* crisis ou flash point **5.** [dans une bibliothèque - sur un livre] shelf mark ; [- sur un périodique] serial mark.

côte [kɔt] nf **1.** [hauteur] slope, incline ; [à monter, à descendre] hill ▸ **descendre la côte** to go downhill / *en haut de la côte* on the top of the hill **2.** [rivage] coast ; [vu d'avion, sur une carte] coastline **3.** ANAT rib **4.** [de porc, d'agneau, de veau] chop ; [de bœuf] rib **5.** ARCHIT, BOT & TEXT rib / *point de côtes* ribbing stitch. ❖ **côte-à-côte** *loc adv* [marcher, s'asseoir] side by side ; [travailler, lutter] side by side, shoulder to shoulder.

Côtes

la Côte d'Amour	the Atlantic coast near
	La Baule-Escoublac
la Côte d'Argent	the Atlantic coast between
	the Gironde and Bidassoa estuaries
la Côte d'Azur	the French Riviera
la côte de Coromandel	the Coromandel Coast
la Côte d'Émeraude	part of the Northern French coast,
	near Saint-Malo
la côte de Malabar	the Malabar Coast
la Côte d'Opale	the coast between Calais
	and Dieppe
la Côte Vermeille	part of the Mediterranean coast,
	between Collioure and Cerbère

coté, e [kɔte] adj [quartier] sought-after ; [produit] highly rated ▸ **être bien / mal coté** to have a good / bad reputation.

côté [kɔte] nm **1.** [d'un tissu, d'une médaille] side **2.** [d'un jardin, d'une pièce, d'une rue] side ▸ **allons de ce côté-ci** let's go this way ▸ **de ce / de l'autre côté de la barrière** *pr & fig* on this side / on the other side of the fence ▸ **côté cour / jardin** THÉÂTRE stage left / right ▸ **côté sous le vent** NAUT leeward side ▸ **côté du vent** NAUT windward side **3.** [du corps] side / *dormir sur le côté* to sleep on one's side **4.** [parti] side / *il s'est mis de mon côté* he sided with me ▸ **être aux côtés de qqn** to be by sb's side **5.** [aspect] side ▸ **côté travail** *fam* on the work front, workwise **6.** [facette - d'une personnalité] side, facet ; [- d'une situation] side, aspect / *chaque emploi a ses bons et ses mauvais côtés* every job has its good and bad sides ou points ▸ **prendre qqch du bon / mauvais côté** to take sthg in good / bad part ▸ **d'un côté** in a way, in some respects. ❖ **à côté** *loc adv* **1.** [tout près] next door ; [pas très loin] nearby ▸ **les voisins d'à côté** the nextdoor neighbours **2.** [mal] ▸ **passer** ou **tomber à côté** to miss. ❖ **à côté de** *loc prép* **1.** [pas loin] next to / *à côté de la cible* off target ▸ **passer à côté de a)** [chemin, difficulté, porte] to miss **b)** [occasion] to miss out on ▸ **à côté de ça** on the other hand ▸ **être à côté de la plaque** *fam* to have (got hold of) the wrong end of the stick **2.** [par rapport à] by ou in comparison with / *il*

fait plutôt avare à côté de son frère he seems rather mean compared to his brother. ❖ **de côté** *loc adv* **1.** [regarder] sideways ; [sauter, tomber] aside, to one side **2.** [en réserve] aside, to one side ▸ **mettre qqch de côté** to put sthg aside ou by ▸ **laisser qqch de côté** to put sthg to one side ▸ **laisser qqn de côté** to leave sb out. ❖ **de mon côté, de son côté** *loc adv* **1.** [en ce qui concerne] for my / his, etc. part **2.** [de la famille] on my / his, etc. side of the family. ❖ **de tous côtés** *loc adv* **1.** [partout - courir] everywhere, all over the place ; [- chercher] everywhere, high and low **2.** [de partout] from all sides. ❖ **du côté de** *loc prép* **1.** [dans l'espace] : *elle est partie du côté du village* she went towards 🇬🇧 ou toward 🇺🇸 the village / *du côté de chez toi* around where you live **2.** [parmi] : *cherchons du côté des auteurs classiques* let's look amongst classical authors.

coteau, x [kɔto] nm **1.** [versant] hillside, slope **2.** [colline] hill.

Côte-d'Ivoire [kotdivwaʀ] npr f ▸ **(la) Côte-d'Ivoire** the Ivory Coast.

côtelé, e [kotle] adj ribbed.

côtelette [kotlɛt] nf [de viande] ▸ **côtelette d'agneau** lamb chop.

coter [3] [kɔte] ❖ vt **1.** BOURSE to list (on the share index) ▸ **coté en Bourse** ≃ listed on the Stock Exchange **2.** COMM to price, to give a list price for. ❖ vi : *les actions Rivetti cotaient autour de 200 euros* Rivetti shares were listed at around 200 euros.

côtier, ère [kotje, ɛʀ] adj [région, navigation] coastal ; [pêche] inshore ; [chemin] coast *(modif)*.

cotillons [kɔtijɔ̃] nmpl party novelties.

cotisation [kɔtizasjɔ̃] nf [pour une fête] contribution ; [à une association] subscription, dues ; [pour la protection sociale] contributions ▸ **cotisation salariale** employees' contribution.

cotiser [3] [kɔtize] vi [par choix] to subscribe ; [par obligation] to pay one's contributions / *cotiser à une caisse de retraite* to contribute to a pension fund. ❖ **se cotiser** *vpi* to club together / *le groupe s'est cotisé* everyone in the group contributed.

coton [kɔtɔ̃] nm **1.** BOT [fibre, culture] cotton ; [plante] cotton plant **2.** TEXT [tissu] cotton ; [fil] (cotton) thread, piece of cotton ▸ **en** ou **de coton** [vêtements] cotton *(modif)* **3.** [ouate] ▸ **coton (hydrophile)** cotton wool 🇬🇧, (absorbent) cotton 🇺🇸 **4.** [tampon de ouate] cotton wool pad 🇬🇧, cotton pad 🇺🇸.

Coton-Tige® [kɔtɔ̃tiʒ] *(pl Cotons-Tiges)* nm cotton bud 🇬🇧, Q-tip® 🇺🇸.

côtoyer [13] [kotwaje] vt **1.** [fréquenter] to mix with **2.** [être confronté à] to deal with / *elle côtoie le danger tous les jours* she faces danger every day.

cou [ku] nm **1.** ANAT neck / *un pendentif autour du cou* a pendant round her neck ▸ **se casser** ou **se rompre le cou a)** *pr* to break one's neck **b)** *fig* to come a cropper 🇬🇧, to take a tumble ▸ **y être jusqu'au cou**: *il y est jusqu'au cou* he's up to his neck in it **2.** VÊT neck.

couac [kwak] ❖ nm [note] false note. ❖ onomat arrk, quack.

couchage [kuʃaʒ] nm [matériel] bed ; [préparatifs] sleeping arrangements.

couchant, e [kuʃɑ̃, ɑ̃t] adj **1.** ⟶ **chien 2.** ⟶ **soleil**. ❖ **couchant** nm *litt* [occident] west.

couche [kuʃ] nf **1.** [épaisseur - de neige, terre, maquillage] layer ; [- de peinture] coat ; [- en cuisine] layer ▸ **avoir** ou **tenir une couche** *fam* to be (as) thick as a brick 🇬🇧 ou as two short planks 🇬🇧, to be as dumb as they come 🇺🇸 ▸ **en remettre** ou **en rajouter une couche** *fam* to lay it on thick

2. ASTRON & GÉOL layer, stratum ▸ **couche d'ozone** ozone layer **3.** SOCIOL level, social stratum **4.** [de bébé] nappy 🇬🇧, diaper 🇺🇸 ▸ **couche jetable** disposable nappy. ❖ **fausse couche** nf miscarriage.

couché, e [kuʃe] adj [allongé] lying down ; [au lit] in bed ▸ **couché !** [à un chien] (lie) down!

couche-culotte [kuʃkylɔt] (pl **couches-culottes**) nf disposable nappy 🇬🇧 ou diaper 🇺🇸.

coucher¹ [kuʃe] nm **1.** [action] going to bed **2.** [moment] bedtime ▸ **au coucher du soleil** at sunset, at sundown 🇬🇧.

coucher² [3] [kuʃe] ▸ vt **1.** [mettre au lit] to put to bed ; [allonger] to lay down (sép) **2.** [héberger] to put up (sép), to accommodate **3.** [poser - par terre] to lay down (sép) / **coucher une bouteille / moto** to lay a bottle / motorbike on its side / **le vent coucha le bateau** the wind made the boat keel over ou keeled the boat over. ▸ vi **1.** [aller dormir] to go to bed **2.** [dormir] to sleep ▸ **on couchera à l'hôtel a)** [une nuit] we'll spend the night ou we'll sleep in a hotel **b)** [plusieurs nuits] we'll stay in a hotel **3.** tfam [sexuellement] to sleep around. ❖ **coucher avec** v + prép fam to go to bed ou sleep with. ❖ **se coucher** vpi **1.** [dans un lit] to go to bed **2.** [s'allonger] to lie down **3.** [soleil, lune] to set, to go down.

couche-tard [kuʃtaʁ] nmf night owl / **c'est un couche-tard** he's always late to bed, he's a night owl.

couche-tôt [kuʃto] nmf : **c'est un couche-tôt** he always goes to bed early.

couchette [kuʃet] nf [d'un train] couchette ; [d'un bateau] bunk.

couci-couça, coucicouça* [kusikusa] loc adv fam so-so.

coucou [kuku] ▸ nm **1.** ZOOL cuckoo ▸ **(pendule à) coucou** cuckoo clock **2.** BOT cowslip **3.** fam [avion] crate, heap. ▸ interj **1.** [cri] hi **2.** JEUX peekaboo, coo-ee.

coude [kud] nm **1.** ANAT elbow ▸ **jusqu'au coude** up to one's elbow ▸ **coude à coude** [marcher, travailler] shoulder to shoulder, side by side ▸ **garder** ou **mettre** ou **tenir qqch sous le coude** to keep sthg shelved indefinitely, to keep sthg on the back burner ▸ **se serrer** ou **se tenir les coudes** to stick together **2.** [d'un tuyau] bend, elbow ; [d'une route] bend.

coudée [kude] nf ▸ **avoir les coudées franches** to have elbow room.

cou-de-pied [kudpje] (pl **cous-de-pied**) nm instep.

coudre [86] [kudʁ] vt COUT [robe] to make up (sép) ; [morceaux] to sew ou to stitch together (sép) ; [bouton] to sew on (sép) ; [semelle] to sew ou to stitch on (sép) ; (en usage absolu) ▸ **j'aime coudre** I enjoy sewing ▸ **coudre à la main / machine** to sew by hand / machine.

couette [kwet] nf **1.** [de cheveux] ▸ **des couettes** bunches 🇬🇧, pigtails 🇺🇸 **2.** [édredon] duvet 🇬🇧, comforter 🇺🇸 (continental) quilt.

couffin [kufɛ̃] nm [pour bébé] Moses basket 🇬🇧, bassinet 🇺🇸.

couille [kuj] nf vulg **1.** [testicule] nut, ball, bollock 🇬🇧 ▸ **avoir des couilles (au cul)** to have balls **2.** [échec, erreur] cock-up 🇬🇧, ball-up 🇺🇸.

couillonner [3] [kujɔne] vt tfam to con.

couiner [3] [kwine] vi **1.** [souris] to squeak ; [lièvre, porc] to squeal **2.** [frein] to squeal.

coulant, e [kulɑ̃, ɑ̃t] adj **1.** fam [personne] easygoing, lax péj **2.** [fromage] runny.

coulée [kule] nf **1.** [de sang, de peinture] streak **2.** [chute] ▸ **coulée de lave** lava flow ▸ **coulée de boue** mudslide.

couler [3] [kule] ▸ vi **1.** [fleuve, eau] to run, to flow ; [larmes] to run down, to flow ▸ **la sueur coulait sur son visage a)** [abondamment] sweat was pouring down his face **b)** [goutte à goutte] sweat was trickling down his face / **le vin coulait à flots** wine flowed freely / **fais couler l'eau** turn on the water ▸ **faire couler un bain** to run a bath / **avoir le nez qui coule** to have a runny nose ▸ **faire couler beaucoup d'encre** fig to cause a lot of ink to flow **2.** [progresser facilement] to flow ▸ **couler de source** to follow (on naturally) ▸ **laisse couler !** fam don't bother!, just drop it! **3.** [avoir une fuite - robinet] to leak, to drip **4.** [se liquéfier - fromage, bougie] to run **5.** [sombrer - nageur] to go under ; [- bateau] to go down, to sink ▸ **couler à pic** to sink straight to the bottom ; [entreprise, politicien] to sink, to go down. ▸ vt **1.** [faire sombrer - bateau] to sink ; [- entreprise, concurrent] to sink, to bring down (sép) **2.** litt [passer] ▸ **couler des jours heureux** to spend some happy days. ❖ **se couler** vpi [se glisser] ▸ **se couler dans** [lit, foule] to slip into. ▸ vpt ▸ **se la couler douce** fam to have an easy time (of it).

couleur [kulœʁ] nf **1.** [impression visuelle] colour 🇬🇧, color 🇺🇸 ▸ **de couleur vive** brightly-coloured ▸ **une jolie couleur verte** a pretty shade of green / **de quelle couleur est sa voiture ?** what colour is his car? / **je n'ai jamais vu la couleur de son argent** fig I've never seen the colour of his money **2.** [pour les cheveux] tint, colour 🇬🇧, color 🇺🇸 / **se faire faire une couleur** to have one's hair tinted, to have some colour put in one's hair **3.** JEUX suit **4.** [vivacité] colour 🇬🇧, color 🇺🇸 ▸ **couleur locale** local colour **5.** [aspect - général] light, colour 🇬🇧, color 🇺🇸 ▸ **quelle sera la couleur politique de votre nouveau journal ?** what will be the political colour of your new newspaper? **6.** [d'une personne] shade, colour 🇬🇧, color 🇺🇸 ; [carnation] : **la couleur de la peau** skin colour **7.** [linge] coloureds 🇬🇧, coloreds 🇺🇸 **8.** HÉRALD & MUS colour 🇬🇧, color 🇺🇸. ❖ **couleurs** nfpl **1.** [linge] coloureds 🇬🇧, coloreds 🇺🇸 **2.** [peintures] coloured paints **3.** [bonne mine] (healthy) glow, colour 🇬🇧, color 🇺🇸 ▸ **prendre des couleurs** to get a tan ou a bit of colour in one's cheeks ▸ **avoir des couleurs** to look well **4.** SPORT [d'une équipe] colours 🇬🇧, colors 🇺🇸 ; [d'un jockey, d'un cheval] livery **5.** HÉRALD colour 🇬🇧 ou color 🇺🇸. ❖ **de couleur** loc adj coloured 🇬🇧, colored 🇺🇸 ▸ **une personne de couleur** a coloured 🇬🇧 ou colored 🇺🇸 person, a nonwhite.

couleuvre [kulœvʁ] nf ▸ **couleuvre (à collier)** grass snake.

coulis [kuli] nm CULIN purée, coulis.

coulissant, e [kulisɑ̃, ɑ̃t] adj sliding.

coulisse [kulis] nf THÉÂTRE ▸ **les coulisses** the wings ▸ **les coulisses du pouvoir** the corridors of power ▸ **dans les coulisses, en coulisse a)** THÉÂTRE in the wings **b)** fig behind the scenes. ❖ **à coulisse** loc adj sliding.

coulisser [3] [kulise] vi to slide.

couloir [kulwaʁ] nm **1.** [d'un bâtiment] corridor, passage ; [d'un wagon] corridor ▸ **bruits de couloirs** rumours **2.** TRANSP ▸ **couloir aérien** air traffic lane ▸ **couloir d'autobus** bus lane **3.** [entre des régions, des pays] corridor ▸ **couloir humanitaire** humanitarian corridor **4.** GÉOGR gully, couloir spéc ▸ **couloir d'avalanche** avalanche corridor **5.** SPORT lane ; TENNIS tramlines, alley 🇺🇸.

coup [ku]
nm

A. HEURT, DÉFLAGRATION 1. [gén] blow, knock ; [avec le poing] punch, blow ; [avec le pied] kick ▸ **frapper à coups redoublés** to hit twice as hard ▸ **donner un coup sec sur qqch** to give sthg a (hard ou smart) tap / **donner un coup sur la table** [avec le poing] to bang one's fist (down) on the table ▸ **prendre des coups** to get knocked about ▸ **recevoir un**

coup to get hit ▸ **coups et blessures** DR grievous bodily harm ▸ **porter un coup à qqn** *pr & fig* to deal sb a blow **2.** [attaque, choc] blow, shock ▸ **ça m'a fait un coup a)** [émotion] it gave me a shock **b)** [déception] it was a blow ▸ **tenir le coup:** *j'ai trop de travail, je ne sais pas si je tiendrai le coup* I've got too much work, I don't know if I'll be able to cope **3.** BOXE punch, blow ▸ **coup bas a)** *pr* blow ou punch below the belt **b)** *fig* blow below the belt ▸ **tous les coups sont permis** *pr & fig* (there are) no holds barred **4.** ARM shot, blast ▸ **un coup de revolver** a shot, a gunshot ▸ **le coup est parti a)** [revolver] the gun went off **b)** [fusil] the rifle went off **5.** [bruit -gén] knock ; [-sec] rap ; [craquement] snap / *des coups au carreau* knocking ou knocks on the window ; [heure sonnée] stroke **6.** *vulg* [éjaculation] ▸ **tirer un** ou **son coup** to shoot one's load.

B. GESTE, ACTION 1. ▸ **coup de griffe** ou **patte a)** *pr* swipe of the paw **b)** *fig* cutting remark **2.** [emploi d'un instrument] : *donner un (petit) coup de brosse / chiffon à qqch* to give sthg a (quick) brush / wipe / *je vais me donner un coup de peigne* I'll just comb my hair ou give my hair a (quick) comb / *je viens pour un coup de peigne* [chez le coiffeur] I just want a quick comb through / *passe un coup d'aspirateur au salon* give the living room a quick vacuum / *passe un coup d'éponge sur la table* give the table a wipe (with the sponge) / *un coup de marteau* a blow with a hammer ▸ **bois un coup** drink something ou have a drink ▸ **un coup de rouge** a glass of red wine **3.** [lancer] throw ; [aux dés] throw (of the dice) ; JEUX [action] move ; CARTES go.

C. ÉVÉNEMENT PARTICULIER 1. *fam* [mauvais tour] trick ▸ **(faire) un mauvais** ou **sale coup (à qqn)** (to play) a dirty trick (on sb) ▸ **monter un coup contre qqn** to set sb up, to frame sb ▸ **coup monté** put-up job, frame-up ▸ **faire un coup en douce:** *elle a fait un coup en douce* she's cooked up something behind everybody's back / *il fait toujours ses coups en douce* he's always going behind people's backs **2.** *arg* crime [vol, escroquerie] job **3.** *fam* [affaire] : *je suis sur un coup* I'm onto something ▸ **rattraper le coup** to sort things out ▸ **il a manqué** ou **raté son coup** he didn't pull it off ▸ **elle a réussi son coup** she pulled it off ; *vulg* [personne -sexuellement] ▸ **c'est un bon coup** he / she's a good lay **4.** [action remarquable, risquée] coup ▸ **faire un beau** ou **joli coup** to pull off a coup ▸ **tenter le coup** to have a go, to give it a try **5.** [circonstance marquante] ▸ **marquer le coup** to mark the occasion ▸ **un coup de chance** ou **de pot** *fam* ou **de bol** *fam* a stroke of luck, a lucky break.

D. FOIS time, go ▸ **du premier coup** first time, at the first attempt ▸ **un bon coup** *fam: c'est ça, pleure un bon coup* that's it, have a good cry ▸ **souffle un grand coup !** *fam* [en se mouchant, sur des bougies] blow hard! ⬦ **à coups de** *loc prép* : *démoli à coups de marteau* smashed to pieces with a hammer / *la productivité a été augmentée à coups de primes spéciales* productivity was increased through ou by dint of special bonuses. ⬦ **à coup sûr** *loc adv* undoubtedly, certainly, for sure. ⬦ **après coup** *loc adv* afterwards, later on / *son attitude, après coup, s'expliquait bien* it was easy to explain her attitude afterwards ou in retrospect. ⬦ **à tous les coups** *loc adv* **1.** [chaque fois] every time / *ça marche à tous les coups* it never fails **2.** [sans aucun doute] : *à tous les coups, il a oublié* he's bound to have forgotten. ⬦ **coup sur coup** *loc adv* one after the other, in quick succession. ⬦ **du coup** *loc adv* so, as a result / *elle ne pouvait pas venir, du coup j'ai reporté le dîner* as she couldn't come, I put the dinner off, she couldn't come so I put the dinner off. ⬦ **d'un (seul) coup** *loc adv* **1.** [en une seule fois] in one (go), all at once **2.** [soudainement] all of a sudden. ⬦ **sous le coup de** *loc prép* ▸ **faire qqch sous le coup de la colère** to do sthg in anger / *il est encore sous le coup de l'émotion* he still hasn't got

over the shock ▸ **tomber sous le coup de qqch** to come within the scope of sthg / *tomber sous le coup de la loi* to be punishable by law, to be a statutory offence UK ou offense US. ⬦ **sur le coup** *loc adv* **1.** [mourir] instantly **2.** [à ce moment-là] straightaway, there and then / *je n'ai pas compris sur le coup* I didn't understand immediately ou straightaway. ⬦ **sur le coup de** *loc prép* ▸ **sur le coup de 6 h / de midi** roundabout ou around 6 o'clock / midday. ⬦ **coup de balai** *nm* : *donner un coup de balai* to sweep up / *le comité aurait besoin d'un bon coup de balai* *fig* the committee could do with a shake-up. ⬦ **coup de barre** *nm fam* : *j'ai un coup de barre* I feel shattered UK ou pooped US. ⬦ **coup de chapeau** *nm* praise ▸ **donner un coup de chapeau à qqn** to praise sb. ⬦ **coup de cœur** *nm* ▸ **avoir un** ou **le coup de cœur pour qqch** to fall in love with sthg, to be really taken with sthg. ⬦ **coup de coude** *nm* ▸ **donner un coup de coude à qqn a)** [en signe] to nudge sb **b)** [agressivement] to dig one's elbow into sb. ⬦ **coup d'éclat** *nm* feat ▸ **faire un coup d'éclat** to pull off a coup. ⬦ **coup d'État** *nm* [putsch] coup (d'état). ⬦ **coup de feu** *nm* [tir] shot ▸ **tirer un coup de feu** to fire a shot, to shoot / *on a entendu des coups de feu* we heard shots being fired ou gunshots. ⬦ **coup de fil = coup de téléphone.** ⬦ **coup de filet** *nm* [poissons] draught, haul ; [suspects] haul. ⬦ **coup de foudre** *nm* **1.** MÉTÉOR flash of lightning **2.** *fig* love at first sight. ⬦ **coup de fouet** *nm* ▸ **donner un coup de fouet à qqn a)** *pr* to lash ou to whip sb **b)** *fig* to give sb a boost. ⬦ **coup fourré** *nm fig* low trick. ⬦ **coup franc** *nm* free kick. ⬦ **coup de fusil** *nm* [acte] shot ; [bruit] shot, gunshot. ⬦ **coup de jeune** *nm* ▸ **donner un coup de jeune à a)** [bâtiment] to give a face-lift to **b)** [émission] to give a new look to. ⬦ **coup de main** *nm* **1.** [raid] smash-and-grab (attack) ; MIL coup de main **2.** [aide] ▸ **donner un coup de main à qqn** to give ou to lend sb a hand **3.** [savoir-faire] : *avoir le coup de main* to have the knack ou the touch. ⬦ **coup d'œil** *nm* **1.** [regard] look, glance ▸ **donner** ou **jeter un petit coup d'œil à** to have a quick look ou glance at ▸ **avoir le coup d'œil** to have a good eye ▸ **valoir le coup d'œil** to be (well) worth seeing **2.** [panorama] view. ⬦ **coup de pied** *nm* [d'une personne, d'un cheval] kick ▸ **donner un coup de pied à qqn** ou **dans qqch** to kick sb / sthg. ⬦ **coup de poing** *nm* punch ▸ **donner un coup de poing à qqn** to give sb a punch, to punch sb. ◀ *adj inv* ▸ **'opération coup de poing'** 'prices slashed'. ⬦ **coup de poker** *nm* (bit of a) gamble / *on peut tenter la chose, mais c'est un coup de poker* we can try it but it's a bit risky. ⬦ **coup de pompe** *nm fam* sudden feeling of exhaustion / *j'ai un coup de pompe* I suddenly feel completely shattered UK ou beat US. ⬦ **coup de pouce** *nm* bit of help ▸ **donner un coup de pouce à qqn** to pull (a few) strings for sb ▸ **donner un coup de pouce à qqch** to give sthg a bit of a boost. ⬦ **coup de sang** *nm* **1.** MÉD stroke **2.** *fig* angry outburst. ⬦ **coup de soleil** *nm* sunburn (U) ▸ **prendre** ou **attraper un coup de soleil** to get sunburnt. ⬦ **coup de téléphone** *nm* (phone) call ▸ **donner** ou **passer un coup de téléphone** to make a call ▸ **donner** ou **passer un coup de téléphone à qqn** to phone ou to call ou to ring UK sb. ⬦ **coup de tête** *nm* **1.** [dans une bagarre] head butt **2.** SPORT header **3.** *fig* (sudden) impulse ▸ **sur un coup de tête** on (a sudden) impulse. ⬦ **coup de théâtre** *nm* THÉÂTRE coup de théâtre, sudden twist in the action ; *fig* sudden turn of events. ⬦ **coup de vent** *nm* **1.** [rafale] gust (of wind) **2.** EXPR **coup de vent:** *entrer / partir en coup de vent* to rush in / off / *elle est passée par Lausanne en coup de vent* she paid a flying visit to Lausanne.

coupable [kupabl] ◆ adj **1.** [fautif] guilty **2.** [responsable] guilty, culpable *sout*; DR guilty **3.** *litt* [amour, rêve, pensée] sinful, reprehensible ; [action] culpable *sout*. ◆ nmf [élément responsable] culprit.

coupant, e [kupɑ̃, ɑ̃t] adj **1.** [tranchant - ciseaux] sharp **2.** [caustique - ton, remarque] cutting, biting.

coupe [kup] nf **1.** [action] cutting (out) ; [coiffure] ▸ **coupe (de cheveux)** cut, haircut **2.** COUT [forme] cut ; [action] cutting ; [tissu] length **3.** [au microscope] section **4.** [sciage] cutting (down) ; [étendue] felling area ; [entaille] section ▸ **coupes budgétaires** budget cuts ▸ **coupe sombre a)** *pr* thinning out **b)** *fig* drastic cut **5.** [verre, contenu - à boire] glass ; [- à entremets] dish ▸ **coupe de glace / fruits** [dessert] ice cream / fruit *(presented in a dish)* / *je t'offre une coupe* [de champagne] let me buy you a glass of champagne ▸ **coupe à glace** sundae dish. ◈ **à la coupe** *loc adj* ▸ **fromage / jambon à la coupe** cheese cut / ham sliced at the request of the customer. ◈ **sous la coupe de** *loc prép* [soumis à] ▸ **être sous la coupe de qqn** to be under sb's thumb.

coupé [kupe] nm AUTO & DANSE coupé.

coupe-circuit [kupsiʀkɥi] *(pl* coupe-circuit *ou* coupe-circuits)* nm cutout.

coupe-faim *(pl* coupe-faim *ou* coupe-faims*)* [kupfɛ̃] nm MÉD appetite suppressant.

coupe-feu *(pl* coupe-feu *ou* coupe-feux*)* [kupfø] nm **1.** [espace] firebreak, fire line **2.** [construction] fireguard.

coupe-gorge *(pl* coupe-gorge *ou* coupe-gorges*)* [kupgɔʀʒ] nm [quartier] dangerous area ; [bâtiment] death trap.

coupe-ongles *(pl* coupe-ongles)*, **coupe-ongle***** *(pl* coupe-ongles*)* [kupɔ̃gl] nm (pair of) nail clippers.

coupe-papier [kuppapje] *(pl* coupe-papier *ou* coupe-papiers)* nm paper knife.

couper [3] [kupe] ◆ vt **1.** [entailler - légèrement] to cut ; [- gravement] to slash ▸ **couper le souffle** ou **la respiration à qqn** to take sb's breath away **2.** [membre] to cut off *(sép)* ; [tête] to cut off, to chop (off) / *couper la tête* ou *le cou à un canard* to chop a duck's head off **3.** [mettre en morceaux - ficelle] to cut ; [- gâteau] to cut up *(sép)* ; [- saucisson] to cut up, to slice (up) ; [- bois] to chop (up) / *couper en tranches* to cut up, to cut into slices, to slice ▸ **couper les cheveux en quatre** to split hairs **4.** [tailler - fleurs] to cut ; [- bordure] to cut off *(sép)* ; [- arbre] to cut ou to chop down *(sép)*, to fell ▸ **couper les cheveux à qqn** to cut ou to trim sb's hair / *se faire couper les cheveux* to have one's hair cut **5.** COUT [robe] to cut out *(sép)* ; [tissu] to cut ▸ **bien / mal coupé** [vêtement] well / badly cut **6.** [écourter - film, texte] to cut ; [ôter - remarque, séquence] to cut (out), to edit out *(sép)* **7.** [arrêter - crédit] to cut **8.** [interrompre - relations diplomatiques, conversation] to break off ▸ **couper la parole à qqn** to cut sb short ▸ **couper l'appétit à qqn** to ruin ou spoil sb's appetite ▸ **couper la chique** ou **le sifflet à qqn** *fam* to shut sb up **9.** [barrer - route] to cut off *(sép)* ; [- retraite] to block off *(sép)*, to cut off **10.** [diviser - surface] to cut ; [- ligne] to cut, to intersect ; [- voie] to cross, to cut across / *la voiture nous a coupé la route* the car cut across in front of us **11.** [diluer - lait] to add water to, to thin ou to water down *(sép)* ▸ **coupé d'eau** diluted, watered down ▸ **couper du vin a)** [à l'eau] to water wine down **b)** [avec d'autres vins] to blend wine **12.** CINÉ ▸ **coupez !** cut ! **13.** TÉLÉC to cut off *(sép)* **14.** JEUX [partager] to cut ; [jouer l'atout] to trump **15.** SPORT [balle] to slice. ◆ vi **1.** [être tranchant] to cut, to be sharp **2.** [prendre un raccourci] ▸ **couper à travers champs** to cut across country ou the fields. ◈ **couper à** v + prép ▸ **couper court à qqch** [mettre fin à] to cut sthg short, to curtail sthg ▸ **couper à qqch** to get out of sthg / *tu dois y aller, tu ne peux pas y*

couper *!* you've got to go, there's no way you can get out of it! ◈ **se couper** vp *(emploi réfléchi)* to cut o.s. ▸ **se couper les ongles** to cut ou to trim one's nails.

couper-coller [kupekɔle] vt & vi to cut-and-paste.

couperet [kupʀɛ] nm **1.** [d'une guillotine] blade, knife **2.** [à viande] cleaver, chopper.

couperose [kupʀoz] nf red blotches (on the face), rosacea *spéc*.

couperosé, e [kupʀoze] adj blotchy and red, affected by rosacea *spéc*.

coupe-vent *(pl* coupe-vent *ou* coupe-vents*)* [kupvɑ̃] nm VÊT windcheater , Windbreaker® .

couple [kupl] ◆ nm [d'amoureux, de danseurs] couple ; [de patineurs, d'animaux] pair / *ils ont des problèmes de couple* they've got problems in their relationship. ◆ nf ▸ **une couple de** *fam* a couple of.

couplet [kuplɛ] nm [strophe] verse ; [chanson] song.

coupole [kupɔl] nf ARCHIT dome ▸ **la Coupole a)** [Académie] the Académie française **b)** [restaurant] *restaurant in Paris famous as a former meeting place for artists*.

coupon [kupɔ̃] nm **1.** TEXT remnant **2.** [de papier] coupon **3.** TRANSP ▸ **coupon annuel / mensuel** yearly / monthly pass ; rail ou train ticket.

coupon-réponse [kupɔ̃ʀepɔ̃s] *(pl* coupons-réponse)* nm reply coupon.

coupure [kupyʀ] nf **1.** [blessure] cut **2.** [trêve, repos] break **3.** ÉLECTR ▸ **coupure (de courant)** power cut, blackout ▸ **il y a une coupure de gaz / d'eau** the gas / the water has been cut off **4.** FIN note , bill ▸ **grosses coupures** large denominations ou bills ▸ **petites coupures** small denominations ou bills .

cour [kuʀ] nf **1.** [d'immeuble] courtyard ; [de ferme] yard, farmyard ▸ **cour de récréation** ÉDUC playground , schoolyard ▸ **jouer dans la cour des grands** *fig* to be up there with the leaders **2.** [d'un roi] court ; *fig* [admirateurs] following, inner circle (of admirers) **3.** DR [magistrats] court ; [tribunal] ▸ **cour d'appel** Court of Appeal ou Appeals , appellate court ▸ **cour d'assises** ≃ Crown Court ; ≃ Circuit court ▸ **Cour de cassation** final Court of Appeal ou Appeals ▸ **Cour européenne des droits de l'homme** European Court of Human Rights ▸ **Cour Internationale de justice** International Court of Justice **4.** EXPR ▸ **faire la cour à qqn** to court sb, to woo sb.

Cour d'assises

This is the court which hears criminal cases. It is made up of a president, two assessors, and a jury of laymen. Normally the court meets every three months in each **département**.

Cour de cassation

The highest court of civil and criminal appeal in France. The court has the power to overturn the decisions of lower courts when it believes the law has been misinterpreted. It does not rehear cases but simply analyses the way the law was applied.

---

courage [kuʀaʒ] nm **1.** [bravoure] courage, bravery / *je n'ai pas eu le courage de le lui dire* [mauvaise nouvelle] I didn't have the heart to tell him ▸ **avoir le courage de ses opinions** to have the courage of one's convictions ▸ **prendre son courage à deux mains** to muster all one's courage **2.** [énergie] will, spirit / *je n'ai pas le courage* *d'aller travailler* / *de le lui dire* I don't feel up to going to work / to telling her ▸ **bon courage !** good luck!, hope it goes well! ▸ **prendre courage** to take heart ▸ **perdre courage** to lose heart, to become discouraged.

courageusement [kuraʒøzmɑ̃] adv **1.** [se battre, parler] courageously, bravely **2.** [travailler] with a will.

courageux, euse [kuraʒø, øz] adj courageous, brave / *je ne me sens pas très courageux aujourd'hui* I don't feel up to much today.

couramment [kuramɑ̃] adv **1.** [bien] fluently / *elle parle le danois couramment* she speaks Danish fluently ou fluent Danish **2.** [souvent] commonly ▸ **ça se dit couramment** it's a common ou an everyday expression ▸ **cela se fait couramment** it's common practice.

courant¹ [kurɑ̃] nm **1.** ÉLECTR ▸ **courant (électrique)** (electric) current ▸ **couper le courant** to cut the power off ▸ **le courant passe bien entre...** : *le courant passe bien entre nous* we're on the same wavelength **2.** [dans l'eau] current, stream / *il y a trop de courant* the current is too strong ▸ **nager contre** ou **remonter le courant a)** pr to swim against the current **b)** fig to go against the tide **3.** [dans l'air] current ▸ **courant d'air** draught UK, draft US **4.** [tendance] current, trend / *les courants de l'opinion* currents ou trends in public opinion ▸ **un courant d'optimisme** a wave of optimism. ◈ **au courant** loc adj [informé] : *je ne suis pas au courant* I don't know anything about it / *oui, je suis au courant* yes, I know. ◂ loc adv ▸ **se tenir au courant** to keep abreast of things ou o.s. informed ▸ **mettre qqn au courant** to let sb know, to fill sb in ▸ **tenir qqn au courant** to keep sb posted ou informed. ◈ **au courant de** loc prép [informé de] : *au courant des nouvelles méthodes* well up on new methods. ◈ **dans le courant de** loc prép in ou during the course of.

courant², e [kurɑ̃, ɑ̃t] adj **1.** [quotidien -vie, dépenses] everyday ; [-travail] everyday, routine ▸ **en anglais courant** in everyday ou conversational English **2.** [commun -problème, maladie] common ; [-incident] everyday **3.** [normal -modèle, pointure] standard **4.** [actuel] current / *votre lettre du 17 courant* your letter of the 17th instant UK ou the 17th of this month. ◈ **courante** nf fam [diarrhée] ▸ **la courante** the runs.

courbature [kurbatyr] nf ache / *plein de courbatures* aching (and stiff) all over.

courbaturé, e [kurbatyre] adj aching (and stiff).

courbe [kurb] nf **1.** [forme] curve **2.** GÉOM curve, curved ou rounded line **3.** [sur un graphique] curve **4.** GÉOGR ▸ **courbe de niveau** contour line.

courber [3] [kurbe] vt **1.** [plier] to bend **2.** [personne] ▸ **courber la tête** to bow ou to bend one's head. ◂ **se courber** vpi **1.** [ployer -arbre, barre] to bend **2.** [personne -gén] to bend down ; [-de vieillesse] to stoop ; [-pour saluer] to bow (down) ; [-par soumission] ▸ **se courber devant qqch** to bow before sthg, to submit to sthg.

coureur, euse [kurœr, øz] nm, f **1.** SPORT runner ; [sauteur de haies] hurdler ▸ **coureur de fond / demi-fond** long-distance / middle-distance runner ▸ **coureur cycliste** (racing) cyclist ▸ **coureur automobile** racing driver **2.** fam [séducteur] womanizer (maneater) ▸ **coureur de jupons** womanizer, philanderer **3.** Québec ▸ **coureur des bois** fur trader.

courge [kurʒ] nf CULIN (vegetable) marrow UK, squash US ; [plante, fruit] gourd, squash.

courgette [kurʒɛt] nf courgette UK, zucchini US.

courir [45] [kurir] ◆ vi **1.** [gén] to run ; [sportif, lévrier] to run, to race ▸ **entrer / sortir / traverser en courant** to run in / out / across ▸ **courir après qqn** to run after sb **2.** [se déplacer -nuée] to race along ou by ; [-eau] to rush, to run /

ses doigts couraient sur les touches his fingers ran up and down the keyboard ▸ **laisser courir sa plume** to let one's pen run freely **3.** [se précipiter] to rush, to run / *j'ai couru toute la journée* I've been in a rush ou I've been run off my feet all day / *qu'est-ce qui le fait courir ?* fig what drives him? / *la pièce qui fait courir tout Paris* the play all Paris is flocking to see **4.** [se propager -rumeur, idée] ▸ **le bruit court que...** rumour UK ou rumor US has it that... **5.** [temps] : *l'année qui court* the current year **6.** FIN [intérêt] to accrue / *laisser courir des intérêts* to allow interest to accrue **7.** EXPR ▸ **tu peux (toujours) courir !** fam no way! ▸ **laisser courir** fam [abandonner] to give up ▸ **laisse courir !** drop it!, forget it! ▸ **courir sur le système** tfam ou **le haricot** tfam **à qqn** [l'énerver] to get up sb's nose UK ou on sb's nerves. ◆ vt **1.** SPORT [course] to compete in, to run **2.** [sillonner -ville, mers] to roam, to rove / *cela court les rues* [idée, style] it's run-of-the-mill / *quelqu'un comme ça, ça ne court pas les rues* people like that are hard to come by **3.** [fréquenter] to go round ▸ **courir les filles / les garçons** to chase girls / boys **4.** [rechercher -honneurs, poste] to seek ; [encourir] ▸ **courir un risque** to run a risk ▸ **faire courir un risque** ou **danger à qqn** to put sb at risk ; [tenter] ▸ **courir sa chance** to try one's luck. ◈ **courir à** v + prép [faillite, désastre] to be heading for / *elle court à sa perte* she's on the road to ruin. ◈ **courir après** v + prép [rechercher] : *courir après qqn* fam to bug sb.

couronne [kurɔn] nf **1.** [coiffure -d'un souverain] crown ; [-d'un pair] coronet ▸ **couronne de lauriers** crown of laurels, laurel wreath ▸ **couronne d'épines** crown of thorns ▸ **couronne royale** royal crown ▸ **couronne funéraire** ou **mortuaire** (funeral) wreath **2.** HIST & POL ▸ **la Couronne d'Angleterre / de Belgique** the English / Belgian Crown **3.** [périphérie] ▸ **la petite couronne** the suburbs adjacent to Paris ▸ **la grande couronne** the outerlying Parisian suburbs **4.** [pain] ring ou ring-shaped loaf **5.** [prothèse dentaire] crown **6.** [monnaie] crown.

couronnement [kurɔnmɑ̃] nm **1.** [cérémonie] coronation, crowning **2.** [réussite] crowning achievement **3.** [récompense] : *cette année a vu le couronnement de ses efforts* this year her efforts were finally rewarded.

couronner [3] [kurɔne] vt **1.** [roi] to crown / *elle fut couronnée reine / impératrice* she was crowned queen / empress ; ANTIQ & HIST [orateur, soldat] to crown with a laurel wreath **2.** [récompenser -poète, chercheur] to award a prize to ; [-œuvre, roman] to award a prize for **3.** [conclure -carrière, recherches, vie] to crown / *sa nomination vient couronner sa carrière* her nomination is the crowning achievement of her career / *et pour couronner le tout* fam and to crown it all, and on top of all that.

courre [kur] ⟶ chasse.

courriel [kurjɛl] nm email.

courrier [kurje] nm **1.** [correspondance -reçue] mail, letters, post UK ; [-à envoyer] letters (to be sent) **2.** [lettre] ▸ **un courrier** a letter **3.** [chronique] column ▸ **courrier du cœur** agony UK ou advice US column, problem page ▸ **courrier des lecteurs** letters (to the editor) **4.** INFORM ▸ **courrier électronique** email ▸ **courrier indésirable** spam, junk email.

⚠ Le mot anglais **courier** ne signifie jamais courrier.

courroie [kurwa] nf **1.** [gén] belt strap **2.** TECHNOL belt ▸ **courroie de transmission** driving belt ▸ **courroie de ventilateur** AUTO fan belt.

cours [kuʀ]
nm

A. ÉCOULEMENT, SUCCESSION 1. GÉOGR [débit] flow ; [parcours] course ▸ **cours d'eau a)** [ruisseau] stream **b)** [rivière] river **2.** [déroulement - des années, des saisons, de pensées] course ; [- d'événements] course, run ; [- de négociations, d'une maladie, de travaux] course, progress ▸ **donner ou laisser (libre) cours à a)** [joie, indignation] to give vent to **b)** [imagination, chagrin] to give free rein to ▸ **suivre son cours** [processus] to continue **3.** [dans des noms de rue] avenue. **B. FINANCE 1.** [de devises] rate ▸ **cours des devises** ou **du change** foreign exchange rate ou rate of exchange ▸ **avoir cours a)** [monnaie] to be legal tender ou legal currency **b)** [pratique] to be common **2.** [d'actions] price, trading rate ▸ **cours des actions** share price ▸ **cours de Bourse** stock price ▸ **au cours du marché** at the market ou trading price. **C. ENSEIGNEMENT 1.** ÉDUC [classe] class, lesson ; UNIV class, lecture ; [ensemble des leçons] course ▸ **aller en cours** to go to one's class ▸ **être en cours** to be in class ▸ **suivre des cours** to attend a course ▸ **prendre des cours** to take lessons ou a course / *j'ai cours tout à l'heure* [élève, professeur] I have a class later / *j'ai quatre heures de cours aujourd'hui* I've got four hours of classes today ▸ **faire cours** to teach / *c'est moi qui vous ferai cours cette année* I'll be teaching you this year ▸ **cours par correspondance** a) correspondence course **b)** UNIV ≃ Open University course 🇬🇧 ▸ **cours magistral** lecture ▸ **donner / prendre des cours particuliers** to give / to have private tuition ▸ **cours du soir** evening class **2.** [manuel] course, coursebook, textbook ; [notes] notes **3.** [degré - dans l'enseignement primaire] ▸ **cours préparatoire** ≃ year one 🇬🇧 ; ≃ nursery school 🇺🇸 ▸ **cours élémentaire** ≃ years two and three 🇬🇧 ; ≃ first and second grades 🇺🇸 ▸ **cours moyen** ≃ years four and five 🇬🇧 ; ≃ third and fourth grades 🇺🇸 **4.** [établissement] school. ❖ **au cours de** loc prép during, in ou during the course of ▸ **au cours des siècles** over the centuries / *au cours de notre dernier entretien* when we last spoke. ❖ **en cours** loc adj [actuel] ▸ **l'année / le tarif en cours** the current year / price ▸ **affaire / travail en cours** business / work in hand ▸ **être en cours** [débat, réunion, travaux] to be under way, to be in progress. ❖ **en cours de** loc prép in the process of ▸ **en cours de route** on the way.

course [kuʀs] nf **1.** SPORT [compétition] race ▸ **faire la course avec qqn** to race (with) sb / *c'est toujours la course au bureau* fig we're always run off our feet at the office ▸ **course de fond** ou **d'endurance** long-distance race ▸ **course automobile** motor ou car race ▸ **course de chevaux** (horse) race ▸ **course de demi-fond** middle-distance race ▸ **course d'obstacles** ÉQUIT steeplechase ▸ **course à pied** race ▸ **course aux armements** arms race ▸ **course de relais** race ▸ **course en sac** sack race ▸ **course contre la montre a)** pr race against the clock, time-trial **b)** fig race against time ▸ **être dans la course** fam to be hip ou with it vieilli **2.** [activité] ▸ **la course a)** [à pied] running **b)** [en voiture, à cheval] racing / *la course au pouvoir / à la présidence* the race for power / the presidency **3.** [randonnée] : *faire une course en montagne* to go for a trek in the mountains **4.** [d'un taxi - voyage] journey ; [- prix] fare **5.** [commission] errand / *j'ai une course à faire* I've got to buy something ou to get something from the shops ; [d'un coursier] errand **6.** [trajectoire - d'un astre, d'un pendule] course, trajectory ; [- d'un missile] flight ; [- d'un piston] stroke **7.** 🇨🇭 [trajet] trip *(by train or boat)* ; [excursion] excursion. ❖ **courses** nfpl **1.** [commissions] ▸ **faire les / des courses** to do the / some shopping **2.** [de chevaux] races ▸ **jouer aux courses** to bet on the races ou on the horses.

courser [3] [kuʀse] vt *fam* to chase, to run after *(insép)*.

coursier, ère [kuʀsje, ɛʀ] nm, f errand boy (girl) ; [à moto] dispatch rider. ❖ **coursier** nm [transporteur] ▸ **envoyer qqch par coursier** to send sthg by courier.

court, e [kuʀ, kuʀt]
adj

A. DANS L'ESPACE 1. [en longueur - cheveux, ongles] short ▸ **court sur pattes a)** *fam* [chien] short-legged **b)** [personne] short / *il y a un chemin plus court* there's a shorter ou quicker way **2.** ANAT [os, muscle] short **3.** RADIO [onde] short. **B. DANS LE TEMPS 1.** [bref, concis - discours, lettre, séjour, durée, etc.] short, brief ▸ **pendant un court instant** for a brief ou fleeting moment **2.** [proche] ▸ **à court terme** short-term *(avant nom)*. **C. FAIBLE, INSUFFISANT 1.** [faible - avance, avantage] small ; [- majorité] small, slender ▸ **gagner d'une courte tête** pr & fig to win by a short head **2.** [restreint] ▸ **avoir la respiration courte** ou **le souffle court** to be short of breath ou wind **3.** *fam* [insuffisant - connaissances] slender, slim ; [- quantité, mesure] meagre, skimpy ▸ **avoir la vue courte** pr & fig to be shortsighted 🇬🇧 ou nearsighted 🇺🇸 ▸ **avoir la mémoire courte** to have a short memory. ❖ **court** ◆ adv **1.** [en dimension] : *je me suis fait couper les cheveux court* I had my hair cut short **2.** [en durée] ▸ **pour faire court** *fam* to cut a long story short **3.** [brusquement] ▸ **tourner court** [discussion, projet] to come to an abrupt end. ◆ nm **1.** [terrain] ▸ **court (de tennis)** tennis court / *sur le court* on (the) court **2.** COUT & VÊT ▸ **le court** short fashions ou hemlines ou styles. ❖ **à court** loc adv *fam* short on cash, hard-up, a bit short. ❖ **à court de** loc prép ▸ **être à court d'idées / de vivres** to have run out of ideas / food ▸ **être à court d'argent** to be short of money. ❖ **de court** loc adv ▸ **prendre qqn de court a)** [ne pas lui laisser de délai de réflexion] to give sb (very) short notice **b)** [le surprendre] to catch sb unawares ou napping. ❖ **tout court** loc adv : *appelez-moi Jeanne, tout court* just call me Jeanne.

court-bouillon [kuʀbujɔ̃] *(pl* courts-bouillons) nm court-bouillon / *faire cuire au* ou *dans un court-bouillon* to cook in a court-bouillon.

court-circuit [kuʀsiʀkɥi] *(pl* courts-circuits) nm ÉLECTR short circuit.

court-circuiter [3] [kuʀsiʀkɥite] vt **1.** ÉLECTR to short, to short-circuit **2.** *fam* [assemblée, personnel] to bypass ; [procédure] to bypass, to short-circuit.

courtier, ère [kuʀtje, ɛʀ] nm, f **1.** BOURSE broker **2.** COMM ▸ **courtier en assurances / vins** insurance / wine broker.

courtiser [3] [kuʀtize] vt [femme] to court, to woo, to pay court to.

court-jus [kuʀʒy] *(pl* courts-jus) nm *fam* [électrique] short.

court(-)métrage [kuʀmetʀaʒ] *(pl* courts métrages ou courts-métrages) nm short film, short.

courtois, e [kuʀtwa, az] adj [poli - personne, manières] civil, courteous.

courtoisie [kuʀtwazi] nf courteousness.

couru, e [kuʀy] ◆ pp ⟶ **courir.** ◆ adj **1.** [populaire] fashionable, popular ; [spectacle] popular **2.** *fam* [certain] ▸ **c'est couru (d'avance) !** it's a (dead) cert! 🇬🇧, it's a sure thing! 🇺🇸

couscous [kuskus] nm couscous.

cousin, e [kuzɛ̃, in] nm, f cousin ▸ **cousin germain** first ou full cousin. ◆ nm ENTOM [insecte] daddy-longlegs, mosquito.

coussin [kusɛ̃] nm **1.** [de siège, de meuble] cushion ; 🇧🇪 [oreiller] pillow **2.** TECHNOL ▸ **coussin d'air** air cushion.

cousu, e [kuzy] pp ⟶ **coudre.**

coût, cout* [ku] nm [prix] cost, price ▶ **coût de la vie** cost of living ▶ **coût salarial** cost of an employee for his employer.

coûtant, coutant* [kutã] adj m cost *(modif)*.

couteau, x [kuto] nm [à main] knife ; [d'une machine, d'un mixer] blade ▶ **couteau à beurre / pain** butter / bread knife ▶ **couteau à poisson** fish knife ▶ **couteau de cuisine / de table** kitchen / table knife ▶ **couteau Économe** ou **éplucheur** ou **à éplucher** potato peeler ▶ **couteau électrique** electric carving knife ▶ **coup de couteau** stab (with a knife) ▶ **remuer** ou **retourner le couteau dans la plaie** to twist the knife in the wound ▶ **avoir le couteau sous la gorge** to have a gun pointed at one's head ▶ **être à couteaux tirés avec qqn** to be at daggers drawn with sb.

coutellerie [kutɛlʁi] nf QUÉBEC cutlery.

coûter, couter* [3] [kute] vt **1.** [somme] to cost ▶ **combien ça coûte ?** *fam* how much is it?, how much does it cost? / **cela m'a coûté 200 euros** it cost me 200 euros ▶ **coûter la peau des fesses** *fam* ou **une fortune** ou **les yeux de la tête** to cost a fortune ou the earth ou an arm and a leg ▶ **coûter cher** [produit, service] to be expensive, to cost a lot of money / **ça va lui coûter cher !** *fig* she's going to pay for this! **2.** [exiger - efforts] to cost / **ça ne coûte rien d'être aimable !** it doesn't cost anything to be kind! **3.** [entraîner la perte de - carrière, membre, vote] to cost / **ça a failli lui coûter la vie** it nearly cost him his life. ❖ **coûte que coûte, coute que coute*** *loc adv* at all costs, whatever the cost, no matter what.

coûteux, euse, couteux*, euse [kutø, øz] adj **1.** [onéreux] expensive, costly **2.** [lourd de conséquences] costly.

coutume [kutym] nf **1.** [tradition] custom ▶ **d'après** ou **selon la coutume** as custom dictates **2.** [habitude, manie] habit, custom / **avoir (pour) coutume de faire** to be in the habit of ou accustomed to doing / **il pleuvait, comme de coutume** as usual, it was raining.

coutumier, ère [kutymje, ɛʁ] adj [habitué à] ▶ **coutumier de**: *il ne m'a pas rendu toute ma monnaie — il est coutumier du fait !* he short-changed me — that wouldn't be the first time ou that's one of his usual tricks! / *j'ai oublié et pourtant je ne suis pas coutumier du fait* I forgot, and yet it's not something I usually do.

couture [kutyʁ] nf **1.** [action de coudre, passe-temps, produit] / *j'ai de la couture à faire* I've got some sewing to do ; [confection] ▶ **la haute couture** (haute) couture, fashion design **2.** [suite de points] seam. ❖ **sans coutures** *loc adj* [bas, collant] seamless. ❖ **sous toutes les coutures** *loc adv* from every angle, very closely, under a microscope *fig*.

couturier, ère [kutyʁje, ɛʁ] nm, f [fabricant - de complets] tailor ; [- de chemises] shirtmaker ; [- de robes] dressmaker. ❖ **couturier** nm [de haute couture] ▶ **(grand) couturier** fashion designer.

couvée [kuve] nf **1.** [œufs] clutch **2.** *fam* [famille] ▶ **sa couvée** her brood.

couvent [kuvã] nm **1.** [de religieuses] convent ; [de religieux] monastery / *entrer au couvent* to enter a convent ou nunnery *vieilli* **2.** [pensionnat] convent school.

couver [3] [kuve] ❖ vt **1.** [suj : oiseau] to sit on *(insép)* ; [suj : incubateur] to hatch, to incubate **2.** [protéger - enfant] to overprotect, to cocoon ▶ **couver des yeux** ou **du regard a)** [personne aimée] to gaze fondly at **b)** [friandise, bijou] to look longingly at **3.** [maladie] to be coming down with / *je crois que je couve quelque chose* I can feel something coming on. ❖ vi **1.** [feu] to smoulder **2.** [rébellion] to be brewing (up) ; [sentiment] to smoulder.

couvercle [kuvɛʁkl] nm [qui se pose, s'enfonce] lid, cover ; [qui se visse] top, screw-top, cap.

couvert¹ [kuvɛʁ] nm **1.** [cuiller, fourchette, couteau] knife, fork and spoon ; [avec assiette et verre] place setting ▶ **mettre le couvert** to lay ou to set the table / *j'ai mis trois couverts* I've laid three places ou the table for three **2.** [prix d'une place au restaurant] cover charge. ❖ **couverts** nmpl cutlery *(U)* UK, silverware *(U)* US.

couvert², e [kuvɛʁ, ɛʁt] ❖ pp ⟶ **couvrir.** ❖ adj **1.** [abrité - allée, halle, marché] covered ; [- piscine] indoor *(avant nom)* **2.** [vêtu - chaudement] warmly-dressed, (well) wrapped-up ou muffled-up ; [- décemment] covered (up) **3.** MÉTÉOR [temps] dull, overcast ; [ciel] overcast, clouded-over. ❖ **sous le couvert de** *loc prép* [sous l'apparence de] in the guise of.

couverte [kuvɛʁt] nf QUÉBEC blanket.

couverture [kuvɛʁtyʁ] nf **1.** [morceau de tissu] blanket ▶ **couverture chauffante** electric blanket ▶ **amener** ou **tirer la couverture à soi a)** [après un succès] to take all the credit **b)** [dans une transaction] to get the best of the deal **2.** CONSTR [activité] roofing ; [ouvrage] (type of) roof **3.** PRESSE [activité] coverage / *assurer* ou *faire la couverture d'un événement* to give coverage of ou to cover an event ; [d'un magazine] cover, front page **4.** [d'un livre] cover **5.** [assurance] cover ▶ **couverture sociale** Social Security cover **6.** [prétexte] disguise, façade / *le financier / la société qui leur servait de couverture* the financier / company they used as a front.

couveuse [kuvøz] nf [machine] ▶ **couveuse (artificielle)** incubator.

couvre-feu [kuvʁəfø] *(pl* couvre-feux*)* nm curfew.

couvre-lit [kuvʁəli] *(pl* couvre-lits*)* nm bedspread.

couvre-pied(s) *(pl* couvre-pieds*)*, **couvrepied*** [kuvʁəpje] nm quilt.

couvreur [kuvʁœʁ] nm roofer.

couvrir [34] [kuvʁiʁ] vt **1.** [d'une protection, d'une couche - meuble] to cover ; [- livre, cahier] to cover, to put a dust cover on ; [d'un couvercle - poêle] to cover, to put a lid on ▶ **couvrir de** [surface]: *couvrir un mur de peinture* to paint a wall ▶ **couvrir avec** ou **de** [protéger] to cover with ▶ **couvrir qqn de** [lui donner en abondance]: *couvrir qqn de cadeaux / d'injures / de louanges / de reproches* to shower sb with gifts / insults / praise / reproaches ▶ **couvrir qqn de caresses / baisers** to stroke / to kiss sb all over **2.** [vêtir] to wrap ou to cover ou to muffle up *(sép)* / *couvre bien ta gorge !* make sure your throat is covered up! ; [envelopper] to cover **3.** [dissimuler - erreur] to cover up *(sép)* ; [protéger - complice] to cover up for **4.** [voix] to drown (out) **5.** [assurer - dégâts, frais, personne, risque] to cover, to insure **6.** [parcourir] to cover **7.** PRESSE [événement] to cover, to give coverage to. ❖ **se couvrir** ❖ vp *(emploi réfléchi)* **1.** [se vêtir] to dress warmly, to wrap up (well) **2.** [se garantir] to cover o.s. ❖ vpi [ciel] to become overcast, to cloud over. ❖ **se couvrir de** *vp + prép* ▶ **se couvrir de fleurs / bourgeons / feuilles** to come into bloom / bud / leaf ▶ **se couvrir de ridicule** to make o.s. look ridiculous ▶ **se couvrir de honte / gloire** to cover o.s. with shame / glory.

covoiturage [kovwatyʁaʒ] nm car-pooling, car-sharing.

cow-boy *(pl* cow-boys*)*, **cowboy*** [kɔbɔj] nm cowboy / *jouer aux cow-boys et aux Indiens* to play (at) cowboys and Indians.

coyote [kɔjɔt] nm coyote.

CP (abr de **cours préparatoire**) nm *first year of primary school.*

CPAM (abr de **caisse primaire d'assurances maladie**) nf *national health insurance office.*

CPGE, cpge (abr de classe préparatoire aux grandes écoles) nf *preparatory course for "grandes écoles".*

CQFD (abr de ce qu'il fallait démontrer) QED.

crabe [kʀab] nm CULIN & ZOOL crab. ❖ **en crabe** loc adv : *marcher / se déplacer en crabe* to walk / to move sideways.

crac [kʀak] onomat [bois, os] crack, snap ; [biscuit] snap ; [tissu] rip.

crachat [kʀaʃa] nm [salive] spit.

craché, e [kʀaʃe] adj *fam* ▶ **tout craché**: *c'est son père tout craché !* he's the spitting image of his dad!

cracher [3] [kʀaʃe] ❖ vi **1.** [personne] to spit ▶ **cracher sur qqn a)** *pr* to spit at sb **b)** *fig* to spit on sb ▶ **il ne faut pas cracher dans la soupe** don't bite the hand that feeds you ▶ **cracher sur qqch** *fam*: *il ne crache pas sur le champagne* he doesn't turn his nose up at champagne **2.** [nasiller - haut-parleur, radio] to crackle. ❖ vt **1.** [rejeter - sang] to spit ; [- aliment] to spit out *(sép)* **2.** [suj : volcan, canon] to belch (forth) ou out ; [suj : fusil] to shoot a burst of, to spit ; [suj : robinet] to spit ou to splutter out *(sép)* **3.** [énoncer - insultes] to spit out *(sép)*, to hiss **4.** *fam* [donner - argent] to cough up *(sép)*, to fork out *(sép)*.

cracheur, euse [kʀaʃœʀ, øz] nm, f spitter ▶ **cracheur (de feu)** fire-eater.

crachin [kʀaʃɛ̃] nm (fine) drizzle.

crack [kʀak] nm **1.** ÉQUIT crack **2.** *fam* [personne - gén] wizard ; [- en sport] ace / *c'est un crack en ski* he's an ace skier **3.** [drogue] crack.

cracra [kʀakʀa] *fam*, **crade** [kʀad], **cradingue** [kʀadɛ̃g] *tfam*, **crado** [kʀado] *fam* adj inv [personne, objet] filthy ; [restaurant] grotty 🇬🇧, lousy 🇺🇸.

craie [kʀɛ] nf chalk, limestone ▶ **écrire qqch à la craie** to chalk sthg, to write sthg in chalk.

craindre [80] [kʀɛ̃dʀ] vt **1.** [redouter - personne] to fear, to be frightened ou afraid of ; [- événement] to fear, to be frightened ou scared of ▶ **craindre le pire** to fear the worst ▶ **ne crains rien** have no fear, never fear, don't be afraid **2.** [tenir pour probable] to fear / *alors, je suis renvoyé ? — je le crains* so, I'm fired? — I'm afraid so / *je crains qu'elle nous dénonce — c'est à craindre* she might give us away — unfortunately, (I think) it's likely / *je crains de l'avoir blessée* I'm afraid I've hurt her / *je crains fort qu'il (ne) soit déjà trop tard* I fear ou I'm very much afraid it's already too late **3.** [être sensible à] : *ça craint le froid* [plante] it's sensitive to cold, it doesn't like the cold **4.** [EXPR] **ça craint** *tfam* **a)** [c'est louche] it's dodgy 🇬🇧 **b)** [c'est ennuyeux] it's a real pain. ❖ **craindre pour** v + prép ▶ **craindre pour qqn / qqch** to fear for sb / sthg.

craint, e [kʀɛ̃, ɛ̃t] pp —→ **craindre.** ❖ **crainte** nf [anxiété] fear / *la crainte de l'échec* fear of failure ou failing / *n'aie aucune crainte* ou *sois sans crainte, tout se passera bien* don't worry ou never fear, everything will be all right. ❖ **de crainte de** loc prép *(suivi de l'infinitif)* for fear of. ❖ **de crainte que** loc conj *(suivi du subjonctif)* for fear of, fearing that / *de crainte qu'on (ne) l'accuse* for fear of being accused, fearing that she might be accused.

craintif, ive [kʀɛ̃tif, iv] adj [facilement effarouché - personne] timid, shy ; [- animal] timid.

cramer [3] [kʀame] *fam* ❖ vi [immeuble] to be on fire ; [rôti, tissu] to burn ; [circuit électrique, prise] to burn out. ❖ vt [rôti] to burn (to a cinder), to let burn ; [vêtement] to burn, to scorch.

cramoisi, e [kʀamwazi] adj [velours] crimson ; [visage] flushed, crimson.

crampe [kʀɑ̃p] nf MÉD cramp / *j'ai une crampe au pied !* I have cramp 🇬🇧 ou a cramp 🇺🇸 in my foot ▶ **crampe d'estomac a)** [gén] stomach cramp **b)** [de faim] hunger pang.

crampon [kʀɑ̃pɔ̃] nm **1.** [de chaussures - de sport] stud ; [- de montagne] crampon ; [de fer à cheval] calk **2.** *fam & péj* [personne] : *c'est un / une crampon* he / she sticks like a leech.

cramponner [3] [kʀɑ̃pɔne] ❖ **se cramponner** vpi **1.** [s'agripper] to hold on, to hang on ▶ **se cramponner à a)** [branche, barre] to cling (on) ou to hold on to **b)** [personne] to cling (on) to **2.** *fam* [s'acharner - malade] to cling ou to hang on ; [- étudiant] to stick with it ▶ **se cramponner à la vie / à un espoir** to cling to life / hope.

cran [kʀɑ̃] nm **1.** [entaille - d'une étagère, d'une crémaillère] notch ; [trou - d'une ceinture] hole, notch ▶ **baisser / monter d'un cran a)** [dans une hiérarchie] to come down / to move up a peg **b)** [voix] to fall / to rise slightly **2.** [mèche] wave **3.** TECHNOL catch ▶ **cran de sûreté** ou **sécurité** safety catch ▶ **cran d'arrêt** *fam* [couteau] flick-knife **4.** *fam* [courage] ▶ **avoir du cran** to have guts. ❖ **à cran** loc adj *fam* uptight, edgy, on edge.

crâne [kʀɑn] nm **1.** ANAT skull, cranium *spéc* **2.** *fam* [tête] ▶ **avoir mal au crâne** to have a headache.

crâner [3] [kʀɑne] vi *fam* to show off, to swank 🇬🇧.

crâneur, euse [kʀɑnœʀ, øz] *fam & péj* ❖ adj ▶ **être crâneur** to be a bit of a show-off. ❖ nm, f show-off, hotshot 🇺🇸 / *faire le crâneur* to show off, to swank 🇬🇧.

crânien, enne [kʀɑnjɛ̃, ɛn] adj cranial.

crapaud [kʀapo] nm ZOOL toad.

crapule [kʀapyl] ❖ nf [individu] crook, villain / *petite crapule !* you little rat! ❖ adj roguish.

craqueler [24] [kʀakle] vt [fendiller] to crack ; [poterie] to crackle. ❖ **se craqueler** vpi [peinture, peau] to crack ; [poterie] to crackle.

📖 In reformed spelling (see p. 16-18), this verb is conjugated like *peler : il craquèlera, elle se craquèlerait.*

craquelure [kʀaklyʀ] nf [accidentelle] crack.

craquement [kʀakmɑ̃] nm [de bois qui casse] snap, crack ; [d'un plancher] creak ; [d'herbes sèches] crackle ; [de chaussures] squeak, creak.

craquer [3] [kʀake] ❖ vi **1.** [plancher] to creak ; [bois qui casse] to snap, to crack ; [cuir, soulier] to squeak, to creak ; [herbes sèches] to crackle ▶ **faire craquer ses doigts** to crack one's knuckles **2.** [se fendre - couture, tissu] to split ; [- sac] to split open ; [- fil, lacets] to break, to snap off ; [- fermeture éclair] to crack, to split (up) ; [- collant] to rip **3.** *fam* [psychologiquement] to break down, to crack up ▶ **ses nerfs ont craqué** she had a nervous breakdown, she cracked up **4.** *fam* [être séduit] to go wild / *j'ai craqué pour cette robe* I went wild over that dress. ❖ vt **1.** [couture] to split, to tear **2.** [allumette] to strike.

crash [kʀaʃ] nm **1.** [accident] crashing (to the ground) **2.** [atterrissage forcé] crash landing.

crasse [kʀas] ❖ nf **1.** [saleté] filth **2.** *fam* [mauvais tour] dirty ou nasty trick ▶ **faire une crasse à qqn** to play a dirty ou nasty trick on sb. ❖ adj *fam* [stupidité] crass ▶ **d'une ignorance crasse** abysmally ignorant, pig-ignorant.

crasseux, euse [kʀaso, øz] adj [mains, vêtements] filthy, grimy, grubby ; [maison] filthy, squalid ; [personne] filthy.

cratère [kʀatɛʀ] nm ANTIQ & GÉOGR crater.

cravache [kʀavaʃ] nf riding crop, horsewhip. ❖ **à la cravache** loc adv ruthlessly, with an iron hand.

cravacher [3] [kʀavaʃe] vt [cheval] to use the whip on ; [personne] to horsewhip.

cravate [kʀavat] nf tie, necktie 🇺🇸 / *en costume (et) cravate* wearing a suit and a tie.

crawl [kʀol] nm crawl / *faire du* ou *nager le crawl* to do ou to swim the crawl.

crayon [kʀɛjɔ̃] nm **1.** [pour écrire, dessiner] pencil ; [stylo] pen ▸ **crayon gras** ou **à mine grasse** soft lead pencil ▸ **crayon à** ou **de papier** lead pencil ▸ **crayon de couleur** coloured pencil, crayon ▸ **crayon à lèvres** lipliner pencil ▸ **crayon noir** [à papier] (lead) pencil ▸ **crayon pour les yeux** eye ou eyeliner pencil ▸ **crayon à sourcils** eyebrow pencil ▸ **coup de crayon** a) [rature] pencil stroke b) [d'un artiste] drawing style / *avoir un bon coup de crayon* to be good at drawing **2.** ART [œuvre] pencil drawing, crayon-sketch. ❖ **au crayon** loc adv [dessiner, écrire] in pencil ▸ **écrire** / **dessiner qqch au crayon** to write / to draw sthg in pencil.

crayon-feutre [kʀɛjɔ̃føtʀ] (*pl* **crayons-feutres**) nm felt-tip (pen).

crayonné [kʀɛjone] nm pencil drawing.

crayonner [3] [kʀɛjone] vt **1.** [dessiner rapidement] to sketch (in pencil) **2.** [écrire - au crayon] to pencil ; [- rapidement] to jot down *(sép)*.

CRDP (abr de **centre régional de documentation pédagogique**) nm *local centre for educational resources.*

créance [kʀeɑ̃s] nf **1.** FIN & DR [dette] claim, debt ; [titre] letter of credit **2.** *litt* [foi] credence.

créancier, ère [kʀeɑ̃sje, ɛʀ] nm, f creditor.

créateur, trice [kʀeatœʀ, tʀis] ◆ adj creative ▸ **imagination créatrice** creativity ▸ **les secteurs créateurs d'emploi** job-creating sectors. ◆ nm, f designer ▸ **les créateurs d'entreprise** entrepreneurs, business creators.

créatif, ive [kʀeatif, iv] ◆ adj [esprit] creative, imaginative, inventive. ◆ nm, f [gén] creative person ; [de publicité] designer.

création [kʀeasjɔ̃] nf **1.** [œuvre originale - bijou, parfum, vêtement] creation ; COMM & INDUST new product **2.** THÉÂTRE [d'un rôle] creation ; [d'une pièce] first production, creation **3.** [fait de créer - une mode, un style] creation ; [- un vêtement] designing, creating ; [- une entreprise] setting up ; [- une association] founding, creating ; [- des emplois] creating, creation ▸ **il y a eu 3 000 créations d'emplois en mai** 3,000 new jobs were created in May.

créationnisme [kʀeasjɔnism] nm creationism.

créativité [kʀeativite] nf **1.** [qualité] creativity, creativeness, creative spirit **2.** LING creativity.

créature [kʀeatyʀ] nf [personne ou bête créée] creature.

crécelle [kʀesɛl] nf rattle.

crèche [kʀɛʃ] nf **1.** [établissement préscolaire] crèche 🇬🇧, day nursery 🇬🇧, child-care center 🇺🇸 ; [dans un centre sportif, un magasin] crèche 🇬🇧, day-care center 🇺🇸 ▸ **crèche familiale** crèche in the home of a registered child minder ▸ **crèche parentale** crèche run by parents **2.** [de la Nativité] ▸ **crèche de Noël** (Christ Child's) crib 🇬🇧, crèche 🇺🇸 ; *litt* [mangeoire] manger, crib.

crécher [18] [kʀeʃe] vi *tfam* [habiter] to live.

✏️ In reformed spelling (see p. 16-18), this verb is conjugated like **semer** : *il crèchera, il crècherait.*

crédibiliser [3] [kʀedibilize] vt to give credibility to.

crédibilité [kʀedibilite] nf credibility.

crédible [kʀedibl] adj credible, believable.

crédit [kʀedi] nm **1.** BANQUE [actif] credit ; [en comptabilité] credit, credit side ▸ **porter 100 euros au crédit de qqn** to credit sb ou sb's account with 100 euros, to credit 100 euros to sb's account / *j'ai 2 890 euros à mon crédit* I am 2,890 euros in credit **2.** COMM [paiement différé, délai] credit ; [prêt] credit ▸ **faire crédit à qqn** to give sb credit, to give credit to sb / **'la maison ne fait** ou **nous ne faisons pas crédit'** 'no credit' / *accorder* | *obtenir un crédit* to grant / to obtain credit / *j'ai pris un crédit sur 25 ans pour la maison* I've got a 25-year mortgage on the house ▸ **crédit immobilier à taux variable** adjustable-rate mortgage ▸ **crédit d'impôt** tax rebate ou credit (for bondholders) ▸ **crédit renouvelable** revolving credit **3.** *sout* [confiance, estime] credibility, esteem ▸ **jouir d'un grand crédit auprès de qqn** to be high in sb's esteem ▸ **donner du crédit aux propos de qqn** to give credence to what sb says **4.** 🇨🇦 UNIV credit. ❖ **crédits** nmpl [fonds] funds / *accorder des crédits* to grant ou to allocate funds ; [autorisation de dépenses] ▸ **crédits budgétaires** supplies. ❖ **à crédit** loc adv ▸ **acheter à crédit** to buy on credit. ❖ **à mon crédit, à son crédit** loc adv to my / her, etc. credit ▸ **c'est à mettre** ou **porter à son crédit** one must credit him with it.

crédit-bail [kʀedibaj] (*pl* **crédits-bails**) nm leasing.

créditer [3] [kʀedite] vt **1.** BANQUE [somme] to credit / *mon compte a été crédité de 800 euros* 800 euros were credited to my account **2.** *fig* ▸ **être crédité de** to be given credit ou to get the praise for.

créditeur, trice [kʀeditœʀ, tʀis] ◆ adj [solde] credit (modif) ▸ **avoir un compte créditeur** to have an account in credit. ◆ nm, f customer in credit, creditworthy customer.

credo (*pl* **credo**), **crédo*** [kʀedo] nm [principe] credo, creed.

crédule [kʀedyl] adj gullible, credulous.

crédulité [kʀedylite] nf gullibility, credulity.

créer [15] [kʀee] vt **1.** [inventer - personnage, style] to create ; [- machine] to invent ; [- vêtement] to create, to design ; [- mot] to invent, to coin **2.** THÉÂTRE [rôle] to create, to play for the first time ; [pièce] to produce for the first time **3.** [occasionner, engendrer - emploi, différences, difficultés] to create ; [- poste] to create, to establish ; [- atmosphère] to create, to bring about (insép) ; [- tension] to give rise to ; [- précédent] to set ▸ **créer des ennuis** ou **difficultés à qqn** to create problems for ou to cause trouble to sb **4.** [fonder - association, mouvement] to create, to found ; [- entreprise] to set up (sép) ; [- État] to establish, to create.

crémaillère [kʀemajɛʀ] nf **1.** [de cheminée] trammel (hook) **2.** AUTO & MÉCAN rack **3.** RAIL rack.

crémation [kʀemasjɔ̃] nf cremation.

crématoire [kʀematwaʀ] ◆ adj crematory. ◆ nm cremator 🇬🇧, cinerator 🇺🇸.

crématorium [kʀematɔʀjɔm] nm crematorium 🇬🇧, crematory 🇺🇸.

crème [kʀɛm] ◆ nf **1.** CULIN [préparation] cream ; [entremets] cream (dessert) ▸ **crème anglaise** custard ▸ **crème au beurre** butter cream ▸ **crème brûlée** crème brûlée ▸ **crème (au) caramel** crème caramel ▸ **crème fraîche épaisse** double 🇬🇧 ou heavy 🇺🇸 cream ▸ **crème fleurette** ≃ low-fat single cream ▸ **crème fouettée** whipped cream ▸ **crème fraîche** crème fraîche ▸ **crème glacée** ice-cream ▸ **crème pâtissière** confectioner's custard ▸ **crème renversée** custard cream 🇬🇧, cup custard 🇺🇸 ▸ **la crème de** : *c'est la crème des maris* he's the perfect husband **2.** [potage] : *crème de poireaux* cream of leek soup **3.** [boisson] ▸ **crème de cassis** crème de cassis **4.** [cosmétique] cream ▸ **crème dépilatoire** hair removing cream ▸ **crème à raser** shaving cream. ◆ adj inv off-white, cream, cream-coloured. ◆ nm *fam* [café] white coffee 🇬🇧, coffee with milk ou cream / *un grand* | *petit crème* a large / small cup of white coffee. ❖ **à la crème** loc adj [gâteau] cream (modif) ▸ **framboises à la crème** raspberries and cream ▸ **escalopes à la crème** escalopes with cream sauce.

crémerie [kʀemʀi] nf [boutique] *shop selling cheese and other dairy products.*

* In reformed spelling (see p. 16-18).

crémeux, euse [kʀemø,øz] adj **1.** [onctueux] creamy, unctuous, smooth **2.** [gras - fromage] soft.

créneau, x [kʀeno] nm **1.** ARCHIT [creux] crenel (embrasure), crenelle ; [bloc de pierre] crenellation ▸ **monter au créneau** fam to step into the breach **2.** AUTO [espace] gap, (parking) space ▸ **faire un créneau** to reverse into a (parking) space 🇬🇧, to parallel park 🇺🇸 **3.** RADIO & TV [temps d'antenne] slot ▸ **créneau horaire / publicitaire** time / advertizing slot ; [dans un emploi du temps] slot, gap **4.** ÉCON gap (in the market), opening ▸ **trouver un bon créneau** to find a good opening (in the market).

créole [kʀeɔl] adj creole. **⋄ Créole** nmf Creole. **⋄ créole** nm LING creole. **⋄ créoles** nfpl hoop earrings.

crêpe¹ [kʀɛp] nm **1.** TEXT crepe, crêpe **2.** [caoutchouc] crepe rubber. **⋄ de crêpe** loc adj **1.** [funéraire] mourning **2.** [chaussures, semelle] rubber (modif).

crêpe² [kʀɛp] nf CULIN pancake.

crêper [4] [kʀepe] vt [cheveux] to backcomb 🇬🇧, to tease 🇺🇸. **⋄ se crêper** vpt ▸ **se crêper les cheveux** to backcomb one's hair ▸ **se crêper le chignon** fam to have a go at each other ou a bust-up.

crêperie [kʀepʀi] nf [restaurant] pancake restaurant, creperie ; [stand] pancake stall.

crépi, e [kʀepi] adj roughcast (modif). **⋄ crépi** nm roughcast.

crépir [32] [kʀepiʀ] vt to roughcast.

crépiter [3] [kʀepite] vi **1.** [feu, coups de feu] to crackle ; [pluie] to patter ; [friture] to splutter ; [flashs] to go off **2.** MÉD to crepitate.

crépon [kʀepɔ̃] nm **1.** [papier] crepe paper **2.** TEXT crepon, seersucker.

crépu, e [kʀepy] adj [cheveux] frizzy.

crépuscule [kʀepyskyl] nm **1.** [fin du jour] twilight, dusk **2.** ASTRON [lumière - du soir] twilight ; [- du matin] dawn light. **⋄ au crépuscule de** loc prép litt ▸ **au crépuscule de sa vie / du siècle** in the twilight of his life / the closing years of the century.

crescendo [kʀeʃendo, kʀeʃɛ̃do] **◆** nm MUS crescendo. **◆** adv crescendo ▸ **aller crescendo a)** [notes] to go crescendo **b)** [bruits, voix] to grow louder and louder **c)** [violence] to rise, to escalate **d)** [mécontentement] to reach a climax.

cresson [kʀesɔ̃] nm f BOT & CULIN cress.

Crète [kʀɛt] npr f ▸ **(la) Crète** Crete.

crête [kʀɛt] nf **1.** ORNITH [d'oiseau] crest ; [de volaille] comb **2.** [d'une montagne, d'un toit] crest, ridge ; [d'un mur] crest, top ; [d'une vague] crest.

crétin, e [kʀetɛ̃, in] **◆** adj moronic. **◆** nm, f **1.** [imbécile] moron, cretin **2.** vieilli MÉD cretin.

crétois, e [kʀetwa, az] adj Cretan. **⋄ Crétois, e** nm, f Cretan.

creuser [3] [kʀøze] vt **1.** [excaver - puits, mine] to dig, to sink ; [- canal] to dig, to cut ; [- tranchée] to dig, to excavate ; [- sillon] to plough ; [- passage souterrain, tunnel] to make, to bore, to dig **2.** [faire un trou dans - gén] to hollow (out) ; [- avec une cuillère] to scoop (out) **3.** fam [ouvrir l'appétit de] to make hungry / **la marche m'a creusé** (l'estomac) the walk gave me an appetite ou whetted my appetite ou made me feel hungry **4.** [approfondir - idée] to look ou to go into (insép) ; [- problème, question] to look ou to delve into (insép) ; (en usage absolu) : **il paraît intelligent, mais il vaut mieux ne pas creuser (trop loin)** he seems intelligent, but it might be better not to go into it too deeply. **⋄ se creuser** vp (emploi réfléchi) : **tu ne t'es pas beaucoup creusé pour écrire ce texte !** you didn't overtax yourself when you wrote this text! ▸ **se creuser la tête** ou

la cervelle fam to rack one's brains. **◆** vpi **1.** [yeux, visage] to grow hollow ; [joues] to grow gaunt ou hollow ; [fossettes, rides] to appear / **la mer commence à se creuser** the sea's starting to swell **2.** [augmenter - écart] to grow bigger / **le fossé entre eux se creuse** the gap between them is widening.

creuset [kʀøze] nm **1.** PHARM & TECHNOL crucible, melting pot ; [d'un haut-fourneau] crucible, hearth **2.** [rassemblement] melting pot, mixture.

Creutzfeldt-Jakob [kʀøtsfeltʒakɔb] npr ▸ **maladie de Creutzfeldt-Jakob** Creutzfeldt-Jakob disease.

creux, euse [kʀø, kʀøz] adj **1.** [évidé - dent, tronc] hollow ; fig ▸ **j'ai le ventre creux** my stomach feels hollow, I feel hungry **2.** péj [inconsistant - discours, phrases] empty, meaningless ; [- promesses] hollow, empty ; [- argumentation] weak **3.** [sans activité] ▸ **périodes creuses a)** [au travail] slack periods **b)** [dans une tarification] off-peak periods ▸ **pendant la saison creuse a)** [pour le commerce] during the slack season **b)** [pour les vacanciers] during the off-peak season ▸ **heures creuses** : **la communication / le trajet aux heures creuses ne vous coûtera que 3 €** the phone call / journey will cost you only 3 € off-peak. **⋄ creux** nm **1.** [trou - dans un roc] hole, cavity ; [- d'une dent, d'un tronc] hollow (part), hole, cavity / **avoir un creux (à l'estomac)** fam to feel peckish 🇬🇧 ou a bit hungry **2.** [concavité - d'une main, d'une épaule] hollow ; [- de l'estomac] pit / **il a bu dans le creux de ma main** it drank out of my hand ▸ **j'ai mal dans le creux du dos** ou **des reins** I've a pain in the small of my back **3.** [dépression - d'une courbe, d'une vague] trough **4.** [inactivité] slack period / **il y a un creux des ventes en janvier** business slows down ou slackens off in January. **⋄ au creux de** loc prép ▸ **au creux de la vague** pr in the trough of the wave ▸ **être au creux de la vague** fig [entreprise, personne] to be going through a bad patch.

crevaison [kʀøvezɔ̃] nf puncture 🇬🇧, flat 🇺🇸.

crevant, e [kʀøvɑ̃, ɑ̃t] adj fam **1.** [pénible - travail] exhausting, backbreaking ; [- enfant] exhausting **2.** [drôle - personne] killing, priceless ; [- histoire, spectacle] killing, side-splitting / **elle est crevante, sa gamine** her kid's a scream ou riot.

crevasse [kʀøvas] nf **1.** GÉOGR [dans le sol] crevice, fissure, split ; [sur un roc] crack, crevice, fissure ; [d'un glacier] crevasse **2.** [sur les lèvres, les mains] crack, split / **j'ai des crevasses aux doigts** my fingers are badly chapped.

crève [kʀɛv] nf fam [rhume] bad cold / **tu vas attraper la crève** you'll catch your death (of cold).

crevé, e [kʀøve] adj **1.** [pneu] flat, punctured ; [tympan] pierced ; [yeux] gouged-out ; [ballon] burst / **j'ai un pneu crevé** I've got a puncture 🇬🇧 ou flat 🇺🇸 **2.** [mort - animal] dead **3.** [fatigué] shattered 🇬🇧, bushed 🇺🇸.

crever [19] [kʀøve] **◆** vt **1.** [faire éclater - abcès] to burst (open) ; [- bulle, ballon, sac] to burst ; [- pneu] to puncture, to burst ; [- tympan] to puncture, to pierce ▸ **crever un œil à qqn a)** [agression] to gouge ou to put out sb's eye **b)** [accident] to blind sb in one eye ▸ **ça crève les yeux a)** [c'est évident] it's as plain as the nose on your face, it sticks out a mile **b)** [c'est visible] it's staring you in the face, it's plain for all to see ▸ **crever l'écran** [acteur] to have great presence (on the screen) **2.** fam [fatiguer] to wear out **3.** (EXPR) **crever la faim** fam [par pauvreté] to be starving. **◆** vi **1.** [éclater - pneu] to puncture ; [- ballon, bulle, nuage] to burst ; [- abcès] to burst **2.** tfam [mourir] to snuff it 🇬🇧, to kick the bucket / **qu'il crève !** to hell with him ! **3.** [mourir - animal, végétal] to die (off). **◆ crever de** v + prép fam **1.** [éprouver] ▸ **crever de faim a)** [par pauvreté] to be starving **b)** [être en appétit] to be starving ou famished ▸ **crever de soif** to be parched / **je crève de chaud !**

I'm baking ou boiling! / *on crève de froid ici* it's freezing cold ou you could freeze to death here **2.** [être plein de] ▶ **crever de jalousie** to be eaten up with jealousy ▶ **crever d'envie de faire qqch** to be dying to do sthg. ❖ **se crever** vp *(emploi réfléchi) fam* ▶ **se crever au boulot** ou **à la tâche** to work o.s. ou **se crever le cul** *tfam* to bust a gut 🇬🇧, to bust one's ass 🇺🇸.

crevette [krəvɛt] nf ▶ **crevette grise** shrimp ▶ **crevette rose** (common) prawn.

cri [kri] nm **1.** [éclat de voix - gén] cry ; [-puissant] shout, yell ; [-perçant] shriek, scream ▶ **un petit cri aigu** a squeak ▶ **pousser un cri de joie / douleur** to cry out with joy / in pain ▶ **pousser des cris d'orfraie** a) [hurler] to screech like a thing possessed b) [protester] to raise the roof **2.** ZOOL [d'un oiseau] call ; [d'un petit oiseau] chirp ; [d'une chouette, d'un paon, d'un singe] screech ; [d'une mouette] cry ; [d'un dindon] gobble ; [d'un perroquet] squawk ; [d'un canard] quack ; [d'une oie] honk ; [d'une souris] squeak ; [d'un porc] squeal **3.** [parole] cry ▶ **cri du cœur** cri de cœur, cry from the heart. ❖ **dernier cri** *loc adj* [voiture, vidéo] state-of-the-art / *il s'est acheté des chaussettes dernier cri* he bought the latest thing in socks. ❖ nm inv ▶ **c'est le dernier cri** a) [vêtement] it's the (very) latest vogue ou fashion ou thing b) [machine, vidéo] it's state-of-the-art.

criant, e [krijã, ãt] adj [erreur] glaring ; [mauvaise foi, mensonge] blatant, glaring, rank *(adj)* ; [parti pris] blatant ; [différence, vérité] obvious, striking ; [injustice] flagrant, blatant, rank ; [preuve] striking, glaring.

criard, e [krijar, ard] adj [couleur] loud, garish ; [tenue] garish, gaudy.

crible [kribl] nm [pour des graines, du sable] riddle, sift ; [pour un charbon, un minerai] screen ▶ **passer au crible** a) [charbon] to riddle, to screen, to sift b) [grains, sable] to riddle, to sift c) [fruits, œufs] to grade d) [région] to go over with a fine-tooth comb, to comb e) [preuves] to sift ou to examine closely f) [document] to examine closely, to go over with a fine-tooth comb g) [candidat] to screen (for a job).

cribler [3] [krible] vt **1.** : *la façade est criblée d'impacts de balles* the facade is riddled with bullet holes **2.** ▶ **cribler qqn de questions** to bombard sb with questions, to fire questions at sb ▶ **cribler qqn de reproches** to heap reproaches on sb **3.** ▶ **être criblé de** [accablé de] to be covered in ▶ **être criblé de dettes** to be crippled with debt, to be up to one's eyes in debt.

cric [krik] nm AUTO (car) jack.

cricket [krikɛt] nm SPORT cricket.

criée [krije] nf fish market *(where auctions take place)*. ❖ **à la criée** *loc adv* by auction / *vendre du thon à la criée* to auction off tuna.

crier [10] [krije] ◆ vi **1.** [gén] to cry (out) ; [d'une voix forte] to shout, to yell ; [d'une voix perçante] to scream, to screech, to shriek / *ne fais pas crier ta mère !* don't get your mother angry! ▶ **crier de douleur** to scream with ou to cry out in pain ▶ **crier à** : *crier à l'injustice* to call it an injustice ▶ **crier au miracle** to hail it as a miracle ▶ **crier au scandale** to call it a scandal, to cry shame ▶ **crier à l'assassin** to cry blue murder **2.** ZOOL [oiseau] to call ; [souris] to squeak ; [porc] to squeal ; [chouette, singe] to call, to screech ; [perroquet] to squawk ; [paon] to screech ; [oie] to honk. ◆ vt **1.** [dire d'une voix forte - avertissement] to shout ou to cry (out) ; [-insultes, ordres] to bawl ou to yell out *(sép)* ▶ **sans crier gare** a) [arriver] without warning b) [partir] without so much as a by-your-leave **2.** [faire savoir] ▶ **crier contre** to complain ou to shout about *(insép)* **3.** ▶ **crier grâce** a) *pr* to beg for mercy b) *fig* to cry for mercy. ❖ **crier après** v + prép *fam* **1.** [s'adresser à] to shout ou to yell at **2.** [réprimander] to scold.

crime [krim] nm **1.** DR [infraction pénale] crime, (criminal) offence ▶ **crime contre l'humanité** crime against humanity ▶ **crime de guerre** war crime **2.** [meurtre] murder ▶ **crime crapuleux** heinous crime ▶ **crime passionnel** crime passionnel, crime of passion ▶ **crime (à motif) sexuel** sex crime ou murder **3.** [acte immoral] crime, act / *ce n'est pas un crime !* it's not a crime!

⚠ Le mot anglais **crime** a un sens plus large que le mot français et recouvre à la fois les sens de « crime », « meurtre », « délit » et « infraction ».

Crimée [krime] npr f ▶ **(la) Crimée** (the) Crimea.

criminalité [kriminalite] nf **1.** SOCIOL crime ▶ **la grande / petite criminalité** serious / petty crime **2.** *sout* [caractère criminel] criminality, criminal nature.

criminel, elle [kriminɛl] ◆ adj **1.** [répréhensible - action, motif] criminal **2.** [relatif aux crimes - droit, enquête] criminal ; [-brigade] crime *(modif)* **3.** [condamnable - acte] criminal, reprehensible. ◆ nm, f [gén] criminal ; [meurtrier] murderer ▶ **criminel de guerre** war criminal. ❖ **criminel** nm DR [juridiction criminelle] ▶ **poursuivre qqn au criminel** to institute criminal proceedings against sb.

crin [krɛ̃] nm [de cheval] hair.

crinière [krinjɛr] nf **1.** ZOOL mane **2.** *fam* [chevelure] mane, mop *péj* ou *hum*.

crique [krik] nf GÉOGR creek, inlet, (small) rocky beach.

criquet [krikɛ] nm ZOOL locust.

crise [kriz] nf **1.** [période, situation difficile] crisis ▶ **la crise de la quarantaine** the midlife crisis ▶ **crise de confiance** crisis of confidence ▶ **crise de conscience** crisis of conscience ▶ **crise d'identité** identity crisis **2.** ÉCON & POL crisis ▶ **crise du logement / papier** housing / paper shortage ▶ **crise économique** economic crisis ou slump, recession **3.** [accès] outburst, fit ▶ **être pris d'une crise de rire** to laugh uproariously ; [de colère] (fit of) rage ▶ **piquer une crise** *fam* to throw ou to have a fit **4.** MÉD ▶ **crise épileptique** ou **d'épilepsie** epileptic fit ▶ **une crise cardiaque** a heart attack ▶ **crise de foie** queasy feeling ▶ **crise de nerfs** fit of hysterics, attack of nerves / *elle a fait une crise de nerfs* she went into hysterics.

criser [krize] vi *fam* to have a fit.

crispant, e [krispã, ãt] adj [attente] nerve-racking ; [stupidité, personne] exasperating, irritating, infuriating ; [bruit] irritating / *arrête de me dire comment jouer, c'est crispant à la fin !* stop telling me how to play, it's getting on my nerves!

crispation [krispasjɔ̃] nf **1.** [du visage] tension ; [des membres] contraction **2.** [anxiété] nervous tension.

crispé, e [krispe] adj **1.** [contracté - sourire, rire] strained, tense ; [-personne, visage, doigts] tense **2.** *fam* [irrité] irritated, exasperated.

crisper [3] [krispe] vt **1.** [traits du visage] to contort, to tense ; [poings] to clench / *le visage crispé par la souffrance* his face contorted ou tense with pain **2.** *fam* [irriter] ▶ **crisper qqn** to get on sb's nerves. ❖ **se crisper** vpi [se contracter - visage] to tense (up) ; [-personne] to become tense ; [-doigts] to contract ; [-sourire] to become strained ou tense ; [-poings] to clench.

crisser [3] [krise] vi [pneus, freins] to squeal, to screech ; [cuir] to squeak ; [neige, gravillons] to crunch ; [étoffe, papier] to rustle ; [craie, scie] to grate.

cristal, aux [kristal, o] nm **1.** MINÉR ▶ **du cristal** crystal **2.** [objet] piece of crystalware ou of fine glassware / *des cristaux* crystalware, fine glassware / [d'un lustre] crystal droplets. ❖ **de cristal** *loc adj* [vase] crystal *(modif)*.

cristallin, e [kʀistalɛ̃, in] adj litt [voix] crystal-clear, crystalline ; [eau] crystalline. ❖ **cristallin** nm ANAT crystalline lens.

cristalliser [3] [kʀistalize] vt to crystallize. ❖ **se cristalliser** vpi to crystallize.

critère [kʀitɛʀ] nm **1.** [principe] criterion / **critère moral** / **religieux** moral / religious criterion ▸ **critères d'âge** age requirements ▸ **critères de qualité** quality requirements ▸ **critères de sélection** selection criteria **2.** [référence] reference (point), standard.

critiquable [kʀitikabl] adj which lends itself to criticism.

critique [kʀitik] ◆ adj **1.** [qui condamne - article, personne] critical ; péj [personne] faultfinding / **se montrer très critique envers** ou **à l'égard de** to be very critical towards **2.** [plein de discernement - analyse, œuvre, personne] critical **3.** [crucial - étape, période] critical, crucial ; [- opération, seuil] critical **4.** [inquiétant - état de santé, situation] critical. ◆ nmf [commentateur] critic, reviewer ▸ **critique d'art** art critic ▸ **critique de cinéma** film 🇬🇧 ou movie 🇺🇸 critic ou reviewer. ◆ nf **1.** PRESSE review ; UNIV critique, appreciation **2.** [activité] : la critique littéraire literary criticism **3.** [personnes] : très bien / mal accueilli par la critique acclaimed / panned by the critics **4.** [blâme] criticism / adresser ou faire une critique à un auteur to level criticism at an author.

critiquer [3] [kʀitike] vt **1.** [blâmer - initiative, mesure, personne] to criticize, to be critical of **2.** [analyser] to critique, to criticize.

croasser [3] [kʀɔase] vi to caw.

croate [kʀɔat] adj Croat, Croatian. ❖ **Croate** nmf Croat, Croatian. ❖ **croate** nm LING Croat, Croatian.

Croatie [kʀɔasi] npr f ▸ **(la) Croatie** Croatia.

croc [kʀo] nm **1.** ZOOL [de chien] tooth, fang ; [d'ours, de loup] fang ▸ **montrer les crocs** [animal] to bare its teeth ou fangs **2.** fam [dent] (long) tooth ▸ **avoir les crocs** : j'ai les crocs I could eat a horse.

croc-en-jambe [kʀɔkɑ̃ʒɑ̃b] (pl **crocs-en-jambe**) nm = croche-pied.

croche[1] [kʀɔʃ] nf MUS quaver 🇬🇧, eighth note 🇺🇸 ▸ **double croche** semiquaver 🇬🇧, sixteenth note 🇺🇸.

croche[2] [kʀɔʃ] 🇨🇦 ◆ adj fam & fig crooked. ◆ adv litt [de travers] crooked.

croche-pied (pl **croche-pieds**), **crochepied**[*] [kʀɔʃpje] nm ▸ **faire un croche-pied à qqn** pr & fig to trip sb up.

crochet [kʀɔʃɛ] nm **1.** [attache, instrument] hook ; [pour volets] catch ▸ **crochet de boucher** ou **boucherie** meathook, butcher's hook **2.** COUT [instrument] crochet hook ; [technique] crochet ; [ouvrage] crochetwork ▸ **faire du crochet** to crochet **3.** SPORT hook ▸ **crochet du droit** / **gauche** right / left hook **4.** [détour] detour, roundabout way ▸ **faire un crochet** to make a detour, to go a roundabout way **5.** [virage brusque - d'une voie] sudden ou sharp turn ; [- d'une voiture] sudden swerve ▸ **faire un crochet a)** [rue] to bend sharply **b)** [conducteur] to swerve suddenly **6.** IMPR square bracket ▸ **entre crochets** in square brackets. ❖ **au crochet** loc adv : faire un vêtement au crochet to crochet a garment.

crocheter [28] [kʀɔʃte] vt [serrure] to pick ; [porte] to pick the lock on.

crochu, e [kʀɔʃy] adj [nez] hooked, hook (modif) ; [doigts, mains] claw-like.

croco [kʀɔko] nm fam crocodile, crocodile-skin. ❖ **en croco** loc adj fam crocodile (modif).

crocodile [kʀɔkɔdil] nm **1.** ZOOL crocodile **2.** [peau] crocodile, crocodile skin. ❖ **en crocodile** loc adj crocodile (modif).

crocus [kʀɔkys] nm crocus.

croire [107] [kʀwaʀ] vt **1.** [fait, histoire, personne] to believe / je te crois sur parole I'll take your word for it / je te crois ! iron I believe you! / je n'en crois pas un mot I don't believe a word of it ▸ **en croire** [se fier à]: croyez-en ceux qui ont l'expérience take it from those who know ▸ **à l'en croire** if he is to be believed ▸ **je n'en crois pas mes yeux** / **oreilles** I can't believe my eyes / ears **2.** [penser] to believe, to think ▸ **on croit rêver !** it's unbelievable! / on l'a crue enceinte she was believed ou thought to be pregnant / je ne suis pas celle que vous croyez I'm not that kind of person / il faut croire que tu avais tort it looks like you were wrong ▸ **je crois que oui** I believe ou think so ▸ **il croit que non** he doesn't think so, he thinks not ▸ **on croirait qu'il dort** he looks as if he's asleep ▸ **il faut croire** (it) looks like it, it would seem so. ❖ **croire à** v + prép **1.** [avoir confiance en] to believe in / il faut croire à l'avenir one must have faith in the future **2.** [accepter comme réel] to believe in / tu crois encore au Père Noël ! fig you're so naive! / c'est à n'y pas croire ! you just wouldn't believe ou credit it! / elle voulait faire croire à un accident she wanted it to look like an accident **3.** RELIG to believe in / croire à la vie éternelle to believe in eternal life **4.** [dans la correspondance] : je vous prie de croire à mes sentiments les meilleurs yours sincerely. ❖ **croire en** v + prép **1.** [avoir confiance en] to believe in **2.** RELIG ▸ **croire en Dieu** to believe in God. ❖ **se croire** ◆ vpt [penser avoir] ▸ **il se croit tous les droits** ou **tout permis** he thinks he can get away with anything. ◆ vpi **1.** [se juger] ▸ **il se croit beau** / **intelligent** he thinks he's handsome / intelligent / où te crois-tu ? where do you think you are? **2.** fam EXPR ▸ **se croire sorti de la cuisse de Jupiter** to think one is God's gift (to mankind) ▸ **s'y croire**: il s'y croit ! he really thinks a lot of himself!

croisade [kʀwazad] nf fig [campagne] campaign, crusade / partir en croisade contre l'injustice to go on a crusade ou to mount a campaign against injustice.

croisé, e [kʀwaze] adj [bras] folded ; [jambes] crossed / il était debout, les bras croisés he was standing with his arms folded ▸ **assis les jambes croisées** sitting cross-legged. ❖ **croisée** nf [intersection] crossing ▸ **être à la croisée des chemins** to be at the parting of the ways.

croisement [kʀwazmɑ̃] nm **1.** [intersection] crossroads, junction **2.** [hybridation] crossbreeding, crossing, interbreeding.

croiser [3] [kʀwaze] ◆ vt **1.** [mettre en croix - baguettes, fils] to cross ▸ **croiser les jambes** to cross one's legs **2.** [traverser] to cross, to intersect, to meet ▸ **croiser la route** ou **le chemin de qqn** fig to come across sb **3.** [rencontrer] to pass, to meet / ses yeux ont croisé les miens her eyes met mine. ◆ vi NAUT to cruise. ❖ **se croiser** ◆ vp (emploi réciproque) **1.** [se rencontrer] to come across ou to meet ou to pass each other / leurs regards se sont croisés their eyes met **2.** [aller en sens opposé - trains] to pass (each other) ; [- lettres] to cross ; [- routes] to cross, to intersect ▸ **nos chemins se sont croisés, nos routes se sont croisées** our paths met. ◆ vpt ▸ **se croiser les bras a)** pr to fold one's arms **b)** fig [être oisif] to twiddle one's thumbs.

croisière [kʀwazjɛʀ] nf cruise / faire une croisière aux Bahamas to go on a cruise to the Bahamas.

croissance [kʀwasɑ̃s] nf **1.** PHYSIOL growth / elle est en pleine croissance she's growing fast **2.** [développement - d'une plante] growth ; [- d'un pays] development, growth ; [- d'un marché] growth ; [- d'une entreprise] growth, expansion.

---

[*] In reformed spelling (see p. 16-18).

croissant¹ [kʀwasɑ̃] nm **1.** CULIN croissant **2.** [forme incurvée] crescent **3.** ASTRON crescent ▸ **croissant de lune** crescent moon.

croissant², e [kʀwasɑ̃, ɑ̃t] adj growing, increasing / *tension croissante dans le sud du pays* increasing tension in the south of the country.

croître, croitre* [93] [kʀwatʀ] vi **1.** PHYSIOL to grow **2.** [augmenter - rivière] to swell ; [- lune] to wax ▸ **croître en** : *croître en beauté et en sagesse* to grow wiser and more beautiful.

croix [kʀwa] nf **1.** [gibet] cross ▸ **porter sa croix** to have one's cross to bear **2.** [objet cruciforme] cross ▸ **c'est la croix et la bannière pour...** : *c'est la croix et la bannière pour le faire manger* it's an uphill struggle to get him to eat **3.** [emblème] cross ▸ **croix gammée** swastika **4.** [récompense] cross, medal ; [de la Légion d'honneur] Cross of the Legion of Honour **5.** [signe écrit] cross ▸ **faire** ou **mettre une croix sur qqch** to forget ou to kiss goodbye to sthg. ❖ **en croix** loc adv ▸ **placer** ou **mettre deux choses en croix** to lay two things crosswise.

Croix-Rouge [kʀwaʀuʒ] npr f ▸ **la Croix-Rouge** the Red Cross.

croquant, e [kʀokɑ̃, ɑ̃t] adj crisp, crunchy.

croque-madame (*pl* croque-madame), **croque-madame*** [kʀɔkmadam] nm *toasted cheese and ham sandwich with a fried egg on top.*

croque-monsieur (*pl* croque-monsieur), **croquemonsieur*** [kʀɔkməsjø] nm *toasted cheese and ham sandwich.*

croque-mort (*pl* croque-morts), **croquemort*** [kʀɔkmɔʀ] nm *fam* undertaker's assistant.

croquer [3] [kʀɔke] ❖ vt **1.** [pomme, radis, sucre d'orge] to crunch **2.** *fam* [dépenser - héritage] to squander **3.** [esquisser] to sketch ; [décrire] to outline ▸ **il est (joli)** ou **mignon à croquer** *fam* he looks good enough to eat. ❖ vi to be crisp ou crunchy. ❖ **croquer dans** v + prép to bite into.

croquette [kʀɔkɛt] nf CULIN croquette. ❖ **croquettes** nfpl [pour animal] dry food.

croquis [kʀɔki] nm sketch.

cross [kʀɔs], **cross-country** (*pl* cross-countrys ou cross-countries), **crosscountry*** (*pl* cross-countrys) [kʀɔskuntʀi] nm [à pied] cross-country running ; [à cheval] cross-country riding ▸ **faire du cross a)** [à pied] to go cross-country running **b)** [à cheval] to go cross-country riding.

crosse [kʀɔs] nf **1.** SPORT [canne - de hockey] stick ; [- de golf] club **2.** QUÉBEC [jeu] lacrosse **3.** [extrémité - d'un violon] scroll **4.** ARM [d'un revolver] grip, butt ; [d'un fusil] butt.

crotale [kʀɔtal] nm rattlesnake.

crotte [kʀɔt] nf **1.** [d'un animal] dropping ; [d'un bébé] poo (U) **2.** CULIN ▸ **crotte au chocolat** chocolate **3.** [morve] **crotte de nez** bogey.

crottin [kʀɔtɛ̃] nm **1.** [de cheval] dung, manure **2.** CULIN *small round goat's milk cheese.*

croulant, e [kʀulɑ̃, ɑ̃t] nm, f *fam & péj* old fogey.

crouler [3] [kʀule] vi [tomber - édifice] to collapse, to crumble, to topple ▸ **crouler sous** : *l'étagère croule sous le poids des livres* the shelf is sagging under the weight of the books ▸ **crouler sous le poids des ans / soucis** *fig* to be weighed down by age / worry / *la salle croula sous les applaudissements* *fig* the auditorium thundered with applause.

croupe [kʀup] nf **1.** ZOOL croup, rump / *monter en croupe* to ride pillion **2.** *fam* ANAT behind.

croupier, ère [kʀupje, ɛʀ] nm, f JEUX croupier.

croupion [kʀupjɔ̃] nm **1.** CULIN parson's UK ou pope's US nose **2.** *(comme adjectif, avec ou sans trait d'union)* ▸ **Parlement Croupion** HIST Rump Parliament.

croupir [32] [kʀupiʀ] vi **1.** [eau] to stagnate, to grow foul **2.** *fig* [s'encroûter, moisir] : *je ne vais pas croupir ici toute ma vie* I'm not going to rot here all my life.

CROUS, Crous [kʀus] (*abr de* Centre régional des œuvres universitaires et scolaires) npr m *student representative body dealing with accommodation, catering, etc.*

croustillant, e [kʀustijɑ̃, ɑ̃t] adj **1.** CULIN [biscuit, gratin] crisp, crunchy ; [baguette, pain] crusty **2.** [osé] saucy.

croustiller [3] [kʀustije] vi [biscuit, gratin] to be crisp ou crunchy ; [baguette, pain] to be crusty.

croûte, croute* [kʀut] nf **1.** [partie - du pain] crust ; [- du fromage] rind ▸ **une croûte de pain** a crust ; [préparation] pastry shell **2.** [dépôt] layer **3.** GÉOL ▸ **la croûte terrestre** the earth's crust **4.** MÉD scab **5.** *fam & péj* [tableau] bad painting **6.** [de cuir] hide.

croûton, crouton* [kʀutɔ̃] nm **1.** CULIN [frit] crouton ; [quignon] (crusty) end, crust **2.** *fam & péj* [personne] ▸ **vieux croûton** fossil.

croyable [kʀwajabl] adj believable, credible / *c'est à peine croyable* it's hardly credible / *son histoire n'est pas croyable* his story is incredible ou unbelievable.

croyance [kʀwajɑ̃s] nf **1.** [pensée] belief **2.** [fait de croire] faith.

croyant, e [kʀwajɑ̃, ɑ̃t] ❖ adj : *il est / n'est pas croyant* he's a believer / non-believer, he believes / he doesn't believe in God. ❖ nm, f believer.

CRS (*abr de* compagnie républicaine de sécurité) nm [policier] state security policeman / *les CRS ont chargé les manifestants* the security police charged the demonstrators.

cru¹ [kʀy] nm ŒNOL [terroir] vineyard ; [vin] vintage, wine. ❖ **de mon cru, de son cru** loc adj : *une histoire de son cru* a story of his own invention. ❖ **du cru** loc adj : *un vin du cru* a local wine.

cru², e [kʀy] adj **1.** [non cuit - denrée] raw, uncooked ; [- céramique] unfired **2.** [aveuglant - couleur] crude, harsh, glaring ; [- éclairage] harsh, blinding, glaring **3.** [osé] coarse, crude. ❖ **à cru** loc adv ÉQUIT bareback.

cruauté [kʀyote] nf **1.** [dureté] cruelty **2.** [acte] cruel act, act of cruelty.

cruche [kʀyʃ] nf **1.** [récipient] jug UK, pitcher US **2.** *fam & péj* [personne] nitwit, dumbbell.

crucial, e, aux [kʀysjal, o] adj crucial, vital.

crucifix [kʀysifi] nm crucifix.

crucifixion [kʀysifiksjɔ̃] nf crucifixion.

cruciverbiste [kʀysivɛʀbist] nmf crossword (puzzle) enthusiast.

crudités [kʀydite] nfpl CULIN raw vegetables ; [sur un menu] mixed salads, assorted raw vegetables.

crue [kʀy] nf **1.** [élévation de niveau] rise in the water level **2.** [inondation] ▸ **en période de crue** when there are floods.

cruel, elle [kʀyɛl] adj [méchant - personne] cruel ; [dur - propos] cruel, harsh.

cruellement [kʀyɛlmɑ̃] adv **1.** [méchamment] cruelly ▸ **traiter qqn cruellement** to be cruel to sb **2.** [péniblement] sorely ▸ **faire cruellement défaut** to be sorely lacking.

crumble [kʀœmbœl] nm crumble ▸ **crumble aux pommes** apple crumble.

crûment, crument* [kʀymɑ̃] adv **1.** [brutalement] bluntly **2.** [grossièrement] coarsely.

crustacé [krystase] nm **1.** ZOOL crustacean **2.** CULIN ▶ **des crustacés** seafood.

cryoconservation [krijɔkɔ̃sɛrvasjɔ̃] nf cryogenic preservation.

cryogénie [krijɔʒeni] nf cryogenics *(sg)*.

cryothérapie [krijɔterapi] nf cryotherapy.

crypte [kript] nf ARCHIT & ANAT crypt.

crypter [kripte] vt [message, données] to encrypt.

CSA (abr de **Conseil supérieur de l'audiovisuel**) npr m *French broadcasting supervisory body.*

CSG (abr de **contribution sociale généralisée**) nf *income-related tax contribution.*

Cuba [kyba] npr Cuba ▶ **à Cuba** in Cuba. ⟶ **île**

cubain, e [kybɛ̃, ɛn] adj Cuban. ✧ **Cubain, e** nm, f Cuban.

cube [kyb] ✦ adj cubic ▶ **centimètre cube** cubic centimetre ou centimeter US. ✦ nm **1.** GÉOM & MATH cube **2.** JEUX (building) block **3.** *fam* [cylindrée] ▶ **un gros cube** [moto] a big bike.

cubique [kybik] adj **1.** [en forme de cube] cube-shaped, cube-like, cubic **2.** MATH & MINÉR cubic.

cubisme [kybism] nm Cubism.

cubitus [kybitys] nm ulna.

cucul [kyky] adj inv *fam* ▶ **cucul (la praline)** silly, goofy.

cueillette [kœjɛt] nf **1.** [ramassage - de fruits] gathering, picking ; [- de fleurs] picking **2.** [récolte] crop, harvest.

cueillir [41] [kœjir] vt **1.** [récolter - fruits] to gather, to pick ; [- fleurs] to pick, to pluck **2.** *fam* [arrêter] to nab, to collar.

cuillère, cuiller [kɥijɛr] nf **1.** [instrument] spoon ▶ **cuillère à café** ou **à moka** teaspoon ▶ **cuillère à dessert** dessert spoon ▶ **cuillère à soupe** tablespoon ▶ **petite cuillère** teaspoon **2.** [contenu] spoonful. ✧ **à la cuillère** loc adv [en mangeant] ▶ **nourrir** ou **faire manger qqn à la cuillère** to spoon-feed sb.

cuillerée [kɥijere] nf spoonful / *une cuillerée à café de* a teaspoonful of / *une cuillerée à soupe de* a tablespoonful of.

cuir [kɥir] nm **1.** [peau - traitée] leather ; [- brute] hide ▶ **le cuir** a) VÊT leather clothes b) COMM & INDUST leather goods **2.** [peau humaine] skin ▶ **cuir chevelu** scalp. ✧ **de cuir, en cuir** loc adj leather *(modif).*

cuirasse [kɥiras] nf **1.** HIST [armure] breastplate, cuirass, corselet **2.** MIL [d'un char] armour UK, armor US.

cuirassé [kɥirase] nm battleship.

cuire [98] [kɥir] ✦ vt **1.** CULIN [viande, légumes] to cook ; [pain] to bake **2.** [brûler - peau] to burn. ✦ vi **1.** CULIN [aliment] to cook ▶ **cuire à feu doux** ou **petit feu** to simmer ▶ **faire cuire qqch** to cook sth ▶ **faire cuire qqch au four** to bake sth ▶ **faire trop cuire qqch** to overcook sth **2.** *fam* [souffrir de la chaleur] : *on cuit dans cette voiture !* it's boiling hot in this car! **3.** [brûler] to burn, to sting ▶ **les yeux me cuisent** my eyes are burning ou stinging. ✧ **à cuire** loc adj ▶ **chocolat à cuire** cooking chocolate.

cuisant, e [kɥizɑ̃, ɑ̃t] adj **1.** [douleur, sensation] burning, stinging **2.** [affront, injure] stinging, bitter.

cuiseur [kɥizœr] nm cooker ▶ **cuiseur (vapeur)** steam cooker ▶ **cuiseur à riz** rice cooker ▶ **cuiseur solaire** solar cooker.

cuisine [kɥizin] nf **1.** [lieu] kitchen ▶ **cuisine américaine** open-plan kitchen **2.** [activité] cooking, cookery UK ▶ **faire la cuisine** to cook / *elle fait très bien la cuisine* she's an excellent cook **3.** [ensemble de mets] cuisine, food, dishes ▶ **cuisine allégée** ou **minceur** lean cuisine **4.** [meubles]

kitchen (furniture) ▶ **cuisine intégrée** fitted kitchen **5.** *fam* & *péj* [complications] complicated ou messy business ; [malversations] wheeler-dealing.

cuisiné, e [kɥizine] adj ⟶ **plat**.

cuisiner [3] [kɥizine] ✦ vt **1.** [plat, dîner] to cook **2.** *fam* [interroger - accusé, suspect] to grill. ✦ vi to cook ▶ **j'aime cuisiner** I like cooking.

cuisinier, ère [kɥizinje, ɛr] nm, f cook. ✧ **cuisinière** nf stove, cooker UK.

cuisiniste [kɥizinist] nmf **1.** [fabricant] kitchen manufacturer **2.** [installateur] kitchen installer.

cuissardes [kɥisard] nfpl **1.** [de femme] thigh boots **2.** [de pêcheur] waders.

cuisse [kɥis] nf **1.** ANAT thigh **2.** CULIN leg ▶ **cuisses de grenouille** frogs' legs ▶ **cuisse de poulet** chicken leg.

cuisson [kɥisɔ̃] nf **1.** CULIN [fait de cuire - le pain, les gâteaux] baking ; [- un rôti] roasting, cooking ; [manière de cuire] cooking technique **2.** TECHNOL [du ciment] burning, kilning ; [de la céramique, du verre, de l'émail] firing ; [du plastique] heating.

cuistot [kɥisto] nm *fam* cook, chef.

cuit, e [kɥi, kɥit] adj **1.** [aliment] cooked ▶ **viande bien cuite** well-done meat ▶ **viande cuite à point** medium rare meat ▶ **mal cuit** undercooked ▶ **trop cuit** overcooked ▶ **attendre que ça tombe tout cuit (dans le bec)** to wait for things to fall into one's lap **2.** *fam* [usé] worn down, threadbare **3.** *fam* [perdu] : *je suis cuit !* I'm done for!, I've had it! **4.** *tfam* [ivre] loaded, plastered. ✧ **cuit** nm EXPR **du tout cuit** : *c'est du tout cuit* it's as good as done (already). ✧ **cuite** nf *tfam* [beuverie] : *(se) prendre une cuite* to get plastered.

cuiter [3] [kɥite] ✧ **se cuiter** vpi *tfam* to get plastered.

cuit-vapeur [kɥivapœr] nm inv steamer, steam cooker.

cuivre [kɥivr] nm MÉTALL copper ▶ **cuivre jaune** brass ▶ **cuivre rouge** copper. ✧ **cuivres** nmpl **1.** [casseroles] copper (pots and) pans **2.** MUS brass instruments.

cuivré, e [kɥivre] adj [rouge] copper-coloured ▶ **avoir le teint cuivré** ou **la peau cuivrée** a) [par le soleil] to be tanned b) [naturellement] to be swarthy.

cul [ky] nm **1.** *vulg* [fesses] arse UK, ass US, bum UK ▶ **avoir du cul** to be a jammy UK ou lucky bastard ▶ **l'avoir dans le cul** : *tu l'as dans le cul* you're screwed ▶ **(en) tomber** ou **rester sur le cul** to be flabbergasted **2.** *vulg* [sexe] sex ▶ **un film de cul** a porn film **3.** [fond d'une bouteille] bottom ▶ **cul sec !** bottoms up! **4.** EXPR **gros cul** *fam* [camion] juggernaut UK, big truck US.

culasse [kylas] nf **1.** ARM breech **2.** MÉCAN cylinder head.

culbute [kylbyt] nf **1.** [pirouette] somersault ▶ **faire des culbutes** to do somersaults **2.** [chute] fall, tumble.

culbuter [3] [kylbyte] vt [faire tomber - personne] to knock over *(sép).*

cul-de-jatte [kydʒat] (pl **culs-de-jatte**) nmf legless person.

cul-de-sac [kydsak] (pl **culs-de-sac**) nm **1.** [rue] dead end, cul-de-sac **2.** [situation] blind alley, no-win situation.

culinaire [kyliner] adj culinary.

culminant, e [kylminɑ̃, ɑ̃t] adj ⟶ **point**.

culminer [3] [kylmine] vi **1.** GÉOGR : *l'Everest culmine à 8 848 mètres* Everest is 8,848 metres at its highest point **2.** [être à son maximum] to reach its peak, to peak **3.** ASTRON to culminate.

culot [kylo] nm **1.** *fam* [aplomb] cheek UK, nerve / *tu as un sacré culot !* you've got a nerve ou a cheek! **2.** [partie inférieure - d'une lampe] base, bottom ; [- d'une cartouche] base, cap ; [-d'une ampoule] base. ❖ **au culot** loc adv *fam* ▸ **faire qqch au culot** to bluff one's way through sthg.

culotte [kylɔt] nf **1.** [sous-vêtement - de femme] (pair of) knickers UK ou panties US ; [- d'enfant] (pair of) knickers UK ou pants ▸ **petite culotte** panties ▸ **faire dans sa culotte a)** *fam* to dirty one's pants **b)** [avoir peur] to be scared stiff **2.** [pantalon] trousers UK, pants US ; HIST breeches ▸ **culottes courtes** shorts ▸ **porter la culotte** to wear the trousers UK ou pants US ▸ **culotte de cheval a)** VÊT riding breeches, jodhpurs **b)** MÉD cellulite *(on the tops of the thighs).*

culotté, e [kylɔte] adj *fam* [effronté] cheeky UK, sassy US.

culpabiliser [3] [kylpabilize] vt ▸ **culpabiliser qqn** to make sb feel guilty. ❖ **se culpabiliser** vp *(emploi réfléchi)* to feel guilty, to blame o.s.

culpabilité [kylpabilite] nf **1.** PSYCHOL guilt, guilty feeling **2.** DR guilt.

culte [kylt] nm **1.** RELIG [religion] religion, faith ; [cérémonie] service **2.** [adoration] cult, worship ▸ **culte du Soleil** sun-worship ▸ **lculte de la personnalité** personality cult **3.** *(comme adj)* cult ▸ **film culte** cult film UK ou movie US.

cultivateur, trice [kyltivatœʀ,tʀis] nm, f farmer. ❖ **cultivateur** nm [machine] cultivator.

cultivé, e [kyltive] adj **1.** AGR cultivated **2.** [éduqué] cultured, educated, well-educated.

cultiver [3] [kyltive] vt **1.** AGR [champ, terres] to cultivate, to farm ; [plantes] to grow **2.** [conserver obstinément - accent] to cultivate / *elle cultive le paradoxe* she cultivates a paradoxical way of thinking **3.** [entretenir - relations, savoir] to keep up. ❖ **se cultiver** vpt : *se cultiver l'esprit* to cultivate the mind.

culture [kyltyʀ] nf **1.** [production - de blé, de maïs] farming ; [- d'arbres, de fleurs] growing ▸ **culture biologique** organic farming **2.** [terrains] arable land **3.** [espèce] crop **4.** [connaissance] ▸ **la culture** culture ▸ **culture d'entreprise** corporate culture ▸ **culture générale** general knowledge **5.** [civilisation] culture, civilization. ❖ **en culture** loc adv [terres] under cultivation.

culturel, elle [kyltyʀɛl] adj cultural.

culturisme [kyltyʀism] nm bodybuilding.

cumin [kymɛ̃] nm [plante] cumin.

cumul [kymyl] nm **1.** [de plusieurs activités] multiple responsibilities ou functions ; [de plusieurs salaires] concurrent drawing ▸ **le cumul des mandats** ou **fonctions** POL multiple office-holding **2.** DR plurality, combination ▸ **cumul des peines** cumulative sentence.

cumuler [3] [kymyle] vt **1.** [réunir - fonctions] to hold concurrently ; [- retraites, salaires] to draw concurrently **2.** DR to accrue ▸ **intérêts cumulés** accrued interest.

cumulus [kymylys] nm **1.** MÉTÉOR cumulus **2.** [citerne] hot water tank.

cupide [kypid] adj *litt* grasping, greedy.

cupidité [kypidite] nf *litt* greed.

curable [kyʀabl] adj curable, which can be cured.

curatif, ive [kyʀatif, iv] adj healing.

cure [kyʀ] nf **1.** MÉD [technique, période] treatment ▸ **cure d'amaigrissement** slimming UK ou weight-loss US course, reducing treatment US ▸ **cure de sommeil** sleep therapy ▸ **cure de thalassothérapie** course of thalassotherapy ▸ **cure thermale** treatment at a spa **2.** *fig* : *faire une cure de romans policiers* to go through a phase of reading nothing but detective novels.

⚠ Le mot anglais **cure** signifie généralement « remède », « guérison » et non **cure** au sens de traitement.

curé [kyʀe] nm (Catholic) priest.

cure-dent(s) [kyʀdɑ̃] *(pl* cure-dents) nm toothpick.

curer [3] [kyʀe] vt to scrape clean. ❖ **se curer** vpt ▸ **se curer les ongles** to clean one's nails ▸ **se curer les dents** to pick one's teeth (clean) ▸ **se curer les oreilles** to clean (out) one's ears.

curieusement [kyʀjøzmɑ̃] adv [avec curiosité - regarder] curiously.

curieux, euse [kyʀjø,øz] ❖ adj **1.** [indiscret] curious, inquisitive **2.** [étrange] curious, odd, strange **3.** [avide de savoir] inquiring, inquisitive ▸ **avoir un esprit curieux** to have an inquiring mind ▸ **soyez curieux de tout** let your interests be wide-ranging. ❖ nm, f **1.** [badaud] bystander, onlooker **2.** [indiscret] inquisitive person. ❖ **curieux** nm [ce qui est étrange] : *c'est là le plus curieux de l'affaire* that's what's so strange. ❖ **en curieux** loc adv : *je suis venu en curieux* I just came to have a look.

curiosité [kyʀjozite] nf **1.** [indiscrétion] inquisitiveness, curiosity ▸ **par (pure) curiosité** out of (sheer) curiosity, just for curiosity's sake ▸ **la curiosité est un vilain défaut** *prov* curiosity killed the cat *prov* **2.** [intérêt] curiosity.

curiste [kyʀist] nmf *person taking the waters at a spa.*

curriculum vitae *(pl* **curriculum vitae** *ou* **curriculums vitae***) [kyʀikylɔmvite] nm curriculum vitae, CV, résumé US.

curry [kyʀi] = **cari.**

curseur [kyʀsœʀ] nm cursor.

cursus [kyʀsys] nm degree course ▸ **cursus universitaire** degree course.

customiser [3] [kystɔmize] vt to customize.

cutané, e [kytane] adj cutaneous *spéc*, skin *(modif).*

cuti-réaction *(pl* cuti-réactions), **cutiréaction*** [kytiʀeaksjɔ̃] nf skin test *(for detecting TB or allergies).*

cutter [kœtœʀ ou kytɛʀ], **cutteur*** [kœtœʀ] nm Stanley® knife.

cuve [kyv] nf **1.** [réservoir] tank, cistern **2.** [pour le blanchissage, la teinture] vat.

cuvée [kyve] nf ŒNOL vintage / *la cuvée 2003 était excellente* the 2003 vintage was excellent / *la dernière cuvée de Polytechnique* hum the latest batch of graduates from the École Polytechnique.

cuver [3] [kyve] vt ▸ **cuver son vin** to sleep off the booze.

cuvette [kyvɛt] nf **1.** [récipient - gén] basin, bowl, washbowl ; [- des WC] pan ; [- d'un lavabo] basin **2.** GÉOGR basin.

CV ❖ nm (abr de curriculum vitae) CV UK, résumé US. ❖ (abr écrite de cheval) [puissance fiscale] *classification for scaling of car tax.*

cyanure [sjanyʀ] nm cyanide.

cyberattaque [siberatak] nf cyberattack.

cybercafé [siberkafe] nm cybercafé.

cybercommerce [siberkɔmɛʀs] nm e-commerce.

cybercrime [siberkrim] nm cybercrime.

cybercriminalité [siberkriminalite] nf cybercrime.

cyberespace [siberɛspas] nm cyberspace.

cyberharcèlement [siberarsɛlmɑ̃] nm [gén] cyberbullying.

cyberjargon [siberʒaʀgɔ̃] nm INFORM netspeak.

cybermonde [sibermɔ̃d] nm cyberworld.

cybernaute [sibernot] nm cybernaut.

cybernétique [sibernetik] nf cybernetics *(sg).*

cybernovice [sibernɔvis] nmf *fam* INFORM newbie.

cybersquatter, cybersquatteur [siberskwatœʀ] nm cybersquatter.

cybersquatting [siberskwatiŋ] nm cybersquatting.

cyberterrorisme [sibɛʀtɛʀɔʀism] nm cyberterrorism.

cyborg [sibɔʀg] nm cyborg.

cyclable [siklabl] adj cycle *(modif)*.

cyclamen [siklamɛn] nm cyclamen.

cycle [sikl] nm **1.** [série] cycle **2.** [évolution] cycle ▶ **cycle de vie** [de produit] life cycle **3.** ÉDUC & UNIV cycle ▶ **il suit un cycle court / long** ≃ he'll leave school at sixteen / go on to higher education ▶ **cycle élémentaire** *the years spent at primary school between the ages of 7 and 9* ▶ **cycle moyen** *the years spent at primary school between the ages of 9 and 11* ▶ **premier cycle a)** ÉDUC lower secondary school years 🇬🇧, junior high school 🇺🇸 **b)** UNIV first and second years 🇬🇧, freshman and sophomore years 🇺🇸 ▶ **second cycle a)** ÉDUC last three years of secondary school 🇬🇧 ou high school 🇺🇸 **b)** UNIV last two years of a degree course ; ≃ final year 🇬🇧 ; ≃ senior year 🇺🇸 ▶ **troisième cycle** postgraduate studies ▶ **être en troisième cycle** to be a postgraduate student / **un étudiant de troisième cycle** a postgraduate **4.** PHYSIOL ▶ **cycle menstruel** menstrual cycle.

cyclique [siklik] adj cyclic, cyclical.

cyclisme [siklism] nm cycling.

cycliste [siklist] ◆ adj ▶ **coureur cycliste** racing cyclist, cycler 🇺🇸 ▶ **course cycliste** cycle race. ◆ nmf cyclist, cycler 🇺🇸. ◆ nm [short] (pair of) cycling shorts.

cyclomoteur [siklɔmɔtœʀ] nm small motorcycle, scooter.

cyclone [siklon] nm [dépression] cyclone ; [typhon] cyclone, hurricane.

cyclothymique [siklɔtimik] adj & nmf cyclothymic, cyclothymiac.

cyclotourisme [siklɔtuʀism] nm cycle touring ▶ **faire du cyclotourisme** to go on a cycling holiday 🇬🇧 ou vacation 🇺🇸.

cygne [siɲ] nm swan. ❖ **Cygne** nm ASTRON ▶ **le Cygne** Cygnus, the Swan.

cylindre [silɛ̃dʀ] nm **1.** AUTO & GÉOM cylinder ▶ **une six cylindres** a six-cylinder car **2.** MÉCAN roller.

cylindrée [silɛ̃dʀe] nf cubic capacity, capacity displacement 🇺🇸 ▶ **une petite cylindrée** a small ou small-engined car.

cymbale [sɛ̃bal] nf cymbal.

cynique [sinik] adj cynical.

cynisme [sinism] nm [attitude] cynicism.

cyprès [sipʀɛ] nm cypress.

cypriote [sipʀijɔt] adj [paysan, village] Cypriot, Cypriote ; [paysage] Cypriot, Cyprus *(modif)*. ❖ **Cypriote** nmf Cypriot, Cypriote.

cyrillique [siʀilik] adj Cyrillic.

cystite [sistit] nf cystitis.

d' [d] ⟶ **de.**

DAB [deabe, dab] (abr de **distributeur automatique de billets**) nm ATM.

d'abord [dabɔʀ] = **abord.**

d'accord [dakɔʀ] = **accord.**

dactylo [daktilo] nmf typist.

dactylographier [9] [daktilɔgʀafje] vt to type (up).

dada [dada] nm **1.** [cheval] gee-gee , horsie **2.** fam [passe-temps] hobby ; [idée] hobbyhorse.

dadais [dadɛ] nm oaf ▶ **grand dadais** clumsy oaf.

dahlia [dalja] nm dahlia.

daigner [4] [deɲe] vt ▶ **daigner faire qqch** to deign to do sthg.

daim [dɛ̃] nm **1.** ZOOL (fallow) deer **2.** [cuir suédé] buckskin, doeskin. ✦ **de daim, en daim** loc adj suede (modif).

dais [dɛ] nm canopy.

Dakar [dakaʀ] npr Dakar.

dallage [dalaʒ] nm [action] paving ; [surface] pavement.

dalle [dal] nf **1.** [plaque] flagstone ▶ **dalle funéraire** tombstone **2.** CONSTR slab ▶ **dalle de béton** concrete slab **3.** fam [faim] ▶ **avoir** ou **crever la dalle** to be starving ou famished. ✦ **que dalle** loc adv fam damn all , zilch / **on n'y voit que dalle** you can't see a damn thing.

dalmatien [dalmasjɛ̃] nm ZOOL Dalmatian.

daltonien, enne [daltɔnjɛ̃, ɛn] ✦ adj daltonic spéc, colour-blind , color-blind . ✦ nm, f colour-blind ou color-blind person.

dam [dam] nm ▶ **au grand dam de qqn** to the great displeasure of sb.

Damas [damas] npr Damascus.

damassé, e [damase] adj damask (modif).

dame [dam] ✦ nf **1.** [femme] lady / **qu'est-ce que je vous sers, ma petite dame ?** fam what would you like, love ou miss? ▶ **dame de compagnie** lady's companion ▶ **la Dame de fer** the Iron Lady ▶ **dame pipi** fam lavatory attendant **2.** [titre] lady ▶ **dame d'honneur** lady-in-waiting ▶ **la première dame de France** France's First Lady **3.** JEUX [aux dames] king ▶ **aller à la** ou **mener un pion à dame** to crown a king ; [aux cartes et aux échecs] queen. ✦ interj régional ou vieilli of course, well / **dame oui !** yes, indeed! ✦ **dames** nfpl ▶ **(jeu de) dames** draughts , checkers .

damer [3] [dame] vt **1.** [tasser - terre] to ram down (sép), to pack down (sép) ; [- neige] to pack down ; [- piste] to groom **2.** JEUX [pion] to crown ▶ **damer le pion à qqn** fig to outwit sb.

damier [damje] nm JEUX draughtboard , checkerboard ▶ **un tissu à** ou **en damier** checked material.

damner [3] [dane] vt RELIG to damn. ✦ **se damner** vp (emploi réfléchi) to damn o.s. / **je me damnerais pour un chocolat** I'd give anything for a chocolate.

dancing [dɑ̃siŋ] nm dance hall.

dandiner [3] [dɑ̃dine] ✦ **se dandiner** vpi [canard, personne] to waddle / **il est entré / sorti en se dandinant** he waddled in / out.

Danemark [danmaʀk] npr m ▶ **le Danemark** Denmark.

danger [dɑ̃ʒe] nm danger / **attention danger !** danger! / **les dangers de la route** the hazards of the road ▶ **en danger de mort** in danger of one's life ▶ **pas de danger** fam: **il n'y a pas de danger qu'il dise oui** it's not likely he'll say yes / **moi, t'accompagner ? pas de danger !** you mean I'd have to go with you? no way! ▶ **danger public** fam public menace. ✦ **en danger** loc adj ▶ **être en danger a)** [personne] to be in danger **b)** [paix, honneur] to be jeopardized / **ses jours sont en danger** there are fears for his life ▶ **mettre qqn en danger** to put sb's life at risk. ✦ **sans danger** ✦ loc adj [médicament] safe. ✦ loc adv safely / **tu peux y aller sans danger** it's quite safe (to go there).

dangereusement [dɑ̃ʒʀøzmɑ̃] adv dangerously, perilously.

dangereux, euse [dɑ̃ʒʀø, øz] adj **1.** [risqué] dangerous, perilous, hazardous ▶ **zone dangereuse** danger area ou zone **2.** [nuisible] dangerous, harmful.

danois, e [danwa, az] adj Danish. ✦ **Danois, e** nm, f Dane. ✦ **danois** nm LING Danish.

dans [dɑ̃] prép **1.** [dans le temps - gén] in ; [- insistant sur la durée] during ; [- dans le futur] in ; [- indiquant un délai] within / **dans son enfance** in ou during her childhood, when she was a child / **je n'ai qu'un jour de libre dans la semaine** I only have one day off during the week / **vous serez livré dans la semaine** you'll get the delivery within the week ou some time this week **2.** [dans l'espace - gén] in ; [- avec des limites] within ; [- avec mouvement] into / **ils ont cherché partout dans la maison** they looked through the whole house, they looked everywhere in the house ▶ **dans le métro a)** [wagon] on the underground **b)** [couloirs] in the underground ▶ **dans le train / l'avion** on the train / the plane ▶ **monte dans la voiture** get in ou into the car / **je suis bien dans ces chaussures** I feel comfortable in these shoes, these shoes are comfortable / **avoir mal dans le dos** to have backache / **dans un rayon de 15 km** within a 15 km radius ▶ **entrer dans une pièce** to go into a room / **je ne pouvais pas l'entendre dans ce vacarme** I couldn't hear him in all that noise / **c'est dans le journal** it's in the paper **3.** [à partir de - prendre, boire, manger] out of, from / **la phrase a été prise dans mon discours** the quote was lifted from my speech **4.** [à travers] through ▸ *un murmure a couru dans la foule* a murmur ran through the crowd **5.** [indiquant l'appartenance à un groupe] : *il est dans le commerce* he's in business / *il est dans mon équipe* he's on ou in my team **6.** [indiquant la manière, l'état] ▸ **dans son sommeil** in his sleep ▸ **mettre qqn dans l'embarras** to put sb in an awkward situation ▸ **dans le but de** in order to, with the aim of / *c'est quelqu'un dans ton genre* it's somebody like you **7.** [indiquant une approximation] : *ça coûtera dans les 40 euros* it'll cost around 40 euros / *il doit avoir dans les 50 ans* he must be about 50.

dansant, e [dɑ̃sɑ̃, ɑ̃t] adj **1.** [qui danse] dancing **2.** [où l'on danse] ▸ **soirée dansante** dance ▸ **thé dansant** tea dance.

danse [dɑ̃s] nf [activité] dance ▸ *il aime la danse* he likes dancing ▸ **danse classique** ballet ou classical dancing ▸ **danse du ventre** belly dancing ▸ **danse sur glace** ice dancing ▸ **école de danse a)** [classique] ballet school **b)** [moderne] dance school.

danser [3] [dɑ̃se] ◆ vi DANSE to dance / *on danse ?* shall we (have a) dance? ▸ **faire danser qqn a)** [suj : cavalier] to (have a) dance with sb **b)** [suj : musicien] to play dance tunes for sb. ◆ vt to dance / *danser une valse / un tango* to (dance a) waltz / tango.

danseur, euse [dɑ̃sœʀ, øz] nm, f **1.** [gén] dancer ; [de ballet] ballet dancer ▸ **danseur étoile** principal dancer ▸ **danseuse étoile** prima ballerina **2.** [cavalier] ▸ **mon danseur** my partner. ❖ **en danseuse** loc adv : *monter la colline en danseuse* to cycle up the hill standing on the pedals.

dard [daʀ] nm ENTOM [d'une abeille, d'une guêpe] sting.

darder [3] [daʀde] vt [lancer] to shoot / *le soleil du matin dardait ses rayons sur la plage* shafts of morning sunlight fell on the beach.

dare-dare, daredare* [daʀdaʀ] loc adv *fam* double-quick, on the double / *va chercher la boîte, et dare-dare !* go and get the box, and get a move on!

darne [daʀn] nf fish steak, thick slice of fish *(cut across the body)*.

dartre [daʀtʀ] nf dartre ▸ **avoir des dartres** to have dry patches on one's skin.

datation [datasjɔ̃] nf dating ▸ **datation au carbone 14** carbon dating.

date [dat] nf **1.** [moment précis] date ▸ **une lettre sans date** an undated letter / *se retrouver chaque année à date fixe* to meet on the same day every year ▸ **prenons date** let's decide on ou let's fix a date ▸ **date limite** [pour un projet] deadline ▸ **date limite de consommation** best before date ▸ **date de naissance** date of birth ▸ **date de péremption a)** [d'un document] expiry date **b)** [d'un aliment] sell-by date **2.** [période] date / *à la date dont tu me parles, j'étais encore aux États-Unis* at the time you're talking about, I was still in the United States ▸ **faire date** : *c'est une réalisation qui fera date (dans l'histoire)* it's an achievement which will stand out (in history) ▸ **de longue date** long-standing / *ils se connaissent de longue date* they've known each other for a long time **3.** BANQUE ▸ **date de valeur** value date. ❖ **en date du** loc prép : *lettre en date du 28 juin* letter dated June 28th.

dater [3] [date] ◆ vt [inscrire la date] to date, to put a date on / *carte datée de mardi* postcard dated Tuesday. ◆ vi [être désuet - tenue] to look dated ou old-fashioned ; [- film] to show its age, to have aged, to be dated. ❖ **dater de** v + prép to date from, to go back to / *un livre qui date du XVIIᵉ siècle* a book dating back to the 17th century / *de quand date votre dernière visite ?* when was your last visit? / *notre amitié ne date pas d'hier* we go ou our friendship goes back a long way. ❖ **à dater de**

loc prép : *à dater du 1ᵉʳ mars, vous ne faites plus partie du service* as of ou effective from March 1st, you are no longer on the staff.

datte [dat] nf date.

dattier [datje] nm date palm.

daube [dob] nf CULIN stew ▸ **bœuf en daube** stewed beef.

dauphin [dofɛ̃] nm **1.** ZOOL dolphin **2.** [successeur] heir apparent, successor.

daurade [dɔʀad] nf sea bream.

davantage [davɑ̃taʒ] adv **1.** [plus] more ▸ **donne-m'en davantage** give me some more / *le droit l'intéresse davantage que l'économie* law interests him more than economics / *je ne lui ferai pas davantage de reproches* I won't reproach him any more / *il a eu davantage de chance que les autres* he was luckier than the others **2.** [de plus en plus] : *chaque jour qui passe nous rapproche davantage* each day that goes by brings us closer together **3.** [plus longtemps] : *je n'attendrai pas davantage* I won't wait any longer.

DCRI (abr de **Direction centrale du renseignement intérieur**) nf *French intelligence service.*

DDASS, Ddass [das] (abr de **Direction départementale d'action sanitaire et sociale**) npr f *department of health and social security* / *un enfant de la DDASS* a state orphan.

de [də] (devant voyelle ou « h » muet *d'*, contraction de *de* avec *le* : *du*, contraction de *de* avec *les* : *des* [de]) ◆ prép

A. INDIQUANT L'ORIGINE **1.** [indiquant la provenance] from / *il n'est pas d'ici* he's not from (around) here / *il a sorti un lapin de son chapeau* he produced ou pulled a rabbit out of his hat **2.** [à partir de] : *de quelques fleurs des champs, elle a fait un bouquet* she made a posy out of ou from a few wild flowers **3.** [indiquant l'auteur] by **4.** [particule] ▸ **Madame de Sévigné** Madame de Sévigné.

B. DANS LE TEMPS **1.** [à partir de] from **2.** [indiquant le moment] ▸ **de jour** during the ou by day ▸ **travailler de nuit** to work nights / *il n'a pas travaillé de l'année* he hasn't worked all year / *le train de 9 h 30* the 9.30 train.

C. INDIQUANT LA CAUSE ▸ **mourir de peur / de faim** to die of fright / of hunger ▸ **pleurer de joie** to cry for joy ▸ **se tordre de douleur / de rire** to be doubled up in pain / with laughter.

D. INDIQUANT LE MOYEN : *faire signe de la main* to wave / *il voit mal de l'œil gauche* he can't see properly with his left eye.

E. INDIQUANT LA MANIÈRE ▸ **manger de bon appétit** to eat heartily ▸ **de toutes ses forces** with all one's strength.

F. AVEC DES NOMBRES **1.** [emploi distributif] ▸ **15 euros de l'heure** 15 euros per ou an hour **2.** [introduisant une mesure] : *un appartement de 60 &m2* ; a 60 &m2; flat / *une femme de 30 ans* a 30-year-old woman / *une équipe de 15 personnes* a team of 15 **3.** [indiquant une différence dans le temps, l'espace, la quantité] ▸ **distant de cinq kilomètres** five kilometres away / *ma montre retarde de 10 mn* my watch is 10 minutes slow.

G. INDIQUANT L'APPARTENANCE ▸ **la maison de mes parents** / **Marie** my parents' / Marie's house / *les pays membres de l'Union européenne* the countries in the EU, EU member states / *les élèves de sa classe* the pupils in his class.

H. MARQUANT LA DÉTERMINATION **1.** [indiquant la matière, la qualité, le genre, etc.] ▸ **un buffet de chêne** an oak dresser ▸ **un bonhomme de neige** a snowman ▸ **une réaction d'horreur** a horrified reaction **2.** [indiquant le contenu, le contenant] ▸ **l'eau de la citerne** the water in the tank

▸ **un pot de fleurs** a) [récipient] a flowerpot b) [fleurs] a pot of flowers **3.** [dans un ensemble] : *le plus jeune de la classe* the youngest pupil in the class **4.** [avec une valeur emphatique] ▸ **l'as des as** the champ.

I. SERVANT DE LIEN SYNTAXIQUE 1. [après un verbe] ▸ **parler de qqch** to speak about ou of sthg ▸ **se séparer de qqn** to leave sb / *ce champ est entouré d'une palissade* this field is surrounded by a fence **2.** [après un substantif] ▸ **l'amour de qqch** the love of sthg ▸ **troubles de l'audition** hearing problems **3.** [après un adjectif] ▸ **sûr de soi** sure of o.s. **4.** [après un pronom] ▸ **rien de nouveau** nothing new **5.** [devant un adjectif, participe ou adverbe] : *restez une semaine de plus* stay (for) one more ou an extra week **6.** [introduisant un nom en apposition] ▸ **le mois de janvier** the month of January ▸ **cet imbécile de Pierre** that idiot Pierre **7.** *litt* [introduisant un infinitif] : *et tous de rire* they all burst into laughter.

◆ *art partitif* **1.** [dans une affirmation] : *j'ai acheté de la viande* I bought (some) meat / *c'est de la provocation / de l'entêtement !* it's sheer provocation / pig-headedness ! / *manger de la viande* to eat meat ; [dans une interrogation] : *prends-tu du sucre dans ton café ?* do you take sugar in your coffee ? ; [dans une négation] : *il n'y a pas de place* there's no room, there isn't any room **2.** ▸ **ça c'est du Julien tout craché** ou **du pur Julien** that's Julien all over, that's typical of Julien.

◆ *art déf* [dans une affirmation] : *il a de bonnes idées* he has ou he's got (some) good ideas. ◆ **de... à** *loc corrélative* **1.** [dans l'espace] from... to **2.** [dans le temps] from... to ▸ **d'un instant à l'autre** a) [progressivement] from one minute to the next b) [bientôt] any minute ou time now **3.** [dans une énumération] from... to **4.** [dans une évaluation] : *ça vaut de 80 à 100 euros* it's worth between 80 and 100 euros. ◆ **de... en** *loc corrélative* **1.** [dans l'espace] from... to **2.** [dans le temps] ▸ **de jour en jour** from day to day / *le nombre d'étudiants augmente d'année en année* the number of students is getting bigger by the year ou every year ou from one year to the next **3.** [dans une évolution] : *aller de déception en déception* to go from one disappointment to the next.

dé [de] *nm* **1.** JEUX die ▸ **des dés** dice ▸ **jouer aux dés** to play dice ▸ **les dés (en) sont jetés** the die is cast **2.** CULIN cube / *couper du lard en dés* to dice bacon **3.** COUT ▸ **dé (à coudre)** thimble.

DEA (*abr de* **diplôme d'études approfondies**) *nm litt* former postgraduate diploma.

dealer[1] [dilœʀ] *nm fam* pusher.

dealer[2] [dile] ◆ *vt fam* to push. ◆ *vi* to push drugs.

déambulateur [deãbylatœʀ] *nm* walking frame, Zimmer®.

déambuler [3] [deãbyle] *vi* to stroll, to amble (along).

débâcle [debakl] *nf* **1.** MIL rout **2.** [faillite - d'une institution, d'un système] collapse / *c'est la débâcle !* it's absolute chaos!

déballer [3] [debale] *vt* **1.** [bagages] to unpack **2.** [exposer - produits] to display **3.** *fam* [sentiments] to unload.

débandade [debãdad] *nf* **1.** [déroute] rout **2.** [panique] panic, rush.

débaptiser [3] [debatize] *vt* [place, rue] to change the name of, to give another name to.

débarbouiller [3] [debaʀbuje] *vt* [enfant, visage] to wash. ◆ **se débarbouiller** *vp (emploi réfléchi) fam* to wash one's face.

débarcadère [debaʀkadɛʀ] *nm* **1.** [de passagers] landing stage ; [de marchandises] wharf **2.** Québec [pour livraison] delivery area.

débardeur [debaʀdœʀ] *nm* VÊT [tricot] tank top ; [tee-shirt] sleeveless T-shirt.

débarquement [debaʀkəmã] *nm* **1.** [déchargement - de marchandises] unloading ; [- de passagers] landing **2.** HIST ▸ **le (jour du) débarquement** D-day, the Normandy landings. ◆ **de débarquement** *loc adj* [quai] arrival *(modif)* ; [navire, troupe, fiche] landing *(modif)*.

débarquer [3] [debaʀke] ◆ *vt* [décharger - marchandises] to unload ; [- voyageurs] to land. ◆ *vi* **1.** NAUT to disembark, to land ; MIL to land **2.** [descendre] ▸ **débarquer de** [train] to get off, to alight from **3.** *fam* [arriver] to turn ou to show up **4.** *fam* [être ignorant] : *tu débarques ou quoi ?* where have you been?

débarras [debaʀa] *nm* **1.** [dépôt] storage room **2.** EXPR ▸ **bon débarras !** *fam* good riddance!

débarrasser [3] [debaʀase] *vt* **1.** [nettoyer - table] to clear ; [enlever - assiette] to clear (away) **2.** [désencombrer] ▸ **débarrasser qqn / qqch de** : *je vais te débarrasser de ta valise* I'll take your case ▸ **débarrasser qqn de ses mauvaises habitudes** to rid sb of his bad habits. ◆ **se débarrasser de** *vp + prép* **1.** [se défaire de] to get rid of **2.** [éloigner - importun] to get rid of ; [- serviteur] to get rid of, to dismiss **3.** [veste, gants] to take off, to remove ; [sac à main, éventail] to put down ; *(en usage absolu)* : *débarrasse-toi, tu vas avoir trop chaud* take your coat ou jacket off, you'll be too hot.

débat [deba] *nm* [controverse] debate, discussion ▸ **débat d'idées** debate of ideas ▸ **débat télévisé** televised debate. ◆ **débats** *nmpl* POL & DR proceedings.

débattre [83] [debatʀ] *vt* [discuter - thème, question] to discuss, to thrash out *(sép)*. ◆ **débattre de, débattre sur** *v + prép* to debate, to discuss. ◆ **se débattre** *vpi* [s'agiter - victime] to struggle ; [- poisson] to thrash about. ◆ **à débattre** *loc adj* / **'500 € à débattre'** '500 € or nearest offer'.

débauche [debo∫] *nf* **1.** [dévergondage] debauchery ▸ **inciter qqn à la débauche** to debauch sb **2.** [profusion] ▸ **une débauche de couleurs** a riot of colours. ◆ **de débauche** *loc adj* [passé, vie] dissolute.

débauché, e [debo∫e] *nm, f* debauched person, libertine.

débaucher [3] [debo∫e] *vt* [licencier] to lay off, to make redundant UK ; *(en usage absolu)* : *on débauche dans le textile* there are lay-offs in the textile industry.

débile [debil] ◆ *adj* **1.** *fam* [inepte - livre, film, décision] stupid, daft UK, dumb US ; [- personne, raisonnement] stupid, moronic **2.** *litt* [faible - corps] frail, weak, feeble ; [- intelligence] deficient. ◆ *nmf* **1.** *fam* [idiot] moron, cretin, idiot **2.** PSYCHOL ▸ **débile léger / moyen / profond** mildly / moderately / severely retarded person ▸ **débile mental** *vieilli* retarded person.

débilitant, e [debilitã, ãt] *adj* **1.** [affaiblissant] debilitating, enervating **2.** *fam* [abrutissant] mindnumbing.

débilité [debilite] *nf* **1.** *fam* [caractère stupide] stupidity, silliness, inanity **2.** PSYCHOL ▸ **débilité (mentale)** (mental) retardation.

débiner [3] [debine] *vt fam* to run down *(sép)*. ◆ **se débiner** *vpi fam* [s'enfuir] to clear out.

débit [debi] *nm* **1.** [d'eau, de passagers] flow ; [de vapeur] capacity ; [de gaz] output ; [de marchandises, de clients] turnover ; GÉOGR flow **2.** [élocution] (speed of) delivery / *il a un sacré débit fam* he talks nineteen to the dozen **3.** ÉLECT output **4.** COMM ▸ **débit de boissons** bar ▸ **débit de tabac** tobacconist UK, tobacco store US **5.** FIN debit ; [sur un relevé] debit side ▸ **débit différé** deferred debit. ◆ **au débit de** *loc prép* : *porter une somme au débit d'un compte* to debit an account.

débitant, e [debitã, ãt] *nm, f* ▸ **débitant de boissons** publican UK, bar owner US ▸ **débitant de tabac** tobacconist UK, tobacco dealer US.

débiter [3] [debite] vt **1.** [couper -matériau, tissu, bœuf] to cut up (sép) ; [-bois] to cut ou to saw up (sép) **2.** COMM to retail, to sell (retail) **3.** péj [texte] to reel off (sép) ; [sermon] to deliver ; [banalité] to trot out ▸ **débiter des mensonges** to come out with a pack of lies **4.** FIN to debit / *votre compte sera débité à la fin du mois* your account will be debited at the end of the month.

débiteur, trice [debitœʀ, tʀis] ◆ adj [colonne, compte, solde] debit (modif) ; [personne, société] debtor (modif). ◆ nm, f sout [obligé] ▸ **être débiteur de qqn** to be indebted to sb ou in sb's debt.

déblatérer [18] [deblateʀe] ❖ **déblatérer contre** v + prép péj to rant (and rave) about, to sound off about.

  🖉 In reformed spelling (see p. 16-18), this verb is conjugated like *semer*: *il déblatèrera, elle déblatèrerait.*

déblayer [11] [debleje] vt **1.** [dégager -neige, terre] to clear away ; [-lieu] to clear out **2.** fig [travail] to do the groundwork ou spadework on ▸ **déblayer le terrain** [se débarrasser des détails] to do the groundwork.

débloquer [3] [debloke] ◆ vt **1.** MÉCAN [écrou, dispositif] to release, to unblock, to free ; [freins] to unjam, to release **2.** [rouvrir - rue] to clear (of obstructions) / *débloquer les discussions* fig to get the negotiations back on course ▸ **débloquer la situation a)** [après un conflit] to break the stalemate **b)** [la sortir de l'enlisement] to get things moving again **3.** ÉCON [prix, salaires] to unfreeze ; BANQUE [compte, crédit] to free, to unfreeze ; COMM [stock] to release. ◆ vi fam **1.** [en parlant] to talk rubbish 🇬🇧 ou nonsense **2.** [être déraisonnable] to be nuts ou cracked.

déboguer [deboge] vt to debug.

déboires [debwaʀ] nmpl disappointments, setbacks, (trials and) tribulations.

déboisement [debwazmã] nm deforestation, clearing (of trees).

déboiser [3] [debwaze] vt [couper les arbres de] to deforest, to clear of trees.

déboîter, déboiter* [3] [debwate] vi [véhicule] to pull out. ❖ **se déboîter, se déboiter*** vpt ▸ **se déboîter le genou / l'épaule** to dislocate one's knee / shoulder.

débonnaire [debɔnɛʀ] adj [air] kindly, debonair ; [personne] good-natured, easy-going, debonair.

débordant, e [debɔʀdã, ãt] adj [extrême - affection] overflowing ; [-activité] tireless ; [-imagination] wild, unbridled, boundless ▸ **d'un enthousiasme débordant** bubbling with enthusiasm ▸ **débordant de santé / de vie** bursting with health / with vitality.

débordé, e [debɔʀde] adj **1.** [peu disponible] (very) busy **2.** [surmené] overworked.

débordement [debɔʀdəmã] nm [profusion - de paroles] rush, torrent ; [-d'injures] outburst, volley ; [-de joie] outburst, explosion. ❖ **débordements** nmpl [agitation] wild ou uncontrolled ou extreme behaviour ▸ *afin d'éviter les débordements* to prevent things from getting out of hand.

déborder [3] [debɔʀde] ◆ vi **1.** [rivière] to overflow ; [bouillon, lait] to boil over / *les pluies ont fait déborder la rivière* the rain made the river burst its banks ▸ **déborder de** to overflow ou to be bursting with / *déborder d'énergie* to be overflowing with energy / *déborder de joie* to be bursting with joy **2.** [récipient] to overflow, to run over ; [tiroir, sac] to be crammed, to spill over / *la casserole est pleine à déborder* the saucepan's full to the brim ou to overflowing / *laisser déborder la baignoire* to let the bath overflow **3.** [faire saillie] to stick ou to jut out, to project / *déborder en coloriant un dessin* to go over the edges while colouring in a picture. ◆ vt **1.** [dépasser] to stick ou to jut out from **2.** [s'écarter de] : *vous débordez le sujet* you've

gone beyond the scope of the topic **3.** [submerger -troupe, parti, équipe] to outflank ▸ **être débordé**: *être débordé de travail* to be up to one's eyes in ou snowed under with work / *être débordé par les événements* to let things get on top of one.

débouché [debuʃe] nm **1.** [possibilité d'emploi] career prospect **2.** [perspective de vente] outlet, avenue for products ; [marché] market **3.** [issue] end / *avoir un débouché sur la mer* to have an outlet to the sea.

déboucher [3] [debuʃe] ◆ vt **1.** [ouvrir -bouteille de bière, tube] to uncap, to take the top off, to open ; [-bouteille de vin] to uncork, to open ; [-flacon] to unstop, to remove the stopper from **2.** [débloquer -pipe, trou, gicleur] to clear, to clean out (sép) ; [-lavabo] to unblock, to unstop, to clear ; [-tuyau, conduit] to clear, to unclog ; [-nez] to unblock ; [-oreille] to clean out (sép). ◆ vi **1.** [aboutir] ▸ **déboucher de** to emerge from, to come out of ▸ **déboucher sur** to open into, to lead to **2.** fig ▸ **déboucher sur** to lead to ▸ **déboucher sur des résultats** to have positive results. ❖ **se déboucher** vpt ▸ **se déboucher le nez** to clear one's nose.

débouler [3] [debule] ◆ vi [surgir] to emerge suddenly / *ils ont déboulé dans le couloir* they charged ou hurtled into the passage. ◆ vt ▸ **débouler les escaliers a)** [en courant] to race ou to hurtle down the stairs **b)** [après être tombé] to tumble down the stairs.

déboulonner [3] [debulɔne] vt TECHNOL to unbolt, to remove the bolts (from) ▸ **déboulonner une statue** to take down a statue.

débourser [3] [debuʀse] vt to spend, to lay out (sép).

déboussoler [3] [debusɔle] vt to confuse, to disorientate, to bewilder.

debout [dəbu] adv **1.** [en parlant des personnes -en station verticale] standing up ▸ **debout !** get ou stand up! / *il était debout sur la table* he was standing on the table ▸ **se mettre debout** to stand (up), to rise / *je préfère rester debout* I'd rather stand ▸ **ne restez pas debout** (please) sit down ▸ **il ne tient plus debout a)** [fatigué] he's dead on his feet **b)** [ivre] he's legless **2.** [en parlant d'objets] upright, vertical / *mettre une chaise debout* to stand a chair up ; fig : *ça ne tient pas debout* it doesn't make sense **3.** [éveillé] up ▸ **debout !** get up! / *être debout à 5 h* to be up at 5 o'clock **4.** [en bon état] standing / *les murs sont encore debout* the walls are still standing / *la maison de mon enfance est encore debout* the house where I lived as a child is still there **5.** [guéri] up on one's feet (again), up and about ; [sorti de chez soi, de l'hôpital] out and about **6.** litt [dignement] uprightly, honourably.

débouter [3] [debute] vt to nonsuit, to dismiss / *être débouté de sa plainte* to be nonsuited, to have one's suit dismissed.

déboutonner [3] [debutɔne] vt to unbutton.

débraillé, e [debʀaje] adj [allure, vêtements, personne] dishevelled 🇬🇧, disheveled 🇺🇸, slovenly, sloppy, scruffy ; [manières] slovenly ; [conversation] unrestrained.

débrancher [3] [debʀãʃe] vt [déconnecter -tuyau] to disconnect ; [-appareil électrique] to unplug.

débrayage [debʀejaʒ] nm **1.** AUTO disengaging the clutch **2.** [grève] stoppage, walkout.

débrayer [11] [debʀeje] vi **1.** AUTO to declutch 🇬🇧, to disengage the clutch **2.** [faire grève] to stop work, to come out ou to go on strike.

débridé, e [debʀide] adj **1.** [libre] unbridled, unrestrained, unfettered **2.** MÉCAN [moto] derestricted.

débrider [3] [debʀide] vt MÉCAN [moto] to derestrict.

débriefer [debʀife] vt to debrief.

débriefing [debʁifiŋ] nm debrief ▶ **faire un débriefing** to debrief.

débris [debʁi] nm **1.** *(gén au pl)* [fragment - de verre] piece, splinter, shard ; [- de vaisselle] (broken) piece ou fragment ; [- de roche] crumb, debris *(sg)* ; [- de métal] scrap ; [- de végétal] piece ou crumb of vegetable matter, debris *(sg)* **2.** *(gén au pl)* [nourriture] scraps, crumbs ; *litt* [restes - d'une fortune, d'un royaume] last shreds, remnants ; [détritus] litter, rubbish 🇬🇧 **3.** *tfam* [vieillard] ▶ **(vieux) débris** old codger.

débrouillard, e [debʁujaʁ, aʁd] adj resourceful.

débrouillardise [debʁujaʁdiz] nf resourcefulness.

débrouiller [3] [debʁuje] vt **1.** [démêler - fils] to unravel, to untangle, to disentangle ; [- énigme] to puzzle out *(sép)*, to untangle, to unravel ▶ **débrouiller les affaires de qqn** to sort out sb's business affairs **2.** *fam* [enseigner les bases à] to teach the basics to. ❖ **se débrouiller** vpi **1.** [faire face aux difficultés] to manage / *débrouille-toi* you'll have to manage by yourself / *comment vas-tu te débrouiller maintenant qu'elle est partie ?* how will you cope now that she's gone ? / *elle se débrouille très bien dans Berlin* she really knows her way around Berlin / *tu parles espagnol ? — je me débrouille* do you speak Spanish? — I get by **2.** [subsister financièrement] to make ends meet, to manage.

débroussailler [3] [debʁusaje] vt [terrain] to clear (of brambles).

débuguer [3] [debœge] vt = **déboguer**.

débusquer [3] [debyske] vt **1.** CHASSE to start, to flush **2.** [découvrir] to hunt out *(sép)*.

début [deby] nm **1.** [commencement] beginning, start / *il y a un début à tout* you have to start sometime ▶ **un début de** : *ressentir un début de fatigue* to start feeling tired ▶ **un début de grippe** the first signs of flu **2.** [dans l'expression des dates] ▶ **début mars** at the beginning of ou in early March. ❖ **débuts** nmpl [dans une carrière] start ; [dans le spectacle] debut / *mes débuts dans le journalisme* my first steps ou early days as a journalist ▶ **en être à ses débuts** a) [projet] to be in its early stages b) [personne] to have just started (out) ; [en société] debut / *faire ses débuts* to make one's debut ; [première période] beginnings. ❖ **au début** loc adv at first, to begin with. ❖ **au début de** loc prép ▶ **au début du printemps / de l'année** at the beginning of spring / of the year. ❖ **dès le début** loc adv from the outset ou very start ou very beginning. ❖ **du début à la fin** loc adv [d'un livre, d'une histoire] from beginning to end ; [d'une course, d'un événement] from start to finish.

débutant, e [debytã, ãt] nm, f [dans un apprentissage] beginner, novice ; [dans une carrière] beginner ▶ **grand débutant** absolute beginner.

débuter [3] [debyte] ◆ vi **1.** [commencer] to start, to begin ▶ **débuter par** to start (off) with **2.** [être inexpérimenté] to be a beginner, to begin **3.** [commencer à travailler] to start (out), to begin / *il a débuté comme serveur dans un restaurant* he started out as a waiter in a restaurant **4.** [artiste] to make one's debut. ◆ vt *fam* : *c'est nous qui débutons le concert* we're on first, we're opening the show.

deçà [dəsa] ❖ **en deçà de** loc prép **1.** [de ce côté-ci de] (on) this side of **2.** *fig* : *en deçà d'un certain seuil* below a certain level / *rester en deçà de la vérité* to be short of the truth.

déca [deka] nm *fam* decaffeinated coffee, decaf.

décacheter [27] [dekaʃte] vt [ouvrir - en déchirant] to open, to tear open ; [- en rompant le cachet] to unseal, to break open.

🖉 In reformed spelling (see p. 16-18), this verb is conjugated like **acheter** : *il décachètera, elle décachèterait*.

décade [dekad] nf [dix jours] period of ten days.

décadence [dekadãs] nf decadence, decline, decay. ❖ **en décadence** loc adv : *tomber* ou *entrer en décadence* to become decadent, to start to decline.

décadent, e [dekadã, ãt] adj **1.** [en déclin] decadent, declining, decaying **2.** ART & LITTÉR decadent.

décaféiné, e [dekafeine] adj decaffeinated. ❖ **décaféiné** nm decaffeinated coffee.

décalage [dekalaʒ] nm **1.** [dans l'espace] space, interval, gap **2.** [dans le temps] interval, time-lag, lag ▶ **décalage horaire** time difference / *souffrir du décalage horaire* to have jet lag **3.** [manque de concordance] discrepancy, gap. ❖ **en décalage** loc adj [sans harmonie] : *on est en complet décalage* we're on completely different wavelengths.

décalcomanie [dekalkɔmani] nf [image] transfer 🇬🇧, decal 🇺🇸, decalcomania *spéc*.

décalé, e [dekale] adj **1.** [style, humour] off-beat, quirky **2.** [personne] quirky / *être décalé par rapport à la réalité* to be out of phase with reality.

décaler [3] [dekale] vt **1.** [dans l'espace] to pull ou to shift (out of line) / *les sièges sont décalés* the seats are staggered **2.** [dans le temps - horaire] to shift ▶ **l'horaire a été décalé d'une heure** a) [avancé] the schedule was brought forward an hour b) [reculé] the schedule was brought ou moved one hour back. ❖ **se décaler** vpi to move (out of line) / *décalez-vous d'un rang en avant / arrière* move forward / back a row.

décalquer [3] [dekalke] vt to trace, to transfer.

décamper [3] [dekãpe] vi to make o.s. scarce, to buzz off.

décan [dekã] nm decan.

décanter [3] [dekãte] vt **1.** [purifier - liquide] to allow to settle, to clarify ; [- argile] to wash ; [- produit chimique] to decant **2.** [éclaircir] to clarify ▶ **décanter ses idées** to think things over. ❖ **se décanter** vpi **1.** [liquide] to settle **2.** [situation] to settle down.

décapant, e [dekapã, ãt] adj [incisif - remarque] caustic, vitriolic ; [- roman, article] corrosive. ❖ **décapant** nm CONSTR stripper.

décaper [3] [dekape] vt [nettoyer - gén] to clean off *(sép)* ; [- en grattant] to scrape clean ; [- avec un produit chimique] to strip ; [- à la chaleur] to burn off *(sép)* / *décaper un parquet* to sand (down) floorboards.

décapiter [3] [dekapite] vt [personne] ▶ **décapiter qqn** a) [le supplicier] to behead sb, to cut sb's head off, to decapitate sb b) [accidentellement] to cut sb's head off, to decapitate sb.

décapotable [dekapɔtabl] adj & nf convertible.

décapsuler [3] [dekapsyle] vt to uncap, to take the top off.

décapsuleur [dekapsylœʁ] nm bottle opener.

décarcasser [3] [dekaʁkase] ❖ **se décarcasser** vpi *fam* to go through a lot of hassle, to sweat (blood).

décéder [18] [desede] vi *sout* DR to die, to pass away *euphém*.

🖉 In reformed spelling (see p. 16-18), this verb is conjugated like **semer** : *il décédera, elle décèderait*.

déceler [25] [desle] vt **1.** [repérer - erreur] to detect, to spot, to discover ; [percevoir] to detect, to discern, to perceive **2.** [révéler] to reveal, to betray, to give away *(sép)*.

décembre [desãbʁ] nm December. **Voir aussi mars.**

décemment [desamã] adv **1.** [correctement] decently, properly **2.** [suffisamment] properly **3.** [raisonnablement] decently / *on ne peut pas décemment lui raconter ça* we can't very well ou we can hardly tell him that.

décence [desɑ̃s] nf decency.

décennie [deseni] nf decade, decennium.

décent, e [desɑ̃, ɑ̃t] adj **1.** [convenable] decent / *il serait plus décent de ne rien lui dire* it would be more fitting ou proper not to tell him anything **2.** [acceptable] decent, reasonable / *un prix décent* a reasonable ou fair price / *un repas décent* a decent meal.

décentralisation [desɑ̃tralizasjɔ̃] nf decentralization, decentralizing.

 Décentralisation

The shifting of a degree of administrative power from Paris to regional bodies has been a key aspect of French domestic policy. This policy led to the creation of the 26 administrative regions in 1982 which are overseen by regional councils.

décentraliser [3] [desɑ̃tralize] vt to decentralize.

déception [desɛpsjɔ̃] nf disappointment.

⚠ Le mot anglais **deception** signifie « tromperie » et non déception.

décerner [3] [desɛrne] vt [prix, médaille] to award ; [titre, distinction] to confer on.

décès [desɛ] nm *sout* ou DR death.

décevant, e [desəvɑ̃, ɑ̃t] adj disappointing.

décevoir [52] [desəvwar] vt to disappoint.

⚠ **Deceive** signifie « tromper » et non décevoir.

déchaîné, e, déchainé*, e [deʃene] adj [mer, vent] raging, wild ; [passions] unbridled, raging ; [personne] wild ; [public] raving, delirious ; [opinion publique] outraged ; [foule] riotous, uncontrollable.

déchaîner, déchainer* [4] [deʃene] vt [déclencher - violence, colère] to unleash, to arouse ; [- enthousiasme] to arouse ; [- rires] to trigger off *(sép)* / *déchaîner l'hilarité générale* to set off a storm of laughter / *son article a déchaîné les passions* his article caused an outcry ou aroused strong passions. **se déchaîner, se déchainer*** vpi **1.** [tempête, vent] to rage **2.** [hilarité, applaudissements] to break ou to burst out ; [instincts] to be unleashed **se déchaîner contre** to rave at ou against / *la presse s'est déchaînée contre le gouvernement* the press railed at the government / *elle s'est déchaînée contre son frère* she lashed out ou let fly at her brother.

déchanter [3] [deʃɑ̃te] vi to be disillusioned, to become disenchanted.

décharge [deʃarʒ] nf **1.** ARM [tir] shot **2.** ÉLECTR discharge **décharge électrique** electric ou field discharge / *prendre une décharge fam* to get an electric 🇬🇧 ou electrical 🇺🇸 shock **3.** [écrit, quittance] discharge paper, chit **4.** [dépotoir] **décharge (publique** ou **municipale)** dump, rubbish tip 🇬🇧, garbage dump 🇺🇸 **5.** PHYSIOL rush **décharge d'adrénaline** rush of adrenaline. **à la décharge de** loc prép : *à sa décharge, il faut dire que...* in his / her defence, it has to be said that...

déchargement [deʃarʒəmɑ̃] nm [d'une arme, d'un véhicule] unloading.

décharger [17] [deʃarʒe] vt **1.** [débarrasser de sa charge - véhicule, animal] to unload ; [- personne] to unburden **je vais te décharger a)** [à un voyageur] let me take your luggage **b)** [au retour des magasins] let me take your parcels for you **2.** [enlever - marchandises] to unload, to take off *(sép)* ; [- passagers] to set down *(sép)* **3.** [soulager] to relieve, to unburden **décharger qqn de qqch** to relieve sb of sthg / *être déchargé de ses fonctions* to be discharged ou dismissed **4.** ARM [tirer avec] to fire, to discharge **décharger son arme sur qqn** to fire one's gun at sb ; [ôter la charge de] to unload. **se décharger** vpi **1.** ÉLECTR [batterie] to run down, to go flat ; [accumulateur] to run down, to lose its charge **2.** [se débarrasser] **se décharger (de qqch) sur** : *je vais essayer de me décharger de cette corvée sur quelqu'un* I'll try to hand over the chore to somebody else.

décharné, e [deʃarne] adj [maigre - personne] emaciated, gaunt, wasted ; [- visage] emaciated, gaunt, haggard ; [- main] bony.

déchausser [3] [deʃose] vt [personne] **déchausser qqn** to take off sb's shoes ; [retirer] **déchausser ses skis** to take off one's skis ; *(en usage absolu)* to lose one's skis. **se déchausser** vp *(emploi réfléchi)* [personne] to take off one's shoes. **vpi** [dent] to get loose.

dèche [deʃ] nf *tfam* dire poverty **être dans la dèche** to be skint 🇬🇧 ou broke.

déchéance [deʃeɑ̃s] nf **1.** [avilissement] (moral) degradation / *tomber dans la déchéance* to go into (moral) decline **2.** POL [d'un monarque] deposition, deposing ; [d'un président] removal *(after impeachment)*.

déchet [deʃɛ] nm [portion inutilisable] : *dans un ananas il y a beaucoup de déchet* there's a lot of waste in a pineapple. **déchets** nmpl [résidus] waste **déchets domestiques / industriels** household / industrial waste **déchets radioactifs / toxiques** radioactive / toxic waste.

déchetterie, déchèterie* [deʃɛtri] nf waste collection centre *(for sorting and recycling)*, recycling centre 🇬🇧 ou center 🇺🇸.

déchiffrer [3] [deʃifre] vt **1.** [comprendre - inscription, manuscrit] to decipher ; [- langage codé] to decipher, to decode **2.** [lire] to spell out *(sép)* **3.** MUS to sight-read **4.** [élucider - énigme] to puzzle out *(sép)*, to make sense of.

déchiqueter [27] [deʃikte] vt [papier, tissu] to rip (to shreds), to tear (to bits) / *les corps ont été déchiquetés par l'explosion* the bodies were torn to pieces by the explosion.

✐ In reformed spelling (see p. 16-18), this verb is conjugated like **acheter** : *il déchiquètera, elle déchiquèterait*.

déchiqueteur [deʃiktœr] nm shredder.

déchirant, e [deʃirɑ̃, ɑ̃t] adj [spectacle] heartbreaking, heartrending ; [cri] agonizing, harrowing ; [séparation] unbearably painful.

déchirement [deʃirmɑ̃] nm **1.** [arrachement] tearing, ripping, rending **2.** [souffrance] wrench **3.** [désunion] rift / *un pays en proie à des déchirements politiques* a country torn apart by internal strife.

déchirer [3] [deʃire] vt **1.** [lacérer] to tear, to rip **2.** [mettre en deux morceaux] to tear / *déchirer une page en deux* to tear a page into two ; [mettre en morceaux] to tear up ou to pieces **3.** [arracher] to tear off *(sép)* **4.** [ouvrir] : *déchirer une enveloppe* to tear ou to rip open an envelope **5.** *litt* [interrompre - nuit, silence] to rend, to pierce **6.** [diviser] to tear apart / *le pays est déchiré par la guerre depuis 10 ans* the country has been torn apart by war for 10 years / *je suis déchiré entre eux deux* I'm torn between the two of them. **se déchirer** vp *(emploi réciproque)* [se faire souffrir] to tear each other apart. **vpi** [vêtement, tissu, papier] to tear, to rip ; [membrane] to break. **vpt** MÉD **se déchirer un muscle / tendon / ligament** to tear a muscle / tendon / ligament.

* In reformed spelling (see p. 16-18).

déchirure [deʃiʀyʀ] nf **1.** [accroc] tear, rip, split **2.** MÉD tear ▸ **déchirure musculaire** pulled muscle.

déchoir [71] [deʃwaʀ] ◆ vi *(aux être)* : *il est déchu de son rang* he has lost ou forfeited his social standing. ◆ vt [priver] ▸ **déchoir qqn d'un droit** to deprive sb of a right ▸ **déchoir qqn de sa nationalité / son titre** to strip sb of his / her nationality / title.

déchu, e [deʃy] ◆ pp —→ **déchoir.** ◆ adj [prince, roi] deposed, dethroned ; [président] deposed ; [ange, humanité] fallen.

décibel [desibɛl] nm decibel.

décidé, e [deside] adj **1.** [résolu] resolute, determined, decided **2.** [réglé] settled.

décidément [desidemɑ̃] adv definitely, clearly / *décidément, ça ne marchera jamais* obviously it'll never work out ▸ **décidément, c'est une manie** you're really making a habit of it, aren't you? / *j'ai encore cassé un verre — décidément !* I've broken another glass — it's not your day, is it!

décider [3] [deside] vt **1.** [choisir] to decide (on) / *décider de faire* to decide ou to resolve to do ▸ **décider que** : *il a décidé que nous irions demain* he's decided that we'll go tomorrow ▸ **c'est décidé** it's settled ; *(en usage absolu)* ▸ **c'est toi qui décides** it's your decision, it's up to you **2.** [entraîner] ▸ **décider qqn à** to convince ou to persuade sb to. ◆ **se décider de** v + prép **1.** [influencer] to determine **2.** [choisir - lieu, date] to choose, to determine, to decide on **3.** [juger] : *le sort en décida autrement* fate decreed otherwise. ◆ **se décider** ◆ vp *(emploi passif)* to be decided (on) / *les choses se sont décidées très vite* things were decided very quickly. ◆ vpi [faire son choix] to make up one's mind ▸ **se décider à** : *je me suis décidé à l'acheter* I decided ou resolved to buy it / *elle s'est décidée à déménager* she's made up her mind to move out / *la voiture s'est enfin décidée à démarrer* the car finally decided to start.

décideur, euse [desidœʀ, øz] nm, f decision-maker.

décilitre [desilitʀ] nm decilitre 🇬🇧, deciliter 🇺🇸.

décimal, e, aux [desimal, o] adj decimal. ◆ **décimale** nf decimal place ▸ **nombre à trois décimales** number given to three decimal places.

décimer [3] [desime] vt to decimate.

décimètre [desimetʀ] nm decimetre 🇬🇧, decimeter 🇺🇸.

décisif, ive [desizif, iv] adj [déterminant - influence, intervention] decisive ; [- preuve] conclusive ; [- élément] decisive, deciding ; [- coup] decisive / *il a eu un argument décisif* what he said clinched the argument / *le facteur décisif* the deciding factor / *à un moment décisif de ma vie* at a decisive moment ou at a watershed in my life.

décision [desizjɔ̃] nf **1.** [résolution] decision / *arriver à une décision* to come to ou to reach a decision ▸ **prendre une décision** to make a decision / *la décision t'appartient* the decision is yours, it's for you to decide **2.** DR ▸ **décision judiciaire** court ruling / *par décision judiciaire* by order of the court. ◆ **de décision** loc adj [organe, centre] decision-making.

décisionnaire [desizjɔnɛʀ] nmf decision-maker.

déclamer [3] [deklame] vt to declaim.

déclaration [deklaʀasjɔ̃] nf **1.** [communication] statement ; [proclamation] declaration / *faire une déclaration à la presse* to issue a statement to the press / *je ne ferai aucune déclaration !* no comment! ▸ **déclaration de guerre / d'indépendance** declaration of war / of independence ▸ **la Déclaration des droits de l'homme et du citoyen** the Declaration of Human Rights *(of 1791)* **2.** [témoignage] statement **3.** ADMIN declaration / *faire une déclaration à la douane* to declare something at customs / *faire une déclaration à son assurance* to file a claim with one's insur-ance company ▸ **déclaration de perte** : *faire une déclaration de perte de passeport à la police* to report the loss of one's passport to the police ▸ **déclaration d'impôts** tax return ▸ **déclaration de naissance** birth registration **4.** [aveu] declaration ▸ **faire une déclaration d'amour** ou **sa déclaration (à qqn)** to declare one's love (to sb).

déclarer [3] [deklaʀe] vt **1.** [proclamer] to declare, to announce, to assert ▸ **déclarer forfait a)** SPORT to withdraw **b)** *fig* to throw in the towel ▸ **déclarer la guerre à** *pr & fig* to declare war on **2.** *(avec un adj ou une loc adj)* [juger] ▸ **déclarer qqn coupable** to find sb guilty **3.** [affirmer] to profess, to claim **4.** [révéler - intention] to state, to declare ▸ **déclarer son amour** ou **sa flamme à qqn** *litt* to declare one's love to sb **5.** [dire officiellement] to declare ▸ **déclarer ses revenus / employés** to declare one's income / employees / *déclarer un enfant à la mairie* to register the birth of a child ▸ **rien à déclarer** nothing to declare. ◆ **se déclarer** vpi **1.** [se manifester - incendie, épidémie] to break out ; [- fièvre, maladie] to set in **2.** [se prononcer] to take a stand **3.** *(avec un adj ou une loc adj)* [se dire] to say / *il s'est déclaré ravi* he said how pleased he was **4.** *litt* [dire son amour] to declare one's love.

déclasser [3] [deklase] vt **1.** [déranger] to put out of order **2.** [rétrograder] to downgrade **3.** [déprécier] to demean **4.** [changer de catégorie - hôtel] to downgrade ; RAIL to change to a lower class.

déclenchement [deklɑ̃ʃmɑ̃] nm [début - d'un événement] starting point, start, trigger ; [- d'une attaque] launching.

déclencher [3] [deklɑ̃ʃe] vt **1.** [provoquer - attaque] to launch ; [- révolte, conflit] to trigger (off), to bring about *(sép)* ; [- grève, émeute, rires] to trigger ou to spark off *(sép)* **2.** TECHNOL [mettre en marche - mécanisme, minuterie] to trigger ; [- activate] ; [- sonnerie, alarme] to set off *(sép)*.

❖ **se déclencher** vpi **1.** [commencer - douleur, incendie] to start **2.** [se mettre en marche - sirène, sonnerie, bombe] to go off ; [-mécanisme] to be triggered off ou released.

déclencheur [deklɑ̃ʃœʀ] nm PHOT shutter release ▸ **déclencheur automatique** time release, self-timer.

déclic [deklik] nm **1.** [bruit] click **2.** [prise de conscience] : *il s'est produit un déclic et elle a trouvé la solution* things suddenly fell into place ou clicked and she found the answer.

déclin [deklɛ̃] nm [diminution] decline, waning. ❖ **en déclin** loc adj on the decline. ❖ **sur le déclin** loc adj [prestige, puissance] declining, on the wane ; [malade] declining.

déclinaison [deklinɛzɔ̃] nf GRAM declension.

décliner [3] [dekline] ◆ vt **1.** GRAM to decline **2.** [énoncer - identité] to give, to state **3.** [refuser - invitation] to decline, to refuse ; [-offre] to decline, to refuse, to reject ▸ **décliner toute responsabilité** to accept no responsibility. ◆ vi [soleil] to set ; [vieillard] to decline ; [malade] to decline, to fade ; [santé, vue] to deteriorate ; [prestige] to wane, to decline ; [jour] to draw to a close.

déclivité [deklivite] nf [descente] downward slope, declivity *spéc*, incline.

déco [deko] (abr de **décoratif**) nf *fam* : *je vais refaire la déco de mon appartement* I'm going to redo the interior design of my flat.

décocher [3] [dekɔʃe] vt **1.** [flèche] to shoot, to fire ; [coup] to throw / *il m'a décoché un coup de pied* he kicked me / *le cheval lui a décoché une ruade* the horse lashed out ou kicked at him **2.** [regard, sourire] to dart, to flash, to shoot ; [plaisanterie, méchanceté] to fire, to shoot.

décoder [3] [dekɔde] vt **1.** [texte] to decode **2.** INFORM & TV to decode, to unscramble.

décodeur [dekɔdœʀ] nm decoder.

décoiffer [3] [dekwafe] vt **1.** [déranger la coiffure de] ▸ **décoiffer qqn** to mess up sb's hair / *elle est toute décoiffée* her hair's in a mess **2.** EXPR *ça décoiffe fam* it takes your breath away.

décoincer [16] [dekwɛse] vt [débloquer - objet] to unjam, to free ; [-vertèbre, articulation] to loosen up *(sép)*. ❖ **se décoincer** vpi **1.** [objet] to unjam, to work loose **2.** *fam* [personne] to relax, to let one's hair down.

décolérer [18] [dekɔleʀe] vi ▸ **ne pas décolérer** : *il n'a pas décoléré de la journée* he's been furious ou fuming all day.

📖 In reformed spelling (see p. 16-18), this verb is conjugated like *semer* : *il décolèrera, elle décolèrerait*.

décollage [dekɔlaʒ] nm **1.** AÉRON takeoff ; ASTRONAUT lift-off, blast-off ▸ **au décollage a)** AÉRON at ou on takeoff **b)** ASTRONAUT on takeoff ou lift-off **2.** ÉCON & SOCIOL takeoff.

décoller [3] [dekɔle] ◆ vi **1.** AÉRON to take off ; ASTRONAUT to take ou to lift ou to blast off **2.** [progresser - exportation, pays] to take off. ◆ vt **1.** [détacher - papier] to unstick, to unglue, to peel off *(sép)* / *décoller à la vapeur* to steam off / *décoller dans l'eau* to soak off **2.** *fam* [faire partir] to tear ou to prise away *(sép).* ❖ **se décoller** ◆ vp *(emploi passif)* to come off. ◆ vpi [se détacher] to come ou to peel off.

décolleté, e [dekɔlte] adj VÊT low-cut, low-necked, décolleté / *robe décolletée dans le dos* dress cut low in the back. ❖ **décolleté** nm **1.** VÊT low neckline ▸ **décolleté en V** V-neck ▸ **décolleté rond** round-neck **2.** [d'une femme] cleavage.

décolorant, e [dekɔlɔʀɑ̃, ɑ̃t] adj [pour cheveux] decolorizing *(avant nom)*, decolorant, bleaching *(avant nom)*.

❖ **décolorant** nm [pour cheveux] decolorizing agent, bleaching agent.

décoloration [dekɔlɔʀasjɔ̃] nf **1.** [atténuation de la couleur] fading, discolouration **2.** [disparition de la couleur] bleaching, discolouring **3.** [des cheveux] bleach treatment / *faire une décoloration* to bleach someone's hair.

décolorer [3] [dekɔlɔʀe] vt **1.** [affaiblir la couleur de] to fade **2.** [éclaircir - cheveux] to bleach / *cheveux décolorés par le soleil* hair lightened ou bleached by the sun. ❖ **se décolorer** vp *(emploi réfléchi)* [personne] to bleach one's hair.

décombres [dekɔ̃bʀ] nmpl [d'un bâtiment] debris *(sg)*, rubble, wreckage.

décommander [3] [dekɔmɑ̃de] vt [commande] to cancel ; [invitation, rendez-vous] to cancel, to call off *(sép)* ; [invité] to put off *(sép).* ❖ **se décommander** vpi to cancel (one's appointment).

décomplexer [4] [dekɔ̃plɛkse] vt to encourage, to reassure / *ça m'a décomplexé* it made me feel more confident ou less inadequate.

décomposer [3] [dekɔ̃poze] vt **1.** PHYS [force] to resolve ; [lumière] to disperse **2.** [analyser - texte, raisonnement] to break down *(sép)*, to analyse ; [-mouvement, processus] to decompose, to break up *(sép)* ; [-exercice, mélodie] to go through (step by step) *(insép)* / *décomposer un pas de danse* to go through a dance step ; GRAM [phrase] to parse **3.** [pourrir - terre, feuilles] to decompose, to rot. ❖ **se décomposer** ◆ vp *(emploi passif)* : *le texte se décompose en trois parties* the text can be broken down ou divided into three parts ; GRAM [phrase] to be parsed ; MATH to be factorized. ◆ vpi **1.** [pourrir] to decompose, to decay, to rot **2.** [s'altérer - visage] to become distorted / *soudain son visage s'est décomposé* his face suddenly fell.

décomposition [dekɔ̃pozisjɔ̃] nf [pourrissement - de la matière organique] decomposition, decay, rot ; [- de la société] decline, decay, decadence ▸ **en (état de) décomposition a)** [cadavre] decomposing, decaying, rotting **b)** [société] declining, decaying.

décompresser [4] [dekɔ̃pʀese] vi **1.** *fam* [se détendre] to relax, to unwind **2.** INFORM to unzip, to decompress.

décompression [dekɔ̃pʀesjɔ̃] nf **1.** MÉD & TECHNOL decompression **2.** *fam* [détente] unwinding, relaxing **3.** AUTO & MÉCAN decompression.

décompte [dekɔ̃t] nm **1.** [calcul] working out, reckoning, calculation / *faire le décompte des voix* to count the votes / *faire le décompte des points* to add ou to reckon up the score **2.** [déduction] deduction.

décompter [3] [dekɔ̃te] vt [déduire] to deduct.

déconcentrer [3] [dekɔ̃sɑ̃tʀe] vt [distraire] ▸ **déconcentrer qqn** to distract sb's attention. ❖ **se déconcentrer** vpi to lose (one's) concentration.

déconcertant, e [dekɔ̃sɛʀtɑ̃, ɑ̃t] adj disconcerting, off-putting.

déconcerter [3] [dekɔ̃sɛʀte] vt to disconcert.

déconfit, e [dekɔ̃fi, it] adj crestfallen.

déconfiture [dekɔ̃fityʀ] nf [échec] collapse, defeat, rout.

décongeler [25] [dekɔ̃ʒle] vt to defrost, to thaw.

décongestionnant, e [dekɔ̃ʒɛstjɔnɑ̃, ɑ̃t] adj MÉD decongestant. ❖ **décongestionnant** nm [médicament] decongestant.

décongestionner [3] [dekɔ̃ʒɛstjɔne] vt **1.** [dégager - route] to relieve congestion in, to ease the traffic load in **2.** MÉD to decongest, to relieve congestion in ou the congestion of.

déconnade [dekɔnad] nf *tfam* : *elle adore la franche déconnade* she loves having a laugh.

déconnecter [4] [dekɔnɛkte] vt **1.** [débrancher - tuyau, fil électrique] to disconnect **2.** *fam & fig* to disconnect, to cut off *(sép)* / *il est totalement déconnecté de la réalité* he's totally cut off from reality. ❖ **se déconnecter** vp INFORM to log off.

déconner [3] [dekɔne] vi *tfam* **1.** [dire des bêtises] to talk rubbish 🇬🇧, to bullshit **2.** [s'amuser] to horse ou to fool around **3.** [faire des bêtises] to mess around / *déconne pas !* stop messing about! **4.** [mal fonctionner] to be on the blink.

déconseiller [4] [dekɔseje] vt to advise against ▸ **déconseiller qqch à qqn / à qqn de faire qqch** to advise sb against sthg / against doing sthg ▸ **c'est déconseillé** it's not (to be) recommended, it's to be avoided.

déconsidérer [18] [dekɔsidere] vt to discredit. ❖ **se déconsidérer** vp *(emploi réfléchi)* to discredit o.s., to bring discredit upon o.s., to lose one's credibility.

📝 In reformed spelling (see p. 16-18), this verb is conjugated like *semer* : *il déconsidèrera, elle déconsidèrerait.*

décontaminer [3] [dekɔtamine] vt to decontaminate.

décontenancer [16] [dekɔtnɑ̃se] vt to disconcert, to discountenance *sout.* ❖ **se décontenancer** vpi to lose one's composure.

décontracté, e [dekɔ̃trakte] adj **1.** [détendu - muscle, corps] relaxed ; [- caractère] easy-going, relaxed ; [- attitude] relaxed, composed, unworried ; [- style, vêtements] casual **2.** *péj* [désinvolte] casual, off-hand.

décontracter [3] [dekɔ̃trakte] ❖ **se décontracter** vpi to relax.

décor [dekɔr] nm **1.** [décoration - d'un lieu] interior decoration, decor ; [- d'un objet] pattern, design **2.** [environs] setting **3.** CINÉ, THÉÂTRE & TV set, scenery, setting / *décor de cinéma* film 🇬🇧 ou movie 🇺🇸 set / *décor de théâtre* stage set ; [toile peinte] backdrop, backcloth. ❖ **dans le(s) décor(s)** loc adv *fam* ▸ **aller** ou **entrer** ou **valser dans le décor** [voiture, automobiliste] to go off the road.

décorateur, trice [dekɔratœr, tris] nm, f **1.** [d'intérieur] interior decorator ou designer **2.** THÉÂTRE [créateur] set designer ou decorator ; [peintre] set painter.

décoratif, ive [dekɔratif, iv] adj decorative, ornamental.

décoration [dekɔrasjɔ̃] nf **1.** [ornement] decoration *(U)* ▸ **décorations de Noël** Christmas decorations **2.** [technique] decoration, decorating **3.** [médaille] medal, decoration.

décorer [3] [dekɔre] vt **1.** [orner - intérieur, vase, assiette] to decorate ; [- table, arbre] to decorate, to adorn **2.** [personne] to decorate.

décortiquer [3] [dekɔrtike] vt **1.** [éplucher - crevette] to peel, to shell ; [- grain] to hull, to husk ; [- noix, amande] to shell **2.** [analyser] to dissect, to analyse 🇬🇧 ou analyze 🇺🇸.

découcher [3] [dekuʃe] vi to stay out all night.

découdre [86] [dekudr] vt [vêtement, couture] to undo, to unpick ; [point] to take out *(sép)* ; [bouton] to take ou to cut off *(sép)*. ❖ **se découdre** vpi [vêtement] to come unstitched ; [bouton] to come off.

découler [3] [dekule] ❖ **découler de** v + prép to follow from ; *(tournure impersonnelle)* : *il découle de cette idée que...* it follows from this idea that...

découpage [dekupaʒ] nm **1.** [partage - d'un tissu, d'un gâteau] cutting (up) ; [- d'une volaille, d'une viande] carving ; [- en tranches] slicing (up) **2.** [image - à découper] figure *(for cutting out)* ; [- découpée] cut-out (picture) **3.** POL ▸ **découpage électoral** division into constituencies 🇬🇧 ou districts 🇺🇸, apportionment 🇺🇸.

découper [3] [dekupe] vt **1.** [détacher - image] to cut out *(sép)* **2.** [partager - gâteau, papier, tissu] to cut up *(sép)* ; [- viande, volaille] to carve. ❖ **se découper sur** vp + prép to be outlined against.

décourageant, e [dekuraʒɑ̃, ɑ̃t] adj [nouvelle, situation] discouraging, disheartening, depressing.

découragement [dekuraʒmɑ̃] nm discouragement, despondency, despondence.

décourager [17] [dekuraʒe] vt [abattre] to discourage, to dishearten ▸ **décourager qqn de faire qqch** to discourage sb from doing sthg. ❖ **se décourager** vpi to get discouraged, to lose heart.

décousu, e [dekuzy] ◆ pp ⟶ **découdre.** ◆ adj **1.** COUT [défait - vêtement] undone, unstitched ; [- ourlet] undone **2.** [incohérent - discours] incoherent, disjointed ; [- conversation] desultory, disjointed ; [- style] disjointed, rambling ; [- idées] disjointed, disconnected, random.

découvert, e [dekuvɛr, ɛrt] ◆ pp ⟶ **découvrir.** ◆ adj [terrain, allée, voiture] open ; [tête, partie du corps] bare, uncovered. ❖ **découvert** nm BANQUE overdraft ▸ **avoir un découvert de** to be overdrawn by. ❖ **à découvert** loc adj BANQUE overdrawn ▸ **être à découvert** to be overdrawn, to have an overdraft. ◆ loc adv [sans dissimuler] openly.

découverte [dekuvɛrt] nf **1.** [détection] discovery, discovering ; [chose détectée] discovery, find **2.** [prise de conscience] discovery, discovering **3.** [personne de talent] discovery, find. ❖ **à la découverte de** loc prép [à la recherche de] in search of / *aller à la découverte d'un trésor* to go in search of a treasure.

découvrir [34] [dekuvrir] vt **1.** [dénicher] to discover, to find / *il m'a fait découvrir beaucoup de choses* he showed me so many things / *elle m'a fait découvrir la région* she took me around the area **2.** [solution - en réfléchissant] to discover, to work out *(sép)* ; [- subitement] to hit on ou upon *(insép)* **3.** [détecter] to discover, to detect **4.** [surprendre - voleur, intrus] to discover ; [- secret, complot] to discover, to uncover ▸ **découvrir le pot aux roses** to discover the truth **5.** [faire connaître] to uncover, to disclose, to reveal **6.** [apercevoir] to uncover, to expose ▸ / *le rideau levé, on découvrit une scène obscure* the raised curtain revealed a darkened stage **7.** [ôter ce qui couvre - fauteuil] to uncover ; [- statue] to uncover, to unveil ; [- casserole] to uncover, to take the lid off **8.** [mettre à nu - épaule, cuisse] to uncover, to bare, to expose ; [- mur, pierre] to uncover, to expose / *sa robe lui découvrait le dos* her dress revealed her back. ❖ **se découvrir** ◆ vp *(emploi réfléchi)* **1.** [se déshabiller] to dress less warmly, to take a layer ou some layers off ; [au lit] to throw off one's bedclothes **2.** [ôter son chapeau] to take off one's hat **3.** [s'exposer] to expose o.s. to attack / *un boxeur ne doit pas se découvrir* a boxer mustn't lower his guard. ◆ vpt ▸ *il s'est découvert un don pour la cuisine* he found he had a gift for cooking. ◆ vpi ▸ **ça se découvre** it's clearing up.

décrasser [3] [dekrase] vt [nettoyer - peigne, tête de lecture] to clean ; [- poêle, casserole] to scour, to clean out *(sép)* ; [- linge] to scrub ; [- enfant] to scrub (down), to clean up *(sép)*.

décrépit, e [dekrepi, it] adj decrepit.

décrépitude [dekrepityd] nf **1.** [décadence] decay **2.** [mauvais état] decrepitude, decrepit state.

décret [dekrɛ] nm DR decree, edict ▸ **décret d'application** *presidential decree affecting the application of a law.*

décréter [18] [dekrete] vt **1.** [ordonner - nomination, mobilisation] to order ; [- mesure] to decree, to enact **2.** [décider] : *le patron a décrété qu'on ne changerait rien* the boss decreed ou ordained that nothing would change / *quand il a décrété quelque chose, il ne change* *pas d'avis* when he's made up his mind about something, he doesn't change it.

🖋️ In reformed spelling (see p. 16-18), this verb is conjugated like *semer* : *il décrètera, elle décrèterait.*

décrier [10] [dekʁije] vt [collègues, entourage] to disparage ; [livre, œuvre, théorie] to criticize, to censure, to decry *sout.*

décrire [99] [dekʁiʁ] vt **1.** [représenter] to describe, to portray **2.** [former - cercle, ellipse] to describe, to draw ; [- trajectoire] to follow, to describe / *décrire des cercles dans le ciel* to fly in circles.

📋 Notez que le verbe describe n'est jamais suivi immédiatement d'un complément d'objet indirect :
Décris-moi ta nouvelle maison. Describe your new house [to me].
Pouvez-vous nous décrire la personne ? Can you describe the person [to us]?
Dans l'usage, «to us», «to me», etc., sont le plus souvent omis.

décrochement [dekʁɔʃmɑ̃] nm ARCHIT [retrait] recess **▸ faire un décrochement a)** [bâtiment] to form an angle **b)** [mur] to form ou to have a recess.

décrocher [3] [dekʁɔʃe] ◆ vt **1.** [dépendre] to unhook, to take down *(sép)* **2.** TÉLÉC **▸ décrocher le téléphone a)** [le couper] to take the phone off the hook **b)** [pour répondre] to pick up the phone / *tu décroches ?* could you answer ou get it? **3.** *fam* [obtenir] to land, to get. ◆ vi **1.** *fam* [abandonner] to opt out **2.** *fam* [se déconcentrer] to switch off **3.** *fam* [se désintoxiquer] to kick the habit. ◆ **se décrocher** vpi **▸ le tableau s'est décroché** the painting came unhooked.

décroissant, e [dekʁwasɑ̃, ɑ̃t] adj MATH decreasing.

décroître, décroitre* [94] [dekʁwatʁ] vi **1.** [diminuer - nombre, intensité, force] to decrease, to diminish ; [- eaux] to subside, to go down ; [- fièvre] to abate, to subside, to decrease ; [- bruit] to die down, to lessen, to decrease ; [- son] to fade, to die down ; [- vent] to let up, to die down ; [- intérêt, productivité] to decline, to drop off ; [- vitesse] to slacken off, to drop ; [- taux d'écoute] to drop ; [- lumière] to grow fainter, to grow dimmer, to fade ; [- influence] to decline, to wane **2.** ASTRON to wane.

décrotter [3] [dekʁɔte] vt **1.** [nettoyer] to scrape the mud off **2.** *fam* [dégrossir] to refine, to take the rough edges off.

décrue [dekʁy] nf decrease ou dropping of the water level.

décrypter [3] [dekʁipte] vt [décoder - message, texte ancien] to decode, to decipher.

déçu, e [desy] ◆ pp —→ **décevoir.** ◆ adj [personne] disappointed.

déculotter [3] [dekylɔte] ◆ **se déculotter** ◆ vp *(emploi réfléchi)* [enlever - sa culotte] to take one's pants 🇺🇸 ou underpants 🇺🇸 down ; [- son pantalon] to drop one's trousers 🇬🇧 ou pants 🇺🇸. ◆ vpi *fam* [se montrer lâche] to lose one's nerve ou bottle 🇬🇧.

déculpabiliser [3] [dekylpabilize] vt **▸ déculpabiliser qqn** to stop sb feeling guilty.

décupler [3] [dekyple] ◆ vt **1.** [rendre dix fois plus grand] to increase tenfold **2.** [augmenter] to increase greatly / *la rage décuple les forces* rage greatly increases one's strength. ◆ vi to increase tenfold.

dédaignable [dedɛɲabl] adj **▸ ce n'est pas dédaignable** it's not to be scoffed at.

dédaigner [4] [dedɛɲe] vt **1.** [mépriser - personne] to look down on *(sép)*, to despise, to scorn ; [- compliment, richesse] to despise, to disdain **2.** [refuser - honneurs, argent] to despise, to disdain, to spurn / *ne dédaignant pas la bonne chère* not being averse to good food.

dédaigneusement [dedɛɲøzmɑ̃] adv contemptuously, disdainfully.

dédaigneux, euse [dedɛɲø, øz] adj [méprisant - sourire, moue, remarque] contemptuous, scornful, disdainful.

dédain [dedɛ̃] nm contempt, scorn, disdain.

dédale [dedal] nm maze.

dedans [dədɑ̃] ◆ adv [reprenant 'dans' + substantif] inside, in it / them, etc. ; [par opposition à 'dehors'] inside, indoors ; [à partir de - prendre, boire, manger] out of, from / *il y a de l'anis dedans* there's aniseed in it / *le tiroir était ouvert, j'ai pris l'argent dedans* the drawer was open, I took the money out of ou from it **▸ en plein dedans** *fam* : *ne me parle pas de comptes, je suis en plein dedans* don't talk to me about the accounts, I'm right in the middle of them ou up to my eyeballs in them **▸ je me suis fichu dedans** *fam* I got it wrong / *le piège, il est tombé en plein dedans* he fell right into the trap. ◆ nm inside.
❖ **en dedans** loc adv : *c'est creux en dedans* it's hollow inside / *marcher les pieds en dedans* to be pigeon-toed.

dédicace [dedikas] nf **1.** [formule manuscrite - d'un ami] (signed) dedication ; [- d'une personnalité] autograph, (signed) dedication **2.** [formule imprimée] dedication **3.** RADIO dedication.

dédicacer [16] [dedikase] vt **1.** [ouvrage, photo] **▸ dédicacer un livre à qqn** to autograph ou to sign a book for sb **2.** RADIO to dedicate.

dédié, e [dedje] adj INFORM dedicated.

dédier [9] [dedje] vt [livre, symphonie] to dedicate.

dédire [103] [dediʁ] ❖ **se dédire** vpi **1.** [se rétracter - délibérément] to recant, to retract **2.** [manquer - à sa promesse] to go back on ou to fail to keep one's word ; [- à son engagement] to fail to honour one's commitment.

dédommagement [dedɔmaʒmɑ̃] nm compensation. ❖ **en dédommagement** loc adv as compensation.

dédommager [17] [dedɔmaʒe] vt **1.** [pour une perte] to compensate, to give compensation to **▸ dédommager qqn d'une perte** to compensate sb for a loss, to make good sb's loss **2.** [pour un désagrément] to compensate.

dédouaner [3] [dedwane] vt **1.** ADMIN [marchandise] to clear through customs **2.** [personne] to clear (the name of).

dédoublement [dedublɑ̃mɑ̃] nm **1.** [d'un groupe, d'une image] splitting ou dividing in two **2.** PSYCHOL **▸ dédoublement de la personnalité** dual personality.

dédoubler [3] [deduble] vt **1.** [diviser - groupe] to split ou to divide in two ; [- brin de laine] to separate into strands **2.** TRANSP **▸ dédoubler un train** to put on ou to run an extra train.

dédramatiser [3] [dedʁamatize] vt [situation] to make less dramatic.

déductible [dedyktibl] adj deductible **▸ frais déductibles des revenus** expenditure deductible against tax.

déduction [dedyksjɔ̃] nf **1.** [d'une somme] deduction **▸ déduction faite de** after deduction of, after deducting **2.** [enchaînement d'idées] deduction.

déduire [98] [deduiʁ] vt **1.** [frais, paiement] to deduct, to take off *(sép)* **2.** [conclure] to deduce, to infer.

déesse [deɛs] nf MYTH & RELIG goddess.

défaillance [defajɑ̃s] nf **1.** [évanouissement] blackout ; [malaise] feeling of faintness **▸ avoir une défaillance**

a) [s'évanouir] to faint, to have a blackout **b)** [être proche de l'évanouissement] to feel faint **2.** [faiblesse] weakness **3.** [lacune] lapse, slip **4.** [mauvais fonctionnement] failure, fault **▪ défaillance mécanique** mechanical fault **5.** MÉD **▪ défaillance cardiaque / rénale** heart / kidney failure.

défaillant, e [defajã, ãt] adj **1.** [près de s'évanouir] : *des spectateurs défaillants* spectators about to faint ou on the verge of fainting **2.** [faible - santé] declining, failing ; [- cœur, poumon] weak, failing ; [- force, mémoire] failing ; [- détermination] weakening, faltering ; [- voix] faltering **3.** [qui ne remplit pas son rôle - appareil] malfunctioning.

défaillir [47] [defajiʀ] vi *litt* **1.** [être près de s'évanouir] to be about to faint ou on the verge of fainting **2.** [forces, mémoire] to fail ; [détermination] to weaken, to falter, to flinch.

défaire [109] [defɛʀ] vt **1.** [détacher - nœud] to untie, to unfasten ; [- fermeture] to undo, to unfasten ; [- cravate] to undo, to untie **2.** [déballer - paquet] to open, to unwrap **▪ défaire ses valises** to unpack **3.** [mettre en désordre] **▪ défaire le lit a)** [pour changer les draps] to strip the bed **b)** [en jouant] to rumple the bedclothes **▪ le lit défait** [pas encore fait] the unmade bed. **❖ se défaire** vpi [se détacher - nœud] to come loose ou undone ; [- coiffure, paquet] to come undone ; [- tricot] to fray, to come undone, to unravel. **❖ se défaire de** vp + prép *sout* [employé, dettes, meuble] to get rid of, to rid o.s. of *sout* ; [idée] to put out of one's mind ; [habitude] to break.

défait, e [defɛ, ɛt] adj **1.** [accablé] **▪ être défait** to be broken **2.** [décomposé] : *il se tenait là, le visage défait* he stood there, looking distraught.

défaite [defɛt] nf MIL, POL & SPORT defeat.

défaitiste [defetist] **◆** adj defeatist. **◆** nmf **1.** MIL defeatist **2.** [pessimiste] defeatist.

défalquer [3] [defalke] vt to deduct.

défaut [defo] nm **1.** [imperfection - d'un visage, de la peau] blemish, imperfection ; [- d'un tissu, d'un appareil] defect, flaw ; [- d'un diamant, d'une porcelaine] flaw ; [- d'un projet] drawback, snag **▪ défaut d'élocution** ou **de prononciation** speech defect ou impediment **▪ défaut de fabrication** manufacturing defect **2.** [tache morale] fault, failing / *son plus gros défaut, c'est qu'il est égoïste* his biggest fault is that he's selfish **3.** [manque] **▪ défaut de** luck ou want of **▪ faire défaut** to be lacking / *si ma mémoire ne me fait pas défaut* if my memory serves me right **4. ▪ le défaut de la cuirasse** ou **de l'armure** the chink in one's ou the armour **5.** DR default **▪ faire défaut** to default. **❖ à défaut** loc adv if not, failing that / *des roses ou, à défaut, des tulipes* roses or, failing that, tulips. **❖ à défaut de** loc prép for lack ou for want of. **❖ en défaut** loc adv [en faute] **▪ être en défaut** to be at fault **▪ prendre qqn en défaut** to catch sb out, to fault sb. **❖ par défaut** loc adv **1.** [sans agir] by default **2.** DR by default **3.** INFORM by default. **❖ sans défaut** loc adj flawless.

défaveur [defavœʀ] nf discredit, disfavour 🇬🇧, disfavor 🇺🇸.

défavorable [defavɔʀabl] adj unfavourable 🇬🇧, unfavorable 🇺🇸 **▪ voir qqch d'un œil défavorable** to view sthg unfavourably.

défavorisé, e [defavɔʀize] adj **▪ régions défavorisées** depressed areas **▪ classes défavorisées** underprivileged social classes.

défavoriser [3] [defavɔʀize] vt [dans un partage] to treat unfairly ; [dans un examen, une compétition] to put at a disadvantage.

défection [defɛksjɔ̃] nf [désistement - d'un allié, d'un partisan] withdrawal of support, defection ; [- d'un touriste, d'un client] cancellation **▪ faire défection a)** [allié] to withdraw support **b)** [invité] to fail to appear.

défectueux, euse [defɛktɥø, øz] adj [appareil, produit] faulty, defective, substandard ; [loi] defective.

défendable [defãdabl] adj [justifiable - position] defensible ; [- comportement] justifiable ; [- idée] tenable, defensible.

défendeur, eresse [defãdœʀ, dʀɛs] nm, f defendant.

défendre [73] [defãdʀ] vt **1.** [interdire] to forbid **▪ défendre à qqn de faire qqch** to forbid sb to do sthg **▪ défendre qqch à qqn** : *elle lui défend les bonbons* she doesn't allow him to eat sweets **▪ c'est défendu** it's not allowed, it's forbidden **2.** MIL [pays, population] to defend ; [forteresse] to defend, to hold **3.** [donner son appui à - ami] to defend, to protect, to stand up for ; [- idée, cause] to defend, to champion, to support. **❖ se défendre ◆** vp *(emploi réfléchi)* **1.** [en luttant - physiquement] to defend o.s. **▪ se défendre de** ou **contre** to protect o.s. from ou against. **◆** vp *(emploi passif)* [être plausible] to make sense. **◆** vpi *fam* [être compétent] to get by / *il se défend bien en maths* he's quite good at maths. **❖ se défendre de** vp + prép **1.** [s'interdire de] : *se défendant de penser du mal d'elle* refusing to think ill of her ; [s'empêcher de] to refrain from **2.** [nier] : *il se défend de vouloir la quitter* he won't admit that he wants to leave her.

⚠ **Attention, to defend ne peut être employé pour traduire défendre au sens d'«interdire».**

défense [defãs] nf **1.** [interdiction] prohibition / **'défense d'entrer'** 'no admittance ou entry' / **'défense d'afficher'** 'stick 🇬🇧 ou post no bills' / **'défense de fumer'** 'no smoking' **2.** [protection] defence 🇬🇧, defense 🇺🇸 / *pour la défense des institutions* in order to defend ou to safeguard institutions ; [moyen de protection] defence 🇬🇧, defense 🇺🇸 / *la défense de l'emploi* job protection **3.** [dans un débat] défense 🇬🇧, defense 🇺🇸 **▪ prendre la défense de qqn / qqch** to stand up for ou to defend sb / sthg **4.** MIL défense 🇬🇧, defense 🇺🇸 **▪ la défense nationale** national defence **5.** PHYSIOL & PSYCHOL defence 🇬🇧, defense 🇺🇸 **▪ défenses immunitaires** immune defence system **6.** DR defence 🇬🇧, defense 🇺🇸 **7.** SPORT **▪ jouer la défense** to play a defensive game **8.** ZOOL tusk. **❖ défenses** nfpl MIL defences 🇬🇧, defenses 🇺🇸. **❖ pour ma défense, pour sa défense** loc adv in my / his, etc. defence 🇬🇧 ou defense 🇺🇸. **❖ sans défense** loc adj **1.** [animal, bébé] defenceless 🇬🇧, defenseless 🇺🇸, helpless **2.** MIL undefended.

défenseur [defãsœʀ] nmf **1.** [partisan - de la foi] defender / *les défenseurs de ces idées* advocates ou supporters of these ideas **▪ défenseur de l'environnement** conservationist **2.** SPORT defender.

défensif, ive [defãsif, iv] adj [armes, mesures] defensive. **❖ défensive** nf : *être* ou *se tenir sur la défensive* to be (on the) defensive.

déféquer [18] [defeke] vi to defecate.

✒ In reformed spelling (see p. 16-18), this verb is conjugated like *semer : il défèquera, elle défèquerait*.

déférence [defeʀãs] nf respect, deference **▪ avec déférence** deferentially **▪ par déférence pour** in deference to.

déférer [18] [defeʀe] vt [affaire] to refer to a court ; [accusé] to bring before a court **▪ déférer qqn à la justice** to hand sb over to the law.

✒ In reformed spelling (see p. 16-18), this verb is conjugated like *semer : il déférera, elle déférerait*.

déferlement [defɛʀləmã] nm **1.** [de vagues] breaking **2.** [invasion] **▪ déferlement de a)** [soudain] flood of **b)** [continu] stream of **3.** [accès] **▪ un déferlement d'émotion** a surge ou wave of emotion.

déferler [3] [defɛʀle] vi **1.** [vague] to break **2.** [se répandre] to rush into / *ils déferlaient dans la rue* they flooded into the streets **3.** [fuser - émotion, applaudissements] to erupt.

défi [defi] nm **1.** [appel provocateur] challenge ▶ **jeter** ou **lancer un défi à qqn** to throw down the gauntlet to sb, to challenge sb ▶ **relever un défi** to take up the gauntlet ou a challenge ; [attitude provocatrice] defiance **2.** [remise en question] : *c'est un défi au bon sens* it defies common sense. ❖ **au défi** loc adv ▶ **mettre qqn au défi (de faire)** to challenge sb (to do).

défiance [defjɑ̃s] nf [méfiance] mistrust, distrust.

déficience [defisjɑ̃s] nf MÉD deficiency.

déficient, e [defisjɑ̃, ɑ̃t] adj **1.** MÉD deficient **2.** [insuffisant - théorie] weak, feeble.

déficit [defisit] nm **1.** ÉCON & FIN deficit / *société en déficit* company in deficit **2.** MÉD ▶ **déficit immunitaire** immunodeficiency **3.** [manque] gap, lack.

déficitaire [defisitɛʀ] adj **1.** ÉCON & FIN in deficit **2.** [insuffisant - production, récolte] poor.

défier [9] [defje] vt **1.** [dans un duel, un jeu] to challenge / *je te défie de trouver moins cher* I defy you to find a better price **2.** [affronter - danger] to defy, to brave ▶ **prix / qualité défiant toute concurrence** absolutely unbeatable prices / quality. ❖ **se défier de** vp + prép *litt* to mistrust, to distrust.

défigurer [3] [defigyʀe] vt **1.** [personne] to disfigure **2.** [ville, environnement] to blight, to ruin **3.** [caricaturer - vérité, faits] to distort.

défilé [defile] nm **1.** [procession - pour une fête] procession ; [- de militaires] march, parade ; [- de manifestants] march ▶ **un défilé de mode** a fashion show **2.** [multitude - d'invités, de pensées] stream ; [- de souvenirs] string ; [- d'images] succession **3.** GÉOGR defile, narrow pass.

défiler [3] [defile] vi **1.** [marcher en file - militaires] to march, to parade ; [- pour manifester] to march ▶ **défiler devant...** a) [gén] to file past b) [troupes, manifestants] to march past **2.** [être nombreux] : *les journalistes ont défilé au ministère toute la journée* the journalists were in and out of the ministry all day **3.** [se dérouler - bande magnétique] to unwind ; [- texte informatique] to scroll ; [- souvenirs, publicité] to stream past ▶ **faire défiler** [données sur écran] to scroll. ❖ **se défiler** vpi *fam* [esquiver une responsabilité] : *n'essaie pas de te défiler* don't try to get out of it.

défini, e [defini] adj **1.** [qui a une définition] defined ; [précis] precise **2.** GRAM ▶ **article défini** definite article.

définir [32] [definiʀ] vt **1.** [donner la définition de] to define **2.** [décrire - sensation] to define, to describe ; [- personne] to describe, to portray **3.** [circonscrire - objectif, politique, condition] to define.

définitif, ive [definitif, iv] adj [irrévocable - décision] final ; [- acceptation] definitive ▶ **à titre définitif** permanently / **'soldes avant fermeture définitive'** 'closing-down sale'. ❖ **en définitive** loc adv **1.** [somme toute] finally, when all's said and done, in the final analysis **2.** [après tout] after all.

définition [definisjɔ̃] nf **1.** [d'une idée, d'un mot] definition **2.** [de mots croisés] clue **3.** PHOT & TÉLÉC definition ▶ **la haute définition** high definition.

définitivement [definitivmɑ̃] adv for good.

> ⚠ **Definitely** a le sens de « sans aucun doute » et ne peut être employé pour traduire *définitivement*.

déflagration [deflagʀasjɔ̃] nf [explosion] explosion ; [combustion] deflagration.

déflation [deflasjɔ̃] nf FIN & GÉOL deflation.

déflationniste [deflasjɔnist] adj [principe] deflationist ; [mesure] deflationary.

déflecteur [deflɛktœʀ] nm AUTO quarter-light ⓊⓀ, vent ⓊⓈ.

déflocage [deflɔkaʒ] nm CONSTR asbestos removal, insulation removal.

déflorer [3] [deflɔʀe] vt **1.** [fille] to deflower **2.** *litt* [sujet] to corrupt, to spoil.

défoncé, e [defɔ̃se] adj **1.** [cabossé - lit, sofa] battered ; [- chemin] rutted **2.** *tfam* [drogué] stoned, high / *des mecs défoncés* guys on drugs.

défoncer [16] [defɔ̃se] vt [démolir - porte] to smash in (sép), to knock down (sép) ; [- mur] to smash ou to knock down (sép), to demolish ; [- chaussée] to break up (sép) ; [- caisse, tonneau] to smash ou to stave in (sép). ❖ **se défoncer** vpi **1.** *fam* [se démener - au travail] to work flat out ; [- en se distrayant] to have a wild time **2.** *tfam* [se droguer] to get high.

déformant, e [defɔʀmɑ̃, ɑ̃t] adj distorting.

déformation [defɔʀmasjɔ̃] nf [travestissement - d'une pensée, de la réalité] distortion, misrepresentation ; [- d'une image] distortion, warping ▶ **déformation professionnelle** : *elle pose toujours des questions, c'est une déformation professionnelle* she's always asking questions because she's used to doing it in her job.

déformer [3] [defɔʀme] vt **1.** [changer la forme de - planche] to warp ; [- barre] to bend (out of shape) ; [- parechocs] to knock out of shape, to buckle ; [- chaussure, pantalon] to put out of shape, to ruin the shape of **2.** [transformer - corps] to deform ; [- visage, voix] to distort **3.** [fausser - réalité, pensée] to distort, to misrepresent ; [- image] to distort ; [- goût] to warp ; [- paroles] to misquote. ❖ **se déformer** vpi [vêtement] to become shapeless, to go out of ou to lose its shape ; [planche] to become warped ; [barre] to become bent.

défoulement [defulmɑ̃] nm release.

défouler [3] [defule] ❖ **se défouler** vpi to let steam off, to unwind ▶ **se défouler sur qqn / qqch** to take it out on sb / sthg.

défouloir [defulwaʀ] nm *fam* way of letting off steam / *sortir en boîte, c'est son défouloir* going out clubbing is his way of letting off steam.

défragmenter [3] [defʀagmɑ̃te] vt INFORM to defragment, to defrag *fam*.

défraîchi, e [defʀeʃi] adj : *des articles défraîchis* shopsoiled articles / *les fleurs sont défraîchies* the flowers are past their best.

défrayer [11] [defʀeje] vt **1.** [indemniser] ▶ **défrayer qqn de** to meet sb's expenses for **2.** ⟨EXPR⟩ **défrayer la chronique** to be the talk of the town, to be widely talked about.

défricher [3] [defʀiʃe] vt **1.** [nettoyer - terrain] to clear / *défricher le terrain avant de négocier* *fig* to clear the way for negotiations **2.** [préparer - texte] to have a first look at ; [- enquête] to do the spadework for.

défrisage [3] [defʀizaj] nm straightening.

défrisant [3] [defʀizɑ̃] nm hair straightener.

défriser [3] [defʀize] vt **1.** [cheveux, moustache] to straighten out (sép), to take the curl ou curls out of **2.** *fam* [contrarier] to bug.

défroisser [3] [defʀwase] vt to smooth out (sép), to take the creases out of.

défunt, e [defœ̃, œ̃t] *litt* ◆ adj [décédé - parent, mari] late. ◆ nm, f deceased person ▶ **le défunt** the deceased.

dégagé, e [degaʒe] adj **1.** [vue] open ; [pièce, passage] cleared **2.** [épaules] bare / *je la préfère avec le front dégagé* I prefer her with her hair back **3.** [désinvolte - air, ton] casual **4.** MÉTÉOR clear, cloudless.

dégagement [degaʒmã] nm **1.** [émanation - d'odeur] emanation ; [- de chaleur] release, emission, emanation **2.** [espace - dans une maison] passage, hall ; [- dans une ville] open space ; [- dans un bois] clearing **3.** SPORT [d'un ballon] clearance.

dégager [17] [degaʒe] vt **1.** [sortir] to free **2.** [enlever - arbres tombés, ordures] to remove, to clear **3.** [désencombrer - couloir, table, salle] to clear (out) ; [- sinus] to clear, to unblock ; [- poitrine, gorge] to clear ; [- ouverture, chemin] to open **4.** FIN [crédit] to release ▸ **dégager des bénéfices** to make a profit **5.** [libérer] ▸ **dégager sa responsabilité** to deny responsibility **6.** [émettre - odeur] to give off *(insép.)*, to emit ; [- gaz] to release, to emit **7.** [manifester - quiétude] to radiate **8.** [extraire - règle, principe] to draw ; [- vérité] to draw, to bring out *(sép.)*, to extract **9.** SPORT [ballon] to clear ; *(en usage absolu)* ▸ **dégager en touche** to put ou kick the ball into touch **10.** *(en usage absolu)* fam [partir] ▸ **dégage !** clear off!, get lost! ◈ **se dégager** ◆ vp *(emploi passif)* [conclusion] to be drawn ; [vérité] to emerge, to come out. ◆ vp *(emploi réfléchi)* **1.** [s'extraire] ▸ **se dégager d'un piège** to free o.s. from a trap **2.** [se libérer - d'un engagement] : *se dégager d'une affaire / d'une association* to drop out of a deal / an association / *se dégager d'une obligation* to free o.s. from an obligation. ◆ vpi **1.** [se vider - route] to clear ; [- ciel] to clear ; [- sinus] to become unblocked, to clear **2.** [émaner - odeur, gaz, fumée] to emanate, to be given off ; [se manifester - quiétude] to emanate, to radiate.

dégaine [degɛn] nf fam [démarche] (peculiar) gait ; [aspect ridicule] (gawky) look / *tu parles d'une dégaine !* just look at that!

dégainer [4] [degene] vt ARM [épée] to unsheathe, to draw ; [revolver] to draw ; *(en usage absolu)* : *avant que le gangster ait pu dégainer* before the gangster could draw his gun.

dégarnir [32] [degaʀniʀ] ◈ **se dégarnir** vpi **1.** [se vider - boîte, collection, rayonnage] to become depleted ; [- groupe] to become depleted, to thin out **2.** [devenir chauve] to go bald, to start losing one's hair **3.** [arbre] to lose its leaves ; [forêt] to become depleted ou thinner.

dégât [dega] nm damage *(U)* / *faire des dégâts* to cause damage.

dégazer [3] [degaze] vi [pétrolier] to degas.

dégel [deʒɛl] nm **1.** MÉTÉOR thaw **2.** [après un conflit] thaw.

dégeler [25] [deʒle] ◆ vt **1.** fam [mettre à l'aise] to thaw (out), to relax **2.** [améliorer - relations diplomatiques] to thaw. ◆ vi **1.** [se réchauffer - banquise, étang] to thaw **2.** [décongeler] to defrost. ◈ **se dégeler** vpi **1.** fam [être moins timide] to thaw (out), to relax **2.** [s'améliorer - relations] to improve.

dégénéré, e [deʒeneʀe] adj & nm, f degenerate.

dégénérer [18] [deʒeneʀe] vi **1.** [perdre ses qualités - race, plante] to degenerate **2.** [s'aggraver - situation] to worsen, to deteriorate ; [- discussion] to get out of hand ; MÉD [tumeur] to become malignant **3.** [se changer] ▸ **dégénérer en** to degenerate into.

🖉 In reformed spelling (see p. 16-18), this verb is conjugated like *semer* : *il dégénèrera, elle dégénèrerait.*

dégénérescence [deʒeneʀesãs] nf **1.** BIOL degeneration **2.** litt [déclin] degeneration, becoming degenerate.

dégingandé, e [deʒɛ̃gãde] adj gangling, lanky.

dégivrer [3] [deʒivʀe] vt [congélateur] to defrost ; [surface] to de-ice.

déglinguer [3] [deglɛ̃ge] vt fam [mécanisme] to break, to bust. ◈ **se déglinguer** vpi fam **1.** [ne plus fonctionner] to be bust ; [mal fonctionner] to go on the blink ; [se détacher] to come ou to work loose **2.** [santé] to get worse ; [poumons, reins] to go to pieces.

déglutir [32] [deglytiʀ] vi to swallow, to gulp.

dégobiller [3] [degɔbije] fam ◆ vt to throw up *(sép.)*. ◆ vi to throw up.

dégonflé, e [degɔ̃fle] ◆ adj **1.** [ballon] deflated ; [pneu] flat **2.** fam [lâche] chicken fam *(modif)*. ◆ nm, f fam chicken.

dégonfler [3] [degɔ̃fle] vt **1.** [ballon, bouée, pneu] to deflate, to let air out of **2.** MÉD [jambes, doigt] to bring down ou to reduce the swelling in. ◈ **se dégonfler** vpi **1.** [ballon] to go down, to deflate **2.** MÉD [jambes, doigt] to become less swollen / *ma cheville se dégonfle* the swelling in my ankle's going down **3.** fam [perdre courage] to chicken ou to bottle 🇬🇧 out.

dégorger [17] [degɔʀʒe] ◆ vt [déverser] to disgorge. ◆ vi CULIN [ris de veau, cervelle] to soak (in cold water) ; [concombre] to drain (having been sprinkled with salt) ▸ **faire dégorger a)** [ris de veau, cervelle] to (leave to) soak **b)** [concombre] to drain of water (by sprinkling with salt) **c)** [escargot] to clean (by salting and starvation).

dégoter [3], **dégotter** [3] [degɔte] vt fam [objet rare] to unearth ; [idée originale] to hit on *(insép.)*.

dégouliner [3] [deguline] vi [peinture, sauce] to drip ; [larmes, sang] to trickle down / *son maquillage dégoulinait* her make-up was running.

dégourdi, e [deguʀdi] fam adj ▸ **être dégourdi** to be smart ou on the ball.

dégourdir [32] [deguʀdiʀ] vt [ranimer - membres] to bring the circulation back to. ◈ **se dégourdir** vpt [remuer] ▸ **se dégourdir les jambes** to stretch one's legs.

dégoût, dégout* [degu] nm [aversion] disgust, distaste ▸ **éprouver du dégoût pour qqch / qqn** to have an aversion to sthg / sb.

dégoûtant, e, dégoutant*, e [degutã, ãt] ◆ adj [sale] disgusting, disgustingly dirty ; [salace - film, remarque] disgusting, dirty ▸ **c'est dégoûtant !** [injuste] it's disgusting ou awful! ◆ nm, f **1.** [personne sale] : *petit dégoûtant !* you little pig! **2.** [vicieux] : *vieux dégoûtant !* you dirty old man! **3.** fam [personne injuste] : *quelle dégoûtante !* that wretched woman! tfam / *quel dégoûtant !* the swine!

dégoûté, e, dégouté*, e [degute] ◆ adj **1.** [écœuré] repulsed, disgusted / *il n'est pas dégoûté !* hum he's not very fussy! **2.** [indigné] outraged, revolted, disgusted. ◆ nm, f ▸ **faire le dégoûté** to be fussy, to make a fuss.

dégoûter, dégouter* [3] [degute] vt **1.** [écœurer] to disgust, to repel, to be repugnant to **2.** [indigner] to disgust, to outrage, to be (morally) repugnant to **3.** [lasser] to put off ▸ **dégoûter qqn de qqch** to put sb off sthg / *c'est à vous dégoûter d'être serviable* it's enough to put you (right) off being helpful.

dégoutter [3] [degute] vi to drip / *son front dégoutte de sueur* his forehead is dripping with sweat, sweat is dripping off his forehead.

dégradant, e [degʀadã, ãt] adj degrading.

dégradation [degʀadasjɔ̃] nf **1.** [destruction - d'un objet] wear and tear ; [- d'un bâtiment] dilapidation **2.** [détérioration - de rapports, d'une situation] deterioration, worsening ; [- de l'environnement] degradation **3.** [avilissement] degradation.

dégradé [degʀade] nm [technique] shading off ; [résultat] gradation ▸ **un dégradé de verts** greens shading off into each other.

dégrader [3] [degʀade] vt **1.** [abîmer] to damage **2.** [avilir] to degrade **3.** [couleurs] to shade (into one another) ; [lumières] to reduce gradually. ❖ **se dégrader** vpi [meuble, bâtiment] to deteriorate ; [relation] to deteriorate ; [santé] to decline ; [langage] to deteriorate, to become debased ; [temps] to get worse.

dégrafer [3] [degʀafe] vt [papiers] to unstaple ; [col, robe] to undo, to unfasten ; [ceinture] to undo ; [bracelet] to unclasp, to unhook / *tu veux que je te dégrafe ?* *fam* shall I undo your dress? ❖ **se dégrafer** vpi [jupe] to come undone ; [papiers] to come unstapled ; [collier] to come unhooked.

dégraissage [degʀesaʒ] nm *fam* [diminution du personnel] shedding staff.

dégraisser [4] [degʀese] vt *fam* [entreprise] to make cutbacks in ; [personnel] to cut back *(sép)*, to shed.

degré [dəgʀe] nm **1.** [échelon - d'une hiérarchie] degree, grade ; [- d'un développement] stage ▸ **second degré**: *une remarque à prendre au second degré* a remark not to be taken at face value **2.** [point] degree / *compréhensif jusqu'à un certain degré* understanding up to a point ou to a degree **3.** [unité] degree / *du gin à 47,5 degrés* 83° proof gin, 47,5 degree gin *(on the Gay-Lussac scale)* ▸ **degré alcoolique** ou **d'alcool** alcohol content ▸ **degré Baumé / Celsius / Fahrenheit** degree Baumé / Celsius / Fahrenheit **4.** ASTRON, GÉOM & MATH degree ▸ **équation du premier / second degré** equation of the first / second degree **5.** [de parenté] degree. ❖ **par degrés** loc adv by ou in degrees, gradually.

dégressif, ive [degʀesif, iv] adj [tarif] on a sliding scale ; [impôt] on a sliding scale according to income.

dégrèvement [degʀɛvmã] nm FIN ▸ **dégrèvement fiscal a)** [d'une entreprise] tax relief **b)** [d'un produit] reduction of tax ou duty.

dégriffé, e [degʀife] adj reduced *(and with the designer label removed)* ▸ **robe dégriffée** designer dress with the label removed sold at a reduced price. ❖ **dégriffé** nm reduced (and unlabelled) designer item.

dégringolade [degʀɛ̃gɔlad] nf **1.** [chute] tumbling (down) **2.** [baisse - des prix] slump ; [- des cours] collapse ; [- d'une réputation] plunge / *l'industrie est en pleine dégringolade* the industry is in the middle of a slump.

dégringoler [3] [degʀɛ̃gɔle] ❖ vi **1.** [chuter] to tumble down ; [bruyamment] to crash down **2.** [baisser - prix] to slump, to tumble ; [- réputation] to plunge / *ça a fait dégringoler les prix* it sent prices plummeting. ❖ vt ▸ **dégringoler l'escalier a)** [courir] to run ou to race down the stairs **b)** [tomber] to tumble down the stairs.

dégriser [3] [degʀize] vt [désillusionner] to bring back down to earth, to sober up *(sép)* ; [après l'ivresse] to sober up *(sép)*. ❖ **se dégriser** vpi to sober up.

dégrossir [32] [degʀosiʀ] vt **1.** [apprenti, débutant] to polish, to smooth the rough edges of / *des jeunes gens mal dégrossis* uncouth young men **2.** [théorie, question] to do the groundwork on ; [texte du programme] to have a first look at **3.** [bloc de pierre, de bois] to rough-hew.

déguenillé, e [degnije] adj ragged, tattered.

déguerpir [32] [degɛʀpiʀ] vi to run away, to decamp.

dégueulasse [degœlas] ❖ adj *tfam* **1.** [sale] disgusting, filthy, yucky **2.** [injuste] disgusting, lousy **3.** [vicieux] disgusting, filthy **4.** [sans valeur] lousy, crappy / *c'est pas dégueulasse comme cadeau* it's a pretty nice present, it's not a bad present. ❖ nmf *tfam* **1.** [personne sale] filthy pig

2. [pervers] : *un gros dégueulasse* a filthy lecher **3.** [personne immorale - homme] swine ; [- femme] bitch.

dégueuler [5] [degœle] ❖ vi *tfam* to throw up, to puke. ❖ vt *tfam* to throw up *(sép)*, to puke up *(sép)*.

déguisé, e [degize] adj **1.** [pour une fête] in fancy dress ; [pour duper] in disguise, disguised **2.** [changé - voix] disguised **3.** [caché - intention] disguised, masked, veiled ; [- agressivité] veiled.

déguisement [degizmã] nm [pour une fête] fancy dress, costume ; [pour duper] disguise.

déguiser [3] [degize] vt **1.** [pour une fête] to dress up *(sép)* ▸ **déguisé en**: *déguisé en pirate* dressed (up) as a pirate, wearing a pirate costume ; [pour duper] to disguise **2.** [changer - voix] to disguise. ❖ **se déguiser** vp *(emploi réfléchi)* [pour une fête] to dress up ; [pour duper] to put on a disguise, to disguise o.s.

dégustation [degystasjɔ̃] nf **1.** [par un convive] tasting *(U)* ; [par un dégustateur] tasting, sampling **2.** [dans une cave] (free) tasting / *dégustation (de vins)* wine-tasting **3.** [à un étalage, dans un restaurant] tasting *(U)* / '**dégustation de fruits de mer à toute heure**' 'seafood served all day'.

déguster [3] [degyste] ❖ vt **1.** [manger, boire - suj : convive] to taste ; [- suj : dégustateur professionnel] to taste, to sample **2.** [écouter, lire, regarder] to savour. ❖ vi *fam* [recevoir des coups] to get a bashing ; [être mal traité] to have a rough time ; [souffrir] to be in agony, to go through hell.

déhancher [3] [deɑ̃ʃe] ❖ **se déhancher** vpi **1.** [en marchant] to sway (one's hips) **2.** [sans bouger] to stand with one's weight on one leg.

dehors[1] [dəɔʀ] ❖ nm **1.** [surface extérieure d'une boîte, d'un bâtiment] outside **2.** [plein air] outside / *les bruits du dehors* the noises from outside **3.** [étranger] : *menace venue du dehors* threat from abroad. ❖ nmpl [apparences] appearances ▸ **sous des dehors égoïstes** beneath a selfish exterior.

dehors[2] [dəɔʀ] ❖ adv [à l'extérieur] outside ; [en plein air] outside, outdoors, out of doors ; [hors de chez soi] out ▸ **mettre qqn dehors a)** *fam* to kick sb out **b)** [renvoyer] to sack sb. ❖ **en dehors** loc adv **1.** [à l'extérieur] outside **2.** [vers l'extérieur] : *avoir* ou *marcher les pieds en dehors* to walk with one's feet turned out. ❖ **en dehors de** loc prép **1.** [excepté] apart from **2.** [à l'écart de] : *reste en dehors de leur dispute* don't get involved in ou stay out of their quarrel.

déjà [deʒa] adv **1.** [dès maintenant, dès lors] already / *il doit être déjà loin* he must be far away by now / *il savait déjà lire à l'âge de 4 ans* he already knew how to read at the age of 4 **2.** [précédemment] : *je vous l'ai déjà dit* I've told you already / *tu l'as déjà vu sur scène ?* have you ever seen him on stage? **3.** [emploi expressif] : *il est d'accord sur le principe, c'est déjà beaucoup* he's agreed on the principle, that's something / *ce n'est déjà pas si mal* you could do worse ▸ **c'est déjà quelque chose** it's better than nothing / *on a perdu une valise, mais ni l'argent ni les passeports, c'est déjà ça !* we lost a case, but not our money or passports, which is something at least! **4.** *fam* [pour réitérer une question] again / *elle s'appelle comment déjà ?* what did you say her name was?, what's she called again?

déjanté, e [deʒɑ̃te] adj *fam* : *il est complètement déjanté* he's off his trolley 🇬🇧 *tfam* ou out of his tree.

déjà-vu [deʒavy] nm inv **1.** [banalité] commonplace / *c'est du déjà-vu comme idée* that idea's a bit banal **2.** [sensation] ▸ **(sensation** ou **impression de) déjà-vu** (feeling of) déjà-vu.

déjeuner[1] [deʒœne] vi [le midi] to (have) lunch / *invite-le à déjeuner* invite him for ou to lunch ▸ **j'ai déjeuné**

d'une salade I had a salad for lunch / *j'ai fait déjeuner les enfants plus tôt* I gave the children an early lunch.

déjeuner² [deʒœne] nm **1.** [repas de la mi-journée] lunch, luncheon *sout* ▸ **prendre son déjeuner** to have lunch / *un déjeuner d'affaires* a business lunch **2.** [tasse et soucoupe] (large) breakfast cup and saucer.

déjouer [6] [deʒwe] vt [vigilance] to evade, to elude ; [complot, machination] to thwart, to foil ; [plan] to thwart, to frustrate ; [feinte] to outsmart.

delà [dəla] adv ⟶ **deçà**.

délabré, e [delabʀe] adj [en ruine - maison, mur] dilapidated, crumbling.

délabrement [delabʀəmɑ̃] nm **1.** [d'un bâtiment] disrepair, ruin, dilapidation **2.** [d'un esprit, d'un corps] deterioration / *les patients étaient dans un état de délabrement total* the patients were in a state of total neglect.

délacer [16] [delase] vt [soulier, botte] to undo (the laces of) ; [corset] to unlace.

délai [dele] nm **1.** [répit] extension (of time) ▸ **délai de réflexion a)** [avant réponse] time to think **b)** [avant de signer un contrat] cooling-off period **2.** [temps fixé] time limit / *quel est le délai à respecter ?* what is the deadline? ▸ **respecter** ou **tenir les délais** to meet the deadline ▸ **délai de livraison** delivery time ▸ **délai de paiement** repayment period **3.** [période d'attente] waiting period / *il faut un délai de trois jours avant que votre compte soit crédité* the cheque will be credited to your account after a period of three working days. ❖ **dans les délais** loc adv within the (prescribed ou allotted) time limit, on time. ❖ **dans les meilleurs délais, dans les plus brefs délais** loc adv in the shortest possible time, as soon as possible / *j'y serai dans les plus brefs délais* I'll be there very shortly. ❖ **dans un délai de** loc prép within (a period of). ❖ **sans délai** loc adv without delay, immediately, forthwith.

⚠ **Delay** signifie « retard » ; il est rarement employé pour traduire le mot **délai**.

délaisser [4] [delese] vt **1.** [quitter - époux] to desert ; [- ami] to neglect **2.** [ne plus exercer - temporairement] to neglect ; [- définitivement] to give up *(sép)*.

délassement [delasmɑ̃] nm [état] relaxation, rest.

délasser [3] [delase] vt [physiquement] to relax, to refresh, to soothe ; [mentalement] to relax, to soothe. ❖ **se délasser** vpi to relax.

délateur, trice [delatœʀ, tʀis] nm, f *sout & péj* informer *péj*.

délation [delasjɔ̃] nf *sout* denouncing, informing.

délavé, e [delave] adj [tissu] faded ; [aquarelle] toned down ; [terres] waterlogged.

délayage [deleja] nm **1.** [mélange - de farine, de poudre] mixing **2.** *fig & péj* [d'un exposé] toning down ; [d'une idée] watering down / *faire du délayage* to waffle 🇬🇧, to spout off 🇺🇸.

délayer [11] [deleje] vt **1.** [diluer - poudre] to mix **2.** *péj* [une idée, un discours] to pad ou to spin out *(sép)* ; [un exposé] to thin ou to water down *(sép)*.

Delco® [dɛlko] nm AUTO distributor.

délectation [delɛktasjɔ̃] nf *litt* delight, delectation *litt*.

délecter [4] [delɛkte] ❖ **se délecter** vpi *litt* ▸ **se délecter à qqch / à faire qqch** to take great delight in sthg / in doing sthg.

délégation [delegasjɔ̃] nf **1.** [groupe envoyé] delegation **2.** [fait de mandater] delegation ▸ **délégation de pouvoirs** delegation of powers.

délégué, e [delege] nm, f delegate ▸ **délégué de classe** *pupil elected to represent his or her class at "conseils de classe"* ; ≃ class rep ▸ **délégué des parents** parents' representative ▸ **délégué du personnel** staff representative ▸ **délégué syndical** union representative, shop steward.

déléguer [18] [delege] vt **1.** [envoyer - groupe, personne] to delegate **2.** [transmettre - pouvoir] to delegate.

✑ In reformed spelling (see p. 16-18), this verb is conjugated like *semer : il délèguera, elle délèguerait*.

délestage [delɛsta] nm TRANSP relief / *itinéraire de délestage* relief route.

délester [3] [delɛste] vt **1.** AÉRON & NAUT to unballast **2.** TRANSP to relieve traffic congestion on, to set up a diversion on.

délibération [deliberasjɔ̃] nf **1.** [discussion] deliberation ▸ **après délibération du jury** after due deliberation by the jury **2.** [réflexion] deliberation, thinking.

délibéré, e [delibere] adj [intentionné] deliberate, wilful. ❖ **délibéré** nm deliberation of the court ▸ **mettre en délibéré** to adjourn for further deliberation.

délibérément [deliberemɑ̃] adv **1.** [intentionnellement] deliberately, intentionally, wilfully **2.** [après réflexion] after thinking it over (long and hard), after due consideration.

délibérer [18] [delibeʀe] vi [discuter] to deliberate.

✑ In reformed spelling (see p. 16-18), this verb is conjugated like *semer : il délibèrera, elle délibèrerait*.

délicat, e [delika, at] ◆ adj **1.** [fragile - tissu] delicate ; [- peau] sensitive ; [- santé] delicate, frail ; [- intestin, estomac] sensitive, delicate ; [- enfant, plante] fragile **2.** [sensible - palais] discerning **3.** [subtil - forme, aquarelle, nuance, travail] delicate, fine ; [- doigts, traits] delicate, dainty ; [- mets] dainty, delicate ; [- saveur, odeur] delicate **4.** [difficile - situation] delicate, awkward, tricky ; [- opération chirurgicale, problème] difficult, tricky ; [- question] delicate, sensitive ▸ **c'est délicat** it's rather delicate ou awkward **5.** [courtois] thoughtful, considerate **6.** [difficile à contenter] fussy, particular **7.** [scrupuleux - conscience, procédé] scrupulous. ◆ nm, f ▸ **faire le délicat a)** to be fussy **b)** [devant le sang, la malhonnêteté] to be squeamish.

délicatement [delikatmɑ̃] adv **1.** [sans brusquerie - poser, toucher] delicately, gently ; [- travailler, orner] dacately, daintily **2.** [agréablement et subtilement - peindre, écrire] delicately, finely ; [- parfumer] delicately, subtly **3.** [avec tact] delicately, tactfully.

délicatesse [delikatɛs] nf **1.** [subtilité - d'une saveur, d'un coloris] delicacy, subtlety ; [- d'une dentelle, d'un geste, d'un visage] delicacy, fineness, daintiness ; [- d'un travail artisanal] delicacy ; [- d'une mélodie] subtlety **2.** [tact] delicacy, tact, tactfulness / *il n'en a rien dit, par délicatesse* he kept quiet out of tact, he tactfully said nothing **3.** [difficulté - d'une situation, d'une opération] delicacy, sensitiveness, trickiness.

délice [delis] nm [source de plaisir] delight ▸ **c'est un délice a)** [mets, odeur] it's delicious **b)** [d'être au soleil, de nager] it's sheer delight.

délicieusement [delisjøzmɑ̃] adv [agréablement] deliciously, delightfully, exquisitely.

délicieux, euse [delisjø, øz] adj **1.** [qui procure du plaisir - repas, parfum, sensation] delicious ; [- lieu, promenade, chapeau] lovely, delightful **2.** [qui charme - femme, geste] lovely, delightful.

délié, e [delje] adj [agile - esprit] sharp ; [- doigt] nimble, agile / *avoir la langue déliée* to be chatty.

délier [9] [delje] vt [dénouer -ruban, mains] to untie ; [-gerbe, bouquet] to undo. ❖ **se délier** vpi [langue] to loosen / *après quelques verres, les langues se délient* a few drinks help to loosen people's tongues.

délimitation [delimitasjɔ̃] nf **1.** [fait de circonscrire -un terrain] demarcation, delimitation ; [-un sujet, un rôle] defining, delineating, delimitation **2.** [limites] delimitation.

délimiter [3] [delimite] vt [espace, frontière] to demarcate, to delimit, to circumscribe ; [sujet] to define, to delimit.

délinquance [delɛ̃kɑ̃s] nf ▸ **la délinquance** criminality ▸ **la délinquance juvénile** juvenile delinquency ▸ **la petite délinquance** petty crime.

délinquant, e [delɛ̃kɑ̃, ɑ̃t] ❖ adj delinquent. ❖ nm, f offender ▸ **jeune délinquant, délinquant juvénile** juvenile delinquent.

délirant, e [deliʀɑ̃, ɑ̃t] adj *fam* [insensé -accueil, foule] frenzied, tumultuous ; [-imagination] frenzied, wild ; [-luxe, prix] unbelievable, incredible / *c'est délirant de travailler dans de telles conditions* working in such conditions is sheer madness ou lunacy.

délire [deliʀ] nm **1.** MÉD delirium, delirious state ▸ **délire de persécution** persecution mania **2.** *fam* EXPR. c'est le ou du délire : *partout où il se produit, c'est le ou du délire* wherever he performs, audiences go wild ou crazy / *ce n'est plus de la mise en scène, c'est du délire !* it's no longer stage production, it's sheer madness! ❖ **en délire** loc adj delirious, ecstatic.

délirer [3] [deliʀe] vi [malade] to be delirious, to rave ▸ **tu délires !** *fig* you're out of your mind!

délit [deli] nm **1.** DR [infraction] crime, offence UK, offense US, misdemeanor US ▸ **délit de faciès** : *il s'est fait arrêter pour délit de faciès* they arrested him because of the colour of his skin ▸ **délit de fuite** failure to stop after causing a road accident / *être incarcéré pour délit d'opinion* to be put in prison because of one's beliefs **2.** BOURSE ▸ **délit d'initié** insider trading ou dealing.

délivrance [delivʀɑ̃s] nf **1.** *litt* [libération -d'une ville] liberation, deliverance ; [-d'un captif] release **2.** [soulagement] relief **3.** [d'un visa, d'un certificat] issue.

délivrer [3] [delivʀe] vt **1.** [libérer -prisonnier] to release, to (set) free **2.** [soulager] to relieve / *ainsi délivré de ses incertitudes, il décida de...* thus freed from doubt, he decided to... **3.** [visa, titre] to issue ; [ordonnance, autorisation] to give, to issue **4.** [faire parvenir -paquet, courrier] to deliver ; [-signal] to put out *(sép).*

délocalisation [delɔkalizasjɔ̃] nf relocation.

délocaliser [3] [delɔkalize] vt to relocate.

déloger [17] [delɔʒe] vt [congédier -locataire] to throw ou to turn out *(sép)*, to oust.

déloyal, e, aux [delwajal, o] adj **1.** [infidèle -ami] disloyal, unfaithful, untrue *litt* **2.** [malhonnête -concurrence] unfair ; [-méthode] dishonest, underhand ; [-coup] foul, below-the-belt.

delta [dɛlta] (*pl* **deltas**) nm GÉOGR ▸ **delta (littoral)** delta.

deltaplane [dɛltaplan] nm **1.** [véhicule] hang-glider **2.** [activité] hang-gliding / *faire du deltaplane* to go hang-gliding.

déluge [delyʒ] nm **1.** [averse] downpour, deluge **2.** [abondance -de paroles, de larmes, de plaintes] flood, deluge ; [-de coups] shower.

déluré, e [delyʀe] adj **1.** [malin -enfant, air] quick, sharp, resourceful **2.** *péj* [effronté -fille] forward, brazen.

démago [demago] adj & nmf *fam* **abr de** **démagogue**.

démagogie [demagɔʒi] nf demagogy, demagoguery.

démagogique [demagɔʒik] adj demagogic, demagogical.

démagogue [demagɔg] ❖ adj demagogic *sout*, rabble-rousing. ❖ nmf demagogue.

demain [dəmɛ̃] adv [lendemain] tomorrow ▸ **salut, à demain !** bye, see you tomorrow! ❖ **de demain** loc adj [futur] : *les architectes / écoles de demain* the architects / schools of tomorrow.

démancher [3] [demɑ̃ʃe] vt Québec *fam* to take apart.

demande [dəmɑ̃d] nf **1.** [requête] request / *adresser toute demande de renseignements à...* send all inquiries to... ▸ **demande (en mariage)** (marriage) proposal ▸ **demande de rançon** ransom demand **2.** ADMIN & ÉCON application / *remplir une demande* to fill in an application (form) ▸ **faire une demande de bourse / visa** to apply for a scholarship / visa ▸ **faire une demande de remboursement** to make a claim for reimbursement ▸ **demande d'adhésion** application for membership ▸ **demande d'asile** application for asylum ▸ **demande d'emploi** job application / **'demandes d'emploi'** 'situations wanted' **3.** ÉCON demand **4.** [expression d'un besoin] need. ❖ **à la demande** loc adj & loc adv on demand. ❖ **à la demande générale** loc adv by popular request.

⚠ **Demand** signifie « exigence », « revendication ». C'est **request** qu'il faut employer pour traduire une demande au sens large.

demandé, e [dəmɑ̃de] adj sought-after, in demand / *le modèle B est très demandé* model B is in great demand, demand for model B is high.

demander [3] [dəmɑ̃de] vt **1.** [solliciter -rendez-vous, conseil, addition] to ask for *(insép)*, to request ; [-emploi, visa] to apply for ▸ **demander le divorce** to petition ou to file for divorce ▸ **demander la main de qqn** to ask for sb's hand (in marriage) ▸ **demander qqn en mariage** to propose to sb ▸ **demander pardon** to apologize ▸ **je te demande pardon** I'm sorry / *je vous demande pardon ?* (I beg your) pardon? ▸ **demander qqch à qqn** : *demander une faveur ou un service à qqn* to ask sb a favour ▸ **demander à qqn de faire** : *il m'a demandé de lui prêter ma voiture* he asked me to lend him my car **2.** [exiger -indemnité, dommages] to claim, to demand ; [-rançon] to demand, to ask for / *demander l'impossible* to ask for the impossible ▸ **demander justice** to demand justice ou fair treatment ▸ **demander qqch à qqn** to ask sthg of sb ▸ **demander que** : *tout ce que je demande, c'est qu'on me laisse seul* all I want ou ask is to be left alone **3.** [réclamer la présence de -gén] to want ; [-médecin] to send for *(insép)*, to call (for) ; [-prêtre] to ask for *(insép)* ▸ **on te demande au téléphone / aux urgences** you're wanted on the telephone / in casualty **4.** [chercher à savoir] to ask ▸ **demander qqch à qqn** : *demander l'heure à qqn* to ask sb the time ▸ **demander son chemin à qqn** to ask sb for directions ▸ **demander des nouvelles de qqn** to ask after sb ; *(en usage absolu)* : *demandez à votre agent de voyages* ask your travel agent **5.** [faire venir -ambulance, taxi] to send for *(sép)*, to call (for) **6.** [chercher à recruter -vendeur, ingénieur] to want, to require **7.** [nécessiter] to need, to require, to call for *(insép)* ▸ **ça demande réflexion** it needs thinking about, it needs some thought. ❖ **demander à** v + prép to ask to / *il demande à voir le chef de rayon* he wants to see the department supervisor / *je demande à voir !* *fam* I'll believe it when I see it! ▸ **ne demander qu'à...** : *je ne demande qu'à vous embaucher / aider* I'm more than willing to hire /

help you. ❖ **se demander** ◆ vp *(emploi passif)* : *cela ne se demande pas !* need you ask! *iron.* ◆ vpi to wonder, to ask o.s.

⚠ Le verbe anglais **to demand** signifie « exiger », « réclamer » et non simplement demander.

📝 Notez les différentes constructions du verbe demander :

• demander qqch (au sens de « solliciter ») = **ask for sthg.**
J'ai demandé un verre de vin rouge. *I asked for a glass of red wine.*
Thomas demande une guitare pour Noël. *Thomas has asked for a guitar for Christmas.*
Attention à la présence de la préposition **for** en anglais.
Notez cependant l'emploi de **ask the way, ask the time** (sans **for**) :
Demande-lui le chemin. *Ask him the way.*
Je peux vous demander l'heure ? *Can I ask you the time, please?*

• demander (qqch) à qqn = **ask sb (for sthg).**
Je vais demander son avis à Luc. *I'll ask Luc for some advice.*

• demander à qqn de faire qqch = **ask sb to do sthg.**
Elle a demandé à Marc de venir l'aider. *She asked Marc to come and help her.*
Notez l'absence de préposition en anglais avant le COI.

• demander à faire qqch = **ask to do sthg.**
Il a demandé à voir le directeur. *He asked to see the manager.*

demandeur, euse [dəmãdœʀ, øz] nm, f ADMIN ▸ **demandeur d'asile** asylum seeker, asylee 🇺🇸 ▸ **demandeur d'emploi** job seeker.

démangeaison [demãʒɛzɔ̃] nf [irritation] itch / *j'ai des démangeaisons partout* I'm itching all over.

démanger [17] [demãʒe] vt to itch, to be itching / *ce pull me démange* that pullover makes me itch ▸ **la langue le** ou **lui démangeait** *fam & fig* he was itching ou dying to say something / *ça la* ou *lui démangeait de dire la vérité* she was itching ou dying to tell the truth.

démanteler [25] [demãtle] vt [désorganiser - réseau, secte] to break up *(sép)* ; [- entreprise, service] to dismantle.

démaquillant, e [demakijã, ãt] adj ▸ **crème / lotion démaquillante** cleansing cream / lotion. ❖ **démaquillant** nm cleanser, make-up remover.

démaquiller [3] [demakije] vt to remove the make-up from. ❖ **se démaquiller** vp *(emploi réfléchi)* to remove ou to take off one's make-up / *se démaquiller les yeux* to remove one's eye make-up.

démarcation [demaʀkasjɔ̃] nf [limite] demarcation, dividing line.

démarchage [demaʀʃaʒ] nm COMM door-to-door selling / 'démarchage interdit' 'no hawkers' ▸ **démarchage électoral** POL canvassing.

démarche [demaʀʃ] nf **1.** [allure] gait, walk / *avoir une démarche gracieuse* to have a graceful gait, to walk gracefully **2.** [initiative] step, move / *faire toutes les démarches nécessaires* to take all the necessary steps / *faire une démarche auprès d'un organisme* to approach an organisation **3.** [approche - d'un problème] approach.

démarcheur, euse [demaʀʃœʀ, øz] nm, f COMM door-to-door salesman (saleswoman).

démarque [demaʀk] nf COMM marking down, markdown.

démarquer [3] [demaʀke] vt **1.** [enlever la marque de] ▸ **démarquer des vêtements** to remove the designer labels from clothes **2.** COMM to mark down *(sép)*. ❖ **se démarquer** vp *(emploi réfléchi)* SPORT to shake off one's marker. ❖ **se démarquer de** vp + prép to distinguish o.s. ou to be different from.

démarrage [demaʀaʒ] nm **1.** AUTO & MÉCAN [mouvement] moving off ; [mise en marche] starting ▸ **démarrage en côte** hill-start **2.** [commencement] start.

démarrer [3] [demaʀe] ◆ vt *fam* to start. ◆ vi **1.** AUTO & MÉCAN [se mettre à fonctionner] to start (up) ; [s'éloigner] to move off / *je n'arrive pas à faire démarrer la voiture* I can't get the car started **2.** [débuter] to start **3.** [dans une progression - économie] to take off, to get off the ground / *les ventes ont bien démarré* sales have got off to a good start.

démarreur [demaʀœʀ] nm starter.

démasquer [3] [demaske] vt **1.** [ôter le masque de] to unmask **2.** [confondre - traître, menteur] to unmask, to expose **3.** [dévoiler - hypocrisie] to unmask, to reveal. ❖ **se démasquer** vp *(emploi réfléchi)* *fig* to throw off ou to drop one's mask.

démêlant [demelã] nm hair conditioner.

démêlé [demele] nm [querelle] quarrel ▸ **avoir des démêlés avec qqn** to have a bit of trouble ou a few problems with sb.

démêler [4] [demele] vt **1.** [cheveux] to untangle, to disentangle, to comb out *(sép)* ; [nœud, filet] to disentangle, to untangle **2.** [éclaircir - mystère, affaire] to clear up *(sép)*, to disentangle, to see through *(insép)* / *démêler la vérité du mensonge* ou *le vrai du faux* to disentangle truth from falsehood, to sift out the truth from the lies.

déménagement [demenaʒmã] nm **1.** [changement de domicile] move / *on les a aidés à faire leur déménagement* we helped them move house 🇬🇧 ou to move ▸ **camion de déménagement** removal 🇬🇧 ou moving 🇺🇸 van ▸ **entreprise de déménagement** removal company ou firm 🇬🇧, mover 🇺🇸 **2.** [déplacement des meubles] : *le déménagement du salon est fini* we've finished moving the furniture out of the living room.

déménager [17] [demenaʒe] ◆ vt [salon] to move the furniture out of, to empty of its furniture ; [piano, meubles] to move. ◆ vi **1.** [changer de maison] to move, to move (house) 🇬🇧 **2.** [changer de lieu] to move **3.** *tfam* [déraisonner] to be off one's nut ou rocker **4.** *tfam* [faire de l'effet] : *t'as vu la blonde ? elle déménage !* did you see that blonde? she's a knockout! / *un rock qui déménage* a mind-blowing rock number.

déménageur [demenaʒœʀ] nm [ouvrier] removal man 🇬🇧, (furniture) mover 🇺🇸 ; [entrepreneur] furniture remover 🇬🇧, mover 🇺🇸.

démence [demãs] nf **1.** MÉD dementia **2.** *fam* [conduite déraisonnable] : *c'est de la démence !* it's madness!

démener [19] [demne] ❖ **se démener** vpi **1.** [s'agiter] to thrash about, to struggle ▸ **se démener comme un beau diable** to thrash about, to struggle violently **2.** [faire des efforts] ▸ **se démener pour** to exert o.s. ou to go out of one's way (in order) to.

dément, e [demã, ãt] adj **1.** [gén] mad, insane **2.** *fam* [remarquable] fantastic, terrific, ace **3.** *fam & péj* [inacceptable] incredible, unbelievable.

démenti [demãti] nm denial / *publier un démenti* to print a denial / *opposer un démenti formel à une rumeur* to deny a rumour categorically.

démentiel, elle [demãsjɛl] adj [excessif, extravagant] insane *fig.*

démentir [37] [demãtiʀ] vt **1.** [contredire - témoin] to contradict **2.** [nier - nouvelle, rumeur] to deny, to refute / *son regard démentait ses paroles* the look in his eyes belied his words. ❖ **se démentir** vpi : *son amitié pour moi ne s'est jamais démentie* his friendship has been unfailing / *des méthodes dont l'efficacité ne s'est jamais démentie* methods that have proved consistently efficient.

démerder [3] [demɛʀde] ❖ **se démerder** vpi *tfam* to get by, to manage / *et moi, comment je vais me démerder ?* and how the hell am I supposed to cope?

démériter [3] [demeʀite] vi *sout* [s'abaisser] : *il n'a jamais démérité* he has never proved unworthy of the trust placed in him.

démesure [deməzyʀ] nf [d'un personnage] excessiveness, immoderation ; [d'une passion, d'une idée] outrageousness.

démesurément [deməzyʀemã] adv excessively, immoderately, inordinately.

démettre [84] [demɛtʀ] vt [destituer] to dismiss ▶ **démettre qqn de ses fonctions** to dismiss sb from his duties. ❖ **se démettre** vpt ▶ **se démettre le poignet** to dislocate one's wrist, to put one's wrist out of joint.

demeurant [dəmœʀã] ❖ **au demeurant** loc adv [du reste] for all that, notwithstanding.

demeure [dəmœʀ] nf **1.** [maison] residence **2.** DR delay ▶ **mettre qqn en demeure de payer** to give sb notice to pay ▶ **mettre qqn en demeure de témoigner / de s'exécuter** to order sb to testify / to comply. ❖ **à demeure** loc adv : *il s'est installé chez elle à demeure* he moved in with her permanently ou for good.

demeuré, e [dəmœʀe] ◆ adj half-witted, backward. ◆ nm, f half-wit.

demeurer [5] [dəmœʀe] vi **1.** *(aux être)* [rester - dans tel état] to remain / *demeurer silencieux / inconnu* to remain silent / unknown **2.** *(aux être)* [subsister] to remain, to be left **3.** *(aux avoir)* *sout* [habiter] to live, to stay.

demi, e [dəmi] adj inv *(devant le nom, avec trait d'union)* **1.** [moitié de] half ▶ *une demi-pomme* half an apple **2.** [incomplet] : *cela n'a été qu'un demi-succès* it wasn't a complete ou it was only a partial success. ❖ **demi** nm **1.** [bière] ▶ **demi (de bière)** ≃ half UK ; ≃ half-pint UK **2.** RUGBY ▶ **demi de mêlée** scrum half ▶ **demi d'ouverture** fly ou stand-off half. ❖ **demie** nf ▶ **la demie** half past / *je te rappelle à la demie* I'll call you back at half past. ❖ **à demi** loc adv **1.** *(avec un adjectif)* : *à demi mort* half-dead **2.** *(avec un verbe)* : *ouvrir la porte à demi* to half-open the door. ❖ **et demi, et demie** loc adj **1.** [dans une mesure] and a half / *ça dure deux heures et demie* it lasts two and a half hours / *boire une bouteille et demie* to drink a bottle and a half **2.** [en annonçant l'heure] : *à trois heures et demie* at three thirty, at half past three.

demi-bouteille [dəmibutɛj] *(pl* demi-bouteilles) nf half-bottle, half bottle.

demi-cercle [dəmisɛʀkl] *(pl* demi-cercles) nm half-circle, semicircle. ❖ **en demi-cercle** loc adv in a semi-circle.

demi-douzaine [dəmiduzɛn] *(pl* demi-douzaines) nf [six] half-dozen, half-a-dozen ▶ **une demi-douzaine de tomates** a half-dozen ou half-a-dozen tomatoes.

demi-écrémé, e [dəmiekʀeme] adj semi-skimmed.

demi-finale [dəmifinal] *(pl* demi-finales) nf semifinal.

demi-frère [dəmifʀɛʀ] *(pl* demi-frères) nm half-brother.

demi-gros [dəmigʀo] nm inv wholesale *(dealing in retail quantities)*.

demi-heure [dəmijœʀ] *(pl* demi-heures) nf half-hour ▶ **une demi-heure** half an hour.

demi-journée [dəmiʒuʀne] *(pl* demi-journées) nf half-day, half-a-day ▶ **une demi-journée de travail** half a day's work, a half-day's work.

démilitariser [3] [demilitaʀize] vt to demilitarize.

demi-litre [dəmilitʀ] *(pl* demi-litres) nm half-litre UK, half-liter US, half a litre UK ou liter US / *un demi-litre de lait, s'il vous plaît* half a litre of milk please.

demi-mal [dəmimal] *(pl* demi-maux [-mo]) nm : *il n'y a que demi-mal* there's no great harm done.

demi-mesure [dəmiməzyʀ] *(pl* demi-mesures) nf [compromis] half measure ▶ **elle ne connaît pas les demi-mesures** ou **ne fait pas de** *fam* **demi-mesures** she doesn't do things by halves.

demi-mot [dəmimo] ❖ **à demi-mot** loc adv ▶ **il comprend à demi-mot** he doesn't need to have things spelled out for him / *on se comprend à demi-mot* we know how each other's mind works.

déminage [deminaʒ] nm [sur la terre] mine clearance ; [en mer] mine sweeping.

déminer [3] [demine] vt to clear of mines.

demi-pension [dəmipãsjɔ̃] *(pl* demi-pensions) nf [à l'hôtel] half-board ▶ **être en demi-pension** ÉDUC to have school lunches ou dinners.

demi-pensionnaire [dəmipãsjɔnɛʀ] *(pl* demi-pensionnaires) nmf pupil who has school dinners.

demi-saison [dəmisɛzɔ̃] *(pl* demi-saisons) nf [printemps] spring ; [automne] autumn, fall US.

demi-sel [dəmisɛl] nm inv [beurre] slightly salted butter.

demi-sœur [dəmisœʀ] *(pl* demi-sœurs) nf half-sister.

démission [demisjɔ̃] nf **1.** [départ] resignation / *donner sa démission* to hand in ou to tender *sout* one's resignation, to resign **2.** [irresponsabilité] abdication of responsibility / *à cause de la démission des parents* because of the refusal of parents to shoulder their responsibilities.

démissionner [3] [demisjɔne] vi **1.** [quitter son emploi] to resign, to hand in one's resignation ou notice **2.** [refuser ses responsabilités] to fail to shoulder one's responsibilities / *c'est trop difficile, je démissionne* it's too hard, I give up.

demi-tarif [dəmitaʀif] *(pl* demi-tarifs) nm [billet] half-price ticket ; [carte] half-price card ; [abonnement] half-price subscription / *voyager à demi-tarif* to travel at half-fare.

demi-teinte [dəmitɛ̃t] *(pl* demi-teintes) nf ❖ **en demi-teinte** loc adj [subtil] subtle, delicate.

demi-tour [dəmituʀ] *(pl* demi-tours) nm **1.** [pivotement] about-face, about-turn **2.** AUTO U-turn ▶ **faire demi-tour a)** [piéton] to retrace one's steps **b)** [conducteur] to turn back.

démo (abr de démonstration) nf *fam* demo.

démobiliser [3] [demɔbilize] vt **1.** MIL to demobilize **2.** [démotiver] to cause to lose interest, to demotivate.

démocrate [demɔkrat] nmf [gén] democrat.

démocrate-chrétien, enne [demɔkratkʀetjɛ̃, ɛn] *(mpl* démocrates-chrétiens, *fpl* démocrates-chrétiennes) adj & nm, f Christian Democrat.

démocratie [demɔkʀasi] nf **1.** [système] democracy ▶ **démocratie populaire** people's democracy **2.** [pays] democracy, democratic country.

démocratique [demɔkratik] adj **1.** POL democratic. **2.** [respectueux des désirs de tous] democratic.

démocratisation [demɔkratizasjɔ̃] nf **1.** POL democratization, making more democratic. **2.** [mise à la portée de tous] ▸ **la démocratisation du ski** putting skiing holidays within everyone's reach.

démocratiser [3] [demɔkratize] vt POL to democratize, to make more democratic. ⬦ **se démocratiser** vpi POL to become more democratic.

démodé, e [demɔde] adj [style, technique] old-fashioned, outdated, out-of-date ; [parents] old-fashioned.

démographie [demɔgrafi] nf [science] demography ; [croissance de la population] population growth.

démographique [demɔgrafik] adj demographic, population (modif) ▸ **poussée / explosion démographique** population increase / explosion.

demoiselle [dəmwazɛl] nf **1.** [jeune femme] young lady ▸ **demoiselle d'honneur** bridesmaid ▸ **demoiselle de compagnie** lady's companion **2.** vieilli [célibataire] maiden lady.

démolir [32] [demɔlir] vt **1.** [détruire - immeuble, mur] to demolish, to pull ou to tear down (sép) ; [- jouet, voiture] to wreck, to smash up (sép) **2.** [anéantir - argument, théorie] to demolish ; [- projet] to ruin, to play havoc with ; [- réputation, autorité] to shatter, to destroy **3.** fam [anéantir - auteur, roman] to pan **4.** fam [battre] to thrash, to beat up (sép) ▸ **démolir le portrait à qqn** to beat ou to smash sb's face in **5.** fam [épuiser - physiquement] to do in (sép) ; [- moralement] to shatter.

démolisseur [demɔlisœr] nm **1.** [ouvrier] demolition worker, wrecker US **2.** [entrepreneur] demolition contractor.

démolition [demɔlisjɔ̃] nf demolition, pulling ou tearing down. ⬦ **de démolition** loc adj : chantier / entreprise de démolition demolition site / contractors / une campagne de démolition systématique fig a systematic campaign of destruction.

démon [demɔ̃] nm **1.** RELIG ▸ **le démon** the Devil **2.** MYTH daemon, daimon ▸ **son démon intérieur a)** fig [mauvais] the evil ou demon within (him) **b)** [bon] the good spirit within (him) **3.** [tentation] demon ▸ **le démon de midi** lust affecting a man in mid-life **4.** [enfant turbulent] ▸ **(petit) démon** (little) devil ou demon.

démoniaque [demɔnjak] adj [ruse, rire] demonic sout, diabolical, fiendish.

démonstrateur, trice [demɔ̃stratœr, tris] nm, f COMM demonstrator, salesperson (in charge of demonstrations).

démonstratif, ive [demɔ̃stratif, iv] adj [expressif] demonstrative, expressive, effusive ▸ **peu démonstratif** reserved, undemonstrative.

démonstration [demɔ̃strasjɔ̃] nf **1.** LOGIQUE & MATH [preuve] demonstration, proof ; [ensemble de formules] demonstration **2.** COMM demonstration **3.** [prestation] display, demonstration **4.** [fait de manifester] demonstration, show / faire une démonstration de force to display one's strength.

démontable [demɔ̃tabl] adj which can be dismantled ou taken to pieces.

démonté, e [demɔ̃te] adj [mer] raging, stormy.

démonte-pneu [demɔ̃tpnø] (pl démonte-pneus) nm tyre lever UK, tire iron US.

démonter [3] [demɔ̃te] vt **1.** [désassembler - bibliothèque, machine] to dismantle, to take down (sép) ; [- moteur] to strip down (sép), to dismantle ; [- fusil, pendule] to dismantle, to take to pieces, to take apart (sép) ; [- manche de vêtement, pièce rapportée] to take off (sép) **2.** [détacher - pneu, store, persienne] to remove, to take off (sép) ; [- ri-

deau] to take down (sép) **3.** [décontenancer] to take aback (sép) / ne te laisse pas démonter par son ironie don't be flustered by his ironic remarks. ⬦ **se démonter** ⬥ vp (emploi passif) to be taken to pieces, to be dismantled. ⬥ vpi [se troubler] to lose countenance, to get flustered.

démontrer [3] [demɔ̃tre] vt **1.** MATH to prove **2.** [montrer par raisonnement] to prove, to demonstrate **3.** [révéler] to show, to reveal, to indicate.

démoralisant, e [demɔralizɑ̃, ɑ̃t] adj [remarque, nouvelle] demoralizing, disheartening, depressing.

démoraliser [3] [demɔralize] vt to demoralize, to dishearten. ⬦ **se démoraliser** vpi to become demoralized, to lose heart.

démordre [76] [demɔrdr] ⬦ **démordre de** vp + prép ▸ **elle n'en démord pas** she won't have it any other way.

démotiver [3] [demɔtive] vt to demotivate, to discourage.

démouler [3] [demule] vt [statuette] to remove from the mould UK ou mold US ; [gâteau] to turn out (sép) ; [tarte] to remove from its tin.

démuni, e [demyni] adj **1.** [pauvre] destitute **2.** [sans défense] powerless, resourceless.

démunir [32] [demynir] vt to deprive ▸ **démunir qqn de qqch** to deprive ou to divest sb of sthg. ⬦ **se démunir de** vp + prép to part with, to give up.

démystifier [9] [demistifje] vt [rendre plus clair] to explain, to demystify.

dénatalité [denatalite] nf fall ou drop in the birth rate.

dénationaliser [3] [denasjɔnalize] vt to denationalize.

dénaturé, e [denatyre] adj **1.** [alcool] denatured **2.** [pervers - goût] unnatural, perverted.

dénaturer [3] [denatyre] vt **1.** [modifier - alcool] to adulterate, to denature ; [- saveur] to alter, to adulterate **2.** [fausser - propos, faits, intention] to distort, to misrepresent, to twist.

déneiger [23] [deneʒe] vt to clear of snow, to clear snow from.

déneigeuse [deneʒøz] nf snowblower.

déni [deni] nm **1.** DR denial **2.** PSYCHOL ▸ **déni de réalité** denial.

dénicher [3] [denife] vt fam [trouver - collier, trésor] find, to unearth ; [- informations] to dig up ou out (sép) ; [- chanteur, cabaret] to discover, to spot.

denier [dənje] nm HIST [monnaie - romaine] denarius ; [- française] denier ▸ **le denier du culte** contribution to parish costs ▸ **les deniers publics** ou **de l'État** public money.

dénigrer [3] [denigre] vt to disparage, to denigrate, to run down (sép).

dénivelé [denivle] nm difference in level ou height.

dénivelée [denivle] nf = **dénivelé**.

dénivellation [denive(l)lasjɔ̃], **dénivelation*** [denivelasjɔ̃] nf [pente] slope.

dénombrable [denɔ̃brabl] adj countable ▸ **non dénombrable** uncountable.

dénombrer [3] [denɔ̃bre] vt to count (out) / on dénombre 130 morts à ce jour at the latest count there were 130 dead.

dénominateur [denɔminatœr] nm MATH denominator ▸ **plus grand dénominateur commun** highest common denominator.

dénomination [denɔminasjɔ̃] nf [nom] designation, denomination, name.

---

dénommé, e [denɔme] adj : *le dénommé Joubert* the man called Joubert.

dénoncer [16] [denɔ̃se] vt **1.** [complice, fraudeur] to denounce, to inform on *(insép)* ; [camarade de classe] to tell on *(insép)* ▸ **dénoncer qqn aux autorités** to denounce sb ou to give sb away to the authorities **2.** [condamner - pratiques, dangers, abus] to denounce, to condemn **3.** [annuler - armistice, traité] to renege on *(insép)* ; [-contrat] to terminate **4.** *sout* [dénoter] to indicate, to betray. ❖ **se dénoncer** vp *(emploi réfléchi)* to give o.s. up.

dénonciation [denɔ̃sjasjɔ̃] nf **1.** [accusation] denunciation **2.** [révélation - d'une injustice] exposure, denouncing, castigating **3.** [rupture - d'un traité] denunciation, reneging on ; [- d'un contrat] termination.

dénoter [3] [denɔte] vt [être signe de] to denote, to indicate.

dénouement [denumã] nm [d'un film, d'une histoire, d'une pièce] dénouement ; [d'une crise, d'une affaire] outcome, conclusion ▸ **un heureux dénouement** a happy ending, a favourable outcome.

dénouer [6] [denwe] vt **1.** [défaire - ficelle, lacet] to undo, to untie, to unknot ; [- cheveux] to let down *(sép)*, to loosen **2.** [résoudre - intrigue] to unravel, to untangle. ❖ **se dénouer** vpi **1.** [cheveux] to come loose ou undone ; [lacet] to come undone ou untied **2.** [crise] to end, to be resolved.

dénoyauter [3] [denwajote] vt to stone 🇬🇧, to pit 🇺🇸.

denrée [dɑ̃ʀe] nf commodity ▸ **denrées de première nécessité** staple foods, staples ▸ **denrées alimentaires** foodstuffs ▸ **denrées périssables** perishable goods, perishables.

dense [dɑ̃s] adj **1.** [épais - brouillard, végétation] thick, dense **2.** [serré - foule] thick, tightly packed ; [- circulation] heavy.

densité [dɑ̃site] nf **1.** PHYS density **2.** [du brouillard, de la foule] denseness, thickness / *selon la densité de la circulation* depending on how heavy the traffic is ▸ **pays à faible / forte densité de population** sparsely / densely populated country.

dent [dɑ̃] nf **1.** ANAT tooth ▸ **faire** ou **percer ses dents** to cut one's teeth, to teethe / *avoir les dents en avant* to have buck teeth ▸ **dents du bas / haut** lower / upper teeth ▸ **dents de devant / du fond** front / back teeth ▸ **dent de lait** baby ou milk 🇬🇧 tooth ▸ **dent de sagesse** wisdom tooth ▸ **fausses dents** false teeth ▸ **avoir la dent** *fam* to be ravenous ou starving ▸ **avoir** ou **garder une dent contre qqn** *fam* to have a grudge against sb, to bear sb a grudge ▸ **avoir les dents longues** to fix one's sights high ▸ **être sur les dents** a) *fam* [occupé] to be frantically busy b) [anxieux] to be stressed out ▸ **parler entre ses dents** to mutter ▸ **se faire les dents** to cut one's teeth / *on n'avait rien à se mettre sous la dent* we didn't have a thing to eat **2.** [de roue, d'engrenage] cog ; [de courroie] tooth **3.** [pointe - d'une scie, d'une peigne] tooth ; [- d'une fourchette, d'une herse] tooth, prong **4.** BOT serration. ❖ **en dents de scie** loc adj [couteau] serrated / *évolution en dents de scie* uneven development.

dentaire [dɑ̃tɛʀ] adj [hygiène] oral, dental ; [cabinet, études, école] dental.

dentelé, e [dɑ̃tle] adj [contour] jagged, indented ; [feuille] dentate, serrate.

dentelle [dɑ̃tɛl] ❖ nf [tissu] lace, lacework / *des gants de* ou *en dentelle* lace gloves ▸ **ne pas faire dans la dentelle** *fam*: *il ne fait pas dans la dentelle* he doesn't go in for subtleties. ❖ adj inv CULIN ▸ **crêpes dentelle** paper-thin pancakes.

dentier [dɑ̃tje] nm denture, dentures, dental plate.

dentifrice [dɑ̃tifʀis] ❖ adj ▸ **eau dentifrice** mouthwash ▸ **pâte dentifrice** toothpaste. ❖ nm toothpaste.

dentiste [dɑ̃tist] nmf dentist.

dentition [dɑ̃tisjɔ̃] nf [dents] teeth, dentition *spéc.*

denturologie [dɑ̃tyʀɔlɔʒi] nf 🇶🇧 MÉD denturism.

dénuder [3] [denyde] vt [dos, épaules] to leave bare ; [sol, câble, os, veine] to strip. ❖ **se dénuder** vpi **1.** [se déshabiller] to strip (off) **2.** [se dégarnir - crâne] to be balding ; [- arbre] to become bare ; [- fil électrique] to show through.

dénué, e [denɥe] adj ▸ **dénué de** lacking in, devoid of ▸ **dénué d'intérêt** utterly uninteresting, devoid of interest.

dénuement [denymã] nm destitution / *être dans le dénuement le plus complet* to be utterly destitute.

déodorant [deɔdɔʀã] ❖ adj m deodorant *(modif)*. ❖ nm deodorant.

déontologie [deɔ̃tɔlɔʒi] nf professional code of ethics, deontology.

dépannage [depanaʒ] nm [réparation] fixing, repairing, repair job. ❖ **de dépannage** loc adj ▸ **voiture de dépannage** breakdown lorry 🇬🇧, tow truck 🇺🇸 / *service de dépannage* breakdown service.

dépanner [3] [depane] vt **1.** [réparer - voiture, mécanisme] to repair, to fix ▸ **dépanner qqn sur le bord de la route** *fam* to help sb who's broken down on the side of the road ; *(en usage absolu)* : *nous dépannons 24 heures sur 24* we have a 24-hour breakdown service **2.** *fam* [aider] to help out *(sép)*, to tide over *(sép)*.

dépanneur, euse [depanœʀ, øz] nm, f [d'appareils] repairman (repairwoman) ; [de véhicules] breakdown mechanic. ❖ **dépanneur** nm 🇶🇧 ≃ corner shop 🇬🇧 ; ≃ convenience store 🇺🇸. ❖ **dépanneuse** nf breakdown truck 🇬🇧, breakdown lorry 🇬🇧, tow truck 🇺🇸, wrecker 🇺🇸.

dépaqueter [depakte] vt to unpack.

✏ In reformed spelling (see p. 16-18), this verb is conjugated like *acheter* : *il dépaquètera, elle dépaquèterait.*

dépareillé, e [depaʀeje] adj **1.** [mal assorti - serviettes, chaussettes] odd ▸ **articles dépareillés** oddments **2.** [incomplet - service, collection] incomplete.

déparer [3] [depaʀe] vt [paysage] to disfigure, to spoil, to be a blight on ; [visage] to disfigure.

déparler [3] [depaʀle] vi 🇶🇧 [dire n'importe quoi] to babble away.

départ [depaʀ] nm **1.** TRANSP departure / *le départ du train est à 7 h* the train leaves at 7 a.m. / *le départ est dans une heure* we're leaving in an hour **2.** [fait de quitter un lieu] going / *on en a parlé après son départ* we discussed it after he went ▸ **être sur le départ** to be ready to go **3.** [d'une course] start ▸ **douze chevaux / voitures / coureurs ont pris le départ (de la course)** there were twelve starters ▸ **prendre un bon / mauvais départ** *pr & fig* to get off to a good / bad start **4.** [son travail] departure ; [démission] resignation / *au départ du directeur* when the manager left ou quit (the firm) / *départ en préretraite* early retirement **5.** [origine] start, beginning ▸ **au départ** at first, to begin with. ❖ **au départ de** loc prép : *visites au départ des Tuileries* tours departing from the Tuileries. ❖ **de départ** loc adj **1.** [gare, quai, heure] departure *(modif)* **2.** [initial] : *salaire de départ* initial ou starting salary.

départager [17] [depaʀtaʒe] vt **1.** [séparer - ex-æquo] to decide between **2.** ADMIN & POL to settle the voting, to give the casting vote.

département [depaʀtəmã] nm **1.** [du territoire français] département, department ▸ **les départements**

d'outre-mer French overseas departments **2.** [service] department, service, division **3.** [ministère] department, ministry.

 Département

One of the three main administrative divisions in France. There are a hundred in all. Each is run by a **conseil général**, which has its headquarters in the principal town of the **département**.

Départements are numbered in alphabetical order (with a few exceptions in Île-de-France and overseas). The number is often used to refer to the department, particularly for the Paris area, and it is not uncommon to hear people say **j'habite dans le 91**, meaning **j'habite dans l'Essonne**.

---

départemental, e, aux [dɛpaʀtəmɑ̃tal, o] adj [des départements français] of the département, departmental. ❖ **départementale** nf [route] secondary road ; ≃ B-road UK.

départir [32] [depaʀtiʀ] ❖ **se départir de** vp + prép to depart from, to abandon, to lose / *sans se départir de sa bonne humeur* without losing his good humour.

dépassé, e [depase] adj [mentalité, technique] outdated, old-fashioned.

dépassement [depasmɑ̃] nm **1.** AUTO overtaking UK, passing US **2.** [excès] exceeding, excess ▸ **être en dépassement budgétaire** to be over budget **3.** [surpassement] ▸ **dépassement (de soi-même)** surpassing o.s., transcending one's own capabilities **4.** ADMIN *charging, by a medical practitioner, of more than the standard fee recognized by the social services.*

dépasser [3] [depase] ❖ vt **1.** [doubler - voiture] to pass, to overtake UK ; [- coureur] to outrun, to outdistance **2.** [aller au-delà de - hôtel, panneau] to pass, to go ou to get past ; [- piste d'atterrissage] to overshoot **3.** [déborder sur] to go over ou beyond / *il a dépassé son temps de parole* he talked longer than had been agreed, he went over time **4.** [suivi d'une quantité, d'un chiffre] to exceed, to go beyond / **'ne pas dépasser la dose prescrite'** 'do not exceed the stated dose' / *les socialistes nous dépassent en nombre* the socialists outnumber us, we're outnumbered by the socialists / *dépasser le budget de 15 millions* to go 15 million over budget / *je n'ai pas dépassé 60 km/h* I did not exceed ou I stayed below 60 km/h **5.** [surpasser - adversaire] to surpass, to do better than, to be ahead of ▸ **dépasser l'attente de qqn** to surpass ou to exceed sb's expectations / *cela dépasse tout ce que j'avais pu espérer* this is beyond all my hopes ou my wildest dreams ▸ **dépasser qqn / qqch en** : *dépasser qqn / qqch en drôlerie / stupidité* to be funnier / more stupid than sb / sthg **6.** [outrepasser - ordres, droits] to go beyond, to overstep / *la tâche dépasse mes forces* the task is beyond me / *les mots ont dépassé ma pensée* I got carried away and said something I didn't mean ▸ **dépasser les bornes** ou **les limites** ou **la mesure** ou **la dose** *fam* to go too far, to overstep the mark **7.** [dérouter] : *les échecs, ça me dépasse !* chess is (quite) beyond me ! ❖ vi **1.** AUTO to pass, to overtake UK ▸ **'interdiction de dépasser'** 'no overtaking UK ', 'no passing US ' **2.** [étagère, balcon, corniche] to jut out, to protrude **3.** [chemisier, doublure] to be hanging out ou untucked / *ton jupon dépasse !* your slip's showing! ▸ **dépasser de** to be sticking out

ou protruding *sout* from (under). ❖ **se dépasser** vpi [se surpasser] to surpass ou to excel o.s.

dépassionner [3] [depasjɔne] vt [débat] to take the heat out of, to calm ou to cool down.

dépatouiller [3] [depatuje] ❖ **se dépatouiller** vpi *fam* to manage to get by / *qu'il se* ou *s'en dépatouille tout seul !* he can get out of this one by himself!

dépaysement [depeizmɑ̃] nm **1.** [changement de cadre] change of scene ou scenery **2.** [malaise] feeling of unfamiliarity.

dépayser [3] [depeize] vt **1.** [changer de cadre] to give a change of scenery ou surroundings to ▸ **laissez-vous dépayser** treat yourself to a change of scene ou scenery **2.** [désorienter] to disorientate.

dépecer [29] [depəse] vt [démembrer - proie] to tear limb from limb ; [- volaille] to cut up (sép).

dépêche [depɛʃ] nf **1.** ADMIN dispatch **2.** TÉLÉC ▸ **dépêche (télégraphique)** telegram, wire ▸ **envoyer une dépêche à qqn** to wire ou to telegraph sb **3.** [nouvelle] news item *(sent through an agency)*.

dépêcher [4] [depeʃe] vt *sout* [enquêteur] to send, to dispatch. ❖ **se dépêcher** vpi to hurry (up) / *mais dépêche-toi donc !* come on, hurry up! / *dépêche-toi de finir cette lettre* hurry up and finish that letter.

dépeindre [81] [depɛ̃dʀ] vt to depict, to portray.

dépénalisation [depenalizasjɔ̃] nf decriminalization.

dépénaliser [3] [depenalize] vt to decriminalize.

dépendance [depɑ̃dɑ̃s] nf **1.** [subordination] dependence ▸ **vivre dans la dépendance** to be dependent, to lead a dependent life ; [d'un drogué] addiction **2.** [annexe] outhouse, outbuilding **3.** [territoire] dependency.

dépendant, e [depɑ̃dɑ̃, ɑ̃t] adj **1.** [subordonné] dependent ▸ **être dépendant de qqn / qqch** to be dependent on sb / sthg **2.** [drogué] dependent.

dépendre [73] [depɑ̃dʀ] ❖ **dépendre de** v + prép **1.** [suj : employé, service] to be answerable to / *il dépend du chef de service* he's answerable to, he reports to the departmental head **2.** [suj : propriété, domaine, territoire] to be a dependency of, to belong to **3.** [financièrement] to depend on ou upon, to be dependent on ▸ **dépendre (financièrement) de qqn** to be financially dependent on ou upon sb / *je ne dépends que de moi-même* I'm my own boss **4.** [suj : décision, choix, résultat] to depend on / *notre avenir en dépend* our future depends ou rests on it / *ça ne dépend pas que de moi* it's not entirely up to me ; *(en usage absolu)* ▸ **ça dépend !** it (all) depends!

dépens [depɑ̃] nmpl DR costs. ❖ **aux dépens de** loc prép at the expense of / *je l'ai appris à mes dépens* I learnt it to my cost.

dépense [depɑ̃s] nf **1.** [frais] expense, expenditure / *je ne peux pas me permettre cette dépense* I can't afford to lay out ou to spend so much money ▸ **dépenses publiques** public ou government spending ▸ **dépenses de santé** [de l'État] health expenditure **2.** [fait de dépenser] spending ▸ **pousser qqn à la dépense** to push ou to encourage sb to spend (money) / *ne regardez pas à la dépense* spare no expense **3.** [consommation] consumption ▸ **dépense physique** physical exertion.

dépenser [3] [depɑ̃se] vt **1.** [argent] to spend ; *(en usage absolu)* ▸ **dépenser sans compter** to spend (money) lavishly ou without counting the cost **2.** [consommer - mazout] to use **3.** [employer - temps] to spend ; [- énergie] to expend. ❖ **se dépenser** vpi **1.** [se défouler] to let off steam / *elle a besoin de se dépenser* she needs an outlet for her (pent-up) energy **2.** [se démener] to expend a lot of energy, to work hard ▸ **se dépenser sans compter pour qqch** to put all one's energies into sthg, to give sthg one's all.

dépensier, ère [depãsje,ɛʀ] ◆ adj extravagant. ◆ nm, f spendthrift.

dépérir [32] [deperiʀ] vi [malade] to fade ou to waste away ; [de tristesse] to pine away ; [plante] to wilt, to wither ; [industrie] to decline.

dépêtrer [4] [depetʀe] vt ▸ **dépêtrer qqn / qqch de** to extricate sb / sthg from. ⬥ **se dépêtrer de** vp + prép **1.** [de filets, de pièges] to free o.s. from **2.** [d'un gêneur] to shake off *(sép)* ; [d'une situation] to get out of / *il nous a dit tant de mensonges qu'il ne peut plus s'en dépêtrer* he's told us so many lies that he can no longer extricate himself from them.

dépeuplement [depœpləmã] nm SOCIOL depopulation.

dépeupler [5] [depœple] ⬥ **se dépeupler** vpi SOCIOL to become depopulated.

déphasé, e [defaze] adj [désorienté] disorientated.

dépilatoire [depilatwaʀ] adj depilatory.

dépistage [depistaʒ] nm MÉD screening ▸ **le dépistage du cancer** screening for cancer ▸ **le dépistage du sida** AIDS testing.

dépister [3] [depiste] vt MÉD to screen for / *des techniques pour dépister le cancer* cancer screening techniques.

dépit [depi] nm pique ▸ **faire qqch par dépit** to do sthg in a fit of pique ou out of spite. ⬥ **en dépit de** loc prép despite, in spite of ▸ **faire qqch en dépit du bon sens a)** [sans logique] to do sthg with no regard for common sense **b)** [n'importe comment] to do sthg any old how.

dépité, e [depite] adj (greatly) vexed, piqued.

déplacé, e [deplase] adj **1.** [malvenu - démarche, remarque, rire] inappropriate **2.** [de mauvais goût - plaisanterie] indelicate, shocking **3.** SOCIOL displaced.

déplacement [deplasmã] nm **1.** [mouvement] moving, shifting ▸ **déplacement d'air** displacement of air **2.** [sortie] moving about ; [voyage d'affaires] (business) trip / *merci d'avoir fait le déplacement* thanks for coming all this way / *joli panorama, ça vaut le déplacement !* fam what a lovely view, it's definitely worth going out of your way to see it ! **3.** [mutation - d'un employé] transfer **4.** MÉD ▸ **déplacement de vertèbre** slipped disc, slipped disk US. ⬥ **en déplacement** loc adv away / *la directrice est en déplacement* the manager's away (on business).

déplacer [16] [deplase] vt **1.** [objet, pion, voiture] to move, to shift **2.** [élève, passager] to move ; [population] to displace **3.** [infléchir] : *ne déplaçez pas le problème* ou *la question* don't change the question **4.** MÉD [os] to displace, to put out of joint ; [vertèbre] to slip **5.** [muter - fonctionnaire] to transfer **6.** [faire venir - médecin, dépanneur] to send for / *son concert a déplacé des foules* crowds flocked to his concert. ⬥ **se déplacer** ◆ vpi **1.** [masse d'air, nuages] to move, to be displaced spéc ; [aiguille d'horloge] to move **2.** [marcher] to move about ou around, to get about ou around / *avec notre messagerie, faites vos courses sans vous déplacer* do your shopping from home with our Teletext service ▸ **cela ne vaut pas / vaut le coup de se déplacer** fam it's not worth / it's worth the trip **3.** [voyager] to travel, to get about. ◆ vpt ▸ **se déplacer une vertèbre** to slip a disc ou disk US.

déplaire [110] [deplɛʀ] ⬥ **déplaire à** v + prép [rebuter] to put off *(sép)* / *il m'a tout de suite déplu* I took an instant dislike to him / *je lui déplais tant que ça ?* does he dislike me as much as that? / *il m'a parlé franchement, ce qui n'a pas été pour me déplaire* he was frank with me, which I liked / *il ne lui déplairait pas de vivre à la campagne* he wouldn't object to living in the country.

déplaisant, e [deplɛzã, ãt] adj **1.** [goût, odeur, atmosphère] unpleasant, nasty **2.** [personne, comportement] unpleasant, offensive.

déplaisir [depleziʀ] nm [mécontentement] displeasure, disapproval / *je fais les corvées ménagères sans déplaisir* I don't mind doing the housework.

déplâtrer [3] [deplatʀe] vt MÉD to take out of a plaster cast.

dépliant [deplijã] nm **1.** [brochure] brochure, leaflet ▸ **dépliant touristique** travel brochure **2.** IMPR foldout.

déplier [10] [deplije] vt [journal, lettre] to open out ou up *(sép)*, to unfold ; [bras, jambes] to stretch.

déploiement [deplwamã] nm **1.** MIL deployment / *un grand déploiement* ou *tout un déploiement de police* a large deployment of police **2.** [manifestation] ▸ **déploiement de** show ou demonstration ou display of.

déplorable [deplɔʀabl] adj **1.** [regrettable] deplorable, regrettable, lamentable **2.** [mauvais - résultat] appalling ; [- plaisanterie] awful, terrible, appalling.

déplorer [3] [deplɔʀe] vt **1.** sout [regretter] to object to, to regret, to deplore / *je déplore que vous n'ayez pas compris* I find it regrettable that you didn't understand **2.** [constater] : *nous n'avons eu que peu de dégâts à déplorer* fortunately, we suffered only slight damage / *on déplore la mort d'une petite fille dans l'accident* sadly, a little girl was killed in the accident.

déployer [13] [deplwaje] vt **1.** [déplier] to spread out *(sép)*, to unfold, to unroll ▸ **déployer les voiles** NAUT to unfurl ou to extend the sails **2.** [faire montre de] to display, to exhibit / *il m'a fallu déployer des trésors de persuasion auprès d'elle* I had to work very hard at persuading her **3.** MIL to deploy. ⬥ **se déployer** vpi **1.** [foule] to extend, to stretch out **2.** MIL to be deployed.

dépolluant, e [depɔlyã, ãt] adj depolluting, antipollutant. ⬥ **dépolluant** nm depollutant, anti-pollutant.

dépolluer [7] [depɔlye] vt to cleanse, to clean up *(sép)* / *dépolluer les plages* to clean up the beaches.

déportation [depɔʀtasjõ] nf **1.** HIST [exil] transportation, deportation **2.** [en camp] deportation, internment / *pendant mes années de déportation* during my years in a concentration camp.

déporté, e [depɔʀte] nm, f [prisonnier] deportee, internee ; [en camp de concentration] concentration camp prisoner.

déporter [3] [depɔʀte] vt **1.** [exiler] to deport, to send to a concentration camp **2.** [déplacer] : *la voiture a été déportée sur la gauche* the car swerved to the left. ⬥ **se déporter** vpi [doucement] to move aside ; [brusquement] to swerve ▸ **se déporter vers la droite / gauche** to veer (off) to the right / left.

déposé, e [depoze] adj ▸ **marque déposée** registered trademark ▸ **modèle déposé** patented design.

déposer [3] [depoze] ◆ vt **1.** [poser] to lay ou to put down *(sép)* **2.** [laisser - gerbe] to lay ; [- objet livré] to leave, to drop off *(sép)* ; [- valise] to leave **3.** [décharger - matériel] to unload, to set down *(sép)* **4.** [conduire en voiture] to drop (off) / *je te dépose ?* can I drop you off?, can I give you a lift? **5.** [argent, valeurs] to deposit / *déposer de l'argent sur son compte* to pay money into one's account, to deposit money in one's account **6.** ADMIN ▸ **déposer son bilan** to file for bankruptcy, to go into (voluntary) liquidation ▸ **déposer un brevet** to file a patent application, to apply for a patent ▸ **déposer une plainte** to lodge a complaint / *déposer un projet de loi* to introduce ou to table a bill **7.** [destituer - roi] to depose **8.** [démonter - radiateur, étagère] to remove, to take out ou down *(sép)*. ◆ vi DR to give evidence, to testify. ⬥ **se déposer** vpi to settle.

dépositaire [depozitɛʀ] nmf **1.** DR depositary, trustee **2.** COMM agent ▸ **dépositaire exclusif** sole agent.

déposition [depozisjɔ̃] nf **1.** [témoignage] deposition, evidence, statement ▸ **faire une déposition** to testify **2.** [destitution - d'un roi] deposition.

déposséder [18] [deposede] vt to dispossess ▸ **déposséder qqn de** to deprive sb of.

⟶ In reformed spelling (see p. 16-18), this verb is conjugated like *semer* : *il dépossèdera, elle dépossèderait*.

dépôt [depo] nm **1.** ADMIN [inscription] application, filing ; [enregistrement] filing, registration ▸ **dépôt de bilan** petition in bankruptcy ▸ **dépôt légal** copyright deposit *(in France, copies of published or recorded documents have to be deposited at the Bibliothèque nationale de France)* **2.** FIN [démarche] depositing ; [somme] deposit **3.** GÉOL deposit ; [couche] layer ; [sédiment] deposit, sediment ▸ **dépôt calcaire** ou **de tartre** layer of scale ou fur ▸ **dépôt marin** silt **4.** [entrepôt] store, warehouse ▸ **dépôt d'ordures** rubbish dump ou tip 🇬🇧, garbage dump 🇺🇸 **5.** MIL depot ▸ **dépôt de munitions** ammunition dump **6.** TRANSP depot, station 🇺🇸 **7.** [boutique] retail outlet ▸ **dépôt de pain** *shop that sells bread (but which is not a bakery)* **8.** [prison] (police) cells *(in Paris)* ▸ **au dépôt** in the cells. ⟶ **en dépôt** loc adv FIN in trust, in safe custody ▸ **avoir en dépôt** to have on bond.

dépoter [3] [depote] vt HORT to plant out *(sép)*, to transplant.

dépotoir [depotwaʀ] nm **1.** [décharge] rubbish dump 🇬🇧, garbage dump 🇺🇸 ; [usine] disposal plant, sewage works 🇬🇧, sewage plant 🇺🇸 **2.** *péj* [lieu sale] pigsty **3.** *fam* [débarras] dumping ground.

dépouille [depuj] nf **1.** [cadavre] ▸ **dépouille (mortelle)** (mortal) remains **2.** [peau - d'un mammifère] hide, skin ; [- d'un reptile] slough.

dépouillement [depujmɑ̃] nm **1.** [analyse] breakdown, collection and analysis ▸ **dépouillement d'un scrutin** tally ou counting of the votes **2.** [ouverture] ▸ **dépouillement du courrier** opening of the mail **3.** [simplicité - d'un décor] bareness, soberness **4.** [dénuement] dispossession, destitution.

dépouiller [3] [depuje] vt **1.** [lapin] to skin **2.** [câble] to strip **3.** [voler] to deprive, to dispossess, to despoil *litt* / *ils m'ont dépouillé de tout ce que j'avais sur moi* they stripped me of ou took everything I had on me **4.** [lire - journal, courrier, inventaire] to go through *(insép)* ; [analyser - questionnaire, réponses] to analyse, to study, to scrutinize ; [- données] to process ▸ **dépouiller le scrutin** POL to count the votes.

dépourvu, e [depuʀvy] adj [manquant] ▸ **dépourvu de** devoid of, lacking in / *c'est dépourvu de tout intérêt* it is of ou holds no interest at all. ⟶ **au dépourvu** loc adv ▸ **prendre qqn au dépourvu** to catch sb off guard ou unawares.

dépoussiérer [18] [depusjeʀe] vt **1.** [nettoyer] to dust (off) **2.** [rajeunir] to rejuvenate, to give a new lease of life to.

⟶ In reformed spelling (see p. 16-18), this verb is conjugated like *semer* : *il dépoussièrera, elle dépoussièrerait*

dépravé, e [depʀave] ◆ adj immoral, depraved, perverted. ◆ nm, f degenerate, pervert.

dépraver [3] [depʀave] vt [corrompre] to deprave, to corrupt, to pervert. ⟶ **se dépraver** vpi to become depraved ou perverted.

déprécier [9] [depʀesje] vt **1.** FIN to depreciate, to cause to drop in value **2.** [dénigrer] to run down *(sép)*, to belittle, to disparage. ⟶ **se déprécier** ◆ vp *(emploi réfléchi)* [se déconsidérer] to belittle ou to disparage o.s., to run o.s. down. ◆ vpi FIN to depreciate.

dépressif, ive [depʀesif, iv] adj [personne] depressive, easily depressed out ; [caractère] depressive.

dépression [depʀesjɔ̃] nf **1.** MÉD & PSYCHOL depression, depressiveness ▸ **dépression nerveuse** nervous breakdown / *avoir* ou *faire fam une dépression (nerveuse)* to have a nervous breakdown **2.** GÉOGR depression **3.** [absence de pression] vacuum ; [différence de pression] suction **4.** MÉTÉOR cyclone, barometric depression, low **5.** ÉCON depression, slump.

déprimant, e [depʀimɑ̃, ɑ̃t] adj [démoralisant] depressing, disheartening, demoralizing.

déprime [depʀim] nf *fam* ▸ **faire une déprime** to be depressed.

déprimé, e [depʀime] adj [abattu] dejected, depressed / *je suis plutôt déprimé aujourd'hui* I feel rather down today.

déprimer [3] [depʀime] ◆ vt [abattre] to depress, to demoralize. ◆ vi *fam* to be depressed.

déprogrammer [3] [depʀɔgʀame] vt RADIO & TV to withdraw ou to remove from the schedule.

dépuceler [24] [depysle] vt to deflower / *se faire dépuceler* to lose one's virginity.

⟶ In reformed spelling (see p. 16-18), this verb is conjugated like *peler* : *il dépucèlera, elle dépucèlerait*.

depuis [dəpɥi] ◆ prép **1.** [à partir d'une date ou d'un moment précis] since ▸ **depuis le 10 mars** since March 10th ▸ **depuis le début** from the very beginning, right from the beginning / *je ne fais du golf que depuis cette année* I only started to play golf this year **2.** [exprimant une durée] for ▸ **depuis 10 ans** for 10 years / *depuis longtemps* for a long time ▸ **depuis quelque temps** of late ▸ **depuis peu** recently, not long ago / *depuis combien de temps le connais-tu ?* how long have you known him for? ▸ **depuis le temps**: *et tu ne sais toujours pas t'en servir depuis le temps !* and you still don't know how to use it after all this time! **3.** [dans l'espace, un ordre, une hiérarchie] from / *il lui a fait signe depuis sa fenêtre* he waved to him from his window. ◆ adv : *je ne l'ai rencontré qu'une fois, je ne l'ai jamais revu depuis* I only met him once and I've not seen him again since (then). ⟶ **depuis... jusqu'à** loc corrélative **1.** [dans le temps] from... to / *depuis 12 h jusqu'à 20 h* from 12 to ou till 8 p.m. **2.** [dans l'espace, un ordre, une hiérarchie] from... to / *ils vendent de tout, depuis les parapluies jusqu'aux sandwiches* they sell everything, from umbrellas to sandwiches. ⟶ **depuis le temps que** loc conj : *depuis le temps que tu me le promets...* you've been promising me that for such a long time... / *depuis le temps que tu le connais, tu pourrais lui demander* considering how long you've known him you could easily ask him. ⟶ **depuis quand** loc adv **1.** [pour interroger sur la durée] how long / *depuis quand m'attends-tu ?* how long have you been waiting for me? **2.** [exprimant l'indignation, l'ironie] since when / *depuis quand est-ce que tu me donnes des ordres ?* since when do you give me orders? ⟶ **depuis que** loc conj since / *je ne l'ai pas revu depuis qu'il s'est marié* I haven't seen him since he got married.

députation [depytasjɔ̃] nf POL office of Deputy, membership of the Assemblée nationale / *se présenter à la députation* to stand for the position of Deputy.

député, e [depyte] nm, f POL [en France] deputy ; [en Grande-Bretagne] member of Parliament, woman MP ; [aux États-Unis] Congressman (Congresswoman), representative ▸ **député européen** Euro-MP.

déraciner [3] [deʀasine] vt BOT to uproot ▸ **déraciner qqn** *fig* to uproot sb, to deprive sb of his roots.

déraillement [deʀajmɑ̃] nm RAIL derailment.

dérailler [3] [deʀaje] vi **1.** RAIL to go off ou to leave the rails ▸ **faire dérailler un train** to derail a train **2.** *fam* [fonctionner mal] to be on the blink / *faire dérailler les* *négociations* to derail the talks **3.** *fam* [déraisonner] to go off the rails ; [se tromper] to talk through one's hat / *tu dérailles complètement !* you're talking utter nonsense!

dérailleur [deʀajœʀ] nm derailleur (gear).

déraisonnable [deʀɛzɔnabl] adj foolish, senseless.

dérangé, e [deʀɑ̃ʒe] adj **1.** *fam* [fou] deranged / *il a l'esprit un peu dérangé* he's lost his marbles, he's lost the plot 🇬🇧 **2.** [malade] upset / *il a l'estomac* ou *il est dérangé* he's got an upset stomach.

dérangement [deʀɑ̃ʒmɑ̃] nm **1.** [gêne] trouble, inconvenience **2.** [déplacement] trip ▸ *cela m'épargnera le dérangement* it'll save me having to go / *cela ne vaut pas / vaut le dérangement* it isn't / it's worth the trip. ❖ **en dérangement** loc adj [appareil, téléphone] out of order, faulty.

déranger [17] [deʀɑ̃ʒe] ◆ vt **1.** [mettre en désordre] to mix ou to muddle up *(sép)*, to make a mess of **2.** [gêner] to bother, to disturb / 'ne pas déranger' 'do not disturb' / *si cela ne vous dérange pas* if you don't mind ▸ *est-ce que cela vous dérange si* ou *que...* do you mind if... / *ça ne te dérange pas de poster ma lettre ?* would you mind posting my letter for me? / *et alors, ça te dérange ?* *fam* so, what's it to you? **3.** [interrompre] to interrupt, to intrude upon ▸ *désolé de vous déranger* sorry to disturb you **4.** [perturber - projets] to interfere with, to upset / *ça lui a dérangé l'esprit* she was badly shaken up by it. ◆ vi ▸ *ses livres dérangent* his books are challenging. ❖ **se déranger** vpi **1.** [venir] to come ; [sortir] to go out / *il a refusé de se déranger* he wouldn't come (out) ▸ *se déranger pour rien* to have a wasted journey **2.** [se pousser] to move (aside) / *ne te dérange pas, je passe très bien* stay where you are, I can get through **3.** [se donner du mal] to put o.s. out / *ne vous dérangez pas, je reviendrai* please don't go to any trouble, I'll come back later.

dérapage [deʀapaʒ] nm **1.** SPORT [en ski] side-slipping / *faire du dérapage* to sideslip ; [en moto] skidding **2.** AÉRON & AUTO skid ▸ *dérapage contrôlé* controlled skid **3.** [dérive] (uncontrolled) drifting / *le dérapage des prix* the uncontrolled increase in prices **4.** [erreur] mistake, slip-up.

déraper [3] [deʀape] vi **1.** [gén] to skid **2.** [au ski] to sideslip **3.** *fig* to go wrong / *ça a complètement dérapé* it went completely wrong / *la conversation a vite dérapé sur la politique* the conversation soon got round to politics.

dératisation [deʀatizasjɔ̃] nf rodent control.

déréglement [deʀɛɡləmɑ̃] nm [dérangement] disturbance, trouble / *déréglement des saisons* upsetting of the seasons.

déréglementation[deʀɛɡləmɑ̃tasjɔ̃], **dérèglementation*** [deʀɛɡləmɑ̃tasjɔ̃] nf deregulation.

déréglementer [deʀɛɡləmɑ̃te], **dérèglementer*** [deʀɛɡləmɑ̃te] [3] vt to deregulate.

dérégler [18] [deʀeɡle] vt **1.** MÉCAN [mécanisme] to disturb, to put out *(sép)* ; [carburateur] to put ou to throw out of tuning ▸ *le compteur est déréglé* the meter's not working properly **2.** [perturber] to unsettle, to upset. ❖ **se dérégler** vpi MÉCAN to go wrong, to start malfunctioning / *le carburateur s'est déréglé* the carburettor's out, the idling needs adjusting.

✏ In reformed spelling (see p. 16-18), this verb is conjugated like *semer* : *il dérèglera, elle dérèglerait.*

dérembourser [deʀɑ̃buʀse] vt [les médicaments] to no longer reimburse (the cost of).

déresponsabilisation [deʀɛspɔ̃sabilizasjɔ̃] nf : *on constate une déresponsabilisation des parents* parents clearly have less of a sense of responsibility.

dérider [3] [deʀide] vt [détendre] to cheer up *(sép)*. ❖ **se dérider** vpi to brighten, to cheer up.

dérision [deʀizjɔ̃] nf [moquerie] derision, mockery ▸ *avec dérision* mockingly, derisively ▸ *tourner qqn / qqch en dérision* to scoff at sb / sthg.

dérisoire [deʀizwaʀ] adj **1.** [risible] ridiculous, laughable **2.** [piètre - salaire, prix] derisory, ridiculous **3.** [sans effet] inadequate, trifling, pathetic.

dérivatif [deʀivatif] nm distraction / *le travail sert de dérivatif à son chagrin* work is an outlet for his grief.

dérivation [deʀivasjɔ̃] nf **1.** ÉLECTR shunt, branch circuit **2.** CHIM, LING & MATH derivation.

dérive [deʀiv] nf **1.** [dérapage] drifting, drift ▸ *la dérive de l'économie* the downward spiral of the economy ▸ *aller à la dérive* **a)** *pr* to drift, to go adrift **b)** *fig* to go downhill **2.** NAUT [déplacement] drift, drifting off course ; [quille] centreboard 🇬🇧, centerboard 🇺🇸, keel ▸ *partir à la dérive* to drift **3.** GÉOGR ▸ *dérive des continents* continental drift.

dérivé, e [deʀive] adj LING & MATH derived. ❖ **dérivé** nm **1.** CHIM derivative **2.** [sous-produit] by-product.

dériver [3] [deʀive] vi NAUT to drift, to be adrift. ◆ vt **1.** ÉLECTR to shunt **2.** CHIM & MATH to derive. ❖ **dériver de** v + prép **1.** [être issu de] to derive ou to come from **2.** LING to stem ou derive from.

dériveur [deʀivœʀ] nm [bateau] sailing dinghy *(with a centreboard)*.

dermato [dɛʀmato] nmf *fam* dermatologist, skin-specialist.

dermatologie [dɛʀmatɔlɔʒi] nf dermatology.

dermatologiste [dɛʀmatɔlɔʒist], **dermatologue** [dɛʀmatɔlɔɡ] nmf dermatologist, skin-specialist.

dernier, ère [dɛʀnje, dɛʀnjɛʀ] *(devant nm commençant par voyelle ou « h » muet* [dɛʀnjɛʀ]*)* ◆ adj

🔲 **A. DANS LE TEMPS 1.** *(avant nom)* [qui vient après tous les autres - avion, bus, personne] last / [- détail, préparatif] final / *un dernier mot / point !* one final word / point ! / *il vient de terminer ses derniers examens* [en fin de cycle d'études] he's just taken his final exams ou finals ▸ *jusqu'à son dernier jour* to his dying day, until the day he died ▸ *ses dernières volontés* his last wishes ▸ *dernier arrivant* ou *arrivé* ou *venu* latecomer ▸ *la dernière édition* the late edition ▸ *la dernière séance* the last ou late performance **2.** *(avant nom)* [arrêté, ultime] final ▸ *c'est mon dernier prix* **a)** [vendeur] it's the lowest I'll go **b)** [acheteur] that's my final offer **3.** [précédent] last, previous / *la nuit dernière* last night ▸ *ces dix dernières années* these last ten years **4.** *(avant nom)* [le plus récent] last, latest / *je ferai mes valises au dernier moment* I'll pack at the last minute ou possible moment / *une nouvelle de dernière minute* a late newsflash ▸ *ces derniers temps* lately, of late / *tu connais la dernière nouvelle ?* have you heard the latest? / *aux dernières nouvelles, le mariage aurait été annulé* according to the latest news, the wedding's been cancelled ▸ *de dernière heure* [changement] last-minute.

🔲 **B. DANS L'ESPACE 1.** [du bas - étagère] bottom **2.** [du haut] top ▸ *au dernier étage* on the top floor **3.** [du bout] last / *un siège au dernier rang* a seat in the back (row).

🔲 **C. DANS UN CLASSEMENT 1.** [dans une série] last / *suite à la dernière page* continued on the back page **2.** [le plus mauvais] last, bottom / *en dernière position* in last position, last ▸ *arriver bon dernier* to come in last **3.** [le meilleur] top, highest / *le dernier échelon* the highest level.

🔲 **D. EN INTENSIF 1.** *(avant nom)* [extrême, sens positif] ▸ *du dernier chic* extremely smart / *atteindre le dernier degré de la perfection* to attain the summit of perfection

* In reformed spelling (see p. 16-18).

2. *(avant nom)* [extrême, sens négatif] : *un acte de la dernière lâcheté* the most cowardly of acts ▸ **traiter qqn avec le dernier mépris** to treat sb with the greatest contempt / *il est la dernière personne à qui je penserais* he's the last person I'd have thought of!

◆ nm, f **1.** [dans le temps] last ou final one / *je suis partie la dernière* I left last, I was the last one to leave ; [dans une famille] youngest ▸ **le petit dernier** the youngest son / *la petite dernière* the youngest daughter **2.** [dans l'espace - celui du haut] top one ; [- celui du bas] last ou bottom one ; [- celui du bout] last one / *son dossier est le dernier de la pile* her file is at the bottom of the pile **3.** [dans une hiérarchie - le pire] : *j'étais toujours le dernier en classe* I was always (at the) bottom of the class / *tu arrives le dernier avec 34 points* you come last with 34 points / *tu es le dernier des imbéciles* fam you're a complete idiot ; [dans une série] last one / *allez, on en prend un dernier !* [verre] let's have a last one (for the road)! **4.** [dans une narration] ▸ **ce dernier, cette dernière a)** [de deux] the latter **b)** [de plusieurs] this last, the last-mentioned. ◆ **dernier** nm **1.** [étage] top floor **2.** [dans une charade] ▸ **mon dernier est / a...** my last is / has... ◆ **dernière** nf **1.** THÉÂTRE last performance **2.** *fam* [nouvelle] : *tu connais la dernière ?* have you heard the latest? ◆ **au dernier degré, au dernier point** loc adv extremely, to the highest ou last degree. ◆ **en dernier** loc adv last ▸ **entrer en dernier** to go in last, to be the last one to go in / *son nom a été mentionné en dernier* his name was mentioned last ou was the last one to be mentioned.

dernièrement [dɛʀnjɛʀmɑ̃] adv lately, not long ago, (quite) recently.

dernier-né, dernière-née [dɛʀnjene, dɛʀnjɛʀne] *(mpl* derniers-nés, *fpl* dernières-nées) nm, f **1.** [benjamin] last-born (child), youngest child **2.** COMM : *le dernier-né de notre gamme d'ordinateurs* the latest addition to our range of computers.

dérobé, e [deʀɔbe] adj *sout* [caché] hidden, concealed, secret ▸ **couloir / escalier dérobé** secret corridor / staircase. ◆ **à la dérobée** loc adv secretly, on the sly, furtively ▸ **regarder qqn à la dérobée** to steal a glance at sb.

dérober [3] [deʀɔbe] vt *sout* **1.** [voler] to steal ▸ **dérober qqch à qqn** to steal sthg from sb **2.** [cacher] ▸ **dérober qqch à la vue** to hide ou to conceal sthg from view. ◆ **se dérober** vpi **1.** [éluder la difficulté] to shy away / *n'essaie pas de te dérober* don't try to be evasive **2.** ÉQUIT to jib, to refuse **3.** [s'effondrer] to collapse, to give way / *ses jambes se sont dérobées sous lui* his legs gave way under him. ◆ **se dérober à** vp + prép to avoid, to evade.

dérogation [deʀɔgasjɔ̃] nf (special) dispensation ou exemption.

déroger [17] [deʀɔʒe] ◆ **déroger à** v + prép [manquer à] to depart from / *sans déroger à ses habitudes* without departing from one's usual practices.

dérouiller [3] [deʀuje] vi *fam* **1.** [être battu] to get it / *tu vas dérouiller !* you're for it ou going to get it! **2.** [souffrir] to be in agony. ◆ **se dérouiller** vpt : *se dérouiller les jambes* to stretch one's legs.

déroulant, e [deʀulɑ̃, ɑ̃t] adj ▸ **menu déroulant** INFORM pull-down menu.

déroulé [deʀule] nm sequence, proceedings *pl* / *le déroulé d'un procès* court proceedings.

déroulement [deʀulmɑ̃] nm [cours - d'une cérémonie, d'un discours] course / *le déroulement des événements* the course ou sequence of events.

dérouler [3] [deʀule] vt [débobiner - câble] to unroll, to unwind, to uncoil ; [- tapis, rouleau] to unroll. ◆ **se dérouler** vpi **1.** [se déployer - câble, bande] to unwind, to uncoil, to unroll / *le paysage se déroule sous nos yeux* the landscape unfolds before our eyes **2.** [avoir lieu] to take place, to be going on / *les spectacles qui se déroulent en ce moment* the shows currently running **3.** [progresser] to develop, to progress.

déroutant, e [deʀutɑ̃, ɑ̃t] adj perplexing, disconcerting, puzzling.

déroute [deʀut] nf **1.** MIL retreat, rout ▸ **mettre qqn en déroute** to disconcert sb **2.** [débâcle] ruin.

dérouter [3] [deʀute] vt **1.** [changer l'itinéraire de] to reroute, to divert UK, to detour US **2.** [étonner] to disconcert, to perplex.

derrick [deʀik] nm derrick.

derrière [dɛʀjɛʀ] ◆ prép **1.** [en arrière de] behind / *ça s'est passé derrière chez moi* it happened behind my house / *il y a un chien derrière la grille* there's a dog (on) the other side of the gate ; *fig* : *ne sois pas toujours derrière moi !* [à me surveiller] stop watching everything I do all the time! ▸ **derrière le dos de qqn** : *je sais bien ce qu'elle dit derrière mon dos* I'm quite aware of what she says behind my back **2.** [à la suite de - dans un classement] behind **3.** [sous] beneath, under / *derrière son indifférence apparente* beneath his apparent indifference. ◆ adv **1.** [en arrière] behind, the other side / *tu vois le bureau de poste ? la bibliothèque est juste derrière* do you see the post office? the library's just behind it **2.** [du côté arrière] at the back ; [sur la face arrière] on the back / *écris le nom de l'expéditeur derrière* write the sender's name on the back **3.** [dans le fond] at the rear ou back ▸ **installe-toi derrière** [dans une voiture] sit in the back. ◆ nm **1.** [d'un objet, d'un espace] back **2.** *fam* [fesses] bottom, posterior *hum* / *pousse ton derrière !* shift your backside! ▸ **coup de pied au derrière** kick up the backside ou US in the pants **3.** ZOOL rump / *le chien assis sur son derrière* the dog sitting on its haunches. ◆ **de derrière** loc adj [dent, jardin, roue, etc.] back *(modif)* / *voici une vue de derrière* here's a rear view. ◆ loc prép **1.** [par l'arrière de] from behind **2.** [EXPR] **de derrière les fagots** very special. ◆ **par derrière** loc adv from behind / *il est passé par derrière* [la maison] he went round the back ▸ **dire du mal de qqn par derrière** to criticize sb behind his / her back.

des [de] ◆ dét *(art indéf)* ⟶ **un.** ◆ prép ⟶ **de.**

dès [dɛ] prép **1.** [dans le temps] from / *dès son retour, il faudra y penser* as soon as he comes back, we'll have to think about it ▸ **dès le début** from the (very) beginning ▸ **prêt dès 8 h** ready by 8 o'clock / *pouvez-vous commencer dès maintenant ?* can you start straight away? **2.** [dans un ordre, une hiérarchie] ▸ **dès la seconde année** from the second year onwards ▸ **dès sa nomination** as soon as he was appointed **3.** [dans l'espace] : *dès la frontière* on reaching the border. ◆ **dès lors** loc adv **1.** [à partir de là] from then on, since (then) **2.** [en conséquence] consequently, therefore. ◆ **dès lors que** loc conj **1.** [étant donné que] as, since ; [du moment où] from the moment (that) **2.** [puisque] as soon as. ◆ **dès que** loc conj **1.** [aussitôt que] as soon as / *dès que possible* as soon as possible **2.** [chaque fois que] whenever / *dès qu'il peut, il part en vacances* whenever he can, he goes off on holiday.

désabusé, e [dezabyze] adj **1.** [déçu] disillusioned, disenchanted **2.** [amer] embittered.

désaccord [dezakɔʀ] nm **1.** [litige] conflict, disagreement, dissension *(U)* **2.** [contraste] discrepancy, disharmony *litt.* ◆ **en désaccord** loc adj ▸ **être en désaccord avec qqn sur qqch** to be in conflict with sb over sthg.

désaccorder [3] [dezakɔʀde] vt MUS to detune ▸ **le piano est désaccordé** the piano's out of tune.

désactiver [3] [dezaktive] vt INFORM to disable.

désaffecté, e [dezafɛkte] adj [église] deconsecrated, secularized ; [gare, entrepôt] disused.

désaffection [dezafɛksjɔ̃] nf disaffection, loss of interest.

désagréable [dezagʀeabl] adj **1.** [déplaisant] disagreeable, unpleasant **2.** [peu sociable] bad-tempered, rude.

désagréablement [dezagʀeabləmã] adv unpleasantly, offensively.

désagréger [22] [dezagʀeʒe] ⇌ **se désagréger** vpi **1.** [s'effriter] to powder ; GÉOL to be weathered **2.** [groupe, équipe] to break up, to disband.

📖 In reformed spelling (see p. 16-18), this verb is conjugated like *semer : il désagrègera, elle désagrègerait.*

désagrément [dezagʀemã] nm trouble *(U)*, inconvenience *(U)* ▶ **causer des désagréments à qqn** to cause trouble for sb, to inconvenience sb.

désalinisation, dessalinisation [desalinizasjɔ̃] nf desalination.

désaltérant, e [dezalteʀã, ãt] adj refreshing, thirst-quenching.

désaltérer [18] [dezalteʀe] ⇌ **se désaltérer** vpi to quench ou to slake one's thirst.

📖 In reformed spelling (see p. 16-18), this verb is conjugated like *semer : il désaltèrera, elle désaltèrerait.*

désamiantage [dezamjãtaʒ] nm removal of asbestos.

désamorcer [16] [dezamɔʀse] vt **1.** ARM [grenade] to defuse ; [arme] to unprime **2.** [contrecarrer] to defuse, to forestall, to inhibit.

désapprobateur, trice [dezapʀɔbatœʀ, tʀis] adj censorious *sout*, disapproving.

désapprobation [dezapʀɔbasjɔ̃] nf disapproval.

désapprouver [3] [dezapʀuve] vt **1.** [condamner] to disapprove of **2.** [s'opposer à - projet, idée] to object to, to reject.

désarçonner [3] [dezaʀsɔne] vt **1.** ÉQUIT to unseat, to unhorse **2.** [déconcerter] to throw, to put off one's stride.

désargenté, e [dezaʀʒãte] adj *fam* penniless.

désarmant, e [dezaʀmã, ãt] adj [touchant] disarming.

désarmement [dezaʀməmã] nm MIL & POL disarmament.

désarmer [3] [dezaʀme] ◆ vt **1.** MIL & POL to disarm **2.** [attendrir] to disarm **3.** NAUT to lay up *(sép)*, to put out of commission. ◆ vi EXPR **il ne désarme pas** he won't give in, he keeps battling on.

désarroi [dezaʀwa] nm dismay, (utter) confusion / *être dans le désarroi le plus profond* to be utterly dismayed, to be in utter confusion.

désastre [dezastʀ] nm **1.** [calamité] calamity, catastrophe, disaster **2.** [échec] disaster, failure.

désastreux, euse [dezastʀø, øz] adj [résultat, effet] disastrous, awful, terrible.

désavantage [dezavãtaʒ] nm **1.** [inconvénient] disadvantage, drawback **2.** [infériorité] disadvantage, handicap. ⇌ **au désavantage de** loc prép ▶ **tourner au désavantage de qqn** to go against sb, to turn out to be a handicap for sb.

désavantager [17] [dezavãtaʒe] vt [défavoriser] to (put at a) disadvantage, to penalize / *il est désavantagé par son jeune âge* he is handicapped by his youth, his youth is against him / *elle est désavantagée simplement parce que c'est une femme* she's at a disadvantage simply because she is a woman.

désavantageux, euse [dezavãtaʒø, øz] adj detrimental, disadvantageous, unfavourable 🇬🇧, unfavorable 🇺🇸.

désaveu, x [dezavø] nm **1.** [reniement] disavowal, retraction **2.** [condamnation] repudiation.

désavouer [6] [dezavwe] vt **1.** [renier - propos] to disavow, to repudiate ; [- dette] to repudiate **2.** [refuser de reconnaître - représentant, candidat] to challenge the authority ou legitimacy of.

désaxé, e [dezakse] ◆ adj [dérangé] mentally deranged, unbalanced, unhinged. ◆ nm, f (dangerous) lunatic, psychopath.

descendance [desãdãs] nf [progéniture] descendants.

descendant, e [desãdã, ãt] ◆ adj down *(avant nom)*, downward, descending. ◆ nm, f [dans une famille] descendant.

descendre [73] [desãdʀ]
◆ vi *(aux être)*

A. ALLER VERS LE BAS **1.** [personne, mécanisme, avion - vu d'en haut] to go down ; [- vu d'en bas] to come down ; [oiseau] to fly ou to swoop down / *j'ai rencontré la concierge en descendant* I met the caretaker on my way down / *aide-moi à descendre* help me down / *son chapeau lui descendait jusqu'aux yeux* his hat came down over his eyes ▶ **faire descendre** : *fais descendre la malade* help the patient down / *ils nous ont fait descendre du train* they made us get off the train ▶ **descendre de qqch** a) [échafaudage, échelle] to come ou to climb down from, to get down from b) [arbre] to climb ou to come down out of c) [balançoire] to get off ▶ **descendre dans la rue** [manifester] to take to the streets **2.** [air froid, brouillard] to come down ; [soleil] to go down ▶ **la nuit** ou **le soir descend** night is closing in ou falling **3.** [se rendre - dans un lieu d'altitude inférieure, dans le Sud, à la campagne] to go down **4.** [poser pied à terre - d'un véhicule] to get off, to alight *sout* ▶ **descendre à terre** ou **to go ashore** ▶ **descendre de bateau** to get off a boat, to land ▶ **descendre de voiture** to get out of a car / *à quelle station descendez-vous ?* where do you get off? **5.** [faire irruption] : *la police est descendue chez elle* / *dans son bar* the police raided her place / her bar **6.** [se loger] to stay / *descendre dans un hôtel* to put up at ou to stay at a hotel.

B. ÊTRE EN PENTE [suivre une pente - rivière] to flow down ; [- route] to go down ou downwards 🇬🇧 ou downward 🇺🇸 ; [- toit] to slope down / *le jardin descend en pente douce jusqu'à la plage* the garden slopes gently down to the beach ▶ **descendre en pente raide** [route, terrain, toit] to drop sharply.

C. ALLER JUSQU'À **1.** ▶ **descendre à** ou **jusqu'à** a) [cheveux, vêtement] to come down to b) [puits] to go down to / *la jupe doit descendre jusqu'au-dessous du genou* the skirt must cover the knee **2.** [baisser - marée, mer] to go out *(insép)*, to ebb ; [- prix] to go down, to fall / *la température est descendue au-dessous de zéro* the temperature has dropped ou fallen below zero ▶ **le thermomètre descend** *fam* the weather's ou it's getting colder ▶ **faire descendre** [inflation, prix] to bring ou to push down *(sép)* / *faire descendre la fièvre* to bring down sb's temperature / *ça a fait descendre les prix* it brought prices down **3.** [s'abaisser moralement] to stoop **4.** MUS to go ou to drop an octave.

◆ vt *(aux avoir)* **1.** [parcourir - escalier, montagne] to go down *(insép)* ▶ **descendre un fleuve** a) [en nageant] to swim downstream b) [en bateau] to sail down a river **2.** [placer plus bas - tableau] to lower ; [- store] to pull down *(sép)*, to lower / *il faudrait descendre le cadre de deux centimètres* the frame should be taken down two centimetres **3.** [porter vers le bas - colis] to take down *(sép)*, to get down *(sép)* ; [- porter vers soi] to bring down *(sép)* **4.** [amener en voiture] to take ou to drive down *(sép)* **5.** *fam* [abattre - gangster] to gun ou to shoot down *(sép)* ; [- avion] to bring ou to shoot

down *(sép)* ▸ **se faire descendre** to get shot **6.** *fam* [critiquer] to pan, to slate **7.** *fam* [boire - bouteille] to down, to knock back *(sép).* ❖ **descendre de** v + prép [être issu de] to be descended from.

descente [desɑ̃t] nf **1.** [pente] slope, hill / *courir / déraper dans la descente* to run / to skid down / *on ira vite, il n'y a que des descentes* we'll do it in no time, it's all downhill **2.** [progression] going down ; [chute] drop, fall **3.** [sortie d'un véhicule] getting off, alighting ▸ **à sa descente d'avion** as he disembarked ou got off the aircraft **4.** SKI downhill race ; ALPINISME ▸ **descente en rappel** abseiling **5.** AÉRON descent **6.** [contrôle] inspection ; [attaque] raid ▸ **descente de police** police raid. ❖ **descente de lit** nf [tapis] bedside rug.

descriptif, ive [dɛskʀiptif, iv] adj [présentation, texte] descriptive. ❖ **descriptif** nm [d'un appartement] description ; [de travaux] specification.

description [dɛskʀipsjɔ̃] nf **1.** [fait de décrire] description ▸ **faire la description de qqch** to describe sthg **2.** ART & LITTÉR description, descriptive passage.

désectoriser [desɛktɔʀize] vt [l'école, un département] to remove catchment area boundaries from.

désemparé, e [dezɑ̃paʀe] adj [perdu] ▸ **être désemparé** to be lost.

désemplir [32] [dezɑ̃pliʀ] vi : *leur maison ne désemplit pas* their house is always full.

désencombrer [3] [dezɑ̃kɔ̃bʀe] vt to clear, to unblock.

désendettement [dezɑ̃dɛtmɑ̃] nm clearing of debts, debt-clearing.

désenfler [3] [dezɑ̃fle] vi to become less swollen / *ma cheville désenfle* the swelling in my ankle's going down.

désengagement [dezɑ̃gaʒmɑ̃] nm disengagement, backing out.

désensibiliser [3] [desɑ̃sibilize] vt MÉD & PHOT to desensitize.

déséquilibre [dezekilibʀ] nm **1.** [inégalité] imbalance ; ÉCON disequilibrium, imbalance **2.** PSYCHOL ▸ **déséquilibre mental** ou **psychique** derangement. ❖ **en déséquilibre** loc adj [mal posé] off balance ; [branlant] unsteady, wobbly.

déséquilibré, e [dezekilibʀe] ◆ adj [personne, esprit] unbalanced, deranged. ◆ nm, f maladjusted person.

déséquilibrer [3] [dezekilibʀe] vt **1.** [faire perdre l'équilibre à] to throw off balance ; [faire tomber] to tip over / *le vent l'a déséquilibré* the wind blew him off balance **2.** [déstabiliser - système, économie] to throw off balance, to destabilize **3.** [faire déraisonner] ▸ **déséquilibrer qqn** to disturb the balance of sb's mind.

désert, e [dezɛʀ, ɛʀt] adj [abandonné] deserted, empty ; [inhabité] desolate, uninhabited. ❖ **désert** nm **1.** GÉOGR desert **2.** [lieu inhabité] desert, wilderness, wasteland.

Déserts

le désert de Gobi	the Gobi Desert
le désert du Kalahari	the Kalahari Desert
le désert du Sahara	the Sahara Desert

déserter [3] [dezɛʀte] ◆ vi MIL to desert. ◆ vt **1.** [quitter sans permission] to desert **2.** [suj : touristes, clients] to desert.

déserteur [dezɛʀtœʀ] nm deserter.

désertification [dezɛʀtifikasjɔ̃] nf GÉOGR desertification.

désertion [dezɛʀsjɔ̃] nf MIL desertion.

désertique [dezɛʀtik] adj [du désert] desert *(modif)* ; [sans végétation] infertile.

désespérant, e [dezɛspeʀɑ̃, ɑ̃t] adj **1.** [navrant] hopeless **2.** [très mauvais - temps] appalling, dreadful **3.** [douloureux] appalling, distressing, terrible.

désespéré, e [dezɛspeʀe] adj **1.** [au désespoir] desperate, despairing **2.** [extrême - tentative] desperate, reckless ; [- mesure, situation] desperate **3.** [sans espoir] hopeless / *être dans un état désespéré* [malade] to be in a critical condition.

désespérément [dezɛspeʀemɑ̃] adv **1.** [avec désespoir] desperately **2.** [extrêmement] hopelessly, desperately.

désespérer [18] [dezɛspeʀe] ◆ vi to despair, to give up hope. ◆ vt **1.** [exaspérer] to drive to despair **2.** [décourager] to drive ou to reduce to despair. ❖ **désespérer de** v + prép ▸ **désespérer de qqch** to have lost faith in sthg ▸ **désespérer de faire qqch** to despair of doing sthg. ❖ **se désespérer** vpi to (be in) despair.

✎ In reformed spelling (see p. 16-18), this verb is conjugated like *semer* : *il désespèrera, elle désespèrerait*.

désespoir [dezɛspwaʀ] nm despair ▸ **faire le désespoir de qqn** to drive ou to reduce sb to despair. ❖ **au désespoir** loc adj ▸ **être au désespoir** [être désespéré] to be desperate, to have lost all hope. ❖ **en désespoir de cause** loc adv in desperation, as a last resort.

déshabillé [dezabije] nm négligé.

déshabiller [3] [dezabije] vt [dévêtir] ▸ **déshabiller qqn** to undress sb, to take sb's clothes off. ❖ **se déshabiller** vp *(emploi réfléchi)* **1.** [se dénuder] to strip (off), to take one's clothes off **2.** [ôter un vêtement] : *déshabille-toi* take off your coat.

déshabituer [7] [dezabitɥe] vt ▸ **déshabituer qqn du tabac** to make sb give up (using) tobacco ▸ **déshabituer qqn de faire qqch** to break sb of the habit of doing sthg.

désherbant [dezɛʀbɑ̃] nm weedkiller.

désherber [3] [dezɛʀbe] vt to weed.

déshérité, e [dezeʀite] ◆ adj **1.** [pauvre] underprivileged, deprived **2.** [région] poor *(lacking natural advantages).* ◆ nm, f deprived person ▸ **les déshérités** the destitute.

déshériter [3] [dezeʀite] vt [priver d'héritage] to cut out of one's will, to disinherit.

déshonneur [dezɔnœʀ] nm **1.** [perte de l'honneur] disgrace, dishonour 🇬🇧, dishonor 🇺🇸 **2.** [honte] disgrace.

déshonorant, e [dezɔnɔʀɑ̃, ɑ̃t] adj **1.** [qui prive de l'honneur] dishonourable 🇬🇧, dishonorable 🇺🇸, disgraceful **2.** [humiliant] degrading, shameful.

déshonorer [3] [dezɔnɔʀe] vt [nuire à l'honneur de] to dishonour, to bring shame upon, to bring into disrepute. ❖ **se déshonorer** vp *(emploi réfléchi)* to bring disgrace upon o.s.

déshumaniser [3] [dezymanize] vt to dehumanize.

déshydratation [dezidʀatasjɔ̃] nf **1.** PHYSIOL dehydration ; [de la peau] loss of moisture, dehydration **2.** TECHNOL dehydration, dewatering **3.** CHIM dehydration.

déshydraté, e [dezidʀate] adj **1.** PHYSIOL dehydrated **2.** [aliment] desiccated, dehydrated.

déshydrater [3] [dezidʀate] ❖ **se déshydrater** vpi [personne] to become dehydrated ; [peau] to lose moisture, to become dehydrated.

desiderata, désidérata* [dezideʀata] nmpl *sout* requirements, wishes.

design [dizajn] nm [création] design ▸ **design industriel** industrial design ; *(comme adj inv)* designer *(modif)* ▸ **mobilier design** designer furniture.

désignation [deziɲasjɔ̃] nf **1.** DR ▸ **désignation du défendeur / requérant** name of the defendant / plaintiff **2.** [nomination] appointment, nomination.

désigner [3] [deziɲe] vt **1.** [montrer] to indicate, to point at ou to (sép), to show ▸ **désigner qqn du doigt** to point at sb **2.** [choisir] to choose, to single out (sép) ▸ **désigner qqn comme héritier** to name sb as one's heir **3.** [nommer - expert, président] to appoint ; [-représentant] to nominate ; [élire] to elect ▸ **désigner qqn pour un poste** to appoint sb to a post **4.** [s'appliquer à] to designate, to refer to / le mot «félin» désigne de nombreux animaux the word "feline" refers to many animals.

désigneur, euse [dezaɲnœr, øz] nm, f designer.

désillusion [dezilyzjɔ̃] nf disappointment, disillusionment, disillusion.

désinence [dezinɑ̃s] nf GRAM inflection, ending.

désinfectant, e [dezɛ̃fɛkta, ɑ̃t] adj disinfecting (avant nom). ❖ **désinfectant** nm disinfectant.

désinfecter [4] [dezɛ̃fɛkte] vt to disinfect.

désinformation [dezɛ̃fɔrmasjɔ̃] nf disinformation.

désinhiber [dezinibe] vt ▸ **désinhiber qqn** to free sb from their inhibitions.

désinstaller [3] [dezɛ̃stale] vt INFORM to uninstall, to deinstall.

désintégration [dezɛ̃tegrasjɔ̃] nf **1.** [d'un matériau, d'un groupe] disintegration, breaking-up, splitting **2.** NUCL disintegration.

désintégrer [18] [dezɛ̃tegre] vt **1.** [matériau] to crumble, to disintegrate ; [groupe, famille] to break up (sép), to split (up) (sép) **2.** NUCL to disintegrate. ❖ **se désintégrer** vpi **1.** [exploser] to disintegrate **2.** [groupe, famille, théorie] to disintegrate, to collapse.

📖 In reformed spelling (see p. 16-18), this verb is conjugated like semer : *il désintègrera, elle désintègrerait.*

désintéressé, e [dezɛ̃terese] adj **1.** [conseil, jugement] disinterested, objective, unprejudiced **2.** [personne] selfless, unselfish.

désintéresser [4] [dezɛ̃terese] ❖ **se désintéresser de** vp + prép ▸ **se désintéresser de qqch a)** [ignorer] to be uninterested in **b)** [perdre son intérêt pour] to lose interest in sthg.

désintérêt [dezɛ̃terɛ] nm indifference, lack of interest.

désintoxication [dezɛ̃tɔksikasjɔ̃] nf MÉD detoxification.

désintoxiquer [3] [dezɛ̃tɔksike] vt MÉD to detoxify ▸ **se faire désintoxiquer** to be weaned off drugs.

désinvestir [32] [dezɛ̃vɛstir] ❖ **se désinvestir** vp [perdre sa motivation] to lose interest.

désinvolte [dezɛ̃vɔlt] adj [sans embarras] casual, nonchalant.

désinvolture [dezɛ̃vɔltyr] nf [légèreté] casualness ; péj [sans-gêne] off-handedness ▸ **avec désinvolture** offhandedly.

désir [dezir] nm **1.** [aspiration] want, wish, desire / j'ai toujours eu le désir d'écrire I've always wanted ou had a desire to write / tu prends tes désirs pour des réalités ! wishful thinking! ; [souhait exprimé] wish **2.** [motivation] desire, drive **3.** [appétit sexuel] desire.

désirable [dezirabl] adj **1.** [souhaitable] desirable ▸ **peu désirable** undesirable **2.** [séduisant] desirable, (sexually) exciting.

désirer [3] [dezire] vt **1.** [aspirer à -paix, bonheur] to wish for ; (suivi d'un infinitif) : elle a toujours désiré posséder un piano she's always wanted to own a piano ▸ **laisser à désirer** to leave something to be desired, to fail to come up to expectations **2.** [vouloir] ▸ **désirer faire** to want ou to wish to do **3.** [dans un achat, une prestation de service] ▸ **vous désirez ?** can I help you? **4.** [sexuellement] to desire.

désireux, euse [deziro, øz] adj ▸ **désireux de faire** inclined ou willing to do / très désireux de faire eager to do.

désistement [dezistəmɑ̃] nm POL withdrawal, standing down.

désister [3] [deziste] ❖ **se désister** vpi POL to stand down, to withdraw.

désobéir [32] [dezɔbeir] vi **1.** [être désobéissant] to be disobedient **2.** [enfreindre un ordre] to disobey / désobéir aux ordres / à ses parents to disobey orders / one's parents.

désobéissance [dezɔbeisɑ̃s] nf [manque de discipline] disobedience, rebelliousness.

désobéissant, e [dezɔbeisɑ̃, ɑ̃t] adj [enfant] disobedient, rebellious ; [chien] disobedient.

désobligeant, e [dezɔbliʒɑ̃, ɑ̃t] adj [désagréable -personne] disagreeable, unkind ; [-propos] unkind.

désodorisant, e [dezɔdɔrizɑ̃, ɑ̃t] adj deodorizing (avant nom). ❖ **désodorisant** nm deodorizer, airfreshener.

désodoriser [3] [dezɔdɔrize] vt to deodorize.

désœuvré, e [dezœvre] adj ▸ **être désœuvré** to have nothing to do.

désœuvrement [dezœvrəmɑ̃] nm idleness.

désolant, e [dezɔlɑ̃, ɑ̃t] adj **1.** [triste -spectacle] wretched, pitiful, awful **2.** [contrariant] annoying, irritating.

désolation [dezɔlasjɔ̃] nf **1.** [chagrin] desolation, grief / être plongé dans la désolation to be disconsolate **2.** litt [d'un lieu, d'un paysage] desolation, desolateness, bleakness.

désolé, e [dezɔle] adj **1.** [contrit] apologetic, contrite ; [pour s'excuser] sorry / désolé de vous déranger sorry to disturb you **2.** litt [aride] desolate, bleak.

désoler [3] [dezɔle] vt **1.** [attrister] to distress, to sadden **2.** [irriter] : tu me désoles ! I despair!

désolidariser [3] [desɔlidarize] ❖ **se désolidariser de** vp + prép to dissociate o.s. from.

désopilant, e [dezɔpilɑ̃, ɑ̃t] adj hilarious, hysterically funny.

désordonné, e [dezɔrdɔne] adj **1.** [désorganisé -dossier, esprit] confused, untidy **2.** [personne] disorderly **3.** [irrégulier] helter-skelter (modif) / le chien faisait des bonds désordonnés the dog was leaping about all over the place **4.** litt [immoral] disorderly, disordered.

désordre [dezɔrdr] nm **1.** [fouillis] mess / quel désordre là-dedans ! what a mess ou it's chaos in there! / mettre le désordre dans une pièce to mess up a room **2.** [manque d'organisation] muddle, confusion, disarray **3.** [agitation] disorder, disturbance ▸ **désordre sur la voie publique** DR disorderly conduct. ❖ **désordres** nmpl [émeutes] riots. ❖ **en désordre** ◆ loc adj [lieu] messy, untidy ; [cheveux] unkempt, dishevelled. ◆ loc adv ▸ **mettre en désordre** to mess ou to muddle up.

désorganiser [3] [dezɔrganize] vt [service] to disorganize, to disrupt ; [fiches] to disrupt the order of.

désorienter [3] [dezɔrjɑ̃te] vt **1.** [faire s'égarer] to cause to become disoriented, to disorientate **2.** [déconcerter] to confuse, to throw into confusion ou disarray, to disorientate.

désormais [dezɔrmɛ] adv [à partir de maintenant] from now on, henceforth sout ; [dans le passé] from that moment on, from then on, from that time (on).

désosser [3] [dezɔse] vt [viande] to bone.

despote [dɛspɔt] nm **1.** POL despot, tyrant **2.** [personne autoritaire] tyrant, bully.

despotique [dɛspɔtik] adj **1.** POL despotic, tyrannical, dictatorial **2.** [autoritaire] despotic, domineering, bullying.

despotisme [dɛspɔtism] nm **1.** POL despotism **2.** [autorité] tyranny, bullying.

desquels [dekɛl] pron mpl & dét mpl ⟶ **lequel.**

DESS (abr de **diplôme d'études supérieures spécialisées**) nm *former postgraduate diploma.*

dessaisir [32] [desezir] vt DR ▸ **dessaisir qqn de** to deny sb jurisdiction over.

dessaler [3] [desale] ◆ vt (ôter le sel de) to desalinate, to remove the salt from ▸ **dessaler du poisson** to freshen fish. ◆ vi NAUT to overturn, to capsize.

dessalinisation [desalinizasjɔ̃] nf = **désalinisation.**

dessécher [18] [deseʃe] vt **1.** [peau, cheveux] to dry out *(sép)* ; [pétale, feuille] to wither **2.** [endurcir] ▸ **dessécher le cœur de qqn** to harden sb's heart. ◈ **se dessécher** vpi [peau, cheveux] to go dry.

✐ In reformed spelling (see p. 16-18), this verb is conjugated like *semer* : *il dessèchera, elle dessècherait.*

dessein [desɛ̃] nm *litt* intention, goal, purpose / *son dessein est de prendre ma place* his intention is to ou he has determined to take my place ▸ **former** ou **avoir le dessein de faire qqch** to determine to do sthg. ◈ **à dessein** loc adv deliberately, purposely. ◈ **dans le dessein de** loc prép in order ou with a view to.

desserrer [4] [desere] vt **1.** [vis, cravate, ceinture] to loosen **2.** [relâcher - étreinte, bras] to relax ; [dents] to unclench ▸ **il n'a pas desserré les dents** ou **lèvres** *fig* he didn't utter a word, he never opened his mouth **3.** [frein] to release. ◈ **se desserrer** vpi [se dévisser] to come loose.

dessert [desɛr] nm dessert, pudding 🇬🇧, sweet 🇬🇧.

desserte [desɛrt] nf **1.** [meuble] sideboard ; [table roulante] tea-trolley 🇬🇧, tea wagon 🇺🇸 **2.** TRANSP (transport) service 🇬🇧, (transportation) service 🇺🇸 / *la desserte du village est très mal assurée* the village is poorly served by public transport.

desservir [38] [deservir] vt **1.** [débarrasser] to clear (away) ; *(en usage absolu)* ▸ **puis-je desservir ?** may I clear the table? **2.** [désavantager] to be detrimental ou harmful to, to go against ▸ **son intervention m'a desservi** he did me a disservice by intervening **3.** TRANSP to serve / *le village est mal desservi* public transport to the village is poor / *ce train dessert les stations suivantes* this train stops at the following stations.

dessin [desɛ̃] nm **1.** [croquis] drawing ▸ **dessin humoristique** ou **de presse** cartoon *(in a newspaper)* ▸ **dessin animé** cartoon ▸ **dessin au fusain** charcoal drawing ▸ **dessin à la plume** pen and ink drawing ▸ [art] ▸ **le dessin** drawing **3.** TECHNOL ▸ **dessin industriel** draughtsmanship 🇬🇧, draftsmanship 🇺🇸, industrial design ▸ **dessin assisté par ordinateur** computer-aided design **4.** [forme, ligne] line, outline **5.** [ornement] design, pattern / *un tissu à dessins géométriques* a fabric with geometric patterns. ◈ **de dessin** loc adj ▸ **cours / école de dessin** art class / school.

dessinateur, trice [desinatœr, tris] nm, f **1.** [technicien] ▸ **dessinateur (industriel)** draughtsman (draughtswoman) 🇬🇧, draftsman (draftswoman) 🇺🇸 **2.** [concepteur] designer **3.** ART *artist who specializes in drawing* ▸ **dessinateur de bandes dessinées** cartoonist ▸ **dessinateur humoristique** cartoonist.

dessiner [3] [desine] vt **1.** ART to draw ; *(en usage absolu)* ▸ **il dessine bien** he's good at drawing ▸ **dessiner à la plume / au crayon / au fusain** to draw in pen and ink / in pencil / in charcoal **2.** TECHNOL [meuble, robe, bâtiment] to design ; [paysage, jardin] to landscape. ◈ **se dessiner** vpi **1.** [devenir visible] to stand out / *un sourire se dessina sur ses lèvres* a smile formed on his lips **2.** [apparaître - solution] to emerge.

dessoûler, dessouler* [3] [desule] ◆ vt to sober up *(sép).* ◆ vi to sober up / *il ne dessoûle pas de la journée* he's drunk all day.

dessous [dəsu] ◆ adv underneath ▸ **mets-toi dessous** get under it. ◆ nm [d'un meuble, d'un objet] bottom ; [d'une feuille] underneath ▸ **les gens du dessous** the people downstairs, the downstairs neighbours ▸ **les dessous de la politique / de la finance** the hidden agenda in politics / in finance ▸ **avoir le dessous** to come off worst, to get the worst of it. ◆ nmpl [sous-vêtements] underwear. ◈ **de dessous** loc prép from under, from underneath. ◈ **en dessous** loc adv underneath / *la feuille est verte en dessous* the leaf is green underneath / *les gens qui habitent en dessous, les gens d'en dessous* *fam* the people downstairs, the people in the flat 🇬🇧 ou apartment 🇺🇸 below. ◈ **en dessous de** loc prép below / *vous êtes très en dessous de la vérité* you're very far from the truth.

dessous-de-plat [dəsudpla] nm inv table mat *(to protect the table from hot dishes)*, hot pad 🇺🇸.

dessous-de-table [dəsudtabl] nm inv *péj* bribe.

dessus [dəsy] ◆ adv [placer, monter] on top ; [marcher, écrire] on it / them, etc. ; [passer, sauter] over it / them, etc. ▸ **ils lui ont tiré / tapé dessus** they shot at him / hit him ▸ **ne compte pas trop dessus** don't count on it too much ▸ **ça nous est tombé dessus à l'improviste** it was like a bolt out of the blue. ◆ nm **1.** [d'un objet, de la tête, du pied] top ; [de la main] back ▸ **avoir / prendre le dessus** to have / to get the upper hand ▸ **reprendre le dessus** [gagner] to get back on top (of the situation), to regain the upper hand ▸ **le dessus du panier a)** [personnes] the cream, the elite **b)** [choses] the top of the pile ou heap **2.** [étage supérieur] ▸ **les voisins du dessus** the people upstairs, the upstairs neighbours.

dessus-de-lit [dəsydli] nm inv bedspread.

déstabiliser [3] [destabilize] vt [pays, régime] to destabilize.

destin [dɛstɛ̃] nm **1.** [sort] fate, destiny **2.** [vie personnelle] life, destiny, fate **3.** [évolution] destiny, fate.

destinataire [dɛstinatɛr] nmf [d'une lettre] addressee ; [de produits] consignee.

destination [dɛstinasjɔ̃] nf [lieu] destination ▸ **arriver à destination** to reach one's destination. ◈ **à destination de** loc prép ▸ **avion / vol à destination de Nice** plane / flight to Nice / *les voyageurs à destination de Paris* passengers for Paris, passengers travelling to Paris.

destinée [dɛstine] nf **1.** [sort] ▸ **la destinée** fate ▸ **la destinée de qqn / qqch** the fate in store for sb / sthg **2.** [vie] destiny.

destiner [3] [dɛstine] vt **1.** [adresser] ▸ **destiner qqch à qqn** to intend sthg for sb / *voici le courrier qui lui est destiné* here is his mail ou the mail for him **2.** [promettre] ▸ **destiner qqn à** to destine sb for / *il était destiné à régner* he was destined to reign **3.** [affecter] ▸ **destiner qqch à** to set sthg aside for. ◈ **se destiner à** vp + prép ▸ **se destiner au journalisme** to want to become a journalist.

destituer [7] [dɛstitɥe] vt [fonctionnaire] to relieve from duties, to dismiss ; [roi] to depose ; [officier] to demote.

destitution [dɛstitysjɔ̃] nf [d'un fonctionnaire] dismissal ; [d'un roi] deposition, deposal ; [d'un officier] demotion.

déstockage [destɔkaʒ] nm COMM destocking ▸ **déstockage massif** clearance sale.

déstresser [destrese] vi & vt to relax.

destructeur, trice [dɛstryktœr, tris] adj destructive.

destruction [dɛstryksjɔ̃] nf **1.** [fait d'anéantir] destroying, destruction **2.** [dégâts] damage.

déstructurer [3] [destʀyktyʀe] vt to remove the structure from.

désuet, ète [dezɥɛ, ɛt] adj [mot, vêtement] outdated, old-fashioned, out-of-date ; [technique] outmoded, obsolete.

désuétude [dezɥetyd] nf obsolescence ▪ **tomber en désuétude a)** [mot] to fall into disuse, to become obsolete **b)** [technique, pratique] to become obsolete.

désuni, e [dezyni] adj [brouillé - famille, ménage] disunited, divided.

détachable [detaʃabl] adj [feuillet, capuchon] removable, detachable.

détachant [detaʃɑ̃] nm stain remover.

détaché, e [detaʃe] adj **1.** [air, mine] detached, casual, offhand **2.** ADMIN ▪ **fonctionnaire détaché** civil servant on secondment UK ou on a temporary assignment US.

détachement [detaʃmɑ̃] nm **1.** [désintéressement] detachment **2.** [troupe] detachment **3.** ADMIN secondment UK, temporary assignment US. ◆ **en détachement** loc adv on secondment UK, on a temporary assignment US.

détacher [3] [detaʃe] vt **1.** [libérer] to untie ▪ **détacher une caravane** to unhitch ou to unhook a caravan **2.** [séparer] : **détacher une recette d'un magazine / un timbre d'un carnet** to tear a recipe out of a magazine / a stamp out of a book ; *(en usage absolu)* ▪ **détacher suivant le pointillé** tear (off) along the dotted line **3.** [défaire - ceinture] to unfasten ; [- col] to unfasten, to loosen **4.** [détourner] ▪ **détacher ses yeux** ou **son regard de qqn** to take one's eyes off sb **5.** ADMIN to send on secondment UK ou on temporary assignment US **6.** [faire ressortir] to separate (out) ▪ **détachez bien chaque mot / note** make sure every word / note stands out (clearly). ◆ **se détacher** ◆ vp *(emploi réfléchi)* [se libérer] to untie ou to free o.s. ◆ vpi **1.** [sandale, lacet] to come undone ; [étiquette] to come off ; [page] to come loose **2.** SPORT [se séparer - du peloton] to break away **3.** [se profiler] to stand out. ◆ **se détacher de** vp + prép [s'éloigner de] : **il a eu du mal à se détacher d'elle** he found it hard to leave her behind / **puis je me suis détachée de ma famille / de l'art figuratif** later, I grew away from my family / from figurative art.

détacheur [detaʃœʀ] nm [produit] stain remover.

détail [detaj] nm **1.** [exposé précis] breakdown, detailed account, itemization / **faites-moi le détail de ce qui s'est passé** tell me in detail what happened / **il n'a pas fait le détail !** *fam* he was a bit heavy-handed ! **2.** [élément - d'un récit, d'une information] detail, particular / **jusque dans les moindres détails** down to the smallest detail ; [point sans importance] detail, minor point / **ne nous arrêtons pas à ces détails** let's not worry about these minor details **3.** COMM retail **4.** [petite partie - d'un meuble, d'un édifice] detail. ◆ **au détail** loc adv ▪ **vendre qqch au détail** to sell sthg retail, to retail sthg / **vous vendez les œufs au détail ?** do you sell eggs separately ? ◆ **en détail** loc adv in detail.

détaillant, e [detajɑ̃, ɑ̃t] nm, f retailer.

détaillé, e [detaje] adj [récit] detailed ; [facture] itemized.

détailler [3] [detaje] vt **1.** [dévisager] to scrutinize, to examine ▪ **détailler qqn de la tête aux pieds** to look sb over from head to foot, to look sb up and down **2.** [énumérer - faits, facture] to itemize, to detail.

détaler [3] [detale] vi [animal] to bolt ; [personne] to decamp, to cut and run US.

détartrant [detaʀtʀɑ̃] nm descaling agent.

détartrer [3] [detaʀtʀe] vt [dents] to scale ; [bouilloire] to descale.

détaxe [detaks] nf **1.** [levée] ▪ **la détaxe des tabacs a)** [réduction] the reduction of duty ou tax on tobacco **b)** [suppression] the lifting of tax ou duty on tobacco **2.** [remboursement] : **cela m'a fait 80 euros de détaxe** the reduction of duty charges saved me 80 euros.

détecter [4] [detɛkte] vt to detect, to spot.

détecteur [detɛktœʀ] nm detector ▪ **détecteur de faux billets** forged banknote detector ▪ **détecteur de fumée** smoke detector, smoke alarm ▪ **détecteur de mensonges** lie detector.

détection [detɛksjɔ̃] nf [gén] detection, detecting, spotting.

détective [detɛktiv] nm detective ▪ **détective privé** private detective ou investigator.

déteindre [81] [detɛ̃dʀ] ◆ vi **1.** [se décolorer] to run / **déteindre au lavage** to run in the wash / **le noir va déteindre sur le rouge** the black will run into the red **2.** *fam* [humeur, influence] ▪ **déteindre sur qqn** to rub off on sb, to influence sb. ◆ vt [linge] to discolour UK, to discolor US ; [tenture, tapisserie] to fade.

dételer [24] [detle] vt [cheval] to unharness, to unhitch ; [bœuf] to unyoke.

✎ In reformed spelling (see p. 16-18), this verb is conjugated like *peler : il détèle, elle détèlera.*

détendre [73] [detɑ̃dʀ] vt **1.** [relâcher - corde] to ease, to loosen, to slacken ; [- ressort] to release **2.** [décontracter] to relax / **il a réussi à détendre l'atmosphère avec quelques plaisanteries** he made things more relaxed by telling a few jokes. ◆ **se détendre** vpi **1.** [corde, courroie] to ease, to slacken **2.** [se décontracter] to relax ▪ **détends-toi !** relax! **3.** [s'améliorer - ambiance] to become more relaxed.

détendu, e [detɑ̃dy] adj **1.** [calme] relaxed **2.** [corde, courroie] slack.

détenir [40] [detniʀ] vt **1.** [posséder - record] to hold, to be the holder of ; [- actions] to hold ; [- document, bijou de famille] to hold, to have (in one's possession) ; [- secret] to hold **2.** DR [emprisonner] to detain.

détente [detɑ̃t] nf **1.** [relaxation] relaxation ▪ **j'ai besoin de détente** I need to relax **2.** POL ▪ **la détente** détente **3.** ARM trigger **4.** SPORT spring.

détenteur, trice [detɑ̃tœʀ, tʀis] nm, f holder.

détention [detɑ̃sjɔ̃] nf **1.** [emprisonnement] detention ▪ **en détention préventive** ou **provisoire** in detention awaiting trial, on remand ▪ **mettre qqn en détention préventive** to remand sb in custody **2.** [possession] possession ▪ **arrêté pour détention d'armes** arrested for illegal possession of arms.

détenu, e [detny] nm, f prisoner.

détergent, e [detɛʀʒɑ̃, ɑ̃t] adj detergent *(modif).* ◆ **détergent** nm [gén] detergent ; [en poudre] washing powder ; [liquide] liquid detergent.

détérioration [deteʀjoʀasjɔ̃] nf [de la santé, des relations] worsening, deterioration ; [des locaux] deterioration.

détériorer [3] [deteʀjoʀe] vt to cause to deteriorate, to damage, to harm. ◆ **se détériorer** vpi [temps, climat social] to deteriorate, to worsen.

déterminant, e [detɛʀminɑ̃, ɑ̃t] adj deciding, determining. ◆ **déterminant** nm LING determiner.

détermination [detɛʀminasjɔ̃] nf **1.** [résolution] determination, decision / **agir avec détermination** to show determination **2.** [de causes, de termes] determining, establishing.

déterminé, e [detɛʀmine] adj **1.** [défini] determined, defined, circumscribed / **il n'a pas d'opinion déterminée à ce sujet** he doesn't really have a strong opinion on the matter / **dans un but bien déterminé** for a definite reason / **à un prix bien déterminé** at a set price **2.** [décidé] determined, resolute.

déterminer [3] [detɛʀmine] vt **1.** [définir] to ascertain, to determine **2.** [inciter] to incite, to encourage ▪ **déterminer qqn à faire qqch** to encourage sb to do sthg **3.** [causer] to determine **4.** BIOL [sexe] to determine ; [groupe sanguin] to type.

déterminisme [detɛrminism] nm determinism.

déterrer [4] [detere] vt **1.** [os, trésor] to dig up *(sép)*, to unearth **2.** [exhumer - cadavre] to dig up *(sép)*, to disinter **3.** [dénicher - secret, texte] to dig out *(sép)*, to unearth.

détestable [detɛstabl] adj dreadful, detestable, foul.

détester [3] [detɛste] vt **1.** [personne] to hate, to detest, to loathe **2.** [viande, jazz, politique, etc.] to hate, to detest, to loathe / *il déteste devoir se lever tôt* he hates having to get up early.

détonant, e [detɔnɑ̃, ɑ̃t] adj detonating.

détonateur [detɔnatœr] nm **1.** ARM detonator **2.** *fig* [déclencheur] detonator, trigger ▶ **servir de détonateur à qqch** to trigger off sthg.

détonation [detɔnasjɔ̃] nf **1.** [coup de feu - gén] shot ; [- d'un canon] boom, roar **2.** AUTO backfiring.

détonner [3] [detɔne] vi [contraster - couleurs, styles] to clash.

détour [detur] nm **1.** [tournant] bend, curve, turn ; [méandre] wind, meander / *faire un brusque détour* to make a sharp turn **2.** [crochet] detour, diversion / *faire un détour par un village* to make a detour through a village ▶ **valoir le détour** [restaurant, paysage] to be worth the detour. ❖ **au détour de** loc prép **1.** [en cheminant le long de] : *au détour du chemin* as you follow the path **2.** [en consultant, en écoutant] : *au détour de la conversation* in the course of the conversation. ❖ **sans détour** loc adv [parler, répondre] straightforwardly, without beating about the bush.

détourné, e [deturne] adj **1.** [route, voie] roundabout *(avant nom)*, circuitous *sout* **2.** [façon, moyen] indirect, roundabout, circuitous *sout*.

détournement [deturnəmɑ̃] nm **1.** [dérivation - d'une rivière] diverting, diversion **2.** AÉRON ▶ **détournement d'avion** hijacking **3.** FIN misappropriation ▶ **détournement de fonds** embezzlement **4.** DR ▶ **détournement de mineur** corruption of a minor.

détourner [3] [deturne] vt **1.** TRANSP [circulation] to redirect, to divert, to detour [US], to reroute ; [fleuve] to divert **2.** [avion, autocar] to hijack **3.** [éloigner - coup] to parry ; [- arme] to turn aside ou away *(sép)* ▶ **détourner les yeux ou le regard** to avert one's eyes, to look away / *détourner la tête* to turn one's head away ▶ **détourner l'attention de qqn** to divert sb's attention ▶ **détourner les soupçons sur qqn** to divert suspicion toward sb **4.** [déformer - paroles, texte] to distort, to twist **5.** [détacher] to take away *(sép)* ▶ **détourner qqn du droit chemin** to lead sb astray **6.** [extorquer] to misappropriate. ❖ **se détourner** vpi [tourner la tête] to turn (one's head), to look away. ❖ **se détourner de** vp + prép to turn away from / *en grandissant, je me suis détourné de la natation* I got tired of swimming as I grew older.

détracteur, trice [detraktœr, tris] nm, f disparager, detractor / *tous ses détracteurs* all his critics ou those who have attacked him.

détraqué, e [detrake] ❖ adj **1.** [cassé] broken **2.** *fam* [dérangé] : *elle a les nerfs complètement détraqués* she's a nervous wreck **3.** *fam* [désaxé] crazy, psychotic. ❖ nm, f *fam* maniac, psychopath.

détraquer [3] [detrake] vt **1.** [appareil] to damage **2.** *fam* [déranger] : *toutes ces études lui ont détraqué le cerveau* *hum* all that studying has addled his brain. ❖ **se détraquer** ❖ vpi [mal fonctionner] to go wrong ; [cesser de fonctionner] to break down. ❖ vpt *fam* : *se détraquer le foie / le système* to ruin one's liver / health.

détremper [3] [detrɑ̃pe] vt [mouiller - chiffon, papier] to soak (through).

détresse [detrɛs] nf **1.** [désespoir] distress, anxiety **2.** [pauvreté] distress / *les familles dans la détresse* families in dire need ou straits. ❖ **en détresse** loc adj [navire, avion] in distress.

détriment [detrimɑ̃] ❖ **au détriment de** loc prép to the detriment of, at the cost of.

détritus [detrity(s)] nm piece of rubbish [UK] ou garbage [US] ▶ **des détritus** refuse.

détroit [detrwa] nm GÉOGR strait.

Détroits

| le détroit de Béring | the Bering Strait |
| le détroit de Gibraltar | the Strait of Gibraltar |

détromper [3] [detrɔ̃pe] vt to disabuse ▶ **détromper qqn** to put ou to set sb right. ❖ **se détromper** vpi ▶ **détrompez-vous !** don't be so sure!

détrôner [3] [detrone] vt [roi] to dethrone, to depose ; [personne, produit] to oust, to push into second position.

détruire [98] [detrɥir] vt **1.** [démolir, casser] to destroy ▶ **détruire par le feu a)** [maison] to burn down **b)** [objet, documents] to burn **2.** [éliminer - population, parasites] to destroy, to wipe out *(sép)* ; [tuer - ennemi] to kill ; [- animal malade, chien errant] to destroy **3.** [porter préjudice à - santé, carrière] to ruin, to destroy, to wreck. ❖ **se détruire** vp *(emploi réfléchi)* *vieilli* to do away with o.s.

dette [dɛt] nf **1.** [d'argent] debt ▶ **avoir des dettes** to be in debt / *faire des dettes* to get ou to run into debt ▶ **dette de l'État** ou **publique** national debt **2.** [obligation morale] debt / *régler sa dette envers la société* to pay one's debt to society.

deuil [dœj] nm **1.** [chagrin] grief, mourning ▶ **faire son deuil de** *fam* : *j'en ai fait mon deuil* I've resigned myself to not having it **2.** [décès] bereavement. ❖ **en deuil** loc adj [personne] bereaved ▶ **une femme en deuil** a woman in mourning.

deux [dø] ❖ dét **1.** two ▶ **eux / nous deux** both of them / us ▶ **des deux côtés** on both sides / *deux fois plus de livres* twice as many books / *deux fois moins de livres* half as many books ▶ **à deux pas** close by, not far away ▶ **à deux pas de** close by, not far away from ▶ **être à deux doigts de** to come very close to doing ▶ **pour lui il y a deux poids (et) deux mesures** he has double standards ▶ **deux avis valent mieux qu'un** two heads are better than one ▶ **deux précautions valent mieux qu'une** *prov* better safe than sorry **2.** [dans des séries] two, second ▶ **à la page deux** on page two ▶ **le deux novembre** on November (the) second, on the second of November. ❖ nm **1.** [gén] two ▶ **venez, tous les deux** come along, both of you ▶ **à nous deux !** right, let's get on with it! ▶ **ça fait deux !** *fam : lui et le dessin, ça fait deux !* he can't draw to save his life! / *elle et la propreté, ça fait deux !* *fam* she doesn't know the meaning of the word "clean"! **2.** JEUX ▶ **le deux de trèfle** the two of clubs. Voir aussi **cinq**. ❖ **à deux** loc adv [vivre] as a couple ; [travailler] in pairs / *il faudra s'y mettre à deux* it'll take two of us. ❖ **deux à deux** loc adv in twos ou pairs. ❖ **deux par deux** loc adv in twos ou pairs.

deuxième [døzjɛm] ❖ adj num second. ❖ nmf second. Voir aussi **cinquième**.

deuxièmement [døzjɛmmɑ̃] adv secondly, in second place.

deux-pièces [døpjɛs] nm **1.** [maillot de bain] two-piece **2.** [costume] two-piece **3.** [appartement] two-room flat [UK] ou apartment [US].

deux-points [døpwɛ̃] nm IMPR colon.

deux-roues [døru] nm two-wheeled vehicle.

deux-temps [døtɑ̃] nm two-stroke.

dévaler [3] [devale] vt [en courant] to run ou to race ou to hurtle down ; [en roulant] to tumble down.

dévaliser [3] [devalize] vt **1.** [voler - banque, diligence] to rob / *il s'est fait dévaliser* he was robbed **2.** *fam* [vider] to raid / *tous les marchands de glaces ont été dévalisés* all the ice-cream vendors have sold out.

dévalorisant, e [devalɔrizɑ̃, ɑ̃t] adj [humiliant] humbling, humiliating.

dévaloriser [3] [devalɔrize] vt **1.** [discréditer - personne, talent] to depreciate, to devalue **2.** COMM to cause a drop in the commercial value of **3.** FIN to devalue. ❖ **se dévaloriser** ◆ vp *(emploi réfléchi)* [se discréditer] to lose credibility. ◆ vpi FIN to become devalued.

dévaluation [devaluasjɔ̃] nf devaluation, devaluing.

dévaluer [7] [devalɥe] vt **1.** FIN to devalue **2.** [déprécier] to devalue / *il t'a fait pour te dévaluer à tes propres yeux* he did it to make you feel cheap. ❖ **se dévaluer** vpi to drop in value.

devancer [16] [dəvɑ̃se] vt **1.** [dans l'espace - coureur, peloton] to get ahead of, to outdistance / *je la devançais de quelques mètres* I was a few metres ahead of her **2.** [dans le temps] to arrive ahead of / *elle m'avait devancé de deux jours* she had arrived two days before me **3.** [agir avant - personne] : *tu m'as devancé, c'est ce que je voulais lui offrir / lui dire* you beat me to it, that's just what I wanted to give her / to say to her / *il s'est fait devancer par les autres* the others got there before him.

devant [dəvɑ̃] ◆ v → **devoir.** ◆ prép **1.** [en face de] in front of ; [avec mouvement] past / *il a déposé le paquet devant la porte* he left the parcel outside the door / *elle est passée devant moi sans me voir* she walked right past (me) without seeing me **2.** [en avant de] in front of ; [en avance sur] ahead of / *nous passerons devant lui pour lui montrer le chemin* we'll go ahead of him to show him the way ▸ **devant soi**: *aller droit devant soi* **a)** to go straight on ou ahead **b)** *fig* to carry on regardless / *elle avait une belle carrière devant elle* she had a promising career ahead of her **3.** [en présence de] ▸ **pleurer devant tout le monde a)** [devant les gens présents] to cry in front of everyone **b)** [en public] to cry in public / *porter une affaire devant la justice* to bring a case before the courts ou to court ▸ **je jure devant Dieu…** I swear to God… **4.** [face à] in the face of, faced with ; [étant donné] given. ◆ adv **1.** [à l'avant] : *mettez les plus petits de la classe devant* put the shortest pupils at the ou in front ▸ **installe-toi devant** sit in the front (of the car) / *faites passer la pétition devant* pass the petition forward ▸ **devant derrière** back to front, the wrong way round **2.** [en face] ▸ **tu es juste devant** it's right in front of you / *je suis passé devant sans faire attention* I went past without paying attention **3.** [en tête] ▸ **elle est loin devant** she's a long way ahead / *passe devant, tu verras mieux* come ou go through you'll get a better view. ◆ nm [gén] front ; NAUT bow, bows, fore / *sur le devant de la scène fig* in the lime light ▸ **prendre les devants** to make the first move, to be the first to act.

devanture [dəvɑ̃tyr] nf **1.** [vitrine] shop window UK, store window US **2.** [étalage] (window) display **3.** [façade] frontage, shopfront UK, storefront US. ❖ **en devanture** loc adv in the window.

dévastateur, trice [devastatœr, tris] adj devastating / *de manière dévastatrice* devastatingly.

dévastation [devastasjɔ̃] nf devastation, havoc.

dévaster [3] [devaste] vt [pays, ville] to devastate, to lay waste ; [récolte] to ruin, to destroy.

déveine [devɛn] nf bad luck / *avec ma déveine habituelle* with my (usual) luck.

développement [devlɔpmɑ̃] nm **1.** [fait de grandir] development ; [fait de progresser] development, growth **2.** ÉCON : *une région en plein développement* a fast-developing area / *le développement de nouveaux produits* new product development ▸ **développement durable** ÉCOL sustainable development **3.** [exposé] exposition / *entrer dans des développements superflus* to go into unnecessary detail ; MUS development (section) **4.** [perfectionnement] developing / *nous leur avons confié le développement du prototype* we asked them to develop the prototype for us **5.** PHOT [traitement complet] processing, developing ; [étape du traitement] developing **6.** MÉCAN gear / *vélo avec un développement de six mètres* bicycle with a six metre gear. ❖ **développements** nmpl [prolongements - d'une affaire] developments / *à la lumière des récents développements* in the light of recent developments.

développer [3] [devlɔpe] vt **1.** [faire croître - faculté] to develop ; [- usine, secteur] to develop, to expand ; [- pays, économie] to develop **2.** [exposer - argument, plan] to develop, to enlarge on **3.** [symptôme, complexe, maladie] to develop **4.** PHOT [traiter] to process ; [révéler] to develop / *faire développer une pellicule* to have a film processed / *faire développer des photos* to have some photos developed **5.** MATH to develop. ❖ **se développer** vpi **1.** [croître - enfant, plante] to develop, to grow ; [- usine, secteur] to develop, to expand ; [- pays, économie] to develop, to become developed / *une région qui se développe* a developing area **2.** [apparaître - membrane, moisissure] to form, to develop **3.** [se déployer - armée] to be deployed ; [- cortège] to spread out ; [- argument] to develop, to unfold ; [- récit] to develop, to progress, to unfold **4.** [se diversifier - technique, science] to improve, to develop **5.** [s'aggraver - maladie] to develop.

développeur [devlɔpœr] nm [INFORM - entreprise] software development ou design company ; [- personne] software developer ou designer ▸ **développeur de sites Web** web developer.

devenir¹ [dəvnir] nm *litt* **1.** [évolution] evolution **2.** [avenir] future. ❖ **en devenir** loc adj *litt* [société, œuvre] evolving, changing ▸ **en perpétuel devenir** constantly changing, ever-changing.

devenir² [40] [dəvnir] vi **1.** [acquérir telle qualité] to become ▸ **devenir professeur** to become a teacher ▸ **devenir vieux** to get ou to grow old ▸ **devenir rouge / bleu** to go red / blue / *l'animal peut devenir dangereux lorsqu'il est menacé* the animal can be dangerous when threatened **2.** [avoir tel sort] : *que sont devenus tes amis de jeunesse ?* what happened to the friends of your youth? / *et moi, qu'est-ce que je vais devenir ?* what's to become of me? **3.** *fam* [pour demander des nouvelles] ▸ **que devenez-vous ?** how are you getting on? / *et lui, qu'est-ce qu'il devient ?* what about him?, what's he up to these days? **4.** *(tournure impersonnelle)* : *il devient difficile de…* it's getting difficult to…

dévergondé, e [devɛrgɔ̃de] adj licentious, shameless.

déverrouiller [3] [devɛruje] vt **1.** ARM & INFORM to unlock **2.** [porte] to unbolt.

déverser [3] [devɛrse] vt **1.** [répandre - liquide] to pour, to discharge ; [- décharger] to discharge / *les paysans ont déversé des tonnes de fruits sur la chaussée* the farmers dumped tons of fruit on the road. ❖ **se déverser** vpi [couler] to flow / *se déverser dans la mer* to flow into the sea.

dévêtir [44] [devetir] vt to undress. ❖ **se dévêtir** vp *(emploi réfléchi)* to undress o.s., to get undressed, to take one's clothes off.

déviant, e [devjɑ̃, ɑ̃t] adj & nm, f deviant.

déviation [devjasjɔ̃] nf **1.** TRANSP detour, diversion UK **2.** [écart] swerving, deviating / *il ne se permet aucune* *déviation par rapport à la ligne du parti* he will not deviate from ou be deflected away from the party line **3.** NAUT [d'un compas] deviation.

dévider [3] [devide] vt [dérouler -bobine] to unwind ; [-câble, corde] to uncoil.

dévier [9] [devje] ◆ vi **1.** [s'écarter] to swerve, to veer / *le bus a brusquement dévié sur la droite / gauche* the bus suddenly veered off to the right / left ▸ **dévier de** to move away, to swerve from **2.** [dans un débat, un projet] to diverge, to deviate ▸ **faire dévier la conversation** to change the subject ▸ **dévier de** to move away from, to stray off. ◆ vt **1.** [balle, projectile] to deflect, to turn away ou aside *(sép)* ; [coup] to parry ; [circulation] to divert, to detour US, to redirect, to reroute **2.** [distraire -attention] to divert.

devin, devineresse [dəvɛ̃, dəvinrɛs] nm, f soothsayer / *il n'est pas devin !* he's not a mind-reader!

deviner [3] [dəvine] vt **1.** [imaginer] to guess, to work out *(sép)*, to figure (out) *(sép)* / *devine qui est là !* guess who's here ! **2.** [découvrir -énigme, mystère] : *tu ne devineras jamais ce qui m'est arrivé* you'll never guess what happened to me **3.** [prédire -avenir] to foresee, to foretell **4.** [apercevoir] : *on devinait son soutien-gorge sous son chemisier* her bra showed through slightly under her blouse.

devinette [dəvinɛt] nf riddle ▸ **poser une devinette (à qqn)** to ask (sb) a riddle ▸ **jouer aux devinettes a)** *pr* to play (at) riddles **b)** *fig* to speak in riddles.

devis [dəvi] nm ▸ **devis (estimatif)** estimate, quotation ▸ **faire** ou **établir un devis** to draw up an estimate / *il a fait un devis de 12 000 €* he quoted 12,000 € (in his estimate).

dévisager [17] [deviʒaʒe] vt to stare (persistently) at.

devise [dəviz] nf **1.** [maxime] motto / *laisser faire les autres, c'est sa devise !* let the others do the work, that's his motto! **2.** FIN currency ▸ **acheter des devises** to buy foreign currency.

dévisser [3] [devise] ◆ vt [desserrer -écrou, vis] to loosen ; [détacher] to undo, to unscrew, to screw off *(sép)* / *dévissez le bouchon* unscrew the top off the bottle. ◆ vi [en montagne] to fall ou to come off. ◆ **se dévisser** ◆ vp *(emploi passif)* [se détacher] to unscrew, to undo / *le bouchon se dévisse facilement* the top twists off the bottle easily. ◆ vpt : *se dévisser le cou / la tête* to screw one's neck / one's head round.

dévoiler [3] [devwale] vt [exprimer -intention, sentiment] to disclose, to reveal, to unveil.

devoir¹ [dəvwaʀ] nm **1.** ÉDUC assignment, exercise / *devoir de chimie* chemistry assignment ou exercise ▸ **devoir de français** French essay ▸ **faire ses devoirs** to do one's homework ▸ **devoir sur table** (written) class test ▸ **devoirs de vacances** holiday UK ou vacation US homework **2.** [impératifs moraux] duty ▸ **le devoir m'appelle** duty calls / *je ne l'ai prévenu que par devoir* I warned him only because I thought it was my duty **3.** [tâche à accomplir] duty, obligation / *faire* ou *accomplir* ou *remplir son devoir* to carry out ou to do one's duty ▸ **avoir le devoir de** to have the duty to ▸ **se faire un devoir de faire qqch** to make it one's duty to do sthg ▸ **se mettre en devoir de faire qqch** to set about (doing) sthg ▸ **devoir conjugal** conjugal duties ▸ **devoir de diligence** duty of care ▸ **devoir de mémoire** duty of memory ▸ **devoir de secours** duty of assistance. ◆ **devoirs** nmpl ▸ **rendre les derniers devoirs à qqn** to pay sb a final homage ou tribute ▸ **rendre ses devoirs à qqn** to pay one's respects to sb. ◆ **de devoir** loc adj : *homme / femme de devoir* man / woman with a (strong) sense of duty. ◆ **du devoir de** loc prép : *il est du devoir de tout citoyen de voter* it is the duty of every citizen to vote / *j'ai cru de mon devoir de l'aider* I felt duty-bound to help him.

devoir² [53] [dəvwaʀ] ◆ v aux **1.** [exprime l'obligation] ▸ **il doit** he has to, he needs to, he must ▸ **il ne doit pas** he must not, he mustn't / *on ne doit pas fumer* smoking is forbidden ou is not allowed **2.** [dans des conseils, des suggestions] ▸ **il devrait** he ought to, he should / *tu ne devrais pas boire* you shouldn't drink **3.** [indique une prévision, une intention] : *il doit m'en donner demain* he's due to ou he should give me some tomorrow ; [dans le passé] : *il devait venir mais je ne l'ai pas vu* he was supposed to come ou to have come but I didn't see him **4.** [exprime une probabilité] ▸ **il / cela doit** he / it must, he's / it's got to ▸ **il doit être fatigué** he must be tired, he's probably tired **5.** [exprime l'inévitable] : *nous devons tous mourir un jour* we all have to die one day ; [exprime une norme] : *un bon chanteur doit savoir chanter en direct* a good singer should be able to sing live. ◆ vt **1.** [avoir comme dette] to owe ▸ **devoir qqch à qqn** to owe sb sthg, to owe sthg to sb / *je te dois l'essence* I owe you for the petrol **2.** [être moralement obligé de fournir] ▸ **devoir qqch à qqn** to owe sb sthg / *je te dois bien ça* that's the least I can do for you ▸ **traiter qqn avec le respect qu'on lui doit** to treat sb with due respect **3.** [être redevable de] ▸ **devoir qqch à qqn** to owe sb sthg, to owe sthg to sb / *c'est à Guimard que l'on doit cette découverte* we have Guimard to thank ou we're indebted to Guimard for this discovery / *c'est à lui que je dois d'avoir trouvé du travail* it's thanks to him that I found a job. ◆ **se devoir** vp *(emploi réciproque)* [avoir comme obligation mutuelle] : *les époux se doivent fidélité* spouses ou husbands and wives must be faithful to each other. ◆ **se devoir de** vp + prép to have it as one's duty to / *tu es grand, tu te dois de donner l'exemple* you're a big boy now, it's your duty to show a good example.

📋 **Devoir qqch à qqn** *Owe sthg to sb* ou *owe sb sthg.*

Notez la construction à double complément qui en anglais peut prendre deux formes dont le sens est le même :

• une structure identique à celle du français :

verbe + COD + préposition + COI

owe sthg to sb

• une structure qui diffère de celle du français, sans préposition, et dans laquelle l'ordre des compléments est inversé :

verbe + COI + COD

owe sb sthg

Il doit encore beaucoup d'argent à son associé. *He still owes a lot of money to his business partner* ou *He still owes his business partner a lot of money.*

---

dévolu, e [devɔly] adj [destiné] : *argent dévolu à cet usage* money allocated to that purpose. ◆ **dévolu** nm EXPR **jeter son dévolu sur a)** [chose] to go for, to choose **b)** [personne] to set one's cap at.

dévorer [3] [devɔʀe] vt **1.** [manger -suj : animal, personne] to devour ; *(en usage absolu)* ▸ **il dévore !** he eats like a horse! / *fig* ▸ **dévorer qqn** ou **qqch des yeux** ou **du regard** to stare hungrily ou to gaze greedily at sb / sthg **2.** [lire] to devour, to read avidly **3.** [tenailler] to devour / *l'ambition le dévore* he's eaten ou devoured by ambition / *être dévoré par l'envie / la curiosité / les remords* to be eaten up with envy / curiosity / remorse.

dévot, e [devo, ɔt] adj devout.

dévotion [devosjɔ̃] nf **1.** RELIG devoutness, religiousness, piety **2.** *litt* [attachement] devotion / *il voue une véritable dévotion à sa mère* he worships his mother.

dévoué, e [devwe] adj [fidèle] devoted, faithful / *être dévoué à ses amis* to be devoted to one's friends.

dévouement [devumã] nm **1.** [abnégation] dedication, devotedness, devotion ▸ **soigner qqn avec dévouement** to look after sb devotedly **2.** [loyauté] devotion.

dévouer [6] [devwe] ❖ **se dévouer** vpi [proposer ses services] : *allez, dévoue-toi pour une fois !* come on, make a sacrifice for once! / *qui va se dévouer pour faire le ménage ?* who's going to volunteer to clean up? ❖ **se dévouer à** vp + prép [se consacrer à] to dedicate o.s. to.

dévoyé, e [devwaje] ◆ adj perverted, corrupted. ◆ nm, f corrupt individual.

dévoyer [13] [devwaje] vt *litt* to lead astray.

dextérité [dɛksteʀite] nf dexterity, deftness ▸ **avec dextérité** dexterously, deftly, skilfully 🇬🇧, skillfully 🇺🇸.

dézipper [3] [dezipe] vt INFORM to unzip.

DG (abr de **directeur général**) nm GM, CEO 🇺🇸.

DGSE (abr de **Direction générale de la sécurité extérieure**) npr f *the arm of the French Defence Ministry in charge of international intelligence* ; ≃ MI6 🇬🇧 ; ≃ CIA 🇺🇸.

diabète [djabɛt] nm diabetes.

diabétique [djabetik] adj & nmf diabetic.

diable [djabl] ◆ nm **1.** RELIG devil ▸ **le diable** the Devil ▸ **envoyer qqn au diable** to send sb packing ▸ **au diable l'avarice !** hang the expense! ▸ **comme un beau diable a)** [courir, sauter] like the (very) devil, like a thing possessed **b)** [hurler] like a stuck pig ▸ **tirer le diable par la queue** to live from hand to mouth ▸ **c'est le diable qui bat sa femme et marie sa fille** *prov* it's rainy and sunny at the same time ▸ **c'est bien le diable si je ne récupère pas mon argent !** I'll be damned if I don't get my money back! **2.** [enfant] (little) devil ; [homme] ▸ **un mauvais diable** a bad sort ▸ **un pauvre diable** a wretched man, a poor wretch **3.** [chariot] trolley **4.** [jouet] jack-in-the-box. ◆ adv : *qui / que / comment diable ?* who / what / how the devil?, who / what / how on earth?

diablement [djabləmã] adv *fam & vieilli* damned / *cette pièce est diablement longue !* this play's interminable!

diablotin [djablɔtɛ̃] nm **1.** [enfant] imp **2.** [pétard] cracker.

diabolique [djabɔlik] adj diabolic, diabolical, devilish.

diaboliser [djabɔlize] vt to diabolize.

diabolo [djabɔlo] nm **1.** [jouet] diabolo **2.** CULIN ▸ **diabolo menthe** lemon soda with mint syrup.

diacre [djakʀ] nm deacon.

diadème [djadɛm] nm tiara.

diagnostic [djagnɔstik] nm MÉD diagnosis.

diagnostiquer [3] [djagnɔstike] vt to diagnose / *on lui a diagnostiqué un diabète* he's been diagnosed as suffering from diabetes.

diagonale [djagɔnal] nf diagonal (line). ❖ **en diagonale** loc adv **1.** [en biais] diagonally **2.** [vite] ▸ **lire** ou **parcourir un livre en diagonale** to skim through a book.

diagramme [djagʀam] nm **1.** [graphique] graph ▸ **diagramme à bâtons** bar chart ou graph ▸ **diagramme en secteurs** pie chart **2.** [croquis] diagram.

dialecte [djalɛkt] nm dialect.

dialectique [djalɛktik] ◆ adj dialectic, dialectical. ◆ nf dialectic, dialectics *(aussi au sg)*.

dialogue [djalɔg] nm **1.** [discussion] dialogue 🇬🇧, dialog 🇺🇸 / *entre eux, c'était un véritable dialogue de sourds* they were not on the same wavelength at all **2.** CINÉ & THÉÂTRE dialogue.

dialoguer [3] [djalɔge] vi **1.** [converser] to converse **2.** [négocier] to have ou to hold talks **3.** INFORM ▸ **dialoguer avec un ordinateur** to interact with a computer.

dialyse [djaliz] nf dialysis ▸ **être sous dialyse** to be on dialysis.

diamant [djamã] nm diamond.

diamétralement [djametʀalmã] adv diametrically.

diamètre [djamɛtʀ] nm diameter / *le fût fait 30 cm de diamètre* the barrel is 30 cm across ou in diameter.

diapason [djapazɔ̃] nm **1.** [instrument] tuning fork ; [registre] range, diapason. ❖ **au diapason** loc adv in tune ; *fig* ▸ **se mettre au diapason (de qqn)** to fall ou to step into line (with sb).

diaphragme [djafʀagm] nm **1.** ANAT & TECHNOL diaphragm **2.** MÉD diaphragm *spéc*, (Dutch) cap **3.** PHOT stop, diaphragm.

diaporama [djapoʀama] nm slide show.

diapositive [djapozitiv] nf PHOT slide.

diarrhée [djaʀe] nf diarrhoea 🇬🇧, diarrhea 🇺🇸 / *avoir la diarrhée* to have diarrhoea.

diatribe [djatʀib] nf diatribe *sout*, (vicious) attack.

dichotomie [dikɔtɔmi] nf dichotomy.

dico [diko] nm *fam* dictionary.

dictateur [diktatœʀ] nm dictator.

dictatorial, e, aux [diktatɔʀjal, o] adj dictatorial.

dictature [diktatyʀ] nf dictatorship / *la dictature du prolétariat* the dictatorship of the proletariat / *la dictature de la mode* the edicts of fashion.

dictée [dikte] nf [à des élèves] dictation.

dicter [3] [dikte] vt **1.** [courrier, lettre, résumé] to dictate **2.** [imposer - choix] to dictate, to impose, to force ; [- condition] to dictate / *on lui a dicté ses réponses* his replies had been dictated to him.

diction [diksjɔ̃] nf diction ▸ **avoir une diction parfaite** to speak with total clarity. ❖ **de diction** loc adj speech *(modif)*.

dictionnaire [diksjɔnɛʀ] nm **1.** [livre] dictionary ▸ **dictionnaire bilingue** bilingual dictionary ▸ **dictionnaire électronique** electronic dictionary **2.** INFORM dictionary.

dicton [diktɔ̃] nm dictum *sout*, (popular) saying / *comme dit le dicton* as they say, as the saying goes.

didacticiel [didaktisjɛl] nm piece of educational software, teachware 🇺🇸.

didactique [didaktik] ◆ adj **1.** [de l'enseignement] didactic **2.** [instructif] didactic, educational. ◆ nf didactics *(sg)*.

dièse [djɛz] ◆ adj ▸ **la dièse** A sharp. ◆ nm sharp ; [symbole] hash 🇬🇧, pound sign 🇺🇸 / *appuyez sur la touche dièse* press the hash key 🇬🇧 ou pound key 🇺🇸.

diesel, diésel* [djezɛl] nm **1.** [moteur] diesel engine ou motor **2.** [véhicule] diesel **3.** [combustible] diesel (oil).

diète [djɛt] nf **1.** [régime] diet **2.** [absence de nourriture] fasting *(for health reasons)* ▸ **à la diète** loc adv **1.** [au régime] on a diet **2.** [sans nourriture] ▸ **mettre qqn à la diète** to prescribe a fast for sb.

diététicien, enne [djetetisjɛ̃, ɛn] nm, f dietician, dietitian, nutrition specialist.

diététique [djetetik] ◆ adj [aliment] health *(modif)* ; [boutique] health food *(modif)*. ◆ nf nutrition science, dietetics *(sg)* *spéc*.

dieu, x [djø] nm **1.** [divinité] god **2.** [héros] god, idol **3.** [objet de vénération] god. ❖ **Dieu** npr **1.** [gén] God / *Dieu le père* God the father ▸ **le bon Dieu** the good Lord ▸ **on lui donnerait le bon Dieu sans confession** he looks as if butter wouldn't melt in his mouth **2.** [dans des exclamations] ▸ **Dieu vous bénisse / entende !** *litt* may God bless / hear you! ▸ **Dieu seul le sait !** God (only) knows! ▸ **Dieu merci !** thank God ou the Lord! ▸ **mon Dieu !** my God!, my goodness!, good Lord!

diffamation [difamasjɔ̃] nf **1.** [accusation -gén] defamation ; [-par un texte] libelling ; [-par des discours] slandering **2.** [texte] libel ; [geste, parole] slander. ❖ **de diffamation** loc adj [campagne] smear *(modif).*

diffamatoire [difamatwaʀ] adj [texte] defamatory, libellous ; [geste, parole] slanderous / *parler / agir de façon diffamatoire* to speak / to act slanderously.

différé, e [difeʀe] adj **1.** [paiement, rendez-vous, réponse] deferred, postponed **2.** RADIO & TV prerecorded. ❖ **en différé** loc adj RADIO & TV prerecorded.

différemment [difeʀamɑ̃] adv differently.

différence [difeʀɑ̃s] nf **1.** [distinction] difference, dissimilarity ▸ **faire la différence entre** to make the distinction between, to distinguish between **2.** [écart] difference ▸ **différence d'âge** age difference ou gap **3.** [particularité -culturelle, sexuelle] ▸ **revendiquer sa différence** to be proud to be different **4.** MATH [d'une soustraction] result ; [ensemble] difference / *je paierai la différence* I'll make up ou pay the difference. ❖ **à la différence de** loc prép unlike. ❖ **à cette différence (près) que, à la différence que** loc conj except that.

différencié, e [difeʀɑ̃sje] adj differentiated.

différencier [9] [difeʀɑ̃sje] vt **1.** [distinguer] to distinguish, to differentiate **2.** BIOL to differentiate.

différend [difeʀɑ̃] nm disagreement, dispute ▸ **avoir un différend avec qqn** to be in dispute with sb.

différent, e [difeʀɑ̃, ɑ̃t] ◆ adj **1.** [distinct] different ▸ **différent de** unlike, different from 🇬🇧 ou than 🇺🇸 **2.** [original] different / *un week-end un peu différent* a weekend with a difference. ◆ dét *(adj indéf, devant un nom au pl)* different, various.

> 📋 **Différent de** *Different from* ou *different than* 🇺🇸.
> **Il a des opinions politiques très différentes de celles de son frère.** *His political opinions are very different from his brother's* ou *His political opinions are very different than his brother's* 🇺🇸.
> Attention, on ne dit pas «different of». La forme «different to», souvent employée à l'oral en anglais britannique, est également à éviter car il s'agit d'un usage critiqué.

différentiel, elle [difeʀɑ̃sjɛl] adj differential. ❖ **différentiel** nm [pourcentage] differential.

différer [18] [difeʀe] ◆ vt [repousser - rendez-vous, réponse, réunion] to defer, to postpone ▸ *différer le paiement d'une dette* to put off ou to delay paying a debt. ◆ vi [se différencier] to differ, to vary.

> 📝 In reformed spelling (see p. 16-18), this verb is conjugated like *semer : il différa, elle différerait.*

difficile [difisil] adj **1.** [route, montée] difficult, hard, tough **2.** [tâche] difficult, hard / *il est difficile de dire si...* it's hard to say whether... **3.** [douloureux] difficult, hard, tough **4.** [personne - d'un tempérament pénible] difficult, demanding ; [-pointilleuse] particular, awkward, fussy / *être difficile (sur la nourriture)* to be fussy about one's

food / *il est si difficile à satisfaire !* he's so hard to please! **5.** [moralement] difficult, tricky ; [financièrement] difficult, tough **6.** [impénétrable - œuvre, auteur] difficult, abstruse **7.** [banlieue, quartier] tough.

difficilement [difisilmɑ̃] adv with difficulty ▸ **il s'endort difficilement** he has a hard time getting to sleep / *je peux difficilement accepter* I find it difficult ou it's difficult for me to accept.

difficulté [difikylte] nf **1.** [caractère ardu] difficulty ; [gêne] difficulty ▸ **avoir de la difficulté à faire qqch** to find it difficult to do sthg **2.** [problème] problem, difficulty ▸ **avoir des difficultés avec qqn** to have difficulties ou problems with sb ; [ennui - financier] ▸ **avoir des difficultés financières** to be in financial difficulties ou straits **3.** [point difficile] difficulty. ❖ **en difficulté** loc adj & loc adv [nageur] in difficulties ; [navire, avion] in distress ▸ **un enfant en difficulté a)** [scolairement] a child with learning difficulties **b)** [psychologiquement] a child with behavioural problems ▸ **mettre qqn en difficulté** to put sb in a difficult ou an awkward situation. ❖ **sans difficulté** loc adv easily, with no difficulty.

difforme [difɔʀm] adj deformed, misshapen.

diffus, e [dify, yz] adj [gén & BOT] diffuse.

diffuser [3] [difyze] vt **1.** [répandre - chaleur, lumière] to spread, to diffuse, to disseminate *sout* **2.** AUDIO, RADIO, TV & INTERNET to broadcast ▸ **émission diffusée en direct / différé** live / prerecorded broadcast ▸ **diffuser sur Internet** to webcast **3.** [propager - nouvelle, rumeur] to spread **4.** [distribuer - tracts] to hand out *(sép)*, to distribute ; [dans l'édition] to distribute, to sell.

diffuseur [difyzœʀ] nm **1.** COMM distributing agent, distributor **2.** [de parfum] *decorative object containing scent used as an air freshener.*

diffusion [difyzjɔ̃] nf **1.** ACOUST diffusion, diffusivity **2.** PHYS [d'une particule] diffusion **3.** OPT diffusion **4.** MÉD spreading **5.** AUDIO, RADIO, TV & INTERNET broadcasting **6.** [propagation - du savoir, d'une théorie] spreading **7.** [distribution - de tracts] distribution, distributing ; [- de livres] distribution, selling.

digérer [18] [diʒeʀe] vt **1.** PHYSIOL to digest / *je ne digère pas le lait* milk doesn't agree with me, I can't digest milk ; *(en usage absolu)* ▸ **prendre qqch pour digérer** to take sthg to help one's digestion **2.** [assimiler - connaissances, lecture] to digest, to assimilate **3.** *fam* [supporter] to stomach, to take.

> 📝 In reformed spelling (see p. 16-18), this verb is conjugated like *semer : il digèrera, elle digèrerait.*

digeste [diʒɛst] adj : *un aliment digeste* an easily digested foodstuff.

digestif, ive [diʒɛstif, iv] adj digestive. ❖ **digestif** nm [alcool] digestif.

digestion [diʒɛstjɔ̃] nf digestion / *avoir une digestion lente* to digest one's food slowly.

digital, e, aux [diʒital, o] adj **1.** ANAT digital **2.** [numérique] digital.

digitale [diʒital] nf foxglove, digitalis.

digne [diɲ] adj **1.** [noble] dignified / *d'un air très digne* in a dignified manner **2.** ▸ **digne de** [qui mérite] worthy ou deserving of / *toute amie digne de ce nom aurait accepté* a true friend would have accepted / *je n'ai pas eu de vacances dignes de ce nom depuis une éternité* I haven't had any holidays as such for ages ▸ **digne de confiance** trustworthy ▸ **digne de foi** credible **3.** ▸ **digne de** [en conformité avec] worthy of / *ce n'est pas digne de toi* it's unworthy of you.

dignement [diɲmɑ̃] adv **1.** [noblement] with dignity, in a dignified manner **2.** *litt* [justement] ▸ **dignement récompensé** justly rewarded.

dignitaire [diɲitɛʀ] nm dignitary.

dignité [diɲite] nf **1.** [noblesse] dignity ; [maintien] poise **2.** [respect] dignity / *une atteinte à la dignité de l'homme* an affront to human dignity **3.** [fonction] dignity.

digression [digʀesjɔ̃] nf digression.

digue [dig] nf [mur] dyke, seawall ; [talus] embankment.

diktat, dictat* [diktat] nm diktat.

dilapider [3] [dilapide] vt [gén] to waste, to fritter away *(sép)*, to squander ; [fonds publics] to embezzle.

dilatation [dilatasjɔ̃] nf **1.** PHYS expansion **2.** [des narines, des pupilles] dilation ; [de l'estomac] distension ; [du col de l'utérus] dilation, opening.

dilater [3] [dilate] vt **1.** PHYS to cause to expand **2.** [remplir d'air - tuyau, pneu] to inflate, to blow up *(sép)* **3.** [élargir - narine, pupille, veine] to dilate ; [- col de l'utérus] to open ; [- poumons] to expand. ◆ **se dilater** vpi **1.** PHYS to expand **2.** [être gonflé - tuyau, pneu] to blow up, to inflate **3.** [être élargi - narine, pupille, veine] to dilate ; [- col de l'utérus] to dilate, to open ; [- poumons] to expand.

dilatoire [dilatwaʀ] adj delaying, dilatory *sout*, procrastinating *sout* ▸ **user de moyens dilatoires** to play for time.

dilemme [dilɛm] nm dilemma / *être devant un dilemme* to face a dilemma.

dilettante [diletɑ̃t] nmf dilettante, dabbler. ◆ **en dilettante** loc adv : *il fait de la peinture en dilettante* he dabbles in painting.

diligence [diliʒɑ̃s] nf **1.** [véhicule] stagecoach **2.** *litt* haste, dispatch *litt* ▸ **avec diligence** hastily, promptly, with dispatch *litt*.

diligent, e [diliʒɑ̃, ɑ̃t] adj *litt* **1.** [actif] prompt, speedy, active **2.** [assidu - soins] constant, assiduous ; [- élève] diligent ; [- employé] conscientious, scrupulous.

diluant [dilɥɑ̃] nm diluent.

diluer [7] [dilɥe] vt **1.** [allonger - d'eau] to dilute, to water down *(sép)* ; [- d'un liquide] to dilute **2.** [délayer] to thin down *(sép)* **3.** *péj* [discours, exposé] to pad ou to stretch out *(sép)* ; [idée, argument] to dilute.

diluvien, enne [dilyvjɛ̃, ɛn] adj [pluie] torrential.

dimanche [dimɑ̃ʃ] nm Sunday ▸ **le dimanche de Pâques** Easter Sunday. **Voir aussi** mardi. ◆ **du dimanche** loc adj **1.** [journal] Sunday **2.** *fam & péj* [amateur] ▸ **chauffeur du dimanche** Sunday driver.

dimension [dimɑ̃sjɔ̃] nf **1.** [mesure] dimension, measurement ▸ **prendre les dimensions de qqch** to measure sthg (up) **2.** [taille] size, dimension / *une pièce de petite / grande dimension* a small-size(d) / large-size(d) room **3.** [importance] dimension / *cela donne une nouvelle dimension au problème* this gives a new dimension to the problem / *un groupe de dimension internationale* a group of international standing **4.** MATH & PHYS dimension ▸ **la troisième / quatrième dimension** the third / fourth dimension. ◆ **à la dimension de** loc prép corresponding ou proportionate to / *un salaire à la dimension du travail requis* wages proportionate to ou commensurate with *sout* the work involved. ◆ **à trois dimensions** loc adj three-dimensional.

diminué, e [diminɥe] adj [affaibli] ▸ **il est très diminué a)** [physiquement] his health is failing **b)** [mentalement] he's losing his faculties.

diminuer [7] [diminɥe] ◆ vt **1.** [réduire - prix, impôts, frais, ration] to reduce, to cut ; [- longueur] to shorten ; [- taille, effectifs, volume, vitesse, consommation] to reduce ; [atténuer - douleurs, souffrance] to alleviate, to lessen **2.** [af-faiblir - personne] : *la maladie l'a beaucoup diminué* his illness has affected him very badly **3.** [humilier - personne] to belittle, to cut down to size **4.** [en tricot] to decrease. ◆ vi **1.** [pression] to fall, to drop ; [volume] to decrease ; [prix] to fall, to come down ; [chômage, accidents, criminalité] to decrease, to be on the decrease ou wane **2.** [s'affaiblir - forces] to ebb away, to wane, to lessen ; [- peur] to lessen ; [- intérêt, attention] to drop, to lessen, to dwindle **3.** [raccourcir] ▸ **les jours diminuent** the days are getting shorter ou drawing in.

⚠ Attention, **diminish** est d'un usage beaucoup plus restreint que **diminuer** et ne doit pas être employé systématiquement pour traduire ce verbe. Voir l'article pour des traductions plus naturelles.

diminutif [diminytif] nm [nom] diminutive / *Greg est le diminutif de Gregory* Greg is short for Gregory.

diminution [diminysjɔ̃] nf **1.** [réduction - de prix, d'impôts, des frais, des rations] reduction, cutting ; [- de longueur] shortening ; [- de taille] reduction, shortening ; [- de volume] decrease, decreasing ; [- de pression] fall ; [- de vitesse, de consommation, des effectifs] reduction ; [- du chômage, de la violence] drop, decrease ▸ **une diminution des effectifs** a reduction in the number of staff **2.** [affaiblissement - d'une douleur] alleviation ; [- des forces] waning, lessening ; [- de l'intérêt, de l'attention] drop, lessening ; [- de l'appétit] decrease **3.** [en tricot] decrease / *faire une diminution* to decrease.

dinde [dɛ̃d] nf **1.** ORNITH turkey (hen) **2.** CULIN turkey.

dindon [dɛ̃dɔ̃] nm **1.** ORNITH turkey (cock) **2.** [sot] fool ▸ **être le dindon de la farce a)** [dupe] to be taken for a ride **b)** [victime de railleries] to end up a laughing stock.

dîner¹, diner* [dine] nm **1.** [repas du soir] dinner **2.** ⬛BELG & ⬛SUISSE *régional ou vieilli* [déjeuner] lunch.

dîner², diner* [3] [dine] vi **1.** [faire le repas du soir] to dine, to have dinner / *avoir des amis à dîner* to have friends to dinner ou round for dinner / *j'ai fait dîner les enfants plus tôt* I gave the children an early dinner **2.** ⬛BELG & ⬛SUISSE *régional ou vieilli* [déjeuner] to have lunch.

dînette, dinette* [dinɛt] nf [jouet] toy ou doll's tea set ▸ **jouer à la dînette** to play (at) tea-parties.

dingue [dɛ̃g] *fam* adj **1.** [fou] nuts, crazy, screwy ⬛US **2.** [incroyable - prix, histoire] crazy, mad / *c'est dingue ce qu'il peut faire chaud ici* it's hot as hell here.

dinosaure [dinozɔʀ] nm ZOOL & *fig* dinosaur.

diocèse [djɔsɛz] nm diocese.

diode [djɔd] nf diode.

dioxine [djɔksin] nf dioxin.

diphtérie [difteʀi] nf diphtheria.

diphtongue [diftɔ̃g] nf diphthong.

diplômant, e [diplomɑ̃, ɑ̃t] adj [cursus, formation] that leads to a qualification.

diplomate [diplɔmat] ◆ adj diplomatic. ◆ nmf POL & *fig* diplomat.

diplomatie [diplɔmasi] nf **1.** POL [relations, représentation] diplomacy ▸ **la diplomatie** [corps] the diplomatic corps ou service **2.** [tact] diplomacy, tact.

diplomatique [diplɔmatik] adj **1.** POL diplomatic **2.** [adroit] diplomatic, tactful, courteous.

diplôme [diplom] nm **1.** [titre] diploma, qualification / *un diplôme d'ingénieur* an engineering diploma ▸ **elle a des diplômes** she's highly qualified **2.** [examen] exam.

diplômé, e [diplome] adj qualified ▸ **il est diplômé d'HEC** he has an HEC degree.

dire¹ [diʀ] nm DR [mémoire] statement. ❖ **dires** nmpl statement ▸ **confirmer les dires de qqn** to confirm what sb says / **d'après** ou **selon les dires de son père** according to his father ou to what his father said. ❖ **au dire de** loc prép : **au dire de son professeur** according to his teacher ou to what his teacher says.

dire² [102] [diʀ]
vt

A. ARTICULER, PRONONCER 1. [énoncer] to say / **quel nom dis-tu ? Castagnel ?** what name did you say ou what's the name again? Castagnel? / **il n'arrive pas à dire ce mot** he cannot pronounce that word / **vous avez dit « démocratie » ?** "democracy", did you say? / **si (l')on peut dire** in a way, so to speak ▸ **disons-le** let's not mince words ▸ **dire non** to say no, to refuse / **dire non au nucléaire** to say no to nuclear energy ▸ **dire oui a)** [gén] to say yes **b)** [à une proposition] to accept **c)** [au mariage] to say I do / **dire bonjour de la main** to wave (hello) / **dire oui de la tête** to nod / **dire non de la tête** to shake one's head 2. [réciter - prière, table de multiplication] to say ; [- texte] to say, to recite, to read ; [- rôle] to speak ▸ **dire la / une messe** to say mass / a mass ▸ **dire des vers** to recite verse, to give a recitation.

B. EXPRIMER 1. [oralement] to say / **que dis-tu là ?** what did you say?, what was that you said? / **bon, bon, je n'ai rien dit !** OK, sorry I spoke! / **pourquoi ne m'as-tu rien dit de tout cela ?** why didn't you speak to me ou tell me about any of this? ▸ **faire dire** : **impossible de lui faire dire l'âge de sa sœur** he won't say ou give his sister's age / **impossible de lui faire dire la vérité** he just refuses to tell the truth ▸ **laisser qqn dire qqch** to let sb say sthg ▸ **laissez-la dire !** let her speak! ▸ **pouvoir dire** : **je peux dire que tu m'as fait peur !** you certainly frightened me! / **j'ai failli faire tout rater ! — ça, tu peux le dire !** I nearly messed everything up — you can say that again! ; *(en usage absolu)* ▸ **comment dire** ou **dirais-je ?** how shall I put it ou say? ▸ **bien dit !** well said! ▸ **dis** fam : **tu te fiches de moi, dis !** you're pulling my leg, aren't you? / **je peux y aller, dis ?** can I go, please? ▸ **dites** : **vous lui parlerez de moi, dites ?** you will talk to her about me, won't you? / **tu es bien habillé, ce soir, dis donc !** my word, aren't you smart tonight! ▸ **dites donc** ou **dites-moi** : **dites donc, pour demain, on y va en voiture ?** by the way, are we driving there tomorrow? ▸ **disons** : **il nous faut, disons, deux secrétaires** we need, (let's) say, two secretaries ▸ **c'est tout dire** : **il ne m'a même pas répondu, c'est tout dire** he never even answered me, that says it all ▸ **pour tout dire** in fact, to be honest ▸ **il va sans dire que...** needless to say (that)... ▸ **ça va sans dire** it goes without saying ▸ **je te dis pas** fam : **il y avait un monde, je te dis pas !** you wouldn't have believed the crowds! 2. [symboliquement] to express, to tell of / **je voudrais dire mon espoir** I'd like to express my hope ▸ **vouloir dire** [signifier] to mean 3. [écrire] to say / **dans sa lettre, elle dit que...** in her letter she says that... 4. [annoncer - nom, prix] to give / **cela t'a coûté combien ? — dis un prix !** how much did it cost you? — have a guess! 5. [prédire] to foretell, to tell / **je te l'avais bien dit !** I told you so ▸ **tu vas le regretter, moi je** fam ou **c'est moi qui** fam **te le dis !** you'll be sorry for this, let me tell you ou mark my words! 6. [ordonner] to tell / **il m'a dit d'arrêter** he told me to stop ; [conseiller] to tell / **tu me dis d'oublier, mais...** you tell me I must forget, but... 7. [objecter] to say, to object / **sa mère ne lui dit jamais rien** her mother never tells her off / **toi, on ne peut jamais rien te dire !** you can't take the slightest criticism! / **c'est tout ce que tu as trouvé à dire ?** is that the best you could come up with? 8. [affirmer] to say, to state / **puisque je vous le dis !** I'm telling you!, you can take it from me! / **c'est le bon train ? — je te dis que oui** is it the right train? — yes it is! ou I'm telling you it is! / **on dit qu'il a un autre fils** rumour has it that ou it's rumoured that ou it's said that he has another son ▸ **on dit ça** fam : **je m'en moque — on dit ça** I don't care — that's what you say ou that's what they all say 9. [prétendre] to claim, to allege / **elle disait ne pas savoir qui le lui avait donné** she claimed ou alleged that she didn't know who'd given it to her ; [dans des jeux d'enfants] : **on dirait qu'on serait des rois** let's pretend we're kings 10. [admettre] to say, to admit / **il faut dire qu'elle a des excuses** (to) give her her due, there are mitigating circumstances ▸ **disons que...** let's say (that)... 11. [décider] : **il est dit que...** fate has decreed that... / **il ne sera pas dit que...** let it not be said that... ▸ **tout est dit a)** [il n'y a plus à discuter] the matter is closed **b)** [l'avenir est arrêté] the die is cast.

C. PENSER, CROIRE 1. [penser] to say, to think ▸ **dire de** : **que dis-tu de ma perruque ?** what do you think of ou how do you like my wig? / **et comme dessert ? — que dirais-tu d'une mousse au chocolat ?** and to follow? — what would you say to ou how about a chocolate mousse? 2. [croire] ▸ **on dirait** [introduit une comparaison, une impression] : **si livide qu'on eût dit un fantôme** so pale he looked like a ghost ▸ **on dirait du thé a)** [au goût] it tastes like tea **b)** [à l'odeur] it smells like tea **c)** [d'apparence] it looks like tea ; [exprime une probabilité] : **on dirait sa fille, au premier rang** it looks like her daughter there in the front row.

D. INDIQUER 1. [indiquer - suj : instrument] to say ; [- suj : attitude, regard] to say, to show / **que dit le baromètre ?** what does the barometer say? ▸ **mon intuition** ou **quelque chose me dit qu'il reviendra** I have a feeling (that) he'll be back 2. [stipuler par écrit] to say.

E. RAPPELER, FAIRE ENVIE 1. [faire penser à] ▸ **dire quelque chose** : **son visage me dit quelque chose** I've seen her face before, her face seems familiar ▸ **cela ne me dit rien de bon** ou **qui vaille** I'm not sure I like (the look of) it 2. [tenter] : **ta proposition me dit de plus en plus** your suggestion's growing on me / **tu viens ? — ça ne me dit rien** are you coming? — I'm not in the mood ou I don't feel like it. ❖ **se dire** ◆ vp (emploi réciproque) [échanger - secrets, paroles] to tell each other ou one another / **nous n'avons plus rien à nous dire** we've got nothing left to say to each other. ◆ vp (emploi passif) 1. [être formulé] : **comment se dit « bonsoir » en japonais ?** how do you say "goodnight" in Japanese?, what's the Japanese for "goodnight"? / **il est vraiment hideux — peut-être, mais ça ne se dit pas** he's really hideous — maybe, but it's not the sort of thing you say 2. [être en usage] to be in use, to be accepted usage. ◆ vpt [penser] to think (to o.s.), to say to o.s. / **maintenant, je me dis que j'aurais dû accepter** now I think I should have accepted. ◆ vpi [estimer être] to say / **il se dit flatté de l'intérêt que je lui porte** he says he's ou he claims to be flattered by my interest in him ; [se présenter comme] to say, to claim / **ils se disent attachés à la démocratie** they claim to ou (that) they care about democracy.

direct, e [diʀɛkt] adj 1. [sans détour - voie, route, chemin] direct, straight 2. TRANSP direct, without a change / **un vol direct Paris-New York** a direct ou nonstop flight from Paris to New York / **c'est un train direct jusqu'à Genève** the train is nonstop to Geneva 3. [franc - question] direct ; [- langage] straightforward ; [- personne] frank, straightforward 4. [sans intermédiaire - cause, conséquence] immediate ; [- supérieur, descendant] direct 5. ASTRON, GRAM & MÉCAN direct. ❖ **direct** nm 1. RAIL through ou nonstop train 2. TV live / **il préfère le direct au playback** he prefers performing live to lipsynching. ❖ **en direct** loc adj & loc adv live.

directement [diʀɛktəmɑ̃] adv 1. [tout droit] straight / **va directement au lit** go straight to bed 2. [franchement]

▸ **allez directement au fait** come straight to the point **3.** [inévitablement] straight, inevitably **4.** [sans intermédiaire] direct ▸ **adresse-toi directement au patron** go straight to the boss ▸ **vendre directement au public** to sell direct to the public **5.** [personnellement] : *cela ne vous concerne pas directement* this doesn't affect you personally ou directly.

directeur, trice [dirɛktœr, tris] ◆ adj [principal - force] controlling, driving ; [- principe] guiding ; [- idée, ligne] main, guiding. ◆ nm, f **1.** [dans une grande entreprise] manager (manageress), director ; [dans une petite entreprise] manager (manageress) ▸ **directeur artistique** creative ou artistic director ▸ **directeur de cabinet** principal private secretary ▸ **directeur commercial** sales manager ▸ **directeur général** managing director 🇬🇧, chief executive officer 🇺🇸 ▸ **directeur de prison** prison governor 🇬🇧 ou warden 🇺🇸 ▸ **directeur des ressources humaines** human resources manager **2.** ÉDUC ▸ **directeur d'école** head teacher 🇬🇧, headmaster 🇬🇧, principal 🇺🇸 ▸ **directrice d'école** head teacher 🇬🇧, headmistress 🇬🇧, (lady) principal 🇺🇸 **3.** UNIV [d'un département] head of department ▸ **directeur de thèse** (thesis) supervisor **4.** CINÉ, THÉÂTRE & TV director ▸ **directeur artistique** artistic director.

directif, ive [dirɛktif, iv] adj [entretien, méthode] directive / *il est très directif* he likes telling people what to do. ❖ **directive** nf ADMIN, MIL & POL directive. ❖ **directives** nfpl orders, instructions.

direction [dirɛksjɔ̃] nf **1.** [fonction de chef - d'une entreprise] management, managing ; [- d'un orchestre] conducting, direction 🇺🇸 ; [- d'un journal] editorship ; [- d'une équipe sportive] captaining ▸ **prendre la direction de a)** [société, usine] to take over the running ou management of **b)** [journal] to take over the editorship of / *orchestre (placé) sous la direction de* orchestra conducted by **2.** ▸ **direction centrale** ADMIN headquarters of a branch of the civil service **3.** [sens] direction, way / *il est parti dans la direction de la gare* he went towards the station / *vous êtes dans la bonne direction* you're going the right way / *vous allez dans quelle direction ?* which way are you going?, where are you heading for? ▸ **prenez la direction Nation** [dans le métro] take the Nation line / **'toutes directions'** 'all routes' ▸ **partir dans toutes les directions a)** [coureurs, ballons] to scatter **b)** [pétards] to go off in all directions **c)** [conversation] to wander **4.** AUTO & MÉCAN steering ▸ **direction assistée** power steering. ❖ **en direction de** loc prép in the direction of, towards / *embouteillages en direction de Paris* holdups for Paris-bound traffic ▸ **les trains / avions / vols en direction de Marseille** trains / planes / flights to Marseille.

dirigeable [diriʒabl] ◆ adj dirigible. ◆ nm airship, dirigible.

dirigeant, e [diriʒɑ̃, ɑ̃t] ◆ adj ruling. ◆ nm, f POL [d'un parti] leader ; [d'un pays] ruler, leader ▸ **dirigeant syndical** union leader.

diriger [17] [diriʒe] vt **1.** [être à la tête de - usine, entreprise] to run, to manage ; [- personnel, équipe] to manage ; [- service, département] to be in charge of, to be head of ; [- école] to be head of ; [- orchestre] to conduct, to direct 🇺🇸 ; [- journal] to edit ; [- pays] to run ; [- parti, mouvement] to lead **2.** [superviser - travaux] to supervise, to oversee ; [- débat] to conduct ; [- thèse, recherches] to supervise ; [- circulation] to direct ; [- opérations] to direct, to oversee **3.** [piloter - voiture] to steer ; [- bateau] to navigate, to steer ; [- avion] to fly, to pilot ; [- cheval] to drive ; [guider - aveugle] to guide ; [- dans une démarche] to direct, to steer ▸ **diriger qqn vers la sortie** to direct sb to the exit / *elle a été mal dirigée dans son choix de carrière* she had poor career guidance **4.** [acheminer - marchandises] to send **5.** [orienter - pensée] to direct ▸ **diriger son regard vers qqn** to look in the direc-

tion of sb **6.** [adresser hostilement] to level, to direct ▸ **diriger des accusations contre qqn** to level accusations at sb / *leurs moqueries étaient dirigées contre lui* he was the butt of their jokes **7.** [braquer] : *une antenne dirigée vers la tour Eiffel* an aerial trained on the Eiffel tower / *lorsque la flèche est dirigée vers la droite* when the arrow points to the right ; ARM [tir] to aim / *diriger un canon vers* ou *sur une cible* to aim ou to level ou to point a cannon at a target. ❖ **se diriger** vpi **1.** [aller] ▸ **se diriger sur** ou **vers** [frontière] to head ou to make for, to go towards 🇬🇧 ou toward 🇺🇸, to head towards 🇬🇧 ou toward 🇺🇸 / *se diriger vers la sortie* to make one's way to the exit **2.** [trouver son chemin] to find one's way.

dirigisme [diriʒism] nm state control, state intervention.

discernement [disɛrnəmɑ̃] nm [intelligence] (good) judgement, discernment *sout* / *il a agi avec discernement* he showed (good) judgement in what he did.

discerner [3] [disɛrne] vt **1.** [voir] to discern, to distinguish, to make out *(insép)* **2.** [différencier] ▸ **discerner qqch de qqch** : *discerner le bien du mal* to distinguish (between) right and wrong, to tell right from wrong.

disciple [disipl] nm **1.** RELIG & ÉDUC disciple **2.** [partisan] follower, disciple.

disciplinaire [disiplinɛr] adj disciplinary.

discipline [disiplin] nf **1.** [règlement] discipline **2.** [obéissance] discipline ▸ **avoir de la discipline** to be disciplined **3.** ÉDUC & UNIV [matière] subject, discipline.

discipliné, e [disipline] adj [personne] obedient, disciplined.

discipliner [3] [disipline] vt [faire obéir - élèves, classe] to discipline, to (bring under) control. ❖ **se discipliner** vp *(emploi réfléchi)* to discipline o.s.

disco [disko] ◆ adj invar ▸ **musique disco** disco (music). ◆ nm [musique] disco (music) ; [danse, chanson] disco number. ◆ nf *fam & vieilli* [discothèque] disco.

discographique [diskɔɡrafik] adj : *l'industrie discographique française* the French record industry.

discompte [diskɔ̃t] nm discount.

discontinu, e [diskɔ̃tiny] adj [ligne] broken ; [effort] discontinuous, intermittent ▸ **le bruit est discontinu** the noise occurs on and off.

discordant, e [diskɔrdɑ̃, ɑ̃t] adj **1.** MUS discordant ; [criard] harsh, grating **2.** [opposé - styles, couleurs, avis, diagnostics] clashing.

discorde [diskɔrd] nf discord, dissension, dissention.

discothèque [diskɔtɛk] nf **1.** [collection] record collection **2.** [établissement de prêt] record ou music library **3.** [boîte de nuit] disco, night club.

discount [diskaunt] nm **1.** [rabais] discount / *un discount de 20 %* (a) 20% discount, 20% off **2.** [technique] discount selling.

discourir [45] [diskurir] vi **1.** *litt* [bavarder] to talk **2.** *péj* [disserter] to speechify.

discours [diskur] nm **1.** [allocution] speech, address / *faire un discours* to make a speech ▸ **discours du trône** POL inaugural speech *(of a sovereign before a Parliamentary session)*, King's Speech, Queen's Speech **2.** LING [langage réalisé] speech ; [unité supérieure à la phrase] discourse ▸ **discours direct** GRAM direct speech ▸ **discours indirect** GRAM reported ou indirect speech **3.** [expression d'une opinion] discourse / *tenir un discours de droite* to talk like a rightwinger.

discrédit [diskredi] nm discredit, disrepute ▸ **jeter le discrédit sur qqn / qqch** to discredit sb / sthg.

discréditer [3] [diskredite] vt to discredit, to bring into disrepute. ❖ **se discréditer** vp *(emploi réfléchi)* [personne] to bring discredit upon o.s. / *se discréditer auprès du public* to lose one's good name.

discret, ète [diskʀɛ, ɛt] adj **1.** [réservé - personne, attitude] reserved, discreet **2.** [délicat - personne] tactful, discreet, diplomatic **3.** [qui sait garder un secret] discreet.

discrètement [diskʀɛtmã] adv **1.** [sans être remarqué] quietly, discreetly, unobtrusively **2.** [se maquiller, se parfumer] discreetly, lightly, subtly ; [s'habiller] discreetly, quietly, soberly.

discrétion [diskʀesjɔ̃] nf **1.** [réserve] discretion, tact, tactfulness **2.** [silence] discretion / **'discrétion assurée'** 'write in confidence'. ❖ **à discrétion** loc adv : *vous pouvez manger à discrétion* you can eat as much as you like. ❖ **à la discrétion de** loc prép at the discretion of.

discrimination [diskʀiminasjɔ̃] nf [ségrégation] ▶ **discrimination raciale** racial discrimination.

discriminatoire [diskʀiminatwaʀ] adj discriminatory.

disculper [3] [diskylpe] vt ▶ **disculper qqn de qqch** to exonerate sb from sthg. ❖ **se disculper** vp *(emploi réfléchi)* ▶ **se disculper de qqch** to exonerate o.s. from sthg.

discussion [diskysjɔ̃] nf **1.** [négociation] talk, discussion ; [querelle] quarrel, argument ▶ **pas de discussion !** no arguing!, don't argue! **2.** [débat] debate, discussion **3.** [conversation] discussion, conversation.

discutable [diskytabl] adj [fait, théorie, décision] debatable, questionable ; [sincérité, authenticité] questionable, doubtful ; [goût] dubious.

discutailler [3] [diskytaje] vi *fam & péj* to quibble.

discuter [3] [diskyte] ❖ vt **1.** [débattre - projet de loi] to debate, to discuss ; [- sujet, question] to discuss, to argue, to consider **2.** [contester - ordres] to question, to dispute ; [- véracité] to debate, to question ; [- prix] to haggle over ; *(en usage absolu)* ▶ **tu discutes ?** no ifs and buts! US, no ifs ands or buts! US. ❖ vi **1.** [parler] to talk, to have a discussion ▶ **discuter de** to talk about *(insép)*, to discuss **2.** [négocier] to negotiate. ❖ **se discuter** vp *(emploi passif)* [point de vue] ▶ **ça se discute** *fam* that's debatable.

disette [dizɛt] nf [pénurie - gén] shortage, dearth ; [- de nourriture] scarcity of food, food shortage.

diseur, euse [dizœʀ, øz] nm, f ▶ **diseur de bonne aventure** fortune-teller.

disgrâce [disgʀas] nf *sout* [défaveur] disgrace, disfavour ▶ **tomber en disgrâce** to fall into disfavour, to fall from grace.

disgracieux, euse [disgʀasjø, øz] adj [laid - visage] ugly, unattractive ; [- geste] awkward, ungainly ; [- comportement] uncouth ; [- personne] unattractive, unappealing ; [- objet] unsightly.

disjoncter [3] [disʒɔ̃kte] vi to short-circuit, *fig : il disjoncte complètement fam* he's losing his marbles.

disjoncteur [disʒɔ̃ktœʀ] nm circuit breaker, cutout (switch).

dislocation [dislɔkasjɔ̃] nf [d'une caisse] breaking up ; [d'un empire] dismantling ; [d'un parti] breaking up, disintegration ; [d'une manifestation] breaking up, dispersal.

disloquer [3] [dislɔke] vt **1.** [faire éclater - empire] to dismantle ; [- parti] to break up *(sép)* **2.** MÉD to dislocate. ❖ **se disloquer** vpi **1.** [meuble] to come ou to fall apart, to fall to pieces **2.** MÉD to be dislocated.

disparaître, disparaitre* [91] [dispaʀɛtʀ] vi **1.** [se dissiper - peur, joie] to evaporate, to fade, to disappear ; [- douleur, problème, odeur] to disappear ; [- bruit] to stop, to subside ; [- brouillard] to clear, to vanish ▶ **faire disparaître qqch** a) [gén] to remove sthg b) [supprimer] to get rid of sthg / *il a fait disparaître tous mes doutes* he dispelled all my doubts **2.** [devenir invisible - soleil, lune] to disappear ; [- côte, bateau] to vanish, to disappear **3.** [être inexplicablement absent] to disappear, to vanish ▶ **faire disparaître qqn / qqch** to conceal sb / sthg **4.** [ne plus exister - espèce,

race] to die out, to become extinct ; [- langue, coutume] to die out, to disappear ; [mourir] to pass away, to die ▶ **disparaître en mer** to be lost at sea.

disparate [dispaʀat] adj **1.** [hétérogène - objets, éléments] disparate, dissimilar **2.** [mal accordé - mobilier] ill-assorted, non-matching ; [- couple] ill-assorted, ill-matched.

disparité [dispaʀite] nf disparity ▶ **disparité de** [sommes d'argent] disparity in.

disparition [dispaʀisjɔ̃] nf **1.** [du brouillard] lifting, clearing ; [du soleil] sinking, setting ; [d'une côte, d'un bateau] vanishing ; [de la peur, du bruit] fading away ; [du doute] disappearance **2.** [absence - d'une personne, d'un porte-monnaie] disappearance **3.** [extinction - d'une espèce] extinction ; [- d'une langue, d'une culture] dying out, disappearance.

disparu, e [dispaʀy] ❖ adj **1.** [mort] dead ▶ **porté disparu** a) [soldat] missing (in action) b) [marin] lost at sea c) [passager, victime] missing believed dead **2.** [langue] dead ; [coutume, culture] vanished, dead ; [ère, époque] bygone. ❖ nm, f **1.** [défunt] dead person ▶ **les disparus** the dead / *les disparus en mer* [marins] men lost at sea **2.** [personne introuvable] missing person.

dispatcher [3] [dispatʃe] vt to dispatch, to send around *(sép)*.

dispendieux, euse [dispɑ̃djø, øz] adj *litt* expensive, costly.

dispensaire [dispɑ̃sɛʀ] nm community clinic UK, free clinic US.

dispense [dispɑ̃s] nf [exemption] exemption / *dispense d'oral* exemption from an oral exam.

dispenser [3] [dispɑ̃se] vt **1.** [exempter] ▶ **dispenser qqn de qqch** to exempt sb from sthg / *se faire dispenser de gymnastique* to be excused (from) gym ▶ **dispenser qqn de faire** to exempt sb from doing / *je te dispense de tes sarcasmes* spare me your sarcasm **2.** [donner - charité] to dispense, to administer ; [- parole] to utter. ❖ **se dispenser de** vp + prép [obligation] to get out of / *je me dispenserais bien de cette corvée !* I could do without this chore!

disperser [3] [dispɛʀse] vt **1.** [répandre - cendres, graines] to scatter **2.** [brume, brouillard] to disperse, to lift **3.** [efforts] to dissipate ; [attention] to divide **4.** [foule, manifestants] to disperse, to break up *(sép)*, to scatter ; [collection] to break up, to scatter. ❖ **se disperser** vpi [manifestation, foule] to disperse, to break up.

dispersion [dispɛʀsjɔ̃] nf **1.** [de cendres, de débris] scattering **2.** [de troupes, de policiers] spreading out **3.** [d'une foule, de manifestants] dispersal.

disponibilité [dispɔnibilite] nf **1.** [d'une fourniture, d'un service] availability **2.** [liberté] availability *(for an occupation)* **3.** ADMIN ▶ **mise en disponibilité** (extended) leave / *se mettre en disponibilité* to take (extended) leave. ❖ **disponibilités** nfpl available funds, liquid assets.

disponible [dispɔnibl] adj **1.** [utilisable - article, service] available ▶ **non disponible** unavailable **2.** [libre - personnel, employé] free, available **3.** [ouvert - personne] receptive, open-minded.

dispos, e [dispo, oz] adj in good form ou shape ▶ **frais et dispos** fresh (as a daisy).

disposé, e [dispoze] adj **1.** [arrangé] : *bien / mal disposé* well- / poorly-laid out **2.** [personne] : *bien / mal disposé* in a good / bad mood ▶ **être bien / mal disposé à l'égard de qqn** to be well-disposed / ill-disposed towards UK ou toward US sb.

disposer [3] [dispoze] ❖ vt **1.** [arranger - verres, assiettes] to lay, to set ; [- fleurs] to arrange ; [- meubles] to place, to arrange / *j'ai disposé la chambre autrement* I've changed the layout of the bedroom **2.** [inciter] ▶ **disposer qqn à** to incline sb to ou towards **3.** [préparer] ▶ **disposer**

qqn à to prepare sb for ▸ **être disposé à faire qqch** to feel disposed ou to be willing to do sthg. ◆ vi [partir] ▸ **vous pouvez disposer** you may leave ou go. ◆ **disposer de** v + prép **1.** [avoir] to have (at one's disposal ou available) **2.** [utiliser] to use **3.** DR ▸ **disposer de ses biens** to dispose of one's property. ◆ **se disposer à** vp + prép to prepare to.

⚠ Attention, **to dispose of** signifie « se débarrasser de » et non disposer de.

dispositif [dispozitif] nm **1.** [appareil, mécanisme] machine, device ▸ **dispositif antibuée** demister 🇬🇧, defogger 🇺🇸 **2.** [mesures] plan, measure **3.** MIL plan **4.** CINÉ, THÉÂTRE & TV ▸ **dispositif scénique** set.

disposition [dispozisjɔ̃] nf **1.** [arrangement - de couverts] layout ; [- de fleurs, de livres, de meubles] arrangement **2.** [tendance - d'une personne] tendency / **avoir une disposition à la négligence / à grossir** to have a tendency to carelessness / to put on weight **3.** [aptitude] aptitude, ability, talent ▸ **avoir une disposition pour** to have a talent for **4.** DR clause, stipulation ▸ **les dispositions testamentaires de...** the last will and testament of... ; [jouissance] disposal **5.** ADMIN ▸ **mise à la disposition** secondment 🇬🇧, temporary transfer 🇺🇸. ◆ **dispositions** nfpl **1.** [humeur] mood / **être dans de bonnes / mauvaises dispositions** to be in a good / bad mood **2.** [mesures] measures ▸ **prendre des dispositions a)** [précautions, arrangements] to make arrangements, to take steps **b)** [préparatifs] to make preparations. ◆ **à la disposition de** loc prép at the disposal of ▸ **mettre** ou **tenir qqch à la disposition de qqn** to place sthg at sb's disposal, to make sthg available to sb / **se tenir à la disposition de** to make o.s. available for / **je suis à votre disposition** I am at your service.

disproportionné, e [dispʀɔpɔʀsjɔne] adj [inégal] disproportionate / **un prix disproportionné avec** ou **à la qualité** a price out of (all) proportion to the quality.

dispute [dispyt] nf quarrel, argument.

⚠ Le mot anglais **dispute** signifie « discussion », « débat » ou « conflit ». Il ne doit pas être employé pour traduire le mot français dispute.

disputer [3] [dispyte] vt **1.** [participer à - match, tournoi] to play ; [- combat] to fight **2.** [tenter de prendre] ▸ **disputer qqch à qqn** to fight with sb over sthg ▸ **disputer la première place à qqn** to contend ou to vie with sb for first place **3.** fam [réprimander] to scold, to tell off (sép) / **tu vas te faire disputer !** you're in for it ! **4.** litt [contester] to deny. ◆ **se disputer** ◆ vp (emploi réciproque) to quarrel, to argue, to fight. ◆ vpt ▸ **se disputer qqch** to fight over sthg.

disquaire [diskɛʀ] nmf [commerçant] record dealer.

disqualification [diskalifikasjɔ̃] nf disqualification.

disqualifier [9] [diskalifje] vt SPORT to disqualify.

disque [disk] nm **1.** [cercle plat] disc, disk 🇺🇸 **2.** ANAT, ASTRON & MATH disc, disk 🇺🇸 **3.** SPORT discus **4.** AUDIO record, disc, disk 🇺🇸 ▸ **disque compact** compact disc, compact disk 🇺🇸 **5.** INFORM disk ▸ **disque dur** hard disk.

disquette [diskɛt] nf floppy disk, diskette.

dissemblable [disɑ̃blabl] adj different, dissimilar.

disséminer [3] [disemine] vt [graines] to scatter. ◆ **se disséminer** vpi [graines] to scatter ; [personnes] to spread (out).

dissension [disɑ̃sjɔ̃] nf disagreement, difference of opinion.

disséquer [18] [diseke] vt MÉD to dissect.
✍ In reformed spelling (see p. 16-18), this verb is conjugated like semer : **il dissèquera, elle dissèquerait.**

dissert' [disɛʀt] (abr de dissertation) nf arg scol essay.

dissertation [disɛʀtasjɔ̃] nf ÉDUC & UNIV essay.

disserter [3] [disɛʀte] vi **1.** ▸ **disserter sur** ÉDUC & UNIV to write an essay on **2.** fig & péj to hold forth on ou about.

dissidence [disidɑ̃s] nf **1.** [rébellion] dissidence **2.** [dissidents] dissidents, rebels.

dissident, e [disidɑ̃, ɑ̃t] ◆ adj [rebelle] dissident (avant nom), rebel (avant nom) ▸ **un groupe dissident** a splinter ou breakaway group. ◆ nm, f [rebelle] dissident, rebel.

dissimulation [disimylasjɔ̃] nf **1.** [fait de cacher] concealment **2.** [hypocrisie] deceit, dissimulation, hypocrisy ; [sournoiserie] dissembling, secretiveness.

dissimulé, e [disimyle] adj [invisible - haine, jalousie] concealed ▸ **non dissimulé** open.

dissimuler [3] [disimyle] vt **1.** [cacher à la vue] to hide (from sight) **2.** [ne pas révéler - identité] to conceal ; [- sentiments, difficultés] to hide, to conceal, to cover up (sép) ; [- fait] to conceal, to disguise. ◆ **se dissimuler** vp (emploi réfléchi) [se cacher] to hide ou to conceal o.s.

dissipation [disipasjɔ̃] nf **1.** [de nuages] dispersal, clearing ; [du brouillard] lifting ; [de craintes] dispelling **2.** [indiscipline] lack of discipline, misbehaviour 🇬🇧, misbehavior 🇺🇸.

dissipé, e [disipe] adj [indiscipliné - classe] unruly, rowdy, undisciplined.

dissiper [3] [disipe] vt **1.** [nuages, brouillard, fumée] to disperse ; [malentendu] to clear up (sép) ; [crainte, inquiétude] to dispel **2.** [dilapider - héritage, patrimoine] to dissipate, to squander **3.** [distraire] to distract, to divert. ◆ **se dissiper** vpi **1.** [orage] to blow over ; [nuages] to clear away, to disperse ; [brouillard] to lift, to clear ; [fumée] to disperse **2.** [craintes] to disappear, to vanish ; [migraine, douleur] to go, to disappear **3.** [s'agiter - enfant] to misbehave, to be undisciplined ou unruly.

dissocier [9] [disɔsje] vt [questions, chapitres] to separate ; [famille] to break up (sép). ◆ **se dissocier** vp (emploi réciproque) to break up, to split / **je tiens à me dissocier de cette action** I am eager to dissociate myself from what they're doing.

dissolu, e [disɔly] adj litt dissolute.

dissolution [disɔlysjɔ̃] nf **1.** [d'un produit, d'un comprimé] dissolving **2.** [d'une société] dissolution ; [d'un groupe] splitting, breaking up **3.** DR [d'un mariage, d'une association] dissolution ; POL [d'un parlement] dissolution.

dissolvant, e [disɔlvɑ̃] nm **1.** [détachant] solvent **2.** [de vernis à ongles] ▸ **dissolvant (gras)** nail polish remover.

dissoudre [87] [disudʀ] vt **1.** [diluer - sel, sucre, comprimé] to dissolve **2.** [désunir - assemblée, mariage] to dissolve ; [- parti] to break up (sép), to dissolve ; [- association] to dissolve, to break up (sép), to bring to an end. ◆ **se dissoudre** vpi **1.** [sel, sucre, comprimé] to dissolve **2.** [groupement] to break up, to come to an end.

dissuader [3] [disɥade] vt ▸ **dissuader qqn de (faire) qqch** to dissuade sb from (doing) sthg.

dissuasif, ive [disɥazif,iv] adj [qui décourage] dissuasive, discouraging, off-putting 🇬🇧.

dissuasion [disɥazjɔ̃] nf dissuasion. ◆ **de dissuasion** loc adj [puissance] dissuasive.

distance [distɑ̃s] nf **1.** [intervalle - dans l'espace] distance ▸ **garder ses distances** to stay aloof, to remain distant ▸ **prendre ses distances a)** SPORT to space out **b)** MIL to spread out in ou to form open order ▸ **prendre ses distances**

envers ou **à l'égard de qqn** to hold o.s. aloof ou to keep one's distance from sb **2.** [parcours] distance ▶ **tenir la distance** *pr & fig* to go the distance, to stay the course **3.** [intervalle -dans le temps] : *ils sont nés à deux mois de distance* they were born within two months of each other **4.** [écart, différence] gap, gulf, great difference / *ce malentendu a mis une certaine distance entre nous* we've become rather distant from each other since that misunderstanding. ◆ **à distance** loc adv **1.** [dans l'espace] at a distance, from a distance, from afar ▶ **tenir qqn à distance** to keep sb at a distance ou at arm's length / *se tenir à distance (de)* to keep one's distance (from) **2.** [dans le temps] with time.

distancer [16] [distɑ̃se] vt SPORT to outdistance, to leave behind ; *fig* to outdistance, to outstrip ▶ **se laisser distancer a)** SPORT to fall behind **b)** *fig* to be left behind / *se faire distancer économiquement* to lag behind economically.

distanciation [distɑ̃sjasjɔ̃] nf [gén] detachment.

distancier [9] [distɑ̃sje] ◆ **se distancier de** vp + prép ▶ **se distancier de qqch / qqn** to distance o.s. from sthg / sb.

distant, e [distɑ̃, ɑ̃t] adj [dans l'espace] far away, distant ▶ **être distant de qqch** to be far ou some distance from sthg / *les deux écoles sont distantes de 5 kilomètres* the (two) schools are 5 kilometres away from each other.

distendre [73] [distɑ̃dʀ] vt [étirer -ressort] to stretch, to overstretch ; [-peau] to stretch, to distend *spéc* ; [-muscle] to strain. ◆ **se distendre** vpi [s'étirer -peau, ventre] to stretch, to become distended *spéc*.

distillation [distilasjɔ̃] nf distillation, distilling.

distiller [3] [distile] vt [alcool, pétrole, eau] to distil UK, to distill US.

distillerie [distilʀi] nf **1.** [usine, atelier] distillery **2.** [activité] distilling.

distinct, e [distɛ̃, ɛ̃kt] adj **1.** [clair, net] distinct, clear **2.** [différent] distinct, different.

distinctement [distɛ̃ktəmɑ̃] adv distinctly, clearly.

distinctif, ive [distɛ̃ktif, iv] adj [qui sépare] distinctive, distinguishing.

distinction [distɛ̃ksjɔ̃] nf [différence] distinction / *faire une distinction entre deux choses* to make ou to draw a distinction between two things. ◆ **sans distinction de** loc prép irrespective of.

distingué, e [distɛ̃ge] adj **1.** [élégant -personne] distinguished ; [-manières, air] refined, elegant, distinguished **2.** [brillant, éminent] distinguished, eminent.

distinguer [3] [distɛ̃ge] vt **1.** [différencier] to distinguish / *distinguer le vrai du faux* to distinguish truth from falsehood / *je n'arrive pas à les distinguer* I can't tell which is which, I can't tell them apart **2.** [honorer] to single out (for reward), to honour. ◆ **se distinguer** ◆ vp *(emploi passif)* **1.** [être vu] to be seen ou distinguished **2.** [différer] to distinguish par: *ces vins se distinguent par leur robe* you can tell these wines are different because of their colour. ◆ vpi [se faire remarquer] to distinguish o.s. / *son fils s'est distingué en musique* his son has distinguished himself ou done particularly well in music.

distraction [distʀaksjɔ̃] nf **1.** [caractère étourdi] absent-mindedness ▶ **par distraction** inadvertently ; [acte] lapse in concentration **2.** [détente] : *il lui faut de la distraction* he needs to have his mind taken off things ; [activité] source of entertainment.

distraire [112] [distʀɛʀ] vt **1.** [déranger] to distract **2.** [amuser] to entertain, to divert **3.** [détourner] ▶ **distraire qqn de**: *distraire un ami de ses soucis* to take a friend's mind off his worries. ◆ **se distraire** vpi **1.** [s'amuser] to have fun, to enjoy o.s. **2.** [se détendre] to relax, to take a break.

distrait, e [distʀɛ, ɛt] adj [gén] absent-minded ; [élève] inattentive ▶ **d'un air distrait** abstractedly, absent-mindedly ▶ **avoir l'air distrait** to look preoccupied.

distraitement [distʀɛtmɑ̃] adv absent-mindedly, abstractedly.

distrayant, e [distʀɛjɑ̃, ɑ̃t] adj amusing, entertaining.

distribuer [7] [distʀibɥe] vt **1.** [donner -feuilles, cadeaux, bonbons] to distribute, to give ou to hand out *(sép)* ; [-cartes] to deal ; [-courrier] to deliver ; [-vivres] to dispense, to share out *(sép)*, to distribute ; [-argent] to apportion, to distribute, to share out *(sép)* **2.** [attribuer -rôles] to allocate, to assign ; [-tâches, travail] to allot, to assign.

distributeur, trice [distʀibytœʀ, tʀis] nm, f distributor. ◆ **distributeur** nm [non payant] dispenser ▶ **distributeur de savon / gobelets** soap / cup dispenser ▶ **distributeur automatique de billets** cash dispenser ou machine, cashpoint, automatic teller machine, ATM ; [payant] ▶ **distributeur (automatique)** vending ou slot machine.

distribution [distʀibysjɔ̃] nf **1.** [remise -de vêtements, de cadeaux] distribution, giving ou handing out ; [-de cartes] dealing ; [-de secours] dispensing, distributing ; [-de tâches, du travail] allotment, assignment ; [-du courrier] delivery ▶ **la distribution des prix** ÉDUC prize-giving day **2.** [approvisionnement] supply / *distribution d'eau / de gaz* water / gas supply **3.** CINÉ & THÉÂTRE [des rôles] cast ; CINÉ [des films] distribution **4.** COMM distribution ; [par des grandes surfaces] retail ▶ **la grande distribution** supermarkets and hypermarkets.

district [distʀikt] nm **1.** [région] district, region **2.** [d'une ville] district.

dit, e [di, dit] adj **1.** [surnommé] (also) known as **2.** [fixé] appointed, indicated ▶ **le jour dit** on the agreed ou appointed day.

dithyrambique [ditiʀɑ̃bik] adj eulogistic, laudatory.

DIU [deiy] *(abr de* **dispositif intra-utérin***)* nm MÉD IUD.

diurétique [djyʀetik] adj & nm diuretic.

diurne [djyʀn] adj diurnal.

divaguer [3] [divage] vi **1.** [malade] to ramble, to be delirious **2.** *fam & péj* [déraisonner] to be off one's head.

divan [divɑ̃] nm **1.** [meuble] divan, couch **2.** HIST ▶ **le divan** the divan.

divergence [diveʀʒɑ̃s] nf [différence] ▶ **divergence (d'idées ou de vues)** difference of opinion.

divergent, e [diveʀʒɑ̃, ɑ̃t] adj [opinions, interprétations, intérêts] divergent, differing.

diverger [17] [diveʀʒe] vi [intérêts, opinions] to differ, to diverge ▶ **diverger de** to diverge ou to depart from.

divers, e [diveʀ, ɛʀs] ◆ dét *(adj indéf)* [plusieurs] various, several ▶ **à usages divers** multipurpose *(avant nom)*. ◆ adj [variés -éléments, musiques, activités] diverse, varied ▶ **pour diverses raisons** for a variety of reasons.

diversement [diveʀsəmɑ̃] adv **1.** [différemment] in different ways **2.** [de façon variée] in diverse ou various ways.

diversification [diveʀsifikasjɔ̃] nf diversification.

diversifier [9] [diveʀsifje] vt **1.** [production, tâches] to diversify **2.** [varier] to make more varied. ◆ **se diversifier** vpi [entreprise, économie, centres d'intérêt] to diversify.

diversion [diveʀsjɔ̃] nf *sout* [dérivatif] diversion, distraction ▶ **faire diversion** to create a distraction.

diversité [diveʀsite] nf [variété] diversity, variety ; [pluralité -de formes, d'opinions, de goûts] diversity.

divertir [32] [diveʀtiʀ] vt [amuser -suj : clown, spectacle, lecture] to entertain, to amuse. ◆ **se divertir** vpi [se distraire] to amuse ou to entertain o.s.

divertissant, e [diveʀtisɑ̃, ɑ̃t] adj amusing, entertaining.

divertissement [divɛʀtismɑ̃] nm **1.** [jeu, passe-temps] distraction ; [spectacle] entertainment **2.** [amusement] entertaining, distraction.

dividende [dividɑ̃d] nm FIN & MATH dividend.

divin, e [divɛ̃, in] adj **1.** RELIG divine **2.** [parfait - beauté, corps, repas, voix] divine, heavenly, exquisite.

divinité [divinite] nf [dieu] deity, divinity.

diviser [3] [divize] vt **1.** [fragmenter - territoire] to divide up *(sép)*, to partition ; [- somme, travail] to divide up *(sép)* ; [- cellule, molécule] to divide, to split **2.** MATH to divide **3.** [opposer] to divide, to set against each other ▸ *c'est diviser pour (mieux) régner* it's (a case of) divide and rule. ❖ **se diviser** vpi **1.** [cellule] to divide ou to split (up) ; [branche, voie] to divide, to fork / *le texte se divise en cinq parties* the text is divided into five parts **2.** [opposition, parti] to split.

divisible [divizibl] adj divisible.

division [divizjɔ̃] nf **1.** MATH division ▸ **faire une division** to do a division **2.** [fragmentation - d'un territoire] splitting, division, partition ; PHYS splitting **3.** [désaccord] division, rift **4.** FOOT division / *un club de première | deuxième | troisième division* a first / second / third division club ; BASEBALL league.

divisionnaire [divizjɔnɛʀ] ❖ adj ADMIN [service] divisional. ❖ nm **1.** MIL major general **2.** [commissaire] ≃ chief superintendent 🇬🇧 ; ≃ police chief 🇺🇸.

divorce [divɔʀs] nm DR divorce ▸ **demander le divorce** to ask ou to petition for a divorce ▸ **divorce par consentement mutuel** divorce by mutual consent, no-fault divorce 🇺🇸.

divorcé, e [divɔʀse] adj divorced.

divorcer [16] [divɔʀse] vi DR to get a divorce, to get divorced.

divulgation [divylgasjɔ̃] nf divulgation, disclosure.

divulguer [3] [divylge] vt to divulge, to disclose, to reveal.

dix [dis *(devant consonne* [di]*, devant voyelle ou «* h *» muet* [diz]*)*] ❖ dét ten. ❖ nm ten. **Voir aussi cinq.**

dix-huit [dizɥit] dét & nm inv eighteen. **Voir aussi cinq.**

dix-huitième [dizɥitjɛm] adj num & nmf eighteenth. **Voir aussi cinquième.**

dixième [dizjɛm] adj num & nmf tenth. **Voir aussi cinquième.**

dix-neuf [diznœf] ((diznœv) *devant an, heure et homme)* dét & nm inv nineteen. **Voir aussi cinq.**

dix-neuvième [diznœvjɛm] adj num & nmf nineteenth. **Voir aussi cinquième.**

dix-sept [dis(s)ɛt] dét & nm inv seventeen. **Voir aussi cinq.**

dix-septième [dis(s)ɛtjɛm] adj num & nmf seventeenth. **Voir aussi cinquième.**

dizaine [dizɛn] nf **1.** [dix] ten **2.** [environ dix] about ou around ten, ten or so.

Djakarta [dʒakaʀta] npr Djakarta, Jakarta.

Djibouti [dʒibuti] npr **1.** [État] Djibouti ▸ **à Djibouti** in Djibouti **2.** [ville] Djibouti City.

djiboutien, enne [dʒibusjɛ̃, ɛn] adj Djiboutian. ❖ **Djiboutien, enne** nm, f Djiboutian.

djihad [dʒiad] nm jihad.

djihadiste [dʒiadist] adj & nmf jihadist.

dl (abr écrite de **décilitre**) dl.

do [do] nm inv C ; [chanté] doh 🇬🇧, do 🇺🇸. **Voir aussi fa.**

doberman [dɔbɛʀman] nm Doberman (pinscher).

doc [dɔk] (abr de **documentation**) nf *fam* literature, brochures.

docile [dɔsil] adj [animal] docile, tractable *sout* ; [enfant, nature] docile, obedient ; [cheveux] manageable.

docilité [dɔsilite] nf [d'un animal, d'une personne] docility.

dock [dɔk] nm **1.** [bassin] dock **2.** [bâtiments, chantier] ▸ **les docks** the docks, the dockyard.

docker [dɔkɛʀ] nm docker 🇬🇧, longshoreman 🇺🇸, stevedore 🇺🇸.

docte [dɔkt] adj *litt* learned, erudite.

docteur, e [dɔktœʀ] nm, f **1.** [médecin] ▸ **le docteur Jacqueline R.** Dr Jacqueline R. **2.** UNIV Doctor ▸ **docteur en histoire / physique** PhD in history / physics ▸ **Vuibert, docteur ès lettres** Vuibert, PhD.

doctoral, e, aux [dɔktɔʀal, o] adj **1.** [pédant] pedantic **2.** UNIV doctoral.

doctorat [dɔktɔʀa] nm doctorate ▸ **doctorat en droit / chimie** PhD in law / chemistry ▸ **doctorat d'État** doctorate *(leading to high-level research)*.

doctoresse [dɔktɔʀɛs] nf *vieilli* (woman) doctor.

doctrinaire [dɔktʀinɛʀ] ❖ adj doctrinaire, dogmatic. ❖ nmf doctrinaire.

doctrine [dɔktʀin] nf doctrine.

docudrame [dɔkydʀam] nm docudrama.

docu-fiction (pl docu-fictions), **docufiction** [dɔkyfiksjɔ̃] nm docufiction, fictional documentary.

document [dɔkymɑ̃] nm **1.** [d'un service de documentation] document **2.** [de travail] document, paper **3.** [témoignage] document.

documentaire [dɔkymɑ̃tɛʀ] ❖ adj **1.** [qui témoigne - livre] documentary **2.** [de documentation] document *(modif)*. ❖ nm CINÉ & TV documentary.

documentaliste [dɔkymɑ̃talist] nmf **1.** [gén] archivist **2.** ÉDUC (school) librarian.

documentation [dɔkymɑ̃tasjɔ̃] nf **1.** [informations] (written) evidence **2.** [opération] documentation.

documenter [3] [dɔkymɑ̃te] vt [thèse] to document ; [avocat] to supply ou to provide with documents, to document. ❖ **se documenter** vpi to inform o.s. ▸ **se documenter sur** to gather information ou material about.

dodeliner [3] [dɔdəline] ❖ **dodeliner de** v + prép : *dodeliner de la tête* to nod gently.

dodo [dodo] nm *langage enfantin* [sommeil] sleep, beddy-byes ▸ **faire dodo** to go beddy-byes ou bybyes ; [lit] bed / *va au dodo* (time to) go to beddy-byes.

dodu, e [dɔdy] adj [oie] plump ; [personne, visage] plump, fleshy, chubby ; [bébé] chubby.

dogmatique [dɔgmatik] adj dogmatic.

dogme [dɔgm] nm dogma.

dogue [dɔg] nm mastiff.

doigt [dwa] nm **1.** ANAT finger, digit *spéc* ▸ **lever le doigt** to put one's hand up / *manger avec ses doigts* to eat with one's fingers ▸ **mettre ses doigts dans** ou **se mettre les doigts dans le nez** to pick one's nose ▸ **mettre son doigt dans l'œil de qqn** to poke sb in the eye ▸ **doigt de pied** toe ▸ **petit doigt** little finger ▸ **glisser** ou **filer entre les doigts de qqn** to slip through sb's fingers ▸ **se mettre** *fam* ou **se mettre,** *fam* ou **se foutre** *tfam* **le doigt dans l'œil (jusqu'au coude)** to be barking up the wrong tree ▸ **mener** ou **faire marcher qqn au doigt et à l'œil** to have sb toe the line, to rule sb with a rod of iron ▸ **obéir au doigt et à l'œil** : *il lui obéit au doigt et à l'œil* she rules him with a rod of iron ▸ *c'est mon petit doigt qui me l'a dit* a little bird told me ▸ **il ne bougera** ou **lèvera pas le petit doigt pour faire…** he won't lift a finger to do… **2.** [mesure] little bit ▸ **servez-m'en un doigt** just pour me out a drop. ❖ **à un doigt de, à deux doigts de** loc prép close to, within an inch / *j'ai été à deux doigts de le renvoyer* I came very close to ou I was within inches of firing him.

doigté [dwate] nm **1.** [adresse] dexterity **2.** [tact] tact, diplomacy ▶ **ne pas avoir de / avoir du doigté** to be tactless / tactful.

doléances [dɔleɑ̃s] nfpl complaints, grievances.

dollar [dɔlaʀ] nm [en Amérique du Nord] dollar.

DOM [dɔm] (**abr de département d'outre-mer**) nm *French overseas département.*

domaine [dɔmɛn] nm **1.** [propriété] estate, (piece of) property **2.** [lieu préféré] domain **3.** DR ▶ **domaine privé** private ownership ▶ **domaine public** public ownership (of rights) ▶ **être dans le domaine public** to be out of copyright **4.** [secteur d'activité] field, domain, area ▶ **dans tous les domaines** in every field ou domain ; [compétence, spécialité] field.

domanial, e, aux [dɔmanjal, o] adj [de l'État] national, state *(modif).*

dôme [dom] nm ARCHIT dome, cupola *spéc.*

domestique [dɔmɛstik] ◆ adj **1.** [familial - problème, vie] family *(modif)* ; [- lieu] household *(modif)* **2.** [du ménage - affaires, devoirs, tâches] household *(modif)*, domestic **3.** [animal] domesticated ▶ **les animaux domestiques** pets. ◆ nmf domestic, servant.

domestiquer [3] [dɔmɛstike] vt [animal] to domesticate ; [plante] to turn into a cultivated variety ; [énergie] to harness.

domicile [dɔmisil] nm **1.** [lieu de résidence] home, place of residence *sout* ; ADMIN & DR domicile *sout* ; [adresse] (home) address ▶ **domicile fiscal / légal** address for tax / legal purposes ▶ **domicile conjugal** marital home **2.** [d'une entreprise] registered address. ◆ **à domicile** ◆ loc adj ▶ **soins à domicile** domiciliary care, home treatment. ◆ loc adv [chez soi] at home ▶ **travailler à domicile** to work from home. ◆ **sans domicile fixe** ◆ adj of no fixed abode ou address. ◆ nmf inv homeless person.

domicilié, e [dɔmisilje] adj : *être fiscalement domicilié dans un pays* to be liable to pay tax in a country ▶ **domicilié à Tokyo / en Suède** domiciled in Tokyo / in Sweden.

domicilier [9] [dɔmisilje] vt ADMIN to domicile / *je me suis fait domicilier chez mon frère* I gave my brother's place as an accommodation address.

dominant, e [dɔminɑ̃, ɑ̃t] adj [principal - facteur, thème, trait de caractère] dominant, main ; [- espèce] dominant ; [- couleur] dominant, main, predominant ; [- intérêt] main, chief ; [- idéologie] prevailing ; [- position] commanding. ◆ **dominante** nf **1.** [aspect prépondérant] dominant ou chief ou main characteristic **2.** [teinte] predominant colour 🇬🇧 ou color 🇺🇸.

domination [dɔminasjɔ̃] nf **1.** [politique, militaire] domination, dominion, rule / *territoires sous domination allemande* territories under German domination ou rule **2.** [ascendant personnel, influence] domination, influence / *il exerçait sur eux une étrange domination* he had a strange hold over them.

dominer [3] [dɔmine] vt **1.** POL [nation, peuple] to dominate, to rule **2.** [contrôler - marché] to control, to dominate **3.** [influencer - personne] to dominate / *elle domine complètement son patron* she's got her boss under her thumb **4.** [surclasser] to outclass / *ils se sont fait dominer en mêlée* they were weaker in the scrums **5.** [colère] to control ; [complexe, dégoût, échec, timidité] to overcome ; [passion] to master, to control ; [matière, question] to master ▶ **dominer la situation** to be in control of the situation **6.** [prédominer dans - œuvre, style, débat] to predominate in, to dominate ; *(en usage absolu)* [couleur, intérêt] to predominate, to be predominant ; [caractéristique] to dominate, to be dominant ;

[idéologie, opinion] to prevail **7.** [surplomber] to overlook, to dominate ▶ **dominer qqn de la tête et des épaules a)** *pr* to be taller than sb by a head **b)** *fig* to tower above sb, to be head and shoulders above sb. ◆ **se dominer** vp *(emploi réfléchi)* to control o.s. / *ne pas savoir se dominer* to have no self-control.

dominicain¹, e [dɔminikɛ̃, ɛn] adj & nm, f RELIG Dominican.

dominicain², e [dɔminikɛ̃, ɛn] adj [de Saint-Domingue] Dominican. ◆ **Dominicain, e** nm, f Dominican.

dominical, e, aux [dɔminikal, o] adj Sunday *(modif)*, dominical *sout.*

Dominique [dɔminik] npr f ▶ **la Dominique** Dominica.

domino [dɔmino] nm **1.** JEUX & VÊT domino ▶ **jouer aux dominos** to play dominoes **2.** ÉLECTR connecting block.

dommage [dɔmaʒ] nm **1.** DR [préjudice] harm, injury ▶ **dommage corporel** physical injury ▶ **dommages de guerre** war damage ▶ **dommages et intérêts** ou **dommages-intérêts** damages **2.** *(gén au pl)* [dégât matériel] ▶ **dommage matériel, dommages matériels** (material) damage ▶ **causer des dommages à** to cause damage to **3.** [expression d'un regret] ▶ **(c'est) dommage !** what a shame ou pity! / *c'est vraiment dommage de devoir abattre ce chêne* it's a real shame to have to cut down this oak / *dommage que tu n'aies pas pu venir !* what a pity ou shame you couldn't come!

domotique [dɔmɔtik] nf home automation.

dompter [3] [dɔ̃te] vt **1.** [animal] to tame **2.** *litt* [révoltés] to quash ; [peuple] to subjugate.

dompteur, euse [dɔ̃tœʀ, øz] nm, f tamer, liontamer.

DOM-TOM [dɔmtɔm] (**abr de départements et territoires d'outre-mer**) npr mpl *French overseas départements and territories.*

 DOM-TOM

This is the abbreviation that is still commonly used for French overseas possessions, although the **départements d'outre-mer** are now officially called **DROM (départements et Régions d'outre-mer)** and the **territoires d'outre-mer** are now officially called **COM (collectivités d'outre-mer)**. Guadeloupe, Martinique, Guyane and La Réunion have **département** status, and their inhabitants are French citizens. The **collectivités** include two islands in the French West Indies (Saint-Barthélemy and the French part of Saint-Martin), Wallis and Futuna, French Polynesia, New Caledonia and French territories at the Poles. The territories are independent, though supervised by a French government representative.

don [dɔ̃] nm **1.** [aptitude naturelle] talent, gift / *avoir le don de voyance* to be clairvoyant / *tu as le don d'envenimer les situations !* you have a knack for stirring up trouble! **2.** [cadeau] gift, donation / *la collection dont elle m'a fait don* the collection she gave me as a present **3.** DR donation ▶ **faire don d'un bien à qqn** to donate a piece of property to sb **4.** MÉD donation, donating ▶ **encourager les dons d'organes** to promote organ donation.

donateur, trice [dɔnatœʀ, tʀis] nm, f donor.

donation [dɔnasjɔ̃] nf [gén] donation, disposition ; [d'argent] donation.

donc [dɔ̃k] conj **1.** [par conséquent] so, therefore / *je n'en sais rien, inutile donc de me le demander* I don't know anything about it, so there's no use asking me / *il faudra donc envisager une autre solution* we should therefore think of another solution **2.** [indiquant une transition] so ▸ **nous disions donc que...** so, we were saying that... **3.** [indiquant la surprise] so ▸ **c'était donc toi !** so it was you! **4.** [renforçant une interrogation, une assertion, une injonction] : *mais qu'y a-t-il donc ?* what's the matter, then? / *allons donc, vous vous trompez* come on (now), you're mistaken / *eh ben dis donc !* well, really! / *essaie donc !* go on, try! ▸ **tiens donc !** well, well, well! / *dis donc, à propos, tu l'as vue hier soir ?* oh, by the way, did you see her yesterday evening?

donf [dɔ̃f] ⬧ **à donf** loc adv *(verlan de à fond)* : *il écoute ce morceau en boucle à donf* he listens to that song over and over again at full blast.

donjon [dɔ̃ʒɔ̃] nm keep, donjon.

> ⚠ **Dungeon** signifie le plus souvent « cachot » et non donjon.

donnant-donnant [dɔnɑ̃dɔnɑ̃] nm : *c'est du donnant-donnant* it's give and take.

donne [dɔn] nf CARTES deal ▸ **il y a eu fausse** ou **mauvaise donne** there was a misdeal.

donné, e [dɔne] adj **1.** [heure, lieu] fixed, given / *sur un parcours donné* on a given ou certain route **2.** [bon marché] ▸ **c'est donné !** it's dirt cheap! ▸ **c'est pas donné !** it's hardly what you'd call cheap! ⬧ **donnée** nf **1.** INFORM, MATH & SCI piece of data, datum *sout* ▸ **données** data **2.** [information] piece of information ▸ **données** facts, information.

donner [3] [dɔne]
◆ vt

A. **CÉDER, ACCORDER 1.** [offrir] to give ; [se débarrasser de] to give away *(sép)* ; [distribuer] to give out *(sép)* ▸ **donner qqch à qqn** to give sthg to sb, to give sb sthg ▸ **donner qqch en cadeau à qqn** to make sb a present of sthg ▸ **donner qqch en souvenir à qqn** to give ou to leave sb sthg as a souvenir ▸ **donner sa place à qqn dans le train** to give up one's seat to sb on the train / *donner à boire à un enfant* to give a child a drink ou something to drink ▸ **donner à manger aux enfants / chevaux** to feed the children / horses ; *(en usage absolu)* to give / *donner aux pauvres* to give to the poor ▸ **donner de son temps** to give up one's time **2.** DR [léguer] to leave ; [faire don public de - argent, œuvre d'art, organe] to donate, to give **3.** [accorder - subvention] to give, to hand out *(sép)* ; [- faveur, interview, liberté] to give, to grant ; [- prix, récompense] to give, to award ▸ **donner la permission à qqn de faire qqch** to allow sb to do sthg, to give sb permission to do sthg ▸ **donner rendez-vous à qqn a)** ADMIN to make an appointment with sb **b)** [ami, amant] to make a date with sb ▸ **donner à qqn l'occasion de faire qqch** to give sb the opportunity to do sthg ou of doing sthg **4.** [laisser - délai] to give, to leave **5.** [confier] to give, to hand, to pass ▸ **donner une tâche à qqn** to entrust sb with a job / *donner ses enfants à garder* to have one's children looked after **6.** [remettre - gén] to give ; [- devoir] to give, to hand in *(sép)* **7.** [vendre - suj : commerçant] to give **8.** [payer] to give / *combien t'en a-t-on donné ?* how much did you get for it? / *je donnerais n'importe quoi pour le retrouver* I'd give anything to find it again **9.** [administrer - médicament, sacrement] to give, to administer *sout* ; [- bain] to give ▸ **donner une punition à qqn** to punish sb **10.** [appliquer - coup, baiser] to give ▸ **donner une fessée à qqn** to smack sb's bottom, to spank sb ▸ **donner un coup de rabot / râteau /**

pinceau à qqch to go over sthg with a plane / rake / paintbrush **11.** [passer, transmettre] to give, to pass on *(sép)* / *son père lui a donné le goût du théâtre* she got her liking for the theatre from her father **12.** [organiser - dîner, bal] to give, to throw.

B. **CONFÉRER 1.** [assigner] to give ▸ **donner un nom à qqn** to give sb a name, to name sb / *je donne peu d'importance à ces choses* I attach little importance to these things **2.** [attribuer] : *on ne lui donnerait pas son âge* he doesn't look his age **3.** [prédire] to give ▸ **je ne lui donne pas trois mois a)** [à vivre] I give her less than three months to live **b)** [avant d'échouer] I'll give it three months at the most.

C. **PROVOQUER, ABOUTIR À 1.** [suj : champ] to yield ; [suj : arbre fruitier] to give, to produce **2.** [susciter, provoquer - courage, énergie, espoir] to give ; [- migraine] to give, to cause ; [- sensation] to give, to create ; [- impression] to give, to produce ▸ **donner du souci à qqn** to worry sb ▸ **donner des boutons à qqn** to make sb come out in spots / *ça donne la diarrhée* it gives you ou causes diarrhoea ▸ **donner chaud / froid / faim / soif à qqn** to make sb hot / cold / hungry / thirsty **3.** [conférer - prestige] to confer, to give ; [- aspect, charme] to give, to lend / *le grand air t'a donné des couleurs* the fresh air has brought colour to your cheeks **4.** [aboutir à - résultats] to give, to yield ; [- effet] to result in / *en ajoutant les impôts, cela donne la somme suivante* when you add (in) ou on the tax, it comes to the following amount ▸ **donner quelque chose** : *et ta candidature, ça donne quelque chose ?* have you had anything about your application? ▸ **ne rien donner** : *les recherches n'ont rien donné* the search was fruitless.

D. **EXPRIMER, COMMUNIQUER 1.** [présenter, fournir - garantie, preuve, précision] to give, to provide ; [- explication] to give ; [- argument] to put forward *(sép)* ; [- ordre, consigne] to give ▸ **donner un conseil à qqn** to give sb a piece of advice, to advise sb **2.** [dire] to give ▸ **donner des nouvelles à qqn** to give sb news ▸ **donnez-moi de ses nouvelles** tell me how he is **3.** [indiquer - suj : instrument] to give, to indicate, to show **4.** *fam* [dénoncer] to give away *(sép)*, to rat on, to shop UK **5.** [rendre public - causerie, cours] to give ; [- œuvre, spectacle] to put on.

◆ vi **1.** [produire - arbre] to bear fruit, to yield ; [- potager, verger, terre] to yield / *la vigne a bien / mal donné cette année* the vineyard had a good / bad yield this year ▸ **donner à plein a)** [radio] to be on full blast, to be blaring (out) **b)** [campagne de publicité, soirée] to be in full swing **2.** CARTES to deal ▸ **à toi de donner** your deal. ⬧ **donner dans** v + prép **1.** [tomber dans] to fall into, *fig* to have a tendency towards UK ou toward US / *sans donner dans le mélodrame* without becoming too melodramatic **2.** [déboucher sur] to give out onto / *l'escalier donne dans une petite cour* the staircase gives out onto ou leads to ou leads into a small courtyard. ⬧ **donner de** v + prép **1.** [cogner avec] : *donner du coude / de la tête contre une porte* to bump one's elbow / one's head against a door **2.** [utiliser] : *donner du cor* to sound the horn ▸ **donner de la voix** to raise one's voice ▸ **ne plus savoir où donner de la tête** *fig* to be run off one's feet. ⬧ **donner sur** v + prép **1.** [se cogner contre] : *la barque alla donner sur le rocher* the boat crashed into the rock **2.** [être orienté vers] ▸ **la chambre donne sur le jardin / la mer** the room overlooks the garden / the sea. ⬧ **se donner** ◆ vp *(emploi passif)* [film, pièce] to be on. ◆ vpi **1.** [employer son énergie] : *monte sur scène et donne-toi à fond* get on the stage and give it all you've got ▸ **se donner à** : *se donner à une cause* to devote o.s. ou one's life to a cause **2.** *sout* [sexuellement] ▸ **se donner à qqn** to give o.s. to sb. ◆ vpt **1.** [donner à soi-même] : *se donner un coup de marteau sur les doigts* to hit one's fingers with a hammer ▸ **se donner les moyens de faire qqch** to give o.s. the means to do sthg **2.** [échanger] to give one another ou each other / *se donner un baiser* to give each other a kiss, to kiss / *ils se sont donné leurs impressions* they swapped views **3.** [se doter de] to give o.s. ❖ **donnant donnant** ◆ loc adv that's fair, fair's fair ▸ *d'accord, mais c'est donnant donnant* OK, but I want something in return. ◆ nm = **donnant-donnant**.

📋 **Donner qqch à qqn** Give sthg to sb ou *give sb sthg.*

Notez la construction à double complément qui en anglais peut prendre deux formes dont le sens est le même :

• une structure identique à celle du français :
verbe + COD + préposition + COI
give sthg to sb

• une structure qui diffère de celle du français, sans préposition, et dans laquelle l'ordre des compléments est inversé :
verbe + COI + COD
give sb sthg

Elle a donné tous ses tableaux à ses petits-enfants. She gave all her paintings to her grandchildren ou She gave her grandchildren all her paintings. **Donne ton adresse à François.** Give your address to François ou Give François your address.

---

donneur, euse [dɔnœr, øz] nm, f **1.** MÉD donor ▸ **donneur d'organe / de sang** organ / blood donor ▸ **donneur universel** universal blood donor **2.** ▸ **donneur de leçons** : *je ne veux pas me transformer en donneur de leçons, mais…* I don't want to lecture you, but… **3.** fam [délateur] squealer, informer. ❖ **donneur** nm ÉCON & FIN ▸ **donneur d'ordres** principal.

dont [dɔ̃] pron rel **1.** [exprimant le complément du nom - personne] whose ; [-chose] whose, of which *sout* / *le club dont je suis membre* the club to which I belong ou of which I'm a member *sout*, the club I belong to **2.** [exprimant la partie d'un tout - personnes] of whom ; [-choses] of which / *deux personnes ont téléphoné, dont ton frère* two people phoned, including your brother **3.** [exprimant le complément de l'adjectif] : *le service dont vous êtes responsable* the service for which you are responsible **4.** [exprimant l'objet indirect] : *une corvée dont je me passerais bien* a chore (which) I could well do without **5.** [exprimant le complément du verbe - indiquant la provenance, l'agent, la manière, etc.] : *une personne dont on ne sait rien* a person nobody knows anything about / *la famille dont je viens* the family (which) I come from / *les amis dont il est entouré* the friends he is surrounded by.

dopage [dɔpaʒ] nm drug use *(in sport).*

dopant, e [dɔpɑ̃, ɑ̃t] adj stimulant *(modif)*. ❖ **dopant** nm drug *(used as stimulant in competitions).*

doper [3] [dɔpe] vt [droguer] to dope *(in a competition)* ▸ **doper les ventes** to boost sales. ❖ **se doper** vp *(emploi réfléchi)* to take drugs *(in a competition).*

dorade [dɔrad] = **daurade**.

doré, e [dɔre] adj **1.** [bouton, robinetterie] gilt, gilded **2.** [chevelure, lumière] golden ; [peau] golden brown ; [gâteau, viande] browned, golden brown.

dorénavant [dɔrenavɑ̃] adv [à partir de maintenant] from now on, henceforth *sout*, henceforward *sout* ; [dans le passé] from then on.

dorer [3] [dɔre] ◆ vt **1.** [couvrir d'or] to gild ▸ **faire dorer qqch** to have sthg gilded ▸ **dorer la pilule à qqn** fam

to sugar the pill for sb **2.** [brunir - peau] to give a golden colour to, to tan ; [-blés, poires] to turn gold ; [-paysage] to shed a golden light on. ◆ vi CULIN to turn golden ▸ **faites dorer les oignons** cook ou fry the onions until golden / *je faire dorer au soleil* to sunbathe. ❖ **se dorer** vp *(emploi réfléchi)* [touriste] to sunbathe ▸ **se dorer la pilule a)** fam [bronzer] to lie in the sun getting o.s. cooked to a turn *hum* **b)** [ne rien faire] to do sweet FA 🇬🇧 ou zilch 🇺🇸.

dorloter [3] [dɔrlɔte] vt to pamper, to cosset.

dormant, e [dɔrmɑ̃, ɑ̃t] adj [eau] still. ❖ **dormant** nm CONSTR [bâti] fixed frame, casing *(U)* ; [vitre] fixed.

dormeur, euse [dɔrmœr, øz] nm, f sleeper ▸ *c'est un grand* ou *gros dormeur* he likes his sleep.

dormir [36] [dɔrmir] vi **1.** PHYSIOL to sleep ; [à un moment précis] to be asleep, to be sleeping ▸ **dors bien !** sleep tight! / *je n'ai pas dormi de la nuit* I didn't sleep a wink all night ▸ **la situation m'inquiète, je n'en dors pas** ou **plus (la nuit)** the situation worries me, I'm losing sleep over it ▸ **avoir envie de dormir** to feel sleepy ▸ **dormir d'un sommeil léger a)** [habituellement] to be a light sleeper **b)** [à tel moment] to be dozing ▸ **dormir à poings fermés** to be fast asleep, to be sleeping like a baby ▸ **dormir comme une bûche** ou **un loir** ou **une marmotte** ou **une souche** ou **un sabot** to sleep like a log ▸ **dormir debout** : *tu dors debout* you can't (even) keep awake, you're dead on your feet ▸ **dormir sur ses deux oreilles** : *tu peux dormir sur tes deux oreilles* there's no reason for you to worry, you can sleep soundly in your bed at night **2.** [être sans activité - secteur] to be dormant ou asleep ; [-volcan] to be dormant ; [-économies personnelles] to lie idle ; [-économie nationale] to be stagnant / *ils ont laissé dormir le projet* they left the project on the back burner **3.** [être inattentif] : *ce n'est pas le moment de dormir !* now's the time for action!

dorsal, e, aux [dɔrsal, o] adj ANAT & ZOOL dorsal, back *(modif).*

dortoir [dɔrtwar] nm dormitory ▸ **cité** ou **ville dortoir** dormitory town.

dorure [dɔryr] nf [en or] gilt ; [artificielle] gold-effect finish.

doryphore [dɔrifɔr] nm Colorado ou potato beetle.

dos [do] nm **1.** ANAT back / *être sur le dos* to be (lying) on one's back ▸ **tourner le dos à qqn a)** [assis] to sit with one's back to sb **b)** [debout] to stand with one's back to sb **c)** [l'éviter] to turn one's back on sb / *je ne l'ai vu que de dos* I only saw him from behind ou the back / *dès que j'ai le dos tourné, il fait des bêtises* as soon as my back is turned, he gets into mischief ▸ **avoir qqch sur le dos** fam : *ce gosse n'a rien sur le dos !* that kid's not dressed warmly enough! ▸ **faire qqch dans** ou **derrière le dos de qqn** to do sthg behind sb's back ▸ **être sur le dos de qqn** fam : *tu es toujours sur le dos de ce gosse, laisse-le un peu !* you're always nagging that kid, leave him alone! ▸ **avoir qqn sur le dos** : *vous aurez les syndicats sur le dos* the unions will be breathing down your necks ▸ **faire le gros dos a)** [chat] to arch its back **b)** fig to lie low ▸ **faire qqch sur le dos de** : *ils ont bâti leur empire sur le dos des indigènes* they built their empire at the expense of the natives ▸ **l'avoir dans le dos** *tfam* : *il l'a dans le dos !* he's been had ou done! ▸ **avoir qqn à dos** : *il les avait tous à dos* they were all after him ▸ **se mettre qqn à dos** to put sb's back up ▸ **mettre qqch sur le dos de qqn** fam [crime, erreur] to pin sthg on sb ▸ **n'avoir rien / pas grand-chose à se mettre sur le dos** : *je n'ai rien / pas grand-chose à me mettre sur le dos* I have got nothing / virtually nothing to wear ▸ **avoir le dos au mur** to have one's back to the wall **2.** [d'une fourchette, d'un habit] back ; [d'un couteau] blunt edge ; [d'un livre] spine ▸ **ne pas y être allé avec le dos de la cuillère** : *il n'y est pas allé avec le dos de la cuillère* **a)** fam [dans une action] he didn't go in for half-measures! **b)** [dans une discussion] he didn't mince words! **3.** SPORT ▸ **dos crawlé** back crawl. ⬧ **au dos** loc adv [d'une feuille] on the other side ou the back, overleaf. ⬧ **au dos de** loc prép [d'une feuille] on the back of / *signer au dos d'un chèque* to endorse a cheque. ⬧ **dos à dos** loc adv with their backs to one another ▸ **mettez-vous dos à dos** *pr* stand back to back ou with your backs to one another ▸ **mettre** ou **renvoyer deux personnes dos à dos** *fig* to refuse to get involved in an argument between two people.

dosage [dozaʒ] nm **1.** [détermination] measurement of ou measuring a quantity **2.** [dose précise de médicaments] (prescribed) dose **3.** [équilibre] balance.

dos-d'âne [dodan] nm inv sleeping policeman ⓊⓀ, speed bump ⓊⓈ.

dose [doz] nf **1.** PHARM dose ; MÉD dose, dosage **2.** COMM [quantité prédéterminée - gén] dose, measure ; [- en sachet] sachet **3.** [quantité - d'un aliment, d'un composant] amount, quantity / *il a une dose de paresse peu commune* he's uncommonly lazy **4.** EXPR avoir sa dose *fam*: *il a sa dose* he's had a bellyful ou as much as he can stand. ⬧ **à petite dose, à petites doses** loc adv in small doses ou quantities / *j'aime le sport / ma sœur, mais à petites doses* I like sport / my sister, but (only) in small doses.

doser [3] [doze] vt **1.** [médicament] to measure a dose of ; [composant, ingrédient] to measure out *(sép)* **2.** [équilibrer - cocktail, vinaigrette] to use the correct proportions for **3.** [utiliser avec mesure] : *il faut savoir doser ses critiques* you have to know how far you can go in your criticism.

dosette [dozɛt] nf sachet.

doseur [dozœʀ] nm measure ; *(comme adj)* ▸ **bouchon doseur** measuring cap.

dossard [dosaʀ] nm SPORT number *(worn by a competitor)* / *portant le dossard numéro 3* wearing number 3.

dossier [dosje] nm **1.** [d'une chaise, d'un canapé] back **2.** [documents] file, dossier ▸ **avoir un dossier sur qqn** to keep a file on sb, to keep sb on file ; DR [d'un prévenu] record ; [d'une affaire] case ; ADMIN [d'un cas social] case file ▸ **dossier de candidature** application ▸ **dossier d'inscription** UNIV registration forms **3.** ▸ **dossier de presse** press pack **4.** [chemise cartonnée] folder, file.

dot [dɔt] nf [d'une mariée] dowry ; [d'une religieuse] (spiritual) dowry.

doter [3] [dɔte] vt **1.** [équiper] ▸ **doter qqch de** to provide ou to equip sthg with **2.** [gratifier] : *pays doté d'une puissante industrie* country with a strong industrial base **3.** [donner une dot à] to give a dowry to **4.** [financer - particulier, collectivité] to endow ; [- service public] to fund.

douane [dwan] nf **1.** [à la frontière] ▸ **poste de douane** customs ▸ **passer à la douane** to go through customs **2.** [administration] ▸ **la douane, les douanes, le service des douanes a)** [gén] the Customs (service) **b)** [en Grande-Bretagne] Customs and Excise (department) **3.** [taxe] ▸ **(droits de) douane** customs duty ou dues ▸ **exempté de douane** duty-free, non-dutiable.

douanier, ère [dwanje, ɛʀ] ◆ adj [tarif, visite] customs *(modif)*. ◆ nm, f customs officer.

doublage [dublaʒ] nm CINÉ [d'un film] dubbing ; [d'un acteur] : *il n'y a pas de doublage pour les cascades* there's no stand-in for the stunts.

double [dubl] ◆ adj **1.** [deux fois plus grand - mesure, production] double ▸ **chambre / lit double** double room / bed **2.** [à deux éléments identiques] double ▸ **faute** TENNIS double fault / *je suis en double file* I'm double-parked ▸ **à double fond** [mallette] double-bottomed, false-bottomed ▸ **double page** double page spread ▸ **faire double emploi** to be redundant **3.** [à éléments différents - avantage, objectif] double, twofold ; [- fonction, personna-

lité, tarification] dual ▸ **à double effet** double acting ▸ **avoir la double nationalité** to have dual nationality ▸ **mener une double vie** to lead a double life. ◆ nm **1.** [en quantité] : *six est le double de trois* six is twice three ou two times three ▸ **coûter le double de** to cost twice as much as **2.** [exemplaire - d'un document] copy ; [- d'un timbre de collection] duplicate, double / *tu as un double de la clé ?* have you got a spare ou duplicate key? **3.** [sosie] double, doppelgänger **4.** ▸ **double messieurs / dames / mixte** men's / women's / mixed doubles. ◆ adv [compter] twice as much, double ; [voir] double. ⬧ **à double sens** ◆ loc adj : *une phrase à double sens* a double-entendre. ◆ loc adv : *on peut prendre la remarque à double sens* you can interpret ou take that remark two ways. ⬧ **à double tour** loc adv ▸ **enfermer qqn à double tour** to lock sb up. ⬧ **à double tranchant** loc adj [couteau, action] double-edged, two-edged. ⬧ **en double** loc adv : *j'ai une photo en double* I've got two of the same photograph ▸ **jouer en double** SPORT to play (a) doubles (match).

doublé, e [duble] adj **1.** COUT lined **2.** CINÉ dubbed. ⬧ **doublé** nm [succès] double.

double-clic [dubləklik] *(pl* **doubles-clics***)* nm INFORM double-click.

double-cliquer [3] [dubləklike] vi INFORM ▸ **double-cliquer (sur)** to double-click (on).

doublement [dubləmɑ̃] adv doubly.

doubler [3] [duble] ◆ vt **1.** [dépasser - coureur, véhicule] to overtake ⓊⓀ, to pass **2.** [porter au double - bénéfices, personnel, quantité] to double **3.** [garnir d'une doublure - coffret, jupe, tenture] to line **4.** CINÉ [voix] to dub ; [acteur] to stand in for, to double / *il se fait doubler pour les cascades* he's got a stand-in for his stunts **5.** [mettre en double - corde, fil] to double ; [- couverture] to fold (in half), to double (over) **6.** ÉDUC to repeat. ◆ vi [bénéfices, poids, quantité] to double, to increase twofold. ⬧ **se doubler de** vp + prép to be coupled with.

doublure [dublyʀ] nf **1.** [garniture] lining *(U)* **2.** CINÉ stand-in ; THÉÂTRE understudy.

doucement [dusmɑ̃] adv **1.** [avec délicatesse, sans brusquerie - caresser, poser, prendre] gently ; [- manier] gently, with care ; [- démarrer] smoothly ▸ **doucement !** gently!, careful! ▸ **doucement avec le champagne / poivre !** (go) easy on the champagne / pepper! **2.** [lentement - marcher, progresser, rouler] slowly **3.** [graduellement - augmenter, s'élever] gently, gradually **4.** [sans bruit - chantonner] softly.

doucereux, euse [dusʀø, øz] adj [goût, liqueur] sweetish ; *péj* sickly sweet ; [voix, ton, paroles] sugary, honeyed ; [manières, personne] suave, smooth.

douceur [dusœʀ] nf **1.** [toucher - d'une étoffe, d'une brosse] softness ; [- des cheveux, de la peau] softness, smoothness ; [goût - d'un vin] sweetness ; [- d'un fromage] mildness **2.** [délicatesse - de caresses, de mouvements, de manières] gentleness ; [- d'une voix] softness ▸ **prendre qqn par la douceur** to use the soft approach with sb ▸ **la douceur de vivre** the gentle pleasures of life **3.** [bonté - d'une personne] sweetness, gentleness ; [- d'un regard, d'un sourire] gentleness **4.** [d'un relief] softness **5.** MÉTÉOR mildness **6.** [friandise] sweet. ⬧ **en douceur** ◆ loc adj [décollage, démarrage] smooth. ◆ loc adv [sans brusquerie - gén] gently ; [- démarrer, s'arrêter] smoothly / *réveille-moi en douceur la prochaine fois* next time, wake me up gently.

douche [duʃ] nf [jet d'eau] shower / *prendre une douche* to have ou to take a shower / *il est sous la douche* he's in the shower ▸ **douche écossaise** *pr* hot and cold shower *(taken successively)*.

doucher [3] [duʃe] vt [laver] to shower, to give a shower to. ⬧ **se doucher** vp *(emploi réfléchi)* to have ou to take a shower.

douchette [duʃɛt] nf shower rose.

doudou [dudu] nm security blanket.

doudoune [dudun] nf (thick) quilted jacket ou anorak.

doué, e [dwe] adj **1.** [acteur, musicien] gifted, talented ▸ **être doué en dessin** to have a gift for ou to be good at drawing ▸ **être doué pour tout** to be an all-rounder **2.** [doté] ▸ **doué de** a) [obj : intelligence, raison] endowed with b) [obj : mémoire] gifted ou blessed ou endowed with.

douille [duj] nf **1.** [de cuisine] piping nozzle **2.** ARM (cartridge) case **3.** [d'une ampoule] (lamp) socket.

douillet, ette [dujɛ, ɛt] adj **1.** [très sensible à la douleur] oversensitive ; [qui a peur de la douleur] afraid of getting hurt ▸ *que tu es douillet !* péj don't be so soft! **2.** [confortable - vêtement, lit] (nice and) cosy 🇬🇧 ou cozy 🇺🇸, snug. ❖ **douillette** nf [robe de chambre] quilted dressing gown.

douillettement [dujɛtmɑ̃] adv cosily, snugly.

douleur [dulœr] nf **1.** [physique] pain **2.** [psychologique] grief, sorrow, pain ▸ *nous avons la douleur de vous faire part du décès de…* it is with great ou deep sorrow (and regret) that we have to announce the death of…

douloureux, euse [dulurø, øz] adj **1.** [brûlure, coup, coupure] painful ; [articulation, membre] painful, sore **2.** [humiliation, souvenirs] painful ; [circonstances, sujet, période] painful, distressing ; [nouvelle] grievous, painful, distressing ; [poème, regard] sorrowful. ❖ **douloureuse** nf fam & hum [au restaurant] bill, check 🇺🇸 ; [facture] bill.

doute [dut] nm **1.** [soupçon] doubt ▸ **avoir des doutes sur** ou **quant à** ou **au sujet de qqch** to have (one's) doubts ou misgivings about sthg ▸ *je n'ai pas le moindre doute là-dessus* I haven't the slightest doubt about it **2.** [perplexité, incertitude] doubt, uncertainty ; PHILOS doubt. ❖ **dans le doute** loc adv : *être dans le doute* to be doubtful ou uncertain ▸ **laisser qqn dans le doute** [suj : personne, circonstances] to leave sb in a state of uncertainty. ❖ **en doute** loc adv ▸ **mettre en doute** a) [suj : personne] to question, to challenge b) [suj : circonstances, témoignage] to cast doubt on. ❖ **sans doute** loc adv **1.** [probablement] most probably, no doubt **2.** [assurément] ▸ **sans aucun** ou **nul doute** without (a) doubt, undoubtedly, indubitably sout **3.** [certes] : *tu me l'avais promis — sans doute, mais…* you'd promised me — that's true ou I know, but…

douter [3] [dute] ❖ **douter de** v + prép **1.** [ne pas croire à - succès, victoire] to be doubtful of ; [- fait, éventualité] to doubt ▸ *tu viendras ? — j'en doute fort* will you come? — I very much doubt it ▸ *elle ne doute de rien* she has no doubt about anything ▸ *je doute que le projet voie le jour* I have (my) doubts about the future of the project, I doubt whether the project will ever be realized **2.** [traiter avec défiance - ami, motivation] to have doubts about ▸ **douter de la parole de qqn** to doubt sb's word ▸ **douter de soi** a) [habituellement] to have doubts about ou to lack confidence in o.s. b) [à un moment] to have doubts about o.s. ❖ **se douter de** vp + prép [s'attendre à] to know, to suspect ▸ **j'aurais dû m'en douter** I should have known ▸ *comme tu t'en doutes sûrement* as you've probably guessed ▸ **se douter de qqch** [soupçonner qqch] to suspect sthg ▸ **se douter que** : *je ne me serais jamais douté que c'était possible* I'd never have thought it (was) possible ▸ *je lui ai proposé de travailler pour moi, tout en me doutant bien qu'il refuserait* I suggested the work for him, but I knew he wouldn't accept.

douteux, euse [dutø, øz] adj **1.** [non certain, non assuré - authenticité, fait] doubtful, uncertain, questionable ; [- avenir, issue, origine, etc.] doubtful, uncertain ; [- signature] doubtful ▸ *il est douteux que…* it's doubtful whether… **2.** péj [inspirant la méfiance - individu] dubious-looking ;

[- comportement, manœuvres, passé, etc.] dubious, questionable ▸ *d'une manière douteuse* dubiously ▸ **le portrait / sa plaisanterie était d'un goût douteux** the portrait / her joke was in dubious taste **3.** [sale, dangereux] dubious ▸ **du linge douteux** clothes that are none too clean.

Douvres [duvr] npr Dover.

doux, douce [du, dus] adj **1.** [au toucher - cheveux, peau, vêtements] soft, smooth ; [- brosse à dents] soft **2.** [au goût - vin] sweet ; [- fromage] mild **3.** [détergent, savon, shampooing] mild ; [énergie, technique] alternative ; [drogue] soft ▸ **médecines douces** alternative medicine **4.** [sans brusquerie - geste, caresse, personne] gentle ; [- pression] soft, gentle ; [- balancement, pente] gentle ; [- accélération] smooth ; [- véhicule] smooth-running ▸ *il a eu une mort douce* he died peacefully **5.** [bon, gentil - personne, sourire, tempérament, etc.] gentle **6.** MÉTÉOR [air, climat] mild ; [chaleur, vent] gentle **7.** [plaisant - rêves, souvenir] sweet, pleasant ; [- paix, succès] sweet. ❖ **doux** adv [tiède] ▸ **il fait doux** it's mild out. ❖ **en douce** loc adv fam [dire, donner, partir, etc.] on the quiet, sneakily.

doux-amer, douce-amère [duzamɛr, dusamɛr] (mpl **doux-amers**, fpl **douces-amères**) adj bittersweet.

douzaine [duzɛn] nf **1.** [douze] dozen **2.** [environ douze] ▸ **une douzaine de** a dozen, around twelve ▸ *une douzaine d'escargots* a dozen snails. ❖ **à la douzaine** loc adv [acheter, vendre] by the dozen.

douze [duz] dét & nm inv twelve. **Voir aussi cinq.**

douzième [duzjɛm] adj num & nmf twelfth. **Voir aussi cinquième.**

douzièmement [duzjɛmmɑ̃] adv in twelfth place. **Voir aussi cinquièmement.**

doyen, enne [dwajɛ̃, ɛn] nm, f **1.** [d'un club, d'une communauté] most senior member ; [d'un pays] eldest ou oldest citizen ; [d'une profession] doyen (doyenne) ▸ **doyen (d'âge)** oldest person **2.** UNIV dean.

Dr (abr écrite de **docteur**) Dr.

draconien, enne [drakɔnjɛ̃, ɛn] adj [mesure] drastic, draconian, stringent ; [règlement] harsh, draconian ; [régime] strict.

dragée [draʒe] nf [confiserie] sugared almond ; PHARM (sugar-coated) pill ▸ **tenir la dragée haute à qqn** [dans une discussion, un match] to hold out on sb.

Dragée

A small paper cone or box filled with sugared almonds is a traditional gift for guests at christenings and weddings in France.

---

dragon [dragɔ̃] nm MYTH dragon.

drague [drag] nf fam [flirt] : *pour la drague, il est doué !* he's always on the pull 🇬🇧 ou on the make 🇺🇸 ▸ *la drague sur Internet* picking people up via Internet, cruising the chatlines.

draguer [3] [drage] ◆ vt **1.** [nettoyer - fleuve, canal, port] to dredge **2.** [retirer - mine] to sweep ; [- ancre] to drag (anchor) **3.** fam [fille, garçon] to chat up (sép) 🇬🇧, to sweet-talk 🇺🇸, to try to pick up (sép) ; [en voiture] to cruise ▸ *je me suis fait draguer par le serveur* the waiter chatted me up 🇬🇧 ou was giving me a line 🇺🇸. ◆ vi to be on the pull 🇬🇧 ou on the make 🇺🇸.

dragueur, euse [dragœr, øz] nm, f fam : *c'est un dragueur* he's always on the pull 🇬🇧 ou on the make 🇺🇸 ▸ *sa sœur est une sacrée dragueuse* her sister's always chasing after boys.

drainer [4] [dʀene] vt **1.** [assécher] to drain **2.** [rassembler - capital, ressources] to tap **3.** [canaliser - foule] to channel.

dramatique [dʀamatik] ◆ adj **1.** THÉÂTRE [musique, œuvre] dramatic **2.** [grave - conséquences, issue, période, situation] horrendous, appalling / *j'ai raté mon permis de conduire — ce n'est pas dramatique !* I've failed my driving test — it's not the end of the world! **3.** [tragique - dénouement, événement] dramatic. ◆ nf TV television play ou drama ; RADIO radio play ou drama.

dramatiser [3] [dʀamatize] vt [exagérer - histoire] to dramatize ▶ **ne dramatise pas !** don't make a drama out of it!

dramaturge [dʀamatyʀʒ] nmf playwright, dramatist.

drame [dʀam] nm **1.** THÉÂTRE [œuvre] drama ; [genre] drama **2.** RADIO & TV drama, play **3.** [événement] drama / *il l'a renversé, mais ce n'est pas un drame* he spilt it but it's not the end of the world.

drap [dʀa] nm **1.** [pour lit] ▶ **drap (de lit)** (bed) sheet ▶ **des draps** sheets, bedlinen ▶ **dans de beaux** ou **vilains draps** : *se retrouver* ou *se trouver dans de beaux draps* to find o.s. up the creek (without a paddle) **2.** [serviette] ▶ **drap de bain** bathtowel ▶ **drap de plage** beach towel.

drapeau, x [dʀapo] nm [pièce d'étoffe] flag ; MIL flag, colours 🇬🇧, colors 🇺🇸 ▶ **le drapeau tricolore** the French flag, the tricolour 🇬🇧 ou tricolor 🇺🇸 (flag). ◆ **sous les drapeaux** loc adv ▶ **être sous les drapeaux a)** [au service militaire] to be doing one's military service **b)** [en service actif] to serve in one's country's armed forces.

draper [3] [dʀape] vt **1.** [couvrir - meuble] to drape, to cover with a sheet **2.** [arranger - châle, rideaux] to drape. ◆ **se draper** vp *(emploi réfléchi)* : *se draper dans sa dignité* to stand on one's dignity.

drap-housse [dʀaus] *(pl* **draps-housses)** nm fitted sheet.

drastique [dʀastik] adj [mesure] harsh, drastic ; [règlement] strict.

drave [dʀav] nf 🇶🇧🇨 drive *(of floating logs)*.

draver [dʀave] vt 🇶🇧🇨 to drive, to raft.

draveur, euse [dʀavœʀ, øz] nm, f 🇶🇧🇨 raftsman (raftswoman).

dreadlocks [dʀɛdlɔks] nfpl dreadlocks, dreads.

dressage [dʀesaʒ] nm [d'un fauve] taming *(U)* ; [d'un cheval sauvage] breaking in *(U)* ; [d'un chien de cirque, de garde] training *(U)* ; [d'un cheval de parade] dressage.

dresser [4] [dʀese] vt **1.** [ériger - mât, pilier] to put up *(sép)*, to raise, to erect ; [- statue] to put up *(sép)*, to erect ; [- tente, auvent] to pitch, to put up *(sép)* **2.** [construire - barricade, échafaudage] to put up *(sép)*, to erect ; [- muret] to erect, to build **3.** [installer - autel] to set up *(sép)* ▶ **dresser le couvert** ou **la table** to lay ou to set the table **4.** [lever - bâton] to raise, to lift ; [- menton] to stick out ; [- tête] to raise, to lift ▶ **dresser les oreilles a)** [suj : chien] to prick up ou to cock its ears ▶ **dresser l'oreille** [suj : personne] to prick up one's ears **5.** [dompter - fauve] to tame ; [- cheval sauvage] to break in *(sép)* ; [- cheval de cirque, chien de garde] to train **6.** [établir - liste, inventaire] to draw up *(sép)*, to make out *(sép)* ; [- bilan] to draw up, to prepare / *dresser le bilan d'une situation* to take stock of a situation **7.** [opposer] ▶ **dresser qqn contre qqn / qqch** to set sb against sb / sthg. ◆ **se dresser** vpi **1.** [se mettre debout] to stand up, to rise / *se dresser sur la pointe des pieds* to stand on tiptoe **2.** [oreille de chien] to prick up ▶ **c'est à vous faire dresser les cheveux sur la tête !** it makes your hair stand on end! **3.** [être vertical - montagne, tour] to stand, to rise ; [dominer] to tower **4.** [surgir - obstacles] to rise, to stand. ◆ **se dresser contre** vp + prép to rise up ou to rebel against.

dresseur, euse [dʀesœʀ, øz] nm, f [de fauves] tamer ; [de chiens de cirque, de garde] trainer ; [de chevaux sauvages] horsebreaker.

dressing [dʀesiŋ] nm dressing room *(near a bedroom)*.

DRH ◆ nf (abr de **direction des ressources humaines**) personnel department. ◆ nm (abr de **directeur des ressources humaines**) personnel manager.

dribbler [3] [dʀible] vi SPORT to dribble.

driver [3] [dʀajve] vt SPORT to drive.

drogue [dʀɔg] nf **1.** [narcotique] drug *(U)* ▶ **drogue douce / dure** soft / hard drug **2.** [usage] ▶ **la drogue** drug-taking, drugs.

drogué, e [dʀɔge] nm, f drug addict.

droguer [3] [dʀɔge] vt [toxicomane] to drug. ◆ **se droguer** vpi to take drugs, to be on drugs.

droguerie [dʀɔgʀi] nf **1.** [boutique] hardware shop 🇬🇧 ou store 🇺🇸 **2.** [activité] hardware trade.

droguiste [dʀɔgist] nmf keeper of a hardware shop 🇬🇧 ou store 🇺🇸.

droit¹ [dʀwa] nm **1.** DR ▶ **le droit** [lois, discipline] law ▶ **faire son droit** to study law / *avoir le droit pour soi* to have right ou the law on one's side ▶ **droit civil / commercial / constitutionnel** civil / commercial / constitutional law ▶ **droit commun** ou **coutumier** common law **2.** [prérogative particulière] right ▶ **avoir des droits sur qqch** to have rights to sthg ▶ **droit d'asile** right of asylum ▶ **droit de chasse** hunting rights ▶ **droits civiques** civil rights ▶ **droit de grève** right to strike ▶ **les droits de l'homme** human rights ▶ **droit de passage** right of way 🇬🇧 ou easement 🇺🇸 ▶ **droit de visite** right of access ▶ **le droit de vote** (the) franchise, the right to vote **3.** [autorisation sociale ou morale] right / *de quel droit l'a-t-il lue ?* what gave him the right to read it?, what right had he to read it? ▶ **donner droit à** : *le billet donne droit à une consommation gratuite* the ticket entitles you to one free drink ▶ **donner le droit à qqn de faire qqch** to give sb the right to ou to entitle sb to do sthg / *être en droit de faire* to be entitled ou to have the right to do ▶ **reprendre ses droits** [idée, habitude, nature] to reassert itself ▶ **avoir droit à a)** [explications] to be entitled to **b)** [bourse, indemnité] to be entitled to, to be eligible for **c)** [reconnaissance, respect] to deserve ▶ **avoir droit de regard sur a)** [comptabilité, dossier] to have the right to examine ou to inspect **b)** [activités] to have the right to control ▶ **avoir le droit de faire a)** [gén] to be allowed ou to have the right to do **b)** [officiellement] to have the right ou to be entitled to do / *tu n'as pas le droit de parler ainsi !* you've no right to talk like that! **4.** [impôt, taxe] duty, tax ▶ **droits de douane** customs duties ▶ **droits de succession** death duties **5.** [frais] fee ▶ **droit d'enregistrement** registration fee *(for legal documents)* ▶ **droit d'entrée** entrance fee ▶ **droits d'inscription** registration fee ou fees **6.** EXPR **à qui de droit** to whom it may concern. ◆ **droits** nmpl ▶ **droits (d'auteur) a)** [prérogative] rights, copyright **b)** [somme] royalties ▶ **tous droits (de reproduction) réservés** copyright ou all rights reserved.

droit², e [dʀwa, dʀwat] adj **1.** [rectiligne - allée, bâton, nez] straight **2.** [vertical, non penché - mur] upright, straight, plumb *spéc* ; [- dossier, poteau] upright, straight ▶ **être** ou **se tenir droit a)** [assis] to sit up straight **b)** [debout] to stand up straight **3.** [loyal - personne] upright, honest **4.** [sensé - raisonnement] sound, sane. ◆ **droit** adv [écrire] in a straight line ; [couper, rouler] straight *(adv)* / *après le carrefour, c'est toujours tout droit* after the crossroads, keep going straight on ou ahead ▶ **aller droit à** : *j'irai droit au but* I'll come straight to the point, I won't beat about the bush / *aller droit à la catastrophe / l'échec* to be heading straight for disaster / a failure. ◆ **droite** nf GÉOM straight line.

droit³, e [dʀwa, dʀwat] adj [ailier, jambe, œil] right ▸ **le côté droit** the right-hand side. ❖ **droit** nm right / *crochet du droit* right hook. ❖ **droite** nf **1.** [côté droit] ▸ **la droite** the right (side), the right-hand side ▸ **tenir sa droite** AUTO to keep to the right / *de droite et de gauche* from all quarters ou sides **2.** POL ▸ **la droite** the right wing. ❖ **à droite** loc adv [du côté droit] : *conduire à droite* to drive on the right-hand side / *à droite et à gauche* fig here and there, hither and thither *litt* ou *hum*, all over the place. ❖ **à droite de** loc prép to ou on the right of. ❖ **de droite** loc adj **1.** [du côté droit] : *la porte de droite* the door on the right, the right-hand door **2.** POL ▸ **les gens de droite** rightwingers, people on the right / *être de droite* to be right-wing.

droitier, ère [dʀwatje, ɛʀ] ◆ adj right-handed. ◆ nm, f right-handed person, right-hander.

droitiste [dʀwatist] adj & nmf POL rightist.

droiture [dʀwatyʀ] nf [d'une personne] uprightness, honesty ; [d'intentions, de motifs] uprightness.

drôle [dʀol] adj **1.** [amusant - personne, film, situation, etc.] comical, funny, amusing ▸ **ce n'est pas drôle !** a) [pas amusant] it's not funny!, I don't find that funny ou amusing! b) [pénible] it's no joke! **2.** [étrange] strange, funny, peculiar / **(tout)** ou **toute drôle** fam : *ça me fait (tout) drôle de revenir ici* it feels really strange to be back ▸ **se sentir (tout) drôle** to feel (really) weird ▸ **drôle de :** *en voilà une drôle d'idée !* what a strange ou funny ou weird idea! / *ça fait un drôle de bruit* it makes a strange ou funny noise / *drôles de gens !* what peculiar ou strange people! ▸ **avoir un drôle d'air** to look strange ou funny **3.** [en intensif] ▸ **drôle de** fam : *il a de drôles de problèmes en ce moment* he hasn't half got some problems at the moment / *il faut un drôle de courage pour faire ça !* you need a hell of a lot of courage to do that!

drôlement [dʀolmã] adv **1.** fam [vraiment] ▸ **drôlement ennuyeux** awfully ou terribly boring ▸ **j'ai eu drôlement peur** I had quite a fright **2.** [bizarrement - regarder, parler] in a strange ou funny ou peculiar way **3.** [de façon amusante] amusingly, comically.

drôlerie [dʀolʀi] nf **1.** [d'une personne, d'un spectacle, d'une remarque] drollness, funniness, comicalness, humour 🇬🇧, humor 🇺🇸 **2.** [acte] funny ou amusing ou comical thing (to do) ; [remarque] funny ou amusing ou comical thing (to say).

DROM [dʀɔm] nm abr de **Département et Région d'outre-mer.**

dromadaire [dʀɔmadɛʀ] nm dromedary.

drone [dʀɔn] nm MIL drone.

dru, e [dʀy] adj [cheveux, végétation] dense, thick ; [pluie] heavy. ❖ **dru** adv [croître, pousser] densely, thickly ; [pleuvoir] heavily / *les mauvaises herbes ont poussé dru* there has been a thick growth of weeds.

drugstore [dʀœgstɔʀ] nm small shopping centre 🇬🇧 ou mall 🇺🇸.

druide [dʀɥid] nm druid.

dsl (abr écrite de **désolé**) SMS Sry.

DTV (abr de **digital television**) nf DTV.

dû, due [dy] ◆ pp ⟶ **devoir.** ◆ adj [à payer] owed / *quelle est la somme due ?* what's the sum owed ou due? ❖ **dû** nm due. ❖ **en bonne et due forme** loc adv DR in due form.

dubitatif, ive [dybitatif, iv] adj dubious, sceptical.

Dublin [dyblɛ̃] npr Dublin.

dublinois, e [dyblinwa, az] adj from Dublin. ❖ **Dublinois, e** nm, f Dubliner.

duc [dyk] nm [titre] duke.

duchesse [dyʃɛs] nf [titre] duchess.

dudit [dydi] (pl **desdits**) adj : *la justice dudit pays* the justice system of the aforesaid country.

duel [dɥɛl] nm **1.** [entre deux personnes] duel / *se battre en duel avec un rival* to fight a duel ou to duel with a rival **2.** [conflit - entre États, organisations] battle.

duffle-coat (pl **duffle-coats**), **duffel-coat** (pl **duffel-coats**) [dœfœlkot] nm duffel coat.

dûment, dument* [dymã] adv duly.

dumping [dœmpiŋ] nm ÉCON dumping ▸ **faire du dumping** to dump (goods).

dune [dyn] nf dune.

duo [dɥo] nm **1.** [spectacle - chanté] duet ; [- instrumental] duet, duo ▸ **chanter en duo** to sing a duet **2.** [dialogue] exchange.

dupe [dyp] ◆ nf dupe ▸ **prendre qqn pour dupe** to dupe sb, to take sb for a ride. ◆ adj : *elle ment, mais je ne suis pas dupe* she's lying but it doesn't fool me.

duper [3] [dype] vt *litt* to dupe, to fool.

duplex [dyplɛks] nm **1.** ▸ **(appartement en) duplex** split-level flat 🇬🇧 ; ≃ maisonette 🇬🇧 duplex (apartment) 🇺🇸 **2.** TÉLÉC duplex ▸ **(émission en) duplex** linkup **3.** 🇶🇨 [maison] duplex.

duplicata [dyplikata] nm duplicate.

duplicité [dyplisite] nf duplicity, falseness, hypocrisy.

dupliquer [3] [dyplike] vt [document] to duplicate.

duquel [dykɛl] ⟶ **lequel.**

dur, e [dyʀ] ◆ adj **1.** [ferme - viande] tough ; [- muscle] firm, hard ; [- lit, mine de crayon] hard **2.** [difficile] hard, difficult **3.** [pénible à supporter - climat] harsh ▸ **les temps sont durs** these are hard times **4.** [cruel] : *ne sois pas dur avec lui* don't be nasty to ou mean to him **5.** [rude, froid] harsh **6.** [endurci] tough ▸ **dur à :** *il est dur à la douleur* he's tough, he can bear a lot of (physical) pain ▸ **être dur d'oreille** ou **de la feuille** fam to be hard of hearing. ◆ nm, f fam [personne sans faiblesse] toughie, tough nut 🇬🇧 ou cookie 🇺🇸 / *un dur en affaires* a hard-nosed businessman ▸ **c'est un dur à cuire** he's a hard nut to crack. ❖ **dur** adv [avec force] hard / *il croit dur comme fer qu'elle va revenir* he believes doggedly ou he's adamant that she'll come back. ❖ **à la dure** loc adv : *élever ses enfants à la dure* to bring up one's children the hard way. ❖ **en dur** loc adj ▸ **construction / maison en dur** building / house built with non-temporary materials.

durable [dyʀabl] adj **1.** [permanent] enduring, lasting, long-lasting ▸ **agriculture durable** sustainable agriculture **2.** ÉCON ▸ **biens durables** durable goods, durables.

durablement [dyʀabləmã] adv durably, enduringly, for a long time.

durant [dyʀã] prép **1.** (avant nom) [au cours de] during, in the course of **2.** (après le nom) [insistant sur la durée] for / *il peut parler des heures durant* he can speak for hours (on end) ▸ **toute sa vie durant** his whole life through, throughout his whole life.

durcir [32] [dyʀsiʀ] ◆ vt [rendre plus dur] to harden, to make firmer ; fig to harden, to toughen / *cette coupe de cheveux lui durcit le visage* that haircut makes her look severe. ◆ vi [sol, plâtre] to harden, to go hard. ❖ **se durcir** vpi [personne] to harden o.s. ; [cœur] to become hard.

durcissement [dyʀsismã] nm **1.** [raffermissement - du sol, du plâtre] hardening **2.** [renforcement] ▸ **le durcissement de l'opposition** the tougher stance taken by the opposition.

durée [dyʀe] nf **1.** [période] duration, length ▸ **pendant la durée de** during, for the duration of **2.** [persistance] lasting quality. ⋙ **de courte durée** loc adj short-lived. ⋙ **de longue durée** loc adj [chômeur, chômage] long-term.

durement [dyʀmɑ̃] adv **1.** [violemment - frapper] hard **2.** [avec sévérité] harshly, severely **3.** [douloureusement] : *durement éprouvé par la mort de* deeply distressed by the death of.

durer [3] [dyʀe] vi **1.** [événement, tremblement de terre] to last, to go ou to carry on / *ça a duré toute la journée* it lasted all day ▸ *ça ne peut plus durer* ! it can't go on like this! ▸ *ça fait longtemps que ça dure* it's been going on for a long time **2.** [rester, persister] to last ▸ **faire durer** : *faire durer les provisions* to stretch supplies, to make supplies last.

dureté [dyʀte] nf **1.** [du sol, du plâtre] hardness, firmness **2.** [du climat, de conditions] harshness **3.** [d'un maître, d'une règle] severity, harshness ; [d'une grève] bitterness, harshness ▸ **traiter qqn avec dureté** to be harsh to ou tough on sb **4.** [d'une teinte, d'une voix, d'une lumière] harshness.

durillon [dyʀijɔ̃] nm callus.

Durit®, **durite*** [dyʀit] nf flexible pipe ▸ **péter une Durit** *fam* to go off the rails.

DUT (abr de **diplôme universitaire de technologie**) nm *diploma taken after two years at an institute of technology.*

duvet [dyvɛ] nm **1.** [plumes] down / *un oreiller en duvet* a down pillow **2.** [sac de couchage] sleeping bag ; [couette] duvet, quilt **3.** BELG & SUISSE eiderdown.

DVD (abr de **digital video disc** ou **digital versatile disc**) nm inv DVD.

DVD-ROM [devedeʀɔm] (abr de **digital video disc-read only memory** OU **digital versatile disc-read only memory**) nm DVD-ROM.

DVI (abr de **digital video interface**) nf DVI.

DVR (abr de **digital video recorder**) nm DVR.

dynamique [dinamik] ◆ adj **1.** [énergique] dynamic, energetic **2.** [non statique] dynamic. ◆ nf **1.** MUS & SCI dynamics *(sg)* **2.** PSYCHOL ▸ **dynamique de groupe** group dynamics.

dynamisant, e [dinamizɑ̃, ɑ̃t] adj stimulating.

dynamiser [3] [dinamize] vt [équipe] to make more dynamic, to inject enthusiasm into ; [économie, entreprise] to stimulate.

dynamisme [dinamism] nm [entrain] energy, enthusiasm.

dynamite [dinamit] nf dynamite.

dynamiter [3] [dinamite] vt **1.** [détruire à l'explosif] to blow up ou to blast (with dynamite) **2.** [abolir - préjugé] to do away with, to sweep away.

dynamo [dinamo] nf dynamo, generator.

dynastie [dinasti] nf [de rois] dynasty.

dysenterie [disɑ̃tʀi] nf dysentery.

dysfonctionnement [disfɔ̃ksjɔnmɑ̃] nm malfunction, malfunctioning / *on constate de nombreux dysfonctionnements dans la gestion de l'entreprise* there are many things wrong with the way the company is managed.

dysfonctionner [disfɔ̃ksjɔne] vi [personne, groupe] to become dysfunctional ; [machine, système] to go wrong.

dyslexique [dislɛksik] adj & nmf dyslexic.

E (abr écrite de **est**) E.

eau, x [o] nf **1.** [liquide incolore] water ▶ **se mettre à l'eau** [pour se baigner] to go in the water (for a swim) ▶ **des légumes / melons pleins d'eau** watery vegetables / melons ▶ **prendre l'eau** [chaussure, tente] to leak, to be leaky, to be leaking ▶ **eau courante** running water ▶ **eau douce** fresh water ▶ **d'eau douce** freshwater, river *(modif)* ▶ **eau de mer** seawater ▶ **eau de pluie** rainwater ▶ **eau de vaisselle** dish ou washing-up water ▶ **eau vive** white water ▶ **jeu d'eau** ou **d'eaux** fountains ▶ **comme l'eau et le feu** as different as chalk and cheese UK ou as night and day US ▶ **ça doit valoir 15 000 euros, enfin, c'est dans ces eaux-là !** *fam* it costs around 15,000 euros more or less ▶ **apporter de l'eau au moulin de qqn**: *tu apportes de l'eau à mon moulin* you're adding weight to my argument ▶ **il est passé / il passera beaucoup d'eau sous les ponts** a lot of water has gone / will flow under the bridge ▶ **il y a de l'eau dans le gaz** *fam* there's trouble brewing ▶ **j'en ai l'eau à la bouche** my mouth is watering **2.** [boisson] water ▶ **eau plate** still water ▶ **eau gazeuse** soda ou fizzy water ▶ **eau minérale** mineral water ▶ **eau du robinet** tap water ▶ **eau de source** spring water ▶ **mettre de l'eau dans son vin** to climb down, to back off **3.** CULIN water ▶ **eau de cuisson** cooking water ▶ **eau de fleur d'oranger** orange flower water ▶ **finir** ou **partir** ou **tourner** ou **s'en aller en eau de boudin** *fam* to peter ou to fizzle out **4.** PHARM [parfum] ▶ **eau de Cologne** (eau de) Cologne ▶ **eau de parfum** perfume ▶ **eau de rose** rose water ▶ **eau de toilette** toilet water **5.** CHIM ▶ **eau de Javel** bleach, Clorox® US ▶ **eau oxygénée** hydrogen peroxide **6.** [limpidité - d'un diamant] water / *de la plus belle eau* pr & fig of the first water **7.** NAUT ▶ **faire de l'eau** [s'approvisionner] to take on water ▶ **faire eau** [avoir une fuite] to take on water / *faire eau de toutes parts* fig to go under. ❖ **eaux** nfpl **1.** [masse] water ▶ **les eaux se retirent** [mer] the tide's going out **b)** [inondation] the (flood) water's subsiding ▶ **eaux d'égouts** sewage ▶ **eaux ménagères** waste water ▶ **eaux usées** sewage ▶ **hautes / basses eaux** GÉOGR high / low water ▶ **grandes eaux**: *les grandes eaux de Versailles* the fountains of Versailles / *on a eu droit aux grandes eaux (de Versailles)* fam & fig she turned on the waterworks **2.** NAUT [zone] waters ▶ **eaux internationales / territoriales** international / territorial waters ▶ **eaux côtières** inshore waters ▶ **dans les eaux de** in the wake of **3.** [d'une accouchée] waters **4.** [thermes] : *prendre les eaux* to take the waters, to stay at a spa *(for one's health)*. ❖ **à grande eau** loc adv ▶ **laver à grande eau a)** [au jet] to hose down **b)** [dans un évier, une bassine] to wash in a lot of water ▶ **rincer à grande eau** to rinse (out) thoroughly ou in a lot of water. ❖ **à l'eau** ◆ loc adj **1.** CULIN boiled **2.** [perdu] : *mon week-end est à l'eau* bang goes my weekend. ◆ loc adv **1.** CULIN ▶ **cuire à l'eau a)** [légumes] to boil **b)** [fruits] to poach **2.** EXPR **se jeter** ou **se lancer à l'eau** to take the plunge ▶ **tomber à l'eau** to fall through. ❖ **à l'eau de rose** loc adj *péj* sentimental. ❖ **de la même eau** loc adj *péj* of the same ilk. ❖ **en eau** loc adj sweating profusely / *ils étaient en eau* the sweat was pouring off them ❖ **en eau profonde** loc adv NAUT in deep (sea) waters.

EAU (abr de **Émirats arabes unis**) nmpl UAE.

eau-de-vie [odvi] *(pl* **eaux-de-vie**) nf eau de vie.

eau-forte [ofɔrt] *(pl* **eaux-fortes**) nf ART etching.

ébahi, e [ebai] adj flabbergasted, stunned.

ébats [eba] nmpl frolics, frolicking ▶ **ébats amoureux** love making.

ébattre [83] [ebatR] ❖ **s'ébattre** vpi to frolic.

ébauche [eboʃ] nf **1.** [première forme - d'un dessin] rough sketch ou draft ; [- d'un plan] outline ▶ **projet à l'éta d'ébauche** project in its early stages **2.** [début] ▶ **l'ébauche de**: *l'ébauche d'un sourire* the beginning of a ou an incipi ent smile.

ébaucher [3] [eboʃe] vt **1.** [esquisser - dessin, portrait] t rough ou to sketch out ; [- plan] to outline **2.** [commencer to begin, to start ▶ **elle ébaucha un vague sourire / geste** she made as if to smile / to move.

ébène [ebɛn] nf ebony.

ébéniste [ebenist] nm cabinetmaker.

ébénisterie [ebenistəri] nf **1.** [métier] cabinetmaking **2.** [placage] veneer.

éberlué, e [eberlye] adj dumbfounded, flabbergasted stunned.

éblouir [32] [ebluir] vt **1.** [aveugler] to dazzle **2.** [impressionner] to dazzle, to stun.

éblouissant, e [ebluisɑ̃, ɑ̃t] adj **1.** [aveuglant - couleur lumière] dazzling **2.** [impressionnant - femme, performance dazzling, stunning.

éblouissement [ebluismɑ̃] nm **1.** [fait d'être aveuglé being dazzled **2.** [vertige] dizziness / *avoir un éblouissement* to have a dizzy spell **3.** [enchantement] dazzlement bedazzlement.

e-book [ibuk] *(pl* **e-books**) nm e-book.

éborgner [3] [ebɔrɲe] vt to blind in one eye ❖ **s'éborgner** vp *(emploi réfléchi)* to put one's eye out

éboueur [ebwœr] nm dustman UK, garbage collector US.

ébouillanter [3] [ebujɑ̃te] vt to scald. ❖ **s'ébouillanter** vp *(emploi réfléchi)* to scald o.s.

éboulement [ebulmɑ̃] nm **1.** [chute] crumbling, sub siding, collapsing ▶ **un éboulement de terrain** a landslid **2.** [éboulis - de terre] mass of fallen earth ; [- de rochers mass of fallen rocks, rock slide ; [- en montagne] scree.

éboulis [ebuli] nm [de terre] mass of fallen earth ; [de rochers] mass of fallen rocks, rock slide ; [en montagne] scree

ébouriffer [3] [eburife] vt **1.** [décoiffer] to ruffle, to tousle **2.** *fam* [ébahir] to amaze, to dumbfound, to stun.

ébranler [3] [ebrɑ̃le] vt **1.** [faire trembler] to shake, to rattle **2.** [affaiblir] to shake, to weaken **3.** [atteindre moralement] to shake / *très ébranlé par la mort de son fils* shattered by the death of his son. **s'ébranler** vpi [cortège, train] to move ou to set off, to pull away.

ébrécher [18] [ebreʃe] vt [assiette, vase] to chip ; [couteau, lame] to nick, to notch.

In reformed spelling (see p. 16-18), this verb is conjugated like semer : *il ébrèchera, elle s'ébrècherait.*

ébriété [ebrijete] nf *sout* intoxication ▸ **être en état d'ébriété** to be under the influence (of drink).

ébrouer [3] [ebrue] **s'ébrouer** vpi **1.** [cheval] to snort **2.** [personne, chien] to shake o.s.

ébruiter [3] [ebrɥite] vt to disclose, to spread. **s'ébruiter** vpi to spread.

ébullition [ebylisjɔ̃] nf boiling. **à ébullition** loc adv ▸ **porter de l'eau / du lait à ébullition** to bring water / milk to the boil. **en ébullition** loc adj [liquide] boiling ; *fig* in turmoil.

écaille [ekaj] nf ZOOL [de poisson, de serpent] scale ; [matière] tortoiseshell. **en écaille** loc adj tortoiseshell *(modif)*.

écailler¹ [3] [ekaje] vt **1.** CULIN [poisson] to scale ; [huître] to open **2.** [plâtre, vernis] to cause to flake off ou to chip. **s'écailler** vpi [vernis, plâtre] to flake off ; [peinture] to peel off.

écailler², **ère** [ekaje, ɛr] nm, f [vendeur] oyster seller ; [dans un restaurant] *person who opens oysters and prepares seafood platters at a restaurant.*

écarlate [ekarlat] adj scarlet.

écarquiller [3] [ekarkije] vt ▸ **écarquiller les yeux** to open one's eyes wide, to stare (wide-eyed).

écart [ekar] nm **1.** [variation] difference, discrepancy ▸ **écart de prix** price differential **2.** [intervalle] gap, distance / *un écart de huit ans les sépare, il y a huit ans d'écart entre eux* there's an eight-year gap between them / *réduire* ou *resserrer l'écart entre* to close ou to narrow the gap between **3.** [déviation] swerving ▸ **faire un écart** a) [cheval] to shy b) [voiture, vélo] to swerve **4.** DANSE & SPORT ▸ **faire le grand écart** a) to do the splits b) *fig* to do a balancing act. **à l'écart** loc adv [de côté] aside ▸ **mettre qqn à l'écart** to put sb on the sidelines ▸ **tenir qqn à l'écart** a) [éloigné] to hold ou keep sb back b) [empêcher de participer] to keep sb out of things ▸ **rester** ou **se tenir à l'écart** a) [éloigné] to stand apart b) [ne pas participer] to stay on the sidelines ou in the background, to keep out of things. **à l'écart de** loc prép : *nous sommes un peu à l'écart du village* we live a little way away from the village / *il essaie de la tenir à l'écart de tous ses problèmes* he's trying not to involve her in all his problems / *se tenir à l'écart de la vie politique* to keep out of politics.

écarté, **e** [ekarte] adj **1.** [isolé] isolated, remote **2.** [loin l'un de l'autre] : *mettez-vous debout les jambes écartées* stand up with your legs wide apart ▸ **gardez les bras écartés** keep your arms outspread ▸ **avoir les dents écartées** to be gap-toothed.

écarteler [25] [ekartəle] vt **1.** [torturer] to quarter, to tear apart *(sép)* **2.** [partager] to tear apart *(sép)* / *écartelé entre le devoir et l'amour* torn between duty and love.

écartement [ekartəmɑ̃] nm RAIL ▸ **écartement (des rails** ou **de voie)** gauge.

écarter [3] [ekarte] vt **1.** [séparer - objets] to move apart *(sép)* ; [- personnes] to separate **2.** [éloigner] to move away ou aside *(sép)*, to pull away ou aside *(sép)* **3.** [refuser - idée] to dismiss, to set aside *(sép)*, to rule out *(sép)* **4.** [tenir à

distance] ▸ **écarter qqn de** [succession, conseil d'administration] to keep sb out of. **s'écarter** vpi to move away ou out of the way, to step ou to draw aside ▸ **s'écarter du droit chemin** to go off the straight and narrow (path) ▸ **s'écarter du sujet** to stray ou to wander from the subject.

ecchymose [ekimoz] nf bruise, ecchymosis *spéc.*

ecclésiastique [eklezjastik] nm priest, ecclesiastic.

écervelé, **e** [esɛrvəle] adj scatterbrained. nm, f scatterbrain.

échafaud [eʃafo] nm scaffold ▸ **monter sur l'échafaud** to be executed.

échafaudage [eʃafodaʒ] nm **1.** CONSTR scaffolding **2.** [élaboration - de systèmes] elaboration, construction.

échafauder [3] [eʃafode] vt **1.** [entasser] to stack ou to heap up *(sép)*, to pile (up) **2.** [construire - systèmes, théories] to build up, to construct ▸ **échafauder des projets** to make plans.

échalas [eʃala] nm *fam* [personne] beanpole / *c'est un grand échalas* he's a real beanpole.

échalote [eʃalɔt] nf **1.** shallot **2.** QUÉBEC [jeune oignon] spring onion **3.** QUÉBEC *fam* [personne grande et maigre] ▸ *c'est une échalote* he's all skin and bones.

échancré, **e** [eʃɑ̃kre] adj VÊT low-necked / *une robe très échancrée sur le devant* a dress with a plunging neckline.

échancrure [eʃɑ̃kryr] nf VÊT low neckline.

échange [eʃɑ̃ʒ] nm **1.** [troc] swap, exchange / *faire un échange* to swap, to do a swap ▸ **échange standard** replacement *(of a spare part)* **2.** ÉCON trade ▸ **échanges internationaux** international trade **3.** [aller et retour] exchange / *avoir un échange de vues* to exchange opinions ▸ **c'est un échange de bons procédés** one good turn deserves another, exchange of favours 🇬🇧 ou favors 🇺🇸. **en échange** loc adv in exchange, in return. **en échange de** loc prép in exchange ou return for.

échangeable [eʃɑ̃ʒabl] adj exchangeable.

échanger [17] [eʃɑ̃ʒe] vt **1.** [troquer] to exchange, to swap / *échanger un stylo contre* ou *pour un briquet* to exchange ou to swap a pen for a lighter **2.** [se donner mutuellement] to exchange ▸ **échanger un regard / sourire** to exchange glances / smiles **3.** SPORT ▸ **échanger des balles** [avant le match] to knock up. **s'échanger** vp *(emploi passif)* [être troqué] to be swapped ; BOURSE to trade / *le dollar s'échange aujourd'hui à 0,74 euro* today the dollar is trading at 0.74 euro.

échangeur [eʃɑ̃ʒœr] nm TRANSP [carrefour] interchange ; [donnant accès à l'autoroute] feeder.

échantillon [eʃɑ̃tijɔ̃] nm **1.** COMM & SCI sample, specimen ▸ **échantillon gratuit** free sample ▸ **échantillon type** representative sample **2.** [cas typique] example, sample.

échantillonnage [eʃɑ̃tijonaʒ] nm **1.** [de parfum] selection ; [de papier peint, de moquette] sample book **2.** INFORM & TÉLÉC sampling.

échappatoire [eʃapatwar] nf loophole, way out.

échappé, **e** [eʃape] nm, f *competitor who has broken away* / *les échappés du peloton* runners breaking away from the rest of the field. **échappée** nf SPORT breakaway.

échappement [eʃapmɑ̃] nm [de gaz] exhaust.

échapper [3] [eʃape] vi EXPR ▸ **l'échapper belle** to have a narrow escape. vi **1.** [s'enfuir] ▸ **faire échapper** a) [animal] to let out b) [détenu] to help to escape / *il a laissé échapper le chien* he let the dog loose **2.** [secret, paroles] ▸ **laisser échapper** to let slip **3.** [glisser] to slip / *le vase lui a échappé des mains* the vase slipped out of her hands **4.** [erreur, occasion] ▸ **laisser échapper** : *j'ai pu *laisser échapper quelques fautes* I may have overlooked a few mistakes ▸ **laisser échapper une occasion** to miss an opportunity. ⟐ **échapper à** v + prép **1.** [se soustraire à] to avoid, to evade **2.** [éviter] to escape from, to get away from / *elle sent que sa fille lui échappe* she can feel (that) her daughter's drifting away from her **3.** [être dispensé de] ▸ **échapper à l'impôt a)** [officiellement] to be exempt from taxation **b)** [en trichant] to evade income tax **4.** [être oublié par] ▸ **rien ne lui échappe** she doesn't miss a thing ▸ **ce détail m'a échappé** that detail escaped me / *son nom m'échappe* his name escapes me ou has slipped my mind / *je me souviens de l'air mais les paroles m'échappent* I remember the tune but I forget the lyrics **5.** [être prononcé par] : *la phrase lui aura échappé* the remark must have slipped out. ⟐ **s'échapper** vpi **1.** [s'enfuir] to escape, to get away / *s'échapper d'un camp* to escape from a camp **2.** [se rendre disponible] to get away **3.** [jaillir] to escape, to leak **4.** SPORT [coureur] to break ou to draw away.

écharde [eʃaʀd] nf splinter.

écharpe [eʃaʀp] nf **1.** VÊT scarf ; [d'un député, d'un maire] sash **2.** [pansement] sling. ⟐ **en écharpe** loc adv : *avoir le bras en écharpe* to have one's arm in a sling.

écharper [3] [eʃaʀpe] vt to tear to pieces / *il s'est fait écharper par sa femme quand il est rentré* his wife really laid into him when he got home.

échasse [eʃas] nf [bâton] stilt.

échassier [eʃasje] nm wader, wading bird.

échauder [3] [eʃode] vt [décevoir] : *l'expérience de l'année dernière m'a échaudé* my experience last year taught me a lesson / *il a déjà été échaudé une fois* he's had his fingers burned once already.

échauffement [eʃofmɑ̃] nm SPORT [processus] warming-up ; [exercices, période] warm-up.

échauffer [3] [eʃofe] vt **1.** [exciter] to heat, to fire, to stimulate ▸ **les esprits sont échauffés** feelings are running high ▸ **échauffer la bile** ou **les oreilles à qqn** fam : *il m'échauffe la bile* ou *les oreilles* he really gets my goat ou on my nerves **2.** MÉCAN to overheat ; [fermenter] to cause fermentation. ⟐ **s'échauffer** vpi **1.** SPORT to warm up **2.** [s'exciter] to become heated.

échauffourée [eʃofuʀe] nf clash, skirmish.

échéance [eʃeɑ̃s] nf **1.** [date - de paiement] date of payment ; [- de maturité] date of maturity ; [- de péremption] expiry date ▸ **venir à échéance** to fall due **2.** [somme d'argent] financial commitment **3.** [moment] term / *un mois avant l'échéance de l'examen* one month before the exam (is due to take place). ⟐ **à brève échéance, à courte échéance** loc adv in the short run. ⟐ **à longue échéance** loc adv in the long run.

échéancier [eʃeɑ̃sje] nm [délais] ▸ **échéancier (de paiement)** payment schedule.

échec [eʃɛk] nm **1.** [revers] failure / *la réunion s'est soldée par un échec* nothing came out of the meeting ▸ **l'échec scolaire** underperforming at school **2.** [défaite] defeat **3.** JEUX ▸ **échec (au roi)** ! check! ▸ **échec et mat** ! checkmate! ⟐ **échecs** nmpl chess (U) ▸ **jouer aux échecs** to play chess. ⟐ **en échec** loc adv ▸ **mettre / tenir qqn en échec** to put / to hold sb in check.

échelle [eʃɛl] nf **1.** [outil] ladder / *monter dans l'échelle sociale* fig to climb the social ladder ▸ **échelle d'incendie** fireman's ladder ▸ **faire la courte échelle à qqn** to give sb a leg up **2.** [mesure] scale / *une carte à l'échelle 1/10 000* a map on a scale of 1/10,000 **3.** GÉOL scale ▸ **sur l'échelle de Richter** on the Richter scale **4.** [dimension] scale / *des événements à l'échelle mondiale* world events / *des villes à l'échelle humaine* cities (built) on a human scale **5.** DR & ADMIN scale ▸ **échelle des valeurs** scale of values ▸ **échelle**

(mobile) **des salaires** ou **traitements** (sliding) salary scale. ⟐ **à l'échelle** loc adv : *la façade n'est pas à l'échelle* the façade isn't (drawn) to scale. ⟐ **à l'échelle de** loc prép at the level ou on a scale of / *à l'échelle de la région / planète* on a regional / world(-wide) scale.

échelon [eʃlɔ̃] nm **1.** [barreau] rung **2.** ADMIN grade / *grimper d'un échelon* to go up one step ou grade / *grimper les échelons de la hiérarchie* to make one's way up the ladder **3.** [niveau] level ▸ **à l'échelon local** at local level.

échelonner [3] [eʃlɔne] vt **1.** [dans l'espace - arbres, poteaux] to space out (sép), to place at regular intervals **2.** [dans le temps - livraisons, remboursements, publication] to spread (out), to stagger, to schedule at regular intervals ▸ **paiements échelonnés** payments in instalments, staggered payments **3.** [graduer - difficultés, problèmes] to grade, to place on a sliding scale.

écheveau, x [eʃvo] nm TEXT hank, skein.

échevelé, e [eʃəvle] adj **1.** [ébouriffé] dishevelled 🇬🇧, disheveled 🇺🇸, tousled **2.** [effréné] frantic, wild, unbridled / *une danse échevelée* a wild dance.

échine [eʃin] nf CULIN chine.

échiner [3] [eʃine] ⟐ **s'échiner à** vp + prép ▸ **s'échiner à faire qqch** to wear ou s. out doing sthg.

échiquier [eʃikje] nm **1.** JEUX chessboard ▸ **le rôle que nous jouons sur l'échiquier européen / mondial** fig the part we play on the European / world scene **2.** POL ▸ **l'Échiquier** the (British) Exchequer.

écho [eko] nm **1.** ACOUST echo / *il y a de l'écho* there is an echo **2.** fig : *j'en ai eu des échos* I heard something about it / *sa proposition n'a pas trouvé d'écho* his offer wasn't taken into consideration / *aucun journal ne s'en est fait l'écho* the story was not picked up by any newspaper **3.** [rubrique de journal] gossip column.

échographie [ekɔgʀafi] nf (ultrasound) scan / *se faire faire une échographie* to have a scan ou an ultrasound scan.

échouer [6] [eʃwe] vi **1.** [rater - projet, tentative] to fail, to fall through / *ils ont échoué dans leur tentative de coup d'État* their attempted coup failed ▸ **échouer à un examen** to fail an exam ▸ **faire échouer** to foil, to frustrate **2.** fam [finir] to end ou to wind up. ⟐ **s'échouer** vpi NAUT to run aground / *quelques caisses échouées sur la plage* a few boxes washed up ou stranded on the beach.

échu, e [eʃy] adj : *payer un loyer à terme échu* to pay at the end of the rental term.

éclabousser [3] [eklabuse] vt **1.** [asperger] to splash, to spatter ▸ **éclaboussé de** : *éclaboussé de boue* mud-spattered **2.** [nuire à la réputation de] ▸ **éclabousser qqn** to malign sb, to tarnish sb's reputation.

éclaboussure [eklabusyʀ] nf **1.** [tache - de boue, de peinture] splash, spatter ▸ **des éclaboussures de sang** bloodstains **2.** [retombée] smear.

éclair [eklɛʀ] nm **1.** MÉTÉOR flash of lightning ▸ **éclairs** lightning ▸ **ses yeux jetaient** ou **lançaient des éclairs** fig her eyes were flashing / *le peloton est passé comme un éclair* the pack of cyclists flashed past ▸ **prompt** ou **rapide** ou **vif comme l'éclair** (as) quick as a flash **2.** [bref instant] : *dans un éclair de lucidité* in a flash of lucidity ▸ **un éclair de génie** a flash of inspiration **3.** CULIN éclair **4.** (comme adj) [lightning (modif) ▸ **visite éclair** lightning ou flying visit. ⟐ **en un éclair** loc adv in a flash ou a trice ou an instant.

éclairage [eklɛʀaʒ] nm **1.** [illumination artificielle] lighting ▸ **éclairage public** street lighting **2.** [intensité de lumière] light **3.** [aspect] light, perspective ▸ **apporter à qqch un éclairage nouveau** to throw new light on sthg.

éclairagiste [eklɛʀaʒist] nmf CINÉ, THÉÂTRE & TV lighting engineer.

éclaircie [eklɛʀsi] nf MÉTÉOR sunny spell, bright interval.

éclaircir [32] [eklɛʀsiʀ] vt **1.** [rendre moins sombre] to make lighter ▸ **éclaircir ses cheveux a)** to make one's hair (look) lighter **b)** [par mèches] to put highlights in one's hair **2.** CULIN [sauce, soupe] to thin (down), to dilute **3.** [forêt] to thin (out) **4.** [élucider - affaire, mystère] to clear up ; [- situation] to clarify. ❖ **s'éclaircir** ❖ vpi **1.** MÉTÉOR to clear (up), to brighten up **2.** [pâlir - cheveux] to go lighter ou paler ou blonder **3.** [se raréfier] to thin (out) **4.** [être clarifié - mystère] to be solved ; [- situation] to become clearer. ❖ vpt ▸ **s'éclaircir la voix** ou **gorge** to clear one's throat.

éclaircissement [eklɛʀsismɑ̃] nm [explication] explanation / *je voudrais des éclaircissements sur ce point* I would like some further clarification on this point.

éclairé, e [eklere] adj [intelligent] enlightened.

éclairer [4] [eklere] ❖ vt **1.** [chemin, lieu] to light (up) / *marchez derrière moi, je vais vous éclairer* walk behind me, I'll light the way for you **2.** [égayer] to brighten ou to light up (*sép*), to illuminate / *le visage éclairé par un sourire* his face lit up by a smile **3.** [rendre compréhensible] to clarify, to throw light on **4.** [informer] to enlighten ▸ **éclairer la lanterne de qqn** to put sb in the picture. ❖ vi ▸ **cette ampoule éclaire bien / mal** this bulb throws out a lot of / doesn't throw out much light. ❖ **s'éclairer** ❖ vp (*emploi réfléchi*) : *s'éclairer à l'électricité* to have electric lighting / *s'éclairer à la bougie* to use candlelight / *tiens, prends ma lampe électrique pour t'éclairer* here, take my flashlight to light your way. ❖ vpi **1.** [visage, regard] to brighten ou to light up **2.** [se résoudre] to get clearer ▸ **enfin, tout s'éclaire !** it's all clear (to me) now!

éclaireur, euse [eklɛʀœʀ, øz] nm, f [scout] boy scout (girl scout). ❖ **éclaireur** nm MIL scout. ❖ **en éclaireur** loc adv : *partir en éclaireur* to go (off) and scout around.

éclat [ekla] nm **1.** [fragment - de verre, de métal] splinter, shard ; [- de bois] splinter, sliver ▸ **des éclats d'obus** shrapnel **2.** [bruit] burst ▸ **éclat de rire** burst ou roar of laughter ▸ **on entendait des éclats de voix** loud voices could be heard **3.** [scandale] scandal / *faire un éclat en public* to cause a public scandal ou embarrassment **4.** [de la lumière, du jour] brightness ; [du soleil, de projecteur] glare ▸ **l'éclat d'un diamant** the sparkle of a diamond **5.** [du regard, d'un sourire, d'une couleur] brightness ; [du teint] radiance, bloom **6.** [splendeur] splendeur 🇬🇧, splendor 🇺🇸, glamour 🇬🇧, glamor 🇺🇸, glitter ▸ **donner de l'éclat à** to make glamorous.

éclatant, e [eklatɑ̃, ɑ̃t] adj **1.** [soleil, couleur] dazzling, brilliant ; [miroir, surface] sparkling ; [dents] gleaming / *draps d'une blancheur éclatante* ou *éclatants de blancheur* dazzling white sheets ▸ **aux couleurs éclatantes** [tissus] brightly coloured ▸ **un sourire éclatant** a dazzling smile **2.** [excellent - santé, teint] radiant, glowing ▸ **éclatant de** : *éclatante de beauté* radiantly beautiful **3.** [spectaculaire - revanche] spectacular ; [- triomphe, victoire] resounding.

éclater [3] [eklate] vi **1.** [exploser] to explode, to blow up, to burst / *j'ai l'impression que ma tête / mon cœur / ma poitrine va éclater* I feel as if my head / heart / chest is going to burst / *mon pneu a éclaté* my tyre burst **2.** [se fractionner] to split, to break up **3.** [retentir] ▸ **l'orage a enfin éclaté** the thunderstorm finally broke / *des coups de feu ont éclaté* shots rang out ▸ **éclater de** : *éclater de rire* to burst out laughing ▸ **éclater en** : *éclater en larmes / sanglots* to burst into tears / sobs **4.** [se déclencher - guerre, scandale] to break out **5.** [apparaître] to stand out **6.** [de colère] to explode. ❖ **s'éclater** vpi *fam* to have a whale of a time ou a ball / *il s'éclate en faisant de la photo* he gets his kicks from photography.

éclectique [eklɛktik] adj [distraction, goût, opinion] eclectic, varied.

éclipse [eklips] nf **1.** ASTRON eclipse **2.** [éloignement] eclipse, decline.

éclipser [3] [eklipse] vt **1.** ASTRON to eclipse **2.** [surclasser] to eclipse, to overshadow, to outshine. ❖ **s'éclipser** vpi *fam* to slip away ou out, to sneak off.

éclopé, e [eklɔpe] adj lame, limping.

éclore [113] [eklɔʀ] vi (*aux être ou avoir*) [œuf, poussin] to hatch (out) ; *litt* [fleur] to open out.

éclosion [eklozjɔ̃] nf [d'un œuf] hatching ; *litt* [d'une fleur] opening (out).

écluse [eklyz] nf lock.

écobilan [ekɔbilɑ̃] nm life cycle analysis.

écocertifié, e [ekɔsɛʀtifje] adj eco-certified.

écocitoyen, enne [ekɔsitwajɛ̃, ɛn] adj eco-responsible / *ayez des gestes écocitoyens* behave like eco-citizens.

écœurant, e [ekœʀɑ̃, ɑ̃t] adj **1.** [nauséeux] nauseating, cloying, sickly **2.** [indigne] disgusting **3.** *fam* [démoralisant] sickening, disheartening.

écœurement [ekœʀmɑ̃] nm **1.** [nausée] nausea **2.** [aversion] disgust, aversion, distaste **3.** *fam* [découragement] discouragement.

écœurer [5] [ekœʀe] vt **1.** [donner la nausée] to sicken / *la vue de ce gâteau m'écœure* looking at that cake makes me feel sick **2.** [inspirer le mépris à] to disgust, to sicken **3.** *fam* [décourager] to dishearten, to discourage.

écolabel [ekɔlabɛl] nm eco-label.

école [ekɔl] nf **1.** [établissement] school ▸ **aller à l'école** to go to school ▸ **école élémentaire** *vieilli* primary school ▸ **école hôtelière** catering school, hotel management school ▸ **école maternelle** nursery school ▸ **école militaire** military academy ▸ **école primaire** primary school 🇬🇧, grade school 🇺🇸 ▸ **école secondaire** secondary school 🇬🇧, high school 🇺🇸 ▸ **faire l'école buissonnière** to play truant 🇬🇧 ou hooky 🇺🇸 **2.** [cours] school / *l'école recommencera le 9 septembre* school will reopen on September 9th **3.** [système] ▸ **l'école laïque** secular education ▸ **l'école libre** sectarian education **4.** [établissement supérieur] ▸ **école de commerce** business school ▸ **grande école** *competitive-entrance higher education establishment* ▸ **École (centrale) des arts et manufactures** ou **École centrale** *prestigious engineering school* ▸ **École nationale d'administration = ENA** ▸ **École normale** HIST teacher training college 🇬🇧, teachers college 🇺🇸 ▸ **École normale supérieure** *prestigious "grande école" for teachers and researchers* **5.** [lieu spécialisé] school ▸ **école de conduite** driving school ▸ **école de danse** ballet school ▸ **école de ski** skiing school **6.** [disciples] school ▸ **il est de la vieille école** he's one of the old school ou guard ▸ **faire école** to attract a following **7.** ▸ **être à bonne école** to learn a lot ▸ **être à rude école** to learn the hard way.

L'école laïque

The separation of Church and State, which reflects the republican ideal and became law in 1905, is an important aspect of French culture. Since that date state education has been independent of the Church, and explicitly excludes religious instruction and religious ceremony.

écolier, ère [ekɔlje, ɛʀ] nm, f ÉDUC [garçon] schoolboy ; [fille] schoolgirl.

écolo [ekɔlo] *fam* ◆ adj green. ◆ nmf environmentalist.

écologie [ekɔlɔʒi] nf ecology.

écologique [ekɔlɔʒik] adj [gén] ecological ; [politique, parti] green.

écologiste [ekɔlɔʒist] nmf **1.** [expert] ecologist, environmentalist **2.** [partisan] ecologist, green.

écomusée [ekɔmyze] nm ecomuseum.

éconduire [98] [ekɔ̃dɥiʀ] vt [importun, vendeur] to get rid of ; [soupirant] to jilt, to reject.

économe [ekɔnɔm] ◆ adj [avec l'argent] thrifty ▸ **être économe** to be careful with money. ◆ nm [couteau] (vegetable) peeler.

économie [ekɔnɔmi] nf **1.** [système] economy ▸ **économie dirigée** ou **planifiée** planned economy ▸ **économie de marché** market economy, market-driven economy **2.** [discipline] economics **3.** [épargne] economy, thrift / *par économie, il y a à pied* he walks to save money ▸ **une économie de**: *nous avons fait une économie de deux euros par livre* we saved two euros on each book ▸ **faire des économies d'énergie** to conserve ou to save energy ▸ **ce sera une économie de temps / d'argent** it'll save time / money ▸ **faire l'économie de** to save ▸ **une économie** ou **des économies de bouts de chandelles** *péj* cheeseparing. ◆ **économies** nfpl savings ▸ **faire des économies** to save money ▸ **elle a quelques économies** she has some savings.

économique [ekɔnɔmik] adj **1.** ÉCON economic **2.** [peu coûteux] economical, cheap, inexpensive ▸ **classe économique** economy class ▸ **taille économique** economy size.

economic ou economical ?

Economic désigne tout ce qui se rapporte à l'économie, tandis que **economical** signifie « peu onéreux ».

économiquement [ekɔnɔmikmɑ̃] adv ÉCON economically, from an economic point of view ▸ **les économiquement faibles** the lower-income groups.

économiser [3] [ekɔnɔmize] ◆ vt **1.** [épargner - argent, temps] to save **2.** [ménager - force] to save ; [- ressources] to husband **3.** [énergie, électricité, denrée] to save, to conserve. ◆ vi to save money, to economize ▸ **économiser sur l'habillement** to cut down on buying clothes, to spend less on clothes.

économiseur [ekɔnɔmizœʀ] nm ▸ **économiseur d'écran** screen saver.

économiste [ekɔnɔmist] nmf economist.

écoparticipation [ekɔpaʀtisipasjɔ̃] nf eco-participation.

écoper [3] [ekɔpe] ◆ vt [barque, bateau] to bail out. ◆ vi *fam* [recevoir une sanction, une réprimande] to take the rap / *c'est lui qui a écopé* he was the one who took the rap. ◆ **écoper de** v + prép *fam* to cop 🇺🇸, to get / *il a écopé de cinq ans de prison* he got five years inside.

écoproduit [ekɔpʀɔdɥi] nm green product.

écoquartier [ekɔkaʀtje] nm *environmentally friendly area.*

écorce [ekɔʀs] nf **1.** [d'un arbre] bark ; [d'un fruit] peel **2.** GÉOGR ▸ **l'écorce terrestre** the earth's crust.

écorcher [3] [ekɔʀʃe] vt **1.** [blesser] to scratch, to graze / *la musique lui écorchait les oreilles* the music grated on his ears **2.** [mal prononcer - mot] to mispronounce. ◆ **s'écorcher** vp *(emploi réfléchi)* to scrape ou to scratch o.s. / *je me suis écorché le pied* I scraped ou scratched my foot.

écorecharge [ekɔʀəʃaʀʒ] nf eco-refill.

écoresponsable [ekɔʀɛspɔ̃sabl] adj eco-responsible.

écorner [3] [ekɔʀne] vt [endommager - cadre, meuble] to chip a corner off ; [- livre, page] to fold down the corner of, to dog-ear / *un livre tout écorné* a dog-eared book.

écossais, e [ekɔsɛ, ɛz] adj **1.** GÉOGR [coutume, lande] Scottish ▸ **whisky écossais** Scotch (whisky) **2.** TEXT tartan. ◆ **Écossais, e** nm, f Scot, Scotsman (Scotswoman) ▸ **les Écossais** Scottish people, the Scots.

Écosse [ekɔs] npr f ▸ **(l')Écosse** Scotland.

écosser [3] [ekɔse] vt [petits pois] to shell, to pod ; [fèves] to shell.

écosystème [ekɔsistɛm] nm ecosystem.

écotaxe [ekɔtaks] nf green tax.

écoterrorisme [ekɔtɛʀɔʀism] nm ecoterrorism.

écotourisme [ekɔtuʀism] nm eco-tourism.

écouler [3] [ekule] vt **1.** [vendre] to sell **2.** [se débarrasser de - fausse monnaie, bijoux volés] to dispose ou to get rid of. ◆ **s'écouler** vpi **1.** [se déverser - liquide] to flow (out) ; [- foule] to pour out **2.** [passer - année, temps] to go by, to pass (by).

écourter [3] [ekuʀte] vt [rendre plus court] to shorten, to cut short.

écoutant, e [ekutɑ̃, ɑ̃t] nm, f helpline volunteer, trained listener.

écoute [ekut] nf **1.** RADIO listening ▸ **heure** ou **période de grande écoute** a) RADIO peak listening time b) TV peak viewing time, prime time / *aux heures de grande écoute* RADIO & TV in prime time **2.** [détection] listening (in) ▸ **écoutes (téléphoniques)** phone tapping ▸ **mettre** ou **placer qqn sur écoutes** to tap sb's phone **3.** [attention] ability to listen. ◆ **à l'écoute de** loc prép **1.** RADIO ▸ **rester à l'écoute** to stay tuned **2.** [attentif à] ▸ **être à l'écoute de** [opinion publique, revendications] to listen to.

écouter [3] [ekute] vt **1.** [entendre - chanson, discours, émission] to listen to *(insép)* / *c'est un des jeux les plus écoutés en France* it's one of the most popular radio games in France / *je vais te faire écouter un truc génial* I'm going to play you something really great / *écoute ça !* check this out! ▸ **n'écouter que d'une oreille** : *je n'écoutais que d'une oreille* I was only half listening ▸ **écouter de toutes ses oreilles** to be all ears ▸ **écouter aux portes** to eavesdrop ; [à l'impératif, à valeur d'insistance] : *écoutez, nous n'allons pas nous disputer !* listen ou look, let's not quarrel! **2.** [porter attention] to listen to / *écoutez-moi avant de vous décider* listen to what I have to say before you make up your mind ; *(en usage absolu)* ▸ **il sait écouter** he's a good listener **3.** [obéir à] to listen to ▸ **n'écoutant que sa colère / sa douleur / son cœur** guided by his anger / pain / heart alone. ◆ **s'écouter** vp *(emploi réfléchi)* ▸ **il s'écoute trop** he's a bit of a hypochondriac / *si je m'écoutais, je le mettrais dehors* if I had any sense, I'd throw him out ▸ **s'écouter parler** to love the sound of one's own voice.

écouteur [ekutœʀ] nm **1.** TÉLÉC earpiece **2.** AUDIO earphone.

écoutille [ekutij] nf hatch, hatchway.

écovolontaire [ekɔvɔlɔ̃tɛʀ] nmf ecovolunteer.

écrabouiller [3] [ekʀabuje] vt *fam* to crush, to squash / *se faire écrabouiller* to get squashed.

écran [ekʀɑ̃] nm **1.** [d'une console, d'un ordinateur] screen ▸ **écran de contrôle** monitor (screen) ▸ **écran (à) plasma** plasma screen ▸ **écran plat** flat screen ▸ **écran tactile** touch-sensitive screen ▸ **écran de visualisation** (visual) display screen **2.** CINÉ cinema screen ▸ **à l'écran** ou **sur les écrans, cette semaine** what's on this week at the cinema ou movies 🇺🇸 ▸ **vedettes de l'écran** movie stars, stars of the big screen ▸ **le grand écran** the big screen, the cinema 🇬🇧

3. TV ▶ **le petit écran** television **4.** [protection] screen, shield ▶ **écran solaire** sun screen ▶ **crème écran total** total protection sun cream ou block.

écrasant, e [ekʀazɑ̃, ɑ̃t] adj **1.** [insupportable - gén] crushing, overwhelming ; [-chaleur] unbearable ; [-responsabilité] weighty, burdensome **2.** [charge de travail, proportion] overwhelming / *une majorité écrasante en faveur de* an overwhelming majority in favour of.

écraser [3] [ekʀaze] ◆ vt **1.** [appuyer sur] to crush **2.** [fruit, pomme de terre] to mash ▶ **écraser un moustique** to swat a mosquito ▶ **écraser une cigarette** to stub a cigarette out **3.** [piéton, chat] to run over / *il s'est fait écraser* he was run over **4.** [faire mal à] to crush, to squash ▶ **tu m'écrases les pieds** you're treading on my feet **5.** [accabler] to crush ▶ **écraser de** : *écraser un pays d'impôts* to overburden a country with taxes / *être écrasé de fatigue* to be overcome by fatigue **6.** [anéantir] to crush / *se faire écraser par l'équipe adverse* to get crushed by the opposing team **7.** [dominer] to outdo / *il écrase tout le monde de son luxe* he flaunts his luxurious lifestyle everywhere. ◆ vi *tfam* [se taire] : *écrase, tu veux bien !* shut up, will you! ◆ **s'écraser** ◆ vp *(emploi passif)* to be crushed. ◆ vpi **1.** [fruit, légume] to get crushed ou mashed ou squashed **2.** [tomber - aviateur, avion] to crash ; [-alpiniste] to crash to the ground **3.** *tfam* [se taire] to shut up, to pipe down ▶ **il vaut mieux s'écraser** better keep quiet ou mum.

écrémer [18] [ekʀeme] vt **1.** CULIN to skim **2.** [sélectionner] to cream off *(sép).*

🖉 In reformed spelling (see p. 16-18), this verb is conjugated like **semer** : *il écrèmera, elle écrèmerait.*

écrevisse [ekʀəvis] nf crayfish, crawfish US.

écrier [10] [ekʀije] ◆ **s'écrier** vpi to cry ou to shout (out), to exclaim.

écrin [ekʀɛ̃] nm [gén] box, case ; [à bijoux] casket.

écrire [99] [ekʀiʀ] vt **1.** [tracer - caractère, mot] to write ; *(en usage absolu)* : *mon crayon écrit mal* my pen doesn't write properly ▶ **tu écris mal** [illisiblement] your handwriting is bad **2.** [rédiger - lettre, livre] to write ; [-chèque, ordonnance] to write (out) ▶ **c'est écrit noir sur blanc** ou **en toutes lettres** *fig* it's written (down) in black and white ; *(en usage absolu)* : *écrire pour demander des renseignements* to write in ou off for information **3.** [noter] to write down **4.** [épeler] to spell. ◆ **s'écrire** vp *(emploi passif)* [s'épeler] to be spelled ▶ **ça s'écrit comment ?** how do you spell it? ◆ vp *(emploi réciproque)* [échanger des lettres] to write to each other.

🖋 **Écrire qqch à qqn** Write sthg to sb ou write sb sthg.

Notez la construction à double complément qui en anglais peut prendre deux formes dont le sens est le même :

• une structure identique à celle du français :
    verbe + COD + préposition + COI
        write sthg to sb

• une structure qui diffère de celle du français, sans préposition, et dans laquelle l'ordre des compléments est inversé :
    verbe + COI + COD
        write sb sthg

Elle a écrit une très belle lettre d'adieu à ses collègues. She wrote a lovely farewell letter to her colleagues ou She wrote her colleagues a lovely farewell letter.

écrit, e [ekʀi, it] adj written / *épreuves écrites d'un examen* written part of an examination. ◆ **écrit** nm **1.** [document] document **2.** [œuvre] written work **3.** ENS [examen] written examination ou papers ; [partie] written part (of the examination). ◆ **par écrit** loc adv in writing.

écriteau, x [ekʀito] nm board, notice, sign.

écriture [ekʀityʀ] nf **1.** [calligraphie] writing ; [tracé] handwriting, writing / *avoir une écriture élégante* to have elegant handwriting, to write (in) an elegant hand *sout* **2.** [système] writing **3.** [style] writing ; [création] writing.

écrivain, e [ekʀivɛ̃, ɛn] nm, f writer ▶ **écrivain public** public letter writer.

écrou [ekʀu] nm **1.** MÉCAN nut **2.** DR committal.

écrouer [3] [ekʀue] vt to imprison, to jail.

écroulement [ekʀulmɑ̃] nm [d'un édifice, d'une théorie] collapse.

écrouler [3] [ekʀule] ◆ **s'écrouler** vpi **1.** [tomber - mur] to fall (down), to collapse ; [-plafond, voûte] to cave in **2.** [être anéanti - empire, monnaie] to collapse / *tous ses espoirs se sont écroulés* all her hopes vanished **3.** [défaillir - personne] to collapse ▶ **s'écrouler de sommeil / fatigue** to be overcome by sleep / weariness.

écru, e [ekʀy] adj **1.** TEXT raw **2.** [couleur] ecru.

ecsta [eksta] **(abr de ecstasy)** nm ecstasy, E.

écueil [ekœj] nm **1.** NAUT reef **2.** *litt* [difficulté] pitfall, danger, hazard.

éculé, e [ekyle] adj **1.** [botte, chaussure] down at heel, worn down at the heel **2.** [plaisanterie] hackneyed, well-worn.

écume [ekym] nf [de la bière] foam, froth ; [de la mer] foam, spume / *ôter l'écume des confitures* to remove the scum from jam.

écumer [3] [ekyme] ◆ vi [cheval] to lather / *écumer (de rage* ou *colère)* to be foaming at the mouth (with rage), to foam with anger. ◆ vt CULIN [confiture] to remove the scum from ; [bouillon] to skim.

écumoire [ekymwaʀ] nf skimmer, skimming ladle.

écureuil [ekyʀœj] nm squirrel.

écurie [ekyʀi] nf **1.** [local à chevaux, mulets, ânes] stable / *mettre à l'écurie* to stable **2.** [chevaux] stable ; SPORT stable, team.

écusson [ekysɔ̃] nm **1.** [écu] badge **2.** HIST escutcheon, coat of arms.

écuyer, ère [ekɥije, ɛʀ] nm, f **1.** [acrobate de cirque] circus rider **2.** [cavalier] rider. ◆ **écuyer** nm HIST [d'un chevalier] squire ; [d'un souverain] (royal) equerry.

eczéma, exéma* [ɛgzema] nm eczema.

éden [edɛn] nm BIBLE ▶ **l'Éden** (the Garden of) Eden.

édenté, e [edɑ̃te] adj [vieillard, peigne, sourire] toothless.

EDF (abr de **Électricité de France**) npr *French national electricity company.*

édifiant, e [edifjɑ̃, ɑ̃t] adj **1.** [lecture] instructive, improving, edifying **2.** *hum* [révélateur] edifying, instructive.

édification [edifikasjɔ̃] nf **1.** [construction] erection, construction **2.** [instruction] edification, enlightenment.

édifice [edifis] nm CONSTR building.

édifier [9] [edifje] vt **1.** [construire - temple] to build, to construct, to erect **2.** [instruire] to edify, to enlighten.

Édimbourg [edɛ̃buʀ] npr Edinburgh.

édit [edi] nm edict, decree.

éditer [3] [edite] vt **1.** COMM [roman, poésie] to publish ; [disque] to produce, to release ; [meuble, robe] to produce, to present **2.** INFORM to edit.

* In reformed spelling (see p. 16-18).

éditeur, trice [editœʀ,tʀis] nm, f publisher, editor ▸ **éditeur de disques** record producer. ❖ **éditeur** nm INFORM ▸ **éditeur de textes** text editor.

⚠ **Editor** ne doit pas être employé pour traduire éditeur au sens d'une personne ou d'une entreprise qui publie.

édition [edisjɔ̃] nf **1.** [activité, profession] publishing **2.** [livre] edition ▸ **édition revue et corrigée** revised edition **3.** [disque - classique] edition, release ; [- de rock] release **4.** [de journaux] edition ▸ **édition spéciale a)** [de journal] special edition **b)** [de revue] special issue **5.** TV : *dans la dernière édition de notre journal* in our late news bulletin ▸ **édition spéciale en direct de Budapest** special report live from Budapest **6.** INFORM editing ▸ **édition électronique** electronic publishing.

⚠ Le mot anglais **edition** désigne un ouvrage publié. Il ne peut être employé pour traduire édition lorsqu'on veut parler de l'activité ou de la profession.

édito [edito] nm *fam* editorial.

éditorial [editɔʀjal] nm [de journal] editorial, leader 🇬🇧.

éditorialiste [editɔʀjalist] nmf leader 🇬🇧 ou editorial writer.

édredon [edʀədɔ̃] nm eiderdown 🇬🇧, comforter 🇺🇸, quilt.

éducateur, trice [edykatœʀ,tʀis] nm, f teacher, youth leader ▸ **éducateur spécialisé** teacher for special needs.

éducatif, ive [edykatif,iv] adj educational ▸ **le système éducatif** the education system.

éducation [edykasjɔ̃] nf **1.** [instruction] education ▸ **l'Éducation nationale** the (French) Education Department ▸ **éducation permanente** continuing education ▸ **éducation physique (et sportive)** physical education, PE ▸ **éducation sexuelle** sex education **2.** [d'un enfant] upbringing ; [bonnes manières] good manners ▸ **manque d'éducation** bad manners ▸ **avoir de l'éducation** to be well-bred ou well-mannered.

édulcorant [edylkɔʀɑ̃] nm sweetener, sweetening agent.

édulcorer [3] [edylkɔʀe] vt **1.** [sucrer] to sweeten **2.** *litt* [modérer - propos, compte rendu] to soften, to water down *(sép)* ; [- texte] to bowdlerize.

éduquer [3] [edyke] vt **1.** [instruire - élève, masses] to teach, to educate **2.** [exercer - réflexe, volonté] to train ▸ **éduquer le goût de qqn** to shape ou to influence sb's taste **3.** [élever - enfant] to bring up *(sép)*, to raise / *être bien éduqué* to be well brought up ou well-bred ou well-mannered / *être mal éduqué* to be badly brought up ou ill-bred ou ill-mannered.

effacé, e [efase] adj [personne] self-effacing, retiring.

effacer [16] [efase] vt **1.** [ôter - tache, graffiti] to erase, to remove, to clean off *(sép)* ; [- mot] to rub out 🇬🇧 *(sép)*, to erase 🇺🇸 ; [nettoyer - ardoise] to clean, to wipe **2.** AUDIO & INFORM to erase, to wipe off *(sép)* **3.** [occulter - rêve, image] to erase ; [- bêtise] to erase, to obliterate. ❖ **s'effacer** ◆ vp *(emploi passif)* : *le crayon à papier s'efface très facilement* pencil rubs out easily ou is easily erased. ◆ vpi **1.** [encre, lettres] to fade, to wear away ; [couleur] to fade **2.** [s'écarter] to move ou to step aside **3.** [disparaître - souvenir, impression] to fade, to be erased.

effaceur [efasœʀ] nm ▸ **effaceur (d'encre)** ink rubber 🇬🇧 ou eraser 🇺🇸.

effarant, e [efaʀɑ̃,ɑ̃t] adj [cynisme, luxe] outrageous, unbelievable ; [étourderie, maigreur] unbelievable, stunning.

effaré, e [efaʀe] adj **1.** [effrayé] alarmed **2.** [troublé] bewildered, bemused / *elle le regarda d'un air effaré* she looked at him with a bewildered air.

effarement [efaʀmɑ̃] nm **1.** [peur] alarm **2.** [trouble] bewilderment, bemusement.

effarer [3] [efaʀe] vt [effrayer] to alarm.

effaroucher [3] [efaʀuʃe] vt [intimider] to frighten away ou off, to scare away ou off. ❖ **s'effaroucher** vpi [prendre peur] to take fright ▸ **s'effaroucher de** to shy at, to take fright at.

effectif, ive [efɛktif,iv] adj [réel - travail, gain, participation] real, actual, effective ; FIN effective. ❖ **effectif** nm [d'un lycée] size, (total) number of pupils ; [d'une armée] strength ; [d'un parti] size, strength / *réduction de l'effectif des classes* reduction in the number of pupils per class ▸ **réduire ses effectifs** to de-man, to downsize. ❖ **effectifs** nmpl MIL numbers, strength.

effectivement [efɛktivmɑ̃] adv **1.** [véritablement] actually, really / *c'est effectivement le cas* this is actually the case **2.** [en effet] actually / *j'ai dit cela, effectivement* I did indeed say so / *on pourrait effectivement penser que...* one may actually ou indeed think that...

⚠ **Effectively** signifie « efficacement » et non effectivement.

effectuer [7] [efɛktɥe] vt [expérience, essai] to carry out *(sép)*, to perform ; [trajet, traversée] to make, to complete ; [saut, pirouette] to make, to execute ; [service militaire] to do ; [retouche, enquête, opération] to carry out *(sép)*. ❖ **s'effectuer** vpi [avoir lieu] to take place / *l'aller-retour s'effectue en une journée* the return trip 🇬🇧 ou round trip 🇺🇸 can be made in one day.

efféminé, e [efemine] adj effeminate.

effervescence [efɛʀvesɑ̃s] nf [agitation] agitation, turmoil. ❖ **en effervescence** loc adj bubbling ou buzzing with excitement.

effervescent, e [efɛʀvesɑ̃,ɑ̃t] adj CHIM effervescent.

effet [efɛ] nm **1.** [résultat] effect, result, outcome ▸ **avoir un effet** : *cela n'a pas eu l'effet escompté* it didn't have the desired ou intended effect ▸ **avoir pour effet de** : *ton insistance n'aura pour effet que de l'agacer* the only thing you'll achieve ou do by insisting is (to) annoy him ▸ **faire un effet** : *le whisky lui fait toujours cet effet* whisky always has ou produces this effect on him / *attends que le médicament fasse son effet* wait for the medicine to take effect ▸ **être sans effet** : *le produit est sans effet sur les taches de fruit* the product does not work on fruit stains ▸ **prendre effet** : *prendre effet à partir de* to take effect ou to come into operation as of ▸ **effet d'annonce** : *créer un effet d'annonce* to create hype ▸ **effet secondaire** MÉD side-effect ▸ **relation de cause à effet** cause and effect relationship **2.** [impression] impression ▸ **faire beaucoup d'effet / peu d'effet** to be impressive / unimpressive ▸ **faire l'effet de** : *il me fait l'effet d'un jeune homme sérieux* he strikes me as (being) a reliable young man / *elle me fait l'effet d'un personnage de bande dessinée* she reminds me of a cartoon character **3.** [procédé] effect ▸ **effet de contraste / d'optique** contrasting / visual effect ▸ **effet (de) domino** domino effect ▸ **effet de style** stylistic effect ▸ **effet de perspective** 3-D ou 3-dimensional effect / *créer un effet de surprise* to create a surprise effect ▸ **effets spéciaux** CINÉ special effects **4.** SCI effect ▸ **effet de serre** greenhouse effect **5.** SPORT spin / *donner de l'effet à une balle* to put a spin on a ball. ❖ **effets** nmpl [affaires] things ;

[vêtements] clothes ▶ **effets personnels** personal effects ou belongings. ⋙ **à cet effet** loc adv to that effect ou end ou purpose. ⋙ **en effet** loc adv **1.** [effectivement] : *oui, je m'en souviens en effet* yes, I do remember / *c'est en effet la meilleure solution* it's actually ou in fact the best solution **2.** [introduisant une explication] : *je ne pense pas qu'il vienne ; en effet il est extrêmement pris ces derniers temps* I don't think he'll come, he's really very busy these days **3.** [dans une réponse] : *drôle d'idée ! — en effet !* what a funny idea! — indeed ou isn't it! ⋙ **sous l'effet de** loc prép : *être sous l'effet d'un calmant / de l'alcool* to be under the effect of a tranquillizer / the influence of alcohol / *j'ai dit des choses regrettables sous l'effet de la colère* anger made me say things which I later regretted.

efficace [efikas] adj **1.** [utile - politique, intervention] effective, efficient, efficacious sout **2.** [actif - employé] efficient ; [- médicament] effective, efficacious sout.

efficacement [efikasmã] adv effectively, efficiently, efficaciously sout.

efficacité [efikasite] nf effectiveness, efficiency, efficaciousness sout ▶ **manquer d'efficacité** to be inefficient.

efficience [efisjãs] nf sout efficiency.

effigie [efiʒi] nf effigy. ⋙ **à l'effigie de** loc prép bearing the effigy of, in the image of. ⋙ **en effigie** loc adv in effigy.

effilé, e [efile] adj [mince - doigt] slender, tapering ; [- main] slender ; [- cheveux] thinned ▶ **amandes effilées** CULIN split almonds.

effilocher [3] [efilɔʃe] ⋙ **s'effilocher** vpi to fray, to unravel.

efflanqué, e [eflãke] adj [animal] raw-boned ; [homme] lanky, tall and skinny.

effleurer [5] [eflœʀe] vt **1.** [frôler - cime, eau] to skim, to graze ; [- peau, bras] to touch lightly, to brush (against) **2.** [aborder - sujet] to touch on ou upon *(insép)* / *ça ne m'a même pas effleuré* it didn't even occur to me ou cross my mind.

effluve [eflyv] nm [odeur] ▶ **effluves a)** [bonnes odeurs] fragrance, exhalations **b)** [mauvaises odeurs] effluvia, miasma.

effondrement [efɔ̃dʀəmã] nm **1.** [chute - d'un toit, d'un pont] collapse, collapsing, falling down ; [- d'une voûte, d'un plafond] falling ou caving in **2.** [anéantissement - des prix, du dollar] collapse, slump ; [- d'un empire] collapse **3.** [abattement] dejection.

effondrer [3] [efɔ̃dʀe] vt fig ▶ **être effondré** : *après la mort de sa femme, il était effondré* he was prostrate with grief after his wife's death. ⋙ **s'effondrer** vpi **1.** [tomber - mur] to fall (down), to collapse ; [- plafond, voûte] to collapse, to fall ou to cave in **2.** [être anéanti - monnaie] to collapse, to plummet, to slump ; [- empire] to collapse, to crumble, to fall apart ; [- rêve, projet] to collapse, to fall through ; [- raisonnement] to collapse **3.** [défaillir] to collapse, to slump / *s'effondrer dans un fauteuil* to slump ou to sink into an armchair.

efforcer [16] [efɔʀse] ⋙ **s'efforcer** vpi ▶ **s'efforcer de** : *s'efforcer de faire qqch* to endeavour to do sthg / *s'efforcer de sourire* to force o.s. to smile.

effort [efɔʀ] nm [dépense d'énergie] effort ▶ **sans effort** effortlessly / *encore un (petit) effort !* one more try! / *fournir un gros effort* to make a great deal of effort ▶ **tu aurais pu faire l'effort d'écrire / de comprendre** you could (at least) have tried to write / to understand ▶ **faire un effort** to make an effort / *chacun doit faire un petit effort* everybody must do their share / *faire un effort sur soi-même pour rester poli* to force o.s. to remain polite ▶ **faire un effort d'imagination** to try to use one's imagination.

effraction [efʀaksjɔ̃] nf DR breaking and entering, housebreaking / *entrer par effraction dans une maison* to break into a house.

effrayant, e [efʀɛjã, ãt] adj **1.** [qui fait peur] frightening, fearsome sout **2.** [extrême - chaleur, charge de travail] frightful, appalling.

effrayer [11] [efʀeje] vt [faire peur à] to frighten, to scare. ⋙ **s'effrayer** vpi [avoir peur] to become frightened, to take fright sout ▶ **s'effrayer de qqch** to be frightened of sthg.

effréné, e [efʀene] adj [poursuite, recherche] wild, frantic ; [orgueil, curiosité, luxe] unbridled, unrestrained ; [vie, rythme] frantic, hectic.

effriter [3] [efʀite] vt to cause to crumble. ⋙ **s'effriter** vpi **1.** [se fragmenter - roche, bas-relief] to crumble away, to be eroded **2.** [diminuer - majorité, popularité] to crumble, to be eroded ; [- valeurs, cours] to decline (in value).

effroi [efʀwa] nm terror, dread / *regard plein d'effroi* frightened look.

effronté, e [efʀɔ̃te] ◆ adj [enfant, manières, réponse] impudent, cheeky UK ; [menteur, mensonge] shameless, barefaced, brazen. ◆ nm, f **1.** [enfant] impudent ou cheeky child / *petite effrontée !* you cheeky UK ou sassy US little girl! **2.** [adulte] impudent fellow (brazen hussy).

effrontément [efʀɔ̃temã] adv impudently, cheekily UK ▶ **mentir effrontément** to lie shamelessly ou barefacedly ou brazenly.

effronterie [efʀɔ̃tʀi] nf [d'un enfant, d'une attitude] insolence, impudence, cheek UK ; [d'un mensonge] shamelessness, brazenness.

effroyable [efʀwajabl] adj **1.** [épouvantable] frightening, appalling, horrifying **2.** [extrême - maigreur, misère] dreadful, frightful.

effusion [efyzjɔ̃] nf effusion, outpouring, outburst ▶ **effusion de sang** bloodshed ▶ **effusions de joie / tendresse** demonstrations of joy / affection ▶ **remercier qqn avec effusion** to thank sb effusively.

égal, e, aux [egal, o] ◆ adj **1.** [identique] equal / *à prix égal, tu peux trouver mieux* for the same price, you can find something better / *à égale distance de A et de B* equidistant from A and B, an equal distance from A and B ▶ **toutes choses égales d'ailleurs** all (other) things being equal ▶ **égal à lui-même / soi-même** : *être* ou *rester égal à soi-même* to remain true to form, to be still one's old self **2.** [régulier - terrain] even, level ; [- souffle, pouls] even, regular ; [- pas] even, regular, steady ; [- climat] equable, unchanging ▶ **être de caractère égal** ou **d'humeur égale** to be even-tempered **3.** EXPR *ça m'est (complètement) égal* **a)** [ça m'est indifférent] I don't care either way **b)** [ça ne m'intéresse pas] I don't care at all, I couldn't care less. ◆ nm, f [personne] equal. ⋙ **d'égal à égal** loc adv [s'entretenir] on equal terms ; [traiter] as an equal. ⋙ **sans égal** loc adj matchless, unequalled UK, unequaled US, unrivalled UK, unrivaled US.

également [egalmã] adv **1.** [autant] equally / *je crains également le froid et la chaleur* I dislike the cold as much as the heat **2.** [aussi] also, too, as well.

égaler [3] [egale] vt **1.** [avoir la même valeur que] to equal, to match **2.** MATH : *3 fois 2 égale 6* 3 times 2 equals 6.

égalisation [egalizasjɔ̃] nf [nivellement - des salaires, d'un terrain] levelling.

égaliser [3] [egalize] ◆ vt [sentier] to level (out) ; [frange] to trim ; [conditions, chances] to make equal, to balance (out) / *se faire égaliser les cheveux* to have one's hair trimmed. ◆ vi SPORT to equalize UK, to tie US.

égalitaire [egalitɛʀ] adj egalitarian.

égalitarisme [egalitaʀism] nm egalitarianism.

égalité [egalite] nf **1.** ÉCON & SOCIOL equality ▸ **politique / principe d'égalité des chances** equal opportunities policy / principle **2.** MATH equality **3.** TENNIS deuce ; FOOT draw, tie. ❖ **à égalité** loc adv TENNIS at deuce ; [dans des jeux d'équipe] in a draw ou tie / **ils ont fini le match à égalité** they tied / **ils sont à égalité avec Riom** they're lying equal with Riom.

égard [egaʀ] nm [point de vue] ▸ **à bien des égards** in many respects ▸ **à cet / aucun égard** in this / no respect. ❖ **égards** nmpl [marques de respect] consideration ▸ **être plein d'égards** ou **avoir beaucoup d'égards pour qqn** to show great consideration for ou to be very considerate towards sb ▸ **manquer d'égards envers qqn** to show a lack of consideration for ou to be inconsiderate towards sb. ❖ **à l'égard de** loc prép **1.** [envers] towards 🇬🇧, toward 🇺🇸 ▸ **être dur / tendre à l'égard de qqn** to be hard on / gentle with sb / **ils ont fait une exception à mon égard** they made an exception for me ou in my case **2.** [à l'encontre de] against **3.** [quant à] with regard to. ❖ **à tous égards** loc adv in all respects ou every respect. ❖ **par égard pour** loc prép out of consideration ou respect for. ❖ **sans égard pour** loc prép with no respect ou consideration for, without regard for.

égaré, e [egaʀe] adj **1.** [perdu - dossier, touriste] lost ; [- chat] lost, stray **2.** [affolé - esprit] distraught ; [- regard] wild, distraught.

égarement [egaʀmã] nm [folie] distraction, distractedness / **dans son égarement, il a oublié de...** he was so distraught he forgot to... ❖ **égarements** nmpl litt : **revenir de ses égarements** to see the error of one's ways.

égarer [3] [egaʀe] vt **1.** [perdre - bagage, stylo] to lose, to mislay **2.** [tromper - opinion, lecteur] to mislead, to deceive ; [- jeunesse] to lead astray. ❖ **s'égarer** vpi **1.** [se perdre - promeneur] to lose one's way, to get lost ; [- dossier, clef] to get lost ou mislaid **2.** [sortir du sujet] to wander / **ne nous égarons pas !** let's not wander off the point!, let's stick to the subject!

égayer [11] [egeje] vt [convives] to cheer up (sép) ; [chambre, robe, vie] to brighten up (sép) ; [ambiance, récit] to brighten up (sép), to liven up (sép), to enliven.

Égée [eʒe] npr ▸ **la mer Égée** the Aegean Sea.

égérie [eʒeʀi] nf [inspiratrice] muse.

égide [eʒid] ❖ **sous l'égide de** loc prép sout under the aegis of.

églantier [eglãtje] nm wild ou dog rose (bush).

églantine [eglãtin] nf wild ou dog rose.

églefin [egləfɛ̃] nm haddock.

Église [egliz] nf ▸ **l'Église** the Church.

église [egliz] nf [édifice] church ▸ **aller à l'église** [pratiquer] to go to church, to be a churchgoer / **se marier à l'église** to be married in church, to have a church wedding.

ego, ego* [ego] nm ego.

égocentrique [egosãtʀik] ❖ adj egocentric, self-centred 🇬🇧, self-centered 🇺🇸. ❖ nmf egocentric ou self-centred 🇬🇧 ou self-centered 🇺🇸 person.

égocentrisme [egosãtʀism] nm egocentricity, self-centredness 🇬🇧, self-centeredness 🇺🇸.

égoïsme [egoism] nm selfishness.

égoïste [egoist] ❖ adj selfish. ❖ nmf selfish man (woman).

égoïstement [egoistəmã] adv selfishly.

égorger [17] [egoʀʒe] vt to cut ou to slit the throat of.

égosiller [3] [egozije] ❖ **s'égosiller** vpi **1.** [crier] to shout o.s. hoarse **2.** [chanter fort] to sing at the top of one's voice.

égout [egu] nm sewer.

égoutter [3] [egute] ❖ vt [linge] to leave to drip ; [vaisselle] to drain / **égoutter des légumes dans une passoire** to strain vegetables in a sieve. ❖ vi [vaisselle] to drain ; [linge] to drip ▸ **faire égoutter les haricots** to strain the beans. ❖ **s'égoutter** vpi [linge] to drip ; [légumes, vaisselle] to drain.

égouttoir [egutwaʀ] nm **1.** [passoire] strainer, colander **2.** [pour la vaisselle] draining rack ou board, drainer.

égratigner [3] [egʀatiɲe] vt **1.** [jambe, carrosserie] to scratch, to scrape ; [peau] to graze **2.** fam [critiquer] to have a dig ou a go at / **il s'est fait égratigner par la presse à propos de sa dernière déclaration** the papers had a real go at him about his latest statement. ❖ **s'égratigner** vp (emploi réfléchi) ▸ **s'égratigner le genou** to scrape ou to scratch ou to skin one's knee.

égratignure [egʀatiɲyʀ] nf [écorchure] scratch, scrape, graze / **il s'en est sorti sans une égratignure** he escaped without a scratch.

égrillard, e [egʀijaʀ, aʀd] adj [histoire] bawdy, ribald ; [personne] ribald.

Égypte [eʒipt] npr f ▸ **(l')Égypte** Egypt.

égyptien, enne [eʒipsjɛ̃, ɛn] adj Egyptian. ❖ **Égyptien, enne** nm, f Egyptian.

égyptologie [eʒiptɔlɔʒi] nf Egyptology.

eh [e] interj hey. ❖ **eh bien** loc adv **1.** [au début d'une histoire] well, right **2.** [pour exprimer la surprise] well, well. ❖ **eh non** loc adv well no. ❖ **eh oui** loc adv well(, actually,) yes / **c'est fini ? — eh oui !** is it over? — I'm afraid so!

éhonté, e [eɔ̃te] adj [menteur, tricheur] barefaced, brazen, shameless ; [mensonge, hypocrisie] brazen, shameless.

Eire [ɛʀ] npr f ▸ **(l')Eire** Eire.

éjaculation [eʒakylasjɔ̃] nf ejaculation ▸ **éjaculation précoce** premature ejaculation.

éjaculer [3] [eʒakyle] vt & vi to ejaculate.

éjecter [4] [eʒɛkte] vt **1.** AÉRON & AUTO to eject **2.** fam [renvoyer] well, right **2.** fam [renvoyer] to kick ou to chuck ou to boot out / **il s'est fait éjecter de l'équipe** he was kicked out of the team / **se faire éjecter d'une boîte de nuit** to get kicked ou chucked ou booted out of a night club. ❖ **s'éjecter** vp (emploi réfléchi) AÉRON to eject.

élaboration [elabɔʀasjɔ̃] nf [d'une théorie, d'une idée] working out / **l'élaboration d'un projet de loi** drawing up a bill.

élaboré, e [elabɔʀe] adj [complexe - dessin] elaborate, intricate, ornate ; [perfectionné - système] elaborate, sophisticated ; [détaillé - carte, schéma] elaborate, detailed.

élaborer [3] [elabɔʀe] vt [préparer - plan, système] to develop, to design, to work out (sép).

élaguer [3] [elage] vt HORT to prune.

élan [elã] nm **1.** [dans une course] run-up, impetus ▸ **prendre son élan** to take a run-up **2.** [énergie] momentum ▸ **prendre de l'élan** to gather speed ou momentum ▸ **être emporté par son propre élan** pr & fig to be carried along by one's own momentum **3.** [impulsion] impulse, impetus / **donner de l'élan à une campagne** to give an impetus ou to provide an impetus for a campaign **4.** [effusion] outburst, surge, rush / **élans de tendresse** surges ou rushes of affection ▸ **élan de générosité** generous impulse **5.** ZOOL elk, moose 🇺🇸.

élancé, e [elãse] adj slim, slender.

élancement [elãsmã] nm sharp ou shooting ou stabbing pain.

élancer [16] [elãse] ❖ **s'élancer** vpi **1.** [courir] to rush ou to dash forward ▸ **s'élancer à la poursuite de qqn** to dash after sb ▸ **s'élancer vers qqn** to dash ou to rush towards sb **2.** SPORT to take a run-up.

élargir [32] [elaʀʒiʀ] vt **1.** [rendre moins étroit - veste] to let out *(sép)* ; [-chaussure] to stretch, to widen ; [-route] to widen **2.** [débat] to broaden ou widen the scope of / *élargir son horizon* to broaden ou to widen one's outlook **3.** DR [libérer - détenu] to free, to release. ❖ **s'élargir** vpi **1.** [être moins étroit - sentier, rivière] to widen, to get wider, to broaden (out) ; [-sourire] to widen **2.** [se relâcher - vêtement] to stretch **3.** [horizon, débat] to broaden out, to widen.

élargissement [elaʀʒismɑ̃] nm **1.** [agrandissement - d'une route] widening **2.** [extension - d'un débat] broadening, widening.

élasticité [elastisite] nf **1.** [extensibilité] stretchiness, stretch, elasticity **2.** ANAT elasticity **3.** *fam & péj* [laxisme - d'une conscience, d'un règlement] accommodating nature **4.** [variabilité] flexibility / *l'élasticité de l'offre | de la demande* the elasticity of supply / of demand.

élastique [elastik] ❖ adj **1.** [ceinture, cuir, tissu] stretchy, elastic ; [badine] supple **2.** *fam & péj* [peu rigoureux - conscience, règlement] accommodating, elastic **3.** [variable - horaire] flexible ; [-demande, offre] elastic. ❖ nm **1.** [bracelet] elastic band **2.** [ruban] ▶ **de l'élastique** elastic.

élastomère [elastɔmɛʀ] nm elastomer.

Eldorado [ɛldɔʀado] npr m ▶ **l'Eldorado** Eldorado.

e-learning [ilœʀniŋ] nm e-learning.

électeur, trice [elɛktœʀ, tʀis] nm, f POL voter ▶ **les électeurs** the voters, the electorate.

élection [elɛksjɔ̃] nf **1.** [procédure] election, polls / *les élections ont lieu aujourd'hui* it's election ou polling day today ▶ **se présenter aux élections** to stand in the elections 🇬🇧, to run for office ou as a candidate 🇺🇸 ▶ **élections européennes** European elections ▶ **élections législatives** general elections *(held every five years)* ▶ **élection partielle** by-election 🇬🇧, off-year election 🇺🇸 ▶ **élection présidentielle** presidential election **2.** [nomination] election. ❖ **d'élection** loc adj [choisi - patrie, famille] of one's own choice ou choosing, chosen.

🏛 **Élections**

All French citizens aged eighteen or over are entitled to vote in elections, after they have registered on the electoral rolls. Elections usually take place on a Sunday and polling stations are often set up in local schools. Voters go to a booth and put their voting slip in an envelope which is placed in the ballot box (**l'urne**) supervised by an **assesseur**, who then utters the words **a voté!**

électoral, e, aux [elɛktɔʀal, o] adj [liste] electoral ; [succès] electoral, election *(modif)* ; [campagne] election *(modif)* ▶ **en période électorale** at election time.

électoralisme [elɛktɔʀalism] nm *péj* electioneering.

électorat [elɛktɔʀa] nm [électeurs] electorate ▶ **l'importance de l'électorat féminin / noir** the importance of the women's / the black vote.

électricien, enne [elɛktʀisjɛ̃, ɛn] nm, f [artisan] electrician.

électricité [elɛktʀisite] nf **1.** INDUST, SCI & TECHNOL electricity ▶ **électricité statique** static (electricity) **2.** [installation domestique] wiring / *faire installer l'électricité dans une maison* to have a house wired ▶ **allumer l'électricité** [au compteur] to switch on (at) the mains **3.** *fam* [tension] tension, electricity / *il y a de l'électricité dans l'air !* there's a storm brewing!

électrifier [9] [elɛktʀifje] vt [ligne de chemin de fer] to electrify.

électrique [elɛktʀik] adj TECHNOL [moteur, radiateur, guitare] electric ; [appareil, équipement] electric, electrical ; [système, énergie] electrical ▶ **atmosphère électrique** *fig* highly-charged atmosphere ▶ **chaise électrique** electric chair.

électro [elɛktʀo] nf inv electro.

électrocardiogramme [elɛktʀokaʀdjɔgʀam] nm electrocardiogram.

électrochoc [elɛktʀoʃɔk] nm electric shock *(for therapeutic purposes)* ▶ **faire des électrochocs à qqn** to give sb electroconvulsive therapy.

électrocuter [3] [elɛktʀokyte] vt to electrocute. ❖ **s'électrocuter** vp *(emploi réfléchi)* to electrocute o.s., to be electrocuted.

électrode [elɛktʀɔd] nf electrode.

électroencéphalogramme [elɛktʀoɑ̃sefalɔgʀam] nm electroencephalogram.

électromagnétique [elɛktʀomaɲetik] adj electromagnetic.

électroménager [elɛktʀomenaʒe] ❖ adj (domestic ou household) electrical. ❖ nm ▶ **l'électroménager a)** [appareils] domestic ou household electrical appliances **b)** [activité] the domestic ou household electrical appliance industry.

électron [elɛktʀɔ̃] nm electron.

électronicien, enne [elɛktʀonisjɛ̃, ɛn] nm, f electronics engineer.

électronique [elɛktʀonik] ❖ adj **1.** INDUST & TECHNOL [équipement] electronic ; [microscope] electron *(modif)* ; [industrie] electronics *(modif)* **2.** MUS electronic. ❖ nf electronics *(sg)*.

électrophone [elɛktʀofɔn] nm record player.

élégamment [elegamɑ̃] adv [s'habiller] elegantly, smartly ; [écrire, parler] stylishly, elegantly.

élégance [elegɑ̃s] nf **1.** [chic] elegance, smartness **2.** [délicatesse - d'un geste, d'un procédé] elegance **3.** [harmonie] grace, elegance, harmoniousness.

élégant, e [elegɑ̃, ɑ̃t] adj **1.** [chic - personne, mobilier] elegant, smart, stylish **2.** [courtois - procédé, excuse] handsome, graceful **3.** [harmonieux - architecture, proportions] elegant, harmonious, graceful ; [-démonstration] elegant, neat.

élément [elemɑ̃] nm **1.** [donnée] element, factor, fact / *il n'y a aucun élément nouveau* there are no new developments **2.** [personne] element / *c'est un des meilleurs éléments de mon service* he's one of the best people in my department / *il y a de bons éléments dans ma classe* there are some good students in my class **3.** [de mobilier] ▶ **élément (de cuisine)** kitchen unit ▶ **éléments de rangement** storage units **4.** [milieu] element ▶ **être dans son élément** to be in one's element ▶ **se sentir dans son élément** : *je ne me sens pas dans mon élément ici* I don't feel at home ou I feel like a fish out of water here.

élémentaire [elemɑ̃tɛʀ] adj **1.** [facile - exercice] elementary **2.** [fondamental - notion, principe] basic, elementary.

éléphant [elefɑ̃] nm **1.** elephant ▶ **éléphant d'Asie / d'Afrique** Indian / African elephant **2.** 🇧🇪 & 🇶🇨 ▶ **éléphant blanc** white elephant. ❖ **éléphant de mer** nm sea elephant, elephant seal.

élevage [ɛlvaʒ] nm **1.** [activité] animal husbandry, breeding ou rearing *(of animals)* ▶ **faire de l'élevage** to breed animals ▶ **élevage de poulets** ou **volaille a)** [intensif] battery-farming of chickens **b)** [extensif] rearing free-range chickens, free-range chicken-farming ▶ **élevage industriel** factory farming **2.** [entreprise] farm. ❖ **d'élevage** loc adj [poulet] battery-reared.

élévation [elevasjɔ̃] nf **1.** [augmentation] rise / *éléva-tion du niveau de vie* rise in the standard of living **2.** ARCHIT [construction] erection, putting up ; [plan] elevation.

élève [elɛv] nmf **1.** ÉDUC [enfant] pupil ; [adolescent] student ▸ **élève professeur** student ou trainee teacher **2.** [disciple] disciple, pupil **3.** MIL cadet.

élevé, e [elve] adj **1.** [fort -prix, niveau de vie] high ▸ **taux peu élevé** low rate **2.** [étage] high ; [arbre] tall, lofty *litt* **3.** [important -position] high, high-ranking ; [-rang, condition] high, elevated **4.** [éduqué] ▸ **bien élevé** well-mannered, well-bred, well brought-up ▸ **mal élevé** bad-mannered, ill-mannered, rude / *c'est très mal élevé de répondre* it's very rude ou it's bad manners to answer back.

élever [19] [elve] vt **1.** [éduquer -enfant] to bring up *(sép)*, to raise **2.** [nourrir -bétail] to breed, to raise ; [-moutons, chiens] to breed ; [-abeilles] to keep **3.** [hisser -fardeau] to raise, to lift (up) *(sép)* **4.** [ériger -statue, chapiteau] to erect, to raise, to put up *(sép)* **5.** [augmenter -prix, niveau, volume] to raise ▸ **élever la voix** ou **le ton** to raise one's voice **6.** [manifester -objection, protestation] to raise ; [-critique] to make **7.** [ennoblir] to elevate, to uplift ▸ **élever le débat** to raise the tone of the debate **8.** [vin] to mature. ❖ **s'élever** vpi **1.** [augmenter -taux, niveau] to rise, to go up **2.** [se manifester] ▸ **s'élever contre a)** [protester contre] to protest against **b)** [s'opposer à] to oppose **3.** [monter -oiseau] to soar, to fly ou to go up, to ascend ; [-cerf-volant] to go up, to soar **4.** [être dressé -falaise, tour] to rise ; [-mur, barricades] to stand **5.** *fig* [moralement, socialement] to rise ▸ **s'élever dans l'échelle sociale** to work one's way up ou to climb the social ladder. ❖ **s'élever à** vp + prép [facture, bénéfices, pertes] to total, to add up to, to amount to.

éleveur, euse [elvœʀ, øz] nm, f stockbreeder ▸ **éleveur de bétail** cattle breeder ou farmer, cattle rancher US / *éleveur de chiens* dog breeder / *éleveur de moutons* / *volaille* sheep / chicken farmer.

elfe [ɛlf] nm elf.

éligible [eliʒibl] adj POL eligible.

élimé, e [elime] adj worn, threadbare.

élimination [eliminasjɔ̃] nf [exclusion] elimination, eliminating, excluding / *procéder par élimination* to use a process of elimination.

éliminatoire [eliminatwaʀ] ◆ adj [note, épreuve] eliminatory ; [condition, vote] disqualifying. ◆ nf *(souvent au pl)* SPORT preliminary heat.

éliminer [3] [elimine] vt **1.** [se débarrasser de] to remove, to get rid of ; PHYSIOL [déchets, urine] to eliminate ; *(en usage absolu)* : *il faut boire pour éliminer* you have to drink to clean out your system **2.** SPORT to eliminate, to knock out *(sép)* **3.** [rejeter -hypothèse, possibilité] to eliminate, to dismiss, to rule out *(sép)*.

élire [106] [eliʀ] vt **1.** POL to elect / *élire un nouveau président* to elect ou to vote in a new president **2.** [EXPR] **élire domicile à** to take up residence ou to make one's home in.

élision [elizjɔ̃] nf elision.

élite [elit] nf [groupe] elite. ❖ **d'élite** loc adj elite *(modif)*, top *(avant nom)*.

élitiste [elitist] adj & nmf elitist.

élixir [eliksiʀ] nm MYTH & PHARM elixir / *élixir d'amour* / *de longue vie* elixir of love / life.

elle [ɛl] *(pl* **elles)** pron pers f **1.** [sujet d'un verbe -personne] she ; [-animal, chose] it ; [-animal de compagnie] she ▸ **elles** they **2.** [emphatique -dans une interrogation] : *ta mère est-elle rentrée ?* has your mother come back? **3.** [emphatique -avec «qui» et «que»] : *c'est elle qui me l'a dit* she's the one who told me, it was she who told me **4.** [complément -personne] her ; [-animal, chose] it ; [-animal de compagnie] her / *dites-le-lui à elle* tell it to her, tell her it.

elle-même [ɛlmɛm] pron pers [désignant -une personne] herself ; [-une chose] itself / **elles-mêmes** themselves.

ellipse [elips] nf **1.** MATH ellipse **2.** LING ellipsis.

elliptique [eliptik] adj MATH elliptic, elliptical.

élocution [elɔkysjɔ̃] nf [débit] delivery ; [diction] diction, elocution.

éloge [elɔʒ] nm [compliment] praise ▸ **digne d'éloges** praiseworthy ▸ **faire l'éloge de** to speak highly of ou in praise of.

élogieux, euse [elɔʒjø, øz] adj laudatory, complimentary, eulogistic / *parler en termes élogieux de* to speak very highly of, to be full of praise for.

éloigné, e [elwaɲe] adj **1.** [loin de tout -province, village] distant, remote, faraway **2.** [distant] : *les deux villes sont éloignées de 50 kilomètres* the two towns are 50 kilometres apart ▸ **éloigné de** [à telle distance de] : *ce n'est pas très éloigné de l'aéroport* it's not very far (away) from the airport / *se tenir éloigné du feu* to keep away from the fire **3.** [dans le temps] distant, remote, far-off / *dans un passé / avenir pas si éloigné que ça* in the not-too-distant past / future **4.** [par la parenté] distant.

éloignement [elwaɲmã] nm [distance dans l'espace] distance, remoteness.

éloigner [3] [elwaɲe] vt **1.** [mettre loin] to move ou to take away *(sép)* **2.** [séparer] ▸ **éloigner qqn de** to take sb away from **3.** [repousser -insectes, mauvaises odeurs] to keep off *(sép)*, to keep at bay **4.** [dissiper -idée, souvenir] to banish, to dismiss ; [-danger] to ward off *(sép)* ▸ **éloigner les soupçons de qqn** to avert suspicion from sb. ❖ **s'éloigner** vpi **1.** [partir -tempête, nuages] to pass, to go away ; [-véhicule] to move away ; [-personne] to go away / *ne vous éloignez pas trop, les enfants* don't go too far (away), children / *éloignez-vous du bord de la falaise* move away ou get back from the edge of the cliff ▸ **s'éloigner du sujet** to wander away from ou off the point **2.** [affectivement] : *il la sentait qui s'éloignait de lui* he could feel that she was growing away from him ou becoming more and more distant.

élongation [elɔ̃gasjɔ̃] nf MÉD [d'un muscle] strained ou pulled muscle ; [d'un ligament] pulled ligament ▸ **se faire une élongation a)** [d'un muscle] to strain ou to pull a muscle **b)** [d'un ligament] to pull a ligament.

éloquence [elɔkãs] nf **1.** [art de parler] eloquence, fine oratory **2.** [expressivité] eloquence, expressiveness ▸ **avec éloquence** eloquently.

éloquent, e [elɔkã, ãt] adj **1.** [parlant bien] eloquent **2.** [convaincant -paroles] eloquent, persuasive ; [-chiffres, réaction] eloquent **3.** [expressif] eloquent, expressive ▸ **ces images sont éloquentes** these pictures speak volumes ou for themselves.

élu, e [ely] ◆ adj **1.** RELIG chosen **2.** POL elected. ◆ nm, f **1.** POL [député] elected representative ; [conseiller] elected representative, councillor ▸ **les élus locaux** local councillors **2.** *hum* [bien-aimé] : *qui est l'heureux élu ?* who's the lucky man? ▸ **l'élu de mon / ton cœur** my / your beloved.

élucider [3] [elyside] vt [mystère] to elucidate, to explain, to clear up *(sép)* ; [problème, texte] to elucidate, to clarify.

éluder [3] [elyde] vt to elude, to evade.

Élysée [elize] npr m POL ▸ **(le palais de) l'Élysée** the Élysée Palace *(the official residence of the French President).*

 L'Élysée

This eighteenth-century palace near the Champs-Élysées in Paris is the official residence of the French President. The name is often used to refer to the presidency itself.

émacié, e [emasje] adj emaciated, wasted.

e-mail [imel] nm email (message).

émail [emaj] (*pl* **émaux** [emo]) nm [matière] enamel. ❖ **émaux** nmpl coloured enamels. ❖ **d'émail, en émail** loc adj enamel (*modif*), enamelled UK, enameled US.

émanations [emanasjɔ̃] nfpl [vapeurs] smells, emanations ▸ **émanations toxiques** toxic fumes.

émancipation [emɑ̃sipasjɔ̃] nf [libération - gén] emancipation ; [- de la femme] emancipation, liberation.

émancipé, e [emɑ̃sipe] adj [peuple] emancipated ; [femme] emancipated, liberated.

émanciper [3] [emɑ̃sipe] vt **1.** [libérer - gén] to emancipate ; [- femmes] to emancipate, to liberate **2.** DR to emancipate. ❖ **s'émanciper** vpi [se libérer - gén] to become emancipated ; [- femme] to become emancipated ou liberated.

émaner [3] [emane] ❖ **émaner de** v + prép [suj : odeur, lumière] to emanate *sout* ou to come from ; [suj : demande, mandat] to come from, to be issued by ; [suj : autorité, pouvoir] to issue from / *il émanait d'elle un charme mélancolique* she had an aura of melancholy charm.

émarger [17] [emaʁʒe] vt [signer] to sign ; [annoter] to annotate.

emballage [ɑ̃balaʒ] nm [gén] packaging ; [papier] wrapper ; [matière] wrapping ou packing materials. ❖ **d'emballage** loc adj [papier] packing, wrapping.

emballement [ɑ̃balmɑ̃] nm **1.** [d'un cheval] bolting ; [d'un moteur] racing / *l'emballement des cours à la Bourse* the Stock-Exchange boom **2.** [enthousiasme] sudden passion, flight ou burst of enthusiasm **3.** [emportement] ▸ **dans un moment d'emballement** without thinking.

emballer [3] [ɑ̃bale] vt **1.** [empaqueter - marchandises] to pack (up) ; [- cadeau] to wrap (up) **2.** *fam* [enthousiasmer - projet, livre] to grab, to thrill (to bits) / *ça n'a pas l'air de l'emballer* he doesn't seem to think much of the idea **3.** *tfam* [séduire] to chat up, to pull UK. ❖ **s'emballer** vpi **1.** [cheval] to bolt ; [moteur] to race ; [cours, taux] to take off **2.** *fam* [s'enthousiasmer] to get carried away **3.** [s'emporter] to flare ou to blow up.

embarcadère [ɑ̃baʁkadɛʁ] nm landing stage, pier.

embarcation [ɑ̃baʁkasjɔ̃] nf (small) boat ou craft.

embardée [ɑ̃baʁde] nf [d'une voiture] swerve, lurch ; [d'un bateau] yaw, lurch ▸ **faire une embardée a)** [voiture] to swerve, to lurch **b)** [bateau] to yaw, to lurch.

embargo [ɑ̃baʁgo] nm ÉCON embargo / *lever l'embargo sur les ventes d'armes* to lift ou to raise the embargo on arms sales.

embarqué, e [ɑ̃baʁke] adj [équipement automobile] in-car.

embarquement [ɑ̃baʁkəmɑ̃] nm **1.** [de marchandises] loading **2.** [des passagers - d'un navire] embarkation, boarding ; [- d'un avion] boarding ▸ **embarquement immédiat porte 16** now boarding at gate 16.

embarquer [3] [ɑ̃baʁke] ❖ vt **1.** TRANSP [matériel, troupeau] to load ; [passagers] to embark, to take on board **2.** *fam* [emporter - voiture, chien] to cart off ou away (*sép*) **3.** *fam* [voler] to pinch, to filch, to nick UK **4.** *fam* [arrêter - gang, manifestant] to pull in / *se faire embarquer par les flics* to get pulled in by the police **5.** *fam* [entraîner] to lug ou to take off (*sép*) / *c'est eux qui l'ont embarqué dans cette affaire* they're the ones who got him involved ou mixed up in this business. ❖ vi **1.** [aller à bord] to board, to go aboard ou on board **2.** [partir en bateau] to embark / *nous embarquons demain pour Rio* we're embarking ou sailing for Rio tomorrow. ❖ **s'embarquer** vpi [aller à bord] to embark, to go on board, to board. ❖ **s'embarquer**

dans vp + prép to embark on ou upon, to begin, to undertake / *dans quelle histoire me suis-je embarqué !* what sort of a mess have I got myself into!

embarras [ɑ̃baʁa] nm **1.** [malaise] embarrassment, confusion **2.** [souci] ▸ **l'embarras, les embarras** trouble ▸ **être dans l'embarras** [dans la pauvreté] to be short of money **3.** [cause de souci] nuisance, cause of annoyance **4.** [position délicate] predicament, awkward position ou situation ▸ **être dans l'embarras a)** [mal à l'aise] to be in a predicament ou in an awkward position **b)** [face à un dilemme] to be in ou caught on the horns of a dilemma ▸ **mettre dans l'embarras** : *ma question l'a mis dans l'embarras* my question put him on the spot ▸ **avoir l'embarras du choix** ou **n'avoir que l'embarras du choix** : *on les a en dix teintes, vous avez l'embarras du choix* ou *vous n'avez que l'embarras du choix* they come in ten different shades, you're spoilt for choice.

embarrassant, e [ɑ̃baʁasɑ̃, ɑ̃t] adj **1.** [gênant - silence, situation] embarrassing, awkward **2.** [difficile - problème, question] awkward, thorny, tricky **3.** [encombrant - colis, vêtement] cumbersome.

embarrassé, e [ɑ̃baʁase] adj **1.** [gêné - personne] embarrassed ; [- sourire, regard] embarrassed, uneasy **2.** [encombré] : *avoir les mains embarrassées* to have one's hands full.

embarrasser [3] [ɑ̃baʁase] vt **1.** [mettre mal à l'aise] to embarrass / *ça m'embarrasse de lui demander son âge* I'm embarrassed to ask her how old she is **2.** [rendre perplexe] : *ce qui m'embarrasse le plus c'est l'organisation du budget* what I find most awkward is how to organize the budget **3.** [encombrer] to clutter up (*sép*), to obstruct / *laisse ta valise ici, elle va t'embarrasser* leave your suitcase here, it'll get in your way. ❖ **s'embarrasser de** vp + prép **1.** [s'encombrer de] to burden o.s. with **2.** [s'inquiéter de] to trouble o.s. with / *sans s'embarrasser de présentations* without bothering with the (usual) introductions.

embauche [ɑ̃boʃ] nf hiring / *il n'y a pas d'embauche (chez eux)* they're not hiring anyone, there are no vacancies.

embaucher [3] [ɑ̃boʃe] vt to take on (*sép*), to hire.

embaumer [3] [ɑ̃bome] ❖ vt **1.** [parfumer - air] to make fragrant / *la lavande embaumait la salle* the scent of lavender filled the room **2.** [sentir - parfum] to be fragrant with the scent of ; [- odeur de cuisine] to be fragrant with the aroma of **3.** [momifier] to embalm. ❖ vi [femme] to be fragrant ; [mets] to fill the air with a pleasant smell ou a delicious aroma ; [fleur, plante] to fill the air with a lovely fragrance ou a delicate scent.

embellie [ɑ̃beli] nf MÉTÉOR [de soleil] bright interval ; [du vent] lull.

embellir [32] [ɑ̃beliʁ] ❖ vt **1.** [enjoliver - rue] to make prettier ; [- pièce] to decorate, to adorn / *embellir une femme* to make a woman prettier ou more beautiful **2.** [exagérer - histoire] to embellish, to embroider on (*insép*), to add frills to. ❖ vi (*aux avoir ou être*) to grow prettier ou more beautiful.

embellissement [ɑ̃belismɑ̃] nm **1.** [fait d'améliorer] embellishment, embellishing **2.** [apport - à un décor] embellishment ; [- à une histoire] embellishment, frill.

emberlificoter [3] [ɑ̃beʁlifikote] vt *fam* [compliquer] to muddle up (*sép*). ❖ **s'emberlificoter dans** vp + prép *fam* [récit, calcul] to get muddled ou mixed up with.

embêtant, e [ɑ̃bɛtɑ̃, ɑ̃t] adj *fam* **1.** [importun - enfant] annoying **2.** [gênant] tricky, awkward.

embêtement [ɑ̃bɛtmɑ̃] nm *fam* problem, hassle ▸ **embêtements** trouble ▸ **avoir des embêtements** : *va les voir* *au commissariat, sinon tu peux avoir des embêtements* go and see them at the police station or you could get into trouble.

embêter [4] [ãbɛte] vt *fam* **1.** [importuner] to annoy, to bother **2.** [lasser] to bore **3.** [mettre mal à l'aise] to annoy. ❖ **s'embêter** vpi *fam* **1.** [s'ennuyer] to be bored **2.** EXPR **il s'embête pas !** a) [il est sans scrupules] he's got a nerve ! b) [il est riche] he does pretty well for himself ! ❖ **s'embêter à** vp + prép : *je ne vais pas m'embêter à les éplucher* I'm not going to bother peeling them.

emblée [ãble] ❖ **d'emblée** loc adv straightaway, right away.

emblématique [ãblematik] adj emblematic.

emblème [ãblɛm] nm **1.** [blason] emblem **2.** [insigne] emblem, symbol.

embobiner [3] [ãbɔbine] vt **1.** [enrouler] to wind onto a bobbin **2.** *fam* [tromper] to take in *(sép)*, to hoodwink / *il t'a bien embobiné !* he really took you for a ride ! **3.** *fam* [manipuler] to get round *(insép)*.

emboîter, emboiter* [3] [ãbwate] vt [ajuster -tuyaux] to fit together ; [-poupées russes] to fit into each other. ❖ **s'emboîter, s'emboiter*** vpi to fit together ou into each other.

embolie [ãbɔli] nf embolism ▶ **embolie pulmonaire** pulmonary embolism.

embonpoint [ãbɔ̃pwɛ̃] nm stoutness, portliness ▶ **prendre de l'embonpoint** to flesh out, to become stout, to put on weight.

embouché, e [ãbuʃe] adj ▶ **mal embouché** *fam* a) [grossier] foulmouthed b) [de mauvaise humeur] in a foul mood.

embouchure [ãbuʃyʀ] nf **1.** GÉOGR mouth **2.** MUS mouthpiece, embouchure **3.** ÉQUIT mouthpiece.

embourber [3] [ãbuʀbe] ❖ **s'embourber** vpi [dans la boue] to get bogged down ou stuck in the mud.

embourgeoiser [3] [ãbuʀʒwaze] ❖ **s'embourgeoiser** vpi *péj* [gén] to become fonder and fonder of one's creature comforts ; [jeune couple] to settle down to a comfortable married life.

embout [ãbu] nm [bout -d'un tuyau] nozzle ; [-d'une seringue] adapter.

embouteillage [ãbutejaʒ] nm AUTO traffic jam ; [à un carrefour] gridlock 🇺🇸.

emboutir [32] [ãbutiʀ] vt [heurter] to crash into *(insép)* / *je me suis fait emboutir par un bus* I was hit by a bus / *l'aile est toute emboutie* the wing's all dented.

embranchement [ãbʀãʃmã] nm **1.** [carrefour -routier] fork ; [-intérieur] junction **2.** [voie annexe -routière] side road ; [-ferroviaire] branch line **3.** [d'égout] junction.

embraser [3] [ãbʀaze] vt *litt* **1.** [incendier] to set ablaze ou on fire, to set fire to **2.** [illuminer] to set ablaze ou aglow. ❖ **s'embraser** vpi *litt* **1.** [prendre feu] to catch fire, to blaze ou to flare up **2.** [s'illuminer] to be set ablaze.

embrassade [ãbʀasad] nf : *des embrassades* hugging and kissing, hugs and kisses.

embrasse [ãbʀas] nf tieback.

embrasser [3] [ãbʀase] vt **1.** [donner un baiser à] to kiss ▶ **je t'embrasse** a) [dans une lettre] with love b) [au téléphone] kiss kiss ! **2.** [adopter -idée] to embrace, to take up *(sép)* ; [-carrière] to take up. ❖ **s'embrasser** vp *(emploi réciproque)* to kiss (one another).

embrasure [ãbʀazyʀ] nf [de porte] door-frame ; [de fenêtre] window-frame ▶ **se tenir dans l'embrasure d'une porte / fenêtre** to be framed in a doorway / window.

embrayage [ãbʀɛjaʒ] nm **1.** [mécanisme] clutch **2.** [pédale] clutch (pedal).

embrayer [11] [ãbʀeje] ❖ vt AUTO to put in the clutch of. ❖ vi **1.** AUTO to put in ou to engage the clutch **2.** *fam* [commencer] to get cracking, to go into action ▶ **embrayer sur** to get straight into.

embrigader [3] [ãbʀigade] vt *péj* [faire adhérer] to press-gang.

embringuer [3] [ãbʀɛ̃ge] vt *fam* ▶ **embringuer qqn dans** to drag sb into.

embrocher [3] [ãbʀɔʃe] vt **1.** CULIN to spit, to spit-roast **2.** *fam* [transpercer] ▶ **embrocher qqn avec qqch** to run sthg through sb.

embrouillamini [ãbʀujamini] nm (hopeless) muddle ou mix-up.

embrouille [ãbʀuj] nf *fam* ▶ **des embrouilles** shenanigans, funny business.

embrouiller [3] [ãbʀuje] vt **1.** [emmêler] to tangle up ; *fig* ▶ **embrouiller qqn** to muddle sb, to confuse sb **2.** [compliquer] to complicate. ❖ **s'embrouiller** vpi to get muddled (up), to get confused.

embruns [ãbʀœ̃] nmpl ▶ **les embruns** the sea spray ou spume.

embryon [ãbʀijɔ̃] nm **1.** BIOL & BOT embryo **2.** *fig* [commencement] embryo, beginning / *un embryon de projet* embryonic project.

embryonnaire [ãbʀijɔnɛʀ] adj **1.** BIOL & BOT embryonic **2.** *fig* [non développé] embryonic, incipient / *idée encore à l'état embryonnaire* idea still at the embryonic stage.

embûche, embuche* [ãbyʃ] nf [difficulté] pitfall, hazard.

embuer [7] [ãbɥe] vt to mist (up ou over) / *des lunettes embuées* misted-up spectacles / *les yeux embués de larmes* eyes misty with tears.

embuscade [ãbyskad] nf ambush ▶ **se tenir en embuscade** to lie in ambush ▶ **tomber dans une embuscade** *pr & fig* to be caught in an ambush ▶ **tendre une embuscade à qqn** *pr & fig* to set up an ambush for sb.

embusquer [3] [ãbyske] ❖ **s'embusquer** vpi [pour attaquer] to lie in ambush.

éméché, e [emeʃe] adj tipsy.

émeraude [emʀod] ❖ nf emerald. ❖ adj inv emerald *(modif)*, emerald-green.

émergent, e [emɛʀʒã, ãt] adj *sout* [idée] emerging, developing.

émerger [17] [emɛʀʒe] vi **1.** *fam* [d'une occupation, du sommeil] to emerge ▶ **émerger de** to emerge from, to come out of **2.** [dépasser] ▶ **émerger de** [eau] to float (up) to the top of, to emerge from ▶ **une bonne copie / un bon élève qui émerge du lot** a paper / pupil standing out from the rest.

émeri [ɛmʀi] nm emery.

émérite [emeʀit] adj **1.** [éminent] (highly experienced and) skilled, expert *(avant nom)* **2.** ▶ **professeur émérite** emeritus professor.

émerveillement [emɛʀvɛjmã] nm [émotion] wonder, wonderment *litt*.

émerveiller [4] [emɛʀveje] vt to fill with wonder ou wonderment *litt*. ❖ **s'émerveiller** vpi to be filled with wonder, to marvel / *il s'émerveillait d'un rien* he marvelled at the smallest thing.

émetteur, trice [emetœʀ, tʀis] ❖ adj **1.** RADIO transmitting **2.** FIN issuing. ❖ nm, f FIN drawer. ❖ **émetteur** nm RADIO [appareil] transmitter ; [élément] emitter.

émettre [84] [emɛtʀ] ❖ vt **1.** [produire -rayon, son] to emit, to give out *(sép)* ; [-odeur] to give off *(sép)*, to produce **2.** [exprimer -hypothèse, opinion] to venture, to put forward ; [-doute, réserve] to express

3. FIN [billet] to issue ; [emprunt] to float **4.** RADIO & TV to broadcast, to transmit ; [onde, signal] to send out. ◆ vi : *émettre sur grandes ondes* to broadcast on long wave.

émeute [emøt] nf riot.

émeutier, ère [emøtje, ɛʀ] nm, f rioter.

émietter [4] [emjete] vt [mettre en miettes - gâteau] to crumble, to break up *(sép)* (into crumbs).

émigrant, e [emigʀɑ̃, ɑ̃t] nm, f emigrant.

émigration [emigʀasjɔ̃] nf emigration, emigrating *(U)*.

émigré, e [emigʀe] ◆ adj migrant. ◆ nm, f emigrant.

émigrer [3] [emigʀe] vi [s'expatrier] to emigrate.

émincé [emɛ̃se] nm émincé ▶ **émincé de veau** émincé of veal, veal cut into slivers *(and served in a sauce)*.

éminemment [eminamɑ̃] adv eminently.

éminence [eminɑ̃s] nf EXPR *c'est l'éminence grise du patron* he's the power behind the boss.

Éminence [eminɑ̃s] nf [titre] : *Son Éminence le cardinal Giobba* His Eminence Cardinal Giobba.

éminent, e [eminɑ̃, ɑ̃t] adj eminent, prominent, noted / *mon éminent collègue* sout my learned colleague.

émir [emiʀ] nm emir, amir.

émirat [emiʀa] nm emirate ▶ **les Émirats arabes unis** the United Arab Emirates.

émissaire [emiseʀ] nm [envoyé] emissary, envoy.

émission [emisjɔ̃] nf **1.** PHYS [de son, de lumière, de signaux] emission **2.** RADIO & TV [transmission de sons, d'images] transmission, broadcasting ; [programme] programme UK, program US ▶ **émission en direct / en différé** live / recorded broadcast **3.** FIN [de monnaie, d'emprunt] issuing.

emmagasiner [3] [ɑ̃magazine] vt **1.** COMM [marchandises - dans une arrière-boutique] to store ; [- dans un entrepôt] to warehouse **2.** [accumuler - connaissances] to store up *(sép)*, to accumulate ; [- provisions] to stock up on, to stockpile ▶ **emmagasiner la chaleur** to keep in the heat.

emmanchure [ɑ̃mɑ̃ʃyʀ] nf armhole.

emmêler [4] [ɑ̃mele] vt **1.** [mêler - cheveux, fils, brins de laine] to entangle, to tangle (up), to get into a tangle ▶ **complètement emmêlé** all tangled up **2.** [rendre confus, confondre] to mix up *(sép)* / *des explications emmêlées* confused ou muddled explanations. ◆ **s'emmêler** ◆ vpi [être mêlé] to be tangled ou knotted ou snarled up. ◆ vpt ▶ **s'emmêler les pieds dans** to get one's feet caught in ▶ **s'emmêler les pieds** ou **pédales** ou **pinceaux** ou **crayons dans qqch** fam & fig to get sthg all muddled up.

emménagement [ɑ̃menaʒmɑ̃] nm moving in.

emménager [17] [ɑ̃menaʒe] vi to move in.

emmener [19] [ɑ̃mne] vt **1.** [inviter à aller] to take along *(sép)* ▶ **emmener qqn dîner** to take sb out to dinner **2.** [forcer à aller] to take away *(sép)* **3.** [accompagner] ▶ **emmener qqn à la gare a)** [en voiture] to give sb a lift to ou to drop sb off at the station **4.** fam [emporter] to take (away) **5.** SPORT [sprint, peloton] to lead.

emmerdant, e [ɑ̃mɛʀdɑ̃, ɑ̃t] adj tfam **1.** [importun] : *il est emmerdant* he's a pain (in the neck) **2.** [gênant] bloody UK ou damn awkward **3.** [ennuyeux] bloody UK ou godawful US boring.

emmerdement [ɑ̃mɛʀdəmɑ̃] nm tfam hassle / *être dans les emmerdements jusqu'au cou* to be up the creek.

emmerder [3] [ɑ̃mɛʀde] vt tfam **1.** [gêner] to bug / *d'y aller, ça m'emmerde !* it's a bloody UK ou goddam US nuisance having to go! ▶ **se faire emmerder par qqn** to be hassled by sb **2.** *(comme exclamation)* : *je t'emmerde !* sod UK ou screw US you! ◆ **s'emmerder** vpi tfam

1. [s'ennuyer] to be bored stiff ou rigid / *on s'emmerde (à cent sous de l'heure) ici !* it's so bloody boring here! **2.** EXPR *il s'emmerde pas !* **a)** [il est sans scrupules] he's got a (bloody) nerve! **b)** [il est riche] he does pretty well for himself!

emmerdeur, euse [ɑ̃mɛʀdœʀ, øz] nm, f tfam bloody UK ou damn pain, pain in the arse UK ou ass US.

emmitoufler [3] [ɑ̃mitufle] vt to wrap up (well) *(sép)*. ◆ **s'emmitoufler** vp *(emploi réfléchi)* to wrap up well / *s'emmitoufler dans une cape* to wrap o.s. up in a cape.

émoi [emwa] nm litt [émotion] agitation ; [tumulte] commotion / *elle était tout en émoi* she was all in a fluster / *la population est en émoi* there's great agitation among the population.

émoluments [emɔlymɑ̃] nmpl [d'un employé] salary, wages ; [d'un notaire] fees.

émoticon [emotikɔ̃] nm INFORM emoticon, smiley.

émotif, ive [emɔtif, iv] ◆ adj [personne] emotional, sentimental ; [trouble, choc] psychological. ◆ nm, f : *c'est un grand émotif* he's very emotional.

émotion [emosjɔ̃] nf **1.** [sensation] feeling ▶ **émotions fortes** strong feelings **2.** [affectivité] emotion, emotionality. ◆ **émotions** nfpl fam ▶ **donner des émotions à qqn** to give sb a (nasty) turn ou a fright.

émotionnel, elle [emosjɔnel] adj [réaction] psychological.

émotivité [emɔtivite] nf emotionalism.

émousser [3] [emuse] ◆ **s'émousser** vpi [faiblir - appétit, peine] to dull ; [- curiosité] to become tempered.

émoustiller [3] [emustije] vt [animer] to excite, to exhilarate.

émouvant, e [emuvɑ̃, ɑ̃t] adj moving, touching / *de façon émouvante* movingly.

émouvoir [55] [emuvwaʀ] vt **1.** [attendrir] to touch, to move / *ému jusqu'aux larmes* moved to tears **2.** [perturber] to disturb, to unsettle. ◆ **s'émouvoir** vp **1.** [s'attendrir] to be touched ou moved / *s'émouvoir à la vue de* to be affected by the sight of **2.** [être perturbé] to be disturbed ou perturbed. ◆ **s'émouvoir de** vp + prép to pay attention to / *le gouvernement s'en est ému* it came to the notice ou attention of the government.

empailler [3] [ɑ̃paje] vt **1.** [animal] to stuff **2.** [chaise] to bottom with straw.

empaler [3] [ɑ̃pale] vt [supplicier] to impale. ◆ **s'empaler** vpi : *s'empaler sur une fourche / un pieu* to impale o.s. on a pitchfork / stake.

empaqueter [27] [ɑ̃pakte] vt **1.** COMM to pack, to package **2.** [envelopper] to wrap up *(sép)*.

✎ In reformed spelling (see p. 16-18), this verb is conjugated like *acheter : il empaquète, elle empaquèterait.*

emparer [3] [ɑ̃paʀe] ◆ **s'emparer de** vp + prép **1.** [avec la main - gén] to grab (hold of), to grasp, to seize ; [- vivement] to snatch **2.** [prendre de force - territoire] to take over *(sép)*, to seize ; [- véhicule] to commandeer **3.** [tirer parti de - prétexte, idée] to seize (hold of) **4.** [envahir] : *la colère s'est emparée d'elle* anger swept over her.

empâté, e [ɑ̃pate] adj [langue, voix] slurred.

empâter [3] [ɑ̃pate] ◆ **s'empâter** vpi to put on weight / *sa taille / figure s'est empâtée* he's grown fatter round the waist / fatter in the face.

empathie [ɑ̃pati] nf sout empathy.

empêchement [ɑ̃pɛʃmɑ̃] nm [obstacle] snag, hitch, holdup ▶ **si tu as un empêchement, téléphone a)** [si tu as un problème] if you hit a snag, phone **b)** [si tu ne viens pas] if you can't make it, phone **c)** [si tu es retenu] if you're held up, phone.

empêcher [4] [ɑ̃peʃe] ◆ vt **1.** [ne pas laisser] ▶ **empêcher qqn de faire qqch** to prevent sb (from) ou to keep sb from ou to stop sb (from) doing sthg ▶ **empêcher que qqn / qqch (ne) fasse** to stop sb / sthg from doing, to prevent sb / sthg from doing ▶ **empêcher qqn de dormir** pr : *le café m'empêche de dormir* coffee keeps me awake / *ce n'est pas ça qui va l'empêcher de dormir !* fig he's not going to lose any sleep over that! **2.** [pour renforcer une suggestion] to stop, to prevent ▶ **cela ne t'empêche pas** ou **rien ne t'empêche de l'acheter à crédit** you could always buy it in instalments **3.** [prévenir - mariage, famine] to prevent, to stop. ◆ v impers : *il n'empêche qu'elle ne l'a jamais compris* the fact remains that she's never understood him. **❖ s'empêcher de** vp + prép ▶ **s'empêcher de faire** to refrain from ou to stop o.s. doing / *je ne peux pas m'empêcher de penser qu'il a raison* I can't help thinking he's right. **❖ n'empêche** loc adv fam all the same, though / *n'empêche, tu aurais pu (me) prévenir !* all the same ou even so, you could have let me know!

empêcheur, euse [ɑ̃peʃœʀ, øz] nm, f ▶ **un empêcheur de danser** ou **tourner en rond** fam a spoilsport.

empereur [ɑ̃pʀœʀ] nm emperor.

empester [3] [ɑ̃peste] ◆ vt [pièce] to stink out *(sép)* 🇬🇧, to make stink ; [parfum] to stink of. ◆ vi to stink.

empêtrer [4] [ɑ̃petʀe] **❖ s'empêtrer** vpi **1.** [s'entortiller] to become tangled up ou entangled **2.** [s'enferrer] ▶ **s'empêtrer dans** [mensonges, explications] to get bogged down ou tied up in.

emphase [ɑ̃faz] nf péj [grandiloquence] pomposity, bombast ▶ **avec emphase** pompously, bombastically.

emphatique [ɑ̃fatik] adj **1.** péj [grandiloquent] pompous, bombastic **2.** LING emphatic.

empiéter [18] [ɑ̃pjete] **❖ empiéter sur** v + prép **1.** [dans l'espace, le temps] to encroach on ou upon *(insép)*, to overlap with *(insép)* **2.** [droit, liberté] to encroach on ou upon *(insép)*, to cut ou to eat into *(insép)*.

✍ In reformed spelling (see p. 16-18), this verb is conjugated like *semer* : *il empiétera, elle empiéterait.*

empiffrer [3] [ɑ̃pifʀe] **❖ s'empiffrer** vpi fam to stuff o.s.

empiler [3] [ɑ̃pile] vt [mettre en tas] to pile ou to heap up *(sép)* ; [ranger en hauteur] to stack (up). **❖ s'empiler** ◆ vp (emploi passif) to be stacked up. ◆ vpi [s'entasser] to pile up ▶ **s'empiler dans** [entrer nombreux dans] to pile ou to pack into.

empire [ɑ̃piʀ] nm **1.** [régime, territoire] empire ▶ **je ne m'en séparerais pas pour (tout) un empire !** I wouldn't be without it for the world! **2.** COMM & INDUST empire **3.** sout [influence] influence ▶ **avoir de l'empire sur qqn** to have a hold on ou over sb. **❖ sous l'empire de** loc prép sout [poussé par] ▶ **sous l'empire de l'alcool** under the influence of alcohol / *sous l'empire de la jalousie* in the grip of jealousy.

empirer [3] [ɑ̃piʀe] ◆ vi [santé] to become worse, to worsen, to deteriorate ; [mauvais caractère] to become worse ; [problème, situation] to get worse. ◆ vt to make worse, to cause to deteriorate.

empirique [ɑ̃piʀik] adj **1.** PHILOS & SCI empirical **2.** péj [non rigoureux] empirical, purely practical.

emplacement [ɑ̃plasmɑ̃] nm **1.** [position - d'un édifice, d'un monument] site, location ; [- d'une démarcation] position, place ▶ **emplacement publicitaire** advertising space **2.** [pour véhicule] parking space.

emplâtre [ɑ̃plɑtʀ] nm PHARM plaster.

emplette [ɑ̃plɛt] nf [fait d'acheter] ▶ **faire ses / des emplettes** to do one's / some shopping.

emploi [ɑ̃plwa] nm **1.** [travail] job ▶ **il est sans emploi** he is unemployed ou out of a job **2.** ÉCON ▶ **l'emploi** employment ▶ **la situation de l'emploi** the job ou employment situation **3.** [au spectacle] part ▶ **avoir le physique** ou **la tête de l'emploi** to look the part **4.** [utilisation] use **5.** ÉDUC ▶ **emploi du temps a)** [de l'année] timetable 🇬🇧, schedule 🇺🇸 **b)** [d'une journée, des vacances] timetable 🇬🇧, schedule 🇺🇸 / *un emploi du temps chargé* a busy timetable ou schedule **6.** 🇶🇧 ▶ **être à l'emploi de qqn** to be employed by sb.

employable [ɑ̃plwajabl] adj [personne] employable ; [objet] usable.

employé, e [ɑ̃plwaje] nm, f employee ▶ **employé de banque** bank clerk ▶ **employé de bureau** office worker ▶ **employé du gaz** : *j'attends un employé du gaz* I'm expecting someone from the gas board 🇬🇧 ou company 🇺🇸 ▶ **employé de maison** servant ▶ **employé des postes** postal worker.

employer [13] [ɑ̃plwaje] vt **1.** [professionnellement] to employ ▶ **employer qqn à faire qqch** [l'assigner à une tâche] to use sb to do sthg **2.** [manier - instrument, machine] to use **3.** [mettre en œuvre - méthode, ruse] to employ, to use ▶ **employer son énergie à faire qqch** to devote ou to apply one's energy to doing sthg ▶ **de l'argent bien employé** money well spent, money put to good use **4.** [expression] to use / *mal employer un mot* to misuse a word, to use a word incorrectly **5.** [temps, journée] to spend ▶ **bien employer son temps** to make good use of one's time ▶ **mal employer son temps** to misuse one's time, to use one's time badly, to waste one's time.

employeur, euse [ɑ̃plwajœʀ, øz] nm, f employer.

empocher [3] [ɑ̃pɔʃe] vt **1.** [mettre dans sa poche] to pocket **2.** [s'approprier] to snap up *(sép)*.

empoignade [ɑ̃pwaɲad] nf **1.** [coups] brawl, set-to **2.** [querelle] row, set-to.

empoigner [3] [ɑ̃pwaɲe] vt [avec les mains] to grab, to grasp.

empoisonnant, e [ɑ̃pwazɔnɑ̃, ɑ̃t] adj fam [exaspérant] annoying.

empoisonnement [ɑ̃pwazɔnmɑ̃] nm PHYSIOL poisoning.

empoisonner [3] [ɑ̃pwazɔne] vt **1.** [tuer] to poison **2.** ÉCOL to contaminate, to poison **3.** [dégrader - rapports] to poison, to taint, to blight ; [- esprit] to poison ▶ **empoisonner l'existence à qqn** to make sb's life a misery **4.** [importuner] to bother. **❖ s'empoisonner** vpi **1.** PHYSIOL to get food poisoning **2.** fam [s'ennuyer] to be bored stiff. **❖ s'empoisonner à** vp + prép [se donner du mal pour] : *je ne vais pas m'empoisonner à coller toutes ces enveloppes !* I can't be bothered to seal all those envelopes!

emporté, e [ɑ̃pɔʀte] adj [coléreux - homme] quick-tempered ; [- ton] angry.

emportement [ɑ̃pɔʀtəmɑ̃] nm [colère] anger *(U)* ; [accès de colère] fit of anger ▶ **avec emportement** angrily.

emporte-pièce [ɑ̃pɔʀtəpjɛs] *(pl* emporte-pièces*)* nm TECHNOL punch. **❖ à l'emporte-pièce** loc adj incisive.

emporter [3] [ɑ̃pɔʀte] vt **1.** [prendre avec soi] to take ▶ **ne pas l'emporter au paradis** : *il ne l'emportera pas au paradis !* he's not getting away with that! **2.** [transporter - stylo, parapluie, chaton] to take ; [- bureau, piano, blessé] to carry (off ou away) **3.** [retirer - livre, stylo] to take (away), to remove ; [- malle, piano] to carry away *(sép)*, to remove **4.** [endommager] to tear off / *il a eu le bras emporté par l'explosion* he lost an arm in the explosion, the explosion blew his arm off / *cette sauce emporte la bouche* this sauce takes the roof of your mouth off **5.** [émouvoir - suj :

amour, haine] to carry (along) *(sép)* ; [-suj : élan] to carry away *(sép)* / *il s'est laissé emporter par son imagination* he let his imagination run away with him **6.** [tuer - suj : maladie] : *il a été emporté par un cancer* he died of cancer **7.** [gagner - victoire] to win, to carry off *(sép)* ▶ **emporter la décision** to win ou to carry the day ▶ **emporter l'adhésion de qqn** to win sb's support ▶ **l'emporter sur** to win ou to prevail over. ⬦ **s'emporter** vpi [personne] to lose one's temper, to flare up. ⬦ **à emporter** loc adj to take away 🇬🇧, to take out 🇺🇸, to go 🇺🇸 ▶ **nous faisons des plats à emporter** we have a takeaway 🇬🇧 ou takeout 🇺🇸 service.

empoté, e [ɑ̃pɔte] *fam* ◆ adj clumsy, awkward. ◆ nm, f clumsy oaf.

empreinte [ɑ̃pʀɛ̃t] nf **1.** [du pas humain] footprint ; [du gibier] track ▶ **empreintes (digitales)** fingerprints **2.** [influence] mark, stamp **3.** [d'une dent] impression **4.** BIOL ▶ **empreinte génétique** genetic fingerprint **5.** ÉCOL ▶ **empreinte écologique** ecological footprint ▶ **empreinte carbone** carbon footprint.

empressé, e [ɑ̃pʀese] adj [fiancé] thoughtful, attentive ; [serveuse, garde-malade] attentive ; *péj* overzealous.

empressement [ɑ̃pʀɛsmɑ̃] nm **1.** [zèle] assiduousness, attentiveness ▶ **montrer de l'empressement** to be eager to please **2.** [hâte] enthusiasm, eagerness, keenness / *il est allé les chercher avec empressement / sans (aucun) empressement* he went off to get them enthusiastically / (very) reluctantly.

empresser [4] [ɑ̃pʀese] ⬦ **s'empresser** vpi ▶ **s'empresser autour** ou **auprès de qqn** a) [s'activer] to bustle around sb b) [être très attentif] to surround sb with attentions, to attend to sb's needs / *les hommes s'empressent autour d'elle* she always has men hovering around her. ⬦ **s'empresser de** vp + prép ▶ **s'empresser de faire qqch** to hasten to do sthg.

emprise [ɑ̃pʀiz] nf [intellectuelle, morale] hold / *l'emprise du désir* the ascendancy of desire / *sous l'emprise de la peur* in the grip of fear ▶ **être sous l'emprise de qqn** to be under sb's thumb.

emprisonnement [ɑ̃pʀizɔnmɑ̃] nm imprisonment / *condamné à 5 ans d'emprisonnement* sentenced to 5 years in prison, given a 5-year sentence ▶ **emprisonnement à perpétuité** life imprisonment.

emprisonner [3] [ɑ̃pʀizɔne] vt [incarcérer - malfaiteur] to imprison, to put in jail, to put in prison.

emprunt [ɑ̃pʀœ̃] nm **1.** FIN [procédé] borrowing ; [argent] loan ▶ **faire un emprunt** to borrow money, to take out a loan ▶ **emprunt d'État / public** national / public loan **2.** LING [processus] borrowing ; [mot] loan (word). ⬦ **d'emprunt** loc adj [nom] assumed.

emprunté, e [ɑ̃pʀœ̃te] adj [peu naturel - façon] awkward ; [-personne] awkward, self-conscious.

emprunter [3] [ɑ̃pʀœ̃te] vt **1.** FIN to borrow **2.** [outil, robe] to borrow **3.** [imiter - élément de style] to borrow, to take **4.** [route] to take ; [circuit] to follow / *vous êtes priés d'emprunter le souterrain* you are requested to use the underpass **5.** LING to borrow ▶ **mot emprunté** loan (word).

emprunteur, euse [ɑ̃pʀœ̃tœʀ, øz] nm, f borrower.

ému, e [emy] adj [de gratitude, de joie, par une musique, par la pitié] moved ; [de tristesse] affected ; [d'inquiétude] agitated ; [d'amour] excited ▶ **ému jusqu'aux larmes** moved to tears ▶ **parler d'une voix émue** to speak with (a voice full of) emotion ▶ **trop ému pour parler** too overcome by emotion to be able to speak.

émulation [emylasjɔ̃] nf **1.** [compétition] emulation **2.** INFORM emulation.

émule [emyl] nmf emulator.

émulsion [emylsjɔ̃] nf CHIM, CULIN & PHOT emulsion.

en [ɑ̃]
◆ prép

A. DANS LE TEMPS [indiquant - le moment] in ; [-la durée] in, during ▶ **en soirée** in the evening / *en 40 ans de carrière...* in my 40 years in the job...

B. DANS L'ESPACE 1. [indiquant - la situation] in ; [-la direction] to ▶ **se promener en forêt / en ville** to walk in the forest / around the town ▶ **aller en Espagne** to go to Spain ▶ **partir en forêt** to go off into the forest **2.** *fig* : *en moi-même, j'avais toujours cet espoir* deep down ou in my heart of hearts, I still had that hope / *ce que j'apprécie en lui* what I like about him.

C. DANS UN DOMAINE ▶ **bon en latin / physique** good at Latin / physics / *je ne m'y connais pas en peinture* I don't know much about painting ▶ **en cela** ou **ce en quoi il n'a pas tort** and I have to say he's right ou not wrong there.

D. INDIQUE LA COMPOSITION ▶ **chaise en bois / fer** wooden / iron chair / *c'est en quoi ?* *fam* what's it made of?

E. INDIQUE LA FAÇON, LE MOYEN 1. [marquant l'état, la forme, la manière] ▶ **être en colère / en rage** to be angry / in a rage / *être en forme* to be on (good) form / *en vacances* on holiday 🇬🇧 ou vacation 🇺🇸 / *je suis venu en ami* I came as a friend ▶ **peint en bleu** painted blue / *il était en pyjama* he was in his pyjamas, he had his pyjamas on ▶ **en (forme de) losange** diamond-shaped / *j'ai passé Noël en famille* I spent Christmas with my family ▶ **faire qqch en cachette / en vitesse / en douceur** to do sthg secretly / quickly / smoothly ▶ **du sucre en morceaux** sugar cubes **2.** [introduisant une mesure] / *auriez-vous la même robe en 38 ?* do you have the same dress in a 38? **3.** [indiquant une transformation] into / *l'eau se change en glace* water turns into ice ▶ **se déguiser en fille** to dress up as a girl **4.** [marquant le moyen] ▶ **j'y vais en bateau** I'm going by boat ▶ **en voiture / train** by car / train ▶ **avoir peur en avion** to be scared of flying ▶ **payer en liquide** to pay cash.

F. AVEC LE GÉRONDIF 1. [indiquant la simultanéité] : *il est tombé en courant* he fell while running / *nous en parlerons en prenant un café* we'll talk about it over a cup of coffee / *c'est en le voyant que j'ai compris* when I saw him I understood **2.** [indiquant la concession, l'opposition] : *en étant plus conciliant, il ne changeait toujours pas d'avis* whilst ou although he was more conciliatory, he still wouldn't change his mind **3.** [indiquant la cause, le moyen, la manière] : *il est parti en courant* he ran off / *retapez en changeant toutes les majuscules* type it out again and change all the capitals **4.** [introduisant une condition, une supposition] if ▶ **en supposant que...** supposing that...

G. DANS DES TOURNURES VERBALES in ▶ **croire en qqn / qqch** to believe in sb / sthg.

◆ pron

A. COMPLÉMENT DU VERBE 1. [indiquant le lieu] : *il faudra que tu ailles à la poste — j'en viens* you'll have to go to the post office — I've just got back from ou just been there **2.** [indiquant la cause, l'agent] : *elle était en dors plus* it's keeping me awake at nights / *elle était tellement fatiguée qu'elle en pleurait* she was so tired (that) she was crying **3.** [complément d'objet] : *passe-moi du sucre — il n'en reste plus* give me some sugar — there's none left ▶ **si tu n'aimes pas la viande / les olives, n'en mange pas** if you don't like meat / olives, don't eat any / *tu en as acheté beaucoup* you've bought a lot (of it / of them) **4.** [avec une valeur emphatique] : *tu en as de la chance !* you really are lucky, you are! **5.** [complément d'objet indirect] about it / *ne vous en souciez plus* don't worry about it any more.

B. COMPLÉMENT DU NOM : *j'en garde un bon souvenir* I have good memories of it.

C. COMPLÉMENT DE L'ADJECTIF : *sa maison en est pleine* his house is full of it / them **/ tu en es sûr ?** are you sure (of that)?

D. DANS DES LOCUTIONS VERBALES : *il en va de même pour lui* the same goes for him **▸ s'en prendre à qqn** to blame ou to attack sb.

EN nf abr de Éducation nationale.

ENA, Ena [ena] (abr de École nationale d'administration) npr f *prestigious grande école training future government officials.*

énarque [enaʀk] nmf *student or former student of the ENA.*

encadré [ɑ̃kadʀe] nm IMPR box.

encadrement [ɑ̃kadʀəmɑ̃] nm **1.** [mise sous cadre] framing ; [cadre] frame **2.** [embrasure - d'une porte] door frame ; [-d'une fenêtre] window frame / *il apparut dans l'encadrement de la porte* he appeared (framed) in the doorway **3.** [responsabilité - de formation] training ; [-de surveillance] supervision ; [-d'organisation] backing ; [personnel] **▸ l'encadrement a)** [pour former] the training staff **b)** [pour surveiller] the supervisory staff.

encadrer [3] [ɑ̃kadʀe] vt **1.** [dans un cadre] to (put into a) frame **2.** [border] to frame, to surround **3.** [flanquer] to flank **4.** [surveiller, organiser] to lead, to organize, to supervise **5.** *fam* [supporter - personne] to stand.

encaissé, e [ɑ̃kese] adj [vallée] deep, steep-sided.

encaisser [4] [ɑ̃kese] vt **1.** FIN [argent] to receive ; [chèque] to cash **2.** *fam* [gifle, injure, échec] to take / *encaisser un coup* SPORT to take a blow / *il n'a pas encaissé que tu lui mentes / ce que tu lui as dit* he just can't stomach the fact that you lied to him / what you told him ; *(en usage absolu)* : *ne dis rien, encaisse !* take it, don't say anything! **3.** *fam* [tolérer] : *je ne peux pas l'encaisser* I can't stand him.

encart [ɑ̃kaʀ] nm insert, inset **▸ encart publicitaire** advertising insert.

en-cas, encas [ɑ̃ka] nm inv snack, something to eat.

encastrable [ɑ̃kastʀabl] adj built-in.

encastrer [3] [ɑ̃kastʀe] vt **1.** [placard] to build in *(sép)*, to slot in *(sép)* ; [interrupteur] to recess, to fit flush ; [coffre-fort] to recess **2.** [dans un boîtier, un mécanisme] to fit. **◈ s'encastrer** vp [voiture] : *la voiture est venue s'encastrer sous le camion* the car jammed itself under the lorry.

encaustique [ɑ̃kostik] nf polish, wax.

enceinte¹ [ɑ̃sɛ̃t] nf **1.** [mur] **▸ (mur d')enceinte** surrounding wall **2.** [ceinture] enclosure, fence **3.** ACOUST speaker. **◈ dans l'enceinte de** loc prép within (the boundary of) / *dans l'enceinte du parc* within ou inside the park.

enceinte² [ɑ̃sɛ̃t] adj f [femme] pregnant / *enceinte de son premier enfant* expecting her first child **▸ enceinte de trois mois** three months pregnant.

encens [ɑ̃sɑ̃] nm [résine] incense.

encenser [3] [ɑ̃sɑ̃se] vt [louer - mérites] to praise to the skies ; [- écrivain] to praise to the skies, to shower praise upon.

encéphalogramme [ɑ̃sefalɔgʀam] nm encephalogram.

encéphalopathie [ɑ̃sefalɔpati] nf encephelopathy **▸ encéphalopathie spongiforme bovine** bovine spongiform encephalopathy.

encercler [3] [ɑ̃sɛʀkle] vt **1.** [entourer] to surround, to encircle, to form a circle around **2.** [cerner] to surround, to encircle, to hem in *(sép)*.

enchaînement, enchainement* [ɑ̃ʃɛnmɑ̃] nm **1.** [série] sequence, series *(sg)* / *un enchaînement de circonstances favorables* a series of favourable circumstances **2.** DANSE enchaînement, linked-up steps **3.** SPORT linked-up movements **▸ faire un enchaînement** to perform a sequence.

enchaîner, enchainer* [4] [ɑ̃ʃene] **◆** vt **1.** [lier - personne] to put in chains, to chain **▸ enchaîner à** to chain (up) to **2.** [relier - idées, mots] to link (up), to link ou to string together **3.** [dans une conversation] : *« c'est faux », enchaîna-t-elle* "it's not true", she went on. **◆** vi **1.** [poursuivre] to move ou to follow on **2.** RADIO & TV to link up two items of news **▸ enchaînons** let's go on to the next item. **◈ s'enchaîner, s'enchainer*** vpi [idées] to follow on (from one another) 🇬🇧, to be connected ; [images, épisodes] to form a (logical) sequence ; [événements] to be linked together.

enchanté, e [ɑ̃ʃɑ̃te] adj **1.** [magique] enchanted **2.** [ravi] delighted, pleased **▸ enchanté !** pleased to meet you! / *je serais enchanté de...* I'd be delighted ou very pleased to... / *enchanté de faire votre connaissance !* how do you do!, pleased to meet you!

enchantement [ɑ̃ʃɑ̃tmɑ̃] nm **1.** [en magie] (magic) spell, enchantment **▸ comme par enchantement** as if by magic **2.** [merveille] delight, enchantment / *la soirée fut un véritable enchantement* the evening was absolutely delightful ou enchanting.

enchanter [3] [ɑ̃ʃɑ̃te] vt [faire plaisir à] to enchant, to charm, to delight **▸ cela ne l'enchante pas (beaucoup)** ou **guère** he's none too pleased ou happy (at having to do it).

enchère [ɑ̃ʃɛʀ] nf **1.** [vente] auction **▸ vendre aux enchères** to sell by auction **▸ mettre aux enchères** to put up for auction **2.** [offre d'achat] bid **▸ faire monter les enchères a)** pr to raise the bidding **b)** fig to raise the stakes **3.** JEUX bid.

enchérir [32] [ɑ̃ʃeʀiʀ] **◈ enchérir sur** v + prép [dans une enchère] **▸ enchérir sur une offre** to make a higher bid **▸ enchérir sur qqn** to bid higher than sb.

enchevêtrer [4] [ɑ̃ʃəvetʀe] vt [mêler - fils, branchages] to tangle (up), to entangle. **◈ s'enchevêtrer** vpi **1.** [être emmêlé - fils] to become entangled, to get into a tangle ; [- branchages] to become entangled **2.** [être confus - idées, événements] to become confused ou muddled.

enclave [ɑ̃klav] nf **1.** [lieu] enclave **2.** [groupe, unité] enclave.

enclencher [3] [ɑ̃klɑ̃ʃe] vt **1.** MÉCAN to engage **2.** [commencer - démarche, procédure] to set in motion, to get under way, to set off *(sép)*. **◈ s'enclencher** vpi **1.** MÉCAN to engage **2.** [démarche, procédure] to get under way, to get started.

enclin, e [ɑ̃klɛ̃, in] adj **▸ enclin à qqch / à faire qqch** inclined to sthg / to do sthg / *peu enclin à partager ses secrets* reluctant to share his secrets.

enclos [ɑ̃klo] nm [terrain] enclosed plot of land ; [à moutons] pen, fold ; [à chevaux] paddock.

encoche [ɑ̃kɔʃ] nf [entaille] notch.

encoder [3] [ɑ̃kɔde] vt to encode.

encodeur, euse [ɑ̃kɔdœʀ, øz] nm, f encoder.

encoller [3] [ɑ̃kɔle] vt to paste, to size.

encolure [ɑ̃kɔlyʀ] nf ANAT, VÊT & ZOOL neck.

encombrant, e [ɑ̃kɔ̃bʀɑ̃, ɑ̃t] adj **1.** [volumineux] bulky, cumbersome / *j'ai dû m'en débarrasser, c'était trop encombrant* I had to get rid of it, it was taking up too much space ou it was getting in the way **2.** [importun] inhibiting, awkward / *le jeune couple trouvait la petite sœur encombrante* the young couple felt the little sister was in the way.

encombre [ãkɔ̃bʀ] ❖ **sans encombre** loc adv safely, without mishap.

encombré, e [ãkɔ̃bʀe] adj **1.** [route] ▸ **l'autoroute est très encombrée** traffic on the motorway is very heavy, there is very heavy traffic on the motorway **2.** [plein d'objets] ▸ **avoir les mains encombrées** to have one's hands full ▸ **un salon encombré** a cluttered living room **3.** [bronches] congested.

encombrement [ãkɔ̃bʀəmã] nm **1.** [embouteillage] traffic jam **2.** [fait d'obstruer] jamming, blocking ▸ **par suite de l'encombrement des lignes téléphoniques / de l'espace aérien** because the telephone lines are overloaded / the air space is overcrowded **3.** [dimension] size ▸ **meuble de faible encombrement** small ou compact piece of furniture.

encombrer [3] [ãkɔ̃bʀe] vt **1.** [remplir] to clutter (up), to fill ou to clog up *(sép)* ▸ **encombrer qqch de** to clutter sthg (up) with **2.** [obstruer - couloir] to block (up) ; [- route] to block ou to clog up *(sép)* ; [-circulation] to hold up *(sép)* **3.** [saturer] : *les logiciels encombrent le marché* there's a surplus ou glut of software packages on the market **4.** [charger - d'un objet lourd] to load (down), to encumber ▸ **encombrer qqn de** to load sb down with **5.** [suj : objet gênant] : *tiens, je te donne ce vase, il m'encombre* here, have this vase, I don't know what to do with it / *que diable de ces sacs qui nous encombrent ?* what shall we do with these bags that are in the way? **6.** [gêner] to burden, to encumber. ❖ **s'encombrer** vpi [avoir trop de bagages, de vêtements] to be loaded ou weighed down ▸ *laisse ta valise là si tu ne veux pas t'encombrer* leave your case there if you don't want to be weighed down / *il ne s'encombre pas de scrupules* he's not exactly overburdened with scruples.

encontre [ãkɔ̃tʀ] ❖ **à l'encontre de** loc prép *sout* ▸ **aller à l'encontre de** to go against, to run counter to / *cette décision va à l'encontre du but recherché* this decision is self-defeating ou counterproductive.

encore [ãkɔʀ] adv **1.** [toujours] still / *ils en sont encore à taper tout à la machine* they're still using typewriters **2.** [pas plus tard que] only / *ce matin encore, il était d'accord* only this morning he was in agreement **3.** [dans des phrases négatives] : *je n'ai pas encore fini* I haven't finished yet ▸ **encore rien** still nothing, nothing yet / *vous n'avez encore rien vu !* you haven't seen anything yet! **4.** [de nouveau] ▸ **tu manges encore !** you're not eating again, are you! / *si tu fais ça encore une fois…* if you do that again ou one more time ou once more… / *je te sers encore un verre ?* will you have another drink? ▸ **quoi encore ? a)** [dans une énumération] what else? **b)** *fam* [ton irrité] now what? ▸ **et puis quoi encore ? a)** [dans une émunération] what else? **b)** *iron* what the hell? **c)** [marquant l'incrédulité] whatever next? / *encore un qui ne sait pas ce qu'il veut !* another one who doesn't know what he wants! **5.** [davantage] : *il faudra encore travailler cette scène* that scene still needs more work on it ; [devant un comparatif] : *il est encore plus gentil que je n'imaginais* he is even nicer than I'd imagined (he'd be) ▸ **encore pire** even ou still worse **6.** [introduisant une restriction] : *c'est bien beau d'avoir des projets, encore faut-il les réaliser* it's all very well having plans, but the important thing is to put them into practice ▸ **et encore :** *je t'en donne 100 euros, et encore !* I'll give you 100 euros for it, if that! ▸ **encore heureux !** thank goodness for that! ▸ **encore une chance :** *encore une chance qu'il n'ait pas été là !* thank goodness ou it's lucky he wasn't there! ❖ **encore que** loc conj : *j'aimerais y aller, encore qu'il soit tard* I'd like to go even though it's late ▸ **encore que…** but then again…

encornet [ãkɔʀnɛ] nm squid.

encourageant, e [ãkuʀaʒã, ãt] adj [paroles] encouraging ; [succès, résultat] encouraging, promising.

encouragement [ãkuʀaʒmã] nm encouragement, support / *quelques mots d'encouragement* a few encouraging words ou words of encouragement.

encourager [ãkuʀaʒe] vt [inciter] to encourage ▸ **encourager qqn du geste** to wave to sb in encouragement ▸ **encourager qqn de la voix** to cheer sb (on) ▸ **encourager qqn à faire qqch** to encourage sb to do sthg.

encourir [45] [ãkuʀiʀ] vt [dédain, reproche, critique] to incur, to bring upon o.s.

encrasser [3] [ãkʀase] vt [obstruer - filtre] to clog up *(sép)* ; [-tuyau] to clog ou to foul up *(sép)* ; [-arme] to foul up *(sép)*. ❖ **s'encrasser** vpi **1.** [s'obstruer - filtre] to become clogged (up) ; [-tuyau] to become clogged (up), to become fouled up ; [-arme] to become fouled up **2.** [se salir] to get dirty.

encre [ãkʀ] nf **1.** [pour écrire] ink / *écrire à l'encre* to write in ink ▸ **encre de Chine** Indian ou India ink ▸ **encre électronique** electronic ink, e-ink **2.** ZOOL ink.

encrier [ãkʀije] nm [pot] inkpot ; [accessoire de bureau] inkstand ; [récipient encastré] inkwell.

encroûter, encrouter* [3] [ãkʀute] ❖ **s'encroûter, s'encrouter*** vpi *fam* [devenir routinier] to be in a rut / *il s'encroûte dans son métier* he's really in a rut in that job.

enculé, e [ãkyle] nm, f *vulg* bastard, arsehole , asshole .

enculer [3] [ãkyle] vt *vulg* to bugger, to fuck / *je t'encule !, va te faire enculer !* fuck off!

encyclopédie [ãsiklɔpedi] nf encyclopedia.

encyclopédique [ãsiklɔpedik] adj **1.** [d'une encyclopédie] encyclopedic **2.** [connaissances] exhaustive, extensive, encyclopedic.

endémique [ãdemik] adj [gén & MÉD] endemic.

endettement [ãdɛtmã] nm indebtedness / *le fort endettement des ménages* the high level of household debt ▸ **endettement extérieur** foreign debt.

endetter [4] [ãdete] vt FIN to get into debt / *il est lourdement endetté* he's heavily in debt. ❖ **s'endetter** vpi to get ou to run into debt / *je me suis endetté de 10 000 euros* I got 10,000 euros in debt.

endeuiller [5] [ãdœje] vt **1.** [famille, personne] to plunge into mourning **2.** [réception, course] to cast a tragic shadow over.

endiguer [3] [ãdige] vt **1.** [cours d'eau] to dyke (up) **2.** [émotion, développement] to hold back *(sép)*, to check ; [chômage, excès] to curb.

endimanché, e [ãdimãʃe] adj in one's Sunday best.

endive [ãdiv] nf chicory , (French) endive .

endoctrinement [ãdɔktʀinmã] nm indoctrination.

endoctriner [3] [ãdɔktʀine] vt to indoctrinate.

endolori, e [ãdɔlɔʀi] adj painful, aching.

endommager [17] [ãdɔmaʒe] vt [bâtiment] to damage ; [environnement, récolte] to damage, to harm.

endormi, e [ãdɔʀmi] adj **1.** [sommeillant] sleeping / *il est endormi* he's asleep ou sleeping / *à moitié endormi* half asleep **2.** [apathique] sluggish, lethargic.

---

asleep ou **sleeping ?**

On peut utiliser indifféremment **asleep** ou **sleeping** pour traduire *endormi*, mais attention, **asleep** s'emploie toujours comme attribut, alors que **sleeping** peut s'employer comme épithète ("a sleeping child" mais jamais "an asleep child").

endormir [36] [ɑ̃dɔʀmiʀ] vt **1.** [d'un sommeil naturel] to put ou to send to sleep ; [avec douceur] to lull to sleep / *j'ai eu du mal à l'endormir* I had a job getting him off to sleep **2.** [anesthésier] to anaesthetize, anesthetize US, to put to sleep **3.** [ennuyer] to send to sleep, to bore **4.** [affaiblir - douleur] to deaden ; [- scrupules] to allay. **❖ s'endormir** vpi **1.** [d'un sommeil naturel] to drop off ou to go to sleep, to fall asleep **2.** [sous anesthésie] to go to sleep **3.** [se relâcher] to let up, to slacken off.

endosser [3] [ɑ̃dose] vt **1.** [revêtir] to put ou to slip on *(sép)*, to don *sout* **2.** [assumer] to assume ▸ **endosser la responsabilité de qqch** to shoulder ou to assume the responsibility for sthg **3.** BANQUE & FIN to endorse.

endroit [ɑ̃dʀwa] nm **1.** [emplacement] place / *à quel endroit tu l'as mis ?* where ou whereabouts did you put it? / *ce n'est pas au bon endroit* it's not in the right place **2.** [localité] place, spot **3.** [partie - du corps, d'un objet] place ; [- d'une œuvre, [- d'une histoire] place, point / *cela fait mal à quel endroit ?* where does it hurt? / *en plusieurs endroits* in several places / *c'est l'endroit le plus drôle du livre* it's the funniest part ou passage in the book **4.** [d'un vêtement] right side. **❖ à l'endroit** loc adv **1.** [le bon côté en haut] right side up **2.** [le bon côté à l'extérieur] right side out **3.** [le bon côté devant] right side round / *remettre son pull à l'endroit* to put one's pullover on again the right way round **4.** TRICOT [dans les explications] ▸ **deux mailles à l'endroit** two plain, knit two. **❖ par endroits** loc adv in places, here and there.

enduire [98] [ɑ̃dɥiʀ] vt [recouvrir] to coat ou to spread ou to cover with *(sép)* ▸ **enduire de** : *enduire de beurre le fond d'un plat* to smear the bottom of a dish with butter. **❖ s'enduire de** v + prép ▸ **s'enduire de crème solaire** to cover oneself with suntan lotion.

enduit [ɑ̃dɥi] nm **1.** [revêtement] coat, coating, facing **2.** [plâtre] plaster.

endurance [ɑ̃dyʀɑ̃s] nf **1.** [d'une personne] endurance, stamina **2.** SPORT endurance.

endurci, e [ɑ̃dyʀsi] adj **1.** [invétéré] hardened, inveterate ▸ **célibataire endurci** confirmed bachelor **2.** [insensible - âme, caractère] hardened.

endurcir [32] [ɑ̃dyʀsiʀ] vt **1.** [rendre résistant - corps, personne] to harden, to toughen **2.** [rendre insensible] to harden. **❖ s'endurcir** vpi **1.** [devenir résistant] to harden o.s., to become tougher **2.** [devenir insensible] to harden one's heart.

endurer [3] [ɑ̃dyʀe] vt to endure, to bear, to stand.

énergétique [enɛʀʒetik] adj **1.** ÉCOL & ÉCON energy *(modif)* **2.** [boisson, aliment] energy-giving ; [besoins, apport] energy *(modif)*.

énergétiquement [enɛʀʒetikmɑ̃] adv in energy terms / *des logements énergétiquement performants* ou *efficaces* energy-efficient housing.

énergie [enɛʀʒi] nf **1.** [dynamisme] energy, stamina, drive / *se mettre au travail avec énergie* to start work energetically / *mettre toute son énergie à* to put all one's energy ou energies into **2.** [force] energy, vigour, strength **3.** SCI & TECHNOL energy, power ▸ **énergie alternative** alternative energy ▸ **énergie atomique** atomic energy ▸ **les énergie douces** alternative energy ▸ **énergie électrique / solaire** electrical / solar energy ▸ **les énergies fossiles** fossil fuels ▸ **énergie éolienne** wind power ▸ **énergie nucléaire** nuclear power ou energy ▸ **les énergies nouvelles** new sources of energy ▸ **énergie renouvelable** renewable energy ▸ **énergies de substitution** alternative energies ▸ **source d'énergie** source of energy.

énergique [enɛʀʒik] adj **1.** [fort - mouvement, intervention] energetic, vigorous ; [- mesure] energetic, drastic, extreme ; [- paroles] emphatic ; [- traitement] strong, powerful **2.** [dynamique - personne, caractère] energetic, forceful, active ; [- visage] determined-looking.

énergiquement [enɛʀʒikmɑ̃] adv [bouger, agir] energetically, vigorously ; [parler, refuser] energetically, emphatically.

énergisant, e [enɛʀʒizɑ̃, ɑ̃t] adj energizing, energy-giving.

énergivore [enɛʀʒivɔʀ] adj [secteur, activité, produit] energy-guzzling.

énergumène [enɛʀgymɛn] nmf energumen *litt*, wild-eyed fanatic ou zealot.

énervant, e [enɛʀvɑ̃, ɑ̃t] adj irritating, annoying, trying.

énervé, e [enɛʀve] adj **1.** [irrité] irritated, annoyed **2.** [agité] agitated, restless.

énervement [enɛʀvəmɑ̃] nm **1.** [agacement] irritation, annoyance **2.** [agitation] restlessness.

énerver [3] [enɛʀve] vt **1.** [irriter] to annoy, to irritate ▸ **cette musique m'énerve** this music is getting on my nerves **2.** [agiter] to make restless, to excite, to overexcite. **❖ s'énerver** vpi **1.** [être irrité] to get worked up ou annoyed ou irritated **2.** [être excité] to get worked up ou excited ou overexcited.

enfance [ɑ̃fɑ̃s] nf **1.** [période de la vie - gén] childhood ; [- d'un garçon] boyhood ; [- d'une fille] girlhood ▸ **la petite enfance** infancy, babyhood, early childhood **2.** [enfants] children / *l'enfance délinquante / malheureuse* delinquant / unhappy children.

enfant [ɑ̃fɑ̃] ◆ adj **1.** [jeune] : *il était encore enfant quand il comprit* he was still a child when he understood **2.** [naïf] childlike. ◆ nmf **1.** [jeune - gén] child ; [- garçon] little boy ; [- fille] little girl / *ne fais pas l'enfant !* act your age!, don't be such a baby!, grow up! ▸ **enfant de chœur** pr choirboy, altarboy ▸ **ce n'est pas un enfant de chœur** fig he's no angel ▸ **enfant gâté** spoilt child ▸ **l'enfant Jésus** Baby Jesus ▸ **enfant naturel / légitime** illegitimate / legitimate child ▸ **enfant unique** only child ▸ **grand enfant** overgrown child, big kid *fam* **2.** [descendant] child ▸ **faire un enfant** to have a child ▸ **enfant du pays** a) [homme] son of the soil b) [femme] daughter of the soil **3.** [en appellatif] child / *alors, les enfants, encore un peu de champagne ? fam* bit more champagne, guys ou folks?

enfantillage [ɑ̃fɑ̃tijaʒ] nm [action, parole] piece of childishness ▸ **arrête ces enfantillages !** don't be so childish!, do grow up!

enfantin, e [ɑ̃fɑ̃tɛ̃, in] adj **1.** [de l'enfance] childlike ; [adulte] childlike **2.** [simple] easy ▸ **c'est enfantin** there's nothing to it, it's child's play **3.** [puéril] childish, infantile, puerile.

enfarger [17] [ɑ̃faʀʒe] Québec vt [faire trébucher] to trip. **❖ s'enfarger** vp [s'empêtrer] to get bogged down.

enfer [ɑ̃fɛʀ] nm **1.** RELIG hell **2.** [lieu, situation désagréable] hell / *sa vie est un véritable enfer* his life is absolute hell. **❖ d'enfer** loc adv **1.** [très mauvais - vie] hellish ; [- bruit] deafening ; [- feu] blazing, raging **2.** [très bien] great / *il est d'enfer ton blouson !* what a brilliant ou wicked jacket!

enfermer [3] [ɑ̃fɛʀme] vt **1.** [mettre dans un lieu clos - personne, animal] to shut up ou in *(sép)* ▸ **il s'est fait enfermer** [chez lui] he got locked in **2.** [emprisonner - criminel] to lock up ou away *(sép)*, to put under lock and key ; [- fou] to lock up **3.** [ranger] to put ou to shut away *(sép)* ; [en verrouillant] to lock up ou away *(sép)* **4.** [confiner] to confine, to coop up *(sép)* / *ne restez pas enfermés, voilà le soleil !* don't stay indoors, the sun's come out! **❖ s'enfermer** vp *(emploi réfléchi)* **1.** [se cloîtrer - dans un couvent] to shut o.s. up ou away **2.** [verrouiller sa porte] to shut o.s. up ou in, to lock o.s. in ▸ **s'enfermer dehors**

to lock ou to shut o.s. out **3.** [s'isoler] to shut o.s. away ▸ **s'enfermer dans le silence** to retreat into silence ▸ **s'enfermer dans un rôle** to stick to a role.

enfilade [ɑ̃filad] nf [rangée] row, line. ❖ **en enfilade** loc adj ▸ **des pièces en enfilade** a suite of adjoining rooms.

enfiler [3] [ɑ̃file] vt **1.** [faire passer] : **enfiler un élastique dans un ourlet** to thread a piece of elastic through a hem **2.** [disposer - sur un fil] to thread ou to string (on) *(sép)* ; [- sur une tige] to slip on *(sép)* / **enfiler une aiguille** to thread a needle / **elle enfila ses bagues** she slipped her rings on **3.** [mettre - vêtement] to pull ou to slip on *(sép)*, to slip into *(sép)* / **enfiler son collant** to slip on one's tights. ❖ **s'enfiler** vpt *fam* [avaler - boisson] to knock back, to put away ; [- nourriture] to guzzle, to gobble up *(sép)*, to put away *(sép)*.

enfin [ɑ̃fɛ̃] adv **1.** [finalement] at last ▸ **enfin seuls !** alone at last ! / **un accord a été enfin conclu** an agreement has at last been reached ▸ **enfin bref...** [à la fin d'une phrase] anyway... / **il ne s'est pas excusé, comme d'habitude, enfin bref...** as usual he didn't apologize, but anyway / **enfin bref, je n'ai pas envie d'y aller** well, basically, I don't want to go **2.** [en dernier lieu] finally / **enfin, j'aimerais vous remercier de votre hospitalité** finally, I would like to thank you for your hospitality **3.** [en un mot] in short, in brief, in a word **4.** [cependant] still, however, after all / **elle est triste, mais enfin, elle s'en remettra** she's sad, but still, she'll get over it **5.** [avec une valeur restrictive] well, at least / **elle est jolie, enfin, à mon avis** she's pretty, (or) at least I think she is **6.** [emploi expressif] : **enfin ! c'est la vie !** oh well, such is life! ▸ **enfin, reprends-toi !** come on, pull yourself together! / **enfin qu'est-ce qu'il y a ?** what on earth is the matter? / **c'est son droit, enfin !** it's his right, after all! / **tu ne peux pas faire ça, enfin !** you can't ᴅo that!

enflammer [3] [ɑ̃flame] vt **1.** [mettre le feu à - bois] to light, to kindle, to ignite ; [- branchages] to ignite ; [- allumette] to light, to strike ; [- papier] to ignite, to set on fire, to set alight **2.** [exalter - imagination, passion] to kindle, to fire ; [- foule] to inflame **3.** MÉD to inflame. ❖ **s'enflammer** vpi **1.** [prendre feu - forêt] to go up in flames, to catch fire, to ignite ; [- bois] to burst into flame, to light **2.** [s'intensifier - passion] to flare up **3.** [s'enthousiasmer] to be fired with enthusiasm.

enflé, e [ɑ̃fle] adj [cheville, joue] swollen ; *fig* [style] bombastic, pompous.

enfler [3] [ɑ̃fle] vi [augmenter de volume - cheville] to swell (up) ; [- voix] to boom (out).

enflure [ɑ̃flyʀ] nf **1.** [partie gonflée] swelling **2.** *tfam* [personne détestable] jerk.

enfoiré, e [ɑ̃fwaʀe] nm, f *tfam* bastard.

enfoncer [16] [ɑ̃fɔ̃se] vt **1.** [faire pénétrer - piquet, aiguille] to push in *(sép)* ; [- vis] to drive ou to screw in *(sép)* ; [- clou] to drive ou to hammer in *(sép)* ; [- épingle, punaise] to push ou to stick in *(sép)* ; [- couteau] to stick ou to thrust in *(sép)* / **il a enfoncé le pieu d'un seul coup** he drove ou stuck the stake home in one ▸ **il faut enfoncer le clou** it's important to ram the point home **2.** [faire descendre] to push ou to ram (on) / **il enfonça son chapeau jusqu'aux oreilles** he rammed his hat onto his head **3.** [briser - côte, carrosserie] to stave in *(sép)*, to crush ; [- porte] to break down *(sép)*, to bash in *(sép)*, to force open *(sép)* ; [- barrière, mur] to smash, to break down *(sép)* / **la voiture a enfoncé la barrière** the car crashed through the fence ▸ **enfoncer une porte ouverte** ou **des portes ouvertes** to labour 🇬🇧 ou to labor 🇺🇸 the point **4.** [vaincre - armée, troupe] to rout, to crush / **enfoncer un adversaire** *fam* to crush an opponent. ❖ **s'enfoncer** ◆ vpi **1.** [dans l'eau, la boue, la terre] to sink (in) / **ils s'enfoncèrent dans la neige jusqu'aux genoux** they sank knee-deep into the snow /

les vis s'enfoncent facilement dans le bois screws go ou bore easily through wood **2.** [se lover] ▸ **s'enfoncer dans** to sink into **3.** [s'engager] ▸ **s'enfoncer dans** to penetrate ou to go into / **le chemin s'enfonce dans la forêt** the path runs into the forest / **plus on s'enfonce dans la forêt plus le silence est profond** the further you walk into the forest the quieter it becomes **4.** [s'affaisser - plancher, terrain] to give way, to cave in **5.** [aggraver son cas] to get into deep ou deeper waters, to make matters worse. ◆ vpt : **s'enfoncer une épine dans le doigt** to get a thorn (stuck) in one's finger / **s'enfoncer une idée dans la tête** *fam* to get an idea into one's head.

enfouir [32] [ɑ̃fwiʀ] vt **1.** [mettre sous terre - os, trésor] to bury **2.** [blottir] to nestle / **elle a enfoui sa tête dans l'oreiller** she buried her head in the pillow **3.** [cacher] to stuff, to bury. ❖ **s'enfouir** vpi **1.** [s'enterrer] to bury o.s. **2.** [se blottir] to burrow / **s'enfouir dans un terrier** / **sous les couvertures** to burrow in a hole / under the blankets.

enfourcher [3] [ɑ̃fuʀʃe] vt [vélo, cheval] to mount, to get on *(insép)* ; [chaise] to straddle ▸ **enfourcher son cheval de bataille** ou **son dada** to get on one's hobbyhorse.

enfourner [3] [ɑ̃fuʀne] vt **1.** [mettre dans un four] to put into an oven ▸ **enfourner des briques** to feed a kiln (with bricks) **2.** *fam* [entasser] to shove ou to cram ou to push (in) **3.** *fam* [manger] to put away *(sép)*, to wolf down *(sép)*.

enfreindre [81] [ɑ̃fʀɛ̃dʀ] vt to infringe.

enfuir [35] [ɑ̃fɥiʀ] ❖ **s'enfuir** vpi to run away, to flee ▸ **s'enfuir de chez soi** to run away from home.

enfumé, e [ɑ̃fyme] adj [pièce] smoky, smoke-filled ; [paroi] sooty.

enfumer [3] [ɑ̃fyme] vt **1.** [abeille, renard] to smoke out *(sép)* **2.** [pièce] to fill with smoke ; [paroi] to soot up *(insép)*.

engagé, e [ɑ̃gaʒe] ◆ adj [artiste, littérature] political, politically committed, engagé *sout*. ◆ nm, f MIL volunteer.

engageant, e [ɑ̃gaʒɑ̃, ɑ̃t] adj [manières, sourire] engaging, winning ; [regard] inviting ; [perspective] attractive, inviting.

engagement [ɑ̃gaʒmɑ̃] nm **1.** [promesse] commitment, undertaking, engagement *sout* / **faire honneur à** / **manquer à ses engagements** to honour / fail to honour one's commitments ▸ **passer un engagement avec qqn** to come to an agreement with sb ▸ **prendre l'engagement de** to undertake ou to agree to ▸ **respecter ses engagements envers qqn** to fulfil 🇬🇧 ou to fulfill 🇺🇸 one's commitments ou obligations towards sb ▸ **sans engagement de votre part a)** with no obligation on your part **b)** [dans une publicité] no obligation to buy **2.** [dette] (financial) commitment, liability / **faire face à ses engagements** to meet one's commitments **3.** [embauche] appointment, hiring ; CINÉ & THÉÂTRE job **4.** [prise de position] commitment **5.** SPORT [participation] entry ; FOOT kickoff.

engager [17] [ɑ̃gaʒe] vt **1.** [insérer - clef] to insert, to put in *(sép)* ; [- CD, disquette] to insert, to put ou to slot in *(sép)* **2.** [lier] to bind, to commit / **voilà ce que je pense, mais ça n'engage que moi** that's how I see it, but it's my own view / **cela ne vous engage à rien** it doesn't commit you to anything **3.** [mettre en jeu - énergie, ressources] to invest, to commit ; [- fonds] to put in *(sép)* ▸ **engager sa parole** to give one's word (of) honour 🇬🇧 ou honor 🇺🇸 **4.** [entraîner] to involve **5.** [inciter] ▸ **engager qqn à faire qqch** to advise sb to do sthg **6.** [commencer] to open, to start, to begin ▸ **engager la conversation avec qqn** to engage sb in conversation, to strike up a conversation with sb ▸ **l'affaire est mal engagée** the whole thing is off to a bad start **7.** [embaucher] to take on *(sép)*, to hire **8.** MIL [envoyer] to commit to military action ; [recruter] to enlist. ❖ **s'engager** vpi **1.** [commencer - négociations, procédure, tournoi] to start, to begin **2.** [prendre position] to take a stand **3.** MIL to enlist. ❖ **s'engager à** vp + prép ▸ **s'engager à faire qqch** [promettre] to commit o.s. to doing sthg, to undertake to do sthg / *tu sais à quoi tu t'engages ?* do you know what you're letting yourself in for? ❖ **s'engager dans** vp + prép **1.** [avancer dans - suj : véhicule, piéton] to go ou to move into / *la voiture s'est engagée dans une rue étroite* the car drove ou turned into a narrow street ▸ **s'engager dans un carrefour** to pull ou to draw out into a crossroads **2.** [entreprendre] to enter into, to begin **3.** SPORT ▸ **s'engager dans une course / compétition** to enter a race / an event.

engelure [ɑ̃ʒlyʀ] nf chilblain.

engendrer [3] [ɑ̃ʒɑ̃dʀe] vt **1.** [procréer] to beget ; BIBLE to father **2.** [provoquer - sentiment, situation] to generate, to create, to breed *péj.*

engin [ɑ̃ʒɛ̃] nm **1.** [appareil] machine, appliance **2.** ASTRONAUT ▸ **engin spatial** spacecraft. **3.** MIL weaponry ▸ **engin blindé** armoured vehicle 🇬🇧, armored vehicle 🇺🇸 ▸ **engin explosif** explosive device **4.** *fam* [chose] contraption, thingamabob, thingamajig.

englober [3] [ɑ̃glɔbe] vt **1.** [réunir] to encompass **2.** [inclure] to include.

engloutir [32] [ɑ̃glutiʀ] vt **1.** [faire disparaître] to swallow up *(sép)*, to engulf **2.** [manger] to gobble up *(sép)*, to gulp ou to wolf down *(sép)* **3.** [dépenser] to squander / *les travaux ont englouti tout mon argent* the work swallowed up all my money / *ils ont englouti des sommes énormes dans la maison* they sank vast amounts of money into the house.

engluer [3] [ɑ̃glye] ❖ **s'engluer** vpi *fig* ▸ **s'engluer dans qqch** to get bogged down in sthg.

engoncer [16] [ɑ̃gɔ̃se] vt to cramp, to restrict / *être engoncé dans ses vêtements* to be restricted by one's clothes.

engorger [17] [ɑ̃gɔʀʒe] vt [canalisation] to flood ; [route] to congest, to jam ; [organe] to engorge ; [sol] to saturate ; [marché] to saturate, to glut. ❖ **s'engorger** vpi **1.** [tuyau] to become blocked, to get blocked **2.** [route] to get congested.

engouement [ɑ̃gumɑ̃] nm [pour une activité, un type d'objet] keen interest / *un engouement pour le jazz* a keen interest in jazz.

engouffrer [3] [ɑ̃gufʀe] vt **1.** [avaler] to wolf ou to shovel (down), to cram (in) **2.** [dépenser] to swallow up *(sép)*. ❖ **s'engouffrer** vpi [foule] to rush, to crush ; [personne] to rush, to dive ; [mer] to surge, to rush ; [vent] to blow, to sweep, to rush ▸ **s'engouffrer dans un taxi a)** [seul] to dive into a taxi **b)** [à plusieurs] to pile into a taxi.

engourdi, e [ɑ̃guʀdi] adj [doigt, membre] numb, numbed.

engourdir [32] [ɑ̃guʀdiʀ] vt **1.** [insensibiliser - doigt, membre] to numb, to make numb ; [- sens] to deaden / *être engourdi par le froid* to be numb with cold **2.** [ralentir - esprit, faculté] to blunt, to dull / *la fatigue lui engourdissait l'esprit* he was so tired he couldn't think straight. ❖ **s'engourdir** vpi to go numb.

engrais [ɑ̃gʀɛ] nm fertilizer ▸ **engrais chimique** artificial fertilizer ▸ **engrais verts** ou **végétaux** green ou vegetable manure.

engraisser [4] [ɑ̃gʀese] ◆ vt AGR [bétail] to fatten up *(sép)* ; [terre] to feed. ◆ vi to grow fat ou fatter, to put on weight. ❖ **s'engraisser** vpi to get fat / *il s'engraisse sur le dos de ses employés fig* he lines his pockets by underpaying his employees.

engranger [17] [ɑ̃gʀɑ̃ʒe] vt **1.** AGR to gather, to get in *(sép)* **2.** [documents] to store (up), to collect.

engrenage [ɑ̃gʀənaʒ] nm **1.** MÉCAN gear ▸ **les engrenages d'une machine** the wheelwork ou train of gears ou gearing of a machine **2.** *fig* trap ▸ **être pris dans l'engrenage** to be caught in a trap / *être pris dans l'engrenage du jeu* to be trapped in the vicious circle of gambling.

engrosser [3] [ɑ̃gʀose] vt *tfam* to knock up *(sép)*.

engueulade [ɑ̃gœlad] nf *tfam* **1.** [réprimande] rollicking 🇬🇧, bawling out 🇺🇸 **2.** [querelle] slanging match 🇬🇧, run-in 🇺🇸 ▸ **avoir une engueulade avec qqn** to have a slanging match 🇬🇧 ou a run-in 🇺🇸 with sb.

engueuler [5] [ɑ̃gœle] vt *tfam* ▸ **engueuler qqn** to give sb a rollicking 🇬🇧, to bawl sb out 🇺🇸 ▸ **se faire engueuler** to get a rollicking 🇬🇧, to get chewed out 🇺🇸. ❖ **s'engueuler** *tfam* vpi ▸ **s'engueuler avec qqn** to have a row with sb.

enguirlander [3] [ɑ̃giʀlɑ̃de] vt *fam* [réprimander] to tick off *(sép)* 🇬🇧, to chew out *(sép)* 🇺🇸 / **se faire enguirlander** to get a ticking-off 🇬🇧 ou a chewing-out 🇺🇸.

enhardir [32] [ɑ̃aʀdiʀ] vt to embolden, to make bolder, to encourage. ❖ **s'enhardir** vpi : *l'enfant s'enhardit et entra dans la pièce* the child plucked up courage and went into the room.

énième [enjɛm] adj umpteenth, nth.

énigmatique [enigmatik] adj enigmatic.

énigme [enigm] nf **1.** [mystère] riddle, enigma, puzzle **2.** [devinette] riddle.

enivrant, e [ɑ̃nivʀɑ̃, ɑ̃t] adj **1.** [qui rend ivre] intoxicating **2.** [exaltant] heady, exhilarating.

enivrer [3] [ɑ̃nivʀe] vt **1.** [soûler - suj : vin] to make drunk, to intoxicate **2.** [exalter] to intoxicate, to exhilarate, to elate / *le succès l'enivrait* he was intoxicated by his success. ❖ **s'enivrer** vpi to get drunk.

enjambée [ɑ̃ʒɑ̃be] nf stride / *avancer à grandes enjambées dans la rue* to stride along the street ▸ **faire de grandes enjambées** to take long steps ou strides.

enjamber [3] [ɑ̃ʒɑ̃be] vt [muret, rebord] to step over *(insép)* ; [fossé] to stride across ou over *(insép)* ; [tronc d'arbre] to stride ou to step over *(insép)* / *le pont enjambe le Gard* the bridge spans the river Gard.

enjeu [ɑ̃ʒø] nm **1.** [dans un jeu] stake, stakes **2.** [défi] challenge / *c'est un enjeu de taille pour l'entreprise* it's a major challenge for the company / *c'est un enjeu important* the stakes are high / *quel est l'enjeu de cet accord ?* what's at stake in this agreement? / *il n'y a pas vraiment d'enjeu dans cette élection* there's not much at stake in this election ▸ **mesurer l'enjeu** to be aware of what is at stake.

enjoindre [82] [ɑ̃ʒwɛ̃dʀ] vt *litt* ▸ **enjoindre à qqn de faire qqch** to enjoin sb to do sthg.

enjôler [3] [ɑ̃ʒole] vt to cajole, to wheedle / *il a réussi à m'enjôler* he managed to cajole me (into accepting).

enjôleur, euse [ɑ̃ʒolœʀ, øz] ◆ adj cajoling, wheedling / *un sourire enjôleur* a wheedling smile. ◆ nm, f cajoler, wheedler.

enjoliver [3] [ɑ̃ʒolive] vt **1.** [décorer - vêtement] to embellish, to adorn **2.** [travestir - histoire, récit, vérité] to embellish, to embroider.

enjoliveur [ɑ̃ʒolivœʀ] nm hubcap.

enjoué, e [ɑ̃ʒwe] adj [personne, caractère] cheerful, jolly, genial ; [remarque, ton] playful, cheerful, jolly.

enlacer [16] [ɑ̃lase] vt [étreindre] to clasp ▸ **enlacer qqn** to embrace sb (tenderly) ▸ **ils étaient tendrement enlacés** they were locked in a tender embrace. ❖ **s'enlacer** *(emploi réciproque)* [amoureux] to embrace, to hug.

enlaidir [32] [ɑ̃lediʀ] ◆ vt to make ugly ▸ **enlaidir le paysage** to be a blot on the landscape ou an eyesore. ◆ vi to become ugly. ❖ **s'enlaidir** vpi to make o.s. (look) ugly.

enlevé, e [ãlve] adj [style, rythme] lively, spirited.

enlèvement [ãlɛvmã] nm **1.** [rapt] abduction, kidnapping ▸ **enlèvement de bébé** babysnatching **2.** [fait d'ôter] removal, taking away **3.** [ramassage] : *l'enlèvement des ordures a lieu le mardi* rubbish is collected on Tuesdays.

enlever [19] [ãlve] vt **1.** [ôter - couvercle, housse, vêtement] to remove, to take off *(sép)* ; [- étagère] to remove, to take down *(sép)* ▸ **enlever les pépins** to take the pips out / *ils ont enlevé le reste des meubles ce matin* they took away ou collected what was left of the furniture this morning **2.** [arracher] to remove, to pull out **3.** [faire disparaître] to remove ▸ **enlever une tache a)** [gén] to remove a stain **b)** [en lavant] to wash out a stain **c)** [en frottant] to rub out a stain **d)** [à l'eau de Javel] to bleach out a stain **4.** DENT & MÉD : *se faire enlever une dent* to have a tooth pulled out ou extracted **5.** [soustraire] ▸ **enlever qqch à qqn** to take sthg away from sb, to deprive sb of sthg / *j'ai peur qu'on ne m'enlève la garde de mon enfant* I'm afraid they'll take my child away from me / *ne m'enlevez pas tous mes espoirs* don't deprive ou rob me of all hope **6.** [kidnapper] to abduct, to kidnap, to snatch. ❖ **s'enlever** ❖ vp *(emploi passif)* **1.** [vêtement, étiquette] to come off ; [écharde] to come out / *comment ça s'enlève ?* how do you take it off? **2.** [s'effacer - tache] to come out ou off. ❖ vpt : *s'enlever une écharde du doigt* to pull a splinter out of one's finger.

enliser [3] [ãlize] vt : *enliser ses roues* to get one's wheels stuck. ❖ **s'enliser** vpi **1.** [s'embourber] to get bogged down ou stuck, to sink **2.** *fig* to get bogged down.

enneigé, e [ãneʒe] adj [champ, paysage] snow-covered ; [pic] snow-capped ▸ **les routes sont enneigées** the roads are snowed up.

enneigement [ãnɛʒmã] nm snow cover ▸ **l'enneigement annuel** yearly ou annual snowfall ▸ **bulletin d'enneigement** snow report.

ennemi, e [ɛnmi] ❖ adj **1.** MIL enemy *(modif)*, hostile **2.** ▸ **ennemi de** [opposé à] : *être ennemi du changement* to be opposed ou averse to change. ❖ nm, f **1.** MIL enemy, foe *litt* **2.** [individu hostile] enemy ▸ **se faire des ennemis** to make enemies ▸ **ennemi public (numéro un)** public enemy (number one) **3.** [antagoniste] ▸ **l'ennemi de:** *le bien est l'ennemi du mal* good is the enemy of evil.

ennui [ãnɥi] nm **1.** [problème] problem, difficulty ▸ **des ennuis** trouble, troubles, problems ▸ **attirer des ennuis à qqn** to get sb into trouble ▸ **avoir des ennuis** : *avoir de gros ennuis* to be in bad trouble / *avoir des ennuis avec la police* to be in trouble with the police ▸ **des ennuis de:** *avoir des ennuis d'argent* to have money problems / *avoir des ennuis de santé* to have health problems ▸ **faire des ennuis à qqn** to get sb into trouble ▸ **l'ennui c'est que...** the trouble is that... **2.** [lassitude] boredom / *c'était à mourir d'ennui* it was dreadfully ou deadly boring.

ennuyer [14] [ãnɥije] vt **1.** [contrarier] to worry, to bother / *ça m'ennuie de les laisser seuls* I don't like to leave them alone / *ça m'ennuie de te le dire mais...* I'm sorry to have to say this to you but... / *cela m'ennuierait d'être en retard* I'd hate to be late **2.** [déranger] to bother, to trouble / *si cela ne vous ennuie pas* if you don't mind / *je ne voudrais pas vous ennuyer mais...* I don't like to bother ou trouble you but... **3.** [agacer] to annoy / *tu l'ennuies avec tes questions* you're annoying him with your questions **4.** [lasser] to bore. ❖ **s'ennuyer** vpi to be bored / *avec lui on ne s'ennuie pas !* hum he's great fun! ▸ **s'ennuyer comme un rat mort** fam to be bored to death. ❖ **s'ennuyer de** vp + prép ▸ **s'ennuyer de qqn / qqch** to miss sb / sthg.

ennuyeux, euse [ãnɥijø, øz] adj **1.** [lassant - travail, conférencier, collègue] boring, dull **2.** [fâcheux] annoying, tiresome ▸ *c'est ennuyeux qu'il ne puisse pas venir*

a) [regrettable] it's a pity (that) he can't come **b)** [contrariant] it's annoying ou a nuisance that he can't come.

énoncé [enɔse] nm **1.** [libellé - d'un sujet de débat] terms ; [- d'une question d'examen, d'un problème d'arithmétique] wording **2.** [lecture] reading, declaration **3.** LING utterance.

énoncer [16] [enɔse] vt [formuler] to formulate, to enunciate *sout*, to express.

énonciation [enɔ̃sjasjɔ̃] nf **1.** [exposition] statement, stating **2.** LING enunciation.

enorgueillir [32] [ãnɔrgœjir] ❖ **s'enorgueillir de** vp + prép to be proud of.

énorme [enɔrm] adj **1.** [gros] enormous, huge **2.** [important] huge, enormous, vast / *20 euros, ce n'est pas énorme* 20 euros isn't such a huge amount / *elle n'a pas dit non, c'est déjà énorme !* she didn't say no, that's a great step forward! **3.** [exagéré - mensonge] outrageous.

énormément [enɔrmemã] adv enormously, hugely / *le spectacle m'a énormément plu* I liked the show very much indeed ▸ **s'amuser énormément** to enjoy o.s. immensely ou tremendously ▸ **énormément de** [argent, bruit] an enormous ou a huge ou a tremendous amount of / *il y avait énormément de monde dans le train* the train was extremely crowded.

énormité [enɔrmite] nf **1.** [ampleur - d'une difficulté] enormity ; [- d'une tâche, d'une somme, d'une population] enormity, size **2.** [extravagance] outrageousness, enormity **3.** [propos] piece of utter ou outrageous nonsense.

enquérir [39] [ãkerir] ❖ **s'enquérir de** vp + prép *sout* to inquire about ou after ▸ **s'enquérir de la santé de qqn** to inquire to ou to ask after sb's health.

enquête [ãkɛt] nf **1.** [investigation] investigation, inquiry ▸ **faire** ou **mener sa petite enquête** to make discreet inquiries / *il a fait l'objet d'une enquête* he was the subject of an investigation / *mener une enquête sur un meurtre* to investigate a murder ▸ **ouvrir / conduire une enquête** to open ou to conduct an investigation ▸ **enquête judiciaire a)** [gén] judicial inquiry **b)** [suite à un décès] inquest **2.** [étude] survey, investigation ▸ **faire une enquête** to conduct a survey.

enquêter [4] [ãkete] vi to investigate ▸ **enquêter sur un meurtre** to inquire into ou to investigate a murder.

enquêteur, euse ou **trice** [ãketœr, øz, tris] nm, f **1.** [de police] officer in charge of investigations, investigator **2.** [de sondage] pollster **3.** [sociologue] researcher.

enquiquinant, e [ãkikinã, ãt] adj *fam* irritating / *des voisins enquiquinants* awkward neighbours.

enquiquiner [3] [ãkikine] vt *fam* **1.** [irriter] to bug / *je les enquiquine !* to hell with them! **2.** [importuner] : *se faire enquiquiner* to be hassled. ❖ **s'enquiquiner** vpi *fam* **1.** [s'ennuyer] to be bored (stiff) **2.** [se préoccuper] : *ne t'enquiquine pas avec ça* don't bother (yourself) with that. ❖ **s'enquiquiner à** vp + prép *fam* : *je ne vais pas m'enquiquiner à tout recopier* I can't be fagged 🇬🇧 ou bothered to copy it out again.

enraciner [3] [ãrasine] vt **1.** BOT to root **2.** [fixer - dans un lieu, une culture] to root **3.** [fixer dans l'esprit] to fix, to implant. ❖ **s'enraciner** vpi **1.** BOT to root, to take root **2.** [se fixer] to take root, to become firmly fixed / *s'enraciner profondément dans une culture / l'esprit* to become deeply rooted in a culture / the mind.

enragé, e [ãraʒe] ❖ adj **1.** MÉD rabid **2.** [furieux] enraged, livid. ❖ nm, f [passionné] ▸ **un enragé de:** *un enragé de football / ski / musique* a football / skiing / music fanatic.

enrager [17] [ãraʒe] vi [être en colère] to be furious ou infuriated ▸ **faire enrager qqn a)** [l'irriter] to annoy sb **b)** [le taquiner] to tease sb mercilessly.

enrayer [11] [ɑ̃ʀeje] vt **1.** ARM to jam **2.** MÉCAN to block **3.** [empêcher la progression de - processus] to check, to stop, to call a halt to ▸ **enrayer la crise** to halt the economic recession ▸ **enrayer l'inflation** to check ou to control ou to curb inflation. ❖ **s'enrayer** vpi to jam.

enrégimenter [3] [ɑ̃ʀeʒimɑ̃te] vt **1.** [dans l'armée] to enlist ; [dans un groupe] to enrol 🇬🇧, to enroll 🇺🇸 **2.** to press-gang.

enregistrement [ɑ̃ʀəʒistʀəmɑ̃] nm **1.** TRANSP [à l'aéroport] check-in ▸ **se présenter à l'enregistrement** to go to the check-in desk ▸ **comptoir d'enregistrement** check-in desk ; [à la gare] registration **2.** AUDIO recording ▸ **enregistrement audio / vidéo / sur cassette** audio / video / cassette recording ▸ **enregistrement numérique** digital recording.

enregistrer [3] [ɑ̃ʀəʒistʀe] vt **1.** [inscrire - opération, transaction, acte] to enter, to record ; [- déclaration] to register, to file ; [- note, mention] to log ; [- commande] to book (in) **2.** [constater] to record, to note / *l'entreprise a enregistré un bénéfice de...* the company showed a profit of... / *on enregistre une baisse du dollar* the dollar has fallen in value **3.** INFORM / **'enregistrer sous'** 'save as' / *j'ai dû enregistrer le fichier sur ma clé* I had to save the file on my USB stick ; AUDIO [cassette audio, disque] to record, to tape ; [cassette vidéo] to record, to video, to video-tape ; [pour commercialiser - disque, émission, dialogue] to record ; *(en usage absolu)* : *ils sont en train d'enregistrer* they're doing ou making a recording **4.** [afficher] to register, to record, to show ▸ **l'appareil n'a rien enregistré** nothing registered on the apparatus, the apparatus did not register anything **5.** [retenir] to take in *(sép)* ▸ **d'accord, c'est enregistré** all right, I've got that **6.** TRANSP [à l'aéroport] to check in *(sép)* ; [à la gare] to register.

enregistreur, euse [ɑ̃ʀəʒistʀœʀ, øz] adj recording *(modif).* ➡ **enregistreur** nm recorder, recording device ▸ **enregistreur de vol** flight recorder.

enrhumé, e [ɑ̃ʀyme] adj ▸ **être enrhumé** to have a cold / *je suis un peu / très enrhumé* I have a bit of a cold / a bad cold.

enrhumer [3] [ɑ̃ʀyme] vt ❖ **s'enrhumer** vpi to catch cold, to get a cold.

enrichir [32] [ɑ̃ʀiʃiʀ] vt **1.** [rendre riche] to enrich, to make rich ou richer **2.** [améliorer - savon, minerai, culture] to enrich ; [- esprit] to enrich, to improve. ❖ **s'enrichir** vpi **1.** [devenir riche] to grow rich ou richer, to become rich ou richer **2.** [se développer - collection] to increase, to develop ; [- esprit] to be enriched, to grow.

enrichissant, e [ɑ̃ʀiʃisɑ̃, ɑ̃t] adj [rencontre] enriching ; [travail] rewarding ; [lecture] enriching, improving.

enrichissement [ɑ̃ʀiʃismɑ̃] nm NUCL enrichment.

enrobé, e [ɑ̃ʀɔbe] adj [personne] plump, chubby.

enrober [3] [ɑ̃ʀɔbe] vt **1.** [enduire] to coat ▸ **enrober qqch de** to coat sthg with **2.** [adoucir] to wrap ou to dress up *(sép)* / *il a enrobé son reproche de mots affectueux* he wrapped his criticism in kind words.

enrôlement [ɑ̃ʀolmɑ̃] nm **1.** MIL enlistment **2.** ADMIN & DR enrolment.

enrôler [3] [ɑ̃ʀole] vt ❖ **s'enrôler** vpi to enrol 🇬🇧, to enroll 🇺🇸, to enlist, to sign up.

enroué, e [ɑ̃ʀwe] adj ▸ **je suis enroué** I'm hoarse.

enrouler [3] [ɑ̃ʀule] vt [mettre en rouleau - corde] to wind, to coil (up) ; [- ressort] to coil ; [- papier, tapis] to roll up *(sép).* ❖ **s'enrouler** ◆ vp *(emploi réfléchi)* : *s'enrouler dans une couverture* to wrap o.s. up in a blanket. ◆ vpi [corde, fil] to be wound ou to wind (up) ; [serpent] to coil (itself).

ENS npr f abr de **École normale supérieure.**

ensabler [3] [ɑ̃sable] ❖ **s'ensabler** vpi **1.** [chenal] to silt up **2.** [véhicule] to get stuck in the sand.

ensanglanter [3] [ɑ̃sɑ̃glɑ̃te] vt [tacher] to bloody ▸ **un mouchoir ensanglanté** a bloodstained handkerchief.

enseignant, e [ɑ̃sɛɲɑ̃, ɑ̃t] ◆ adj → **corps.** ◆ nm, f teacher.

enseigne [ɑ̃sɛɲ] nf [panneau] sign ▸ **enseigne lumineuse** ou **au néon** neon sign.

enseignement [ɑ̃sɛɲmɑ̃] nm **1.** [instruction] education ▸ **enseignement par correspondance** correspondence courses ▸ **enseignement à distance** distance learning **2.** [méthodes d'instruction] teaching (methods) ▸ **l'enseignement des langues** language teaching / *l'enseignement des langues est excellent dans mon collège* languages are taught very well at my school **3.** [système scolaire] ▸ **enseignement primaire / supérieur** primary / higher education ▸ **enseignement professionnel** vocational education ▸ **enseignement public** state education ou schools ▸ **enseignement technique** technical education **4.** [profession] ▸ **l'enseignement** teaching, the teaching profession ▸ **entrer dans l'enseignement** to go into teaching ▸ **être dans l'enseignement** to be a teacher **5.** [leçon] lesson, teaching ▸ **tirer un enseignement de qqch** to learn (a lesson) from sthg.

enseigner [4] [ɑ̃sɛɲe] vt to teach ▸ **enseigner qqch à qqn** to teach sb sthg ou sthg to sb ; *(en usage absolu)* : *elle enseigne depuis trois ans* she's been teaching for three years.

ensemble[1] [ɑ̃sɑ̃bl] nm **1.** [collection - d'objets] set, collection ; [- d'idées] set, series ; [- de données, d'informations, de textes] set, body, collection **2.** [totalité] whole / *la question dans son ensemble* the question as a whole ▸ **l'ensemble de:** *l'ensemble des joueurs* all the players / *l'ensemble des réponses montre que...* the answers taken as a whole show that... / *il s'est adressé à l'ensemble des employés* he spoke to all the staff ou the whole staff **3.** [simultanéité] unity ▸ **manquer d'ensemble** to lack unity / *ils ont protesté dans un ensemble parfait* they protested unanimously **4.** [groupe] group ▸ **ensemble instrumental** (instrumental) ensemble ▸ **ensemble vocal** vocal group **5.** [d'immeubles] ▸ **grand ensemble** housing scheme 🇬🇧 ou project 🇺🇸 **6.** VÊT suit, outfit ▸ **ensemble pantalon** trouser suit **7.** MATH set ▸ **ensemble fermé** closed set ▸ **ensemble vide** empty set. ❖ **dans l'ensemble** loc adv on the whole, by and large, in the main. ❖ **d'ensemble** loc adj **1.** [général] overall, general ▸ **mesures d'ensemble** comprehensive ou global measures ▸ **vue d'ensemble** overall ou general view **2.** MUS : *faire de la musique d'ensemble* to play in an ensemble.

ensemble[2] [ɑ̃sɑ̃bl] adv **1.** [l'un avec l'autre] together / *elles en sont convenues ensemble* they agreed (between themselves) / *nous en avons parlé ensemble* we spoke ou we had a talk about it ▸ **aller bien ensemble a)** [vêtements, couleurs] to go well together **b)** [personnes] to be well-matched ▸ **ils vont mal ensemble a)** [vêtements] they don't match **b)** [couple] they're ill-matched **2.** [en même temps] at once, at the same time.

ensevelir [32] [ɑ̃səvliʀ] vt [enfouir] to bury / *l'éruption a enseveli plusieurs villages* the eruption buried several villages.

ensoleillé, e [ɑ̃sɔleje] adj sunny, sunlit.

ensoleillement [ɑ̃sɔlejmɑ̃] nm (amount of) sunshine, insolation *spéc* ▸ **l'ensoleillement annuel** the number of days of sunshine per year.

ensorceler [24] [ɑ̃sɔʀsəle] vt to bewitch, to cast a spell over.

✐ In reformed spelling (see p. 16-18), this verb is conjugated like *peler : il ensorcèle, elle ensorcèlera.*

ensuite [ãsɥit] adv **1.** [dans le temps - puis] then, next ; [- plus tard] later, after, afterwards **/** *et ensuite, que s'est-il passé ?* and what happened next?, and then what happened? **/** *ils ne sont arrivés qu'ensuite* they didn't arrive until later **2.** [dans l'espace] then, further on.

ensuivre [89] [ãsɥivʀ] ❖ **s'ensuivre** vpi **1.** [en résulter] to follow, to ensue ; *(tournure impersonnelle)* ▶ *il s'ensuit que* it follows that **2.** EXPR **et tout ce qui s'ensuit** and so on (and so forth).

ENT nm abr de **espace numérique de travail**.

entaille [ãtaj] nf **1.** [encoche] notch, nick **2.** [blessure] gash, slash, cut ▶ **petite entaille** nick.

entailler [3] [ãtaje] vt **1.** [fendre] to notch, to nick **2.** [blesser] to gash, to slash, to cut. ❖ **s'entailler** vpt ▶ **s'entailler le doigt** to cut one's finger.

entame [ãtam] nf [morceau - de viande] first slice ou cut ; [- de pain] crust.

entamer [3] [ãtame] vt **1.** [jambon, fromage] to start ; [bouteille, conserve] to open **2.** [durée, repas] to start, to begin ; [négociation] to launch, to start, to initiate ; [poursuites] to institute, to initiate **3.** [ébranler] to shake.

entarter [ãtaʀte] vt fam to pie **/** *il s'est fait entarter* he got pied.

entartrer [3] [ãtaʀtʀe] vt **1.** [chaudière, tuyau] to scale, to fur (up) 🇬🇧 **2.** [dent] to cover with tartar ou scale. ❖ **s'entartrer** vpi **1.** [chaudière, tuyau] to scale, to fur up 🇬🇧 **2.** [dent] to become covered in tartar ou scale.

entasser [3] [ãtase] vt **1.** [mettre en tas] to heap ou to pile ou to stack (up) **2.** [accumuler - vieilleries, journaux] to pile ou to heap (up) **3.** [serrer] to cram ou to pack (in) **/** *ils vivent entassés à quatre dans une seule pièce* the four of them live in one cramped room. ❖ **s'entasser** vpi [neige, terre] to heap ou to pile up, to bank ; [vieilleries, journaux] to heap ou to pile up ; [personnes] to crowd (in) ou together, to pile in **/** *s'entasser dans une voiture* to pile into a car.

entendement [ãtãdmã] nm comprehension, understanding ▶ **cela dépasse l'entendement** it's beyond all comprehension ou understanding.

entendre [73] [ãtãdʀ] vt **1.** [percevoir par l'ouïe] to hear **/** *parlez plus fort, on n'entend rien* speak up, we can't hear a word (you're saying) **/** *silence, je ne veux pas vous entendre !* quiet, I don't want to hear a sound from you! ▶ **j'entends pleurer à côté** I can hear someone crying next door ▶ **entendre dire** to hear **/** *j'ai entendu dire qu'il était parti* I heard that he had left **/** *c'est la première fois que j'entends (dire) ça* that's the first I've heard of it ▶ **entendre parler de** to hear about ou of **/** *il ne veut pas entendre parler d'informatique* he won't hear of computers **/** *je ne veux plus entendre parler de lui* I don't want to hear him mentioned again ; *(en usage absolu)* : *j'entends mal de l'oreille droite* my hearing's bad in the right ear ▶ **j'aurai tout entendu !** whatever next? **2.** [écouter] to hear, to listen to **/** *essayer de se faire entendre* to try to make o.s. heard **/** *il ne veut rien entendre* he won't listen ▶ **entendre raison** to see sense ▶ **faire entendre raison à qqn** to make sb listen to reason, to bring sb to his / her senses ▶ **il va m'entendre !** I'll give him hell! **3.** [accepter - demande] to agree to (insép) ; [- vœu] to grant **/** *nos prières ont été entendues* our prayers were answered **4.** RELIG ▶ **entendre la messe** to attend ou to hear mass ▶ **entendre une confession** to hear ou to take a confession **5.** DR [témoin] to hear, to interview **6.** sout [comprendre] to understand ▶ **donner qqch à entendre** ou **laisser entendre qqch à qqn** : *elle m'a laissé* ou *donné à entendre que...* she gave me to understand that... ▶ **entendre qqch à** : *y entendez-vous quelque chose ?* do you know anything about it? **7.** [apprendre] to hear **8.** [vouloir] to want,

to intend ▶ **fais comme tu l'entends** do as you wish ou please **/** *il entend bien partir demain* he's determined to go tomorrow. ❖ **s'entendre** ◆ vp *(emploi passif)* **1.** [être perçu] to be heard **/** *cela s'entend de loin* you can hear it ou it can be heard from far off ; [être utilisé - mot, expression] to be heard **/** *cela s'entend encore dans la région* you can still hear it said ou used around here **2.** [être compris] to be understood. ◆ vp *(emploi réciproque)* **1.** [pouvoir s'écouter] to hear each other ou one another **2.** [s'accorder] to agree **/** *s'entendre sur un prix* to agree on a price ▶ **entendons-nous bien** let's get this straight **3.** [sympathiser] to get on ▶ **s'entendre comme larrons en foire** to be as thick as thieves. ◆ vp *(emploi réfléchi)* [percevoir sa voix] to hear o.s. **/** *on ne s'entend plus tellement il y a de bruit* there's so much noise, you can't hear yourself think. ◆ vpi ▶ **s'y entendre** [s'y connaître] : *il s'y entend en mécanique* he's good at ou he knows (a lot) about mechanics ▶ **s'y entendre pour** to know how to. ❖ **s'entendre avec** vp + prép **1.** [s'accorder avec] to reach an agreement with **2.** [sympathiser avec] to get on with.

entendu, e [ãtãdy] adj **1.** [complice - air, sourire] knowing **/** *hocher la tête d'un air entendu* to nod knowingly **2.** [convenu] agreed ▶ **(c'est) entendu, je viendrai** all right ou very well, I'll come.

entente [ãtãt] nf **1.** [harmonie] harmony ▶ **vivre en bonne entente** to live in harmony **2.** POL agreement, understanding ; ÉCON agreement, accord.

entériner [3] [ãteʀine] vt DR to ratify, to confirm.

enterrement [ãtɛʀmã] nm **1.** [funérailles] funeral **2.** [ensevelissement] burial. ❖ **d'enterrement** loc adj [mine, tête] gloomy, glum ▶ **faire une tête d'enterrement** to wear a gloomy or long expression.

enterrer [4] [ãteʀe] vt **1.** [ensevelir] to bury **2.** [inhumer] to bury, to inter sout ▶ **vous nous enterrerez tous** you'll outlive us all ▶ **enterrer sa vie de garçon** to celebrate one's last night as a bachelor, to hold a stag party **3.** [oublier - scandale] to bury, to hush (up) ; [- souvenir, passé, querelle] to bury, to forget (about) ; [- projet] to shelve, to put aside. ❖ **s'enterrer** vp *(emploi réfléchi) pr* to bury o.s. ; *fig* to hide o.s. away.

en-tête *(pl* **en-têtes)**, **entête*** [ãtɛt] nm **1.** [sur du papier à lettres] letterhead, heading **2.** IMPR head, heading. ❖ **à en-tête**, **à entête*** loc adj [papier, bristol] headed.

entêté, e [ãtete] ◆ adj obstinate, stubborn. ◆ nm, f stubborn ou obstinate person.

entêtement [ãtɛtmã] nm stubbornness, obstinacy.

entêter [4] [ãtete] ❖ **s'entêter** vpi ▶ **s'entêter à faire** to persist in doing ▶ **s'entêter dans** : *s'entêter dans l'erreur* to persist in one's error.

enthousiasmant, e [ãtuzjasmã, ãt] adj exciting, thrilling.

enthousiasme [ãtuzjasm] nm enthusiasm, keenness.

enthousiasmer [3] [ãtuzjasme] ❖ **s'enthousiasmer** vpi ▶ **s'enthousiasmer pour qqn / qqch** to be enthusiastic about sb / sthg.

enthousiaste [ãtuzjast] ◆ adj enthusiastic, keen. ◆ nmf enthusiast.

enticher [3] [ãtiʃe] ❖ **s'enticher de** vp + prép ▶ **s'enticher de qqn** [s'amouracher de qqn] to become infatuated with sb ▶ **s'enticher de qqch** [s'enthousiasmer pour qqch] to become very keen on sthg.

entier, ère [ãtje, ɛʀ] adj **1.** [complet] whole, entire ▶ **pendant des journées / des heures entières** for days / hours on end ▶ **dans le monde entier** in the whole world, throughout the world ▶ **payer place entière** to pay the full price

tout entier, tout entière : *je le voulais tout entier pour moi* I wanted him all to myself ▪ **tout entier à, tout entière à** : *être tout entier à son travail* to be completely wrapped up ou engrossed in one's work **2.** *(avant nom)* [en intensif] absolute, complete ▪ **donner entière satisfaction à qqn** to give sb complete satisfaction **3.** *(après le verbe)* [intact] intact ▪ **le problème reste entier** the problem remains unresolved **4.** [absolu - personne] : *c'est quelqu'un de très entier* she is someone of great integrity. ❖ **en entier** loc adv : *manger un gâteau en entier* to eat a whole ou an entire cake / *je l'ai lu en entier* I read all of it, I read the whole of it, I read it right through.

entièrement [ɑ̃tjɛʁmɑ̃] adv entirely, completely.

entonner [3] [ɑ̃tɔne] vt [hymne, air] to strike up *(insép)*, to start singing.

entonnoir [ɑ̃tɔnwaʁ] nm [ustensile] funnel.

entorse [ɑ̃tɔʁs] nf **1.** [foulure] sprain / *se faire une entorse au poignet* to sprain one's wrist **2.** [exception] infringement (of) / *faire une entorse au règlement* to bend the rules.

entortiller [3] [ɑ̃tɔʁtije] vt **1.** [enrouler - ruban, mouchoir] to twist, to wrap **2.** [compliquer] ▪ **être entortillé** to be convoluted **3.** *fam* [tromper] to hoodwink, to con. ❖ **s'entortiller** vpi **1.** [s'enrouler - lierre] to twist, to wind **2.** [être empêtré] to get caught ou tangled up.

entourage [ɑ̃tuʁaʒ] nm [gén] circle ; [d'un roi, d'un président] entourage ▪ **entourage familial** family circle / *on dit dans l'entourage du Président que...* sources close to the President say that...

entouré, e [ɑ̃tuʁe] adj **1.** [populaire] : *une actrice très entourée* an actress who is very popular ou who is the centre of attraction **2.** [par des amis] : *heureusement, elle est très entourée* fortunately, she has a lot of friends around her.

entourer [3] [ɑ̃tuʁe] vt **1.** [encercler - terrain, mets] to surround ▪ **entourer qqch / qqn de** : *entourer un champ de barbelés* to surround a field with barbed wire, to put barbed wire around a field **2.** [environner] : *le monde qui nous entoure* the world around us ou that surrounds us **3.** [soutenir - malade, veuve] to rally round *(insép)*. ❖ **s'entourer de** vp + prép **1.** [placer autour de soi] to surround o.s. with, to be surrounded by **2.** [vivre au sein de] : *s'entourer de beaucoup de précautions* to take elaborate precautions.

entourloupe [ɑ̃tuʁlup], **entourloupette** [ɑ̃tuʁlupɛt] nf *fam* nasty ou dirty trick ▪ **faire une entourloupe à qqn** to play a dirty trick on sb.

entournure [ɑ̃tuʁnyʁ] nf armhole.

entracte [ɑ̃tʁakt] nm CINÉ & THÉÂTRE interval 🇬🇧, intermission 🇺🇸.

entraide [ɑ̃tʁɛd] nf mutual aid.

entraider [4] [ɑ̃tʁede] ❖ **s'entraider** vp *(emploi réciproque)* to help one another ou each other.

entrailles [ɑ̃tʁaj] nfpl **1.** ANAT & ZOOL entrails, guts **2.** [profondeur - de la terre] depths, bowels ; [- d'un piano, d'un navire] innards.

entrain [ɑ̃tʁɛ̃] nm **1.** [fougue] spirit / *avoir beaucoup d'entrain, être plein d'entrain* to be full of life ou energy **2.** [animation] liveliness ▪ **la fête manquait d'entrain** the party wasn't very lively. ❖ **avec entrain** loc adv with gusto, enthusiastically. ❖ **sans entrain** loc adv half-heartedly, unenthusiastically.

entraînant, e, entraînant*, e [ɑ̃tʁɛnɑ̃, ɑ̃t] adj [chanson] catchy, swinging ; [rythme] swinging, lively ; [style, éloquence] rousing, stirring.

entraînement, entrainement* [ɑ̃tʁɛnmɑ̃] nm **1.** [d'un sportif] training, coaching ; [d'un cheval] training / *il est à l'entraînement* he's training / *il est à l'entraînement de rugby* he's at rugby practice ▪ **séance d'entraînement** training session ▪ **manquer d'entraînement** to be out of training **2.** [habitude] practice. ❖ **d'entraînement, d'entrainement*** loc adj ÉQUIT & SPORT [séance, matériel] training *(modif)*.

entraîner, entrainer* [4] [ɑ̃tʁene] vt **1.** [emporter] to carry ou to sweep along *(sép)* ; *fig* to carry away *(sép)* / *les nageurs se sont fait entraîner par le courant* the swimmers were carried away by the current / *se laisser entraîner par la musique* to let o.s. be carried away by the music ; [tirer - wagons] to pull, to haul ; [actionner - bielle] to drive **2.** [conduire] to drag (along) ▪ **entraîner qqn dans sa chute** a) *pr* to pull ou to drag sb down in one's fall b) *fig* to pull sb down with one **3.** [occasionner] to bring about *(sép)*, to lead to *(insép)*, to involve **4.** ÉQUIT & SPORT [équipe, boxeur] to train, to coach ; [cheval] to train. ❖ **s'entraîner, s'entrainer*** vpi SPORT to train ▪ **s'entraîner à faire qqch** a) [gén] to teach o.s. to do sthg, to practise 🇬🇧 ou practice 🇺🇸 doing sthg b) SPORT to train o.s. to do sthg.

entraîneur, euse, entraîneur*, euse [ɑ̃tʁenœʁ, øz] nm, f [d'un cheval] trainer ; [d'un sportif] trainer, coach. ❖ **entraîneuse, entraineuse*** nf hostess *(in a bar)*.

entrapercevoir [52], **entr'apercevoir** [52] [ɑ̃tʁapɛʁsɔvwaʁ] vt to catch a (fleeting) glimpse of.

entrave [ɑ̃tʁav] nf [obstacle] hindrance, obstacle / *cette mesure est une entrave au libre-échange* this measure is an obstacle ou a hindrance to free trade.

entraver [3] [ɑ̃tʁave] vt **1.** [gêner - circulation] to hold up *(sép)* **2.** [contrecarrer - initiative, projet] to hinder, to hamper, to get in the way of **3.** *arg crime* : *j'y entrave rien ou que dalle ou que couic* I don't get this at all.

entre [ɑ̃tʁ] prép **1.** [dans l'espace] between ; [dans] in ; [à travers] through, between / *Lyon est à la cinquième place, entre Marseille et Bordeaux* Lyon is in fifth place, between Marseille and Bordeaux ▪ **tenir qqch entre ses mains** to hold sthg in one's hands **2.** [dans le temps] between / *entre le travail et le transport, je n'ai plus de temps à moi* between work and travel, I haven't any time left **3.** [indiquant un état intermédiaire] : *elle était entre le rire et les larmes* she didn't know whether to laugh or cry / *le cidre est doux ou sec ? — entre les deux* is the cider sweet or dry? — it's between the two ou in between **4.** [exprimant une approximation] between / *il y a entre 10 et 12 km* it's between 10 and 12 kms / *ils ont invité entre 15 et 20 personnes* they've invited 15 to 20 people **5.** [parmi] among / *ceux d'entre vous qui désireraient venir* those among you ou of you who'd like to come / *lequel est le plus âgé d'entre vous ?* who is the oldest amongst you? / *tu as le choix entre trois réponses* you've got a choice of three answers ▪ **je le reconnaîtrais entre tous** a) [personne] I'd know him anywhere b) [objet] I couldn't fail to recognize it **6.** [dans un groupe] : *parle, nous sommes entre amis* you can talk, we're among friends / *ils ont tendance à rester entre eux* they tend to keep themselves to themselves ▪ **entre nous, il n'a pas tort** a) [à deux] between you and me, he's right b) [à plusieurs] between us, he's right ▪ **entre vous et moi** between you and me **7.** [indiquant une relation] between / *les clans se battent entre eux* the clans fight (against) each other, there are fights between the clans. ❖ **entre autres** loc adv : *sont exposés, entre autres, des objets rares, des œuvres de jeunesse du peintre, etc.* the exhibition includes, among other things, rare objects, examples of the artist's early work, etc.

entrebâiller [3] [ɑ̃tʁəbaje] vt [porte, fenêtre] to half-open / *laisse la porte entrebâillée* leave the door half-open ou ajar.

entrechoquer [3] [ãtrəʃɔke] vt to knock ou to bang together. ❖ **s'entrechoquer** vp *(emploi réciproque)* [se heurter -verres] to clink (together) ; [-épées] to clash (together) ; [-dents] to chatter.

entrecôte [ãtrəkot] nf entrecôte (steak).

entrecoupé, e [ãtrəkupe] adj [voix] broken.

entrecouper [3] [ãtrəkupe] vt **1.** [interrompre] : *la conversation a été entrecoupée de sonneries de téléphone* the phone kept interrupting the conversation / *une voix entrecoupée de sanglots* a voice broken by sobs **2.** [émailler] ▸ **entrecouper qqch de** to intersperse ou to pepper sthg with.

entrecroiser [3] [ãtrəkrwaze] vt to intertwine. ❖ **s'entrecroiser** vp *(emploi réciproque)* to intersect.

entre-déchirer [3] [ãtrədeʃire] ❖ **s'entre-déchirer, s'entredéchirer*** vp *(emploi réciproque)* pr & fig to tear one another to pieces.

entre-deux-guerres [ãtrədøɡɛr] nm inv ou nf inv ▸ **l'entre-deux-guerres** the interwar period.

entrée [ãtre] nf **1.** [arrivée] entrance, entry / *à son entrée, tout le monde s'est levé* everybody stood up as she walked in ou entered / *il a fait une entrée remarquée* he made quite an entrance, he made a dramatic entrance ▸ **entrée en** : *entrée en action* coming into play **2.** THÉÂTRE entrance ▸ **entrée en scène** entrance ▸ **rater son entrée** to miss one's cue **3.** [adhésion] entry, admission / *l'entrée de l'Espagne dans le Marché commun* Spain's entry into the Common Market **4.** [accès] entry, admission / *l'entrée est gratuite pour les enfants* there is no admission charge for children / **'entrée'** 'way in' / **'entrée libre'** a) [dans un magasin] 'no obligation to buy' b) [dans un musée] 'free admission' / **'entrée interdite'** a) [dans un local] 'no entry', 'keep out' b) [pour empêcher le passage] 'no way in', 'no access' c) [dans un bois] 'no trespassing' **5.** [voie d'accès -à un immeuble] entrance (door) ; [-à un tunnel, une grotte] entry, entrance, mouth ▸ **entrée des artistes** stage door ▸ **entrée principale** main entrance ▸ **entrée de service** service ou tradesmen's entrance **6.** [vestibule -dans un lieu public] entrance (hall), lobby ; [-dans une maison] hall, hallway **7.** LOISIRS [billet] ticket ; [spectateur] spectator ; [visiteur] visitor **8.** CULIN first course, starter ; [dans un repas de gala] entrée **9.** INFORM ▸ **entrée des données** a) [gén] inputting of data, data input b) [par saisie] keying in ou keyboarding of data **10.** [inscription] entry ; [dans un dictionnaire] headword, entry word US. ❖ **à l'entrée de** loc prép [dans l'espace] at the entrance ou on the threshold of.

entrefaites [ãtrəfɛt] nfpl ▸ **sur ces entrefaites** at that moment ou juncture.

entrefilet [ãtrəfilɛ] nm short piece, paragraph *(in a newspaper)*.

entrejambe [ãtrəʒãb] nm crotch.

entrelacer [16] [ãtrəlase] vt to intertwine, to interlace ▸ **initiales entrelacées** intwined initials. ❖ **s'entrelacer** vp *(emploi réciproque)* to intertwine, to interlace.

entremêler [4] [ãtrəmele] vt [mêler -rubans, fleurs] to intermingle, to mix together *(sép)*. ❖ **s'entremêler** vp *(emploi réciproque)* [fils, cheveux] to become entangled ; [idées, intrigues] to become intermingled.

entremets [ãtrəmɛ] nm entremets.

entremetteur, euse [ãtrəmɛtœr, øz] nm, f **1.** *vieilli* [intermédiaire] mediator, go-between **2.** *péj* [dans des affaires galantes] procurer (procuress).

entreposer [3] [ãtrəpoze] vt [mettre en entrepôt] to store, to put in a warehouse, to warehouse.

entrepôt [ãtrəpo] nm warehouse.

entreprenant, e [ãtrəprənã, ãt] adj **1.** [dynamique] enterprising **2.** [hardi] forward.

entreprendre [79] [ãtrəprãdr] vt [commencer -lecture, étude] to begin, to start (on) ; [-croisière, carrière] to set out on ou upon *(insép)* ; [-projet, démarche] to undertake, to set about *(insép)*.

entrepreneur, euse [ãtrəprənœr, øz] nm, f **1.** CONSTR ▸ **entrepreneur en bâtiment** ou **construction** (building) contractor, builder **2.** [chef d'entreprise] entrepreneur ▸ **petit entrepreneur** small businessman ▸ **entrepreneur de pompes funèbres** funeral director, undertaker.

entrepreneuriat [ãtrəprənœrja] nm entrepreneurship.

entreprise [ãtrəpriz] nf **1.** [société] firm, concern, business ▸ **entreprise agricole** farm ▸ **entreprise familiale** family business ou firm ▸ **entreprise de pompes funèbres** funeral director's, undertaker's ▸ **entreprise de transports** transport company ▸ **entreprise de travaux publics** civil engineering firm ▸ **entreprise d'utilité publique** public utility company **2.** [monde des affaires] ▸ **l'entreprise** business, the business world **3.** [régime économique] enterprise (U) ▸ **l'entreprise publique / privée** public / private enterprise **4.** [initiative] undertaking, initiative.

entrer [ãtre]
◆ vi *(aux être)*

A. PÉNÉTRER **1.** [personne -gén] to enter ; [-vu de l'intérieur] to come in ; [-vu de l'extérieur] to go in ; [-à pied] to walk in ; [-à cheval, à bicyclette] to ride in ; [véhicule] to drive in / *toc, toc !* — *entrez !* knock, knock! — come in! / *la cuisine est à droite en entrant* the kitchen is on the right as you come ou go in ▸ **entrez sans frapper** go (straight) in / *il me fit signe d'entrer* he beckoned me in ▸ **entrer en gare** to pull in (to the station) ▸ **entrer au port** to come into ou to enter harbour UK ou harbor US ▸ **faire entrer qqn** to let sb in ▸ **faites-la entrer** a) [en lui montrant le chemin] show her in b) [en l'appelant] call her in ; [vent, eau] : *le vent entrait par rafales* the wind was blowing in in gusts ▸ **laisser entrer** : *ce genre de fenêtre laisse entrer plus de lumière* this kind of window lets more light in **2.** [adhérer] ▸ **entrer à l'université** to go to university UK ou college US ▸ **elle entre à la maternelle / en troisième année** she's going to nursery school / moving up into the third year ▸ **entrer à l'hôpital** to go into hospital UK, to enter the hospital US **3.** ÉCON [devises, produits] to enter ▸ **faire entrer des marchandises** a) [gén] to get goods in b) [en fraude] to smuggle goods in **4.** [tenir, trouver sa place] ▸ **je peux faire entrer un autre sac sous le siège** a) [gén] I can fit another bag under the seat b) [en serrant] I can squeeze another bag under the seat **5.** RELIG ▸ **entrer en religion** to enter the religious life.

B. DÉBUTER ▸ **entrer en** : *entrer en pourparlers* to start ou to enter negotiations ▸ **entrer en conversation avec qqn** to strike up a conversation with sb ▸ **entrer en guerre** to go to war.

◆ vt *(aux avoir)* **1.** [produits -gén] to take in *(sép)*, to bring in *(sép)*, to import ; [-en fraude] to smuggle in *(sép)* **2.** [enfoncer] to dig **3.** [passer] : *entre la tête par ce trou-là* get your head through that hole **4.** INFORM to enter. ❖ **entrer dans** v + prép **1.** [pénétrer dans -obj : lieu] to enter, to come into, to go into ; [à pied] to walk into ▸ **entrer dans l'eau** to get into the water / *un rayon de soleil entra dans la chambre* a ray of sunlight entered the room **2.** [adhérer à -obj : club, association, parti] to join, to become a member of ; [-obj : entreprise] to join / *entrer dans le monde du travail* to start work / *il l'a fait entrer dans la société* he got him a job with the firm **3.** [heurter -pilier, mur] to crash into, to hit ; [-voiture] to collide with **4.** [constituant] : *entrer dans la composition de* to go into

5. [se mêler de] to enter into ; [se lancer dans] : *sans entrer dans les détails* without going into details **6.** [être inclus dans] : *c'est entré dans les mœurs* it's become accepted / *elle est entrée dans la légende de son vivant* she became a living legend **7.** [s'enfoncer, pénétrer dans] ▸ **la balle / flèche est entrée dans son bras** the bullet / arrow lodged itself in her arm ▸ **faire entrer qqch de force dans** to force sthg into **8.** [tenir dans] to get in, to go in, to fit in ▸ **faire entrer** [en poussant] : *faire entrer des vêtements dans une valise* to press clothes in ou down in a suitcase **9.** [obj : période] to enter / *elle entre dans sa 97ᵉ année* she's entering her 97th year **10.** [relever de - rubrique] to fall into, to come into ; [- responsabilités] to be part of / *cela n'entre pas dans mes attributions* this is not within my responsibilities.

entresol [ɑ̃tʀəsɔl] nm mezzanine, entresol.

entre(-)temps, entretemps* [ɑ̃tʀətɑ̃] adv meanwhile, in the meantime.

entretenir [40] [ɑ̃tʀətniʀ] vt **1.** [tenir en bon état - locaux, château] to maintain, to look after *(insép)*, to see to the upkeep of ; [- argenterie, lainage] to look after *(insép)* ; [- matériel, voiture, route] to maintain ; [- santé, beauté] to look after *(insép)*, to maintain ▸ **entretenir sa forme** ou **condition physique** to keep o.s. fit ou in shape **2.** [maintenir - feu] to keep going ou burning ; [- querelle, rancune] to foster, to feed ; [- enthousiasme] to foster, to keep alive *(sép)* ; [- espoirs, illusions] to cherish, to entertain ; [- fraîcheur, humidité] to maintain ▸ **entretenir une correspondance avec qqn** to keep up ou to carry on a correspondence with sb **3.** [payer les dépenses de - enfants] to support ; [- maîtresse] to keep, to support ; [- troupes] to keep, to maintain ▸ **se faire entretenir par qqn** to be kept by sb **4.** ▸ **entretenir qqn de** [lui parler de] to converse with *sout* ou to speak to sb about. ❖ **s'entretenir** vp *(emploi réciproque)* to have a discussion, to talk / *ils se sont longuement entretenus de...* they had a lengthy discussion about... ❖ **s'entretenir avec** vp + prép to converse with, to speak to.

entretenu, e [ɑ̃tʀətny] adj **1.** [personne] kept **2.** [lieu] ▸ **maison bien entretenue a)** [où le ménage est fait] well-kept house **b)** [en bon état] house in good repair ▸ **maison mal entretenue a)** [sale et mal rangée] badly kept house **b)** [en mauvais état] house in bad repair / *jardin bien / mal entretenu* well-kept / neglected garden.

entretien [ɑ̃tʀətjɛ̃] nm **1.** [maintenance] maintenance, upkeep **2.** [discussion - entre employeur et candidat] interview ; [colloque] discussion ▸ **solliciter / accorder un entretien** to request / to grant an interview ▸ **entretien d'embauche** job interview ▸ **entretien d'évaluation** [au travail] appraisal **3.** RADIO & TV [questions] interview.

entre-tuer [7] [ɑ̃tʀətɥe] ❖ **s'entre-tuer, s'entretuer*** vp *(emploi réciproque)* to kill one another.

entrevoir [62] [ɑ̃tʀəvwaʀ] vt **1.** [apercevoir] to catch sight ou a glimpse of **2.** [pressentir - solution, vie meilleure] to glimpse ; [- difficultés, issue] to foresee, to anticipate.

entrevue [ɑ̃tʀəvy] nf [réunion] meeting ; [tête-à-tête] interview.

entrouvert, e [ɑ̃tʀuvɛʀ, ɛʀt] adj [porte] half-open, ajar.

entrouvrir [34] [ɑ̃tʀuvʀiʀ] vt to half-open. ❖ **s'entrouvrir** vpi [porte] to half-open ; [rideau] to draw back *(sép)* (slightly) ; [lèvres] to part.

énumération [enymeʀasjɔ̃] nf [énonciation] enumeration, enumerating.

énumérer [18] [enymeʀe] vt to enumerate, to itemize, to list.

✐ In reformed spelling (see p. 16-18), this verb is conjugated like *semer : il énumèrera, elle énumèrerait.*

env. abr écrite de **environ**.

---

envahir [32] [ɑ̃vaiʀ] vt **1.** [occuper - pays, palais] to invade, to overrun **2.** [se répandre dans] to overrun / *plate-bande envahie par les mauvaises herbes* border overrun with weeds.

envahissant, e [ɑ̃vaisɑ̃, ɑ̃t] adj **1.** [qui s'étend - végétation] overgrown, rampant ; [- ambition, passion] invasive **2.** [importun - voisin, ami] interfering, intrusive.

envahisseur [ɑ̃vaisœʀ] nm invader.

enveloppe [ɑ̃vlɔp] nf **1.** [pour lettre] envelope ▸ **enveloppe autoadhésive** self-sealing envelope ▸ **enveloppe matelassée** ou **rembourrée** padded envelope, Jiffy bag® **2.** FIN [don] sum of money, gratuity ; [don illégal] bribe ; [crédits] budget / *l'enveloppe (budgétaire) du ministère de la Culture* the Arts budget / *il a touché une enveloppe* [pot-de-vin] he got a backhander. ❖ **sous enveloppe** loc adv ▸ **mettre / envoyer sous enveloppe** to put / to send in an envelope / *envoyer un magazine sous enveloppe* [pour le dissimuler] to send a magazine under plain cover.

enveloppé, e [ɑ̃vlɔpe] adj **1.** *fam & hum* [personne] : *il est un peu enveloppé* he's a bit chubby **2.** *fam* [propos] : *c'était très bien enveloppé* it was phrased nicely.

envelopper [3] [ɑ̃vlɔpe] vt **1.** [empaqueter] to wrap (up) **2.** [emmailloter] to wrap (up) **3.** [voiler - suj : brume, obscurité] to shroud, to envelop. ❖ **s'envelopper dans** vp + prép [vêtement] to wrap o.s. in.

envenimer [3] [ɑ̃vnime] vt [aggraver - conflit] to inflame, to fan the flames of ; [- rapports] to poison, to spoil. ❖ **s'envenimer** vpi **1.** MÉD to fester, to become septic **2.** [empirer - relation] to grow more bitter ou acrimonious ; [- situation] to get worse, to worsen.

envergure [ɑ̃vɛʀgyʀ] nf **1.** [d'un oiseau, d'un avion] wingspan, wingspread **2.** NAUT breadth **3.** [importance - d'une manifestation, d'une œuvre] scale, scope ▸ **de petite** ou **faible envergure** small ▸ **de grande envergure** large-scale **4.** [d'un savant, d'un président] calibre 🇬🇧, caliber 🇺🇸 ▸ **il manque d'envergure** he doesn't have a strong personality.

envers [ɑ̃vɛʀ] ◆ prép [à l'égard de] towards 🇬🇧, toward 🇺🇸, to ▸ **son attitude envers moi** his attitude towards me ▸ **envers et contre tous** ou **tous** in the face of ou despite all opposition. ◆ nm **1.** [autre côté] ▸ **l'envers a)** [d'un papier] the other side, the back **b)** [d'une peau] the inside **2.** [mauvais côté] wrong side ▸ **l'envers du décor** ou **tableau** the other side of the coin **3.** GÉOGR cold northern slope *(of valley)*. ❖ **à l'envers** loc adv **1.** [dans le mauvais sens] ▸ **mettre à l'envers a)** [chapeau] to put on the wrong way round, to put on back to front **b)** [chaussettes] to put on inside out **2.** [mal, anormalement] ▸ **tout va** ou **marche à l'envers** everything is upside down ou topsy-turvy **3.** [dans l'ordre inverse] backwards, in reverse.

enviable [ɑ̃vjabl] adj enviable ▸ **peu enviable** unenviable.

envie [ɑ̃vi] nf **1.** [souhait, désir] desire ▸ **avoir envie de** : *j'avais (très) envie de ce disque* I wanted that record (very much) / *j'ai envie d'une bière* I feel like a beer ▸ **avoir envie de rire / pleurer** to feel like laughing / crying / *j'ai presque envie de ne pas y aller* I have half a mind not to go / *il avait moyennement envie de la revoir* he didn't really feel like seeing her again ▸ **mourir** ou **crever** *fam* **d'envie de faire qqch** to be dying to do sthg ▸ **avoir envie que** : *elle n'a pas envie que tu restes* she doesn't want you to stay ▸ **faire envie à qqn** : *la robe beige me fait vraiment envie* I'm really tempted by the beige dress ▸ **ôter** ou **faire passer à qqn l'envie de faire...** : *voilà qui lui ôtera l'envie de revenir* this'll make sure he's not tempted to come back ▸ **envie de femme enceinte** (pregnant woman's) craving **2.** [désir sexuel] desire ▸ **j'ai envie de toi** I want you **3.** [besoin] urge ▸ **être pris d'une envie (pressante** ou

---

naturelle) to feel the call of nature, to be taken short ⓤ **4.** [jalousie] envy **5.** ANAT [tache] birthmark ; [peau] hangnail.

envier [9] [ãvje] vt ▸ **envier qqch à qqn** to envy sb (for) sthg / *vous n'avez rien à lui envier* you have no reason to be envious of her ▸ **envier qqn d'avoir fait qqch** to envy sb for having done sthg.

envieux, euse [ãvjø, øz] ◆ adj envious. ◆ nm, f envious person ▸ **faire des envieux** to arouse ou to excite envy.

environ [ãvirɔ̃] adv about, around / *il y a environ six mois* about six months ago / *il était environ midi* it was around ou about 12 / *il habite à environ 100 m* ou *à 100 m environ d'ici* he lives about 100 m from here.

environnant, e [ãvirɔnã, ãt] adj surrounding.

environnement [ãvirɔnmã] nm **1.** [lieux avoisinants] environment, surroundings, surrounding area **2.** [milieu] background ▸ **l'environnement culturel / familial** the cultural / family background **3.** ÉCOL ▸ **l'environnement** the environment.

environnemental, e, aux [ãvirɔnmãtal, o] adj environmental.

environnementaliste [ãvirɔnmãtalist] nmf environmentalist.

environner [3] [ãvirɔne] vt to surround, to encircle.

environs [ãvirɔ̃] nmpl surroundings, surrounding area. ◆ **aux environs de** loc prép **1.** [dans l'espace] near, close to **2.** [dans le temps] around, round about / *aux environs de midi* around noon, at noon or thereabouts. ◆ **dans les environs** loc adv in the local ou surrounding area. ◆ **dans les environs de** loc prép in the vicinity of, near.

envisageable [ãvizaʒabl] adj conceivable.

envisager [17] [ãvizaʒe] vt **1.** [examiner] to consider **2.** [prévoir] to envisage, to contemplate, to consider / *j'envisage d'aller vivre là-bas* I'm contemplating going ou I'm thinking of going to live there.

envoi [ãvwa] nm **1.** [de marchandises, d'argent] sending ▸ **faire un envoi** a) [colis] to send a parcel ⓤ ou package ⓤ b) [lettre] to send a letter **2.** [colis] parcel, consignment ; [lettre] letter **3.** SPORT ▸ **coup d'envoi** kick-off.

envol [ãvɔl] nm **1.** [d'un oiseau] taking flight ▸ **l'aigle prit son envol** the eagle took flight **2.** AÉRON taking off (U), takeoff.

envolée [ãvɔle] nf **1.** [élan] flight / *il s'est lancé dans une grande envolée lyrique* hum he waxed lyrical **2.** [augmentation] sudden rise.

envoler [3] [ãvɔle] ◆ **s'envoler** vpi **1.** [oiseau] to fly off ou away **2.** AÉRON [avion] to take off / *je m'envole pour Tokyo demain* I'm flying (off) to Tokyo tomorrow **3.** [passer - temps] to fly **4.** [augmenter - cours, dollar] to soar **5.** [être emporté - écharpe] to blow off ou away / *le vent a fait s'envoler tous les papiers* the wind sent all the documents flying (everywhere) **6.** [disparaître - voleur, stylo] to disappear, to vanish (into thin air).

envoûtant, e, envoutant*, e [ãvutã, ãt] adj spellbinding, bewitching, entrancing.

envoûter, envouter* [3] [ãvute] vt to bewitch, to cast a spell on ▸ **être envoûté par une voix / femme** to be under the spell of a voice / woman.

envoyé, e [ãvwaje] nm, f [gén] messenger ; POL envoy ; PRESSE correspondent / *de notre envoyé spécial à Londres* from our special correspondent in London.

envoyer [30] [ãvwaje] vt **1.** [expédier - gén] to send (off) ; [- message radio] to send out (sép) ; [- marchandises] to send, to dispatch ; [- invitation] to send (out) ; [- vœux, condoléances] to send ; [- CV, candidature] to send (in) ; [- argent, mandat] to send, to remit ▸ **envoyer qqch par bateau**

to ship sthg, to send sthg by ship ▸ **envoyer un (petit) mot à qqn** to drop sb a line **2.** [personne] to send / *envoyer un enfant à l'école* to send a child (off) to school / *on m'a envoyé aux nouvelles* I've been sent to find out whether there's any news / *envoyer des soldats à la mort* to send soldiers to their deaths ; *(suivi d'un infinitif)* ▸ **envoyer chercher un médecin** to send for a doctor ▸ **envoyer promener** ou **balader** ou **paître** ou **bouler qqn** *fam*, **envoyer qqn au diable**, *fam*, **envoyer qqn sur les roses** *fam* to send sb packing ▸ **tout envoyer promener** *fam* ou **valser** *fam*: *j'avais envie de tout envoyer promener* ou *valser* I felt like chucking the whole thing in **3.** [projeter] : *envoyer un adversaire à terre* ou *au tapis* to knock an opponent down ou to the ground **4.** [lancer - projectile] to throw, to fling ; [- ballon] to throw ; [- balle de tennis] to send ▸ **envoyer sa fumée dans les yeux de qqn** to blow smoke into sb's eyes ▸ **envoyer des baisers** to blow sb kisses **5.** [donner - coup] ▸ **envoyer des coups de pied / poing à qqn** to kick / to punch sb **6.** [hisser - pavillon] to hoist. ◆ **s'envoyer** ◆ vpt **1.** *fam* [subir - corvée] to get saddled with **2.** *fam* [consommer - bière, bouteille] to knock back *(sép)*, to down ; [- gâteau] to wolf down ; *tfam* [sexuellement] ▸ **s'envoyer qqn** to get off with sb. ◆ vpi EXPR ▸ **s'envoyer en l'air** *tfam* to have it off.

> 📋 **Envoyer qqch à qqn** *Send sthg to sb* ou *send sb sthg.*
>
> Notez la construction à double complément qui en anglais peut prendre deux formes dont le sens est le même :
>
> • une structure identique à celle du français :
> verbe + COD + préposition + COI
> *send sthg to sb*
>
> • une structure qui diffère de celle du français, sans préposition, et dans laquelle l'ordre des compléments est inversé :
> verbe + COI + COD
> *send sb sthg*
>
> **Marie envoie toujours des cartes postales à ses parents lorsqu'elle est en voyage.** *Marie always sends postcards to her parents when she's travelling* ou *Marie always sends her parents postcards when she's travelling.*

envoyeur, euse [ãvwajœr, øz] nm, f sender.

éolien, enne [eɔljɛ̃, ɛn] adj aeolian *spéc*, wind *(modif)*. ◆ **éolienne** nf windmill, wind pump.

épagneul [epaɲœl] nm spaniel ▸ **épagneul breton** Breton spaniel.

épais, aisse [epɛ, ɛs] adj **1.** [haut - livre, strate, tranche] thick ; [- couche de neige] thick, deep / *une planche épaisse de 10 centimètres* a board 10 centimetres thick **2.** [charnu - lèvres, cheville, taille] thick ; [- corps] thickset, stocky / *il n'est pas (bien) épais* *fam* he's thin (as a rake) **3.** [dense - fumée, sauce, foule] thick ; [- sourcil] thick, bushy.

épaisseur [epɛsœr] nf **1.** [d'un mur, d'un tissu, d'une strate] thickness / *un mur de 30 centimètres d'épaisseur* a wall 30 centimetres thick **2.** [couche] layer, thickness ▸ **plier un papier en quatre / cinq épaisseurs** to fold a piece of paper in four / five **3.** [densité - du brouillard, d'une soupe, d'un feuillage] thickness.

épaissir [32] [epesir] ◆ vt **1.** [sauce, enduit] to thicken (up) **2.** [grossir] to thicken. ◆ vi **1.** [fumée, peinture, mayonnaise] to thicken, to get thicker **2.** [grossir - taille] to get thicker ou bigger ; [- traits du visage] to get coarser, to coarsen / *il a beaucoup épaissi* he's put on a lot of weight. ❖ **s'épaissir** vpi **1.** [fumée, crème] to thicken, to get thicker **2.** [grossir - traits] to get coarse ou coarser ; [- taille] to get thicker ou bigger ; [- personne] to grow stout ou stouter **3.** fig [mystère, ténèbres] to deepen ▸ **le mystère s'épaissit a)** [dans un fait divers] the mystery deepens **b)** [dans un roman] the plot thickens.

épancher [3] [epɑ̃ʃe] vt [tendresse, craintes] to pour out (sép) ; [colère] to vent, to give vent to. ❖ **s'épancher** vpi [se confier] ▸ **s'épancher auprès d'un ami** to open one's heart to ou to pour out one's feelings to a friend.

épanoui, e [epanwi] adj [rose, jeunesse] blooming ; [sourire] beaming, radiant ; [personne] radiant.

épanouir [32] [epanwiʀ] ❖ **s'épanouir** vpi **1.** [fleur] to bloom, to open **2.** [personne] to blossom.

épanouissant, e [epanwisɑ̃, ɑ̃t] adj fulfilling.

épanouissement [epanwismɑ̃] nm **1.** [d'une plante] blooming, opening up **2.** [d'un visage] lighting up ; [d'un enfant, d'une personnalité] fulfilment, self-fulfilment.

épargnant, e [epaʀɲɑ̃, ɑ̃t] nm, f saver, investor ▸ **petits épargnants** small investors.

épargne [epaʀɲ] nf **1.** [économies] ▸ **l'épargne** savings **2.** [fait d'économiser] saving ▸ **épargne salariale** employee savings.

épargner [3] [epaʀɲe] ❖ vt **1.** [économiser - argent, essence, forces] to save **2.** [éviter] : *tu m'as épargné un déplacement inutile* you spared ou saved me a wasted journey / *je vous épargnerai les détails* I'll spare you the details **3.** [ménager - vieillard, adversaire] to spare. ❖ vi to save (money), to put money aside ▸ **épargner sur qqch** péj to save on sthg.

éparpiller [3] [epaʀpije] vt **1.** [disperser - lettres, graines] to scatter ; [- troupes, famille] to disperse / *éparpillés un peu partout dans le monde* scattered about the world **2.** [dissiper - attention, forces] to dissipate. ❖ **s'éparpiller** vpi **1.** [se disperser - foule, élèves] to scatter, to disperse **2.** [disperser son énergie] to dissipate one's energies.

épars, e [epaʀ, aʀs] adj scattered.

épatant, e [epatɑ̃, ɑ̃t] adj fam & vieilli splendid.

épate [epat] nf fam & péj showing off ▸ **faire de l'épate** to show off.

épaté, e [epate] adj [aplati - nez, forme] flat, snub.

épater [3] [epate] vt fam **1.** [étonner] to amaze ▸ **ça t'épate, hein ?** how about that then? **2.** péj [impressionner] to impress.

épaule [epol] nf **1.** ANAT shoulder ▸ **être large d'épaules** to be broad-shouldered ▸ **donner un coup d'épaule à qqn** to knock sb with one's shoulder ▸ **reposer sur les épaules de qqn** to rest on sb's shoulders **2.** CULIN shoulder ▸ **épaule d'agneau** shoulder of lamb.

épauler [3] [epole] vt **1.** [fusil] to raise (to the shoulder) **2.** [aider] to support, to back up (sép).

épaulette [epolɛt] nf **1.** MIL epaulette **2.** VÊT shoulder pad **3.** [bretelle] shoulder strap.

épave [epav] nf [véhicule, bateau] wreck.

épeautre [epotʀ] nm spelt (wheat).

épée [epe] nf ARM sword ▸ **l'épée de Damoclès** the sword of Damocles ▸ **c'est un coup d'épée dans l'eau** it's a waste of time.

épeler [24] [eple] vt [nom] to spell (out). ❖ **s'épeler** vp (emploi passif) : *comment ça s'épelle ?* how do you spell it?, how is it spelt?

✎ In reformed spelling (see p. 16-18), this verb is conjugated like **peler** : *il épèle, elle épèlera.*

éperdu, e [epɛʀdy] adj **1.** [fou - regard, cri] wild, distraught / *une fuite éperdue* a headlong flight ▸ **éperdu de douleur** frantic ou distraught with grief **2.** [intense - gratitude] boundless ; [- besoin] violent, intense.

éperdument [epɛʀdymɑ̃] adv **1.** [à la folie] madly, passionately **2.** [en intensif] ▸ **je m'en moque** ou **fiche** fam **éperdument** I couldn't care less ou give a damn.

éperlan [epɛʀlɑ̃] nm smelt.

éperon [epʀɔ̃] nm ÉQUIT & TRAV PUB spur.

éperonner [3] [epʀɔne] vt ÉQUIT to spur (on).

épervier [epɛʀvje] nm ORNITH sparrowhawk.

épeurant, e [epœʀɑ̃, ɑ̃t] adj Québec scary.

épeurer [5] [epœʀe] vt Québec to scare, to frighten.

éphémère [efemɛʀ] ❖ adj [gloire, sentiment] short-lived, ephemeral, transient ; [mode] short-lived ; [regret] passing. ❖ nm ZOOL mayfly, dayfly, ephemera spéc.

éphéméride [efemeʀid] nf [calendrier] tear-off calendar.

épi [epi] nm **1.** [de fleur] spike ; [de céréale] ear ▸ **épi de maïs** corncob **2.** [de cheveux] tuft.

épice [epis] nf spice.

épicé, e [epise] adj CULIN highly spiced, hot, spicy.

épicéa [episea] nm spruce.

épicerie [episʀi] nf **1.** [magasin] grocery shop UK ou store US ▸ **à l'épicerie du coin** at the local grocer's ▸ **épicerie fine** delicatessen **2.** [profession] grocery trade **3.** [aliments] provisions, groceries.

épicier, ère [episje, ɛʀ] nm, f grocer.

épidémie [epidemi] nf epidemic / *épidémie de typhus* epidemic of typhus, typhus epidemic.

épiderme [epidɛʀm] nm skin, epidermis spéc.

épidermique [epidɛʀmik] adj **1.** ANAT epidermic spéc, epidermal spéc, skin (modif) ; [blessure] surface (modif) ; [greffe] skin (modif) **2.** [immédiat - sentiment, réaction] instant.

épier [9] [epje] vt **1.** [espionner] to spy on (insép) **2.** [réaction, mouvement] to watch closely ; [bruit] to listen out for ; [occasion] to be on the look-out, to watch for (insép).

épieu, x [epjø] nm MIL pike ; CHASSE hunting spear.

épilateur [epilatœʀ] nm hair remover ▸ **épilateur à cire** wax hair remover ▸ **épilateur électrique** electric hair remover.

épilation [epilasjɔ̃] nf hair removal ▸ **épilation à la cire** waxing ▸ **épilation au laser** ou **définitive** laser ou permanent hair removal.

épilepsie [epilɛpsi] nf epilepsy.

épiler [3] [epile] vt [aisselles, jambes] to remove unwanted hair from ; [sourcils] to pluck / *se faire épiler les jambes* to have one's legs waxed. ❖ **s'épiler** vp (emploi réfléchi) to remove unwanted hair / *s'épiler les jambes à la cire* to wax one's legs.

épilogue [epilɔg] nm **1.** LITTÉR & THÉÂTRE epilogue **2.** [issue] conclusion, dénouement.

épiloguer [3] [epilɔge] vi ▸ **épiloguer sur qqch** to hold forth about ou to go over (and over) sthg.

épinard [epinaʀ] nm spinach ▸ **épinards en branches** spinach leaves.

épine [epin] nf **1.** [de fleur] thorn, prickle ; [de hérisson] spine, prickle ▸ **tirer** ou **ôter une épine du pied à qqn** to get sb out of a spot **2.** [buisson] thorn bush. ❖ **épine dorsale** nf backbone.

épinette [epinɛt] nf Québec [épicéa] spruce.

épineux, euse [epinø, øz] ❖ adj **1.** BOT thorny, prickly **2.** [délicat - problème, contexte] thorny, tricky. ❖ nm thorn bush.

épingle [epɛ̃gl] nf COUT pin ▸ **épingle anglaise** ou **à nourrice** ou **de sûreté** safety pin ▸ **épingle à cheveux** hairpin ▸ **épingle à linge** clothes peg 🇬🇧 ou pin 🇺🇸 ▸ **épingle de cravate** tie clip, tiepin ▸ **tirer** ou **retirer son épingle du jeu** to pull out.

épingler [3] [epɛ̃gle] vt **1.** [attacher - badge, papier] to pin (on) **2.** fam [arrêter] to nab / **se faire épingler** to get nabbed **3.** [critiquer] to criticize severely.

épinglette [epɛ̃glɛt] nf 🇶🇧ᴜᴇᴮᴇᴄ **1.** [broche] brooch **2.** [petit insigne] pin.

épinière [epinjɛʀ] adj f ⟶ **moelle**.

épiphanie [epifani] nf [fête] ▸ **l'Épiphanie** Twelfth Night, the Epiphany.

épique [epik] adj **1.** LITTÉR epic **2.** [extraordinaire - discussion, scène] epic.

épiscopal, e, aux [episkɔpal, o] adj episcopal.

épiscopat [episkɔpa] nm episcopate, episcopacy.

épisode [epizɔd] nm **1.** [partie] episode, instalment ▸ **feuilleton en six épisodes** six-part serial **2.** [circonstance] episode **3.** MÉTÉOR ▸ **épisode de neige** ou **neigeux a)** [gén] snowy period **b)** [chute de neige] snowfall. ⟐ **à épisodes** loc adj serialized.

épisodique [epizɔdik] adj [ponctuel] occasional ▸ **de façon épisodique** occasionally.

épitaphe [epitaf] nf epitaph.

épithète [epitɛt] ⟐ adj attributive. ⟐ nf **1.** GRAM attribute **2.** [qualificatif] epithet.

éploré, e [eplɔʀe] adj [parent, veuve] tearful, weeping ; [voix] tearful ; [visage] bathed ou covered in tears.

épluche-légumes [eplyʃlegym] nm inv potato peeler.

éplucher [3] [eplyʃe] vt **1.** [peler - pomme] to peel ; [- poireau] to clean **2.** [analyser - texte] to dissect, to go over (insép) with a fine-tooth comb ; [- liste, statistiques] to go through (insép).

épluchure [eplyʃyʀ] nf piece of peeling / **épluchures de pommes** apple peelings.

éponge [epɔ̃ʒ] nf **1.** ZOOL sponge **2.** [pour nettoyer] sponge ▸ **éponge métallique** scouring pad, scourer / **effacer une tache d'un coup d'éponge** to sponge a stain out ou away ▸ **jeter l'éponge** to throw in the sponge ▸ **passer l'éponge sur qqch** to forget all about sthg **3.** BOT ▸ **éponge végétale** loofah, vegetable sponge.

éponger [17] [epɔ̃ʒe] vt **1.** [absorber - encre, vin] to soak ou to sponge (up) ▸ **éponger ses dettes** fig to pay off one's debts **2.** [nettoyer - table] to wipe, to sponge (down) ; [- visage] to sponge, to wipe. ⟐ **s'éponger** vpt ▸ **s'éponger le front** to mop one's brow.

épopée [epɔpe] nf [poème] epic (poem) ; [récit] epic (tale) ; [saga] saga.

époque [epɔk] nf **1.** [moment, date] time / **à l'époque des Grecs** at the time of the Greeks ▸ **à la même époque** at the same time, during the same period ▸ **à cette époque-là** at that time, in those days / **les jeunes de notre époque** the young people of today ▸ **être de** ou **vivre avec son époque** to move with the times / **on vit une drôle d'époque** we live in strange times **2.** [période historique] age, era, epoch ▸ **la Belle Époque** the Belle Epoque **3.** [style] period **4.** GÉOL period ▸ **à l'époque glaciaire** in the ice age. ⟐ **d'époque** loc adj period (modif) ▸ **la pendule est d'époque** it's a period clock.

époumoner [3] [epumɔne] ⟐ **s'époumoner** vpi to shout o.s. hoarse.

épouse [epuz] nf wife, spouse sout / **voulez-vous prendre Maud Jolas pour épouse ?** do you take Maud Jolas to be your lawful wedded wife?

épouser [3] [epuze] vt **1.** [se marier avec] to marry **2.** [adopter - idées] to espouse, to embrace ; [- cause] to take up (sép) **3.** [suivre] : **une robe qui épouse la forme du corps** a figure-hugging ou close-fitting dress.

épousseter [27] [epuste] vt **1.** [nettoyer] to dust **2.** [enlever - poussière] to dust ou to flick off (sép). ✎ In reformed spelling (see p. 16-18), this verb is conjugated like *acheter* : **il époussète, elle époussètera**.

époustouflant, e [epustuflɑ̃, ɑ̃t] adj fam stunning, astounding, staggering.

époustoufler [3] [epustufle] vt fam to stun, to astound, to flabbergast.

épouvantable [epuvɑ̃tabl] adj **1.** [très désagréable] awful, horrible, terrible / **elle a un caractère épouvantable** she has a foul temper **2.** [effrayant] frightening, dreadful.

épouvantail [epuvɑ̃taj] nm **1.** [pour oiseaux] scarecrow **2.** [menace] bogey, bogeyman / **agiter l'épouvantail de la drogue** to use the threat of drugs as a bogey.

épouvante [epuvɑ̃t] nf terror, dread. ⟐ **d'épouvante** loc adj [film, roman] horror (modif).

épouvanter [3] [epuvɑ̃te] vt to terrify, to fill with terror ou dread.

époux [epu] nm husband, spouse sout / **voulez-vous prendre Paul Hilbert pour époux ?** do you take Paul Hilbert to be your lawful wedded husband? ▸ **les époux Bertier** Mr and Mrs Bertier.

éprendre [79] [epʀɑ̃dʀ] ⟐ **s'éprendre de** vp + prép litt ▸ **s'éprendre de qqn** to fall for sb, to become enamoured of sb litt.

épreuve [epʀœv] nf **1.** [test] test ▸ **l'épreuve du temps** the test of time ▸ **épreuve de force** trial of strength **2.** [obstacle] ordeal, trial ▸ **vie remplie d'épreuves** life of hardship **3.** ÉDUC & UNIV [examen] test, examination ▸ **épreuve écrite** paper, written test ▸ **épreuve orale** oral (test) ; [copie] paper, script ▸ **corriger des épreuves** to mark exam papers **4.** SPORT event ▸ **épreuves d'athlétisme** track events ▸ **épreuve d'endurance** heat, endurance trial ▸ **épreuve de sélection** heat ▸ **épreuve contre la montre** time trial **5.** IMPR proof **6.** PHOT print. ⟐ **à l'épreuve** loc adv ▸ **mettre qqn à l'épreuve** to put sb to the test. ⟐ **à l'épreuve de** loc prép proof against ▸ **à l'épreuve du feu** fireproof. ⟐ **à rude épreuve** loc adv ▸ **mettre les nerfs de qqn à rude épreuve** to put sb's nerves to the test. ⟐ **à toute épreuve** loc adj [mécanisme] foolproof ; [patience, bonne humeur] unfailing.

épris, e [epri, iz] ⟐ pp ⟶ **éprendre**. ⟐ adj litt ▸ **être épris de qqn** to be in love with sb ▸ **être épris de liberté** to be in love with freedom.

éprouvant, e [epʀuvɑ̃, ɑ̃t] adj trying, testing.

éprouvé, e [epʀuve] adj [méthode, matériel] well-tested, tried and tested, proven ; [compétence, courage] proven ; [spécialiste] proven, experienced.

éprouver [3] [epʀuve] vt **1.** [ressentir - douleur, haine] to feel, to experience **2.** [tester - procédé] to try ou to test (out) ; [- courage, personne] to test ▸ **éprouver la patience de qqn** to try sb's patience, to put sb's patience to the test **3.** [subir - pertes] to suffer, to sustain **4.** [faire souffrir] to try, to test / **une région durement éprouvée par la crise** an area that has been hard-hit by the recession.

éprouvette [epʀuvɛt] nf test tube.

EPS (abr de **éducation physique et sportive**) nf PE.

épuisant, e [epɥizɑ̃, ɑ̃t] adj exhausting.

épuisé, e [epɥize] adj **1.** [fatigué] exhausted, worn-out, tired-out **2.** COMM [article] sold-out ; [livre] out of print ; [stock] exhausted.

épuisement [epqizmã] nm **1.** [fatigue] exhaustion **2.** COMM & INDUST exhaustion ▪ **jusqu'à épuisement des stocks** while stocks last.

épuiser [3] [epqize] vt [fatiguer] to exhaust, to wear ou to tire out *(sép)*. ❖ **s'épuiser** vpi **1.** [être très réduit - provisions, munitions] to run out, to give out ; [-source] to dry up ; [-filon] to be worked out **2.** [se fatiguer - athlète] to wear o.s. out, to exhaust o.s. ; [-corps] to wear itself out, to run out of steam ▪ **s'épuiser à faire qqch** [s'évertuer à faire qqch] to wear o.s. out doing sthg.

épuisette [epqizɛt] nf [filet] landing net.

épuration [epyʀasjɔ̃] nf [de l'eau] purification, filtering.

Équateur [ekwatœʀ] npr m ▪ **(la république de) l'Équateur** (the Republic of) Ecuador.

équateur [ekwatœʀ] nm equator ▪ **sous l'équateur** at the equator.

équation [ekwasjɔ̃] nf MATH equation.

équato-guinéen, enne [ekwatɔgineɛ̃, ɛn] adj from Equatorial Guinea. ❖ **Équato-Guinéen, enne** nm, f Equatorial Guinean.

équatorial, e, aux [ekwatɔʀjal, o] adj ASTRON & GÉOGR equatorial.

équatorien, enne [ekwatɔʀjɛ̃, ɛn] adj Ecuadoran, Ecuadorian. ❖ **Équatorien, enne** nm, f Ecuadoran, Ecuadorian.

équerre [ekɛʀ] nf [instrument] set square ᴜᴷ, triangle ᴜˢ. ❖ **à l'équerre, d'équerre** loc adj [mur] straight ; [pièce] square. ❖ **en équerre** loc adj at right angles.

équestre [ekɛstʀ] adj [statue, peinture] equestrian ; [exercice, centre] horseriding *(modif)* ▪ **le sport équestre** (horse) riding.

équeuter [3] [ekøte] vt [fruit] to pull the stalk off, to remove the stalk from.

équilibre [ekilibʀ] nm **1.** [stabilité du corps] balance ▪ **garder / perdre l'équilibre** to keep / to lose one's balance **2.** [rapport de force] balance ▪ **rétablir l'équilibre** to restore the balance **3.** ÉCON & FIN ▪ **équilibre budgétaire** balance in the budget **4.** PSYCHOL ▪ **manquer d'équilibre** to be (mentally ou emotionally) unbalanced ▪ **équilibre mental** (mental) equilibrium **5.** CHIM & PHYS equilibrium. ❖ **en équilibre** loc adv : *marcher en équilibre sur un fil* to balance on a tightrope ▪ **mettre qqch en équilibre** to balance sthg.

équilibré, e [ekilibʀe] adj **1.** PSYCHOL balanced, stable **2.** [budget] balanced ; [alimentation, emploi du temps] balanced, well-balanced ▪ **mal équilibré** unbalanced, unstable ; [vie] well-regulated.

équilibrer [3] [ekilibʀe] vt **1.** [contrebalancer - poids, forces] to counterbalance **2.** [rendre stable - balance, budget] to balance. ❖ **s'équilibrer** vp *(emploi réciproque)* to counterbalance each other ou one another, to even out.

équilibriste [ekilibʀist] nmf [acrobate] acrobat ; [funambule] tightrope walker.

équinoxe [ekinɔks] nm equinox.

équipage [ekipaʒ] nm AÉRON & NAUT crew.

équipe [ekip] nf **1.** [groupe - de chercheurs, de secouristes] team ▪ **travailler en équipe** to work as a team ▪ **faire équipe avec qqn** to team up with sb **2.** INDUST ▪ **équipe de jour / nuit** day / night shift ▪ **travailler en** ou **par équipes a)** [à l'usine] to work in shifts **b)** [sur un chantier] to work in gangs **3.** SPORT [gén] team ; [sur un bateau] crew ▪ **jouer en** ou **par équipes** to play in teams ▪ **l'équipe de France de rugby / hockey** the French rugby / hockey team **4.** [bande] crew, gang. ❖ **d'équipe** loc adj **1.** [collectif] ▪ **esprit d'équipe** team ou group spirit **2.** [sport, jeu] team *(modif)*.

équipement [ekipmã] nm **1.** [matériel -léger] equipment, supplies ; [-lourd] equipment ▪ **équipement électrique** electrical supplies **2.** [infrastructure] ▪ **équipements collectifs** public amenities ▪ **équipements sportifs / scolaires** sports / educational facilities ▪ **l'équipement routier / ferroviaire du pays** the country's road / rail infrastructure.

équiper [3] [ekipe] vt [pourvoir de matériel - armée, élève, skieur] to kit out *(sép)*, to fit out ; [-navire] to fit out *(sép)*, to commission ; [-salle] to equip, to fit out *(sép)* ; [-usine] to equip, to tool up ▪ **cuisine tout** ou **entièrement équipée** fully-equipped kitchen. ❖ **s'équiper** vp *(emploi réfléchi)* to equip o.s., to kit o.s. out ᴜᴷ.

équipier, ère [ekipje, ɛʀ] nm, f team member.

équitable [ekitabl] adj **1.** [verdict, répartition] fair, equitable ; [juge] fair, fair-minded, even-handed **2.** ÉCON [coton, thé, cacao] fair-trade.

équitation [ekitasjɔ̃] nf horse-riding ᴜᴷ, horseback riding ᴜˢ, riding ▪ **faire de l'équitation** to go horse-riding. ❖ **d'équitation** loc adj [école, professeur] riding *(modif)*.

équité [ekite] nf equity, fairness, fair-mindedness. ❖ **en toute équité** loc adv very equitably ou fairly.

équivalent [ekivalɑ̃, ɑ̃t] adj [gén & MATH] equivalent / *le prix de vente est équivalent au prix de revient* the selling price is equivalent to the cost price. ❖ **équivalent** nm [élément comparable] equivalent.

équivaloir [60] [ekivalwaʀ] ❖ **équivaloir à** v + prép [être égal à] to be equal ou equivalent to ; [revenir à] to amount to / *ça équivaut à s'avouer vaincu* it amounts to admitting defeat.

équivoque [ekivɔk] ◆ adj **1.** [ambigu - terme, réponse] equivocal, ambiguous ; [-compliment] double-edged, backhanded **2.** [suspect - fréquentation, comportement] questionable, dubious ; [-personnage] shady. ◆ nf **1.** [caractère ambigu] ambiguity *(U)* ▪ **déclaration sans équivoque** unambiguous ou unequivocal statement **2.** [malentendu] misunderstanding *(C)* **3.** [doute] doubt / *pour lever ou dissiper l'équivoque sur mes intentions* so as to leave no doubt as to my intentions.

érable [eʀabl] nm maple.

éradiquer [3] [eʀadike] vt to eradicate, to root out *(sép)*.

érafler [3] [eʀafle] vt **1.** [écorcher - peau, genou] to scrape, to scratch ; [rayer - peinture, carrosserie] to scrape, to scratch.

éraflure [eʀaflyʀ] nf scratch, scrape.

éraillé, e [eʀaje] adj [rauque] rasping, hoarse.

ère [ɛʀ] nf **1.** [époque] era / *270 ans avant notre ère* 270 BC / *en l'an 500 de notre ère* in the year 500 AD, in the year of our Lord 500 ▪ **l'ère atomique** the atomic age ▪ **l'ère chrétienne** the Christian era **2.** GÉOL era.

érection [eʀɛksjɔ̃] nf PHYSIOL erection.

éreintant, e [eʀɛ̃tɑ̃, ɑ̃t] adj gruelling, backbreaking.

éreinter [3] [eʀɛ̃te] vt **1.** [épuiser] to exhaust, to wear out *(sép)* ▪ **être éreinté** to be worn out **2.** [critiquer - pièce, acteur] to slate ᴜᴷ, to pan.

érémiste [eʀemist] nmf *person receiving the RMI benefit*.

ergonomie [ɛʀgɔnɔmi] nf ergonomics *(sg)*.

ergonomique [ɛʀgɔnɔmik] adj ergonomic.

ergot [ɛʀgo] nm [de coq] spur ; [de chien] dewclaw.

ergoter [3] [ɛʀgɔte] vi to quibble / *ergoter sur des détails* to quibble about details.

ergothérapeute [ɛʀgɔteʀapøt] nmf occupational therapist.

ergothérapie [ɛʀgɔteʀapi] nf occupational therapy.

ériger [17] [eʀiʒe] vt **1.** [édifier - statue, temple] to erect, to raise ▪ **ériger qqch / qqn en** *fig* [le transformer en] : *le cynisme érigé en art* cynicism raised to the status of fine art

2. [instituer - comité, tribunal] to set up *(sép)*, to establish. ❖ **s'ériger** vpi ▸ **s'ériger en moraliste / censeur** to set o.s. up as a moralist / a censor.

ermite [ɛʀmit] nm **1.** RELIG hermit **2.** [reclus] hermit, recluse.

éroder [3] [eʀɔde] vt to erode.

érogène [eʀɔʒɛn] adj erogenous, erogenic.

érosion [eʀozjɔ̃] nm **1.** GÉOGR & MÉD erosion **2.** [dégradation] erosion ▸ **érosion monétaire** erosion of the value of money.

érotique [eʀɔtik] adj erotic.

érotisme [eʀɔtism] nm eroticism.

errant, e [ɛʀɑ̃, ɑ̃t] adj wandering, roaming ▸ **chien errant** stray dog.

erratum [eʀatɔm] *(pl* **errata** [eʀata] *ou* **erratums** [eʀatɔm]**)* nm erratum.

errements [ɛʀmɑ̃] nmpl *litt* erring ways *litt,* bad habits.

errer [4] [eʀe] vi **1.** [marcher] to roam, to wander **2.** *litt* [se tromper] to err.

erreur [ɛʀœʀ] nf **1.** [faute] mistake, error ▸ *il doit y avoir une erreur* there must be a ou some mistake ▸ *il y a erreur sur la personne* you've got the wrong person, it's a case of mistaken identity / *ce serait une erreur (que) de penser cela* it would be wrong ou a mistake to think that ▸ **faire** ou **commettre une erreur** to make a mistake ou an error ▸ **faire erreur** to be wrong ou mistaken ▸ **erreur de calcul** miscalculation ▸ **erreur typographique** ou **d'impression** misprint, printer's error ▸ **l'erreur est humaine** to err is human **2.** [errement] error ▸ **des erreurs de jeunesse** youthful indiscretions / *retomber dans les mêmes erreurs* to lapse back into the same old bad habits **3.** DR ▸ **erreur judiciaire** miscarriage of justice **4.** INFORM ▸ **erreur système** system error. ❖ **par erreur** loc adv by mistake. ❖ **sauf erreur** loc adv : *sauf erreur de ma part, ce lundi-là est férié* unless I'm (very much) mistaken, that Monday is a public holiday. ❖ **sauf erreur ou omission** loc adv COMM & DR errors and omissions excepted.

erroné, e [eʀɔne] adj erroneous, mistaken.

ersatz [ɛʀzats] nm ersatz, substitute ▸ **un ersatz de café** ersatz coffee.

érudit, e [eʀydi, it] ◆ adj erudite, learned, scholarly. ◆ nm, f scholar, erudite ou learned person.

érudition [eʀydisjɔ̃] nf erudition, scholarship.

éruption [eʀypsjɔ̃] nf **1.** ASTRON & GÉOL eruption ▸ **entrer en éruption** to erupt ▸ **volcan en éruption** erupting volcano ▸ **éruption (solaire)** solar flare **2.** MÉD outbreak ▸ **éruption cutanée** rash ▸ **éruption de boutons** outbreak of spots **3.** *fig* outbreak / *éruption de colère* fit of anger, angry outburst.

érythème [eʀitɛm] nm erythema ▸ **érythème fessier** nappy UK ou diaper US rash ▸ **érythème solaire** sunburn.

Érythrée [eʀitʀe] npr f ▸ **(l')Érythrée** Eritrea.

érythréen, enne [eʀitʀeɛ̃, ɛn] adj Eritrean. ❖ **Érythréen, enne** nm, f Eritrean.

ESB (abr de encéphalopathie spongiforme bovine) nf BSE.

esbroufe [ɛzbʀuf] nf *fam* bluff ▸ **faire de l'esbroufe** to bluff.

escabeau, x [ɛskabo] nm [échelle] stepladder.

escadrille [ɛskadʀij] nf **1.** NAUT squadron **2.** AÉRON flight, squadron.

escadron [ɛskadʀɔ̃] nm [dans la cavalerie] squadron ; [dans l'armée blindée] squadron ; [dans la gendarmerie] company ▸ **escadron de la mort** POL death squad.

escalade [ɛskalad] nf **1.** SPORT [activité] rock climbing *(U)* ▸ **faire de l'escalade** to go rock climbing ; [ascension] climb **2.** [d'un mur, d'une grille] climbing *(U)*, scaling *(U)* ; DR illegal entry **3.** [aggravation] escalation ▸ **l'escalade de la violence** the escalation of violence ▸ **l'escalade des prix** the soaring of prices.

escalader [3] [ɛskalade] vt [portail] to climb, to scale, to clamber up *(insép)* ; [montagne] to climb ; [grille] to climb over ; [muret] to scramble up *(insép)*.

Escalator® [ɛskalatɔʀ] nm escalator, moving staircase.

escale [ɛskal] nf **1.** NAUT [lieu] port of call ; AÉRON stop **2.** NAUT [halte] call ; AÉRON stop, stopover ▸ **faire escale à a)** [navire] to call at, to put in at **b)** [avion] to stop over at ▸ **escale technique** refuelling stop. ❖ **sans escale** loc adj nonstop, direct.

escalier [ɛskalje] nm staircase, (flight of) stairs ▸ **les escaliers** the staircase ou stairs ▸ **être dans l'escalier** ou **les escaliers** to be on the stairs ▸ **escalier mécanique** ou **roulant** escalator ▸ **escalier de secours** fire escape ▸ **escalier de service** backstairs, service stairs.

escalope [ɛskalɔp] nf escalope.

escamotable [ɛskamɔtabl] adj [train d'atterrissage] retractable ; [lit, table] collapsible, foldaway ; [antenne] retractable.

escamoter [3] [ɛskamɔte] vt **1.** [faire disparaître - mouchoir, carte] to conjure ou to spirit away *(sép)* ; [- placard, lit] to fold away *(sép)* **2.** [éluder - difficultés] to evade, to skirt round *(insép)* ; [- question] to dodge ; [- mot, note] to skip.

escapade [ɛskapad] nf **1.** [fugue] ▸ **faire une escapade** to run off ou away **2.** [séjour] jaunt / *une escapade de deux jours à Deauville* a two-day visit ou jaunt to Deauville.

escarbille [ɛskaʀbij] nf piece of soot.

escargot [ɛskaʀgo] nm snail ▸ **avancer comme un escargot** ou **à une allure d'escargot** to go at a snail's pace.

escarmouche [ɛskaʀmuʃ] nf skirmish.

escarpé, e [ɛskaʀpe] adj steep.

escarpement [ɛskaʀpəmɑ̃] nm [pente] steep slope.

escarpin [ɛskaʀpɛ̃] nm court shoe UK, pump US.

escarre [ɛskaʀ] nf scab.

escient [esjɑ̃] nm ▸ **à bon escient** advisedly, judiciously ▸ **à mauvais escient** injudiciously, unwisely.

esclaffer [3] [ɛsklafe] ❖ **s'esclaffer** vpi to burst out laughing, to guffaw.

esclandre [ɛsklɑ̃dʀ] nm scene, scandal ▸ **faire un esclandre** to make a scene.

esclavage [ɛsklavaʒ] nm **1.** SOCIOL slavery ▸ **réduire qqn en esclavage** to reduce sb to slavery, to make a slave out of sb **2.** [dépendance] ▸ **vivre dans l'esclavage de** to be a slave to.

esclavagisme [ɛsklavaʒism] nm SOCIOL slavery.

esclave [ɛsklav] nm **1.** SOCIOL slave **2.** *fig* slave ▸ **l'esclave de** a slave to, the slave of.

escompte [ɛskɔ̃t] nm **1.** BANQUE : *faire un escompte à 2 %* to allow a discount of 2 % **2.** COMM discount.

escompter [3] [ɛskɔ̃te] vt **1.** [espérer] ▸ **escompter qqch** to rely ou to count ou to bank on sthg / *c'est mieux que ce que j'escomptais* it's better than what I expected **2.** BANQUE to discount.

escorte [ɛskɔʀt] nf **1.** AÉRON, MIL & NAUT escort **2.** [personne, groupe] escort. ❖ **sous bonne escorte** loc adv ▸ **être sous bonne escorte** to be in safe hands / *reconduit sous bonne escorte jusqu'à la prison* brought back to prison under heavy escort.

escorter [3] [ɛskɔʀte] vt [ami, président, célébrité] to escort ; [femme] to escort, to be the escort of.

---

* In reformed spelling (see p. 16-18).

escrime [ɛskʀim] nf fencing *(U)* ▸ **faire de l'escrime** to fence.

escrimer [3] [ɛskʀime] ❖ **s'escrimer** vpi ▸ **s'escrimer à faire qqch** to strive to do sthg ▸ **s'escrimer sur qqch** *fig* to plug away at sthg.

escroc [ɛskʀo] nm swindler, crook.

escroquer [3] [ɛskʀɔke] vt [voler - victime, client] to swindle, to cheat ; [- argent, milliard] to swindle ▸ **escroquer de l'argent à qqn** to swindle money out of sb, to swindle sb out of (his / her) money.

escroquerie [ɛskʀɔkʀi] nf **1.** [pratique malhonnête] swindle / 6 € le kilo, c'est de l'escroquerie ! 6 € a kilo, it's daylight **UK** ou highway **US** robbery! **2.** DR fraud.

eskimo [ɛskimo] = **esquimau**.

ésotérique [ezɔteʀik] adj esoteric.

espace¹ [ɛspas] nm **1.** [gén & ASTRON] ▸ **l'espace** space **2.** [place, volume] space, room ▸ **espace disque** INFORM disk space ▸ **espace vital** living space **3.** [distance - physique] space, gap ; [- temporelle] gap, interval, space **4.** [lieu] space ▸ **l'Espace économique européen** the European Economic Area ▸ **espaces verts** park, public gardens and planted areas : *il y a peu d'espaces verts dans ce quartier* there isn't much greenery in this neighbourhood. ❖ **dans l'espace de, en l'espace de** loc prép [dans le temps] within (the space of).

espace² [ɛspas] nf IMPR space.

espacer [16] [ɛspase] vt **1.** [séparer - lignes, mots, arbustes] to space out *(sép)* **2.** [dans le temps] to space out. ❖ **s'espacer** vpi [dans le temps - visites] to become less frequent.

espadon [ɛspadɔ̃] nm swordfish.

espadrille [ɛspadʀij] nf espadrille.

Espagne [ɛspaɲ] npr f ▸ **(l')Espagne** Spain.

espagnol, e [ɛspaɲɔl] adj Spanish. ❖ **Espagnol, e** nm, f Spaniard ▸ **les Espagnols** the Spanish. ❖ **espagnol** nm LING Spanish.

espalier [ɛspalje] nm **1.** HORT espalier **2.** SPORT gym ladder.

espèce [ɛspɛs] nf **1.** SCI species *(sg)* ▸ **l'espèce humaine** the human race, mankind ▸ **des espèces animales / végétales** animal / plant species ▸ **espèce menacée** endangered species ▸ **espèce en voie de disparition** endangered species **2.** [sorte] sort, kind / c'est un menteur de la pire espèce he's the worst kind of liar, he's a terrible liar / ça n'a aucune espèce d'importance ! that is of absolutely no importance ! ▸ **une espèce / l'espèce de** péj : c'était une espèce de ferme it was a sort of farm ou a farm of sorts ▸ **espèce de** fam & péj : espèce d'idiot ! you idiot! ❖ **espèces** nfpl FIN cash ▸ **payer en espèces** to pay cash.

espérance [ɛspeʀɑ̃s] nf **1.** [espoir] hope, expectation **2.** [cause d'espoir] hope **3.** SOCIOL ▸ **espérance de vie** life expectancy **4.** RELIG hope. ❖ **contre toute espérance** loc adv contrary to (all) ou against all expectations.

espérer [18] [ɛspeʀe] vt [souhaiter] to hope / espérer le succès to hope for success, to hope to succeed / j'espère que vous viendrez I hope (that) you will come ; *(en usage absolu)* ▸ **j'espère (bien)** ! I (do ou certainly) hope so !

✏ In reformed spelling (see p. 16-18), this verb is conjugated like *semer* : *il espèrera, elle espèrerait.*

espiègle [ɛspjɛgl] adj [personne] impish, mischievous ; [regard, réponse] mischievous / d'un air espiègle mischievously.

espièglerie [ɛspjɛgləʀi] nf **1.** [caractère] impishness, mischievousness **2.** [farce] prank, trick, piece of mischief.

espiogiciel [ɛspjɔʒisjɛl] nm INFORM : des espiogiciels spyware.

espion, onne [ɛspjɔ̃, ɔn] nm, f spy.

espionnage [ɛspjɔnaʒ] nm [activité] espionage ▸ **espionnage industriel** industrial espionage. ❖ **d'espionnage** loc adj [film, roman] spy *(modif)*.

espionner [3] [ɛspjɔne] vt to spy on *(insép)*.

esplanade [ɛsplanad] nf esplanade.

espoir [ɛspwaʀ] nm **1.** [espérance] hope / j'ai l'espoir de le voir revenir I'm hopeful that he'll return ▸ **j'ai bon espoir qu'il va gagner** ou **de le voir gagner** I'm confident that he'll win **2.** [cause d'espérance] hope / c'est un des espoirs du tennis français he's one of France's most promising young tennis players. ❖ **dans l'espoir de** loc conj in the hope of / dans l'espoir de vous voir bientôt hoping to see you soon. ❖ **sans espoir** loc adj hopeless.

esprit [ɛspʀi] nm **1.** [manière de penser] mind ▸ **avoir l'esprit clair** to be a clear thinker ▸ **avoir l'esprit critique** to have a critical mind ▸ **avoir l'esprit étroit / large** to be narrow-minded / broad-minded / avoir l'esprit lent / vif to be slow-witted / quick-witted ▸ **avoir l'esprit mal tourné** fam to have a dirty mind ▸ **esprit de** : esprit d'analyse analytical mind **2.** [facultés, cerveau] mind, head ▸ **j'ai l'esprit ailleurs** I'm not concentrating / il n'a pas l'esprit à ce qu'il fait his mind is elsewhere ou isn't on what he's doing ▸ **ça m'a traversé l'esprit** it occurred to me, it crossed my mind / dans son esprit nous devrions voter according to him we should vote / dans mon esprit, la chambre était peinte en bleu in my mind's eye, I saw the bedroom painted in blue **3.** [mentalité] spirit ▸ **esprit de compétition / d'équipe** competitive / team spirit ▸ **avoir l'esprit de famille** to be family-minded ▸ **faire preuve de mauvais esprit** to be a troublemaker **4.** [personne] mind ▸ **un des esprits marquants de ce siècle** one of the great minds ou leading lights of this century ▸ **un bel esprit** a wit ▸ **les grands esprits se rencontrent** hum great minds think alike **5.** [humour] wit ▸ **avoir de l'esprit** to be witty ▸ **faire de l'esprit** to try to be witty ou funny **6.** RELIG spirit ; [ange] ▸ **l'Esprit Saint** the Holy Spirit ou Ghost **7.** [fantôme] ghost, spirit ▸ **esprit frappeur** poltergeist.

Esquimau® [ɛskimo] nm choc-ice on a stick **UK**, Eskimo **US**.

esquimau, aude, x [ɛskimo, od] adj Eskimo. ❖ **Esquimau, aude, x** nm, f Eskimo ▸ **les Esquimaux** the Eskimos. ❖ **esquimau** nm LING Eskimo.

esquinter [3] [ɛskɛ̃te] vt fam [endommager - chose] to ruin, to mess up ; [- voiture] to smash up, to total **US** **CAN** ; [- santé] to ruin. ❖ **s'esquinter** vp *(emploi réfléchi)* fam [s'abîmer] ▸ **s'esquinter la santé** to ruin one's health / tu vas t'esquinter les yeux avec cet écran you'll strain your eyes with that screen.

esquisse [ɛskis] nf ART sketch.

esquisser [3] [ɛskise] vt **1.** ART to sketch **2.** [geste, mouvement] to give a hint of ▸ **esquisser un sourire** to give a faint ou slight smile.

esquiver [3] [ɛskive] vt **1.** [éviter - coup] to dodge **2.** [se soustraire à - question] to evade, to avoid, to skirt ; [- difficulté] to skirt, to avoid, to side step ; [- démarche, obligation] to shirk, to evade. ❖ **s'esquiver** vpi to slip ou to sneak out (unnoticed).

essai [ɛsɛ] nm **1.** [expérimentation - d'un produit, d'un appareil] test, testing, trial ; [- d'une voiture] test, testing, test-driving ▸ **période d'essai** trial period ▸ **essais nucléaires** nuclear tests **2.** [tentative] attempt, try / nous avons fait plusieurs essais we had several tries, we made several attempts ▸ **coup d'essai** first attempt ou try **3.** LITTÉR essay **4.** RUGBY try. ❖ **à l'essai** loc adv **1.** [à l'épreuve] ▸ **mettre qqn / qqch à l'essai** to put sb / sthg to the test **2.** COMM & DR ▸ **engager** ou **prendre qqn à l'essai** to appoint sb for a trial period.

⚠️ **Essay** signifie toujours un texte écrit. Il ne doit pas être employé pour traduire les autres sens du mot **essai**.

essaim [esɛ̃] nm ENTOM swarm.

essaimer [4] [eseme] vi **1.** ENTOM to swarm **2.** litt [se disperser - groupe] to spread, to disperse ; [- firme] to expand.

essayage [esɛjaʒ] nm COUT & VÊT [séance] fitting ; [action] trying on.

essayer [11] [eseje] vt **1.** [tenter] ▶ **essayer de faire** to try to do, to try and do ; *(en usage absolu)* ▶ **essaie un peu !** fam just you try! **2.** [utiliser pour la première fois] to try (out) *(sép)* **3.** [mettre - vêtement, chaussures] to try on **4.** [expérimenter] to try, to test ▶ **essayer une voiture** [pilote, client] to test-drive a car. ❖ **s'essayer à** vp + prép ▶ **s'essayer à (faire) qqch** to try one's hand at (doing) sthg.

📝 **Essayer de faire qqch**

Notez l'emploi de try and do sthg qui a le même sens que try to do sthg mais qui est d'un registre plus familier :
Essaie de deviner ce qu'il y a dans mon sac. *Try and guess what's in my bag.*
J'essaierai de lui en parler. *I'll try and talk to him about it.*

La construction try and do sthg ne peut pas être employée au prétérit :
J'ai essayé de lui en parler. *I tried to talk to him about it.*

essence [esɑ̃s] nf **1.** PÉTR petrol 🇬🇧, gas 🇺🇸, gasoline 🇺🇸 ▶ **prendre de l'essence** to get petrol 🇬🇧 ou gas 🇺🇸 ▶ **à essence** petrol-driven 🇬🇧, gasoline-powered 🇺🇸 ▶ **essence ordinaire** two-star petrol 🇬🇧, regular gas 🇺🇸 ▶ **essence sans plomb** unleaded petrol 🇬🇧 ou gasoline 🇺🇸 **2.** [solvant] spirit, spirits ▶ **essence de térébenthine** spirit ou spirits of turpentine, turps **3.** PHARM [cosmétique] (essential) oil, essence **4.** BOT species **5.** PHILOS essence **6.** sout [contenu fondamental] essence, gist.

essentiel, elle [esɑ̃sjɛl] adj **1.** [indispensable] essential **2.** [principal] main, essential. ❖ **essentiel** nm **1.** [l'indispensable] ▶ **l'essentiel** the basic essentials **2.** [le plus important] : *l'essentiel c'est que tu comprennes* the most important ou the main thing is that you should understand **3.** [la plus grande partie] : *elle passe l'essentiel de son temps au téléphone* she spends most of her time on the phone.

essentiellement [esɑ̃sjɛlmɑ̃] adv **1.** [par nature] in essence, essentially **2.** [principalement] mainly, essentially.

essieu, x [esjø] nm axle, axletree.

essor [esɔʀ] nm **1.** [d'un oiseau] flight ; [d'une entreprise, d'une industrie] rise, development ▶ **en plein essor** booming, fast-growing ▶ **prendre son essor a)** [oiseau] to soar **b)** [adolescent] to fend for o.s., to become self-sufficient **c)** [économie, entreprise] to grow.

essorage [esɔʀaʒ] nm [à la machine] spinning ; [à l'essoreuse à rouleaux] mangling ; [à la main] wringing / **'pas d'essorage'** 'do not spin'.

essorer [3] [esɔʀe] vt [sécher] ▶ **essorer le linge a)** [à la machine] to spin-dry the laundry **b)** [à l'essoreuse à rouleaux] to put the laundry through the mangle **c)** [à la main] to wring the laundry.

essoreuse [esɔʀøz] nf **1.** [pour le linge] ▶ **essoreuse (à tambour)** spin-drier **2.** [pour la salade] salad drier.

essouffler [3] [esufle] vt to make breathless ▶ **être essoufflé** to be breathless ou out of breath. ❖ **s'essouffler** vpi **1.** PHYSIOL to get breathless **2.** [s'affaiblir - moteur] to get weak ; [- production, économie] to lose momentum ; [- inspiration, écrivain] to dry up.

essuie [esɥi] nm 🇧🇪 [essuie-mains] hand towel ; [torchon] cloth, tea towel ; [serviette de bain] bath towel.

essuie-glace [esɥiɡlas] *(pl* **essuie-glaces)** nm windscreen 🇬🇧 ou windshield 🇺🇸 wiper.

essuie-mains *(pl* essuie-mains), **essuie-main*** *(pl* essuie-mains*)* [esɥimɛ̃] nm hand towel.

essuie-tout *(pl* essuie-tout), **essuietout*** *(pl* essuietouts*)* [esɥitu] nm kitchen paper.

essuyer [14] [esɥije] vt **1.** [sécher - vaisselle] to wipe, to dry (up) ; [- sueur] to wipe, to mop up *(sép)*, to wipe (off) ; [- main] to dry, to wipe dry ; [- surface] to wipe (down) ; [- sol] to wipe, to dry ▶ **essuyer les plâtres** fam to have to endure initial problems **2.** [nettoyer - surface poussiéreuse] to dust (down) ; [- tableau noir] to wipe (clean), to clean / *essuie tes pieds sur le paillasson* wipe your feet on the doormat **3.** [subir - reproches] to endure ; [- refus] to meet with *(insép)* ; [- défaite, échec, pertes] to suffer ; [- tempête] to weather, to bear up against / *essuyer un coup de feu* to be shot at. ❖ **s'essuyer** vp *(emploi réfléchi)* [se sécher] to dry o.s. ▶ **s'essuyer les mains** to dry ou to wipe one's hands.

est [ɛst] ◆ nm inv **1.** [point cardinal] east / *le soleil se lève à l'est* the sun rises in the east / *la bise souffle de l'est* it's a harsh eastern wind **2.** [partie d'un pays, d'un continent] east, eastern area ou regions ▶ **l'Est a)** HIST & POL Eastern Europe, Eastern European countries **b)** [en France] the East (of France) ▶ **l'Europe de l'Est** Eastern Europe ▶ **les pays de l'Est** the Eastern Bloc. ◆ adj inv [façade] east *(modif)*, east-facing ; [secteur, banlieue] east *(modif)*, eastern. ❖ **à l'est de** loc prép (to the) east of.

est-allemand, e [ɛstalmɑ̃, ɑ̃d] adj East German.

estampe [ɛstɑ̃p] nf [image] engraving, print.

est-ce que [ɛskə] *(devant voyelle ou « h » muet est-ce qu')* adv interr **1.** [suivi d'un verbe plein] [au présent] : *est-ce que vous aimez le thé ?* do you like tea? ; [au passé] : *est-ce que vous avez acheté la maison ?* did you buy the house? **2.** [suivi d'un auxiliaire] [au présent] : *est-ce que tu as une enveloppe ?* do you have ou have you got an envelope? ; [au futur proche] : *est-ce que tu vas lui téléphoner ?* are you going to ou will you phone her? **3.** [avec un autre adverbe interrogatif] : *quand est-ce qu'il arrive ?* when does he arrive?

esthète [ɛstɛt] nmf aesthete, esthete 🇺🇸.

esthéticien, enne [ɛstetisjɛ̃, ɛn] nm, f [en institut de beauté] beautician.

esthétique [ɛstetik] ◆ adj ART & PHILOS aesthetic, esthetic 🇺🇸. ◆ nf ART & PHILOS [science] aesthetics *(sg)*, esthetics *(U)* 🇺🇸 ; [code] aesthetic, esthetic 🇺🇸.

estimable [ɛstimabl] adj [digne de respect - personne] respectable.

estimation [ɛstimasjɔ̃] nf **1.** [évaluation - d'un vase] appraisal, valuation ; [- de dégâts] estimation, assessment ; [- d'une distance] gaging, gauging **2.** [montant] estimate, estimation **3.** [prévision] projection.

estime [ɛstim] nf esteem, respect ▶ **avoir de l'estime pour qqn / qqch** to have a great deal of respect for sb / sthg, to hold sb / sthg in high esteem ▶ **baisser / monter dans l'estime de qqn** to go down / up in sb's esteem.

estimer [3] [ɛstime] vt **1.** [expertiser - valeur, dégâts] to appraise, to evaluate, to assess / *les dégâts ont été estimés à mille euros* the damage was estimated at a thousand euros ▶ **faire estimer un tableau** to have a painting valued

2. [évaluer approximativement - quantité] to estimate ; [- distance] to gage, to gauge **3.** [apprécier - ami, écrivain, collègue] to regard with esteem *sout*, to esteem *sout*, to think highly of / *je l'estime trop pour ça* I respect him too for that much **4.** [juger] to think, to consider, to believe. ❖ **s'estimer** vpi *(suivi d'un adj)* ▶ **s'estimer satisfait de / que** to be happy with / that.

estival, e, aux [ɛstival, o] adj summer *(modif)* ▶ **la période estivale** the summer season.

estivant, e [ɛstivɑ̃, ɑ̃t] nm, f summer tourist, holidaymaker 🇬🇧, vacationer 🇺🇸.

estomac [ɛstɔma] nm ANAT stomach ▶ **j'ai mal à l'estomac** I have a stomach ache ▶ *il a pris de l'estomac fam* he's developed a paunch ou potbelly ▶ **avoir l'estomac dans les talons** *fam* to be famished ou ravenous ▶ **partir l'estomac vide** to set off on an empty stomach.

estomaquer [3] [ɛstɔmake] vt *fam* to stagger, to flabbergast.

estomper [3] [ɛstɔ̃pe] vt **1.** ART to stump, to shade off *(sép)* **2.** [ride] to smoothe over *(sép)* ; [silhouette] to dim, to blur **3.** [souvenir, sentiment] to dim, to blur. ❖ **s'estomper** vpi **1.** [disparaître - contours] to become blurred **2.** [s'affaiblir - souvenir] to fade away ; [- douleur, rancune] to diminish, to die down.

Estonie [ɛstɔni] npr f ▶ **(l')Estonie** Estonia.

estonien, enne [ɛstɔnjɛ̃, ɛn] adj Estonian. ❖ **Estonien, enne** nm, f Estonian. ❖ **estonien** nm LING Estonian.

estrade [ɛstʀad] nf [plancher] platform, rostrum, dais.

estragon [ɛstʀagɔ̃] nm tarragon.

estropié, e [ɛstʀɔpje] ◆ adj crippled, maimed. ◆ nm, f cripple, disabled ou maimed person.

estropier [ɛstʀɔpje] vt **1.** *pr* to cripple, to maim **2.** *fig* [en prononçant] to mispronounce ; [à l'écrit] to misspell ; [texte] to mutilate.

estuaire [ɛstɥɛʀ] nm estuary.

estudiantin, e [ɛstydjɑ̃tɛ̃, in] adj *litt* student *(avant nom)*.

esturgeon [ɛstyʀʒɔ̃] nm sturgeon.

et [e] conj **1.** [reliant des termes, des propositions] and / *une belle et brillante jeune fille* a beautiful, clever girl / *toi et moi, nous savons ce qu'il faut faire* you and I know what should be done / *il y a mensonge et mensonge* there are lies, and then there are lies / *il connaît l'anglais, et très bien* he speaks English, and very well at that **2.** [exprimant une relation de simultanéité, de succession ou de conséquence] : *il s'est levé et il a quitté la pièce* he got up and left the room / *j'ai bien aimé ce film, et toi ?* I really liked the film, how ou what about you? **3.** [reliant des propositions comparatives] : *plus ça va, et plus la situation s'aggrave* as time goes on, the situation just gets worse **4.** [avec une valeur emphatique] : *et d'un, je n'ai pas faim, et de deux, je n'aime pas ça* for one thing I'm not hungry and for another I don't like it / *je l'ai dit et répété* I've said it over and over again, I've said it more than once / *et les dix euros que je t'ai prêtés ?* and (what about) the ten euros I lent you? / *et pourquoi pas ?* (and) why not? ▶ **et pourtant...** and yet ou still... ▶ **et voilà !** there you are!, there you go! / *et moi je vous dis que je n'irai pas !* and I'm telling you that I won't go! **5.** [dans les nombres composés, les horaires, les poids et les mesures] ▶ **vingt et un** twenty one ▶ **deux heures et demie** half past two.

étable [etabl] nf cowshed.

établi [etabli] nm workbench.

établir [32] [etabliʀ] vt **1.** [duplex, liaison téléphonique] to set up *(sép)*, to establish **2.** [implanter - usine, locaux, quartier général] to establish, to set ou to put up *(sép)* ;

[- filiale] to establish / *établir son domicile à Paris* to take up residence in Paris **3.** [instaurer - règlement] to introduce, to promulgate *sout* ; [- usage] to pass ; [- pouvoir] to install, to implement ; [- ordre, relation] to establish **4.** [bâtir - réputation] to establish ; [- empire] to build **5.** [prouver] ▶ **établir l'innocence de qqn** to establish sb's innocence, to vindicate sb **6.** [dresser - organigramme] to set out *(sép)* ; [- liste] to draw up *(sép)* ; [- devis] to provide ; [- chèque] to make out ; [- programme, prix] to fix **7.** SPORT ▶ **établir un record** to set a record. ❖ **s'établir** vpi **1.** [vivre] : *ils ont préféré s'établir en banlieue* they chose to live in the suburbs **2.** [professionnellement] to set (o.s.) up (in business) ▶ **s'établir à son compte** to set (o.s.) up in business, to become self-employed **3.** [être instauré] : *une relation stable s'est établie entre nous* a stable relationship has developed between the two of us.

établissement [etablismɑ̃] nm

A. ORGANISME, ENTITÉ **1.** [institution] establishment, institution ; [école] school ; [université] university ▶ **établissement hospitalier** hospital ▶ **établissement pénitentiaire** prison, penitentiary 🇺🇸 ▶ **établissement religieux a)** [monastère] monastery **b)** [couvent] convent **c)** [collège] religious ou denominational school **d)** [séminaire] seminary ▶ **établissement scolaire** school **2.** COMM firm ▶ **établissement financier** financial institution.

B. MISE EN PLACE, INSTALLATION **1.** [instauration - d'un empire] setting up, establishing ; [- d'un régime, d'une république] installing ; [- d'un usage] establishing **2.** [préparation - d'un devis] drawing up, preparation ; [- d'une liste] drawing up ; [- d'un organigramme] laying out, drawing up.

étage [etaʒ] nm **1.** [dans une maison] floor, storey 🇬🇧, story 🇺🇸 ; [dans un parking] level ▶ **au troisième étage a)** [maison] on the third floor 🇬🇧, on the fourth floor 🇺🇸 **b)** [aéroport] on level three ▶ **habiter au premier / dernier étage** to live on the first / top floor / *un immeuble de cinq étages* a five-storey building, a five-storey block of flats 🇬🇧, a six-story block of apartments 🇺🇸 **2.** [division - d'une pièce montée] tier ; [- d'un buffet, d'une bibliothèque] shelf ; [- de fusée] stage. ❖ **étages** nmpl [escaliers] : *grimper / monter les étages* to climb / to go upstairs. ❖ **à l'étage** loc adv upstairs, on the floor above.

étagère [etaʒɛʀ] nf [planche] shelf ; [meuble] (set of) shelves.

étain [etɛ̃] nm **1.** [métal blanc] tin **2.** [vaisselle] piece of pewter ware. ❖ **en étain** loc adj pewter *(modif)*.

étal, als [etal] nm **1.** [au marché] (market) stall **2.** [de boucher] block.

étalage [etalaʒ] nm **1.** [vitrine] (display) window ; [stand] stall ; [marchandises exposées] display **2.** *péj* [démonstration] : *faire étalage de son argent* to flaunt one's wealth.

étalement [etalmɑ̃] nm **1.** [déploiement - de papiers, d'objets] spreading (out) ; [- de marchandises] displaying **2.** [des vacances, des horaires, des paiements] staggering, spreading out.

étaler [3] [etale] vt **1.** [exposer - marchandise] to display, to lay out *(sép)* **2.** [exhiber - richesse, luxe] to flaunt, to show off *(sép)* ▶ **étaler ses connaissances** to show off one's knowledge **3.** [disposer à plat - tapis, tissu] to spread (out) ; [- plan, carte, journal] to open ou to spread (out) ; [- pâte à tarte] to roll out *(sép)* ▶ **étaler ses cartes** ou **son jeu** to show one's hand **4.** [appliquer en couche - beurre, miel] to spread ; [- pommade, fond de teint] to rub ou to smooth on ; [- enduit] to apply **5.** [dates, paiements, rendez-vous] to spread out *(sép)* / *les entreprises essaient d'étaler les vacances de leurs employés* firms try to stagger their employees' holidays **6.** *arg scol* : *se faire étaler (à un examen)* to flunk an exam. ❖ **s'étaler** ◆ vp *(emploi passif)* [s'appliquer] to spread / *une peinture qui s'étale facilement* a paint which goes on easily. ◆ vpi **1.** [s'étendre - ville, plaine] to stretch ou to spread out **2.** [être exhibé : *son nom s'étale à la une de tous les journaux* his name is in ou is splashed over all the papers **3.** *fam* [tomber] to fall (down), to take a tumble **4.** *fam & péj* [prendre trop de place] to spread o.s. out. ◆ **s'étaler sur** vp + prép [suj : vacances, paiements] to be spread over.

étalon [etalɔ̃] nm **1.** ZOOL [cheval] stallion ; [âne, taureau] stud **2.** [référence] standard ▸ **étalon-or** gold standard.

étalonner [3] [etalɔne] vt **1.** TECHNOL [graduer] to calibrate ; [vérifier] to standardize **2.** SCI [test] to table, to grade.

étamine [etamin] nf **1.** BOT stamen **2.** COUT etamine, etamin ; CULIN muslin.

étanche [etɑ̃ʃ] adj [chaussure, montre] waterproof ; [réservoir] watertight ; [surface] water-resistant, water-repellent ▸ **étanche à l'air** airtight ▸ **rendre étanche** to waterproof.

étanchéité [etɑ̃ʃeite] nf [d'une montre, de chaussures] waterproofness ; [d'un réservoir] watertightness ; [d'un revêtement] water-resistance / *étanchéité à l'air* airtightness.

étang [etɑ̃] nm pond.

étant [etɑ̃] nm PHILOS being.

étant donné [etɑ̃dɔne] loc prép given, considering ▸ **étant donné les circonstances** given ou in view of the circumstances. ◆ **étant donné que** loc conj since, given the fact that ▸ **étant donné qu'il pleuvait...** since ou as it was raining...

étape [etap] nf **1.** [arrêt] stop, stopover / *nous avons fait étape à Lille* we stopped off ou over at Lille **2.** [distance] stage **3.** SPORT stage **4.** [phase] phase, stage, step.

État [eta] nm **1.** POL state ▸ **l'État français** the French state ou nation ▸ **l'État de Washington** the State of Washington ▸ **les États membres** the member states ▸ **l'État-providence** the Welfare state **2.** ADMIN & ÉCON state ▸ **géré par l'État** state-run, publicly run ▸ **entreprise d'État** state-owned ou public company 🇬🇧.

état [eta]
nm

A. MANIÈRE D'ÊTRE PHYSIQUE **1.** [d'une personne - condition physique] state, condition ; [- apparence] state / *le malade est dans un état grave* the patient's condition is serious ▸ **être dans un état second a)** [drogué] to be high **b)** [en transe] to be in a trance ▸ **en état de** : *être en état d'ivresse ou d'ébriété* to be under the influence (of alcohol), to be inebriated ▸ **être en état de faire qqch** to be fit to do sthg / *être hors d'état de, ne pas être en état de* to be in no condition to ou totally unfit to ▸ **état général** general state of health ▸ **état de santé** (state of) health, condition **2.** [d'un appartement, d'une route, d'une machine, d'un colis] condition, state ▸ **être en bon / mauvais état a)** [meuble, route, véhicule] to be in good / poor condition **b)** [bâtiment] to be in a good / bad state of repair ; [colis, marchandises] to be undamaged / damaged ▸ **en état de marche** in working order ▸ **remettre en état a)** [appartement] to renovate, to refurbish **b)** [véhicule] to repair **c)** [pièce de moteur] to recondition ▸ **maintenir qqch en état** [bâtiment, bateau, voiture] to keep sthg in good repair **3.** [situation particulière - d'un développement, d'une technique] state / *dans l'état actuel des choses* as things stand at the moment, in the present state of affairs ▸ **(en) état d'alerte / d'urgence** (in a) state of alarm / emergency ▸ **être en état d'arrestation** to be under arrest ▸ **être en état de siège** to be under siege **4.** CHIM & PHYS : *état gazeux / liquide / solide* gaseous / liquid / solid state ▸ **à l'état naturel** in its natural state ▸ **à l'état pur** [gemme, métal] pure **5.** LING ▸ **verbe d'état** stative verb.

B. MANIÈRE D'ÊTRE MORALE state ▸ **ne te mets pas dans cet état !** **a)** [à une personne inquiète, déprimée] don't worry!

b) [à une personne énervée] don't get so worked up! ▸ **état d'esprit** state ou frame of mind ▸ **être dans tous ses états a)** [d'anxiété] to be beside o.s. with anxiety **b)** [de colère] to be beside o.s. (with anger) ▸ **se mettre dans tous ses états** [en colère] to go off the deep end 🇬🇧, to go off at the deep end 🇺🇸, to go spare 🇬🇧.

C. CONDITION SOCIALE **1.** [profession] trade, profession ; [statut social] social position, standing, station **2.** ADMIN ▸ **(bureau de l')état civil** registry office.

D. DOCUMENT [compte rendu] account, statement ; [inventaire] inventory / *l'état des dépenses / des recettes* statement of expenses / takings ▸ **état des lieux** inventory (of fixtures) ▸ **états de service a)** MIL service record **b)** [professionnellement] professional record. ◆ **état d'âme** nm mood ▸ **avoir des états d'âme** to suffer from angst *hum* ▸ **faire qqch sans états d'âme** to do sthg without any qualms. ◆ **état de grâce** nm RELIG state of grace ; POL honeymoon period.

étatique [etatik] adj under state control, state-controlled.

étatiser [3] [etatize] vt to bring under state control ▸ **une firme étatisée** a state-owned company.

état-major [etamaʒɔʀ] (pl états-majors) nm **1.** MIL [officiers] general staff ; [locaux] headquarters **2.** [direction - d'une entreprise] management ; [- d'un parti politique] leadership.

États-Unis [etazyni] npr mpl ▸ **les États-Unis (d'Amérique)** the United States (of America) ▸ **aux États-Unis** in the United States.

> 📋 Attention, l'expression the United States se comporte comme un nom singulier ; le verbe qui lui est associé est par conséquent toujours au singulier :
> **Les États-Unis ont décidé d'abandonner le projet.** *The United States has decided to abandon the project.*
> **Les États-Unis sont un acteur majeur dans ce domaine.** *The United States is a key player in this field.*

étau, x [eto] nm vice 🇬🇧, vise 🇺🇸 ▸ **l'étau se resserre** *fig* the noose is tightening.

étayer [11] [eteje] vt **1.** [mur] to prop ou to shore up **2.** [raisonnement] to support, to back up ; [thèse, argument] to support.

etc. (abr écrite de **et cetera**) etc.

et cetera, et cætera, etcétéra* [ɛtseteʀa] loc adv et cetera, and so on (and so forth).

été [ete] nm summer ▸ **été indien** Indian summer. ◆ **d'été** loc adj ▸ **robe d'été** summer dress ▸ **nuit d'été** summer's night ▸ **l'heure d'été** daylight-saving time.

éteindre [81] [etɛ̃dʀ] vt **1.** [arrêter la combustion de - cigarette, incendie] to put out (sép), to extinguish ; [- bougie] to put out ou to blow out (sép) ; [- gaz, chauffage] to turn off (sép) **2.** ÉLECTR [phare, lampe] to turn ou to switch off (sép) ; [radio, télévision] to turn off / *va éteindre (dans) la chambre* *fam* switch off the light in the bedroom. ◆ **s'éteindre** vpi **1.** [feu, gaz, chauffage] to go out ; [bougie] to blow out ; [cigarette] to burn out ; [volcan] to die down **2.** ÉLECTR [lampe] to go out ; [radio, télévision] to go off **3.** *euphém* [mourir - personne] to pass away.

éteint, e [etɛ̃, ɛ̃t] adj [sans éclat - regard] dull, lacklustre ; [- visage, esprit] dull ; [- couleur] faded ▸ **d'une voix éteinte** faintly.

étendard [etɑ̃daʀ] nm MIL standard / **lever l'étendard de la révolte** fig to raise the standard of revolt.

étendre [73] [etɑ̃dʀ] vt **1.** [beurre, miel] to spread ; [pommade, fond de teint] to rub ou to smooth on **2.** [tapis, tissu] to unroll ; [plan, carte, journal] to open ou to spread (out) ; [pâte à tarte] to roll out (sép) ▸ **étendre ses bras / jambes** to stretch (out) one's arms / legs **3.** [faire sécher] ▸ **étendre du linge a)** [dehors] to put the washing out to dry, to hang out the washing **b)** [à l'intérieur] to hang up the washing **4.** [allonger - personne] to stretch out (sép) **5.** [élargir - pouvoir] to extend ; [- recherches] to broaden, to extend ; [- cercle d'amis] to extend, to widen ▸ **étendre qqch à :** étendre une grève au secteur privé to extend a strike to the private sector **6.** [diluer - peinture] to dilute, to thin down (sép) ; [- sauce] to thin out ou down (sép), to water down (sép) ; [- vin] to water down (sép) **7.** fam [vaincre] to thrash ▸ **se faire étendre a)** [à un match de boxe] to get knocked ou laid out **b)** [aux élections] to be trounced **c)** [à un examen] to be failed. ◆ **s'étendre** vpi **1.** [dans l'espace] to extend, to stretch / les banlieues s'étendaient à l'infini the suburbs stretched out endlessly / son ambition s'étendait aux plus hautes sphères de la politique his ambition extended to the highest echelons of politics **2.** [dans le temps] to extend / les vacances s'étendent sur trois mois the vacation stretches over three months **3.** [se développer - épidémie, grève] to spread ; [- cercle d'amis] to widen ; [- pouvoir] to widen, to increase, to expand ; [- culture, vocabulaire] to increase, to broaden **4.** [s'allonger - malade] to stretch out, to lie down. ◆ **s'étendre sur** vp + prép ▸ je ne m'étendrai pas davantage sur ce sujet I won't discuss this subject at any greater length.

étendu, e [etɑ̃dy] adj **1.** [vaste - territoire] big, wide, spread-out ; [- banlieue] sprawling **2.** [considérable - pouvoir, connaissances] extensive, wide-ranging **3.** [étiré] ▸ **les jambes étendues** with legs stretched out. ◆ **étendue** nf **1.** [surface] area, stretch **2.** [dimension] area / un domaine d'une grande étendue a large estate **3.** [durée] : sur une étendue de 10 ans over a period of 10 years **4.** [ampleur] extent.

éternel, elle [etɛʀnɛl] adj **1.** [sans fin] eternal, endless / cette situation ne sera pas éternelle this situation won't last for ever **2.** (avant nom) [invariable] ▸ **c'est un éternel mécontent** he's perpetually discontented, he's never happy ▸ **l'éternel féminin** womankind. ◆ **Éternel** npr m ▸ **l'Éternel** the Eternal ▸ **grand voyageur / menteur devant l'Éternel** fam great ou inveterate traveller / liar.

éternellement [etɛʀnɛlmɑ̃] adv eternally / je ne l'attendrai pas éternellement I'm not going to wait for him for ever.

éterniser [3] [etɛʀnize] ◆ **s'éterniser** vpi péj **1.** [durer - crise, discussion] to drag on **2.** fam [s'attarder] : on ne va pas s'éterniser ici we're not going to stay here for ever / ne nous éternisons pas sur ce sujet let's not dwell forever on that subject.

éternité [etɛʀnite] nf **1.** PHILOS & RELIG eternity **2.** [longue durée] eternity / il y avait une éternité que je ne l'avais vu I hadn't seen him for ages ou an eternity / la construction du stade va durer une éternité it will take forever to build the stadium.

éternuement [etɛʀnymɑ̃] nm sneeze.

éternuer [7] [etɛʀnɥe] vi to sneeze.

éther [etɛʀ] nm litt ou CHIM ether.

Éthiopie [etjɔpi] npr f ▸ (l')Éthiopie Ethiopia.

éthiopien, enne [etjɔpjɛ̃, ɛn] adj Ethiopian. ◆ **Éthiopien, enne** nm, f Ethiopian.

éthique [etik] ◆ adj ethic, ethical. ◆ nf **1.** PHILOS ethics (sg) **2.** [code moral] ethic.

ethnie [ɛtni] nf ethnic group.

ethnique [ɛtnik] adj ethnic.

ethnographie [ɛtnɔgʀafi] nf ethnography.

ethnologie [ɛtnɔlɔʒi] nf ethnology.

ethnologue [ɛtnɔlɔg] nmf ethnologist.

éthylique [etilik] ◆ adj ethyl (modif), ethylic. ◆ nmf alcoholic.

éthylotest [etilɔtɛst] nm Breathalyser UK, Breathalyzer US.

étincelant, e [etɛ̃slɑ̃, ɑ̃t] adj **1.** [brillant - diamant, étoile] sparkling, gleaming, twinkling ; [- soleil] brightly shining ; [bien lavé - vaisselle] shining, sparkling, gleaming **2.** [vif - regard, œil] twinkling ▸ **les yeux étincelants de colère / de haine** eyes glinting with rage / with hate.

étinceler [24] [etɛ̃sle] vi **1.** [diamant, étoile] to sparkle, to gleam, to twinkle ; [soleil] to shine brightly ; [vaisselle] to shine, to sparkle, to gleam **2.** [regard, œil] to sparkle, to glitter / ses yeux étincelaient de colère / jalousie / passion her eyes glittered with anger / jealousy / passion / ses yeux étincelaient de bonheur / fierté her eyes were sparkling with happiness / pride.

In reformed spelling (see p. 16-18), this verb is conjugated like **peler : il étincèle, elle étincèlera**.

étincelle [etɛ̃sɛl] nf **1.** [parcelle incandescente] spark ▸ **faire des étincelles a)** pr to throw off sparks **b)** fig to cause a huge sensation, to be a big success ▸ **c'est l'étincelle qui a mis le feu aux poudres** it was this which sparked everything off **2.** [lueur] spark, sparkle ▸ **jeter des étincelles** to sparkle ▸ **ses yeux jettent des étincelles a)** [de joie] his eyes shine with joy **b)** [de colère] his eyes flash with rage **3.** [bref élan] ▸ **l'étincelle du génie** the spark of genius.

étioler [3] [etjɔle] ◆ **s'étioler** vpi **1.** AGR & BOT to blanch, to wither **2.** [s'affaiblir - personne] to decline, to fade away, to become weak ; [- esprit] to become lacklustre ou dull.

étiqueter [27] [etikte] vt **1.** [marchandise] to mark, to label ; [colis] to ticket, to label **2.** péj [cataloguer] to label.

In reformed spelling (see p. 16-18), this verb is conjugated like **acheter : il étiquète, elle étiquètera**.

étiquette [etikɛt] nf **1.** [marque - portant le prix] ticket ▸ **étiquette autocollante** sticky label, sticker **2.** [appartenance] label ▸ **mettre une étiquette à qqn** to label sb ▸ **sans étiquette politique** [candidat, journal] independent **3.** [protocole] ▸ **l'étiquette** etiquette.

étirement [etiʀmɑ̃] nm [des membres, du corps] stretching ▸ **faire des étirements** to do stretching exercises.

étirer [3] [etiʀe] vt [allonger - membres, cou] to stretch ; [- peloton, convoi] to stretch out (sép). ◆ **s'étirer** vpi [personne, animal] to stretch (out).

étoffe [etɔf] nf **1.** TEXT material, fabric **2.** [calibre - d'un professionnel, d'un artiste] calibre / il a l'étoffe d'un héros he has the makings of a hero, he's the stuff heroes are made of ▸ **avoir l'étoffe d'un chef** to be leadership material.

étoffer [3] [etɔfe] vt **1.** [faire grossir] to put weight on **2.** [développer - roman, personnage] to flesh ou to fill out (sép), to give substance to. ◆ **s'étoffer** vpi **1.** [personne] to fill out, to put on weight **2.** [carnet de commandes] to fill up.

étoile [etwal] nf **1.** ASTRON star ▸ **étoile du berger** morning star ▸ **étoile filante** shooting star ▸ **étoile Polaire** pole star **2.** [insigne] star ▸ **hôtel trois / quatre étoiles** three-star / four-star hotel **3.** vieilli [célébrité] star **4.** ZOOL ▸ **étoile de mer** starfish. ◆ **à la belle étoile** loc adv [coucher, dormir] (out) in the open, outside.

étoilé, e [etwale] adj [ciel] starry, star-studded ; [nuit] starry.

étole [etɔl] nf COUT & RELIG stole.

étonnamment [etɔnamɑ̃] adv amazingly, astonishingly.

étonnant, e [etɔnɑ̃, ɑ̃t] adj **1.** [remarquable - personne, acteur, mémoire] remarkable, astonishing ; [- roman] great, fantastic ; [- voyage] fabulous **2.** [surprenant] surprising, amazing ▶ **ça n'a rien d'étonnant** it's no wonder.

étonné, e [etɔne] adj astonished, amazed / *il avait l'air étonné* he looked astonished ou amazed.

étonnement [etɔnmɑ̃] nm surprise, astonishment, amazement.

étonner [3] [etɔne] vt to amaze, to surprise / *je suis étonné de ses progrès* I'm amazed at the progress he's made / *ça m'étonne qu'elle ne t'ait pas appelé* I'm surprised she didn't call you ▶ **cela m'étonnerait** I'd be surprised / *ça ne m'étonne pas de toi !* you do surprise me! *iron* / *tu vas y aller ? — tu m'étonnes !* *fam* are you going to go? — of course I am! **◆ s'étonner** vpi to be surprised / *je ne m'étonne plus de rien* nothing surprises me anymore.

étouffant, e [etufɑ̃, ɑ̃t] adj [oppressant - lieu, climat, ambiance] stifling.

étouffée [etufe] **◆ à l'étouffée ◆** loc adj steamed *(in a tightly shut pot).* **◆** loc adv ▶ **cuire qqch à l'étouffée** to steam sthg *(in a tightly shut steamer).*

étouffement [etufmɑ̃] nm **1.** [asphyxie] suffocation **2.** [respiration difficile] breathlessness / *avoir une sensation d'étouffement* to have a feeling of breathlessness ou suffocation ; [crise] fit of breathlessness.

étouffer [3] [etufe] **◆** vt **1.** [asphyxier - personne, animal] ▶ **le bébé a été étouffé a)** [accident] the baby suffocated to death **b)** [meurtre] the baby was smothered ▶ **mourir étouffé** to die of suffocation, to choke to death ▶ **ne pas étouffer qqn** *fam & hum* : *ce n'est pas la politesse qui l'étouffe* politeness isn't exactly his strong point / *ça t'étoufferait de dire bonjour / de ranger ta chambre ?* would it kill you to say hello / to tidy your room? **2.** [oppresser - suj : famille, entourage] to smother ; [- suj : ambiance] to stifle **3.** [arrêter, atténuer - feu] to put out *(sép)*, to smother ; [- bruit] to muffle, to deaden ; [- cris, pleurs, sentiment, rire] to stifle, to hold back *(sép)* ; [- voix] to lower ; [- révolte, rumeur] to quash ; [- scandale] to hush ou to cover up *(sép)* ▶ **rires étouffés** suppressed laughter. **◆** vi **1.** [s'asphyxier] to suffocate, to choke / *j'ai failli étouffer en avalant de travers* I almost choked on my food **2.** [avoir chaud] to suffocate, to be gasping for air / *on étouffe dans cette pièce* it's stifling in here **3.** [être oppressé] to feel stifled. **◆ s'étouffer** vpi to choke.

étourderie [eturdəri] nf **1.** [faute] careless mistake **2.** [caractère] carelessness.

étourdi, e [eturdi] **◆** adj [personne] careless ; [acte, réponse] thoughtless. **◆** nm, f scatterbrain.

étourdir [32] [eturdir] vt **1.** [assommer] to stun, to daze **2.** [griser - suj : vertige, sensation, alcool] to make dizzy ou light-headed ; [- suj : odeur] to overpower ▶ **le succès l'étourdissait** success had gone to his head **3.** [abasourdir - suj : bruit] to deafen / *ces enfants m'étourdissent !* these children are making me dizzy (with their noise)!

étourdissement [eturdismɑ̃] nm [vertige] fit of giddiness ou dizziness, dizzy spell ; MÉD fainting fit, blackout / *j'ai eu un léger étourdissement dû à la chaleur* I felt slightly dizzy on account of the heat.

étourneau, x [eturno] nm ORNITH starling.

étrange [etrɑ̃ʒ] adj [personne] strange, odd ; [chose, fait] strange, funny, odd / *chose étrange, elle a dit oui* strangely enough, she said yes.

étrangement [etrɑ̃ʒmɑ̃] adv [bizarrement] oddly, strangely ; [inhabituellement] strangely.

étranger, ère [etrɑ̃ʒe, ɛʀ] **◆** adj **1.** [visiteur, langue, politique] foreign **2.** [extérieur à un groupe] outside *(adj)*

▶ **étranger à** : *je suis étranger à leur communauté* I'm not a member of ou I don't belong to their community **3.** [non familier - voix, visage, région, sentiment] unknown, unfamiliar **4.** *sout* ▶ **étranger à** [inconnu de] unknown to. **◆** nm, f **1.** ADMIN [habitant d'un autre pays] foreigner, alien **2.** [inconnu] stranger. **◆ étranger** nm ▶ **l'étranger** foreign countries ▶ **ça vient de l'étranger** it comes from abroad. **◆ à l'étranger** loc adv abroad.

 stranger ou **foreigner ?**

Stranger signifie « inconnu », tandis que **foreigner** désigne un « habitant d'un autre pays ».

étrangeté [etrɑ̃ʒte] nf [singularité - d'un discours, d'un comportement] strangeness, oddness.

étranglement [etrɑ̃gləmɑ̃] nm [strangulation] strangling, strangulation.

étrangler [3] [etrɑ̃gle] vt **1.** [tuer - intentionnellement] to strangle ; [- par accident] to strangle, to choke **2.** [faire balbutier - suj : colère, peur] to choke **3.** *litt* [restreindre - libertés] to stifle. **◆ s'étrangler** vpi **1.** [personne] to choke / *s'étrangler avec un os* to choke on a bone ▶ **s'étrangler de** : *s'étrangler de rire* to choke with laughter ▶ **s'étrangler d'indignation** to be speechless with indignation **2.** [voix] to choke.

étrave [etrav] nf stem.

être¹ [2] [etr] **◆** vi

A. EXISTER 1. [exister] to be, to exist / *mon fils n'est plus litt* my son is no more *litt* ou has died ou passed away / *la nounou la plus patiente qui soit* the most patient nanny that ever was ou in the world **2.** MATH ▶ **soit une droite AB** let AB be a straight line.

B. COMME LIEN 1. [suivi d'un attribut] to be ▶ **elle est professeur** she's a teacher / *je suis comme je suis* I am what I am / *elle n'est plus rien pour lui* she no longer matters to him ▶ **qui était-ce ?** who was it? **2.** [suivi d'une préposition] ▶ **être à** [se trouver à] : *être à l'hôpital* to be in hospital / *je suis à la gare* I'm at the station / *je suis à vous dans un instant* I'll be with you in a moment / *la Sardaigne est au sud de la Corse* Sardinia is (situated) south of Corsica ▶ **tout le monde est à la page 15 / au chapitre 9 ?** is everybody at page 15 / chapter 9? ▶ **être à** [appartenir à] : *ce livre est à moi* the book's mine ▶ **être à** [être occupé] : *il est tout à son travail* he's busy with his work ▶ **être à** [être en train de] : *il est toujours à me questionner* he's always asking me questions ▶ **être de** [provenir de] to be from, to come from ▶ **être de** [dater de] : *l'église est du XVIe* the church is from ou dates back to the 16th century ▶ **les œufs sont d'hier** the eggs were laid yesterday ▶ **être de** [se joindre à] : *acceptez-vous d'être (un) des nôtres ?* would you care to join us? ▶ **être en** [lieu] : *être en prison / en France* to be in prison / in France ▶ **être en** [matériau] : *la table est en chêne* the table is made of oak ▶ **être en** [pour exprimer l'état] : *être en bonne santé* to be in good health / *les dossiers qui sont en attente* the pending files.

C. DANS DES LOCUTIONS VERBALES 1. ▶ **en être à** : *les joueurs en sont à deux sets partout* the players are two sets all / *le projet n'en est qu'au début* the project has only just started / *où en es-tu avec Michel ?* how is it going with Michel? ▶ **où en étais-je ?** [après une interruption dans une conversation] where was I? / *où en sont les travaux ?* how's the work coming along? ▶ **en être à faire qqch** : *j'en suis à me demander si...* I'm beginning to wonder if...

ne plus savoir où l'on en est : *je ne sais plus du tout où j'en suis dans tous ces calculs* I don't know where I am any more with all these calculations / *j'ai besoin de faire le point, je ne sais plus où j'en suis* I've got to take stock, I've completely lost track of everything ▶ **y être** [être prêt] : *tout le monde y est ?* is everyone ready? **2.** [dans l'expression du temps] to be ▶ **nous sommes le 8 / jeudi** today is the 8th / Thursday ▶ **on était en avril** it was April.

D. SUBSTITUT DE ALLER, PARTIR to go / *tu y as déjà été ?* have you already been there? / *elle s'en fut lui porter la lettre* *litt* she went to take him the letter.

◆ v impers **1.** [exister] ▶ **il est** [il y a] *(suivi d'un sg)* there is / *(suivi d'un pl)* there are / *il était une fois un prince...* once (upon a time) there was a prince... **2.** [pour exprimer l'heure] ▶ **il est 5 h** it's 5 o'clock ▶ **quelle heure est-il ?** what time is it? **3.** *sout* : *il en est ainsi de toutes les démocraties* that's how it is in all democracies.

◆ v aux **1.** [sert à former les temps composés] ▶ **je suis / j'étais descendu** I came / had come down **2.** [sert à former le passif] : *des arbres ont été déterrés par la tempête* trees were uprooted during the storm **3.** [sert à exprimer une obligation] : *ce dossier est à préparer pour lundi* the file must be ready for Monday. ❖ **cela étant** *loc adv* [dans ces circonstances] things being what they are ; [cela dit] having said that.

être² [εtr] *nm* **1.** BIOL & PHILOS being ▶ **l'être** PHILOS being ▶ **être humain** human being ▶ **être de raison** rational being ▶ **être vivant** living thing **2.** RELIG ▶ **l'Être éternel** ou **infini** ou **suprême** the Supreme Being **3.** [personne] person ▶ **un être cher** a loved one **4.** [cœur, âme] being, heart, soul / *je le crois de tout mon être* I believe it with all my heart.

étreindre [81] [etrɛ̃dr] *vt* **1.** [serrer entre ses bras - ami, amant, adversaire] to hug, to clasp *litt*, to embrace **2.** *sout* [oppresser - suj : émotion, colère, peur] to seize, to grip.

étreinte [etrɛ̃t] *nf* **1.** [embrassement] hug, embrace **2.** [d'un boa] constriction ; [d'un lutteur] grip / *les troupes ennemies resserrent leur étreinte autour de la ville* the enemy troops are tightening their grip ou stranglehold on the city.

étrenner [4] [etrene] *vt* [machine] to use for the first time ; [robe, chaussures] to wear for the first time.

étrennes [etrεn] *nfpl* [cadeau] New Year's Day present.

étrier [etrije] *nm* ÉQUIT stirrup ▶ **coup de l'étrier** stirrup cup, one for the road.

étriller [3] [etrije] *vt* [cheval] to curry, to currycomb.

étriper [3] [etripe] *vt* **1.** [poisson] to gut ; [volaille, gibier] to draw, to clean out *(sép)* **2.** *fam* [tuer] : *je vais l'étriper, celui-là !* I'm going to kill him ou to make mincemeat of him ou to have his guts for garters! ❖ **s'étriper** *vp* *(emploi réciproque)* to tear each other to pieces.

étriqué, e [etrike] *adj* **1.** [trop petit - vêtement] skimpy **2.** [mesquin - vie, habitudes, caractère] mean, petty / *un point de vue très étriqué* a very narrow outlook.

étroit, e [etrwa, at] *adj* **1.** [rue, bande, sentier] narrow ; [vêtement] tight **2.** [mesquin - esprit] narrow ; [- idées] limited / *être étroit d'esprit* to be narrow-minded **3.** [liens, rapport, complicité, collaboration] close **4.** [surveillance] close, strict, tight ; [acception, interprétation] narrow, strict. ❖ **à l'étroit** *loc adv* : *on est un peu à l'étroit ici* it's rather cramped in here ▶ **ils vivent** ou **sont logés à l'étroit** they haven't much living space.

étroitement [etrwatmã] *adv* **1.** [strictement - respecter] strictly ; [- surveiller] closely, strictly **2.** [intimement - relier] closely.

étroitesse [etrwatεs] *nf* [mesquinerie] ▶ **étroitesse d'esprit** ou **de vues** narrow-mindedness.

étude [etyd] *nf* **1.** [apprentissage] study **2.** [analyse, essai] study, paper ▶ **étude de cas** case study **3.** [travail préparatoire] study / *ce projet est à l'étude* this project is under consideration ou being studied ▶ **étude de marché** market research *(U)* **4.** ÉDUC [salle] study ou UK prep room ; [période] study-time / *elle reste à l'étude le soir* she stays on to study in the evenings **5.** DR [charge] practice ; [locaux] office **6.** MUS study, étude **7.** ART study. ❖ **études** *nfpl* ÉDUC & UNIV studies / *il a fait ses études à Bordeaux* he studied in Bordeaux ▶ **payer ses études** to pay for one's education ▶ **études secondaires / supérieures** secondary / higher education.

étudiant, e [etydjã, ãt] ◆ *adj* student *(modif)*. ◆ *nm, f* [avant la licence] undergraduate, student ; [après la licence] postgraduate, student ▶ **étudiant en droit / médecine** law / medical student ▶ **étudiant de première année** first year (student).

étudié, e [etydje] *adj* **1.** [bien fait - plan, dessin] specially ou carefully designed ; [- discours] carefully composed ; [- tenue] carefully selected **2.** COMM [prix] reasonable.

étudier [9] [etydje] *vt* **1.** [apprendre - matière] to learn, to study ; [- leçon] to learn ; [- piano] to learn (to play), to study ; [- auteur, période] to study ; [observer - insecte] to study **2.** [examiner - contrat] to study, to examine ; [- proposition] to consider, to examine ; [- liste, inventaire] to go through *(insép)*, to check over *(insép)* **3.** [concevoir - méthode] to devise ; [- modèle, maquette] to design ▶ **c'est étudié pour** *fam* that's what it's for.

étui [etɥi] *nm* [à lunettes, à cigares, de violon] case ▶ **étui de revolver** holster.

étuvée [etyve] = **étouffée**.

étymologie [etimɔlɔʒi] *nf* **1.** [discipline] etymology, etymological research **2.** [origine] etymology, origin.

étymologique [etimɔlɔʒik] *adj* etymological.

E-U (abr de **États-Unis (d'Amérique)**) *npr mpl* US, USA.

eucalyptus [økaliptys] *nm* eucalyptus.

eucharistie [økaristi] *nf* ▶ **l'eucharistie** the Eucharist, Holy Communion.

euh [ø] *interj* er.

eunuque [ønyk] *nm* eunuch.

euphémisme [øfemism] *nm* euphemism.

euphorie [øfɔri] *nf* euphoria.

euphorique [øfɔrik] *adj* euphoric.

euphorisant, e [øfɔrizã, ãt] *adj* [atmosphère, succès] heady. ❖ **euphorisant** *nm* [médicament] antidepressant ; [drogue] euphoriant.

eurasien, enne [ørazjɛ̃, εn] *adj* Eurasian. ❖ **Eurasien, enne** *nm, f* Eurasian.

euro [øro] *nm* euro.

eurochèque [ørɔʃεk] *nm* Eurocheque.

eurodéputé, e [ørɔdepyte] *nmf* Euro-MP.

Europe [ørɔp] *npr f* GÉOGR ▶ **(l')Europe** Europe ▶ **(l')Europe centrale / occidentale** Central / Western Europe ▶ **(l')Europe de l'Est** East ou Eastern Europe ▶ **l'Europe des 27** the 27 countries of the European Union.

européaniser [3] [ørɔpeanize] *vt* to Europeanize, to make European.

européanisme [ørɔpeanism] *nm* Europeanism.

européen, enne [ørɔpeɛ̃, εn] *adj* European. ❖ **Européen, enne** *nm, f* European.

europhile [ørɔfil] *adj & nmf* Europhile.

eurosceptique [ørɔsεptik] *nmf* Eurosceptic.

Eurostar® [ørɔstar] *npr m* Eurostar®.

Eurovision [ørɔvizjɔ̃] *nf* Eurovision.

euthanasie [øtanazi] nf euthanasia.

eux [ø] pron pers **1.** [sujet] they **▸ nous sommes invités, eux pas** ou **non** we are invited but they aren't ou but not them / *eux, voter ? cela m'étonnerait* them? vote? I doubt it very much! **2.** [après une préposition] them / *avec eux, on ne sait jamais* you never know with them ; *(en fonction de pronom réfléchi)* themselves / *ils ne pensent qu'à eux* they only think of themselves.

eux-mêmes [ømɛm] pron pers themselves.

évacuation [evakɥasjɔ̃] nf **1.** PHYSIOL [de toxines] elimination, eliminating *(U)* ; [du pus] draining off **2.** [écoulement] draining **3.** [d'une ville, d'un lieu] evacuation **4.** [sauvetage] evacuation, evacuating **▸ organiser l'évacuation des habitants** to evacuate the local people.

évacuer [7] [evakɥe] vt **1.** [navire, hôpital] to evacuate **▸ faire évacuer un bâtiment** to evacuate ou to clear a building **2.** [personne, population] **▸ évacuer qqn de** to evacuate sb from.

évadé, e [evade] nm, f escaped prisoner, escapee.

évader [3] [evade] **⬦ s'évader** vpi **1.** [s'enfuir] **▸ s'évader de** to escape from, to break out of **2.** [pour oublier ses soucis] to escape, to get away from it all.

évaluateur, trice [evalɥatœr, tʀis] nm, f Québec appraiser.

évaluation [evalɥasjɔ̃] nf [estimation] assessment, evaluation, valuation / *faire l'évaluation d'un tableau* to estimate the value of ou to evaluate a painting.

évaluer [7] [evalɥe] vt **1.** [estimer - bijou, tableau] to appraise, to assess / *la propriété a été évaluée à trois millions* the estate has been valued at ou the value of the estate has been put at three million **2.** [mesurer - dégâts, volume, débit] to estimate **▸ évaluer qqch à** to estimate ou to evaluate sthg at **3.** [estimer approximativement - distance] to gauge / *on évalue sa fortune à trois millions de dollars* his fortune is estimated at three million dollars **4.** [juger - qualité] to weigh up *(sép)*, to gauge, to assess **▸ mal évaluer les risques** to miscalculate the risks.

évangélique [evɑ̃zelik] adj [de l'Évangile] evangelic, evangelical.

évangéliser [3] [evɑ̃zelize] vt to evangelize.

évangéliste [evɑ̃zelist] nm Evangelist.

évangile [evɑ̃zil] nm **1.** RELIG **▸ l'Évangile** the Gospel **▸ l'Évangile selon saint...** the Gospel according to Saint... **2.** [credo] gospel.

évanoui, e [evanwi] adj MÉD unconscious.

évanouir [32] [evanwiʀ] **⬦ s'évanouir** vpi **1.** MÉD to faint, to pass out **2.** [disparaître - personne] to vanish (into thin air) ; [- craintes, illusions] to vanish, to disappear, to evaporate *litt*.

évanouissement [evanwismɑ̃] nm [syncope] fainting *(U)*, blackout.

évaporation [evapɔʀasjɔ̃] nf evaporation.

évaporer [3] [evapɔʀe] **⬦ s'évaporer** vpi **1.** [liquide] to evaporate **2.** fam [disparaître] to vanish (into thin air).

évasé, e [evaze] adj [robe] flared ; [ouverture, tuyau] splayed ; [récipient] tapered.

évasif, ive [evazif, iv] adj evasive, non-committal.

évasion [evazjɔ̃] nf **1.** [d'un prisonnier] escape **2.** [distraction] : *j'ai besoin d'évasion* I need to get away from it all **3.** FIN & DR **▸ évasion fiscale** tax avoidance **4.** ÉCON **▸ évasion de capitaux** flight of capital.

⚠ Le mot anglais **evasion** signifie « dérobade ». Il ne doit pas être employé pour traduire *évasion*.

évasivement [evazivmɑ̃] adv evasively.

éveil [evɛj] nm **1.** *sout* [fin du repos] awakening *(C)* **2.** [déclenchement] **▸ l'éveil de qqn à qqch** sb's awakening to sthg **3.** ENS **▸ activité** ou **matière d'éveil** early-learning *(U)* **4.** [alerte] **▸ donner l'éveil** to raise the alarm. **⬦ en éveil** loc adv **1.** [sur ses gardes] **▸ être en éveil** to be on the alert **2.** [actif] : *à quatre ans, leur curiosité est en éveil* by the time they're four, their curiosity is fully roused.

éveillé, e [eveje] adj **1.** [vif - enfant, esprit] alert, bright, sharp ; [- intelligence] sharp **2.** [en état de veille] awake **▸ tout éveillé** wide awake **▸ tenir qqn éveillé** to keep sb awake.

éveiller [4] [eveje] vt **1.** *litt* [tirer du sommeil] to awaken, to waken, to arouse *sout* **2.** [susciter - désir, jalousie, passion] to kindle, to arouse ; [- amour, méfiance] to arouse ; [- curiosité, soupçons] to arouse, to awaken ; [- espoir] to awaken ; [- attention, intérêt] to attract **3.** [stimuler - intelligence] to stimulate, to awaken. **⬦ s'éveiller** vpi **1.** [animal, personne] to awaken, to wake up, to waken **2.** [se révéler - intelligence, talent] to reveal itself, to come to light **3.** [naître - curiosité, jalousie, méfiance] to be aroused ; [- amour] to dawn, to stir. **⬦ s'éveiller à** vp + prép : *s'éveiller à l'amour* to discover love.

événement, évènement [evɛnmɑ̃] nm **1.** [fait] event, occurrence, happening *(C)* **▸ vacances pleines d'événements** eventful holidays **2.** POL : *les événements de mai 68* the events of May 68 **3.** [fait important] event **▸ événement sportif** sporting event **▸ faire** ou **créer l'événement** to be news ou a major event.

événementiel, elle, évènementiel, elle [evɛnmɑ̃sjɛl] adj **▸ communication événementielle** events. **⬦ événementiel, évènementiel** nm **▸ l'événementiel** events.

éventail [evɑ̃taj] nm **1.** [accessoire] fan **2.** [gamme] range, spectrum / *éventail des salaires* salary range ou spread **3.** COMM range. **⬦ en éventail** loc adj [queue] spread-out.

éventaire [evɑ̃tɛʀ] nm [étalage] stall.

éventer [3] [evɑ̃te] vt **1.** [avec un éventail, un magazine] to fan **2.** [révéler - secret] to disclose, to give away *(sép)*. **⬦ s'éventer** vp *(emploi réfléchi)* [pour se rafraîchir] to fan o.s. **⬦** vpi [s'altérer - parfum, vin] to go musty ou stale ; [- limonade, eau gazeuse] to go flat ou stale.

éventrer [3] [evɑ̃tʀe] vt **1.** [personne - avec un couteau] to disembowel / *il a été éventré par le taureau* he was gored by the bull **2.** [canapé, outre, oreiller, sac] to rip (open) ; [boîte en carton] to tear open ; [coffret] to break open **3.** [champ] to rip open *(sép)*, to rip holes in ; [immeuble] to rip apart *(sép)*. **⬦ s'éventrer** **⬦** vp *(emploi réfléchi)* to disembowel o.s. **⬦** vpi [se fendre - oreiller, sac] to burst open.

éventualité [evɑ̃tɥalite] nf **1.** [possibilité] possibility, contingency **2.** [circonstance] eventuality, possibility, contingency **▸ pour parer** ou **être prêt à toute éventualité** to be ready for anything that might crop up **▸ dans cette éventualité** in such an ou in this event. **⬦ dans l'éventualité de** loc prép in the event of.

éventuel, elle [evɑ̃tɥel] adj [potentiel - client] potential, prospective ; [- bénéfice] possible, potential ; [- issue, refus, remplaçant, etc.] possible.

⚠ **Eventual** signifie « final », « ultime » et non *éventuel*.

éventuellement [evɑ̃tɥɛlmɑ̃] adv : *tu me le prêterais ? — éventuellement* would you lend it to me?
— maybe ou if need be / *les entreprises qui pourraient
éventuellement nous racheter* the companies which might
ou could buy us out.

⚠ **Eventually** signifie « finalement », « en
fin de compte » et non éventuellement.

évêque [evɛk] nm bishop.
évertuer [7] [evɛrtɥe] ❖ **s'évertuer à** vp + prép
▶ **s'évertuer à faire qqch** to strive ou to endeavour to do
sthg.
éviction [eviksjɔ̃] nf **1.** DR eviction **2.** ▶ **éviction scolaire** expulsion, suspension.
évidemment [evidamɑ̃] adv [bien entendu] of course ;
[manifestement] obviously / *bien évidemment !* of course!

⚠ **Evidently** signifie « apparemment »,
« manifestement » et non évidemment.

évidence [evidɑ̃s] nf **1.** [caractère certain] obviousness
2. [fait manifeste] obvious fact / *c'est une évidence* it's
obvious **3.** [ce qui est indubitable] ▶ **accepter** ou **se rendre
à l'évidence** to face facts ▶ **c'est l'évidence même !** it's
quite obvious ou evident! ▶ **refuser** ou **nier l'évidence**
to deny the facts ou obvious. ❖ **en évidence** loc adv
[chose, personne] : *j'ai laissé le message bien en évidence sur la table* I left the message on the table where
it couldn't be missed ▶ **mettre en évidence a)** [expo-
ser] to display **b)** [détail, talent] to bring out ▶ **se mettre
en évidence** [se faire remarquer] to make o.s. conspicuous.
❖ **à l'évidence, de toute évidence** loc adv evidently,
obviously.

⚠ **Attention, le mot anglais evidence** signifie « preuve », « témoignage » et ne peut
être employé pour traduire évidence que
dans des expressions telles que **in evidence**
ou **against all the evidence.**

évident, e [evidɑ̃, ɑ̃t] adj **1.** [manifeste -manque, plai-
sir] obvious, evident ; [-choix, raison] obvious, evident, self-
evident **2.** [certain] obvious, certain ▶ **c'est évident !** of
course!, obviously!, that's obvious! / *il est évident que...*
it's obvious ou evident that... **3.** fam [EXPR] **ce n'est pas
évident a)** [ce n'est pas facile] it's not that easy **b)** [ce n'est
pas sûr] I wouldn't bank on it.
évider [3] [evide] vt [rocher, fruit] to hollow ou to scoop
out (sép).
évier [evje] nm (kitchen) sink.
évincer [16] [evɛ̃se] vt **1.** [concurrent, rival] to oust, to
supplant **2.** DR to evict.
éviter [3] [evite] vt **1.** [ne pas subir -coup] to avoid ;
[-danger] to avoid, to steer clear of ; [-corvée] to avoid,
to shun **2.** [ne pas heurter -ballon] to avoid, to dodge, to
stay out of the way of ; [-obstacle] to avoid **3.** [regard,
personne] to avoid, to shun **4.** [lieu, situation] to avoid
5. [maladresse, impair] to avoid ▶ **éviter de faire qqch**
to avoid doing sthg, to try not to do sthg **6.** [aliment] to
avoid **7.** [épargner] ▶ **éviter qqch à qqn** to spare sb sthg /
cela lui évitera d'avoir à sortir that'll save him having to
go out. ❖ **s'éviter** ❖ vp (emploi réciproque) to avoid
each other ou one another, to stay out of each other's way.
❖ vpt ▶ **s'éviter qqch** to save ou to spare o.s. sthg.

📋 Notez la différence entre les construc-
tions française et anglaise :
éviter de + infinitif
avoid + -ing
Évitez de manger trop de graisses animales.
Avoid eating too much animal fat.
J'ai évité de parler de la situation avec elle.
I avoided talking to her about the situation.

évocation [evɔkasjɔ̃] nf [rappel -du passé, d'une personne, d'un paysage, etc.] evocation, recalling / *la simple
évocation de cette scène la faisait pleurer* just recalling this
scene made her weep.
évolué, e [evɔlɥe] adj **1.** [civilisé -peuple, société]
advanced, sophisticated **2.** [progressiste -parents] broad-
minded ; [-idées] progressive **3.** [méthode, technologie] advanced, sophisticated.
évoluer [7] [evɔlɥe] vi **1.** [changer -maladie] to develop ;
[-mœurs, circonstances] to change, to develop **2.** [progres-
ser -pays] to develop ; [-civilisation, technique] to develop,
to advance ; [-personne] to mature / *ce stage l'a fait évoluer de manière significative* the traineeship really brought
him on **3.** [danseur] to perform ; [cerf-volant] to fly around ;
[poisson] to swim (about) / *les cercles dans lesquels elle
évoluait* fig the circles in which she moved **4.** MIL & NAUT to
manoeuvre **5.** BIOL to evolve.
évolutif, ive [evɔlytif, iv] adj **1.** [poste] with career
prospects **2.** MÉD [maladie] progressive.
évolution [evɔlysjɔ̃] nf **1.** [changement -de mœurs]
change ; [-d'une institution, de la mode] evolution ; [-d'idées,
d'événements] development **2.** [progrès -d'un pays] development ; [-d'une technique] development, advancement,
evolution **3.** MÉD [d'une maladie] development, progression ;
[d'une tumeur] growth **4.** BIOL evolution **5.** (souvent au pl)
SPORT linked-up dance movements ▶ **les évolutions** [d'un
joueur, d'un patineur] movements.
évoquer [3] [evɔke] vt **1.** [remémorer -image, journée] to
conjure up (sép), to evoke ; [-souvenirs] to call up (sép), to
recall, to evoke ▶ **évoquer qqch à qqn** to remind sb of sthg
2. [recréer -pays, atmosphère] to call to mind, to conjure up
(sép), to evoke **3.** [rappeler par ressemblance] to be reminiscent of / *elle m'évoque un peu ma tante* she reminds me
of my aunt a little **4.** [aborder -affaire, question] to refer to
(insép), to mention.
ex- [ɛks] préf ex- ▶ **mon ex-mari** my ex-husband ou former husband.
ex. abr écrite de **exemple.**
exacerber [3] [ɛgzasɛrbe] vt sout [douleur, tension] to
exacerbate sout, to aggravate, to sharpen ; [colère, curiosité, désir] to exacerbate, to heighten ; [mépris, remords] to
deepen. ❖ **s'exacerber** vpi to intensify.
exact, e [ɛgzakt] adj **1.** [conforme à la réalité -descrip-
tion, information] exact, accurate ; [-copie, réplique] exact,
true ; [-prédiction] correct, accurate / *c'est exact, je t'avais
promis de t'y emmener* quite right ou true ou correct, I'd
promised I'd take you there **2.** [précis -mesure, poids] exact, precise ; [-expression, mot] exact, right ▶ **as-tu l'heure
exacte ?** have you got the right ou correct time? / *pour
être exact, disons que...* to be accurate, let's say that... ;
MATH right, correct, accurate **3.** [fonctionnant avec précision
-balance, montre] accurate **4.** [ponctuel] punctual, on time /
être très exact to be always on time ou very punctual.

exactement [ɛgzaktəmã] adv **1.** [précisément] exactly, precisely / *ce n'est pas exactement ce que je cherchais* it's not exactly ou quite what I was looking for / *il est très exactement 2 h 13* it is 2:13 precisely **2.** [tout à fait] ▸ **exactement !** exactly!, precisely!

exaction [ɛgzaksjɔ̃] nf exaction, extortion. ◂▸ **exactions** nfpl *sout* violent acts, acts of violence.

exactitude [ɛgzaktityd] nf **1.** [conformité à la réalité] exactness, accuracy **2.** [expression précise - d'une mesure] exactness, precision ; [- d'une localisation] exactness **3.** [d'un instrument de mesure] accuracy **4.** [justesse - d'une traduction, d'une réponse] exactness, correctness **5.** [ponctualité] punctuality.

ex aequo [ɛgzeko] ◂ loc adj placed equal ▸ **être ex aequo (avec)** to tie ou to be placed equal (with) ▸ **premiers ex aequo, Maubert et Vuillet a)** [à un concours] the joint winners are Maubert and Vuillet **b)** ÉDUC top marks 🇬🇧 ou highest grades 🇺🇸 have been awarded to Maubert and to Vuillet. ◂ nmf : *il y a deux ex aequo pour la troisième place* there's a tie for third place.

exagération [ɛgzaʒeʁasjɔ̃] nf **1.** [amplification] exaggeration, overstating *(U)* **2.** [écrit, parole] exaggeration, overstatement **3.** [outrance - d'un accent, d'une attitude] exaggeration.

exagéré, e [ɛgzaʒeʁe] adj [excessif - dépense, prix] excessive ; [- éloge, critique] exaggerated, overblown ; [- optimisme, prudence] excessive, exaggerated ; [- hâte, mécontentement] undue ; [- ambition, confiance en soi] excessive, overweening / *80 € par personne, c'est un peu exagéré !* 80 € per person, that's a bit much! / *il n'est pas exagéré de parler de menace* it wouldn't be an overstatement to call it a threat.

exagérément [ɛgzaʒeʁemã] adv excessively, exaggeratedly.

exagérer [18] [ɛgzaʒeʁe] ◂ vt [amplifier - importance, dangers, difficultés] to exaggerate, to overemphasize, to overstate ; [- mérites, pouvoir] to exaggerate, to overrate, to overstate ▸ **tu exagères mon influence** you're crediting me with more influence than I have ▸ **n'exagérons rien** let's not get carried away ; *(en usage absolu)* ▸ **sans exagérer** without any exaggeration. ◂ vi : *ça fait deux heures que j'attends, il ne faut pas exagérer !* I've been waiting for two hours, that's a bit much! / *j'étais là avant vous, faut pas exagérer !* fam I was there before you, you've got a nerve!

📎 In reformed spelling (see p. 16-18), this verb is conjugated like *semer : il exagèrera, elle s'exagèrerait.*

exaltant, e [ɛgzaltã, ãt] adj [expérience, perspective] exciting ; [harangue] elating, stirring.

exalté, e [ɛgzalte] ◂ adj [excité - personne] excited ; [- esprit] excited, inflamed ; [- imagination] wild. ◂ nm, f *péj* fanatic, hothead *péj.*

exalter [3] [ɛgzalte] vt **1.** [intensifier - désir] to excite, to kindle ; [- enthousiasme] to fire, to excite ; [- imagination] to fire, to stimulate, to stir up *(sép)* **2.** [exciter - foule, partisan] to excite ▸ **exalté à l'idée de** carried away by the idea of **3.** *litt* [faire l'éloge de - beauté, bienfaits, talent] to glorify, to extol, to exalt *litt.* ◂▸ **s'exalter** vpi to become excited.

examen [ɛgzamɛ̃] nm **1.** ÉDUC & UNIV examination, exam ▸ **passer un examen a)** [série d'épreuves] to take an exam **b)** [écrit] to sit 🇬🇧 ou to write 🇺🇸 a paper **c)** [oral] to take a viva 🇬🇧 ou an oral (exam) ▸ **examen blanc** mock exam 🇬🇧, practice test 🇺🇸 ▸ **examen écrit** written exam ▸ **examen oral** viva 🇬🇧, oral (exam) ▸ **examen de passage** end-of-year ou sessional exam 🇬🇧, final exam 🇺🇸 *(for admission to the year above)* **2.** MÉD [auscultation] ▸ **examen médical** (medical) examination ▸ **examen de santé** medical check-up ; [analyse] test ▸ **se faire faire un examen / des examens** to have a test / some tests done **3.** [inspection] inspection,

examination **4.** [de documents, d'un dossier, d'un projet de loi] examination ; [d'une requête] examination, consideration ; [d'un texte] study ; [d'une comptabilité] checking inspection / *son argumentation ne résiste pas à l'examen* his arguments don't stand up to examination ou under scrutiny ▸ **examen de conscience** examination of (one's) conscience. ◂▸ **à l'examen** loc adv under consideration.

examinateur, trice [ɛgzaminatœʁ, tʁis] nm, f examiner.

examiner [3] [ɛgzamine] vt **1.** [réfléchir sur - dossier, documents] to examine, to go through *(insép)* ; [- circonstances] to examine ; [- requête] to examine, to consider ; [- affaire] to investigate, to examine, to go into *(insép)* **2.** [regarder de près - meuble, signature, etc.] to examine ; [- personne] to look carefully at, to study ; [- appartement] to have a look around ▸ **examiner qqch à la loupe a)** *pr* to look at sthg through a magnifying glass **b)** *fig* to have a very close look at, to scrutinize **3.** MÉD [lésion, malade] to examine. ◂▸ **s'examiner** ◂ vp *(emploi réfléchi)* to examine o.s. ◂ vp *(emploi réciproque)* to scrutinize one another ou each other ▸ **ils s'examinaient avec méfiance** they were eyeing each other up.

exaspérant, e [ɛgzaspeʁã, ãt] adj exasperating, infuriating.

exaspérer [18] [ɛgzaspeʁe] vt [irriter] to infuriate, to exasperate ▸ **être exaspéré contre qqn** to be exasperated with sb.

📎 In reformed spelling (see p. 16-18), this verb is conjugated like *semer : il exaspèrera, elle s'exaspèrerait.*

exaucer [16] [ɛgzose] vt **1.** [vœu] to grant, to fulfil ; [prière] to answer, to grant **2.** [personne] to grant the wish of.

excédant, e [ɛksedã, ãt] adj exasperating, infuriating.

excédent [ɛksedã] nm **1.** [surplus] surplus, excess / *vous avez un excédent de bagages* your luggage is overweight **2.** ÉCON & FIN ▸ **excédent commercial** trade surplus. ◂▸ **en excédent** loc adj surplus *(modif)*, excess.

excédentaire [ɛksedãtɛʁ] adj [budget, balance commerciale] surplus *(modif)* ; [solde] positive ; [poids] excess.

excéder [18] [ɛksede] vt **1.** [dépasser - poids, prix] to exceed, to be over, to be in excess of ; [- durée] to exceed, to last more than ; [- limite] to go beyond *(insép)* **2.** [outrepasser - pouvoirs, responsabilités] to exceed, to go beyond *(insép)*, to overstep ; [- forces, ressources] to overtax **3.** [exaspérer] to exasperate, to infuriate **4.** *litt* [épuiser] ▸ **excédé de** : *excédé de fatigue* exhausted, overtired / *excédé de travail* overworked.

📎 In reformed spelling (see p. 16-18), this verb is conjugated like *semer : il excèdera, elle excèderait.*

excellence [ɛkselãs] nf **1.** [qualité - d'une prestation, d'un produit] excellence **2.** [titre] : *Son / Votre Excellence* His / Your Excellency. ◂▸ **par excellence** loc adv par excellence *sout*, archetypal.

excellent, e [ɛkselã, ãt] adj [très bon - artiste, directeur, nourriture] excellent, first-rate ; [- article, devoir, note] excellent ; [- santé] excellent, perfect ; [- idée] excellent.

exceller [4] [ɛksele] vi to excel, to shine / *elle excelle dans la pâtisserie* she excels at baking, she's an excellent pastry cook ▸ **exceller en** : *je n'excelle pas en latin* Latin isn't my strong point ▸ **exceller à faire** to be particularly good at doing.

excentré, e [ɛksãtʁe] adj [quartier, stade] outlying.

excentrique [ɛksãtʁik] ◂ adj [bizarre] eccentric. ◂ nmf [personne] eccentric.

excepté¹, e [ɛksɛpte] adj *(après le nom)* ▸ *elle exceptée* except her, apart from her.

excepté² [ɛksɛpte] prép except, apart from.
❖ **excepté que** loc conj except for ou apart from the fact that.
exception [ɛksɛpsjɔ̃] nf **1.** [chose, être ou événement hors norme] exception / *ils sont tous très paresseux, à une exception / quelques exceptions près* all of them with one exception / a few exceptions are very lazy ▸ **faire exception** to be an exception ▸ **être l'exception** to be the ou an exception ▸ **l'exception confirme la règle** the exception proves the rule ▸ **l'exception culturelle** cultural exception *(idea that cultural exports should not be treated in the same way as other goods in trade negotiations in order to protect national cultures)* **2.** [dérogation] exception ▸ **faire une exception à** to make an exception to. ❖ **à l'exception de, exception faite de** loc prép except, with the exception of. ❖ **d'exception** loc adj **1.** [mesure] exceptional ; [loi] emergency *(modif)* **2.** [remarquable] remarkable, exceptional. ❖ **sans (aucune) exception** loc adv without (any) exception.
exceptionnel, elle [ɛksɛpsjɔnɛl] adj **1.** [très rare - faveur, chance, circonstances] exceptional ; [- accident, complication] exceptional, rare ; [- mesure] exceptional, special ; [unique - concert] special, one-off 🇬🇧 ▸ **offre exceptionnelle** special offer / **'ouverture exceptionnelle dimanche 22 décembre'** 'open Sunday 22nd December' **2.** [remarquable - intelligence, œuvre] exceptional ; [- personne] remarkable, exceptional **3.** POL [assemblée, conseil, mesures] special, emergency *(modif)*.
exceptionnellement [ɛksɛpsjɔnɛlmɑ̃] adv **1.** [beau, doué] exceptionally, extremely **2.** [contrairement à l'habitude] exceptionally / *notre magasin sera ouvert lundi exceptionnellement* next week only, our shop will be open on Monday.
excès [ɛksɛ] ◆ nm **1.** [surabondance] surplus, excess ▸ **excès de zèle** overzealousness **2.** TRANSP : *faire un excès de vitesse* to exceed ou to break the speed limit **3.** [abus] ▸ **excès de pouvoir** DR abuse of power, action ultra vires *spéc* **4.** [manque de mesure] ▸ **tomber dans l'excès** to be extreme ▸ **tomber dans l'excès inverse** to go to the opposite extreme. ◆ nmpl ▸ **excès (de table)** overindulgence ▸ **faire des excès** to eat and drink too much, to overindulge ; [violences] excesses ; [débauche] excesses. ❖ **à l'excès** loc adv to excess, excessively. ❖ **sans excès** loc adv with moderation, moderately.
excessif, ive [ɛksesif, iv] adj **1.** [chaleur, sévérité, prix] excessive ; [colère] excessive ; [enthousiasme, optimisme] undue, excessive / *75 €, ce n'est pas excessif* 75 € is quite a reasonable amount to pay **2.** [personne] extreme / *c'est quelqu'un de très excessif* he's given to extremes of behaviour.
excessivement [ɛksesivmɑ̃] adv **1.** [trop - raffiné] excessively ▸ **excessivement cher** overpriced **2.** [extrêmement] extremely / *il fait excessivement froid* it's hideously cold.
excision [ɛksizjɔ̃] nf excision, female genital mutilation.
excitant, e [ɛksitɑ̃, ɑ̃t] adj **1.** [stimulant - boisson] stimulating **2.** [aguichant - femme, homme, tenue] arousing **3.** [passionnant - aventure, projet, vie] exciting, thrilling ; [- film, roman] exciting. ❖ **excitant** nm stimulant.
excitation [ɛksitasjɔ̃] nf **1.** [exaltation] excitement / *en proie à une grande excitation* very excited, in a state of great excitement **2.** [stimulation - d'un sens] excitation ; [- sexuelle] sexual arousal ou excitement **3.** PHYSIOL excitation, stimulation.
excité, e [ɛksite] ◆ adj **1.** [enthousiasmé] excited, thrilled / *nous étions tout excités à l'idée de la revoir* we were really excited ou thrilled by the idea of seeing her

again **2.** [agité - enfant, chien] excited, restless ; [- candidat] tense, excited **3.** [sexuellement - organe, personne] aroused. ◆ nm, f *péj* hothead.
exciter [3] [ɛksite] vt **1.** [exalter] to excite, to exhilarate / *n'excite pas les enfants avant le coucher* don't get the children excited before bed **2.** [rendre agité - drogue, café] to make excited, to overstimulate, to stimulate **3.** [pousser] ▸ **exciter qqn contre qqn** to work sb up against sb **4.** [attiser - admiration, envie] to provoke ; [- curiosité, intérêt, soupçons] to arouse, to stir up *(sép)* ; [- amour, jalousie] to arouse, to inflame, to kindle **5.** [intensifier - appétit] to whet ; [- rage] to whip up *(sép)* ; [- désir] to increase, to sharpen ; [- douleur] to intensify **6.** [sexuellement] to excite, to arouse **7.** *fam* [intéresser] to excite, to thrill, to get worked up **8.** BIOL to stimulate. ❖ **s'exciter** vpi **1.** *fam* [se mettre en colère] to get worked up **2.** [s'exalter] to get carried away ou excited ou overexcited.
exclamation [ɛksklamasjɔ̃] nf **1.** [cri] exclamation, cry **2.** LING exclamation.
exclamer [3] [ɛksklame] ❖ **s'exclamer** vpi to exclaim, to cry out.
exclu, e [ɛkskly] ◆ adj **1.** [non compris] excluded, left out / *du 15 au 30 exclu* from the 15th to the 30th exclusive **2.** [rejeté - hypothèse, solution] ruled out, dismissed, rejected / *une victoire de la gauche n'est pas exclue* a victory for the left is not to be ruled out / *il est exclu que je m'y rende* my going there is totally out of the question / *il n'est pas exclu qu'on les retrouve* it's not impossible that they might be found **3.** [renvoyé - définitivement] expelled ; [- provisoirement] suspended. ◆ nm, f : *le grand exclu du palmarès à Cannes* the big loser in the Cannes festival. ❖ **exclus** nmpl ▸ **les exclus a)** [gén] the underprivileged **b)** [SDF] the homeless.
exclure [96] [ɛsklyʀ] vt **1.** [expulser - membre, élève] to expel ; [- étudiant] to send down 🇬🇧 *(sép)*, to expel ; [- sportif] to ban / *elle s'est fait exclure de l'école pour 3 jours* she's been suspended from school for 3 days **2.** [être incompatible avec] to exclude, to preclude **3.** [rejeter - hypothèse] to exclude, to rule out *(sép)*, to reject. ❖ **s'exclure** vp *(emploi réciproque)* [solutions, traitements] to exclude ou to preclude one another, to be incompatible ou mutually exclusive.
exclusif, ive [ɛksklyzif, iv] adj **1.** [droit, modèle, privilège] exclusive ; [droits de reproduction, usage] exclusive, sole ; [dépositaire, concessionnaire] sole **2.** [absolu - amour, relation] exclusive / *dans le but exclusif de* with the sole aim of **3.** [dossier, image, reportage] exclusive.
exclusion [ɛksklyzjɔ̃] nf **1.** [renvoi] expulsion ▸ **exclusion temporaire** suspension ▸ **exclusion définitive** expulsion **2.** [mise à l'écart] exclusion **3.** SOCIOL exclusion / *les victimes de l'exclusion sociale* those rejected by society. ❖ **à l'exclusion de** loc prép except, apart from, with the exception of.
exclusivement [ɛksklyzivmɑ̃] adv [uniquement] exclusively, solely ▸ **ouvert le lundi exclusivement** open on Mondays only.
exclusivité [ɛksklyzivite] nf **1.** COMM [droit] exclusive rights / *avoir l'exclusivité d'une interview* to have (the) exclusive coverage of an interview **2.** [objet unique] : *ce modèle est une exclusivité* this is an exclusive design ; [article] exclusive (article) ; [interview] exclusive interview **3.** CINÉ film 🇬🇧 ou movie 🇺🇸 on general release. ❖ **en exclusivité** loc adv **1.** COMM exclusively **2.** [diffusé, publié] exclusively **3.** CINÉ ▸ **en première exclusivité** on general release.
excrément [ɛkskʀemɑ̃] nm excrement ▸ **excréments** excrement, faeces.

excroissance [ɛkskʀwasɑ̃s] nf MÉD growth, excrescence *spéc.*

excursion [ɛkskyʀsjɔ̃] nf [voyage - en car] excursion, trip ; [- à pied] ramble, hike ; [- à bicyclette] ride, tour ; [- en voiture] drive ▸ **faire une excursion a)** [avec un véhicule] to go on an excursion **b)** [à pied] to go on ou for a hike / *excursions de deux jours au pays de Galles* two-day tours ou trips to Wales.

excusable [ɛkskyzabl] adj excusable, forgivable / *tu n'es pas excusable* you have no excuse.

excuse [ɛkskyz] nf [motif allégué] excuse, pretext / *elle a donné pour excuse le manque d'argent* she used lack of money as an excuse. ❖ **excuses** nfpl apology ▸ **faire** ou **présenter ses excuses à qqn** to offer one's apologies ou to apologize to sb / *tu me dois des excuses* you owe me an apology.

excuser [3] [ɛkskyze] vt **1.** [pardonner - conduite] to excuse, to forgive ; [- personne] to forgive ▸ **excuse-moi d'appeler si tard** forgive me ou I do apologize for phoning so late ▸ **excusez-moi a)** [regret] forgive me, I'm sorry, I do apologize **b)** [interpellation, objection, après un hoquet] excuse me ▸ **tu es tout excusé** you are forgiven, please don't apologize **2.** [justifier - attitude, personne] to excuse, to find excuses ou an excuse for / *sa grossièreté ne peut être excusée* his rudeness is inexcusable, there is no excuse for his rudeness **3.** [accepter l'absence de] to excuse ▸ **se faire excuser** to ask to be excused **4.** [présenter les excuses de] ▸ **excuse-moi auprès de lui** apologize to him for me. ❖ **s'excuser** vpi [demander pardon] to apologize ▸ **s'excuser auprès de qqn** to apologize to sb ▸ **je m'excuse de mon retard / de vous interrompre** sorry for being late / for interrupting you.

exécrable [ɛgzekʀabl] adj [mauvais - dîner, goût, spectacle] abysmal, awful, foul ; [- temps] awful, rotten, wretched ; [- travail] abysmal.

exécrer [18] [ɛgzekʀe] vt *sout* to loathe, to abhor.
📝 In reformed spelling (see p. 16-18), this verb is conjugated like *semer : il exècrera, elle exècrerait.*

exécutant, e [ɛgzekytɑ̃, ɑ̃t] nm, f **1.** [musicien] performer **2.** *péj* [subalterne] subordinate, underling *péj.*

exécuter [3] [ɛgzekyte] vt **1.** [mouvement, cabriole] to do, to execute **2.** [confectionner - maquette, statue] to make ; [- tableau] to paint **3.** [interpréter - symphonie] to perform, to play ; [- chorégraphie] to perform, to dance **4.** [mener à bien - consigne, ordre, mission] to carry out *(sép)*, to execute ; [- projet] to carry out **5.** [commande] to carry out *(sép)* **6.** [tuer - condamné] to execute, to put to death ; [- victime] to execute, to kill **7.** INFORM to run.

exécutif, ive [ɛgzekytif, iv] adj executive. ❖ **exécutif** nm ▸ **l'exécutif** the executive.

exécution [ɛgzekysjɔ̃] nf **1.** [d'une maquette] execution, making ; [d'un tableau] execution, painting *(U)* **2.** [d'une symphonie, d'une chorégraphie] performance, performing **3.** [d'une menace, d'une décision] carrying out ; [d'un projet] execution ▸ **mettre qqch à exécution** to carry sthg out / *va ranger ta chambre, exécution !* *hum* go and tidy up your bedroom, NOW ou on the double! **4.** [d'un condamné] ▸ **exécution (capitale)** execution.

exemplaire¹ [ɛgzɑ̃plɛʀ] adj **1.** [qui donne l'exemple - conduite] exemplary, perfect ; [- personne] exemplary, model **2.** [qui sert d'exemple - punition] exemplary.

exemplaire² [ɛgzɑ̃plɛʀ] nm **1.** [d'un document] copy ▸ **exemplaire gratuit** presentation copy ▸ **en deux exemplaires** in duplicate / *le livre a été tiré à 10 000 exemplaires* 10,000 copies of the book were published **2.** [d'un coquillage, d'une plante] specimen, example.

exemple [ɛgzɑ̃pl] nm **1.** [d'architecture, d'un défaut, d'une qualité] example ; [d'une situation] example, instance ▸ **citer qqch en exemple** to quote sthg as an example **2.** [modèle] example, model ▸ **donner l'exemple** to give ou to set the example ▸ **prendre exemple sur qqn** to take sb as a model ou an example / *que cela vous serve d'exemple* let this be a warning to you ▸ **suivre l'exemple de qqn** to follow sb's example, to take one's cue from sb **3.** GRAM & LING (illustrative) example. ❖ **à l'exemple de** loc prép : *à l'exemple de son maître* following his master's example. ❖ **par exemple** loc adv **1.** [comme illustration] for example ou instance **2.** [marque la surprise] : *(ça) par exemple, c'est Pierre !* Pierre ! well I never!

exempt, e [ɛgzɑ̃, ɑ̃t] adj [dispensé] ▸ **exempt de** [d'une obligation] exempt from ▸ **produits exempts de taxes** duty-free ou non dutiable goods.

exempter [3] [ɛgzɑ̃te] vt ▸ **exempter qqn d'impôts** to exempt sb from taxes.

exercer [16] [ɛgzɛʀse] vt **1.** [pratiquer - talent] to exercise ; [- profession] to exercise ; [- art] to practise UK, to practice US ▸ **exercer le métier de dentiste / forgeron** to work as a dentist / blacksmith ; *(en usage absolu)* [suj : dentiste, avocat, médecin] to be in practice, to practise **2.** [autorité, influence] to exercise, to exert ; [droit, privilège] to exercise ; [sanctions] to carry out **3.** [entraîner - oreille, esprit, mémoire] to exercise, to train ▸ **exercer qqn à faire qqch** to train sb to do sthg. ❖ **s'exercer** vpi **1.** [s'entraîner] to practise UK, to practice US / *s'exercer au piano* to practise (playing) the piano **2.** [s'appliquer] ▸ **s'exercer sur** [force, pression] to be brought to bear on, to be exerted on.

exercice [ɛgzɛʀsis] nm **1.** [mouvement] exercise ▸ **exercices d'assouplissement / d'échauffement** stretching / warm-up exercises **2.** [activité physique] ▸ **l'exercice (physique)** (physical) exercise ▸ **faire de l'exercice** to take exercise, to exercise **3.** ÉDUC exercise ▸ **faire un exercice** to do an exercise / *exercice de chimie* chemistry exercise **4.** MIL drill, exercise **5.** [usage] ▸ **l'exercice du pouvoir** / d'un **droit** exercising power / a right / *condamné pour exercice illégal de la médecine* condemned for illegal practice of medicine / *dans l'exercice de ses fonctions* in the exercise of her duties **6.** FIN year / *les impôts pour l'exercice 2007* taxes for the 2007 fiscal ou tax year ▸ **exercice budgétaire** budgetary year ▸ **exercice financier** accounting period. ❖ **en exercice** loc adj [député, juge] sitting ; [membre de comité] serving ; [avocat, médecin] practising ▸ **être en exercice** [diplomate, magistrat] to be in ou to hold office.

exergue [ɛgzɛʀg] nm [dans un livre] inscription ▸ **mettre qqch en exergue** : *mettre une citation en exergue à un* ou *d'un texte* to head a text with quotation, to write a quotation as an epigraph to a text / *mettre un argument en exergue* *fig* to underline ou to stress an argument.

exfoliant, e [ɛksfɔljɑ̃, ɑ̃t] adj exfoliative. ❖ **exfoliant** nm exfoliant.

exhaler [3] [ɛgzale] vt **1.** [dégager - parfum] to exhale ; [- gaz, effluves, vapeur] to exhale, to give off *(sép)* **2.** [en respirant] to exhale.

exhaustif, ive [ɛgzostif, iv] adj exhaustive.

exhiber [3] [ɛgzibe] vt **1.** [afficher - décorations, muscles] to display, to show off *(insép)* ; [- richesses] to display, to make a (great) show of ; [- savoir] to show off **2.** [au cirque, à la foire] to show, to exhibit **3.** [document officiel] to produce, to show, to present. ❖ **s'exhiber** vpi [parader] to parade (around) ; [impudiquement] to expose o.s.

exhibitionniste [ɛgzibisjɔnist] nmf exhibitionist.

exhortation [ɛgzɔʀtasjɔ̃] nf exhortation.

exhorter [3] [ɛgzɔʀte] vt to urge ▸ **exhorter qqn à la prudence** to urge ou to exhort sb to be careful ▸ **exhorter qqn à faire qqch** to exhort ou to urge sb to do sthg.

exhumer [3] [ɛgzyme] vt **1.** [déterrer - cadavre] to exhume ; [- objets enfouis] to excavate, to dig out *(sép)* **2.** [sentiments] to unearth ; [vieux documents] to dig out ou up *(sép)*, to rescue from oblivion.

exigeant, e [ɛgziʒɑ̃, ɑ̃t] adj [pointilleux - maître, professeur] demanding, exacting ; [- malade] demanding ; [- client] demanding, particular, hard to please / *je suis très exigeant sur la qualité* I'm very particular about quality / *tu es trop exigeante avec tes amis* you ask ou expect too much from your friends.

exigence [ɛgziʒɑ̃s] nf **1.** [demande - d'un client] requirement ; [- d'un ravisseur] demand **2.** [nécessité] demand, requirement **3.** [caractère exigeant - d'un client] particularity ; [- d'un professeur, d'un parent] strictness, exactingness / *devant l'exigence de son client* faced with such a demanding customer. ❖ **exigences** nfpl [salaire] expected salary.

exiger [17] [ɛgziʒe] vt **1.** [compensation, dû] to demand, to claim **2.** [excuse] to require, to demand, to insist on *(insép)* ▸ **exiger beaucoup / trop de qqn** to expect a lot / too much from sb **3.** [déclarer obligatoire] to require / *la connaissance du russe n'est pas exigée* knowledge of Russian is not a requirement **4.** [nécessiter] to require, to need / *un métier qui exige beaucoup de précision* a job requiring great accuracy.

exigible [ɛgziʒibl] adj [impôt] due (for payment), payable.

exigu, exiguë ou **exigüe*** [ɛgzigy] adj [appartement, pièce] very small, tiny ; [couloir] very narrow.

exiguïté, exigüité* [ɛgziguite] nf [d'une pièce] smallness ; [d'un couloir] narrowness.

exil [ɛgzil] nm exile. ❖ **en exil** loc adv [vivre] in exile ▸ **envoyer qqn en exil** to exile sb.

exilé, e [ɛgzile] nm, f exile.

exiler [3] [ɛgzile] vt to exile. ❖ **s'exiler** vpi **1.** [quitter son pays] to go into self-imposed exile **2.** [s'isoler] to cut o.s. off.

existant, e [ɛgzistɑ̃, ɑ̃t] adj [modèle, loi, tarif] existing, current, currently in existence.

existence [ɛgzistɑ̃s] nf [vie] life, existence ; [mode de vie] lifestyle.

existentialisme [ɛgzistɑ̃sjalism] nm existentialism.

existentiel, elle [ɛgzistɑ̃sjɛl] adj existential.

exister [3] [ɛgziste] vi **1.** [être réel] to exist, to be real / *le savon, ça existe !* fam there is such a thing as soap, you know! **2.** [subsister] to exist ▸ **l'hôtel existe toujours / n'existe plus** the hotel is still there / isn't there anymore **3.** [vivre - personne] to live **4.** *(tournure impersonnelle)* ▸ *il existe (suivi d'un sg)* there is, there's / *(suivi d'un pl)* there are.

exode [ɛgzɔd] nm **1.** [départ] exodus ▸ **l'exode des cerveaux** the brain drain ▸ **l'exode des capitaux** the flight of capital ▸ **l'exode rural** the drift from the land, the rural exodus **2.** BIBLE ▸ **l'Exode** the Exodus.

exonération [ɛgzɔnerasjɔ̃] nf exemption, exempting *(U)* ▸ **exonération fiscale** ou **d'impôt** tax exemption.

exonérer [18] [ɛgzɔneʀe] vt [contribuable, revenus] to exempt ▸ **exonérer qqn d'impôts** to exempt sb from income tax ▸ **intérêt : 12 %, exonéré d'impôts** 12% interest rate, non-taxable ou free of tax.

✒ In reformed spelling (see p. 16-18), this verb is conjugated like *semer : il exonèrera, elle exonèrerait.*

exoplanète [ɛgzɔplanɛt] nf exoplanet, extrasolar planet.

exorbitant, e [ɛgzɔʀbitɑ̃, ɑ̃t] adj **1.** [trop cher - loyer] exorbitant, extortionate **2.** [démesuré - requête] outrageous ; [- prétention] absurd.

exorbité, e [ɛgzɔʀbite] adj bulging.

exorciser [3] [ɛgzɔʀsize] vt to exorcize.

exorciste [ɛgzɔʀsist] nmf exorcist.

exotique [ɛgzɔtik] adj [produit, fruit, pays] exotic.

exotisme [ɛgzɔtism] nm exoticism.

expansif, ive [ɛkspɑ̃sif, iv] adj [caractère, personne] expansive, exuberant, effusive / *il n'est pas très expansif* he's never very forthcoming.

expansion [ɛkspɑ̃sjɔ̃] nf **1.** ÉCON ▸ **expansion (économique)** (economic) growth **2.** [augmentation - d'un territoire, de l'univers] expansion, expanding *(U)*. ❖ **en (pleine) expansion** loc adj ÉCON expanding, booming.

expansionniste [ɛkspɑ̃sjɔnist] adj & nmf expansionist.

expatrié, e [ɛkspatʀije] adj & nm, f expatriate.

expatrier [10] [ɛkspatʀije] vt to expatriate. ❖ **s'expatrier** vpi to become an expatriate, to leave one's country (of origin).

expectative [ɛkspɛktativ] nf [attente - incertaine] state of uncertainty ; [- prudente] cautious wait ; [- pleine d'espoir] expectancy, expectation. ❖ **dans l'expectative** loc adv ▸ **être dans l'expectative a)** [espérer] to be in a state of expectation **b)** [être incertain] to be in a state of uncertainty.

expectorant [ɛkspɛktɔʀɑ̃] nm expectorant.

expédient, e [ɛkspedjɑ̃, ɑ̃t] adj *sout* expedient. ❖ **expédient** nm **1.** [moyen] expedient **2.** EXPR user ou **vivre d'expédients** to live by one's wits.

expédier [9] [ɛkspedje] vt **1.** [envoyer - colis, lettre] to send, to dispatch ▸ **expédier par bateau a)** [lettre, paquet] to send surface mail **b)** [marchandises] to send by sea, to ship ▸ **expédier par la poste** to send through the post UK ou mail **2.** [personne] to send off *(sép)* / *je vais l'expédier en colonie de vacances* I'm going to send her off to a summer camp **3.** [bâcler, finir sans soin - dissertation, lettre] to dash off *(sép)* ; [- corvée, travail] to make short work of, to dispatch **4.** [avaler vite - repas] to dispatch, to swallow ; [- verre de vin] to knock back *(sép)* **5.** EXPR **expédier les affaires courantes a)** [employé] to deal with day-to-day matters (only) **b)** [président] to be a caretaker president.

expéditeur, trice [ɛkspeditœʀ, tʀis] nm, f **1.** [d'un colis, d'une lettre] sender, forwarder **2.** COMM [de marchandises] shipper, consigner ; [par bateau] shipper.

expéditif, ive [ɛkspeditif, iv] adj **1.** [efficace et rapide - procédé] expeditious *sout*, quick ; [- personne] expeditious *sout*, prompt **2.** *péj* [trop rapide - procès, justice] hasty.

expédition [ɛkspedisjɔ̃] nf **1.** [voyage] expedition / *pour traverser la capitale, quelle expédition !* fam it's quite an expedition to get across the capital! ; [équipe] (members of the) expedition **2.** [raid] ▸ **expédition punitive** punitive raid ou expedition **3.** [envoi] sending, dispatch, dispatching ▸ **expédition par bateau** [de marchandises] shipping.

expérience [ɛkspeʀjɑ̃s] nf **1.** [connaissance] experience ▸ **avoir de l'expérience (en)** to have experience ou to be experienced (in) **2.** [apprentissage] experience / *ses premières expériences amoureuses* his first amorous experiences / *faire l'expérience de la haine* to experience hatred **3.** [test] experiment / *faire des expériences (sur des rats)* to carry out experiments ou to experiment (on rats). ❖ **par expérience** loc adv from experience. ❖ **sans expérience** loc adj inexperienced.

 experience ou experiment ?

Pour parler d'un « ensemble de connaissances », de « la pratique d'une activité » ou du « vécu », on emploie **experience**. Pour désigner une expérience de type scientifique, on emploie **experiment**.

---

* In reformed spelling (see p. 16-18).

expérimental, e, aux [ɛkspeʀimɑ̃tal, o] adj [méthode, sciences] experimental ▸ **à titre expérimental** experimentally, as an experiment.

expérimentation [ɛkspeʀimɑ̃tasjɔ̃] nf experimentation ▸ **expérimentation animale a)** [pratique] animal experimentation **b)** [tests] animal experiments.

expérimenté, e [ɛkspeʀimɑ̃te] adj experienced, practised.

expérimenter [3] [ɛkspeʀimɑ̃te] vt to try out *(sép)*, to test.

expert, e [ɛkspeʀ, ɛʀt] ◆ adj **1.** [agile] expert **2.** [savant] highly knowledgeable / **être expert en la matière** to be a specialist in the subject. ◆ nm, f [connaisseur] expert, connoisseur ▸ **expert de** ou **en** expert on, specialist in. ❖ **expert** nm [chargé d'expertise] expert, specialist ; [en bâtiments] surveyor ; [en assurances] valuer.

expert-comptable, experte-comptable [ɛkspeʀkɔ̃tabl] *(mpl* **experts-comptables**, *fpl* **expertes-comptables)** nm, f ≃ chartered accountant 🇬🇧 ; ≃ certified public accountant 🇺🇸.

expertise [ɛkspeʀtiz] nf **1.** [examen - d'un meuble, d'une voiture] (expert) appraisal ou evaluation ou valuation ; [-de bijou] valuation ; [de dommages] (expert) assessment ▸ **expertise médicale et psychiatrique** DR expert opinion *(by a doctor)* **2.** [document] expert's ou valuer's report.

expertiser [3] [ɛkspeʀtize] vt [véhicule, bijou] to value ; [dommages, meuble, tableau] to appraise, to assess, to value.

expier [9] [ɛkspje] vt [crime, péché] to expiate, to atone for *(insép)* ; *sout* [erreur, faute] to pay ou to atone for *(insép)*.

expiration [ɛkspiʀasjɔ̃] nf **1.** [d'air] breathing out **2.** [fin] expiry 🇬🇧, expiration 🇺🇸 / **le bail arrive à expiration le 30 août** the lease expires by August 30th. ❖ **à l'expiration de** loc prép ▸ **à l'expiration du délai** at the end of the stated period.

expirer [3] [ɛkspiʀe] ◆ vi *(aux avoir ou être)* [cesser d'être valide - abonnement, bail, délai] to expire, to end ; [-carte de crédit] to expire. ◆ vt [air] to breathe out *(sép)*.

explicable [ɛksplikabl] adj explainable, explicable / **c'est un phénomène difficilement explicable** it's a phenomenon which is difficult to explain ou which is not easily explained.

explicatif, ive [ɛksplikatif, iv] adj **1.** [brochure, lettre] explanatory **2.** GRAM ▸ **proposition relative explicative** non-restrictive relative clause.

explication [ɛksplikasjɔ̃] nf **1.** [éclaircissement - d'un fait, d'une situation] explanation **2.** ÉDUC & UNIV [d'une œuvre] commentary, analysis ▸ **explication de texte** critical analysis, appreciation of a text **3.** [discussion] discussion ; [querelle] argument ▸ **avoir une explication avec qqn sur qqch a)** [discussion] to talk sthg over with sb **b)** [querelle] to have an argument with sb about sthg. ❖ **explications** nfpl [mode d'emploi] instructions ou directions (for use).

explicite [ɛksplisit] adj explicit ▸ **suis-je assez explicite ?** do I make myself plain (enough)?

expliciter [3] [ɛksplisite] vt **1.** [intentions] to make explicit ou plain **2.** [phrase] to clarify, to explain.

expliquer [3] [ɛksplike] vt **1.** [faire comprendre - événement, réaction, fonctionnement, etc.] to explain ▸ **expliquer qqch à qqn** to explain sthg to sb **2.** ÉDUC & UNIV [texte] to analyse, to make a critical analysis of, to comment on *(insép)*. ❖ **s'expliquer** ◆ vp *(emploi passif)* to be explained ▸ **tout s'explique !** that explains it! ◆ vp *(emploi réciproque)* : *sors, on va s'expliquer !* fam we'll talk this over outside! ◆ vpi [s'exprimer] to explain o.s., to make o.s. clear ▸ **explique-toi mieux** make yourself clearer **>** **s'expliquer sur** [éclaircir] : *s'expliquer sur ses inten-*

tions to make plain ou to explain one's intentions. ◆ vpt [comprendre] to understand / *je n'arrive pas à m'expliquer son silence* I can't understand why he remains silent. ❖ **s'expliquer avec** vp + prép **1.** [avoir une discussion avec] to talk things over with **2.** [se disputer avec] to have it out with.

> 📝 Notez que le verbe explain n'est jamais suivi immédiatement d'un complément d'objet indirect :
> **Explique-nous comment ça marche.** Explain [to us] how it works.
> **Pouvez-vous m'expliquer comment cela s'est passé ?** Can you explain [to me] how it happened?
> Dans l'usage, « to us », « to me », etc., sont le plus souvent omis.

exploit [ɛksplwa] nm [acte] exploit, feat ▸ **exploit sportif** remarkable sporting achievement / *ses exploits amoureux* his amorous exploits.

exploitable [ɛksplwatabl] adj [idée, mine, terre, etc.] exploitable, workable ; [énergie] exploitable.

exploitant, e [ɛksplwatɑ̃, ɑ̃t] nm, f [d'une carrière, d'un cinéma] owner ▸ **exploitant (agricole)** farmer ▸ **petit exploitant** smallholder 🇬🇧, small farmer ▸ **exploitant forestier** forestry agent.

exploitation [ɛksplwatasjɔ̃] nf **1.** [entreprise] ▸ **exploitation agricole** farm (estate) ▸ **exploitation familiale** family holding ▸ **exploitation vinicole a)** [vignes] vineyard **b)** [société] wine-producing establishment **2.** [d'un réseau ferroviaire] operating ; [d'un cinéma] running ; [d'une carrière, d'une forêt, d'une mine, d'un sol] exploitation, working **3.** [utilisation - d'une idée, d'un talent] exploitation, exploiting (U), utilizing (U) **4.** [fait d'abuser] exploitation, exploiting ; [de la main-d'œuvre] exploitation / *l'exploitation de l'homme par l'homme* man's exploitation of man.

exploiter [3] [ɛksplwate] vt **1.** [mettre en valeur - forêt, mine, terre, etc.] to work, to work ; [faire fonctionner - cinéma] to run ; [- tunnel, réseau ferroviaire] to run, to operate **2.** [tirer avantage de - talent] to exploit, to make use of ; [- thème] to exploit ; [- situation] to exploit, to make capital out of, to take advantage of.

exploiteur, euse [ɛksplwatœʀ, øz] nm, f exploiter.

explorateur, trice [ɛksplɔʀatœʀ, tʀis] nm, f explorer.

exploration [ɛksplɔʀasjɔ̃] nf **1.** GÉOGR & MÉD exploration **2.** [analyse] exploration, examination.

exploratoire [ɛksplɔʀatwaʀ] adj exploratory, tentative.

explorer [3] [ɛksplɔʀe] vt **1.** [voyager dans - contrée, île] to explore **2.** [examiner - possibilité] to explore, to examine.

exploser [3] [ɛksploze] vi **1.** [détoner - grenade, mine, maison] to explode, to blow up ; [- dynamite, gaz] to explode ▸ **faire exploser une bombe** to set off ou to explode ou to detonate a bomb **2.** [augmenter - population] to explode ; [- prix] to shoot up, to soar **3.** [se révéler soudain - mécontentement, joie] to explode ; [- rage] to explode ; to burst out ; [- rires] to burst out ; [- artiste] to burst onto the scene ▸ **exploser (de colère)** to explode (with anger) ▸ **laisser exploser sa colère** to give vent to one's anger.

explosif, ive [ɛksplozif, iv] adj **1.** [mélange, puissance] explosive ; [obus] high-explosive **2.** [dangereux - situation, sujet] explosive, highly sensitive ; [- atmosphère] explosive, charged. ❖ **explosif** nm ARM explosive.

explosion [ɛksplozjɔ̃] nf **1.** [détonation - d'une bombe, d'une chaudière, d'une mine] explosion, blowing up ; [d'un gaz] explosion **2.** [manifestation] ▸ **explosion d'enthousiasme** / **d'indignation** burst of enthusiasm / indignation

▶ **explosion de joie** outburst ou explosion of joy **3.** [accroissement] ▶ **explosion démographique** population boom ou explosion.

expo [ɛkspo] nf *fam* exhibition.

exportateur, trice [ɛkspɔʀtatœʀ,tʀis] ◆ adj exporting ▶ **être exportateur de** to be an exporter of, to export. ◆ nm, f exporter.

exportation [ɛkspɔʀtasjɔ̃] nf [sortie] export, exportation. ◆ **d'exportation** loc adj export *(modif)*.

exporter [3] [ɛkspɔʀte] vt **1.** COMM & ÉCON to export **2.** [répandre à l'étranger - idées, culture] to export, to spread abroad.

exposant, e [ɛkspozɑ̃, ɑ̃t] nm, f [dans une galerie, une foire] exhibitor. ◆ **exposant** nm MATH exponent.

exposé, e [ɛkspoze] adj **1.** [orienté] : *la chambre est exposée au nord* the room faces north **2.** [non abrité] exposed, wind-swept **3.** [montré] on show, on display ▶ **objet exposé** [dans une galerie, une foire] item on show, exhibit. ◆ **exposé** nm **1.** [compte rendu] account, exposition *sout* ▶ **faire un exposé sur** to give an account of **2.** ÉDUC & UNIV [écrit] (written) paper ; [oral] talk, lecture ▶ **faire un exposé sur** a) [oral] to give a talk ou to read a paper on b) [écrit] to write a paper on.

exposer [3] [ɛkspoze] vt **1.** [dans un magasin] to display, to put on display, to set out *(sép)* ; [dans une galerie, dans une foire] to exhibit, to show **2.** [soumettre] ▶ **exposer qqch à** : *exposer qqch à l'air* to expose sthg to the air ▶ **exposer qqn à** [critiques, ridicule] to lay sb open to, to expose sb to **3.** [mettre en danger - honneur, vie] to endanger, to put at risk **4.** [faire connaître - arguments, motifs] to expound, to put forward *(sép)* ; [-intentions] to set forth ou out *(sép)*, to explain ; [-revendications] to set forth, to put forward, to make known **5.** LITTÉR & MUS to set out *(sép)* ; [thème] to introduce. ◆ **s'exposer** vp *(emploi réfléchi)* **1.** [se compromettre] to leave o.s. exposed ▶ **s'exposer à des représailles** to expose o.s. to retaliation **2.** [se placer] ▶ **s'exposer au soleil** to expose one's skin to the sun.

exposition [ɛkspozisjɔ̃] nf **1.** [d'œuvres d'art] show, exhibition ; [de produits manufacturés] exhibition, exposition ▶ **l'exposition universelle** the World Fair **2.** [d'arguments, de motifs] exposition, expounding *(U)* ; [d'une situation, d'une théorie] exposition **3.** [soumission] ▶ **exposition à** [danger, radiation, risque] exposure to **4.** [orientation] orientation, aspect **5.** PHOT exposure.

exposition-vente [ɛkspozisjɔ̃vɑ̃t] *(pl* **expositions-ventes)** nf [gén] exhibition *(where items are for sale)* ; [d'objets d'artisanat] craft fair.

expo-vente [ɛkspovɑ̃t] = **exposition-vente.**

exprès¹ [ɛkspʀɛ] adv **1.** [délibérément] on purpose, intentionally, deliberately ▶ **faire exprès** : *tu l'as vexé — je ne l'ai pas fait exprès* you've offended him — I didn't mean to ou it wasn't intentional / *il y a du papier à l'intérieur — c'est fait exprès* there's some paper inside — it's meant to be like that **2.** [spécialement] especially, specially.

exprès², expresse [ɛkspʀɛs] adj **1.** [avertissement, autorisation, ordre] express, explicit ; [recommandation] express, strict ▶ **défense expresse de fumer** smoking strictly prohibited **2.** [lettre, paquet] express 🇬🇧, special delivery 🇺🇸 *(modif)*. ◆ **en exprès, par exprès** loc adv ▶ **envoyer qqch en exprès** to send sthg by express post 🇬🇧 ou special delivery 🇺🇸.

express [ɛkspʀɛs] ◆ adj inv **1.** TRANSP ⟶ **train 2.** [café] espresso. ◆ nm **1.** RAIL express ou fast train **2.** [café] espresso (coffee).

expressément [ɛkspʀɛsemɑ̃] adv **1.** [catégoriquement - défendre, ordonner] expressly, categorically ; [-conseiller, prévenir] expressly **2.** [spécialement] specially, specifically.

expressif, ive [ɛkspʀɛsif,iv] adj [suggestif - style] expressive, vivid ; [-regard, visage] expressive, meaningful ; [-ton] expressive.

expression [ɛkspʀɛsjɔ̃] nf **1.** [mot, tournure] expression, phrase, turn of phrase ▶ **expression figée** set phrase ou expression, fixed expression, idiom ▶ **expression toute faite** a) [figée] set phrase ou expression b) [cliché] hackneyed phrase, cliché **2.** [pratique de la langue] : *des enfants d'expression française* French-speaking children ▶ **expression écrite / orale** written / oral expression **3.** [extériorisation - d'un besoin, d'un sentiment] expression, self-expression ▶ **expression corporelle** self-expression through movement **4.** [vivacité] expression / **geste / regard plein d'expression** expressive gesture / look **5.** [du visage] expression, look.

expressionnisme [ɛkspʀɛsjɔnism] nm expressionism.

expresso [ɛkspʀɛso] nm espresso.

exprimer [3] [ɛkspʀime] vt **1.** [dire - sentiment] to express ; [-idée, revendication] to express, to voice **2.** [manifester - mécontentement, surprise] to express, to show. ◆ **s'exprimer** ◆ vp *(emploi passif)* [idée, sentiment] to be expressed, to express itself ; [opinion] to be heard. ◆ vpi **1.** [dire sa pensée] to express o.s. / *je me suis exprimée sur ce sujet* I've expressed myself ou made my opinions known on the subject ▶ **s'exprimer par signes** to use sign language **2.** [choisir ses mots] to express o.s. ▶ **exprime-toi clairement** express yourself clearly, make yourself clear / *si je peux m'exprimer ainsi* if I can put it that way **3.** [se manifester - talent, sentiment] to express ou show itself.

exproprier [10] [ɛkspʀɔpʀije] vt **1.** [personne] to expropriate / **se faire exproprier** to have one's property expropriated, to have a compulsory purchase order placed on one's property 🇬🇧 **2.** [maison, terre] to expropriate, to place a compulsory purchase order on 🇬🇧.

expulser [3] [ɛkspylse] vt [renvoyer - locataire] to evict, to throw out *(sép)* ; [-membre, participant] to expel ; [-immigrant] to expel, to deport ; [-joueur] to send off *(sép)*.

expulsion [ɛkspylsjɔ̃] nf [d'un locataire] eviction ; [d'un membre de comité] expulsion ; [d'un étudiant] sending down 🇬🇧, expulsion 🇺🇸 ; [d'un immigrant] expulsion, deportation ; [d'un joueur] sending off ▶ **décider l'expulsion d'un élève** a) [définitive] to decide to expel a pupil b) [temporaire] to decide to suspend a pupil.

expurger [17] [ɛkspyʀʒe] vt to expurgate, to bowdlerize.

exquis, e [ɛkski, iz] adj [saveur, vin, gentillesse, etc.] exquisite ; [personne] delightful.

extase [ɛkstaz] nf [exaltation] ecstasy, rapture / **être** ou **rester en extase devant** to be in raptures ou ecstasies over ▶ **tomber en extase devant qqch / qqn** to go into ecstasies at the sight of sthg / sb.

extasier [9] [ɛkstazje] ◆ **s'extasier** vpi ▶ **s'extasier devant** to go into raptures ou ecstasies over.

extensible [ɛkstɑ̃sibl] adj [organe] extensible ; [matière] tensible, extensible ; [tissu] stretch ; [liste] extendable / *mon budget n'est pas extensible* I can't stretch my budget any further, I can't make my budget go any further.

extensif, ive [ɛkstɑ̃sif,iv] adj AGR extensive.

extension [ɛkstɑ̃sjɔ̃] nf **1.** [étirement - d'un élastique, d'un muscle] stretching ; [-d'une matière] extension ; MÉD traction, extension **2.** [agrandissement - d'un territoire] expansion, enlargement ; [-d'une entreprise, d'un marché, d'un réseau] expansion, extension ; [-de pouvoirs, d'un incendie, d'une infection] spreading ; [-de droits] extension ▶ **prendre de l'extension** a) [territoire] to get bigger, to expand b) [secteur] to grow, to develop c) [infection] to extend, to spread d) [incendie] to spread **3.** [élargissement] : *on a décidé l'extension des mesures à toute la population* it has been decided to extend the scope of the measures to include the entire population **4.** [de cheveux] ▶ **se faire faire**

des extensions to get extensions done. ◆ **en extension** loc adj **1.** [secteur] developing, expanding ; [production] increasing **2.** [muscle, ressort] stretched. ◆ **par extension** loc adv by extension.

exténuant, e [ɛkstenɥɑ̃, ɑ̃t] adj exhausting.

exténuer [7] [ɛkstenɥe] vt to exhaust, to tire out *(sép).* ◆ **s'exténuer** vpi to exhaust o.s., to tire ou to wear o.s. out ▶ **s'exténuer à faire qqch** to exhaust o.s. doing sthg.

extérieur, e [ɛksteʀjœʀ] adj **1.** [escalier, bruit] outside ; [cour, poche, mur, orbite, bord] outer ; [porte] external, outer **2.** [excentré - quartier] outlying, out-of-town 🇺🇸 **3.** [non subjectif - monde, réalité] external **4.** [étranger à la personne, la chose considérée - influence, aide] outside, external ▶ **extérieur à** outside (of) **5.** ÉCON & POL [dette, politique] foreign, external **6.** TÉLÉC outside. ◆ **extérieur** nm **1.** ▶ **l'extérieur** [le plein air] the outside ou outdoors **2.** ▶ **l'extérieur** [à une personne] the outside (world) ▶ **l'extérieur** ÉCON & POL abroad **3.** [apparence] outward appearance, exterior **4.** SPORT ▶ **l'extérieur** [d'une piste, d'un circuit] the outside **5.** CINÉ location shot ▶ **extérieurs tournés à Rueil** shot on location in Rueil. ◆ **à l'extérieur** loc adv **1.** [en plein air] outside, outdoors ▶ **manger à l'extérieur a)** [en plein air] to eat outside ou outdoors **b)** [hors de chez soi] to eat out **2.** SPORT [sur une piste] on the outside ; [dans une autre ville] away ▶ **match joué à l'extérieur** away match **3.** ÉCON & POL abroad **4.** TÉLÉC outside / *téléphoner à l'extérieur* to make an outside call. ◆ **à l'extérieur de** loc prép outside (of) / *à l'extérieur de l'Afrique* outside Africa. ◆ **de l'extérieur** loc adv **1.** [dans l'espace] from (the) outside **2.** [dans un système] from the outside / *considérer un problème de l'extérieur* to look at a problem from the outside.

extérieurement [ɛksteʀjœʀmɑ̃] adv **1.** [au dehors] on the outside, externally **2.** [apparemment] outwardly.

extérioriser [3] [ɛksteʀjɔʀize] vt **1.** [montrer - sentiment] to express, to show **2.** PSYCHOL to exteriorize, to externalize. ◆ **s'extérioriser** ◆ vp *(emploi passif)* [joie, mécontentement] to be expressed, to show. ◆ vpi [personne] to show one's feelings.

extermination [ɛkstɛʀminasjɔ̃] nf extermination.

exterminer [3] [ɛkstɛʀmine] vt [tuer - peuple, race] to exterminate.

externaliser [3] [ɛkstɛʀnalize] vt to outsource.

externat [ɛkstɛʀna] nm **1.** ÉDUC [école] day school ; [élèves] day pupils ; [statut] non-residency **2.** [en médecine] non-resident (medical) studentship.

externe [ɛkstɛʀn] ◆ adj **1.** [cause, facteur] external **2.** [orbite, bord] outer, external. ◆ nmf **1.** ÉDUC day-pupil, non-boarder **2.** [en médecine] non-resident (medical) student 🇺🇸, extern 🇺🇸.

extincteur, trice [ɛkstɛ̃ktœʀ, tʀis] adj extinguishing *(avant nom).* ◆ **extincteur** nm (fire) extinguisher.

extinction [ɛkstɛ̃ksjɔ̃] nf **1.** [arrêt - d'un incendie] extinction *sout*, extinguishment *sout*, putting out ▶ **extinction des feux** lights out **2.** [suppression - d'une dette] extinguishment ▶ **espèce animale menacée** ou **en voie d'extinction** endangered animal species **3.** ▶ **avoir une extinction de voix** to have lost one's voice.

extirper [3] [ɛkstiʀpe] vt [ôter - tumeur] to remove, to extirpate *spéc* ; [- épine, racine] to pull out *(sép)* ; [- plante] to root up ou out *(sép)*, to uproot, to pull up *(sép)* ▶ **extirper qqn d'un fauteuil / piège** to drag sb out of an armchair / a trap. ◆ **s'extirper** vp *(emploi réfléchi)* : *s'extirper du lit* to drag ou to haul o.s. out of bed.

extorquer [3] [ɛkstɔʀke] vt [fonds] to extort ▶ **extorquer de l'argent à qqn** to extort money from sb.

extorsion [ɛkstɔʀsjɔ̃] nf extortion ▶ **extorsion de fonds** extortion of money.

extra [ɛkstʀa] ◆ adj inv **1.** *fam* [exceptionnel - journée, personne, spectacle] great, terrific, super **2.** COMM ▶ **poires (de qualité) extra** first class pears. ◆ nm **1.** [gâterie] (special) treat ▶ **faire** ou **s'offrir un extra** to give o.s. a treat, to treat o.s. **2.** [emploi ponctuel] : *faire des extra(s) comme ouvreuse* to earn extra money by working (occasionally) as an usherette **3.** [serveur] help.

extrader [3] [ɛkstʀade] vt to extradite.

extradition [ɛkstʀadisjɔ̃] nf extradition.

extrafin, e [ɛkstʀafɛ̃, in] adj [haricots] extra(-)fine ; [collants] sheer ; [chocolats] superfine.

extraire [112] [ɛkstʀɛʀ] vt **1.** MIN & PÉTR [charbon] to extract, to mine ; [pétrole] to extract ; [pierre] to extract, to quarry **2.** [ôter - dent, écharde] to extract, to remove, to pull out *(sép)* / *extraire un ticket de sa poche* to take ou to dig a ticket out of one's pocket **3.** CHIM, CULIN & PHARM to extract ; [en pressant] to squeeze out *(sép)* ; [en écrasant] to crush out *(sép)* ; [en tordant] to wring out *(sép)* **4.** [citer - passage, proverbe] ▶ **extraire de** to take ou to extract from. ◆ **s'extraire** vp *(emploi réfléchi)* ▶ **s'extraire de qqch** to climb ou to clamber out of sthg.

extrait [ɛkstʀɛ] nm **1.** [morceau choisi - gén] extract ; [- de film, de livre] excerpt, extract / *un petit extrait de l'émission d'hier soir* a short sequence ou a clip from last night's programme **2.** ADMIN ▶ **extrait (d'acte) de naissance** birth certificate **3.** BANQUE ▶ **extrait de compte** abstract of accounts **4.** CULIN & PHARM extract, essence / *extrait de viande* meat extract ou essence.

extralucide [ɛkstʀalysid] adj & nmf clairvoyant.

extranet [ɛkstʀanɛt] nm extranet.

extraordinaire [ɛkstʀaɔʀdinɛʀ] adj **1.** [inhabituel - histoire] extraordinary, amazing ; [- cas, personne, intelligence] extraordinary, exceptional ; [- talent, courage] extraordinary, exceptional, rare ; [- circonstances] extraordinary, special **2.** [remarquable - artiste, joueur, spectacle] remarkable, outstanding ; [- temps] wonderful / *le repas n'avait rien d'extraordinaire* ou *n'était pas extraordinaire* there was nothing special about the meal **3.** [étrange] extraordinary, strange.

extraplat, e [ɛkstʀapla, at] adj extraflat, very slim, slimline.

extrapoler [3] [ɛkstʀapole] vt & vi [gén & SCI] to extrapolate ▶ **extrapoler qqch d'un fait** to extrapolate sthg from a fact.

extrascolaire [ɛkstʀaskɔlɛʀ] adj [activités] extracurricular.

extraterrestre [ɛkstʀatɛʀɛstʀ] ◆ adj extraterrestrial. ◆ nmf extraterrestrial (being ou creature).

extravagance [ɛkstʀavagɑ̃s] nf **1.** [outrance - d'une attitude, d'une personne, d'une réponse] extravagance ; [- d'une demande, de dépenses] extravagance, unreasonableness ; [- d'une tenue] extravagance, eccentricity **2.** [acte] extravagance ; [parole] foolish thing (to say) ▶ **faire des extravagances** to behave extravagantly, to do eccentric things.

extravagant, e [ɛkstʀavagɑ̃, ɑ̃t] adj **1.** [déraisonnable - attitude, personne, tenue] extravagant, eccentric ; [- idée] extravagant, wild, crazy **2.** [excessif - demande, exigence, dépenses] extravagant, unreasonable.

extraverti, e [ɛkstʀavɛʀti] ◆ adj extroverted. ◆ nm, f extrovert.

extrême [ɛkstʀɛm] ◆ adj **1.** [intense - confort, importance, soin, etc.] extreme, utmost ; [- froid] extreme, intense ▶ **d'une complexité / maigreur extrême** extremely complex / skinny **2.** [radical - idée] extreme ; [- mesures] extreme, drastic / *être extrême dans ses idées* to hold extreme views

3. [le plus éloigné] : *la limite extrême, l'extrême limite* the furthest point ▸ **l'extrême droite / gauche** POL the extreme right / left. ◆ nm [cas limite] extreme / *passer d'un extrême à l'autre* to go from one extreme to the other ou to another. ❖ **à l'extrême** loc adv extremely, in the extreme.

extrêmement [ɛkstʀɛmmɑ̃] adv extremely.

Extrême-Orient [ɛkstʀɛmɔʀjɑ̃] npr m ▸ **(l')Extrême-Orient** the Far East.

extrémiste [ɛkstʀemist] adj & nmf extremist.

extrémité [ɛkstʀemite] nf **1.** [d'un bâtiment, d'une table, d'une jetée] end ; [d'un bâton] end, tip ; [d'un doigt, de la langue] tip ; [d'un champ] edge, end ; [d'un territoire] (furthest) boundary **2.** ANAT & MATH extremity **3.** [acte radical] extreme act ▸ **pousser qqn à des extrémités** to drive sb to extremes.

exubérant, e [ɛgzybeʀɑ̃, ɑ̃t] adj **1.** [joyeux - attitude, personne] exuberant **2.** [vigoureux - végétation, style] luxuriant ; [- imagination] wild, exuberant.

exulter [3] [ɛgzylte] vi to exult, to rejoice.

exutoire [ɛgzytwaʀ] nm [dérivatif] ▸ **un exutoire à** an outlet for.

eye-liner [ajlajnœʀ] (*pl* eye-liners) nm eyeliner.

F 1. (abr écrite de **franc**) F **2.** [appartement] ▸ **un F3** ≃ a two-bedroomed flat 🇬🇧 ou apartment & 🇺🇸.

fa [fa] nm inv F ; [chanté] fa, fah.

fable [fabl] nf LITTÉR fable.

fabricant, e [fabrikɑ̃, ɑ̃t] nm, f manufacturer, maker.

fabrication [fabrikasjɔ̃] nf **1.** INDUST manufacture, production ▸ **fabrication en série** mass production **2.** [production] workmanship ▸ **de fabrication maison** home-made.

fabrique [fabrik] nf INDUST factory, works, mill.

fabriquer [3] [fabrike] vt **1.** INDUST to make, to produce, to manufacture ; [gâteau, pull-over, guirlande] to make **2.** fam [faire] to do, to cook up (sép) / qu'est-ce qu'il fabrique, ce bus ? what's that bus up to? **3.** péj [histoire] to concoct ; [personnalité] to build up (sép) ▸ **fabriquer qqch de toutes pièces** to make sthg up, to fabricate sthg.

fabuleusement [fabyløzmɑ̃] adv fabulously, fantastically.

fabuleux, euse [fabylø, øz] adj **1.** [de légende] fabulous, legendary **2.** [hors du commun] incredible, fabulous.

fac [fak] nf fam : **en fac, à la fac** at university ou college.

façade [fasad] nf **1.** ARCHIT ▸ **façade principale** façade, (main) frontage **2.** [paroi] front wall ou panel **3.** [apparence] outward appearance, façade ▸ **ce n'est qu'une façade** it's all show ou a façade ; péj [faux-semblant] cover, pretence **4.** tfam [visage] mug ; face / **se refaire la façade** to touch up one's make-up / **se faire refaire la façade** to have a face-lift **5.** GÉOGR ▸ **la façade atlantique** the Atlantic coast.

face [fas] nf **1.** [visage] face ▸ **tomber face contre terre** to fall flat on one's face ▸ **perdre / sauver la face** to lose / to save face **2.** [aspect] ▸ **changer la face de** to alter the face of **3.** [côté - d'une médaille] obverse ; [- d'une monnaie] head, headside ; [- d'une montagne] face / **la face B d'un disque** the B-side ou flipside of a record ▸ **face !** heads! **4.** GÉOM & MÉCAN face, side ▸ **face portante** bearing face **5.** EXPR **faire face** to face up to things, to cope ▸ **faire face à a)** pr to stand opposite to, to face **b)** [danger] to face up to ou to **c)** [obligations, dépense] to meet. ⬦ **de face** loc adj face (modif), facing ▸ **photo / portrait de face** ART & PHOT full-face photograph / portrait ▸ **vue de face** ARCHIT front view ou elevation. ⬦ **d'en face** loc adj ▸ **ceux d'en face a)** [adversaires] the opposition **b)** [voisins] the people opposite. ⬦ **en face** loc adv [de front] : **regarder la mort en face** to face up to death / **regarder les choses en face** to face facts. ⬦ **en face de** loc prép : **juste en face de moi** right in front of me / **sa maison est en face de l'église** his house is opposite ou faces the church / **en face l'un de l'autre**, **l'un en face de l'autre** face to face. ⬦ **face à** loc prép [dans l'espace] in front of ▸ **face à l'ennemi / aux médias** faced with the enemy / media. ⬦ **face à face** loc adv face to face.

face-à-face [fasafas] nm inv [conversation] (face-to-face) meeting ; [conflit] (one-to-one) confrontation ▸ **face-à-face télévisé** television debate (between two politicians).

facétieux, euse [fasesjø, øz] adj facetious, humorous.

facette [faset] nf **1.** ENTOM & JOAILL facet **2.** [aspect] facet, aspect, side. ⬦ **à facettes** loc adj **1.** GÉOL & JOAILL multifaceted **2.** [personnalité, talent] multifaceted, many-sided.

fâché, e [faʃe] adj **1.** [contrarié] angry, cross / **je suis fâché de l'avoir manqué** I'm really sorry I missed him ; (à la forme négative) ▸ **n'être pas fâché de** : **je ne serais pas fâché d'avoir une réponse** I wouldn't mind getting an answer **2.** [brouillé] ▸ **ils sont fâchés** they're not on speaking terms **3.** fig & hum ▸ **être fâché avec qqch** [sans goût pour] : **je suis fâché avec les langues / les chiffres** languages / figures are not my line.

fâcher [3] [faʃe] ⬦ **se fâcher** vpi **1.** [se brouiller] to fall out ou to quarrel (with one another) ▸ **se fâcher avec qqn** to quarrel ou to fall out with sb **2.** [se mettre en colère] to get cross ou angry, to lose one's temper ▸ **se fâcher contre qqn** to get angry with sb.

fâcheux, euse [faʃø, øz] adj regrettable, unfortunate / **une fâcheuse habitude** an unfortunate habit.

facho [faʃo] adj & nmf fam & péj fascist.

faciès [fasjes] nm [traits] facial aspect, features.

facile [fasil] ⬦ adj **1.** [aisé] easy ▸ **rien de plus facile** nothing easier ▸ **facile à faire** easy to do, easily done / **c'est facile à dire (mais moins facile à faire), c'est plus facile à dire qu'à faire** easier said than done ▸ **facile d'accès** easy to reach, easily reached, readily accessible ▸ **facile comme bonjour** easy as pie **2.** [spontané, naturel] : **elle a la parole / plume facile** speaking / writing comes easily to her / **avoir l'argent facile** to be very casual about money / **avoir la larme facile** to be easily moved to tears **3.** [souple - caractère] easy, easy-going **4.** péj [libertin] : **une femme facile ou de mœurs faciles** a woman of easy virtue. ⬦ adv fam : **je te fais ça en deux heures facile** I can have it done for you in two hours, no problem.

facilement [fasilmɑ̃] adv **1.** [sans difficulté] easily, readily **2.** [au moins] at least.

facilité [fasilite] nf **1.** [simplicité] easiness, ease **2.** [aisance] gift, talent / **facilité à s'exprimer** fluency / **avoir beaucoup de facilité pour** to have a gift for ▸ **avec facilité** easily, with ease. ⬦ **facilités** nfpl **1.** [capacités] ability, aptitude **2.** FIN facilities ▸ **facilités de paiement** payment facilities.

faciliter [3] [fasilite] vt to ease, to help along (sép), to make easy / **ça ne va pas faciliter les choses entre eux** it won't make things easier ou smoother between them.

façon [fasɔ̃] nf **1.** [manière] manner, way / *la phrase peut se comprendre de plusieurs façons* the sentence can be interpreted in several ways / *je vais lui dire ma façon de penser, moi !* I'll give him a piece of my mind! / *ça dépend de la façon de voir les choses* it depends on your way of looking at things ou on how you lode at things ▸ **d'une façon générale** generally speaking ▸ **sa façon d'être** the way he is ▸ **ce n'est qu'une façon de parler** ou dire it's just a manner of speaking **2.** [moyen] way **3.** [fabrication] making, fashioning ; [facture] craftsmanship, workmanship ; [main-d'œuvre] labour **4.** COUT & VÊT cut. ❖ **façons** nfpl [manières] manners, behaviour / *en voilà des façons !* manners!, what a way to behave! ▸ **faire des façons a)** [se faire prier] to make a fuss **b)** [se pavaner] to put on airs. ❖ **à la façon de** loc prép like, in the manner of. ❖ **à ma façon, à sa façon** loc adv ▸ **chante-le à ta façon** sing it your way ou any way you like. ❖ **de façon à** loc prép so as to, in order to / *j'ai fermé la fenêtre de façon à éviter les courants d'air* I shut the window in order to prevent draughts. ❖ **de façon (à ce) que** loc conj so that / *il s'est levé de bonne heure de façon à ce que tout soit prêt* he got up early so that everything would be ready in time. ❖ **de telle façon que** loc conj so that, in such a way that. ❖ **de toute façon, de toutes les façons** loc adv anyway, in any case. ❖ **d'une certaine façon** loc adv in a way, in a manner of speaking, so to speak. ❖ **d'une façon ou d'une autre** loc adv somehow. ❖ **sans façon(s)** loc adv **1.** [familièrement] ▸ **elle m'a pris le bras sans façon** ou **façons** she took my arm quite naturally **2.** [non merci] no thank you.

façonner [3] [fasɔne] vt **1.** [modeler - argile] to shape, to fashion ; [- métal] to shape, to work **2.** fig [caractère] to mould, to shape **3.** [fabriquer] to manufacture, to produce, to make.

fac-similé (*pl* fac-similés), **facsimilé*** [faksimile] nm [reproduction] facsimile.

facteur[1] [faktœʀ] nm **1.** [élément] element, factor ▸ **facteur de risque** risk factor **2.** MUS instrument maker ▸ **facteur de pianos** piano maker ▸ **facteur d'orgues** organ builder.

facteur[2]**, trice** [faktœʀ, tʀis] nm, f ADMIN postman 🇬🇧 (postwoman), mailman 🇺🇸 (mailwoman), mail ou letter carrier 🇺🇸.

factice [faktis] adj **1.** [imité - diamant] artificial, false ; [- marchandise de présentation] dummy *(modif)* **2.** [inauthentique] artificial, simulated, false.

faction [faksjɔ̃] nf **1.** [groupe] faction **2.** MIL sentry ou guard duty / *être en* ou *de faction* to be on sentry ou guard duty.

factuel, elle [faktɥɛl] adj [gén & PHILOS] factual.

facturation [faktyʀasjɔ̃] nf [action] invoicing, billing ▸ **facturation détaillée** itemized bill.

facture [faktyʀ] nf **1.** COMM invoice, bill ▸ **fausse facture** faked ou forged invoice ▸ **payer la facture** to pay the price **2.** [technique] craftsmanship, workmanship.

facturer [3] [faktyʀe] vt [article, service] ▸ **facturer qqch à qqn** to bill ou to invoice sb for sthg.

facturette [faktyʀɛt] nf (credit card sales) receipt, record of charge form.

facultatif, ive [fakyltatif, iv] adj **1.** [au choix] optional **2.** [sur demande] ▸ **arrêt facultatif** request stop.

faculté [fakylte] nf **1.** [capacité] ability, capability ▸ **faculté d'adaptation** adaptability, ability to adapt **2.** *sout* [droit] freedom, right ▸ **avoir la faculté de** to have the right to ou the option of ; [autorité] power **3.** UNIV [avant 1968] faculty ▸ **la faculté des sciences** the science faculty ; [depuis

1969] university, college. ❖ **facultés** nfpl [esprit] faculties, powers / *avoir* ou *jouir de toutes ses facultés* to be of sound mind ou in full possession of one's faculties.

fade [fad] adj **1.** [sans saveur] insipid, tasteless, bland **2.** [banal] dull, pointless, vapid *sout*.

fagot [fago] nm [branches] bundle (of wood).

fagoté, e [fagɔte] adj fam & péj ▸ **mal fagoté** badly dressed.

faible [fɛbl] ◆ adj **1.** [malade, vieillard] weak, frail / *se sentir faible* to feel weak ; [fonction organique] ▸ **être de faible constitution** to have a weak constitution **2.** [esprit] weak, deficient **3.** [médiocre - étudiant, résultat] weak, poor, mediocre / *elle est faible en travaux manuels* she's not very good at handicrafts **4.** [trop tempéré - style, argument, réforme] weak ; [- jugement] mild ; [- prétexte] feeble, flimsy **5.** [complaisant] weak, lax ; [sans volonté] weak, spineless **6.** [impuissant - nation, candidat] weak **7.** COMM & ÉCON [demande] slack ; [marge] low ; [monnaie] weak ; [revenus] low ; [ressources] scant, thin **8.** [léger - lumière] dim, faint ; [- bruit] faint ; [- brise] light ; [- odeur] faint **9.** [peu important] low, small / *aller à faible vitesse* to proceed at low speed / *avoir de faibles chances de succès* to have slight ou slender chances of succeeding. ◆ nmf weak-willed person / *c'est un faible* he's weak-willed ▸ **faible d'esprit** simpleton. ◆ nm [préférence] ▸ **avoir un faible pour qqch** to be partial to sthg ▸ **avoir un faible pour qqn** to have a soft spot for sb.

faiblement [fɛbləmɑ̃] adv **1.** [sans force] feebly, weakly **2.** [légèrement] faintly.

faiblesse [fɛblɛs] nf **1.** [manque de vigueur physique] weakness, frailty / *la faiblesse de sa constitution* his weak constitution **2.** [médiocrité - d'un élève] weakness ; [- d'une œuvre, d'un argument] feebleness, weakness ▸ **faiblesse d'esprit** feeblemindedness **3.** [insignifiance - d'une différence, d'un écart] insignificance ▸ **la faiblesse des effectifs a)** [employés] a shortage of staff **b)** [élèves] insufficient numbers **4.** *litt* [lâcheté] weakness, spinelessness ▸ **avoir la faiblesse de croire / dire** to be foolish enough to believe / to say **5.** [défaut] failing, flaw, shortcoming / *c'est là la grande faiblesse du scénario* this is the script's major flaw.

faiblir [32] [fɛbliʀ] vi **1.** [perdre de sa force - personne, pouls] to get weaker ; [- mémoire, mécanisme] to fail **2.** [diminuer - vent, orage, bourrasque] to drop ; [- lumière] to dwindle ; [- enthousiasme, colère, intérêt] to wane, to dwindle **3.** [plier - paroi, tige] to show signs of weakening ; [- résistance] to weaken **4.** *litt* [défaillir] to have a fainting fit.

faïence [fajɑ̃s] nf faience *spéc*, (glazed) earthenware ▸ **faïence fine** china.

faignant, e [fɛɲɑ̃, ɑ̃t] = **feignant**.

faille [faj] nf **1.** GÉOL fault **2.** [faiblesse] flaw, weakness ; [incohérence] inconsistency, flaw / *il y a une faille dans votre démonstration* your demonstration is flawed. ❖ **sans faille** loc adj [logique] faultless, flawless ; [fidélité, dévouement] unfailing, unwavering.

faillible [fajibl] adj fallible.

faillir [46] [fajiʀ] vi [être sur le point de] : *j'ai failli rater la marche* I nearly missed the step. ❖ **faillir à** v + prép *sout* ▸ **faillir à une promesse** to fail to keep a promise / *faillir à son devoir* to fail in one's duty. ❖ **sans faillir** loc adv unfailingly.

faillite [fajit] nf **1.** COMM bankruptcy, insolvency ▸ **faire faillite** to go bankrupt **2.** [échec] failure. ❖ **en faillite** loc adj bankrupt, insolvent.

faim [fɛ̃] nf **1.** [appétit] hunger ▸ **avoir faim** to be hungry / *j'ai une de ces faims, je meurs de faim, je crève de faim* I'm famished ou starving / *merci, je n'ai plus faim* I've had enough, thank you ▸ **ça me donne faim** it makes me hungry ▶ **manger à sa faim** to eat one's fill ▶ **rester sur sa faim a)** pr to be still hungry **b)** fig to be left unsatisfied ou frustrated **2.** [famine] ▶ **la faim** hunger, famine.

fainéant, e [feneɑ̃, ɑ̃t] ◆ adj idle, lazy. ◆ nm, f idler, layabout.

faire [109] [fɛʀ]
◆ vt

A. FABRIQUER, RÉALISER **1.** [confectionner - objet, vêtement] to make ; [- construction] to build ; [- tableau] to paint ; [- film] to make ; [- repas, café] to make, to prepare ; [- gâteau, pain] to make, to bake ; [- vin] to make ; [- bière] to brew ; [concevoir - thèse, dissertation] to do / *qu'as-tu fait (à manger) pour ce soir ?* what have you prepared for dinner ? / *c'est elle qui fait ses chansons* she writes her own songs **2.** [produire, vendre] : *faire de l'élevage de bétail* to breed cattle / *faire du blé / de la vigne* to grow wheat / grapes / *je vous fais les deux à 60 €* fam you can have both for 60 €, I'll take 60 € for both **3.** [obtenir, gagner - bénéfices] to make / *faire de l'argent* to earn ou to make money **4.** [mettre au monde] : *faire un enfant* to have a child **5.** PHYSIOL : *faire ses besoins* euphém to do one's business.

B. ACCOMPLIR, EXÉCUTER **1.** [effectuer - mouvement, signe] to make ; [saut périlleux, roue] to do ▶ **fais-moi un bisou** fam / *un sourire* give me a kiss / a smile ▶ **faire la tête** ou **la gueule** tfam to sulk **2.** [accomplir - choix, erreur, réforme, proposition] to make ; [- inventaire] to do ; [- discours] to deliver, to make, to give ; [- conférence] to give ; [- exercice] to do ; [- recherches] to do, to carry out *(sép)* ; [- enquête] to carry out *(sép)* ▶ **faire ses études** to study / *faire son devoir* to do one's duty ▶ **faire une blague à qqn** to play a joke on sb / *faire son lit* to make one's bed **3.** [étudier - matière, œuvre] to study, to do ; [suivre les cours de] ▶ **elle voulait faire l'ENA** she wanted to go to the ENA **4.** [pratiquer] ▶ **faire de la flûte / du violon** to play the flute / the violin ▶ **faire de la danse** [cours] to go to dance classes / *faire de l'équitation / de la natation / de la voile* to go horseriding / swimming / sailing **5.** [écrire - lettre] to write ; [- contrat, testament] to write, to make **6.** [dire] to say ▶ **il fit oui / non de la tête** he nodded / he shook his head ▶ **«non», fit-elle** "no", she said **7.** [nettoyer - chambre, vitres] to clean, to do ; [- chaussures] to polish, to clean ; [tapisser, aménager - pièce, maison] to do, to decorate **8.** [action non précisée] to do / *que fais-tu dans la vie ?* what do you do (for a living) ? / *je ne t'ai jamais rien fait !* I've never done you any harm ! ▶ **faire qqch de qqn / qqch**: *qu'ai-je fait de mes clefs ?* what have I done with ou where did I put my keys ? / *que vais-je faire de toi ?* what am I going to do with you ?

C. AVEC IDÉE DE DÉPLACEMENT **1.** [se déplacer à la vitesse de] : *le train peut faire jusqu'à 400 km/h* the train can do 400 km/h **2.** [couvrir - distance] : *il y a des cars qui font Londres-Glasgow* there's a coach service between London and Glasgow **3.** [visiter - pays, ville] to do, to go to, to visit ; [inspecter, passer au crible] : *j'ai fait tous les étages avant de vous trouver* I looked on every floor before I found you.

D. AVEC IDÉE DE TRANSFORMATION **1.** [nommer] : *elle l'a fait baron* she gave him the title of Baron, she made him a baron **2.** [transformer en] ▶ **faire qqch de qqn / qqch**: *des rats, la fée fit des laquais* the fairy changed the rats into footmen / *garde les restes, j'en ferai une soupe* keep the leftovers, I'll make a soup with them **3.** [devenir] : *«cheval» fait «chevaux» au pluriel* the plural of "cheval" is "chevaux" **4.** [servir de] : *une fois plié, le billard fait table* the billiard table, when folded, can be used ou can serve as a normal table **5.** [remplir un rôle, une fonction] : *il fera un bon mari* he'll make ou be a good husband ; CINÉ & THÉÂTRE to play the part of, to be ; [imiter - personne] to imitate, to

take off, to impersonate ; [- automate, animal] to imitate ▶ **ne fais pas l'innocent** don't play the innocent, don't come the innocent with me UK.

E. INDIQUE UN RÉSULTAT **1.** [provoquer] : *faire de la poussière* to raise dust / *l'accident a fait cinq morts* the accident left five dead ou claimed five lives ▶ **faire quelque chose à qqn** [l'émouvoir] to move sb, to affect sb / *la vue du sang ne me fait rien* I don't mind the sight of blood, the sight of blood doesn't bother me ▶ **faire que**: *la gravitation, force qui fait que les objets s'attirent* gravitation, the force which causes objects to be attracted towards each other ; [pour exprimer un souhait] : *faites qu'il ne lui arrive rien !* please don't let anything happen to him ! **2.** [importer] : *qu'est-ce que cela peut te faire ?* what's it to (do with) you ? ▶ **cela ne fait rien** it doesn't matter, never mind.

F. INDIQUE UNE FORME, UNE MESURE **1.** [former] : *la route fait un coude* the road bends **2.** [coûter] to be, to cost ▶ **ça fait combien ?** how much is it ? **3.** [valoir, égaler] to be, to make / *2 et 2 font 4* 2 and 2 are 4 / *on a 18 euros, ça ne fait pas assez* we've got 18 euros, that's not enough **4.** [taille, pointure] ▶ **je fais du 38** I take size 38 **5.** [indique la durée, le temps] : *ça fait deux jours qu'il n'a pas mangé* he hasn't eaten for two days ; fam [durer - suj : vêtement, objet] to last / *ton cartable te fera encore bien cette année* your schoolbag will last ou do you this year.

G. VERBE ATTRIBUTIF **1.** [paraître] : *la broche fait bien* ou *joli* ou *jolie sur ta robe* the brooch looks nice on your dress ▶ **ça fait bizarre** it looks strange ▶ **faire son âge** to look one's age **2.** fam [devenir, embrasser la carrière de] to be / *je veux faire pompier* I want to be a fireman.

H. VERBE DE SUBSTITUTION : *range ta chambre — je l'ai déjà fait* go and tidy up your room — I've already done it / *vous le lui expliquerez mieux que je ne saurais le faire* you'll explain it to her better than I could.
◆ vi [agir] to do / *fais comme chez toi, surtout !* iron you've got a nerve!, don't mind me! iron ▶ **faites comme vous voulez** do as you please / *fais comme tu veux !* [ton irrité] suit yourself! / *je le lui ai rendu — tu as bien fait !* I gave it back to him — you did the right thing ou you did right! / *tu ferais bien d'y réfléchir* you'd do well to ou you should ou you'd better think about it! / *ça commence à bien faire !* enough is enough!
◆ v impers MÉTÉOR ▶ **il fait chaud / froid** it's hot / cold ▶ **il faisait nuit** it was dark.
◆ v aux **1.** [provoquer une réaction] ▶ **tu l'as fait rougir** you made her blush ▶ **ça me fait dormir** it puts ou sends me to sleep **2.** [forcer à] to make, to have / *fais-moi penser à le lui demander* remind me to ask him / *n'essaie pas de me faire croire que...* don't try to make ou to have me believe that... / *il me faisait faire ses dissertations* he had me write his essays for me **3.** [commander à] ▶ **faire faire qqch par qqn** to have sb do ou make sthg, to have sthg done ou made by sb / *il fait faire ses costumes sur mesure* he has his suits tailormade ▶ **se faire faire qqch** to have sthg made. ◆ **faire dans** v + prép fam : *il ne fait pas dans le détail* he doesn't bother about details / *son entreprise fait maintenant dans les produits de luxe* her company now produces luxury items. ◆ **se faire** ◆ vp (emploi réfléchi) **1.** [réussir] ▶ **elle s'est faite seule** she's a self-made woman **2.** [se forcer à] ▶ **se faire pleurer / vomir** to make o.s. cry / vomit. ◆ vp (emploi réciproque) ▶ **se faire la guerre** to wage war on each other. ◆ vp (emploi passif) **1.** [être à la mode] to be fashionable, to be in fashion / *les salopettes ne se font plus* dungarees UK ou overalls US are out of fashion **2.** [être convenable] : *ça ne se fait pas de demander son âge à une femme* it's rude ou it's not done to ask a woman her age **3.** [être réalisé] : *sans argent le film ne se fera pas* without money the film will never be made ;

(tournure impersonnelle) : *comment se fait-il que...* how come ou how is it that... ◆ vpi **1.** [se former] : *les couples se font et se défont* people get together and separate **2.** (suivi d'un infinitif) ❯ **se faire opérer** to have an operation ❯ **se faire tuer** to get killed ❯ **se faire couper les cheveux** to have one's hair cut **3.** [devenir] to become / *sa voix se fit plus grave* his voice became deeper ; (tournure impersonnelle) ❯ **il se fait tard** it's getting late **4.** [s'améliorer - fromage] to ripen ; [-vin] to mature / *mes chaussures me serrent — elles vont se faire* my shoes feel tight — they'll stretch. ◆ vpt **1.** [fabriquer] : *elle se fait ses vêtements* she makes her own clothes **2.** [effectuer sur soi] : *il se fait ses piqûres seul* he gives himself his own injections ; [se maquiller] ❯ **se faire les ongles** to do one's nails **3.** fam [gagner] : *elle se fait 10 000 euros par mois* she earns 10,000 euros per month, she gets 10,000 euros every month. **4.** fam [s'accorder] ❯ **on se fait un film / un petit café ?** what about going to see a film / going for a coffee? **5.** fam [supporter] : *il faut se la faire !* she's a real pain! ◆ **se faire à** vp + prép to get used to. ◆ **s'en faire** vpi to worry / *je ne m'en fais pas pour lui* I'm not worried about him / *elle s'en souviendra, ne t'en fais pas !* she'll remember, don't you worry!

📝 **Faire qqch pour / à qqn** Make sthg for sb ou make sb sthg.

Notez la construction à double complément qui en anglais peut prendre deux formes dont le sens est le même :

• une structure identique à celle du français :
verbe + COD + préposition + COI
make sthg for sb

• une structure qui diffère de celle du français, sans préposition, et dans laquelle l'ordre des compléments est inversé :
verbe + COI + COD
make sb sthg

Elle a fait un superbe gâteau d'anniversaire pour Vincent. She made a lovely birthday cake for Vincent ou She made Vincent a lovely birthday cake.
Avec le tissu qu'il lui restait elle a fait une robe à Léa. With the remaining fabric she made a dress for Léa ou With the remaining fabric she made Léa a dress.

---

faire-part (pl faire-part), **fairepart*** [fɛʀpaʀ] nm [dans la presse] announcement ❯ **faire-part de décès** death notice ❯ **faire-part de mariage** wedding announcement ; [carte] card sent to family or friends announcing a birth, wedding, death, etc.

faire-valoir [fɛʀvalwaʀ] nm inv THÉÂTRE stooge, straight man / *c'est lui le faire-valoir de Robert* he acts as straight man to Robert.

fair-play (pl fair-play), **fairplay*** [fɛʀplɛ] ◆ nm fair play, fair-mindedness. ◆ adj fair-minded ❯ **il est fair-play a)** [joueur] he plays fair **b)** fig he has a sense of fair play.

faisabilité [fəzabilite] nf feasibility.

faisable [fəzabl] adj [réalisable] feasible ; [possible] possible, practicable.

faisan [fəzɑ̃] nm ZOOL (cock) pheasant.

faisandé, e [fəzɑ̃de] adj CULIN gamy, high.

faisceau, x [fɛso] nm **1.** [rayon] beam, ray ❯ **faisceau hertzien** radio beam ❯ **faisceau lumineux** light beam **2.** [gerbe] cluster, bundle ❯ **faisceau de preuves** fig accumulation of evidence.

* In reformed spelling (see p. 16-18).

faiseur, euse [fəzœʀ, øz] nm, f péj ❯ **faiseuse d'anges** back-street abortionist.

fait¹ [fɛ] nm **1.** [action] act, deed ❯ **les faits et gestes de qqn** everything sb says and does, sb's every move ❯ **prendre qqn sur le fait** to catch sb red-handed ❯ **prendre fait et cause pour qqn** to side with sb **2.** [événement] event, fact, occurrence ❯ **fait nouveau** new development ❯ **au moment des faits** at the time / *les faits qui lui sont reprochés* the charge laid against him ❯ **de ce fait** thereby **3.** [réalité] fact ❯ **c'est un fait** it's a (matter of) fact / *le fait est que nous étions en retard* the fact is we were late ❯ **placer** ou **mettre qqn devant le fait accompli** to present sb with a fait accompli **4.** [sujet, question] point ❯ **aller (droit) au fait** to go straight to the point / *venons-en au fait* let's come ou get to the point **5.** EXPR dire son fait à qqn to give sb a piece of one's mind. ◆ **au fait** loc adv by the way, incidentally. ◆ **au fait de** loc prép well aware of, fully informed about. ◆ **de fait** loc adj DR actual, de facto. ◆ **de fait, en fait** loc adv in fact, actually, as a matter of fact. ◆ **du fait de** loc prép because of, due to, on account of. ◆ **du fait que** loc conj because (of the fact that). ◆ **en fait de** loc prép **1.** [en guise de] by way of / *en fait de nourriture, il n'y a qu'une boîte de sardines* there's only a can of sardines by way of food **2.** [au lieu de] instead of / *en fait de chien, c'était un loup* it wasn't a dog at all, it was a wolf.

fait², e [fɛ, fɛt] adj **1.** [formé] : *elle a la jambe bien faite* she's got shapely ou nice legs / *une femme fort bien faite* a very good-looking woman **2.** [mûr] mature, ripe ❯ **un fromage fait** a fully ripened cheese **3.** [maquillé] made-up / *elle a les yeux faits* she's wearing eye make-up **4.** [prêt] ❯ **tout fait a)** [vêtement] ready-made, ready-to-wear **b)** [tournure] set, ready-made.

fait divers (pl faits divers), **fait-divers** (pl faits-divers) [fɛdivɛʀ] nm **1.** [événement] news story, news item **2.** [rubrique] (news) in brief ; [page] news in brief.

faîte, faite* [fɛt] nm **1.** GÉOGR crest, top **2.** [sommet] top, summit **3.** [summum] climax, acme sout / *le faîte de la gloire* the height of glory.

faitout, fait-tout (nm inv) [fɛtu] nm stewpot, cooking pot.

falaise [falɛz] nf cliff.

fallacieux, euse [falasjø, øz] adj [trompeur] deceptive, misleading, fallacious.

falloir [69] [falwaʀ]
v impers

A. EXPRIME LE BESOIN 1. [gén] : *pour ce tricot, il faut des aiguilles n° 6* to knit this jumper, you need number 6 needles / *il faut deux heures pour y aller* it takes two hours to get there / *je crois que nous avons trouvé l'homme qu'il nous faut* [pour un poste] I think we've found the right person for the job / *c'est tout ce qu'il vous fallait ?* [dans une boutique] anything else? / *j'ai plus d'argent qu'il n'en faut* I've got more money than I need ❯ **il t'a fait ses excuses, qu'est-ce qu'il te faut de plus ?** fam he apologized, what more do you want? / *ce n'est pas très cher — qu'est-ce qu'il te faut !* fam it's not very expensive — well, what do you call expensive then? ❯ **je suis satisfait de lui — il t'en faut peu !** fam I'm satisfied with him — you're not hard to please! **2.** (suivi d'une complétive au subjonctif) : *il faudrait que nous nous réunissions plus souvent* we should have more regular meetings.

B. EXPRIME L'OBLIGATION 1. [gén] : *je lui ai dit — le fallait-il vraiment ?* I told him — was it really necessary ou did you really have to? ❯ **il ne fallait pas** fam [en recevant un cadeau] you shouldn't have ❯ **s'il le faut** if I / we must, if necessary **2.** (suivi de l'infinitif) ❯ **il faut m'excuser** please forgive me, you must forgive me / *c'est un film qu'il faut voir* *(absolument)* this film's a must / *il ne fallait pas commencer !* you shouldn't have started! / *j'ai faim — il fallait le dire !* I'm hungry — why didn't you say so? **3.** *(suivi d'une complétive au subjonctif)* : *il a fallu que je m'absente* I had to go out for a while **4.** *(au conditionnel, sens affaibli)* : *il aurait fallu prévenir la police* the police should have been called / *il ne faudrait pas me prendre pour une idiote !* do you think I'm stupid? **5.** [en intensif] : *il faut le voir pour le croire !* it has to be seen to be believed! / *ne pas fermer sa voiture, faut le faire !* it takes a fool ou you've got to be completely stupid to leave your car unlocked! ▸ **il fallait l'entendre !** you should have heard him!

C. EXPRIME UNE FATALITÉ : *il a fallu que le téléphone sonne juste à ce moment-là !* the phone had to ring just then!

D. EXPRIME LA PROBABILITÉ : *il faut que tu aies fait mal à Rex pour qu'il t'ait mordu !* you must have hurt Rex to make him bite you! **❖ s'en falloir** v impers : *peu s'en est fallu que je ne manque le train !* I very nearly ou almost missed the train! ▸ **il s'en est fallu de rien** ou **d'un cheveu** *fam* ou **d'un doigt** *fam* **qu'il ne fût décapité** he came within inches of having his head chopped off.

falot, e [falo, ɔt] adj colourless, bland, vapid *sout* / *c'est un personnage assez falot* he's rather insipid.

falsification [falsifikasjɔ̃] nf falsification, faking, forgery.

falsifier [9] [falsifje] vt [vin, lait] to adulterate ; [document, signature] to forge, to falsify.

famé, e [fame] adj ⟶ **mal famé.**

famélique [famelik] adj [chat] scrawny ; [prisonnier] half-starved.

fameux, euse [famø, øz] adj **1.** [célèbre] famous, renowned, well-known **2.** *fam* [bon - gén] excellent, brilliant ; [- repas, mets] excellent, delicious **3.** [en intensif] : *c'est un fameux mystère* it's quite a mystery / *un fameux exemple de courage* an outstanding example of courage **4.** [dont on parle] famous / *et où as-tu acheté ce fameux bouquin ?* where did you buy the book you were talking about? **5.** *iron* so-called / *c'est ça, ton fameux trésor ?* is THAT your famous treasure?

familial, e, aux [familjal, o] adj [de famille] domestic, family *(modif)*. **❖ familiale** nf estate (car) 🇬🇧, station wagon 🇺🇸.

familiariser [3] [familjaʀize] **❖ se familiariser avec** vp + prép to familiarize o.s. with ▸ **se familiariser avec une technique / langue** to master a technique / language.

familiarité [familjaʀite] nf **1.** [désinvolture] familiarity, casualness **2.** [connaissance] : *il a une grande familiarité avec l'œuvre de Proust* he has a close ou an intimate knowledge of the work of Proust. **❖ familiarités** nfpl liberties, undue familiarity.

familier, ère [familje, ɛʀ] adj **1.** [connu] familiar / *la maison lui était familière* he remembered the house quite clearly **2.** [apprivoisé] domestic, tame **3.** *péj* [cavalier] overfamiliar **4.** LING colloquial, informal. **❖ familier** nm [client] habitué, regular / *les familiers de ce café* this café's regulars.

famille [famij] nf **1.** [foyer] family ▸ **famille d'accueil** foster family ▸ **famille monoparentale** single-parent ou lone-parent family ▸ **famille nombreuse**, 🇨🇭 grande famille large family ▸ **famille recomposée** reconstituted family, blended family **2.** [enfants] family, children / *comment va la petite famille ?* *fam* how are the children? **3.** [tous les parents] family, relatives / *ils sont de la même famille* they're related ▸ **prévenir la famille a)** to inform sb's relatives **b)** DR to inform the next of kin / *c'est une famille de danseurs* they're all dancers in their family, they're a fam-

ily of dancers **4.** [idéologie] obedience, persuasion / *de la même famille politique* of the same political persuasion. **❖ de famille ❖** loc adj [cercle, médecin, biens] family *(modif)*. **❖** loc adv ▸ **c'est** ou **cela tient de famille** it runs in the family, it's in the blood. **❖ en famille** loc adv **1.** [en groupe] ▸ **passer Noël en famille** to spend Christmas with one's family ou at home **2.** [en confiance] ▸ **se sentir en famille** to feel at home.

famine [famin] nf famine, starvation.

fan [fan] nmf fan.

fanatique [fanatik] **❖** adj **1.** *péj* RELIG fanatical, bigoted, zealous **2.** [passionné] enthusiastic. **❖** nmf [partisan] fan, fanatic.

fanatisme [fanatism] nm fanaticism.

fan-club [fanklœb] *(pl* **fans-clubs)** nm **1.** [d'un artiste] fan club **2.** *hum* admirers, supporters, fan club *fig*.

fane [fan] nf [de légumes] top / *fanes de carotte / radis* carrot / radish tops.

faner [3] [fane] **❖ se faner** vpi **1.** BOT to fade, to wither **2.** [perdre son éclat] to wane, to fade / *sa beauté s'est fanée* her beauty has lost its bloom ou faded.

fanfare [fɑ̃faʀ] nf [air] fanfare ; [orchestre - civil] brass band ; [- militaire] military band. **❖ en fanfare** loc adv [réveiller] noisily, brutally / *annoncer la nouvelle en fanfare* to trumpet the news.

fanfaron, onne [fɑ̃faʀɔ̃, ɔn] nm, f boaster, braggart, swaggerer.

fanfreluche [fɑ̃fʀəlyʃ] nf ▸ **des fanfreluches** frills (and furbelows).

fange [fɑ̃ʒ] nf *litt* mire.

fanion [fanjɔ̃] nm flag, pennant.

fantaisie [fɑ̃tezi] nf **1.** [imagination] imagination ▸ **être plein de fantaisie** to be fanciful ▸ **manquer de fantaisie a)** [personne] to lack imagination, to be lacking in imagination **b)** [vie] to be monotonous ou uneventful ; *péj* fantasy **2.** [lubie] whim ▸ **s'offrir une fantaisie** to give o.s. a treat, to treat o.s. **3.** [bibelot] fancy / *un magasin de fantaisies* a novelty shop **4.** ART & LITTÉR [piece of] fantasy ; MUS fantasy, fantasia **5.** *(comme adj inv)* [simulé] imitation ▸ **bijou fantaisie** piece of costume jewellery 🇬🇧 ou jewelry 🇺🇸 ; [peu classique] fancy.

> ⚠ Attention, **fantasy** ne peut être employé pour traduire **fantaisie** que dans le sens littéraire ou musical.

fantaisiste [fɑ̃tezist] adj **1.** [farfelu] eccentric, unconventional **2.** [inventé] fanciful.

fantasme [fɑ̃tasm] nm fantasy.

fantasmer [3] [fɑ̃tasme] vi to fantasize ▸ **fantasmer sur qqch / qqn** to fantasize about sthg / sb.

fantasque [fɑ̃task] adj [capricieux] capricious, whimsical.

fantastique [fɑ̃tastik] **❖** adj **1.** [fabuleux - animal, personnage] fantastical, fabulous, fantasy *(modif)* **2.** CINÉ & LITTÉR ▸ **roman fantastique** gothic novel ▸ **cinéma fantastique** science-fiction ou fantasy films **3.** [étonnant] extraordinary, unbelievable. **❖** nm ▸ **le fantastique a)** [l'étrange] the fantastic, the supernatural **b)** [genre] the gothic (genre).

fantoche [fɑ̃tɔʃ] nm *péj* puppet.

fantomatique [fɑ̃tɔmatik] adj phantom *(modif)*, ghostly.

fantôme [fɑ̃tom] nm **1.** [revenant] ghost, phantom, spirit **2.** *(comme adj)* ▸ **cabinet fantôme** shadow cabinet ▸ **société fantôme** bogus company.

fanzine [fɑ̃zin] nm fanzine.

faon [fɑ̃] nm fawn.

FAQ [fak] (abr de Foire aux Questions) nf FAQ.

faramineux, euse [faʀaminø, øz] adj *fam* [somme, fortune] huge, tremendous.

farce¹ [faʀs] nf **1.** [tour] practical joke, prank, trick **▶ faire une farce à qqn** to play a trick on sb **2.** LITTÉR & THÉÂTRE farce / *la vie n'est qu'une farce* life is nothing but a farce. **✲ farces et attrapes** nfpl assorted tricks.

farce² [faʀs] nf CULIN forcemeat, stuffing.

farceur, euse [faʀsœʀ, øz] **◆** adj mischievous / *il a l'œil farceur* he has a waggish look. **◆** nm, f practical joker, prankster **▶ petit farceur !** you rascal!

farci, e [faʀsi] adj CULIN stuffed.

farcir [32] [faʀsiʀ] vt CULIN to stuff. **✲ se farcir** vpt **▶ se farcir qqn a)** *fam* [le subir] to have to put up with ou to have to take sb / *son beau-frère, faut se le farcir !* his brother-in-law is a real pain ! **b)** *vulg* [sexuellement] to get off with 🇬🇧 ou to screw sb **▶ se farcir qqch a)** *fam* [le subir] to have to put up with ou to have to take sth **b)** [le boire] to knock sth back, to down sth **c)** [le manger] to stuff o.s. with sth, to scoff 🇬🇧 ou scarf 🇺🇸 sth.

fard [faʀ] nm **1.** [produit] colour *(for make-up)* **▶ fard à joues** blusher **▶ fard à paupières** eyeshadow **2.** *vieilli* [maquillage] **▶ le fard a)** [gén] make-up **b)** THÉÂTRE greasepaint. **✲ sans fard** loc adv straightforwardly, frankly.

fardeau, x [faʀdo] nm **1.** [poids] burden, load **2.** [contrainte] burden, millstone.

farder [3] [faʀde] vt [maquiller] to make up *(sép).* **✲ se farder** vp *(emploi réfléchi)* to make up one's face, to put one's make-up on.

farfelu, e [faʀfəly] *fam* adj crazy, strange, cranky.

farfouiller [3] [faʀfuje] *fam* vi to grope ou to rummage about.

farine [faʀin] nf CULIN flour **▶ farine complète** wholemeal flour 🇬🇧, wholewheat flour **▶ farine de froment / seigle** wheat / rye flour **▶ farine de maïs** cornflour **▶ farines animales** bone meal.

fariner [3] [faʀine] vt to flour, to sprinkle flour over.

farineux, euse [faʀinø, øz] adj **1.** [fariné] floury, flour-covered **2.** [pâteux - poire] mealy ; [- pomme de terre] floury **3.** [au goût de farine] chalky, floury.

farniente [faʀnjɛnte, faʀnjãt] nm idleness, laziness.

farouche [faʀuʃ] adj **1.** [caractère] fierce, unflinching ; [volonté] fierce **2.** [animal] wild **▶ un animal peu farouche** a tame animal ; [personne] shy, coy.

farouchement [faʀuʃmã] adv [violemment] fiercely, savagely.

fart [faʀ(t)] nm skiing wax.

farter [3] [faʀte] vt to wax *(skis).*

fascicule [fasikyl] nm [partie d'un ouvrage] instalment 🇬🇧, installment 🇺🇸, part, section.

fascinant, e [fasinã, ãt] adj captivating, fascinating.

fascination [fasinasjɔ̃] nf fascination **▶ exercer une fascination sur** to be fascinating to.

fasciner [3] [fasine] vt [charmer - suj : spectacle] to captivate, to fascinate.

fascisant, e [faʃizã, ãt] adj fascist, fascistic, pro-fascist.

fascisme [faʃism] nm [gén] fascism.

fasciste [faʃist] adj & nmf [gén] fascist.

fashionista [faʃjɔnista] nmf *(parfois péj)* fashionista.

faste [fast] **◆** adj [favorable - année] good ; [- jour] good, lucky. **◆** nm [luxe] sumptuousness, splendour 🇬🇧, splendor 🇺🇸 **▶ sans faste** simply, quietly, plainly.

fast-food, fastfood* [fastfud] nm fast-food restaurant.

fastidieux, euse [fastidjø, øz] adj boring, tiresome, tedious.

⚠ Fastidious signifie « pointilleux », « méticuleux », et non **fastidieux**.

fastoche [fastɔʃ] adj *fam* dead easy **▶ c'est fastoche** it's dead easy, it's a doddle.

fastueux, euse [fastɥø, øz] adj magnificent, munificent *sout*, sumptuous.

fatal, e, als [fatal] adj **1.** [fixé par le sort] fateful **▶ l'instant fatal** the fatal moment **2.** [mortel - collision, blessure] fatal, mortal **▶ porter un coup fatal à a)** [frapper] to deliver a deadly ou mortal blow to **b)** *fig* to administer the coup de grâce to **3.** [inévitable] inevitable.

fatalement [fatalmã] adv inevitably **▶ il devait fatalement perdre** he was bound to lose.

⚠ Fatally signifie « mortellement » et non **fatalement**.

fataliste [fatalist] **◆** adj fatalist, fatalistic. **◆** nmf fatalist.

fatalité [fatalite] nf **1.** [sort] destiny, fate / *la fatalité s'acharne contre eux* they're dogged by misfortune **2.** [circonstance fâcheuse] mischance.

fatidique [fatidik] adj [marqué par le destin - date, jour] fated, fateful.

fatigant, e [fatigã, ãt] adj **1.** [épuisant] tiring, wearing **2.** [agaçant] tiresome, tedious, annoying.

 tiring ou **tiresome ?**
Au sens d'« épuisant », **fatigant** se traduit par **tiring**. Si l'on veut signifier que quelqu'un ou quelque chose est ennuyeux, c'est **tiresome** qu'il faut employer.

fatigue [fatig] nf **1.** [lassitude] tiredness, weariness **▶ je tombe** ou **je suis mort de fatigue** I'm dead on my feet **2.** [tension - physique] strain ; [- nerveuse] stress **▶ fatigue oculaire** eyestrain.

fatigué, e [fatige] adj [las] tired, weary / *fatigué de rester debout / d'attendre* tired of standing / waiting.

fatiguer [3] [fatige] **◆** vt **1.** [épuiser] to tire ou to wear out *(sép)* **2.** [lasser] to annoy / *tu me fatigues avec tes critiques !* your constant criticism is getting on my nerves! **◆** vi **1.** [peiner] to grow tired, to flag / *dépêche-toi, je fatigue !* hurry up, I'm getting tired! **2.** MÉCAN [faiblir] to become weakened ; [forcer] to bear a heavy strain. **✲ se fatiguer ◆** vpi **1.** [s'épuiser] to get tired, to tire o.s. out **▶ se fatiguer à :** *tu ne vas pas te fatiguer à tout nettoyer !* don't tire yourself out cleaning everything! **2.** [faire un effort] to push o.s. / *ils ne se sont pas fatigués* they didn't exactly kill themselves **3.** [faire des efforts inutiles] **▶ ne te fatigue pas** don't waste your time / *je me fatigue à le lui répéter* I wear myself out telling her. **◆** vpt **▶ se fatiguer la vue** ou **les yeux** to put a strain on ou to strain one's eyes. **✲ se fatiguer de** vp + prép to get tired of.

fatras [fatʀa] nm *péj* [tas] clutter, jumble.

fatuité [fatɥite] nf complacency, conceit, smugness.

faubourg [fobuʀ] nm suburb.

fauché, e [foʃe] adj *fam* [sans argent] broke, skint 🇬🇧, cleaned out.

faucher [3] [foʃe] vt **1.** AGR to reap **2.** [renverser] to knock ou to mow down *(sép)* / *se faire faucher par une voiture* to be knocked down by a car **3.** [tuer] : *tous ces jeunes artistes fauchés à la fleur de l'âge* all these young artists struck down in the prime of life **4.** *fam* [voler] to pinch, to swipe / *qui a fauché le sel ?* who's got the salt?

faucille [fosij] nf sickle, reaping hook.

faucon [fokɔ̃] nm ORNITH falcon, hawk.

faufil [fofil] nm basting ou tacking thread.

faufiler [3] [fofile] vt COUT to baste, to tack. ❖ **se faufiler** vpi to slip through, to edge / *se faufiler dans la foule* to weave through the crowd / *se faufiler entre les voitures* to weave one's way through the traffic.

faune [fon] nf **1.** ZOOL fauna, animal life / *la faune et la flore* flora and fauna, wildlife **2.** *péj* [groupe] mob, bunch, crowd.

faussaire [fosɛR] nmf faker, forger, falsifier.

faussement [fosmɑ̃] adv [à tort] wrongfully.

fausser [3] [fose] vt **1.** [déformer - clef, lame] to bend, to put out of true ; [détériorer - serrure] to damage **2.** [diminuer la justesse de - esprit, raisonnement] to distort, to twist **3.** EXPR **fausser compagnie à qqn** to give sb the slip.

fausset [fosɛ] nm MUS falsetto (voice).

faute [fot] nf **1.** [erreur] error, mistake / *faire une faute* to make a mistake ▶ **faute de frappe** typing error ▶ **commettre une faute de goût** to show a lack of taste ▶ **faute de grammaire** grammatical error ou mistake ▶ **faute d'impression** misprint ▶ **faute d'orthographe** spelling mistake **2.** [manquement] misdeed, transgression ▶ **commettre une faute** to go wrong **3.** [responsabilité] fault / *c'est (de) ma / ta faute* it's my / your fault ▶ **c'est la faute à pas de chance** *fam* it's just bad luck **4.** ADMIN & DR offence UK, offense US ▶ **faute grave** [motif de licenciement] serious misconduct ▶ **faute légère** minor offence ▶ **faute professionnelle** professional misconduct **5.** TENNIS fault ; FOOT foul. ❖ **en faute** loc adv ▶ **prendre qqn en faute** to catch sb out. ❖ **faute de** loc prép for want of ▶ **faute de mieux** for want of anything better ▶ **faute de quoi** otherwise. ❖ **par la faute de** loc prép because of, owing to. ❖ **sans faute** loc adj faultless, offenceless ▶ **faire un parcours sans faute a)** ÉQUIT to get a clear round **b)** [coureur] to run a perfect race **c)** [dans un jeu télévisé] to get all the answers right **d)** [dans sa carrière] not to put a foot wrong. ❖ loc adv without fail / *à demain sans faute* see you tomorrow without fail ▶ **écris-moi sans faute** do write to me / *je le ferai sans faute* I'll do it without fail / *tu me donneras la clef sans faute* be sure and give me the key.

fauteuil [fotœj] nm **1.** [meuble] armchair, chair, seat ▶ **fauteuil à bascule** rocking-chair ▶ **fauteuil de dentiste** dentist's chair ▶ **fauteuil de jardin** garden chair ▶ **fauteuil roulant** wheelchair **2.** THÉÂTRE ▶ **fauteuil d'orchestre** seat in the stalls UK ou the orchestra US **3.** [à l'Académie française] numbered seat occupied by a member of the Académie française.

fauteur, trice [fotœʀ, tʀis] nm, f ▶ **fauteur de troubles** trouble-maker.

fautif, ive [fotif, iv] ❖ adj **1.** [défectueux - liste] incorrect ; [- citation] inaccurate **2.** [coupable] offending, responsible. ❖ nm, f offender / *qui est le fautif ?* who's to blame?, who's the culprit?

fauve [fov] ❖ adj [couleur] fawn-coloured, tawny. ❖ nm **1.** ZOOL big cat / *ça sent le fauve dans cette pièce* this room stinks of sweat **2.** ART Fauve, Fauvist.

fauvette [fovɛt] nf warbler.

faux¹ [fo] nf AGR scythe / *couper de l'herbe à la faux* to scythe through grass.

faux², fausse [fo, fos]

adj

A. NON VRAI, EXACT **1.** [mensonger - réponse] wrong ; [- affirmation] untrue ; [- excuse, prétexte] false ; [- nouvelle, promesse, témoignage] false **2.** [inexact - raisonnement] false, faulty ; [- calcul] wrong ; [- balance] faulty ▶ **t'as tout faux** *fam* you're completely wrong **3.** [non vérifié - argument] false ; [- impression] mistaken, wrong, false ; [- espoir] false ▶ **c'est un faux problème** ou **débat** this is not the issue **4.** MUS [piano, voix] out of tune.

B. CONTRAIRE AUX APPARENCES **1.** [dent, nez, barbe, poche] false ; [bijou, cuir, fourrure, marbre] imitation ; [plafond, poutre] false **2.** [falsifié - monnaie] false, counterfeit, forged ; [- carte à jouer] trick ; [- papiers, facture] forged, false ; [- testament] spurious ▶ **c'est un faux Renoir** it's a fake Renoir **3.** [feint - candeur, émotion] feigned **4.** [pseudo - policier] bogus ; [- intellectuel] pseudo **5.** [hypocrite - caractère, personne] false, deceitful ; [- regard] deceitful, treacherous. ❖ **faux** ❖ adv MUS [jouer, chanter] out of tune, off-key ▶ **sonner faux** [excuse] to have a hollow ou false ring. ❖ nm **1.** DR [objet, activité] forgery ▶ **c'est un faux** [document, tableau] it's a fake ou a forgery **2.** [imitation] : *c'est du cuir ? — non, c'est du faux* is it leather? — no, it's imitation. ❖ **faux ami** nm false friend. ❖ **fausse couche** nf miscarriage / *faire une fausse couche* to have a miscarriage. ❖ **faux-cul** ❖ adj *tfam* : *il est faux-cul* he's a two-faced bastard. ❖ nmf *tfam* two-faced bastard (two-faced bitch). ❖ **faux départ** nm *pr & fig* false start. ❖ **faux frère** nm false friend. ❖ **faux jeton** *fam* ❖ adj inv hypocritical. ❖ nmf hypocrite. ❖ **faux pas** nm **1.** [en marchant] ▶ **faire un faux pas** to trip, to stumble **2.** [erreur] false move **3.** [maladresse] faux pas, gaffe.

faux-filet [fofilɛ] *(pl* faux-filets*)* nm sirloin.

faux-fuyant [fofɥijɑ̃] *(pl* faux-fuyants*)* nm excuse, subterfuge ▶ **user de faux-fuyants** to prevaricate.

faux-monnayeur [fomɔnɛjœʀ] *(pl* faux-monnayeurs*)* nm forger, counterfeiter.

faux-semblant [fosɑ̃blɑ̃] *(pl* faux-semblants*)* nm : *ne vous laissez pas abuser par des faux-semblants* don't let yourself be taken in by pretence UK ou pretense US.

faux-sens [fosɑ̃s] nm inv mistranslation.

faveur [favœʀ] nf **1.** [plaisir] favour UK, favor US ▶ **faire une faveur à qqn** to do sb a favour **2.** [bienveillance] favour UK, favor US / *elle a eu la faveur de la presse / du public* she found favour with the press / with the public. ❖ **faveurs** nfpl *sout* favours ▶ **accorder / refuser ses faveurs à qqn** *euphém* to give / to refuse sb one's favours. ❖ **à la faveur de** loc prép owing to, with the help of / *à la faveur de la nuit* under cover of darkness. ❖ **de faveur** loc adj preferential. ❖ **en faveur de** loc prép **1.** [à cause de] on account of **2.** [au profit de] to the benefit of, in favour of / *en ma / votre faveur* in my / your favour.

favorable [favɔʀabl] adj **1.** [propice] favourable UK, favorable US, right ▶ **saisir le moment favorable** to take the opportunity **2.** [bien disposé] favourable UK, favorable US / *se montrer sous un jour favorable* to show o.s. in a favourable light ▶ **regarder qqch d'un œil favorable** to be favourable to sthg ▶ **je suis favorable à cette décision / à vos idées** I approve of this decision / of your ideas.

favorablement [favɔʀabləmɑ̃] adv favourably UK, favorably US ▶ **répondre favorablement** to say yes / *il a répondu favorablement à mon invitation* he accepted my invitation / *si les choses tournent favorablement* if things turn out all right.

favori, ite [favɔʀi, it] ❖ adj [mélodie, dessert] favourite UK, favorite US ; [idée, projet] favourite UK, favorite US, pet *(modif)*. ❖ nm, f SPORT favourite UK, favorite US. ❖ **favoris** nmpl sideboards, sideburns.

favoriser [3] [favɔʀize] vt **1.** [être avantageux pour] to favour 🇬🇧, to favor 🇺🇸, to be to the advantage of **2.** [faciliter] to further, to promote / *favoriser le développement de l'économie* to promote economic development.

favoritisme [favɔʀitism]nm favouritism 🇬🇧, favoritism 🇺🇸.

fax [faks] (abr de **Téléfax**) nm **1.** [machine] fax (machine) **2.** [message] fax ▸ **par fax** by fax.

faxer [3] [fakse] vt to fax.

fayot, e [fajo, ɔt] nm, f *fam péj* [employé] toady, bootlicker ; [élève] swot 🇬🇧, apple-polisher 🇺🇸. ❖ **fayot** nm [haricot] bean.

fayoter [3] [fajɔte] vi *fam* to lick sb's boots / *il est toujours à fayoter* he's always bootlicking.

FB (abr écrite de **franc belge**) BF.

FBI [ɛfbiaj] (abr de **Federal Bureau of Investigation**) npr m FBI.

fébrile [febʀil] adj **1.** MÉD febrile ▸ **état fébrile** feverishness **2.** [agité] feverish, restless.

fébrilement [febʀilmã] adv [avec inquiétude] feverishly.

fécal, e, aux [fekal, o] adj faecal.

fécond, e [fekɔ̃, ɔ̃d] adj **1.** BIOL fecund, fertile **2.** [prolifique - terre] rich, fertile ; [- écrivain, inventeur] prolific, productive ; [- imagination] lively, powerful.

fécondation [fekɔ̃dasjɔ̃] nf **1.** BIOL [des mammifères] fertilization, impregnation ; [des ovipares] fertilization ▸ **fécondation artificielle / in vitro** artificial / in vitro fertilization **2.** BOT fertilization, fertilizing.

féconder [3] [fekɔ̃de] vt BIOL [femme, femelle] to impregnate ; [œuf] to fertilize.

fécondité [fekɔ̃dite] nf **1.** BIOL fecundity **2.** *litt* [d'une terre, d'un jardin] fruitfulness.

fécule [fekyl] nf starch ▸ **fécule de pomme de terre** potato flour.

féculent [fekylɑ̃] nm starchy food, starch / *évitez les féculents* avoid starch ou starchy foods.

fédéral, e, aux [federal, o] adj **1.** POL federal **2.** 🇨🇭 federal *(relative to the Swiss Confederation)*.

fédéralisme [federalism] nm POL federalism.

fédérateur, trice [federatœʀ, tʀis] ◆ adj federative, federating. ◆ nm, f unifier.

fédératif, ive [federatif, iv] adj federative.

fédération [federasjɔ̃] nf **1.** POL [gén] federation ; [au Canada] confederation ▸ **la Fédération de Russie** the Federation of Russia **2.** [groupe] federation ▸ **fédération syndicale** trade union.

fée [fe] nf fairy / *sa bonne fée* his good fairy, his fairy godmother ▸ **la méchante fée** the wicked fairy ▸ **c'est une fée du logis** she's a wonderful housewife.

feed-back [fidbak] nm inv TECHNOL feedback.

feeling [filiŋ] nm *fam* : *on va y aller au feeling* we'll play it by ear / *j'ai un bon feeling* I have a good feeling about it.

féerie [fe(e)ʀi], **féerie*** [feeʀi] nf [merveille] enchantment.

féerique [fe(e)ʀik], **féerique*** [feeʀik] adj [beau - vue, spectacle] enchanting, magical.

feignant, e [fɛɲã, ãt] *fam* ◆ adj lazy, idle. ◆ nm, f loafer.

feindre [81] [fɛ̃dʀ] vt to feign / *feindre la joie* to feign joy.

feinte [fɛ̃t] nf **1.** [ruse] ruse **2.** SPORT [à la boxe et à l'escrime] feint ; [au football, au rugby, etc.] dummy 🇬🇧, fake 🇺🇸.

fêlé, e [fele] adj **1.** [voix, son] hoarse, cracked **2.** *fam* [fou] nuts.

fêler [4] [fele] ❖ **se fêler** vpi [tasse] to crack.

* In reformed spelling (see p. 16-18).

---

félicitations [felisitasjɔ̃] nfpl congratulation, congratulations / *(toutes mes) félicitations* congratulations! ▸ **adresser** ou **faire ses félicitations à qqn** to congratulate sb ▸ **recevoir les félicitations de qqn pour qqch** to be congratulated by sb on sthg / *avec les félicitations du jury* UNIV with the examining board's utmost praise, summa cum laude.

féliciter [3] [felisite] vt to congratulate ▸ **féliciter qqn de qqch** to congratulate sb on sthg / *je ne vous félicite pas !* you'll get no thanks from me! ❖ **se féliciter de** vp + prép **1.** [se réjouir de] ▸ **se féliciter de qqch** to be glad ou pleased about sthg **2.** [se louer de] : *je me félicite d'être resté calme* I'm pleased to say I remained calm.

félin, e [felɛ̃, in] adj ZOOL feline. ❖ **félin** nm cat ▸ **les félins** the cat family ▸ **grand félin** big cat.

fêlure [felyʀ] nf **1.** [d'un objet] crack **2.** [de la voix] crack.

femelle [fəmɛl] ◆ adj ZOOL female. ◆ nf ZOOL female.

féminin, e [feminɛ̃, in] adj **1.** BIOL ▸ **la morphologie féminine** the female body **2.** [composé de femmes] ▸ **l'équipe féminine** the women's team **3.** [considéré comme typique de la femme] ▸ **elle est très féminine** she's very feminine **4.** GRAM & LITTÉR [nom, rime] feminine. ❖ **féminin** nm GRAM feminine (gender).

féminiser [3] [feminize] vt **1.** BIOL to feminize **2.** GRAM [mot] to put into the feminine gender **3.** SOCIOL : *il faut féminiser ces professions* more women must be encouraged to enter those professions. ❖ **se féminiser** vpi SOCIOL ▸ **notre profession se féminise** more and more women are entering our profession.

féminisme [feminism] nm [mouvement] feminism.

féministe [feminist] adj & nmf feminist.

féminité [feminite] nf femininity.

femme [fam] nf **1.** [personne] woman ▸ **femme ingénieur / soldat** woman engineer / soldier ▸ **femme de ménage** cleaning lady, daily (woman) 🇬🇧, maid 🇺🇸 ▸ **femme d'affaires** businesswoman ▸ **femme de chambre** maid, chambermaid ▸ **femme fatale** femme fatale **2.** [adulte] : *à treize ans elle fait déjà très femme* at thirteen she already looks very much a woman **3.** [ensemble de personnes] ▸ **la femme** woman ▸ **les femmes** women **4.** [épouse] wife **5.** *(comme adj)* [féminine] ▸ **être très femme** to be very feminine.

fémur [femyʀ] nm thigh bone, femur *spéc*.

fendiller [3] [fãdije] ❖ **se fendiller** vpi [miroir, mur, tableau] to crack ; [bois] to spring ; [verre, poterie, émail, vernis] to craze, to crackle.

fendre [73] [fãdʀ] vt **1.** [couper - bois, roche] to split, to cleave ; [- lèvre] to cut ou to split (open) / *fendre une bûche en deux* to split ou to chop a log down the middle ▸ **ça vous fend** ou **c'est à vous fendre le cœur** it breaks your heart, it's heartbreaking, it's heartrending **2.** [fissurer - terre, sol, mur] to crack. ❖ **se fendre** vpi **1.** [s'ouvrir - bois] to split ; [- terre, sol, mur] to crack **2.** *fam* [se ruiner] : *tu ne t'es pas trop fendu !* this really didn't ruin ou break you, did it! ▸ **se fendre de** : *se fendre de 30 euros* to fork out ou to shell out 30 euros **3.** ESCRIME to lunge. ◆ vpt ▸ **se fendre qqch** : *elle s'est fendu la lèvre* she cut her lip (open) / *se fendre le crâne* to crack one's skull (open) ▸ **se fendre la gueule** *tfam* ou **pêche**, *fam* ou **pipe**, *fam* ou **poire** *fam* **a)** [rire] to split one's sides **b)** [s'amuser] to have a ball.

fendu, e [fɑ̃dy] adj [robe, jupe] slit ; [yeux] almond-shaped / *une bouche fendue jusqu'aux oreilles* a broad grin ou smile.

fenêtre [fənɛtʀ] nf **1.** CONSTR window / *regarder par la fenêtre* to look out of the window ▶ **ouvrir une fenêtre sur** *fig* to open a window on ▶ **fenêtre à coulisse** ou **à guillotine** sash window ▶ **fenêtre de tir** *fig* window of opportunity **2.** [d'une enveloppe] window **3.** INFORM window ▶ **fenêtre active** ou **activée** active window ▶ **fenêtre de dialogue** dialogue box ▶ **fenêtre de lecture-écriture** read-write slot.

feng shui [fɛ̃gʃwi] nm inv feng shui.

fennec [fenɛk] nm fennec.

fenouil [fənuj] nm fennel.

fente [fɑ̃t] nf **1.** [fissure - dans du bois] cleft, split ; [- dans un sol, un mur] crack, fissure ; [- dans une roche] cleft **2.** [ouverture - d'une jupe, des volets] slit ; [- dans une boîte, sur une vis] slot ; [- dans une veste] vent ; [- pour passer les bras] armhole.

féodal, e, aux [feɔdal, o] adj feudal.

fer [fɛʀ] nm **1.** CHIM iron *(U)* **2.** MÉTALL iron *(U)* ▶ **fer forgé** wrought iron **3.** [dans les aliments] iron *(U)* **4.** [lame] blade ▶ **fer de lance** *pr & fig* spearhead ▶ **tourner** ou **retourner le fer dans la plaie** to twist the knife in the wound **5.** [pour repassage] ▶ **fer à repasser** iron / *passer un coup de fer sur un pantalon* to give a pair of trousers 🇬🇧 ou pants 🇺🇸 a quick iron ▶ **fer à vapeur** steam iron **6.** [instrument] ▶ **fer à friser** curling tongs 🇬🇧 ou iron 🇺🇸 ▶ **fer à lisser** (hair) straighteners ▶ **fer à souder** soldering iron. ◆ **de fer** loc adj [moral, santé] cast-iron *(modif)* ; [discipline, volonté] iron *(modif)*. ◆ **fer à cheval** nm horseshoe.

fer-blanc [fɛʀblɑ̃] (*pl* **fers-blancs**) nm tin, tinplate. ◆ **en fer-blanc** loc adj tin *(modif)* ▶ **boîte en fer-blanc** can, tin can.

férié, e [feʀje] adj ▶ **c'est un jour férié** it's a (public) holiday.

férir [feʀiʀ] vt *litt* ▶ **sans coup férir** without any problem ou difficulty.

ferme¹ [fɛʀm] nf [maison] farmhouse ; [exploitation] farm ▶ **ferme éolienne** wind farm.

ferme² [fɛʀm] ◆ adj **1.** [dur - sol] solid, firm ; [- corps, chair, fruit, muscle] firm **2.** [décidé - ton, pas] firm, steady **3.** [inébranlable - volonté, décision] firm ; [- réponse] definite / *des prix fermes et définitifs* firm ou definite prices. ◆ adv **1.** [solidement] ▶ **tenir ferme a)** [clou] to hold **b)** [personne, troupe] to stand firm, to hold on **2.** [beaucoup - travailler, boire] hard / *il boit ferme* he's a heavy ou a hard drinker ▶ **s'ennuyer ferme** to be bored stiff *fam* **3.** [avec passion - discuter] with passion, passionately.

fermé, e [fɛʀme] adj **1.** [passage] closed, blocked **2.** [porte, récipient] closed, shut ; [à clef] locked ▶ **fermé à clef** locked **3.** [radiateur, robinet] off **4.** [bouche, œil] shut, closed (up) **5.** [magasin, bureau, restaurant] closed **6.** [méfiant - visage] closed, inscrutable, impenetrable ; [- regard] impenetrable ▶ **être fermé à qqch** to have no feeling for ou no appreciation of sthg **7.** [exclusif - milieu, ambiance] exclusive, select.

fermement [fɛʀməmɑ̃] adv [avec force] firmly, solidly, steadily.

ferment [fɛʀmɑ̃] nm CHIM ferment, leaven ▶ **ferments lactiques** bacilli used in making yoghurt.

fermentation [fɛʀmɑ̃tasjɔ̃] nf CHIM fermentation, fermenting.

fermenter [3] [fɛʀmɑ̃te] vi CHIM to ferment.

fermer [3] [fɛʀme] ◆ vt **1.** [yeux] to shut, to close ; [poing, main] to seal, to shut, to close ; [enveloppe] to close ;

[éventail] to fold, to close ; [col, jupe] to fasten, to do up *(sép)* ; [sac, valise, bocal, livre] to shut, to close ; [robinet] to turn off *(sép)* ▶ **fermer les yeux sur qqch** to turn a blind eye to sthg ▶ **ne pas fermer l'œil de la nuit** : *je n'ai pas fermé l'œil de la nuit* I didn't get a wink (of sleep) all night ▶ **fermer sa bouche** *fam* ou **sa gueule**, *tfam* ou **son bec** *fam* to shut up, to shut one's trap ▶ **la fermer** *tfam* : *je le savais mais je l'ai fermée* I knew it but I didn't let on ▶ **la ferme !** *tfam* shut up!, shut your face! **2.** [porte] to close, to shut / *fermer une porte à clef* to lock a door / *fermer une porte à double tour* to double-lock a door ▶ **fermer ses portes** [boutique, musée] to shut, to close ; *(en usage absolu)* ▶ **on ferme !** closing now! **3.** [éteindre - électricité, lumière, compteur] to turn ou to switch off *(sép)* ; [- robinet] to turn off *(sép)* **4.** [rendre inaccessible - rue, voie] to block, to bar, to obstruct **5.** [faire cesser l'activité de] ▶ **fermer un restaurant / théâtre a)** [pour un congé] to close a restaurant / theatre **b)** [définitivement] to close a restaurant / theatre (down) ▶ **fermer boutique a)** [pour un congé] to shut up shop **b)** [pour cause de faillite] to stop ou to cease trading, to close down **c)** *fig* to give up. ◆ vi **1.** [se verrouiller - couvercle, fenêtre, porte] to close / *le portail ferme mal* the gate is difficult to close ou won't close properly **2.** [cesser son activité - temporairement] to close ; [- définitivement] to close down. ◆ **se fermer** vpi **1.** [être verrouillé - porte, fenêtre] to close **2.** [se serrer, se plier - bras, fleur, huître, main] to close (up) ; [- aile] to fold ; [- bouche, œil, paupière, livre, rideau] to close (up) ; [- blessure] to close (up), to heal **3.** [être impénétrable] : *on ne peut pas lui parler, elle se ferme aussitôt* there's no talking to her, she just switches off ou freezes up.

fermeté [fɛʀməte] nf **1.** [solidité - d'un objet] solidness, firmness ; [- d'un corps] firmness **2.** [assurance - d'un geste] assurance, steadiness ; [- d'une voix] firmness **3.** [autorité] firmness ▶ **faire preuve de fermeté à l'égard de qqn** to be firm with sb ▶ **avec fermeté** firmly, resolutely, steadfastly.

fermeture [fɛʀmətyʀ] nf **1.** [obstruction] : *après la fermeture du puits / tunnel* once the well / tunnel is blocked off **2.** [rabattement] closing / **'ne pas gêner la fermeture des portes'** 'please do not obstruct the doors' **3.** COMM [arrêt des transactions] ▶ **au moment de la fermeture a)** [du bureau] at the end of the day's work **b)** [de la banque, du magasin, du café] at closing time / **'fermeture annuelle'** 'closed for annual holiday' ▶ **à la fermeture** BOURSE at the close of trading ; ADMIN & FIN closing ▶ **jour de fermeture a)** [hebdomadaire] closing day **b)** [férié] public holiday **4.** VÊT ▶ **fermeture Éclair®** ou **à glissière** zip (fastener) 🇬🇧, zipper 🇺🇸.

fermier, ère [fɛʀmje, ɛʀ] adj COMM ▶ **poulet / œuf fermier** free-range chicken / egg ▶ **lait / beurre fermier** dairy milk / butter. ◆ **fermier** nm AGR [locataire] tenant farmer ; [propriétaire, agriculteur] farmer. ◆ **fermière** nf [cultivatrice] woman farmer.

fermoir [fɛʀmwaʀ] nm [de collier, de sac] clasp, fastener.

féroce [feʀɔs] adj **1.** [acerbe - humour, examinateur] cruel, harsh, ferocious **2.** [qui tue - animal, bête] ferocious **3.** [extrême - appétit] ravenous, voracious **4.** [concurrence] fierce.

férocité [feʀɔsite] nf **1.** [brutalité] cruelty, bloodlust **2.** [intransigeance] harshness, ferociousness **3.** [d'une bête] ferocity **4.** [de concurrence] fierceness.

Féroé [feʀɔe] npr fpl ▶ **les (îles) Féroé** the Faeroes, the Faeroe Islands. ⟶ **île**

ferraille [feʀaj] nf **1.** [débris] ▶ **de la ferraille** scrap (iron) ▶ **un bruit de ferraille** a clanking noise **2.** [rebut] ▶ **la ferraille** : *mettre une machine à la ferraille* to sell a machine for scrap / *bon pour la* ou *à mettre à la ferraille* ready for the scrapheap, good for scrap **3.** *fam* [monnaie] small change.

ferré, e [fɛʀe] adj **1.** [muni de fers -cheval] shod ; [-chaussure] hobnailed ; [-roue] rimmed ; [-lacets] tagged **2.** *fam* EXPR **être ferré sur qqch** to be a genius at sthg ▸ **être ferré en qqch** to be well up on sthg.

ferrer [4] [fɛʀe] vt **1.** [cheval, bœuf] to shoe **2.** PÊCHE to strike.

ferreux, euse [fɛʀø, øz] adj ferrous.

ferronnerie [fɛʀɔnʀi] nf **1.** [art] ▸ **ferronnerie (d'art)** wrought-iron craft **2.** [ouvrage] : *une belle ferronnerie du XVIII* siècle a fine piece of 18th-century wrought ironwork ou wrought-iron work.

ferroutage [fɛʀutaʒ] nm piggyback traffic.

ferroviaire [fɛʀɔvjɛʀ] adj [trafic, tunnel, réseau] rail *(modif)*, railway UK *(modif)*, railroad US *(modif)*.

ferrure [fɛʀyʀ] nf [garniture] metal hinge.

ferry [fɛʀi] *(pl* **ferries)** nm [pour voitures] car-ferry, ferry ; [pour voitures ou trains] ferry, ferry-boat.

ferry-boat *(pl* **ferry-boats),** **ferryboat*** [fɛʀibot] nm ferry-boat.

fertile [fɛʀtil] adj **1.** AGR & GÉOGR fertile, rich ▸ **fertile en** rich in **2.** *fig* ▸ **fertile en** rich in / *une année fertile en événements* a very eventful year / *un épisode fertile en rebondissements* an action-packed episode.

fertiliser [3] [fɛʀtilize] vt AGR to fertilize.

fertilité [fɛʀtilite] nf **1.** AGR fertility, fruitfulness **2.** BIOL [d'un couple, d'une femme] fertility.

féru, e [feʀy] adj ▸ **être féru de qqch** to be keen on ou highly interested in sthg.

férule [feʀyl] nf EXPR **être sous la férule de qqn** to be under sb's strict authority.

fervent, e [fɛʀvɑ̃, ɑ̃t] ◆ adj fervent, ardent. ◆ nm, f devotee, enthusiast, addict.

ferveur [fɛʀvœʀ] nf fervour UK, fervor US, ardour UK, ardor US, enthusiasm ▸ **avec ferveur** with fervour, fervently, enthusiastically.

fesse [fɛs] nf **1.** ANAT buttock ▸ **les fesses** the buttocks ▸ **avoir qqn aux fesses** *fam* to have sb on one's back **2.** : *raconter des histoires de fesses* *fam* to tell dirty jokes.

fessée [fese] nf spanking ▸ **donner une fessée à qqn** to spank sb.

fessier, ère [fesje, ɛʀ] adj buttocks *(modif)*, gluteal *spéc*.

festif, ive [fɛstif, iv] adj *sout* festive.

festin [fɛstɛ̃] nm feast, banquet / *faire un festin* to have ou hold a feast.

festival, als [fɛstival] nm festival ▸ **un festival de** *fig* a brilliant display of.

festivalier, ère [fɛstivalje, ɛʀ] nm, f festival-goer.

festivités [fɛstivite] nfpl festivities.

festoyer [3] [fɛstwaje] vi to feast.

feta [feta] nf feta (cheese).

fêtard, e [fetaʀ, aʀd] nm, f party animal.

fête [fɛt] nf **1.** [célébration -civile] holiday ; [-religieuse] feast / *demain c'est fête* tomorrow we have a day off ▸ **fête légale** public holiday ▸ **la fête des Mères** Mother's Day, Mothering Sunday UK ▸ **la fête nationale** a) [gén] the national holiday b) [en France] Bastille Day c) [aux États-Unis] Independence Day ▸ **la fête de Noël** (the celebration of) Christmas ▸ **la fête des Pères** Father's Day ▸ **la fête des Rois** Twelfth Night, Epiphany ▸ **la fête du Travail** May Day **2.** [d'un saint] saint's day, name day ▸ **souhaiter sa fête à qqn** to wish sb a happy saint's ou name day ▸ **ça va être ta fête !** you'll cop it UK ou catch hell US **3.** [réunion -d'amis] party ▸ **une fête de famille** a family celebration ou gathering / *vous serez de la fête ?* will you be joining us / them? ▸ **être à la fête** *fig* : *il n'a jamais été à pareille fête* he's

never had such a good time ▸ **que la fête commence !** let the festivities begin! **4.** [foire] fair ; [kermesse] fête, fete ; [festival] festival, show / *ce n'est pas tous les jours (la) fête !* it's not everyday you've got something to celebrate! ▸ **faire la fête** to have a party ou (some) fun ou a good time ▸ **la fête de la bière** the beer festival ▸ **fête foraine** [attractions] funfair UK, carnival US **5.** EXPR **faire (la) fête à qqn** to greet sb warmly ▸ **se faire une fête de** to look forward eagerly to **6.** QUÉBEC & SUISSE [anniversaire] birthday. ⬧ **fêtes** nfpl [gén] holidays ; [de Noël et du jour de l'an] the Christmas and New Year celebrations.

Fête

The French traditionally wish **bonne fête** to the person who has the same name as the saint commemorated on a particular day.

Fête-Dieu [fɛtdjø] *(pl* **Fêtes-Dieu)** nf ▸ **la Fête-Dieu** Corpus Christi.

fêter [4] [fete] vt **1.** [célébrer -anniversaire, événement] to celebrate / *une promotion ? il faut fêter ça !* a promotion? that's worth celebrating! **2.** [accueillir -personne] to fête, to fete.

fétiche [fetiʃ] nm **1.** [objet de culte] fetish, fetich **2.** [porte-bonheur] mascot ; *(comme adj)* lucky ▸ **mon numéro fétiche** my lucky number.

fétichisme [fetiʃism] nm [culte] fetishism, fetichism.

fétide [fetid] adj fetid.

fétu [fety] nm ▸ **fétu (de paille)** (wisp of) straw.

feu[1], x [fø] ◆ nm **1.** [combustion] fire ▸ **faire du un feu** to make a fire / *allumer un feu* to light a fire ▸ **feu de bois** (wood) fire ▸ **cuire qqch au feu de bois** to cook sthg in a wood-burning oven ▸ **feu de cheminée** chimney fire / *mettre le feu à une maison* to set a house on fire ▸ **au feu !** fire! ▸ **feu de camp** campfire ▸ **feu de joie** bonfire ▸ **feu de paille** flash in the pan ▸ **prendre feu** to catch fire ▸ **avoir le feu sacré** to burn with enthusiasm ▸ **il n'y a pas le feu (au lac) !** *hum* what's the big hurry?, where's the fire? ▸ **jouer avec le feu** to play with fire ▸ **il n'y a vu que du feu** he never saw a thing, he was completely taken in ▸ **avoir le feu au derrière** *fam* ou **aux fesses,** *fam* ou **au cul** *vulg* a) [être pressé] to be in a tearing hurry b) [sexuellement] to be horny **2.** [brûleur] ring UK, burner US ▸ **à feu doux** a) [plaque] on a gentle ou slow heat b) [four] in a slow oven ▸ **faire cuire à petit feu** to cook slowly ▸ **à feu vif** on a fierce heat ▸ **avoir qqch sur le feu** to be (in the middle of) cooking sthg **3.** [briquet] ▸ **avez-vous du feu ?** have you got a light? **4.** [en pyrotechnie] ▸ **feu d'artifice** [spectacle] fireworks display / *son récital, un vrai feu d'artifice !* *fig* his recital was a virtuoso performance! **5.** MIL [tir] fire, shooting ; [combats] action ▸ **ouvrir le feu (sur)** to open fire (on), to start firing (at) ▸ **cesser le feu** to cease fire ▸ **faire feu** to fire, to shoot ▸ **feu !** fire! ▸ **un feu croisé, des feux croisés** *pr* crossfire ▸ **mettre le feu aux poudres** a) *pr* to spark off an explosion b) *fig* to spark things off **6.** TRANSP [signal] ▸ **feu (tricolore** ou **de signalisation)** traffic lights ▸ **feu rouge/orange/vert** red / amber / green light ▸ **donner le feu vert à qqn / qqch** *fig* to give sb / sthg the green light ou the go-ahead **7.** AÉRON, AUTO & NAUT light ▸ **feu arrière** taillight ▸ **feux de brouillard** fog lamps ▸ **feu de position** sidelight ▸ **feux de croisement** dipped UK ou dimmed US headlights ▸ **feux de détresse** warning lights ▸ **feux de route** headlights ou full beam UK ou high beams US **8.** CINÉ & THÉÂTRE ▸ **les feux de la rampe** the footlights ▸ **être sous le feu des projecteurs** a) *pr* to be in front of the spotlights **b)** *fig* to be in the limelight **9.** *litt* [ardeur] fire, passion, ardour **10.** *litt* [éclat, lumière] fire, light / *les cristaux brillaient de tous leurs feux* the crystals sparkled brightly ▶ **le feu d'un diamant** the blaze ou fire of a diamond **11.** [sensation de brûlure] burn ▶ **le feu du rasoir** razor burn **12.** *arch* [maison] house, homestead **13.** *fam* [pistolet] gun, rod US. ◆ adj inv flame *(modif)*, flame-coloured. ◈ **à feu et à sang** loc adv : *mettre un pays à feu et à sang* to ransack and pillage a country. ◈ **dans le feu de** loc prép in the heat of / *dans le feu de l'action* in the heat of the moment. ◈ **en feu** loc adj **1.** [incendié] on fire, burning **2.** [brûlant] ▶ **j'ai la bouche / gorge en feu** my mouth / throat is burning. ◈ **tout feu tout flamme** loc adj burning with enthusiasm. ◈ **feu follet** nm will-o'-the-wisp.

feu², **e** [fø] adj *(inv avant l'article ou le possessif)* *sout* late ▶ **feu la reine** the late Queen.

feuillage [fœjaʒ] nm **1.** [sur l'arbre] foliage *spéc*, leaves **2.** [coupé] foliage *spéc*, greenery.

feuille [fœj] nf **1.** BOT leaf **2.** [morceau de papier] sheet / *les feuilles d'un cahier* the sheets ou leaves ou pages of a notebook ▶ **feuille volante** (loose) sheet of paper **3.** PRESSE ▶ **feuille à sensation** gossip sheet **4.** [imprimé] form, slip ▶ **feuille de maladie** ou **de soins** claim form for reimbursement of medical expenses ▶ **feuille d'heures** time sheet ▶ **feuille d'impôts** tax form, tax return ▶ **feuille de paie** payslip ▶ **feuille de présence** attendance sheet **5.** [plaque] leaf, sheet / *feuille de métal / d'or* metal / gold leaf **6.** INFORM sheet. ◈ **feuille de chou** nf PRESSE rag. ◈ **feuille de vigne** nf **1.** BOT vine leaf **2.** ART fig-leaf.

feuillet [fœjɛ] nm [d'un formulaire] page, leaf.

feuilleté, **e** [fœjte] adj **1.** CULIN puff *(modif)* **2.** TECHNOL laminated. ◈ **feuilleté** nm **1.** [dessert] puff pastry **2.** [hors-d'œuvre] puff pastry case / *feuilleté aux asperges* asparagus in puff pastry.

feuilleter [27] [fœjte] vt [album, magazine] to leaf ou flip ou to flick through *(insép)*, to skim (through).

🖉 In reformed spelling (see p. 16-18), this verb is conjugated like **acheter** : *il feuillète, elle feuillètera*.

feuilleton [fœjtɔ̃] nm **1.** PRESSE series *(sg)*, serial **2.** TV ▶ **feuilleton (télévisé) a)** [sur plusieurs semaines] TV serial, mini-series **b)** [sur plusieurs années] soap opera **3.** *fig* saga.

feuillu, **e** [fœjy] adj leafy. ◈ **feuillu** nm lobed-leaved tree.

feutre [føtʀ] nm **1.** TEXT [étoffe] felt **2.** [chapeau] felt hat ; ≃ fedora **3.** [stylo] felt-tip (pen).

feutré, **e** [føtʀe] adj **1.** [pull, vêtement] felted **2.** [silencieux - salon, atmosphère] quiet ; [- voix] muffled ▶ **marcher à pas feutrés** to creep stealthily.

feutrer [3] [føtʀe] vt TEXT to felt. ◈ **se feutrer** vpi to felt, to become felted ou matted.

feutrine [føtʀin] nf felt.

fève [fɛv] nf **1.** BOT bean **2.** [des Rois] lucky charm or token made of porcelain and hidden in a "galette des Rois".

février [fevʀije] nm February. **Voir aussi mars.**

FF (abr écrite de de franc français) FF.

fg abr écrite de **faubourg.**

fi [fi] interj EXPR ▶ **faire fi de a)** [mépriser] to turn one's nose up at, to spurn **b)** [ignorer] to ignore.

fiabilité [fjabilite] nf [crédibilité] reliability.

fiable [fjabl] adj [crédible] reliable.

fiacre [fjakʀ] nm fiacre, (horse-drawn) carriage.

fiançailles [fijɑ̃saj] nfpl [promesse] engagement.

fiancé, **e** [fijɑ̃se] nm, f fiancé (fiancée) ▶ **les fiancés** the betrothed *litt hum*, the engaged couple.

fiancer [16] [fijɑ̃se] ◈ **se fiancer** vpi to get engaged ▶ **se fiancer avec qqn** to get engaged to sb.

fiasco [fjasko] nm [entreprise, tentative] fiasco, flop ; [film, ouvrage] flop.

fibre [fibʀ] nf **1.** [du bois] fibre UK, fiber US, woodfibre **2.** OPT & TECHNOL fibre UK, fiber US ▶ **fibre de verre** fibreglass ▶ **fibre optique** fibre optics *(sg)* **3.** TEXT & BIOL ▶ **une fibre textile** a fibre UK, a fiber US ▶ **riche en fibres (alimentaires)** rich in (dietary) fibre **4.** [sentiment] feeling / *avoir la fibre paternelle* to have strong paternal feelings.

fibreux, **euse** [fibʀø, øz] adj **1.** [dur - viande] stringy, tough **2.** [à fibres - tissu, muscle] fibrous.

fibrome [fibʀom] nm [tumeur] fibroma ; [dans l'utérus] fibroid.

ficelé, **e** [fisle] adj ▶ **bien ficelé a)** [histoire, scénario] tight, seamless **b)** [dossier] well put together.

ficeler [24] [fisle] vt to tie up *(sép)*.

🖉 In reformed spelling (see p. 16-18), this verb is conjugated like *peler : il ficèle, elle ficèlera.*

ficelle [fisɛl] nf **1.** [corde] piece of string ▶ **de la ficelle** string ▶ **connaître toutes les ficelles du métier** to know the ropes ▶ **tirer les ficelles** to pull the strings **2.** [pain] *very thin baguette*.

fiche [fiʃ] nf **1.** [carton] piece of (stiff) card, (index) card ▶ **fiche cuisine** recipe card **2.** [papier] sheet, slip ▶ **fiche de paie** pay slip UK, paystub US ▶ **fiche technique** COMM product specification **3.** [formulaire] form ▶ **mettre qqn en** ou **sur fiche** to open a file on sb **4.** ÉLECTR plug ▶ **fiche multiple** multiple adaptor ou adapter.

ficher¹ [3] [fiʃe] vt **1.** [enfoncer] to drive ou to stick (in) **2.** [information] to file, to put on file ; [suspect] to put on file.

ficher² [3] [fiʃe] *(pp fichu)* vt *fam* **1.** [mettre] : *fiche-le à la porte !* throw ou kick him out! / *fiche-moi ça dehors !* get rid of this! ▶ **ficher dedans** : *c'est cette phrase qui m'a fichu dedans* it was that phrase that got me into trouble ou hot water / *ce contretemps fiche tout en l'air* this last-minute hitch really messes everything up / *c'est le genre de remarque qui me fiche en rogne* that's the kind of remark that drives me mad / *si c'est fermé mardi, ça fiche tout par terre !* if it's closed on Tuesday, everything's ruined! **2.** [faire] to do / *qu'est-ce que tu fiches ici ?* what on earth ou the heck are you doing here? / *je n'ai rien fichu aujourd'hui* I haven't done a thing today **3.** [donner] : *ça m'a fichu la chair de poule / la trouille* it gave me the creeps / the willies ▶ **fiche-moi la paix !** leave me alone! / *je t'en ficherai, moi, du champagne !* champagne? I'll give you champagne! ▶ **ficher le camp** to clear off. ◈ **se ficher** vpi *fam* [se mettre] ▶ **se ficher dedans** to land o.s. right in it. ◈ **se ficher de** vp + prép *fam* **1.** [railler] : *elle n'arrête pas de se ficher de lui* she keeps making fun of him, she's forever pulling his leg / *tu te fiches de moi ou quoi ?* are you kidding me? / *eh bien, tu ne t'es pas fichu de nous !* well, you've really done things in style! ▶ **se ficher de qqch** to make fun of sthg **2.** [être indifférent à] : *je me fiche de ce que disent les gens* I don't care what ou I don't give a damn about what people say ▶ **je m'en fiche comme de ma première chemise** ou **comme de l'an quarante** ou **complètement** I don't give a damn (about it), I couldn't care less.

fichier [fiʃje] nm **1.** [fiches] (card index) file, catalogue / *le fichier de nos clients* our file of customers ▶ **fichier d'adresses** mailing list **2.** INFORM file ▶ **fichier natif** native file.

fichu, **e** [fiʃy] adj *fam* **1.** [perdu] ▶ **il est fichu** he's had it / *pour samedi soir, c'est fichu* Saturday evening's up the spout UK ou down the drain US **2.** *(avant nom)* [mauvais] lousy, rotten / *quel fichu temps !* what lousy weather!

3. *(avant nom)* [important] : *j'ai un fichu mal de dents* I've got one hell of a nasty toothache **4.** [capable] ▶ **fichu de** : *il n'est même pas fichu de prendre un message correctement* he can't even take a message properly **5.** ▶ **bien fichu** : *il est bien fichu* he's got a nice body / *ce système est très bien fichu* it's a very clever device / *je suis mal fichu aujourd'hui* [malade] I feel lousy today.

fictif, ive [fiktif, iv] adj [imaginaire] imaginary, fictitious.

fiction [fiksjɔ̃] nf **1.** [domaine de l'imaginaire] ▶ **la fiction** fiction **2.** [histoire] story, (piece of) fiction ; TV [film] TV drama.

fidèle [fidɛl] ◆ adj **1.** [constant - ami] faithful, loyal, true ; [- employé, animal] loyal, faithful ; [- conjoint] faithful ; [- client] regular ; *être fidèle à une idée* to stand by ou to be true to an idea ▶ **fidèle à elle-même** true to herself / *elle est toujours fidèle au poste* you can always rely ou depend on her **2.** [conforme - copie, description] true, exact ; [- traduction] faithful, close ; [- historien, narrateur] faithful ; [- mémoire] reliable, correct ; [- balance] reliable, accurate. ◆ nmf **1.** RELIG believer ▶ **les fidèles a)** [croyants] the believers **b)** [pratiquants] the faithful **c)** [assemblée] the congregation **2.** [adepte] devotee, follower ; [client] regular.

fidèlement [fidɛlmɑ̃] adv **1.** [loyalement] faithfully, loyally **2.** [conformément] exactly, faithfully.

fidéliser [3] [fidelize] vt : *fidéliser ses clients* ou *sa clientèle* to foster customer loyalty *(by a marketing policy)* / *fidéliser un public* to maintain a regular audience *(by a commercial policy).*

fidélité [fidelite] nf [loyauté - d'un ami, d'un employé, d'un animal] faithfulness, loyalty ; [- d'un conjoint] faithfulness, fidelity ; [- d'un client] loyalty.

Fidji [fidʒi] npr fpl ▶ **les (îles) Fidji** Fiji, the Fiji Islands. ⟶ **île**

fidjien, enne [fidʒjɛ̃, ɛn] adj Fijian. ❖ **Fidjien, enne** nm, f Fijian.

fief [fjɛf] nm **1.** HIST fief **2.** [domaine réservé] fief, kingdom.

fieffé, e [fjefe] adj *fam & péj* [extrême] complete, utter ▶ **un fieffé menteur / voleur** an arrant liar / thief.

fiente [fjɑ̃t] nf : *de la fiente* droppings.

fier¹ [9] [fje] ❖ **se fier à** vp + prép **1.** [avoir confiance en] to trust (in) ▶ **se fier aux apparences** to go by ou on appearances **2.** [compter sur] to rely on.

fier², fière [fjɛʀ] ◆ adj **1.** [satisfait] proud / *il n'y a pas de quoi être fier* it's nothing to be proud of / *j'étais fier d'avoir gagné* I was proud (that) I won / *je n'étais pas fier de moi* I wasn't pleased with ou proud of myself **2.** [arrogant - personnage] proud, arrogant, haughty ; [- regard] haughty, supercilious ▶ **avoir fière allure** to cut (quite) a dash ▶ **être fier comme Artaban** ou **comme un coq** to be as proud as a peacock, to be puffed up with pride. ◆ nm, f proud person ▶ **faire le fier** to put on airs and graces.

fièrement [fjɛʀmɑ̃] adv proudly.

fierté [fjɛʀte] nf **1.** [dignité] pride **2.** [satisfaction] (source of) pride ▶ **tirer fierté** ou **une grande fierté de** to take (a) pride in, to pride o.s. on.

fièvre [fjevʀ] nf **1.** MÉD fever, temperature ▶ **avoir de la fièvre** to have a temperature ou a fever / *il a 40 de fièvre* his temperature is up to 40 (°C), he has a temperature of 40 ° ▶ **fièvre jaune** yellow fever ▶ **fièvre typhoïde** typhoid fever **2.** *sout* [agitation] excitement / *dans la fièvre du moment* in the heat of the moment.

fiévreusement [fjevʀøzmɑ̃] adv MÉD & *fig* feverishly.

fiévreux, euse [fjevʀø, øz] adj MÉD & *fig* feverish, febrile.

figé, e [fiʒe] adj set / *dans une attitude figée* motionless.

figer [17] [fiʒe] vi [huile] to congeal ; [sang] to coagulate, to clot. ❖ **se figer** vpi **1.** [être coagulé - huile] to congeal ; [- sang] to coagulate, to clot / *mon sang s'est figé dans mes veines* my blood froze **2.** [s'immobiliser - attitude, sourire] to stiffen ; [- personne] to freeze.

fignoler [3] [fiɲɔle] vt to perfect, to polish ou to touch up *(sép).*

figue [fig] nf fig ▶ **figue de Barbarie** prickly pear.

figuier [figje] nm fig tree.

figurant, e [figyʀɑ̃, ɑ̃t] nm, f CINÉ extra ; THÉÂTRE extra, walk-on actor ; DANSE figurant.

figuratif, ive [figyʀatif, iv] adj [art] figurative, representational ; [artiste] representational ; [plan] figurative.

figuration [figyʀasjɔ̃] nf [métier] ▶ **faire de la figuration a)** CINÉ to work as an extra **b)** THÉÂTRE to do walk-on parts **c)** DANSE to dance as a figurant.

figure [figyʀ] nf **1.** [visage] face ; [mine] face, features ▶ **faire triste** ou **piètre figure** to cut a sad figure, to be a sad ou sorry sight ▶ **faire bonne figure** to look contented ▶ **faire figure de** : *il faisait figure de riche* he was looked on ou thought of as a rich man ▶ **prendre figure** to take shape **2.** [personnage] figure / *une grande figure de la politique* a great political figure **3.** NAUT & *fig* ▶ **figure de proue** figurehead **4.** [illustration] figure, illustration ; [schéma, diagramme] diagram, figure ▶ **figure géométrique** geometrical figure **5.** DANSE, MUS & SPORT figure ▶ **figures imposées** compulsory figures ▶ **figures libres** freestyle **6.** LING ▶ **figure de style** stylistic device.

figuré, e [figyʀe] adj LING [langage, sens] figurative. ❖ **au figuré** loc adv figuratively.

figurer [3] [figyʀe] ◆ vt [représenter] to represent, to show, to depict. ◆ vi [apparaître] to appear / *votre nom ne figure pas sur la liste* your name doesn't appear ou isn't on the list / *j'ai oublié de faire figurer son nom sur l'affiche* I forgot to include his name on the poster. ❖ **se figurer** vpt **1.** [imaginer] to imagine **2.** [croire] to believe / *figure-toi qu'il n'a même pas appelé !* he didn't even call, can you believe it! / *eh bien figure-toi que moi non plus, je n'ai pas le temps !* surprising though it may seem, I haven't got the time either!

figurine [figyʀin] nf figurine, statuette.

fil [fil] nm **1.** TEXT [matière - de coton, de soie] thread ; [- de laine] yarn *(U)* ; [brin - de coton, de soie] piece of thread ; [- de laine] strand ▶ **fil à bâtir / à coudre** basting / sewing thread ▶ **fil dentaire** dental floss ▶ **fil d'Écosse** lisle ▶ **fil de Nylon** nylon thread ▶ **fil de fil en aiguille** one thing leading to another ▶ **donner du fil à retordre à qqn** to cause sb (no end of) trouble **2.** [lin] linen **3.** [filament - de haricot] string **4.** [corde - à linge] line ; [- d'équilibriste] tightrope, high wire ; [- pour marionnette] string ▶ **fil conducteur** ou **d'Ariane a)** [d'une enquête] (vital) lead **b)** [dans une histoire] main theme ▶ **sa vie ne tient qu'à un fil** his life hangs by a thread ▶ **un fil de la Vierge** a gossamer thread ▶ **avoir un fil à la patte** to be tied down, to have one's hands tied **5.** [câble] wire / *fil de cuivre / d'acier* copper / steel wire ▶ **fil électrique** wire ▶ **fil de fer** wire ▶ **fil de fer barbelé** barbed wire ▶ **fil à plomb** plumbline **6.** *fam* [téléphone] ▶ **au bout du fil** on the phone, on the line **7.** [tranchant] edge ▶ **être sur le fil du rasoir** to be on a knife-edge **8.** [cours - de l'eau] current, stream ; [- de la pensée, d'une discussion] thread / *perdre / reprendre le fil d'une histoire* to lose / to pick up the thread of a story ▶ **fil de discussion** INFORM discussion thread. ❖ **au fil de** loc prép **1.** [le long de] : *aller au fil de l'eau* to go with the current ou stream **2.** [au fur et à mesure de] ▶ **au fil du temps** as time goes by / *au fil des semaines* as the weeks go by, with the passing weeks. ❖ **sans fil** loc adj [télégraphie, téléphonie] wireless *(modif)* ; [rasoir, téléphone] cordless.

filaire [filɛʀ] nf filaria.

filament [filamɑ̃] nm [fibre] filament.

filandreux, euse [filɑ̃dʀø, øz] adj [fibreux -viande] stringy.

filasse [filas] ◆ nf tow. ◆ adj inv : *cheveux (blonds) filasse* péj dirty blond hair.

filature [filatyʀ] nf **1.** TEXT [opérations] spinning ; [usine] (spinning) mill **2.** [surveillance] shadowing, tailing ▸ **prendre qqn en filature** to shadow ou to tail sb.

file [fil] nf **1.** [suite -de véhicules] line, row ; [-de personnes] line ▸ **se mettre en file** to queue up UK, to line up, to stand in line ▸ **file d'attente** queue UK, line US ▸ **en file indienne** in single file **2.** TRANSP lane / *la file de droite* the right-hand lane / *sur deux files* in two lanes. ◆ **à la file** loc adv in a row, one after another ou the other.

filer [3] [file] ◆ vt **1.** TECHNOL & TEXT to spin ▸ **filer un mauvais coton a)** fam [être malade] to be in bad shape **b)** [se préparer des ennuis] to be heading for trouble **2.** [dérouler -câble, amarre] to pay out (sép), to release **3.** [développer -image, métaphore] to draw ou to spin out (sép) ; [tenir -note, son] to draw out (sép) **4.** [suivre -suj : détective] to tail, to shadow **5.** [déchirer -collant, bas] to ladder UK, to run US **6.** fam [donner] to give / *il m'a filé un coup de poing* he landed UK ou beaned US me one / *elle m'a filé la grippe* she's given me the flu ▸ **filer une gifle à qqn** to smack ou to slap sb in the face **7.** EXPR **filer le parfait amour** to live a great romance. ◆ vi **1.** NAUT **filer (à) 20 nœuds** to sail ou to proceed at 20 knots **2.** [collants, bas] to ladder UK, to run ; [maille] to run **3.** [passer vite -coureur, véhicule] to dash ; [-nuage] to fly (past) ; [-temps] to fly ▸ **filer à toute vitesse** [voiture] to bomb along ▸ **il a filé dans sa chambre a)** [gén] he dashed ou flew into his bedroom **b)** [après une réprimande] he stormed off to his room ▸ **bon, je file !** right, I'm off! / *l'argent lui file entre les doigts* money just slips through his fingers **4.** fam [disparaître -cambrioleur] to scram, to scarper UK, to skedaddle US / *je t'ai assez vu, file !* I've had enough of you, scram! ou clear off! ▸ **filer à l'anglaise** to sneak off, to take French leave **5.** fam [argent] to go, to disappear, to vanish **6.** EXPR **filer doux** to behave o.s.

filet [filɛ] nm **1.** TECHNOL thread **2.** [petite quantité] ▸ **un filet de** : *un filet d'eau* a trickle of water / *un filet de sang* a trickle of blood ▸ **un filet de lumière** a (thin) shaft of light ▸ **un filet de citron / vinaigre** a dash of lemon / vinegar **3.** CULIN [de viande, de poisson] fillet, filet US / *un morceau dans le filet* [de bœuf] ≃ a sirloin ou porterhouse steak ▸ **filet mignon** filet mignon **4.** [ouvrage à mailles] net ▸ **filet (de pêche)** (fishing) net ▸ **filet (à bagages)** (luggage) rack ▸ **filet dérivant** drift net ▸ **filet à provisions** string shopping bag **5.** SPORT [au football, au hockey, au tennis] net ; [d'acrobate] safety net ▸ **monter au filet** to come to the net ▸ **travailler sans filet a)** pr to perform without a safety net **b)** fig to take risks.

filial, e, aux [filjal, o] adj filial. ◆ **filiale** nf subsidiary (company).

filiation [filjasjɔ̃] nf **1.** [entre individus] line of descent, filiation sout ; DR filiation **2.** [entre des mots, des idées] relationship.

filière [filjɛʀ] nf **1.** [procédures] procedures, channels / *passer par la filière administrative* to go through administrative channels **2.** [réseau -de trafiquants, de criminels] network, connection **3.** ÉDUC & UNIV ▸ **la filière technique / scientifique** technical / scientific subjects **4.** MÉTALL ▸ **filière (à machine) a)** [pour étirage] draw, drawing plate **b)** [pour tréfilage, filage] die **5.** INDUST industry.

filiforme [filifɔʀm] adj **1.** [maigre] lanky, spindly **2.** MÉD [pouls] thready.

filigrane [filigʀan] nm [d'un papier] watermark. ◆ **en filigrane** loc adv between the lines / *le problème du racisme apparaissait en filigrane dans la discussion* the problem of racism was implicit in the discussion.

filin [filɛ̃] nm rope.

fille [fij] nf **1.** [enfant] girl / *c'est une belle / gentille fille* she's a good-looking / nice girl / *tu es une grande fille maintenant* you're a big girl now / *c'est encore une petite fille* she's still a little girl **2.** [jeune fille] girl ; [femme] woman / *une fille de la campagne* a country girl **3.** [descendante] daughter ▸ **tu es bien la fille de ton père !** you're just like your father! **4.** vieilli [prostituée] whore ▸ **fille publique** ou **de joie** ou **des rues** ou **perdue** litt prostitute.

fillette [fijɛt] nf [enfant] little girl.

filleul, e [fijœl] nm, f godchild, godson (goddaughter).

film [film] nm **1.** CINÉ [pellicule] film ; [œuvre] film UK, movie US ▸ **film d'animation** animated film ▸ **film d'horreur** ou **d'épouvante** horror film ▸ **film muet** silent film ▸ **film parlant** talking film, talkie fam **2.** PHOT film **3.** [couche] film **4.** [emballage] film / *sous film plastique* shrink-wrapped ▸ **film alimentaire** clingfilm **5.** [déroulement] sequence / *le film des événements* the sequence of events.

filmer [3] [filme] vt [scène, événement] to film, to shoot ; [personnage] to film.

filon [filɔ̃] nm **1.** GÉOL seam, vein **2.** fam EXPR **trouver le filon a)** [moyen] *il a trouvé le filon pour gagner de l'argent* he found an easy way to make money **b)** [situation lucrative] to strike it rich, to find the right connection US / *j'ai enfin trouvé le filon* I've found a cushy number at last, I'm on the gravy train at last US ▸ **c'est un bon filon** it's a gold mine ou a money-spinner.

filou [filu] nm [voleur] crook, rogue.

fils [fis] nm [enfant] son, boy ▸ **il est bien le fils de son père !** he's just like his father! ▸ **un fils de famille** a wealthy young man.

filtrage [filtʀaʒ] nm [d'un liquide] filtering ; [de l'information, de personnes] screening ▸ **filtrage d'appels** call screening.

filtrant, e [filtʀɑ̃, ɑ̃t] adj [matériau, dispositif] filtering (avant nom) ; [crème, huile solaire] sunscreen (modif) ; [verre] filter (modif).

filtre [filtʀ] nm filter ▸ **filtre à café / huile** coffee / oil filter ▸ **filtre solaire** sunscreen ▸ **filtre à air** air filter.

filtrer [3] [filtʀe] ◆ vt **1.** [liquide, air, lumière] to filter **2.** [visiteurs, informations] to screen. ◆ vi **1.** [liquide] to seep ou to filter through ; [lumière, bruit] to filter through **2.** [nouvelles] to filter through.

fin¹, e [fɛ̃, fin] adj **1.** [mince -sable, pinceau] fine ; [-cheveu, fil] fine, thin ; [-écriture] fine, small ; [-doigt, jambe, taille, main] slim, slender ; [peu épais -papier, tranche] thin ; [-collant, bas] sheer ▸ **pluie fine** drizzle ▸ **haricots verts fins** high quality green beans **2.** [délicat -visage, traits] delicate **3.** [aiguisé -pointe] sharp **4.** [de qualité -aliments, produit] high-quality, top-quality ; [-mets, repas] delicate, exquisite, refined ; [-dentelle, lingerie] delicate, fine ; [-or, pierre, vin] fine **5.** [subtil -observation, description] subtle, clever ; [-personne] perceptive, subtle ; [-esprit] sharp, keen, shrewd ; [-plaisanterie] witty / *ce n'était pas très fin de ta part* it wasn't very smart ou clever of you ▸ **c'est fin !** fam & iron very clever! / *ne joue pas au plus fin avec moi* don't try to outwit ou to outsmart me **6.** [sensible -ouïe, vue] sharp, keen, acute ; [-odorat] discriminating, sensitive **7.** (avant nom) [extrême] : *au fin fond de la campagne* in the depths of the countryside, in the middle of nowhere péj / *on ne connaîtra jamais le fin mot de l'histoire* we'll never know what really happened ou the real story **8.** *(avant nom)* [excellent] ▸ **fin connaisseur** (great) connoisseur ▸ **la fine équipe !** what a team ! ▸ **un fin gourmet** a gourmet. ❖ **fin** adv **1.** [finement -moulu] finely ; [-taillé] sharply ▸ **c'est écrit trop fin** it's written too small **2.** [tout à fait] ▸ **être fin prêt** to be ready. ❖ **fine bouche** nf [EXPR] **faire la fine bouche:** *tu ne vas pas faire la fine bouche !* don't be so choosy!

fin² [fɛ̃] nf **1.** [terme -d'une période, d'un mandat] end ; [-d'une journée, d'un match] end, close ; [-d'une course] end, finish ; [-d'un film, d'un roman] end, ending *(C)* ▸ **jusqu'à la fin des temps** ou **des siècles** until the end of time / *par une fin d'après-midi de juin* late on a June afternoon ▸ **fin mai / 2009** (at the) end of May / 2009 ▸ **mettre fin à qqch** to put an end to sthg ▸ **prendre fin** to come to an end ▸ **tirer** ou **toucher à sa fin** to come to an end, to draw to a close ▸ **fin de semaine** [QUEBEC] weekend ▸ **en voir la fin** there doesn't seem to be any end to it ▸ **avoir** ou **connaître des fins de mois difficiles** to find it hard to make ends meet (at the end of the month) **2.** [disparition] end / *ce n'est quand même pas la fin du monde !* it's not the end of the world, is it ! ▸ **c'est la fin de tout** ou **des haricots** *fam & hum* our goose is cooked! **3.** [mort] death, end ▸ **avoir une fin tragique / lente** to die a tragic / slow death **4.** [objectif] end, purpose ▸ **à cette fin** to this end, for this purpose, with that aim in mind ▸ **arriver** ou **parvenir à ses fins** to achieve one's aim ▸ **fin en soi** end in itself **5.** COMM ▸ **fins de série** oddments. ❖ **à la fin** loc adv **1.** [finalement] in the end, eventually **2.** *fam* [ton irrité] : *tu es énervant à la fin !* you're beginning to get on my nerves! ❖ **à la fin de** loc prép at the end ou close of. ❖ **à toutes fins utiles** loc adv **1.** [pour information] : *je vous signale à toutes fins utiles que...* for your information, let me point out that... **2.** [le cas échéant] just in case / *dans la boîte à gants j'avais mis à toutes fins utiles une carte de France* I had put a map of France in the glove compartment just in case. ❖ **en fin de** loc prép ▸ **en fin de soirée / match** towards [UK] ou toward [US] the end of the evening / match / *être en fin de droits* to come to the end of one's entitlement *(to an allowance)*. ❖ **en fin de compte** loc adv in the end, when all is said and done. ❖ **sans fin** ◆ loc adj [interminable] endless, interminable, never-ending. ◆ loc adv endlessly, interminably.

final, e, als ou **aux** [final, o] adj [qui termine] final, end *(modif)*. ❖ **finale** nf SPORT final. ❖ **au final** loc adv in the end.

finalement [finalmɑ̃] adv **1.** [à la fin] finally, eventually, in the end **2.** [tout compte fait] after all, when all is said and done.

finaliser [3] [finalize] vt to finalize.

finaliste [finalist] nmf JEUX, PHILOS & SPORT finalist.

finalité [finalite] nf [but] aim, purpose, end.

finance [finɑ̃s] nf [profession] : *entrer dans la finance* to enter the world of finance. ❖ **finances** nfpl **1.** ▸ **finances publiques** public finance **2.** *fam* [budget] : *mes finances sont à zéro* my finances have hit rock-bottom.

financement [finɑ̃smɑ̃] nm financing *(U)*, finance.

financer [16] [finɑ̃se] vt [journal, projet] to finance, to back (financially), to put up the finance for.

financier, ère [finɑ̃sje, ɛʀ] adj [crise, politique] financial ▸ **problèmes financiers a)** [d'un État] financial problems **b)** [d'une personne] money problems.

financièrement [finɑ̃sjɛʀmɑ̃] adv financially.

finasser [3] [finase] vi *fam* to scheme.

finaud, e [fino, od] ◆ adj cunning, shrewd, wily. ◆ nm, f : *c'est un (petit) finaud* he's a crafty ou sly one.

fine [fin] nf **1.** [eau-de-vie] ≃ brandy **2.** [huître] ▸ **fines de claire** *specially fattened greenish oysters.*

finement [finmɑ̃] adv **1.** [de façon fine -hacher, dessiner] finely **2.** [subtilement] subtly, with finesse.

finesse [finɛs] nf **1.** [délicatesse -d'un mets, d'un vin] delicacy ; [-d'une étoffe] delicacy, fineness **2.** [perspicacité] flair, finesse, shrewdness **3.** [subtilité] subtlety *(U)* ▸ **finesse d'esprit** intellectual refinement ▸ **finesse de goût** refined taste **4.** [acuité] sharpness, keenness **5.** [minceur -de la taille] slenderness, slimness ; [-des cheveux, d'une poudre] fineness ; [-du papier, d'un fil] thinness. ❖ **finesses** nfpl [subtilités] subtleties, niceties / *les finesses du français* the subtleties of the French language.

fini, e [fini] adj **1.** [perdu] finished ▸ **c'est un homme fini** he's finished **2.** *péj* [en intensif] complete, utter / *un imbécile fini* a complete ou an utter fool **3.** [accompli, terminé] finished, accomplished. ❖ **fini** nm [perfection] finish.

finir [32] [finiʀ] ◆ vt **1.** [achever -tâche, ouvrage] to finish (off) ; [-guerre, liaison] to end ; [-études] to complete ; [-période, séjour] to finish, to complete ▸ **finir de faire qqch** to finish doing sthg / *finis de faire tes devoirs* finish your homework ; *(en usage absolu) : je n'ai pas fini !* I haven't finished (what I was saying)! ▸ **c'en est fini de** sout: *c'en est bien fini de mes rêves !* that's the end of all my dreams! ▸ **en finir:** *finissons-en* let's get it over with / *il faut en finir, cette situation ne peut plus durer* we must do something to put an end to this situation / *nous devons en finir avec la crise économique* we must end the slump / *j'en aurai bientôt fini avec lui* I'll be done with him soon **2.** [plat, boisson, etc.] to finish (off ou up) / *finis ton assiette fam* eat up ou finish off what's on your plate **3.** [en réprimande] : *vous n'avez pas fini de vous plaindre ?* haven't you done enough moaning?, can't you stop moaning? / *tu n'as pas bientôt fini ?* will you stop it! ◆ vi **1.** [arriver à son terme] to finish, to end / *la route finit au pont* the road stops at the bridge / *la réunion a fini dans les hurlements* the meeting ended in uproar / *je finirai sur ce vers de Villon* let me end with this line from Villon ▸ **pour finir** in the end, finally ▸ **finir par** *(suivi d'un infinitif):* *il a fini par renoncer / réussir* he eventually ou finally gave up / succeeded / *ça finit par coûter cher* it costs a lot of money in the end ▸ **fini de rire:** *et maintenant, fini de se croiser les bras !* and now let's see some action! ▸ **n'en pas finir, n'en plus finir:** *cette journée / son discours n'en finit pas* there's no end to this day / his speech / *des plaintes à n'en plus finir* endless ou never-ending complaints **2.** [avoir telle issue] ▸ **elle a fini juge** she ended up a judge ▸ **il a mal fini** [délinquant] he came to a bad end ▸ **ça va mal finir** no good will come of it, it will all end in disaster **3.** [mourir] to die.

✏ Notez la différence entre les constructions française et anglaise :

finir de + infinitif
finish + -ing

Je dois finir de ranger mon bureau avant de partir. *I've got to finish tidying up my desk before I leave.*
As-tu fini de trier ces vieux journaux ? *Have you finished sorting through those old newspapers?*

---

finition [finisjɔ̃] nf **1.** [détail] ▸ **les finitions** the finishing touches **2.** [perfectionnement] finishing off *(U)* / *les travaux de finition prendront plusieurs jours* it will take several days to finish off the work.

finlandais, e [fɛlɑ̃dɛ,ɛz] adj Finnish. ❖ **Finlandais, e** nm, f Finn. ❖ **finlandais** nm LING Finnish.

Finlande [fɛlɑ̃d] npr f ▸ **(la) Finlande** Finland.

finnois, e [finwa,az] adj Finnish. ❖ **finnois** nm LING Finnish.

fiole [fjɔl] nf [bouteille] phial.

fioul [fjul] nm fuel oil.

firmament [fiʀmamɑ̃] nm *litt* firmament *litt*, heavens.

firme [fiʀm] nf firm, company.

fisc [fisk] nm ≃ Inland 🇬🇧 ou Internal & 🇺🇸 Revenue / *des problèmes avec le fisc* problems with the taxman.

fiscal, e, aux [fiskal, o] adj fiscal, tax *(modif)* ▸ **l'administration fiscale** the tax authorities.

fiscaliser [3] [fiskalize] vt to tax.

fiscalité [fiskalite] nf [système, législation] tax system.

fission [fisjɔ̃] nf fission.

fissure [fisyʀ] nf [fente] crack, fissure *spéc.*

fissurer [3] [fisyʀe] ❖ **se fissurer** vpi to crack.

fiston [fistɔ̃] nm *fam* son.

fitness [fitnɛs] nm fitness.

FIVETE, fivete [fivɛt] **(abr de fécondation in vitro et transfert d'embryon)** nf GIFT.

fixateur, trice [fiksatœʀ,tʀis] adj fixative. ❖ **fixateur** nm **1.** PHOT fixer **2.** ART fixative.

fixation [fiksasjɔ̃] nf **1.** [accrochage] fixing, fastening **2.** PSYCHOL fixation, obsession ▸ **faire une fixation sur qqch** to be obsessed with ou by sthg **3.** [de ski] binding.

fixe [fiks] ❖ adj **1.** [invariable - repère] fixed / *prendre un médicament à heure fixe* to take (a) medicine at a set time **2.** MIL : *(à vos rangs,) fixe !* attention! **3.** [immobile - œil, regard] fixed, staring **4.** [durable - emploi] permanent, steady **5.** ÉCON, FIN & DR [droit] fixed duty *(modif)* ; [prix] set ; [revenu, salaire] fixed. ❖ nm (fixed) ou regular salary.

fixement [fiksəmɑ̃] adv fixedly.

fixer [3] [fikse] vt **1.** [accrocher - gén] to fix ; [- par des épingles, des punaises] to pin (on) ; [- avec de l'adhésif] to tape (on) ; [- avec un fermoir, un nœud] to fasten **2.** [en regardant] to stare ▸ **fixer qqn du regard** to stare at sb / *tout le monde avait les yeux fixés sur elle* everybody was staring at her, all eyes were on her **3.** [concentrer] ▸ **fixer son attention / esprit sur qqch** to focus one's attention / mind on sthg ▸ **fixer son choix sur qqch** to decide ou to settle on sthg **4.** [définir - date, lieu] to fix, to set, to decide on *(insép)* ▸ **fixer un rendez-vous à qqn** to arrange a meeting with sb ; [règle, conditions] to lay down ; [prix] to fix, to set **5.** [informer] : *cette conversation m'a fixé sur son compte* that conversation set me straight about him ▸ **te voilà fixé !** now you know! ❖ **se fixer** vpi **1.** [s'installer] to settle / *elle s'est fixée en Irlande* she settled (permanently) in Ireland. ❖ vpt : *il s'est fixé un but dans la vie, réussir* he has (set himself) one aim in life, to succeed.

fixette [fikset] nf *fam* obsession / *elle fait une fixette sur la forme de ses oreilles* she's obsessed about the shape of her ears.

fjord, fiord* [fjɔʀd] nm fjord.

flacon [flakɔ̃] nm [de parfum, de solvant] (small) bottle ; [de spiritueux] flask.

flageller [4] [flaʒele] vt [battre] to whip.

flageoler [3] [flaʒɔle] vi [jambes] to shake, to tremble, to wobble ▸ **flageoler sur ses jambes** to sway to and fro.

flageolet [flaʒɔle] nm BOT (flageolet) bean.

flagornerie [flagɔʀnəʀi] nf *litt* fawning, flattering, toadying.

flagrant, e [flagʀɑ̃, ɑ̃t] adj **1.** [évident] blatant, obvious, flagrant **2.** DR ▸ **en flagrant délit a)** in flagrante delicto **b)** *fig* in the act, red-handed / *pris en flagrant délit de mensonge* caught lying.

flair [flɛʀ] nm **1.** [odorat] scent **2.** [perspicacité] flair / *il a du flair* he has flair.

flairer [4] [flɛʀe] vt **1.** [humer - suj : chien] to scent, to sniff at *(insép)* ; [- suj : personne] to smell **2.** [deviner] to sense ▸ **flairer le danger** to have a sense of impending danger.

flamand, e [flamɑ̃, ɑ̃d] adj Flemish. ❖ **Flamand, e** nm, f Fleming ▸ **les Flamands** the Flemish. ❖ **flamand** nm LING Flemish.

flamant [flamɑ̃] nm flamingo ▸ **flamant rose** (pink) flamingo.

flambant, e [flɑ̃bɑ̃, ɑ̃t] adj EXPR **flambant neuf** brand new.

flambé, e [flɑ̃be] adj CULIN flambéed. ❖ **flambée** nf **1.** [feu] blaze, fire / *faire une bonne flambée* to get a roaring fire going **2.** *fig* [poussée] ▸ **une flambée de violence** an outbreak ou a sudden wave of violence ▸ **la flambée des prix** the leap in prices.

flambeau, x [flɑ̃bo] nm [torche] torch ; [chandelier] candlestick ; *fig* torch ▸ **passer** ou **transmettre le flambeau** to pass on the torch ▸ **reprendre le flambeau** to take up the torch.

flamber [3] [flɑ̃be] ❖ vt CULIN [lapin, volaille] to singe ; [omelette] to flambé. ❖ vi **1.** [se consumer] to burn (brightly) **2.** [briller] to flash **3.** *fam* [augmenter - prix] to rocket, to soar **4.** *fam* [jouer] to gamble (for big stakes).

flamboyant, e [flɑ̃bwajɑ̃, ɑ̃t] adj **1.** [brillant - foyer] blazing, flaming ; [- regard] flashing **2.** ARCHIT flamboyant *spéc* ▸ **le gothique flamboyant** high Gothic style.

flamme [flam] nf **1.** [feu] flame ▸ **la flamme olympique** the Olympic flame **2.** [litt] [éclat] fire / *dans la flamme de son regard* in her fiery eyes **3.** [ferveur] fervour 🇬🇧, fervor 🇺🇸, fire ▸ **discours plein de flamme** impassioned speech **4.** *arch* ou *litt* [amour] ardour 🇬🇧, ardor 🇺🇸. ❖ **en flammes** ❖ loc adj burning, blazing. ❖ loc adv : *l'avion est tombé en flammes* the plane went down in flames.

flan [flɑ̃] nm **1.** CULIN (baked) egg custard **2.** *fam* EXPR *c'est du flan !* it's a load of bunkum ou bunk!

flanc [flɑ̃] nm **1.** ANAT [entre les côtes et le bassin] flank ; [côté du corps] side **2.** ZOOL flank, side **3.** [côté - d'un navire] side ; [- d'une colline] side, slope **4.** MIL flank **5.** EXPR **tirer au flanc** to be bone-idle. ❖ **à flanc de** loc prép ▸ **à flanc de coteau** on the hillside.

flancher [3] [flɑ̃ʃe] vi **1.** [faiblir] to give out, to fail **2.** [manquer de courage] to waver / *ce n'est vraiment pas le moment de flancher* this is really no time for weakness.

Flandre [flɑ̃dʀ] npr f ▸ **(la) Flandre, (les) Flandres** Flanders.

flanelle [flanɛl] nf TEXT flannel.

flâner [3] [flane] vi [se promener] to stroll ou to amble (along).

flânerie [flɑnʀi] nf stroll, wander.

flâneur, euse [flɑnœʀ, øz] nm, f stroller.

flanquer [3] [flɑ̃ke] vt **1.** *fam* [lancer] to fling, to throw, to chuck ▸ **flanquer qqn dehors** ou **à la porte a)** [l'expulser] to kick sb out **b)** [le licencier] to kick 🇬🇧 ou to can 🇺🇸 sb ▸ **flanquer qqch par terre** : *il a flanqué les bouquins par terre* **a)** [volontairement] he chucked the books on the floor **b)** [par maladresse] he knocked the books onto the floor / *j'ai tellement voulu réussir et toi tu vas tout flanquer par terre* fig I wanted to succeed so badly and now you're going to mess it all up (for me) **2.** *fam* [donner]

* In reformed spelling (see p. 16-18).

▸ **flanquer une gifle à qqn** to smack ou to slap sb ▸ **flanquer la trouille** ou **frousse à qqn** to scare the pants off sb **3.** [être à côté de] to flank **4.** *fam & péj* [accompagner] ▸ **être flanqué de** : *elle est arrivée, flanquée de ses deux frères* she came in with her two brothers at her side ou flanked by her two brothers.

flaque [flak] nf puddle ▸ **une large flaque d'huile** a pool of oil.

flash [flaʃ] (*pl* **flashs** ou **flashes**) nm **1.** PHOT [éclair] flash ; [ampoule] flash bulb / *prendre une photo au flash* to take a picture using a flash **2.** RADIO & TV ▸ **flash (d'informations)** newsflash.

Flash-Ball® [flaʃbol] nm [arme] ≃ baton gun ; [projectile] ≃ baton round.

flasher [3] [flaʃe] ◆ vi **1.** [clignoter] to flash (on and off) **2.** *fam* [craquer] : *elle me fait flasher, cette nana !* that girl really turns me on! ◆ vt AUTO ▸ **se faire flasher** to be caught on a speed camera. ◆ **flasher sur** v + prép *fam* to go crazy over.

flashy [flaʃi] adj inv flashy.

flasque¹ [flask] adj [muscle, peau] flaccid, flabby.

flasque² [flask] nf [pour whisky] (hip) flask.

flatter [3] [flate] vt **1.** [encenser] to flatter **2.** [toucher] to touch, to flatter. ◆ **se flatter** vpi : *sans vouloir me flatter, je crois que j'ai raison* though I say it myself, I think I'm right / *elle se flatte de savoir recevoir* she prides herself on knowing how to entertain ou on her skills as a hostess.

flatterie [flatʀi] nf **1.** [adulation] flattery **2.** [propos] flattering remark ▸ **flatteries** sweet talk.

flatteur, euse [flatœʀ, øz] ◆ adj flattering. ◆ nm, f flatterer.

flatulence [flatylɑ̃s] nf flatulence.

fléau, x [fleo] nm [désastre] curse, plague.

flèche [flɛʃ] nf **1.** ARM [projectile] arrow ▸ **partir comme une flèche** to shoot off ; [d'un canon] trail **2.** [signe] arrow **3.** ARCHIT [d'un arc] broach ; [d'un clocher] spire **4.** MÉCAN [d'une grue] boom. ◆ **en flèche** loc adv [spectaculairement] : *les tarifs montent en flèche* prices are rocketing.

flécher [18] [fleʃe] vt to mark with arrows, to signpost.

✐ In reformed spelling (see p. 16-18), this verb is conjugated like *semer* : *il flèchera, elle flècherait.*

fléchette [fleʃɛt] nf dart / *jouer aux fléchettes* to play darts.

fléchir [32] [fleʃiʀ] ◆ vt **1.** [ployer] to bend, to flex **2.** [apitoyer - juge, tribunal] to move to pity ▸ **se laisser fléchir** to relent. ◆ vi **1.** [se ployer] to bend / *elle sentait ses genoux fléchir sous elle* she could feel her knees giving way **2.** [baisser] to fall / *le dollar a de nouveau fléchi* the dollar has fallen again **3.** [céder] to weaken / *leur père ne fléchissait jamais* their father was utterly inflexible.

fléchissement [fleʃismɑ̃] nm **1.** [flexion - d'une partie du corps] flexing, bending **2.** [affaiblissement - des genoux] sagging ; [- de la nuque] drooping **3.** [baisse] fall ▸ **fléchissement de la demande** drop in demand / *fléchissement de la production / natalité* fall in production / in the birthrate.

flegmatique [flɛgmatik] adj phlegmatic.

flegme [flɛgm] nm phlegm, composure.

flemmard, e [flemaʀ, aʀd] *fam* ◆ adj idle, lazy, workshy. ◆ nm, f idler, loafer.

flemmarder [3] [flemaʀde] vi *fam* to loaf about.

flemme [flɛm] nf *fam* idleness, laziness.

flétan [fletɑ̃] nm halibut.

flétrir [32] [fletʀiʀ] vt BOT to wither, to wilt. ◆ **se flétrir** vpi **1.** BOT to wither, to wilt **2.** *litt* [peau] to wither ; [couleur, beauté] to fade.

fleur [flœʀ] nf **1.** BOT flower ; [d'un arbre] blossom ▸ **une robe à fleurs** a flowery dress, a dress with a flower motif ▸ **fleur d'oranger a)** [fleur] orange flower **b)** [essence] orange flower water **2.** *fig* ▸ **la fleur de** [le meilleur de] : *la fleur de l'âge* the prime of life ▸ **la fine fleur de** [l'élite de] : *c'est la fine fleur de l'école* he's the pride of his school **3.** HÉRALD ▸ **fleur de lis** ou **lys** fleur-de-lis **4.** EXPR arriver comme une fleur to turn up out of the blue ▸ **faire une fleur à qqn** *fam* to do sb an unexpected favour ou a favour ▸ **faire qqch comme une fleur** to do sthg almost without trying. ◆ **fleurs** nfpl [louanges] ▸ **couvrir qqn de fleurs** to praise sb highly ▸ **s'envoyer** ou **se jeter des fleurs a)** *fam* [mutuellement] to sing one another's praises, to pat one another on the back **b)** [à soi-même] to pat o.s. on the back. ◆ **à fleur de** loc prép on the surface of ▸ **à fleur d'eau** just above the surface (of the water) / *une sensibilité à fleur de peau* hypersensitivity. ◆ **en fleur(s)** loc adj [rose, pivoine] in flower ou bloom, blooming ; [arbre, arbuste] blossoming, in blossom. ◆ **fleur bleue** loc adj sentimental.

fleurer [5] [flœʀe] ◆ vt *litt* to smell of. ◆ vi ▸ **fleurer bon** to smell nice.

fleuret [flœʀɛ] nm ESCRIME foil.

fleuri, e [flœʀi] adj **1.** [arbre, arbuste] in bloom ou blossom ▸ **un balcon fleuri** a balcony decorated with flowers **2.** [orné de fleurs] flowered, flowery **3.** [conversation, style] flowery, overornate.

fleurir [32] [flœʀiʀ] ◆ vi **1.** BOT [rose, pivoine] to flower, to bloom ; [arbre, arbuste] to flower, to blossom **2.** [apparaître] to burgeon **3.** [se développer - affaire, commerce] to flourish, to thrive. ◆ vt to decorate with flowers ▸ **fleurir la tombe de qqn** to put flowers on sb's grave.

fleuriste [flœʀist] nmf [vendeur] florist.

fleuron [flœʀɔ̃] nm [ornement - de reliure] flower, fleuron ; [- en pierre] finial / *le (plus beau) fleuron de...* *fig* the jewel of... / *on a volé le fleuron de sa collection d'émeraudes* the finest emerald in his collection has been stolen.

fleuve [flœv] nm **1.** [rivière] river *(flowing into the sea)* **2.** [écoulement] ▸ **un fleuve de** : *un fleuve de boue* a river of mud, a mudslide **3.** *(comme adjectif, avec ou sans trait d'union)* ▸ **une lettre fleuve** a very long letter.

flexibilité [fleksibilite] nf [d'un arrangement, d'un horaire] flexibility, adaptability ; [d'un dispositif] versatility.

flexible [fleksibl] adj **1.** [pliable] pliable, flexible **2.** [variable - arrangement, horaire] flexible ; [- dispositif] versatile.

flexion [fleksjɔ̃] nf **1.** [des membres] flexing *(U)* ▸ **flexion, extension !** bend, stretch! **2.** LING inflection.

flibustier [flibystje] nm freebooter, buccaneer.

flic [flik] nmf *fam* cop.

flicage [flikaʒ] nm *fam & péj* surveillance / *le flicage des réseaux* network surveillance / *le patron parle de contrôle qualité, les employés parlent de flicage* the boss calls it quality control but the staff think it's just a way of keeping tabs on them.

flingue [flɛ̃g] nm *tfam* piece, gat US.

flinguer [3] [flɛ̃ge] vt *tfam* to blow away *(sép)*, to waste.

flipper¹ [flipœʀ] nm pinball machine.

flipper² [3] [flipe] vi *tfam* **1.** [être déprimé] to feel down / *lui raconte pas tes malheurs, tu vas le faire flipper* don't go telling him your troubles, it'll only get him down **2.** [paniquer] to flip.

fliquer [3] [flike] vt *fam* to keep under surveillance / *son chef n'arrête pas de le fliquer* his boss is always keeping tabs on him.

flirt [flœʀt] nm *vieilli* **1.** [relation] (little) fling **2.** [ami] boyfriend ; [amie] girlfriend.

flirter [3] [flœʀte] vi [badiner] to flirt.

flocon [flɔkɔ̃] nm [parcelle - de laine, de coton] flock ; [- de neige] snowflake, flake ▸ **flocons d'avoine** oatmeal ▸ **flocons de pommes de terre** instant mashed potato mix.

flop [flɔp] nm *fam* flop.

flopée [flɔpe] nf *fam* ▸ **une flopée de** a whole bunch of.

floraison [flɔʀezɔ̃] nf **1.** BOT [éclosion] blooming, blossoming, flowering ; [saison] flowering time **2.** [apparition - d'artistes, d'œuvres] : *il y a actuellement une floraison de publicités pour des banques* at present there is something of a rash of advertisements for banks.

floral, e, aux [flɔʀal, o] adj [décor] floral ; [exposition] flower *(modif)*.

floralies [flɔʀali] nfpl flower show.

flore [flɔʀ] nf **1.** [végétation] flora **2.** MÉD ▸ **flore intestinale** intestinal flora.

Florence [flɔʀɑ̃s] npr Florence.

florentin, e [flɔʀɑ̃tɛ̃, in] adj Florentine. ❖ **Florentin, e** nm, f Florentine.

Floride [flɔʀid] npr f ▸ **(la) Floride** Florida.

florilège [flɔʀilɛʒ] nm anthology.

florissant, e [flɔʀisɑ̃, ɑ̃t] adj [affaire, plante] thriving, flourishing ; [santé] blooming.

flot [flo] nm [de larmes, de paroles] flood ; [de boue] stream ▸ **un flot de gens** a stream of people. ❖ **flots** nmpl *litt* ▸ **les flots** the waves. ❖ **à flot** loc adv **1.** NAUT : *remettre un bateau à flot* to refloat a boat ; [sorti de difficultés financières] : *je suis à flot maintenant* I'm back on an even keel now ▸ **remettre à flot** [personne, entreprise] to get back on an even keel. ❖ **à flots** loc adv in floods ou torrents / *le champagne coulait à flots* champagne flowed like water.

flottaison [flɔtezɔ̃] nf **1.** [sur l'eau] buoyancy **2.** FIN floating.

flottant, e [flɔtɑ̃, ɑ̃t] adj **1.** [sur l'eau - épave, mine] floating **2.** [ondoyant - chevelure] flowing ; [- drapeau] billowing **3.** FIN floating.

flotte [flɔt] nf **1.** AÉRON & NAUT fleet **2.** *fam* [pluie] rain ; [eau] water.

flottement [flɔtmɑ̃] nm **1.** [incertitude] indecisiveness, wavering *(U)* / *on note un certain flottement dans ses réponses* his answers seem hesitant ou indecisive **2.** [imprécision] looseness, imprecision.

flotter [3] [flɔte] ❖ vi **1.** [surnager] to float **2.** [être en suspension] to hang / *une bonne odeur de soupe flottait dans la cuisine* the kitchen was filled with a delicious smell of soup **3.** [ondoyer - banderole] to flap, to flutter ▸ **ses cheveux flottent au vent / sur ses épaules** her hair is streaming in the wind / hangs loose over her shoulders **4.** [être trop large] to flap (around) ; [être au large] : *elle flotte dans sa robe* she's lost in that dress, her dress is too big for her **5.** [hésiter] to hesitate. ❖ v impers *fam* [pleuvoir] to rain.

flotteur [flɔtœʀ] nm ball, float.

flou, e [flu] adj **1.** [imprécis - souvenir] blurred, hazy ; [- renseignements] vague **2.** [souple - vêtement] ample, flowing, loose-fitting ; [- coiffure] soft. ❖ **flou** nm **1.** CINÉ & PHOT blurredness, fuzziness / *il entretient un certain flou artistique* *fig* he's being fairly vague about it **2.** [imprécision] vagueness.

flouer [3] [flue] vt *fam* to rook, to con / *il s'est fait flouer* he was conned.

flouter [flute] vt PHOT & TV to blur.

fluctuant, e [flyktɥɑ̃, ɑ̃t] adj fluctuating.

fluctuation [flyktɥasjɔ̃] nf fluctuation.

fluctuer [3] [flyktɥe] vi to fluctuate.

fluet, ette [flyɛ, ɛt] adj [personne] slender, slim ; [voix] reedy.

fluide [flɥid] ❖ adj **1.** CHIM fluid **2.** [qui coule facilement] fluid, smooth / *la circulation est fluide* there are no hold-ups (in the traffic) / *en un style fluide* in flowing style **3.** [fluctuant - situation] fluctuating, changeable ; [- pensée] elusive **4.** [flou - forme, blouse, robe] flowing. ❖ nm **1.** CHIM fluid **2.** [d'un médium] aura ▸ **il a du fluide** he has occult powers.

fluidité [flɥidite] nf [qualité - d'une crème, d'une sauce] smoothness, fluidity / *grâce à la fluidité de la circulation* because there were no hold-ups in the traffic.

fluo [flyo] adj fluorescent, Day-Glo®.

fluor [flyɔʀ] nm fluorine ▸ **dentifrice au fluor** fluoride toothpaste.

fluoré, e [flyɔʀe] adj fluoridated.

fluorescent, e [flyɔʀesɑ̃, ɑ̃t] adj fluorescent.

flûte, flute* [flyt] ❖ nf **1.** [instrument] flute ▸ **flûte à bec** recorder ▸ **flûte de Pan** panpipe ▸ **flûte traversière** flute **2.** [verre] flute (glass) **3.** [pain] thin loaf of French bread. ❖ interj *fam* drat, damn.

flûtiste, flutiste* [flytist] nmf flautist, flutist US.

fluvial, e, aux [flyvjal, o] adj [érosion] fluvial ; [navigation] river *(modif)*.

flux [fly] nm **1.** [marée] incoming tide / *le flux et le reflux* the ebb and flow **2.** [écoulement - d'un liquide] flow ; [- du sang menstruel] menstrual flow **3.** [abondance] ▸ **un flux de** : *noyé dans un flux de paroles* carried away by a stream of words **4.** PHYS flux ▸ **flux magnétique** magnetic flux **5.** ÉCON ▸ **travailler en flux tendus** to use just-in-time methods ou planning **6.** FIN ▸ **flux monétaire** flow of money ▸ **flux de trésorerie** cash flow.

FM (abr de **frequency modulation**) nf FM.

FMI (abr de **Fonds monétaire international**) npr m IMF.

fo SMS abr écrite de **faut**.

FO (abr de **Force ouvrière**) npr f *moderate workers' union (formed out of the split with Communist CGT in 1948)*.

foc [fɔk] nm jib.

focal, e, aux [fɔkal, o] adj [central] : *point focal d'un raisonnement* main ou central point in an argument. ❖ **focale** nf OPT & PHOT focal distance ou length.

focaliser [3] [fɔkalize] ❖ **se focaliser sur** vp + prép to be focussed ou to focus on.

fœtus [fetys] nm foetus UK, fetus US.

foi [fwa] nf **1.** RELIG faith ▸ **avoir la foi** to have faith ▸ **n'avoir ni** ou **être sans foi ni loi** to fear neither God nor man **2.** [confiance] faith, trust ▸ **avoir foi en** ou **dans qqn** to have faith in ou to trust (in) sb **3.** [preuve] : *il n'y a qu'une pièce officielle qui fasse foi* only an official paper is valid ▸ **EXPR** **ma foi!** well! ❖ **sous la foi de** loc prép : *sous la foi du serment* on ou under oath. ❖ **sur la foi de** loc prép ▸ **sur la foi de ses déclarations / de sa réputation** on the strength of his statement / of his reputation. ❖ **bonne foi** nf ▸ **être de bonne foi** to be sincere / *il a agi en toute bonne foi* he acted in good faith. ❖ **mauvaise foi** nf ▸ **être de mauvaise foi** to be insincere.

foie [fwa] nm **1.** ANAT liver **2.** CULIN liver ▸ **foie gras** foie gras ▸ **foie de veau** calf's liver *(from a milk-fed animal)* ▸ **foie de volaille** chicken liver.

foin [fwɛ̃] nm **1.** AGR hay **2.** **EXPR** **faire du foin a)** *fam* [être bruyant] to make a din **b)** [faire un scandale] to kick up a fuss.

foire [fwaʀ] nf **1.** [marché] fair **2.** [exposition] trade fair **3.** [fête foraine] funfair UK, carnival US **4.** *fam* [désordre] mess / *c'est une vraie foire dans cette maison !* this house is a real dump! / *faire la foire* to live it up 5. EXPR **foire d'empoigne** free-for-all.

foire-exposition [fwaʀɛkspozisjɔ̃] (*pl* foires-expositions) nf trade fair.

foirer [3] [fwaʀe] vi *fam* [rater] to fall through.

foireux, euse [fwaʀø, øz] adj *fam & péj* [mal fait] : *cette bagnole foireuse* this wreck of a car.

fois [fwa] nf 1. [exprime la fréquence] **une fois** once **deux fois** twice **trois fois** three times, thrice *litt* **payer en plusieurs fois** to pay in instalments **payez en six fois** pay in six instalments / *neuf fois sur dix, quatre-vingt-dix-neuf fois sur cent* nine times out of ten, ninety-nine times out of a hundred **pour une fois** for once / *une (bonne) fois pour toutes* once and for all / *cette fois, je gagnerai* this time, I'll win / *(à) chaque fois que, toutes les fois que* every ou each time / *la fois suivante* ou *d'après* the time after that **deux cents euros une fois, deux fois, trois fois, adjugé, vendu !** two hundred euros, going, going, gone! **une fois n'est pas coutume** just the once won't hurt **il était une fois** : *il était une fois un roi* once upon a time there was a king 2. [dans les comparaisons] time / *c'est trois fois plus grand* it's three times as big / *il y a dix fois moins de spectateurs que l'année dernière* there are ten times fewer spectators than last year 3. (*comme distributif*) **deux fois par mois** twice a month **une fois par semaine** once a week / *trois fois par an, trois fois l'an* three times a year 4. MATH times / *15 fois 34* 15 times 34 5. EXPR *tu n'as qu'à venir une fois ton travail terminé* just come as soon as your work is finished **une fois que:** *une fois que tu auras compris, tout sera plus facile* once you've understood, you'll find everything's easier **des fois** *fam* [parfois] sometimes / *non mais des fois !* honestly! / *je préfère l'appeler, des fois qu'elle aurait oublié* I'd rather call her in case she's forgotten. ❖ **à la fois** loc adv together, at a time, at the same time / *pas tous à la fois !* one at a time!, not all at once!

foison [fwazɔ̃] ❖ **à foison** loc adv *litt* galore, plenty / *il y a de quoi boire à foison* there's drinks galore.

foisonnement [fwazɔnmɑ̃] nm [de la végétation, d'idées] abundance, proliferation.

foisonner [3] [fwazɔne] vi [abonder] to abound / *une œuvre où les idées foisonnent* a work rich in ideas / *notre littérature foisonne en jeunes auteurs de talent* our literature abounds in ou is full of talented young authors.

fol [fɔl] m ⟶ fou.

folâtrer [3] [fɔlatʀe] vi to frolic, to fool around.

folichon, onne [fɔliʃɔ̃, ɔn] adj *fam* **pas folichon** not much fun.

folie [fɔli] nf 1. MÉD [démence] madness 2. [déraison] madness, lunacy **c'est de la folie**: *c'est de la folie douce que de vouloir la raisonner* it's sheer lunacy to try to reason with her / *sortir par ce temps, c'est de la folie furieuse !* it's (sheer) madness to go out in weather like this! **avoir la folie des grandeurs** to suffer from ou to have delusions of grandeur 3. [acte déraisonnable] crazy thing to do, folly *litt* **faire des folies** [dépenser] to be extravagant. ❖ **à la folie** loc adv passionately, to distraction **aimer qqn à la folie** to be madly in love with sb, to love sb to distraction.

folk [fɔlk] ❖ adj folk (*modif*). ❖ nm folk music.

folklo [fɔlklo] adj inv *fam* weird / *c'est un type plutôt folklo* he's a bit of a weirdo.

folklore [fɔlklɔʀ] nm DANSE & MUS **le folklore** folklore.

folklorique [fɔlklɔʀik] adj 1. DANSE & MUS folk (*modif*) 2. *fam* [insolite, ridicule] bizarre, weird.

folle [fɔl] f ⟶ fou.

follement [fɔlmɑ̃] adv 1. [excessivement] madly **s'amuser follement** to have a great time 2. [déraisonnablement] madly, wildly.

follet [fɔlɛ] adj m ⟶ feu.

fomenter [3] [fɔmɑ̃te] vt *litt* to foment *litt*, to cause.

foncé, e [fɔ̃se] adj dark, deep.

foncer [16] [fɔ̃se] ❖ vi 1. [s'élancer] to charge **foncer contre** ou **sur son adversaire** to rush at one's adversary 2. *fam* [se déplacer très vite] to speed along / *il a foncé à l'hôpital* he rushed straight to the hospital 3. *fam* [se hâter] : *nous avons tous foncé pour boucler le journal* we all rushed to finish the newspaper in time 4. [teinte] to go darker. ❖ vt [teinte] to make darker, to darken.

fonceur, euse [fɔ̃sœʀ, øz] nm, f dynamic type.

foncier, ère [fɔ̃sje, ɛʀ] adj 1. ADMIN & FIN [impôt, politique, problème] land (*modif*) **propriétaire foncier** landowner 2. [fondamental] fundamental, basic.

foncièrement [fɔ̃sjɛʀmɑ̃] adv 1. [fondamentalement] fundamentally, basically 2. [totalement] deeply, profoundly.

fonction [fɔ̃ksjɔ̃] nf 1. [emploi] office **entrer en fonction** ou **fonctions** to take up one's post **faire fonction de** to act as / *est-ce que cela entre dans tes fonctions ?* is this part of your duties? **prendre ses fonctions** to take up one's post 2. [rôle] function / *la pièce a pour fonction de maintenir l'équilibre de la balance* the part serves to keep the scales balanced 3. **être fonction de** [dépendre de]: *sa venue est fonction de son travail* whether he comes or not depends on his work. ❖ **de fonction** loc adj **appartement** ou **logement de fonction** tied accommodation 🇬🇧, accommodation that goes with the job **voiture de fonction** company car. ❖ **en fonction de** loc prép according to. ❖ **fonction publique** nf **la fonction publique** the civil ou public service.

fonctionnaire [fɔ̃ksjɔnɛʀ] nmf civil servant **haut fonctionnaire** senior civil servant.

Fonctionnaire

This term covers a broader range of public service employees than the term "civil servant": from high-ranking members of the state administration to public-sector teachers and post-office workers.

fonctionnalité [fɔ̃ksjɔnalite] nf [de téléphone, d'ordinateur] feature.

fonctionnel, elle [fɔ̃ksjɔnɛl] adj 1. MATH, MÉD & PSYCHOL functional 2. [adapté] practical, functional.

fonctionnement [fɔ̃ksjɔnmɑ̃] nm functioning, working / *pour assurer le bon fonctionnement de votre machine à laver* to keep your washing machine in good working order ; [d'une entreprise] running.

fonctionner [3] [fɔ̃ksjɔne] vi [mécanisme, engin] to function, to work ; [métro, véhicule] to run / *le moteur fonctionne mal / bien* the engine isn't / is working properly **faire fonctionner une machine** to operate a machine / *je n'arrive pas à faire fonctionner la machine à laver* I can't get the washing machine to work / *les freins n'ont pas fonctionné* the brakes failed ; [personne] to function ; [entreprise] to run.

fond [fɔ̃] nm 1. [d'un récipient] bottom ; [d'un placard] back ; [extrémité] bottom, far end ; [de la gorge] back ; [d'une pièce] far end, back ; [d'un jardin] far end, bottom **sans fond** bottomless / *il y a cinq mètres de fond* [de profondeur] the water is five metres deep ou in depth / *couler par 100 m de fond* to sink to a depth of 100 m **les grands**

fonds marins the depths of the ocean ▸ **gratter** ou **vider** ou **racler les fonds de tiroir** *fam & fig* to scrape around *(for money, food, etc.)* **2.** *fig* depths / *toucher le fond (du désespoir)* to reach the depths of despair / *je vous remercie du fond du cœur* I thank you from the bottom of my heart **3.** [cœur, substance] heart, core, nub / *puis-je te dire le fond de ma pensée ?* can I tell you what I really think? / *le fond et la forme* LITTÉR substance and form **4.** [tempérament] : *il a un bon fond* he's basically a good ou kind person **5.** [arrière-plan] background ▸ **fond de vérité**: *il y a un fond de vérité dans ce que vous dites* there's some truth in what you're saying ▸ **fond sonore** background music ▸ **le fond de l'air est frais** there's a chill ou nip in the air **6.** [reste] drop **7.** CULIN ▸ **fond d'artichaut** artichoke heart ▸ **fond de tarte** pastry case. ❖ **à fond** *loc adv* in depth ▸ **respirer à fond** to breathe deeply / *faire le ménage à fond dans la maison* to clean the house thoroughly, to spring-clean. ❖ **au fond** *loc adv* basically. ❖ **au fond de** *loc prép* ▸ **au fond de soi-même** deep down ▸ *c'est au fond du couloir / de la salle* it's at the (far) end of the corridor / of the hall / *au fond de la rivière* at the bottom of the river. ❖ **dans le fond** = **au fond**. ❖ **de fond** *loc adj* **1.** SPORT [épreuve, coureur, course] long-distance *(avant nom)* ▸ **ski de fond** cross-country skiing **2.** [analyse, remarque, texte] basic, fundamental. ❖ **de fond en comble** *loc adv* [nettoyer, fouiller] from top to bottom / *revoir un texte de fond en comble* *fig* to revise a text thoroughly. ❖ **fond de teint** *nm* (make-up) foundation.

fondamental, e, aux [fɔ̃damɑ̃tal, o] *adj* **1.** SCI fundamental, basic **2.** [de base] elementary, basic **3.** [important] fundamental, essential, crucial.

fondamentalement [fɔ̃damɑ̃talmɑ̃] *adv* fundamentally / *c'est fondamentalement la même chose* it's basically the same thing ▸ **fondamentalement opposés** radically opposed.

fondamentalisme [fɔ̃damɑ̃talism] *nm* (religious) fundamentalism.

fondamentaliste [fɔ̃damɑ̃talist] ◆ *adj* fundamentalist, fundamentalistic. ◆ *nmf* fundamentalist.

fondant, e [fɔ̃dɑ̃, ɑ̃t] *adj* **1.** [glace, neige] melting, thawing **2.** [aliment] ▸ **un rôti fondant** a tender roast ▸ **un bonbon / chocolat fondant** a sweet / chocolate that melts in the mouth.

fondateur, trice [fɔ̃datœr, tʀis] *nm, f* [gén] founder.

fondation [fɔ̃dasjɔ̃] *nf* **1.** [création - d'une ville, d'une société] foundation ; [- d'une bourse, d'un prix] establishment, creation **2.** [institution] foundation. ❖ **fondations** *nfpl* CONSTR foundations.

fondé, e [fɔ̃de] *adj* [argument, peur] justified / *un reproche non fondé* an unjustified reproach. ❖ **fondé de pouvoir** *nm* proxy.

fondement [fɔ̃dmɑ̃] *nm* [base] foundation / *jeter les fondements d'une nouvelle politique* to lay the foundations of a new policy. ❖ **sans fondement** *loc adj* [crainte, rumeur] groundless, unfounded.

fonder [3] [fɔ̃de] *vt* **1.** [construire - empire, parti] to found ▸ **fonder un foyer** ou **une famille** *sout* to start a family **2.** COMM to found, to set up / **'maison fondée en 1930'** 'Established 1930' **3.** [appuyer]: *elle fondait tous ses espoirs sur son fils* she pinned all her hopes on her son **4.** [légitimer - réclamation, plainte] to justify. ❖ **se fonder sur** *vp + prép* **1.** [se prévaloir de] to base o.s. on **2.** [remarque, théorie] to be based on.

fonderie [fɔ̃dʀi] *nf* [atelier] foundry.

fondeur, euse [fɔ̃dœr, øz] *nm, f* SPORT langläufer, cross-country skier.

fondre [75] [fɔ̃dʀ] ◆ *vt* **1.** [rendre liquide] to melt ▸ **fondre de l'or / de l'argent** to smelt gold / silver **2.** [fabriquer - statue, canon, cloche] to cast, to found **3.** [dissoudre] to dissolve **4.** [combiner - couleurs] to blend, to merge ; [- sociétés] to combine, to merge. ◆ *vi* **1.** [se liquéfier] to melt / *faites fondre le chocolat* melt the chocolate ▸ **fondre comme cire** ou **neige au soleil** to vanish into thin air **2.** [se dissoudre] to dissolve ▸ **faire fondre du sucre** to dissolve sugar ▸ **fondre dans la bouche** to melt in the mouth **3.** [s'affaiblir - animosité, rage] to melt away, to disappear ▸ **fondre en larmes** to dissolve into tears **4.** *fam* [maigrir] to get thin / *il fond à vue d'œil* the weight's dropping off him. ❖ **fondre sur** *v + prép* to sweep ou to swoop down on. ❖ **se fondre** *vpi* [se mêler] to merge, to mix ▸ **se fondre dans la nuit / le brouillard** to disappear into the night / mist.

fonds [fɔ̃] ◆ *nm* **1.** [propriété] business ▸ **un fonds de commerce** a business **2.** FIN fund ▸ **fonds de pension** pension fund ▸ **fonds de prévoyance** contingency fund **3.** [ressources] collection. ◆ *nmpl* **1.** FIN funds / *prêter de l'argent à fonds perdus* to loan money without security ▸ **fonds publics** public funds **2.** [argent] money.

fondu, e [fɔ̃dy] ◆ *pp* ⟶ **fondre**. ◆ *adj* **1.** [liquéfié] melted ; MÉTALL molten ▸ **de la neige fondue** slush **2.** [ramolli] melted **3.** ART [teinte] blending. ❖ **fondu** *nm* CINÉ dissolve ▸ **fondu enchaîné** fade-in fade-out. ❖ **fondue** *nf* CULIN ▸ **fondue bourguignonne** meat fondue ▸ **fondue savoyarde** (Swiss) cheese fondue.

fongicide [fɔ̃ʒisid] *nm* fungicide.

fontaine [fɔ̃tɛn] *nf* **1.** [édifice] fountain **2.** [source] spring.

fonte [fɔ̃t] *nf* **1.** MÉTALL cast iron **2.** [fusion - gén] melting ; [- du métal] smelting ; [- des neiges] thawing ▸ **à la fonte des neiges** when the snow thaws.

fonts [fɔ̃] *nmpl* ▸ **fonts (baptismaux)** (baptismal) font.

foot [fut] *nm fam* football UK, soccer / *jouer au foot* to play football.

football [futbol] *nm* football UK, soccer ▸ **jouer au football** to play football ▸ **football américain** American football UK, football US.

footballeur, euse [futbolœr, øz] *nm, f* footballer UK, soccer player US.

footballistique [futbalistik] *adj* football-related.

footeux, euse [futø, øz] *nm, f fam* footy-fan.

footing [futiŋ] *nm* ▸ **le footing** jogging / *faire un footing* to go jogging, to go for a jog.

for [fɔr] *nm* ▸ **en mon for intérieur** deep down ou inside, in my heart of hearts.

forage [fɔraʒ] *nm* [d'un puits de pétrole] boring, drilling ; [d'un puits, d'une mine] sinking.

forain, e [fɔrɛ̃, ɛn] ◆ *adj* [boutique] fairground *(modif)*. ◆ *nm, f* stallholder.

forçat [fɔrsa] *nm* HIST [sur une galère] galley slave ; [dans un bagne] convict ▸ **travailler comme un forçat** to work like a slave.

force [fɔrs] *nf* **1.** [puissance - d'une tempête, d'un coup] strength, force ; [- d'un sentiment] strength ; [- d'une idée, d'un argument] strength, power ▸ **avec force** forcefully / *un vent (de) force 7* MÉTÉOR a force 7 wind ▸ **les forces du mal** the forces of evil **2.** [vigueur physique] strength ▸ **avoir beaucoup de force** to be very strong ▸ **avoir la force de faire qqch** to have the strength to do sthg / *reprendre des forces* to regain one's strength / *c'est au-dessus de mes forces* it's beyond me ▸ **de toutes mes / ses forces** with all my / his strength, with all my / his might ▸ **être une force de la nature** to be a mighty force ▸ **être dans la force de l'âge** to be in the prime of life **3.** [contrainte, autorité] force /

vaincre par la force to win by (using) force / *avoir recours à la force* to resort to force ▸ **force majeure** DR force majeure / *c'est un cas de force majeure* it's completely unavoidable ▸ **un coup de force** POL & ÉCON a takeover by force **4.** [puissance morale] strength / *ce qui fait sa force, c'est sa conviction politique* his political commitment is his strength ; [groupe de personnes] ▸ **force de vente** sales force ▸ **force de caractère** strength of character **5.** ADMIN & MIL ▸ **la force nucléaire stratégique** ou **la force de frappe** ou **la force de dissuasion de la France** France's nuclear strike capacity ▸ **les forces armées** the (armed) forces ▸ **force d'intervention** task force ▸ **la force publique, les forces de l'ordre** the police **6.** [suprématie] strength, might / *occuper une position de force* to be in a position of strength **7.** PHYS force ▸ **force centrifuge / centripète** centrifugal / centripetal force. ❖ **à force** loc adv *fam* : *tu vas le casser, à force !* you'll break it if you go on like that! / *à force, je suis fatigué* I'm getting tired. ❖ **à force de** loc prép by dint of / *à force de parler* by dint of talking. ❖ **à la force de** loc prép by the strength of / *s'élever à la force du poignet* fig to go up in the world by the sweat of one's brow. ❖ **de force** loc adv by force / *on les a fait sortir de force* they were made to leave. ❖ **en force** loc adv [en nombre] in force, in large numbers / *ils sont arrivés en force* they arrived in force ou in great numbers.

forcé, e [fɔʀse] adj **1.** [obligé] forced ▸ **atterrissage forcé** emergency ou forced landing **2.** [inévitable] inevitable **3.** [sans spontanéité] strained ▸ **rire forcé** forced laugh.

forcément [fɔʀsemã] adv inevitably, necessarily ▸ **ça devait forcément arriver** it was bound to happen ▸ **pas forcément** not necessarily / *elle est très mince — forcément, elle ne mange rien !* she's very slim — that's hardly surprising, she never eats a thing!

forcené, e [fɔʀsəne] ❖ adj **1.** [passionné] fanatical, frenzied **2.** [violent] frenzied. ❖ nm, f [fou] maniac.

forceps [fɔʀsɛps] nm forceps ▸ **au forceps** fig : *ils ont fait adopter la loi au forceps* the law was painfully adopted.

forcer [16] [fɔʀse] ❖ vt **1.** [obliger] to compel, to force ▸ **forcer qqn à faire qqch** : *l'ennemi a forcé l'avion à atterrir* the enemy forced the plane down / *il l'a forcée à quitter la société* he forced her out of the firm ▸ **être forcé de faire qqch** to be forced to do sthg **2.** [ouvrir de force -tiroir, valise] to force (open) ; [-serrure, mécanisme] to force / *forcer un coffre-fort* to force a safe open ▸ **forcer la porte de qqn** fig to barge ou to force one's way into sb's house ▸ **forcer le passage** to force (one's way) through **3.** [outrepasser] ▸ **forcer la dose a)** PHARM to prescribe too large a dose **b)** fig to go too far **4.** [susciter] ▸ **son courage a forcé l'admiration / le respect de tous** his courage commanded everybody's admiration / respect **5.** [influencer -destin, événements] to influence **6.** [presser] ▸ **forcer le pas** to force the pace **7.** AGR & HORT to force. ❖ vi to force, to strain / *ne force pas, tu vas casser le mécanisme* don't force the mechanism, you'll break it. ❖ **forcer sur** v + prép to overdo ▸ **forcer sur la bouteille** fam to drink too much. ❖ **se forcer** vp *(emploi réfléchi)* [gén] to make an effort ; [en mangeant] to force o.s. / *se forcer à lire / travailler* to force o.s. to read / to work.

forcing [fɔʀsiŋ] nm SPORT pressure ▸ **faire le forcing** pr to put the pressure on ▸ **faire du forcing** fam & fig to use fair means and foul.

forcir [32] [fɔʀsiʀ] vi to get bigger.

forer [3] [fɔʀe] vt [puits de pétrole] to bore, to drill ; [puits, mine] to sink.

forestier, ère [fɔʀɛstje, ɛʀ] ❖ adj [chemin, code] forest *(modif)*. ❖ nm, f forester.

foret [fɔʀɛ] nm drill.

forêt [fɔʀɛ] nf [arbres] forest ▸ **forêt pluviale (tropicale)** (tropical) rainforest ▸ **forêt vierge** virgin forest.

Forêt-Noire [fɔʀɛnwaʀ] npr f ▸ **la Forêt-Noire** the Black Forest. ❖ **forêt-noire** *(pl* forêts-noires*)* nf CULIN Black Forest gateau.

forfait [fɔʀfɛ] nm **1.** [abonnement -de transport, à l'opéra] season ticket ; [-au ski] pass, ski-pass ▸ **forfait train plus hôtel** package deal including train ticket and hotel reservation **2.** COMM ▸ **travailler au forfait** to work for a flat rate **3.** SPORT [somme] withdrawal ▸ **gagner par forfait** to win by default **4.** *litt* [crime] infamy *litt*, (heinous) crime.

forfaitaire [fɔʀfetɛʀ] adj inclusive ▸ **somme** ou **montant forfaitaire** lump sum ▸ **prix forfaitaires** inclusive prices ▸ **voyage à prix forfaitaire** package tour.

forge [fɔʀʒ] nf **1.** [atelier] forge, smithy **2.** [fourneau] forge.

forger [17] [fɔʀʒe] vt **1.** TECHNOL to forge ▸ **c'est en forgeant qu'on devient forgeron** *prov* practice makes perfect *prov* **2.** [inventer -alibi] to make up *(sép)* ; [-phrase] to coin / *une histoire forgée de toutes pièces* a fabricated story **3.** [aguerrir -personnalité, caractère] to form, to forge. ❖ **se forger** vpt : *se forger une réputation* to earn o.s. a reputation.

forgeron [fɔʀʒəʀɔ̃] nm blacksmith.

formaliser [3] [fɔʀmalize] vt [idée, théorie] to formalize. ❖ **se formaliser de** vp + prép to take offence 🇬🇧 ou offense 🇺🇸 at.

formaliste [fɔʀmalist] adj [guindé] strict about etiquette.

formalité [fɔʀmalite] nf **1.** ADMIN formality **2.** [acte sans importance] : *cet examen n'est qu'une formalité* this medical test is a mere formality **3.** [cérémonial] formality.

format [fɔʀma] nm **1.** [dimension] size **2.** IMPR format ▸ **papier format A4/A3** A4/A3 paper **3.** INFORM format.

formater [3] [fɔʀmate] vt INFORM to format.

formateur, trice [fɔʀmatœʀ, tʀis] adj [rôle, influence] formative / *ce stage a été très formateur* this training course was very instructive.

formation [fɔʀmasjɔ̃] nf **1.** [naissance] development, formation, forming **2.** [groupe] group ▸ **formation musicale a)** [classique] orchestra **b)** [moderne] band ▸ **formation politique** political group **3.** ENS [apprentissage] training *(U)* ; [connaissances] cultural background / *elle a une bonne formation littéraire / scientifique* she has a good literary / scientific background / *il n'a aucune formation musicale* he has no musical training / *architecte de formation, elle est devenue cinéaste* having trained as an architect, she turned to making films ▸ **formation continue** ou **permanente** day release or night school education for employees provided by companies ▸ **formation des maîtres** ou **pédagogique** teacher training 🇬🇧, teacher education 🇺🇸 ▸ **formation accélérée** crash course ▸ **formation en alternance** training given partly in an educational institution and partly in the workplace ▸ **formation interne** in-house training ▸ **formation professionnelle** vocational training.

⚠ Attention, le mot anglais **formation** ne peut être employé pour traduire formation au sens d'«apprentissage», «connaissances».

forme [fɔʀm] nf **1.** [configuration] shape, form ▸ **mettre en forme** : *mettez vos idées en forme* give your ideas some shape / *mettre un écrit en forme* to structure a piece of writing ▸ **prendre la forme de** to take (on) the form of, to assume the shape of ▸ **prendre forme** to take shape, to shape up **2.** [état] form / *se présenter sous forme gazeuse* to come in gaseous form ou in the form of a gas / *nous voulons combattre la misère sous toutes ses formes* we want to fight poverty in all its forms **3.** [silhouette] figure, shape **4.** [type] form **5.** [style] form / *sacrifier à la forme* to put form above content **6.** LING form / *mettre un verbe à la forme interrogative / négative* to put a verb into the interrogative / in the negative (form) **7.** DR form **8.** [condition physique] form ▶ **être en forme** to be on form / *être au mieux* ou *sommet de sa forme*, être en pleine forme to be on top form / *être en bonne forme physique* to be fit / *avoir* ou *tenir la forme* fam to be in great shape / *je n'ai* ou *ne tiens pas la forme* I'm in poor shape ▶ **centre de remise en forme** health farm. ❖ **formes** nfpl ▶ **respecter les formes** : *elle a toujours respecté les formes* she has always respected convention. ❖ **dans les formes** loc adv according to form. ❖ **de pure forme** loc adj purely formal. ❖ **en bonne (et due) forme** loc adv [établir un document] in due form, according to the proper form. ❖ **en forme de** loc prép [ressemblant à] ▶ **en forme de poisson** shaped like a fish, fish-shaped. ❖ **pour la forme** loc adv for the sake of form, as a matter of form. ❖ **sous forme de**, **sous la forme de** loc prép in the form of, as / *un médicament qui existe sous forme de comprimés* a drug available in tablet form.

formel, elle [fɔʀmɛl] adj **1.** [net - ordre, refus] definite ; [- identification, preuve] positive / *le médecin a été formel, pas de laitages !* no milk products, the doctor was quite clear about that! **2.** [de la forme] formal.

formellement [fɔʀmɛlmɑ̃] adv [affirmer] categorically ; [interdire] strictly / *il m'a formellement interdit de fumer* he strictly forbade me to smoke ; [identifier] positively.

⚠ Attention, **formally** ne peut être employé pour traduire **formellement** au sens de « catégoriquement ».

former [3] [fɔʀme] vt **1.** [donner un contour à - lettre] to shape, to form ; [- phrase] to put together, to shape **2.** [créer - gouvernement, association] to form **3.** [se constituer en] to form / *ils ont formé un cortège / attroupement* they formed a procession / a mob **4.** [dessiner] to form **5.** [constituer] to form / *ils forment un couple étrange* they make a strange couple **6.** [faire apparaître] to make, to form **7.** *sout* [créer, faire par la pensée] ▶ **former un projet** to think up a plan **8.** ENS & INDUST to train / *former son personnel à l'informatique* to train one's staff to use computers **9.** [développer - caractère, goût] to develop. ❖ **se former** vpi **1.** [apparaître - croûte, pellicule, peau] to form ; [- couche, dépôt] to form, to build up **2.** [se perfectionner] to train o.s.

⚠ Attention, **to form** ne peut être employé pour traduire **former** au sens d'« instruire ».

formidable [fɔʀmidabl] adj **1.** [imposant] tremendous ; *litt* formidable **2.** *vieilli* [invraisemblable] incredible, unbelievable **3.** [admirable] great, wonderful.

formidablement [fɔʀmidabləmɑ̃] adv tremendously / *elle sait formidablement bien s'occuper des enfants* she's great with children.

formol [fɔʀmɔl] nm formalin.

formulaire [fɔʀmylɛʀ] nm form.

formulation [fɔʀmylasjɔ̃] nf formulation, wording.

formule [fɔʀmyl] nf **1.** [tournure] expression, (turn of) phrase ▶ **belle formule / formule toute faite** : *elle a terminé sa lettre par une belle formule / une formule*

toute faite she ended her letter with a well-turned phrase / a ready-made phrase ▶ **la formule magique** the magic words ▶ **formule de politesse** [dans une lettre] letter ending **2.** CHIM & MATH formula **3.** [solution] formula, trick **4.** [en langage publicitaire] way / *une formule économique* way for *vos vacances* an economical way to spend your holidays ᴜᴋ ou vacation ᴜs / *nous vous proposons plusieurs formules de crédit* we offer you several credit options / *notre restaurant vous propose sa formule à 20 €* ou *sa carte* our restaurant offers you a set menu at 20 € or an à la carte menu **5.** AUTO formula.

formuler [3] [fɔʀmyle] vt [exprimer - doctrine, revendication] to formulate, to express.

forniquer [3] [fɔʀnike] vi *litt* ou *hum* to fornicate.

fort, e [fɔʀ, fɔʀt]
adj

Ⓐ **PUISSANT 1.** [vigoureux - personne, bras] strong, sturdy ; [- vent] strong, high ; [- courant, jet] strong ; [- secousse] hard ; [- pluies] heavy ▶ **mer forte** MÉTÉOR rough sea ▶ **fort comme un Turc** ou **un bœuf** as strong as an ox **2.** [d'une grande résistance morale] ▶ **rester fort dans l'adversité** to remain strong ou to stand firm in the face of adversity **3.** [autoritaire, contraignant - régime] strong-arm *(avant nom)* **4.** [puissant - syndicat, parti, économie] strong, powerful ; [- monnaie] strong, hard ; [- carton, loupe, tranquillisant] strong ▶ **colle (très) forte** (super) ou extra strong glue / *c'est plus fort que moi* I can't help it ▶ **fort de** : *fort de son expérience* with a wealth of experience behind him ▶ **fort de leur protection** reassured by their protection **5.** [de grand impact - œuvre, film] powerful ; [- argument] weighty, powerful, forcible.

Ⓑ **MARQUÉ 1.** [épais, corpulent - jambes] big, thick ; [- personne] stout, large ; [- hanches] broad, large, wide **2.** [important quantitativement - dénivellation] steep, pronounced ; [- accent] strong, pronounced, marked ; [- fièvre, taux] high ; [- hausse] large ; [- somme] large, big ; [- bruit] loud ; [- différence] great, big **3.** [grand, intense - amour, haine] strong, intense ; [- douleur] intense, great ; [- influence] strong, big, great ; [- propension] marked / *elle a une forte personnalité* she's got a strong personality **4.** [café, thé, moutarde, tabac] strong ; [sauce] hot, spicy ; [odeur] strong ▶ *fam* ᴇxᴘʀ **c'est trop fort** : *et c'est moi qui devrais payer ? alors ça c'est trop fort !* and I should pay? that's a bit much!

Ⓒ **HABILE** : *le marketing, c'est là qu'il est fort / que sa société est forte* marketing is his / his company's strong point / *fort en gymnastique / en langues* very good at gymnastics / at languages. ❖ **fort** ◆ adv **1.** [avec vigueur - taper, tirer] hard / *pousse plus fort* push harder ; [avec intensité] ▶ **sentir fort** to smell ▶ **mets le gaz plus / moins fort** turn the gas up / down ▶ **y aller un peu fort** : *tu y vas un peu fort !* you're going a bit far! **2.** [bruyamment - parler] loudly, loud / *parle plus fort, on ne t'entend pas* speak up, we can't hear you ▶ **parle moins fort** lower your voice ▶ **mets le son plus / moins fort** turn the sound up / down **3.** *sout* [très] ▶ **fort désagréable** most disagreeable ▶ **fort joli** very pretty **4.** ᴇxᴘʀ **faire très fort** : *là, tu as fait très fort !* you've really excelled yourself! ◆ nm **1.** [physiquement, moralement] : *les forts et les faibles* the strong and the weak **2.** [spécialité] forte / *la politesse n'est pas son fort !* politeness isn't his strongest point! **3.** [forteresse] fort. ❖ **au (plus) fort de** loc prép : *au (plus) fort de l'hiver* in the depths of winter / *au (plus) fort de l'été* in the height of summer.

fortement [fɔʀtəmɑ̃] adv **1.** [avec force] hard ▶ **fortement salé** heavily salted ▶ **fortement épicé** highly spiced

2. [avec netteté] strongly **3.** [beaucoup] strongly ▶ **être fortement tenté** to be sorely tempted ▶ **être fortement intéressé par qqch** to be most interested in sthg.

forteresse [fɔʀtəʀɛs] nf **1.** [citadelle] fortress **2.** [prison] fortress.

fortifiant [fɔʀtifjɑ̃] nm tonic.

fortification [fɔʀtifikasjɔ̃] nf [mur] fortification, wall.

fortifier [9] [fɔʀtifje] vt **1.** [affermir - muscle, santé] to fortify, to strengthen ; [- amitié, volonté, opinion] to strengthen **2.** [protéger] to fortify / *une ville fortifiée* a walled ou fortified town.

fortiori [fɔʀsjɔʀi] → **a fortiori.**

fortuit, e [fɔʀtɥi, it] adj [événement] fortuitous.

fortune [fɔʀtyn] nf **1.** [biens] wealth, fortune ▶ **faire fortune** to make one's fortune **2.** *litt* [hasard] good fortune, luck ▶ **faire contre mauvaise fortune bon cœur** to make the best of a bad job **3.** *litt* [sort] fortune / *leurs livres ont connu des fortunes très diverses* their books had varying success. ❖ **de fortune** loc adj [lit] makeshift ; [installation, réparation] temporary.

fortuné, e [fɔʀtyne] adj [riche] rich, wealthy.

forum [fɔʀɔm] nm ANTIQ & ARCHIT forum ; [débat] forum ▶ **forum de discussion** INFORM discussion forum ▶ **participer à un forum de discussion** to participate in a discussion forum.

fosse [fos] nf **1.** [cavité] pit ▶ **fosse aux lions** lions' den ▶ **fosse septique** septic tank **2.** AUTO & SPORT pit **3.** MUS ▶ **fosse d'orchestre** orchestra pit **4.** [tombe] grave ▶ **fosse commune** common grave.

fossé [fose] nm **1.** [tranchée] ditch **2.** *fig* gulf, gap ▶ **fossé culturel** culture gap.

fossette [fosɛt] nf dimple.

fossile [fosil] ◆ adj *pr* fossil *(modif)* ; *fig* fossil-like, fossilized. ◆ nm *pr & fig* fossil.

fossoyeur [foswajœʀ] nm gravedigger.

fou, folle [fu, fɔl] *(devant nm commençant par voyelle ou «h» muet* **fol** [fɔl]) ◆ adj **1.** [dément] insane, mad / *devenir fou* to go mad ou insane ▶ **être fou de bonheur /** **joie / douleur** to be beside o.s. with happiness / joy / grief ▶ **être fou furieux** ou **à lier** to be (stark) raving mad **2.** [déraisonnable] mad **3.** [hors de soi] wild, mad ▶ **rendre qqn fou** to drive ou to send sb mad **4.** [passionné] ▶ **être fou de qqn / qqch** to be mad ou wild about sb / sthg **5.** [intense] mad, wild / *entre eux, c'est l'amour fou* they're crazy about each other, they're madly in love **6.** [incontrôlé] wild ▶ **camion / train fou** runaway truck / train ▶ **avoir** ou **être pris d'un fou rire** to have a fit of the giggles **7.** *fam* [très important] tremendous / *il y avait un monde fou* there was a huge crowd ▶ **un prix fou** an extortionate price / *nous avons mis un temps fou pour venir* it took us ages to get here ▶ **gagner un argent fou** to make piles ou a lot of money **8.** [incroyable] incredible / *c'est fou, ce qui lui est arrivé* what happened to him is incredible. ◆ nm, f **1.** [dément] madman (madwoman) ▶ **comme un fou** *pr* dementedly **b)** [intensément] like mad ou crazy **2.** [excité] lunatic, fool ▶ **faire le fou** to act the fool ou idiot **3.** [passionné] : *c'est un fou de moto* he's mad on ou crazy about bikes. ❖ **fou** nm JEUX bishop. ❖ **folle** nf *fam & péj* [homosexuel] queen ▶ **grande folle** raving queen.

foudre [fudʀ] nf MÉTÉOR lightning / *il est resté comme frappé par la foudre* he looked as if he had been struck by lightning. ❖ **foudres** nfpl *litt* wrath, ire *litt* / *il a tout fait pour s'attirer les foudres du public* he did everything to bring down the public's wrath upon ou to incur the public's wrath.

foudroyant, e [fudʀwajɑ̃, ɑ̃t] adj **1.** [soudain] violent ▶ **une mort foudroyante** (an) instant death **2.** [extraordinaire] striking, lightning *(modif)* / *la pièce a connu un succès foudroyant* the play was a massive success / *à une vitesse foudroyante* with lightning speed.

foudroyer [13] [fudʀwaje] vt **1.** MÉTÉOR to strike / *deux personnes ont été foudroyées hier pendant l'orage* two people were struck by lightning yesterday during the thunderstorm **2.** [tuer] to strike down *(sép)* ▶ **foudroyer qqn du regard** ou **des yeux** *fig* to look daggers at sb **3.** [anéantir] to strike down *(sép)*.

fouet [fwɛ] nm **1.** [instrument] whip **2.** CULIN whisk.

fouetter [4] [fwete] vt **1.** [frapper] to whip, to flog **2.** CULIN [crème] to whip ; [blanc d'œuf] to beat, to whisk **3.** [cingler - suj : pluie] to lash.

fougasse [fugas] nf *flat loaf traditionally cooked in wood-ash and sometimes flavoured with olives or anchovies.*

fougère [fuʒɛʀ] nf fern ▶ **fougère arborescente** tree fern.

fougue [fug] nf [ardeur] passion, spirit, ardour 🇬🇧, ardor 🇺🇸 ▶ **un discours rempli** ou **plein de fougue** a fiery speech / *se battre avec fougue* to fight with spirit, to put up a spirited fight.

fougueux, euse [fugø, øz] adj [personne] ardent, fiery, impetuous ; [cheval] spirited ; [réponse, résistance] spirited, lively.

fouille [fuj] nf **1.** [d'un lieu] search ▶ **fouille corporelle a)** [rapide] frisking **b)** [approfondie] body search. ❖ **fouilles** nfpl ARCHÉOL dig, excavations / *participer à des fouilles* to take part in a dig.

fouillé, e [fuje] adj [enquête] thorough, wide-ranging ; [étude] detailed ; [détails] elaborate.

fouiller [3] [fuje] ◆ vt **1.** [explorer - tiroir] to search (through) ; [au cours d'une vérification] to search, to go through *(insép)* ▶ **fouiller des voyageurs a)** [rapidement] to frisk travellers **b)** [de façon approfondie] to search travellers **2.** [creuser - suj : cochon, taupe] to dig ▶ **fouiller un site** ARCHÉOL to excavate a site **3.** [approfondir] to go deeply ou thoroughly. ◆ vi [faire une recherche] ▶ **fouiller dans qqch a)** [légitimement] to go through sthg, to search sthg **b)** [par indiscrétion] to rifle through sthg *péj*, to go through sthg *péj* ▶ **fouiller dans sa mémoire** to search one's memory ▶ **fouiller dans le passé de qqn** to delve into sb's past.

fouillis [fuji] nm jumble / *quel fouillis dans ta chambre !* what a dump your room is! / *se perdre dans un fouillis de détails* to get bogged down in (a mass of) details.

fouine [fwin] nf ZOOL stone marten.

fouiner [3] [fwine] vi *fam* **1.** [explorer] to go through / *fouiner au marché aux puces* to go hunting for bargains at the flea market **2.** *péj* [être indiscret] to nose about ou around.

foulard [fulaʀ] nm VÊT scarf ▶ **le foulard islamique** the muslim headscarf.

foule [ful] nf **1.** [gens] crowd, mob *péj* ▶ **il y a foule** *fam* there are crowds ou masses of people / *il n'y a pas foule* *fam* there's hardly anyone around **2.** [masses populaires] ▶ **la foule, les foules** the masses **3.** [grand nombre] ▶ **une foule d'amis** a host of friends / *j'ai une foule d'histoires à te raconter* I've got lots of stories to tell you. ❖ **en foule** loc adv [venir, se présenter] in huge numbers.

foulée [fule] nf stride / *avancer à longues foulées* to stride along. ❖ **dans la foulée** loc adv *fam* : *dans la foulée, j'ai fait aussi le repassage* I did the ironing while I was at it.

fouler [3] [fule] vt **1.** [écraser - raisin] to press, to tread ; [- céréale] to tread **2.** [marcher sur] to tread ou to walk on *(insép)* / *fouler le sol natal* *litt* to tread the native soil.

❖❖ **se fouler** ◆ vpi *fam* [se fatiguer] to strain o.s. / *tu ne t'es pas beaucoup foulé* you didn't exactly strain ou overexert yourself, did you? ◆ vpt ▶ **se fouler qqch** [se faire mal] : *se fouler la cheville* to sprain ou to twist one's ankle.

foulure [fulyʀ] nf sprain.

four [fuʀ] nm **1.** CULIN oven / *un plat allant au four* an ovenproof dish ▶ **four à chaleur tournante** fan-assisted oven ▶ **four à micro-ondes** microwave oven ▶ **four à pyrolyse** self-cleaning oven **2.** TECHNOL furnace, kiln ▶ **four à céramique** pottery kiln **3.** *fam* [fiasco] flop / *sa pièce a été ou a fait un four* his play was a flop.

fourbe [fuʀb] *litt* adj deceitful, treacherous.

fourbi [fuʀbi] nm *fam* [ensemble hétéroclite] paraphernalia.

fourbu, e [fuʀby] adj [personne] exhausted.

fourche [fuʀʃ] nf **1.** AGR fork **2.** [embranchement] fork **3.** [d'une bicyclette, d'un arbre] fork.

fourcher [3] [fuʀʃe] vi EXPR **sa langue a fourché** he made a slip (of the tongue).

fourchette [fuʀʃɛt] nf **1.** [pour manger] fork ▶ **elle a un bon coup de fourchette** she's a hearty eater **2.** [écart] bracket / *une fourchette comprise entre 1 000 et 1 500 euros* prices ranging from 1,000 to 1,500 euros / *dans une fourchette de prix acceptable* within an acceptable price range ou bracket.

fourchu, e [fuʀʃy] adj **1.** [cheveux] ▶ **avoir les cheveux fourchus** to have split ends **2.** [tronc, route] forked.

fourgon [fuʀgɔ̃] nm [voiture] van ▶ **fourgon blindé** armoured van ▶ **fourgon cellulaire** police van UK, patrol ou police wagon US ▶ **fourgon postal** mail van UK, mail truck US.

fourgonnette [fuʀgɔnɛt] nf (small) van.

fourguer [3] [fuʀge] vt *fam & péj* [donner] : *qui t'a fourgué ces vieilles nippes ?* who palmed off those old clothes on you?

fourmi [fuʀmi] nf **1.** ENTOM ant **2.** EXPR ▶ **avoir des fourmis dans les jambes** to have pins and needles in one's legs.

fourmilière [fuʀmiljɛʀ] nf **1.** ENTOM anthill, antheap **2.** [lieu animé] hive of activity.

fourmillement [fuʀmijmɑ̃] nm **1.** [picotement] tingle / *j'ai des fourmillements dans les doigts* I've got pins and needles in my fingers **2.** [foisonnement - de promeneurs] swarming ; [- d'idées] swarm.

fourmiller [3] [fuʀmije] vi **1.** [s'agiter] to swarm **2.** [être abondant] to abound ▶ **fourmiller de** a) [insectes, personnes] to swarm with b) [fautes, idées] to be full of, to be packed with.

fournaise [fuʀnɛz] nf **1.** *litt* [feu] blaze **2.** [lieu caniculaire] : *la ville est une fournaise en été* the city's like an oven in the summer **3.** QUÉBEC furnace.

fourneau, x [fuʀno] nm [cuisinière] stove ▶ **être aux** ou **derrière les fourneaux** to be cooking.

fournée [fuʀne] nf [du boulanger] batch.

fourni, e [fuʀni] adj **1.** [touffu - cheveux] thick ; [- barbe] heavy, thick ; [- sourcils] bushy ; [- haie] luxuriant **2.** [approvisionné] ▶ **abondamment** ou **bien fourni** well supplied ou stocked.

fournir [32] [fuʀniʀ] vt **1.** [ravitailler] to supply / *fournir une entreprise en matières premières* to supply a firm with raw materials **2.** [procurer] to provide ▶ **fournir un alibi à qqn** to provide sb with an alibi / *la brochure vous fournira tous les renseignements nécessaires* the brochure will give you all the necessary information / *fournissez-moi l'argent demain* let me have the money tomorrow **3.** [produire] to produce **4.** [accomplir] ▶ **fournir un effort** to make an effort. ❖❖ **se fournir** vpi ▶ **se fournir chez qqn** to get

one's supplies from sb / *je me fournis toujours chez le même boucher* I always shop at the same butcher's, I get all my meat from the same place.

fournisseur [fuʀnisœʀ] nm **1.** [établissement, marchand] supplier **2.** INFORM ▶ **fournisseur d'accès Internet** Internet service provider.

fourniture [fuʀnityʀ] nf [action] supplying, providing. ❖❖ **fournitures** nfpl [objets] materials ▶ **fournitures (de bureau)** office supplies ▶ **fournitures scolaires** school stationery.

fourrage [fuʀaʒ] nm AGR fodder.

fourrager¹ [17] [fuʀaʒe] ❖❖ **fourrager dans** v + prép to rummage through (*insép*).

fourrager², ère [fuʀaʒe, ɛʀ] adj fodder (*modif*).

fourré¹ [fuʀe] nm [bois] thicket.

fourré², e [fuʀe] adj **1.** [doublé de fourrure] fur-lined **2.** CULIN filled / *bonbons fourrés à la fraise* sweets UK ou candy US with strawberry-flavoured centres / *des dates fourrées à la pâte d'amandes* marzipan-filled dates, dates stuffed with marzipan.

fourreau, x [fuʀo] nm **1.** [d'une arme] sheath ; [d'un parapluie] cover **2.** VÊT sheath dress.

fourrer [3] [fuʀe] vt **1.** [doubler de fourrure] to line with fur **2.** CULIN [fruit, gâteau] to fill **3.** *fam* [mettre] to stick, to shove **4.** *fam* [laisser - papier, vêtement] to put, to leave **5.** *fam* [placer - personne, animal] to stick, to put ▶ **être toujours fourré dans** ou **chez** : *il est toujours fourré chez ses parents / à l'église* he's always at his parents' / in the church. ❖❖ **se fourrer** *fam* ◆ vpi **1.** [se mettre] : *où est-il allé se fourrer ?* wherever has he got to? ▶ **se fourrer au lit / sous les couvertures / dans son sac de couchage** to snuggle down in bed / under the blankets / into one's sleeping bag ▶ **ne plus savoir où se fourrer** : *il ne savait plus où se fourrer* he wished the earth would open up and swallow him **2.** [s'engager] : *se fourrer dans une sale affaire* to get mixed up in a nasty business. ◆ vpt : *se fourrer une idée dans la tête* to get an idea into one's head.

fourre-tout (*pl* fourre-tout), **fourretout*** (*pl* fourretouts) [fuʀtu] nm [sac léger] holdall UK, carryall US ; [trousse] pencil case.

fourreur [fuʀœʀ] nm furrier.

fourrière [fuʀjɛʀ] nf [pour chiens, voitures] pound ▶ **emmener une voiture à la fourrière** to tow away a car ▶ **mettre une voiture en** ou **à la fourrière** to impound a car.

fourrure [fuʀyʀ] nf **1.** VÊT fur / *un manteau / une veste de fourrure* a fur coat / jacket **2.** [peau préparée] fur **3.** ZOOL fur, coat.

fourvoyer [13] [fuʀvwaje] vt *litt* to lead astray, to mislead. ❖❖ **se fourvoyer** vpi to be in error, to make a mistake, to go astray. ❖❖ **se fourvoyer dans** vp + prép to get o.s. involved in.

foutaise [futɛz] nf *tfam* crap, bull US / *tout ça, c'est de la foutaise !* that's just a load of rubbish UK ou crap!

foutoir [futwaʀ] nm *tfam* dump, tip UK / *sa chambre est un vrai foutoir* her room is a complete tip.

foutre [116] [futʀ] vt *tfam* **1.** [envoyer, mettre] ▶ **foutre un rêve / un projet par terre** to wreck a dream / a project ▶ **foutre qqn à la porte** to throw ou to chuck sb out **2.** [donner] to give ▶ **foutre la trouille à qqn** to give sb the creeps ▶ **foutre la paix à qqn** to leave sb alone, to get out of sb's hair **3.** [faire] to do ▶ **qu'est-ce que ça peut te / lui foutre ?** what the hell does it matter to you / him? **4.** EXPR **ça la fout mal** it looks pretty bad ▶ **foutre le camp** : *mon mec a foutu le camp* my man's buggered off (and left me) UK ou run out on me US / *fous le camp de chez moi !* get the hell out of my house! ▶ **tout fout**

le camp ! this place is going to the dogs! ❖ **se foutre** *tfam* vpi ❱ **se foutre dedans** to blow it. ❖ **se foutre de** vp + prép *tfam* **1.** [se moquer de] to laugh at, to make fun of / *tu te fous de moi ou quoi ! are you taking the piss? / ils se foutent du monde !* they really take people for idiots! **2.** [être indifférent à] not to give a damn ou a toss 🇬🇧 about.

foutu, e [futy] *tfam* ◆ pp ⟶ **foutre.** ◆ adj **1.** [abîmé] buggered 🇬🇧, screwed-up 🇺🇸 ; [gâché] ruined **2.** *(avant nom)* [considérable] bloody 🇬🇧, damned / *tu as eu une foutue chance* you were damned lucky **3.** *(avant nom)* [détestable] bloody 🇬🇧, god-awful ❱ **quel foutu caractère !** what a nasty individual! **4.** ⟨EXPR⟩ **bien foutu:** *cette machine est bien foutue* what a clever machine / *une fille très bien foutue* a girl with a great figure ❱ **mal foutu:** *il est mal foutu* **a)** [de corps] he's got an ugly body **b)** [malade] he feels awful ❱ **foutu de** [en mesure de]: *pas foutu de planter un clou dans un mur !* can't even be bothered to hammer a nail into a wall! / *il est foutu de réussir* he just might succeed.

fox-terrier [fɔksteʀje] *(pl* **fox-terriers)** nm fox terrier.

foyer [fwaje] nm **1.** [chez soi] home ❱ **femme au foyer** housewife ❱ **être mère au foyer** to be a housewife and mother ❱ **être père au foyer:** *il est père au foyer* he keeps house and looks after the children, he's a house husband **2.** [résidence collective] hall / *foyer pour le troisième âge* retirement home ❱ **foyer d'étudiants** (students') hall of residence ❱ **foyer d'immigrés** immigrant workers' hostel **3.** [lieu de réunion - gén] hall ; [- pour le public d'un théâtre] foyer ❱ **foyer socio-éducatif** ≃ community centre 🇬🇧, center & 🇺🇸 **4.** [âtre] hearth **5.** [centre] centre 🇬🇧, center 🇺🇸 ❱ **un foyer d'incendie** a fire **6.** MÉD ❱ **foyer infectieux** ou **d'infection** source of infection **7.** OPT & PHYS focus, focal point / *des lunettes à double foyer* bifocals **8.** ADMIN ❱ **foyer fiscal** household.

fracas [fʀaka] nm [bruit] crash, roar. ❖ **à grand fracas** loc adv **1.** [bruyamment] with a great deal of crashing and banging **2.** [spectaculairement] with a lot of fuss.

fracassant, e [fʀakasɑ̃, ɑ̃t] adj **1.** [assourdissant] deafening, thunderous / *la porte s'ouvrit avec un bruit fracassant* the door opened with a deafening bang **2.** [qui fait de l'effet] sensational, staggering.

fracasser [3] [fʀakase] vt to smash ❱ **fracasser qqch en mille morceaux** to smash sthg into pieces.

fraction [fʀaksjɔ̃] nf **1.** MATH fraction **2.** [partie] fraction, part ❱ **une fraction de seconde** a fraction of a second.

fractionner [3] [fʀaksjɔne] vt [diviser] to divide, to split up *(sép).*

fracture [fʀaktyʀ] nf **1.** MÉD fracture ❱ **fracture du crâne** fractured skull **2.** SOCIOL ❱ **fracture numérique** digital divide ❱ **la fracture sociale** social inequalities.

fracturer [3] [fʀaktyʀe] vt **1.** [briser] to break open *(sép)* **2.** PÉTR to fracture. ❖ **se fracturer** vpt : *je me suis fracturé le bras / poignet* I fractured my arm / wrist.

fragile [fʀaʒil] adj **1.** [peu solide] fragile / *'attention, fragile'* 'fragile', 'handle with care' / *c'est une pendule très fragile* it's a very delicate clock **2.** [constitution] frail / *il est de santé fragile* his health is rather delicate / *il a l'estomac très fragile* he has a delicate stomach **3.** [équilibre] fragile, frail.

fragiliser [3] [fʀaʒilize] vt PSYCHOL to weaken.

fragilité [fʀaʒilite] nf **1.** [d'une horloge, d'une construction] fragility, weakness **2.** [d'un organe, d'un malade] weakness.

fragment [fʀagmɑ̃] nm **1.** [débris] chip, fragment, piece ❱ **des fragments de verre** bits of shattered glass, shards of glass **2.** [morceau - d'une œuvre en partie perdue] fragment ; [- d'un air, d'une conversation] snatch / *il nous a lu quelques fragments de son dernier roman* he read a few extracts of his last novel for us.

fragmentaire [fʀagmɑ̃tɛʀ] adj fragmentary, sketchy, incomplete.

fragmenter [3] [fʀagmɑ̃te] vt to divide, to split (up).

fraîche, fraiche* [fʀɛʃ] f ⟶ **frais.**

fraîchement, fraichement* [fʀɛʃmɑ̃] adv **1.** [nouvellement] freshly, newly ❱ **fraîchement coupé** [herbe] new-mown **2.** [froidement] coolly **3.** ⟨EXPR⟩ **ça va plutôt fraîchement aujourd'hui** *fam* it's a bit chilly today.

fraîcheur, fraicheur* [fʀɛʃœʀ] nf **1.** [température] coolness / *dans la fraîcheur du petit jour* in the cool of early dawn **2.** [bonne qualité] freshness **3.** [intensité - des couleurs] freshness, brightness / *la robe n'est plus de la première fraîcheur* the dress isn't exactly brand new **4.** [éclat] freshness **5.** [indifférence] coolness.

fraîchir, fraichir* [32] [fʀɛʃiʀ] vi **1.** [se refroidir] to get cooler **2.** NAUT [vent] to freshen, to get stronger.

frais¹ [fʀɛ] nmpl **1.** [dépenses] expenditure, expense, costs ❱ **à grands frais** with much expense, (very) expensively ❱ **à peu de frais** cheaply ❱ **frais de déplacement** ou **de mission** ou **de voyage** travelling expenses ❱ **frais d'entretien** maintenance costs ❱ **frais de fonctionnement** running costs ❱ **frais de garde** child-minding costs ❱ **frais de gestion** running costs ❱ **frais de représentation** entertainment allowance ❱ **frais médicaux** medical expenses ❱ **frais professionnels** professional expenses ❱ **tous frais payés** all expenses paid ❱ **faire les frais de la conversation** to be the centre of the conversation ❱ **rentrer dans ses frais** to break even, to recoup one's expenses ❱ **se mettre en frais** to spend money ❱ **aux frais de la princesse** *fam*: *hôtel cinq étoiles, restaurants de luxe, tout ça aux frais de la princesse* five-star hotel, smart restaurants, all on expenses **2.** COMPTA outgoings ❱ **frais bancaires** bank charges ❱ **frais divers** miscellaneous costs ❱ **frais d'envoi** ou **d'expédition** postage ❱ **frais généraux** overheads 🇬🇧, overhead 🇺🇸 ❱ **faux frais** incidental costs **3.** ADMIN fees ❱ **frais de dossier** administrative charges ❱ **frais d'inscription** registration fee, membership fee ❱ **frais de scolarité** school fees.

frais², fraîche ou **fraiche*** [fʀɛ, fʀɛʃ] adj **1.** [un peu froid] cool, fresh **2.** [rafraîchissant] cooled, chilled ❱ **des boissons fraîches** cold drinks **3.** [récent - œuf, huître] fresh ; [- encre, peinture] wet / *j'ai reçu des nouvelles fraîches* I've got some recent news **4.** [reposé] fresh / *je ne me sens pas trop frais ce matin* fam I don't feel too good ou well this morning **5.** [éclatant] fresh **6.** [indifférent - accueil, réception] cool **7.** *fam* [en mauvais état] ❱ **me voilà frais** I'm in a mess! ❖ **frais** ◆ adv **1.** [nouvellement] newly ❱ **frais émoulu:** *frais émoulu de la faculté de droit* freshly graduated from law school **2.** [froid] : *il fait frais dans la maison* it's chilly in the house ❱ **boire frais** drink chilled ❱ **servir frais** serve cold ou chilled. ◆ nm [air frais] ❱ **le frais** the fresh air. ❖ **fraîche, fraiche*** nf [heure] cool (of evening) ❱ **à la fraîche** in the cool evening air. ❖ **au fraîche** loc adv [dans un lieu froid] in a cool place.

fraise [fʀɛz] nf **1.** BOT strawberry ❱ **fraise des bois** wild strawberry **2.** DENT drill.

fraiser [4] [fʀɛze] vt [usiner] to mill ; [évaser - trou] to ream ; [- trou de vis] to countersink, to knead.

fraisier [fʀɛzje] nm **1.** BOT strawberry plant **2.** CULIN strawberry cream cake.

framboise [fʀɑ̃bwaz] nf BOT raspberry.

---

framboisier [fʀɑ̃bwazje] nm **1.** BOT raspberry cane **2.** [gâteau] raspberry cream cake.

franc¹ [fʀɑ̃] nm [monnaies] franc ▸ **franc belge** Belgian franc ▸ **franc suisse** Swiss franc.

franc², franche [fʀɑ̃, fʀɑ̃ʃ] adj **1.** [honnête - réponse] frank, straightforward, honest ▸ **un rire franc** an open laugh / **pour être franc avec vous** to be honest with you **2.** [pur] strong ▸ **un rouge franc** a strong red **3.** DR ▸ **jour franc** : *le jugement est exécutable au bout de trois jours francs* the decision of the court to be carried out within three clear days **4.** COMM & FIN free ▸ **zone franche** free zone. ❖ **franc** ❖ adv ▸ **parlons franc** let's be frank. ❖ adj m : *franc de port (et d'emballage)* postage paid.

français, e [fʀɑ̃sɛ, ɛz] adj French. ❖ **Français, e** nm, f Frenchman (Frenchwoman) ▸ **les Français a)** [la population] French people, the French **b)** [les hommes] Frenchmen ▸ **les Françaises** French women ▸ **le Français n'aime pas...** the average Frenchman ou French person doesn't like... ❖ **français** nm LING French. ❖ **à la française** loc adj [jardin, parquet] French, French-style.

France [fʀɑ̃s] npr f ▸ **(la) France** France / *vivre en France* to live in France ▸ **la France profonde** grassroots France.

Francfort [fʀɑ̃kfɔʀ] npr ▸ **Francfort (sur-le-Main)** Frankfurt (am Main).

franche [fʀɑ̃ʃ] f ⟶ franc *(adj).*

franchement [fʀɑ̃ʃmɑ̃] adv **1.** [sincèrement] frankly ▸ **parlons franchement** let's be frank / *pour vous parler franchement, je ne sais pas de quoi il s'agit* to be honest with you, I don't know what it's all about **2.** [sans équivoque] clearly, definitely **3.** [résolument] boldly ▸ **ils y sont allés franchement a)** [dans un projet] they got right down to it **b)** [dans une conversation, une négociation] they didn't mince words **4.** [vraiment] really / *elle est devenue franchement jolie* she became really pretty.

franchir [32] [fʀɑ̃ʃiʀ] vt **1.** [passer par-dessus - barrière, mur] to get over *(insép)* ▸ **franchir un obstacle** *fig* to get over an obstacle ▸ **franchir une difficulté** to overcome a difficulty **2.** [outrepasser - ligne, limite, date] to cross / *au moment de franchir le seuil, je m'arrêtai* I halted just as I was stepping across the threshold / *franchir le mur du son* to break through the sound barrier / *il y a certaines limites à ne pas franchir* there are certain limits which should not be overstepped ▸ **franchir un cap** *fig* to reach a milestone ou turning point ▸ **franchir le cap de la trentaine / cinquantaine** to turn thirty / fifty **3.** [dans le temps] to last through / *sa renommée a franchi les siècles* his reputation has lasted ou come down intact through the centuries.

franchise [fʀɑ̃ʃiz] nf **1.** COMM & FIN [exploitation] franchise agreement ; [exonération] exemption ▸ **magasin en franchise** franchised shop 🇬🇧 ou store 🇺🇸 ▸ **franchise de bagages** baggage allowance ▸ **franchise douanière** exemption from customs duties ▸ **en franchise postale** official paid **2.** [d'une assurance] excess 🇬🇧, deductible 🇺🇸 **3.** [honnêteté] frankness, straightforwardness ▸ **en toute franchise** quite frankly, to be honest with you.

franchiser [fʀɑ̃ʃize] vt to franchise.

francilien, enne [fʀɑ̃siljɛ̃, ɛn] adj from the Île-de-France *(region around Paris).* ❖ **Francilien, enne** nm, f inhabitant of or person from the Île-de-France.

franciser [3] [fʀɑ̃size] vt LING [mot, terme] to gallicize.

franc-jeu [fʀɑ̃ʒø] *(pl* francs-jeux) nm fair play.

franc-maçon, onne [fʀɑ̃masɔ̃, ɔn] *(mpl* francs-maçons, fpl franc-maçonnes) nm, f Freemason.

franc-maçonnerie [fʀɑ̃masɔnʀi] *(pl* franc-maçonneries) nf [société secrète] ▸ **la franc-maçonnerie** Freemasonry.

franco [fʀɑ̃ko] ❖ adj inv & adv [dans un envoi] ▸ **franco (de port)** postage paid. ❖ adv *fam* [franchement] ▸ **y aller franco** to go straight ou right ahead.

franco-français, e [fʀɑ̃kofʀɑ̃sɛ, ɛz] *(mpl* franco-français, fpl franco-françaises) adj *fam & péj* typically French.

francophile [fʀɑ̃kofil] ❖ adj Francophil, Francophile. ❖ nmf Francophile.

francophone [fʀɑ̃kofɔn] ❖ adj Francophone, French-speaking. ❖ nmf Francophone, French speaker.

francophonie [fʀɑ̃kofɔni] nf ▸ **la francophonie** *French-speaking countries.*

Francophonie

This is a wide-ranging cultural and political concept involving the promotion of the French language in French-speaking communities around the world.

franc-parler [fʀɑ̃paʀle] *(pl* francs-parlers) nm outspokenness ▸ **il a son franc-parler** he doesn't mince (his) words.

franc-tireur [fʀɑ̃tiʀœʀ] *(pl* francs-tireurs) nm **1.** MIL franc-tireur, irregular (soldier) **2.** [indépendant] maverick.

frange [fʀɑ̃ʒ] nf **1.** [de cheveux] fringe, bangs 🇺🇸 **2.** [de tissu] fringe **3.** [minorité] fringe.

frangin [fʀɑ̃ʒɛ̃] nm *fam* brother, bro.

frangine [fʀɑ̃ʒin] nf *fam* [sœur] sister, sis.

frangipane [fʀɑ̃ʒipan] nf CULIN [crème, gâteau] frangipane.

franquette [fʀɑ̃kɛt] nf ▸ **à la bonne franquette** *fam* simply, informally ▸ **recevoir qqn à la bonne franquette** to have sb round for a simple meal (among friends).

frappant, e [fʀapɑ̃, ɑ̃t] adj [ressemblance, exemple] striking.

frappe [fʀap] nf **1.** [d'une secrétaire, d'un pianiste] touch **2.** SPORT [d'un footballeur] kick ; [d'un boxeur] punch **3.** *tfam* [voyou] hooligan, hoodlum ▸ **une petite frappe** a young hooligan **4.** MIL ▸ **frappe aérienne** airstrike ▸ **frappe de précision** precision strike.

frappé, e [fʀape] adj [boisson] iced ▸ **café frappé** iced coffee ▸ **servir bien frappé** serve chilled.

frapper [3] [fʀape] ❖ vt **1.** [battre - adversaire] to hit, to strike **2.** [donner] to hit, to strike / *frapper un grand coup* ou *un coup décisif* *fig* to strike a decisive blow **3.** [percuter] to hit ▸ **frapper la terre** ou **le sol du pied** to stamp (one's foot) **4.** [affecter] to strike ou to bring down, to hit ▸ **le deuil / mal qui nous frappe** the bereavement / pain we are suffering **5.** [s'appliquer à - suj : loi, sanction, taxe] to hit **6.** [surprendre] to strike / *ce qui me frappe chez lui, c'est sa désinvolture* what strikes me about him is his offhandedness ; [impressionner] to upset, to shock ▸ **être frappé de stupeur** to be stupefied ou struck dumb **7.** ART & TEXT to emboss **8.** MÉTALL to stamp. ❖ vi **1.** [pour entrer] to knock ▸ **frapper à la porte / fenêtre** to knock on the door / window / *on a frappé* someone knocked at the door / *frapper à toutes les portes* *fig* to try every avenue ▸ **frapper à la bonne / mauvaise porte** *fig* to go to the right / wrong place **2.** [pour exprimer un sentiment] ▸ **frapper dans ses mains** to clap one's hands ▸ **frapper du pied** to stamp one's foot **3.** [cogner] to strike ▸ **frapper dur** ou **sec** to strike hard ▸ **frapper fort a)** *pr* to hit hard **b)** *fig* to hit hard, to act decisively. ❖ **se frapper** ◆ vp *(emploi réfléchi)* to hit o.s. ▶ **se frapper le front** to slap one's forehead. ◆ vpi *fam* [s'inquiéter] to worry, to get (o.s.) worked up.

frasil [fʀazil] nm ᵩᵤᵉᵇᵉᶜ frazil.

frasques [fʀask] nfpl escapades, pranks.

fraternel, elle [fʀatɛʀnɛl] adj brotherly, fraternal.

fraterniser [3] [fʀatɛʀnize] vi to fraternize.

fraternité [fʀatɛʀnite] nf [lien] brotherhood, fraternity.

fratricide [fʀatʀisid] adj [guerre, haine] fratricidal.

fratrie [fʀatʀi] nf siblings, brothers and sisters.

fraude [fʀod] nf **1.** [tromperie] fraud ▶ **la fraude aux examens** cheating at exams **2.** DR ▶ **fraude électorale** electoral fraud, vote ou ballot rigging ▶ **fraude fiscale** tax evasion. ❖ **en fraude** loc adv [vendre] fraudulently ▶ **entrer / sortir en fraude** to smuggle o.s. in / out ▶ **passer qqch en fraude** to smuggle sthg in.

frauder [3] [fʀode] ◆ vt [état] to defraud ▶ **frauder le fisc** to evade taxation. ◆ vi to cheat / *frauder à* ou *dans un examen* to cheat at an exam.

fraudeur, euse [fʀodœʀ, øz] nm, f [envers le fisc] tax evader ; [à la douane] smuggler ; [à un examen] cheat ; [dans le métro, le bus] fare dodger.

frauduleux, euse [fʀodylø, øz] adj fraudulent.

frayer [11] [fʀeje] ◆ vt [route, voie] to clear / *frayer un chemin en abattant les arbres* to clear a path by felling the trees ▶ **frayer la voie à qqch / qqn** *fig* to pave the way for sthg / sb. ◆ vi ZOOL to spawn. ❖ **frayer avec** v + prép to associate with *(sép)*. ❖ **se frayer** vpt ▶ **se frayer un chemin** ou **un passage dans la foule** to force ou to push one's way through the crowd.

frayeur [fʀejœʀ] nf fright ▶ **faire une frayeur à qqn** to give sb a fright ▶ **se remettre de ses frayeurs** to recover from one's fright.

fredonner [3] [fʀədɔne] vt [air, chanson] to hum.

free-lance [fʀilɑ̃s] *(pl* **free-lances)** ◆ adj inv freelance. ◆ nmf freelance, freelancer. ◆ nm freelancing, freelance work ▶ **travailler** ou **être en free-lance** to work on a freelance basis ou as a freelancer.

freezer, freezeur* [fʀizœʀ] nm freezer compartment.

frégate [fʀegat] nf **1.** ORNITH frigate bird **2.** NAUT frigate.

frein [fʀɛ̃] nm AUTO brake ▶ **frein à disque** disc brake ▶ **frein à main** handbrake ▶ **frein moteur** engine brake ▶ **coup de frein**: *donner un brusque coup de frein* to brake sharply ou suddenly / *c'est un coup de frein à l'économie fig* this will act as a brake on the economy ▶ **mettre un frein à** to block.

freinage [fʀɛnaʒ] nm braking.

freiner [4] [fʀene] ◆ vt **1.** [ralentir - véhicule] to slow down *(sép)* ; [-évolution] to check **2.** [amoindrir - impatience] to curb ; [-enthousiasme] to dampen. ◆ vi [conducteur, auto] to brake ▶ **ta voiture freine bien / mal** your car brakes are good / bad.

frelaté, e [fʀəlate] adj [nourriture, vin] adulterated.

frêle [fʀɛl] adj [fragile - corps, santé] frail, fragile ; [-voix] thin, reedy.

frelon [fʀəlɔ̃] nm hornet.

frémir [32] [fʀemiʀ] vi **1.** [trembler] to shiver, to shudder ▶ **frémir de colère** to quiver with anger ▶ **frémir d'impatience** to tremble with impatience **2.** *litt* [vibrer - tige, herbe] to quiver, to tremble ; [-surface d'un lac] to ripple **3.** [avant l'ébullition] to simmer.

frémissement [fʀemismɑ̃] nm **1.** [d'indignation, de colère] quiver, shiver, shudder / *un frémissement d'impatience la parcourut* a thrill of impatience ran through her **2.** [avant l'ébullition] simmer, simmering.

frêne [fʀɛn] nm **1.** [arbre] ash (tree) **2.** [bois] ash.

frénésie [fʀenezi] nf frenzy.

frénétique [fʀenetik] adj [agitation, hurlement] frantic ; [joie, passion] frenzied.

fréquemment [fʀekamɑ̃] adv frequently, often.

fréquence [fʀekɑ̃s] nf **1.** [périodicité] frequency **2.** ACOUST frequency ▶ **basse / moyenne / haute fréquence** low / middle / high frequency ; TÉLÉC wavelength, (wave) band, frequency.

fréquent, e [fʀekɑ̃, ɑ̃t] adj [répété] frequent.

fréquentable [fʀekɑ̃tabl] adj : *sa famille n'est guère fréquentable* her family isn't exactly the kind you'd care to associate with.

fréquentation [fʀekɑ̃tasjɔ̃] nf **1.** [d'un lieu] frequenting **2.** COMM attendance **3.** [relation] acquaintance ▶ **avoir de mauvaises fréquentations** to keep bad company.

fréquenté, e [fʀekɑ̃te] adj ▶ **un endroit bien / mal fréquenté** a place with a good / bad reputation / *c'est un café très fréquenté par les jeunes* it's a café that's very popular with young people.

fréquenter [3] [fʀekɑ̃te] vt **1.** [lieu] to frequent **2.** [personne] to see frequently, to associate with ; [courtiser] : *elle fréquente mon frère depuis un an* she's been going out with my brother for a year. ❖ **se fréquenter** vp *(emploi réciproque)* : *ils se fréquentent depuis deux ans* they've been going out for two years / *ils se fréquentent assez peu* they don't see much of each other.

frère [fʀɛʀ] nm **1.** [dans une famille] brother ▶ **frère aîné / cadet** older / younger brother ▶ **ce sont des frères ennemis** a friendly rivalry exists between them **2.** [compagnon] brother **3.** RELIG brother, friar / *aller à l'école chez les frères* to go to a Catholic boys' school.

fresque [fʀɛsk] nf ART fresco.

fret [fʀɛt] nm **1.** [chargement - d'un avion, d'un navire] cargo, freight ; [-d'un camion] load ▶ **fret aérien** air freight **2.** [prix - par air, mer] freight, freightage ; [-par route] carriage.

fret, frette [fʀɛt] adj ᵩᵤᵉᵇᵉᶜ *fam* cold.

frétiller [3] [fʀetije] vi [ver, poisson] to wriggle ; [queue] to wag ▶ **il frétille d'impatience** *fig* he's quivering with impatience.

fretin [fʀətɛ̃] nm fry.

friable [fʀijabl] adj [roche] crumbly, friable ; [biscuit] crumbly.

friand, e [fʀijɑ̃, ɑ̃d] adj ▶ **friand de** [sucreries] fond of ▶ **être friand de compliments** to enjoy receiving compliments. ❖ **friand** nm [salé] ≃ meat pie (in puff pastry).

friandise [fʀijɑ̃diz] nf sweetmeat, (sweet) delicacy, titbit ▶ **aimer les friandises** to have a sweet tooth.

fric [fʀik] nm *fam* cash, money / *il est bourré de fric* he's loaded.

fricassée [fʀikase] nf [ragoût] fricassee.

friche [fʀiʃ] nf **1.** AGR piece of fallow land, fallow **2.** INDUST ▶ **friche industrielle** industrial wasteland. ❖ **en friche** loc adj **1.** AGR ▶ **terre en friche** plot of fallow land **2.** [inactif] unused.

fricoter [3] [fʀikɔte] vt *fam* [manigancer] to cook up / *je me demande ce qu'il fricote* I wonder what he's up to ou what he's cooking up. ❖ **fricoter avec** v + prép *fam* [sexuellement] to knock around with.

friction [fʀiksjɔ̃] nf **1.** [massage - gén] rub (down) ; [- du cuir chevelu] scalp massage **2.** [désaccord] friction / *il y a des frictions entre eux* they don't see eye to eye.

frictionner [3] [fʀiksjɔne] vt to rub (down).

Frigidaire® [fʀiʒidɛʀ] nm **1.** [portant la marque] Frigidaire® (refrigerator) **2.** [appareil quelconque] refrigerator, fridge.

frigide [fʀiʒid] adj frigid.

frigidité [fʀiʒidite] nf frigidity.

frigo [fʀigo] nm *fam* [réfrigérateur] fridge.

frigorifié, e [fʀigɔʀifje] adj *fam & fig* frozen stiff.

frigorifique [fʀigɔʀifik] adj refrigerated.

frileux, euse [fʀilø, øz] adj **1.** [qui a froid] sensitive to cold **2.** [prudent] timid, unadventurous.

frime [fʀim] nf *fam* put-on ▶ **pour la frime** for show *ou* effect.

frimer [3] [fʀime] vi *fam* to show off, to put on an act.

frimeur, euse [fʀimœʀ, øz] *fam* nm, f show-off.

frimousse [fʀimus] nf (sweet) little face.

fringale [fʀɛ̃gal] nf *fam* [faim] hunger / *j'ai une de ces fringales !* I'm starving!

fringant, e [fʀɛ̃gɑ̃, ɑ̃t] adj **1.** [personne] dashing **2.** [cheval] frisky, spirited.

fringuer [3] [fʀɛ̃ge] **⇌ se fringuer** vp *(emploi réfléchi) fam* **1.** [s'habiller] to dress o.s. / *être bien / mal fringué* to be well / badly dressed **2.** [s'habiller bien] to do *ou* to get o.s. up.

fringues [fʀɛ̃g] nfpl *fam* gear, clobber 🇬🇧, threads 🇺🇸.

fripe [fʀip] nf : *la fripe, les fripes* secondhand clothes.

friper [3] [fʀipe] vt [chiffonner] to crumple *ou* to crease (up).

fripier, ère [fʀipje, ɛʀ] nm, f secondhand clothes dealer.

fripon, onne [fʀipɔ̃, ɔn] **◆** adj [enfant] mischievous, roguish ; [sourire] roguish. **◆** nm, f rogue / *tu n'es qu'un petit fripon !* you little rogue *ou* scamp!

fripouille [fʀipuj] nf *péj* [scélérat] rascal, rogue.

frire [115] [fʀiʀ] **◆** vt CULIN to fry ; [en friteuse, dans un bain d'huile] to deep-fry. **◆** vi to fry / *faire frire des poissons* to fry fish.

Frisbee® [fʀizbi] nm Frisbee®.

frise [fʀiz] nf ARCHIT & ART frieze.

frisé, e [fʀize] adj [barbe, cheveux] curly ; [personne] curly-haired. **⇌ frisée** nf [chicorée] curly endive.

friser [3] [fʀize] **◆** vt **1.** [barbe, cheveux] to curl / *se faire friser (les cheveux)* to have one's hair curled **2.** [être proche de - ridicule, insolence] to verge on / *elle doit friser la quarantaine* she must be getting on for forty / *nous avons frisé la catastrophe* we came within an inch of disaster. **◆** vi to have curly hair.

frisette [fʀizet] nf [de cheveux] small curl.

frisquet, ette [fʀiskɛ, ɛt] adj *fam* [temps, vent] chilly / *il fait plutôt frisquet aujourd'hui* it's rather chilly *ou* there's a nip in the air today.

frisson [fʀisɔ̃] nm [de froid, de fièvre] shiver ; [de peur] shudder ▶ **être pris** *ou* **saisi de frissons** to get the shivers.

frissonner [3] [fʀisɔne] vi [de froid, de fièvre] to shiver ; [de peur] to shudder ; [de joie] to quiver ▶ **elle frissonnait de bonheur** she was trembling with happiness.

frit, e [fʀi, fʀit] adj fried.

frite [fʀit] nf **1.** CULIN chip 🇬🇧, French fry 🇺🇸 ▶ **des frites** chips 🇬🇧, French fries 🇺🇸 **2.** EXPR **avoir la frite** *fam* to be on top form.

friterie [fʀitʀi] nf [restaurant] ≃ fast-food restaurant ; [ambulante] chip van 🇬🇧, French fry vendor 🇺🇸.

friteuse [fʀitøz] nf deep fryer, chip pan 🇬🇧 ▶ **friteuse électrique** electric fryer.

friture [fʀityʀ] nf **1.** [aliments frits] fried food ; [poissons] fried fish **2.** CULIN [cuisson] frying ; [matière grasse] deep fat **3.** ACOUST static / *il y a de la friture* we're getting some interference **4.** 🇧🇪 [friterie] ≃ chip van 🇬🇧, French fry vendor & 🇺🇸.

frivole [fʀivɔl] adj [personne] frivolous, shallow ; [sujet] frivolous.

frivolité [fʀivɔlite] nf [légèreté] frivolity, frivolousness ; [manque de sérieux - d'un projet, d'une œuvre] triviality.

froc [fʀɔk] nm **1.** *fam* [pantalon] trousers 🇬🇧, pants 🇺🇸 **2.** RELIG [habit] habit, frock.

froid, e [fʀwa, fʀwad] adj **1.** [boisson, temps, moteur] cold **2.** [indifférent - personne] cold, insensitive, unfeeling ; [- tempérament] cold ; [- accueil] cold, chilly ; [- réponse] cold, cool ; [- attitude] cold, unfriendly ▶ **ton / regard froid** hostile tone / stare ▶ **ça me laisse froid** it leaves me cold **3.** [triste] cold, bleak **4.** [couleur] cold, cool. **⇌ froid** nm **1.** [température] ▶ **le froid** a) [climat] cold weather, the cold b) [air] the cold (air) ▶ **coup de froid** cold spell *ou* snap ▶ **il fait un froid de canard** *ou* **sibérien** it's freezing *ou* bitterly cold ▶ **froid polaire** arctic cold **2.** [sensation] ▶ **avoir froid** to be *ou* to feel cold ▶ **j'ai froid aux mains** my hands are cold ▶ **attraper** *ou* **prendre froid** to get *ou* to catch a cold ▶ **donner froid dans le dos à qqn** : *ça me donne froid dans le dos* it makes my blood run cold, it sends shivers down my spine ▶ **ne pas avoir froid aux yeux** : *il n'a pas froid aux yeux* he's bold *ou* plucky **3.** [malaise] : *il y a un froid entre eux* things have gone cool between them ▶ **être en froid avec qqn** to be on bad terms with sb. **◆** adv ▶ **il fait froid dehors** it's cold out. **⇌ à froid** loc adv [sans préparation] ▶ **prendre qqn à froid** to catch sb unawares *ou* off guard.

froidement [fʀwadmɑ̃] adv **1.** [avec réserve] coldly, coolly **2.** [lucidement] dispassionately **3.** [avec indifférence] cold-bloodedly ▶ **abattre qqn froidement** to shoot down sb in cold blood.

froideur [fʀwadœʀ] nf **1.** [indifférence méprisante] coldness, cold indifference **2.** [manque de sensualité] coldness.

froisser [3] [fʀwase] vt **1.** [friper - tissu] to crease, to crumple ; [- papier] to crumple, to crease **2.** [blesser - orgueil] to ruffle, to bruise ; [- personne] to offend. **⇌ se froisser** **◆** vpi **1.** [vêtement] to crush, to crease **2.** [personne] to take offence 🇬🇧 *ou* offense 🇺🇸, to be offended. **◆** vpt ▶ **se froisser un muscle** to strain a muscle.

frôler [3] [fʀole] vt **1.** [effleurer] to brush, to touch lightly, to graze / *l'avion a frôlé les arbres* the plane skimmed *ou* grazed the treetops **2.** [passer très près de] to come close to touching **3.** [échapper à] to come within a hair's breadth *ou* an ace of, to escape narrowly / *frôler la mort* to come within a hair's breadth of death *ou* dying.

fromage [fʀomaʒ] nm [laitage] cheese ▶ **un fromage** a cheese ▶ **plusieurs sortes de fromages** several kinds of cheese ▶ **fromage de vache / brebis / chèvre** cow's / sheep's / goat's milk cheese ▶ **fromage blanc** fromage frais ▶ **fromage frais** ≃ cream cheese ▶ **fromage à pâte molle** soft cheese ▶ **fromage à pâte pressée** hard cheese ▶ **fromage à tartiner** cheese spread ▶ **en faire tout un fromage** *fam* to kick up a (huge) fuss, to make a mountain out of a molehill ▶ **fromage de tête** brawn 🇬🇧, headcheese 🇺🇸.

fromager, ère [fʀomaʒe, ɛʀ] **◆** adj cheese *(modif)*. **◆** nm, f [commerçant] cheesemonger 🇬🇧, cheese seller 🇺🇸.

fromagerie [fʀomaʒʀi] nf **1.** [boutique] cheese shop 🇬🇧 *ou* store 🇺🇸 **2.** [fabrique] dairy.

froment [fʀɔmɑ̃] nm wheat.

fronce [fʀɔ̃s] nf [de tissu] gather. ❖ **à fronces** loc adj gathered.

froncement [fʀɔ̃smɑ̃] nm ▶ **froncement de sourcils** frown.

froncer [16] [fʀɔ̃se] vt **1.** COUT to gather **2.** [rider] ▶ **froncer les sourcils** to knit one's brow, to frown.

fronde [fʀɔ̃d] nf **1.** ARM sling **2.** [lance-pierres] catapult UK, slingshot US **3.** litt [révolte] rebellion, revolt.

frondeur, euse [fʀɔ̃dœʀ, øz] adj insubordinate, rebellious.

front [fʀɔ̃] nm **1.** ANAT forehead, brow ▶ **le front haut** proudly, with one's head held high **2.** [d'une montagne] face ; [d'un monument] frontage, façade ▶ **front de mer** seafront **3.** POL front ▶ **faire front commun contre qqn / qqch** to make common cause against sb / sthg **4.** MIL [zone] front ; [ligne] front line **5.** MIN [gén] face ; [dans une houillère] coalface ▶ **front de taille** working face **6.** MÉTÉOR front. ❖ **de front** loc adv **1.** [attaquer] head-on / aborder une difficulté de front to tackle a problem head-on **2.** [en vis-à-vis] head-on ▶ **se heurter de front** a) [véhicules] to collide head-on b) [adversaires] to come into direct confrontation **3.** [côte à côte] abreast / nous marchions de front we were walking next to one another **4.** [en même temps] at the same time, at a time.

frontal, e, aux [fʀɔ̃tal, o] adj [conflit, attaque] head-on.

frontalier, ère [fʀɔ̃talje, ɛʀ] ❖ adj border (modif). ❖ nm, f cross-border commuter.

frontière [fʀɔ̃tjɛʀ] nf **1.** POL border ▶ **poste / ville / zone frontière** border post / town / area **2.** [démarcation] boundary / la frontière entre la veille et le sommeil the borderline between sleeping and waking ▶ **frontière naturelle / linguistique** natural / linguistic boundary.

frontispice [fʀɔ̃tispis] nm [titre, illustration] frontispiece.

fronton [fʀɔ̃tɔ̃] nm ARCHIT pediment.

frottement [fʀɔtmɑ̃] nm **1.** [friction] rubbing (U), friction **2.** [bruit] rubbing ou scraping noise.

frotter [3] [fʀɔte] ❖ vt **1.** [pour nettoyer] to rub, to scrub / frotter une tache avec une brosse / avec du savon to scrub a stain with a brush / with soap ▶ **frotter une casserole** to scour a saucepan **2.** [mettre en contact] ▶ **frotter une allumette** to strike a match **3.** [frictionner] to rub ▶ **frotter le dos de qqn** to give sb's back a rub, to rub sb's back. ❖ vi to scrape, to rub. ❖ **se frotter** vp (emploi réfléchi) [se frictionner] to rub o.s. (down) ▶ **se frotter les mains** a) pr to rub one's hands (together) b) fig to rub one's hands. ❖ **se frotter à** vp + prép **1.** [effleurer] : ne te frotte pas à lui quand il est en colère fig steer clear of him when he's angry ▶ **s'y frotter** : ne vous y frottez pas, c'est trop dangereux don't interfere ou meddle, it's too dangerous **2.** [se confronter à] to face.

frottis [fʀɔti] nm MÉD smear.

froufrou, frou-frou (pl **frous-frous**) [fʀufʀu] nm [bruit] swish, rustle, froufrou. ❖ **froufrous, frous-frous** nmpl VÊT frills (and furbelows).

froussard, e [fʀusaʀ, aʀd] fam nm, f coward, chicken, yellow-belly.

frousse [fʀus] nf fam fright ▶ **avoir la frousse** to be scared.

fructifier [9] [fʀyktifje] vi **1.** AGR to be productive ; BOT to bear fruit, to fructify sout **2.** ÉCON to yield a profit / faire fructifier son capital to make one's capital yield a profit **3.** [produire des résultats] to bear fruit, to be productive ou fruitful.

fructueux, euse [fʀyktɥø, øz] adj **1.** [fécond] fruitful, productive **2.** [profitable] profitable.

frugal, e, aux [fʀygal, o] adj **1.** [simple] frugal **2.** [qui mange peu] frugal.

fruit [fʀɥi] nm **1.** BOT ▶ **un fruit** : après ton fromage, veux-tu un fruit ? would you like some fruit ou a piece of fruit after your cheese? ▶ **des fruits** fruit ▶ **manger des fruits** to eat fruit ▶ **fruit défendu** forbidden fruit ▶ **fruit de la passion** passion fruit ▶ **un fruit sec** a) pr a piece of dried fruit b) fig a failure ▶ **fruits confits** candied ou crystallized fruit ▶ **fruits rouges** red berries **2.** CULIN ▶ **fruits de mer** seafood **3.** [résultat] fruit / le fruit de son travail the fruit ou result of his labours / cela a porté ses fruits it bore fruit.

fruitages [fʀɥitaʒ] nmpl QUÉBEC wild berries.

fruité, e [fʀɥite] adj fruity.

fruitier, ère [fʀɥitje, ɛʀ] ❖ adj fruit (modif). ❖ nm, f fruiterer, greengrocer UK, fruit seller US. ❖ **fruitière** nf cooperative cheese dairy.

frusques [fʀysk] nfpl fam togs, gear.

fruste [fʀyst] adj **1.** [grossier - personne] uncouth, rough **2.** [sans élégance - style] unpolished, crude, rough.

frustrant, e [fʀystʀɑ̃, ɑ̃t] adj frustrating.

frustration [fʀystʀasjɔ̃] nf frustration.

frustré, e [fʀystʀe] adj frustrated.

frustrer [3] [fʀystʀe] vt **1.** [décevoir] to frustrate, to thwart **2.** [priver] ▶ **frustrer qqn de** to rob sb of **3.** PSYCHOL to frustrate.

FS (abr de franc suisse) SFr.

fudge [fœdʒ] nm QUÉBEC fudge.

fuel [fjul], **fuel-oil** [fjulɔjl] (pl **fuel-oils**) nm (fuel ou heating) oil ▶ **fuel domestique** domestic heating oil.

fugace [fygas] adj [beauté] transient, evanescent, ephemeral ; [impression, souvenir, pensée] transient, fleeting.

fugitif, ive [fyʒitif, iv] ❖ adj [fugace - vision, idée] fleeting, transient ; [- bonheur] short-lived ; [- souvenir] elusive. ❖ nm, f runaway, fugitive.

fugue [fyg] nf **1.** MUS fugue **2.** [fuite] ▶ **faire une fugue** a) [de chez soi] to run away from home b) [d'une pension] to run away from boarding school c) [pour se marier] to elope.

fuguer [1] [fyge] vi to run away, to do a bunk UK.

fuir [35] [fɥiʀ] ❖ vi **1.** [s'enfuir] to run away, to flee ▶ **fuir devant le danger** to flee in the face of danger **2.** [se dérober] to run away ▶ **fuir devant ses responsabilités** to shirk ou evade one's responsibilities **3.** [se répandre - eau] to leak ; [- gaz] to leak, to escape **4.** [perdre son contenu - tonneau, stylo] to leak, to be leaky. ❖ vt **1.** [abandonner] to flee (from) / elle a fui le pays she fled the country **2.** [éviter] to avoid, to shun ▶ **fuir le danger** to keep away from ou avoid danger **3.** [se soustraire à, s'éloigner de] to shirk, to evade / fuir la tentation to flee from ou avoid temptation.

fuite [fɥit] nf **1.** [départ] escape, flight ▶ **prendre la fuite** [prisonnier] to run away, to (make one's) escape ▶ **mettre qqn / un animal en fuite** to put sb / an animal to flight ▶ **la fuite des cerveaux** the brain drain **2.** FIN ▶ **fuite de capitaux** flight of capital (abroad) **3.** [écoulement - de liquide] leak, leakage ; [- de gaz] leak ; [- de courant] escape **4.** [d'un pneu] puncture ; [d'une canalisation, d'un récipient] leak **5.** [indiscrétion] leak.

fulgurant, e [fylgyʀɑ̃, ɑ̃t] adj **1.** [rapide - réponse] lightning (modif) ; [- idée] sudden ; [- carrière] dazzling **2.** [intense - douleur] shooting, fulgurating spéc ; [- lumière] blinding, dazzling, fulgurant sout.

fulminer [3] [fylmine] vi litt to fulminate, to rail / fulminer contre le gouvernement to fulminate ou rail against the government.

fumant, e [fymɑ̃, ɑ̃t] adj **1.** [cheminée, feu] smoking, smoky ; [cendres, décombres] smouldering **2.** [liquide, nourriture] steaming **3.** *fam* [remarquable] brilliant ▸ **un coup fumant** a masterstroke.

fumé, e [fyme] adj smoked.

fumée [fyme] nf [de combustion] smoke ▸ **partir** ou **s'en aller en fumée** to go up in smoke.

fumer [3] [fyme] ◆ vt **1.** [tabac] to smoke ▸ **fumer la pipe** to smoke a pipe ▸ **fumer comme un pompier** ou **un sapeur** to smoke like a chimney **2.** CULIN to smoke **3.** AGR to manure, to dung, to fatten. ◆ vi **1.** [feu, cheminée] to smoke, to give off smoke ; [cendres, décombres] to smoke, to smoulder **2.** [liquide, nourriture] to steam, to give off steam.

fumet [fymɛ] nm [odeur - d'un plat] (pleasant) smell, aroma ; [- d'un vin] bouquet.

fumette [fymɛt] nf *fam* smoking marijuana / *se faire une fumette* to get stoned.

fumeur, euse [fymœʀ, øz] nm, f [adepte du tabac] smoker ▸ **compartiment fumeurs** smoking compartment ou car US.

fumeux, euse [fymø, øz] adj [confus] hazy, woolly UK ou wooly US.

fumier [fymje] nm **1.** AGR manure **2.** *tfam* [personne] bastard.

fumiste [fymist] ◆ nm **1.** [installateur] heating specialist **2.** [ramoneur] chimney sweep. ◆ nmf *péj* shirker.

fumisterie [fymistəʀi] nf *fam & péj* humbug, sham, farce / *une vaste fumisterie* an absolute farce.

funambule [fynɑ̃byl] nmf tightrope walker, funambulist *sout*.

funèbre [fynɛbʀ] adj **1.** [relatif aux funérailles] funeral *(modif)* **2.** [lugubre] gloomy, lugubrious, funereal.

funérailles [fyneʀaj] nfpl funeral.

funéraire [fyneʀɛʀ] adj funeral *(modif)*, funerary *spéc*.

funeste [fynɛst] adj [désastreux] disastrous, catastrophic / *l'ignorance est souvent funeste* ignorance is often dangerous ou harmful ▸ **être funeste à qqn** to have terrible consequences for sb.

funiculaire [fynikylɛʀ] nm funicular (railway).

furax [fyʀaks] adj inv *fam* livid, hopping mad.

furet [fyʀɛ] nm ZOOL ferret.

fur et à mesure [fyʀeamzyʀ] ◈ **au fur et à mesure** loc adv gradually / *donnez-les-moi au fur et à mesure* give them to me gradually ou as we go along / *il s'adaptera au fur et à mesure* he'll get used to it in time / *je préfère faire mon travail au fur et à mesure plutôt que de le laisser s'accumuler* I prefer to do my work as and when it comes rather than letting it pile up. ◈ **au fur et à mesure de** loc prép as / *au fur et à mesure de l'avance des travaux* as work proceeds / *au fur et à mesure des besoins* as needed / *je vous les enverrai au fur et à mesure de leur disponibilité* I'll send them to you as and when they are available. ◈ **au fur et à mesure que** loc conj as / *l'eau s'écoule au fur et à mesure que je remplis l'évier* the water drains away as (soon as) I fill up the sink.

fureter [28] [fyʀte] vi [fouiller] to ferret (around ou about), to snoop (around ou about).

fureur [fyʀœʀ] nf **1.** [colère] rage, fury / *accès de fureur* fit of anger ou rage **2.** [passion] passion ▸ **la fureur de vivre** a lust for life ▸ **faire fureur** to be all the rage.

furibond, e [fyʀibɔ̃, ɔ̃d] adj furious.

furie [fyʀi] nf **1.** [colère] fury, rage **2.** [mégère] fury. ◈ **en furie** loc adj furious, enraged / *les éléments en furie litt* the raging elements.

furieusement [fyʀjøzmɑ̃] adv **1.** [avec colère] furiously, angrily **2.** [extrêmement] hugely, tremendously, extremely.

furieux, euse [fyʀjø, øz] adj **1.** [enragé - personne] furious, (very) angry ; [- geste, cri] furious ▸ **être furieux contre qqn** to be furious with sb ▸ **furieux de** : *être furieux de son échec* to be enraged ou infuriated at one's failure / *il est furieux d'avoir attendu* he's furious at having been kept waiting **2.** *litt* [violent] raging, wild **3.** [extrême] tremendous / *avoir une furieuse envie de dormir* to have an overwhelming desire to go to sleep.

furoncle [fyʀɔ̃kl] nm boil, furuncle *spéc*.

furtif, ive [fyʀtif, iv] adj **1.** [comportement] furtive ; [geste, action] furtive, surreptitious, stealthy ; [regard] furtive, sly ; [sourire] quiet, secret ; [larme] hidden **2.** MIL anti-radar.

furtivement [fyʀtivmɑ̃] adv stealthily, surreptitiously, furtively.

fusain [fyzɛ̃] nm **1.** BOT spindle (tree) **2.** ART [crayon] piece of charcoal ; [dessin] charcoal.

fuseau, x [fyzo] nm **1.** [bobine] spindle ▸ **dentelle / ouvrage aux fuseaux** bobbin lace / needlework **2.** VÊT stirrup pants. ◈ **fuseau horaire** nm time zone.

fusée [fyze] nf **1.** ASTRONAUT rocket ▸ **fusée orbitale** orbital rocket **2.** [signal] rocket ▸ **fusée de détresse** flare.

fuselage [fyzlaʒ] nm fuselage.

fuselé, e [fyzle] adj [doigt] slender, tapered, tapering ; [jambe] slender ; [muscle] well-shaped ; [colonne] tapered, tapering, spindle-shaped.

fuser [3] [fyze] vi **1.** [jaillir - vapeur] to gush ou to spurt (out) ; [- liquide] to jet ou to gush ou to spurt (out) ; [- lumière] to stream out ; [- étincelle] to fly **2.** [retentir - rire, voix] to burst out.

fusible [fyzibl] nm fuse ▸ **un fusible a grillé** a fuse blew.

fusil [fyzi] nm **1.** ARM gun, rifle ▸ **fusil à air comprimé** airgun ▸ **fusil à canon scié** sawn-off shotgun ▸ **fusil de chasse** shotgun ▸ **fusil à lunette** rifle with telescopic sight ▸ **fusil sous-marin** speargun **2.** [affiloir] ▸ **fusil (à aiguiser)** steel.

fusillade [fyzijad] nf **1.** [bruit] shooting *(U)*, gunfire **2.** [combat] gunfight, gun battle.

fusiller [3] [fyzije] vt [exécuter] to shoot ▸ **fusiller qqn du regard** to look daggers ou to glare at sb.

fusil-mitrailleur [fyzimitʀajœʀ] *(pl* fusils-mitrailleurs*)* nm light machine gun.

fusion [fyzjɔ̃] nf **1.** MÉTALL fusion, melting **2.** NUCL ▸ **fusion (nucléaire)** fusion ▸ **fusion du cœur** nuclear meltdown **3.** [union - d'idées, de sentiments] fusion ; [- de groupes] fusion, merging ; [- de peuples, de cultures] fusion, merging **4.** ÉCON merger, merging **5.** INFORM merge, merging. ◈ **en fusion** loc adj molten.

fusionnel, elle [fyzjɔnɛl] adj [couple] inseparable, intense ; [relation] intense.

fusionner [3] [fyzjɔne] ◆ vt to merge. ◆ vi ÉCON to amalgamate, to merge.

fustiger [17] [fystiʒe] vt *litt* **1.** [battre] to thrash **2.** [critiquer - personne, attitude] to censure, to criticize harshly ; [- vice] to castigate *sout*.

fût, fut* [fy] nm **1.** [d'un arbre] bole **2.** [tonneau] cask **3.** [partie - d'une vis, d'un poteau] shaft ; [- d'une colonne] shaft, body.

futaie [fytɛ] nf forest, (piece of) timberland US.

futé, e [fyte] adj sharp, smart, clever / *il n'est pas très futé* he's not very bright.

futile [fytil] adj **1.** [frivole - raison] frivolous, trifling ; [- occupation, lecture, personne] frivolous **2.** [sans valeur - vie] pointless, futile.

futilité [fytilite] nf [caractère futile] triviality / *ils ne se racontaient que des futilités* their conversation consisted of nothing but trivialities.

futur, e [fytyʀ] ◆ adj **1.** [à venir - difficulté, joie] future *(modif)* ▸ **la vie future** RELIG the afterlife **2.** *(avant nom)* ▸ **future mère** mother-to-be ▸ **mon futur époux** my future husband ▸ **un futur client** a prospective client / *un futur mathématicien* a future ou budding mathematician. ◆ nm, f *hum* intended *hum*, husband-to-be (wife-to-be).

◆◆ **futur** nm **1.** [avenir] ▸ **le futur** the future ▸ **le futur proche** the immediate future **2.** GRAM future (tense).

futuriste [fytyʀist] adj [d'anticipation] futuristic.

futurologue [fytyʀɔlɔg] nmf futurologist.

fuyant, e [fɥijɑ̃, ɑ̃t] adj **1.** [insaisissable - caractère] elusive ; [- regard] shifty, elusive **2.** [menton, front] receding / *un homme au menton fuyant* a weak-chinned man.

fuyard, e [fɥijaʀ, aʀd] nm, f runaway, fugitive.

g, G [ʒe] nm (abr écrite de **gramme**) g.

G SMS abr écrite de **j'ai**.

G8 nm ▸ **le G8** G8 *(the eight most industrialised countries)*.

G20 nm ▸ **le G20** G20.

gabardine [gabaʀdin] nf **1.** [tissu] gabardine, gaberdine **2.** [vêtement] gabardine (coat).

gabarit [gabaʀi] nm **1.** [dimension] size **2.** *fam* [carrure] size, build ▸ **c'est un tout petit gabarit a)** he / she is very slightly built **b)** [stature] he's a bit on the short side **3.** *fam & fig* calibre ▸ **il a / n'a pas le gabarit** he is / isn't up to it **4.** TECHNOL [pour mesure] gauge ; [maquette] template.

gabegie [gabʒi] nf ▸ **la gabegie administrative** bureaucratic waste.

Gabon [gabɔ̃] npr m ▸ **le Gabon** Gabon.

gabonais, e [gabɔnɛ, ɛz] adj Gabonese. ✢ **Gabonais, e** nm, f Gabonese.

gâcher [3] [gaʃe] vt **1.** [gaspiller - argent, talent, temps] to waste **2.** [abîmer] to spoil, to ruin / *ne va pas me gâcher le plaisir fam* don't go spoiling ou ruining it for me **3.** CONSTR [plâtre, ciment] to mix.

gâchette [gaʃɛt] nf [d'arme à feu] trigger / *appuyez sur la gâchette* pull the trigger ▸ **avoir la gâchette facile / rapide** to be trigger-happy / quick on the draw.

gâchis [gaʃi] nm **1.** [gaspillage] waste / *sa vie est un véritable gâchis* her life has been completely wasted **2.** [désordre] mess.

gadelle [gadɛl] nf QUÉBEC currant.

gadget [gadʒɛt] nm **1.** [appareil] gadget **2.** [idée, projet] gimmick.

gadgétiser [gadʒetize] vt to fill with gadgets.

gadin [gadɛ̃] nm *tfam* ▸ **prendre** ou **ramasser un gadin** to come a cropper UK, to fall flat on one's face.

gadoue [gadu] nf *fam* [boue] mud, muck.

gaélique [gaelik] ✦ adj Gaelic. ✦ nm LING Gaelic.

gaffe [gaf] nf **1.** *fam* [bêtise - en paroles] gaffe ; [- en actions] blunder, boob UK, goof US / *tu as fait une gaffe en le lui racontant* you put your foot in it ou you dropped a clanger UK ou you goofed US when you told her that **2.** *fam* EXPR⟩ **faire gaffe** [faire attention] to be careful.

gaffer [3] [gafe] vi **1.** [en parlant] to drop a clanger UK, to make a gaffe ; [en agissant] to put one's foot in it, to boob UK, to goof US.

gaffeur, euse [gafœʀ, øz] nm, f *fam* blunderer.

gag [gag] nm gag, joke.

gaga [gaga] *fam* adj senile, gaga.

gage [gaʒ] nm **1.** [caution] security, collateral *(U)* ; [au mont-de-piété] pledge ▸ **laisser qqch en gage** to leave sthg as security ▸ **mettre qqch en gage** to pawn ou US to hock sthg **2.** *fig* [garantie] guarantee **3.** [témoignage] proof, token / *en gage de mon amour* as proof ou a pledge of my love / *en gage de ma bonne volonté* as a token of my goodwill **4.** JEUX forfeit.

gager [17] [gaʒe] vt *litt* [parier] to wager / *gageons qu'il l'épousera* I wager he'll marry her.

gageure, gageüre* [gaʒyʀ] nf *sout* challenge / *pour le gouvernement, c'est une gageure* the government is attempting the impossible.

gagnant, e [gaɲɑ̃, ɑ̃t] ✦ adj [ticket, coupon] winning *(avant nom)* ▸ **partir gagnant** *fig* : *elle part gagnante* all the odds are in her favour. ✦ nm, f winner.

gagnant-gagnant [gaɲɑ̃gaɲɑ̃] ✦ adj inv [accord, stratégie, partenariat] win-win. ✦ nm : *c'est du gagnant-gagnant pour l'entreprise et le salarié* it's a win-win for the firm and the employee.

gagne-pain [gaɲpɛ̃] (*pl* gagne-pain ou gagne-pains*) nm livelihood ▸ **c'est mon seul gagne-pain** it's my only means of existence.

gagner [3] [gaɲe] ✦ vt **1.** [partie, match, élection, prix] to win / *ce n'est pas gagné d'avance* it's a bit early to start talking about success ▸ **c'est gagné !** *iron* now you've got what you asked for! ▸ **gagner le gros lot** *pr & fig* to win ou to hit the jackpot **2.** [argent - comme rémunération] to earn, to make ; [- comme récompense] to earn ; [- dans une transaction] to make a profit of, to make ▸ **gagner gros** *fam* to earn ou to make big money / *gagner une fortune à la loterie* to win a fortune on the lottery / *allez, prends, tu l'as bien gagné !* go on, take it, you've earned it! ▸ **gagner des mille et des cents** to earn a fortune ▸ **gagner sa vie** ou **son pain** ou **son bifteck** *fam* ou **sa croûte** *fam* to earn a living ou one's daily bread ▸ **eh bien, j'ai gagné ma journée !** *fam & iron* I should have stayed in bed today! **3.** [avantage] to gain ▸ **il y a tout à gagner à faire cette démarche** there's everything to gain ou to be gained from making this move / *et si j'accepte, qu'est-ce que j'y gagne ?* and if I accept, what do I get out of it? ▸ **c'est toujours ça de gagné** that's something, anyway! **4.** [économiser] to save / *gagner de la place* to save space ▸ **gagner du temps a)** [en allant très vite] to save time **b)** [en atermoyant] to play for time **5.** ÉCON to gain / *l'indice a gagné deux points* the index has gone up by ou has gained two points **6.** [conquérir - ami] to win ; [- partisan] to win over *(sép)* ▸ **gagner l'amitié / l'appui de qqn** to win sb's friendship / support ▸ **gagner qqn à une cause** to win sb over (to a cause) **7.** [suj : sentiment, sensation] to overcome / *je sentais la panique me gagner* I could feel panic coming ou creeping over me ; [suj : épidémie, feu, nuages] to spread to ▸ **gagner du terrain** *pr & fig* to gain ground **8.** [rejoindre] to reach, to get to / *le ferry gagna le port* / *le large* the ferry reached port / got out into the open sea. ✦ vi **1.** [l'emporter] to win / *on a gagné (par) 3 buts à 2* we won (by) 3 goals to 2, we won 3-2 / *gagner aux courses* to win at the races **2.** [avancer - incendie, érosion] to gain ground ▸ **gagner sur** to gain ou to advance on ▸ **gagner en** to increase ou to gain in / *notre production gagne en qualité* the quality of our product is improving. ◆ **gagner à** v + prép : *elle gagne à être connue* once you get to know her a bit she grows on you / *vin qui gagne à vieillir* wine for laying down ou which improves with age / *ils gagneraient à ce que nul ne l'apprenne* it would be to their advantage if nobody found out.

gagneur, euse [ɡaɲœʀ, øz] nm, f winner, go-getter.

gai, e [ɡɛ] ◆ adj **1.** [mine, décor, personnalité] cheerful, happy ; [musique] cheerful, jolly ; [couleur] bright, cheerful / *il pleut encore, c'est gai !* iron great, it's raining again! ▸ **gai comme un pinson** happy as a lark ou a sandboy 🇬🇧 **2.** [un peu ivre] merry, tipsy **3.** [homosexuel] = **gay.** ◆ nm, f = **gay.**

gaiement, gaiment* [ɡemɑ̃] adv **1.** [avec joie] cheerfully, cheerily **2.** [avec enthousiasme] cheerfully, heartily ▸ **allons-y gaiement** let's get on with it!

gaieté, gaîté* [ɡete] nf **1.** [bonne humeur] cheerfulness, gaiety / *elle a retrouvé sa gaieté* she's cheered up again **2.** [d'une couleur] brightness, gaiety. ◆ **de gaieté de cœur, de gaîté de cœur*** loc adv willingly, gladly / *je ne l'ai pas fait de gaieté de cœur !* it's not something I enjoyed doing!

gaillard, e [ɡajaʀ, aʀd] nm, f [personne forte] ▸ *c'est un sacré gaillard !* **a)** [homme viril] he's a lusty ou red-blooded fellow! **b)** [costaud] he's a great strapping lad! ▸ *c'est une (rude) gaillarde* she's no shrinking violet. ◆ **gaillard** nm fam [avec menace] : *toi mon gaillard, tu n'as pas intérêt à bouger !* you'd better not move, mate! 🇬🇧 ou buddy! 🇺🇸 ; [avec amitié] : *c'est un gaillard qui promet* he's a promising lad 🇬🇧 ou boy.

gain [ɡɛ̃] nm **1.** [succès] winning ▸ **gain de cause**: *elle a eu* ou *obtenu gain de cause* **a)** [dans un procès] she won the case **b)** fig it was agreed that she was in the right **2.** [économie] saving ▸ *cela permet un (énorme) gain de place / temps* it saves (a lot of) space / time **3.** [progrès] benefit / *un gain de 30 sièges aux élections* a gain of 30 seats in the elections **4.** [bénéfice financier] profit, gain / *faire des gains importants à la Bourse* to make a big profit on the stock exchange ; [rémunération] earnings / *l'amour du gain* the love of gain.

gaine [ɡɛn] nf **1.** [étui - de poignard] sheath ; [- de parapluie] cover **2.** CONSTR [conduit vertical] shaft, duct ; [de climatisation] duct ▸ **gaine d'aération** ou **de ventilation** ventilation shaft **3.** VÊT girdle.

gainer [4] [ɡene] vt [câble] to sheathe, to encase ; [cylindre, tuyau] to lag.

gala [ɡala] nm gala / *gala de charité* charity gala. ◆ **de gala** loc adj gala (*modif*).

galant, e [ɡalɑ̃, ɑ̃t] adj **1.** [courtois] gallant, gentlemanly ▸ **un galant homme** courteous ou an honourable man, a gentleman **2.** litt [amoureux] ▸ **un rendez-vous galant** a date, a rendezvous, a lover's tryst vieilli ▸ **en galante compagnie** in the company of the opposite sex.

galanterie [ɡalɑ̃tʀi] nf [courtoisie] courteousness, gallantry, chivalry.

galaxie [ɡalaksi] nf galaxy.

galbe [ɡalb] nm curve.

galbé, e [ɡalbe] adj **1.** [commode, poterie] curved, with a curved outline **2.** [mollet - de femme] shapely ; [- de sportif] muscular.

gale [ɡal] nf **1.** MÉD scabies **2.** VÉTÉR [du chien, du chat] mange ; [du mouton] scab.

galère [ɡalɛʀ] ◆ nf **1.** [navire] galley **2.** fam [situation pénible] hassle ▸ *c'est la galère pour obtenir des places*

de théâtre it's a real hassle getting theatre tickets ▸ **mais qu'allais-tu faire dans cette galère ?** (*allusion à Molière*) why on earth did you have to get mixed up in this? ◆ adj fam : *il est vraiment galère, ce mec* he's nothing but trouble ▸ *c'est un peu galère* it's a bit of a hassle.

galérer [18] [ɡaleʀe] vi fam [avoir du mal] : *j'ai galéré toute la journée pour m'inscrire* I've been running around (like mad) all day sorting out my enrolment / *elle a vraiment galéré avant d'être connue* she had a hard time of it before she made it.

🖉 In reformed spelling (see p. 16-18), this verb is conjugated like *semer : il galèrera, elle galèrerait.*

galerie [ɡalʀi] nf **1.** [local - d'expositions, de ventes] (art) gallery, private gallery ▸ **galerie d'art** ou **de peinture** ou **de tableaux** art gallery **2.** [salle d'apparat] hall, gallery ▸ **la galerie des Glaces** the Hall of Mirrors **3.** [passage couvert] gallery ; [arcade] arcade ▸ **galerie marchande** ou **commerciale** shopping arcade 🇬🇧, shopping mall 🇺🇸 **4.** ▸ **les deuxièmes galeries a)** [qui ne sont pas les plus hautes] the dress circle **b)** [les plus hautes] the upper circle ▸ **tout ce qu'il fait, c'est pour la galerie** everything he does is to show off ou is calculated to impress **5.** [souterrain - de taupe] tunnel ; [- de termites] gallery **6.** MIN gallery, level **7.** AUTO roof rack.

galeriste [ɡalʀist] nmf gallery owner.

galet [ɡalɛ] nm [caillou] pebble / *sur les galets* on the shingle ou the pebble beach.

galette [ɡalɛt] nf **1.** [crêpe - épaisse] pancake, griddle cake ; [- de froment, de sarrasin] pancake ; [pain azyme] matzo bread ; [biscuit] shortbread ▸ **galette de maïs** corn bread (U) ▸ **la galette des Rois** pastry traditionally eaten on Twelfth Night (in France) **2.** fam [disque, CD] disk.

galeux, euse [ɡalø, øz] adj [qui a la gale] mangy.

galimatias [ɡalimatja] nm gibberish (U), gobbledegook (U), nonsense (U).

galipette [ɡalipɛt] nf forward roll, somersault / *les enfants dévalaient la colline en faisant des galipettes* the children were tearing down the hill doing somersaults.

Galles [ɡal] npr ▸ **le pays de Galles** Wales.

gallicisme [ɡalisism] nm LING (calque du français) gallicism ; [emprunt au français] French idiom, gallicism.

gallois, e [ɡalwa, az] adj Welsh. ◆ **Gallois, e** nm, f Welshman (Welshwoman) ▸ **les Gallois** the Welsh. ◆ **gallois** nm LING Welsh.

galon [ɡalɔ̃] nm **1.** TEXT [ruban] braid (U), trimming (U) **2.** MIL [insigne] stripe ▸ **prendre du galon** to take a step up the ladder, to get a promotion **3.** 🍁QUÉBEC COUT tape measure.

galop [ɡalo] nm ÉQUIT gallop ▸ **prendre le galop** to break into a gallop ▸ **galop d'essai a)** pr warm-up gallop **b)** fig dry run. ◆ **au galop** loc adv at a gallop ▸ **il a descendu la colline au galop** he galloped down the hill ▸ **au triple galop** fig at top speed.

galopant, e [ɡalɔpɑ̃, ɑ̃t] adj [consommation, inflation] galloping ; [urbanisation] uncontrolled, unplanned.

galoper [3] [ɡalɔpe] vi **1.** ÉQUIT to gallop **2.** [aller trop vite - idées, images] to race ; [- enfants] to charge ▸ **galoper après qqn / qqch** fam to chase (around) after sb / sthg.

galopin [ɡalɔpɛ̃] nm fam (street) urchin, scamp / *espèce de petit galopin !* you little devil!, you little brat!

galvaniser [3] [ɡalvanize] vt [stimuler] to galvanize ou to spur into action.

galvauder [3] [ɡalvode] vt [mot, sens] to debase / *le mot a été galvaudé* the word has become clichéd ou hackneyed through overuse.

gambader [3] [ɡɑ̃bade] vi to gambol, to leap ou to caper about.

gamberger [17] [gɑ̃bɛʁʒe] *tfam* vi [penser] to think ✦ *ça m'a fait gamberger, cette histoire* this business really made me think.

gambette [gɑ̃bɛt] nf *fam* [jambe] leg, pin 🇬🇧, gam 🇺🇸.

Gambie [gɑ̃bi] npr f [pays] ▸ **(la) Gambie** the Gambia.

gambien, enne [gɑ̃bjɛ̃, ɛn] adj Gambian. ❖ **Gambien, enne** nm, f Gambian.

gamelle [gamɛl] nf **1.** [récipient - d'un soldat] mess tin 🇬🇧 ou kit 🇺🇸; [- d'un ouvrier] lunch box 🇬🇧 ou pail 🇺🇸 **2.** [d'un chien] bowl **3.** EXPR **ramasser** ou **prendre une gamelle** *tfam* to fall flat on one's face, to come a cropper 🇬🇧.

gamin, e [gamɛ̃, in] ✦ nm, f kid. ✦ adj [puéril] childish; [espiègle] childlike, impish, playful.

gaminerie [gaminʁi] nf [acte] childish ou silly prank; [comportement] childishness, infantile behaviour ▸ *ses gamineries m'exaspéraient* his childish ways were driving me mad.

gamme [gam] nf **1.** MUS scale, gamut *spéc* ▸ **faire ses gammes a)** *pr* to play one's scales **b)** *fig* to go through the basics, to learn the ropes **2.** [de produits] range; [de sentiments] gamut **3.** COMM ▸ **bas / haut de gamme**: *produits bas / haut de gamme* down-market / up-market products.

Gand [gɑ̃] npr Ghent.

gang [gɑ̃g] nm gang.

ganglion [gɑ̃glijɔ̃] nm MÉD ganglion ▸ **ganglion lymphatique** lymph gland.

gangrène [gɑ̃gʁɛn] nf MÉD gangrene.

gangster [gɑ̃gstɛʁ] nm **1.** [bandit] gangster **2.** [escroc] cheat, swindler.

gant [gɑ̃] nm [accessoire] glove ▸ **gant de boxe / d'escrime** boxing / fencing glove ▸ **gant de crin** massage glove ▸ **gant de toilette** flannel 🇬🇧, washcloth 🇺🇸, facecloth 🇺🇸 ▸ *ça te / lui va comme un gant* it fits you / him like a glove ▸ **mettre** ou **prendre des gants avec qqn** to handle sb with kid gloves ▸ *pour lui annoncer la nouvelle je te conseille de prendre des gants* I'd advise you to break the news to him very gently ▸ **relever** ou **ramasser le gant** to take up the gauntlet, to accept the challenge.

garage [gaʁaʒ] nm **1.** [de voitures] garage; [de bateaux] boathouse; [de vélos] shed; [d'avions] shed, hangar; [de bus] garage, depot ▸ *la voiture est au garage* the car is in the garage **2.** [atelier] garage, car repair shop 🇺🇸.

garagiste [gaʁaʒist] nmf [propriétaire] garage owner; [gérant] garage manager; [mécanicien] (garage) mechanic.

garant, e [gaʁɑ̃, ɑ̃t] ✦ adj **1.** DR ▸ **être garant d'une dette** to stand guarantor ou surety for a debt **2.** [responsable] ▸ **être / se porter garant de** to vouch ou to answer for ▸ *désormais, vous serez garante de ses faits et gestes* from now on, you'll be answerable ou responsible for his conduct. ✦ nm, f [responsable] guarantor. ❖ **garant** nm **1.** DR [personne] guarantor; [somme, bien, document] surety, security ▸ **être le garant de qqn** to stand surety for sb **2.** [garantie] guarantee, warranty.

garantie [gaʁɑ̃ti] nf **1.** COMM [assurance] guarantee ▸ **contrat de garantie** guarantee **2.** DR [obligation] guarantee ▸ **garantie de paiement** guarantee of payment **3.** [gage] guarantee ▸ *c'est sans garantie* I'm not promising ou guaranteeing anything! **4.** POL ▸ **garantie individuelle, garanties individuelles** guarantee of individual liberties. ❖ **sous garantie** *loc adj* under guarantee.

garantir [32] [gaʁɑ̃tiʁ] vt **1.** [veiller sur] to guarantee, to safeguard **2.** [assurer - appareil] to guarantee **3.** [promettre] to guarantee, to assure ▸ *il m'a garanti que ça serait livré demain* he assured me that it would be delivered tomorrow ▸ *je te garantis que tu le regretteras !* I can assure you you'll regret it! **4.** [protéger] ▸ **garantir qqn de** to protect sb from **5.** DR ▸ **garantir qqn contre** to cover sb against

6. FIN [paiement] to guarantee; [emprunt] to guarantee, to back; [créance] to secure.

garce [gaʁs] nf *tfam péj* bitch.

garçon [gaʁsɔ̃] nm **1.** [enfant] boy ▸ **grand garçon**: *un grand garçon comme toi, ça ne pleure pas* big boys like you don't cry ▸ **garçon manqué** tomboy **2.** [homme] boy ▸ **garçon d'honneur** best man ▸ **bon** ou **brave garçon**: *c'est un bon* ou *brave garçon* he's a good sort ▸ **joli garçon**: *il est plutôt joli garçon* he's quite good-looking **3.** [employé] ▸ **garçon de bureau / courses** office / errand boy ▸ **garçon (de café** ou **de salle)** waiter.

garçonnet [gaʁsɔnɛ] nm [petit garçon] (little) boy.

garde¹ [gaʁd] nf

A. SURVEILLANCE, PROTECTION 1. [surveillance - d'un bien, d'un lieu]: *je te confie la garde du manuscrit* I am entrusting you with the manuscript, I am leaving the manuscript in your safekeeping ou care ▸ **assurer la garde d'un immeuble a)** [police] to guard a building **b)** [concierge] to look after a building, to be caretaker 🇬🇧 ou janitor 🇺🇸 of a building ▸ **monter la garde** to stand guard **2.** [protection - d'un enfant, d'un animal] care ▸ *je confierai la garde des enfants à ma tante* I will leave the children in the care of my aunt **3.** MÉD [service de surveillance]: *interne qui fait des gardes* locum 🇬🇧, locum tenens 🇺🇸, intern on duty 🇺🇸 ▸ **garde de nuit** night duty **4.** DR custody ▸ *la garde des enfants fut confiée à la mère* the mother was given custody of the children, the children were left in the custody of their mother ▸ **garde à vue** police custody ▸ **droit de garde** (right of) custody ▸ **garde alternée** shared custody.

B. VIGILANCE SPORT guard ▸ *tenir la garde haute* to keep one's guard up ▸ **baisser sa garde** to drop one's guard ▸ **prendre garde**: *prends garde !* watch out! ▸ **prendre garde à**: *prenez garde à la marche* mind 🇬🇧 ou watch 🇺🇸 the step ▸ **prendre garde de**: *prenez garde de ne rien oublier* make sure ou take care you don't leave anything behind.

C. ARMES 1. [escorte, milice] guard ▸ **garde mobile** (State) security police ▸ **garde rapprochée** close guard ▸ **la vieille garde** the old guard *(of a political party)* **2.** [soldats en faction] guard ▸ **garde montante / descendante** relief / old guard **3.** [d'une arme blanche] hilt ▸ **jusqu'à la garde** *fig* up to the hilt. ❖ **gardes** nfpl iguard *(civil militia, 1789-1871)* ▸ **être** ou **tenir sur ses gardes** to be ou to stay on one's guard. ❖ **de garde** *loc adj* **1.** → **chien 2.** MÉD duty *(modif)* ▸ **médecin de garde** duty doctor, doctor on duty. ❖ **en garde** *loc adv* **1.** MIL & SPORT on (your) guard! ▸ **mettez-vous en garde** take your guard **2.** DR in care 🇬🇧, in custody 🇺🇸 **3.** EXPR **mettre qqn en garde** to warn sb. ❖ **sous bonne garde** *loc adv*: *le stade est sous bonne garde* the stadium is under (heavy) guard.

garde² [gaʁd] ✦ nmf [personne] ▸ **garde d'enfants** baby-sitter, childminder 🇬🇧 ▸ *la garde des enfants est une jeune Allemande* the childminder 🇬🇧 ou baby-sitter is a young German girl ▸ **garde des Sceaux** (French) Minister of Justice; ≃ Lord Chancellor 🇬🇧; ≃ Attorney General 🇺🇸. ✦ nm **1.** [surveillant] warden ▸ **garde du corps** bodyguard ▸ **garde forestier** forest warden 🇬🇧, forest ranger 🇺🇸 ▸ **garde mobile** member of the (State) security police ▸ **garde de nuit** night watchman ▸ **garde républicain** Republican guardsman *(on duty at French state occasions)* **2.** [soldat - en faction] guard; [- en service d'honneur] guardsman ▸ **garde rouge** Red Guard. ✦ nf MÉD nurse.

garde-à-vous [gaʁdavu] nm inv: *garde-à-vous, fixe !* attention!, 'shun! ▸ *se mettre au garde-à-vous* to stand to attention.

garde-barrière [ɡaʁdəbaʁjɛʁ] (*pl* gardes-barrière *ou* gardes-barrières *ou* garde-barrières*) nmf signalman (at a level crossing 🇬🇧 *ou* a grade crossing 🇺🇸).

garde-boue [ɡaʁdəbu] (*pl* garde-boue *ou* garde-boues*) nm mudguard.

garde-chasse [ɡaʁdəʃas] (*pl* gardes-chasse *ou* gardes-chasses *ou* garde-chasses*) nm gamekeeper.

garde-côte(s)[1] [ɡaʁdəkot] (*pl* garde-côtes) nm [bateau] coastguard ship.

garde-côte(s)[2] [ɡaʁdəkot] (*pl* gardes-côtes *ou* garde-côtes*) nm [personne] coastguard.

garde-fou [ɡaʁdəfu] (*pl* garde-fous) nm **1.** [barrière] railing, guardrail ; [talus] (raised) bank **2.** fig [défense] ▶ **servir de garde-fou contre** to safeguard against.

garde-malade [ɡaʁdəmalad] (*pl* gardes-malade *ou* gardes-malades *ou* garde-malades*) nmf nurse.

garde-manger [ɡaʁdəmɑ̃ʒe] (*pl* garde-manger *ou* garde-mangers*) nm [placard] meat safe ; [réserve] pantry, larder.

garde-meuble(s) [ɡaʁdəmœbl] (*pl* garde-meubles) nm furniture depository 🇬🇧 *ou* storehouse ▶ **mettre qqch au garde-meubles** to put sthg in storage.

garde-pêche [ɡaʁdəpɛʃ] ◆ nm (*pl* gardes-pêche *ou* garde-pêches*) water bailiff 🇬🇧, fish warden 🇺🇸. ◆ nm inv [en mer] fisheries protection vessel ; [sur rivière] bailiff's boat 🇬🇧, fish warden's boat 🇺🇸.

garder [3] [ɡaʁde]
vt

A. SURVEILLER, PROTÉGER **1.** [veiller sur - personne, animal] to look after *(insép)* ; [-boutique] to keep an eye on, to mind / **il doit faire garder les enfants le soir** he has to get somebody to look after the children in the evening ▶ **elle garde des enfants** she does some childminding 🇬🇧 *ou* babysitting **2.** [surveiller - personne, lieu] to guard **3.** DR ▶ **garder qqn à vue** to keep *ou* to hold sb in custody.

B. RESTER **1.** [suj : malade] ▶ **garder le lit** to be confined to bed, to be laid up **2.** MIL ▶ **garder les arrêts** to remain under arrest.

C. MAINTENIR, PRÉSERVER **1.** [conserver - aliment] to keep **2.** [ne pas se dessaisir de] to keep / *j'ai gardé toutes ses lettres* I kept all his letters **3.** [conserver sur soi] to keep on *(sép)* / *puis-je garder mon chapeau / manteau ?* may I keep my hat / coat on? **4.** [conserver en dépôt] to keep / *la voisine garde mon courrier pendant mon absence* my neighbour keeps my mail for me when I'm away **5.** [réserver] to save, to keep / *ne te fatigue pas trop, il faut garder des forces pour ce soir* don't overtire yourself, save some of your energy for tonight ▶ **garder une poire pour la soif** to keep something for a rainy day **6.** [retenir - personne] to keep ▶ **garder qqn à dîner** to have sb stay for dinner / *va-t-elle garder le bébé ?* [femme enceinte] is she going to keep the baby? **7.** [ne pas révéler] to keep ▶ **garder le secret sur qqch** to keep sthg secret **8.** [avoir à l'esprit] : *je n'ai pas gardé de très bons souvenirs de cette époque* my memories of that time are not very happy ones ▶ **garder qqch présent à l'esprit** to bear *ou* to keep sthg in mind **9.** [maintenir - attitude, sentiment] to keep ▶ **garder son calme** to keep calm *ou* cool ▶ **garder le silence** to keep silent ▶ **garder la tête froide** to keep one's head *ou* a cool head **10.** [ne pas perdre - qualité] : *le mot garde encore toute sa valeur* the word still retains its full meaning. ◆ **se garder** vp *(emploi passif)* [aliment] to keep / *les framboises ne se gardent pas (longtemps)* raspberries do not keep (long). ◆ **se garder de** vp + prép *sout* **1.** [éviter de] : *je me garderai bien de lui en parler* I'll be very careful not to talk to him about it **2.** [se méfier de] : *il faut se garder des gens trop expansifs* one should beware *ou* be wary of over-effusive people.

garderie [ɡaʁdəʁi] nf [de quartier] day nursery 🇬🇧, day-care center 🇺🇸 ; [liée à une entreprise] crèche 🇬🇧, baby-sitting services 🇺🇸.

garde-robe [ɡaʁdəʁɔb] (*pl* garde-robes) nf [vêtements] wardrobe.

gardien, enne [ɡaʁdjɛ̃, ɛn] nm, f **1.** [surveillant - d'une usine, d'une société] (security) guard ; [-d'un cimetière] caretaker ; [-d'un domaine] warden ; [-d'un zoo] keeper ▶ **gardien d'immeuble** caretaker 🇬🇧, porter 🇬🇧, janitor 🇺🇸 ▶ **gardien de musée** museum attendant ▶ **gardien de nuit** night watchman ▶ **gardien de prison** prison warder 🇬🇧, prison guard 🇺🇸 **2.** Québec [d'enfants] baby-sitter **3.** fig [protecteur] guardian, custodian. ◆ **gardien** nm ▶ **gardien de but** goalkeeper ▶ **gardien de la paix** police officer. ◆ **gardienne** nf ▶ **gardienne d'enfants** nursery help *ou* helper 🇬🇧, day-care assistant 🇺🇸.

gardiennage [ɡaʁdjenaʒ] nm : *assurer le gardiennage d'un entrepôt* to be in charge of security in a warehouse ▶ **société de gardiennage** security firm / *assurer le gardiennage d'une résidence* to be the caretaker *ou* porter in a block of flats 🇬🇧, to be the doorman *ou* janitor in an apartment block 🇺🇸.

gardon [ɡaʁdɔ̃] nm ZOOL roach.

gare [ɡaʁ] ◆ nf RAIL [installations et voies] station ; [hall] (station) concourse ; [bâtiments] station building *ou* buildings / *le train de 14 h 30 à destination de Paris va entrer en gare voie 10* the train now arriving at platform 10 is the two-thirty to Paris ▶ **gare frontière / maritime** border / harbour 🇬🇧 *ou* harbor 🇺🇸 station ▶ **gare de passagers / marchandises** passenger / goods station ▶ **gare routière** a) [d'autobus] coach 🇬🇧 *ou* bus 🇺🇸 station b) [de camions] haulage depot ▶ **gare de triage** marshalling yard 🇬🇧, switchyard 🇺🇸 ▶ **romans de gare** cheap *ou* trashy novels. ◆ interj : *gare à toi !, gare à tes fesses !* fam you just watch it! / *gare à vous si vous rentrez après minuit !* if you come home after midnight, there'll be trouble!, you'd better be in by midnight, or else!

garer [3] [ɡaʁe] vt [véhicule] to park ▶ **garé en double file** double-parked. ◆ **se garer** vpi **1.** [en voiture] to park **2.** [s'écarter] ▶ **gare-toi !** get out of the way!

gargariser [3] [ɡaʁɡaʁize] ◆ **se gargariser** vpi to gargle. ◆ **se gargariser de** vp + prép to delight in *(insép)* / *il se gargarise volontiers de mots à la mode / de noms célèbres* he delights in trotting out fashionable words / in dropping famous names.

gargarisme [ɡaʁɡaʁism] nm [rinçage] gargling ; [produit] mouthwash / *faire des gargarismes* to gargle.

gargote [ɡaʁɡɔt] nf péj cheap restaurant.

gargouille [ɡaʁɡuj] nf ARCHIT gargoyle.

gargouillement [ɡaʁɡujmɑ̃] nm **1.** [d'une fontaine] gurgling **2.** [de l'estomac] rumbling.

gargouiller [3] [ɡaʁɡuje] vi **1.** [liquide] to gurgle **2.** [estomac] to rumble.

gargouillis [ɡaʁɡuji] = **gargouillement**.

garnement [ɡaʁnəmɑ̃] nm brat, rascal.

garni, e [ɡaʁni] adj CULIN [plat du jour, viande] with vegetables.

garnir [32] [ɡaʁniʁ] vt **1.** [décorer] : *ils ont garni la table de fleurs et de bougies* they decorated the table with flowers and candles **2.** [remplir] : *nous vendons la corbeille garnie de fruits* the basket is sold (complete) with an assortment of fruit / *il est bien garni, ton frigo !* your fridge is very well stocked! **3.** [équiper] : *les semelles sont garnies de pointes d'acier* the soles are steel-tipped ; AUTO & RAIL [aménager - intérieur d'un véhicule] to fit **4.** [de tissu - siège] to cover, to upholster ; [-vêtement, coffret] to line **5.** CULIN [remplir] to fill ; [pour accompagner] : *toutes nos* *viandes sont garnies de pommes sautées* all our meat dishes come with ou are served with sautéed potatoes **6.** [remplir du nécessaire] to fill (up).

garnison [ɡaʀnizɔ̃] nf garrison / *le régiment est en garnison à Nancy* the regiment is garrisoned ou stationed in Nancy.

garniture [ɡaʀnityʀ] nf **1.** [ensemble] (matching) set ▶ **garniture de cheminée** (set of) mantelpiece ornaments ▶ **une garniture de lit** a matching set of sheets and pillowcases **2.** [ornementation] : *avec une garniture de dentelle* trimmed with lace **3.** [protection] ▶ **garniture de frein / d'embrayage** brake / clutch lining **4.** CULIN [d'un feuilleté] filling ; [accompagnement - décoratif] garnish ; [- de légumes] garnish, fixings *(pl)* 🇺🇸 / *c'est servi sans garniture* it is served without vegetables ou on its own.

garrigue [ɡaʀig] nf scrubland, garigue.

garrocher [3] [ɡaʀɔʃe] 🇶🇧 vt *fam* [jeter, lancer] to throw. ◆ **se garrocher** vp *fam* [se précipiter] to hurry.

garrot [ɡaʀo] nm **1.** MÉD tourniquet ▶ **mettre un garrot** to apply a tourniquet **2.** ZOOL withers.

garrotter, garroter* [3] [ɡaʀɔte] vt [attacher] to tie up *(sép)*, to bind.

gars [ɡa] nm *fam* **1.** [garçon, fils] boy, lad 🇬🇧 / *qu'est-ce qui ne va pas, mon petit gars ?* what's the matter, kid ou sonny? **2.** [jeune homme] boy, lad 🇬🇧, guy 🇺🇸 / *c'est un gars bizarre* he's a weird bloke 🇬🇧 ou guy 🇺🇸.

gaspillage [ɡaspijaʒ] nm waste / *évitez le gaspillage de nourriture / d'électricité* don't waste food / electricity.

gaspiller [3] [ɡaspije] vt [denrée, temps, talent] to waste ; [économies] to squander.

gastrique [ɡastʀik] adj gastric, stomach *(modif)*.

gastro-entérite *(pl* gastro-entérites*)*, **gastroentérite*** [ɡastʀoɑ̃teʀit] nf gastroenteritis *(U)*.

gastro-entérologue *(pl* gastro-entérologues*)*, **gastroentérologue*** [ɡastʀoɑ̃teʀɔlɔg] nmf gastroenterologist.

gastronome [ɡastʀɔnɔm] nmf gastronome, gourmet.

gastronomie [ɡastʀɔnɔmi] nf gastronomy.

gastronomique [ɡastʀɔnɔmik] adj gastronomic, gastronomical ▶ **buffet gastronomique** gourmet buffet.

gâteau, x [ɡato] nm **1.** CULIN [pâtisserie] cake ; [biscuit] biscuit 🇬🇧, cookie 🇺🇸 ▶ **gâteau d'anniversaire** birthday cake ▶ **gâteau apéritif** savoury biscuit 🇬🇧, cracker 🇺🇸 *(to eat with drinks)* ▶ **gâteau marbré** marble cake ▶ **gâteau de riz / de semoule** ≃ rice / semolina pudding ▶ **gâteau sec** (sweet) biscuit 🇬🇧 ou cookie 🇺🇸 ▶ *c'est du gâteau fam* it isn't as easy as it looks ▶ *c'est du gâteau fam* it's a piece of cake ou a walkover **2.** 🇨🇭 tart **3.** 🇶🇧 ▶ **gâteau des anges** angel food cake. ◆ **gâteau** adj inv *fam* ▶ *c'est un papa gâteau* he's a soft touch with his children.

gâter [3] [ɡate] vt **1.** [combler - ami, enfant] to spoil / *quel beau temps, nous sommes vraiment gâtés* we're really lucky with the weather / *nous sommes gâtés avec cette pluie !* *iron* lovely weather for ducks! / *il n'est pas gâté par la nature* nature wasn't very kind to him **2.** [abîmer] to spoil / *l'humidité gâte les fruits* moisture makes fruit go bad ou spoils fruit **3.** [gâcher] to spoil / *il est beau et riche, ce qui ne gâte rien* he's good-looking and wealthy, which does him no harm. ◆ **se gâter** vpi **1.** [pourrir - viande, poisson, lait] to go off 🇬🇧 ou bad ; [- fruit] to go bad **2.** [se carier - dent] to decay, to go rotten **3.** [se détériorer - situation] to go wrong / *regarde le ciel, le temps se gâte* look at the sky, it's starting to cloud over ou the weather's changing for the worse.

gâterie [ɡatʀi] nf **1.** [cadeau] treat, present **2.** [friandise] treat, titbit.

gâteux, euse [ɡatø, øz] ◆ adj [sénile] doddering, doddery. ◆ nm, f : *un vieux gâteux* *péj* a silly ou doddering old fool.

gâtisme [ɡatism] nm MÉD senility.

gauche [ɡoʃ] ◆ adj **1.** [dans l'espace] left / *la partie gauche du tableau est endommagée* the left ou left-hand side of the painting is damaged **2.** [maladroit - adolescent] awkward, gawky ; [- démarche] ungainly ; [- manières] awkward, gauche ; [- geste, mouvement] awkward, clumsy. ◆ nm SPORT [pied gauche] : *marquer un but du gauche* to score a goal with one's left (foot) ; [poing gauche] : *il a un gauche imparable* he has an unstoppable left. ◆ nf **1.** [côté gauche] ▶ **la gauche** the left ou left-hand side / *il confond sa droite et sa gauche* he mixes up (his) right and left / *la page de gauche* the left-hand page / *l'église est à gauche de l'hôtel* the church is to the left of the hotel / *la deuxième rue sur votre gauche* the second street on your left **2.** POL left ▶ **elle vote à gauche** she votes (for the) left ▶ **la gauche caviar** champagne Socialism. ◆ **à gauche** loc adv [sur le côté gauche] on the left ▶ **tournez à gauche** turn left. ◆ **de gauche** loc adj left-wing / *être de gauche* to be left-wing ou a left-winger.

gaucher, ère [ɡoʃe, ɛʀ] ◆ adj left-handed. ◆ nm, f [gén] left-hander ; [boxeur] southpaw.

gauchisme [ɡoʃism] nm POL [gén] leftism ; [depuis 1968] New Leftism.

gauchiste [ɡoʃist] ◆ adj [gén & POL] left ; [depuis 1968] (New) Leftist. ◆ nmf [gén & POL] leftist ; [depuis 1968] (New) Leftist.

gaufre [ɡofʀ] nf CULIN waffle.

gaufrer [3] [ɡofʀe] vt **1.** [imprimer un relief sur - cuir, métal, papier] to emboss, to boss ; [- étoffe] to diaper **2.** [plisser - tissu] to goffer ; [- cheveux] to crimp.

gaufrette [ɡofʀɛt] nf wafer.

gaule [ɡol] nf **1.** [perche] pole **2.** PÊCHE fishing rod.

gauler [3] [ɡole] vt **1.** [arbre] to beat ; [fruit] to beat down *(sép)* (from the tree) **2.** EXPR se faire gauler *tfam* to be nicked 🇬🇧 ou busted 🇺🇸.

gaulliste [ɡolist] adj & nmf Gaullist.

gaulois, e [ɡolwa, az] adj **1.** HIST Gallic, Gaulish **2.** [grivois] bawdy ▶ **l'humour gaulois** bawdy humour. ◆ **Gaulois, e** nm, f Gaul.

gauloiserie [ɡolwazʀi] nf [plaisanterie] bawdy joke ; [remarque] bawdy remark.

gausser [3] [ɡose] ◆ **se gausser** vpi *litt* to mock.

gaver [3] [ɡave] vt **1.** AGR to force-feed **2.** [bourrer] : *la télévision nous gave de publicités* we get an overdose of commercials on television / *ça me gave* *fam* it really hacks me off. ◆ **se gaver** vp + prép to fill ou stuff o.s. up with / *cet été je me suis gavé de romans policiers* *fig* this summer I indulged myself with detective stories.

gay [ɡɛ] adj & nmf gay.

gaz [ɡaz] ◆ nm inv **1.** [pour le chauffage, l'éclairage] gas / *avoir le gaz* to have gas, to be on gas 🇬🇧 / *employé du gaz* gasman ▶ **gaz de ville** town gas **2.** CHIM gas ▶ **gaz asphyxiant / hilarant / lacrymogène** asphyxiating / laughing / tear gas ▶ **gaz carbonique** carbon dioxide ▶ **gaz à effet de serre** greenhouse effect gas ▶ **gaz naturel** natural gas **3.** MÉD [pour anesthésie] gas. ◆ nmpl **1.** PHYSIOL ▶ **avoir des gaz** to have wind 🇬🇧 ou gas 🇺🇸 **2.** [carburant] ▶ **gaz brûlés** ou **d'échappement** exhaust fumes ▶ **mettre les gaz** *fam* to put one's foot down 🇬🇧, to step on the gas 🇺🇸.

Gaza [ɡaza] npr Gaza ▶ **la bande de Gaza** the Gaza Strip.

gaze [ɡaz] nf **1.** TEXT gauze **2.** MÉD gauze ▶ **gaze stérilisée** aseptic gauze.

gazelle [ɡazɛl] nf gazelle.

gazer [3] [gaze] ◆ vt [asphyxier] to gas. ◆ vi *fam* [aller bien] ▶ **alors, ça gaze ? — ça gaze !** how's things? ou how's it going? — great! / *ça ne gaze pas du tout en ce moment* things aren't too great at the moment.

gazeux, euse [gazø,øz] adj **1.** CHIM gaseous **2.** [boisson] fizzy, sparkling ; [eau] sparkling, carbonated, fizzy.

gazinière [gazinjɛʀ] nf gas stove, gas cooker UK.

gazoduc [gazɔdyk] nm gas pipeline.

gazole [gazɔl] nm [pour moteur Diesel] diesel (oil), derv UK.

gazon [gazɔ̃] nm **1.** [herbe] : *du gazon* turf **2.** [pelouse] lawn.

gazouillement [gazujmɑ̃] nm **1.** [d'oiseau] chirping *(U)*, warbling *(U)* **2.** [d'un bébé] babbling *(U)*, gurgling *(U)*.

gazouiller [3] [gazuje] vi **1.** [oiseau] to chirp, to warble **2.** [bébé] to babble, to gurgle **3.** *litt* [ruisseau, eau] to babble, to murmur, to gurgle.

gazouillis [gazuji] = gazouillement.

GDF npr abr de Gaz de France.

geai [ʒɛ] nm jay.

géant, e [ʒeɑ̃, ɑ̃t] ◆ adj **1.** [énorme] giant / *un écran géant* a giant screen **2.** *fam* [formidable] ▶ **c'est géant !** it's wicked ou brill! ◆ nm, f **1.** [personne, chose de grande taille] giant **2.** *fig* : *c'est un des géants de l'électronique* ÉCON it's one of the giants of the electronics industry.

geek [gik] nmf geek.

geignard, e [ʒɛɲaʀ, aʀd] *fam* ◆ adj [personne, voix] whining, whingeing UK, whiny US. ◆ nm, f [enfant] crybaby ; [adulte] moaner, whinger UK, bellyacher US.

geindre [81] [ʒɛ̃dʀ] vi **1.** [gémir] to groan, to moan **2.** *fam* [pour des riens] to whine, to gripe.

gel [ʒɛl] nm **1.** MÉTÉOR frost **2.** [suspension] : *le gel des opérations militaires* the suspension of military operations **3.** ÉCON freezing ▶ **le gel des salaires** the wage freeze **4.** CHIM gel ▶ **gel coiffant** hair gel.

gélatine [ʒelatin] nf CULIN gelatine.

gélatineux, euse [ʒelatinø,øz] adj **1.** [contenant de la gélatine] gelatinous **2.** [flasque] gelatinous, jellylike, flaccid.

gelé, e [ʒəle] adj **1.** AGR & MÉTÉOR [sol] frozen **2.** *fig* [glacé] frozen / *des draps gelés* ice-cold sheets **3.** MÉD frostbitten **4.** ÉCON & FIN frozen. ◆ **gelée** nf **1.** MÉTÉOR frost ▶ **gelée blanche** white frost, hoarfrost **2.** CULIN jelly. ◆ **gelée royale** nf royal jelly.

geler [25] [ʒəle] ◆ vt **1.** [transformer en glace - eau, sol] to freeze **2.** [paralyser - négociations] to halt ; [- projet] to halt, to block ; [- capitaux, salaires, prix] to freeze. ◆ vi **1.** [eau, liquide] to freeze ; [lac] to freeze over **2.** [tuyau, serrure] to freeze up **3.** [pousses, légumes] to freeze, to be nipped by the frost **4.** [personne] to freeze ▶ **je gèle** I'm frozen (stiff) / *ferme la porte, on gèle ici* shut the door, it's freezing in here. ◆ v impers ▶ **il gèle** it's freezing. ◆ **se geler** vpi [personne] : *je me suis gelé là-bas* I got (absolutely) frozen down there.

gélule [ʒelyl] nf PHARM capsule.

Gémeaux [ʒemo] npr mpl ASTROL Gemini ▶ **elle est Gémeaux** she's (a) Gemini.

gémir [32] [ʒemiʀ] vi **1.** [blessé, malade] to moan, to groan **2.** [vent] to moan, to wail ; [parquet, gonds] to creak **3.** [se plaindre] to moan, to whine.

gémissement [ʒemismɑ̃] nm [gén] moan, groan / *le gémissement du vent* the moaning ou wailing of the wind ▶ **gémissements** [plaintes] whimpering, whining.

gemme [ʒɛm] nf [pierre précieuse] gem.

gênant, e [ʒenɑ̃, ɑ̃t] adj **1.** [ennuyeux] annoying / *c'est gênant qu'elle ne soit pas là* it's annoying ou it's a bit of a nuisance that she's not here ▶ **ce n'est pas gênant** it doesn't matter **2.** [embarrassant] awkward, embarrassing.

gencive [ʒɑ̃siv] nf ANAT gum / *prendre un coup dans les gencives* fam to get socked in the jaw, to get a kick in the teeth.

gendarme [ʒɑ̃daʀm] nmf [policier] gendarme, policeman, policewoman, police officer ▶ **jouer au gendarme et au voleur** ou **aux gendarmes et aux voleurs** to play cops and robbers. ◆ **gendarme** nm *fam* [personne autoritaire] ▶ **faire le gendarme** to lay down the law / *leur mère est un vrai gendarme* their mother's a real ou UK right battle-axe.

gendarmerie [ʒɑ̃daʀməʀi] nf **1.** [corporation] gendarmerie, police force ▶ **gendarmerie mobile** riot police **2.** [bureaux] gendarmerie, police station ; [caserne] police ou gendarmerie barracks.

Gendarmerie

In France, while the police are especially present in larger towns, the **gendarmerie** patrols the road network, small towns and the countryside. The **gendarmes** fulfil the same role as police officers, ensuring law and order and recording declarations of theft.

gendre [ʒɑ̃dʀ] nm son-in-law.

gène [ʒɛn] nm gene.

gêne [ʒɛn] nf **1.** [matérielle] : *je resterais bien un jour de plus si ça ne vous cause aucune gêne* I would like to stay for another day if it doesn't put you to any trouble ou if that's no bother **2.** [morale] embarrassment ▶ **un moment de gêne** an awkward moment / *'nous vous prions de nous excuser pour la gêne occasionnée'* 'we apologize for the inconvenience caused' **3.** [physique] difficulty, discomfort ▶ **éprouver** ou **avoir de la gêne à faire qqch** to find it difficult to do sthg **4.** [pauvreté] ▶ **être dans la gêne** to be in need.

gêné, e [ʒene] adj **1.** [personne, sourire] embarrassed / *pourquoi prends-tu cet air gêné ?* why are you looking so embarrassed? / *il n'est pas gêné, lui !* fam he's got a nerve ou UK a cheek! **2.** [serré] ill at ease, uncomfortable **3.** [financièrement] : *les personnes momentanément gênées peuvent demander une avance* people with temporary financial difficulties can ask for an advance.

généalogie [ʒenealɔʒi] nf [science] genealogy.

généalogique [ʒenealɔʒik] adj genealogical.

gêner [4] [ʒene] vt **1.** [incommoder - suj : chose] to bother **2.** [encombrer] to be in the way of **3.** [empêcher] : *la neige gênait la visibilité* visibility was hindered ou impaired by the snow / *ce camion gêne la circulation* that lorry is holding up the traffic **4.** [importuner - suj : personne] to put out (sép), to bother, to inconvenience / *ça ne le gênerait pas que j'arrive après minuit ?* would it bother him ou put him out if I arrived after midnight? / *ça vous gêne si j'ouvre la fenêtre ?* do you mind if I open the window? / *oui pourquoi, ça te gêne ?* fam yes why, what's it to you ou you got any objections? / *(en usage absolu) : ça ne gêne pas que tu viennes, il y a de la place* it'll be no bother ou trouble at all if you come, there's enough room **5.** [intimider] to embarrass / *les plaisanteries de son ami la gênaient* her friend's jokes embarrassed her ou made her feel uncomfortable **6.** [mettre en difficulté financière] : *en ce moment, cela me gênerait un peu de vous prêter cet argent* I can't really afford to lend you the money at the moment. ◆ **se gêner** ◆ vp *(emploi réciproque)* : *la chambre est trop petite, on se gêne les uns les autres* the room is too small, we're in each other's way. ◆ vpi *fam* : *je vais me gêner, tiens !* just watch me! ▶ **ne pas se gêner**: *continuez votre repas, ne vous gênez pas pour moi* go on with your meal, don't mind me / *vous avez pris ma place, surtout ne vous gênez pas !* *iron* go on, take my seat, don't mind me! / *il y en a qui ne se gênent pas !* some people have got a nerve!

général, e, aux [ʒeneʀal, o] adj **1.** [d'ensemble] general / *la situation générale* the general ou overall situation ▶ **le phénomène est général** the phenomenon is widespread, it's a general phenomenon **2.** [imprécis] general / *il s'en est tenu à des remarques générales* he confined himself to generalities ou to some general remarks **3.** [collectif] general, common ▶ **à la surprise / l'indignation générale** to everybody's surprise / indignation **4.** ADMIN & POL [assemblée, direction] general **5.** [discipline, science] general. ❖ **général, e, aux** nm, f MIL general ▶ **général en chef** commander in chief ▶ **général de brigade** brigadier 🇬🇧, brigadier general 🇺🇸 ▶ **général de corps d'armée** lieutenant general ▶ **général de division** major general. ❖ **générale** nf THÉÂTRE (final) dress rehearsal. ❖ **en général** loc adv **1.** [habituellement] generally **2.** [globalement] : *tu parles en général ou (tu parles) de nous ?* are you talking generally ou in general terms ou (are you talking) about us?

généralement [ʒeneʀalmã] adv **1.** [habituellement] generally, usually **2.** [globalement] generally.

généralisation [ʒeneʀalizasjɔ̃] nf **1.** [propos, idée] generalization **2.** [extension] generalization ▶ **nous assistons à la généralisation du conflit / de la maladie** the conflict / the disease is spreading.

généraliser [3] [ʒeneʀalize] vt **1.** [répandre] ▶ **cette méthode / interdiction a été généralisée** this method / ban now applies to everybody / *cette mesure a été généralisée en 1969* this measure was extended across the board in 1969 **2.** [globaliser] to generalize. ❖ **se généraliser** vpi [conflit, grève, infection] to spread ; [crise, famine] to become widespread / *l'usage de la carte de crédit s'est généralisé* credit cards are now in general use.

généraliste [ʒeneʀalist] ◆ adj : *une chaîne de télévision généraliste* a general-interest TV channel / *le caractère généraliste de l'entreprise* the diversity of the company's activities. ◆ nmf MÉD general practitioner, GP.

généralités [ʒeneʀalite] nfpl [points généraux] general remarks ; [banalités] generalities.

générateur, trice [ʒeneʀatœʀ, tʀis] adj [créateur] : *la nouvelle politique salariale sera génératrice d'emplois* the new wages policy will create jobs ou generate employment ▶ **une industrie génératrice d'emplois** a job-creating industry. ❖ **générateur** nm **1.** ÉLECTR ▶ **générateur d'électricité** electricity generator **2.** INFORM ▶ **générateur automatique de programmes** report program generator. ❖ **génératrice** nf ÉLECTR generator.

génération [ʒeneʀasjɔ̃] nf **1.** BIOL generation **2.** [groupe d'âge] generation / *les jeunes de ma génération* young people my age ou of my generation / *des immigrés de la seconde génération* second-generation immigrants.

générationnel, elle [ʒeneʀasjɔnɛl] adj generational ▶ **marketing générationnel** generational marketing ▶ **le dialogue générationnel** intergenerational dialogue ▶ **le fossé générationnel** the generation gap.

génératrice [ʒeneʀatʀis] f ⟶ **générateur**.

générer [18] [ʒeneʀe] vt to generate.

📝 In reformed spelling (see p. 16-18), this verb is conjugated like *semer* : *il génèrera, elle génèrerait*.

généreusement [ʒeneʀøzmã] adv **1.** [avec libéralité] generously **2.** [avec noblesse] generously **3.** [en grande quantité] : *se servir à manger généreusement* to help o.s. to a generous portion.

généreux, euse [ʒeneʀø, øz] adj **1.** [prodigue] generous / *il a été très généreux* he gave very generously, he was very generous **2.** [noble - geste, tempérament] noble **3.** [fertile - terre] generous, fertile **4.** [abondant - portion] generous ; [- repas] lavish **5.** [plantureux] : *une femme à la poitrine généreuse* a woman with an ample bosom.

générique [ʒeneʀik] ◆ adj generic. ◆ nm **1.** CINÉ & TV credits **2.** MÉD ▶ **(médicament) générique** generic medecine 🇬🇧 ou drug 🇺🇸.

générosité [ʒeneʀozite] nf **1.** [largesse] generosity **2.** [bonté] generosity, kindness.

genèse [ʒənɛz] nf **1.** [élaboration] genesis **2.** BIBLE ▶ **la Genèse** (the Book of) Genesis.

genêt [ʒənɛ] nm BOT broom (U).

génétique [ʒenetik] ◆ adj genetic ▶ **d'origine génétique** genetically-transmitted. ◆ nf genetics (sg).

Genève [ʒənɛv] npr Geneva.

genevois, e [ʒənvwa, az] adj Genevan, Genevese. ❖ **Genevois, e** nm, f Genevan, Genevese.

génial, e, aux [ʒenjal, o] adj **1.** [qui a du génie] of genius **2.** [ingénieux] brilliant **3.** *fam* [sensationnel] brilliant, great, fantastic / *je n'ai pas trouvé cette exposition géniale* I didn't think much of that exhibition ▶ **génial !** brilliant ou great!

génie [ʒeni] nm **1.** [don] genius ▶ **avoir du génie** to be a genius / *elle a le génie des affaires* she has a genius for business **2.** [personne] genius / *c'est loin d'être un génie* he's no genius **3.** [essence] genius / *le génie de la langue française* the genius ou spirit of the French language **4.** LITTÉR & MYTH [magicien] genie ; [esprit] spirit ▶ **être le bon / mauvais génie de qqn** to be a good / bad influence on sb **5.** TECHNOL ▶ **le Génie** engineering / *les officiers du Génie* ≃ the Royal Engineers 🇬🇧 ; ≃ the (Army) Corps of Engineers 🇺🇸 ▶ **génie atomique / chimique / civil** / **génétique** nuclear / chemical / civil / genetic engineering ▶ **génie maritime / militaire** marine / military engineering. ❖ **de génie** loc adj [musicien, inventeur] of genius ; [idée] brilliant.

genièvre [ʒənjɛvʀ] nm BOT [arbre] juniper ; [fruit] juniper berry.

génisse [ʒenis] nf heifer.

génital, e, aux [ʒenital, o] adj ANAT & PSYCHOL genital.

géniteur, trice [ʒenitœʀ, tʀis] nm, f *hum* progenitor.

génitif [ʒenitif] nm GRAM genitive (case).

génocide [ʒenɔsid] nm genocide.

génoise [ʒenwaz] nf CULIN sponge cake.

génome [ʒenom] nm genome.

génothérapie [ʒenoteʀapi] nf MÉD gene therapy.

genou, x [ʒənu] nm ANAT knee / *on était dans la neige jusqu'aux genoux* we were knee-deep ou up to our knees in snow / *assis sur les genoux de sa mère* sitting on his mother's lap ou knee ▶ **faire du genou à qqn** to play footsie with sb ▶ **être sur les genoux** to be exhausted. ❖ **à genoux** loc adv **1.** [sur le sol] ▶ **mets-toi à genoux** get down on your knees, kneel down **2.** *fig* ▶ **être à genoux devant qqn** a) [lui être soumis] to be on one's knees before sb b) [être en adoration devant lui] to worship sb.

genouillère [ʒənujɛʀ] nf [protection] knee pad.

genre [ʒɑ̃ʀ] nm **1.** [sorte, espèce] kind, sort, type / *ce n'est pas le genre à renoncer* she's not the sort to give up ou who gives up / *partir sans payer, ce n'est pas son genre* it's not like him to leave without paying / *il a exigé qu'on lui rembourse le dessert, tu vois le genre !* he had the dessert deducted from the bill, you know the sort! ▶ **un genre de** [une sorte de] a kind ou sort of **2.** [comportement, manières] type, style / *le genre intellectuel* the intellectual type

▶ **genre de vie** lifestyle / *avoir un drôle de genre* to be an odd sort ▶ **avoir bon / mauvais genre** : *leurs enfants ont vraiment bon genre* their children really know how to behave ▶ **il a mauvais genre** he's a bit vulgar / *il est romantique, tout à fait mon genre !* he's a romantic, just my type! **3.** BIOL genus ▶ **le genre humain** mankind, the human race **4.** ART genre **5.** GRAM gender **6.** LITTÉR genre ▶ **le genre romanesque** the novel. ◆ **dans son genre** loc adv [à sa façon] in his / her (own) way. ◆ **en tout genre, en tous genres** loc adv of all kinds ▶ **travaux en tous genres** all kinds of work undertaken.

gens [ʒɑ̃] nmpl ou nfpl **1.** *(adjectif au féminin si placé avant ; adjectif au masculin si placé après)* [personnes] people ▶ **beaucoup de gens** many people, a lot of people ▶ **les gens d'ici** people from around here, the locals / *les gens de la ville* townspeople, townsfolk ▶ **petites gens** people of limited means / *les bonnes gens murmurent que…* people are saying ou whispering that… **2.** ▶ **gens de lettres** men and women of letters ▶ **gens du spectacle** stage ou showbusiness people ▶ **les gens du voyage a)** [artistes] travelling players ou performers **b)** [gitans] travellers.

gentiane [ʒɑ̃sjan] nf [plante] gentian.

gentil, ille [ʒɑ̃ti, ij] adj **1.** [serviable] kind / *ils sont gentils avec moi* they're kind ou nice to me / *sois gentil, apporte-moi mes lunettes* do me a favour and get my glasses for me / *vous serez gentil de me prévenir de leur arrivée* be kind enough to let me know when they are arriving / *merci, c'est gentil* thanks, that's very kind of you **2.** [aimable] nice, sweet / *elle a pris mon idée sans me le dire, ce n'est pas très gentil* she stole my idea without telling me, that's not very nice (of her) **3.** [joli] nice, pretty, cute / *un gentil petit minois* a cute little face **4.** [exprimant l'impatience] : *c'est bien gentil tout ça mais si on parlait affaires ?* that's all very well but what about getting down to business? **5.** [obéissant] good / *si tu es gentil / gentille* if you're a good boy / girl.

gentillesse [ʒɑ̃tijɛs] nf **1.** [d'une personne] kindness (U) / *j'étais touché par la gentillesse de leur accueil* I was moved by their kind welcome **2.** [dans des formules de politesse] : *ayez la gentillesse de me prévenir à l'avance* be so kind as to let me know beforehand **3.** [acte] act of kindness / *elle est toujours prête à toutes les gentillesses* she's always ready to help people out.

gentillet, ette [ʒɑ̃tijɛ, ɛt] adj **1.** [mignon] : *il est gentillet, leur appartement* they've got a lovely little flat 🇬🇧 ou apartment 🇺🇸 **2.** *péj* : *c'est un film gentillet, sans plus* it's a pleasant enough film, but that's about it.

gentiment [ʒɑ̃timɑ̃] adv **1.** [aimablement] kindly **2.** [sagement] : *on discutait gentiment quand…* we were chatting away nicely ou quietly chatting away when…

génuflexion [ʒenyflɛksjɔ̃] nf genuflection / *faire une génuflexion* to genuflect.

géo [ʒeo] nf *arg scol* geography.

géographe [ʒeɔgʀaf] nmf geographer.

géographie [ʒeɔgʀafi] nf [science] geography ▶ **géographie humaine / physique / politique** human / physical / political geography.

géographique [ʒeɔgʀafik] adj geographic, geographical.

géolocalisation [ʒeɔlɔkalizasjɔ̃] nf geolocalization.

géolocaliser [ʒeɔlɔkalize] vt to geolocate.

géologie [ʒeɔlɔʒi] nf geology.

géologique [ʒeɔlɔʒik] adj geologic, geological.

géologue [ʒeɔlɔg] nmf geologist.

géomètre [ʒeɔmɛtʀ] nmf [arpenteur] land surveyor.

géométrie [ʒeɔmetʀi] nf MATH geometry. ◆ **à géométrie variable** loc adj *fig* [susceptible d'évoluer] variable-geometry.

géométrique [ʒeɔmetʀik] adj **1.** MATH geometric, geometrical **2.** ART geometric.

géopolitique [ʒeɔpɔlitik] ◆ adj geopolitical. ◆ nf geopolitics *(sg)*.

Géorgie [ʒeɔʀʒi] npr f ▶ **(la) Géorgie** Georgia.

gérance [ʒeʀɑ̃s] nf management / *prendre / reprendre un fonds en gérance* to take on / to take over the management of a business.

géranium [ʒeʀanjɔm] nm geranium.

gérant, e [ʒeʀɑ̃, ɑ̃t] nm, f manager (manageress) ▶ **gérant d'immeubles** managing agent *(for an apartment block)* ▶ **gérant de société** managing director *(of a company)* ▶ **gérant de magasin** store manager.

gerbe [ʒɛʀb] nf **1.** [de blé] sheaf ; [de fleurs] wreath **2.** [de feu d'artifice] spray, gerbe *spéc* **3.** [jaillissement -d'eau] spray ; [-d'étincelles] shower.

gerber [3] [ʒɛʀbe] vi *tfam* [vomir] to throw up, to puke.

gercer [16] [ʒɛʀse] ◆ vi [peau, mains, lèvres] to chap, to crack / *chaque hiver, j'ai les mains qui gercent* every winter I get chapped hands. ◆ vt to chap, to crack.

gerçure [ʒɛʀsyʀ] nf [des mains, des lèvres] crack, chapping *(U)*.

gérer [18] [ʒeʀe] vt **1.** [budget, fortune] to administer, to manage / *ils se contentent de gérer la crise* *fig* they're (quite) happy to sit out the crisis **2.** [entreprise, hôtel, magasin] to manage, to run ; [stock, production] to control **3.** INFORM to manage / *gérer des données / un fichier* to manage data / a file.

In reformed spelling (see p. 16-18), this verb is conjugated like semer : il gèrera, elle gèrerait.

gériatrie [ʒeʀjatʀi] nf geriatrics *(sg)*.

gériatrique [ʒeʀjatʀik] adj geriatric.

germain, e [ʒɛʀmɛ̃, ɛn] adj [ayant un grand-parent commun] ▶ **cousine germaine** first cousin.

germanique [ʒɛʀmanik] ◆ adj [allemand] Germanic. ◆ nm LING Germanic ; HIST & LING Germanic, Proto-Germanic.

germaniste [ʒɛʀmanist] nmf Germanist.

germe [ʒɛʀm] nm **1.** ANAT, BIOL & MÉD germ **2.** [pousse] germe de pomme de terre potato sprout ▶ **germe de blé** wheat germ ▶ **germes de soja** (soya) bean sprouts.

germer [3] [ʒɛʀme] vi **1.** AGR & HORT [graine] to germinate ; [bulbe, tubercule] to shoot, to sprout **2.** [idées] to germinate / *le concept a d'abord germé dans l'esprit des urbanistes* the notion first took shape in the minds of town planners.

gérondif [ʒeʀɔ̃dif] nm [en latin] gerundive ; [en français] gerund.

gérontologie [ʒeʀɔ̃tɔlɔʒi] nf gerontology.

gésier [ʒezje] nm gizzard.

gésir [49] [ʒeziʀ] vi **1.** [être étendu] to lie, to be lying **2.** [être épars] to lie.

gestation [ʒɛstasjɔ̃] nf BIOL gestation. ◆ **en gestation** loc adj **1.** BIOL [fœtus] gestating **2.** *fig* ▶ **un roman en gestation** a novel in preparation.

geste [ʒɛst] nm **1.** [mouvement] movement ; [signe] gesture / *faire des gestes en parlant* to speak with one's hands / *faire un geste de la main* to wave / *il a eu un geste de désespoir* he did something desperate ▶ **faire un geste approbateur** to nod one's assent ou approval / *d'un geste de la main, il refusa le whisky* he waved aside the glass of whisky / *pas un geste ou je tire !* don't move or I'll shoot! **2.** [action] gesture / *un geste politique / diplomatique* a political / diplomatic gesture ▶ **faire un beau geste** to make a noble gesture.

gesticuler [3] [ʒɛstikyle] vi to gesticulate, to wave one's arms about.

gestion [ʒɛstjɔ̃] nf **1.** [d'une entreprise, de biens, de carrière, du temps, du stress] management / *chargé de la gestion de l'hôtel* in charge of running ou managing the hotel / *par une mauvaise gestion* through bad management, through mismanagement ▸ **gestion d'affaires** (day-to-day) running of affairs ou business ▸ **gestion de stock** inventory ou stock control **2.** INFORM management ▸ **gestion de fichiers** file management ▸ **système de gestion de base de données** database management system.

gestionnaire [ʒɛstjɔnɛʀ] ◆ nmf **1.** ADMIN administrator **2.** COMM & INDUST manager, administrator. ◆ nm INFORM manager ▸ **gestionnaire de base de données** database administrator ▸ **gestionnaire de fichiers** file manager.

gestuelle [ʒɛstɥɛl] nf **1.** [gén] non-verbal communication **2.** DANSE & THÉÂTRE gesture.

geyser [ʒɛzɛʀ] nm geyser.

Ghana [gana] npr m ▸ **le Ghana** Ghana.

ghanéen, enne [ganeɛ̃, ɛn] adj Ghanaian, Ghanian. ◆ **Ghanéen, enne** nm, f Ghanaian, Ghanian.

ghetto [gɛto] nm ghetto.

ghettoïser [gɛtɔize] vt [quartier] to make into a ghetto ; [population] to marginalize.

Ght SMS abr écrite de **j'ai acheté**.

gibet [ʒibɛ] nm [potence] gibbet, gallows.

gibier [ʒibje] nm **1.** [animaux] game (U) ▸ **gros / petit gibier** big / small game ▸ **gibier à plume** game birds ou fowl (U) **2.** CULIN [viande] game.

giboulée [ʒibule] nf shower ▸ **giboulées de mars** April showers.

giboyeux, euse [ʒibwajø, øz] adj abounding ou rich in game, well stocked with game.

Gibraltar [ʒibʀaltaʀ] npr Gibraltar.

gicler [ʒikle] vi [liquide] to spurt, to squirt.

gicleur [ʒiklœʀ] nm AUTO (carburettor) jet.

gifle [ʒifl] nf **1.** [coup] slap (in the face) ▸ **donner une gifle à qqn** to slap sb's face, to box sb's ears **2.** [humiliation] (burning) insult, slap in the face.

gifler [3] [ʒifle] vt [suj : personne] ▸ **gifler qqn** to slap sb's face ou sb in the face.

gigantesque [ʒigɑ̃tɛsk] adj **1.** [animal, plante, ville] gigantic, giant (modif) **2.** [projet] gigantic, giant (modif) ; [erreur] huge, gigantic.

gigaoctet [ʒigaɔktɛ] nm INFORM gigabyte.

GIGN (abr de **Groupe d'intervention de la gendarmerie nationale**) npr m special crack force of the gendarmerie ; ≃ SAS [UK] ; ≃ SWAT [US].

gigogne [ʒigɔɲ] adj **1.** → **lit 2.** → **poupée 3.** → **table**.

gigolo [ʒigolo] nm fam gigolo.

gigot [ʒigo] nm CULIN leg ▸ **gigot (d'agneau)** leg of lamb.

gigoter [3] [ʒigɔte] vi [bébé] to wriggle (about) ; [enfant] to fidget.

gilet [ʒilɛ] nm **1.** [vêtement - taillé] waistcoat [UK], vest [US] ; [- tricoté] cardigan **2.** [sous-vêtement] vest [UK], undershirt [US] **3.** [protection] ▸ **gilet pare-balles** bulletproof vest ▸ **gilet de sauvetage** life jacket.

gin [dʒin] nm gin.

gingembre [ʒɛ̃ʒɑ̃bʀ] nm ginger.

gingivite [ʒɛ̃ʒivit] nf gum disease, gingivitis spéc.

girafe [ʒiʀaf] nf ZOOL giraffe.

giratoire [ʒiʀatwaʀ] adj gyrating, gyratory ▸ **sens giratoire** roundabout [UK], traffic circle [US].

girofle [ʒiʀɔfl] nm clove.

giroflée [ʒiʀɔfle] nf BOT gillyflower.

girolle, girole* [ʒiʀɔl] nf chanterelle.

giron [ʒiʀɔ̃] nm **1.** [d'une personne] lap **2.** litt [communauté] bosom ▸ **le giron familial** the family fold / *accepté dans le giron de l'Église* accepted into the fold ou the bosom of the Church.

girouette [ʒiʀwɛt] nf **1.** [sur un toit] weathercock, weather vane **2.** fam [personne] weathercock / *c'est une vraie girouette !* he keeps changing his mind!, he's a real weathercock !

gisement [ʒizmɑ̃] nm GÉOL & MIN deposit ▸ **gisement houiller** a) [filon] coal deposit ou measures b) [bassin] coalfield ▸ **gisement de pétrole** ou **pétrolifère** oilfield.

gitan, e [ʒitɑ̃, an] adj Gypsy (modif). ◆ **Gitan, e** nm, f Gypsy.

gîte, gite* [ʒit] ◆ nm **1.** [foyer] home / *le gîte et le couvert* room and board ▸ **gîte d'étape** [pour randonneurs] halt ▸ **gîte rural** gîte **2.** [viande] shin [UK] ou shank [US] (of beef) ▸ **gîte à la noix** topside [UK], round [US]. ◆ nf NAUT list.

givre [ʒivʀ] nm [glace] frost.

givré, e [ʒivʀe] adj **1.** [arbre] covered with frost ; [serrure] iced up **2.** CULIN **orange givrée** orange sorbet [UK] ou sherbet [US] (served inside the fruit) **3.** fam [fou] screwy, nuts, crazy, round the twist [UK].

glabre [glabʀ] adj **1.** [imberbe] smooth-chinned ; [rasé] clean-shaven **2.** BOT glabrous, hairless.

glace [glas] nf **1.** [eau gelée] ice ▸ **rompre** ou **briser la glace** to break the ice **2.** [crème glacée] ice cream, ice [UK] ; [sucette] ice lolly [UK], popsicle [US] ; [cône] ice cream (cone) ▸ **glace à la vanille / à l'abricot** vanilla / apricot ice cream **3.** [miroir] mirror **4.** [vitre - d'un véhicule, d'une boutique] window. ◆ **glaces** nfpl [du pôle] ice fields ; [sur un fleuve] ice sheets ; [en mer] ice floes, drift ice / *le navire est pris dans les glaces* the ship is icebound. ◆ **de glace** loc adj [accueil, visage, regard] icy, frosty ▸ **être** ou **rester de glace** to remain unmoved.

glacé, e [glase] adj **1.** [transformé en glace] frozen **2.** [lieu] freezing ou icy (cold) **3.** [personne] frozen, freezing cold / *j'ai les pieds glacé* my feet are frozen **4.** [hostile] frosty, icy **5.** CULIN [dessert, soufflé, café] iced ; [petit-four] glacé ; [oignon, viande, poisson] glazed.

glacer [16] [glase] vt **1.** [transformer en glace] to freeze **2.** [transir] : *un froid qui vous glace jusqu'aux os* weather that chills you to the bone **3.** fig [pétrifier] ▸ **son regard me glace** the look in his eye turns me cold / *un hurlement à vous glacer le sang* a blood-curdling scream **4.** CULIN [petit-four, oignon, poisson, etc.] to glaze ; [gâteau] to ice, to frost [US] **5.** INDUST & TECHNOL to glaze, to glacé. ◆ **se glacer** vpi : *leur sang se glaça dans leurs veines* their blood ran cold.

glaciaire [glasjɛʀ] ◆ adj glacial. ◆ nm ▸ **le glaciaire** the Ice Age, the glacial period ou epoch.

glacial, e, als ou **aux** [glasjal, o] adj **1.** [climat] icy, freezing ; [vent] bitter, freezing ; [pluie] freezing (cold) **2.** [sourire] frosty ; [abord, personne] cold.

glacier [glasje] nm **1.** GÉOL glacier **2.** [confiseur] ice cream man ou salesman ; [fabricant] ice-cream maker.

glacière [glasjɛʀ] nf [armoire] refrigerated cabinet ; [récipient] cool box.

glaçon [glasɔ̃] nm [pour boisson] ice cube ▸ **voulez-vous un glaçon ?** would you like some ice? ▸ **servi avec des glaçons** served with ice ou on the rocks.

glaïeul [glajœl] nm gladiolus ▸ **des glaïeuls** gladioli.

glaire [glɛʀ] nf **1.** PHYSIOL mucus ▸ **glaire cervicale** cervical mucus **2.** [d'œuf] white.

---

* In reformed spelling (see p. 16-18).

glaise [glɛz] nf clay.

glaive [glɛv] nm glaive *arch*, broadsword.

glamour [glamuʀ] adj inv glamorous.

gland [glɑ̃] nm **1.** [du chêne] acorn **2.** COUT tassel **3.** ANAT glans **4.** *tfam* [imbécile] prat 🇬🇧, jerk 🇺🇸.

glande [glɑ̃d] nf ANAT gland.

glander [3] [glɑ̃de] vi *tfam* **1.** [ne rien faire] to loaf about **2.** [attendre] to hang around **3.** EXPR **n'en avoir rien à glander** : *j'en ai rien à glander* I don't give a damn.

glaner [3] [glane] vt **1.** [ramasser - épis] to glean ; [- bois] to gather ; [- fruits] to gather, to pick up *(sép)* **2.** *fig* [renseignements, détails] to glean, to gather.

glapir [32] [glapiʀ] vi **1.** [renard] to bark ; [chiot] to yelp, to yap **2.** [personne] to yelp, to squeal.

glas [gla] nm knell.

glauque [glok] adj **1.** [louche - lieu] shabby ; [ambiance] murky ; [personne] creepy **2.** *fam* [lugubre] dreary.

glissade [glisad] nf **1.** [jeu] sliding *(U)* **2.** [glissoire] slide.

glissant, e [glisɑ̃, ɑ̃t] adj [sol] slippery.

glisse [glis] nf [d'un ski] friction coefficient **♦ sports de glisse** *generic term referring to sports such as skiing, surfing, windsurfing, etc.*

glissement [glismɑ̃] nm **1.** [déplacement] sliding *(U)* **2.** [évolution] shift / *la politique du gouvernement a connu un net glissement à droite* there's been a marked shift to the right in government policy **3.** LING **♦ glissement de sens** shift in meaning **4.** GÉOL **♦ glissement de terrain** landslide, landslip.

glisser [3] [glise] **♦** vi **1.** [déraper - personne] to slip ; [- voiture] to skid / *mon pied a glissé* my foot slipped / *attention, ça glisse par terre* watch out, it's slippery underfoot ou the ground's slippery **2.** [s'échapper accidentellement] to slip / *ça m'a glissé des mains* it slipped out of my hands **3.** [tomber] to slide / *il se laissa glisser à terre* he slid to the ground **4.** [avancer sans heurt - skieur, patineur] to glide along ; [- péniche, ski] to glide **5.** [passer] : *glissons sur ce sujet !* let's say no more about it **♦ sur toi, tout glisse comme l'eau sur les plumes d'un canard** it's like water off a duck's back with you **6.** *fig* [s'orienter] **♦ glisser à** ou **vers** to shift to ou towards / *une partie de l'électorat a glissé à gauche* part of the electorate has shifted ou moved to the left. **♦** vt **1.** [introduire] to slip / *glisser une lettre sous la porte* to slip a letter under the door ; [dire furtivement] : *j'ai glissé ton nom dans la conversation* I managed to slip ou to drop your name into the conversation **2.** [confier] **♦ glisser un petit mot / une lettre à qqn** to slip sb a note / a letter **♦ glisser qqch à l'oreille de qqn** to whisper sthg in sb's ear. **♦ se glisser** vpi **1.** [se faufiler] : *se glisser au premier rang* [rapidement] to slip into the front row **♦ glisse-toi là** [sans prendre de place] squeeze (yourself) in there **2.** [erreur] : *des fautes ont pu se glisser dans l'article* some mistakes may have slipped ou crept into the article.

glissière [glisjɛʀ] nf **1.** TECHNOL slide, runner / *porte à glissière* sliding door **2.** TRAV PUB **♦ glissière de sécurité** crash barrier.

global, e, aux [glɔbal, o] adj [résultat, vision] overall, global ; [somme] total.

> ⚠ Attention, l'adjectif anglais **global** n'a pas les mêmes emplois que l'adjectif français. Voir article.

globalement [glɔbalmɑ̃] adv all in all, overall / *globalement, l'entreprise se porte bien* all in all ou by and large, the company is doing well.

globalisation [glɔbalizasjɔ̃] nf [d'un marché, d'un conflit] globalization.

globalité [glɔbalite] nf [ensemble] : *envisageons le processus dans sa globalité* let's view the process as a whole / *si l'on envisage les problèmes dans leur globalité* if we look at all the problems together.

globe [glɔb] nm **1.** [sphère] globe **♦ le globe** [la Terre] the globe, the world / *sur toute la surface du globe* all over the globe **♦ le globe terrestre** the terrestrial globe **2.** [d'une lampe] (glass) globe **3.** [pour protéger] glass dome **4.** ANAT **♦ globe oculaire** eye.

globe-trotteur, euse *(mpl* globe-trotteurs, *fpl* globe-trotteuses)*, **globetrotteur*, euse** [glɔbtʀɔtœʀ, øz] nm, f globe-trotter.

globule [glɔbyl] nm BIOL & PHYSIOL corpuscle **♦ globule blanc** white corpuscle, white blood cell **♦ globule rouge** red corpuscle, red blood cell.

globuleux, euse [glɔbylø, øz] adj **1.** [forme] globular, globulous **2.** [œil] protruding, bulging.

gloire [glwaʀ] nf **1.** [renom] fame **♦ au faîte** ou **sommet de sa gloire** at the height ou pinnacle of his fame / *ne t'attends pas à être payé, on fait ça pour la gloire* don't expect payment, we're doing it for love **2.** [mérite] glory, credit / *toute la gloire vous en revient* the credit is all yours **♦ c'est pas la gloire** *fam* it's not exactly brilliant **3.** [éloge] praise / *écrit à la gloire de...* written in praise of... **♦ rendre gloire au courage de qqn** to praise sb's courage / *gloire à Dieu* praise be to ou glory to God **4.** [personne] celebrity.

glorieux, euse [glɔʀjø, øz] adj [remarquable] glorious / *une page peu glorieuse de notre histoire* an event in our history we can be less than proud of **♦ ce n'est pas glorieux** *fam & fig* it's not exactly brilliant.

glorifier [9] [glɔʀifje] vt [exploit, qualité, héros] to glorify, to praise ; [Dieu] to glorify. **♦ se glorifier de** vp + prép **♦ se glorifier de qqch** to glory in sthg.

gloriole [glɔʀjɔl] nf vainglory **♦ faire qqch par gloriole** to do sthg to show off ou for show.

glose [gloz] nf gloss.

gloss [glɔs] nm lipgloss.

glossaire [glɔsɛʀ] nm glossary, vocabulary.

glotte [glɔt] nf ANAT glottis.

glouglou [gluglu] nm *fam* [d'une fontaine] gurgle, gurgling ; [d'une bouteille] glug-glug.

glousser [3] [gluse] vi **1.** [personne] to chuckle **2.** [poule] to cluck.

glouton, onne [glutɔ̃, ɔn] **♦** adj greedy, gluttonous. **♦** nm, f glutton.

gloutonnerie [glutɔnʀi] nf gluttony.

glu [gly] nf **1.** [substance visqueuse] birdlime **2.** *fam* [personne] : *c'est une vraie glu* she sticks to you like glue.

gluant, e [glyɑ̃, ɑ̃t] adj sticky, slimy.

glucide [glysid] nm carbohydrate.

glucose [glykoz] nm glucose.

gluten [glytɛn] nm gluten.

glycémie [glisemi] nf blood-sugar level, glycaemia 🇬🇧 ou glycemia 🇺🇸 *spéc*.

glycérine [gliseʀin] nf glycerin, glycerine.

glycine [glisin] nf BOT wisteria.

gnangnan [nɑ̃nɑ̃] *fam* adj inv *péj* [œuvre, style] : *j'ai vu le film, que c'était gnangnan !* I saw the film, it was so soppy!

gnognot(t)e [nɔɲɔt] nf *fam* **♦ c'est de la gnognotte a)** [c'est facile] that's ou it's a cinch **b)** [c'est sans valeur] that's ou it's rubbish 🇬🇧 ou garbage 🇺🇸.

gnole, gnôle [ɲɔl] nf tfam hard stuff, hooch US.

gnome [gnom] nm **1.** [génie] gnome **2.** sout [nabot] dwarf, gnome.

gnon [ɲɔ̃] nm fam **1.** [coup] thump **2.** [enflure] bruise.

G.N.V., gnv (abr de **gaz naturel (pour) véhicules**) nm natural gas for vehicles.

Go (abr écrite de **gigaoctet**) nm INFORM Gb.

goal [gol] nm [gardien] goalkeeper.

gobelet [gɔblɛ] nm [timbale] tumbler, beaker ▸ **gobelet jetable a)** [en papier] paper cup **b)** [en plastique] plastic cup.

gober [3] [gɔbe] vt **1.** [avaler - huître] to swallow ; [- œuf] to suck ; [- insecte] to catch (and eat) **2.** fam [croire] to swallow / **ils ont tout gobé !** they swallowed it (all), hook, line and sinker!

goberge [gɔbɛʀʒ] nf QUÉBEC [genre de morue] pollock.

godasse [gɔdas] nf fam shoe.

godendart [gɔdɑ̃daʀ] nm QUÉBEC two-handed saw.

godet [gɔdɛ] nm **1.** [petit récipient] jar ; [verre] tumbler **2.** [pour peinture] pot **3.** [nacelle - d'une noria] scoop ; [- d'une roue à eau, en manutention] bucket **4.** COUT [à ondulation] flare ; [à découpe] gore ; [défaut] pucker, ruck.

godiller [3] [gɔdije] vi [au ski] to wedeln.

goéland [gɔelɑ̃] nm seagull.

goélette [gɔelɛt] nf schooner.

goémon [gɔemɔ̃] nm wrack.

gogo [gogo] nm fam sucker. ◆ **à gogo** loc adv fam galore.

goguenard, e [gɔgnaʀ, aʀd] adj mocking, jeering.

goguette [gɔgɛt] ◆ **en goguette** loc adj merry, a little tiddly / **des commerciaux en goguette** some salesmen having a boozy get-together.

goinfre [gwɛ̃fʀ] nmf fam pig.

goinfrer [3] [gwɛ̃fʀe] ◆ **se goinfrer** vpi fam to pig ou to stuff o.s.

goitre [gwatʀ] nm goitre.

golf [gɔlf] nm **1.** SPORT ▸ **le golf** golf / **jouer au golf** to play golf **2.** [terrain] (golf) links, golf course.

golfe [gɔlf] nm gulf.

Golfes

le golfe d'Aden	the Gulf of Aden
le golfe de Gascogne	the Bay of Biscay
le golfe du Lion	the Gulf of Lions
le golfe du Mexique	the Gulf of Mexico
le golfe Persique	the Persian Gulf

Golfe [gɔlf] npr m : **les États / la Guerre du Golfe** the Gulf States / War.

golfeur, euse [gɔlfœʀ, øz] nm, f golfer.

gominer [3] [gɔmine] ◆ **se gominer** vp (emploi réfléchi) to put Brylcreem® ou hair cream on.

gommage [gɔmaʒ] nm [de la peau] exfoliation / **se faire faire un gommage** to have one's skin deep-cleansed.

gomme [gɔm] nf **1.** [pour effacer] rubber UK, eraser **2.** [substance] gum.

gommé, e [gɔme] adj [papier] gummed.

gommer [3] [gɔme] vt **1.** [avec une gomme] to rub out UK (sép), to erase **2.** [faire disparaître] to chase away (sép), to erase.

gond [gɔ̃] nm hinge ▸ **sortir de ses gonds** to blow one's top, to fly off the handle.

gondole [gɔ̃dɔl] nf COMM & NAUT gondola ▸ **tête de gondole** COMM gondola head.

gondoler [3] [gɔ̃dɔle] ◆ vi [bois] to warp, to get warped ; [tôle] to buckle. ◆ vt to wrinkle, to crinkle. ◆ **se gondoler** vpi tfam [rire] to fall about (laughing).

gonflable [gɔ̃flabl] adj [canot] inflatable ; [ballon, poupée] blow-up.

gonflé, e [gɔ̃fle] adj **1.** [enflé] swollen, puffed up **2.** fam EXPR **être gonflé**: **t'es gonflé !** [effronté] you've got a nerve ou some cheek! **b)** [courageux] you've got guts!

gonfler [3] [gɔ̃fle] ◆ vt **1.** [remplir d'un gaz - bouée, pneu] to inflate, to blow up (sép) ; [- poumons] to fill ▸ **avoir le cœur gonflé de peine / de chagrin / de joie** to be heartbroken / grief-stricken / overjoyed **2.** [faire grossir - voiles] to fill / **un abcès lui gonflait la joue** his cheek was swollen with an abscess **3.** [augmenter - prix, devis] to inflate, to push up (sép) ; [- frais, statistiques] to exaggerate, to inflate ; [- importance, impact] to exaggerate, to blow out of all proportion ; [- moteur] to soup up **4.** tfam [irriter] ▸ **gonfler qqn** to get on sb's nerves ou UK wick. ◆ vi **1.** CULIN [pâte] to rise ; [riz] to swell (up) **2.** [enfler] to be puffed up ou bloated ▸ **le bois a gonflé** the wood has warped. ◆ **se gonfler** vpi fig : **son cœur se gonfle d'allégresse** her heart is bursting with joy.

gonflette [gɔ̃flɛt] nf fam & péj ▸ **faire de la gonflette** to pump iron.

gong [gɔ̃g] nm SPORT bell.

gonzesse [gɔ̃zɛs] nf tfam [femme] bird UK, chick US.

gore [gɔʀ] ◆ adj (pl gore ou gores*) gory. ◆ nm ▸ **le gore** gore / **il aime le gore** he likes gore.

goret [gɔʀɛ] nm [porcelet] piglet.

GORE-TEX® [gɔʀtɛks] nm Gore-Tex®.

gorge [gɔʀʒ] nf **1.** [gosier] throat ▸ **rester en travers de la gorge a)** pr **l'arête m'est restée en travers de la gorge** the bone got stuck in my throat **b)** fig **son refus m'est resté en travers de la gorge** his refusal stuck in my throat ▸ **l'odeur / la fumée vous prenait à la gorge** the smell / smoke made you gag ▸ **rire à gorge déployée** to roar with laughter ▸ **prendre qqn à la gorge** pr to grab ou to take sb by the throat / **pris à la gorge, ils ont dû emprunter** fig they had a gun to their heads, so they had to borrow money ▸ **faire des gorges chaudes de qqn / qqch** to have a good laugh about sb / sthg **2.** litt [seins] bosom **3.** GÉOGR gorge.

gorgée [gɔʀʒe] nf mouthful ▸ **à petites gorgées** in little sips ▸ **à grandes gorgées** in great gulps.

gorger [17] [gɔʀʒe] vt ▸ **des champs gorgés d'eau** waterlogged fields. ◆ **se gorger de** vp + prép [se remplir de] : **au moment de la mousson, les rizières se gorgent d'eau** during the monsoon the rice paddies fill to overflowing with water.

gorille [gɔʀij] nm **1.** ZOOL gorilla **2.** fam [garde] bodyguard, gorilla.

gosier [gozje] nm [gorge] throat, gullet ▸ **rester en travers du gosier** fam : **ça m'est resté en travers du gosier** it really stuck in my throat.

gosse [gɔs] nmf fam **1.** [enfant] kid ▸ **sale gosse !** you brat! **2.** [fils, fille] kid **3.** [jeune] ▸ **il est beau gosse** he's a good-looking chap.

gothique [gɔtik] adj **1.** ART & HIST Gothic **2.** LITTÉR Gothic **3.** [mouvement] gothic, goth.

gouache [gwaʃ] nf gouache.

gouaille [gwaj] nf vieilli cheeky humour UK, sassy humor US.

goudron [gudʀɔ̃] nm tar.

goudronner [3] [gudʀɔne] vt [route] to tar, to surface (with tar).

gouffre [gufʀ] nm GÉOL [dû à l'effondrement] trough fault (valley) ; [dû à un fleuve] swallow hole ; [abîme] chasm, abyss, pit / *cette affaire sera un gouffre financier* this business will just swallow up money, we'll have to keep on pouring money into this business / *être au bord du gouffre* to be on the edge of the abyss.

goujat [guʒa] nm *sout* boor.

goujon [guʒɔ̃] nm **1.** ZOOL gudgeon **2.** MÉCAN [de poulie] pin.

goulet [gulɛ] nm [rétrécissement] narrowing ▶ **goulet d'étranglement** bottleneck.

goulot [gulo] nm **1.** [de bouteille] neck ▶ **boire au goulot** to drink straight from the bottle **2.** *fig* ▶ **goulot d'étranglement** bottleneck.

goulu, e [guly] adj greedy, gluttonous.

goulûment, goulument* [gulymɑ̃] adv greedily.

goupille [gupij] nf (joining) pin, cotter (pin).

goupiller [3] [gupije] vt *fam* [combiner] to set up *(sép)* / *elle avait bien goupillé son coup* she'd set it up neatly ou planned it just right. ❖ **se goupiller** vpi *fam* [se dérouler] to turn out / *ça s'est bien / mal goupillé* things turned out well / badly.

gourde [guʀd] nf **1.** [récipient -en peau] leather flask, wineskin ; [-en métal ou plastique] bottle, flask **2.** *fam* [personne] blockhead, twit.

gourdin [guʀdɛ̃] nm cudgel.

gourer [3] [guʀe] ❖ **se gourer** vpi *fam* [se tromper] : *je me suis gouré d'adresse* I made a slip-up with the address / *je me suis gouré dans les horaires* I got the times mixed up.

gourgane [guʀgan] nf Québec broad bean.

gourmand, e [guʀmɑ̃, ɑ̃d] adj [personne] greedy ▶ **gourmand de chocolat** fond of chocolate.

gourmandise [guʀmɑ̃diz] nf fondness for food ; *péj* greediness, greed.

gourmet [guʀmɛ] nm gourmet, epicure.

gourmette [guʀmɛt] nf JOAILL (chain) bracelet.

gourou [guʀu] nm **1.** RELIG guru **2.** *fig* guru, mentor.

gousse [gus] nf [de haricot] pod, husk ; [de petit pois] pod ; [d'ail] clove ; [de vanille] bean, pod.

goût, gout* [gu] nm **1.** [sens] taste **2.** [saveur] taste / *avoir un drôle de goût* to taste funny ▶ **ça a un goût de miel / moutarde** it tastes of honey / mustard / *ça n'a aucun goût* it's tasteless, it's got no taste / *ajoutez du sucre selon votre goût* add sugar to taste **3.** [préférence] taste / *avoir des goûts de luxe* to have expensive tastes ▶ **prendre goût à qqch** to develop a taste for sthg ▶ **c'est (une) affaire ou question de goût** it's a matter of taste ▶ **des goûts et des couleurs on ne discute pas** *prov* there's no accounting for taste **4.** [intérêt] taste, liking ▶ **ne plus avoir goût à qqch** to have lost one's taste for sthg ▶ **faire qqch par goût** to do sthg out of ou by inclination **5.** [jugement esthétique] taste ▶ **les gens de goût** people of taste / *elle a bon / mauvais goût* she has good / bad taste / *une décoration de bon goût* a tasteful decoration / *cette plaisanterie est d'un goût douteux* that joke is in poor ou doubtful taste / *une remarque de mauvais goût* a remark in poor ou bad taste **6.** [mode] : *être au goût du jour* to be in line with current tastes ▶ **dans ce goût-là** : *c'était une fourrure en renard, ou quelque chose dans ce goût-là* it was a fox fur, or something of the sort. ❖ **à mon goût, à ton goût, à mon gout*, à son gout*** loc adj & loc adv to my / his, etc. liking.

goûter¹, gouter* [3] [gute] ❖ vt **1.** [aliment, boisson] to taste, to try ▶ **fais-moi goûter** let me have a taste, give me a taste **2.** *sout* [apprécier] to savour, to enjoy **3.** Belg [avoir un goût de] to taste. ❖ vi **1.** [prendre une collation] to have an afternoon snack, to have tea UK **2.** Belg [avoir bon goût] to taste nice. ❖ **goûter à, gouter à*** v + prép [manger] : *goûtez donc à ces biscuits* do try some of these biscuits. ❖ **goûter de, gouter de*** v + prép [faire l'expérience de] to have a taste of.

goûter², gouter* [gute] nm [collation] afternoon snack for children, typically consisting of bread, butter, chocolate, and a drink ; [fête] children's party.

goutte [gut] nf **1.** [d'eau, de lait, de sang] drop ; [de sueur] drop, bead ; [de pluie] drop (of rain), raindrop / *il est tombé une goutte (ou deux)* there was a drop (or two) of rain ▶ **goutte de rosée** dewdrop ▶ **avoir la goutte au nez** to have a runny nose ▶ **être la goutte d'eau qui fait déborder le vase** : *c'est la goutte d'eau qui fait déborder le vase* it's the straw that broke the camel's back **2.** [petite quantité] ▶ **une goutte de** a (tiny) drop of **3.** MÉD [maladie] gout. ❖ **gouttes** nfpl PHARM ▶ **gouttes pour le nez / les oreilles / les yeux** nose / ear / eye drops. ❖ **à grosses gouttes** loc adv ▶ **suer à grosses gouttes** to be running with sweat ▶ **pleuvoir à grosses gouttes** to rain heavily. ❖ **goutte à goutte** loc adv drop by drop ▶ **tomber goutte à goutte** to drip.

goutte-à-goutte [gutagut] nm inv MÉD (intravenous) drip UK, IV US.

gouttelette [gutlɛt] nf droplet.

gouttière [gutjɛʀ] nf CONSTR gutter ▶ **gouttière verticale** drainpipe.

gouvernail, s [guvɛʀnaj] nm NAUT rudder.

gouvernant, e [guvɛʀnɑ̃, ɑ̃t] adj ruling / *les classes gouvernantes* the ruling classes. ❖ **gouvernante** nf [préceptrice] governess.

gouverne [guvɛʀn] nf *sout* [instruction] ▶ **pour ma / ta gouverne** for my / your information.

gouvernement [guvɛʀnəmɑ̃] nm **1.** [régime] government / *il est au gouvernement depuis 15 ans* he has been in government ou in power for 15 years **2.** [ensemble des ministres] Government / *le Premier ministre a formé son gouvernement* the Prime Minister has formed his government ou cabinet / *le gouvernement a démissionné* the Government has resigned.

gouvernemental, e, aux [guvɛʀnəmɑ̃tal, o] adj [parti] ruling, governing ; [presse] pro-government ; [politique, décision, crise] government *(modif)* ▶ **l'équipe gouvernementale** the Government ou Cabinet UK ou Administration US.

gouverner [3] [guvɛʀne] vt **1.** POL to rule, to govern **2.** *litt* [maîtriser] to govern, to control / *ne nous laissons pas gouverner par la haine* let us not be governed ou ruled by hatred **3.** NAUT to steer.

gouverneur, e [guvɛʀnœʀ] nm, f ADMIN & POL governor ▶ **Gouverneur général** Québec Governor general.

goyave [gɔjav] nf guava.

GPL (abr de gaz de pétrole liquéfié) nm LPG.

GPS (abr de global positioning system) nm [système] GPS ; [appareil] satnav.

gr abr écrite de **grade**.

GR nm abr de (sentier de) grande randonnée.

grabataire [gʀabatɛʀ] nmf (bedridden) invalid.

grabuge [gʀabyʒ] nm *fam* : *ça va faire du grabuge* that's going to cause havoc.

grâce [gʀɑs] ❖ nf **1.** [beauté -d'un paysage] charm ; [-d'une personne] grace ▶ **avec grâce** gracefully ▶ **plein de**

grâce graceful **2.** [volonté] **‣ de bonne grâce** with good grace, willingly / **de mauvaise grâce** with bad grace **‣ vous auriez mauvaise grâce à** ou **de vous plaindre** it would be ungracious of you to complain **3.** [faveur] favour 🇬🇧, favor 🇺🇸 **‣ trouver grâce aux yeux de qqn** to find favour with sb **4.** [sursis - de peine] pardon ; [-dans un délai] grace **‣ crier** ou **demander grâce** to beg for mercy / **je te fais grâce du récit complet** I'll spare you the full story / **une semaine / un mois de grâce** one week's / month's grace **‣ grâce présidentielle** presidential pardon **5.** RELIG grace **‣ à la grâce de Dieu a)** [advienne que pourra] come what may **b)** [n'importe comment] any old way ; [pour exprimer la reconnaissance] **‣ grâce à Dieu !** thanks be to God ! ◆ interj arch mercy **‣ de grâce !** for God's ou pity's sake ! ⬥ **grâces** nfpl [faveurs] **‣ être / entrer dans les bonnes grâces de qqn** to be / to get in favour with sb. ⬥ **grâce à** loc prép thanks to.

gracier [9] [gʀasje] vt to reprieve.

gracieusement [gʀasjøzmɑ̃] adv **1.** [joliment] gracefully **2.** [aimablement] graciously, kindly **3.** [gratuitement] free (of charge), gratis.

gracieuseté [gʀasjøzte] nf 🇶 QUÉBEC [bien ou service] freebie **‣ (être une) gracieuseté de** (to be) courtesy of.

gracieux, euse [gʀasjø, øz] adj **1.** [joli] charming, graceful **2.** [aimable] affable, amiable, gracious.

gracile [gʀasil] adj litt slender.

gradation [gʀadasjɔ̃] nf [progression] : **il y a une gradation dans nos exercices** we grade our exercises **‣ gradation ascendante / descendante** gradual increase / decrease.

grade [gʀad] nm **1.** [rang] rank **‣ avancer** ou **monter en grade** to be promoted **‣ en prendre pour son grade** fam to get it in the neck 🇬🇧, to get hauled over the coals **2.** GÉOM (centesimal) grade **3.** CHIM grade.

gradé, e [gʀade] nm, f non-commissioned officer, NCO.

gradin [gʀadɛ̃] nm [dans un amphithéâtre] tier, (stepped) row of seats ; [dans un stade] **‣ les gradins** the terraces.

graduation [gʀaduasjɔ̃] nf **1.** [repère] mark **2.** [échelle de mesure] scale **3.** [processus] graduating.

gradué, e [gʀadɥe] adj **1.** [à graduations] graduated **2.** [progressif] graded **‣ exercices gradués** graded exercises.

graduel, elle [gʀadɥɛl] adj gradual, progressive.

graduer [7] [gʀadɥe] vt **1.** [augmenter] to increase gradually / **il faut graduer la difficulté des tests** the tests should become gradually more difficult **2.** [diviser] to graduate.

graff [gʀaf] (abr de graffiti) nm (piece of) graffiti.

graffeur, euse [gʀafœʀ, øz] nm, f graffiti artist, graffitist.

graffiteur, euse [gʀafitœʀ, øz] nm, f graffiti artist.

graffiti [gʀafiti] (pl graffiti ou graffitis) nm [inscription] graffiti **‣ un graffiti** a piece of graffiti **‣ des graffitis** graffiti (U).

graillon [gʀajɔ̃] nm fam [friture] **‣ une odeur de graillon** a smell of grease.

grain [gʀɛ̃] nm **1.** [de sel, de sable] grain, particle ; [de riz] grain ; [de poussière] speck ; fig **‣ un grain de folie** a touch of madness / **il n'a pas un grain de bon sens** he hasn't got an ounce ou a grain of common sense **‣ avoir un grain** fam : **elle a un grain** she's got a screw loose tfam **‣ mettre son grain de sel** fam to stick one's oar in **2.** [céréales] **‣ le grain, les grains** (cereal) grain **3.** [d'un fruit, d'une plante] **‣ grain de café a)** [avant torréfaction] coffee berry **b)** [après torréfaction] coffee bean **‣ grain de poivre** peppercorn **‣ grain de raisin** grape **4.** [aspect - de la peau] grain, texture ; [-du bois, du papier] grain **5.** MÉTÉOR squall **6.** PHOT grain. ⬥ **grain de beauté** nm beauty spot, mole.

graine [gʀɛn] nf [semence] seed **‣ monter en graine a)** pr to go to seed **b)** fig to shoot up **‣ en prendre de la

graine fam : **ton frère a réussi tous ses examens, prends-en de la graine** your brother has passed all his exams, take a leaf out of his book.

graisse [gʀɛs] nf **1.** [corps gras] fat **‣ régime pauvre en graisses** low-fat diet **‣ graisse animale / végétale** animal / vegetable fat **2.** MÉCAN grease.

graisser [4] [gʀese] vt **1.** [enduire - moteur] to lubricate ; [-pièce, mécanisme] to grease, to oil ; [-fusil] to grease ; [-chaussures] to dub ; [-moule] to grease / **une crème qui ne graisse pas les mains** a non-greasy cream **‣ graisser la patte à qqn** to grease sb's palm **2.** [tacher] to grease, to soil with grease.

graisseux, euse [gʀesø, øz] adj **1.** [cheveux, col] greasy **2.** [tumeur] fatty.

graminée [gʀamine], **graminacée** [gʀaminase] nf grass **‣ les graminées** (the) grasses, the gramineae spéc.

grammaire [gʀamɛʀ] nf **1.** [règles] grammar **‣ faute de grammaire** grammatical mistake **‣ règle de grammaire** grammatical rule, rule of grammar **2.** [livre] grammar (book).

grammatical, e, aux [gʀamatikal, o] adj **1.** [de grammaire] grammatical **‣ exercice grammatical** grammar exercise **2.** [correct] grammatical **‣ non grammatical** ungrammatical.

gramme [gʀam] nm gramme / **je n'ai pas pris un gramme pendant les fêtes !** I didn't put on an ounce over the Christmas holidays!

grand, e [gʀɑ̃, gʀɑ̃d] (devant nm commençant par voyelle ou « h » muet [gʀɑ̃t])
◆ adj

A. ASPECT QUANTITATIF 1. [de taille élevée - adulte] tall ; [-enfant] tall, big **2.** [de grandes dimensions - objet, salle, ville] big, large ; [-distance] long / **une grande tour** a high ou tall tower / **un grand fleuve** a long ou big river / **de grandes jambes** long legs / **avoir de grands pieds** to have big ou large feet **‣ marcher à grands pas** to walk with great ou long strides **3.** [d'un certain âge - être humain] big / **tu es un grand garçon maintenant** you're a big boy now ; [aîné - frère, sœur] big ; [au terme de sa croissance - personne] grown-up ; [-animal] fully grown, adult **‣ quand je serai grand** when I'm grown-up ou big **4.** [qui dure longtemps] long **5.** [intense, considérable] great / **un grand cri** a loud cry / **les risques sont grands** there are considerable risks **‣ une grande fortune** great wealth, a large fortune **‣ les grands froids** intense cold **‣ pendant les grandes chaleurs** in high summer, in ou at the height of summer / **un grand incendie** a large ou great fire **‣ grande consommation :** **ce sont des articles de grande consommation** they are everyday consumer articles **6.** [pour qualifier une mesure] large, great **‣ la grande majorité de** the great ou vast majority of / **son grand âge explique cette erreur** this mistake can be put down to her being so old / **un grand nombre de passagers** a large number of passengers **7.** [entier] : **une grande cuillerée de sucre** a heaped spoonful of sugar.

B. ASPECT QUALITATIF 1. [important] great, major / **les grands problèmes de notre temps** the main ou major ou key issues of our time **2.** [acharné, invétéré] great, keen **‣ c'est un grand travailleur** he's a hard worker, he's hard-working / **ce sont de grands amis** they're great ou very good friends **‣ les grands blessés / brûlés / invalides** the seriously wounded / burned / disabled **3.** [puissant, influent - banque] top ; [-industriel] top, leading, major ; [-propriétaire, famille] important ; [-personnage] great **4.** [dans une hiérarchie] : **les grands dignitaires du régime** the leading ou important dignitaries of the regime **5.** [généreux] : **il a un grand cœur** he's big-hearted, he has a big heart **6.** [exagéré] big **‣ grands mots** high-sounding words, high-flown language **7.** [fameux, reconnu] great / *un grand journaliste* a great ou top journalist ▸ **le grand jour** the big day ▸ **un grand nom** a great name ▸ **les grands couturiers** the top fashion designers. **C. EN INTENSIF** : *avec une (très) grande facilité* with (the greatest of) ease ▸ **sans grand enthousiasme / intérêt** without much enthusiasm / interest / *un grand merci à ta sœur* lots of thanks to ou a big thank you to your sister ▸ **le grand amour**: *c'est le grand amour !* it's true love! / *cette cuisine a grand besoin d'être nettoyée* this kitchen really needs ou is in dire need of a clean ▸ **faire grand bien**: *ça m'a fait le plus grand bien* it did me a power of ou the world of good / *toute la famille au grand complet* the whole family, every single member of the family / *pour notre plus grand plaisir* to our (great) delight ▸ **prendre grand soin de** to take great care of ▸ **à sa grande surprise** much to his surprise, to his great surprise.

◆ nm, f **1.** [enfant - d'un certain âge] ▸ **l'école des grands** primary school ; [en appellatif] ▸ **merci mon grand !** thanks, son! ▸ **comme un grand**: *je me débrouillerai tout seul, comme un grand / toute seule, comme une grande* I'll manage on my own, like a big boy / a big girl **2.** [adulte - gén] grown-up, adult / *un jeu pour petits et grands* a game for young and old (alike); [personne de grande taille] : *pour la photo, les grands se mettront derrière* for the photo, tall people ou the taller people will stand at the back. ◆ **grand** ◆ adv **1.** VÊT ▸ **chausser grand**: *c'est un modèle qui chausse grand* this is a large-fitting shoe **2.** [largement] ▸ **grand ouvert** wide-open **3.** EXPR *ils ont vu trop grand* they bit off more than they could chew / *deux rôtis ! tu as vu grand !* two roasts! you don't do things by halves! ◆ nm [entrepreneur, industriel] : *un grand de la mode* a leading light in the fashion business. ◆ **grands** nmpl ÉCON & POL ▸ **les grands** [les puissants] the rich (and powerful). ◆ **en grand** loc adv [complètement] on a large scale / *il faut aérer la maison en grand* the house needs a thorough ou good airing ▸ **il a fait les choses en grand** *fig* he really did things properly. ◆ **grande école** nf *competitive-entrance higher education establishment.* ◆ **grand ensemble** nm housing scheme 🇬🇧, housing project 🇺🇸. ◆ **grande surface** nf hypermarket.

📖 Grande école

The **grandes écoles** are relatively small and highly respected higher education establishments. Admission is usually only possible after two years of intensive preparatory studies and a competitive entrance examination. Most have close links with industry. The **grandes écoles** include l'École des hautes études commerciales or HEC (management and business), l'École polytechnique or l'X (engineering) and l'École normale supérieure (teacher training and research).

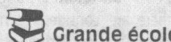

grand-angle [grɑ̃tɑ̃gl] (*pl* grands-angles [grɑ̃zɑ̃gl]), **grand-angulaire** [grɑ̃tɑ̃gylɛr] (*pl* grands-angulaires [grɑ̃zɑ̃gylɛr]) nm wide-angle lens.

Grand Canyon [grɑ̃kanjɔ̃] npr ▸ **le Grand Canyon** the Grand Canyon.

grand-chose [grɑ̃ʃoz] pron indéf ▸ **pas grand-chose** not much / *je n'y comprends pas grand-chose* I don't understand much of it / *il ne me reste plus grand-chose à dire* there's not much more (left) to say.

Grande-Bretagne [grɑ̃dbrətaɲ] npr f ▸ **(la) Grande-Bretagne** (Great) Britain.

grandement [grɑ̃dmɑ̃] adv **1.** [largement] absolutely / *vous avez grandement raison / tort* you are quite right / wrong **2.** [beaucoup] a great deal, greatly ▸ **être grandement reconnaissant à qqn de qqch** to be truly grateful to sb for sthg.

grandeur [grɑ̃dœr] nf **1.** [taille] size ▸ **(en) grandeur nature** life-size **2.** [noblesse] greatness ▸ **avec grandeur** nobly ▸ **grandeur d'âme** magnanimity **3.** [splendeur] greatness, splendour / *grandeur et décadence de Byzance* rise and fall of Byzantium.

grandiloquent, e [grɑ̃dilɔkɑ̃, ɑ̃t] adj grandiloquent, pompous *péj*.

grandiose [grɑ̃djoz] adj grandiose.

grandir [32] [grɑ̃dir] ◆ vi **1.** [devenir grand] to grow / *sa fille a grandi de cinq centimètres* her daughter is five centimetres taller (than when I last saw her) / *je te trouve grandie* you've grown ou you look taller since I last saw you **2.** [mûrir] to grow up / *j'ai compris en grandissant* I understood as I grew up ou older **3.** [s'intensifier - bruit] to increase, to grow louder; [-influence] to increase **4.** [s'étendre - ville] to spread **5.** *fig* ▸ **grandir en force / sagesse / beauté** to get stronger / wiser / more beautiful, to grow in strength / wisdom / beauty. ◆ vt **1.** [faire paraître plus grand] : *ces talons hauts la grandissent encore* these high-heeled shoes make her (look) even taller **2.** [ennoblir] : *ils n'en sortent pas vraiment grandis* they don't come out of it terribly well, it hasn't done much for their reputation.

grandissant, e [grɑ̃disɑ̃, ɑ̃t] adj [effectifs, douleur, renommée] growing, increasing ; [vacarme] growing ; [pénombre] deepening.

grand-mère [grɑ̃mɛr] (*pl* grand-mères *ou* grands-mères) nf [aïeule] grandmother.

grand-oncle [grɑ̃tɔ̃kl] (*pl* grands-oncles [grɑ̃zɔ̃kl]) nm great-uncle.

grand-peine [grɑ̃pɛn] ◆ **à grand-peine** loc adv with great difficulty.

grand-père [grɑ̃pɛr] (*pl* grands-pères) nm [parent] grandfather.

grands-parents [grɑ̃parɑ̃] nmpl grandparents.

grand-tante [grɑ̃tɑ̃t] (*pl* grand-tantes *ou* grands-tantes) nf great-aunt.

grand-voile [grɑ̃vwal] (*pl* grand-voiles *ou* grands-voiles) nf mainsail.

grange [grɑ̃ʒ] nf barn.

granit(e) [granit] nm GÉOL granite.

granule [granyl] nm **1.** [particule] (small) grain, granule **2.** PHARM (small) tablet, pill.

granulé [granyle] nm granule ; [pour animaux] pellet.

granuleux, euse [granylø, øz] adj [aspect] granular, grainy.

graphie [grafi] nf written form.

graphique [grafik] ◆ adj [relatif au dessin] graphic. ◆ nm MATH [courbe] graph ; [tracé] diagram, chart ▸ **graphique à bandes** bar chart ▸ **graphique circulaire** pie chart.

graphisme [grafism] nm **1.** [écriture] handwriting **2.** [dessin] ▸ **un graphisme vigoureux** a vigorously executed drawing ▸ **le graphisme de Dürer** Dürer's draughtsmanship.

graphiste [grafist] nmf graphic artist, artworker.

graphologie [grafɔlɔʒi] nf graphology.

graphologue [grafɔlɔg] nmf graphologist.

grappe [gʀap] nf [de fleurs, de fruit] ▶ **grappe de glycine** wisteria flowerhead ▶ **grappe de raisins** bunch of grapes. ❖ **en grappe(s)** loc adv [tomber - fleurs] in bunches.

grappiller [3] [gʀapije] ❖ vi [faire de petits profits] to be on the take ou the fiddle 🇬🇧. ❖ vt **1.** fam [argent] to fiddle 🇬🇧, to chisel 🇺🇸 **2.** fam [informations] to pick up (sép) / on n'a pu grappiller que quelques détails insignifiants we could only pick up a few minor clues.

grappin [gʀapɛ̃] nm **1.** NAUT [ancre] grapnel ; [d'abordage] grappling iron **2.** fam EXPR mettre le grappin sur qqn : une fois qu'il t'a mis le grappin dessus... once he's got his hands on you... / il m'a mis le grappin dessus à la sortie he grabbed me on the way out.

gras, grasse [gʀa, gʀas] adj **1.** CULIN fatty / ne mettez pas trop de matière grasse do not add too much fat ▶ **fromage gras** full-fat cheese **2.** [dodu] fat, plump **3.** [huileux] greasy, oily ; [taché] greasy **4.** [peau, cheveux] greasy **5.** [terre, boue] sticky, slimy **6.** [voix, rire] throaty **7.** [vulgaire] crude, coarse **8.** litt [abondant - récompense] generous ; [- pâturage] rich ▶ **ce n'est pas gras** fam a) [peu de chose] that's not much b) [profit médiocre] it's not a fortune **9.** [épais - gén] thick ; [- trait] bold ; [- caractère] bold, bold-faced ▶ **en gras** IMPR in bold (type) **10.** MÉD [toux] phlegmy **11.** EXPR faire la grasse matinée to stay in bed (very) late, to have a long lie-in 🇬🇧. ❖ **gras** ❖ nm **1.** [d'une viande] fat **2.** [du corps] fleshy part **3.** [substance] grease / des taches de gras greasy stains. ❖ adv [dans l'alimentation] ▶ **il mange trop gras** he eats too much fatty food.

grassement [gʀasmɑ̃] adv **1.** [largement] handsomely **2.** [vulgairement] coarsely, crudely.

grassouillet, ette [gʀasujɛ, ɛt] adj podgy 🇬🇧, pudgy 🇺🇸.

gratifiant, e [gʀatifjɑ̃, ɑ̃t] adj gratifying, rewarding.

gratification [gʀatifikasjɔ̃] nf **1.** [pourboire] tip ; [prime] bonus **2.** [satisfaction] gratification.

gratifier [9] [gʀatifje] vt iron ▶ **gratifier qqn de qqch** : elle m'a gratifié d'un sourire she favoured me with a smile.

gratin [gʀatɛ̃] nm **1.** CULIN [plat - recouvert de fromage] gratin (dish with a topping of toasted cheese) ; [- recouvert de chapelure] dish with a crispy topping ▶ **gratin dauphinois** sliced potatoes baked with cream and browned on top ; [croûte - de fromage] cheese topping ; [- de chapelure] crispy topping **2.** fam [élite] ▶ **le gratin** the upper crust.

gratiné, e [gʀatine] adj **1.** CULIN [doré] browned ; [cuit au gratin] (cooked) au gratin **2.** fam [addition] huge, steep / c'était un sujet d'examen gratiné ! it was a pretty tough exam question!

gratis [gʀatis] fam ❖ adv free (of charge). ❖ adj free.

gratitude [gʀatityd] nf gratitude, gratefulness.

grattage [gʀata3] nm [loterie] ▶ **gagner au grattage** to win on the scratchcards.

gratte-ciel [gʀatsjɛl] (pl gratte-ciel ou gratte-ciels*) nm sky-scraper.

gratte-papier [gʀatpapje] (pl gratte-papier ou gratte-papiers*) nm fam & péj penpusher.

gratter [3] [gʀate] ❖ vt **1.** [avec des griffes, des ongles, une plume] to scratch ; [avec un sabot] to paw **2.** [frotter - allumette] to strike ; [- métal oxydé] to scrape, to rub ; [- couche de saleté] to scrape ou to rub off (sép) **3.** [effacer] to scratch out (sép) **4.** [irriter] ▶ **ça (me) gratte** fam it's itchy **5.** fam [grappiller] to fiddle 🇬🇧, to chisel 🇺🇸 **6.** fam [devancer] to overtake **7.** fam [jouer de] ▶ **gratter du violon** to scrape away at the violin. ❖ vi **1.** [plume] to scratch **2.** [tissu, laine, pull] to itch, to be itchy. ❖ **se gratter** vp (emploi réfléchi) to scratch (o.s.), to have a scratch / se gratter la tête / le bras to scratch one's head / arm.

grattoir [gʀatwaʀ] nm **1.** [de bureau] erasing-knife **2.** [de graveur] scraper **3.** [allumettes] striking surface.

gratuit, e [gʀatɥi, it] adj **1.** [non payant] free / 'entrée gratuite' 'free admission' ▶ **c'est gratuit** it's free, there's no charge **2.** [sans fondement] unwarranted **3.** [absurde - violence] gratuitous ; [- cruauté] wanton, gratuitous **4.** [désintéressé] ▶ **aide gratuite** free help.

gratuité [gʀatɥite] nf [accès non payant] ▶ **nous voulons la gratuité de l'enseignement / des livres scolaires** we want free education / schoolbooks.

gratuitement [gʀatɥitmɑ̃] adv **1.** [sans payer] free (of charge) **2.** [sans motif] gratuitously, for no reason.

gravats [gʀava] nmpl [décombres] rubble.

grave [gʀav] ❖ adj **1.** [sérieux - motif, problème, maladie, accident] serious ; [- opération] serious, major / ce n'est pas grave ! never mind!, it doesn't matter! **2.** (après le nom) [solennel] grave, solemn / il la dévisageait, l'air grave he stared at her gravely **3.** ACOUST & MUS [note] low ; [voix] deep **4.** fam [stupide] : il est grave ce mec this guy's just too much. ❖ adv fam [beaucoup] : je le kiffe grave I'm completely crazy about him / je suis grave à la bourre I'm really late. ❖ nm MUS ▶ **le grave** the low register / les graves et les aigus low and high notes, the low and high registers. ❖ **graves** nmpl ACOUST bass.

gravement [gʀavmɑ̃] adv **1.** [solennellement] gravely, solemnly **2.** [en intensif] ▶ **gravement handicapé** severely handicapped ▶ **gravement malade** seriously ill.

graver [3] [gʀave] vt **1.** [tracer - sur métal, sur pierre] to carve, to engrave ; [- sur bois] to carve **2.** fig ▶ **à jamais gravé (en lettres d'or) dans mon esprit / mon souvenir** indelibly printed on my mind / memory **3.** [disque] to cut ; [CD, DVD] to burn.

graveur, euse [gʀavœʀ, øz] nm, f [personne] engraver, carver ▶ **graveur sur bois** wood engraver ou cutter. ❖ **graveur** nm ▶ **graveur de CD** CD burner ▶ **graveur de DVD** DVD burner ou writer.

gravier [gʀavje] nm [petits cailloux] gravel / allée de gravier gravel path.

gravillon [gʀavijɔ̃] nm **1.** [caillou] piece of gravel ou grit **2.** [revêtement] grit, fine gravel / 'gravillons' 'loose chippings'.

gravir [32] [gʀaviʀ] vt sout [grimper] to climb / gravir une montagne / un escalier to climb up a mountain / a staircase.

gravité [gʀavite] nf **1.** [sérieux, dignité] seriousness, solemnity / l'enfant la dévisagea avec gravité the child stared at her solemnly **2.** [importance] seriousness, gravity **3.** [caractère alarmant] seriousness ; [d'une blessure] severity / un accident sans gravité s'est produit en gare d'Orléans there was a minor accident at the station in Orléans **4.** [pesanteur] gravity.

graviter [3] [gʀavite] vi **1.** ASTRON ▶ **graviter autour de** to revolve ou to orbit around **2.** sout [évoluer] : il a toujours gravité dans les sphères gouvernementales he has always moved in government circles.

gravure [gʀavyʀ] nf **1.** [tracé en creux] ▶ **gravure sur bois** a) [procédé] woodcutting b) [objet] woodcut ▶ **gravure sur pierre** stone carving **2.** IMPR [processus] engraving, imprinting ▶ **gravure à l'eau-forte** etching ; [image] engraving, etching ▶ **gravure de mode** fashion plate.

gré [gʀe] nm **1.** [goût, convenance] : prenez n'importe quelle chaise, à votre gré sit down wherever you wish ou please **2.** [volonté, accord] ▶ **je suis venue de mon plein** ou **propre gré** I came of my own free will / il la suivit de bon gré he followed her willingly ou of his own accord / on l'a fait signer contre son gré they made her sign against her will ▶ **bon gré mal gré** : bon gré mal gré il faudra que tu *m'écoutes* whether you like it or not you'll have to listen to me ‣ **de gré ou de force** : *ramenez-le de gré ou de force !* bring him back by fair means or foul! ❖ **au gré de** loc prép : *se laisser aller au gré du courant* to let o.s. drift along with the current / *ballotté au gré des événements* tossed about ou buffeted by events.

grec, grecque [gʀɛk] adj Greek ‣ **profil grec** Grecian profile. ❖ **Grec, Grecque** nm, f Greek. ❖ **grec** nm LING Greek.

Grèce [gʀɛs] npr f ‣ **(la) Grèce** Greece.

grecque [gʀɛk] ❖ adj ⟶ **grec**. ❖ nf ⟶ **grec**.

gréement [gʀemɑ̃] nm [voilure] rigging, rig ; [processus] rigging ‣ **les vieux gréements** [voiliers] old sailing ships.

greffe [gʀɛf] ❖ nm DR clerk's office, clerk of the court's office. ❖ nf **1.** HORT [processus] grafting ; [pousse] graft **2.** MÉD [organe, moelle osseuse] transplant ; [os] graft.

greffer [4] [gʀefe] vt **1.** HORT to graft **2.** MÉD [os, peau] to graft ; [organe, moelle osseuse] to transplant. ❖ **se greffer sur** vp + prép : *puis d'autres problèmes sont venus se greffer là-dessus* then additional problems came along ou arose.

greffier [gʀefje] nm DR clerk (of the court), registrar.

grégaire [gʀegeʀ] adj gregarious ‣ **l'instinct grégaire** the herd instinct.

grège [gʀɛʒ] adj [soie] raw, unbleached, undyed.

grégorien, enne [gʀegɔʀjɛ̃, ɛn] adj Gregorian.

grêle [gʀɛl] ❖ adj **1.** [mince et long] spindly, thin **2.** [aigu - voix] reedy. ❖ nf MÉTÉOR hail ‣ **une averse de grêle** a hailstorm.

grêlé, e [gʀele] adj [peau, visage] pockmarked, pitted.

grêler [4] [gʀele] v impers ‣ **il grêle** it's hailing.

grêlon [gʀelɔ̃] nm hailstone.

grelot [gʀəlo] nm [clochette] (small sleigh ou jingle) bell.

grelotter, greloter* [3] [gʀəlɔte] vi [trembler] ‣ **grelotter de froid** to shiver ou to tremble with cold.

grenade [gʀənad] nf **1.** ARM grenade ‣ **grenade fumigène / incendiaire / lacrymogène** smoke / incendiary / teargas grenade **2.** BOT pomegranate.

Grenade [gʀənad] ❖ npr f [île] ‣ **la Grenade** Grenada. ❖ npr [ville d'Espagne] Granada.

grenadier [gʀənadje] nm **1.** MIL grenadier **2.** BOT pomegranate tree.

grenadine [gʀənadin] nf [sirop] grenadine *(bright red fruit syrup used in making drinks)*.

grenat [gʀəna] ❖ nm [pierre, couleur] garnet. ❖ adj inv garnet, garnet-coloured.

grenier [gʀənje] nm **1.** [combles] attic ‣ **grenier aménagé** converted loft **2.** [à grain] loft.

grenouille [gʀənuj] nf ZOOL frog ‣ **c'est une vraie grenouille de bénitier** *fam* she's very churchy.

grenouillère [gʀənujeʀ] nf VÊT sleepsuit, sleeping-suit.

grenu, e [gʀəny] adj [surface] grainy, grained.

grès [gʀɛ] nm **1.** GÉOL sandstone **2.** [vaisselle] ‣ **grès (cérame)** stoneware.

grésil [gʀezil] nm fine hail.

grésillement [gʀezijmɑ̃] nm [de l'huile] sizzling ; [du téléphone] crackling.

grésiller [3] [gʀezije] ❖ v impers ‣ **il grésille** it's hailing. ❖ vi [huile] to sizzle ; [feu, téléphone] to crackle.

grève [gʀɛv] nf **1.** [cessation d'une activité] strike ‣ **être en grève** to be on strike ‣ **faire grève** to strike ‣ **se mettre en grève** to go on strike ‣ **grève de la faim** hunger strike ‣ **grève générale** general strike ‣ **grève perlée** go-slow Uk, slowdown Uk ‣ **grève sauvage** ou **illégale** wildcat strike ‣ **grève de solidarité** sympathy strike ‣ **grève surprise**

lightning strike ‣ **grève sur le tas** sit-down strike ‣ **grève du zèle** work-to-rule **2.** *litt* [plage] shore, strand *litt* ; [rive] bank, strand *litt*.

grever [19] [gʀəve] vt **1.** *sout* [économie] to put a strain on **2.** DR : *sa propriété est grevée d'hypothèques* he's mortgaged up to the hilt.

gréviste [gʀevist] nmf striker, striking worker.

gribouillage [gʀibujaʒ] nm **1.** [dessin] doodle **2.** [écriture illisible] scrawl, scribble.

gribouiller [3] [gʀibuje] ❖ vt to scribble. ❖ vi to doodle, to scribble.

gribouillis [gʀibuji] = **gribouillage**.

grief [gʀijɛf] nm *litt* grievance ‣ **faire grief à qqn de qqch** to hold sthg against sb.

grièvement [gʀijɛvmɑ̃] adv [blessé] severely, seriously / *quinze blessés dont trois grièvement* fifteen wounded, three of them seriously.

griffe [gʀif] nf **1.** ZOOL claw ‣ **rentrer / sortir ses griffes** to draw into / show one's claws ‣ **arracher qqn des griffes de qqn** : *il faut l'arracher des griffes de sa mère* he needs to be rescued from his mother's clutches ‣ **donner un coup de griffe à qqn** *pr* to scratch ou to claw sb **2.** [d'un couturier] label, signature ; [d'un auteur] stamp **3.** JOAILL claw.

griffé, e [gʀife] adj [vêtement] designer *(modif)*.

griffer [3] [gʀife] vt [suj : personne, animal] to scratch.

griffonner [3] [gʀifɔne] vt [mal écrire] to scribble.

griffure [gʀifyʀ] nf [d'une personne, d'une ronce] scratch ; [d'un animal] scratch, claw mark.

grignoter [3] [gʀiɲɔte] ❖ vt **1.** [ronger] to nibble (at ou on) **2.** *fig* [amoindrir] to erode **3.** [acquérir] to acquire gradually. ❖ vi to nibble / *ne grignotez pas entre les repas* don't eat between meals.

grignotines [gʀiɲɔtin] nfpl Québec CULIN savoury snacks.

gril [gʀil] nm CULIN grill, broiler Us / *faire cuire du poisson sur le gril* to grill fish, to broil fish Us ‣ **être sur le gril** *fig* to be on tenterhooks, to be like a cat on hot bricks Uk ou a hot tin roof Us.

grillade [gʀijad] nf grill, grilled meat.

grillage [gʀijaʒ] nm **1.** [matériau] wire netting ou mesh **2.** [clôture] wire fence ou fencing.

grillager [17] [gʀijaʒe] vt **1.** [fenêtre] to put wire mesh ou netting on **2.** [terrain] to surround with a wire fence.

grille [gʀij] nf **1.** [porte] (iron) gate ; [barrière] railing ; [d'une fenêtre] bars **2.** [d'un égout, d'un foyer] grate ; [d'un parloir, d'un comptoir, d'un radiateur] grill, grille **3.** [programme] schedule **4.** JEUX : *une grille de mots croisés* a crossword grid ou puzzle ‣ **la grille du Loto** Loto card **5.** DR & ÉCON ‣ **grille des salaires** payscale.

grillé, e [gʀije] adj *fam* [personne] : *il est grillé* his cover's blown.

grille-pain [gʀijpɛ̃] *(pl* grille-pain *ou* grille-pains*) nm toaster.

griller [3] [gʀije] ❖ vt **1.** CULIN [pain] to toast ; [cacahuète, café] to roast ; [poisson, viande] to grill, to broil Us **2.** [cultures, végétation] ‣ **grillé par la chaleur** scorched by the heat **3.** *fam* [ampoule, fusible] to blow ; [moteur] to burn out **4.** TEXT to singe **5.** *fam* [dépasser] ‣ **griller un feu rouge** to go through a red light ‣ **griller quelques étapes** to jump a few stages ‣ **griller qqn (à l'arrivée)** to pip sb at the post Uk, to beat out sb Us **6.** *fam* [fumer] : *griller une cigarette, en griller une* to have a smoke. ❖ vi **1.** CULIN ‣ **faire griller du pain** to toast some bread / *faire griller de la viande* to grill meat, to broil meat Us **2.** *fam* [avoir trop chaud] to roast, to boil. ❖ **se griller** ❖ vp *(emploi réfléchi)* [se démasquer] : *il s'est grillé en disant cela* he gave himself away by saying that. ❖ vpt : *se griller les orteils devant la cheminée* to toast one's feet in front of the fire.

grillon [gʀijɔ̃] nm cricket.

grimace [gʀimas] nf [expression - amusante] funny face ; [-douloureuse] grimace / *une grimace de dégoût* a disgusted look ▸ **faire la grimace** to make a face.

grimacer [16] [gʀimase] vi **1.** [de douleur] to grimace, to wince ; [de dégoût] to make a face **2.** [pour faire rire] to make a funny face.

grimer [3] [gʀime] vt to make up *(sép)*. ✤ **se grimer** vp *(emploi réfléchi)* ▸ **se grimer en** to make o.s. up as.

grimoire [gʀimwaʀ] nm [livre de sorcellerie] book of magic spells.

grimpant, e [gʀɛ̃pɑ̃, ɑ̃t] adj [arbuste] climbing ; [fraisier] creeping.

grimper [3] [gʀɛ̃pe] ✦ vi **1.** [personne, animal, plante] to climb ▸ **grimper à un arbre a)** to climb (up) a tree **b)** [en s'aidant des jambes] to shin up a tree / *grimpe dans la voiture* get into the car **2.** [s'élever en pente raide] to climb / *ça grimpe à cet endroit-là* there's a steep climb at that point **3.** [température, inflation] to soar. ✦ vt [escalier, pente] to climb (up) *(insép)*.

grimpeur, euse [gʀɛ̃pœʀ, øz] nm, f SPORT climber.

grinçant, e [gʀɛ̃sɑ̃, ɑ̃t] adj [humour] sardonic.

grincement [gʀɛ̃smɑ̃] nm [bruit] grating, creaking / *dans un grincement de freins* with a squeal of brakes ▸ **il y a eu des grincements de dents** fig there was much gnashing of teeth.

grincer [16] [gʀɛ̃se] vi **1.** [bois] to creak ; [frein] to squeal ; [métal] to grate ; [ressort] to squeak **2.** [personne] ▸ **grincer des dents** pr to gnash one's teeth / *le bruit de la craie sur le tableau me fait grincer des dents* fig the noise the chalk makes on the board sets my teeth on edge.

grincheux, euse [gʀɛ̃ʃø, øz] adj grumpy, grouchy.

gringalet [gʀɛ̃galɛ] nm [enfant] puny child ; [adulte] puny man.

griotte [gʀijɔt] nf BOT morello (cherry).

grippal, e, aux [gʀipal, o] adj flu *(modif)*, influenzal spéc ▸ **état grippal** influenza, flu.

grippe [gʀip] nf MÉD flu, influenza spéc ▸ **avoir la grippe** to have (the) flu ▸ **grippe A H1N1** H1N1 A influenza ▸ **grippe aviaire** bird flu, avian influenza ▸ **grippe intestinale** gastric flu ▸ **grippe porcine** swine influenza ▸ **prendre qqn / qqch en grippe** to take a (strong) dislike to sb / sthg.

grippé, e [gʀipe] adj MÉD ▸ **être grippé** to have (the) flu.

gripper [3] [gʀipe] ✦ vt to block, to jam. ✦ vi to jam, to seize up.

grippe-sou [gʀipsu] *(pl* **grippe-sou** *ou* **grippe-sous)** fam nm skinflint.

gris, e [gʀi, gʀiz] adj **1.** [couleur] grey UK, gray US ▸ **gris acier / anthracite / ardoise / argent / fer / perle** steel / charcoal / slate / silver / iron / pearl grey ▸ **gris bleu / vert** bluish / greenish grey ▸ **avoir les cheveux gris** to have grey hair, to be grey-haired **2.** MÉTÉOR overcast / *nous sommes partis par un matin gris* we left on a dull (grey) morning **3.** [terne] dull, grey UK, gray US / *en apprenant la nouvelle, il a fait grise mine* his face fell when he heard the news **4.** fam [ivre] tipsy. ✤ **gris** ✦ adv : *il a fait gris toute la journée* it's been grey ou dull all day. ✦ nm [couleur] grey UK, gray US.

grisaille [gʀizaj] nf **1.** [morosité] dullness, greyness UK, grayness US **2.** MÉTÉOR dull weather.

grisant, e [gʀizɑ̃, ɑ̃t] adj **1.** [enivrant] intoxicating, heady **2.** [excitant] exhilarating.

grisâtre [gʀizatʀ] adj greyish UK, grayish US.

griser [3] [gʀize] vt **1.** [enivrer] to intoxicate **2.** [étourdir, exciter] to intoxicate, to fascinate / *le luxe ambiant l'a grisé* the luxuriousness of the place went to his head.

grisonnant, e [gʀizɔnɑ̃, ɑ̃t] adj greying UK, graying US / *elle est grisonnante, elle a les cheveux grisonnants* she's going grey.

grisonner [3] [gʀizɔne] vi [barbe, cheveux] to be going grey, to turn grey UK ou gray US.

grisou [gʀizu] nm firedamp ▸ **coup de grisou** firedamp explosion.

grive [gʀiv] nf thrush.

grivois, e [gʀivwa, az] adj risqué, bawdy.

Groenland [gʀɔɛnlɑ̃d] npr m ▸ **le Groenland** Greenland.

grog [gʀɔg] nm hot toddy ▸ **grog au rhum** rum toddy.

groggy [gʀɔgi] adj inv **1.** [boxeur] groggy **2.** fam [abruti] stunned, dazed.

grogne [gʀɔɲ] nf dissatisfaction, discontent.

grognement [gʀɔɲmɑ̃] nm **1.** [d'une personne] grunt, growl **2.** [d'un cochon] grunt, grunting *(U)* ; [d'un chien] growl, growling *(U)*.

grogner [3] [gʀɔɲe] vi **1.** [personne] to grumble, to grouse **2.** [cochon] to grunt ; [chien] to growl.

grognon, onne [gʀɔɲɔ̃, ɔn] adj fam grumpy, crotchety.

groin [gʀwɛ̃] nm [d'un porc] snout.

grommeler [24] [gʀɔmle] ✦ vi [personne] to grumble, to mumble. ✦ vt to mutter.

✍ In reformed spelling (see p. 16-18), this verb is conjugated like **peler** : *il grommèle, elle grommèlera*.

grondement [gʀɔ̃dmɑ̃] nm **1.** [du tonnerre, du métro] rumbling / *le grondement de la foule se fit de plus en plus fort* the angry murmur of the crowd grew louder and louder **2.** [d'un chien] growling.

gronder [3] [gʀɔ̃de] ✦ vi **1.** [rivière, tonnerre, métro] to rumble **2.** [chien] to growl **3.** litt [révolte] to be brewing. ✦ vt [réprimander] to scold, to tell off *(insép)*.

groom [gʀum] nm [employé d'hôtel] bellboy, bellhop US.

gros, grosse [gʀo, gʀos] *(devant nm commençant par voyelle ou « h » muet* [gʀoz]*)* ✦ adj **1.** [grand] large, big ; [épais, solide] big, thick / *le paquet n'est pas (très) gros* the parcel is / isn't (very) big ▸ **de grosses chaussures** heavy shoes ▸ **de grosses lèvres** thick lips ▸ **un gros pull** a thick ou heavy jumper ▸ **une grosse tranche** a thick slice **2.** [corpulent] big, fat / *un homme grand et gros* a tall fat man ▸ **de grosses jambes** fat ou stout legs **3.** [en intensif] ▸ **un gros appétit / mangeur** a big ou hearty appetite / eater ▸ **un gros bisou** fam a big kiss ▸ **un gros bruit** a loud ou big noise ▸ **un gros buveur** a heavy drinker ▸ **par les grosses chaleurs** in the hot season **4.** [abondant] heavy / *une grosse averse* a heavy shower **5.** [important] big ▸ **de gros dégâts** extensive ou widespread damage / *une grosse entreprise* a large ou big company ▸ **avoir de gros moyens** to have a large income ou considerable resources ▸ **une grosse somme** a large sum of money ▸ **un gros rhume** a bad ou heavy cold ▸ **de gros ennuis** serious trouble, lots of trouble ▸ **de grosses pertes** heavy losses **6.** [prospère] big / *un gros producteur d'Hollywood* a big Hollywood producer ▸ **les gros actionnaires** the major shareholders **7.** [rude] ▸ **une grosse voix** a rough ou gruff voice ▸ **un gros rire** coarse laughter ▸ **l'astuce / la supercherie était un peu grosse** the trick / the hoax was a bit obvious **8.** MÉTÉOR ▸ **par gros temps / grosse mer** in heavy weather / seas **9.** sout [rempli] ▸ **gros de:** *un ciel gros d'orage* stormy skies / *un cœur gros de tendresse* a heart full of tenderness. ✦ nm, f fat person / *un petit gros* a fat little man. ✤ **gros** ✦ nm **1.** [majorité] ▸ **le gros de:** *le gros de la classe a du mal à suivre* most of the class has trouble keeping up ▸ **le gros du chargement** the bulk of the cargo **2.** COMM ▸ **le gros** the wholesale business. ✦ adv ▸ **couper gros** to cut in thick slices ▸ **écrire gros** to write big ▸ **jouer** ou **miser** ou **risquer gros** *fig* to take ou to run a big risk, to stick one's neck out. ❖ **de gros** *loc adj* [commerce, prix] wholesale. ❖ **en gros** ◆ *loc adj* bulk *(modif)* ▸ **vente en gros** wholesaling. ◆ *loc adv* **1.** [approximativement] roughly **2.** [en lettres capitales] ▸ *c'est imprimé en gros* it's printed in big letters **3.** COMM wholesale ▸ **acheter en gros** to buy wholesale. ❖ **gros bonnet** *nm fam* bigwig, big shot. ❖ **grosse légume** *nf fam* [personne influente] bigwig, big shot ; [officier] brass (hat).

groseille [gʀozɛj] *nf* ▸ **groseille rouge** redcurrant ▸ **groseille blanche** white currant ▸ **groseille à maquereau** gooseberry.

groseillier [gʀozeje] *nm* currant bush.

grosse [gʀos] *f* ⟶ **gros**.

grossesse [gʀosɛs] *nf* pregnancy ▸ **grossesse nerveuse** phantom pregnancy.

grosseur [gʀosœʀ] *nf* **1.** [taille] size ; [de fil, bâton] thickness **2.** *sout* [obésité] weight, fatness **3.** MÉD lump.

grossier, ère [gʀosje, ɛʀ] *adj* **1.** [impoli] rude, crude ; [vulgaire] vulgar, uncouth **2.** [peu raffiné] coarse, rough / *des traits grossiers* coarse features **3.** [approximatif] rough, crude *péj* ▸ *c'est du travail grossier* it's shoddy work **4.** [flagrant - erreur] gross, stupid ; [- manœuvre, procédé] unsubtle.

grossièrement [gʀosjɛʀmɑ̃] *adv* **1.** [approximativement] roughly (speaking) **2.** [sans délicatesse] roughly **3.** [injurieusement] rudely **4.** [beaucoup] : *tu te méprends grossièrement* you're grossly ou wildly mistaken.

grossièreté [gʀosjɛʀte] *nf* **1.** [impolitesse] coarseness, rudeness **2.** [manque de finesse - d'une personne] coarseness ; [- d'une chose] crudeness, coarseness **3.** [gros mot] coarse remark ; [obscénité] rude joke.

grossir [32] [gʀosiʀ] ◆ *vi* **1.** [prendre du poids] to put on weight / *j'ai grossi d'un kilo* I've put on a kilo **2.** [augmenter en taille - tumeur, entreprise, somme, troupeau] to grow, to get bigger ; [- vague, nuages] to get bigger ; [- effectifs] to increase ; [- rumeur] to grow ▸ *les bourgeons / ruisseaux grossissent* the buds / streams are swelling ▸ *le bruit grossit* the noise is getting louder. ◆ *vt* **1.** [faire paraître gros] : *ta robe te grossit* your dress makes you look fatter **2.** [augmenter] to raise, to swell / *grossir le nombre / les rangs des manifestants* to join the growing numbers of demonstrators, to swell the ranks of the demonstrators **3.** [exagérer] to exaggerate, to overexaggerate **4.** [à la loupe] to magnify, to enlarge.

grossissant, e [gʀosisɑ̃, ɑ̃t] *adj* [verre] magnifying.

grossissement [gʀosismɑ̃] *nm* [avec une loupe] magnifying.

grossiste [gʀosist] *nmf* wholesaler.

grosso modo [gʀosomodo] *loc adv* roughly, more or less.

grotesque [gʀɔtɛsk] ◆ *adj* **1.** [burlesque] ridiculous **2.** [absurde] ridiculous, ludicrous. ◆ *nm* ART & LITTÉR ▸ **le grotesque** the grotesque.

grotte [gʀɔt] *nf* GÉOL cave.

grouiller [3] [gʀuje] *vi* **1.** [clients, touristes] to mill ou to swarm about **2.** ▸ **grouiller de** [être plein de] to be swarming ou crawling with. ❖ **se grouiller** *vpi fam* to get a move on.

groupe [gʀup] *nm* **1.** [de gens, d'objets] group ▸ **groupe armé** armed group ▸ **groupe hospitalier / scolaire** hospital / school complex ▸ **groupe de discussion** discussion group ▸ **groupe parlementaire** parliamentary group ▸ **groupe de parole** support group ▸ **groupe de pression** pressure group ▸ **groupe de rock** rock band ou group ▸ **groupe de travail** working group ou party **2.** ÉCON group ▸ **groupe de presse** press consortium ou group

3. ART group **4.** ÉLECTR set ▸ **groupe électrogène** generator **5.** LING ▸ **groupe de mots** word group ▸ **groupe du verbe** ou **verbal** verbal group ▸ **groupe du nom** ou **nominal** nominal group **6.** MATH group **7.** MÉD & BIOL ▸ **groupe sanguin** blood group **8.** MIL group **9.** BOT & ZOOL [classification] group. ❖ **de groupe** *loc adj* group *(modif)* ▸ **psychologie / psychothérapie de groupe** group psychology / therapy. ❖ **en groupe** *loc adv* in a group.

groupement [gʀupmɑ̃] *nm* [association] group ▸ **groupement d'achat (commercial)** bulk-buying group ▸ **groupement d'intérêt économique** intercompany management syndicate ▸ **groupement professionnel** professional organization.

grouper [3] [gʀupe] *vt* **1.** [réunir - personnes] to group together *(sép)* ; [- ressources] to pool **2.** [classer] to put ou to group together *(sép)*. ❖ **se grouper** *vpi* **1.** [dans un lieu] to gather **2.** [dans une association] to join together / **se grouper autour d'un chef** to join forces under one leader.

groupuscule [gʀupyskyl] *nm péj* POL small group.

grue [gʀy] *nf* ORNITH crane.

gruger [17] [gʀyʒe] *vt litt* [tromper] to deceive, to swindle / **se faire gruger** to get swindled.

grumeau, x [gʀymo] *nm* lump.

grumeleux, euse [gʀymlø, øz] *adj* [sauce] lumpy.

gruyère [gʀyjɛʀ] *nm* ▸ **gruyère, fromage de Gruyère** Gruyere (cheese).

GSM (*abr de* Global System for Mobile Communication) *nm* TÉLÉC GSM.

Guadeloupe [gwadlup] *npr f* ▸ **la Guadeloupe** Guadeloupe.

guadeloupéen, enne [gwadlupeɛ̃, ɛn] *adj* Guadeloupean. ❖ **Guadeloupéen, enne** *nm, f* Guadeloupean.

Guatemala [gwatemala] *npr m* ▸ **le Guatemala** Guatemala.

guatémaltèque [gwatemaltɛk] *adj* Guatemalan. ❖ **Guatémaltèque** *nmf* Guatemalan.

gué [ge] *nm* [passage] ford / **passer un ruisseau à gué** to ford a stream.

guenilles [gənij] *nfpl* rags (and tatters) / **être vêtu de guenilles** to wear old rags.

guenon [gənɔ̃] *nf* ZOOL female monkey, she-monkey.

guépard [gepaʀ] *nm* cheetah.

guêpe [gɛp] *nf* ZOOL wasp.

guêpier [gepje] *nm* [situation périlleuse] sticky situation.

guère [gɛʀ] *adv sout* **1.** [employé avec 'ne'] ▸ *il n'est guère aimable* he's not very nice ▸ *je n'aime guère cela* I don't much like that, I don't like that much / *il n'est guère plus aimable qu'elle* he's not much nicer than she is / *il n'y a guère de monde* there's hardly anyone / *le beau temps ne dura guère* the fine weather lasted hardly any time at all ou didn't last very long / *il ne vient guère nous voir* he hardly ever comes to see us / *je ne suis plus guère qu'à une heure de Paris* I'm only an hour away from Paris **2.** [dans une réponse] : *aimez-vous l'art abstrait ? guère* do you like abstract art? — not really / *comment allez-vous ? — guère mieux* how are you? — not much better ou hardly any better.

guéridon [geʀidɔ̃] *nm* [table] occasional table.

guérilla [geʀija] *nf* [guerre] guerrilla warfare.

guérir [32] [geʀiʀ] ◆ *vt* MÉD [malade, maladie] to cure ; [blessure] to heal. ◆ *vi* **1.** MÉD [convalescent] to recover, to be cured / *elle est guérie de sa rougeole* she's cured of ou recovered from her measles ; [blessure] to heal, to mend **2.** *fig* : *il est guéri de sa timidité* he is cured of ou he has got over his shyness. ❖ **se guérir** ◆ *vp* [emploi réfléchi] to cure o.s. ◆ *vpi* **1.** [maladie] : *est-ce que ça* *se guérit facilement ?* is it easy to cure? **2.** [personne] : *il ne s'est jamais guéri de sa jalousie* he never got over his jealousy.

guérison [geʀizɔ̃] nf MÉD [d'un patient] recovery ; [d'une blessure] healing / *il est maintenant en voie de guérison* he's now on the road to recovery.

guérissable [geʀisabl] adj MÉD [patient, mal] curable.

guérisseur, euse [geʀisœʀ, øz] nm, f healer ; péj quack.

guérite [geʀit] nf **1.** [sur un chantier] site office **2.** MIL sentry box.

Guernesey [gɛʀnəzɛ] npr Guernsey.

guerre [gɛʀ] nf **1.** [conflit] war ▸ **des pays en guerre** countries at war, warring countries ▸ **déclarer la guerre (à)** to declare war (against ou on) ▸ **guerre atomique / nucléaire** atomic / nuclear war ▸ **la guerre de Cent Ans** the Hundred Years War ▸ **guerre civile** civil war ▸ **guerre d'embuscade** guerrilla war ▸ **la guerre des étoiles** Star Wars ▸ **la guerre froide** the Cold War ▸ **guerre des nerfs** war of nerves ▸ **guerre ouverte** open war ▸ **guerre de religion** war of religion ▸ **guerre sainte** Holy War ▸ **la guerre de Sécession** the American Civil War ▸ **guerre d'usure** war of attrition ▸ **la Grande Guerre** ou **la Première Guerre (mondiale)** ou **la guerre de 14** the Great War, the First World War, World War I ▸ **la Seconde Guerre mondiale** ou **la guerre de 40** World War II, the Second World War ▸ **faire la guerre (à) a)** pr to wage war (against) **b)** fig to battle (with) / *il a fait la guerre en Europe* he was in the war in Europe / *je fais la guerre aux moustiques / fumeurs* I've declared war on mosquitoes / smokers ▸ **partir en guerre (contre) a)** pr to go to war (against) **b)** fig to launch an attack (on) ▸ **c'est de bonne guerre** all's fair in love and war prov ▸ **de guerre lasse :** *de guerre lasse je l'ai laissé sortir* in the end I let him go out just to have some peace (and quiet) **2.** [technique] warfare ▸ **guerre biologique / chimique** biological / chemical warfare ▸ **guerre éclair** blitzkrieg ▸ **guerre économique** economic warfare ▸ **guerre psychologique** psychological warfare ▸ **guerre de tranchées** trench warfare.

guerrier, ère [geʀje, ɛʀ] ▸ adj [peuple] warlike ▸ **un chant guerrier** a battle song ou chant. ▸ nm, f warrior.

guerroyer [13] [geʀwaje] vi sout to (wage) war.

guet [gɛ] nm watch ▸ **faire le guet** to be on the lookout.

guet-apens [gɛtapɑ̃] (pl **guets-apens** [gɛtapɑ̃]) nm ambush, trap / *tomber dans un guet-apens* to fall into a trap, to be ambushed.

guetter [4] [gete] vt **1.** [surveiller] to watch **2.** fig [menacer] : *les ennuis la guettent* there's trouble in store for her **3.** [attendre] to watch out for (insép) ▸ **il guette le facteur** he is on the lookout for the postman / *guetter l'occasion propice* to watch out for the right opportunity.

gueulante [gœlɑ̃t] nf tfam ▸ **pousser une gueulante** to raise the roof.

gueule [gœl] nf **1.** tfam [bouche] gob 🇬🇧, yap 🇺🇸 ▸ **c'est une grande gueule** ou **un fort en gueule** he's a big mouth ou a loudmouth, he's always shooting his mouth off ▸ **(ferme) ta gueule !** shut your mouth ou trap ou gob 🇬🇧! **2.** tfam [visage] mug, face / *il va faire une sale gueule quand il saura la vérité* he's going to be mad ou livid when he finds out the truth / *avoir ou faire une drôle de gueule* to look funny ou weird ▸ **faire la gueule** : *il nous fait la gueule depuis notre arrivée* he's been in a huff ou in a bad mood with us ever since we arrived **3.** fam [apparence] : *cette pizza a une sale gueule* that pizza looks disgusting **4.** tfam [charme] : *leur maison a vraiment de la gueule* their house really has got style **5.** [d'un animal]

mouth ▸ **se jeter dans la gueule du loup** to throw o.s. into the lion's mouth ou jaws. ❖ **gueule de bois** nf fam hangover.

gueule-de-loup [gœldəlu] (pl **gueules-de-loup**) nf BOT snapdragon.

gueuler [5] [gœle] fam ▸ vi **1.** [personne - de colère] to shout ; [- de douleur] to yell out / *faudrait gueuler !* we should kick up a fuss ▸ **gueuler sur qqn** to shout at sb **2.** [radio, haut-parleur] to blare out (insép) / *faire gueuler sa radio* to turn the radio up full blast **3.** [chien] to howl. ❖ vt to bellow out (sép), to bawl out (sép).

gueuleton [gœltɔ̃] nm tfam [repas] nosh-up 🇬🇧, blowout.

gui [gi] nm BOT mistletoe.

guichet [giʃɛ] nm [d'une banque] counter ; [d'un théâtre] ticket office ; [d'une poste] counter, window / **'guichet fermé'** 'position closed' ▸ **guichet automatique** autobank, cash dispenser ▸ **jouer à guichets fermés** to play to packed houses.

guichetier, ère [giʃtje, ɛʀ] nm, f counter clerk.

guide [gid] ▸ nmf **1.** SPORT ▸ **guide (de haute montagne)** mountain guide **2.** [pour touristes] (tour) guide. ▸ nm **1.** [personne] guide, leader **2.** [principe] guiding principle **3.** [livre] guidebook ▸ **guide touristique** guidebook. ▸ nf **1.** [scout] girl guide 🇬🇧, girl scout 🇺🇸 **2.** [rêne] rein.

guider [3] [gide] vt **1.** [diriger] to guide **2.** [conseiller] to guide / *guidée par son expérience* guided by her experience / *nous sommes là pour vous guider dans vos recherches* we're here to help you find what you're looking for.

guidon [gidɔ̃] nm [d'un vélo] handlebars ▸ **avoir le nez** ou **la tête dans le guidon** fig to have one's nose to the ground.

guigne [giɲ] nf **1.** BOT sweet cherry **2.** fam [malchance] bad luck ▸ **avoir la guigne** to be jinxed, to have rotten luck.

guignol [giɲɔl] nm **1.** [pantin] (glove) puppet ; [théâtre] puppet theatre ; [spectacle] Punch and Judy show **2.** fam & fig ▸ **faire le guignol** to clown around / *ce nouveau ministre est un guignol* that new minister is a (real) clown.

guignolée [giɲɔle] nf 🇶🇧 guignolée (annual Christmas charity event in Canada).

guillemet [gijmɛ] nm quotation mark, inverted comma 🇬🇧 / *tu connais son sens de la «justice», entre guillemets* you know his so-called sense of justice.

guilleret, ette [gijʀɛ, ɛt] adj jolly, cheerful.

guillotine [gijɔtin] nf guillotine.

guillotiner [3] [gijɔtine] vt to guillotine.

guimauve [gimov] nf **1.** BOT & CULIN marshmallow **2.** fig & péj : *ses chansons, c'est de la guimauve* his songs are all soppy ou schmaltzy.

guimbarde [gɛ̃baʀd] nf **1.** fam [voiture] (old) banger 🇬🇧, jalopy 🇺🇸 **2.** MUS jew's-harp.

guindé, e [gɛ̃de] adj [personne] stiff, starchy ; [discours] stilted / *d'un air guindé* starchily, stiffly.

Guinée [gine] npr f ▸ **(la) Guinée** Guinea ▸ **(la) Guinée-Bissau** Guinea-Bissau ▸ **(la) Guinée-Équatoriale** Equatorial Guinea.

guinéen, enne [gineɛ̃, ɛn] adj Guinean. ❖ **Guinéen, enne** nm, f Guinean.

guingois [gɛ̃gwa] ❖ **de guingois** loc adv [de travers] ▸ **marcher de guingois** to walk lop-sidedly.

guinguette [gɛ̃gɛt] nf open-air café or restaurant with dance floor.

guirlande [giʀlɑ̃d] nf **1.** [de fleurs] garland **2.** [de papier] paper garland ▶ **guirlande de Noël** (length of) tinsel **3.** [de lumières] ▶ **guirlande électrique a)** [de Noël] Christmas tree lights, fairy lights **b)** [pour une fête] fairy lights.

guise [giz] ⬥ **à ma guise, à ta guise** loc adv as I / you, etc. please ▶ **il n'en fait qu'à sa guise** he just does as he pleases ou likes. ⬥ **en guise de** loc prép by way of.

guitare [gitaʀ] nf guitar / *jouer de la guitare* to play the guitar ▶ **guitare basse / électrique** bass / electric guitar ▶ **guitare hawaïenne / sèche** Hawaiian / acoustic guitar.

guitariste [gitaʀist] nmf guitar player, guitarist.

gustatif, ive [gystatif, iv] adj gustatory, gustative.

guttural, e, aux [gytyʀal, o] adj [ton] guttural ; [voix] guttural, throaty.

Guyana [gɥijana] npr f ou npr m ▶ **(la** ou **le) Guyana** Guyana.

guyanais, e [gɥijanɛ, ɛz] adj **1.** [région, département] Guianese, Guianian **2.** [république] Guyanan, Guyanese. ⬥ **Guyanais, e** nm, f **1.** [région, département] Guianese, Guianian ▶ **les Guyanais** the Guianese, the Guianians **2.** [république] Guyanan, Guyanese ▶ **les Guyanais** the Guyanans, the Guyanese.

Guyane [gɥijan] npr f ▶ **la Guyane, les Guyanes** Guiana, the Guianas / *(la) Guyane française* French Guiana.

gym [ʒim] nf [à l'école] PE ; [pour adultes] gym / *aller à la gym* to go to gym class / *faire de la gym* to do exercises.

gymkhana [ʒimkana] nm SPORT rally.

gymnase [ʒimnaz] nm **1.** [salle] gym, gymnasium **2.** Suisse [lycée] secondary school UK, high school US.

gymnaste [ʒimnast] nmf gymnast.

gymnastique [ʒimnastik] nf **1.** SPORT physical education, gymnastics *(sg)* ▶ **faire de la gymnastique** to do exercises ▶ **gymnastique aquatique** aquaerobics ▶ **gymnastique corrective** remedial gymnastics **2.** fig gymnastics *(sg)* / *gymnastique mentale* ou *intellectuelle* mental gymnastics.

gynéco [ʒineko] (abr de **gynécologue**) nmf fam gynaecologist UK, gynecologist US.

gynécologie [ʒinekɔlɔʒi] nf gynaecologist UK, gynecologist US.

gynécologique [ʒinekɔlɔʒik] adj gynaecological UK, gynecological US.

gynécologue [ʒinekɔlɔg] nmf gynaecologist UK, gynecologist US.

gypse [ʒips] nm gypsum.

gyrophare [ʒiʀɔfaʀ] nm rotating light ou beacon.

h, H [aʃ] nm h, H ▸ **h aspiré / muet** aspirate / silent h.

ha [ˈa] interj [rire] : *ha, ha, que c'est drôle !* ha-ha, very funny!

habile [abil] adj **1.** [adroit] skilful UK, skillful US / *être habile de ses mains* to be good ou clever with one's hands **2.** [intelligent, fin - personne] clever, bright ; [- ouvrage] clever **3.** [rusé] clever, cunning.

habilement [abilmɑ̃] adv [travailler] skilfully UK, skillfully US ; [répondre] cleverly.

habileté [abilte] nf **1.** [dextérité] skill, dexterity *sout* **2.** [ingéniosité] cleverness, smartness.

habiliter [3] [abilite] vt **1.** DR to entitle, to empower **2.** UNIV to accredit, to authorize, to habilitate *sout*.

habillage [abijaʒ] nm **1.** [revêtement - d'une machine] casing ; [- d'un produit] packaging ; [- d'un ordinateur] cabinetry ; [AUTO - d'un siège] covering ; [- d'un plafond] lining ; [- d'un intérieur] trim **2.** [d'un acteur] dressing.

habillé, e [abije] adj [vêtements] smart, dressy ▸ *dîner habillé* dinner in evening dress.

habillement [abijmɑ̃] nm [vêtements] clothes, clothing ; [action d'habiller] dressing, clothing.

habiller [3] [abije] vt **1.** [vêtir] to dress / *toujours habillé de ou en vert* always dressed in green **2.** [équiper - famille, groupe] to clothe ; [- skieur, écolier] to kit out (*sép*) ; [suj : couturier, tailleur] to design clothes for / *elle est habillée par un grand couturier* she gets her clothes from a top designer **3.** [décorer, recouvrir] to cover / *habiller un mur de toile de jute* to cover a wall with hessian. ❖ **s'habiller** vp (*emploi réfléchi*) **1.** [se vêtir] to get dressed, to dress ▸ *tu t'habilles mal* you have no dress sense ▸ *habille-toi chaudement* wrap up well ou warm **2.** [se déguiser en] to dress up as **2.** [se parer] to dress up / *s'habiller pour le dîner* to dress for dinner.

habit [abi] nm **1.** [déguisement] costume, outfit ▸ *habit d'arlequin* Harlequin suit ou costume **2.** [vêtement de cérémonie] tails ▸ *en habit* wearing tails **3.** RELIG habit. ❖ **habits** nmpl clothes.

habitable [abitabl] adj : *la maison est tout à fait habitable* the house is perfectly fit to live in.

habitacle [abitakl] nm **1.** AÉRON cockpit **2.** AUTO passenger compartment **3.** NAUT binnacle.

habitant, e [abitɑ̃, ɑ̃t] nm, f **1.** [d'une ville, d'un pays] inhabitant ; [d'un immeuble] occupant ; [d'un quartier] inhabitant, resident / *nous avons dormi chez l'habitant* we stayed with a family **2.** QUÉBEC farmer.

habitat [abita] nm **1.** BOT & ZOOL habitat **2.** ANTHR & SOCIOL settlement.

habitation [abitasjɔ̃] nf **1.** [immeuble] house, building ▸ *groupe d'habitations* housing estate UK ou development US ▸ **habitation à loyer modéré** = HLM **2.** [domicile] residence.

habité, e [abite] adj [maison] occupied ; [planète] inhabited ▸ **engin spatial habité** manned spacecraft.

habiter [3] [abite] ◆ vt **1.** [maison, ville, quartier] to live in ; [ferme] to live on **2.** *fig & sout* to inhabit, to be ou to dwell in ▸ **les craintes / démons qui l'habitent** the fears / demons within him. ◆ vi to live / *habiter en ville / à la campagne* to live in town / in the country / *j'habite au 15, rue de Javel* I live at number 15 rue de Javel / *habiter à l'hôtel* to live ou to stay in a hotel / *habiter chez des amis* to be staying with friends.

habitude [abityd] nf [manière d'agir] habit / *je n'ai pas l'habitude d'attendre !* I am not in the habit of being kept waiting ! / *elle a l'habitude de la conduite sur circuit* she's used to race track driving ▸ **prendre l'habitude de faire qqch** to get into the habit of doing sthg ▸ **prendre de mauvaises habitudes** to get into bad habits / *elle a ses petites habitudes* she's got her own (little) ways ou habits / *ce n'est pas dans mes habitudes d'insister ainsi* I don't usually insist on things like that. ❖ **d'habitude** loc adv usually ▸ **comme d'habitude** as usual. ❖ **par habitude** loc adv out of habit.

habitué, e [abitɥe] nm, f regular / *ça va déplaire aux habitués* the regulars won't like it.

habituel, elle [abitɥɛl] adj [ordinaire, courant] usual.

habituellement [abitɥɛlmɑ̃] adv usually, normally.

habituer [7] [abitɥe] vt to accustom ▸ **habituer qqn à qqch** to get sb used to sthg, to accustom sb to sthg / *on l'a habitué à se taire* he's been taught to keep quiet / *il est habitué* [il a l'habitude] he's used to it / *c'est facile quand on est habitué* it's easy once you're used to it ou once you get used to it ▸ **être habitué à faire qqch** to be used to doing sthg. ❖ **s'habituer à** vp + prép to get ou to grow ou to become used to.

hach* [ˈaʃ] = hasch.

hache [ˈaʃ] nf [instrument tranchant] axe, ax US / *abattre un arbre à la hache* to chop a tree down ▸ **hache de guerre** tomahawk ▸ **enterrer la hache de guerre** *pr & fig* to bury the hatchet ▸ **déterrer la hache de guerre** *pr & fig* to be on the warpath (again).

haché, e [ˈaʃe] adj **1.** CULIN [légume, amandes] chopped ; [viande] minced UK, ground US **2.** [style, tirade] jerky. ❖ **haché** nm mince UK, ground meat US.

hacher [3] [ˈaʃe] vt [légumes, fines herbes] to chop (up) ▸ **hacher de la viande** to mince UK ou to grind US meat / *le persil doit être haché menu* the parsley should be chopped finely.

hachette [ˈaʃɛt] nf [outil] hatchet.

hachich* [ˈaʃiʃ] = haschisch.

hachis [ˈaʃi] nm [de viande] mince 🇬🇧, ground meat 🇺🇸; [pour farce] (meat) stuffing, forcemeat ; [de légumes] chopped vegetables ▸ **hachis Parmentier** CULIN hachis Parmentier *(dish similar to shepherd's pie)*.

hachisch, hachich* [ˈaʃiʃ] = haschisch.

hachoir [ˈaʃwaʀ] nm **1.** [couteau] chopping knife, chopper **2.** [planche] chopping board 🇬🇧, cutting board 🇺🇸; [machine] (meat) mincer 🇬🇧 ou grinder 🇺🇸.

hachure [ˈaʃyʀ] nf [dessin, gravure] hatching *(U).*

hachurer [3] [ˈaʃyʀe] vt [dessin, gravure] to hatch.

hacker [akœʀ] nm = hackeur.

hackeur, euse [akœʀ, øz] nm, f INFORM hacker.

haddock [ˈadɔk] nm smoked haddock.

hagard, e [ˈagaʀ, aʀd] adj wild, crazed ▸ **avoir l'air hagard** to look crazed, to have a wild look in one's eyes.

haie [ˈɛ] nf **1.** HORT hedge **2.** SPORT hurdle / *courir le 400 mètres haies* to run the 400 metres 🇬🇧 ou meters 🇺🇸 hurdles ; ÉQUIT fence ▸ **course de haies** hurdles race **3.** [file de gens] line, row ▸ **haie d'honneur** guard of honour 🇬🇧 ou honor 🇺🇸.

haillons [ˈajɔ̃] nmpl rags, torn and tattered clothes.

haine [ˈɛn] nf hatred, hate ▸ **être plein de haine envers qqn** to be full of hatred ou filled with hatred for sb ▸ **prendre qqn / qqch en haine** to take an immense dislike to sb / sthg ▸ **avoir la haine** *fam* to be full of hatred.

haineux, euse [ˈɛnø, øz] adj full of hatred ou hate.

haïr [33] [ˈaiʀ] vt **1.** [personne] to hate / *il me hait de lui avoir menti* he hates me for having lied to him **2.** [attitude, comportement] to hate, to detest.

haïssable [ˈaisabl] adj *sout* [préjugé, attitude, personne] hateful, loathsome, detestable.

Haïti [aiti] npr Haiti.

haïtien, enne [aisjɛ̃, ɛn] adj Haitian. ❖ **Haïtien, enne** nm, f Haitian.

halal [alal] *(pl* halal *ou* halals*) adj halal.

hâle [ˈal] nm suntan, tan.

hâlé, e [ˈale] adj suntanned, tanned 🇬🇧, tan 🇺🇸.

haleine [alɛn] nf **1.** [mouvement de respiration] breath, breathing ▸ **hors d'haleine** out of breath ▸ **reprendre haleine** to get one's breath back ▸ **tenir qqn en haleine** to keep sb in suspense ou on tenterhooks **2.** [air expiré] breath / *avoir mauvaise haleine* to have bad breath. ❖ **de longue haleine** *loc* adj long-term / *des recherches de longue haleine* long-term research.

haletant, e [ˈaltɑ̃, ɑ̃t] adj [chien] panting / *il est entré, tout haletant* he came in, all out of breath.

haleter [28] [ˈalte] vi [chien] to pant ; [asthmatique] to gasp for breath ; [pendant l'accouchement] to breathe hard, to pant.

hall [ˈol] nm [d'un hôtel] hall, lobby, foyer ; [d'une banque] lobby, hall ▸ **hall de gare** concourse ▸ **hall d'exposition** exhibition hall.

hallali [alali] nm ▸ **l'hallali** [sonnerie] the mort.

halle [ˈal] nf [édifice] (covered) market / *elle fait ses courses aux halles* she goes to the central food market to do her shopping.

Halloween [aloˈwin] npr Halloween.

hallucinant, e [alysinɑ̃, ɑ̃t] adj [frappant] staggering, incredible.

hallucination [alysinasjɔ̃] nf hallucination ▸ **avoir des hallucinations** to hallucinate.

halluciner [3] [alysine] vi *fam & fig* : *mais j'hallucine ou quoi ?* I don't believe this!

hallucinogène [alysinɔʒɛn] ◆ adj hallucinogenic. ◆ nm hallucinogen.

halo [ˈalo] nm **1.** ASTRON halo, corona **2.** *litt* aureole, halo / *un halo de lumière / de gloire* a halo of light / of glory.

halogène [alɔʒɛn] ◆ adj halogenous. ◆ nm [éclairage] ▸ **(lampe à) halogène** halogen lamp.

halte [ˈalt] ◆ nf **1.** [arrêt] stop, break ▸ **faire halte** to halt, to stop ▸ **faire une halte** to have a break, to pause **2.** [lieu] stopping ou resting place ; RAIL halt 🇬🇧 ▸ **halte routière** 🇨🇦 [sur autoroute] rest area. ◆ interj stop ; MIL halt / *halte à la pollution !* no more pollution! / *halte-là, ne t'emballe pas trop* hold on, don't get carried away.

halte-garderie [ˈaltəgaʀdəʀi] *(pl* haltes-garderies*)* nf ≃ day nursery.

haltère [altɛʀ] nm [avec des sphères] dumbbell ; [avec des disques] barbell ▸ **faire des haltères** to do weight-lifting.

haltérophile [alteʀɔfil] nmf weight-lifter.

haltérophilie [alteʀɔfili] nf weight-lifting.

hamac [ˈamak] nm hammock.

hamburger [ˈɑ̃bœʀgœʀ] nm hamburger.

hameau, x [ˈamo] nm hamlet.

hameçon [amsɔ̃] nm (fish) hook.

hameçonnage [amsɔnaʒ] nm 🇨🇦 [par courriel] phishing.

hammam [ˈamam] nm Turkish ou steam bath, hammam.

hampe [ˈɑ̃p] nf [d'un drapeau] pole.

hamster [ˈamstɛʀ] nm hamster.

hanche [ˈɑ̃ʃ] nf ANAT hip / *mettre les mains* ou *les poings sur les hanches* to put one's hands on one's hips.

handball [ˈɑ̃dbal] nm handball.

handicap [ˈɑ̃dikap] nm **1.** [gén] handicap, disability / *son poids est un grand handicap* her weight is a great handicap ▸ **handicap léger / moyen / lourd** minor / moderate / severe disability ; SPORT handicap **2.** *(comme adjectif, avec ou sans trait d'union)* handicap *(modif).*

handicapant, e [ˈɑ̃dikapɑ̃, ɑ̃t] adj [maladie] disabling / *c'est (très) handicapant* it's a (great) handicap.

handicapé, e [ˈɑ̃dikape] ◆ adj handicapped / *enfants handicapés mentaux* mentally handicapped children. ◆ nm, f handicapped ou disabled person ▸ **les handicapés** the disabled ▸ **un handicapé moteur** a spastic ▸ **handicapé mental** mentally handicapped person ▸ **handicapé physique** physically handicapped person.

handicaper [3] [ˈɑ̃dikape] vt to handicap.

handisport [ˈɑ̃dispɔʀ] adj ▸ **activité handisport** sport for the disabled.

hangar [ˈɑ̃gaʀ] nm [gén] shed ; [pour avions] (aircraft) hangar ▸ **hangar à bateaux** boathouse.

hanneton [ˈantɔ̃] nm cockchafer, maybug.

hanté, e [ˈɑ̃te] adj [maison, forêt] haunted.

hanter [3] [ˈɑ̃te] vt to haunt / *ce souvenir le hante* he's haunted by the memory.

hantise [ˈɑ̃tiz] nf obsession, obsessive fear / *avoir la hantise de la mort* to be haunted ou obsessed by the fear of death / *chez lui, c'est une hantise* he's obsessed by it, it's an obsession with him.

happer [3] [ˈape] vt **1.** [avec le bec ou la bouche] to snap up ; [avec la main ou la patte] to snatch, to grab **2.** [accrocher violemment] to strike ou to hit violently ▸ **être happé par un train / une voiture** to be mown down ou hit by a train / car.

harangue [ˈaʀɑ̃g] nf [discours solennel] harangue.

haranguer [3] [ˈaʀɑ̃ge] vt to harangue.

haras [ˈaʀa] nm stud farm.

harassant, e [ˈaʀasɑ̃, ɑ̃t] adj exhausting, wearing.

harasser [3] [ˈaʀase] vt to exhaust, to wear out *(sép)*.

harcèlement [ˈaʀsɛlmɑ̃] nm harassing, pestering ▸ **harcèlement moral / sexuel** moral / sexual harassment.

harceler [25] [ˈaʀsəle] vt to harass ▸ **harceler qqn de questions** to plague ou to pester sb with questions ▸ **harceler l'ennemi** to harass ou to harry the enemy.

harceleur, euse [aʀsəlœʀ, øz] nm, f [verbalement] bully ; [sexuellement] sex pest ; ; [qui suit sa victime obsessionnellement] stalker / **harceleur téléphonique** phone pest.

hard [ˈaʀd] *fam* **1.** = **hard-core 2.** = **hard-rock**.

hard-core [ˈaʀdkɔʀ] adj inv hard-core / *un film hardcore* a hard-core (porn) movie.

hardi, e [ˈaʀdi] adj **1.** [intrépide] bold, daring / *l'hypothèse est un peu hardie* fig the supposition is a bit rash ou hasty **2.** [licencieux] daring, bold.

hardiesse [ˈaʀdjɛs] nf **1.** [intrépidité] boldness, daring, audacity *sout* ▸ **avoir la hardiesse de faire qqch** to be forward ou daring enough to do sthg **2.** [indécence] boldness, raciness.

hard-rock [ˈaʀdʀɔk] (*pl* **hard-rocks**), **hard** [ˈaʀd] nm MUS hard rock, heavy metal.

hardware [ˈaʀdwɛʀ] nm INFORM hardware.

hareng [ˈaʀɑ̃] nm CULIN & ZOOL herring ▸ **hareng saur** smoked herring, kipper.

hargne [ˈaʀɲ] nf **1.** [colère] aggressiveness ▸ **avec hargne** aggressively, cantankerously **2.** [ténacité] fierce determination.

hargneux, euse [ˈaʀɲø, øz] adj **1.** [caractère] aggressive, quarrelsome **2.** [ton] scathing, caustic **3.** [animal] vicious.

haricot [ˈaʀiko] nm **1.** [légume] bean ▸ **haricot blanc** white (haricot) bean ▸ **haricot rouge** red ou kidney bean ▸ **haricot vert** French 🇬🇧 ou green 🇺🇸 ou string bean **2.** CULIN [ragoût] ▸ **haricot de mouton** mutton haricot ou stew.

harissa [ˈaʀisa] nf harissa (sauce).

harki [ˈaʀki] nm *Algerian who fought for the French during the Franco-Algerian War and who was subsequently given French nationality.*

harmonica [aʀmɔnika] nm harmonica, mouth organ.

harmonie [aʀmɔni] nf **1.** [élégance] harmony **2.** [entente] harmony **3.** MUS [accords] harmony ; [instruments à vent et percussions] wind section (with percussion) ; [fanfare] brass band. ❖ **en harmonie** ◆ loc adv in harmony, harmoniously. ◆ loc adj in harmony / *le tapis n'est pas en harmonie avec les meubles* the carpet doesn't go with ou match the furniture.

harmonieusement [aʀmɔnjøzmɑ̃] adv harmoniously, in harmony.

harmonieux, euse [aʀmɔnjø, øz] adj **1.** [mélodieux - son, instrument] harmonious ; [- voix] harmonious, tuneful, melodious **2.** [équilibré] harmonious, balanced / *des teintes harmonieuses* well-matched colours.

harmonisation [aʀmɔnizasjɔ̃] nf [mise en accord] harmonization.

harmoniser [3] [aʀmɔnize] vt MUS to harmonize ; [styles, couleurs] to match / *harmoniser les salaires du public et du privé* to bring public and private sector salaries into line.

harmonium [aʀmɔnjɔm] nm harmonium.

harnachement [ˈaʀnaʃmɑ̃] nm **1.** [équipement] harness ; [action] harnessing **2.** *hum* [accoutrement] outfit, getup ; [attirail] paraphernalia.

harnacher [3] [ˈaʀnaʃe] vt **1.** [cheval] to harness **2.** *hum* [accoutrer] to deck ou to rig out (sép) ; [équiper] to kit out *(sép)*. ❖ **se harnacher** vp *(emploi réfléchi)* [s'équiper] to get kitted out / *ils s'étaient harnachés de cordes et de piolets pour l'ascension* they were kitted out with ropes and ice axes for the climb.

harnais [ˈaʀnɛ] nm **1.** [d'un cheval] harness **2.** [sangles] ▸ **harnais (de sécurité)** (safety) harness.

harpe [ˈaʀp] nf MUS harp.

harpon [ˈaʀpɔ̃] nm PÊCHE harpoon.

harponner [3] [ˈaʀpɔne] vt **1.** PÊCHE to harpoon **2.** *fam* [arrêter] to nab, to collar.

hasard [ˈazaʀ] nm **1.** [providence] chance, fate / *ne rien laisser au hasard* to leave nothing to chance / *le hasard a voulu que je sois à l'étranger* as luck would have it I was abroad / *le hasard fait bien les choses* there are some lucky coincidences **2.** [incident imprévu] ▸ **quel heureux hasard !** what a stroke of luck ou piece of good fortune! ▸ **un hasard malheureux** a piece of bad luck **3.** [coïncidence] ▸ **quel heureux hasard !** what a fantastic coincidence! / *par un heureux hasard* by a happy coincidence / *par un curieux hasard, il était né le même jour* by a strange coincidence he was born on the same day / *par quel hasard étiez-vous là ce jour-là ?* how come you happened to be there that day? / *par le plus grand des hasards* by the most extraordinary ou incredible coincidence. ❖ **hasards** nmpl **1.** [aléas] : *les hasards de la vie* life's ups and downs, life's vicissitudes *sout* **2.** *litt* [périls] hazards, dangers. ❖ **à tout hasard** loc adv on the off chance, just in case. ❖ **au hasard** loc adv at random / *j'ai ouvert le livre au hasard* I opened the book at random ▸ **tirez une carte au hasard** pick a card(, any card). ❖ **par hasard** loc adv by chance ou accident / *je l'ai appris par hasard* I heard about it completely by chance / *si par hasard vous la voyez* if by any chance you should see her, should you happen to see her ▸ **comme par hasard !** *iron* that's a surprise, surprise, surprise! / *comme par hasard, elle n'a rien entendu* surprisingly enough, she didn't hear a thing!

⚠️ **Hazard** signifie « risque », « danger » et non hasard.

hasarder [3] [ˈazaʀde] vt [opinion, démarche] to hazard, to venture, to risk. ❖ **se hasarder** vpi [s'aventurer] to venture / *il se hasarda dans l'obscurité* he ventured into the darkness ▸ **se hasarder à**: *la nouvelle élève se hasarda à répondre* the new student plucked up courage to answer / *je ne m'y hasarderais pas* I wouldn't risk it ou chance it.

hasardeux, euse [ˈazaʀdø, øz] adj **1.** [douteux] dubious **2.** [dangereux] hazardous, dangerous / *une affaire hasardeuse* a risky business.

haschisch, haschich, hachisch, hachich* [ˈaʃiʃ] nm hashish.

hâte [ˈat] nf **1.** [précipitation] haste, hurry, rush ▸ **sans hâte** at a leisurely pace, without hurrying **2.** ▸ **avoir hâte de** [être impatient de] : *avoir hâte de faire qqch* to be looking forward to doing sthg ▸ **j'ai hâte que vous veniez / Noël arrive** I can't wait for you to come / Christmas to come round / *il n'a qu'une hâte, c'est d'avoir un petit-fils* he's dying to have a grandson. ❖ **à la hâte** loc adv hurriedly, hastily, in a rush. ❖ **en hâte, en grande hâte, en toute hâte** loc adv hurriedly, in (great) haste.

hâter [3] [ˈate] vt **1.** [accélérer] to speed up, to hasten *sout* ▸ **hâter le pas** to quicken one's pace *sout*, to walk quicker **2.** *sout* [avancer - date] to bring forward / [- naissance, mort, mariage] to precipitate / *je dois hâter mon* *départ* I must go sooner than I thought. ❖ **se hâter** vpi *sout* to hurry (up), to hasten *sout*, to make haste *sout* / *elle s'est hâtée de répandre la nouvelle* she hastened to spread the news.

hâtif, ive ['atif, iv] adj **1.** [rapide - travail, repas] hurried, rushed ; [- décision] hasty, rash **2.** [précoce - croissance] early.

hauban ['obã] nm **1.** AÉRON & NAUT shroud **2.** TECHNOL stay.

hausse ['os] nf **1.** [augmentation] rise, increase / *la hausse du coût de la vie* the rise in the cost of living **2.** [élévation] rise. ❖ **à la hausse** loc adv **1.** [au maximum] : *réviser le budget à la hausse* to increase the budget **2.** BOURSE ▸ **jouer à la hausse** to speculate on the rising market ou on the bull market ▸ **le marché est à la hausse** there is an upward trend in the market. ❖ **en hausse** loc adj increasing, rising / *être en hausse* to be on the increase, to be rising.

hausser [3] ['ose] vt **1.** ÉCON to raise, to increase, to put up (sép) **2.** [partie du corps] ▸ **hausser les épaules** to shrug (one's shoulders) **3.** [intensifier] ▸ **hausser la voix** ou **le ton** to raise one's voice. ❖ **se hausser** vpi **1.** [se hisser] to reach up / *se hausser sur la pointe des pieds* to stand on tiptoe **2.** [atteindre un degré supérieur] : *elle est parvenue à se hausser au niveau de la classe* she managed to reach the level of the other students in her class.

haut, e ['o, 'ot] (devant nm commençant par voyelle ou « h » muet ['ot]) adj **1.** [de grande dimension] high, tall / *les pièces sont hautes de plafond* the rooms have high ceilings ; BOT [tige, tronc] tall ; [qui a poussé] high **2.** [d'une certaine dimension] ▸ **haut de:** *la maison est haute de trois mètres* the house is three metres high **3.** [situé en hauteur] high / *la partie haute de l'arbre* the upper part of the tree **4.** [extrême, intense] high / *c'est de la plus haute importance* it's of the utmost ou greatest importance ▸ **à haut risque** high-risk ▸ **haut débit** INFORM & TÉLÉC broadband ▸ **haute technologie** high technology **5.** [dans une hiérarchie] high, top (avant nom) ▸ **de haut niveau** top-level, high-level ▸ **athlète de haut niveau** top athlete ▸ **les hauts fonctionnaires** top ou top-ranking civil servants ▸ **les hauts salaires** the highest ou top salaries **6.** [dans une échelle de valeurs] high / *d'une haute intelligence* highly intelligent ▸ **tenir qqn / qqch en haute estime** to hold sb / sthg in high esteem **7.** BOURSE & COMM high **8.** MUS & PHON high **9.** *litt* [noble] lofty, high-minded. ◆ **haut** ◆ adv **1.** [dans l'espace] high / *levez haut la jambe* raise your leg (up) high ou high up **2.** [dans le temps] far (back) ; [dans un livre] ▸ **voir plus haut** see above **3.** [fort, avec puissance] ▸ **(tout) haut** aloud ▸ **parlez plus haut** speak up, speak louder **4.** MUS high **5.** [dans une hiérarchie] high ▸ **être haut placé** to be highly placed, to hold high office **6.** BOURSE & COMM high. ◆ nm **1.** [partie supérieure] top ; [sur une caisse, un emballage] ▸ **'haut'** '(this way ou side) up' **2.** VÊT [gén] top ; [de robe] bodice **3.** [hauteur] : *un mur d'un mètre de haut* a one metre (high) wall. ◆ **hauts** nmpl **1.** [dans des noms de lieux] heights **2.** EXPR avoir ou **connaître des hauts et des bas** to have one's ups and downs. ❖ **de haut** loc adv **1.** [avec détachement] casually, unconcernedly ▸ **prendre** ou **voir les choses de haut** to look at things with an air of detachment **2.** [avec mépris] ▸ **regarder qqn de haut** to look down on sb **3.** EXPR **tomber de haut a)** [être surpris] to be flabbergasted **b)** [être déçu] to come down (to earth) with a bump. ❖ **de haut en bas** loc adv **1.** [sans mouvement] from top to bottom **2.** [avec mouvement, vers le bas] from top to bottom, downwards. ❖ **d'en haut** loc adv **1.** [depuis la partie élevée] from above / *d'en haut on voit la mer* you can see the sea from above **2.** *fig* [du pouvoir] from on high. ❖ **du haut** loc adj ▸ **les gens du haut a)** [de la partie haute du village] the people

up the top end (of the village) **b)** [des étages supérieurs] the people upstairs / *les chambres du haut* the upstairs bedrooms. ❖ **du haut de** loc prép [depuis la partie élevée de - échelle, colline] from the top of. ❖ **en haut** loc adv **1.** [à l'étage supérieur] upstairs **2.** [dans la partie élevée] at the top **3.** [en l'air] up in the sky. ❖ **en haut de** loc prép at the top of / *tout en haut d'une colline* high up on a hill.

hautain, e ['otɛ̃, ɛn] adj haughty.

hautbois ['obwa] nm **1.** [instrument] oboe **2.** [instrumentiste] oboe (player).

haut-commissaire ['okɔmisɛʀ] (pl **hauts-commissaires**) nmf high commissioner.

haut-commissariat ['okɔmisaʀja] (pl **hauts-commissariats**) nm [bureaux] high commission.

haut-de-forme ['odfɔʀm] (pl **hauts-de-forme**) nm top hat.

haut de gamme [odgam] ◆ adj upmarket, high-end, top-of-the-line US / *une chaîne haut de gamme* a state-of-the-art hi-fi system. ◆ nm top of the range, top of the line US.

haute-fidélité (pl **hautes-fidélités**), **hautefidélité*** ['otfidelite] nf **1.** [technique] high fidelity, hi-fi **2.** (comme adj) high-fidelity (avant nom), hi-fi.

hautement ['otmã] adv *sout* [fortement] highly, extremely.

hauteur ['otœʀ] nf **1.** [mesure verticale] height / *il est tombé de toute sa hauteur* he fell headlong / *la pièce fait trois mètres de hauteur (sous plafond)* the ceiling height in the room is three metres ; CONSTR height ; COUT length **2.** [altitude] height, altitude ▸ **prendre de la hauteur** to gain altitude ou height **3.** MUS & PHON height, pitch **4.** [arrogance] haughtiness, arrogance. ◆ **hauteurs** nfpl heights / *il y a de la neige sur les hauteurs* there's snow on the higher slopes. ❖ **à hauteur de** loc prép [jusqu'à] ▸ **à hauteur des yeux** at eye level / *vous serez remboursé à hauteur de 600 euros* you'll be reimbursed up to 600 euros. ❖ **à la hauteur** loc adj *fam* : *tu ne t'es pas montré à la hauteur* you weren't up to it ou equal to the task. ❖ **à la hauteur de** loc prép **1.** [à côté de] : *arrivé à sa hauteur, je m'aperçus qu'il parlait tout seul* when I was ou drew level with him, I noticed he was talking to himself / *elle habite à la hauteur de l'église* she lives near the church ou up by the church / *arrivés à la hauteur du cap* when we were in line with ou when we were off the cape **2.** [digne de] worthy of / *être à la hauteur d'une situation* to be equal to ou up to a situation.

haut-fond ['ofɔ̃] (pl **hauts-fonds**) nm shallow, shoal.

haut-le-cœur ['olkœʀ] nm inv [nausée] ▸ **avoir un** ou **des haut-le-cœur** to retch.

haut-parleur (pl **haut-parleurs**), **hautparleur*** ['opaʀlœʀ] nm loudspeaker, speaker ▸ **haut-parleur d'aigus** tweeter.

havre ['avʀ] nm *litt* haven, harbour ▸ **havre de paix** haven of peace.

Hawaii [awaj] npr Hawaii.

hawaïen, enne [awajɛ̃, ɛn] adj Hawaiian.

Haye ['ɛ] npr f ▸ **La Haye** The Hague.

hayon ['ajɔ̃] nm AUTO tailgate ▸ **véhicule à hayon arrière** hatchback (car).

HCR (abr de Haut-Commissariat des Nations unies pour les réfugiés) nm UNHCR.

hé ['e] interj **1.** [pour interpeller quelqu'un] hey / *hé, vous, là !* hey! you! **2.** [d'étonnement] hey, well (well, well).

heavy metal [ɛvimetal] nm inv MUS heavy metal.

hebdo [ɛbdo] nm *fam* PRESSE weekly.

hebdomadaire [ɛbdɔmadɛʀ] adj & nm weekly.

hébergement [ebɛʀʒəmɑ̃] nm **1.** [lieu] accommodation 🇬🇧, accommodations *(pl)* 🇺🇸 **2.** [action] lodging **3.** INTERNET [d'un site Web] hosting.

héberger [17] [ebɛʀʒe] vt **1.** [pour une certaine durée] to lodge, to accommodate ; [à l'improviste] to put up *(sép)* ; [réfugié, vagabond] to take in *(sép)*, to shelter ; [criminel] to harbour, to shelter / *notre bâtiment hébergera le secrétariat pendant les travaux* the secretarial offices will be housed in our building during the alterations **2.** INTERNET to host.

hébergeur [ebɛʀʒœʀ] nm INTERNET ‣ **hébergeur (Web)** web host.

hébété, e [ebete] adj dazed, in a daze / *il avait un air hébété* he looked dazed.

hébraïque [ebʀaik] adj Hebraic, Hebrew *(modif)*.

hébreu, x [ebʀø] adj m Hebrew. ✦ **Hébreux** nmpl ‣ **les Hébreux** the Hebrews. ✦ **hébreu** nm **1.** LING Hebrew **2.** EXPR *être de l'hébreu* fam: *pour moi, c'est de l'hébreu* I can't make head or tail of it, it's all Greek to me.

HEC (abr de **Hautes études commerciales**) npr *grande école for management and business studies.*

hécatombe [ekatɔb] nf [carnage] slaughter, massacre / *l'hécatombe annuelle des blessés de la route* the carnage that occurs every year on the roads.

hectare [ɛktaʀ] nm hectare.

hégémonie [eʒemɔni] nf hegemony.

hein [ɛ̃] interj fam **1.** [quoi] ‣ **hein ?** eh?, what? **2.** [n'est-ce pas] eh / *c'est drôle, hein !* funny, eh ou isn't it! **3.** [exprimant la colère] OK, right / *on se calme, hein !* cool it, will you!, that's enough, OK?

hélas [elas] interj unfortunately, unhappily, alas *litt*.

héler [18] [ele] vt to call out to *(insép)*, to hail.
✐ In reformed spelling (see p. 16-18), this verb is conjugated like *semer* : *il hèlera, elle hèlerait.*

hélice [elis] nf MÉCAN & NAUT propeller, screw, screwpropeller.

hélico [eliko] nm *fam* AÉRON chopper.

hélicoptère [elikɔptɛʀ] nm helicopter.

héliport [elipɔʀ] nm heliport.

héliporté, e [elipɔʀte] adj **1.** [transporté par hélicoptère] helicoptered ‣ **troupes héliportées** airborne troops *(brought in by helicopter)* **2.** [exécuté par hélicoptère] ‣ **une opération héliportée** a helicopter mission.

hélitreuiller [5] [elitʀœje] vt to winch up *(sép)* *(into a helicopter in flight).*

hélium [eljɔm] nm helium.

helvétique [ɛlvetik] adj Swiss, Helvetian.

helvétisme [ɛlvetism] nm LING *characteristic word or expression used by French-speaking Swiss.*

hématome [ematom] nm bruise, haematoma 🇬🇧 *spéc*, hematoma 🇺🇸 *spéc*.

hémicycle [emisikl] nm **1.** [espace en demi-cercle] semicircle **2.** [salle garnie de gradins] semicircular amphitheatre ‣ [hémicycle **a)** POL [salle] the benches ou chamber of the French National Assembly **b)** [Assemblée] the French National Assembly.

hémiplégie [emipleʒi] nf hemiplegia.

hémiplégique [emipleʒik] adj & nmf hemiplegic.

hémisphère [emisfɛʀ] nm GÉOGR & ANAT hemisphere.

hémoglobine [emɔglɔbin] nf BIOL haemoglobin 🇬🇧, hemoglobin 🇺🇸.

hémophile [emɔfil] nmf haemophiliac 🇬🇧, hemophiliac 🇺🇸.

hémorragie [emɔʀaʒi] nf **1.** MÉD haemorrhage 🇬🇧, hemorrhage 🇺🇸, bleeding *(U)* ‣ **hémorragie cérébrale** cerebral haemorrhage ‣ **hémorragie interne / externe** internal / external haemorrhage **2.** fig [perte] drain ‣ **l'hémorragie des capitaux** the drain ou haemorrhage of capital.

hémorroïdes [emɔʀɔid] nfpl haemorrhoids 🇬🇧, hemorrhoids 🇺🇸 / *avoir des hémorroïdes* to suffer from haemorrhoids, to have piles.

henné [ene] nm henna / *les cheveux teints au henné* hennaed hair ‣ **se faire un henné** to henna one's hair.

hennir [32] [eniʀ] vi [cheval] to neigh, to whinny.

hennissement ['enismɑ̃] nm [d'un cheval] neigh, whinny.

hep ['ɛp] interj hey.

hépatique [epatik] adj hepatic, liver *(modif)*.

hépatite [epatit] nf hepatitis.

herbe [ɛʀb] nf **1.** [plante, gazon] grass ‣ **herbes folles** wild grass ‣ **une mauvaise herbe** a weed ‣ **couper ou faucher l'herbe sous le pied à qqn** to cut the ground ou to pull the rug from under sb's feet **2.** fam [marihuana] grass. ✦ **herbes** nfpl ‣ **herbes de Provence** herbes de Provence ‣ **fines herbes** CULIN herbs, fines herbes. ✦ **en herbe** loc adj BOT green ; fig in the making / *c'est un musicien en herbe* he has the makings of a musician, he's a budding musician.

herbicide [ɛʀbisid] nm weedkiller, herbicide *spéc*.

herbier [ɛʀbje] nm [collection] dried flower collection, herbarium *spéc*.

herbivore [ɛʀbivɔʀ] ✦ adj herbivorous. ✦ nm herbivore.

herboriste [ɛʀbɔʀist] nmf herbalist, herb doctor.

herboristerie [ɛʀbɔʀistəʀi] nf herbalist's (shop).

héréditaire [eʀeditɛʀ] adj **1.** DR hereditary **2.** BIOL inherited, hereditary / *c'est héréditaire* it runs in the family / *il est toujours grincheux, c'est héréditaire !* hum he's always moaning, it's congenital!, he was born moaning!

hérédité [eʀedite] nf BIOL heredity.

hérésie [eʀezi] nf **1.** [erreur] sacrilege, heresy / *une table Régence dans la cuisine, c'est de l'hérésie !* a Regency table in the kitchen, that's (a) sacrilege! **2.** RELIG heresy.

hérétique [eʀetik] ✦ adj heretical. ✦ nmf heretic.

hérissé, e ['eʀise] adj **1.** [cheveux, poils - naturellement raides] bristly ; [- dressés de peur] bristling, standing on end / *un chien à l'échine hérissée* a dog with its hackles up **2.** [parsemé] ‣ **hérissé de** full of, stuffed with / *un texte hérissé de difficultés* a text bristling with ou full of difficult points.

hérisser [3] ['eʀise] vt [irriter] ‣ **cette question le hérisse** ou **lui hérisse le poil** that question gets his back up ou really makes his hackles rise. ✦ **se hérisser** vpi [s'irriter] to bristle ‣ **elle se hérisse facilement** she's easily ruffled.

hérisson ['eʀisɔ̃] nm ZOOL hedgehog.

héritage [eʀitaʒ] nm **1.** DR [destiné à une personne] inheritance ; [- une institution] bequest ‣ **faire un héritage** to inherit ‣ **faire un gros héritage** to come into a fortune / *elle m'a laissé ses bijoux en héritage* she left me her jewels **2.** fig heritage, legacy / *nos problèmes sont l'héritage de la décennie précédente* our problems are the legacy of the previous decade.

hériter [3] [eʀite] ✦ vi to inherit ‣ **hériter de qqch** [recevoir en legs] to inherit sthg. ✦ vt **1.** [bien matériel] to inherit ; *(en usage absolu)* ‣ **hériter de qqn** to inherit from sb **2.** [trait physique ou moral] ‣ **hériter qqch de qqn** *elle* *a hérité sa bonne humeur de sa famille paternelle* she inherited her even temper from her father's side of the family.

héritier, ère [eritje, ɛʀ] nm, f **1.** DR heir (heiress) ▸ **l'héritier d'une fortune / d'une grosse entreprise** the heir to a fortune / to a big firm **2.** *fam* [enfant] heir ; [fils] son and heir ; [fille] daughter **3.** [disciple] heir, follower.

hermétique [ɛʀmetik] adj **1.** [étanche - gén] hermetically sealed, hermetic *sout* ; [-à l'eau] watertight ; [-à l'air] airtight **2.** [incompréhensible] abstruse **3.** [impénétrable - visage] inscrutable, impenetrable / *son expression était parfaitement hermétique* his face was totally expressionless **4.** [insensible] ▸ **être hermétique à** to be unreceptive ou impervious to / *je suis complètement hermétique à l'art moderne* modern art is a closed book to me.

hermétiquement [ɛʀmetikmɑ̃] adv hermetically / *fermer un bocal hermétiquement* to hermetically seal a jar.

hermine [ɛʀmin] nf ZOOL [brune] stoat ; [blanche] ermine.

hernie [ʼɛʀni] nf MÉD hernia, rupture ▸ **hernie discale** slipped disc ou disk US.

héroïne [eʀɔin] nf **1.** [drogue] heroin **2.** [femme]
⟶ **héros**.

héroïnomane [eʀɔinɔman] nmf heroin addict.

héroïque [eʀɔik] adj **1.** [courageux] heroic **2.** [mémorable] : *l'époque héroïque des machines volantes* the pioneering ou great days of the flying machines.

héroïquement [eʀɔikmɑ̃] adv heroically.

héroïsme [eʀɔism] nm heroism.

héron [ʼeʀɔ̃] nm heron.

héros, héroïne [ʼeʀo, eʀɔin] nm, f hero (heroine) / *il est mort en héros* he died a hero's death ou like a hero.

herpès [ɛʀpɛs] nm herpes (U) / *avoir de l'herpès à la bouche* to have a cold sore (on one's mouth).

herse [ʼɛʀs] nf AGR harrow.

hertz [ʼɛʀts] nm hertz.

hésitant, e [ezitɑ̃, ɑ̃t] adj **1.** [indécis] hesitant / *je suis encore un peu hésitant* I haven't quite made up my mind yet **2.** [peu assuré] hesitant, faltering.

hésitation [ezitasjɔ̃] nf **1.** [atermoiement] hesitation / *après moult hésitation* after much hesitation **2.** [arrêt] pause ▸ **marquer** ou **avoir une hésitation** to pause, to hesitate **3.** [doute] doubt / *pas d'hésitation, c'est lui !* it's him, no doubt about it ou without a doubt ! ❖ **sans hésitation** loc adv unhesitatingly, without hesitation.

hésiter [3] [ezite] vi **1.** [être dans l'incertitude] to hesitate ▸ **sans hésiter** without hesitating ou hesitation **2.** [être réticent] ▸ **hésiter à** to hesitate to ▸ **j'hésite à lui dire** I'm not sure whether to tell him **3.** [marquer un temps d'arrêt] to pause, to falter / *il a hésité en prononçant le nom* he faltered ou stumbled over the name.

hétéro [eteʀo] adj & nmf *fam* hetero, straight.

hétéroclite [eteʀɔklit] adj disparate / *tout le mobilier est hétéroclite* none of the furniture matches.

hétérogène [eteʀɔʒɛn] adj [mêlé] heterogeneous *sout*, mixed.

hétérogénéité [eteʀɔʒeneite] nf heterogeneousness, heterogeneity.

hétérosexuel, elle [eteʀɔsɛksyɛl] adj & nm, f heterosexual.

hêtre [ʼɛtʀ] nm **1.** BOT beech (tree) **2.** MENUIS beech (wood).

heu [ʼø] interj **1.** [exprime le doute] h'm, um, er **2.** [exprime l'hésitation] er, um.

heure [œʀ] nf **1.** [unité de temps] hour / *à 45 km à l'heure* at 45 km an ou per hour ▸ **24 heures sur 24** round-the-clock, 24 hours a day ▸ **d'heure en heure** by the hour

2. [durée d'un trajet] hour ▸ **à deux heures (de voiture** ou **de route) de chez moi** two hours' (drive) from my home **3.** [unité de travail ou de salaire] hour / *un travail (payé) à l'heure* a job paid by the hour ▸ **dix euros de l'heure** ten euros an ou per hour ▸ **une heure de chimie** ÉDUC a chemistry period ou class ▸ **des heures supplémentaires** overtime (U) **4.** [point précis de la journée] time ▸ **15 heures locale** 3 p.m. local time / *elle est passée sur le coup de huit heures* fam she dropped in at about eight ▸ **c'est l'heure !** **a)** [de partir] it's time (to go)! **b)** [de rendre sa copie] time's up! ▸ **quelle heure est-il ?** what time is it?, what's the time? ▸ **vous avez l'heure ?** do you have the time? ▸ **quelle heure avez-vous ?** what time do you make it? ▸ **l'heure d'été** British Summer Time UK, daylight (saving) time US ▸ **passer à l'heure d'été / d'hiver** to put the clocks forward / back ▸ **l'heure H** zero hour **5.** [moment] time ▸ **à une heure indue** at some ungodly ou godforsaken hour ▸ **elle est romancière à ses heures** she writes the odd novel (now and again) ▸ **l'heure d'aller au lit** bedtime ▸ **l'heure du déjeuner** lunchtime ▸ **les heures de pointe** [où il y a foule] peak time, the rush hour ▸ **heures de réception** office / surgery UK hours ▸ **pendant les heures d'ouverture a)** COMM when the shops are open, during (normal) opening hours **b)** ADMIN during (normal) office ou working hours ▸ **les heures d'affluence** the rush hour ▸ **heures de bureau** office hours ▸ **les heures creuses a)** [sans foule] off-peak period **b)** [sans clients] slack period ▸ **à l'heure qu'il est** fam, **à l'heure actuelle** : *ils ont dû atterrir à l'heure qu'il est* they must have landed by now / *à l'heure qu'il est* ou *à l'heure actuelle, je ne sais pas si les otages ont été libérés* at this (point in) time I don't know whether the hostages have been freed **6.** [période d'une vie] hour ▸ **son heure de gloire** his moment of glory ▸ **l'heure de vérité** the moment of truth. ❖ **heures** nfpl RELIG hours ▸ **livre d'heures** Book of Hours. ❖ **à la bonne heure** loc adv good / *elle est reçue, à la bonne heure !* so she passed, good ou marvellous! ❖ **à l'heure** ◆ loc adj **1.** [personne] on time **2.** [montre] : *la montre est à l'heure* the watch is keeping good time. ◆ loc adv ▸ **mettre sa montre / une pendule à l'heure** to set one's watch / a clock right. ❖ **à l'heure de** loc prép in the era ou age of. ❖ **de bonne heure** loc adv [tôt] early ; [en avance] in good time. ❖ **pour l'heure** loc adv for now ou the time being ou the moment. ❖ **tout à l'heure** loc adv **1.** [dans un moment] later, in a (short ou little) while / *tout à l'heure !* see you later! **2.** [il y a un moment] earlier (today).

⌖ Notez qu'on dit plus couramment what time... que at what time...
À quelle heure sors-tu du bureau ? *What time do you leave the office?*
À quelle heure veux-tu partir ? *What time do you want to leave?*

---

heureusement [œʀøzmɑ̃] adv **1.** [par chance] fortunately, luckily / *il a freiné à temps — oh, heureusement !* he braked in time — thank God ou goodness for that! ▸ **heureusement que** : *la soirée fut une catastrophe, heureusement que tu n'es pas venu* the party was a total flop, (it's a) good thing you didn't come **2.** [favorablement] well **3.** [dans le bonheur] happily.

heureux, euse [œʀø, øz] ◆ adj **1.** [qui éprouve du bonheur] happy / *elle a tout pour être heureuse* she has everything going for her ▸ **ils vécurent heureux et eurent beaucoup d'enfants** they lived happily ever after **2.** [satisfait] happy, glad / *il était trop heureux de partir* he was only too glad to leave / *(très) heureux de faire votre* *connaissance* pleased ou nice to meet you **3.** [chanceux] lucky, fortunate / *il est heureux que... * it's fortunate ou it's a good thing that... **‣ heureux au jeu, malheureux en amour** *prov* lucky at cards, unlucky in love **4.** [bon] good **‣ un heureux événement** *euphém* a happy event **5.** [réussi] good, happy, felicitous *sout* ou *hum* **‣ c'est un choix heureux** it's well-chosen. **◆** nm, f happy man (woman) **‣ faire des heureux** to make some people happy.

heurt ['œʀ] nm [conflit] clash, conflict / *il y a eu des heurts entre le président et le secrétaire* the chairman and the secretary crossed swords / *le concert / débat s'est déroulé sans heurts* the concert / debate went off smoothly.

heurter [3] ['œʀte] vt **1.** [cogner] to strike, to hit, to knock / *en descendant du train, je l'ai heurté avec mon sac* I caught him with my bag ou I bumped into him with my bag as I got off the train **2.** [aller à l'encontre de] to run counter to *sout*, to go against **3.** [choquer] to shock, to offend **‣ heurter la sensibilité de qqn** to hurt sb's feelings. **◆ se heurter** vp *(emploi réciproque)* **1.** [passants, véhicules] to collide, to bump ou to run into each other **2.** [être en désaccord] to clash (with each other). **◆ se heurter à** vp + prép [rencontrer] to come up against / *il s'est heurté à un refus catégorique* he met with a categorical refusal. **◆ se heurter contre** vp + prép [se cogner à] to bump into.

hexagonal, e, aux [ɛgzagɔnal, o] adj **1.** GÉOM & SCI hexagonal **2.** *fig* [français] French ; *péj* chauvinistically French.

hexagone [ɛgzagɔn] nm **1.** GÉOM hexagon **2.** *fig* **‣ l'Hexagone** [la France] (metropolitan) France.

hiatus [jatys] nm **1.** [interruption] break, hiatus *sout*, gap **2.** LING hiatus **3.** MÉD hiatus.

hibernation [ibɛʀnasjɔ̃] nf ZOOL hibernation.

hiberner [3] [ibɛʀne] vi to hibernate.

hibiscus [ibiskys] nm hibiscus.

hibou, x ['ibu] nm owl.

hic ['ik] nm inv *fam* snag **‣ c'est bien là** ou **voilà le hic** there's the rub, that's the trouble.

hideux, euse ['idø, øz] adj hideous.

hidjab [idʒab] nm hidjab, hijab.

hier [ijɛʀ] adv [désignant le jour précédent] yesterday / *hier (au) soir* yesterday evening / *j'y ai consacré la journée / l'après-midi d'hier* I spent all (day) yesterday / all yesterday afternoon doing it.

hiérarchie ['jeʀaʀʃi] nf **1.** [structure] hierarchy **2.** *fam* [supérieurs] **‣ la hiérarchie** the top brass.

hiérarchique ['jeʀaʀʃik] adj hierarchic, hierarchical.

hiérarchiser [3] ['jeʀaʀʃize] vt **1.** ADMIN to organize along hierarchical lines **2.** [classer - données] to structure, to classify ; [-besoins] to grade or to assess according to importance.

hiéroglyphe ['jeʀɔglif] nm hieroglyph. **◆ hiéroglyphes** nmpl *hum* [écriture illisible] hieroglyphics.

hi-fi (*pl* hi-fi), **hifi*** ['ifi] nf hi-fi.

hilare [ilar] adj laughing, smiling, joyful.

hilarité [ilaʀite] nf hilarity, mirth, gaiety.

Himalaya [imalaja] npr m **‣ l'Himalaya** the Himalayas.

himalayen, enne [imalajɛ̃, ɛn] adj Himalayan.

hindou, e [ɛ̃du] adj hindu. **◆ Hindou, e** nm, f Hindu.

hindouisme [ɛ̃duism] nm Hinduism.

hindouiste [ɛ̃duist] adj Hindu.

hip-hop [ipɔp] adj inv & nm inv hip-hop.

hippie ['ipi] adj & nmf hippie, hippy.

hippique [ipik] adj horse *(modif)*.

hippisme [ipism] nm equestrian sports, equestrianism *sout*, horse riding 🇬🇧, horseback riding 🇺🇸.

hippocampe [ipɔkɑ̃p] nm ZOOL sea horse.

hippodrome [ipɔdʀom] nm [champ de courses] racecourse.

hippopotame [ipɔpɔtam] nm **1.** ZOOL hippopotamus **2.** *fam* [personne] elephant / *c'est un vrai hippopotame !* what an elephant!

hippy ['ipi] = hippie.

hirondelle [iʀɔ̃dɛl] nf ORNITH swallow.

hirsute [iʀsyt] adj [échevelé] bushy-haired ; [touffu - sourcils] bushy ; [-barbe, cheveux] unkempt.

hispanique [ispanik] adj **1.** [gén] Hispanic **2.** [aux États-Unis] Spanish-American.

hispano-américain, e [ispanoameʀikɛ̃, ɛn] (*mpl* hispano-américains, *fpl* hispano-américaines) adj Spanish-American.

hispanophone [ispanɔfɔn] **◆** adj Spanish-speaking. **◆** nmf Spanish speaker.

hisser [3] ['ise] vt [lever - drapeau] to run up *(sép)* ; [-voile] to hoist ; [-ancre] to raise ; [-épave] to raise, to haul up *(sép)* ; [soulever - personne] to lift up *(sép)* **‣ hisser qqn sur ses épaules** to lift sb onto one's shoulders. **◆ se hisser** vpi [s'élever] to hoist o.s. / *se hisser sur la pointe des pieds* to stand up on tiptoe / *se hisser sur une balançoire* to heave ou to hoist o.s. (up) onto a swing.

histoire [istwaʀ] nf **1.** [passé] history **‣ un lieu chargé d'histoire** a place steeped in history **2.** [mémoire, postérité] history **3.** [période précise] history / *l'histoire et la préhistoire* history and prehistory **4.** [discipline] **‣ l'Histoire avec un grand H** History with a capital H **‣ l'histoire ancienne / du Moyen Âge** Ancient / Medieval History / *tout ça, c'est de l'histoire ancienne fig* that's all ancient history **‣ licence d'histoire** ≃ History degree 🇬🇧 ; ≃ BA in History **5.** [récit, écrit] story / *je leur raconte une histoire tous les soirs* every night I tell them a story **‣ c'est une histoire vraie** it's a true story / *nous avons vécu ensemble une belle histoire d'amour* we had a wonderful romance **‣ une histoire drôle** a joke, a funny story **‣ histoire à dormir debout** *fam* cock and bull story, tall story **6.** [mensonge] : *tout ça, c'est des histoires* that's a load of (stuff and) nonsense, that's all hooey ou baloney 🇺🇸 **‣ raconter des histoires** to tell tall stories / *allez, tu me racontes des histoires !* come on, you're pulling my leg! **7.** *fam* [complications] trouble, fuss **‣ faire des histoires** to make a fuss / *ça va faire toute une histoire* there'll be hell to pay / *elle en a fait (toute) une histoire* she kicked up a (huge) fuss about it **8.** [ennuis] trouble **‣ faire des histoires (à qqn)** to cause ou to make trouble (for sb) / *si tu ne veux pas d'histoires* if you want to keep ou to stay out of trouble **9.** [question, problème] : *pourquoi démissionne-t-elle ?* — oh, une histoire de contrat why is she resigning? — oh, something to do with her contract / *qu'est-ce que c'est que cette histoire ?* what's this I hear?, what's all this about? **10.** *fam* EXPR **histoire de** [afin de] just to / *on va leur téléphoner, histoire de voir s'ils sont là* let's ring them up, just to see if they're there. **◆ sans histoires** loc adj [gens] ordinary ; [voyage] uneventful, trouble-free.

historien, enne [istɔʀjɛ̃, ɛn] nm, f [spécialiste] historian.

historique [istɔʀik] **◆** adj **1.** [relatif à l'histoire - méthode, roman] historical ; [-fait, personnage] historical **2.** [célèbre] historic **3.** [mémorable] historic. **◆** nm background history, (historical) review / *faire l'historique des jeux Olympiques* to trace the (past) history of the Olympic Games.

hit-parade ['itparad] (*pl* **hit-parades**) nm MUS charts / *ils sont premiers au hit-parade* they're (at the) top of *ou* they're number one in the charts.

HIV (*abr de* human immunodeficiency virus) nm HIV / *être atteint du virus HIV* to be HIV-positive.

hiver [ivɛʀ] nm [saison] winter.

hivernal, e, aux [ivɛʀnal, o] adj [propre à l'hiver] winter *(modif)* ; [qui rappelle l'hiver] wintry / *un paysage hivernal* a winter landscape / *un temps hivernal* wintry weather.

hivernement [ivɛʀnəmɑ̃] nm 🇶🇧 wintering.

hiverner [3] [ivɛʀne] vi [passer l'hiver] to winter.

HLM (*abr de* habitation à loyer modéré) nm *ou* nf low rent, state-owned housing ; ≃ council house / flat 🇬🇧 ; ≃ public housing unit 🇺🇸.

ho ['o] interj **1.** [de surprise] oh **2.** [pour interpeller] hey.

hobby ['ɔbi] (*pl* hobbys *ou* hobbies) nm hobby.

hochement ['ɔʃmɑ̃] nm ▶ **hochement de tête a)** [approbateur] nod **b)** [désapprobateur] shake of the head.

hocher [3] ['ɔʃe] vt ▶ **hocher la tête a)** [pour accepter] to nod **b)** [pour refuser] to shake one's head.

hochet ['ɔʃɛ] nm [jouet] rattle.

hockey ['ɔkɛ] nm hockey / *faire du hockey* to play hockey ▶ **hockey sur glace** ice hockey 🇬🇧, hockey 🇺🇸 ▶ **hockey sur gazon** hockey 🇬🇧, field hockey 🇺🇸.

holà ['ɔla] ◆ interj hey, whoa. ◆ nm ▶ **mettre le holà à qqch** to put a stop to sthg.

holding ['ɔldiŋ] nm *ou* nf ▶ **holding (financier)** holding company.

hold-up (*pl* **hold-up**), **holdup*** ['ɔldœp] nm raid, hold-up / *un hold-up à la banque / poste* a bank / post office raid.

hollandais, e ['ɔlɑ̃dɛ, ɛz] adj Dutch. ◆❖ **Hollandais, e** nm, f Dutchman (Dutchwoman) ▶ **les Hollandais** the Dutch. ◆❖ **hollandais** nm LING Dutch.

Hollande ['ɔlɑ̃d] npr f ▶ **(la) Hollande** Holland.

holocauste [ɔlɔkost] nm **1.** HIST ▶ **l'holocauste, l'Holocauste** the Holocaust **2.** RELIG burnt offering / *offrir un animal en holocauste* to offer an animal in sacrifice.

hologramme [ɔlɔgʀam] nm hologram.

homard ['ɔmaʀ] nm lobster.

home cinéma [omsinema] (*pl* home cinémas) nm home cinema.

homéopathe [ɔmeɔpat] nmf homoeopath, homoeopathist.

homéopathie [ɔmeɔpati] nf homoeopathy.

homéopathique [ɔmeɔpatik] adj homoeopathic.

homicide [ɔmisid] nm **1.** [acte] killing (U) **2.** DR homicide ▶ **homicide involontaire** *ou* **par imprudence** involuntary manslaughter *ou* homicide ▶ **homicide volontaire** murder.

hommage [ɔmaʒ] nm [marque de respect] tribute, homage *sout* ▶ **rendre hommage à qqn / qqch** to pay homage *sout ou* (a) tribute to sb / sthg. ◆❖ **hommages** nmpl *sout* : *(je vous présente) mes hommages, Madame* my respects, Madam ▶ **veuillez agréer, Madame, mes hommages respectueux** *ou* **mes respectueux hommages** yours faithfully 🇬🇧, yours truly 🇺🇸.

homme [ɔm] nm **1.** [individu de sexe masculin] man / *sors si t'es un homme !* step outside if you're a man! ▶ **trouver son homme** [pour un travail] to find one's man / *une discussion d'homme à homme* a man-to-man talk ▶ **homme d'action** man of action ▶ **homme d'affaires** businessman ▶ **homme d'État** statesman ▶ **homme à femmes** lady's *ou* ladies' man, womanizer *péj* ▶ **homme**

au foyer househusband ▶ **homme de paille** man of straw ▶ **homme de peine** labourer ▶ **homme à tout faire** jack-of-all-trades ▶ **un magazine pour hommes** a men's magazine ▶ **un homme averti en vaut deux** *prov* forewarned is forearmed *prov* **2.** [être humain] man ▶ **les hommes** man, mankind, human beings ▶ **l'homme des cavernes** caveman ▶ **l'homme de la rue** the man in the street **3.** *fam* [amant, époux] ▶ **mon / son homme** my / her man ▶ **elle a rencontré l'homme de sa vie** she's met the love of her life ▶ **l'homme idéal** Mr Right **4.** NAUT [marin] ▶ **homme d'équipage** crew member, crewman **5.** MIL : *les officiers et leurs hommes* the officers and their men.

homme-grenouille [ɔmgʀənuj] (*pl* **hommes-grenouilles**) nm frogman, diver.

homme-orchestre [ɔmɔʀkɛstʀ] (*pl* **hommes-orchestres**) nm **1.** MUS one-man band **2.** *fig* jack-of-all-trades.

homme-sandwich [ɔmsɑ̃dwitʃ] (*pl* **hommes-sandwichs**) nm sandwich man.

homo [ɔmo] adj & nmf *fam* [homosexuel] gay.

homogène [ɔmɔʒɛn] adj **1.** [substance, liquide] homogeneous / *ayant obtenu une pâte bien homogène* when you have a nice smooth mixture **2.** [gouvernement, classe] uniform, consistent, coherent **3.** CHIM & MATH homogeneous.

homogénéisé, e [ɔmɔʒeneize] adj homogenized.

homogénéité [ɔmɔʒeneite] nf **1.** [d'une substance] homogeneity, homogeneousness **2.** [d'une œuvre, d'une équipe] coherence, unity.

homologue [ɔmɔlɔg] nmf [personne] counterpart, opposite number.

homologuer [3] [ɔmɔlɔge] vt **1.** [déclarer conforme] to approve, to accredit **2.** DR [entériner] to sanction, to ratify **3.** SPORT to ratify.

homonyme [ɔmɔnim] ◆ adj homonymous. ◆ nmf [personne, ville] namesake. ◆ nm LING homonym.

homoparental, e, aux [ɔmɔpaʀɑ̃tal, o] adj relating to gay parenting, homoparental.

homoparentalité [ɔmɔpaʀɑ̃talite] nf gay parenting.

homophobe [ɔmɔfɔb] adj homophobe.

homophobie [ɔmɔfɔbi] nf homophobia.

homosexualité [ɔmɔsɛksɥalite] nf homosexuality.

homosexuel, elle [ɔmɔsɛksɥɛl] adj & nm, f homosexual, gay.

Honduras ['ɔ̃dyʀas] npr m ▶ **le Honduras** Honduras.

hondurien, enne ['ɔ̃dyʀjɛ̃, ɛn] adj Honduran. ◆❖ **Hondurien, enne** nm, f Honduran.

Hong Kong ['ɔ̃gkɔ̃g] npr Hong Kong.

Hongrie ['ɔ̃gʀi] npr f ▶ **(la) Hongrie** Hungary.

hongrois, e ['ɔ̃gʀwa, az] adj Hungarian. ◆❖ **Hongrois, e** nm, f Hungarian. ◆❖ **hongrois** nm LING Hungarian, Magyar.

honnête [ɔnɛt] adj **1.** [scrupuleux - vendeur, associé] honest **2.** [franc] honest / *il faut être honnête, elle n'a aucune chance de réussir* let's face it ou we might as well face facts, she hasn't got a hope of succeeding **3.** [acceptable - prix] fair, reasonable ; [- résultat] decent, reasonable ; [- repas] decent / *12 sur 20, c'est honnête* 12 out of 20, that's not bad **4.** [respectable] honest, respectable, decent / *des gens honnêtes* respectable people.

honnêtement [ɔnɛtmɑ̃] adv **1.** [sincèrement] honestly, frankly, sincerely / *non mais, honnêtement, tu la crois ?* come on now, be honest, do you believe her? **2.** [décemment] fairly, decently / *elle a terminé honnêtement son année scolaire* she finished the year with reasonable marks **3.** [de façon morale] honestly ▶ **vivre honnêtement** to live ou to lead an honest life / *c'est de l'argent honnêtement gagné* it's money honestly earned.

honnêteté [ɔnɛtte] nf **1.** [franchise] honesty, candour ‣ **avec honnêteté** honestly, candidly **2.** [intégrité - d'une conduite] honesty, decency ; [- d'une personne] integrity, decency. ◈ **en toute honnêteté** loc adv **1.** [avec sincérité] in all honesty, frankly **2.** [pour être honnête] to tell the truth, to be perfectly honest.

honneur [ɔnœʀ] nm **1.** [dignité] honour **UK**, honor **US** ‣ **mettre un point d'honneur à** ou **se faire un point d'honneur de faire qqch** to make a point of honour of doing sth **2.** [mérite] : *c'est tout à son honneur* it's entirely to his credit ‣ **faire honneur à qqn** to do sb credit **3.** [marque de respect] honour ‣ **à vous l'honneur !** after you ! ; *sout* [dans des formules de politesse] privilege, honour / *c'est un honneur pour moi de vous présenter… it's a great privilege for me to introduce to you… / j'ai l'honneur de solliciter votre aide* I would be most grateful for your assistance ‣ *nous avons l'honneur de vous informer que… we have the pleasure of informing you that… / à qui ai-je l'honneur ?* to whom do I have the honour (of speaking)? **4.** [titre] ‣ **Votre / Son Honneur** Your / His Honour **5.** **EXPR** **faire honneur à qqch**: *faire honneur à ses engagements / sa signature* to honour one's commitments / signature / *ils ont fait honneur à ma cuisine / mon gigot* they did justice to my cooking / leg of lamb. ◈ **honneurs** nmpl **1.** [cérémonie] honours **UK**, honors **US 2.** ‣ **faire à qqn les honneurs de qqch** to show sb round sthg. ◈ **à l'honneur** loc adj ‣ **être à l'honneur** to have the place of honour / *les organisateurs de l'exposition ont voulu que la sculpture soit à l'honneur* the exhibition organizers wanted sculpture to take pride of place. ◈ **d'honneur** loc adj [invité, place, tour] of honour ; [membre, président] honorary ; [cour, escalier] main. ◈ **en l'honneur** loc prép in honour of ‣ **en quel honneur ?** *fam* why, for goodness' sake?

honorable [ɔnɔʀabl] adj **1.** [digne de respect] respectable, honourable **UK**, honorable **US 2.** [satisfaisant] fair, decent / *son bulletin scolaire est tout à fait honorable / est honorable sans plus* her school report is quite satisfactory / is just satisfactory.

honorablement [ɔnɔʀabləmã] adv **1.** [de façon respectable] decently, honourably **UK**, honorably **US 2.** [de façon satisfaisante] creditably, honourably ‣ **gagner honorablement sa vie** to earn an honest living.

honoraire [ɔnɔʀɛʀ] adj **1.** [conservant son ancien titre] ‣ **professeur honoraire** professor emeritus **2.** [ayant le titre mais non les fonctions] honorary.

honoraires [ɔnɔʀɛʀ] nmpl fee, fees.

honorer [3] [ɔnɔʀe] vt **1.** [rendre hommage à] to honour **UK**, to honor **US 2.** [respecter, estimer] to honour **UK**, to honor **US 3.** [contribuer à la réputation de] to honour **UK**, to honor **US** ‣ *il vous ferait un honneur* ou an honour to ‣ **votre sincérité vous honore** your sincerity does you credit **4.** [gratifier] to honour **UK**, to honor **US** ‣ **votre présence m'honore** you honour me with your presence.

honorifique [ɔnɔʀifik] adj honorary **UK**, ceremonial **US** ‣ *c'est un poste honorifique* it's an honorary position.

honte [ˈɔt] nf **1.** [sentiment d'humiliation] shame ‣ **avoir honte (de qqn / qqch)** to be ou to feel ashamed (of sb / sthg) / *vous devriez avoir honte !* you should be ashamed! ‣ **faire honte à qqn** to make sb (feel) ashamed, to shame sb *sout* **2.** [indignité, scandale] disgrace, (object of) shame / *être la honte de sa famille* to be a disgrace to one's family / *la société laisse faire, c'est une honte !* it's outrageous ou it's a crying shame that society just lets it happen! **3.** [déshonneur] shame, shamefulness / *à ma grande honte* to my shame.

honteusement [ˈɔtøzmã] adv **1.** [avec gêne] shamefully, ashamedly / *elle cacha honteusement son visage dans ses mains* she hid her face in shame **2.** [scandaleusement] shamefully, disgracefully.

honteux, euse [ˈɔtø, øz] adj **1.** [déshonorant] shameful, disgraceful **2.** [scandaleux - exploitation, politique] disgraceful, outrageous, shocking / *c'est honteux de lui prendre le peu qu'elle a* it's disgraceful ou a disgrace to take from her the little she has **3.** [qui a des remords] ashamed / *je suis honteux de ce que j'ai fait* I'm ashamed of what I did.

hooliganisme, houliganisme [uliganism] nm hooliganism.

hop [ˈɔp] interj ‣ **allez, hop !** [à un enfant] come on, upsadaisy! / *et* ou *allez hop, on s'en va !* (right,) off we go!

hôpital, aux [ɔpital, o] nm [établissement] hospital ‣ **hôpital de jour a)** [pour traitement] day hospital **UK**, outpatient clinic **US b)** [psychiatrique] day hospital **c)** [pour activités] daycare centre.

hoquet [ˈɔkɛ] nm [spasme] hiccup, hiccough ‣ **avoir le hoquet** to have the hiccups.

hoqueter [27] [ˈɔkte] vi [personne] to hiccup, to have (the) hiccups.

🖉 In reformed spelling (see p. 16-18), this verb is conjugated like *acheter* : *il hoquète, elle hoquètera*.

horaire [ɔʀɛʀ] ◈ adj hourly. ◈ nm **1.** [de travail] schedule, timetable **UK** / *nous n'avons pas les mêmes horaires* we don't work the same hours ‣ **je n'ai pas d'horaire** I don't have any particular schedule ‣ **horaire individualisé** ou **souple** ou **à la carte** flexible working hours, flexitime **UK** / *nous avons un horaire à la carte* we work flexitime **UK**, we have flexible working hours ‣ **horaires aménagés a)** [au bureau] flexible working hours **b)** [à l'école] flexible timetable / *classe à horaires aménagés* class with a flexible timetable ‣ **horaires de bureau / de travail** office / working hours **2.** [de train, d'avion] schedule, timetable **UK** / *je ne connais pas l'horaire des trains* I don't know the train times.

horde [ˈɔʀd] nf horde.

horizon [ɔʀizɔ̃] nm **1.** [ligne] horizon ‣ **à l'horizon** pr & fig on the horizon ‣ **rien à l'horizon** pr & fig nothing in sight ou view **2.** [paysage] horizon, view, vista ‣ **changer d'horizon** to have a change of scene ou scenery **3.** [domaine d'activité] horizon / *élargir ses horizons* to broaden one's horizons **4.** [perspectives d'avenir] : *les prévisions à l'horizon 2012* the forecast for 2012 ‣ **ouvrir des horizons** to open up new horizons ou prospects ‣ **horizon économique / politique** ÉCON economic / political prospects.

horizontal, e, aux [ɔʀizɔ̃tal, o] adj horizontal ‣ **mettez-vous en position horizontale** lie down (flat) ‣ **le un horizontal** [aux mots croisés] one across. ◈ **horizontale** nf horizontal. ◈ **à l'horizontale** loc adv horizontally, in a horizontal position ‣ **placer qqch à l'horizontale** to lay sthg down (flat).

horizontalement [ɔʀizɔ̃talmã] adv horizontally / *horizontalement : un, en six lettres, oiseau* one across, six letters, bird.

horloge [ɔʀlɔʒ] nf [pendule] clock ‣ **horloge parlante** speaking clock **UK**, time (telephone) service **US**.

horloger, ère [ɔʀlɔʒe, ɛʀ] nm, f watchmaker, clockmaker ‣ **horloger bijoutier** jeweller.

horlogerie [ɔʀlɔʒʀi] nf [technique, métier] clock (and watch) ou timepiece making.

hormis [ˈɔʀmi] prép *litt* save (for) / *le stade était vide, hormis quelques rares spectateurs* the stadium was empty, save for ou apart from a handful of spectators.

hormonal, e, aux [ɔʀmɔnal, o] adj [gén] hormonal ; [traitement, crème] hormone *(modif)*.

hormone [ɔʀmɔn] nf hormone ‣ **hormone de croissance / sexuelle** growth / sex hormone.

horodateur [ɔʀɔdatœʀ] nm [administratif] time-stamp ; [de parking] ticket machine.

horoscope [ɔʀɔskɔp] nm horoscope.

horreur [ɔʀœʀ] nf **1.** [effroi] horror ▸ **avoir qqch en horreur** [dégoût] to have a horror of ou to loathe sthg ▸ **avoir qqn en horreur** to loathe sb / *j'ai horreur qu'on me dérange* I hate ou I can't stand being disturbed ▸ **faire horreur à qqn** to horrify ou to terrify sb, to fill sb with horror **2.** [cruauté] horror, ghastliness / *il décrit la guerre des tranchées dans toute son horreur* he describes trench warfare in all its horror **3.** *fam* [chose ou personne laide] ▸ **c'est une horreur a)** [personne] he's / she's repulsive **b)** [objet] it's hideous / *jette-moi toutes ces vieilles horreurs* throw away all these horrible old things **4.** [dans des exclamations] ▸ **oh, quelle horreur !** that's awful ou terrible! / *quelle horreur, cette odeur !* what a disgusting ou vile smell! ❖ **horreurs** nfpl **1.** [crimes] horrors / *les horreurs de la guerre* the horrors of war / *les horreurs dont il est responsable* the horrible ou dreadful deeds he is responsible for **2.** [calomnies] : *on m'a raconté des horreurs sur lui* I've heard horrible things about him.

horrible [ɔʀibl] adj **1.** [effroyable -cauchemar] horrible, dreadful ; [-mutilation, accident] horrible, horrific ; [-crime] horrible, ghastly ; [-cri] horrible, frightful **2.** [laid -personne] horrible, hideous, repulsive ; [-vêtement] ghastly, frightful ; [-décor, style] horrible, hideous, ghastly **3.** [méchant] horrible, nasty, horrid ▸ **être horrible avec qqn** to be nasty ou horrible to sb **4.** [infect] horrible, disgusting, frightful **5.** [temps] terrible ; [douleur] terrible, awful.

horriblement [ɔʀibləmã] adv **1.** [en intensif] horribly, terribly, awfully **2.** [atrocement] horribly.

horrifier [9] [ɔʀifje] vt ▸ **horrifier qqn** to horrify sb, to fill sb with horror.

horripilant, e [ɔʀipilã, ãt] adj *fam* infuriating, exasperating, irritating.

horripiler [3] [ɔʀipile] vt *fam* [exaspérer] to exasperate.

hors [ɔʀ] prép **1.** *litt* [hormis] except (for), save (for) *sout* **2.** EXPR **hors antenne** off the air ▸ **hors catégorie** outstanding, exceptional ▸ **hors circuit** : *mettre une lampe hors circuit* to disconnect a lamp ▸ **être hors circuit** *fig* to be out of circulation ▸ **être hors course** to be out of touch ▸ **hors jeu** SPORT : *il est hors jeu* he's offside ▸ **hors la loi** : *mettre qqn hors la loi* to declare sb an outlaw, to outlaw sb ▸ **hors normes a)** non-standard **b)** [personnage] unconventional ▸ **hors pair** exceptional, outstanding ▸ **hors saison** off-season ▸ **numéro hors série** [publication] special issue ▸ **hors service** out of order ▸ **hors sujet** irrelevant, off the subject ▸ **hors taxe** ou **taxes a)** excluding tax **b)** [à la douane] duty-free ▸ **hors tout** overall. ❖ **hors de** loc prép **1.** [dans l'espace -à l'extérieur de] out of, outside ; [-loin de] away from ▸ **hors de ma vue** out of my sight ▸ **hors d'ici !** *sout* get out of here! **2.** [dans le temps] ▸ **hors du temps** timeless **3.** EXPR **mettre qqch hors d'action** to disable sthg ▸ **hors de portée (de) a)** [trop loin] out of reach ou range (of) **b)** *fig* out of reach (of) ▸ **mettre qqn hors de combat** to disable sb ▸ **hors du commun** outstanding, exceptional ▸ **hors de danger** : *ici, vous êtes hors de danger* you're safe ou out of harm's reach here ▸ **être hors d'état de nuire** : *il est hors d'état de nuire* **a)** he's been rendered harmless **b)** *euphém* [tué] he's been taken care of ▸ **hors de prix** prohibitively ou ruinously expensive ▸ **hors de propos** inopportune, untimely ▸ **hors de question** : *c'est hors de question* it's out of the question ▸ **hors de soi** : *il était hors de lui* he was beside himself ▸ **hors d'usage** out of service.

hors-bord [ɔʀbɔʀ] (*pl* hors-bord ou hors-bords*) nm **1.** [moteur] outboard motor **2.** [bateau] speedboat, outboard.

hors-d'œuvre [ɔʀdœvʀ] nm inv CULIN starter, hors d'œuvre *sout* ▸ **hors-d'œuvre variés** (assorted) cold meats and salads.

hors-jeu [ɔʀʒø] (*pl* hors-jeu ou hors-jeux*) ◆ adj offside / *le joueur est hors-jeu* the player is offside. ◆ nm offside.

hors-la-loi [ɔʀlalwa] nmf inv outlaw.

hors-piste(s) [ɔʀpist] ◆ nm ▸ **faire du hors-pistes** to ski off piste. ◆ adj ▸ **le ski hors-pistes** off-piste skiing.

hors-série [ɔʀseʀi] nm (*pl* hors-séries) special issue ou edition.

hortensia [ɔʀtãsja] nm hydrangea.

horticole [ɔʀtikɔl] adj horticultural.

horticulteur, trice [ɔʀtikyltœʀ, tʀis] nm, f horticulturist.

horticulture [ɔʀtikyltyʀ] nf horticulture.

hospice [ɔspis] nm [asile] ▸ **hospice (de vieillards)** (old people's) home.

hospitalier, ère [ɔspitalje, ɛʀ] adj **1.** ADMIN [frais, service, personnel] hospital *(modif)* ▸ **établissement hospitalier** hospital **2.** [personne, peuple, demeure] hospitable, welcoming ; *sout* [rivage, île] inviting.

hospitalisation [ɔspitalizasjɔ̃] nf hospitalization ▸ **hospitalisation à domicile** home care.

hospitaliser [3] [ɔspitalize] vt to hospitalize ▸ **se faire hospitaliser** to be admitted ou taken to hospital.

hospitalité [ɔspitalite] nf [hébergement] hospitality ▸ **offrir / donner l'hospitalité à qqn** to offer / to give sb hospitality.

hostie [ɔsti] nf RELIG host.

hostile [ɔstil] adj **1.** [inamical] hostile, unfriendly **2.** [opposé] hostile ▸ **être hostile à qqn** to be hostile to ou opposed to ou against sb **3.** ÉCOL hostile.

hostilité [ɔstilite] nf hostility. ❖ **hostilités** nfpl MIL : *reprendre les hostilités* to reopen ou to resume hostilities.

hot dog (*pl* hot dogs), **hotdog*** [ɔtdɔg] nm hot dog.

hôte, hôtesse [ot, otɛs] nm, f *sout* [personne qui reçoit] host (hostess). ❖ **hôte** nm [invité] guest ; [client dans un hôtel] patron, guest. ❖ **hôtesse** nf [responsable de l'accueil -dans un hôtel] receptionist ; [-dans une exposition] hostess ▸ **hôtesse d'accueil** receptionist ▸ **hôtesse de caisse** check-out assistant 🇬🇧, checker 🇺🇸 ▸ **hôtesse de l'air** air hostess 🇬🇧, stewardess.

hôtel [otɛl] nm [proposant des chambres] hotel ▸ **aller / descendre à l'hôtel** to stay in a hotel. ❖ **hôtel particulier** nm (private) mansion, town house. ❖ **hôtel des ventes** nm sale room ou rooms, auction room ou rooms. ❖ **hôtel de ville** nm town 🇬🇧 ou city 🇺🇸 hall.

hôtelier, ère [otalje, ɛʀ] ◆ adj [relatif à l'hôtellerie] hotel *(modif)*. ◆ nm, f COMM & LOISIRS hotelier, hotel manager ou owner.

hôtellerie [otɛlʀi] nf COMM & LOISIRS hotel trade ou business ou industry.

hôtesse [otɛs] f → hôte.

hot line [ɔtlain] (*pl* hot lines) nf hot line.

hotte [ɔt] nf **1.** [de cheminée, de laboratoire] hood ▸ **hotte aspirante** ou **filtrante** [de cuisine] extractor hood **2.** [de vendangeur] basket / *la hotte du Père Noël* Father Christmas's sack.

houblon [ublɔ̃] nm BOT hop (plant) ; [de bière] hops.

houille [uj] nf **1.** MIN coal **2.** ÉLECTR ▸ **houille blanche** hydroelectric power *(from waterfalls)*.

houiller, ère [uje, ɛʀ] adj [bassin, production] coal *(modif)* ; [sol, roche] coal-bearing, carboniferous *spéc*. ❖ **houillère** nf coalmine.

houle [ul] nf [mouvement de la mer] swell.

houlette [ulɛt] nf ❖ **sous la houlette de** loc prép under the leadership ou direction ou aegis *sout* of.

houleux, euse ['ulø,øz] adj **1.** [mer] rough, choppy **2.** [débat, réunion] stormy.

houligan ['uligan] nm (football) hooligan.

houliganisme [uliganism] = **hooliganisme**.

hourra ['uʀa] ◆ interj hurrah, hooray. ◆ nm cheer (of joy) **/ pousser des hourras** to cheer.

house [(a)ws], **house music** [awsmjusik] nf **▸ la house (music)** house music.

houspiller [3] ['uspije] vt to tell off *(sép)*.

housse ['us] nf [de coussin] cover ; [de meubles - pour protéger] dustsheet ; [- pour décorer] cover 🇬🇧, slipcover 🇺🇸 ; [de vêtements] suit sack **▸ housse de couette** duvet 🇬🇧 ou comforter 🇺🇸 cover.

houx ['u] nm holly.

HS (abr de **hors service**) adj *fam* [appareil] out of order ; [personne] shattered.

HT adj (abr de **hors taxe**) *not including tax* **▸ 50 € HT** ≃ 50 € plus VAT.

huard, huart ['yaʀ] nm 🇶🇧 **1.** [oiseau] (black-throated) diver 🇬🇧 ou loon 🇺🇸 **2.** [pièce de un dollar canadien] Canadian dollar, loonie 🇨🇦.

hub [œb] nm AÉRON & INFORM hub.

hublot ['yblo] nm [de bateau] porthole ; [d'avion] window ; [de machine à laver] (glass) door.

huche ['yʃ] nf chest **▸ huche à pain** bread bin 🇬🇧, bread box 🇺🇸.

hue ['y] interj gee up.

huer [7] ['ɥe] ◆ vt [par dérision] to boo. ◆ vi [hibou] to hoot ; [héron] to croak.

huile [ɥil] nf **1.** CULIN oil **▸ cuit à l'huile** cooked in oil **▸ à l'huile**: *pommes à l'huile* potatoes (done) in an oil dressing **▸ huile d'arachide / de coco / de colza / d'olive / de maïs / de noix / de tournesol** groundnut 🇬🇧 ou peanut 🇺🇸 / coconut / rapeseed ou colza / olive / corn / walnut / sunflower oil **▸ huile vierge** unrefined ou virgin oil **▸ jeter** ou **mettre** ou **verser de l'huile sur le feu** to add fuel to the flames **2.** [pour chauffer, pour lubrifier] oil **▸ huile de chauffage** 🇶🇧 domestic fuel **▸ huile de coude** *fam* elbow grease **3.** PHARM **▸ huile essentielle** ou **volatile** essential oil **▸ huile de lin / ricin** linseed / castor oil **▸ huile solaire** suntan oil **▸ huile de foie de morue** cod-liver oil **4.** ART [œuvre] oil (painting) **5.** *fam* [personne importante] bigwig, VIP, big shot. ◆ **d'huile** *loc adj* [mer] glassy **▸ la mer était d'huile** the sea was like glass ou a mill pond.

huiler [3] ['ɥile] vt to oil, to lubricate.

huileux, euse [ɥilø,øz] adj **1.** [substance] oily **2.** [cheveux, doigts] oily, greasy.

huis clos ['ɥiklo] ◆ **à huis clos** *loc adv* : *le procès se déroulera à huis clos* the trial will be held in camera.

huissier, ère [ɥisje,ɛʀ] nm, f DR **▸ huissier (de justice)** ≃ bailiff.

huit ['ɥit] *(devant consonne* ['ɥi]*)* ◆ dét eight **▸ huit jours** [une semaine] a week **/** *dans huit jours* in a week. ◆ nm inv [nombre] eight **/** *nous avons rendez-vous le huit (mars)* we are meeting on the eighth (of March) **▸ jeudi en huit** a week on 🇬🇧 ou from 🇺🇸 Thursday. **Voir aussi cinq.**

huitaine ['ɥitɛn] nf **▸ une huitaine** about eight, eight or so **▸ une huitaine (de jours)** about a week, a week or so.

huitième ['ɥitjɛm] ◆ adj num ord eighth **▸ la huitième merveille du monde** the eighth wonder of the world. ◆ nmf : *il est arrivé huitième* he finished eighth. ◆ nm eighth **▸ les huitièmes de finale** SPORT the round before the quarterfinals. ◆ nf ENS & *vieilli* ≃ Year 5 *(at junior school)* 🇬🇧 ; ≃ fourth grade 🇺🇸. **Voir aussi cinquième.**

huître, huitre* [ɥitʀ] nf ZOOL oyster.

hululer [3] ['ylyle] vi to hoot.

hum ['œm] interj **1.** [marquant le doute] er, um, h'mm **2.** [pour signaler sa présence] ahem.

humain, e [ymɛ̃,ɛn] adj **1.** [propre à l'homme - corps, race, condition] human **/** *il cherche à se venger, c'est humain* he's looking for revenge, it's only human **2.** [bienveillant] humane. ◆ **humain** nm [être] **▸ un humain** a human (being).

human ou **humane ?**
Ce qui se rapporte à l'être humain se traduit par **human**. Au sens de « bon », « compréhensif », humain se traduit par **humane**.

humainement [ymɛnmɑ̃] adv **1.** [avec bienveillance] humanely **2.** [par l'homme] humanly **/** *faire tout ce qui est humainement possible* to do everything that is humanly possible.

humaniser [3] [ymanize] vt [environnement] to humanize, to adapt to human needs ; [personne] to make more human. ◆ **s'humaniser** vpi to become more human.

humaniste [ymanist] ◆ adj humanist, humanistic. ◆ nmf humanist.

humanitaire [ymanitɛʀ] ◆ adj humanitarian **▸ organisation humanitaire** humanitarian ou relief ou aid organization. ◆ nmf [personne] humanitarian (aid) worker. ◆ nm **▸ l'humanitaire** the humanitarian sector.

humanité [ymanite] nf **1.** [êtres] **▸ l'humanité** humanity, mankind, humankind **2.** [compassion] humanity, humaneness.

humanoïde [ymanɔid] adj & nmf humanoid.

humble [œbl] adj **1.** [effacé - personne] humble, meek **2.** [par déférence] humble **▸ à mon humble avis** in my humble opinion **3.** [pauvre, simple - demeure, origine] humble ; [- employé] humble, lowly, obscure.

humblement [œbləmɑ̃] adv humbly.

humecter [4] [ymɛkte] vt [linge] to dampen ; [visage - avec un liquide] to moisten ; [- avec un linge mouillé] to dampen. ◆ **s'humecter** vpt **▸ s'humecter les lèvres** to moisten one's lips.

humer ['yme] vt [sentir] to smell ; [inspirer] to inhale, to breathe in *(sép)*.

humérus [ymeʀys] nm humerus.

humeur [ymœʀ] nf **1.** [état d'esprit] mood **▸ être d'humeur changeante** to be moody **▸ être de bonne / mauvaise humeur** to be in a good / bad mood **▸ être d'une humeur noire** to be in a foul mood **2.** [caractère] temper **/** *être d'humeur égale / inégale* to be even-tempered / moody **3.** *litt* [acrimonie] bad temper, ill humour **/** *répondre avec humeur* to answer testily ou moodily **▸ accès / mouvement d'humeur** outburst / fit of temper.

humide [ymid] adj [linge, mur] damp ; [éponge] damp, moist ; [cave] damp, dank ; [chaussée] wet ; [chaleur, air, climat] humid, moist ; [terre] moist **/** *j'ai les mains humides* my hands are wet **▸ temps chaud et humide** muggy weather.

humidificateur [ymidifikatœʀ] nm humidifier.

humidifier [9] [ymidifje] vt **1.** [air] to humidify, to moisturize **2.** [linge] to dampen, to moisten.

humidité [ymidite] nf [de l'air chaud] humidity, moisture ; [de l'air froid, d'une terre] dampness ; [d'une cave] dampness, dankness **/** *il y a des taches d'humidité au plafond* there are damp patches on the ceiling.

humiliant, e [ymiljɑ̃, ɑ̃t] adj humiliating.

humiliation [ymiljasjɔ̃] nf humiliation.

humilier [9] [ymilje] vt to humiliate, to shame.

humilité [ymilite] nf [d'une personne] humility, humbleness, modesty. ❖ **en toute humilité** loc adv *sout* in all humility.

humoriste [ymɔʀist] nmf humorist.

humoristique [ymɔʀistik] adj [récit, ton] humorous.

humour [ymuʀ] nm humour 🇬🇧, humor 🇺🇸 ▸ **avec humour** humorously ▸ **sans humour** humourless ▸ **plein d'humour** humorous ▸ **avoir de l'humour** ou **le sens de l'humour** to have a sense of humour ▸ **humour noir** black humour.

humus [ymys] nm humus.

huppé, e ['ype] adj **1.** *fam* [personne, restaurant, soirée] posh 🇬🇧, smart **2.** ORNITH crested.

hurlement ['yʀləmɑ̃] nm **1.** [humain] yell, roar / *des hurlements de joie* whoops of joy / *des hurlements d'indignation* howls of indignation **2.** [d'un chien, d'un loup] howl **3.** *litt* [de la tempête] roar ; [du vent] howling, screaming ; [d'une sirène] howl.

hurler [3] ['yʀle] ❖ vi **1.** [crier] to yell, to scream / *hurler de rage* to howl with rage / *ça me fait hurler d'entendre ça !* it makes me so mad to hear things like that! / *il me fait hurler de rire !* *fam* he creases me up! **2.** [parler fort] to shout, to bellow **3.** [singe] to howl, to shriek ; [chien, loup, sirène] to howl. ❖ vt **1.** [ordre] to bawl out *(sép)*, to yell out *(sép)* **2.** [douleur, indignation, réponse] to howl out *(sép)*.

hurluberlu, e [yʀlybɛʀly] nm, f *fam* crank, weirdo.

husky [œski] *(pl* **huskies)** nm husky.

hutte ['yt] nf hut, cabin.

hybride [ibʀid] ❖ adj **1.** BOT, ZOOL & LING hybrid **2.** [mêlé] hybrid, mixed **3.** AUTO hybrid ▸ **voiture hybride** hybrid car. ❖ nm hybrid.

hydratant, e [idʀatɑ̃, ɑ̃t] adj [crème, lotion] moisturizing. ❖ **hydratant** nm moisturizer.

hydratation [idʀatasjɔ̃] nf **1.** [de la peau] moisturizing **2.** CHIM hydration.

hydrate [idʀat] nm hydrate / *hydrate de carbone* carbohydrate.

hydrater [3] [idʀate] vt **1.** [peau] to moisturize **2.** CHIM to hydrate. ❖ **s'hydrater** vpi **1.** [peau] to become moisturized **2.** CHIM to become hydrated, to hydrate.

hydraulique [idʀolik] adj hydraulic.

hydravion [idʀavjɔ̃] nm seaplane, hydroplane, float plane 🇺🇸.

hydrocarbure [idʀɔkaʀbyʀ] nm hydrocarbon.

hydroélectrique [idʀɔelɛktʀik] adj hydroelectric.

hydrogène [idʀɔʒɛn] nm [élément] hydrogen.

hydroglisseur [idʀɔglisœʀ] nm hydroplane (boat).

hyène [jɛn] nf ZOOL hyena, hyaena.

hygiène [iʒjɛn] nf [principes] hygiene ▸ **hygiène alimentaire / corporelle** food / personal hygiene ▸ **hygiène mentale / publique** mental / public health ▸ **avoir une bonne hygiène de vie** to live healthily.

hygiénique [iʒjenik] adj hygienic.

hymne [imn] nm LITTÉR & RELIG hymn ▸ **hymne national** national anthem.

hype [ajp] ❖ adj inv [quartier, créateur] trendy. ❖ nf ▸ **la hype a)** [dernière mode] the new hip thing **b)** [personnes] the hip crowd, the fashionistas.

hyperactif, ive [ipɛʀaktif, iv] adj hyperactive.

hyperbole [ipɛʀbɔl] nf **1.** [figure de style] hyperbole **2.** GÉOM hyperbola.

hypercalorique [ipɛʀkalɔʀik] adj hypercalorific.

hypermarché [ipɛʀmaʀʃe] nm hypermarket.

hypermétrope [ipɛʀmetʀɔp] ❖ adj longsighted 🇬🇧, farsighted 🇺🇸, hypermetropic *spéc.* ❖ nmf longsighted 🇬🇧 ou farsighted 🇺🇸 ou hypermetropic *spéc* person.

hypernerveux, euse [ipɛʀnɛʀvø, øz] adj overexcitable.

hyperpuissance [ipɛʀpɥisɑ̃s] nf hyperpower.

hyperréaliste [ipɛʀealist] adj hyperrealistic.

hypersensible [ipɛʀsɑ̃sibl] adj hypersensitive.

hypersympa [ipɛʀsɛ̃pa] adj really nice.

hypertension [ipɛʀtɑ̃sjɔ̃] nf ▸ **hypertension (artérielle)** high blood pressure, hypertension *spéc.*

hypertexte [ipɛʀtɛkst] nm hypertext.

hypertrophié, e [ipɛʀtʀɔfje] adj hypertrophied *spéc*, abnormally enlarged.

hypnose [ipnoz] nf hypnosis ▸ **sous hypnose** under hypnosis.

hypnothérapie [ipnɔteʀapi] nf hypnotherapy.

hypnotique [ipnɔtik] adj MÉD hypnotic.

hypnotiser [3] [ipnɔtize] vt MÉD to hypnotize.

hypoallergénique [ipɔalɛʀʒenik] = hypoallergique *(adj)*.

hypoallergique [ipɔalɛʀʒik] adj & nm hypoallergenic.

hypocondriaque [ipɔkɔ̃dʀijak] ❖ adj hypochondriac, hypochondriacal. ❖ nmf hypochondriac.

hypocrisie [ipɔkʀizi] nf [attitude] hypocrisy.

hypocrite [ipɔkʀit] ❖ adj **1.** [sournois - personne] hypocritical, insincere **2.** [mensonger - attitude, regard] hypocritical ; [- promesse] hollow. ❖ nmf hypocrite.

hypocritement [ipɔkʀitmɑ̃] adv hypocritically.

hypodermique [ipɔdɛʀmik] adj hypodermic.

hypoglycémie [ipɔglisemi] nf hypoglycaemia 🇬🇧, hypoglycemia 🇺🇸.

hypokhâgne [ipɔkaɲ] nf *arg scol* 1st year of a two-year Arts course, preparing for entrance to the *École normale supérieure.*

hypotension [ipɔtɑ̃sjɔ̃] nf low blood pressure, hypotension *spéc.*

hypoténuse [ipɔtenyz] nf hypotenuse.

hypothécaire [ipɔtekɛʀ] adj mortgage *(modif).*

hypothèque [ipɔtɛk] nf **1.** DR mortgage ▸ **prendre une hypothèque** to take out a mortgage **2.** *fig* ▸ **lever l'hypothèque** to remove the stumbling block ou the obstacle.

hypothéquer [18] [ipɔteke] vt **1.** [propriété] to mortgage **2.** *fig* ▸ **hypothéquer son avenir** to mortgage one's future.

📝 In reformed spelling (see p. 16-18), this verb is conjugated like *semer* : *il hypothèquera, elle hypothèquerait.*

hypothèse [ipɔtɛz] nf **1.** [supposition] hypothesis, assumption / *dans la meilleure des hypothèses* at best / *dans l'hypothèse où il refuserait, que feriez-vous ?* supposing he refuses, what would you do? **2.** LOGIQUE hypothesis.

hypothétique [ipɔtetik] adj **1.** [supposé] hypothetical, assumed **2.** [peu probable] hypothetical, unlikely, dubious **3.** LOGIQUE hypothetical.

hystérie [isteʀi] nf hysteria ▸ **hystérie collective** mass hysteria.

hystérique [isteʀik] ❖ adj hysterical. ❖ nmf hysteric.

Hz (abr écrite de hertz) Hz.

IA (abr de **intelligence artificielle**) nf AI.

ibérique [iberik] adj Iberian.

iceberg [ajsbɛʀg] nm **1.** GÉOGR iceberg **2.** *fig* : *la partie immergée de l'iceberg* the hidden aspects of the problem.

ici [isi] adv **1.** [dans ce lieu, à cet endroit] here ; [dans un écrit, un discours] here, at this point **▸ vous ici !** what are you doing here? / *pour toute demande, s'adresser ici* please enquire within / *c'est ici que j'ai mal* this is where it hurts **▸ les gens d'ici** the locals, the people from around here **2.** [dans le temps] : *d'ici demain ce sera terminé* it will be finished by tomorrow **▸ d'ici peu** before (very) long / *d'ici là, tout peut arriver !* in the meantime ou until then ou between now and then anything can happen! / *vous serez guéri d'ici là* you'll be better by then **▸ je vois ça d'ici** I can just see that! **3.** [au téléphone, à la radio] **▸ allô, ici Paul** hello, (it's) Paul here ou Paul speaking. **⬥ par ici** loc adv **1.** [dans cette direction] this way / *elle est passée par ici avant d'aller à la gare* she stopped off here on her way to the station **2.** [dans les environs] around here.

icône [ikon] nf icon.

iconoclaste [ikɔnɔklast] **◆** adj iconoclastic. **◆** nmf iconoclast.

iconographie [ikɔnɔgʀafi] nf **1.** [étude théorique] iconography **2.** [illustrations] artwork.

idéal, e, als ou **aux** [ideal, o] adj [demeure, société, solution] ideal, best, perfect. **⬥ idéal, als** ou **aux** nm **1.** [modèle parfait] ideal **2.** [valeurs] ideal, ideals **3.** [solution parfaite] **▸ l'idéal serait de / que...** the ideal ou best solution would be to / if... **▸ dans l'idéal** ideally.

idéalement [idealmɑ̃] adv ideally.

idéaliser [3] [idealize] vt to idealize.

idéaliste [idealist] **◆** adj [gén] idealistic. **◆** nmf idealist.

idée [ide] nf **1.** [pensée] idea, thought / *rien qu'à l'idée de la revoir, je tremble* the mere thought ou the very idea of seeing her again makes me nervous **▸ je me faisais une autre idée de la Tunisie / de sa femme** I had imagined Tunisia / his wife to be different / *moi, t'en vouloir ? en voilà une idée !* me, hold it against you? where did you get that idea (from)? **▸ se faire des idées** to imagine things **▸ donner des idées à qqn** to give sb ideas ou to put ideas in ou into sb's head **▸ avoir une idée derrière la tête** to be up to sthg **▸ avoir des idées noires** to be down in the dumps, to have the blues **2.** [inspiration, création] idea / *qui a eu l'idée du barbecue ?* whose idea was it to have ou who suggested having a barbecue? ; [imagination] ideas, imagination / *pas mal ce dessin, il y a de l'idée* fam not bad this drawing, it's got something **3.** [gré, convenance] **▸ fais à ton idée** do as you see fit ou as you please **4.** *(toujours au sg)* [esprit] : *avoir dans l'idée que...* to have an idea that..., to think that... / *tu la connais, quand elle a dans*

l'idée de faire quelque chose ! you know her, when she's got it into her head to do something ou when she's set her mind on doing something! / *t'est-il jamais venu à l'idée que...* has it never occurred to you ou entered your head that... **5.** [point de vue] : *avoir des idées bien arrêtées sur* to have set ideas ou definite views about / *je préfère me faire moi-même une idée de la situation* I'd rather assess the situation for myself **▸ idée fixe** idée fixe *sout*, obsession **▸ idée reçue** commonplace, received idea *sout*, idée reçue *sout* **▸ avoir les idées larges / étroites** to be broad- / narrow-minded **6.** [aperçu, impression] idea / *donnez-moi une idée du prix que ça va coûter / du temps que ça va prendre* give me a rough idea ou some idea of the price / of the time it will take **▸ tu n'as pas idée de son entêtement !** you have no idea ou you can't imagine how stubborn he is! **▸ je n'en ai pas la moindre idée** I haven't the slightest ou faintest idea **▸ une vague** ou **une petite idée** an inkling **▸ aucune idée !** I haven't got a clue!, no idea!

idem [idɛm] adv idem, ditto.

identifiant [idɑ̃tifjɑ̃] nm INFORM user name, login name.

identification [idɑ̃tifikasjɔ̃] nf **1.** [reconnaissance] identification **2.** [assimilation] identification **▸ identification à** identification with **3.** [d'un cadavre] identification ; [d'un tableau] identification, attribution.

identifier [9] [idɑ̃tifje] vt **1.** [reconnaître] to identify **2.** [assimiler] **▸ identifier qqn / qqch à** to identify sb / sthg with. **⬥ s'identifier à** vp + prép **▸ s'identifier à qqn / qqch** to identify o.s. with sb / sthg.

identique [idɑ̃tik] adj identical **▸ identique à qqn / qqch** identical to sb / sthg.

identitaire [idɑ̃titɛʀ] adj **▸ crise identitaire** identity crisis **▸ démarche / revendication identitaire** assertion of (one's) identity.

identité [idɑ̃tite] nf **1.** [personnalité, état civil] identity **2.** [similitude] identity, similarity **3.** LOGIQUE, MATH & PSYCHOL identity.

idéogramme [ideɔgʀam] nm ideogram.

idéologie [ideɔlɔʒi] nf ideology.

idéologique [ideɔlɔʒik] adj ideological.

idiomatique [idjɔmatik] adj idiomatic.

idiot, e [idjo, ɔt] **◆** adj [stupide -individu, réponse] idiotic, stupid ; [-sourire] idiotic ; [-accident, mort] stupid. **◆** nm, f **1.** [imbécile] idiot **▸ arrête de faire l'idiot !** **a)** [de faire le pitre] stop fooling around ou about! **b)** [à un enfant] stop being stupid! **c)** [à un simulateur] stop acting stupid! **2.** *vieilli* MÉD idiot **▸ l'idiot du village** the village idiot.

idiotie [idjɔsi] nf **1.** [caractère] idiocy, stupidity **2.** [acte, parole] stupid thing / *arrête de dire des idioties* stop talking nonsense.

idolâtrer [3] [idɔlatʀe] vt **1.** RELIG to idolize **2.** [adorer] to idolize.

idole [idɔl] nf **1.** RELIG idol **2.** [personne] idol / *mon frère était mon idole* I used to idolize my brother.

idylle [idil] nf [amourette] romantic idyll.

idyllique [idilik] adj [amour, couple, paysage] idyllic, perfect.

if [if] nm **1.** BOT yew (tree) **2.** MENUIS yew.

IFOP, Ifop [ifɔp] (abr de **Institut français d'opinion publique**) npr m *French market research institute.*

igloo, iglou [iglu] nm igloo.

ignare [iɲaʀ] ◆ adj ignorant, uncultivated. ◆ nmf ignoramus.

ignifuge [iɡnifyʒ ou iɲify3], **ignifugeant, e** [iɡnify3ɑ̃, ɑ̃t ou iɲify3ɑ̃, ɑ̃t] adj fire-retardant.

ignoble [iɲɔbl] adj **1.** [vil - individu] low, base ; [- crime] infamous, heinous ; [- accusation] shameful ; [- conduite] unspeakable, disgraceful, shabby **2.** *fam* [bâtisse] hideous ; [nourriture] revolting, vile ; [logement] squalid.

ignorance [iɲɔʀɑ̃s] nf ignorance ▸ **être dans l'ignorance de qqch** to be unaware of sthg ▸ **tenir qqn dans l'ignorance de qqch** to keep sb in ignorance of sthg.

ignorant, e [iɲɔʀɑ̃, ɑ̃t] ◆ adj **1.** [inculte] ignorant, uncultivated **2.** [incompétent] : *il est ignorant en informatique* he doesn't know anything about computers **3.** [pas au courant] ▸ **ignorant de** ignorant ou unaware of. ◆ nm, f ignoramus ▸ **ne fais pas l'ignorant** don't pretend you don't know.

ignorer [3] [iɲɔʀe] vt **1.** [cause, événement, etc.] to be unaware of ▸ **j'ignore son adresse / où il est / quand elle revient** I don't know her address / where he is / when she's coming back / *il ignorait tout de son passé / d'elle* he knew nothing about her past / her / *j'ignorais qu'il était malade* I was unaware that he was ill **2.** [personne, regard] to ignore, to take no notice of ; [avertissement, panneau] to ignore, to take no heed of ; [ordre, prière] to ignore **3.** *sout* [faim, pauvreté] to have had no experience of. ◆ **s'ignorer** ◆ vp *(emploi réciproque)* to ignore each other. ◆ vpi : *c'est un comédien qui s'ignore* he is unaware of his talent as an actor, he's an actor without knowing it.

⚠ Attention, **to ignore** ne peut être employé pour traduire **ignorer** au sens de « ne pas savoir ».

il [il] *(pl* **ils**) pron pers m **1.** [sujet d'un verbe - homme] he ; [- animal, chose] it ; [- animal de compagnie] he ▸ **ils** they **2.** [sujet d'un verbe impersonnel] ▸ **il pleut** it's raining ▸ **il faut patienter** you / we have to wait **3.** [emphatique - dans une interrogation] : *ton père est-il rentré ?* has your father come back?

île, ile* [il] nf **1.** GÉOGR island, isle *litt* ▸ **ile déserte** desert island ▸ **l'île de Beauté** Corsica **2.** CULIN ▸ **île flottante** floating island.

🌎 **îles**

les îles Anglo-Normandes	the Channel Islands
les îles Britanniques	the British Isles
l'île de Man	the Isle of Man
les îles Marshall	the Marshall Islands
l'île Maurice	Mauritius
l'île de Pâques	Easter Island
les îles Salomon	the Solomon Islands
les îles Sous-le-Vent	a) [aux Antilles] the Netherlands (and Venezuelan) Antilles
	b) [en Polynésie] the Leeward Islands, the Western Society Islands
les îles Vierges	the Virgin Islands

illégal, e, aux [ilegal, o] adj [contre la loi] illegal, unlawful ; [sans autorisation] illicit / *de façon illégale* illegally.

illégalité [ilegalite] nf [caractère] illegality, unlawfulness ▸ **être dans l'illégalité** to be in breach of the law.

illégitime [ileʒitim] adj **1.** DR [enfant, acte] illegitimate **2.** [requête, prétention] illegitimate ; [frayeur] groundless.

illettré, e [iletʀe] ◆ adj [analphabète] illiterate. ◆ nm, f [analphabète] illiterate.

illettrisme [iletʀism] nm illiteracy ▸ **campagne contre l'illettrisme** literacy campaign.

illicite [ilisit] adj illicit.

illico [iliko] adv ▸ **illico (presto)** right away, pronto.

illimité, e [ilimite] adj **1.** [en abondance - ressources, espace] unlimited ; [- patience, bonté] boundless, limitless **2.** [non défini - durée] unlimited, indefinite / *en congé illimité* on indefinite leave.

illisible [ilizibl] adj [écriture] illegible, unreadable.

illogique [ilɔʒik] adj illogical.

illumination [ilyminasjɔ̃] nf **1.** [d'un monument] floodlighting **2.** [lumière] illumination, lighting (up) **3.** [idée] flash of inspiration ou understanding ; [révélation] illumination. ◆ **illuminations** nfpl illuminations, lights / *les illuminations de Noël* the Christmas lights.

illuminé, e [ilymine] ◆ adj [monument] lit up, floodlit, illuminated ; [rue] lit up, illuminated. ◆ nm, f **1.** [visionnaire] visionary, illuminate *arch* **2.** *péj* [fou] lunatic.

illuminer [3] [ilymine] vt **1.** [ciel - suj : étoiles, éclairs] to light up *(sép)* ; [monument] to floodlight ; [pièce] to light **2.** [visage, regard] to light up *(sép)* / *un sourire illumina son visage* a smile lit up her face. ◆ **s'illuminer 1.** *sout* [ciel, regard, visage] to light up ▸ **illuminer de** to light up with **2.** [vitrine] to be lit up ; [guirlande] to light up.

illusion [ilyzjɔ̃] nf **1.** [idée fausse] illusion / *ne lui donne pas d'illusions* don't give him (any) false ideas / *perdre ses illusions* to lose one's illusions ▸ **se faire des illusions** to delude o.s. **2.** [erreur de perception] illusion, trick ▸ **son aisance fait illusion** his apparent ease is deceptive ▸ **illusion d'optique** optical illusion.

illusionner [ilyzjɔne] ◆ **s'illusionner** vpi to delude ou to deceive o.s. / *tu t'illusionnes sur ses intentions* you're deluding yourself ou you're mistaken about his intentions.

illusionniste [ilyzjɔnist] nmf conjurer, illusionist.

illusoire [ilyzwaʀ] adj [promesse] deceptive, illusory ; [bonheur, victoire] illusory, fanciful.

illustrateur, trice [ilystʀatœʀ, tʀis] nm, f illustrator.

illustration [ilystʀasjɔ̃] nf **1.** [image, activité] illustration ; [ensemble d'images] illustrations **2.** *fig* [démonstration] illustration ; [exemple] illustration, example.

illustre [ilystʀ] adj illustrious.

illustré, e [ilystʀe] adj illustrated. ◆ **illustré** nm pictorial, illustrated magazine.

illustrer [3] [ilystʀe] vt **1.** [livre] to illustrate **2.** [définition, théorie] to illustrate. ◆ **s'illustrer** vpi to become renowned ou famous.

îlot, ilot* [ilo] nm **1.** GÉOGR small island, islet **2.** [espace] island ▸ **îlot de résistance** pocket of resistance.

ils [il] pl ⟶ **il**.

image [imaʒ] nf **1.** [représentation] picture ▸ **image de la mère / du père** mother / father figure **2.** [réflexion] image, reflection ; PHYS image ▸ **image réelle / virtuelle** real / virtual image **3.** TV image ; CINÉ frame ▸ **image d'archives** library picture ▸ **l'image est floue** [télévision] the picture is fuzzy **4.** LITTÉR image **5.** [idée] image, picture ▸ **donner une fausse image de qqch** to misrepresent sthg, to give a false impression of sthg **6.** INFORM [imprimée] hard copy ; [sur l'écran] image ▸ **image de synthèse** computer-generated image ou picture. ✧ **image de marque** nf [d'un produit] brand image ; [d'une entreprise] corporate image ; [d'une personnalité, d'une institution] (public) image.

imagé, e [imaʒe] adj full of imagery / **elle a un langage très imagé** she uses colourful imagery.

imagerie [imaʒʀi] nf MÉD ▸ **imagerie par résonance magnétique / par ultrasons** magnetic resonance / ultrasound imaging.

imaginable [imaʒinabl] adj imaginable, conceivable ▸ **c'est difficilement imaginable** it's hard to imagine / **ce n'est plus imaginable à notre époque** it's just unthinkable nowadays.

imaginaire [imaʒinɛʀ] ◆ adj **1.** [fictif - pays, personnage] imaginary **2.** MATH imaginary. ◆ nm imagination ▸ **le domaine de l'imaginaire** the realm of fancy ▸ **l'imaginaire collectif** PSYCHOL the collective imagination.

imaginatif, ive [imaʒinatif, iv] adj imaginative, fanciful.

imagination [imaʒinasjɔ̃] nf [faculté] imagination / **avoir beaucoup d'imagination** to have a lot of imagination, to be very imaginative.

imaginer [3] [imaʒine] vt **1.** [concevoir] to imagine / **la maison est plus grande que je l'imaginais** the house is bigger than I imagined it (to be) / **tu imagines sa tête quand je lui ai dit ça !** you can imagine ou picture his face when I told him that ! **2.** [supposer] to imagine, to suppose **3.** [inventer - personnage] to create, to imagine ; [- gadget, mécanisme] to devise, to think up (*sép*). ✧ **s'imaginer** ◆ vp (*emploi réfléchi*) to imagine o.s. / **j'ai du mal à m'imaginer grand-mère** I have a hard job picturing ou seeing myself as a grandmother. ◆ vpt [se représenter] to imagine, to picture ▸ **s'imaginer que** to imagine ou to think that / **tu t'imagines bien que je n'ai pas vraiment apprécié** as you can imagine, I wasn't too pleased.

imam [imam] nm imam.

imbattable [ɛ̃batabl] adj unbeatable.

imbécile [ɛ̃besil] ◆ adj [niais] stupid. ◆ nmf [niais] idiot, fool ▸ **ne fais pas l'imbécile a)** [ne fais pas le pitre] stop fooling about ou around **b)** [ne simule pas] stop acting stupid ou dumb / **le premier imbécile venu peut comprendre ça** fam any (old) fool can understand that.

imbécillité, imbécilité* [ɛ̃besilite] nf **1.** [caractère] stupidity, idiocy **2.** [parole] nonsense (*U*) ; [acte] stupid behaviour (*U*).

imberbe [ɛ̃bɛʀb] adj beardless.

imbiber [3] [ɛ̃bibe] vt to soak / **imbiber une éponge d'eau** to soak a sponge with water. ✧ **s'imbiber** vpi [s'imprégner] to become soaked ▸ **s'imbiber de a)** [suj : gâteau] to become soaked with ou in **b)** [suj : terre] to become saturated with.

imbriqué, e [ɛ̃brike] adj **1.** [écailles, pièces] imbricated ; [cercles] overlapping **2.** [questions] overlapping, interlinked.

imbriquer [3] [ɛ̃brike] ✧ **s'imbriquer** vpi **1.** CONSTR [pièces] to fit into ou over each other ; [tuiles, feuilles, écailles] to overlap, to imbricate *spéc* **2.** [être lié] to be interlinked ou closely linked.

imbroglio [ɛ̃brɔljo] nm imbroglio.

imbu, e [ɛ̃by] adj ▸ **être imbu de sa personne** ou **de soi-même** to be full of o.s., to be full of a sense of one's own importance *sout*.

imbuvable [ɛ̃byvabl] adj **1.** [boisson] undrinkable **2.** *fam* [individu] unbearable.

IMC, imc (abr de **indice de masse corporelle**) nm BMI.

IMG (abr de **interruption médicale de grossesse**) nf medical abortion.

imitateur, trice [imitatœʀ, tʀis] nm, f imitator ; [de personnalités connues] impersonator, mimic ; [de cris d'animaux] imitator, mimic.

imitation [imitasjɔ̃] nf **1.** [parodie] imitation, impersonation / **elle a un talent d'imitation** she's a talented mimic **2.** ART imitation, copy ; LITTÉR imitation **3.** [matière artificielle] imitation ▸ **imitation marbre** imitation marble.

imiter [3] [imite] vt **1.** [copier - bruit, personne] to imitate ; [- mouvements, façon de parler] to imitate, to mimic ▸ **imiter la signature de qqn a)** to imitate sb's signature **b)** [à des fins criminelles] to forge sb's signature **2.** [suivre l'exemple de] to imitate, to copy / **si elle démissionne, d'autres l'imiteront** if she resigns, others will do the same ou follow suit ou do likewise **3.** [ressembler à] to look like / **c'est une matière qui imite le liège** it's imitation cork.

immaculé, e [imakyle] adj *sout* [blanc, neige] immaculate ; [réputation] immaculate, unsullied, spotless ▸ **l'Immaculée Conception** RELIG the Immaculate Conception.

immanent, e [imanɑ̃, ɑ̃t] adj immanent.

immangeable [ɛ̃mɑ̃ʒabl] adj uneatable, inedible.

immanquablement [ɛ̃mɑ̃kabləmɑ̃] adv definitely, certainly.

immatriculation [imatrikylasjɔ̃] nf registration ▸ **numéro d'immatriculation** registration number 🇬🇧, license number 🇺🇸.

 Immatriculation

A new vehicle registration system was introduced in France in 2009. The new number consists of a series of seven characters: 2 letters, three numbers, and 2 letters, separated by dashes (e.g. AA - 123 - AA). The number of the **département** (which used to form the last two figures of the registration number) continues to be shown on the number plate, but it now appears on the right hand side, along with the logo of the **Région**. However, this local reference no longer relates to the owner's home address, and car owners can choose the **département** they want to appear on the plate for personal reasons.

immatriculer [3] [imatrikyle] vt ▸ **(faire) immatriculer** to register ▸ **car immatriculé à Paris** coach with a Paris registration 🇬🇧 ou license 🇺🇸 number.

immature [imatyr] adj immature.

immédiat, e [imedja, at] adj **1.** [avenir] immediate ; [réponse] immediate, instantaneous ; [effet] immediate, direct ; [soulagement] immediate, instant **2.** [voisins] immediate, next-door (*avant nom*) ; [environs] immediate. ✧ **dans l'immédiat** loc adv for the time being, for the moment, for now.

immédiatement [imedjatmɑ̃] adv **1.** [dans le temps] immediately, at once, forthwith *sout hum* **2.** [dans l'espace] directly, immediately.

immense [imɑ̃s] adj [forêt, bâtiment, plaine] vast, huge ; [talent] immense, towering ; [soulagement, impact] immense, great, tremendous ; [sacrifice, dévotion] immense, boundless ▸ **dans l'immense majorité des cas** in the vast majority of cases.

immensément [imɑ̃semɑ̃] adv immensely, hugely.

immensité [imɑ̃site] nf **1.** [d'un lieu] immensity, vastness ; [de la mer] immensity **2.** [d'une tâche, d'un problème] enormity ; [d'un talent, d'un chagrin] immensity.

immerger [17] [imɛʀʒe] vt [oléoduc, bombes] to lay under water, to submerge ; [produits radioactifs] to dump ou to deposit at sea ; [cadavre] to bury at sea. ❖ **s'immerger** vpi [sous-marin] to dive, to submerge.

immersion [imɛʀsjɔ̃] nf **1.** [d'un sous-marin] diving, submersion ; [d'un oléoduc, de bombes] underwater laying, submersion ; [de déchets] dumping at sea ; [d'un cadavre] burying at sea **2.** ASTRON & RELIG immersion.

immettable [ɛ̃metabl] adj [abîmé] no longer fit to wear ; [indécent] unwearable.

immeuble [imœbl] nm CONSTR [gén] building ▸ **immeuble de bureaux** office block 🇬🇧 ou building ▸ **immeuble d'habitation** residential building, block of flats 🇬🇧, apartment building 🇺🇸.

immigrant, e [imigʀɑ̃, ɑ̃t] adj & nm, f immigrant.

immigration [imigʀasjɔ̃] nf immigration.

immigré, e [imigʀe] ❖ adj immigrant ▸ **travailleur immigré** immigrant worker, guest worker. ❖ nm, f immigrant.

immigrer [3] [imigʀe] vi to immigrate.

imminence [iminɑ̃s] nf imminence.

imminent, e [iminɑ̃, ɑ̃t] adj imminent, impending.

immiscer [16] [imise] ❖ **s'immiscer dans** vp + prép [intervenir dans] ▸ **s'immiscer dans une affaire** to interfere with ou in a matter.

immobile [imɔbil] adj [mer, surface] still, calm ; [nuit, air] still ; [feuillage, animal, personne] still, motionless ; [visage] immobile.

immobilier, ère [imɔbilje, ɛʀ] adj COMM & DR [marché, opération] property (modif) ; [action] real ; [fortune] real estate (modif) ▸ **biens immobiliers** immovables, real estate 🇺🇸 ▸ **société immobilière** property ou real estate 🇺🇸 company. ❖ **immobilier** nm ▸ **l'immobilier** COMM the property ou real estate 🇺🇸 business, realty.

immobilisation [imɔbilizasjɔ̃] nf **1.** [d'un adversaire, de forces armées] immobilization **2.** MÉD immobilization. ❖ **immobilisations** nfpl FIN fixed assets.

immobiliser [3] [imɔbilize] vt **1.** [membre] to strap up (sép), to immobilize ; [adversaire, forces armées] to immobilize ; [balancier] to stop ; [circulation] to bring to a standstill ou to a halt ▸ **il est resté immobilisé au lit pendant cinq semaines** he was laid up in bed for five weeks **2.** FIN [des capitaux] to tie up (sép), to immobilize. ❖ **s'immobiliser** vpi [personne] to stand still ou stock-still ; [véhicule] to come to a halt, to pull up.

immobilisme [imɔbilism] nm [gén] opposition to change ; POL immobilism.

immobilité [imɔbilite] nf [d'un lac, d'une personne] stillness, motionlessness ; [d'un regard] immobility, steadiness ▸ **je suis contraint à l'immobilité totale** I've been confined to bed.

immodéré, e [imɔdeʀe] adj immoderate, inordinate.

immoler [3] [imɔle] vt RELIG [sacrifier] to immolate ▸ **immoler qqn à** to sacrifice sb to. ❖ **s'immoler** vp (emploi réfléchi) litt to sacrifice o.s. ▸ **il s'immola par le feu** he set fire to himself.

immonde [imɔ̃d] adj **1.** [sale] foul, filthy, obnoxious **2.** [ignoble - crime, pensées, propos] sordid, vile, base ; [- individu] vile, base, obnoxious.

immondices [imɔ̃dis] nfpl refuse, rubbish 🇬🇧, trash 🇺🇸.

immoral, e, aux [imɔʀal, o] adj immoral.

immortaliser [3] [imɔʀtalize] vt to immortalize.

immortalité [imɔʀtalite] nf immortality.

immortel, elle [imɔʀtɛl] ❖ adj [dieu] immortal ; [bonheur, gloire] immortal, everlasting, eternal. ❖ nm, f fam [académicien] ▸ **les Immortels** the members of the Académie française. ❖ **immortelle** nf BOT everlasting (flower), immortelle.

immuable [imɥabl] adj [principes, vérités, amour] immutable sout, unchanging ; [sourire] unchanging, fixed ; [politesse] eternal, unfailing ; [opinion] unwavering, unchanging.

immunisation [imynizasjɔ̃] nf immunization.

immuniser [3] [imynize] vt MÉD to immunize / **depuis le temps qu'elle me critique, je suis immunisé !** she's been criticizing me for so long, I'm immune to it now!

immunitaire [imynitɛʀ] adj immune ▸ **système immunitaire** immune system.

immunité [imynite] nf **1.** DR immunity **2.** MÉD immunity.

immunodéficience [imynɔdefisjɑ̃s] nf immunodeficiency.

immunologique [imynɔlɔʒik] adj immunological.

impact [ɛ̃pakt] nm **1.** [choc - de corps] impact, collision ; [- de projectiles] impact ▸ **au moment de l'impact** on impact **2.** [influence, effet - de mesures] impact, effect ; [- d'un mouvement, d'un artiste] impact, influence.

impair, e [ɛ̃pɛʀ] adj [chiffre] odd, uneven / **les jours impairs** odd ou odd-numbered days ▸ **le côté impair** [dans la rue] the uneven numbers. ❖ **impair** [ɛ̃pɛʀ] nm [bévue] blunder / **faire** ou **commettre un impair** to (make a) blunder.

imparable [ɛ̃paʀabl] adj **1.** [coup, ballon] unstoppable **2.** [argument] unanswerable ; [logique] irrefutable.

impardonnable [ɛ̃paʀdɔnabl] adj [erreur, oubli] unforgivable, inexcusable.

imparfait, e [ɛ̃paʀfɛ, ɛt] adj **1.** [incomplet] imperfect, partial **2.** [personne] imperfect. ❖ **imparfait** nm LING : **l'imparfait** the imperfect (tense).

impartial, e, aux [ɛ̃paʀsjal, o] adj impartial, unprejudiced, unbiased.

impartialité [ɛ̃paʀsjalite] nf impartiality, fairness ▸ **juger avec impartialité** to judge impartially.

impartir [32] [ɛ̃paʀtiʀ] vt **1.** [temps] : **le temps qui vous était imparti est écoulé** you have used up the time allotted to you **2.** litt [pouvoir] : **en vertu des pouvoirs qui me sont impartis** by virtue of the powers (that are) vested in me.

impasse [ɛ̃pas] nf **1.** [rue] dead end, cul-de-sac / '**impasse**' 'no through road' **2.** [situation] impasse, blind alley / **il faut absolument faire sortir les négociations de l'impasse** we must break the deadlock in the negotiations **3.** arg scol : **j'ai fait une impasse sur la Seconde Guerre mondiale** I missed out 🇬🇧 ou skipped (over) 🇺🇸 World War II in my revision.

impassible [ɛ̃pasibl] adj impassive, imperturbable.

impatiemment [ɛ̃pasjamɑ̃] adv impatiently.

impatience [ɛ̃pasjɑ̃s] nf impatience.

impatient, e [ɛ̃pasjɑ̃, ɑ̃t] adj [personne, geste] impatient / **êtes-vous impatient de rentrer ?** are you anxious ou eager to get home?

impatienter [3] [ɛ̃pasjɑ̃te] vt to annoy, to irritate. ❖ **s'impatienter** vpi [dans une attente] to grow ou to become impatient ; [dans une discussion] to lose one's patience ▸ **s'impatienter de qqch** to get impatient with sthg.

impayable [ɛ̃pɛjabl] adj fam priceless / il est vraiment impayable ! he's priceless ou a scream!

impayé, e [ɛ̃pɛje] adj [facture] unpaid ; [dette] outstanding. ❖ **impayé** nm [somme] unpaid ou dishonoured bill / **'les impayés'** 'payments outstanding'.

impeccable [ɛ̃pekabl] adj **1.** [propre et net - intérieur, vêtement] spotless, impeccable ; [- coiffure, ongles] impeccable **2.** [parfait - manières, travail] impeccable, flawless, perfect / 10 heures, ça te va? — oui, impeccable! fam would 10 o'clock suit you? — yes, great ou perfect!

impénétrable [ɛ̃penetrabl] adj impenetrable.

impénitent, e [ɛ̃penitɑ̃, ɑ̃t] adj **1.** RELIG impenitent, unrepentant **2.** [buveur, fumeur] inveterate.

impensable [ɛ̃pɑ̃sabl] adj [inconcevable] unthinkable, inconceivable ; [incroyable] unbelievable.

imper [ɛ̃pɛʀ] nm raincoat, mac UK.

impératif, ive [ɛ̃peratif, iv] adj **1.** [qui s'impose - mesure, intervention] imperative, urgent, vital ; [- besoin, date] imperative / il est impératif de... it is imperative ou essential to... **2.** [de commandement - appel, geste, voix] imperative, peremptory **3.** LING imperative. ❖ **impératif** nm **1.** (souvent au pl) [exigence] requirement, necessity / les impératifs de la mode the dictates of fashion ▸ **les impératifs du direct** fam the constraints of live broadcasting **2.** LING ▸ **l'impératif** the imperative (mood) / verbe à l'impératif imperative verb, verb in the imperative.

impérativement [ɛ̃perativmɑ̃] adv : il faut que je termine impérativement pour ce soir it's essential that I should finish tonight.

impératrice [ɛ̃peratris] nf empress.

imperceptible [ɛ̃pɛʀsɛptibl] adj imperceptible.

imperceptiblement [ɛ̃pɛʀsɛptibləmɑ̃] adv imperceptibly.

imperfection [ɛ̃pɛʀfɛksjɔ̃] nf **1.** [défaut - d'un tissu, d'un cuir] imperfection, defect ; [- d'une personne] imperfection, shortcoming ; [- d'un style, d'une œuvre] imperfection, weakness ; [- d'un système] shortcoming / toutes les petites imperfections de la peau all the small blemishes on the skin **2.** [état] imperfection.

impérial, e, aux [ɛ̃perjal, o] adj **1.** HIST & POL imperial **2.** fig [allure, manières] imperial, majestic. ❖ **impériale** nf [étage] top deck ▸ **bus / rame à impériale** double-decker bus / train.

impérialisme [ɛ̃perjalism] nm imperialism.

impérialiste [ɛ̃perjalist] adj & nmf imperialist.

impérieusement [ɛ̃perjøzmɑ̃] adv **1.** [impérativement] absolutely **2.** [autoritairement] imperiously, peremptorily.

impérieux, euse [ɛ̃perjø, øz] adj **1.** [irrésistible - désir] urgent, compelling, pressing / un besoin impérieux a pressing need **2.** [de commandement - appel, personne, voix] imperious, peremptory ▸ **d'un ton impérieux** in a commanding tone.

impérissable [ɛ̃perisabl] adj sout [vérité] eternal, imperishable sout ; [splendeur] undying ; [souvenir] enduring.

imperméabiliser [3] [ɛ̃pɛʀmeabilize] vt to (make) waterproof ou rainproof.

imperméable [ɛ̃pɛʀmeabl] ◆ adj **1.** GÉOL impermeable **2.** [combinaison de plongée] waterproof ; [enduit intérieur] waterproof, water-resistant spéc ; [vêtement, chaussure, enduit extérieur] waterproof, rainproof. ◆ nm [vêtement] raincoat.

impersonnel, elle [ɛ̃pɛʀsɔnɛl] adj **1.** [atmosphère, décor, ton] impersonal, cold **2.** [approche, texte] impersonal **3.** LING impersonal.

impertinence [ɛ̃pɛʀtinɑ̃s] nf **1.** [caractère] impertinence, impudence, effrontery **2.** [parole] impertinence, impertinent remark.

impertinent, e [ɛ̃pɛʀtinɑ̃, ɑ̃t] adj [impudent] impertinent, impudent.

imperturbable [ɛ̃pɛʀtyʀbabl] adj imperturbable.

impétueux, euse [ɛ̃petɥø, øz] adj **1.** [personne] impetuous, rash, impulsive ; [tempérament] fiery, impetuous **2.** litt [flot, rythme] impetuous, wild.

impitoyable [ɛ̃pitwajabl] adj [juge, adversaire] merciless, pitiless ; [haine, combat] merciless, relentless.

impitoyablement [ɛ̃pitwajabləmɑ̃] adv mercilessly, ruthlessly, pitilessly.

implacable [ɛ̃plakabl] adj [acharné, inflexible] implacable sout.

implant [ɛ̃plɑ̃] nm implant ▸ **implant capillaire** hair graft.

implantation [ɛ̃plɑ̃tasjɔ̃] nf **1.** [établissement] establishment, setting up **2.** [des cheveux] hairline **3.** MÉD (lateral) implantation ; [en odontologie] implant **4.** ÉLECTRON implantation.

implanter [3] [ɛ̃plɑ̃te] vt [bâtiment] to locate ; [entreprise] to set up, to establish, to locate ; [idées] to implant ; [coutumes, mode] to introduce ; [parti politique] to establish / implanter un produit sur le marché to establish a product on the market. ❖ **s'implanter** vpi [entreprise, ville] to be set up ou located ou established ; [peuple] to settle.

implémenter [ɛ̃plemɑ̃te] vt INFORM to implement.

implication [ɛ̃plikasjɔ̃] nf [participation] involvement, implication.

implicite [ɛ̃plisit] adj [tacite] implicit.

implicitement [ɛ̃plisitmɑ̃] adv [tacitement] implicitly.

impliquer [3] [ɛ̃plike] vt **1.** [compromettre] to implicate, to involve ▸ **impliquer qqn dans qqch** to implicate sb in sthg ▸ **être impliqué dans qqch** to be involved in sthg **2.** [supposer - suj : terme, phrase] to imply **3.** [entraîner - dépenses, remaniements] to imply, to involve, to entail. ❖ **s'impliquer dans** vp + prép ▸ **s'impliquer dans qqch** to get (o.s.) involved in sthg.

imply ou **implicate** ?
Attention à ne pas confondre **to imply**, qui signifie impliquer au sens de « supposer », « entraîner », et **to implicate** qui a le sens de « compromettre ».

implorer [3] [ɛ̃plɔʀe] vt **1.** [solliciter] to implore, to beseech ▸ **implorer le pardon de qqn** to beg sb's forgiveness **2.** sout [supplier] ▸ **implorer qqn de faire qqch** to implore ou to beg sb to do sthg.

imploser [3] [ɛ̃ploze] vi to implode.

implosion [ɛ̃plozjɔ̃] nf PHON & PHYS implosion.

impoli, e [ɛ̃pɔli] adj impolite, rude, uncivil ▸ **être impoli envers qqn** to be impolite ou rude to sb.

impoliment [ɛ̃pɔlimɑ̃] adv impolitely, rudely.

impolitesse [ɛ̃pɔlitɛs] nf **1.** [caractère] impoliteness, rudeness **2.** [acte, parole] impolite thing.

impondérable [ɛ̃pɔ̃deʀabl] ◆ adj imponderable. ◆ nm (gén au pl) unknown quantity, imponderable.

impopulaire [ɛ̃pɔpylɛʀ] adj [mesure, dirigeant] unpopular.

importance [ɛ̃pɔʀtɑ̃s] nf **1.** [qualitative - d'une décision, d'un discours, d'une personne] importance, significance ▶ **avoir de l'importance** to be of importance, to matter ▶ **sans importance a)** [personne] unimportant, insignificant **b)** [fait] of no importance, irrelevant **c)** [somme] insignificant, trifling / *que disais-tu ? — c'est sans importance* what were you saying? — it's of no importance ou it doesn't matter ▶ **accorder** ou **attacher trop d'importance à qqch** to attach too much importance ou significance to sthg ▶ **se donner de l'importance** to act important **2.** [quantitative - d'un effectif, d'une agglomération] size ; [- de dégâts, de pertes] extent ▶ **prendre de l'importance** to expand.

important, e [ɛ̃pɔʀtɑ̃, ɑ̃t] ◆ adj **1.** [qualitativement - découverte, témoignage, rencontre, personnalité] important ; [- date, changement] important, significant ; [- conséquence] important, serious, far-reaching ; [- position] important, high ▶ **peu important a)** [petit] small **b)** [insignifiant] unimportant **2.** [quantitativement - collection, effectif] sizeable, large ; [- augmentation, proportion] substantial, significant, large ; [- somme] substantial, considerable, sizeable ; [- retard] considerable ; [- dégâts] considerable, extensive **3.** [présomptueux] ▶ **prendre** ou **se donner des airs importants** to act important, to give o.s. airs. ◆ nm, f [personne] ▶ **faire l'important** to act important. ◆ **important** nm ▶ **l'important, c'est de...** the important thing is to..., the main thing is to...

⚠️ Attention, l'adjectif anglais **important** ne peut pas être employé systématiquement pour traduire **important**, notamment au sens quantitatif.

importateur, trice [ɛ̃pɔʀtatœʀ, tʀis] ◆ adj importing / *les pays importateurs de pétrole* oil-importing countries. ◆ nm, f importer.

importation [ɛ̃pɔʀtasjɔ̃] nf ÉCON importation, importing ▶ **produit d'importation** imported product, import.

importer [3] [ɛ̃pɔʀte] ◆ vt **1.** [marchandises, main-d'œuvre, brevets] to import ; [mode] to introduce, to import ; [animal, végétal] to import, to introduce into the country ; [idée] to import, to bring in *(sép)* **2.** INFORM to import. ◆ vi [avoir de l'importance] to matter ▶ **peu importe** it doesn't matter ▶ **qu'importe !** what does it matter! / *ce qui importe avant tout c'est que tu sois heureuse* the most important thing ou what matters most is your happiness ▶ **peu m'importe !** it doesn't matter to me!

import-export [ɛ̃pɔʀɛkspɔʀ] *(pl* **imports-exports)** nm import-export.

importun, e [ɛ̃pɔʀtœ̃, yn] ◆ adj [question] importunate *sout*, untimely ; [visite, visiteur] unwelcome, importunate *sout*. ◆ nm, f pest, nuisance.

importuner [3] [ɛ̃pɔʀtyne] vt *sout* [suj : musique, insecte] to bother, to disturb, to annoy ; [suj : personne] to importune *sout*, to bother.

imposable [ɛ̃pozabl] adj taxable.

imposant, e [ɛ̃pozɑ̃, ɑ̃t] adj imposing, impressive.

imposé, e [ɛ̃poze] ◆ adj **1.** SPORT ⟶ **figure 2.** COMM ⟶ **prix.** ◆ nm, f [contribuable] taxpayer. ❖ **imposé** nm SPORT [exercice] compulsory exercise.

imposer [3] [ɛ̃poze] vt **1.** [fixer - règlement, discipline] to impose, to enforce ; [- méthode, délai, corvée] to impose ▶ **imposer qqch à qqn** to force sthg on sb / *imposer sa volonté / son point de vue* to impose one's will / one's ideas **2.** [provoquer] ▶ **imposer l'admiration / le respect** to command admiration / respect ▶ **cette affaire impose la prudence / la discrétion** this matter requires prudence / discretion **3.** ÉCON to tax **4.** EXPR **en imposer** to be impressive ▶ **en imposer à qqn** to impress sb. ❖ **s'imposer** ◆ vpi **1.** [se faire accepter de force] to impose o.s. **2.** [se faire reconnaître] to stand out ▶ **s'imposer dans un domaine** to make a name for o.s. in a field / *elle s'impose par son talent* her talent makes her stand out **3.** [être inévitable] to be necessary / *cette dernière remarque ne s'imposait pas* that last remark was unnecessary ou uncalled for. ◆ vpt [se fixer] ▶ **s'imposer qqch** to impose sthg on o.s.

imposition [ɛ̃pozisjɔ̃] nf ÉCON [procédé] taxation ; [impôt] tax.

impossibilité [ɛ̃pɔsibilite] nf impossibility ▶ **être dans l'impossibilité de faire qqch** to be unable to do sthg.

impossible [ɛ̃pɔsibl] ◆ adj **1.** [infaisable] impossible / *il est impossible de...* it's impossible ou not possible to... / *il m'est impossible de te répondre* it's impossible for me to give you an answer, I can't possibly answer you ▶ **désolé, cela m'est impossible** I'm sorry but I can't (possibly) / *il n'est pas impossible que je vienne aussi* I might (just) ou there's a chance I might come too **2.** [insupportable - personne] impossible, unbearable ; [- situation, vie] impossible, intolerable **3.** *fam* [extravagant] impossible, ridiculous, incredible ▶ **à des heures impossibles** at the most ungodly hours. ◆ nm : *ne me demande pas l'impossible* don't ask me to do the impossible ou to perform miracles ▶ **nous ferons l'impossible** we will do our utmost, we will move heaven and earth ▶ **à l'impossible nul n'est tenu** *prov* nobody is expected to do the impossible.

imposteur [ɛ̃pɔstœʀ] nm impostor.

imposture [ɛ̃pɔstyʀ] nf *litt* fraud, (piece of) trickery, deception.

impôt [ɛ̃po] nm [prélèvement] tax / *payer des impôts* to pay (income) tax / *payer 300 euros d'impôt* to pay 300 euros in taxes ou (in) tax ▶ **impôt sur les bénéfices** tax on profits ▶ **impôt sur le chiffre d'affaires** turnover ou cascade 🇬🇧 tax ▶ **impôt direct / indirect** direct / indirect tax ▶ **impôt foncier** property tax ▶ **impôt sur les grandes fortunes** former wealth tax ▶ **impôts locaux** ≃ council tax 🇬🇧 ; ≃ local property tax 🇺🇸 ▶ **impôt sur les plus-values** capital gains tax ▶ **impôt sur le revenu** income tax ▶ **impôt de solidarité sur la fortune** wealth tax ▶ **impôt sur les sociétés** corporation tax.

 Impôts locaux

These are taxes levied to finance local, departmental or regional government. The best-known are the **taxe d'habitation** (paid by homeowners and rent-paying tenants), the **taxe foncière** (paid by homeowners) and the **taxe professionnelle** (levied on businesses). The rate of each tax is decided at local level.

impotent, e [ɛ̃pɔtɑ̃, ɑ̃t] ◆ adj [personne] infirm ; [membre] withered. ◆ nm, f [personne] cripple.

impraticable [ɛ̃pʀatikabl] adj **1.** [col] inaccessible, impassable ; [fleuve] unnavigable ; [aérodrome] unfit for use ; [route] impassable **2.** *litt* [méthode, idée] unfeasible, unworkable, impracticable.

imprécation [ɛ̃pʀekasjɔ̃] nf *litt* imprecation *litt*, curse.

imprécis, e [ɛ̃pʀesi, iz] adj **1.** [témoignage, souvenir] imprecise, vague **2.** [appareil, instrument] imprecise, inaccurate.

imprécision [ɛ̃pʀesizjɔ̃] nf [d'un souvenir, d'un témoignage] vagueness, imprecision.

imprégner [18] [ɛ̃pʀeɲe] vt **1.** [imbiber] to soak, to impregnate ▸ **être imprégné de** to be soaked in, to be impregnated with **2.** [être présent dans] to permeate, to pervade, to fill. ❖ **s'imprégner de** vp + prép [éponge, bois] to become soaked ou impregnated with ; [air] to become permeated ou filled with ; [personne, esprit] to become immersed in ou imbued with.
📝 In reformed spelling (see p. 16-18), this verb is conjugated like *semer* : *il imprègnera, elle s'imprègnerait.*

imprenable [ɛ̃pʀənabl] adj **1.** MIL [ville] impregnable ; [position] unassailable **2.** [gén] : *vue imprenable sur la baie* uninterrupted view of the bay.

imprésario, impresario (*pl* **impresarii** [-ʀi]) [ɛ̃pʀesaʀjo] nm impresario.

impression [ɛ̃pʀesjɔ̃] nf **1.** [effet, réaction] impression ▸ **faire bonne / mauvaise impression** to make a good / a bad impression ▸ **faire une forte** ou **grosse impression** to make quite a strong impression **2.** [sensation] feeling ▸ **avoir l'impression** [croire] : *j'ai l'impression qu'elle ne viendra plus* I have a feeling (that) she won't come **3.** [motif, dessin] pattern **4.** IMPR printing / *envoyer un manuscrit à l'impression* to send a manuscript off to press ou the printer's.

impressionnable [ɛ̃pʀesjɔnabl] adj [émotif] impressionable.

impressionnant, e [ɛ̃pʀesjɔnɑ̃, ɑ̃t] adj [imposant - œuvre, personnalité] impressive ; [- portail, temple] awe-inspiring ; [- exploit] impressive, stunning, sensational ; [- somme] considerable.

impressionner [3] [ɛ̃pʀesjɔne] vt **1.** [frapper] to impress / *se laisser impressionner* to let o.s. be impressed **2.** [bouleverser] to distress, to upset **3.** PHOT to expose.

impressionnisme [ɛ̃pʀesjɔnism] nm impressionism.

impressionniste [ɛ̃pʀesjɔnist] ◆ adj ART impressionist. ◆ nmf impressionist.

imprévisible [ɛ̃pʀevizibl] adj unpredictable, unforeseeable.

imprévoyant, e [ɛ̃pʀevwajɑ̃, ɑ̃t] adj [gén] lacking (in) foresight ; [financièrement] improvident.

imprévu, e [ɛ̃pʀevy] adj [inattendu] unexpected, unforeseen. ❖ **imprévu** nm **1.** ▸ **l'imprévu** [les surprises] : *j'adore l'imprévu !* I love surprises ! **2.** [événement] unexpected event ▸ **sauf imprévu** ou **à moins d'un imprévu, je serai à l'heure** unless anything unforeseen happens ou barring accidents, I'll be on time.

imprimante [ɛ̃pʀimɑ̃t] nf printer ▸ **imprimante matricielle** ou **par points** (dot) matrix printer ▸ **imprimante à jet d'encre** ink jet printer.

imprimé [ɛ̃pʀime] nm **1.** [brochure, livre] printed book ou booklet / **'imprimés'** 'printed matter' **2.** [formulaire] (printed) form **3.** [étoffe] printed fabric ou material.

imprimer [3] [ɛ̃pʀime] vt **1.** IMPR [fabriquer] to print (out) (sép) ; [publier] to print, to publish **2.** TEXT to print **3.** [transmettre] to transmit, to impart, to give.

imprimerie [ɛ̃pʀimʀi] nf **1.** [technique] printing **2.** [établissement] printing works (sg), printer's ; [atelier] printing office ou house ; PRESSE print room **3.** [industrie] ▸ **l'imprimerie** the printing industry.

imprimeur [ɛ̃pʀimœʀ] nm [industriel] printer ; [ouvrier] printer, print worker.

impro [ɛ̃pʀo] (abr de **improvisation**) nf fam impro.

improbable [ɛ̃pʀɔbabl] adj unlikely, improbable.

improductif, ive [ɛ̃pʀɔdyktif, iv] adj unproductive.

impromptu, e [ɛ̃pʀɔ̃pty] adj [improvisé] impromptu, unexpected, surprise (modif) / **faire un discours impromptu** to give an impromptu ou off-the-cuff speech. ❖ **impromptu** nm LITTÉR & MUS impromptu.

imprononçable [ɛ̃pʀɔnɔ̃sabl] adj unpronounceable.

impropre [ɛ̃pʀɔpʀ] adj **1.** [personne, produit] unsuitable, unsuited, unfit ▸ **produits impropres à la consommation** products not fit ou unfit for human consumption **2.** [terme] inappropriate.

improvisation [ɛ̃pʀɔvizasjɔ̃] nf **1.** [gén] improvisation, improvising **2.** MUS & THÉÂTRE improvisation ▸ **faire de l'improvisation** to improvise.

improvisé, e [ɛ̃pʀɔvize] adj [discours] improvised, extempore sout ; [explication] off-the-cuff, ad hoc ; [mesure, réforme] hurried, makeshift, improvised ; [décision] snap.

improviser [3] [ɛ̃pʀɔvize] ◆ vt to improvise ▸ **improviser une explication** to give an off-the-cuff explanation. ◆ vi **1.** [parler spontanément] to improvise **2.** MUS to improvise. ❖ **s'improviser** vpi : *on ne s'improvise pas peintre* you don't become a painter overnight ou just like that.

improviste [ɛ̃pʀɔvist] ❖ **à l'improviste** loc adv unexpectedly, without warning.

imprudemment [ɛ̃pʀydamɑ̃] adv recklessly, carelessly, imprudently.

imprudence [ɛ̃pʀydɑ̃s] nf **1.** [caractère] imprudence, carelessness, foolhardiness **2.** [acte] careless act ou action / *il a commis l'imprudence d'en parler aux journalistes* he was stupid enough to talk to the press about it ▸ **pas d'imprudences !** be careful!, don't do anything silly!

imprudent, e [ɛ̃pʀydɑ̃, ɑ̃t] ◆ adj **1.** [conducteur] careless ; [joueur] reckless **2.** [acte, comportement] unwise, imprudent ; [remarque] foolish, careless, unwise ; [projet] foolish, ill-considered ; [décision] rash, unwise, ill-advised. ◆ nm, f [personne] careless ou reckless person.

impudence [ɛ̃pydɑ̃s] nf **1.** [caractère] impudence, insolence, brazenness **2.** [action] impudent act ; [remarque] impudent remark.

impudent, e [ɛ̃pydɑ̃, ɑ̃t] ◆ adj impudent, insolent, brazen. ◆ nm, f impudent person.

impudique [ɛ̃pydik] adj **1.** [immodeste] immodest, shameless **2.** [indécent] shameless, indecent.

impuissance [ɛ̃pɥisɑ̃s] nf **1.** [faiblesse] powerlessness, helplessness **2.** [incapacité] inability, powerlessness **3.** MÉD & PSYCHOL impotence.

impuissant, e [ɛ̃pɥisɑ̃, ɑ̃t] adj **1.** [vain] powerless, helpless ▸ **être impuissant à faire qqch** to be powerless to do sthg **2.** MÉD & PSYCHOL impotent.

impulsif, ive [ɛ̃pylsif, iv] ◆ adj impulsive. ◆ nm, f impulsive person.

impulsion [ɛ̃pylsjɔ̃] nf **1.** MÉCAN & PHYS impulse ; ÉLECTRON pulse, impulse **2.** fig [dynamisme] impetus, impulse / *donner une impulsion au commerce* to give an impetus to ou to boost trade / *sous l'impulsion des dirigeants syndicaux* spurred on by the union leaders **3.** [élan] impulse ▸ **sur** ou **sous l'impulsion du moment** on the spur of the moment.

impulsivité [ɛ̃pylsivite] nf impulsiveness.

impunément [ɛ̃pynemɑ̃] adv with impunity.

impuni, e [ɛ̃pyni] adj unpunished.

impunité [ɛ̃pynite] nf impunity ▸ **en toute impunité** with impunity.

impur, e [ɛ̃pyʀ] adj sout [pensée, sentiment] impure, unclean ; [air, eau] impure, foul ; [style] impure ; [race] mixed, mongrel.

impureté [ɛ̃pyʀte] nf **1.** [caractère] impurity, foulness **2.** [élément] impurity.

imputable [ɛ̃pytabl] adj **1.** [attribuable] ▸ **imputable à** imputable ou ascribable ou attributable to **2.** FIN ▸ **imputable sur a)** [crédit] chargeable ou to be credited to **b)** [débit] to be debited from.

imputer [3] [ɛ̃pyte] vt **1.** [attribuer] ▸ **imputer un crime à qqn** to impute a crime to sb **2.** FIN : *imputer des frais à un budget* [déduire] to deduct expenses from a budget / *imputer une somme à un budget* to allocate a sum to a budget.

imputrescible [ɛ̃pytʀesibl] adj rot-resistant, antirot.

INA [ina] (abr de **Institut national de l'audiovisuel**) npr m *national television archive.*

inabordable [inabɔʀdabl] adj [lieu] inaccessible ; [personne] unapproachable, inaccessible ; [prix] exorbitant ; [produit, service] exorbitantly priced.

inacceptable [inaksɛptabl] adj [mesure, proposition] unacceptable ; [propos, comportement] unacceptable, intolerable, inadmissible.

inaccessible [inaksesibl] adj [hors d'atteinte - sommet] inaccessible, out-of-reach, unreachable ; [irréalisable - objectif, rêve] unfeasible, unrealizable ; [inabordable - personne] unapproachable, inaccessible ; [obscur - ouvrage] inaccessible, opaque.

inachevé, e [inaʃve] adj [non terminé] unfinished, uncompleted ; [incomplet] incomplete.

inactif, ive [inaktif, iv] ◆ adj **1.** [personne - oisive] inactive, idle ; [- sans travail] non-working **2.** BOURSE & COMM slack, slow. ◆ nm, f ▸ **les inactifs** SOCIOL the non-working population, those not in active employment.

inaction [inaksjɔ̃] nf [absence d'activité] inaction ; [oisiveté] idleness, lethargy.

inactivité [inaktivite] nf inactivity.

inadapté, e [inadapte] adj **1.** [enfant] with special needs, maladjusted / *enfants inadaptés au système scolaire* children who fail to adapt to the educational system **2.** [outil, méthode] ▸ **inadapté à** unsuited ou not adapted to.

inadéquat, e [inadekwa, at] adj *sout* inadequate, inappropriate.

inadéquation [inadekwasjɔ̃] nf *sout* inadequacy, inappropriateness.

inadmissible [inadmisibl] adj inadmissible, intolerable, unacceptable.

inadvertance [inadvɛʀtɑ̃s] nf *sout* oversight, slip (up), inadvertence. ◆❖ **par inadvertance** loc adv inadvertently, by mistake.

inaliénable [inaljenabl] adj inalienable, unalienable.

inaltérable [inalteʀabl] adj **1.** [métal] stable ; [couleur] permanent, fast ▸ **inaltérable à l'air** air-resistant **2.** [amitié] steadfast ; [haine] eternal ; [espoir] unfailing, steadfast ; [humeur, courage] unfailing ; [optimisme] steadfast, unshakeable.

inamovible [inamɔvibl] adj **1.** ADMIN [fonctionnaire] permanent, irremovable **2.** [fixé] fixed.

inanimé, e [inanime] adj **1.** [mort] lifeless ; [évanoui] unconscious **2.** LING inanimate ▸ **objets inanimés** inanimate objects.

inanité [inanite] nf futility, pointlessness.

inanition [inanisjɔ̃] nf [faim] starvation ; [épuisement] total exhaustion, inanition *spéc* ▸ **tomber / mourir d'inanition a)** *pr* to faint / to die with hunger **b)** *fig & hum* to be starving.

inaperçu, e [inapɛʀsy] adj unnoticed ▸ **passer inaperçu** to go unnoticed.

inapplicable [inaplikabl] adj inapplicable, not applicable.

inappréciable [inapʀesjabl] adj [précieux] invaluable, priceless.

inapproprié, e [inapʀopʀije] adj inappropriate.

inapte [inapt] adj **1.** [incapable] unsuitable ▸ **être inapte à qqch** to be unsuitable ou unfit for sthg ▸ **être inapte à faire qqch** to be unfit to do sthg **2.** MIL ▸ **inapte (au service militaire)** unfit (for military service).

inaptitude [inaptityd] nf [incapacité - physique] incapacity, unfitness ; [- mentale] (mental) inaptitude ▸ **inaptitude à qqch** unfitness for sthg ▸ **inaptitude à faire qqch** unfitness for doing ou to do sthg.

inarticulé, e [inaʀtikyle] adj inarticulate.

inassouvi, e [inasuvi] adj *sout* [passion] unappeased, unsatiated ; [désir] unfulfilled.

inattaquable [inatakabl] adj [personne] beyond reproach ou criticism ; [conduite] unimpeachable, irreproachable ; [argument, preuve] unassailable, irrefutable, unquestionable ; [forteresse, lieu] impregnable.

inattendu, e [inatɑ̃dy] adj [personne] unexpected ; [réflexion, événement] unexpected, unforeseen.

inattentif, ive [inatɑ̃tif, iv] adj inattentive.

inattention [inatɑ̃sjɔ̃] nf lack of attention ou concentration, inattentiveness ▸ **un moment** ou **une minute d'inattention** a momentary lapse of concentration.

inaudible [inodibl] adj [imperceptible] inaudible.

inaugural, e, aux [inogyʀal, o] adj [discours, cérémonie] opening (modif), inaugural ; [voyage] maiden (modif).

inauguration [inogyʀasjɔ̃] nf **1.** [cérémonie] inauguration **2.** [commencement] beginning, inauguration, initiation.

inaugurer [3] [inogyʀe] vt **1.** [route, monument, exposition] to inaugurate ; *fig* [système, méthode] to initiate, to launch **2.** [marquer le début de] to usher in.

inavouable [inavwabl] adj unmentionable, shameful.

INC (abr de **Institut national de la consommation**) npr m *consumer protection body.*

incalculable [ɛ̃kalkylabl] adj **1.** [considérable] incalculable, countless ▸ **un nombre incalculable de** a countless number of **2.** [imprévisible] incalculable.

incandescence [ɛ̃kɑ̃desɑ̃s] nf incandescence ▸ **porté à incandescence** heated until glowing, incandescent.

incandescent, e [ɛ̃kɑ̃desɑ̃, ɑ̃t] adj incandescent.

incantation [ɛ̃kɑ̃tasjɔ̃] nf incantation.

incapable [ɛ̃kapabl] ◆ adj **1.** [par incompétence] incapable, incompetent, inefficient ▸ **incapable de:** *être incapable de faire qqch* to be incapable of doing sthg / *elle était incapable de répondre* she was unable to answer, she couldn't answer **2.** [par nature] ▸ **incapable de:** *être incapable de qqch* to be incapable of sthg. ◆ nmf [incompétent] incompetent.

incapacité [ɛ̃kapasite] nf **1.** [impossibilité] incapacity, inability ▸ **être dans l'incapacité de faire qqch** to be unable to do sthg / *son incapacité à se décider* his incapacity ou inability to make up his mind **2.** MÉD disablement, disability ▸ **incapacité permanente** permanent disablement ou disability ▸ **incapacité de travail** industrial disablement **3.** DR (legal) incapacity.

incarcération [ɛ̃kaʀseʀasjɔ̃] nf imprisonment, jailing, incarceration *sout.*

incarcérer [18] [ɛ̃kaʀseʀe] vt to incarcerate *sout.*
✐ In reformed spelling (see p. 16-18), this verb is conjugated like *semer : il incarcèrera, elle incarcèrerait.*

incarnation [ɛ̃kaʀnasjɔ̃] nf **1.** MYTH & RELIG incarnation **2.** [manifestation] embodiment / *elle est l'incarnation de la bonté* she's the embodiment ou personification of goodness.

incarné, e [ɛ̃kaʀne] adj **1.** [personnifié] incarnate, personified **2.** MÉD ▸ **ongle incarné** ingrowing 🇬🇧 ou ingrown toenail.

incarner [3] [ɛ̃kaʀne] vt **1.** [symboliser] to embody, to personify **2.** [interpréter - personnage] to play. ✧ **s'incarner** vpi RELIG to become incarnate.

incartade [ɛ̃kaʀtad] nf [écart de conduite] misdemeanour 🇬🇧, misdemeanor 🇺🇸, escapade.

incassable [ɛ̃kasabl] adj unbreakable.

incendiaire [ɛ̃sɑ̃djɛʀ] ◆ adj **1.** ARM incendiary **2.** [propos] incendiary, inflammatory. ◆ nmf fire-raiser 🇬🇧, arsonist.

incendie [ɛ̃sɑ̃di] nm [feu] fire / *maîtriser un incendie* to bring a fire ou blaze under control ▸ **incendie criminel** (act of deliberate) arson ▸ **incendie de forêt** forest fire.

incendier [9] [ɛ̃sɑ̃dje] vt **1.** [mettre le feu à] to set fire to, to set on fire **2.** *fam* [invectiver] ▸ **incendier qqn** to give sb hell.

incertain, e [ɛ̃sɛʀtɛ̃, ɛn] adj **1.** [peu sûr - personne] uncertain, unsure ▸ **être incertain de qqch** to be uncertain ou unsure of sthg **2.** [indéterminé - durée, date, quantité] uncertain, undetermined ; [- fait] uncertain, doubtful **3.** [aléatoire - gén] uncertain ; [- temps] unsettled.

incertitude [ɛ̃sɛʀtityd] nf [doute, précarité] uncertainty ▸ **nous sommes dans l'incertitude** we're uncertain, we're not sure / *il est seul face à ses incertitudes* he's left alone with his doubts.

incessamment [ɛ̃sesamɑ̃] adv shortly, soon ▸ **il doit arriver incessamment** he'll be here any minute now.

incessant, e [ɛ̃sesɑ̃, ɑ̃t] adj [effort] ceaseless, continual ; [bruit, bavardage] incessant, ceaseless, continual ; [douleur, pluie] unremitting, constant.

inceste [ɛ̃sɛst] nm incest.

incestueux, euse [ɛ̃sɛstɥø, øz] adj **1.** [personne, relation] incestuous **2.** [né d'un inceste] ▸ **enfant incestueux** child born of an incestuous relationship.

inchangé, e [ɛ̃ʃɑ̃ʒe] adj unchanged, unaltered.

incidemment [ɛ̃sidamɑ̃] adv [accessoirement] incidentally, in passing ; [par hasard] by chance.

incidence [ɛ̃sidɑ̃s] nf [répercussion] effect, repercussion, impact ▸ **avoir une incidence sur** to affect.

incident [ɛ̃sidɑ̃] nm [événement] incident, event ; [accrochage] incident ▸ **sans incident** safely ▸ **incident diplomatique / de frontière** diplomatic / border incident ▸ **incident technique** technical hitch ou incident / *sa démission n'est qu'un incident de parcours* his resignation is only a minor incident ▸ **l'incident est clos** the matter is (now) closed.

incinérateur [ɛ̃sineʀatœʀ] nm incinerator.

incinération [ɛ̃sineʀasjɔ̃] nf [de chiffons, de papiers] incineration ; [de cadavres] cremation.

incinérer [18] [ɛ̃sineʀe] vt [linge, papier] to incinerate ; [cadavre] to cremate.

✍ In reformed spelling (see p. 16-18), this verb is conjugated like *semer : il incinèrera, elle incinèrerait.*

inciser [3] [ɛ̃size] vt MÉD to incise, to make an incision in ; [abcès] to lance.

incisif, ive [ɛ̃sizif, iv] adj [ironie, remarque, ton] cutting, incisive, biting ; [regard] piercing.

incision [ɛ̃sizjɔ̃] nf **1.** MÉD cut, incision *spéc* **2.** HORT notch, incision *spéc.*

incisive [ɛ̃siziv] ◆ f ⟶ **incisif.** ◆ nf incisor.

incitatif, ive [ɛ̃sitatif, iv] adj : *mesures incitatives* incentive measures.

incitation [ɛ̃sitasjɔ̃] nf [encouragement] incitement, encouragement / *c'est une incitation à la violence* it's incitement to ou it encourages violence ▸ **incitation fiscale** ÉCON tax incentive.

inciter [3] [ɛ̃site] vt [encourager] ▸ **inciter qqn à faire qqch** to prompt ou to encourage sb to do sthg ▸ **inciter qqn à qqch** : *cela vous incite à la réflexion / prudence* it makes you stop and think / makes you cautious.

incivilité [ɛ̃sivilite] nf **1.** [manque de courtoisie] rudeness, disrespect **2.** [insultes, vandalismes] antisocial behaviour 🇬🇧 ou behavior 🇺🇸.

incivisme [ɛ̃sivism] nm incivility.

inclassable [ɛ̃klasabl] adj unclassifiable.

inclinaison [ɛ̃klinɛzɔ̃] nf **1.** [d'un plan] incline, slant ; [d'un avion] tilt, tilting ; [d'un toit, des combles, d'un pignon] pitch, slope ; [d'un navire] list, listing **2.** [d'une partie du corps] ▸ **l'inclinaison de la tête** the tilt of the head.

inclination [ɛ̃klinasjɔ̃] nf **1.** [tendance] inclination, tendency ; [goût] inclination, liking / *suivre son inclination* to follow one's (natural) inclination **2.** *litt* [attirance] ▸ **avoir de l'inclination pour qqn** to have a liking for sb.

incliné, e [ɛ̃kline] adj [en pente] sloping ; [penché - mur] leaning ; [- dossier, siège] reclining.

incliner [3] [ɛ̃kline] vt [courber] to bend ▸ **incliner la tête** ou **le front a)** to bow ou to incline *litt* one's head **b)** [pour acquiescer ou saluer] to nod (one's head) ; [pencher - dossier, siège] to tilt. ✧ **incliner à** v + prép to tend to ou towards, to incline towards / *j'incline à penser qu'elle a tort* I tend ou I'm inclined to think she's wrong. ✧ **s'incliner** vpi **1.** [être penché - mur] to lean (over) ; [- toit, route] to slope ; [- avion] to tilt, to bank ; [- navire] to list ; [- siège] to tilt ; [se courber - personne] to bend forward ; [- personne qui salue] to bow ; [- cime d'arbre] to bend (over) **2.** *fig* [se soumettre] ▸ **s'incliner devant le talent** to bow before talent ▸ **s'incliner devant la supériorité de qqn** to yield to sb's superiority / *le Racing s'est incliné devant Toulon par 15 à 12* SPORT Racing Club lost ou went down to Toulon 15 to 12 **3.** [se recueillir] ▸ **s'incliner devant la dépouille mortelle de qqn** to pay one's last respects to sb.

inclure [96] [ɛ̃klyʀ] vt **1.** [ajouter] to include, to add, to insert **2.** [joindre] to enclose **3.** [comporter] to include.

inclus, e [ɛ̃kly, yz] adj **1.** [contenu] enclosed **2.** [compris] included / *du 1er au 12 juin inclus* from June 1st to June 12th inclusive, from June 1 through June 12 🇺🇸 ▸ **jusqu'au dimanche inclus** up to and including Sunday **3.** MATH : *l'ensemble X est inclus dans l'ensemble Z* the set X is included in the set Z ou is a subset of Z.

inclusion [ɛ̃klyzjɔ̃] nf [action] inclusion.

incognito [ɛ̃kɔɲito] ◆ adv incognito. ◆ nm incognito ▸ **garder l'incognito** to remain anonymous ou incognito.

incohérence [ɛ̃kɔeʀɑ̃s] nf **1.** [manque d'unité] inconsistency, incoherence **2.** [contradiction] inconsistency, contradiction, discrepancy.

incohérent, e [ɛ̃kɔeʀɑ̃, ɑ̃t] adj [confus, décousu] incoherent, inconsistent.

incollable [ɛ̃kɔlabl] adj **1.** CULIN ▸ **riz incollable** nonstick rice **2.** *fam* [connaisseur] unbeatable / *elle est incollable en géographie* you can't trip her up in geography.

incolore [ɛ̃kɔlɔʀ] adj [transparent - liquide] colourless 🇬🇧, colorless 🇺🇸 ; [- vernis, verre] clear ; [- cirage] neutral.

incomber [3] [ɛ̃kɔ̃be] ◆ **incomber à** v + prép [revenir à] : *à qui ce droit incombe la responsabilité ?* who is responsible for it? ▸ **cette tâche vous incombe** this task is your responsibility ; *(tournure impersonnelle)* : *il vous incombe de la recevoir* it's your duty ou it's incumbent *sout* upon you to see her.

incombustible [ɛ̃kɔ̃bystibl] adj non-combustible.

incommensurable [ɛ̃kɔmɑ̃syʀabl] adj [énorme] immeasurable.

incommodant, e [ɛ̃kɔmɔdɑ̃, ɑ̃t] adj [chaleur] unpleasant, uncomfortable ; [bruit] irritating, irksome ; [odeur] offensive, nauseating.

incommode [ɛ̃kɔmɔd] adj [inconfortable - position] uncomfortable, awkward ; [- fauteuil] uncomfortable.

incommoder [3] [ɛ̃kɔmɔde] vt to bother / *la chaleur commence à m'incommoder* the heat is beginning to bother me ou to make me feel uncomfortable.

incomparable [ɛ̃kɔ̃paʀabl] adj **1.** [très différent] not comparable, unique, singular **2.** [inégalable] incomparable, matchless, peerless.

incompatibilité [ɛ̃kɔ̃patibilite] nf **1.** [opposition] incompatibility ▶ **incompatibilité d'humeur** mutual incompatibility **2.** BOT, MÉD & PHARM incompatibility.

incompatible [ɛ̃kɔ̃patibl] adj incompatible.

incompétence [ɛ̃kɔ̃petɑ̃s] nf **1.** [incapacité] incompetence **2.** [ignorance] ignorance, lack of knowledge.

incompétent, e [ɛ̃kɔ̃petɑ̃, ɑ̃t] ◆ adj **1.** [incapable] incompetent, inefficient **2.** [ignorant] ignorant. ◆ nm, f incompetent.

incomplet, ète [ɛ̃kɔ̃plɛ, ɛt] adj [fragmentaire] incomplete ; [inachevé] unfinished.

incompréhensible [ɛ̃kɔ̃pʀeɑ̃sibl] adj incomprehensible, impossible to understand.

incompréhensif, ive [ɛ̃kɔ̃pʀeɑ̃sif, iv] adj unsympathetic, unfeeling.

incompréhension [ɛ̃kɔ̃pʀeɑ̃sjɔ̃] nf lack of understanding ou comprehension / *leur incompréhension était totale* they found it totally impossible to understand.

incompressible [ɛ̃kɔ̃pʀesibl] adj **1.** [dépenses] which cannot be reduced **2.** DR ▶ **peine incompressible** irreducible sentence.

incompris, e [ɛ̃kɔ̃pʀi, iz] adj [méconnu] misunderstood.

inconcevable [ɛ̃kɔ̃svabl] adj inconceivable, unthinkable, unimaginable.

inconciliable [ɛ̃kɔ̃siljabl] adj [incompatible] incompatible, irreconcilable.

inconditionnel, elle [ɛ̃kɔ̃disjɔnɛl] ◆ adj [appui] unconditional, unreserved, wholehearted ; [reddition] unconditional. ◆ nm, f ▶ **un inconditionnel de** a fan of / *pour les inconditionnels de l'informatique* for computer buffs ou enthusiasts.

inconfort [ɛ̃kɔ̃fɔʀ] nm [d'une maison] lack of comfort ; [d'une posture] discomfort ; [d'une situation] awkwardness.

inconfortable [ɛ̃kɔ̃fɔʀtabl] adj **1.** [maison, siège] uncomfortable **2.** [situation, posture] uncomfortable, awkward.

incongru, e [ɛ̃kɔ̃gʀy] adj [remarque, réponse] incongruous, out of place ; [bruit] unseemly, rude ; [personne] uncouth.

incongruité [ɛ̃kɔ̃gʀɥite] nf **1.** [caractère incongru] incongruity, incongruousness **2.** [parole] unseemly remark.

inconnu, e [ɛ̃kɔny] ◆ adj **1.** [personne - dont on ignore l'existence] unknown ; [- dont on ignore l'identité] ou '**inconnu à cette adresse**' 'not known at this address' **2.** [destination] unknown **3.** [étranger] unknown / *ce visage ne m'est pas inconnu* I've seen that face before **4.** [sans notoriété] unknown. ◆ nm, f [étranger] unknown person, stranger. ◆ **inconnu** nm ▶ **l'inconnu** the unknown. ◆ **inconnue** nf **1.** [élément ignoré] unknown quantity ou factor **2.** MATH unknown.

inconsciemment [ɛ̃kɔ̃sjamɑ̃] adv [machinalement] unconsciously, unwittingly ; [dans l'inconscient] unconsciously.

inconscience [ɛ̃kɔ̃sjɑ̃s] nf **1.** [insouciance] recklessness, thoughtlessness ; [folie] madness, craziness **2.** [perte de connaissance] unconsciousness.

inconscient, e [ɛ̃kɔ̃sjɑ̃, ɑ̃t] ◆ adj **1.** ▶ **être inconscient de qqch** [ne pas s'en rendre compte] to be unaware of sthg **2.** [insouciant] reckless, rash ; [irresponsable] thoughtless, careless **3.** [automatique] mechanical, unconscious ; PSYCHOL unconscious **4.** [évanoui] unconscious. ◆ nm, f reckless ou thoughtless ou crazy person. ◆ **inconscient** nm PSYCHOL ▶ **l'inconscient** the unconscious ▶ **l'inconscient collectif** the collective unconscious.

inconséquent, e [ɛ̃kɔ̃sekɑ̃, ɑ̃t] adj [incohérent] incoherent, inconsistent ; [imprudent] thoughtless, unthinking, reckless.

inconsidéré, e [ɛ̃kɔ̃sideʀe] adj thoughtless, rash, foolhardy.

inconsistant, e [ɛ̃kɔ̃sistɑ̃, ɑ̃t] adj [roman, argument] flimsy, weak, shallow ; [personne, caractère] shallow, superficial, indecisive.

⚠ **Inconsistent** signifie « incohérent », « inégal » et non inconsistant.

inconsolable [ɛ̃kɔ̃sɔlabl] adj inconsolable.

inconstance [ɛ̃kɔ̃stɑ̃s] nf [infidélité, variabilité] inconstancy, fickleness.

inconstant, e [ɛ̃kɔ̃stɑ̃, ɑ̃t] adj [infidèle, d'humeur changeante] inconstant, fickle.

incontestable [ɛ̃kɔ̃tɛstabl] adj incontestable, indisputable, undeniable.

incontestablement [ɛ̃kɔ̃tɛstabləmɑ̃] adv indisputably, undeniably, beyond any shadow of (a) doubt.

incontesté, e [ɛ̃kɔ̃tɛste] adj uncontested, undisputed.

incontinence [ɛ̃kɔ̃tinɑ̃s] nf MÉD incontinence.

incontinent, e [ɛ̃kɔ̃tinɑ̃, ɑ̃t] adj MÉD incontinent.

incontournable [ɛ̃kɔ̃tuʀnabl] adj : *c'est un problème incontournable* this problem can't be ignored / *son œuvre est incontournable* her work cannot be overlooked.

incontrôlable [ɛ̃kɔ̃tʀolabl] adj [sentiment, colère] uncontrollable, ungovernable, wild ; [personne] out of control.

inconvenance [ɛ̃kɔ̃vnɑ̃s] nf **1.** [caractère] impropriety, indecency **2.** [parole] impropriety, rude remark ; [acte] impropriety, rude gesture.

inconvenant, e [ɛ̃kɔ̃vnɑ̃, ɑ̃t] adj [déplacé] improper, indecorous, unseemly ; [indécent] indecent, improper.

inconvénient [ɛ̃kɔ̃venjɑ̃] nm [désagrément] disadvantage, drawback, inconvenience ; [danger] risk ▶ **y voyez-vous un inconvénient ?** **a)** [désagrément] can you see any difficulties ou drawbacks in this? **b)** [objection] do you have any objection to this?, do you mind?

incorporation [ɛ̃kɔʀpɔʀasjɔ̃] nf **1.** MIL recruitment, conscription 🇬🇧, induction 🇺🇸 **2.** [d'un produit] blending, incorporating, mixing ; [d'un territoire] incorporation.

incorporé, e [ɛ̃kɔʀpɔʀe] adj built-in, integrated.

incorporer [3] [ɛ̃kɔʀpɔʀe] vt **1.** [mêler] to blend, to mix / *incorporez le sucre peu à peu* gradually mix in the sugar **2.** [intégrer] to incorporate, to integrate.

incorrect, e [ɛ̃kɔʀɛkt] adj **1.** [erroné] incorrect, wrong ▶ **l'emploi incorrect d'un mot** the improper use of a word **2.** [indécent] improper, impolite, indecent **3.** [impoli] rude, discourteous, impolite.

incorrection [ɛ̃kɔʀɛksjɔ̃] nf **1.** [propos] impropriety, improper remark ; [acte] improper act **2.** [emploi fautif] impropriety.

incorrigible [ɛ̃kɔʀiʒibl] adj **1.** [personne] incorrigible / *c'est un incorrigible paresseux* he's incorrigibly lazy **2.** [défaut] incorrigible.

incorruptible [ɛ̃kɔʀyptibl] ◆ adj [honnête] incorruptible. ◆ nmf incorruptible.

incrédule [ɛ̃kʀedyl] adj [sceptique] incredulous, disbelieving, sceptical UK, skeptical US / *d'un air incrédule* incredulously, in disbelief.

incrédulité [ɛ̃kʀedylite] nf [doute] incredulity, scepticism UK, skepticism US, disbelief, unbelief.

increvable [ɛ̃kʀəvabl] adj **1.** [pneu, ballon] punctureproof **2.** *fam* [personne] tireless / *cette voiture est increvable* this car will last for ever.

incriminer [3] [ɛ̃kʀimine] vt [rejeter la faute sur] to put the blame on, to incriminate.

incroyable [ɛ̃kʀwajabl] adj **1.** [peu vraisemblable] incredible, unbelievable **2.** [étonnant] incredible, amazing / *d'une bêtise incroyable* incredibly stupid.

incroyablement [ɛ̃kʀwajabləmɑ̃] adv incredibly, unbelievably, amazingly.

incroyant, e [ɛ̃kʀwajɑ̃, ɑ̃t] nm, f unbeliever.

incrustation [ɛ̃kʀystasjɔ̃] nf **1.** [décoration] inlay ; [procédé] inlaying **2.** TV (image) inlay, cut-in.

incruste [ɛ̃kʀyst] nf ▸ **taper l'incruste** *fam* to make o.s. at home / *il faut toujours qu'elle tape l'incruste quand je suis avec mes amis* she's impossible to get rid of when I'm with my friends.

incruster [3] [ɛ̃kʀyste] vt **1.** [orner] to inlay ▸ **incruster qqch de** to inlay sthg with **2.** CONSTR [pierre] to insert. ⬦ **s'incruster** vpi **1.** [se couvrir de calcaire] to become incrusted, to become covered in scale, to fur up **2.** *fam* [personne] : *ne t'incruste pas* don't stick around too long.

incubateur [ɛ̃kybatœʀ] nm incubator.

incubation [ɛ̃kybasjɔ̃] nf **1.** [d'œufs] incubation **2.** [d'une maladie] incubation / *l'incubation dure trois jours* the incubation period is three days.

inculpation [ɛ̃kylpasjɔ̃] nf indictment, charge / *être sous le coup d'une inculpation (pour)* to be indicted (for) ou on a charge (of).

inculper [3] [ɛ̃kylpe] vt to charge / *inculpé de meurtre* charged with murder.

inculquer [3] [ɛ̃kylke] vt to inculcate ▸ **inculquer qqch à qqn** to inculcate sthg in sb, to instil UK ou instill US sthg in sb.

inculte [ɛ̃kylt] adj **1.** [campagne, pays] uncultivated **2.** [esprit, intelligence, personne] uneducated, uncultured, uncultivated.

incurable [ɛ̃kyʀabl] adj **1.** MÉD incurable **2.** [incorrigible - personne, défaut] incurable, inveterate.

incursion [ɛ̃kyʀsjɔ̃] nf **1.** [exploration] foray, incursion **2.** MIL foray, raid.

incurver [3] [ɛ̃kyʀve] vt to curve (inwards), to make into a curve. ⬦ **s'incurver** vpi [trajectoire] to curve (inwards ou in), to bend.

Inde [ɛ̃d] npr f ▸ **l'Inde** India.

indécelable [ɛ̃deslabl] adj undetectable.

indécence [ɛ̃desɑ̃s] nf **1.** [manque de pudeur] indecency **2.** [propos, acte] indecence, impropriety.

indécent, e [ɛ̃desɑ̃, ɑ̃t] adj **1.** [honteux] indecent / *c'est un gaspillage presque indécent* the waste is almost obscene **2.** [licencieux] indecent, obscene.

indéchiffrable [ɛ̃deʃifʀabl] adj **1.** [code] undecipherable, indecipherable **2.** [écriture] illegible, unreadable **3.** [visage, mystère, pensée] inscrutable, impenetrable.

indécis, e [ɛ̃desi, iz] ◆ adj **1.** [flou] vague, indistinct **2.** [hésitant] undecided, unsure, uncertain ; [irrésolu] indecisive, irresolute / *je suis indécis (sur la solution à choisir)*

I'm undecided (as to the best solution), I can't make up my mind (which solution is the best). ◆ nm, f indecisive person ; [électeur] floating voter, don't-know.

indécision [ɛ̃desizjɔ̃] nf [caractère irrésolu] indecisiveness ; [hésitation] indecision.

indécrottable [ɛ̃dekʀɔtabl] adj *fam* hopeless / *c'est un indécrottable imbécile !* he's hopelessly stupid!

indéfendable [ɛ̃defɑ̃dabl] adj **1.** [condamnable - personne, comportement] indefensible **2.** [insoutenable - théorie, opinion] indefensible, untenable.

indéfini, e [ɛ̃defini] adj **1.** [sans limites] indefinite, unlimited **2.** [confus] ill-defined, vague **3.** LING indefinite.

indéfiniment [ɛ̃definimɑ̃] adv indefinitely, for ever.

indéfinissable [ɛ̃definisabl] adj indefinable.

indélébile [ɛ̃delebil] adj **1.** [ineffaçable - encre] indelible, permanent ; [- tache] indelible **2.** [indestructible - souvenir] indelible.

indélicat, e [ɛ̃delika, at] adj **1.** [grossier] coarse, indelicate, rude **2.** [véreux] dishonest, unscrupulous.

indemne [ɛ̃dɛmn] adj **1.** [physiquement] unhurt, unharmed **2.** [moralement] unscathed.

indemnisation [ɛ̃dɛmnizasjɔ̃] nf **1.** [argent] compensation, indemnity **2.** [procédé] compensating.

indemniser [3] [ɛ̃dɛmnize] vt **1.** [après un sinistre] to compensate, to indemnify ▸ **se faire indemniser** to receive compensation **2.** [après une dépense] : *être indemnisé de ses frais* to have one's expenses paid for ou reimbursed.

indemnité [ɛ̃dɛmnite] nf **1.** [après un sinistre] compensation ; [dommages et intérêts] damages **2.** [allocation] allowance ▸ **indemnité de chômage** unemployment benefit ▸ **indemnité journalière** sickness ou maternity benefit ▸ **indemnité de licenciement** redundancy payment UK, severance pay ▸ **indemnité parlementaire** ≃ MP's salary UK ▸ **indemnité de rupture** severance pay ▸ **indemnité de vie chère** cost of living allowance.

indémodable [ɛ̃demɔdabl] adj perenially fashionable.

indéniable [ɛ̃denjabl] adj undeniable.

indéniablement [ɛ̃denjabləmɑ̃] adv undeniably.

indépendamment [ɛ̃depɑ̃damɑ̃] adv **1.** [séparément] independently **2.** ▸ **indépendamment de** [outre, mis à part] apart from.

indépendance [ɛ̃depɑ̃dɑ̃s] nf [d'un pays, d'une personne] independence ▸ **prendre son indépendance** to assume one's independence.

indépendant, e [ɛ̃depɑ̃dɑ̃, ɑ̃t] ◆ adj **1.** [gén & POL] independent ▸ **pour des raisons indépendantes de notre volonté** for reasons beyond our control **2.** [distinct] : *ces deux problèmes sont indépendants l'un de l'autre* these two problems are separate ou distinct from each other ▸ **une chambre indépendante** a self-contained room **3.** LING & MATH independent. ◆ nm, f POL independent. ⬦ **en indépendant** loc adv ▸ **travailler en indépendant** to work on a freelance basis.

indépendantiste [ɛ̃depɑ̃dɑ̃tist] adj ▸ **mouvement indépendantiste** independence ou separatist movement.

indéracinable [ɛ̃deʀasinabl] adj [préjugé, habitude] entrenched, ineradicable *sout*.

indescriptible [ɛ̃dɛskʀiptibl] adj indescribable.

indésirable [ɛ̃deziʀabl] ◆ adj undesirable, unwanted. ◆ nmf undesirable.

indestructible [ɛ̃dɛstʀyktibl] adj [bâtiment, canon] indestructible, built to last ; [amour, lien] indestructible.

indéterminé, e [ɛ̃detɛʀmine] adj [non défini] indeterminate, unspecified / *à une date indéterminée* at an unspecified date / *l'origine du mot est indéterminée* the origin of the word is uncertain ou not known.

index [ɛ̃dɛks] nm **1.** [doigt] index finger, forefinger **2.** [liste] index **3.** ▸ **mettre qqch à l'index** to blacklist sthg.

indexation [ɛ̃dɛksasjɔ̃] nf indexation, indexing.

indexer [4] [ɛ̃dɛkse] vt **1.** [gén & ÉCON] to index / *indexer les salaires sur le coût de la vie* to index salaries to the cost of living **2.** [ouvrage, mot] to index **3.** INFORM to index.

indicateur, trice [ɛ̃dikatœʀ, tʀis] nm, f [informateur] (police) informer ou spy. ❖ **indicateur** nm **1.** [plan, liste] ▸ **indicateur des chemins de fer** railway 🇬🇧 ou railroad 🇺🇸 timetable **2.** [appareil] indicator, gauge **3.** [indice] indicator, pointer ▸ **indicateur économique** economic indicator.

indicatif, ive [ɛ̃dikatif, iv] adj [état, signe] indicative ; GRAM [mode] indicative. ❖ **indicatif** nm **1.** GRAM indicative **2.** RADIO & TV theme ou signature tune **3.** TÉLÉC [de zone] (dialling) code ▸ **indicatif du pays** international dialling code.

indication [ɛ̃dikasjɔ̃] nf **1.** [recommandation] instruction / *les indications du mode d'emploi* the directions for use **2.** [information, renseignement] information (U), piece of information **3.** [signe] sign, indication **4.** MÉD & PHARM ▸ **indication thérapeutique** indication **5.** COMM ▸ **indication d'origine** label of origin.

indice [ɛ̃dis] nm **1.** [symptôme - d'un changement, d'un phénomène] indication, sign ; [- d'une maladie] sign, symptom **2.** [d'une enquête policière] clue ; [d'une énigme] clue, hint **3.** ÉCON, OPT & PHYS index ; BOURSE index, average ▸ **indice du coût de la vie** cost of living index ▸ **indice de pollution (atmosphérique)** air quality index ▸ **indice des prix à la consommation** consumer price index **4.** RADIO & TV ▸ **l'indice d'écoute** the audience rating, the ratings **5.** MATH index.

indicible [ɛ̃disibl] adj indescribable, unutterable *sout.*

indien, enne [ɛ̃djɛ̃, ɛn] adj Indian. ❖ **Indien, enne** nm, f **1.** [de l'Inde] Indian **2.** [amérindien] ▸ **indien (d'Amérique)** American Indian, Native American.

indifféremment [ɛ̃difeʀamɑ̃] adv **1.** [aussi bien] : *elle joue indifféremment de la main droite ou de la main gauche* she plays equally well with her right or left hand **2.** [sans discrimination] indiscriminately.

indifférence [ɛ̃difeʀɑ̃s] nf [détachement - envers une situation, un sujet] indifference, lack of interest ; [- envers qqn] indifference / *son roman est paru dans la plus grande indifférence* the publication of his novel went completely unnoticed.

indifférent, e [ɛ̃difeʀɑ̃, ɑ̃t] adj **1.** [insensible, détaché] indifferent / *elle ne le laisse pas indifférent* he's not blind ou indifferent to her charms / *être indifférent à la politique* to be indifferent towards politics **2.** [insignifiant] indifferent, uninteresting, of no interest ▸ **ça m'est indifférent** it's (all) the same to me ou I don't care either way / *la suite des événements m'est indifférente* what happens next is of no concern ou interest to me.

indifférer [18] [ɛ̃difeʀe] ❖ **indifférer à** v + prép **1.** [n'inspirer aucun intérêt à] : *il m'indiffère complètement* I'm totally indifferent to him, I couldn't care less about him **2.** [être égal à] to be of no importance to ▸ **ça m'indiffère** I don't mind, it's all the same to me.

✐ In reformed spelling (see p. 16-18), this verb is conjugated like *semer* : *cela l'indiffère, cela l'indiffèrerait.*

indigence [ɛ̃diʒɑ̃s] nf **1.** [matérielle] poverty, indigence *sout* / *vivre dans l'indigence* to be destitute **2.** [intellectuelle] paucity, poverty.

indigène [ɛ̃diʒɛn] ❖ adj **1.** [d'avant la colonisation - droits, pratique] native, indigenous **2.** [autochtone - popu-

lation] native, indigenous **3.** BOT & ZOOL indigenous, native. ❖ nmf **1.** [autochtone] native **2.** BOT & ZOOL indigen, indigene, native.

indigent, e [ɛ̃diʒɑ̃, ɑ̃t] ❖ adj **1.** [pauvre] destitute, poor, indigent *sout* **2.** [insuffisant] poor. ❖ nm, f pauper ▸ **les indigents** the destitute, the poor.

indigeste [ɛ̃diʒɛst] adj **1.** [nourriture] indigestible, heavy **2.** [livre, compte-rendu] heavy-going.

indigestion [ɛ̃diʒɛstjɔ̃] nf **1.** MÉD indigestion (U) **2.** fig ▸ **avoir une indigestion de** to get a surfeit ou an overdose of.

indignation [ɛ̃diɲasjɔ̃] nf indignation / *protester avec indignation* to protest indignantly.

indigne [ɛ̃diɲ] adj **1.** ▸ **indigne de** [honneur, confiance] unworthy of / *un mensonge / une corvée indigne de lui* a lie / chore unworthy of him **2.** [choquant - action, propos] disgraceful, outrageous, shameful ; [méprisable - personne] unworthy ▸ **c'est une mère indigne** she's not fit to be a mother.

indigné, e [ɛ̃diɲe] adj indignant, shocked, outraged.

indigner [3] [ɛ̃diɲe] vt to make indignant, to incense, to gall. ❖ **s'indigner** vpi [se révolter] to be indignant ▸ **s'indigner de** to be indignant about.

indigo [ɛ̃digo] adj inv indigo (blue).

indiqué, e [ɛ̃dike] adj **1.** [recommandé - conduite] advisable **2.** [approprié - personne, objet] : *tu es tout indiqué pour le rôle* you're exactly the right person ou the obvious choice for the part ▸ **ce médicament est / n'est pas indiqué dans ce cas** this drug is appropriate / inappropriate in this case.

indiquer [3] [ɛ̃dike] vt **1.** [montrer d'un geste - chose, personne, lieu] to show, to point out *(sép)* **2.** [musée, autoroute, plage] to show the way to ; [chemin] to indicate, to show / *pouvez-vous m'indiquer (le chemin de) la gare ?* could you show me the way to ou direct me to the station? **3.** [suj : carte, enseigne, pancarte, statistiques] to show, to say, to indicate ; [suj : flèche, graphique] to show ; [suj : horaire] to show, to say, to give ; [suj : dictionnaire] to say, to give ▸ **l'horloge indique 6 h** the clock says ou shows that it's 6 o'clock **4.** [noter - date, prix] to note ou to write (down) ; [- repère] to mark, to draw / *ce n'est pas indiqué dans le contrat* it's not written ou mentioned in the contract **5.** [conseiller - ouvrage, professionnel, restaurant] to suggest, to recommend ; [- traitement] to prescribe, to give **6.** [dire - marche à suivre, heure] to tell ; [fixer - lieu de rendez-vous, jour] to give, to name **7.** [être le signe de - phénomène] to point to *(insép)*, to indicate ; [- crainte, joie] to show, to betray / *tout indique que nous allons vers une crise* everything suggests that we are heading towards a crisis.

indirect, e [ɛ̃diʀɛkt] adj **1.** [approche - indirect, roundabout ; [influence] indirect / *elle m'a fait des reproches indirects* she told me off in a roundabout way **2.** GRAM ▸ **complément indirect a)** [d'un verbe transitif] indirect complement **b)** [d'un verbe intransitif] prepositional complement.

indirectement [ɛ̃diʀɛktəmɑ̃] adv indirectly / *je l'ai su indirectement* I heard about it indirectly ou in a roundabout way.

indiscipline [ɛ̃disiplin] nf [dans un groupe] lack of discipline, indiscipline ; [d'un enfant] disobedience ; [d'un soldat] insubordination.

indiscipliné, e [ɛ̃disipline] adj [dans un groupe] undisciplined, unruly ; [enfant] unruly, disobedient ; [soldat] undisciplined, insubordinate.

indiscret, ète [ɛ̃diskʀe, ɛt] adj **1.** [curieux - personne] inquisitive ; [- demande, question] indiscreet ; [- regard] inquisitive, prying / *sans (vouloir) être indiscret, combien est-ce* *que ça vous a coûté ?* could I possibly ask you how much you paid for it? ▶ **loin des oreilles indiscrètes** far from ou out of reach of eavesdroppers **2.** [révélateur - propos, geste] indiscreet, telltale ; [- personne] indiscreet, garrulous.

indiscrétion [ɛ̃diskʀesjɔ̃] nf **1.** [d'une personne] inquisitiveness, curiosity ; [d'une question] indiscreetness, tactlessness ▶ **pardonnez mon indiscrétion** forgive me for asking / *sans indiscrétion, avez-vous des enfants ?* do you mind if I ask you if you've got any children? **2.** [révélation] indiscretion / *commettre une indiscrétion* to commit an indiscretion, to say something one shouldn't.

indiscutable [ɛ̃diskytabl] adj indisputable, unquestionable.

indiscutablement [ɛ̃diskytabləmɑ̃] adv indisputably, unquestionably.

indiscuté, e [ɛ̃diskyte] adj undisputed.

indispensable [ɛ̃dispɑ̃sabl] adj [fournitures, machine] essential, indispensable ; [mesures] essential, vital, indispensable ; [précautions] essential, required, necessary ; [personne] indispensable / *tes réflexions n'étaient pas indispensables!* we could have done without your remarks! ▶ **il est indispensable de / que...** it's essential to / that... / *son fils lui est indispensable* he can't do without his son.

indisponible [ɛ̃dispɔnibl] adj [marchandise, personne] not available, unavailable.

indisposé, e [ɛ̃dispoze] adj [légèrement souffrant] unwell, indisposed *sout.*

indisposer [3] [ɛ̃dispoze] vt **1.** [irriter] to annoy **2.** [rendre malade] to upset, to make (slightly) ill, to indispose *sout.*

indisposition [ɛ̃dispozisjɔ̃] nf [malaise] discomfort, ailment, indisposition *sout /* *j'ai eu une indisposition passagère* I felt slightly off colour for a little while.

indissociable [ɛ̃disɔsjabl] adj indissociable, inseparable.

indissoluble [ɛ̃disɔlybl] adj [lien, union] indissoluble.

indistinct, e [ɛ̃distɛ̃(kt), ɛ̃kt] adj [chuchotement] indistinct, faint ; [forme] indistinct, unclear, vague / *prononcer des paroles indistinctes* to mumble inaudibly.

indistinctement [ɛ̃distɛ̃ktəmɑ̃] adv **1.** [confusément - parler] indistinctly, unclearly ; [- se souvenir] indistinctly, vaguely **2.** [sans distinction] indiscriminately / *recruter indistinctement hommes et femmes* to recruit people regardless of sex.

individu [ɛ̃dividy] nm **1.** [quidam] individual, person / *un drôle d'individu* a strange character **2.** BIOL, BOT & LOGIQUE individual.

individualiser [3] [ɛ̃dividɥalize] vt [système] to adapt to individual needs, to tailor.

individualiste [ɛ̃dividɥalist] ◆ adj individualistic. ◆ nmf individualist.

individuel, elle [ɛ̃dividɥɛl] adj **1.** [personnel] individual, personal **2.** [particulier] individual, private ▶ **chambre individuelle** (private) single room **3.** SPORT ▶ **épreuve individuelle** individual event.

individuellement [ɛ̃dividɥɛlmɑ̃] adv [séparément] individually, separately, one by one.

indivisible [ɛ̃divizibl] adj indivisible.

Indochine [ɛ̃dɔʃin] npr f ▶ **(l')Indochine** Indochina.

indo-européen, enne [ɛ̃dɔœʀɔpeɛ̃, ɛn] *(mpl* **indo-européens,** *fpl* **indo-européennes)** adj Indo-European.

indolence [ɛ̃dɔlɑ̃s] nf [mollesse - dans le travail] indolence, apathy, lethargy ; [- dans l'attitude] indolence, languidness.

indolent, e [ɛ̃dɔlɑ̃, ɑ̃t] adj **1.** [apathique] indolent, apathetic, lethargic **2.** [languissant] indolent, languid.

indolore [ɛ̃dɔlɔʀ] adj painless.

indomptable [ɛ̃dɔ̃tabl] adj **1.** [qu'on ne peut dompter] untamable, untameable **2.** *fig* [courage, volonté] indomitable, invincible.

Indonésie [ɛ̃dɔnezi] npr f ▶ **(l')Indonésie** Indonesia.

indonésien, enne [ɛ̃dɔnezjɛ̃, ɛn] adj Indonesian. ❖ **Indonésien, enne** nm, f Indonesian. ❖ **indonésien** nm LING Indonesian.

indu, e [ɛ̃dy] adj **1.** [inopportun] undue, excessive **2.** DR [non fondé - réclamation] unjustified, unfounded.

indubitable [ɛ̃dybitabl] adj undoubted, indubitable, undisputed ▶ **c'est indubitable** it's beyond doubt ou dispute.

indubitablement [ɛ̃dybitabləmɑ̃] adv undoubtedly, indubitably.

induction [ɛ̃dyksjɔ̃] nf PHILOS & PHYS induction.

induire [98] [ɛ̃dɥiʀ] vt **1.** [inciter] ▶ **induire qqn en erreur** to mislead sb **2.** [avoir pour conséquence] to lead to.

induit, e [ɛ̃dɥi, it] adj [résultant] resulting.

indulgence [ɛ̃dylʒɑ̃s] nf [clémence] leniency, tolerance, indulgence *sout.* ❖ **sans indulgence** ◆ loc adj [traitement, critique] severe, harsh ; [regard] stern, merciless. ◆ loc adv [traiter, critiquer] severely, harshly ; [regarder] sternly, mercilessly.

indulgent, e [ɛ̃dylʒɑ̃, ɑ̃t] adj **1.** [qui pardonne] lenient, forgiving **2.** [sans sévérité - personne] indulgent, lenient ; [- verdict] lenient ▶ **sois indulgent avec elle** go easy on her.

indûment, indument* [ɛ̃dymɑ̃] adv unjustifiably, without due ou just cause.

industrialisation [ɛ̃dystʀijalizasjɔ̃] nf industrialization.

industrialisé, e [ɛ̃dystʀijalize] adj [pays] industrialized ▶ **nouveaux pays industrialisés** new industrialized countries ; [agriculture] industrial.

industrialiser [3] [ɛ̃dystʀijalize] vt [doter d'industries] to industrialize. ❖ **s'industrialiser** vpi [se doter d'industries] to industrialize, to become industrialized.

industrie [ɛ̃dystʀi] nf **1.** [secteur de production] industry ▶ **industrie aéronautique** aviation industry ▶ **industrie automobile** car 🇬🇧 ou automobile 🇺🇸 industry ▶ **industrie chimique** chemical industry ▶ **industrie cinématographique** film industry, movie industry 🇺🇸 ▶ **industrie légère** light industry ▶ **industrie lourde** heavy industry ▶ **industrie de luxe** luxury goods industry ▶ **industrie pharmaceutique** pharmaceutical ou drug industry ▶ **industrie de pointe** hightech industry ▶ **industrie du spectacle** entertainment business, show business **2.** [secteur commercial] industry, trade, business ▶ **l'industrie hôtelière** the hotel industry ou trade ou business / *l'industrie des loisirs* the leisure industry.

industriel, elle [ɛ̃dystʀijɛl] adj **1.** [procédé, secteur, zone, révolution, société] industrial ; [pays] industrial, industrialized **2.** [destiné à l'industrie - véhicule, équipement, rayonnage] industrial, heavy, heavy-duty **3.** [non artisanal] mass-produced, factory-made / *des crêpes industrielles* ready-made ou factory-made pancakes. ❖ **industriel** nm industrialist, manufacturer.

inébranlable [inebʀɑ̃labl] adj [ferme] steadfast, unshakeable, unwavering ▶ **elle a été inébranlable** there was no moving her, she was adamant.

inédit, e [inedi, it] adj **1.** [correspondance, auteur] (hitherto) unpublished / *ce film est inédit en France* this film has never been released in France **2.** [jamais vu] new, original.

ineffable [inefabl] adj **1.** [indicible] ineffable, indescribable **2.** [amusant] hilarious.

ineffaçable [inefasabl] adj [marque] indelible ; [souvenir, traumatisme] unforgettable, enduring.

inefficace [inefikas] adj [méthode, médicament] ineffective ; [personne] inefficient, ineffective.

inefficacité [inefikasite] nf [d'une méthode] inefficacy, ineffectiveness ; [d'une personne] inefficiency, ineffectiveness.

inégal, e, aux [inegal, o] adj **1.** [varié - longueurs, salaires] unequal, different ; [mal équilibré] uneven, unequal ▸ **le combat était inégal** the fight was one-sided **2.** [changeant - écrivain, élève, pouls] uneven, erratic ; [- humeur] changeable, uneven ▸ **la qualité est inégale** it varies in quality **3.** [rugueux] rough, uneven, bumpy.

inégalable [inegalabl] adj incomparable, matchless, peerless.

inégalé, e [inegale] adj unequalled 🇬🇧, unequaled 🇺🇸, unmatched, unrivalled.

inégalité [inegalite] nf **1.** [disparité] difference, disparity ∕ **l'inégalité des chances** the lack of equal opportunities ▸ **combattre les inégalités sociales** to fight social injustice **2.** [qualité variable - d'une surface] roughness, unevenness ; [- d'un travail, d'une œuvre] uneven quality, unevenness ; [- du caractère] changeability.

inélégant, e [inelegã, ãt] adj sout [indélicat] indelicate, inelegant ∕ **ce fut très inélégant de ta part** that was very indelicate of you.

inéligible [ineliʒibl] adj DR ineligible.

inéluctable [inelyktabl] adj inevitable, unavoidable, ineluctable litt.

inéluctablement [inelyktabləmã] adv inevitably, inescapably, unavoidably.

inénarrable [inenaRabl] adj hilarious.

inenvisageable [inãvizaʒabl] adj inconceivable, unthinkable.

inepte [inɛpt] adj [personne] inept, incompetent ; [réponse, raisonnement] inept, foolish ; [plan] inept, ill-considered.

ineptie [inɛpsi] nf **1.** [caractère d'absurdité] ineptitude, stupidity **2.** [acte, parole] piece of nonsense ∕ **dire des inepties** to talk nonsense.

inépuisable [inepҷizabl] adj **1.** [réserves] inexhaustible, unlimited ; [courage] endless, unlimited **2.** [bavard] inexhaustible ∕ **elle est inépuisable sur mes imperfections** once she gets going about my faults, there's no stopping her.

inerte [inɛRt] adj **1.** [léthargique] inert, apathetic, lethargic **2.** [semblant mort] inert, lifeless **3.** CHIM & PHYS inert.

inertie [inɛRsi] nf [passivité] lethargy, inertia, passivity.

inespéré, e [inɛspeRe] adj unhoped-for.

inesthétique [inɛstetik] adj unsightly, unattractive.

inestimable [inɛstimabl] adj **1.** [impossible à évaluer] incalculable, inestimable **2.** [précieux] inestimable, invaluable, priceless.

inévitable [inevitabl] adj [auquel on ne peut échapper] unavoidable, inevitable ▸ **c'était inévitable !** it was bound to happen ou inevitable!

inévitablement [inevitabləmã] adv inevitably, predictably.

inexact, e [inɛgza(kt), akt] adj [erroné] inexact, incorrect, inaccurate ∕ **il serait inexact de dire...** it would be wrong ou incorrect to say...

inexactitude [inɛgzaktityd] nf [d'un raisonnement] inaccuracy, imprecision ; [d'un récit] inaccuracy, inexactness ; [d'un calcul] inaccuracy, inexactitude.

inexcusable [inɛkskyzabl] adj [action] inexcusable, unforgivable ; [personne] unforgivable.

inexistant, e [inɛgzistã, ãt] adj [très insuffisant] nonexistent, inadequate ∕ **les structures de base sont inexistantes** the basic structures are lacking, there are hardly any basic structures.

inexorable [inɛgzɔRabl] adj [inévitable] inexorable, inevitable.

inexorablement [inɛgzɔRabləmã] adv [inévitablement] inexorably, inevitably.

inexpérience [inɛkspeRjãs] nf lack of experience.

inexpérimenté, e [inɛkspeRimãte] adj [sans expérience] inexperienced.

inexplicable [inɛksplikabl] ◆ adj [comportement] inexplicable ; [raison, crainte] inexplicable, unaccountable. ◆ nm ▸ **l'inexplicable** the inexplicable.

inexpliqué, e [inɛksplike] adj [décision] unexplained ; [phénomène] unexplained, unsolved ; [agissements, départ] unexplained, mysterious.

inexploré, e [inɛksplɔRe] adj unexplored.

inexpressif, ive [inɛkspResif, iv] adj [visage, regard] inexpressive, expressionless, blank.

inexprimable [inɛkspRimabl] adj inexpressible, ineffable, indescribable.

in extremis, in extrémis* [inɛkstRemis] loc adv [de justesse] at the last minute, in the nick of time, at the eleventh hour ▸ **réussir qqch in extremis** to (only) just manage to do sthg.

inextricable [inɛkstRikabl] adj inextricable.

infaillible [ɛ̃fajibl] adj **1.** [efficace à coup sûr] infallible **2.** [certain] infallible, reliable, guaranteed **3.** [qui ne peut se tromper] infallible.

infaisable [ɛ̃fəzabl] adj [choix] impossible.

infamant, e [ɛ̃famã, ãt] adj sout [déshonorant - acte, crime] heinous, infamous, abominable ∕ **tu peux réclamer ton argent, ce n'est pas infamant** you can go and ask for your money, there's no shame in that.

infâme [ɛ̃fam] adj **1.** [vil - crime] despicable, loathsome, heinous ; [- criminel] vile, despicable ; [- traître] despicable **2.** [répugnant - odeur, nourriture] revolting, vile, foul ; [- endroit] disgusting, revolting.

infamie [ɛ̃fami] nf sout **1.** [déshonneur] infamy, disgrace **2.** [caractère abject - d'une action, d'une personne] infamy, vileness **3.** [acte révoltant] infamy, loathsome deed **4.** [propos] piece of (vile) slander, smear.

infanterie [ɛ̃fãtRi] nf infantry.

infantile [ɛ̃fãtil] adj **1.** MÉD & PSYCHOL child (modif), infantile spéc **2.** péj [puéril] infantile, childish.

infantiliser [3] [ɛ̃fãtilize] vt to infantilize.

infarctus [ɛ̃faRktys] nm infarct ▸ **avoir un infarctus** to have a heart attack ou a coronary ▸ **infarctus du myocarde** myocardial infarction.

infatigable [ɛ̃fatigabl] adj [toujours dispos] tireless, untiring, indefatigable sout.

infect, e [ɛ̃fɛkt] adj [répugnant - repas] rotten, revolting, disgusting ; [- odeur] foul, rank, putrid.

infecter [4] [ɛ̃fɛkte] vt **1.** PHYSIOL to infect **2.** [rendre malsain] to contaminate, to pollute. ◆ **s'infecter** vpi to become infected, to go septic.

infectieux, euse [ɛ̃fɛksjø, øz] adj [maladie] infectious.

infection [ɛ̃fɛksjɔ̃] nf **1.** MÉD infection **2.** [puanteur] (foul) stench ∕ **c'est une infection, ce marché !** this market stinks (to high heaven)!

inférer [18] [ɛ̃feRe] vt sout to infer ∕ **que pouvons-nous en inférer ?** what can we infer ou gather from this?

 ✎ In reformed spelling (see p. 16-18), this verb is conjugated like **semer : il inférera, elle inférerait**.

inférieur, e [ɛ̃feRjœR] ◆ adj **1.** [du bas - étagères, membres] lower ; [- lèvre, mâchoire] lower, bottom (avant nom) ; [situé en dessous] lower down, below ∕ **c'est à l'étage inférieur** it's on the floor below ou on the next floor down

▸ **être inférieur à** to be lower than ou below **2.** [moins bon - niveau] lower ; [-esprit, espèce] inferior, lesser ; [-qualité] inferior, poorer ▸ **inférieur à** inferior to, poorer than / *en physique il est très inférieur à sa sœur* he's not nearly as good as his sister at physics **3.** [plus petit - chiffre, salaire] lower, smaller ; [- poids, vitesse] lower ; [- taille] smaller ▸ **inférieur à** a) [chiffre] lower ou smaller ou less than b) [rendement] lower than, inferior to / *des températures inférieures à 10 °C* temperatures below 10 °C ou lower than 10 °C **4.** [dans une hiérarchie - le plus bas] lower. ◆ nm, f [gén] inferior ; [subalterne] inferior, subordinate, underling *péj.*

infériorité [ɛ̃feʀjɔʀite] nf **1.** [inadéquation - en grandeur, en valeur] inferiority ; [- en effectif] (numerical) inferiority **2.** [handicap] weakness, inferiority, deficiency / *être en situation d'infériorité* to be in a weak position.

infernal, e, aux [ɛ̃fɛʀnal, o] adj **1.** *fam* [insupportable] infernal, hellish, diabolical / *cet enfant est infernal !* that child's a real terror! / *il mettent de la musique toute la nuit, c'est infernal* they've got music on all night, it's absolute hell **2.** *litt* [de l'enfer] infernal **3.** [diabolique - engrenage, logique] infernal, devilish, diabolical ▸ **cycle infernal** vicious circle.

infester [3] [ɛ̃fɛste] vt [suj : rats] to infest, to overrun ; [suj : pillards] to infest / *la région est infestée de sauterelles / moustiques* the area is infested with locusts / mosquitoes.

infichu, e [ɛ̃fiʃy] adj *fam* incapable / *il est infichu de répondre à la moindre question* he's incapable of answering the simplest question.

infidèle [ɛ̃fidɛl] ◆ adj **1.** [gén] disloyal, unfaithful ; [en amour] unfaithful, untrue *litt* ; [en amitié] disloyal **2.** [inexact - témoignage, texte] inaccurate, unreliable ; [- mémoire] unreliable. ◆ nmf RELIG infidel.

infidélité [ɛ̃fidelite] nf **1.** [inconstance] infidelity, unfaithfulness ; [aventure adultère] infidelity, affair ▸ **faire une infidélité à qqn** to be unfaithful to sb **2.** [déloyauté] disloyalty, unfaithfulness.

infiltration [ɛ̃filtʀasjɔ̃] nf **1.** [gén & PHYSIOL] infiltration / *il y a des infiltrations dans le plafond* there are leaks in the ceiling, water is leaking ou seeping through the ceiling **2.** [d'un agitateur] infiltration.

infiltrer [3] [ɛ̃filtʀe] vt [organisation, réseau] to infiltrate. ◆ **s'infiltrer** vpi [air, brouillard, eau] to seep ; [lumière] to filter in / *s'infiltrer dans un réseau d'espions* to infiltrate a spy network.

infime [ɛ̃fim] adj [quantité, proportion] infinitesimal, minute, tiny ; [détail] minor.

infini, e [ɛ̃fini] adj **1.** [étendue] infinite, vast, boundless ; [ressources] infinite, unlimited **2.** [extrême - générosité, patience, reconnaissance] infinite, boundless, limitless ; [- charme, douceur] infinite ; [- précautions] infinite, endless ; [- bonheur, plaisir] infinite, immeasurable ; [- difficulté, peine] immense, extreme ▸ **mettre un soin infini à faire qqch** to take infinite pains to do sthg **3.** [interminable] never-ending, interminable, endless. ◆ **infini** nm **1.** MATH, OPT & PHOT infinity **2.** PHILOS ▸ **l'infini** the infinite. ◆ **à l'infini** loc adv **1.** [discuter, reproduire] endlessly, ad infinitum ; [varier] infinitely ; [s'étendre] endlessly **2.** MATH to ou towards infinity.

infiniment [ɛ̃finimɑ̃] adv [extrêmement - désolé, reconnaissant] extremely, infinitely ; [- généreux] immensely, boundlessly ; [- agréable, douloureux] immensely, extremely ; [- long, grand] infinitely, immensely ▸ **je vous remercie infiniment** thank you so much ▸ **avec infiniment de patience / de précautions** with infinite patience / care.

infinité [ɛ̃finite] nf [très grand nombre] ▸ **une infinité de** an infinite number of / *on me posa une infinité de questions* I was asked endless ou a great many questions.

infinitésimal, e, aux [ɛ̃finitezimal, o] adj infinitesimal.

infinitif, ive [ɛ̃finitif, iv] adj infinitive. ◆ **infinitif** nm infinitive (mood).

infirme [ɛ̃fiʀm] ◆ adj disabled, crippled. ◆ nmf disabled person ▸ **les infirmes** the disabled.

infirmer [3] [ɛ̃fiʀme] vt **1.** [démentir] to invalidate, to contradict **2.** DR [arrêt] to revoke ; [jugement] to quash.

infirmerie [ɛ̃fiʀməʀi] nf [dans une école, une entreprise] sick bay ou room ; [dans une prison] infirmary ; [dans une caserne] infirmary, sick bay ; [sur un navire] sick bay.

infirmier, ère [ɛ̃fiʀmje, ɛʀ] nm, f male nurse (nurse) ▸ **infirmier** ou **infirmière en chef** charge nurse (nurse), head nurse US.

infirmité [ɛ̃fiʀmite] nf [invalidité] disability, handicap.

inflammable [ɛ̃flamabl] adj [combustible] inflammable, flammable.

inflammation [ɛ̃flamasjɔ̃] nf MÉD inflammation.

inflation [ɛ̃flasjɔ̃] nf ÉCON inflation.

inflationniste [ɛ̃flasjɔnist] adj [tendance] inflationary ; [politique] inflationist.

infléchir [32] [ɛ̃fleʃiʀ] vt *sout* [influer sur] to modify, to influence / *infléchir le cours des événements* to affect ou to influence the course of events. ◆ **s'infléchir** vpi *fig* [changer de but] to shift, to change course / *la politique du gouvernement s'infléchit dans le sens du protectionnisme* government policy is shifting ou veering towards protectionism.

inflexible [ɛ̃flɛksibl] adj **1.** [matériau] rigid, inflexible **2.** [personne] inflexible, rigid, unbending.

inflexion [ɛ̃flɛksjɔ̃] nf **1.** [modulation - de la voix] inflection, modulation **2.** [changement de direction] shift, change of course **3.** LING & MATH inflection **4.** [inclination] : *avec une gracieuse inflexion de la tête* with a graceful nod.

infliger [17] [ɛ̃fliʒe] vt ▸ **infliger une punition / une défaite / des souffrances / des pertes à qqn** to inflict a punishment / a defeat / sufferings / losses on sb ▸ **infliger une amende / corvée à qqn** to impose a fine / chore on sb.

influençable [ɛ̃flyɑ̃sabl] adj : *elle est beaucoup trop influençable* she's far too easily influenced ou swayed.

influence [ɛ̃flyɑ̃s] nf **1.** [marque, effet] influence / *cela n'a eu aucune influence sur ma décision* it didn't influence my decision at all, it had no bearing (at all) on my decision **2.** [emprise - d'une personne, d'une drogue, d'un sentiment] influence ▸ **avoir de l'influence sur qqn** to have influence over sb / *avoir une bonne influence sur* to be ou to have a good influence on ▸ **être sous l'influence de la boisson / drogue** to be under the influence of drink / drugs **3.** [poids social ou politique] influence ▸ **avoir de l'influence** to have influence, to be influential.

influencer [16] [ɛ̃flyɑ̃se] vt to influence / *ne te laisse pas influencer par la publicité* don't let advertising influence you, don't let yourself be influenced by advertising.

influent, e [ɛ̃flyɑ̃, ɑ̃t] adj influential.

influer [3] [ɛ̃flye] ◆ **influer sur** v + prép to have an influence on, to influence, to affect.

info [ɛ̃fo] nf *fam* info (U). ◆ **infos** nfpl *fam* ▸ **les infos** the news (U).

infobulle [ɛ̃fobyl] nf INFORM tooltip.

infogérance [ɛ̃foʒeʀɑ̃s] nf outsourcing.

infographie® [ɛ̃fogʀafi] nf computer graphics.

infographiste [ɛ̃fogʀafist] nmf computer graphics artist.

infondé, e [ɛ̃fɔ̃de] adj unfounded, groundless.

informateur, trice [ɛ̃fɔʀmatœʀ, tʀis] nm, f informer.

informaticien, enne [ɛ̃fɔʀmatisjɛ̃, ɛn] nm, f [dans une entreprise] data processor ; [à l'université] computer scientist.

information [ɛ̃fɔʀmasjɔ̃] nf **1.** [indication] piece of information ▸ **demander des informations sur** to ask (for information) about, to inquire about **2.** [diffusion de renseignements] information ▸ **réunion d'information** briefing session ▸ *pour ton information, sache que...* for your (own) information you should know that... **3.** PRESSE, RADIO & TV news item, piece of news / *voici une information de dernière minute* here is some last minute news ▸ **journal d'information** quality newspaper **4.** ▸ **traitement de l'information** data processing **5.** ▸ **information judiciaire** preliminary investigation ou inquiry. ❖ **informations** nfpl RADIO & TV [émission] ▸ **les informations** the news (bulletin) / *informations télévisées* / *radiodiffusées* television / radio news / *c'est passé aux informations* it was on the news.

> 📋 **Attention ! Le mot anglais information est indénombrable.** Il ne s'emploie jamais ni au pluriel ni avec l'article indéfini an :
> **Je recherche des informations sur l'histoire de cette église.** *I'm looking for* information *about the history of the church* ou *I'm looking for* some *information about the history of the church.*
> **Ces informations me seront très précieuses.** *This* information *will be extremely useful.*
> **Chaque information est payante.** *Each* piece / item *of* information *has to be paid for.*

informatique [ɛ̃fɔʀmatik] ◆ adj computer *(modif)* ▸ **un système informatique** a computer system. ◆ nf [science] computer science, information technology ; [traitement des données] data processing ▸ **faire de l'informatique** to work ou to be in computing.

informatisation [ɛ̃fɔʀmatizasjɔ̃] nf computerization.

informatiser [3] [ɛ̃fɔʀmatize] vt to computerize.

informe [ɛ̃fɔʀm] adj **1.** [qui n'a plus de forme - chaussure] shapeless, battered **2.** [sans contours nets] formless, shapeless.

informé, e [ɛ̃fɔʀme] adj well-informed, informed ▸ **nous sommes mal informés a)** [peu renseignés] we don't get enough information, we're not sufficiently informed **b)** [avec de fausses informations] we're being misinformed ▸ **se tenir informé de** to keep o.s. informed about ▸ **tenir qqn informé (de qqch)** to keep sb informed (of sthg).

informel, elle [ɛ̃fɔʀmɛl] adj **1.** [non officiel, décontracté] informal **2.** ART informal.

informer [3] [ɛ̃fɔʀme] vt **1.** [aviser] ▸ **informer qqn de** to inform ou to tell ou to advise *sout* sb of / *si le notaire téléphone, vous voudrez bien m'en informer* if the lawyer phones, will you please let me know ou inform me ▸ **informer qqn que** to inform ou to tell sb that **2.** [renseigner] to inform, to give information to. ❖ **s'informer** vpi ▸ **s'informer de** [droit, horaire, résultats] to inquire ou to ask about / *je vais m'informer sur la marche à suivre* I'm going to find out what the procedure is.

inforoute [ɛ̃fɔʀut] nf information superhighway.

infortune [ɛ̃fɔʀtyn] nf *litt* **1.** [événement] misfortune **2.** [malheur] misfortune / *dans son infortune, elle a au moins une consolation* she has at least one consolation in the midst of her misfortune.

infortuné, e [ɛ̃fɔʀtyne] *litt* adj *(avant nom)* [malchanceux - gén] unfortunate, luckless ; [- mari] hapless, wretched.

infoutu, e [ɛ̃futy] adj *fam* ▸ **être infoutu de faire qqch** to be incapable of doing sthg / *il est infoutu d'être à l'heure* he's incapable of being on time.

infraction [ɛ̃fʀaksjɔ̃] nf DR breach of the law, offence ⓤⓚ ou offense ⓤⓢ / *infraction au code de la route* driving offence / *je n'ai jamais été en infraction* I've never committed an ou any offence.

infranchissable [ɛ̃fʀɑ̃ʃisabl] adj **1.** [col] impassable ; [rivière] which cannot be crossed **2.** [difficulté] insuperable, insurmountable.

infrarouge [ɛ̃fʀaʀuʒ] adj infrared.

infrastructure [ɛ̃fʀastʀyktyʀ] nf [ensemble d'équipements] infrastructure.

infréquentable [ɛ̃fʀekɑ̃tabl] adj : *ils sont infréquentables* they're not the sort of people you'd want to associate with.

infroissable [ɛ̃fʀwasabl] adj crease-resistant.

infructueux, euse [ɛ̃fʀyktɥø, øz] adj fruitless.

infuse [ɛ̃fyz] adj f ⟶ **science.**

infuser [3] [ɛ̃fyze] vi *(aux être ou avoir)* [macérer - thé] to brew, to infuse ; [- tisane] to infuse ▸ **faire infuser** to brew ▸ **laissez infuser quelques minutes** leave to infuse for a few minutes.

infusion [ɛ̃fyzjɔ̃] nf [boisson] herbal tea, infusion *sout.*

ingénier [9] [ɛ̃ʒenje] ❖ **s'ingénier à** vp + prép to try hard ou to endeavour ou to strive to / *s'ingénier à trouver une solution* to work hard at finding ou to do all one can to find a solution.

ingénierie [ɛ̃ʒeniʀi] nf engineering.

ingénieur, e [ɛ̃ʒenjœʀ] nm, f engineer ▸ **ingénieur agronome** agricultural engineer ▸ **ingénieur informaticien** computer engineer ▸ **ingénieur du son** sound engineer ▸ **ingénieur système** systems engineer ▸ **ingénieur des travaux publics** construction engineer.

ingénieux, euse [ɛ̃ʒenjø, øz] adj [personne] ingenious, clever, inventive ; [plan, appareil, procédé] ingenious.

ingéniosité [ɛ̃ʒenjozite] nf ingenuity, inventiveness, cleverness.

ingénu, e [ɛ̃ʒeny] ◆ adj ingenuous, naive. ◆ nm, f ingenuous ou naive person. ❖ **ingénue** nf THÉÂTRE ingénue ou ingénue (role) / *cesse de jouer les ingénues* fig stop acting ou playing the innocent.

ingénuité [ɛ̃ʒenɥite] nf ingenuousness, naivety.

ingérable [ɛ̃ʒeʀabl] adj *fam* unmanageable.

ingérence [ɛ̃ʒeʀɑ̃s] nf interference ; POL interference, intervention.

ingérer [18] [ɛ̃ʒeʀe] vt to absorb, to ingest.

> 📝 In reformed spelling (see p. 16-18), this verb is conjugated like *semer : il ingèrera, elle s'ingèrerait.*

ingrat, e [ɛ̃gʀa, at] ◆ adj **1.** [sans grâce - visage] unattractive, unpleasant, coarse **2.** [tâche, travail] unrewarding, thankless ; [terre] unproductive **3.** [sans reconnaissance] ungrateful ▸ **être ingrat avec** ou **envers qqn** to be ungrateful towards sb. ◆ nm, f ungrateful person.

ingratitude [ɛ̃gʀatityd] nf [d'une personne] ingratitude, ungratefulness.

ingrédient [ɛ̃gʀedjɑ̃] nm **1.** [dans une recette, un mélange] ingredient **2.** *fig* [élément] ingredient.

ingurgiter [3] [ɛ̃gyʀʒite] vt *fam* **1.** [avaler - aliments] to wolf ou to gulp down *(sép)* ; [- boisson] to gulp down *(sép)*, to knock back *(sép)* **2.** *fig* to take in *(sép)* ▸ **faire ingurgiter des faits** / **dates à qqn** to stuff sb's head full of facts / dates.

inhabitable [inabitabl] adj [maison, grenier] uninhabitable ; [quartier] unpleasant to live in.

inhabité, e [inabite] adj [maison, chambre] uninhabited, unoccupied ; [contrée] uninhabited.

⚠ **Inhabited** signifie « habité » et non inhabité.

inhabituel, elle [inabitɥɛl] adj unusual, odd.

inhalation [inalasjɔ̃] nf 1. [respiration] breathing in, inhalation spéc 2. [traitement] (steam) inhalation / je (me) fais des inhalations avec ce produit I use this product as an inhalant.

inhaler [3] [inale] vt to inhale, to breathe in (sép).

inhérent, e [inerɑ̃, ɑ̃t] adj inherent ▸ **inhérent à** inherent in.

inhiber [3] [inibe] vt to inhibit.

inhibition [inibisjɔ̃] nf PHYSIOL & PSYCHOL inhibition.

inhospitalier, ère [inɔspitalje, ɛʀ] adj inhospitable.

inhumain, e [inymɛ̃, ɛn] adj inhuman.

inhumation [inymasjɔ̃] nf burial, interment sout, inhumation sout.

inhumer [3] [inyme] vt to bury, to inter.

inimaginable [inimaʒinabl] adj unimaginable / un paysage d'une beauté inimaginable an unbelievably beautiful landscape.

inimitable [inimitabl] adj inimitable.

inimitié [inimitje] nf sout enmity, hostility.

ininflammable [inɛ̃flamabl] adj [produit] non-flammable ; [revêtement] flame-proof.

inintelligible [inɛ̃teliʒibl] adj unintelligible, impossible to understand.

inintéressant, e [inɛ̃teʀesɑ̃, ɑ̃t] adj uninteresting.

ininterrompu, e [inɛ̃teʀɔ̃py] adj [série, flot] unbroken, uninterrupted ; [bruit] continuous ; [tradition] continuous, unbroken ; [effort] unremitting, steady ; [bavardage] continuous, ceaseless / nous diffusons aujourd'hui cinq heures de musique ininterrompue today we are broadcasting five hours of non-stop ou uninterrupted music.

inique [inik] adj sout iniquitous sout, unjust, unfair.

iniquité [inikite] nf sout iniquity sout, injustice.

initial, e, aux [inisjal, o] adj initial. ❖ **initiale** nf [première lettre] initial.

initialement [inisjalmɑ̃] adv initially, at first, originally.

initialer [3] [inisjale] vt QUÉBEC to initial.

initialiser [3] [inisjalize] vt INFORM to initialize.

initiateur, trice [inisjatœʀ, tʀis] nm, f 1. [maître] initiator 2. [novateur] pioneer.

initiation [inisjasjɔ̃] nf 1. [approche] initiation, introduction / initiation à la psychologie / au russe introduction to psychology / to Russian 2. ANTHR initiation.

initiatique [inisjatik] adj initiatory, initiation (modif).

initiative [inisjativ] nf 1. [esprit de décision] initiative / avoir de l'initiative to have initiative ou drive ▸ **plein d'initiative** enterprising 2. [idée] initiative ▸ **à** ou **sur l'initiative de qqn** on sb's initiative ▸ **prendre l'initiative de qqch** to initiate sthg, to take the initiative for sthg 3. [action spontanée] initiative ▸ **faire qqch de sa propre initiative** to do sthg on one's own initiative ▸ **prendre des initiatives** to show initiative ▸ **prendre l'initiative de faire qqch** to take the initiative in doing sthg ▸ **initiative de paix** POL peace initiative ou overture.

initié, e [inisje] ❖ adj initiated. ❖ nm, f [connaisseur] initiated person, initiate sout ▸ **pour les initiés** not for the uninitiated.

initier [9] [inisje] vt 1. [novice] to initiate ▸ **initier qqn à qqch** to initiate sb into sthg, to introduce sb to sthg 2. [faire démarrer] to initiate, to get going. ❖ **s'initier à** vp + prép to learn the basics of, to get to know.

injecté, e [ɛ̃ʒɛkte] adj [rougi] ▸ **yeux injectés de sang** bloodshot eyes.

injecter [4] [ɛ̃ʒɛkte] vt 1. CONSTR, GÉOL & MÉD to inject 2. [introduire] to inject, to infuse, to instil / injecter des millions dans une affaire to inject ou to pump millions into a business.

injection [ɛ̃ʒɛksjɔ̃] nf 1. CONSTR, GÉOL & MÉD injection 2. ÉCON [apport - d'argent] injection 3. MÉCAN injection ▸ **à injection** (fuel) injection (modif).

injoignable [ɛ̃ʒwaɲabl] adj : j'ai essayé de l'appeler toute la matinée mais il était injoignable I tried to phone him all morning, but I couldn't get through (to him) ou get hold of him.

injonction [ɛ̃ʒɔ̃ksjɔ̃] nf 1. sout [ordre] order ▸ **sur l'injonction de qqn** at sb's behest 2. DR injunction, (judicial) order ▸ **injonction de payer** order to pay.

injure [ɛ̃ʒyʀ] nf 1. [insulte] insult, abuse (U) / un chapelet d'injures a stream of abuse ou insults 2. sout [affront] affront, insult / il m'a fait l'injure de refuser mon invitation he insulted me by refusing my invitation.

⚠ **Injury** signifie « blessure » et non injure.

injurier [9] [ɛ̃ʒyʀje] vt [adresser des insultes à] to insult, to abuse.

⚠ **To injure** signifie « blesser » et non injurier.

injurieux, euse [ɛ̃ʒyʀjø, øz] adj abusive, insulting, offensive.

injuste [ɛ̃ʒyst] adj 1. [décision] unjust, unfair 2. [personne] unfair, unjust / ne sois pas injuste ! be fair!, don't be unfair!

injustement [ɛ̃ʒystəmɑ̃] adv [avec iniquité] unfairly, unjustly.

injustice [ɛ̃ʒystis] nf 1. [caractère inique] injustice, unfairness 2. [acte inique] injustice, wrong ▸ **commettre une injustice envers qqn** to do sb wrong ou an injustice.

injustifiable [ɛ̃ʒystifjabl] adj unjustifiable.

injustifié, e [ɛ̃ʒystifje] adj [critique, punition] unjustified, unwarranted ; [crainte] unfounded, groundless ; [absence] unexplained.

inlassable [ɛ̃lasabl] adj [infatigable - personne] indefatigable, tireless, untiring ; [- énergie] tireless.

inlassablement [ɛ̃lasabləmɑ̃] adv indefatigably, tirelessly, untiringly.

inné, e [ine] adj 1. [don] inborn, innate 2. PHILOS innate. ❖ **inné** nm ▸ **l'inné et l'acquis** nature and nurture.

innocemment [inɔsamɑ̃] adv innocently.

innocence [inɔsɑ̃s] nf [gén] innocence / en toute innocence in all innocence, quite innocently.

innocent, e [inɔsɑ̃, ɑ̃t] ❖ adj 1. [non responsable - inculpé, victime] innocent ▸ **être innocent de qqch** to be innocent of sthg 2. [plaisanterie, question, plaisirs] innocent, harmless ; [baiser, jeune fille] innocent 3. [candide - enfant, âge] innocent. ❖ nm, f 1. [personne non coupable] innocent person 2. [personne candide] innocent ▸ **faire l'innocent** to play ou to act the innocent.

innocenter [3] [inɔsɑ̃te] vt DR [suj : jury] to clear, to find innocent ou not guilty ; [suj : témoignage, document] to prove innocent, to show to be innocent.

innocuité [inɔkɥite] nf harmlessness, inoffensiveness, innocuousness sout.

innombrable [inɔ̃bʀabl] adj innumerable, countless / *une foule innombrable* a vast ou huge crowd.

innommable [inɔmabl] adj unspeakable, loathsome, nameless.

innovant, e [in(n)ɔvɑ̃, ɑ̃t] adj innovative.

innovateur, trice [inɔvatœʀ, tʀis] ◆ adj innovative, innovatory. ◆ nm, f innovator.

innovation [inɔvasjɔ̃] nf 1. [créativité] innovation 2. [changement] innovation 3. COMM innovation.

innover [3] [inɔve] vi to innovate.

inoccupé, e [inɔkype] adj 1. [vide - maison, local] unoccupied, empty 2. [vacant - poste] unoccupied, vacant, available ; [- taxi, fauteuil] empty, free 3. [inactif] inactive, unoccupied, idle.

inoculer [3] [inɔkyle] vt MÉD to inoculate / *on inocule le virus à un cobaye* a guinea pig is injected with the virus / *les volontaires se font inoculer le vaccin* the volunteers are injected with the vaccine.

inodore [inɔdɔʀ] adj [sans odeur] odourless 🇬🇧, odorless 🇺🇸.

inoffensif, ive [inɔfɑ̃sif, iv] adj [personne] harmless, inoffensive ; [animal] harmless ; [remarque] innocuous.

inondation [inɔ̃dɑsjɔ̃] nf [d'eau] flood, flooding, inundation sout.

inonder [3] [inɔ̃de] vt 1. [champs, maison, ville] to flood, to inundate sout / *tu ne peux donc pas prendre un bain sans tout inonder ?* can't you have a bath without flooding the bathroom ? 2. [tremper] to soak / *les yeux inondés de pleurs* his eyes full of ou swimming with tears / *le front inondé de sueur* his forehead bathed in sweat 3. fig [envahir - marché] to flood, to inundate, to swamp ; [- suj : foule] to flood into, to swarm ; [- suj : lumière] to flood ou to pour into, to bathe.

inopérable [inɔpeʀabl] adj inoperable.

inopiné, e [inɔpine] adj [inattendu] unexpected.

inopinément [inɔpinemɑ̃] adv unexpectedly.

inopportun, e [inɔpɔʀtœ̃, yn] adj ill-timed, inopportune, untimely.

inoubliable [inublijabl] adj unforgettable, never to be forgotten.

inouï, e [inwi] adj 1. [incroyable] incredible, amazing, unbelievable 2. litt [sans précédent - prouesse, performance] unheard of, unprecedented.

Inox® [inɔks] nm stainless steel / *couverts en Inox* stainless steel cutlery.

inoxydable [inɔksidabl] ◆ adj MÉTALL stainless. ◆ nm stainless steel.

inqualifiable [ɛ̃kalifjabl] adj unspeakable.

inquiet, ète [ɛ̃kjɛ, ɛt] adj 1. [personne] worried, anxious, concerned ; [regard] worried, uneasy, nervous ; [attente] anxious / *je suis inquiet de l'avoir laissé seul* I'm worried ou uneasy about having left him alone 2. litt [activité, curiosité] restless.

inquiétant, e [ɛ̃kjetɑ̃, ɑ̃t] adj worrying, disquieting, disturbing.

inquiéter [18] [ɛ̃kjete] vt 1. [troubler - suj : personne, situation] to worry, to trouble / *son silence m'inquiète beaucoup* I find her silence quite disturbing ou worrying / *qu'est-ce qui t'inquiète ?* what are you worried about?, what's worrying you? 2. [ennuyer, harceler] to disturb, to bother, to harass / *le magistrat ne fut jamais inquiété par la police* the police never troubled the magistrate / *il n'a*

jamais inquiété le champion du monde he's never posed any threat to the world champion. ❖ **s'inquiéter** vpi [être soucieux] to worry, to be worried / *il y a de quoi s'inquiéter* that's something to be worried about, there's real cause for concern ▸ **s'inquiéter au sujet de** ou **pour qqn** to be worried ou concerned about sb. ❖ **s'inquiéter de** vp + prép 1. [tenir compte de] to bother ou to worry about 2. [s'occuper de] to see to sthg 3. [se renseigner sur] to inquire ou to ask about.

✍ In reformed spelling (see p. 16-18), this verb is conjugated like **semer** : *il inquiètera, elle s'inquièterait.*

inquiétude [ɛ̃kjetyd] nf worry, anxiety, concern ▸ **un sujet d'inquiétude** a cause for concern ou anxiety ▸ **n'ayez aucune inquiétude** ou **soyez sans inquiétude** rest easy, have no fear.

inquisiteur, trice [ɛ̃kizitœʀ, tʀis] adj inquisitive, prying. ❖ **inquisiteur** nm inquisitor.

INRA, Inra [inʀa] (abr de Institut national de la recherche agronomique) npr m *national institute for agronomic research.*

insaisissable [ɛ̃sezisabl] adj 1. [imprenable - terroriste, voleur] elusive 2. [imperceptible] imperceptible, intangible 3. [fuyant] unfathomable, elusive.

insalubre [ɛ̃salybʀ] adj [immeuble] insalubrious ; [climat] insalubrious, unhealthy.

insalubrité [ɛ̃salybʀite] nf [d'un immeuble] insalubrity ; [du climat] insalubrity, unhealthiness.

insanité [ɛ̃sanite] nf 1. [folie] insanity 2. [remarque] insane ou nonsensical remark ; [acte] insane act, insane thing to do / *tu n'es pas forcé d'écouter ses insanités* you don't have to listen to his ravings.

insatiable [ɛ̃sasjabl] adj insatiable.

insatisfait, e [ɛ̃satisfɛ, ɛt] ◆ adj 1. [inassouvi - curiosité, besoin] unsatisfied, frustrated 2. [mécontent - personne] unsatisfied, dissatisfied, displeased. ◆ nm, f discontented person ▸ *c'est un perpétuel insatisfait* he's never satisfied ou happy.

inscription [ɛ̃skʀipsjɔ̃] nf 1. [ensemble de caractères] inscription, writing (U) / *il y avait une inscription sur le mur* there was an inscription ou something written on the wall 2. [action d'inclure] : *une question dont l'inscription à l'ordre du jour s'impose* a question which must go (down) ou be placed on the agenda 3. [formalité] ▸ **inscription à** a) [cours, concours] registration for, enrolment 🇬🇧 ou enrollment 🇺🇸 in b) [club, parti] enrolment 🇬🇧 ou enrollment 🇺🇸 in, joining (of) / *inscription sur les listes électorales* registration on the electoral roll 🇬🇧, voter registration 🇺🇸 ▸ **dossier d'inscription** UNIV admission form ; ≃ UCCA form 🇬🇧 ▸ **droits d'inscription** UNIV registration fees 4. [personne inscrite] ▸ *il y a une trentaine d'inscriptions au club / pour le rallye* about 30 people have joined the club / entered the rally.

inscrire [99] [ɛ̃skʀiʀ] vt 1. [écrire - chiffre, détail] to write ou to note (down) / *inscris ton nom au tableau / sur la feuille* write your name (up) on the board / (down) on the sheet ; [graver] to engrave, to inscribe 2. [enregistrer - étudiant] to register, to enrol 🇬🇧, to enroll 🇺🇸 ; [- électeur, membre] to register / *(faire) inscrire un enfant à l'école* to register ou to enrol a child for school, to put a child's name down for school / *les étudiants inscrits en droit* the students enrolled on 🇬🇧 ou in 🇺🇸 the law course / *se faire inscrire sur les listes électorales* to register as a voter, to put one's name on the electoral register ▸ **inscrire qqn (pour un rendez-vous)** to put sb ou sb's name down for an appointment 3. [inclure] to list, to include / *ces sommes sont inscrites au budget de la culture* these amounts are listed in the arts budget / *inscrire une question à l'ordre du jour* to put ou to place a question on the agenda

4. SPORT [but, essai] to score. ❖ **s'inscrire** ❖ vp *(emploi réfléchi)* ❱ **s'inscrire à a)** [club, parti, bibliothèque] to join **b)** [université] to register ou to enrol at **c)** [concours, rallye] to enter ou to put one's name down for. ❖ vpi **1.** [apparaître] to appear, to come up / *le numéro de téléphone va s'inscrire sur vos écrans* the phone number will come up ou be displayed ou appear on your screens **2.** DR : *s'inscrire en faux contre une politique* / *des allégations* fig to strongly denounce a policy / deny allegations. ❖ **s'inscrire dans** vp + prép *sout* [suj : événement, attitude] to be consistent with, to be in keeping with, to be in line with ; [suj : auteur] to belong to, to rank amongst ; [suj : œuvre] to take its place in / *cette mesure s'inscrit dans le cadre de notre campagne* this measure comes ou lies within the framework of our campaign.

inscrit, e [ɛ̃skʀi, it] ❖ adj [étudiant, membre d'un club] enrolled, registered, matriculated 🇬🇧 ; [chômeur] registered ; POL [candidat, électeur] registered ; [orateur] scheduled. ❖ nm, f [sur une liste] registered person ; [à un club, à un parti] registered member ; [étudiant] registered student ; [candidat] registered candidate ; [électeur] registered elector.

insecte [ɛ̃sɛkt] nm insect.

insecticide [ɛ̃sɛktisid] ❖ adj insecticide *(modif)*, insecticidal. ❖ nm insecticide.

insécurité [ɛ̃sekyʀite] nf **1.** [manque de sécurité] lack of safety **2.** [précarité - de l'emploi] insecurity, precariousness ; [- de l'avenir] uncertainty **3.** [angoisse] insecurity.

INSEE, Insee [inse] (abr de **Institut national de la statistique et des études économiques**) npr m *national institute of statistics and information about the economy.*

insémination [ɛ̃seminasjɔ̃] nf insemination ❱ **insémination artificielle** artificial insemination.

insensé, e [ɛ̃sɑ̃se] adj **1.** [déraisonnable - projet, initiative] foolish, insane ; [- espoir] unrealistic, mad ❱ **c'est insensé !** this is absurd ou preposterous! **2.** [excessif] enormous, considerable.

insensibiliser [3] [ɛ̃sɑ̃sibilize] vt MÉD to anaesthetize, to anesthetize 🇺🇸.

insensibilité [ɛ̃sɑ̃sibilite] nf **1.** [absence de réceptivité] ❱ **insensibilité à** insensitiveness ou insensitivity to **2.** MÉD insensitivity, numbness.

insensible [ɛ̃sɑ̃sibl] adj **1.** [privé de sensation, de sentiment] ❱ **insensible à** insensitive to / *insensible à la douleur* insensitive to pain / *elle demeura insensible à ses prières* she remained indifferent to ou unmoved by his pleas **2.** [imperceptible] imperceptible.

⚠ L'adjectif anglais **insensible** signifie « inconscient ». Il ne doit pas être employé pour traduire **insensible**.

inséparable [ɛ̃separabl] adj inseparable / *le vice et le crime sont inséparables* vice and crime are inseparable ou go hand in hand.

insérer [18] [ɛ̃seʀe] vt **1.** [ajouter - chapitre, feuille] to insert ❱ **insérer qqch dans** / **entre** to insert sthg into / between / *faire insérer une clause dans un contrat* to have a clause added to ou put in ou inserted into a contract **2.** [introduire - clé, lame] to insert ❱ **insérer qqch dans** to insert sthg into. ❖ **s'insérer dans** vp + prép **1.** [socialement] to become integrated into / *les jeunes ont souvent du mal à s'insérer dans le monde du travail* young people often find it difficult to find their place in ou to fit into a work environment **2.** [s'inscrire dans] to be part of.

🖉 In reformed spelling (see p. 16-18), this verb is conjugated like *semer : il insèrera, elle s'insèrerait.*

insertion [ɛ̃sɛʀsjɔ̃] nf **1.** [introduction] insertion, introduction **2.** [intégration] integration ❱ **insertion sociale** social integration.

insidieusement [ɛ̃sidjøzmɑ̃] adv insidiously.

insidieux, euse [ɛ̃sidjø, øz] adj **1.** [perfide - question] insidious, treacherous / *un raisonnement insidieux* a specious argument ; *litt* [personne] insidious **2.** MÉD insidious.

insigne [ɛ̃siɲ] nm [marque distinctive - d'un groupe] badge, emblem, symbol ; [- d'une dignité] insignia / *les insignes de la royauté* royal insignia.

insignifiant, e [ɛ̃siɲifjɑ̃, ɑ̃t] adj **1.** [sans intérêt] insignificant, trivial / *des gens insignifiants* insignificant ou unimportant people **2.** [minime] insignificant, negligible ❱ **somme insignifiante** trifling ou petty sum.

insinuation [ɛ̃sinɥasjɔ̃] nf [allusion] insinuation, innuendo.

insinuer [7] [ɛ̃sinɥe] vt to insinuate / *que veut-elle insinuer ?* what's she hinting at ou trying to insinuate? ❖ **s'insinuer** vpi ❱ **s'insinuer dans a)** [suj : arôme, gaz] to creep in **b)** [suj : eau] to filter ou to seep in **c)** [suj : personne] to make one's way in, to infiltrate, to penetrate ❱ **le doute** / **une idée diabolique s'insinua en lui** doubt / an evil thought crept into his mind.

insipide [ɛ̃sipid] adj **1.** [sans goût] insipid, tasteless **2.** [sans relief - personne] insipid, bland, vapid ; [- conversation, livre] insipid, uninteresting, dull.

insistance [ɛ̃sistɑ̃s] nf [obstination] insistence / *il lui demanda avec insistance de chanter* he insisted that she should sing ❱ **regarder qqn avec insistance** to stare at sb insistently.

insistant, e [ɛ̃sistɑ̃, ɑ̃t] adj [persévérant] insistent.

insister [3] [ɛ̃siste] vi **1.** [persévérer] to insist / *je ne vous dirai rien, inutile d'insister !* I'm not telling you anything, so there's no point pressing me any further! / *ça ne répond pas — insistez !* there's no answer — keep trying ou try again! / *il a tellement insisté que j'ai fini par accepter* he was so insistent about it that I ended up accepting / *il était en colère, alors je n'ai pas insisté* he was angry, so I didn't push the matter (any further) ou I didn't insist **2.** [demander instamment] to insist / *j'insiste pour que vous m'écoutiez jusqu'au bout* I insist that you hear me out. ❖ **insister sur** v + prép **1.** [mettre l'accent sur - idée, problème] to stress, to emphasize, to underline / *dans notre école, nous insistons beaucoup sur la discipline* in our school, we attach great importance to ou lay great stress on discipline **2.** [s'attarder sur - anecdote] to dwell on *(insép)* ; [- tache, défaut] to pay particular attention to.

insolation [ɛ̃sɔlasjɔ̃] nf MÉD sunstroke, insolation *spéc*.

insolence [ɛ̃sɔlɑ̃s] nf **1.** [irrespect] insolence ❱ **avec insolence** insolently **2.** [remarque] insolent remark ; insolent act.

insolent, e [ɛ̃sɔlɑ̃, ɑ̃t] adj **1.** [impoli] insolent **2.** [extraordinaire - luxe, succès] outrageous / *vous avez eu une chance insolente* you've been outrageously ou incredibly lucky.

insolite [ɛ̃sɔlit] ❖ adj unusual, strange. ❖ nm ❱ **l'insolite** the unusual, the bizarre.

insoluble [ɛ̃sɔlybl] adj **1.** CHIM insoluble **2.** [problème] insoluble, insolvable 🇺🇸.

insolvable [ɛ̃sɔlvabl] adj & nmf insolvent.

insomniaque [ɛ̃sɔmnjak] adj & nmf insomniac.

insomnie [ɛ̃sɔmni] nf insomnia *(U)* ❱ **des nuits d'insomnie** sleepless nights.

insondable [ɛ̃sɔ̃dabl] adj **1.** [impénétrable - desseins, mystère] unfathomable, impenetrable ; [- regard, visage] inscrutable **2.** [très profond] unfathomable **3.** [infini] abysmal / *il est d'une bêtise insondable* he's abysmally stupid.

insonoriser [3] [ɛ̃sɔnɔʀize] vt to soundproof, to insulate.

insortable [ɛ̃sɔʀtabl] adj : *il est vraiment insortable !* you can't take him anywhere!

insouciance [ɛ̃susjɑ̃s] nf lack of concern, carefree attitude, casualness ▸ *vivre dans l'insouciance* to live a carefree ou untroubled existence.

insouciant, e [ɛ̃susjɑ̃, ɑ̃t] adj **1.** [nonchalant] carefree, unconcerned, casual **2.** ▸ *insouciant de* [indifférent à] : *insouciant du danger* oblivious of ou to the danger.

insoumis, e [ɛ̃sumi, iz] adj **1.** [indiscipliné - jeunesse, partisan] rebellious ; [- enfant] unruly, refractory *sout* **2.** [révolté - tribu] rebel, rebellious ; [- pays] unsubdued, undefeated, rebellious **3.** MIL ▸ *soldat insoumis* **a)** [réfractaire au service militaire] draft dodger 🇺🇸 **b)** [déserteur] soldier absent without leave. ✦ **insoumis** nm [réfractaire au service militaire] draft dodger 🇺🇸 ; [déserteur] soldier absent without leave.

insoumission [ɛ̃sumisjɔ̃] nf **1.** [indiscipline] rebelliousness, insubordination **2.** [révolte] rebelliousness, rebellion.

insoupçonné, e [ɛ̃supsɔne] adj [vérité] unsuspected ; [richesses] undreamt-of, unheard-of.

insoutenable [ɛ̃sutnabl] adj [insupportable - douleur, scène, température] unbearable, unendurable ; [- lumière] blinding.

inspecter [4] [ɛ̃spɛkte] vt [contrôler - appartement, bagages, engin, travaux] to inspect, to examine ; [MIL - troupes] to review, to inspect ; [- école, professeur] to inspect.

inspecteur, trice [ɛ̃spɛktœʀ, tʀis] nm, f **1.** [contrôleur] inspector ▸ *inspecteur des impôts* FIN tax inspector ▸ *inspecteur du travail* factory inspector **2.** [policier] inspector, detective ▸ *inspecteur de police* detective sergeant 🇬🇧, lieutenant 🇺🇸 ▸ *inspecteur principal* ≃ detective inspector **3.** ENS ▸ *inspecteur d'Académie* ≃ inspector of schools 🇬🇧 ; ≃ Accreditation officer 🇺🇸.

inspection [ɛ̃spɛksjɔ̃] nf **1.** [vérification] inspection ; [surveillance] overseeing, supervising ▸ *les douaniers soumirent la valise / le passager à une inspection en règle* the customs officers subjected the suitcase / the passenger to a thorough search ▸ *passer une inspection* **a)** [l'organiser] to carry out an inspection, to inspect **b)** [la subir] to undergo an inspection, to be inspected **2.** ADMIN inspectorate ▸ *inspection académique* ≃ Schools Inspectorate 🇬🇧 ; ≃ Accreditation Agency 🇺🇸 ▸ *inspection du travail* ≃ Health and Safety Executive 🇬🇧 ; ≃ Labor Board 🇺🇸 **3.** [inspectorat] inspectorship.

inspiration [ɛ̃spiʀasjɔ̃] nf **1.** [esprit créatif] inspiration / *je n'ai pas d'inspiration ce matin* I don't feel inspired ou I don't have any inspiration this morning **2.** [idée, envie] inspiration, (bright) idea, brainwave 🇬🇧, brainstorm 🇺🇸 / *agir selon l'inspiration du moment* to act on the spur of the moment **3.** [influence] influence, instigation / *une architecture d'inspiration nordique* an architecture with a Scandinavian influence, a Scandinavian-inspired architecture **4.** PHYSIOL breathing in, inspiration *spéc*.

inspiré, e [ɛ̃spiʀe] adj **1.** [artiste, air, livre] inspired **2.** [avisé] : *j'ai été bien inspiré de lui résister* I was well-advised ou to resist him, I did the right thing in resisting him.

inspirer [3] [ɛ̃spiʀe] ◆ vt **1.** [provoquer - décision, sentiment] to inspire ; [- remarque] to inspire, to give rise to *(insép)* ; [- conduite] to prompt ; [- complot] to instigate ▸ *inspirer confiance à qqn* to inspire confidence in sb, to inspire sb with confidence / *cette viande ne m'inspire pas confiance !* I don't much like the look of that meat! **2.** [influencer - œuvre, personne] to inspire / *le sujet de dissertation ne m'inspire guère !* the subject of the essay doesn't really fire my imagination! ◆ vi to breathe in, to inspire *spéc*. ✦ **s'inspirer de** vp + prép to draw one's inspiration from, to be inspired by.

instabilité [ɛ̃stabilite] nf **1.** CHIM & PHYS instability **2.** [précarité] instability, precariousness **3.** PSYCHOL instability.

instable [ɛ̃stabl] adj **1.** [branlant] unsteady, unstable ; [glissant - terrain] unstable, shifting **2.** [fluctuant - situation, régime politique, prix] unstable ; [- personnalité] unsteady, unreliable ; [- population] shifting, unsettled, unstable ; [- temps] unsettled **3.** CHIM, PHYS & PSYCHOL unstable.

installateur, trice [ɛ̃stalatœʀ, tʀis] nm, f [d'appareils sanitaires] fitter ; ÉLECTR, RADIO & TV installer.

installation [ɛ̃stalasjɔ̃] nf **1.** [dispositif, équipement] installation ; [aménagement] set-up ▸ *installation électrique* wiring ▸ *installation informatique* computer facility ▸ *installation téléphonique* telephone installation **2.** [d'un dentiste, d'un médecin] setting up (practice) ; [d'un commerçant] opening, setting up (shop) ; [d'un locataire] moving in **3.** [mise en service - de l'électricité, du gaz, du chauffage] installation, installing, putting in ; [- d'un appareil ménager] installation, installing ; [- d'une grue] setting up ; [- d'une antenne] installing ; [- d'une cuisine, d'un atelier, d'un laboratoire] fitting out / *refaire l'installation électrique (d'une maison)* to rewire (a house) **4.** INFORM [d'un programme] installation **5.** [implantation - d'une usine] setting up. ✦ **installations** nfpl [dans une usine] machinery and equipment ; [complexe, bâtiment] installations ▸ *installations portuaires* port installations.

installé, e [ɛ̃stale] adj [aménagé] : *elle est bien installée* she has a really nice place / *ils sont mal installés* their place isn't very comfortable.

installer [3] [ɛ̃stale] vt **1.** [mettre en service - chauffage, eau, gaz, électricité, téléphone] to install, to put in *(sép)* ; [- appareil ménager] to install ▸ *nous avons dû faire installer l'eau / le gaz / l'électricité* we had to have the water laid on / the gas put in / the house wired **2.** [faire asseoir, allonger] to put, to place / *une fois qu'il est installé devant la télévision, il n'y a plus moyen de lui parler* once he's settled himself down ou planted himself ou installed (himself) in front of the TV, there's no talking to him **3.** [pièce, logement - aménager] to fit out *(sép)* ; [- disposer] to lay out *(sép)* / *nous avons installé la salle de jeu au grenier* we've turned the attic into a playroom **4.** [loger - jeune couple] to set up *(sép)* ; [- visiteur] to put up *(sép)*, to install *sout* **5.** INFORM [programme] to install. ✦ **s'installer** vpi **1.** [s'asseoir, s'allonger] : *installez-vous comme il faut, je reviens tout de suite* make yourself comfortable ou at home, I'll be right back / *s'installer dans un canapé* to settle down on a couch **2.** [s'implanter - cirque, marché] to (be) set up ; [- usine] to be set up / *quand nous nous installés* when we settled in / *s'installer à la campagne* [emménager] to set up house ou to go and live ou to settle in the country / *s'installer dans une maison* to move into a house **3.** [pour exercer - médecin, dentiste] to set up a practice ; [- commerçant] to set up shop, to open ▸ *s'installer à son compte* to set up one's own business ou on one's own **4.** [se fixer - statu quo] to become established ; [- maladie] to take a hold ou a grip ; [- doute, peur] to creep in ; [- silence] to take over / *le pays s'installe peu à peu dans la crise* the country is gradually learning to live with the crisis.

⚠ **To install** ne doit pas être employé systématiquement pour traduire **installer**, comme le montre l'article.

instamment [ɛ̃stamɑ̃] adv *sout* insistently.

instance [ɛ̃stɑ̃s] nf **1.** [organisme] authority / *les plus hautes instances du parti* the leading bodies of the party / *le dossier sera traité par une instance supérieure* the file will be dealt with at a higher level ou by a higher authority 2. DR ((legal) proceedings ▸ **en première instance** on first hearing ▸ **en seconde instance** on appeal. ❖ **instances** nfpl *sout* entreaties. ❖ **en instance** loc adj [dossier] pending, waiting to be dealt with ; DR [affaire] pending, sub judice UK ; [courrier] ready for posting. ❖ **en instance de** loc prép : *être en instance de divorce* to be waiting for a divorce ou in the middle of divorce proceedings.

instant [ɛ̃stɑ̃] nm [courte durée] moment, instant ▸ *j'ai pensé, pendant un instant* ou *l'espace d'un instant, que.... for half a minute* ou *for a split second, I thought that..... / je n'en doute pas un seul instant* I don't doubt it at all, I've never doubted it for a minute / *je reviens dans un instant* I'll be right back, I'll be back in a minute / *c'est prêt en un instant* it's ready in an instant ou in no time at all. ❖ **à l'instant (même)** loc adv this instant, this minute / *je l'apprends à l'instant (même)* I've just this moment heard about it / *nous devons partir à l'instant (même)* we must leave right now ou this instant ou this very minute *sout*. ❖ **à tout instant** loc adv [continuellement] all the time ; [d'une minute à l'autre] any time (now), any minute. ❖ **dans l'instant** loc adv at this moment, instantly. ❖ **de tous les instants** loc adj constant. ❖ **dès l'instant que** loc conj [si] if ; [puisque] since ; [aussitôt que] as soon as, from the moment. ❖ **pour l'instant** loc adv for the moment, for the time being.

instantané, e [ɛ̃stɑ̃tane] adj 1. [immédiat] instantaneous 2. [soluble] ▸ **café instantané** instant coffee. ❖ **instantané** nm snap, snapshot.

instantanément [ɛ̃stɑ̃tanemɑ̃] adv instantaneously, instantly.

instar [ɛ̃star] ❖ **à l'instar de** loc prép *sout* following (the example of).

instaurer [3] [ɛ̃stɔre] vt to institute, to found, to establish / *instaurer une nouvelle mode* to introduce ou to start a new fashion / *instaurer le couvre-feu dans une ville* to impose a curfew in a town ; *fig* [peur, confiance] to instil UK, to instill US.

instigateur, trice [ɛ̃stigatœr, tris] nm, f instigator.

instigation [ɛ̃stigasjɔ̃] nf instigation ▸ **à** ou **sur l'instigation de qqn** at sb's instigation.

instiller [3] [ɛ̃stile] vt 1. MÉD to instil 2. *litt* [insuffler] to instil UK, to instill US ▸ **instiller le doute dans l'esprit de qqn** to instil doubt into sb's mind.

instinct [ɛ̃stɛ̃] nm 1. PSYCHOL & ZOOL instinct ▸ **instinct de conservation** instinct of self-preservation ▸ **instinct maternel** maternal instinct 2. [intuition] instinct / *se fier à son instinct* to trust one's instincts ou intuition. ❖ **d'instinct** loc adv instinctively, by instinct.

instinctif, ive [ɛ̃stɛ̃ktif, iv] adj 1. [irraisonné] instinctive 2. [impulsif] instinctive, impulsive, spontaneous.

instinctivement [ɛ̃stɛ̃ktivmɑ̃] adv instinctively.

instituer [7] [ɛ̃stitɥe] vt [instaurer, créer] to institute, to establish.

institut [ɛ̃stity] nm [établissement] institute / *institut de recherches / scientifique* research / scientific institute ▸ **institut de beauté** beauty salon ou parlour ▸ **institut médico-légal** mortuary ▸ **institut de sondage** polling organization ▸ **institut universitaire de formation des maîtres** teacher training college ▸ **institut universitaire de technologie** ≃ polytechnic UK ; ≃ technical school US.

instituteur, trice [ɛ̃stitytœr, tris] nm, f [de maternelle] (nursery school) teacher ; [d'école primaire] (primary school) teacher.

institution [ɛ̃stitysjɔ̃] nf 1. [établissement privé] institution ▸ **institution religieuse** a) [catholique] Catholic school

b) [autre] denominational school 2. [coutume] institution 3. [mise en place] institution, establishment ; [d'une loi] introduction ; [d'une règle] laying down. ❖ **institutions** nfpl institutions ▸ **les institutions politiques** political institutions.

institutionnaliser [3] [ɛ̃stitysjɔnalize] vt to institutionalize.

institutionnel, elle [ɛ̃stitysjɔnɛl] adj institutional.

instructeur, trice [ɛ̃stryktœr, tris] nm, f instructor. ❖ **instructeur** nm AÉRON (flying) instructor ; MIL instructor.

instructif, ive [ɛ̃stryktif, iv] adj informative, instructive.

instruction [ɛ̃stryksjɔ̃] nf 1. [formation] education, teaching / *l'instruction que j'ai reçue à l'école* the teaching ou education I was given at school ▸ **instruction religieuse** a) [gén] religious education b) ENS religious instruction 2. DR preliminary investigation ou inquiry (of a case by an examining magistrate) / *qui est chargé de l'instruction ?* who's setting up the inquiry? 3. INFORM instruction, statement 4. [ordre] instruction / *sur les instructions de ses supérieurs* following orders from his superiors. ❖ **instructions** nfpl [d'un fabricant] instructions, directions.

instruire [98] [ɛ̃strɥir] vt 1. [enseigner à] to teach, to instruct ; [former] to educate ; MIL [recrue] to train / *une émission destinée à instruire en distrayant* a programme designed to be both entertaining and educational 2. DR ▸ **instruire une affaire** ou **un dossier** to set up a preliminary inquiry. ❖ **s'instruire** vp *(emploi réfléchi)* [se cultiver] to educate o.s., to improve one's mind / *il s'est instruit tout seul* he's a self-educated man. ◆ vpi [apprendre] to learn.

instruit, e [ɛ̃strɥi, it] adj well-educated, educated.

instrument [ɛ̃strymɑ̃] nm 1. [outil, matériel] instrument ▸ **instruments de bord** instruments ▸ **instrument de mesure / d'observation** measuring / observation instrument / *c'est un de mes instruments de travail* it's a tool of my trade 2. MUS ▸ **instrument (de musique)** (musical) instrument ▸ **instrument à cordes / à percussion / à vent** string / percussion / wind instrument 3. *fig* [agent] instrument, tool ▸ **être l'instrument de qqn** to be sb's instrument ou tool.

instrumental, e, aux [ɛ̃strymɑ̃tal, o] adj instrumental.

instrumentaliser [3] [ɛ̃strymɑ̃talize] vt to use, to manipulate.

instrumentiste [ɛ̃strymɑ̃tist] nmf MUS instrumentalist.

insu [ɛ̃sy] ❖ **à l'insu de** loc prép 1. [sans être vu de] without the knowledge of, unbeknown ou unbeknownst to / *sortir à l'insu de ses parents* to go out without one's parents' knowing ou knowledge 2. ▸ **à mon / son insu** [sans m'en/s'en apercevoir] unwittingly, without being aware of it.

insubmersible [ɛ̃sybmɛrsibl] adj [canot] insubmersible ; [jouet] unsinkable.

insubordination [ɛ̃sybɔrdinasjɔ̃] nf insubordination.

insubordonné, e [ɛ̃sybɔrdɔne] adj insubordinate.

insuffisamment [ɛ̃syfizamɑ̃] adv insufficiently, inadequately.

insuffisance [ɛ̃syfizɑ̃s] nf 1. [manque] insufficiency, deficiency / *insuffisance de ressources* lack of ou insufficient resources 2. [point faible] weakness, deficiency 3. MÉD ▸ **elle est morte d'une insuffisance cardiaque** she died from heart failure ▸ **insuffisance rénale** kidney failure ou insufficiency *spéc*.

insuffisant, e [ɛ̃syfizɑ̃, ɑ̃t] adj **1.** [en quantité] insuffisant **2.** [en qualité] inadequate **3.** [inapte] incompetent / *la plupart de nos élèves sont insuffisants en langues* most of our pupils are poor ou weak at languages.

insuffler [3] [ɛ̃syfle] vt **1.** MÉD & TECHNOL to insufflate / *insuffler de l'air dans un corps* to blow ou to insufflate air into a body **2.** *sout* [inspirer] : *la terreur lui insuffla du courage* terror inspired her to be brave.

insulaire [ɛ̃sylɛʀ] ◆ adj island (*modif*), insular / *la population insulaire* the population of the island, the island population. ◆ nmf islander.

insuline [ɛ̃sylin] nf insulin.

insultant, e [ɛ̃syltɑ̃, ɑ̃t] adj insulting / *c'est insultant pour moi* it's an insult to me, I'm insulted by it.

insulte [ɛ̃sylt] nf **1.** [parole blessante] insult **2.** *fig & sout* [atteinte, outrage] insult / *une insulte au bon sens* an insult to common sense.

insulter [ɛ̃sylte] vt to insult.

insupportable [ɛ̃sypɔʀtabl] adj **1.** [insoutenable -démangeaison, vision] unbearable, unendurable ; [-bruit] unbearable, insufferable ; [-lumière] unbearably bright ; [-situation] intolerable **2.** [turbulent -enfant, élève] impossible, insufferable, unbearable.

insurgé, e [ɛ̃syʀʒe] nm insurgent.

insurger [17] [ɛ̃syʀʒe] ❖ s'insurger vpi ▸ **s'insurger contre qqn** to rise up ou to rebel against sb ▸ **s'insurger contre qqch** to rebel against ou to strongly oppose sthg.

insurmontable [ɛ̃syʀmɔ̃tabl] adj **1.** [infranchissable -obstacle] insurmountable, insuperable **2.** [invincible -aversion, angoisse] uncontrollable, unconquerable.

insurrection [ɛ̃syʀɛksjɔ̃] nf **1.** [révolte] insurrection **2.** *litt* [indignation] revolt, rising up.

intact, e [ɛ̃takt] adj [réputation, économies] intact.

intangible [ɛ̃tɑ̃ʒibl] adj [impalpable] intangible.

intarissable [ɛ̃taʀisabl] adj **1.** [inépuisable -source] inexhaustible, unlimited ; [-mine] inexhaustible ; [-imagination] inexhaustible, boundless, limitless **2.** [bavard] inexhaustible, unstoppable, tireless / *sur le vin, il est intarissable* if you get him talking on wine, he'll go on for ever.

intégral, e, aux [ɛ̃tegral, o] adj [complet] complete / *remboursement intégral d'une dette* full ou complete repayment of a debt ▸ **texte intégral** unabridged version ▸ **version intégrale** [film] uncut version. ❖ **Intégrale** nf [œuvre] complete works.

intégralement [ɛ̃tegralmɑ̃] adv in full, fully, completely.

intégralité [ɛ̃tegralite] nf whole ▸ **l'intégralité de la dette** the entire debt, the debt in full.

intégration [ɛ̃tegʀasjɔ̃] nf **1.** [insertion] integration **2.** [entrée dans une école, une organisation] entry **3.** MATH, PHYS & PSYCHOL integration **4.** ÉCON integration.

intègre [ɛ̃tɛgʀ] adj **1.** [honnête] honest **2.** [équitable, impartial] upright, righteous, upstanding.

intégré, e [ɛ̃tegʀe] adj **1.** [appareil] built-in **2.** [entreprise] integrated **3.** NUCL integrated **4.** INFORM integrated ▸ **traitement intégré de l'information** integrated (data) processing.

intégrer [8] [ɛ̃tegʀe] vt **1.** [inclure] to integrate, to incorporate, to include ▸ **intégrer qqch à** ou **dans un ensemble** to integrate ou to incorporate sthg into a whole **2.** [entrer à -école] to get into, to enter ; [-entreprise] to enter ; [-club] to join. ❖ **s'intégrer** vpi **1.** [élément d'un kit] to fit ▸ **s'intégrer à** to fit into **2.** [personne] to become integrated ou assimilated / *ils se sont mal intégrés à la vie du village* they never really fitted into village life.

▱ In reformed spelling (see p. 16-18), this verb is conjugated like *semer : il intègrera, elle s'intègrerait*.

intégrisme [ɛ̃tegʀism] nm RELIG fundamentalism.

intégriste [ɛ̃tegʀist] adj & nmf RELIG fundamentalist.

intégrité [ɛ̃tegʀite] nf **1.** [totalité] integrity / *dans son intégrité* as a whole, in its integrity **2.** [état originel] soundness, integrity *sout* **3.** [honnêteté] integrity, uprightness, honesty.

intellect [ɛ̃telɛkt] nm intellect, understanding.

intellectuel, elle [ɛ̃telɛktɥɛl] ◆ adj **1.** [mental -capacité] intellectual, mental **2.** [abstrait] intellectual, cerebral. ◆ nm, f intellectual.

intellectuellement [ɛ̃telɛktɥɛlmɑ̃] adv intellectually.

intelligemment [ɛ̃teliʒamɑ̃] adv intelligently, cleverly.

intelligence [ɛ̃teliʒɑ̃s] nf **1.** [intellect, discernement] intelligence ▸ **avec intelligence** intelligently / *il a eu l'intelligence de ne pas recommencer* he was bright ou intelligent enough not to try again ; [personne] ▸ **c'est une grande intelligence** he's a great mind ou intellect **2.** *sout* [compréhension] : *elle a l'intelligence des affaires* she has a good understanding ou grasp of what business is all about **3.** [relation] ▸ **vivre en bonne / mauvaise intelligence avec qqn** to be on good / bad terms with sb **4.** INFORM ▸ **intelligence artificielle** artificial intelligence.

intelligent, e [ɛ̃teliʒɑ̃, ɑ̃t] adj **1.** [gén] intelligent, bright, clever ▸ *c'est intelligent !* *iron* brilliant!, that was clever! **2.** INFORM intelligent.

intelligible [ɛ̃teliʒibl] adj **1.** [compréhensible -explication, raisonnement] intelligible, comprehensible **2.** [audible] intelligible, clear, audible / *parler à haute et intelligible voix* to speak loudly and clearly.

intello [ɛ̃telo] *fam & péj* ◆ adj highbrow. ◆ nmf intellectual.

intempéries [ɛ̃tɑ̃peʀi] nfpl bad weather.

intempestif, ive [ɛ̃tɑ̃pɛstif, iv] adj untimely, ill-timed, inopportune.

intenable [ɛ̃tnabl] adj **1.** [insupportable] unbearable, intolerable **2.** [indiscipliné] uncontrollable, unruly, badly-behaved **3.** [non défendable -thèse] untenable ; [-position] indefensible.

intendance [ɛ̃tɑ̃dɑ̃s] nf **1.** MIL [pour l'ensemble de l'armée de terre] Supply Corps ; [dans un régiment] quartermaster stores **2.** ÉDUC [service, bureau] (domestic) bursar's office ; [gestion] school management / *nous avons eu des problèmes d'intendance* we had supply problems.

intense [ɛ̃tɑ̃s] adj **1.** [extrême -chaleur] intense, extreme ; [-froid] intense, extreme, severe ; [-bruit] loud, intense ; [-plaisir, désir, passion] intense, keen ; [-douleur] intense, severe, acute ; [-émotion] intense **2.** [très vif -couleur] intense, bright, strong **3.** [abondant, dense -circulation, bombardement] heavy.

intensément [ɛ̃tɑ̃semɑ̃] adv intensely.

intensif, ive [ɛ̃tɑ̃sif, iv] adj **1.** [soutenu] intensive **2.** LING [pronom, verbe] intensive ; [préfixe] intensifying **3.** AGR & ÉCON intensive.

intensification [ɛ̃tɑ̃sifikasjɔ̃] nf intensification.

intensifier [9] [ɛ̃tɑ̃sifje] vt to intensify, to step up (*sép*). ❖ **s'intensifier** vpi [passion, recherche] to intensify, to become ou to grow more intense ; [douleur] to become more intense, to worsen ; [bombardements, circulation] to become heavier.

intensité [ɛ̃tɑ̃site] nf **1.** [de la chaleur, du froid] intensity ; [d'une douleur] intensity, acuteness ; [d'une couleur, d'une émotion] intensity, depth, strength ; [de la circulation] density, heaviness ; [des bombardements] severity **2.** OPT & PHYS intensity ; [d'un son] loudness ▸ **intensité de courant** ÉLECTR current.

intenter [3] [ɛ̃tɑ̃te] vt ▸ **intenter une action en justice à** ou **contre qqn** to bring an action against sb ▸ **intenter un procès à** ou **contre qqn** to institute (legal) proceedings against sb *sout*, to take sb to court.

intention [ɛ̃tɑ̃sjɔ̃] nf intention ▸ **c'est l'intention qui compte** it's the thought that counts ▸ **avoir l'intention de faire qqch** to intend to do sthg, to have the intention of doing sthg ▸ **dans l'intention de** with the intention of, with a view to ▸ **sans intention de donner la mort** DR without intent to kill ▸ **intention de vote** voting intention. ❖ **à l'intention de** loc prép for / *film à l'intention des enfants* film for ou aimed at children / *collecte à l'intention des aveugles* fund-raising for ou in aid of the blind.

intentionné, e [ɛ̃tɑ̃sjɔne] adj : *bien / mal intentionné* well- / ill-intentioned.

intentionnel, elle [ɛ̃tɑ̃sjɔnɛl] adj intentional, deliberate.

intentionnellement [ɛ̃tɑ̃sjɔnɛlmɑ̃] adv intentionally, deliberately.

interactif, ive [ɛ̃tɛʀaktif, iv] adj interactive.

interaction [ɛ̃tɛʀaksjɔ̃] nf 1. [gén] interaction, interplay 2. PHYS interaction.

intercalaire [ɛ̃tɛʀkalɛʀ] nm 1. [feuillet] inset, insert 2. [fiche] divider.

intercaler [3] [ɛ̃tɛʀkale] vt 1. IMPR to insert, to inset 2. [insérer] to insert, to fit ou to put in (*sép.*). ❖ **s'intercaler** vpi ▸ **s'intercaler entre** to come (in) ou to fit in between.

intercéder [8] [ɛ̃tɛʀsede] vi ▸ **intercéder (auprès de qqn) en faveur de qqn** to intercede (with sb) for ou on behalf of sb.

✐ In reformed spelling (see p. 16-18), this verb is conjugated like *semer* : *il intercèdera, elle intercèderait.*

intercepter [4] [ɛ̃tɛʀsɛpte] vt 1. [arrêter - véhicule] to stop ; [- lettre, message] intercept 2. MIL [avion] to intercept 3. SPORT [ballon] to intercept.

interchangeable [ɛ̃tɛʀʃɑ̃ʒabl] adj interchangeable.

interclasse [ɛ̃tɛʀklas], **intercours** [ɛ̃tɛʀkuʀ] nm break 🇬🇧, recess 🇺🇸 ▸ **à l'interclasse** at ou during the break.

intercontinental, e, aux [ɛ̃tɛʀkɔ̃tinɑ̃tal, o] adj intercontinental.

intercours [ɛ̃tɛʀkuʀ] nm = interclasse.

interdépendance [ɛ̃tɛʀdepɑ̃dɑ̃s] nf interdependence.

interdépendant, e [ɛ̃tɛʀdepɑ̃dɑ̃, ɑ̃t] adj interdependent, mutually dependent.

interdiction [ɛ̃tɛʀdiksjɔ̃] nf 1. [prohibition] ban, banning ▸ **passer outre à / lever une interdiction** to ignore / to lift a ban / *l'interdiction du livre en 1953 a assuré son succès* the banning of the book in 1953 guaranteed its success / '**interdiction de marcher sur les pelouses**' 'keep off the grass', 'do not walk on the grass' / '**interdiction de stationner**' 'no parking' / '**interdiction de déposer des ordures**' 'no dumping' 2. [suspension - d'un fonctionnaire] suspension (from duty) ; [- d'un aviateur] grounding ; [- d'un prêtre] interdict, interdiction ▸ **interdiction bancaire** stopping of payment on all cheques 🇬🇧 ou checks 🇺🇸 ▸ **interdiction de séjour** banning order.

interdire [103] [ɛ̃tɛʀdiʀ] vt 1. [défendre] to forbid ▸ **interdire l'alcool / le tabac à qqn** to forbid sb to drink / to smoke ▸ **interdire à qqn de faire qqch** a) [suj : personne] to forbid sb to do sthg b) [suj : règlement] to prohibit sb from doing sthg ; *(tournure impersonnelle) : il m'est interdit d'en dire plus* I am not allowed ou at liberty to say any more 2. DR [prohiber - circulation, stationnement, arme à feu, médicament] to prohibit, to ban ; [- manifestation, revue] to ban 3. [empêcher] to prevent, to preclude / *le mauvais temps interdit toute opération de sauvetage* bad weather is preventing any rescue operations. ❖ **s'interdire** vpt :

s'interdire l'alcool / le tabac to abstain from drinking / smoking / *elle s'interdit tout espoir de la revoir* she denies herself all hope of seeing her again.

interdisciplinaire [ɛ̃tɛʀdisiplinɛʀ] adj interdisciplinary.

interdit, e [ɛ̃tɛʀdi, it] ◆ adj 1. [non autorisé] / '**décharge / baignade interdite**' 'no dumping / bathing' / *la zone piétonne est interdite aux véhicules* vehicles are not allowed in the pedestrian area / '**interdit au public**' 'no admittance' / '**interdit aux moins de 18 ans**' CINÉ adults only, '18 🇬🇧 ', 'NC-17 🇺🇸 ' / '**interdit aux moins de 13 ans**' CINÉ 'PG 🇬🇧 ', 'PG-13 🇺🇸 ' 2. [privé d'un droit] : *interdit de séjour en France* DR banned ou prohibited from entering France 3. [frappé d'interdiction - film, revue] banned 4. [stupéfait] dumbfounded, flabbergasted ▸ **laisser qqn interdit** to take sb aback. ◆ nm, f DR ▸ **interdit de séjour en Suisse** person banned from ou not allowed to enter Switzerland. ❖ **interdit** nm 1. [de la société] (social) constraint ; [tabou] taboo ▸ **lever un interdit** to lift a restriction 2. ANTHR prohibition 3. BANQUE ▸ **interdit bancaire** stopping of payment on all cheques 🇬🇧 ou checks 🇺🇸.

intéressant, e [ɛ̃teʀesɑ̃, ɑ̃t] ◆ adj 1. [conversation, œuvre, personne, visage, etc.] interesting / *elle cherche toujours à se rendre intéressante* she's always trying to attract attention, she's an attention-seeker ▸ **de manière intéressante** interestingly 2. [avantageux] attractive, favourable ; [lucratif] profitable, worthwhile ▸ **pas intéressant** a) [offre, prix] not attractive, not worthwhile b) [activité] not worthwhile, unprofitable / *il n'est vraiment pas intéressant* he's not worth knowing. ◆ nm, f ▸ **faire l'intéressant** ou **son intéressant** *péj* to show off.

⚠ **Attention, interesting ne doit pas être employé pour traduire** intéressant **au sens d'« avantageux ».**

intéressé, e [ɛ̃teʀese] adj 1. [personne] self-interested, self-seeking, calculating ; [comportement] motivated by self-interest 2. [concerné] concerned, involved ▸ **les parties intéressées** a) [gén] the people concerned ou involved b) DR the interested parties.

intéressement [ɛ̃teʀesmɑ̃] nm profit-sharing scheme.

intéresser [4] [ɛ̃teʀese] vt 1. [passionner - suj : activité, œuvre, professeur, etc.] to interest / *l'histoire l'intéresse beaucoup* he's very interested in history / *notre offre peut peut-être vous intéresser* our offer might interest you ou might be of interest to you / *le débat ne m'a pas du tout intéressé* I didn't find the debate at all interesting / *continue, tu m'intéresses !* go on, you're starting to interest me! / *ça m'intéresserait de savoir ce qu'il en pense* I'd be interested to know what he thinks 2. [concerner - suj : loi, réforme] to concern, to affect / *un problème qui intéresse la sécurité du pays* a problem which is relevant to ou concerns national security. ❖ **s'intéresser à** vp + prép : *elle ne s'intéresse à rien* she is not interested ou she takes no interest in anything / *à quoi vous intéressez-vous ?* what are your interests (in life)? / *personne ne s'intéresse à moi* ! nobody cares about me!, nobody's interested in me!

intérêt [ɛ̃teʀɛ] nm 1. [attention, curiosité] interest ▸ **prendre intérêt à qqch** to take an interest in sthg, [bienveillance] interest, concern ▸ **porter de l'intérêt à qqn** to take an interest in sb ▸ **témoigner de l'intérêt à qqn** to show an interest in sb, to show concern for sb 2. [ce qui éveille l'attention] : *son essai offre peu d'intérêt* her essay is of no great interest 3. [utilité] point, idea / *je ne vois pas l'intérêt de continuer cette discussion* I see no point in carrying on this discussion ; [importance] importance, significance ▸ **ses observations sont du plus haut** ou **grand intérêt** his comments are of the greatest interest ou importance **4.** [avantage - d'une personne, d'une cause] inter-est **/** *elle sait où se trouve son intérêt* she knows what's in her best interests **/** *agir dans / contre son intérêt* to act in **/** against one's own interest **▸ dans l'intérêt général** in the general interest **▸ d'intérêt public** of public interest **5.** [égo-isme] self-interest **/** *il l'a fait par intérêt* he did it out of self-interest **6.** ÉCON & FIN interest **▸ à 5 % d'intérêt** 5% interest (rate). **❖ intérêts** nmpl [d'une personne, d'un pays] interests **/** *avoir des intérêts dans une société* ÉCON & FIN to have a stake ou a financial interest in a company. **❖ sans intérêt ◆** loc adj [exposition, album] uninter-esting, of no interest, devoid of interest **/** *que disais-tu ? — c'est sans intérêt* what were you saying? — it's not impor-tant ou it doesn't matter. **◆** loc adv uninterestedly, without interest **/** *je fais mon travail sans intérêt* I take no interest in my work.

interface [ɛ̃tɛʀfas] nf **1.** INFORM interface **2.** [personne] **▸ servir d'interface entre** to act as an interface between, to liaise between.

interférence [ɛ̃tɛʀfeʀɑ̃s] nf MÉTÉOR, RADIO & PHYS interference *(U)*.

interférer [18] [ɛ̃tɛʀfeʀe] vi **1.** PHYS to interfere **2.** [in-tervenir] **▸ interférer dans la vie de qqn** to interfere ou to meddle in sb's life.

🖉 In reformed spelling (see p. 16-18), this verb is conjugated like **semer** *: il interfèrera, elle interfèrerait.*

intergénérationnel, elle [ɛ̃tɛʀʒeneʀasjɔnɛl] adj intergenerational **▸ le fossé intergénérationnel** the gener-ation gap.

intérieur, e [ɛ̃teʀjœʀ] adj **1.** [du dedans] inside, inner, interior **/** *les peintures intérieures de la maison* the inter-ior decoration of the house **2.** [sentiment, vie] inner **/** *des voix intérieures* inner voices **3.** [national - ligne aérienne] domestic, internal ; [- politique, marché] domestic **▸ la dette intérieure** the national debt **4.** [interne] internal **/** *les pro-blèmes intérieurs d'un parti* a party's internal problems **5.** GÉOGR [désert, mer] inland. **❖ intérieur** nm **1.** [d'un objet] inside, interior ; [d'un continent, d'un pays] **▸ l'inté-rieur (des terres)** the interior **▸ les villages de l'intérieur** inland villages **2.** [foyer, décor] interior, home **▸ tenir un intérieur** to housekeep, to keep house **▸ homme d'inté-rieur, femme d'intérieur** homebody **3.** CINÉ interior (shot) **/** *entièrement tourné en intérieur* with interior shots only. **❖ à l'intérieur** loc adv **1.** [dedans] inside **2.** [dans la maison] inside, indoors. **❖ à l'intérieur de** loc prép **1.** [lieu] in, inside **/** *reste à l'intérieur de la voiture* stay in ou inside the car **▸ à l'intérieur des frontières** within ou inside the frontiers **▸ à l'intérieur des terres** inland **2.** [groupe] within. **❖ de l'intérieur** loc adv **1.** [d'un lieu] from (the) inside **2.** [d'un groupe] from within.

intérieurement [ɛ̃teʀjœʀmɑ̃] adv [secrètement] in-wardly.

intérim [ɛ̃teʀim] nm **1.** [période] interim (period) **▸ dans l'intérim** meanwhile, in the meantime, in the interim **2.** [remplacement] : *j'assure l'intérim de la secrétaire en chef* I'm deputizing ou covering for the chief secretary **3.** [emploi] temporary work **▸ faire de l'intérim** to temp **▸ agence d'intérim** temping agency. **❖ par intérim** loc adj [président, trésorier] interim *(modif)*, acting *(modif)* **▸ gouvernement par intérim** caretaker government.

intérimaire [ɛ̃teʀimɛʀ] **◆** adj **1.** [assurant l'intérim - directeur, trésorier, ministre] acting ; [- personnel, employé] temporary ; [- gouvernement, cabinet] caretaker **2.** [non durable - fonction] interim *(modif)* ; [- commission] provi-sional, temporary, stopgap. **◆** nmf [cadre] deputy ; [secré-taire] temp **▸ travailler comme intérimaire** to temp, to do temping work.

intérioriser [3] [ɛ̃teʀjɔʀize] vt **1.** PSYCHOL to internal-ize, to interiorize **2.** [garder pour soi] to internalize, to keep in *(sép)*.

interjection [ɛ̃tɛʀʒɛksjɔ̃] nf [exclamation] interjection.

interjeter [27] [ɛ̃tɛʀʒəte] vt **▸ interjeter appel** to lodge an appeal.

interligne [ɛ̃tɛʀliɲ] nm [blanc] space (between the lines) ; IMPR & INFORM line spacing **▸ simple / double inter-ligne** single / double spacing.

interlocuteur, trice [ɛ̃tɛʀlɔkytœʀ, tʀis] nm, f **1.** [gén] *person speaking or being spoken to* ; LING speaker, interlocu-tor *sout* ; [dans un débat] speaker **2.** [dans une négociation] negotiating partner.

interlope [ɛ̃tɛʀlɔp] adj **1.** [frauduleux] unlawful, illegal, illicit **2.** [louche] shady, dubious.

interloquer [3] [ɛ̃tɛʀlɔke] vt [décontenancer] to take aback *(sép)*, to disconcert ; [stupéfier] to stun **/** *elle resta interloquée* she was dumbfounded ou flabbergasted ou stunned.

interlude [ɛ̃tɛʀlyd] nm interlude.

intermède [ɛ̃tɛʀmɛd] nm **1.** MUS interlude, intermedio, intermezzo *spéc* ; THÉÂTRE interlude, interval piece **2.** *fig* interlude, interval.

intermédiaire [ɛ̃tɛʀmedjɛʀ] **◆** adj [moyen] inter-mediate, intermediary **▸ solution intermédiaire** com-promise (solution). **◆** nmf **1.** [médiateur] intermediary, mediator, go-between **2.** COMM intermediary, middleman. **❖ par l'intermédiaire de** loc prép [personne] through, via. **❖ sans intermédiaire** loc adv **1.** [directement] dir-ectly **2.** COMM direct, directly.

interminable [ɛ̃tɛʀminabl] adj interminable, never-ending, endless.

interministériel, elle [ɛ̃tɛʀministeʀjɛl] adj POL interdepartmental, joint ministerial UK.

intermittence [ɛ̃tɛʀmitɑ̃s] nf [irrégularité] intermit-tence, irregularity. **❖ par intermittence** loc adv inter-mittently.

intermittent, e [ɛ̃tɛʀmitɑ̃, ɑ̃t] **◆** adj [irrégulier - tir] intermittent, sporadic ; [- travail] casual, occasional ; [- pulsa-tion] irregular, periodic ; [- éclairage] intermittent ; [- averses] occasional. **◆** nm, f **▸ les intermittents du spectacle** *people working in the performing arts (and thus entitled to so-cial security benefits designed for people without regular em-ployment)*.

internat [ɛ̃tɛʀna] nm **1.** ÉDUC [école] boarding school **2.** MÉD [concours] *competitive examination leading to intern-ship* ; [stage] hospital training, time as a houseman UK, in-ternship US.

international, e, aux [ɛ̃tɛʀnasjɔnal, o] **◆** adj [gén] international. **◆** nm, f international (player ou athlete). **❖ internationaux** nmpl SPORT internationals **/** *les in-ternationaux de France de tennis* the French Open.

internationalement [ɛ̃tɛʀnasjɔnalmɑ̃] adv interna-tionally **▸ connu internationalement** world famous.

internationalisation [ɛ̃tɛʀnasjɔnalizasjɔ̃] nf inter-nationalization.

internationaliser [3] [ɛ̃tɛʀnasjɔnalize] vt to interna-tionalize. **❖ s'internationaliser** vpi to take on an inter-national dimension.

internaute [ɛ̃tɛʀnot] nmf net surfer, Internet surfer, Internet user.

interne [ɛ̃tɛʀn] **◆** adj [intérieur - paroi] internal, in-side ; [- face] internal ; [- raison, cause, logique] internal, in-ner ; [- conflit] internal ; [- personnel] in-house ; [hémorragie, organe] internal **▸ médecine interne** internal medicine. **◆** nmf **1.** MÉD **▸ interne (des hôpitaux)** houseman UK, junior hospital doctor 🇬🇧, intern 🇺🇸 **2.** ÉDUC boarder / *c'est un interne* he's at boarding school. **❖ en interne** loc adv [dans l'entreprise] in-house, on an in-house basis.

internement [ɛ̃tɛʀnəmɑ̃] nm **1.** MÉD commitment, sectioning 🇬🇧 spéc **2.** [emprisonnement] internment.

interner [3] [ɛ̃tɛʀne] vt **1.** MÉD to commit, to section 🇬🇧 spéc **2.** POL to intern.

Internet, internet [ɛ̃tɛʀnɛt] nm ▸ **(l')Internet** (the) Internet.

interpellation [ɛ̃tɛʀpelasjɔ̃] nf [par la police] (arrest for) questioning / *la police a procédé à plusieurs interpellations* several people were detained ou taken in by police for questioning.

interpeller [26], **interpeler*** [24] [ɛ̃tɛʀpəle] vt **1.** [appeler] to call out, to hail **2.** [suj : police] to call in ou to stop for questioning **3.** [concerner] to call out *(insép)* to ▸ **ça m'interpelle quelque part** hum it says something to me **4.** POL to put a question to, to interpellate *sout*.

Interphone® [ɛ̃tɛʀfɔn] nm [dans un bureau] intercom ; [à l'entrée d'un immeuble] entry ou security phone.

interplanétaire [ɛ̃tɛʀplanetɛʀ] adj interplanetary.

INTERPOL, Interpol [ɛ̃tɛʀpɔl] npr Interpol.

interposer [3] [ɛ̃tɛʀpoze] **❖ s'interposer** vpi [intervenir] to intervene, to step in *(insép)*, to make o.s. *sout* / *il s'est interposé pour l'empêcher de me frapper* he stepped in ou intervened to stop her hitting me.

interprétariat [ɛ̃tɛʀpʀetaʀja] nm interpreting.

interprétation [ɛ̃tɛʀpʀetasjɔ̃] nf **1.** [exécution - d'une œuvre musicale] interpretation, rendering, performance ; [-d'un rôle] interpretation ; [-d'un texte] reading **2.** [analyse] interpretation, analysis **3.** [interprétariat] interpreting ▸ **interprétation simultanée** simultaneous translation.

interprète [ɛ̃tɛʀpʀɛt] nmf **1.** [musicien, acteur] performer, player ; [chanteur] singer ; [danseur] dancer ▸ **les interprètes** [d'un film, d'une pièce] the cast **2.** [traducteur] interpreter ▸ **servir d'interprète à** to act as interpreter for **3.** [représentant] spokesperson, spokesman (spokeswoman).

interpréter [18] [ɛ̃tɛʀpʀete] vt **1.** [exécuter, jouer] to perform, to interpret *sout* ▸ **interpréter un rôle** to play a part / *interpréter une sonate au piano* to play a sonata on the piano ▸ **interpréter un air** to perform ou to sing a tune **2.** [comprendre - texte] to interpret ▸ **mal interpréter qqch** to misinterpret sthg ▸ **interpréter qqch en bien / mal** to take sthg well / the wrong way **3.** [traduire] to interpret.

✐ In reformed spelling (see p. 16-18), this verb is conjugated like semer : il interprètera, elle interprèterait.

interro [ɛ̃teʀo] nf ENS test.

interrogateur, trice [ɛ̃teʀɔgatœʀ, tʀis] adj [geste, regard] questioning, inquiring, probing / *sur un ton interrogateur* questioningly, searchingly.

interrogatif, ive [ɛ̃teʀɔgatif, iv] adj **1.** [interrogateur] questioning, inquiring **2.** LING interrogative.

interrogation [ɛ̃teʀɔgasjɔ̃] nf **1.** [question] question, questioning ; [doute] questioning, questions, doubts **2.** ÉDUC test, quiz 🇺🇸 ▸ **interrogation écrite / orale** written / oral test **3.** LING ▸ **interrogation directe / indirecte** direct / indirect question **4.** INFORM & TÉLÉC search ▸ **système d'interrogation à distance** remote access system.

interrogatoire [ɛ̃teʀɔgatwaʀ] nm **1.** [par la police - d'un prisonnier, d'un suspect] interrogation, questioning **2.** DR [dans un procès] examination, cross-examination, cross-questioning ; [par un juge d'instruction] hearing ; [procès-verbal] statement.

interrogeable [ɛ̃teʀɔgabl] adj fam : *répondeur interrogeable à distance* answering machine with remote-access facility.

interroger [17] [ɛ̃teʀɔge] vt **1.** [questionner - ami] to ask, to question ; [-guichetier] to ask, to inquire of ; [-suspect] to question, to interrogate, to interview ▸ **interroger qqn pour savoir si** to ask sb whether, to inquire of sb whether *sout* ▸ **interroger qqn du regard** to look questioningly ou inquiringly at sb **2.** SOCIOL to poll, to question ▸ **personne interrogée** respondent **3.** ENS [avant l'examen] to test, to quiz ; [à l'examen] to examine ▸ **être interrogé par écrit** to be given a written test ou exam **4.** INFORM to interrogate, to search (through) **5.** DR to examine, to cross-examine. **❖ s'interroger** vpi ▸ **s'interroger sur qqch** to wonder about sthg.

interrompre [78] [ɛ̃tɛʀɔ̃pʀ] vt **1.** [perturber - conversation, études] to interrupt **2.** [faire une pause dans - débat] to stop, to suspend ; [-session] to interrupt, to break off ; [-voyage] to break **3.** [définitivement] to stop. **❖ s'interrompre** vpi [dans une conversation] to break off, to stop ; [dans une activité] to break off.

interrupteur [ɛ̃tɛʀyptœʀ] nm [dispositif] switch.

interruption [ɛ̃tɛʀypsjɔ̃] nf **1.** [arrêt définitif] breaking off / *interruption des relations diplomatiques* breaking off ou severance *sout* of diplomatic relations ▸ **sans interruption** continuously, uninterruptedly, without stopping / 'ouvert sans interruption de 9 h à 20 h' 'open all day 9 a.m.-8 p.m.' ▸ **interruption volontaire de grossesse** voluntary termination of pregnancy **2.** [pause - dans un spectacle] break ; [-dans la journée] interruption ▸ **interruption de courant** ÉLECTR power cut.

intersection [ɛ̃tɛʀsɛksjɔ̃] nf [de routes] intersection, crossroads, junction.

interstice [ɛ̃tɛʀstis] nm crack, chink, interstice *sout*.

intertitre [ɛ̃tɛʀtitʀ] nm PRESSE subheading.

interurbain, e [ɛ̃tɛʀyʀbɛ̃, ɛn] adj [gén] intercity, inter urban ; *vieilli* TÉLÉC long-distance *(avant nom)*, trunk 🇬🇧 *(modif)*.

intervalle [ɛ̃tɛʀval] nm **1.** [durée] interval / *un intervalle de trois heures* a three-hour interval ou gap / *ils se sont retrouvés à trois mois d'intervalle* they met again after an interval of three months / *dans l'intervalle, je ferai le nécessaire* meanwhile ou in the meantime, I'll do what has to be done **2.** [distance] interval, space.

intervenant, e [ɛ̃tɛʀvənɑ̃, ɑ̃t] nm, f [dans un débat, un congrès] contributor, speaker.

intervenir [40] [ɛ̃tɛʀvəniʀ] vi **1.** [agir] to intervene, to step in ▸ **intervenir en faveur de qqn** to intercede ou to intervene on sb's behalf / *on a dû faire intervenir la police* the police had to be brought in ou called in **2.** MÉD to operate **3.** [prendre la parole] to speak **4.** MIL to intervene **5.** [jouer un rôle - circonstance, facteur] ▸ **intervenir dans** to influence, to affect **6.** [survenir - accord, décision] to be reached ; [-incident, changement] to take place.

intervention [ɛ̃tɛʀvɑ̃sjɔ̃] nf **1.** [entrée en action] intervention / *malgré l'intervention rapide des secours* despite swift rescue action ▸ **intervention en faveur de qqn** intervention in sb's favour 🇬🇧 ou favor 🇺🇸 **2.** MIL intervention ▸ **intervention aérienne** air strike ▸ **intervention armée** armed intervention **3.** [ingérence] interference ; POL intervention **4.** [discours] talk / *j'ai fait deux interventions* I spoke twice **5.** MÉD ▸ **intervention (chirurgicale)** (surgical) operation, surgery (U).

interventionnisme [ɛ̃tɛʀvɑ̃sjɔnism] nm interventionism.

interventionniste [ɛ̃tɛʀvɑ̃sjɔnist] **◆** adj interventionist. **◆** nmf interventionist.

intervertir [32] [ɛ̃tɛʀvɛʀtiʀ] vt to invert (the order of) / *intervertir les rôles* to reverse roles.

interview [ɛ̃tɛʀvju] nf ou nm PRESSE interview.

interviewer¹ [3] [ɛ̃tɛʀvjuve] vt PRESSE to interview.

interviewer² [ɛ̃tɛʀvjuvœʀ] nm PRESSE interviewer.

intervieweur, euse [ɛ̃tɛʀvjuvœʀ, øz] nm, f interviewer.

intestin¹ [ɛ̃tɛstɛ̃] nm ANAT intestine, bowel, gut ▸ **les intestins** the intestines, the bowels ▸ **intestin grêle** small intestine ▸ **gros intestin** large intestine.

intestin², e [ɛ̃tɛstɛ̃, in] adj *sout* [interne] internal ▸ **luttes intestines** internecine struggles.

intestinal, e, aux [ɛ̃tɛstinal, o] adj intestinal.

intime [ɛ̃tim] ◆ adj **1.** [proche] close / *un ami intime* a close friend, an intimate *sout* **2.** [privé - pensée, vie] intimate ▸ **avoir des relations intimes avec qqn** to be on intimate terms with sb ▸ **avoir l'intime conviction que** to have no doubt in one's mind that **3.** *euphém* [génital] ▸ **hygiène intime** personal hygiene **4.** [discret] quiet, intimate ▸ **soirée intime** a) [entre deux personnes] quiet dinner b) [entre plusieurs] quiet get-together **5.** [profond] inner, intimate / *il a une connaissance intime de la langue* he has a thorough knowledge of the language, he knows the language inside out. ◆ nmf [ami] close friend, intimate *sout*.

intimement [ɛ̃timmɑ̃] adv [connaître] intimately / *ces deux faits sont intimement liés* these two facts are closely connected ▸ **intimement convaincu** ou **persuadé** profoundly convinced.

intimer [3] [ɛ̃time] vt [ordonner] to instruct, to order, to tell ▸ **intimer à qqn l'ordre de se taire / de rester** to tell sb to be quiet / to stay.

intimidant, e [ɛ̃timidɑ̃, ɑ̃t] adj intimidating.

intimidation [ɛ̃timidasjɔ̃] nf intimidation.

intimider [3] [ɛ̃timide] vt **1.** [faire pression sur] to intimidate **2.** [troubler] to intimidate, to overawe.

intimité [ɛ̃timite] nf **1.** [vie privée, caractère privé] privacy / *ils se sont mariés dans la plus stricte intimité* they were married in the strictest privacy **2.** [familiarité] intimacy ▸ **l'intimité conjugale** the intimacy of married life **3.** [confort] intimacy, cosiness, snugness.

intitulé [ɛ̃tityle] nm [d'un livre] title ; [d'un chapitre] heading, title.

intituler [3] [ɛ̃tityle] vt to call, to entitle. ❖ **s'intituler** vpi [œuvre] to be entitled ou called.

intolérable [ɛ̃tɔleʀabl] adj **1.** [insupportable] intolerable, unbearable **2.** [inadmissible] intolerable, inadmissible, unacceptable.

intolérance [ɛ̃tɔleʀɑ̃s] nf **1.** [sectarisme] intolerance **2.** MÉD intolerance ▸ **intolérance alimentaire** allergy (to food).

intolérant, e [ɛ̃tɔleʀɑ̃, ɑ̃t] adj intolerant.

intonation [ɛ̃tɔnasjɔ̃] nf **1.** [inflexion de la voix] tone, intonation **2.** LING intonation.

intouchable [ɛ̃tuʃabl] ◆ adj [qui ne peut être - touché, sanctionné] untouchable ; [-critiqué] untouchable, beyond criticism, uncriticizable. ◆ nmf [paria] untouchable.

intox [ɛ̃tɔks] nf *fam* propaganda, brainwashing.

intoxication [ɛ̃tɔksikasjɔ̃] nf **1.** MÉD poisoning ▸ **intoxication alimentaire** food poisoning **2.** *fig* propaganda, brainwashing.

intoxiquer [3] [ɛ̃tɔksike] vt **1.** MÉD to poison **2.** *fig* to brainwash, to indoctrinate. ❖ **s'intoxiquer** vpi to poison o.s.

intraduisible [ɛ̃tʀadɥizibl] adj [texte, mot] untranslatable.

intraitable [ɛ̃tʀɛtabl] adj uncompromising, inflexible.

intra-muros, intramuros* [ɛ̃tʀamyʀos] ◆ loc adj inv ▸ **Londres intra-muros** inner London. ◆ loc adv ▸ **habiter intra-muros** to live in the city itself.

intranet [ɛ̃tʀanɛt] nm intranet.

intransigeance [ɛ̃tʀɑ̃ziʒɑ̃s] nf intransigence ▸ **faire preuve d'intransigeance** to be uncompromising ou intransigent *sout*.

intransigeant, e [ɛ̃tʀɑ̃ziʒɑ̃, ɑ̃t] adj uncompromising, intransigent *sout* ▸ **se montrer intransigeant envers** ou **vis-à-vis de qqn** to take a hard line ou to be uncompromising with sb.

intransitif, ive [ɛ̃tʀɑ̃zitif, iv] adj intransitive.

intransportable [ɛ̃tʀɑ̃spɔʀtabl] adj **1.** [objet] untransportable **2.** [blessé] ▸ **il est intransportable** he shouldn't be moved, he's unfit to travel.

intraveineux, euse [ɛ̃tʀavɛnø, øz] adj intravenous. ❖ **intraveineuse** nf intravenous injection.

intrépide [ɛ̃tʀepid] adj [courageux] intrepid, bold, fearless.

intrépidité [ɛ̃tʀepidite] nf [courage] intrepidness, intrepidity *sout*, boldness.

intrigant, e [ɛ̃tʀigɑ̃, ɑ̃t] nm, f schemer, plotter, intriguer *sout*.

intrigue [ɛ̃tʀig] nf **1.** [scénario] plot **2.** [complot] intrigue, plot, scheme.

intriguer [3] [ɛ̃tʀige] vt to intrigue, to puzzle / *son appel m'a intrigué* his call puzzled me.

intrinsèque [ɛ̃tʀɛ̃sɛk] adj intrinsic.

intro [ɛ̃tʀo] **(abr de introduction)** nf *fam* intro / **'passer l'intro'** [sur site Web] 'skip intro'.

introduction [ɛ̃tʀɔdyksjɔ̃] nf **1.** [préambule] introduction ▸ **quelques mots d'introduction** a few introductory remarks **2.** [contact] introduction / *après leur introduction auprès de l'attaché* after they were introduced to the attaché **3.** [importation] importing ; [adoption - d'un mot, d'un règlement] introduction ▸ **introduction en France de techniques nouvelles / de drogues dures** introducing new techniques / smuggling hard drugs into France.

introduire [98] [ɛ̃tʀɔdɥiʀ] vt **1.** [insérer] to insert, to introduce / *introduire une clé dans une serrure* to put ou to insert a key into a lock **2.** [faire adopter - idée, mot] to introduce, to bring in (sép) ; [-règlement] to institute ; [-mode, produit] to introduce, to launch ; [illégalement] to smuggle in (sép), to bring in (sép) / *introduire un produit sur le marché* ÉCON to bring out (sép) ou to launch a product onto the market **3.** [présenter] to introduce ▸ **introduire qqn auprès de** to introduce sb to ; [faire entrer - visiteur] to show in (sép). ❖ **s'introduire dans** vp + prép **1.** [pénétrer dans - suj : clé, piston] to go ou to fit into ; [-suj : eau] to filter ou to seep into ; [-suj : cambrioleur] to break into ; *fig* [suj : date, erreur] to creep into **2.** [être accepté par - suj : idée] to penetrate (into), to spread throughout, to infiltrate *péj* / *l'expression s'est introduite dans la langue* the expression entered the language.

introduit, e [ɛ̃tʀɔdɥi, it] adj : *il est très bien introduit dans ce milieu* he's well established in these circles.

introspection [ɛ̃tʀɔspɛksjɔ̃] nf introspection.

introuvable [ɛ̃tʀuvabl] adj nowhere ou no-place US to be found ▸ **elle reste introuvable** she's still missing, her whereabouts are still unknown / *ces pendules sont introuvables aujourd'hui* you can't get hold of these clocks anywhere these days.

introverti, e [ɛ̃tʀovɛʀti] ◆ adj introverted. ◆ nm, f introvert.

intrus, e [ɛ̃tʀy, yz] ◆ adj intruding, intrusive. ◆ nm, f intruder.

intrusion [ɛ̃tʀyzjɔ̃] nf [ingérence] intrusion/ *intrusion dans les affaires d'un pays étranger* interference ou intervention in the affairs of a foreign country.

intuitif, ive [ɛ̃tɥitif, iv] ◆ adj [perspicace] intuitive, instinctive. ◆ nm, f intuitive person.

intuition [ɛ̃tɥisjɔ̃] nf **1.** [faculté] intuition **2.** [pressentiment] : *il en a eu l'intuition* he knew it intuitively, he intuited it *sout*.

intuitivement [ɛ̃tɥitivmɑ̃] adv intuitively, instinctively.

inusable [inyzabl] adj which will never wear out, hardwearing.

inusité, e [inyzite] adj **1.** LING [mot] uncommon, not in use (any longer) **2.** *sout* [inhabituel] unusual, uncommon.

inutile [inytil] adj **1.** [gadget] useless ; [digression] pointless ; [effort] useless, pointless, vain / *(il est) inutile de m'interroger* there's no point in questioning me ▶ **inutile de mentir !** it's no use lying!, lying is useless! **2.** [superflu] needless, unnecessary / *quelques précisions ne seront pas inutiles* a few explanations will come in useful / *inutile de préciser qu'il faut arriver à l'heure* I hardly need to point out that ou needless to say you have to turn up on time ▶ **inutile de demander, sers-toi** just help yourself, there's no need to ask.

inutilement [inytilmɑ̃] adv needlessly, unnecessarily, to no purpose.

inutilisable [inytilizabl] adj unusable, useless.

inutilisé, e [inytilize] adj unused.

inutilité [inytilite] nf [d'un objet] uselessness ; [d'un argument] pointlessness ; [d'un effort, d'une tentative] uselessness, pointlessness ; [d'un remède] uselessness, ineffectiveness.

invaincu, e [ɛ̃vɛ̃ky] adj [équipe] unbeaten, undefeated ; [armée] unvanquished, undefeated ; [maladie] unconquered.

invalide [ɛ̃valid] ◆ adj [infirme] disabled. ◆ nmf [infirme] disabled person, invalid. ◆ nm ▶ **(grand) invalide de guerre** officially recognized war invalid.

invalider [3] [ɛ̃valide] vt [élection] to invalidate, to make invalid, to nullify ; [décision juridique] to quash ; [élu] to remove from office.

invalidité [ɛ̃validite] nf disability, disablement.

invariable [ɛ̃vaʀjabl] adj **1.** [constant] invariable, unchanging **2.** GRAM invariable.

invariablement [ɛ̃vaʀjabləmɑ̃] adv invariably.

invasion [ɛ̃vazjɔ̃] nf **1.** MIL invasion **2.** [arrivée massive] invasion, influx.

invective [ɛ̃vɛktiv] nf invective *(U)*, insult / *il s'est répandu en invectives contre moi* he started hurling abuse at me.

invectiver [3] [ɛ̃vɛktive] vt to curse, to insult, to heap insults ou abuse upon.

invendable [ɛ̃vɑ̃dabl] adj unsaleable, unsellable.

invendu [ɛ̃vɑ̃dy] nm [gén] unsold article ou item ; [journal] unsold copy.

inventaire [ɛ̃vɑ̃tɛʀ] nm **1.** [liste] inventory / *faire l'inventaire des ressources d'un pays* to assess a country's resources **2.** COMM [procédure] stocktaking 🇬🇧 ; [liste] stocklist, inventory 🇺🇸 / *faire l'inventaire de la marchandise* to take stock of the goods.

inventer [3] [ɛ̃vɑ̃te] vt **1.** [créer - machine] to invent ; [- mot] to coin **2.** [imaginer - jeu] to think ou to make up (sép), to invent ; [- système] to think ou to dream up (sép),

to work out (sép), to concoct *péj* / *je ne sais plus quoi inventer pour les amuser* I've run out of ideas trying to keep them amused / *qu'est-ce que tu vas inventer là ?* whatever gave you that idea?, where on earth did you get that idea from? **3.** [forger] to think ou to make up (sép), to invent / *une histoire inventée de toutes pièces* an entirely made-up story, a complete fabrication. ❖ **s'inventer** vp *(emploi passif)* ▶ **ça ne s'invente pas** nobody could make up a thing like that, you don't make that sort of thing up.

inventeur, trice [ɛ̃vɑ̃tœʀ, tʀis] nm, f [d'un appareil, d'un système] inventor.

inventif, ive [ɛ̃vɑ̃tif, iv] adj inventive, creative, resourceful.

invention [ɛ̃vɑ̃sjɔ̃] nf **1.** SCI & TECHNOL invention **2.** [créativité] inventiveness, creativeness / *un modèle de mon invention* a pattern I designed myself, one of my own designs **3.** [idée] invention ; [mensonge] invention, fabrication / *c'est (de la) pure invention* it's all made up ou sheer invention ou pure fabrication.

inventorier [9] [ɛ̃vɑ̃tɔʀje] vt **1.** [gén] to list, to make a list of **2.** COMM to take stock of, to list (for stocktaking) **3.** DR to make an inventory of, to inventory *sout*.

invérifiable [ɛ̃veʀifjabl] adj unverifiable, uncheckable.

inverse [ɛ̃vɛʀs] ◆ adj **1.** [opposé] opposite / *les voitures qui viennent en sens inverse* cars coming the other way ou from the opposite direction ▶ **dans l'ordre inverse** in (the) reverse order, the other way round / *dans le sens inverse des aiguilles d'une montre* anticlockwise 🇬🇧, counterclockwise 🇺🇸 **2.** MATH inverse. ◆ nm [contraire] ▶ **l'inverse** the opposite, the reverse. ❖ **à l'inverse** loc adv conversely. ❖ **à l'inverse de** loc prép contrary to.

inversement [ɛ̃vɛʀsəmɑ̃] adv **1.** [gén] conversely / *vous pouvez l'aider, et inversement il peut vous renseigner* you can help him, and in return he can give you some information **2.** MATH inversely.

inverser [3] [ɛ̃vɛʀse] vt **1.** [intervertir] to reverse, to invert ▶ **inverser les rôles** to swap parts ou roles **2.** ÉLECTR & PHOT to reverse.

inversion [ɛ̃vɛʀsjɔ̃] nf [changement] reversal, inversion.

invertébré, e [ɛ̃vɛʀtebʀe] adj invertebrate. ❖ **invertébré** nm invertebrate.

investigation [ɛ̃vɛstigasjɔ̃] nf investigation ▶ **investigations** a) [policières] inquiries, investigation b) [scientifiques] research, investigations.

investir [32] [ɛ̃vɛstiʀ] vt **1.** FIN to invest ; *(en usage absolu)* ▶ **investir à court / long terme** to make a short- / long-term investment **2.** [engager - ressources, temps, efforts] to invest, to commit / *j'avais beaucoup investi dans notre amitié* I had put a lot into our friendship **3.** [encercler - suj : armée] to surround, to besiege ; [suj : police] to block off (sép), to surround. ❖ **s'investir dans** vp + prép ▶ **s'investir dans son métier** to be involved ou absorbed in one's job / *je me suis énormément investie dans le projet* the project really meant a lot to me.

investissement [ɛ̃vɛstismɑ̃] nm **1.** FIN investment **2.** [effort] investment, commitment / *un important investissement en temps* a big commitment in terms of time.

investisseur [ɛ̃vɛstisœʀ] nm investor.

investiture [ɛ̃vɛstityʀ] nf POL [d'un candidat] nomination, selection ; [d'un gouvernement] vote of confidence.

invétéré, e [ɛ̃vetere] adj [habitude] ingrained, deeprooted ; [préjugé] deeply-held, deep-seated, confirmed ; [buveur] inveterate, habitual / *un coureur invétéré* an inveterate ou incorrigible womanizer.

invincible [ɛ̃vɛ̃sibl] adj **1.** [imbattable - héros, nation] invincible, unconquerable **2.** [irréfutable - argument] invincible, unbeatable.

inviolable [ɛ̃vjɔlabl] adj **1.** [droit, serment] inviolable **2.** [imprenable] impregnable, inviolable *sout.*

invisible [ɛ̃vizibl] adj [imperceptible] invisible ▸ **invisible à l'œil nu** invisible ou not visible to the naked eye.

invitation [ɛ̃vitasjɔ̃] nf **1.** [requête] invitation / *à* ou *sur l'invitation de nos amis* at the invitation of ou invited by our friends / **'sur invitation'** 'by invitation only' ▸ **lettre d'invitation** letter of ou written invitation **2.** [incitation] invitation, provocation / *ce film est une invitation au voyage* this film makes you want to travel.

invité, e [ɛ̃vite] nm, f guest ▸ **invité de marque** distinguished guest.

inviter [3] [ɛ̃vite] vt **1.** [ami, convive] to invite ▸ **inviter qqn à déjeuner** to invite ou to ask sb to lunch ▸ **inviter qqn chez soi** to invite sb (over) to one's house ; *(en usage absolu)* [payer] : *allez, c'est moi qui invite !* fam it's on me! **2.** [exhorter] ▸ **inviter qqn à** : *d'un signe de la tête, il m'invita à me taire* he nodded to me to keep quiet / *je vous invite à observer une minute de silence* I invite you ou call upon you to observe a minute's silence.

invivable [ɛ̃vivabl] adj [personne] impossible, unbearable, insufferable.

involontaire [ɛ̃vɔlɔ̃tɛR] adj **1.** [machinal] involuntary **2.** [non délibéré] unintentional ▸ **c'était involontaire** it was unintentional, I didn't do it on purpose **3.** [non consentant] unwilling, reluctant.

involontairement [ɛ̃vɔlɔ̃tɛRmɑ̃] adv unintentionally, unwittingly, without meaning to.

invoquer [3] [ɛ̃vɔke] vt **1.** [avoir recours à - argument, prétexte] to put forward *(sép)* / *invoquer l'article 15 du Code pénal* to refer to ou to cite Article 15 of the Penal Code ▸ **invoquer son ignorance** to plead ignorance **2.** [en appeler à - personne] to invoke, to appeal to *(insép)* ; [- dieu] to invoke ; [- aide] to call upon *(insép)*.

invraisemblable [ɛ̃vRɛsɑ̃blabl] adj **1.** [improbable - hypothèse] unlikely, improbable, implausible **2.** [incroyable - histoire] incredible, unbelievable, amazing **3.** [bizarre - tenue] weird, incredible, extraordinary **4.** [en intensif] : *elle a un toupet invraisemblable !* she has an amazing cheek!

invraisemblance [ɛ̃vRɛsɑ̃blɑ̃s] nf **1.** [caractère improbable] unlikelihood, unlikeliness, improbability **2.** [fait] improbability / *le scénario est truffé d'invraisemblances* the script is filled with implausible details.

invulnérable [ɛ̃vylneRabl] adj **1.** [physiquement] invulnerable **2.** [moralement] invulnerable **3.** [socialement] invulnerable.

iode [jɔd] nm iodine.

iodé, e [jɔde] adj iodized, iodated.

ion [jɔ̃] nm ion.

IRA [iRa] **(abr de** Irish Republican Army**)** npr f IRA.

Irak [iRak] npr m ▸ **(l')Irak** Iraq.

Irakien, enne [iRakjɛ̃, ɛn] adj Iraqi. ⬦ **Irakien, enne** nm, f Iraqi. ⬦ **Irakien** nm LING Iraqi.

Iraq [iRak] = **Irak.**

iraquien [iRakjɛ̃] = **Irakien.**

irascible [iRasibl] adj irascible *sout*, short-tempered, testy.

IRC (abr de Internet Relay Chat**)** nm IRC.

iris [iRis] nm **1.** ANAT iris **2.** BOT iris, flag.

irisé, e [iRize] adj iridescent.

irlandais, e [iRlɑ̃dɛ, ɛz] adj Irish. ⬦ **Irlandais, e** nm, f Irishman (Irishwoman) ▸ **les Irlandais** the Irish. ⬦ **irlandais** nm LING Irish (Gaelic).

Irlande [iRlɑ̃d] npr f ▸ **(l')Irlande** Ireland ▸ **(l')Irlande du Nord / Sud** Northern / Southern Ireland ▸ **la République d'Irlande** the Irish Republic.

IRM [iɛRɛm] **(abr de** imagerie par résonance magnétique**)** nm MÉD MRI.

ironie [iRɔni] nf irony / *l'ironie du sort a voulu que je le rencontre* as fate would have it, I bumped into him.

ironique [iRɔnik] adj ironic, ironical.

ironiser [3] [iRɔnize] vi to be sarcastic ▸ **ironiser sur** to be sarcastic about.

irradiation [iRadjasjɔ̃] nf **1.** [rayonnement] radiation, irradiation **2.** [exposition - d'une personne, d'un tissu] irradiation, exposure to radiation **3.** MÉD [traitement] irradiation.

irradier [9] [iRadje] ⬥ vi **1.** PHYS to radiate **2.** [se propager] to spread. ⬥ vt [soumettre à un rayonnement] to irradiate / *se faire irradier* to be exposed to radiation.

irrationnel, elle [iRasjɔnɛl] adj [gén & MATH] irrational. ⬦ **irrationnel** nm **1.** [gén] ▸ **l'irrationnel** the irrational **2.** MATH irrational (number).

irréalisable [iRealizabl] adj [ambition] unrealizable, unachievable ; [idée] unworkable, unfeasible, impracticable.

irréaliste [iRealist] adj unrealistic.

irrecevable [iRəsəvabl] adj **1.** [inacceptable] unacceptable **2.** DR inadmissible.

irrécupérable [iRekypeRabl] adj [objet] beyond repair ; [personne] irremediable, beyond redemption.

irréductible [iRedyktibl] ⬥ adj [inflexible] invincible, implacable, uncompromising. ⬥ nmf diehard, hardliner / *les irréductibles de (la) gauche / droite* the left-wing / right-wing diehards.

irréel, elle [iReɛl] adj unreal. ⬦ **irréel** nm [gén & PHILOS] ▸ **l'irréel** the unreal.

irréfléchi, e [iRefleʃi] adj [acte, parole] thoughtless, rash, reckless ; [personne] unthinking, rash, reckless.

irréfutable [iRefytabl] adj irrefutable.

irrégularité [iRegylaRite] nf **1.** [de forme, de rythme] irregularity, unevenness ; [en qualité] unevenness, patchiness **2.** [surface irrégulière - bosse] bump ; [- creux] hole **3.** [infraction] irregularity.

irrégulier, ère [iRegylje, ɛR] adj **1.** [dessin, rythme, surface] irregular, uneven ; [traits] irregular / *nous avons des horaires irréguliers* we don't work regular hours **2.** [qualité, travail] uneven / *j'étais un étudiant irrégulier* my work was erratic when I was a student **3.** [illégal] irregular / *ils sont en situation irrégulière dans le pays* their residence papers are not in order **4.** MIL irregular **5.** BOT, GÉOM & GRAM irregular.

irrégulièrement [iRegyljɛRmɑ̃] adv **1.** [de façon non uniforme] irregularly, unevenly **2.** [de façon illégale] irregularly, illegally **3.** [de façon inconstante] irregularly, erratically.

irrémédiable [iRemedjabl] adj [rupture] irreparable, irretrievable ; [dégâts] irreparable, irreversible ; [maladie] incurable, fatal.

irrémédiablement [iRemedjabləmɑ̃] adv irremediably, irretrievably.

irremplaçable [iRɑ̃plasabl] adj irreplaceable ▸ **personne n'est irremplaçable** no one is indispensable.

irréparable [iRepaRabl] ⬥ adj **1.** [montre, voiture] unrepairable, beyond repair **2.** [erreur] irreparable. ⬥ nm ▸ **l'irréparable est arrivé** irreparable harm has been done.

irrépressible [irepresibl] adj irrepressible.

irréprochable [ireprɔʃabl] adj **1.** [personne, conduite] irreproachable **2.** [tenue] impeccable / *un travail irréprochable* an impeccable ou a faultless piece of work.

irrésistible [irezistibl] adj **1.** [séduisant] irresistible **2.** [irrépressible - besoin] compelling, pressing ; [- envie] irresistible, uncontrollable, compelling.

irrésistiblement [irezistibləmã] adv irresistibly.

irrésolu, e [irezɔly] adj [personne] irresolute *sout*, indecisive, unresolved.

irrespirable [irespirabl] adj **1.** [qu'on ne peut respirer] ▶ **à l'intérieur, l'air est irrespirable a)** [trop chaud] it's close ou stifling ou stuffy inside **b)** [toxique] the air inside is unsafe ou not fit to breathe **2.** [oppressant - ambiance] unbearable, stifling.

irresponsable [irespɔ̃sabl] ◆ adj [inconséquent] irresponsible. ◆ nmf irresponsible person.

irrévérencieux, euse [ireverãsjø, øz] adj irreverent.

irréversible [ireversibl] adj **1.** [gén] irreversible **2.** CHIM & PHYS irreversible.

irrévocable [irevɔkabl] adj irrevocable.

irrigation [irigasjɔ̃] nf AGR & MÉD irrigation.

irriguer [3] [irige] vt **1.** AGR to irrigate **2.** PHYSIOL to supply (blood to).

irritabilité [iritabilite] nf [irascibilité] irritability, quick temper.

irritable [iritabl] adj **1.** [colérique] irritable, easily annoyed **2.** MÉD irritable.

irritant, e [iritã, ãt] adj **1.** [agaçant] irritating, annoying, aggravating **2.** MÉD irritant.

irritation [iritasjɔ̃] nf **1.** [agacement] irritation, annoyance **2.** MÉD irritation ▶ **irritation cutanée** skin irritation.

irriter [3] [irite] vt **1.** [agacer] to irritate, to annoy **2.** MÉD to irritate.

irruption [irypsjɔ̃] nf **1.** [entrée] breaking ou bursting ou storming in **2.** [émergence] upsurge, sudden development.

islam [islam] nm ▶ **l'islam** [religion] Islam.

Islam [islam] nm ▶ **l'Islam** [civilisation] Islam.

islamique [islamik] adj Islamic.

islamisation [islamizasjɔ̃] nf Islamization.

islamiste [islamist] ◆ adj Islamic. ◆ nmf Islamic fundamentalist.

islamophobe [islamɔfɔb] ◆ adj Islamophobic. ◆ nmf Islamophobe.

islamophobie [islamɔfɔbi] nf islamophobia.

islandais, e [islãdɛ, ɛz] adj Icelandic. ◆ **Islandais, e** nm, f Icelander. ◆ **islandais** nm LING Icelandic.

Islande [islãd] npr f ▶ **(l')Islande** Iceland.

isolant, e [izɔlã, ãt] adj CONSTR & ÉLECTR insulating ; [insonorisant] soundproofing. ◆ **isolant** nm insulator, insulating material.

isolation [izɔlasjɔ̃] nf **1.** CONSTR insulation ▶ **isolation thermique** heat ou thermal insulation ▶ **isolation phonique** ou **acoustique** soundproofing, sound insulation **2.** ÉLECTR insulation **3.** PSYCHOL isolation.

⚠ Le mot anglais **isolation** signifie avant tout « isolement ». Il ne correspond au terme français isolation que dans le domaine de la psychologie.

isolé, e [izɔle] adj **1.** [unique - cas, exemple] isolated **2.** [coupé du monde - personne] isolated ; [- hameau] isolated, cut-off, remote ; [- maison] isolated, secluded, remote ; [- forêt] remote, lonely **3.** GÉOM & PHYS isolated.

isolement [izɔlmã] nm **1.** [éloignement - géographique] isolation, seclusion, remoteness ; [- affectif] isolation, loneliness ; [sanction] solitary (confinement) ; ÉCON & POL isolation **2.** BIOL & MÉD isolation **3.** ÉLECTR insulation.

isolément [izɔlemã] adv separately, individually.

isoler [3] [izɔle] vt **1.** [séparer] to isolate, to separate off ou out *(sép)*, to keep separate / *isoler une citation de son contexte* to lift a quotation out of context, to isolate a quotation from its context **2.** [couper du monde - personne] to isolate, to leave isolated ; [- endroit] to isolate, to cut off *(sép)* **3.** [distinguer] to isolate, to single ou to pick out *(sép)* / *on n'a pas pu isoler la cause de la déflagration* it was not possible to identify the cause of the explosion **4.** CONSTR [du froid, de la chaleur] to insulate ; [du bruit] to insulate (against sound), to soundproof **5.** ÉLECTR to insulate **6.** MÉD [malade, virus] to isolate **7.** CHIM to isolate **8.** ADMIN [prisonnier] to put into ou to place in solitary confinement. ◆ **s'isoler** vp *(emploi réfléchi)* to isolate o.s., to cut o.s. off / *s'isoler pour travailler* to find somewhere private to work.

⚠ **Attention à ne pas confondre** to isolate, **qui signifie** « mettre à part », **et** to insulate, **qui a le sens d'**« isoler du froid, du bruit », **etc.**

isoloir [izɔlwar] nm polling 🇬🇧 ou voting 🇺🇸 booth.

isotherme [izɔtɛrm] adj isothermal.

Israël [israɛl] npr Israel.

israélien, enne [israeljɛ̃, ɛn] adj Israeli. ◆ **Israélien, enne** nm, f Israeli.

israélite [israelit] adj [juif] Jewish. ◆ **Israélite** nmf **1.** [Juif] Jew (Jewess) **2.** BIBLE Israelite.

issu, e [isy] adj ▶ **être issu de** [résulter de] to stem ou to derive ou to spring from / *être issu d'une famille pauvre / nombreuse* to be born into a poor / large family.

issue [isy] nf **1.** [sortie] exit ; [déversoir] outlet ▶ **issue de secours** emergency exit **2.** [solution] solution, way out **3.** [fin] outcome ▶ **cet épisode a eu une issue heureuse / tragique** the incident had a happy / tragic ending. ◆ **à l'issue de** loc prép at the end ou close of. ◆ **sans issue** loc adj **1.** [sans sortie] with no way out ▶ **ruelle sans issue** dead end / 'sans issue' 'no exit' **2.** [voué à l'échec] hopeless, doomed ; [discussions] deadlocked.

⚠ Le mot anglais **issue** signifie « problème », « question » et non issue.

Istanbul [istãbul] npr Istanbul.

isthme [ism] nm ANAT & GÉOGR isthmus.

Italie [itali] npr f ▶ **(l')Italie** Italy.

italien, enne [italjɛ̃, ɛn] adj Italian. ◆ **Italien, enne** nm, f Italian. ◆ **italien** nm LING Italian.

italique [italik] nm IMPR italics / *écrire un mot en italique* to write a word in italics, to italicize a word.

itinéraire [itinerɛr] nm [trajet] itinerary, route ▶ **itinéraire bis** diversion ▶ **itinéraire de dégagement** alternative route.

itinérant, e [itineʀɑ̃, ɑ̃t] ◆ adj [main-d'œuvre] itinerant, travelling ; [inspecteur] peripatetic ; [comédien, exposition] travelling. ◆ nm, f QUÉBEC homeless person.

IUT (abr de **institut universitaire de technologie**) nm *institute of technology offering two-year vocational courses leading to the DUT qualification.*

IVG nf abr de **interruption volontaire de grossesse.**

ivoire [ivwaʀ] nm **1.** [matière] ivory *(U)* / *statuette d'ivoire* ou *en ivoire* ivory statuette **2.** [objet] (piece of) ivory.

ivoirien, enne [ivwaʀjɛ̃, ɛn] adj Ivorian. ◆ **Ivoirien, enne** nm, f Ivorian.

ivre [ivʀ] adj [saoul] drunk, intoxicated ▸ **ivre mort** blind drunk.

ivresse [ivʀɛs] nf **1.** [ébriété] drunkenness, intoxication **2.** [excitation] ecstasy, euphoria, exhilaration / *la vitesse procure un sentiment d'ivresse* speed is exhilarating.

ivressomètre [ivʀɛsɔmɛtʀ] nm QUÉBEC ≃ Breathalyser® UK ; ≃ Breathalyzer® US.

ivrogne [ivʀɔɲ] nmf drunk, drunkard.

J (abr écrite de jour) ▸ **le jour J** a) HIST D-day b) [le grand jour] the big day.

j' [ʒ] ⟶ je.

jacasser [3] [ʒakase] vi **1.** ZOOL to chatter **2.** péj [bavarder] to chatter, to prattle.

jachère [ʒaʃɛʀ] nf [pratique] (practice of) following land / *mettre la terre en jachère* to let the land lie fallow.

jacinthe [ʒasɛ̃t] nf hyacinth ▸ **jacinthe sauvage** ou **des bois** bluebell, wild hyacinth.

jackpot [dʒakpɔt] nm **1.** [combinaison] jackpot ▸ **toucher le jackpot** pr & fig to hit the jackpot **2.** [machine] slot machine.

Jacuzzi® [ʒakuzi] nm Jacuzzi®.

jade [ʒad] nm **1.** [matière] jade **2.** [objet] jade (object) ou artefact.

jadis [ʒadis] ◆ adv sout formerly, long ago, in olden days. ◆ adj littr ▸ **au temps jadis** in times past, in the old days.

jaguar [ʒagwaʀ] nm jaguar.

jaillir [32] [ʒajiʀ] vi **1.** [personne, animal] to spring ou to shoot ou to bolt out **2.** [liquide, sang, source] to spurt (out), to gush (forth), to spout ; [flamme] to leap ou to shoot ou to spring up ; [larmes] to gush, to start flowing ; [rire] to burst out ou forth **3.** [se manifester - doute] to spring up, to arise (suddenly) / *une pensée jaillit dans son esprit* a thought suddenly came into his mind.

jais [ʒɛ] nm MINÉR jet ▸ **des yeux de jais** fig jet black eyes.

jalon [ʒalɔ̃] nm **1.** [piquet] ranging pole ou rod **2.** [référence] milestone, landmark ▸ **planter** ou **poser des jalons** fig to prepare the ground, to clear the way.

jalonner [3] [ʒalɔne] vt **1.** [terrain] to mark out ou off (insép) **2.** [longer] to line / *une carrière jalonnée de succès* a career marked by a series of successes.

jalousement [ʒaluzmɑ̃] adv **1.** [avec jalousie] jealously **2.** [soigneusement] jealously ▸ **un secret jalousement gardé** a closely ou jealously guarded secret.

jalouser [3] [ʒaluze] vt to be jealous of.

jalousie [ʒaluzi] nf [envie] jealousy, envy ; [possessivité] jealousy / *tourmenté par la jalousie* tormented by jealousy.

jaloux, ouse [ʒalu, uz] ◆ adj **1.** [possessif] jealous ▸ **rendre qqn jaloux** to make sb jealous **2.** [envieux] jealous, envious ▸ **jaloux de** jealous ou envious of--. ◆ nm, f jealous person ▸ **faire des jaloux** to make people jealous ou envious.

jamaïquain, e, jamaïcain, e [ʒamaikɛ̃, ɛn] adj Jamaican. ◈ **Jamaïquain, e, Jamaïcain, e** nm, f Jamaican.

Jamaïque [ʒamaik] npr f ▸ **(la) Jamaïque** Jamaica.

jamais [ʒamɛ] adv **1.** [sens négatif] never / *il n'a jamais su à quoi s'en tenir* he never knew where he stood / *il travaille sans jamais s'arrêter* he works without ever stopping / *vous ne le verrez plus jamais, plus jamais vous ne le verrez* you'll never (ever) see him again / *ah non ! plus jamais ça !* oh no, never again! / *jamais (une) si grande émotion ne m'avait envahi* never before had I been so overcome with emotion ▸ **presque jamais** hardly ever, almost never / *c'est du jamais vu !* it's never happened before!, it's totally unheard of! ▸ **c'est le moment ou jamais !** it's now or never! / *c'est le moment ou jamais d'y aller* now it's the best time to go ▸ **on ne sait jamais !** you never know!, who knows? ▸ **jamais deux sans trois** everything comes in threes, if it's happened twice, it'll happen a third time ▸ **jamais de la vie !** not on your life! / *jamais, au grand jamais, je n'ai fait une telle promesse !* I never ever made such a promise!, I never made such a promise, never on your life! **2.** [sens positif] ever / *si jamais il reste des places, tu en veux ?* if by any chance there are tickets left, do you want any? ▸ **si jamais je t'y reprends !** if I ever catch you at it again! ▸ **plus / moins / pire que jamais** more / less / worse than ever / *le seul / le plus beau que j'aie jamais vu* the only one / the most beautiful I have ever seen. ◈ **à jamais** loc adv sout for good, forever ▸ **à tout jamais** forever, for evermore litt.

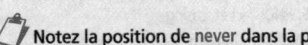 Notez la position de never dans la phrase.

• Avec un verbe autre que be conjugué, never s'insère comme suit :

sujet + [aux/modal] + never + verbe

Je n'ai jamais su si elle était sincère. *I never knew if she was sincere.*

Il ne doit jamais l'apprendre, c'est un secret. *He must never find out, it's a secret.*

• Avec le verbe be conjugué, never se place comme suit :

sujet + be + never

C'est très difficile de le joindre, il n'est jamais chez lui. *It's really hard to reach him, he's never at home.*

Elle n'est jamais contente, c'est pénible ! *She's never happy, it's really annoying!*

Dans un style recherché, never peut se placer en début de phrase. Le sujet et l'auxiliaire ou le modal qui suit sont alors inversés :

Il n'avait jamais imaginé que la maison serait vendue. *Never had he imagined that the house might be sold.*

Il ne devait jamais la revoir. *Never would he see her again.*

---

jamais-vu [ʒamɛvy] nm inv : *c'est du jamais-vu à Marseille !* it's a first for Marseille!

jambe [ʒɑ̃b] nf **1.** ANAT leg ▸ **avoir les jambes nues** to be bare-legged ▸ **avoir un bon jeu de jambes** SPORT : *il a un bon jeu de jambes* his footwork is good ▸ **ne plus avoir de jambes** ou **ne plus sentir ses jambes** : *je n'ai plus de* ou *je ne sens plus mes jambes* I'm totally exhausted, my legs have gone ▸ **avoir les jambes en coton** : *il avait les jambes en coton* his legs were like jelly ou cotton wool ▸ **être (toujours) dans les jambes de qqn** [enfant] : *il est toujours dans mes jambes* he's always under my feet ou in my way ▸ **faire une belle jambe à qqn** : *ça me / lui fait une belle jambe !* a fat lot of good that does me / him! ▸ **prendre ses jambes à son cou** to take to one's heels ▸ **se mettre en jambes** (to do a) warm up ▸ **tenir la jambe à qqn** *fam* to drone on (and on) at sb ▸ **traiter qqn par-dessus la jambe** to treat sb offhandedly **2.** [du cheval] leg **3.** VÊT (trouser) leg.

jambette [ʒɑ̃bɛt] nf ᵠᵘᴱᴮᴱᶜ [croc-en-jambe] ▸ **faire une jambette à qqn** to trip sb up.

jambière [ʒɑ̃bjɛʀ] nf **1.** [pour la danse] legwarmer **2.** [guêtre] legging, gaiter **3.** SPORT [de football] shin pads ou guards **4.** [pièce d'armure] greave, jambeau.

jambon [ʒɑ̃bɔ̃] nm [viande] ham ▸ **jambon blanc** ou **de Paris** boiled ou cooked ham ▸ **jambon cru** ou **de pays** raw ham ▸ **jambon de Bayonne** / **Parme** Bayonne / Parma ham ▸ **un jambon beurre** *fam* a ham sandwich (*in buttered baguette*).

jambonneau [ʒɑ̃bɔno] nm [petit jambon] knuckle of ham.

jante [ʒɑ̃t] nf (wheel) rim ▸ **jantes en aluminium** AUTO (aluminium) alloy wheels.

janvier [ʒɑ̃vje] nm January. **Voir aussi** mars.

Japon [ʒapɔ̃] npr m ▸ **le Japon** Japan.

japonais, e [ʒaponɛ, ɛz] adj Japanese. ❖ **Japonais, e** nm, f Japanese (person). ❖ **japonais** nm LING Japanese.

japper [3] [ʒape] vi **1.** [chien] to yelp, to yap ; [chacal] to bark **2.** ᵠᵘᴱᴮᴱᶜ to bark.

jaquette [ʒakɛt] nf **1.** VÊT [d'homme] morning coat ; [de femme] jacket **2.** [de livre] (dust) cover ou jacket, book jacket **3.** TECHNOL jacket, casing.

jardin [ʒaʀdɛ̃] nm [terrain clos - gén] garden ; [- d'une maison] garden, yard ᵁˢ ▸ **jardin botanique** botanical garden ou gardens ▸ **jardin à la française** / **à l'anglaise** formal / landscape garden ▸ **jardin zoologique** ou **d'acclimatation** zoological garden ou gardens, zoo ▸ **jardin d'hiver** winter garden ▸ **jardin ouvrier** allotment ▸ **jardin paysager** landscaped garden ▸ **jardin potager** vegetable ou kitchen garden ▸ **jardin public** public garden ou gardens, park ▸ **jardin secret** : *c'est mon jardin secret* that's my little secret. ❖ **jardin d'enfants** nm kindergarten, playgroup ou pre-school nursery ᵁᴷ.

jardinage [ʒaʀdinaʒ] nm [d'un potager, de fleurs] gardening / *faire un peu de jardinage* to potter ᵁᴷ ou to putter ᵁˢ around in the garden.

jardiner [3] [ʒaʀdine] vi to garden / *elle est dehors en train de jardiner* she's out doing some gardening.

jardinet [ʒaʀdinɛ] nm small garden.

jardinier, ère [ʒaʀdinje, ɛʀ] nm, f gardener. ❖ **jardinière** nf **1.** [sur un balcon] window box ; [pour fleurs coupées] jardiniere ; [meuble] plant holder **2.** CULIN ▸ **jardinière (de légumes)** (diced) mixed vegetables, jardiniere.

jargon [ʒaʀgɔ̃] nm **1.** [langage incorrect] jargon ; [langage incompréhensible] jargon, mumbo jumbo **2.** [langue spécialisée] jargon, argot ▸ **jargon administratif / des journalistes** officialese / journalese.

jarret [ʒaʀɛ] nm ANAT back of the knee, ham ; ZOOL hock ▸ **jarret de veau** CULIN knuckle of veal, veal shank ᵁˢ.

jarretelle [ʒaʀtɛl] nf suspender ᵁᴷ, garter ᵁˢ.

jarretière [ʒaʀtjɛʀ] nf VÊT garter.

jaser [3] [ʒaze] vi **1.** [médire] to gossip / *ça va faire jaser dans le quartier* that'll set the neighbours' tongues wagging **2.** [gazouiller - pie, geai] to chatter ; [- ruisseau, bébé] to babble ; [- personne] to chatter **3.** ᵠᵘᴱᴮᴱᶜ *fam* [bavarder] to chat.

jasette [ʒazɛt] nf ᵠᵘᴱᴮᴱᶜ *fam* chit-chat.

jasmin [ʒasmɛ̃] nm jasmine.

jatte [ʒat] nf [petite] bowl ; [grande] basin.

jauge [ʒoʒ] nf **1.** [pour calibrer] gauge **2.** [indicateur] gauge ▸ **jauge d'essence** AUTO petrol gauge ᵁᴷ, gas gauge ᵁˢ ▸ **jauge (de niveau) d'huile** AUTO dipstick.

jauger [17] [ʒoʒe] vt *litt* [juger - dégâts] to assess ▸ **jauger qqn** to size sb up / *jauger la situation* to size ou to weigh up the situation.

jaunâtre [ʒonatʀ] adj [couleur] yellowish, yellowy ; [teint] yellowish, sallow, waxen.

jaune [ʒon] ❖ adj [couleur] yellow ▸ **jaune moutarde** mustard-coloured ▸ **jaune d'or** golden yellow ▸ **jaune paille** straw-coloured. ❖ nm **1.** [couleur] yellow **2.** CULIN ▸ **jaune (d'œuf)** (egg) yolk.

jaunir [32] [ʒoniʀ] ❖ vt **1.** [rendre jaune] to turn yellow / *ses dents sont jaunies par le tabac* his teeth have been turned yellow by smoking **2.** [défraîchir] to yellow, to turn yellow / *le soleil a jauni les pages* the sun has made the pages go ou turn yellow. ❖ vi **1.** [devenir jaune] to turn ou to become yellow, to yellow **2.** [se défraîchir] to fade.

jaunisse [ʒonis] nf MÉD jaundice ▸ **en faire une jaunisse** *fam* : *tu ne vas pas en faire une jaunisse !* there's no need to get into a state ou to get worked up about it!

java [ʒava] nf **1.** [danse] java **2.** *fam* [fête] knees-up ᵁᴷ, shindig ᵁˢ / *faire la java* to have a (good old) knees-up.

Javel [ʒavɛl] npr ▸ **eau de Javel** bleach.

javelliser [3] [ʒavelize] vt to chlorinate.

javelot [ʒavlo] nm javelin.

jazz [dʒaz] nm jazz.

J.-C. (abr écrite de Jésus-Christ) J.C. ▸ **en (l'an) 180 avant / après J.-C.** in (the year) 180 BC / AD.

je [ʒə] ❖ pron pers I / *puisse-je me tromper !* *sout* let us hope I am wrong! ❖ nm inv ▸ **le je** a) LING the first person b) PHILOS the self.

jean [dʒin] nm **1.** [tissu] ▸ **(toile de) jean** denim **2.** [pantalon] (pair of) jeans.

Jeanne [ʒan] npr ▸ **Jeanne d'Arc** ou **la Pucelle** Joan of Arc ▸ **elle est coiffée à la Jeanne d'Arc** she wears her hair in a pageboy cut.

jeans [dʒins] = **jean**.

je-m'en-foutisme [ʒmɑ̃futism] nm *fam* couldn't-give-a-damn approach ou attitude.

je-ne-sais-quoi [ʒənsɛkwa] nm inv ▸ **un je-ne-sais-quoi** a certain je ne sais quoi, a certain something ▸ **un je-ne-sais-quoi de qqch** a certain hint of sthg.

jérémiades [ʒeʀemjad] nfpl [lamentations] wailing ▸ **assez de jérémiades !** stop whining ou moaning ou complaining!

jerrican(e), jerrycan [ʒeʀikan] nm jerrycan.

jersey [ʒɛʀze] nm **1.** VÊT jersey, sweater **2.** TEXT jersey, jersey knit.

Jersey [ʒɛʀze] npr Jersey. ⟶ **île**

Jérusalem [ʒeʀyzalɛm] npr Jerusalem.

jésuite [ʒezɥit] ❖ adj RELIG Jesuitic, Jesuitical. ❖ nm RELIG Jesuit.

Jésus-Christ [ʒezykʀi] npr Jesus Christ ▸ **en (l'an) 180 avant / après Jésus-Christ** in (the year) 180 BC / AD.

jet¹ [dʒɛt] nm AÉRON jet (plane).

jet² [ʒɛ] nm **1.** [jaillissement - de flammes, de sang] spurt, jet ; [- d'eau, de vapeur] jet, gush ; [- de gaz] gush **2.** [lancer - de cailloux] throwing *(U)* ▸ **à un jet de pierre** a stone's throw away **3.** SPORT throw. ❖ **d'un (seul) jet** loc adv in one go / *elle nous raconta tout d'un seul jet* she told us everything in one go ou breath. ❖ **jet d'eau** nm [filet d'eau] fountain, spray.

jetable [ʒətabl] adj [couche, briquet, gobelet, etc.] disposable.

jetée [ʒəte] nf [en bord de mer] pier, jetty.

jeter [27] [ʒəte] ❖ vt **1.** [lancer - balle, pierre] to throw / *elle m'a jeté la balle* she threw me the ball, she threw the ball to me ▸ **jeter qqch par terre** to throw sthg down (on the ground) / *ne jetez pas de papiers par terre* don't drop litter **2.** [avec un mouvement du corps] to throw / *l'enfant jeta ses bras autour de mon cou* the child threw ou flung his arms around my neck ▸ **jeter un (coup d')œil sur** ou **à qqch** to have a (quick) look at sthg, to glance at sthg **3.** [émettre - étincelle] to throw ou to give out *(sép)* ; [- lumière] to cast, to shed ; [- ombre] to cast ; [- son] to let ou to give out *(sép)* **4.** [dire brusquement] : *la petite phrase jetée par le ministre aux journalistes* the cryptic remark the minister threw at the press ▸ **jeter des injures à la tête de qqn** to hurl ou to fling insults at sb ; [écrire rapidement] to jot down *(sép)*, to scribble (down) **5.** [mettre] to throw ▸ **jeter qqn dehors** ou **à la porte** to throw sb out ▸ **jeter qqn en prison** to throw sb into jail ou prison ▸ **jeter qqch par la fenêtre** to throw sthg out of the window / *jeter un châle sur ses épaules* to throw on a shawl ▸ **se faire jeter** fam [expulser] to get kicked out **6.** [mettre au rebut - ordures, vêtements] to throw away ou out *(sép)* ▸ **jeter qqch à la poubelle** to throw sthg into the (dust) bin ▸ **jeter le bébé avec l'eau du bain** to throw the baby out with the bathwater **7.** [plonger - dans un état, dans une humeur] ▸ **jeter qqn dans l'embarras** to throw ou to plunge sb into confusion **8.** [établir - fondations] to lay ; [- passerelle] to set up ; [- pont] to throw / *jeter les fondements d'une loi / politique* to lay the foundations of a law / policy ; [maille] to make **9.** [répandre - doute] to cast ▸ **jeter le discrédit sur qqn** ou **qqch** to cast discredit on sb / sthg, to discredit sb / sthg **10.** fam [expulser] : *on a essayé d'aller en boîte mais on s'est fait jeter par un videur* we tried to get into a nightclub but got thrown out by a bouncer. ❖ vi [avoir de l'allure] fam ▸ **ça en jette !** it looks fantastic! ❖ **se jeter** ❖ vp *(emploi passif)* : *un rasoir qui se jette* a disposable razor. ❖ vpi **1.** [sauter] to throw ou to hurl o.s., to leap / *se jeter dans le vide* to throw o.s. ou to hurl o.s. into empty space ▸ **se jeter à l'eau** a) [au pr] to leap into the water b) fig to take the plunge **2.** [se précipiter] to rush (headlong) ▸ **se jeter sur qqn** to set about ou to pounce on sb / *les chiens se sont jetés sur la viande* the dogs fell on the meat / *les gens se sont jetés sur le buffet* the people fell on the food **3.** ▸ **se jeter dans** [commencer] : *se jeter à corps perdu dans une aventure* to fling o.s. body and soul into an adventure **4.** [cours d'eau] to run ou to flow into / *là où la Marne se jette dans la Seine* where the river Marne flows ou runs into the Seine.

je t'm (abr écrite de je t'aime) SMS ILU.

jeton [ʒətɔ̃] nm **1.** [pièce] token ▸ **jeton de téléphone** token for the telephone **2.** JEUX counter ; [à la roulette] chip, counter, jetton **3.** tfam [coup de poing] whack. ❖ **jetons** nmpl tfam ▸ **avoir les jetons** to be scared stiff.

jet-set [dʒɛtsɛt], **jet-society** [dʒɛtsɔsajti] nf jet set ▸ **membre de la jet-set** jet-setter.

Jet-ski® [dʒɛtski] nm jet-ski.

jeu, X [ʒø] nm **1.** LOISIRS game ▸ **le jeu** [activité] play ▸ **par jeu** for fun, in play ▸ **jeu d'adresse / de hasard** game of skill / of chance ▸ **jeu électronique / vidéo** electronic / video game ▸ **jeu radiophonique / télévisé** radio / TV quiz (game) ▸ **jeu d'argent** game played for money ▸ **jeu de construction** building set ▸ **jeu éducatif** educational game ▸ **le Jeu des mille euros** *famous radio quiz* ▸ **jeu de l'oie** *board game in the form of a spiral* ▸ **jeu en réseau** multiplayer (online) game ▸ **jeu de rôle** role play ▸ **jeu de société** board game ▸ **c'est un jeu d'enfant !** this is child's play! **2.** [cartes] hand ▸ **avoir du jeu** ou **un bon jeu** to have a good hand ▸ **il a bien caché son jeu** he played his cards very close to his chest! fig **3.** [ensemble de pièces] set ▸ **jeu de 32 / 52 cartes** pack ⬛US ou deck ⬛US of 32 / 52 cards ▸ **un jeu de dames / d'échecs / de quilles** a draughts / chess / skittles set / *un jeu de clés / tournevis* a set of keys / screwdrivers **4.** [manigances] game / *qu'est-ce que c'est que ce petit jeu ?* [ton irrité] what are you playing at?, what's your (little) game? ▸ **se (laisser) prendre au jeu** to get caught up ou involved in what's going on ▸ **voir clair** ou **lire dans le jeu de qqn** to see through sb's little game, to see what sb is up to **5.** SPORT [activité] game ▸ **le jeu à XIII** Rugby League ; [action] play ; [partie] game ▸ **faire jeu égal** to be evenly matched ; [au tennis] game **6.** [terrain] : *la balle est sortie du jeu* the ball has gone out (of play) ▸ **jeu de boules** a) [sur gazon] bowling green b) [de pétanque] ground *(for playing boules)* ▸ **jeu de quilles** skittle alley **7.** [style d'un sportif] game, way of playing / *avoir un bon jeu de jambes* to move well ; [interprétation - d'un acteur] acting ; [- d'un musicien] playing **8.** [activité du parieur] ▸ **le jeu** gambling **9.** [effet] play ▸ **jeu d'eau** fountain ▸ **jeu de mots** play on words, pun ▸ **des jeux de lumière** a) [naturels] play of light b) [artificiels] lighting effects **10.** [espace] play ▸ **la vis a** ou **prend du jeu** the screw is loose **11.** [action] play ▸ **c'est un jeu de ton imagination / ta mémoire** it's a trick of your imagination / your memory ▸ **laisser faire le jeu de la concurrence** to allow the free play of competition. ❖ **jeux** nmpl **1.** [mise] ▸ **faites vos jeux(, rien ne va plus)** faites vos jeux (rien ne va plus) ▸ **les jeux sont faits** a) pr les jeux sont faits b) fig the die is cast, there's no going back now **2.** SPORT ▸ **les Jeux (Olympiques)** the (Olympic) Games ▸ **les Jeux Olympiques d'hiver** the Winter Olympics. ❖ **en jeu** ◀ loc adj **1.** [en question] at stake / *l'avenir de l'entreprise n'est pas en jeu* the company's future is not at stake ou at risk ou in jeopardy **2.** [en action] at play **3.** [parié] at stake / *la somme en jeu* the money at stake ou which has been staked. ◀ loc adv **1.** SPORT : *mettre le ballon en jeu* FOOT to throw in the ball **2.** [en pariant] : *mettre une somme en jeu* to place a bet ▸ **mettre qqch en jeu** [risquer qqch] to put sthg at stake. ❖ **jeu de massacre** nm Aunt Sally / *le débat s'est transformé en jeu de massacre* fig the debate turned into a demolition session.

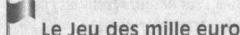

Le Jeu des mille euros

This radio programme formerly called **Jeu des mille francs** was originally broadcast in the 1950s and has become a national institution. The quiz, whose top prize was originally one thousand francs, consists of a series of questions sent in by listeners.

jeudi [ʒødi] nm Thursday ▸ **le jeudi saint** Maundy Thursday. **Voir aussi** mardi.

jeun [ʒœ̃] ❖ **à jeun** ◀ loc adj ▸ **il est à jeun** a) [il n'a rien mangé] he hasn't eaten anything b) [il n'a rien bu] he's sober. ◆ loc adv on an empty stomach ▶ **venez à jeun** don't eat anything before you come / *trois comprimés à jeun* three tablets to be taken on an empty stomach.

jeune [ʒœn] ◆ adj **1.** [peu avancé en âge - personne, génération, population] young / *il n'est plus très jeune* he's not that young any more, he's not as young as he used to be / *ma voiture n'est plus toute jeune fam* my car's got quite a few miles on the clock now ▶ **la jeune génération** the younger generation ▶ **jeune oiseau** fledgling, young bird ▶ **jeune chien** puppy, young dog ▶ **un jeune homme** a young man, a youth ▶ **une jeune femme** a (young) woman ▶ **un jeune garçon** a) [enfant] a boy, a youngster b) [adolescent] a youth, a teenager ▶ **une jeune fille** a girl, a young woman ▶ **jeunes gens** a) [garçons] young men b) [garçons et filles] youngsters, young people / *je suis plus jeune que lui de deux mois* I'm younger than him by two months, I'm two months younger than him / *ma plus jeune sœur* my youngest sister ▶ **faire jeune** : *ils font jeune(s)* they look young **2.** [débutant] : *être jeune dans le métier* to be new to the trade ou business **3.** [du début de la vie] young, early ▶ **mes jeunes années** my youth / *étant donné son jeune âge* given his youth ou how young he is **4.** [qui a l'aspect de la jeunesse - personne] young, young-looking, youthful ; [- couleur, coiffure] young, youthful ▶ **être jeune d'esprit** ou **de caractère** to be young at heart **5.** [récent - discipline, entreprise, État] new, young. ◆ adv [comme les jeunes] ▶ **s'habiller jeune** to wear young-looking clothes. ◆ nm [garçon] young man, youngster ▶ **petit jeune** *fam* young man. ◆ nf [fille] (young) girl ▶ **petite jeune** *fam* young girl. ❖ **jeunes** nmpl : *les jeunes* youngsters, young people, the young / *les jeunes d'aujourd'hui* today's young people, the young people of today, the young generation ▶ **une bande de jeunes** a bunch of kids.

jeûne [ʒøn] nm **1.** [période] fast **2.** [pratique] fast, fasting *(U)*.

jeûner, jeuner* [3] [ʒøne] vi **1.** RELIG to fast **2.** [ne rien manger] to go without food.

jeunesse [ʒœnɛs] nf **1.** [juvénilité - d'une personne] youth, youthfulness ; [- d'une génération, d'une population] youthfulness, young age ; [- d'un arbre, d'un animal] young age ; [- des traits, d'un style] youthfulness ▶ **j'apprécie la jeunesse d'esprit** ou **de caractère** I appreciate a youthful outlook ou frame of mind **2.** [enfance - d'une personne] youth ; [- d'une science] early period, infancy ▶ **dans ma** ou **au temps de ma jeunesse** in my youth, when I was young, in my early years **3.** SOCIOL ▶ **la jeunesse** young people, the young / *la jeunesse étudiante* young students, student youth / *la jeunesse ouvrière* young workers, working-class youth ▶ **émissions pour la jeunesse** a) TV programmes 🇬🇧 ou programs 🇺🇸 for younger viewers b) RADIO programmes 🇬🇧 ou programs 🇺🇸 for younger listeners ▶ **la jeunesse dorée** gilded youth *sout* **4.** *vieilli* [jeune fille] (young) girl / *ce n'est plus une jeunesse* she's no longer young. ❖ **de jeunesse** loc adj : *ses amours / œuvres / péchés de jeunesse* the loves / works / sins of his youth.

jeunisme [ʒœnism] nm discrimination in favour of young people.

JF, jf 1. abr écrite de **jeune fille 2.** abr écrite de **jeune femme.**

JH abr écrite de **jeune homme.**

JO nmpl abr de **jeux Olympiques.**

joaillerie [ʒɔajri] nf **1.** [art] ▶ **la joaillerie** jewelling **2.** [commerce] ▶ **la joaillerie** the jewel trade, jewellery **3.** [magasin] jeweller's shop 🇬🇧, jeweler's store 🇺🇸 **4.** [articles] ▶ **la joaillerie** jewellery.

joaillier, ère, joailler*, ère [ʒɔaje, ɛʀ] nm, f jeweller 🇬🇧, jeweler 🇺🇸.

job [dʒɔb] nm *fam* [travail - temporaire] (temporary) job ; [- permanent] job.

jockey [ʒɔkɛ] nmf jockey.

jogging [dʒɔgiŋ] nm **1.** [activité] jogging ▶ **faire son jogging matinal** to go for one's morning jog **2.** VÊT track suit *(for jogging).*

joie [ʒwa] nf **1.** [bonheur] joy, delight ▶ **être fou de joie** to be wild with joy / *pousser un cri de joie* to shout ou to whoop for joy ▶ **pour la plus grande joie de ses parents, elle a obtenu la bourse** much to the delight of her parents ou to her parent's great delight, she won the scholarship ▶ **joie de vivre** joie de vivre / *c'est pas la joie à la maison fam* life at home isn't exactly a laugh-a-minute ou a bundle of laughs **2.** [plaisir] pleasure ▶ **avec joie !** with great pleasure! / *il a accepté avec joie* he was delighted to accept / *je suis tout à la joie de revoir mes amis sout* I'm overjoyed at the idea of ou I'm greatly looking forward to seeing my friends again / *je me ferai une joie de lui dire ses quatre vérités hum* I shall be only too pleased to tell him a few home truths. ❖ **joies** nfpl [plaisirs] joys / *les joies de la vie / retraite* the joys of life / retirement.

joignable [ʒwaɲabl] adj : *je suis joignable à ce numéro* I can be reached at this number.

joindre [82] [ʒwɛ̃dʀ] ◆ vt **1.** [attacher - ficelles, bâtons] to join (together), to put together ; [- câbler] to join, to connect ▶ **joindre les deux bouts** to make ends meet **2.** [rapprocher] to put ou to bring together / *joindre les mains* [pour prier] to clasp one's hands, to put one's hands together **3.** [ajouter] ▶ **joindre qqch à** to add sthg to / *je joins à ce pli un chèque de 50 euros* please find enclosed a cheque for 50 euros / *voulez-vous joindre une carte aux fleurs ?* would you like to send a card with ou to attach a card to the flowers? **4.** [associer] to combine, to link / *joindre la technique à l'efficacité* to combine technical know-how and efficiency **5.** [contacter] to contact, to get in touch with ▶ **joindre qqn par téléphone** to get through to sb on the phone, to contact sb by phone. ◆ vi [porte, planches, battants] : *les volets qui joignent bien / mal* shutters that close / don't close properly. ❖ **se joindre** à vp + prép [s'associer à] to join / *tu veux te joindre à nous ?* would you like to come with us? / *se joindre à une conversation / partie de rami* to join in a conversation / game of rummy / *Lisa se joint à moi pour vous souhaiter la bonne année* Lisa and I wish you ou Lisa joins me in wishing you a Happy New Year.

joint, e [ʒwɛ̃, ɛ̃t] adj **1.** [rapproché] : *agenouillé, les mains jointes* kneeling with his hands (clasped) together **2.** [attaché] : *planches mal / solidement jointes* loose- / tight-fitting boards. ❖ **joint** nm **1.** CONSTR & MENUIS [garniture d'étanchéité] joint ; [ligne d'assemblage] join **2.** MÉCAN [ligne d'assemblage] joint ▶ **joint de culasse** AUTO (cylinder) head gasket ▶ **joint (d'étanchéité)** gasket, seal **3.** [de robinet] washer **4.** *fam* [drogue] joint.

jointure [ʒwɛtyʀ] nf **1.** ANAT joint ; [chez le cheval] pastern joint, fetlock **2.** [assemblage] joint ; [point de jonction] join.

joker [ʒɔkɛʀ] nm **1.** CARTES joker **2.** INFORM wild card.

joli, e [ʒɔli] adj **1.** [voix, robe, sourire] pretty, lovely, nice ; [poème] pretty, lovely ; [voyage, mariage] lovely, nice ; [personne] attractive ▶ **être joli garçon** : *il est joli garçon* he's nice-looking ou attractive **2.** [considérable] : *une jolie (petite) somme, un joli (petit) pécule* a nice ou tidy ou handsome (little) sum of money **3.** [usage ironique] : *tu nous as mis dans un joli pétrin fam* you got us into a fine mess ou pickle ▶ **tout ça c'est bien joli, mais…** that's all very well ou that's all well and good but… ❖ **joli** *fam* ◆ nm iron

* In reformed spelling (see p. 16-18).

EXPR **faire du joli** : *quand il va voir les dégâts, ça va faire du joli !* when he sees the damage, there'll be all hell to pay! ◆ adv ▸ **faire joli** to look nice ou pretty.

joliment [ʒɔlimɑ̃] adv [élégamment] prettily, nicely.

jonc [ʒɔ̃] nm **1.** BOT rush **2.** [canne] (Malacca) cane, rattan.

joncher [3] [ʒɔ̃ʃe] vt [couvrir] to strew / *les corps jonchaient le sol* the bodies lay strewn on the ground ▸ **jonché de détritus** littered with rubbish.

jonction [ʒɔ̃ksjɔ̃] nf **1.** [réunion] joining, junction ▸ **à la jonction** ou **au point de jonction des deux cortèges** where the two processions meet **2.** ÉLECTRON, INFORM, RAIL & TÉLÉC junction.

jongler [3] [ʒɔ̃gle] vi **1.** [avec des balles] to juggle **2.** *fig* ▸ **jongler avec** [manier avec aisance] to juggle with.

jongleur, euse [ʒɔ̃glœr, øz] nm, f juggler.

jonquille [ʒɔ̃kij] nf (wild) daffodil, jonquil.

Jordanie [ʒɔrdani] npr f ▸ **(la) Jordanie** Jordan.

jordanien, enne [ʒɔrdanjɛ̃, ɛn] adj Jordanian. ◆ **Jordanien, enne** nm, f Jordanian.

jouable [ʒwabl] adj **1.** MUS & THÉÂTRE playable **2.** SPORT [coup] which can be played, feasible / *le coup n'est pas jouable* it's not feasible, it's impossible.

joual [ʒwal] nm ⟨QUÉBEC⟩ joual.

joue [ʒu] nf **1.** [du visage] cheek ▸ **joue contre joue** cheek to cheek. ◆ **en joue** loc adv ▸ **coucher** ou **mettre qqn / qqch en joue** to (take) aim at sb / sthg ▸ **tenir qqn / qqch en joue** to hold sb / sthg in one's sights ▸ **en joue !** take aim!

jouer [6] [ʒwe] ◆ vi **1.** [s'amuser] to play ▸ **jouer au ballon / au train électrique / à la poupée** to play with a ball / an electric train / a doll ▸ **jouer à la marchande / au docteur** to play (at) shops / doctors and nurses ▸ **jouer avec les sentiments de qqn** to play ou to trifle with sb's feelings ▸ **tu joues avec ta santé / vie** you're gambling with your health / life ▸ **je ne joue plus a)** *pr* I'm not playing anymore **b)** *fig* I don't want to have any part of this any more **2.** LOISIRS & SPORT to play / *jouer au golf / football / squash* to play golf / football / squash / *jouer aux cartes / au billard* to play cards / billiards ▸ **(c'est) à toi de jouer a)** [aux cartes] (it's) your turn **b)** [aux échecs] (it's) your move **c)** *fig* now it's your move ▸ **jouer contre qqn / une équipe** to play (against) sb / a team **3.** [parier - au casino] to gamble ; [- en Bourse] to play, to gamble ; [- aux courses] to bet / *jouer à la roulette* to play roulette ▸ **jouer aux courses** to bet on horses ▸ **jouer au loto sportif** ≃ to do the pools ⟨UK⟩ ; ≃ to play the pools ⟨US⟩ **4.** CINÉ & THÉÂTRE to act, to perform ▸ **jouer dans un film / une pièce** to be in a film / a play ▸ **elle joue vraiment bien** she's a really good actress **5.** MUS to play, to perform ▸ **bien / mal jouer a)** [gén] to be a good / bad musician **b)** [dans un concert] to give a good / bad performance, to play well / badly ▸ **elle joue très bien du piano / de la clarinette** she's a very good pianist / a very good clarinet player **6.** [intervenir - facteur] to be of consequence ou of importance ; [- clause] to apply / *il a fait jouer la clause 3 pour obtenir des indemnités* he had recourse to ou made use of clause 3 to obtain compensation / *il a fait jouer ses relations pour obtenir le poste* he pulled some strings to get the job ▸ **jouer pour** ou **en faveur de qqn** to work in sb's favour **7.** [se déformer - bois] to warp ; [avoir du jeu] to work loose **8.** [fonctionner] ▸ **faire jouer une clé (dans une serrure) a)** [pour ouvrir la porte] to turn a key (in a lock) **b)** [pour l'essayer] to try a key (in a lock). ◆ vt **1.** LOISIRS & SPORT [match, carte] to play ; [pièce d'échecs] to move, to play / *ils jouent la balle de match* it's match point ; *fig* : *il joue un drôle de jeu* he's playing a strange ou funny (little) game ▸ **bien joué ! a)** CARTES & SPORT well played! **b)** JEUX good move! **c)** *fig* well done! ▸ **jouer le jeu** to play the game ▸ **rien n'est**

encore **joué** nothing has been decided yet **2.** [au casino - somme] to stake, to wager ; [- numéro] to play (on) (insép) ; [au turf - somme] to bet, to stake ; [- cheval] to bet on (insép), to back / *il joue d'énormes sommes* he gambles vast sums, he plays for high stakes ou big money **3.** [risquer - avenir, réputation] to stake **4.** [interpréter - personnage] to play (the part of), to act ; [- concerto] to play, to perform ▸ **il a très bien joué Cyrano / la fugue** he gave an excellent performance as Cyrano / of the fugue / *jouer du Chopin* to play (some) Chopin ; *fig* ▸ **jouer l'étonnement / le remords** to pretend to be surprised / sorry ▸ **jouer un rôle** *pr & fig* to play a part **5.** [montrer - film, pièce] to put on (sép), to show / *qu'est-ce qu'on joue en ce moment ?* what's on at the moment? ◆ **jouer de** v + prép **1.** [se servir de] to make use of, to use ▸ **jouer du couteau / marteau** to wield a knife / hammer / *elle joue de son infirmité* she plays on ou uses her handicap **2.** [être victime de] ▸ **jouer de malchance** ou **malheur** to be dogged by misfortune ou bad luck. ◆ **jouer sur** v + prép [crédulité, sentiment] to play on (insép) / *arrête de jouer sur les mots !* stop quibbling! ◆ **se jouer** vp (emploi passif) **1.** [film] to be on, to be shown ; [pièce] to be on, to be performed ; [morceau de musique] to be played ou performed / *ce passage se joue legato* this passage should be played legato **2.** SPORT to be played **3.** [être en jeu] to be at stake / *des sommes considérables se jouent chaque soir* huge amounts of money are played for every night. ◆ vpi [dépendre] : *mon sort va se jouer sur cette décision* my fate hangs on this decision. ◆ **se jouer de** vp + prép **1.** [ignorer] to ignore **2.** *litt* [duper] to deceive, to dupe, to fool.

jouet [ʒwɛ] nm **1.** [d'enfant] toy **2.** [victime] plaything / *j'ai été le jouet de leur machination* I was a pawn in their game.

joueur, euse [ʒwœr, øz] ◆ adj [chaton, chiot] playful. ◆ nm, f **1.** MUS & SPORT player / *joueurs de cartes / d'échecs* card / chess players ▸ **joueur de tambour** drummer **2.** [pour l'argent] gambler ▸ **être beau / mauvais joueur** to be a good / bad loser ou sport.

joufflu, e [ʒufly] adj [bébé] chubby-cheeked.

joug [ʒu] nm **1.** AGR yoke **2.** *litt* [assujettissement] yoke.

jouir [32] [ʒwir] vi *tfam* [sexuellement] to come. ◆ **jouir de** v + prép **1.** [profiter de - vie, jeunesse] to enjoy, to get pleasure out of **2.** [se réjouir de - victoire] to enjoy, to delight in (insép) **3.** [avoir - panorama] to command ; [- ensoleillement, droit] to enjoy, to have ; [- privilège, réputation] to enjoy, to command / *il ne jouit pas de toutes ses facultés* he isn't in full possession of his faculties.

jouissance [ʒwisɑ̃s] nf **1.** [plaisir] enjoyment, pleasure ; [orgasme] climax, orgasm **2.** DR [usage] use.

jouisseur, euse [ʒwisœr, øz] nm, f pleasure-seeker.

jouissif, ive [ʒwisif, iv] adj *fam* : *ce film, c'était jouissif* that film ⟨UK⟩ ou movie ⟨US⟩ was a treat!

joujou, x [ʒuʒu] nm [jouet] toy, plaything ▸ **faire joujou avec** *fam* to play with.

jour [ʒur] nm

A. DIVISION TEMPORELLE 1. [division du calendrier] day / *quel jour sommes-nous ?* what day is it today? / *un mois de trente jours* a thirty-day month / *un jour de deuil / joie* a day of mourning / joy / *un jour de fête* **a)** [férié] holiday **b)** [de joie] day of celebration / *un jour de repos* a day of rest / *dans deux / quelques jours* in two / a few days' time / *tous les jours* every day ▸ **jour de semaine** weekday ▸ **un jour de travail** a working day ⟨UK⟩, a workday ▸ **au jour le jour a)** [sans s'occuper du lendemain] from day to day **b)** [précairement] from hand to mouth ▸ **de jour en jour a)** [grandir] daily, day by day **b)** [varier] from day to day, from one day to the next ▸ **d'un jour à l'autre**

a) [incessamment] any day (now) **b)** [de façon imprévisible] from one day to the next ▸ **jour après jour a)** [constamment] day after day **b)** [graduellement] day by day ▸ **jour pour jour** to the day / *cela fait deux ans jour pour jour* it's two years to the day **2.** [exprime la durée] ▸ **un jour de:** *c'est à un jour de marche / voiture* it's one day's walk / drive away / *j'en ai pour deux jours de travail* it's going to take me two days' work **3.** [date précise] day ▸ **l'autre jour** the other day ▸ **le jour où** the day ou time that / *dès le premier jour* from the very first day / *ils sont amoureux comme au premier jour* they're as much in love as when they first met ▸ **le jour viendra où** the day will come when ▸ **un jour** one day ▸ **un jour que** one day when / *le jour de la rentrée* ÉDUC the first day (back) at school ▸ **le jour de l'An** New Year's Day ▸ **le jour des morts** All Souls' Day ▸ **le jour de Noël** Christmas day ▸ **le jour des Rois** Twelfth Night ▸ **le jour du Seigneur** the Lord's Day, the Sabbath ▸ **de tous les jours** everyday *(avant nom)* / *dans la vie de tous les jours* in everyday life ▸ **ce n'est pas mon jour !** it's not my day! ▸ **ce n'est (vraiment) pas le jour !, tu choisis bien ton jour !** *iron* you really picked your day! ▸ **être dans un bon jour:** *elle est dans un bon jour* she's having one of her good days ▸ **être dans un mauvais jour:** *il est dans un mauvais jour* he's having one of his off days ▸ **un beau jour** one (fine) day ▸ **un de ces jours, un jour ou l'autre** one of these days ▸ **à un de ces jours !** see you soon! ▸ **à ce jour** to this day, to date ▸ **au jour d'aujourd'hui** *fam* in this day and age. **B. CLARTÉ 1.** [lumière] daylight ▸ **le jour baisse** it's getting dark ▸ **il fait (encore) jour** it's still light ▸ **le jour se lève** the sun is rising ▸ **avant le jour** before dawn ou daybreak ▸ **au petit jour** at dawn ou daybreak ▸ **jour et nuit** day and night / *je dors le jour* I sleep during the day ou in the daytime **2.** [aspect] : *sous un certain jour* in a certain light / *présenter qqch / qqn sous un jour favorable* to show sthg / sb in a favourable light / *le marché apparaît sous un jour défavorable* the market does not look promising ▸ **voir qqn sous son vrai** ou **véritable jour** to see what sb's really like ▸ **sous un faux jour** in a false light **3.** ▸ **donner le jour à a)** [enfant] to give birth to, to bring into the world **b)** [projet] to give birth to **c)** [mode, tendance] to start ▸ **jeter un jour nouveau sur** to throw ou to cast new light on ▸ **mettre au jour** to bring to light ▸ **voir le jour a)** [bébé] to be born **b)** [journal] to come out **c)** [théorie, invention] to appear **d)** [projet] to see the light of day ▸ **c'est le jour et la nuit** there's no comparison / *elle et son mari, c'est le jour et la nuit* she and her husband are like chalk and cheese. **C. OUVERTURE** [interstice - entre des planches] gap, chink ; [- dans un feuillage] gap. ◆ **jours** nmpl **1.** [vie] days, life / *mettre fin à ses jours* to put an end to one's life / *ses jours ne sont plus en danger* he no longer fear for her life **2.** [époque] : *de la Rome antique à nos jours* from Ancient Rome to the present day ▸ **passer des jours heureux** to have a good time ▸ **ses vieux jours** his old age ▸ **de nos jours** these days, nowadays ▸ **les beaux jours a)** [printemps] springtime **b)** [été] summertime. ◆ **à jour** ◆ [cahier, travail] kept up to date ; [rapport] up-to-date, up-to-the-minute / *être à jour de ses cotisations* to have paid one's subscription. ◆ *loc adv* up to date ▸ **tenir / mettre qqch à jour** to keep / to bring sthg up to date. ◆ **au grand jour** *loc adv* ▸ **faire qqch au grand jour** *fig* to do sthg openly ou in broad daylight / *l'affaire fut étalée au grand jour* the affair was brought out into the open. ◆ **de jour** ◆ *loc adj* [hôpital, unité] day, daytime *(modif)*. ◆ *loc adv* [travailler] during the day ; [conduire] in the daytime, during the day / *voyager de jour* to travel by day ▸ **être de jour** to be on day duty ou on days / *de jour comme de nuit* day and night. ◆ **du jour** *loc adj* [mode, tendance, préoccupation] cur-

rent, contemporary ; [homme] of the moment ▸ **le journal du jour** the day's paper. ◆ **du jour au lendemain** *loc adv* overnight. ◆ **par jour** *loc adv* a day, per day / *trois fois par jour* three times a day.

journal, aux [ʒuʀnal, o] nm **1.** [publication] paper, newspaper ▸ **journal électronique** electronic newspaper ▸ **journal gratuit** free paper [UK] ▸ **journal de mode** fashion magazine ▸ **le Journal officiel (de la République française)** official publication listing all new laws and decrees, transcribing parliamentary debates and publishing public notices ; ≃ Hansard [UK] ; ≃ Federal Register [US] **2.** RADIO & TV [informations] ▸ **journal parlé / télévisé** radio / television news **3.** [carnet] diary, journal ▸ **tenir un journal** to keep a diary ▸ **journal de bord** NAUT log, logbook.

 Le Journal officiel

This bulletin diffuses information about new laws, includes parliamentary debates, and informs the public of any important government business. New companies are obliged by law to publish an announcement in the Journal officiel.

journalier, ère [ʒuʀnalje, ɛʀ] adj daily.

journalisme [ʒuʀnalism] nm journalism ▸ **journalisme d'investigation** investigative journalism.

journaliste [ʒuʀnalist] nmf journalist / *les journalistes de la rédaction* the editorial staff ▸ **journaliste sportif** sports correspondent.

journalistique [ʒuʀnalistik] adj journalistic.

journée [ʒuʀne] nf **1.** [durée] day / *je n'ai rien fait de la journée* I haven't done a thing all day / *en début de journée* early in the morning ou day / *en fin de journée* at the end of the day, in the early evening **2.** ÉCON & INDUST ▸ **une journée de travail** a day's work ▸ **je commence / finis ma journée à midi** I start / stop work at noon ▸ **journée d'action** day of (industrial) action ▸ **faire la journée continue a)** [entreprise] to work a continuous shift **b)** [magasin] to stay open over the lunch hour **3.** [activité organisée] day / *les journées (parlementaires) du parti* POL ≃ the (Parliamentary) Party conference [UK] ; ≃ the party convention [US] ▸ **journée portes ouvertes** open day.

journellement [ʒuʀnɛlmɑ̃] adv **1.** [chaque jour] daily, every day **2.** [fréquemment] every day.

joute [ʒut] nf **1.** HIST joust, tilt **2.** *litt* [rivalité] joust ; [dialogue] sparring match ▸ **joute littéraire / oratoire** literary / verbal contest.

jouter [3] [ʒukste] vt to be adjacent to, to adjoin.

jovial, e, als ou **aux** [ʒɔvjal, o] adj [visage] jovial, jolly ; [rire] jovial, hearty ; [caractère] jovial, cheerful.

joyau, x [ʒwajo] nm **1.** [bijou] gem, jewel / *les joyaux de la Couronne* the crown jewels **2.** *fig* [monument] gem ; [œuvre d'art] jewel.

joyeusement [ʒwajøzmɑ̃] adv joyfully, gladly / *elle accepta joyeusement* she gladly accepted.

joyeux, euse [ʒwajø, øz] adj joyful, joyous, merry ▸ **joyeux drille :** *c'est un joyeux drille* he's a jolly fellow.

joystick [dʒɔjstik] nm joystick.

JPEG [ʒipɛg] (abr de Joint Photographic Experts Group) nm JPEG / *fichier JPEG* JPEG file.

JT nm abr de **journal télévisé**.

jubilaire [ʒybilɛʀ] nmf [BELG], [QUÉBEC] & [SUISSE] person celebrating a jubilee.

jubilation [ʒybilasjɔ̃] nf jubilation, exultation.

jubilé [ʒybile] nm **1.** [célébration de 50 ans d'existence] jubilee **2.** `SUISSE` celebration marking the anniversary of a club, the arrival of a member of staff in a company, etc.

jubiler [3] [ʒybile] vi to be jubilant, to rejoice, to exult.

jucher [3] [ʒyʃe] vt to perch ▶ juchée sur les épaules de son père perched on her father's shoulders. ❖ **se jucher sur** vp + prép to perch (up) on.

judaïque [ʒydaik] adj Judaic, Judaical.

judaïsme [ʒydaism] nm Judaism.

judas [ʒyda] nm [ouverture] judas (hole).

judéo-chrétien, enne [ʒydeɔkretjẽ, ɛn] (mpl judéo-chrétiens, fpl judéo-chrétiennes) adj Judaeo-Christian.

judiciaire [ʒydisjɛʀ] adj judicial, judiciary.

judicieusement [ʒydisjøzmɑ̃] adv [décider] judiciously, shrewdly ; [agencer, organiser] cleverly.

judicieux, euse [ʒydisjø, øz] adj [personne, esprit] judicious, shrewd ; [manœuvre, proposition, décision] shrewd ; [choix] judicious ; [plan] well thought-out.

judo [ʒydo] nm judo ▶ **au judo** in judo.

juge [ʒyʒ] nmf **1.** DR judge ▶ **Madame / Monsieur le Juge X** ≃ Mrs / Mr Justice X `UK` ; ≃ Judge X `US` / jamais, mdfes juonsieur le juge ! never, Your Honour! / être nommé juge to be appointed judge ; ≃ to be raised to the Bench `UK` ; ≃ to be appointed to the Bench `US` ▶ aller / se retrouver devant le juge to appear / to end up in court ▶ **juge d'enfants** children's judge, juvenile magistrate `UK` ▶ **juge d'instruction** ≃ examining magistrate ou justice `UK`; ≃ committing magistrate `US` ▶ **juge de proximité** ≃ lay judge **2.** [personne compétente] ▶ **j'en suis seul juge** I am sole judge (of the matter) / je te laisse juge de la situation I'll let you be the judge of the situation / être bon / mauvais juge en matière de to be a good / bad judge of **3.** SPORT judge ▶ **juge de ligne** linesman, lineswoman ▶ **juge de touche a)** FOOT linesman, lineswoman **b)** RUGBY linesman, lineswoman, touch judge.

jugé [ʒyʒe] ❖ **au jugé** loc adv at a guess / au jugé, je dirais que... at a guess, I would say that... ▶ **tirer au jugé** to fire blind.

jugement [ʒyʒmɑ̃] nm **1.** DR [verdict] sentence, ruling, decision ▶ **prononcer** ou **rendre un jugement** to pass sentence, to give a ruling ▶ **passer en jugement** to stand trial **2.** RELIG ▶ **le Jugement dernier** the Last Judgment, Day of Judgment **3.** [discernement] judgment, flair / faire preuve de jugement to show sound ou good judgment **4.** [évaluation] judgment ▶ **porter un jugement sur qqch / qqn** to pass judgment on sthg / sb ▶ **jugement de valeur** value judgment.

jugeote [ʒyʒɔt] nf fam commonsense.

juger [17] [ʒyʒe] vt **1.** DR [accusé] to try ; [affaire] to judge, to try, to sit in judgment on ▶ **elle a été jugée coupable / non coupable** she was found guilty / not guilty / il s'est fait juger pour atteinte à la vie privée he had to stand trial for violation of privacy **2.** [trancher] to judge, to decide ▶ **à toi de juger (si / quand...)** it's up to you to decide ou to judge (whether / when...) **3.** [se faire une opinion de] to judge ▶ **juger qqch / qqn à sa juste valeur** to form a correct opinion of sthg / sb ; [en usage absolu] ▶ **juger par soi-même** to judge for o.s. ▶ **il ne faut pas juger sur les apparences** don't judge from ou go by appearances **4.** [considérer] ▶ **juger qqn capable / incompétent** to consider sb capable / incompetent ▶ **juger qqn bien / mal** to have a good / poor opinion of sb ▶ **juger bon de faire qqch** to think fit to do sthg. ❖ **juger de** v + prép to judge / à en juger par son large sourire if her broad smile is anything to go by ▶ **jugez-en vous-même** judge ou see for yourself. ❖ **se juger** vp (emploi réfléchi) : elle se juge sévèrement she has a harsh opinion of herself. ◆ vp

(emploi passif) DR ▶ **l'affaire se jugera mardi** the case will be heard on Tuesday.

juguler [3] [ʒygyle] vt [arrêter - hémorragie, maladie] to halt, to check ; [- sanglots] to suppress, to repress ; [- chômage] to curb ▶ **juguler l'inflation** to curb inflation.

juif, ive [ʒɥif, iv] adj Jewish. ❖ **Juif, ive** nm, f Jew (Jewess).

juillet [ʒɥijɛ] nm July ▶ **la fête du 14 Juillet** Bastille day celebrations. Voir aussi mars.

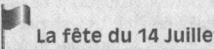

La fête du 14 Juillet

The celebrations to mark the anniversary of the storming of the Bastille begin on July 13th with outdoor public dances (**les bals du 14 Juillet**), and continue on the 14th with a military parade in the morning and a firework display in the evening.

juin [ʒɥɛ̃] nm June. Voir aussi mars.

juke-box (pl juke-box ou juke-boxes), **jukebox*** [dʒukbɔks] nm jukebox.

jumeau, elle, x [ʒymo, ɛl] ◆ adj **1.** BIOL twin (modif) **2.** [symétrique] twin (modif), identical. ◆ nm, f **1.** BIOL twin ▶ **vrais / faux jumeaux** identical / fraternal twins **2.** [sosie] double.

jumelage [ʒymlaʒ] nm [association] twinning.

jumelé, e [ʒymle] adj [villes] twin, twinned.

jumeler [24] [ʒymle] vt [villes] to twin ▶ **être jumelé à** to be twinned with.

✍ In reformed spelling (see p. 16-18), this verb is conjugated like peler : il jumèle, elle jumèlera

jumelle [ʒymɛl] f ⟶ jumeau.

jumelles [ʒymɛl] ◆ fpl ⟶ jumeau. ◆ nfpl OPT binoculars ▶ **jumelles de théâtre** ou **spectacle** opera glasses.

jument [ʒymɑ̃] nf mare.

jungle [ʒœ̃gl] nf **1.** GÉOGR jungle **2.** fig jungle ▶ **la jungle des villes** the concrete jungle.

junior [ʒynjɔʀ] ◆ adj inv **1.** [fils] junior / Douglas Fairbanks junior Douglas Fairbanks Junior **2.** [destiné aux adolescents] junior **3.** [débutant] junior / les équipes juniors the junior teams. ◆ nmf SPORT junior.

junte [ʒœ̃t] nf junta.

jupe [ʒyp] nf VÊT skirt ▶ **jupe cloche / entravée / plissée** bell / hobble / pleated skirt ▶ **jupe portefeuille** wrapover ou wraparound (skirt).

jupe-culotte [ʒypkylɔt] (pl jupes-culottes) nf (pair of) culottes.

Jupiter [ʒypitɛʀ] npr **1.** ASTRON Jupiter **2.** MYTH Jupiter, Jove.

jupon [ʒypɔ̃] nm VÊT petticoat, slip, underskirt.

Jura [ʒyʀa] npr m **1.** [en France] ▶ **le Jura** [chaîne montagneuse] the Jura (Mountains) **2.** [en Suisse] ▶ **le Jura** the Jura (canton).

juré, e [ʒyʀe] ◆ adj [ennemi] sworn / je ne recommencerai plus — (c'est) juré ? I won't do it again — promise? ◆ nm, f DR member of a jury, juror, juryman (jurywoman) / elle a été convoquée comme juré she's had to report for jury service `UK` ou jury duty `US`.

jurer [3] [ʒyʀe] ◆ vt **1.** [promettre] to swear ▶ **jurer allégeance / fidélité / obéissance à qqn** to swear ou to pledge allegiance / loyalty / obedience to sb / je te jure que c'est vrai I swear it's true ▶ **jurer de faire qqch** to swear to do sthg / elle m'a fait jurer de garder le secret she swore

* In reformed spelling (see p. 16-18).

me to secrecy *sout* **2.** DR [suj : témoin] to swear ; *(en usage absolu)* ▶ **jurer sur la Bible / devant Dieu** to swear on the Bible / to God ▶ **jurer sur la tête de qqn** to swear on one's mother's grave. ◆ vi **1.** [blasphémer] to swear, to curse ▶ **jurer après qqn / qqch** to curse ou to swear at sb / sthg **2.** [détonner -couleurs, architecture] to clash, to jar **3.** *fig* : *ils ne jurent que par leur nouvel entraîneur* they swear by their new coach. ❖ **jurer de** v + prép **1.** ▶ **il ne faut jurer de rien** you never can tell **2.** [au conditionnel] ▶ **j'en jurerais** I'd swear to it. ❖ **se jurer** ◆ vp *(emploi réciproque)* : *se jurer fidélité* to swear ou to vow to be faithful to each other. ◆ vp *(emploi réfléchi)* : *se jurer de faire* to promise o.s. ou to vow to do / *se jurer que* to vow to o.s. that.

juridiction [ʒyʀidiksjɔ̃] nf **1.** [pouvoir] jurisdiction **2.** [tribunal] court (of law) ; [tribunaux] courts (of law).

juridique [ʒyʀidik] adj [vocabulaire] legal, juridical / *il a une formation juridique* he studied law.

juridiquement [ʒyʀidikmɑ̃] adv legally, juridically.

jurisprudence [ʒyʀispʀydɑ̃s] nf [source de droit] case law, jurisprudence ▶ **faire jurisprudence** to set ou to create a precedent.

juriste [ʒyʀist] nmf jurist, law ou legal expert ▶ **juriste d'entreprise** company lawyer.

juron [ʒyʀɔ̃] nm swearword, oath.

jury [ʒyʀi] nm **1.** DR jury / *il fait partie du jury* he sits on the jury **2.** ÉDUC board of examiners, jury **3.** ART & SPORT panel ou jury *(of judges)*.

jus [ʒy] nm **1.** [boisson] juice / *ces oranges rendent* ou *donnent beaucoup de jus* these oranges are very juicy ▶ **jus de fruits** fruit juice **2.** CULIN juice, gravy ▶ **jus (de viande)** juice (from the meat) ▶ **c'est du jus de chaussettes, leur café** *fam* their coffee tastes like dishwater **3.** *fam* [café] coffee **4.** *fam* [courant électrique] juice / *attention, tu vas prendre le jus !* watch out, you'll get a shock!

jusqu'au-boutiste [ʒyskobutist] *(pl* **jusqu'au-boutistes)** *fam* ◆ nmf POL hard-liner / *c'est un jusqu'au-boutiste* he's a hard-liner. ◆ adj hard-line.

jusque [ʒyskə] *(devant voyelle ou « h » muet* **jusqu'** [ʒysk], *littéraire devant voyelle* **jusques** [ʒyskəz])**1.** *(suivi d'une prép)* [dans l'espace] : *elle m'a suivi jusque chez moi* she followed me all the way home / *je suis monté jusqu'en haut de la tour* I climbed (right) up to the top of the tower ; *(suivi d'un adverbe)* ▶ **jusqu'où** ? how far? **2.** *(suivi d'une prép)* [dans le temps] : *j'attendrai jusque vers 11 h* I'll wait till ou until about 11 o'clock ; *(suivi d'un adverbe)* ▶ **jusqu'alors** (up) until ou till then **3.** [même, y compris] even / *il y avait du sable jusque dans les rues* there was even sand in the beds. ❖ **jusqu'à** loc prép **1.** [dans l'espace] : *jusqu'à Marseille* as far as Marseille / *le sous-marin peut plonger jusqu'à 3 000 m de profondeur* the submarine can dive (down) to 3,000 m / *elle avait de l'eau jusqu'aux genoux* she was up to her knees in water **2.** [dans le temps] until / *la pièce dure jusqu'à quelle heure ?* what time does the play finish? / *jusqu'à quand peut-on s'inscrire ?* when's the last (possible) date for registering? / *jusqu'à preuve du contraire* as far as I know ▶ **jusqu'à nouvel ordre** until further notice **3.** [indiquant le degré] : *jusqu'à quel point peut-on lui faire confiance ?* to what extent ou how far can we trust him? / *sa désinvolture va jusqu'à l'insolence* he's relaxed to the point of insolence **4.** [même, y compris] even / *il a mangé tous les bonbons jusqu'au dernier* he's eaten all the sweets (down to the last one), he's eaten every last one / *single sweet.* ❖ **jusqu'à ce que** loc conj until / *tout allait bien jusqu'à ce qu'il arrive* everything was going fine until he turned up. ❖ **jusqu'au moment où** loc conj until / *je t'ai attendu jusqu'au moment où j'ai dû partir*

pour mon rendez-vous I waited for you until I had to go to my meeting. ❖ **jusque-là** loc adv **1.** [dans le présent] up to now, (up) until now ou till now ; [dans le passé] up to then, (up) until ou till then ▶ **jusque-là, tout va bien** so far so good **2.** [dans l'espace] : *je ne suis pas allé jusque-là pour rien* I didn't go all that way for nothing / *on avait de l'eau jusque-là* the water was up to here ▶ **en avoir jusque-là de qqch** *fam* : *j'en ai jusque-là de tes caprices !* I've had it up to here with your whims!, I'm sick and tired of your whims! ❖ **jusqu'ici** loc adv **1.** [dans l'espace] (up) to here, as far as here **2.** [dans le temps] so far, until now, up to now.

justaucorps [ʒystokɔʀ] nm [de gymnaste, de danseur] leotard.

juste [ʒyst] ◆ adv **1.** [avec justesse] ▶ **chanter juste** to sing in tune ▶ **tomber juste** to guess right, to hit the nail on the head **2.** [exactement] exactly, just / *il est 9 h juste* it's exactly 9 o'clock ▶ **juste à temps** [à l'heure] just in time / *tu arrives juste à temps* you've come just in time / *juste quand* ou *comme le téléphone sonnait* just as ou when the phone was ringing **3.** [à peine, seulement] just / *il vient juste d'arriver* he's just (this minute) arrived ▶ **tout juste** : *j'ai tout juste le temps de prendre un café* I've just about enough ou I've just got enough time to have a cup of coffee / *c'est tout juste s'il ne m'a pas frappé* he very nearly ou all but hit me / *c'est tout juste s'il dit bonjour* he hardly bothers to say hello, you're lucky if he says hello / *elle a été tout juste polie avec moi* she was barely civil to me **4.** [en quantité insuffisante] : *un gâteau pour 8, ça fait (un peu) juste* one cake for 8 people, that won't go very far / *tu as coupé le tissu un peu juste* you've cut the material a bit on the short side. ◆ adj **1.** [équitable -partage, décision, personne] fair ▶ **être juste envers** ou **avec qqn** to be fair to sb / *c'est pas juste !* *fam* it's not fair ou right! ; *(avant nom)* [justifié -cause, récompense, punition] just ; [-requête] legitimate ; [-colère] just, legitimate **2.** *(après le nom)* [exact -calcul, compte, réponse] right / *as-tu l'heure juste ?* have you got the right ou exact time? ; [dans son fonctionnement -horloge] accurate, right ; [-balance] accurate, true **3.** [précis -terme, expression] appropriate, right **4.** [serré -habit] tight ; [-chaussures] tight, small / *une heure pour aller à l'aéroport, c'est trop juste* an hour to get to the airport, that's not enough / *ses notes sont trop justes pour que vous le laissiez passer* his marks are too borderline for you to pass him ; [de justesse] : *elle a réussi l'examen, mais c'était juste* she passed her exam, but it was a close thing **5.** *(après le nom)* [compétent] good ; [sensé, judicieux -raisonnement] sound ; [-objection, observation] relevant, apt / *ta remarque est tout à fait juste !* your comment is quite right! / *très juste !* quite right!, good point! / *j'ai moins d'expérience que lui — c'est juste* I'm less experienced than he is — that's true ou right ; MUS [voix, instrument] true, in tune ; [note] true, right **6.** *(avant nom)* [approprié] ▶ **apprécier qqn à sa juste valeur** to appreciate the true worth ou value of sb. ❖ **au juste** loc adv exactly / *combien sont-ils au juste ?* how many (of them) are there exactly? ❖ **comme de juste** loc adv of course, needless to say.

justement [ʒystəmɑ̃] adv **1.** [à ce moment précis] : *j'allais justement te téléphoner* I was just going to phone you **2.** [pour renforcer un énoncé] quite, just so / *il se met vite en colère — justement, ne le provoque pas !* he loses his temper very quickly — quite ou exactly ou that's right, so don't provoke him! **3.** [exactement] exactly, precisely / *j'ai justement ce qu'il vous faut* I've got exactly ou just what you need **4.** [pertinemment] rightly, justly / *comme tu l'as dit si justement* as you (so) rightly said **5.** [avec justice] rightly, justly / *elle fut justement récompensée / condamnée* she was justly rewarded / condemned.

justesse [ʒystɛs] nf **1.** [d'un raisonnement, d'un jugement] soundness ; [d'une observation] appropriateness, aptness, relevance ; [d'un terme, d'un ton] appropriateness, aptness **2.** MATH & MUS accuracy ; [d'un mécanisme, d'une horloge, d'une balance] accuracy, precision. ❖ **de justesse** loc adv just, barely, narrowly / *il a gagné de justesse* he won by a narrow margin ou by a hair's breadth / *j'ai eu mon permis de justesse* I only just passed my driving test / *on a évité la collision de justesse* we very nearly had a crash / *rattraper qqn de justesse* to catch sb just in time.

justice [ʒystis] nf **1.** [équité] justice, fairness ▸ **en bonne justice** in all fairness ▸ **ce n'est que justice** it's only fair ▸ **justice sociale** social justice **2.** DR ▸ **la justice** the law ▸ **rendre la justice** to administer ou to dispense justice **3.** [réparation] justice ▸ **demander justice** to ask for justice to be done ▸ **obtenir justice** to obtain justice ▸ **se faire justice** a) [se venger] to take the law into one's own hands b) [se tuer] to take one's (own) life ▸ **rendre justice à qqn** to do sb justice / *la postérité rendra justice à son courage* posterity will recognize his courage. ❖ **en justice** loc adv DR ▸ **aller en justice** to go to court ▸ **passer en justice** to stand trial, to appear in court ▸ **traîner qqn en justice** to take sb to court, to drag sb before the courts.

justiciable [ʒystisjabl] nmf person liable ou subject to trial ▸ **les justiciables** those due to be tried.

justicier, ère [ʒystisje, ɛʀ] ◆ adj **1.** [qui rend la justice] justiciary *(modif)* **2.** [qui fait justice lui-même] : *le jury a condamné le mari justicier* the jury condemned the husband who took the law into his own hands. ◆ nm, f [redresseur de torts] righter of wrongs.

justifiable [ʒystifjabl] adj justifiable / *sa négligence n'est pas justifiable* his negligence is unjustifiable ou cannot be justified.

justificatif, ive [ʒystifikatif, iv] adj [rapport] justificatory, supporting ; [facture] justificatory / *document justificatif d'identité* written proof of one's identity. ❖ **justificatif** nm ADMIN written proof ou evidence ▸ **justificatif de domicile** proof of address ; COMPTA receipt.

justification [ʒystifikasjɔ̃] nf **1.** [motivation - d'une attitude, d'une politique] justification / *la justification de la violence* apology for ou justification of violence **2.** [excuse] justification, reason **3.** ADMIN (written) proof *(of expenses incurred)*.

justifier [9] [ʒystifje] vt **1.** [motiver - conduite, mesure, dépense] to justify, to vindicate / *rien ne saurait justifier de tels propos* there's no possible justification for speaking in such terms **2.** [confirmer - crainte, théorie] to justify, to confirm, to back up *(sép)* **3.** [prouver - affirmation] to prove, to justify ; [- versement] to give proof ou evidence of **4.** [innocenter] to vindicate **5.** IMPR & INFORM to justify. ❖ **justifier de** v + prép ▸ **justifier de son identité** to prove one's identity / *pouvez-vous justifier de ce diplôme ?* can you provide evidence that ou can you prove that you are the holder of this qualification? ❖ **se justifier** vp *(emploi réfléchi)* to justify o.s. ▸ **se justifier d'une accusation** to clear o.s. of an accusation, to clear one's name.

jute [ʒyt] nm jute.

juteux, euse [ʒytø, øz] adj **1.** [fruit, viande] juicy **2.** *fam* [transaction] juicy / *c'est une affaire bien juteuse !* that business is a real gold mine !

juvénile [ʒyvenil] adj **1.** [jeune - silhouette] young, youthful ; [- ardeur, enthousiasme] youthful **2.** PHYSIOL juvenile.

juxtaposer [3] [ʒykstapoze] vt to juxtapose, to place side by side.

juxtaposition [ʒykstapozisjɔ̃] nf juxtaposition.

K7 [kasɛt] (abr de **cassette**) nf fam cassette.
kabyle [kabil] adj Kabylian. ❖ **Kabyle** nmf Kabylian. ❖ **kabyle** nm LING Kabylian.
Kabylie [kabili] npr f ▸ **(la) Kabylie** Kabylia.
kaki [kaki] ◆ adj inv [couleur] khaki. ◆ nm BOT [arbre] (Japanese) persimmon, kaki ; [fruit] persimmon, sharon fruit.
kaléidoscope [kaleidɔskɔp] nm OPT kaleidoscope.
kamikaze [kamikaz] nmf kamikaze.
kanak, e [kanak] = **canaque.**
kangourou [kɑ̃guʀu] nm ZOOL kangaroo.
karaoké [kaʀaɔke] nm karaoke.
karaté [kaʀate] nm karate.
kart [kaʀt] nm kart, go-kart.
karting [kaʀtiŋ] nm karting, go-karting / *faire du karting* to go-kart, to go karting.
kasher [kaʃɛʀ] adj inv kosher.
Katar [kataʀ] npr m ▸ **le Katar** Katar, Qatar.
kayak [kajak] nm kayak ; [sport] kayaking / *faire du kayak* to go kayaking.
kel1 (abr écrite de **quelqu'un**) SMS SUM1.
kendo [kendo] nm kendo.
Kenya [kenja] npr m ▸ **le Kenya** Kenya.
kenyan, e [kenjɑ̃, an] adj Kenyan. ❖ **Kenyan, e** nm, f Kenyan.
képi [kepi] nm kepi.
kermesse [kɛʀmɛs] nf **1.** [de charité] charity fête, bazaar **2.** BELG [dans les Flandres] kermis, kirmess.
kérosène [keʀɔzɛn] nm kerosene, kerosine.
kestudi SMS abr écrite de **qu'est-ce que tu dis?**
kestufé SMS abr écrite de **qu'est-ce que tu fais?**
ketchup¹ [kɛtʃœp] nm ketchup.
ketchup² [kɛtʃɔp] nm QUÉBEC (chunky) ketchup.
keuf [kœf] nm *(verlan de flic)* tfam cop.
keum [kœm] nm *(verlan de mec)* fam guy.
Kfé SMS abr écrite de **café.**
kg (abr écrite de **kilogramme**) kg.
khmer, ère [kmɛʀ] adj Khmerian. ❖ **Khmer, ère** nm, f Khmer. ❖ **khmer** nm LING Khmer.
khôl [kɔl] nm kohl.
kibboutz [kibuts] (pl **kibboutz** ou **kibboutzim** [-tsim]) nm kibbutz.
kick(-starter) [kik(staʀtɛʀ)] nm kick-starter, kick-start.
kidnapper [3] [kidnape] vt [personne] to kidnap.
kidnappeur, euse [kidnapœʀ, øz] nm, f kidnapper.
kidnapping [kidnapiŋ] nm kidnapping.
kiffer, kifer [kife] vt fam to love.

kif-kif, kifkif* [kifkif] adj inv fam ▸ *c'est kif-kif* **(bourricot)** it's all the same, it makes no odds UK, it's six of one and half a dozen of the other.
kilo [kilo] (abr de **kilogramme**) nm kilo.
kilogramme [kilɔgʀam] nm kilogramme.
kilométrage [kilɔmetʀaʒ] nm [d'un véhicule] mileage.
kilomètre [kilɔmetʀ] nm **1.** [distance] kilometre UK, kilometer US **2.** INFORM ▸ *frappe* ou *saisie au kilomètre* straight keying.
kilométrique [kilɔmetʀik] adj ▸ *distance kilométrique* distance in kilometres.
kilooctet [kilɔɔkte] (pl **kilooctets**) nm kilobyte.
kilowatt [kilɔwat] nm kilowatt.
kilt [kilt] nm [d'Écossais, de femme] kilt.
kimono [kimɔno] nm VÊT kimono.
kiné [kine] nmf (abr de **kinésithérapeute**) fam physio UK, physical therapist US.
kinésithérapeute [kineziteʀapøt] nmf physiotherapist UK, physical therapist US.
kiosque [kjɔsk] nm **1.** [boutique] ▸ *kiosque à journaux* newspaper kiosk ou stand, news-stand **2.** [édifice - dans un jardin] pavilion ▸ *kiosque à musique* bandstand.
kir [kiʀ] nm kir ▸ *kir royal* kir royal *(champagne with blackcurrant liqueur).*
kirsch, kirch* [kiʀʃ] nm kirsch.
kit [kit] nm kit / *vendu en kit* sold in kit form ▸ *kit main(s) libre(s)* [pour mobile] hands-free kit.
kitch [kitʃ] = **kitsch.**
kitchenette [kitʃənet] nf kitchenette.
kitesurf [kajtsœʀf], **kite** [kajt] nm kitesurfing.
kitsch, kitch [kitʃ] adj inv kitsch. ❖ **kitsch** (pl **kitsch** ou **kitschs***), **kitch** (pl **kitch** ou **kitchs***) nm kitsch.
kiwi [kiwi] nm **1.** BOT [fruit] kiwi (fruit), Chinese gooseberry ; [arbre] kiwi tree **2.** ZOOL kiwi.
Klaxon® [klaksɔn] nm horn / *donner un coup de Klaxon* to hoot (one's horn) UK, to honk (one's horn) US.
klaxonner [3] [klaksɔne] ◆ vi to honk ou to hoot UK (one's horn). ◆ vt : *il m'a klaxonné* he tooted ou hooted UK ou honked at me.
kleptomane [klɛptɔman] nmf kleptomaniac.
km (abr écrite de **kilomètre**) km.
km/h (abr écrite de **kilomètre par heure**) kmph.
Ko (abr écrite de **kilooctet**) Kb.
K.-O. ◆ nm inv KO. ◆ adj inv **1.** SPORT KO'd ▸ *mettre qqn K.-O.* to knock sb out ▸ *être K.-O.* to be out for the count **2.** fam [épuisé] shattered UK, all in, dead beat.
koala [kɔala] nm koala (bear).

kohol [kɔɔl] = khôl.

koi (abr écrite de quoi) SMS WOT.

koi29 SMS abr écrite de quoi de neuf?

kosovar, e [kɔsɔvaʀ] adj Kosovan. ❖ **Kosovar, e** [kɔsɔvaʀ] nm, f Kosovar.

Kosovo [kɔsɔvo] npr m ▸ **le Kosovo** Kosovo.

kouglof [kuglɔf] nm kugelhopf *(cake)*.

kouign-amann [kwiɲaman] nm inv CULIN Breton cake made with a large quantity of butter.

Koweït [kɔwɛjt] npr m ▸ **le Koweït** Kuwait, Koweit.

koweïtien, enne [kɔwɛjtjɛ̃, ɛn] adj Kuwaiti. ❖ **Koweïtien, enne** nm, f Kuwaiti.

krach [kʀak] nm ▸ **krach (boursier)** crash.

kumquat [kumkwat] nm kumquat, cumquat.

kung-fu [kuŋfu] nm inv kung fu.

kurde [kyʀd] adj Kurd. ❖ **Kurde** nmf Kurd.

Kurdistan [kyʀdistɑ̃] npr m ▸ **le Kurdistan** Kurdistan.

kwa (abr écrite de quoi) SMS WOT.

K-way® [kawɛ] nm cagoule.

kyrielle [kiʀjɛl] nf : *une kyrielle de bambins* fam a whole bunch of kids / *une kyrielle d'insultes* a string of insults.

kyste [kist] nm cyst.

L SMS abr écrite de **elle**.

l' [l] ⟶ **le**.

la¹ [la] nf ⟶ **le**.

la² [la] nm inv **1.** MUS A ; [chanté] lah **2.** [EXPR] **donner le la** to set the tone. **Voir aussi fa**.

là [la] adv **1.** [dans l'espace - là-bas] there ; [-ici] here / *elle habite Paris maintenant, c'est là qu'elle a trouvé du travail* she lives in Paris now, that's where she found work / *à quelques kilomètres de là* a few kilometres away / *je ne suis là pour personne* if anybody asks I'm not in ou here **2.** [dans le temps] : *c'est là que j'ai paniqué* that's when I panicked / *attendons demain et là nous déciderons* let's wait until tomorrow and then (we'll) decide / *là, je n'ai pas le temps de lui en parler* I don't have time to tell him about it right now **3.** [dans cette situation] : *c'est justement là où je ne vous suis plus* that's just where you've lost me / *pour l'instant nous en sommes là* that's how things stand at the moment ▸ **en rester là** : *je n'ai pas l'intention d'en rester là* I don't intend leaving it at that **4.** [dans cela] : *ne voyez là aucune malice de ma part* please don't take it the wrong way **5.** [pour renforcer] ▸ **c'est là le problème / la difficulté** that's where the problem / the difficulty lies **6.** [emploi expressif] : *alors là, je ne sais pas !* well that I really don't know! / *alors là, tu exagères !* you've got a nerve! / *que me chantes-tu là ?* *fam* what are you on about? ❖ **de là** loc adv **1.** [dans l'espace] : *de là je me suis dirigée vers l'église* from there I headed towards the church **2.** [marquant la conséquence] ▸ **de là son amertume** that's why he's bitter, that explains his bitterness, hence his bitterness. ❖ **par là** loc adv **1.** [dans l'espace] ▸ **c'est par là** it's over there / *vous devriez passer par là* you should go that way **2.** *fig* : *qu'entendez-vous* ou *que voulez-vous dire par là ?* what do you mean by that?

là-bas [laba] adv **1.** [en bas] down ou under there **2.** [en un lieu éloigné] there **3.** [endroit indiqué] over there / *je le vois là-bas* I can see him over there.

label [label] nm **1.** [étiquette, marque] label ▸ **label de qualité / d'exportation** quality / export label **2.** [maison de disques] label.

labelliser, labéliser [labelize] vt [un produit] to label.

labo [labo] nm *fam* lab ▸ **labo photo** darkroom.

laborantin, e [labɔʀɑ̃tɛ̃, in] nm, f laboratory assistant, laboratory operator [US].

laboratoire [labɔʀatwaʀ] nm **1.** SCI [lieu] laboratory ; [équipe] (research) team ▸ **laboratoire d'analyses (médicales)** analytical laboratory **2.** ÉDUC ▸ **laboratoire de langue** ou **langues** language laboratory.

laborieusement [labɔʀjøzmɑ̃] adv [péniblement] laboriously, with great difficulty.

laborieux, euse [labɔʀjø, øz] adj **1.** [long et difficile - procédure, tâche, manœuvre] laborious **2.** [lourd - style] heavy, laboured / *trois heures pour écrire une lettre, ce fut laborieux !* three hours to write a letter, that's slow going! ▸ **dans un anglais laborieux** in halting English **3.** [industrieux] hardworking, industrious ▸ **la classe laborieuse** the working ou labouring class.

labour [labuʀ] nm AGR tilling, ploughing [UK], plowing [US] ▸ **les labours** the ploughed [UK] ou plowed [US] fields.

labourer [3] [labuʀe] vt AGR to plough [UK], to plow [US] ; HORT to dig (over).

labrador [labʀadɔʀ] nm ZOOL Labrador retriever, labrador.

labyrinthe [labiʀɛ̃t] nm **1.** [dédale] labyrinth, maze **2.** *fig* maze / *le labyrinthe des lois* the intricacies of the law.

lac [lak] nm [pièce d'eau] lake.

le lac Léman	Lake Geneva
le lac Majeur	Lake Maggiore
les Grands Lacs	the Great Lakes

lacer [16] [lase] vt [vêtement] to lace (up) *(sép)* ; [chaussure] to lace up *(sép)*, to tie up *(sép)*.

lacérer [18] [laseʀe] vt **1.** [affiche, rideau] to rip up *(sép)*, to tear (to shreds), to slash **2.** [blesser] to lacerate, to gash.
✐ In reformed spelling (see p. 16-18), this verb is conjugated like **semer** : *il lacèrera, elle lacèrerait*.

lacet [lasɛ] nm [de chaussure] (shoe) lace ; [de botte] (boot) lace. ❖ **à lacets** loc adj ▸ **chaussures à lacets** lace-ups, lace-up shoes. ❖ **en lacets** loc adj [route] winding, twisting. ◆ loc adv : *la route monte en lacets* the road winds ou twists upwards.

lâche [laʃ] ◆ adj **1.** [poltron] cowardly, spineless / *se montrer lâche* to behave like a coward **2.** *(avant nom)* [méprisable] cowardly / *un lâche attentat* a cowardly ou despicable attack **3.** [non serré - nœud] loose, slack ; [- vêtement] loose, baggy **4.** [sans rigueur - loi, règlement] lax, overlenient. ◆ nmf coward.

lâchement [laʃmɑ̃] adv [sans courage] in a cowardly manner.

lâcher [3] [laʃe] ◆ vt **1.** [cesser de tenir] to let go of *(insép)* / *lâcher la pédale du frein* to take one's foot off the brake (pedal) / *lâche-moi !* let me go!, let go of me! ▸ **tu me lâches, oui ?** *fam* get out of my sight, will you? ▸ **lâche-moi les baskets !** *fam* leave me alone!, get off my back! ▸ **lâcher prise** to let go **2.** AÉRON [bombe] to drop ; [ballon] to launch **3.** [libérer - oiseau] to let loose, to release, to let go ; [- chien] to let off, to unleash ; [- animal dangereux] to set loose ; [- meute, faucon] to slip ▸ **lâcher les chiens**

sur qqn to set the dogs on sb / *le prof nous a lâchés plus tôt fam* the teacher let us out earlier **4.** *fam* [abandonner - ami, amant] to drop ; [-emploi] to quit / *lâcher ses études* to drop out of school / *le moteur nous a lâchés le deuxième jour* the engine broke down on us on the second day **5.** [émettre] to let out, to come out with *(insép)* / *lâcher un juron* to let out an oath. ◆ vi [se casser - câble] to snap, to break, to give (way) ; [-embrayage, frein] to fail. ◆ **se lâcher** vp **1.** [se comporter librement] to let o.s. go **2.** [parler librement] to say what's on one's mind.

lâcheté [laʃte] nf **1.** [manque de courage] cowardice **2.** [caractère vil] baseness, lowness ; [procédé vil] low ou dirty trick.

lâcheur, euse [laʃœr, øz] nm, f *fam* : *quel lâcheur, il n'est pas venu !* what an unreliable so-and-so, he didn't come!

laconique [lakɔnik] adj [lettre, réplique] laconic *sout*, terse ; [personne] laconic.

lacté, e [lakte] adj [produit, alimentation, régime] milk *(modif)* ▶ **farine lactée** milk-enriched cereal.

lacunaire [lakynɛʀ] adj [incomplet] incomplete, with gaps, lacunary *litt* / *il a des connaissances lacunaires* his knowledge is full of gaps.

lacune [lakyn] nf [omission] gap / *il y a des lacunes dans cette encyclopédie* there are some omissions in this encyclopedia / *j'ai des lacunes en mathématiques* there are gaps in my knowledge of mathematics.

lacustre [lakystʀ] adj CONSTR ▶ **cité lacustre** lakeside pile dwellings.

là-dedans [laddɑ̃] adv **1.** [ici] in here ; [là-bas] in there / *le tiroir est sens dessus dessous, je ne trouve rien là-dedans* the drawer is in a mess, I can't find anything in here **2.** [dans ce texte] in here ; [dans ce qui est dit] : *il y a du vrai là-dedans* there's some truth in it **3.** [dans cette affaire] : *quel est son rôle là-dedans ?* what part does he play in all this?

là-dessous [ladsu] adv **1.** [sous cet objet-ci] under here ; [sous cet objet-là] under there **2.** [dans cette affaire] : *il y a quelque chose de bizarre là-dessous* there's something strange ou odd about all this.

là-dessus [ladsy] adv **1.** [sur cet objet-ci] on here ; [sur cet objet-là] on there / *ne t'appuie pas là-dessus !* don't lean on it! **2.** [à ce sujet] about this ou it / *je n'en sais pas plus que toi là-dessus* I don't know any more than you about it **3.** [sur ce] : *là-dessus, elle se tut* at which point ou whereupon, she stopped talking.

ladite [ladit] nf ⟶ **ledit**.

lagon [lagɔ̃] nm [coral reef] lagoon.

lagune [lagyn] nf lagoon.

là-haut [lao] adv [au-dessus] up there / *leur maison est là-haut sur la colline* their house is up there on the hill / *mais que fait-elle là-haut ?* [à l'étage] what's she doing upstairs?

laïc, laïque [laik] nm, f layman (laywoman). ◆ **laïque** adj **1.** [non clérical] secular, lay, laic *litt* **2.** [indépendant du clergé] ▶ **un État laïque** a secular state ▶ **l'école laïque** secular education.

laïcisation [laisizasjɔ̃] nf secularization, laicization.

laïcité [laisite] nf secularism.

laid, e [lɛ, lɛd] adj [inesthétique - bâtisse] ugly, unsightly ; [-vêtement, tableau, décoration] ugly, unattractive, awful ; [-personne] unattractive, ugly.

laideur [lɛdœʀ] nf **1.** [physique - d'une personne, d'une chose] ugliness / *ce nouveau bâtiment est d'une laideur !* that new building is so ugly! **2.** [morale - d'un crime] heinousness ; [- d'une accusation] meanness, baseness *litt*.

lainage [lɛnaʒ] nm **1.** TEXT [tissu] woollen 🇬🇧 ou woolen 🇺🇸 fabric ou material ; [procédé] napping / *une robe de ou en lainage* a woollen dress **2.** [pull] woollen jumper 🇬🇧, woollen sweater 🇺🇸 **3.** [gilet] wool cardigan.

laine [lɛn] nf **1.** [poil - du mouton, de l'alpaga, etc.] wool **2.** TEXT wool ▶ **laine à tricoter** knitting wool ▶ **laine polaire** fleece ▶ **laine vierge** new wool **3.** [fibre] ▶ **laine de verre** glass wool. ◆ **de laine** loc adj wool *(modif)*, woollen.

laïque [laik] nf ⟶ **laïc**.

laisse [lɛs] nf [lien] leash, lead 🇬🇧 / *tenir un chien en laisse* to keep a dog on the leash ou lead ▶ **mener** ou **tenir qqn en laisse** *fig* to keep a tight rein on sb.

laissé-pour-compte, laissée-pour-compte [lesepuʀkɔ̃t] *(mpl* **laissés-pour-compte,** *fpl* **laissées-pour-compte)** nm, f [personne] social reject ou outcast / *les laissés-pour-compte de la société* the casualties ou victims of society.

laisser [4] [lese]
vt

🅰 **ABANDONNER 1.** [ne pas prendre, renoncer à] to leave / *elle a laissé son dessert* she left her pudding (untouched), she didn't touch her pudding **2.** [quitter momentanément - personne, chose] to leave / *j'ai laissé mes enfants chez mon frère* I left my children at my brother's / *j'ai laissé la voiture à la maison* I left the car at home ▶ **je vous laisse** a) [au téléphone] I must hang up ou go now b) [dans une lettre] that's all for now, I'll leave you now **3.** [quitter définitivement] to leave, to abandon / *il a laissé femme et enfants* he abandoned his wife and children, he walked out on his wife and children ; [après sa mort - famille] to leave / *elle a laissé une œuvre considérable* she left (behind her) a vast body of work **4.** [oublier] to leave, to forget / *j'ai laissé mon sac à la maison* I left my bag at home **5.** [perdre - membre, personne, bien matériel] to lose ▶ **y laisser sa santé** to ruin one's health **6.** [déposer - trace, marque] to leave / *ce vin laisse un arrière-goût désagréable* this wine has an unpleasant aftertaste ▶ **il laisse un bon / un mauvais souvenir** we have good / bad memories of him **7.** [négliger] to leave / *laisse ton livre et viens avec moi* put down ou leave your book and come with me / *laisse tes soucis et viens avec nous* forget your worries and come with us.

🅱 **DONNER, CRÉER 1.** [accorder] to leave ▶ **laisser qqch à qqn** to leave sthg for sb, to leave sb sthg ▶ **laisser sa place à qqn** [siège] to give up one's seat to sb / *laisse-nous un peu de place !* let us have ou leave us some room! / *laisse-lui le temps de faire* leave ou give her time to do it **2.** [confier] to leave ▶ **laisser des consignes à qqn** to leave instructions with sb, to leave sb with instructions / *laissez les clés chez le gardien* drop the keys off at the caretaker's, leave the keys with the caretaker ▶ **laisser qqch à faire à qqn** to leave sb to do sthg, to leave sthg for sb to do **3.** [vendre] to let have / *je vous le laisse pour 100 euros* I'll let you have it for 100 euros **4.** [transmettre] : *après l'insurrection, il dut laisser le pouvoir à son fils* after the rebellion, he had to hand over power to his son ; [après sa mort] to leave, to bequeath *sout* **5.** [réserver] to leave / *laissez une marge pour les corrections* leave a margin for corrections **6.** ᴱˣᴾᴿ **laisser à penser que** [suj : chose] to make one think ou suppose that, to lead one to believe that / *cette note laisse à penser qu'elle est fâchée* this message would lead you to believe ou from this message you would think she's angry / *ta lettre laisse à penser que tu ne pourras pas venir* your letter implies that you won't be coming.

🅲 **DANS UN ÉTAT, UNE SITUATION 1.** [faire demeurer] to leave, to keep / *laisse la fenêtre fermée / ouverte* leave the window shut / open ▶ **laisser un crime impuni** to let a crime go unpunished, to leave a crime unpunished / *cela me laisse* froid ou *indifférent* it leaves me cold ou unmoved ▸ **laisser qqn tranquille** ou **en repos** ou **en paix** to leave sb alone ou in peace ▸ **laisser derrière soi** *pr & fig* to leave behind / *laisser derrière soi tous ses concurrents* to leave all one's competitors behind / *il a laissé le peloton loin derrière* he left the pack well behind him / *elle laisse les autres loin derrière elle* she puts all the others to shame, she leaves all the others way behind **2.** *(en usage absolu)* [s'abstenir d'intervenir] : *laisse, je vais le faire tout seul, I'll do it myself / laisse, je vais me débrouiller, ça va aller* I'll be all right / *laisse, c'est moi qui paie* put your money away, I'll pay for this.

D. SUIVI D'UN INFINITIF **1.** [autoriser] to let, to allow, to permit ▸ **laisser qqn faire qqch** to let sb do sthg, to allow sb to do sthg **2.** [ne pas empêcher de] to let, to allow ▸ **laisser qqn faire** to let sb do, to leave sb to do, to allow sb to do ▸ **laisse-le dormir** let him sleep, leave him to sleep ▸ **laisser tomber qqch** to drop sthg ▸ **laisser voir** [montrer] to show, to reveal / *laisser échapper un cri de douleur* to let out a cry of pain ▸ **laissez bouillir quelques secondes** let it boil for a few seconds / *ceci laisse supposer que… this implies that…,* this makes one think that… **3.** EXPR ▸ **laisser dire** : *laissez dire et faites ce que vous avez à faire* let them talk and do what you have to do ▸ **laisser faire** : *on n'y peut rien, il faut laisser faire* there's nothing we can do (about it), you just have to let things take their course ▸ **laisser le temps** to let time take its course ▸ **laisser tomber** *fam* : *laisser tomber un ami* to drop a friend / *tu devrais laisser tomber, ça ne marchera jamais* you should give up ou drop it ou forget it, it'll never work. ◆ **se laisser** ◆ vp *(emploi passif)* ▸ **ça se laisse regarder** [à la télévision] it's watchable / *il se laisse boire, ton petit vin* your little wine goes down nicely ou is very drinkable. ◆ vpi : *elle s'est laissé accuser injustement* she allowed herself to be ou she let herself be unjustly accused / *il s'est laissé séduire* he let himself be seduced ▸ **se laisser tomber sur une chaise / dans un fauteuil** to collapse onto a chair / into an armchair ▸ **se laisser aller a)** [se négliger] to let o.s. go **b)** [se détendre] to let o.s. go, to relax ▸ **se laisser faire** : *on l'accuse injustement et elle se laisse faire* she's unjustly accused, and she just stands by and lets it happen / *ne te laisse pas faire !* stand up for yourself!, don't let yourself be taken advantage of! ▸ **se laisser vivre** *fam* to live for the moment, to take life as it comes.

📝 **Laisser qqch à qqn** *Leave sthg for / to / with sb* ou *leave sb sthg*.

Notez la construction à double complément qui en anglais peut prendre deux formes dont le sens est le même :

• une structure identique à celle du français :
verbe + COD + préposition + COI
leave sthg for / to / with sb

• une structure qui diffère de celle du français, sans préposition, et dans laquelle l'ordre des compléments est inversé :
verbe + COI + COD
leave sb sthg

Ils laissent toujours une clé de leur appartement aux voisins. *They always leave a key to their flat with the neighbours* ou *They always leave the neighbours a key to their flat.*

Il a laissé toute sa collection de timbres à ses petits-enfants. *He left his entire stamp collection to his grandchildren* ou *He left his grandchildren his entire stamp collection.*

---

laisser-aller [leseale] nm inv : *il y a du laisser-aller dans cette maison !* things are a bit too easy-going ou slack in this house! / *il y a du laisser-aller dans sa tenue* he dresses a bit too casually, he's a bit of a sloppy dresser.

laissez-passer [lesepase] nm inv [autorisation] pass.

lait [lɛ] nm **1.** [des mammifères] milk / *avec ou sans lait ?* black or white? 🇬🇧, with or without milk? ▸ **lait concentré** ou **condensé sucré** (sweetened) condensed milk ▸ **lait écrémé** skimmed ou skim 🇺🇸 milk ▸ **lait entier** full-cream milk 🇬🇧, whole milk ▸ **lait fraise** milk with strawberry syrup ▸ **lait maternel** mother's ou breast milk ▸ **lait en poudre** dried ou powdered milk **2.** [de certains fruits] milk ▸ **lait de soja** soya milk **3.** [pour la toilette] milk ▸ **lait démaquillant** cleansing milk.

laitage [lɛtaʒ] nm dairy product.

laiteux, euse [lɛtø, øz] adj **1.** [semblable au lait] milky **2.** [de la couleur du lait] milk white, milky white.

laitier, ère [lɛtje, ɛʀ] ◆ adj [du lait] dairy *(modif)* ▸ **des produits laitiers** dairy produce. ◆ nm, f [livreur] milkman (milkwoman).

laiton [lɛtɔ̃] nm brass.

laitue [lety] nf lettuce.

laïus [lajys] nm *fam* long spiel, long-winded speech.

lama [lama] nm **1.** RELIG lama **2.** ZOOL llama.

lambda [lɑ̃bda] *(pl* lambda *ou* lambdas*)* nm *(comme adj)* *fam* ▸ **un individu lambda** your average bloke 🇬🇧 ou Joe 🇺🇸.

lambeau, x [lɑ̃bo] nm [morceau] scrap, strip, bit / *lambeaux de chair* strips of flesh. ◆ **en lambeaux** loc adj [déchiré] in tatters, in shreds.

lambiner [3] [lɑ̃bine] vi *fam* to dawdle.

lambris [lɑ̃bri] nm [en bois] panelling 🇬🇧, paneling 🇺🇸, wainscoting.

lame [lam] nf **1.** [de couteau] blade ; [de scie] web ; [de tournevis] shaft ▸ **lame de rasoir** razor blade **2.** CONSTR [de store] slat ; [en bois] lath, strip ▸ **lames de parquet** floorboards **3.** OPT slide **4.** [vague] wave ▸ **lame de fond** *pr & fig* ground swell.

lamelle [lamɛl] nf **1.** CULIN [de viande] thin strip ; [de fromage, de pomme] thin slice, sliver **2.** MINÉR flake, lamella *spéc* **3.** OPT coverslip, cover glass. ◆ **en lamelles** loc adj CULIN sliced.

lamentable [lamɑ̃tabl] adj **1.** [désolant - accident] deplorable, frightful, lamentable ; [pitoyable - plainte, vie] pathetic, pitiful ; [- état] awful, terrible **2.** [mauvais - performance, résultat] pathetic, appalling ▸ **c'est lamentable !** [comportement, action] it's pathetic!

lamentablement [lamɑ̃tabləmɑ̃] adv miserably, dismally.

lamentation [lamɑ̃tasjɔ̃] nf **1.** [pleurs] wailing *(U)*, lamentation **2.** [récrimination] moaning *(U)*, complaining *(U)* / *se répandre en lamentations* to burst into a torrent of complaints.

lamenter [3] [lamɑ̃te] ◆ **se lamenter** vpi [gémir] to moan, to whine ▸ **se lamenter sur qqch** to moan about sthg, to bemoan sthg *sout* / *il se lamente sur la dégradation des valeurs morales* he deplores ou regrets the decline in moral values / *il ne cesse de se lamenter sur son propre sort* he keeps moaning about how things are for him.

laminer [3] [lamine] vt **1.** [plastique, métal, verre] to roll, to laminate **2.** [parti politique, équipe] to annihilate **3.** *fam* [personne] to exhaust.

lampadaire [lɑ̃padɛʀ] nm **1.** [dans une maison] standard lamp 🇬🇧, floor lamp 🇺🇸 **2.** [dans la rue] street lamp, streetlight.

---

lampe [lɑ̃p] nf **1.** [luminaire] lamp, light / *à la lumière de la lampe* by lamplight ▶ **lampe de bureau** desk lamp ▶ **lampe de chevet** bedside lamp ▶ **lampe électrique** flashlight ▶ **lampe à pétrole** paraffin lamp 🇬🇧, kerosene lamp 🇺🇸 ▶ **lampe de poche** torch 🇬🇧, flashlight 🇺🇸 ▶ **lampe témoin** warning light **2.** [appareil] ▶ **lampe à souder** blowlamp 🇬🇧, blowtorch 🇺🇸.

lampe-tempête [lɑ̃ptɑpɛt] nf storm lamp.

lampion [lɑ̃pjɔ̃] nm paper ou Chinese lantern.

lance [lɑ̃s] nf **1.** ARM spear **2.** [tuyau] ▶ **lance à eau** hose, pipe ▶ **lance d'arrosage** garden hose ▶ **lance d'incendie** fire hose.

lancé, e [lɑ̃se] adj [personne] : *le voilà lancé !* he's made it! ❖ **lancée** nf [vitesse acquise] momentum. ❖ **sur sa lancée** loc adv : *il courait et sur sa lancée, il dribbla ses deux adversaires* he ran up the field, dribbling around two attackers as he went / *sur sa lancée, il s'en prit même à son père* he even took his father to task while he was at it / *continuer sur sa lancée* to keep going.

lancée [lɑ̃se] nf ⟶ **lancé**.

lancement [lɑ̃smɑ̃] nm **1.** ASTRONAUT & NAUT launch, launching ▶ **créneau** ou **fenêtre de lancement** firing ou launch window **2.** [en publicité - opération] launching ; [- cérémonie, réception] launch ▶ **le lancement d'un produit** the launching of a product ▶ **prix de lancement** launch price.

lancer¹ [lɑ̃se] nm **1.** PÊCHE casting ▶ **lancer léger** / **lourd** fixed / free reel casting **2.** SPORT throw ▶ **le lancer du disque** the discus ▶ **le lancer du poids** the shot ▶ **pratiquer le lancer du poids** to put the shot.

lancer² [16] [lɑ̃se]

◆ vt

A. ENVOYER, ÉMETTRE 1. [jeter] to throw / *elle m'a lancé la balle* she threw me the ball, she threw the ball to me ▶ **lancer le poids** to put the shot / *ils nous lançaient des regards curieux* they looked at us curiously ▶ **lancer qqch à la figure de qqn** to throw sthg in sb's face **2.** [à l'aide d'un instrument] to fire, to shoot ; [bombe] to drop ; ASTRONAUT to launch **3.** [émettre - cri] to let out *(insép)* ; [- accusation] to level / *lancer un bon mot* to crack a joke ▶ **lancer des injures à qqn** to hurl insults at sb **4.** [diffuser - décret, consigne] to send ou to put out *(sép)*, to issue ▶ **lancer des invitations** to send ou to give out invitations ▶ **lancer un SOS / un appel à la radio** to send out an SOS / an appeal on the radio ▶ **lancer un mandat d'amener / un ultimatum** to issue a summons / an ultimatum **5.** PÊCHE to cast.

B. FAIRE DÉBUTER, PARTIR 1. [faire partir brusquement] : *ils lancèrent les chiens sur les rôdeurs* they set the dogs on the prowlers / *lancer des troupes à l'attaque* to send troops into the attack ; [mettre en train - campagne] to launch ; [-affaire] to set up ; [-idée] to float ; [-mode] to start **2.** [INFORM - programme] to start ▶ **lancer une application** to launch an application ▶ **lancer une impression** to start printing **3.** [faire connaître - produit] to launch ▶ **lancer une mode** to start a fashion ▶ *c'est ce roman / cette émission qui l'a lancé* this novel / programme made him famous **4.** fam [orienter - discussion] to get going / *une fois qu'il est lancé sur ce sujet, on ne peut plus l'arrêter* once he gets going on the subject, there's no stopping him.

◆ vi [élancer - douleur] to stab / *ça me lance dans l'épaule, l'épaule me lance* I've got a sharp stabbing pain in my shoulder. ❖ **se lancer** ◆ vp *(emploi réciproque)* [balle] to throw at one another / *elles se lançaient des injures* they were hurling insults back and forth, they were exchanging insults. ◆ vpi **1.** [se précipiter] to throw o.s. ; [courir] to rush (headlong), to dash / *se lancer à la poursuite de* to set off

in pursuit of ▶ **se lancer à la conquête de qqch** to set out to conquer sthg **2.** [se mettre à parler] : *se lancer sur un sujet* to get going on a topic **3.** [prendre l'initiative] : *allez, lance-toi et demande une augmentation* go on, take the plunge and ask for a rise. ❖ **se lancer dans** vp + prép **1.** [s'aventurer dans - explication, aventure] to embark on **2.** [se mettre à pratiquer] to get involved in.

lance-roquettes *(pl* lance-roquettes), **lance-roquette*** *(pl* lance-roquettes) [lɑ̃srɔkɛt] nm (hand held) rocket launcher ou gun.

lanceur, euse [lɑ̃sœr, øz] nm, f [au baseball] pitcher ; [au cricket] bowler ▶ **lanceur de javelot** javelin thrower ▶ **lanceur de poids** shot putter. ❖ **lanceur** nm ASTRONAUT launch vehicle, launcher.

lancinant, e [lɑ̃sinɑ̃, ɑ̃t] adj **1.** [douleur] throbbing **2.** [obsédant - souvenir] haunting **3.** [répétitif] nerve-shattering.

landau, s [lɑ̃do] nm [pour bébés] pram 🇬🇧, baby carriage 🇺🇸.

lande [lɑ̃d] nf moor.

langage [lɑ̃gaʒ] nm **1.** LING & PSYCHOL language ▶ **langage écrit / parlé** written / spoken language ▶ **troubles du langage** speech ou language disorders **2.** [code] language / *le langage du corps* body language, body talk ▶ **le langage des signes** sign language **3.** [jargon] language ▶ **langage administratif / technique** administrative / technical language **4.** [style] language ▶ **langage familier / populaire** colloquial / popular language ▶ **langage argotique** slang ▶ **langage poétique** poetic language **5.** [discours] language, talk / *c'est le langage de la raison* that's a sensible thing to say ▶ **tenir un double langage** to speak out of both sides of one's mouth **6.** INFORM & TÉLÉC language ▶ **langage machine** internal ou machine language ▶ **langage de programmation** programming language.

langer [17] [lɑ̃ʒe] vt [bébé] to change ▶ **table / matelas à langer** changing table / mat.

langoureusement [lɑ̃gurøzmɑ̃] adv languorously.

langoureux, euse [lɑ̃gurø, øz] adj [alangui] languishing ; [mélancolique] languid, languorous.

langouste [lɑ̃gust] nf ZOOL crayfish ; CULIN (spiny) lobster.

langoustine [lɑ̃gustin] nf langoustine ; ≃ Dublin bay prawn.

langue [lɑ̃g] nf

A. ORGANE 1. ANAT tongue ▶ **une mauvaise langue, une langue de vipère** a (malicious) gossip ▶ **tirer la langue à qqn** to stick one's tongue out at sb ▶ **tirer la langue a)** fam & fig [avoir soif] to be gasping (for a drink) **b)** [avoir du mal] to have a hard ou rough time **c)** [être fatigué] to be worn out ▶ **avoir avalé** ou **perdu sa langue** : *as-tu avalé* ou *perdu ta langue ?* have you lost ou (has the) cat got your tongue? ▶ **avoir la langue bien affilée** ou **bien pendue** fam to be a chatterbox, to have the gift of the gab ▶ **coup de langue** lick / *donner des coups de langue* to lick ▶ **ne pas avoir sa langue dans sa poche** fam : *elle n'a pas la langue dans sa poche* she's never at a loss for something to say ou for words ▶ **donner sa langue au chat** to give up (guessing) ▶ **tenir sa langue** to keep a secret ▶ **tourner sept fois sa langue dans sa bouche avant de parler** fam to think twice before you open your mouth **2.** CULIN tongue ▶ **langue de bœuf** ox tongue.

B. LINGUISTIQUE 1. [moyen de communication] language, tongue ▶ **un professeur de langues** a language teacher ▶ **langue cible** ou **d'arrivée** target language ▶ **langue maternelle** mother tongue ▶ **langue officielle** official language ▶ **dans la langue parlée** colloquially, in the spoken language ▸ **langue source** ou **de départ** source language ▸ **langues étrangères** foreign languages ▸ **les langues vivantes a)** ÉDUC modern languages **b)** [utilisées de nos jours] living languages **2.** [jargon] language ▸ **la langue populaire / littéraire** popular / literary language ▸ **langue de bois** hackneyed phrases / *la langue de bois des politiciens* the clichés politicians come out with **3.** [style - d'une époque, d'un écrivain] language ▸ **dans la langue de Molière / Shakespeare** in French / English.

C. FORME 1. [gén] tongue / *des langues de feu léchaient le mur* tongues of fire were licking the wall **2.** GÉOGR ▸ **une langue de terre** a strip of land, a narrow piece of land.

languette [lɑ̃gɛt] nf [petite bande] strip / *les dossiers sont séparés par une languette de papier* the files are separated by a strip of paper ou a paper marker.

languir [32] [lɑ̃giʀ] vi **1.** litt [personne, animal] to languish, to pine ▸ **languir (d'amour) pour qqn** to be consumed ou languishing with love for sb **2.** [attendre] ▸ **faire languir qqn** to keep sb waiting / *ne nous fais pas languir !* don't keep us waiting for too long! ⬦ **se languir** vpi [personne] to pine / *il se languit de toi* he's pining for you.

lanière [lanjɛʀ] nf **1.** [sangle] strap **2.** CULIN ▸ **découper qqch en lanières** to cut sthg into strips.

lanterne [lɑ̃tɛʀn] nf **1.** [lampe] lantern **2.** PHOT ▸ **lanterne magique** magic lantern. ⬦ **lanterne rouge** nf EXPR ▸ **être la lanterne rouge a)** [gén] to bring up the rear **b)** SPORT [dans une course] to come (in) last **c)** [équipe] to get the wooden spoon **d)** [à l'école] to be bottom of the class.

Laos [laos] npr m ▸ **le Laos** Laos.

laotien, enne [laosjɛ̃, ɛn] adj Laotian. ⬦ **Laotien, enne** nm, f Laotian. ⬦ **laotien** nm LING Lao, Laotian.

lapalissade [lapalisad] nf truism ▸ **c'est une lapalissade** that's self-evident, that's stating the obvious.

laper [3] [lape] vt to lap (up).

lapidaire [lapidɛʀ] adj [concis] terse, lapidary *sout*.

lapider [3] [lapide] vt **1.** [tuer] to stone to death, to lapidate *sout* **2.** litt [critiquer] to lambast.

lapin [lapɛ̃] nm **1.** ZOOL rabbit ▸ **poser un lapin à qqn** fam to stand sb up **2.** CULIN rabbit **3.** [fourrure] rabbit (skin) UK, cony (skin) US **4.** fam [terme d'affection] poppet UK, honey US.

laps [laps] nm ▸ **un laps de temps** a lapse of time, a while.

lapsus [lapsys] nm **1.** [faute] slip (of the tongue), lapsus linguae *spéc* ▸ **lapsus calami** slip (of the pen) **2.** PSYCHOL Freudian slip ▸ **lapsus révélateur** hum Freudian slip.

laque [lak] nf **1.** [vernis] lacquer **2.** [pour cheveux] hair spray, (hair) lacquer UK **3.** [peinture] gloss paint.

laqué, e [lake] adj **1.** CONSTR gloss / *cuisine laquée (en) rouge* kitchen in red gloss **2.** CULIN ▸ **canard**.

laquelle [lakɛl] nf ⟶ **lequel**.

larbin [laʀbɛ̃] nm tfam, pr & fig flunkey.

lard [laʀ] nm **1.** CULIN ▸ **lard fumé** smoked bacon ▸ **lard salé** salt pork **2.** EXPR ▸ **un gros lard** tfam a fatso, a fat slob.

larder [3] [laʀde] vt CULIN to lard.

lardon [laʀdɔ̃] nm CULIN lardon ▸ **petits lardons** diced bacon.

large [laʀʒ] ⬦ adj **1.** [grand - gén] broad, wide ; [- plaine] big, wide ; [- rue] broad ; [- tache] large ▸ **large de 5 cm** 5 cm wide ▸ **large d'épaules** broad-shouldered ▸ **un large sourire** a broad smile **2.** [ample - vêtement] big, baggy ; [- chaussures] wide **3.** [considérable] large / *elle a une large part de responsabilité* she must bear a large ou ma-

jor share of the blame / *une large majorité* a big majority ▸ **remporter une large victoire** to win by a large margin ▸ **jouissant d'une large diffusion** widely distributed ▸ **destiné à un large public** designed for a wide audience **4.** [général] : *prendre un mot dans son sens large* to take a word in its broadest sense **5.** [généreux] generous **6.** [ouvert] open ▸ **avoir l'esprit large** ou **les idées larges** to be broad-minded ou open-minded **7.** [excessif] : *ton estimation était un peu large* your estimate was a bit wide of the mark. ⬦ nm **1.** [dimension] width / *5 mètres de large* 5 metres UK ou meters US wide **2.** NAUT ▸ **le large** the open sea ▸ **le vent du large** offshore wind ▸ **au large de Hong Kong** off Hong Kong ▸ **gagner** ou **prendre le large** pr to head for the open sea ▸ **il est temps de prendre le large** fam & fig it's time we were off. ⬦ adv ▸ **calculer** ou **prévoir large** to allow a good margin for error ▸ **voir large** to think big.

⚠ L'adjectif anglais **large** signifie « grand » et ne doit pas être employé systématiquement pour traduire large. Voir article.

largement [laʀʒəmɑ̃] adv **1.** [amplement] : *tu auras largement le temps* you'll easily have enough time, you'll have more than enough time / *elle a largement 60 ans* she's well over 60 ▸ **une opinion largement répandue** a widely held opinion / *il était largement cinq heures* it was well past five / *il vit largement au-dessus de ses moyens* he lives well above his means **2.** [généreusement] generously **3.** [de beaucoup] greatly / *la demande excède largement notre capacité* demand greatly exceeds our capacity **4.** [facilement] easily / *il vaut largement son frère* he's easily as good as his brother.

largeur [laʀʒœʀ] nf **1.** [dimension] width / *quelle est la largeur de la pièce ?* how wide is the room? ▸ **une remorque barrait la route dans** ou **sur toute sa largeur** there was a trailer blocking the entire width of the road **2.** fig broadness, breadth ▸ **largeur d'esprit** ou **de vues** broadness of mind, broad-mindedness. ⬦ **en largeur** loc adv widthways, widthwise, crosswise / *la table fait 30 cm en largeur* the table is 30 cm widthways ou across.

largué, e [laʀge] adj fam ▸ **être largué** to be out of one's depth.

larguer [3] [laʀge] vt **1.** NAUT [voile] to slip, to let out (sép), to unfurl ; [amarre] to slip ; (en usage absolu) ▸ **larguez !** let go! **2.** AÉRON [bombe, charge, parachutiste, vivres] to drop ; [réservoir, étage de fusée] to jettison ; [fusée, satellite] to release **3.** tfam [abandonner - poste] to quit, to chuck (on) (insép), to walk out on (insép) ; [- vieillerie, projet] to chuck, to bin UK ; [- amant] to dump, to jilt ; [- personne avec qui l'on vit] to walk out on (insép) ▸ **se faire larguer** to be dumped.

larme [laʀm] nf **1.** PHYSIOL tear / *retenir ses larmes* to hold back one's tears ▸ **être en larmes** to be in tears / *avoir les larmes aux yeux* to have tears in one's eyes ▸ **larmes de crocodile** crocodile tears **2.** [petite quantité] ▸ **une larme (de)** a drop (of).

larve [laʀv] nf **1.** ZOOL larva ; [ver] maggot **2.** sout & péj ▸ **larve (humaine)** worm.

larvé, e [laʀve] adj **1.** MÉD latent, larvate *spéc* **2.** [latent] latent, concealed.

laryngite [laʀɛ̃ʒit] nf laryngitis.

larynx [laʀɛ̃ks] nm voice-box, larynx *spéc*.

las, lasse [la, las] adj **1.** litt [fatigué] weary **2.** [découragé, écœuré] weary ▸ **être las de qqch** to be weary of sthg.

lascif, ive [lasif, iv] adj **1.** [sensuel] lascivious, sensual **2.** [lubrique] lustful, lewd.

dans la mesure du possible as far as possible / **dans la mesure où cela peut lui être agréable** insofar as ou inasmuch as he might enjoy it ▸ **dans une certaine mesure** to some ou a certain extent ▸ **dans une large mesure** to a large extent, in large measure *sout* ▸ **être en mesure de** to be able ou in a position to **9.** MUS [rythme] time, tempo ▸ **être en mesure** to be in time **10.** LITTÉR metre. ⬦ **à la mesure de** loc prép worthy of / **elle a un adversaire à sa mesure** she's got an opponent worthy of her ou who is a match for her. ⬦ **à mesure que** loc conj as. ⬦ **outre mesure** loc adv excessively, overmuch / **ils ne s'aiment pas outre mesure** they're not overkeen ou excessively keen on each other. ⬦ **sur mesure** loc adj **1.** COUT made-to-measure / **fabriquer des vêtements sur mesure** to make clothes to measure ▸ **fait sur mesure** custom-made **2.** *(comme nom)* ▸ **c'est du sur mesure a)** COUT it's made to measure **b)** *fig* it fits the bill.

mesuré, e [məzyʀe] adj **1.** [lent] measured ▸ **à pas mesurés** at a measured pace **2.** [modéré] steady, moderate.

mesurer [3] [məzyʀe] ◆ vt **1.** [déterminer la dimension de] to measure ▸ **mesurer qqch en hauteur / largeur** to measure the height / width of sthg / **je vais vous en mesurer le double** [obj : coupon, liquide] I'll measure out twice as much for you **2.** [difficulté, qualité] to assess / **il ne mesure pas sa force** ou **ses forces** he doesn't know his own strength / **mesure-t-elle la portée de ses paroles ?** is she aware of the consequences of what she's saying? **3.** [limiter] to limit ▸ **mesurer ses paroles** to be careful what one says, to weigh one's words. ◆ vi to measure ▸ **combien mesures-tu ?** how tall are you? / **le sapin mesure 2 mètres** the fir tree is 2 metres high / **la cuisine mesure 2 mètres sur 3** the kitchen is ou measures 2 metres by 3. ⬦ **se mesurer** à vp + prép to have a confrontation with, to pit o.s. against / **je n'ai pas envie de me mesurer à lui** I don't feel like tackling him.

métabolisme [metabɔlism] nm metabolism.

métal, aux [metal, o] nm **1.** MÉTALL metal ▸ **en métal argenté / doré** silver- / gold-plated ▸ **le métal jaune** gold **2.** FIN & HÉRALD metal.

métallique [metalik] adj **1.** [en métal] metal *(modif)* **2.** [semblable au métal] metallic, steel *(modif)*, steely.

métallisé, e [metalize] adj [couleur, finition] metallic.

métallurgie [metalyʀʒi] nf metallurgy.

métallurgiste [metalyʀʒist] nm **1.** [ouvrier] metalworker ; [dans une aciérie] steelworker **2.** [industriel, expert] metallurgist.

métamorphose [metamɔʀfoz] nf **1.** BIOL & MYTH metamorphosis **2.** [transformation] metamorphosis, transformation.

métamorphoser [3] [metamɔʀfoze] vt [transformer] to transform, to change. ⬦ **se métamorphoser** vpi [se transformer] to change, to transform.

métaphore [metafɔʀ] nf metaphor.

métaphorique [metafɔʀik] adj metaphoric, metaphorical, figurative.

métaphysique [metafizik] ◆ adj ART & PHILOS metaphysical. ◆ nf PHILOS metaphysics *(sg)* ; [système de pensée] metaphysic.

métayer, ère [meteje, ɛʀ] nm, f sharecropper, sharecropping tenant.

météo [meteo] ◆ adj inv **(abr de météorologique)** ▸ **bulletin météo** weather report ▸ **prévisions météo** (weather) forecast. ◆ nf **(abr de météorologie)** [service] Met Office 🇬🇧 ; ≃ National Weather Service 🇺🇸 ; [temps prévu] weather forecast / **la météo a dit que...** the weatherman said…

météore [meteɔʀ] nm ASTRON meteor.

météorite [meteɔʀit] nf [aérolithe] meteorite.

météorologie [meteɔʀɔlɔʒi] nf **1.** SCI meteorology **2.** [organisme] Meteorological Office 🇬🇧 ; ≃ National Weather Service 🇺🇸.

météorologique [meteɔʀɔlɔʒik] adj meteorological, weather *(modif)*.

méthadone [metadɔn] nf methadone.

méthane [metan] nm methane (gas).

méthode [metɔd] nf **1.** [système] method ; SCI & TECHNOL method, technique / **c'est une bonne méthode pour apprendre l'anglais** it's a good way of learning English / **j'ai ma méthode pour le convaincre** I have my own way of convincing him ▸ **méthode de travail** working method, modus operandi *fam* **2.** [organisation] method / **vous manquez de méthode** you lack method, you aren't methodical enough ▸ **avec méthode** methodically **3.** *fam* [astuce] : **lui, il a la méthode !** he's got the hang of it ou the knack ! **4.** [manuel] ▸ **méthode de lecture** primer ▸ **méthode de solfège** music handbook ou manual.

méthodique [metɔdik] adj methodical.

méthodiste [metɔdist] adj & nmf Methodist.

méthodologie [metɔdɔlɔʒi] nf methodology.

méticuleux, euse [metikylø, øz] adj **1.** [minutieux - personne] meticulous ; [- enquête] probing, searching **2.** [scrupuleux] meticulous, scrupulous.

métier [metje] nm **1.** [profession] trade ▸ **mon métier** my job ou occupation ou trade ▸ **les métiers manuels** the manual trades / **j'ai fait tous les métiers** I've done every sort of job there is / **la soudure ne tiendra pas, et je connais mon métier !** the welding won't hold, and I know what I'm talking about ou what I'm doing! **2.** [expérience] skill, experience ▸ **avoir du métier** to have job experience **3.** [machine] ▸ **métier à tisser** loom. ⬦ **de métier** ◆ loc adj [homme, femme, armée] professional ; [argot] technical ; [technique] of the trade. ◆ loc adv : **avoir 15 ans de métier** to have been in the job ou business for 15 years. ⬦ **de son métier** loc adv by trade / **être boulanger / journaliste de son métier** to be a baker / journalist by trade. ⬦ **du métier** loc adj of the trade / **demande à quelqu'un du métier** ask a professional ou an expert.

métis, isse [metis] adj, f [personne] person of mixed race.

métissage [metisaʒ] nm **1.** BIOL [de personnes] interbreeding ; [d'animaux] crossbreeding, hybridization ; [de plantes] hybridation **2.** SOCIOL intermarrying / **le métissage de la salsa et du rock** the mixing of salsa with rock music ▸ **le métissage culturel** the mixing of cultures.

métrage [metʀaʒ] nm **1.** [longueur] length ; COUT & COMM length, yardage / **quel métrage faut-il pour un manteau ?** how many yards are needed to make an overcoat? **2.** CINÉ footage, length ▸ **long métrage** feature film ▸ **court métrage** short (film 🇬🇧 ou movie 🇺🇸).

mètre [mɛtʀ] nm **1.** [unité] metre 🇬🇧, meter 🇺🇸 ▸ **mètre carré / cube** square / cubic metre **2.** SPORT ▸ **le 400 mètres** the 400 metres, the 400-metre race **3.** [instrument] (metre) rule ▸ **mètre à ruban** tape measure, measuring tape.

métrique [metʀik] adj GÉOM & LITTÉR metric.

métro [metʀo] nm underground 🇬🇧, subway 🇺🇸 / **prendre le métro** to take the underground 🇬🇧 ou subway 🇺🇸 ▸ **le dernier métro** the last train ▸ **métro aérien** elevated ou overhead railway ▸ **avoir toujours un métro de retard** : **elle a toujours un métro de retard** she's slow to catch on ▸ **métro, boulot, dodo** *fam* the daily grind ou routine.

métronome [metʀɔnɔm] nm metronome / **avec la régularité d'un métronome** like clockwork, (as) regular as clockwork.

métropole [metʀɔpɔl] nf **1.** [ville] metropolis **2.** ADMIN mother country.

métropolitain, e [metʀɔpɔlitɛ̃, ɛn] adj ADMIN & RELIG metropolitan.

mets [mɛ] nm [aliment] dish.

mettable [mɛtabl] adj wearable / *je n'ai plus rien de mettable* I don't have anything decent left to wear.

metteur, euse [mɛtœʀ, øz] nm, f ▶ **metteur en scène a)** CINÉ director **b)** THÉÂTRE producer.

mettre [84] [mɛtʀ] vt **1.** [placer] to put / *mettre sa confiance / tout son espoir en* to put one's trust / all one's hopes in / *j'avais mis beaucoup de moi-même dans le projet* I'd put a lot into the project ▶ **mettre à** : *mettre une pièce à l'affiche* to bill a play / *mettre un enfant au lit* to put a child to bed / *on m'a mis au standard* they put me on the switchboard ▶ **mettre qqn dans** : *mettre qqn dans l'avion / le train* to put sb on the plane / the train ▶ **mettre qqn en** : *mettre un enfant en pension* to put a child in a ou to send a child to boarding school ▶ **mettre qqch sur** : *mettre 10 euros sur un cheval* to put ou to lay 10 euros on a horse ▶ **mettre qqn en boîte** *fam* to pull sb's leg **2.** [poser horizontalement] to lay, to put ▶ **mettre la main sur le bras de qqn** to lay ou to put one's hand on sb's arm **3.** [disposer] : *mettre le loquet* to put the latch down **4.** [ajuster] to set ▶ **mettre qqch droit** to set sthg straight *pr* / *mets la sonnerie à 20 h 30* set the alarm for 8:30 p.m. **5.** [établir - dans un état, une situation] ▶ **mettre qqch à** : *mettre un étang à sec* to drain a pond / *mettez les verbes à l'infinitif* put the verbs into the infinitive ▶ **mettre qqn dans l'embarras a)** [perplexité] to put sb in a predicament **b)** [pauvreté] to put sb in financial difficulty ▶ **mettre qqn dans l'obligation de faire qqch** to oblige sb to do sthg ▶ **mettre en** : *mettre une maison en vente* to put a house up for sale ▶ **mettre qqn en examen** DR to indict sb ▶ **mettre qqn sous qqch** : *mettre qqn sous tranquillisants* to put sb on tranquillizers / *mettre une plante en pot* to pot a plant ▶ **mettre qqch en miettes** to smash sthg to bits ▶ **mettre qqch à** : *mettre qqch à cuire* to put sthg on to cook / *mettre du linge à sécher* to hang ou to hang clothes up to dry **6.** [fixer] to put / *mettre une pièce à un pantalon* to put a patch on ou to patch a pair of trousers ; [ajouter] to put / *il faut lui mettre des piles* you have to put batteries in it **7.** [se vêtir, se coiffer, se chausser de] to put on (sép) ; [porter régulièrement] to wear / *je lui ai mis son manteau / ses gants* I put his coat / his gloves on (for him) **8.** [faire fonctionner - appareil] to turn ou to put ou to switch on (sép) / *mettre un CD* to put a CD on / *mets de la musique* put some music on, play some music **9.** [installer] to put in (sép), to install ▶ **mettre du papier peint / de la moquette dans une pièce** to wallpaper / to carpet a room **10.** [consacrer - temps] to take / *elle a mis trois mois à me répondre* she took three months ou it took her three months to answer me ▶ **nous y mettrons le temps / le prix qu'il faudra** we'll spend as much time / money as we have to / *tu en as mis du temps pour te décider !* you took some time to make up your mind! **11.** [écrire] to put / *on met un accent sur le «e»* "e" takes an accent **12.** [supposer] ▶ **mettons** (let's) say / *et mettons que tu gagnes ?* suppose ou let's say you win? / *mettons que j'aie mal compris !* [acceptation] let's just say I got it wrong! **13.** [donner] to give / *le prof m'a mis 18* ≃ the teacher gave me an A **14.** *fam* [infliger] : *qu'est-ce qu'il m'a mis au ping-pong !* he really hammered me ou he didn't half thrash me at table tennis! / *qu'est-ce que son père va lui mettre !* his father is really going to give it to him! ❖ **se mettre** ❖ vp (emploi passif) **1.** [dans une position, un endroit - chose] to go / *les pieds, ça ne se met pas sur la table !* tables aren't made to put your feet on! **2.** [aller - vêtement] to go / *le noir se met avec tout* black goes with everything. ❖ vpi **1.** [s'installer, s'établir - dans une position] ▶ **se mettre debout** to stand up ▶ **mets-toi près de la fenêtre a)** [debout] stand near the window **b)** [assis] sit near the window **2.** [entrer - dans un état, une situation] : *ne te mets pas dans un tel état !* don't get (yourself) into such a state! / *il s'est mis dans une position difficile* he's got ou put himself in a difficult situation **3.** [s'habiller] ▶ **se mettre en** to put on / *elle se met toujours en jupe* she always wears a skirt **4.** [s'unir] ▶ **se mettre avec qqn a)** [pour un jeu] to team up with sb **b)** [pour vivre] to move in with sb **c)** [dans une discussion] to side with sb / *on s'est mis par équipes de 6* we split up into ou we formed teams of 6 (people) / *ils ont dû s'y mettre à 4 pour porter le buffet* it took 4 of them to carry the dresser. ❖ vpt to put on (sép) / *se mettre une belle robe / du parfum* to put on a nice dress / some perfume. ❖❖ **se mettre à** vp + prép **1.** [passer à] : *quand le feu se met au rouge* when the lights turn ou go red ; MÉTÉOR : *le temps se met au beau* it's turning sunny **2.** [commencer] ▶ **se mettre au judo** to take up judo / *voilà qu'il se met à pleuvoir !* now it's started to rain ou raining! ▶ **s'y mettre a)** [au travail] to get down to it **b)** [à une activité nouvelle] to have a try.

meuble¹ [mœbl] adj AGR & HORT loose, light.

meuble² [mœbl] nm **1.** [élément du mobilier] ▶ **un meuble** a piece of furniture ▶ **des meubles** furniture ▶ **meuble de rangement** cupboard ▶ **faire partie des meubles** *fam* to be part of the furniture **2.** DR movable.

> 📎 Attention ! Le mot furniture est indénombrable. Il ne s'emploie jamais ni au pluriel ni avec l'article indéfini a :
> **C'est un très joli meuble art déco.** *It's a fine piece of art deco furniture.*
> **Ils ont dû déplacer tous les meubles.** *They had to move all the furniture.*
> **Je dois acheter des meubles pour mon nouvel appartement.** *I've got to buy some furniture for my new flat.*

meublé, e [mœble] adj furnished / *une maison meublée / non meublée* a furnished / an unfurnished house. ❖❖ **meublé** nm [une pièce] furnished room ; [plusieurs pièces] furnished flat 🇬🇧 ou apartment 🇺🇸 / *habiter ou vivre en meublé* to live in furnished accommodation.

meubler [5] [mœble] vt **1.** [garnir de meubles] to furnish **2.** [remplir] to fill / *pour meubler la conversation* to stop the conversation from flagging, for the sake of conversation.

meuf [mœf] nf *tfam* girl ("verlan" form of the word "femme").

meugler [5] [møgle] vi to moo.

meule [møl] nf **1.** AGR stack, rick ▶ **meule de foin** hayrick, haystack ▶ **meule de paille** stack of straw **2.** TECHNOL (grinding) wheel ▶ **meule à aiguiser** ou **affûter** grindstone **3.** CULIN ▶ **une meule de fromage** a (whole) cheese **4.** [d'un moulin] millstone.

meunier, ère [mønje, ɛʀ] consiste en adj milling (modif). ❖❖ **meunier** nm [artisan] miller. ❖❖ **meunière** nf CULIN ▶ **sole (à la) meunière** sole meunière.

meurt v ⟶ **mourir**.

meurtre [mœʀtʀ] nm murder / *crier au meurtre* to scream blue murder.

meurtrier, ère [mœʀtʀije, ɛʀ] ❖ adj [qui tue - engin, lame] deadly, lethal, murderous ; [- avalanche] deadly, fatal ; [- route] lethal, murderous ; [- folie, passion] murderous / *une chasse à l'homme meurtrière* a bloody ou murderous manhunt. ❖ nm, f [meurtrier (murderess)]. ❖❖ **meurtrière** nf ARCHIT (arrow) loophole.

meurtrir [32] [mœʀtʀiʀ] vt **1.** [contusionner] to bruise / *elle avait le visage tout meurtri* her face was all black and blue ou all bruised **2.** [poire, fleur] to bruise.

meute [møt] nf [de chiens] pack ; [de gens] mob, crowd.

mexicain, e [mɛksikɛ̃, ɛn] adj Mexican.
❖ **Mexicain, e** nm, f Mexican.

Mexico [mɛksiko] npr Mexico City.

Mexique [mɛksik] npr m ▸ **le Mexique** Mexico ▸ **au Mexique** in Mexico.

mezzanine [mɛdzanin] nf **1.** ARCHIT [entresol] mezzanine ; [fenêtre] mezzanine window **2.** THÉÂTRE [corbeille] mezzanine, lower balcony.

MF nf (**abr de modulation de fréquence**) FM.

mi [mi] nm inv E ; [chanté] mi, me. **Voir aussi fa.**

mi- [mi] préf **1.** [moitié] half- **2.** EXPR ▸ **mi-figue mi-raisin** a) [accueil] somewhat mixed b) [réponse] ambiguous, enigmatic c) [sourire] quizzical, wry.

miam-miam [mjammjam] interj *fam* yum-yum.

miaou [mjau] nm miaow UK, meow ▸ **faire miaou** to miaow.

miaulement [mjolmɑ̃] nm miaowing UK, mewing, meowing.

miauler [3] [mjole] vi to miaow UK, to mew, to meow.

mi-bas [miba] nm inv knee-high ou knee-length sock.

mi-carême [mikaʀɛm] (*pl* mi-carêmes) nf ▸ **à la mi-carême** on the third Thursday of Lent.

miche [miʃ] nf [pain] round loaf. ❖ **miches** nfpl *tfam* [fesses] bum UK, butt US, fanny UK ; [seins] knockers, tits.

mi-chemin [miʃmɛ̃] ❖ **à mi-chemin** loc adv halfway, midway. ❖ **à mi-chemin de** loc prép halfway to / *à mi-chemin de l'église et de l'école* halfway ou midway between the church and the school.

mi-clos, e [miklo, mikloz] adj half-closed.

micmac [mikmak] nm *fam* [affaire suspecte] funny ou fishy business, strange carry-on ; [complications] mix-up / *ça a été tout un micmac pour pouvoir entrer* getting in was a real hassle.

micro [mikʀo] nm **1.** (abr de **microphone**) mike ▸ **parler dans le micro** to speak into the mike **2.** (abr de **micro-ordinateur**) *fam* PC.

microbe [mikʀɔb] nm **1.** [germe] microbe, germ **2.** *fam* [personne] shrimp, (little) runt ou pipsqueak.

microblog [mikʀoblɔg] nm microblog.

microbrasserie [mikʀobʀasʀi] nf microbrewery.

microclimat [mikʀoklima] nm microclimate.

microcosme [mikʀokɔsm] nm microcosm.

microcrédit [mikʀokʀedi] (*pl* micro-crédits) nm microcredit.

microédition [mikʀoedisjɔ̃] nf desktop publishing.

microélectronique [mikʀoelɛktʀonik] ❖ adj microelectronic. ❖ nf microelectronics (U).

microentreprise [mikʀoɑ̃tʀəpʀiz] nf microenterprise, microbusiness.

microfilm [mikʀofilm] nm microfilm.

micro-informatique [mikʀoɛ̃fɔʀmatik] (*pl* micro-informatiques) nf computer science.

micro-ondable [mikʀoɔ̃dabl] (*pl* micro-ondables) adj microwavable.

micro-ondes [mikʀoɔ̃d] nm inv microwave ▸ **faire cuire qqch au micro-ondes** to cook sthg in the microwave, to microwave sthg.

micro-ordinateur [mikʀoɔʀdinatœʀ] (*pl* micro-ordinateurs) nm microcomputer.

microphone [mikʀofɔn] nm microphone.

microprocesseur [mikʀopʀosesœʀ] nm microprocessor.

microscope [mikʀoskɔp] nm microscope ▸ **étudier qqch au microscope** a) *pr* to examine sthg under ou through a microscope b) *fig* to put sthg under the microscope ▸ **microscope électronique / optique** electron / optical microscope.

microscopique [mikʀoskɔpik] adj SCI microscopic ; [petit] microscopic, tiny, minute.

microsillon [mikʀosijɔ̃] nm [sillon] microgroove ▸ **(disque) microsillon** microgroove record.

microvoiture [mikʀovwatyʀ] nf microcar.

midi [midi] nm **1.** [milieu du jour] midday, lunchtime, noon ▸ **je m'arrête à midi** a) I stop at lunchtime b) [pour déjeuner] I stop for lunch ▸ **tous les midis** every day at lunchtime, every lunchtime / *il mange des pâtes tous les midis* he has pasta for lunch every day **2.** [heure] midday, twelve (o'clock), (twelve) noon ▸ **il est midi** it's midday, it's twelve (noon) ▸ **il est midi passé** it's after twelve, it's past midday / *midi et quart* a quarter past twelve / *entre midi et deux (heures)* between twelve and two, during lunch ou lunchtime **3.** [sud] south ▸ **exposé au midi** south-facing, facing south. ❖ **Midi** nm [région du sud] South / *le Midi (de la France)* the South of France. ❖ **de midi** loc adj [repas, informations] midday (modif) ▸ **la pause de midi** the lunch break.

midinette [midinɛt] nf *péj* [jeune fille] starry-eyed girl / *des amours de midinette* the loves of some starry-eyed young girl.

mi-distance [midistɑ̃s] ❖ **à mi-distance** loc adv halfway, midway. ❖ **à mi-distance de** loc prép halfway ou midway between.

mie [mi] nf [de pain] white ou soft ou doughy part (of bread).

miel [mjɛl] nm [d'abeilles] honey.

mielleux, euse [mjɛlø, øz] adj [doucereux] sickly sweet ; [personne] sugary ▸ **un sourire mielleux** a saccharine smile / *d'un ton mielleux* in a syrupy voice.

mien, mienne [mjɛ̃, mjɛn] (*mpl* miens [mjɛ̃], *fpl* miennes [mjɛn]) adj poss *sout* : *j'ai fait mien ce mot d'ordre* I've adopted this slogan as my own. ❖ **le mien, la mienne** (*mpl* les miens, *fpl* les miennes) pron poss mine / *je suis parti avec une valise qui n'était pas la mienne* I left with a suitcase that wasn't mine ou that didn't belong to me ▸ **ton jour / ton prix sera le mien** name the day / your price ; (emploi nominal) ▸ **les miens** my family and friends ▸ **j'y mets du mien** a) [en faisant des efforts] I'm making an effort b) [en étant compréhensif] I'm trying to be understanding.

miette [mjɛt] nf **1.** [d'aliment] crumb / *des miettes de pain* breadcrumbs ▸ **des miettes de thon** tuna flakes **2.** [petite quantité] ▸ **pas une miette de** not a shred of. ❖ **miettes** nfpl [restes] leftovers, crumbs, scraps ; [morceaux] piece, fragment, bit / *sa voiture est en miettes* her car's a wreck / *son rêve est en miettes* his dream is in shreds ou tatters.

mieux [mjø]
❖ adv

A. COMPARATIF DE « BIEN » **1.** [d'une manière plus satisfaisante] better ▸ **elle va mieux** she's better ▸ **qui dit mieux ?** a) [aux enchères] any advance on that?, any more bids? b) *fig* who can top that? ▸ **mieux assis** a) [plus confortablement] sitting more comfortably b) [au spectacle] in a better seat / *moins je le vois, mieux je me porte !* the less I see of him, the better I feel! **2.** [conformément à la raison, à la morale] better / *son frère ne fait que des bêtises, et elle ce* *n'est pas mieux* her brother is always misbehaving and she's no better ▶ *il ferait mieux de travailler / de se taire* he'd do better to work / to keep quiet. **B. SUPERLATIF DE « BIEN »** ▶ **le mieux a)** [de deux] the better **b)** [de plusieurs] the best ▶ *c'est le mannequin le mieux payé* **a)** [des deux] she's the better-paid model **b)** [de plusieurs] she's the best-paid model / *voilà ce qui me convient le mieux* this is what suits me best / *le mieux qu'il peut* the best he can ▶ **le mieux du monde** *sout* beautifully. **C. EMPLOI NOMINAL** better / *c'est pas mal, mais il y a mieux* it's not bad, but there's better / *en attendant / espérant mieux* while waiting / hoping for better (things) / *faute de mieux, je m'en contenterai* since there's nothing better, I'll make do with it / *changer en mieux* to take a turn for ou to change for the better.

◆ *adj* **1.** [plus satisfaisant] better / *on ne se voit plus, c'est mieux ainsi* we don't see each other any more, it's better that way **2.** [du point de vue de la santé, du bien-être] better / *on sent qu'il est mieux dans sa peau* you can feel he's more at ease with himself / *on est mieux dans ce fauteuil* this armchair is more comfortable **3.** [plus beau] better / *elle est mieux avec les cheveux courts* she looks better with short hair.

◆ *nm* **1.** [amélioration] improvement / *il y a du mieux* things have got better, there's some improvement **2.** [ce qui est préférable] : *le mieux est de ne pas y aller* it's best not to go ▶ **faire de son mieux** to do one's (level) best. ◆ **à qui mieux mieux** *loc adv* : *les enfants répondaient à qui mieux mieux* the children were trying to outdo each other in answering. ◆ **au mieux** *loc adv* ▶ **faire au mieux** to do whatever's best, to act for the best / *au mieux de sa forme* on top form, in prime condition / *j'ai agi au mieux de vos intérêts* I acted in your best interest. ◆ **de mieux** *loc adj* [de plus satisfaisant] : *c'est ce que nous avons de mieux* it's the best we have / *si tu n'as rien de mieux à faire, viens avec moi* if you've got nothing better to do, come with me. ◆ **de mieux en mieux** *loc adv* better and better / *et maintenant, de mieux en mieux, j'ai perdu mes clefs !* *iron* and now, to cap it all, I've lost my keys! ◆ **pour le mieux** *loc adv* for the best / *tout va pour le mieux* everything is for the best.

mieux-être [mjøzɛtʀ] *nm inv* better quality of life.

mièvre [mjɛvʀ] *adj péj* **1.** [fade] insipid, vapid, bland ; [sentimental] mawkish, syrupy ▶ **un roman mièvre** a mushy novel **2.** [maniéré] mawkish, precious **3.** [joli sans vrai talent - dessin] pretty-pretty, flowery.

mignon, onne [miɲɔ̃, ɔn] *adj* **1.** [joli] sweet, pretty, cute / *il est mignon, ton appartement* you've got a lovely little flat **2.** *fam* [gentil] sweet, nice, lovely / *allez, sois mignonne, va te coucher* come on, be a darling ou sweetie ou dear and go to bed.

migraine [migʀɛn] *nf* MÉD migraine ; [mal de tête] (bad) headache / *ces formulaires à remplir, c'est à vous donner la migraine* filling in these forms is a real headache.

migrant, e [migʀɑ̃, ɑ̃t] *adj & nm, f* migrant.

migrateur, trice [migʀatœʀ, tʀis] *adj* BIOL & ORNITH migratory.

migration [migʀasjɔ̃] *nf* [des oiseaux, des travailleurs] migration.

migrer [3] [migʀe] *vi* to migrate.

mi-hauteur [mi'otœʀ] ◆ **à mi-hauteur** *loc adv* halfway up ou down.

mijaurée [miʒɔʀe] *nf* [pimbêche] (stuck-up) little madam ▶ **faire la mijaurée** to put on airs.

mijoter [3] [miʒɔte] ◆ *vt* **1.** CULIN to simmer, to slow-cook / *il est mignon, ton appartement* ; *mijoter des petits plats* to spend a lot of time cooking delicious meals **2.** *fam* [coup, plan] to plot, to cook up

(sép) / *qu'est-ce que tu mijotes ?* what are you up to? ◆ *vi* **1.** CULIN to simmer, to stew gently **2.** *fam & fig* : *laisse-la mijoter dans son coin* leave her awhile to mull it over.

mi-journée [miʒuʀne] *nf* : *les informations de la mi-journée* the lunchtime news.

mildiou [mildju] *nm* mildew.

milice [milis] *nf* **1.** HIST militia **2.** [organisation paramilitaire] militia.

milicien, enne [milisjɛ̃, ɛn] *nm, f* militiaman (militia woman).

milieu, x [miljø] *nm* **1.** [dans l'espace] middle, centre / *sciez-la par le* ou *en son milieu* saw it through ou down the middle / *celui du milieu* the one in the middle, the middle one **2.** [dans le temps] middle / *l'incendie s'est déclaré vers le milieu de la nuit* the fire broke out in the middle of the night ▶ **en milieu de trimestre** in mid-term **3.** [moyen terme] middle way ou course / *il faut trouver un juste milieu* we have to find a happy medium **4.** [entourage] environment, milieu / *des gens de tous les milieux* people from all walks of life ou backgrounds ▶ **les milieux scientifiques** scientific circles / *ne pas se sentir / se sentir dans son milieu* to feel out of place / at home **5.** BIOL [environnement] environment, habitat ▶ **milieu naturel** natural habitat ▶ **en milieu stérile** in a sterile environment **6.** [pègre] ▶ **le milieu** the underworld. ◆ **au beau milieu de** *loc prép* right in the middle of. ◆ **au (beau) milieu** *loc adv* (right) in the middle, (right) in the centre. ◆ **au milieu de** *loc prép* **1.** [dans l'espace] in the middle of, in the centre of **2.** [dans le temps] in the middle of / *elle est partie au milieu de mon cours* she left in the middle of ou halfway through my lesson ▶ **au milieu de l'hiver / l'été** in midwinter / midsummer / *au milieu du mois de mars* in mid-March **3.** [parmi] amongst, in the midst of, surrounded by. ◆ **milieu de terrain** *nm* [zone] midfield (area) ; [joueur] midfield player.

militaire [militɛʀ] ◆ *adj* [gén] military ; [de l'armée de terre] army (*modif*), service (*modif*) ; [de l'armée de l'air, de la marine] service (*modif*). ◆ *nm* [soldat - gén] soldier ; [- de l'armée de terre] soldier, serviceman ; [- de l'armée de l'air, de la marine] serviceman.

militant, e [militɑ̃, ɑ̃t] ◆ *adj* militant. ◆ *nm, f* militant / *les militants de base sont d'accord* the grassroots militants agree ▶ **militant syndical** trade union militant ou activist.

militariser [3] [militaʀize] *vt* to militarize.

militariste [militaʀist] ◆ *adj* militaristic. ◆ *nmf* militarist.

militer [3] [milite] *vi* **1.** [agir en militant] to be a militant ou an activist / *militer au* ou *dans le parti socialiste* to be a socialist party activist ▶ **militer pour / contre qqch** to fight for / against sthg **2.** [plaider] to militate / *ces témoignages ne militent pas en votre faveur* this evidence goes ou militates against you.

mille [mil] ◆ *dét* **1.** [dix fois cent] a ou one thousand ▶ **dix / cent mille** ten / a hundred thousand ▶ **en l'an mille cinquante** ou **mil cinquante** in the year one thousand and fifty **2.** [beaucoup de] : *c'est mille fois trop grand* it's miles too big ▶ **mille excuses** ou **pardons si je t'ai blessé** I'm dreadfully sorry if I've hurt you ▶ **en mille morceaux** in pieces / *il y a mille et une manières de réussir sa vie* there are thousands of ways ou a thousand and one ways of being successful in life. ◆ *nm inv* **1.** [nombre] a ou one thousand / *y a une chance sur mille que ça marche* there's a one-in-a-thousand chance that it'll work ▶ **je te le donne en mille !** *fam* I bet you'll never guess! **2.** [centre d'une cible] bull's eye ▶ **mettre** ou **taper (en plein) dans le mille a)** *fam & pr* to hit the bull's-eye **b)** *fam & fig* to score a bull's-eye, to be bang on target. ◆ *nm* **1.** NAUT ▶ **mille (marin)** nautical mile **2.** [Québec] (statute) mile.

mille-feuille (*pl* mille-feuilles), **millefeuille*** [milfœj] nm CULIN mille feuilles ; ≈ vanilla slice 🇬🇧 ou napoleon 🇺🇸.

millénaire [milenɛʀ] ◆ adj thousand-year-old. ◆ nm [période] millennium.

mille-pattes (*pl* mille-pattes), **millepatte*** [milpat] nm millipede.

millésime [milezim] nm ŒNOL [date de récolte] year, vintage / *le millésime 1976 est l'un des meilleurs* the 1976 vintage is among the best.

millésimé, e [milezime] adj vintage (*modif*) / *une bouteille millésimée 1880* a bottle dated 1880.

millet [mijɛ] nm millet.

milliard [miljaʀ] nm billion (*one thousand million*) / *cela a coûté deux milliards (d'euros)* it cost two billion (euros) / *des milliards de globules rouges* billions of red corpuscles.

milliardaire [miljaʀdɛʀ] ◆ adj : *sa famille est plusieurs fois milliardaire* his family is worth billions. ◆ nmf multimillionaire, billionaire 🇺🇸.

millième [miljɛm] ◆ adj num thousandth. ◆ nm thousandth / *il ne fournit pas le millième du travail nécessaire* he isn't doing a fraction of the work that has to be done.

millier [milje] nm thousand / *un millier de badges / livres ont été vendus* a thousand badges / books have been sold ‣ **des milliers de** thousands of. ❖ **par milliers** loc adv [arriver] in their thousands ; [envoyer, commander] by the thousand / *des ballons ont été lâchés par milliers* thousands (upon thousands) of balloons have been released.

milligramme [miligʀam] nm milligram, milligramme.

millilitre [mililitʀ] nm millilitre 🇬🇧, milliliter 🇺🇸.

millimètre [milimɛtʀ] nm millimetre 🇬🇧, millimeter 🇺🇸.

million [miljɔ̃] nm million / *un million de personnes* a ou one million people ‣ **des millions de** millions of.

millionnaire [miljɔnɛʀ] ◆ adj millionaire, millionnaire ‣ **être / devenir millionnaire** to be / to become a millionaire / *elle est plusieurs fois millionnaire (en dollars)* she's a (dollar) millionaire ou millionairess several times over. ◆ nmf millionaire (millionairess).

mi-long, mi-longue [milɔ̃, milɔ̃g] (*mpl* **mi-longs**, *fpl* **mi-longues**) adj [jupe] half-length ; [cheveux] shoulder-length.

mime [mim] ◆ nmf [artiste] mime (artist). ◆ nm **1.** [art] mime ‣ **faire du mime** to be a mime (artist) / *un spectacle de mime* a mime show **2.** [action de mimer] miming (*U*).

mimer [3] [mime] vt **1.** THÉÂTRE to mime **2.** [imiter] to mimic.

mimétisme [mimetism] nm [imitation] mimicry, mimicking.

mimique [mimik] nf **1.** [gestuelle] gesture **2.** [grimace] facial expression.

mimosa [mimɔza] nm BOT mimosa.

min (*abr écrite de* minute) min.

minable [minabl] *fam* ◆ adj **1.** [médiocre, laid - costume] shabby, tatty 🇬🇧, tacky 🇺🇸 ; [-chambre] dingy, shabby ; [-film] third-rate, rotten, lousy ; [-situation, salaire] pathetic **2.** [mesquin] petty, mean **3.** [sans envergure] small-time, third-rate. ◆ nmf nonentity, no-hoper, loser / *pauvre minable, va !* you pathetic little nobody!

minaret [minaʀɛ] nm minaret.

minauder [3] [minode] vi to mince, to simper / *elle répondait aux questions en minaudant* she answered the questions with a simper.

mince [mɛ̃s] ◆ adj **1.** [sans épaisseur] thin **2.** [personne - svelte] slim, slender **3.** *fig* [faible] small, meagre 🇬🇧, meager 🇺🇸 ; [négligeable] slim, slender / *de minces bénéfices* slender profits / *ce n'est pas une mince affaire* this is no trifling matter / *un demi-chapitre sur la Révolution, c'est un peu mince* half a chapter on the French Revolution is a bit feeble. ◆ interj *fam* damn.

minceur [mɛ̃sœʀ] nf [sveltesse] slimness, slenderness / *régime minceur* slimming diet / *cuisine minceur* cuisine minceur ; [finesse] slimness, thinness.

mincir [32] [mɛ̃siʀ] ◆ vi [personne] to get slimmer ou thinner. ◆ vt [suj : vêtement, couleur] : *cette robe te mincit* that dress makes you look slimmer.

mine [min] nf **1.** [apparence] appearance, exterior ‣ **faire mine de** : *elle fit mine de raccrocher, puis se ravisa* she made as if to hang up, then changed her mind / *ne fais pas mine de ne pas comprendre* don't act as if you pretend you don't understand ‣ **mine de rien** *fam* : *mine de rien, ça finit par coûter cher* it may not seem much but when you add it all up, it's expensive / *mine de rien, elle était furieuse* although ou though she didn't show it, she was furious **2.** [teint] ‣ **avoir bonne mine** to look well ‣ **avoir mauvaise mine** : *il a mauvaise mine* he doesn't look very well / *tu as bonne mine, avec ta veste à l'envers !* *fig & iron* you look great with your jacket on inside out! ‣ **avoir une mine superbe** to be the (very) picture of health ‣ **avoir une sale mine** *fam* to look dreadful ou awful ‣ **avoir une petite mine** *fam* to look peaky ‣ **avoir une mine de papier mâché** *fam* to look like death warmed up / *je lui trouve meilleure mine* I think she looks better ou in better health ; [visage, contenance] look, countenance *litt* / *avoir une mine réjouie* to beam, to be beaming / *ne fais pas cette mine !* don't look so downhearted! **3.** GÉOL deposit ; [installations - de surface] pithead ; [-en sous-sol] pit ‣ **mine de charbon** ou **de houille** coal mine ‣ **mine à ciel ouvert** opencast mine ‣ **une mine d'or** *pr & fig* a gold mine **4.** [source importante] ‣ **une mine de** a mine ou source of / *une mine d'informations* a mine of information **5.** [d'un crayon] lead ‣ **mine de plomb** graphite ou black lead ‣ MIL [galerie] mine, gallery, sap ; [explosif] mine.

miner [3] [mine] vt **1.** [poser des mines] to mine / **'danger ! zone minée'** 'beware of mines' **2.** [ronger] to undermine, to erode, to eat away (at) ou into **3.** [affaiblir] to undermine, to sap ‣ **miner les forces / la santé de qqn** to sap sb's strength / health ‣ **miné par le chagrin** consumed ou worn down by grief.

minerai [minʀɛ] nm ore ‣ **minerai de fer / d'uranium** iron / uranium ore.

minéral, e, aux [mineʀal, o] adj mineral. ❖ **minéral, aux** nm mineral.

minéralogique [mineʀalɔʒik] adj **1.** GÉOL mineralogical **2.** AUTO ‣ **numéro minéralogique** registration 🇬🇧 ou license 🇺🇸 number ‣ **plaque minéralogique** numberplate 🇬🇧, license plate 🇺🇸.

minerve [minɛʀv] nf MÉD neck brace, (surgical) collar.

minet, ette [minɛ, ɛt] nm, f *fam* **1.** [jeune personne superficielle] (young) trendy **2.** [chat] puss, pussy, pussycat.

mineur, e [minœʀ] ◆ adj **1.** [insignifiant] minor **2.** DR below the age of criminal responsibility ‣ **enfants mineurs** under age children, minors ‣ **être mineur** to be under age ou a minor **3.** MUS minor. ◆ nm, f DR minor / **'interdit aux mineurs'** 'adults only'. ❖ **mineur** nm [ouvrier] miner, mineworker ‣ **mineur de fond** underground worker.

mini [mini] ◆ adj inv VÊT : *la mode mini* the mini-length ou thigh-length fashion. ◆ nm VÊT mini / *le mini est de retour* minis ou miniskirts are back.

miniature [minjatуʀ] ◆ adj miniature / *un train miniature* a model ou miniature train. ◆ nf ART miniature. ❖ **en miniature** loc adj miniature *(avant nom)*.

miniaturiser [3] [minjatуʀize] vt to miniaturize.

minibar [minibaʀ] nm minibar.

minibus [minibys], **minicar** [minikaʀ] nm minibus.

minichaîne, minichaine* [miniʃεn] nf mini (stereo) system.

minier, ère [minje, εʀ] adj mining.

minijupe [miniʒyp] nf miniskirt.

minimal, e, aux [minimal, o] adj [seuil, peine] minimum *(avant nom)*.

minime [minim] ◆ adj [faible] minimal, minor / *la différence est minime* the difference is negligible. ◆ nmf SPORT (school) Junior.

minimiser [3] [minimize] vt [rôle] to minimize, to play down *(sép)* ; [risque] to minimize, to cut down *(sép)*.

minimum [minimɔm] *(pl* minimums *ou* minima [minima])* ◆ adj minimum / **poids / service minimum** minimum weight / service / **prix minimum a)** minimum ou bottom price **b)** [aux enchères] reserve price. ◆ nm **1.** [le plus bas degré] minimum / *températures proches du minimum saisonnier* temperatures approaching the minimum ou the lowest recorded for the season / *mets le chauffage au minimum* turn the heating down as low as it'll go / *j'ai réduit les matières grasses au minimum* I've cut down on fat as much as possible, I've cut fat down to a minimum / **avoir le minimum vital** [financier] to be on subsistence level, to earn the minimum living wage / *ils n'ont même pas le minimum vital* they don't even have the bare minimum **2.** DR [peine la plus faible] / **le minimum** the minimum sentence **3.** [une petite quantité] / **un minimum (de)** a minimum (of) / *tu en as vraiment fait un minimum !* you really have done just the bare minimum! / *s'il avait un minimum de bon sens / d'honnêteté* if he had a minimum of common sense / of decency **4.** ADMIN / **minimum vieillesse** basic state pension. ◆ adv minimum / *il fait 3 °C minimum* the temperature is 3 °C minimum. ❖ **au minimum** loc adv [au moins] at the least / *deux jours au minimum* at least two days, a minimum of two days.

mini-ordinateur [miniɔʀdinatœʀ] *(pl* mini-ordinateurs)* nm minicomputer.

minipilule [minipilyl] nf low dose (contraceptive) pill, minipill.

minisérie [miniseʀi] nf miniseries *(sg)*.

ministère [ministεʀ] nm **1.** POL [charge] ministry 🇬🇧, administration 🇺🇸 / *elle a refusé le ministère qu'on lui proposait* she turned down the government position she was offered **2.** [cabinet] government, ministry **3.** [bâtiment] ministry 🇬🇧, department (offices) 🇺🇸 ; [département] ministry 🇬🇧, department 🇺🇸 / **ministère des Affaires étrangères** ≃ Ministry of Foreign Affairs ; ≃ Foreign Office 🇬🇧 ; ≃ State Department 🇺🇸 / **ministère des Finances** ≃ Ministry of Finance ; ≃ Treasury Department 🇺🇸 & 🇬🇧 / **ministère de la Défense** ≃ Ministry of Defence 🇬🇧 ; ≃ Department of Defense 🇺🇸 / **ministère de l'Intérieur** ≃ Ministry of the Interior ; ≃ Home Office 🇬🇧 ; ≃ Department of the Interior 🇺🇸 **4.** / **ministère public** ≃ (office of the) Director of Public Prosecutions / ≃ Crown Prosecution Service 🇬🇧 ; ≃ District Attorney's office 🇺🇸

ministériel, elle [ministeʀjεl] adj **1.** [émanant d'un ministre] ministerial 🇬🇧, departmental 🇺🇸 **2.** [concernant le gouvernement] ministerial 🇬🇧, cabinet *(modif)*.

ministre [ministʀ] ◆ nmf POL minister 🇬🇧, secretary 🇺🇸 / **ministre de l'Écologie** ministry responsible for legislation relating to environmental issues / **ministre de l'Intérieur** ≃ Ministry of the Interior ; ≃ Home Office 🇬🇧 ; ≃ De-

partment of the Interior 🇺🇸 / **ministre d'État** minister 🇬🇧, secretary of state / **Premier ministre** Prime Minister ; [ambassadeur] / **ministre plénipotentiaire (auprès de)** minister plenipotentiary (to). ◆ nm RELIG [pasteur] / **ministre du culte** minister.

minois [minwa] nm (sweet little) face.

minorer [3] [minɔʀe] vt [baisser] to reduce, to cut, to mark down / *minorer les prix de 2 %* to cut prices by 2%.

minoritaire [minɔʀitεʀ] adj **1.** [moins nombreux] minority *(modif)* / **parti minoritaire** minority party / *les femmes sont minoritaires dans cette profession* women are a minority in this profession **2.** [non reconnu] minority *(modif)*.

minorité [minɔʀite] nf **1.** [le plus petit nombre] minority / **une minorité de** a minority of **2.** [groupe] minority (group) / **minorité ethnique** ethnic minority / **minorité nationale** national minority **3.** [âge légal] minority ; DR nonage. ❖ **en minorité** ◆ loc adj in a ou the minority / *nous sommes en minorité* we're in a minority. ◆ loc adv : *mettre le gouvernement en minorité* to force the government into a minority.

Minorque [minɔʀk] npr Minorca / **à Minorque** in Minorca.

minoterie [minɔtʀi] nf [lieu] flourmill.

minou [minu] nm *fam* [chat] pussy, pussycat.

minuit [minɥi] nm **1.** [milieu de la nuit] midnight **2.** [heure] midnight, twelve midnight, twelve o'clock (at night) / **il est minuit passé** it's after ou past midnight / *minuit et quart* a quarter past twelve ou past midnight / **à minuit** at midnight, at twelve o'clock (at night). ❖ **de minuit** loc adj midnight *(modif)*.

minuscule [minyskyl] ◆ adj **1.** [très petit] minute, minuscule, tiny **2.** IMPR / **un b minuscule** a small b. ◆ nf small letter ; IMPR lower-case letter / **écrire en minuscules** to write in small letters.

minutage [minytaʒ] nm timing.

minute [minyt] ◆ nf **1.** [mesure - du temps] minute / **une minute de silence** a minute's silence, a minute of silence / **à la minute près** on the dot, right on time / **on n'est pas à la minute près** ou **à la minute !** *fam* there's no hurry! / *à deux minutes de voiture / de marche de chez moi* two minutes' drive / walk away from my house **2.** [moment] minute, moment / *revenez dans une petite minute* come back in a minute ou moment (or two) / *il y a une minute* ou *il n'y a pas même une minute, tu disais tout le contraire* just a minute ou moment ago, you were saying the very opposite / *je n'ai pas une minute à moi* I haven't got a minute ou moment to myself **3.** GÉOM minute. ◆ interj *fam* wait a minute ou moment / *minute, je n'ai pas dit ça !* hang on *fam* ou wait a minute, I never said that! / **minute, papillon !** hold your horses!, not so fast! ❖ **à la minute** loc adv **1.** [il y a un instant] a moment ago / *elle est sortie à la minute* she's just this minute gone out **2.** [toutes les 60 secondes] per minute. ❖ **d'une minute à l'autre** loc adv any time / *il sera là d'une minute à l'autre* he'll be arriving any minute, he won't be a minute.

minuter [3] [minyte] vt [spectacle, cuisson] to time / *sa journée de travail est soigneusement minutée* she works to a very tight ou strict schedule.

minuterie [minytʀi] nf **1.** ÉLECTR time switch **2.** [d'une horloge] motion work ; [d'un compteur] counter mechanism **3.** [minuteur] timer.

minuteur [minytœʀ] nm AUDIO & ÉLECTR timer.

minutie [minysi] nf meticulousness, thoroughness / **avec minutie a)** [travailler] meticulously, carefully **b)** [examiner] in minute detail, thoroughly.

minutieusement [minysjøzmɑ̃] adv **1.** [avec précision] meticulously, carefully **2.** [en détail] in minute detail.

minutieux, euse [minysjø, øz] adj **1.** [personne] meticulous, thorough / *déjà enfant, il était très minutieux* even as a child, he used to do everything with great thoroughness **2.** [travail] meticulous, detailed, thorough.

mioche [mjɔʃ] nmf *fam* kid, nipper [UK].

mirabelle [miʀabɛl] nf [fruit] mirabelle (plum) ; [liqueur] mirabelle *(plum brandy)*.

miracle [miʀakl] nm **1.** [intervention divine] miracle / *sa guérison tient du miracle* his recovery is (nothing short of) a miracle **2.** [surprise] miracle, marvel **3.** THÉÂTRE miracle play **4.** *(comme adjectif, avec ou sans trait d'union)* miracle *(modif)*, wonder *(modif)* ▶ **médicament miracle** miracle ou wonder drug / *la solution-miracle à vos problèmes de rangement* the miracle solution to your storage problems. ❖ **par miracle** loc adv by a ou some miracle, miraculously.

miraculé, e [miʀakyle] nm, f **1.** RELIG : *c'est un miraculé de Lourdes* he was miraculously cured at Lourdes **2.** [survivant] miraculous survivor / *un des rares miraculés du tremblement de terre* one of the few (people) who miraculously survived the earthquake.

miraculeusement [miʀakyløzmɑ̃] adv miraculously, (as if) by a ou some miracle.

miraculeux, euse [miʀakylø, øz] adj **1.** [qui tient du miracle] miraculous, miracle *(modif)* **2.** [très opportun] miraculous, wonderful **3.** [prodigieux] miraculous, miracle *(modif)*.

mirador [miʀadɔʀ] nm MIL watchtower, mirador.

mirage [miʀaʒ] nm **1.** [illusion optique] mirage **2.** *sout* [chimère] mirage, delusion.

mire [miʀ] nf ARM ▶ **point de mire** pr aim, target / *pendant les Jeux, la ville sera le point de mire du monde entier* fig the eyes of the world will be on the city during the Games.

miro [miʀo] *fam* adj [myope] short-sighted / *sans mes lunettes, je suis complètement miro* I'm as blind as a bat without my glasses.

mirobolant, e [miʀobɔlɑ̃, ɑ̃t] adj *fam* [mirifique] fabulous, stupendous, amazing.

miroir [miʀwaʀ] nm **1.** [verre réflecteur] mirror ▶ **miroir déformant / grossissant** distorting / magnifying mirror ▶ **miroir aux alouettes a)** CHASSE decoy **b)** fig trap for the unwary ▶ **miroir de courtoisie** AUTO vanity mirror **2.** *litt* [image, reflet] mirror, reflection.

miroiter [3] [miʀwate] vi **1.** *sout* [luire] to glisten, to gleam **2.** fig ▶ **faire miroiter qqch à qqn** to (try and) lure sb with the prospect of sthg / *on lui a fait miroiter une augmentation* they dangled the prospect of a rise before him.

mis, e [mi, miz] adj [vêtu] ▶ **bien mis** well dressed, nicely turned out.

misaine [mizɛn] nf ▶ **(voile de) misaine** foresail.

misanthrope [mizɑ̃tʀɔp] adj misanthropic.

mise [miz] nf **1.** JEUX stake / *doubler sa mise* to double one's stake **2.** *sout* [tenue] attire, dress ▶ **soigner sa mise** to take care over one's appearance **3.** [dans des expressions] ▶ **mise à jour a)** updating **b)** INFORM maintenance ▶ **mise à pied a)** [disciplinaire] suspension **b)** [économique] laying off ▶ **mise en ondes** RADIO production. ❖ **de mise** loc adj appropriate / *ta colère n'est plus de mise* your anger is out of place now, there's no point in your being angry any more. ❖ **mise à prix** nf reserve [UK] ou upset [US] price. ❖ **mise au point** nf **1.** OPT & PHOT focusing, focussing **2.** TECHNOL tuning, adjustment **3.** INFORM trouble-shooting, debugging **4.** fig clarification, correction /

après cette petite mise au point now that the record has been set straight. ❖ **mise de fonds** nf capital outlay.

❖ **mise en page(s)** nf INFORM editing / *je n'aime pas la mise en page de la revue* I don't like the layout of the review. ❖ **mise en plis** nf set. ❖ **mise en scène** nf CINÉ & THÉÂTRE production.

miser [3] [mize] ◆ vt [parier] to stake, to bet. ◆ vi [Suisse] [acheter] to buy *(at an auction sale)* ; [vendre] to put up for auction. ❖ **miser sur** v + prép **1.** JEUX [cheval] to bet on, to back / *j'ai misé 10 euros sur le numéro 29* I've staked 10 euros on number 29 ; [numéro] to bet on ▶ **miser sur les deux tableaux** to back both horses, to hedge one's bets **2.** [compter sur - quelque chose] to bank ou to count on *(insép)* ; [- quelqu'un] to count on *(insép)*.

misérabilisme [mizeʀabilism] nm miserabilism.

misérable [mizeʀabl] adj **1.** *(après le nom)* [sans ressources] impoverished, poverty-stricken, poor **2.** [pitoyable] pitiful, miserable, wretched **3.** [insignifiant] miserable, paltry / *travailler pour un salaire misérable* to work for a pittance.

misérablement [mizeʀabləmɑ̃] adv **1.** [pauvrement] in poverty, wretchedly **2.** [lamentablement] pitifully, miserably, wretchedly.

misère [mizɛʀ] nf **1.** [indigence] poverty, destitution *sout* ▶ **être dans la misère** to be destitute ou poverty-stricken / *être réduit à la misère* to be reduced to poverty **2.** fig poverty ▶ **misère sexuelle** sexual deprivation **3.** [malheur] : *c'est une misère de les voir se séparer* it's pitiful ou it's a shame to see them break up **4.** [somme dérisoire] pittance / *je l'ai eu pour une misère* I got ou bought it for next to nothing **5.** [EXPR] ▶ **avoir de la misère** [Québec] to be having a hard time. ❖ **misères** nfpl fam [ennuis] ▶ **faire des misères à qqn** to give sb a hard time, to make sb's life a misery / *raconte-moi tes misères* tell me all your troubles ou woes. ❖ **de misère** loc adj ▶ **un salaire de misère** a starvation wage, a pittance.

⚠ Misery ne doit pas être employé pour traduire misère car il n'a pas le même sens que le mot français.

miséreux, euse [mizeʀø, øz] nm, f *sout* poor person, pauper *vieilli* / *aider* ou *secourir les miséreux* to help the poor.

miséricorde [mizeʀikɔʀd] nf *litt* [pitié] mercy, forgiveness ▶ **implorer miséricorde** to beg ou to cry for mercy.

misogyne [mizɔʒin] ◆ adj misogynous, misogynistic. ◆ nmf misogynist, woman-hater.

misogynie [mizɔʒini] nf misogyny.

miss [mis] *(pl* miss ou misses [mis]) nf *fam & hum* : *ça va, la miss ?* how's things, beauty? ❖ **Miss** nf [reine de beauté] : *Miss Japon / Monde* Miss Japan / World.

missile [misil] nm missile ▶ **missile antichar / antiaérien** antitank / antiaircraft missile ▶ **missile balistique** ballistic missile.

mission [misjɔ̃] nf **1.** [charge] mission, assignment ; [dans le cadre d'une entreprise] assignment ▶ **mission accomplie** mission accomplished ▶ **être en mission** to be on an assignment ▶ **recevoir pour mission de faire qqch** to be commissioned to do sthg **2.** [devoir] mission, task / *la mission du journaliste est d'informer* a journalist's task is to inform **3.** [groupe] mission ▶ **mission diplomatique** diplomatic mission **4.** RELIG [organisation] mission ; [lieu] mission (station).

missionnaire [misjɔnɛʀ] adj & nmf missionary.

missionner [misjɔne] vt to task / *un expert a été missionné pour évaluer les dégâts* a consultant has been tasked with assessing the damage.

mistral [mistʀal] nm mistral.

mite [mit] nf [papillon] (clothes) moth / *rongé par les ou aux mites* moth-eaten.

mité, e [mite] adj moth-eaten.

mi-temps [mitɑ̃] ◆ nf inv SPORT **1.** [moitié] half ▶ **la première mi-temps** the first half **2.** [pause] halftime / *le score est de 0 à 0 à la mi-temps* the halftime score is nil nil / *siffler la mi-temps* to blow the whistle for halftime. ◆ nm inv part-time job / *faire un mi-temps* to work part-time. ◆ **à mi-temps** loc adv ▶ **travailler à mi-temps** to work part-time / *elle travaille à mi-temps comme serveuse* she's a part-time waitress.

miteux, euse [mitø, øz] fam adj [costume] shabby, tatty 🇬🇧, tacky 🇺🇸 ; [chambre] dingy, crummy ; [situation, salaire] pathetic ; [escroc] small-time.

mitigé, e [mitiʒe] adj [modéré] mixed / *des critiques mitigées* mixed reviews / *manifester un enthousiasme mitigé* to be reserved in one's enthusiasm.

mitonner [3] [mitɔne] ◆ vt CULIN to simmer, to slow-cook / *je vous ai mitonné une petite recette à moi* I've cooked you one of my tasty little recipes. ◆ vi CULIN to simmer, to stew gently.

mitoyen, enne [mitwajɛ̃, ɛn] adj **1.** [commun] common, shared **2.** [jouxtant] bordering, neighbouring / *le jardin mitoyen du nôtre* the garden (immediately) next to ours, the neighbouring garden (to ours) ▶ **deux maisons mitoyennes** semi-detached houses / *une rue de maisons mitoyennes* a street of terrace (d) houses **3.** [en copropriété] commonly-owned, jointly-owned ▶ **mur mitoyen** party wall.

mitrailler [3] [mitʀaje] vt **1.** MIL to machine-gun **2.** fam [photographier] to snap (away) at **3.** fig [assaillir] ▶ **mitrailler qqn de questions** to fire questions at sb, to bombard sb with questions.

mitraillette [mitʀajɛt] nf submachine gun.

mitrailleuse [mitʀajøz] nf machine gun.

mi-voix [mivwa] ◆ **à mi-voix** loc adv in a low ou hushed voice, in hushed tones.

mix [miks] nm inv **1.** [morceau de musique] mix **2.** [mélange] mixture, combination.

mixage [miksaʒ] nm AUDIO, RADIO, TV & MUS mixing.

mixer[1] [mikse] vt **1.** CULIN [à la main] to mix ; [au mixer] to blend, to liquidize **2.** MUS to mix.

mixer[2] [miksɛʀ], **mixeur** [miksœʀ] nm mixer, blender, liquidizer.

mixité [miksite] nf ENS coeducation, coeducational system ▶ **la mixité sociale** social diversity.

mixte [mikst] adj **1.** [des deux sexes] mixed ▶ **classe mixte** ENS mixed class ▶ **double mixte** SPORT mixed doubles **2.** [de nature double] mixed **3.** [à double usage] ▶ **cuisinière mixte** combined gas and electric cooker 🇬🇧 ou stove 🇺🇸.

mixture [mikstyʀ] nf [boisson ou nourriture] mixture, concoction.

MJC nf abr de **maison des jeunes et de la culture**.

 MJC

The **maisons des jeunes et de la culture** or **MJC** are leisure clubs run in part by local authorities. They are funded by **communes**, the **conseil général** and also by the sports ministry. They offer all sorts of activities, some more specifically for youngsters (sports, music, art) and some for adults (keep fit, folk dancing, pottery, photography, etc.) ; their mission is to develop citizenship through education and culture.

ml (abr écrite de **millilitre**) ml.

MLF (abr de **Mouvement de libération de la femme**) npr m *women's movement* ; ≃ NOW 🇺🇸.

Mlle abr écrite de **Mademoiselle**.

mm (abr écrite de **millimètre**) mm.

MM. (abr écrite de **Messieurs**) Messrs.

Mme (abr écrite de **Madame**) [femme mariée] Mrs ; [femme mariée ou célibataire] Ms.

MMS (abr de **multimedia message service**) nm TÉLÉC MMS.

mnémotechnique [mnemɔtɛknik] adj mnemonic ▶ **formule mnémotechnique** mnemonic.

Mo (abr écrite de **mégaoctet**) Mb.

mob [mɔb] (abr de **Mobylette®**) nf fam moped.

mobile [mɔbil] ◆ adj **1.** [qui se déplace - pont] moving ; [- main-d'œuvre] mobile ; [- panneau] sliding ; [amovible] movable, removable **2.** MIL [unité] mobile. ◆ nm **1.** [téléphone] mobile **2.** [de sculpteur, pour enfant] mobile **3.** [motif] motive ▶ **le mobile d'un crime** the motive for a crime / *quel mobile l'a poussé à agir ainsi ?* what motivated ou prompted him to act this way?

mobilier, ère [mɔbilje, ɛʀ] adj DR [propriété] personal, movable ; [titre] transferable. ◆ **mobilier** nm **1.** [d'une habitation] furniture, furnishings / *du mobilier Louis XIII / Renaissance* Louis XIII / Renaissance (style) furniture **2.** [pour un usage particulier] ▶ **mobilier de bureau** office furniture ▶ **mobilier de jardin** garden ou lawn furniture.

mobilisation [mɔbilizasjɔ̃] nf **1.** MIL [action] mobilization, mobilizing, calling up ; [état] mobilization **2.** [d'une force politique] mobilization ; [d'énergie, de volonté] mobilization, summoning up / *il appelle à la mobilisation de tous les syndicats* he is calling on all the unions to mobilize.

mobiliser [3] [mɔbilize] vt **1.** MIL [population] to call up (sép), to mobilize ; [armée] to mobilize / *toute la famille fut mobilisée pour préparer la fête* the whole family was put to work to organize the party **2.** [syndicalistes, consommateurs, moyens techniques] to mobilize ; [volontés] to mobilize, to summon up (sép) / *mobiliser l'opinion en faveur des réfugiés politiques* to rally public opinion for the cause of the political refugees. ◆ **se mobiliser** vpi to mobilize / *tout le village s'est mobilisé contre le projet* the whole village rose up in arms against the plan ou mobilized to fight the plan.

mobilité [mɔbilite] nf **1.** [dans l'espace - d'une personne] mobility ; [expression - d'un regard] expressiveness **2.** SOCIOL [dans une hiérarchie] mobility ▶ **mobilité géographique** geographical mobility ▶ **mobilité sociale** upward mobility.

Mobylette® [mɔbilɛt] nf Mobylette®, moped.

mocassin [mɔkasɛ̃] nm [chaussure] moccasin.

moche [mɔʃ] adj fam **1.** [laid - personne] ugly ; [- objet, vêtement] ugly, awful, horrible **2.** [détestable] lousy, rotten / *c'est moche, ce qu'elle lui a fait* it was rotten, what she did to him **3.** [pénible] : *tu ne peux pas prendre de congé ? c'est moche, dis donc !* can't you take any time off? that's terrible! / *c'est moche qu'il pleuve aujourd'hui !* it's a real drag ou pain that it had to rain today!

modalité [mɔdalite] nf **1.** [façon] mode ▶ **modalités de paiement** conditions ou terms of payment **2.** [circonstances] ▶ **les modalités de l'accord** the terms of the agreement ▸ **modalités d'intervention** procedure **3.** LING, MUS & PHILOS modality ▸ **adverbe de modalité** modal adverb.

mode¹ [mɔd] ◆ nf **1.** VÊT ▸ **la mode** fashion / *la mode (de) printemps* / *(d')hiver* the spring / winter fashion ▸ **c'est la dernière** ou **c'est la grande mode** it's the latest fashion / *c'est la mode des bas résille* fishnet stockings are in fashion ou in vogue ▸ **c'est passé de mode** it's out of fashion, it's no longer fashionable ▸ **lancer une mode** to set a fashion ou a trend **2.** [activité] ▸ **la mode a)** [gén] the fashion industry ou business **b)** [stylisme] fashion designing **3.** [goût du jour] fashion / *ce n'est plus la mode de se marier* marriage is outdated ou has gone out of fashion / *la mode des années 80* the style of the eighties. ◆ adj inv [coloris, coupe] fashion *(modif)*, fashionable. ◈ **à la mode** ◆ loc adj [vêtement] fashionable, in fashion ; [personne, sport] fashionable ; [chanson] (currently) popular / *ce n'est plus à la mode* it's out of fashion. ◆ loc adv : *revenir à la mode* to come back into fashion.

mode² [mɔd] nm **1.** [méthode] ▸ **mode de a)** [méthode] mode ou method of **b)** [manière personnelle] way of / *on ne connaît pas le mode d'action de cette substance* we don't know how this substance works ▸ **mode d'emploi** directions ou instructions for use ▸ **mode de paiement** mode ou method of payment ▸ **mode de scrutin** voting system ▸ **mode de transport** mode of transport ▸ **mode de vie a)** [gén] life style **b)** SOCIOL pattern of living **2.** LING mood, mode **3.** INFORM & TÉLÉC mood ▸ **mode avion** [sur téléphone mobile] airplane mode ▸ **mode autonome** ou **local** ou **hors ligne** off-line mode ▸ **mode connecté** ou **en ligne** on-line mode ▸ **mode utilisateur** user mode **4.** MATH, MUS & PHILOS mode. ◈ **en mode** loc prép : *la ministre est passée en mode silencieux* fig the minister went into silent mode.

modelage [mɔdlaʒ] nm [action] modelling 🇬🇧, modeling 🇺🇸 ; MÉTALL moulding.

modèle [mɔdɛl] ◆ nm **1.** [référence à reproduire - gén] model ; [- de tricot, de couture] pattern ; ÉDUC [corrigé] model answer **2.** [bon exemple] model, example ▸ **prendre qqn pour modèle** to model o.s. on sb / *c'est un modèle de discrétion* he's a model of discretion / *c'est un modèle du genre* it's a perfect example of its type **3.** COMM [prototype, version] model ▸ **modèle déposé** registered design **4.** VÊT model, style, design **5.** [maquette] model ▸ **modèle réduit** small-scale model ▸ **modèle réduit d'avion** model aeroplane **6.** ART model **7.** INFORM model **8.** ÉCON model ▸ **modèle économique** business model **9.** LING pattern. ◆ adj **1.** [parfait] model *(modif)* / *il a eu un comportement modèle* he was a model of good behaviour 🇬🇧 ou behavior 🇺🇸 **2.** [qui sert de référence] : *ferme* / *prison modèle* model farm / prison.

modeler [25] [mɔdle] vt **1.** [argile] to model, to shape, to mould ; [figurine] to model, to mould, to fashion **2.** fig [idées, caractère, opinion publique] to shape, to mould ▸ **modeler sa conduite sur (celle de) qqn** to model one's behaviour on sb ou sb's. ◈ **se modeler sur** vp + prép to model o.s. on.

modélisme [mɔdelism] nm scale model making.

modem [mɔdɛm] nm modem.

modération [mɔdeʁasjɔ̃] nf **1.** [mesure] moderation, restraint ▸ **avec modération a)** [boire, manger, utiliser] in moderation **b)** [agir] moderately, with moderation / *une réponse pleine de modération* a very restrained answer **2.** [réduction - de dépenses] reduction, reducing ; [atténuation - d'un sentiment] restraint, restraining.

modéré, e [mɔdeʁe] adj **1.** [prix] moderate, reasonable ; [vent, température] moderate ; [enthousiasme, intérêt, succès] moderate **2.** [mesuré, raisonnable] moderate ; [plein de retenue] moderate, restrained **3.** POL moderate.

modérément [mɔdeʁemã] adv **1.** [sans excès] in moderation **2.** [relativement] moderately, relatively / *je ne suis que modérément surpris* I'm only moderately surprised, I'm not really all that surprised.

modérer [18] [mɔdeʁe] vt [ardeur, enthousiasme, impatience, dépenses] to moderate, to restrain, to curb ; [vitesse] to reduce ; [exigences] to moderate, to restrain ▸ **modérez vos propos !** please tone down ou moderate your language! ◈ **se modérer** vp *(emploi réfléchi)* **1.** [se contenir] to restrain o.s. **2.** [se calmer] to calm down.

📝 In reformed spelling (see p. 16-18), this verb is conjugated like *semer : il modèrera, elle modèrerait*.

moderne [mɔdɛʁn] ◆ adj **1.** [actuel, récent - mobilier, bâtiment, technique, théorie] modern / *le mode de vie moderne* modern living, today's way of life **2.** [progressiste - artiste, opinions, théoricien] modern, progressive / *c'est une grand-mère très moderne* she's a very modern ou up-to-date grandmother **3.** ART modern, contemporary **4.** ENS [maths] modern, new ; [études, histoire] modern, contemporary. ◆ nmf ART modern artist ; LITTÉR modern writer, modern poet. ◆ nm ▸ **le moderne a)** [genre] modern style **b)** [mobilier] modern furniture.

modernisation [mɔdɛʁnizasjɔ̃] nf modernization, modernizing, updating.

moderniser [3] [mɔdɛʁnize] vt to modernize, to bring up to date. ◈ **se moderniser** vp *(emploi réfléchi)* to modernize.

modernité [mɔdɛʁnite] nf modernity.

modeste [mɔdɛst] ◆ adj **1.** [logement] modest ; [revenu] modest, small ; [goût, train de vie] modest, unpretentious ; [tenue] modest, simple ; [milieu] modest, humble / *être d'origine très modeste* to come from a very modest ou humble background **2.** *(avant nom)* [modique] modest, humble, small / *ce n'est qu'un modeste présent* it's only a very modest ou small gift, it's just a little something **3.** [sans vanité] modest. ◆ nmf : *allons, ne fais pas la* ou *ta modeste !* come on, don't be (so) modest!

modestement [mɔdɛstəmã] adv **1.** [simplement] modestly, simply **2.** [sans vanité] modestly.

modestie [mɔdɛsti] nf **1.** [humilité] modesty ▸ **en toute modestie** in all modesty ▸ **fausse modestie** false modesty **2.** *vieilli* [réserve] modesty, self-effacement ; [pudeur] modesty.

modeux, euse [mɔdø, øz] *fam* ◆ adj into fashion. ◆ nm, f stylist.

modicité [mɔdisite] nf lowness, smallness, paltriness.

modification [mɔdifikasjɔ̃] nf [processus] modification, modifying, changing ; [altération] modification, alteration, change.

modifier [9] [mɔdifje] vt [transformer - politique, texte] to modify, to change, to alter ; [- vêtement] to alter ; [- loi] to amend, to change. ◈ **se modifier** vpi to change, to alter, to be modified.

modique [mɔdik] adj [peu élevé - prix, rémunération] modest, small / *et pour la modique somme de 20 euros, mesdames, je vous donne deux couvertures !* and for the modest sum of 20 euros, ladies, I'll give you two blankets!

modulable [mɔdylabl] adj **1.** [équipement, installation] modular, flexible **2.** [horaires, tarif] flexible **3.** [chauffage, éclairage] adjustable.

modulation [mɔdylasjɔ̃] nf **1.** [tonalité - de la voix] modulation ; ACOUST & MUS modulation **2.** ÉLECTRON, INFORM, RADIO & TÉLÉC modulation ▸ **modulation d'amplitude** / **de fréquence** amplitude / frequency modulation **3.** [nuance] modulation, variation.

module [mɔdyl] nm [élément - gén] module, unit ; ARCHIT & CONSTR module.

moduler [3] [mɔdyle] ◆ vt **1.** TECHNOL to modulate **2.** [adapter] to adjust **3.** [nuancer] to vary. ◆ vi MUS to modulate.

moelle [mwal] nf ANAT marrow, medulla *spéc* ▸ **moelle épinière** spinal chord ▸ **moelle osseuse / jaune / rouge** bone / yellow / red marrow ▸ **être gelé** ou **transi jusqu'à la moelle des os** to be frozen to the marrow ou to the bone.

moelleux, euse [mwalø, øz] adj [au toucher] soft / *des coussins moelleux* soft ou comfortable cushions ; [à la vue, à l'ouïe] mellow, warm ; [au palais - vin] mellow, well-rounded ; [- viande] tender ; [- gâteau] moist.

mœurs [mœR(s)] nfpl **1.** [comportement social] customs, habits ▸ **les mœurs politiques** political practice / *c'est entré dans les mœurs* it's become part of everyday life **2.** [comportement personnel] manners, ways / *quelles drôles de mœurs !* what a strange way to behave! ; [style de vie] life-style **3.** [principes moraux] morals, moral standards / *des mœurs particulières* euphém particular tastes ▸ **être contraire aux bonnes mœurs** : *c'est contraire aux bonnes mœurs* it goes against accepted standards of behaviour 🇬🇧 ou behavior 🇺🇸 ▸ **la police / brigade des mœurs, les Mœurs** fam ≃ the vice squad. ◆ **de mœurs** loc adj [sexuel] ▸ **affaire de mœurs** sex case.

mohair [mɔɛR] nm mohair.

moi [mwa] ◆ pron pers **1.** [sujet] : *qui est là ? — moi* who's there? — me / *je l'ai vue hier — moi aussi* I saw her yesterday — so did I ou me too / *je n'en sais rien — moi non plus* I have no idea — neither do I ou me neither / *et vous voulez que moi, j'y aille ?* you want ME to go? / *et moi qui te faisais confiance !* and to think (that) I trusted you! **2.** [avec un présentatif] : *c'est moi qui lui ai dit de venir* I was the one who ou it was me who told him to come ▸ **salut, c'est moi !** hi, it's me! / *c'est moi qui te le dis !* I'm telling you! **3.** [complément] ▸ **dites-moi** tell me ▸ **donne-le-moi** give it to me / *il nous a invités, ma femme et moi* he invited both my wife and myself ; [avec une préposition] : *c'est à moi qu'il l'a donné* he gave it to ME / *un ami à moi* fam a friend of mine / *plus âgé que moi* older than me / *tu as d'aussi bonnes raisons que moi* you have just as good reasons as me ou as I have ▸ **à moi ! a)** [au secours] help! **b)** [de jouer] it's my turn! **c)** [d'essayer] let me have a go! **4.** [en fonction de pronom réfléchi] myself / *je suis contente de moi* I'm pleased with myself **5.** [emploi expressif] ▸ **regardez-moi ça !** just look at that! ◆ nm ▸ **le moi a)** PHILOS the self **b)** PSYCHOL the ego.

moignon [mwaɲɔ̃] nm stump *(of a limb)*.

moi-même [mwamɛm] pron pers myself ▸ **mon épouse et moi-même** my wife and I / *j'y suis allé de moi-même* I went there on my own initiative.

moindre [mwɛ̃dR] adj **1.** *(compar)* [perte] lesser, smaller ; [qualité] lower, poorer ; [prix] lower / *de moindre importance* less important, of lesser importance ▸ **c'est un moindre mal** it's the lesser evil **2.** *(superl)* ▸ **le moindre, la moindre a)** [de deux] the lesser **b)** [de trois ou plus] the least, the slightest / *le moindre mouvement / danger* the slightest movement / danger ▸ **la moindre chance** the slightest ou remotest chance / *je n'en ai pas la moindre idée* I haven't got the slightest ou faintest ou remotest idea ▸ **jusqu'au moindre détail** down to the last ou smallest detail / *il n'a pas fait la moindre remarque* he didn't say a single word ▸ **c'est la moindre des choses !** : *je vous en prie, c'est la moindre des choses !* don't mention it, it was the least I could do! / *dis merci, c'est la moindre des choses !* you could at least say thank you!

moine [mwan] nm RELIG monk, friar.

moineau, x [mwano] nm ORNITH sparrow.

moins [mwɛ̃] ◆ adv

A. COMPARATIF D'INFÉRIORITÉ 1. [avec un adjectif, un adverbe] less ▸ **deux fois moins cher** half as expensive, twice as cheap ▸ **en moins rapide** but not so ou as fast / *c'est moins bien que l'an dernier* it's not as good a last year ▸ **beaucoup / un peu moins** a lot / a little less / *il est moins timide que réservé* he's not so much shy as reserved **2.** [avec un verbe] less, not… so ou as much ▸ **je souffre moins** I'm not in so much ou I'm in less pain ▸ **tu devrais demander moins** you shouldn't ask for so much / *j'y pense moins que tu ne le crois* I think about it less than you think.

B. SUPERLATIF D'INFÉRIORITÉ 1. [avec un adjectif, un adverbe] : *c'est lui le moins riche des trois* he's the least wealthy of the three / *c'est le modèle le moins cher qu'on puisse trouver* it's the least expensive (that) you can find ▸ **le moins possible** as little as possible ▸ **pas le moins du monde :** *je ne suis pas le moins du monde surpris* I'm not at all ou not in the least bit surprised / *je vous dérange ? — mais non, pas le moins du monde* am I disturbing you? — of course not ou not in the slightest **2.** [avec un verbe] ▸ **le moins** (the) least ▸ **le moins qu'on puisse faire / dire :** *le moins qu'on puisse faire, c'est de les inviter* the least we could do is invite them / *c'est le moins qu'on puisse dire !* that's the least you can say!

◆ prép **1.** [en soustrayant] : *dix moins huit font deux* ten minus ou less eight makes two **2.** [indiquant l'heure] ▸ **il est moins vingt** it's twenty to ou of 🇺🇸 / *il est 3 h moins le quart* it's (a) quarter to ou of 🇺🇸 3 **3.** [introduisant un nombre négatif] ▸ **il fait moins 25** it's 25 below ou minus 25. ◆ nm minus (sign). ◆ **à moins de** loc prép **1.** [excepté] ▸ **à moins d'un miracle** short of ou barring a miracle / *nous n'arriverons pas à temps, à moins de partir demain* we won't get there on time unless we leave tomorrow **2.** [pour moins de] for less than **3.** [dans le temps, l'espace] : *il habite à moins de 10 minutes / 500 m d'ici* he lives less than 10 minutes / 500 m from here. ◆ **à moins que** loc conj unless. ◆ **au moins** loc adv **1.** [en tout cas] at least **2.** [au minimum] at least. ◆ **de moins** loc adv : *il y a 10 euros de moins dans le tiroir* there are 10 euros missing from the drawer ; *(en corrélation avec «que»)* : *j'ai un an de moins qu'elle* I'm a year younger than her. ◆ **de moins en moins** loc adv less and less / *de moins en moins souvent* less and less often. ◆ **de moins en moins de** loc dét [suivi d'un nom comptable] fewer and fewer ; [suivi d'un nom non comptable] less and less / *il y a de moins en moins de demande pour ce produit* there is less and less demand for this product. ◆ **du moins** loc adv at least / *ils devaient venir samedi, c'est du moins ce qu'ils nous avaient dit* they were supposed to come on Saturday, at least that's what they told us. ◆ **en moins** loc adv : *il y a une chaise en moins* there's one chair missing, we're one chair short. ◆ **en moins de** loc prép in less than ▸ **en moins de temps qu'il n'en faut pour le dire** before you can say Jack Robinson ▸ **en moins de deux** fam in a jiffy, in two ticks. ◆ **moins de** loc dét **1.** *(compar)* [avec un nom comptable] fewer ; [avec un nom non comptable] less / *un peu moins de bruit !* a little less noise! / *il a moins de 18 ans* he's under 18 / *il ne me faudra pas moins de 3 heures pour tout faire* I'll need no less than ou at the very least 3 hours to do everything **2.** *(superl)* ▸ **le moins de a)** [avec un nom comptable] the fewest **b)** [avec un nom non comptable] the least. ◆ **moins… moins** loc corrélative the less… the less. ◆ **moins… plus** loc corrélative the less… the more. ◆ **moins que rien** ◆ loc adv next to nothing. ◆ nmf nobody ▸ **il est un / une moins que rien** he's / she's a nobody. ◆ **pour le moins** loc adv at the very least, to say the least.

moiré, e [mwaʀe] adj **1.** TEXT moiré, watered **2.** [irisé] iridescent, irisated, moiré.

mois [mwa] nm **1.** [division du calendrier] month / *le mois de mai / décembre* the month of May / December ▸ *au début / à la fin du mois d'avril* in early / late April ▸ *le 15 de ce* ou *du mois* COMM the 15th inst 🆄🅺 ou instant 🆄🆂, the 15th of this month **2.** [durée] month ▸ *tous les mois* every ou each month, monthly ▸ *dans un mois* in a month, in a month's time **3.** [somme] monthly wage ou salary ou pay ; [versement] monthly instalment ▸ *je vous dois trois mois* **a)** [de salaire] I owe you three months' wages **b)** [de loyer] I owe you three months' rent ▸ *mois double, treizième mois* extra month's pay *(income bonus equal to an extra month's salary and paid annually)*. ❖ *au mois* loc adv by the month, monthly, on a monthly basis.

Moïse [mɔiz] npr Moses.

moisi, e [mwazi] adj [papier, tissu] mildewy, mouldy 🆄🅺, moldy 🆄🆂 ; [fruit, pain] mouldy 🆄🅺, moldy 🆄🆂 ; [logement] mildewy, fusty. ❖ **moisi** nm [moisissure] mildew, mould 🆄🅺, mold 🆄🆂 ▸ *ça sent le moisi* it smells musty.

moisir [32] [mwaziʀ] ❖ vt to make (go) mouldy 🆄🅺 ou moldy 🆄🆂. ❖ vi **1.** [pourrir] to go mouldy **2.** *fam* [s'éterniser] to rot / *moisir en prison* to rot in prison.

moisissure [mwazisyʀ] nf [champignon] mould 🆄🅺, mold 🆄🆂, mildew ; [tache] patch of mould.

moisson [mwasɔ̃] nf **1.** AGR harvest / *faire la moisson* to harvest (the crops) **2.** [grande quantité] ▸ *une moisson de* an abundance ou a wealth of.

moissonner [3] [mwasɔne] vt **1.** AGR to harvest, to reap **2.** *sout* [recueillir - informations, documents] to amass ; [remporter - prix] to carry off.

moissonneuse [mwasɔnøz] nf [machine] harvester.

moissonneuse-batteuse [mwasɔnøzbatøz] *(pl* moissonneuses-batteuses) nf combine (harvester).

moite [mwat] adj [air] muggy, clammy ; [mains] sticky, sweaty ; [front] damp, sweaty.

moitié [mwatje] nf [part] half ▸ *une moitié de* ou *la moitié d'un poulet* half a chicken ▸ *la moitié des élèves* half (of) the pupils / *quelle est la moitié de douze ?* what's half of twelve? / *nous ferons la moitié du trajet* ou *chemin ensemble* we'll do half the journey together ▸ *partager qqch en deux moitiés* to divide sthg in half ou into (two) halves, to halve sthg ; *(comme modificateur)* half / *je suis moitié français, moitié canadien* I'm half French, half Canadian. ❖ *à moitié* loc adv half / *je ne suis qu'à moitié surpris* I'm only half surprised / *le travail n'est fait qu'à moitié* only half the work's been done, the work's only half done ▸ *vendre à moitié prix* to sell (at) half-price. ❖ *à moitié chemin* loc adv halfway. ❖ *de moitié* loc adv by half ▸ *réduire qqch de moitié* to reduce sthg by half, to halve sthg.

moitié-moitié [mwatjemwatje] adv **1.** [à parts égales] half-and-half ▸ *faire moitié-moitié* **a)** [dans une affaire] to go halves ou fifty-fifty **b)** [au restaurant] to go halves, to split the bill **2.** *fam* [ni bien ni mal] so-so / *elle est contente ? — moitié-moitié* is she pleased? — so-so.

moit-moit [mwatmwat] adv *fam* : *faire moit-moit* to go halves.

moka [mɔka] nm **1.** [gâteau] mocha cake, coffee cream cake **2.** [café] mocha (coffee).

moi [mɔl] m ⟶ **mou.**

molaire [mɔlɛʀ] nf [dent] molar.

Moldavie [mɔldavi] npr f ▸ *(la)* **Moldavie** Moldavia.

môle [mol] nm [jetée] mole, (stone) jetty ou breakwater.

moléculaire [mɔlekylɛʀ] adj molecular ▸ *cuisine moléculaire* molecular cuisine.

molécule [mɔlekyl] nf molecule.

molester [3] [mɔleste] vt to maul, to manhandle, to molest / *la police a molesté les manifestants* the demonstrators were manhandled by the police.

mollasson, onne [mɔlasɔ̃, ɔn] *fam* ❖ adj wet 🆄🅺, wimpy, soft. ❖ nm, f wimp.

molle [mɔl] f ⟶ **mou.**

mollement [mɔlmã] adv **1.** [sans énergie] listlessly, limply / *il m'a serré mollement la main* he gave me a limp handshake **2.** [sans conviction] feebly, weakly / *elle protesta mollement* she protested feebly ou made a feeble protest.

mollesse [mɔlɛs] nf **1.** [d'une substance, d'un objet] softness ; [des chairs] flabbiness ; [d'une poignée de main] limpness **2.** [apathie] feebleness, weakness.

mollet [mɔlɛ] nm ANAT calf.

molletonné, e [mɔltɔne] adj [garni] covered with swansdown ; [doublé] lined with swansdown.

mollir [32] [mɔliʀ] vi **1.** [chanceler] : *j'ai senti mes jambes mollir* I felt my legs give way (under me) **2.** [vent] to drop, to abate *sout* **3.** [volonté, résolution] ▸ *sa détermination mollissait* her determination began to flag ou to wane.

mollo [mɔlo] adv *fam* easy / *vas-y mollo sur cette route !* take it easy on that road!

mollusque [mɔlysk] nm ZOOL mollusc 🆄🅺, mollusk 🆄🆂.

molosse [mɔlɔs] nm [chien] watchdog.

môme [mom] *fam* nmf [enfant] kid / *sale môme !* you little brat!

moment [mɔmã] nm **1.** [laps de temps] moment, while / *il y a un (bon) moment que j'attends* I've been waiting for (quite) a while / *j'en ai pour un petit moment* I'll be a (little) while **2.** [instant] moment, minute ▸ *c'est l'affaire d'un moment* it'll only take a minute ou moment / *il eut un moment d'hésitation* he hesitated for a moment ▸ *un moment !* just a moment ou minute! **3.** [période] moment, time ▸ *nous avons passé* ou *eu de bons moments* we had some good times / *c'est un mauvais moment à passer* it's just a bad patch 🆄🅺 ou a difficult spell ▸ *à mes moments perdus* in my spare time **4.** [occasion] moment, opportunity ▸ *à quel moment ?* when? ▸ *c'est le moment d'intervenir* now's the time to speak up / *c'est le moment ou jamais* it's now or never ▸ *le moment venu* when the time comes ▸ *arriver au bon moment* to come at the right time / *au mauvais moment* at the wrong time. ❖ *à aucun moment* loc adv at no time. ❖ *à ce moment-là* loc adv **1.** [dans le temps] at that time, then **2.** [dans ce cas] in that case, if that's so. ❖ *à tout moment* loc adv **1.** [n'importe quand] (at) any time ou moment **2.** [sans cesse] constantly, all the time. ❖ *au moment de* loc prép : *au moment de mon divorce* when I was getting divorced, at the time of my divorce. ❖ *au moment où* loc conj as, when / *juste au moment où le téléphone a sonné* just when ou as the phone rang. ❖ *à un moment donné* loc adv at one point, at a certain point. ❖ *dès le moment où* loc conj **1.** [dans le temps] from the time ou moment that, as soon as **2.** [dans un raisonnement] as soon as, once. ❖ *du moment que* loc conj [puisque] since / *du moment que je te le dis !* *fam* you can take my word for it! ❖ *d'un moment à l'autre* loc adv [très prochainement] any moment ou minute ou time now. ❖ *en ce moment* loc adv at the moment, just now. ❖ *par moments* loc adv at times, from time to time, every now and then. ❖ *pour le moment* loc adv for the moment, for the time being. ❖ *sur le moment* loc adv at the time.

momentané, e [mɔmãtane] adj momentary, brief.

momentanément [mɔmɑ̃tanemɑ̃] adv **1.** [en ce moment] for the time being, for the moment **2.** [provisoirement] momentarily, for a short while.

momie [mɔmi] nf ARCHÉOL mummy.

mon, ma [mɔ̃, ma] (*pl* **mes** [me]) *(devant nf ou adj f commençant par voyelle ou « h » muet* [mɔ̃n]) dét *(adj poss)* **1.** [indiquant la possession] my / **mon père et ma mère** my father and mother ‣ **mes frères et sœurs** my brothers and sisters **2.** [dans des appellatifs] ‣ **mon cher Pierre** my dear Pierre / **mes enfants, au travail !** time to work, children! / **mais mon pauvre vieux, vous n'y arriverez jamais !** fam look, mate, you'll never manage it! **3.** [emploi expressif] ‣ **j'ai mon vendredi** I've got Friday off / **ah ben mon salaud** tfam! ou **cochon** tfam! lucky bastard!

monacal, e, aux [mɔnakal, o] adj monastic, monachal *sout.*

Monaco [mɔnako] npr ‣ **(la principauté de) Monaco** (the principality of) Monaco.

monarchie [mɔnaʁʃi] nf monarchy.

monarchiste [mɔnaʁʃist] ◆ adj monarchist, monarchistic. ◆ nmf monarchist.

monarque [mɔnaʁk] nm monarch.

monastère [mɔnastɛʁ] nm monastery.

monceau, x [mɔ̃so] nm [amas] heap, pile.

mondain, e [mɔ̃dɛ̃, ɛn] ◆ adj **1.** [de la haute société] society *(modif)* / **il mène une vie très mondaine** he moves in society circles ‣ **carnet mondain, rubrique mondaine** society ou gossip column ‣ **soirée mondaine** society ou high-society evening **2.** [qui aime les mondanités] : **elle est très mondaine** she likes moving in fashionable circles ou society, she's a great socialite. ◆ nm, f socialite, society person.

monde [mɔ̃d] nm **1.** [univers] world ‣ **dans le monde entier** all over the world ‣ **venir au monde** to come into the world / **mettre un enfant au monde** to bring a child into the world ‣ **en ce bas monde** here on earth, here below **2.** [humanité] world / **le monde entier attend cet événement** the whole world is awaiting this event / **tout le monde sait cela** everybody ou the whole world knows that ‣ **il faut de tout pour faire un monde** it takes all sorts (to make a world) **3.** [pour intensifier] ‣ **le plus célèbre au** ou **du monde** the most famous in the world ‣ **le plus simplement / gentiment du monde** in the simplest / kindest possible way ‣ **c'est ce que j'aime / je veux le plus au monde** it's what I love / want most in the world / **je vous dérange ? — pas le moins du monde !** am I interrupting? — not in the least! ‣ **pour rien au monde** not for anything, not for the world ‣ **nul** ou **personne au monde** no one in the world **4.** [communauté] world ‣ **le monde des affaires** the business world ‣ **le monde du spectacle** (the world of) show business ‣ **le monde animal / végétal** the animal / plant world **5.** [gens] people (*pl*) / **il y a un monde fou, c'est noir de monde** the place is swarming ou alive with people / **il n'y avait pas grand monde au spectacle** there weren't many people at the show / **il ne voit plus beaucoup de monde** he doesn't socialize very much any more / **j'ai du monde à dîner** fam I've got people coming for dinner / **c'est qu'il faut s'en occuper de tout ce petit monde !** [enfants] all that little lot takes some looking after! ‣ **se moquer** ou **se ficher** fam ou **se foutre** fam **du monde** : **tu te moques** ou **fiches** ou **fous du monde !** you've got a nerve ou a bloody nerve! **6.** [société] world / **se retirer du monde** to withdraw from society ‣ **le monde** RELIG the world ; [groupe social] circle, set / **ils ne sont pas du même monde** they don't move in the same circles ; [classes élevées] : **aller dans le monde** to mix in society / **fréquenter le beau** ou **grand monde** to mix with high society ou in

society ‣ **femme du monde** socialite ‣ **homme du monde** man-about-town **7.** [domaine] world, realm / **le monde de l'imaginaire** the realm of imagination / **le monde du silence** litt the silent world (under the sea).

mondial, e, aux [mɔ̃djal, o] adj world *(modif)*, global ‣ **crise à l'échelle mondiale** worldwide crisis, crisis on a world scale. ❖ **mondial** nm ‣ **le Mondial de football** the World Cup ‣ **le Mondial de l'athlétisme** the World Athletics Championship.

mondialement [mɔ̃djalmɑ̃] adv throughout ou all over the world ‣ **mondialement renommé** famous all over the world, world-famous.

mondialisation [mɔ̃djalizasjɔ̃] nf globalization / **on assiste à la mondialisation de la reprise économique** a worldwide economic revival is taking place.

mondialiste [mɔ̃djalist] adj pro-globalization.

monégasque [mɔnegask] adj Monegasque, Monacan. ❖ **Monégasque** nmf Monegasque, Monacan.

monétaire [mɔnetɛʁ] adj monetary ‣ **marché / masse monétaire** money market / supply.

mongol, e [mɔ̃gɔl] adj Mongol, Mongolian. ❖ **Mongol, e** nm, f Mongol, Mongolian.

Mongolie [mɔ̃gɔli] npr f ‣ **(la) Mongolie** Mongolia.

mongolien, enne [mɔ̃gɔljɛ̃, ɛn] *vieilli* ◆ adj mongol *péj vieilli.* ◆ nm, f mongol *péj vieilli.*

moniteur, trice [mɔnitœʁ, tʁis] nm, f SPORT instructor (instructress) ; [de colonie de vacances] (group) supervisor ou leader, (camp) counsellor 🇺🇸 ‣ **moniteur d'auto-école** driving instructor ‣ **moniteur de ski** skiing instructor. ❖ **moniteur** nm **1.** INFORM [écran] display unit ; [dispositif matériel ou logiciel] monitor **2.** MÉD monitor.

monnaie [mɔnɛ] v ⟶ **monnayer.** ◆ nf **1.** ÉCON & FIN currency, money / **les monnaies étrangères** foreign currencies / **le yen est la monnaie du Japon** the yen is Japan's (unit of) currency ou monetary unit ‣ **monnaie d'échange** fig bargaining counter ‣ **monnaie électronique** electronic ou plastic money ‣ **monnaie légale** legal tender ‣ **monnaie unique** single currency ‣ **fausse monnaie** counterfeit ou false money ‣ **c'est monnaie courante** it's common practice, it's a common ou an everyday occurrence **2.** [appoint] change ‣ **faire de la monnaie** to get (some) change / **faire la monnaie de 20 euros** to get change for 20 euros, to change a 20 euro note / **il m'a rendu la monnaie sur 10 euros** he gave me the change out of ou from 10 euros ‣ **menue / petite monnaie** small / loose change ‣ **rendre à qqn la monnaie de sa pièce** : **je lui rendrai la monnaie de sa pièce !** I'll give him a taste of his own medicine!

monnayer [11] [mɔneje] vt **1.** [convertir en monnaie] to mint **2.** [vendre] to sell, to make money out of ‣ **monnayer son expérience / savoir-faire** to cash in on one's experience / know-how **3.** [échanger] to exchange / **il a monnayé ses services contre une lettre d'introduction** he asked for a letter of introduction in exchange for his services.

monochrome [mɔnɔkʁom] adj monochrome, monochromic.

monocoque [mɔnɔkɔk] ◆ adj AÉRON monocoque. ◆ nm NAUT monohull.

monocorde [mɔnɔkɔʁd] adj monotonous, droning.

monogame [mɔnɔgam] adj monogamous.

monogamie [mɔnɔgami] nf monogamy.

monologue [mɔnɔlɔg] nm **1.** [discours] monologue ; THÉÂTRE monologue, soliloquy **2.** LITTÉR ‣ **monologue intérieur** stream of consciousness, interior monologue.

mononucléose [mɔnɔnykleoz] nf mononucleosis ▸ **mononucléose infectieuse** glandular fever **UK**, mono **US**, infectious mononucleosis *spéc* **US**.

monoparental, e, aux [mɔnɔparɑ̃tal, o] adj single-parent.

monoplace [mɔnɔplas] ◆ adj one-seater *(avant nom)*, single-seater *(avant nom)*. ◆ nm one-seater ou single-seater (vehicle).

monopole [mɔnɔpɔl] nm **1.** ÉCON monopoly ▸ **monopole d'État** state monopoly **2.** *fig* monopoly / *vous pensez avoir le monopole de la vérité ?* do you think you have a monopoly of the truth?

monopoliser [3] [mɔnɔpɔlize] vt ÉCON & *fig* to monopolize / *ne monopolisez pas notre jeune amie* don't keep our young friend to yourself.

monoski [mɔnɔski] nm monoski.

monospace [mɔnɔspas] nm people carrier **UK**, minivan **US**.

monotone [mɔnɔtɔn] adj **1.** [voix, bruit] monotonous **2.** [discours, style] monotonous, dull **3.** [vie] monotonous, dreary, humdrum ; [paysage] monotonous, dreary.

monotonie [mɔnɔtɔni] nf monotony, dullness, dreariness.

Monseigneur [mɔ̃sɛɲœr] (*pl* **Messeigneurs** [mesɛɲœr]) nm [en s'adressant à un - archevêque] Your Grace ; [- évêque] My Lord (Bishop) ; [- cardinal] Your Eminence ; [- prince] Your Royal Highness ; [en parlant d'un - archevêque] His Grace ; [- évêque] His Lordship ; [- cardinal] His Eminence (Cardinal) ; [- prince] His Royal Highness.

monsieur [məsjø] (*pl* **messieurs** [mesjø]) nm man, gentleman.

Monsieur [məsjø] (*pl* **Messieurs** [mesjø]) nm **1.** [dans une lettre] ▸ **Monsieur** Sir *sout*, Dear Sir ▸ **Cher Monsieur Duval** Dear Mr. Duval ▸ **Messieurs** Dear Sirs / *Monsieur le Maire* Dear Sir ; [sur l'enveloppe] ▸ **Monsieur Duval** Mr. Duval ▸ **Messieurs Thon et Lamiel** Messrs Thon and Lamiel **2.** [terme d'adresse - suivi du nom du titre] : *bonjour Monsieur Leroy !* good morning Mr. Leroy ! ▸ **bonjour Messieurs Duval !** good morning, gentlemen! / *bonjour Monsieur le Ministre !* good morning Sir! ▸ **Monsieur le Président, et l'inflation ?** a) [au chef de l'État] Sir ou Mr. President **US**, what about inflation? b) [au directeur] Sir ou Mr. Chairman, what about inflation? ; [à un inconnu] : *bonjour Monsieur !* good morning! ▸ **bonjour Messieurs** good morning (, gentlemen) / *bonjour Messieurs Dames* *fam* morning all ou everybody ▸ **Mesdames, Mesdemoiselles, Messieurs** Ladies and Gentlemen! / *Monsieur désirerait voir les pantalons ?* would you like to see the trousers, Sir? ; *sout & hum* : *vous n'y pensez pas, cher* ou *mon bon* ou *mon pauvre Monsieur !* my dear Sir, you can't be serious! / *peux-tu prêter un instant ton stylo à Monsieur ?* could you lend the gentleman your pen for a minute? ; [au téléphone] : *bonjour Monsieur, je voudrais parler à quelqu'un de la comptabilité, s'il vous plaît* hello, I'd like to speak to somebody in the accounts department, please **3.** [en se référant à une tierce personne] ▸ **adressez-vous à Monsieur Duval** apply to Mr. Duval ▸ **Monsieur le Président regrette de ne pas pouvoir venir** a) [chef de l'État] the President regrets he is unable to come b) [directeur] the Chairman ou Mr. X regrets he is unable to come **4.** ÉDUC : *Monsieur, j'ai fini mon addition !* (please) Sir, I've done my addition! **5.** *fam* [en appellatif] : *et en plus, Monsieur exige des excuses !* His Lordship wants an apology as well, does he? **6.** [EXPR] **il a été nommé Monsieur sécurité routière** he was made Mr. Road Safety ▸ **Monsieur Tout le Monde** the man in the street, Joe Public **UK** *hum*, Joe Blow **US**.

monstre [mɔ̃str] ◆ nm **1.** BIOL, MYTH & ZOOL monster ▸ **monstre sacré** superstar **2.** [chose énorme] monster

3. [personne laide] monster, monstrously ugly ou hideous person ; [brute] monster, brute / *un monstre d'ingratitude / d'égoïsme* an ungrateful / a selfish brute **4.** *fam* [enfant insupportable] monster, little terror, perisher **UK** / *sortez d'ici, petits monstres !* out of here, you little monsters! ◆ adj *fam* [erreur, difficulté, déficit] monstrous, enormous, colossal ; [rassemblement] monstrous, mammoth ; [répercussions, succès, effet] tremendous, enormous ; [soldes] gigantic, huge, colossal / *il y a une queue monstre chez le boucher* there's a huge ou massive queue at the butcher's / *j'ai un boulot monstre !* I've got loads ou tons ou piles of work to do! / *il a un culot monstre* he's got a bloody cheek **UK** ou a damned nerve.

monstrueusement [mɔ̃stryøzmɑ̃] adv [laid] monstrously, hideously ; [intelligent] prodigiously, stupendously.

monstrueux, euse [mɔ̃stryø, øz] adj **1.** [difforme] monstrous, deformed / *un être monstrueux, une créature monstrueuse* a freak **2.** [laid] monstrous, hideous, ghastly **3.** [abject, cruel] monstrous, wicked, vile / *un crime monstrueux* a heinous ou monstrous crime **4.** [très grave] monstrous, dreadful, ghastly / *une monstrueuse erreur* an awful ou a dreadful mistake.

mont [mɔ̃] nm GÉOGR mountain ; *litt* mount ▸ **mont sous-marin** seamount / *il est toujours par monts et par vaux* he's always on the move.

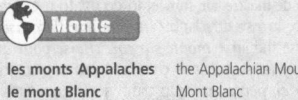

Monts	
les monts Appalaches	the Appalachian Mountains
le mont Blanc	Mont Blanc
le mont Cervin	the Matterhorn
le mont Everest	Mount Everest

montage [mɔ̃taʒ] nm **1.** [assemblage - d'un meuble, d'un kit] assembly, assemblage ; [- d'une tente] pitching, putting up ; [- d'un vêtement] assembling, sewing together ; [- d'un col] setting in ; IMPR (page) makeup, pasting up **2.** FIN ▸ **montage financier** financial arrangement **3.** AUDIO & CINÉ [processus] editing ; [avec effets spéciaux] montage ; [résultat] montage ▸ **montage audiovisuel** ou **sonorisé** sound slide show **4.** PHOT mounting ▸ **montage de photos** photomontage.

montagnard, e [mɔ̃taɲar, ard] ◆ adj mountain *(modif)*, highland *(modif)*. ◆ nm, f mountain dweller.

montagne [mɔ̃taɲ] nf **1.** [mont] mountain ▸ **montagnes russes** LOISIRS big dipper **UK**, roller coaster **US** / *moi, en ce moment, c'est les montagnes russes* [moral, santé] I'm a bit up and down at the moment ▸ **déplacer** ou **soulever des montagnes** to move heaven and earth ▸ **(se) faire une montagne de qqch** to make a great song and dance about sthg ▸ **(se) faire une montagne de rien** ou **d'un rien** to make a mountain out of a molehill ▸ **gros comme une montagne** a) [mensonge] huge, colossal b) [canular] mammoth *(modif)* **2.** [région] ▸ **la montagne** a) the mountains b) [en Écosse] the highlands ▸ **de montagne** mountain *(modif)* **3.** [grosse quantité] ▸ **une montagne de** lots ou mountains ou a mountain of.

montagneux, euse [mɔ̃taɲø, øz] adj mountainous.

montant, e [mɔ̃tɑ̃, ɑ̃t] adj **1.** [qui grimpe - sentier] rising, uphill **2.** VÊT [col] high ; [corsage] high-necked, high-neckline *(modif)*. ◆ **montant** nm **1.** [d'une échelle, d'un châssis] upright ; [d'une tente] pole ; [d'une porte, d'une fenêtre] stile ; [d'un lit] post **2.** FIN amount, sum, total ▸ **chèque / facture d'un montant de 80 euros** cheque / invoice for 80 euros ou *le montant total des réparations s'élève à...*, *les réparations s'élèvent à un montant total de...* the total cost of the repairs adds up to... / **'montant à régler'** 'amount due'.

monté, e [mɔ̃te] adj **1.** MIL mounted ▶ **troupes montées** mounted troops **2.** CULIN ▶ **œufs montés en neige** whipped egg whites. ◆ **montée** nf **1.** [pente] climb, uphill ou upward slope **2.** [ascension] climb / *la montée des escaliers lui fut très pénible* he climbed ou struggled up the stairs with great difficulty **3.** [élévation - d'une fusée, d'un dirigeable] ascent ; [- de la sève] rise ; [- des eaux] rise, rising **4.** [augmentation - de violence] rise ; [- de mécontentement] rise, increase, growth ▶ **la montée des prix / températures** the rise in prices / temperatures ▶ **devant la montée de la violence / du racisme** faced with the rising tide of violence / racism **5.** [accession] rise, ascension *sout*.

monte-charge [mɔ̃tʃaʁʒ] (*pl* monte-charge *ou* monte-charges) nm hoist, goods lift 🇬🇧, freight elevator 🇺🇸, service elevator 🇺🇸.

montée [mɔ̃te] f ⟶ **monté**.

Monténégro [mɔ̃tenegʁo] npr m ▶ **le Monténégro** Montenegro.

monte-plat(s) [mɔ̃tpla] (*pl* monte-plats) nm service lift 🇬🇧, dumbwaiter.

monter [3] [mɔ̃te] ◆ vi (aux être ou avoir) **1.** [personne, animal - vu d'en bas] to go up ; [- vu d'en haut] to come up ; [avion, soleil] to rise, to climb (up) ; [drapeau] to go up ; [rideau de théâtre, air, fumée] to go up, to rise ; [chemin] to go up, to rise, to climb / *monte par l'ascenseur* go up in ou use the lift / *monte sur une chaise pour que j'épingle ton ourlet* stand on a chair so I can pin up your hem / *monter en pente douce* to climb gently (upwards) / *monter en pente raide* to climb steeply ou sharply ▶ **monter de** [suj : odeur, bruit] to rise (up) from, to come from **2.** [dans un moyen de transport] ▶ **monter dans a)** [avion, train] to get on ou onto, to board **b)** [bus] to get on, to board **c)** [voiture] to get into ▶ **monter sur un cheval** to get on ou to mount a horse ▶ **monter sur un vélo** to get on a bicycle ; ÉQUIT to ride / *monter à cheval* to ride horses **3.** [apparaître suite à une émotion] : *les larmes lui sont montées aux yeux* tears welled up in his eyes, his eyes filled with tears **4.** [s'élever - température] to rise, to go up ; [- fièvre] to rise ; [- prix, taux] to rise, to go up, to increase ; [- action] to rise ; [- rivière] to rise ; [- mer, marée] to come in ; [- anxiété, mécontentement] to grow, to increase ▶ **faire monter** [tension, peur] to increase ▶ **faire monter les prix a)** [surenchère] to send ou to put prices up **b)** [marchand] to put up ou to increase prices / *les loyers ont monté de 25 %* rents have gone up ou increased by 25% ▶ **le lait monte a)** [il bout] the milk is boiling **b)** [chez une femme qui allaite] lactation has started / *faire monter des blancs en neige* CULIN to whisk up egg whites ▶ **le ton montait a)** [de colère] voices were being raised, the discussion was becoming heated **b)** [d'animation] the noise level was rising **5.** [atteindre un certain niveau] : *la cloison ne monte pas assez haut* the partition isn't high enough ▶ **monter à** ou **jusqu'à** [eau, vêtement, chaussures] to come up to / *son plâtre monte jusqu'au genou* his leg is in a plaster cast up to the knee / *l'hectare de vigne peut monter jusqu'à 5 000 euros* one hectare of vineyard can cost up to ou fetch as much as 5,000 euros **6.** MUS [voix] to go up, to rise / *il peut monter jusqu'au «si»* he can go ou sing up to B **7.** [pour attaquer] : *monter à l'abordage* NAUT to board / *monter à l'attaque* ou *à l'assaut* MIL to go into the attack ▶ **monter au filet** [au tennis, au volle-yball] to go up to the net **8.** [dans une hiérarchie] to rise ▶ **monter en grade** to be promoted **9.** [aller vers le nord] : *je monte à Paris demain* I'm going (up) to Paris tomorrow **10.** JEUX : *monter sur le valet de trèfle* to play a club higher than the jack. ◆ vt (aux avoir) **1.** [gravir]

to go up (insép) ▶ **monter l'escalier** to go ou to climb up the stairs, to go upstairs / *la voiture a du mal à monter la côte* the car has difficulty getting up the hill **2.** [porter en haut - bagages, colis] to take ou to carry up (sép) ; [- courrier] to take up (sép) / *je lui ai monté son journal* I took the newspaper up to him **3.** [mettre plus haut] ▶ **monte l'étagère d'un cran** put the shelf up a notch / *monte la vitre, j'ai froid* wind up the (car) window, I'm cold **4.** [augmenter - son] to turn up (sép) ; [- prix] to put up (sép) / *monte la télé* fam turn the TV up ; [mettre en colère] ▶ **monter qqn contre** to set sb against **5.** [assembler - kit] to assemble, to put together (sép) ; [- tente] to pitch, to put up (sép) ; [- abri] to rig up (sép) **6.** [fixer - radiateur] to fit, to mount ; [- store] to put up (sép), to mount / *il a monté un moteur plus puissant sur sa voiture* he has put a more powerful engine into his car ; JOAILL to mount, to set **7.** [organiser - gén] to organize ; [- pièce, spectacle] to put on (sép), to stage, to produce ; [- canular] to think up (sép) ; [- complot, machination] to set up (sép) **8.** [pourvoir - bibliothèque, collection, cave] to set up (sép) **9.** ÉQUIT ▶ **monter un cheval** to ride a horse **10.** CINÉ [bobine] to mount ; [film] to edit **11.** COUT to fit (on) ▶ **monter une manche** to sew on ou to attach a sleeve ; [tricoter - maille] to cast on (sép) **12.** CULIN ▶ **monter une mayonnaise** to make some mayonnaise **13.** VÉTÉR & ZOOL to cover, to serve. ◆ **se monter** vp (emploi passif) : *cette bibliothèque se monte facilement* these bookshelves are easy to assemble. ◆ **se monter à** vp + prép [coût, dépenses] to come ou to amount ou to add up to.

monteur, euse [mɔ̃tœʁ, øz] nm, f **1.** INDUST & TECHNOL fitter **2.** AUDIO & CINÉ editor.

montgolfière [mɔ̃gɔlfjɛʁ] nf hot-air balloon, montgolfier (balloon).

monticule [mɔ̃tikyl] nm **1.** [colline] hillock, mound, monticule *sout* **2.** [tas] heap, mound.

montre [mɔ̃tʁ] nf **1.** [instrument] watch / *il est 11 heures à ma montre* it's 11 o'clock by my watch ▶ **montre de plongée** diver's watch ▶ **montre en main** : *il a mis une heure montre en main* it took him ou he took exactly one hour (by the clock) ▶ **jouer la montre** FOOT to play for time **2.** [preuve] ▶ **faire montre de prudence** to show caution, to behave cautiously.

Montréal [mɔ̃real] npr Montreal, Montréal.

montre-bracelet [mɔ̃tʁəbʁaslɛ] (*pl* montres-bracelets) nf wristwatch.

montrer [3] [mɔ̃tʁe] vt **1.** [gén] to show ; [passeport, ticket] to show ; [document secret] to show, to disclose ; [spectacle, œuvre] to show, to exhibit ▶ **montrer qqch à qqn** to show sth to sb, to show sb sth ▶ **montrer le poing à qqn** to shake one's fist at sb ▶ **montrer patte blanche** to produce one's credentials *fig* **2.** [faire preuve de - courage, impatience, détermination] to show, to display ; [laisser apparaître - émotion] to show **3.** [signaler] to point out (sép), to show ▶ **montrer l'exemple** to set an example, to give the lead **4.** [marquer - suj : aiguille, curseur, cadran] to show, to point to (insép) ; [- suj : écran] to show, to display **5.** [prouver] to show, to prove / *ça montre bien que...* fam it (just) goes to show that... **6.** [enseigner - technique, procédé] to show, to demonstrate ; [- recette, jeu] to show / *la brochure montre comment s'en servir* the booklet explains ou shows how to use it. ◆ **se montrer** vpi **1.** [se présenter] to show o.s., to appear (in public) / *le voilà, ne te montre pas !* here he is, stay out of sight ! / *elle ne s'est même pas montrée au mariage de sa fille* she never even showed up ou showed her face ou turned up at her daughter's wedding **2.** [s'afficher] to appear ou to be seen (in public) / *elle adore se montrer* she loves to be seen (in public) **3.** [se révéler] : *ce soir-là, il s'est montré odieux / charmant* he was obnoxious / charming that evening.

Montrer qqch à qqn Show sthg to sb ou show sb sthg.

Notez la construction à double complément qui en anglais peut prendre deux formes dont le sens est le même :

• une structure identique à celle du français :
verbe + COD + préposition + COI
show sthg to sb

• une structure qui diffère de celle du français, sans préposition, et dans laquelle l'ordre des compléments est inversé :
verbe + COI + COD
show sb sthg

Marie a montré ses photos de Chine à tous ses amis. Marie showed her photos of China to all her friends ou Marie showed all her friends her photos of China.
Montre ta main au médecin. Show your hand to the doctor ou Show the doctor your hand.

monture [mɔ̃tyʀ] nf **1.** JOAILL setting ; [de lunettes] frame ▶ **des lunettes à monture d'écaille / de plastique** horn- / plastic-rimmed glasses **2.** ÉQUIT mount.

monument [mɔnymɑ̃] nm **1.** [stèle, statue] monument ▶ **monument aux morts** war memorial **2.** ADMIN & LOISIRS monument, building ▶ **monument historique** historic monument ou building **3.** litt [travail admirable] monument, masterpiece.

monumental, e, aux [mɔnymɑ̃tal, o] adj **1.** [grandiose] monumental, incredible **2.** fam [canular, erreur] monumental, phenomenal, mammoth (modif).

moquer [3] [mɔke] ❖ **se moquer de** vp + prép **1.** [railler] to laugh at, to make fun of / les gens vont se moquer d'elle people will laugh at her ou make fun of her, she'll be a laughing stock **2.** [ignorer - danger, conseil] to disregard, to ignore **3.** [être indifférent à] : je me moque que tu sois mécontent I don't care if you're not pleased / elle s'en moque pas mal she couldn't care less **4.** [duper] to dupe, to deceive, to trick / on s'est moqué de toi you've been taken for a ride ▶ **elle ne s'est pas moquée de toi ! a)** fam [repas, réception] she did you proud (there)! **b)** [cadeau] she didn't skimp on your present! / ce type se moque du monde ! fam that guy's got a real nerve!

moquerie [mɔkʀi] nf jeering, mocking / il était en butte à des moqueries continuelles he was always being mocked ou made fun of.

moquette [mɔkɛt] nf wall-to-wall carpet, fitted carpet **UK** / faire poser de la ou une moquette to have a (wall-to-wall) carpet laid.

moqueur, euse [mɔkœʀ, øz] adj mocking / d'un ton moqueur mockingly, derisively / elle est très moqueuse she likes to make fun of people.

moral, e, aux [mɔʀal, o] adj **1.** [éthique - conscience, jugement] moral / il n'a aucun sens moral he has no sense of morality ▶ **prendre l'engagement moral de faire qqch** to be morally committed to do sthg [édifiant - auteur, conte, réflexion] moral **2.** [spirituel - douleur] mental ; [- soutien, victoire, résistance] moral. ❖ **moral** nm morale, spirits / toutes les épreuves n'ont pas affecté son moral these ordeals failed to shake her morale ▶ **son moral est bas** his spirits are low, he's in low spirits ▶ **avoir le moral, avoir bon moral** to be in good ou high spirits / il n'a pas le moral en ce moment he's a bit depressed ou low at the moment ▶ **allez, il faut garder le moral !** come on, keep your chin ou spirits up! ▶ **remonter le moral de qqn a)** [conso-

ler] to raise sb's spirits, to boost sb's morale **b)** [égayer] to cheer sb up ▶ **avoir le moral à zéro** fam: j'ai le moral à zéro I feel down in the dumps ou really low.

morale [mɔʀal] nf **1.** [règles - de la société] moral code ou standards, morality ; [- d'une religion] moral code, ethic ; [- personnelles] morals, ethics ▶ **faire la morale à qqn** to lecture sb, to preach at sb **2.** [d'une fable, d'une histoire] moral.

moralement [mɔʀalmɑ̃] adv **1.** [du point de vue de la morale] morally **2.** [sur le plan psychique] ▶ **moralement, elle va mieux** she's in better spirits ▶ **physiquement et moralement** physically and mentally.

moralisateur, trice [mɔʀalizatœʀ, tʀis] adj **1.** [personne, propos] moralizing, moralistic **2.** [histoire] edifying.

moraliser [3] [mɔʀalize] ❖ vt **1.** [rendre conforme à la morale] to moralize sout, to improve the morals of **2.** [réprimander] to lecture. ❖ vi [prêcher] to moralize, to preach.

moraliste [mɔʀalist] nmf moralist.

moralité [mɔʀalite] nf **1.** [éthique] morality, ethics (sg) / d'une moralité douteuse of questionable morals **2.** [comportement] morals, moral standing ou standards **3.** [conclusion] : moralité, il faut toujours... and the moral (of the story) is, you must always... / moralité, on ne l'a plus revu fam and the result was, we never saw him again.

moratoire [mɔʀatwaʀ] nm moratorium.

morbide [mɔʀbid] adj **1.** [malsain] morbid, unhealthy **2.** MÉD morbid.

morceau, x [mɔʀso] nm **1.** [de nourriture] piece, bit ▶ **morceau de sucre** lump of sugar, sugar lump / si on allait manger un morceau ? fam what about a snack?, how about a bite to eat? ; [de viande] cut, piece ▶ **cracher** ou **lâcher le morceau** fam to spill the beans, to come clean **2.** [de bois, de métal - petit] piece, bit ; [- gros] lump, chunk ; [de papier, de verre] piece ; [d'étoffe, de câble - gén] piece ; [- mesuré] length ▶ **en morceaux** in bits ou pieces ▶ **mettre en morceaux a)** [papier, étoffe] to tear up (sép) **b)** [jouet] to pull to pieces ou bits **3.** [extrait] passage, extract, excerpt ▶ **cette scène est un véritable morceau d'anthologie** it's a truly memorable scene ▶ **(recueil de) morceaux choisis** (collection of) selected passages ou extracts **4.** MUS [fragment] passage ; [œuvre] piece.

morceler [24] [mɔʀsəle] vt [partager] to parcel out (sép) ; [démembrer] to divide (up), to break up (sép).
In reformed spelling (see p. 16-18), this verb is conjugated like acheter : il morcèle, elle morcèlera.

mordant, e [mɔʀdɑ̃, ɑ̃t] adj **1.** [caustique] biting, caustic, scathing **2.** [froid] biting, bitter.

mordicus [mɔʀdikys] adv fam stubbornly, doggedly.

mordiller [3] [mɔʀdije] vt to nibble ou to chew (at).

mordoré, e [mɔʀdɔʀe] adj golden brown, bronze (modif).

mordre [76] [mɔʀdʀ] ❖ vt **1.** [suj : animal, personne] to bite / mordre un fruit to bite into a piece of fruit / il s'est fait mordre à la main he was bitten on the hand **2.** [empiéter sur] ▶ **mordre la ligne a)** [saut en longueur] to cross the (take-off) board **b)** [sur la route] to cross the white line. ❖ vi PÊCHE to bite / ça ne mord pas beaucoup par ici the fish aren't biting ou rising much around here ▶ **mordre (à l'appât)** ou **à l'hameçon** pr & fig to rise (to the bait), to bite ▶ **il ou ça n'a pas mordu** fam & fig he wasn't taken in, he didn't fall for it. ❖ **mordre dans** v + prép to bite into. ❖ **mordre sur** v + prép [ligne, marge] to go ou to cross over ; [économies] to make a dent in, to eat into (insép) ; [période] to overlap / le stage mordra sur la deuxième semaine de mars the course will go over into the second week in March. ❖ **se mordre** vpt ▶ **se mordre la langue** to bite one's tongue pr ▶ **s'en mordre les doigts** fig: je m'en suis mordu les doigts I could have kicked myself.

mordu, e [mɔʀdy] ◆ adj *fam* **1.** [passionné] : *il est mordu de jazz* he's mad ou crazy about jazz **2.** [amoureux] madly in love, completely smitten. ◆ nm, f *fam* [passionné] addict *hum*, fan ▸ **un mordu de cinéma / d'opéra** a film / an opera buff / *les mordus de la télé* TV addicts.

more [mɔʀ] = **maure**.

moresque [mɔʀɛsk] = **mauresque** *(adj)*.

morfler [3] [mɔʀfle] vi *tfam* : *il a morflé !* he copped it! 🇬🇧, he caught it! 🇺🇸

morfondre [75] [mɔʀfɔ̃dʀ] ◆ **se morfondre** vpi to mope.

morgue [mɔʀg] nf [établissement] morgue ; [dans un hôpital] mortuary 🇬🇧, morgue 🇺🇸

moribond, e [mɔʀibɔ̃, ɔ̃d] ◆ adj dying, moribund *sout*. ◆ nm, f dying person.

morille [mɔʀij] nf morel.

mormon, e [mɔʀmɔ̃, ɔn] adj & nm, f Mormon.

morne [mɔʀn] adj **1.** [triste - personne] glum, gloomy **2.** [monotone - discussion] dull ; [- paysage] bleak, drab, dreary **3.** [maussade - climat] dull, dreary, dismal.

morose [mɔʀoz] adj **1.** [individu, air, vie] glum, morose ; [temps, année] miserable ; [paysage] gloomy **2.** [économie] sluggish, slack.

morosité [mɔʀozite] nf **1.** [d'une personne] glumness, sullenness, moroseness **2.** [d'un marché] slackness, sluggishness.

morphine [mɔʀfin] nf morphine, morphia.

morphologie [mɔʀfɔlɔʒi] nf morphology.

morpion [mɔʀpjɔ̃] nm **1.** *fam & péj* [enfant] brat, perisher 🇬🇧 **2.** *fam* [pou] crab **3.** JEUX ≃ noughts and crosses 🇬🇧 ; ≃ tic tac toe 🇺🇸

mors [mɔʀ] nm [d'un cheval] bit ▸ **prendre le mors aux dents** *fig* to take the bit between one's teeth, to swing into action.

morse [mɔʀs] nm **1.** ZOOL walrus **2.** [code] Morse (code).

morsure [mɔʀsyʀ] nf [d'un animal] bite / *une morsure de serpent* a snakebite.

mort, e [mɔʀ, mɔʀt] ◆ adj **1.** [décédé - personne] dead ; [arbre, cellule, dent] dead / *elle est morte depuis longtemps* she died a long time ago, she's been dead (for) a long time ▸ **tu es un homme mort !** *fam* you're dead meat! ▸ **mort sur le champ de bataille** ou **au champ d'honneur** killed in action **2.** [en intensif] ▸ **mort de:** *il était mort de fatigue* he was dead tired / *on était morts de froid* we were freezing cold ▸ **j'étais morte de rire** *fam* I nearly died laughing **3.** [inerte - regard] lifeless, dull ; [- quartier, bistrot] dead ; [- eau] stagnant **4.** *fam* [hors d'usage - appareil, voiture] dead, finished **5.** *fam* [épuisé] ▸ **je suis mort !** I'm dead! ◆ nm, f [personne] dead person / *les émeutes ont fait 300 morts* 300 people died ou were killed in the rioting ▸ **les morts** the dead ▸ **jour** ou **fête des Morts** All Souls' Day ▸ **faire le mort** *pr* to pretend to be dead, to play dead / *tu as intérêt à faire le mort* *fam & fig* you'd better lie low. ◆ **mort** nf [décès] death ▸ **la mort** death / *il a vu la mort de près* he saw death staring him in the face ▸ **se donner la mort** *sout* to commit suicide, to take one's own life ▸ **il y a eu mort d'homme a)** [une victime] somebody was killed **b)** [plusieurs victimes] lives were lost ▸ **périr de mort violente** to die a violent death ▸ **mort aux traîtres !** death to the traitors! ▸ **mort subite du nourrisson** sudden infant death syndrome *spéc*, cot death ▸ **avoir la mort dans l'âme** to have a heavy heart ▸ **son cours, c'est vraiment la mort !** *fam* his class is deadly boring! ◆ **à mort** ◆ loc adj [lutte, combat] to the death. ◆ loc adv **1.** *fam* [en intensif] ▸ **j'ai freiné à mort** I braked like hell, I jammed on the brakes ▸ **ils sont brouillés** ou **fâchés à mort** they're mortal

enemies ou enemies for life / *je lui en veux à mort* I hate his guts **2.** [mortellement] ▸ **blesser qqn à mort** to mortally wound sb ▸ **frapper qqn à mort** to strike sb dead / *mettre un animal à mort* to kill an animal. ◆ **de mort** loc adj [silence, pâleur] deathly, deathlike ▸ **être en danger** ou **péril de mort** to be in mortal danger. ◆ **jusqu'à la mort** loc adv *pr* to the death ; *fig* to the bitter end.

📋 Attention à ne pas confondre **be dead** et **have died.**

Dead est la traduction de l'adjectif **mort** :
Il me semble que ses deux parents sont morts. *I think both his parents are dead.*

Died (prétérit et participe passé de **die**) sert à traduire le verbe **mourir** :
Sa grand-mère est morte cet été. *His grandmother died this summer.*

Comparez les deux traductions possibles de la phrase suivante :
Toutes mes roses sont mortes. a) *All my roses have died.* (ici, l'emploi du verbe **mort** sert sur l'action de **mourir** = les fleurs sont mortes récemment) b) *All my roses are dead.* (ici, l'emploi de l'adjectif met l'accent sur l'état des fleurs = celles-ci sont sans vie).

---

mortadelle [mɔʀtadɛl] nf mortadella.

mortalité [mɔʀtalite] nf [gén] mortality ; [dans des statistiques] death rate, mortality (rate).

mort-aux-rats [mɔʀoʀa] nf inv rat poison.

mortel, elle [mɔʀtɛl] ◆ adj **1.** [qui tue - accident] fatal ; [- dose, poison] deadly, lethal ; [- coup, blessure] fatal, lethal, mortal *sout* ; [- maladie] fatal / *c'est un coup mortel porté à notre communauté* *fig* this is a deathblow for our little community **2.** [dangereux] lethal, deadly / *tu as raté l'examen mais ça n'est pas mortel !* *fam* you've failed the exam but it's not the end of the world! **3.** *fam* [ennuyeux] deadly ou excruciatingly boring **4.** [qui rappelle la mort - pâleur, silence] deathly **5.** [acharné - ennemi] mortal, deadly **6.** [qui n'est pas éternel] mortal. ◆ nm, f [être humain] mortal.

mortellement [mɔʀtɛlmɑ̃] adv **1.** [à mort] ▸ **être mortellement blessé** to be fatally ou mortally *sout* wounded **2.** [en intensif] : *le film est mortellement ennuyeux* the film is deadly boring.

morte-saison [mɔʀtsɛzɔ̃] (*pl* **mortes-saisons**) nf slack ou off season / *à la morte-saison* in the off season.

mortier [mɔʀtje] nm **1.** ARM mortar **2.** CONSTR mortar.

mort-né, e [mɔʀne] (*mpl* **mort-nés,** *fpl* **mort-nées**) adj *pr & fig* stillborn.

mortuaire [mɔʀtyɛʀ] adj [rituel] mortuary *(modif)*, funeral *(modif)* ; [cérémonie, chambre] funeral *(modif)*.

morue [mɔʀy] nf CULIN & ZOOL cod.

morve [mɔʀv] nf [mucus] nasal mucus.

morveux, euse [mɔʀvø, øz] ◆ adj [sale] snotty-nosed. ◆ nm, f *fam* [enfant] (snotty-nosed) little kid.

mosaïque [mɔzaik] nf **1.** ART mosaic **2.** [mélange - de couleurs] patchwork, mosaic ; [- de cultures] mixture, mosaic **3.** INFORM ▸ **afficher en mosaïque** [fenêtres] to tile.

Moscou [mɔsku] npr Moscow.

moscovite [mɔskɔvit] adj Muscovite.

mosquée [mɔske] nf mosque.

mot [mo] nm **1.** LING word / *orgueilleux, c'est bien le mot* arrogant is the (right) word ▸ **le mot de Cambronne**

ou **de cinq lettres** *euphém* the word "merde" ▶ **mot composé** compound (word) ▶ **mot d'emprunt** loanword ▶ **mot de passe** password ▶ **gros mot** swearword **2.** [parole] word / *il n'a pas dit un mot* he didn't say a word ▶ **dire un mot à qqn** to have a word with sb / *pas un mot à qui que ce soit !* not a word to anybody! ▶ **les mots me manquent** words fail me / *je ne trouve pas les mots (pour le dire)* I cannot find the words (to say it) ▶ **à ces mots** at these words ▶ **sur ces mots** with these words / *ce ne sont que des mots !* it's just talk!, it's all hot air! ▶ **mot d'ordre a)** slogan **b)** MIL watchword ▶ **mot d'ordre de grève** call for strike action ▶ **c'est mon dernier mot** it's my last ou final offer ▶ **avoir le dernier mot** to have the last word ▶ **je n'ai pas dit mon dernier mot** you / they, etc. haven't heard the last of me ▶ **grand mot** : *voleur, c'est un bien grand mot* thief, that would be putting it a bit too strongly ou going a bit too far / *avec toi, c'est tout de suite* ou *toujours les grands mots* you're always exaggerating ▶ **avoir des mots (avec qqn)** to have words (with sb) ▶ **avoir son mot à dire** to have one's say ▶ **avoir toujours le mot pour rire** to be a (great) laugh ou joker ▶ **dire un mot de travers** to say something wrong, to put one's foot in it ▶ **n'avoir jamais un mot plus haut que l'autre** : *il n'a jamais un mot plus haut que l'autre* he never raises his voice ▶ **pas le premier** ou **un traître mot** de not a single word of ▶ **prendre qqn au mot** to take sb at his word ▶ **je vais lui en toucher** ou **je lui en toucherai un mot** I'll have a word with him about it ▶ **dire deux mots à qqn** to give sb a piece of one's mind **3.** [parole mémorable] saying ▶ **mot d'esprit** ou **bon mot** witticism, witty remark ▶ **mot d'auteur** (author's) witty remark ▶ **mot d'enfant** child's remark **4.** [message écrit] note, word ▶ **écrire un mot à qqn** to write sb a note, to drop sb a line ▶ **mot d'excuse** word of apology ▶ **mot de remerciements** thank-you note. ❖ **à mots couverts** loc adv in veiled terms. ❖ **au bas mot** loc adv at (the very) least. ❖ **en un mot** loc adv in a word. ❖ **mot à mot** loc adv [littéralement] word for word ; : *traduire mot à mot* to translate word for word. ❖ **mot pour mot** loc adv word for word / *c'est ce qu'elle a dit, mot pour mot* those were her very words, that's what she said, word for word. ❖ **sans mot dire** loc adv without (uttering) a word.

motard, e [mɔtaʀ, aʀd] nm, f *fam* motorcyclist, biker. ❖ **motard** nm [policier] motorcycle policeman.

mot-clé (*pl* **mots-clés**), **mot-clef** (*pl* **mots-clefs**) [mokle] nm keyword.

motel [mɔtɛl] nm motel.

moteur, trice [mɔtœʀ, tʀis] adj **1.** MÉCAN [force] driving, motive **2.** ANAT [nerf, neurone, muscle] motor (*modif*). ❖ **moteur** nm **1.** MÉCAN engine ▶ **moteur électrique** (electric) motor **2.** [cause] mainspring, driving force ▶ **être le moteur de qqch** to be the driving force behind sthg **3.** CINÉ ▶ **moteur !** action! **4.** INTERNET ▶ **moteur de recherche** search engine. ❖ **à moteur** loc adj power-driven, motor (*modif*).

motif [mɔtif] nm **1.** [raison] reason / *peur* / *soupçons sans motifs* groundless fear / suspicions ; DR [jugement] grounds ▶ **motif d'inquiétude** cause for concern **2.** [intention] motive **3.** [dessin] pattern, design / *un motif à petites fleurs* a small flower pattern ou design.

motion [mɔsjɔ̃] nf motion / *voter une motion* to pass a motion ▶ **motion de censure** vote of no confidence.

motivant, e [mɔtivɑ̃, ɑ̃t] adj motivating.

motivation [mɔtivasjɔ̃] nf [justification] motivation, justification, explanation ; [raison] motivation, motive, reason.

motivé, e [mɔtive] adj **1.** [personne] motivated **2.** [justifié] well-founded, justified ▶ **non motivé** unjustified, unwarranted ▶ **un refus motivé** a justifiable refusal.

motiver [3] [mɔtive] vt **1.** [inciter à agir] to spur on (*sép*), to motivate **2.** [causer] to be the reason for / *qu'est-ce qui a motivé votre retard ?* what's the reason for your being late? **3.** [justifier] to justify, to explain.

moto [mɔto] nf motorbike, bike ▶ **moto de course** race bike ▶ **moto tout-terrain** ou **verte** trail bike.

motocross [mɔtokʀɔs] nm (motorcycle) scramble 🇬🇧, moto-cross.

motoculteur [mɔtokyltœʀ] nm (motor) cultivator.

motocyclette [mɔtosiklɛt] nf *vieilli* motorcycle.

motocyclisme [mɔtosiklism] nm motorcycle racing.

motocycliste [mɔtosiklist] nmf motorcyclist.

motomarine [mɔtomaʀin] nf 🇨🇦 jet ski.

motoneige [mɔtonɛʒ] = **motoski**.

motorisé, e [mɔtoʀize] adj **1.** [agriculture, troupes] motorized **2.** *fam* [personne] ▶ **être motorisé** to have transport 🇬🇧 ou transportation 🇺🇸 / *tu es motorisé ?* have you got a car?

motoriste [mɔtoʀist] nmf [industriel] engine manufacturer.

motoski [mɔtoski] nf snowbike.

moto-taxi [mɔtotaksi] nf motorbike taxi.

motrice [mɔtʀis] f ⟶ **moteur**.

motricité [mɔtʀisite] nf motor functions.

motte [mɔt] nf **1.** AGR ▶ **motte (de terre)** clod ou clump (of earth) ▶ **motte de gazon** sod **2.** CULIN ▶ **motte de beurre** slab of butter.

motton [mɔtɔ̃] nm 🇨🇦 lump ▶ **avoir le motton** [émotion] to be all choked up ▶ **faire le motton** [s'enrichir] to make a fortune.

motus [mɔtys] interj *fam* ▶ **motus (et bouche cousue) !** not a word (to anybody)!, mum's the word!

mou, molle [mu, mɔl] (*devant nm commençant par voyelle ou « h » muet mol* [mɔl]) ◆ adj **1.** [souple - pâte, cire, terre, fruit] soft ; [- fauteuil, matelas] soft ; [sans tenue - étoffe, vêtement] limp ; [- joues, chair] flabby **2.** [sans vigueur physique - mouvement] limp, lifeless, feeble ; [- poignée de main] limp / *j'ai les jambes toutes molles* *fam* my legs feel all weak ou feel like jelly ; [estompé - contour] soft **3.** [sans conviction - protestation, excuse, tentative] feeble, weak ; [- doigté, style] lifeless, dull ; [- élève] apathetic, lethargic ; [sans force de caractère] spineless ▶ **être mou comme une chiffe** *fam* ou **chique** *fam* to be a real wimp **4.** [trop tolérant - parents, gouvernement] lax, soft. ◆ nm, f *fam* **1.** [moralement] spineless individual **2.** [physiquement] weak ou feeble individual. ❖ **mou** nm [jeu] slack, give, play ▶ **avoir du mou a)** [cordage] to be slack **b)** [vis, charnière] to be loose, to have a bit of play / *donner du mou à un câble* to give a cable some slack.

mouchard, e [muʃaʀ, aʀd] nm, f *fam & péj* **1.** [rapporteur] sneak **2.** [indic] informer, grass 🇬🇧, stoolpigeon 🇺🇸. ❖ **mouchard** nm [enregistreur - d'un avion] black box, flight recorder ; [- d'un camion] tachograph.

moucharder [3] [muʃaʀde] *fam & péj* ◆ vt **1.** [suj : enfant] to sneak on (*insép*) 🇬🇧, to tell tales about **2.** [suj : indic] to inform on (*insép*), to grass on (*insép*) 🇬🇧, to fink on (*insép*) 🇺🇸. ◆ vi [enfant] to sneak 🇬🇧, to tell tales.

mouche [muʃ] nf **1.** ENTOM fly ▶ **quelle mouche te pique ?** *fam* what's up ou wrong with you (all of a sudden)? ▶ **prendre la mouche** : *elle prend facilement la mouche* she's very touchy **2.** ESCRIME button ▶ **faire mouche a)** *pr* to hit the ou to score a bull's eye **b)** *fig* to hit the nail on the head.

moucher [3] [muʃe] vt **1.** [nettoyer] : *moucher son nez* to blow one's nose ▶ **moucher qqn** to blow sb's nose **2.** *fam* [rabrouer] ▶ **moucher qqn** to put sb in his

place, to teach sb a lesson **3.** [chandelle] to snuff (out).
❖ **se moucher** vp *(emploi réfléchi)* to blow one's nose.

moucheron [muʃʀɔ̃] nm ENTOM midge.

moucheté, e [muʃte] adj [œuf, fourrure, laine, etc.] mottled, flecked.

mouchoir [muʃwaʀ] nm handkerchief ▸ **mouchoir en papier** (paper) tissue ▸ **leur jardin est grand comme un mouchoir de poche** their garden is the size of a pocket handkerchief.

moudre [85] [mudʀ] vt [café, poivre] to grind ; [blé] to mill, to grind.

moue [mu] nf pout / **faire une moue de dépit** to pull a face ▸ **faire la moue** to pout.

mouette [mwɛt] nf gull, seagull.

moufle [mufl] nf [gant] mitt, mitten.

mouflet, ette [muflɛ, ɛt] nm, f *tfam* kid, sprog UK.

mouflon [muflɔ̃] nm mouflon, moufflon.

mouillage [mujaʒ] nm NAUT [emplacement] anchorage, moorings, moorage ; [manœuvre] mooring.

mouillasser [mujase] v impers QUÉBEC to drizzle.

mouillé, e [muje] adj [surface, vêtement, cheveux] wet, damp / **je suis tout mouillé** I'm all wet ou drenched ou soaked.

mouiller [3] [muje] ❖ vt **1.** [accidentellement - vêtement, personne] to wet / **ne mouille pas tes chaussons !** don't get your slippers wet ! / **se faire mouiller** [par la pluie] to get wet **2.** [humecter - doigt, lèvres] to moisten ; [- linge] to dampen **3.** *fam* [compromettre] to drag in *(sép)* **4.** NAUT [ancre] to cast, to drop ; MIL [mine] to lay ; PÊCHE [ligne] to cast **5.** *(en usage absolu)* CULIN ▸ **mouillez avec du vin / bouillon** moisten with wine / stock ; [lait, vin] to water down *(sép)*. ❖ vi NAUT [jeter l'ancre] to cast ou to drop anchor ; [stationner] to ride ou to lie ou to be at anchor.
❖ **se mouiller** vp *(emploi réfléchi)* **1.** [volontairement] ▸ **se mouiller les cheveux** to wet one's hair **2.** [accidentellement] to get wet **3.** *fam* [prendre un risque] to commit o.s.

mouillette [mujɛt] nf [de pain] finger of bread *(for dunking)*, soldier UK.

mouise [mwiz] nf ▸ **être dans la mouise** *fam* **a)** [être dans la misère] to be hard up, to be on one's uppers **b)** [avoir des ennuis] to be in a hole, to be behind the eight ball US.

moulage [mulaʒ] nm **1.** ART [processus] casting ; [reproduction] cast **2.** MÉTALL casting, moulding UK, molding US.

moulant, e [mulɑ̃, ɑ̃t] adj close-fitting, tight-fitting, clinging.

moule [mul] ❖ nm **1.** [récipient, matrice] mould UK, mold US ▸ **moule à gaufre** ou **gaufres** waffle iron ▸ **moule à gâteau** cake ou baking tin UK, cake ou baking pan US ▸ **moule à manqué** sandwich tin UK, deep cake pan US ▸ **moule à tarte** flan case UK, pie pan US **2.** [modèle imposé] mould ▸ **être coulé dans le même moule** *pr & fig* to be cast in the same mould. ❖ nf [mollusque] mussel ▸ **moules marinières** moules marinières, mussels in white wine.

mouler [3] [mule] vt **1.** [former - buste, statue] to cast ; [- brique, lingot, fromage] to mould UK, to mold US **2.** [serrer - hanches, jambes] to hug, to fit closely (round) / **cette jupe te moule trop** this skirt is too tight ou tight-fitting for you.

moulin [mulɛ̃] nm **1.** [machine, bâtiment] mill ▸ **moulin à eau** water mill ▸ **moulin à vent** windmill **2.** [instrument] ▸ **moulin à café** coffee grinder ▸ **moulin à légumes** vegetable mill ▸ **moulin à poivre** peppermill **3.** TEXT [pour la soie] thrower ; [pour retordre] doubling frame, twister

4. QUÉBEC : **moulin à viande** mincer / **moulin à bois** sawmill. ❖ **moulin à paroles** nm *fam* windbag *péj*, chatterbox.

mouliner [3] [muline] vt **1.** [aliment] to mill **2.** PÊCHE to reel in *(sép)*.

Moulinette® [mulinɛt] nf **1.** CULIN (hand-held) vegetable mill, Moulinette / *passer de la viande à la Moulinette* to put some meat through a food mill **2.** *fam & fig* ▸ **passer qqch à la Moulinette** to make mincemeat of sthg.

moulu, e [muly] adj **1.** [en poudre] ground / *café fraîchement moulu* freshly ground coffee **2.** *fam* [épuisé] ▸ **moulu (de fatigue)** dead beat.

moulure [mulyʀ] nf moulding UK, molding US.

mourant, e [muʀɑ̃, ɑ̃t] ❖ adj [personne, animal, plante] dying. ❖ nm, f dying man (woman) ▸ **les mourants** the dying.

mourir [42] [muʀiʀ] vi **1.** BIOL to die / *mourir d'une crise cardiaque / de vieillesse / d'un cancer* to die of a heart attack / of old age / of cancer ▸ **mourir de mort naturelle** ou **de sa belle mort** to die a natural death ▸ **mourir en héros** to die a hero's death ou like a hero / *tu n'en mourras pas !* *fam* it won't kill you ! ▸ **plus rapide / bête que lui, tu meurs !** *fam* you'd be hard put to be quicker / more stupid than him ! **2.** *sout* [disparaître - culture] to die out ; [- flamme, bougie] to die out ou down ; [- bruit] to die away ou down **3.** [pour intensifier] ▸ **mourir d'envie de faire qqch** to be dying to do sthg / *mourir d'ennui, s'ennuyer à mourir* to be bored to death ou to tears / *la pièce est à mourir de rire* the play's hilarious ou a scream ▸ **mourir de faim** to be starving ou famished ▸ **mourir de froid** to be freezing cold ▸ **mourir de soif** to be dying of thirst, to be parched ▸ **mourir de peur** to be scared to death.

mouron [muʀɔ̃] nm *fam* EXPR ▸ **se faire du mouron** to worry o.s. sick.

mousquetaire [muskətɛʀ] nm musketeer.

mousse [mus] ❖ adj **1.** TEXT ▸ **collant mousse** stretch tights **2.** CHIM ▸ **caoutchouc mousse** foam rubber. ❖ nm cabin boy. ❖ nf **1.** [bulles - de shampoing, de crème à raser] lather, foam ; [- d'un bain] bubbles, foam ; [- de savon] suds, lather ; [- de champagne, de cidre] bubbles ; [- de bière] froth ▸ **mousse coiffante** styling mousse ▸ **mousse à raser** shaving foam **2.** CULIN mousse ▸ **mousse au chocolat** chocolate mousse **3.** *fam* [bière] (glass of) beer **4.** [dans les matériaux synthétiques] foam ▸ **balle en mousse** rubber ball **5.** BOT moss.

mousseline [muslin] nf [de coton] muslin ; [de soie, de Nylon, de laine] chiffon, mousseline.

mousser [3] [muse] vi **1.** [champagne, cidre] to bubble, to sparkle ; [bière] to froth ; [savon, crème à raser] to lather ; [détergent, shampooing] to foam, to lather **2.** *fam & fig* ▸ **faire mousser qqn a)** [le mettre en colère] to wind sb up, to rile sb **b)** [le mettre en valeur] to sing sb's praises ▸ **se faire mousser** to sell o.s. **3.** QUÉBEC [promouvoir] to promote.

mousseux, euse [musø, øz] adj [vin, cidre] sparkling ; [bière] frothy ; [eau] foamy ; [sauce, jaunes d'œufs] (light and) frothy / *un chocolat mousseux* a cup of frothy hot chocolate. ❖ **mousseux** nm sparkling wine.

mousson [musɔ̃] nf monsoon.

moustache [mustaʃ] nf **1.** [d'un homme] moustache, mustache US / *porter la moustache* ou *des moustaches* to have a moustache / *elle a de la moustache* she's got a bit of a moustache **2.** ZOOL whiskers.

moustachu, e [mustaʃy] adj : *il est moustachu* he's got a moustache. ❖ **moustachu** nm man with a moustache.

moustiquaire [mustikɛʀ] nf [d'un lit] mosquito net ; [d'une ouverture] mosquito screen.

moustique [mustik] nm **1.** ENTOM mosquito **2.** fam [gamin] kid, mite ; [petite personne] (little) squirt.

moutard [mutaʀ] nm fam kid.

moutarde [mutaʀd] ◆ nf **1.** CULIN mustard **2.** fam ⟨EXPR⟩ **la moutarde me / te / lui monte au nez** : *la moutarde lui est montée au nez* he lost his temper, he saw red. ◆ adj inv mustard *(modif)*, mustard-coloured.

mouton [mutɔ̃] nm **1.** ZOOL sheep ▶ **mouton à cinq pattes** rare bird *fig* ▶ **revenons** ou **retournons à nos moutons** let's get back to the point **2.** [fourrure, cuir] sheepskin ▶ **veste en (peau de) mouton** sheepskin jacket **3.** CULIN mutton **4.** fam [individu] sheep ▶ **c'est un vrai mouton de Panurge** he's easily led, he follows the herd. ◆ **moutons** nmpl [poussière] (bits of) fluff ; [nuages] fleecy ou fluffy clouds ; [écume sur la mer] white horses 🇬🇧, whitecaps 🇺🇸.

mouture [mutyʀ] nf **1.** [version] version / *ma première mouture était meilleure* my first draft was better **2.** AGR & CULIN [des céréales] milling, grinding ; [du café] grinding / *ayant obtenu une mouture fine* [farine, café] once it has been finely ground.

mouvance [muvɑ̃s] nf *sout* [domaine d'influence] circle of influence / *ils se situent dans la mouvance socialiste* they belong to the socialist camp.

mouvant, e [muvɑ̃, ɑ̃t] adj **1.** [instable - surface] unsteady, moving **2.** [changeant - situation] unstable, unsettled.

mouvement [muvmɑ̃] nm **1.** [geste] movement ▶ **un mouvement de tête a)** [affirmatif] a nod **b)** [négatif] a shake of the head / *avoir un mouvement de recul* to start (back) / *faire des mouvements de gymnastique* to do some exercises **2.** [impulsion] ▶ **mouvement de colère** fit ou burst of anger ▶ **avoir un bon mouvement** to make a nice gesture **3.** [déplacement - d'un astre, d'un pendule] movement ; [- de personnes] movement ; PHYS motion ▶ **mouvements de capitaux** ou **de fonds** movement of capital ▶ **mouvements de troupes** troop movements / *il y eut un mouvement de foule* the crowd surged forward **4.** [évolution - des prix, des taux] trend, movement ; [- du marché] fluctuation ▶ **le mouvement des idées** the evolution of ideas ▶ **mouvement de la population** SOCIOL demographic changes **5.** POL [action collective] movement / *mouvement de contestation* protest movement ▶ **mouvement de grève** strike (movement) ▶ **le mouvement syndical** the trade-union 🇬🇧 ou labor-union 🇺🇸 movement ▶ **Mouvement de libération de la femme** Women's Liberation Movement **6.** [animation - d'un quartier] bustle, liveliness ; [- dans un aéroport, un port] movement **7.** [impression de vie - d'une peinture, d'une sculpture] movement ; [- d'un vers] flow, movement ; [- d'une robe] drape ; [- d'un paysage] undulations **8.** [mécanisme] movement. ◆ **en mouvement** loc adj [athlète] moving, in motion ; [population, troupes] on the move. ◆ loc adv : *mettre un mécanisme en mouvement* to set a mechanism going ou in motion / *le cortège se mit en mouvement* the procession started ou set off.

mouvementé, e [muvmɑ̃te] adj [débat] (very) lively, heated, stormy ; [voyage, vie] eventful ; [match] (very) lively, eventful.

mouvoir [54] [muvwaʀ] vt *sout* **1.** [bouger - membre, objet] to move **2.** [activer - machine] to drive, to power **3.** fig [pousser] to move, to prompt. ◆ **se mouvoir** vpi *sout* [se déplacer] to move.

moyen[1] [mwajɛ̃] nm **1.** [méthode] way / *il n'y a pas d'autre moyen* there's no other way ou solution / *par quel moyen peut-on le contacter ?* how can he be contacted? ▶ **trouver (le) moyen de faire qqch** to manage to do sthg ▶ **moyen de locomotion** ou **de transport** means

of transport ▶ **avec les moyens du bord** : *il faudra faire avec les moyens du bord* we'll have to manage with what we've got ▶ **moyen d'expression** means of expression ▶ **moyen de pression** : *ils n'ont utilisé aucun moyen de pression* they didn't apply any pressure ▶ **employer** ou **utiliser les grands moyens** to take drastic steps ▶ **tous les moyens** : *tous les moyens lui sont bons* he'll stop at nothing **2.** [pour intensifier] : *il n'y a pas moyen d'ouvrir la porte !* there's no way of opening the door!, the door won't open! / *je voulais me reposer, mais non, pas moyen !* fam I wanted to get some rest, but no such luck! **3.** GRAM ▶ **adverbe de moyen** adverb of means. ◆ **moyens** nmpl [financiers] means / *je n'ai pas les moyens de m'acheter un ordinateur* I haven't got the means to ou I can't afford to buy a computer ▶ **avoir de gros moyens** to be very well-off / *c'est au-dessus de mes moyens* it's beyond my means, I can't afford it ; [intellectuels, physiques] ▶ **perdre (tous) ses moyens** to go to pieces ▶ **je suis venu par mes propres moyens** I made my own way here. ◆ **au moyen de** loc prép by means of, with. ◆ **par tous les moyens** loc adv by all possible means ; [même immoraux] by fair means or foul / *j'ai essayé par tous les moyens* I've tried everything.

moyen[2]**, enne** [mwajɛ̃, ɛn] adj **1.** [intermédiaire - selon des mesures] medium *(avant nom)*, average ; [- selon une évaluation] medium / *un arbre de taille moyenne* a medium-sized tree ▶ **classes moyennes** middle classes **2.** [prix, taille, consommation, distance] average ; [température] average, mean ; [aptitudes, niveau, service] average / *ses notes sont trop moyennes* his marks are too poor / *il est moyen en maths* he's average at maths **3.** [ordinaire] : *le Français moyen* the average Frenchman.

Moyen Âge [mwajɛnaʒ] nm ▶ **le Moyen Âge** the Middle Ages.

moyenâgeux, euse [mwajɛnaʒø, øz] adj medieval / *ils utilisent des techniques moyenâgeuses* hum they use methods out of the Dark Ages.

moyen-courrier [mwajɛ̃kurje] *(pl* moyen-courriers*)* nm medium-haul aeroplane.

moyennant [mwajɛnɑ̃] prép : *elle garde ma fille moyennant trente euros par jour* she looks after my daughter for thirty euros a day ▶ **moyennant finance** for a fee ou a consideration ▶ **moyennant quoi** in return for which.

moyenne [mwajɛn] ◆ adj f ⟶ **moyen**. ◆ nf **1.** [gén] average / *la moyenne d'âge des candidats est de 21 ans* the average age of the applicants is 21 / *calculer* ou *faire la moyenne de* to work out the average of ; MATH mean, average **2.** [vitesse moyenne] average speed **3.** ÉDUC [absolue] pass mark 🇬🇧, passing grade 🇺🇸 *(of fifty per cent)* ▶ **notes au-dessus / au-dessous de la moyenne** marks above / under half / *j'ai eu tout juste la moyenne* [à un examen] I just got a pass ; [relative] average (mark) **4.** [ensemble] : *d'une intelligence au-dessus de la moyenne* of above-average intelligence. ◆ **en moyenne** loc adv on average.

moyennement [mwajɛnmɑ̃] adv moderately, fairly / *c'est moyennement intéressant* it's not that interesting / *j'ai moyennement aimé ce qu'elle a dit* I didn't think much of what she said ▶ **il a moyennement apprécié** he was not amused.

Moyen-Orient [mwajɛnɔʀjɑ̃] npr m ▶ **le Moyen-Orient** the Middle East ▶ **au Moyen-Orient** in the Middle East.

moyeu [mwajø] nm **1.** [d'une roue - de voiture] (wheel) hub ; [- de charrue] nave **2.** [d'une hélice] boss, hub.

mozambicain, e [mɔzɑ̃bikɛ̃, ɛn] adj Mozambican. ◆ **Mozambicain, e** nm, f Mozambican.

Mozambique [mɔzãbik] npr m ▶ **le Mozambique** Mozambique ▶ **au Mozambique** in Mozambique.

MP3 (abr de moving picture experts group audio layer 3) nm INFORM MP3 ▶ **lecteur (de) MP3** MP3 player.

MP4 (abr de moving picture experts group audio layer 4) nm INFORM MP4 ▶ **lecteur (de) MP4** MP4 player.

MRAP [mʀap] (abr de Mouvement contre le racisme, l'antisémitisme et pour la paix) npr m *pacifist anti-racist organization*.

MST nf (abr de maladie sexuellement transmissible) STD.

mue [my] nf **1.** ZOOL [transformation - d'un reptile] sloughing ; [- d'un volatile] moulting 🇬🇧, molting 🇺🇸 ; [- d'un mammifère à poils] shedding hair, moulting 🇬🇧, molting 🇺🇸 ; [- d'un mammifère sans poils] shedding ou casting (of skin) ; [- d'un cerf] shedding (of antlers) **2.** PHYSIOL [de la voix] breaking, changing.

muer [7] [mɥe] ◆ vi **1.** ZOOL [reptile] to slough, to moult 🇬🇧, to molt 🇺🇸 ; [volatile] to moult 🇬🇧, to molt 🇺🇸 ; [mammifère à fourrure] to shed hair, to moult 🇬🇧, to molt 🇺🇸 ; [mammifère sans poils] to shed skin, to moult 🇬🇧, to molt 🇺🇸 ; [cerf] to shed (antlers) **2.** PHYSIOL [voix] to break, to change ▶ **il mue** his voice is breaking. ◆ vt *litt* ▶ **muer qqch en** to change ou to turn sth into. ❖ **se muer en** vp + prép *litt* to change ou to turn into.

muesli [mɥesli ou mysli], **musli** [mysli] nm muesli.

muet, ette [mɥɛ, ɛt] ◆ adj **1.** [qui ne parle pas] dumb **2.** *fig* [silencieux] silent, mute, dumb ▶ **muet d'admiration** in mute admiration ∕ **il en resta muet d'étonnement** he was struck dumb with astonishment **3.** *sout* [non exprimé - douleur, reproche] unspoken, mute, silent **4.** CINÉ [film, cinéma] silent ; [rôle, acteur] non-speaking, walk-on **5.** LING mute, silent. ◆ nm, f [personne] mute, dumb person. ❖ **muet** nm CINÉ ▶ **le muet** the silent cinema 🇬🇧 ou movies 🇺🇸.

muffin [mœfin] nm muffin.

mufle [myfl] nm **1.** ZOOL [d'un ruminant] muffle ; [d'un félin] muzzle **2.** *fam & péj* [malotru] boor, lout.

mugir [32] [myʒiʀ] vi **1.** [vache] to moo, to low *litt* **2.** *litt* [vent] to howl, to roar ; [océan] to roar, to thunder.

muguet [mygɛ] nm BOT lily of the valley, May lily.

 Muguet

On May Day in France, bunches of lilies of the valley are sold in the streets and given as presents. The flowers are supposed to bring good luck.

mulâtre, mulâtresse [mylatʀ, mylatʀɛs] nm, f mulatto.

mule [myl] nf **1.** ZOOL mule *(female)* **2.** [chausson] mule.

mulet [mylɛ] nm **1.** ZOOL mule *(male)* **2.** [poisson] grey mullet.

mulot [mylo] nm field mouse.

multi- [mylti] préf multi-.

multicolore [myltikɔlɔʀ] adj multicoloured 🇬🇧, multicolored 🇺🇸, many-coloured.

multiconfessionnel, elle [myltikɔ̃fɛsjɔnɛl] adj multifaith.

multicoque [myltikɔk] nm multihull.

multicritère [myltikʀitɛʀ] adj INFORM multicriteria ∕ *recherche multicritère* multicriteria search.

multiculturel, elle [myltikyltyʀɛl] adj multicultural.

multiethnique [myltiɛtnik] adj multi-ethnic.

multifonction [myltifɔ̃ksjɔ̃] adj multifunction.

multimédia [myltimedja] ◆ adj multimedia *(avant nom)*. ◆ nm ▶ **le multimédia** multimedia.

multimilliardaire [myltimiljaʀdɛʀ] adj & nmf multimillionaire.

multimillionnaire [myltimiljɔnɛʀ] adj & nmf multimillionaire.

multinational, e, aux [myltinasjɔnal, o] adj multinational. ❖ **multinationale** nf multinational (company).

multiplateforme [myltiplatfɔʀm] nf INFORM [logiciel, jeu] cross-platform.

multiple [myltipl] ◆ adj **1.** [nombreux - exemples, incidents, qualités] many, numerous ; [- fractures] multiple ▶ **à de multiples reprises** repeatedly, time and (time) again **2.** [divers - raisons, intérêts] many, multiple, manifold *sout* **3.** *sout* [complexe - problème, difficulté] many-sided, multifaceted, complex. ◆ nm MATH multiple.

multiplexe [myltiplɛks] nm CINÉ multiplex (cinema), multiscreen cinema.

multiplication [myltiplikasjɔ̃] nf BIOL, MATH & NUCL multiplication ▶ **la multiplication des accidents** *fig* the increase in the number of accidents.

multiplicité [myltiplisite] nf multiplicity.

multiplier [10] [myltiplije] vt **1.** [contrôles, expériences, efforts, etc.] to multiply, to increase ∕ *nous avons multiplié les avertissements* we have issued repeated warnings **2.** MATH to multiply ∕ *la production a été multipliée par trois fig* output has tripled. ❖ **se multiplier** vpi [attentats, menaces] to multiply, to increase.

multiprise [myltipʀiz] nf adapter.

multipropriété [myltipʀɔpʀijete] nf timeshare (system), time-sharing ∕ *investir dans la multipropriété* to invest in a timeshare.

multiracial, e, aux [myltiʀasjal, o] adj multiracial.

multirécidiviste [myltiʀesidivist] nmf habitual offender.

multirésistant, e [myltiʀezistã, ãt] adj multi-resistant.

multirisque [myltiʀisk] adj multiple risk *(modif)*.

multitude [myltityd] nf [grande quantité] ▶ **une multitude de** a multitude of, a vast number of.

municipal, e, aux [mynisipal, o] adj [élection, conseil] local, municipal ; [bibliothèque, parc, théâtre] public, municipal. ❖ **municipales** nfpl POL local ou council 🇬🇧 elections *(to elect the conseil municipal)*.

 Municipales

These elections, held every six years, are for the town councils (**conseils municipaux**). Electors vote for a list of council members headed by the **tête de liste**, who will then become the mayor.

municipalité [mynisipalite] nf **1.** [communauté] town, municipality ▶ **municipalité régionale de comté** 🇶🇦Québec regional county municipality **2.** [représentants] ≃ (town) council.

munir [32] [myniʀ] vt ▶ **munir qqn de** to provide ou to supply sb with ∕ *munie d'un plan de la ville, elle se mit en route* equipped ou armed with a map of the town, she set off ▶ **munir qqch de** to equip ou to fit sth with. ❖ **se munir de** vp + prép : *se munir de vêtements* chauds / d'un parapluie to equip o.s. with warm clothes / an umbrella ▸ **munissez-vous de votre passeport** carry your passport ou take your passport with you.

munitions [mynisjɔ̃] nfpl ammunition (U), munitions.

mur [myʀ] nm **1.** [construction] wall ▸ **mur d'escalade** climbing wall ▸ **faire le mur** fam [soldat, interne] to go ou to jump over the wall ▸ **parler à un mur** : c'est comme si tu parlais à un mur it's (just) like talking to a brick wall ▸ **se heurter à un mur** to come up against a brick wall ▸ **les murs ont des oreilles** walls have ears **2.** fig [de flammes, de brouillard, de pluie, etc.] wall, sheet ; [de silence] wall ; [de haine, d'incompréhension] wall, barrier **3.** AÉRON ▸ **passer le mur du son** to break the sound barrier.

mûr, mûre [myʀ] (mpl **mûrs,** fpl **mûres**), **mur*, mure** ou **mure*** (mpl **murs,** fpl **mures**) adj **1.** [fruit, graine, abcès, etc.] ripe ▸ **trop mûr** overripe, too ripe ▸ **pas mûr** unripe, not ripe **2.** [personne] mature **3.** [prêt - révolte, plan] ripe, ready / le pays est mûr pour la guerre civile the country is ripe for civil war ▸ **après mûre réflexion** after careful thought ou consideration.

muraille [myʀaj] nf [d'une ville, d'un château, de rocs] wall ▸ **la Grande Muraille (de Chine)** the Great Wall of China.

mural, e, aux [myʀal, o] adj wall (modif).
❖ **mural, als** nm [peinture] mural.

mûre, mure* [myʀ] ❖ f ⟶ **mûr.** ❖ nf [fruit] mulberry ▸ **mûre sauvage** blackberry, bramble.

mûrement, murement* [myʀmɑ̃] adv : après avoir mûrement réfléchi after careful thought ou consideration / un projet mûrement réfléchi a carefully thought-out plan.

murène [myʀɛn] nf moray (eel).

murer [3] [myʀe] vt **1.** [entourer de murs] to wall in (sép) **2.** [boucher - porte] to wall up (sép). ❖ **se murer** vpi to shut o.s. away / se murer dans le silence fig & sout to retreat ou to withdraw into silence, to build a wall of silence around o.s.

mûrier, murier* [myʀje] nm mulberry tree ou bush ▸ **mûrier sauvage** bramble (bush), blackberry bush.

mûrir, murir* [32] [myʀiʀ] ❖ vi **1.** BOT to ripen ▸ **faire mûrir** to ripen **2.** [abcès] to come to a head **3.** [évoluer - pensée, projet] to mature, to ripen, to develop ; [- personne] to mature. ❖ vt [pensée, projet, sentiment] to nurture, to nurse / une année à l'étranger l'a mûri a year abroad has made him more mature.

murmure [myʀmyʀ] nm **1.** [d'une personne] murmur ; litt [d'une source, de la brise] murmur, murmuring **2.** [commentaire] ▸ **un murmure de protestation / d'admiration** a murmur of protest / admiration. ❖ **murmures** nmpl [plaintes] murmurs, murmurings.

murmurer [3] [myʀmyʀe] ❖ vi **1.** [parler à voix basse] to murmur **2.** [se plaindre] ▸ **murmurer (contre)** to mutter ou to grumble (about). ❖ vt to murmur ▸ **on murmure que...** there is a rumour (going about) that...

musaraigne [myzaʀɛɲ] nf shrew.

musarder [3] [myzaʀde] vi sout [flâner] to dawdle, to saunter ; [ne rien faire] to dillydally.

musc [mysk] nm musk.

muscade [myskad] nf BOT ⟶ **noix.**

muscat [myska] nm [fruit] muscat grape ; [vin] Muscat, Muscatel (wine).

muscle [myskl] nm ANAT muscle ▸ **avoir des muscles** ou **du muscle** fam to be muscular.

musclé, e [myskle] adj **1.** [corps, personne] muscular **2.** fam [énergique] powerful, forceful ▸ **mener une politique musclée contre qqch** to take a hard line ou a tough stance on sthg.

muscler [3] [myskle] vt **1.** SPORT : muscler ses jambes / épaules to develop one's leg / shoulder muscles **2.** fig [renforcer] to strengthen. ❖ **se muscler** vp (emploi réfléchi) to develop (one's) muscles.

muscu [mysky] (abr de **musculation**) nf fam bodybuilding.

musculaire [myskylɛʀ] adj muscular, muscle (modif).

musculation [myskylasjɔ̃] nf bodybuilding / faire de la musculation to do bodybuilding.

musculature [myskylatyʀ] nf musculature, muscles.

muse [myz] nf [inspiratrice] muse.

museau, x [myzo] nm **1.** ZOOL [d'un chien, d'un ours] muzzle ; [d'un porc] snout ; [d'une souris] nose **2.** fam [figure] face **3.** CULIN ▸ **museau (de porc)** brawn UK, headcheese US.

musée [myze] nm **1.** [d'œuvres d'art] art gallery UK, museum US ; [des sciences, des techniques] museum **2.** (comme adjectif, avec ou sans trait d'union) ▸ **une ville musée** a historical town.

museler [24] [myzle] vt **1.** [chien] to muzzle **2.** sout [presse, opposition] to muzzle, to gag, to silence.
✍ In reformed spelling (see p. 16-18), this verb is conjugated like *peler : il musèle, elle musèlera.*

muselière [myzǝljɛʀ] nf muzzle / mettre une muselière à un chien to muzzle a dog.

muséum [myzeɔm] nm ▸ **muséum (d'histoire naturelle)** natural history museum.

musical, e, aux [myzikal, o] adj [voix, événement] musical ▸ **critique musical** music critic.

music-hall [myzikol] (pl **music-halls**) nm [local] music hall ; [activité] ▸ **le music-hall** music hall UK, vaudeville US ▸ **numéro de music-hall** variety act.

musicien, enne [myzisjɛ̃, ɛn] nm, f musician.

musique [myzik] nf [art, notation ou science] music / texte mis en musique text set ou put to music ▸ **faire de la musique** a) [personne] to play (an instrument) b) [objet] to play a tune ▸ **étudier / dîner en musique** to study / to have dinner with music playing ▸ **musique d'ambiance** ou **de fond** background music ▸ **musique contemporaine / classique** contemporary / classical music ▸ **musique folklorique / militaire** folk / military music ▸ **musique instrumentale** instrumental music ▸ **musique sacrée / de chambre** sacred / chamber music ▸ **une musique de film** a film UK ou movie US theme ou score ▸ **ça va, je connais la musique** fam I've heard it all before.

musli [mysli] = **muesli.**

must [mœst] nm fam must / ce film est un must this film is compulsory viewing ou a must.

musulman, e [myzylmɑ̃, an] adj & nm, f Muslim.

mutant, e [mytɑ̃, ɑ̃t] adj & nm, f mutant.

mutation [mytasjɔ̃] nf **1.** [d'une entreprise, d'un marché] change, transformation ▸ **industrie en pleine mutation** industry undergoing major change ou a radical transformation **2.** ADMIN & DR transfer **3.** BIOL mutation.

muter [3] [myte] vt ADMIN to transfer, to move / il s'est fait muter en province he's been transferred to the provinces.

mutilation [mytilasjɔ̃] nf [du corps] mutilation.

mutilé, e [mytile] nm, f disabled person ▸ **mutilés de guerre** disabled ex-servicemen.

mutiler [3] [mytile] vt [personne, animal] to mutilate, to maim. ❖ **se mutiler** vp (emploi réfléchi) to mutilate o.s.

mutin¹ [mytɛ̃] nm sout rebel, mutineer.

* In reformed spelling (see p. 16-18).

mutin², e [mytɛ̃, in] adj *litt* [enfant] impish, mischievous, cheeky ; [air] mischievous.

mutiner [3] [mytine] ❖ **se mutiner** vpi [marin, soldat] to mutiny, to rebel, to revolt ; [employés, élèves, prisonniers] to rebel, to revolt.

mutinerie [mytinʀi] nf [de marins, de soldats] mutiny, revolt, rebellion ; [d'employés, de prisonniers] rebellion, revolt.

mutisme [mytism] nm **1.** [silence] silence / *s'enfermer dans un mutisme complet* to retreat into absolute silence **2.** MÉD muteness, dumbness ; PSYCHOL mutism.

mutualiser [mytɥalize] vt [risques, coûts, compétences] to mutualise.

mutuel, elle [mytɥɛl] adj [partagé, réciproque] mutual. ❖ **mutuelle** nf mutual (benefit) insurance company ; ≈ friendly society ; ≈ benefit society US.

🏛️ **Mutuelle**

An insurance company which provides complementary health cover and guarantees payment of all or part of the expenses not covered by the **Sécurité sociale**. These companies are often organized around professions. There is a **mutuelle** for students, one for teachers, etc.

---

mutuellement [mytɥɛlmã] adv one another, each other.

mwa SMS abr écrite de **moi.**

Myanmar [mjãmaʀ] npr Myanmar.

mycose [mikoz] nf [gén] mycosis *(U)* spéc, thrush *(U)* ; [aux orteils] athlete's foot.

mygale [migal] nf mygale spéc, tarantula ▶ **mygale aviculaire / maçonne** bird / trapdoor spider.

myopathie [mjɔpati] nf [gén] myopathy ; [dystrophie musculaire] muscular dystrophy.

myope [mjɔp] ◆ adj short-sighted , nearsighted US, myopic spéc ▶ **myope comme une taupe** fam (as) blind as a bat. ◆ nmf short-sighted ou nearsighted US person, myope spéc.

myopie [mjɔpi] nf short-sightedness , nearsightedness US, myopia spéc.

myosotis [mjozɔtis] nm forget-me-not, myosotis spéc.

myrtille [miʀtij] nf bilberry , blueberry US.

mystère [mistɛʀ] nm **1.** [atmosphère] mystery ▶ **mystère et boule de gomme** fam : *où est-elle ? — mystère et boule de gomme !* where is she ? — I haven't got a clue ou search me ! **2.** [secret] mystery / *ne fais pas tant de mystères* don't be so mysterious / *si tu avais travaillé, tu aurais réussi l'examen, il n'y a pas de mystère !* if you'd worked, you'd have passed your exam, it's as simple as that ! / *ce n'est un mystère pour personne* it's no secret, it's an open secret / *je n'en fais pas (un) mystère* I make no mystery ou secret of it **3.** HIST & THÉÂTRE mystery (play).

mystérieusement [misteʀjøzmã] adv mysteriously.

mystérieux, euse [misteʀjø, øz] adj **1.** [inexplicable] mysterious, strange **2.** [confidentiel] secret **3.** [énigmatique] mysterious.

mystifier [9] [mistifje] vt **1.** [duper, se jouer de] to fool, to take in *(sép)* **2.** [leurrer] to fool, to deceive.

mystique [mistik] ◆ adj mystic, mystical. ◆ nmf mystic.

mythe [mit] nm myth.

mythifier [9] [mitifje] vt to mythicize.

mythique [mitik] adj mythic, mythical.

mytho [mito] (abr de **mythomane**) adj fam : *il est complètement mytho* you can't believe anything he says.

mythologie [mitɔlɔʒi] nf mythology.

mythologique [mitɔlɔʒik] adj mythological.

mythomane [mitɔman] ◆ adj PSYCHOL mythomaniac / *il est un peu mythomane* he has a tendency to make things up (about himself). ◆ nmf PSYCHOL mythomaniac, compulsive liar.

n' [n] ⟶ ne.

na [na] interj *fam* so there, and that's that.

NAC [ɛnase, nak] **(abr de nouveaux animaux de compagnie)** nmpl unusual pets.

nacelle [nasɛl] nf [d'un aérostat] basket, nacelle, gondola ; [d'un avion] nacelle, pod ; [d'un landau] carriage ; [pour un ouvrier] basket.

nacre [nakʀ] nf ▶ **la nacre** mother-of-pearl, nacre *spéc.*

nacré, e [nakʀe] adj pearly, nacreous *litt.*

nage [naʒ] nf SPORT [activité] swimming ; [style] stroke ▶ **nage indienne** sidestroke ▶ **nage libre** freestyle. ❖ **à la nage** ◆ loc adv : *s'éloigner à la nage* to swim off ou away / *traverser un lac à la nage* to swim across a lake. ◆ loc adj CULIN à la nage *(cooked in a court-bouillon).* ❖ **en nage** loc adj ▶ **être en nage** to be dripping with sweat.

nageoire [naʒwaʀ] nf ZOOL [de poisson] fin ; [d'otarie, de phoque, etc.] flipper.

nager [17] [naʒe] ◆ vi **1.** SPORT to swim ▶ **elle nage très bien** she's a very good swimmer **2.** *fig* ▶ **nager dans le bonheur** to be basking in bliss / *on nageait dans le mystère* we were totally bewildered / *tu nages dans ce pantalon !* those trousers are miles too big for you ! **3.** [ne rien comprendre] to be completely lost ou out of one's depth. ◆ vt : *nager le 200 mètres* to swim the 200 metres.

nageur, euse [naʒœʀ, øz] nm, f [personne] swimmer.

naguère [nagɛʀ] adv *litt* [autrefois] long ago, formerly ; [il y a peu de temps] not long ago.

naïf, ïve [naif, iv] ◆ adj **1.** [candide - enfant, remarque] innocent, naïve, ingenuous **2.** [trop crédule] naïve, gullible. ◆ nm, f (gullible) ou naïve fool.

nain, naine [nɛ̃, nɛn] ◆ adj dwarf *(modif).* ◆ nm, f dwarf ▶ **nain de jardin** garden gnome.

naissance [nɛsɑ̃s] nf **1.** BIOL birth ▶ **donner naissance à** to give birth to **2.** *sout* [début - d'un sentiment, d'une idée] birth ; [- d'un mouvement, d'une démocratie, d'une ère] birth, dawn / *à la naissance du jour* at daybreak ▶ **donner naissance à qqch** to give birth ou rise to sthg ▶ **prendre naissance a)** [mouvement] to arise, to originate **b)** [idée] to originate, to be born **c)** [sentiment] to arise, to be born **3.** *sout* [endroit] ▶ **la naissance du cou** the base of the neck ▶ **la naissance d'un fleuve** the source of a river. ❖ **à la naissance** loc adv at birth. ❖ **de naissance** loc adv **1.** [congénitalement] congenitally, from birth / *elle est aveugle de naissance* she was born blind, she's been blind from birth **2.** [d'extraction] ▶ **italien de naissance** Italian by birth.

naissant, e [nɛsɑ̃, ɑ̃t] adj *sout* [révolte] incipient ; [sentiment] growing, budding *litt* ; [beauté] budding *litt*, nascent *litt* ;

[jour] dawning ▶ **une barbe naissante** the beginnings of a beard.

naître, naïtre* [92] [nɛtʀ] vi *(aux être)* **1.** BIOL to be born / *mon bébé devrait naître en mars* my baby is due in March / *le bébé qui vient de naître* the newborn baby ▶ **ne pas être né d'hier** ou **de la dernière couvée** ou **de la dernière pluie** : *je ne suis pas né d'hier* ou *de la dernière couvée* ou *de la dernière pluie* I wasn't born yesterday ▶ **être né coiffé** ou **sous une bonne étoile** : *il est né coiffé* ou *sous une bonne étoile* he was born under a lucky star **2.** ▶ **être né pour** [être destiné à] to be born ou destined ou meant to **3.** [apparaître - sentiment, doute, espoir] to arise, to be born *sout* ; [- problème] to crop ou to come up ; [- projet] to be conceived ; [- communauté, entreprise] to spring up ; [- mouvement] to spring up, to arise / *faire naître des soupçons / la sympathie* to arouse suspicion / sympathy ▶ **naître de** [provenir de] to arise ou to spring from **4.** *litt* [fleur] to spring ou to come up ; [jour] to break, to dawn.

> 📋 Attention, naître se traduit par be born :
> **Certains enfants naissent avec des dents.** *Some babies are born with teeth.*
> **Je suis né en Afrique du Nord.** *I was born in North Africa.*

naïvement [naivmɑ̃] adv **1.** [innocemment] innocently, naively, ingenuously **2.** [avec crédulité] naively, gullibly.

naïveté [naivte] nf **1.** [innocence] innocence, naivety **2.** [crédulité] naivety, gullibility / *j'ai eu la naïveté de lui faire confiance* I was naive enough to trust him.

Namibie [namibi] npr f ▶ **(la) Namibie** Namibia.

namibien, enne [namibjɛ̃, ɛn] adj Namibian. ❖ **Namibien, enne** nm, f Namibian.

nana [nana] nf *fam* girl / *c'est sa nana* she's his girlfriend.

nanoparticule [nanopaʀtikyl] nf PHYS nanoparticule.

nanotechnologie [nanotɛknɔlɔʒi] nf nanotechnology.

nanti, e [nɑ̃ti] ◆ adj [riche] affluent, well-to-do, well-off. ◆ nm, f affluent person ▶ **les nantis** the well-to-do.

nantir [32] [nɑ̃tiʀ] vt [doter] ▶ **nantir qqn de** to provide sb with. ❖ **se nantir de** vp + prép to equip o.s. with.

naphtaline [naftalin] nf ▶ **(boules de) naphtaline** mothballs.

nappe [nap] nf **1.** [linge] tablecloth **2.** [couche] ▶ **nappe de pétrole / gaz** layer of oil / gas ▶ **nappe de brouillard** blanket of fog ▶ **nappe d'eau a)** [en surface] stretch ou expanse ou sheet of water **b)** [souterraine] groundwater **3.** GÉOL ▶ **nappe phréatique** groundwater ou phreatic table.

napper [3] [nape] vt ▶ **napper qqch de** to coat sthg with.

napperon [napʀɔ̃] nm [sous un vase, un bougeoir] mat ; [sous un plat, un gâteau] doily.

narcisse [naʀsis] nm BOT narcissus.

narcissique [naʀsisik] adj narcissistic.

narcissisme [naʀsisism] nm narcissism.

narcodollars [naʀkɔdɔlaʀ] nmpl narcodollars, drug money.

narcotique [naʀkɔtik] ◆ adj narcotic. ◆ nm narcotic.

narcotrafic [naʀkɔtʀafik] nm narcotrafficking.

narcotrafiquant, e [naʀkɔtʀafikɑ̃, ɑ̃t] nm, f drug trafficker.

narguer [3] [naʀge] vt **1.** [se moquer de, provoquer] to scoff at *(insép)* **2.** *sout* [braver, mépriser] to scorn, to spurn, to deride.

narine [naʀin] nf nostril.

narquois, e [naʀkwa, az] adj mocking, derisive.

narrateur, trice [naʀatœʀ, tʀis] nm, f narrator.

narration [naʀasjɔ̃] nf [exposé] narrative, narration ; [partie du discours] narration.

NASA, Nasa [naza] **(abr de National Aeronautics and Space Administration)** npr f NASA, Nasa.

nasal, e, aux [nazal, o] adj nasal.

nase [naz] *tfam* adj [inutilisable - appareil, meuble] kaput, bust ; [fou] cracked, screwy ; [fatigué, malade] knackered.

naseau, x [nazo] nm ZOOL nostril.

nasillard, e [nazijaʀ, aʀd] adj [ton] nasal ; [radio, haut-parleur] tinny.

nasse [nas] nf PÊCHE (conical) lobster pot.

natal, e, als [natal] adj [pays, ville] native ▶ **sa maison natale** the house where he was born.

nataliste [natalist] adj ▶ **politique nataliste** policy to increase the birth rate.

natalité [natalite] nf birth rate, natality US.

natation [natasjɔ̃] nf swimming ▶ **natation synchronisée** ou **artistique** synchronized swimming.

natif, ive [natif, iv] ◆ adj [originaire] native ▶ **je suis natif de Paris / Pologne** I was born in Paris / Poland. ◆ nm, f native.

nation [nasjɔ̃] nf nation ▶ **les Nations Unies** the United Nations.

national, e, aux [nasjɔnal, o] adj [de la nation] national ▶ **l'économie nationale** the domestic economy ▶ **funérailles** ou **obsèques nationales** state funeral. ◆ **nationale** nf ≃ A road UK ; ≃ highway US.

nationalisation [nasjɔnalizasjɔ̃] nf nationalization.

nationaliser [3] [nasjɔnalize] vt to nationalize.

nationalisme [nasjɔnalism] nm nationalism.

nationaliste [nasjɔnalist] ◆ adj nationalist, nationalistic. ◆ nmf nationalist.

nationalité [nasjɔnalite] nf nationality ▶ **être de nationalité française / nigériane** to be French / Nigerian.

nativité [nativite] nf **1.** RELIG ▶ **la Nativité** the Nativity **2.** ART Nativity scene.

natte [nat] nf [de cheveux] pigtail, braid US, plait UK.

natter [3] [nate] vt [cheveux] to braid US, to plait UK.

naturalisation [natyʀalizasjɔ̃] nf **1.** ADMIN naturalization, acquired citizenship US **2.** [empaillage] stuffing **3.** BOT & LING naturalization.

naturaliser [3] [natyʀalize] vt **1.** ADMIN to naturalize / **il s'est fait naturaliser français** he was granted French citizenship **2.** [empailler] to stuff.

naturaliste [natyʀalist] nmf **1.** BOT & ZOOL naturalist **2.** [empailleur] taxidermist.

nature [natyʀ] ◆ nf **1.** [univers naturel] ▶ **la nature** nature ▶ **laisser faire** ou **agir la nature** let nature take its course **2.** [campagne] ▶ **la nature** nature, the country, the countryside / **tomber en panne en pleine nature** to break down in the middle of nowhere ▶ **disparaître** ou **s'évanouir dans la nature** to vanish into thin air **3.** [caractère] nature / **ce n'est pas dans sa nature** it's not like him, it's not in his nature / **c'est dans la nature des choses** it's in the nature of things, that's the way the world is ▶ **la nature humaine** human nature **4.** [type de personne] type, sort ▶ **une heureuse nature** a happy person ▶ **c'est une petite nature** he's the feeble type ou a weakling **5.** [sorte] nature, type, sort / **les raisonnements de cette nature** this kind of argument, arguments of this kind **6.** ART ▶ **d'après nature** from life ▶ **nature morte** still life. ◆ adj inv **1.** [bœuf, choucroute] plain, with no trimmings ; [salade, avocat] plain, with no dressing ; [café] black ; ŒNOL still **2.** *fam* [simple] natural. ◆ **contre nature** loc adj against nature, unnatural. ◆ **de nature** loc adj by nature / **il est généreux de nature** he's generous by nature, it's (in) his nature to be generous. ◆ **de nature à** loc conj likely ou liable to / **je ne suis pas de nature à me laisser faire** I'm not the kind ou type of person you can push around. ◆ **de toute nature** loc adj of all kinds ou types. ◆ **en nature** loc adv in kind.

naturel, elle [natyʀɛl] adj **1.** [du monde physique - phénomène, ressource, frontière] natural **2.** [physiologique - fonction, processus] natural, bodily **3.** [inné - disposition, talent] natural, inborn ; [- boucles, blondeur] natural **4.** [sans affectation] natural / **c'est bien** ou **tout naturel que je t'aide** it's only natural that I should help you / **je vous remercie — je vous en prie, c'est tout naturel !** thank you — please don't mention it, it's the least I could do ! ▶ **trouver naturel de faire qqch** to think nothing of doing sthg **6.** [pur - fibre] pure ; [- nourriture] natural ; COMM natural, organic. ◆ **naturel** nm **1.** [tempérament] nature / **il est d'un naturel anxieux** he's the worrying kind, it's (in) his nature to worry **2.** [authenticité] naturalness / **ce que j'aime chez elle c'est son naturel** what I like about her is she's so natural ▶ **avec beaucoup de naturel** with perfect ease, completely naturally. ◆ **au naturel** loc adj CULIN plain / **poires au naturel** pears in natural fruit juice.

naturellement [natyʀɛlmɑ̃] adv **1.** [de façon innée] naturally **2.** [simplement] naturally, unaffectedly **3.** [bien sûr] naturally, of course.

naturisme [natyʀism] nm [nudisme] naturism.

naturiste [natyʀist] ◆ adj [nudiste] naturist. ◆ nmf [nudiste] naturist, nudist.

naturopathe [natyʀɔpat] nmf naturopath.

naturopathie [natyʀɔpati], **naturothérapie** [natyʀɔteʀapi] nf naturopathy.

naufrage [nofʀaʒ] nm **1.** [d'un navire] wreck, shipwreck ▶ **faire naufrage a)** [personne] to be shipwrecked **b)** [navire] to be wrecked **2.** *fig* ruin, wreckage.

naufragé, e [nofʀaʒe] ◆ adj **1.** [personne - gén] shipwrecked ; [- sur une île] castaway *(modif)* **2.** [navire] wrecked. ◆ nm, f [gén] shipwreck victim ; [sur une île] castaway.

nauséabond, e [nozeabɔ̃, ɔ̃d] adj **1.** [qui sent mauvais] putrid, foul, foul-smelling **2.** [répugnant] nauseating, sickening, repulsive.

nausée [noze] nf **1.** [envie de vomir] nausea ▶ **avoir la nausée** to feel sick ▶ **avoir des nausées** to have bouts of sickness **2.** *fig* [dégoût] : **une telle hypocrisie me donne la nausée** such hypocrisy makes me sick.

nautique [notik] adj nautical / **le salon nautique** ≃ the Boat Show.

nautisme [notism] nm water sports, aquatics *(sg)*.

naval, e, als [naval] adj naval ▸ **construction navale** shipbuilding (industry).

navarin [navaʀɛ̃] nm navarin *(mutton and vegetable stew)*.

navet [navɛ] nm **1.** BOT turnip **2.** QUÉBEC [rutabaga] turnip, swede **3.** *fam* [œuvre] : *c'est un navet* it's (a load of) tripe.

navette [navɛt] nf AÉRON & TRANSP shuttle ▸ **faire la navette (entre)** to shuttle back and forth ou to and fro (between) / *un bus fait la navette entre la gare et l'aéroport* there is a shuttle bus (service) between the station and the airport / *il fait la navette entre Paris et Marseille* he comes and goes ou goes to and fro between Paris and Marseille ▸ **navette gratuite** courtesy bus ▸ **navette spatiale** space shuttle.

navetteur, euse [navɛtœʀ, øz] nm, f BELG commuter.

navigable [navigabl] adj navigable.

navigant, e [navigɑ̃, ɑ̃t] ◆ adj NAUT seafaring ▸ **personnel navigant** AÉRON flight personnel, aircrew, crew. ◆ nm, f ▸ **les navigants a)** NAUT the crew **b)** AÉRON the aircrew, the crew.

navigateur, trice [navigatœʀ, tʀis] nm, f **1.** NAUT [voyageur] sailor, seafarer ; [membre de l'équipage] navigator **2.** AÉRON & AUTO navigator, copilot *(in charge of navigation)*.

navigation [navigasjɔ̃] nf **1.** NAUT navigation, sailing ▸ **interdit à la navigation a)** [des gros bateaux] closed to shipping **b)** [des petits bateaux] no sailing ou boating ▸ **navigation côtière** coastal navigation ▸ **navigation de plaisance** yachting, pleasure sailing **2.** AÉRON navigation, flying ▸ **navigation aérienne** aerial navigation. ◆ **de navigation** loc adj [registre] navigational ; [terme, école] nautical ; [instrument] navigation *(modif)*.

naviguer [3] [navige] vi **1.** NAUT to sail ▸ **depuis que je navigue a)** [plaisancier] since I first went sailing **b)** [marin] since I first went to sea **2.** AÉRON to fly **3.** *fig* [se déplacer] to get about ▸ **savoir naviguer** to know one's way around.

navire [naviʀ] nm ship, vessel *litt* ▸ **navire marchand** ou **de commerce** merchant ship, merchantman ▸ **navire de guerre** warship.

navire-école [naviʀekɔl] *(pl* **navires-écoles)** nm training ship.

navire-usine [naviʀyzin] *(pl* **navires-usines)** nm factory ship.

navrant, e [navʀɑ̃, ɑ̃t] adj **1.** [attristant - spectacle] distressing, upsetting, harrowing / *tu es navrant !* you're pathetic ou hopeless! / *sa bêtise est navrante* he's hopelessly stupid **2.** [regrettable] : *c'est navrant, mais il n'y a rien à faire* it's a terrible shame, but there's nothing we can do.

navré, e [navʀe] adj sorry / *je suis navré de vous l'entendre dire* I'm so sorry to hear you say that.

navrer [3] [navʀe] vt to upset, to distress, to sadden.

naze [naz] *tfam* = **nase**.

nazi, e [nazi] adj & nm, f Nazi.

nazisme [nazism] nm Nazism.

NDLR (abr écrite de **note de la rédaction**) Ed.

ne [nə] *(devant voyelle ou « h » muet n')* adv

A. AVEC UN MOT NÉGATIF ▸ **je n'ai rien vu** I saw nothing, I didn't see anything / *ce n'est ni bleu ni vert* it's neither blue nor green ▸ **ne… jamais** : *il ne répond jamais au téléphone* he never answers the phone ▸ **ne… plus** : *le téléphone ne marche plus* the telephone doesn't work any more ▸ **ne… pas** : *ne le dérange pas !* don't disturb him!

B. AVEC « QUE » ▸ *je n'ai pas que cette idée-là* that's not the only idea I have / *tu ne sais dire que des mensonges* all you ever do is tell lies.

C. EMPLOYÉ SEUL **1.** *sout* [avec une valeur négative] : *il ne cesse de m'appeler* he won't stop calling me / *quel père n'aiderait son fils ?* what father would refuse to help his son? / *prenez garde qu'on ne vous voie* be careful (that) nobody sees you / *que ne ferais-je pour vous ?* what wouldn't I do for you? **2.** *sout* [avec une valeur explétive] ▸ **je crains qu'il n'accepte** I'm afraid he might say yes / *évite qu'il ne te rencontre* try to avoid meeting him / *il se porte mieux que je ne croyais* he's better than I'd imagined.

né, e [ne] ◆ pp ⟶ **naître**. ◆ adj born ▸ **Clara Brown, née Moore** Clara Brown, née ou nee Moore ▸ *c'est une musicienne née* she's a born musician, she was born (to be) a musician.

néanmoins [neɑ̃mwɛ̃] adv nevertheless, nonetheless.

néant [neɑ̃] nm **1.** [non-être] nothingness / *une voix sortie du néant* a voice that seemed to come from nowhere **2.** [superficialité] vacuousness **3.** ADMIN ▸ **enfants : néant** children: none.

Nebraska [nebraska] npr m ▸ **le Nebraska** Nebraska ▸ **au Nebraska** in Nebraska.

nébuleux, euse [nebylø, øz] adj *fig* [obscur] obscure, nebulous. ◆ **nébuleuse** nf ASTRON nebula.

nécessaire [neseseʀ] ◆ adj **1.** [indispensable] necessary ▸ **si (c'est) nécessaire** if necessary, if need be / *est-il nécessaire de la mettre* ou *qu'elle soit au courant ?* does she have ou need to know? **2.** [requis - aptitude] necessary, requisite. ◆ nm **1.** [choses indispensables] bare necessities / *n'emportez que le strict nécessaire* just take the basic essentials ou what's absolutely necessary **2.** [démarche requise] : *ne vous inquiétez pas, j'ai fait le nécessaire* don't worry, I've taken care of things ou I've done what had to be done **3.** [trousse, étui] ▸ **nécessaire à couture** needlework basket ▸ **nécessaire à ongles** manicure set ▸ **nécessaire de voyage** grip, travel ou overnight bag UK.

nécessairement [neseseʀmɑ̃] adv **1.** [inévitablement] necessarily, unavoidably, inevitably **2.** [obligatoirement] necessarily, of necessity *sout* ▸ **pas nécessairement** not necessarily / *il y a nécessairement une explication à tout cela* there must be an explanation for all this.

nécessité [nesesite] nf **1.** [caractère nécessaire] necessity, need / *elle ne voit pas la nécessité de se marier* she doesn't see any need to get married ▸ **être dans la nécessité de** to find it necessary to, to have no choice but to ; [chose indispensable] necessity ▸ **de première nécessité a)** [dépenses, fournitures] basic **b)** [objets, denrées] essential **2.** *vieilli* [indigence] destitution, poverty ▸ **être dans la nécessité** to be in need. ◆ **nécessités** nfpl : *des nécessités financières nous obligent à…* we are financially bound to… ◆ **par nécessité** loc adv of necessity, necessarily, unavoidably / *on dut par nécessité vendre la moto* there was no choice but to sell the motorbike.

nécessiter [nesesite] vt to require, to demand.

nec plus ultra [nɛkplyzyltʀa] nm inv last word, ultimate / *le nec plus ultra des cuisines intégrées* the last word in built-in kitchens.

nécrologie [nekʀɔlɔʒi] nf **1.** [notice biographique] obituary **2.** [rubrique] obituary column.

nécrologique [nekʀɔlɔʒik] adj obituary *(modif)*.

nectar [nɛktaʀ] nm [gén] nectar.

nectarine [nɛktaʀin] nf nectarine.

néerlandais, e [neɛʀlɑ̃dɛ, ɛz] adj Dutch. ◆ **Néerlandais, e** nm, f Dutchman (Dutchwoman) ▸ **les Néerlandais** the Dutch. ◆ **néerlandais** nm LING Dutch.

nef [nɛf] nf ARCHIT nave ▸ **nef latérale** (side) aisle.

néfaste [nefast] adj [nuisible] harmful, noxious / *une influence néfaste* a bad influence.

négatif, ive [negatif, iv] adj **1.** [réponse, attitude] negative **2.** ÉLECTR, LING & MÉD negative **3.** MATH ▸ **un nombre négatif** a negative ou minus number. ❖ **négatif** nm PHOT negative. ❖ **négative** nf : *répondre par la négative* to give a negative answer, to answer in the negative.

négation [negasjɔ̃] nf **1.** [gén & PHILOS] negation **2.** GRAM negative (form).

négationniste [negasjɔnist] adj negationist.

négativement [negativmɑ̃] adv negatively / *ils ont répondu négativement* they said no.

négligé, e [neɡliʒe] adj [tenue, personne] sloppy, scruffy, slovenly ; [coiffure] unkempt, untidy. ❖ **négligé** nm **1.** [débraillé, laisser-aller] scruffiness, slovenly ou untidy appearance **2.** [robe d'intérieur] negligee, négligé.

négligeable [neɡliʒabl] adj [somme] trifling ; [détail] unimportant, trifling ; [différence] negligible, insignificant / *elle a une influence non négligeable sur lui* she has a not inconsiderable influence over him.

négligemment [neɡliʒamɑ̃] adv **1.** [sans soin] negligently, carelessly **2.** [avec nonchalance] negligently, casually.

négligence [neɡliʒɑ̃s] nf **1.** [manque de soin] negligence, carelessness **2.** [manque d'attention] negligence, neglect ; [oubli] oversight / *l'erreur est due à une négligence de ma secrétaire* the error is due to an oversight on the part of my secretary **3.** DR ▸ **négligence criminelle** criminal negligence.

négligent, e [neɡliʒɑ̃, ɑ̃t] adj **1.** [non consciencieux] negligent, careless, neglectful **2.** [nonchalant] negligent, casual, nonchalant.

négliger [17] [neɡliʒe] vt **1.** [se désintéresser de - études, santé, ami] to neglect **2.** [dédaigner] to disregard ; [élément, détail] to overlook, to disregard / *il ne faut rien négliger* you mustn't leave anything to chance **3.** [omettre] to neglect / *les enquêteurs n'ont rien négligé pour retrouver l'assassin* the police left no stone unturned in their efforts to find the murderer. ❖ **se négliger** vpi **1.** [être mal habillé] to be careless about ou to neglect one's appearance **2.** [se désintéresser de sa santé] to be neglectful of ou to neglect one's health.

négoce [neɡɔs] nm *sout* [activité] business, trade, trading.

négociable [neɡɔsjabl] adj negotiable ▸ **non négociable** non-negotiable.

négociant, e [neɡɔsjɑ̃, ɑ̃t] nm, f **1.** [commerçant] merchant, trader **2.** [grossiste] wholesaler.

négociateur, trice [neɡɔsjatœʀ, tʀis] nm, f COMM & POL negotiator.

négociation [neɡɔsjasjɔ̃] nf negotiation ▸ **négociations salariales** wage bargaining.

négocier [9] [neɡɔsje] ❖ vt **1.** COMM, FIN & POL to negotiate **2.** AUTO ▸ **négocier un virage** to negotiate a bend. ❖ vi to negotiate.

nègre, négresse [nɛɡʀ, neɡʀɛs] nm, f Negro, Negress (note: the terms "nègre" and "négresse", like their English equivalents, are considered racist in most contexts). ❖ **nègre** nm [écrivain] ghost (writer).

négrier nm **1.** [marchand d'esclaves] slave trader, slaver **2.** péj [employeur] slave driver.

neige [nɛʒ] nf **1.** MÉTÉOR snow ▸ **neige fondue a)** [pluie] sleet **b)** [boue] slush ▸ **les neiges éternelles** permanent snow ▸ **pneu neige** snow tyre **2.** CHIM ▸ **neige carbonique** dry ice **3.** CULIN : *battez les blancs en neige* whisk the whites until they form peaks / *œufs en neige* stiffly-beaten egg whites. ▸ **à la neige** loc adv fam LOISIRS on a skiing holiday 🇬🇧 ou vacation 🇺🇸.

neiger [23] [neʒe] v impers ▸ **il neige** it's snowing.

nem [nɛm] nm CULIN (Vietnamese) small spring roll.

nénuphar, nénufar* [nenyfaʀ] nm water lily.

néo-calédonien, enne (mpl néo-calédoniens, fpl néo-calédoniennes), **néocalédonien*, enne** [neɔkaledɔ̃njɛ̃, ɛn] adj New Caledonian. ❖ **Néo-Calédonien, enne, Néocalédonien*, enne** nm, f New Caledonian.

néocolonialiste [neɔkɔlɔnjalist] ◆ adj neocolonial, neocolonialist. ◆ nmf neocolonialist.

néofasciste [neɔfaʃist] adj & nmf neofascist.

néologisme [neɔlɔʒism] nm LING & PSYCHOL neologism.

néon [neɔ̃] nm **1.** [gaz] neon **2.** [éclairage] neon (lighting) ; [lampe] neon (lamp).

néonazi, e [neɔnazi] adj & nm, f neo-Nazi.

néophyte [neɔfit] nmf [nouvel adepte] neophyte, novice.

néo-zélandais, e (mpl néo-zélandais, fpl néo-zélandaises), **néozélandais*, e** [neɔzelɑ̃dɛ, ɛz] adj from New Zealand. ❖ **Néo-Zélandais, e, Néozélandais*, e** nm, f New Zealander.

Népal [nepal] npr m ▸ **le Népal** Nepal.

népalais, e [nepalɛ, ɛz] adj Nepalese, Nepali. ❖ **Népalais, e** nm, f Nepalese (person), Nepali.

nerf [nɛʀ] nm **1.** ANAT nerve ▸ **avoir les nerfs à fleur de peau** ou **à vif** to be a bundle of nerves ▸ **avoir les nerfs solides** ou **des nerfs d'acier** to have nerves of steel ▸ **être sur les nerfs** to be worked up ▸ **ne passe pas tes nerfs sur moi** fam don't take it out on me ▸ **porter** fam ou **taper** fam **sur les nerfs de qqn** to get on sb's nerves **2.** (toujours au sg) [énergie] : *elle manque de nerf pour diriger l'entreprise* she hasn't got what it takes to run the company ▸ **allez, du nerf !** come on, put some effort into it! **3.** [tendon] piece of gristle.

nerveusement [nɛʀvøzmɑ̃] adv **1.** MÉD nervously / *elle est fatiguée nerveusement* she's suffering from nervous exhaustion **2.** [de façon agitée] nervously, restlessly ; [avec impatience] nervously, impatiently.

nerveux, euse [nɛʀvø, øz] ◆ adj **1.** ANAT & MÉD [système, dépression, maladie] nervous ; [centre, influx] nerve (modif) **2.** [énervé - de nature] nervous, highly-strung ; [- passagèrement] on edge / *tu me rends nerveux* you're making me nervous **3.** [toux, rire] nervous **4.** [énergique - cheval] spirited, vigorous ; [- voiture] responsive ; [- style] energetic, forceful, vigorous **5.** [dur - viande] gristly, stringy. ◆ nm, f nervous ou highly-strung person.

nervosité [nɛʀvozite] nf **1.** [excitation - passagère] nervousness, tension, agitation ; [- permanente] nervousness / *la nervosité du candidat* the candidate's uneasiness **2.** [vigueur] responsiveness.

nervure [nɛʀvyʀ] nf BOT vein, nervure.

n'est-ce pas [nɛspa] loc adv [sollicitant l'acquiescement] : *vous savez, n'est-ce pas, ce qu'il en est* you know what the situation is, don't you? / *n'est-ce pas qu'ils sont mignons ?* aren't they cute ou sweet?

net, nette [nɛt] adj **1.** [nettoyé] clean, neat ; [ordonné] (clean and) tidy, neat (and tidy) **2.** [pur - peau, vin] clear **3.** [bien défini] clear / *la cassure est nette* the break is clean ▸ **une réponse nette** a straight answer ▸ **un refus net** a flat refusal / *j'ai la nette impression que...* I have the distinct ou clear impression that... ; [évident] distinct, definite, striking / *il y a une nette amélioration* there's a marked improvement **4.** PHOT sharp ▸ **l'image n'est pas nette** the picture isn't very clear **5.** COMM & FIN net ▸ **net d'impôt** tax-free ▸ **revenu net** net income **6.** fam 〔EXPR〕 *ce mec n'est pas net* **a)** [suspect] there's something shifty ou shady about that guy **b)** [fou] that guy's a bit funny ou weird. ❖ **net** adv **1.** [brutalement] ▸ **s'arrêter net** to stop dead ▸ **être tué net** to be killed outright **2.** [sans mentir] frankly, plainly ; [sans tergiverser] frankly, bluntly / *je vous le dis tout*

* In reformed spelling (see p. 16-18).

net I'm telling you straight **3.** COMM & FIN net. **⤸ au net** loc adv **▶ mettre qqch au net** to make a fair copy of sthg / *après mise au net (du texte)* after tidying up (the text).

Net [nɛt] nm **▶ le Net** the Net.

netéconomie [nɛtekɔnomi] nf net economy.

nettement [nɛtmã] adv **1.** [distinctement] clearly, distinctly **2.** [avec franchise] clearly, frankly, bluntly **3.** [beaucoup] definitely, markedly / *il est nettement plus fort que Paul* he's much stronger than Paul / *j'aurais nettement préféré ne pas y être* I would definitely have preferred not to be there.

netteté [nɛtte] nf **1.** [propreté] cleanness, cleanliness **2.** [clarté] clearness, clarity **3.** [précision - de l'écriture] neatness, clearness ; [- d'une image, d'un contour] sharpness, clearness.

nettoyage [netwajaʒ] nm **1.** [d'une maison, d'un vêtement] cleaning **▶ nettoyage de peau** skin cleansing **▶ nettoyage de printemps** spring-cleaning **▶ nettoyage à sec a)** [sur une étiquette] 'dry clean only' **▶ entreprise de nettoyage** cleaning firm **▶ produits de nettoyage** cleaning agents **▶ faire le nettoyage par le vide** to make a clean sweep **2.** *fam & fig* [d'un quartier, d'une ville] clean-up.

nettoyant [netwajã] nm [gén] cleaning product, cleanser ; [détachant] stain remover.

nettoyer [13] [netwaje] vt **1.** [rendre propre - gén] to clean ; [- plaie] to clean, to cleanse / *nettoyer une maison à fond* to spring-clean a house **▶ nettoyer à sec** to dry-clean **2.** [enlever - tache] to remove **3.** *fam* [vider] to clean out (sép) / *je me suis fait nettoyer au poker* I got cleaned out at poker.

nettoyeur, euse [netwajœR,øz] nm, f [employé] cleaner. **⤸ nettoyeur** nm ᴏᵁᴱᴮᴇᴄ dry cleaner's.

neuf[1] [nœf] **◆ dét 1.** nine **2.** [dans des séries] **▶ Charles IX** Charles the Ninth. **◆** nm inv nine. **Voir aussi** **cinq.**

neuf[2], **neuve** [nœf, nœv] *(devant an, heure et homme* [nœv]*)* adj **1.** [n'ayant jamais servi] new **▶ flambant neuf** brand-new **2.** [récemment créé - pays] new, young **3.** [original - point de vue, idée] new, fresh, original **▶ porter un regard neuf sur qqn / qqch** to take a fresh look at sb / sthg. **⤸ neuf** nm **1.** [objets nouveaux] : *ici, on vend du neuf et de l'occasion* here we sell both new and second-hand items **2.** [informations nouvelles] **▶ qu'est-ce qu'il y a de** ou **quoi de neuf ?** what's new? / *rien de neuf depuis la dernière fois* nothing new since last time. **⤸ à neuf** loc adv : *j'ai remis* ou *refait la maison à neuf* I did up the house like new.

neuneu [nønø] *(pl neuneus)* fam **◆** adj stupid, dumb fam. **◆** nmf idiot, dummy fam.

neuroleptique [nøʀɔleptik] adj & nm neuroleptic.

neurologie [nøʀɔlɔʒi] nf neurology.

neurologique [nøʀɔlɔʒik] adj neurologic, neurological.

neurologiste [nøʀɔlɔʒist], **neurologue** [nøʀɔlɔg] nmf neurologist.

neurone [nøʀɔn] nm neuron, neurone.

neutralisation [nøtralizasjɔ̃] nf [gén] neutralization.

neutraliser [3] [nøtralize] vt **1.** [annuler] to neutralize, to cancel out *(sép)* **2.** [maîtriser] to overpower, to bring under control / *les agents ont neutralisé le forcené* the police overpowered the maniac **3.** [bloquer] to close **4.** POL [déclarer neutre] to neutralize **5.** CHIM, ÉLECTR, LING & MÉD to neutralize.

neutralité [nøtralite] nf [d'une attitude] neutrality.

neutre [nøtʀ] **◆** adj **1.** [couleur, décor, attitude, pays] neutral **▶ rester neutre** : *je veux rester neutre* I don't want

to take sides **2.** CHIM, ÉLECTR & PHYS neutral **3.** LING & ZOOL neuter. **◆** nm **1.** LING neuter **2.** ÉLECTR neutral (wire).

neutron [nøtʀɔ̃] nm neutron.

neuve [nœv] f **⟶ neuf.**

neuvième [nœvjɛm] **◆** adj num ord ninth. **◆** nmf ninth / *elle est la neuvième de la classe* she's ninth in the class. **◆** nf ÉDUC third form ᵁᴷ ou grade ᵁˢ *(in French primary school).* **◆** nm ninth. **Voir aussi** **cinquième.**

neveu [nəvø] nm nephew.

névralgie [nevralʒi] nf neuralgia / *avoir une névralgie* [un mal de tête] to have a headache.

névralgique [nevralʒik] adj **1.** MÉD neuralgic **2.** *fig* **⟶ point.**

névrose [nevʀoz] nf neurosis.

névrosé, e [nevʀoze] adj & nm, f neurotic.

news [njuz] nmpl news / *quelles sont les news ?* what's new? / *voilà les dernières news* that's the latest news.

New York [nujɔʀk] npr **1.** [ville] New York (City) **2.** [état] New York State.

new-yorkais, e [nujɔʀkɛ, ɛz] *(mpl new-yorkais, fpl new-yorkaises)* adj from New York. **⤸ New-Yorkais, e** nm, f New Yorker.

nez [ne] nm **1.** ANAT nose / *avoir le nez qui coule* to have a runny nose **2.** [jugement] flair *(U)*, good judgment *(U)*, intuition *(U)* **▶ avoir du nez** to have good judgment / *il a du nez pour acheter des antiquités* he's got a flair for buying antiques **3.** [flair d'un chien] nose **4.** ŒNOL nose **5.** ᴇˣᴾᴿ **avoir le nez dans qqch** : *il a toujours le nez dans une BD* he's always got his nose buried in a comic **▶ montrer (le bout de) son nez** to show one's face, to put in an appearance **▶ fermer / claquer la porte au nez à qqn** to shut / to slam the door in sb's face **▶ avoir le nez sur qqch**, **être sous le nez de qqn** : *tu as le nez dessus !, il est sous ton nez !* it's right under your nose! **▶ passer sous le nez de qqn** : *le dernier billet m'est passé sous le nez* I just missed the last ticket **▶ se trouver nez à nez avec qqn** to find o.s. face to face with sb **▶ avoir qqn dans le nez** *fam* : *ce type, je l'ai dans le nez* that guy gets right up my nose ᵁᴷ, I can't stand that guy **▶ se voir comme le nez au milieu de la figure** : *ça se voit comme le nez au milieu de la figure* it's as plain as the nose on your face **▶ se manger** ou **se bouffer** *fam* **le nez** to be at each other's throats **▶ mettre le nez quelque part** : *elle ne met jamais le nez ici* she never shows her face in here / *je n'ai pas mis le nez dehors depuis une semaine* I haven't put my nose outside the door for a week **▶ mettre** ou **fourrer son nez dans les affaires de qqn** *fam* to poke ou to stick one's nose in sb's business **▶ mettre à qqn le nez dans son caca** *tfam* ou **sa merde** *vulg* : *je lui mettre le nez dans son caca* ou *sa merde, moi !* I'm going to rub his nose right in it! **▶ à plein nez** loc adv *fam* : *ça sent le fromage à plein nez* there's a strong smell of cheese.

NF (abr de **Norme française**) nf *label indicating compliance with official French standards* ; ≃ BS ᵁᴷ ; ≃ US standard ᵁˢ.

ni [ni] conj nor / *il ne veut pas qu'on l'appelle, ni même qu'on lui écrive* he doesn't want anyone to phone him or even to write to him / *il est sorti sans pull ni écharpe* he went out without either his jumper or his scarf. **⤸ ni... ni** loc corrélative neither… nor **▶ ni lui ni moi** neither of us / *ni l'un ni l'autre n'est tout à fait innocent* neither (one) of them is completely innocent / *il n'a répondu ni oui ni non* he didn't say yes and he didn't say no / *il n'est ni plus sot, ni plus paresseux qu'un autre* he's no more silly or lazy than the next man **▶ ni vu ni connu** without anybody noticing.

niais, e [njɛ, njɛz] ◆ adj [sot] simple, simple-minded, inane. ◆ nm, f *sout* simpleton, halfwit.

niaiserie [njɛzʀi] nf **1.** [caractère] simpleness, inanity, foolishness **2.** [parole] stupid ou inane remark / *cesse de raconter des niaiseries* stop talking such silly nonsense.

niaiseux, euse [njɛzø, øz] nm, f Québec idiot.

niaque, gnaque [njak] nf *fam* determination / *les joueurs ont manqué de niaque* the players lacked drive ▶ **avoir la niaque** to be determined to succeed / *toute l'équipe a la niaque* the whole team is determined to win.

Nicaragua [nikaʀagwa] npr m ▶ **le Nicaragua** Nicaragua.

nicaraguayen, enne [nikaʀagwejɛ̃, ɛn] adj Nicaraguan. ◆ **Nicaraguayen, enne** nm, f Nicaraguan.

niche [niʃ] nf **1.** [pour chien] kennel UK, doghouse US **2.** [renfoncement] niche, (small) alcove **3.** ÉCON niche ▶ **marché de niche** niche market.

nicher [3] [niʃe] vi **1.** [faire son nid] to nest **2.** *fam* [habiter] to hang out, to doss UK. ◆ **se nicher** vpi **1.** [faire son nid] to nest **2.** [se blottir] to nestle.

nichons [niʃɔ̃] nmpl *tfam* tits, boobs.

nickel [nikɛl] ◆ nm nickel. ◆ adj inv *fam* : *c'est nickel chez toi !* your house is so spick-and-span ou spotless!

niçois, e [niswa, az] adj from Nice.

nicotine [nikɔtin] nf nicotine.

nid [ni] nm **1.** [d'oiseau, de guêpes, etc.] nest **2.** *fig* [habitation] (little) nest **3.** [repaire] : *un nid d'espions* a spy hideout, a den of spies. ◆ **nid d'aigle** nm *pr* eyrie, eagle's nest ; *fig* eyrie.

nid-de-poule [nidpul] (*pl* **nids-de-poule**) nm pothole.

nièce [njɛs] nf niece.

nième [enjɛm] adj = **énième**.

nier [9] [nje] ◆ vt **1.** [démentir] to deny / *il nie l'avoir tuée* he denies that he killed her, he denies killing her **2.** [rejeter, refuser] to deny. ◆ vi : *il continue de nier* he continues to deny it.

nigaud, e [nigo, od] ◆ adj simple, simple-minded, stupid. ◆ nm, f simpleton, halfwit / *quel nigaud !* what an idiot!

Niger [niʒɛʀ] npr m [État] ▶ **le Niger** Niger.

Nigeria [niʒeʀja] npr m ▶ **le Nigeria** Nigeria.

nigérian, e [niʒeʀjɑ̃, an] adj Nigerian. ◆ **Nigérian, e** nm, f Nigerian.

nigérien, enne [niʒeʀjɛ̃, ɛn] adj Nigerien, Nigerian.

night-club [najtklœb] (*pl* **night-clubs**) nm nightclub.

Nil [nil] npr m ▶ **le Nil** the Nile.

n'importe [nɛ̃pɔʀt] loc adv [indique l'indétermination] : *quel pull mets-tu ? — n'importe* which pullover are you going to wear? — any of them ou I don't mind. ◆ **n'importe comment** loc adv **1.** [sans soin] any old how **2.** [de toute façon] anyway, anyhow. ◆ **n'importe lequel, n'importe laquelle** pron indéf any ▶ **n'importe lequel d'entre eux** any (one) of them / *tu veux le rouge ou le vert ? — n'importe lequel* do you want the red one or the green one? — either ou I don't mind. ◆ **n'importe où** loc adv anywhere / *ne laisse pas traîner tes affaires n'importe où* don't leave your things just anywhere. ◆ **n'importe quand** loc adv anytime / *il peut arriver n'importe quand* he could come at any time ou moment. ◆ **n'importe quel, n'importe quelle** adj indéf any / *n'importe quel débutant sait ça* any beginner knows that. ◆ **n'importe qui** pron indéf anybody, anyone / *ce n'est pas n'importe qui !* *fam* she's not just anybody! / *demande à n'importe qui dans la rue* ask the first person you meet in the street. ◆ **n'importe quoi**

pron indéf anything / *il ferait n'importe quoi pour obtenir le rôle* he'd do anything ou he would go to any lengths to get the part / *tu dis vraiment n'importe quoi !* you're talking absolute nonsense!

nippon, one ou **onne** [nipɔ̃, ɔn] adj Japanese.

niquer [3] [nike] vt **1.** *vulg* [sexuellement] to fuck, to screw **2.** *tfam* [rouler] to con, to have **3.** *fam* [abîmer] to bugger, to knacker.

nirvana [niʀvana] nm Nirvana.

nitrate [nitʀat] nm nitrate.

nitroglycérine [nitʀɔɡliseʀin] nf nitroglycerin, nitroglycerine.

niveau, x [nivo] nm **1.** [hauteur] level / *fixer les étagères au même niveau que la cheminée* put up the shelves level with ou on the same level as the mantelpiece **2.** [étage] level, storey **3.** [degré] level / *la décision a été prise au plus haut niveau* the decision was made at the highest level ▶ **niveau social** social level ▶ **niveau de langue** LING register **4.** [étape] level, stage **5.** [qualité] level, standard / *son niveau scolaire est-il bon ?* is she doing well at school? / *j'ai un bon niveau / un niveau moyen en russe* I'm good / average at Russian / *les élèves sont tous du même niveau* the pupils are all on a par ou on the same level ▶ **remettre à niveau** to bring up to standard ▶ **niveau de vie** standard of living **6.** GÉOGR level ▶ **niveau de la mer** sea level **7.** [instrument] level (tube) ▶ **niveau d'eau** water level. ◆ **au niveau** ◆ loc adj up to standard, of the required level. ◆ loc adv ▶ **se mettre au niveau** to catch up. ◆ **au niveau de** loc prép **1.** [dans l'espace] : *au niveau de la mer* at sea level / *l'eau lui arrivait au niveau du genou* the water came up to his knees / *j'habite à peu près au niveau de l'église* I live by the church **2.** [dans une hiérarchie] on a par with, at the level of / *ce problème sera traité au niveau du syndicat* this problem will be dealt with at union level. ◆ **de niveau** loc adj level / *les deux terrains ne sont pas de niveau* the two plots of land are not level (with each other).

niveler [24] [nivle] vt **1.** [aplanir] to level (off) (*sép*) **2.** *fig* [égaliser] to level (off) (*sép*), to even out (*sép*) ▶ **niveler par le bas** to level down, to dumb donwn.

🖉 In reformed spelling (see p. 16-18), this verb is conjugated like *acheter* : *il nivèle, elle nivèlera.*

nivellement, nivèlement* [nivɛlmɑ̃] nm **1.** [aplanissement] evening out, levelling UK ou leveling US (out) ou off **2.** *fig* [égalisation] equalizing, levelling UK, leveling US / *le nivellement par le bas de la télévision* dumbing down television.

Nobel [nɔbɛl] npr m : *le Nobel de la paix* the Nobel peace prizewinner.

noble [nɔbl] ◆ adj **1.** [de haute naissance] noble **2.** *fig* noble / *un geste noble* a noble deed. ◆ nmf noble, nobleman (noblewoman) ▶ **les nobles** the nobility.

noblesse [nɔblɛs] nf **1.** [condition sociale] nobleness, nobility ▶ **noblesse terrienne** landed gentry ▶ **la petite noblesse** the gentry **2.** [générosité] nobleness, nobility / *par noblesse de cœur / d'esprit* through the nobleness of his heart / spirit.

noce [nɔs] nf **1.** [fête] wedding ▶ **ne pas être à la noce** *fam* : *il n'était pas à la noce* he felt far from comfortable ▶ **faire la noce** *fam* to live it up **2.** [ensemble des invités] : *regarder passer la noce* to watch the wedding procession go by. ◆ **noces** nfpl wedding / *elle l'a épousé en troisièmes noces* he was her third husband ▶ **noces d'argent / de diamant / d'or** silver / diamond / golden wedding (anniversary). ◆ **de noces** loc adj wedding (*modif*).

nocif, ive [nɔsif, iv] adj noxious, harmful.

nocivité [nɔsivite] nf noxiousness, harmfulness.

noctambule [nɔktɑ̃byl] nmf night owl.

nocturne [nɔktyʀn] ◆ adj **1.** [gén] nocturnal, night *(modif)* **2.** BOT & ZOOL nocturnal. ◆ nf **1.** SPORT evening fixture 🇬🇧 ou meet 🇺🇸 **2.** COMM late-night closing / *le magasin fait nocturne* ou *ouvre en nocturne le jeudi* the shop stays open late on Thursdays ▶ **nocturne le mardi** late-night opening: Tuesday.

Noël [nɔɛl] nm **1.** [fête] Christmas ▶ **joyeux Noël !** Merry Christmas! ▶ **la veille de Noël** Christmas Eve **2.** [période] Christmas time.

nœud [nø] nm **1.** [lien] knot / *faire un nœud* to tie ou to make a knot / *faire un nœud de cravate* to knot ou to tie a tie ▶ **nœud coulant** slipknot, running knot **2.** [étoffe nouée] bow ▶ **nœud papillon** ou **pap** *fam* bow tie **3.** NAUT [vitesse] knot **4.** [point crucial] crux / *le nœud du problème* the crux ou heart of the problem **5.** TRAV PUB ▶ **nœud ferroviaire** rail junction ▶ **nœud routier** interchange.

noir, e [nwaʀ] adj **1.** [gén] black ▶ **noir de monde** *fig* teeming with people **2.** [sale] black, dirty, grimy **3.** [obscur] black, dark / *un ciel noir* a dark ou leaden sky **4.** [maléfique] black / *il m'a regardé d'un œil noir* he gave me a black look ▶ **de noirs desseins** dark intentions **5.** [pessimiste] black, gloomy, sombre 🇬🇧, somber 🇺🇸 **6.** [extrême] ▶ **saisi d'une colère noire** livid with rage / *être dans une misère noire* to live in abject poverty. ◆ **Noir, e** nm, f Black, Black man (woman) ▶ **les Noirs** (the) Blacks ▶ **Noir américain** African American. ❖ **noir** ◆ nm **1.** [couleur] black / *se mettre du noir aux yeux* to put on eyeliner / *une photo* | *un film en noir et blanc* a black and white photo / film 🇬🇧 ou movie 🇺🇸 **2.** [saleté] dirt, grime / *tu as du noir sur la joue* you've got a black mark on your face **3.** [obscurité] darkness ▶ **dans le noir** in the dark, in darkness / *avoir peur dans le noir* to be afraid ou scared of the dark **4.** fam [café] (black) coffee. ◆ adv dark / *il fait noir de bonne heure* it gets dark early. ❖ **noire** nf MUS crotchet 🇬🇧, quarter note 🇺🇸. ❖ **au noir** ◆ loc adj ▶ **travail au noir** a) undeclared work b) [en plus de l'activité principale] moonlighting. ◆ loc adv [illégalement] : *je l'ai eu au noir* I got it on the black market ▶ **travailler au noir** a) to do undeclared work b) [en plus de l'activité principale] to moonlight. ❖ **en noir** loc adv **1.** [colorié, teint] black **2.** *fig* ▶ **voir tout en noir** to look on the dark side of things.

noirâtre [nwaʀɑtʀ] adj blackish.

noiraud, e [nwaʀo, od] adj dark, dark-skinned, swarthy.

noirceur [nwaʀsœʀ] nf **1.** [couleur noire] blackness, darkness **2.** *litt* [d'un acte, d'un dessein] blackness, wickedness.

noircir [32] [nwaʀsiʀ] ◆ vt **1.** [rendre noir] to blacken / *noirci par le charbon* blackened with coal **2.** [dramatiser] ▶ **noircir la situation** to make the situation out to be darker ou blacker than it is. ◆ vi to go black, to darken / *le ciel noircit à l'horizon* the sky is darkening on the horizon.

noise [nwaz] nf ▶ **chercher noise** ou **des noises à qqn** to try to pick a quarrel with sb.

noisetier [nwaztje] nm hazel, hazelnut tree.

noisette [nwazɛt] ◆ nf **1.** BOT hazelnut **2.** [petite portion] ▶ **une noisette de beurre** a knob of butter. ◆ adj inv hazel *(modif)*.

noix [nwa] nf **1.** BOT walnut ▶ **noix du Brésil** Brazil nut ▶ **noix de cajou** cashew (nut) ▶ **noix de coco** coconut ▶ **noix (de) muscade** nutmeg **2.** CULIN ▶ **noix de veau** cushion of veal, noix de veau **3.** [petite quantité] ▶ **une noix de beurre** a knob of butter. ❖ **à la noix (de coco)** loc adj fam lousy, crummy / *toi et tes idées à la noix (de coco) !* you and your lousy ideas!

noliser [3] [nɔlize] vt 🇶🇨 [avion, navire] to charter.

nom [nɔ̃] nm **1.** [patronyme] name ; [prénom] (Christian) ou first name ▶ **quelqu'un du nom de** ou **qui a pour nom Kregg vous demande** someone called Kregg ou someone by the name of Kregg is asking for you / *je n'arrive pas à mettre un nom sur son visage* I can't put a name to her (face) / *je la connais de nom* I (only) know her by name ▶ **en son** / **mon** / **ton nom** in his / my / your name, on his / my / your behalf ▶ **nom de baptême** Christian ou first name, given name 🇺🇸 ▶ **nom d'emprunt** assumed name ▶ **nom de famille** surname ▶ **nom de jeune fille** maiden name ▶ **nom de guerre** nom de guerre, alias ▶ **traiter** ou **appeler qqn de tous les noms d'oiseaux** to call sb all the names under the sun ▶ **nom de plume** nom de plume, pen name ▶ **nom de scène** stage name ▶ **se faire un nom** to make a name for o.s. **2.** [appellation - d'une rue, d'un animal, d'un objet, d'une fonction] name / *il n'est roi que de nom* he is king in name only ▶ **cruauté** / **douleur sans nom** unspeakable cruelty / pain ▶ **nom de lieu** place name ▶ **nom commercial** ou **de marque** trade name ▶ **nom déposé** trademark ▶ **nom de fichier** filename ▶ **appeler** ou **nommer les choses par leur nom** to call things by their names, to call a spade a spade **3.** GRAM & LING noun ▶ **nom commun** common noun ▶ **nom composé** compound (noun) ▶ **nom propre** proper noun ou name **4.** ᴇxᴘʀ **nom de Dieu** *tfam*: *nom de Dieu, les voilà !* bloody hell 🇬🇧 ou goddam 🇺🇸, here they come! / *je t'avais pourtant dit de ne pas y toucher, nom de Dieu !* *tfam* for Christ's sake, I did tell you not to touch it! ▶ **nom d'un chien** ou **d'une pipe** ou **de Zeus** ou **d'un petit bonhomme !** *fam* good heavens! ❖ **au nom de** loc prép in the name of / *au nom de la loi, je vous arrête* I arrest you in the name of the law / *au nom de notre longue amitié* for the sake of our long friendship / *au nom de toute l'équipe* on behalf of the whole team.

nomade [nɔmad] ◆ adj [peuple] nomad, nomadic. ◆ nmf nomad.

nombre [nɔ̃bʀ] nm **1.** MATH [gén] number ; [de 0 à 9] number, figure ▶ **nombre entier** whole number, integer ▶ **nombre premier** prime (number) **2.** [quantité] number / *inférieur* / *supérieur en nombre* inferior / superior in number ou numbers / *nous ne sommes pas en nombre suffisant* there aren't enough of us / *je te l'ai déjà dit (un) bon nombre de fois* I've already told you several times ▶ **un grand nombre de** a lot of, a great number of, a great many / *le plus grand nombre d'entre eux a accepté* the majority of them accepted **3.** [masse] numbers ▶ **vaincre par le nombre** to win by sheer weight ou force of numbers / *dans le nombre, il y en aura bien un pour te raccompagner* there's bound to be one of them who will take you home ▶ **faire nombre** : *tous ceux-là n'ont été invités que pour faire nombre* those people over there have just been invited to make up the numbers **4.** ASTRON & PHYS number **5.** GRAM number. ❖ **au nombre de** loc prép : *les invités sont au nombre de cent* there are a hundred guests / *tu peux me compter au nombre des participants* you can count me among the participants, you can count me in. ❖ **du nombre de** loc prép amongst / *étiez-vous du nombre des invités ?* were you amongst ou one of those invited?

nombreux, euse [nɔ̃bʀø, øz] adj **1.** [comportant beaucoup d'éléments] : *une foule nombreuse* a large ou huge crowd **2.** [en grand nombre] many, numerous / *ils étaient peu nombreux* there weren't many of them / *nombreux sont ceux qui croient que...* many people believe that... / *avoir de nombreux clients* to have a great number of ou many ou numerous customers / *les étudiants sont plus nombreux qu'avant* there are more students than before / *les fumeurs sont de moins en moins nombreux* there are fewer and fewer smokers, the number of smokers is decreasing / *nous espérons que vous viendrez nombreux* we hope that a large number of you will come.

nombril [nɔ̃bʀil] nm **1.** ANAT navel **2.** *fam* EXPR> **se prendre pour le nombril du monde** : *il se prend pour le nombril du monde* he thinks he's the centre of the universe.

nombrilisme [nɔ̃bʀilism] nm navel-gazing, self-centredness.

nomenclature [nɔmãklatyʀ] nf [liste - gén] list ; [- d'un dictionnaire] word list.

nominal, e, aux [nɔminal, o] adj **1.** [sans vrai pouvoir] nominal ▸ *j'assume les fonctions purement nominales de recteur* I'm the rector in title only **2.** [par le nom] of names, nominal *sout* ▸ **appel nominal** roll call **3.** GRAM nominal ; [en grammaire transformationnelle] noun *(modif)*.

nominatif, ive [nɔminatif, iv] adj **1.** [contenant les noms] ▸ **liste nominative** nominative list of names **2.** [ticket, carte] non-transferable.

nomination [nɔminasjɔ̃] nf **1.** [à un poste] appointment, nomination ▸ *elle a obtenu* ou *reçu sa nomination au poste de directrice* she was appointed (to the post of) manager **2.** [pour un prix, une récompense] nomination.

nominé, e [nɔmine] nm, f nominee.

nommé, e [nɔme] ◆ adj [appelé] named. ◆ nm, f : *elle fréquente un nommé Paul* she's going out with a man called Paul. ◈ **à point nommé** *loc adv* [au bon moment] (just) at the right moment ou time ; [au moment prévu] at the appointed time.

nommément [nɔmemã] adv **1.** [par le nom - citer, féliciter] by name **2.** [spécialement] especially, notably, in particular.

nommer [3] [nɔme] vt **1.** [citer] to name, to list / *ceux qui sont responsables, pour ne pas les nommer, devront payer* those who are responsible and who shall remain nameless, will have to pay / *c'est la faute de Nina, pour ne pas la nommer* without mentioning any names, it's Nina's fault **2.** [prénommer] to name, to call ; [dénommer] to name, to call, to term **3.** [désigner à une fonction] to appoint / *être nommé à Paris* to be appointed to a post in Paris. ◈ **se nommer** *vpi* to be called ou named / *comment se nomme-t-il ?* what's his name?, what's he called?

non [nɔ̃] ◆ adv **1.** [en réponse négative] : *veux-tu venir ? non* do you want to come? — no! ▸ **non merci !** no, thank you! ▸ **mais non !** no!, absolutely not! / *oh que non !* definitely not!, certainly not! ▸ **ah ça non !** definitely not! / *non, non et non !* no, no and no again! **2.** [pour annoncer ou renforcer la négation] no / *non, je ne veux pas y aller* no, I don't want to go there **3.** [dans un tour elliptique] : *que tu le veuilles ou non* whether you like it or not **4.** [comme complément du verbe] : *il me semble que non* I think not, I don't think so ▸ **il a fait signe que non a)** [de la main] he made a gesture of refusal **b)** [de la tête] he shook his head **5.** [en corrélation avec 'pas'] ▸ **non pas** not / *il l'a fait par gentillesse et non (pas) par intérêt* he did it out of kindness and not out of self-interest **6.** [n'est-ce pas] : *il devait prendre une semaine de vacances, non ?* he was supposed to take a week's holiday 🇬🇧 ou vacation 🇺🇸, wasn't he? / *j'ai le droit de dire ce que je pense, non ?* I am entitled to say what I think, am I not? *sout* ou aren't I? **7.** [emploi expressif] : *non ! pas possible !* no ou never! I don't believe it! / *non mais celui-là, pour qui il se prend ?* who on earth does he think he is? **8.** [devant un nom, un adjectif, un participe] : *un bagage non réclamé* an unclaimed piece of luggage / *il a bénéficié d'une aide non négligeable* he received not insubstantial help. ◆ nm inv [réponse] no / *les non de la majorité* the majority no votes *(modif)*.

non-agression [nɔnagʀesjɔ̃] nf non-aggression.

non-alcoolisé, e [nɔnalkɔlize] adj non-alcoholic.

non(-)aligné, e [nɔnaliɲe] adj nonaligned.

nonante [nɔnãt] dét *régional* ninety.

non-assistance [nɔnasistãs] nf ▸ **non-assistance à personne en danger** failure to assist a person in danger.

nonchalance [nɔ̃ʃalãs] nf [indifférence, insouciance] nonchalance ; [lenteur] listlessness.

nonchalant, e [nɔ̃ʃalã, ãt] adj [insouciant] nonchalant ; [lent] listless.

non(-)combattant, e [nɔ̃kɔbatã, ãt] adj & nm, f noncombatant.

non(-)conformiste [nɔ̃kɔ̃fɔʀmist] adj & nmf [original] nonconformist.

non(-)croyant, e [nɔ̃kʀwajã, ãt] nm, f unbeliever.

non-dit [nɔ̃di] nm : *il y avait trop de non-dits dans notre famille* too much was left unsaid in our family.

non-droit [nɔ̃dʀwa] nm : *ce quartier est une zone de non-droit* the district is a no-go area.

non-fumeur, euse [nɔ̃fymœʀ, øz] nm, f nonsmoker ▸ **compartiment non-fumeurs** nonsmoking ou no smoking compartment.

non-intervention [nɔ̃ɛ̃tɛʀvãsjɔ̃] nf nonintervention.

non-lieu [nɔ̃ljø] *(pl* non-lieux) nm : *il a bénéficié d'un non-lieu* charges against him were dismissed.

non-paiement [nɔ̃pɛmã] nm nonpayment, failure to pay.

non-prolifération [nɔ̃pʀolifeʀasjɔ̃] nf nonproliferation.

non-résident [nɔ̃ʀezidã] nm foreign national, nonresident.

non-respect [nɔ̃ʀɛspɛ] nm failure to respect.

non-sens [nɔ̃sãs] nm inv **1.** [absurdité] nonsense **2.** LING meaningless word or phrase *(in a translation)*.

non-stop [nɔnstɔp] adj inv nonstop.

non-violence [nɔ̃vjɔlãs] nf nonviolence.

non-voyant, e [nɔ̃vwajã, ãt] nm, f visually impaired person.

nord [nɔʀ] ◆ nm inv **1.** [point cardinal] north / *le vent vient du nord* it's a north ou northerly wind, the wind is coming from the north / *nous allons vers le nord* we're heading north ou northwards ▸ **la cuisine est en plein nord** ou **exposée au nord** the kitchen faces due north **2.** [partie d'un pays, d'un continent] north ▸ **le nord de l'Italie** northern Italy / **les gens du nord** (the) Northerners. ◆ adj inv [septentrional] north *(modif)*, northern. ◈ **Nord** ◆ adj inv North. ◆ npr m GÉOGR ▸ **le Nord** the North ▸ **le grand Nord** the Far North ▸ **la mer du Nord** the North Sea. ◈ **au nord de** *loc prép* (to the) north of. ◈ **du nord** *loc adj* north *(modif)*.

nord-africain, e [nɔʀafʀikɛ̃, ɛn] *(mpl* nord-africains, *fpl* nord-africaines) adj North African. ◈ **Nord-Africain, e** nm, f North African.

nord-américain, e [nɔʀameʀikɛ̃, ɛn] *(mpl* nord-américains, *fpl* nord-américaines) adj North American. ◈ **Nord-Américain, e** nm, f North American.

nord-coréen, enne [nɔʀkɔʀeɛ̃, ɛn] *(mpl* nord-coréens, *fpl* nord-coréennes) adj North Korean. ◈ **Nord-Coréen, enne** nm, f North Korean.

nord-est [nɔʀɛst] nm inv & adj inv northeast.

nordicité [nɔʀdisite] nf QUÉBEC northerliness.

nordique [nɔʀdik] adj [pays, peuple] Nordic ; [langue] Nordic, Scandinavian.

nord-ouest [nɔʀwɛst] nm inv & adj inv northwest.

normal, e, aux [nɔʀmal, o] adj **1.** [ordinaire - vie, personne] normal ; [- taille] normal, standard ; [- accouchement, procédure] normal, straightforward / *la situation est redevenue normale* the situation is back to normal ▸ **ce n'est pas normal** : *la lampe ne s'allume pas, ce n'est pas nor-*

mal the light isn't coming on, there's something wrong (with it) **2.** [habituel] normal, usual / *elle n'était pas dans son état normal* she wasn't her normal self / *en temps normal* in normal circumstances, normally **3.** [compréhensible] normal, natural / *mais c'est bien normal, voyons* it's only natural, don't worry about it / *ce n'est pas normal* that's not right **4.** *fam* [mentalement] normal. ❖ **normale** *nf* **1.** [situation] normal (situation) / *un retour à la normale* a return to normal **2.** GÉOM normal **3.** MÉTÉOR normal **4.** [moyenne] average / *intelligence supérieure à la normale* above average intelligence **5.** ENS ▶ **Normale (Sup)** *fam* nickname of the **École normale Supérieure 6.** GOLF par.

⚠ Attention, l'adjectif anglais **normal** ne peut être employé pour traduire normal au sens de « compréhensible ».

normalement [nɔrmalmɑ̃] *adv* **1.** [de façon ordinaire] normally **2.** [sauf changement] if all goes well **3.** [habituellement] normally, usually, generally.

⚠ Attention, lorsque normalement signifie « sauf changement », il ne doit pas être traduit par **normally**.

normalien, enne [nɔrmaljɛ̃, ɛn] *nm, f* [de l'École normale supérieure] student at the École Normale Supérieure ; [ancien de l'École normale supérieure] graduate of the École Normale Supérieure.

normalisation [nɔrmalizasjɔ̃] *nf* **1.** [d'un produit] standardization **2.** [d'une situation] normalization / *jusqu'à la normalisation de la situation* until the situation becomes normal.

normaliser [3] [nɔrmalize] *vt* **1.** [produit] to standardize **2.** [rapport, situation] to normalize. ❖ **se normaliser** *vpi* to get back to normal.

normalité [nɔrmalite] *nf* normality, normalcy US.

normand, e [nɔrmɑ̃, ɑ̃d] *adj* **1.** [de Normandie] Normandy *(modif)* / *je suis normand* I'm from Normandy **2.** HIST Norman. ❖ **Normand, e** *nm, f* [en France] Norman.

Normandie [nɔrmɑ̃di] *npr f* ▶ **la Normandie** Normandy.

normatif, ive [nɔrmatif, iv] *adj* normative.

norme [nɔrm] *nf* **1.** INDUST norm, standard / *produit conforme aux normes de fabrication* product conforming to manufacturing standards ▶ **normes de sécurité** safety standards **2.** [règle] : *rester dans la norme* to keep within the norm.

Norvège [nɔrvɛʒ] *npr f* ▶ **la Norvège** Norway.

norvégien, enne [nɔrveʒjɛ̃, ɛn] *adj* Norwegian. ❖ **Norvégien, enne** *nm, f* Norwegian.

nos [no] *pl* ⟶ **notre**.

nosocomial, e, aux [nozɔkɔmjal, nozɔkɔmjo] *adj* nosocomial, contracted in hospital.

nostalgie [nɔstalʒi] *nf* [regret] nostalgia ▶ **avoir la nostalgie de** to feel nostalgic about.

nostalgique [nɔstalʒik] *adj* nostalgic.

notable [nɔtabl] ◆ *adj* [fait] notable ; [différence] appreciable, noticeable. ◆ *nm* notable.

notaire [nɔtɛr] *nmf* [qui reçoit actes et contrats] notary (public), lawyer ; [qui surveille les transactions immobilières] lawyer, solicitor UK.

notamment [nɔtamɑ̃] *adv* especially, in particular, notably.

notation [nɔtasjɔ̃] *nf* **1.** ▶ **la notation d'un devoir** marking UK ou grading US ou correcting homework **2.** FIN ▶ **notation financière** credit ratings, rating **3.** CHIM, DANSE, LING, MATH & MUS notation.

note [nɔt] *nf* **1.** MUS [son] note ; [touche] key ▶ **faire une fausse note a)** MUS [pianiste] to hit a wrong note ou key **b)** [violoniste] to play a wrong note **c)** [chanteur] to sing a wrong note ▶ **donner la note a)** MUS to give the keynote **b)** *fig* to give the lead ▶ **être dans la note** to hit just the right note *fig* **2.** [annotation] note / *prendre des notes* to take ou to make notes ▶ **note de** ou **en bas de page** footnote ▶ **prendre bonne note de qqch** to take good note of sthg **3.** [communication] ▶ **note de service** memo, memorandum **4.** ENS mark UK, grade US / *avoir la meilleure note* to get the best ou highest ou top mark **5.** [nuance] note, touch, hint / *avec une note de tristesse dans la voix* with a note ou hint of sadness in his voice **6.** [facture] bill, check US ▶ **la note, s'il vous plaît !** may I have the bill, please? ▶ **note de frais** [à remplir] expense ou expenses claim (form) ▶ **note d'honoraires** invoice *(for work done by a self-employed person)*.

noter [3] [nɔte] *vt* **1.** [prendre en note] to note ou to write (down) / *veuillez noter notre nouvelle adresse* please note ou make a note of our new address **2.** [faire ressortir - gén] to mark ; [- en cochant] to tick ; [- en surlignant] to highlight **3.** [remarquer] to note, to notice / *notez que je ne dis rien* please note that I'm making no comment / *je ne veux pas que tu recommences, c'est noté ?* fam I don't want you to do it again, do you understand ou have you got that ou is that clear? / *notez bien, il a fait des progrès* mind you, he's improved **4.** [évaluer] to mark UK, to grade US ; ENS [élève] to give a mark to UK, to grade US ; [devoir, examen] to mark UK, to grade US *(en usage absolu)* ▶ **noter sur 20** to mark UK ou grade US out of 20 / *elle note généreusement / sévèrement* she gives high / low marks UK ou grades.

notice [nɔtis] *nf* **1.** [résumé] note ▶ **notice bibliographique** bibliographical details **2.** [instructions] ▶ **notice explicative** ou **d'emploi** directions for use ▶ **notice de fonctionnement** instructions.

⚠ Attention à ne pas traduire notice par le mot anglais **notice** qui n'a pas les mêmes sens.

notification [nɔtifikasjɔ̃] *nf* [avis] notification.

notifier [9] [nɔtifje] *vt* to notify / *on vient de lui notifier son renvoi* he's just received notice of his dismissal, he's just been notified of his dismissal.

notion [nɔsjɔ̃] *nf* [idée] notion / *perdre la notion du temps* to lose all notion ou sense of time. ❖ **notions** *nfpl* [rudiments] ▶ **notions de base** basics, basic knowledge / **'anglais : notions'** [sur un CV] 'basic knowledge of English' ; [comme titre d'ouvrage] primer.

notoire [nɔtwar] *adj* recognized ▶ **le fait est notoire** it's an acknowledged ou accepted fact ▶ **un criminel notoire** a notorious criminal.

notoirement [nɔtwarmɑ̃] *adv* : *ses ressources sont notoirement insuffisantes* it's widely known that she has limited means / *notoirement connu* for notorious for.

notoriété [nɔtɔrjete] *nf* [renommée] fame, renown / *sa thèse lui a valu une grande notoriété* ou *a fait sa notoriété* his thesis made him famous / *il est de notoriété publique que...* it's public ou common knowledge that...

notre [nɔtr] *(pl* **nos** [no]*) dét (adj poss)* **1.** [indiquant la possession] our ▶ **un de nos amis** a friend of ours, one of our friends / *notre fils et notre fille* our son and daughter **2.** RELIG ▶ **Notre Père** Our Father **3.** [se rapportant au 'nous' de majesté ou de modestie] : *car tel est notre bon plaisir* for such is our pleasure **4.** [emploi expressif] our / *comment se porte notre petit malade ?* how's our little invalid, then?

nôtre [notʀ] dét *(adj poss) sout* ours / *l'objectif que je considère comme nôtre* the aim which I consider to be ours. ❖ **le nôtre, la nôtre** (*pl* les nôtres) pron poss ours / *amenez vos enfants, les nôtres ont le même âge* bring your children, ours are the same age ; *(emploi nominal)* ▸ **les nôtres** our family and friends / *serez-vous des nôtres demain soir ?* will you be joining us tomorrow evening?

nouer [6] [nwe] vt **1.** [attacher ensemble - lacets, cordes] to tie ou to knot (together) **2.** [faire un nœud à] to tie (up), to knot / *laisse-moi nouer ta cravate* let me knot your tie / *elle noua ses cheveux avec un ruban* she tied her hair back ou up with a ribbon ▸ **la peur lui nouait la gorge / les entrailles** *fig* his throat / stomach tightened with fear **3.** [établir] ▸ **nouer des relations avec qqn** to enter into a relationship with sb. ❖ **se nouer** ❖ vp *(emploi passif)* [ceinture] to fasten, to do up. ❖ vpi **1.** [s'entrelacer] to intertwine **2.** [s'instaurer] to develop, to build up / *c'est à cet âge que beaucoup d'amitiés se nouent* it's at that age that a lot of friendships are made.

noueux, euse [nwø, øz] adj **1.** [tronc, bois] knotty, gnarled **2.** [doigt] gnarled.

nougat [nuga] nm CULIN nougat.

nouille [nuj] nf **1.** CULIN noodle **2.** *fam* [nigaud] nitwit, dumbo ; [mollasson] drip, wimp. ❖ **nouilles** nfpl pasta *(U)*.

nounou [nunu] nf *fam* nanny.

nounours [nunuʀs] nm *fam* teddy (bear).

nourri, e [nuʀi] adj **1.** [dense - fusillade] sustained, heavy **2.** [ininterrompu - applaudissements] prolonged, sustained.

nourrice [nuʀis] nf [qui garde] nanny, childminder 🇬🇧, nurse 🇺🇸, nursemaid 🇺🇸.

nourrir [32] [nuʀiʀ] vt **1.** [alimenter] to feed, to nourish *sout* ▸ **nourrir un bébé au sein / au biberon / à la cuillère** to breast-feed / to bottle-feed / to spoon-feed a baby ▸ **être bien nourri** to be well-fed ▸ **être mal nourri** [sous-alimenté] to be undernourished **2.** [faire subsister] to feed / *j'ai trois enfants à nourrir* I've got three children to feed ou to provide for ▸ **(ne pas) nourrir son homme :** *la chanson / sculpture ça ne nourrit pas son homme* you can't live off singing / sculpture alone **3.** *litt* [espoir] to nourish ; [pensée] to entertain ; [illusion, rancœur] to harbour, to nurse, to nourish *sout* ; [haine] to feel, to harbour feelings of / *nourrir des doutes au sujet de* to entertain doubts ou to be doubtful about. ❖ **se nourrir** vp *(emploi réfléchi)* **1.** [s'alimenter] to feed (o.s.) / *il se nourrit mal* he doesn't feed himself ou eat properly / *elle ne se nourrit que de bananes* she eats only bananas **2.** *fig* : *se nourrir d'illusions* to revel in illusions.

nourrissant, e [nuʀisɑ̃, ɑ̃t] adj nourishing, nutritious.

nourrisson [nuʀisɔ̃] nm [bébé] baby, infant.

nourriture [nuʀityʀ] nf **1.** [alimentation] food ▸ **donner à qqn une nourriture saine** to provide sb with a healthy diet **2.** [aliment] food / *nourriture pour animaux* pet food.

nous [nu] ❖ pron pers *(1ère pers pl)* **1.** [sujet ou attribut d'un verbe] we / *toi et moi, nous comprenons* you and I understand ▸ **c'est nous qui déciderons** we are the ones who'll decide / *nous, nous restons* ou on reste *fam là* we are staying here / *nous autres médecins pensons que…* we doctors think that… **2.** [complément d'un verbe ou d'une préposition] us / *à nous six, on a fini la paella* between the six of us we finished the paella / *ces anoraks ne sont pas à nous* these anoraks aren't ours ou don't be-

long to us ▸ **chez nous** a) [dans notre foyer] at home, in our house b) [dans notre pays] at ou back home **3.** [sujet ou complément, représentant un seul locuteur] we / *dans notre thèse, nous traitons le problème sous deux aspects* in our thesis we deal with the problem in two ways / *alors, à nous, qu'est-ce qu'il nous fallait ?* [chez un commerçant] now, what can I do for you? ❖ pron réfléchi : *nous nous amusons beaucoup* we're having a great time, we're really enjoying ourselves. ❖ pron réciproque each other / *nous nous aimons* we love each other.

nous-mêmes [numɛm] pron pers ourselves.

nouveau, nouvelle [nuvo, nuvɛl] (*mpl* nouveaux [nuvo], *fpl* nouvelles [nuvɛl]) *(devant nm commençant par voyelle ou « h » muet* nouvel [nuvɛl]) adj **1.** [de fraîche date - appareil, modèle] new ; [- pays] new, young ▸ **c'est tout nouveau, ça vient de sortir** a) it's new, it's just come out b) *fig* that's a new one on me ▸ **nouveaux mariés** newlyweds, newly married couple ▸ **les nouveaux pauvres** the new poor ▸ **nouveau riche** nouveau riche ▸ **nouveau venu** newcomer ▸ **nouvelle venue** newcomer **2.** [dernier en date] new, latest ▸ **pommes de terre nouvelles** new potatoes ▸ **Nouvel An, nouvelle année** New Year ▸ **le Nouveau Monde** the New World **3.** [autre] further, new **4.** [original - découverte, idée] new, novel, original ▸ **porter un regard nouveau sur qqn / qqch** to take a fresh look at sb / sthg / *elle est mécontente — ce n'est pas nouveau !* she's not happy — there's nothing new about that! **5.** [inhabituel] new / *ce dossier est nouveau pour moi* this case is new to me, I'm new to this case **6.** [novateur] ▸ **nouvelle critique** new criticism ▸ **nouvelle cuisine** nouvelle cuisine. ❖ **nouveau, elle** nm, f [élève] new boy (girl) ; [adulte] new man (woman). ❖ **nouveau** nm : *rien de nouveau depuis la dernière fois* nothing new ou special since last time / *il y a eu du nouveau dans l'affaire Perron* there are new developments in the Perron case. ❖ **à nouveau** loc adv [encore] (once) again, once more / *recommence à nouveau* start again. ❖ **de nouveau** loc adv again, once again, once more.

Nouveau-Mexique [nuvomɛksik] npr m ▸ **le Nouveau-Mexique** New Mexico ▸ **au Nouveau-Mexique** in New Mexico.

nouveau-né, e [nuvone] (*mpl* nouveau-nés, *fpl* nouveau-nées) ❖ adj newborn *(modif)*. ❖ nm, f **1.** [bébé] newborn baby **2.** [appareil, technique] new arrival.

nouveauté [nuvote] nf **1.** [chose nouvelle] novelty, new thing ▸ **les nouveautés discographiques / littéraires** new releases / books / *le racisme a toujours existé, ce n'est pas une nouveauté* racism has always existed, there's nothing new ou recent about it **2.** [originalité] novelty, newness / *l'exposition a l'attrait de la nouveauté* the exhibition has novelty appeal **3.** COUT fashion / *nouveautés de printemps* new spring fashions.

nouvel [nuvɛl] m ⟶ nouveau.

nouvelle [nuvɛl] ❖ f ⟶ nouveau. ❖ nf **1.** [information] (piece of) news *(U)* ▸ **j'ai une bonne / mauvaise nouvelle pour toi** I have (some) good / bad news for you / *voici une excellente nouvelle !* this is good news! / *tu ne connais pas la nouvelle ? elle est renvoyée* haven't you heard (the news)? she's been fired ▸ **fausse nouvelle** false report ▸ **première nouvelle !** that's news to me! **2.** LITTÉR short story, novella. ❖ **nouvelles** nfpl **1.** [renseignements] news *(U)* / *je n'ai pas eu de ses nouvelles depuis* I haven't had any news from him ou heard from him since / *donne vite de tes nouvelles* write soon ▸ **prendre des nouvelles de qqn** to ask after sb / *j'ai eu de tes nouvelles par ta sœur* your sister told me how you were getting on ▸ **aller aux nouvelles** to go and find out what's (been) happening / *on est sans nouvelles des trois alpinistes* there's been no news of the three climbers ▶ **tu auras de mes nouvelles !** *fam*: *tu ferais mieux de signer, ou tu auras de mes nouvelles !* you'd better sign, or else! ▶ **pas de nouvelles, bonnes nouvelles** no news is good news **2.** RADIO & TV news *(U)* / *à quelle heure sont les nouvelles ?* when's the news on?

> 🏷️ Attention ! Le mot anglais news est singulier et indénombrable. Il est suivi d'un verbe au singulier et ne s'emploie jamais avec l'article indéfini a :
> **Les nouvelles ne sont pas bonnes.** *The news isn't very good.*
> **En voilà une bonne nouvelle !** *That's good news!*
> **Il m'a rapporté une nouvelle intéressante.** *He told me an interesting piece of news* ou *He told me some interesting news.*

Nouvelle-Calédonie [nuvɛlkaledɔni] npr f ▶ **la Nouvelle-Calédonie** New Caledonia.

Nouvelle-Écosse [nuvɛlekɔs] npr f ▶ **la Nouvelle-Écosse** Nova Scotia.

Nouvelle-Guinée [nuvɛlgine] npr f ▶ **la Nouvelle-Guinée** New Guinea.

nouvellement [nuvɛlmã] adv newly, recently, freshly.

Nouvelle-Orléans [nuvɛlɔrleã] npr ▶ **La Nouvelle-Orléans** New Orleans.

Nouvelle-Zélande [nuvɛlzelãd] npr f ▶ **la Nouvelle-Zélande** New Zealand.

novateur, trice [nɔvatœr, tris] adj innovative, innovatory.

novembre [nɔvãbr] nm November. **Voir aussi mars.**

novice [nɔvis] ◆ adj inexperienced, green ▶ **être novice dans** ou **en qqch** to be inexperienced in ou a novice at sthg. ◆ nmf [débutant] novice, beginner.

noyade [nwajad] nf **1.** [fait de se noyer] drowning *(U)* **2.** [accident] drowning *(C)* / *il y a eu beaucoup de noyades ici l'été dernier* many people (were) drowned here last summer.

noyau, x [nwajo] nm **1.** [de fruit] stone, pit 🇺🇸 / *noyau de cerise* / *pêche* cherry / peach stone **2.** [centre] nucleus ▶ **noyau familial** family nucleus **3.** [petit groupe] small group ▶ **le noyau dur** [d'un parti, de l'actionnariat] the hard core ▶ **noyau de résistance** pocket ou centre of resistance **4.** ANAT, ASTRON, BIOL & PHYS nucleus **5.** ÉLECTR, GÉOL & NUCL core.

noyauter [3] [nwajote] vt POL to infiltrate.

noyé, e [nwaje] ◆ pp **1.** [personne] drowned ▶ **mourir noyé** to drown **2.** [moteur] flooded **3.** *fig* : *les yeux noyés de larmes* his eyes bathed with tears / *être noyé dans la foule* to be lost in the crowd / *l'essentiel est noyé dans les détails* the essentials have been buried ou lost in a mass of detail. ◆ nm, f drowned person.

noyer² [13] [nwaje] vt **1.** [personne, animal] to drown ; [moteur, vallée] to flood ▶ **noyer son chagrin (dans l'alcool)** to drown one's sorrows (in drink) ▶ **noyer le poisson a)** PÊCHE to play the fish **b)** *fam & fig* ne cherche pas à noyer le poisson don't try to confuse the issue **2.** [faire disparaître] : *une épaisse brume noie la vallée* the valley is shrouded in fog. ◆ **se noyer** ◆ vp *(emploi réfléchi)* [se suicider] to drown o.s. ◆ vpi [accidentellement] to drown. ◆ **se noyer dans** vp + prép **1.** [se plonger dans] to bury ou to absorb o.s. in **2.** [s'empêtrer dans] to get tangled up ou bogged down ou trapped in / *vous vous noyez*

dans des considérations hors sujet you're getting tangled up in ou lost in a series of side issues ▶ **se noyer dans un verre d'eau** to make a mountain out of a molehill.

NRV SMS abr écrite de **énervé**.

NTIC (abr de **nouvelles technologies de l'information et de la communication**) nfpl (N)ICT.

nu, e [ny] adj **1.** [sans habits - personne] naked, nude ▶ **être nu** to be naked ou in the nude / *poser nu pour un photographe* to pose in the nude for a photographer ▶ **se mettre (tout) nu** to take off all one's clothes, to strip naked ▶ **être nu comme un ver** ou **la main** to be stark naked **2.** [découvert - partie du corps] ▶ **avoir les bras nus / fesses nues** to be barearmed / bare-bottomed / *se promener les jambes nues* to walk about bare-legged ou with bare legs ▶ **être pieds nus** to be barefoot ou barefooted ▶ **la tête nue** bareheaded ou without a hat on ▶ **mettez-vous torse nu** strip to the waist ▶ **à l'œil nu**: *ça ne se voit pas / ça se voit à l'œil nu* you can't / you can see it with the naked eye **3.** [dégarni - sabre] naked ; [-paysage] bare, empty ; [-mur] bare. ◆ **nu** nm ART nude. ◆ **à nu** ◆ loc adj bare ▶ **le fil est à nu a)** [accidentellement] the wire is bare **b)** [exprès] the wire has been stripped. ◆ loc adv ▶ **mettre à nu** to expose / *mettre un fil électrique à nu* to strip a wire / *mettre son cœur à nu* to bare one's soul.

nuage [nɥaʒ] nm **1.** MÉTÉOR cloud ▶ **ciel chargé de nuages** cloudy ou overcast sky / *nuage toxique / radioactif* toxic / radioactive cloud **2.** [menace, inquiétude] cloud / *il y a de gros nuages à l'horizon économique* the economic outlook is very gloomy ou bleak ; [rêverie] ▶ **être dans les nuages** to have one's head in the clouds, to be daydreaming **3.** [masse légère] : *un nuage de tulle* a mass ou swathe of tulle ; [petite quantité] ▶ **un nuage de lait** a drop of milk **4.** JOAILL cloud. ◆ **sans nuages** loc adj **1.** MÉTÉOR cloudless **2.** [amitié] untroubled, perfect ; [bonheur] unclouded, perfect.

nuageux, euse [nɥaʒø, øz] adj MÉTÉOR ▶ **ciel nuageux** cloudy ou overcast sky.

nuance [nɥãs] nf **1.** [différence - de couleur] shade, hue ; [- de son] nuance ▶ **nuance de sens** shade of meaning, nuance / *il y a une nuance entre indifférence et lâcheté* there's a (slight) difference between indifference and cowardice / *j'ai dit que je l'aimais bien et non que je l'aimais, nuance !* I said I liked him and not that I loved him, that's not the same thing! **2.** [subtilité] nuance, subtlety / *toutes les nuances de sa pensée* the many subtleties ou all the finer aspects of his thinking ▶ **personne / personnage tout en nuances** very subtle person / character **3.** [trace légère] touch, tinge / *il y avait une nuance d'amertume dans sa voix* there was a touch ou hint of bitterness in his voice.

nuancer [16] [nɥãse] vt **1.** [couleur] to shade **2.** [critique, jugement] to nuance, to qualify.

nucléaire [nykleɛr] ◆ adj BIOL, MIL & PHYS nuclear. ◆ nm [énergie] nuclear power ou energy ; [industrie] nuclear industry.

nudisme [nydism] nm nudism, naturism.

nudiste [nydist] ◆ adj nudist *(modif).* ◆ nmf nudist.

nudité [nydite] nf **1.** [d'une personne] nakedness, nudity **2.** [d'un lieu] bareness.

nuée [nɥe] nf [multitude] horde, host / *nuée de paparazzi / d'admirateurs* a horde of paparazzi / admirers ▶ **nuée d'insectes** horde ou swarm of insects.

nues [ny] nfpl ▶ **porter qqn / qqch aux nues** to praise sb / sthg to the skies ▶ **tomber des nues**: *nous sommes tombés des nues* we were flabbergasted ou dumbfounded.

nugget [nœgɛt] nm nugget.

nuire [97] [nɥiʀ] ❖ **nuire à** v + prép [être néfaste pour]
▸ **nuire à qqn** to harm ou to injure sb ▸ **nuire à qqch** to be
harmful to ou to damage ou to harm sthg. ❖ **se nuire**
vp *(emploi réfléchi)* to do o.s. harm.

nuisance [nɥizɑ̃s] nf (environmental) nuisance ▸ **nuisance sonore** noise pollution.

nuisette [nɥizɛt] nf short ou babydoll nightgown.

nuisible [nɥizibl] adj harmful ▸ **gaz / fumées nuisibles**
noxious gases / fumes. ❖ **nuisibles** nmpl ZOOL vermin,
pests.

nuit [nɥi] nf **1.** [obscurité] night *(U)*, dark, darkness ▸ **il
fait nuit** it's dark / **il fait nuit noire** it's pitch-dark ou
pitch-black / *la nuit tombe* it's getting dark, night is falling
sout / *rentrer avant la nuit* to get back before nightfall
ou dark / *à la nuit tombante* ou *à la tombée de la nuit*
at nightfall, at dusk ▸ **la nuit des temps** : *remonter à / se
perdre dans la nuit des temps* to go back to the dawn of /
to be lost in the mists of time **2.** [intervalle entre le coucher
et le lever du soleil] night, nighttime / *je dors la nuit* I sleep
at ou during the night ▸ **faire sa nuit** to sleep through the
night ▸ **bonne nuit !** goodnight! / *une nuit d'insomnie* a
sleepless night ▸ **la nuit de noces** the wedding night ▸ **la
nuit porte conseil** *prov* I'd / you'd, etc. better sleep on it
3. [dans des expressions de temps] ▸ **cette nuit** : *que s'est-il
passé cette nuit ?* what happened last night? ▸ **nous partons cette nuit** we're leaving tonight / *des nuits entières*
nights on end / *en pleine nuit* in the middle of the night /
il y a deux nuits the night before last ▸ **la nuit** : *l'émission
passe tard la nuit* the programme is on late at night, it's
a late-night programme / *dans la nuit de mardi à mercredi* during Tuesday night, during the night of Tuesday to
Wednesday ▸ **l'autre nuit** the other night / *stationnement
interdit nuit et jour* no parking day or night ▸ **toute la
nuit** all night (long), through the night **4.** [dans des noms
de dates] ▸ **la nuit de Noël** Christmas night ▸ **la nuit de
la Saint-Sylvestre** New Year's Eve night **5.** [nuitée] :
c'est combien la nuit ? how much is it for one night? /
la chambre est à 49 € la nuit rooms are 49 € a night.
❖ **de nuit** ◆ loc adj **1.** ZOOL ▸ **animaux / oiseaux de
nuit** nocturnal animals / birds **2.** [pharmacie] night *(modif)*, all-night *(avant nom)*, twenty-four hour *(avant nom)*
3. [qui a lieu la nuit] night *(modif)* / *aujourd'hui je suis
de nuit à l'hôpital* I'm on night-duty at the hospital tonight.
◆ loc adv : *travailler de nuit* to work nights ou the night
shift ou at night / *conduire de nuit* to drive at ou by night.
❖ **nuit blanche** nf sleepless night.

nuitée [nɥite] nf bed-night, person-night *spéc* / *le gérant
de l'hôtel nous a facturé deux nuitées* the hotel manager
charged us for two nights.

nul, nulle [nyl] ◆ adj **1.** [inexistant] nil, nonexistent
2. *fam* [très mauvais] useless, rubbish, hopeless / *être nul
en maths* to be hopeless ou useless at maths / *c'est vraiment nul de dire une chose pareille* what a pathetic thing
to say ▸ **t'es nul !** a) [mauvais] you're useless! b) [méchant]
you're pathetic! **3.** DR null ▸ **rendre nul** to nullify, to annul
4. SPORT nil / *le score est nul* the score is nil-nil ▸ **match
nul** draw 🇬🇧, tie. ◆ nm, f *fam* prat.

nul, nulle [nyl] *sout* ◆ dét *(adj indéf, avant le nom)*
no, not any / *nul autre que lui n'aurait pu y parvenir*
nobody (else) but he could have done it ▸ **sans nul doute**
undoubtedly, without any doubt. ◆ pron indéf no one,
nobody / *nul mieux que lui n'aurait su analyser la
situation* no one could have analyzed the situation better
than him ▸ **nul n'est parfait** nobody's perfect ▸ **nul n'est**

censé ignorer la loi ignorance of the law is no defence.
❖ **nulle part** loc adv nowhere, no place 🇺🇸 / *on ne l'a
trouvé nulle part* he was nowhere to be found.

nullement [nylmɑ̃] adv *litt* not at all, not in the least.

nullité [nylite] nf **1.** [manque de valeur] incompetence,
uselessness / *ce film est d'une parfaite nullité* this film is
really terrible **2.** [personne] incompetent, nonentity / *c'est
une nullité* he's useless **3.** DR nullity.

numéraire [nymeʀɛʀ] nm cash.

numéral, e, aux [nymeʀal, o] adj numeral.
❖ **numéral, aux** nm numeral.

numérique [nymeʀik] ◆ adj **1.** [gén] numerical **2.** INFORM
digital. ◆ nm ▸ **le numérique** digital technology.

numérisé, e [nymeʀize] adj digitalised.

numéro [nymeʀo] nm **1.** [nombre] number ▸ **numéro
de compte (bancaire)** account number ▸ **numéro d'immatriculation** registration number 🇬🇧, license number 🇺🇸
▸ **numéro de vol** flight number ▸ **le numéro un / deux
chinois** the Chinese number one / two / *le numéro un
du parti républicain* the leader of the Republican party
2. TÉLÉC ▸ **numéro (de téléphone)** TÉLÉC (telephone)
number / *faire un faux numéro* to dial a wrong number
▸ **numéro d'appel gratuit** ou **vert** ≃ Freefone number 🇬🇧 ;
≃ 800 ou toll-free number 🇺🇸 **3.** [habitation, place] number / *j'habite Rue Froment — à quel numéro ?* I live in
rue Froment — what number? **4.** [exemplaire] issue / *il
faudra chercher dans de vieux numéros* we'll have to
look through some back issues ou numbers **5.** MUS number ; [dans un spectacle] act, turn / *elle a fait son numéro
habituel* she went into her usual routine **6.** JEUX [nombre]
number / *un numéro gagnant* a winning number / *tirer le
bon / mauvais numéro* to pick the right / wrong number /
lui, il a tiré le bon numéro ! *fig* he's really picked a winner! **7.** [personne] : *quel numéro !* *fam* [hurluberlu] what
a character **8.** *(comme adj, après le nom)* : *le lot numéro 12*
lot 12.

numérologie [nymeʀɔlɔʒi] nf numerology.

numérotation [nymeʀɔtasjɔ̃] nf **1.** [attribution d'un
numéro] numbering **2.** TÉLÉC dialling ▸ **numérotation vocale** voice dialing.

numéroter [3] [nymeʀɔte] vt to number.

numerus clausus, numérus clausus* [nymeʀys-
klozys] nm numerus clausus.

nu-pieds [nypje] ◆ loc adv barefoot. ◆ nmpl sandals.

nuptial, e, aux [nypsjal, o] adj [de mariage] wedding
(modif) ▸ **robe nuptiale** wedding dress, bridal gown.

nuque [nyk] nf nape *(of the neck)* ▸ **saisir qqn par la
nuque** to grab sb by the scruff of the neck.

nurse [nœʀs] nf *vieilli* nanny, governess.

nursery [pl nurserys ou nurseries), **nurserie*** [nœʀ-
səʀi] nf nursery.

nutrithérapie [nytʀiteʀapi] nf nutritional therapy.

nutritif, ive [nytʀitif, iv] adj **1.** [nourrissant -aliment]
nourishing, nutritious **2.** [relatif à la nutrition] nutritive, nutritional ▸ **valeur nutritive** food ou nutritional value.

nutrition [nytʀisjɔ̃] nf PHYSIOL nutrition, feeding.

nutritionniste [nytʀisjɔnist] nmf nutritionist, dietary
expert.

Nylon® [nilɔ̃] nm nylon / *en* ou *de Nylon* nylon *(modif)*.

nymphe [nɛ̃f] nf MYTH nymph.

nymphomane [nɛ̃fɔman] adj f & nf nymphomaniac.

* In reformed spelling (see p. 16-18).

ô [o] interj *litt* oh, O.

oasis [ɔazis] nf oasis.

obédience [ɔbedjɑ̃s] nf [adhésion] allegiance.

obéir [32] [ɔbeiʀ] ❖ v + prép **1.** [se soumettre à] ▶ **obéir à qqn / qqch** to obey sb / sthg ▶ **savoir se faire obéir de qqn** to command ou to compel obedience from sb / *obéir à un ordre* to comply with ou to obey an order ; *(en usage absolu)* ▶ **vas-tu obéir ?** will you do as you're told! **2.** [être régi par] ▶ **obéir à qqch** to submit to ou to obey sthg / *obéir à une théorie* / *un principe* to obey ou to follow a theory / principle / *obéir à une impulsion* to follow an impulse.

obéissance [ɔbeisɑ̃s] nf **1.** [action d'obéir] obedience, submission / *obéissance à une règle* adherence to a rule **2.** [discipline] obedience.

obéissant, e [ɔbeisɑ̃, ɑ̃t] adj obedient.

obélisque [ɔbelisk] nm obelisk.

obèse [ɔbɛz] ◆ adj obese. ◆ nmf obese person.

obésité [ɔbezite] nf obesity, obeseness.

objecter [4] [ɔbʒɛkte] vt [opposer - un argument] ▶ **objecter qqch à qqn** to put sthg forward as an argument against sb / *on nous objectera le coût trop élevé de l'opération* they will object to the high cost of the operation.

objecteur [ɔbʒɛktœʀ] nm ▶ **objecteur de conscience** conscientious objector.

objectif, ive [ɔbʒɛktif, iv] adj **1.** [impartial] objective, unbiased **2.** [concret, observable] objective. ❖ **objectif** nm **1.** [but à atteindre] objective, goal, aim ; COMM [de croissance, de production] target / *se fixer / atteindre un objectif* to set o.s. / to reach an objective **2.** MIL [cible] target, objective **3.** OPT & PHOT lens, objective.

objection [ɔbʒɛksjɔ̃] nf **1.** [gén] objection / *faire* ou *soulever une objection* to make ou to raise an objection / *tu as* ou *tu y vois une objection ?* do you have any objection? **2.** DR : *objection accordée / refusée* objection sustained / overruled.

objectivement [ɔbʒɛktivmɑ̃] adv objectively.

objectivité [ɔbʒɛktivite] nf objectivity ▶ **en toute objectivité** (quite) objectively.

objet [ɔbʒɛ] nm **1.** [chose] object, item ▶ **objet sexuel** sex object ▶ **objets personnels** personal belongings ou effects ▶ **objets trouvés** lost property *(U)* ▶ **objets de valeur** valuables ▶ **objet volant non identifié** = OVNI ▶ **homme-objet** : *c'est un homme-objet* he's a sex object **2.** [thème] subject / *l'objet de leurs discussions était toujours la politique* politics was always the subject of their discussions **3.** [personne] object ; [raison] cause / *l'objet de sa curiosité / passion* the object of her curiosity / passion **4.** [but] object, purpose, aim / *exposer l'objet de sa visite* to explain the purpose of ou reason for one's visit ▶ **faire** ou

être l'objet de : *faire* ou *être l'objet de soins particuliers* to receive ou to be given special care / *faire l'objet d'une fouille corporelle* to be subjected to a body search ▶ **faire l'objet de controverses** to be a controversial subject / *faire l'objet de vives critiques* to be the object ou target of sharp criticism **5.** GRAM object **6.** DR matter / *l'objet de la plainte* the matter of the complaint. ❖ **sans objet** loc adj **1.** [sans but] aimless, pointless **2.** [non justifié] unjustified, groundless, unfounded.

obligation [ɔbligasjɔ̃] nf **1.** [contrainte] obligation ▶ **obligation de** : *je suis* ou *je me vois dans l'obligation de vous expulser* I'm obliged ou forced to evict you / *'sans obligation d'achat'* 'no purchase necessary' **2.** [devoir] obligation, duty, commitment / *mes obligations de président de la société* my duties as the chairman of the company ▶ **obligations familiales** family obligations ou commitments ▶ **obligations militaires** military obligations ou duties **3.** DR obligation / *faire honneur à ses obligations* to fulfil one's obligations, to carry out one's duties **4.** BOURSE & FIN bond, debenture ▶ **obligation hypothécaire** mortgage bond ▶ **obligation au porteur** bearer bond.

obligatoire [ɔbligatwaʀ] adj **1.** [exigé, imposé] compulsory, obligatory / *(le port de) la ceinture de sécurité est obligatoire* the wearing of seat belts is compulsory / *'tenue de soirée obligatoire'* 'formal dress required' **2.** [inéluctable] : *un jour ou l'autre ils en viendront aux mains, c'est obligatoire* one of these days they're bound to come to blows.

obligatoirement [ɔbligatwaʀmɑ̃] adv **1.** [par nécessité] : *il doit obligatoirement avoir la licence pour s'inscrire* he must have a degree to enrol / *nous devons obligatoirement fermer les portes à 20 h* we're obliged ou required to close the doors at 8 p.m **2.** *fam* [immanquablement] inevitably / *il va obligatoirement tout aller lui répéter* he's bound to go and tell her everything.

obligé, e [ɔbliʒe] adj **1.** [inévitable] : *c'était obligé !* *fam* it was bound to happen! **2.** [nécessaire - conséquence] necessary.

obligeance [ɔbliʒɑ̃s] nf *sout* ▶ **avoir l'obligeance de faire qqch** : *veuillez avoir l'obligeance de me répondre rapidement* please be so kind as to ou be kind enough to reply as quickly as possible.

obliger [17] [ɔbliʒe] vt **1.** [mettre dans la nécessité de] to oblige, to force ▶ **obliger qqn à faire qqch** to force sb to do sthg / *ne m'oblige pas à te punir* don't force me to ou don't make me punish you ▶ **être obligé de faire qqch** to be forced to do sthg, to have to do sthg ▶ **se croire obligé de** to feel obliged to ; *(en usage absolu)* : *irez-vous ? — bien obligé !* are you going? — I don't have any choice, do I? / *j'ai mis une cravate, réunion oblige* I had to wear a tie, what with the meeting and all **2.** [contraindre moralement ou juridiquement] : *la loi oblige les candidats à se* *soumettre à un test* applicants are legally required to take a test **3.** *sout* [faire plaisir à] to oblige / *vous m'obligeriez en venant* ou *si vous veniez* you would oblige me by coming, I would be obliged if you came. ❖ **s'obliger à** vp + prép **1.** [se forcer à] to force o.s. to **2.** [s'engager à] to commit o.s. to.

⚠ D'un registre plus soutenu, **to oblige** ne peut être utilisé systématiquement pour traduire obliger. Voir article.

oblique [ɔblik] ◆ adj [ligne] oblique ; [pluie, rayon] slanting ; [regard] sidelong. ◆ nf GÉOM oblique (line). ❖ **en oblique** loc adv diagonally.

obliquer [3] [ɔblike] vi to turn ou to veer off *(insép)* / *la route oblique à gauche* the road veers left.

oblitérer [18] [ɔblitere] vt [timbre] to postmark, to cancel ▸ **timbre oblitéré** used stamp.
  🖉 In reformed spelling (see p. 16-18), this verb is conjugated like *semer : il oblitèrera, elle oblitèrerait.*

obnubiler [3] [ɔbnybile] vt *sout* [obséder] to obsess / *être obnubilé par une idée* to be obsessed by an idea.

obole [ɔbɔl] nf [somme d'argent] (small) contribution ou donation / *chacun verse son obole* each person is making a contribution.

obscène [ɔpsɛn] adj [licencieux] obscene, lewd.

obscénité [ɔpsenite] nf **1.** [caractère licencieux] obscenity, lewdness **2.** [parole, geste] obscenity / *raconter* ou *dire des obscénités* to utter obscenities.

obscur, e [ɔpskyʀ] adj **1.** [sombre] dark / *une nuit obscure* a pitch-black night **2.** [incompréhensible] obscure, abstruse **3.** [indéfini] obscure, vague, indefinite / *un obscur pressentiment* a vague premonition **4.** [peu connu] obscure ▸ **une vie obscure** a modest existence.

obscurcir [32] [ɔpskyʀsiʀ] vt **1.** [priver de lumière] to darken, to make dark **2.** [rendre confus - discours, raisonnement] to make obscure / *le jugement obscurci par l'alcool* his judgement clouded ou obscured ou confused by drink. ❖ **s'obscurcir** vpi [ciel] to darken / *soudain, tout s'obscurcit et je m'évanouis* suddenly everything went dark ou black and I fainted.

obscurément [ɔpskyʀemɑ̃] adv obscurely, vaguely, dimly.

obscurité [ɔpskyʀite] nf **1.** [manque d'éclairage] dark, darkness ▸ **dans l'obscurité** in darkness, in the dark / *soudain, l'obscurité se fit dans la chambre* it suddenly became ou went dark in the room **2.** *litt* [anonymat] : *vivre / tomber dans l'obscurité* to live in / to fall into obscurity.

obsédant, e [ɔpsedɑ̃, ɑ̃t] adj [souvenir, musique] haunting, obsessive ; [besoin] obsessive.

obsédé, e [ɔpsede] nm, f **1.** [victime d'obsessions] obsessive ▸ **obsédé sexuel** sex maniac **2.** *fam* [fanatique] : *les obsédés de l'hygiène* hygiene freaks.

obséder [18] [ɔpsede] vt [suj : image, souvenir, peur] to haunt, to obsess / *obsédé par la pensée de la mort* obsessed ou gripped with the idea of death.
  🖉 In reformed spelling (see p. 16-18), this verb is conjugated like *semer : il obsèdera, elle obsèderait.*

obsèques [ɔpsɛk] nfpl funeral.

obséquieux, euse [ɔpsekjø, øz] adj obsequious.

observateur, trice [ɔpsɛʀvatœʀ, tʀis] ◆ adj [perspicace] observant / *avoir un esprit très observateur* to be very perceptive. ◆ nm, f **1.** [témoin] observer **2.** POL observer.

observation [ɔpsɛʀvasjɔ̃] nf **1.** [remarque] observation, remark, comment / *avez-vous des observations à faire*

sur ce premier cours ? do you have any comments to make about this first class? **2.** [critique] (piece of) criticism, critical remark / *je te prie de garder tes observations pour toi* please keep your remarks to yourself / *j'ai horreur qu'on me fasse des observations* I hate people criticizing me ou making remarks to me **3.** SCI [investigation, exposé] observation ; [exposé] observation ; [méthode d'étude] observation, observing ▸ **avoir l'esprit d'observation** to be observant **4.** MIL observation **5.** [observance] observance, observing, keeping **6.** MÉD [description] notes ; [surveillance] observation / *mettre un malade en observation* to put a patient under observation.

observatoire [ɔpsɛʀvatwaʀ] nm **1.** ASTRON & MÉTÉOR observatory **2.** MIL & *fig* observation ou lookout post **3.** ÉCON ▸ **observatoire économique** economic research institute.

observer [3] [ɔpsɛʀve] vt **1.** [examiner] to observe, to examine ; SCI to observe **2.** [surveiller] to watch, to keep a watch ou an eye on ▸ **observer qqn avec attention / du coin de l'œil** to watch sb attentively / out of the corner of one's eye **3.** [respecter - trêve] to observe ; [- accord] to observe, to respect, to abide by / *observer une minute de silence* to observe a minute's silence **4.** [constater] to observe, to notice, to note / *on observe un changement d'attitude chez les jeunes* there is a noticeable change in attitude amongst young people **5.** [dire] to observe, to remark / *tu ne portes plus d'alliance, observa-t-il* you're not wearing a wedding ring any more, he observed ou remarked / *je te ferai observer que tu t'es trompé* let me point out to you that you were wrong. ❖ **s'observer** ◆ vp *(emploi réciproque)* to observe ou to watch each other. ◆ vp *(emploi passif)* to be seen ou observed.

obsession [ɔpsesjɔ̃] nf **1.** [hantise] obsession / *il croit qu'on veut le tuer, c'est devenu une obsession* he believes people want to kill him, it's become a real obsession (with him) **2.** [idée fixe] obsession.

obsessionnel, elle [ɔpsesjɔnɛl] adj [répétitif] obsessive, obsessional.

obsolète [ɔpsɔlɛt] adj LING obsolete.

obstacle [ɔpstakl] nm **1.** [objet bloquant le passage] obstacle **2.** SPORT hurdle ; ÉQUIT fence **3.** [difficulté] obstacle, difficulty, problem / *buter sur un obstacle* to come up against an obstacle / *être un* ou *faire obstacle à* to be an obstacle to, to hinder, to impede.

obstétricien, enne [ɔpstetʀisjɛ̃, ɛn] nm, f obstetrician.

obstétrique [ɔpstetʀik] nf obstetrics (U).

obstination [ɔpstinasjɔ̃] nf **1.** [persévérance] persistence, perseverance **2.** [entêtement] obstinacy, obstinateness, stubbornness.

obstiné, e [ɔpstine] adj **1.** [entêté] obstinate, stubborn ; [persévérant] persevering, determined **2.** [assidu] obstinate / *un travail obstiné* unyielding ou obstinate work.

obstinément [ɔpstinemɑ̃] adv **1.** [avec entêtement] obstinately, stubbornly **2.** [avec persévérance] perseveringly, persistently.

obstiner [3] [ɔpstine] ❖ **s'obstiner** vpi to persist, to insist / *elle s'obstine à vouloir partir* she persists in wanting to leave ou insists on leaving.

obstruction [ɔpstʀyksjɔ̃] nf **1.** [obstacle] obstruction, blockage ; [blocage] obstruction, obstructing, blocking **2.** [action délibérée] ▸ **faire de l'obstruction a)** [gén] to be obstructive **b)** POL to obstruct (legislation) **c)** FOOT to obstruct.

obstructionnisme [ɔpstʀyksjɔnism] nm obstructionism.

obstructionniste [ɔpstʀyksjɔnist] adj & nmf obstructionist.

obstruer [3] [ɔpstʀye] vt [passage] to obstruct, to block. ❖ **s'obstruer** vpi to become blocked ou obstructed.

obtempérer [18] [ɔptɑ̃peʀe] ❖ **obtempérer à** v + prép [se soumettre à] to comply with *(insép)* / *obtempérer à un ordre* to obey an order ; *(en usage absolu)* : *le soldat s'empressa d'obtempérer* the soldier hurriedly obeyed.

📎 In reformed spelling (see p. 16-18), this verb is conjugated like semer : il obtempèrera, elle obtempèrerait.

obtenir [40] [ɔptəniʀ] vt **1.** [acquérir - baccalauréat, licence, note, point] to obtain, to get ; [- prix, nomination] to receive, to win, to get ; [- consentement] to get, to win ; [- prêt] to secure, to obtain, to get ; [- accord] to reach, to obtain, to get / *obtenir la garde d'un enfant* to get ou to win custody of a child / *obtenir le droit de vote* to win the right to vote, to get the vote / *j'ai enfin obtenu qu'elle mette ses gants pour sortir* I eventually got her to wear her gloves to go out **2.** [procurer] ▶ **obtenir qqch à qqn** to obtain ou to get ou to procure *sout* sthg for sb / *elle lui a obtenu une augmentation* she got him a raise **3.** [arriver à - résultat] to get, to obtain ; [- effet, succès] to achieve / *en divisant par deux on obtient 24* if you divide by two you get 24.

> ⚠ Attention, **to obtain**, d'un registre plus soutenu qu'obtenir, ne doit pas être employé systématiquement pour traduire ce verbe. Voir l'article pour des traductions plus naturelles, notamment à l'oral.

> 📋 **Obtenir qqch pour qqn** *Get sthg for sb* ou *get sb sthg.*
>
> Notez la construction à double complément qui en anglais peut prendre deux formes dont le sens est le même :
>
> • une structure identique à celle du français :
> verbe + COD + préposition + COI
> *get sthg for sb*
>
> • une structure qui diffère de celle du français, sans préposition, et dans laquelle l'ordre des compléments est inversé :
> verbe + COI + COD
> *get sb sthg*
>
> **Elle a obtenu une invitation pour Anne.** *She got an invitation for Anne* ou *She got Anne an invitation.*

obtention [ɔptɑ̃sjɔ̃] nf **1.** [acquisition] obtaining, getting **2.** [production] creation, production / *l'obtention d'un nouveau vaccin* the production of a new vaccine.

obturer [3] [ɔptyʀe] vt **1.** TECHNOL [boucher] to seal, to stop up *(sép)* **2.** MÉD to fill.

obtus, e [ɔpty, yz] adj **1.** MATH obtuse **2.** [borné] obtuse, dull, slow-witted.

obus [ɔby] nm ARM shell.

occasion [ɔkazjɔ̃] nf **1.** [circonstance favorable] opportunity, chance / *c'est l'occasion rêvée* it's an ideal opportunity ▶ *si l'occasion se présente* if the opportunity arises ▶ *laisser passer l'occasion* to let the opportunity slip (by) / *saisir l'occasion au vol, sauter sur l'occasion* to seize the opportunity, to jump at the chance ▶ *je le lui dirai à la première occasion* I'll tell him as soon as I get a chance ▶ *l'occasion de : ça te donnera l'occasion de la rencontrer* it'll give you the opportunity ou the chance to meet her ▶ *il a manqué*

ou **perdu** ou **raté une belle occasion de se taire** *fam* he could have kept his mouth shut **2.** [moment] occasion / *en plusieurs / maintes occasions* several / many times / *dans les grandes occasions* on big ou important ou special occasions **3.** [article non neuf] secondhand ou used item / *le marché de l'occasion* the secondhand market ; [affaire] bargain. ❖ **à l'occasion** loc adv **1.** [un de ces jours] one of these days **2.** [éventuellement] should the opportunity arise / *à l'occasion, passez nous voir* drop by some time ou if you get the chance. ❖ **à l'occasion de** loc prép on the occasion of, upon. ❖ **d'occasion** ◆ loc adj [non neuf] secondhand ▶ **voiture d'occasion** secondhand ou used car. ◆ loc adv [acheter, vendre] secondhand *(adv)* / *j'ai fini par le trouver d'occasion* in the end I found a secondhand one. ❖ **par la même occasion** loc adv at the same time.

> ⚠ Attention, le mot anglais **occasion** signifie une occasion au sens de « moment important ». Il ne peut être employé systématiquement pour traduire les autres sens du mot français occasion.

occasionnel, elle [ɔkazjɔnɛl] adj **1.** [irrégulier] casual, occasional **2.** [fortuit] chance *(avant nom)* ▶ **rencontre occasionnelle** chance meeting.

occasionner [3] [ɔkazjɔne] vt [causer] to cause, to bring about *(sép)*, to occasion *sout* ▶ **occasionner des ennuis à qqn** to cause trouble for sb, to get sb into trouble.

occident [ɔksidɑ̃] nm POL ▶ **l'Occident** the West, the Occident *sout*.

occidental, e, aux [ɔksidɑtal, o] adj **1.** GÉOGR west, western ▶ **Europe occidentale** Western Europe **2.** POL Western, Occidental *sout* ▶ **les pays occidentaux** Western countries. ❖ **Occidental, e, aux** nm, f POL Westerner, Occidental *sout*.

occidentaliser [3] [ɔksidɑtalize] ❖ **s'occidentaliser** vpi to become westernized.

occulte [ɔkylt] adj **1.** [surnaturel] occult **2.** [secret] occult, secret ▶ **financements occultes** secret ou mystery funding ▶ **fonds** ou **réserves occultes** slush funds.

occulter [3] [ɔkylte] vt [réalité, problème] to cover up *(sép)*, to hush up *(sép)*, to gloss over *(insép)* ; [sentiment, émotion] to deny / *votre récit occulte un détail essentiel* your story glosses over ou overlooks an essential detail.

occupant, e [ɔkypɑ̃, ɑ̃t] nm, f **1.** [d'un véhicule] occupant ; [d'un lieu] occupant, occupier **2.** MIL occupier, occupying force / *collaborer avec l'occupant* to collaborate with the occupying forces.

occupation [ɔkypasjɔ̃] nf **1.** [professionnelle] occupation, job ; [de loisirs] occupation **2.** ▶ **occupation des lieux** occupancy **3.** MIL occupation ▶ **les troupes d'occupation** the occupying troops **4.** HIST ▶ **l'Occupation** the (German) Occupation (of France).

> 🏛 **L'Occupation**
>
> The military occupation of part of France after the French-German armistice on 22nd June 1940, which spread throughout to the whole country in 1942. Under the terms of the armistice, France had to contribute financially to the upkeep of German troops in France and provide labour for German factories. Thousands of French Jews were deported during this period by the Vichy government.

occupé, e [ɔkype] adj **1.** [non disponible -ligne de téléphone] engaged 🇬🇧, busy 🇺🇸 ; [-toilettes] engaged 🇬🇧, occupied 🇺🇸 ▶ **ça sonne occupé** fam I'm getting the engaged tone 🇬🇧, the line is busy 🇺🇸 / **ces places sont occupées** these seats are taken **2.** MIL & POL occupied **3.** [personne] busy / **j'ai des journées très occupées** my days are full.

occuper [3] [ɔkype] vt **1.** [donner une activité à] ▶ **occuper qqn** to keep sb busy ou occupied ▶ **cela l'occupe beaucoup** it takes up a lot of his time / **la question qui nous occupe** the matter in hand **2.** [envahir] to occupy, to take over (sép) ▶ **occuper le terrain** MIL & fig to have the field **3.** [remplir - un espace, une durée] to take up (insép) / **le bar occupe le fond de la pièce / trop de place** the bar stands at the back of the room / takes up too much space **4.** [consacrer] to spend / **j'occupe mes loisirs à lire** I spend my free time reading **5.** [habiter] to occupy, to live (in) **6.** [détenir - poste, place] to hold, to occupy. ❖ **s'occuper** vp (emploi réfléchi) to keep o.s. busy ou occupied, to occupy o.s. / **à quoi s'occupent les citadins au mois d'août ?** how do city dwellers spend their time in August? / **tu n'as donc pas de quoi t'occuper ?** haven't you got something to be getting on with? ❖ **s'occuper de** vp + prép **1.** [avoir pour responsabilité ou tâche] to deal with, to be in charge of, to take care of / **qui s'occupe de votre dossier ?** who's dealing with ou handling your file? / **je m'occupe de jeunes délinquants** I'm in charge of young offenders / **je m'en occuperai dès demain matin** I'll see to ou attend to ou take care of it first thing in the morning / **t'es-tu occupé des réservations / de ton inscription ?** did you see about the reservations / registering for your course? ▶ **s'occuper de ses affaires** ou **oignons** fam : **occupe-toi de tes affaires** ou **oignons** mind your own business ▶ **t'occupe !** fam none of your business!, don't be so nosy! **2.** [entourer de soins] to look after, to care for / **s'occuper d'un malade** to care for a patient / **s'occuper d'un bébé** to look after a baby / **peux-tu t'occuper des invités pendant que je me prépare ?** would you look after ou see to the guests while I get ready? / **on s'occupe de vous, Madame ?** are you being served, Madam?

occurrence [ɔkyRɑ̃s] ❖ **en l'occurrence** loc adv as it happens.

OCDE (abr de **Organisation de coopération et de développement économiques**) npr f OECD.

océan [ɔseɑ̃] nm GÉOGR ocean.

l'océan Antarctique ou Austral	the Antarctic ou Southern Ocean
l'océan Arctique	the Arctic Ocean
l'océan Atlantique	the Atlantic Ocean
l'océan Indien	the Indian Ocean
l'océan Pacifique	the Pacific Ocean

Océanie [ɔseani] npr f ▶ **(l')Océanie** Oceania, the (Central and) South Pacific.

océanien, enne [ɔseanjɛ̃, ɛn] adj Oceanian, Oceanic. ❖ **Océanien, enne** nm, f Oceanian.

océanique [ɔseanik] adj oceanic.

océanographie [ɔseanɔgRafi] nf oceanography.

ocre [ɔkR] ❖ nf ochre, ocher 🇺🇸. ❖ adj inv & nm ochre.

octane [ɔktan] nm octane.

octante [ɔktɑ̃t] dét régional eighty.

octave [ɔktav] nf ESCRIME, MUS & RELIG octave.

octet [ɔktɛ] nm INFORM octet, (eight-bit) byte.

octobre [ɔktɔbR] nm October. **Voir aussi mars**.

octogénaire [ɔktɔʒenɛR] adj & nmf octogenarian.

octogonal, e, aux [ɔktɔgɔnal, o] adj octagonal.

octogone [ɔktɔgɔn] nm octagon.

octroyer [13] [ɔktRwaje] vt [accorder] to grant ▶ **octroyer qqch à a)** [faveur] to grant sthg to **b)** [permission, congé] to grant sthg to, to give to / **le patron a octroyé un congé à tout le personnel** the boss granted ou gave a day off to the entire staff. ❖ **s'octroyer** vpt SPORT [médaille, place] to win ; [congé] to allow o.s., to treat o.s. to ; [augmentation] to give o.s. ▶ **s'octroyer le droit de faire qqch** to assume the right to do sthg.

oculaire [ɔkylɛR] adj ocular.

oculiste [ɔkylist] nmf oculist.

ode [ɔd] nf ode.

odeur [ɔdœR] nf [de nourriture] smell, odour ; [de fleur, de parfum] smell, fragrance, scent / **une forte odeur de brûlé / chocolat venait de la cuisine** a strong smell of burning / chocolate was coming from the kitchen / **une odeur de pourriture** a putrid smell / **chasser les mauvaises odeurs** to get rid of (nasty ou unpleasant) smells ▶ **sans odeur** odourless / **ce médicament a une mauvaise odeur** this medicine smells bad ou has a bad smell.

odieusement [ɔdjøzmɑ̃] adv odiously, hatefully, obnoxiously.

odieux, euse [ɔdjø, øz] adj **1.** [atroce -comportement] obnoxious ▶ **crime odieux** heinous crime **2.** [désagréable -personne] hateful, obnoxious / **l'examinateur a été odieux avec moi** the examiner was obnoxious ou vile to me / **elle a deux enfants odieux** she has two unbearable ou obnoxious children.

odorant, e [ɔdɔRɑ̃, ɑ̃t] adj **1.** [qui a une odeur] odorous **2.** sout [parfumé] fragrant, sweet-smelling.

odorat [ɔdɔRa] nm (sense of) smell / **avoir l'odorat développé** to have a keen sense of smell.

odyssée [ɔdise] nf odyssey.

œcuménique [ekymenik] adj ecumenical.

œdème [edɛm] nm oedema 🇬🇧, edema 🇺🇸.

œil [œj] (pl **yeux** [jø] ou **œils**) nm **1.** ANAT eye / **avoir les yeux verts / marron** to have green / brown eyes / **elle a des yeux de biche** she's got doe eyes / **il ne voit plus que d'un œil** he can only see with one eye now ▶ **se faire les yeux** to make up one's eyes ▶ **faire** ou **ouvrir des yeux ronds** to stare wide-eyed ▶ **œil artificiel / de verre** artificial / glass eye ▶ **mauvais œil** evil eye ▶ **jeter le mauvais œil à qqn** to give sb the evil eye / **généreux, mon œil !** generous, my foot! ▶ **avoir de petits yeux a)** pr to have small eyes **b)** fig to look (all) puffy-eyed ou puffy round the eyes ▶ **faire qqch les yeux fermés** pr & fig to do sthg with one's eyes shut ou closed ▶ **avoir un œil poché** ou **au beurre noir** fam to have a black eye ou a shiner hum ▶ **faire les gros yeux à un enfant** to look sternly ou reprovingly at a child ▶ **faire qqch pour les beaux yeux de qqn** to do sthg for the love of sb ▶ **œil pour œil(, dent pour dent)** (allusion à la Bible) an eye for an eye (and a tooth for a tooth) **2.** [vision] sight, eyesight / **avoir de bons yeux** to have good eyesight / **avoir de mauvais yeux** to have bad ou poor eyesight ▶ **avoir des yeux de lynx** to be eagle-eyed **3.** [regard] : **ne me fais pas ces yeux-là !** don't look ou stare at me like that! ▶ **les yeux dans les yeux a)** [tendrement] looking into each other's eyes **b)** [avec franchise] looking each other straight in the eye ▶ **chercher qqn des yeux** to look around for sb ▶ **jeter un œil à** to have a quick look at ▶ **lever les yeux sur qqch / qqn** to look up at sthg / sb ▶ **lever les yeux au ciel a)** [pour regarder] to look up at the sky **b)** [par exaspération] to raise one's eyes heavenwards ▶ **poser un œil sur** to have a look at ▶ **devant les**

yeux de before (the eyes of) / *sous les yeux de, sous l'œil de litt* under the eye ou gaze of / *il l'a volé sous nos yeux* he stole it from under our very eyes / *j'ai votre dossier sous les yeux* I've got your file right here in front of me ou before me **4.** [expression, air] look / *il m'a regardé d'un œil noir / furieux* he gave me a black / furious look ▸ **faire de l'œil à qqn a)** *fam* [pour aguicher] to give sb the eye, to make eyes at sb **b)** [en signe de connivence] to wink knowingly at sb ▸ **faire les yeux doux** ou **des yeux de velours à qqn** to make sheep's eyes at sb **5.** [vigilance] : *rien n'échappait à l'œil du professeur* nothing escaped the teacher's notice ▸ **avoir l'œil** to be vigilant ou watchful ▸ **avoir l'œil sur qqn, avoir** ou **tenir qqn à l'œil** to keep an eye ou a close watch on sb / *toi, je t'ai à l'œil !* I've got my eye on you! **6.** [état d'esprit, avis] ▸ **voir qqch d'un bon / mauvais œil** to look favourably / unfavourably upon sthg ▸ **considérer** ou **voir qqch d'un œil critique** to look critically at sthg / *ça n'a aucun intérêt à mes yeux* it's of no interest to me / *aux yeux de la loi* in the eyes of the law **7.** [trou - dans une porte] Judas hole ; [- au théâtre] peep hole ; [- d'une aiguille, d'un marteau] eye ; MÉTÉOR [d'un cyclone] eye, centre. ❖ **à l'œil** *loc adv fam* (for) free, for nothing, gratis / *j'ai eu deux tickets à l'œil* I got two tickets gratis ou (for) free ou on the house.

œillade [œjad] nf wink, oeillade *litt* ▸ **jeter** ou **lancer des œillades à qqn** to give sb the (glad) eye.

œillère [œjɛʀ] nf [de cheval] blinker UK, blinder US ▸ **avoir des œillères** *fig* to be blinkered, to have a blinkered view of things.

œillet [œjɛ] nm BOT [plante] carnation, pink ; [fleur] carnation ▸ **œillet d'Inde** African marigold.

œnologie [enɔlɔʒi] nf oenology / *un stage d'œnologie* a wine-tasting course.

œnologue [enɔlɔg] nmf oenologist, wine expert.

œsophage [ezɔfaʒ] nm oesophagus UK, esophagus US.

œstrogène [ɛstʀɔʒɛn] nm oestrogen UK, estrogen US.

œuf [œf] (*pl* **œufs** [ø]) nm **1.** CULIN egg ▸ **œuf sur le plat** ou **au plat** ou **(au) miroir** fried egg ▸ **œuf (à la) coque** boiled egg ▸ **œuf dur** hard-boiled egg ▸ **œuf mollet** soft-boiled egg ▸ **œuf de Pâques** Easter egg ▸ **œufs brouillés / pochés** scrambled / poached eggs ▸ **œufs en neige a)** [mets] floating islands **b)** [préparation] beaten egg whites ▸ **écraser** ou **étouffer** ou **tuer qqch dans l'œuf** to nip sthg in the bud ▸ **c'est comme l'histoire de l'œuf et de la poule** it's a chicken and egg situation ▸ **il ne faut pas mettre tous ses œufs dans le même panier** *prov* never put all your eggs in one basket *prov* **2.** [télécabine] cable car.

œuvre [œvʀ] nf **1.** [travail] work / *le troisième but a été l'œuvre de Bergova* FOOT the third goal was the work of Bergova / *elle a fait œuvre durable / utile* she's done a lasting / useful piece of work ▸ **mettre qqch en œuvre** to bring sthg into play ▸ **mettre tout en œuvre pour que** to do everything in one's power to ensure that **2.** [production artistique - unique] work ; [- ensemble de réalisations] works ▸ **œuvre d'art** work of art **3.** [charité] ▸ **œuvre (de bienfaisance)** charity, charitable organization ▸ **(bonnes) œuvres** charity. ❖ **œuvres** nfpl ADMIN ▸ **œuvres sociales** community service. ❖ **à l'œuvre** *loc adv* at work / *être à l'œuvre* to be working ou at work / *se mettre à l'œuvre* to get down to ou to start work ▸ **voir qqn à l'œuvre** to see sb at work.

œuvrer [5] [œvʀe] vi *sout* to work, to strive.

off [ɔf] (*pl* **off** ou **offs***) adj **1.** CINÉ offscreen **2.** [théâtre, spectacle, festival] fringe *(modif)*.

offensant, e [ɔfɑ̃sɑ̃, ɑ̃t] adj offensive.

offense [ɔfɑ̃s] nf [affront] insult ▸ **faire offense à** to offend, to give offence to.

offenser [3] [ɔfɑ̃se] vt [blesser] to offend, to give offence to / *soit dit sans (vouloir) vous offenser, votre fils n'est pas un ange* without wishing to offend you, your son is no angel. ❖ **s'offenser** vpi *sout* [se vexer] to take offence / *s'offenser de la moindre critique* to take exception to the slightest criticism.

offensif, ive [ɔfɑ̃sif, iv] adj offensive / *l'équipe a adopté un jeu très offensif* the team has opted to play an attacking game. ❖ **offensive** nf MIL & *fig* offensive / *passer à / prendre l'offensive* to go on / to take the offensive / *offensive de l'hiver fig* onslaught of winter.

offert, e [ɔfɛʀ, ɛʀt] pp ⟶ **offrir.**

office [ɔfis] ◆ nm **1.** [gén & HIST] office / *le signal d'alarme n'a pas rempli son office* the alarm didn't (fulfil its) function ▸ **faire office de**: *faire office de président* to act as chairman / *qu'est-ce qui peut faire office de pièce d'identité ?* what could serve as proof of identity? ▸ **office ministériel** ministerial office **2.** RELIG service **3.** [agence] agency, bureau ▸ **office du tourisme espagnol** Spanish tourist office ou bureau. ◆ nm *(vieilli au féminin)* [d'une cuisine] pantry ; [d'un hôtel, d'une grande maison] kitchen, kitchens. ❖ **offices** nmpl ▸ **grâce aux bons offices de M. Prat / du gouvernement allemand** thanks to Mr. Prat's good offices / to the good offices of the German government. ❖ **d'office** *loc adv* automatically ▸ **avocat commis d'office** (officially) appointed lawyer.

officialiser [3] [ɔfisjalize] vt to make official, to officialize.

officiel, elle [ɔfisjɛl] adj **1.** [public] official / *rien de ce que je vous dis là n'est officiel* everything I'm telling you is unofficial ou off the record / *il a rendu officielle sa décision de démissionner* he made public ou he officially announced his decision to resign **2.** [réglementaire] formal / *notre rencontre n'avait aucun caractère officiel* our meeting took place on an informal ou unofficial basis. ❖ **officiel** nm [représentant] official.

officiellement [ɔfisjɛlmɑ̃] adv officially.

officier¹ [9] [ɔfisje] vi RELIG to officiate.

officier² [ɔfisje] nm **1.** MIL officer ▸ **officier de marine / de l'armée de terre** naval / army officer **2.** [titulaire - d'une fonction, d'une distinction] ▸ **officier de l'état civil** ≃ registrar ▸ **officier de police judiciaire** police officer in the French Criminal Investigation Department.

officieusement [ɔfisjøzmɑ̃] adv unofficially, informally.

officieux, euse [ɔfisjø, øz] adj unofficial, informal.

⚠ **officious** signifie avant tout « zélé » et non officieux.

officine [ɔfisin] nf PHARM dispensary, pharmacy.

offrande [ɔfʀɑ̃d] nf **1.** RELIG [don] offering ; [cérémonie] offertory **2.** [contribution] offering.

offrant [ɔfʀɑ̃] nm bidder ▸ **vendre qqch au plus offrant** to sell sthg to the highest bidder.

offre [ɔfʀ] nf **1.** [proposition - gén et marketing] offer / *ils lui ont fait une offre avantageuse* they made him a worthwhile offer ▸ **faire une offre à 1 000 euros a)** to make an offer of 1,000 euros **b)** [aux enchères] to bid 1,000 euros / **'offres d'emploi'** 'situations vacant', 'help wanted US ', 'vacancies' / *il y a très peu d'offres d'emploi* there are very few job offers ou openings ▸ **offre de lancement** introductory offer ▸ **offre spéciale** special offer **2.** ÉCON supply ▸ **l'offre et la demande** supply and demand **3.** FIN ▸ **offre publique d'achat** takeover bid.

offrir [34] [ɔfʀiʀ] vt **1.** [faire cadeau de] to give ▸ **offrir qqch en cadeau à qqn** to give sb sthg as a present

▸ **je vous offre un café / un verre ?** can I buy you coffee / a drink? / **ils (nous) ont offert le champagne** they treated us to champagne ; *(en usage absolu)* : *pourriez-vous me faire un paquet-cadeau, c'est pour offrir* could you gift-wrap it for me, please, it's a present ▸ **c'est moi qui offre** I'll pay **2.** [donner - choix, explication, hospitalité] to give, to offer ▸ **offrir une récompense** to offer a reward **3.** [proposer] ▸ **offrir son bras à qqn** to offer ou to lend sb one's arm / **je lui ai montré mon autoradio, il m'en offre 100 €** I showed him my car radio, he's offering me 100 € for it **4.** [présenter - spectacle, vue] to offer, to present / *la conversation n'offrait qu'un intérêt limité* the conversation was of only limited interest / *cette solution offre l'avantage d'être équitable* this solution has ou presents the advantage of being fair. **⬧ s'offrir ⬧** vp *(emploi réfléchi)* [proposer ses services] to offer one's services / *s'offrir à payer les dégâts* to offer to pay for the damage. **⬧** vpi [se présenter - occasion] : *un seul moyen s'offrait à moi* there was only one course of action open to me / *un panorama exceptionnel s'offre au regard* an amazing view meets your eyes. **⬧** vpt [se faire cadeau de] to treat o.s. to.

⚠ Attention, **offer** ne peut être utilisé pour traduire **offrir** lorsque ce que l'on offre est un cadeau. Dans ce cas c'est **give** qu'il faut employer.

off shore, offshore [ɔfʃɔʀ] **⬧** adj inv BANQUE, PÉTR & SPORT offshore. **⬧** nm inv PÉTR offshore technology ; SPORT [activité] powerboat racing ; [bateau] powerboat.

offusquer [3] [ɔfyske] vt to offend, to upset, to hurt. **⬧ s'offusquer** vpi ▸ **s'offusquer de** to take offence UK ou offense US at, to take umbrage at.

ogive [ɔʒiv] nf **1.** ARCHIT ogive, diagonal rib **2.** MIL & NUCL warhead ▸ **ogive nucléaire** nuclear warhead.

OGM (abr de **organisme génétiquement modifié**) nm GMO.

ogre, ogresse [ɔgʀ, ɔgʀɛs] nm, f **1.** [dans les contes] ogre (ogress) **2.** *fam & fig* ogre (ogress), monster.

oh [o] **⬧** interj **1.** [pour indiquer - la surprise, l'admiration, l'indignation] oh **2.** [pour interpeller] hey. **⬧** nm inv ooh, oh ▸ **pousser des oh et des ah devant qqch** to ooh and aah at sthg.

ohé [ɔe] interj hey.

oie [wa] nf **1.** ORNITH goose **2.** *péj* [personne] silly goose.

oignon, ognon* [ɔɲɔ̃] nm **1.** CULIN onion ▸ **soupe à l'oignon** onion soup ▸ **petits oignons** pickling onions ▸ **ce ne sont pas tes oignons** *fam* that's none of your business ▸ **mêle-toi** ou **occupe-toi de tes oignons** *fam* mind your own business **2.** HORT [bulbe] bulb **3.** MÉD bunion.

oiseau, x [wazo] nm ZOOL bird / *oiseau nocturne* ou *de nuit* night bird ▸ **oiseau de proie** bird of prey ▸ **oiseau de mauvais augure** ou **de malheur** bird of ill omen ▸ **oiseau rare** : *il est parfait pour cet emploi, tu as vraiment déniché l'oiseau rare* he's perfect for this job, you've found a rare bird there ▸ **le petit oiseau va sortir !** [photo] watch the birdie!

oiseau-mouche [wazomuʃ] *(pl* **oiseaux-mouches)** nm hummingbird.

oiseux, euse [wazø, øz] adj **1.** [futile] futile **2.** [stérile] irrelevant, pointless.

oisif, ive [wazif, iv] adj [personne, vie] idle.

oisiveté [wazivte] nf idleness.

ola [ɔla] nf Mexican wave UK, wave US.

oléoduc [ɔleɔdyk] nm (oil) pipeline.

olfactif, ive [ɔlfaktif, iv] adj olfactory.

oligoélément [ɔligɔelemɑ̃] nm trace element.

olivaie [ɔlivɛ] nf olive grove.

olive [ɔliv] **⬧** nf BOT olive. **⬧** adj inv [couleur] ▸ **(vert) olive** olive, olive-green.

oliveraie [ɔlivʀɛ] = **olivaie.**

olivier [ɔlivje] nm **1.** BOT olive tree **2.** [bois] olive (wood).

OLP (abr de **Organisation de libération de la Palestine**) npr f PLO.

olympique [ɔlɛ̃pik] adj Olympic / *être dans une forme olympique* to be in great shape ▸ **les jeux Olympiques** the Olympic Games, the Olympics.

Oman [ɔman] npr Oman ▸ **le sultanat d'Oman** the Sultanate of Oman. ⟶ **mer**

ombilical, e, aux [ɔ̃bilikal, o] adj ANAT umbilical.

ombragé, e [ɔ̃bʀaʒe] adj shady.

ombrageux, euse [ɔ̃bʀaʒø, øz] adj *sout* [susceptible] touchy, easily offended.

ombre [ɔ̃bʀ] nf **1.** [pénombre] shade ▸ **faire de l'ombre à qqn a)** *pr* to be in sb's light **b)** *fig* to be in sb's way **2.** [forme - d'une personne, d'un arbre, d'un mur] shadow **3.** [trace - de jalousie, de surprise] hint ; [- d'un sourire] hint, shadow ▸ **pas l'ombre d'un remords / d'une preuve** not a trace of remorse / shred of evidence / *cela ne fait pas ou il n'y a pas l'ombre d'un doute* there's not a shadow of a doubt. **⬧ ombres** nfpl THÉÂTRE ▸ **ombres chinoises, théâtre d'ombres** shadow theatre. **⬧ à l'ombre** loc adv [à l'abri du soleil] in the shade / *il fait 30 °C à l'ombre* it's 30 °C in the shade. **⬧ dans l'ombre** loc adv **1.** [dans la pénombre] in the shade **2.** [dans le secret] ▸ **rester dans l'ombre a)** [raison] to remain obscure ou unclear **b)** [personne] to remain unknown / *l'enquête n'a rien laissé dans l'ombre* the enquiry left no stone unturned. **⬧ ombre à paupières** nf eye shadow.

📝 **shadow** ou **shade ?**

Shadow désigne l'ombre portée au sol par quelqu'un ou quelque chose, tandis que **shade** se réfère à l'ombre au sens d'« absence de lumière ».

ombrelle [ɔ̃bʀɛl] nf [parasol] parasol.

oméga(s) [ɔmega] nmpl ▸ **oméga 3 / 6** omega 3 / 6 *(fatty acids).*

omelette [ɔmlɛt] nf omelette / *omelette aux champignons / au fromage / au jambon* mushroom / cheese / ham omelette / *une omelette baveuse* a runny omelette ▸ **omelette norvégienne** ou **surprise** baked Alaska ▸ **on ne fait pas d'omelette sans casser des œufs** *prov* you can't make an omelette without breaking eggs *prov.*

omerta [ɔmɛʀta] nf law of silence, omertà.

omettre [84] [ɔmɛtʀ] vt to omit, to leave out *(sép)* ▸ **omettre de** to fail ou to neglect ou to omit to.

omission [ɔmisjɔ̃] nf [oubli] omission.

omnibus [ɔmnibys] **⬧** nm RAIL slow ou stopping train UK, local (train) US. **⬧** adj : *le train est omnibus entre Melun et Sens* the train calls at all stations between Melun and Sens.

omniprésence [ɔmnipʀezɑ̃s] nf omnipresence.

omniprésent, e [ɔmnipʀezɑ̃, ɑ̃t] adj [souci, souvenir] omnipresent ; [publicité, pollution] ubiquitous / *il est omniprésent dans l'usine* he's everywhere (at once) in the factory.

omniscient, e [ɔmnisjɑ̃, ɑ̃t] adj *sout* omniscient.

* In reformed spelling (see p. 16-18).

omnisports [ɔmnispɔʀ] adj inv ▸ **rencontre omnisports** all-round sports event ▸ **salle omnisports** sports centre.

omnivore [ɔmnivɔʀ] ◆ adj omnivorous. ◆ nm omnivore.

omoplate [ɔmɔplat] nf shoulder blade, scapula *spéc.*

OMS (abr de **Organisation mondiale de la santé**) npr f WHO.

on [ɔ̃] pron pers *(peut être précédé de l'article l' dans un contexte soutenu)* **1.** [indéterminé] : *on lui a retiré son passeport* they took his passport away (from him), his passport was confiscated / *on vit de plus en plus vieux en Europe* people in Europe are living longer and longer **2.** [avec une valeur généralisante] you, one *sout* / *souvent, on n'a pas le choix* often you don't have any choice, often there's no choice / *on ne sait jamais (ce qui peut arriver)* you never know ou one never knows *sout* (what could happen) / *on dirait qu'il va pleuvoir* it looks like rain **3.** [les gens] people, they / *on dit que la vie là-bas n'est pas chère* they say that the cost of living over there is cheap **4.** [désignant un nombre indéterminé de personnes] they / *en Espagne on dîne plus tard* in Spain they eat later / *on m'a dit que vous partiez bientôt* I've been told you're leaving soon **5.** [quelqu'un] : *on vous a appelé ce matin* somebody called you ou there was a (phone) call for you this morning / *est-ce qu'on vous sert, Monsieur ?* are you being served, Sir? **6.** *fam* [nous] we ▸ **on était très déçus** we were very disappointed **7.** [se substituant à d'autres pronoms personnels] : *alors, on ne répond pas au téléphone ? fam* aren't you going to answer the phone? / *alors les gars, on cherche la bagarre ? fam* are you guys looking for a fight? **8.** [dans des annonces] / **'on cherche un vendeur'** 'salesman wanted ou required'.

oncle [ɔ̃kl] nm uncle.

onctueux, euse [ɔ̃ktɥø,øz] adj **1.** [huileux] smooth, unctuous *sout* **2.** CULIN creamy **3.** *litt* [personne] smooth, unctuous *sout.*

onde [ɔ̃d] nf **1.** PHYS wave ▸ **ondes courtes / moyennes** short / medium wave ▸ **onde de choc** shock wave ▸ **ondes longues, grandes ondes** long wave **2.** *fig* [vague] wave. ◆ **ondes** nfpl RADIO ▸ **sur les ondes** on the air.

ondée [ɔ̃de] nf shower (of rain).

on-dit [ɔ̃di] nm inv : *je ne me soucie guère des on-dit* I don't care about what people say / *fonder son opinion sur des on-dit* to base one's opinion on hearsay.

ondoyer [13] [ɔ̃dwaje] vi [champ de blé] to undulate, to ripple ; [flamme] to dance, to waver ; [lumière, ruisseau] to ripple.

ondulant, e [ɔ̃dylɑ̃, ɑ̃t] adj [terrain] undulating ; [route, rivière] twisting (and turning), winding ; [chevelure] flowing ; [façon de marcher] swaying.

ondulation [ɔ̃dylasjɔ̃] nf **1.** *sout* [de l'eau, du terrain] undulation **2.** [des cheveux] wave.

ondulé, e [ɔ̃dyle] adj [cheveux] wavy ; [carton] corrugated.

onéreux, euse [ɔneʀø,øz] adj costly, expensive.

⚠ Le mot anglais **onerous** signifie « lourd », « pénible » et non onéreux.

ONG (abr de **organisation non gouvernementale**) nf NGO.

ongle [ɔ̃gl] nm **1.** ANAT [des doigts de la main] nail, fingernail ; [des orteils] toenail ▸ **se faire les ongles** a) [les cou-

per] to cut one's nails b) [les vernir] to do ou to paint one's nails **2.** ZOOL claw ; [de rapace] talon. ◆ **à ongles** loc adj [ciseaux, lime, vernis] nail *(modif).*

onglet [ɔ̃glɛ] nm **1.** [entaille] thumb index ; [d'un canif] thumbnail groove, nail nick **2.** IMPR [béquet] tab **3.** CULIN top skirt 🇬🇧 ▸ **onglet à l'échalote** long, narrow steak served fried with chopped shallots **4.** INFORM thumbnail ; [sur Internet] tab.

onguent [ɔ̃gɑ̃] nm ointment, salve.

onirique [ɔniʀik] adj *fig & sout* : *une vision onirique* a dreamlike vision.

onomatopée [ɔnɔmatɔpe] nf onomatopoeia.

ont v ⟶ avoir.

Ontario [ɔ̃taʀjo] ◆ npr ▸ **le lac Ontario** Lake Ontario. ◆ npr m ▸ **(l')Ontario** Ontario.

ONU, Onu [ɔny] (abr de **Organisation des Nations unies**) npr f UN, UNO.

onyx [ɔniks] nm onyx.

onze [ɔ̃z] ◆ dét **1.** eleven **2.** [dans des séries] ▸ **le onze novembre** Armistice 🇬🇧 ou Veterans' 🇺🇸 Day. ◆ nm inv FOOT ▸ **le onze tricolore** the French eleven ou team. **Voir aussi cinq.**

onzième [ɔ̃zjɛm] ◆ adj num eleventh / *elle est onzième* she is in eleventh place. ◆ nmf eleventh. **Voir aussi cinquième.**

OPA (abr de **offre publique d'achat**) nf ▸ **OPA amicale** friendly takeover bid ▸ **OPA hostile** hostile takeover bid.

opale [ɔpal] nf opal.

opaque [ɔpak] adj **1.** PHYS opaque **2.** [sombre] dark, impenetrable **3.** [incompréhensible] opaque, impenetrable.

open-source [ɔpɛnsuʀs] adj INFORM open source.

OPEP, Opep [ɔpɛp] (abr de **Organisation des pays exportateurs de pétrole**) npr f OPEC.

opéra [ɔpeʀa] nm **1.** MUS [œuvre] opera ; [genre] opera ▸ **opéra rock** rock opera **2.** [bâtiment] opera (house).

opérable [ɔpeʀabl] adj operable / *la malade n'est plus opérable* the patient is no longer operable ou is beyond surgery.

opérateur, trice [ɔpeʀatœʀ,tʀis] nm, f **1.** TÉLÉC [employé] (telephone) operator ; [exploitant] telephone company **2.** TECHNOL ▸ **opérateur (sur machine)** (machine) operator **3.** INFORM operator **4.** BOURSE operator, dealer.

opération [ɔpeʀasjɔ̃] nf **1.** MÉD operation / *subir une grave / petite opération* to undergo major / minor surgery, to have a major / minor operation ▸ **une opération (chirurgicale)** surgery, a surgical operation **2.** MATH operation **3.** BANQUE & BOURSE operation, transaction ▸ **opération boursière** ou **de Bourse** stock exchange transaction ou dealing ▸ **opération bancaire** ou **de banque** banking transaction ou operation ▸ **opération immobilière** property deal **4.** [manœuvre] operation, job ▸ **opération de commando / sauvetage** commando / rescue operation ▸ **opération escargot** : *une opération escargot a perturbé la circulation hier* a go-slow 🇬🇧 ou slowdown 🇺🇸 by drivers disrupted traffic yesterday **5.** COMM campaign / **'opération coup de poing sur les chaînes hi-fi'** 'hi-fi prices slashed' ▸ **opération promotionnelle** promotional campaign.

opérationnel, elle [ɔpeʀasjɔnɛl] adj **1.** [en activité] operational **2.** [fournissant le résultat optimal] efficient, operative **3.** MIL operational.

opérer [18] [ɔpeʀe] ◆ vt **1.** MÉD [blessé, malade] to operate on / *elle a été opérée de l'appendicite* she was operated on for appendicitis, she had her appendix removed / *on va l'opérer d'un kyste au poignet* they're going to remove a cyst from her wrist / *elle vient juste d'être opérée* she's just had an operation / *se faire opérer* to undergo ou to have surgery **2.** [procéder à -modification] to carry out *(sép)* ; [-miracle, retour en arrière] to bring about *(sép)* ; [-paiement] to make / *le pays tente d'opérer un redressement économique* the country is attempting to bring about an economic recovery. ◆ vi **1.** [faire effet] to work **2.** [intervenir] to act, to operate. ◆ **s'opérer** vpi to take place. 🖉 In reformed spelling (see p. 16-18), this verb is conjugated like *semer* : *il opèrera, elle opèrerait.*

opérette [ɔpeʀɛt] nf operetta.

ophtalmique [ɔftalmik] adj ophthalmic.

ophtalmo [ɔftalmo] nmf *fam* **abr de** ophtalmologiste.

ophtalmologiste [ɔftalmɔlɔʒist], **ophtalmologue** [ɔftalmɔlɔg] nmf ophthalmologist, eye specialist.

Opinel® [ɔpinɛl] nm *folding knife used especially for outdoor activities, scouting, etc.*

opiniâtre [ɔpinjatʀ] adj [personne] stubborn, obstinate.

opiniâtreté [ɔpinjatʀəte] nf *litt* **1.** [entêtement] stubbornness, obstinacy **2.** [ténacité] relentlessness, doggedness.

opinion [ɔpinjɔ̃] nf **1.** [point de vue] opinion / *j'ai mon opinion sur lui* I have my own opinion about him / *se faire soi-même une opinion* to make up one's own mind / *je ne partage pas votre opinion* I don't agree with you, I don't share your views ▶ **opinions politiques / subversives** political / subversive views ▶ **l'opinion (publique)** public opinion ▶ **informer l'opinion** to inform the public **2.** [jugement] opinion ▶ **avoir une bonne / mauvaise / haute opinion de qqn** to have a good / bad / high opinion of sb.

opium [ɔpjɔm] nm opium.

opportun, e [ɔpɔʀtœ̃, yn] adj opportune, timely / *je vous donnerai ma réponse en temps opportun* I'll give you my answer in due course / *il lui est apparu opportun de partir avant elle* he found it appropriate ou advisable to leave before her.

opportunisme [ɔpɔʀtynism] nm opportunism.

opportuniste [ɔpɔʀtynist] adj & nmf opportunist ▶ **maladie opportuniste** opportunistic infection.

opportunité [ɔpɔʀtynite] nf **1.** [à-propos] timeliness, appropriateness **2.** [occasion] opportunity ▶ **opportunités et menaces** ÉCON opportunities and threats.

opposant, e [ɔpozɑ̃, ɑ̃t] nm, f [adversaire] opponent.

opposé, e [ɔpoze] adj **1.** [en vis-à-vis] opposite / *il est arrivé du côté opposé* he came from the other ou opposite side **2.** [contraire -sens, direction] opposite, other ; [-mouvement] opposing ; [-avis, goût] opposing, conflicting, different / *je suis d'une opinion opposée (à la vôtre)* I am of a different opinion **3.** [contrastant -couleur, ton] contrasting **4.** [contre] : *être opposé à une mesure* to be opposed to a measure **5.** GÉOM & MATH [côté, angle] opposite. ◆ **opposé** nm **1.** [direction] opposite / *vous cherchez l'église ? vous allez à l'opposé* you want the church? you're going in the wrong direction **2.** [contraire] opposite, reverse / *il est tout l'opposé de sa sœur* he's the exact opposite of his sister. ◆ **à l'opposé de** loc prép unlike, contrary to / *à l'opposé de sa mère, elle n'aimait pas la peinture* unlike her mother, she didn't like painting.

opposer [3] [ɔpoze] vt **1.** [objecter -argument] : *je n'ai rien à opposer à cette objection* I've nothing to say against that objection / *elle m'a opposé qu'elle n'avait pas le temps de s'en occuper* she objected that she didn't have time to take care of it **2.** [mettre en confrontation] : *qui peut-on opposer au président sortant ?* who can we put up against the outgoing president? / *le match de demain oppose Bordeaux à Lens* Bordeaux will play against Lens in tomorrow's match / *deux guerres ont opposé nos pays*

two wars have brought our countries into conflict **3.** [disposer vis-à-vis] to set ou to place opposite each other. ◆ **s'opposer** vp [rivaux, partis] to clash ; [opinions, idées] to conflict ; [couleurs] to contrast / *ces deux théories s'opposent* the two theories conflict with each other. ◆ **s'opposer à** vp + prép **1.** [être contre] to object to, to oppose / *le règlement / ma religion s'y oppose* it goes against the rules / my religion / *je m'oppose à ce que tu reviennes* I'm against ou opposed to your coming back **2.** [affronter] to oppose, to be against / *il s'opposera ce soir au président dans un débat télévisé* he'll face the president tonight in a televised debate **3.** [contraster avec -couleur, notion, mot] to be the opposite of.

opposition [ɔpozisjɔ̃] nf **1.** [désaccord] opposition ; [contraste] contrast, difference / *opposition de ou entre deux styles* clash of ou between two styles **2.** [résistance] opposition / *le ministre a fait ou mis opposition au projet* the minister opposed the plan **3.** POL ▶ **l'opposition** the Opposition / *les dirigeants / partis de l'opposition* the leaders / parties of the Opposition **4.** DR : *faire opposition à un chèque* to stop a cheque. ◆ **par opposition à** loc prép as opposed to, in contrast with.

oppressant, e [ɔpʀesɑ̃, ɑ̃t] adj oppressive.

oppresser [4] [ɔpʀese] vt to oppress / *elle était oppressée par l'angoisse* she was gripped ou choked with anxiety.

oppresseur [ɔpʀesœʀ] nm oppressor.

oppression [ɔpʀesjɔ̃] nf **1.** [domination] oppression **2.** [suffocation] suffocation, oppression.

opprimé, e [ɔpʀime] ◆ adj oppressed. ◆ nm, f oppressed person / *elle prend toujours le parti des opprimés* she always sides with the underdog.

opprimer [3] [ɔpʀime] vt [asservir] to oppress.

opter [3] [ɔpte] ◆ **opter pour** v + prép to opt for *(insép)* / *vous devez opter pour une de ces deux possibilités* you'll have to choose between these two possibilities / *le prix m'a fait opter pour une plus petite voiture* the price finally made me come down in favour of a smaller car.

opticien, enne [ɔptisjɛ̃, ɛn] nm, f optician.

optimal, e, aux [ɔptimal, o] adj optimal, optimum *(avant nom)* / *pour un rendement optimal* for optimal results.

optimaliser [3] [ɔptimalize] vt to optimize.

optimiser [ɔptimize] = optimaliser.

optimisme [ɔptimism] nm optimism ▶ **avec optimisme** optimistically.

optimiste [ɔptimist] ◆ adj optimistic. ◆ nmf optimist.

optimum [ɔptimɔm] *(pl* optimums *ou* optima [-ma]*)* ◆ adj optimum *(avant nom)*, optimal. ◆ nm optimum.

option [ɔpsjɔ̃] nf **1.** [choix] option, choice **2.** ÉDUC ▶ **(matière à) option** optional subject **3.** [accessoire facultatif] optional extra ▶ **en option** as an (optional) extra.

optionnel, elle [ɔpsjɔnɛl] adj optional.

optique [ɔptik] ◆ adj **1.** ANAT optic ▶ **nerf optique** optic nerve **2.** OPT optical **3.** INFORM optical. ◆ nf **1.** SCI optics *(U)* **2.** TECHNOL [set of] lenses **3.** [point de vue] point of view / *dans cette optique* from this point of view.

opulence [ɔpylɑ̃s] nf [richesse] opulence, affluence ▶ **vivre dans l'opulence** to live an opulent life ou a life of plenty.

opulent, e [ɔpylɑ̃, ɑ̃t] adj **1.** [riche] affluent, wealthy, opulent **2.** [physiquement -personne] corpulent ; [-forme] generous, full.

or¹ [ɔʀ] conj *sout* : *il faut tenir les délais ; or, ce n'est pas toujours possible* deadlines must be met ; now this is not always possible / *je devais y aller, or au dernier moment j'ai eu un empêchement* I was supposed to go, but then at the last moment something came up.

or² [ɔʀ] ◆ nm **1.** [métal] gold / *le cours de l'or* the price of gold ▶ **or ou jaune** yellow gold ▶ **or massif** solid gold / *la montre est en or massif* the watch is solid gold ▶ **l'étalon-or** the gold standard ▶ **pour tout l'or du monde** for all the tea in China *hum*, for all the money in the world **2.** [couleur] gold, golden colour. ◆ adj inv gold *(modif)*, gold-coloured. ◆ **d'or** loc adj **1.** JOAILL & MINÉR gold *(modif)* **2.** [doré - cheveux] golden, gold *(modif)* ; [- cadre] gold *(modif)* **3.** EXPR un cœur d'or a heart of gold. ◆ **en or** loc adj **1.** JOAILL gold *(modif)* / *une bague en or* a gold ring **2.** [excellent] ▶ **une affaire en or a)** [occasion] a real bargain **b)** [entreprise] a goldmine.

orage [ɔʀaʒ] nm MÉTÉOR storm, thunderstorm / *il va y avoir un orage* there's a storm brewing, there's going to be a storm ▶ **laisser passer l'orage** to let the storm blow over ▶ **orage magnétique / de chaleur** magnetic / heat storm ▶ **pluie d'orage** rainstorm.

orageux, euse [ɔʀaʒø, øz] adj **1.** MÉTÉOR [ciel] stormy, thundery ; [chaleur, averse] thundery / *le temps est orageux* it's thundery ou stormy, the weather's thundery ou stormy **2.** [tumultueux - jeunesse, séance] stormy, turbulent.

oral, e, aux [ɔʀal, o] adj [confession, déposition] verbal, oral ; [message, tradition] oral ; ENS [épreuve] oral. ◆ **oral, aux** nm **1.** [examen - gén] oral (examination) ; [- à l'université] viva (voce) UK, oral (examination) **2.** ÉDUC & UNIV ▶ **l'oral** [l'expression orale]: *il n'est pas très bon à l'oral* his oral work isn't very good.

oralement [ɔʀalmɑ̃] adv orally, verbally.

orange [ɔʀɑ̃ʒ] ◆ nf orange ▶ **orange sanguine** blood orange ▶ **une orange pressée** a glass of freshly squeezed orange juice. ◆ nm **1.** [couleur] orange (colour) **2.** [sur feu de signalisation] amber UK, yellow US / *le feu était à l'orange* the lights were on amber UK, the light was yellow US. ◆ adj inv orange, orange-coloured.

orangé, e [ɔʀɑ̃ʒe] adj orangey, orange-coloured.

orangeade [ɔʀɑ̃ʒad] nf orange drink, orange squash UK.

oranger [ɔʀɑ̃ʒe] nm orange tree.

orangeraie [ɔʀɑ̃ʒʀɛ] nf orange grove.

orangiste [ɔʀɑ̃ʒist] nmf [en Irlande du Nord] Orangeman (Orangewoman).

orang-outan(g) [ɔʀɑ̃utɑ̃] *(pl* **orangs-outans** *ou* **orangs-outangs)** nm orangutang.

orateur, trice [ɔʀatœʀ, tʀis] nm, f [gén] speaker.

orbital, e, aux [ɔʀbital, o] adj orbital.

orbite [ɔʀbit] nf **1.** ANAT (eye) socket, orbit *spéc* **2.** ASTRON orbit / *être sur* ou *en orbite* to be in orbit ▶ **être en orbite autour de qqch** [suj : astre, engin] to be in orbit round sthg, to orbit sthg / *satellite en orbite autour de la Terre* Earth-orbiting satellite ▶ **mettre en** ou **placer sur orbite** to put into orbit **3.** [d'une personne, d'un pays] sphere of influence, orbit.

orbiter [3] [ɔʀbite] vi to orbit ▶ **orbiter autour de** to orbit (round).

Orcades [ɔʀkad] npr fpl ▶ **les Orcades** the Orkney Islands, the Orkneys.

orchestre [ɔʀkɛstʀ] nm **1.** MUS [classique] orchestra ; [de jazz] band, orchestra ▶ **orchestre symphonique / de chambre** symphony / chamber orchestra **2.** CINÉ & THÉÂTRE stalls UK, orchestra US.

orchestrer [3] [ɔʀkɛstʀe] vt **1.** MUS [composer] to orchestrate ; [adapter] to orchestrate, to score **2.** [préparer] to orchestrate, to organize.

orchidée [ɔʀkide] nf orchid.

ordi [ɔʀdi] nm *fam* computer.

ordinaire [ɔʀdinɛʀ] ◆ adj **1.** [habituel - journée] ordinary, normal ; [- procédure] usual, standard, normal ; [- comportement] ordinary, usual, customary ; DR [& POL - session] ordinary ▶ **peu** ou **pas ordinaire a)** [attitude, méthode, journée] unusual **b)** [volonté] unusual, extraordinary **2.** [de tous les jours - habits, vaisselle] ordinary, everyday *(avant nom)* **3.** COMM [qualité, modèle] standard ; [produit] ordinary **4.** [banal - cuisine, goûts] ordinary, plain ; [- gens] ordinary, common *péj* ; [- spectacle] ordinary, run-of-the-mill ; [- conversation] run-of-the-mill, commonplace / *elle mène une existence très ordinaire* she leads a very humdrum existence / *elle n'est pas ordinaire, ton histoire !* your story is certainly an unusual one! ◆ nm [norme] ▶ **sortir de l'ordinaire** to be out of the ordinary, to be unusual / *son mari sort vraiment de l'ordinaire !* her husband is one of a kind! ◆ **d'ordinaire** loc adv usually, ordinarily, normally / *plus tôt que d'ordinaire* earlier than usual.

ordinal, e, aux [ɔʀdinal, o] adj [adjectif, nombre] ordinal. ◆ **ordinal, aux** nm **1.** [nombre] ordinal (number) **2.** [adjectif] ordinal (adjective).

ordinateur [ɔʀdinatœʀ] nm **1.** INFORM computer ▶ **mettre qqch sur ordinateur** to computerize sthg, to put sthg on computer ▶ **ordinateur portable / portatif** portable / laptop computer ▶ **ordinateur de bureau** desktop computer **2.** TECHNOL computer ▶ **ordinateur de bord a)** AUTO dashboard computer **b)** NAUT shipboard computer.

ordonnance [ɔʀdɔnɑ̃s] nf **1.** MÉD prescription / *un médicament vendu sans ordonnance* a drug that can be bought over the counter / *faire une ordonnance* to write a prescription / *'seulement sur ordonnance'* 'on prescription only'* **2.** DR [loi] ordinance, statutory instrument ; [jugement] order, ruling ; [de police] (police) regulation ou order.

ordonné, e [ɔʀdɔne] adj **1.** [méthodique - personne] tidy, neat ; [- esprit] methodical, systematic **2.** [rangé - chambre] tidy, neat, orderly **3.** [régulier - existence, mode de vie] orderly, well-ordered.

ordonnée [ɔʀdɔne] nf MATH ordinate.

ordonner [3] [ɔʀdɔne] vt **1.** [commander - silence, attaque] to order ; MÉD [traitement, repos] to prescribe ▶ **ordonner à qqn de faire qqch** to order ou to command sb to do sthg ▶ **ordonner à qqn d'entrer / de sortir** to order sb in / out **2.** [agencer - documents] to (put in) order ; [- arguments, idées] to (put into) order, to arrange ; [- chambre] to tidy (up) ; MATH [nombres, suite] to arrange in order **3.** RELIG to ordain.

ordre [ɔʀdʀ]
nm

A. INSTRUCTION **1.** [directive, injonction] order ; MIL order, command ▶ **c'est un ordre !** (and) that's an order! ▶ **donner un ordre a)** [parent] to give an order **b)** [officiel, policier, officier] to issue ou to give an order ▶ **donner à qqn l'ordre de faire qqch** to order sb to do sthg, to give sb the order to do sthg ▶ **donner des ordres à qqn a)** *pr* to give sb orders / *il aime bien donner des ordres* he likes giving orders **b)** *fig* to order sb around / *je n'aime pas qu'on me donne des ordres* I don't like being ordered around ▶ **recevoir des ordres a)** *pr* to receive ou to take orders **b)** *fig* to be ordered around / *je n'aime pas recevoir d'ordres !* I don't like to be ordered around! ▶ **recevoir l'ordre de faire qqch** to be ordered ou to receive the order to do sthg / *j'ai reçu l'ordre formel de ne pas le déranger* I've been formally instructed not to disturb him ▶ **par** ou **sur ordre de** by order of, on the orders of ▶ **être sous les ordres de qqn** to be under sb's command ▶ **être aux ordres de qqn** to take orders from sb / *je ne suis pas à tes ordres !* I'm not at your beck and call! ▶ **ordre de grève** strike call ▶ **ordre de mission** MIL orders (for a mission) ▶ **à vos ordres !** *hum* ou MIL yes, Sir! **2.** BANQUE & BOURSE ▶ **à l'ordre de** payable to, to the order of ▶ **ordre de paiement / virement** order to pay / to transfer.

B. HIÉRARCHIE, AGENCEMENT 1. [succession] order, sequence / *l'ordre des mots dans la phrase* the word order in the sentence ▶ **par ordre chronologique / croissant / décroissant** in chronological / ascending / descending order ▶ **en ordre dispersé / serré** MIL in extended / close order ▶ **par ordre alphabétique**: *noms classés par ordre alphabétique* names filed in alphabetical order **2.** [rangement] tidiness, orderliness, neatness / *la pièce était en ordre* the room was tidy ▶ **mettre qqch en ordre** to put sthg in order ▶ **remettre qqch en ordre** to tidy sthg up **3.** [organisation méthodique - de documents] order / *mettre en ordre, mettre de l'ordre dans* [documents, comptabilité] to set in order, to tidy up *(sép)* / *mettre de l'ordre dans ses idées* to order one's ideas **4.** [discipline sociale] : *faire régner l'ordre* to keep ou maintain order ▶ **rappeler qqn à l'ordre** to call sb to order / *la police est chargée du maintien de l'ordre* it's the police's job to keep law and order ▶ **l'ordre public** public order, law and order ▶ **rentrer dans l'ordre**: *puis tout est rentré dans l'ordre* then order was restored, then everything went back to normal.

C. CLASSIFICATION, DOMAINE 1. RELIG order ▶ **entrer dans les ordres** RELIG to take (holy) orders **2.** [confrérie] ▶ **l'ordre des avocats** ≃ the Bar **UK** ; ≃ the Bar Association **US** ▶ **l'ordre des médecins** ≃ the British Medical Association **UK** ; ≃ the American Medical Association **US** ▶ **les ordres de chevalerie** the orders of knighthood **3.** [nature, sorte] nature, order / *des problèmes d'ordre professionnel* problems of a professional nature / *dans le même ordre d'idées* similarly ▶ **du même ordre** [proposition, responsabilités] similar, of the same nature ▶ **c'est dans l'ordre des choses** it's in the order ou nature of things **4.** ARCHIT & BIOL order ▶ **ordre attique / dorique / ionique** Attic / Doric / Ionic order. ❖ **de premier ordre** *loc adj* first-rate. ❖ **de second ordre** *loc adj* [question] of secondary importance ; [artiste, personnalité] second-rate. ❖ **ordre du jour** *nm* [d'un comité] agenda ▶ **être à l'ordre du jour a)** *pr* to be on the agenda **b)** *fig* to be in the news ▶ **mettre qqch à l'ordre du jour** to put ou to place sthg on the agenda.

ordure [ɔʀdyʀ] *nf tfam* [personne abjecte] ▶ **ordure !** bastard! ❖ **ordures** *nfpl* **1.** [déchets] refuse *(U)*, rubbish **UK** *(U)*, garbage **US** *(U)* ▶ **jeter** ou **mettre qqch aux ordures** to throw sthg into the rubbish bin **UK** ou garbage can **US** ▶ **ordures ménagères** household refuse **2.** *fam* [obscénités] obscenities, filth *(U)*.

ordurier, ère [ɔʀdyʀje, ɛʀ] *adj* foul, filthy, obscene.

oreille [ɔʀɛj] *nf* **1.** ANAT & ZOOL ear ▶ **j'ai mal aux oreilles** I've got earache, my ears are hurting ▶ **tirer les oreilles à qqn a)** *pr* to pull sb's ears **b)** [réprimander] to tell sb off ▶ **se faire tirer l'oreille** *fig* to need a lot of persuading **2.** [ouïe] (sense of) hearing / *avoir l'oreille fine* to have an acute sense of hearing ▶ **avoir de l'oreille** ou **l'oreille musicale** to have a good ear for music ▶ **avoir l'oreille absolue** to have perfect pitch **3.** [pour écouter] ear / *dire qqch à l'oreille de qqn* to whisper sthg in sb's ear / *écouter une conversation d'une oreille distraite* to listen to a conversation with only half an ear / *ouvrez bien vos oreilles !* listen very carefully! ▶ **venir** ou **parvenir aux oreilles de qqn** to come to ou to reach sb's ears.

oreiller [ɔʀeje] *nm* pillow.

oreillette [ɔʀejɛt] *nf* **1.** ANAT auricle **2.** [de baladeur] téléphone portable] earphone.

oreillons [ɔʀejɔ̃] *nmpl* MÉD mumps / *avoir les oreillons* to have (the) mumps.

ores [ɔʀ] ❖ **d'ores et déjà** *loc adv* already.

orfèvre [ɔʀfɛvʀ] *nmf* **1.** [artisan qui travaille - l'or] goldsmith ; [- l'argent] silversmith **2.** EXPR **être orfèvre en la matière** to be an expert.

orfèvrerie [ɔʀfɛvʀəʀi] *nf* **1.** [métier - de l'or] goldsmithing, gold work ; [- de l'argent] silversmithing, silver work ▶ **l'orfèvrerie a)** [en or] gold plate **b)** [en argent] silver plate **2.** [boutique - d'objets d'or] goldsmith's shop **UK** ou store **US** ; [- d'objets d'argent] silversmith's shop **UK** ou store **US**.

orfraie [ɔʀfʀɛ] *nf* white-tailed eagle.

organe [ɔʀgan] *nm* **1.** ANAT organ ▶ **organes génitaux** ou **sexuels** genitals, genitalia **2.** [institution] organ ▶ **organe de presse** newspaper, publication **3.** [porte-parole, publication] mouthpiece, organ.

organigramme [ɔʀganigʀam] *nm* **1.** [structure] organization chart **2.** INFORM [de programmation] flow chart ou diagram.

organique [ɔʀganik] *adj* organic.

organisateur, trice [ɔʀganizatœʀ, tʀis] *nm, f* organizer.

organisation [ɔʀganizasjɔ̃] *nf* **1.** [organisme] organization ▶ **organisation internationale** international organization ou agency ▶ **Organisation de libération de la Palestine** Palestine Liberation Organization ▶ **Organisation des Nations unies** United Nations Organization ▶ **organisation non gouvernementale** nongovernmental organization ▶ **organisation patronale** employers' organization ou association ▶ **organisation syndicale** trade union **2.** [mise sur pied - d'une fête, d'une réunion, d'un service] organization ; [- d'une manifestation] organization, staging ; [- d'un attentat] organization, planning / *l'organisation du temps de travail* the organization of working hours **3.** [structure - d'un discours, d'une association, d'un système] organization, structure ; [- du travail] organization **4.** [méthode] organization / *ne pas avoir d'organisation* to be disorganized.

organisé, e [ɔʀganize] *adj* **1.** [regroupé - consommateurs, groupe] organized **2.** [aménagé] : *bien / mal organisé* well- / badly-organized **3.** [méthodique - personne] organized, well-organized, methodical.

organiser [3] [ɔʀganize] *vt* **1.** [mettre sur pied - gén] to organize ; MIL [attaque] to plan **2.** [agencer - association, journée, tâche] to organize / *j'ai organisé mon emploi du temps de façon à pouvoir partir plus tôt* I've organized ou arranged my schedule so that I can leave earlier. ❖ **s'organiser** *vpi* [personne] to get (o.s.) organized, to organize o.s. / *je m'organiserai en fonction d'elle* I'll just fit in with her ▶ **il suffit de s'organiser** all you need is some organization / *la société s'est vite organisée en classes sociales* society rapidly became organized into social classes.

organiseur [ɔʀganizœʀ] *nm* **1.** [agenda] personal organizer, Filofax® **2.** [agenda électronique] electronic organizer.

organisme [ɔʀganism] *nm* **1.** BIOL [animal, végétal] organism ; [humain] body, organism ▶ **organisme génétiquement modifié** genetically modified organism **2.** [institut] organism, body ▶ **organisme de crédit** credit institution ▶ **organisme de formation** training institute.

orgasme [ɔʀgasm] *nm* orgasm.

orge [ɔʀʒ] *nm* barley.

orgelet [ɔʀʒəlɛ] *nm* sty, stye.

orgie [ɔʀʒi] *nf* **1.** ANTIQ orgy **2.** [débauche] orgy.

orgue [ɔʀg] *nm* MUS organ ▶ **orgue de Barbarie** barrel organ. ❖ **orgues** *nfpl* MUS organ.

orgueil [ɔʀgœj] *nm* **1.** [fierté] pride **2.** [amour-propre] pride / *c'est de l'orgueil mal placé* it's just misplaced pride **3.** [sujet de fierté] pride.

orgueilleux, euse [ɔʀgœjø, øz] ◆ *adj* [fier - personne] proud. ◆ *nm, f* [fier] proud person.

orient [ɔʀjɑ̃] *nm* **1.** [est] east, orient *litt* ▶ **parfum / tapis d'Orient** oriental scent / carpet **2.** GÉOGR ▶ **l'Orient** the East ou Orient *litt*.

orientable [ɔʀjɑ̃tabl] adj **1.** [antenne, rétroviseur] adjustable **2.** [lampe] rotating, swivel *(modif)*.

oriental, e, aux [ɔʀjɑ̃tal,o] ◆ adj **1.** GÉOGR eastern, east *(modif)* **2.** [de l'Orient - art, cuisine, civilisation] oriental, eastern. ◆ nm, f Oriental, Easterner.

orientation [ɔʀjɑ̃tasjɔ̃] nf **1.** [direction - d'une enquête, de recherches] direction, orientation ; [- d'un mouvement] orientation / *l'orientation de notre entreprise doit changer* our firm must adopt a new outlook ▸ **orientation politique a)** [d'un journal, d'une personne] political leanings ou tendencies **b)** [d'un parti] political direction **2.** [conseil - pour des études] academic counselling ; [vers un métier] careers guidance ; [direction - des études] course ; [- du métier] career / *changer d'orientation* to change courses ▸ **orientation professionnelle** careers advice ou guidance **3.** [position - d'une antenne] direction ; [- d'une maison] aspect / *l'orientation plein sud de l'appartement est ce qui le rend agréable* what makes the flat so pleasant to live in is the fact that it faces due south ; [positionnement - d'un faisceau, d'une lampe] directing ; [- d'un rétroviseur] adjustment **4.** [aptitude] : *avoir le sens de l'orientation* to have a good sense of direction **5.** [tendance] trend / *orientation à la hausse / baisse* upward / downward trend.

orienté, e [ɔʀjɑ̃te] adj **1.** [positionné] ▸ **orienté à l'ouest a)** [édifice] facing west, with a western aspect **b)** [radar] directed towards the west ▸ **local bien / mal orienté** well- / badly-positioned premises **2.** [idéologiquement - discours, journal] biased, slanted **3.** ENS : *élève bien / mal orienté* pupil who has taken the right / wrong academic advice **4.** BOURSE : *orienté à la hausse* [marché] bullish, rising / *orienté à la baisse* [marché] bearish, falling **5.** INFORM ▸ **orienté objet** object-orientated.

orienter [3] [ɔʀjɑ̃te] vt **1.** [antenne, haut-parleur, spot] to direct, to turn, to point ; [rétroviseur] to adjust, to position ; [plante] to position / *orientez votre tente à l'est* pitch your tent so that it faces east / *la chambre est orientée plein nord* the bedroom faces due north **2.** [mettre sur une voie] ▸ **orienter vers a)** [enquête, recherches] to direct ou to orientate towards **b)** [discussion] to turn toward ou to **c)** [passant] to direct to / *on l'a orienté vers un spécialiste* he was referred to a specialist / *il m'a demandé où était la gare mais je l'ai mal orienté* he asked where the station was, but I misdirected him / *elle a été orientée vers une école technique* she was advised to go to a technical school. ❖ **s'orienter** vpi [se repérer] to take one's bearings. ❖ **s'orienter vers** vp + prép [suj : enquête, recherches] to be directed towards ou toward US ; [suj : discussion] to turn round to ; [suj : parti, entreprise] to move towards ou toward US ; [suj : étudiant] to turn to / *il s'oriente vers une carrière commerciale* he's got his sights set on a career in sales.

orifice [ɔʀifis] nm [ouverture] hole, opening.

origan [ɔʀigɑ̃] nm oregano.

originaire [ɔʀiʒinɛʀ] adj [natif] : *il est originaire de la Martinique* he's from Martinique.

original, e, aux [ɔʀiʒinal,o] ◆ adj **1.** [nouveau - architecture, idée, système] original, novel ; [- cadeau, film, style, personne] original / *il n'y a rien d'original dans son dernier roman* there's nothing original in his latest novel **2.** [excentrique - personne] odd, eccentric **3.** [d'origine - document, manuscrit] original. ◆ nm, f [excentrique] eccentric, character. ❖ **original, aux** nm **1.** [d'une œuvre] original ; [d'un document] original ou master (copy) ; [d'un texte] top copy, original ; [d'un objet, d'un personnage] original **2.** [texte à traduire] original.

⚠ Attention, l'adjectif anglais **original** ne peut être employé pour traduire original au sens d'« excentrique ».

originalité [ɔʀiʒinalite] nf **1.** [caractère] originality, novelty / *cet artiste manque d'originalité* there is nothing new ou original in this artist's work ; [extravagance] eccentricity **2.** [nouveauté] original feature.

origine [ɔʀiʒin] nf **1.** [cause première - d'un feu, d'une maladie, d'une querelle] origin / *avoir son origine dans, tirer son origine de* to have one's origins in, to originate in ▸ **avoir qqch pour origine** to be caused by sthg / *être à l'origine d'un projet de loi* [personne] to be behind a bill ▸ **être à l'origine d'une querelle a)** [personne] to be behind ou to be the cause of an argument **b)** [malentendu] to be at the origin ou root of an argument **2.** [début] origin, beginning / *les origines de la civilisation* the origins of civilization **3.** [provenance - d'un terme] origin, root ; [- d'un produit manufacturé] origin ▸ **graisse d'origine animale** vegetable oil ▸ **graisse d'origine végétale** animal fat **4.** [d'une personne] origin ▸ **d'origine modeste** of humble origin ou birth ▸ **d'origine espagnole** of Spanish origin **5.** GÉOM origin. ❖ **à l'origine** loc adv originally, initially, at the beginning. ❖ **d'origine** loc adj [pays] of origin ; [couleur, emballage, nom, monnaie] original / *ma voiture a encore son moteur d'origine* my car has still got its original engine.

originel, elle [ɔʀiʒinɛl] adj **1.** [primitif - innocence] original **2.** RELIG original **3.** [premier] original.

orignal, aux [ɔʀiɲal,o] nm moose.

ORL ◆ nmf (abr de **oto-rhino-laryngologiste**) ENT specialist. ◆ nf (abr de **oto-rhino-laryngologie**) ENT.

orme [ɔʀm] nm elm (tree).

ornement [ɔʀnəmɑ̃] nm **1.** [objet] ornament **2.** ART embellishment, adornment ▸ **sans ornement** plain, unadorned. ❖ **d'ornement** loc adj [plantes, poupée] ornamental.

ornementer [3] [ɔʀnəmɑ̃te] vt *sout* to ornament.

orner [3] [ɔʀne] vt [décorer - suj : personne] to decorate ; [suj : dessin, plante, ruban] to adorn, to decorate, to embellish ▸ **orner avec** ou **de** to decorate with.

ornière [ɔʀnjɛʀ] nf **1.** [trou] rut **2.** [routine] ▸ **sortir de l'ornière** to get out of a rut **3.** [impasse] ▸ **sortir de l'ornière** to get o.s. out of trouble.

ornithologie [ɔʀnitɔlɔʒi] nf ornithology.

orphelin, e [ɔʀfəlɛ̃,in] ◆ adj [enfant] orphan *(modif)*, orphaned ▸ **être orphelin de père** to be fatherless, to have lost one's father. ◆ nm, f orphan.

orphelinat [ɔʀfəlina] nm [bâtiment] orphanage ; [personnes] orphans.

orque [ɔʀk] nf killer whale.

orteil [ɔʀtɛj] nm toe ▸ **gros / petit orteil** big / little toe.

orthodontiste [ɔʀtɔdɔ̃tist] nmf orthodontist.

orthodoxe [ɔʀtɔdɔks] ◆ adj **1.** RELIG Orthodox **2.** *fig* [méthode, pratique] orthodox / *pas très* ou *peu orthodoxe* rather unorthodox. ◆ nmf RELIG member of the Orthodox church ▸ **les orthodoxes** the Orthodox.

orthodoxie [ɔʀtɔdɔksi] nf orthodoxy.

orthographe [ɔʀtɔgʀaf] nf [graphie] spelling ; [règles] spelling system, orthography *spéc* ; [matière] spelling, orthography *spéc* / *il y a deux orthographes possibles* there are two ways of spelling it ou two possible spellings.

orthographier [9] [ɔʀtɔgʀafje] vt to spell / *mal / bien orthographié* wrongly / correctly spelt.

orthographique [ɔʀtɔgʀafik] adj spelling *(modif)*, orthographic.

orthopédagogie [ɔʀtɔpedagɔʒi] nf QUÉBEC SCOL & MÉD special education.

orthopédie [ɔʀtɔpedi] nf orthopedics (U).

orthopédique [ɔʀtɔpedik] adj orthopedic.

orthopédiste [ɔʀtɔpedist] adj & nmf orthopedist.

orthophonie [ɔʀtɔfɔni] nf MÉD speech therapy.

orthophoniste [ɔʀtɔfɔnist] nmf speech therapist.

ortie [ɔʀti] nf (stinging) nettle ▶ **ortie blanche / rouge** white / red dead-nettle.

orvet [ɔʀvɛ] nm slowworm.

os [ɔs] (pl **os** [o]) nm **1.** ANAT & ZOOL bone ▶ **os de seiche** cuttlebone ▶ **être gelé / trempé jusqu'aux os** to be frozen to the marrow / soaked to the skin **2.** CULIN bone ▶ **os à moelle** marrowbone **3.** fam [difficulté] ▶ **il y a un os** there's a snag ou hitch.

OS nm abr de **ouvrier spécialisé**.

oscar [ɔskaʀ] nm CINÉ Oscar.

oscarisé, e [ɔskaʀize] adj CINÉ Oscar-winning.

oscariser [3] [ɔskaʀize] vt to award an Oscar to.

oscillation [ɔsilasjɔ̃] nf **1.** [variation] fluctuation, variation **2.** ÉLECTR & PHYS oscillation.

osciller [3] [ɔsile] vi **1.** [bouger - pendule, objet suspendu] to oscillate, to swing, to sway ; [-branche, corde] to sway, to swing ; [-arbre, statue] to sway ; [-aiguille aimantée] to flicker ; [- personne, tête] to rock **2.** [varier] ▶ **osciller entre** to vary ou to fluctuate between.

osé, e [oze] adj [audacieux - tentative] bold, daring.

oseille [ozɛj] nf **1.** BOT & CULIN sorrel ▶ **à l'oseille** with sorrel **2.** tfam [argent] dough, cash.

oser [3] [oze] vt **1.** [avoir l'audace de] ▶ **oser faire qqch** to dare (to) do sthg ; (en usage absolu) ▶ **comment oses-tu !** how dare you! ; sout [suggestion, réponse] to risk **2.** [dans les tournures de politesse] ▶ **j'ose croire / espérer que...** I trust / hope that... ▶ **je n'ose y croire** it seems too good to be true ▶ **si j'ose dire** if I may say so / **si j'ose m'exprimer ainsi** if I may say so, if I may put it that way.

osier [ozje] nm BOT willow, osier. ❖ **d'osier, en osier** loc adj [fauteuil, panier] wicker, wickerwork (modif).

Oslo [ɔslo] npr Oslo.

osmose [ɔsmoz] nf **1.** SCI osmosis **2.** fig osmosis.

ossature [ɔsatyʀ] nf ANAT [d'une personne] frame, skeleton ; [du visage] bone structure.

osselet [ɔslɛ] nm JEUX jacks (U), knucklebones (U) / **jouer aux osselets** to play jacks.

ossements [ɔsmɑ̃] nmpl remains, bones.

osseux, euse [ɔsø, øz] adj **1.** ANAT bone (modif), osseous spéc **2.** MÉD ▶ **greffe osseuse** bone graft ▶ **maladie osseuse** bone disease **3.** [aux os apparents] bony.

ostensible [ɔstɑ̃sibl] adj sout conspicuous, open, clear.

ostensiblement [ɔstɑ̃sibləmɑ̃] adv conspicuously, openly, clearly.

ostentation [ɔstɑ̃tasjɔ̃] nf sout [affectation, vanité] ostentation ▶ **avec ostentation** with ostentation, ostentatiously.

ostentatoire [ɔstɑ̃tatwaʀ] adj sout ostentatious / **port ostentatoire de signes religieux** wearing of visible religious symbols.

ostéopathe [ɔsteɔpat] nmf osteopath.

ostéoporose [ɔsteɔpɔʀoz] nf osteoporosis.

ostracisme [ɔstʀasism] nm sout [exclusion] ostracism / **être victime de l'ostracisme** to be ostracized.

ostréiculteur, trice [ɔstʀeikyltœʀ, tʀis] nm, f oyster farmer, oysterman (oysterwoman).

ostréiculture [ɔstʀeikyltyʀ] nf oyster farming.

otage [ɔtaʒ] nmf hostage ▶ **prendre qqn en otage** to take sb hostage.

OTAN, Otan [ɔtɑ̃] (abr de Organisation du traité de l'Atlantique Nord) npr f NATO.

otarie [ɔtaʀi] nf eared seal.

ôte-agrafe (pl **ôte-agrafes**) [otagraf] nm staple remover.

ôter [3] [ote] vt **1.** [retirer] to take off (sép), to remove (from) / **ôte tes pieds du fauteuil** take ou get your feet off the armchair **2.** [mettre hors de portée] to take away / **personne n'a pensé à lui ôter son arme** nobody thought to take his weapon (away) from him **3.** [supprimer] to remove (from) / **son attitude m'a ôté mes dernières illusions** his attitude rid me of my last illusions / **on ne m'ôtera pas de l'idée que...** I can't help thinking that... **4.** MATH to take away (sép) / **20 ôté de 100 égale 80** 20 (taken away) from 100 leaves 80. ❖ **s'ôter** vpt : **ôte-toi cette idée de la tête** get that idea out of your head. ❖ **s'ôter de** vp + prép : **ôtez-vous de là, vous gênez le passage** move, you're in the way.

otite [ɔtit] nf ear infection, otitis spéc.

oto-rhino-laryngologiste (pl **oto-rhino-laryngologistes**), **otorhinolaryngologiste*** [ɔtɔʀinɔlaʀɛ̃gɔlɔʒist] nmf otorhinolaryngologist spéc, ear, nose and throat specialist.

Ottawa [ɔtawa] npr Ottawa.

ou [u] conj **1.** [indiquant une alternative ou une équivalence] or / **tu peux venir aujourd'hui ou demain** you can come (either) today or tomorrow **2.** [indiquant une approximation] or / **ils étaient cinq ou six** there were five or six of them **3.** [indiquant la conséquence] or (else) / **rends-le-moi, ou ça ira très mal** give it back, or else there'll be trouble. ❖ **ou (bien)... ou (bien)** loc corrélative either... or / **ou tu viens, ou tu restes, mais tu arrêtes de te plaindre** you (can) either come or stay, but stop complaining!

où [u] ❖ pron rel **1.** [dans l'espace] where / **pose-le là où tu l'as trouvé** put it back where you found it ▶ **partout où vous irez** everywhere you go ▶ **d'où viens-tu ?** where have you come from? / **le pays d'où je viens** the country which ou where I come from / **les villes par où nous passerons** the towns which we will go through **2.** [dans le temps] : **le jour où je suis venu** the day (that) I came ▶ **à l'époque où...** in the days when... **3.** fig : **c'est une spécialité où il excelle** it's a field in which he excels / **dans l'état où elle est** in her state, in the state she is / **au point où nous en sommes** (at) the point we've reached. ❖ adv rel [dans l'espace] where ; [avec «que»] : **où que vous alliez** wherever you go. ❖ adv interr where / **par où voulez-vous passer ?** which way do you want to go?, which route do you want to take? / **où voulez-vous en venir ?** what point are you trying to make?, what are you trying to say? ❖ **d'où** loc conj : **d'où il suit que...** from which it follows that... / **je ne savais pas qu'il était déjà arrivé, d'où ma surprise** I didn't know that he'd already arrived, which is why I was so surprised.

ouais [wɛ] interj fam yeah.

ouananiche [wananiʃ] nf QUÉBEC Atlantic salmon.

ouaouaron [wawaʀɔ̃] nm QUÉBEC bullfrog.

ouate [wat] nf **1.** [coton] cotton wool UK, (absorbent) cotton US **2.** TEXT wadding, padding.

oubli [ubli] nm **1.** [lacune] omission / **il y a beaucoup d'oublis dans sa liste** she left a lot of items off her list, there are a lot of gaps in her list ; [trou de mémoire] oversight, lapse of memory / **ce n'est qu'un oubli** it's just an oversight **2.** sout [isolement] ▶ **l'oubli** oblivion ▶ **tomber dans l'oubli** to sink into oblivion **3.** litt [indifférence] : **l'oubli de soi** selflessness, self-denial.

oublier [10] [ublije] vt **1.** [ne pas se remémorer - nom, rue, date] to forget / *n'oublie pas le rendez-vous* don't forget (that) you have an appointment / *n'oublie pas que c'est son anniversaire* remember ou don't forget that it's her birthday ; *(en usage absolu)* : *qu'a-t-elle dit ? j'ai oublié* what did she say? I've forgotten ; [ne pas reconnaître - visage, mélodie] to forget **2.** [ne plus penser à - héros, injure, souci] to forget (about) / *j'ai oublié l'heure* I forgot the time / *je veux bien oublier le passé* I'm ready to forget about the past ou to let bygones be bygones / *oublie-moi un peu, veux-tu ? fam* just leave me alone, will you? ▶ **se faire oublier** to keep a low profile, to stay out of the limelight ; *(en usage absolu)* to forget / *il boit pour oublier* he drinks to forget **3.** [omettre] to leave out *(sép)* / *je ferai en sorte de l'oublier dans mon testament* / *sur le registre* I'll make sure she's left out of my will / left off the register **4.** [négliger] to forget (about) / *depuis son mariage, il nous oublie* he's been neglecting us ou he's forgotten (about) us since he got married **5.** [ne pas prendre] to forget, to leave (behind) / *j'ai oublié la lettre à la maison* I left the letter at home **6.** [ne pas mettre] to forget.

oubliettes [ublijet] nfpl [cachot] dungeon, black hole ▶ **le projet est tombé dans les** ou **aux oubliettes** *fig* the project has been shelved.

ouest [wɛst] ◆ nm inv **1.** [point cardinal] west / *nous allons vers l'ouest* we're heading west ou westwards / *aller droit vers l'ouest* to head due west ▶ **la cuisine est plein ouest** ou **exposée à l'ouest** the kitchen faces (due) west **2.** [partie d'un pays, d'un continent] west, western area ou region / *l'ouest de l'Italie* Western Italy / *elle habite dans l'Ouest* she lives in the west **3.** POL ▶ **l'Ouest** Western countries, the West. ◆ adj inv west *(modif)*, western / *la façade ouest d'un immeuble* the west ou west-facing wall of a building. ❖ **à l'ouest de** *loc prép* (to the) west of.

ouest-allemand, e [wɛstalmã, ãd] *(mpl* **ouest-allemands,** *fpl* **ouest-allemandes)** adj West German.

ouf¹ [uf] interj phew / *je n'ai pas eu le temps de dire ouf* I didn't even have time to catch my breath ▶ **pousser un ouf de soulagement** to breathe a sigh of relief.

ouf² [uf] ◆ adj [fou en verlan] nuts / *non, mais t'es ouf ou quoi ?* are you nuts? ◆ nm [fou en verlan] nutter / *j'ai eu une semaine de ouf !* I've had a crazy week / *c'est un truc de ouf* it's crazy.

Ouganda [ugãda] npr m ▶ **(l')Ouganda** Uganda.

ougandais, e [ugãdɛ, ɛz] adj Ugandan. ❖ **Ougandais, e** nm, f Ugandan.

oui [wi] ◆ adv **1.** [en réponse affirmative] yes / *voulez-vous prendre X pour époux ? — oui* do you take X to be your lawful wedded husband? — I do / *tu comprends ? — oui et non* do you understand? — yes and no ou I do and I don't ▶ **mais oui** yes, of course / *c'est vraiment injuste ! — ah ça oui !* that's really unfair! — you've said it! ou that's for sure! **2.** [en remplacement d'une proposition] ▶ **il semblerait que oui** it would seem so / *tu vas voter ? — je crois que oui* are you going to vote? — (yes) I think so ou I think I will / *elle n'a dit ni oui ni non* she didn't say either yes or no, she was very noncommittal / *faire oui de la tête* to nod **3.** [emploi expressif] : *oui, évidemment, elle a un peu raison* of course, she's right in a way / *je suis déçu, oui, vraiment déçu !* I'm disappointed, really disappointed! / *tu viens, oui ?* are you coming then? / *tu viens, oui ou non ?* are you coming or not? / *c'est bientôt fini de crier, oui ?* will you stop shouting?, stop shouting, will you! ◆ nm inv : *il y a eu 5 oui* [dans un vote] there were 5 votes for ou 5 ayes / *il change d'avis pour un oui pour un non* he changes his mind at the drop of a hat.

ouï-dire [widiʀ] nm inv hearsay. ❖ **par ouï-dire** loc adv by hearsay, through the grapevine.

ouïe¹ [wi] nf **1.** ANAT (sense of) hearing ▶ **avoir l'ouïe fine** to have a keen ear ▶ **être tout ouïe** *hum: continue, je suis tout ouïe* go on, I'm all ears **2.** ZOOL gill.

ouïe², ouille [uj] interj ouch.

ouistiti [wistiti] nm ZOOL marmoset.

ouragan [uʀagã] nm MÉTÉOR hurricane.

ourlet [uʀlɛ] nm COUT hem / *faire un ourlet à une jupe* to hem a skirt.

ours [uʀs] nm **1.** ZOOL bear ▶ **ours blanc** ou **polaire** polar bear ▶ **ours brun** brown bear **2.** [personne] : *il est un peu ours* he's a bit grumpy **3.** [jouet] ▶ **ours (en peluche)** teddy bear.

ourse [uʀs] nf ZOOL she-bear.

Ourse [uʀs] npr f ASTRON ▶ **la Grande Ourse** Ursa Major, the Great Bear ▶ **la Petite Ourse** Ursa Minor, the Little Bear.

oursin [uʀsɛ̃] nm sea urchin.

ourson [uʀsɔ̃] nm (bear) cub.

oust(e) [ust] interj *fam* out, scram / *allez, ouste, tout le monde dehors !* come on, get a move on, everybody out!

outarde [utaʀd] nf bustard.

outil [uti] nm *pr & fig* tool ▶ **cabane** / **boîte à outils** tool shed / box ▶ **outil pédagogique** teaching aid ▶ **outil de travail** tool ▶ **savoir utiliser l'outil informatique** *fig* to know how to use computers.

outillage [utijaʒ] nm [ensemble d'outils] (set of) tools ; [pour un jardinier] (set of) tools ou implements.

outillé, e [utije] adj ▶ **être outillé pour faire qqch** to be properly equipped ou to have the proper tools to do sthg ▶ **être bien outillé en qqch** to be well equipped with sthg.

outrage [utʀaʒ] nm **1.** [offense] insult ▶ **faire outrage à l'honneur de qqn** to insult sb's honour / *faire outrage à la raison* to be an insult to reason ▶ **les outrages du temps** the ravages of time **2.** DR ▶ **outrage à agent** insulting behaviour ▶ **outrage aux bonnes mœurs** affront to public decency ▶ **outrage à magistrat** (criminal) contempt of court ▶ **outrage (public) à la pudeur** indecent exposure.

outragé, e [utʀaʒe] adj [personne] deeply offended ▶ **d'un air** / **ton outragé** indignantly.

outrageant, e [utʀaʒã, ãt] adj offensive, insulting, abusive.

outrageusement [utʀaʒøzmã] adv excessively, extravagantly, outrageously.

outrance [utʀãs] nf [exagération] excessiveness, extravagance, outrageousness. ❖ **à outrance** loc adv excessively, extravagantly, outrageously.

outrancier, ère [utʀãsje, ɛʀ] adj excessive, extravagant, extreme / *des propos outranciers* extreme ou wild remarks.

outre¹ [utʀ] nf goatskin, wineskin.

outre² [utʀ] ◆ prép [en plus de] besides, as well as / *outre le fait que…* besides the fact that… ◆ adv : *elle a passé outre malgré l'interdiction* she carried on regardless of ou she disregarded the ban. ❖ **en outre** loc adv besides, furthermore, moreover. ❖ **outre mesure** loc adv overmuch / *le voyage ne l'avait pas fatigué outre mesure* he wasn't overly tired from the journey.

outré, e [utʀe] adj **1.** *litt* [exagéré] excessive, exaggerated, overdone **2.** [choqué] indignant, shocked, outraged.

outre-Atlantique [utʀatlãtik] adv across the Atlantic.

outrecuidance [utʀəkɥidãs] nf *litt* **1.** [fatuité] overconfidence, self-importance **2.** [impertinence] impudence, impertinence.

outre-Manche [utʀəmãʃ] adv across the Channel.

outremer [utʀəmɛʀ] ◆ nm MINÉR lapis lazuli ; [teinte] ultramarine. ◆ adj inv ultramarine.

outre-mer [utrəmɛr] adv overseas / *la France d'Outre-mer* France's overseas territories and departments.

outrepasser [3] [utrəpase] vt [droit] to go beyond ; [ordre] to exceed / *vous outrepassez vos droits* you're going beyond your rights.

outrer [3] [utre] vt [révolter] to outrage.

outre-Rhin [utrərɛ̃] adv across the Rhine.

outre-tombe [utrətɔ̃b] ❖ **d'outre-tombe** loc adj inv ▸ *une voix d'outre-tombe* a voice from beyond the grave.

outsider [awtsajdœr] nm outsider.

ouvert, e [uvɛr, ɛrt] ◆ pp ⟶ **ouvrir**. ◆ adj **1.** [porte, tiroir] open ▸ **grand ouvert, grande ouverte** wide open / *un robinet ouvert peut causer une inondation* a tap that's been left on can cause flooding / *il avait la chemise ouverte* his shirt was open (to the waist) ou undone / *n'achetez pas de tulipes ouvertes* don't buy tulips that are already open **2.** [bouche, yeux] open ; [coupé] cut, open / *elle a eu la lèvre ouverte* her lip was cut **3.** [magasin, bureau, restaurant] open ; CHASSE & PÊCHE open **4.** [réceptif] open / *nous sommes ouverts aux idées nouvelles* we are open to new ideas **5.** INFORM open ; [système] open-ended **6.** MATH open ; GÉOM wide **7.** SPORT [imprévisible] ▸ **un match très ouvert** a wide open game.

ouvertement [uvɛrtəmɑ̃] adv openly.

ouverture [uvɛrtyr] nf **1.** [trou] opening / *une ouverture dans le mur* an opening ou a hole in the wall / *l'événement représente une véritable ouverture pour ces pays* fig this development will open up real opportunities for these countries **2.** [action d'ouvrir] : *l'ouverture des grilles a lieu à midi* the gates are opened ou unlocked at noon / *nous attendons avec impatience l'ouverture du tunnel* we can hardly wait for the tunnel to open **3.** [mise à disposition] : *pour faciliter l'ouverture d'un compte courant* to make it easier to open a current account ▸ **heures d'ouverture** opening hours ▸ **jours d'ouverture** opening days **4.** [d'une session, d'un festival] opening / *je tiens le rayon parfumerie depuis le jour de l'ouverture* I've been in charge of the perfume department since the day we opened ; CHASSE & PÊCHE opening / **cérémonie / match d'ouverture** opening match / ceremony **5.** fig : *l'ouverture vers la gauche / droite* POL broadening the base of government to the left / right ▸ **la politique d'ouverture** consensus politics ▸ **ouverture d'esprit** open-mindedness **6.** RUGBY opening up ; BOXE opening ; CARTES & JEUX opening ▸ **avoir l'ouverture** to have the opening move **7.** MUS overture **8.** PHOT aperture. ❖ **ouvertures** nfpl overtures / *faire des ouvertures de paix* to make peace overtures.

ouvrable [uvrabl] adj ▸ **heures ouvrables** business hours, shop hours ▸ **pendant les heures ouvrables** a) COMM during opening hours b) ADMIN during office hours ▸ **jour ouvrable** working day 🇬🇧, workday.

ouvrage [uvraʒ] nm **1.** [travail] work / *se mettre à l'ouvrage* to get down to work, to start work **2.** [œuvre] (piece of) work ▸ **ouvrage d'art** ARCHIT & CONSTR construction works **3.** [livre] book.

ouvragé, e [uvraʒe] adj [nappe] (finely ou elaborately) embroidered ; [construction] elaborate, ornate.

ouvré, e [uvre] adj ADMIN & COMM ▸ **jour ouvré** working day 🇬🇧, workday.

ouvre-boîte(s) (*pl* ouvre-boîtes), **ouvre-boite*** (*pl* ouvre-boites) [uvrəbwat] nm tin opener 🇬🇧, can opener.

ouvre-bouteille(s) [uvrəbutɛj] (*pl* ouvre-bouteilles) nm bottle opener.

ouvreur, euse [uvrœr, øz] nm, f CINÉ & THÉÂTRE usher (usherette).

ouvrier, ère [uvrije, ɛr] ◆ adj [questions, statut] labour (avant nom) 🇬🇧, labor (avant nom) 🇺🇸 ; [quartier, condition] working-class ▸ **agitation ouvrière** industrial unrest ▸ **la classe ouvrière** the working class. ◆ nm, f (manual) worker ▸ **une ouvrière** a (female) worker / *les ouvriers sur le chantier* the workmen on the site ▸ **ouvrier qualifié / spécialisé** skilled / unskilled worker ▸ **ouvrier agricole** agricultural worker, farm labourer ▸ **ouvrier hautement qualifié** highly-skilled worker.

ouvrir [34] [uvrir] ◆ vt **1.** [portail, tiroir, capot de voiture, fenêtre] to open ; [porte fermée à clé] to unlock, to open ; [porte verrouillée] to unbolt, to open / *il ouvrit la porte d'un coup d'épaule* he shouldered the door open, he forced the door (open) with his shoulder / *ouvrir une porte par effraction* to force a door ; (en usage absolu) : *on a sonné, je vais ouvrir* there's someone at the door, I'll go / *c'est moi, ouvre* it's me, open the door ou let me in **2.** [bouteille, pot, porte-monnaie] to open ; [coquillage] to open (up) (sép) ; [paquet] to open, to unwrap ; [enveloppe] to open, to unseal **3.** [déplier - éventail] to open (up) (sép) ; [- carte routière] to open (up) (sép), to unfold ; [- livre] to open (up) (sép) **4.** [desserrer, écarter - compas, paupières] to open ; [- rideau] to open, to draw back (sép) ; [- aile, bras] to open (out) (sép), to spread (out) (sép) ; [- mains] to open (out) (sép) ; [déboutonner - veste] to undo, to unfasten / *ouvrir les yeux* to open one's eyes ▸ **ouvrir l'œil** a) *pr* to open one's eye b) *fig* to keep one's eyes open ▸ **ouvrir de grands yeux** [être surpris] to be wide-eyed ▸ **ouvrez grands vos yeux** [soyez attentifs] keep your eyes peeled ▸ **ouvrir l'esprit à qqn** to broaden sb's outlook **5.** [commencer - hostilités] to open, to begin ; [- campagne, récit, enquête] to open, to start ; [- bal, festival, conférence, saison de chasse] to open **6.** [rendre accessible - chemin, voie] to open (up), to clear ; [- frontière, filière] to open / *ils refusent d'ouvrir leur marché aux produits européens* they refuse to open up their market to European products **7.** [créer - boutique, cinéma, infrastructure] to open ; [- entreprise] to open, to set up (sép) **8.** [faire fonctionner - radiateur, robinet] to turn on (sép) ; [- circuit électrique] to open ▸ **ouvrir l'eau / l'électricité / le gaz** fam to turn on the water / the electricity / the gas **9.** [être en tête de - défilé, procession] to lead **10.** [inciser - corps] to open (up), to cut open ; [- panaris] to lance, to cut open **11.** SPORT : *ouvrir le jeu* to open play ▸ **ouvrir la marque** ou **le score** a) [gén] to open the scoring b) FOOT to score the first goal **12.** BANQUE [compte bancaire, portefeuille d'actions] to open ; [emprunt] to issue, to float ▸ **ouvrir un crédit à qqn** to give sb credit facilities **13.** JEUX [enchères] to open. ◆ vi **1.** [boutique, restaurant, spectacle] to (be) open **2.** [couvercle, fenêtre, porte] to open / *le portail ouvre mal* the gate is difficult to open ou doesn't open properly. ❖ **ouvrir sur** v + prép **1.** [déboucher sur] to open onto / *le vasistas ouvre sur le parking* the fanlight opens onto ou looks out over the car park **2.** [commencer par] to open with. ❖ **s'ouvrir** ◆ vp (emploi passif) **1.** [boîte, valise] to open ; [chemisier, fermeture] to come undone / *la fenêtre de ma chambre s'ouvre mal* the window in my room is difficult to open ou doesn't open properly **2.** [être inauguré] to open. ◆ vpt [se couper - personne] : *je me suis ouvert le pied sur un bout de verre* I've cut my foot (open) on a piece of glass ▸ **s'ouvrir les veines** to slash ou to cut one's wrists. ◆ vpi **1.** [se desserrer, se déplier - bras, fleur, huître, main] to open ; [- aile] to open (out), to spread, to unfold ; [- bouche, œil, paupière, livre, rideau] to open **2.** [se fendre - foule, flots] to part ; [- sol] to open up **3.** [boîte, valise - accidentellement] to (come) open **4.** [fenêtre, portail] to open / *la fenêtre s'ouvrit brusquement* the window flew ou was flung ou was thrown open **5.** [s'épancher] to open up ▸ **s'ouvrir à qqn de**

qqch to open one's heart to sb about sthg, to confide in sb about sthg **6.** [débuter - bal, conférence] ▶ **s'ouvrir par** to open ou to start with **7.** [se présenter - carrière] to open up. ❖ **s'ouvrir à** vp + prép [des idées, des influences] : *s'ouvrir à des cultures nouvelles* to become aware of new cultures / *leur pays s'ouvre peu à peu au commerce extérieur* their country is gradually opening up to foreign trade.

ovaire [ɔvɛʀ] nm ovary.

ovale [ɔval] ❖ adj [en surface] oval ; [en volume] egg-shaped, ovoid. ❖ nm [forme] oval.

ovation [ɔvasjɔ̃] nf ovation / *le public lui a fait une véritable ovation* the audience gave her a real ovation.

ovationner [3] [ɔvasjɔne] vt ▶ **ovationner qqn** to give sb an ovation / *le groupe s'est fait ovationner pendant 10 minutes* the group were given a 10-minute standing ovation.

overdose [ɔvœʀdoz] nf **1.** [surdose] overdose **2.** *fam & fig* overdose, OD / *j'ai eu une overdose de chocolat à Noël* I overdosed on chocolate at Christmas.

ovin [ɔvɛ̃] nm ovine, sheep.

ovni [ɔvni] (abr de **objet volant non identifié**) nm UFO / *c'est un véritable ovni* it's like something from another planet.

ovule [ɔvyl] nm PHYSIOL ovum.

ovuler [3] [ɔvyle] vi to ovulate.

oxydable [ɔksidabl] adj liable to rust, oxidizable.

oxydation [ɔksidasjɔ̃] nf oxidation.

oxyde [ɔksid] nm oxide ▶ **oxyde de carbone** carbon monoxide.

oxyder [3] [ɔkside] vt to oxidize. ❖ **s'oxyder** vpi to become oxidized.

oxygène [ɔksiʒɛn] nm **1.** CHIM oxygen **2.** *fig* : *j'ai besoin d'oxygène* I need some fresh air.

oxygéner [18] [ɔksiʒene] vt **1.** CHIM to oxygenate **2.** [cheveux] to bleach, to peroxide. ❖ **s'oxygéner** vpi to get some fresh air.

✎ In reformed spelling (see p. 16-18), this verb is conjugated like *semer* : *il oxygènera, elle oxygènerait.*

ozone [ozon] nm ozone ▶ **la couche d'ozone** the ozone layer / *'préserve la couche d'ozone'* [sur produit] 'ozone-friendly'.

p 1. (abr écrite de **pico**) p **2.** (abr écrite de **page**) p **3.** abr écrite de **pièce**.

PAC, Pac [pak] (**abr de politique agricole commune**) nf CAP.

pacemaker [pɛsmekœʀ] nm (cardiac) pacemaker.

pacha [paʃa] nm HIST pasha.

pachyderme [paʃidɛʀm] nm ZOOL elephant, pachyderm *spéc*.

pacification [pasifikasjɔ̃] nf [gén & POL] pacification.

pacifier [9] [pasifje] vt to pacify.

pacifique [pasifik] adj **1.** POL [pays, gouvernement] peace-loving **2.** [non militaire] peaceful, non-military **3.** [fait dans le calme] peaceful.

Pacifique [pasifik] npr m ▶ **le Pacifique** the Pacific (Ocean).

pacifiste [pasifist] adj & nmf pacifist.

pack [pak] nm **1.** SPORT pack **2.** COMM pack / *un pack de bière* a pack of beer.

package [pakadʒ] nm package holiday.

packager, packageur [pakaʒœʀ] nm packager.

packaging [pakadʒiŋ] nm packaging.

pacotille [pakɔtij] nf [camelote] cheap junk. ❖ **de pacotille** loc adj cheap.

PACS [paks] (**abr de pacte civil de solidarité**) nm civil partnership (*between same-sex or opposite-sex couples*).

pacser ❖ **se pacser** vpi *fam* to enter a civil partnership.

pacte [pakt] nm **1.** [gén] agreement **2.** POL pact, treaty, agreement.

pactiser [3] [paktize] ❖ **pactiser avec** v + prép **1.** [conclure un accord avec] to make a deal ou pact with **2.** [transiger avec] to collude with, to connive at ▶ **pactiser avec sa conscience** to stifle one's conscience.

pactole [paktɔl] nm [profit] gold mine *fig* / *on peut se faire un joli pactole dans le pétrole* there are rich pickings to be had in the oil business ; [gros lot] jackpot.

paella [paɛla] nf paella.

paf [paf] adj inv *fam* sloshed, plastered.

PAF [paf] ◆ npr f **abr de Police de l'air et des frontières**. ◆ nm **abr de paysage audiovisuel français**.

pagaie [pagɛ] nf [rame] paddle.

pagaille, pagaïe [pagaj] nf *fam* **1.** [désordre] mess, shambles / *arrête de mettre la pagaille dans mes affaires* stop messing up my things **2.** [confusion] chaos / *c'est la pagaille dans les rues de Paris* the streets of Paris are absolute chaos. ❖ **en pagaille** loc adv **1.** [en désordre]

▶ **mettre qqch en pagaille** to mess sthg up **2.** [en quantité] : *ils ont de l'argent en pagaille* they've got loads of money.

paganisme [paganism] nm paganism.

pagayer [11] [pageje] vi to paddle.

page¹ [paʒ] nm HIST page (boy).

page² [paʒ] nf **1.** [rectangle de papier] page ▶ **page blanche** blank page / *suite de l'article en page cinq* (article) continued on page five / *c'est en bas de page* it's at the bottom of the page / *une lettre de huit pages* an eight-page letter ▶ **tourner la page** to make a fresh start, to put something behind one **2.** [extrait] passage, excerpt ▶ **une page de publicité** RADIO & TV a commercial break **3.** [épisode] page, chapter / *quelques pages de notre histoire* some pages ou chapters in our history **4.** INFORM page ▶ **page d'accueil** home page ▶ **page suivante / précédente** page down / up ▶ **page Web** Web page. ❖ **à la page** loc adj up-to-the-minute, up-to-date / *tu n'es plus à la page du tout !* you're completely out of touch ou out of it!

pagination [paʒinasjɔ̃] nf **1.** IMPR pagination, page numbering **2.** INFORM page numbering, paging.

pagne [paɲ] nm [en tissu] loincloth, pagne ; [en rafia] grass skirt.

pagode [pagɔd] nf ARCHIT pagoda.

paie [pɛ] nf [salaire] pay, wages ▶ **toucher sa paie** to be paid.

paiement [pɛmɑ̃] nm payment / *faire ou effectuer un paiement* to make a payment ▶ **paiement comptant** cash payment ▶ **paiement mensuel** monthly payment ▶ **paiement différé** deferred payment.

païen, enne [pajɛ̃, ɛn] ◆ adj pagan, heathen. ◆ nm, f **1.** [polythéiste] pagan, heathen **2.** *sout* [athée] atheist, pagan.

paillard, e [pajaʀ, aʀd] adj [personne] bawdy, coarse ; [chanson] dirty ; [histoire] dirty, smutty.

paillasse [pajas] nf **1.** [matelas grossier] straw ou straw-filled mattress **2.** [d'un évier] drainer, draining board 🇬🇧, drainboard 🇺🇸.

paillasson [pajasɔ̃] nm [d'une entrée] doormat.

paille [paj] nf **1.** [chaume] straw ▶ **paille de riz** rice straw ▶ **il est sur la paille** he's penniless **2.** [tige] piece of straw, straw ▶ **tirer à la courte paille** to draw straws **3.** [pour boire] (drinking) straw ▶ **boire avec une paille** to drink through a straw **4.** MÉTALL flaw ▶ **paille de fer** steel wool.

paillette [pajɛt] nf **1.** COUT sequin, spangle **2.** [parcelle -d'or] speck ; [-de quartz, de mica] flake ; [-de savon] flake ▶ **savon en paillettes** soap flakes.

paillote [pajɔt] nf straw hut.

pain [pɛ̃] nm **1.** [baguette] French stick 🇬🇧, French loaf ; [boule] round loaf (of bread), cob / *pain de deux / quatre* *livres* long two-pound / four-pound loaf ▸ **pain azyme** unleavened bread ▸ **pain biologique** organic wholemeal 🇬🇧 ou wholewheat 🇺🇸 loaf ▸ **pain bis** ou 🇶🇺🇪🇧🇪🇨 **brun** brown loaf ▸ **pain de blé entier** 🇶🇺🇪🇧🇪🇨 wholemeal, 🇬🇧 ou wholewheat 🇺🇸 loaf ▸ **pain brioché** brioche-like bread ▸ **pain aux céréales** granary bread ▸ **pain de campagne** farmhouse loaf ▸ **pain complet** wholemeal 🇬🇧 ou wholewheat 🇺🇸 loaf ▸ **pain d'épices** ≃ gingerbread ▸ **pain français** 🇶🇺🇪🇧🇪🇨 French loaf, French stick 🇬🇧 ▸ **pain au lait** finger roll *(made with milk)* ▸ **pain de mie** sandwich bread ▸ **pain polaire** ou **suédois** polar bread *(soft flat bread)* ▸ **pain de seigle** rye bread ▸ **pain surprise** pain surprise *(large round loaf that is hollowed out and filled with tasty sandwiches, served on festive occasions)* ▸ **pain viennois** Vienna loaf ▸ **petits pains** (bread) rolls **2.** [substance] bread ▸ **un peu de pain** a bit ou piece of bread ▸ **pain grillé** toast ▸ **pain perdu, pain doré** French toast ▸ **avoir du pain sur la planche** to have one's work cut out ▸ **enlever** ou **retirer** ou **ôter le pain de la bouche à qqn** to take the bread out of sb's mouth **3.** [préparation] loaf / *pain de poisson* fish loaf **4.** [bloc] ▸ **pain de cire / savon** bar of wax / soap.

paintball [pɛntbol] nm paintball.

pair¹ [pɛʀ] nm **1.** [noble] peer **2.** [égal] peer / *jugé par ses pairs* judged by one's peers **3.** BOURSE par (value) / *emprunt émis au-dessus du pair* loan issued above par ; FIN par (rate of exchange) / *pair d'une monnaie* par of a currency. ❖ **au pair** ◆ loc adj : *jeune fille au pair* au pair girl. ◆ loc adv ▸ **travailler au pair** to work as an au pair. ❖ **de pair** loc adv together / *la méchanceté va souvent de pair avec la bêtise* nastiness often goes together ou hand in hand with stupidity. ❖ **hors pair, hors de pair** loc adj outstanding, unrivalled 🇬🇧, unrivaled 🇺🇸 / *c'est un cuisinier hors pair* he's an outstanding cook / *dans son domaine il est hors de pair* he is unequalled in his field.

pair², e [pɛʀ] adj even / *jouer un chiffre pair* to bet on an even number / *stationnement les jours pairs seulement* parking on even dates only.

paire [pɛʀ] nf [de ciseaux, chaussures] pair ; [bœufs] yoke ▸ **ils font la paire** [personnes] they're two of a kind ▸ **c'est une autre paire de manches** that's a different kettle of fish.

paisible [pezibl] adj **1.** [doux] peaceful, quiet **2.** [serein] quiet, calm, peaceful **3.** [silencieux] calm, quiet.

paisiblement [peziblǝmɑ̃] adv **1.** [dormir] peacefully, quietly **2.** [parler, discuter] calmly.

paître, paitre* [91] [pɛtʀ] vi [animaux] to graze.

paix [pɛ] nf **1.** MIL & POL peace / *pourparlers / offres de paix* peace talks / proposals ▸ **en temps de paix** in peacetime ▸ **faire la paix** to make peace / *signer / ratifier un traité de paix* to sign / to ratify a peace treaty **2.** [ordre] peace / *favoriser la paix sociale* to promote social peace **3.** [entente] peace / *vivre en paix* to live in peace **4.** [repos] peace, quiet / *j'ai enfin la paix depuis qu'il est parti* I've at last got some peace and quiet now that he's left ▸ **laisse-moi en paix !** leave me alone! / *fiche-moi la paix !* fam buzz off!, clear off! **5.** [sérénité] peace / *avoir la conscience en paix* to have a clear conscience ▸ **qu'il repose en paix, paix à son âme** may he ou his soul rest in peace.

Pakistan [pakistɑ̃] npr m ▸ **le Pakistan** Pakistan ▸ **au Pakistan** in Pakistan.

pakistanais, e [pakistanɛ, ɛz] adj Pakistani. ❖ **Pakistanais, e** nm, f Pakistani.

palabrer [3] [palabʀe] vi to talk endlessly / *vous ne faites que palabrer* all you ever do is talk.

palace [palas] nm luxury hotel.

 Le mot anglais **palace** signifie « palais » et non **palace**.

palais [palɛ] nm **1.** [bâtiment] palace ▸ **palais des congrès** convention centre ▸ **palais des expositions** exhibition hall ▸ **palais des sports** sports stadium **2.** DR ▸ **le palais de justice** the law courts **3.** ANAT palate **4.** [organe du goût] palate / *elle a le palais fin* she has a refined palate.

Palais des Papes

This historic building, dating from the 13th and 14th centuries, is the prestigious venue for the most important events of the Festival d'Avignon.

Palais-Bourbon [palɛbuʀbɔ̃] npr m the French National Assembly.

palan [palɑ̃] nm hoist.

pale [pal] nf [d'une hélice, d'une rame] blade ; [d'un bateau à aube] paddle.

pâle [pal] adj **1.** [clair] pale ; [exsangue] pale, pallid ▸ **être pâle comme un linge** to be as white as a sheet ▸ **se faire porter pâle** fam to report sick **2.** [couleur] pale / *une robe jaune pâle* a pale yellow dress **3.** [insipide] pale, weak.

palefrenier, ère [palfʀǝnje, ɛʀ] nm, f [homme] stableman, ostler ; [femme] stable girl ; [garçon] stable boy.

paléolithique [paleɔlitik] nm ▸ **le paléolithique** the Paleolithic period.

paléontologie [paleɔ̃tɔlɔʒi] nf paleontology.

Palerme [palɛʀm] npr Palermo.

Palestine [palɛstin] npr f ▸ **(la) Palestine** Palestine.

palestinien, enne [palɛstinjɛ̃, ɛn] adj Palestinian. ❖ **Palestinien, enne** nm, f Palestinian.

palet [palɛ] nm **1.** SPORT puck **2.** JEUX [à la marelle] quoit.

paletot [palto] nm VÊT (short) jacket.

palette [palɛt] nf **1.** ART palette / *proposer toute une palette d'articles* to offer a wide choice ou range of articles **2.** CULIN shoulder ▸ **palette de chocolat** 🇶🇺🇪🇧🇪🇨 chocolate bar **3.** TECHNOL [instrument] pallet ; [pour la manutention] pallet, stillage **4.** 🇶🇺🇪🇧🇪🇨 [d'une casquette] visor.

palétuvier [paletyvje] nm mangrove.

pâleur [palœʀ] nf [d'une couleur] paleness ; [du teint] pallor / *je fus frappé par sa pâleur* I was surprised to see how pale she looked.

pâlichon, onne [paliʃɔ̃, ɔn] adj fam (a bit) pale ou peaky.

palier [palje] nm **1.** [plate-forme] landing **2.** [niveau] stage, level ; [d'un graphique] plateau. ❖ **par paliers** loc adv in stages, step by step.

pâlir [32] [paliʀ] vi [personne] to (turn ou go) pale ▸ **pâlir de jalousie / d'envie** to go green with jealousy / envy.

palissade [palisad] nf [clôture - de pieux] fence, paling, palisade ; [- de planches] hoarding ; [- d'arbres] hedgerow.

palissandre [palisɑ̃dʀ] nm rosewood, palissander.

palliatif [paljatif] nm **1.** MÉD palliative **2.** [expédient] palliative, stopgap measure.

pallier [9] [palje] vt **1.** [manque, erreur, inconvénient] to make up for **2.** [difficulté] to overcome.

palmarès [palmaʀɛs] nm **1.** [liste - de lauréats] prize list, list of prizewinners ; [- de sportifs] winners' list, list of winners ; [- de chansons] charts ▸ **être premier au palmarès** to top the charts, to be top of the pops **2.** [succès] : *avoir* *de nombreuses victoires à son palmarès* to have numerous victories to one's credit / *avoir un beau palmarès* to have an excellent track record.

palme [palm] nf **1.** BOT [feuille] palm leaf ; [palmier] palm tree ▸ **huile / vin de palme** palm oil / wine **2.** [distinction] palm ▸ **remporter la palme a)** [être le meilleur] to be the best **b)** *iron* to win hands down **3.** LOISIRS & SPORT flipper. ❖ **palmes** nfpl ▸ **palmes académiques** *decoration for services to education, the arts or science.*

palmé, e [palme] adj BOT palmate ; ZOOL palmate *spéc*, webbed / *avoir les pieds palmés* to have webbed feet.

palmeraie [palmǝʀɛ] nf palm grove.

palmier [palmje] nm BOT palm (tree) ▸ **palmier dattier** date palm.

palombe [palɔ̃b] nf ringdove, woodpigeon.

pâlot, otte [palo, ɔt] adj *fam* (a bit) pale.

palourde [paluʀd] nf clam.

palper [3] [palpe] vt **1.** MÉD to palpate **2.** [tâter] to feel.

palpitant, e [palpitɑ̃, ɑ̃t] adj [passionnant] thrilling, exciting, exhilarating.

palpitations [palpitasjɔ̃] nfpl palpitations ▸ **avoir des palpitations a)** [une fois] to have (an attack of) palpitations **b)** [souvent] to suffer from palpitations.

palpiter [3] [palpite] vi [artère] to throb ; [paupière] to flutter ; [flancs] to quiver, to heave ▸ **son cœur palpitait violemment a)** PHYSIOL her heart was beating fast ou pounding **b)** [d'émotion] her heart was pounding ou throbbing.

paludisme [palydism] nm malaria, paludism.

pâmer [3] [pame] ❖ **se pâmer** vpi *litt* to swoon ▸ **se pâmer devant qqn** *hum* to swoon over sb.

pampa [pɑ̃pa] nf pampas.

pamphlet [pɑ̃flɛ] nm lampoon, squib.

pamplemousse [pɑ̃plǝmus] nm ou nf grapefruit, pomelo US.

pan¹ [pɑ̃] interj [gifle] wham, whack ; [coup de feu] bang.

pan² [pɑ̃] nm **1.** [d'un vêtement] tail ; [d'une nappe] fold **2.** CONSTR ▸ **pan de mur** (face ou plain of a) wall **3.** [morceau] section, piece / *un pan de ciel bleu* a patch of blue sky / *un pan de sa vie* a chapter of his life / *des pans entiers de la société* whole sections ou strata of society **4.** TECHNOL side, face.

panacée [panase] nf panacea.

panachage [panaʃaʒ] nm **1.** [mélange] blend, blending, mixing **2.** POL *voting for candidates from different lists rather than for a list as a whole.*

panache [panaʃ] nm **1.** [plume] plume, panache ▸ **panache de fumée** *fig* plume of smoke **2.** [brio] panache, style, verve ▸ **avoir du panache** to have panache, to show great verve.

panaché, e [panaʃe] adj [sélection] mixed ; [fleurs] variegated ; [glace] mixed-flavour. ❖ **panaché** nm (lager) shandy.

Panamá [panama] npr m [pays] ▸ **le Panamá** Panama.

panaméen, enne [panameɛ̃, ɛn] adj Panamanian. ❖ **Panaméen, enne** nm, f Panamanian.

panard [panaʀ] nm *tfam* foot.

panaris [panaʀi] nm whitlow.

pan-bagnat [pɑ̃baɲa] (*pl* pans-bagnats) nm filled roll *(containing tomatoes, onions, green peppers, olives, tuna and anchovies and seasoned with olive oil).*

pancarte [pɑ̃kaʀt] nf [gén] sign, notice ; [dans une manifestation] placard.

pancréas [pɑ̃kʀeas] nm pancreas.

panda [pɑ̃da] nm panda.

pané, e [pane] adj breaded.

panégyrique [paneʒiʀik] nm panegyric, eulogy ▸ **faire le panégyrique de qqn** to extol sb's virtues, to eulogize sb.

panel [panɛl] nm **1.** TV panel **2.** [échantillon] panel, sample group.

paner [3] [pane] vt to breadcrumb, to coat with breadcrumbs.

panier [panje] nm **1.** [corbeille] basket ; PÊCHE lobster pot ▸ **panier à provisions** shopping basket ▸ **panier à salade a)** *pr* salad shaker **b)** *fam* [fourgon cellulaire] Black Maria ▸ **bon à mettre** ou **jeter au panier** fit for the bin UK ou trashcan US ▸ **être un (véritable) panier percé** to be a (real) spendthrift ▸ **c'est un (véritable) panier de crabes** they're always at each other's throats **2.** SPORT basket ▸ **réussir un panier** to score a basket **3.** ÉCON ▸ **panier de la ménagère** shopping basket **4.** INTERNET shopping cart ▸ **ajouter au panier** add to shopping cart.

panier-repas [panjeʀǝpa] (*pl* paniers-repas) nm packed lunch.

panique [panik] ◆ nf [terreur] panic / *il s'est enfui, pris de panique* he ran away panic-stricken / *pas de panique !* no need to ou there's no panic! ◆ adj panic / *envahi par une peur panique* overcome by panic.

paniquer [3] [panike] ◆ vt [angoisser] to (throw into a) panic / *il est paniqué à l'idée de la rencontrer* he's panic-stricken at the thought of meeting her, the thought of meeting her fills him with panic. ◆ vi to panic / *elle n'a pas paniqué* she didn't lose her head ou didn't panic.

panne [pan] nf [de voiture] breakdown ▸ **panne d'électricité** ou **de courant** power cut ou failure ▸ **panne d'essence** : *avoir une panne d'essence* to run out of petrol UK ou gas US ▸ **panne de secteur** local mains failure. ❖ **en panne** ◆ loc adj '*en panne*' 'out of order' / *la machine / voiture est en panne* the machine / car has broken down ▸ *je suis en panne de poivre / d'idées* *fig* I've run out of ou I'm out of pepper / ideas. ◆ loc adv ▸ **tomber en panne** : *la machine est tombée en panne* the machine has broken down ▸ *je suis tombé en panne d'essence* ou *sèche* *fam* I've run out of petrol.

panneau, x [pano] nm **1.** [pancarte] sign ▸ **panneau d'affichage** noticeboard UK, bulletin board US ▸ **panneau de configuration** INFORM control panel ▸ **panneau indicateur** signpost ▸ **panneau publicitaire** signboard, hoarding UK, billboard US ▸ **panneau de signalisation** roadsign **2.** [plaque] panel / *un panneau de contreplaqué* a piece ou panel of plywood / *panneau de particules* chipboard ▸ **panneau solaire** solar panel **3.** CHASSE (game) net ▸ **tomber** ou **donner dans le panneau** to fall into the trap.

panoplie [panɔpli] nf **1.** [ensemble d'instruments] (complete) set / *la panoplie du bricoleur* do-it-yourself equipment ou kit **2.** JEUX outfit **3.** *fig* : *une panoplie de mesures contre les chauffards* a full array of measures against dangerous drivers.

panorama [panɔrama] nm **1.** [vue] panorama, view **2.** *fig* [vue d'ensemble] survey, overview.

panoramique [panɔramik] adj panoramic ▸ **écran panoramique** panoramic screen.

panse [pɑ̃s] nf **1.** ZOOL paunch, rumen **2.** *fam* [d'une personne] paunch, belly *tfam* / *s'en mettre plein* ou *se remplir la panse* to make a pig of o.s., to stuff one's face.

pansement [pɑ̃smɑ̃] nm [action] dressing ; [objet] dressing, bandage / *il lui a fait un pansement à la jambe* he bandaged her leg ▸ **pansement adhésif** (sticking) plaster UK, Elastoplast UK, Band Aid US.

panser [3] [pɑ̃se] vt **1.** MÉD to dress (and bandage) / *panser une blessure* to dress ou to put a dressing on a wound ▸ **panser les plaies de qqn** to tend sb's wounds **2.** [toiletter - animal] to groom.

pantacourt [pɑ̃takuʀ] nm capri pants, capris, clamdiggers.

pantalon [pɑ̃talɔ̃] nm (pair of) trousers 🇬🇧 ou pants 🇺🇸 ▸ **mon pantalon** my trousers ▸ **pantalon de golf** (pair of) plus fours ▸ **pantalon de pyjama** pyjama trousers ou bottoms ▸ **pantalon de ski** ski pants.

pantelant, e [pɑ̃tlɑ̃, ɑ̃t] adj panting, gasping for breath.

panthéon [pɑ̃teɔ̃] nm **1.** ANTIQ & RELIG pantheon ▸ **le Panthéon** the Pantheon **2.** fig pantheon, hall of fame.

panthère [pɑ̃tɛʀ] nf ZOOL panther.

pantin [pɑ̃tɛ̃] nm **1.** [jouet] jumping jack **2.** fig puppet.

pantois, e [pɑ̃twa, az] adj speechless / **elle en est restée pantoise** it left her speechless.

pantomime [pɑ̃tɔmim] nf [jeu de mime] mime ; THÉÂTRE [pièce] mime show.

pantouflard, e [pɑ̃tuflaʀ, aʀd] nm, f fam homebody, stay-at-home (type).

pantoufle [pɑ̃tufl] nf slipper.

panure [panyʀ] nf ≃ breadcrumbs (for coating).

PAO (abr de **publication assistée par ordinateur**) nf DTP.

paon [pɑ̃] nm ORNITH peacock.

papa [papa] nm [père] dad, daddy. ❖ **à papa** loc adj fam ▸ **c'est un fils / une fille à papa** he's / she's got a rich daddy. ❖ **de papa** loc adj fam old-fashioned.

papauté [papote] nf papacy.

papaye [papaj] nf papaya, pawpaw.

pape [pap] nm RELIG pope.

paperasse [papʀas] nf péj papers, bumf 🇬🇧 / **je n'ai pas le temps de remplir toute cette paperasse** I don't have the time to fill up all these forms.

paperasserie [papʀasʀi] nf péj [formulaires] paperwork / **toute cette paperasserie va sûrement retarder le projet** all this red tape is bound to delay the project.

papet [papɛ] nm 🇨🇭Suisse Swiss dish made with potatoes, leeks and sausages.

papeterie, papèterie* [papɛtʀi] nf **1.** [boutique] stationer's shop **2.** [matériel] stationery.

papetier, ère [paptje, ɛʀ] nm, f COMM stationer.

papi [papi] fam = **papy.**

papier [papje] nm **1.** [matériau] paper / **sur le papier, le projet paraît réalisable** on paper, the project seems feasible ▸ **papier absorbant** kitchen paper ▸ **papier alu** ou **d'aluminium** aluminium 🇬🇧 ou aluminum 🇺🇸 foil ▸ **papier brouillon** rough paper ▸ **papier buvard** blotting paper ▸ **papier cadeau** wrapping paper ▸ **papier à cigarette** cigarette paper ▸ **papier crépon** crêpe paper ▸ **papier électronique** electronic paper, e-paper ▸ **papier d'emballage** brown (wrapping) paper ▸ **papier à en-tête** headed paper ou notepaper ▸ **papier glacé** glazed paper ▸ **papier hygiénique** toilet paper ▸ **papier journal** newspaper, newsprint ▸ **papier kraft** brown paper ▸ **papier à lettres** writing paper / **envoyer une lettre sur papier libre** apply in writing ▸ **papier mâché** papier-mâché ▸ **papier millimétré** graph paper ▸ **papier à musique** music paper ▸ **papier peint** wallpaper ▸ **papier pelure** onion skin (paper) ▸ **papier de soie** tissue paper ▸ **papier sulfurisé** greaseproof ou spéc sulphurized paper ▸ **papier de verre** glasspaper, sandpaper **2.** [morceau] piece of paper ; [page] sheet of paper, piece of paper ▸ **être dans les petits papiers de qqn** to be in sb's good books **3.** PRESSE article, piece **4.** ADMIN papers ▸ **papiers (d'identité)** (identity) papers ▸ **faux papiers** false ou forged papers. ❖ **de papier, en papier** loc adj paper (modif). ❖ **papiers gras** nmpl litter.

papier-calque [papjekalk] (pl **papiers-calque**) nm tracing paper.

papille [papij] nf papilla ▸ **papilles gustatives** taste buds.

papillon [papijɔ̃] nm **1.** ENTOM butterfly ▸ **papillon de nuit** moth **2.** fam [contravention] (parking) ticket **3.** SPORT butterfly (stroke).

papillonner [3] [papijɔne] vi **1.** [voltiger] to flit ou to flutter about **2.** [être volage] to behave in a fickle manner **3.** [être inattentif] to be inattentive / **son esprit papillonne** he can't keep his mind on things.

papillote [papijɔt] nf CULIN [pour gigot] frill ▸ **en papillotes** en papillote (cooked in foil or paper parcels).

papoter [3] [papɔte] vi fam to chatter, to have a chinwag.

papou, e [papu] adj Papuan. ❖ **Papou, e** nm, f Papuan.

Papouasie-Nouvelle-Guinée [papwazinuvɛlgine] npr f ▸ **(la) Papouasie-Nouvelle-Guinée** Papua New Guinea.

paprika [papʀika] nm paprika.

papy [papi] nm fam grandad.

papy-boom [papibum] nm grey boom, ageing population ; [pour insister sur les effets négatifs] demographic time-bomb.

papy-boomeur [papibumœʀ] nm current retiree born during the baby-boom of the post-war generation.

papyrus [papiʀys] nm ARCHÉOL & BOT papyrus.

Pâque [pak] nf ▸ **la Pâque** Passover, Pesach.

paquebot [pakbo] nm liner.

pâquerette [pakʀɛt] nf daisy.

Pâques [pak] nm Easter ▸ **l'île de Pâques** Easter Island. ❖ **pâques** nfpl ▸ **joyeuses pâques** Happy Easter.

🚩 **Les cloches de Pâques**

In France, Easter is traditionally symbolized not only by eggs but also by bells; according to legend, church bells fly to Rome at Easter.

paquet [pakɛ] nm **1.** [colis, ballot] parcel 🇬🇧, package / **faire un paquet de vieux journaux** to make up a bundle of old newspapers **2.** COMM [marchandise emballée] packet 🇬🇧, package 🇺🇸 ▸ **un paquet de sucre / de farine** a bag of sugar / flour ▸ **un paquet de cigarettes** a packet 🇬🇧 ou a pack 🇺🇸 (of cigarettes) / **je vous fais un paquet-cadeau ?** shall I gift-wrap it for you? **3.** [valise] bag **4.** [quantité importante] : **il y a un paquet d'erreurs dans ce texte** this text is full of mistakes, there are loads of mistakes in this text ▸ **mettre le paquet** : **j'ai mis (tout) le paquet** fig I gave it all I've got **5.** ▸ **un paquet de mer** NAUT a big wave ▸ **un paquet de nerfs** : **sa mère est un paquet de nerfs** her mother's a bundle ou bag of nerves.

paquetage [paktaʒ] nm MIL kit, pack / **ils font leur paquetage** they're getting their kits ready.

par [paʀ] prép **1.** [indiquant la direction, le parcours] by ; [en traversant un lieu] through / **il est arrivé par la route** he came by road ▸ **il est arrivé par la gauche / par la droite / par le nord** he arrived from the left / the right / the north / **il est passé par la maison avant de ressortir** he dropped in before going off again ; [indiquant la position] : **elle est assise par terre** she's sitting on the ground / **la neige avait fondu par endroits** the snow had melted in places **2.** [pendant] : **par un beau jour d'été** on a fine summer's day ▸ **par grand froid / grosse chaleur** in extreme cold / intense heat ▸ **par moments** at times, from time to time ▸ **par deux fois** twice **3.** [indiquant le moyen, la manière] by / *les lettres sont classées par ordre d'arrivée* the letters are filed in order of arrival ▶ **par air / terre / mer** by air / land / sea / *je l'ai appris par la radio* I heard it on the radio ▶ **répondre par oui ou par non / par la négative** to answer yes or no / in the negative ▶ **obtenir qqch par la force / la douceur** to obtain sthg by force / through kindness **4.** [indiquant la cause, l'origine] ▶ **faire qqch par habitude / caprice / plaisir / paresse** to do sthg out of habit / on a whim / for the pleasure of it / out of laziness / *je l'ai rencontré par hasard* I met him by chance / *une tante par alliance* an aunt by marriage **5.** [introduisant le complément d'agent] by / *le logiciel est protégé par un code* the software is protected by ou with a code ▶ **faire faire qqch par qqn** to have sthg done by sb / *je l'ai appris par elle* I heard it from her, I learned of it through her **6.** [emploi distributif] ▶ **une heure par jour** one hour a ou per day / *150 euros par personne* 150 euros per person ▶ **une fois par an** once a year ▶ **un par un** one by one ▶ *ils arrivaient par petits groupes / centaines* they arrived in small groups / in their hundreds **7.** [avec les verbes 'commencer' et 'finir'] ▶ *ça finira par arriver / par ressembler à quelque chose* it will end up happening / looking like something ▶ **commence par travailler** start (off) by working / *il a fini par avouer* he eventually owned up. ❖ **de par** *loc prép* **1.** [par l'ordre de] ▶ **de par la loi** according to the law **2.** *litt* [dans l'espace] throughout / *de par le monde* all over ou throughout the world **3.** [du fait de] by virtue of. ❖ **par-ci par-là** *loc adv* **1.** [dans l'espace] here and there **2.** [dans le temps] now and then, from time to time, every now and then ou again **3.** [marquant la répétition] : *avec lui, c'est mon yacht par-ci, mon avion personnel par-là* it's my yacht this, my plane that, all the time with him.

paraben, parabène [paraben] nm paraben ▶ **sans paraben** paraben-free.

parabole [parabɔl] nf **1.** LITTÉR & RELIG parable **2.** MATH parabola.

parabolique [parabɔlik] adj **1.** LITTÉR & RELIG parabolic, parabolical **2.** TV ▶ **antenne parabolique** satellite dish, disk aerial.

parachever [19] [paraʃve] vt *sout* to complete / *parachever un tableau* to put the finishing touches to a painting.

parachute [paraʃyt] nm parachute ▶ **faire du parachute** to go parachuting ▶ **parachute dorsal** back-pack parachute ▶ **parachute ventral** lap-pack ou chest-pack parachute.

parachuter [3] [paraʃyte] vt **1.** MIL & SPORT to parachute **2.** *fam* POL to bring in from outside the constituency / *ils l'ont parachuté directeur dans une succursale* ADMIN he was unexpectedly given the job of branch manager.

parachutisme [paraʃytism] nm parachuting ▶ **faire du parachutisme** to go parachuting ▶ **parachutisme ascensionnel** parascending.

parachutiste [paraʃytist] nm **1.** LOISIRS & SPORT parachutist **2.** MIL paratrooper.

parade [parad] nf **1.** [défilé] parade ▶ **faire parade de** [faire étalage de] : *faire parade de ses connaissances* to show off ou to parade ou to display one's knowledge **2.** ZOOL (courtship) display **3.** BOXE parry ; ESCRIME parade, parry ; ÉQUIT checking ; FOOT save **4.** [riposte] retort, reply, riposte / *nous devons trouver la parade* we must find a way of counterattacking. ❖ **de parade** *loc adj litt* [ornemental] ceremonial.

parader [3] [parade] vi **1.** [troupes] to parade **2.** [personne] to show off, to pose, to strut about.

paradis [paradi] nm RELIG paradise, heaven ▶ **paradis fiscal** tax haven ▶ **le Paradis terrestre a)** *pr* the Garden of Eden ou Earthly Paradise **b)** *fig* heaven on earth.

paradisiaque [paradizjak] adj heavenly, paradisal *sout*, paradisiacal *sout*.

paradoxal, e, aux [paradɔksal, o] adj **1.** [contradictoire] paradoxical **2.** [déconcertant] unexpected, paradoxical.

paradoxalement [paradɔksalmɑ̃] adv paradoxically.

paradoxe [paradɔks] nm paradox.

parafe [paraf] = **paraphe**.

parafer [parafe] = **parapher**.

paraffine [parafin] nf paraffin ou paraffine (wax).

parages [paraʒ] nmpl [environs] area, surroundings / *il habite dans les parages* he lives around here somewhere.

paragraphe [paragraf] nm [passage] paragraph.

Paraguay [paragɥɛ] npr m ▶ **le Paraguay** Paraguay.

paraguayen, enne [paragwejɛ̃, ɛn] adj Paraguayan.
❖ **Paraguayen, enne** nm, f Paraguayan.

paraître, paraitre* [91] [paretr] ❖ vi **1.** [se montrer - soleil] to appear, to come out ; [- émotion] to show ; [- personne attendue] to appear, to turn up ; [- dignitaire, prince] to appear, to make a public appearance ; [- acteur] to appear / *laisser paraître son émotion* to let one's emotion show **2.** [être publié - livre] to be published, to come out, to appear / *faire paraître une petite annonce dans un journal* to put an advertisement in a paper / **'à paraître'** 'forthcoming' / **'vient de paraître'** 'just published' **3.** [sembler] to appear, to seem, to look / *il parut céder* he looked as though he was giving in ▶ **paraît-il** apparently **4.** [se donner en spectacle] to show off. ❖ v impers ▶ **ça ne paraît pas (mais...)** [ça ne se voit pas] it doesn't look like it (but...) / *dans une semaine il n'y paraîtra plus* in a week it won't show any more / *il me paraît préférable de se décider maintenant* I think it's better ou it seems better to make up our minds now / *vous êtes renvoyé ? — il paraît* have you been fired? — it looks like it ou so it seems ▶ **il paraît que...** I've heard (that)..., it would seem (that)... / *paraît que tu vas te marier ?* fam I hear you're getting married? ▶ **à ce qu'il paraît** apparently.

parallèle [paralɛl] ❖ adj **1.** GÉOM, SPORT & INFORM parallel / *la droite AB est parallèle à la droite CD* line AB is parallel to line CD **2.** [comparable - données, résultats] parallel, comparable, similar **3.** [non officiel - festival] unofficial, fringe (*modif*) ; [- marché, transaction] unofficial ; [- police] unofficial, secret. ❖ nm [comparaison] parallel / *établir un parallèle entre deux phénomènes* to draw a parallel between two phenomena. ❖ nf GÉOM parallel (line).
❖ **en parallèle** *loc adv* [en balance] : *mettre deux faits en parallèle* to draw a parallel between ou to compare two facts.

parallèlement [paralɛlmɑ̃] adv **1.** GÉOM in a parallel to **2.** [simultanément] ▶ **parallèlement à** at the same time as.

parallélisme [paralelism] nm **1.** GÉOM parallelism **2.** AUTO wheel alignment **3.** [concordance] parallel, concordance / *établir un parallélisme entre deux faits* to draw a parallel between two facts.

paralympique [paralɛ̃pik] adj Paralympic ▶ **les Jeux paralympiques** the Paralympics.

paralysé, e [paralize] ❖ adj paralysed UK, paralyzed US. ❖ nm, f MÉD paralytic.

paralyser [3] [paralize] vt **1.** MÉD to paralyse UK, to paralyze US **2.** [figer, inhiber] to paralyse UK, to paralyze US / *paralysé par la peur* crippled with fear / *paralysé par le brouillard* fog-bound.

paralysie [paralizi] nf **1.** MÉD paralysis **2.** [arrêt] paralysis.

paralytique [paralitik] adj & nmf MÉD paralytic.

*** In reformed spelling (see p. 16-18).**

paramédical, e, aux [paʀamedikal, o] adj paramedical.

paramètre [paʀametʀ] nm **1.** MATH parameter **2.** [élément variable] parameter, factor.

parano [paʀano] fam adj paranoid.

paranoïaque [paʀanɔjak] ◆ adj paranoiac, paranoid. ◆ nmf paranoiac.

paranormal, e, aux [paʀanɔʀmal, o] adj paranormal.

parapente [paʀapɑ̃t] nm paragliding.

parapet [paʀapɛ] nm CONSTR parapet.

parapharmacie [paʀafaʀmasi] nf (non-pharmaceutical) chemist's 🇬🇧 ou druggist's 🇺🇸 merchandise.

paraphe [paʀaf] nm [pour authentifier] initials ; [pour décorer] flourish, paraph.

parapher [3] [paʀafe] vt [pour authentifier] to initial.

paraphrase [paʀafʀaz] nf [gén & LING] paraphrase.

paraphraser [3] [paʀafʀaze] vt to paraphrase.

paraplégique [paʀapleʒik] adj & nmf paraplegic.

parapluie [paʀaplɥi] nm [accessoire] umbrella.

parapsychologie [paʀapsikɔlɔʒi] nf parapsychology.

parapublic, ique [paʀapyblik] adj semi-public.

parascolaire [paʀaskɔlɛʀ] adj extracurricular.

parasite [paʀazit] nm **1.** BIOL parasite **2.** [personne] scrounger. ◆ **parasites** nmpl RADIO & TV interference (U), atmospherics 🇬🇧 ; TÉLÉC noise, static.

parasiter [3] [paʀazite] vt BIOL to live as a parasite on, to be parasitical upon / *je me suis fait parasiter par un ancien copain* fam & fig an old friend came around to sponge off me.

parasol [paʀasɔl] nm [en ville, dans un jardin] parasol, sunshade ; [pour la plage] beach umbrella, parasol.

paratonnerre [paʀatɔnɛʀ] nm lightning conductor 🇬🇧 ou rod 🇺🇸.

paravent [paʀavɑ̃] nm [écran] (folding) screen ou partition.

parc [paʀk] nm **1.** LOISIRS [jardin public] park ; [domaine privé] park, grounds ▸ **parc aquatique** water parc ▸ **parc d'attractions** amusement park ▸ **parc de loisirs** leisure park ▸ **parc naturel** nature reserve ▸ [enclos - à bétail] pen, enclosure ; [- à moutons] fold ; [- pour bébé] pen, playpen ▸ **parc de stationnement** car park 🇬🇧, parking lot 🇺🇸 **3.** PÊCHE bed ▸ **parc à huîtres** oyster bed **4.** COMM ▸ **parc d'expositions** showground **5.** [unités d'équipement] stock ▸ **le parc automobile français** the total number of cars in France ▸ **parc immobilier** housing stock **6.** INDUST [entrepôt] depot ▸ **parc industriel** 🇶🇧 industrial estate 🇬🇧 ou park 🇺🇸.

parcelle [paʀsɛl] nf **1.** ADMIN parcel, plot ; [lopin] plot (of land) **2.** [morceau - d'or] particle / *pas une parcelle de vérité* not a grain ou shred of truth.

parce que [paʀskə] (devant voyelle ou « h » muet **parce qu'** [paʀsk]) loc conj because / *pourquoi pleures-tu ? — parce que !* fam why are you crying? — because!

parchemin [paʀʃəmɛ̃] nm [pour écrire] (piece of) parchment.

parcimonie [paʀsimɔni] nf sout parsimony, parsimoniousness. ◆ **avec parcimonie** loc adv parsimoniously, sparingly.

parcimonieux, euse [paʀsimɔnjø, øz] adj sout parsimonious, sparing.

parc(o)mètre [paʀk(ɔ)mɛtʀ] nm (parking) meter.

parcourir [45] [paʀkuʀiʀ] vt **1.** [distance - gén] to cover ; [- en courant] to run ; [- en marchant] to walk ; [- à cheval, à vélo] to ride **2.** [pour visiter] to travel through (insép) ; [dans une quête] to scour, to search (all over) / *je parcou-*

rais la ville à la recherche d'un emploi I was searching all over town for a job **3.** [suj : douleur, frisson] to run through (insép) **4.** [jeter un coup d'œil à - journal, roman, notes de cours] to skim ou to leaf through (insép) / *je n'ai fait que parcourir sa lettre* I've only glanced at her letter.

parcours [paʀkuʀ] nm **1.** [trajet - d'une personne] way, journey ; TRANSP route ▸ **parcours du combattant a)** MIL assault course **b)** fig obstacle course **2.** fig [carrière] career, record, path / *son parcours scolaire a été irréprochable* she had a faultless school record ▸ **parcours professionnel** career **3.** SPORT course.

par-delà [paʀdəla] prép sout beyond / *par-delà les mers* over the seas / *par-delà les siècles* across the centuries.

par-derrière [paʀdɛʀjɛʀ] ◆ prép behind, round 🇬🇧 ou around 🇺🇸 the back of / *passe par-derrière la maison* go round the back of the house. ◆ adv **1.** [par l'arrière] from behind, at the rear **2.** [sournoisement] ▸ *il me critique par-derrière* he criticizes me behind my back.

par-dessous [paʀdəsu] ◆ prép under, underneath / *passe par-dessous la barrière* go under the fence. ◆ adv underneath.

pardessus [paʀdəsy] nm overcoat.

par-dessus [paʀdəsy] ◆ prép **1.** [en franchissant] over, above / *passe par-dessus la grille* go over the railings **2.** [sur] : *porter un manteau par-dessus sa veste* to wear an overcoat on top of one's jacket. ◆ adv [dans l'espace] : *saute par-dessus !* jump over! ◆ **par-dessus tout** loc adv most of all, above all.

par-devant [paʀdəvɑ̃] ◆ prép ADMIN & DR ▸ **par-devant notaire** in the presence of a solicitor 🇬🇧 ou lawyer 🇺🇸, with a solicitor 🇬🇧 ou lawyer 🇺🇸 present. ◆ adv [sur le devant] at ou round the front.

pardon [paʀdɔ̃] nm **1.** [rémission] forgiveness, pardon sout ▸ **demander pardon à qqn** to apologize to sb, to ask for sb's forgiveness / *demander pardon à la dame* say sorry to ou apologize to the lady ▸ **pardon ?** [pour faire répéter] sorry?, (I beg your) pardon? 🇬🇧, pardon me? 🇺🇸 ▸ **oh, pardon ! a)** [pour s'excuser] sorry!, excuse me! **b)** iron (so) sorry! / *la mère est déjà désagréable, mais alors la fille, pardon !* the mother's bad enough, but the daughter! **2.** [en Bretagne] religious festival **3.** RELIG ▸ **Grand Pardon** Yom Kippur, Day of Atonement.

pardonnable [paʀdɔnabl] adj excusable, forgivable, pardonable / *votre erreur n'est pas pardonnable* your mistake is unforgivable ou inexcusable.

pardonner [3] [paʀdɔne] vt **1.** [oublier - offense] to forgive, to excuse ; [- péché] to forgive, to pardon ▸ **pardonner qqch à qqn** to forgive sb for sthg / *allez, je te pardonne tout* all right, I'll let you off (everything) / *il ne me pardonne pas d'avoir eu raison* he won't forgive me for having been right / *se faire pardonner* to be forgiven, to win forgiveness ; (en usage absolu) to be forgiving / *une distraction au volant, ça ne pardonne pas !* one slip in concentration at the wheel is fatal! **2.** [dans des formules de politesse] to forgive, to excuse / *pardonnez ma curiosité* ou *pardonnez-moi si je suis indiscret mais...* I'm sorry if I'm being ou excuse me for being nosy, but... / *pardonnez-moi, mais vous oubliez un détail d'importance* excuse me, but you've forgotten an important point. ◆ **se pardonner** vp (emploi réfléchi) : *je ne me le pardonnerai jamais* I'll never forgive myself.

paré, e [paʀe] adj [prêt] ready.

pare-balles (pl pare-balles), **pare-balle*** (pl pare-balles*) [paʀbal] adj bullet proof.

pare-brise [paʀbʀiz] (pl pare-brise ou pare-brises*) nm windscreen 🇬🇧, windshield 🇺🇸.

pare-chocs, pare-choc* [paʀʃɔk] nm bumper.

pare-feu [paʀfø] (*pl* pare-feu *ou* pare-feux*) nm
1. [en forêt] firebreak **2.** [d'une cheminée] fireguard.

pareil, eille [paʀɛj] ◆ adj **1.** [semblable, équivalent]
the same, alike, similar / *je n'ai jamais rien vu de pareil*
I've never seen anything like it / *comment vas-tu ? — tou-*
jours pareil ! how are you? — same as ever! / *c'est tou-*
jours pareil, personne n'ose se plaindre ! it's always the
same, nobody ever dares complain! ▶ **pareil à** the same
as, just like ▶ **pareil que** *fam* (the) same as **2.** [de cette
nature] such (a) / *on n'avait jamais vu (un) pareil scan-*
dale ! there'd never been such a scandal! / *qui peut bien*
téléphoner à une heure pareille ? who could be phoning at
this hour ou time? ▶ **pareil** nm, f
[semblable] : *ne pas avoir son pareil, ne pas avoir sa*
pareille to be second to none / *il n'a pas son pareil pour*
arriver au mauvais moment ! there's nobody quite like
him for turning up at the wrong moment! ◆ **pareil** adv
fam the same / *on n'a pas dû comprendre pareil* we can't
have understood the same thing. ◆ **pareille** nf ▶ **rendre**
la pareille à qqn to repay sb in kind. ◆ **pareils** nmpl
▶ **nos pareils a)** [semblables] our fellow men **b)** [égaux]
our equals ou peers. ◆ **sans pareil, sans pareille**
loc adj [éclat, beauté, courage] unrivalled, unequalled ; [talent,
habileté] unparalleled, unequalled ; [artiste] peerless *sout*, unequalled.

pareillement [paʀɛjmɑ̃] adv **1.** [de la même manière]
in the same way **2.** [aussi] equally, likewise / *bonne soirée !*
— et à vous pareillement ! have a nice evening! — you
too!

parement [paʀmɑ̃] nm **1.** COUT facing **2.** CONSTR [sur-
face] facing, face ; [revêtement] facing, dressing.

parent, e [paʀɑ̃, ɑ̃t] ◆ adj [de la même famille] related / *je suis parente avec eux, nous sommes parents*
I'm related to them. ◆ nm, f relative, relation / *un proche*
parent a close relative ou relation / *ce sont des parents en*
ligne directe / *par alliance* they're blood relations / related
by marriage ▶ **parent pauvre** poor relation. ◆ **parent**
nm parent ▶ **parent biologique** birth parent. ◆ **parents**
nmpl [père et mère] parents, father and mother ▶ **parents**
adoptifs adoptive ou foster parents.

parental, e, aux [paʀɑ̃tal, o] adj parental.

parenté [paʀɑ̃te] nf [lien familial] relationship, kinship /
il n'y a aucune parenté entre eux they're not related in any
way.

parenthèse [paʀɑ̃tɛz] nf **1.** [signe] parenthesis, bracket
🇬🇧 / *ouvrir* / *fermer la parenthèse* to open / to close the
brackets 🇬🇧 ou parentheses **2.** [digression] digression, parenthesis / *je fais une (brève) parenthèse pour signa-*
ler que... incidentally ou in parenthesis, we may briefly
note that... ▶ **fermons la parenthèse** anyway, enough of
that. ◆ **entre parenthèses** loc adv **1.** [mot, phrase]
▶ **mettre qqch entre parenthèses** to put sthg in parenthesis, to put sthg in ou between brackets 🇬🇧, to bracket sthg
🇬🇧 / *il a dû mettre sa vie privée entre parenthèses* fig he
had to put his private life to one side **2.** [à propos] incidentally, by the way.

parer [3] [paʀe] vt **1.** *litt* [embellir - pièce] to decorate, to
deck out (*sép*), to adorn ; [-personne] to deck out (*sép*), to
adorn ; [vêtir] to dress / *elle ne sort que parée de ses plus*
beaux atours she only goes out attired in her best finery
2. *sout* [attribuer à] ▶ **parer qqn de toutes les vertus** to
attribute many virtues to sb **3.** CULIN [poisson, volaille] to
dress ; [rôti] to trim **4.** [éviter - coup, danger] to ward ou to
fend ou to stave off (*sép*) ; [-attaque] to stave off (*sép*), to
parry ; BOXE & ESCRIME to parry **5.** [protéger] ▶ **parer qqn**
contre qqch to shield ou to protect sb against sthg / *je suis*
paré contre le froid / *l'hiver* I'm prepared for the cold / winter. ◆ **parer à** v + prép **1.** [faire face - incident] to cope
ou to deal with (*insép*), to handle ▶ **parer à toute éven-**

tualité to prepare for ou to guard against any contingency
▶ **parer au plus pressé** [en voyageant, en emménageant] to
deal with basic necessities (first) **2.** [se défendre contre - tir,
attaque] to ward off.

pare-soleil [paʀsɔlɛj] (*pl* pare-soleil *ou* pare-
soleils*) nm sun visor, sunshade.

paresse [paʀɛs] nf **1.** [fainéantise] laziness, idleness
2. [apathie] indolence, laziness **3.** RELIG [péché capital] sloth
4. MÉD ▶ **paresse intestinale**: *souffrir de paresse intesti-*
nale to be slow to digest (one's) food.

paresser [4] [paʀese] vi to laze (about ou around).

paresseusement [paʀɛsøzmɑ̃] adv **1.** [avec paresse]
idly, lazily **2.** *sout* [avec lenteur] lazily, idly, sluggishly.

paresseux, euse [paʀɛsø, øz] ◆ adj **1.** [sans ardeur]
lazy, idle **2.** MÉD [digestion] sluggish. ◆ nm, f lazy person.

parfaire [109] [paʀfɛʀ] vt [peaufiner] to perfect, to bring
to perfection / *parfaire une œuvre* to add the finishing
touches to a work.

parfait, e [paʀfɛ, ɛt] adj **1.** [sans défaut - beauté, crime,
harmonie, conditions] perfect ; [- argumentation, diamant,
maquillage] perfect, flawless ; [- scolarité, savoir-vivre, per-
sonne] perfect, faultless **2.** [en intensif] perfect, utter /
c'est le parfait homme du monde he's a perfect gentleman / *c'est un parfait goujat* / *idiot* he's an utter boor /
fool **3.** [complet, total - bonheur, calme, entente] perfect,
complete, total ; [- ressemblance] perfect ; [- ignorance] utter,
complete, total / *elle s'est montrée d'une parfaite déli-*
catesse she showed exquisite ou perfect tact **4.** [excellent]
perfect, excellent / *il a été parfait* he was perfect ou marvellous / *10 heures, ça vous va ? — c'est parfait !* would
10 o'clock suit you? — that's perfect ou (just) fine!
◆ **parfait** nm CULIN parfait.

parfaitement [paʀfɛtmɑ̃] adv **1.** [très bien] perfectly,
impeccably, faultlessly / *j'avais parfaitement entendu !*
I heard all right! **2.** [absolument] perfectly, absolutely, thoroughly / *cela lui est parfaitement indifférent* it's a matter
of complete indifference to him **3.** [oui] (most) certainly,
definitely / *c'est vrai ? — parfaitement !* is that true? — it
(most) certainly ou definitely is!

parfois [paʀfwa] adv **1.** [quelquefois] sometimes **2.** [dans
certains cas] sometimes, at times, occasionally.

📝 Notez la position de sometimes dans la
phrase.

• **Comme** parfois **et** quelquefois, sometimes
peut être placé en début ou en fin de phrase :
Parfois, il vient me voir en rentrant du travail.
Sometimes, he comes to see me on his way back
from work.
Il m'agaçait parfois. *He got on my nerves some-*
times.

• **Avec un verbe autre que** be **conjugué,** sometimes peut également s'insérer comme suit :
sujet + [aux/modal] + sometimes + verbe
Il m'arrive parfois de penser à elle. / *sometimes*
think about her.
Sa sœur gardait ses enfants parfois. *His sister*
sometimes looked after his children.

• **Avec le verbe** be **conjugué,** sometimes peut
se placer comme suit :
sujet + be + sometimes
Il est malade parfois lorsqu'il mange des fruits
de mer. *He's sometimes ill when he eats seafood.*
Elle est très cassante parfois. *She's sometimes*
very sharp-tongued.

---

* In reformed spelling (see p. 16-18).

parfum [paʀfœ̃] nm **1.** [odeur - d'une lotion, d'une fleur] perfume, scent, fragrance ; [- d'un mets] aroma ; [- d'un fruit] smell **2.** [cosmétique] perfume, scent **3.** [goût] flavour 🇬🇧, flavor 🇺🇸 / *(tu veux une glace) à quel parfum ?* what flavour (ice cream) do you want? ❖ **au parfum** loc adv *fam* ▸ **être au parfum** to be in the know.

parfumé, e [paʀfyme] adj **1.** [savon] scented ; [bougie] perfumed ; [personne] : *elle est parfumée* she's wearing perfume / *parfumé au café* [glace] coffee-flavoured 🇬🇧, coffee-flavored 🇺🇸 **2.** [fleur] fragrant, sweet-smelling ; [fruit] sweet-smelling ; [vin, air] fragrant.

parfumer [3] [paʀfyme] vt **1.** [embaumer] to perfume *sout* **2.** [mettre du parfum sur] to put ou to dab perfume on ▸ **être parfumé** [personne] to have perfume on, to be wearing perfume **3.** CULIN to flavour ▸ **parfumé à** flavoured with. ❖ **se parfumer** vp *(emploi réfléchi)* to put on perfume / *je ne me parfume jamais* I never wear ou use perfume.

parfumerie [paʀfymʀi] nf **1.** [magasin] perfumery (shop) 🇬🇧, perfumery (store) 🇺🇸 **2.** [articles] perfumes (and cosmetics), perfumery.

pari [paʀi] nm **1.** [défi, enjeu] bet, wager ▸ **faire un pari** to lay a bet, to (have a) bet / *cette politique est un pari sur l'avenir* this policy is a gamble on the future **2.** JEUX [mise] bet, stake / *il a gagné son pari* he won his bet ▸ **Pari Mutuel Urbain®** = PMU.

paria [paʀja] nmf [d'un groupe] outcast, pariah.

parier [9] [paʀje] ❖ vt **1.** [somme] to bet, to lay, to stake ; [repas, bouteille] to bet **2.** [exprimant la certitude] to bet / *qu'est-ce que tu paries qu'il va refuser ?* how much do you bet he'll say no? ▸ **je l'aurais parié !** I knew it! ; *(en usage absolu) : tu paries ? fam* want to bet? **3.** [exprimant la probabilité] ▸ **il y a fort** ou **gros à parier que...** the odds are ou it's odds on that... ❖ vi [être parieur] to bet / *parier aux courses* [de chevaux] to bet on the horses.

parieur, euse [paʀjœʀ, øz] nm, f **1.** [qui fait un pari] better **2.** [qui aime parier] betting man (woman).

Paris [paʀi] npr Paris.

Paris

The name **Paris** followed by a number or Roman numeral refers to a Paris university: **Paris-VII** (the science faculty at Jussieu), **Paris-IV** (the Sorbonne), **Paris-X** (Nanterre university), etc.

When **Paris** is followed by an ordinal number, this refers to an arrondissement: **Paris XVᵉ**, **Paris IVᵉ**, etc.

parisien, enne [paʀizjɛ̃, ɛn] adj **1.** [relatif à Paris, sa région] Paris *(modif)* ; [natif de Paris, habitant à Paris] Parisian **2.** [typique de Paris] Parisian. ❖ **Parisien, enne** nm, f Parisian.

paritaire [paʀitɛʀ] adj ▸ **représentation paritaire** parity of representation, equal representation.

parité [paʀite] nf [concordance - entre des rémunérations] parity, equality ; [- entre des monnaies, des prix] parity ; [- entre des concepts] comparability ▸ **la parité hommes-femmes** gender parity.

parjure [paʀʒyʀ] nm [acte] disloyalty, treachery, betrayal.

parjurer [3] [paʀʒyʀe] ❖ **se parjurer** vpi *sout* [manquer à son serment] to break one's word ou promise.

parka [paʀka] nm ou nf parka.

parking [paʀkiŋ] nm [parc de stationnement] car park 🇬🇧, parking lot 🇺🇸 ▸ **une place de parking** a parking space.

parlant, e [paʀlɑ̃, ɑ̃t] adj **1.** CINÉ talking **2.** [significatif - chiffre, exemple, schéma] which speaks for itself ▸ **leurs statistiques sont parlantes** their figures speak volumes **3.** [bien observé - portrait] lifelike ; [- description] vivid, graphic.

parlé, e [paʀle] adj [anglais, langue - oral] spoken ; [- familier] colloquial.

parlement [paʀləmɑ̃] nm POL ▸ **le Parlement a)** [en France] (the French) Parliament **b)** [en Grande-Bretagne] (the Houses of) Parliament ▸ **au parlement** in Parliament.

parlementaire [paʀləmɑ̃tɛʀ] ❖ adj [débat, habitude, régime] parliamentary. ❖ nmf [député] member of Parliament ; [aux États-Unis] Congressman (Congresswoman).

parlementer [3] [paʀləmɑ̃te] vi to negotiate ▸ **parlementer avec** POL to parley with.

parler¹ [paʀle] nm **1.** [vocabulaire] speech, way of speaking / *dans le parler de tous les jours* in common parlance **2.** [langue d'une région] dialect, variety.

parler² [3] [paʀle]

❖ vi

A. FAIRE UN ÉNONCÉ **1.** [articuler des paroles] to talk, to speak / *parler bas* ou *à voix basse* to speak softly ou in a low voice / *parler haut* ou *à voix haute* to speak loudly ou in a loud voice / *parle plus fort* speak louder ou up / *parlez moins fort* keep your voice down, don't speak so loud / *parler par gestes* ou *signes* to use sign language **2.** [s'exprimer] to talk, to speak / *je n'ai pas l'habitude de parler en public* I'm not used to speaking in public ou to public speaking ▸ **les armes ont parlé** weapons were used ▸ **parler pour** ou **à la place de qqn** to speak for sb ou on sb's behalf ▸ **parle pour toi !** speak for yourself! ▸ **parler contre**/**pour** to speak against / for ▸ **politiquement**/**artistiquement parlant** politically / artistically speaking ▸ **parler à qqn** [lui manifester ses sentiments] to talk to ou to speak to ou to have a word with sb ▸ **parler à qqn** [s'adresser à qqn] to talk ou to speak to sb ▸ *puis-je parler à Virginie ?* [au téléphone] may I speak to Virginie? ▸ **parler à qqn** [l'émouvoir, le toucher] to speak ou to appeal to sb **3.** [discuter] to talk ▸ **parler de qqch / qqn** to talk ou to speak about sth / sb / *je sais de quoi je parle* I know what I'm talking about / *parler de choses et d'autres* to talk about this and that / *tiens, en parlant de vacances, Luc a une villa à louer* hey, talking of holidays, Luc has a villa to let ▸ **parler de qqn / qqch** [le mentionner] : *vous ne parlez même pas de Dali dans votre thèse* you don't even mention Dali in your thesis / *le livre parle de la guerre* the book is about ou deals with the war ▸ **parler de faire qqch** to talk about ou of doing sth / *qui parle de laisser tomber ?* who said anything about giving up? ▸ **parler de qqch / qqn comme de** : *on parle d'elle comme d'une candidate possible* she's being talked about ou billed as a possible candidate / *tu en parles comme d'une catastrophe* you make it sound like a catastrophe ▸ **parler de qqn / qqch à qqn** : *n'en parle à personne !* don't mention it to anybody! / *elle nous a parlé de ses projets* she talked to us about her plans ; [jaser] to talk / *tout le monde en parle* everybody's talking about it ▸ **faire parler de soi a)** to get o.s. talked about **b)** [dans la presse] to get one's name in the papers **4.** [avouer] to talk ▸ **faire parler qqn** to make sb talk, to get sb to talk **5.** [être éloquent] to speak volumes ▸ **les chiffres / faits parlent d'eux-mêmes** the figures / facts speak for themselves.

B. LOCUTIONS ▸ **tu parles, vous parlez** *fam: tu parles comme je peux oublier ça !* as if I could ever forget it! ▸ **ça t'a plu ? — tu parles ! a)** [bien sûr] did you like it? — you bet! **b)** [pas du tout] did you like it? — you must be joking! / *tu parles si c'est agréable / intelligent ! iron* that's really nice / clever! ▸ **tu parles de** *fam*, **vous parlez de** *fam: tu parles d'une déception !* talk about a letdown!, it was such a letdown! ▶ **ne m'en parle pas, m'en parle pas** *fam*: *c'est difficile* — *ne m'en parle pas !* it's difficult — don't tell me ou you're telling me ou you don't say! ▶ **parlons-en**: *laisse faire la justice* — *ah, parlons-en, de leur justice !* let justice take its course — justice indeed ou some justice! ▶ **n'en parlons pas**: *la chambre du haut, n'en parlons pas* let's ou we can forget the upstairs bedroom ▶ **n'en parlons plus** let's not mention it again, let's say no more about it.

◆ vt [langue] to speak / *il parle bien (le) russe* he speaks good Russian ▶ **nous ne parlons pas la même langue** ou **le même langage** *fig* we don't speak the same language ▶ **parler affaires / politique** to talk business / politics. ◆ **se parler** ◆ vp *(emploi réciproque)* to talk to one another ou each other / *elles ne se parlent plus* they aren't on speaking terms any more. ◆ vp *(emploi réfléchi)* to talk to o.s. ◆ vp *(emploi passif)* to be spoken. ◆ **sans parler de** loc prép to say nothing of, not to mention, let alone.

parleur, euse [parlœr, øz] nm, f talker ▶ **beau parleur** *sout* fine talker.

parloir [parlwar] nm [d'une prison] visitors' room ; [d'un monastère] parlour [UK], parlor [US].

parlure [parlyr] nf [Québec] way of talking.

parme [parm] ◆ adj inv mauve. ◆ nm [couleur] mauve.

Parme [parm] npr Parma.

parmesan [parməzã] nm Parmesan (cheese).

parmi [parmi] prép among / *elle erra parmi la foule* she wandered in ou among the crowd / *nous souhaitons vous avoir bientôt parmi nous* we hope that you'll soon be with us / *parmi tout ce vacarme* in the midst of all this noise / *c'est une solution parmi d'autres* that's one solution.

parodie [parodi] nf **1.** LITTÉR parody **2.** *fig* ▶ **une parodie de procès** a mockery of a trial.

parodier [9] [parodje] vt **1.** ART to parody **2.** [singer] to mimic, to parody.

paroi [parwa] nf **1.** [d'une chambre] partition (wall) ; [d'un ascenseur] wall ; [d'une citerne] inside **2.** GÉOL & ALPINISME face, wall ▶ **paroi rocheuse** rock face.

paroisse [parwas] nf parish.

paroissial, e, aux [parwasjal, o] adj [fête, église] parish *(modif)* ; [décision, don] parish *(modif)*, parochial.

paroissien, enne [parwasjɛ̃, ɛn] nm, f RELIG parishioner.

parole [parɔl] nf **1.** [faculté de s'exprimer] ▶ **la parole** speech **2.** [fait de parler] ▶ **demander la parole** a) to ask for the right to speak b) DR to request leave to speak ▶ **prendre la parole** a) [gén] to speak b) [au parlement, au tribunal] to take the floor ▶ **vous avez la parole** a) [à un avocat, un député] you have the floor b) [dans un débat] (it's) your turn to speak ou over to you ▶ **adresser la parole à qqn** to talk ou to speak to sb ▶ **couper la parole à qqn** to interrupt sb ▶ **temps de parole** speaking time **3.** *(souvent au pl)* [propos] word, remark / *ce sont ses (propres) paroles* those are his very (own) words / *ce ne sont que des paroles en l'air* all that's just idle talk ▶ **répandre** ou **porter la bonne parole** to spread ou to carry the good word **4.** [engagement] word ▶ **tenir parole** to keep one's word ▶ **c'est un homme de parole** he's a man of his word ▶ **ma parole !** my word! ◆ **paroles** nfpl [d'une chanson] words, lyrics ; [d'une illustration] words / **'sans paroles'** 'no caption'. ◆ **sur parole** loc adv on parole.

parolier, ère [parɔlje, ɛr] nm, f [d'une chanson] lyric writer, lyricist ; [d'un opéra] librettist.

paroxysme [parɔksism] nm **1.** [d'un état affectif] paroxysm, height / *le mécontentement a atteint son paroxysme* discontent is at its height / *les fans étaient au paroxysme du délire* the fans' enthusiasm had reached fever pitch **2.** MÉD paroxysm.

parpaing [parpɛ̃] nm [aggloméré] breezeblock [UK], cinderblock [US].

parquer [3] [parke] vt **1.** [mettre dans un parc - bétail] to pen in ou up *(sép)* ; [- moutons] to pen in ou up *(sép)*, to fold **2.** [enfermer - prisonniers] to shut in ou up *(sép)*, to confine ; [- foule, multitude] to pack ou to cram in *(sép)* **3.** [voiture] to park.

parquet [parke] nm **1.** [revêtement de bois] (wooden) floor ou flooring ; [à chevrons] parquet ▶ **parquet flottant** floating floor **2.** DR public prosecutor's department ; ≃ Crown Prosecution Service [UK] ; ≃ District Attorney's office [US].

parrain [parɛ̃] nm **1.** RELIG godfather **2.** COMM sponsor **3.** [d'un projet] promoter ; [d'une œuvre charitable] patron ; POL proposer, sponsor [US] **4.** [de la mafia] godfather.

parrainer [4] [parɛne] vt **1.** [candidat, postulant] to propose, to sponsor [US] ; [projet] to propose, to support ; [œuvre charitable] to patronize **2.** COMM to sponsor.

parricide [parisid] nm [crime] parricide.

parsemer [19] [parsəme] vt **1.** [semer, saupoudrer] ▶ **parsemer qqch de** to scatter sthg with **2.** [suj : fleurs, étoiles] : *parsemé d'étoiles* studded ou scattered with stars / *parsemé de fleurs* dotted with flowers / *parsemé de difficultés* riddled with difficulties.

part [par] nf **1.** [dans un partage - de nourriture] piece, portion ; [- d'un butin, de profits, de travail, etc.] share ▶ **une part de gâteau** a slice of cake ▶ **faire la part belle à qqn** to give sb a good deal ▶ **vouloir sa part de** ou **du gâteau** to want one's share of the cake ▶ **se réserver** ou **se tailler la part du lion** to keep ou to take the lion's share **2.** DR [pour les impôts] basic unit used for calculating personal income tax **3.** ÉCON & FIN ▶ **part de marché** market share **4.** [fraction] part, portion ▶ **en grande part** for the most part, largely, to a large extent / *les sociétés, pour la plus grande part, sont privatisées* firms, for the most part, are privatized **5.** [participation] ▶ **prendre part à** a) [discussion, compétition, manifestation] to take part in b) [cérémonie, projet] to join in, to play a part in c) [attentat] to take part in, to play a part in ▶ **faire la part des choses** to take things into consideration **6.** [EXPR] **de la part de** [au nom de] : *je viens de la part de Paula* Paula sent me / *donne-le-lui de ma part* give it to her from me ▶ **de la part de** [provenant de] : *de ta part, cela me surprend beaucoup* I'm surprised at you / *c'est très généreux de ta part* that's very generous of you / *c'est de la part de qui ?* [au téléphone, à un visiteur] who (shall I say) is calling? ▶ **pour ma / sa part** (as) for me / him ▶ **faire part de qqch à qqn** to announce sthg to sb, to inform sb of sthg ▶ **prendre qqch en mauvaise part** to take offence at sthg, to take sthg amiss. ◆ **à part** ◆ loc adj **1.** [séparé - comptes, logement] separate **2.** [original, marginal] odd / *ce sont des gens à part* these people are rather special. ◆ loc adv **1.** [à l'écart] : *elle est restée à part toute la soirée* she kept herself to herself all evening / *mets les dossiers bleus à part* put the blue files to one side **2.** [en aparté] ▶ **prendre qqn à part** to take sb aside ou to one side **3.** [séparément] separately. ◆ loc prép [excepté] except for, apart ou aside from / *à part cela* apart from that, that aside. ◆ **à part entière** loc adj : *un membre à part entière* a full ou fully paid up member of / *elle est devenue une actrice à part entière* she's now a proper ou a fully-fledged actress / *c'est un système de communication à part entière* it's a fully-fledged communication system ▶ **citoyen à part entière** person with full citizenship (status). ◆ **à part que** loc conj *fam* except that, if it weren't as except for the fact that. ◆ **autre part** loc adv somewhere ou someplace [US] else. ◆ **de part en part** loc adv from end to end, throughout, right through. ◆ **de part et d'autre** loc adv **1.** [des deux côtés] on both sides, on either side **2.** [partout] on all sides.

❖ **de part et d'autre de** loc prép on both sides of. ❖ **de toute(s) part(s)** loc adv (from) everywhere, from all sides ou quarters. ❖ **d'une part... d'autre part** loc corrélative on the one hand... on the other hand. ❖ **pour une large part** loc adv to a great extent.

partage [paʀtaʒ] nm **1.** [division - d'un domaine] division, dividing ou splitting up ; [-d'un rôti] carving ; [-d'un gâteau] slicing, cutting (up) ▸ **faire le partage de qqch** to divide sthg up **2.** [répartition - d'une fortune, des devoirs, des tâches] sharing out ; [-des torts, des fautes] sharing, apportioning ▸ **partage du travail** jobsharing **3.** INFORM ▸ **partage de fichier** file sharing. ❖ **en partage** loc adv ▸ **donner qqch en partage à qqn** to leave sb sthg (in one's will).

partagé, e [paʀtaʒe] adj **1.** [opposé] split, divided / *j'ai lu des critiques partagées* I've read mixed reviews / *il était partagé entre la joie et la crainte* he was torn between joy and fear **2.** [mutuel - haine] mutual, reciprocal ; [-amour] mutual.

partager [17] [paʀtaʒe] vt **1.** [diviser - propriété] to divide up (sép), to share out (sép) ▸ **partager qqch en deux / par moitié** to divide sthg in two / into two halves **2.** [diviser - pays, société] to divide / *la question du désarmement partage le pays* the country is divided ou split over the question of disarmament ▸ **être partagé entre** to be split ou divided between **3.** [répartir - bénéfices, provisions] to share out (sép) **4.** [avoir avec d'autres] to share ▸ **partager la joie / peine / surprise de qqn** to share (in) sb's joy / sorrow / surprise / *voici une opinion partagée par beaucoup de gens* this is an opinion shared ou held by many (people) ; *(en usage absolu)* : *elle n'aime pas partager* she doesn't like to share. ❖ **se partager** ◆ vpt [biens, travail] to share (out) / *se partager la tâche* to share (out) the work. ◆ vpi **1.** [personne] : *elles se partagent entre leur carrière et leurs enfants* their time is divided between their professional lives and their families **2.** [se diviser] to fork, to divide ▸ **se partager en** to be split ou divided into.

partance [paʀtɑ̃s] ❖ **en partance** loc adj due to leave / *le premier avion en partance* the first plane due to take off / *le dernier bateau en partance* the last boat out ou due to sail / *le dernier train en partance* the last train.

partant, e [paʀtɑ̃, ɑ̃t] ◆ adj ▸ **être partant pour (faire) qqch** to be willing ou ready to do sthg / *aller danser ? je suis partante !* go dancing? I'd love to! ◆ nm, f SPORT [cheval] runner ; [cycliste, coureur] starter.

partenaire [paʀtənɛʀ] nmf [gén] partner ▸ **partenaire économique** business partner ▸ **les partenaires sociaux** management and the workforce, labour 🇬🇧 ou labor 🇺🇸 and management.

partenariat [paʀtənaʀja] nm partnership.

parterre [paʀtɛʀ] nm **1.** HORT [en bordure] border ; [plus large] bed, flowerbed **2.** THÉÂTRE [emplacement] stalls 🇬🇧, orchestra 🇺🇸 ; [spectateurs] (audience in the) stalls 🇬🇧 ou orchestra 🇺🇸.

parti¹ [paʀti] nm **1.** POL ▸ **parti (politique)** (political) party **2.** *sout* [choix, décision] decision, course of action ▸ **prendre le parti de** : *prendre le parti de la modération* to opt for moderation ▸ **prendre le parti de faire qqch** to make up one's mind to do sthg, to decide to do sthg ▸ **prendre parti** [prendre position] to take sides ou a stand ▸ **prendre parti pour qqn** to side ou to take sides with sb ▸ **prendre son parti** : *son parti est pris* her mind is made up, she's made up her mind ▸ **en prendre son parti** : *elle ne sera jamais musicienne, il faut que j'en prenne mon / qu'elle en prenne son parti* she'll never be a musician, I'll / she'll just have to accept it **3.** [avantage] ▸ **tirer parti de a)** [situation] to take advantage of **b)** [équipement] to put to good use **4.** *hum* [personne à marier] ▸ **c'est un beau** ou

bon parti he's / she's a good match. ❖ **parti pris** nm **1.** [prise de position] commitment / *avoir un parti pris de modernisme / clarté* to be committed to modernism / clearthinking **2.** [préjugé] bias ▸ **être de parti pris** to be biased.

parti², e [paʀti] adj *fam* drunk, tight.

partial, e, aux [paʀsjal, o] adj biased, partial.

partialité [paʀsjalite] nf [favorable] partiality ; [défavorable] bias ▸ **partialité en faveur de qqn** partiality for sb, bias in favour of sb ▸ **partialité contre qqn** bias against sb.

participant, e [paʀtisipɑ̃, ɑ̃t] nm, f participant / *les participants au congrès* the participants in ou those taking part in the congress.

participatif, ive [paʀtisipatif, iv] adj [collaboratif] collaborative.

participation [paʀtisipasjɔ̃] nf **1.** [engagement, contribution] participation, involvement / *il nie sa participation à* ou *dans l'enlèvement du prince* he denies having participated ou been involved in the prince's kidnapping / *sa participation aux jeux Olympiques semble compromise* there's a serious question mark hanging over his participation in the Olympic Games **2.** [dans un spectacle] appearance / **'avec la participation des frères Jarry'** 'featuring the Jarry Brothers' / **'avec la participation spéciale de Robert Vann'** 'guest appearance by Robert Vann' **3.** [contribution financière] contribution (to costs) / *il y a 15 euros de participation aux frais* you have to pay 15 euros towards costs / *nous demandons à chacun une petite participation* we're asking every one of you to contribute a small amount ou to make a small contribution **4.** POL ▸ **participation (électorale)** (voter) turnout / *un faible taux de* ou *une faible participation aux élections* a poor ou low turnout at the polls **5.** ÉCON & POL [détention de capital] interest, share / *prendre des participations dans une entreprise* to buy into a company ▸ **participation aux bénéfices** profit-sharing.

participe [paʀtisip] nm participle (form) ▸ **participe passé / présent** past / present participle.

participer [3] [paʀtisipe] ❖ **participer à** v + prép **1.** [prendre part à - concours, négociation, cérémonie] to take part in ; [-discussion] to contribute to ; [-projet] to be involved in ; [-aventure] to be involved in, to be part of ; [-épreuve sportive] to take part ou to be in ; [-attentat, vol] to be involved in, to take part in ; [-jeu] to join in ; [-émission] to take part in ; *(en usage absolu)* [dans un jeu] to take part, to join in ; [à l'école] to contribute (during class) / *l'idée principale du metteur en scène est de faire participer le public* the director's basic idea is to get the public to participate in the show **2.** [financièrement - achat, dépenses] to share in, to contribute to / *tous ses collègues ont participé au cadeau* all her colleagues contributed something towards the present ; ÉCON & FIN [profits, pertes] to share (in).

particularisme [paʀtikylaʀism] nm particularism.

particularité [paʀtikylaʀite] nf [trait distinctif - d'une personne, d'une culture, d'une langue, etc.] particularity, (specific) feature ou characteristic ou trait ; [-d'une région] distinctive feature ; [-d'une machine] special feature.

particule [paʀtikyl] nf GÉOL, GRAM & PHYS particle.

particulier, ère [paʀtikylje, ɛʀ] adj **1.** [précis - circonstance, exemple, point] particular, specific **2.** [caractéristique - odeur, humour, parler, style] particular, distinctive, characteristic / *une odeur particulière au pois de senteur* a fragrance peculiar to sweetpeas / *un trait bien particulier* a highly distinctive feature **3.** [hors du commun] particular, special, unusual ▸ **porter une attention toute particulière à qqch** to pay particular ou special attention to sthg / *il ne s'est rien passé de particulier* nothing special ou particular happened **4.** [bizarre - comportement, goûts, mœurs] peculiar, odd **5.** [privé - avion, intérêts] private.

❖ **particulier** nm **1.** ADMIN private individual / *il loge chez des particuliers* he's in private lodgings 🇬🇧, he rooms with a family 🇺🇸 **2.** [élément individuel] ▸ **le particulier** the particular. ❖ **en particulier** loc adv [essentiellement] in particular, particularly, especially.

particulièrement [paʀtikyljɛʀmɑ̃] adv **1.** [surtout] particularly, specifically, in particular / *nous nous attacherons plus particulièrement à cet aspect de l'œuvre* we shall deal in particular ou more specifically with this aspect of the work **2.** [exceptionnellement] particularly, specially, especially / *il n'est pas particulièrement laid / doué* he's not particularly ugly / gifted / *je n'aime pas particulièrement cela* I'm not particularly keen on it / *tu aimes le whisky ? — pas particulièrement* do you like whisky ? — not particularly.

partie [paʀti] ❖ f ⟶ **parti** (adj). ❖ nf **1.** [élément, composant] part ▸ **faire partie de a)** [comité] to be a member of, to be on, to sit on **b)** [club, communauté] to be a member of, to belong to **c)** [équipe] to belong to, to be one of, to be in **d)** [licenciés] to be among, to be one of **e)** [métier, inconvénients, risques] to be part of ▸ **parties communes / privatives** communal / private areas *(in a building ou an estate)* ▸ **parties génitales** ou **sexuelles** genitals, private parts **2.** [fraction, morceau] part ▸ **couper qqch en deux parties** to cut sthg into two (parts) / *une partie du blé est contaminée* some ou part of the wheat is contaminated / *une grande / petite partie de l'électorat* a large / small part of the electorate, a large / small section of the electorate **3.** JEUX & SPORT game / *faire une partie de cartes* to have a game of cards ▸ **partie d'échecs / de billard / de tennis / de cartes** game of chess / billiards / tennis / cards **4.** [divertissement à plusieurs] ▸ **partie de chasse / pêche** shooting / fishing party / *ça n'est pas une partie de plaisir !* fam it's no picnic ou fun! ▸ **je ne peux pas partir avec toi cette fois, mais ce n'est que partie remise** I can't go with you this time, but there'll be other opportunities **5.** [domaine, spécialité] field, line / *elle est de la partie* it's her line **6.** MUS part **7.** DR [participant] party ▸ **les parties en présence** the parties ▸ **partie civile** private party *(acting jointly with the public prosecutor in criminal cases)*, plaintiff *(for damages)* ▸ **se constituer** ou **se porter partie civile** to act jointly with the public prosecutor ▸ **partie prenante** payee, receiver ▸ **être partie prenante dans qqch** fig to be directly involved ou concerned in sthg **8.** GRAM ▸ **partie du discours** part of speech **9.** EXPR avoir partie liée avec qqn to be hand in glove with sb. ❖ **à partie** loc adv ▸ **prendre qqn à partie a)** [s'attaquer à lui] to set on sb **b)** [l'interpeller] to take sb to task. ❖ **en partie** loc adv in part, partly, partially / *je ne l'ai cru qu'en partie* I only half believed him ▸ **en grande** ou **majeure partie** for the most part, largely, mainly.

partiel, elle [paʀsjɛl] adj partial ▸ **contrôle** ou **examen partiel** mid-year exam ▸ **(emploi à) temps partiel** part-time job. ❖ **partiel** nm ÉDUC mid-year exam.

partiellement [paʀsjɛlmɑ̃] adv partially, partly / *ce n'est que partiellement vrai* it's only partly true.

partir [43] [paʀtiʀ] vi **1.** [s'en aller] to go, to leave ▸ **laisser partir a)** [prisonnier, otage] to set free, to let go, to release **b)** [écolier] to let go **c)** [employé] to let go / *il est parti avec la caisse* he ran away ou off with the till / *le climat les a fait partir* the climate drove them away / *tout son argent part en disques* all his money goes on records **2.** [se mettre en route] to set off ou out, to start off / *pars devant, je te rattrape* go ahead, I'll catch up with you / *le courrier n'est pas encore parti* the post hasn't gone yet ▸ **partir en avion a)** [personne] to fly (off) **b)** [courrier] to go air mail ou by air / *partir en bateau* to go (off) by boat, to sail / *partir en voiture* to go (off) by car, to drive off **3.** [se rendre] to go, to leave / *je pars à* ou *pour Tou-*

lon demain I'm leaving for ou I'm off to Toulon tomorrow ▸ **partir vers le sud** to go south **4.** [aller - pour se livrer à une activité] to go ▸ **partir à la chasse / pêche** to go shooting / fishing ▸ **nous partons en excursion / voyage demain** we're setting off on an excursion / a journey tomorrow ▸ **partir skier / se promener** to go skiing / for a walk **5.** [s'engager] ▸ **partir dans** : *partir dans un discours* to launch into a speech / *partir dans une explication* to embark on an explanation ▸ **partir sur** : *partir sur un sujet* to start off on a topic **6.** [démarrer - machine, moteur, voiture] to start (up) ; [-avion] to take off, to leave ; [-train] to leave, to depart ; [-fusée] to go up ; [-pétard] to go off ; [-balle] to take / *le coup (de feu) est parti tout seul* the gun went off on its own ▸ **faire partir a)** [moteur] to start (up) **b)** [pétard] to set ou let off *(sép)* **c)** [fusil] to let off *(sép)* **d)** [plante] to get started **7.** [se mettre en mouvement, débuter - coureur, match, concert] to start (off) ▸ **être parti pour** : *on est partis pour avoir des ennuis !* we're headed for trouble ! / *le projet est bien parti* the project is off to a good start / *je le vois mal parti pour récupérer son titre* the way he's going, I just can't see him winning back his title **8.** [se vendre] to sell **9.** [disparaître, s'effacer - inscription] to disappear, to be rubbed off ou out, to be worn off ; [-tache] to disappear, to go, to come out ; [-douleur] to go, to disappear ; [-boutons] to come off ; [-pellicules, odeur] to go ▸ **faire partir a)** [salissure] to get rid of, to remove **b)** [odeur] to get rid of, to clear **c)** [douleur] to ease **10.** [se défaire, se détacher - attache, bouton] to come off, to go ; [-maille] to run ; [-étiquette] to come off. ❖ **partir de** v + prép **1.** [dans l'espace] ▸ **le ferry / marathon part de Brest** the ferry sails / the marathon starts from Brest / *la rue part de la mairie* the street starts at the town hall **2.** [dans le temps] : *nous allons faire partir le contrat du 15 janvier* we'll make the contract effective (as) from January the 15th **3.** [dans un raisonnement] ▸ **partir du principe que** to start from the principle that, to start by assuming that **4.** [provenir de] : *tous les problèmes sont partis de là* all the problems stemmed from that / *ça partait d'un bon sentiment* his intentions were good. ❖ **à partir de** loc prép **1.** [dans le temps] (as) from / *à partir de mardi* starting from Tuesday, from Tuesday onwards **2.** [dans l'espace] (starting) from / *le deuxième à partir de la droite* the second (one) from the right **3.** [numériquement] : *imposé à partir de 5 000 euros* taxable from 5,000 euros upwards **4.** [avec, à base de] from / *c'est fait à partir d'huiles végétales* it's made from ou with vegetable oils / *j'ai fait un résumé à partir de ses notes* I've made a summary based on his notes.

partisan, e [paʀtizã, an] adj partisan ▸ **être partisan de** to be in favour 🇬🇧 ou favor 🇺🇸 of. ❖ **partisan** nm [adepte, défenseur] supporter / *c'est un partisan de la censure* he's for ou in favour of censorship.

partition [paʀtisjɔ̃] nf **1.** MUS [symboles] score ; [livret] score, music **2.** HIST & POL partition, partitioning, splitting **3.** INFORM & MATH partition.

partout [paʀtu] adv **1.** [dans l'espace] everywhere / *je ne peux pas être partout à la fois !* I can't be in two places at the same time ! / *il a voyagé un peu partout* he's been all over the place ▸ **j'ai mal partout** I ache all over / *les gens accouraient de partout* people came rushing from all sides **2.** SPORT ▸ **15 partout** 15 all.

parure [paʀyʀ] nf **1.** [ensemble] set ▸ **parure de lit** set of bed linen **2.** JOAILL parure, set of jewels ; [colifichets] matching set of costume jewellery **3.** VÊT finery.

parution [paʀysjɔ̃] nf publication ▸ **juste avant / après la parution du livre** just before / after the book came out.

parvenir [40] [paʀvəniʀ] ❖ **parvenir à** v + prép *(aux être)* **1.** [atteindre - suj : voyageur, véhicule, lettre, son] ▸ **parvenir à** ou **jusqu'à** to get to, to reach ▸ **faire parvenir un**

colis à qqn to send sb a parcel / *si cette carte vous parvient* if you get ou receive this card / *l'histoire est parvenue aux oreilles de sa femme* the story reached his wife's ears **2.** [réussir à] ▶ **parvenir à faire qqch** to succeed in doing ou to manage to do sthg.

parvenu, e [paʀvəny] adj & nm, f *péj* parvenu, upstart, nouveau riche.

parvis [paʀvi] nm parvis *(in front of church)*.

pas¹ [pa] nm **1.** [déplacement] step / *le convalescent fit quelques pas dehors* the convalescent took a few steps outside ▶ **revenir** ou **retourner sur ses pas** to retrace one's steps ou path, to turn back ▶ **avancer à** ou **faire de petits pas** to take short steps ▶ **marcher à grands pas** to stride along ▶ **faire ses premiers pas** *pr* to learn to walk / *il a fait ses premiers pas de comédien dans un film de Hitchcock* fig he made his debut as an actor in a Hitchcock film **2.** [progrès] ▶ **avancer à petits pas** to make slow progress ▶ **avancer à grands pas a)** [enquête] to make great progress **b)** [technique, science] to take big steps forward **c)** [échéance, événement] to be looming / *faire un grand pas en avant* to take a great step ou leap forward / *faire un pas en arrière* to take a step back ou backwards ▶ **faire le premier pas** to make the first move ▶ **franchir** ou **sauter le pas** to take the plunge **3.** [empreinte] footprint / *des pas sur le sable* footprints in the sand **4.** [allure] pace ▶ **hâter** ou **presser le pas** to hurry on / *ralentir le pas* to slow one's pace, to slow down **5.** [démarche] gait, tread / *marcher d'un pas alerte* [léger / élastique] to walk with a sprightly / light / bouncy tread ▶ **avancer d'un pas lourd** ou **pesant** to tread heavily, to walk with a heavy tread **6.** MIL step ▶ **au pas de charge a)** MIL at the charge **b)** fig charging along **7.** DANSE pas, step / *esquisser un pas* to dance a few steps, to do a little dance **8.** SPORT ▶ **pas de patinage** ou **patineur** SKI skating ▶ **au pas de course a)** at a run **b)** fig at a run, on the double **9.** [mesure] pace ; [espace approximatif] pace, step ▶ **à deux** ou **trois** ou **quelques pas:** *l'église est à deux pas* the church is very close at hand ou is only a stone's throw from here / *il se tenait à quelques pas de moi* he was standing just a few yards from me **10.** [marche d'escalier] step ▶ **pas de porte** doorstep ▶ **sur le pas de la porte**: *ne reste pas sur le pas de la porte* don't stand at the door ou on the doorstep ou in the doorway **11.** GÉOGR [en montagne] pass ; [en mer] strait ▶ **le pas de Calais** the Strait of Dover **12.** TECHNOL [d'une vis] thread ; [d'une denture, d'un engrenage] pitch **13.** EXPR ▶ **prendre le pas (sur qqn / qqch)** to take precedence (over sb / sthg), to dominate (sb / sthg) ▶ **céder le pas** to give way ▶ **se tirer d'un mauvais pas** to get o.s. out of a fix. ❖ **à chaque pas** loc adv **1.** [partout] everywhere, at every step **2.** [constamment] at every turn ou step. ❖ **au pas** loc adv **1.** [en marchant] at a walking pace **2.** AUTO ▶ **aller** ou **rouler au pas a)** [dans un embouteillage] to crawl along **b)** [consigne de sécurité] to go dead slow ⟨UK⟩, to go slow **3.** ÉQUIT walking, at a walk / *mettre son cheval au pas* to walk one's horse. ❖ **de ce pas** loc adv straightaway, at once. ❖ **pas à pas** loc adv **1.** [de très près] step by step **2.** [prudemment] step by step, one step at a time **3.** INFORM step by step.

pas² [pa] adv **1.** [avec 'ne', pour exprimer la négation] : *elle ne viendra pas* she won't come / *ils ne sont pas trop inquiets* they're not too worried ▶ **ils n'ont pas de problèmes / d'avenir** they have no problems / no future, they haven't got any problems / a future / *il a décidé de ne pas accepter* he decided not to accept ; *fam* [avec omission du 'ne'] : *elle sait pas* she doesn't know / *t'en fais pas !* don't (you) worry ! / *non, j'aime pas* no, I don't like it **2.** [avec 'non', pour renforcer la négation] : *elle n'est pas belle mais jolie* she's not so much beautiful as pretty **3.** [employé seul] ▶ **sincère ou pas** sincere or not ▶ **pourquoi pas ?**

why not ? ▶ **pas la peine** *fam* (it's) not worth it ▶ **pas assez** not enough **4.** [dans les réponses négatives] : *pas de dessert pour moi, merci* no dessert for me, thank you ▶ **pas du tout** not at all / *pas le moins du monde* not in the least ou slightest, not at all ▶ **absolument pas** not at all. ❖ **pas mal** *fam* ❖ loc adj inv not bad / *c'est pas mal comme idée* that's not a bad idea. ❖ loc adv **1.** [bien] : *je ne m'en suis pas mal tiré* I handled it quite well **2.** [très] : *la voiture est pas mal amochée* the car's pretty battered. ❖ **pas mal de** loc dét *fam* [suivi d'un nom comptable] quite a few, quite a lot of ; [suivi d'un nom non comptable] quite a lot of / *pas mal d'argent* quite a lot of money. ❖ **pas plus mal** loc adv : *il a maigri — c'est pas plus mal* he's lost weight — good thing too ou that's not such a bad thing ou just as well. ❖ **pas un, pas une** ❖ loc dét not a (single), not one / *pas un geste !* not one move! ❖ loc pron not (a single) one / *parmi elles, pas une qui ne veuille y aller* every one of them wants to go there / *pas un n'a bronché* there wasn't a peep out of any of them ▶ **comme pas un** : *il s'y entend comme pas un pour déranger les gens à 2 h du matin* he's a specialist at disturbing you at 2 in the morning / *il sait faire les crêpes comme pas un* he makes pancakes like nobody else (on earth).

pas-de-porte [padpɔʀt] nm inv DR key money.

passable [pasabl] adj **1.** ÉDUC [tout juste moyen] average **2.** ⟨Québec⟩ [praticable] negotiable, passable.

passablement [pasabləmɑ̃] adv **1.** [de façon satisfaisante] passably well, tolerably well **2.** [notablement] fairly, rather, somewhat ▶ **ils avaient passablement bu** they had drunk quite a lot.

passage [pasaʒ]
nm

A. MOUVEMENT 1. [allées et venues] : *prochain passage du car dans deux heures* the coach will be back ou will pass through again in two hours' time ▶ **laisser le passage à qqn / une ambulance** to let sb / an ambulance through, to make way for sb / an ambulance / *les gens se retournent sur son passage* heads turn when he walks by ou past **2.** [circulation] traffic **3.** [arrivée, venue] : *elle attend le passage de l'autobus* she's waiting for the bus **4.** [visite] call, visit / *c'est le seul souvenir qui me reste de mon passage chez eux* that's the only thing I remember of my visit to them / *lors de mon prochain passage à Paris* next time I'm in Paris **5.** [franchissement -d'une frontière, d'un fleuve] crossing ; [-d'un col] passing ; [-de la douane] passing (through) / '**passage interdit**' 'no entry' **6.** [changement, transition] change, transition ▶ **le passage de l'hiver au printemps** the change ou passage from winter to spring **7.** [dans une hiérarchie] move ▶ **passage d'un employé à l'échelon supérieur** promotion of an employee to a higher grade **8.** [voyage sur mer, traversée] crossing / *ils travaillaient durement pour payer leur passage* they worked hard to pay their passage ou to pay for their crossing **9.** INFORM ▶ **passage machine** run **10.** PSYCHOL ▶ **passage à l'acte** acting out **11.** RADIO, THÉÂTRE & TV ▶ **lors de son dernier passage à la télévision a)** [personne] last time he was on TV **b)** [film] last time it was shown on TV.

B. VOIE 1. [chemin] passage, way / *tu es dans le passage !* you're in the way! / *essaye de trouver un passage dans cette foule* try to find a way through the crowd ▶ **passage secret** secret passage **2.** [ruelle] alley, passage ; [galerie commerçante] arcade ▶ **passage couvert** passageway **3.** [tapis de couloir] runner **4.** RAIL ▶ **passage à niveau** level crossing ⟨UK⟩, grade crossing ⟨US⟩ **5.** TRAV PUB ▶ **passage clouté** ou **(pour) piétons** pedestrian ou zebra crossing ⟨UK⟩, crosswalk ⟨US⟩ ▶ **passage protégé** priority over secondary roads ▶ **passage souterrain** (pedestrian) subway ⟨UK⟩, underpass.

C. EXTRAIT, PARTIE passage, section / *tu te souviens du passage où ils se rencontrent ?* do you remember the bit where they meet? ❖ **au passage** loc adv [sur un trajet] on one's ou the way. ❖ **au passage de** loc prép : *au passage du carrosse, la foule applaudissait* when the carriage went past ou through, the crowd clapped. ❖ **de passage** loc adj [client] casual ▸ **être de passage** [voyageur] to be passing through. ❖ **sur le passage de** loc prép : *la foule s'est massée sur le passage du marathon* the crowd gathered on the marathon route. ❖ **passage à tabac** nm beating up. ❖ **passage à vide** nm ▸ **avoir un passage à vide a)** [syncope] to feel faint, to faint **b)** [moralement] to go through a bad patch **c)** [intellectuellement] to have a lapse in concentration.

passager, ère [pasaʒe, ɛʀ] ◆ adj **1.** [momentané] passing, temporary, transient **2.** [très fréquenté] busy. ◆ nm, f passenger ▸ **passager clandestin** stowaway.

passant, e [pasɑ̃, ɑ̃t] ◆ adj [voie, route] busy. ◆ nm, f passer-by.

passation [pasasjɔ̃] nf POL ▸ **passation des pouvoirs** transfer of power.

passe [pas] ◆ nm **1.** [passe-partout] master ou pass key **2.** [laissez-passer] pass. ◆ nf **1.** SPORT [aux jeux de ballon] pass ▸ **faire une passe** to pass (the ball), to make a pass ; [en tauromachie] pass **2.** *tfam* [d'une prostituée] trick / *faire une passe* to turn a trick **3.** [situation] ▸ **bonne / mauvaise passe** [commerce] : *être dans une bonne passe* to be thriving / *leur couple traverse une mauvaise passe* their relationship is going through a rough ou bad period. ❖ **en passe de** loc prép : *ils sont en passe de prendre le contrôle des médias* they're poised ou set to gain control of the media.

passé¹ [pase] prép after ▸ **passé minuit** after midnight.

passé², e [pase] adj **1.** [précédent - année, mois] last, past / *au cours des mois passés* over the last few months **2.** [révolu] : *il est 3 h passées* it's past ou gone UK 3 o'clock / *elle a 30 ans passés* she's over 30 **3.** [qui n'est plus] past, former / *elle songeait au temps passé* she was thinking of times ou days gone by **4.** [teinte, fleur] faded. ❖ **passé** nm **1.** [temps révolu] ▸ **le passé** the past ▸ **oublions le passé** let bygones be bygones, let's forget the past ▸ **c'est du passé, tout ça** it's all in the past ou it's all behind us now **2.** [d'une personne, d'une ville] past **3.** GRAM past tense ▸ **les temps du passé** past tenses ▸ **passé composé** (present) perfect ▸ **passé simple** ou **historique** simple past, past historic.

passe-droit [pasdʀwa] (*pl* passe-droits) nm privilege, special favour.

passéiste [paseist] *péj* adj backward-looking.

passementerie [pasmɑ̃tʀi] nf soft furnishings (and curtain fitments).

passe-montagne [pasmɔ̃taɲ] (*pl* passe-montagnes) nm balaclava.

passe-partout (*pl* passe-partout), **passepartout*** (*pl* passepartouts*) [paspaʀtu] ◆ adj [robe, instrument] versatile, all-purpose (*modif*) ▸ **un discours passe-partout** a speech for all occasions. ◆ nm **1.** [clef] master ou skeleton key **2.** ART & IMPR passe-partout.

passe-passe (*pl* passe-passe), **passepasse*** [paspas] nm ▸ **tour de passe-passe a)** [tour de magie] (magic) trick **b)** [tromperie] trick.

passe-plat [paspla] (*pl* passe-plats) nm serving hatch.

passeport [paspɔʀ] nm **1.** ADMIN passport ▸ **passeport biométrique** biometric passport **2.** *fig* passport / *ce diplôme est un passeport pour la vie professionnelle* this diploma is a passport to a job.

passer [3] [pase]

◆ vi *(aux être)*

A. EXPRIME UN DÉPLACEMENT **1.** [se déplacer - personne, véhicule] to pass (by), to go ou to come past / *regarder passer les coureurs* to watch the runners go past ▸ **passer au-dessus de** : *l'avion est passé au-dessus de la maison* the plane flew over the house ▸ **passer dans** : *un avion passait dans le ciel* a plane was flying in the sky ▸ **passer devant qqch** to go past sthg ▸ **passer sous** : *passer sous une échelle* to go under a ladder ▸ **passer sous une voiture** [se faire écraser] to get run over (by a car) ▸ **passer sur** : *passer sur un pont* to go over ou to cross a bridge ; [fugitivement] : *un sourire passa sur ses lèvres* a smile played about her lips, she smiled briefly ▸ **elle dit tout ce qui lui passe par la tête** she says the first thing that comes into her head **2.** [s'écouler - fluide] to flow, to run ▸ **il y a de l'air qui passe sous la porte** there's a permanent draught coming under the door **3.** [emprunter un certain itinéraire] ▸ **si vous passez à Paris, venez me voir** come and see me if you're in Paris ▸ **passer par** : *le voleur est passé par la fenêtre* the burglar got in through the window ; [fleuve, route] to go, to run ▸ **le tunnel passera sous la montagne** the tunnel will go under the mountain **4.** MATH to pass **5.** [sur un parcours régulier - démarcheur, représentant] to call ; [- bateau, bus, train] to come ou to go past / *le facteur n'est pas encore passé* the postman hasn't been yet / *le bus passe toutes les sept minutes* there's a bus every seven minutes **6.** [aller en visite] to call ▸ **passer chez qqn** to call at sb's place / *j'essaierai de passer dans la soirée* I'll try and call in the evening ; (suivi de l'infinitif) ▸ **passer voir qqn** to call on sb ▸ **je passerai te chercher** I'll come and fetch you **7.** [franchir une limite] to get through ▸ **il est passé au rouge** he went through a red light ▸ **ça passe ou ça casse** it's make or break (time) **8.** [s'infiltrer] to pass ▸ **la lumière passe à travers les rideaux** the light shines through the curtains / *le café doit passer lentement* [dans le filtre] the coffee must filter through slowly **9.** [aller, se rendre] to go / *où est-il passé ?* where's he gone (to)? / *où sont passées mes lunettes ?* where have my glasses got ou disappeared to? ▸ **passons à table** let's eat.

B. EXPRIME UNE ACTION **1.** ▸ **passer à** [se soumettre à] to go for / *ce matin, je suis passé au tableau* I was asked to explain something at the blackboard this morning ▸ **y passer** *fam* : *je ne veux pas me faire opérer — il faudra bien que tu y passes, pourtant !* I don't want to have an operation — you're going to have to! **2.** [être accepté] to pass ▸ **elle est passée à l'écrit mais pas à l'oral** she got through ou she passed the written exam but not the oral / *j'ai mangé quelque chose qui ne passe pas* I've eaten something that won't go down / *ton petit discours est bien passé* your little speech went down well ou was well received ▸ **passe (encore)** : *l'injurier, passe encore, mais le frapper !* it's one thing to insult him, but quite another to hit him **3.** [être transmis] to go ▸ **la ferme est passée de père en fils depuis cinq générations** the farm has been handed down from father to son for five generations / *la carafe passa de main en main* the jug was passed around **4.** [entrer] to pass ▸ **c'est passé dans le langage courant** it's passed into ou it's now part of everyday speech **5.** [être utilisé, absorbé] to go ▸ **tout son salaire passe dans la maison** all her salary goes on the house ▸ **y passer** : *tout le fromage y est passé* every last bit of cheese went (in the end) **6.** POL [être adopté - projet de loi, amendement] to pass, to be passed / *la loi est passée* the law was passed ; [être élu - député] to be elected, to get in **7.** CINÉ & THÉÂTRE to be on, to be showing ; RADIO & TV ▸ **passer à la radio** [émission, personne] to be on the radio ou the air ▸ **passer à la télévision a)** [personne] to be ou to appear on television **b)** [film] to be on television **8.** DR [comparaître] ▸ **passer devant le tribunal** to come up ou to go before the court **9.** JEUX to pass.

C. EXPRIME UN CHANGEMENT D'ÉTAT **1.** [accéder - à un niveau] ▸ **passer dans la classe supérieure** to move up to the next form [UK] ou grade [US] ▸ **passer en seconde** ENS to move up to the fifth form [UK] ou to tenth grade [US] **2.** [devenir] to become ▸ **passer professionnel** to turn professional **3.** [dans des locutions verbales] ▸ **passer à** [aborder] : *passons à l'ordre du jour* let us turn to the business on the agenda ▸ **passer à l'action** to take action ▸ **passer de... à** [changer d'état] : *passer de l'état liquide à l'état gazeux* to pass ou to change from the liquid to the gaseous state / *passer du français au russe* to switch from French to Russian **4.** AUTO ▸ **passer en troisième** to change ou go into third (gear).

D. EXPRIME UNE ÉVOLUTION 1. [s'écouler - temps] to pass, to go by / *comme le temps passe !* how time flies! **2.** [s'estomper - douleur] to fade (away), to wear off ; [-malaise] to disappear ; [-mode, engouement] to die out ; [-enthousiasme] to wear off, to fade ; [-beauté] to fade, to wane ; [-chance, jeunesse] to pass ; [-mauvaise humeur] to pass, to vanish ; [-rage, tempête] to die down ; [-averse] to die down, to stop ▸ **mon envie est passée** I don't feel like it anymore ▸ **faire passer** : *ce médicament fait passer la douleur très rapidement* this medicine relieves pain very quickly **3.** [s'altérer - fruit, denrées] to go off [UK], to spoil, to go bad ; [se faner - fleur] to wilt ; [pâlir - teinte] : *le papier peint a passé au soleil* the sun has faded the wallpaper.

◆ vt *(aux avoir)*

A. EXPRIME UN DÉPLACEMENT 1. [traverser - pont, col de montagne] to go over *(insép)*, to cross ; [-écluse] to go through *(insép)* ▸ **passer une rivière à la nage** to swim across a river **2.** [franchir - frontière, ligne d'arrivée] to cross **3.** [dépasser - point de repère] to pass, to go past *(insép)* / *passer l'arrêt de l'autobus* [le manquer] to miss one's bus stop ▸ **passer le cap Horn** to (go) round Cape Horn, to round the Cape **4.** [transporter] to ferry ou to take across *(sép)* **5.** [introduire] ▸ **passer de la drogue / des cigarettes en fraude** to smuggle drugs / cigarettes **6.** [engager - partie du corps] to put ▸ **passer son bras autour de la taille de qqn** to put ou to slip one's arm round sb's waist ▸ **il a passé la tête par l'entrebâillement de la porte** he poked his head round the door **7.** [faire aller - instrument] to run ▸ **passer une éponge sur la table** to wipe the table ▸ **passer l'aspirateur** to vacuum, to hoover [UK] ▸ **passer le balai** to sweep up **8.** ÉQUIT [haie] to jump, to clear **9.** SPORT [franchir - obstacle, haie] to jump (over).

B. EXPRIME UNE ACTION 1. [se soumettre à - permis de conduire] to take ; [-examen] to take, to sit [UK] ; [-entretien] to have ; [-scanner, visite médicale] to have, to go for *(insép)* **2.** [omettre] to miss ou to leave out *(sép)*, to omit **3.** [tolérer] ▸ **elle lui passe tout** she lets him get away with anything **4.** [assouvir - envie] to satisfy ▸ **passer sa colère sur qqn** to take one's anger out on sb **5.** [soumettre à l'action de] ▸ **passer des légumes au mixeur** to put vegetables through the blender, to blend vegetables ▸ **passer qqch sous l'eau** to rinse sthg ou to give sthg a rinse under the tap ▸ **passer quelque chose à qqn** for to give sb a good dressing-down, to tick sb off [UK] ▸ **se faire passer quelque chose** *fam* to get a good ticking off [UK], to get a good chewing-out [US] **6.** [donner, transmettre - gén] to pass, to hand, to give ; [-maladie] to give ; [-au téléphone] to put through *(sép)* ▸ **passe-moi le sel** pass me the salt / *fais passer à ton voisin* pass it to your neighbour ▸ **je te passe Fred** here's Fred, I'll hand you over to Fred **7.** [rendre public - annonce] ▸ **passer une petite annonce** to place a small ad **8.** *fam* [prêter] to lend **9.** [appliquer - substance] to apply, to put on *(sép)* ▸ **passer de la cire sur qqch** to wax sthg / *passer une couche de peinture sur un mur* to paint a wall **10.** [filtrer, tamiser - thé, potage] to strain ; [-farine] to sieve **11.** [enfiler - vêtement] to slip ou to put on *(sép)* **12.** AUTO ▸ **passer la troisième** to change ou to shift into third gear **13.** CINÉ & TV [film] to show, to screen ; [diapositive] to show ; RADIO [émission] to broadcast ; [disque, cassette] to play, to put on *(sép)* **14.** COMM [conclure - en-

tente] to conclude, to come to *(insép)*, to reach ; [-marché] to agree on *(insép)*, to strike, to reach ; [-commande] to place ▸ **passez commande avant le 12** order before the 12th.

C. EXPRIME LE TEMPS 1. [employer - durée] to spend / *j'ai passé un an en Angleterre* I spent a year in England ▸ **passez un bon week-end / une bonne soirée !** have a nice weekend / evening! ▸ **pour passer le temps** to pass the time **2.** [aller au-delà de - durée] to get through *(insép)*, to survive. ❖ **passer après** v + prép : *il faut le faire libérer, le reste passe après* we must get him released, everything else is secondary. ❖ **passer avant** v + prép to go ou to come before / *ses intérêts passent avant tout* his own interests come before anything else, he puts his own interests before everything else. ❖ **passer par** v + prép **1.** [dans une formation] to go through / *il est passé par une grande école* he studied at a Grande École **2.** [dans une évolution] to go through, to undergo / *elle est passée par des moments difficiles* she's been through some difficult times **3.** [recourir à] to go through / *je passe par une agence pour avoir des billets* I get tickets through an agency ▸ **passer par là** : *je suis passé par là* it's happened to me too, I've been through that too / *pour comprendre, il faut être passé par là* you have to have experienced it to understand. ❖ **passer pour** v + prép **1.** [avec nom] to be thought of as / *dire qu'il passe pour un génie !* to think that he's considered a genius! / *je vais passer pour un idiot* I'll be taken for ou people will take me for an idiot ▸ **se faire passer pour qqn** to pass o.s. off as sb **2.** [avec adj] : *son livre passe pour sérieux* her book is considered to be serious / *il s'est fait passer pour fou* he pretended to be mad. ❖ **passer sur** v + prép [ne pas mentionner] to pass over, to skip ; [excuser] to overlook / *passons sur les détails* let's pass over ou skip the details ▸ **passons !** let's say no more about it!, let's drop it! ❖ **se passer** vpi **1.** [s'écouler - heures, semaines] to go by, to pass / *la soirée s'est passée tranquillement* the evening went by ou passed quietly **2.** [survenir - événement] to take place, to happen / *qu'est-ce qui se passe ?* what's happening?, what's going on? **3.** [se dérouler - dans certaines conditions] to go (off) / *l'opération s'est bien / mal passée* the operation went (off) smoothly / badly / *si tout se passe bien, nous y serons demain* if all goes well, we'll be there tomorrow. ❖ vpt [s'appliquer, se mettre - produit] to apply, to put on *(sép)* ▸ **il se passa un peigne / la main dans les cheveux** he ran a comb / his fingers through his hair. ❖ **se passer de** vp + prép **1.** [vivre sans] to do ou to go without / *il ne peut pas se passer de télévision* he can't live without the television **2.** [s'abstenir] : *je me passerais (volontiers) de ses réflexions !* I can do very well without her remarks! **3.** [ne pas avoir besoin de] : *sa déclaration se passe de tout commentaire* her statement needs no comment. ❖ **en passant** loc adv **1.** [dans la conversation] in passing / *faire une remarque en passant* to remark in passing, to make a casual remark **2.** [sur son chemin] : *il s'arrête de temps à autre en passant* he calls on his way by ou past from time to time. ❖ **en passant par** loc prép **1.** [dans l'espace] via **2.** [dans une énumération] (and) including.

📋 **Passer qqch à qqn** *Pass sthg to sb* ou *pass sb sthg.*

Notez la construction à double complément qui en anglais peut prendre deux formes dont le sens est le même :

• une structure identique à celle du français :
    verbe + COD + préposition + COI
    pass sthg to sb →

→

• une structure qui diffère de celle du français, sans préposition, et dans laquelle l'ordre des compléments est inversé :

verbe + COI + COD

pass sb sthg

Il a discrètement passé un mot à son voisin. *He discreetly passed a note to the person sitting next to him* ou *He discreetly passed the person sitting next to him a note.*
Passe la télécommande à ton père, s'il te plaît. *Pass the remote control to your father, please* ou *Pass your father the remote control, please.*

passerelle [pasʀɛl] nf **1.** [pour piétons] footbridge **2.** NAUT [plan incliné] gangway, gangplank ; [escalier] gangway **3.** ENS [entre deux cycles] link **4.** INFORM gateway.

passe-temps, passetemps* [pastɑ̃] nm inv pastime, hobby.

passe-thé [paste] nm inv tea strainer.

passeur, euse [pasœʀ, øz] nm, f **1.** [sur un bac, un bateau, etc.] ferryman *(nm)* **2.** [de contrebande] smuggler **3.** [d'immigrants clandestins] : *il trouva un passeur qui l'aida à gagner les États-Unis* he found someone to get him over the border into the United States.

passible [pasibl] adj **▶ passible de** liable to / *crime passible de la prison* crime punishable by imprisonment.

passif¹ [pasif] nm FIN liabilities.

passif², ive [pasif, iv] adj [gén & GRAM] passive. **⬦ passif** nm GRAM passive (form).

passion [pasjɔ̃] nf **1.** [amour fou] passion, love **2.** [du jeu, des voyages, etc.] passion **▶ avoir la passion de qqch** to have a passion for sthg, to be passionately interested in sthg **3.** [exaltation] passion, feeling **▶ débattre de qqch avec passion** to argue passionately about sthg.

passionnant, e [pasjɔnɑ̃, ɑ̃t] adj [voyage, débat] fascinating, exciting ; [personne] intriguing, fascinating ; [récit] fascinating, enthralling, gripping / *nous avons eu une discussion passionnante* we had a fascinating discussion.

passionné, e [pasjɔne] ⬥ adj **1.** [aimant - amant, lettre] passionate **2.** [très vif - caractère, tempérament] passionate, emotional ; [- discours] passionate, impassioned ; [- intérêt, sentiment] passionate, keen **3.** [intéressé - spectateur, lecteur] keen, fervent, ardent. ⬥ nm, f **1.** [en amour] passionate person **2.** [fervent] enthusiast, devotee **▶ pour les passionnés de flamenco** for flamenco lovers.

passionnel, elle [pasjɔnɛl] adj passionate.

passionnément [pasjɔnemɑ̃] adv [avec passion] passionately, with passion.

passionner [pasjɔne] vt [intéresser - suj : récit] to fascinate, to enthral, to grip ; [- suj : discussion, idée] to fascinate, to grip **▶ la politique la passionne** politics is her passion, she has a passion for politics. **⬦ se passionner pour** vp + prép [idée] to feel passionately about ; [activité] to have a passion for / *je me passionne pour le reggae* I have a passion for reggae.

passivité [pasivite] nf [attitude] passivity, passiveness.

passoire [paswaʀ] nf [à petits trous] sieve ; [à gros trous] colander **▶ passoire à thé** tea strainer.

pastel [pastɛl] ⬥ nm [crayon] pastel ; [dessin] pastel (drawing) **▶ dessiner au pastel** to draw in pastels. ⬥ adj inv pastel, pastel-hued.

pastèque [pastɛk] nf [plante] watermelon plant ; [fruit] watermelon.

pasteur [pastœʀ] nm RELIG [protestant] minister, pastor ; arch [prêtre] pastor **▶ le Bon Pasteur** the Good Shepherd.

pasteuriser [3] [pastœʀize] vt to pasteurize.

pastiche [pastiʃ] nm pastiche.

pastille [pastij] nf PHARM pastille, lozenge **▶ pastille pour la gorge** throat lozenge ou pastille.

pastis [pastis] nm [boisson] pastis.

pastoral, e, aux [pastɔʀal, o] adj LITTÉR, MUS & RELIG pastoral.

Patagonie [patagɔni] npr f **▶ (la) Patagonie** Patagonia.

patate [patat] nf **1.** BOT & CULIN **▶ patate (douce)** sweet potato **2.** fam [pomme de terre] spud **3.** Québec fam [cœur] ticker UK.

patati [patati] **⬦ et patati, et patata** loc adv and so on and so forth, etc. etc.

pataud, e [pato, od] adj [maladroit] clumsy ; [sans finesse] gauche.

pataugeoire [patoʒwaʀ] nf paddling pool UK, wading pool US.

patauger [17] [patoʒe] vi **1.** [dans une flaque, à la piscine] to splash ou to paddle about ; [dans la gadoue] to wade / *les sauveteurs pataugeaient dans la boue* the members of the rescue party were wading about in the mud **2.** fig [s'empêtrer] to flounder / *il patauge dans ses réponses* he's getting more and more bogged down trying to answer **3.** [ne pas progresser] : *l'enquête policière patauge* the police inquiry is getting bogged down.

patch [patʃ] nm MÉD nicotine patch.

patchwork [patʃwœʀk] nm **1.** COUT [technique] patchwork ; [ouvrage] (piece of) patchwork **2.** [ensemble hétérogène] patchwork.

pâte [pat] nf **1.** [à base de farine - à pain] dough ; [- à tarte] pastry UK, dough US ; [- à gâteau] mixture UK, batter US ; [- à frire] batter **▶ pâte brisée** short ou shortcrust pastry UK, pie dough US **▶ pâte à crêpes** pancake batter **▶ pâte à choux** choux pastry **▶ pâte feuilletée** flaky pastry, puff pastry UK **▶ pâte à frire** batter **▶ pâte sablée** sweet biscuit ou sweet flan pastry UK, sweet ou sugar dough US **2.** [pour fourrer, tartiner] paste **▶ pâte d'amandes** marzipan, almond paste **▶ pâte d'anchois** anchovy paste ou spread **▶ pâte de coing** quince jelly **▶ pâte de fruit** fruit jelly *(made from thick fruit pulp)* **3.** [en fromagerie] **▶ (fromage à) pâte fermentée / molle** fermented / soft cheese **4.** [en cosmétologie] paste **▶ pâte dentifrice** toothpaste **5.** TECHNOL **▶ pâte à papier** pulp **▶ pâte de verre a)** INDUST molten glass **b)** JOAILL paste **6.** JEUX **▶ pâte à modeler** Plasticine®, modelling UK ou modeling US clay. **⬦ pâtes** nfpl CULIN **▶ pâtes (alimentaires)** pasta *(U).*

> 📝 Attention ! Le mot pasta est indénombrable. Il est suivi d'un verbe au singulier et ne s'emploie jamais avec l'article indéfini a :
> **Je n'aime pas les pâtes.** *I don't like pasta.*
> **Ces pâtes sont trop cuites.** *This pasta is overcooked.*
> **Il s'est étouffé en avalant une pâte.** *He choked on a piece of pasta.*

pâté [pate] nm **1.** CULIN pâté **▶ pâté en croûte** pâté en croûte, raised (crust) pie UK **▶ pâté de foie** liver pâté **2.** fam [tache d'encre] (ink) blot **3.** [tas] **▶ pâté de sable** sand pie. **⬦ pâté de maisons** nm block.

pâtée [pate] nf [pour animaux] food, feed / *pâtée pour chat / chien* cat / dog food.

patelin [patlɛ̃] nm fam [village] little village.

patente¹ [patɑ̃t] nf [taxe] trading tax.

patente² [patɑ̃t] nf `QUÉBEC` **1.** [invention] ingenious invention **2.** [objet quelconque] thing **3.** [affaire, histoire] : *c'est quoi cette patente ?* what's going on?

patenté, e [patɑ̃te] adj **1.** *fam* [attesté] established / *un raciste patenté* an out-and-out racist **2.** [qui paie patente] trading under licence, licensed.

patère [patɛʀ] nf [à vêtements] coat peg.

paternalisme [patɛʀnalism] nm paternalism.

paternaliste [patɛʀnalist] adj paternalist, paternalistic.

paternel, elle [patɛʀnɛl] adj [du père] paternal / *cousins du côté paternel* cousins on the father's ou paternal side.

paternité [patɛʀnite] nf **1.** [d'un enfant] paternity *sout*, fatherhood **2.** [d'une œuvre] paternity *sout*, authorship ; [d'une théorie] paternity.

pâteux, euse [patø, øz] adj [peinture, soupe] pasty ; [gâteau] doughy ▶ **avoir la bouche** ou **langue pâteuse** to have a furred tongue ▶ **parler d'une voix pâteuse** to sound groggy.

pathétique [patetik] ◆ adj [émouvant] pathetic, moving, poignant. ◆ nm [émotion] pathos.

pathogène [patɔʒɛn] adj pathogenic.

pathologie [patɔlɔʒi] nf pathology.

pathologique [patɔlɔʒik] adj **1.** MÉD pathologic, pathological **2.** *fam* [excessif, anormal] pathological.

patibulaire [patibylɛʀ] adj sinister ▶ **il avait une mine patibulaire** he looked sinister.

patiemment [pasjamɑ̃] adv patiently.

patience [pasjɑ̃s] ◆ nf **1.** [calme] patience, forbearance *sout* / *aie un peu de patience* be patient for a minute **2.** [persévérance] patience, painstaking care **3.** JEUX [cartes] patience `UK`, solitaire `US`. ◆ interj : *patience, j'ai presque fini !* hold on ou just a minute, I've almost finished!

patient, e [pasjɑ̃, ɑ̃t] ◆ adj patient. ◆ nm, f [malade] patient.

patienter [3] [pasjɑ̃te] vi [attendre] to wait / *faites-la patienter un instant* ask her to wait for a minute / *c'est occupé, vous voulez patienter ?* TÉLÉC it's engaged `UK` ou busy `US`, will you hold?

patin [patɛ̃] nm SPORT skate ▶ **patins à glace / roulettes** ice / roller skates ▶ **faire du patin (à) glace / roulettes** to go ice-skating / roller-skating.

patinage [patinaʒ] nm SPORT skating, ice-skating ▶ **patinage artistique** figure skating ▶ **patinage de vitesse** speed skating.

patine [patin] nf **1.** [d'un meuble] sheen **2.** ART & GÉOL patina.

patiner [3] [patine] ◆ vi **1.** SPORT to skate **2.** AUTO [roue] to spin ; [embrayage] to slip. `EXPR` **savoir patiner** `QUÉBEC` to know how to duck and weave *fig.* ◆ vt [un meuble] to patine, to patinize.

patineur, euse [patinœʀ, øz] nm, f skater.

patinoire [patinwaʀ] nf **1.** SPORT ice ou skating rink **2.** [surface trop glissante] : *ce trottoir est une véritable patinoire* this pavement is like an ice rink.

pâtir [32] [patiʀ] ◆ **pâtir de** v + prép to suffer from, to suffer as a result of.

pâtisserie [patisʀi] nf **1.** [gâteau] cake, pastry **2.** [activité] cake-making ▶ **faire de la pâtisserie** to make ou to bake cakes **3.** [boutique] pâtisserie, cake shop `UK` ou store `US` ▶ **pâtisserie-confiserie** confectioner's.

pâtissier, ère [patisje, ɛʀ] nm, f pastry cook, confectioner.

patois [patwa] nm patois, dialect.

patraque [patʀak] adj *fam* [souffrant] out of sorts, peaky `UK`, peaked `US`.

patriarcal, e, aux [patʀijaʀkal, o] adj patriarchal.

patriarche [patʀijaʀʃ] nm [gén & RELIG] patriarch.

patrie [patʀi] nf [pays natal] homeland, fatherland.

patrimoine [patʀimwan] nm **1.** [possessions héritées] inheritance ▶ **patrimoine immobilier** real estate assets **2.** [artistique, culturel] heritage **3.** BIOL ▶ **patrimoine héréditaire** gene pool ▶ **patrimoine génétique** gene pool.

patriote [patʀijɔt] ◆ adj patriotic. ◆ nmf patriot.

patriotique [patʀijɔtik] adj patriotic.

patriotisme [patʀijɔtism] nm patriotism.

patron¹ [patʀɔ̃] nm **1.** COUT pattern **2.** VÊT ▶ **(taille) patron** medium size / *demi-patron* small size ▶ **grand patron** large size.

patron², onne [patʀɔ̃, ɔn] nm, f **1.** [d'une entreprise - propriétaire] owner ; [-gérant] manager (manageress) ; [-directeur] employer ; [-de café, d'auberge] owner, landlord (landlady) ▶ **les grands patrons de la presse** the press barons ▶ **patron voyou a)** [entreprise] crooked company **b)** [dirigeant] abusive boss **2.** UNIV ▶ **patron de thèse** (doctoral) supervisor ou director **3.** RELIG (patron) saint. ◆ **patron** nm **1.** [d'une entreprise] boss **2.** ANTIQ & HIST patron.

patronage [patʀɔnaʒ] nm **1.** [soutien officiel] patronage ▶ **sous le haut patronage du président de la République** under the patronage of the President of the Republic **2.** [pour les jeunes] youth club.

patronal, e, aux [patʀɔnal, o] adj COMM & INDUST employer's, employers'.

patronat [patʀɔna] nm ▶ **le patronat** the employers.

patronyme [patʀɔnim] nm patronymic.

patrouille [patʀuj] nf **1.** MIL [groupe -d'hommes] patrol ; [-d'avions, de navires] squadron **2.** [mission] patrol ▶ **faire une / être en patrouille** to go / to be on patrol.

patrouiller [3] [patʀuje] vi to patrol.

patte [pat] nf

A. PARTIE DU CORPS **1.** [d'un félin, d'un chien] paw ; [d'un cheval, d'un bœuf] hoof ; [d'un oiseau] foot ▶ **être bas** ou **court sur pattes** [animal, personne] to be short-legged ▶ **pattes de devant a)** [membres] forelegs **b)** [pieds] forefeet ▶ **pattes de derrière a)** [membres] hind legs **b)** [pieds] hind feet ▶ **pattes de mouche** [écriture] (spidery) scrawl ▶ **pantalon (à) pattes d'éléphant** ou **d'éph** bell-bottoms, flares `UK` **2.** *fam* [jambe] leg, pin `UK`, gam `US` **3.** [savoir-faire - d'un peintre] (fine) touch ; [-d'un écrivain] talent.
B. SENS SPÉCIALISÉS **1.** `SUISSE` [torchon] cloth **2.** COUT strap. ◆ **à pattes** loc adv *fam* ▶ **allez, on y va à pattes !** come on, let's hoof it!

patte-d'oie [patdwa] (*pl* **pattes-d'oie**) nf **1.** [rides] crow's-foot **2.** [carrefour] Y-shaped crossroads ou junction.

pâturage [patyʀaʒ] nm [prairie] pasture, pastureland.

pâture [patyʀ] nf **1.** [nourriture] food, feed ▶ **jeter** ou **donner qqn en pâture à qqn** to serve sb up to sb **2.** [lieu] pasture.

paume [pom] nf ANAT palm.

paumé, e [pome] *fam* ◆ adj **1.** [désemparé, indécis] confused ; [marginal] out of it **2.** [isolé] remote, godforsaken / *un patelin complètement paumé* a place in the middle of nowhere **3.** [perdu] lost. ◆ nm, f [marginal] dropout.

paumer [3] [pome] *fam* vt [égarer] to lose. ◆ **se paumer** vpi *fam* to get lost, to lose one's way.

paupérisation [popeʀizasjɔ̃] nf pauperization.

paupière [popjɛʀ] nf eyelid.

paupiette [popjɛt] nf ▸ **paupiette (de veau)** paupiette of veal, veal olive.

pause [poz] nf **1.** [moment de repos] break ▸ **faire une pause** to have ou to take a break ▸ **la pause de midi** the lunch break **2.** [temps d'arrêt - dans une conversation] pause ▸ **marquer une pause** to pause ▸ **pause publicitaire** commercial break **3.** SPORT half-time.

pause-café [pozkafe] (pl **pauses-café**) nf coffee break.

pauvre [povʀ] ◆ adj **1.** [sans richesse - personne, pays, quartier] poor **2.** (avant nom) [pitoyable - demeure, décor] humble, wretched ; [- personne] poor / laisse donc ce pauvre chien tranquille ! do leave that poor ou wretched dog alone! / c'est la vie, mon pauvre vieux ! that's life, my friend! / pauvre crétin, va ! you idiot! **3.** [insuffisant] poor ▸ **pauvre en** : la ville est pauvre en espaces verts the town is short of ou lacks parks / alimentation pauvre en sels minéraux food lacking (in) minerals ▸ **régime pauvre en calories** low-calorie diet. ◆ nmf **1.** [par compassion] poor thing / les pauvres, comme ils ont dû souffrir ! poor things, they must have suffered so much! **2.** [en appellatif] : mais mon pauvre / ma pauvre, il ne m'obéit jamais ! [pour susciter la pitié] but my dear fellow / my dear, he never does as I say! ◆ nm poor man, pauper litt ▸ **les pauvres** the poor.

pauvreté [povʀəte] nf **1.** [manque d'argent] poverty ▸ **il a fini ses jours dans la pauvreté** he ended his days in poverty **2.** [médiocrité] poverty **3.** [déficience] poverty.

pavaner [3] [pavane] ◆◆ **se pavaner** vpi to strut about.

pavé [pave] nm **1.** [surface - dallée] pavement UK, sidewalk US ; [- empierrée] cobbles ▸ **être sur le pavé a)** [sans domicile] to be on the streets **b)** [au chômage] to be jobless **2.** [pierre] paving stone, cobblestone ; [dalle] flag, flagstone ▸ **un** ou **le pavé dans la mare** a bombshell fig **3.** INFORM pad, keypad ▸ **pavé numérique** numeric keypad **4.** fam [livre] huge ou massive tome ; [article] huge article ; [dissertation] huge essay.

paver [3] [pave] vt [avec des pavés] to cobble ; [avec des dalles] to pave.

pavillon [pavijɔ̃] nm

A. BÂTIMENT 1. [maison particulière] detached house ▸ **pavillon de banlieue** detached house (in the suburbs) **2.** [belvédère, gloriette] lodge ▸ **pavillon de chasse** hunting lodge **3.** [dans un hôpital] wing, wards ; [dans une cité universitaire] house ; [dans une exposition] pavilion.

B. DRAPEAU NAUT flag / pavillon en berne flag at half-mast ▸ **pavillon de complaisance** flag of convenience ▸ **pavillon de quarantaine** quarantine flag, yellow jack.

pavoiser [3] [pavwaze] ◆ vt [édifice] to deck with flags ou bunting. ◆ vi fam [faire le fier] ▸ **il n'y a pas de quoi pavoiser** that's nothing to be proud of.

pavot [pavo] nm BOT poppy.

payable [pɛjabl] adj payable / facture payable le 5 du mois invoice payable ou due on the 5th of the month.

payant, e [pɛjɑ̃, ɑ̃t] adj **1.** [non gratuit] ▸ **les consommations sont payantes** you have to pay for your drinks **2.** [qui paie] paying **3.** fam [qui produit - de l'argent] profitable ; [- un résultat] efficient / ses efforts du premier trimestre ont été payants his efforts during the first term have borne fruit.

paye [pɛj] = **paie**.

payé, e [peje] adj : bien / mal payé well- / low-paid.

payement [pɛmɑ̃] = **paiement**.

payer [11] [peje] ◆ vt **1.** [solder, régler] to pay ; (en usage absolu) ▸ **payer comptant / à crédit** to pay cash / by credit ▸ **je paye par chèque / avec ma carte de crédit / en liquide** I'll pay by cheque / with my credit card / (in) cash ▸ **c'est moi qui paie** [l'addition] I'll pay, it's my treat ▸ **payer de ses deniers** ou **de sa poche** to pay out of one's own pocket **2.** [rémunérer] to pay / tu es pourtant payé pour le savoir ! you of all people should know that! **3.** [acheter - repas, voyage] to pay for ▸ **payer à boire à qqn** to buy sb a drink / combien as-tu payé ta maison ? how much did your house cost you?, how much did you pay for your house? / combien il t'a fait payer ? how much did he charge? **4.** [obtenir au prix d'un sacrifice] ▸ **payer qqch de** to pay for sthg with ▸ **payer sa réussite de sa santé** to succeed at the expense ou the cost of one's health / elle me le paiera ! fig she'll pay for this! **5.** [subir les conséquences] to pay for (insép) ; (en usage absolu) ▸ **payer pour les autres** to be punished for others ▸ **payer les pots cassés** to foot the bill fig **6.** [dédommager] to compensate, to repay ▸ **ses félicitations me paient de mes efforts** his congratulations repay me my efforts **7.** [acheter - criminel] to hire ; [- témoin] to buy (off) / payer un tueur to hire a gunman. ◆ vi **1.** [être profitable] to pay / c'est un travail qui paie mal it's badly paid work, it's not a well paid job **2.** EXPR ne pas payer de mine : la maison ne paie pas de mine, mais elle est confortable the house isn't much to look at ou the house doesn't look much but it's very comfortable ▸ **payer de sa personne a)** [s'exposer au danger] to put o.s. on the line **b)** [se donner du mal] to put in a lot of effort. ◆◆ **se payer** vpt **1.** fam [s'offrir] to treat o.s. to / j'ai envie de me payer une robe I feel like treating myself to a dress ou like buying myself a dress ▸ **se payer la tête de qqn** to make fun of sb **2.** fam [recevoir] to get, to land UK / je me suis payé un 2 à l'oral I got a 2 in the oral **3.** fam [percuter] to run ou to bump into / elle s'est payé le mur en reculant she backed into the wall.

Notez les différentes constructions du verbe to pay :

• payer qqn = pay sb.
Elle paie sa femme de ménage 15 euros de l'heure. She pays her cleaner 15 euros an hour.

• Lorsque payer qqch signifie donner de l'argent en échange de qqch, il se traduit par pay for sthg :
Vous pouvez payer vos consommations à la sortie. You can pay for your drinks on the way out.
Vous avez payé ces achats ? Have you paid for these items?

• Lorsque payer signifie régler (un montant), on emploie le verbe pay suivi du montant, et on fait précéder le nom de ce qu'on achète par for :
J'ai payé cette voiture 20 000 euros. I paid 20,000 euros for this car.

Notez également :
Combien l'avez-vous payé ? How much did you pay for it?

payeur, euse [pɛjœʀ, øz] nm, f payer. ◆◆ **payeur** nm [débiteur] ▸ **mauvais payeur** bad debtor, defaulter.

pays [pei] nm **1.** [nation] country ▸ **les nouveaux pays industrialisés** the newly industrialized countries ▸ **le pays d'accueil** the host country ▸ **pays en (voie de) développement** developing country ▸ **se conduire comme en pays conquis** : ils se conduisent comme en pays conquis they're acting ou behaving as if they own the place ▶ **voir du pays** to travel a lot **2.** [zone, contrée] region, area / *pays chaud / sec* hot / dry region ▶ **en pays de connaissance** : *vous serez en pays de connaissance, Tom fait aussi du piano* you'll have something in common because Tom plays the piano too **3.** [peuple] people, country / *tout le pays se demande encore qui est l'assassin* the whole country's still wondering who the murderer might be **4.** [région d'origine] ▶ **le pays a)** [nation] one's country **b)** [région] one's home (region) **c)** [ville] one's home (town) ▶ **avoir le mal du pays** to be homesick **5.** *fig* [berceau, foyer] ▶ **le pays de** : *le pays des tulipes* the country of the tulip. **◆ de pays** loc adj [produits] local.

paysage [peizaʒ] nm **1.** [étendue géographique] landscape **2.** [panorama] view, scenery, landscape **3.** [aspect d'ensemble] landscape, scene / *paysage politique / social* political / social landscape ▶ **le paysage audiovisuel français** French broadcasting ▶ **paysage urbain** townscape, urban landscape **4.** ART landscape (painting) **5.** INFORM ▶ **mode** ou **format paysage** landscape (mode).

paysager, ère [peizaʒe,ɛʀ] adj landscape *(modif)* ▶ **parc paysager** landscaped gardens.

paysagiste [peizaʒist] nmf **1.** ART landscape painter, landscapist **2.** HORT landscape gardener.

paysan, anne [peizɑ̃, an] **◆** adj **1.** SOCIOL peasant *(modif)* ; [population] rural ▶ **le malaise paysan** discontent amongst small farmers **2.** [rustique - décor] rustic ; [- style, vêtements] rustic, country *(modif).* **◆** nm, f [cultivateur] peasant, farmer.

Pays-Bas [peiba] npr mpl ▶ **les Pays-Bas** the Netherlands ▶ **aux Pays-Bas** in the Netherlands.

PC nm **1.** (abr de **Parti communiste**) Communist Party **2.** (abr de **personal computer**) PC, micro.

pck (abr écrite de **parce que**) SMS COS, COZ.

PCV (abr de **à percevoir**) nm reverse-charge call 🇬🇧, collect call 🇺🇸 ▶ **appeler Paris en PCV** to make a reverse-charge call to Paris 🇬🇧, to call Paris collect 🇺🇸.

PDF (abr de **portable document format**) nm INFORM PDF.

P-DG (abr de **président-directeur général**) nmf *fam* chairman and managing director 🇬🇧, Chief Executive Officer 🇺🇸 ; ≃ MD 🇬🇧 ; ≃ CEO 🇺🇸.

péage [peaʒ] nm **1.** [sur une voie publique - taxe] toll ; [- lieu] toll (gate) / **'péage à 5 km'** 'toll 5 km' **2.** TV ▶ **chaîne à péage** pay channel.

peau, x [po] nf **1.** ANAT skin ▶ **avoir la peau sèche / grasse** to have dry / greasy skin ▶ **peau mixte** combination skin ▶ **être** ou **se sentir bien dans sa peau** *fam* to feel good about o.s., to be together ▶ **être mal dans sa peau** to feel bad about o.s., to be unhappy ▶ **entrer** ou **se mettre dans la peau de qqn** to put o.s. in sb's shoes ou place ▶ **faire peau neuve** to get a facelift *fig* / *l'université fait peau neuve* the university system is being completely overhauled ▶ **avoir la peau dure** to be thick-skinned ▶ **si tu tiens à ta peau** *fam* if you value your life ou hide ▶ **un jour, j'aurai ta peau !** *fam* I'll get you one of these days! **2.** ZOOL [gén] skin ; [fourrure] pelt ; [cuir - non tanné] hide ; [- tanné] leather, (tanned) hide / *une valise en peau* a leather suitcase / *mes économies diminuent comme une peau de chagrin* my savings are just melting away ▶ **peau d'ours** bearskin **3.** [d'un fruit, d'un légume, du lait bouilli] skin ; [du fromage] rind ▶ **peau d'orange** orange peel ▶ **peau de banane** *pr & fig* banana skin. **◆ peau d'orange** nf MÉD orange-peel skin *(caused by cellulite).* **◆ peau de vache** nf *tfam* [femme] cow 🇬🇧, bitch ; [homme] bastard.

peaufiner [3] [pofine] vt *fig* to put the finishing touches to.

Peau-Rouge [poʀuʒ] nmf Red Indian, Redskin.

pécan [pekã] nm ▶ **noix de pécan** pecan nut.

peccadille [pekadij] nf [vétille] : *se disputer pour des peccadilles* to argue over trifles.

pêche¹ [pɛʃ] **◆** nf **1.** BOT peach **2.** *fam* [énergie] get-up-and-go / *avoir la pêche* to be full of get-up-and-go, to be on form. **◆** adj inv peach *(modif)*, peach-coloured.

pêche² [pɛʃ] nf **1.** [activité - en mer] fishing ; [- en eau douce] fishing, angling ▶ **aller à la pêche a)** [en mer] to go fishing **b)** [en eau douce] to go angling ▶ **pêche à la baleine** whaling, whale-hunting ▶ **pêche à la ligne** angling ▶ **pêche maritime** sea fishing ▶ **pêche sous-marine** underwater fishing ▶ **aller à la pêche aux informations** to go in search of information **2.** [produit de la pêche] catch / *la pêche a été bonne pr* there was a good catch.

péché [peʃe] nm [faute] sin ▶ **péché mortel / originel / véniel** mortal / original / venial sin / *mon péché mignon, c'est le chocolat* I just can't resist chocolate, chocolate is my little weakness ▶ **les sept péchés capitaux** the seven deadly sins.

pécher [18] [peʃe] vi **1.** RELIG to sin **2.** *sout* [commettre une erreur] : *elle a péché par imprudence* she was too careless, she was overcareless.

✍ In reformed spelling (see p. 16-18), this verb is conjugated like *semer : il pèchera, elle pècherait.*

pêcher¹ [peʃe] nm BOT peach tree.

pêcher² [4] [peʃe] **◆** vt **1.** PÊCHE [essayer de prendre] to fish for *(insép)* ; [prendre] to catch ▶ **pêcher la crevette** to shrimp, to go shrimping **2.** *fam* [dénicher] to seek out *(sép)*, to hunt ou to track down *(sép)*, to unearth / *où a-t-il été pêcher que j'avais démissionné ?* where did he get the idea that I'd resigned ? **◆** vi [aller à la pêche] to fish / *il pêche tous les dimanches* he goes fishing every Sunday ▶ **pêcher à la ligne / traîne** to angle / troll.

pécheresse [peʃʀɛs] f ⟶ **pécheur.**

pécheur, pécheresse ou **pècheresse** [peʃœʀ, peʃʀɛs] nm, f sinner.

pêcheur, euse [pɛʃœʀ, øz] nm, f [en mer] fisherman (fisherwoman) ; [en eau douce] angler ▶ **pêcheur de crevettes** shrimper.

pêchu, e [peʃy] adj *fam* ▶ **être pêchu** to have lots of energy.

pecnot [pekno] = **péquenaud.**

pectoral, e, aux [pɛktɔʀal, o] adj **1.** ANAT pectoral **2.** PHARM throat *(modif)*, cough *(modif).* **◆ pectoral, aux** nm ANAT pectoral muscle.

pécule [pekyl] nm [petit capital] savings, nest egg ▶ **se constituer un (petit) pécule** to put some money aside.

pécuniaire [pekynjɛʀ] adj financial, pecuniary *sout.*

pédagogie [pedagoʒi] nf **1.** [méthodologie] educational methods **2.** [pratique] teaching skills.

pédagogique [pedagoʒik] adj [science, manière] educational, teaching *(modif)*, pedagogical *sout* / *elle n'a aucune formation pédagogique* she's not been trained to teach ou as a teacher / *aides* ou *supports pédagogiques* teaching materials.

pédagogue [pedagog] **◆** adj ▶ **il n'est pas très pédagogue** he's not very good at teaching ▶ **elle est très pédagogue** she's a very good teacher. **◆** nmf [enseignant] teacher.

pédale [pedal] nf **1.** [d'un véhicule] pedal **2.** [d'une poubelle] pedal ; [d'une machine à coudre] treadle **3.** AUTO pedal **4.** MUS pedal ▶ **mettre la pédale douce** *pr & fig* to soft-pedal **5.** *tfam & péj* [homosexuel] queer 🇬🇧, faggot 🇺🇸.

pédaler [3] [pedale] vi **1.** [sur un vélo] to pedal **2.** EXPR **pédaler dans la choucroute** ou **la semoule** ou **le yaourt** *fam* to be all at sea.

pédalier [pedalje] nm [d'une bicyclette] (bicycle) drive.

Pédalo® [pedalo] nm pedalo, pedal-boat.

pédant, e [pedɑ̃, ɑ̃t] ◆ adj [exposé, ton] pedantic. ◆ nm, f pedant.

⚠ Le mot anglais **pedant** signifie « pointilleux » et non « pédant » ; **pedantry** est le fait d'être pointilleux, de couper les cheveux en quatre, et n'a rien à voir avec la pédanterie.

pédé [pede] nm *tfam & péj* queer 🇬🇧, fag 🇺🇸.

pédestre [pedɛstʀ] adj **1.** ⟶ randonnée **2.** ⟶ statue.

pédiatre [pedjatʀ] nmf paediatrician.

pédiatrie [pedjatʀi] nf paediatrics *(U)*.

pédicure [pedikyʀ] nmf chiropodist, podiatrist 🇺🇸.

pedigree, pédigrée* [pedigʀe] nm pedigree.

pédophile [pedɔfil] nmf paedophile.

pédopornographie [pedɔpɔʀnɔgʀafi] nf child pornography.

pédopsychiatre [pedɔpsikjatʀ] nmf child psychiatrist.

peeling [piliŋ] nm exfoliation (treatment) ▶ **se faire faire un peeling** to be given a face (peeling) mask.

peer to peer, peer-to-peer [piʀtupiʀ] ◆ nm ▶ **le peer to peer** peer to peer technology. ◆ adj peer-to-peer.

pègre [pɛgʀ] nf (criminal) underworld.

peigne [pɛɲ] nm [pour les cheveux] comb ▶ **passer une région / un document au peigne fin** to go over an area / a document with a fine-tooth comb.

peigner [4] [peɲe] vt [cheveux, personne] to comb. ◆ **se peigner** vp *(emploi réfléchi)* [se coiffer] to comb one's hair.

peignoir [peɲwaʀ] nm **1.** [sortie de bain] ▶ **peignoir (de bain)** bathrobe **2.** [robe de chambre] dressing gown 🇬🇧, robe 🇺🇸, bathrobe 🇺🇸.

peinard, e [penaʀ, aʀd] adj *tfam* [vie, travail] cushy ▶ **rester** ou **se tenir peinard** to keep one's nose clean / **là-bas, on sera peinards** we'll have it easy there.

peindre [81] [pɛ̃dʀ] vt **1.** [mur, tableau] to paint ▶ **j'ai peint la porte en bleu** I painted the door blue / **peindre à la bombe / au pistolet** to spray-paint ▶ **peindre au pinceau / rouleau** to paint with a brush / roller ▶ **peindre à l'huile / à l'eau** to paint in oils / in watercolours **2.** [décrire] to portray, to depict.

peine [pɛn] nf

A. SANCTION **1.** [châtiment] sentence, penalty ▶ **infliger une lourde peine à qqn** to pass a harsh sentence on sb ▶ **la peine de mort** capital punishment, the death penalty ▶ **peine de prison** prison sentence ▶ **peine de prison avec sursis** suspended (prison) sentence **2.** RELIG [damnation] damnation, suffering.

B. DOULEUR MORALE **1.** [tourment, inquiétude] trouble ▶ **faire peine à voir** to be a sorry sight ▶ **peines de cœur** heartache(s) **2.** [tristesse] sorrow, sadness, grief ▶ **avoir de la peine** to be sad ou upset / **je ne voudrais pas lui faire de la peine en le lui disant** I wouldn't like to upset him by telling him / **il me fait vraiment de la peine** I feel really sorry for him.

C. EFFORT, DIFFICULTÉ **1.** [effort] effort, trouble / **ce n'est pas la peine** it's not worth it, it's pointless ▶ **ce n'est pas**

la peine de tout récrire / que tu y ailles there's no point writing it all out again / your going ▶ **prendre** ou **se donner la peine de** to go to ou to take the trouble to / **il ne s'est même pas donné la peine de répondre** he didn't even bother replying ▶ **valoir la peine** to be worth it / **l'exposition vaut la peine d'être vue** the exhibition is worth seeing ▶ **peine perdue**: *n'essaie pas de le convaincre, c'est peine perdue* don't try to persuade him, it's a waste of time ou you'd be wasting your breath **2.** [difficulté] ▶ **avoir de la peine à**: *avoir de la peine à marcher* to have trouble ou difficulty walking ▶ **avoir toutes les peines du monde à**: *elle a eu toutes les peines du monde à venir à la réunion* she had a terrible time ou the devil's own job getting to the meeting ▶ **être (bien) en peine de**: *je serais bien en peine de vous l'expliquer* I'd have a hard job explaining it to you, I wouldn't really know how to explain it to you. ⟿ **à peine** loc adv **1.** [presque pas] hardly, barely, scarcely / *j'arrive à peine à soulever mon sac* I can hardly ou barely lift my bag **2.** [tout juste] barely / *il y a à peine une semaine / deux heures* not quite a week / two hours ago, barely a week / two hours ago **3.** [à l'instant] just **4.** [aussitôt]: *à peine guérie, elle a repris le travail* no sooner had she recovered than she went back to work ▶ **à peine... que**: *à peine était-elle couchée que le téléphone se mit à sonner* no sooner had she gone to bed than ou she'd only just gone to bed when the phone rang. ⟿ **sous peine de** loc prép / '**défense de fumer sous peine d'amende**' 'smokers will be prosecuted' ▶ **sous peine de mort** on pain of death.

Peine de mort
The death penalty was abolished in France in 1981.

peiner [4] [pene] ◆ vt [attrister] to upset, to distress / *je suis peiné par ton attitude* I'm unhappy about your attitude. ◆ vi **1.** [personne] to have trouble ou difficulty / *j'ai peiné pour terminer dans les délais* I had to struggle to finish ou I had a lot of trouble finishing on time **2.** [machine] to strain, to labour 🇬🇧, to labor 🇺🇸 / *on entendait un moteur peiner dans la montée* you could hear a car engine toiling up the hill.

peintre [pɛ̃tʀ] nmf **1.** [artiste] painter **2.** [artisan, ouvrier] painter ▶ **peintre en bâtiment** house painter.

peinture [pɛ̃tyʀ] nf

A. PRODUIT **1.** [substance] paint ▶ **peinture à l'eau** CONSTR water ou water-based paint ▶ **peinture à l'huile** ART oil paint ▶ **peinture laquée / satinée / mate** gloss / satin-finish / matt paint ▶ **peinture métallisée** metallic paint **2.** [action] painting **3.** [couche de matière colorante] paintwork ▶ **donner un petit coup de peinture à qqch** to freshen sth up, to give sth a lick of paint / '**peinture fraîche**' 'wet paint' / *refaire la peinture d'une porte* to repaint a door / *refaire la peinture d'une pièce* to redecorate a room.

B. COMME ART **1.** ART [art et technique] painting ▶ **peinture au doigt** finger-painting / *peinture sur soie* silk painting, painting **2.** [œuvre] painting, picture, canvas **3.** [ensemble d'œuvres peintes] painting / *la peinture flamande* Flemish painting.

C. DESCRIPTION portrayal, picture / *une peinture de la société médiévale* a picture of mediaeval society.

péjoratif, ive [peʒɔʀatif, iv] adj pejorative, derogatory.

Pékin [pekɛ̃] npr Peking.

pékinois [pekinwa] nm ZOOL Pekinese, Pekingese.

PEL, Pel [pɛl, peœɛl] nm abr de plan d'épargne logement.

pelage [pəlaʒ] nm coat, fur.

pelé, e [pəle] adj **1.** [chat, renard, fourrure] mangy **2.** [sans végétation] bare. ❖ **pelé** nm fam EXPR **trois pelés et un tondu** : il y avait trois pelés et un tondu there was hardly anyone there.

pêle-mêle, pêlemêle* [pɛlmɛl] adv in a jumble, every which way, pell-mell / les draps et les couvertures étaient pêle-mêle sur le lit sheets and covers were all jumbled up ou in a heap on the bed.

peler [25] [pəle] ❖ vt [fruit, légume] to peel. ❖ vi [peau] to peel / j'ai le dos qui pèle my back's peeling. ❖ **se peler** vpi fam : qu'est-ce qu'on se pèle ici ! it's freezing in here!

pèlerin [pɛlʀɛ̃] nm RELIG pilgrim.

pèlerinage [pɛlʀinaʒ] nm [voyage] pilgrimage ▸ **faire un** ou **aller en pèlerinage à Lourdes** to go on a pilgrimage to Lourdes.

pèlerine [pɛlʀin] nf pelerine.

pélican [pelikɑ̃] nm pelican.

pelle [pɛl] nf **1.** [pour ramasser] shovel ; [pour creuser] spade **2.** CULIN ▸ **pelle à poisson** / **tarte** fish / pie slice **3.** TRAV PUB ▸ **pelle mécanique** a) [sur roues] mechanical shovel b) [sur chenilles] excavator **4.** fam EXPR **rouler une pelle à qqn** to give sb a French kiss. ❖ **à la pelle** loc adv **1.** [avec une pelle] : ramasser la neige à la pelle to shovel up the snow **2.** [en grande quantité] in huge numbers / gagner ou ramasser de l'argent à la pelle to earn huge amounts of money.

pelletée [pɛlte] nf **1.** [de terre - ramassée] shovelful ; [- creusée] spadeful **2.** fam [grande quantité] heap, pile.

pelleter [27] [pɛlte] vt to shovel (up).

✏ In reformed spelling (see p. 16-18), this verb is conjugated like acheter : il pellète, elle pelletera.

pelleteuse [pɛltøz] nf mechanical shovel ou digger.

pellicule [pelikyl] nf **1.** [mince croûte] film, thin layer **2.** PHOT film ▸ **une pellicule** a) [bobine] a reel (of film) b) [chargeur] a roll (of) film. ❖ **pellicules** nfpl [dans les cheveux] dandruff (U) / avoir des pellicules to have dandruff.

pelote [pəlɔt] nf **1.** [de ficelle, de coton] ball ▸ **une pelote de laine** a ball of wool **2.** Québec [boule] ▸ **pelote de neige** snowball **3.** COUT [coussinet] pincushion **4.** SPORT pelota ▸ **jouer à la pelote basque** to play pelota.

peloter [3] [pləte] vt fam to grope. ❖ **se peloter** vp (emploi réciproque) fam to neck.

peloton [plɔtɔ̃] nm **1.** MIL [division] platoon ; [unité] squad ▸ **peloton d'exécution** firing squad **2.** SPORT pack ▸ **être dans le peloton de tête** a) to be up with the leaders b) fig to be among the front runners.

pelotonner [3] [plɔtɔne] ❖ **se pelotonner** vpi to curl up ▸ **se pelotonner contre qqn** to snuggle up to sb.

pelouse [pəluz] nf **1.** [terrain] lawn ; [herbe] grass / 'pelouse interdite' 'keep off the grass' **2.** SPORT field, ground ; [d'un champ de courses] paddock.

peluche [pəlyʃ] nf **1.** [jouet] cuddly toy **2.** [poussière] (piece of) fluff (U). ❖ **en peluche** loc adj ▸ **chien** / **canard en peluche** (cuddly) toy dog / duck.

pelucheux, euse [pəlyʃø, øz] adj **1.** [tissu] fluffy **2.** [fruit] downy.

pelure [pəlyʀ] nf [peau] peel (U) ▸ **pelure d'oignon** onionskin (paper).

pénal, e, aux [penal, o] adj [droit] criminal ; [réforme] penal.

pénalisation [penalizasjɔ̃] nf **1.** SPORT penalty (for infringement) ▸ **points de pénalisation** ÉQUIT faults, penalty points **2.** [désavantage] penalization.

pénaliser [3] [penalize] vt **1.** SPORT to penalize **2.** [désavantager] to penalize, to put ou to place at a disadvantage.

pénalité [penalite] nf **1.** FIN penalty **2.** SPORT penalty / coup de pied de pénalité penalty kick.

penalty (pl **penaltys** ou **penalties**), **pénalty*** [penalti] nm penalty (kick) ▸ **siffler** / **tirer un penalty** to award / to take a penalty.

pénates [penat] nmpl fam & fig ▸ **regagner ses pénates** to go home.

penaud, e [pəno, od] adj sheepish, contrite / d'un air tout penaud sheepishly, with a hangdog look.

penchant [pɑ̃ʃɑ̃] nm [pour quelque chose] propensity, liking, penchant / un petit penchant pour le chocolat a weakness for chocolate ▸ **de mauvais penchants** evil tendencies.

penché, e [pɑ̃ʃe] adj [tableau] crooked, askew ; [mur, écriture] sloping, slanting ; [objet] tilting.

pencher [3] [pɑ̃ʃe] ❖ vi **1.** (aux être) [être déséquilibré - entassement] to lean (over), to tilt ; [- bateau] to list / la tour / le mur penche vers la droite the tower / the wall leans to the right ▸ **faire pencher la balance en faveur de / contre qqn** fig to tip the scales in favour of / against sb **2.** (aux avoir) ▸ **pencher pour** [préférer] to be inclined to, to incline towards. ❖ vt to tilt, to tip up (sép) / il pencha la tête en arrière pour l'embrasser he leaned backwards to kiss her / elle pencha la tête au-dessus du parapet she leaned over the parapet. ❖ **se pencher** vpi [s'incliner] to lean, to bend / elle se pencha sur le berceau she leaned over the cradle / 'ne pas se pencher au-dehors' 'do not lean out of the window'. ❖ **se pencher sur** vp + prép to look into.

pendaison [pɑ̃dɛzɔ̃] nf hanging. ❖ **pendaison de crémaillère** nf housewarming (party).

pendant¹ [pɑ̃dɑ̃] prép [au cours de] during ; [insistant sur la durée] for / quelqu'un a appelé pendant l'heure du déjeuner somebody called while you were at lunch ou during your lunch break ▸ **pendant ce temps-là** in the meantime, meanwhile / j'y ai habité pendant un an I lived there for a year / nous avons roulé pendant 20 km we drove for 20 km. ❖ **pendant que** loc conj **1.** [tandis que] while **2.** [tant que] while / pendant que tu y es, pourras-tu passer à la banque ? while you're there ou at it, could you stop off at the bank? / pendant que j'y pense, voici l'argent que je te dois while I think of it, here's the money I owe you **3.** [puisque] since, while / allons-y pendant que nous y sommes let's go, since we're here.

pendant², e [pɑ̃dɑ̃, ɑ̃t] adj **1.** [tombant] hanging ▸ **la langue pendante** a) [de chaleur, de fatigue] panting b) [de convoitise] drooling ▸ **chien aux oreilles pendantes** dog with drooping ou droopy ears **2.** DR [en cours - d'instruction] pending ; [- de résolution] pending, being dealt with. ❖ **pendant** nm **1.** [bijou] pendant ▸ **pendant (d'oreilles)** (pendant) earring **2.** [symétrique - d'une chose] ▸ **faire pendant à qqch** to match sthg ▸ **se faire pendant** to match, to be a matching pair ; [alter ego - d'une personne] counterpart, opposite number.

pendentif [pɑ̃dɑ̃tif] nm [bijou] pendant.

penderie [pɑ̃dʀi] nf [meuble] wardrobe ; [pièce] walk-in wardrobe 🇬🇧 ou closet 🇺🇸.

pendouiller [3] [pɑ̃duje] vi fam to hang down, to dangle.

pendre [73] [pɑ̃dʀ] ❖ vt **1.** [accrocher] to hang (up) / pendre un tableau à un clou to hang a picture from a nail / pendre son linge sur un fil to hang up one's washing on a line ▶ **pendre la crémaillère** to have a housewarming (party) **2.** [exécuter] to hang ▶ **aller se faire pendre ailleurs** *fam: qu'il aille se faire pendre ailleurs* he can go to blazes ou go hang **3.** *fig* ▶ **être (toujours) pendu après qqn** ou **aux basques de qqn** to dog sb's every footstep, to hang around sb / **être pendu au téléphone** to spend hours ou one's life on the phone. ◆ vi **1.** [être accroché] to hang / *du linge pendait aux fenêtres* washing was hanging out of the windows ▶ **prendre au nez de qqn** *fam: ça te pend au nez* you've got it coming to you **2.** [retomber] to hang ; [bras, jambes] to dangle ; [langue d'un animal] to hang out. ◆ **se pendre** ◆ vp *(emploi réfléchi)* [se suicider] to hang o.s. ◆ vpi [s'accrocher] to hang / *les chauves-souris se pendent aux branches* the bats hang from the branches ▶ **se pendre au cou de qqn** to fling one's arms around sb's neck.

pendu, e [pɑ̃dy] adj, f hanged man (woman) ▶ **le jeu du pendu** (the game of) hangman.

pendule [pɑ̃dyl] ◆ nm [instrument, balancier] pendulum. ◆ nf [horloge] clock ▶ **remettre les pendules à l'heure** *fig* to set the record straight.

pendulette [pɑ̃dylɛt] nf small clock ▶ **pendulette de voyage** travel (alarm) clock.

pêne [pɛn] nm bolt (of lock).

pénétrant, e [penetrɑ̃, ɑ̃t] adj **1.** [froid, pluie] : *une petite bruine pénétrante* the kind of drizzle that soaks one through / *le froid était pénétrant* it was bitterly cold **2.** [fort] strong, penetrating **3.** [clairvoyant] sharp, penetrating, acute.

pénétré, e [penetre] adj [rempli] : *pénétré de sa propre importance* *péj* self-important.

pénétrer [18] [penetre] ◆ vi [entrer] to go, to enter / *ils ont réussi à pénétrer en Suisse* they managed to cross into ou to enter Switzerland ▶ **pénétrer dans la maison de qqn** a) [avec sa permission] to enter sb's house b) [par effraction] to break into sb's house ; [passer] to go, to penetrate / *la balle a pénétré dans la cuisse* the bullet entered the thigh ; [s'infiltrer] to seep, to penetrate / *l'eau a très vite pénétré dans la cale* water quickly flooded into the hold / *le vent pénètre par la cheminée* the wind comes in by the chimney / *faire pénétrer la crème en massant doucement* gently rub ou massage the cream in. ◆ vt **1.** [traverser] to penetrate, to go in ou into, to get in ou into / *un froid glacial me pénétra* I was chilled to the bone ou to the marrow **2.** COMM [marché] to penetrate, to break into **3.** [sexuellement] to penetrate **4.** [deviner] to penetrate, to perceive / *pénétrer un mystère* to get to the heart of a mystery. ◆ **se pénétrer de** vp + prép : *se pénétrer d'une vérité* to become convinced of a truth / *il faut vous pénétrer de l'importance du facteur religieux* you must be aware of ou you must understand the importance of the religious element.

✍ In reformed spelling (see p. 16-18), this verb is conjugated like **semer** : *il pénètrera, elle pénètrerait*.

pénible [penibl] adj **1.** [épuisant] hard, tough, tiring ▶ **un travail pénible** a laborious job / *elle trouve de plus en plus pénible de monter les escaliers* it gets harder and harder for her to climb the stairs **2.** [attristant] distressing, painful / *en parler m'est très pénible* I find it difficult to talk about (it) / *ma présence lui est pénible* my being here bothers him **3.** [difficile à supporter] tiresome / *je trouve ça vraiment pénible* I find it a real pain / *tu es pénible, tu sais !* you're a real pain in the neck ou a nuisance !

péniblement [peniblɑ̃] adv **1.** [avec difficulté] laboriously, with difficulty **2.** [tout juste] just about.

péniche [peniʃ] nf [large] barge ; [étroite] narrow boat ▶ **péniche de débarquement** MIL landing craft.

pénicilline [penisilin] nf penicillin.

péninsule [penɛ̃syl] nf peninsula.

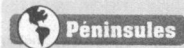 **Péninsules**

la péninsule arabique	the Arabian Peninsula
la péninsule des Balkans ou balkanique	the Balkan Peninsula
la péninsule Ibérique	the Iberian Peninsula
la péninsule italienne	the Italian Peninsula

pénis [penis] nm penis.

pénitence [penitɑ̃s] nf **1.** RELIG [repentir] penitence ; [punition] penance ; [sacrement] penance, sacrament of reconciliation ▶ **faire pénitence** to repent **2.** [punition] punishment.

pénitencier [penitɑ̃sje] nm [prison] prison, jail, penitentiary US.

pénitent, e [penitɑ̃, ɑ̃t] ◆ adj penitent. ◆ nm, f penitent.

pénitentiaire [penitɑ̃sjɛr] adj prison *(modif)*.

pénombre [penɔ̃br] nf [obscurité] half-light, dim light.

pensable [pɑ̃sabl] adj : *à cette époque-là, de telles vitesses n'étaient pas pensables* in those days, such speeds were unthinkable.

pense-bête [pɑ̃sbɛt] *(pl* pense-bêtes) nm reminder.

pensée [pɑ̃se] nf **1.** [idée] thought, idea / *la seule pensée d'une seringue me donne des sueurs froides* the very thought of a needle leaves me in a cold sweat / *tout à la pensée de son rendez-vous, il n'a pas vu arriver la voiture* deeply absorbed in ou by the thought of his meeting, he didn't see the car (coming) ▶ **à la pensée de faire qqch** at the thought of doing sthg ▶ **être tout à ou perdu dans ses pensées** to be lost in thought ▶ **avoir une bonne pensée pour qqn** to spare a kind thought for sb **2.** [façon de raisonner] thought / *avoir une pensée claire* to be clear-thinking **3.** [opinion] thought, (way of) thinking ▶ **aller au bout** ou **au fond de sa pensée** : *pour aller jusqu'au bout ou fond de ma pensée je dirais que...* to be absolutely frank, I'd say that... / *allez donc jusqu'au bout de votre pensée* come on, say what you really think ou what's really on your mind **4.** [esprit] mind ▶ **nous sommes avec vous par la** ou **en pensée** our thoughts are with you **5.** PHILOS thought **6.** BOT pansy.

penser [3] [pɑ̃se] ◆ vt **1.** [croire] to think, to assume, to suppose / *qu'en penses-tu* ? what do you think of it? / *je pense que oui* (yes), I think so / *je pense que non* (no), I don't think so ou I think not / *je pense que tu devrais lui dire* I think you should tell him / *qu'est-ce qui te fait penser qu'il ment* ? what makes you think he's lying? ▶ **quoi qu'on pense** whatever people (may) think ; *(avec un adj attribut)* : *je le pensais diplomate* I thought him tactful, I thought he was tactful **2.** [escompter] ▶ **je pense partir demain** I'm thinking of ou planning on ou reckoning on leaving tomorrow **3.** [avoir à l'esprit] to think / *je ne sais jamais ce que tu penses* I can never tell what you're thinking ou what's on your mind ▶ **dire tout haut ce que certains** ou **d'autres pensent tout bas** to say out loud what others are thinking in private / *il a marché dans ce que je pense* he trod in some you-know-what **4.** [comprendre] to think, to realize, to imagine / *pense qu'elle a près de cent ans* you must realize that she's nearly a hundred **5.** [se rappeler] to remember, to think / *je n'ai plus pensé que c'était lundi* I forgot ou I never thought it was Monday **6.** [pour exprimer la surprise, l'approbation, l'ironie] : *je n'aurais / on n'aurait jamais pensé que...* I'd never / nobody'd ever have thought that... ▶ **quand je pense que...** to think that... / *quand on pense qu'il n'y avait pas le téléphone à l'époque !* when you think that there was no such thing as the phone in those days ! / *lui, me dire merci ? tu penses* ou *penses-tu* ou *pense donc !* fam him? thank me? I should be so lucky ou you must be joking ! ▶ **penser bien** fam: *tu penses bien que je lui ai tout raconté !* I told him everything, as you can well imagine **7.** [concevoir] to think out ou through *(sép)* / *une architecture bien pensée* a well-planned ou well-thought out architectural design. ◆ vi **1.** [réfléchir] to think, to ponder / *donner* ou *laisser à penser* to make one think, to start one thinking **2.** [avoir une opinion] : *je n'ai jamais pensé comme toi* I never did agree with you ou share your views. ◆ **penser à** v + prép **1.** [envisager] to think about ou of *(insép)* / *vous éviteriez des ennuis, pensez-y* you'd save yourself a lot of trouble, think it over ! ▶ **sans y penser** [par automatisme] without thinking ▶ **tu n'y penses pas** fam you can't be serious **2.** [rêver à] to think about ou of *(insép)* **3.** [se préoccuper de] to think of, to care about / *elle ne pense qu'à elle* she only cares about herself **4.** [se remémorer] to think ou to remember to / *n'y pense plus !* forget (all about) it ! ▶ **faire penser à** : *cela me fait penser à mon frère* it reminds me of my brother / *fais-moi penser à l'appeler* remind me to call her.

penseur, euse [pɑ̃sœr, øz] nm, f thinker.

pensif, ive [pɑ̃sif, iv] adj thoughtful, pensive, reflective / *d'un air pensif* thoughtfully.

pension [pɑ̃sjɔ̃] nf **1.** [somme allouée] pension ▶ **pension alimentaire** child maintenance 🆄🅺, alimony 🆄🆂 ▶ **pension d'invalidité** disability pension ▶ **pension de retraite** (retirement ou old-age) pension **2.** [logement et nourriture] board and lodging ▶ **être en pension complète** to be on full board **3.** [hôtel] ▶ **pension (de famille)** ≃ boarding house ; ≃ guesthouse **4.** ÉDUC boarding school / *être en pension* to be a boarder ou at boarding school ▶ **envoyer qqn en pension** to send sb to boarding school.

pensionnaire [pɑ̃sjɔner] nmf **1.** [d'un hôtel] guest, resident ; [d'un particulier] (paying) guest, lodger **2.** ÉDUC boarder.

⚠ **Pensioner** signifie « retraité » et non pensionnaire.

pensionnat [pɑ̃sjɔna] nm [école] boarding school.

pentagone [pɛ̃tagɔn] nm pentagon.

Pentagone [pɛ̃tagɔn] npr m ▶ **le Pentagone** the Pentagon.

pente [pɑ̃t] nf **1.** [inclinaison] slope, incline ; [descente, montée] slope **2.** TRAV PUB slope ▶ **une pente de 10 %** a 1 in 10 gradient **3.** EXPR ▶ **être sur une mauvaise pente** to be heading for trouble ▶ **remonter la pente** : *il a bien remonté la pente* **a)** [en meilleure santé] he's back on his feet again **b)** [financièrement] he's solvent again. ◆ **en pente** ◆ loc adj sloping / *la route est en pente* the road is on a slope ou an incline. ◆ loc adv : *descendre / monter en pente douce* to slope gently down / up / *descendre / monter en pente raide* to slope sharply down / up.

Pentecôte [pɑ̃tkot] nf [fête chrétienne] Whitsun, Pentecost / *la semaine de la Pentecôte* Whit Week, Whitsuntide / *dimanche de Pentecôte* Whit Sunday.

pénurie [penyri] nf [manque] : *pénurie de main-d'œuvre* labour 🆄🅺 ou labor 🆄🆂 shortage / *il y a (une) pénurie de viande* there is a meat shortage, meat is in short supply.

people [pipɔl ou pipœl] adj : *un magazine people* a celebrity magazine / *la presse people* the celebrity press / *c'était une soirée très people* there were lots of A-list celebrities at the event.

pépé [pepe] nm fam [grand-père] granddad, grandpa, gramps 🆄🆂.

pépère [peper] fam adj [tranquille] (nice and) easy / *un petit boulot pépère* a cushy number ou little job / *une petite vie pépère* a cosy little life.

pépier [9] [pepje] vi to chirp, to tweet, to twitter.

pépin [pepɛ̃] nm **1.** [de fruit] pip / *pépins de pomme / poire* apple / pear pips ▶ **des mandarines sans pépins** seedless tangerines **2.** fam [problème] hitch, snag / *il m'arrive un gros pépin* I'm in big trouble / *en cas de pépin* if there's a snag ou hitch **3.** fam [parapluie] umbrella, brolly 🆄🅺.

pépinière [pepinjɛr] nf BOT (tree) nursery.

pépiniériste [pepinjɛrist] nmf nurseryman (nurserywoman).

pépite [pepit] nf nugget ▶ **pépite d'or** gold nugget ▶ **pépites de chocolat** chocolate chips.

pepperoni [peperɔni] nm pepperoni.

peps [pɛps] nm [dynamisme] energy.

péquenaud, e, pèquenaud*, e [pekno, od], **péquenot, otte, pèquenot*, otte** [pekno, ɔt] nm, f tfam [rustre] yokel.

perçant, e [pɛrsɑ̃, ɑ̃t] adj **1.** [voix] piercing, shrill ; [regard] piercing, sharp / *pousser des cris perçants* to scream loudly ▶ **avoir une vue perçante** to have a sharp eye **2.** [froid] : *le froid était perçant* it was bitterly cold.

percée [pɛrse] nf **1.** SPORT break ; MIL breakthrough **2.** ÉCON & TECHNOL breakthrough ▶ **percée technologique** technological breakthrough.

perce-neige [pɛrsənɛʒ] (pl **perce-neige** ou **perce-neiges***) nm ou nf snowdrop.

perce-oreille [pɛrsɔrɛj] (pl **perce-oreilles**) nm earwig.

percepteur, trice [pɛrsɛptœr, tris] nm, f tax inspector.

perceptible [pɛrsɛptibl] adj [sensible] perceptible.

perception [pɛrsɛpsjɔ̃] nf **1.** [notion] perception, notion / *avoir une perception claire des problèmes* to be clearly aware of the problems **2.** PSYCHOL perception **3.** FIN & DR [encaissement] collection, levying / *perception d'un impôt* collection of a tax ; [lieu] tax office 🆄🅺, internal revenue office 🆄🆂 ; [recouvrement] tax collecting.

percer [16] [pɛrse] ◆ vt **1.** [trouer - gén] to pierce (through) / *se faire percer les oreilles* to have one's ears pierced / *il a eu le tympan percé dans l'accident* he suffered a burst ou perforated eardrum in the accident ▶ **percer un trou** to drill a hole **2.** CONSTR & TRAV PUB to open, to build / *percer une porte dans un mur* to put a door in ou into a wall / *percer un tunnel dans la montagne* to drive ou to build a tunnel through the mountain **3.** [pénétrer avec difficulté] to push through / *le soleil perça enfin le brouillard* at last the sun pierced through the fog ▶ **percer un mystère** to solve a mystery ; [déchirer] to pierce, to tear, to rend litt ▶ **percer qqn / qqch à jour** to see right through sb / sthg **4.** MÉD ▶ **il faut percer l'abcès** the abscess will have to be lanced **5.** [suj : bébé] : *percer ses dents* to be teething. ◆ vi **1.** [poindre] to come through / *le soleil perce enfin* the sun's finally broken through / *ses dents ont commencé à percer* his teeth have begun to come through **2.** [filtrer] to filter through, to emerge / *elle ne laisse rien percer de ce qu'elle ressent* she keeps her feelings well hidden **3.** [réussir] to become famous ▶ **commencer à percer** to be on the way up.

perceuse [pɛrsøz] nf [machine-outil] drill ▶ **perceuse électrique** power drill ▶ **perceuse radiale / à percussion** radial / hammer drill.

percevoir [52] [pɛrsəvwar] vt **1.** [vibration, sensation, chaleur] to feel / *j'ai cru percevoir une nuance de mépris dans sa voix* I thought I detected a note of contempt in his voice **2.** [comprendre - situation] to perceive / *leur présence est perçue comme une menace* their presence is perceived as a threat **3.** FIN [rente, intérêt] to receive, to be paid ; [impôt] to collect.

perchaude [pɛʀʃod] nf QUÉBEC yellow ou lake perch.

perche [pɛʀʃ] nf **1.** [pièce de bois] pole ; [tuteur] beanpole, stake ; SPORT pole **2.** CINÉ & TV boom **3.** *fam* [personne] ▸ **grande perche** beanpole **4.** ZOOL perch.

percher [3] [pɛʀʃe] ◆ vi [oiseau] to perch ; [poule] to roost. ◆ vt [placer] to put / *une petite église perchée en haut de la colline* fig a little church perched on top of the hill. ◆ **se percher** vpi [oiseau] to perch ; [poule] to roost.

perchiste [pɛʀʃist] nmf SPORT polevaulter.

perchoir [pɛʀʃwaʀ] nm **1.** [pour les oiseaux] perch ; [pour la volaille] roost **2.** POL *raised platform for the seat of the President of the French National Assembly.*

perclus, e [pɛʀkly, yz] adj crippled, paralysed / *être perclus de rhumatismes* to be stiff ou crippled with rheumatism.

percolateur [pɛʀkɔlatœʀ] nm coffee (percolating) machine.

percussion [pɛʀkysjɔ̃] nf MÉD, MUS & TECHNOL percussion. ◆ **percussions** nfpl percussion ensemble.

percussionniste [pɛʀkysjɔnist] nmf percussionist.

percutant, e [pɛʀkytɑ̃, ɑ̃t] adj [argument, formule] powerful, striking ▸ **titre percutant** hard-hitting headlines / *leur slogan est percutant* their slogan hits you right between the eyes.

percuter [3] [pɛʀkyte] ◆ vt **1.** [heurter] to crash ou to run into *(inség)* **2.** ARM & TECHNOL to strike. ◆ vi *fam* [comprendre] : *il n'a pas percuté* he didn't twig ou catch on.

perdant, e [pɛʀdɑ̃, ɑ̃t] ◆ adj losing ▸ **être perdant a)** [gén] to come off the loser **b)** [perdre de l'argent] to be out of pocket. ◆ nm, f loser ▸ **mauvais perdant** bad loser.

perdition [pɛʀdisjɔ̃] nf RELIG perdition. ◆ **en perdition** loc adj **1.** NAUT in distress **2.** [en danger] lost ▸ **des adolescents en perdition** adolescents heading for trouble.

perdre [77] [pɛʀdʀ] ◆ vt **1.** [égarer - clefs, lunettes] to lose, to mislay **2.** [laisser tomber] : *tu perds des papiers / un gant !* you've dropped some documents / a glove ! ; [laisser échapper] to lose / *perdre sa page* to lose one's page ou place ▸ **perdre la trace de qqn** pr & fig to lose track of sb ▸ **perdre qqn / qqch de vue** pr & fig to lose sight of sb / sthg, to lose track of sb / sthg ▸ **ne pas être perdu pour tout le monde** : *ça ne sera pas perdu pour tout le monde, va !* somebody somewhere will be happy (about it) ! ▸ **perdre les pédales a)** *fam* [ne plus comprendre] to be completely lost **b)** [céder à la panique] to lose one's head ▸ **perdre pied** pr & fig to get out of one's depth **3.** [être privé de - bien, faculté] to lose / *perdre son emploi* ou *sa situation* ou *sa place* to lose one's job / *perdre la mémoire / l'appétit* to lose one's memory / appetite / *perdre du sang / poids* to lose blood / weight / *elle a perdu les eaux* MÉD her waters broke ▸ **perdre le contrôle de** to lose control of ▸ **perdre connaissance** to pass out, to faint ▸ **perdre espoir** to lose hope ▸ **perdre l'habitude de (faire)** to get out of the habit of (doing) ▸ **perdre patience** to run out of ou to lose patience ▸ **perdre (tous) ses moyens** to panic ▸ **perdre la tête** ou **le nord** *fam* ou **la boule** *fam* to go mad **4.** [avoir moins] ▸ **perdre de** : *la tapisserie n'a rien perdu de ses couleurs* the wallpaper has lost none of its colour / *les actions ont perdu de leur valeur* the shares have partially depreciated **5.** [être délaissé par] to lose / *il a perdu toute sa clientèle* he has lost all his customers **6.** [par décès] to lose **7.** [contre quelqu'un] to lose ▸ **perdre l'avantage** to lose the ou one's advan-

tage ▸ **perdre la partie** JEUX : *il a perdu la partie* he lost the game ; SPORT [set] to drop, to lose **8.** [gâcher - temps, argent] to waste **9.** *sout* [causer la ruine de] to ruin (the reputation of) / *c'est le jeu qui le perdra* gambling will be the ruin of him ou his downfall **10.** EXPR) **ne rien perdre pour attendre** : *tu ne perds rien pour attendre !* just (you) wait and see ! ◆ vi **1.** [dans un jeu, une compétition, une lutte, etc.] to lose / *perdre à la loterie / aux élections* to lose at the lottery / polls **2.** [en qualité, psychologiquement] to lose (out) ▸ **perdre en** [avoir moins de] : *le récit perd en précision ce qu'il gagne en puissance d'évocation* what the story loses in precision, it gains in narrative power. ◆ **se perdre** vp *(emploi réciproque)* ▸ **se perdre de vue** to lose sight of each other. ◆ vp *(emploi passif)* [crayon, foulard, clef] to get lost, to disappear. ◆ vpi **1.** [s'égarer - personne] to get lost, to lose one's way ; [- avion, bateau] to get lost ; fig : *se perdre dans les détails* to get bogged down in too much detail / *se perdre en conjectures* to be lost in conjecture **2.** [disparaître] to disappear, to become lost, to fade / *ses appels se perdirent dans la foule* her calls were swallowed up by the crowd **3.** [devenir désuet] to become lost, to die out / *la coutume s'est perdue* the custom is (now) lost **4.** [nourriture, récolte - par pourrissement] to rot ; [- par surabondance] to go to waste.

perdreau, x [pɛʀdʀo] nm young partridge.

perdrix [pɛʀdʀi] nf ▸ **perdrix (grise)** partridge.

perdu, e [pɛʀdy] ◆ pp ⟶ **perdre**. ◆ adj **1.** [balle, coup] stray ; [heure, moment] spare **2.** [inutilisable - emballage] disposable ; [- verre] non-returnable **3.** [condamné] lost / *sans votre intervention, j'étais un homme perdu* if you hadn't intervened, I'd have been finished ou lost **4.** [désespéré] lost **5.** [gaspillé - occasion, temps] wasted **6.** [abîmé - vêtement, chapeau] ruined, spoiled ; [- nourriture] spoiled **7.** [isolé - coin, village] lost, remote, godforsaken *hum*.

perdurer [3] [pɛʀdyʀe] vi *sout* to continue (on), to endure, to last.

père [pɛʀ] nm **1.** [géniteur] father ▸ **devenir père** to become a father ▸ **père célibataire** single father / *le père Viot ne voulait pas que la propriété soit vendue* old Viot didn't want the estate to be sold ▸ **tel père, tel fils** *prov* like father, like son *prov* **2.** [innovateur] father / *le père de la psychanalyse* the father of psychoanalysis **3.** [chef] ▸ **père de famille** : *maintenant que je suis père de famille* now that I've got a family **4.** [homme, enfant] ▸ **petit père** *fam* : *mon petit père* (my) little one ou fellow ▸ **le père Fouettard** the Bogeyman ▸ **le père Noël** Santa Claus, Father Christmas **5.** RELIG father. ◆ **pères** nmpl *litt* [aïeux] forefathers, fathers. ◆ **de père en fils** loc adv : *ils sont menuisiers de père en fils* they've been carpenters for generations / *cette tradition s'est transmise de père en fils* this tradition has been handed down from father to son.

péremption [peʀɑ̃psjɔ̃] nf lapsing.

péremptoire [peʀɑ̃ptwaʀ] adj [impérieux] peremptory.

pérennité [peʀenite] nf perenniality, lasting quality.

perfection [pɛʀfɛksjɔ̃] nf [qualité] perfection. ◆ **à la perfection** loc adv perfectly (well).

perfectionné, e [pɛʀfɛksjone] sophisticated.

perfectionnement [pɛʀfɛksjonmɑ̃] nm **1.** [d'un art, d'une technique] perfecting **2.** [d'un objet matériel] improvement. ◆ **de perfectionnement** adj advanced.

perfectionner [3] [pɛʀfɛksjone] vt **1.** [amener au plus haut niveau] to (make) perfect ▸ **des techniques très perfectionnées** very sophisticated techniques **2.** [améliorer] to improve (upon). ◆ **se perfectionner** vpi to improve o.s. / *il s'est beaucoup perfectionné en français* his French has improved considerably.

perfectionnisme [pɛʀfɛksjonism] nm perfectionism.

perfectionniste [pɛʀfɛksjɔnist] nmf perfectionist.

perfide [pɛʀfid] *litt* adj [personne, conseil] perfidious, treacherous, faithless.

perfidie [pɛʀfidi] nf *sout* **1.** [caractère] perfidy, treacherousness **2.** [acte] piece of treachery, perfidy ; [parole] perfidious ou treacherous remark.

perforation [pɛʀfɔʀasjɔ̃] nf **1.** [trou - dans du papier, du cuir] perforation ; [- dans une pellicule] sprocket hole ; INFORM punch **2.** MÉD perforation.

perforer [3] [pɛʀfɔʀe] vt **1.** [percer] to pierce **2.** INFORM to punch **3.** MÉD to perforate.

performance [pɛʀfɔʀmɑ̃s] nf **1.** SPORT [résultat] result, performance / *les performances de l'année dernière sur le marché japonais* fig last year's results on the Japanese market **2.** [réussite] achievement. **⬧ performances** nfpl [d'ordinateur, de voiture, etc.] (overall) performance.

performant, e [pɛʀfɔʀmɑ̃, ɑ̃t] adj [machine, système] efficient ; [produit, entreprise] successful ; [employé] effective ; [technicien] first-class / *une voiture performante* a car that runs well.

perfusion [pɛʀfyzjɔ̃] nf drip, perfusion ▸ **être sous perfusion** to be on a drip ▸ **nourrir** ou **alimenter qqn par perfusion** to drip-feed sb.

péricliter [3] [peʀiklite] vi to be on a downward slope, to be going downhill / *une industrie qui périclite* an industry with no future.

péridurale [peʀidyʀal] nf epidural (anaesthesia).

périf, périph [peʀif] nm *fam* **abr de périphérique**.

péril [peʀil] nm **1.** *sout* [danger] danger / *au péril de sa vie* at great risk to his (own) life **2.** [menace] peril. **⬧ en péril ◆** loc adj [monuments, animaux] endangered / *être en péril* to be in danger ou at risk. **◆** loc adv ▸ **mettre en péril** to endanger, to put at risk.

périlleux, euse [peʀijø, øz] adj perilous, hazardous, dangerous.

périmé, e [peʀime] adj **1.** [expiré] out-of-date / *mon passeport est périmé* my passport is no longer valid ou has expired **2.** [aliment] past its use-by date.

périmètre [peʀimɛtʀ] nm **1.** [surface] perimeter / *des recherches ont été entreprises dans un vaste périmètre* searches were conducted over a vast area ▸ **périmètre de sécurité** safety zone **2.** DR ▸ **périmètre sensible** ≃ green belt 🇬🇧.

période [peʀjɔd] nf **1.** [époque] period, time / *traverser une période difficile* to go through a difficult period ou time / *pendant la période électorale* during election time / *pendant la période des fêtes* at Christmas time / *dans la période allant de début juin à fin septembre* between the beginning of June and the end of September ▸ **période d'engagement** TÉLÉC commitment period **2.** TRANSP ▸ **période bleue / blanche / rouge** *period during which tickets are cheapest / medium-priced / most expensive.* **⬧ par périodes** loc adv from time to time, every now and then, every so often ▸ **c'est par périodes** it comes and goes.

périodique [peʀjɔdik] **◆** adj **1.** CHIM, MATH, PHYS & PSYCHOL periodic **2.** [publication] periodical. **◆** nm periodical.

périodiquement [peʀjɔdikmɑ̃] adv **1.** CHIM, MATH & PHYS periodically **2.** [régulièrement] periodically, every so often.

péripétie [peʀipesi] nf [événement] event, episode, adventure.

périph [peʀif] nm *fam* **abr de périphérique**.

périphérie [peʀifeʀi] nf **1.** [bord] periphery **2.** [faubourg] outskirts / *à la périphérie des grandes villes* on the outskirts of cities.

périphérique [peʀifeʀik] **◆** adj **1.** [quartier] outlying **2.** PHYSIOL & INFORM peripheral. **◆** nm **1.** [boulevard] ring road 🇬🇧, beltway 🇺🇸 ; [à Paris] ▸ **le périphérique** the Paris orbital 🇬🇧 ou beltway 🇺🇸 **2.** INFORM peripheral device / *périphérique d'entrée / de sortie* input / output device.

périphrase [peʀifʀaz] nf periphrasis.

périple [peʀipl] nm **1.** [voyage d'exploration] voyage, expedition **2.** [voyage touristique] tour, trip.

périr [32] [peʀiʀ] vi *litt* [personne, souvenir] to perish *litt*, to die ▸ **péri en mer** lost at sea ▸ **périr noyé** to drown.

périscolaire [peʀiskɔlɛʀ] adj extracurricular.

périscope [peʀiskɔp] nm periscope.

périssable [peʀisabl] adj perishable.

péritonite [peʀitɔnit] nf peritonitis.

perle [pɛʀl] nf **1.** [bijou] pearl ▸ **perle fine / de culture** natural / cultured pearl **2.** [bille] bead ▸ **perles de verre** glass beads **3.** *litt* [goutte] drop ▸ **des perles de sueur** beads of sweat / *des perles de rosée* dewdrops **4.** [personne] gem, treasure **5.** *fam* [bêtise] howler.

perler [3] [pɛʀle] vi to bead / *la sueur perlait sur son visage* beads of sweat stood out on his face.

permanence [pɛʀmanɑ̃s] nf **1.** [persistance - gén] permanence, lasting quality ; [- d'une tradition] continuity **2.** [service de garde] duty (period) ▸ **être de permanence** to be on duty ou call / *une permanence est assurée à la mairie le mardi matin* council offices are open on Tuesday mornings ▸ **permanence téléphonique** answering service **3.** POL [local, bureau] committee room ; ÉDUC study room 🇬🇧 ou hall 🇺🇸. **⬧ en permanence** loc adv permanently / *elle me harcèle en permanence* she's forever harassing me.

permanent, e [pɛʀmanɑ̃, ɑ̃t] **◆** adj **1.** [constant] permanent / *avec elle, ce sont des reproches permanents* she's forever nagging me **2.** [fixe] permanent / *avoir un emploi permanent* to have a permanent job ▸ **armée permanente** standing army **3.** CINÉ continuous, non-stop. **◆** nm, f [d'un parti] official ; [d'une entreprise] salaried worker, worker on the payroll. **⬧ permanente** nf perm.

perméable [pɛʀmeabl] adj **1.** GÉOL & PHYS permeable **2.** [personne] malleable.

permettre [84] [pɛʀmɛtʀ] vt **1.** [suj : personne] to allow ▸ **permettre à qqn de faire qqch** ou **permettre que qqn fasse qqch** to allow sb to do sthg, to let sb do sthg ; [suj : chose] to allow, to permit, to enable / *le train à grande vitesse permettra d'y aller en moins de deux heures* the high-speed train will make it possible to get there in under two hours / *ce document permet d'entrer dans le secteur turc* this document enables ou entitles you to enter the Turkish sector ▸ **si le temps / sa santé le permet** weather / (his) health permitting **2.** *(tournure impersonnelle)* : *est-il permis d'être aussi mal élevé ?* how can anyone be so rude? **3.** [dans des formules de politesse] : *il reste un sandwich, vous permettez ?* may I have the last sandwich? / *tu n'es pas sincère non plus, permets-moi de te le dire* and you're not being honest either, let me tell you. **⬧ se permettre** vpt **1.** [oser] to dare / *il se permet de petites entorses au règlement* he's not averse to bending the rules now and then / *elle se permettait n'importe quoi* she thought she could get away with anything / *si je peux me permettre, je ne pense pas que ce soit une bonne idée* if you don't mind my saying so, I don't think it's a very good idea **2.** [pouvoir payer] to (be able to) afford. **⬧ se permettre de** vp + prép to take the liberty / *je me permets de vous écrire au sujet de mon fils* I'm writing to you about my son.

⚠ Attention, **to permit** est d'un registre plus soutenu que le verbe permettre. Voir l'article pour des traductions plus naturelles, notamment à l'oral.

permis [pɛʀmi] nm permit, licence UK, license US ▶ **permis (de conduire)** driving licence UK, driver's license US ▶ **rater / réussir le permis (de conduire)** to fail / to pass one's (driving) test ▶ **permis à points** driving licence with a penalty points system, introduced in France in 1992 ▶ **permis de construire** building permit US, planning permission UK ▶ **permis de chasse a)** [chasse à courre] hunting permit **b)** [chasse au fusil] shooting licence ▶ **permis de séjour / travail** residence / work permit.

 Permis de conduire

To get one's driving licence in France one must be at least eighteen. The driving test has both a practical and a theoretical part, the latter taking the form of an exam paper at the test centre.

permissif, ive [pɛʀmisif, iv] adj permissive.

permission [pɛʀmisjɔ̃] nf **1.** [autorisation] permission, leave ▶ **demander / accorder la permission de faire qqch** to ask / to grant permission to do sthg ▶ **avoir la permission de minuit** to have a late pass / *j'ai la permission de minuit* I'm allowed to stay out until midnight **2.** MIL leave, furlough ▶ **être en permission** to be on leave ou furlough.

permuter [3] [pɛʀmyte] ◆ vt **1.** [intervertir] to switch round *(sép)*, to permutate **2.** MATH to permute. ◆ vi [prendre la place de] : *les deux équipes permutent* the two teams swap shifts.

pernicieux, euse [pɛʀnisjø, øz] adj **1.** [néfaste] noxious, injurious, pernicious *sout* **2.** MÉD pernicious.

péroné [peʀɔne] nm fibula.

pérorer [3] [peʀɔʀe] vi [discourir] to hold forth.

Pérou [peʀu] npr m ▶ **le Pérou** Peru ▶ **au Pérou** in Peru.

perpendiculaire [pɛʀpɑ̃dikylɛʀ] ◆ adj [gén & MATH] perpendicular / *la droite A est perpendiculaire à la droite B* line A is perpendicular ou at right angles to line B. ◆ nf perpendicular.

perpendiculairement [pɛʀpɑ̃dikylɛʀmɑ̃] adv perpendicularly / *perpendiculairement à la rue* at right angles ou perpendicular to the street.

perpète [pɛʀpɛt] ◆ **à perpète** loc adv *fam* **1.** [loin] miles away, in the back of beyond **2.** [très longtemps] ▶ **jusqu'à perpète** till Doomsday, till the cows come home, forever and a day.

perpétrer [18] [pɛʀpetʀe] vt *sout* to perpetrate *sout*, to commit.

🖉 In reformed spelling (see p. 16-18), this verb is conjugated like *semer : il perpètrera, elle perpètrerait.*

perpette [pɛʀpɛt] = **perpète.**

perpétuel, elle [pɛʀpetɥɛl] adj **1.** [éternel] perpetual, everlasting **2.** [constant] constant, continual, perpetual.

perpétuellement [pɛʀpetɥɛlmɑ̃] adv forever, constantly, perpetually.

perpétuer [7] [pɛʀpetɥe] vt **1.** [tradition, préjugé] to carry on *(sép)* **2.** [souvenir] to perpetuate, to pass on *(sép).* ◆ **se perpétuer** vpi **1.** [personne] to perpetuate one's name **2.** [tradition] to live on / *certains rites se sont perpétués de père en fils* some rites have been handed down from father to son.

perpétuité [pɛʀpetɥite] nf *litt* perpetuity. ◆ **à perpétuité** ◆ loc adj **1.** [condamnation] life *(modif)* **2.** [concession] in perpetuity. ◆ loc adv ▶ **être condamné à perpétuité** to be sentenced to life imprisonment.

perplexe [pɛʀplɛks] adj perplexed, puzzled.

perplexité [pɛʀplɛksite] nf confusion, perplexity, puzzlement.

perquisition [pɛʀkizisjɔ̃] nf search.

perquisitionner [3] [pɛʀkizisjɔne] ◆ vi DR to (make a) search. ◆ vt DR to search.

perron [pɛʀɔ̃] nm steps *(outside a building)* ▶ **sur le perron de l'Élysée** on the (front) steps of the Élysée palace.

perroquet [pɛʀɔkɛ] nm ORNITH parrot.

perruche [pɛʀyʃ] nf [petit perroquet] parakeet ▶ **perruche (ondulée)** budgerigar UK, budgie UK, parakeet US.

perruque [pɛʀyk] nf [postiche] wig ; HIST periwig, peruke.

persan, e [pɛʀsɑ̃, an] adj Persian. ◆ **Persan, e** nm, f Persian. ◆ **persan** nm LING Persian.

perse [pɛʀs] adj Persian. ◆ **Perse** nmf Persian.

Perse [pɛʀs] npr f ▶ **la Perse** Persia.

persécuter [3] [pɛʀsekyte] vt **1.** [opprimer] to persecute **2.** [harceler] to torment.

persécution [pɛʀsekysjɔ̃] nf **1.** [oppression] persecution **2.** [harcèlement] harassment, harassing, tormenting **3.** PSYCHOL ▶ **délire** ou **manie de la persécution** persecution mania.

persévérance [pɛʀseveʀɑ̃s] nf perseverance, persistence, tenacity.

persévérant, e [pɛʀseveʀɑ̃, ɑ̃t] adj persevering, persistent, tenacious.

persévérer [18] [pɛʀseveʀe] vi to persevere, to persist ▶ **persévérer dans qqch** to continue ou to carry on doing sthg ▶ **persévérer dans l'effort** to sustain one's effort.

🖉 In reformed spelling (see p. 16-18), this verb is conjugated like *semer : il persévèrera, elle persévèrerait.*

persienne [pɛʀsjɛn] nf shutter, Persian blind.

persiflage, persifflage* [pɛʀsiflaʒ] nm [attitude] scoffing, jeering, mocking.

persifleur, euse, persiffleur*, euse [pɛʀsiflœʀ, øz] adj *litt* [moqueur] scoffing, jeering, mocking.

persil [pɛʀsi] nm parsley.

persillé, e [pɛʀsije] adj **1.** [plat] sprinkled with parsley **2.** [viande] marbled **3.** [fromage] (green) ou blue veined.

Persique [pɛʀsik] adj ▶ **le golfe Persique** the Persian Gulf.

persistance [pɛʀsistɑ̃s] nf **1.** [de quelque chose] persistence **2.** [de quelqu'un - dans le travail] persistence, perseverance, tenacity ; [- dans le refus] obdurateness *sout*, obstinacy, stubbornness / *je ne comprends pas sa persistance à vouloir partir ce soir* I don't understand why he persists in wanting to leave tonight.

persistant, e [pɛʀsistɑ̃, ɑ̃t] adj **1.** [tenace] persistent, lasting, enduring **2.** BOT evergreen.

persister [3] [pɛʀsiste] vi **1.** [durer] to last, to continue, to persist / *les doutes qui pouvaient encore persister* any lingering doubts **2.** [s'obstiner] ▶ **persister à** : *je persiste à croire que tu avais tort* I still think you were wrong / *pourquoi persistes-tu à lui faire faire du grec ?* why do you persist in making her learn Greek? / *persister dans une attitude* to continue with ou to maintain an attitude.

perso [pɛʀso] (abr de **personnel**) adj *fam* personal, private.

personnage [pɛʀsɔnaʒ] nm **1.** [de fiction] character ▶ **jouer un personnage a)** CINÉ & THÉÂTRE to play ou to act a part **b)** *fig* to act a part, to put on an act **2.** [individu] character, individual **3.** [personnalité importante] person of note, important figure, big name ; [personne remarquable] character / *ce Frédéric, c'est un personnage !* that Frederic's quite a character!

* In reformed spelling (see p. 16-18).

personnaliser [3] [pɛʀsɔnalize] vt [papier à lettres] to personalize ; [voiture] to customize ; [plan, système] ▸ **personnaliser qqch** to tailor sthg to personal requirements / *comment personnaliser votre cuisine* how to give your kitchen a personal touch.

personnalité [pɛʀsɔnalite] nf **1.** [caractère - d'une personne] personality, character ; [- d'une maison, d'une pièce, etc.] character / *un homme sans aucune personnalité* a man with no personality (whatsoever) **2.** [personne importante] personality.

personne¹ [pɛʀsɔn] nf **1.** [individu] person ▸ **plusieurs personnes a)** [sens courant] several people **b)** ADMIN several persons ▸ **quelques personnes** a few people / *toute personne intéressée peut* ou *les personnes intéressées peuvent s'adresser à Nora* all those interested ou all interested parties should contact Nora ▸ **dix euros par personne** ten euros each ou per person ou a head ▸ **une personne âgée** an elderly person ▸ **les personnes âgées** the elderly ▸ **les personnes à mobilité réduite** people with impaired mobility ▸ **grande personne** grown-up ▸ **les grandes personnes** grown-ups **2.** [être humain] : *s'en prendre aux biens et aux personnes* to attack property and people / *ce qui compte, c'est l'œuvre ; le rang et non la personne* it's the work / the rank that matters and not the individual ▸ **la personne humaine** the individual **3.** [femme] lady / *une jeune personne* a young lady / *une petite personne* a little woman **4.** [corps] ▸ **ma personne** myself ▸ **ta personne** yourself ▸ **sa personne** himself / *il s'occupe un peu trop de sa petite personne fam* he's a little too fond of number one ▸ **la personne de**: *ils s'en sont pris à la personne (même) du diplomate* they attacked the diplomat physically / *un attentat sur la personne du Président* an attempt on the President's life ▸ **en la personne de** in the person of / *venir en personne* to come in person / *j'y veillerai en personne* I'll see to it personally / *il dînait avec Napoléon en personne* he was dining with Napoleon himself ou none other than Napoleon / *c'était lui ! — en personne !* was it him? — none other! / *elle est la beauté en personne* she's the very embodiment of beauty, she's beauty personified ▸ **être bien (fait) de sa personne** to have a good figure **5.** GRAM person / *à la première personne du singulier* in the first person singular **6.** DR ▸ **personne juridique** juristic person ▸ **personne morale** legal entity ▸ **personne physique** natural person ▸ **personne à charge** dependant. ⬧ **par personne interposée** loc adv through ou via a third party / *dis-le-lui par personne interposée* have a go-between tell her.

personne² [pɛʀsɔn] pron indéf **1.** [avec un sens négatif] no one, nobody / *que personne ne sorte !* nobody ou no one leave (the room)! ▸ **personne d'autre que toi** nobody ou no one (else) but you ; [en fonction de complément] anyone, anybody ▸ **il n'y a personne** there's nobody ou no one there, there isn't anybody ou anyone there / *je ne connais personne d'aussi gentil qu'elle* I don't know anyone ou anybody as nice as her / *elle ne parle à personne d'autre* she doesn't speak to anyone ou anybody else **2.** [avec un sens positif] anyone, anybody / *il est parti sans que personne le remarque* he left without anybody ou anyone noticing him / *y a-t-il personne de plus rassurant que lui ?* is there anyone ou anybody more reassuring than him? / *tu le sais mieux que personne* you know it better than anybody ou anyone (else) / *elle réussit les crêpes comme personne* there's no ou nobody who makes pancakes quite like her.

personnel¹ [pɛʀsɔnɛl] nm [d'une entreprise] staff, workforce ; [d'un service] staff, personnel ; MIL personnel ▸ **avoir trop / manquer de personnel** to be overstaffed / understaffed ou short-staffed / *le personnel est autorisé à…* (members of) staff are authorized to… ▸ **personnel au sol /**

navigant AÉRON ground / flight crew ou staff ▸ **personnel (de maison)** (domestic) staff.

personnel², elle [pɛʀsɔnɛl] adj **1.** [privé] personal, individual ▸ *c'est un appel personnel* **a)** [n'intéressant pas le travail] it's a private call **b)** [confidentiel] it's a rather personal call / *avoir son hélicoptère personnel* to have one's own ou a private helicopter **2.** [original] ▸ **très personnel** highly personal ou idiosyncratic *sout* **3.** GRAM [pronom] personal **4.** [égoïste] self-centred 🇬🇧, self-centered 🇺🇸.

personnellement [pɛʀsɔnɛlmɑ̃] adv personally.

personnification [pɛʀsɔnifikasjɔ̃] nf **1.** [symbole] personification **2.** [modèle] : *ma mère est la personnification de la patience* my mother is patience itself ou is the epitome of patience.

personnifier [9] [pɛʀsɔnifje] vt **1.** [symboliser] to personify, to be the personification of **2.** [être le modèle de] to embody, to typify.

perspective [pɛʀspɛktiv] nf **1.** ART perspective **2.** [point de vue] angle, viewpoint, standpoint / *dans une perspective sociologique* from a sociological standpoint **3.** [éventualité] idea, prospect, thought ▸ **perspective d'avenir** outlook, prospects **4.** [avenir] (future) prospect, outlook ▸ **ouvrir de nouvelles** ou **des perspectives (pour)** to open up new horizons (for) **5.** [vue] view. ⬧ **en perspective** loc adv [en vue] on the horizon, in sight / *pas de reprise du travail en perspective* no return to work in sight.

perspicace [pɛʀspikas] adj perceptive, perspicacious *sout* / *être très perspicace* to have a sharp ou clever mind.

perspicacité [pɛʀspikasite] nf (clearness of) insight, perceptiveness, perspicacity ▸ **avec perspicacité** astutely, perceptively.

persuader [3] [pɛʀsɥade] vt to persuade, to convince ▸ **persuader qqn de qqch** to impress sthg on sb, to convince sb of sthg ▸ **persuader qqn de faire qqch** to talk sb into doing sthg / *j'en suis persuadé* I'm convinced ou sure of it. ⬧ **se persuader** vp ▸ **se persuader que** to convince ou persuade oneself that ▸ **se persuader de** to convince o.s. of, to become convinced of.

persuasif, ive [pɛʀsɥazif, iv] adj [personne] persuasive ; [argument] convincing, persuasive.

persuasion [pɛʀsɥazjɔ̃] nf persuasion.

perte [pɛʀt] nf **1.** [décès] loss **2.** [privation d'une faculté] ▸ **perte de mémoire** (memory) blank **3.** [disparition, destruction] loss ▸ **ce n'est pas une grande** ou **grosse perte** it's no great loss **4.** [gaspillage] waste / *quelle perte de temps !* what a waste of time! **5.** [réduction] loss ▸ **perte de poids** weight loss ▸ **en perte de vitesse a)** AUTO losing speed **b)** *fig* losing momentum **6.** *litt* [ruine] ruin, ruination *sout* ▸ **courir** ou **aller (droit) à sa perte** to be on the road to ruin ▸ **ruiner** ou **jurer la perte de qqn** to vow to ruin sb **7.** FIN loss, deficit / *l'entreprise a enregistré une perte de deux millions* the company has chalked up losses of two million ▸ **perte sèche** dead loss. ⬧ **pertes** nfpl MÉD ▸ **pertes (blanches)** whites, (vaginal) discharge. ⬧ **à perte** loc adv at a loss. ⬧ **à perte de vue** loc adv **1.** [loin] as far as the eye can see **2.** [longtemps] endlessly, interminably, on and on.

pertinemment [pɛʀtinamɑ̃] adv [parfaitement] : *je sais pertinemment que ce n'est pas vrai* I know perfectly well ou for a fact that it's not true.

pertinence [pɛʀtinɑ̃s] nf [bien-fondé] pertinence, relevance, appositeness *sout*.

pertinent, e [pɛʀtinɑ̃, ɑ̃t] adj [propos] pertinent, relevant, apt.

perturbant, e [pɛʀtyʀbɑ̃, ɑ̃t] adj disturbing.

perturbateur, trice [pɛʀtyʀbatœʀ, tʀis] adj [élève] disruptive ; [agent, militant] subversive.

perturbation [pɛʀtyʀbasjɔ̃] nf **1.** [désordre] disturbance, disruption ▸ **jeter** ou **semer la perturbation dans qqch** to disrupt sthg **2.** ASTRON perturbation **3.** MÉTÉOR disturbance ▸ **perturbation atmosphérique** (atmospheric) disturbance.

perturber [3] [pɛʀtyʀbe] vt **1.** [interrompre] to disrupt **2.** [rendre perplexe] to trouble, to perturb / *ça m'a un peu perturbé* it bothered me somewhat ; [troubler] to upset, to disconcert, to perturb / *la mort de son frère l'a profondément perturbé* he was severely affected by his brother's death.

péruvien, enne [peʀyvjɛ̃, ɛn] adj Peruvian.
❖ **Péruvien, enne** nm, f Peruvian.

pervenche [pɛʀvɑ̃ʃ] nf **1.** BOT periwinkle **2.** fam [contractuelle] meter maid US, (lady) traffic warden UK ou officer US (in Paris).

pervers, e [pɛʀvɛʀ, ɛʀs] ◆ adj **1.** [obsédé] perverted **2.** litt [malfaisant] wicked **3.** [effet] perverse. ◆ nm, f ▸ **pervers (sexuel)** (sexual) pervert.

perversion [pɛʀvɛʀsjɔ̃] nf **1.** litt [corruption] perversion, corruption **2.** PSYCHOL ▸ **perversion (sexuelle)** (sexual) perversion.

perversité [pɛʀvɛʀsite] nf [caractère] perversity.

pervertir [32] [pɛʀvɛʀtiʀ] vt **1.** litt [corrompre] to pervert, to corrupt **2.** [déformer] to pervert, to impair, to distort.

pesamment [pəzamɑ̃] adv heavily ▸ **marcher pesamment** to walk with a heavy step, to tread heavily.

pesant, e [pəzɑ̃, ɑ̃t] adj **1.** [lourd] heavy, weighty, unwieldy / *marcher à pas pesants* ou *d'une démarche pesante* to tread heavily **2.** [astreignant] hard, heavy, demanding **3.** [grave] heavy, weighty, burdensome litt **4.** [trop orné] heavy, cumbersome **5.** [insupportable] heavy.

pesanteur [pəzɑ̃tœʀ] nf **1.** PHYS gravity **2.** [lourdeur -d'un objet] heaviness, weightiness ; [-d'une démarche] heaviness ; [-d'un style] ponderousness ; [-de l'esprit] slowness, sluggishness.

pèse-bébé [pɛzbebe] (pl **pèse-bébé** ou **pèse-bébés**) nm (pair of) baby scales.

pesée [pəze] nf [avec une balance] weighing.

pèse-personne [pɛzpɛʀsɔn] (pl **pèse-personne** ou **pèse-personnes**) nm (pair of) bathroom scales.

peser [19] [pəze] ◆ vt **1.** [avec une balance] to weigh **2.** [évaluer, choisir] to weigh ▸ **peser ses mots** to weigh ou to choose one's words / *peser le pour et le contre* to weigh (up) the pros and cons / *peser les risques* to weigh up the risk, to evaluate the risks ▸ **tout bien pesé** all things considered, all in all. ◆ vi **1.** [corps, objet] to weigh / *combien pèses-tu / pèse le paquet ?* how much do you / does the parcel weigh? / *ce truc-là pèse une tonne !* fam that thing weighs a ton! **2.** fig [personne, opinion] to weigh ▸ **peser lourd** to weigh a lot / *la question d'argent a pesé très lourd dans mon choix* the question of money was a determining ou major factor in my choice ▸ **ne pas peser lourd dans la balance**: *mes raisons ne pèsent pas lourd dans la balance* my arguments don't carry much weight ou don't matter very much **3.** ▸ **peser sur** [faire pression sur] to press (heavily) on ▸ **peser sur** [accabler] to weigh down, to be a strain on ▸ *les responsabilités qui pèsent sur moi* the responsibilities I have to bear / *des présomptions pèsent sur elle* she's under suspicion ▸ **ça me pèse sur l'estomac / la conscience** it's lying on my stomach / weighing on my conscience ▸ **peser sur** [influer sur] to influence, to affect **4.** ▸ **peser à** [être pénible pour] to weigh down ou heavy on ▸ **ton absence me pèse** I find your absence difficult to bear / *la solitude ne me pèse pas* being alone doesn't bother me. ❖ **se peser** vp (emploi réfléchi) to weigh o.s.

pessimisme [pesimism] nm pessimism.

pessimiste [pesimist] ◆ adj pessimistic. ◆ nmf pessimist.

peste [pɛst] nf **1.** MÉD plague ▸ **se méfier de qqn comme de la peste, fuir qqn comme la peste** to avoid sb like the plague **2.** fam [personne] (regular) pest, pain in the neck.

pester [3] [pɛste] vi ▸ **pester contre qqn / qqch** to complain ou to moan about sb / sthg.

pesticide [pɛstisid] nm pesticide.

pestiféré, e [pɛstifeʀe] nm, f plague victim.

pestilentiel, elle [pɛstilɑ̃sjɛl] adj foul, stinking, pestilential sout.

pet [pɛ] nm [vent] fart / *lâcher un pet* to fart tfam, to break wind.

pétage [petaʒ] nm fam : *il a eu un pétage de plombs* ou *de câble* he went psycho ou ballistic.

pétale [petal] nm petal / *pétales de maïs* cornflakes.

pétanque [petɑ̃k] nf (game of) pétanque.

pétant, e [petɑ̃, ɑ̃t] adj fam ▸ **à 3 heures pétantes** at 3 o'clock sharp ou on the dot.

pétarader [3] [petaʀade] vi [feu d'artifice] to crackle, to bang ; [moteur] to backfire, to put-put.

pétard [petaʀ] nm **1.** [explosif] firecracker, banger UK **2.** tfam [revolver] pistol, gat US **3.** fam [cigarette] joint **4.** tfam [fesses] bum UK, ass US, butt US. ❖ **en pétard** loc adj fam furious, livid, pissed US.

pété, e [pete] adj tfam [ivre] plastered, smashed ; [drogué] stoned, high (as a kite).

péter [18] [pete] fam ◆ vi **1.** [faire un pet] to fart **2.** [exploser] to blow up ; [casser] : *la corde a pété* the rope snapped. ◆ vt **1.** [casser] to break, to bust ▸ **péter la gueule à qqn** to smash sb's face in **2.** [être plein de] ▸ **péter la santé** to be bursting with health ▸ **péter le feu** to be a livewire **3.** EXPR ▸ **péter un câble** to go off the rails ▸ **péter les plombs** to go ballistic ▸ **péter des flammes** to turn nasty. ❖ **se péter** fam vpt ▸ **se péter la gueule a)** [s'enivrer] to get pissed tfam ou plastered UK **b)** [en voiture] to get smashed up ▸ **se la péter**: *il se la pète avec son nouveau portable* he thinks he's it (and a bit) with that new laptop.

✎ In reformed spelling (see p. 16-18), this verb is conjugated like **semer** : *il pètera, elle pèterait.*

pète-sec [pɛtsɛk] adj inv overbearing, high-handed, bossy.

pétillant, e [petijɑ̃, ɑ̃t] adj **1.** [effervescent -eau, vin] sparkling, fizzy **2.** [brillant] : *avoir le regard pétillant* to have a twinkle in one's eye / *une réponse pétillante d'humour* an answer sparkling with wit.

pétiller [3] [petije] vi **1.** [crépiter] to crackle **2.** [faire des bulles] to bubble, to fizz, to effervesce sout **3.** [briller] to sparkle.

petit, e [p(ə)ti] (devant nm commençant par voyelle ou «h» muet [p(ə)tit, it]) ◆ adj **1.** [en hauteur, en largeur] small, little ; [en longueur] little, small, short / *une personne de petite taille* a small ou short person / *un petit gros* a tubby little man / *à petite distance* on voyait *une chaumière* a cottage could be seen a short way ou distance away / *elle a de petits pieds* she's got small ou little feet ▸ **un petit «a»** a lower-case ou small "a" / *un petit bout de papier* a scrap of paper ▸ **une toute petite maison** a tiny little house ▸ **se faire tout petit** [passer inaperçu] to make o.s. inconspicuous, to keep a low profile ▸ **se faire tout petit devant qqn a)** [par respect ou timidité] to humble o.s. before sb **b)** [par poltronnerie] to cower ou to shrink before sb ; [exprime l'approximation] : *ça vaut un petit 12 sur 20* it's only worth 12 out of 20 / *on y sera* *dans une petite heure* we'll be there in a bit less than ou in under an hour **2.** [faible] small / *expédition / émission à petit budget* low-budget expedition / programme / *petite retraite / rente* small pension / annuity **3.** [jeune - personne] small, little ; [- plante] young, baby *(modif)* / *quand j'étais petit* when I was little / *les petits Français* French children / *une petite Chinoise* a young ou little Chinese girl ; [plus jeune] little, younger **4.** [bref, court] short, brief / *un petit séjour* a short ou brief stay / *si on lui faisait une petite visite ?* shall we pop in to see her? **5.** [dans une hiérarchie] : *petite entreprise* small company ❱ **les petites et moyennes entreprises** small and medium-sized businesses ❱ **les petits commerçants** (owners of) small businesses ❱ **les petits salaires a)** [sommes] low salaries, small wages **b)** [employés] low-paid workers **6.** [minime] small, slight, minor / *une petite touche de peinture* a slight touch of paint / *ce n'est qu'un petit détail* it's just a minor detail ; [insignifiant] small, slight / *il y a un petit défaut* there's a slight ou small ou minor defect / *j'ai un petit ennui* I've got a bit of a problem / *j'ai eu un petit rhume* I had a bit of a cold ou a slight cold **7.** [léger] slight / *elle a un petit accent* she's got a slight accent / *dit-elle d'une petite voix* she said in a faint voice / *petite montée* gentle slope / *ça a un petit goût* it tastes a bit strange / *ça a un petit goût d'orange* it tastes slightly of orange **8.** [avec une valeur affective] little / *j'ai trouvé une petite couturière / un petit garagiste* I've found a very good little seamstress / garage / *il y a un petit vent frais pas désagréable* there's a nice little breeze / *ma petite maman* Mummy 🇬🇧, Mommy 🇺🇸, my Mum 🇬🇧 ou Mom 🇺🇸 / *alors, mon petit Paul, comment ça va ?* **a)** [dit par une femme] how's life, Paul, dear? **b)** [dit par un homme plus âgé] how's life, young Paul? ; [pour encourager] : *tu mangeras bien une petite glace !* come on, have an ice cream! ; [avec une valeur admirative] : *c'est une petite futée* she's a clever one ; [avec une valeur dépréciative] : *petit imbécile !* you idiot! **9.** *litt* [mesquin] mean, mean-spirited, petty. ◆ nm, f **1.** [fils, fille] little son (daughter), little boy (girl) / *c'est le petit de Monique* it's Monique's son / [enfant] little ou small child, little ou small boy (girl) / *c'est un livre qui fera les délices des petits comme des grands* this book will delight young and old (alike) **3.** *fam* [adolescent] (young) boy (girl) **4.** [avec une valeur affective -à un jeune] dear ; [-à un bébé] little one ❱ **mon petit a)** [à un homme] dear **b)** [à une femme] dear, darling / *la pauvre petite, comment va-t-elle faire ?* poor thing, however will she manage? ◆ **petit** ◆ nm **1.** [animal] baby ❱ **ses petits a)** [gén] her young **b)** [chatte] her kittens **c)** [chienne] her puppies **d)** [tigresse, louve] her cubs ❱ **faire des petits a)** [chienne] to have pups **b)** [chatte] to have kittens **2.** [dans une hiérarchie] : *c'est toujours les petits qui doivent payer* it's always the little man who's got to pay. ◆ adv COMM ❱ **c'est un 38 mais ce modèle chausse / taille petit** it says 38 but this style is a small fitting 🇬🇧 runs small 🇺🇸. ◆ **en petit** loc adv [en petits caractères] in small characters ou letters ; [en miniature] in miniature / *je voudrais cette jupe (mais) en plus petit* I'd like this skirt (but) in a smaller size. ◆ **petit à petit** loc adv little by little, gradually.

petit déjeuner [p(ə)tideʒœne] *(pl* petits déjeuners) nm breakfast.

petit-déjeuner [5] [p(ə)tideʒœne] vi to have breakfast.

petite-fille [p(ə)titfij] *(pl* petites-filles) nf granddaughter.

petitesse [p(ə)tites] nf **1.** [taille] smallness, small size **2.** [caractère] pettiness, meanness ❱ **petitesse d'esprit** narrow-mindedness.

petit-fils [p(ə)tifis] *(pl* petits-fils) nm grandson.

pétition [petisjɔ̃] nf [texte] petition / *faire une pétition* to organize a petition.

petit-lait [p(ə)tilɛ] *(pl* petits-laits) nm whey.

petit pois [pɔtipwa] *(pl* petits pois) nm (garden) pea.

petits-enfants [p(ə)tizɑ̃fɑ̃] nmpl grandchildren.

petit-suisse [p(ə)tisɥis] *(pl* petits-suisses) nm *thick fromage frais sold in small individual portions.*

pétrifier [9] [petʀifje] vt [abasourdir] to petrify, to transfix / *être pétrifié de terreur* to be rooted to the spot ou rigid with terror. ◆ **se pétrifier** vpi [se figer] : *son visage se pétrifia* his face froze.

pétrin [petʀɛ̃] nm **1.** *fam* [embarras] jam, fix ❱ **être dans le pétrin** to be in a jam ou pickle ❱ **se fourrer dans un beau** ou **sacré pétrin** to get into a real jam **2.** [à pain] kneading trough.

pétrir [32] [petʀiʀ] vt [malaxer] to knead.

pétrochimie [petʀɔʃimi] nf petrochemistry.

pétrochimique [petʀɔʃimik] adj petrochemical.

pétrole [petʀɔl] nm oil, petroleum ❱ **pétrole brut** crude (oil).

⚠ Le mot anglais **petrol** signifie « essence » et non pétrole.

pétrolier, ère [petʀɔlje,ɛʀ] adj oil *(modif)*. ◆ **pétrolier** nm [navire] (oil) tanker.

pétulant, e [petylɑ̃, ɑ̃t] adj exuberant, ebullient.

pétunia [petynja] nm petunia.

peu [pø]
adv

🄰 EMPLOYÉ SEUL **1.** [modifiant un verbe] little, not much / *il mange / parle peu* he doesn't eat / talk much ❱ **je le connais peu** I don't know him well ❱ **il vient très peu** he comes very rarely, he very seldom comes / *j'ai trop peu confiance en elle* I don't trust her enough **2.** [modifiant un adjectif, un adverbe, etc.] not very / *une avenue peu fréquentée* a quiet street / *il est assez peu soigneux* he doesn't take much care ❱ **peu avant** shortly ou not long before ❱ **peu après** soon after, shortly ou not long after.

🄱 EMPLOI NOMINAL **1.** *(avec déterminant)* [indiquant la faible quantité] : *le peu que tu gagnes* the little you earn ; *(sans déterminant)* : *il vit de peu* he lives off very little / *il a raté son examen de peu* *fam* he just failed his exam, he failed his exam by a hair's breadth ❱ **c'est peu** it's not much ❱ **hommes / gens de peu** *litt* worthless men / people ❱ **c'est peu dire** that's an understatement, that's putting it mildly ❱ **très peu pour moi !** *fam* not on your life! **2.** [dans le temps] : *ils sont partis il y a peu* they left a short while ago, they haven't long left ❱ **d'ici peu** very soon, before long / *je travaille ici depuis peu* I've only been working here for a while, I haven't been working here long **3.** [quelques personnes] a few (people) / *nous étions peu à le croire* only a few of us believed it.

🄲 PRÉCÉDÉ DE 'UN' **1.** [modifiant un verbe] ❱ **un peu** a little, a bit / *je le connais un peu* I know him a little ou a bit / *reste un peu avec moi* stay with me for a while / *pousse-toi un (tout) petit peu* move up a (little) bit / *fais voir un peu…* let me have a look… ❱ **un peu** *fam*: *tu l'as vu ? — un peu !* did you see it? — you bet I did ou and how! **2.** [modifiant un adjectif, un adverbe, etc.] ❱ **un peu** a little, a bit / *je suis un peu pressée* I'm in a bit of a hurry ❱ **un peu plus de a)** [suivi d'un nom comptable] a few more **b)** [suivi d'un nom non comptable] a little (bit) more ❱ **un peu moins de a)** [suivi d'un nom comptable] slightly fewer, not so many **b)** [suivi d'un nom non comptable] a little (bit) less / *un peu trop* a little ou bit too (much) / *un peu beaucoup* *fam* a bit much ❱ **un peu plus**: *un peu plus et l'évier débordait !*

another minute and the sink would have overflowed! / *un peu plus et on se serait cru au bord de la mer* you could almost imagine that you were at the seaside / *un peu plus et je me faisais écraser !* I was within an inch of being run over! ❖ **peu à peu** loc adv little by little, bit by bit, gradually / *on s'habitue, peu à peu* you get used to things, bit by bit ou gradually. ❖ **peu de** loc dét **1.** [suivi d'un nom non comptable] not much, little ; [suivi d'un nom comptable] not many, few / *cela a peu d'intérêt* it's of little interest ▶ **peu de temps** : *je ne reste que peu de temps* I'm only staying for a short while, I'm not staying long / *il y avait peu de neige* there wasn't much snow / *j'ai peu d'amis* I have few friends, I don't have many friends ▶ **en peu de mots** in a few words **2.** [avec un déterminant] ▶ **le peu de a)** [suivi d'un nom comptable] the ou what few **b)** [suivi d'un nom non comptable] the ou what little / *le peu de connaissances que j'ai* the ou what few acquaintances I have / *le peu de fois où je l'ai vu* on the few ou rare occasions when I've seen him. ❖ **pour peu que** loc conj : *pour peu qu'il le veuille, il réussira* if he wants to, he'll succeed. ❖ **pour un peu** loc adv : *pour un peu il m'accuserait !* he's all but accusing me! / *pour un peu, j'oubliais mes clés* I nearly forgot my keys. ❖ **quelque peu** loc adv *sout* **1.** [modifiant un verbe] just a little **2.** [modifiant un adjectif] somewhat, rather / *il était quelque peu éméché* he was somewhat ou rather tipsy. ❖ **sous peu** loc adv before long, in a short while / *vous recevrez sous peu les résultats de vos analyses* you will receive the results of your tests in a short while. ❖ **un peu de** loc dét a little (bit) of / *prends un peu de gâteau* have a little ou some cake / *avec un peu de chance...* with a little luck... / *allons, un peu de patience !* come on, let's be patient! / *tu l'as quitté par dépit ? — il y a un petit peu de ça* so you left him in a fit of pique? — that was partly it ou that was part of the reason.

peuplade [pœplad] nf (small) tribe, people.

peuple [pœpl] nm **1.** [communauté] people ▶ **les peuples d'Asie** the people of Asia **2.** ▶ **le peuple** [prolétariat] the people **3.** *fam* [foule] crowd / *il va y avoir du peuple* it's going to be a lot on the crowded side **4.** *fam* EXPR ▶ **que demande le peuple ?** what more do you want?

peuplé, e [pœple] adj populated / *région peu / très peuplée* sparsely / densely populated region.

peupler [5] [pœple] vt **1.** [région, ville] to populate, to people ; [forêt] to plant (with trees) ; [rivière] to stock (with fish) **2.** *fig & littér* to fill.

peuplier [pøplije] nm poplar (tree).

peur [pœr] nf **1.** [sentiment] fear, apprehension, alarm ▶ **avoir peur** to be afraid ou frightened ou scared / *on a eu très peur* we were badly frightened / *on a sonné tard, j'ai eu une de ces peurs !* *fam* someone rang the doorbell late at night and it gave me a terrible fright! ▶ **avoir peur pour qqn** to fear for sb ▶ **avoir peur d'un rien** to scare easily, to be easily frightened ▶ **n'aie pas peur a)** [ne t'effraie pas] don't be afraid **b)** [ne t'inquiète pas] don't worry / *j'ai bien peur qu'elle ne vienne pas* I'm really worried (that) she won't come ▶ **j'en ai (bien) peur** I'm (very much) afraid so ▶ **faire peur** : *des monstres qui font peur* frightening monsters ▶ **faire peur à qqn** to frighten ou to scare sb / *le travail ne lui fait pas peur* he's not work shy ou afraid of hard work ▶ **prendre peur** to get frightened, to take fright ▶ **peur bleue** : *avoir une peur bleue de* to be scared stiff of ▶ **faire une peur bleue à qqn** to give sb a terrible fright ▶ **la peur du gendarme** the fear of authority ▶ **être mort** ou **vert de peur** to be frightened out of one's wits ▶ **plus de peur que de mal** : *on a eu plus de peur que de mal* we weren't hurt, just scared **2.** [phobie] fear ▶ **avoir peur de l'eau / du noir** to be afraid of water / of the dark / *il a peur en avion* he's afraid of flying. ❖ **de peur de** loc prép ▶ **de peur de faire** for fear of doing / *je ne disais rien de peur de lui faire du mal* I said nothing for fear that I might ou in case I hurt her.

peureux, euse [pœrø, øz] ◆ adj [craintif] timorous, fearful. ◆ nm, f [poltron] fearful person.

peut-être [pøtɛtr] adv maybe, perhaps / *ils sont peut-être sortis, peut-être sont-ils sortis* maybe they've gone out, they may ou might have gone out / *peut-être pas* maybe ou perhaps not / *il est peut-être bien déjà parti* he may well have already left ▶ **je suis ta bonne, peut-être ?** what do you take me for? a maid? ▶ **peut-être bien, mais...** perhaps ou maybe so but... ❖ **peut-être que** loc conj perhaps, maybe / *peut-être qu'il est malade* perhaps ou maybe he is ill ▶ **peut-être (bien) qu'il viendra** he may well come.

phalange [falɑ̃ʒ] nf ANAT phalanx.

phallique [falik] adj phallic.

phallocrate [falɔkrat] ◆ adj male-chauvinist. ◆ nm male chauvinist.

phallus [falys] nm ANAT phallus.

phantasme [fɑ̃tasm] = **fantasme**.

pharaon [faraɔ̃] nm HIST pharaoh.

pharaonique [faraɔnik] adj *pr & fig* [gigantesque] Pharaonic.

phare [far] nm **1.** NAUT lighthouse **2.** AUTO headlight, headlamp UK ▶ **phare antibrouillard** fog lamp UK, fog light / *allumer ses phares* to switch one's headlights on **3.** AÉRON light, beacon **4.** (comme adjectif, avec ou sans trait d'union) [exemplaire] landmark (modif) ▶ **industrie phare** flagship ou pioneering industry.

pharmaceutique [farmasøtik] adj pharmaceutic, pharmaceutical.

pharmacie [farmasi] nf **1.** [dans la rue] chemist's (shop) UK, pharmacy US, drugstore US ; [dans un hôpital] dispensary, pharmacy ▶ **pharmacie de garde** duty chemist UK, emergency drugstore US **2.** [meuble] medicine chest ou cabinet ou cupboard UK ; [boîte] first-aid box.

pharmacien, enne [farmasjɛ̃, ɛn] nm, f [titulaire] pharmacist, chemist UK.

pharyngite [farɛ̃ʒit] nf pharyngitis.

pharynx [farɛ̃ks] nm pharynx.

phase [faz] nf **1.** [moment] phase, stage ▶ **phase terminale** final phase **2.** ÉLECTR & TECHNOL phase **3.** ASTRON phase **4.** CHIM phase. ❖ **en phase** loc adj ÉLECTR, PHYS & TECHNOL in phase ▶ **être en phase** *fig* to see eye to eye / *ils ne sont pas en phase* they don't see things the same way.

phénix [feniks] nm **1.** MYTH phoenix **2.** *littér* [prodige] paragon.

phénoménal, e, aux [fenɔmenal, o] adj [prodigieux] phenomenal, tremendous, amazing.

phénomène [fenɔmɛn] nm **1.** SCI phenomenon / *la grêle et autres phénomènes naturels* hail and other natural phenomena **2.** [manifestation] phenomenon ▶ **un phénomène de société** a social phenomenon **3.** [prodige] prodigy, wonder **4.** *fam* [excentrique] character.

philanthrope [filɑ̃trɔp] nmf philanthrope, philanthropist.

philanthropique [filɑ̃trɔpik] adj philanthropic.

philatélie [filateli] nf philately *spéc*, stamp-collecting.

philatéliste [filatelist] nmf philatelist *spéc*, stamp-collector.

philharmonique [filarmɔnik] adj philharmonic.

philippin, e [filipɛ̃, in] adj Filipino. ❖ **Philippin, e** nm, f Filipino.

Philippines [filipin] npr fpl ▶ **les Philippines** the Philippines, the Philippine Islands ▶ **aux Philippines** in the Philippines.

philo [filo] nf *fam* philosophy.

philologie [filɔlɔʒi] nf philology.

philosophe [filɔzɔf] ◆ adj philosophical. ◆ nmf, f PHILOS philosopher.

philosophie [filɔzɔfi] nf **1.** PHILOS philosophy **2.** ENS philosophy **3.** [conception] philosophy / *quelle est votre philosophie de la vie ?* what's your philosophy of life? ❖ **avec philosophie** loc adv philosophically.

philosophique [filɔzɔfik] adj philosophical.

philtre [filtʀ] nm love-potion, philtre.

phishing [fiʃiŋ] nm INFORM phishing.

phlébite [flebit] nf phlebitis.

phobie [fɔbi] nf **1.** PSYCHOL phobia **2.** [aversion] aversion ▶ **avoir la phobie de qqch** to have an aversion to sthg.

phobique [fɔbik] adj phobic.

phocéen, enne [fɔseɛ̃, ɛn] adj [de Marseille] from Marseille ▶ **la cité phocéenne** the city of Marseille.

phonétique [fɔnetik] ◆ adj phonetic. ◆ nf phonetics *(sg)*.

phoque [fɔk] nm **1.** ZOOL seal **2.** [fourrure] sealskin.

phosphate [fɔsfat] nm phosphate.

phosphore [fɔsfɔʀ] nm CHIM phosphorus.

phosphorescent, e [fɔsfɔʀesɑ̃, ɑ̃t] adj [luisant] luminous, glowing.

photo [fɔto] nf **1.** [cliché] photo, shot / *avez-vous fait des photos ?* did you take any pictures? ▶ **photo d'identité** passport photo ▶ **(entre les deux) (il n')y a pas photo** there's no comparison ou contest (between the two) **2.** [activité] photography ▶ **faire de la photo en amateur / professionnel** to be an amateur / professional photographer. ❖ **en photo** loc adv ▶ **prendre qqn en photo** to take sb's picture ▶ **prendre qqch en photo** to take a picture of sthg.

photocomposition [fɔtokɔ̃pozisjɔ̃] nf photocomposition US, photosetting, filmsetting UK.

photocopie [fɔtokɔpi] nf photocopy.

photocopier [9] [fɔtokɔpje] vt to photocopy / *photocopiez-moi ce document en trois exemplaires, s'il vous plaît* please make three photocopies ou copies of this document for me.

photocopieur [fɔtokɔpjœʀ] nm = **photocopieuse**.

photocopieuse [fɔtokɔpjøz] nf photocopier.

photogénique [fɔtoʒenik] adj photogenic.

photographe [fɔtogʀaf] nmf **1.** [artiste] photographer ▶ **photographe de presse / mode** press / fashion photographer **2.** [commerçant] dealer in photographic equipment.

⚠ Le mot anglais **photograph** signifie « photographie » et non photographe.

photographie [fɔtogʀafi] nf **1.** [activité] photography ▶ **faire de la photographie a)** [professionnel] to work as a photographer **b)** [amateur] to do amateur photography **2.** [cliché - de professionnel] photograph, picture ; [- d'amateur] picture, snap, snapshot.

photographier [9] [fɔtogʀafje] vt PHOT to photograph, to take photographs ou pictures of ▶ **se faire photographier** to have one's picture taken.

photographique [fɔtogʀafik] adj PHOT photographic.

Photomaton® [fɔtomatɔ̃] nm photobooth.

photoreportage [fɔtoʀəpɔʀtaʒ] nm PRESSE report *(consisting mainly of photographs)*.

photosensible [fɔtosɑ̃sibl] adj photosensitive.

photothèque [fɔtotɛk] nf picture ou photographic library.

phrase [fʀɑz] nf **1.** LING sentence ; [en grammaire transformationnelle] phrase **2.** ▶ **phrase toute faite** set phrase ▶ **petite phrase** POL soundbite **3.** MUS phrase.

phréatique [fʀeatik] adj phreatic.

physicien, enne [fizisjɛ̃, ɛn] nm, f physicist.

⚠ Le mot anglais **physician** signifie « médecin » et non physicien, physicienne.

physiologie [fizjolɔʒi] nf physiology.

physiologique [fizjolɔʒik] adj physiological.

physionomie [fizjonɔmi] nf **1.** [visage] features, facial appearance, physiognomy *litt* **2.** [aspect] face, appearance / *la physionomie des choses* the face of things / *ceci a modifié la physionomie du marché* this has altered the appearance of the market.

physionomiste [fizjonɔmist] adj good at remembering faces, observant (of people's faces) / *je ne suis pas très physionomiste* I'm not very good at (remembering) faces.

physiothérapeute [fizjoteʀapøt] nmf QUÉBEC & SUISSE physiotherapist.

physiothérapie [fizjoteʀapi] nf natural medicine.

physique¹ [fizik] nf SCI physics *(sg)*.

physique² [fizik] ◆ adj **1.** SCI [propriété] physical **2.** [naturel - monde, univers] physical, natural **3.** [corporel - exercice, force, effort] physical, bodily ; [- symptôme] physical, somatic *spéc* ; [- souffrance] physical, bodily **4.** [sexuel - plaisir, jouissance] physical, carnal. ◆ nm **1.** [apparence] ▶ **un physique avantageux** good looks ▶ **avoir le physique de l'emploi** THÉÂTRE & *fig* to look the part **2.** [constitution] physical condition.

physiquement [fizikmɑ̃] adv physically / *il n'est pas mal physiquement* he's quite good-looking.

phytoplancton [fitoplɑ̃ktɔ̃] nm phytoplankton.

phytothérapie [fitoteʀapi] nf herbal medicine.

piaf [pjaf] nm *fam* [moineau] sparrow.

piaffer [3] [pjafe] vi **1.** [cheval] to paw the ground **2.** [personne] ▶ **piaffer d'impatience** to be champing at the bit, to be seething with impatience.

piaillement [pjajmɑ̃] nm squawking.

piailler [3] [pjaje] vi **1.** [oiseau] to chirrup, to chirp, to tweet ; [volaille] to squawk **2.** *fam* [enfant] to squawk, to screech.

pianiste [pjanist] nmf pianist, piano player.

piano [pjano] ◆ nm [instrument] piano, pianoforte *sout* ▶ **se mettre au piano a)** [s'asseoir] to sit at the piano **b)** [jouer] to go to the piano (and start playing) **c)** [apprendre] to take up the piano ▶ **piano droit / à queue** upright / grand piano. ◆ adv **1.** MUS piano *(adv)* **2.** *fam* [doucement] easy *(adv)*, gently.

pianoter [3] [pjanɔte] vi **1.** [jouer du piano] to tinkle away at the piano **2.** [tapoter sur un objet] to drum one's fingers **3.** *fam* [taper sur un clavier] to tap away.

piaule [pjol] nf *fam* [chambre] room.

PIB (abr de **produit intérieur brut**) nm GDP.

pic [pik] nm **1.** GÉOGR & TECHNOL peak **2.** [outil] pick, pickaxe, pickax US ▶ **pic à glace** ice-pick **3.** ORNITH woodpecker. ❖ **à pic** ◆ loc adj [paroi, falaise] sheer ; [chemin]

steep. ◆ loc adv **1.** [verticalement] straight down / *monter à pic* [chemin] to rise steeply **2.** *fam* [au bon moment] spot on , just at the right time.

pichenette [piʃnɛt] nf flick / *d'une pichenette, elle envoya la miette par terre* she flicked the crumb onto the ground.

pichet [piʃɛ] nm jug , pitcher.

pickpocket [pikpɔkɛt] nm pickpocket.

pick-up (*pl* pick-up), **pickup*** [pikœp] nm [camion] pick-up (truck).

picoler [3] [pikɔle] vi *fam* [boire] to booze.

picorer [3] [pikɔʀe] vt **1.** [oiseau] to peck (at) **2.** [personne] to nibble (away) at (*insép*), to pick at (*insép*).

picotement [pikɔtmɑ̃] nm [dans les yeux] smarting ou stinging (sensation) ; [dans la gorge] tickle ; [sur la peau] tingle, prickle / *j'ai des picotements dans les doigts* my fingers are tingling.

picoter [3] [pikɔte] vt [piquer - yeux] to sting, to smart ; [- gorge] to irritate, to tickle ; [- peau, doigt] to sting.

pictogramme [piktɔgram] nm pictogram, pictograph.

pictural, e, aux [piktyral, o] adj pictorial.

pic-vert [pivɛʀ] (*pl* pics-verts) = pivert.

pie [pi] ◆ adj [couleur] pied ▶ **cheval pie** piebald (horse). ◆ nf ORNITH magpie.

pièce [pjɛs] ◆ nf **1.** [morceau] piece, bit / *je l'ai retrouvé en pièces* I found it in pieces ▶ **d'une seule pièce, tout d'une pièce** *pr* all of a piece ▶ **monter qqch de toutes pièces** : *il n'a jamais travaillé pour nous, il a monté cela de toutes pièces* he never worked for us, he made up ou invented the whole thing **2.** [d'une collection] piece, item ; [d'un mécanisme] part, component ; [d'un jeu] piece ▶ **pièce détachée** (spare) part ▶ **pièces et main-d'œuvre** parts and labour / *la pièce maîtresse de ma collection* the centrepiece of ou choicest piece in my collection ▶ **pièce de musée** *pr & fig* museum piece ▶ **pièce de rechange** spare ou replacement part **3.** COUT patch ▶ **pièce rapportée** a) *pr* patch b) *fig* [personne] odd person out **4.** [salle] room ▶ **un deux-pièces** a one-bedroom flat ou apartment **5.** [document] paper, document ▶ **pièce à conviction** DR exhibit / *avez-vous une pièce d'identité ?* do you have any proof of identity ou any ID? ▶ **pièce jointe** [dans mail] attachment ▶ **pièces jointes** enclosures ▶ **pièces justificatives** supporting documents **6.** LITTÉR & MUS piece ▶ **pièce (de théâtre)** play ▶ **monter une pièce** to put on ou to stage a play **7.** [argent] ▶ **pièce (de monnaie)** coin / *une pièce de 1 euro* a one-euro coin ou piece / *je n'ai que quelques pièces dans ma poche* I've only got some loose change in my pocket **8.** CULIN ▶ **pièce montée** a) [gâteau] ≃ tiered cake b) [pyramide] *pyramid of caramel-covered profiteroles often served at weddings and other special occasions* **9.** MIL ▶ **pièce (d'artillerie)** gun. ◆ adv [chacun] each, apiece / *les roses sont à 2 euros pièce* the roses are 2 euros each ou apiece. ◆ **à la pièce** loc adv [à l'unité] singly, separately / *ceux-ci sont vendus à la pièce* these are sold separately ou individually. ◆ **à la pièce, aux pièces** loc adv : *le travail est payé à la pièce* you get a piecework rate ▶ **on n'est pas aux pièces !** *fam* what's the big hurry?, where's the fire? ◆ **sur pièces** loc adv on evidence ▶ **juger sur pièces** to judge for o.s. ◆ **pièce d'eau** nf **1.** [lac] (ornamental) lake **2.** [bassin] (ornamental) pond.

⚠ Le mot anglais **piece** signifie avant tout « morceau », « bout » et ne peut pas toujours être employé pour traduire **pièce**.

📙 **Pièce**

Flats in France are referred to in terms of the total number of rooms they have (excluding the kitchen and bathroom). Un deux-pièces is a flat with a living room and one bedroom; un cinq-pièces is a flat with five rooms.

---

pied [pje] nm **1.** ANAT & ZOOL foot ▶ **pieds nus** barefoot *(adv)* / *marcher / être pieds nus* to walk / to be barefoot ▶ **sauter à pieds joints** to make a standing jump ▶ **mettre pied à terre** [à cheval, à moto] to dismount ▶ **je n'ai pas mis les pieds dehors / à l'église depuis longtemps** *fam* I haven't been out / to church for a long time ▶ **je ne mettrai** ou **remettrai plus jamais les pieds là-bas** I'll never set foot there again ▶ **avoir les pieds plats** to have flat feet *pr*, to be flat-footed *pr* ▶ **partir du bon / mauvais pied** to start off (in) the right / wrong way ▶ **avoir le pied marin** to be a good sailor ▶ **avoir les (deux) pieds sur terre** to have one's feet (firmly) on the ground ou one's head screwed on (the right way) ▶ **avoir pied** to touch bottom ▶ **avoir un pied dans** : *j'ai déjà un pied dans la place / l'entreprise* I've got a foot in the door / a foothold in the company already ▶ **bien fait pour tes / ses pieds** *fam*, **ça te** / *lui fera les pieds* *fam* serves you / him right! ▶ **faire des pieds et des mains pour** to bend over backwards ou to pull out all the stops in order to ▶ **faire du pied à qqn** a) [flirter] to play footsie with sb b) [avertir] to kick sb (under the table) ▶ **faire le pied de grue** to cool ou to kick one's heels ▶ **avoir le pied au plancher** [accélérer] to have one's foot down ▶ **lever le pied** a) [ralentir] to ease off (on the accelerator), to slow down b) [partir subrepticement] to slip off ▶ **mettre le pied à l'étrier** to get into the saddle / *il a fallu lui mettre le pied à l'étrier* he had to be given a leg up *fig* ▶ **mettre les pieds dans le plat** *fam* to put one's foot in it ▶ **mettre qqch sur pied** to set sthg up ▶ **retomber sur ses pieds** *pr & fig* to fall ou to land on one's feet ▶ **se jeter** ou **se traîner aux pieds de qqn** to throw o.s. at sb's feet, to get down on one's knees to sb ▶ **se lever du pied gauche** to get out of the wrong side of the bed ▶ **comme un pied** [très mal] : *je cuisine comme un pied* I'm a useless cook, I can't cook an egg / *on s'est débrouillés comme des pieds* we went about it the wrong ou in a cackhanded way ▶ **prendre son pied** a) *fam* [s'amuser] to get one's kicks b) [sexuellement] to come ▶ **quel pied !** *fam*: *on a passé dix jours à Hawaï, quel pied !* we really had a ball ou we had the time of our lives during our ten days in Hawaï! **2.** [d'un mur, d'un lit] foot ; [d'une table, d'une chaise] leg ; [d'une lampe, d'une colonne] base ; [d'un verre] stem ; [d'un micro, d'un appareil photo] stand, tripod **3.** IMPR [d'une lettre] bottom, foot **4.** BOT plant ; [de champignon] foot ▶ **pied de vigne** vine (plant), vinestock **5.** [mesure] foot / *le mur fait six pieds de haut* the wall is six-feet high **6.** TECHNOL ▶ **pied de bielle** AUTO end of connecting rod ▶ **pied à coulisse** calliper rule ▶ **pied de roi** QUÉBEC folding ruler **7.** LITTÉR foot / *vers de 12 pieds* 12-foot verse ou line **8.** CULIN ▶ **pied de cochon** pig's trotter ou foot ▶ **pied de veau** calf's foot. ◆ **à pied** loc adv **1.** [en marchant] on foot / *on ira au stade à pied* we'll walk to the stadium **2.** [au chômage] ▶ **mettre qqn à pied** a) [mesure disciplinaire] to suspend sb b) [mesure économique] to lay sb off, to make sb redundant . ◆ **à pied d'œuvre** loc adj ▶ **être à pied d'œuvre** to be ready to get down to the job. ◆ **à pied sec** loc adv on dry land, without getting one's feet wet. ◆ **au pied de** loc prép at the foot ou bottom of / *au pied des Alpes* in the foothills of the Alps ▶ **au pied du mur** : *être au pied du mur* to be faced with no alternative. ◆ **au pied de la lettre** loc adv literally. ❖ **au pied levé** loc adv at a moment's notice / *il faut que tu sois prêt à le faire au pied levé* you must be ready to drop everything and do it. ❖ **de pied ferme** loc adv resolutely / *je t'attends de pied ferme* I'll definitely be waiting for you. ❖ **des pieds à la tête** loc adv from top to toe ou head to foot. ❖ **en pied** loc adj [photo, portrait] full-length ; [statue] full-size standing. ❖ **pied à pied** loc adv inch by inch ▸ **lutter** ou **se battre pied à pied** to fight every inch of the way. ❖ **sur le pied de guerre** loc adv MIL on a war footing ; *hum* ready (for action). ❖ **sur pied** ◆ loc adj [récolte] uncut, standing ; [bétail] on the hoof. ◆ loc adv ▸ **être sur pied** [en bonne santé] to be up and about ▸ **remettre qqn sur pied** to put sb on his / her feet again, to make sb better. ❖ **sur un pied d'égalité** loc adv on an equal footing / *être sur un pied d'égalité avec* to stand on equal terms with.

pied-à-terre [pjetatɛʀ] nm inv pied-à-terre.

pied-de-biche [pjedbiʃ] (*pl* **pieds-de-biche**) nm **1.** [pince] nail puller ou extractor **2.** [levier] crowbar.

pied(-)de(-)nez [pjedne] (*pl* **pieds-de-nez**) nm ▸ **faire un pied-de-nez à qqn** to thumb one's nose at sb.

pied-de-poule [pjedpul] (*pl* **pieds-de-poule**) adj inv : *un tailleur pied-de-poule* a hound's-tooth suit.

pied-de-roi [pjedəʀwa] (*pl* **pieds-de-roi**) nm Québec carpenter's ruler.

piédestal, aux [pjedɛstal, o] nm pedestal ▸ **mettre qqn sur un piédestal** to put ou to set ou to place sb on a pedestal.

pied-noir [pjenwaʀ] (*pl* **pieds-noirs**) nmf pied-noir *(French colonial born in North Africa, most often in Algeria).*

🏛 **Pied-noir**

This is the name given to former French settlers in Algeria who returned to France after Algeria regained its independence in 1962, many of them resettling in cities on the south coast.

---

piège [pjɛʒ] nm **1.** [dispositif] trap, snare / *prendre un animal au piège* to trap an animal ▸ **poser** ou **tendre un piège** to set a trap **2.** [difficulté] trap, snare, pitfall.

piégé, e [pjeʒe] adj ▸ **lettre / voiture piégée** letter / car bomb ▸ **colis piégé** parcel ou mail bomb.

piéger [22] [pjeʒe] vt **1.** [animal] to trap, to ensnare / *la police les a piégés* the police trapped them / *je me suis fait piéger comme un débutant fig* I was taken in ou caught out like a complete beginner **2.** [voiture, paquet] to booby-trap.

✏ In reformed spelling (see p. 16-18), this verb is conjugated like *semer* : *il piègera, elle piègerait.*

piercing [piʀsiŋ] nm piercing.

pierraille [pjɛʀaj] nf loose stones, scree *(U).*

pierre [pjɛʀ] nf **1.** [matière] stone ; [caillou] stone, rock US ; [immobilier] ▸ **investir dans la pierre** to invest in property ou in bricks and mortar ▸ **faire d'une pierre deux coups** to kill two birds (with one stone) ▸ **jeter la pierre à qqn** to cast a stone at sb **2.** CONSTR ▸ **pierre de taille** ou **d'appareil** freestone ▸ **pierre angulaire** *pr & fig* keystone, cornerstone ▸ **poser la première pierre (de)** a) *pr* to lay down the first stone (of) b) *fig* to lay the foundations (of) **3.** ▸ **pierre précieuse** gem, precious stone ▸ **pierre de touche** *pr & fig* touchstone **4.** GÉOL ▸ **pierre ponce** pum-

ice stone **5.** [instrument] ▸ **pierre à briquet** (lighter) flint **6.** [stèle] ▸ **pierre funéraire** ou **tombale** tombstone, gravestone.

pierreries [pjɛʀʀi] nfpl precious stones, gems.

piété [pjete] nf **1.** RELIG piety **2.** [amour] devotion, reverence ▸ **piété filiale** filial devotion.

piétiner [3] [pjetine] ◆ vi **1.** [s'agiter] to walk on the spot / *piétiner de rage* to stamp one's feet in rage ▸ **piétiner d'impatience** *fig* to be fidgeting with impatience, to be champing at the bit **2.** *fig* [stagner] to fail to make (any) progress ou headway / *on piétine, il faut se décider !* we're not getting anywhere ou we're just marking time, let's make up our minds! ◆ vt **1.** [écraser] to trample ou to tread on **2.** *fig* [libertés, traditions] to trample underfoot, to ride roughshod over.

piéton, onne [pjetɔ̃, ɔn] ◆ adj pedestrian *(modif)* / *rue* ou *zone piétonne* pedestrian precinct UK ou mall US. ◆ nm, f pedestrian.

piétonnier, ère [pjetɔnje, ɛʀ] adj pedestrian *(modif).*

piètre [pjɛtʀ] adj *(avant nom)* very poor, mediocre ▸ **faire piètre figure** to be a sorry sight / *de piètre qualité* very mediocre ▸ **c'est une piètre consolation** that's small ou not much comfort.

pieu, x [pjø] nm **1.** [poteau -pour délimiter] post ; [-pour attacher] stake **2.** *fam* [lit] bed.

pieuter [3] [pjøte] ❖ **se pieuter** vpi *tfam* to turn in, to hit the hay ou the sack.

pieuvre [pjœvʀ] nf ZOOL octopus.

pieux, euse [pjø, øz] adj **1.** [dévot] pious, devout **2.** [charitable] ▸ **pieux mensonge** white lie.

pif [pif] nm [nez] conk UK, hooter UK, shnoz(zle) US. ❖ **au pif** loc adv *fam* at random / *au pif, je dirais trois* I'd say three, at a rough guess ou off the top of my head / *j'ai pris celui-là au pif* I just took the first one that came to hand.

pifomètre [pifɔmɛtʀ] nm *fam* ▸ **au pifomètre** : *j'ai dit ça au pifomètre* I was just guessing ▸ **faire qqch au pifomètre** to follow one's hunch in doing sthg.

pige [piʒ] nf **1.** *fam* IMPR & PRESSE : *travailler à la pige, faire des piges* to work freelance **2.** *tfam* [an] year / *pour quarante piges, il est bien conservé* he still looks pretty good for a forty-year-old.

pigeon [piʒɔ̃] nm **1.** ORNITH pigeon ▸ **pigeon ramier** wood pigeon, ringdove ▸ **pigeon voyageur** carrier ou homing pigeon **2.** *fam* [dupe] mug UK, sucker US.

pigeonnant, e [piʒɔnɑ̃, ɑ̃t] adj ▸ **soutien-gorge pigeonnant** uplift (bra) ▸ **poitrine pigeonnante** full bosom.

pigeonner [3] [piʒɔne] vt *fam* [duper] ❖ **se faire pigeonner** a) [tromper] to be led up the garden path, to be taken for a ride b) [pour de l'argent] to get ripped off.

pigeonnier [piʒɔnje] nm [pour pigeons] dovecote.

piger [17] [piʒe] vt *fam* [comprendre] to get, to twig UK / *(t'as) pigé ?* got it?, have you twigged? UK, have you got the picture? US.

pigiste [piʒist] nmf PRESSE freelance journalist.

pigment [pigmɑ̃] nm pigment.

pignon [piɲɔ̃] nm **1.** ARCHIT [de mur] gable ; [de bâtiments] side wall ▸ **avoir pignon sur rue** a) [personne] to be well-off (and respectable) b) [entreprise] to be well established **2.** TECHNOL [roue dentée] cogwheel, gear wheel ; [petite roue] pinion ; [d'un vélo] rear-wheel, sprocket **3.** BOT pine kernel ou nut.

pile [pil] ◆ nf **1.** [tas -désordonné] pile, heap ; [-ordonné] stack **2.** INFORM stack **3.** TRAV PUB [appui] pier ; [pieu] pile **4.** ÉLECTR battery / *une radio à piles* a radio run on batteries, a battery radio ▸ **pile rechargeable** rechargeable battery

5. [côté d'une pièce] ▸ **pile ou face ?** heads or tails? ▸ **jouer ou tirer à pile ou face** to toss a coin. ◆ adv fam **1.** [net] dead ▸ **s'arrêter pile** to stop dead / *ça commence à 8 h pile* it begins at 8 o'clock sharp ou on the dot **2.** [juste] right ▸ **tomber pile** : *tu es tombé pile sur le bon chapitre* you just hit (on) the right chapter / *vous tombez pile, j'allais vous appeler* you're right on cue, I was about to call you.

pile-poil [pilpwal] adv fam just / *ça rentre pile-poil dans la valise* it just fits into the suitcase / *je suis arrivé pile-poil à l'heure* I arrived exactly on time / *c'est pile-poil !* it's just right!

piler [3] [pile] ◆ vt [broyer] to crush, to grind. ◆ vi fam [freiner] to slam (one's foot) on the brakes.

pilier [pilje] nm **1.** ANAT, CONSTR & MIN pillar **2.** fig [défenseur] pillar ; [bastion] bastion, bulwark ▸ **être un pilier de bar** ou **bistrot** fam & péj [habitué] : *c'est un pilier de bar* ou *bistrot* he can always be found propping up the bar, he's a barfly.

pillage [pijaʒ] nm [vol] pillage, looting, plundering / *le pillage de la ville par les soldats* the pillaging of the town by the soldiers.

pillard, e [pijar, ard] nm, f pillager, looter, plunderer.

piller [3] [pije] vt **1.** [dépouiller] to pillage, to loot, to plunder **2.** [détourner] to cream 🇬🇧 ou to siphon off (sép).

pilon [pilõ] nm **1.** [de mortier] pestle ; TECHNOL pounder **2.** IMPR : *mettre un livre au pilon* to pulp a book **3.** [de volaille] drumstick.

pilonner [3] [pilone] vt [bombarder] to bombard, to shell.

pilori [pilɔri] nm **1.** HIST pillory **2.** fig ▸ **clouer** ou **mettre qqn au pilori** to pillory sb.

pilotage [pilɔtaʒ] nm **1.** NAUT piloting **2.** AÉRON pilotage, piloting **3.** fig [direction] : *le pilotage d'une entreprise* running a business.

pilote [pilɔt] ◆ nmf **1.** AÉRON pilot ▸ **pilote de chasse** fighter pilot ▸ **pilote d'essai** test pilot ▸ **pilote de ligne** airline pilot **2.** AUTO driver ▸ **pilote automobile** ou **de course** racing driver **3.** (comme adjectif, avec ou sans trait d'union) [expérimental] experimental ▸ **école pilote** experimental school ; [promotionnel] promotional ▸ **produit pilote** promotional item, special offer. ◆ nm **1.** AÉRON & NAUT pilot ▸ **pilote automatique** autopilot, automatic pilot **2.** INFORM ▸ **pilote (de périphérique)** driver.

piloter [3] [pilɔte] vt **1.** [conduire - avion] to pilot, to fly ; [- bateau] to sail ; [- voiture] to drive **2.** [gérer - entreprise, projet] to run **3.** [guider - personne] to guide, to show around (sép) ; [- outil] to guide ▸ **piloté par ordinateur** computer-driven.

pilotis [pilɔti] nm ▸ **des pilotis** piling ▸ **maison sur pilotis** house built on piles ou stilts.

pilule [pilyl] nf **1.** [médicament] pill ▸ **trouver la pilule amère** fam to find it a bitter pill to swallow **2.** [contraceptif] ▸ **pilule contraceptive** contraceptive pill ▸ **prendre la pilule** to be on the pill ▸ **pilule du lendemain** morning-after pill.

pimbêche [pɛ̃bɛʃ] nf : *c'est une pimbêche* she's really stuck-up.

pimbina [pɛ̃bina] nm QUÉBEC BOT pimbina, highbush cranberry.

piment [pimã] nm **1.** BOT pepper, capsicum spéc ▸ **piment rouge** red pepper **2.** [poudre, purée] chilli, chili **3.** [charme] spice, pizzazz 🇺🇸 ▸ **donner du piment à qqch** to spice sthg up, to add pizzazz to sthg 🇺🇸.

pimenter [3] [pimãte] vt **1.** CULIN to season with chili, to spice up (sép) **2.** [corser] : *pimenter une histoire* to lace a story with spicy details / *pimenter la vie* to add spice to life.

pimpant, e [pɛ̃pã, ɑ̃t] adj [net] spruce, neat, smart ; [frais] fresh, bright.

pin [pɛ̃] nm **1.** BOT pine **2.** MENUIS pine, pinewood.

pinacle [pinakl] nm **1.** ARCHIT pinnacle **2.** fig zenith, acme ▸ **mettre** ou **porter qqn au pinacle** to praise sb to the skies, to put sb on a pedestal.

pinailler [3] [pinaje] vi fam to quibble, to nitpick / *elle pinaille sur tout* she's a real nitpicker.

pinard [pinar] nm tfam vino, plonk 🇬🇧, jug wine 🇺🇸.

pince [pɛ̃s] nf **1.** [outil] (pair of) pliers ou pincers ; [pour un âtre] (fire) tongs ▸ **pince à cheveux** hair clip ▸ **pince coupante** wire cutters ▸ **pince à épiler** (pair of) tweezers ▸ **pince à linge** clothes peg 🇬🇧 ou pin 🇺🇸 ▸ **pince universelle** universal ou all-purpose pliers ▸ **pince à vélo** bicycle clip **2.** ZOOL claw, pincer ; [d'un sabot de cheval] front part (of a horse's hoof) **3.** COUT dart, tuck. ◆ **à pinces** ◆ loc adj COUT pleated ▸ **pantalon à pinces** front-pleated trousers. ◆ loc adv fam [à pied] on foot, on shanks's pony 🇬🇧 ou mare 🇺🇸 / *j'irai à pinces* I'll hoof ou leg it.

pincé, e [pɛ̃se] adj **1.** [dédaigneux] ▸ **un sourire pincé** a thin-lipped smile / *il avait un air pincé* he had a stiff ou starchy manner **2.** [serré] tight / *aux lèvres pincées* tight-lipped.

pinceau, x [pɛ̃so] nm [brosse - de peintre] paintbrush, brush ; [- de maquillage] brush.

pincée [pɛ̃se] ◆ f ⟶ **pincé.** ◆ nf pinch.

pincement [pɛ̃smã] nm [émotion] twinge, pang / *avoir un pincement au cœur* to have a lump in one's throat.

pincer [16] [pɛ̃se] vt **1.** [serrer] to pinch, to nip **2.** [suj : vent, froid] to nip at **3.** fam EXPR ▸ **en pincer pour qqn** to be crazy about sb, to be gone on sb. ◆ **se pincer** ◆ vp (emploi réfléchi) to pinch o.s. / *se pincer le nez* to hold ou to pinch one's nose. ◆ vpt : *je me suis pincé le doigt dans le tiroir* I caught my finger in the drawer, my finger got caught in the drawer.

pince-sans-rire [pɛ̃ssɑ̃rir] nmf person with a deadpan ou dry sense of humour.

pincettes [pɛ̃sɛt] nfpl [pour attiser] (fireplace) tongs ▸ **il n'est pas à prendre avec des pincettes** [très énervé] he's like a bear with a sore head.

pinçon [pɛ̃sõ] nm pinch mark.

pinède [pinɛd] nf pinewood, pine grove.

pingouin [pɛ̃gwɛ̃] nm [alcidé] auk ; [manchot] penguin.

ping-pong, pingpong* [piŋpõg] nm table tennis, ping-pong.

pingre [pɛ̃gr] péj adj [avare] stingy, mean, tight-fisted.

pin's [pins] nm inv badge.

pinson [pɛ̃sõ] nm chaffinch.

pintade [pɛ̃tad] nf guinea fowl.

pinte [pɛ̃t] nf **1.** [verre] pint / *une pinte de bière* a pint of beer **2.** SUISSE bar.

pin-up (pl pin-up), **pinup*** [pinœp] nf pinup.

pioche [pjɔʃ] nf [outil] pick, pickaxe, mattock.

piocher [3] [pjɔʃe] ◆ vt **1.** [creuser] to dig (up) **2.** [tirer] to draw / *piocher une carte* / *un domino* to draw a card / domino (from stock) **3.** fam [étudier] to cram, to swot at 🇬🇧 (insép), to grind away at 🇺🇸 (insép). ◆ vi [puiser] to dig / *les cerises sont fameuses, vas-y, pioche (dans le tas)* the cherries are delicious, go ahead, dig in.

piolet [pjɔlɛ] nm ice-axe, ice ax 🇺🇸.

pion¹ [pjõ] nm JEUX [de dames] draughtsman, checker 🇺🇸 ; [d'échecs] pawn.

pion², pionne [pjõ, pjɔn] nm, f fam ÉDUC (paid) prefect ou monitor.

Pion

In French **collèges** and **lycées**, the pions (officially called **assistants d'éducation**) are responsible for supervising pupils outside class hours; they are often university students who do the job to help finance their studies.

pionnier, ère [pjɔnje, ɛʀ] nm, f **1.** [inventeur] pioneer **2.** [colon] pioneer.

pipe [pip] nf **1.** [à fumer - contenant] pipe ; [- contenu] pipe, pipeful **2.** vulg [fellation] blow-job.

pipeau, X [pipo] nm MUS (reed) pipe ▶ **c'est du pipeau** fig it's all fibs.

pipelette [piplɛt] nf fam gossip (monger) / **mon oncle est une vraie pipelette** my uncle loves a good chin-wag.

pipe-line (pl pipe-lines), **pipeline** [pajplajn, piplin] nm pipeline.

piper [3] [pipe] vt **1.** [truquer - dés] to load ; [- cartes] to mark **2.** EXPR **ne pas piper (mot)** to keep mum.

pipette [pipɛt] nf pipette.

pipeule [pipœl] adj inv & nmf inv = **pipole**.

pipi [pipi] nm fam [urine] (wee) wee, pee ▶ **faire pipi** to do a (wee) wee, to have a pee, to pee / **faire pipi au lit** to wet the bed.

pipole [pipɔl] adj inv & nmf inv celebrity.

pipolisation, peopolisation [pipɔlizasjɔ̃] nf : **elle condamne la pipolisation de la sphère politique** she is critical of the way politics has become dominated by celebrity and glamour.

piquant, e [pikɑ̃, ɑ̃t] adj **1.** [plante] thorny / **sa barbe est piquante** his beard's all prickly **2.** [vif - froid] biting **3.** CULIN [moutarde, radis] hot **4.** sout [excitant - récit, détail] spicy, juicy **5.** fam [eau] fizzy. ◆ **piquant** nm **1.** [de plante] thorn, prickle ; [d'oursin, de hérisson] spine ; [de barbelé] barb, spike / **couvert de piquants** prickly **2.** sout [intérêt] : **des détails qui ne manquent pas de piquant** juicy details.

pique [pik] ◆ nf **1.** [arme] pike ; [de picador] pic **2.** [propos] barb, carping remark. ◆ nm **1.** [carte] spade **2.** [couleur] spades.

piqué, e [pike] adj **1.** [abîmé - vin] sour ; [- miroir] mildewed ; [- bois] wormeater ; [- papier] foxed **2.** fam [fou] nutty, screwy, cracked **3.** CULIN [de lard] larded, piqué ; [d'ail] studded with garlic, piqué. ◆ **piqué** nm AÉRON nose dive ▶ **attaquer en piqué** to dive-bomb.

pique-assiette [pikasjɛt] (pl pique-assiette ou pique-assiettes) nmf fam sponger, scrounger.

pique-nique (pl pique-niques), **piquenique*** [piknik] nm picnic ▶ **faire un pique-nique** to go on ou for a picnic.

pique-niquer, piqueniquer* [3] [piknike] vi to picnic, to go on ou for a picnic / **un bon endroit pour pique-niquer** a nice place to have ou for a picnic.

piquer [3] [pike] ◆ vt **1.** MÉD [avec une seringue] ▶ **piquer qqn** to give sb an injection **2.** VÉTÉR [tuer] : **faire piquer un chien** to have a dog put down **3.** [avec une pointe] to prick ▶ **piquer un morceau de viande avec une fourchette** to stick a fork / **la pointe d'un couteau** to stick the tip of a knife into a piece of meat **4.** [suj : animal, plante] to sting, to bite **5.** [enfoncer] to stick **6.** [brûler] to tickle, to tingle, to prickle / **ça pique la gorge** it gives you a tickle in your ou the throat / **la fumée me pique les yeux** the smoke is making my eyes smart **7.** [stimuler - curiosité, jalousie] to arouse, to awaken ; [- amour-propre] to pique ;

[- intérêt] to stir (up) **8.** fam [faire de manière soudaine] : **piquer une crise (de nerfs)** to get hysterical ▶ **piquer un somme** ou **un roupillon** fam to grab a nap ou some shut-eye **9.** fam [dérober] to steal, to pinch, to grab US **10.** COUT to sew ; [cuir] to stitch. ◆ vi **1.** [brûler - barbe] to prickle ; [- désinfectant, alcool] to sting ; [- yeux] to burn, to smart / **aïe ! ça pique !** ouch! that stings! ▶ **radis / moutarde qui pique** hot radish / mustard ▶ **eau qui pique** fam fizzy water **2.** [descendre - avion] to (go into a) dive ; [- oiseau] to swoop down ; [- personne] to head straight towards **3.** EXPR **piquer du nez a)** [avion] to go into a nosedive **b)** [bateau] to tilt forward **c)** [fleur] to droop **d)** [personne] to (begin to) drop off. ◆ **se piquer** ◆ vp (emploi réfléchi) [avec une seringue - malade] to inject o.s. ; [- drogué] to take drugs (intravenously) / **il se pique à l'héroïne** he shoots ou does heroin. ◆ vpi **1.** [par accident] to prick o.s. **2.** EXPR **se piquer au jeu** : **elle s'est piquée au jeu** it grew on her. ◆ **se piquer de** vp + prép to pride o.s. on.

piquerie [pikʀi] nf QUÉBEC shooting gallery.

piquet [pikɛ] nm **1.** [pieu] post, stake, picket **2.** [groupe - de soldats, de grévistes] picket ▶ **piquet de grève** picket.

piquette [pikɛt] nf [vin] (cheap) wine, plonk.

piqûre, piqure* [pikyʀ] nf **1.** [d'aiguille] prick ▶ **piqûre d'épingle** pinprick **2.** [d'insecte] sting, bite / **piqûre de guêpe / d'abeille** wasp / bee sting / **piqûre de moustique / puce** mosquito / flea bite **3.** [de plante] sting ▶ **piqûres d'orties** nettle stings **4.** MÉD injection, shot ▶ **piqûre de rappel a)** pr booster (injection ou shot) **b)** fig reminder / **les élèves n'ont pas bien assimilé cette notion, une piqûre de rappel s'impose** the students haven't fully grasped this notion, we need to go over it again ▶ **faire une piqûre à qqn** to give sb an injection **5.** COUT [point] stitch ; [rangs, couture] stitching (U) **6.** [saleté] ▶ **piqûres de mouches** fly specks.

piranha [piʀana] nm piranha.

piratage [piʀataʒ] nm pirating (U), piracy ▶ **piratage informatique** hacking ▶ **piratage de musique** music piracy ▶ **piratage téléphonique** phreaking.

pirate [piʀat] nm **1.** [sur les mers] pirate ▶ **pirate de l'air** hijacker **2.** INFORM & INTERNET hacker ▶ **pirate informatique** (computer) hacker **3.** (comme adjectif, avec ou sans trait d'union) pirate (modif).

pirater [3] [piʀate] vt **1.** fam [voler] to rip off (sép), to rob / **pirater des idées** to pinch ou steal ideas **2.** INFORM [ordinateur] to hack into **3.** [copier illégalement] to pirate ▶ **pirater un film / un jeu vidéo** to make a pirate copy of a film / a video game.

piraterie [piʀatʀi] nf **1.** [sur les mers] piracy ▶ **piraterie aérienne** air piracy, hijacking **2.** [plagiat] piracy, pirating ▶ **piraterie commerciale** industrial piracy.

pire [piʀ] ◆ adj **1.** (comparatif) worse / **si je dors, c'est pire encore** if I sleep, it's even worse / **les conditions sont pires que jamais** the conditions are worse than ever / **c'est de pire en pire** it's getting worse and worse **2.** (superl) worst / **mon pire ennemi** my worst enemy. ◆ nm ▶ **le pire** the worst / **je m'attends au pire** I expect the worst / **le pire est qu'elle en aime un autre** the worst (part) of it is that she's in love with someone else / **dans le pire des cas**, **(en mettant les choses) au pire** at worst.

pirogue [piʀɔg] nf pirogue, dugout.

pirouette [piʀwɛt] nf **1.** [tour sur soi-même] pirouette, body spin **2.** DANSE & ÉQUIT pirouette **3.** [dérobade] ▶ **répondre** ou **s'en tirer par une pirouette** to answer flippantly.

pis¹ [pi] nm [de vache] udder.

pis² [pi] *litt* ◆ adj worse. ◆ adv worse ▶ **aller de pis en pis** to get worse and worse. ◆◆ **qui pis est** loc adv what's ou what is worse.

pis-aller [pizale] nm inv [expédient] last resort / *disons lundi, mais ce serait un pis-aller* let's say Monday, but that's if the worst comes to the worst.

pisciculture [pisikyltyʀ] nf fish-farming, pisciculture *spéc.*

piscine [pisin] nf [de natation] (swimming) pool ou baths 🇬🇧 ▶ **piscine couverte / découverte** indoor / outdoor (swimming) pool ▶ **piscine municipale** public (swimming) pool ou baths ▶ **piscine olympique** Olympic-sized (swimming) pool ; [pour s'amuser] ▶ **piscine à balles** ball pit ▶ **piscine à vagues** wave pool.

pisse [pis] nf tfam piss, pee.

pisse-froid (*pl* pisse-froid), **pissefroid*** [pisfʀwa] nm *fam* wet blanket, killjoy.

pissenlit [pisɑ̃li] nm dandelion.

pisser [3] [pise] ◆ vi tfam **1.** [uriner] to piss, to (have a) pee ▶ **ne plus se sentir pisser** : *il ne se sent plus pisser* he's too big for his boots ▶ **faire pisser qqn de rire** : *elle me fait pisser de rire* she has me in stitches **2.** [fuir] to leak. ◆ vt **1.** [uriner] to pass / *pisser du sang* to pass blood **2.** [laisser s'écouler] : *mon nez pissait le sang* I had blood pouring from my nose.

pistache [pistaʃ] nf pistachio (nut).

piste [pist] nf **1.** [trace] track, trail / *ils sont sur la bonne / une fausse piste* they're on the right / wrong track ▶ **jeu de piste** treasure hunt **2.** [indice] lead **3.** SPORT [de course à pied] running track ; [en hippisme - pour la course] track ; [- pour les chevaux] bridle path ; [de patinage] rink ; [de course cycliste] cycling track ; [de course automobile] racing track ; [d'athlétisme] lane ; [d'escrime] piste ▶ **piste de danse** dance floor ▶ **piste de cirque** circus ring ▶ **piste de ski artificielle** dry ski slope **4.** [chemin, sentier] trail, track ▶ **piste cyclable a)** [sur la route] cycle lane **b)** [à côté] cycle track **5.** AÉRON runway ▶ **piste d'envol / d'atterrissage** take-off / landing runway **6.** AUDIO, CINÉ & INFORM track. ◆◆ **en piste** interj off you go. ◆ loc adv ▶ **entrer en piste** to come into play, to join in.

pister [3] [piste] vt [suivre - personne] to tail, to trail ; [- animal] to trail, to track.

pisteur [pistœʀ] nm SKI [pour entretien] ski slope maintenance man ; [pour surveillance] ski patrolman.

pistil [pistil] nm pistil.

pistolet [pistɔlɛ] nm **1.** ARM pistol, gun ▶ **pistolet d'alarme** alarm pistol ▶ **pistolet automatique** pistol ▶ **pistolet à impulsion électronique** stun gun, Taser® **2.** [instrument] ▶ **pistolet agrafeur** staple gun ▶ **pistolet à peinture** spray gun **3.** [jouet] ▶ **pistolet à eau** water pistol.

piston [pistɔ̃] nm **1.** MÉCAN piston **2.** MUS valve **3.** *fam* [recommandation, protection] string-pulling, connections / *il est rentré par piston* he got in by knowing the right people.

pistonner [3] [pistɔne] vt fam to pull strings for / *elle s'est fait pistonner pour entrer au ministère* she used her connections to get into the Ministry.

pistou [pistu] nm *Provençal vegetable soup (with garlic and basil).*

pitbull, pit-bull (*pl* pit-bulls) [pitbul] nm pitbull (terrier).

piteux, euse [pitø, øz] adj **1.** [pitoyable] pitiful, piteous / *être en piteux état* to be in a pitiful condition **2.** [triste] : *faire piteuse mine* to look sad **3.** [honteux] sheepish.

pitié [pitje] ◆ nf **1.** [compassion] pity ▶ **avoir pitié de qqn** to feel pity for ou to pity sb ▶ **faire pitié à qqn** : *elle me fait pitié* I feel sorry for her **2.** [désolation] pity / *quelle pitié !, c'est une pitié !* what a pity ! **3.** [clémence] mercy, pity / *il a eu pitié de ses ennemis* he had mercy on his enemies. ◆ interj ▶ **(par) pitié ! a)** (have) mercy! **b)** [avec agacement] for pity's sake! / *pitié pour ma pauvre carcasse !* hum have mercy on my poor old bones! ◆◆ **sans pitié** loc adj ruthless, merciless ▶ **ils ont été sans pitié a)** [jurés] they showed no mercy **b)** [terroristes] they were ruthless.

piton [pitɔ̃] nm **1.** [clou - gén] eye ou eye-headed nail ; [- d'alpiniste] piton **2.** GÉOGR [dans la mer] submarine mountain ; [pic] piton, needle ▶ **piton rocheux** rocky outcrop **3.** 🇨🇦 fam [touche d'un appareil] button **4.** 🇨🇦 fam [dans les jeux de société] counter **5.** ᴇxᴘʀ **être sur le piton** 🇨🇦 fam to be in great shape.

pitonner [3] [pitɔne] vi **1.** 🇨🇦 fam [sur des touches, un clavier] to tap away ▶ **pitonner sur l'ordinateur** to tap away on a computer **2.** 🇨🇦 fam [avec une télécommande] to zap, to channel-hop.

pitonneux, euse [pitɔnø, øz] nm, f 🇨🇦 fam **1.** [adepte de l'informatique] computer buff **2.** TV channel hopper.

pitoyable [pitwajabl] adj **1.** [triste - destin] pitiful **2.** [mauvais - effort, résultat] pitiful, deplorable, dismal.

pitre [pitʀ] nm [plaisantin] clown ▶ **faire le pitre** to clown ou to fool around.

pitrerie [pitʀəʀi] nf piece of tomfoolery ou buffoonery.

pittoresque [pitɔʀɛsk] adj picturesque, colourful 🇬🇧, colorful 🇺🇸.

pivert [pivɛʀ] nm (green) woodpecker.

pivoine [pivwan] nf peony.

pivot [pivo] nm **1.** [axe] pivot **2.** [centre] pivot, hub / *le pivot de toute son argumentation* the crux of his argument.

pivotant, e [pivotɑ̃, ɑ̃t] adj revolving, swivelling.

pivoter [3] [pivote] vi [autour d'un axe - porte] to revolve ; [- fauteuil] to swivel.

pixel [piksɛl] nm pixel.

pixellisation [pikselizasjɔ̃] nf pixellation.

pixellisé, e [pikselize] adj pixelized.

pizza [pidza] nf pizza.

pizzeria, pizzéria* [pidzeʀja] nf pizzeria.

PJ ◆ npr f (abr de **police judiciaire**) ≃ CID 🇬🇧 ; ≃ FBI 🇺🇸. ◆ (abr écrite de **pièces jointes**) encl.

Pk SMS abr écrite de **pourquoi**.

placage [plakaʒ] nm **1.** [revêtement - de bois] veneering ; [- de pierre, marbre] facing ; [- de métal] cladding, coating **2.** SPORT tackle.

placard [plakaʀ] nm **1.** [armoire] cupboard, closet 🇺🇸 ▶ **placard à balais** broom cupboard **2.** IMPR galley (proof) ▶ **placard publicitaire a)** [grand] large display advertisement **b)** [de pleine page] full-page advertisement.

placarder [3] [plakaʀde] vt [afficher] to plaster / *j'ai placardé des photos sur les murs* I plastered the walls with photos.

placardiser [plakaʀdize] vt to sideline ▶ **se faire placardiser** to be sidelined.

place [plas] nf **1.** [espace disponible] space (U), room (U) / *faire de la place* to make room ou space / *il reste de la place pour quatre personnes* there's enough space ou room left for four people ▶ **ne prends pas toute la place a)** [à table, au lit] don't take up so much room **b)** [sur la page] don't use up all the space ▶ **laisser la** ou **faire place à** to make room ou way for / *les anciens font place aux jeunes* older people give way to the young generation / *et maintenant, place aux artistes* and now, on with the show **2.** [endroit précis] place, spot ▶ **changer les meubles / la cuisinière de place** to move the furniture around / the stove ▸ **mets / remets les clefs à leur place** put the keys / put the keys back where they belong ; [d'une personne] : *savoir rester à sa place* to know one's place / *je ne me sens pas à ma place parmi eux* I feel out of place among them ▸ **reprendre sa place a)** [sa position] to go back to one's place **b)** [son rôle] to go back to where one belongs ▸ **remettre qqn à sa place** to put sb in his / her place **3.** [siège] seat ; [fauteuil au spectacle] seat ; [billet] ticket / *à la place du conducteur* in the driver's seat / *une salle de 500 places* a room that can seat 500 people ▸ **réserver une place d'avion / de train** to make a plane / train reservation / *j'ai trois places de concert* I have three tickets for the concert / *est-ce que cette place est prise ?* is anybody sitting here? ▸ **prendre place** [s'asseoir] to sit down ▸ **place assise** seat **4.** [dans un parking] (parking) space / *un parking de 1 000 places* a car park with space for 1,000 cars **5.** [espace urbain] square / *la place du village* the village square ▸ **sur la place de Paris** : *médecin connu sur la place de Paris* doctor well-known in Paris ▸ **sur la place publique** in public / *porter le débat sur la place publique* to make the debate public **6.** [poste, emploi] position, post ▸ **une bonne place** a good job **7.** [rang - dans une compétition] place, rank ▸ **avoir la première place** to come first ou top ▸ **avoir la dernière place** to come bottom 🇬🇧 ou last / *elle est en bonne place au dernier tour* she's well placed on the last lap **8.** BOURSE ▸ **place boursière** stock market ▸ **place financière** financial centre **9.** MIL ▸ **place (forte)** fortress, stronghold. ◆ **à la place** loc adv instead / *j'ai rapporté la jupe et j'ai pris un pantalon à la place* I returned the skirt and exchanged it for a pair of trousers. ◆ **à la place de** loc prép **1.** [au lieu de] instead of / *j'irai à sa place* I'll go instead of him **2.** [dans la situation de] ▸ **à ma / sa place** in my / his place / *mettez-vous à ma place* put yourself in my place ou shoes / *je ne voudrais pas être à sa place* rather him than me, I wouldn't like to be in his shoes. ◆ **en place** ◆ loc adj [important] established. ◆ loc adv **1.** [là] in position / *est-ce que tout est en place ?* is everything in order ou in its proper place? **2.** EXPR mettre en place **a)** [équipement] to set up (sép), to install **b)** [plan] to set up (sép), to put into action **c)** [réseau] to set up (sép) ▸ **mettre / remettre les idées en place à qqn** : *ça va lui mettre / remettre les idées en place* it'll give him a more realistic view of things / set him thinking straight again ▸ **tenir en place** : *il ne tient pas en place* **a)** [il est turbulent] he can't keep still **b)** [il est anxieux] he's nervous **c)** [il voyage beaucoup] he's always on the move. ◆ **sur place** loc adv there, on the spot / *je serai déjà sur place* I'll already be there.

⚠ Le mot anglais **place** ne traduit que rarement le mot français place. Voir article.

🌐 **Places**

la place Beauvau	square in Paris (also refers to the Ministry of the Interior, whose offices are situated there)
la place de la Concorde	square in Paris (one of the biggest and busiest squares in Paris, laid out in the reign of Louis XV)
la place du Colonel-Fabien	square in Paris (also refers to the Communist party headquarters, which are situated there)
la place Rouge	Red Square
la place Saint-Marc	Saint Mark's Square
la place Tian'anmen	Tiananmen Square
la place Vendôme	square in Paris (the name evokes opulence and luxury because of the Ritz hotel and the jewellery shops situated on the square)
la place des Vosges	elegant and fashionable square in the Marais district of Paris, built under Henri IV

placé, e [plase] adj **1.** *(comme adv)* ▸ **arriver placé** to be placed **2.** [situé] ▸ **bien placé a)** [magasin, appartement] well-situated **b)** [fermeture, bouton, couture] well-positioned ▸ **mal placé a)** [magasin, appartement] badly-located **b)** [fermeture, bouton, couture] poorly-positioned **c)** [coup] below the belt **d)** [abcès] in an awkward spot **e)** *euphém* in an embarrassing place **f)** [orgueil] misplaced / *on était très bien / mal placés* [au spectacle] we had really good / bad seats ▸ **être bien / mal placé pour** *fig* to be in a / no position to ▸ **haut placé** well up ou high up in the hierarchy / *des gens haut placés* people in high places.

placebo, placébo* [plasebo] nm placebo.

placement [plasmɑ̃] nm **1.** [investissement] investment ▸ **placement financier** financial investment **2.** [de chômeurs] placing **3.** [internement] ▸ **placement d'office** hospitalization order.

placenta [plasɛ̃ta] nm placenta.

placer [16] [plase] vt **1.** [mettre dans une position précise] to place ▸ **placer sa voix** MUS to pitch one's voice **2.** [faire asseoir] to seat **3.** [établir - dans une position, un état] to put, to place ▸ **placer qqn devant ses responsabilités** to force sb to face up to his / her responsibilities **4.** [établir - dans une institution] to place **5.** [classer] to put, to place **6.** [situer dans le temps] : *il a placé l'action du film en l'an 2000* he set the film in the year 2000 **7.** [situer dans l'espace] to locate **8.** [mettre] to put / *elle a placé tous ses espoirs dans ce projet* she's pinned all her hopes on this project **9.** [dans la conversation] : *je n'ai pas pu placer un mot* I couldn't get a word in edgeways **10.** [vendre] to sell **11.** FIN to invest. ◆ **se placer** vpi **1.** [dans l'espace] ▸ **place-toi près de la fenêtre a)** [debout] stand near the window **b)** [assis] sit near the window ; [dans un jugement, une analyse] to look at ou to consider things **2.** [occuper un rang] to rank, to finish / *se placer premier / troisième* to finish first / third.

placide [plasid] adj placid, calm.

placotage [plakotaʒ] nm 🇶🇨 *fam* **1.** [bavardage] chatting **2.** [médisance] gossiping.

placoter [3] [plakote] vi 🇶🇨 *fam* **1.** [bavarder] to chat **2.** [médire] to gossip.

plafond [plafɔ̃] nm **1.** CONSTR ceiling ; [d'une voiture] roof ▸ **faux plafond** false ceiling ▸ **bas de plafond** *pr* : *la pièce est basse de plafond* the room has got a low ceiling **2.** [limite supérieure] ▸ **plafond de crédit** credit limit ▸ **plafond de découvert** BANQUE overdraft limit **3.** *(comme adj, avec ou sans trait d'union)* ceiling *(modif)* ▸ **vitesse plafond** maximum speed **4.** MÉTÉOR ▸ **plafond nuageux** cloud ceiling.

plafonnement [plafɔnmɑ̃] nm ▸ **plafonnement des salaires** top-grading of wages ▸ **plafonnement des émissions** ÉCOL emissions cap.

plafonner [3] [plafɔne] ◆ vt **1.** [impôts] to set a ceiling for **2.** ÉCOL ▸ **plafonner les émissions de gaz à effet de serre** to cap greenhouse emissions. ◆ vi [ventes, salaires] to level off ; [taux d'intérêt, prix] to peak / *je plafonne à 3 000 euros depuis un an* my monthly income hasn't exceeded 3,000 euros for over a year.

plafonnier [plafɔnje] nm **1.** [d'appartement] ceiling light **2.** AUTO (overhead) courtesy ou guide light.

plage [plaʒ] nf **1.** GÉOGR beach ▶ **plage de galets / de sable** pebble / sandy beach **2.** [espace de temps] ▶ **plage horaire** (allotted) slot ▶ **plage musicale** musical intermission ▶ **plage publicitaire** commercial break **3.** [écart] range ▶ **plage de prix** price range **4.** AUTO ▶ **plage arrière** back shelf **5.** [d'un disque] track. ❖ **de plage** loc adj beach (modif) ▶ **vêtements de plage** beachwear.

plagiat [plaʒja] nm plagiary, plagiarism.

plagier [9] [plaʒje] vt [œuvre] to plagiarize ▶ **plagier qqn** to plagiarize sb's work.

plagiste [plaʒist] nmf beach attendant.

plaid [plɛd] nm [pièce de tissu] plaid ; [couverture] car rug.

plaider [4] [plede] ◆ vi **1.** DR to plead ▶ **plaider pour qqn** to defend sb **2.** [présenter des arguments] ▶ **plaider en faveur de qqn / qqch** pr & fig to speak in sb's / sthg's favour. ◆ vt to plead ▶ **plaider une cause** a) DR to plead a case b) fig to speak (up) for ou to plead a cause ▶ **plaider coupable / non coupable** to plead guilty / not guilty, to make a plea of guilty / not guilty ▶ **plaider la légitime défense** to plead self-defence.

plaideur, euse [plɛdœʀ, øz] nm, f litigant.

plaidoirie [plɛdwaʀi] nf pr [exposé] speech for the defence 🇬🇧 ou defense 🇺🇸 ; fig defence 🇬🇧, defense 🇺🇸.

plaidoyer [plɛdwaje] nm **1.** DR speech for the defence **2.** [supplication] plea.

plaie [plɛ] nf **1.** [blessure] wound **2.** fam [personne ou chose ennuyeuse] ▶ **quelle plaie !** what a pain!

plaignant, e [plɛɲɑ̃, ɑ̃t] nm, f plaintiff.

plaignard, e [plɛɲaʀ, aʀd] nm, f 🇶🇺🇪🇧🇪🇨 [geignard] moaner, grumbler.

plaindre [80] [plɛ̃dʀ] vt [avoir pitié de] to feel sorry for, to pity ▶ **elle est bien à plaindre avec des enfants pareils !** with children like that, you can't help but feel sorry for her ! / **avec tout l'argent qu'ils gagnent, ils ne sont vraiment pas à plaindre** with all the money they're making, they've got nothing to complain about. ❖ **se plaindre** vpi [protester] to complain, to moan ▶ **se plaindre de** a) [symptôme] to complain of b) [personne, situation] to complain about.

plaine [plɛn] nf plain.

plain-pied [plɛ̃pje] ❖ **de plain-pied** loc adv **1.** [au même niveau] : **une maison construite de plain-pied** [avec le sol extérieur] a bungalow 🇬🇧, a ranch-house 🇺🇸 / **la chambre et le salon sont de plain-pied** the bedroom and the living room are on the same level **2.** [d'emblée] : **entrons de plain-pied dans le sujet** let's get straight down to the subject.

plainte [plɛ̃t] nf **1.** [gémissement] moan, groan **2.** [protestation] complaining, moaning **3.** DR complaint ▶ **porter plainte contre qqn** to bring an action against sb ▶ **plainte contre X** action against person or persons unknown.

plaintif, ive [plɛ̃tif, iv] adj [de douleur] plaintive, mournful / **d'un ton plaintif** querulously.

plaire [110] [plɛʀ] ❖ **plaire à** v + prép **1.** [être apprécié par] ▶ **cela me plaît** I like it / **ça vous plaît, le commerce ?** how do you like business life? / **le nouveau professeur ne me plaît pas du tout** I really don't like ou care for the new teacher / **cette idée ne me plaît pas du tout** I'm not at all keen on this idea ; (en usage absolu) : **offre du parfum, ça plaît toujours** give perfume, it's always appreciated **2.** [convenir à] ▶ **si ça me plaît** if I feel like it / **quand ça me plaît** whenever I feel like it / **elle ne lit que ce qui lui plaît** she only reads what she feels like (reading) **3.** [séduire] to be appealing ou attractive / **c'est le genre de fille qui plaît aux hommes** she's the kind of girl that men find attractive ; (en usage absolu) ▶ **aimer plaire** to take pleasure in being attractive. ❖ **il plaît** v impers

1. ▶ **comme** ou **tant qu'il te plaira, comme** ou **tant qu'il vous plaira** [exprime l'indécision] see if I care **2.** 🇪🇽🇵🇷 **s'il te plaît, s'il vous plaît** please ▶ **s'il vous plaît !** a) [dit par un client] excuse me! b) 🇧🇪🇱🇬 [dit par un serveur] here you are! ❖ **se plaire** vpi [dans un endroit] : **je me plais (bien) dans ma nouvelle maison** I enjoy living in my new house, I like it in my new house / **mes plantes se plaisent ici** my plants are happy here.

plaisance [plɛzɑ̃s] nf (pleasure) boating. ❖ **de plaisance** loc adj pleasure (modif).

plaisancier, ère [plɛzɑ̃sje,ɛʀ] nm, f amateur yachtsman (yachtswoman).

plaisant, e [plɛzɑ̃, ɑ̃t] adj **1.** [agréable] pleasant, nice **2.** [drôle] funny, amusing.

plaisanter [3] [plɛzɑ̃te] vi **1.** [faire - de l'esprit] to joke ; [- une plaisanterie] to (crack a) joke / **elle n'était pas d'humeur à plaisanter** she wasn't in a joking mood **2.** [parler à la légère] to joke / **tu plaisantes, ou quoi ?** you can't be serious!, you've got to be joking! **3.** ▶ **ne pas plaisanter avec qqch** [prendre qqch très au sérieux] : **on ne plaisante pas avec ces choses-là** you mustn't joke about such things.

plaisanterie [plɛzɑ̃tʀi] nf **1.** [parole amusante] joke ; [acte amusant] joke, hoax ▶ **faire une plaisanterie à qqn** to play a joke on sb / **la plaisanterie a assez duré** this has gone far enough **2.** [parole, action non sérieuse] joke **3.** [raillerie] joke, jibe / **il comprend** ou **entend** sout **la plaisanterie** he can take a joke ▶ **mauvaise plaisanterie** cruel joke.

plaisantin [plɛzɑ̃tɛ̃] nm [farceur] joker, clown.

plaisir [plɛziʀ] nm **1.** [joie] pleasure ▶ **avoir (du) plaisir** ou **prendre (du) plaisir à faire qqch** to take pleasure in doing sthg ▶ **faire plaisir à qqn** to please sb / **ça va lui faire plaisir** he'll be pleased ou delighted (with this) **2.** [dans des formules de politesse] : **cela fait plaisir de vous voir en bonne santé** it's a pleasure to see you in good health / **elle se fera un plaisir de vous raccompagner** she'll be (only too) glad to take you home / **j'ai le plaisir de vous informer que...** I am pleased to inform you that... / **au plaisir (de vous revoir)** see you again ou soon **3.** [agrément] pleasure / **les plaisirs de la vie** life's pleasures ▶ **les plaisirs de la table** : **elle aime les plaisirs de la table** she loves good food **4.** [sexualité] pleasures. ❖ **avec plaisir** loc adv with pleasure. ❖ **par plaisir, pour le plaisir** loc adv for its own sake, just for the fun of it.

plan¹ [plɑ̃] nm

🅰️ **SURFACE, PERSPECTIVE 1.** GÉOM plane ▶ **plan horizontal / incliné / médian / tangent** level / inclined / median / tangent plane ▶ **en plan incliné** sloping **2.** CONSTR surface ▶ **plan de cuisson** hob ▶ **plan de travail** [d'une cuisine] worktop 🇬🇧, countertop **3.** ART & PHOT plane **4.** CINÉ shot ▶ **gros plan, plan serré** close-up ▶ **plan général / moyen / rapproché** long / medium / close shot.

🅱️ **PROGRAMME 1.** [projet] plan, project / **ne vous inquiétez pas, j'ai un plan** fam don't worry, I've got a plan / **j'ai un bon plan pour les vacances** I've got a great idea for the holidays ▶ **un plan d'action** a plan of action ▶ **un plan de carrière** a career strategy **2.** [structure] plan, framework, outline / **je veux un plan détaillé de votre thèse** I want a detailed outline ou a synopsis of your thesis **3.** ADMIN plan, project ▶ **plan d'occupation des sols** land use plan 🇬🇧, zoning regulations 🇺🇸 ▶ **plan d'urbanisme** town planning scheme **4.** ÉCON plan ▶ **plan d'épargne** BANQUE savings plan ▶ **plan d'épargne(-)logement** savings scheme offering low-interest mortgages ▶ **plan social** redundancy scheme ou plan 🇬🇧 ▶ **plan de restructuration** restructuring plan.

C. REPRÉSENTATION 1. [carte] map, plan ▸ **plan de métro** underground 🇬🇧 ou subway 🇺🇸 map ▸ **plan de vol** flight plan 2. ARCHIT [dessin] plan, blueprint 🇬🇧 3. INFORM ▸ **plan de site** site map 4. TECHNOL plan, blueprint. ⬩ **de second plan** loc adj [question] of secondary importance ; [artiste, personnalité] second-rate. ⬩ **en plan** loc adv *fam* in the lurch ▸ **laisser qqn en plan** to leave sb in the lurch ▸ **laisser qqch en plan** to drop sthg. ⬩ **sur le plan de** loc prép as regards, as far as… is concerned / *sur le plan intellectuel* intellectually speaking ▸ **sur le plan personnel** at a personal level. ⬩ **plan d'eau** nm [naturel] stretch of water ; [artificiel] reservoir ; [ornemental] (ornamental) lake. ⬩ **premier plan** nm 1. CINÉ foreground ▸ **au premier plan** in the foreground 2. *fig* : *au premier plan de l'actualité* in the forefront of today's news ▸ **de (tout) premier plan** [personnage] leading, prominent.

🚩 **Plan Vigipirate**

Plan Vigipirate is a series of measures to prevent terrorist attacks. There are four levels: **jaune, orange, rouge** and **écarlate**. Vigipirate includes surveillance of public buildings and the public transportation system. Other measures such as no parking near school buildings can also be applied.

plan², **e** [plɑ̃, plan] adj 1. [miroir] plane ; [surface] flat 2. MATH plane, planar ▸ **surface plane** plane.

planche [plɑ̃ʃ] nf 1. [de bois] plank, board ▸ **planche à découper** chopping board ▸ **planche à dessin** drawing board ▸ **planche à pain** *pr* breadboard ▸ **planche à repasser** ironing board ▸ **planche de salut** last hope ▸ **recourir à** ou **faire marcher la planche à billets** *fam* to pump (more) money into the economy 2. *fam* [ski] ski 3. LOISIRS & SPORT ▸ **planche de surf** surf board ▸ **faire la planche** to float on one's back. ⬩ **planches** nfpl THÉÂTRE ▸ **les planches** the boards, the stage. ⬩ **planche à roulettes** nf skateboard. ⬩ **planche à voile** nf sail board / *faire de la planche à voile* to go windsurfing.

plancher¹ [plɑ̃ʃe] nm 1. ARCHIT & CONSTR floor 2. 🇶🇺 [étage] floor, story 3. [limite inférieure] floor ▸ **plancher des salaires** wage floor 4. *(comme adjectif, avec ou sans trait d'union)* minimum ▸ **prix plancher** minimum ou bottom price.

plancher² [3] [plɑ̃ʃe] ⬩ **plancher sur** v + prép *fam* [travailler sur] to work on.

planchiste [plɑ̃ʃist] nmf windsurfer.

plancton [plɑ̃ktɔ̃] nm plankton.

planer [3] [plane] vi 1. [oiseau] to soar ; [avion] to glide ; [fumée, ballon] to float 2. [danger, doute, mystère] to hover ▸ **planer sur** to hover over, to hang over / *le doute plane encore sur cette affaire* this affair is still shrouded in mystery 3. *fam* [être dans un état second] ▸ **il plane complètement** a) [il est drogué] he's high b) [il n'est pas réaliste] he's got his head in the clouds.

planétaire [planetɛr] adj [mondial] worldwide, global / *à l'échelle planétaire* on a global scale.

planétarium [planetarjɔm] nm planetarium.

planète [planɛt] nf planet ▸ **la planète** [la Terre] : *sur la planète tout entière* all over the Earth ou world ▸ **la planète bleue / rouge** the blue / red planet ; *fig* : *la planète informatique* the world of computing.

planeur [planœr] nm AÉRON glider.

planification [planifikasjɔ̃] nf ÉCON (economic) planning.

planifier [9] [planifje] vt [gén & ÉCON] to plan.

planning [planiŋ] nm [programme] schedule ▸ **avoir un planning très serré** to have a very tight schedule ▸ **faire un planning** to work out a schedule. ⬩ **planning familial** nm [méthode] family planning ; [organisme] family planning clinic.

plan-plan [plɑ̃plɑ̃] adj inv *fam* & *péj* [personne, film] boring ; [activité, vie] humdrum.

planque [plɑ̃k] nf *fam* 1. [cachette] hide-out, hideaway 2. [travail - gén] cushy job ; [- en temps de guerre] safe job.

planquer [3] [plɑ̃ke] *fam* vt [cacher] to hide. ⬩ **se planquer** vpi *fam* [se cacher] to hide out ou up.

plant [plɑ̃] nm [jeune végétal] seedling, young plant ▸ **plant de vigne** young vine ▸ **plant de tomate** tomato plant.

plantage [plɑ̃taʒ] nm *fam fam* INFORM crash.

plantaire [plɑ̃tɛr] adj plantar.

plantation [plɑ̃tasjɔ̃] nf 1. [opération] planting 2. [culture] plant, crop 3. [exploitation agricole] plantation.

plante¹ [plɑ̃t] nf 1. BOT plant ▸ **plante verte / à fleurs** green / flowering plant ▸ **plante textile / fourragère** fibre / fodder plant ▸ **plante grasse / vivace** succulent / perennial ▸ **plante d'appartement** ou **d'agrément** house ou pot plant ▸ **plante grimpante** creeper, climbing plant ▸ **plante d'intérieur** pot plant, indoor plant ▸ **plante médicinale** medicinal plant / *se soigner par les plantes* to use herbal remedies 2. EXPR **une belle plante** *fam* : *c'est une belle plante* she's a fine figure of a woman.

plante² [plɑ̃t] nf ANAT ▸ **la plante du pied** the sole of the foot.

planter [3] [plɑ̃te] vt 1. AGR & HORT to plant ▸ **allée plantée d'acacias** avenue lined with acacia trees 2. [enfoncer] to stick ou to drive in *(sép)* ; [avec un marteau] to hammer in *(sép)* 3. [dépeindre - personnage] to sketch (in) ▸ **planter le décor** a) THÉÂTRE to set the scenery b) LITTÉR to set the scene 4. *fam* [abandonner - personne, voiture] to dump, to ditch ; [- travail, projet] to pack in *(sép)*. ⬩ **se planter** vpi 1. *fam* [se tromper] to get it wrong / *on s'est complètement plantés, c'est infaisable* we've got it completely wrong, it can't be done 2. *fam* [dans un accident] to (have a) crash 3. *fam* [échouer] to make a complete mess of things 4. *fam* [ordinateur] to crash.

planteur, euse [plɑ̃tœr, øz] nm, f planter.

planton [plɑ̃tɔ̃] nm MIL orderly ▸ **faire le planton** *fam* to stand about ou around (waiting).

plantureux, euse [plɑ̃tyʀø, øz] adj [aux formes pleines - femme, beauté] buxom ; [- poitrine] full, generous.

plaque [plak] nf 1. [surface - de métal] plate ; [- de marbre] slab ; [- de verre] plate, pane ; [revêtement] plate ; [pour commémorer] plaque ▸ **plaque de cheminée** fire back ▸ **plaque minéralogique** ou **d'immatriculation** number plate 🇬🇧, license plate 🇺🇸 2. ÉLECTR plate ▸ **plaque d'accumulateur** accumulator plate ; ÉLECTRON plate, anode 3. PHOT plate 4. CULIN [de four] baking tray ; 🇨🇭 [moule] cake tin ▸ **plaque chauffante** hot plate ▸ **plaque (de cuisson)** hot plate 5. ANAT & MÉD [sur la peau] patch ▸ **plaque dentaire** (dental) plaque 6. RAIL turntable ; *fig* hub. ⬩ **plaque tournante** nf hub ; *fig* nerve centre.

plaqué, e [plake] adj JOAILL plated / *plaqué d'or* ou gold-plated / *plaqué d'argent* ou *argent* silver-plated. ⬩ **plaqué** nm JOAILL ▸ **c'est du plaqué** a) [or] it's gold-plated b) [argent] it's silver-plated.

plaquer [3] [plake] vt 1. MENUIS to veneer 2. JOAILL to plate 3. MÉTALL to clad 4. [mettre à plat] to lay flat / *les cheveux plaqués sur le front* hair plastered down on the forehead / *je l'ai plaqué contre le mur / au sol* I pinned him to the wall / ground **5.** *fam* [abandonner - personne, travail, situation] to dump, to ditch ; [- amant, conjoint] to jilt / *j'ai envie de tout plaquer* I feel like packing ou chucking it all in **6.** SPORT to tackle ; *fig* [personne en fuite] to rugby-tackle **7.** MUS [accord] to strike, to play.

plaquette [plakɛt] nf **1.** [petite plaque] ▸ **plaquette commémorative** commemorative plaque **2.** COMM ▸ **plaquette de beurre** pack of butter ▸ **plaquette de chocolat** bar of chocolate ▸ **plaquette de pilules** blister-pack of pills **3.** AUTO ▸ **plaquette de frein** brake pad.

plasma [plasma] nm **1.** BIOL plasma ▸ **plasma sanguin** blood plasma **2.** PHYS plasma.

plastic [plastik] nm plastic explosive.

plastifier [9] [plastifje] vt [recouvrir de plastique] to cover in ou with plastic / *une couverture plastifiée* a plastic-coated cover.

plastique [plastik] ◆ adj ART plastic. ◆ nm [matière] plastic. ⬥ **en plastique** loc adj plastic.

plastiquer [3] [plastike] vt to blow up (*sép*), to bomb.

plastronner [3] [plastʀɔne] vi [parader] to swagger ou to strut around.

plat¹ [pla] nm **1.** [contenant] dish **2.** [préparation culinaire] dish ▸ **plat cuisiné** precooked ou ready-cooked dish ▸ **le plat du jour** the dish of the day, today's special / *elle aime les bons petits plats* she enjoys good food **3.** [partie du menu] course ▸ **le plat principal** ou **de résistance** the main course ou dish ▸ **faire (tout) un plat de qqch** *fam* to make a big deal out of ou a great fuss about sthg.

plat², **e** [pla, plat] adj **1.** [plan, horizontal - terrain] flat, level ; [- mer] still **2.** [sans hauteur - casquette] flat ▸ **chaussures plates** ou **à talons plats** flat shoes **3.** [obséquieux] cringing, fawning / *je vous fais mes plus plates excuses* please accept my most humble apologies. ⬥ **plat** nm **1.** [partie plate] (part) ▸ **le plat de la main / d'une épée** the flat of the hand / a sword **2.** [lieu plan] ▸ **sur le plat** on the flat ou level ; ÉQUIT [course] flat race **3.** *fam* [plongeon] belly-flop ▸ **faire un plat** to belly-flop **4.** [EXPR] **faire du plat à qqn** *fam* a) [à une femme] to chat sb up [UK], to give sb a line [US] b) [à son patron] to butter sb up [UK], to sweet-talk sb. ⬥ **à plat** loc adj **1.** *fam* [fatigué] (all) washed out **2.** *fam* [déprimé] down / *il est très à plat* he's feeling very low ou down **3.** [pneu, batterie, pile] flat. ◆ loc adv [horizontalement] flat ▸ **mettre qqch à plat** a) [robe] to unpick (and lay out the pieces) b) [projet, problème] to examine from all angles ▸ **tomber à plat** [plaisanterie] to fall flat.

platane [platan] nm plane tree.

plateau, x [plato] nm **1.** [présentoir] tray ▸ **plateau à fromages** cheeseboard ▸ **plateau de fruits de mer** seafood platter **2.** THÉÂTRE stage ; CINÉ set ; TV panel / *nous avons un beau plateau ce soir* TV we have a wonderful line-up for you in the studio tonight **3.** MÉCAN & TECHNOL [d'un électrophone] turntable ; [d'une balance] plate, pan ; [d'un véhicule] platform **4.** [d'une courbe] plateau / *faire un* ou *atteindre son plateau* to reach a plateau, to level off **5.** GÉOGR plateau, tableland ▸ **plateau continental** continental shelf **6.** [d'une table] top.

plateau-repas [platoʀəpa] (*pl* plateaux-repas) nm TV [à la maison] dinner ; [dans un avion] in-flight meal.

plate-bande [platbɑ̃d] (*pl* plates-bandes) nf HORT [pour fleurs] flowerbed, bed ; [pour arbustes, herbes] bed.

platée [plate] nf [pleine assiette] plate, plateful ; [plein plat] dish, dishful ; *fam* [portion] big helping.

plate-forme (*pl* plates-formes), **plateforme** [platfɔʀm] nf **1.** TRANSP [d'un train, d'un bus] platform **2.** PÉTR rig ▸ **plate-forme de forage en mer** off-shore oil rig **3.** INFORM platform.

platement [platmɑ̃] adv [servilement] cringingly, fawningly ▸ **s'excuser platement** to give a cringing apology.

platine [platin] ◆ nm platinum. ◆ nf ACOUST ▸ **platine laser** CD player.

platitude [platityd] nf [lieu commun] platitude, commonplace, trite remark.

platonique [platɔnik] adj [amour] platonic.

plâtre [plɑtʀ] nm **1.** CONSTR plaster **2.** MÉD [matériau] plaster ; [appareil] plaster cast **3.** ART [matériau] plaster ; [objet] plaster cast ou model.

plâtrer [3] [plɑtʀe] vt MÉD [accidenté] to plaster (up) ; [membre] to put in plaster [UK] ou a cast / *je suis allé à l'hôpital pour me faire plâtrer le bras* I went to hospital to have my arm put in plaster.

plâtrier [plɑtʀije] nm [maçon] plasterer.

plausible [plozibl] adj plausible, credible, believable.

play-back (*pl* play-back), **playback*** [plɛbak] nm ▸ **il chante en play-back** he's miming (to a tape).

playlist, play-list [plɛlist] nf playlist.

plébiscite [plebisit] nm [scrutin] plebiscite.

plébisciter [3] [plebisite] vt **1.** [élire] to elect by (a) plebiscite **2.** [approuver] to approve (by a large majority) / *les spectateurs plébiscitent notre émission* viewers overwhelmingly support our programme.

pléiade [plejad] nf *sout* [grand nombre de] group, pleiad *litt* ▸ **une pléiade de vedettes** a glittering array of stars.

plein, e [plɛ̃, plɛn] adj **1.** [rempli] full / *avoir les mains pleines* to have one's hands full ▸ **plein à ras bord de** brimming with ▸ **plein de** full of / *une pièce pleine de livres* a room full of books / *être plein d'enthousiasme / de bonne volonté* to show great enthusiasm / willingness ▸ **plein aux as** *fam* loaded, stinking rich ▸ **plein à craquer** a) [valise] bulging, bursting, crammed full b) [salle] packed ▸ **être plein (comme) une barrique** ou **une outre** *fam* to be (well) tanked up **2.** [complet] full ▸ **plein temps, temps plein** full-time ▸ **être** ou **travailler à temps plein** to work full-time ▸ **avoir les pleins pouvoirs** to have full powers **3.** [chargé] busy, full / *j'ai eu une journée pleine* I've had a busy day **4.** [en intensif] ▸ **une pleine carafe de** a jugful of ▸ **être en pleine forme** to be on top form ▸ **embrasser qqn à pleine bouche** to kiss sb full on the mouth ▸ **rire à pleine gorge** to laugh one's head off ▸ **respirer à pleins poumons** to take deep breaths ▸ **plein tube** *fam*, **pleins tubes** *fam*: *mettre la radio (à) pleins tubes* to put the radio on full blast / *foncer / rouler (à) plein tube* to go / to drive flat out ▸ **pleins feux sur** spotlight on ▸ **pleins gaz** *fam*, **pleins pots** *fam* full throttle ▸ **pleins phares** full beam [UK], high beams [US] **5.** [arrondi] full / *avoir des joues pleines* to have chubby cheeks, to be chubby-cheeked **6.** ZOOL [vache] in calf ; [jument] in foal ; [chatte] pregnant **7.** JEUX [couleur] full **8.** ASTRON & MÉTÉOR full ▸ **la pleine mer** high tide. ⬥ **plein** ◆ nm **1.** [de carburant] full tank ▸ **faire le plein** to fill up / *le plein, s'il vous plaît* fill her ou it up, please / *faire le plein de vitamines / soleil* *fig* to stock up on vitamins / sunshine ; [de courses] : *on fait le plein une fois par mois au supermarché* we stock up once a month at the supermarket **2.** [en calligraphie] downstroke. ◆ adv *fam* ▸ **tout plein** [très] really / *il est mignon tout plein, ce bébé* what a cute little baby. ◆ prép ▸ **tout dans** all over / *j'ai des plantes plein ma maison* my house is full of plants, I have plants all over the house / *avoir de l'argent plein les poches fig* to have loads of money ▸ **en avoir plein les bottes de qqch** *fam* to be fed up with sthg ▸ **en avoir plein le dos** *fam* ou **le cul** *tfam*: *j'en ai plein le dos* ou *le cul* I've had it up to here ▸ **en mettre plein la vue à qqn** *fam* to put on a show for sb. ⬥ **à plein** loc adv : *les moteurs / usines tournent à plein* the engines / factories are working to full capacity /

utiliser des ressources à plein to make full use of resources. **❖ de plein air, en plein air** loc adj open-air *(modif)*. **❖ de plein droit** loc adv ▸ **exiger** ou **réclamer qqch de plein droit** to demand sthg as of right ou as one's right. **❖ de plein fouet** loc adj head on. ◆ loc adv head on, full on / *les deux véhicules se sont heurtés de plein fouet* the vehicles hit each other head on ou full on. **❖ en plein** loc adv **1.** [en entier] in full, entirely **2.** [complètement, exactement] ▸ **en plein dans /sur** right in the middle of / on top of. **❖ en plein, en pleine** loc prép [au milieu de, au plus fort de] ▸ **en plein air** in the open (air) ▸ **en pleine campagne** right out in the country / *en pleine figure* ou *fam poire* right in the face ▸ **en plein jour** in broad daylight / *en pleine mer* (out) in the open sea / *en pleine nuit* in the middle of the night / *en plein soleil* in full sunlight ▸ **en plein vol** in mid-flight. **❖ plein de** loc dét *fam* lots of / *il y avait plein de gens dans la rue* there were crowds ou masses of people in the street.

pleinement [plɛnmɑ̃] adv wholly, fully, entirely / *je suis pleinement convaincu* I'm fully convinced ▸ **profiter pleinement de qqch** to make the most of sthg.

plein-temps [plɛ̃tɑ̃] (*pl* **pleins-temps**) nm full-time job / *faire un plein-temps* to work full-time, to have a full-time job.

plénier, ère [plenje, ɛʁ] adj plenary.

plénitude [plenityd] nf [satisfaction totale] fulfilment.

pléonasme [pleɔnasm] nm pleonasm.

pléthore [pletɔʁ] nf ▸ **pléthore de** an excess of / *il y a pléthore de candidats à ce poste* far too many candidates have applied for the post.

pléthorique [pletɔʁik] adj excessive, overabundant, plethoric *litt*.

pleurer [5] [plœʁe] ◆ vi **1.** PHYSIOL to cry ; [verser des larmes] to cry, to weep / *pleurer de joie / rage* to cry for joy / with rage / *j'en pleurais de rire* ! I laughed so much that I cried! / *l'histoire est bête / triste à pleurer* the story is so stupid / sad you could weep ▸ **faire pleurer qqn** to make sb cry ▸ **pleurer à chaudes larmes** ou **comme une Madeleine** *fam* ou **comme un veau** *fam* ou **comme une fontaine** *fam* to cry ou to bawl one's eyes out **2.** [se lamenter] ▸ **pleurer sur** to lament, to bemoan, to bewail / *pleurer sur soi-même* ou *son sort* to bemoan one's fate. ◆ vt **1.** [répandre] to cry, to shed, to weep ▸ **pleurer toutes les larmes de son corps** to cry one's eyes out **2.** *sout* [être en deuil de] to mourn / *nous pleurons notre cher père* we're mourning (for) our dear father ; [regretter] to lament, to bemoan.

pleurésie [plœʁezi] nf pleurisy.

pleurnicher [3] [plœʁniʃe] vi [sangloter] to whimper ; [se plaindre] to whine, to whinge 🇬🇧.

pleurnicheur, euse [plœʁniʃœʁ, øz] nm, f [qui sanglote] whimperer ; [qui se plaint] whiner, whinger 🇬🇧.

pleurs [plœʁ] nmpl *litt* tears ▸ **en pleurs** in tears.

pleutre [pløtʁ] *litt* ◆ adj cowardly, faint-hearted, lily-livered. ◆ nm coward.

pleuvoir [68] [pløvwaʁ] ◆ v impers to rain ▸ **il pleut** it's raining / *on dirait qu'il va pleuvoir* it looks like rain ▸ **il pleut à seaux** ou **à verse** ou *fam* **des cordes** ou *fam* **des hallebardes** it's raining cats and dogs ou stair rods 🇬🇧. ◆ vi [coup] to rain down, to fall like rain ; [insulte] to shower down.

pli [pli] nm **1.** [repli - d'un éventail, d'un rideau, du papier] fold ; [- d'un pantalon] crease / *le drap fait des plis* the sheet is creased ou rumpled ▸ **pli d'aisance** inverted pleat ▸ **faux pli** crease / *ça ne fait pas un pli fam* it goes without saying **2.** [habitude] habit / *c'est un pli à prendre* you've (just) got to get into the habit **3.** [ride] wrinkle, line, crease ;

[bourrelet] fold ▸ **pli du bras** bend of the arm **4.** JEUX trick ▸ **faire un pli** to win ou to take a trick **5.** COUT pleat.

pliable [plijabl] adj foldable ▸ **difficilement pliable** hard to fold.

pliant, e [plijɑ̃, ɑ̃t] adj folding, collapsible. **❖ pliant** nm folding stool.

plier [10] [plije] ◆ vt **1.** [journal, carte] to fold ▸ **plier bagage** to pack up and go **2.** [tordre - fil de fer, doigt, genou] to bend ▸ **plié en deux** *fam* ou **en quatre** *fam* (**de rire**) doubled up (with laughter). ◆ vi **1.** [se courber] to bend (over), to bow / *les branches pliaient sous le poids des fruits / de la neige* the branches were weighed down with fruit / snow **2.** [se soumettre] to yield, to give in, to give way ▸ **plier devant qqn** to submit ou to yield to sb. **❖ se plier** vpi [meuble, appareil] to fold up ou away ; [personne, corps] to bend, to stoop. **❖ se plier à** vp + prép [se soumettre à] to submit to ; [s'adapter à] to adapt to / *c'est une discipline à laquelle il faut se plier* you have to accept the discipline.

plinthe [plɛ̃t] nf CONSTR [en bois] skirting (board) 🇬🇧, baseboard 🇺🇸, mopboard 🇺🇸 ; [en pierre] skirting.

plissé, e [plise] adj **1.** VÊT pleated **2.** [ridé - front, visage] wrinkled, creased.

plisser [3] [plise] vt **1.** [froncer - yeux] to screw up (*sép*) ; [- nez] to wrinkle / *la contrariété plissait son front* his brow was furrowed with worry **2.** COUT to pleat. **❖ se plisser** vpi [se rider] to crease, to wrinkle.

pliure [plijyʁ] nf [marque] fold.

plomb [plɔ̃] nm **1.** MÉTALL lead ▸ **il n'a pas de plomb dans la tête** ou **cervelle** he's got nothing between the ears ▸ **ça te mettra un peu de plomb dans la tête** ou **cervelle** that will knock some sense into you ▸ **avoir du plomb dans l'aile a)** [entreprise] to be in a sorry state ou bad way **b)** [personne] to be in bad shape ou on one's last legs **2.** ÉLECTR fuse ▸ **faire sauter les plombs** to blow the fuses **3.** PÊCHE sinker. **❖ de plomb** loc adj lead *(modif)*.

plombage [plɔ̃baʒ] nm [d'une dent] filling.

plombe [plɔ̃b] nf *tfam* hour.

plomber [3] [plɔ̃be] vt [dent] to fill, to put a filling in.

plomberie [plɔ̃bʁi] nf **1.** [installation] plumbing **2.** [profession] plumbing.

plombier [plɔ̃bje] nm [artisan] plumber.

plonge [plɔ̃ʒ] nf washing-up, washing the dishes ▸ **faire la plonge** to wash dishes *(in a restaurant)*.

plongeant, e [plɔ̃ʒɑ̃, ɑ̃t] adj plunging / *il y a une vue plongeante jusqu'à la mer* the view plunges down to the sea.

plongée [plɔ̃ʒe] nf LOISIRS & SPORT (underwater) diving / *il fait de la plongée depuis deux ans* he has been diving for two years ▸ **plongée sous-marine** skin ou scuba diving ▸ **plongée avec tuba** snorkelling.

plongeoir [plɔ̃ʒwaʁ] nm diving board.

plongeon [plɔ̃ʒɔ̃] nm **1.** [dans l'eau] dive **2.** FOOT dive / *faire un plongeon* to dive.

plonger [17] [plɔ̃ʒe] ◆ vi **1.** LOISIRS & SPORT to dive ; [en profondeur] to dive, to go skin ou scuba diving / *il plongea du haut du rocher* he dived off the rock ; FOOT to dive **2.** [descendre - avion] to dive ; [- sous-marin] to dive ; [- oiseau] to dive, to swoop ; [- racine] to go down **3.** ▸ **plonger dans** [s'absorber dans] to plunge into, to absorb o.s. in / *elle plongea dans la dépression* she plunged into depression. ◆ vt [mettre] to plunge / *la panne a plongé la pièce dans l'obscurité* the power failure plunged the room into darkness / *plonger son regard dans* to look deep ou deeply into ▸ **plonger qqn dans l'embarras** to put sb in a difficult spot ▸ **être plongé dans** to be deep in / *j'étais plongé* *dans mes pensées / comptes* I was deep in thought / in my accounts / *être plongé dans le désespoir* to be deep in despair / *je suis plongé dans Proust pour l'instant* at the moment, I'm completely immersed in Proust / *il est plongé dans ses dossiers* he's engrossed in his files / *plongé dans un sommeil profond, il ne nous a pas entendus* as he was sound asleep, he didn't hear us. ❖ **se plonger dans** vp + prép [bain] to sink into ; [études, travail] to throw o.s. into ; [livre] to bury o.s. in.

plongeur, euse [plɔ̃ʒœʀ, øz] nm, f **1.** LOISIRS & SPORT diver ▶ **plongeur sous-marin** skin ou scuba diver **2.** [dans un café] washer-up 🇬🇧, dishwasher 🇺🇸.

plot [plo] nm **1.** ÉLECTR contact ; [dans un commutateur] contact block **2.** [bille de bois] block **3.** SPORT block **4.** 🇨🇭 [billot] wooden block.

plouc [pluk] nm *fam & péj* yokel, bumpkin, hick 🇺🇸.

plouf [pluf] interj splash.

ployer [13] [plwaje] vi *litt* [arbre] to bend ; [étagère, poutre] to sag.

plug-and-play [plœgœndplɛ] nm INFORM plug-and-play.

pluie [plɥi] nf MÉTÉOR rain / *le temps est à la pluie* it looks like rain ▶ **pluie battante** driving rain / *pluie diluvienne* ou *torrentielle* pouring rain / *(petite) pluie fine* drizzle ▶ **pluies acides** ÉCOL acid rain ▶ **faire la pluie et le beau temps** to be powerful. ❖ **en pluie** loc adv : *verser la farine en pluie dans le lait* sprinkle the flour into the milk.

plumage [plyma3] nm plumage, feathers.

plumard [plymaʀ] nm *tfam* bed, sack.

plume [plym] nf **1.** [d'oiseau] feather ▶ **j'y ai laissé des plumes** *fam* I didn't come out of it unscathed **2.** [pour écrire] quill ; [de stylo] nib ▶ **dessiner à la plume** to draw in pen and ink.

plumeau, x [plymo] nm feather duster.

plumer [3] [plyme] vt **1.** [oiseau] to pluck **2.** *fam* [escroquer] to fleece.

plumier [plymje] nm pencil box ou case.

plupart [plypaʀ] ❖ **la plupart** nf most / *quelques-uns sont partis mais la plupart ont attendu* some left but most (of them) waited. ❖ **la plupart de** loc prép most (of) ▶ **la plupart du temps** most of the time / *dans la plupart des cas* in the majority of ou in most cases. ❖ **pour la plupart** loc adv mostly, for the most part / *les clients sont pour la plupart satisfaits* the customers are mostly satisfied ou for the most part satisfied.

pluralisme [plyʀalism] nm pluralism.

pluralité [plyʀalite] nf plurality.

pluriculturel, elle [plyʀikyltyʀɛl] adj multicultural.

pluridisciplinaire [plyʀidisiplinɛʀ] adj [approche, démarche, art]] multidisciplinary.

pluriel, elle [plyʀjɛl] adj GRAM plural. ❖ **pluriel** nm plural / *la troisième personne du pluriel* the third person plural / **au pluriel** in the plural ▶ **le pluriel de majesté** the royal "we".

pluriethnique [plyʀiɛtnik] adj multiethnic.

plurilinguisme [plyʀilɛ̃gɥism] nm multilingualism.

plus [ply(s)]
◆ adv

A. COMPARATIF DE SUPÉRIORITÉ **1.** [suivi d'un adverbe, d'un adjectif] : *viens plus souvent* (do) come more often ▶ **plus tôt** earlier ▶ **plus tard** later ▶ **à plus tard** see you later ▶ **c'est plus loin** it's further ou farther / *tu es plus patient que moi* you're more patient than I am ou than me / *c'est plus fatigant qu'on ne le croit* it's more tiring than it seems / *c'est plus que gênant* it's embarrassing, to say the least / *elle a eu le prix mais elle n'en est pas plus fière pour ça*

she got the award, but it didn't make her any prouder for all that / *je veux la même, en plus large* I want the same, only bigger / *encore plus beau* more handsome still, even more handsome / *cinq fois plus cher* five times dearer ou as dear ou more expensive **2.** [avec un verbe] more / *j'apprécie plus son frère* I like his brother more ou better / *je ne peux vous en dire plus* I can't tell you any more **3.** (avec un nom) : *cela représente plus qu'une simple victoire* it means more than just a victory.

B. SUPERLATIF DE SUPÉRIORITÉ **1.** [suivi d'un adverbe, d'un adjectif] : *le plus loin* the furthest ou farthest / *la montagne la plus haute* the highest mountain / *j'y vais le plus rarement possible* I go there as seldom as possible / *un de ses tableaux les plus connus* one of her best-known paintings / *le plus gros des deux* the bigger of the two / *le plus gros des trois* the biggest of the three / *choisis les fruits les plus mûrs possible* select the ripest possible fruit ▶ **le plus souvent** most of the time ▶ **faites au plus vite** do it as quickly as possible **2.** [précédé d'un verbe] most / *c'est moi qui travaille le plus* I'm the one who works most ou the hardest ▶ **faites-en le plus possible** do as much as you can.

C. ADVERBE DE NÉGATION **1.** [avec 'ne'] ▶ **je n'y retournerai plus** I won't go back there any more / *je ne les vois plus* I don't see them any more **2.** [tour elliptique] ▶ **plus de** no more / *plus de glace pour moi, merci* no more ice cream for me, thanks ▶ **plus un mot !** not another word!

◆ adj ▶ **B plus** ÉDUC B plus.
◆ conj **1.** MATH plus / *3 plus 3 égale 6* 3 plus 3 is ou makes 6 ▶ **il fait plus 5 °C** it's 5 ° above freezing, it's plus 5 ° **2.** [en sus de] plus / *le transport, plus le logement, plus la nourriture, ça revient cher* travel, plus ou and accommodation, plus ou then food, (all) work out quite expensive.
◆ nm **1.** MATH plus (sign) **2.** [avantage, atout] plus, bonus, asset / *la connaissance de l'anglais est toujours un plus* knowledge of English is always a plus. ❖ **au plus** loc adv [au maximum] at the most ou outside / *ça coûtera au plus 40 euros* it'll cost a maximum of 40 euros ou 40 euros at most. ❖ **de plus** loc adv **1.** [en supplément] extra, another, more / *mets deux couverts de plus* lay two extra ou more places / *raison de plus pour y aller* all the more reason for going / *je ne veux rien de plus* I don't want anything more / *un mot / une minute de plus et je m'en allais* another word / minute and I would have left **2.** [en trop] too many / *en recomptant, je trouve trente points de plus* on adding it up again, I get thirty points too many **3.** [en outre] furthermore, what's more, moreover. ❖ **de plus en plus** loc adv **1.** [suivi d'un adjectif] more and more, increasingly ; [suivi d'un adverbe] more and more / *de plus en plus souvent* more and more often / *ça devient de plus en plus facile / compliqué* it's getting easier and easier / more and more complicated **2.** [précédé d'un verbe] : *les prix augmentent de plus en plus* prices are increasing all the time. ❖ **de plus en plus de** loc dét [suivi d'un nom comptable] more and more, a growing number of ; [suivi d'un nom non comptable] more and more / *de plus en plus de gens* more and more people, an increasing number of people / *il y a de plus en plus de demande pour ce produit* demand for this product is increasing, there is more and more demand for this product. ❖ **des plus** loc adv most / *son attitude est des plus compréhensibles* her attitude is most ou quite understandable. ❖ **en plus** loc adv **1.** [en supplément] extra (avant nom) / *c'est le même appartement avec un balcon en plus* it's the same flat with a balcony as well / *les boissons sont en plus* drinks are extra, you pay extra for the drinks / *ça fait 45 minutes de transport en plus* it adds 45 minutes to the journey ; [en trop] spare ▶ **j'ai une carte en plus a)** [à la fin du jeu] I've got one card left over ou **b)** [en distribuant] I've got one card too many ; [en cadeau] as well, on top of that **2.** [en outre] further, furthermore, what's more /

elle a une excellente technique et, en plus, elle a de la force her technique's first-class and she's got strength too / *et elle m'avait menti, en plus !* not only that but she'd lied to me (as well)! **3.** [d'ailleurs] besides, what's more, moreover / *je ne tiens pas à le faire et, en plus, je n'ai pas le temps* I'm not too keen on doing it, and besides ou what's more, I've no time. ❖ **en plus de** loc prép [en supplément de] besides, on top of, in addition to / *en plus du squash, elle fait du tennis* besides (playing) squash, she plays tennis. ❖ **et plus** loc adv over / *les gens de 30 ans et plus* people aged 30 and over. ❖ **ni plus ni moins** loc adv no more no less, that's all / *je te donne une livre, ni plus ni moins* I'll give you one pound, no more no less. ❖ **non plus** loc adv : *moi non plus je n'irai pas* I won't go either / *je ne sais pas — moi non plus !* I don't know — neither do I ou nor do I ou me neither! ❖ **on ne peut plus** loc adv : *je suis on ne peut plus désolé de vous voir partir* I'm ever so sorry you're leaving. ❖ **plus de** loc dét **1.** [comparatif, suivi d'un nom] more / *nous voulons plus d'autonomie !* we want more autonomy! / *je n'ai pas plus de courage qu'elle* I'm no braver than she is ou her ; [suivi d'un nombre] more than, over / *il y a plus de 15 ans de cela* it's more than 15 years ago now / *elle a bien plus de 40 ans* she's well over 40 / *il est plus de 5 h* it's past 5 o'clock ou after 5 **2.** [superlatif, suivi d'un nom] ▸ **le plus de** (the) most / *c'est ce qui m'a fait le plus de peine* that's what hurt me (the) most / *celui qui a le plus de chances de réussir* the one (who's the) most likely to succeed / *le plus d'argent possible* as much money as possible ; *(comme nom)* : *les plus de 20 ans* people over 20, the over-20s. ❖ **plus... moins** loc corrélative the more... the less / *plus il vieillit, moins il a envie de sortir* the older he gets, the less he feels like going out. ❖ **plus... plus** loc corrélative the more... the more / *plus je réfléchis, plus je me dis que...* the more I think (about it), the more I'm convinced that... / *plus ça va, plus il est agressif* he's getting more and more aggressive (all the time). ❖ **plus ou moins** loc adv more or less / *c'est plus ou moins cher, selon les endroits* prices vary according to where you are. ❖ **qui plus est** loc adv what's ou what is more. ❖ **sans plus** loc adv nothing more / *c'était bien, sans plus* it was nice, but nothing more. ❖ **tout au plus** loc adv at the most.

plusieurs [plyzjœʀ] ◆ dét *(adj indéf pl)* several / *en plusieurs endroits* in several places / *plusieurs fois, à plusieurs reprises* several times. ◆ pron indéf pl [désignant des personnes] several people ▸ *se mettre à plusieurs pour faire qqch* to do sthg as a group / *plusieurs (d'entre eux) ont refusé* several of them refused.

plus-que-parfait [plyskəpaʀfɛ] nm pluperfect, past perfect.

plus-value [plyvaly] *(pl* plus-values*)* nf **1.** [augmentation de la valeur] increase (in value), appreciation **2.** [surcoût] surplus value **3.** [bénéfice] capital gain, profit / *réaliser une plus-value* to make a profit.

plutonium [plytɔnjɔm] nm plutonium.

plutôt [plyto] adv **1.** [de préférence] rather ; [à la place] instead ▸ *plutôt mourir !* I'd rather die! / *demande plutôt à un spécialiste* you'd better ask a specialist ▸ *plutôt que* rather than, instead of / *plutôt que de travailler, je vais aller faire des courses* I'm going to do some shopping instead of working **2.** [plus précisément] rather / *la situation n'est pas désespérée, disons plutôt qu'elle est délicate* the situation is not hopeless, let's say rather that it is delicate / *ce n'était pas une maison de campagne, mais plutôt un manoir* it wasn't a country house, it was more of a country house **3.** [assez, passablement] rather, quite **4.** [en inten-

sif] : *il est plutôt collant, ce type !* fam that guy's a bit of a leech! / *il est idiot, ce film ! — plutôt, oui !* it's stupid, this film! — you can say that again ou you're telling me!

pluvial, e, aux [plyvjal,o] adj pluvial *spéc*, rainy.

pluvieux, euse [plyvjø,øz] adj [temps, journée] rainy, wet ; [climat] wet, damp.

pluviosité [plyvjozite] nf (average) rainfall.

PME (abr de **petite et moyenne entreprise**) nf small business ▸ *les* **PME** small and medium-sized firms.

PMR (abr écrite de **personnes à mobilité réduite**) nf PRM.

PMU® (abr de **Pari Mutuel Urbain®**) npr m *French betting authority* ; ≃ tote 🇬🇧 ; ≃ pari-mutuel 🇺🇸.

PMU

These initials, often posted outside bars in France, indicate that there is a counter inside where bets on horse races can be placed.

PNB (abr de **produit national brut**) nm GNP.

pneu [pnø] nm AUTO tyre 🇬🇧, tire 🇺🇸 ▸ **pneu clouté** spiked tyre ▸ **pneu neige** snow tyre.

pneumatique [pnømatik] adj [gonflable] inflatable, blow-up *(avant nom)*.

pneumologue [pnømɔlɔg] nmf pneumologist.

pneumonie [pnømɔni] nf pneumonia.

poche [pɔʃ] ◆ nf **1.** VÊT pocket ; [d'un sac] pocket, pouch ▸ *s'en mettre plein les* ou *se remplir les poches* fam to line one's pockets ▸ **en être de sa poche** : *j'en ai été de ma poche* I was out of pocket ▸ *c'est dans la poche !* fam it's in the bag! **2.** [boursouflure] bag / *avoir des poches sous les yeux* to have bags under one's eyes ▸ *faire des poches aux genoux / coudes* to go baggy at the knees / elbows **3.** [amas] pocket ▸ **poche d'air** air pocket **4.** MIL ▸ **poche de résistance** pocket of resistance **5.** 🇨🇭 [louche] ladle. ◆ nm [livre] paperback (book). ❖ **de poche** loc adj [collection, édition] pocket *(modif)* ; [cuirassé, théâtre] pocket *(modif)*, miniature *(avant nom)*. ❖ **en poche** loc adv **1.** [avec soi - argent] on me / you, etc. / [- diplôme] under one's belt / *elle est repartie, contrat en poche* she left with the contract signed and sealed **2.** [livre] in paperback / *il est sorti en poche* he's come out in paperback.

poché, e [pɔʃe] adj **1.** [œuf] poached **2.** [meurtri] ▸ *avoir un œil poché* to have a black eye.

pocher [3] [pɔʃe] vt CULIN [œuf, poisson] to poach.

pochette [pɔʃɛt] nf **1.** VÊT (breast) pocket handkerchief **2.** [sac - de femme] (small) handbag ; [- d'homme] clutch bag **3.** [sachet] wallet, envelope **4.** [d'un disque] sleeve, cover, jacket 🇺🇸.

pochette-surprise [pɔʃɛtsyʀpʀiz] *(pl* pochettes-surprises*)* nf lucky bag 🇬🇧, surprise pack 🇺🇸.

pochoir [pɔʃwaʀ] nm [plaque évidée] stencil.

podcast [pɔdkast] nm podcast.

podcaster [pɔdkaste] vt [une émission] to podcast.

podcasting [pɔdkastiŋ] nm podcasting.

podiatre [pɔdjatʀ] nmf 🇶🇨 MÉD podiatrist.

podiatrie [pɔdjatʀi] nf 🇶🇨 MÉD podiatry.

podiatrique [pɔdjatʀik] adj 🇶🇨 MÉD podiatric.

podium [pɔdjɔm] nm [plate-forme] podium ▸ **monter sur le podium** SPORT to mount the podium.

podologue [pɔdɔlɔg] nmf chiropodist, podiatrist 🇺🇸.

poêle [pwal] ◆ nm [chauffage] stove ; [en céramique] furnace ▸ **poêle à mazout** oil ou oil-fired stove. ◆ nf [ustensile] ▸ **poêle (à frire)** frying pan.

poêlon [pwalɔ̃] nm casserole.

poème [pɔɛm] nm **1.** LITTÉR poem **2.** fam EXPR *ta fille, c'est un poème !* your daughter's really something else!

poésie [pɔezi] nf **1.** [genre] poetry **2.** [poème] poem.

poète [pɔɛt] ◆ nm [auteur] poet. ◆ adj [allure, air] poetic, of a poet.

poétique [pɔetik] adj poetic, poetical.

pognon [pɔɲɔ̃] nm fam readies ⓊⓀ, dough ⓊⓈ / *ils ont plein de pognon* they're rolling in it ⓊⓀ ou in dough ⓊⓈ.

poids [pwa] nm **1.** PHYS weight ▸ **prendre / perdre du poids** to gain / to lose weight ▸ **poids brut / net** gross / net weight / *il ne fait pas le poids face aux spécialistes* he's no match for ou not in the same league as the experts / *j'ai peur de ne pas faire le poids* I'm afraid of being out of my depth **2.** [objet - gén, d'une horloge] weight / *avoir un poids sur l'estomac* fig to feel bloated / *ça m'a enlevé un poids* it's taken a weight off my mind **3.** SPORT ▸ **poids et haltères** weightlifting ; [lancer] shotputting, shot ; [instrument] shot ; BOXE [catégorie] ▸ **poids coq** bantamweight ▸ **poids léger** lightweight ▸ **poids lourd** heavyweight ▸ **poids mouche** flyweight ▸ **poids moyen** middleweight ▸ **poids plume** featherweight ; [aux courses] weight **4.** [importance] influence, weight / *son avis a du poids auprès du reste du groupe* her opinion carries weight with the rest of the group. ◈ **au poids** loc adv [vendre] by weight. ◈ **de poids** loc adj [alibi, argument] weighty. ◈ **sous le poids de** loc prép [sous la masse de] under the weight of. ◈ **poids lourd** nm **1.** TRANSP heavy (goods) vehicle ou lorry ⓊⓀ ou truck ⓊⓈ **2.** ⟶ **poids**. ◈ **poids mort** nm MÉCAN & fig dead weight.

poignant, e [pwaɲɑ̃, ɑ̃t] adj heartrending, poignant.

poignard [pwaɲaʁ] nm dagger ▸ **coup de poignard** stab / *recevoir un coup de poignard* to get stabbed.

poignarder [3] [pwaɲaʁde] vt to stab, to knife ▸ **poignarder qqn dans le dos** pr & fig to stab sb in the back.

poigne [pwaɲ] nf grip ▸ **avoir de la poigne a)** pr to have a strong grip **b)** fig to rule with a firm hand. ◈ **à poigne** loc adj firm, authoritarian, iron-handed.

poignée [pwaɲe] nf **1.** [contenu] handful, fistful **2.** [petit nombre] handful / *une poignée de manifestants* a handful of demonstrators **3.** [pour saisir - gén] handle ▸ **poignée de porte** door handle. ◈ **par poignées** loc adv in handfuls. ◈ **poignée de main** nf handshake ▸ **donner une poignée de main à qqn** to shake hands with sb, to shake sb's hand.

poignet [pwaɲɛ] nm **1.** ANAT wrist **2.** VÊT cuff ; [bande de tissu] wristband.

poil [pwal] nm **1.** ANAT hair ▸ **sans poils** hairless ▸ **il n'a plus un poil sur le caillou** fam he's bald as a coot ⓊⓀ ou an egg ▸ **avoir un poil dans la main** fam to be bone-idle ▸ **être de bon / mauvais poil** fam to be in a good / foul mood ▸ **reprendre du poil de la bête a)** fam [guérir] to perk up again **b)** [reprendre des forces] to regain some strength for a fresh onslaught **2.** fam [infime quantité] : *c'est un poil trop cher* it's a touch (too) expensive ▸ **un poil de** : *il n'a pas un poil d'intégrité* he doesn't have one ounce ou a shred of integrity / *il n'y a pas un poil de vrai dans ce qu'il dit* there's not an ounce of truth in what he says / *manquer son train d'un poil* ou *à un poil près* to miss one's train by a hair's breadth ou a whisker **3.** [pelage - long] hair, coat ; [- court] coat ▸ **chien à poil ras / long** smooth-haired / long-haired dog ▸ **manteau en poil de chameau** camel-hair coat **4.** [d'une brosse] bristle ; [d'un pinceau] hair, bristle ; [d'un tapis] pile ; [d'un pull angora]

down. ◈ **à poil** fam ◆ loc adj stark naked, starkers. ◆ loc adv starkers ⓊⓀ, in the altogether / *se mettre à poil* to strip (off). ◈ **au poil** fam ◆ loc adj terrific, great / *tu peux venir samedi, au poil !* you can come on Saturday, great! ◆ loc adv terrifically. ◈ **au quart de poil, au petit poil** loc adv fam perfectly / *ça a marché au quart de poil* it's all gone exactly according to plan. ◈ **de tout poil** loc adj fam & hum of all kinds / *voleurs et escrocs de tout poil* all manner of thieves and crooks.

poilant, e [pwalɑ̃, ɑ̃t] adj fam hilarious, side-splitting.

poil de carotte [pwaldəkaʁɔt] adj inv [cheveux] red ; [enfant] red-haired / *être poil de carotte* to be red-haired, to have carroty-red hair.

poiler [3] [pwale] ◈ **se poiler** vpi fam [rire] to laugh fit to burst ; [s'amuser] to have a ball.

poilu, e [pwaly] adj hairy.

poinçon [pwɛ̃sɔ̃] nm **1.** JOAILL [marque] hallmark **2.** [de graveur] stylus ; [de sculpteur] chisel.

poinçonner [3] [pwɛ̃sɔne] vt **1.** [ticket] to punch **2.** JOAILL to hallmark.

poindre [82] [pwɛ̃dʁ] litt vi [lumière] to break / *dès que le jour poindra* as soon as dawn breaks, at daybreak.

poing [pwɛ̃] nm fist / *taper du poing sur la table* to bang one's fist on ou to thump the table ▸ **revolvers / armes au poing** : *ils sont entrés, revolvers / armes au poing* they came in, guns / arms at the ready.

point¹ [pwɛ̃] v ⟶ **poindre**.

point² [pwɛ̃] nm **1.** [marque] point, dot, spot ; [sur un dé, un domino] pip, spot / *un corsage à petits points bleus* a blouse with blue polka dots ▸ **point lumineux** spot ou point of light **2.** [petite quantité] spot, dab, blob / *un point de soudure* a spot ou blob of solder **3.** [symbole graphique - en fin de phrase] full stop ⓊⓀ, period ⓊⓈ ; [- sur un i ou un j] dot ; [- en morse, en musique] dot ; MATH point ▸ **mettre les points sur les i** fig to spell it out ▸ **point d'exclamation** exclamation mark ou ⓊⓈ point ▸ **point d'interrogation** pr & fig question mark ▸ **points de suspension** ellipsis, suspension points ⓊⓈ ▸ **point final** full stop ⓊⓀ, period ⓊⓈ / *j'ai dit non, point final* ou *un point c'est tout !* fig I said no and that's that ou that's final ou there's an end to it! ▸ **point, à la ligne !** pr new paragraph! / *il a fait une bêtise, point à la ligne !* he did something stupid, let's leave it at that! **4.** AÉRON & NAUT [position] position ▸ **faire le point a)** NAUT to take a bearing, to plot one's position **b)** fig to take stock (of the situation) / *on fera le point vendredi* we'll get together on Friday and see how things are progressing / *et maintenant, le point sur la circulation* and now, the latest traffic news **5.** GÉOM point ▸ **point d'intersection / de tangence** intersection / tangential point **6.** [endroit] point, spot, place ▸ **point chaud** trouble spot ▸ **point de non-retour** point of no return ▸ **point de rassemblement** meeting point ▸ **point névralgique a)** MÉD nerve centre **b)** fig sensitive spot ▸ **point de rencontre** meeting point ▸ **point de vente** retail outlet **7.** [douleur] twinge, sharp pain ; MÉD pressure point ▸ **point de côté** stitch **8.** [moment, stade] point, stage / *à ce point de la discussion* at this point in the discussion / *les pourparlers en sont toujours au même point* the negotiations haven't got any further **9.** [degré] point / *si tu savais à quel point je te méprise !* if you only knew how much I despise you! **10.** [élément - d'un texte, d'une théorie] point ; [- d'un raisonnement] point, item ; [- d'une description] feature, trait / *le second point à l'ordre du jour* the second item on the agenda / *un programme social en trois points* a three-point social programme ▸ **point d'entente / de désaccord** point of agreement / of disagreement ▸ **point commun** common feature / *nous n'avons aucun point commun* we have nothing in common ▸ **un**

point de droit DR a point of law **11.** [unité de valeur - dans un sondage, à la Bourse] point ; [- de retraite] unit ; [- du salaire de base] (grading) point ; ENS mark 🇬🇧, point ; JEUX & SPORT point / *sa cote de popularité a gagné / perdu trois points* his popularity rating has gone up / down by three points / *il me manquait 12 points pour avoir l'examen* I was 12 marks short of passing the exam ▸ **bon point** mark (for good behaviour) / *un bon point pour toi !* fig & hum good on 🇬🇧 ou for you!, you get a brownie point! ▸ **mauvais point** ÉDUC black mark (against sb's name) ▸ **marquer un point** pr & fig to score a point **12.** COUT ▸ **faire un point à** to put a stitch ou a few stitches in ▸ **point de couture / crochet / tricot** sewing / crochet / knitting stitch ▸ **point de croix** cross-stitch ▸ **point de jersey** stocking stitch ▸ **point mousse** garter stitch **13.** INFORM [unité graphique] dot **14.** ART & JOAILL point. ❖ **à ce point, à un tel point** loc adv [tellement] so, that / *ton travail est dur à ce point ?* is your job so (very) ou that hard? ❖ **à ce point que, à (un) tel point que** loc conj so much so that, to such a point that / *les choses en étaient arrivées à un tel point que...* things had reached such a pitch that... ❖ **à point** ◆ loc adj [steak] medium ; [rôti] done to a turn ; [fromage] ripe, just right ; [poire] just ou nicely ripe. ◆ loc adv **1.** CULIN : *le gâteau est cuit à point* the cake is cooked (through) **2.** [au bon moment] ▸ **tomber à point** a) [personne] to come (just) at the right time b) [arrivée, décision] to be very timely. ❖ **à point nommé** loc adv ▸ **arriver à point nommé** to arrive (just) at the right moment ou when needed, to arrive in the nick of time. ❖ **au plus haut point** loc adv [énervé, généreux, irrespectueux] extremely, most ; [méfiant] highly, extremely. ❖ **au point** ◆ loc adj PHOT in focus ; [moteur] tuned ; [machine] in perfect running order ; [technique] perfected ; [discours, plaidoyer] finalized ; [spectacle, artiste] ready / *quand ma technique sera au point* when I've perfected my technique. ◆ loc adv ▸ **mettre au point** a) [discours, projet, rapport] to finalize, to put the finishing touches to b) [spectacle] to perfect c) [moteur] to tune d) [appareil photo] to (bring into) focus e) [affaire] to settle, to finalize / *mettre les choses au point* to put ou set the record straight / *tu devrais mettre les choses au point avec lui* you should sort things out between you. ❖ **au point de** loc prép : *il n'est pas stupide au point de le leur répéter* he's not so stupid as to tell them. ❖ **au point du jour** loc adv litt at dawn ou daybreak. ❖ **au point où** loc conj : *nous sommes arrivés au point où...* we've reached the point ou stage where... / *au point où en sont les choses* as things stand, the way things are (now). ❖ **au point que** loc conj so much that, so... that / *il était très effrayé, au point qu'il a essayé de se sauver* he was so frightened that he tried to run away. ❖ **point par point** loc adv point by point. ❖ **sur le point de** loc prép ▸ **être sur le point de faire qqch** to be about to do ou on the point of doing ou on the verge of doing sthg / *j'étais sur le point de partir* I was about to ou going to leave. ❖ **point d'appui** nm **1.** [d'un levier] fulcrum **2.** MIL strongpoint **3.** fig [soutien] support. ❖ **point de chute** nm **1.** ARM point of impact **2.** fig : *j'ai un point de chute à Milan* I have somewhere to stay in Milan. ❖ **point culminant** nm ASTRON zenith ; GÉOGR peak, summit, highest point, fig acme, apex. ❖ **point de départ** nm starting point / *nous voilà revenus au point de départ* pr & fig now we're back where we started. ❖ **point faible** nm weak spot. ❖ **point fort** nm [d'une personne, d'une entreprise] strong point ; [d'un joueur de tennis] best shot / *les maths n'ont jamais été mon point fort* I was never any good at maths, maths was never my strong point. ❖ **point mort** nm **1.** AUTO neutral ▸ **au point mort** a) AUTO in neutral b) fig at a standstill **2.** FIN breakeven. ❖ **point noir** nm

1. MÉD blackhead **2.** [difficulté] difficulty, headache fig. ❖ **point sensible** nm **1.** [endroit douloureux] tender ou sore spot **2.** MIL key ou strategic target.

point³ [pwɛ̃] adv litt **1.** [en corrélation avec 'ne'] : *je ne l'ai point encore vu* I haven't seen him yet **2.** [employé seul] : *du vin il y en avait, mais de champagne point* there was wine, but no champagne ou not a drop of champagne **3.** [en réponse négative] : *point du tout !* not at all!, not in the least!

pointage [pwɛ̃taʒ] nm **1.** [d'une liste, d'un texte] ticking off (U), checking (U), marking (U) **2.** [des ouvriers - à l'arrivée] clocking in ; [- à la sortie] clocking out.

point de vue [pwɛ̃dvy] (pl **points de vue**) nm **1.** [panorama] vista, view **2.** [opinion] point of view, standpoint / *quel est ton point de vue ?* what is your opinion?, where do you stand on this? / *du point de vue des prix, du point de vue prix* pricewise, as far as prices are concerned.

pointe [pwɛ̃t] nf **1.** [extrémité - gén] point, pointed end, tip ; [- d'un cheveu] tip / *la pointe du sein* the nipple / *mets-toi sur la pointe des pieds* stand on tiptoe ou on the tips of your toes / *elle traversa la pièce / monta l'escalier sur la pointe des pieds* she tiptoed across the room / up the stairs / *allons jusqu'à la pointe de l'île* let's go to the farthest point of the island ▸ **pointe d'asperge** asparagus tip **2.** SPORT spike **3.** [accès] peak, burst ▸ **pointe (de vitesse)** burst of speed **4.** sout [moquerie] barb, taunt ; [mot d'esprit] witticism ▸ **lancer des pointes à qqn** to taunt sb **5.** [petite quantité - d'ail] hint ; [- d'ironie, de jalousie] trace, hint, note / *il a une pointe d'accent* he's got a slight accent **6.** [clou] nail, sprig, brad. ❖ **à la pointe de** loc prép to the forefront of / *à la pointe de l'actualité* right up to date / *à la pointe du progrès* in the vanguard (of progress). ❖ **de pointe** loc adj **1.** [puissance, période] peak (avant nom) ▸ **heure de pointe** rush hour ▸ **vitesse de pointe** maximum ou top speed **2.** [secteur, industrie] key (avant nom), leading, growth (modif) ▸ **technologie de pointe** leading-edge technology. ❖ **en pointe** loc adj [menton] pointed ; [décolleté] plunging.

pointer [3] [pwɛ̃te] ◆ vt **1.** [diriger - arme] to aim ; [- doigt] to point / *pointer son fusil vers le plafond* to aim one's rifle at the ceiling **2.** [marquer - liste] to check (off), to tick off (sép) **3.** [contrôler - à l'arrivée] to check in (sép) ; [- à la sortie] to check out (sép). ◆ vi **1.** [apparaître - aube, jour] to be dawning **2.** [ouvrier - arrivant] to clock in ; [- sortant] to clock out ▸ **pointer au chômage** to register unemployed, to sign on 🇬🇧. ❖ **se pointer** vpi fam to show (up), to turn up.

pointillé [pwɛ̃tije] nm [trait] dotted line / *découper suivant le pointillé* cut along the dotted line. ❖ **en pointillé** ◆ loc adj : *les frontières sont en pointillé sur la carte* frontiers are drawn as dotted lines on the map. ◆ loc adv fig in outline / *une solution lui apparaissait en pointillé* he was beginning to see the outline of a solution.

pointilleux, euse [pwɛ̃tijø, øz] adj [personne] fussy, fastidious / *il est très pointilleux sur l'horaire* he's very particular about ou he's a stickler for time-keeping.

pointu, e [pwɛ̃ty] adj **1.** [effilé] sharp, pointed **2.** [perspicace - esprit] sharp, astute ; [- étude] in-depth, astute **3.** [aigu - voix, ton] shrill, sharp ▸ **un accent pointu** [parisien] a clipped Parisian accent **4.** [spécialisé - formation, marché] (very) narrowly-specialized, narrowly-targeted.

pointure [pwɛ̃tyʀ] nf **1.** [de chaussures] size / *quelle est ta pointure ?* what size do you take? **2.** fam & fig : *une grande pointure de la boxe* a big name in boxing.

point-virgule [pwɛ̃viʀgyl] (pl **points-virgules**) nm semicolon.

poire [pwaʀ] nf **1.** [fruit] pear ▸ **nous en avons parlé entre la poire et le fromage** we talked idly about it at the end of the meal **2.** tfam [visage] mug ▸ **prendre qqch en pleine poire** to get smacked in the face ou between the eyes with sthg **3.** fam [imbécile] sucker, mug, dope.

poireau, x [pwaʀo] nm leek.

poireauter [3] [pwaʀote] vi fam to be cooling ou kicking one's heels, to hang around ▸ **faire poireauter qqn** to keep sb hanging around.

poirier [pwaʀje] nm **1.** BOT pear tree **2.** SPORT ▸ **faire le poirier** to do a headstand.

pois [pwa] nm **1.** BOT & CULIN pea **2.** [motif] dot, spot / **un corsage à pois blancs** a blouse with white polka dots. ⬥ **pois chiche** nm chickpea. ⬥ **pois de senteur** nm sweet pea.

poison [pwazɔ̃] nm [substance] poison.

poisse [pwas] nf fam bad ou rotten luck / **quelle poisse !** what rotten luck! ▸ **avoir la poisse** to be really unlucky.

poisseux, euse [pwasø, øz] adj sticky.

poisson [pwasɔ̃] nm **1.** ZOOL fish ▸ **poisson d'eau douce / de mer** freshwater / saltwater fish ▸ **poisson rouge** goldfish ▸ **poisson volant** flying fish ▸ **être comme un poisson dans l'eau** to be in one's element ▸ **engueuler qqn comme du poisson pourri** tfam to scream at sb **2.** CULIN fish. ⬥ **poisson d'avril** nm [farce] April fool ▸ **poisson d'avril !** April fool!

poissonnerie [pwasɔnʀi] nf [magasin] fishmonger's 🇬🇧 ou (fresh) fish shop ; [au marché] fish stall.

poissonneux, euse [pwasɔnø, øz] adj full of fish.

poissonnier, ère [pwasɔnje, ɛʀ] nm, f [personne] fishmonger 🇬🇧, fish merchant 🇺🇸.

Poissons [pwasɔ̃] npr mpl **1.** ASTRON Pisces **2.** ASTROL Pisces / **elle est Poissons** she's Pisces.

poitrail [pwatʀaj] nm ZOOL breast.

poitrine [pwatʀin] nf **1.** [thorax] chest ; [seins] bust, chest / **elle n'a pas beaucoup de poitrine** she's flat-chested **2.** CULIN ▸ **poitrine fumée** ≃ smoked bacon ▸ **poitrine de porc** belly (of) pork ▸ **poitrine salée** ≃ salt belly pork 🇬🇧 ; ≃ salt pork 🇺🇸.

poivre [pwavʀ] nm ▸ **poivre noir** ou **gris** (black) pepper ▸ **poivre blanc** white pepper ▸ **poivre en grains** peppercorns, whole pepper ▸ **poivre moulu** ground pepper. ⬥ **poivre et sel** loc adj inv pepper-and-salt.

poivré, e [pwavʀe] adj **1.** CULIN peppery **2.** [chanson, histoire] spicy, racy.

poivrer [3] [pwavʀe] vt CULIN to pepper.

poivrier [pwavʀije] nm [ustensile] pepper pot 🇬🇧, pepper shaker 🇺🇸.

poivrière [pwavʀijɛʀ] nf [ustensile] pepper pot.

poivron [pwavʀɔ̃] nm sweet pepper, capsicum ▸ **poivron vert / jaune / rouge** green / yellow / red pepper.

poivrot, e [pwavʀo, ɔt] nm, f fam drunkard.

poix [pwa] nf pitch.

poker [pɔkɛʀ] nm JEUX poker ▸ **jouer au poker** to play poker.

polaire [pɔlɛʀ] ◆ adj MATH, SCI & TECHNOL polar. ◆ nf [vêtement] fleece.

polar [pɔlaʀ] nm fam [livre, film] thriller, whodunnit, detective.

polarisé, e [pɔlaʀize] adj [personne] obsessed / **il est complètement polarisé sur sa carrière** he's completely obsessed with his career.

polariser [3] [pɔlaʀize] vt **1.** SCI to polarize **2.** [attention, énergie, ressources] to focus / **il a polarisé l'attention de l'auditoire** he made the audience sit up and listen **3.** [faire se concentrer] ▸ **polariser qqn sur** to make sb concentrate (exclusively) on. ⬥ **se polariser** vpi [se concentrer] ▸ **se polariser sur qqch** to focus on sthg.

pôle [pol] nm **1.** SCI, GÉOGR & MATH pole ▸ **le pôle Nord / Sud** the North / South Pole ▸ **le pôle Nord / Sud magnétique** the magnetic North / South pole / **Toulouse est devenue le pôle (d'attraction) économique de la région** Toulouse has become the focus ou hub of economic development in the region **2.** [centre] ▸ **le Pôle emploi** the body that combines the functions of the former **ASSEDIC** (unemployment benefit office) and **ANPE** (employment office) ▸ **pôle d'activité** [d'entreprise] area of activity ▸ **pôle économique** economic hub ▸ **pôle universitaire** university centre.

polémique [pɔlemik] ◆ adj [article] polemic, polemical, provocative ; [attitude] polemic, polemical, embattled. ◆ nf polemic, controversy.

polémiquer [3] [pɔlemike] vi to be polemical.

poli, e [pɔli] adj **1.** [bien élevé] polite, courteous, well-bred / **ce n'est pas poli de répondre !** it's rude to answer back! / **vous pourriez être poli !** keep a civil tongue in your head! **2.** [pierre] smooth ; [métal] polished ; [marbre] glassed. ◆ **poli** nm [éclat] shine, sheen.

police [pɔlis] nf **1.** [institution] police ▸ **police de l'air et des frontières** airport and border police ▸ **police judiciaire** plain-clothes police force responsible for criminal investigation and arrests ; ≃ CID 🇬🇧 ; ≃ FBI 🇺🇸 ▸ **police mondaine** ou **des mœurs** Vice Squad ▸ **police municipale** ≃ local police ▸ **la Police nationale** the police force (excluding "gendarmes") ▸ **police secours** (police) emergency services ▸ **police technique et scientifique** branch of the French police specialising in forensics ▸ **la police des polices** fam ≃ police complaints committee **2.** [maintien de l'ordre] (enforcement of) law and order / **il n'a jamais voulu faire la police chez lui** he never tried to keep his family in order **3.** IMPR ▸ **police (de caractères)** bill (of fount) **4.** DR ▸ **police d'assurance** insurance policy.

> 📋 Attention, en anglais, police est un nom collectif et le verbe qui lui est associé doit toujours être au pluriel.

polichinelle [pɔliʃinɛl] nm [pantin] (Punch) puppet.

Polichinelle [pɔliʃinɛl] npr [aux marionnettes] Punchinello ; [à la commedia dell'arte] Pulcinella.

policier, ère [pɔlisje, ɛʀ] ◆ adj **1.** [de la police] police (modif) **2.** [roman, film] detective (modif). ◆ nm, f [agent] policeman, police officer / **une policière** a policewoman, a woman police officer. ⬥ **policier** nm [livre] detective story ; [film] detective thriller.

poliment [pɔlimɑ̃] adv politely.

polio [pɔljo] nf polio.

polir [32] [pɔliʀ] vt [métal] to polish (up), to burnish ; [meuble] to polish ; [chaussures] to polish, to clean, to shine ; [ongles] to buff.

polisson, onne [pɔlisɔ̃, ɔn] ◆ adj **1.** [taquin] mischievous, cheeky **2.** [égrillard] saucy, naughty. ◆ nm, f [espiègle] little devil ou rogue ou scamp.

politesse [pɔlites] nf [bonne éducation] politeness, courteousness ▸ **faire / dire qqch par politesse** to do / to say sthg out of politeness.

politicien, enne [pɔlitisjɛ̃, ɛn] ◆ adj [d'habile politique] political / **une manœuvre politicienne** a successful political move. ◆ nm, f politician.

politique [pɔlitik] ◆ adj [de la vie publique] political ▸ **homme politique, femme politique** politician ▸ **les partis politiques** the political parties. ◆ nf **1.** [activité] politics / **faire de la politique** to be involved in politics ▸ **la politique politicienne** péj party politics **2.** [stratégie] policy ▸ **politique intérieure / extérieur** domestic / foreign policy / **une politique de gauche** a left-wing policy ▸ **la poli-**

tique agricole commune the common agricultural policy ▶ **pratiquer la politique de l'autruche** to bury one's head in the sand ▶ **la politique du pire** *deliberately worsening the situation to further one's ends.* ◆ nmf [politicien] politician.

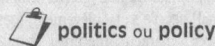 **politics** ou **policy ?**

Politics se réfère à la politique au sens de l'art de gouverner, tandis que a **policy** est une politique au sens d'une stratégie ou d'un ensemble de mesures.

---

politiquement [pɔlitikmɑ̃] adv POL politically.

politiser [3] [pɔlitize] vt to politicize / **ils sont moins / plus politisés** they are less / more interested in politics / **politiser une grève** to give a political dimension to a strike.

pollen [pɔlɛn] nm pollen.

polluant, e [pɔlɥɑ̃, ɑ̃t] adj polluting / **non polluant** non-polluting. ◆ **polluant** nm polluting agent, pollutant.

polluer [7] [pɔlɥe] vt ÉCOL to pollute.

pollueur, euse [pɔlɥœʀ, øz] nm, f polluter.

pollution [pɔlysjɔ̃] nf ÉCOL pollution ▶ **pollution de l'air / des eaux / de l'environnement** air / water / environmental pollution ▶ **pollution acoustique** ou **sonore** noise pollution ▶ **pollution lumineuse** light pollution.

polo [pɔlo] nm **1.** SPORT polo **2.** VÊT polo shirt.

Pologne [pɔlɔɲ] npr f ▶ **(la) Pologne** Poland.

polonais, e [pɔlɔnɛ, ɛz] adj Polish. ◆ **Polonais, e** nm, f Pole. ◆ **polonais** nm LING Polish.

poltron, onne [pɔltʀɔ̃, ɔn] nm, f coward, poltroon *litt.*

polyamide [pɔliamid] nm polyamide.

polyclinique [pɔliklinik] nf polyclinic.

polycopié [pɔlikɔpje] nm [gén] (duplicated) notes ; UNIV lecture handout.

polycopier [9] [pɔlikɔpje] vt to duplicate.

polyculture [pɔlikyltyʀ] nf polyculture, mixed farming.

polyester [pɔliɛstɛʀ] nm polyester.

polygamie [pɔligami] nf polygamy.

polyglotte [pɔliɡlɔt] adj & nmf polyglot.

polyhandicapé, e [pɔliɑ̃dikape] ◆ adj multi-disabled. ◆ nm, f multi-disabled person.

Polynésie [pɔlinezi] npr f ▶ **(la) Polynésie** Polynesia ▶ **(la) Polynésie française** French Polynesia.

polynésien, enne [pɔlinezjɛ̃, ɛn] adj Polynesian. ◆ **Polynésien, enne** nm, f Polynesian. ◆ **polynésien** nm LING Polynesian.

polystyrène [pɔlistiʀɛn] nm polystyrene ▶ **polystyrène expansé** expanded polystyrene.

polytechnicien, enne [pɔliteknisjɛ̃, ɛn] nm, f student or ex-student from the École polytechnique.

polytechnique [pɔliteknik] adj **1.** [polyvalent] polytechnic **2.** ENS polytechnic ▶ **l'École polytechnique** *grande école* for engineers.

 École polytechnique

Founded in 1794, this prestigious engineering college has close connections with the Ministry of Defence. Formerly situated in the heart of the fifth arrondissement, the college moved to Palaiseau, near Paris, in the 1970s. It is popularly known as **l'X**. Students are effectively enlisted in the army and must repay their education through government service.

---

polyvalent, e [pɔlivalɑ̃, ɑ̃t] adj [gén] versatile, adaptable ; [salle] multipurpose ; SCI polyvalent. ◆ **polyvalente** nf **Québec** *secondary school giving both general and vocational courses.*

pommade [pɔmad] nf MÉD [pour brûlures] ointment ; [pour foulures] liniment ; *vieilli* [cosmétique] cream ▶ **pommade pour les lèvres** lip salve ▶ **passer de la pommade à qqn** *fam* to butter sb up.

pomme [pɔm] nf **1.** [fruit] apple ▶ **la pomme de discorde** the bone of contention ▶ **tomber dans les pommes** *fam & fig* to pass out **2.** [légume] potato ▶ **pommes allumettes** *(very thin)* fries ▶ **pommes mousseline** mashed potatoes **3.** ▶ **pomme d'arrosoir** rose *(of a watering can)* ▶ **pomme de douche** shower head. ◆ **pomme d'Adam** nf Adam's apple. ◆ **pomme d'amour** nf [friandise] toffee apple. ◆ **pomme de pin** nf pine ou fir cone.

pommeau, x [pɔmo] nm [d'une canne] knob, pommel.

pomme de terre [pɔmdətɛʀ] *(pl* **pommes de terre)** nf potato / **des pommes de terre frites** chips **UK**, French fries **US**.

pommelé, e [pɔmle] adj **1.** [cheval] dappled **2.** [ciel] mackerel *(modif)*, dappled.

pommette [pɔmɛt] nf cheekbone.

pommier [pɔmje] nm BOT apple tree.

pompe [pɔ̃p] nf **1.** [machine] pump ▶ **pompe à air / chaleur** air / heat pump ▶ **pompe à bicyclette** ou **à vélo** bicycle pump ▶ **pompe à essence a)** [distributeur] petrol pump **UK**, gas pump **US b)** [station] petrol **UK** ou gas **US** station ▶ **pompe à incendie** water pump *(on a fire engine)* **2.** *tfam* [chaussure] shoe ▶ **il est à côté de ses pompes aujourd'hui** he's not quite with it today **3.** [apparat] pomp ▶ **en grande pompe** with great pomp and ceremony. ◆ **pompes** nfpl SPORT press-ups **UK**, push-ups **US**. ◆ **à toute(s) pompe(s)** loc adv *fam* [courir] flat out ; [s'enfuir] like a shot. ◆ **pompes funèbres** nfpl ▶ **(entreprise de) pompes funèbres** undertaker's *(sg)*, funeral director's *(sg)* **UK**, mortician's *(sg)* **US**.

pomper [3] [pɔ̃pe] ◆ vt **1.** [aspirer - pour évacuer] to pump (out) ; [- pour boire] to suck (up) ▶ **pomper l'air à qqn** *fam :* **tu me pompes l'air** you're being a real pain in the neck **2.** *fam* [fatiguer] to wear out *(sép)*, to do in *(sép)* **3.** *arg scol* [copier] to crib. ◆ vi *arg scol* [copier] to crib / **j'ai pompé sur Anne** I cribbed from Anne.

pompette [pɔ̃pɛt] adj *fam* tipsy, tiddly.

pompeux, euse [pɔ̃pø, øz] adj pompous, bombastic.

pompier, ère [pɔ̃pje, ɛʀ] adj ART pompier ; *péj* [style, décor] pretentious, pompous ▶ **art pompier** *official paintings of the second half of the 19th century, today often considered grandiloquent and overconventional (eg certain paintings by Gérôme and Meissonier).* ◆ **pompier** nm [sapeur] fireman ▶ **les pompiers** the fire brigade **UK** ou department **US**.

pompiste [pɔ̃pist] nm petrol pump attendant **UK**, gas station attendant **US**.

pompon [pɔ̃pɔ̃] nm **1.** TEXT & VÊT pompom **2.** *fam* **EXPR** **ça, c'est le pompon !** that's just about the•limit ! ▶ **décerner le pompon à qqn** to give first prize to sb.

pomponner [3] [pɔ̃pɔne] vt ▶ **pomponner qqn** to do sb up nicely, to doll sb up *(sép).* ◆ **se pomponner** vp *(emploi réfléchi)* to do o.s. up nicely, to doll o.s. up.

poncer [16] [pɔ̃se] vt [polir avec un abrasif - mur] to sand-paper, to sand (down) ; [polir avec une machine] to sand (down).

poncif [pɔ̃sif] nm *péj* [cliché] cliché, commonplace, old chestnut.

ponction [pɔ̃ksjɔ̃] nf **1.** MÉD puncture / *ponction lombaire / du ventricule* lumbar / ventricular puncture **2.** [retrait] withdrawal.

ponctionner [3] [pɔ̃ksjɔne] vt [compte en banque] to withdraw money from ; [économies] to make a hole ou dent in / *on nous ponctionne un tiers de notre salaire en impôts* a third of our salary goes in tax.

ponctualité [pɔ̃ktɥalite] nf [exactitude] punctuality, promptness.

ponctuation [pɔ̃ktɥasjɔ̃] nf punctuation.

ponctuel, elle [pɔ̃ktɥɛl] adj **1.** [exact] punctual ▸ **être ponctuel** to be on time **2.** [action] one-off UK, one-shot US ; [problèmes, difficultés] occasional / *l'État accorde une aide ponctuelle aux entreprises en difficulté* the state gives backing to companies to see them through periods of financial difficulty / *nous avons une action ponctuelle dans les entreprises* we visit companies on an irregular basis.

ponctuellement [pɔ̃ktɥɛlmɑ̃] adv **1.** [avec exactitude] punctually **2.** [de façon limitée] on an ad hoc basis ▸ **agir ponctuellement** to take action as the need arises.

ponctuer [7] [pɔ̃ktɥe] vt fig to punctuate.

pondéré, e [pɔ̃dere] adj **1.** [personne] level-headed, steady **2.** [indice, moyenne] weighted.

pondérer [18] [pɔ̃dere] vt **1.** [pouvoirs] to balance (out), to counterbalance **2.** BOURSE & ÉCON to weight.

🖉 In reformed spelling (see p. 16-18), this verb is conjugated like *semer* : *il pondèrera, elle pondèrerait.*

pondre [75] [pɔ̃dʀ] ◆ vt **1.** [suj : oiseau] to lay **2.** [créer - gén] to come up with ; [- en série] to churn out *(sép).* ◆ vi [poule] to lay (an egg) ; [moustique, saumon, etc.] to lay its eggs.

poney [pɔne] nm pony.

pongiste [pɔ̃ʒist] nmf table tennis player.

pont [pɔ̃] nm **1.** TRAV PUB bridge / *dormir* ou *vivre sous les ponts* to sleep under the arches UK, to be homeless ▸ **pont mobile / suspendu** movable / suspension bridge ▸ **pont à péage** toll-bridge ▸ **faire / promettre un pont d'or à qqn** to offer / to promise sb a fortune *(so that they'll take on a job)* **2.** NAUT deck ▸ **pont arrière** aft ou after deck ▸ **pont avant** foredeck ▸ **tout le monde sur le pont !** a) [levez-vous] everybody up! b) [mettez-vous au travail] let's get down to business! ▸ **être sur le pont** fig to be on the ready **3.** [week-end] long weekend ; [jour] day off between a national holiday and a weekend ▸ **faire le pont** to take the intervening working day or days off **4.** [structure de manutention] ▸ **pont élévateur** ou **de graissage** garage ramp, car lift, elevator platform **5.** AÉRON ▸ **pont aérien** airlift. ❖ **Ponts et Chaussées** nmpl ▸ **les Ponts et Chaussées** a) ADMIN Department of Civil Engineering b) ENS College of Civil Engineering.

pontage [pɔ̃taʒ] nm MÉD bypass (operation).

ponte[1] [pɔ̃t] nm fam [autorité] ▸ **un (grand) ponte** a bigshot, a bigwig.

ponte[2] [pɔ̃t] nf ZOOL [action] laying (of eggs).

pontifical, e, aux [pɔ̃tifikal, o] adj RELIG [insignes, cérémonie] pontifical ; [États, trône] papal.

pontifier [9] [pɔ̃tifje] vi to pontificate.

pont-levis [pɔ̃ləvi] (pl ponts-levis) nm drawbridge.

ponton [pɔ̃tɔ̃] nm [d'un port de commerce] pontoon, floating dock ; [d'un port de plaisance] landing stage, jetty ; [pour nageurs] (floating) platform.

pool [pul] nm ▸ **pool génétique** genetic pool.

pop [pɔp] ◆ adj *(pl pop ou pops*)* [art, chanteur, mouvement] pop. ◆ nm ou nf pop (music).

pop-corn (pl pop-corn), **popcorn*** [pɔpkɔʀn] nm popcorn.

pope [pɔp] nm (Eastern Orthodox Church) priest.

popote [pɔpɔt] fam nf [repas] ▸ **faire la popote** to do the cooking.

populace [pɔpylas] nf fam & péj rabble, hoi polloi, plebs.

populaire [pɔpylɛʀ] adj **1.** SOCIOL [du peuple] working-class **2.** [tradition, croyance] popular **3.** POL [gouvernement] popular ; [démocratie, tribunal] people's ; [soulèvement] mass *(modif)* **4.** [qui a du succès - chanteur, mesures] popular **5.** LING [étymologie] popular ; [niveau de langue] colloquial.

populariser [3] [pɔpylaʀize] vt ▸ **populariser qqch** to popularize sthg, to make sthg available to all. ❖ se **populariser** vpi to become more (and more) popular.

popularité [pɔpylaʀite] nf popularity.

population [pɔpylasjɔ̃] nf **1.** SOCIOL population ▸ **population active / civile** working / civilian population ▸ **population carcérale / scolaire** prison / school population **2.** [peuple] people / *la population locale* the local people, the locals.

populiste [pɔpylist] ◆ adj HIST Populist. ◆ nmf HIST Populist.

pop-up [pɔpœp] *(pl pop-ups)* nm inv & nm pop-up.

porc [pɔʀ] nm **1.** ZOOL pig UK, hog US **2.** CULIN pork **3.** [peau] pigskin **4.** fam [personne] pig, swine.

porcelaine [pɔʀsəlɛn] nf [produit] china, porcelain. ❖ **de porcelaine, en porcelaine** loc adj [tasse, objet] china *(modif)*, porcelain *(modif)*.

porcelet [pɔʀsəle] nm piglet.

porc-épic [pɔʀkepik] *(pl porcs-épics)* nm ZOOL porcupine.

porche [pɔʀʃ] nm porch.

porcherie [pɔʀʃəʀi] nf pr & fig pigsty.

porcin, e [pɔʀsɛ̃, in] adj [industrie, production] pig *(modif)*.

pore [pɔʀ] nm pore.

poreux, euse [pɔʀø, øz] adj porous.

porno [pɔʀno] fam ◆ adj [film, magazine, scène] porn, porno. ◆ nm **1.** ▸ **le porno** a) [genre] porn b) [industrie] the porn industry **2.** [film] porno film UK, blue movie.

pornographie [pɔʀnɔgʀafi] nf pornography.

pornographique [pɔʀnɔgʀafik] adj pornographic.

port[1] [pɔʀ] nm **1.** [infrastructure] port UK, harbour ; [ville] port ▸ **port maritime** ou **de mer** sea port ▸ **port d'attache** a) NAUT port of registry, home port b) fig home base ▸ **port fluvial** river port ▸ **port franc** free port ▸ **port de pêche** fishing port ▸ **port de plaisance** marina ▸ **port pétrolier** oil terminal **2.** INFORM port ▸ **port parallèle / série** parallel / serial port ▸ **port USB** USB port. ❖ **à bon port** loc adv safely, safe and sound / *les verres sont arrivés à bon port* the glasses got there in one piece ou without mishap.

port[2] [pɔʀ] nm **1.** [d'une lettre, d'un colis] postage ▸ **frais de port** (cost of) postage **2.** TRANSP [de marchandises] carriage ▸ **franco de port** carriage paid ou included **3.** [possession - d'une arme] carrying ; [- d'un uniforme, d'un casque] wearing / *port d'armes prohibé* illegal carrying of weapons / *le port du casque est obligatoire* a crash helmet must be worn.

portable [pɔʀtabl] ◆ adj **1.** [ordinateur, téléviseur, machine à écrire] portable ; [téléphone] mobile UK, cellular US **2.** [vêtement] wearable. ◆ nm [ordinateur] laptop ; [téléphone] mobile (phone) UK, cell (phone) US.

portail [pɔʀtaj] nm **1.** [d'une église] portal ; [d'un jardin, d'une école] gate **2.** INTERNET gateway.

portant, e [pɔʀtɑ̃, ɑ̃t] adj EXPR ▸ **bien / mal portant** in good / poor health. ❖ **portant** nm [pour vêtements] rail.

portatif, ive [pɔʀtatif, iv] adj [machine à écrire, ordinateur] portable.

porte [pɔʀt] nf **1.** [d'une maison, d'un véhicule, d'un meuble] door ; [d'un passe-plat] hatch ▶ **ouvrir ses portes** [magasin, musée] to open ▶ **porte coupe-feu** firedoor ▶ **porte d'entrée** front door ▶ **porte de service** tradesmen's entrance ▶ **porte de sortie** a) *pr* way out, exit b) *fig* way out ▶ **à ma / sa porte** *pr & fig* at my / his door, on my / his doorstep ▶ **la porte à côté**: *Lyon, ce n'est pas la porte à côté* it's a fair way to Lyon / *il n'habite pas la porte à côté* he doesn't exactly live round the corner ▶ **entrer par la grande / petite porte**: *elle est entrée dans l'entreprise par la grande porte* she went straight in at the top of the company ▶ **prendre la porte** to leave ▶ **trouver porte close**: *j'y suis allé mais j'ai trouvé porte close* I went round but nobody was in ou at home / *il a essayé tous les éditeurs, mais partout il a trouvé porte close* he tried all the publishers, but without success ▶ **être la porte ouverte à qqch**: *c'est la porte ouverte à tous les abus* it leaves the door wide open to all kinds of abuses **2.** [passage dans une enceinte] gate ▶ **porte d'embarquement** (departure) gate **3.** [panneau] door (panel) ▶ **porte basculante / battante** up-and-over / swing door ▶ **porte coulissante** ou **roulante** sliding door ▶ **porte palière** landing door ▶ **porte à tambour** revolving door **4.** SPORT gate. ❖ **à la porte** *loc adv* out ▶ **je suis à la porte de chez moi** a) [sans clefs] I'm locked out b) [chassé] I've been thrown out (of my home) ▶ **mettre qqn à la porte** a) [importun] to throw sb out b) [élève] to expel sb c) [employé] to fire ou to dismiss sb. ❖ **de porte à porte** *loc adv* door-to-door / *je mets 40 minutes de porte à porte* it takes me 40 minutes door-to-door.

porte-à-faux [pɔʀtafo] ❖ **en porte(-)à(-)faux** *loc adv* ▶ **être en porte-à-faux** a) [mur] to be out of plumb, to be out of true b) *fig* to be in an awkward position.

porte-à-porte [pɔʀtapɔʀt] nm inv : *faire du porte-à-porte* to sell from door-to-door, to be a door-to-door salesman (saleswoman).

porte-avions (*pl* porte-avions), **porte-avion*** [pɔʀtavjɔ̃] nm aircraft carrier.

porte-bagages (*pl* porte-bagages), **porte-bagage*** [pɔʀtbagaʒ] nm [d'un vélo] rack ; [d'une voiture, d'un train] (luggage) rack.

porte-bébé [pɔʀtbebe] (*pl* porte-bébés) nm **1.** [nacelle] carry-cot **2.** [harnais] baby sling.

porte-bonheur [pɔʀtbɔnœʀ] (*pl* porte-bonheur ou porte-bonheurs*) nm lucky charm.

porte-bouteilles (*pl* porte-bouteilles), **porte-bouteille*** [pɔʀtbutɛj] nm [châssis] wine rack.

porte-cartes (*pl* porte-cartes), **porte-carte*** [pɔʀtakaʀt] nm [portefeuille] card-holder, wallet 🇬🇧, billfold 🇺🇸 (with spaces for cards, photos, etc.).

porte-clefs (*pl* porte-clefs), **porte-clés** (*pl* porte-clés), **porteclé*** [pɔʀtəkle] nm **1.** [anneau] key ring **2.** [étui] key case.

porte-couteau [pɔʀtkuto] (*pl* porte-couteau ou porte-couteaux) nm knife rest.

porte-documents (*pl* porte-documents), **porte-document*** [pɔʀtdɔkymɑ̃] nm document case.

porte-drapeau [pɔʀtdʀapo] (*pl* porte-drapeau ou porte-drapeaux) nm *pr & fig* standard bearer.

portée [pɔʀte] nf **1.** MIL & OPT range ▶ **à** ou **de moyenne portée** medium-range **2.** [champ d'action - d'une mesure, d'une loi] scope ; [impact - d'une décision] impact, significance ; [- d'un événement] consequences, repercussions / *l'incident a eu une portée considérable* the incident had far-reaching consequences / *une découverte d'une grande portée* a far-reaching discovery **3.** ZOOL litter **4.** MUS staff, stave. ❖ **à la portée de** *loc prép* **1.** [près de] close ou near to ▶ **'ne pas laisser à la portée des enfants'** 'keep out of the reach of children' **2.** [pouvant être compris par] : *son livre est à la portée de tous* her book is easily accessible to the ordinary reader **3.** EXPR *ce n'est pas à la portée de toutes les bourses* not everyone can afford it. ❖ **à portée de** *loc prép* within reach of / **à portée de (la) main** within (easy) reach / ▶ **à portée de voix** within earshot.

porte-fenêtre [pɔʀtfənɛtʀ] (*pl* portes-fenêtres) nf French window ou door 🇺🇸.

portefeuille [pɔʀtəfœj] nm **1.** [étui] wallet 🇬🇧, billfold 🇺🇸 **2.** BOURSE portfolio ▶ **portefeuille de titres** portfolio of securities **3.** POL portfolio **4.** ÉCON ▶ **portefeuille d'activités** business portfolio.

portemanteau, **x** [pɔʀtmɑ̃to] nm **1.** [sur pied] hat stand ; [mural] coat rack **2.** [cintre] coat hanger.

portemine [pɔʀtəmin] nm propelling pencil 🇬🇧, mechanical pencil 🇺🇸.

porte-monnaie (*pl* porte-monnaie), **porte-monnaie*** [pɔʀtmɔnɛ] nm purse 🇬🇧, change purse 🇺🇸.

porte-parapluies [pɔʀtparaplui] nm inv umbrella stand.

porte-parole [pɔʀtparɔl] (*pl* porte-parole ou porte-paroles*) nmf [personne] spokesperson, spokesman (spokeswoman).

porte-plume (*pl* porte-plume ou porte-plumes), **porteplume*** [pɔʀtəplym] nm pen holder.

porter [3] [pɔʀte]

❖ vt

A. TENIR, SUPPORTER 1. [soutenir - colis, fardeau, meuble] to carry ; [- bannière, pancarte, cercueil] to carry, to bear / *deux piliers portent le toit* two pillars take the weight of ou support the roof ▶ **porter qqn sur son dos / dans ses bras** to carry sb on one's back / in one's arms ; *fig* ▶ **porter la responsabilité de** to bear (the) responsibility for **2.** [soutenir moralement - suj : foi, religion] to give strength to, to support / *c'est l'espoir de le retrouver qui la porte* the hope of finding him again keeps her going.

B. METTRE, AMENER 1. [amener] to take, to bring ▶ **porter qqch à qqn** to take sthg to sb / *se faire porter un repas* to have a meal brought (to one) ; [mettre] ▶ **porter une œuvre à l'écran / à la scène** to adapt a work for the screen / the stage / *porter une affaire devant les tribunaux* to take ou to bring a matter before the courts ▶ **porter qqn / qqch à**: *porter qqn au pouvoir* to bring sb to power / *cela porte le total à 306 euros* that brings the total (up) to 306 euros ▶ **porter qqch à ébullition** CULIN to bring sthg to the boil **2.** [diriger] ▶ **porter sa** ou **la main à sa tête** to raise one's hand to one's head / *porter son regard vers* ou *sur* to look towards ou in the direction of **3.** [enregistrer - donnée] to write ou to put down (*sép*) / *porter sa signature sur un registre* to sign a register ▶ **se faire porter absent / malade** to go absent / sick ▶ **porter qqn disparu** to report sb missing **4.** [appliquer - effort, énergie] to direct, to bring, to bear ▶ **porter son attention sur** to focus one's attention on, to turn one's attention to ▶ **porter une accusation contre qqn** to bring a charge against sb **5.** [inciter] ▶ **porter qqn à qqch**: *mon intervention l'a portée à plus de clémence* my intervention made her inclined ou prompted her to be more lenient / *tout porte à croire que...* everything leads one to believe that... ▶ **être porté sur** *fam*: *il est porté sur la boisson* ou *bouteille* he likes a drink **5.** [éprouver] ▶ **porter de l'intérêt à qqn / qqch** to be interested in sb / sthg / *je lui porte beaucoup d'amitié* I hold him very dear ▶ **l'amour qu'il lui portait** the love he felt for her.

C. AVOIR SUR SOI, EN SOI 1. [bijou, chaussures, lunettes, vêtement] to wear, to have on (*sép*) ; [badge, décoration] to wear ; [barbe, couettes, moustache, perruque] to have ;

[cicatrice] to bear, to have, to carry ; [pistolet, stylo] to carry / *porter les cheveux longs / courts / relevés* to wear one's hair long / short / up **2.** [laisser voir - trace] to show, to bear ; [- date, inscription] to bear / *l'étui portait ses initiales gravées* the case was engraved with his initials / *elle portait la résignation sur son visage* resignation was written all over ou on her face **3.** [nom, prénom, patronyme] to have / *il porte le nom de Legrand* he's called Legrand / *c'est un nom difficile à porter* it's not an easy name to be called by **4.** [en soi] to carry, to bear / *l'espoir / la rancune que je portais en moi* the hope / resentment I bore within me **5.** MÉD [virus] to carry / *tous ceux qui portent le virus* all carriers of the virus **6.** [enfant, petit, portée] to carry **7.** AGR & HORT [fruits] to bear ▶ **porter ses fruits** *fig* to bear fruit.
◆ vi **1.** [son, voix] to carry / *aussi loin que porte la vue* as far as the eye can see ; [canon, fusil] ▶ **porter à** to have a range of **2.** [faire mouche - critique, mot, plaisanterie] to hit ou to strike home ; [- observation] to be heard ou heeded ; [- coup] to hit home, to tell **3.** [cogner] : *c'est le crâne qui a porté* the skull took the impact ou the full force **4.** [dans l'habillement masculin] : *porter à droite / gauche* to dress on the right / left. ❖ **porter sur** v + prép **1.** [concerner - suj : discussion, discours, chapitre, recherches] to be about, to be concerned with ; [- suj : critiques] to be aimed at ; [- suj : loi, mesures] to concern ; [- suj : dossier, reportage] to be about ou on **2.** [reposer sur - suj : charpente] to rest on. ❖ **se porter**
◆ vp *(emploi passif)* [bijou, chaussures, vêtement] to be worn / *les manteaux se porteront longs cet hiver* coats will be (worn) long this winter. ◆ vpi **1.** [personne] ▶ **comment vous portez-vous ?** how do you feel?, how are you (feeling)? / *à bientôt, portez-vous bien !* see you soon, look after yourself! **2.** [se proposer comme] ▶ **se porter acquéreur de qqch** to offer to buy sthg ▶ **se porter candidat** to put o.s. up ou to stand 🇬🇧 ou to run 🇺🇸 as a candidate ▶ **se porter caution** to stand security **3.** [aller] ▶ **se porter au-devant de qqn** to go to meet sb / *tout son sang s'est porté à sa tête* the blood rushed to his head. ❖ **se porter sur** vp + prép [choix, soupçon] to fall on ; [conversation] to turn to / *tous les regards se portèrent sur elle* all eyes turned towards her.

porte-savon [pɔʀtsavɔ̃] (*pl* porte-savon ou porte-savons) nm soap dish.

porte-serviettes [pɔʀtsɛʀvjɛt] (*pl* porte-serviettes) nm inv towel rail.

porteur, euse [pɔʀtœʀ, øz] ◆ adj **1.** [plein d'avenir] promising / *un marché porteur* a buoyant market / *une idée porteuse* an idea with great potential **2.** [chargé] : *un vaccin porteur d'espoir* a vaccine which brings new hope. ◆ nm, f **1.** MÉD carrier **2.** [de bagages] porter ; [de nouvelles, d'une lettre] bearer. ❖ **porteur** nm BANQUE & BOURSE bearer / *payable au porteur* payable to bearer ; [actionnaire] shareholder, stockholder 🇺🇸.

porte-voix, portevoix* [pɔʀtəvwa] nm inv [simple] megaphone ; [électrique] loud-hailer 🇬🇧, bullhorn 🇺🇸.

portier, ère [pɔʀtje, ɛʀ] nm, f commissionaire 🇬🇧, doorman (doorwoman). ❖ **portière** nf [d'un véhicule] door.

portillon [pɔʀtijɔ̃] nm [d'une porte cochère] wicket ; [dans le métro] ▶ **portillon automatique** ticket barrier.

portion [pɔʀsjɔ̃] nf [part - de nourriture] portion, helping ; [- d'argent] share, cut ▶ **portion congrue** (income providing) a meagre living. ❖ **en portions** loc adj in individual helpings.

portique [pɔʀtik] nm [dispositif de sécurité] security gate.

porto [pɔʀto] nm port (wine).

portoricain, e [pɔʀtɔʀikɛ̃, ɛn] adj Puerto Rican. ❖ **Portoricain, e** nm, f Puerto Rican.

Porto Rico [pɔʀtoʀiko] npr Puerto Rico.

portrait [pɔʀtʀɛ] nm **1.** [dessin, peinture, photo] portrait ▶ **faire le portrait de qqn** a) [dessinateur] to draw sb's portrait b) [peintre] to paint sb's portrait ▶ **portrait de famille** family portrait ▶ **être tout le portrait** ou **le portrait vivant de qqn** to be the spitting image of sb **2.** *fam* [figure] : *il lui a abîmé le portrait* he rearranged his face (for him) *hum* **3.** [description] portrayal, description, portrait ▶ **faire** ou **tracer le portrait de qqn** to portray sb.

portraitiste [pɔʀtʀetist] nmf portraitist.

portrait-robot [pɔʀtʀeʀɔbo] (*pl* portraits-robots) nm **1.** [d'un criminel] Photofit ou Identikit picture **2.** [caractéristiques] typical profile.

portuaire [pɔʀtɥɛʀ] adj port *(modif)*, harbour *(modif)* 🇬🇧, harbor *(modif)* 🇺🇸.

portugais, e [pɔʀtygɛ, ɛz] adj Portuguese. ❖ **Portugais, e** nm, f Portuguese ▶ **les Portugais** the Portuguese. ❖ **portugais** nm LING Portuguese.

Portugal [pɔʀtygal] npr m ▶ **le Portugal** Portugal.

POS, Pos [pɔs] nm *abr de* plan d'occupation des sols.

pose [poz] nf **1.** [mise en place] putting in, installing / *la pose de la fenêtre vous coûtera 85 €* it will cost you 85 € to have the window put in / *la pose d'un carrelage* laying tiles / *la pose d'une moquette* fitting ou laying (wall-to-wall) carpet **2.** [attitude] position, posture ▶ **prendre une pose avantageuse** to strike a flattering pose ; [pour un artiste] pose **3.** PHOT [cliché, durée] exposure / *24/36 poses* 24/36 exposures.

posé, e [poze] adj [mesuré - personne] self-possessed, collected, composed ; [- manières, ton] calm, cool, tranquil.

posément [pozemã] adv calmly, coolly.

poser [3] [poze] ◆ vt **1.** [mettre] to put, to lay, to place / *poser ses coudes sur la table* to rest ou to put one's elbows on the table / *poser un sac par terre* to put a bag (down) on the floor ; [cesser d'utiliser] to put away ou down *(sép)* **2.** [installer - papier peint, cadre, tentures, affiche] to put up *(sép)* ; [- antenne] to put up ou *(sép)*, to install ; [- radiateur, alarme] to put in ou *(sép)*, to install ; [- verrou] to fit ; [- cadenas] to put on ou *(sép)* ; [- moquette] to fit, to lay ; [- carrelage, câble, mine, rail, tuyau] to lay ; [- vitre] to put in ; [- placard] to put in, to install ; [- prothèse] to fit, to put in ; [- enduit] to put on ; [- bombe] to plant ▶ **faire poser un double vitrage** to have double-glazing put in ou fitted **3.** [énoncer - question] to ask ; [- devinette] to ask, to set ▶ **poser une question à qqn** to ask sb a question, to put a question to sb ▶ **poser sa candidature** a) [à un emploi] to apply b) POL to stand 🇬🇧 ou run 🇺🇸 for election ▶ **poser un problème** a) [causer des difficultés] to raise ou pose a problem b) [l'énoncer] to set a problem / *elle me pose de gros problèmes* she's a great problem ou source of anxiety to me / *si ça ne pose pas de problème, je viendrai avec mon chien* if it's not a problem (for you) I'll bring my dog **4.** [demander] ▶ **poser des jours de congé** to put in a request for leave **5.** [établir - condition] to state, to lay down ; [- principe, règle] to lay ou to set down *(sép)*, to state / *une fois posées les bases du projet* once the foundations of the project have been laid down ▶ **poser qqch comme condition / principe** to lay sthg down as a condition / principle **6.** *fam* [mettre en valeur] to establish the reputation of, to give standing to / *une voiture comme ça, ça vous pose* that kind of car gives you a certain status **7.** MATH to put down *(sép)* / *je pose 2 et je retiens 1* put down 2, carry 1. ◆ vi **1.** [pour un peintre, un photographe] to pose, to sit **2.** [fanfaronner] to put on airs, to show off, to pose. ❖ **se poser** vpi **1.** [descendre - avion, hélicoptère] to land, to touch down ; [- papillon] to land, to alight ; [- oiseau] to land, to perch ▶ **se poser en catastrophe** to make an emergency landing / *tous les regards se posèrent sur elle* all eyes turned to her **2.** *fam* [s'asseoir] ▶ **pose-toi**

là sit (yourself) down here **3.** [surgir - question, problème] to arise, to come up **4.** ▶ **se poser en** ou **comme** [se faire passer pour] to pass o.s. off as / *je ne me suis jamais posé en expert* I never set myself up to be ou I never pretended I was an expert **5.** *fam* EXPR ▶ **se poser là** [il est brillant] : *pour l'intelligence, son frère se pose là !* her brother's got quite a brain ! / *comme gaffe, ça se pose là !* that's what you might call a blunder !

poseur, euse [pozœʀ, øz] nm, f **1.** [m'as-tu-vu] poseur, show-off **2.** [installateur] ▶ **poseur de** : *poseur de parquet / carrelage* floor / tile layer / *les poseurs de bombes se sont enfuis* those responsible for planting the bombs ou the bombers ran away.

positif, ive [pozitif, iv] adj **1.** [constructif - mesures, suggestion, attitude] positive, constructive ; [- réaction, échos, critique] favourable UK, favorable US **2.** [affirmatif - réponse] positive. ◆ **positif** nm **1.** [quelque chose de constructif] : *il nous faut du positif* we need something positive **2.** LING, MATH & PHOT positive.

position [pozizjɔ̃] nf **1.** MIL [lieu d'où l'on mène une action] position ▶ **être en position de combat** to be ready to attack ▶ **position de repli** MIL & *fig* fall-back position **2.** [lieu où l'on se trouve] position **3.** [dans un sondage, une course] position, place ▶ **arriver en première / dernière position** a) [coureur] to come first / last b) [candidat] to come top / be last **4.** [posture] posture, position / *tu as une mauvaise position* you've got bad posture ▶ **dans la** ou **en position verticale** when standing up ▶ **dans la** ou **en position allongée** when lying down ▶ **dans la** ou **en position assise** when sitting, in a sitting position **5.** [opinion] position, stance, standpoint ▶ **prendre position pour** ou **en faveur de qqch** to come down in favour of sthg ▶ **prendre position contre qqch** to come out against sthg ▶ **rester sur ses positions** *pr & fig* to stand one's ground, to stick to one's guns **6.** [situation] position, situation / *vous me mettez dans une position délicate* you're putting me in a difficult situation ou position ▶ **en position de** : *en position de force* in a strong position ou a position of strength ▶ **être en position de faire qqch** to be in a position to do sthg ; [dans une entreprise] position, post.

positionner [3] [pozisjɔne] vt **1.** ÉCON [produit] to position **2.** [localiser] to locate, to determine the position of. ◆ **se positionner** vp *(emploi réfléchi)* to position o.s., to get into position ; [dans un débat] to take a stand.

positivement [pozitivmɑ̃] adv positively.

positiver [pozitive] vi to think positive.

posologie [pozɔlɔʒi] nf [instructions] dosage.

posséder [18] [pɔsede] vt **1.** [détenir - demeure, collection, fortune, terres] to own, to possess, to have ; [- colonies] to have ; [- preuve, document, titre, ticket] to hold, to have ; [- arme, armée] to possess **2.** [être doté de - talent, mémoire] to possess, to have **3.** [maîtriser - art, langue] to have mastered ▶ **(bien) posséder son sujet** to be master ou on top of one's subject **4.** *fam* [tromper - suj : escroc] to con, to have / *je me suis fait posséder* I've been conned ou had.

✏ In reformed spelling (see p. 16-18), this verb is conjugated like *semer* : *il possédera, elle posséderait*.

possesseur [pɔsesœʀ] nm [propriétaire - d'une maison, d'une collection, d'une fortune] owner, possessor ; [- d'un hôtel, d'une ferme] owner, proprietor ; [- d'une charge, d'un ticket] holder ; [- d'un titre] incumbent, holder ; [- de documents] possessor, holder.

possessif, ive [pɔsesif, iv] adj LING & PSYCHOL possessive.

possession [pɔsesjɔ̃] nf **1.** [détention - d'une maison, d'un hôtel, d'une collection, d'une fortune] ownership, possession ; [- d'informations] possession ; [- d'actions, d'un diplôme] holding ; [- charge, d'un titre] possession, hold-

ing ; [- d'un poste] tenure ▶ **avoir qqch en sa possession** to have sthg in one's possession ▶ **être en possession de** to be in possession of ▶ **prendre possession de** a) [maison] to take possession of b) [fonctions] to take up **2.** DR possession **3.** [territoire] possession, dominion.

possibilité [pɔsibilite] nf [chose envisageable ou faisable] possibility. ◆ **possibilités** nfpl [financières] means / *la maison était au-dessus de nos possibilités* we couldn't afford the house ; [intellectuelles, physiques] possibilities, potential ; [techniques] facilities.

possible [pɔsibl] ◆ adj **1.** [réalisable - gén] possible ; [- construction] feasible / *il est possible de dire / de faire* it is possible to say / to do / *il est toujours possible d'annuler la réunion* the meeting can always be cancelled / *j'ai fait tout ce qu'il m'était techniquement possible de faire* I did everything that was technically possible ; [par exagération] : *ce n'est pas possible d'être aussi maladroit !* how can anyone be so clumsy! **2.** [probable] possible / *il est possible que je vous rejoigne plus tard* I may ou might join you later / *il t'aime — c'est bien possible, mais moi pas !* he loves you — quite possibly ou that's as may be, but I don't love him! **3.** [pour exprimer l'étonnement] : *elle est morte hier — c'est pas possible !* fam she died yesterday — I can't believe it! / *pas possible ! c'est ta fille ?* fam is this your daughter? well, I never! **4.** [envisageable - interprétation, explication, option] possible **5.** [potentiel] possible / *je l'ai cherché dans tous les endroits possibles* I looked for it everywhere imaginable ou in every possible place / *il a eu tous les problèmes possibles et imaginables pour récupérer son argent* he had all kinds of problems getting his money back ▶ **bougez le moins possible** move as little as possible / *je veux un rapport aussi détaillé que possible* I want as detailed a report as possible. ◆ nm ▶ **le possible** the possible / *c'est dans le domaine du possible* it's within the bounds of possibility, it's quite possible ▶ **faire (tout) son possible** to do one's best ou all one (possibly) can ou one's utmost. ◆ **au possible** loc adv in the extreme ▶ **ennuyeux au possible** extremely boring.

postal, e, aux [pɔstal, o] adj [colis] (sent) by post UK ou mail ; [frais, service, tarif] postal.

poste[1] [pɔst] nm **1.** RADIO & TV ▶ **poste (de) radio / télévision** (radio) / television set **2.** TÉLÉC [appareil] telephone ; [d'un standard] extension / *passez-moi le poste 1421* give me extension 1421 **3.** [métier] post, job, position / *un poste à pourvoir* a post to be filled, a vacancy **4.** [local, installation] ▶ **poste d'aiguillage** signal box ▶ **poste de douane** customs post ▶ **poste d'incendie** fire point ▶ **poste de péage** tollbooth ▶ **poste de police** police station ▶ **poste de secours** first-aid post **5.** MIL : *être / rester à son poste* pr & *fig* to be / to stay at one's post ▶ **poste de commandement** command post ▶ **poste de contrôle** checkpoint ▶ **poste d'observation / d'écoute / de surveillance** pr & *fig* observation / listening post **6.** FIN [d'un compte] item, entry ; [d'un budget] item **7.** INDUST [division du temps] shift ▶ **poste de travail** a) [emplacement] workplace b) [emploi] job **8.** CHASSE hide.

poste[2] [pɔst] nf **1.** [établissement] post office ▶ **poste restante** poste restante UK, general delivery US **2.** [moyen d'acheminement] post UK, mail US ▶ **envoyer qqch par la poste** to send sthg by post UK, to mail sthg US / *mettre une lettre à la poste* to post UK ou to mail US a letter ▶ **poste aérienne** air-mail **3.** ADMIN ▶ **La Poste** the Post Office.

poster[1] [pɔstɛʀ] nm poster.

poster[2] [3] [pɔste] vt **1.** [envoyer - colis, courrier] to post UK, to mail US ▶ **poster un message sur un blog** to post a message on a blog **2.** [placer - garde, complice] to post, to station. ◆ **se poster** vpi [sentinelle] to station ou to post ou to position o.s.

postérieur, e [pɔsteʀjœʀ] adj **1.** [ultérieur - date, époque] later ; [-fait, invention] subsequent, later **/** *le tableau est postérieur à 1930* the picture was painted after 1930 **2.** [de derrière - pattes] hind, rear, back *(modif)* ; [-partie] back, posterior *sout*. ◆ **postérieur** nm *fam* behind, bottom, posterior.

postérieurement [pɔsteʀjœʀmɑ̃] adv later, subsequently, at a later date ▸ **postérieurement à** later than, after.

posteriori [pɔsteʀjɔʀi] ⟶ **a posteriori**.

postériorité [pɔsteʀjɔʀite] nf *sout* posteriority.

postérité [pɔsteʀite] nf **1.** *litt* [lignée] posterity, descendants **2.** [générations futures] posterity ▸ **passer à la postérité a)** [artiste] to become famous, to go down in history **b)** [mot, œuvre] to be handed down to posterity ou to future generations.

posthume [pɔstym] adj [enfant, ouvrage] posthumous **/** *médaille décernée à titre posthume* posthumously awarded medal.

postiche [pɔstiʃ] ◆ adj [cheveux, barbe, chignon] false. ◆ nm [pour homme] toupee ; [pour femme] hairpiece.

postier, ère [pɔstje, ɛʀ] nm, f postal worker.

postillon [pɔstijɔ̃] nm [de salive] ▸ **postillons** spluttering.

postillonner [3] [pɔstijɔne] vi to splutter.

Post-it® [pɔstit] nm inv Post-it®.

postopératoire [pɔstɔpeʀatwaʀ] adj postoperative.

post-scriptum *(pl* post-scriptum), **postscriptum*** [pɔstskʀiptɔm] nm postscript.

postsynchronisation [pɔstsɛ̃kʀɔnizasjɔ̃] nf postsynchronization.

post-traumatique [pɔstʀomatik] *(pl* post-traumatiques)* adj MÉD post-traumatic.

postulant, e [pɔstylɑ̃, ɑ̃t] nm, f [à un emploi] applicant, candidate.

postuler [3] [pɔstyle] vt LOGIQUE & MATH to postulate, to assume. ◆ **postuler à** v + prép to apply for.

posture [pɔstyʀ] nf **1.** [position du corps] posture, position **2.** [situation] position **/** *être en bonne / en mauvaise posture* to be in a good / in an awkward position.

pot [po] nm **1.** [contenant] pot ▸ **pot de chambre a)** (chamber) pot **b)** [pour enfant] pot, potty ▸ **pot à confiture** ou **à confitures** jam jar ▸ **pot de fleurs a)** [vide] flowerpot, plant pot **b)** [planté] flowers in a pot, potted flowers ▸ **tourner autour du pot** to beat around the bush **2.** [contenu] pot, potful ▸ **pot de confiture / miel** jar of jam / honey ▸ **pot de peinture** pot ou can of paint ▸ **petit pot (pour bébé)** (jar of) baby food **3.** *fam* [boisson] drink, jar 🇬🇧, snort 🇺🇸 ; [fête] ▸ **faire un pot** to have a drinks party 🇬🇧 **/** *ils font un pot pour son départ à la retraite* they're having a little get-together for his retirement **4.** *fam* [chance] luck ▸ **avoir du pot a)** [souvent] to be lucky **b)** [à un certain moment] to be in luck ▸ **pas de pot !** hard ou tough luck! ▸ **coup de pot** stroke of luck ▸ **payer plein pot** to pay full fare ou full whack 🇬🇧 **5.** AUTO ▸ **pot d'échappement** exhaust (pipe) 🇬🇧, tail pipe 🇺🇸 ▸ **pot catalytique** catalytic converter ; [silencieux] silencer 🇬🇧, muffler 🇺🇸. ◆ **en pot** loc adj [plante] pot *(modif)*, potted ; [confiture, miel] in a jar. ◆ **pot de colle** nm *fam & fig* nuisance ; *(comme adj)* : *elle est pot de colle* she sticks to you like glue, you just can't get rid of her.

potable [pɔtabl] adj **1.** [buvable] ▸ **eau potable** drinking water ▸ **eau non potable** water unsuitable for drinking **2.** *fam* [acceptable - travail] passable, reasonable ; [-vêtement] wearable.

potache [pɔtaʃ] nm *fam* schoolkid **/** *blague de potache* schoolboy joke.

potage [pɔtaʒ] nm CULIN soup.

potager, ère [pɔtaʒe, ɛʀ] adj [culture] vegetable *(modif)* ; [plante] grown for food, food *(modif)*. ◆ **potager** nm kitchen garden, vegetable plot.

potasse [pɔtas] nf **1.** [hydroxyde] potassium hydroxide, (caustic) potash **2.** [carbonate] (impure) potassium carbonate, potash.

potasser [3] [pɔtase] vt *fam* [discipline, leçon] to swot up 🇬🇧, to bone up on 🇺🇸 ; [examen] to swot up for 🇬🇧, to bone up for 🇺🇸, to cram for.

potassium [pɔtasjɔm] nm potassium.

pot-au-feu [pɔtofø] nm inv CULIN pot-au-feu, beef and vegetable stew.

pot-de-vin [podvɛ̃] *(pl* pots-de-vin)* nm bribe.

pote [pɔt] nm *fam* pal, mate 🇬🇧, buddy 🇺🇸.

poteau, x [pɔto] nm **1.** [mât] post, pole ▸ **poteau indicateur** signpost ▸ **poteau télégraphique** telegraph pole ou post ▸ **poteau (d'exécution)** (execution) stake **2.** SPORT [support de but] post, goal-post ; [dans une course] ▸ **poteau d'arrivée** winning post.

potée [pɔte] nf pork hotpot *(with cabbage and root vegetables)*.

potelé, e [pɔtle] adj plump, chubby.

potence [pɔtɑ̃s] nf **1.** [supplice, instrument] gallows **2.** CONSTR [d'une charpente] post and braces ; [pour une lanterne, une enseigne] support.

potentiel, elle [pɔtɑ̃sjɛl] adj potential ▸ **un client potentiel** a prospective client. ◆ **potentiel** nm [possibilités] potential, potentiality **/** *avoir un certain potentiel* [personne] to have potential.

potentiellement [pɔtɑ̃sjɛlmɑ̃] adv potentially.

poterie [pɔtʀi] nf **1.** [art] pottery **2.** [article] piece of pottery.

potiche [pɔtiʃ] nf **1.** [vase] rounded vase **2.** *fam* [personne] figurehead *fig*, puppet *fig*.

potier, ère [pɔtje, ɛʀ] nm, f potter.

potimarron [pɔtimaʀɔ̃] nm *variety of small pumpkin.*

potin [pɔtɛ̃] nm *fam* [bruit] racket, rumpus ▸ **faire du potin a)** [machine, personne] to make a racket **b)** [scandale, affaire] to cause a furore. ◆ **potins** nmpl *fam* [ragots] gossip, idle rumours.

potion [pɔsjɔ̃] nf potion, draft ▸ **potion magique** magic potion.

potiron [pɔtiʀɔ̃] nm pumpkin.

pot-pourri *(pl* pots-pourris)*, **potpourri*** [popuʀi] nm MUS potpourri, medley.

pou, x [pu] nm **1.** [parasite de l'homme] louse ▸ **des poux** lice **2.** EXPR ▸ **être laid** ou **moche** *fam* **comme un pou** to be as ugly as sin.

pouah [pwa] interj ugh, yuck.

poubelle [pubɛl] nf **1.** [récipient à déchets] dustbin 🇬🇧, trash ou garbage can 🇺🇸 ▸ **mettre** ou **jeter qqch à la poubelle** to put ou to throw sthg in the dustbin ▸ **faire les poubelles** to go scavenging (from the dustbins) **2.** [dépotoir] dumping-ground, rubbish 🇬🇧 ou garbage 🇺🇸 dump.

pouce [pus] nm **1.** ANAT [doigt] thumb ; [orteil] big toe ▸ **se tourner les pouces** *fam* to twiddle one's thumbs **2.** [mesure] inch **/** *on n'avançait pas d'un pouce sur la route* the traffic was solid **/** *je ne changerai pas d'un pouce les dispositions de mon testament* I won't change one jot ou iota of my will **3.** EXPR ▸ **faire du pouce, voyager sur le pouce** 🇶🇧 to hitchhike.

Poucet [pusɛ] npr ▸ **le Petit Poucet** Tom Thumb.

poudre [pudʀ] nf **1.** [aliment, médicament] powder ; [de craie, d'os, de diamant, d'or] dust, powder ▸ **mettre** ou

réduire qqch en poudre to reduce sthg to powder, to pulverize ou to powder sthg ▸ **poudre à laver** washing 🇬🇧 ou soap powder ▸ **poudre à récurer** scouring powder **2.** ARM powder, gunpowder ▸ **poudre à canon** gunpowder **3.** [cosmétique - pour le visage] (face) powder ; [- pour une perruque] powder / **se mettre de la poudre** to powder one's face ou nose **4.** EXPR **prendre la poudre d'escampette** to decamp ▸ **tout ça c'est de la poudre aux yeux** all that's just for show ▸ **poudre de perlimpinpin** [faux remède] quack remedy. ❖ **en poudre** loc adj [amandes, lait] powdered.

poudrerie [pudʀəʀi] nf 🇶🇧 [neige] flurry of snow.

poudreux, euse [pudʀø, øz] adj [terre] dusty ; [substance] powdery. ❖ **poudreuse** nf [neige] powdery snow, powder.

poudrier [pudʀije] nm (powder) compact.

poudrière [pudʀijɛʀ] nf ARM (gun) powder store / **la maison était une vraie poudrière** the house was packed with explosives ; *fig* power keg.

pouf¹ [puf] nm pouf, pouffe.

pouf² [puf] onomat [dans une chute] thump, bump.

pouffer [3] [pufe] vi : *pouffer (de rire)* to titter.

pouilleux, euse [pujø, øz] adj [pauvre et sale - individu] grubby, filthy ; [- restaurant, quartier] shabby, seedy.

poulailler [pulaje] nm **1.** [hangar] hen house ; [cour] hen-run **2.** fam THÉÂTRE ▸ **le poulailler** the gods 🇬🇧, the peanut gallery 🇺🇸.

poulain [pulɛ̃] nm **1.** ZOOL colt **2.** [protégé] (young) protégé.

poulamon [pulamɔ̃] nm 🇶🇧 tomcod.

poule [pul] nf **1.** ZOOL hen ▸ **poule d'eau** moorhen ▸ **la poule aux œufs d'or** the goose that laid the golden eggs ▸ **poule mouillée** drip, wimp, wet 🇬🇧 **2.** CULIN (boiling) fowl **3.** fam [maîtresse] mistress ; fam & péj [femme] bird 🇬🇧, broad 🇺🇸 **4.** fam [terme d'affection] ▸ **ma poule** (my) pet, (my) love **5.** (comme adj) ▸ **c'est une mère poule** she's a real mother hen ▸ **c'est un papa poule** he's a real mother hen *hum* **6.** SPORT pool (in a round robin) / **en poule A, Metz bat Béziers** in group ou pool A Metz beat Béziers.

poulet [pulɛ] nm **1.** CULIN & ZOOL chicken **2.** tfam [policier] cop, copper 🇬🇧.

poulette [pulɛt] nf **1.** ZOOL pullet **2.** fam [terme d'affection] ▸ **ma poulette** (my) pet, (my) love.

pouliche [puliʃ] nf filly.

poulie [puli] nf [roue] pulley ; [avec enveloppe] block.

poulpe [pulp] nm octopus.

pouls [pu] nm MÉD pulse ▸ **prendre le pouls de** [malade] to feel ou to take the pulse of ▸ **prendre ou tâter le pouls de** a) [électoral] to feel the pulse of, to sound out b) [entreprise, secteur] to feel the pulse of.

poumon [pumɔ̃] nm lung ▸ **poumon artificiel** ou **d'acier** artificial ou iron lung.

poupe [pup] nf stern.

poupée [pupe] nf **1.** [figurine] doll ▸ **jouer à la poupée** to play with dolls **2.** fam [jolie femme] doll, looker **3.** fam [bandage] (large) finger bandage.

poupon [pupɔ̃] nm **1.** [bébé] little baby **2.** [jouet] baby doll.

pouponner [3] [pupɔne] vi fam to look after babies ou a baby.

pouponnière [pupɔnjɛʀ] nf nursery (for babies and toddlers who can neither stay with their parents nor be fostered).

pour [puʀ] ❖ prép **1.** [indiquant le lieu où l'on va] for / *partir pour l'Italie* to leave for Italy / *un billet pour Paris* a ticket for ou to Paris **2.** [dans le temps - indiquant le moment] for / *pourriez-vous avoir fini pour lundi / demain ?* could you have it finished for Monday / tomorrow ? / *pour dans une semaine* for a week's time ; [indiquant la durée] for / *partir pour 10 jours* to go away for 10 days / *j'en ai bien pour cinq heures* it'll take me at least five hours **3.** [exprimant la cause] : *je l'ai remercié pour son amabilité* I thanked him for his kindness / *ils se querellent pour des broutilles* they quarrel over trifles / *désolé pour dimanche* sorry about Sunday ▸ **condamné pour vol** found guilty of theft **4.** [exprimant la conséquence] to / *pour la plus grande joie des enfants* to the children's great delight / *il a erré trois heures en forêt pour se retrouver à son point de départ* he wandered for three hours in the forest, only to find he was back where he'd started from / *ce n'est pas pour me déplaire* I can't say I'm displeased with it **5.** [capable de] : *je me suis trompé et il ne s'est trouvé personne pour me le dire* I made a mistake and nobody was capable of telling me **6.** [par rapport à] for / *il est en avance pour son âge* he's advanced for his age / *c'est cher pour ce que c'est* it's expensive for what it is **7.** [avec une valeur emphatique] ▸ **mot pour mot** word for word / *pour un champion, c'est un champion !* that's what I call a (real) champion! **8.** [indiquant une proportion, un pourcentage] per ▸ **cinq pour cent** five per cent / *il faut 200 g de farine pour une demi-livre de beurre* take 200 g of flour to ou for half a pound of butter **9.** [moyennant] ▸ **pour la somme de** for the sum of **10.** [à la place de] for / *prendre un mot pour un autre* to mistake a word for another **11.** [au nom de] for, on behalf of ▸ **pour le directeur** [dans la correspondance] pp Director **12.** [en guise de, en qualité de] ▸ **prendre qqn pour époux / épouse** to take sb to be one's husband / wife ▸ **avoir qqn pour ami / professeur** to have sb as a friend / teacher ▸ **avoir pour conséquence** to have as a consequence / *il se fait passer pour un antiquaire* he claims to be an antique dealer / *le livre a pour titre...* the book's title is..., the book is entitled... **13.** [indiquant l'attribution, la destination, le but] for / *mes sentiments pour elle* my feelings towards ou for her / *tant pis pour lui !* that's too bad (for him)! / *c'est pour quoi faire, ce truc ?* what's that thing for ? ▸ **sirop pour la toux** cough mixture ▸ **pour 4 personnes** a) [recette] serves 4 b) [couchage] sleeps 4 **14.** (suivi de l'infinitif) [afin de] (in order) to / *je suis venu pour vous voir* I'm here ou I've come to see you ; (elliptiquement) : *si tu veux réussir, il faut tout faire pour* if you want to succeed you have to do everything possible **15.** [en faveur de] for, in favour of ▸ **voter pour qqn** to vote for ou in favour of sb ▸ **être pour** to be in favour **16.** [du point de vue de] : *ça compte peu pour toi, mais pour moi c'est tellement important* it matters little to you but to ou for me it's so important **17.** [en ce qui concerne] : *et pour le salaire ?* and what about the salary ? / *ne t'en fais pas pour moi* don't worry about me / *pour certains de nos collègues, la situation est inchangée* as far as some of our colleagues are concerned, the situation has not changed. ❖ nm inv : *peser le pour et le contre* to weigh up the pros and cons. ❖ **pour que** loc conj **1.** [exprimant le but] so that, in order that *sout* / *j'ai pris des places non-fumeurs pour que vous ne soyez pas incommodés par la fumée* I've got non-smoking seats so that you won't be bothered by the smoke **2.** [exprimant la conséquence] : *mon appartement est trop petit pour qu'on puisse tous y dormir* my flat is too small for us all to be able to sleep there.

pourboire [puʀbwaʀ] nm tip ▸ **donner un pourboire à qqn** to give a tip to sb, to tip sb / *j'ai laissé 5 euros de pourboire* I left a 5 euro tip.

pourcentage [puʀsɑ̃taʒ] nm **1.** FIN & MATH percentage **2.** COMM percentage, commission / *être payé au pourcentage* to be paid by commission.

pourchasser [3] [puʀʃase] vt [criminel] to chase, to pursue.

pourparlers [puʀpaʀle] nmpl negotiations, talks ▶ **être / entrer en pourparlers avec qqn** to have / to enter into talks ou negotiations with sb.

pourpre [puʀpʀ] ◆ adj crimson. ◆ nm [couleur] crimson. ◆ nf [teinte] purple (dye).

pourquoi [puʀkwa] ◆ adv why / *pourquoi m'avoir menti ?* why did you lie to me? / *pourquoi chercher des difficultés ?* why make things more complicated? ▶ **pourquoi pas ?** why not? / *elle a bien réussi l'examen, pourquoi pas moi ?* she passed the exam, why shouldn't I? / *pourquoi ça ?* why? / *je ne sais pas pourquoi tu dis ça* I don't know why you're saying that / *voilà pourquoi je démissionne* that's (the reason) why I am resigning, that's the reason for my resignation ▶ **il boude, va savoir** ou **comprendre pourquoi !** he's sulking, don't ask me why! ◆ nm inv : *nous ne saurons jamais le pourquoi de cette affaire* we'll never get to the bottom of this affair / *il s'interroge toujours sur le pourquoi et le comment des choses* he's always bothered about the whys and wherefores of everything.

pourri, e [puʀi] adj **1.** [nourriture] rotten, bad ; [planche, arbre, plante] rotten ▶ **être pourri** [aliment] to have gone bad **2.** fam [mauvais - climat, saison] rotten ; [- individu, système] stinking, rotten / *elle est complètement pourrie ta voiture !* your car is a wreck ou is nothing but a pile of rust! ◆ **pourri** nm [partie pourrie] rotten ou bad part.

pourriel [puʀjɛl] nm ⁅ᴏᴜᴇ́ʙᴇᴄ⁆ INFORM spam message.

pourrir [32] [puʀiʀ] ◆ vi **1.** [se gâter - fruit, légume, viande, œuf] to go rotten, to go bad ou ⁅ᴜᴋ⁆ off ; [- planche, arbre] to rot ; [- végétation, dent] to decay, to rot ; [- chairs] to decay, to putrefy / *pourrir sur pied* to rot on the stalk **2.** fig ▶ **laisser pourrir une situation** to let a situation deteriorate. ◆ vt **1.** [putréfier - nourriture] to rot, to putrefy ; [- végétation, dent] to decay **2.** [gâter - enfant] to spoil **3.**- [pervertir - individu] to corrupt, to spoil ; [- société] to corrupt **4.** [gâcher] : *ça me pourrit la vie* it's ruining my life.

pourriture [puʀityʀ] nf **1.** [état] rottenness **2.** fam [personne] rotten swine.

poursuite [puʀsɥit] nf **1.** [pour rattraper - animal, fugitif] chase / *poursuite en voiture* car chase ▶ **se mettre** ou **se lancer à la poursuite de qqn** to set off in pursuit of sb, to give chase to sb **2.** [prolongation - de pourparlers, d'études, de recherches] continuation / *ils ont décidé la poursuite de la grève* they've decided to carry on ou to continue with the strike **3.** SPORT pursuit. ◆ **poursuites** nfpl DR ▶ **poursuites (judiciaires) a)** [en droit civil] legal proceedings **b)** [en droit pénal] prosecution.

poursuivant, e [puʀsɥivɑ̃, ɑ̃t] nm, f [dans une course] pursuer.

poursuivre [89] [puʀsɥivʀ] vt **1.** [courir après - animal, voleur, voiture] to chase (after), to pursue *sout* **2.** [s'acharner contre - suj : créancier, rival] to hound, to harry, to pursue ; [- suj : image, passé, remords] to haunt, to hound, to pursue ▶ **poursuivre qqn de ses assiduités** to pester sb with one's attentions **3.** [continuer - interrogatoire, récit, recherche, voyage] to go ou to carry on with (*insép*), to continue ; [- lutte] to continue, to pursue ▶ **poursuivre son chemin** to press on ; *(en usage absolu)* : *veuillez poursuivre, Monsieur* please proceed, Sir **4.** [aspirer à - objectif] to pursue, to strive towards (*insép*) ; [- rêve] to pursue **5.** DR ▶ **poursuivre qqn (en justice) a)** [en droit civil] to institute (legal) proceedings against ou to sue sb **b)** [en droit pénal] to prosecute sb / *être poursuivi pour détournement de fonds* to be prosecuted for embezzlement. ◆ **se poursuivre** vpi [se prolonger - pourparlers, recherches] to go on, to continue ; [- opération] to go on.

pourtant [puʀtɑ̃] adv **1.** [malgré tout] yet, even so, all the same ▶ **et pourtant** and yet **2.** [emploi expressif] : *c'est pourtant simple !* but it's quite simple! / *je t'avais pourtant prévenu...* I did warn you...

pourtour [puʀtuʀ] nm [bordure - d'un plat] edge, rim ; [- d'une feuille] edge ; [- d'une baignoire] surround.

pourvoi [puʀvwa] nm DR appeal ▶ **il a présenté un pourvoi en cassation** he has taken his case to the Appeal Court.

pourvoir [64] [puʀvwaʀ] vt **1.** [équiper] ▶ **pourvoir qqn de** ou **en a)** [outils] to equip ou to provide sb with **b)** [vivres, documents] to provide sb with **2.** [doter] ▶ **pourvoir de** to endow with **3.** [remplir - emploi] to fill / *le poste est toujours à pourvoir* the post is still vacant ou is still to be filled. ◆ **pourvoir à** v + prép [besoin] to provide ou to cater for ; [dépense] to pay for / *nous pourvoirons au transport des médicaments* we will provide for ou deal with the transport of medicine. ◆ **se pourvoir** vpi DR to appeal ▶ **se pourvoir en cassation** to take one's case to the Supreme Court of Appeal.

pourvoirie [puʀvwaʀi] nf ⁅ᴏᴜᴇ́ʙᴇᴄ⁆ hunting ou fishing resort.

pourvoyeur, euse [puʀvwajœʀ, øz] nm, f **1.** [d'armes, de marchandises] supplier ; [de drogue] dealer **2.** ⁅ᴏᴜᴇ́ʙᴇᴄ⁆ [exploitant d'une pourvoirie] outfitter (*in a hunting or fishing resort*).

pourvu, e [puʀvy] ◆ pp → **pourvoir**. ◆ adj ▶ **bien pourvu** well-off, well-provided for.

pourvu que [puʀvyka] *(devant voyelle ou «h» muet* [puʀvyk]*)* loc conj **1.** [exprimant un souhait] ▶ **pourvu qu'il vienne !** I hope ou let's hope he's coming! / *pourvu que ça dure !* let's hope it lasts! **2.** [exprimant une condition] provided (that), so ou as long as.

pousse [pus] nf BOT [bourgeon] (young) shoot, sprout ▶ **pousses de bambou** bamboo shoots ▶ **pousses de soja** beansprouts.

poussé, e [puse] adj [fouillé - interrogatoire] thorough, probing, searching ; [- recherche, technique] advanced ; [- description] thorough, extensive, exhaustive / *je n'ai pas fait d'études poussées* I didn't stay in education very long.

pousse-café [puskafe] *(pl* **pousse-café** ou **pousse-cafés***) nm fam liqueur, pousse-café.

poussée [puse] nf **1.** CONSTR, GÉOL & PHYS thrust **2.** [pression] push, shove, thrust **3.** MÉD eruption, outbreak / *faire une poussée de fièvre* to have a sudden rise in temperature **4.** AÉRON & ASTRONAUT thrust.

pousse-pousse *(pl* pousse-pousse),
poussepousse* [puspus] nm **1.** [en Extrême-Orient] rickshaw **2.** ⁅ꜱᴜɪꜱꜱᴇ⁆ [poussette] pushchair ⁅ᴜᴋ⁆, baby buggy® ⁅ᴜᴋ⁆, stroller ⁅ᴜꜱ⁆.

pousser [3] [puse] ◆ vt **1.** [faire avancer - caddie, fauteuil roulant, landau] to push, to wheel (along) ; [- moto en panne] to push, to walk ; [- caisse] to push (along) ou forward ; [- pion] to move forward / *ils essayaient de pousser les manifestants vers la place* they were trying to drive ou to push the demonstrators towards the square **2.** [enclencher, appuyer sur - bouton, interrupteur] to push (in) (*sép*), to press on (*insép*) / *pousser un levier vers le haut / bas* to push a lever up / down ▶ **pousser une porte a)** [doucement, pour l'ouvrir] to push a door open **b)** [doucement, pour la fermer] to push a door to ou shut **3.** [bousculer] to push, to shove ▶ **pousser qqn du coude** [pour l'alerter, accidentellement] to nudge sb with one's elbow **4.** [enlever] to push (away), to push ou to shove aside (*sép*) **5.** [inciter, entraîner - personne] to spur on (*sép*), to drive ▶ **pousser qqn à qqch** : *pousser qqn à la consommation* to encourage sb to buy ou to consume ▶ **pousser qqn à la dépense** to encourage sb to spend more ▶ **pousser qqn au désespoir / suicide**

to drive sb to despair / suicide ◗ **pousser qqn à faire qqch** a) [suj : curiosité, jalousie] to drive sb to do sthg b) [suj : pitié soudaine] to prompt sb to do sthg c) [suj : personne] to incite sb to do ou to push sb into doing ou to prompt sb to do sthg **6.** [poursuivre - recherches] to press on ou to carry on with *(insép)* ; [- discussion, études, analyse] to continue, to carry on (with) ; [- argumentation] to carry on (with) *(insép)*, to push further ; [- comparaison, interrogatoire] to take further ; [- avantage] to press home *(insép)* / *en poussant plus loin l'examen de leur comptabilité* by probing deeper into their accounts / *elle a poussé l'audace jusqu'à…* she was bold enough to… **7.** [forcer - moteur] to push ; [- voiture] to drive hard ou fast ; [- chauffage] to turn up *(sép)* ; [- son] to turn up *(sép)* ; [exiger un effort de - étudiant, employé] to push ; [- cheval] to urge ou to spur on *(sép)* ; [encourager - candidat, jeune artiste] to push **8.** [émettre] ◗ **pousser un cri** a) [personne] to cry, to utter ou to let out a cry b) [oiseau] to call / *pousser un soupir* to sigh, to heave a sigh / *pousser des cris / hurlements de douleur* to scream / to yell with pain **9.** AGR & BOT [plante, animal] to force. ◆ vi **1.** [grandir - arbre, poil, ongle] to grow ; [- dent] to come through / *les plants de tomates poussent bien* the tomato plants are doing well / *ses dents commencent à pousser* he's cutting his teeth, he's teething / *elle a laissé pousser ses cheveux* she's let her hair grow **2.** [avancer] to push on / *poussons un peu plus loin* let's go ou push on a bit further **3.** *fam* [exagérer] : *deux heures de retard, tu pousses !* you're two hours late, that's a bit much! / *faut pas pousser !* enough's enough! **4.** [bousculer] to push, to shove / *ne poussez pas, il y en aura pour tout le monde !* stop shoving ou pushing, there's plenty for everyone! **5.** [appuyer] to push / *pousser sur ses pieds / jambes* to push with one's feet / legs / *'poussez'* 'push' **6.** PHYSIOL [à la selle] to strain ; [dans l'enfantement] to push. ◆◆ **se pousser** *vp (emploi passif)* to be pushed. ◆ *vp (emploi réciproque)* : *les gens se poussaient pour voir arriver le Président* people were pushing and shoving to get a look at the President. ◆ *vpi* [se déplacer] to move ◗ **tu peux te pousser un peu ?** a) [dans une rangée de chaises] could you move along a bit ou a few places? b) [sur un canapé, dans un lit] could you move over slightly?

poussette [puset] nf [pour enfant] pushchair 🇬🇧, stroller 🇺🇸 ; [à provisions] shopping trolley 🇬🇧 ou cart 🇺🇸.

poussière [pusjɛʀ] nf **1.** [terre sèche, salissures] dust / *tu en fais de la poussière en balayant !* you're making ou raising a lot of dust with your broom! ◗ **faire la poussière** to dust, to do the dusting ◗ **tomber en poussière** to crumble into dust **2.** [dans l'œil] mote *litt*, piece of grit. ◆◆ **poussières** nfpl *fam* : *20 euros et des poussières* just over 20 euros.

poussiéreux, euse [pusjeʀø, øz] adj **1.** [couvert de poussière] dusty, dust-covered **2.** *sout* [dépassé - législation, théorie] outmoded, outdated.

poussif, ive [pusif, iv] adj **1.** [essoufflé - cheval] broken-winded ; [- vieillard] short-winded, wheezy ; [- locomotive] puffing, wheezing **2.** [laborieux - prose] dull, flat, laboured ; [- campagne électorale, émission] sluggish, dull.

poussin [pusɛ̃] nm **1.** ZOOL chick ; COMM poussin **2.** *fam* [terme d'affection] ◗ **mon poussin** my pet ou darling **3.** SPORT under-eleven *(member of junior team or club)*.

poutine [putin] nf 🇶🇧 fried potato topped with grated cheese and brown sauce.

poutre [putʀ] nf CONSTR [en bois] beam ; [en fer] girder ◗ **poutre apparente** exposed beam.

poutrelle [putʀɛl] nf CONSTR [en bois] small beam ; [en fer] small girder.

pouvoir¹ [puvwaʀ] nm **1.** [aptitude, possibilité] power / *avoir un grand pouvoir de concentration / de persuasion*

to have great powers of concentration / persuasion / *je ferai tout ce qui est en mon pouvoir pour t'aider* I'll do everything ou all in my power to help you ◗ **pouvoir d'achat** ÉCON purchasing power **2.** ADMIN & DR [d'un président, d'un tuteur] power ◗ **pouvoir disciplinaire** disciplinary powers **3.** POL ◗ **le pouvoir** a) [exercice] power b) [gouvernants] government / *elle est trop proche du pouvoir pour comprendre* she's too close to the seat of power to understand ◗ **arriver au pouvoir** to come to power ◗ **être au pouvoir** a) [parti élu] to be in power ou office b) [junte] to be in power / *les gens au pouvoir ne connaissent pas nos problèmes* those in power ou the powers that be don't understand our difficulties ◗ **prendre le pouvoir** a) [élus] to take office b) [dictateur] to seize power ◗ **exercer le pouvoir** to exercise power, to govern, to rule ◗ **le pouvoir central** central government ◗ **le pouvoir exécutif** executive power, the executive ◗ **le pouvoir judiciaire** judicial power, the judiciary ◗ **le pouvoir législatif** legislative power, the legislature ◗ **le pouvoir local** local government, the local authorities **4.** [influence] power, influence ◗ **avoir du pouvoir sur qqn** to have power ou influence over sb ◗ **avoir qqn en son pouvoir** to have sb in one's power **5.** PHYS & TECHNOL power, quality ◗ **pouvoir couvrant (d'une peinture)** opacity (of a paint) ◗ **pouvoir isolant** insulating capacity. ◆◆ **pouvoirs** nmpl **1.** [fonctions] powers, authority / *outrepasser ses pouvoirs* to overstep ou to exceed one's authority ◗ **avoir tous pouvoirs pour faire qqch** a) [administrateur] to have full powers to do sthg b) [architecte, animateur] to have carte blanche to do sthg ◗ **pouvoirs exceptionnels** POL special powers *(available to the President of the French Republic in an emergency)* **2.** [gouvernants] ◗ **les pouvoirs constitués** the legally constituted government ◗ **les pouvoirs publics** the authorities **3.** [surnaturels] powers.

pouvoir² [58] [puvwaʀ] ◆ v aux **1.** [avoir la possibilité, la capacité de] : *je peux revenir en France* I'm able to ou I can return to France / *je peux vous aider ?* [gén, dans un magasin] can I help you? / *je ne peux pas dormir* I'm unable to ou I can't sleep / *le projet ne pourra pas se faire sans sa collaboration* the project can't be carried out without her collaboration ◗ **ne pas pouvoir voir qqn (en peinture)** *fam*: *il ne peut pas la voir (en peinture)* he can't stand (the sight of) her **2.** [parvenir à] to manage ou to be able to / *avez-vous pu entrer en contact avec lui ?* did you succeed in contacting ou manage to contact him? **3.** [avoir la permission de] ◗ **vous pouvez disposer** you may ou can go now ◗ **si je peux** ou *sout* **si je puis m'exprimer ainsi** if I may use the phrase ; [avoir des raisons de] : *on ne peut que s'en féliciter* one can't but feel happy about it **4.** [exprime une éventualité, un doute, un risque] : *la maladie peut revenir* the disease can ou may recur / *attention, tu pourrais glisser* careful, you might ou could slip / *après tout, il pourrait bien ne pas avoir menti* he may well have been telling the truth after all / *ça aurait pu être pire* it could have been worse ; *(tournure impersonnelle)* : *il pourrait s'agir d'un suicide* it could ou may ou might be a suicide **5.** [exprime une approximation] : *elle pouvait avoir entre 50 et 60 ans* she could have been between 50 and 60 (years of age) **6.** [exprime une suggestion, une hypothèse] : *tu peux toujours essayer de lui téléphoner* you could always try phoning him / *tu pourrais au moins t'excuser* you could at least apologize!, the least you could do is (to) apologize! / *on peut s'attendre à tout avec elle* anything's possible with her **7.** [en intensif] : *où ai-je bien pu laisser mes lunettes ?* what on earth can I have done with my glasses? **8.** *litt* [exprime le souhait] : *puisse-t-il vous entendre !* let us hope he can hear you! ◆ vt [être capable de faire] ◗ **on n'y peut rien** it can't be helped, nothing can be done about it / *j'ai fait tout ce que j'ai pu* I did my level best ou all I could ◗ **ne plus en pouvoir** : *je n'en peux plus* a) [physiquement] I'm exhausted b) [moralement]

I can't take anymore ou stand it any longer **c)** [je suis rassasié] I'm full (up) / *je n'en peux plus de l'entendre se plaindre sans cesse* I just can't take his continual moaning any more. ❖ **se pouvoir** v impers ▸ **ça se peut** it may ou could be / *il va pleuvoir — ça se pourrait bien !* it's going to rain — that's quite possible! ▸ **il** ou **ça se peut que**: *il se peut qu'il soit malade* he might be ill, maybe he's ill / *il se pourrait bien qu'il n'y ait plus de places* it might ou could well be fully booked.

PQ nm (**abr de papier-cul**) *tfam* bog paper.

pragmatique [pʀagmatik] adj [politique] pragmatic ; [personne, attitude] pragmatic, practical.

praire [pʀɛʀ] nf clam.

prairie [pʀeʀi] nf **1.** [terrain] meadow **2.** [formation végétale] grassland.

praline [pʀalin] nf CULIN [amande] praline, sugared almond ; [chocolat] (filled) chocolate.

praliné, e [pʀaline] adj [glace, entremets] almond-flavoured ; [amande] sugared ; [chocolat] with (toasted) sugared almonds. ❖ **praliné** nm chocolate with (toasted) sugared almonds.

praticable [pʀatikabl] adj **1.** [sentier] passable, practicable **2.** [réalisable - suggestion, solution] practicable, feasible.

praticien, enne [pʀatisjɛ̃, ɛn] nm, f practitioner.

pratiquant, e [pʀatikɑ̃, ɑ̃t] ◆ adj practising UK, practicing US. ◆ nm, f RELIG churchgoer, practising UK ou practicing US Christian / Jew / Muslim, etc.

pratique¹ [pʀatik] adj **1.** [utile - gadget, outil, voiture, dictionnaire] practical, handy ; [- vêtement] practical **2.** [facile] : *il faut changer de bus trois fois, ce n'est pas pratique !* you have to change buses three times, it's very inconvenient! **3.** [concret - application, connaissance, sens, formation] practical **4.** [pragmatique] practical / *avoir le sens* ou *l'esprit pratique* to have a practical turn of mind, to be practical.

pratique² [pʀatik] nf **1.** [application - d'une philosophie, d'une politique] practice ; [- de l'autocritique, d'une vertu] exercise ; [- d'une technique, de la censure] application ▸ **mettre en pratique a)** [conseils, préceptes] to put into practice **b)** [vertu] to exercise ▸ **en** ou **dans la pratique** in (actual) practice **2.** [d'une activité] practice / *la pratique régulière du tennis* / *vélo* playing tennis / cycling on a regular basis / *pratique illégale de la médecine* illegal practice of medicine **3.** [expérience] practical experience **4.** [usage] practice / *des pratiques religieuses* religious practices ▸ **bonnes pratiques** best practices.

pratiquement [pʀatikmɑ̃] adv **1.** [presque] practically, virtually / *il n'y avait pratiquement personne* there was hardly anybody ou practically nobody **2.** [en fait] in practice ou (actual) fact.

pratiquer [3] [pʀatike] ◆ vt **1.** [faire - entaille] to make, to cut ; [- ouverture] to make ; [- passage] to open up ; [- intervention chirurgicale] to carry out (sép), to perform ▸ **pratiquer un trou a)** [à la vrille] to bore ou to drill a hole **b)** [aux ciseaux] to cut (out) a hole **2.** [appliquer - préceptes, politique] to practise UK, to practice US ; [- autocritique, vertu] to practise UK, to practice US ; [- technique] to use, to apply ; [- censure] to apply ; [- sélection] to make **3.** [s'adonner à - jeu de ballon] to play ; [- art martial, athlétisme] to do ; [- art, médecine, religion] to practise UK, to practice US ; [- langue] to speak ; [- humour, ironie] to use ▸ **pratiquer un sport** to do ou practise a sport. ◆ vi RELIG to be a practising UK ou practicing US Christian / Jew / Muslim, etc., to attend church (regularly), to be a (regular) churchgoer. ❖ **se pratiquer** vp *(emploi passif)* : *les prix qui se pratiquent à Paris* current Paris prices / *cela se pratique couramment dans leur pays* it is common practice in their country.

pré [pʀe] nm **1.** AGR meadow **2.** EXPR **pré carré** domain, preserve.

préado [pʀeado] nmf *fam* preadolescent.

préadolescent, e [pʀeadɔlesɑ̃, ɑ̃t] nm, f preadolescent, preteen, pre-teenager.

préaffranchi, e [pʀeafʀɑ̃ʃi] adj prepaid.

préalable [pʀealabl] ◆ adj [discussion, entrevue, sélection] preliminary ; [travail, formation] preparatory ; [accord, avertissement] prior / *sans avertissement préalable* without prior notice. ◆ nm prerequisite, precondition. ❖ **au préalable** loc adv first, beforehand.

préalablement [pʀealabləmɑ̃] adv first, beforehand.

préambule [pʀeɑ̃byl] nm **1.** [d'une constitution, d'une conférence] preamble **2.** [prémices] : *cet incident a été le préambule d'une crise grave* this incident was the prelude to a serious crisis. ❖ **sans préambule** loc adv without warning.

préau, x [pʀeo] nm [d'une école] covered part of the playground ; [d'un pénitencier] yard ; [d'un cloître] inner courtyard.

préavis [pʀeavi] nm (advance) notice / *mon propriétaire m'a donné un mois de préavis* my landlord gave me a month's notice (to move out) ▸ **déposer un préavis de grève** to give strike notice. ❖ **sans préavis** loc adv ADMIN without prior notice ou notification.

précaire [pʀekɛʀ] adj [équilibre] fragile, precarious ; [vie, situation] precarious ; [santé] delicate, frail / *il a un emploi précaire* he's got no job security.

précariser [pʀekaʀize] vt ▸ **précariser l'emploi** to threaten job security / *la crise a précarisé leur situation* the recession has made them more vulnerable.

précarité [pʀekaʀite] nf precariousness / *la précarité de l'emploi* the lack of job security.

précaution [pʀekosjɔ̃] nf **1.** [disposition préventive] precaution ▸ **prendre des** ou **ses précautions** pr & euphém to take precautions ▸ **précautions d'emploi** caution (before use) **2.** [prudence] caution, care. ❖ **avec précaution** loc adv cautiously, warily. ❖ **par (mesure de) précaution** loc adv as a precaution ou precautionary measure. ❖ **pour plus de précaution** loc adv to be on the safe side, to make absolutely certain. ❖ **sans précaution** loc adv carelessly, rashly.

précautionneux, euse [pʀekosjɔnø, øz] adj **1.** [circonspect] cautious, wary **2.** [soigneux] careful.

précédemment [pʀesedamɑ̃] adv before (that), previously.

précédent, e [pʀesedɑ̃, ɑ̃t] adj previous / *la semaine précédente* the week before, the previous week. ❖ **précédent** nm precedent. ❖ **sans précédent** loc adj without precedent, unprecedented.

précéder [18] [pʀesede] ◆ vt **1.** [marcher devant] to precede **2.** [être placé avant] to precede, to be in front of **3.** [avoir lieu avant] to precede / *le jour qui précéda son arrestation* the day before ou prior to his arrest **4.** [arriver en avance sur] to precede, to arrive ahead of ou before / *il précède le favori de trois secondes* he has a three second lead over the favourite. ◆ vi to precede / *les semaines qui précédèrent* the preceding weeks.

✍ In reformed spelling (see p. 16-18), this verb is conjugated like *semer* : *il précédera, elle précéderait.*

précepte [pʀesɛpt] nm precept.

précepteur [pʀesɛptœʀ] nm private ou home tutor.

préchauffer [3] [pʀeʃofe] vt to preheat.

prêcher [4] [pʀeʃe] ◆ vt **1.** RELIG [Évangile, religion] to preach ; [carême, retraite] to preach for *(insép)* ; [personne] to preach to *(insép)* ▸ **vous prêchez un converti** you're preaching to the converted **2.** [recommander - doctrine, bonté, vengeance] to preach ▸ **prêcher le faux pour**

savoir le vrai to make false statements in order to discover the truth. ➙ vi [prêtre] to preach ; [moralisateur] to preach ▸ **prêcher dans le désert** *allusion* BIBLE to preach in the wilderness.

précieusement [pʀesjøzmɑ̃] adv [soigneusement] preciously.

précieux, euse [pʀesjø, øz] adj **1.** [de valeur - temps, santé] precious ; [- pierre, métal] precious ; [- ami, amitié] precious, valued ; [- objet, trésor, bijou] precious, priceless **2.** [très utile] invaluable / **elle fut d'une aide précieuse** her help was invaluable **3.** [maniéré] mannered, affected, precious.

préciosité [pʀesjozite] nf [maniérisme] affectedness, mannered style.

précipice [pʀesipis] nm **1.** [gouffre] precipice **2.** [catastrophe] : **être au bord du précipice** to be on the brink of disaster.

précipitamment [pʀesipitamɑ̃] adv [annuler, changer] hastily, hurriedly.

précipitation [pʀesipitasjɔ̃] nf **1.** [hâte] haste **2.** [irréflexion] rashness. ➙ **précipitations** nfpl MÉTÉOR precipitation / **fortes précipitations sur l'ouest du pays demain** tomorrow, it will rain heavily in the west.

précipité, e [pʀesipite] adj **1.** [pressé - pas] hurried ; [- fuite] headlong **2.** [hâtif - retour] hurried, hasty ; [- décision] hasty, rash. ➙ **précipité** nm precipitate.

précipiter [3] [pʀesipite] vt **1.** [faire tomber] to throw ou to hurl (down) **2.** *fig* [plonger] to plunge **3.** [faire à la hâte] : **il ne faut rien précipiter** we mustn't rush (into) things ou be hasty **4.** [accélérer - pas, cadence] to quicken, to speed up *(sép)* ; [- mouvement, mort] to hasten. ➙ **se précipiter** vpi **1.** [d'en haut] to hurl o.s. / **se précipiter dans le vide** to hurl o.s. into space **2.** [se ruer] to rush ▸ **il s'est précipité dans l'escalier pour la rattraper a)** [vers le bas] he rushed downstairs after her **b)** [vers le haut] he rushed upstairs after her ▸ **se précipiter vers** ou **au-devant de qqn** to rush to meet sb ▸ **se précipiter sur qqn** to rush at sb **3.** [se dépêcher] to rush, to hurry / **ne te précipite pas pour répondre** take your time before answering.

précis, e [pʀesi, iz] adj **1.** [exact - horloge, tir, instrument] precise, exact ; [- description] precise, accurate ▸ **à 20 h précises** at precisely 8 p.m., at 8 p.m. sharp / **il arriva à l'instant précis où je partais** he arrived just as I was leaving **2.** [clair, net] precise, specific / **je n'ai aucun souvenir précis de cette année-là** I don't remember that year clearly at all **3.** [particulier] particular, specific / **sans raison précise** for no particular reason / **sans but précis** with no specific aim in mind / **rien de précis** nothing in particular.

précisément [pʀesizemɑ̃] adv **1.** [exactement] precisely / **il nous reste très précisément 52 euros** we've got precisely ou exactly 52 euros left **2.** [justement, par coïncidence] precisely, exactly / **c'est précisément le problème** that's exactly ou precisely what the problem is.

préciser [3] [pʀesize] vt **1.** [clarifier - intentions, pensée] to make clear **2.** [spécifier] : **j'ai oublié de leur préciser le lieu du rendez-vous** I forgot to tell them where the meeting is taking place / **la Maison-Blanche précise que la rencontre n'est pas officielle** the White House has made it clear that this is not an official meeting / **je dois préciser que** I must point out that. ➙ **se préciser** vpi [idée, projet] to take shape ; [situation, menace] to become clearer.

précision [pʀesizjɔ̃] nf **1.** [exactitude] preciseness, precision **2.** [netteté] precision, distinctness **3.** [explication] point / **nous y reviendrons dès que nous aurons plus de précisions** we'll come back to that as soon as we have further information ou details. ➙ **de précision** loc adj precision *(modif)* ▸ **horlogerie de haute précision** high-precision watchmaking.

précoce [pʀekɔs] adj **1.** [prématuré - surdité, mariage] premature **2.** [en avance - intellectuellement] precocious, mature (beyond one's years) **3.** BOT & MÉTÉOR early.

précocité [pʀekɔsite] nf [d'un enfant] precociousness, precocity.

préconçu, e [pʀekɔ̃sy] adj set, preconceived ▸ **idée préconçue** preconceived idea.

préconiser [3] [pʀekɔnize] vt [recommander - solution, méthode] to advocate ; [- remède] to recommend.

précuit, e [pʀekɥi, it] adj precooked, ready-cooked.

précurseur [pʀekyʀsœʀ] ➙ adj m warning. ➙ nm forerunner, precursor.

prédateur, trice [pʀedatœʀ, tʀis] nm, f BOT & ZOOL predator ▸ **prédateur sexuel** sexual predator.

prédécesseur [pʀedesesœʀ] nm predecessor.

prédestiner [3] [pʀedɛstine] vt [vouer] to prepare, to predestine / **rien ne me prédestinait à devenir acteur** nothing marked me out to become an actor ou for an acting career.

prédicateur, trice [pʀedikatœʀ, tʀis] nm, f preacher.

prédiction [pʀediksjɔ̃] nf [prophétie] prediction.

prédilection [pʀedilɛksjɔ̃] nf predilection, partiality ▸ **avoir une prédilection pour qqch** to be partial to sthg, to have a predilection for sthg. ➙ **de prédilection** loc adj favourite *(avant nom)* 🇬🇧, favorite *(avant nom)* 🇺🇸.

prédire [103] [pʀediʀ] vt to predict, to foretell ▸ **prédire l'avenir a)** [par hasard ou estimation] to predict the future **b)** [voyant] to tell fortunes.

prédisposer [3] [pʀedispoze] vt [préparer] to predispose.

prédisposition [pʀedispozisjɔ̃] nf **1.** [tendance] predisposition / **avoir une prédisposition au diabète** to have a predisposition to diabetes **2.** [talent] gift, talent.

prédominant, e [pʀedɔminɑ̃, ɑ̃t] adj [principal - couleur, trait] predominant, main ; [- opinion, tendance] prevailing ; [- souci] chief, major.

prédominer [3] [pʀedɔmine] vi [couleur, trait] to predominate ; [sentiment, tendance] to prevail.

préemption [pʀeɑ̃psjɔ̃] nf pre-emption ▸ **droit de préemption** pre-emptive right.

préenregistrer [pʀeɑ̃ʀʒistʀe] vt to prerecord / **vous pouvez préenregistrer vos bagages** you can check in your luggage in advance.

préétabli, e [pʀeetabli] adj pre-established.

préexistant, e [pʀeɛgzistɑ̃, ɑ̃t] adj existing.

préfabriqué, e [pʀefabʀike] adj prefabricated. ➙ **préfabriqué** nm **1.** [construction] prefab **2.** [matériau] prefabricated material ▸ **en préfabriqué** prefabricated.

préface [pʀefas] nf preface.

préfacer [16] [pʀefase] vt [livre, texte] to preface.

préfectoral, e, aux [pʀefɛktɔʀal, o] adj prefectoral, prefectural.

préfecture [pʀefɛktyʀ] nf ADMIN [chef-lieu] prefecture ; [édifice] prefecture building ; [services] prefectural office ; [emploi] post of préfet ▸ **préfecture maritime** port prefecture ▸ **préfecture de police** (Paris) police headquarters.

 Préfecture

The main administrative office of each **département** and **Région**. The word has also come to refer to the town where the office is located. One goes to the **préfecture** to get a driving licence or a **carte de séjour**, for example.

préférable [pʀefeʀabl] adj preferable / *ne va pas trop loin, c'est préférable* it'd be better if you didn't go too far away ▸ **préférable à** preferable to, better than.

préféré, e [pʀefeʀe] adj favourite 🇬🇧, favorite 🇺🇸.

préférence [pʀefeʀɑ̃s] nf [prédilection] preference ▸ **donner la préférence à** to give preference to / *ça m'est égal, je n'ai pas de préférence* it doesn't matter to me, I've no particular preference. ❖ **de préférence** loc adv preferably / **'à consommer de préférence avant fin...'** 'best before end ...'. ❖ **de préférence à** loc prép in preference to, rather than.

préférentiel, elle [pʀefeʀɑ̃sjɛl] adj [traitement, tarif, taux, vote] preferential.

préférer [18] [pʀefeʀe] vt to prefer / *ils préfèrent les échecs aux cartes* they prefer chess to playing cards / *préférez-vous du vin ou de la bière ?* would you rather have wine or beer? / *je me préfère avec un chignon* I think I look better with my hair in a bun / *il préférait mourir plutôt que (de) partir* he would rather die than leave / *je préfère que tu n'en dises rien à personne* I'd prefer it if you I'd rather you didn't tell anybody ; *(en usage absolu)* : *si tu préfères, nous allons rentrer* if you'd rather, we'll go home.
🖉 In reformed spelling (see p. 16-18), this verb is conjugated like *semer* : *il préférera, elle préférerait.*

préfet [pʀefɛ] nm **1.** ADMIN préfet, prefect **2.** 🇧🇪 head teacher 🇬🇧 ou principal 🇺🇸 *(of a secondary school).*

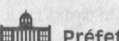 **Préfet**

One of a body of civil servants which was created by Napoleon in 1800. The **préfet**, who is appointed by a **décret** of the **président de la République**, is the government representative of a **département** or a **Région**.

---

préfigurer [3] [pʀefigyʀe] vt *sout* [annoncer] to prefigure.

préfixe [pʀefiks] nm prefix.

préhistoire [pʀeistwaʀ] nf prehistory.

préhistorique [pʀeistɔʀik] adj [ère, temps] prehistoric, prehistorical.

préinscription [pʀeɛ̃skʀipsjɔ̃] nf preregistration.

préinstallé, e [pʀeɛ̃stale] adj INFORM preinstalled.

préjudice [pʀeʒydis] nm harm *(U)*, wrong *(U)* ▸ **subir un préjudice matériel / financier** to sustain damage / financial loss ▸ **subir un préjudice moral** to suffer mental distress ▸ **causer un** ou **porter préjudice à qqn** to harm sb, to do sb harm / *les magnétoscopes ont-ils porté préjudice au cinéma ?* have videorecorders been detrimental to the cinema?

⚠ Le mot anglais **prejudice** signifie généralement « préjugé » et, en dehors du domaine du droit, ne doit pas être employé pour traduire **préjudice**.

préjudiciable [pʀeʒydisjabl] adj *sout* prejudicial, detrimental.

préjugé [pʀeʒyʒe] nm prejudice ▸ **avoir un préjugé contre qqn** to be prejudiced ou biased against sb ▸ **avoir un préjugé favorable pour qqn** to be prejudiced in sb's favour, to be biased towards sb.

préjuger [17] [pʀeʒyʒe] ❖ **préjuger de** v + prép *litt* ▸ **préjuger de qqch** to judge sthg in advance, to prejudge sthg.

prélart [pʀelaʀ] nm 🇶🇨 linoleum.

prélasser [3] [pʀelase] ❖ **se prélasser** vpi to be stretched out, to lounge (around), to laze around.

prélavage [pʀelavaʒ] nm prewash.

prélèvement [pʀelɛvmɑ̃] nm **1.** MÉD [échantillon - de sang] sample ; [-sur les tissus] swab **2.** BANQUE [retrait] ▸ **prélèvement automatique** ou **bancaire** direct debit **3.** FIN [retenue - sur le salaire] deduction ; [-sur les biens] levy ▸ **prélèvements obligatoires** tax and social security contributions.

prélever [19] [pʀeləve] vt **1.** MÉD [échantillon] to take / *prélever du sang* to take a blood sample **2.** FIN [somme - au distributeur] to withdraw ; [-sur un salaire] to deduct, to withdraw / *la somme sera prélevée sur votre compte tous les mois* the sum will be deducted ou debited from your account every month.

préliminaire [pʀeliminɛʀ] adj preliminary. ❖ **préliminaires** nmpl [préparatifs] preliminaries ; [discussions] preliminary talks.

prélude [pʀelyd] nm **1.** MUS prelude **2.** *sout* [préliminaire] prelude.

préluder [3] [pʀelyde] ❖ **préluder à** v + prép to be a prelude to.

prématuré, e [pʀematyʀe] ◆ adj [naissance, bébé] premature. ◆ nm, f premature baby ou infant.

prématurément [pʀematyʀemɑ̃] adv prematurely.

préméditation [pʀemeditasjɔ̃] nf premeditation ▸ **avec préméditation** with malice aforethought.

préméditer [3] [pʀemedite] vt [crime, vol] to premeditate ▸ **préméditer de faire qqch** to plan to do sthg.

prémices [pʀemis] nfpl *litt* [début] beginnings.

premier, ère [pʀəmje, ɛʀ] ◆ adj num **1.** *(souvent avant le nom)* [initial] early ▸ **les premiers hommes** early man / *ses premières œuvres* her early works ▸ **les premiers temps** at the beginning, early on **2.** [proche] nearest ▸ **au premier rang a)** CINÉ & THÉÂTRE in the first ou front row **b)** ÉDUC in the first row **3.** [à venir] next, first / *ce n'est pas le premier venu* he's not just anybody / *on s'est arrêtés dans le premier hôtel venu* we stopped at the first hotel we came to ou happened to come to **4.** [dans une série] first ▸ **chapitre premier** Chapter One ▸ **à la première heure** first thing, at first light / *à première vue* at first (sight) ▸ **au premier abord** at first ▸ **dans un premier temps** (at) first, to start with, to begin with ▸ **du premier coup** *fam* first off, at the first attempt ▸ **premier amour** first love / *le premier arrivé* the first person to arrive ▸ **premier jet** (first) ou rough ou initial draft ▸ **premiers secours a)** [personnes et matériel] emergency services **b)** [soins] first aid ▸ **première fois** : *c'est la première fois que...* it's the first time that... ▸ **première page** PRESSE front page ▸ **première partie a)** [gén] first part **b)** [au spectacle] opening act **5.** [principal] main ▸ **de (toute) première nécessité / urgence** (absolutely) essential / urgent / *le premier pays producteur de vin au monde* the world's leading wine-producing country **6.** [haut placé - clerc, commis] chief ; [-danseur] leading / *sortir premier d'une grande école* to be first on the pass list *(in the final exam of a "grande école")* **7.** *(après le nom)* [originel] first, original, initial / *l'idée première était de...* the original idea was to... **8.** [spontané] first / *son premier mouvement* his first ou spontaneous impulse **9.** *(après le nom)* [fondamental] first ; MATH [nombre] prime ; [polynôme] irreducible **10.** [moindre] : *et ta récitation, tu n'en connais pas le premier mot !* you haven't a clue about your recitation, have you? **11.** GRAM ▸ **première personne du singulier / pluriel** first person singular / plural. ◆ nm, f **1.** [personne] ▸ **le premier** the first ▸ **entre la première** go in first ▸ **elle est la première de sa classe / au hit-parade** she's top of her class / the charts ▸ **jeune**

premier CINÉ & THÉÂTRE juvenile lead **2.** [chose] ▸ **le premier** the first (one) **3.** ▸ **le premier** [celui-là] the former. Voir aussi **cinquième**. ❖ **premier** nm **1.** [étage] first floor 🇬🇧, second floor 🇺🇸 **2.** [dans des dates] : *le premier du mois* the first of the month ▸ **le Premier Mai** May Day. ❖ **première** nf **1.** CINÉ & THÉÂTRE first night, opening night ▸ **première mondiale** world première **2.** [exploit] : *c'est une (grande) première chirurgicale* it's a first for surgery **3.** ÉDUC ≃ lower sixth year ou form 🇬🇧 ; ≃ eleventh grade 🇺🇸 **4.** AUTO first (gear) ▸ *être / passer en première* to be in / to go into first **5.** TRANSP first class ▸ **voyager en première** to travel first class / *billet / wagon de première* first-class ticket / carriage **6.** DANSE first (position) **7.** IMPR [épreuve] first proof ; [édition - d'un livre] first edition ; [- d'un journal] early edition. ❖ **en premier** loc adv first, in the first place, first of all. ❖ **premier de cordée** nm leader *(of a roped climbing team)*. ❖ **premier degré** nm **1.** ÉDUC primary 🇬🇧 ou elementary 🇺🇸 education **2.** [phase initiale] first step ▸ **brûlure au premier degré** first-degree burn **3.** *fig* : *des gags à ne pas prendre au premier degré* jokes which mustn't be taken at face value. ❖ **premier prix** nm **1.** COMM lowest ou cheapest price **2.** [récompense] first prize.

premièrement [prəmjɛrmɑ̃] adv **1.** [dans une énumération] in the first place, first **2.** [pour objecter] firstly, in the first place, to start with. Voir aussi **cinquièmement**.

premier-né, première-née [prəmjene, prəmjɛrne] *(mpl* **premiers-nés,** *fpl* **premières-nées)** adj & nm, f first-born.

prémisse [premis] nf premise.

prémonition [premɔnisjɔ̃] nf premonition.

prémonitoire [premɔnitwar] adj premonitory.

prémunir [32] [premynir] ❖ **se prémunir contre** vp + prép to protect o.s. ou to guard against sthg.

prenant, e [prənɑ̃, ɑ̃t] adj **1.** [captivant] engrossing, gripping **2.** [qui prend du temps] time-consuming.

prénatal, e, als *ou* **aux** [prenatal, o] adj prenatal, antenatal.

prendre [79] [prɑ̃dr]
◆ vt

A. SAISIR **1.** [saisir] to take / *prends la casserole par le manche* pick the pan up by the handle / *il prit son manteau à la patère* he took his coat off the hook ▸ **prendre qqch des mains de qqn** to take sthg off sb ; [saisir et garder] to take (hold of), to hold / *prendre sa tête entre ses mains* to hold one's head in one's hands **2.** [emporter - lunettes, document, en-cas] to take / *tu as pris tes papiers (avec toi) ?* have you got your papers (with you)? / *quand prendrez-vous le colis ?* when will you collect the parcel? ; [emmener] to take (along) ▸ **(passer) prendre qqn:** *je suis passé le prendre chez elle à midi* I picked her up ou collected her from her home at midday ▸ **prendre qqn en voiture** to give sb a lift **3.** [trouver] to get / *où as-tu pris ce couteau ?* where did you get that knife (from)? **4.** [se procurer] ▸ **prendre des renseignements** to get some information **5.** [acheter - nourriture, billet de loterie] to get, to buy ; [- abonnement, assurance] to take out *(sép)* ; [réserver - chambre d'hôtel, place de spectacle] to book / *j'ai pris des artichauts pour ce soir* I've got ou bought some artichokes for tonight **6.** [demander - argent] to charge / *je prends une commission de 3 %* I take a 3% commission / *mon coiffeur ne prend pas cher fam* my hairdresser isn't too expensive ou doesn't charge too much **7.** [retirer] : *les impôts sont pris à la source* tax is deducted at source.

B. AVOIR RECOURS À, SE SERVIR DE **1.** [utiliser - outil] to use / *prends un marteau, ce sera plus facile* use a hammer, you'll find it's easier ; [emprunter] to take, to borrow / *je peux prendre ta voiture ?* can I take ou borrow

your car? **2.** [consommer - nourriture] to eat ; [- boisson] to drink, to have ; [- médicament] to take ; [- sucre] to take / *je ne prends jamais de somnifères* I never take sleeping pills / *je prendrais bien une bière* I could do with a beer / *si on allait prendre un verre ?* how about (going for) a drink? / *tu lui as fait prendre ses médicaments ?* did you make sure he took his medicine? ; [comme ingrédient] to take **3.** [se déplacer en] to take, to go ou to travel by *(insép)* ▸ **prendre l'avion** to take the plane, to fly / *prendre le bateau* to take the boat, to sail, to go by boat / *prendre le bus / le train* to take the bus / train, to go by bus / train **4.** [monter dans - bus, train] to catch, to get on *(insép)* **5.** [louer] : *on a pris une chambre dans un petit hôtel* we took a room in a small hotel **6.** [suivre - voie] to take / *prends la première à droite* take the first (on the) right / *j'ai pris un sens interdit* I drove ou went down a one-way street.

C. PRENDRE POSSESSION DE **1.** [retenir par la force - fugitif] to capture ; [- prisonnier] to take ; [- animal] to catch ; MIL [ville, position] to take ▸ **prendre qqn en otage** to take sb hostage **2.** [voler] to take / *il a tout pris dans la maison* he took everything in the house ▸ **prendre qqch à qqn:** *combien vous a-t-on pris ?* how much was taken ou stolen from you? / *elle m'a pris mon idée / petit ami* she stole my idea / boyfriend **3.** [occuper - temps] to take (up), to require *sout* ; [- place] to take (up) / *pousse-toi, tu prends toute la place* move up, you're taking up all the space / *ça (m')a pris deux heures* it took (me) two hours **4.** [envahir - suj : malaise, rage] to come over *(insép)* ; [- suj : peur] to seize, to take hold of ▸ **l'envie le** ou **lui prit d'aller nager** he felt like going for a swim / *qu'est-ce qui te prend ?* what's wrong with ou what's the matter with ou what's come over you? / *ça te prend souvent ? fam & hum* are you often like this? / *quand ça le* ou **lui prend, il casse tout** *fam* when he gets into this state, he just smashes everything in sight ▸ **prendre la tête à qqn** *tfam* : *ça me prend la tête* it's a real hassle / *arrête de me prendre la tête* stop being such a pain **5.** JEUX [pion, dame] to take ; *(en usage absolu)* CARTES ▸ **je prends** I'll try it **6.** SPORT ▸ **prendre le service de qqn** to break sb's service.

D. SURPRENDRE [surprendre - voleur, tricheur] to catch ▸ **prendre qqn à faire qqch** to catch sb doing sthg.

E. ADMETTRE, RECEVOIR **1.** [recevoir] : *le docteur ne pourra pas vous prendre avant demain* the doctor won't be able to see you before tomorrow **2.** [cours] to take **3.** [accueillir - pensionnaire] to take in *(sép)* ; [- passager] to take ; [admettre par règlement] to allow ; [engager - employé, candidat] to take on *(sép)* / *nous ne prenons pas les cartes de crédit / les bagages en cabine* we don't take credit cards / cabin baggage ▸ **prendre qqn comme stagiaire** to take sb on as a trainee **4.** [acquérir, gagner] ▸ **prendre de l'avance / du retard** to be earlier / later than scheduled / *le projet commence à prendre forme* ou *tournure* the project's starting to take shape ; [terminaison] to take / *le a prend un accent circonflexe* there's a circumflex on the a **5.** [subir] to take / *prendre un coup de soleil* to get sunburnt / *prendre froid* ou *vieilli du mal* to catch ou to get a cold ▸ **c'est elle qui a tout pris a)** *fam* [coups, reproches] she got the worst ou took the brunt of it **b)** [éclaboussures] she got most ou the worst of it ; *(en usage absolu)* : *c'est toujours les mêmes qui prennent !* *fam* they always pick on the same ones, it's always the same ones who get it in the neck!

F. CONSIDÉRER DE TELLE MANIÈRE **1.** [accepter] to take ▸ **bien / mal prendre qqch** to take sthg well / badly ; [interpréter] : *ne prends pas ça pour toi* [ne te sens pas visé] don't take it personally / *elle a pris mon silence pour de la désapprobation* she took my silence as a criticism **2.** [considérer] to take, to consider ▸ **prenons un exemple** let's take ou consider an example ▸ **prendre qqn en pitié** to take pity on sb ▸ **prendre qqch / qqn pour a)** [par méprise] to mistake sthg / sb for **b)** [volontairement] to take sthg / sb for, to consider sthg / sb to be / *pour qui me prenez-vous ?* what do you take me for?, who do you think I am? ▶ **prendre qqch / qqn comme** to take sthg / sb as **3.** [traiter - qqn] to handle, to deal with *(insép)* ▶ **prendre qqn par la douceur** to use gentle persuasion on sb / *prendre l'ennemi de front / à revers* MIL & *fig* to tackle the enemy head on / from the rear.

G. ENREGISTRER 1. [consigner - notes] to take ou to write down *(sép)* ; [- empreintes, mesures, température, tension] to take **2.** PHOT ▶ **prendre qqch / qqn (en photo)** to take a picture ou photo ou photograph of sthg / sb.

H. DÉCIDER DE, ADOPTER 1. [s'octroyer - vacances] to take, to have ; [- bain, douche] to have, to take / *prendre un jour de congé* to take ou to have the day off ▶ **prendre le temps de faire qqch** to take the time to do sthg / *prendre un amant* to take a lover **2.** [s'engager dans - mesure, risque] to take ▶ **prendre une décision a)** [gén] to make a decision **b)** [après avoir hésité] to make up one's mind, to come to a decision ▶ **prendre l'initiative de faire qqch** to take the initiative in doing sthg, to take it upon o.s. to do sthg ▶ **prendre la résolution de** to resolve to **3.** [choisir - sujet d'examen, cadeau] to take, to choose, to have / *j'ai pris le docteur Valiet comme médecin* I chose Dr Valiet to be ou as my GP ▶ **c'est à prendre ou à laisser** (you can) take it or leave it **4.** [se charger de - poste] to take, to accept ▶ **prendre ses fonctions** to start work / *j'ai un appel pour toi, tu le prends ?* I've got a call for you, will you take it? **5.** [adopter - air] to put on *(sép)*, to assume ; [- ton] to assume.

◆ vi **1.** [se fixer durablement - végétal] to take (root) ; [- bouture, greffe, vaccin] to take ; [- mode, slogan] to catch on ▶ **ça ne prendra pas avec elle** [mensonge] it won't work with her, she won't be taken in **2.** [durcir - crème, ciment, colle] to set ; [- lac, étang] to freeze (over) ; [- mayonnaise] to thicken **3.** [passer] : *prends à gauche* [tourne à gauche] turn left / *prendre à travers bois / champs* to cut through the woods / fields **4.** [commencer] to start, to get going. ◆ **prendre sur** v + prép **1.** [entamer] to use (some of) **2.** [EXPR] **prendre sur soi** to grin and bear it ▶ **prendre sur soi de faire qqch** to take (it) upon o.s. to do sthg. ◆ **se prendre** ◆ vp *(emploi passif)* : *ces cachets se prennent avant les repas* the tablets should be taken before meals. ◆ vpi to get caught ou trapped / *le foulard s'est pris dans la portière* the scarf got caught ou shut in the door. ◆ vpt **1.** [se coincer] : *attention, tu vas te prendre les doigts dans la charnière !* careful, you'll trap your fingers ou get your fingers caught in the hinge! **2.** *fam* [choisir] : *prends-toi un gâteau* get yourself a cake. ◆ **se prendre à** vp + prép **1.** [se laisser aller à] : *se prendre à rêver* to find o.s. dreaming **2.** [EXPR] **s'y prendre** : *comment pourrions-nous nous y prendre ?* how could we go about it? / *tu t'y prends un peu tard pour t'inscrire !* you've left it a bit late to enrol! / *elle s'y est prise à trois fois pour faire démarrer la tondeuse* she made three attempts before the lawn mower would start ▶ **s'y prendre bien / mal** : *s'y prendre bien / mal avec qqn* to handle sb the right / wrong way. ◆ **se prendre de** vp + prép ▶ **se prendre d'amitié pour qqn** to grow fond of sb, to feel a growing affection for sb. ◆ **se prendre pour** vp + prép ▶ **il ne se prend pas pour rien** ou **pour n'importe qui** he thinks he's God's gift to humanity. ◆ **s'en prendre à** vp + prép ▶ **s'en prendre à qqn / qqch a)** [l'attaquer] to attack sb / sthg **b)** [le rendre responsable] to put the blame on sb / sthg / *pourquoi faut-il toujours que tu t'en prennes à moi ?* why do you always take it out on me?

preneur, euse [pʀənœʀ, øz] nm, f [acheteur] buyer ▶ **trouver preneur pour qqch** to find someone (willing) to buy sthg, to find a buyer for sthg / *si vous me le laissez*

à 50 €, je suis preneur I'll buy it if you'll take 50 € for it. ◆ **preneur de son, preneuse de son** nm, f sound engineer.

prénom [pʀenɔ̃] nm first ou Christian **UK** ou given **US** name.

prénommer [3] [pʀenɔme] vt to call. ◆ **se prénommer** vpi ▶ **comment se prénomme-t-il ?** what's his first name?

prénuptial, e, aux [pʀenypsjal, o] adj premarital, antenuptial.

préoccupant, e [pʀeɔkypɑ̃, ɑ̃t] adj worrying.

préoccupation [pʀeɔkypasjɔ̃] nf **1.** [souci] concern, worry **2.** [priorité] concern, preoccupation / *depuis qu'elle est partie, il n'a plus qu'une préoccupation, la retrouver* since she left his one thought is to find her again.

préoccupé, e [pʀeɔkype] adj [inquiet] worried, preoccupied, concerned / *elle avait l'air préoccupé* she looked worried, there was a look of concern on her face.

préoccuper [3] [pʀeɔkype] vt [tracasser - suj : avenir, question] to worry. ◆ **se préoccuper de** vp + prép to be concerned with, to care about / *se préoccuper de ses enfants* to worry about one's children / *ne te préoccupe donc pas de ça !* don't you worry ou bother about that!

préparateur, trice [pʀepaʀatœʀ, tʀis] nm, f **1.** ENS *assistant to a professor of science* **2.** PHARM ▶ **préparateur en pharmacie** chemist's assistant **UK**, assistant to a dispensing chemist **UK** ou pharmacist **US**.

préparatifs [pʀepaʀatif] nmpl preparations / *commencer les préparatifs du voyage* to start preparing for the trip.

préparation [pʀepaʀasjɔ̃] nf **1.** [réalisation - d'un plat, d'un médicament] preparation **2.** [organisation - d'un voyage, d'une fête, d'un attentat] preparation **3.** [entraînement - pour un examen] preparation ; [- pour une épreuve sportive] training, preparation.

préparatoire [pʀepaʀatwaʀ] adj ▶ **travail préparatoire** groundwork.

préparer [3] [pʀepaʀe] vt **1.** [réaliser - plat] to prepare, to make ; [- sandwich] to prepare, to make ; [- médicament, cataplasme] to prepare / *qu'est-ce que tu nous as préparé de bon ?* what delicious dish have you cooked for us? **2.** [rendre prêt - valise] to pack ; [- repas, chambre, champ] to prepare, to get ready ; [- peaux, laine] to dress ; [- document] to prepare, to draw up *(sép)* ▶ **plats tout préparés** precooked ou ready-cooked meals / *on dirait qu'il nous prépare une rougeole fam* (it) looks like he's getting the measles ▶ **préparer le terrain (pour) a)** *pr* to prepare the ground ou to lay the ground (for) **b)** *fig* to pave the way (for) **3.** [organiser - attentat, conférence] to prepare, to organize ; [- complot] to prepare, to hatch ▶ **préparer une surprise à qqn** to have a surprise in store for sb **4.** [travailler à - œuvre] to be preparing, to be working on ; [- examen] to be preparing for ; [- épreuve sportive] to be in training for / *il prépare une grande école* he's studying for the entrance exam to a "grande école" **5.** [former - élève] to prepare ; [- athlète] to train ▶ **préparer qqn à qqch** to prepare sb for sthg / *on les prépare intensivement à l'examen* they're being coached for the exam **6.** [habituer] to accustom. ◆ **se préparer** ◆ vp *(emploi réfléchi)* [s'apprêter] to get ready. ◆ vpi *(tournure impersonnelle)* : *je sens qu'il se prépare quelque chose* I can feel there's something afoot ou in the air. ◆ **se préparer à** vp + prép **1.** [être disposé à] to be ready ou prepared for **2.** [être sur le point de] to be about to.

prépayer [pʀepeje] vt to prepay / **'port prépayé'** 'postage paid'.

prépondérance [pʀepɔ̃deʀɑ̃s] nf predominance, preponderance, primacy.

prépondérant, e [pʀepɔ̃deʀɑ̃, ɑ̃t] adj prominent / *jouer un rôle prépondérant* to play a prominent part ou role.

préposé, e [pʀepoze] nm, f **1.** [employé] ▸ **préposé des douanes** customs official ou officer ▸ **préposé au vestiaire** cloakroom attendant **2.** ADMIN ▸ **préposé (aux postes)** postman (postwoman) 🇬🇧, mailman 🇺🇸, mail ou letter carrier 🇺🇸.

préposer [3] [pʀepoze] vt [affecter] ▸ **préposer qqn à** to place ou to put sb in charge of.

préposition [pʀepozisjɔ̃] nf preposition.

préprogrammé, e [pʀepʀɔgʀame] adj pre-programmed.

préréglé, e [pʀeʀegle] adj preset, preprogrammed.

prérequis [pʀeʀəki] nm prerequisite.

préretraite [pʀeʀətʀɛt] nf **1.** [allocation] early retirement allowance **2.** [période] ▸ **partir en préretraite** to take early retirement.

prérogative [pʀeʀɔgativ] nf prerogative, privilege.

près [pʀɛ] adv **1.** [dans l'espace] near, close ▸ **cent mètres plus près** one hundred metres nearer ou closer / *le bureau est tout près* the office is very near ou just around the corner **2.** [dans le temps] near, close, soon / *jeudi c'est trop près, disons plutôt samedi* Thursday is too soon, let's say Saturday. ❖ **à... près** loc corrélative : *c'est parfait, à un détail près* it's perfect but for ou except for one thing / *j'ai raté mon train à quelques secondes près* I missed my train by a few seconds / *on n'est pas à 10 euros près* we can spare 10 euros / *tu n'es plus à cinq minutes près* another five minutes won't make much difference. ❖ **à peu de chose près** loc adv more or less / *à peu de chose près, il y en a cinquante* there are fifty of them, more or less ou give or take a few. ❖ **à peu près** loc adv **1.** [environ] about, around / *on était à peu près cinquante* there were about ou around fifty of us. **2.** [plus ou moins] more or less / *il sait à peu près comment y aller* he knows more or less how to get there. ❖ **de près** loc adv at close range ou quarters / *il est rasé de près* he's clean-shaven ▸ **surveiller qqn de près** to keep a close watch ou eye on sb / *les explosions se sont suivies de très près* the explosions took place within seconds of each other ▸ **regarder qqch de (très) près a)** *pr* to look at sthg very closely **b)** *fig* to look (very) closely at sthg, to look carefully into sthg / *étudions la question de plus près* let's take a closer look at the problem / *tout ce qui touche, de près ou de loin à* everything (which is) even remotely connected with. ❖ **près de** loc prép **1.** [dans l'espace] near / *assieds-toi près de lui* sit near him ou next to him / *vêtements près du corps* close-fitting ou tight-fitting clothes ; [affectivement, qualitativement] close to ▸ **être près de ses sous** ou **de son argent** to be tightfisted **2.** [dans le temps] : *on est près des vacances* it's nearly the holidays / *il doit être près de la retraite* he must be about to retire / *je ne suis pas près d'oublier ça* I'm not about to ou it'll be a long time before I forget that **3.** [environ, presque] nearly, almost / *on était près de cinquante* there were almost ou nearly fifty of us.

présage [pʀezaʒ] nm [signe] omen, portent *litt*, presage *litt*.

présager [17] [pʀezaʒe] vt **1.** [être le signe de] to be a sign of, to portend *litt* / *cela ne présage rien de bon* that's an ominous sign, nothing good will come of it **2.** [prévoir] to predict ▸ **laisser présager qqch** to be a sign of sthg.

presbyte [pʀɛsbit] adj longsighted 🇬🇧, farsighted 🇺🇸, presbyopic *spéc*.

presbytère [pʀɛsbitɛʀ] nm presbytery.

presbytérien, enne [pʀɛsbiteʀjɛ̃, ɛn] adj & nm, f Presbyterian.

presbytie [pʀɛsbisi] nf longsightedness 🇬🇧, farsightedness 🇺🇸, presbyopia *spéc*.

préscolaire [pʀeskɔlɛʀ] adj preschool.

prescription [pʀɛskʀipsjɔ̃] nf **1.** DR prescription / *y a-t-il prescription pour les crimes de guerre ?* is there a statutory limitation relating to war crimes? **2.** [instruction] : *se conformer aux prescriptions* to conform to instructions ou regulations **3.** MÉD [gén] orders, instructions ; [ordonnance] prescription.

prescrire [99] [pʀɛskʀiʀ] vt **1.** [recommander] to prescribe / *on lui a prescrit du repos* she was ordered to rest **2.** [stipuler] to prescribe, to stipulate **3.** DR [propriété] to obtain by prescription ; *(en usage absolu)* : *on ne prescrit pas contre les mineurs* one cannot obtain property from minors by prescription ; [sanction, peine] to lapse.

prescrit, e [pʀɛskʀi, it] adj **1.** [conseillé - dose] prescribed, recommended **2.** [fixé] ▸ **au jour prescrit** on the set day / *dans le délai prescrit* within the agreed time.

préséance [pʀeseɑ̃s] nf [priorité] precedence, priority.

présélection [pʀeseleksjɔ̃] nf **1.** [choix] preselection, short-listing **2.** RADIO ▸ **poste avec / sans présélection** radio with / without preset.

présélectionner [3] [pʀeseleksjɔne] vt **1.** [candidat] to preselect, to short-list **2.** [heure, programme] to preset.

présence [pʀezɑ̃s] nf **1.** [fait d'être là] presence / *réunion à 9 h, présence obligatoire* meeting at 9 o'clock, attendance compulsory **2.** THÉÂTRE [personnalité] presence. ❖ **en présence** loc adj **1.** [en opposition] : *les armées / équipes en présence* the opposing armies / teams **2.** DR : *les parties en présence* the opposing parties, the litigants *spéc*. ❖ **en présence de** loc prép : *je ne parlerai qu'en présence de mon avocat* I will talk unless my lawyer is present. ❖ **présence d'esprit** nf presence of mind / *mon voisin a eu la présence d'esprit de me prévenir* my neighbour had the presence of mind to warn me.

présent, e [pʀezɑ̃, ɑ̃t] ◆ adj **1.** [dans le lieu dont on parle] present ▸ **avoir qqch présent à l'esprit** to bear ou to keep sthg in mind / *des images que nous garderons longtemps présentes à l'esprit* images which will linger in our minds ▸ **répondre présent a)** ÉDUC to answer to one's name, to be present at roll call **b)** *fig* to rise to the challenge **2.** [actif] : *les Français ne sont pas du tout présents dans le jeu* the French team is making no impact on the game at all **3.** *(avant nom)* : *la présente convention* sout this agreement. ◆ nm, f : *il y avait 20 présents à la réunion* 20 people were present at ou attended the meeting. ◆ **présent** nm **1.** [moment] present **2.** GRAM present (tense) ▸ **au présent** in the present ▸ **présent de l'indicatif / du subjonctif** present indicative / subjunctive. ◆ **présente** nf ADMIN [lettre] the present (letter), this letter / *je vous informe par la présente que...* I hereby inform you that... ❖ **à présent** loc adv now.

présentable [pʀezɑ̃tabl] adj presentable.

présentateur, trice [pʀezɑ̃tatœʀ, tʀis] nm, f RADIO & TV [des programmes] announcer, presenter ; [du journal] newscaster, anchorman (anchorwoman) 🇺🇸 ; [de la météo] weatherman (weatherwoman) ; [de variétés] host.

présentation [pʀezɑ̃tasjɔ̃] nf **1.** [dans un groupe] introduction / *Robert, faites donc les présentations* [entre plusieurs personnes] Robert, could you introduce everybody? **2.** COUT fashion show / *aller à une présentation de collection* ou *couture* ou *mode* to attend a fashion show **3.** [exposition] presenting, showing ; COMM [à un client potentiel] presentation **4.** [d'un document, d'un laissez-passer] showing ; [d'un compte, d'une facture] presentation. ❖ **sur présentation de** loc prép on presentation of.

présentement [pʀezɑ̃tmɑ̃] **Québec** adv at present, presently **US**.

présenter [3] [pʀezɑ̃te] ◆ vt **1.** [faire connaître] to introduce / *je te présente ma sœur Blanche* this is ou let me introduce my sister Blanche **2.** [remettre - ticket, papiers] to present, to show ; [- facture, devis] to present **3.** [montrer publiquement] to present **4.** [soumettre - démission] to present, to submit, to hand in *(sép)* ; [- pétition] to put in *(sép)*, to submit ; [- projet de loi] to present, to introduce / *présenter sa candidature à un poste* to apply for a position ; [dans un festival] to present ; [dans un concours] to enter ◗ **présenter l'anglais à l'oral** ÉDUC & UNIV to take English at the oral exam **5.** [expliquer - dossier] to present, to explain ; [- rapport] to present, to bring in *(sép)* / *vous avez présenté votre cas de manière fort convaincante* you have set out ou stated your case most convincingly / *présentez-leur la chose gentiment* put it to them nicely **6.** [dans des formules de politesse] to offer / *je vous présente mes condoléances* please accept ou I'd like to offer my condolences / *présenter ses excuses* to offer (one's) apologies ◗ **présenter ses félicitations à qqn** to congratulate sb **7.** [comporter - anomalie, particularité] to present *sout*, to have ; [- symptômes, traces, signes] to show ; [- difficulté, risque] to involve ◗ **présenter l'avantage de** to have the advantage of / *cette œuvre présente un intérêt particulier* this work is of particular interest / *les deux systèmes présentent peu de différences* the two systems present *sout* ou display very few differences. ◆ vi : *il présente bien, ton ami* your friend looks good. ◈ **se présenter** ◆ vp *(emploi réfléchi)* [décliner son identité] to introduce o.s. ◆ vpi **1.** [se manifester] to appear / *vous devez vous présenter au tribunal à 14 h* you are required to be in court at 2 pm / *elle s'est présentée à son entretien avec une heure de retard* she arrived one hour late for the interview ◗ **se présenter chez qqn** to call on sb, to go to sb's house **2.** [avoir telle tournure] : *les choses se présentent plutôt mal* things aren't looking too good / *tout cela se présente fort bien* it all looks very promising **3.** [être candidat] ◗ **se présenter à la présidentielle** to run for president / *se présenter à un examen* to take an exam / *se présenter à un concours de beauté* to go in for ou to enter a beauty contest **4.** [survenir] to arise / *si une difficulté se présente* if any difficulty should arise / *j'attends que quelque chose d'intéressant se présente* I'm waiting for something interesting to turn up ou to come my way.

présentoir [pʀezɑ̃twaʀ] nm [étagère] (display) shelf ; [support] (display) stand, display unit.

préservatif [pʀezɛʀvatif] nm condom, sheath ◗ **préservatif féminin a)** [gén] female condom, femidom **b)** [diaphragme] diaphragm.

> ⚠ **Preservative** signifie « conservateur » et non préservatif.

préservation [pʀezɛʀvasjɔ̃] nf preservation, protection.

préserver [3] [pʀezɛʀve] vt [maintenir] to preserve, to keep.

présidence [pʀezidɑ̃s] nf POL [fonction] presidency ; UNIV principalship, vice-chancellorship **US**, presidency **US** ; COMM [d'un homme] chairmanship, directorship ; ADMIN chairmanship / *la présidence du jury* UNIV the chief examinership.

président [pʀezidɑ̃] nm **1.** POL president ◗ **le président de la République française** the French President **2.** ADMIN chairman (chairwoman), chairperson **3.** COMM chairman (chairwoman) ◗ **président-directeur général** chairman and managing director **US**, president and chief executive officer

US ◗ **président du conseil d'administration** Chairman of the Board **4.** DR ◗ **président du tribunal** vice-chancellor **US** **5.** UNIV principal, vice-chancellor **US**, president **US** ◗ **président du jury (d'examen)** chief examiner **6.** SPORT : *président d'un club de football* president of a football club / *le président du comité olympique* the chairman of the Olympic Committee ◗ **président du jury** chairman of the panel of judges.

présidente [pʀezidɑ̃t] nf **1.** POL [titulaire] (woman) president **2.** COMM [titulaire] chairwoman **3.** DR presiding judge.

présidentiable [pʀezidɑ̃sjabl] nmf would-be presidential candidate.

présidentiel, elle [pʀezidɑ̃sjɛl] adj [du président] presidential, president's. ◈ **présidentielle** nf presidential election ou elections.

présider [3] [pʀezide] vt [diriger - séance] to preside at ou over *(insép)* ; [- œuvre de bienfaisance, commission] to preside over, to be the president of ; [table] to be at the head of. ◈ **présider à** v + prép *sout* : *présider aux destinées d'un pays* to rule over a country, to steer the ship of state *sout*.

présomption [pʀezɔ̃psjɔ̃] nf **1.** [prétention] presumption, presumptuousness **2.** [supposition] presumption, assumption **3.** DR presumption.

présomptueux, euse [pʀezɔ̃ptɥø, øz] adj presumptuous.

presque [pʀɛsk] adv **1.** [dans des phrases affirmatives] almost, nearly / *l'espèce a presque entièrement disparu* the species is virtually ou all but extinct **2.** [dans des phrases négatives] : *ils ne se sont presque pas parlé* they hardly spoke to each other / *je n'avais presque pas mangé de la journée* I'd eaten next to ou almost ou virtually nothing all day / *est-ce qu'il reste des gâteaux ?* — *non, presque pas* are there any cakes left? — hardly any / *il n'y a presque plus de café* there's hardly any coffee left **3.** *sout* [quasi] : *la presque totalité des électeurs* almost ou nearly all the voters.

presqu'île, presqu'ile* [pʀɛskil] nf peninsula.

pressant, e [pʀesɑ̃, ɑ̃t] adj **1.** [urgent] urgent **2.** [insistant - question, invitation] pressing, insistent.

presse [pʀɛs] nf **1.** [journaux, magazines, etc.] ◗ **la presse (écrite)** the press, the papers ◗ **presse féminine / financière / sportive** women's / financial / sports magazines ◗ **presse à sensation** ou **à scandale** popular press, gutter press ; ≃ tabloids ◗ **presse quotidienne régionale** local daily press ◗ **avoir bonne / mauvaise presse a)** *pr* to have a good / bad press **b)** *fig* to be well / badly thought of **2.** IMPR press / *être mis sous presse* to go to press. ◈ **de presse** loc adj [campagne, coupure, attaché] press *(modif)*.

Presse

The main national newspapers in France are, in alphabetical order:

l'Équipe: a popular daily sports newspaper;

le Figaro: a quality broadsheet newspaper (it has a predominantly conservative readership);

France-Dimanche: a popular weekend broadsheet with a tendency to sensationalism;

Le Canard enchaîné: a weekly satirical newspaper which appears on Wednesdays;

l'Humanité ("l'Huma"): a quality daily broadsheet (it is the organ of the French Communist Party);

Libération ("Libé"): a quality daily tabloid (with a predominantly left-of-centre readership);

le Monde: a quality broadsheet newspaper which appears in the afternoon (its readership is predominantly left-of-centre).

pressé, e [pʀese] adj **1.** [personne] ▶ **être pressé** to be pressed for time, to be in a hurry ou rush / *je suis pressé d'en finir* I'm anxious to get the whole thing over with **2.** [urgent - réparation, achat] urgent / *il n'a rien trouvé de plus pressé que d'aller tout raconter à sa femme* he wasted no time in telling his wife the whole story ; [agrume] freshly squeezed.

presse-citron [pʀesitʀɔ̃] (*pl* presse-citron *ou* presse-citrons) nm lemon squeezer.

pressentiment [pʀesɑ̃timɑ̃] nm premonition, feeling, hunch / *j'ai eu le curieux pressentiment que je reviendrais ici un jour* I had the odd feeling ou a hunch that I'd be back again some day.

pressentir [37] [pʀesɑ̃tiʀ] vt **1.** [prévoir] to sense (in advance), to have a premonition of / *pressentir un danger / des difficultés* to sense danger / trouble **2.** [contacter] to approach, to contact / *toutes les personnes pressenties* all the people who were contacted.

presse-papiers (*pl* presse-papiers), **presse-papier*** [pʀɛspapje] nm paperweight.

presser [4] [pʀese] ◆ vt **1.** [extraire le jus de] to squeeze / *presser le raisin* to press grapes **2.** [faire se hâter] to rush ▶ **presser le pas** to speed up **3.** [accabler] ▶ **presser qqn de questions** to ply ou to bombard sb with questions. ◆ vi ▶ **le temps presse** time is short ▶ **l'affaire presse** it's an urgent matter ▶ **rien ne presse, ça ne presse pas** there's no (need to) rush ou hurry ▶ **pressons !** come on, let's hurry up! ◆ **se presser** vpi [se dépêcher] to hurry / *il n'est que 2 h, il n'y a pas de raison de se presser* it's only 2 o'clock, there's no point in rushing ou no need to hurry / *allons les enfants, pressons-nous un peu* come on children, get a move on.

pressing [pʀesiŋ] nm **1.** [boutique] dry cleaner's **2.** *fam* SPORT ▶ **faire le pressing** to put ou to pile on the pressure.

pression [pʀesjɔ̃] nf **1.** [action] pressure **2.** PHYS pressure ▶ **mettre sous pression** to pressurize ▶ **à haute / basse pression** high- / low-pressure ▶ **pression atmosphérique** MÉTÉOR atmospheric pressure ▶ **être sous pression** to be stressed ou under pressure **3.** [contrainte morale] pressure ▶ **faire pression sur qqn, mettre la pression sur** ou **à qqn** to put pressure on sb ▶ **mettre la pression** to put ou lay on the pressure **4.** [bière] draught 🇬🇧 ou draft 🇺🇸 (beer). ◆ **à la pression** loc adj [bière] draught 🇬🇧, draft 🇺🇸.

pressoir [pʀeswaʀ] nm [appareil] : *pressoir (à vin)* winepress ▶ **pressoir à cidre / huile** cider / oil press.

pressurer [3] [pʀesyʀe] vt **1.** [raisin] to press ; [citron] to squeeze **2.** *fig* [exploiter] to squeeze, to extort, to exploit.

pressuriser [3] [pʀesyʀize] vt to pressurize.

prestance [pʀɛstɑ̃s] nf : *il a de la prestance* he is a fine figure of a man.

prestataire [pʀɛstatɛʀ] nmf **1.** [bénéficiaire] recipient (*of an allowance*) **2.** [fournisseur] ▶ **prestataire de service** service provider.

prestation [pʀɛstasjɔ̃] nf **1.** [allocation] allowance, benefit ▶ **prestations sociales** social security benefits **2.** COMM ▶ **prestation de service** provision ou delivery of a service **3.** [d'un artiste, d'un sportif, etc.] performance / *faire une bonne / mauvaise prestation* to play well / badly.

prestidigitateur, trice [pʀɛstidiʒitatœʀ, tʀis] nm, f conjuror, magician.

prestidigitation [pʀɛstidiʒitasjɔ̃] nf conjuring, prestidigitation *sout*.

prestige [pʀɛstiʒ] nm prestige ▶ **le prestige de l'uniforme** the glamour of the uniform. ◆ **de prestige** loc adj [politique] prestige (*modif*) ; [résidence] luxury (*modif*).

prestigieux, euse [pʀɛstiʒjø, øz] adj [magnifique] prestigious, glamorous.

présumé, e [pʀezyme] adj **1.** [considéré comme] présumed / *tout accusé, en l'absence de preuves, est présumé innocent* in the absence of proof, all defendants are presumed innocent **2.** [supposé] presumed, putative.

présumer [3] [pʀezyme] vt [supposer] to presume, to assume / *je présume que vous êtes sa sœur* I take it ou presume you're his sister. ◆ **présumer de** v + prép [surestimer] : *j'ai un peu présumé de mes forces* I overdid things somewhat ▶ **présumer de qqn** to rely on sb too much.

présupposé [pʀesypoze] nm presupposition.

prêt¹ [pʀe] nm **1.** [bancaire] loan ▶ **prêt à la construction** building loan ▶ **prêt immobilier** mortgage, home loan ; ≃ mortgage **2.** [dans une bibliothèque - document] loan, issue, book issued.

prêt², e [pʀe, pʀɛt] adj **1.** [préparé] ready / *je suis prêt, on peut partir* I'm ready, we can go now ▶ **prêt à** : *prêt à l'envoi* ready for dispatch / *prêt (fin) prêt au départ* to be all set to go ▶ **prêt à l'usage** off-the-shelf **2.** [disposé] ▶ **prêt à** ready ou willing to ▶ **être prêt à tout** to be game for anything.

prêt-à-porter [pʀɛtapɔʀte] (*pl* prêts-à-porter) nm (ready-to-wear) fashion.

prétendant, e [pʀetɑ̃dɑ̃, ɑ̃t] nm, f : *prétendant au trône* pretender to the throne. ◆ **prétendant** nm *hum* [soupirant] suitor, wooer *vieilli*.

prétendre [73] [pʀetɑ̃dʀ] vt **1.** [affirmer] to claim, to say, to maintain / *je ne prétends pas être un expert* I don't pretend to be an expert / *à ce qu'elle prétend, son mari est ambassadeur* according to her, her husband is an ambassador **2.** [avoir l'intention de] to intend, to mean. ◆ **prétendre à** v + prép *litt* [aspirer à] to aspire to.

⚠ En anglais moderne, **pretend** signifie généralement « faire semblant » et ne doit pas être employé systématiquement pour traduire prétendre.

prétendu, e [pʀetɑ̃dy] adj [par soi-même] so-called, self-styled ; [par autrui] so-called, alleged.

prétendument [pʀetɑ̃dymɑ̃] adv [par soi-même] supposedly ; [par autrui] supposedly, allegedly.

prête-nom [pʀɛtnɔ̃] (*pl* **prête-noms**) nm figurehead, man of straw.

prétentieux, euse [pʀetɑ̃sjø, øz] ◆ adj [personne] pretentious ; [style, remarque] pretentious. ◆ nm, f conceited ou self-important person, poseur.

prétention [pʀetɑ̃sjɔ̃] nf **1.** [orgueil] pretentiousness, conceit, self-conceit / *il est plein de prétention* he's so conceited **2.** [ambition] pretension, pretence. ❖ **prétentions** nfpl **1.** [exigences] claims / *avoir des prétentions sur un héritage* / *une propriété* to lay claim to an inheritance / a property **2.** [financières] : *vos prétentions sont trop élevées* you're asking for too high a salary / *envoyez une lettre spécifiant vos prétentions* send a letter specifying your salary expectations. ❖ **sans prétention** loc adj unpretentious.

prêter [4] [pʀete] vt **1.** [argent, bien] to lend / *peux-tu me prêter ta voiture ?* can you lend me ou can I borrow your car? **2.** [attribuer] to attribute, to accord **3.** [offrir] ▸ **prêter assistance** ou **secours à qqn** to give ou to lend assistance to sb ▸ **prêter attention à** to pay attention to ▸ **prêter main forte à qqn** to lend sb a hand ▸ **prêter l'oreille** to listen ▸ **prêter serment** a) to take the oath b) POL to be sworn in ▸ **prêter le flanc à** : *prêter le flanc à la critique* to lay o.s. open to ou to invite criticism. ❖ **prêter à** v + prép [donner lieu à] to give rise to, to invite / *la déclaration prête à équivoque* the statement is ambiguous / *il est d'une naïveté qui prête à rire* he is ridiculously naive. ❖ **se prêter à** vp + prép **1.** [consentir à] to lend o.s. to ▸ **se prêter au jeu** to enter into the spirit of the game **2.** [être adapté à] to be suitable for.

> 📋 **Prêter qqch à qqn** Lend sthg to sb ou lend sb sthg.
>
> Notez la construction à double complément qui en anglais peut prendre deux formes dont le sens est le même :
>
> • une structure identique à celle du français :
>   verbe + COD + préposition + COI
>   lend sthg to sb
>
> • une structure qui diffère de celle du français, sans préposition, et dans laquelle l'ordre des compléments est inversé :
>   verbe + COI + COD
>   lend sb sthg
>
> **Ils nous ont prêté leur appartement.** *They lent their flat to us* ou *They lent us their flat.*
> **Pouvez-vous prêter votre voiture à ma mère pour le week-end ?** *Can you lend your car to my mother for the weekend?* ou *Can you lend my mother your car for the weekend?*

prétérit [pʀeteʀit] nm preterite.

prêteur, euse [pʀetœʀ, øz] ◆ adj : *elle n'est pas prêteuse* she doesn't like lending, she's very possessive about her belongings. ◆ nm, f lender, moneylender ▸ **prêteur sur gages** pawnbroker.

prétexte [pʀetɛkst] nm [excuse] pretext, excuse / *un mauvais prétexte* a lame ou feeble excuse / *pour toi, tous les prétextes sont bons pour ne pas travailler* any excuse is good for avoiding work as far as you are concerned. ❖ **sous aucun prétexte** loc adv on no account. ❖ **sous prétexte de, sous prétexte que** loc conj : *il est sorti sous prétexte d'aller acheter du pain* he went out on the pretext of buying some bread.

prétexter [4] [pʀetɛkste] vt to give as a pretext, to use as an excuse ▸ **prétexter que** to pretend (that).

prétimbré, e [pʀetɛ̃bʀe] adj prepaid.

prêtre [pʀɛtʀ] nm RELIG priest.

prêt relais (*pl* **prêts relais**) [pʀeʀalɛ] nm ▸ **prêt relais** bridging loan.

preuve [pʀœv] nf **1.** [indice] proof, (piece of) evidence / *avoir la preuve que* to have proof that / *avez-vous des preuves de ce que vous avancez ?* can you produce evidence of ou can you prove what you're saying? **2.** [démonstration] proof / *mon avocat fera la preuve de mon innocence* my lawyer will prove that I'm innocent, my lawyer will prove my innocence ▸ **faire preuve de** : *faire preuve d'un grand sang-froid* to show ou to display great presence of mind ▸ **faire ses preuves** : *c'est un produit qui a fait ses preuves* it's a tried and tested product / *il avait fait ses preuves dans le maquis* he'd won his spurs ou proved himself in the Maquis. ❖ **preuve en main** loc adv with cast-iron proof available ▸ **affirmer qqch preuve en main** to back up a statement with cast-iron evidence ou proof.

prévaloir [61] [pʀevalwaʀ] vi [prédominer] to prevail / *nous lutterons pour faire prévaloir nos droits légitimes* we will fight for our legitimate rights. ❖ **se prévaloir de** vp + prép **1.** [profiter de] : *elle se prévalait de son ancienneté pour imposer ses goûts* she took advantage of her seniority to impose her preferences **2.** [se vanter de] : *il se prévalait de ses origines aristocratiques* he boasted of ou about his aristocratic background.

prévenance [pʀevnɑ̃s] nf kindness, consideration, thoughtfulness.

prévenant, e [pʀevnɑ̃, ɑ̃t] adj kindly, considerate, thoughtful ▸ **être prévenant à l'égard de qqn** to be considerate ou thoughtful towards sb.

prévenir [40] [pʀevniʀ] vt **1.** [informer] ▸ **prévenir qqn** to inform sb, to let sb know ▸ **prévenir la police** to call ou to notify the police **2.** [mettre en garde] to warn, to tell / *je te préviens, si tu recommences, c'est la fessée !* I'm warning you, if you do that again I'll spank you! ; *(en usage absolu)* ▸ **partir sans prévenir** to leave without warning ou notice **3.** [empêcher] to prevent, to avert **4.** [anticiper - désir, besoin] to anticipate ; [- accusation, critique] to forestall.

préventif, ive [pʀevɑ̃tif, iv] adj preventive, preventative / *prendre des mesures préventives* to take preventive ou precautionary measures / *prenez ce médicament à titre préventif* take this medicine as a precaution.

prévention [pʀevɑ̃sjɔ̃] nf [ensemble de mesures] prevention ▸ **la prévention routière** the road safety measures ; ≃ Royal Society for the Prevention of Accidents 🇬🇧.

prévenu, e [pʀevny] ◆ pp ⟶ **prévenir.** ◆ nm, f [à un procès] defendant ; [en prison] prisoner.

prévisible [pʀevizibl] adj foreseeable, predictable / *ses réactions ne sont pas toujours prévisibles* his reactions are sometimes unexpected ou unpredictable / *difficilement prévisible* difficult to foresee ▸ **dans un avenir prévisible** in the foreseeable future.

prévision [pʀevizjɔ̃] nf **1.** *(gén au pl)* [calcul] expectation **2.** ÉCON [processus] forecasting ▸ **prévision budgétaire** budget forecast ou projections **3.** MÉTÉOR [technique] (weather) forecasting ▸ **prévisions météorologiques** [bulletin] weather forecast. ❖ **en prévision de** loc prép in anticipation of.

prévisionnel, elle [pʀevizjɔnɛl] adj [analyse, étude] forward-looking ; [coût] estimated ; [budget] projected.

prévoir [63] [pʀevwaʀ] vt **1.** [prédire] to foresee, to expect, to anticipate ; MÉTÉOR to forecast / *on ne peut pas toujours tout prévoir* you can't always think of everything in advance / *rien ne laissait prévoir qu'il nous quitterait* *si rapidement* we never expected him to pass away so soon **2.** [projeter] to plan / *tout s'est passé comme prévu* everything went according to plan ou smoothly / *on a dîné plus tôt que prévu* we had dinner earlier than planned / *tout est prévu pour les invités* everything has been laid on ou arranged for the guests / *j'ai prévu d'apporter des boissons chaudes pour tout le monde* I'm planning to bring hot drinks for everyone **3.** [préparer] to allow, to provide ‣ **prévoyez des vêtements chauds** make sure you bring some warm clothes **4.** DR to provide for / *dans tous les cas prévus par la loi* in all cases provided for by law.

prévoyance [pʀevwajɑ̃s] nf foresight, foresightedness, forethought.

prévoyant, e [pʀevwajɑ̃, ɑ̃t] adj provident, prudent.

prévu, e [pʀevy] pp ⟶ **prévoir**.

prier [10] [pʀije] ◆ vt **1.** [ciel, Dieu] to pray to **2.** [supplier] to beg, to beseech *litt* / *je vous en prie, emmenez-moi* I beg you to take me with you / *je te prie de me pardonner* please forgive me / *les enfants, je vous en prie, ça suffit !* children, please, that's enough! ‣ **se faire prier** : *il adore se faire prier* he loves to be coaxed / *j'ai accepté sans me faire prier* I said yes without any hesitation **3.** [enjoindre] to request / *vous êtes priés d'arriver à l'heure* you're requested to arrive on time / *je vous prie de sortir* will you please leave the room **4.** [dans des formules de politesse orales] : *merci — je vous en prie* thank you — (please) don't mention it / *puis-je entrer ? — je vous en prie* may I come in? — please do ; [par écrit] : *je vous prie de croire à mes sentiments distingués* ou *les meilleurs* yours sincerely. ◆ vi to pray ‣ **prier pour qqn** to pray for sb.

prière [pʀijɛʀ] nf **1.** RELIG prayer / *dire* ou *faire* ou *réciter ses prières* to pray, to say one's prayers **2.** [requête] request, plea, entreaty / *elle a fini par céder aux prières de ses enfants* she finally gave in to her children's pleas / *'prière de ne pas fumer'* 'no smoking (please)'.

primaire [pʀimɛʀ] ◆ adj **1.** [premier - d'une série] primary ‣ **école / enseignement primaire** primary school / education **2.** [borné - personne] simpleminded ; [- attitude] simplistic, unsophisticated. ◆ nm ‣ **le primaire** ENS primary education ‣ **dans le primaire** ENS in primary schools. ◆ nf POL primary (election).

primate [pʀimat] nm ZOOL primate.

primauté [pʀimote] nf [supériorité] primacy.

prime [pʀim] ◆ adj *litt* [premier] ‣ **dès sa prime enfance** ou **jeunesse** from her earliest childhood. ◆ nf **1.** [gratification] bonus ; [indemnité - par un organisme] allowance ; [- par l'État] subsidy ‣ **prime d'ancienneté** seniority bonus ‣ **prime de rendement** ou **de résultat** productivity bonus ‣ **prime de risque** danger money **2.** FIN [assurances - cotisation] premium ‣ **prime d'assurance** insurance premium. ❖ **de prime abord** loc adv at first sight ou glance. ❖ **en prime** loc adv as a bonus.

primer [3] [pʀime] ◆ vt **1.** [récompenser - animal, invention] to award a prize to **2.** *sout* [prédominer sur] to take precedence over. ◆ vi [avoir l'avantage] to be dominant ‣ **primer sur** to take precedence over.

primesautier, ère [pʀimsotje, ɛʀ] adj *sout* [spontané] impulsive, spontaneous.

primeur [pʀimœʀ] nf *sout* [exclusivité] : *notre chaîne a eu la primeur de l'information* our channel was first with the news. ❖ **primeurs** nfpl early fruit and vegetables.

primevère [pʀimvɛʀ] nf [sauvage] primrose ; [cultivée] primula.

primitif, ive [pʀimitif, iv] adj [initial] primitive, original.

primo [pʀimo] adv first (of all), firstly.

primo-accédant, e [pʀimoaksedɑ̃, ɑ̃t] (*mpl* primo-accédants, *fpl* primo-accédantes) nm, f first-time buyer.

primo-délinquant, e [pʀimodelɛ̃kɑ̃, ɑ̃t] (*mpl* primo-délinquants, *fpl* primo-délinquantes) nm, f first offender.

primordial, e, aux [pʀimɔʀdjal, o] adj [essentiel] fundamental, essential / *elle a eu un rôle primordial dans les négociations* she played a crucial role in the negotiations.

prince [pʀɛ̃s] nm [souverain, fils de roi] prince ‣ **le prince héritier** the crown prince ‣ **le prince de Galles** the Prince of Wales ‣ **le Prince charmant** Prince Charming ‣ **être** ou **se montrer bon prince** to behave generously.

princesse [pʀɛ̃sɛs] nf [souveraine, fille de roi] princess.

princier, ère [pʀɛ̃sje, ɛʀ] adj [du prince] prince's, royal.

principal, e, aux [pʀɛ̃sipal, o] ◆ adj [essentiel] main / *c'est lui l'acteur principal* he's the leading man. ◆ nm, f ÉDUC headmaster (headmistress) UK, (school) principal US. ❖ **principal** nm ‣ **le principal** the most important thing / *c'est fini, c'est le principal* it's over, that's the main thing. ❖ **principale** nf LING main clause.

principalement [pʀɛ̃sipalmɑ̃] adv chiefly, mostly, principally.

principauté [pʀɛ̃sipote] nf principality.

principe [pʀɛ̃sip] nm **1.** [règle morale] principle, rule of conduct / *j'ai des principes* I've got principles / *j'ai toujours eu pour principe d'agir honnêtement* I have always made it a principle to act with honesty **2.** [axiome] principle, law, axiom / *je pars du principe que...* I start from the principle ou I assume that... ‣ **le principe d'Archimède** Archimedes' principle. ❖ **de principe** loc adj [accord, approbation] provisional ‣ **c'est une question de principe** it's a matter of principle. ❖ **en principe** loc adv [en théorie] in principle, in theory, theoretically. ❖ **par principe** loc adv on principle. ❖ **pour le principe** loc adv on principle.

printanier, ère [pʀɛ̃tanje, ɛʀ] adj [du printemps] spring ‣ **une température printanière** springlike weather.

printemps [pʀɛ̃tɑ̃] nm [saison] spring ‣ **au printemps** in (the) springtime.

priori [pʀijɔʀi] ⟶ **a priori**.

prioritaire [pʀijɔʀitɛʀ] adj **1.** TRANSP priority (*modif*), having priority / *ce véhicule est prioritaire lorsqu'il quitte son arrêt* this vehicle has the (right of way when leaving a stop **2.** [usager, industrie] priority (*modif*) / *notre projet est prioritaire sur tous les autres* our project has priority over all the others.

priorité [pʀijɔʀite] nf **1.** [sur route] right of way ‣ **avoir la priorité** to have the right of way / *'priorité à droite'* 'give way UK ', 'yield to right US (in France, road law that gives right of way to vehicles coming from the right)* ' **2.** [primauté] priority ‣ **donner** ou **accorder la priorité à qqch** to prioritize sthg, to give priority to sthg. ❖ **en priorité, par priorité** loc adv as a priority, as a matter of urgency.

pris, e [pʀi, iz] ◆ pp ⟶ **prendre**. ◆ adj **1.** [occupé - personne] busy / *aide-moi, tu vois bien que j'ai les mains prises* help me, can't you see my hands are full? **2.** MÉD [gorge] sore ; [nez] blocked **3.** [envahi] ‣ **pris de** : *pris de pitié / peur* stricken by pity / fear / *pris de panique* panic-stricken / *pris d'une violente douleur* seized with a terrible pain ‣ **pris de boisson** *sout* under the influence of alcohol. ❖ **prise** nf **1.** [point de saisie] grip, hold ‣ **avoir prise sur qqn** to have a hold over sb / *je n'ai aucune prise sur mes filles* I can't control my daughters at all ‣ **donner prise à la critique a)** [personne] to lay o.s. open to attack **b)** [idée, réalisation] to be open to attack ‣ **lâcher prise** *pr & fig* to let go **2.** [de judo, de lutte] : *faire une prise de judo à qqn* to get sb in a judo hold **3.** [capture - de contrebande, de drogue] seizure, catch ; JEUX capture ; PÊCHE catch ; MIL ▸ **prises de guerre** spoils of war **4.** ÉLECTR ▸ **prise (de courant)** ou **électrique a)** [mâle] plug **b)** [femelle] socket ▸ **prise multiple** adaptor ▸ **prise de terre** earth 🇬🇧, ground 🇺🇸 **5.** TECHNOL ▸ **prise d'air a)** [ouverture] air inlet **b)** [introduction d'air] ventilation ▸ **prise d'eau** water point **6.** [durcissement - du ciment, de la colle] setting ; [- d'un fromage] hardening / *à prise rapide* [ciment, colle] quicksetting. ❖ **aux prises avec** loc prép fighting ou battling against, grappling with / *je l'ai laissé aux prises avec un problème de géométrie* I left him grappling ou wrestling with a geometry problem. ❖ **en prise** ◆ loc adv AUTO in gear / *mets-toi en prise* put the car in ou into gear. ◆ loc adj : *être en prise (directe) avec la réalité* fig to have a good hold on ou to have a firm grip on reality. ❖ **prise de bec** nf row, squabble. ❖ **prise de sang** blood test. ❖ **prise de son** nf sound (recording). ❖ **prise de vues** nf CINÉ & TV [technique] shooting ; [image] (camera) shot.

prisé, e [pʀize] adj valued / *des qualités très prisées* highly valued qualities.

priser [3] [pʀize] ◆ vt **1.** litt [estimer] to prize, to value highly **2.** [tabac] to take. ◆ vi to take snuff.

prisme [pʀism] nm SCI prism.

prison [pʀizɔ̃] nf **1.** [lieu] prison, jail ▸ **envoyer / mettre qqn en prison** to send sb to / to put sb in jail **2.** [peine] imprisonment ▸ **faire de la prison** to be in prison ou jail, to serve time / *il a été condamné à cinq ans de prison* he was sentenced to five years in jail.

prisonnier, ère [pʀizɔnje, ɛʀ] ◆ adj [séquestré] captive. ◆ nm, f prisoner / *il a été fait prisonnier* he was taken prisoner.

privatif, ive [pʀivatif, iv] adj [privé] private / *avec jardin privatif* with a private garden.

privation [pʀivasjɔ̃] nf [perte] loss, deprivation. ❖ **privations** nfpl [sacrifices] hardship, hardships.

privatisation [pʀivatizasjɔ̃] nf privatization, privatizing.

privatiser [3] [pʀivatize] vt to privatize.

privé, e [pʀive] adj **1.** [personnel] private **2.** [non public] private **3.** [officieux] unofficial. ❖ **privé** nm **1.** INDUST private sector **2.** fam [détective] sleuth, private detective. ❖ **en privé** loc adv in private.

priver [3] [pʀive] vt **1.** [démunir] to deprive ▸ **être privé de** to be deprived of, to have no / *nous sommes privés de voiture depuis une semaine* we've been without a car for a week / *privé d'eau / d'air / de sommeil* deprived of water / air / sleep **2.** [comme sanction] to deprive ▸ **priver qqn de qqch** to make sb go ou do without sthg ▸ **tu seras privé de dessert / télévision** no dessert / television for you. ❖ **se priver de** vp + prép **1.** [renoncer à] to deprive o.s. of, to do without / *il se prive d'alcool* he cuts out drink, he goes without drink ; *(en usage absolu) : il n'aime pas se priver* he hates denying himself anything **2.** [se gêner pour] : *je ne vais pas me priver de le lui dire !* I'll make no bones about telling him!

privilège [pʀivilɛʒ] nm [avantage] privilege.

privilégié, e [pʀivileʒje] ◆ adj [avantagé] privileged / *l'île jouit d'un climat privilégié* the island enjoys an excellent climate / *appartenir aux classes privilégiées* to belong to the privileged classes. ◆ nm, f privileged person / *quelques privilégiés ont assisté à la représentation* a privileged few attended the performance.

privilégier [9] [pʀivileʒje] vt **1.** [préférer] to privilege **2.** [avantager] to favour 🇬🇧, to favor 🇺🇸.

prix [pʀi] nm **1.** [tarif fixe] price, cost / *prix et conditions de transport d'un produit* freight rates and conditions for a product / *le prix de l'essence à la pompe* the cost of pet-

rol 🇬🇧 ou gas 🇺🇸 to the motorist / *ça coûte un prix fou* it costs a fortune ou the earth / *à bas prix* very cheaply / *à ce prix-là* at that price ▸ **dans mes prix** within my (price) range ▸ **le prix fort a)** [maximal] top ou maximum price **b)** [excessif] high price ▸ **un bon prix** : *je l'ai acheté un bon prix* I bought it for a very reasonable price ▸ **prix imposé / libre** fixed / deregulated price ▸ **prix d'achat** purchase price ▸ **prix d'appel** loss leader ▸ **prix conseillé** recommended retail price ▸ **prix coûtant** ou **de revient** cost price ▸ **prix de détail** retail price ▸ **prix de gros** wholesale price ▸ **prix de lancement** introductory price ▸ **prix public** retail price ▸ **prix de revient** cost price ▸ **prix à l'unité** unit price ▸ **prix usine** factory price ▸ **prix de vente** selling price ▸ **oui, mais à quel prix !** fig yes, but at what cost! ▸ **à prix d'or** : *on achète aujourd'hui ses esquisses à prix d'or* his sketches are now worth their weight in gold ou now cost the earth / *je l'ai acheté à prix d'or* I paid a small fortune for it ▸ **y mettre le prix** : *j'ai fini par trouver le cuir que je voulais mais j'ai dû y mettre le prix* I finally found the type of leather I was looking for, but I had to pay top price for it **2.** [étiquette] price (tag) ou label / *il n'y avait pas de prix dessus* it wasn't priced, there was no price tag on it **3.** [barème convenu] price / *votre prix sera le mien* name your price ▸ **faire un prix (d'ami) à qqn** to do a special deal for sb ▸ **mettre qqch à prix** [aux enchères] to set a reserve 🇬🇧 ou an upset 🇺🇸 price on sthg **4.** [valeur] price, value / *le prix de la vie / liberté* the price of life / freedom ▸ **donner du prix à qqch** to make sthg worthwhile / *ça n'a pas de prix* you can't put a price on it **5.** [dans un concours commercial, un jeu] prize ; [dans un concours artistique, un festival] prize, award / *premier / deuxième prix* first / second prize ▸ **prix littéraire** literary prize / *elle a eu le prix de la meilleure interprétation* she got the award for best actress ▸ **le Grand Prix (automobile)** SPORT the Grand Prix ▸ **le prix Goncourt** *the most prestigious French annual literary prize* ▸ **le prix Nobel** the Nobel prize **6.** [œuvre primée - livre] award-winning book ou title ; [- disque] award-winning record ; [- film] award-winning film 🇬🇧 ou movie 🇺🇸 **7.** [lauréat] prizewinner **8.** ÉDUC [distinction] : *jour de la distribution des prix* prize-giving day ▸ **prix d'excellence** first prize. ❖ **à aucun prix** loc adv not at any price, not for all the world, on no account / *je ne quitterais le pays à aucun prix !* nothing would induce me to leave the country! ❖ **à n'importe quel prix** loc adv at any price, no matter what (the cost). ❖ **à tout prix** loc adv **1.** [obligatoirement] at all costs **2.** [coûte que coûte] at any cost, no matter what (the cost). ❖ **au prix de** loc prép at the cost of. ❖ **de prix** loc adj [bijou, objet] valuable. ❖ **sans prix** loc adj invaluable, priceless.

pro [pʀo] (abr de **professionnel**) fam nmf pro / *c'est une vraie pro* she's a real pro / *ils ont fait un vrai travail de pro* they did a really professional job.

probabilité [pʀobabilite] nf **1.** [vraisemblance] probability, likelihood ▸ **selon toute probabilité** in all probability ou likelihood **2.** [supposition] probability **3.** MATH & PHYS probability.

probable [pʀobabl] adj **1.** [vraisemblable] likely, probable / *il est peu probable qu'elle soit sa sœur* it's not very likely that she's his sister **2.** [possible] probable / *est-il à Paris ? — c'est probable* is he in Paris? — quite probably (he is) / *il est probable qu'elle vienne* she'll probably come.

probablement [pʀobabləmã] adv probably.

probant, e [pʀobã, ãt] adj [convaincant - argument, fait, expérience] convincing.

probatoire [pʀobatwaʀ] adj probationary.

probité [pʀobite] nf probity, integrity, uprightness.

problématique [pʀoblematik] ◆ adj problematic, problematical. ◆ nf set of problems ou issues.

problème [pʀɔblɛm] nm **1.** [difficulté] problem, difficulty / *pas de problème, viens quand tu veux* no problem, you can come whenever you want ▸ **un problème personnel** a personal matter ▸ **problème de santé** health problem / *il a toujours eu des problèmes d'argent* he always had money troubles ou problems **2.** [question] problem, issue, question / *soulever un problème* to raise a question ou an issue. ◆ **à problèmes** loc adj problem *(modif)* / *ma cousine, c'est une femme à problèmes* fam my cousin's always got problems.

procédé [pʀɔsede] nm **1.** sout [comportement] conduct, behaviour 🇬🇧, behavior 🇺🇸 / *je n'ai pas du tout apprécié son procédé* I wasn't very impressed with what he did **2.** [technique] process.

procéder [18] [pʀɔsede] vi **1.** [progresser] to proceed ▸ **procéder par ordre** to take things in order **2.** [se conduire] to behave / *j'apprécie sa manière de procéder avec nous* I like the way he deals with us. ◆ **procéder à** v + prép [effectuer] to conduct / *procéder à une étude* to conduct a study / *procéder à l'élection du bureau national du parti* to elect the national executive of the party.

📝 In reformed spelling (see p. 16-18), this verb is conjugated like *semer* : *il procèdera, elle procèderait*.

procédure [pʀɔsedyʀ] nf [démarche] procedure, way to proceed.

procès [pʀɔsɛ] nm **1.** DR [pénal] trial ; [civil] lawsuit, legal proceedings ▸ **faire** ou **intenter un procès à qqn** to institute legal proceedings against sb / *il a gagné / perdu son procès contre nous* he won / lost his case against us **2.** [critique] ▸ **faire le procès de qqn / qqch** to put sb / sthg on trial.

processeur [pʀɔsesœʀ] nm INFORM [organe] (hardware) processor ; [unité centrale] central processing unit.

procession [pʀɔsesjɔ̃] nf **1.** RELIG procession **2.** [cortège] procession.

processus [pʀɔsesys] nm process ▸ **processus de paix** peace process.

procès-verbal, aux [pʀɔsɛvɛʀbal, o] nm **1.** [pour une contravention] parking ticket **2.** [résumé] minutes, proceedings.

prochain, e [pʀɔʃɛ̃, ɛn] adj **1.** [dans le temps] next / *je te verrai la semaine prochaine* I'll see you next week ▸ **à samedi prochain !** see you next Saturday! / *le mois prochain* next month, this coming month / *la prochaine fois, fais attention* next time, be careful **2.** [dans l'espace] next / *je descends au prochain arrêt* I'm getting off at the next stop **3.** [imminent] imminent, near / *on se reverra dans un avenir prochain* we will see each other again in the near future. ◆ **prochain** nm ▸ **son prochain** one's fellow man / *aime ton prochain comme toi-même* love your neighbour as yourself. ◆ **prochaine** nf fam **1.** [arrêt] next stop / *je descends à la prochaine* I'm getting off at the next stop **2.** EXPR ▸ **à la prochaine !** see you (soon)!, be seeing you!, so long! 🇺🇸.

prochainement [pʀɔʃɛnmɑ̃] adv shortly, soon ▸ **'prochainement sur vos écrans**' 'coming soon'.

proche [pʀɔʃ] ◆ adj **1.** [avoisinant] nearby / *le bureau est tout proche* the office is close at hand ou very near / *le village le plus proche est Pigny* Pigny's the nearest village **2.** [dans l'avenir] near, imminent ; [dans le passé] in the recent past ▸ **dans un avenir proche** in the near future / *Noël est proche* we're getting close to Christmas / *la dernière guerre est encore proche de nous* the last war belongs to the not too distant past **3.** [cousin, parent] close / *adresse de votre plus proche parent* address of your next of kin **4.** [intime] close / *l'un des proches conseillers du président* one of the president's trusted ou close advisors. ◆ nm close relative ou relation ▸ **ses proches** his friends

and relatives. ◆ **de proche en proche** loc adv [petit à petit] gradually, step by step. ◆ **proche de** loc prép **1.** [dans l'espace] near (to), close to, not far from / *plus proche de chez lui* closer to his home **2.** [en contact avec] close to / *il est resté proche de son père* he remained close to his father / *d'après des sources proches de la Maison-Blanche* according to sources close to the White House **3.** [semblable à - langage, espèce animale] closely related to ; [-style, solution] similar to.

Proche-Orient [pʀɔʃɔʀjɑ̃] npr m ▸ **le Proche-Orient** the Near East.

proclamation [pʀɔklamasjɔ̃] nf [annonce] (official) announcement ou statement.

proclamer [3] [pʀɔklame] vt **1.** [déclarer - innocence, vérité] to proclaim, to declare ▸ **proclamer que** to declare that **2.** [annoncer publiquement] to publicly announce ou state, to proclaim / *proclamer le résultat des élections* to announce the outcome of the election.

procréation [pʀɔkʀeasjɔ̃] nf procreation ▸ **procréation médicalement assistée** assisted conception.

procréer [15] [pʀɔkʀee] vt litt to procreate.

procuration [pʀɔkyʀasjɔ̃] nf **1.** DR [pouvoir - gén] power ou letter of attorney ; [-pour une élection] proxy (form) ▸ **donner procuration à qqn** to authorize ou to empower sb **2.** BANQUE mandate. ◆ **par procuration** loc adv **1.** [voter] by proxy **2.** fig vicariously.

procurer [3] [pʀɔkyʀe] vt **1.** [fournir] to provide ▸ **procurer de l'argent à qqn** to provide sb with money, to obtain money for sb **2.** [occasionner] to bring. ◆ **se procurer** vpt to get, to obtain.

procureur, e [pʀɔkyʀœʀ] nm, f DR prosecutor ▸ **procureur général** public prosecutor at the *"parquet"* ; ≃ Director of Public Prosecutions 🇬🇧 ; ≃ district attorney 🇺🇸 ▸ **procureur de la République** public prosecutor at a *"tribunal de grande instance"* ; ≃ Attorney General.

prodige [pʀɔdiʒ] ◆ nm **1.** [miracle] marvel, wonder ▸ **faire des prodiges** to work wonders, to achieve miracles ▸ **tenir du prodige** to be nothing short of miraculous ou a miracle **2.** [personne] prodigy. ◆ adj ▸ **musicien prodige** musical prodigy.

prodigieusement [pʀɔdiʒjøzmɑ̃] adv [beaucoup] enormously, tremendously / *il m'agace prodigieusement* he really gets on my nerves.

prodigieux, euse [pʀɔdiʒjø, øz] adj **1.** [extrême] huge, tremendous **2.** [peu commun] prodigious, astounding, amazing.

prodigue [pʀɔdig] adj **1.** [dépensier] extravagant, profligate sout **2.** fig ▸ **prodigue de** generous ou overgenerous with / *prodigue de compliments* lavish with compliments / *tu es toujours prodigue de bons conseils* you're always full of good advice.

prodiguer [3] [pʀɔdige] vt [faire don de] to be lavish with / *elle a prodigué des soins incessants à son fils* she lavished endless care on her son.

producteur, trice [pʀɔdyktœʀ, tʀis] adj producing / *les pays producteurs de pétrole* oil-producing countries. ◆ **producteur** nm AGR & ÉCON producer.

productif, ive [pʀɔdyktif, iv] adj [travailleur] productive ; [auteur] prolific.

production [pʀɔdyksjɔ̃] nf **1.** [activité économique] ▸ **la production** production / *la production ne suit plus la consommation* supply is failing to keep up with demand **2.** INDUST [rendement] output ; AGR yield.

productivité [pʀɔdyktivite] nf [rentabilité] productivity.

produire [98] [pʀɔdyiʀ] vt **1.** [fabriquer - bien de consommation] to produce, to manufacture ; [-énergie, électricité] to produce, to generate ; AGR [faire pousser] to produce, to grow **2.** [fournir - suj : usine] to produce ; [- suj : sol] to produce, to yield ; FIN [bénéfice] to yield, to return **3.** [causer - bruit, vapeur] to produce, to make, to cause ; [- douleur, démangeaison] to produce, to cause ; [- changement] to effect, to bring about *(sép)* ; [- résultat] to produce **4.** [créer - suj : artiste] to produce ; *(en usage absolu)* ▸ **il produit beaucoup a)** [écrivain] he writes a lot **b)** [musicien] he writes ou composes a lot **c)** [cinéaste] he makes a lot of films. ◆ **se produire** vpi **1.** [événement] to happen, to occur **2.** [personne] to appear, to give a performance / *se produire sur scène* to appear on stage.

produit [pʀɔdɥi] nm **1.** INDUST product ; AGR produce ▸ **produits de grande consommation** ou **de consommation courante** consumer goods, consumable goods, consumables ▸ **produits alimentaires** food, foodstuffs ▸ **les produits de beauté** cosmetics, beauty products ▸ **produits chimiques** chemicals ▸ **produit dérivé** by-product ▸ **produit d'entretien** (household) cleaning product ▸ **produits manufacturés** manufactured goods **2.** [résultat] product, outcome / *c'est un pur produit de ton imagination* it's a complete figment of your imagination **3.** [bénéfice] profit / *le produit de la vente* the profit made on the sale **4.** ÉCON ▸ **produit intérieur brut** gross domestic product ▸ **produit national brut** gross national product.

proéminent, e [pʀɔeminɑ̃, ɑ̃t] adj prominent.

prof [pʀɔf] nmf *fam* **1.** ÉDUC teacher **2.** UNIV [sans chaire] lecturer UK, instructor US ; [titulaire de chaire] prof.

profanation [pʀɔfanasjɔ̃] nf [sacrilège] blasphemy, sacrilege, profanation ▸ **profanation de sépultures** desecration of graves.

profane [pʀɔfan] ◆ adj **1.** [ignorant] uninitiated / *je suis profane en la matière* I know nothing about the subject **2.** [non religieux] non-religious, secular, profane *litt*. ◆ nmf **1.** [ignorant] lay person, layman (laywoman) / *pour le profane* to the layman ou uninitiated **2.** [non religieux] lay person, non-initiate.

profaner [3] [pʀɔfane] vt **1.** RELIG [tombe, église, hostie] to desecrate, to violate the sanctity of, to profane *sout* **2.** [dégrader - justice, talent] to debase, to defile, to profane *sout*.

proférer [18] [pʀɔfeʀe] vt [insultes, menaces] to utter. 📖 In reformed spelling (see p. 16-18), this verb is conjugated like *semer* : *il proférera, elle proférerait*.

professer [4] [pʀɔfese] vt *litt* [déclarer] to affirm, to claim, to profess.

professeur, e [pʀɔfesœʀ] nm, f **1.** [du primaire, du secondaire] teacher, schoolteacher / *mon professeur d'anglais* my English teacher ▸ **professeur certifié** qualified schoolteacher *(who has passed the CAPES)* ▸ **professeur des écoles** primary school teacher *(formerly called an "instituteur")* **2.** [de l'enseignement supérieur - assistant] ≃ lecturer ; [- au grade supérieur] professor ▸ **professeur agrégé a)** ÉDUC qualified teacher *(who has passed the "agrégation")* **b)** MÉD *professor qualified to teach medicine* **3.** QUÉBEC ▸ **professeur adjoint** assistant professor ▸ **professeur agrégé** associate professor.

profession [pʀɔfesjɔ̃] nf **1.** [métier] occupation, job, profession ; [d'un commerçant, d'un artisan] trade ; [d'un artiste, d'un industriel] profession ▸ **les professions libérales** the professions **2.** [corporation - de commerçants, d'artisans] trade ; [- d'artistes, d'industriels] profession **3.** RELIG ▸ **profession de foi** profession of faith. ◆ **sans profession** loc adj ADMIN unemployed.

professionnalisme [pʀɔfesjɔnalism] nm professionalism.

professionnel, elle [pʀɔfesjɔnel] ◆ adj **1.** [lié à une profession - maladie, risque] occupational ; [- enseignement] vocational ▸ **école professionnelle** ≃ technical college

2. [qualifié - musicien, sportif] professional **3.** [compétent] professional, accomplished / *elle a réagi d'une manière très professionnelle* she reacted in a very professional way. ◆ nm, f **1.** SPORT professional / *les professionnels de la boxe* professional boxers **2.** [personne expérimentée] professional / *c'est l'œuvre d'un professionnel* this is the work of a professional.

professoral, e, aux [pʀɔfesɔʀal, o] adj [de professeur] professorial ▸ **le corps professoral** the teaching profession.

professorat [pʀɔfesɔʀa] nm teaching / *il a choisi le professorat* he chose teaching as a ou his profession.

profil [pʀɔfil] nm **1.** [côté du visage] profile **2.** [silhouette] profile, outline **3.** [caractéristiques] profile / *elle a le profil de l'emploi* she seems right for the job ▸ **profil psychologique** PSYCHOL psychological profile. ◆ **de profil** loc adv in profile.

profilé, e [pʀɔfile] adj AUTO streamlined.

profiler [3] [pʀɔfile] ◆ **se profiler** vpi **1.** [se découper] to stand out, to be silhouetted **2.** *sout* [apparaître] to emerge / *des périodes difficiles / des ennuis se profilent à l'horizon* a difficult time / trouble is looming on the horizon.

profit [pʀɔfi] nm **1.** [avantage] profit, advantage / *tirer profit de ses lectures* to benefit from one's reading / *j'ai lu ton livre avec profit* reading your book taught me a lot ▸ **mettre qqch à profit** to take advantage of ou to make the most of sthg **2.** COMM & FIN [bénéfice] profit. ◆ **au profit de** loc prép in aid of.

profitable [pʀɔfitabl] adj profitable / *ce séjour en Italie lui a été profitable* the time she spent in Italy did her a lot of good.

profiter [3] [pʀɔfite] ◆ **profiter à** v + prép to benefit, to be beneficial to. ◆ **profiter de** v + prép **1.** [jouir de] to enjoy / *profiter de sa retraite* to enjoy ou make the most of one's retirement **2.** [tirer parti de] to take advantage of / *profiter du soleil* to make the most of the sun ▸ **profiter de la situation** to take advantage of the situation / *profites-en, ça ne va pas durer !* make the most of it, it won't last! **3.** [exploiter] to exploit / *profiter de* to use.

profiteur, euse [pʀɔfitœʀ, øz] nm, f profiteer.

profond, e [pʀɔfɔ̃, ɔ̃d] adj **1.** [enfoncé - lac, racine, blessure] deep ▸ **peu profond** shallow / *un puits profond de 10 mètres* a well 10 metres deep **2.** [intense - respiration] deep ; [- soupir, sommeil] deep, heavy ; [- silence] profound, utter ; [- changement] profound / *absorbé dans de profondes pensées* deep in thought **3.** [sagace] deep, profound **4.** [véritable - cause] deep, underlying, primary. ◆ **profond** ◆ adv [aller, creuser] deep. ◆ nm : *au plus profond de la terre* in the depths ou bowels of the earth.

profondément [pʀɔfɔdemɑ̃] adv **1.** [creuser, enfouir] deep **2.** [respirer] deeply ; [soupirer] heavily, deeply ▸ **dormir profondément** to be sound asleep / *d'habitude, je dors très profondément* I usually sleep very heavily, I'm usually a sound sleeper **3.** [en intensif] profoundly, deeply / *je suis profondément choqué* I'm deeply shocked.

profondeur [pʀɔfɔdœʀ] nf **1.** [dimension] depth / *un trou de trois mètres de profondeur* a hole three metres deep / *on s'est arrêtés à huit mètres de profondeur* we stopped eight metres down **2.** [intensité - d'un sentiment] depth, profundity *sout* **3.** [perspicacité] profoundness, profundity / *sa profondeur d'esprit* her insight **4.** OPT & PHOT ▸ **profondeur de champ** depth of field. ◆ **profondeurs** nfpl *litt* depths. ◆ **en profondeur** ◆ loc adj [étude] in-depth, thorough / *il nous faut des changements en profondeur* we need fundamental changes. ◆ loc adv [creuser] deep / *notre crème antirides agit en profondeur* our anti-wrinkle cream works deep into the skin.

profusion [prɔfyzjɔ̃] nf *sout* [abondance] profusion, abundance. ◆ **à profusion** loc adv galore, plenty / *il y avait à boire et à manger à profusion* there was food and drink galore, there was plenty to eat and drink.

progéniture [prɔʒenityʀ] nf offspring, progeny *sout*, issue *sout*.

progiciel [prɔʒisjɛl] nm INFORM package.

programmable [prɔgramabl] adj programmable.

programmateur, trice [prɔgramatœʀ, tʀis] nm, f RADIO & TV programme 🇬🇧 ou program 🇺🇸 planner. ◆ **programmateur** nm [d'une cuisinière] programmer, autotimer ; [d'une machine à laver] programme selector.

programmation [prɔgramasjɔ̃] nf INFORM programming.

programme [prɔgram] nm **1.** [de cinéma, concert, radio, télévision] programme 🇬🇧, program 🇺🇸 ▶ **au programme** on the programme / *qu'est-ce qu'il y a au programme ce soir à l'Opéra ?* what's on tonight at the Opera? ▶ **programmes d'été** TV summer schedule ou programmes **2.** [brochure - d'un concert, d'une soirée] programme ; [- de cinéma, de télévision] listings, guide **3.** [emploi du temps] schedule / *notre programme est très chargé cette semaine* we have a busy schedule this week ▶ **inscrire qqch au programme** to schedule sthg **4.** ÉDUC [d'une année] curriculum ; [dans une matière] syllabus / *Shakespeare figure au programme cette année* Shakespeare is on this year's syllabus **5.** POL [plate-forme] manifesto 🇬🇧, platform 🇺🇸 **6.** [projet] programme / *programme de travail* work plan / *lancer un programme de réformes* to launch a package ou programme of reforms ▶ **tout un programme** *fam* : *ton voyage, c'est tout un programme !* this trip sounds like it's quite something! **7.** [de lave-linge, etc.] programme 🇬🇧, program 🇺🇸 ; INFORM program.

programmer [3] [prɔgrame] ◆ vt **1.** CINÉ, RADIO, THÉÂTRE & TV to bill, to programme **2.** [planifier] to plan **3.** ÉLECTRON to set, to programme **4.** INFORM to program. ◆ vi INFORM to (write a) program.

programmeur, euse [prɔgramœʀ, øz] nm, f INFORM programmer.

progrès [prɔgʀɛ] nm **1.** [amélioration] progress ▶ **faire des progrès** to make progress ▶ **être en progrès** to be making progress, to be improving / *il y a du progrès, continuez* that's better, keep it up **2.** [avancée] breakthrough, advance / *le XXᵉ siècle a connu de grands progrès scientifiques* the 20th century has witnessed some great scientific breakthroughs ▶ **le progrès** progress **3.** [développement] : *les progrès de la médecine* advances in medecine.

> 📋 Attention ! Le mot progress est indénombrable. Il ne s'emploie jamais ni au pluriel ni avec l'article indéfini a.

progresser [4] [prɔgʀese] vi **1.** [s'améliorer] to improve, to (make) progress **2.** [gagner du terrain - ennemi] to advance, to gain ground / *je progresse lentement dans ma lecture* I'm getting on ou progressing slowly in my reading ; [maladie] to progress ; [inflation] to creep up, to rise / *nos bénéfices ont progressé de 2 % l'année dernière* our profits rose by 2% last year / *la recherche scientifique progresse de jour en jour / à grands pas* scientific research is making progress every day / is advancing by leaps and bounds.

progressif, ive [prɔgʀesif, iv] adj [graduel] gradual, progressive.

progression [prɔgʀesjɔ̃] nf **1.** [avancée] progress, advance **2.** [développement - d'une maladie] progression, progress ; [- du racisme] development / *notre chiffre d'affaires est en constante progression* our turnover is constantly increasing ou improving / *un chiffre d'affaires en progression de 22 %* turnover up by 22% **3.** MATH & MUS progression.

progressiste [prɔgʀesist] ◆ adj [politique, parti] progressive. ◆ nmf progressive.

progressivement [prɔgʀesivmɑ̃] adv progressively, gradually.

prohiber [3] [prɔibe] vt to prohibit, to ban.

prohibitif, ive [prɔibitif, iv] adj [prix, tarif] prohibitive.

prohibition [prɔibisjɔ̃] nf [interdiction] prohibition, ban, banning.

proie [pʀwa] nf **1.** [animal] prey **2.** [victime] prey / *la ville devint rapidement la proie des flammes* the city rapidly became engulfed in flames. ◆ **en proie à** loc prép in the grip of ▶ **en proie au doute** racked with ou beset by doubt / *être en proie à des hallucinations* to suffer from hallucinations.

projecteur [pʀɔʒɛktœʀ] nm **1.** [pour illuminer - un spectacle] spotlight ; [- un édifice] floodlight ; [pour surveiller] searchlight / *sous les projecteurs de l'actualité* fig in the spotlight **2.** [d'images] projector / *projecteur (de diapositives)* slide projector.

projectile [pʀɔʒɛktil] nm **1.** ARM projectile **2.** [objet lancé] projectile, missile.

projection [pʀɔʒɛksjɔ̃] nf **1.** CINÉ & PHOT screening, projection, showing / *une projection de diapos* a slide show **2.** [jet] splash, spatter ▶ **projection de cendres** GÉOL ash fall **3.** [prévision] forecast **4.** PSYCHOL projection **5.** MATH projection.

projectionniste [pʀɔʒɛksjɔnist] nmf projectionist.

projet [pʀɔʒɛ] nm **1.** [intention] plan ▶ **faire des projets** to make plans **2.** [esquisse] plan, outline / *ma pièce n'est encore qu'à l'état de projet* my play is still only a draft ou at the planning stage **3.** ARCHIT & TECHNOL plan **4.** [travail] project. ◆ **en projet** loc adv : *nous avons un nouveau modèle d'avion en projet* we're working on (the plans for) a new design of aircraft. ◆ **projet de loi** nm bill. ◆ **projet de société** nm vision of society.

> ⚠ Project ne peut pas toujours être employé pour traduire projet. Voir article.

projeter [27] [pʀɔʃte] vt **1.** [prévoir] to plan, to arrange **2.** [lancer] to throw, to hurl **3.** [faire apparaître - ombre, lumière] to project, to cast, to throw **4.** CINÉ & PHOT to show, to project **5.** PSYCHOL to project **6.** MATH to project. ◆ **se projeter** vpi [ombre] to be outlined ou silhouetted.

prolétaire [pʀɔletɛʀ] nmf proletarian, member of the proletariat.

prolétariat [pʀɔletaʀja] nm proletariat.

prolifération [pʀɔlifeʀasjɔ̃] nf [gén] proliferation, multiplication.

proliférer [18] [pʀɔlifeʀe] vi to proliferate.

> ✏ In reformed spelling (see p. 16-18), this verb is conjugated like *semer* : *il proliférera, elle proliférerait*.

prolifique [pʀɔlifik] adj **1.** [fécond] prolific **2.** fig [auteur, peintre] prolific, productive.

prolixe [pʀɔliks] adj **1.** [description, style] wordy, verbose, prolix *sout* **2.** [écrivain] verbose, prolix *sout*.

prolo [pʀɔlo] fam nmf ▶ **les prolos** the working class.

prologue [pʀɔlɔg] nm **1.** LITTÉR, MUS & THÉÂTRE prologue **2.** [début] prologue, prelude, preamble.

prolongation [pʀɔlɔ̃gasjɔ̃] nf **1.** [allongement] extension **2.** SPORT extra time 🇬🇧, overtime 🇺🇸 ▸ **jouer les prolongations** pr to play ou to go into extra time.

prolongé, e [pʀɔlɔ̃ʒe] adj **1.** [long - applaudissements, séjour] lengthy, prolonged ▸ **week-end prolongé** long weekend **2.** [trop long] protracted, prolonged / *le séjour prolongé au soleil abîme la peau* prolonged exposure to the sun is harmful to the skin.

prolongement [pʀɔlɔ̃ʒmɑ̃] nm [extension - d'une route] continuation ; [- d'un mur, d'une période] extension. **◈ prolongements** nmpl [conséquences] effects, consequences, repercussions. **◈ dans le prolongement de** loc prép : *les deux rues sont dans le prolongement l'une de l'autre* the two streets are a continuation of each other / *c'est tout à fait dans le prolongement de mes préoccupations actuelles* that's along exactly the same lines as what I'm concerned with at the moment.

prolonger [17] [pʀɔlɔ̃ʒe] vt **1.** [dans le temps] to extend, to prolong **2.** [dans l'espace] to extend, to continue / *la route sera prolongée de deux kilomètres* the road will be made 2 km longer ou will be extended by 2 km / *la ligne de métro n° 7 a été prolongée jusqu'en banlieue* the no. 7 underground line was extended to the suburbs. **◈ se prolonger** vpi **1.** [dans le temps] to persist, to go on / *notre discussion s'est prolongée tard* our conversation went on until late **2.** [dans l'espace] to go on, to continue.

promenade [pʀɔmnad] nf **1.** [à pied] walk, stroll ; [à vélo, à cheval] ride ; [en voiture] ride, drive ▸ **aller faire une promenade a)** [à pied] to go for a walk ou stroll **b)** [à vélo, à cheval] to go for a ride **2.** [allée] walk ; [front de mer] promenade. **◈ en promenade** loc adv out walking, out for a walk.

promener [19] [pʀɔmne] vt **1.** [sortir - à pied] to take (out) for a walk ou stroll ; [- en voiture] to take (out) for a drive / *j'ai passé le week-end à promener un ami étranger dans Paris* I spent the weekend showing a foreign friend around Paris ▸ **promener le chien** to walk the dog, to take the dog for a walk **2.** [déplacer] : *elle promène son regard sur la foule* her eyes scan the crowd. **◈ se promener** vpi **1.** [à pied] to go for a walk ou stroll ; [en voiture] to go for a drive ; [à vélo, à cheval] to go for a ride ; [en bateau] to go for a sail / *viens te promener avec moi* come for ou on a walk with me **2.** [mains, regard] : *ses doigts se promenaient sur le clavier* her fingers wandered over the keyboard.

promeneur, euse [pʀɔmnœʀ, øz] nm, f walker, stroller.

promesse [pʀɔmɛs] nf **1.** [engagement] promise, assurance ▸ **faire une promesse** to (make a) promise ▸ **manquer à / tenir sa promesse** to break / to keep one's promise ▸ **encore une promesse en l'air** ou **d'ivrogne** ou **de Gascon !** promises, promises! **2.** FIN commitment ▸ **promesse (unilatérale) d'achat / de vente** (unilateral) commitment ou undertaking to buy / to sell. **◈ promesses** nfpl [avenir] promise / *un jeune joueur plein de promesses* a young player showing great promise, a very promising young player.

prometteur, euse [pʀɔmɛtœʀ, øz] adj **1.** [début, situation] promising, encouraging **2.** [musicien, acteur] promising, of promise.

promettre [84] [pʀɔmɛtʀ] **◈** vt **1.** [jurer] to promise / *je ne peux rien vous promettre* I can't promise anything / *je te promets de ne pas lui en parler* I promise I won't say a word to him about it / *je te promets que je ne dirai rien* I promise (you) I won't say anything / *on nous a promis de l'aide* we were promised help / *je te rembourserai, c'est promis* I'll pay you back, I promise ▸ **comme promis** as promised **2.** [annoncer] to promise / *la météo nous promet du beau temps pour toute la semaine* the weather forecast promises nice weather for the whole week / *tout cela ne*

promet rien de bon it doesn't look ou sound too good. **◈** vi **1.** [faire naître des espérances] to promise / *un jeune auteur qui promet* a promising young author / *être promis à un bel avenir* [personne] to be destined for great things **2.** fam [laisser présager des difficultés] : *ce gamin promet !* that kid's got a great future ahead of him! / *eh bien, ça promet !* iron that's a good start! **◈ se promettre ◈** vp (emploi réciproque) : *ils se sont promis de se revoir* they promised (each other) that they would meet again. **◈** vpt [se jurer à soi-même] to swear, to promise (to) o.s. / *je me suis bien promis de ne jamais recommencer* I swore never to do it again, I promised myself I would never do it again.

> 📋 **Promettre qqch à qqn** Promise sthg to sb ou promise sb sthg.
>
> Notez la construction à double complément qui en anglais peut prendre deux formes dont le sens est le même :
>
> • une structure identique à celle du français :
> verbe + COD + préposition + COI
> promise sthg to sb
>
> • une structure qui diffère de celle du français, sans préposition, et dans laquelle l'ordre des compléments est inversé :
> verbe + COI + COD
> promise sb sthg
>
> **Il a promis monts et merveilles à sa femme.** He promised the moon to his wife ou He promised his wife the moon.
>
> **Promets-moi une dernière chose.** Promise one last thing to me ou Promise me one last thing.

promis, e [pʀɔmi, iz] adj promised.

promiscuité [pʀɔmiskɥite] nf promiscuity.

promo [pʀɔmo] nf fam **1.** MIL, ÉDUC & UNIV year 🇬🇧, class 🇺🇸 **2.** COMM special offer ▸ **en promo** : *les canapés sont en promo chez X* sofas are on special offer at X.

promontoire [pʀɔmɔ̃twaʀ] nm GÉOGR headland, promontory.

promoteur, trice [pʀɔmɔtœʀ, tʀis] nm, f **1.** litt [créateur] promoter, instigator **2.** CONSTR developer.

promotion [pʀɔmɔsjɔ̃] nf **1.** [avancement] promotion **2.** COMM promotion **3.** MIL, ÉDUC & UNIV year 🇬🇧, class 🇺🇸. **◈ en promotion** loc adj COMM on special offer.

promotionnel, elle [pʀɔmɔsjɔnɛl] adj promotional / *tarifs promotionnels sur ce voyage en Israël !* special offer on this trip to Israel! ▸ **offre promotionnelle** special 🇬🇧, special 🇺🇸.

promouvoir [56] [pʀɔmuvwaʀ] vt **1.** [faire monter en grade] to promote / *il a été promu capitaine* he was promoted (to the rank of) captain **2.** [encourager - réforme] to advocate, to push for.

prompt, e [pʀɔ̃, pʀɔ̃t] adj prompt, quick, swift.

promptitude [pʀɔ̃tityd] nf quickness, swiftness.

promulguer [3] [pʀɔmylge] vt to promulgate.

prôner [3] [pʀone] vt sout to advocate, to extol.

pronom [pʀɔnɔ̃] nm pronoun.

pronominal, e, aux [pʀɔnɔminal, o] adj [adjectif, adverbe] pronominal ; [verbe] reflexive.

prononcé, e [pʀɔnɔ̃se] adj pronounced, strongly marked.

prononcer [16] [pʀɔnɔ̃se] vt **1.** [dire - parole] to say, to utter ; [- discours] to make, to deliver ▸ **sans prononcer un**

mot without a word **2.** [proclamer - jugement] to pronounce **3.** [articuler - mot, langue] to pronounce ; *(en usage absolu)* ❯ **il prononce mal** his pronunciation is poor. ❖ **se prononcer** ❯ vp *(emploi passif)* [mot] to be pronounced / *ça s'écrit comme ça se prononce* it's spelled as it sounds. ❯ vpi **1.** [se décider] to come to a decision, to decide / *je ne peux pas encore me prononcer* I can't decide yet **2.** [s'exprimer - gén] to give one's opinion ; [- médecin] to give one's prognosis ❯ **ils se sont prononcés pour / contre la peine de mort** they pronounced ou declared themselves in favour of / against the death penalty / **'ne se prononcent pas'** 'don't know'.

prononciation [pʀɔnɔ̃sjasjɔ̃] nf **1.** [d'un mot] pronunciation **2.** [d'une personne] pronunciation / *elle a une bonne / mauvaise prononciation en allemand* her German pronunciation is good / bad.

pronostic [pʀɔnɔstik] nm **1.** SPORT forecast ; [pour les courses] forecast, (racing) tip / *vos pronostics sur le match Bordeaux-Marseille ?* what is your prediction for the Bordeaux-Marseille match? **2.** [conjecture] forecast **3.** MÉD prognosis.

pronostiquer [3] [pʀɔnɔstike] vt [prévoir] to forecast, to prognosticate *sout*.

propagande [pʀɔpagɑ̃d] nf **1.** [politique] propaganda **2.** [publicité] publicity, plugging. ❖ **de propagande** loc adj [film, journal] propaganda *(modif)*.

propagation [pʀɔpagasjɔ̃] nf **1.** *litt* [reproduction] propagation, spreading **2.** [diffusion - d'un incendie, d'une doctrine, etc.] spreading.

propager [17] [pʀɔpaʒe] vt [répandre - foi, idées] to propagate, to disseminate, to spread ; [- épidémie, feu, rumeur] to spread. ❖ **se propager** vpi **1.** [s'étendre - nouvelle, épidémie, etc.] to spread **2.** PHYS [onde, son] to be propagated **3.** BOT to propagate, to reproduce.

propension [pʀɔpɑ̃sjɔ̃] nf [tendance] proclivity, propensity ❯ **avoir une forte propension à faire qqch** to have a strong tendency to do sthg.

prophète [pʀɔfɛt] nm prophet ❯ **prophète de malheur** prophet of doom.

prophétie [pʀɔfesi] nf prophecy.

prophétique [pʀɔfetik] adj **1.** RELIG prophetic **2.** *fig & sout* prophetic, premonitory *sout*.

prophétiser [3] [pʀɔfetize] vt **1.** RELIG to prophesy **2.** *fig & sout* to foretell, to predict, to prophesy.

propice [pʀɔpis] adj **1.** *sout* [temps, période, vent] favourable 🇬🇧, favorable 🇺🇸 / *l'automne est propice à la méditation* autumn is conducive to ou is an appropriate time for meditation **2.** [opportun] suitable ❯ **au moment propice** at the right moment.

proportion [pʀɔpɔʀsjɔ̃] nf [rapport] proportion, ratio / *dans une juste proportion* in the correct proportion. ❖ **proportions** nfpl **1.** [importance] (great) importance / *prendre des proportions énormes* to grow out of all proportions **2.** [dimensions] dimensions, size ❯ **toutes proportions gardées**: *c'est la même chose, toutes proportions gardées* it's the same thing but on a different scale. ❖ **à proportion de** loc prép in proportion to. ❖ **en proportion** loc adj in proportion / *il a de gros frais, mais son salaire est en proportion* he has a lot of expenses, but he has a correspondingly high salary. ❖ **en proportion de** loc prép : *il est payé en proportion des risques qu'il court* he is payed in proportion to the risks he takes.

proportionné, e [pʀɔpɔʀsjɔne] adj [harmonieux] ❯ **bien proportionné** well-proportioned.

proportionnel, elle [pʀɔpɔʀsjɔnɛl] adj ❯ **proportionnel à** [en rapport avec] proportional to, in proportion

with, commensurate with ❯ **directement / inversement proportionnel (à)** directly / inversely proportional (to). ❖ **proportionnelle** nf POL ❯ **la proportionnelle a)** [processus] proportional system **b)** [résultat] proportional representation / *être élu à la proportionnelle* to be elected by proportional representation.

proportionnellement [pʀɔpɔʀsjɔnɛlmɑ̃] adv [gén] proportionately ; MATH & ÉCON proportionally, in direct ratio.

propos [pʀɔpo] ❯ nm [sujet] subject, topic ❯ **à ce propos** in this respect ou connection / *c'est à quel propos ?* what's it about? ❯ nmpl [paroles] words, talk ❯ **tenir des propos injurieux** to make offensive remarks. ❖ **à propos** loc adv **1.** [opportunément] at the right moment / *arriver* ou *tomber à propos* to occur at the right time ❯ **mal à propos** at the wrong moment ou time **2.** [au fait] by the way, incidentally / *à propos, as-tu reçu ma carte ?* by the way ou incidentally, did you get my postcard? ❖ **à propos de** loc prép about, concerning, regarding / *j'ai quelques remarques à faire à propos de votre devoir* I have a few things to say to you about your homework. ❖ **à tout propos** loc adv constantly, at the slightest provocation. ❖ **de propos délibéré** loc adv deliberately, on purpose.

proposer [3] [pʀɔpoze] vt **1.** [suggérer] to suggest / *qu'est-ce que tu proposes ?* what would ou do you suggest? / *je vous propose de rester dîner* I suggest (that) you stay for dinner / *l'agence nous a proposé un projet original* the agency submitted an original project to us **2.** [offrir] to offer / *il a proposé sa place à la vieille dame* he offered the old lady his seat / *on m'en propose un bon prix* I've been offered a good price for it / *elle m'a proposé de m'aider* she offered to help me. ❖ **se proposer** vpi [être volontaire] to offer one's services / *je me propose pour coller les enveloppes* I'm volunteering to stick the envelopes. ❖ **se proposer de** vp + prép [avoir l'intention de] to intend to / *ils se proposaient de passer ensemble une semaine tranquille* they intended to spend a quiet week together.

⚠ Attention à ne pas traduire systématiquement **proposer** par **to propose**. L'article indique les différentes traductions qui s'imposent selon le contexte.

📋 **Proposer qqch à qqn** *Offer sthg to sb* ou *offer sb sthg*.

Notez la construction à double complément qui en anglais peut prendre deux formes dont le sens est le même :

• une structure identique à celle du français :
   verbe + COD + préposition + COI
      offer sthg to sb

• une structure qui diffère de celle du français, sans préposition, et dans laquelle l'ordre des compléments est inversé :
   verbe + COI + COD
      offer sb sthg

Ils ont proposé un poste plutôt intéressant à Pierre. *They offered quite an interesting job to Pierre* ou *They offered Pierre quite an interesting job*.

proposition [pʀɔpozisjɔ̃] nf **1.** [suggestion] suggestion ❯ **faire une proposition à qqn** to make sb a proposition

2. [offre] offer / *refuser une proposition* to turn down an offer ▶ **faire des propositions à qqn** *euphém* to proposition sb **3.** [recommandation] recommendation / *sur proposition du comité* on the committee's recommendation **4.** POL ▶ **proposition de loi** private member's bill 🇬🇧, private bill 🇺🇸 **5.** GRAM clause.

propre [pʀɔpʀ]
◆ adj

A. NET **1.** [nettoyé, lavé] clean ; [rangé] neat, tidy / *chez eux c'est bien propre* their house is neat and tidy ▶ **propre sur lui** *hum* neat and proper ▶ **propre comme un sou neuf** spick and span, clean as a new pin **2.** *euphém* [éduqué - bébé] toilet-trained, potty-trained ; [- chiot] house-trained 🇬🇧, house-broken 🇺🇸 **3.** [honnête] honest / *une affaire pas très propre* a shady business **4.** [bien exécuté - travail] neat, well done **5.** ÉCOL clean, non-polluting, non-pollutant ; NUCL clean.
B. PARTICULIER, ADAPTÉ **1.** *(avant nom)* [en intensif] own / *de mes propres yeux* with my own eyes ▶ **de son propre chef** on his own initiative ou authority ; [privé] own, private / *son propre hélicoptère* his own helicopter, a helicopter of his own, his private helicopter **2.** [caractéristique] ▶ **propre à** specific ou peculiar to / *pour des raisons qui lui sont propres* for reasons of his / her own **3.** [adapté] proper ▶ **propre à** suited to, fit for, appropriate to / *mesures propres à stimuler la production* appropriate measures for boosting production **4.** LING [nom] proper ; [sens] literal **5.** FIN ▶ **capitaux** ou **fonds propres** capital stock.
◆ nm **1.** [propreté] cleanliness, tidiness ▶ **sentir le propre** to smell clean ▶ **c'est du propre !** a) *fam & iron* [gâchis] what a mess! b) [action scandaleuse] shame on you! **2.** [caractéristique] peculiarity, distinctive feature. ◇ **au propre** *loc adv* **1.** [en version définitive] ▶ **mettre qqch au propre** to copy sthg out neatly, to make a fair copy of sthg **2.** LING literally / *le mot peut s'employer au propre et au figuré* the word can be used both literally and figuratively.

proprement [pʀɔpʀəmɑ̃] adv **1.** [avec propreté] cleanly ; [avec netteté] tidily, neatly ▶ **mange proprement !** eat properly! **2.** [spécifiquement] specifically, strictly **3.** [absolument] truly, totally, absolutely / *elle est proprement insupportable !* she's absolutely unbearable! ◇ **à proprement parler** *loc adv* strictly speaking. ◇ **proprement dit,** **proprement dite** *loc adj* actual / *la maison proprement dite* the house proper, the actual house, the house itself.

propreté [pʀɔpʀəte] nf **1.** [absence de saleté] cleanness, cleanliness ; [fait d'être rangé] tidiness ; [hygiène] hygiene **2.** *euphém :* *l'apprentissage de la propreté* [chez l'enfant] toilet-training, potty-training.

propriétaire [pʀɔpʀijetɛʀ] nmf **1.** [celui qui possède] owner / *tous les propriétaires seront soumis à la taxe* all householders ou homeowners will be liable to tax ▶ **propriétaire terrien** landowner **2.** [celui qui loue] landlord (landlady).

propriété [pʀɔpʀijete] nf **1.** [biens] estate, property / *une très belle / une grande / une petite propriété* an excellent / a large / a small property ▶ **propriété foncière / immobilière** landed / real estate ▶ **propriété de l'État** government ou state property ▶ **propriété privée** private (property) **2.** [fait de posséder] ownership **3.** DR ownership ▶ **propriété industrielle** patent rights ▶ **propriété littéraire et artistique** copyright **4.** [qualité] property, characteristic, feature.

propulser [3] [pʀɔpylse] vt **1.** ASTRONAUT to propel **2.** [pousser] to push ; to fling / *elle s'est trouvée propulsée à la tête de l'entreprise* *fig* she suddenly found herself in charge of the business.

propulsion [pʀɔpylsjɔ̃] nf AÉRON, MÉCAN & NAUT [phénomène] propulsion, propelling force ; [résultat] propulsion, propulsive motion, drive ▶ **fusée à propulsion atomique / nucléaire** atomic-powered / nuclear-powered rocket.

prorata [pʀɔʀata] (*pl* **prorata** *ou* **proratas***) nm proportion. ◇ **au prorata de** *loc prép* in proportion to.
prorogation [pʀɔʀɔgasjɔ̃] nf ADMIN & DR [d'un délai] extension ; [d'un visa] renewal.
proroger [17] [pʀɔʀɔʒe] vt ADMIN & DR [délai, compétence] to extend ; [traité] to renew ; [échéance] to defer.
prosaïque [pʀɔzaik] adj mundane, pedestrian, prosaic.
proscrire [99] [pʀɔskʀiʀ] vt **1.** [exiler] to banish, to proscribe *sout* **2.** [interdire - gén] to forbid ; [- par la loi] to outlaw ; [déconseiller] to advise against.
proscrit, e [pʀɔskʀi, it] adj *sout* **1.** [exilé] proscribed *sout* **2.** [interdit] forbidden.
prose [pʀoz] nf LITTÉR prose.
prosélytisme [pʀɔzelitism] nm **1.** RELIG proselytism **2.** *sout* [propagande] proselytism, missionary zeal / *faire du prosélytisme* to proselytize 🇬🇧, to proselyte 🇺🇸.
prospecter [4] [pʀɔspɛkte] vt **1.** COMM & ÉCON [région] to comb ; [clientèle] to canvass ; [marché] to explore, to investigate **2.** MIN to prospect.
prospection [pʀɔspɛksjɔ̃] nf **1.** MIN prospecting ▶ **prospection minière / pétrolière** mining / oil exploration **2.** COMM [de la clientèle] canvassing ; [des tendances] exploring ▶ **prospection téléphonique** telephone canvassing.
prospective [pʀɔspɛktiv] nf **1.** ÉCON (long-term) forecasting **2.** [science] futurology.
prospectus [pʀɔspɛktys] nm COMM [feuillet publicitaire] leaflet, handout.
prospère [pʀɔspɛʀ] adj **1.** [fructueux] flourishing, thriving **2.** [riche] prosperous.
prospérer [18] [pʀɔspeʀe] vi [entreprise] to flourish, to thrive ; [personne] to fare well, to thrive ; [plante] to thrive.
  In reformed spelling (see p. 16-18), this verb is conjugated like **semer** *: il prospèrera, elle prospèrerait.*
prospérité [pʀɔspeʀite] nf prosperity, success.
prostate [pʀɔstat] nf prostate (gland).
prosterner [3] [pʀɔstɛʀne] ◇ **se prosterner** vpi RELIG to bow down ▶ **se prosterner devant qqn** *fig* to grovel to sb.
prostitué, e [pʀɔstitɥe] nm, f [femme] prostitute ; [homme] male prostitute.
prostituer [7] [pʀɔstitɥe] ◇ **se prostituer** vp *(emploi réfléchi)* *pr & fig* to prostitute o.s.
prostitution [pʀɔstitysjɔ̃] nf *pr & fig* prostitution.
prostré, e [pʀɔstʀe] adj **1.** [accablé] prostrate, despondent **2.** MÉD prostrate.
protagoniste [pʀɔtagɔnist] nmf **1.** [principal participant] protagonist **2.** CINÉ & LITTÉR (chief) protagonist, main character.
protecteur, trice [pʀɔtɛktœʀ, tʀis] ◆ adj **1.** [qui protège] protective ▶ **crème protectrice** barrier cream **2.** [condescendant] patronizing. ◆ nm, f [gardien] custodian, guardian, guarantor.
protection [pʀɔtɛksjɔ̃] nf **1.** [défense] protection ▶ **assurer la protection de qqn** to protect sb ▶ **prendre qqn sous sa protection** to take sb under one's wing ▶ **protection civile** a) [en temps de guerre] civil defence b) [en temps de paix] disaster management ▶ **protection de l'enfance** child welfare ▶ **protection de l'environnement** environmental protection ▶ **protection maternelle et infantile** mother and child care *(including antenatal and postnatal clinics and family planning)* ▶ **protection de la nature** nature conservation ou conservancy ▶ **protection sociale** social welfare **2.** [soutien] ▶ **solliciter la protection de qqn** to ask for sb's support, to ask sb to use their influence on one's behalf **3.** ART & SPORT patronage **4.** [serviette hygiénique]

protection (féminine) sanitary towel 🇬🇧, sanitary napkin 🇺🇸. ❖ **de protection** loc adj protective, safety (modif).

protectionnisme [pʀɔtɛksjɔnism] nm protectionism.

protégé, e [pʀɔteʒe] ◆ adj **1.** ÉCOL [espèce, zone] protected **2.** ÉLECTRON protected **3.** INFORM [logiciel] copy-protected **4.** [relations sexuelles] protected ▸ **rapports non protégés** unprotected sex **5.** [pour handicapé] ▸ **atelier protégé** sheltered workshop. ◆ nm, f protégé.

protège-cahier [pʀɔtɛʒkaje] (pl **protège-cahiers**) nm exercise-book cover 🇬🇧, notebook cover 🇺🇸.

protège-dents (pl **protège-dents**), **protège-dent*** [pʀɔtɛʒdɑ̃] nm gum-shield.

protège-poignets [pʀɔtɛʒpwaɲɛ] nm inv wrist guard, wrist protector.

protéger [22] [pʀɔteʒe] vt [assurer - la sécurité de] to protect, to defend ; [-la santé, la survie de] to protect, to look after (insép), to shield against. ❖ **se protéger** vp (emploi réfléchi) to protect o.s. / **protégez-vous contre la grippe** protect yourself against the flu / **se protéger contre le** ou **du soleil** to shield o.s. from the sun.

📖 In reformed spelling (see p. 16-18), this verb is conjugated like semer : **il protègera, elle protègerait.**

protège-slip [pʀɔtɛʒslip] (pl **protège-slips**) nm panty liner.

protège-tibia [pʀɔtɛʒtibja] (pl **protège-tibias**) nm shin pad.

protéine [pʀɔtein] nf protein.

protestant, e [pʀɔtɛstɑ̃, ɑ̃t] adj & nm, f Protestant.

protestantisme [pʀɔtɛstɑ̃tism] nm Protestantism.

protestataire [pʀɔtɛstatɛʀ] nmf protester, protestor.

protestation [pʀɔtɛstasjɔ̃] nf **1.** [mécontentement] protest, discontent / **grand mouvement** / **grande manifestation de protestation demain à 14 h** a big protest rally / demonstration will be held tomorrow at 2 pm **2.** [opposition] protest ▸ **en signe de protestation** as a protest. ❖ **protestations** nfpl litt [déclarations] ▸ **protestations d'amitié** protestations ou assurances of friendship.

protester [3] [pʀɔtɛste] vi [dire non] to protest / **je proteste !** I protest!, I object! ❖ **protester de** v + prép litt ▸ **protester de son innocence** to protest one's innocence.

prothèse [pʀɔtɛz] nf **1.** [technique] prosthetics (U) ▸ **prothèse dentaire** prosthodontics (U) **2.** [dispositif] prosthesis.

protocolaire [pʀɔtɔkɔlɛʀ] adj [respectueux des usages] formal ; [conforme à l'étiquette] mindful of ou conforming to etiquette.

protocole [pʀɔtɔkɔl] nm **1.** DR & POL protocol ▸ **protocole d'accord a)** POL draft agreement **b)** ÉCON agreement in principle **2.** INFORM protocol **3.** [cérémonial] ▸ **le protocole** protocole, etiquette **4.** SCI ▸ **protocole d'une expérience** experimental procedure.

prototype [pʀɔtɔtip] nm **1.** INDUST prototype **2.** [archétype] standard.

protubérance [pʀɔtybeʀɑ̃s] nf **1.** [bosse] bump ; [enflure] bulge, protuberance spéc **2.** ANAT protuberance.

protubérant, e [pʀɔtybeʀɑ̃, ɑ̃t] adj [muscle] bulging ; [menton, front] prominent ; [œil, ventre] protruding, bulging.

proue [pʀu] nf NAUT bow, bows, prow.

prouesse [pʀuɛs] nf exploit, feat ▸ **faire des prouesses a)** [briller] to perform outstandingly **b)** [faire des efforts] to do one's utmost.

prouver [3] [pʀuve] vt **1.** [faire la preuve de] to prove / **cela n'est pas encore prouvé** it remains to be proved / **il est prouvé que...** it has been proved that... / **il n'est pas prouvé que...** there's no proof that... **2.** [mettre en évidence] to show / **son désintéressement n'est plus à**

prouver her impartiality is no longer open to question. ❖ **se prouver** vpt ▸ **se prouver qqch (à soi-même)** to prove sthg (to o.s.).

provenance [pʀɔvnɑ̃s] nf [d'un mot] origin ; [d'une rumeur] source / **quelle est la provenance de ces légumes ?** where do these vegetables come from? ❖ **en provenance de** loc prép (coming) from / **le train en provenance de Genève** the train from Geneva, the Geneva train.

provençal, e, aux [pʀɔvɑ̃sal, o] adj Provençal. ❖ **Provençal, e, aux** nm, f Provençal. ❖ **provençal** nm LING Provençal. ❖ **à la provençale** loc adj CULIN à la provençale.

Provence [pʀɔvɑ̃s] npr f ▸ **(la) Provence** Provence.

provenir [40] [pʀɔvniʀ] ❖ **provenir de** v + prép **1.** [lieu] to come from (insép) / **d'où provient cette statuette ?** where does this statuette come from? **2.** [résulter de] to arise ou to result from, to arise out of.

proverbe [pʀɔvɛʀb] nm proverb, adage ▸ **comme dit le proverbe** as the proverb goes.

proverbial, e, aux [pʀɔvɛʀbjal, o] adj [de proverbe] proverbial.

providence [pʀɔvidɑ̃s] nf RELIG Providence.

providentiel, elle [pʀɔvidɑ̃sjɛl] adj providential, miraculous / **c'est l'homme providentiel !** he's the man we need!

province [pʀɔvɛ̃s] nf [régions en dehors de la capitale] ▸ **la province a)** [en France] provincial France **b)** [dans d'autres pays] the provinces / **Bordeaux est une grande ville de province** Bordeaux is a major provincial town.

provincial, e, aux [pʀɔvɛ̃sjal, o] ◆ adj [en dehors de Paris] provincial. ◆ nm, f provincial. ❖ **provincial, aux** nm 🇶🇨 ▸ **le Provincial** the Provincial Government.

proviseur, e [pʀɔvizœʀ] nm, f **1.** [directeur] ≃ head 🇬🇧, head teacher 🇬🇧, headmaster (headmistress) 🇬🇧, principal 🇺🇸 **2.** 🇧🇪 [adjoint] deputy head (with overall responsibility for discipline within the school).

provision [pʀɔvizjɔ̃] nf [réserve] stock, store, supply ▸ **faire provision de sucre** / **d'enveloppes** to stock up with sugar / envelopes ▸ **faire des provisions** to stock up on food, to lay in stocks of food. ❖ **à provisions** loc adj [filet, sac] shopping (modif).

provisoire [pʀɔvizwaʀ] ◆ adj **1.** [momentané] temporary, provisional **2.** [précaire] makeshift **3.** [intérimaire - gouvernement] provisional ; [- directeur] acting. ◆ nm : **c'est du provisoire** it's only temporary, it's only for the time being.

provisoirement [pʀɔvizwaʀmɑ̃] adv temporarily, provisionally / **provisoirement, je fais des ménages** for the time being, I do cleaning for people.

provocant, e [pʀɔvɔkɑ̃, ɑ̃t] adj **1.** [agressif] aggressive, provoking **2.** [excitant] exciting, provocative, teasing.

provocateur, trice [pʀɔvɔkatœʀ, tʀis] ◆ adj [discours, propagande] inflammatory ; [argument, propos] provocative. ◆ nm, f POL provocateur.

provocation [pʀɔvɔkasjɔ̃] nf [stratégie] provocation, incitement ; [acte] provocation / **c'est un acte de provocation !** it's an act of provocation ! ▸ **faire qqch par provocation** to do sthg as an act of provocation / **provocation à la haine raciale** incitement to racial hatred.

provoquer [3] [pʀɔvɔke] vt **1.** [défier] to provoke, to push (to breaking point) ▸ **provoquer qqn en duel** to challenge sb to a duel **2.** [sexuellement] to tease **3.** [occasionner - maladie, sommeil] to cause, to induce ; [sentiment] to arouse, to stir up (sép), to give rise to / **il ne se doutait pas qu'il allait provoquer sa jalousie** he didn't realize that he would make her jealous / **ses dénégations ne provoquèrent aucune réaction chez le juge** his denials brought no reaction from the judge / *l'explosion provoqua la panique générale* the explosion caused general panic ; [réaction, explosion, changement] to cause ; [événement] to cause, to be the cause of, to bring about *(sép)* **4.** MÉD ▸ **provoquer l'accouchement** to induce labour.

proxénète [pʀɔksenɛt] nmf procurer (procuress).

proxénétisme [pʀɔksenetism] nm procuring.

proximité [pʀɔksimite] nf **1.** [dans l'espace] closeness, nearness, proximity **2.** [dans le temps] closeness, imminence / *la proximité du départ les rend fébriles* the approaching departure is making them excited. ❖ **à proximité** loc adv nearby, close at hand. ❖ **à proximité de** loc prép near, close to, not far from. ❖ **de proximité** loc adj [de quartier] ▸ **commerces de proximité** local shops ▸ **services de proximité** local community-based services.

proxy [pʀɔksi] nm INFORM proxy.

pr tjr (abr écrite de **pour toujours**) SMS 4eva, 4E.

prude [pʀyd] ❖ adj prudish, prim and proper. ❖ nf prude, puritan.

prudemment [pʀydamɑ̃] adv **1.** [avec précaution] carefully, cautiously, prudently **2.** [avec sagesse] wisely, prudently.

prudence [pʀydɑ̃s] nf [précaution] caution, carefulness.

prudent, e [pʀydɑ̃, ɑ̃t] adj **1.** [attentif] careful, prudent / *sois prudent !* be careful! **2.** [mesuré] discreet, circumspect, cautious **3.** [prévoyant] judicious, wise / *tu sors sans écharpe, ce n'est pas prudent* you're going out without a scarf, it's not very sensible / *c'est plus prudent* it's wiser **4.** [préférable] advisable, better / *il est prudent de réserver ses places* advance booking is advisable.

prud'hommes, prudhommes* [pʀydɔm] nmpl [tribunal] ▸ **les prud'hommes, le conseil de prud'hommes** the elected industrial tribunal.

prune [pʀyn] ❖ nf **1.** BOT plum **2.** [alcool] plum brandy **3.** *fam* EXPR pour des prunes for nothing. ❖ adj inv plum-coloured UK, plum-colored US.

⚠ Le mot anglais **prune** signifie « pruneau » et non **prune**.

pruneau, x [pʀyno] nm **1.** [fruit sec] prune **2.** Suisse [prune] red plum **3.** *arg crime* [balle] bullet, slug.

prunelle [pʀynɛl] nf **1.** BOT sloe **2.** ANAT pupil **3.** [regard] eye.

prunier [pʀynje] nm plumtree.

prurit [pʀyʀit] nm pruritus.

Prusse [pʀys] npr f ▸ **(la) Prusse** Prussia.

PS ❖ npr m (abr de **Parti socialiste**) French socialist party. ❖ nm (abr de **post-scriptum**) PS, ps.

psalmodier [9] [psalmɔdje] vi RELIG to chant.

psaume [psom] nm psalm.

pseudonyme [psødɔnim] nm [nom d'emprunt - gén] assumed name ; [-d'un écrivain] pen name, pseudonym ; [-d'acteur] stage name ; [-Internet] nickname.

psy [psi] *fam* ❖ nmf [psychanalyste] analyst, shrink / *elle va chez son psy une fois par semaine* she goes to see her analyst ou shrink once a week. ❖ nf [psychanalyse] : *il est très branché psy* he's really into psychoanalysis.

psychanalyse [psikanaliz] nf analysis, psychoanalysis / *il fait une psychanalyse* he's undergoing psychoanalysis.

psychanalyser [3] [psikanalize] vt to psychoanalyse UK, to psychoanalyze US, to analyse.

psychanalyste [psikanalist] nmf analyst, psychoanalyst.

psychanalytique [psikanalitik] adj analytical, psychoanalytical.

psychédélique [psikedelik] adj psychedelic.

psychiatre [psikjatʀ] nmf psychiatrist.

psychiatrie [psikjatʀi] nf psychiatry.

psychiatrique [psikjatʀik] adj psychiatric.

psychique [psiʃik] adj MÉD [blocage] mental ; [troubles] mental, psychic *spéc.*

psychisme [psiʃism] nm psyche, mind.

psychologie [psikɔlɔʒi] nf **1.** [étude] psychology **2.** [intuition] perception / *tu manques de psychologie* you're not very perceptive **3.** [mentalité] psychology.

psychologique [psikɔlɔʒik] adj MÉD [état, troubles] psychological, mental / *il suffit qu'elle aille parler à son médecin pour aller mieux, c'est psychologique* she only has to talk to her doctor to feel better, it's all in her mind.

psychologiquement [psikɔlɔʒikmɑ̃] adv psychologically.

psychologue [psikɔlɔg] ❖ adj insightful, perceptive. ❖ nmf psychologist ▸ **psychologue scolaire** educational psychologist.

psychomoteur, trice [psikɔmɔtœʀ, tʀis] adj psychomotor.

psychopathe [psikɔpat] nmf psychopath.

psychose [psikoz] nf **1.** PSYCHOL psychosis **2.** [angoisse - individuelle] (obsessive) fear ; [-collective] fear.

psychosomatique [psikɔsɔmatik] adj [médecine, trouble] psychosomatic.

psychothérapeute [psikɔteʀapøt] nmf psychotherapist.

psychothérapie [psikɔteʀapi] nf psychotherapy ▸ **faire une psychothérapie** to be in therapy.

PTDR *fam* SMS abr écrite de **pété de rire**.

puant, e [pɥɑ̃, ɑ̃t] adj *fam* [prétentieux] insufferably conceited / *tu es vraiment puant !* you really think you're something special!

puanteur [pɥɑ̃tœʀ] nf foul smell, stench.

pub¹ [pyb] nf *fam* **1.** [publicité] advertising / *il travaille dans la pub* he's in advertising / *faire de la pub pour un produit* to plug ou to push a product ▸ **un coup de pub** a plug **2.** [annonce - gén] ad, advertisement ; RADIO & TV commercial.

pub² [pœb] nm [bar] bar *(in the style of an English pub)*.

pubère [pybɛʀ] adj pubescent.

puberté [pybɛʀte] nf puberty.

public, ique [pyblik] adj **1.** [ouvert à tous] public **2.** [connu] public, well-known ▸ **l'homme public** the man the public sees **3.** [de l'État] public, state *(modif)*. ❖ **public** nm **1.** [population] public ▸ **le grand public** the general public, the public at large **2.** [audience - d'un spectacle] public, audience ; [-d'un écrivain] readership, readers ; [-d'un match] spectators / *s'adresser à un vaste public* / *à un public restreint* to address a vast / limited audience / *c'est un excellent livre, mais qui n'a pas encore trouvé son public* although the book is excellent, it hasn't yet found the readership it deserves ▸ **être bon public** to be easy to please **3.** [secteur] ▸ **le public** the public sector. ❖ **en public** loc adv publicly, in public. ❖ **grand public** ▸ **produits grand public** consumer goods ▸ **film grand public** blockbuster ▸ **l'électronique grand public** consumer electronics.

publication [pyblikasjɔ̃] nf **1.** [d'un livre, d'un journal] publication, publishing ▸ **publication assistée par ordinateur** = PAO **2.** [document] publication, magazine.

publiciste [pyblisist] nmf [publicitaire] advertiser, advertising man *(nm)*.

publicitaire [pyblisitɛʀ] ◆ adj advertising, promotional. ◆ nmf : *c'est un publicitaire* he's an advertising man, he's in advertising / *c'est une publicitaire* she's in advertising.

publicité [pyblisite] nf **1.** [action commerciale, profession] advertising ▸ **publicité sur le lieu de vente** point-of-sale advertising **2.** [annonce commerciale] advertisement ; RADIO & TV commercial ; [pour une association] publicity / *ça ne peut que lui faire de la publicité* it's bound to be publicity for him / *faire sa propre publicité* to sell o.s. / *faire de la publicité pour* to publicize ▸ **publicité mensongère** misleading advertising.

publier [10] [pyblije] vt **1.** [éditer - auteur, texte] to publish **2.** [rendre public - communiqué] to make public, to release ; [- brochure] to publish, to issue, to release ; [- bans] to publish, to announce ; [- décret, loi] to promulgate, to publish.

publipostage [pyblipɔstaʒ] nm mailshot, mailing.

publiquement [pyblikmɑ̃] adv publicly, in public.

puce [pys] ◆ nf **1.** ZOOL flea / *ce nom m'a mis la puce à l'oreille* the name gave me a clue ou set me thinking **2.** fam [par affection] ▸ **ma puce** sweetie **3.** ÉLECTRON chip. ◆ adj inv [couleur] puce. ◆ **puces** nfpl [marché] flea market.

puceau, elle [pyso, ɛl] adj fam : *il est puceau* he's a virgin. ◆ **puceau** nm virgin. ◆ **pucelle** nf virgin, maid litt.

puceron [pysʀɔ̃] nm greenfly, aphid, plant louse.

pudding [pudiŋ] nm bread pudding.

pudeur [pydœʀ] nf **1.** [décence] modesty, decency, propriety ▸ **avec pudeur** modestly / *manquer de pudeur* to have no sense of decency ▸ **fausse pudeur** false modesty **2.** [délicatesse] tact, sense of propriety.

pudibond, e [pydibɔ̃, ɔ̃d] adj prudish, prim.

pudique [pydik] adj **1.** [chaste] chaste, modest **2.** [discret] discreet.

pudiquement [pydikmɑ̃] adv **1.** [avec pudeur] modestly **2.** [avec tact] discreetly.

puer [7] [pɥe] ◆ vi to stink / *ça pue ici !* what a stink ou stench ! ◆ vt [répandre - odeur] to stink of / *il pue de la gueule* his breath stinks.

puériculteur, trice [pɥeʀikyltœʀ, tʀis] nm, f [dans une crèche] nursery nurse.

puériculture [pɥeʀikyltyʀ] nf **1.** [gén] child care ou welfare **2.** ENS nursery nursing.

puéril, e [pɥeʀil] adj [immature, naïf] childish, infantile, puerile.

puérilité [pɥeʀilite] nf [non-maturité] childishness, puerility. ◆ **puérilités** nfpl childish ou petty trifles.

pugilat [pyʒila] nm [bagarre] brawl, scuffle, (bout of) fisticuffs hum.

puis [pɥi] adv **1.** [indiquant la succession] then **2.** [dans une énumération] then. ◆ **et puis** loc adv **1.** [indiquant la succession] : *il a dîné rapidement et puis il s'est couché* he ate quickly and then he went to bed ▸ **et puis après ?** **a)** [pour solliciter la suite] what then?, what happened next? **b)** fam [pour couper court] it's none of your business! **c)** fam [exprimant l'indifférence] so what! ▸ **et puis après tout** and after all ▸ **et puis quoi encore ?** [tu exagères] whatever next? **2.** [dans une énumération] : *il y avait ses parents, ses frères et puis aussi ses cousins* there were his parents, his brothers and also his cousins.

puiser [3] [pɥize] ◆ vt **1.** [eau] to draw **2.** sout [extraire] to get, to take, to derive ▸ **puiser son inspiration dans** to take ou to draw one's inspiration from. ◆ vi [avoir recours à] to draw / *puiser dans ses économies* to draw on ou upon one's savings.

puisque [pɥiskə] *(devant voyelle **puisqu'**)* conj **1.** [parce que] since, because / *tu ne peux pas acheter de voiture, puisque tu n'as pas d'argent* you can't buy a car because ou since you don't have any money **2.** [étant donné que] since / *je viendrai dîner, puisque vous insistez* I will come to dinner, since you insist ▸ **bon, puisque tu le dis** / y tiens alright, if that's what you say / want / *puisque c'est comme ça, je m'en vais !* if that's how it is, I'm leaving! **3.** [emploi exclamatif] : *mais puisque je te dis que je ne veux pas !* but I'm telling you that I don't want to! / *tu vas vraiment y aller ? — puisque je te le dis !* so are you really going? — isn't that what I said?

puissamment [pɥisamɑ̃] adv **1.** [avec efficacité] greatly / *puissamment raisonné !* iron brilliant thinking! **2.** [avec force] powerfully, mightily sout.

puissance [pɥisɑ̃s] nf **1.** [force physique] power, force, strength **2.** [pouvoir, autorité] power **3.** [capacité] power, capacity / *une grande puissance de travail* a great capacity for work / *une grande puissance de séduction* great powers of seduction **4.** [d'un appareil] power, capacity, capability ; [d'une arme nucléaire] yield ▸ **puissance fiscale** AUTO engine rating **5.** COMM power ▸ **puissance commerciale** sales power **6.** MATH ▸ **six puissance cinq** six to the power (of) five **7.** ADMIN ▸ **la puissance publique** the authorities **8.** [pays puissant] power ▸ **puissance économique** economic power ▸ **puissance mondiale** world power. ◆ **en puissance** loc adj [virtuel] potential, prospective / *un client en puissance* a prospective customer / *c'est un fasciste en puissance* he's got latent fascist tendencies ▸ **montée en puissance a)** [de pays, mouvement, personne] increase in power **b)** [de secteur] increase in importance.

puissant, e [pɥisɑ̃, ɑ̃t] adj **1.** [efficace - remède] powerful, potent, efficacious sout ; [- antidote, armée, ordinateur] powerful ; [- membre, mouvement] strong, powerful, mighty litt **2.** [intense - odeur, voix] strong, powerful. ◆ **puissants** nmpl ▸ **les puissants** the powerful.

puits [pɥi] nm **1.** [pour l'eau] well **2.** PÉTR ▸ **puits de pétrole** oil well **3.** MIN shaft, pit **4.** fig ▸ **un puits de science** a walking encyclopedia, a fount of knowledge, a mine of information.

pull [pyl] = **pull-over**.

pull-over [pylɔvɛʀ] *(pl pull-overs)*, **pulloveur*** [pylɔvœʀ] nm sweater, pullover, jumper 🇬🇧.

pulluler [3] [pylyle] vi **1.** [abonder] to congregate, to swarm **2.** [se multiplier] to multiply, to proliferate.

pulmonaire [pylmɔnɛʀ] adj MÉD pulmonary, lung *(modif)*.

pulpe [pylp] nf [de fruit] pulp.

pulpeux, euse [pylpø, øz] adj [charnu - lèvres, formes] fleshy, voluptuous / *une blonde pulpeuse* a curvaceous blonde.

pulsation [pylsasjɔ̃] nf ANAT ▸ **pulsations cardiaques** heartbeats.

pulsion [pylsjɔ̃] nf PSYCHOL drive, urge ▸ **pulsions sexuelles** sexual desire, sexual urge.

pulvérisateur [pylveʀizatœʀ] nm [vaporisateur] spray.

pulvériser [3] [pylveʀize] vt **1.** [broyer] to pulverise, to turn into powder **2.** fig [détruire] to demolish, to smash to pieces ▸ **pulvériser un record** to smash a record **3.** [vaporiser] to spray.

puma [pyma] nm puma, cougar, mountain lion.

punaise [pynez] ◆ nf **1.** ZOOL bug **2.** [clou] tack, drawing pin 🇬🇧, thumbtack 🇺🇸. ◆ interj fam ▸ **punaise !** blimey! 🇬🇧, gee whizz! 🇺🇸.

punch¹, ponch* [pɔ̃ʃ] nm [boisson] punch.

punch² [pœnʃ] nm fam [dynamisme] pep, get-up-and-go / *avoir du punch* to be full of get-up-and-go.

punching-ball [pœnʃiŋbol] (*pl* punching-balls) nm punch ball, speed ball 🇬🇧.

punir [32] [pyniʀ] vt **1.** [élève, enfant] to punish **2.** DR to punish, to penalize / *être puni par la loi* to be punished by law, to be prosecuted ▸ **être puni de prison** to be sentenced to prison / *elle est bien punie de sa méchanceté* she's paying the price for her spitefulness.

punition [pynisjɔ̃] nf [sanction] punishment / *en guise de punition* as (a) punishment.

punk [pœnk] adj inv & nmf punk.

pupille [pypij] ◆ nmf **1.** [en tutelle] ward (of court) **2.** [orphelin] orphan ▸ **pupille de l'État** child in care ▸ **pupilles de la nation** war orphans. ◆ nf ANAT pupil.

pupitre [pypitʀ] nm MUS [support - sur pied] music stand ; [- sur un instrument] music rest ; [de professeur] desk.

pur, e [pyʀ] ◆ adj **1.** [non pollué - eau] pure, clear, uncontaminated ; [- air] clean, pure **2.** [sans mélange - liquide] undiluted ; [- race] pure ; [- bonheur, joie] unalloyed, pure ; [- note, voyelle, couleur] pure / *il parle un anglais très pur* he speaks very refined ou polished English ▸ **biscuits pur beurre** (100%) butter biscuits / *c'est un pur produit de la bourgeoisie* he's a genuine middle-class product ▸ **pur et dur a)** [fidèle] strict **b)** [intransigeant] hard-line **3.** [en intensif] sheer, utter, pure / *c'est de la folie pure !* it's sheer lunacy ! ▸ **par pure méchanceté** out of sheer malice / *c'était un pur hasard de le trouver là* I found him there purely by chance / *c'est de la lâcheté pure et simple* it's sheer cowardice, it's cowardice pure and simple. ◆ nm, f POL [fidèle] dedicated follower ; [intransigeant] hardliner.

purée [pyʀe] ◆ nf CULIN [de légumes] purée / *purée de tomates* / *carottes* tomato / carrot purée / *purée (de pommes de terre)* mashed potatoes. ◆ interj *fam* crumbs, crikey. ❖ **purée de pois** nf *fam* [brouillard] peasouper.

purement [pyʀmã] adv **1.** [uniquement] purely, only, solely **2.** [entièrement] purely, wholly ▸ **purement et simplement** purely and simply.

pureté [pyʀte] nf **1.** [propreté] cleanness, purity **2.** [harmonie - d'un contour] neatness, purity ; [- d'une langue, d'un style] purity, refinement / *la pureté de ses traits* the perfection in her face ou of her features.

purgatif, ive [pyʀgatif, iv] adj purgative. ❖ **purgatif** nm purgative.

purgatoire [pyʀgatwaʀ] nm RELIG & *fig* purgatory.

purge [pyʀʒ] nf **1.** TECHNOL [processus] draining, bleeding ; [d'un radiateur] bleeding **2.** MÉD purge, purgative **3.** *fig* [au sein d'un groupe] purge.

purger [17] [pyʀʒe] vt **1.** TECHNOL [radiateur] to bleed **2.** DR [peine] to serve, to purge *sout*.

purification [pyʀifikasjɔ̃] nf CHIM purifying ; *fig* cleansing ▸ **purification ethnique** ethnic cleansing.

purifier [9] [pyʀifje] vt **1.** [rendre pur - air] to purify, to clear **2.** MÉTALL to refine. ❖ **se purifier** vpi *sout* RELIG to be cleansed ou purified.

purin [pyʀɛ̃] nm liquid manure.

puriste [pyʀist] adj & nmf [gén & LING] purist.

puritain, e [pyʀitɛ̃, ɛn] ◆ adj [strict] puritan, puritanical. ◆ nm, f [personne stricte] puritan.

puritanisme [pyʀitanism] nm [austérité] puritanism, austerity.

pur-sang [pyʀsã] nm inv ZOOL thoroughbred.

purulent, e [pyʀylɑ̃, ɑ̃t] adj MÉD [plaie] suppurating ; [sinusite] purulent.

pus [py] nm pus.

pusillanime [pyzilanim] adj *sout* pusillanimous *sout*, spineless.

pustule [pystyl] nf MÉD pustule *spéc*, pimple.

putain [pytɛ̃] *tfam* ◆ nf [prostituée] whore. ◆ interj shit / *putain de voiture !* that bloody 🇬🇧 ou goddam 🇺🇸 car !

pute [pyt] nf *vulg* whore.

putois [pytwa] nm ZOOL polecat.

putréfaction [pytʀefaksjɔ̃] nf putrefaction, decomposition.

putréfier [9] [pytʀefje] ❖ **se putréfier** vpi to putrify, to become putrid.

putride [pytʀid] adj **1.** *sout* [pourri - viande, cadavre] decomposed, putrid ; [- eau] putrid, contaminated **2.** [nauséabond] foul, putrid.

putsch [putʃ] nm military coup, putsch.

puzzle [pœzl] nm JEUX (jigsaw) puzzle.

P-V (*abr de* procès-verbal) nm *fam* (parking) ticket ▸ **mettre un P-V à qqn** to give sb a ticket.

pygmée [pigme] adj Pygmy. ❖ **Pygmée** nmf ANTHR & MYTH Pygmy.

pyjama [piʒama] nm ▸ **un pyjama** (a pair of) pyjamas 🇬🇧, pajamas (*pl*) 🇺🇸.

pylône [pilon] nm ÉLECTR & TÉLÉC pylon.

pyramide [piʀamid] nf **1.** ARCHIT & GÉOM pyramid **2.** ▸ **pyramide humaine** human pyramid.

Pyrénées [piʀene] npr fpl ▸ **les Pyrénées** the Pyrenees.

Pyrex® [piʀɛks] nm Pyrex® ▸ **en Pyrex** Pyrex.

pyromane [piʀɔman] nmf arsonist, pyromaniac.

pyrotechnique [piʀɔteknik] adj pyrotechnic, pyrotechnical / *un spectacle pyrotechnique* a firework display.

python [pitɔ̃] nm ZOOL python.

qch SMS abr écrite de **quelque chose**.

QCM (abr de **questionnaire à choix multiple**) nm multiple-choice questionnaire.

qd SMS abr écrite de **quand**.

QG (abr de **quartier général**) nm HQ.

QI (abr de **quotient intellectuel**) nm IQ.

qqch (abr écrite de **quelque chose**) sthg.

qqn (abr écrite de **quelqu'un**) sb.

quad [kwad] nm [moto] quad bike ; [rollers] roller skate.

quadra [k(w)adʀa] nmf fortysomething.

quadragénaire [k(w)adʀaʒenɛʀ] ◆ adj ▸ **être quadragénaire** a) [avoir de 40 à 50 ans] to be in one's forties b) [avoir 40 ans] to be forty. ◆ nmf [de 40 à 50 ans] person in his / her forties ; [de 40 ans] forty-year-old man (woman), quadragenarian.

quadribande [kwadʀibɑ̃d] adj INFORM quad-band.

quadriceps [kwadʀisɛps] nm quadriceps.

quadrillage [kadʀijaʒ] nm 1. [tracé] grid ou criss-cross pattern 2. [contrôle] surveillance.

quadrillé, e [kadʀije] adj squared, cross-ruled.

quadriller [3] [kadʀije] vt 1. [papier] to criss-cross, to mark into squares 2. [surveiller] to surround / *la police quadrille le quartier* police presence is heavy in the district.

quadruple [k(w)adʀypl] ◆ adj quadruple. ◆ nm quadruple.

quadrupler [3] [k(w)adʀyple] ◆ vi to quadruple, to increase fourfold. ◆ vt to increase fourfold, to quadruple.

quadruplés, ées [k(w)adʀyple] nmf pl quadruplets, quads.

quai [kɛ] nm 1. [d'une gare] platform / *le train est à quai* the train is in 2. NAUT quay, wharf / *le navire est à quai* the ship has berthed 3. [berge] bank, embankment 4. [rue bordant un fleuve] street ▸ **le Quai a)** [le Quai d'Orsay] the (French) Foreign Ministry **b)** [le Quai des Orfèvres] Police Headquarters *(in Paris)* 5. TECHNOL platform.

🏛 **Quai**

The names **Quai d'Orsay** and **Quai des Orfèvres** are often used to refer to the government departments situated on the streets of the same name (the foreign office and the police department respectively). **Le Quai de Conti** is sometimes used to refer to the **Académie française**.

---

qualifiant, e [kalifjɑ̃, ɑ̃t] adj [formation, stage] leading to a qualification.

qualificatif, ive [kalifikatif, iv] adj qualifying. ❖ **qualificatif** nm 1. [mot] term, word 2. LING qualifier, modifier.

qualification [kalifikasjɔ̃] nf 1. [formation] qualification, skill ▸ **sans qualification** unskilled / *il n'a pas les qualifications requises pour ce poste* he's not qualified ou he hasn't got the right qualifications for this job ▸ **qualification professionnelle** professional qualifications 2. SPORT preliminary, qualifying ▸ **obtenir sa qualification** to qualify ▸ **épreuves / match de qualification** qualifying heats / match.

qualifié, e [kalifje] adj 1. [compétent] skilled, qualified / *elle est qualifiée pour remplir cette tâche* she's qualified to do this task 2. SPORT [choisi] qualifying 3. DR aggravated.

qualifier [9] [kalifje] vt 1. [appeler] ▸ **qualifier qqn / qqch de...** to describe sb / sthg as... / *il qualifie tout le monde de snob* he calls ou dubs everybody a snob 2. SPORT to qualify 3. LING to qualify, to modify. ❖ **se qualifier** vpi [être choisi] to qualify / *se qualifier pour une finale* to qualify for ou to get through to a final.

qualitatif, ive [kalitatif, iv] adj qualitative.

qualité [kalite] nf 1. [côté positif - d'une personne] quality, virtue ; [- d'une chose] good point, positive feature ▸ **qualités humaines** ou **de cœur** human qualities ▸ **qualités personnelles** personal qualities ▸ **qualités professionnelles** professional skills 2. [niveau] quality, grade ▸ **de mauvaise qualité** poor quality, substandard ▸ **de première qualité** top-quality, first-rate ▸ **qualité de vie** quality of life 3. [statut] position ; DR quality, capacity ▸ **nom, prénom, âge et qualité** name, first name, age and occupation. ❖ **qualités** nfpl [mérites] skills, qualifications. ❖ **de qualité** loc adj [de luxe] quality *(modif)*, high-standard. ❖ **en qualité de** loc prép : *en qualité de tuteur, je peux intervenir* (in my capacity) as guardian, I can intervene.

quand [kɑ̃] ◆ conj 1. [lorsque] when / *réveille-moi quand tu partiras* wake me when you leave / *quand je pense à l'argent que j'ai dépensé !* when I think ou to think of the money I spent! 2. [alors que] when / *pourquoi rester enfermé quand il fait si beau dehors ?* why stay cooped up when it's so lovely outside? 3. [introduisant une hypothèse] even if. ◆ adv when / *quand viendras-tu nous voir ?* when will you come and visit us? / *depuis quand es-tu là ?* how long have you been here? / *à quand le mariage ?* when's the wedding? / *quand est-ce que tu y vas ?* fam when are you going there? ❖ **quand bien même** loc conj even if. ❖ **quand même** ◆ loc conj *sout* even though, even if. ◆ loc adv 1. [malgré tout] all the same, even so / *c'était quand même bien* it was still good, it was good all the same / *je pense qu'il ne viendra pas, mais je* *l'inviterai quand même* I don't think he'll come but I'll invite him all the same **2.** [en intensif] : *tu pourrais faire attention quand même !* you really should be more careful!

quant [kɑ̃] ❖ **quant à** loc prép as for ou to / *je partage votre opinion quant à ses capacités* I share your opinion about his ability ▶ **quant à lui** as for him.

quantifier [9] [kɑ̃tifje] vt [gén & PHILOS] to quantify.

quantitatif, ive [kɑ̃titatif, iv] adj LING quantitative.

quantitativement [kɑ̃titativmɑ̃] adv quantitatively.

quantité [kɑ̃tite] nf **1.** [mesure] amount, quantity / *quelle quantité de lessive faut-il mettre ?* how much detergent do you have to put in? ▶ **une quantité de, des quantités de** lots of, a lot of, a great many ▶ **en quantités industrielles** ou **en grandes quantités** in large quantities **2.** EXPR **traiter qqn / qqch comme une quantité négligeable** to treat sb / sthg as unworthy of consideration. ❖ **en quantité** loc adv in abundance, in great amounts ▶ **du vin / des prix en quantité** lots of wine / prizes. ❖ **quantité de** loc dét *sout* a great many, lots of / *elle trouve quantité de raisons pour ne pas le faire* she finds any amount ou lots of reasons not to do it.

quarantaine [kaRɑ̃tɛn] nf **1.** [nombre] about forty **2.** [âge] ▶ **avoir la quarantaine** to be in one's forties **3.** [isolement] quarantine. ❖ **en quarantaine** loc adv ▶ **mettre en quarantaine a)** MÉD & VÉTÉR to quarantine **b)** *fig* to ostracize, to exclude.

quarante [kaRɑ̃t] ❖ dét forty. ❖ nm inv [numéro] forty ▶ **les Quarante** the French Academy.

quarantenaire [kaRɑ̃tnɛR] ❖ adj [qui dure quarante ans] forty-year *(avant nom)*. ❖ nmf [personne de quarante ans] forty-year-old.

quarantième [kaRɑ̃tjɛm] ❖ adj num & nmf fortieth. ❖ nm **1.** [fraction] fortieth **2.** NAUT ▶ **les quarantièmes rugissants** the roaring forties. Voir aussi **cinquième**.

quart [kaR] nm **1.** [quatrième partie] quarter / *un quart de beurre* a quarter (of a pound) of butter / *un quart de la tarte* one quarter of the tart ▶ **quart de finale** quarter final ▶ **un quart de tour** a quarter turn ▶ **démarrer** ou **partir au quart de tour** *pr* to start first go / *il a réagi au quart de tour* he reacted straight away ▶ **au quart de poil** *fam* perfectly / *le frigo rentre au quart de poil* the fridge just fits **2.** [période de quinze minutes] quarter of an hour, quarter hour US / *c'est le quart qui sonne* that's the bell for quarter past ▶ **une heure et quart** (a) quarter past one, (a) quarter after one US / *une heure moins le quart* (a) quarter to one, (a) quarter of one US / *j'étais là à moins le quart fam* I was there at (a) quarter to ou (a) quarter of US **3.** NAUT [garde] watch / *être de quart* to be on watch ou duty **4.** [gobelet] (quarter litre) mug ou beaker.

quart d'heure [kaRdœR] *(pl* **quarts d'heure)** nm **1.** [quinze minutes] quarter of an hour / *je suis resté un quart d'heure devant la porte* I stood at the door for a quarter of an hour / *cela va te prendre au moins trois quarts d'heure* it'll take you at least three quarters of an hour **2.** EXPR **passer un mauvais quart d'heure** *fam* to have a bad time of it.

Quarté® [kaRte] nm forecast *(of the first four horses).*

quartette [kwaRtɛt] nm MUS quartet, quartette.

quartier [kaRtje] nm **1.** [division d'une ville] district, area / *le quartier des affaires* the business district ▶ **le quartier chinois** Chinatown ▶ **le quartier** the neighbourhood / *je ne suis pas du quartier* I'm not from around here ▶ **les vieux quartiers** the old town ou quarter (of town) ▶ **le Quartier latin** the Latin Quarter *(area on the Left Bank of the Seine traditionally associated with students and artists)* **2.** MIL quarters ▶ **quartier général** *pr & fig* headquarters ▶ **avoir quartier libre a)** MIL to be off duty **b)** *fig* to be free **3.** [partie d'une prison] wing ▶ **quartier de haute sé-**curité ou **de sécurité renforcée** high- ou top-security wing **4.** [quart] quarter / *un quartier de pomme* a quarter of an apple ; [morceau] portion, section / *un quartier d'orange* an orange segment / *un quartier de bœuf* a quarter of beef **5.** [pitié] mercy, quarter / *l'armée victorieuse n'a pas fait de quartier* the victorious army gave no quarter. ❖ **de quartier** loc adj [médecin, cinéma] local.

quart-monde [kaRmɔ̃d] *(pl* **quarts-mondes)** nm ▶ **le quart-monde a)** [ensemble de pays] the least developed countries, the Fourth World **b)** [dans un pays] the poor.

quartz [kwaRts] nm quartz.

quasi [kazi] adv = **quasiment**.

quasi- [kazi] préf quasi-, near, almost ▶ **j'en ai la quasi-certitude** I'm virtually certain ▶ **la quasi-totalité de...** almost the whole...

quasiment [kazimɑ̃] adv *fam* almost, practically ▶ **quasiment jamais** hardly ever.

quatorze [katɔRz] ❖ dét **1.** fourteen **2.** [dans des séries] fourteenth ▶ **à quatorze heures** at 2 p.m. ▶ **le 14 Juillet** Bastille Day, the fourteenth of July ▶ **la guerre de quatorze** World War I, the First World War. ❖ nm inv fourteen. Voir aussi **cinq**.

quatorzième [katɔRzjɛm] adj num, nmf & nm fourteenth. Voir aussi **cinquième**.

quatre [katR] ❖ dét **1.** four **2.** EXPR **faire les quatre cents coups** : *il a fait les quatre cents coups dans sa jeunesse* he sowed his wild oats when he was young ▶ **ne pas y aller par quatre chemins** : *il n'y est pas allé par quatre chemins* he came straight to the point ou didn't beat about the bush / *ils viennent des quatre coins du monde* they come from the four corners of the world ▶ **être tiré à quatre épingles** to be immaculately dressed ou dressed to the nines ▶ **les quatre fers en l'air** *fam* flat on one's back ▶ **un de ces quatre matins** one of these days ▶ **être enfermé entre quatre murs** to be shut away indoors ▶ **dire ses quatre vérités à qqn** to tell sb a few home truths ▶ **faire les quatre volontés de qqn** to pander to sb's every whim ▶ **se mettre en quatre pour qqn** to go to no end of trouble ou to bend over backwards for sb ▶ **se mettre en quatre pour faire qqch** to go out of one's way to do sthg. ❖ nm inv [nombre] four. Voir aussi **cinq**. ❖ **à quatre pattes** loc adv on all fours / *se mettre à quatre pattes* to go down on all fours. ❖ **comme quatre** loc adv ▶ **boire / manger / parler comme quatre** to eat / to drink / to talk a lot.

quatre-heures, quatre heures [katRœR] nm inv *fam* afternoon snack.

quatre-quarts [katkaR] nm inv ≈ pound cake.

quatre-quatre [katkatR] ❖ adj inv four-wheel drive. ❖ nm inv ou nf inv four-wheel drive (vehicle).

quatre-vingt-dix [katRəvɛ̃dis] ❖ dét ninety. ❖ nm inv [nombre] ninety. Voir aussi **cinquante**.

quatre-vingts, quatre-vingt [katRəvɛ̃] *(si suivi d'un autre adj num)* ❖ dét eighty / *page quatre-vingt* page eighty / *quatre-vingts personnes* eighty people / *quatre-vingt-quatre euros* eighty-four euros. ❖ nm eighty. Voir aussi **cinquante**.

quatrième [katRijɛm] ❖ adj num & nmf fourth. ❖ nf ENS ≈ year 9 UK ; ≈ eighth grade US ; [vitesse] fourth gear. Voir aussi **cinquième**. ❖ **en quatrième vitesse** loc adv *fam* in a hurry, at breakneck speed / *rapporte ce livre à la bibliothèque, et en quatrième vitesse !* take this book back to the library and be quick about it!

quatrièmement [katRijɛmmɑ̃] adv fourthly, in (the) fourth place. Voir aussi **cinquièmement**.

que [kə] *(devant voyelle ou «h» muet qu')* ❖ adv **1.** [combien] : *que tu es naïf !* you're so naive!, aren't you naive! **/** *que de bruit ici !* it's so noisy here!, what a lot of noise there is in here! **/** *qu'il a un grand nez !* he's got such a big nose! **/** *qu'est-ce que tu es bête !* *fam* you're (ever) so stupid! **2.** [exprimant l'indignation] : *que m'importent ses états d'âme !* what do I care about what he feels! ◆ pron rel **1.** [représente une personne] whom *sout*, who, that **/** *la fille qu'il a épousée* the girl (whom) he married **/** *la femme qu'elle était devenue* the woman (that) she'd become **2.** [représente une chose, une idée] which, that **/** *le contrat que j'ai signé* the contract (which) ou that I signed **4.** [pour souligner une caractéristique] : *malheureux que vous êtes !* you unfortunate man! **/** *de timide qu'il était, il est devenu expansif* once a shy man, he's now an extrovert **/** *en bon père / électricien qu'il était* being the good father / electrician he was **/** *bel exploit que le sien !* what he's done is quite a feat! **5.** [dans des expressions de temps, de durée] : *ça fait deux heures que j'attends* I've been waiting for two hours **/** *le temps que tu te prépares, il sera trop tard* by the time you're ready it'll be too late **/** *il y a bien longtemps que je le sais* I've known for a long time **/** *chaque fois que je m'absente, il téléphone* every time I'm out he phones. ◆ pron interr **1.** [dans le discours direct] what **/** *qu'y a-t-il ?* what's the matter? **/** *que devient-elle ?* what's become of her? **/** *qu'est-ce qui t'arrive ?* what's the matter with you? **2.** [dans le discours indirect] what. ◆ conj **1.** [après les verbes déclaratifs ou des verbes d'évaluation] that **/** *je sais que je peux le faire* I know (that) I can do it **/** *il est possible que je revienne* I may come back ; [en début de proposition] : *que leur fils ait fugué, cela ne devrait pas nous surprendre* the fact that their son ran away shouldn't come as a surprise to us **2.** (à valeur circonstancielle) [et déjà] than **/** *il n'a pas fini de lire un roman qu'il en commence un autre* no sooner has he finished one novel than he starts reading another ; [afin que] so that **/** *approche-toi, que je te voie mieux* come closer so that I can see you better **3.** (suivi du subjonctif) [pour formuler un ordre, un souhait, une éventualité] ▶ **qu'elle parle !** **a)** [faites-la parler] make her talk! **b)** [laissez-la parler] let her speak! **/** *que l'on apporte à boire !* bring some drinks! **/** *eh bien, qu'il s'en aille s'il n'est pas content !* he can leave if he doesn't like it! **4.** [répète la conjonction précédente] : *quand je serai grande et que j'aurai un métier* when I'm grown up and (I) have a job **5.** [formule de présentation et d'insistance] : *je croyais l'affaire faite et voilà qu'elle n'est pas d'accord* I thought the deal was clinched and now I find she disagrees **/** *si je n'ai rien dit, c'est que je craignais de te vexer* if I said nothing, it was because I was afraid of upsetting you ▶ **que tu crois / dis !** *fam* that's what you think / say! ◆ **que... ou non** loc conj whether... or not **/** *que tu me croies ou non* whether you believe me or not. ◆ **que... (ou) que** loc conj whether... or **/** *qu'il fasse beau, qu'il pleuve, je sors me promener* come rain or come shine, I go out for a walk.

Québec [kebɛk] npr m **1.** [province] ▶ **le Québec** Quebec **2.** [ville] Quebec.

québécois, e [kebekwa, az] adj from Quebec. ◆ **Québécois, e** nm, f Québécois, Quebecker. ◆ **québécois** nm LING Canadian French.

quel, quelle [kɛl] (*mpl* **quels**, *fpl* **quelles**) ◆ dét (adj interr) [personne] which ; [animal, chose] which, what **/** *de quel côté es-tu ?* which ou whose side are you on? **/** *je ne sais quels sont ses projets* I don't know what his plans are **/** *quelle heure est-il ?* what's the time?, what time is it? ◆ dét (adj excl) what **/** *quel idiot !* what a fool! **/** *quel sale temps !* what terrible weather! ◆ dét (adj rel) [en corrélation avec «que» - personne] whoever ; [-animal] whichever ; [-chose] whichever, whatever **/** *les mammifères quels qu'ils soient* all mammals **/** *quelle que soit l'assu-*

rance que vous choisissiez... whichever the insurance policy you choose... **/** *il se baigne quel que soit le temps* he goes swimming whatever the weather. ◆ pron interr which (one) **/** *de tous vos matches, quel fut le plus difficile ?* of all the matches you've played, which (one) was the most difficult ou which was the most difficult one?

quelconque [kɛlkɔ̃k] ◆ dét (adj indéf) [quel qu'il soit] any, some or other **/** *si, pour une raison quelconque, tu ne pouvais pas venir* if, for some reason or other ou if, for any reason, you can't come **/** *as-tu une quelconque idée du prix ?* have you got any idea of the price? ◆ adj [insignifiant, banal - nourriture, visage] ordinary, plain ; [-personne] average, ordinary ; [-comédien, film, spectacle] run-of-the-mill, second-rate, (pretty) average.

quelque [kɛlk(ə)] ◆ dét (adj indéf) **1.** [un peu de] some **/** *elle est bizarre depuis quelque temps* she's been acting strangely for a ou some time now **2.** *sout* [n'importe quel] some **3.** [en corrélation avec «que»] : *dans quelque pays que tu sois* whichever ou whatever country you may be in. ◆ adv *sout* [approximativement] around, about **/** *il y a quelque 40 ans de cela* that was about 40 years ago, that was 40 or so years ago. ◆ **quelques** dét (adj indéf pl) **1.** (sans déterminant) a few, some **/** *amène quelques amis* bring some ou a few friends along ▶ **et quelques** *fam:* *ça pèse deux kilos et quelques* it's a little ou a bit over two kilos **/** *il était cinq heures et quelques* it was just after five o'clock **2.** (avec déterminant) few **/** *les quelques millions de téléspectateurs qui nous regardent* the few million viewers watching us. ◆ **en quelque sorte** loc adv **1.** [en un sens] as it were, so to speak, in a manner of speaking **2.** [en résumé] in a nutshell, in fact. ◆ **quelque chose** pron indéf **1.** [dans une affirmation] something **/** *elle a quelque chose aux poumons* she's got something wrong with her lungs **/** *quand il est parti, ça m'a vraiment fait quelque chose* when he left, it really affected me **2.** [dans une question, une négation, une hypothèse] anything, something **/** *s'il m'arrivait quelque chose, contactez mon notaire* if anything ou something should happen to me, contact my solicitor **3.** *fam* [dans une approximation] : *elle a quelque chose comme 80 ans* she's about 80 ou 80 or so **/** *Anne quelque chose a téléphoné* *fam* Anne something phoned **4.** *fam* [emploi expressif] ▶ **je vais te corriger, quelque chose de bien !** I'm going to give you a good ou proper hiding! ▶ **c'est quelque chose !** that's a bit much! ◆ **quelque part** loc adv **1.** [dans un lieu] somewhere, someplace 🇺🇸 **/** *l'as-tu vu quelque part ?* did you see him anywhere ou anyplace 🇺🇸? **/** *tu vas quelque part à Noël ?* are you going anywhere (special) for Christmas? **2.** *fam & euphém* [aux toilettes] : *elle est allée quelque part* she went to wash her hands *euphém* **3.** *fam & euphém* [au derrière] : *c'est mon pied quelque part que tu veux ?* do you want a kick up the backside?

quelquefois [kɛlkəfwa] adv sometimes, from time to time.

quelques-uns, quelques-unes [kɛlkəzœ̃, yn] pron indéf pl **1.** [certains] some **/** *quelques-uns de ses collaborateurs étaient au courant* some of his colleagues knew about it **2.** [un petit nombre] a few **/** *tu connais ses pièces ? — seulement quelques-unes* do you know his plays? — only a few of them.

quelqu'un, e [kɛlkœ̃, yn] pron indéf *litt* : *quelqu'une de ces demoiselles va vous conduire* one of these young ladies will show you the way. ◆ **quelqu'un** pron indéf m **1.** [dans une affirmation] someone, somebody **/** *quelqu'un te demande au téléphone* there's someone ou somebody on the phone for you **/** *quelqu'un de très grand est venu* somebody very tall called ▶ **c'est quelqu'un de bien** he's a nice person ▶ **c'est quelqu'un !** [ton admiratif] she's quite somebody! **/** *elle veut devenir quelqu'un (dans le* *monde de l'art)* she wants to become someone famous (in the world of art) **2.** [dans une question, une négation, une hypothèse] anybody, anyone / *il y a quelqu'un ?* is (there) anybody in?

quémander [3] [kemɑ̃de] vt [aide, argent, nourriture] to beg for *(insép)* ; [compliment] to fish ou to angle for *(insép)*.

qu'en-dira-t-on [kɑ̃diʀatɔ̃] nm inv gossip / *elle a peur du qu'en-dira-t-on* she's afraid of what people will say.

quenelle [kənɛl] nf ▶ **quenelle (de poisson)** (fish) quenelle.

querelle [kəʀɛl] nf quarrel ; [verbale] quarrel, argument / *ce n'est qu'une querelle d'amoureux* it's only a lovers' tiff.

quereller [4] [kəʀele] ❖ **se quereller** vp *(emploi réciproque)* to quarrel (with one another) / *elles se querellent pour des riens* they quarrel ou squabble over nothing. ❖ **se quereller avec** vp + prép to have an argument ou to quarrel with.

qu'est-ce que [kɛskə], **qu'est-ce qui** [kɛski] ⟶ **que** *(pron interr)*.

question [kɛstjɔ̃] nf **1.** [interrogation] question ▶ **je ferme la porte à clé ? — bien sûr, quelle ou cette question !** shall I lock the door? — of course, what a question! ▶ **poser une question à qqn** to ask sb a question / *je commence à me poser des questions sur sa compétence* I'm beginning to have (my) doubts about ou to wonder how competent he is / *se poser la question de savoir si* to ask o.s. whether ▶ **question piège a)** JEUX trick question **b)** [dans un interrogatoire] loaded ou leading question ▶ **question subsidiaire** JEUX tiebreaker **2.** [sujet] question, topic ▶ **être question de** : *de quoi est-il question dans ce paragraphe ?* what is this paragraph about? / *dans notre prochaine émission, il sera question de l'architecture romane* in our next programme, we will examine Roman architecture / *il n'est jamais question de la répression dans son livre* repression is never mentioned in his book ▶ **pas question !** *fam* : *prête-moi 1 000 euros — pas question !* lend me 1,000 euros — no way *fam* ou nothing doing *fam!* ▶ **il n'en est pas question !, c'est hors de question !** it's out of the question! ▶ **question salaire, je ne me plains pas** *fam* as far as the salary is concerned ou salarywise, I'm not complaining **3.** [affaire, difficulté] question, matter, point (at issue) / *là n'est pas la question* that's not the point (at issue) ou the issue / *ce n'est plus qu'une question de temps* it's only a question ou matter of time / *ils se sont disputés pour des questions d'argent* they had an argument over ou about money ▶ **je ne lis pas les critiques, question de principe !** I don't read reviews on principle! ❖ **en question** ⧫ loc adj in question, concerned. ⧫ loc adv ▶ **mettez-vous mon honnêteté en question ?** are you questioning my honesty? ▶ **remettre en question a)** [mettre en doute] to (call into) question, to challenge **b)** [compromettre] to call into question ▶ **se remettre en question** to do some soul searching.

questionnaire [kɛstjɔnɛʀ] nm questionnaire ▶ **questionnaire à choix multiple = QCM.**

questionner [3] [kɛstjɔne] vt [interroger] ▶ **questionner qqn** to question sb, to ask sb questions.

quétaine [keten] adj QUÉBEC *fam* corny, naff UK.

quétainerie [ketɛnʀi] nf QUÉBEC *fam* [objet] piece of junk.

quête [kɛt] nf **1.** [d'argent] collection ▶ **faire la quête a)** [à l'église] to take (the) collection **b)** [dans la rue] to go round with the hat, to pass the hat round **2.** CHASSE search. ❖ **en quête de** loc prép *sout* in search ou pursuit of, searching for / *se mettre en quête de* to go in search of.

quetsche [kwɛtʃ] nf BOT quetsch (plum).

queue [kø] nf **1.** ZOOL tail ▶ **faire une queue de poisson à qqn** AUTO to cut in in front of sb / *leur relation a fini en queue de poisson* their relationship fizzled out ▶ **il est parti la queue basse** *fam* ou **entre les jambes** *fam* he left with his tail between his legs **2.** BOT [d'une cerise, d'une feuille] stalk ; [d'une fleur] stalk, stem **3.** [extrémité - d'une poêle] handle ; [- d'un avion, d'une comète, d'un cerf-volant] tail ; [- d'une étoile filante] trail ; [- d'un cortège] back, tail (end) ; [- d'un orage, d'un tourbillon] tail (end) ; [- d'une procession, d'un train] rear / *je monte toujours en queue* I always get on at the rear (of the train) / *il est en queue de peloton* SPORT he is at the back ou rear of the bunch ▶ **n'avoir ni queue ni tête** : *ce que tu dis n'a ni queue ni tête* you make no sense at all, you're talking nonsense / *une histoire sans queue ni tête* a shaggy-dog story **4.** [dans un classement] bottom / *être à la queue de la classe / du championnat* to be at the bottom of the class / league **5.** [file d'attente] queue UK, line US ▶ **faire la queue** to queue (up) *(insép)* UK, to stand in line US **6.** *vulg* [pénis] cock, prick **7.** JEUX ▶ **queue (de billard)** (billiard) cue **8.** IMPR [d'une lettre] stem, tail, descender *spéc* ; [d'une note de musique] stem ; [d'une page] tail, foot. ❖ **à la queue leu leu** loc adv in single ou Indian file.

queue-de-cheval [køtʃəval] *(pl* **queues-de-cheval)** nf [cheveux] ponytail.

queue-de-pie [kødpi] *(pl* **queues-de-pie)** nf tail coat.

qui [ki] ⧫ pron rel **1.** [représente une personne] who, that / *il y a des gens qui aiment ça* there are people who like that / *toi qui connais le problème, tu pourras m'aider* you who ou as you are acquainted with the problem, you can help me out ; *(après une prép)* whom, who / *la personne à qui je l'ai prêté* the person to whom I lent it *sout*, the person I lent it to / *c'est à qui aura le dernier mot* each tries ou they all try to have the last word / *c'était à qui crierait le plus fort* it was down to who could shout the loudest / *l'amie par qui j'ai eu cette adresse* the friend from whom I got this address *sout*, the friend I got this address from / *c'est rebutant pour qui n'est pas habitué* it's disconcerting for somebody who isn't ou for whoever isn't used to it ; [sans antécédent] whoever, anyone (who) / *qui tu sais, qui vous savez* you know who **2.** [représente un animal] which, that **3.** [représente une chose, une idée] which, that / *le festival, qui débutera en mai* the festival, which will start in May ▶ **donne-moi le magazine qui est sur la table** give me the magazine (that) ou which is on the table **4.** [formule de présentation] : *le voilà qui pleure, maintenant !* now he's crying! **5.** [en corrélation avec «que»] : *qui que tu sois, qui que vous soyez* whoever you are ou you may be *sout* ▶ **qui que ce soit a)** [sujet] whoever **b)** [objet] anybody, anyone. ⧫ pron interr **1.** [sujet ou attribut dans le discours direct] who / *qui donc t'a frappé ?* who hit you? ▶ **qui est-ce qui** who / *qui est-ce qui en veut ?* who wants some? ; [objet dans le discours direct] who, whom *sout* / *qui cherchez-vous ?* who are you looking for? / *c'est à qui ?* whose is it, to whom does it belong? *sout* / *à qui le tour ?* whose turn (is it)? / *de qui parles-tu ?* who ou whom *sout* are you talking about? ▶ **qui est-ce que** who, whom *sout* / *qui est-ce que tu connais ici ?* who do you know around here? **2.** [sujet dans le discours indirect] who / *je ne vois pas qui pourrait t'aider* I can't see who could ou I can't think of anyone who could help you ; [objet dans le discours indirect] who, whom *sout* / *sais-tu qui j'ai rencontré ce matin ?* do you know who I met this morning?

quiche [kiʃ] nf quiche ▶ **quiche lorraine** quiche lorraine.

quiconque [kikɔ̃k] ⧫ pron rel whoever. ⧫ pron indéf anyone ou anybody (else) / *il connaît les volcans mieux que quiconque* he knows volcanoes better than anybody else ou than anyone alive.

qui est-ce que [kiɛskø], **qui est-ce qui** [kiɛski] —→ **qui** (pron interr).

quiétude [kjetyd] nf litt [d'esprit] peace of mind / elle attendait les résultats en toute quiétude she was calmly waiting for the results.

quignon [kiɲɔ̃] nm ▸ **quignon (de pain)** a) [morceau] (crusty) chunk of bread b) [extrémité] heel (of the loaf).

quille [kij] nf **1.** JEUX skittle / jouer aux quilles to play ninepins ou skittles **2.** arg mil [fin du service] demob 🇬🇧, discharge **3.** NAUT keel.

quincaillerie [kɛ̃kajʀi] nf **1.** [articles, commerce] ironmongery 🇬🇧, hardware **2.** [boutique] ironmonger's 🇬🇧, hardware store 🇺🇸 ou shop 🇬🇧 **3.** fam [bijoux, décorations] (cheap) baubles péj.

quincaillier, ère, **quincailler*, ère** [kɛ̃kaje, ɛʀ] nm, f hardware dealer, ironmonger 🇬🇧.

quinconce [kɛ̃kɔ̃s] nm HORT quincunx ▸ **en quinconce** quincuncial, arranged in a quincunx.

quinine [kinin] nf quinine.

quinoa [kinɔa] nm quinoa.

quinqua [kɛ̃ka] nmf fiftysomething.

quinquagénaire [kɛ̃kaʒenɛʀ] ◆ adj ▸ **être quinquagénaire** a) [avoir de 50 à 60 ans] to be in one's fifties b) [avoir 50 ans] to be fifty. ◆ nmf [de 50 à 60 ans] person in his / her fifties ; [de 50 ans] 50-year-old man (woman).

quinquennal, e, aux [kɛ̃kenal, o] adj [plan] five-year (avant nom) ; [élection, foire] five-yearly, quinquennial.

quinquennat [kɛ̃kena] nm five-year period, quinquennium, lustrum.

quinte [kɛ̃t] nf MÉD ▸ **quinte (de toux)** coughing fit, fit of coughing.

Quinté® [kɛ̃te] nm French forecast system involving betting on five horses.

quintette [kɛ̃tɛt] nm quintet, quintette.

quintuple [kɛ̃typl] ◆ adj [somme, quantité] quintuple, five-fold. ◆ nm quintuple / le quintuple de sa valeur five times its value.

quintupler [3] [kɛ̃typle] ◆ vt to quintuple, to increase fivefold. ◆ vi to quintuple, to increase fivefold.

quinzaine [kɛ̃zɛn] nf **1.** [durée] ▸ **une quinzaine de jours** a fortnight, two weeks **2.** [quantité] ▸ **une quinzaine de** about fifteen **3.** COMM ▸ **quinzaine commerciale** two-week sale.

quinze [kɛ̃z] ◆ dét fifteen ▸ **quinze jours** two weeks, a fortnight. ◆ nm inv **1.** [nombre] fifteen ▸ **lundi en quinze** a fortnight on 🇬🇧 ou two weeks from Monday **2.** SPORT ▸ **le quinze de France** the French Fifteen. Voir aussi **cinq**.

quinzième [kɛ̃zjɛm] adj num, nmf & nm fifteenth. Voir aussi **cinquième**.

quiproquo [kipʀɔko] nm [sur l'identité d'une personne] mistake / l'intrigue est fondée sur un quiproquo the plot revolves round a case of mistaken identity ; [sur le sujet d'une conversation] misunderstanding / il y a quiproquo, nous ne parlons pas du même étudiant there is a misunderstanding, we're not talking about the same student.

quittance [kitɑ̃s] nf ▸ **quittance de gaz / d'électricité** gas / electricity bill ▸ **quittance de loyer** rent receipt.

quitte [kit] adj **1.** [libéré -d'une dette, d'une obligation] ▸ **être quitte envers qqn** to be even ou quits ou (all) square with sb / être quitte envers la société [après une peine de prison] to have paid one's debt to society **2.** [au même niveau] ▸ **être quittes** to be quits ou all square **3.** : il en a été quitte pour quelques égratignures / la peur he got away with a few scratches / a bit of a fright **4.** JEUX ▸ **quitte ou double** double or quits 🇬🇧, double or nothing 🇺🇸 ▸ **c'est jouer à quitte ou double** fig it's a big gamble ou risk.

◆ **quitte à** loc prép **1.** [au risque de] : je lui dirai, quitte à me faire renvoyer I'll tell him, even if it means being fired **2.** [puisqu'il faut] since it is necessary to / quitte à les inviter, autant le faire dans les règles since we have to invite them, we may as well do things properly.

quitter [3] [kite] vt **1.** [lieu] to leave ; [ami, époux] to leave, to split up with (insép) ; [emploi] to leave, to quit, to give up (sép) ; [habitude] to drop, to get rid of (insép) / je quitte (le bureau) à 5 h I leave the office ou I finish at 5 o'clock / la voiture a quitté la route the car came off ou ran off ou left the road / il faut que je te quitte I must be going, I must go / il ne la quitta pas des yeux ou du regard he never took his eyes off her, he watched her every move / elle a quitté ce monde euphém she has departed this world ou this life **2.** [au téléphone] ▸ **ne quittez pas** hold on, hold the line. ◆ **se quitter** vp (emploi réciproque) [amis] to part ; [époux] to part, to break ou to split up / quittons-nous bons amis let's part on good terms / depuis qu'ils se sont rencontrés, ils ne se quittent plus ever since they met they have been inseparable / nous nous sommes quittés à 9 heures we left each other at 9.

qui-vive [kiviv] nm inv ▸ **être sur le qui-vive** a) [soldat] to be on the alert ou the qui vive b) [animal] to be on the alert.

quiz [kwiz] nm quiz.

quoi [kwa] ◆ pron rel what, which / il a refusé, ce en quoi il a eu raison he refused, which was quite right of him / on est allés au jardin, après quoi il a fallu rentrer we went to the garden, and then we had to come back in ▸ **prends de quoi boire / écrire / payer** get something to drink / to write / to pay with / il y a de quoi nourrir au moins 10 personnes there's enough to feed at least 10 people / je suis en colère — il y a de quoi ! fam I'm angry — it's no wonder ou with good reason ! ▸ **merci ! — il n'y a pas de quoi** thank you! — not at all ou you're welcome ou don't mention it. ◆ adv interr **1.** [quelle chose] what / c'est quoi ? what's that? / tu fais quoi ce soir ? fam what are you doing this evening? / en quoi puis-je vous être utile ? how can I help you? / par quoi se sent-il concerné ? what does he feel concerned about? / sur quoi va-t-elle travailler ? what is she going to work on? / quoi de plus naturel ? what could be more natural? ▸ **à quoi bon ?** what's the use? ▸ **quoi encore ?** a) what else? b) [ton irrité] what is it now? **2.** fam [pour faire répéter] ▸ **quoi ?** what? **3.** [emplois expressifs] : eh bien quoi, qu'est-ce que tu as ? well, what's the matter with you? / enfin quoi, ou eh bien quoi, tu pourrais regarder où tu vas ! come on now, watch where you're going! / tu viens (oui) ou quoi ? are you coming or not? / décide-toi, quoi ! well make up your mind! ◆ **quoi que** loc conj ▸ **quoi qu'il arrive** whatever happens ▸ **quoi qu'il en soit** be that as it may, however that may be / je te défends de lui dire quoi que ce soit ! I forbid you to tell her / him anything (whatsoever)!

quoique [kwakə] (devant voyelle quoiqu') conj **1.** [bien que] though, although / quoiqu'il fût déjà minuit though ou although it was already midnight **2.** [introduisant une restriction] : il a l'air compétent… quoique… he seems competent… mind you…

quota [k(w)ɔta] nm quota.

quote-part (pl **quotes-parts**), **quotepart*** [kɔtpaʀ] nf share.

quotidien, enne [kɔtidjɛ̃, ɛn] adj [de chaque jour - entraînement, promenade, repas] daily ; [- préoccupations] everyday. ◆ **quotidien** nm daily (paper) ▸ **un grand quotidien** a (major) national daily. ◆ **au quotidien** loc adv fam on a day-to-day basis / vivre sa vie au quotidien to live from day to day.

quotidiennement [kɔtidjɛnmɑ̃] adv daily, every day.

quotient [kɔsjɑ̃] nm **1.** MATH quotient **2.** PSYCHOL ▸ **quotient intellectuel** intelligence quotient.

* In reformed spelling (see p. 16-18).

r1 (abr écrite de rien) SMS nufn.

rab [ʀab] nm *fam* : *qui veut du rab ?* [à table] anyone for seconds? / *alors, on fait du rab ?* [au travail] doing some overtime, are we?

rabâcher [3] [ʀabaʃe] *fam* vt [conseils] to keep (on) repeating ; [malheurs] to keep harping on about / *tu n'arrêtes pas de rabâcher la même chose* you're like a record that's got stuck, you do go on.

rabais [ʀabɛ] nm reduction, discount / *faire un rabais de 10 % sur le prix* to knock 10% off the price. **au rabais** ◆ loc adj [vente] cut-price ; *péj* [formation] second-rate ; [travail] underpaid. ◆ loc adv : *elle travaille au rabais* she works for a pittance.

rabaisser [4] [ʀabese] vt **1.** [diminuer - prétentions] to moderate, to reduce ; [- niveau] to lower ; [- orgueil] to humble ; [- prix] to reduce, to lower **2.** [dévaloriser - mérites, personne] to devalue, to belittle. **se rabaisser** vp *(emploi réfléchi)* [se dévaloriser] to belittle o.s., to sell o.s. short.

rabat [ʀaba] nm [d'un sac, d'une poche] flap.

rabat-joie [ʀabaʒwa] *(pl* rabat-joie *ou* rabat-joies*)* nmf killjoy, spoilsport.

rabattable [ʀabatabl] adj [siège] folding.

rabattre [83] [ʀabatʀ] vt **1.** [toit ouvrant, strapontin - pour baisser] to pull down *(sép)* ; [- pour lever] to pull up *(sép)* ; [couvercle] to shut down *(sép)*, to close ; [chapeau] to pull down *(sép)* ; [col, visière] to turn down *(sép)* / *rabats le drap sur la couverture* fold the sheet back over the blanket / *les cheveux rabattus sur le front* hair brushed forward *ou* down over the forehead / *rabats le capot de la voiture* close the bonnet of the car / *le vent rabattait la pluie contre son visage* the wind was driving the rain against his face **2.** CHASSE to drive **3.** ▶ **en rabattre** *sout* [modérer ses exigences] to climb down *(insép)*, to lower one's sights **4.** COUT to stitch down *(sép)* ; [en tricot] : *rabattre toutes les mailles* to cast off. **se rabattre** vpi **1.** [véhicule - graduellement] to move back into position ; [- brusquement] to cut in / *le car s'est rabattu juste devant moi* the bus cut in just in front of me **2.** [se fermer - volet] to slam shut ; [- table] to fold away. **se rabattre sur** vp + prép [se contenter de] to fall back on, to make do with.

rabbin [ʀabɛ̃] nm rabbi ▶ **grand rabbin** Chief Rabbi.

rabibocher [3] [ʀabibɔʃe] vt *fam* [réconcilier] to patch things up between, to bring together again. **se rabibocher** vpi to make up ▶ **se rabibocher avec qqn** to patch things up with sb.

rabiole [ʀabjɔl] nf QUÉBEC turnip.

râble [ʀabl] nm ZOOL back ▶ **râble de lièvre** CULIN saddle of hare ▶ **tomber** *ou* **sauter sur le râble de qqn** a) *fam* [attaquer] to lay into sb, to go for sb b) [critiquer] to go for sb.

râblé, e [ʀable] adj [personne] stocky.

rabot [ʀabo] nm MENUIS plane.

raboter [3] [ʀabɔte] vt to plane (down).

rabougri, e [ʀabugʀi] adj **1.** [étiolé] scraggy ; [desséché] shrivelled **2.** *fam* [chétif] stunted ; [ratatiné] shrivelled, wizened.

rabrouer [3] [ʀabʀue] vt to send packing ▶ **se faire rabrouer par qqn** to feel the sharp end of sb's tongue.

racaille [ʀakaj] nf *péj* rabble, riff-raff ▶ **une racaille** a scumbag.

raccommodage [ʀakɔmɔdaʒ] nm [de linge, d'un filet] mending, repairing ; [d'une chaussette] darning, mending / *j'ai du raccommodage à faire* I've got some mending to do.

raccommoder [3] [ʀakɔmɔde] vt [réparer - linge, filet] to repair, to mend ; [- chaussette] to darn, to mend. **se raccommoder** vpi *fam* [se réconcilier] to be reconciled, to get together (again).

raccompagnateur, trice [ʀakɔ̃paɲatœʀ, tʀis] nm, f QUÉBEC [personne qui raccompagne] *person who walks or drives sb home.*

raccompagnement [ʀakɔ̃paɲmɑ̃] nm QUÉBEC [action de reconduire] *walking or driving sb home.*

raccompagner [3] [ʀakɔ̃paɲe] vt **1.** [reconduire à la porte] ▶ **raccompagner qqn** to show *ou* to see sb out **2.** [accompagner] : *je vais te raccompagner chez toi* a) [à pied] I'll walk *ou* take you back home b) [en voiture] I'll give you a lift home, I'll drive *ou* run you home / *je me suis fait raccompagner en voiture après la soirée* I asked someone to give me a lift home after the party / *raccompagner qqn à la gare / à l'aéroport* to see sb off at the station / airport.

raccord [ʀakɔʀ] nm **1.** [en décoration] join / *papier avec raccord* wallpaper with pattern match **2.** [retouche] touch-up / *la peinture de la cuisine a besoin de quelques raccords* the kitchen paintwork needs some touching up / *elle s'est fait un petit raccord devant la glace* *fam* she touched up her make-up in front of the mirror.

raccordement [ʀakɔʀdǝmɑ̃] nm RAIL [opération de connexion] linking, joining ; TRAV PUB connecting, linking, joining ; ÉLECTR joining, connecting / *faire le raccordement (au réseau)* TÉLÉC to connect the phone.

raccorder [3] [ʀakɔʀde] vt **1.** ÉLECTR [au secteur] to couple ; [à un circuit] to join **2.** TÉLÉC ▶ **raccorder qqn au réseau** to connect (up) sb's phone.

raccourci [ʀakuʀsi] nm [trajet] shortcut.

raccourcir [32] [ʀakuʀsiʀ] ◆ vt [vêtement, rideau] to shorten, to take up *(sép)* ; [cheveux, barbe] to trim ; [discours] to shorten ; [film] to shorten ; [trajet] to shorten / *le sentier raccourcit le trajet de deux kilomètres* the path shortens the trip by two kilometres ; [séjour] to cut short / *elle a dû raccourcir ses vacances d'une semaine* she had to come back from her holidays a week early. ◆ vi [durée] : *les jours raccourcissent* the days are growing shorter ou drawing in.

raccroc [ʀakʀo] ❖ **par raccroc** loc adv by a stroke of good luck.

raccrocher [3] [ʀakʀɔʃe] ◆ vt **1.** [remettre en place - habit, rideau] to hang back up ; [-tableau] to put back on the hook, to put back up ; [-téléphone] to put down, to hang up ▶ **raccrocher les gants** fam [boxeur] to hang up one's glove, to retire **2.** [relier - wagons] to couple, to hitch together. ◆ vi **1.** [au téléphone] to hang up, to put the receiver down / *elle m'a raccroché au nez* she hung up ou put the phone down on me **2.** fam [prendre sa retraite - boxeur] to hang up one's gloves. ❖ **se raccrocher à** vp + prép [se rattraper à] to grab ou to catch hold of / *il se raccrochait à cet espoir* he hung on to that hope.

race [ʀas] nf **1.** ANTHR race / *de race blanche* white / *de race noire* black **2.** [catégorie] : *la race des honnêtes gens est en voie de disparition* decent people are a dying breed **3.** ZOOL breed. ❖ **de race** loc adj [chien, chat] purebred, pedigree (modif) ; [cheval] thoroughbred.

racé, e [ʀase] adj **1.** ZOOL [chien] purebred, pedigree (modif) ; [cheval] thoroughbred **2.** [personne] wellbred **3.** [voilier, voiture] handsome.

rachat [ʀaʃa] nm **1.** [de ce qu'on avait vendu] repurchase, buying back **2.** [achat] / **'nous vous proposons le rachat de votre ancienne voiture !'** COMM 'we offer to take your old car in part-exchange 🇬🇧 ou as a trade-in 🇺🇸' **3.** FIN [d'actions, d'obligations] buying up ou in ; [d'une affaire] take over ; [d'une franchise, d'une rente] redemption ▶ **rachat d'une entreprise par ses salariés** ≃ leveraged buyout.

racheter [28] [ʀaʃte] vt **1.** [en plus] to buy some more (of) / *je vais racheter un service à café* I'm going to buy another ou a new coffee set **2.** [acheter] to buy / **'on vous rachète vos anciens meubles'** COMM your old furniture taken in part-exchange 🇬🇧 ou as a trade-in 🇺🇸 ▶ **j'ai racheté sa part** / **son affaire** FIN I've bought him out (of the business) / bought him up ▶ **racheter une entreprise** to take over a company **3.** [erreur, défaut] to make up for (insép), to compensate for (insép) ; [péché] to atone for (insép), to expiate sout ; [vie dissolue] to make amends for, to make up for (insép) ; [pécheur] to redeem ▶ **il n'y en a pas un pour racheter l'autre** one's as bad as the other. ❖ **se racheter** vp (emploi réfléchi) [gén] to make amends, to redeem o.s. ; [pécheur] to redeem o.s.

rachitique [ʀaʃitik] adj [chétif - plante] stunted ; [- chien, personne] puny, scrawny.

racial, e, aux [ʀasjal, o] adj racial, race (modif) ▶ **émeute raciale** race riot.

racine [ʀasin] nf **1.** BOT root ▶ **il prend racine** fam [il s'installe] he's getting a bit too comfortably settled / *tu vas prendre racine !* fam [l'attente est longue] you'll take root! **2.** ANAT [d'un cheveu, d'un poil, d'une dent] root **3.** LING & MATH root. ❖ **racines** nfpl [origines] roots / *retrouver ses racines* to go back to one's roots.

racisme [ʀasism] nm racism, racial prejudice / *c'est du racisme antivieux* that's ageism / *c'est du racisme anti-jeunes* that's prejudice against young people.

raciste [ʀasist] ◆ adj racist, prejudiced. ◆ nmf racist.

racket [ʀakɛt] nm (protection) racket ▶ **racket scolaire** bullying other children for money, etc. ▶ *c'est du racket !* it's daylight robbery!

racketter [4] [ʀakɛte] vt to racketeer, to run a (protection) racket ▶ *il est inadmissible que les enfants se fassent racketter dans les écoles* it is unacceptable for children to be subject to racketeering in schools.

racketteur, euse [ʀakɛtœʀ, øz] nm, f racketeer.

raclée [ʀakle] nf fam **1.** [coups] thrashing, hiding / *donner une raclée à qqn* to give sb a good thrashing ou hiding **2.** [défaite] thrashing, hammering / *mettre une raclée à qqn* to thrash sb / *il a pris sa raclée en finale* he got thrashed ou hammered in the final.

racler [3] [ʀakle] vt [frotter] to scrape / *un petit vin blanc qui racle le gosier* a white wine that is rough on ou that burns your throat. ❖ **se racler** vpt : *se racler la gorge* to clear one's throat.

raclette [ʀaklɛt] nf **1.** CULIN [plat] Swiss speciality consisting of melted cheese prepared at the table using a special heater or grill, served with potatoes and cold meats ; [fromage] raclette (cheese) **2.** [grattoir] scraper.

racloir [ʀaklwaʀ] nm **1.** MIN scraper **2.** MENUIS scraper plane.

racolage [ʀakɔlaʒ] nm [par une prostituée] soliciting ; [par un vendeur] touting (for customers) ; [par un militant] canvassing ▶ **faire du racolage a)** [prostituée] to solicit **b)** [commerçant] to tout (for customers).

racoler [3] [ʀakɔle] vt [clients - suj : prostituée] to accost ; [- suj : vendeur] to tout for.

racoleur, euse [ʀakɔlœʀ, øz] adj [sourire] enticing ; [affiche] eye-catching ; [titre, journal] sensationalist ; [campagne électorale] vote-catching.

racontar [ʀakɔ̃taʀ] nm fam piece of gossip / *n'écoute pas les racontars* don't listen to gossip.

raconter [3] [ʀakɔ̃te] vt **1.** [conte, histoire] to tell / *il a raconté l'histoire à son voisin* he told his neighbour the story, he told the story to his neighbour **2.** [événement, voyage] to tell, to relate / *il a raconté l'accident à sa mère* he told his mother about the accident ▶ **raconter ses malheurs à qqn** to tell sb all one's troubles, to pour one's heart out to sb ▶ **raconter sa vie** fam to tell one's (whole) life story **3.** [dire] to tell / *on raconte beaucoup de choses sur lui* you hear all sorts of stories about him / *on raconte qu'il a été marié plusieurs fois* people say he's been married several times / *mais enfin qu'est-ce que tu racontes ?* what (on earth) are you on about? / *ne raconte pas de bêtises* don't be silly ; (en usage absolu) ▶ **vite, raconte !** go on!, quick, tell me! ▶ **je te raconte pas** fam I can't imagine! ❖ **se raconter** vpi **1.** [personne - parler de soi] to talk about o.s. **2.** fam ▶ **se raconter des histoires** [se leurrer] to fool oneself ▶ **se la raconter** to show off.

racorni, e [ʀakɔʀni] adj [vieillard] wizened, shrivelled ; [mains] gnarled ; [plante] shrivelled ; [parchemin] dried-up.

radar [ʀadaʀ] nm radar ▶ **contrôle radar** [sur la route] radar (speed) trap (on a road) ▶ **aujourd'hui je suis** ou **je marche au radar** fam I'm on automatic pilot today.

rade [ʀad] nf **1.** [bassin] (natural) harbour 🇬🇧 ou harbor 🇺🇸, roads spéc / *en rade de San Francisco* in San Francisco harbour **2.** fam ⓔⓧⓟ laisser qqn en rade [l'abandonner] to leave sb in the lurch ▶ **rester en rade** : *on est restés en rade* we were left stranded ▶ **tomber en rade** fam to break down.

radeau, x [ʀado] nm raft ▶ **radeau de sauvetage** life raft ▶ **radeau pneumatique** inflatable raft.

radiateur [ʀadjatœʀ] nm [à eau, d'un véhicule] radiator ▶ **radiateur électrique** electric radiator ou heater ▶ **radiateur soufflant** fan heater.

radiation [ʀadjasjɔ̃] nf **1.** BIOL & PHYS radiation **2.** [élimination] removal, striking off / *ils ont demandé sa radiation de l'ordre des médecins* / *du barreau* they asked that he should be struck off the register / that he should be struck off.

radical, e, aux [ʀadikal, o] ◆ adj **1.** [complet] radical, drastic / *une réorganisation radicale* a thoroughgoing ou root and branch reorganization **2.** [efficace] : *l'eucalyptus* *c'est radical contre le rhume* eucalyptus is just the thing for colds. ◆ nm, f POL Radical.

radicalement [ʀadikalmã] adv radically, completely / *il a radicalement changé* he's completely different, he's a different person.

radicaliser [3] [ʀadikalize] vt to radicalize, to make more radical. ◆ **se radicaliser** vpi : *le mouvement étudiant s'est radicalisé* the student movement has become more radical.

radier [9] [ʀadje] vt to strike off *(sép)* / *elle a été radiée de l'ordre des médecins / du barreau* she was struck off the register / struck off.

radieux, euse [ʀadjø, øz] adj [matinée, temps] glorious ; [soleil, beauté] brilliant, radiant ; [visage, personne] radiant, glowing (with happiness).

radin, e [ʀadɛ̃, in] fam ◆ adj tightfisted, stingy. ◆ nm, f skinflint.

radiner [3] [ʀadine] ◆ **se radiner** vpi tfam [arriver] to turn ou to show up *(insép)* ; : *allez, vite, radine-toi !* come on, get a move on!

radio [ʀadjo] nf **1.** [récepteur] radio **2.** [diffusion] **)** **à la radio** on the radio **)** **passer à la radio a)** [personne] to be on the radio **b)** [chanson] to be played on the radio **c)** [jeu, concert] to be broadcast (on the radio), to be radiocast US **3.** [station] radio station **)** **radio locale privée** ou **libre** independent local radio station **)** **radio privée** independent ou commercial radio station **4.** *(comme adj inv)* MIL **)** **message radio** radio message **5.** MÉD X-ray (photograph) **)** **passer une radio** to have an X-ray (done), to be X-rayed.

radioactif, ive [ʀadjoaktif, iv] adj radioactive.

radioactivité [ʀadjoaktivite] nf radioactivity.

radioamateur [ʀadjoamatœʀ] nm radio ham.

radiocassette [ʀadjokasɛt] nf radio cassette player.

radiodiffuser [3] [ʀadjodifyze] vt to broadcast (on radio), to radiocast US.

radioélectrique [ʀadjoelɛktʀik] adj ÉLECTR radio *(modif)*.

radiographie [ʀadjoɡʀafi] nf [technique] radiography ; [image] X-ray, radiograph.

radiographier [9] [ʀadjoɡʀafje] vt to X-ray.

radiologie [ʀadjolɔʒi] nf radiology.

radiophonique [ʀadjofɔnik] adj [émission, feuilleton] radio *(modif)* ; [studio] broadcasting *(modif)*.

radioréveil, radio-réveil *(pl* radios-réveils*)* [ʀadjoʀevɛj] nm radio alarm (clock).

radio-taxi *(pl* radio-taxis*)*, **radiotaxi*** [ʀadjotaksi] nm radio cab, radio-taxi.

radiotélévisé, e [ʀadjotelevize] adj broadcast simultaneously on radio and TV, simulcast.

radiothérapie [ʀadjoteʀapi] nf radiotherapy.

radis [ʀadi] nm **1.** BOT radish **2.** EXPR **n'avoir plus un radis** tfam: *je n'ai plus un radis* I haven't got a bean US ou a red cent US.

radium [ʀadjɔm] nm radium.

radoter [3] [ʀadɔte] fam vi to witter on / *là, il radote !* he's going soft in the head!

radoucir [32] [ʀadusiʀ] ◆ **se radoucir** vpi **1.** [voix] to soften, to become gentler ; [personne] to yield, to soften **2.** [température] to get milder.

radoucissement [ʀadusismã] nm MÉTÉOR (slight) rise in temperature / *net radoucissement des températures ce matin* a marked rise in temperature this morning.

raf SMS abr écrite de **rien à faire.**

rafale [ʀafal] nf **1.** MÉTÉOR blast, gust / *le vent souffle en rafales* it's blustery **2.** ARM burst **)** **une rafale de mitraillette** a burst of machine-gun fire **3.** fig burst / *par* ou *en rafales* intermittently.

raffermir [32] [ʀafɛʀmiʀ] vt **1.** [muscle, peau] to tone ou to firm up *(sép)* **2.** [consolider] to strengthen, to reinforce **)** **raffermir le courage de qqn** to bolster up sb's courage. ◆ **se raffermir** vpi **1.** [muscle, peau] to tone ou to firm up **2.** [se consolider] to get stronger **3.** FIN [monnaie, prix] to strengthen.

raffinage [ʀafinaʒ] nm refining.

raffiné, e [ʀafine] adj **1.** INDUST refined **2.** [élégant] refined, sophisticated.

raffinement [ʀafinmã] nm [élégance] refinement, sophistication.

raffiner [3] [ʀafine] vt INDUST to refine. ◆ **raffiner sur** v + prép to be overparticular about / *je n'ai pas eu le temps de raffiner sur les détails* I didn't have time to pay that much attention to the details.

raffinerie [ʀafinʀi] nf refinery.

raffoler [3] [ʀafole] ◆ **raffoler de** v + prép to be crazy ou mad about / *chic, des glaces, j'en raffole !* ooh, ice cream, I LOVE ice cream!

raffut [ʀafy] nm fam **1.** [bruit] racket **2.** [esclandre] to-do **)** **faire du raffut à propos de qqch** to make a big to-do about sthg.

rafiot [ʀafjo] nm fam [bateau] **)** **vieux rafiot** old tub.

rafistoler [3] [ʀafistɔle] vt fam to patch up *(sép)*, to fix temporarily.

rafle [ʀafl] nf [arrestation] raid **)** **une rafle de police** a police raid.

rafler [3] [ʀafle] vt fam **1.** [voler] to nick UK, to swipe **2.** [saisir] to grab ; COMM to buy up *(sép)* / *les clients ont tout raflé en moins de deux heures* the customers cleared the shelves in less than two hours **3.** [remporter - prix] to walk off with / *le film a raflé toutes les récompenses* the film made a clean sweep of the awards.

rafraîchir, rafraichir* [32] [ʀafʀeʃiʀ] ◆ vt **1.** [refroidir] to cool (down) **2.** [remettre en état - vêtement] to smarten ou to brighten up *(sép)* ; [-barbe, coupe de cheveux] to trim ; [-peintures] to freshen up *(sép)* ; [-logement] to smarten up / **'à rafraîchir'** [logement] 'needs some redecoration' **3.** fig [raviver - connaissances] to brush up **)** **rafraîchir la mémoire à qqn** to refresh ou to jog sb's memory **4.** INFORM to refresh ; [navigateur] to reload. ◆ vi **1.** MÉTÉOR to get cooler ou colder **2.** CULIN to chill. ◆ **se rafraîchir, se rafraichir*** vpi **1.** [se refroidir] to get colder **2.** [faire sa toilette] to freshen up **3.** [boire] to have a cool drink.

rafraîchissant, e, rafraichissant*, e [ʀafʀeʃisã, ãt] adj [froid] cool, refreshing ; [tonique] refreshing, invigorating.

rafraîchissement, rafraichissement* [ʀafʀeʃismã] nm **1.** [refroidissement] cooling / *net rafraîchissement des températures sur tout le pays* temperatures are noticeably cooler throughout the country **2.** [boisson] cool ou cold drink **)** **rafraîchissements** [glaces, fruits] refreshments.

raft(ing) [ʀaft(iŋ)] nm white water rafting.

ragaillardir [32] [ʀaɡajaʀdiʀ] vt fam to buck ou to perk up *(sép)* / *ragaillardi par une nuit de sommeil* refreshed after a good night's sleep.

rage [ʀaʒ] nf **1.** MÉD & VÉTÉR **)** **la rage** rabies **)** **rage de dents** (severe) toothache **2.** [colère - d'adulte] rage, fury ; [-d'enfant] tantrum **)** **être fou de rage** to be absolutely furious **)** **mettre qqn en rage** to infuriate sb / *elle est repartie la rage au cœur* she went off boiling ou seething with rage

---

* In reformed spelling (see p. 16-18).

3. [passion] passion, mania ▸ **avoir la rage de vivre** to have an insatiable lust for life **4.** ⟨EXPR⟩ **faire rage a)** [feu, ouragan] to rage **b)** [mode] to be all the rage.

rageant, e [ʀaʒɑ̃, ɑ̃t] adj infuriating, exasperating.

rager [17] [ʀaʒe] vi : *ça me fait rager de voir tout cet argent dépensé pour rien* it makes my blood boil to see all that money just wasted.

ragnagnas [ʀaɲaɲa] nmpl *fam* period / *elle a ses ragnagnas* she's on the rag.

ragot [ʀago] nm piece of gossip ▸ **des ragots** *fam* gossip, (malicious) rumour 🇬🇧 ou rumor 🇺🇸, tittle-tattle.

ragoût, ragout* [ʀagu] nm stew, ragout.

⬦ **en ragoût, en ragout*** loc adj stewed.

raid [ʀɛd] nm **1.** MIL raid, surprise attack ▸ **raid aérien** air raid **2.** SPORT [avec des véhicules] long-distance rally ; [à pied] trek **3.** BOURSE raid.

raide [ʀɛd] ◆ adj **1.** [rigide - baguette, matériau] stiff, rigid ; [tendu - fil, ficelle] taut, tight ; [droit] straight / *avoir une jambe raide* to have a stiff leg ▸ **avoir les cheveux raides (comme des baguettes de tambour)** to have straight hair ▸ **se tenir raide comme un piquet** to stand as stiff as a pole ou a poker **2.** [abrupt] steep / *la côte est (en pente) raide* the hill climbs steeply **3.** *fam* [fort - café] strong ; [- alcool] rough **4.** *fam* [osé - détail, récit] risqué ; [- scène] explicit, daring **5.** *fam* [surprenant] ▸ **elle est raide, celle-là !** that's a bit far-fetched ou hard to believe **6.** *tfam* [désargenté] broke, skint 🇬🇧. ◆ adv **1.** [à pic] steeply **2.** [en intensif] ▸ **tomber raide** to drop dead ▸ **raide mort** stone dead 🇬🇧, dead as a doornail.

raideur [ʀɛdœʀ] nf [d'un muscle] stiffness / *avoir une raideur dans l'épaule* to have a stiff shoulder.

raidir [32] [ʀɛdiʀ] vt [tendre] to stiffen. ⬦ **se raidir** vpi **1.** [perdre sa souplesse] to stiffen, to go stiff, to become stiffer **2.** [se tendre - muscle, corps] to tense (up), to stiffen ; [- cordage] to tighten, to grow taut.

raie [ʀɛ] nf **1.** [trait] line ; [rayure] stripe ; [griffure] scratch, mark **2.** [dans les cheveux] parting 🇬🇧, part 🇺🇸 / *une raie sur le côté* a side parting **3.** ANAT slit / *raie des fesses* cleft of the buttocks **4.** ZOOL ray, skate ; CULIN skate.

rail [ʀaj] nm **1.** [barre d'acier] rail ▸ **les rails** [la voie] the tracks, the rails ▸ **être sur les rails** *fig* to be under way ▸ **sortir des rails** to leave the rails, to go ou to come off the rails ▸ **remettre qqch / qqn sur les rails** *fig* to put sthg / sb back on the rails **2.** [glissière] ▸ **rail de sécurité** guardrail.

railler [3] [ʀaje] *litt* vt to mock, to laugh ou to scoff at (*insép.*)

raillerie [ʀajʀi] nf **1.** [attitude] mocking, raillery *litt* **2.** [remarque] jibe, jest *arch* ou *hum.*

rainure [ʀɛnyʀ] nf [sillon] groove ; [guide] channel, slot / *les rainures du parquet* the gaps between the floorboards.

raisin [ʀɛzɛ̃] nm **1.** [en grappes] grapes ▸ **raisin blanc / noir** white / black grapes ▸ **raisin de cuve / table** wine / eating grapes **2.** CULIN ▸ **raisins de Corinthe** currants ▸ **raisins secs** raisins ▸ **raisins de Smyrne** sultanas.

raison [ʀɛzɔ̃] nf **1.** [motif] reason / *il n'y a aucune raison pour que vous partiez* there's no reason for you to leave / *y a-t-il une raison de s'inquiéter ?* is there any reason to worry? / *quelle est la raison de son départ ?* why is she leaving? / *la raison pour laquelle je vous écris* the reason (why) ou that I'm writing to you ▸ **pour quelle raison ?** why? ▸ **pour des raisons familiales / personnelles** for family / personal reasons / *pour raisons de santé* for reasons of ill-health, for health reasons ▸ **avoir de bonnes raisons** ou **des raisons (de faire qqch)** to have good reasons (for doing sthg) ▸ **avec raison** with good reason ▸ **sans raison** for no reason (at all) ▸ **pour une raison ou pour une autre** for one reason or another / *pour la (bonne) et*

simple raison que for the simple reason that / *ce n'est pas une raison !, c'est pas une raison !* that's no excuse! ▸ **raison de vivre** reason to live / *cet enfant c'est sa raison de vivre* he lives for that child ▸ **à plus forte raison** all the more so / *raison de plus pour le faire* that's one more reason for doing so **2.** [lucidité] ▸ **perdre la raison** to lose one's mind **3.** [bon sens] reason ▸ **faire entendre raison à qqn, ramener qqn à la raison** to make sb see reason ▸ **plus que de raison** to excess, more than is reasonable **4.** [faculté de penser] reason / *l'homme est un être doué de raison* man is a thinking being **5.** ⟨EXPR⟩ **avoir raison** to be right ▸ **donner raison à qqn a)** [personne] to agree that sb is right **b)** [événement] to prove sb right ▸ **se faire une raison** to resign o.s. ▸ **avoir raison de qqn / qqch** *sout* to get the better of sb / sthg, to overcome sb / sthg ▸ **la raison du plus fort est toujours la meilleure** *prov* might is right *prov.* ⬦ **à raison de** loc prép at the rate of. ⬦ **en raison de** loc prép [à cause de] on account of, because of. ⬦ **raison d'État** nf : *le gouvernement a invoqué la raison d'État pour justifier cette mesure* the government said that it had done this for reasons of State. ⬦ **raison d'être** nf raison d'être. ⬦ **raison sociale** nf corporate ou company name.

raisonnable [ʀɛzɔnabl] adj **1.** [sensé - personne, solution, décision] sensible / *il devrait être plus raisonnable* he should know better / *est-ce bien raisonnable ?* *hum* is that wise? **2.** [acceptable - prix, taux, heure] reasonable ; [- salaire] decent.

raisonnablement [ʀɛzɔnabləmɑ̃] adv **1.** [de manière sensée] sensibly, properly **2.** [normalement] reasonably **3.** [modérément] in moderation.

raisonné, e [ʀɛzɔne] adj **1.** [analyse, projet, décision] reasoned **2.** [grammaire, méthode] structured.

raisonnement [ʀɛzɔnmɑ̃] nm **1.** [faculté, réflexion] ▸ **le raisonnement** reasoning **2.** [argumentation] reasoning / *je ne suis pas bien votre raisonnement* I don't follow your line of argument ou thought / *il ne faudra pas tenir ce raisonnement avec lui* we mustn't use that argument with him.

raisonner [3] [ʀɛzɔne] ◆ vi **1.** [penser] to think **2.** [enchaîner des arguments] : *non, là vous raisonnez mal !* no, your reasoning isn't sound there! **3.** [discuter] ▸ **raisonner sur** to argue about ▸ **raisonner avec qqn** to reason with sb. ◆ vt [faire appel à la raison de] to reason with (*insép*). ⬦ **se raisonner** vp (*emploi réfléchi*) : *raisonne-toi, essaie de manger moins* be reasonable and try not to eat so much.

rajeunir [32] [ʀaʒœniʀ] ◆ vi **1.** [redevenir jeune] to grow young again **2.** [paraître plus jeune] to look ou to seem younger. ◆ vt **1.** [rendre jeune] ▸ **rajeunir qqn a)** *pr* to rejuvenate sb, to make sb younger **b)** *fig* to make sb look younger / *rajeunir le personnel d'une société* to bring new blood into a company **2.** [faire se sentir plus jeune] : *ça me rajeunit !* it makes me feel younger! **3.** [moderniser - mobilier, équipement] to modernize. ⬦ **se rajeunir** vp (*emploi réfléchi*) **1.** [se faire paraître plus jeune] to make o.s. look younger **2.** [se dire plus jeune] to lie about one's age.

rajeunissement [ʀaʒœnismɑ̃] nm **1.** BIOL & PHYSIOL rejuvenation **2.** [abaissement de l'âge] : *le rajeunissement de la population* the decreasing average age of the population.

rajouter [3] [ʀaʒute] vt **1.** [ajouter] ▸ **rajouter qqch (à)** to add sthg (to) **2.** [dire en plus] ▸ **rajouter qqch (à)** to add sthg (to) / *je n'ai rien à rajouter* I have nothing to add, I have nothing more to say **3.** *fam* ⟨EXPR⟩ **en rajouter** to lay it on a bit thick.

rajustement [ʀaʒystəmɑ̃] nm adjustment / *un rajustement des salaires* a wage adjustment.

rajuster [3] [ʀaʒyste] vt **1.** [prix, salaires, vêtements] to adjust **2.** [rectifier] : *rajuster le tir* to adjust ou to correct one's aim. ❖ **se rajuster** vpi to tidy o.s. up / *il avait oublié de se rajuster* he'd forgotten to do up his fly ou to adjust his dress *hum*.

râlant, e [ʀɑlɑ̃, ɑ̃t] adj *fam* infuriating, exasperating / *c'est râlant !* it's enough to drive you mad!

râle [ʀal] nm [d'un agonisant] ▶ **râle (d'agonie)** death rattle.

ralenti, e [ʀalɑ̃ti] adj : *mener une vie ralentie* to live quietly. ❖ **ralenti** nm **1.** CINÉ slow motion **2.** AUTO & MÉCAN idling speed ▶ **régler le ralenti** to adjust the idling speed. ❖ **au ralenti** loc adv **1.** CINÉ in slow motion **2.** [à vitesse réduite] ▶ **tourner au ralenti** [moteur] to idle ▶ **l'usine tourne au ralenti** the factory is running under capacity / *depuis qu'il est à la retraite, il vit au ralenti* now that he's retired, he doesn't do as much as he used to.

ralentir [32] [ʀalɑ̃tiʀ] ◆ vi to slow down / **'ralentir, travaux'** 'slow, roadworks ahead'. ◆ vt [mouvement, effort] to slow down / *ralentir sa course* ou *l'allure* to reduce speed, to slow down ▶ **ralentir le pas** to slow down. ❖ **se ralentir** vpi to slow down.

ralentissement [ʀalɑ̃tismɑ̃] nm **1.** [décélération] decrease in speed / *un ralentissement de 10 km sur la N10* slow-moving traffic for 6 miles on the N10 **2.** [diminution] reduction ▶ **un ralentissement de l'économie** economic turndown.

ralentisseur [ʀalɑ̃tisœʀ] nm **1.** [sur route] speed bump, sleeping policeman **UK** **2.** AUTO & MÉCAN idler, speed reducer.

râler [3] [ʀale] vi *fam* [se plaindre] to grumble, to moan.

râleur, euse [ʀalœʀ, øz] *fam* nm, f grouch, moaner / *quel râleur !* he never stops moaning!

ralliement [ʀalimɑ̃] nm **1.** [adhésion] : *lors de son ralliement à notre parti / notre cause* when he came over to our party / cause **2.** [rassemblement] rally, gathering ▶ **signe / cri de ralliement** rallying sign / cry / *point de ralliement* rallying point.

rallier [9] [ʀalje] vt **1.** [rejoindre - groupe, poste] to go back to **2.** [adhérer à] to join **3.** [rassembler - autour de soi, d'un projet] to win over *(sép)* ; [- des troupes] to gather together, to rally ▶ **rallier tous les suffrages** to win general approval ▶ **rallier qqn à sa cause** to win sb over **4.** NAUT : *rallier la terre* to haul in for the coast. ❖ **se rallier à** vp + prép **1.** [se joindre à] ▶ **se rallier à qqn** to join forces with sb / *se rallier à un parti* to join a party **2.** [se montrer favorable à] ▶ **se rallier à un avis / un point de vue** to come round to an opinion / a point of view.

rallonge [ʀalɔ̃ʒ] nf **1.** [électrique] extension (cable) **2.** [planche] extension **3.** *fam* [délai] extra time *(U)* / *une rallonge de quelques jours* a few extra days **4.** *fam* [supplément] extra money *(U)* / *il nous a donné une rallonge de quarante euros* he gave us an extra forty euros **5.** **Québec** ARCHIT extension. ❖ **à rallonge(s)** loc adj ▶ **table à rallonge** ou **rallonges** extending table.

rallonger [17] [ʀalɔ̃ʒe] ◆ vt **1.** [gén] to extend ; [durée, liste] to lengthen, to make longer, to extend **2.** [vêtement - en défaisant l'ourlet] to let down *(sép)* ; [- en ajoutant du tissu] to make longer **3.** *fam* [suj : trajet, itinéraire] : *en passant par Lille, ça te rallonge d'une heure* if you go via Lille, it'll add an hour to your journey time. ◆ vi : *les jours rallongent* the days are getting longer.

rallumer [3] [ʀalyme] vt **1.** [feu] to rekindle, to light again ; [lampe, télévision] to put back on, to switch on again ; [électricité] to turn on again ▶ **rallumer une cigarette a)** [éteinte] to relight a cigarette **b)** [une autre] to light

up another cigarette ; *(en usage absolu)* ▶ **rallume !** put the light back on! **2.** *sout* [faire renaître - haine, passion] to rekindle. ❖ **se rallumer** vpi [feu, incendie] to flare up again ; [lampe] to come back on.

rallye [ʀali] nm **1.** [course] ▶ **rallye (automobile)** rally, car-rally **2.** [soirée] *exclusive upper-class ball for young people*.

RAM, Ram [ʀam] (abr de **Random Access Memory**) nf Ram, ram.

ramadan [ʀamadɑ̃] nm Ramadan, Ramadhan ▶ **faire** ou **observer le ramadan** to observe Ramadan.

ramassage [ʀamasaʒ] nm **1.** [collecte] ▶ **ramassage des ordures** rubbish **UK** ou garbage **US** collection **2.** [transport] picking up ▶ **ramassage scolaire** school bus service.

ramasse [ʀamas] nf *fam* ▶ **être à la ramasse** [fatigué] to be shattered / *après la compétition, il était complètement à la ramasse* he was completely shattered after the competition / *l'entreprise est à la ramasse face à ses concurrents* the company is lagging way behind the competition.

ramasser [3] [ʀamase] vt **1.** [objet à terre] to pick up *(sép)* **2.** [cueillir - champignons] to pick, to gather ; [- pommes de terre] to dig ; [- marrons] to gather **3.** [rassembler - copies] to collect, to take in *(sép)* ; [- cartes à jouer] to gather up *(sép)* ; [- feuilles mortes] to sweep up *(sép)* / *il a ramassé pas mal d'argent fam* he's picked up ou made quite a bit of money **4.** [élèves, ouvriers] to collect **5.** *fam* [trouver] to pick up, to dig up **6.** *fam* [arrêter] : to collar, to nab / *se faire ramasser* to get nabbed, to get collared **7.** *fam* [recevoir - mauvais coup, gifle] to get **8.** *fam* [attraper - maladie] to catch **9.** *arg scol* : *se faire ramasser* to fail. ❖ **se ramasser** vpi **1.** [avant de bondir] to crouch **2.** *fam* [tomber] to come a cropper **UK**, to fall flat on one's face ; [échouer] to fail.

ramassis [ʀamasi] nm *péj* [d'objets] jumble ; [de personnes] bunch.

rambarde [ʀɑ̃baʀd] nf rail, guardrail.

rame [ʀam] nf **1.** [aviron] oar **2.** [de papier] ream **3.** [train] train / *rame (de métro)* (underground) train **UK**, subway train **US 4.** **EXPR** ▶ **ne pas en ficher une rame** *fam* : *il n'en a pas fichu une rame* he hasn't done a stroke (of work).

rameau, x [ʀamo] nm [branche] (small) branch. ❖ **Rameaux** nmpl ▶ **les Rameaux, le dimanche des Rameaux** Palm Sunday.

ramener [19] [ʀamne] vt **1.** [personne, véhicule - au point de départ] to take back *(sép)* ; [- à soi] to bring back *(sép)* / *son chauffeur le ramène tous les soirs* his chauffeur drives him back every evening ▶ **ramener à** [un endroit] to take back to / *ramener les enfants à l'école* to take the children back to school **2.** [rapporter] : *il faut que je ramène les clefs à l'agence* I've got to take the keys back to the estate agent **3.** [rétablir] to bring back *(sép)*, to restore / *ramener la paix* to restore peace **4.** [placer] : *elle ramena le châle sur ses épaules* she pulled the shawl around her shoulders / *ramener ses cheveux en arrière* to draw one's hair back **5.** [faire revenir] : *le film m'a ramené dix ans en arrière* the film took me back ten years ▶ **ramener la conversation à** ou *sur qqch* to bring the conversation back (round) to sthg ▶ **ramener qqn à la vie** to bring sb back to life, to revive sb **6.** [réduire] : *ramener tout à soi* to bring everything back to ou to relate everything to o.s. **7.** [diminuer] : *ramener à* to bring down to. **EXPR** ▶ **la ramener, ramener sa fraise a)** *fam* [vouloir s'imposer] to stick one's oar in **b)** [faire l'important] to show off. ❖ **se ramener** vpi *fam* [arriver] to turn up ou to show up / *ramène-toi en vitesse !* come on, hurry up!

ramer [3] [ʀame] vi **1.** [pagayer] to row **2.** *fam* [peiner] : *j'ai ramé trop longtemps, maintenant je veux en* *vrai boulot* I've been slaving away for too long, now I want a decent job / *qu'est-ce qu'on a ramé pour trouver cet appartement !* it was such a hassle finding this flat!

rameuter [3] [ʀamøte] vt **1.** [regrouper - foule] to draw **2.** [mobiliser - militants, partisans] to rouse.

ramier [ʀamje] adj m & nm ▸ **(pigeon) ramier** ringdove, wood pigeon.

ramification [ʀamifikasjɔ̃] nf **1.** BOT ramification *spéc*, offshoot **2.** [d'un fleuve] ramification, distributary ; [d'une voie ferrée] branch line ; [d'un réseau, d'une organisation] branch.

ramolli, e [ʀamɔli] adj **1.** [mou] soft **2.** *fam* [gâteux] soft ▸ **il est un peu ramolli du cerveau** he's gone a bit soft (in the head) ou soft-headed.

ramollir [32] [ʀamɔliʀ] vt **1.** *fam* [rendre mou] to soften **2.** [affaiblir] to weaken. ❖ **se ramollir** vpi **1.** [devenir mou] to go soft **2.** *fam* [perdre son tonus]: *depuis que j'ai arrêté le sport, je me suis ramolli* I've been out of condition since I stopped doing sport **3.** *fam* [devenir gâteux] : *j'ai l'impression que je me ramollis* I feel like I'm going senile.

ramoner [3] [ʀamɔne] vt [cheminée] to sweep ; [machine] to clean ; [pipe] to clean (out).

ramoneur [ʀamɔnœʀ] nm chimney sweep.

rampant, e [ʀɑ̃pɑ̃, ɑ̃t] adj **1.** [animal] creeping, crawling **2.** BOT creeping **3.** [évoluant lentement] ▸ **inflation rampante** creeping inflation.

rampe [ʀɑ̃p] nf **1.** [main courante] handrail, banister ▸ **rampe (d'escalier)** banister ▸ **lâcher la rampe** *fam & euphém* to kick the bucket **2.** [plan incliné] slope, incline ▸ **rampe d'accès** approach ramp **3.** THÉÂTRE footlights ▸ **passer la rampe** to get across to the audience **4.** TECHNOL ▸ **rampe de lancement a)** ASTRONAUT launchpad, launching pad **b)** *fig* launchpad.

ramper [3] [ʀɑ̃pe] vi **1.** [lierre] to creep ; [personne] to crawl ; [serpent] to slither, to crawl ; [doute, inquiétude] to lurk **2.** *fig* [s'abaisser] to grovel ▸ **ramper devant qqn** to grovel before sb.

rampon [ʀɑ̃pɔ̃] nm Suisse lamb's lettuce.

rancard [ʀɑ̃kaʀ] nm *tfam* **1.** [rendez-vous - gén] meeting ; [- amoureux] date / *j'ai rancard avec lui à 15 h* I'm meeting him at 3 ▸ **filer (un) rancard à qqn** to arrange to meet sb **2.** *arg crime* [renseignement] info *(U)*, gen *(U)* UK ; [tuyau] tip, tip-off.

rancarder [3] [ʀɑ̃kaʀde] vt *arg crime* [renseigner] to fill in *(sép)*, to clue up *(sép)* / *qui t'a rancardé ?* who tipped you off? ❖ **se rancarder** vpr *(emploi réfléchi) arg crime* to get information.

rancart [ʀɑ̃kaʀ] nm *fam* EXPR⟩ **mettre qqch au rancart** to chuck sthg out, to bin sthg UK / *on a mis le projet au rancart* we scrapped the project.

rance [ʀɑ̃s] adj [beurre, huile] rancid ; [noix] stale.

rancir [32] [ʀɑ̃siʀ] vi [beurre, huile] to go rancid ; [noix] to go stale.

rancœur [ʀɑ̃kœʀ] nf *sout* resentment, rancour UK, rancor US ▸ **avoir de la rancœur envers qqn** to feel resentful towards sb.

rançon [ʀɑ̃sɔ̃] nf **1.** [somme d'argent] ransom **2.** [contrepartie] ▸ **c'est la rançon de la gloire / du succès** that's the price you have to pay for being famous / successful.

rancune [ʀɑ̃kyn] nf rancour UK, rancor US, spite, grudge ▸ **garder rancune à qqn** to bear ou to harbour a grudge against sb ▸ **sans rancune !** let's shake hands and forget it!

rancunier, ère [ʀɑ̃kynje, ɛʀ] adj spiteful ▸ **être rancunier** to bear grudges.

rando [ʀɑ̃do] nf *fam* hiking ▸ **ski de rando** cross-country skiing.

randonnée [ʀɑ̃dɔne] nf ▸ **faire une randonnée** [à pied] to go for a hike / *faire une randonnée à vélo* to go for a (long) bike ride / *faire une randonnée à skis* to go cross-country skiing ▸ **la randonnée (pédestre)** walking, hiking ▸ **grande randonnée** long-distance hiking.

randonneur, euse [ʀɑ̃dɔnœʀ, øz] nm, f hiker.

rang [ʀɑ̃] nm **1.** [rangée - de personnes] row, line ; [- de fauteuils] row ; [- de crochet, de tricot] row (of stitches) / *on était au premier rang* we were in the front row **2.** [dans une hiérarchie] rank / *notre ville occupe le premier rang dans le respect de l'environnement* our city leads the field in terms of environment-friendly policy **3.** [condition sociale] (social) standing ▸ **tenir son rang** to maintain one's position in society **4.** MIL ▸ **le rang** the ranks **5.** Québec long strip of farmland *(at right angles to a road or a river)*. ❖ **rangs** nmpl ranks ▸ **être** ou **se mettre sur les rangs** to line up ▸ **servir dans les rangs d'un parti / syndicat** to be a member ou to serve in the ranks of a party / union. ❖ **au rang de** loc prép **1.** [dans la catégorie de] : *une habitude élevée* ou *passée au rang de rite sacré* a habit which has been raised to the status of a sacred rite **2.** [au nombre de] ▸ **mettre qqn au rang de ses amis** to count sb among one's friends. ❖ **en rang** loc adv in a line ou row ▸ **se mettre en rang** to line up, to form a line.

rangé, e [ʀɑ̃ʒe] adj **1.** [en ordre - chambre, vêtements] tidy **2.** [raisonnable - personne] steady, level-headed ; [- vie] settled / *une jeune personne rangée* a very sober ou well-behaved young person.

rangée [ʀɑ̃ʒe] nf row.

rangement [ʀɑ̃ʒmɑ̃] nm **1.** [mise en ordre - d'une pièce] tidying (up) / *faire du rangement* to tidy up **2.** [d'objets, de vêtements] putting away **3.** [meuble] storage unit ; [cagibi] storage room ; [espace] storage space.

ranger¹ [ʀɑ̃dʒœʀ] nm MIL ranger. ❖ **rangers** nmpl combat boots.

ranger² [17] [ʀɑ̃ʒe] vt **1.** [mettre en ordre - pièce] to tidy (up) **2.** [mettre à sa place - vêtement, objets] to put away *(sép)* ; [- document] to file away *(sép)* / *j'ai rangé la voiture au garage* I've put the car in the garage **3.** [classer] to sort (out) / *ranger des dossiers par année* to file documents according to year ; *fig* ▸ **ranger qqn parmi** to rank sb amongst. ❖ **se ranger** ◈ vp *(emploi passif)* : *où se rangent les serviettes ?* where do the towels go?, where are the towels kept? ◈ vpi **1.** [s'écarter - piéton] to stand aside ; [- véhicule] to pull over **2.** [se mettre en rang - élèves, coureurs] to line up / *rangez-vous deux par deux* get into rows of two, line up in twos **3.** [se placer] ▸ **se ranger du côté de qqn** to side with sb **4.** [s'assagir] to settle down. ❖ **se ranger à** vp + prép [adhérer à] ▸ **se ranger à l'avis / au choix de qqn** to go along with sb's opinion / decision.

ranimer [3] [ʀanime] vt **1.** [feu] to rekindle, to relight **2.** [conversation] to bring back to life ; [haine, passion] to rekindle, to revive ; [douleur] to bring back / *ranimer le moral des troupes* to restore the morale of the troops **3.** [malade] to revive, to bring round *(sép)* ; *fig* [passé] to bring back.

rap [ʀap] nm MUS rap.

rapace [ʀapas] nm ORNITH bird of prey.

rapatrié, e [ʀapatʀije] nm, f repatriate ▸ **les rapatriés d'Algérie** French settlers in Algeria who were repatriated as a result of Algerian independence in 1962.

rapatriement [ʀapatʀimɑ̃] nm repatriation ▸ **rapatriement sanitaire** repatriation on medical grounds.

rapatrier [10] [ʀapatʀije] vt [personnes, capitaux] to repatriate ; [objets] to send ou to bring home / *se faire rapatrier* to be sent back to one's home country.

râpe [ʀap] nf **1.** [de cuisine] grater ▶ **râpe à fromage / muscade** cheese / nutmeg grater **2.** [en outillage] rasp ou rough file.

râpé, e [ʀape] adj **1.** [carotte, fromage, etc.] grated **2.** [vêtement] worn out, threadbare **3.** *fam* EXPR‹ *c'est râpé !* that's the end of that! ❖ **râpé** nm [fromage] grated cheese.

râper [3] [ʀape] vt **1.** [carotte, fromage, etc.] to grate **2.** *fig* : *un vin qui râpe la gorge* a rough wine.

rapetisser [3] [ʀaptise] vi to get smaller.

raphia [ʀafja] nm TEXT raffia, raphia.

rapide [ʀapid] ❖ adj **1.** [véhicule, sportif] fast ; [cheval] fast ; [courant] fast flowing ▶ **rapide comme l'éclair** quick as lightning **2.** [esprit, intelligence, travail] quick ; [progrès, réaction] rapid / *c'est l'homme des décisions rapides* he's good at reaching quick decisions / *une réponse rapide* a quick ou speedy reply **3.** [rythme] quick, fast / *marcher d'un pas rapide* to walk at a brisk ou quick pace ▶ **battements de cœur rapides** MÉD rapid heartbeat **4.** [court, sommaire] quick / *le chemin le plus rapide* the shortest ou quickest way / *un examen rapide des dossiers* a quick ou cursory glance through the documents **5.** [hâtif - jugement, décision] hurried, hasty. ❖ nmf *fam* [personne qui comprend vite] : *c'est un rapide* he's really quick on the uptake / *ce n'est pas un rapide* he's a bit slow on the uptake. ❖ nm **1.** [cours d'eau] rapid **2.** [train] express (train), fast train.

rapidement [ʀapidmɑ̃] adv [vite] quickly, rapidly.

rapidité [ʀapidite] nf **1.** [vitesse - d'une course, d'une attaque] speed ; [- d'une réponse] quickness ▶ **avec rapidité** quickly, speedily, rapidly ▶ **avec la rapidité de l'éclair** in a flash, with lightning speed **2.** [du pouls] rapidity.

rapiécer [20] [ʀapjese] vt to patch up *(sép)*.

✍ In reformed spelling (see p. 16-18), this verb is conjugated like *semer : il rapiècera, elle rapiècerait.*

rappel [ʀapɛl] nm **1.** [remise en mémoire] reminder / *rappel des titres de l'actualité* a summary of today's news ▶ **rappel à l'ordre a)** [gén] call to order **b)** POL ≃ naming 🇬🇧 **2.** [d'un ambassadeur] recalling ; [de produits défectueux] recalling **3.** THÉÂTRE curtain call **4.** MÉD booster / *ne pas oublier le rappel l'an prochain* don't forget to renew the vaccination next year **5.** [arriéré] ▶ **rappel de salaire** back pay **6.** [en alpinisme] abseiling 🇬🇧, rapelling 🇺🇸 ▶ **descendre en rappel** to rope ou to abseil 🇬🇧 down.

rappeler [24] [ʀaple] vt **1.** [remettre en mémoire] ▶ **rappeler qqch à qqn** to remind sb of sthg ▶ **rappelez-moi votre nom** what was your name again, please? ▶ **il faut rappeler que…** it should be borne in mind ou remembered that… / *ça me rappelle quelque chose* that rings a bell / **'numéro à rappeler dans toute correspondance'** 'please quote this number in all correspondence' **2.** [faire revenir] to recall, to call back *(sép)* / *rappelez donc votre chien !* call your dog off! ▶ **rappeler un ambassadeur** to recall an ambassador / *rappeler des réservistes* MIL to recall reservists / *l'acteur a été rappelé plusieurs fois* the actor has had several curtain calls / *la mort de sa mère l'a rappelé à Aix* the death of his mother took him back to Aix **3.** [au téléphone] to call back *(sép)*, to ring 🇬🇧 ou to phone back *(sép)* **4.** [faire écho à] : *son collier de turquoise rappelle la couleur de ses yeux* her turquoise necklace echoes the colour of her eyes **5.** EXPR‹ **rappeler qqn à la vie** to bring sb back to life ▶ **rappeler qqn à l'ordre** to call sb to order. ❖ **se rappeler** vpt [se souvenir de] to remember / *elle se rappelle avoir reçu une lettre* she remembers receiving a letter.

 to remember ou **to remind ?**

To remember s'emploie lorsqu'on se rappelle quelque chose :
I've just remembered where I put them. *Je viens de me rappeler où je les ai mis.*

To remind est employé pour rappeler quelque chose à quelqu'un :
Remind him of the time of the meeting. *Rappelez-lui l'heure de la réunion.*

rappeur, euse [ʀapœʀ, øz] nm, f rapper.

rappliquer [3] [ʀaplike] vi *tfam* to show ou to turn up (again).

rapport [ʀapɔʀ] nm **1.** [compte rendu - gén] report ; MIL briefing ▶ **rapport de police** police report **2.** [profit] profit ▶ **d'un bon rapport** profitable / *cette terre est d'un bon rapport* this land gives a good yield **3.** [ratio] ratio ▶ **rapport qualité-prix a)** [gén] value for money **b)** COMM quality-price ratio / *c'est d'un bon rapport qualité-prix* it's good value for money **4.** [relation] connection, link ▶ **n'avoir aucun rapport avec qqch** to have no connection with ou to bear no relation to sthg / *son dernier album n'a aucun rapport avec les précédents* her latest record is nothing like her earlier ones / *c'est sans rapport avec le sujet* that's beside the point, that's irrelevant / *je ne vois pas le rapport* I don't see the connection / *mais ça n'a aucun rapport !* but that's got nothing to do with it! ▶ **rapport de forces** : *le rapport de forces entre les deux pays* the balance of power between the two countries. ❖ **rapports** nmpl [relations] relationship, relations ▶ **cesser tous rapports avec qqn** to break off all relations with sb / *nous n'avons plus de rapports avec cette société* we no longer deal with that company ▶ **entretenir de bons rapports avec qqn** to be on good terms with sb ▶ **rapports sexuels** (sexual) intercourse ▶ **avoir des rapports (avec qqn)** to have sex (with sb). ❖ **en rapport avec** loc prép **1.** [qui correspond à] in keeping with **2.** [en relation avec] ▶ **mettre qqn en rapport avec** to put sb in touch with sb ▶ **se mettre en rapport avec qqn** to get in touch ou contact with sb ▶ **être en rapport avec qqn** to be in touch with sb. ❖ **par rapport à** loc prép **1.** [en ce qui concerne] regarding **2.** [comparativement à] compared with, in comparison to / *on constate un retrait du yen par rapport aux autres devises* the yen has dropped sharply against other currencies. ❖ **sous tous (les) rapports** loc adv in every respect / **'jeune homme bien sous tous rapports'** 'respectable young man'.

rapporter [3] [ʀapɔʀte] ❖ vt **1.** [apporter avec soi] to bring / *as-tu rapporté le journal ?* did you get ou buy the paper? / *le chien rapporte la balle* the dog brings back the ball ; [apporter de nouveau ou en plus] : *rapporte-nous un peu plus de vin* bring us a little more wine ; CHASSE to retrieve **2.** [rendre] to take back *(sép)*, to return / *quelqu'un a rapporté le sac que tu avais oublié* somebody has brought ou returned the bag you left behind **3.** [ajouter] to add ; COUT to sew on *(sép)* **4.** [produire] to produce, to yield / *le compte d'épargne vous rapporte 3,5 %* the savings account has a yield of 3.5% ou carries 3.5% interest / *sa boutique lui rapporte beaucoup d'argent* her shop brings in a lot of money **5.** [répéter - propos] to tell, to say **6.** [faire le compte rendu de] to report (on) / *rapporter les décisions d'une commission* POL to report on the decisions of a committee **7.** ▶ **rapporter qqch à** [rattacher à] to relate sthg to / *elle rapporte tout à elle* she always brings everything back to herself. ❖ vi **1.** [être rentable] to yield a profit ▶ **ça rapporte** *fam* it pays **2.** CHASSE to retrieve

3. *fam* [enfant] to tell tales, to sneak. ❖ **se rapporter à** vp + prép **1.** [avoir un lien avec] to refer ou to relate to **2.** *sout* ▶ **s'en rapporter à** [s'en remettre à] to rely on.

rapporteur, euse [ʀapɔʀtœʀ, øz] ◆ nm, f telltale, sneak UK, tattletale US. ◆ nm, f ADMIN & POL [porte-parole] rapporteur, reporter ▶ **rapporteur de la commission** *committee member who acts as spokesman.* ❖ **rapporteur** nm GÉOM protractor.

rapproché, e [ʀapʀɔʃe] adj **1.** [proche] close **2.** [répété - incidents, crises, grossesses] frequent.

rapprochement [ʀapʀɔʃmã] nm **1.** [réconciliation - entre groupes, personnes] rapprochement, reconciliation **2.** [comparaison] link, connection / *tu n'avais pas fait le rapprochement ?* hadn't you made the connection? / *le rapprochement de ces deux textes établit le plagiat* comparing the two texts provides proof of plagiarism **3.** [convergence] coming together / *on assiste à un rapprochement des thèses des deux parties* the arguments of the two parties are coming closer together.

rapprocher [3] [ʀapʀɔʃe] vt **1.** [approcher] to bring closer ou nearer **2.** [faire paraître proche] to bring closer **3.** ▶ **rapprocher qqn** [de sa destination] to take ou to bring sb closer **4.** [affectivement] to bring (closer) together / *ça m'a rapproché de mon père* it's brought me closer to my father, it's brought my father and me closer together **5.** [comparer] to compare. ❖ **se rapprocher** vpi [venir près] to come close ou closer / *la date du mariage / le vacarme des moteurs se rapproche* the wedding day / the roar of the engines is getting closer / *rapprochez-vous de l'estrade* move closer to the stage. ❖ **se rapprocher de** vp + prép **1.** [se réconcilier avec] : *j'ai essayé sans succès de me rapprocher d'elle avant sa mort* I tried in vain to get closer to her before she died **2.** [être comparable à] to be similar to.

rapt [ʀapt] nm [kidnapping] abduction, kidnapping.

raquette [ʀaket] nf **1.** TENNIS racket ; [au ping-pong] bat **2.** [pour la neige] snowshoe.

rare [ʀaʀ] adj **1.** [difficile à trouver] rare, uncommon / *ce qui est rare est cher* anything that is in short supply is expensive / *plantes / timbres rares* rare plants / stamps ▶ **être d'une beauté rare** to be uncommonly beautiful **2.** [peu fréquent] rare / *tes visites sont trop rares* you don't visit us nearly often enough / *ça n'a rien de rare* there's nothing unusual about that / *il n'est pas rare de le voir ici* it's not uncommon ou unusual to see him here / *tu te fais rare ces derniers temps* fam you've become quite a stranger lately, where have you been hiding lately? **3.** [peu nombreux] few / *les rares électeurs qui ont voté pour lui* the few who voted for him / *à de rares exceptions près* with only ou apart from a few exceptions / *elle est une des rares personnes que je connaisse à aimer le jazz* she's one of the very few people I know who enjoys jazz / *les visiteurs se font rares* there are fewer and fewer visitors ; [peu abondant] scarce **4.** PHYS [raréfié] rare.

raréfaction [ʀaʀefaksjɔ̃] nf **1.** PHYS [de l'air] rarefaction **2.** [des denrées, de l'argent] increasing scarcity.

raréfier [9] [ʀaʀefje] ❖ **se raréfier** vpi **1.** PHYS [air] to rarefy, to rarify **2.** [argent, denrées] to become scarce ; [visites] to become less frequent.

rarement [ʀaʀmã] adv rarely, seldom / *elle téléphone rarement, pour ne pas dire jamais* she seldom, if ever, calls / *cela arrive plus rarement* it happens less often.

rareté [ʀaʀte] nf **1.** [d'un fait, d'un phénomène] rarity ; [d'une denrée] scarcity **2.** [objet - rare] rarity, rare object ; [- bizarre] curio.

rarissime [ʀaʀisim] adj extremely rare, most unusual.

ras, e [ʀa, ʀaz] adj **1.** [cheveux] close-cropped, very short ; [barbe] very short **2.** [végétation] short ; [pelouse] closely-mown **3.** TEXT short-piled **4.** EXPR **en rase campagne** in the open countryside. ❖ **ras** adv **1.** [très court] short / *avoir les ongles coupés ras* to keep one's nails cut short / *une haie taillée ras* a closely-clipped hedge **2.** EXPR **en avoir ras le bol** fam ou **ras le cul** vulg **de qqch** to be fed up to the (back) teeth with sthg, to have had it up to here with sthg ▶ **ras le bol !** fam enough is enough! ❖ **à ras** loc adv ▶ **coupé à ras** cut short. ❖ **à ras bord(s)** loc adv to the brim ou top. ❖ **à ras de** loc prép level with. ❖ **au ras de** loc prép : *au ras de l'eau* just above water level, level with the water / *le débat était au ras des pâquerettes* fam the discussion isn't exactly highbrow.

RAS abr de rien à signaler.

rasage [ʀazaʒ] nm [de la barbe] shaving.

rasant, e [ʀazɑ̃, ɑ̃t] adj **1.** [bas] : *un soleil rasant* a low sun **2.** fam [assommant] boring / *il est vraiment rasant !* he's so boring!, he's such a bore!

ras(-)du(-)cou [ʀadyku] ◆ adj inv round neck (modif) ▶ **un pull ras-du-cou** a round neck sweater. ◆ nm inv round neck sweater.

rase-mottes (pl rase-mottes), **rase-motte**[*] [ʀazmɔt] nm AÉRON hedgehopping ▶ **voler en** ou **faire du rase-mottes** to hedgehop.

raser [3] [ʀaze] vt **1.** [cheveux, poils] to shave off (sép) ; [crâne] to shave ▶ **raser qqn** to give sb a shave, to shave sb ▶ **mal rasé** ill-shaven ▶ **être rasé de près** to be close-shaven **2.** [détruire] to raze **3.** [frôler] : *l'hirondelle rase le sol* the swallow is skimming the ground / *la balle lui rasa l'épaule* the bullet grazed his shoulder ▶ **raser les murs** to hug the walls **4.** fam [lasser] to bore. ❖ **se raser** ◆ vp (emploi réfléchi) to shave / *se raser les jambes* to shave one's legs / *se raser la barbe* to shave off one's beard. ◆ vpi fam [s'ennuyer] to get bored. ❖ **à raser** loc adj shaving (modif) ▶ **mousse à raser** shaving foam.

raseur, euse [ʀazœʀ, øz] nm, f fam : *c'est un raseur* he's a real drag ou pain.

ras-le-bol [ʀalbɔl] nm inv fam : *il y a un ras-le-bol général dans la population* people in general are sick and tired of ou fed up with the way things are going.

rasoir [ʀazwaʀ] ◆ nm razor ▶ **rasoir électrique** (electric) shaver ▶ **rasoir mécanique** ou **de sûreté** safety razor. ◆ adj fam boring.

rassasier [9] [ʀasazje] vt **1.** [faim] to satisfy ▶ **je suis rassasié** I'm full **2.** fig : *alors, vous êtes rassasiés de plein air ?* so, have you had your fill of fresh air? ❖ **se rassasier** vpi **1.** [apaiser sa faim] to eat one's fill **2.** [assouvir son désir] ▶ **se rassasier de qqch** to get one's fill of sthg.

rassemblement [ʀasɑ̃bləmɑ̃] nm **1.** [réunion sur la voie publique] gathering, group ; [en politique] rally / *rassemblement pour la paix* peace rally **2.** [fait de se rassembler] gathering / *tous les rassemblements sont strictement interdits* all rallies ou gatherings are strictly forbidden.

rassembler [3] [ʀasɑ̃ble] vt **1.** [objets, idées, preuves] to collect, to gather ; [documents] to collect, to assemble / *j'eus à peine le temps de rassembler quelques affaires* I hardly had enough time to gather ou to put a few things together / *rassembler ses forces* to gather ou to muster one's strength / *rassembler ses esprits* to gather ou to collect one's wits ▶ **rassembler son courage** to summon up one's courage **2.** [personnes] to gather together (sép) ; [animaux] to round up (sép) / *leur manifestation a rassemblé des milliers de personnes* their demonstration drew ou attracted thousands of people. ❖ **se rassembler** vpi to gather together, to assemble / *ils se sont rassemblés devant chez moi* they gathered together ou assembled outside my home.

* In reformed spelling (see p. 16-18).

rasseoir, rassoir* [65] [ʀaswaʀ] vt [asseoir de nouveau] ▸ **rasseoir qqn** to sit sb down (again). ❖ **se rasseoir, se rassoir*** vpi to sit down again / *allez vous rasseoir* go back to your seat, go and sit down again.

rasséréner [18] [ʀaseʀene] vt *litt* to make calm / *ses déclarations m'ont complètement rasséréné* what he said put my mind completely at rest.

In reformed spelling (see p. 16-18), this verb is conjugated like semer : *il rassérèna, elle rassérènerait.*

rassir [32] [ʀasiʀ] ❖ **se rassir** vpi to go stale.

rassis, e [ʀasi, iz] adj [gâteau, pain] stale ; [viande] properly hung.

rassurant, e [ʀasyʀɑ̃, ɑ̃t] adj **1.** [personne] reassuring / *le président n'a pas été très rassurant dans ses dernières déclarations* the president's most recent statements were not very reassuring **2.** [nouvelle, déclaration, ton, voix] reassuring, comforting.

rassuré, e [ʀasyʀe] adj confident, at ease.

rassurer [3] [ʀasyʀe] vt to reassure / *va vite rassurer ta mère* go and tell your mother she has nothing to worry about, go and set your mother's mind at ease / *je n'étais pas très rassuré* I felt rather worried. ❖ **se rassurer** ◆ vp *(emploi réfléchi)* to reassure o.s. / *j'essaie de me rassurer en me disant que tout n'est pas fini* I try to reassure myself by saying it's not all over. ◆ vpi : *elle a mis longtemps à se rassurer* it took her a while to calm down ▸ **rassure-toi** don't worry.

rat [ʀa] nm **1.** ZOOL rat **2.** *fig* ▸ **rat de bibliothèque** bookworm **3.** DANSE ▸ **petit rat de l'Opéra** ballet student *(at the Opéra de Paris)* **4.** *fam & péj* [avare] miser, skinflint.

ratage [ʀata3] nm failure.

ratatiné, e [ʀatatine] adj **1.** [fruit] shrivelled 🇬🇧 ou shriveled 🇺🇸 (up) **2.** [visage] wrinkled, wizened **3.** *fam* [voiture, vélo] smashed up ; [soufflé] flat.

ratatiner [3] [ʀatatine] vt **1.** *fam* [démolir] : *le bâtiment a été ratatiné en quelques secondes* the building was reduced to a pile of rubble within seconds / *la voiture a été complètement ratatinée* the car was completely smashed up **2.** *fam* [battre] : *je me suis fait ratatiner au tennis / aux échecs* I got thrashed at tennis / chess ; [assassiner] : *il s'est fait ratatiner* he got done in. ❖ **se ratatiner** vpi **1.** [se dessécher] to shrivel **2.** *fam* [personne - rapetisser] to shrink / *elle se ratatine en vieillissant* she's shrinking with age ; [flétrir] to become wizened.

ratatouille [ʀatatuj] nf CULIN ▸ **ratatouille (niçoise)** ratatouille.

rate [ʀat] nf ANAT spleen.

raté, e [ʀate] ◆ adj **1.** [photo, sauce] spoilt ; [coupe de cheveux] disastrous / *il est complètement raté, ce gâteau* this cake is a complete disaster **2.** [attentat] failed ; [vie] wasted ; [occasion] missed ; [tentative] failed, abortive, unsuccessful / *un musicien raté* a failed musician. ◆ nm, f failure, loser. ❖ **raté** nm [bruit] misfiring *(U)* / *le moteur a des ratés* the engine is misfiring.

râteau, x [ʀato] nm rake.

râtelier [ʀatəlje] nm **1.** [support] rack **2.** *fam* [dentier] dentures, (set of) false teeth.

rater [3] [ʀate] ◆ vi *fam* [échouer] to fail / *je t'avais dit qu'elle serait en retard, et ça n'a pas raté !* I told you she'd be late, and sure enough she was! / *ça ne rate jamais* it never fails / *tais-toi, tu vas tout faire rater !* shut up or you'll ruin everything! ◆ vt **1.** [but] to miss / *elle a raté la marche* she missed the step ▸ **rater son coup** *fam*: *j'ai raté mon coup* I made a mess of it ▸ **ne pas rater qqn** *fam*: *s'il recommence, je te jure que je ne le raterai pas !* if he does it again, I swear I'll get him! **2.** [avion, rendez-vous, visiteur, occasion] to miss / *c'est une émission à ne pas rater* this programme is a must ▸ **ne pas en rater une** *fam*:

tu n'en rates pas une ! you're always putting your foot in it! **3.** [ne pas réussir] : *il a raté son effet* he didn't achieve the desired effect / *il rate toujours les mayonnaises* his mayonnaise always goes wrong / *rater sa vie* to make a mess of one's life. ❖ **se rater** vp *(emploi réfléchi) fam* : *elle s'est ratée pour la troisième fois* that's her third (unsuccessful) suicide attempt.

ratification [ʀatifikasjɔ̃] nf ratification.

ratifier [9] [ʀatifje] vt DR to ratify.

ration [ʀasjɔ̃] nf **1.** [portion] ration / *sa ration de problèmes* *fig* his share of problems **2.** [quantité nécessaire] daily intake ▸ **ration alimentaire** food (intake) **3.** MIL rations.

rationalisation [ʀasjɔnalizasjɔ̃] nf rationalization.

rationaliser [3] [ʀasjɔnalize] vt to rationalize.

rationnel, elle [ʀasjɔnɛl] adj **1.** MATH & PHILOS rational **2.** [sensé] rational.

rationnellement [ʀasjɔnɛlmɑ̃] adv **1.** MATH & PHILOS rationally **2.** [avec bon sens] rationally, sensibly, logically.

rationnement [ʀasjɔnmɑ̃] nm rationing.

rationner [3] [ʀasjɔne] vt [quelque chose] to ration. ❖ **se rationner** vp *(emploi réfléchi)* to ration o.s.

ratisser [3] [ʀatise] ◆ vt **1.** [gravier, allée] to rake ; [feuilles, herbe coupée] to rake up *(sép)* **2.** *fam* [voler] to pinch, to nick 🇬🇧 ; [ruiner] to clean out *(sép)* / *il s'est fait ratisser au poker* he got cleaned out playing poker **3.** [fouiller] to comb **4.** SPORT to heel. ◆ vi ▸ **ratisser large** *fam* to cast one's net wide *fig*.

raton [ʀatɔ̃] nm ZOOL young rat ▸ **raton laveur** raccoon.

RATP (abr de **Régie autonome des transports parisiens**) npr f *Paris transport authority.*

rattachement [ʀataʃmɑ̃] nm : *demander son rattachement à un service* to ask to be attached to a department.

rattacher [3] [ʀataʃe] vt **1.** [paquet] to tie up *(sép)* again, to do up *(sép)* again ; [ceinture, lacet] to do up *(sép)* again ; [chien] to tie up *(sép)* again ; [plante grimpante] to tie back *(sép)* **2.** ADMIN & POL : *rattacher plusieurs services à une même direction* to bring several departments under the same management / *rattacher un territoire à un pays* to bring a territory under the jurisdiction of a country **3.** [lier - idée, fait] ▸ **rattacher qqch à** to connect ou to link sthg with, to relate sthg to **4.** [relier - personne] : *c'était la seule chose qui nous rattachait l'un à l'autre* it was the only thing that bound us together.

rattrapage [ʀatʀapa3] nm **1.** [d'un étudiant] passing, letting through ; [remise à niveau] ▸ **rattrapage scolaire** ≃ remedial teaching ▸ **cours de rattrapage** extra class for pupils who need to catch up ▸ **session de rattrapage** resit **2.** ÉCON ▸ **rattrapage des salaires** wage adjustment.

rattraper [3] [ʀatʀape] vt **1.** [animal, prisonnier] to recapture, to catch again **2.** [objet qui tombe] to catch (hold of) / *rattraper la balle au vol* / *bond* to catch the ball in the air / on the bounce **3.** [quelqu'un parti plus tôt] to catch up with **4.** [compenser] ▸ **rattraper le temps perdu** to make up for lost time / *rattraper du sommeil* to catch up on one's sleep **5.** [erreur, maladresse] to put right **6.** [étudiant] to let through **7.** [maille] to pick up *(sép)*. ❖ **se rattraper** vpi **1.** [éviter la chute] to catch o.s. (in time) ▸ **se rattraper à qqn / qqch** to grab ou to catch hold of sb / sthg to stop o.s. falling **2.** [compenser] : *la limonade est en promotion, mais ils se rattrapent sur le café* lemonade is on special offer, but they've put up the price of coffee to make up for it.

rature [ʀatyʀ] nf crossing out, deletion / *tu as fait trop de ratures* you've crossed too many things out.

raturer [3] [ʀatyʀe] vt to cross out *(sép)*, to delete.

rauque [ʁok] adj **1.** [voix] husky **2.** [cri] raucous.

ravage [ʁavaʒ] nm **1.** [destruction] devastation ▸ **faire des ravages** pr to wreak havoc / *l'alcoolisme faisait des ravages* fig alcoholism was rife / *notre cousin fait des ravages (dans les cœurs) !* our cousin is a heartbreaker! **2.** ᵠᵘᵉᵇᵉᶜ deeryard.

ravagé, e [ʁavaʒe] adj **1.** [par la fatigue, le désespoir] haggard ; [par la maladie, la douleur] ravaged **2.** fam [fou] loopy, barmy ᵁᴷ, nuts / *c'est un mec complètement ravagé !* he's completely loopy!

ravager [17] [ʁavaʒe] vt [région, ville] to ravage, to lay waste (insép), to devastate / *la guerre a ravagé leur vie* the war wreaked havoc upon their lives.

ravalement [ʁavalmã] nm [d'une façade] cleaning.

ravaler [3] [ʁavale] vt **1.** CONSTR to clean ▸ **se faire ravaler la façade** tfam ou **le portrait** tfam to have a facelift **2.** [salive] to swallow ; [larmes] to hold ou to choke back ; [colère] to stifle, to choke back ; [fierté] to swallow ▸ **faire ravaler ses paroles à qqn** fam to make sb eat his words **3.** [abaisser] to lower. **❖ se ravaler ◆** vp (emploi réfléchi) [s'abaisser] to debase ou to lower o.s. ◆ vpt tfam ▸ **se ravaler la façade** [se maquiller] to slap some make-up on, to put on one's warpaint.

ravi, e [ʁavi] adj delighted ▸ **être ravi de qqch** to be delighted with sthg / *ravi (de faire votre connaissance)* (I'm) delighted ou very pleased to meet you.

ravigoter [3] [ʁavigɔte] vt fam to buck up (sép).

ravin [ʁavɛ̃] nm gully, ravine.

raviner [3] [ʁavine] vt **1.** GÉOGR to gully **2.** fig & sout to furrow / *un visage raviné* a deeply lined face.

ravir [82] [ʁaviʁ] vt **1.** [enchanter] to delight **2.** litt [enlever] ▸ **ravir qqch à qqn** to rob sb of sthg / *il s'est fait ravir la première place par un jeune inconnu* he was beaten to first place by a youngster nobody had heard of. **❖ à ravir** loc adv [merveilleusement] : *la robe lui va à ravir* the dress looks lovely on her.

raviser [3] [ʁavize] **❖ se raviser** vpi to change one's mind / *il s'est ravisé* he changed his mind, he thought better of it, he had second thoughts.

ravissant, e [ʁavisã, ãt] adj [vêtement] gorgeous, beautiful ; [endroit, maison] delightful, beautiful ; [femme] strikingly ou ravishingly beautiful.

ravissement [ʁavismã] nm [enchantement] ▸ **mettre** ou **plonger qqn dans le ravissement** to send sb into raptures.

ravisseur, euse [ʁavisœʁ, øz] nm, f abductor sout, kidnapper.

ravitaillement [ʁavitajmã] nm **1.** MIL & NAUT supplying ▸ **assurer le ravitaillement de qqn en munitions / carburant / vivres** to supply sb with ammunition / fuel / food **2.** AÉRON refuelling ᵁᴷ, refueling ᵁˢ ▸ **ravitaillement en vol** in-flight ou mid-air refuelling **3.** [denrées] food supplies / *je vais au ravitaillement* fam I'm off to buy some food, I'm going for fresh supplies.

ravitailler [3] [ʁavitaje] vt **1.** MIL to supply / *ravitailler un régiment en vivres* to supply a regiment with food, to supply food to a regiment **2.** AÉRON to refuel. **❖ se ravitailler** vp (emploi réfléchi) **1.** [en nourriture] to get (fresh) supplies **2.** [en carburant] to refuel.

raviver [3] [ʁavive] vt **1.** [feu] to rekindle, to revive ; [couleur] to brighten up (sép) **2.** [sensation, sentiment] to rekindle, to revive.

ravoir [ʁavwaʁ] vt (à l'infinitif seulement) **1.** [récupérer] to get back **2.** fam [vêtement] : *ravoir une chemise* to get a shirt clean.

rayé, e [ʁeje] adj **1.** [à raies - papier] lined, ruled ; [- vêtement] striped **2.** [éraflé - verre, disque] scratched.

rayer [11] [ʁeje] vt **1.** [abîmer] to scratch **2.** [éliminer - faute, coquille] to cross ou to score out (sép) ; [- clause, codicille] to cancel / *'rayer la mention inutile'* 'delete where inapplicable' / *j'ai rayé son souvenir de ma mémoire* I've erased his memory from my mind ▸ **rayé de la carte** wiped off the face of the earth.

rayon [ʁejɔ̃]
nm

🅰 **TRAIT, AMPLITUDE 1.** OPT & PHYS ray ▸ **rayon laser** laser beam **2.** [de lumière] beam, shaft ; [du soleil] ray ▸ **un rayon de soleil a)** a ray of sunshine, a sunbeam **b)** MÉTÉOR a brief sunny spell **c)** fig a ray of sunshine **3.** MATH [d'un cercle] radius **4.** [de roue] spoke **5.** [distance] radius / *dans un rayon de vingt kilomètres* within (a radius of) twenty kilometres **6.** MIL ▸ **rayon d'action** range.

🅱 **SUPERPOSITION 1.** [étagère - gén] shelf ; [- à livres] shelf, bookshelf **2.** COMM department / *nous n'en avons plus en rayon* we're out of stock **3.** fam [domaine] : *demande à ton père, c'est son rayon* ask your father, that's his department / *il en connaît un rayon en électricité* he really knows a thing or two about electricity **4.** ZOOL comb ; [d'abeilles] honeycomb. **❖ rayons** nmpl **1.** MÉD X-ray treatment (U) (for cancer) **2.** PHYS ▸ **rayons X** X-rays.

rayonnage [ʁejɔnaʒ] nm [étagères] shelving (U), shelves.

rayonnant, e [ʁejɔnã, ãt] adj [radieux] radiant / *rayonnant de joie* radiant with joy / *rayonnant de santé* glowing ou blooming with health.

rayonnement [ʁejɔnmã] nm **1.** [influence] influence **2.** litt [éclat] radiance **3.** [lumière - d'une étoile, du feu] radiance **4.** SCI radiation ▸ **chauffage par rayonnement** radiant heating.

rayonner [3] [ʁejɔne] vi **1.** [personne, physionomie] to be radiant / *rayonner de joie* to be radiant with joy **2.** [circuler - influence] to spread ; [- touriste] to tour around ; [- chaleur] to radiate / *nos cars rayonnent dans toute la région* our coaches cover every corner of the region **3.** OPT & PHYS to radiate.

rayure [ʁejyʁ] nf **1.** [ligne] line, stripe ; [du pelage] stripe / *papier à rayures* lined ou ruled paper / *tissu à rayures* striped fabric / *une chemise à rayures bleues* a blue-striped shirt **2.** [éraflure] score, scratch.

raz(-)de(-)marée [ʁadmaʁe] nm inv **1.** GÉOGR tidal wave, tsunami spéc **2.** fig tidal wave ▸ **raz-de-marée électoral** landslide victory.

razzia [ʁazja] nf **1.** MIL foray, raid **2.** fam & fig raid ▸ **faire une razzia sur qqch** to raid sthg.

RdC abr écrite de rez-de-chaussée.

rdv SMS abr écrite de rendez-vous.

ré [ʁe] nm inv D ; [chanté] re, ray. **Voir aussi fa.**

réabonner [3] [ʁeabɔne] vt ▸ **réabonner qqn à une revue** to renew sb's subscription to a magazine. **❖ se réabonner** vp (emploi réfléchi) [à un cinéma, théâtre, etc.] to renew one's season ticket ; [à une revue] to renew one's subscription.

réac [ʁeak] adj & nmf fam & péj reactionary.

réaccoutumer [3] [ʁeakutyme] vt sout to reaccustom. **❖ se réaccoutumer à** vp + prép to reaccustom o.s. to, to become reaccustomed to.

réacheminer [3] [ʁeaʃmine] vt to forward.

réacteur [ʁeaktœʁ] nm **1.** AÉRON jet (engine) **2.** CHIM, NUCL & PHYS reactor ▸ **réacteur nucléaire** nuclear reactor.

réaction [ʁeaksjɔ̃] nf **1.** [réponse] reaction, response / *la nouvelle l'a laissée sans réaction* she showed no reaction to the news **2.** [riposte] reaction ▸ **en réaction contre**

as a reaction against **3.** AÉRON, ASTRONAUT, CHIM & PHYS reaction ▶ **réaction en chaîne a)** *pr* chain reaction **b)** *fig* chain reaction, domino effect.

réactionnaire [ʀeaksjɔnɛʀ] adj & nmf reactionary.

réactiver [3] [ʀeaktive] vt [feu] to rekindle ; [circulation sanguine] to restore ; [système] to reactivate ; [négociations] to revive.

réactualiser [3] [ʀeaktɥalize] vt **1.** [moderniser -diction-naire] to update, to bring up to date **2.** INFORM to refresh.

réadaptation [ʀeadaptasjɔ̃] nf [rééducation] reeducation.

réadapter [3] [ʀeadapte] ❖ **se réadapter** vpi [han-dicapé, exilé] to readjust ▶ **se réadapter à qqch** to readjust to sthg.

réaffirmer [3] [ʀeafiʀme] vt to reaffirm, to reassert.

réagir [32] [ʀeaʒiʀ] vi **1.** [répondre] to react / *il a bien / mal réagi à son départ* he reacted well / badly to her leav-ing ▶ **il faut absolument réagir** we really have to do some-thing / *au moins ça l'a fait réagir* at least it got a reaction from him / her **2.** MÉD to respond.

réajustement [ʀeaʒystəmɑ̃] = rajustement.

réajuster [ʀeaʒyste] = rajuster.

réalisable [ʀealizabl] adj [projet] feasible, workable ; [rêve] attainable.

réalisateur, trice [ʀealizatœʀ,tʀis] nm, f CINÉ direc-tor, film-maker ; RADIO & TV producer.

réalisation [ʀealizasjɔ̃] nf **1.** [d'un projet] carrying out, execution ; [d'un rêve] fulfilment ; [d'un exploit] achievement **2.** [chose réalisée] achievement / *être en cours de réalisa-tion* to be under way **3.** CINÉ & TV [mise en scène] directing, filmmaking ; [film] production, film 🇬🇧, movie 🇺🇸 / **'réali-sation (de) George Cukor'** 'directed by George Cukor' **4.** RADIO [émission] production ; [enregistrement] recording.

réaliser [3] [ʀealize] vt **1.** [rendre réel -projet] to carry out (*sép*) ; [-rêve] to fulfil, to realize ; [-espoir] to real-ize **2.** [accomplir -œuvre] to complete, to carry out (*sép*) ; [-exploit] to achieve, to perform **3.** COMM [vente] to make ; FIN [capital, valeurs] to realize ; [bénéfice] to make **4.** CINÉ, RADIO & TV to direct **5.** [comprendre] to realize ; (*en usage absolu*) : *je ne réalise pas encore* it hasn't sunk in yet. ❖ **se réaliser** vpi **1.** [s'accomplir -projet] to be carried out ; [-rêve, vœu] to come true, to be fulfilled ; [-prédiction] to come true **2.** [personne] to fulfil 🇬🇧 ou fulfill 🇺🇸 o.s.

⚠ Attention, **to realize** ne peut être employé systématiquement pour traduire réaliser. Voir article.

réalisme [ʀealism] nm [gén] realism.

réaliste [ʀealist] ◆ adj **1.** [gén] realistic **2.** ART & LITTÉR realist. ◆ nmf realist.

réalité [ʀealite] nf **1.** [existence] reality / *douter de la réalité d'un fait* to doubt the reality of a fact **2.** [univers réel] ▶ **la réalité** reality ▶ **quand la réalité dépasse la fic-tion** when fact is stranger than fiction ▶ **réalité augmentée** augmented reality ▶ **réalité virtuelle** virtual reality **3.** [fait] fact / *prendre conscience des réalités (de la vie)* to face facts. ❖ **en réalité** loc adv [en fait] in (actual) fact.

reality-show, reality show [ʀealitiʃo] (*pl* reality(-)shows) nm *talk show focussing on real-life drama.*

réaménagement [ʀeamenaʒmɑ̃] nm [modification -d'un bâtiment] refitting (*U*) ; [-d'un projet] reorganization, replanning (*U*) ▶ **réaménagement urbain** urban redevelop-ment.

réaménager [17] [ʀeamenaʒe] vt **1.** [espace, salle] to re-fit, to refurbish **2.** [horaire] to replan, to readjust ; [politique] to reshape.

réamorcer [16] [ʀeamɔʀse] vt **1.** [pompe] to prime again ▶ **réamorcer la pompe** *fig* to get things rolling again **2.** [discussion] to begin ou to start again, to reinitiate.

réanimation [ʀeanimasjɔ̃] nf [action] resuscitation ▶ **service de réanimation (intensive)** intensive care unit.

réanimer [3] [ʀeanime] vt [malade] to resuscitate, to re-vive.

réapparaître, réapparaitre* [91] [ʀeapaʀɛtʀ] vi (*aux être ou avoir*) to come back, to reappear, to appear again.

réapparition [ʀeapaʀisjɔ̃] nf **1.** [du soleil] reappear-ance **2.** [d'une vedette] comeback.

réapprendre [79] [ʀeapʀɑ̃dʀ] vt to learn again.

réapprovisionner [3] [ʀeapʀɔvizjɔne] vt COMM [magasin] to restock ; [commerçant] to resupply. ❖ **se réapprovisionner** vp to stock up again.

réarmement [ʀeaʀməmɑ̃] nm **1.** MIL rearmament, re-arming ; POL rearmament **2.** NAUT refitting **3.** ARM cocking.

réarmer [3] [ʀeaʀme] ◆ vt **1.** MIL & POL to rearm **2.** NAUT to refit **3.** ARM to cock. ◆ vi [pays] to rearm.

rébarbatif, ive [ʀebaʀbatif, iv] adj **1.** [personne] can-tankerous, surly **2.** [idée] off-putting 🇬🇧, daunting.

rebâtir [32] [ʀɔbɑtiʀ] vt to rebuild.

rebattre [83] [ʀɔbatʀ] vt 〈EXPR〉 **rebattre les oreilles à qqn de qqch** : *elle m'a rebattu les oreilles de son divorce* she went on and on ou she kept harping on about her di-vorce.

rebattu, e [ʀɔbaty] adj [éculé] hackneyed, worn out.

rebelle [ʀɔbɛl] ◆ adj **1.** POL rebel (*modif*) **2.** [indompt-able -cheval] rebellious ; [-cœur, esprit] rebellious, intrac-table ; [-enfant] rebellious, wilful ; [-mèche] unruly, wild **3.** ▶ **rebelle à** [réfractaire à] impervious to / *rebelle à tout conseil* unwilling to heed advice, impervious to advice **4.** [acné, fièvre] stubborn, refractory *spéc*. ◆ nmf rebel.

rebeller [4] [ʀɔbele] ❖ **se rebeller** vpi to rebel.

rébellion [ʀebeljɔ̃] nf [révolte] rebellion.

rebiffer [3] [ʀɔbife] ❖ **se rebiffer** vpi *fam* ▶ **se rebif-fer contre qqch** to kick out against sthg.

rebiquer [3] [ʀɔbike] vi *fam* to stick up.

reboiser [3] [ʀɔbwaze] vt to reafforest, to reforest.

rebond [ʀɔbɔ̃] nm bounce, rebound / *je l'ai attrapé au rebond* I caught it on the rebound.

rebondi, e [ʀɔbɔ̃di] adj [joue, face] chubby, plump ; [formes] well-rounded / *à la poitrine rebondie* buxom.

rebondir [32] [ʀɔbɔ̃diʀ] vi **1.** [balle, ballon] to bounce **2.** [conversation] to get going again ; [intérêt] to be revived ou renewed ; [procès, scandale] to get new impetus ▶ **faire rebondir qqch** to give sthg a fresh start ou a new lease of life **3.** [intrigue] to take off again **4.** [actions, marché, mon-naie] to recover, to pick up again.

rebondissement [ʀɔbɔ̃dismɑ̃] nm [d'une affaire] (new) development.

rebord [ʀɔbɔʀ] nm [d'un fossé, d'une étagère] edge ; [d'une assiette, d'un verre] rim ; [d'une cheminée] mantel-piece ; [d'une fenêtre] (window) ledge ou sill.

reboucher [3] [ʀɔbuʃe] vt **1.** [bouteille de vin] to recork ; [flacon, carafe] to restopper **2.** CONSTR [trou] to fill, to plug ; [fissure] to fill, to stop.

rebours [ʀɔbuʀ] ❖ **à rebours** loc adv [à l'envers -compter, lire] backwards ; [dans le mauvais sens] the wrong way.

rebouteur, euse [ʀəbutœʀ, øz], **reboute ux, euse** [ʀəbutø, øz] nm, f bonesetter.

reboutonner [3] [ʀəbutɔne] vt to button up *(sép)* again, to rebutton.

rebrousse-poil [ʀəbʀuspwal] ❖ **à rebrousse-poil** loc adv [maladroitement] the wrong way / *mieux vaut ne pas prendre le patron à rebrousse-poil* better not rub the boss up the wrong way.

rebrousser [3] [ʀəbʀuse] vt EXPR▷ **rebrousser chemin** to turn back, to retrace one's steps.

rébus [ʀebys] nm rebus.

rebut [ʀəby] nm [poubelle, casse] ▶ **mettre** ou **jeter au rebut** to throw away, to discard.

rebutant, e [ʀəbytɑ̃, ɑ̃t] adj **1.** [repoussant] repulsive **2.** [décourageant] off-putting UK, disheartening.

rebuter [3] [ʀəbyte] vt **1.** [décourager] to discourage, to put off *(sép)* **2.** [dégoûter] to put off *(sép)*.

recadrer [ʀəkadʀe] vt **1.** CINÉ & PHOT to crop **2.** *fig* [action, projet] to redefine ; [collaborateur] : *j'ai été obligé de le recadrer car il prenait des décisions intempestives* I had to bring him back into line because he kept making rush decisions.

récalcitrant, e [ʀekalsitʀɑ̃, ɑ̃t] adj [animal] stubborn ; [personne] recalcitrant, rebellious.

recalé, e [ʀəkale] fam ◆ adj : *recalée en juin, j'ai réussi en septembre* I failed in June but passed in September. ◆ nm, f failed candidate.

recaler [3] [ʀəkale] vt fam [candidat] to fail / *il s'est fait recaler à l'examen pour la deuxième fois* he failed the exam for the second time.

récapitulatif, ive [ʀekapitylatif, iv] adj [note] summarizing ; [tableau] summary *(modif)*. ❖ **récapitulatif** nm summary, recapitulation, résumé.

récapituler [3] [ʀekapityle] vt [résumer] to summarize, to recapitulate.

recaser [3] [ʀəkaze] vt fam [personne] to find a new job for. ❖ **se recaser** vp *(emploi réfléchi)* fam [retrouver un emploi] to get fixed up with a new job ; [se remarier] to get hitched again.

recel [ʀəsɛl] nm DR **1.** [d'objets] possession of stolen goods **2.** [de personnes] ▶ **recel de déserteur / malfaiteur** harbouring a deserter / a (known) criminal.

receler [25] [ʀəsəle], **recéler*** [18] [ʀəsele] vt **1.** [bijoux, trésor] to receive ; [personne] to harbour **2.** [mystère, ressources] to hold.

receleur, euse [ʀəsəlœʀ, øz], **recéleur*, euse** [ʀəselœʀ, øz] nm, f receiver (of stolen goods).

récemment [ʀesamɑ̃] adv **1.** [dernièrement] recently, not (very) long ago ▶ **l'as-tu rencontrée récemment ?** have you met her lately? **2.** [nouvellement] recently, newly / *membres récemment inscrits* newly registered members.

recensement [ʀəsɑ̃smɑ̃] nm [de population] census / *faire le recensement de la population* to take a census of the population.

recenser [3] [ʀəsɑ̃se] vt **1.** [population] to take ou to make a census of ; [votes] to count, to register **2.** [biens] to inventory, to make an inventory of ; [marchandises] to check, to take stock of **3.** [malades, victimes] to make a list of.

récent, e [ʀesɑ̃, ɑ̃t] adj **1.** [événement] recent ▶ **jusqu'à une date récente** until recently **2.** [bourgeois, immigré] new.

recentrer [3] [ʀəsɑ̃tʀe] vt POL to revise, to realign.

récepteur [ʀesɛptœʀ] nm [téléphonique] receiver.

réceptif, ive [ʀesɛptif, iv] adj [ouvert] receptive ▶ **réceptif à** open ou receptive to.

réception [ʀesɛpsjɔ̃] nf **1.** [du courrier] receipt **2.** RADIO & TV reception **3.** [accueil] welcome, reception **4.** [fête, dîner] party, reception **5.** [d'un hôtel, d'une société - lieu] reception area ou desk, front desk UK ; [- personnel] reception staff / *demandez à la réception* ask at reception **6.** CONSTR ▶ **réception des travaux** acceptance (of work done) **7.** SPORT [d'un sauteur] landing.

réceptionner [3] [ʀesɛpsjɔne] vt **1.** [article] to check and sign for **2.** [recevoir] to receive. ❖ **se réceptionner** vpi to land / *il s'est bien / mal réceptionné* he made a good / poor landing.

réceptionniste [ʀesɛpsjɔnist] nmf receptionist, desk clerk UK.

récession [ʀesɛsjɔ̃] nf [crise économique] recession.

recette [ʀəsɛt] nf **1.** COMM takings UK, take US ▶ **faire recette a)** [idée] to catch on **b)** [mode] to be all the rage **c)** [personne] to be a great success, to be a hit **2.** DR & FIN [recouvrement] collection **3.** CULIN ▶ **recette (de cuisine)** recipe / *elle m'a donné la recette des crêpes* she gave me the recipe for pancakes **4.** *fig* [méthode] : *elle a une recette pour enlever les taches* she's got a formula for getting rid of stains. ❖ **recettes** nfpl [sommes touchées] income *(U)*, receipts, incomings.

receveur, euse [ʀəsəvœʀ, øz] nm, f **1.** TRANSP ▶ **receveur (d'autobus)** (bus) conductor **2.** ADMIN ▶ **receveur (des postes)** postmaster ▶ **receveuse (des postes)** postmistress ▶ **receveur des contributions** income tax collector **3.** MÉD recipient.

recevoir [52] [ʀəsəvwaʀ] ❖ vt **1.** [courrier, coup de téléphone, compliments] to receive, to get ; [salaire, somme] to receive, to get, to be paid ; [cadeau] to get, to receive, to be given ; [prix, titre] to receive, to get, to be awarded ; [déposition, réclamation, ordre] to receive / *voilà longtemps que je n'ai pas reçu de ses nouvelles* it's a long time since I last heard from him / *nous avons bien reçu votre courrier du 12 mai* we acknowledge receipt ou confirm receipt of your letter dated May 12th **2.** [obtenir - attention] to receive, to get ; [- affection, soins] to receive ; [- éducation] to receive **3.** [subir - coups] to get ; [recevoir] to get ; to get hit on the head / *recevoir un coup sur la tête* to receive a blow to ou to get hit on the head / *la bouteille est tombée et c'est lui qui a tout reçu* the bottle fell over and it went all over him **4.** [chez soi - accueillir] to greet, to welcome ; [- inviter] to entertain ; [- héberger] to take in *(sép)*, to put up *(sép)* ▶ **recevoir qqn à dîner a)** [avec simplicité] to have sb round for dinner, to invite sb to dinner **b)** [solennellement] to entertain sb to dinner / *j'ai été très bien reçu* I was made (to feel) most welcome ▶ **j'ai été mal reçu** I was made to feel unwelcome **5.** [à son lieu de travail - client, représentant] to see / *ils furent reçus par le Pape* they had an audience with ou were received by the Pope **6.** [dans un club, une société - nouveau membre] to admit **7.** [abriter] : *l'école peut recevoir 800 élèves* the school can take up to 800 pupils / *le chalet peut recevoir six personnes* the chalet sleeps six (people) **8.** [eaux de pluie] to collect ; [lumière] to receive. ❖ vi *(surtout au passif)* [candidat] to pass / *elle a été reçue à l'épreuve de français* she passed her French exam **10.** RADIO & TV to receive, to get **11.** RELIG [sacrement, vœux] to receive ; [confession] to hear. ❖ vi **1.** [donner une réception] to entertain / *elle sait merveilleusement recevoir* she's marvellous at entertaining, she's a marvellous hostess **2.** [avocat, conseiller, médecin] to be available (to see clients) / *le médecin reçoit / ne reçoit pas aujourd'hui* the doctor is / isn't seeing patients today. ❖ **se recevoir** vpi SPORT to land.

rechange [ʀəʃɑ̃ʒ] ❖ **de rechange** loc adj **1.** [de secours] spare ; [pour se changer] extra / *elle n'avait même pas de linge de rechange* she didn't even have a change of clothes / *apporte un maillot de rechange* bring an extra ou a spare swimming costume **2.** [de remplacement - solution] alternative.

réchapper [3] [ʀeʃape] ❖ **réchapper à, réchapper de** v + prép to come ou to pull through ▸ **en réchapper** [rester en vie] to come through, to escape alive.

recharge [ʀəʃaʀʒ] nf [d'arme] reload ; [de stylo, briquet, parfum] refill.

rechargeable [ʀəʃaʀʒabl] adj [briquet, stylo] refillable ; [batterie, appareil électrique, carte à puce] rechargeable.

recharger [17] [ʀəʃaʀʒe] vt [réapprovisionner - arme, appareil photo] to reload ; [- un téléphone portable, un ordinateur] to charge ; [- briquet, stylo] to refill ; [- poêle à bois, à mazout, à charbon] to refill ; [- batterie] to recharge.

réchaud [ʀeʃo] nm [de cuisson] (portable) stove ▸ **réchaud à gaz** (portable) gas stove.

réchauffement [ʀeʃofmɑ̃] nm warming up *(U)* / *on annonce un léger réchauffement pour le week-end* temperatures will rise slightly this weekend ▸ **réchauffement climatique** ou **global** ou **de la planète** global warming.

réchauffer [3] [ʀeʃofe] vt **1.** [nourriture] to heat ou to warm up *(sép)* (again) / *je vais faire réchauffer la soupe* I'll heat up the soup **2.** [personne, salle] to warm up *(sép)* **3.** *fig* [ambiance] to warm up *(sép)* ; [ardeur] to rekindle / *ça vous réchauffe le cœur de les voir* it warms (the cockles of) your heart to see them. ❖ **se réchauffer** vpi **1.** [personne] to warm up **2.** [pièce, sol, temps] to warm up, to get warmer.

rêche [ʀɛʃ] adj **1.** [matière, vin] rough ; [fruit] bitter **2.** *fig* [voix, ton] harsh, rough.

recherche [ʀəʃɛʀʃ] nf **1.** [d'un objet, d'une personne, d'un emploi, etc.] search ; [du bonheur, de la gloire, du plaisir] pursuit ; [d'informations] research **2.** SCI & UNIV ▸ **la recherche** research / *bourse / travaux de recherche* research grant / work ▸ **faire de la recherche** to do research **3.** [raffinement] sophistication, refinement / *vêtu avec recherche* elegantly dressed ▸ **sans recherche** simple, plain ; [affectation] affectation, ostentatiousness. ❖ **recherches** nfpl [enquête] search ▸ **faire des recherches sur qqch a)** [gén] to inquire into sthg **b)** [chercheur] to do research on sthg ; [travaux - gén] work, research ; [- de médecine] research. ❖ **à la recherche de** loc prép in search of, looking ou searching for / *être / partir / se mettre à la recherche de* to be / to set off / to go in search of / *depuis combien de temps êtes-vous à la recherche d'un emploi ?* how long have you been looking for a job?

> 📋 Attention ! Le mot research est indénombrable. Il ne s'emploie jamais ni au pluriel ni avec l'article indéfini a :
> **Ces recherches sont financées par le conseil général.** *This research is financed by the local council.*

recherché, e [ʀəʃɛʀʃe] adj **1.** [prisé - mets] choice *(modif)* ; [- comédien] in demand, much sought-after ; [- objet rare] much sought-after **2.** [raffiné - langage] studied ; [- tenue] elegant ; [- style] ornate.

rechercher [3] [ʀəʃɛʀʃe] vt **1.** [document, objet] to look ou to search for *(insép)* ; [disparu] to search for *(insép)* ; [assassin] to look for *(insép)* / *il est recherché par la police* the police are looking for him / **'on recherche pour meurtre homme brun, 32 ans'** 'wanted for murder brown-haired, 32-year-old man' **2.** [dans une annonce] : *(on) recherche jeunes gens pour travail bien rémunéré* young people wanted for well-paid job **3.** [cause] to look

into *(insép)*, to investigate **4.** [compliment, pouvoir, gloire] to seek (out) ; [sécurité] to look for *(insép)* ; [fortune, plaisirs] to be in search of ; [beauté, pureté] to strive for *(insép)*, to aim at *(insép)* **5.** [récupérer - une personne] to collect, to fetch back (again) **6.** INFORM to search.

rechigner [3] [ʀəʃiɲe] vi [protester] to grumble. ❖ **rechigner à** v + prép : *elle rechigne à faire cette vérification* she's reluctant to carry out this check.

rechute [ʀəʃyt] nf MÉD relapse.

rechuter [3] [ʀəʃyte] vi MÉD to (have a) relapse.

récidive [ʀesidiv] nf DR [après première condamnation] second offence 🇬🇧 ou offense 🇺🇸 ; [après deuxième condamnation] subsequent offence.

récidiver [3] [ʀesidive] vi **1.** DR [après première condamnation] to commit a second offence 🇬🇧 ou offense 🇺🇸 ; [après deuxième condamnation] to commit a subsequent offence 🇬🇧 ou offense 🇺🇸 **2.** [recommencer] : *il récidive dans ses plaintes* he's bringing up the same complaints again.

récidiviste [ʀesidivist] nmf [pour la première fois] second offender, recidivist *spéc* ; [de longue date] habitual offender, recidivist *spéc*.

récif [ʀesif] nm reef ▸ **récif corallien** ou **de corail** coral reef.

récipient [ʀesipjɑ̃] nm container, receptacle *sout*, vessel *litt*.

réciproque [ʀesipʀɔk] ❖ adj **1.** [mutuel] mutual / *je vous hais ! — c'est réciproque !* I hate you! — I hate you too ou the feeling's mutual! **2.** [bilatéral - accord] reciprocal. ❖ nf **1.** ▸ **la réciproque** [l'inverse] the reverse, the opposite **2.** ▸ **la réciproque** [la même chose] the same.

réciproquement [ʀesipʀɔkmɑ̃] adv **1.** [mutuellement] : *ils ont le devoir de se protéger réciproquement* it is their duty to protect each other ou one another, they must provide each other with mutual protection **2.** [inversement] vice versa.

récit [ʀesi] nm **1.** [histoire racontée] story, tale, narration *sout* ▸ **faire le récit de qqch** to narrate sthg **2.** LITTÉR & THÉÂTRE narrative ▸ **récit de voyage** [livre] travel book.

récital, als [ʀesital] nm recital.

récitation [ʀesitasjɔ̃] nf [d'un texte] recitation.

réciter [3] [ʀesite] vt [dire par cœur - leçon] to repeat, to recite ; [- discours] to give ; [- poème, prière] to say, to recite ; [- formule] to recite.

réclamation [ʀeklamasjɔ̃] nf ADMIN [plainte] complaint / *pour toute réclamation, s'adresser au guichet 16* all complaints should be addressed ou referred to desk 16 / *faire une réclamation* to lodge a complaint ▸ **service / bureau des réclamations** complaints department / office. ❖ **réclamations** nfpl TÉLÉC [service] ▸ **appeler les réclamations** to call the (telephone) engineer.

réclamer [3] [ʀeklame] vt **1.** [argent, augmentation] to demand ; [attention, silence] to call for *(insép)*, to demand ; [personne] to ask ou to clamour for *(insép)* / *je réclame le silence !* silence, please! / *elle me doit encore de l'argent mais je n'ose pas le lui réclamer* she still owes me money but I daren't ask for it back **2.** [revendiquer - droit] to claim ; [- somme due] to put in for *(insép)*, to claim **3.** [nécessiter - précautions] to call for *(insép)* ; [- soins] to require ; [- explication] to require, to demand. ❖ **se réclamer de** vp + prép ▸ **se réclamer de qqn a)** [utiliser son nom] to use sb's name **b)** [se prévaloir de lui] to invoke sb's name / *elle ne se réclame d'aucun mouvement politique* she doesn't identify with any political movement / *les organisations se réclamant du marxisme* organizations calling ou labelling themselves Marxist.

reclasser [3] [ʀəklase] vt **1.** [ranger] to put back, to re-file ; [réorganiser] to reclassify, to reorganize **2.** [chômeur] to place ; [handicapé, ex-détenu] to rehabilitate.

reclus, e [ʀəkly, yz] ◆ adj solitary, secluded. ◆ nm, f recluse.

réclusion [ʀeklyzjɔ̃] nf DR imprisonment ▸ **réclusion criminelle** imprisonment with labour / *condamné à la réclusion criminelle à perpétuité* sentenced to life (imprisonment), given a life sentence.

recoiffer [3] [ʀəkwafe] vt : *recoiffer ses cheveux* to do ou to redo one's hair ▸ **recoiffer qqn** to do sb's hair (again). ❖ **se recoiffer** vp *(emploi réfléchi)* [se peigner] to do ou to redo one's hair.

recoin [ʀəkwɛ̃] nm **1.** [coin] corner, nook / *chercher dans le moindre recoin* ou *dans tous les (coins et) recoins* to search every nook and cranny **2.** fig [partie secrète] recess.

recoller [3] [ʀəkɔle] vt **1.** [objet brisé] to stick ou to glue back together ; [timbre] to stick back on ; [enveloppe] to stick back down, to restick ; [semelle] to stick ou to glue back on ▸ **recoller les morceaux a)** [avec de la colle] to stick ou to glue the pieces back together (again) **b)** [avec de l'adhésif] to tape the pieces back together (again) **c)** fig to patch things up **2.** fam [redonner] : *on nous a recollé un prof nul* we've been landed with another useless teacher. ❖ **se recoller** vpi [se ressouder - os] to knit (together), to mend ; [- objet] to stick (together).

récolte [ʀekɔlt] nf **1.** [des céréales] harvest (U) ; [des fruits, des choux] picking (U) ; [des pommes de terre] lifting (U) ; [du miel] gathering, collecting (U) / *ils ont déjà commencé à faire la récolte* they've already started harvesting **2.** [quantité récoltée] harvest ; [denrées récoltées] crop **3.** [de documents, d'information] gathering, collecting.

récolter [3] [ʀekɔlte] vt **1.** [céréales] to harvest, to gather ; [légumes, fruits] to pick ; [miel] to collect, to gather ; [tubercules] to lift, to pick **2.** [informations, argent] to collect, to gather / *récolter des voix* to get sb's votes *(in a transferable vote system)* **3.** fam [ennuis, maladie, etc.] to get.

recommandable [ʀəkɔmɑ̃dabl] adj commendable ▸ **un individu peu recommandable** a rather disreputable character / *le procédé est peu recommandable* that isn't a very commendable thing to do.

recommandation [ʀəkɔmɑ̃dasjɔ̃] nf [conseil] advice, recommendation ▸ **faire qqch sur la recommandation de qqn** to do sthg on sb's recommendation / *je lui ai fait mes dernières recommandations* I gave him some last-minute advice.

recommandé, e [ʀəkɔmɑ̃de] adj **1.** [conseillé] advisable ▸ **il est recommandé de...** it is advisable to... **2.** [courrier - avec avis de réception] recorded [UK], certified [US] ; [- à valeur assurée] registered. ❖ **recommandé** nm [courrier - avec avis de réception] recorded [UK] ou certified [US] delivery item ; [- à valeur assurée] registered item ▸ **en recommandé a)** [avec avis de réception] by recorded delivery [UK] ou certified mail [US] **b)** [à valeur assurée] by registered post [UK] ou mail [US].

recommander [3] [ʀəkɔmɑ̃de] vt **1.** [conseiller - produit, personne] to recommend / *je te recommande vivement mon médecin* I (can) heartily recommend my doctor to you **2.** [exhorter à] to recommend, to advise / *je vous recommande la prudence* I recommend ou I advise you to be cautious ; *je vous recommande d'être vigilant* I cannot advise you too strongly to be watchful.

> 📝 Notez que le verbe recommend n'est jamais suivi immédiatement d'un complément d'objet indirect :
> **Ils m'ont recommandé un hôtel dans le centre.**
> *They recommended a good hotel in the centre.*
> **Pouvez-vous nous recommander un médecin ?**
> *Can you recommend a good doctor?*
>
> Comme le montrent ces exemples, le complément d'objet indirect (« to me », « to us ») est sous-entendu et par conséquent omis.

recommencement [ʀəkɔmɑ̃smɑ̃] nm renewal, resumption / *la vie est un éternel recommencement* every day is a new beginning.

recommencer [16] [ʀəkɔmɑ̃se] ◆ vt [refaire - dessin, lettre, travail, etc.] to start ou to begin again ; [- attaque] to renew, to start again ; [- expérience] to repeat ; [- erreur] to repeat, to make again / *tout est à recommencer, il faut tout recommencer* we have to start ou to begin all over again ; *(en usage absolu)* ▸ **ne recommence pas !** don't do that again! ◆ vi **1.** [depuis le début] to start ou to begin again ; [après interruption] to resume / *pour moi, la vie va recommencer* my life is about to begin anew, a new life is beginning for me / *ça y est, ça recommence !* here we go again! **2.** [se remettre] ▸ **recommencer à faire qqch** to start doing ou to do sthg again ; *(tournure impersonnelle)* : *il a recommencé à neiger dans la nuit* it started snowing again during the night.

récompense [ʀekɔ̃pɑ̃s] nf **1.** [d'un acte] reward, recompense sout ▸ **en récompense de** as a reward ou in return for **2.** [prix] award, prize.

récompenser [3] [ʀekɔ̃pɑ̃se] vt **1.** [pour un acte] to reward, to recompense sout **2.** [primer] to give an award ou a prize to, to reward / *le scénario a été récompensé à Cannes* the script won an award at Cannes.

recomposé, e [ʀəkɔ̃poze] adj [famille] blended.

recomposer [3] [ʀəkɔ̃poze] vt **1.** [reconstituer] to piece ou to put together *(sép)* (again), to reconstruct / *recomposer une famille* to build another family **2.** TÉLÉC : *recomposer un numéro* to dial a number again.

recompter [3] [ʀəkɔ̃te] vt to count again.

réconciliation [ʀekɔ̃siljasjɔ̃] nf [entente] reconciliation.

réconcilier [9] [ʀekɔ̃silje] vt **1.** [deux personnes] to reconcile / *réconcilier qqn avec qqch* to reconcile sb to ou with sthg. ❖ **se réconcilier** vpi [personnes] to make up ; [pays] to make peace.

reconduction [ʀəkɔ̃dyksjɔ̃] nf [d'un contrat, d'un budget] renewal ; [d'un bail] renewal, extension.

reconduire [98] [ʀəkɔ̃dɥiʀ] vt **1.** [accompagner] ▸ **reconduire qqn** to see sb home ▸ **reconduire qqn à pied / en voiture** to walk / to drive sb home ; [vers la sortie] to show to the door **2.** [expulser] to escort / *ils ont été reconduits à la frontière sous bonne escorte* they were escorted (back) to the border by the police ou were taken (back) to the border under police escort **3.** [renouveler - contrat, budget, mandat] to renew ; [-bail] to renew, to extend.

reconduite [ʀəkɔ̃dɥit] nf ▸ **reconduite à la frontière** escorting back to the border.

reconfigurer [ʀəkɔ̃figyʀe] vt to reconfigure.

réconfort [ʀekɔ̃fɔʀ] nm comfort / *tu m'es d'un grand réconfort* you're a great comfort to me.

réconfortant, e [ʀekɔ̃fɔʀtɑ̃, ɑ̃t] adj **1.** [rassurant] comforting, reassuring **2.** [revigorant] fortifying, invigorating, stimulating.

réconforter [3] [ʀekɔ̃fɔʀte] vt **1.** [consoler] to comfort, to reassure **2.** [revigorer] : *bois ça, ça va te réconforter* drink this, it'll make you feel better.

reconnaissable [ʀəkɔnɛsabl] adj recognizable ▸ **reconnaissable à** identifiable by.

reconnaissance [ʀəkɔnɛsɑ̃s] nf **1.** [gratitude] gratitude ▸ **avoir / éprouver de la reconnaissance envers qqn** to be / to feel grateful to ou towards sb **2.** [exploration] reconnaissance / *envoyer des hommes en reconnaissance* to send men out on reconnaissance / *elle est partie en reconnaissance* ou *est allée faire une reconnaissance des lieux fig* she went to check the place out ▸ **patrouille de reconnaissance** reconnaissance patrol **3.** [identification] recognition **4.** POL [d'un gouvernement] recognition ▸ **reconnaissance d'un État** recognition (of statehood) **5.** DR [d'un droit] recognition, acknowledgment ▸ **reconnaissance de dette** acknowledgment of a debt **6.** [reçu] ▸ **acte de reconnaissance (du mont-de-piété)** pawn ticket **7.** INFORM recognition ▸ **reconnaissance de formes / de caractères** pattern / character recognition ▸ **reconnaissance vocale** ou **de la parole** speech recognition.

reconnaissant, e [ʀəkɔnɛsɑ̃, ɑ̃t] adj grateful ▸ **se montrer reconnaissant** to show gratitude / *je te suis reconnaissant de ta patience* I'm most grateful to you for your patience / *je vous serais reconnaissant de me fournir ces renseignements dans les meilleurs délais* I would be (most) obliged ou grateful if you would provide me with this information as soon as possible.

reconnaître, reconnaitre* [91] [ʀəkɔnɛtʀ] vt **1.** [air, personne, pas] to recognize / *je t'ai reconnu à ta démarche* I recognized you ou I could tell it was you by your walk / *je te reconnais bien (là) !* that's just like you!, that's you all over! / *tu veux fonder une famille ? je ne te reconnais plus !* you want to start a family? that's not like you at all ou you've changed your tune! **2.** [admettre - torts] to recognize, to acknowledge, to admit ; [- aptitude, talent, vérité] to acknowledge, to recognize / *l'accusé reconnaît-il les faits ?* does the accused acknowledge the facts? / *sa prestation fut décevante, il faut bien le reconnaître* it has to be admitted that his performance was disappointing / *je reconnais que j'ai eu tort* I admit I was wrong / *il n'a jamais reconnu avoir falsifié les documents* he never admitted to having falsified the documents **3.** DR & POL [État, chef de file] to recognize ; [enfant] to recognize legally ; [dette, document, signature] to authenticate / *tous le reconnaissent comme leur maître* they all acknowledge him as their master ▸ **être reconnu coupable** to be found guilty **4.** [explorer] to reconnoitre / *l'équipe de tournage est allée reconnaître les lieux* the film crew went to have a look round (the place). ▸ **se reconnaître, se reconnaitre*** vp *(emploi réfléchi)* [physiquement, moralement] to see o.s. / *je ne me reconnais pas dans votre description* I don't see myself as fitting your description. ◆ vp *(emploi réciproque)* to recognize each other. ◆ vp *(emploi passif)* to be recognizable / *un poisson frais se reconnaît à l'odeur* you can tell a fresh fish by the smell. ◆ vpi [se retrouver] : *je ne me reconnais plus dans ma propre ville* I can't even find my way about ou around my own home town any more.

reconnecter [ʀəkɔnɛkte] ◆ **se reconnecter** vpi INFORM to reconnect o.s., to get back on line.

reconnu, e [ʀəkɔny] ◆ pp ⟶ **reconnaître.** ◆ adj **1.** [admis] recognized, accepted **2.** [célébré] famous, well-known.

reconquérir [39] [ʀəkɔ̃keʀiʀ] vt **1.** [territoire, peuple] to reconquer, to recapture **2.** [honneur, avantage] to win back *(sép)*, to recover **3.** [personne] to win back *(sép)*.

reconquête [ʀəkɔ̃kɛt] nf **1.** [d'un territoire, d'un peuple] reconquest, recapture **2.** [de l'honneur, d'un avantage] winning back *(U)*, recovery.

reconsidérer [18] [ʀəkɔ̃sideʀe] vt to reconsider.
In reformed spelling (see p. 16-18), this verb is conjugated like semer : *il reconsidèrera, elle reconsidèrerait.*

reconstituer [7] [ʀəkɔ̃stitɥe] vt **1.** [reformer - groupe] to bring together *(sép)* again, to reconstitute ; [- capital] to rebuild, to build up *(sép)* again ; [- fichier] to recreate ; [- histoire, meurtre] to reconstruct / *ils ont reconstitué un décor d'époque* they created a period setting ▸ **lait reconstitué** reconstituted milk **2.** [réparer] to piece together *(sép)* (again).

reconstitution [ʀəkɔ̃stitysjɔ̃] nf **1.** [d'un groupe] reconstituting *(U)*, bringing together *(sép)* again *(U)* ; [d'un capital] rebuilding, building up *(sép)* again ; [d'un fichier] recreating *(U)* ; [d'une histoire, d'un meurtre] reconstruction **2.** [réparation] piecing together (again).

reconstruction [ʀəkɔ̃stʀyksjɔ̃] nf **1.** [gén] reconstruction, rebuilding ▸ **en reconstruction** being rebuilt **2.** LING reconstruction.

reconstruire [98] [ʀəkɔ̃stʀɥiʀ] vt **1.** [bâtiment] to reconstruct, to rebuild ; [fortune, réputation] to rebuild, to build up *(sép)* again **2.** LING to reconstruct.

recontacter [3] [ʀ(ə)kɔ̃takte] vt ▸ **recontacter qqn** to get in touch with sb again.

reconversion [ʀəkɔ̃vɛʀsjɔ̃] nf [d'une usine] reconversion ; [d'un individu] retraining.

reconvertir [32] [ʀəkɔ̃vɛʀtiʀ] vt [usine] to reconvert. ◆ **se reconvertir** vpi to retrain / *il s'est reconverti dans l'informatique* he retrained and went into computing.

recopier [9] [ʀəkɔpje] vt **1.** [mettre au propre] to write up *(sép)*, to make ou to take a fair copy of **2.** [copier à nouveau] to copy again, to make another copy of.

record [ʀəkɔʀ] nm **1.** SPORT & *fig* record / *battre un record de vitesse* to break a speed record / *tu bats tous les records d'idiotie ! fam* they don't come any more stupid than you! ▸ **le record du monde** the world record ▸ **bat tous les records** *fam* that beats everything ou the lot **2.** (comme adj, avec ou sans trait d'union) record *(modif)* ▸ **l'inflation a atteint le chiffre-record de 200 %** inflation has risen to a record ou record-breaking 200% ▸ **en un temps-record** in record time.

recordman [ʀəkɔʀdman] *(pl* recordmans *ou* recordmen [-mɛn]) nm (men's) record holder.

recordwoman [ʀəkɔʀdwuman] *(pl* recordwomans *ou* recordwomen [-mɛn]) nf (women's) record holder.

recoucher [3] [ʀəkuʃe] vt [personne] to put back to bed ; [objet] to lay down again. ◆ **se recoucher** vpi to go back to bed.

recoudre [86] [ʀəkudʀ] vt **1.** [bouton, badge, etc.] to sew on *(sép)* again ; [accroc, ourlet, etc.] to sew up *(sép)* again **2.** MÉD to sew ou to stitch up *(sép)* (again).

recoupement [ʀəkupmɑ̃] nm [vérification] crosschecking ▸ **procéder par recoupements** to carry out a crosscheck.

recouper [3] [ʀəkupe] vt **1.** [couper à nouveau] : *recouper de la viande* to cut ou to carve some more meat **2.** [concorder avec] to tally with *(insép)*, to match up with *(insép)*. ◆ **se recouper** vp *(emploi réciproque)* [statistiques, témoignages] to tally, to confirm one another / *les deux versions ne se recoupent pas* the two stories don't tally.

recourbé, e [ʀəkuʀbe] adj [cils] curved ; [nez] hooked.

recourir [45] [ʀəkuʀiʀ] vi SPORT to run ou to race again. ◆ **recourir à** v + prép **1.** [personne] ▸ **recourir à qqn** to appeal ou to turn to sb **2.** [objet, méthode, etc.] ▸ **recourir à qqch** to resort to sthg.

---

* In reformed spelling (see p. 16-18).

recours [ʀəkuʀ] nm **1.** [ressource] recourse, resort ▶ **avoir recours à** a) [moyen] to resort to b) [personne] to turn to **2.** DR appeal ▶ **recours en cassation** appeal (to the appellate court) ▶ **recours en grâce** a) [pour une remise de peine] petition for pardon b) [pour une commutation de peine] petition for clemency ou remission. ❖ **en dernier recours** loc adv as a last resort.

recouvrer [3] [ʀəkuvʀe] vt **1.** [récupérer] to recover / *laissez-lui le temps de recouvrer ses esprits* give her time to recover her wits ou to get her wits back ▶ **recouvrer la liberté** to regain one's freedom **2.** FIN [percevoir] to collect, to recover.

recouvrir [34] [ʀəkuvʀiʀ] vt [couvrir] to cover / *recouvrir un gâteau de chocolat* to coat a cake with chocolate. ❖ **se recouvrir** vpi [surface] : *la glace s'est recouverte de buée* the mirror steamed up.

recracher [3] [ʀəkʀaʃe] ❖ vt [cracher] to spit out (sép) (again). ❖ vi to spit again.

récréation [ʀekʀeasjɔ̃] nf ÉDUC [dans le primaire] play-time 🇬🇧, recess 🇺🇸 ; [dans le secondaire] break 🇬🇧, recess 🇺🇸.

recréer [15] [ʀəkʀee] vt [suivant un modèle] to recreate.

récrimination [ʀekʀiminasjɔ̃] nf recrimination, protest.

récriminer [3] [ʀekʀimine] vi [critiquer] ▶ **récriminer (contre qqn)** to recriminate (against sb).

récrire [ʀekʀiʀ] = **réécrire**.

recroquevillé, e [ʀəkʀɔkvije] adj **1.** [confortablement] curled up ; [dans l'inconfort] hunched ou huddled up **2.** [feuille, pétale] curled ou shrivelled up.

recroqueviller [3] [ʀəkʀɔkvije] ❖ **se recroqueviller** vpi **1.** [confortablement] to curl up ; [dans l'inconfort] to hunch ou to huddle up **2.** [feuille, pétale] to shrivel ou to curl (up).

recrudescence [ʀəkʀydesɑ̃s] nf [aggravation - d'une maladie] aggravation, worsening ; [- de la fièvre] new bout ; [- d'une épidémie] fresh ou new outbreak ; [- du froid] new spell.

recrue [ʀəkʀy] nf **1.** MIL recruit **2.** fig recruit, new member.

recrutement [ʀəkʀytmɑ̃] nm recruiting, recruitment (U).

recruter [3] [ʀəkʀyte] vt [engager] to recruit. ❖ **se recruter** vp (emploi passif) [être engagé] to be recruited.

rectangle [ʀɛktɑ̃gl] nm GÉOM rectangle.

rectangulaire [ʀɛktɑ̃gylɛʀ] adj [forme] rectangular, oblong.

recteur, trice [ʀɛktœʀ, tʀis] nm, f **1.** ENS [d'académie] *chief administrative officer of an education authority* ; ≃ (Chief) Education Officer 🇬🇧, 🇶🇧 UNIV dean.

rectificatif [ʀɛktifikatif] nm correction, rectification.

rectification [ʀɛktifikasjɔ̃] nf **1.** [action] rectification, correction **2.** [rectificatif] correction / *apporter une rectification à une déclaration* to correct a statement.

rectifier [9] [ʀɛktifje] vt **1.** [rajuster] to adjust, to rectify **2.** [corriger] to correct, to rectify.

rectiligne [ʀɛktiliɲ] adj rectilinear.

recto [ʀɛkto] nm first side ou front of a page, recto *sout*. ❖ **recto verso** loc adv on both sides.

rectorat [ʀɛktɔʀa] nm ENS [d'une académie - administration] ≃ Education Office 🇬🇧 ; [- bâtiment] ≃ Education offices 🇬🇧 ; [chez les jésuites] rectorship.

reçu, e [ʀəsy] ❖ pp ⟶ **recevoir**. ❖ nm, f [candidat] pass ▶ **les reçus** the successful candidates, the passes. ❖ **reçu** nm [quittance] receipt.

recueil [ʀəkœj] nm collection / *un recueil de poèmes* a collection ou a selection ou an anthology of poems.

recueillement [ʀəkœjmɑ̃] nm contemplation, meditation ▶ **écouter qqch avec recueillement** to listen reverently to sthg.

recueillir [41] [ʀəkœjiʀ] vt **1.** [récolter] to gather, to pick / *elle espère recueillir plus de la moitié des suffrages* she hopes to win more than half the votes **2.** [renseignements] to collect, to obtain ; [argent] to collect **3.** [personne] to take in (sép) / *recueillir un oiseau tombé du nid* to take care of a bird which has fallen from its nest. ❖ **se recueillir** vpi [penser] to spend some moments in silence ; [prier] to pray ▶ **aller se recueillir sur la tombe de qqn** to spend some moments in silence at sb's graveside.

recuire [98] [ʀəkɥiʀ] ❖ vt CULIN [à l'eau] to cook longer ; [au four] to cook longer in the oven. ❖ vi : *faire recuire un rôti* to recook a joint.

recul [ʀəkyl] nm **1.** [mouvement] moving back, backward movement ; ARM recoil, kick / *il eut un mouvement de recul* he stepped back **2.** [distance] : *as-tu assez de recul pour juger du tableau / prendre la photo ?* are you far enough away to judge the painting / to take the photograph? **3.** [réflexion] ▶ **avec le recul** retrospectively, with (the benefit of) hindsight / *prendre du recul par rapport à un événement* to stand back (in order) to assess an event / *nous n'avons pas assez de recul pour juger des effets à long terme* it's too early ou there's not been enough time to assess what long-term effects there might be **4.** [baisse] fall, drop / *le recul de l'industrie textile* the decline of the textile industry / *le recul du yen par rapport au dollar* the fall of the yen against the dollar.

reculé, e [ʀəkyle] adj **1.** [dans l'espace] remote, far-off **2.** [dans le temps] remote, far-off, distant.

reculer [3] [ʀəkyle] ❖ vt **1.** [dans l'espace] to push ou to move back (sép) **2.** [dans le temps - rendez-vous] to delay, to postpone, to defer ; [- date] to postpone, to put back (sép) ; [- décision] to defer, to postpone, to put off (sép). ❖ vi **1.** [aller en arrière - à pied] to step ou to go ou to move back ; [- en voiture] to reverse, to move back / *recule d'un pas !* take one step backwards! **2.** [renoncer] to retreat, to shrink (back), to draw back / *reculer devant l'ennemi* to retreat in the face of the enemy ▶ **c'est reculer pour mieux sauter** that's just putting off the inevitable **3.** [faiblir - cours, valeur] to fall, to weaken ; [- épidémie, criminalité, mortalité] to recede, to subside / *le yen recule par rapport au dollar* the yen is losing ground ou falling against the dollar / *l'isolement des malades a fait reculer l'épidémie* they managed to get the epidemic under control by putting people in quarantine. ❖ **se reculer** vpi fam ▶ **recule-toi !** get back!

reculons [ʀəkylɔ̃] ❖ **à reculons** loc adv **1.** [en marche arrière] backwards ▶ **sortir à reculons** to back out ▶ **avancer à reculons** hum to be getting nowhere **2.** [avec réticence] reluctantly, under protest / *je le fais à reculons* I'm reluctant to do it.

récup [ʀekyp] (abr de **récupération**) nf fam **1.** [jour de congé] compensatory time off work due to previous overtime **2.** [chiffons, papier, ferraille, etc.] second-hand object.

récupération [ʀekypeʀasjɔ̃] nf **1.** [après séparation, perte] recovery **2.** ÉCOL recycling, reclaiming ▶ **matériau de récupération** scrap (U) **3.** POL takeover / *il y a eu récupération du mouvement par les extrémistes* the extremists have taken over and manipulated the movement **4.** [au travail] making up / *quand je fais des heures supplémentaires, j'ai des jours de récupération* when I work overtime, I get time off in exchange ou in lieu.

récupérer [18] [ʀekypeʀe] ❖ vt **1.** [retrouver] to get back (sép) / *il doit récupérer son chien au chenil* he's got to pick up ou to collect his dog from the kennels / *je passe te récupérer en voiture* I'll come and pick you up / *veux-tu* *récupérer ton anorak ?* do you want your anorak back? **/** *il a récupéré toutes ses forces* [il s'est reposé] he has recuperated, he's back to normal **2.** [pour utiliser - chiffons, papier, verre, ferraille] to salvage ; [- chaleur, énergie] to save **/** *j'ai récupéré des chaises dont personne ne voulait* I've rescued some chairs no one wanted **3.** [jour de congé] to make up for, to compensate for **4.** POL to take over *(sép)* **/** *le mouvement a été récupéré par le gouvernement* the movement has been taken over by the government for its own ends. ❖ vi [se remettre] to recover, to recuperate.

🖋 In reformed spelling (see p. 16-18), this verb is conjugated like *semer* : *il récupèrera, elle récupèrerait.*

récurer [3] [Rekyʀe] vt [casserole, évier] to scour, to scrub.

récurrent, e [Rekyʀɑ̃, ɑ̃t] adj [à répétition] recurrent, recurring.

récuser [3] [Rekyze] vt **1.** DR [juge, juré, expert] to challenge **2.** [décision, témoignage] to challenge, to impugn *sout.* ❖ **se récuser** vpi **1.** [lors d'un procès] to declare o.s. incompetent **2.** [lors d'une entrevue, d'un débat] to refuse to give an opinion, to decline to (make any) comment.

recyclable [Rəsiklabl] adj recyclable.

recyclage [Rəsiklaʒ] nm **1.** INDUST recycling **2.** ENS [perfectionnement] refresher course ; [reconversion] retraining **3.** [stage - pour employés] retraining course ; [- pour chômeurs] retraining course, restart (course) 🇬🇧 **4.** ÉCOL ▶ **recyclage des déchets** waste recycling.

recycler [3] [Rəsikle] vt **1.** INDUST to recycle ▶ **papier recyclé** recycled paper **2.** [perfectionner] to send on a refresher course ; [reconvertir] to retrain. ❖ **se recycler** vpi [pour se perfectionner] to go on a refresher course ; [pour se reconvertir] to retrain **/** *le vocabulaire des jeunes change, j'ai dû me recycler* hum young people speak differently nowadays, I've had to bring myself up to date.

rédacteur, trice [Redaktœʀ, tʀis] nm, f **1.** [auteur - d'un livre] writer ; [- d'un guide] compiler ▶ **les rédacteurs de l'encyclopédie** the contributors to the encyclopedia **2.** PRESSE writer, contributor ▶ **rédacteur en chef a)** [d'une revue] (chief) editor **b)** [du journal télévisé] television news editor.

rédaction [Redaksjɔ̃] nf **1.** [écriture] writing ▶ **équipe chargée de la rédaction d'un guide / dictionnaire** team responsible for compiling a guide / dictionary ▶ **la rédaction d'un projet de loi / d'un contrat d'assurance** the drafting of a bill / of an insurance contract **2.** PRESSE [lieu] editorial office ; TV newsdesk, newsroom ; [équipe] editorial staff **3.** ÉDUC [composition] ≃ essay ; ≃ composition.

reddition [Redisjɔ̃] nf MIL surrender.

redécouvrir [34] [Rədekuvʀiʀ] vt to rediscover.

redéfinir [32] [Rədefiniʀ] vt to redefine.

redemander [3] [Rədəmɑ̃de] vt **1.** [demander à nouveau] to ask again **2.** [demander davantage] to ask for more **/** *sa correction ne lui a pas suffi, il en redemande* one spank obviously wasn't enough because he's asking for another one **3.** [après un prêt] to ask for *(insép).*

redémarrer [3] [Rədemaʀe] vi **1.** [moteur] to start up *(sép)* again **2.** [processus] to get going ou to take off again ▶ **l'économie redémarre** the economy is looking up again.

redéploiement [Rədeplwamɑ̃] nm **1.** MIL redeployment **2.** ÉCON reorganization, restructuring.

redescendre [73] [Rədesɑ̃dʀ] ❖ vt **1.** [colline, montagne, etc. - en voiture] to drive (back) down ; [- à pied] to walk (back) down ; [suj : alpiniste] to climb back down *(insép)* **2.** [passager, fret] to take ou to drive (back) down *(sép)* ▶ **je redescendrai les cartons plus tard a)** [je suis en haut] I'll take the cardboard boxes back down later **b)** [je suis en bas] I'll bring the cardboard boxes back down later. ❖ vi

(aux être) **1.** [descendre] to go ou to come ou to get (back) down **/** *la température / le niveau de l'eau redescend* the temperature / the water level is falling (again) **2.** [descendre à nouveau] to go down again.

redevable [Rədəvabl] adj **1.** FIN : *vous êtes redevable d'un acompte provisionnel* you are liable for an interim payment **2.** *fig* ▶ **être redevable de qqch à qqn** to be indebted to sb for sthg.

redevance [Rədəvɑ̃s] nf **1.** TV licence 🇬🇧 ou license 🇺🇸 fee ; TÉLÉC rental charge **2.** COMM & FIN [pour un service] dues, fees ; [royalties] royalties **3.** HIST tax.

redevenir [40] [Rədəvniʀ] vi *(aux être)* to become again ▶ **redevenir amis** to become friends again.

rédhibitoire [Redibitwaʀ] adj *fig* : *une mauvaise note à l'écrit, c'est rédhibitoire* a bad mark in the written exam is enough to fail the candidate.

rediffuser [3] [Rədifyze] vt to rebroadcast, to repeat, to rerun.

rediffusion [Rədifyzjɔ̃] nf repeat, rerun, rebroadcast.

rédiger [17] [Rediʒe] vt [manifeste, contrat] to write, to draw up ; [thèse, rapport] to write up *(sép)* ; [lettre] to write, to compose ; [guide, manuel] to write, to compile ; *(en usage absolu)* ▶ **il rédige bien** he writes well.

redingote [Rədɛ̃gɔt] nf **1.** [de femme] tailored ou fitted coat **2.** [d'homme] frock coat.

redire [102] [RədiR] vt **1.** [répéter] to say ou to tell again, to repeat ; [rabâcher] to keep saying, to repeat **/** *on lui a dit et redit* he's been told again and again **2.** EXPR *il n'y avait rien à redire à cela* there was nothing wrong with ou nothing to object to in that ▶ **trouver à redire (à)** to find fault (with).

rediriger [RədiʀiʒE] vt to redirect.

rediscuter [3] [Rədiskyte] ❖ **rediscuter de** v + prép to talk about ou to discuss again.

redistribuer [7] [RədistʀibyE] vt [cartes] to deal again ; [fortune] to redistribute ; [emplois] to reallocate ▶ **redistribuer les rôles a)** *pr* to recast the show **b)** *fig* to reallocate the tasks.

redistribution [Rədistʀibysjɔ̃] nf [des revenus, des terres, des richesses] redistribution.

redite [Rədit] nf superfluous ou needless repetition.

redondance [Rədɔ̃dɑ̃s] nf [répétition] redundancy.

redondant, e [Rədɔ̃dɑ̃, ɑ̃t] adj [mot] redundant, superfluous ; [style] redundant, verbose, wordy.

redonner [3] [RədɔnE] vt **1.** [donner de nouveau] to give again **2.** [rendre] to give back *(sép)* ▶ **ça m'a redonné confiance** it restored my confidence in myself.

redorer [3] [Rədɔʀe] vt ▶ **redorer son blason** to regain prestige.

redoublant, e [Rədublɑ̃, ɑ̃t] nm, f pupil repeating a year 🇬🇧 ou grade 🇺🇸.

redoubler [3] [Rəduble] ❖ vt **1.** [rendre double] : *redoubler une consonne* to double a consonant **2.** ÉDUC : *redoubler une classe* to repeat a year 🇬🇧 ou grade 🇺🇸. ❖ vi [froid, tempête] to increase, to intensify, to become more intense. ❖ **redoubler de** v + prép to increase in ▶ **redoubler d'efforts** to strive doubly hard, to redouble one's efforts **/** *redoubler de patience* to be doubly ou extra patient.

redoutable [Rədutabl] adj [dangereux] formidable **/** *un ennemi redoutable* a fearsome or formidable enemy **/** *une maladie redoutable* a dreadful illness.

redoutablement [Rədutabləmɑ̃] adv extremely **/** *redoutablement efficace / intelligent* extremely effective / intelligent.

redouter [3] [Rədute] vt to dread.

redoux [Rədu] nm mild spell *(during winter).*

redressement [ʀədʀɛsmɑ̃] nm **1.** COMM & ÉCON recovery ▸ **plan de redressement** recovery programme **2.** FIN ▸ **redressement fiscal** payment of back taxes ▸ **être placé en redressement judiciaire** to be put into receivership ou administration.

redresser [4] [ʀədʀese] vt **1.** [arbre, poteau] to straighten (up), to set upright ; [véhicule, volant] to straighten (up) ; [bateau] to right ▸ **redresser la tête a)** [la lever] to lift up one's head **b)** [avec fierté] to hold one's head up high **2.** [corriger - courbure] to put right, to straighten out *(sép)* ; [- anomalie] to rectify, to put right ; [- situation] to sort out *(sép)*, to put right, to put back on an even keel. ❖ **se redresser** vpi **1.** [personne assise] to sit up straight ; [personne allongée] to sit up ; [personne voûtée ou penchée] to straighten up ▸ **redresse-toi !** [personne assise] sit up straight! **b)** [personne debout] stand up straight! **2.** *fig* [remonter] to recover / *la situation se redresse un peu* the situation is on the mend.

redresseur de torts [ʀədʀesœʀdətɔʀ] nm *hum* ou HIST righter of wrongs.

réducteur, trice [ʀedyktœʀ, tʀis] adj [limitatif] simplistic / *une analyse réductrice* an over-simplistic analysis. ❖ **réducteur** nm MÉCAN reduction gear.

réduction [ʀedyksjɔ̃] nf **1.** [remise] discount, rebate ▸ **carte de réduction** discount card **2.** [baisse] cut, drop / *ils nous ont imposé une réduction des dépenses / salaires* they've cut our expenditure / wages / *ils ont promis une réduction des impôts* they promised to reduce ou to lower taxes **3.** DR : *il a eu une réduction de peine* he got his sentence cut ou reduced.

réduire [98] [ʀedɥiʀ] ◆ vt **1.** [restreindre - consommation] to reduce, to cut down on ; [- inflation] to reduce, to bring down *(sép)*, to lower ; [- dépenses, effectifs] to reduce, to cut back on ; [- distance] to reduce, to decrease ; [- chauffage] to lower, to turn down *(sép)* **2.** [changer] ▸ **réduire qqch à l'essentiel** to boil sthg down ▸ **réduire qqch en miettes** to smash sthg to bits ou pieces ▸ **réduire qqch en cendres** to reduce sthg to ashes ▸ **réduire qqch à sa plus simple expression** to reduce sthg to its simplest expression **3.** [forcer] ▸ **réduire qqn à** to reduce sb to ▸ **réduire qqn à faire** to force ou to compel ou to drive sb to do **4.** Suisse [ranger] to put away *(sép)*. ◆ vi CULIN ▸ **faire réduire** to reduce. ❖ **se réduire à** vp + prép [consister en] to amount to.

réduit, e [ʀedɥi, it] adj **1.** [échelle, format, etc.] scaled-down, small-scale **2.** [taille] small ; [tarif] reduced, cut / *à vitesse réduite* at reduced ou low speed ▸ **à prix réduit** cut price **3.** [peu nombreux - débouchés] limited, restricted. ❖ **réduit** nm *péj* [logement] cubbyhole.

redynamiser [3] [r(ə)dinamize] vt [économie, secteur, activité] to give a new boost to.

rééchelonner [ʀeeʃlɔne] vt [dette] to reschedule.

réécrire [99] [ʀeekʀiʀ] vt to rewrite.

rééditer [3] [ʀeedite] vt **1.** IMPR to republish **2.** *fam* [refaire] to repeat.

réédition [ʀeedisjɔ̃] nf IMPR [nouvelle édition] new edition ; [action de rééditer] republishing, republication.

rééducation [ʀeedykasjɔ̃] nf **1.** MÉD [d'un membre] reeducation ; [d'un malade] rehabilitation, reeducation / *faire de la rééducation* to undergo physiotherapy UK ou physical therapy US **2.** [morale] reeducation ; DR [d'un délinquant] rehabilitation.

rééduquer [3] [ʀeedyke] vt **1.** MÉD [malade] to give physiotherapy UK ou physical therapy US to, to reeducate ; [membre] to reeducate **2.** [délinquant] to rehabilitate.

réel, elle [ʀeɛl] adj **1.** [concret] real ; [prix, profit, salaire] real ; [date] effective **2.** *(avant nom)* [appréciable] genuine, real / *elle a fait preuve d'un réel talent* she's shown true ou genuine talent. ❖ **réel** nm ▸ **le réel** reality, the real.

réélection [ʀeelɛksjɔ̃] nf reelection.

réélire [106] [ʀeeliʀ] vt to reelect.

réellement [ʀeɛlmɑ̃] adv really.

réembaucher [ʀeɑ̃boʃe], **rembaucher** [ʀɑ̃boʃe] [3] vt to take back on, to take on *(sép)* again, to reemploy.

réemploi [ʀeɑ̃plwa] = **remploi**.

réemployer [ʀeɑ̃plwaje] = **remployer**.

réenregistrer [ʀeɑ̃ʀəʒistʀe] vt to rerecord.

rééquilibrer [3] [ʀeekilibʀe] vt [budget] to balance again ; [situation] to restabilize.

réessayer [11] [ʀeeseje] vt [voiture, produit, méthode] to try again ; [vêtement] to try on *(sép)* again.

réévaluer [7] [ʀeevalɥe] vt **1.** FIN [devise, monnaie] to revalue ; [salaire, taux] to reappraise ; [à la hausse] to upgrade ; [à la baisse] to downgrade **2.** [qualité, travail] to reassess, to reevaluate.

réexaminer [3] [ʀeɛgzamine] vt to reexamine, to reassess.

réexpédier [9] [ʀeɛkspedje] vt [courrier - à l'expéditeur] to return (to sender), to send back *(sép)* ; [- au destinataire] to forward.

réf. (abr écrite de **référence**) ref.

refaire [109] [ʀəfɛʀ] vt **1.** [à nouveau] to redo, to do again / *j'ai dû refaire le trajet* I had to make the same journey again / *quand pourras-tu refaire du sport ?* when will you be able to do some sport again? ; *fig* : *vous ne la referez pas* you won't change her ▸ **refaire sa vie** to start a new life, to make a fresh start (in life) / *si c'était à refaire ? — je suis prête à recommencer* — I would do the same thing **2.** [réparer] to redo ▸ **ils refont la route** they are resurfacing the road / *le moteur a été complètement refait à neuf* the engine has had a complete overhaul ; MÉD : *se faire refaire le nez* to have a nose job **3.** *fam* [berner] to take in *(sép)* / *il m'a refait de quinze euros* he did me out of fifteen euros. ❖ **se refaire** ◆ vp *(emploi réfléchi)* [se changer] : *on ne se refait pas* you can't change the way you are. ◆ vpi *fam* [financièrement] to recoup one's losses / *j'ai besoin de me refaire* I need to get hold of some more cash. ◆ vpt : *se refaire une tasse de thé* to make o.s. another cup of tea ▸ **se refaire une beauté** to powder one's nose ▸ **se refaire une santé** to recuperate. ❖ **se refaire à** vp + prép ▸ **se refaire à qqch** to get used to sthg again.

réfection [ʀefɛksjɔ̃] nf [gén] redoing ; [d'une pièce] redecorating ; [d'une maison] redoing, doing up ; [d'une route] repairs.

réfectoire [ʀefɛktwaʀ] nm [dans une communauté] refectory ; ÉDUC dining hall, canteen ; UNIV (dining) hall.

référé [ʀefere] nm [procédure] special hearing ; [arrêt] temporary ruling ; [ordonnance] temporary injunction.

référence [ʀefeʀɑ̃s] nf **1.** ADMIN & COMM reference number / **'référence à rappeler dans toute correspondance'** 'reference number to be quoted when replying ou in all correspondence' **2.** [base d'évaluation] reference / *un prix littéraire, c'est une référence* a literary prize is a good recommendation for a book ▸ **faire référence à** to refer to, to make (a) reference to **3.** LING reference. ❖ **références** nfpl [pour un emploi - témoignages] references, credentials *fig* ; [- document] reference letter, testimonial. ❖ **de référence** loc adj reference *(modif)* ▸ **prix de référence** reference price.

référencement [ʀefeʀɑ̃smɑ̃] nm **1.** COMM listing **2.** INTERNET referencing.

référencer [16] [ʀefeʀɑ̃se] vt INTERNET to reference.

référendum [ʀefeʀɛdɔm] nm referendum.

référent [ʀefeʀ] nm referent.

référer [18] [ʀefeʀe] ❖ **en référer à** v + prép to refer back to / *il ne peut rien décider sans en référer à son supérieur* he can't decide anything without referring back to his boss. ❖ **se référer à** vp + prép to refer to.

📝 In reformed spelling (see p. 16-18), this verb is conjugated like *semer : il (se) référera, elle (se) référerait.*

refermable [ʀ(ə)fɛʀmabl] adj [sachet] resealable.

refermer [3] [ʀəfɛʀme] vt to close ou to shut (again). ❖ **se refermer** vpi [porte] to close ou to shut (again) ; [blessure] to close ou to heal up ; [piège] to snap shut.

refiler [3] [ʀəfile] vt *fam* [donner] to give.

réfléchi, e [ʀefleʃi] adj **1.** [caractère, personne] reflective, thoughtful / *une analyse réfléchie* a thoughtful ou well thought-out analysis **2.** LING reflexive.

réfléchir [32] [ʀefleʃiʀ] ❖ vt PHOT & PHYS to reflect. ❖ vi to think, to reflect / *je n'ai pas eu le temps de réfléchir* I haven't had time to think / *il fallait réfléchir avant de parler !* you should have thought before you spoke! ▸ **j'ai longuement réfléchi** I gave it a lot of thought / *quand on voit comment ça se passe, ça fait réfléchir* when you see what's happening, it makes you think. ❖ **se réfléchir** vpi [lumière, son] to be reflected.

reflet [ʀəflɛ] nm **1.** [lumière] reflection, glint, light **2.** [couleur] tinge, glint, highlight / *se faire faire des reflets* to have highlights put in.

refléter [18] [ʀəflete] vt **1.** [renvoyer -lumière] to reflect ; [-image] to reflect, to mirror **2.** [représenter] to reflect, to mirror. ❖ **se refléter** vpi **1.** [lumière, rayon] to be reflected **2.** [se manifester] to be reflected.

📝 In reformed spelling (see p. 16-18), this verb is conjugated like *semer : il reflètera, elle reflèterait.*

refleurir [32] [ʀəflœʀiʀ] vi [plante] to flower again, to blossom again.

reflex, réflex* [ʀeflɛks] ❖ adj inv reflex (*modif*). ❖ nm inv reflex (camera).

réflexe [ʀeflɛks] ❖ nm **1.** BIOL & PHYSIOL reflex ▸ **réflexe inné / conditionné** instinctive / conditioned reflex **2.** [réaction] reaction ▸ **il a eu / n'a pas eu le réflexe de tirer le signal d'alarme** he instinctively pulled / he didn't think to pull the alarm. ❖ adj reflex (*modif*).

réflexion [ʀeflɛksjɔ̃] nf **1.** [méditation] thought / *leur proposition demande réflexion* their offer will need thinking over ▸ **réflexion faite, à la réflexion** on reflection **2.** [remarque] remark, comment, reflection *sout* ▸ **faire des réflexions à qqn** to make remarks to sb / *elle a eu des réflexions de la direction* the management have had a word with her *euphém*.

⚠️ Le mot anglais **reflection** ne doit pas être employé systématiquement pour traduire réflexion, notamment au sens de « pensée » et de « remarque ». Voir article.

refluer [3] [ʀəflye] vi **1.** [liquide] to flow back ; [marée] to ebb ; [foule, public] to surge back **2.** *fig & litt* [pensée, souvenir] to come flooding ou rushing back.

reflux [ʀəfly] nm **1.** [de la marée] ebb **2.** [d'une foule] backward surge.

refondre [75] [ʀəfɔ̃dʀ] vt *fig* [remanier] to recast, to reshape, to refashion / *la 3ᵉ édition a été entièrement refondue* the third edition has been entirely revised.

reforestation [ʀəfɔʀɛstasjɔ̃] nf reforestation.

reformater [3] [ʀ(ə)fɔʀmate] vt INFORM to reformat.

réformateur, trice [ʀefɔʀmatœʀ, tʀis] nm, f reformer.

réforme [ʀefɔʀm] nf [modification] reform.

réformé, e [ʀefɔʀme] ❖ adj [religion] Reformed, Protestant. ❖ nm, f [calviniste] Protestant ; [moine] member of a Reformed Order.

reformer [3] [ʀəfɔʀme] vt [à nouveau] to re-form, to form again.

réformer [3] [ʀefɔʀme] vt **1.** [modifier] to reform **2.** MIL [recrue] to declare unfit for service ; [soldat] to discharge ; [tank, arme] to scrap.

refoulé, e [ʀəfule] adj [instinct, sentiment] repressed ; [ambition] frustrated ; [personne] inhibited.

refoulement [ʀəfulmɑ̃] nm **1.** [d'assaillants] pushing ou forcing back ; [d'immigrants] turning back ou away **2.** PSYCHOL repression.

refouler [3] [ʀəfule] ❖ vt **1.** [assaillants] to drive ou to push back (*sép*), to repulse ; [immigrants] to turn back ou away (*sép*) / *ils se sont fait refouler à la frontière* they were driven back at the border **2.** [retenir] ▸ **refouler ses larmes** to hold ou to choke back one's tears ▸ **refouler sa colère** to keep one's anger in check **3.** PSYCHOL to repress. ❖ vi [mal fonctionner] ▸ **l'égout refoule** a stench is coming up from the sewer / *la cheminée refoule* the fire is blowing back.

réfractaire [ʀefʀaktɛʀ] adj **1.** [matériau] refractory, heat-resistant **2.** [personne] ▸ **réfractaire à** resistant ou unamenable to / *je suis réfractaire aux mathématiques* I'm incapable of understanding mathematics, mathematics is a closed book to me **3.** MÉD resistant.

refrain [ʀəfʀɛ̃] nm **1.** [d'une chanson] chorus, refrain ; [chanson] tune, song **2.** *péj* [sujet] : *change de refrain* can't you talk about something else? / *avec toi c'est toujours le même refrain* it's always the same old story with you.

réfréner [18] [ʀefʀene], **refréner** [ʀəfʀene] vt to hold back (*sép*), to hold in check, to curb.

📝 In reformed spelling (see p. 16-18), this verb is conjugated like *semer : il réfrènera, elle réfrènerait.*

réfrigérateur [ʀefʀiʒeʀatœʀ] nm refrigerator *sout*, fridge, icebox 🇺🇸.

refroidir [32] [ʀəfʀwadiʀ] ❖ vt **1.** TECHNOL to cool **2.** *fig* [personne] to cool (down) ; [sentiment] to dampen, to put a damper on **3.** *tfam* [assassiner] to bump off. ❖ vi **1.** [devenir froid] to cool (down), to get cold ou colder / *faites refroidir pendant deux heures dans le réfrigérateur* cool ou leave to cool in the refrigerator for two hours **2.** *fam & fig* ▸ **laisser refroidir qqch** to leave ou to keep ou to put sthg on ice. ❖ **se refroidir** vpi [devenir froid] to get cold ou colder, to cool down ▸ **le temps va se refroidir a)** [légèrement] it'll get cooler **b)** [sensiblement] it'll get cold ou colder.

refroidissement [ʀəfʀwadismɑ̃] nm **1.** TECHNOL cooling **2.** *fig* [dans une relation] cooling (off).

refuge [ʀəfyʒ] nm **1.** [abri] refuge ▸ **chercher / trouver refuge dans une grange** to seek / to find shelter in a barn ; [en montagne] (mountain) refuge **2.** (comme adj) ⟶ **valeur**.

réfugié, e [ʀefyʒje] nm, f refugee ▸ **réfugié climatique** climate refugee.

réfugier [9] [ʀefyʒje] ❖ **se réfugier** vpi [s'abriter] to take refuge ou shelter.

* In reformed spelling (see p. 16-18).

refus [Rəfy] nm [réponse négative] refusal, rebuff ▶ **refus de vente / de priorité / d'obéissance** refusal to sell / to give way / to comply ▶ **ce n'est pas de refus !** fam I wouldn't say no!, I don't mind if I do!

refuser [3] [Rəfyze] vt **1.** [don, livraison] to refuse to accept, to reject ; [offre, proposition] to turn down, to refuse / refuser une invitation to turn down ou to decline an invitation / le restaurant refuse du monde tous les soirs the restaurant turns people away every evening **2.** [autorisation] to refuse, to turn down ; [service] to refuse, to deny / refuser de payer une somme to withhold a sum of money / il refuse de sortir de sa chambre he refuses to leave his room / il ne peut rien lui refuser he can refuse him nothing **3.** [objet] : le tiroir refuse de s'ouvrir the drawer refuses to ou won't open **4.** ÉQUIT to refuse **5.** [maladie, responsabilité] to refuse, to reject / refuser le combat to refuse battle ou to fight. ❖ **se refuser** ◆ vp (emploi passif) (à la forme négative) : une telle offre ne se refuse pas such an offer is not to be refused ou can't be turned down / un séjour au bord de la mer, ça ne se refuse pas a stay at the seaside, you can't say no to that. ◆ vpt to deny o.s. / des vacances au Brésil, on ne se refuse rien ! fam & hum a holiday in Brazil, no less! ❖ **se refuser à** vp + prép : je me refuse à croire de pareilles sornettes ! I refuse to believe such twaddle! / l'avocat se refuse à tout commentaire the lawyer is refusing to make any comment ou is declining to comment.

réfuter [3] [Refyte] vt [en prouvant] to refute, to disprove.

regagner [3] [Rəɡaɲe] vt **1.** [gagner - à nouveau] to win back (sép), to regain ; [- après perte] to win back ▶ **regagner du terrain** to recover lost ground **2.** [retourner à] to go back ou to return to / regagner sa place to get back to one's seat ou place.

regain [Rəɡɛ̃] nm [retour, accroissement] renewal, revival.

régal, als [Reɡal] nm [délice] delight, treat / ce repas est un vrai régal this meal is a real treat.

régaler [3] [Reɡale] vt [offrir à manger, à boire] to treat / aujourd'hui, c'est moi qui régale fam today it's on me ou I'm treating you ou it's my treat. ❖ **se régaler** vpi **1.** [en mangeant] ▶ **je me suis régalé** it was a real treat, I really enjoyed it **2.** fig : je me régale à l'écouter it's a real treat for me to listen to her.

regard [RəɡaR] nm **1.** [expression] look, expression / son regard était haineux he had a look of hatred in his eye ou eyes, his eyes were full of hatred **2.** [coup d'œil] look, glance, gaze / ils échangèrent un regard de connivence they exchanged knowing looks ▶ **lancer un regard à qqn** to look at sb, to glance at sb **3.** [d'égout] manhole ; [de four] peephole. ❖ **au regard de** loc prép [aux termes de] in the eyes of / mes papiers sont en règle au regard de la loi my papers are in order from a legal point of view. ❖ **en regard** loc adv : un texte latin avec la traduction en regard a Latin text with a translation on the opposite page. ❖ **en regard de** loc prép [en comparaison avec] compared with.

regardant, e [RəɡaRdɑ̃, ɑ̃t] adj **1.** [avare] careful with money euphém, sparing, grudging **2.** [pointilleux] demanding / elle n'est pas très regardante sur la propreté she's not very particular when it comes to cleanliness.

regarder [3] [RəɡaRde] ◆ vt **1.** [voir] to look at (insép), to see ; [observer] to watch, to see ▶ **regarder qqch rapidement** to glance at sthg ▶ **regarder qqch fixement** to stare at sthg ▶ **regarder qqch longuement** to gaze at sthg / regarde s'il arrive see if he's coming / si tu veux t'instruire, regarde-le faire if you want to learn something, watch how he does it / as-tu regardé le match ? did you watch ou

see the match? / regarde-moi ça ! fam just look at that! **2.** [examiner - moteur, blessure] to look at (insép), to check ; [- notes, travail] to look over ou through (sép) ; [- causes] to examine, to consider, to look into (insép) / as-tu eu le temps de regarder le dossier ? did you have time to look at ou to examine the file? **3.** [vérifier] to look up (sép) / je vais regarder quelle heure il est ou l'heure I'm going to see ou to check what time it is ; (en usage absolu) : regarde à la lettre D look through the D's, look at the letter D **4.** [concerner] to concern / ceci ne regarde que toi et moi this is (just) between you and me / ça ne te regarde pas ! that's ou it's none of your business! **5.** [considérer - sujet, situation] to look at (insép), to view / il regarde avec envie la réussite de son frère he casts an envious eye upon his brother's success, he looks upon his brother's success with envy ▶ **regarder qqn comme** to consider sb as, to regard sb as, to look upon sb as ▶ **regarder qqch comme** to regard sthg as, to look upon sthg as, to think of sthg as. ◆ vi [personne] to look / nous avons regardé partout we looked ou searched everywhere. ❖ **regarder à** v + prép [morale, principes] to think of ou about, to take into account ; [apparence, détail] to pay attention to ▶ **regarder à la dépense** to be careful with one's money ▶ **y regarder à deux** ou **à plusieurs fois avant de faire qqch** to think twice before doing sthg ▶ **à y bien regarder, à y regarder de plus près** when you think it over, on thinking it over. ❖ **se regarder** ◆ vp (emploi réfléchi) pr & fig to look at oneself ▶ **tu ne t'es pas regardé !** fam you should take a (good) look at yourself ! ◆ vp (emploi réciproque) [personnes] to look at each other ou at one another. ◆ vp (emploi passif) [spectacle] : cette émission se regarde en famille this is a family show, this show is family viewing.

régate [Reɡat] nf NAUT regatta.

régence [Reʒɑ̃s] nf regency. ❖ **Régence** adj inv (French) Regency / un fauteuil Régence a Regency armchair.

régénérant, e [ReʒeneRɑ̃, ɑ̃t] adj regenerative.

régénérer [18] [ReʒeneRe] vt **1.** BIOL & CHIM to regenerate **2.** litt [rénover] to regenerate, to restore.
✎ In reformed spelling (see p. 16-18), this verb is conjugated like semer : il régénèrera, elle régénèrerait.

régent [Reʒɑ̃] nm BELG qualified secondary school teacher.

régenter [3] [Reʒɑ̃te] vt to rule over (insép), to run / il veut régenter tout le monde he wants everybody to be at his beck and call.

régie [Reʒi] nf **1.** [d'une entreprise publique] ▶ **(société) en régie a)** [par l'État] state-controlled (corporation) **b)** [par le département] local authority controlled (company) **c)** [par la commune] ≃ local district controlled (company) **2.** [pièce - dans un studio de télévision ou de radio] control room ; [- dans un théâtre] lighting box **3.** CINÉ, THÉÂTRE & TV [équipe] production team.

régime [Reʒim] nm **1.** POL [système] regime, (system of) government ; [gouvernement] regime **2.** ADMIN & DR [système] system, scheme ; [règlement] rules, regulations ▶ **régime de Sécurité sociale** subdivision of the French social security system applying to certain professional groups ▶ **être marié sous le régime de la communauté** to opt for a marriage based on joint ownership of property **3.** MÉD : être au régime to be on a diet, to be dieting ▶ **régime (alimentaire)** diet ▶ **régime amaigrissant** slimming UK ou reducing US diet ▶ **régime sans sel** salt-free diet **4.** INDUST & MÉCAN engine speed ▶ **fonctionner à plein régime** [usine] to work to full capacity / à ce régime vous ne tiendrez pas longtemps at this rate you won't last long **5.** GÉOGR ▶ **régime d'un fleuve** rate of flow, regimen of a river ▶ **régime**

des pluies rainfall pattern **6.** BOT ▶ **un régime de bananes** a hand ou stem ou bunch of bananas ▶ **un régime de dattes** a bunch ou cluster of dates.

 Régime de Sécurité sociale

The French **Sécurité sociale** system is divided into the following types of **régimes:**

1. **Le régime général des salariés,** which provides social security cover for people in paid employment.

2. **Le régime agricole,** for farmers.

3. **Le régime social des indépendants,** for the self-employed.

In addition to these main **régimes,** there are the **régimes spéciaux,** which provide tailor-made cover for certain socioprofessional groups (civil servants, miners, students, etc.), and the **régimes complémentaires,** which provide additional retirement cover for wage-earners.

---

régiment [ʀeʒimɑ̃] nm MIL [unité] regiment.

région [ʀeʒjɔ̃] nf **1.** GÉOGR region / *les habitants de Paris et sa région* the inhabitants of Paris and the surrounding region ou area / *le nouveau médecin n'est pas de la région* the new doctor isn't from the area ou from around here ▶ **la région parisienne** the Paris area, the area around Paris **2.** ANAT ▶ **région cervicale / lombaire** cervical / lumbar region. ❖ **Région** nf ADMIN region *(French administrative area made up of several departments).*

 Région

One of the three main administrative divisions in France, the **Région** was created in 1982. There are twenty-six in all, four of which are overseas. Each **Région** groups together several **départements** and is administered by a **conseil régional,** headed by the **président du conseil régional.**

---

régional, e, aux [ʀeʒjɔnal, o] adj [de la région] regional ; [de la localité] local.

régir [32] [ʀeʒiʀ] vt to govern.

régisseur, euse [ʀeʒisœʀ, øz] nm, f **1.** [d'un domaine] steward **2.** CINÉ & TV assistant director ; THÉÂTRE stage manager / *régisseur de plateau* floor manager.

registre [ʀəʒistʀ] nm **1.** ADMIN & DR register ▶ **s'inscrire au registre du commerce** to register one's company ▶ **registre de l'état civil** ≃ register of births, marriages and deaths **2.** IMPR & INFORM register **3.** MUS [d'un orgue] stop ; [d'une voix] range, register / *un registre aigu / grave* a high / low pitch **4.** LING register, level of language.

réglage [ʀeglaʒ] nm **1.** [mise au point] adjustment, regulation **2.** AUTO, RADIO & TV tuning.

règle [ʀɛgl] nf **1.** [instrument] ruler ▶ **règle à calcul** slide rule **2.** [principe, code] rule / *les règles de l'honneur* the rules ou code of honour / *il est de règle de porter une cravate ici* it's usual to wear a tie here / *les règles de base en grammaire* the basic rules of grammar ▶ **la règle du jeu** the rules of the game ▶ **règle d'or** golden rule ▶ **dans les règles**

(de l'art) according to the (rule) book. ❖ **règles** nfpl PHYSIOL [en général] periods ; [d'un cycle] period / *avoir ses règles* to be menstruating, to be having one's period / *avoir des règles douloureuses* to suffer from period ou pains [UK], to suffer from menstrual cramps [US], to have painful periods. ❖ **en règle** loc adj ▶ **être en règle a)** [document] to be in order **b)** [personne] to have one's papers in order, to be in possession of valid papers. ❖ **en règle générale** loc adv generally, as a (general) rule.

réglé, e [ʀegle] adj **1.** [organisé] regular, well-ordered **2.** [rayé ou quadrillé] ▶ **papier réglé** ruled ou lined paper. ❖ **réglée** adj f ▶ **être réglée** [avoir ses règles] : *depuis combien de temps êtes-vous réglée ?* how long have you been having your periods?

règlement [ʀɛgləmɑ̃] nm **1.** ADMIN regulation, rules / *d'après le règlement, il est interdit de...* it's against the regulations to... ▶ **règlement intérieur** house rules **2.** [paiement] payment, settlement / *règlement par carte de crédit* payment by credit card **3.** [résolution] settlement, settling ▶ **règlement de compte** ou **comptes** settling of scores.

réglementaire, règlementaire* [ʀɛgləmɑ̃tɛʀ] adj [conforme] regulation *(modif).*

réglementation, règlementation* [ʀɛgləmɑ̃tasjɔ̃] nf **1.** [mesures] regulations **2.** [limitation] control, regulation / *la réglementation des prix* price controls.

réglementer, règlementer* [3] [ʀɛgləmɑ̃te] vt to regulate, to control / *la vente des boissons alcoolisées est très réglementée* the sale of alcoholic drinks is under strict control ou is strictly controlled.

régler [18] [ʀegle] vt **1.** [résoudre -litige] to settle, to resolve ; [-problème] to solve, to iron out *(sép)*, to sort out *(sép)* / *c'est une affaire réglée* it is (all) settled now **2.** [payer -achat] to pay (for) ; [-facture, mensualité] to settle ; [-créancier] to settle up *(insép)* with ▶ **régler l'addition** to pay ou settle the bill ▶ **régler qqch en espèces** to pay cash for sthg ▶ **régler qqch par chèque / par carte de crédit** to pay for sthg by cheque / by credit card ▶ **avoir un compte à régler avec qqn** : *j'ai un compte à régler avec toi* I've got a bone to pick with you ▶ **régler son compte à qqn a)** *fam* [se venger de lui] to get even with sb **b)** [le tuer] to take care of sb *euphém* **3.** [volume, allumage, phare, etc.] to adjust ; [vitesse, thermostat] to set ; [température] to regulate ; [circulation] to control ; [moteur] to tune / *j'ai réglé mon réveil sur 7 h / le four à 200 °* I've set my alarm for seven o'clock / the oven at 200 degrees ▶ **régler qqch sur** [accorder par rapport à] to set sthg by / *régler son rythme sur celui du soleil* to model one's rhythm of life on the movement of the sun.

✍ In reformed spelling (see p. 16-18), this verb is conjugated like *semer : il règlera, elle règlerait.*

réglisse [ʀeglis] nf liquorice [UK], licorice [US] / *bâton / rouleau de réglisse* stick / roll of liquorice.

réglo [ʀeglo] adj inv *tfam* regular, OK, on the level.

régnant, e [ʀeɲɑ̃, ɑ̃t] adj [qui règne] reigning.

règne [ʀɛɲ] nm **1.** [gouvernement] reign / *sous le règne de Catherine II* in the reign of Catherine II **2.** BIOL ▶ **règne animal / végétal** animal / plant kingdom.

régner [8] [ʀeɲe] vi **1.** [gouverner] to reign, to rule **2.** [dominer -idée] to predominate, to prevail ; [-ordre, silence] to reign, to prevail / *le chaos règne* chaos reigns ou prevails ▶ **régner sur** to rule over / *faire régner le silence* to keep everybody quiet ▶ **faire régner l'ordre** to keep things under control / *un dictateur qui a fait régner la terreur* a dictator who established a reign of terror.

✍ In reformed spelling (see p. 16-18), this verb is conjugated like *semer : il règnera, elle règnerait.*

---

* In reformed spelling (see p. 16-18).

regonfler [3] [ʀəgɔ̃fle] vt **1.** [gonfler de nouveau - ballon, bouée] to blow up *(sép)* (again), to reinflate ; [- matelas pneumatique] to pump up *(sép)* (again), to reinflate / *son séjour à la mer l'a regonflée à bloc* fam & fig her stay at the seaside has bucked her up (no end) **2.** [gonfler davantage - pneus] to put more air in ou into.

regorger [17] [ʀəgɔʀʒe] ❖ **regorger de** v + prép to overflow with *(insép)*, to abound in *(insép)* / *la terre regorge d'eau* the ground is waterlogged / *les vitrines regorgent de marchandises* the shop windows are packed with goods.

régresser [4] [ʀegʀese] vi **1.** [baisser - chiffre, population] to drop / *le chiffre d'affaires a régressé* there has been a drop in turnover ; [civilisation] to regress **2.** PSYCHOL to regress.

régression [ʀegʀesjɔ̃] nf **1.** [recul] decline, decrease, regression **2.** PSYCHOL & SCI regression.

regret [ʀəgʀɛ] nm **1.** [remords] regret / *sans un regret* without a single regret / **'regrets éternels'** 'deeply regretted', 'greatly lamented' **2.** [tristesse] regret ▶ **nous sommes au** ou **nous avons le regret de vous annoncer que...** we are sorry ou we regret to have to inform you that... ❖ **à regret** loc adv [partir, sévir] regretfully, with regret.

regrettable [ʀəgʀetabl] adj regrettable, unfortunate / *il est regrettable que tu n'aies pas été informée à temps* it is unfortunate ou a pity (that) you were not informed in time.

regretter [4] [ʀəgʀete] vt **1.** [éprouver de la nostalgie pour - personne, pays] to miss ; [- jeunesse, passé] to be nostalgic for / *son regretté mari* her late lamented husband **2.** [se repentir de] to be sorry about, to regret / *je ne regrette rien* I've no regrets / *vous regretterez vos paroles !* you'll be sorry that you said that!, you'll regret those words! ❖ **regretter de** v + prép [dans des expressions de politesse] : *nous regrettons de ne pouvoir donner suite à votre appel* we regret ou we are sorry we are unable to connect you.

⚠ Attention, **to regret** ne doit pas être employé systématiquement pour traduire regretter. Voir article.

regroupement [ʀəgʀupmɑ̃] nm : *regroupement de troupes* gathering ou grouping together of troops / *le regroupement des différentes tendances politiques* the rallying (together) of various shades of political opinion.

regrouper [3] [ʀəgʀupe] vt [rassembler] to bring together *(sép)*, to group ou to gather together *(sép)*. ❖ **se regrouper** vpi [institutions] to group together ; [foule] to gather.

régularisation [ʀegylaʀizasjɔ̃] nf **1.** [d'une situation] straightening out, regularization **2.** FIN : *paiement de dix mensualités avec régularisation annuelle* ten monthly payments with end-of-year adjustments.

régulariser [3] [ʀegylaʀize] vt **1.** [rendre légal] to regularize / *il a fait régulariser son permis de séjour* he got his residence permit sorted out ou put in order **2.** [rendre régulier] to regulate.

régularité [ʀegylaʀite] nf **1.** [dans le temps] regularity, steadiness / *les factures tombent avec régularité* there's a steady flow of bills to pay **2.** [dans l'espace - de la dentition] evenness ; [- d'une surface] smoothness ; [- de plantations] straightness **3.** [en valeur, en intensité] consistency **4.** [légalité] lawfulness, legality.

régulateur [ʀegylatœʀ] nm [dispositif, horloge] regulator.

régulation [ʀegylasjɔ̃] nf [contrôle] control, regulation ; [réglage] regulation, correction / *régulation de la circulation* traffic control.

réguler [3] [ʀegyle] vt to control.

régulier, ère [ʀegylje, ɛʀ] adj **1.** [fixe] regular / *manger à heures régulières* to eat regularly ou at regular intervals ; [permanent] regular ▶ **les vols réguliers** scheduled flights ▶ **armée régulière** regular ou standing army **2.** [dans l'espace - gén] regular, even ; [- plantations] evenly distributed / *une écriture régulière* regular ou neat handwriting **3.** [montée, déclin] steady ; [distribution] even / *être régulier dans son travail* to be a steady worker **4.** [harmonieux - traits] regular **5.** [conforme à la règle - transaction] legitimate ; [- procédure] correct, fair ; [conforme à la loi] legal ▶ **être en situation régulière** to be in line with the law **6.** fam [honnête] on the level, straight **7.** BOT, GÉOM, LING & ZOOL regular. ❖ **régulière** nf fam & hum ▶ **ma régulière a)** [épouse] my missus, my old lady **b)** [maîtresse] my girlfriend.

régulièrement [ʀegyljɛʀmɑ̃] adv **1.** [dans l'espace - disposer] evenly, regularly, uniformly **2.** [dans le temps - progresser] steadily / *je la vois assez régulièrement* I see her quite regularly ou quite frequently **3.** [selon la règle] lawfully.

réhabilitation [ʀeabilitasjɔ̃] nf **1.** DR rehabilitation **2.** [d'une personne] rehabilitation, clearing the name of **3.** [d'un quartier] rehabilitation.

réhabiliter [3] [ʀeabilite] vt **1.** DR [condamné] to rehabilitate ; [failli] to discharge **2.** [revaloriser - profession] to rehabilitate, to restore to favour 🇬🇧 ou favor 🇺🇸 ; [- quartier] to rehabilitate.

réhabituer [7] [ʀeabitɥe] vt ▶ **réhabituer qqn à qqch** to get sb used to sthg again. ❖ **se réhabituer à** vp + prép to get used to again ▶ **se réhabituer à faire qqch** to get back into the habit of doing sthg.

rehausser [3] [ʀəose] vt **1.** [surélever - plafond] to raise ; [- mur] to make higher **2.** [faire ressortir - goût] to bring out ; [- beauté, couleur] to emphasize, to enhance.

réhydrater [3] [ʀeidʀate] vt [peau] to moisturize, to rehydrate spéc.

réimpression [ʀeɛ̃pʀesjɔ̃] nf [processus] reprinting ; [résultat] reprint / *ce livre est en cours de réimpression* this book is being reprinted.

réimprimer [3] [ʀeɛ̃pʀime] vt to reprint.

rein [ʀɛ̃] nm **1.** ANAT kidney ▶ **rein artificiel** artificial kidney, kidney machine **2.** CONSTR springer. ❖ **reins** nmpl [dos] back, loin sout ; litt [taille] waist ▶ **avoir mal aux reins** to have (a) backache ▶ **avoir les reins solides** to have good financial backing.

réincarnation [ʀeɛ̃kaʀnasjɔ̃] nf RELIG reincarnation.

réincarner [3] [ʀeɛ̃kaʀne] ❖ **se réincarner** vpi to be reincarnated / *il voulait se réincarner en oiseau* he wanted to be reincarnated as a bird.

reine [ʀɛn] nf **1.** [femme du roi] queen (consort) ; [souveraine] queen / *la reine de Suède / des Pays-Bas* the Queen of Sweden / of the Netherlands ▶ **la reine mère** the Queen Mother **2.** fig [qui domine] queen / *la reine de la soirée* the belle of the ball, the star of the party / *tu es vraiment la reine des imbéciles* you're the most stupid woman I've ever come across ▶ **reine de beauté** beauty queen ▶ **la petite reine** vieilli the bicycle.

reine-claude [ʀɛnklod] (*pl* **reines-claudes**) nf (Reine Claude) greengage.

réinitialiser [ʀeinisjalize] vt INFORM to reinitialize.

réinscriptible [ʀeɛ̃skʀiptibl] adj [disque compact] rewritable.

réinscrire [99] [ʀeɛ̃skʀiʀ] vt [étudiant] to reregister, to reenroll 🇬🇧, re-enroll 🇺🇸 ; [électeur] to reregister ; [sur un agenda] to put down *(sép)* again. ❖ **se réinscrire** vp *(emploi réfléchi)* to reregister, to re-enrol 🇬🇧 ou reenroll 🇺🇸.

réinsérer [18] [ʀeɛ̃seʀe] vt **1.** [paragraphe] to reinsert **2.** [détenu, drogué] to rehabilitate, to reintegrate. ❖ **se réinsérer** vp (emploi réfléchi) to rehabilitate o.s., to become rehabilitated.

✍ In reformed spelling (see p. 16-18), this verb is conjugated like semer : il réinsèrera, elle réinsèrerait.

réinsertion [ʀeɛ̃sɛʀsjɔ̃] nf [d'un détenu] rehabilitation ▸ **la réinsertion sociale** social rehabilitation, reintegration into society.

réinstaller [3] [ʀeɛ̃stale] vt [chauffage, électricité, téléphone] to reinstall, to put back (sép) / j'ai réinstallé mon bureau au premier étage I've moved my office back to the first floor. ❖ **se réinstaller** vpi **1.** [retourner] to go back, to settle again / il s'est réinstallé dans son ancien bureau he's gone ou moved back to his old office **2.** [se rasseoir] to settle (back) down in one's seat.

réintégrer [18] [ʀeɛ̃tegʀe] vt [employer à nouveau] to reinstate.

✍ In reformed spelling (see p. 16-18), this verb is conjugated like semer : il réintègrera, elle réintègrerait.

réitérer [18] [ʀeiteʀe] vt sout [interdiction, demande] to reiterate, to repeat.

✍ In reformed spelling (see p. 16-18), this verb is conjugated like semer : il réitèrera, elle réitèrerait.

rejaillir [32] [ʀəʒajiʀ] vi **1.** [gicler - gén] to splash (back) ; [- violemment] to spurt (up) **2.** sout [se répercuter] : sa notoriété a rejailli sur nous tous his fame reflected on ou was shared by all of us / la honte rejaillit sur lui he was covered in shame.

rejet [ʀəʒɛ] nm **1.** [physique] throwing back ou up, driving back / interdire le rejet de substances polluantes to prohibit the discharge of pollutants **2.** [refus] rejection ▸ **phénomène de rejet** : les enfants handicapés sont parfois victimes d'un phénomène de rejet à l'école handicapped children are sometimes rejected by other children at school **3.** LITTÉR [enjambement] run-on / il y a rejet du verbe à la fin de la proposition subordonnée GRAM the verb is put ou goes at the end of the subordinate clause **4.** MÉD rejection ▸ **rejet d'une greffe** rejection of a transplant **5.** GÉOL throw **6.** BOT shoot.

rejeter [27] [ʀəʒte] vt **1.** [relancer] to throw back (sép) ; [violemment] to hurl back (sép) ; fig : elle rejeta ses cheveux en arrière she tossed her hair back / rejeter la tête en arrière to throw one's head back **2.** [repousser - ennemi] to drive ou to push back (sép) / rejeter une armée audelà des frontières to drive an army back over the border ; [bannir] to reject, to cast out (sép), to expel / la société les rejette society rejects them ou casts them out **3.** [rendre - nourriture] to spew out (sép), to throw up (sép), to reject ; [- déchets] to throw out (sép), to expel / la mer a rejeté plusieurs épaves several wrecks were washed up ou cast up by the sea **4.** [refuser] to reject, to turn down (sép) / rejeter un projet de loi to throw out a bill **5.** [déplacer] ▸ **rejeter la faute / la responsabilité sur qqn** to shift the blame / responsibility on to sb. ❖ **se rejeter** ◆ vpi : se rejeter en arrière to jump backwards. ◆ vpt [se renvoyer] : ils se rejettent mutuellement la responsabilité de l'accident they blame each other for the accident.

rejeton [ʀəʒtɔ̃] nm péj **ou** hum [enfant] kid.

rejoindre [82] [ʀəʒwɛ̃dʀ] vt **1.** [retrouver] to meet (up with) (insép), to join ; [avec effort] to catch up with **2.** [retourner à] to get back ou to return to / il a reçu l'ordre de rejoindre son régiment he was ordered to rejoin his regiment **3.** [aboutir à] to join ou to meet (up with) **4.** [être d'accord avec] to agree with / je ne peux vous rejoindre sur ce point I cannot agree ou see eye to eye with you (on this matter) ; POL [adhérer à] to join / elle a fini par rejoindre l'opposition she ended up joining the opposition.

❖ **se rejoindre** vp (emploi réciproque) **1.** [se réunir] to meet again ou up / nous nous rejoindrons à Marseille we'll meet up in Marseille **2.** [concorder] : nos opinions se rejoignent entièrement our views concur perfectly, we are in total agreement.

réjoui, e [ʀeʒwi] adj joyful, happy, pleased.

réjouir [32] [ʀeʒwiʀ] vt to delight / ça ne me réjouit guère d'y aller I'm not particularly keen on ou thrilled at going. ❖ **se réjouir** vpi to be delighted / se réjouir du malheur des autres to gloat over other people's misfortunes / je me réjouis de votre succès I'm glad to hear of your success / je me réjouis à la pensée de les retrouver I'm thrilled at the idea of meeting them again / je m'en réjouis d'avance I'm really looking forward to it.

réjouissance [ʀeʒwisɑ̃s] nf [gaieté] rejoicing. ❖ **réjouissances** nfpl [fête] festivities / quel est le programme des réjouissances ? hum what exciting things lie in store for us today?

réjouissant, e [ʀeʒwisɑ̃, ɑ̃t] adj joyful, cheerful.

relâche [ʀəlɑʃ] nf **1.** CINÉ & THÉÂTRE [fermeture] : nous ferons relâche en août no performances in August / 'relâche le mardi' 'no performance on Tuesdays' **2.** ⒬ SCOL break. ❖ **sans relâche** loc adv without respite, continuously.

relâché, e [ʀəlɑʃe] adj [négligé - discipline, effort] lax, loose ; [- style] flowing, loose péj.

relâchement [ʀəlɑʃmɑ̃] nm **1.** [laisser-aller] laxity, loosening / il y a du relâchement dans votre travail you're letting your work slide / le relâchement des mœurs the laxity of ou decline in moral standards **2.** MÉD [de l'intestin] loosening ; [d'un muscle] relaxation **3.** [d'une corde, d'un lien] loosening, slackening.

relâcher [3] [ʀəlɑʃe] vt **1.** [libérer - animal] to free ; [- prisonnier] to release, to set free (sép) **2.** [diminuer] to relax, to slacken / relâcher son attention to let one's attention wander **3.** [détendre - câble] to loosen, to slacken ; [- muscle] to relax / elle a relâché son étreinte she relaxed ou loosened her grip **4.** MÉD [intestin] to loosen. ❖ **se relâcher** vpi **1.** [muscle] to relax, to loosen ; [câble] to loosen, to slacken **2.** [devenir moins rigoureux] to become lax ou laxer / se relâcher dans son travail to become lax about one's work.

relais, relai* [ʀəlɛ] nm **1.** [succession] shift ▸ **prendre le relais (de qqn)** to take over (from sb) **2.** SPORT relay **3.** [auberge] inn, post house ▸ **relais autoroutier** motorway café ⓤⓚ, truck stop ⓤⓢ **4.** (comme adjectif, avec ou sans trait d'union) ÉLECTR [appareil, station] relay (modif) ; [processus] relaying **5.** TÉLÉC ▸ **relais hertzien** radio relay **6.** BANQUE ▸ **(crédit) relais** bridging loan.

relance [ʀəlɑ̃s] nf **1.** [nouvelle impulsion] revival, boost **2.** ÉCON : il y a une relance de la production sidérurgique steel production is being boosted ou increased ▸ **politique de relance** reflationary policy ▸ **relance économique** reflation **3.** ADMIN & COMM : lettre de relance follow-up letter.

relancer [16] [ʀəlɑ̃se] vt **1.** [donner un nouvel essor à] to relaunch, to revive ▸ **relancer l'économie d'un pays** to give a boost to ou to boost ou to reflate a country's economy **2.** [solliciter] to chase up ⓤⓚ, to chase after fig / elle s'est déjà fait relancer trois fois par la banque she's already had three reminders from her bank.

relater [3] [ʀəlate] vt **1.** sout [raconter] to relate, to recount **2.** DR [consigner] to record.

relatif, ive [ʀəlatif, iv] adj **1.** [gén & GRAM & MATH] relative ▸ **tout est relatif** it's all relative **2.** ▸ **relatif à** [concernant] relating to, concerning **3.** [approximatif] : nous avons goûté un repos tout relatif we enjoyed a rest of sorts. ❖ **relatif** nm GRAM relative pronoun. ❖ **relative** nf relative clause.

* In reformed spelling (see p. 16-18).

relation [rəlasjɔ̃] nf **1.** [corrélation] relationship, connection / *relation de cause à effet* relation ou relationship of cause and effect / *c'est sans relation avec..., il n'y a aucune relation avec...* there's no connection with..., it's nothing to do with... **2.** [rapport] relationship ▶ **avoir de bonnes / mauvaises relations avec qqn** to be on good / bad terms with sb ▶ **en relation** ou **relations** : *nous sommes en relation d'affaires depuis des années* we've had business dealings ou a business relationship for years / *en excellentes / mauvaises relations avec ses collègues* on excellent / bad terms with one's colleagues ▶ **entrer en relation avec qqn** [le contacter] to get in touch ou to make contact with sb ▶ **mettre qqn en relation avec un ami / une organisation** to put sb in touch with a friend / an organization ▶ **relations diplomatiques** diplomatic relations ou links ▶ **relations humaines a)** [gén] dealings between people **b)** SOCIOL human relations ▶ **relations publiques** public relations ▶ **relations sexuelles** sexual relations **3.** [connaissance] acquaintance ▶ **avoir de nombreuses relations** to know a lot of people.

 relation ou **relationship ?**

Attention à ne pas traduire une relation par a **relation**, qui signifie « un parent ». Une relation est le plus souvent a **relationship**. Le nom pluriel **relations** en anglais se réfère principalement aux échanges diplomatiques ou professionnels (**public relations, customer relations, diplomatic relations**).

relationnel, elle [rəlasjɔnɛl] adj **1.** PSYCHOL relationship *(modif)* / *avoir des difficultés relationnelles* to have trouble relating to people **2.** LING relational, relation *(modif)*.

relativement [rəlativmɑ̃] adv [passablement] relatively, comparatively, reasonably. ❖ **relativement à** loc prép **1.** [par rapport à] compared to, in relation to **2.** [concernant] concerning.

relativiser [3] [rəlativize] vt ▶ **relativiser qqch** to consider sthg in context, to relativize sthg *spéc* / *il faut relativiser tout ceci, ça pourrait être pire* you've got to keep things in perspective, it could be worse.

relativité [rəlativite] nf [gén] relativity.

relax [rəlaks] adj inv *fam* [personne, ambiance] easy-going, laid back ; [activité, vacances] relaxing ▶ **fauteuil relax** reclining chair.

relaxant, e [rəlaksɑ̃, ɑ̃t] adj relaxing, soothing.

relaxation [rəlaksasjɔ̃] nf [détente] relaxation, relaxing / *faire de la relaxation* to do relaxation exercises.

relaxe [rəlaks] ❖ adj *fam* = **relax.** ❖ nf DR discharge, release.

relaxer [3] [rəlakse] vt **1.** [relâcher - muscle] to relax **2.** DR [prisonnier] to discharge, to release. ❖ **se relaxer** vpi to relax.

relayer [11] [rəleje] vt **1.** [suppléer] to relieve, to take over from **2.** RADIO & TV to relay. ❖ **se relayer** vp *(emploi réciproque)* to take turns.

relecture [rələktyr] nf : *à la relecture, j'ai trouvé que...* on reading it again ou when I reread it, I found that...

relégation [rəlegasjɔ̃] nf SPORT relegation.

reléguer [18] [rəlege] vt [cantonner] to relegate ▶ **reléguer qqn au second plan** to put sb in the background / *leur équipe a été reléguée en deuxième division cette*

année SPORT their team went down into the second division this year.

✎ In reformed spelling (see p. 16-18), this verb is conjugated like *semer* : *il relèguera, elle reléguerait.*

relent [rəlɑ̃] nm *(gén au pl)* [mauvaise odeur] stink *(U)*, stench *(U)* / *des relents de tabac froid* a stench of stale tobacco.

relève [rəlɛv] nf [manœuvre] relieving, changing ▶ **prendre la relève (de qqn)** to take over (from sb) ▶ **la relève de la garde** the changing of the guard.

relevé, e [rəlve] adj **1.** [redressé - col, nez] turned-up **2.** CULIN [assaisonné] seasoned, well-seasoned ; [pimenté] spicy, hot **3.** *sout* [distingué] elevated, refined. ❖ **relevé** nm **1.** [de recettes, de dépenses] summary, statement ; [de gaz, d'électricité] reading ; [de noms] list ▶ **relevé mensuel** BANQUE monthly statement ▶ **relevé d'identité bancaire** ≃ particulars of one's bank account ; ≃ bank details ▶ **relevé de notes** ÉDUC examination results **2.** ARCHIT layout.

relèvement [rəlɛvmɑ̃] nm **1.** [rétablissement] recovery, restoring **2.** [fait d'augmenter] raising ; [résultat] increase, rise / *le relèvement des impôts / des salaires* tax / salary increase.

relever [19] [rəlve] ❖ vt **1.** [redresser - lampe, statue] to stand up *(sép)* again ; [-chaise] to pick up *(sép)* ; [-tête] to lift up *(sép)* again ▶ **ils m'ont relevé a)** [debout] they helped me (back) to my feet **b)** [assis] they sat me up ou helped me to sit up **2.** [remonter - store] to raise ; [-cheveux] to put up *(sép)* ; [-col, visière] to turn up *(sép)* ; [-pantalon, manches] to roll up *(sép)* ; [-rideaux] to tie back *(sép)* ; [-strapontin] to lift up *(sép)* **3.** [augmenter - prix, salaires] to increase, to raise, to put up *(sép)* ; [-notes] to put up, to raise **4.** [ramasser, recueillir] to pick up *(sép)* / *relever les copies* ÉDUC to collect the papers **5.** [remettre en état - mur] to rebuild, to re-erect ; [-pylône] to re-erect, to put up *(sép)* again / *c'est lui qui a relevé la nation* fig he's the one who put the country back on its feet (again) ou got the country going again ▶ **relever l'économie** to rebuild the economy / *relever le moral des troupes* to boost the troops' morale **6.** [mettre en valeur] to enhance **7.** CULIN to season, to spice up *(sép)* **8.** [remarquer] to notice ▶ **elle n'a pas relevé l'allusion a)** [elle n'a pas réagi] she didn't pick up the hint **b)** [elle l'a sciemment ignorée] she pretended not to notice the hint **9.** [enregistrer - empreinte digitale] to record ; [-cote, mesure] to take down *(sép)*, to plot ; [-informations] to take ou to note down ; [-plan] to sketch ▶ **relever l'eau** *fam* ou **le compteur d'eau** to read the water meter / *relever le gaz* *fam* ou *le compteur de gaz* to read the gas meter / *températures relevées à 16 h* MÉTÉOR temperatures recorded at 4 p.m. **10.** [relayer - garde] to relieve ; [-coéquipier] to take over *(insép)* from ▶ **relever qqn de ses fonctions** to relieve sb of his / her duties. ❖ vi [remonter - vêtement] to ride up. ❖ **relever de** v + prép **1.** [être de la compétence de - juridiction] to fall ou to come under ; [-spécialiste] to be a matter for ; [-magistrat] to come under the jurisdiction of / *cela relève des tribunaux / de la psychiatrie* it's a matter for the courts / the psychiatrists **2.** [tenir de] ▶ **cela relève du miracle** it's truly miraculous **3.** *sout* [se rétablir de] : *relever de couches* to come out of confinement *sout* / *elle relève d'une grippe* she is recovering from flu. ❖ **se relever** ❖ vp *(emploi passif)* [être inclinable] to lift up. ❖ vpi [se remettre - debout] to get ou to stand up again ; [-assis] to sit up again / *il l'aida à se relever* he helped her to her feet again. ❖ **se relever de** vp + prép to recover from, to get over / *le parti se relève de ses cendres* ou *ruines* the party is rising from the ashes / *je ne m'en relèverai / ils ne s'en relèveront pas l'II / they'll never get over it.*

relief [rəljef] nm ART, GÉOGR & OPT relief / *la région a un relief accidenté* the area is hilly. ❖ **en relief**

◆ loc adj ART & IMPR relief *(modif)*, raised ▸ **lettres en relief** embossed letters / *motif en relief* raised design, design in relief. ◆ loc adv [en valeur] ▸ **mettre qqch en relief** to bring sthg out.

relier [9] [Rǝlje] vt **1.** [faire communiquer] to link up *(sép)*, to link (together), to connect / *la route qui relie Bruxelles à Ostende* the road running from ou linking Brussels to Ostend **2.** [mettre en rapport] to connect, to link (together), to relate **3.** [livre] to bind / *relié en cuir* leatherbound.

religieusement [Rǝliʒjøzmã] adv **1.** [pieusement] religiously ▸ **se marier religieusement** to get married in church **2.** [soigneusement] religiously, rigorously, scrupulously ; [avec vénération] reverently, devoutly.

religieux, euse [Rǝliʒjø, øz] adj [cérémonie, éducation, ordre, art] religious. ❖ **religieux** nm member of a religious order. ❖ **religieuse** nf **1.** RELIG nun **2.** CULIN cream puff.

religion [Rǝliʒjɔ̃] nf [croyance] religion ▸ **entrer en religion** to join a religious order.

reliquat [Rǝlika] nm remainder, balance.

relique [Rǝlik] nf RELIG relic.

relire [106] [RǝliR] vt to read again, to reread. ❖ **se relire** vp *(emploi réfléchi)* to read (over) what one has written / *j'ai du mal à me relire* I have difficulty reading my own writing.

relish [Rǝliʃ] nf QUÉBEC CULIN relish.

reliure [RǝljyR] nf **1.** [technique] binding, bookbinding **2.** [couverture] binding.

relocalisation [Rǝlokalizasjɔ̃] nf relocation.

relocaliser [Rǝlokalize] vt to relocate.

reloger [17] [RǝlɔƷe] vt to rehouse.

relookage [RǝlukaƷ] nm makeover ▸ *ils ont fait un relookage de leur site* they've given their website a makeover.

relooker [Rǝluke] vt [personne] to give a makeover to ; [produit, journal, site Web] to give a new look to.

relou [Rǝlu] adj fam [idiot] stupid / *tu deviens relou avec tes questions* [agaçant] your questions are starting to get on my nerves.

reluire [97] [RǝlɥiR] vi [casque, casserole] to gleam, to shine ; [pavé mouillé] to glisten.

reluisant, e [Rǝlɥizã, ãt] adj **1.** *(gén nég)* fam : *peu* ou *pas reluisant* [médiocre] shabby / *notre avenir n'apparaît guère reluisant* our future hardly looks bright **2.** [brillant] shining, shiny, gleaming.

reluquer [3] [Rǝlyke] vt fam [personne] to ogle, to eye up ; [objet] to have one's eye on, to covet.

remake [Rimɛk] nm CINÉ remake.

remaniement [Rǝmanimã] nm **1.** [d'un projet de loi] redrafting, altering, amending ; [d'un discours] revision, altering ; [d'un programme] modification **2.** [d'un gouvernement, d'un ministère] reshuffle ▸ **remaniement ministériel** cabinet reshuffle.

remanier [9] [Rǝmanje] vt **1.** [texte, discours] to revise ; [projet de loi] to draft again, to redraft **2.** [gouvernement, ministère] to reshuffle.

remaquiller [3] [Rǝmakije] vt to make up *(sép)* again. ❖ **se remaquiller** vp *(emploi réfléchi)* [entièrement] to reapply one's make-up ; [partiellement] to touch up one's make-up.

remarier [9] [RǝmaRje] ❖ **se remarier** vpi to get married ou to marry again, to remarry.

remarquable [RǝmaRkabl] adj **1.** [marquant] striking, notable, noteworthy / *un événement remarquable* a noteworthy event **2.** [émérite - personne] remarkable, outstanding, exceptional.

remarquablement [RǝmaRkablǝmã] adv remarkably, strikingly, outstandingly.

remarque [RǝmaRk] nf [opinion exprimée] remark, comment ; [critique] (critical) remark / *je l'ai trouvée insolente et je lui en ai fait la remarque* I thought she was insolent and (I) told her so / *j'en ai assez de tes remarques* I've had enough of your criticisms ▸ **faire une remarque à qqn sur qqch** to pass a remark to sb about sthg.

remarqué, e [RǝmaRke] adj conspicuous, noticeable, striking / *il a fait une intervention très remarquée* the speech he made attracted a great deal of attention / *une entrée remarquée* a conspicuous entrance.

remarquer [3] [RǝmaRke] vt **1.** [constater] to notice ▸ **faire remarquer qqch à qqn** to point sthg out to sb / *on m'a fait remarquer que... it's been pointed out to me ou it's been drawn to my attention that...* ▸ **je te ferais remarquer qu'il est déjà minuit** look, it's already midnight ▸ **remarque, je m'en moque éperdument** mind you, I really couldn't care less ; [distinguer] to notice ▸ **se faire remarquer** to draw attention to o.s. / *elle partit sans se faire remarquer* she left unnoticed ou without drawing attention to herself **2.** [marquer de nouveau - date, adresse] to write ou to note down *(sép)* again ; [- linge] to tag ou to mark again. ❖ **se remarquer** vp *(emploi passif)* [être visible] to be noticed, to show / *le défaut du tissu se remarque à peine* the flaw in the material is scarcely noticeable ou hardly shows.

> ⚠ Attention, **to remark** signifie remarquer au sens de « dire ». Il ne doit pas être employé systématiquement pour traduire les autres sens de remarquer.

rembarrer [3] [RãbaRe] vt fam ▸ **rembarrer qqn** to put sb in his place, to tell sb where to get off.

rembaucher [Rãboʃe] = réembaucher.

remblai [Rãblɛ] nm RAIL & TRAV PUB embankment ; [terre rapportée] ballast.

remblayer [11] [Rãbleje] vt TRAV PUB to bank up *(sép)* / *remblayer un fossé* to fill up a ditch.

rembobiner [3] [Rãbɔbine] vt [film, bande magnétique] to rewind, to spool back *(sép)*.

rembourrage [RãbuRaƷ] nm [d'un vêtement] padding ; [d'un siège] stuffing.

rembourrer [3] [RãbuRe] vt [coussin, manteau] to pad ; [siège] to stuff ; [personne] well-padded / *il est bien rembourré* fam & hum he's very well-padded.

remboursable [RãbuRsabl] adj [billet] refundable ; [prêt] repayable.

remboursement [RãbuRsǝmã] nm [d'un billet, d'un achat] refund ; [d'un prêt] repayment, settlement ; [d'une dépense] reimbursement ; FIN [d'une obligation] redemption.

rembourser [3] [RãbuRse] vt [argent] to pay back ou off *(sép)*, to repay ; [dépense, achat] to reimburse, to refund ; [personne] to pay back, to reimburse ; FIN [obligation] to redeem / *est-ce que tu peux me rembourser ?* can you pay me back? ▸ **se faire rembourser** to get a refund / *ce médicament n'est remboursé qu'à 40 % (par la Sécurité sociale)* only 40% of the price of this drug is refunded (by the Health Service).

rembrunir [32] [RãbRyniR] ❖ **se rembrunir** vpi [se renfrogner] to darken / *son visage s'est rembruni à l'annonce de la nouvelle* his face darkened when he heard the news.

remède [Rǝmɛd] nm **1.** [solution] remedy, cure **2.** [thérapeutique] cure, remedy / *le remède est pire que le mal* fig the remedy is worse than the disease **3.** *vieilli* [médicament] remedy ▸ **un remède de bonne femme** a traditional ou an old-fashioned remedy ▸ **un remède de cheval** a drastic remedy.

remédier [9] [ʀəmedje] ❖ **remédier à** v + prép **1.** [maladie] to cure ; [douleur] to alleviate, to relieve **2.** *sout* [problème] to remedy, to find a remedy ou solution for / *nous ne savons pas comment remédier à la situation* we don't know how to remedy the situation.

remémorer [3] [ʀəmemɔʀe] ❖ **se remémorer** vpt *sout* to recollect, to recall, to remember.

remerciement [ʀəmɛʀsimɑ̃] nm **1.** [action] thanks, thanking / *une lettre de remerciement* a letter of thanks, a thank-you letter **2.** [parole] *(je vous adresse) tous mes remerciements pour ce que vous avez fait* (I) thank you for what you did / *avec mes remerciements* with (many) thanks.

remercier [9] [ʀəmɛʀsje] vt **1.** [témoigner sa gratitude à] to thank ▸ **je te remercie** thank you **2.** [pour décliner une offre] : *encore un peu de thé ? — je vous remercie* would you like some more tea? — no, thank you **3.** *euphém* [licencier] to dismiss, to let go.

remettre [84] [ʀəmɛtʀ] vt **1.** [replacer - gén] to put back *(sép)* ; [- horizontalement] to lay, to put / *remets le livre où tu l'as trouvé* put the book back where you found it ; [personne] ▸ **remettre qqn debout** to stand sb up again ou sb back up / *je l'ai remis en pension* I sent him back to boarding school ▸ **remettre qqn sur le droit chemin** to set sb on the straight and narrow again **2.** [rétablir dans un état] ▸ **remettre qqch en marche** to get sthg going again ▸ **remettre qqch en état** to repair sthg ▸ **remettre qqch à neuf** to restore sthg **3.** [rajouter] to add / *il est assez puni comme ça, n'en remets pas* fam he's been punished enough already, no need to rub it in **4.** [vêtements, chaussures] to put on *(sép)* again, to put back on *(sép)* **5.** ▸ **remettre ça** fam: *voilà qu'elle remet ça !* there she goes again!, she's at it again! / *allez, on remet ça !* [au café] come on, let's have another round ou another one! **6.** [donner - colis, lettre, message] to deliver, to hand over *(sép)* ; [- objet, dossier à régler, rançon] to hand over *(sép)*, to give ; [- dossier d'inscription, dissertation] to hand ou to give in *(sép)* ; [- pétition, rapport] to present, to hand in ; [- démission] to hand in, to tender ; [- médaille, récompense] to present, to give / *on nous a remis 20 euros à chacun* we were each given 20 euros / *on lui a remis le prix Nobel* he was presented with ou awarded the Nobel prize **7.** [confier] to place **8.** [rendre - copies] to hand ou to give back *(sép)* ; [- clés] to hand back *(sép)*, to return / *l'enfant a été remis à sa famille* the child was returned to his family **9.** [ajourner - entrevue] to put off *(sép)*, to postpone, to put back *(sép)* ; [- décision] to put off *(sép)*, to defer / *la réunion a été remise à lundi* the meeting has been put off ou postponed until Monday **10.** MÉD [replacer - articulation, os] to put back *(sép)* **11.** [reconnaître - personne] to remember. ❖ **se remettre** ◆ vp *(emploi réfléchi)* [se livrer] ▸ **se remettre entre les mains de qqn** to put ou to place o.s. in sb's hands. ◆ vpi **1.** [se replacer - dans une position, un état] : *se remettre au lit* to go back to bed / *se remettre debout* to stand up again, to get back up / *se remettre en route* to get started ou going again ▸ **se remettre avec qqn a)** [se réconcilier] to make it up with sb **b)** [se réinstaller] to go ou to be back with sb again **2.** [guérir] to recover, to get better ▸ **se remettre de qqch** to get over sthg. ❖ **se remettre à** vp + prép **1.** [recommencer à] ▸ **se remettre à (faire) qqch** to start (doing) sthg again, to take up (doing) sthg again **2.** MÉTÉOR : *la pluie se remet à tomber, il se remet à pleuvoir* the rain's starting again, it's started raining again. ❖ **s'en remettre à** vp + prép [se fier à] to

rely on, to leave it (up) to ▸ **s'en remettre à la décision de qqn** to leave it (up) to sb to decide.

réminiscence [ʀeminisɑ̃s] nf [souvenir] reminiscence, recollection.

remis, e [ʀəmi, iz] pp ⟶ **remettre**. ❖ **remise** nf **1.** [livraison] delivery / *remise d'une lettre / d'un paquet en mains propres* personal delivery of a letter / package / *la remise des clés sera faite par l'agence* the agency will be responsible for handing over the keys / *la remise de la rançon aura lieu derrière le garage* the ransom will be handed over ou paid behind the garage ▸ **remise des prix** ÉDUC prize-giving **2.** COMM [réduction] discount, reduction, remittance *spéc* / *une remise de 15 %* a 15% discount ▸ **faire une remise à qqn** to give sb a discount ou a reduction **3.** DR remission ▸ **remise de peine** reduction of (the) sentence **4.** [resserre] shed.

rémission [ʀemisjɔ̃] nf MÉD remission.

remixé, e [ʀəmikse] adj remastered / *remixé en numérique* digitally remastered.

remixer [ʀəmikse] vt to remix.

remmener [19] [ʀɑ̃mne] vt [au point de départ] to take back ; [à soi] to bring back *(sép)* / *je te remmènerai chez toi en voiture* I'll drive you back home.

remodeler [25] [ʀəmɔdle] vt [silhouette, traits] to remodel.

remontant, e [ʀəmɔ̃tɑ̃, ɑ̃t] adj **1.** BOT [fraisier] double-cropping, remontant *spéc* ; [rosier] remontant **2.** [fortifiant] invigorating. ❖ **remontant** nm tonic.

remonté, e [ʀəmɔ̃te] adj *fam* **1.** [plein d'énergie] full of beans **2.** [irrité] ▸ **remonté contre qqn / qqch** up in arms about sb / sthg. ❖ **remontée** nf [rattrapage] catching up / *le coureur colombien a fait une belle remontée face à ses adversaires* the Colombian competitor is catching up with his opponents / *on constate une brusque remontée de la cote du président* the popularity of the President has shot up. ❖ **remontée mécanique** nf ski lift.

remonte-pente [ʀəmɔ̃tpɑ̃t] *(pl* remonte-pentes*)* nm ski tow.

remonter [3] [ʀəmɔ̃te] ◆ vt **1.** [côte, étage] to go ou to climb back up **2.** [porter - à nouveau] to take back up **3.** [parcourir - en voiture, en bateau, etc.] to go up *(insép)* / *les saumons remontent le fleuve* the salmon are swimming upstream / *nous avons remonté la Seine en voiture jusqu'à Rouen* we drove along the Seine (up-river) to Rouen / *remonter la rue* to go ou to walk back up the street ▸ **en remontant le cours des siècles** ou **du temps** going back several centuries **4.** [relever - chaussette] to pull up *(sép)* ; [- manche] to roll up *(sép)* ; [- col, visière] to raise, to turn up *(sép)* ; [- robe] to raise, to lift ; [- store] to pull up, to raise ▸ **remonter qqch** to put sthg higher up, to raise sthg / *remonte ton pantalon* pull your trousers UK ou pants US up / *elle a remonté la vitre* she wound the window up ; [augmenter - salaire, notation] to increase, to raise, to put up *(sép)* **5.** [assembler à nouveau - moteur, kit] to reassemble, to put back *(sép)* together (again) ; [- étagère] to put back *(sép)* up ; CINÉ [film] to reedit **6.** COMM [rouvrir] to set up *(sép)* again **7.** [renouveler] to restock, to stock up again **8.** [mécanisme, montre] to wind (up) **9.** [ragaillardir - physiquement] to pick up *(sép)* ; [- moralement] to cheer up *(sép)* ▸ **remonter le moral à qqn** to cheer sb up **10.** SPORT [concurrent] to catch up (with) **11.** THÉÂTRE to stage again, to put on (the stage) again. ◆ vi *(surtout aux être)* **1.** [monter de nouveau] to go back up, to go up again / *remonte dans ta chambre* go back up to your room **2.** TRANSP ▸ **remonter dans a)** [bateau, bus, train] to get back onto **b)** [voiture] to get back into ▸ **remonter à cheval a)** [se remettre en selle] to remount **b)** [refaire de l'équitation] to take up riding again **3.** [s'élever - route] to go back up, to go up again / *le sentier remonte jusqu'à la villa* the path goes up to the villa ; [avoir un niveau supérieur] **▸ le baromètre remonte** the barometer is rising / *tu remontes dans mon estime* you've gone up in my esteem **▸ ses actions remontent** *fig* things are looking up ou picking up for him **4.** [jupe] to ride ou to go up **5.** [faire surface - mauvaise odeur] to come back up **▸ remonter à la surface a)** [noyé] to float back (up) to the surface **b)** [plongeur] to resurface **c)** [scandale] to reemerge, to resurface **6.** [retourner vers l'origine] **▸ remonter dans le temps** to go back in time **▸ remonter à** [se reporter à] to go back to, to return to **▸ remonter à** [dater de] to go ou to date back to / *on fait généralement remonter la crise à 1910* the crisis is generally believed to have started in 1910 **7.** NAUT [navire] to sail north ; [vent] to come round the north. **◆ se remonter ◆** vp *(emploi passif)* : *ces nouvelles montres ne se remontent pas* these new watches don't have to be wound up. **◆** vp *(emploi réfléchi)* [physiquement] to recover one's strength ; [moralement] to cheer o.s. up / *se remonter le moral* to cheer o.s. up.

remontoir [Rəmɔ̃twaR] nm [d'une montre] winder.

remontrance [Rəmɔ̃tRɑ̃s] nf *(gén au pl)* *sout* [reproche] remonstrance, reproof **▸ faire des remontrances à qqn** to reprimand ou to admonish sb.

remontrer [3] [Rəmɔ̃tRe] vt **1.** [montrer de nouveau] to show again / *j'aimerais que tu me remontres comment tu as fait* I'd like you to show me again ou once more how you did it **2.** EXPR **en remontrer à qqn** : *crois-tu vraiment pouvoir m'en remontrer ?* do you really think you have anything to teach me?

remords [Rəmɔʀ] nm [repentir] remorse / *avoir des remords* to be full of remorse / *il a été pris de remords* his conscience got the better of him **▸ sans aucun remords** without a qualm, without any compunction, without (the slightest) remorse.

remorque [Rəmɔʀk] nf **1.** [traction - d'une voiture] towing ; [-d'un navire] tugging, towing / *câble de remorque* towline, towrope / *prendre une voiture en remorque* to tow a car / *'véhicule accidenté en remorque'* 'on tow' **2.** *fig* **être à la remorque de qqn** to tag (along) behind sb / *il est toujours à la remorque* he always lags behind.

remorquer [3] [Rəmɔʀke] vt [voiture] to tow ; [navire] to tug, to tow ; [masse] to haul / *se faire remorquer jusqu'au garage* to get a tow to the garage.

remorqueur [Rəmɔʀkœʀ] nm NAUT towboat, tug.

remous [Rəmu] nm **1.** [tourbillon] swirl, eddy ; [derrière un bateau] wash, backwash **2.** *sout* [réaction] stir, flurry / *l'article va sûrement provoquer quelques remous dans la classe politique* the article will doubtless cause a stir ou raise a few eyebrows in the political world.

rempailler [3] [Rɑ̃paje] vt [chaise] to reseat (with rushes).

rempart [Rɑ̃paR] nm **1.** [enceinte] rampart, bulwark **▸ les remparts** [d'une ville] ramparts, city walls **2.** *fig & litt* bulwark, bastion.

rempiler [3] [Rɑ̃pile] **◆** vt to pile (up) again. **◆** vi *arg mil* to re-enlist, to sign up again.

remplaçant, e [Rɑ̃plasɑ̃, ɑ̃t] nm, f **1.** [gén] replacement, stand-in ; UNIV supply 🇬🇧 ou substitute 🇺🇸 teacher ; [d'un médecin] replacement, locum 🇬🇧 **2.** SPORT reserve ; [au cours du match] substitute **3.** MUS, THÉÂTRE & TV understudy.

remplacement [Rɑ̃plasmɑ̃] nm **1.** [substitution] replacement **2.** [suppléance] **▸ faire des remplacements a)** [gén] to do temporary replacement work **b)** [comme secrétaire] to do temporary secretarial work **c)** [comme enseignant] to work as a supply 🇬🇧 ou substitute 🇺🇸 teacher. **◆ de remplacement** *loc adj* **▸ produit de remplacement** substitute product **▸ solution de remplacement** alternative ou fallback (solution).

remplacer [16] [Rɑ̃plase] vt **1.** [renouveler - pièce usagée] to replace, to change **2.** [mettre à la place de] to replace **3.** [prendre la place de] to replace, to take the place of / *dans de nombreuses tâches, la machine remplace maintenant l'homme* in a lot of tasks, machines are now taking over from men **4.** [suppléer] to stand in ou to substitute for / *je me suis fait remplacer par une collègue pendant mon absence* I got a colleague to replace me while I was away.

rempli, e [Rɑ̃pli] adj : *j'ai eu une journée bien remplie* I've had a very full ou busy day / *j'ai le ventre bien rempli, ça va mieux !* *fam* I feel a lot better for that meal!

remplir [32] [Rɑ̃pliR] vt **1.** [emplir] to fill **2.** [compléter - questionnaire, dossier] to fill in ou out *(sép)* ; [-chèque] to fill ou to make out *(sép)* **3.** [combler - trou] to fill in *(sép)* **4.** [accomplir - engagement] to fulfil ; [-fonction, mission] to carry out *(sép)* **5.** [satisfaire - condition] to fulfil, to satisfy, to meet ; [-besoin] to meet, to satisfy **6.** [d'émotion] **▸ remplir qqn de joie / d'espoir** to fill sb with joy / with hope. **◆ se remplir** vpi to fill (up).

remplissage [Rɑ̃plisaʒ] nm **1.** [d'une fosse, d'un récipient] filling (up) **2.** *fig* [d'un texte] padding / *faire du remplissage* to pad.

remploi [Rɑ̃plwa] nm **1.** [d'un travailleur] re-employment **2.** [d'une machine, de matériaux] reuse **3.** FIN reinvestment.

remployer [13] [Rɑ̃plwaje] vt **1.** [travailleur] to take on *(sép)* again, to re-employ **2.** [machine] to reuse, to use again **3.** FIN to reinvest.

remplumer [3] [Rɑ̃plyme] **◆ se remplumer** vpi *fam* **1.** [physiquement] to fill out again, to put weight back on **2.** [financièrement] to improve one's cash flow, to straighten out one's cash situation.

rempocher [3] [Rɑ̃pɔʃe] vt to pocket again, to put back in one's pocket.

remporter [3] [Rɑ̃pɔʀte] vt **1.** [reprendre] to take back *(sép)* **2.** [obtenir] to win, to get / *remporter un prix* to carry off ou to win a prize **▸ remporter un succès** to be successful **3.** SPORT to win.

rempoter [3] [Rɑ̃pɔte] vt to repot.

remuant, e [Rəmɥɑ̃, ɑ̃t] adj [agité] restless, fidgety.

remue-ménage [Rəmymenaʒ] *(pl* **remue-ménage** *ou* **remue-ménages****)* nm **1.** [d'objets] jumble, disorder **2.** [agitation bruyante] commotion, hurly-burly, rumpus.

remuer [7] [Rəmɥe] **◆** vt **1.** [agiter] to move, to shift / *la brise remue les branches / les herbes* the breeze is stirring the branches / the grass / *le chien remuait la queue* the dog was wagging its tail **2.** [déplacer - objet] to move, to shift **3.** [retourner - cendres] to poke ; [-terre, compost] to turn over *(sép)* ; [-salade] to toss ; [-boisson, préparation] to stir **▸ remuer ciel et terre** to move heaven and earth, to leave no stone unturned **4.** *sout* [ressasser] to stir up *(sép)*, to brood over *(sép)* **▸ remuer des souvenirs** to turn ou to go over memories **5.** [troubler] to move. **◆** vi **1.** [s'agiter - nez, oreille] to twitch **2.** [branler - dent, manche] to be loose **3.** [bouger] to move ; [gigoter] to fidget / *les gosses, ça remue tout le temps* *fam* kids can't stop fidgeting ou never keep still. **◆ se remuer** vpi **1.** [bouger] to move **2.** [se démener] to put o.s. out / *remue-toi un peu !* *fam* get a move on!, shift yourself!

rémunération [Remynerasjɔ̃] nf remuneration, payment.

rémunérer [18] [Remynere] vt to remunerate, to pay / *travail bien / mal rémunéré* well-paid / badly-paid work / *vous êtes-vous fait rémunérer pour ce travail ?* did you get paid for this job?

🖉 In reformed spelling (see p. 16-18), this verb is conjugated like *semer* : *il rémunèrera, elle rémunèrerait.*

renâcler [3] [ʀənakle] vi [personne] to grumble, to moan ▸ **renâcler à faire qqch** to be (very) loath ou reluctant to do sthg.

renaissance [ʀənɛsɑ̃s] nf **1.** [réincarnation] rebirth **2.** [renouveau] revival, rebirth.

Renaissance [ʀənɛsɑ̃s] ◆ nf ▸ **la Renaissance** the Renaissance (period). ◆ adj inv ARCHIT & ART Renaissance *(modif)*.

renaître, renaitre* [92] [ʀənɛtʀ] vi *(inusité aux temps composés)* **1.** [naître de nouveau - gén] to come back to life, to come to life again ; [- végétation] to spring up again ▸ **se sentir renaître** to feel like a new person ▸ **renaître de ses cendres** to rise from the ashes **2.** [revenir - jour] to dawn ; [- courage, économie] to revive, to recover ; [- bonheur, espoir] to return ▸ *faire renaître le passé / un antagonisme* to revive the past / an antagonism.

rénal, e, aux [ʀenal, o] adj kidney *(modif)*, renal *spéc*.

renard [ʀənaʀ] nm **1.** ZOOL fox **2.** *fig* ▸ **vieux renard** (sly) old fox, cunning old devil.

rencard [ʀɑ̃kaʀ] *tfam* = **rancard**.

rencarder [ʀɑ̃kaʀde] *tfam* = **rancarder**.

renchérir [32] [ʀɑ̃ʃeʀiʀ] vi [faire une surenchère] to make a higher bid, to bid higher. ◆ **renchérir sur** v + prép [obj : personne] to outbid ; [obj : enchère] to bid higher than ; [en actes ou en paroles] to go further than, to outdo / *il renchérit toujours sur ce que dit sa femme* he always goes further ou one better than his wife.

rencontre [ʀɑ̃kɔ̃tʀ] nf **1.** [entrevue] meeting, encounter ▸ **faire la rencontre de qqn** to meet sb / *faire des mauvaises rencontres* to meet the wrong kind of people ▸ **aller** ou **marcher à la rencontre de qqn** to go to meet sb **2.** [conférence] meeting, conference ▸ **rencontre au sommet** summit meeting **3.** SPORT match, game, fixture 🇬🇧 ▸ **une rencontre d'athlétisme** an athletics meeting. ◆ **de rencontre** loc adj [liaison] passing, casual ; [amitié] chance *(modif)*.

rencontrer [3] [ʀɑ̃kɔ̃tʀe] vt **1.** [croiser] to meet, to encounter *sout* ; [faire la connaissance de] to meet / *je l'ai rencontré (par hasard) au marché* I met him (by chance) ou ran into him at the market **2.** [affronter] to meet ; SPORT to play against *(insép)*, to meet **3.** [trouver] to meet with, to come across / *sans rencontrer la moindre résistance* without meeting with ou experiencing the least resistance. ◆ **se rencontrer** ◆ vp *(emploi réciproque)* [se trouver en présence] to meet / *c'est elle qui les a fait se rencontrer* she arranged for them to meet. ◆ vp *(emploi passif)* : *un homme intègre, ça ne se rencontre pas souvent* it's not often you come across ou meet an honest man.

rendement [ʀɑ̃dmɑ̃] nm **1.** [production] output **2.** [rentabilité] productivity / *le rendement de cette machine est supérieur* this machine is more productive **3.** AGR yield **4.** FIN yield, return.

rendez-vous [ʀɑ̃devu] nm [rencontre] appointment ▸ **prendre rendez-vous** to make an appointment / *j'ai rendez-vous chez le médecin* I have an appointment with the doctor ▸ **donner rendez-vous à qqn** to make an appointment with sb ▸ **se donner rendez-vous** to arrange to meet ▸ **son premier rendez-vous** [amoureux] her first date.

rendormir [36] [ʀɑ̃dɔʀmiʀ] vt to put ou to send back to sleep. ◆ **se rendormir** vpi to go back to sleep, to fall asleep again.

rendre [73] [ʀɑ̃dʀ] ◆ vt **1.** [restituer - objet prêté ou donné] to give back *(sép)*, to return ; [- objet volé] to give back *(sép)*, to return ; [- objet défectueux] to take back *(sép)*, to return ; [- somme] to pay back *(sép)* ; [- réponse] to give / *il est venu rendre la chaise* he brought the chair back / *donne-moi cinq euros, je te les rendrai demain*

give me five euros, I'll pay you back ou I'll give it back to you tomorrow ▸ **rendre un devoir a)** [élève] to hand ou to give in a piece of work **b)** [professeur] to hand ou to give back a piece of work **2.** [donner en retour] to return ▸ **rendre la monnaie (sur)** to give change (out of ou from) / *elle me méprise, mais je le lui rends bien* she despises me, but the feeling's mutual **3.** *(suivi d'un adj)* [faire devenir] to make ▸ **rendre qqch public** to make sthg public ▸ **rendre qqn fou** to drive ou to make sb mad **4.** [faire recouvrer] ▸ **rendre l'ouïe / la santé / la vue à qqn** to restore sb's hearing / health / sight, to give sb back his hearing / health / sight ▸ **tu m'as rendu l'espoir** you've given me new hope **5.** [exprimer - personnalité] to portray, to capture ; [- nuances, pensée] to convey, to render *sout*, to express / *l'enregistrement ne rend pas la qualité de sa voix* the recording doesn't do justice to the quality of her voice **6.** [produire] : *ici le mur rend un son creux* the wall sounds hollow here / *mes recherches n'ont encore rien rendu* my research hasn't come up with anything yet ou hasn't produced any results yet **7.** CULIN to give out *(sép)* **8.** [vomir - repas] to vomit, to bring up *(sép)* **9.** [prononcer - jugement, arrêt] to pronounce ; [- verdict] to deliver, to return / *rendre une sentence* to pass ou to pronounce sentence **10.** AGR & HORT [produire] to yield, to have a yield of. ◆ vi **1.** AGR & HORT to be productive / *les vignes ont bien rendu* the vineyards have given a good yield ou have produced well **2.** [ressortir] to be effective / *ce tapis rend très bien / ne rend pas très bien avec les rideaux* this carpet looks really good / doesn't look much with the curtains **3.** [vomir] to vomit, to be sick. ◆ **se rendre** vpi **1.** [criminel] to give o.s. up, to surrender ; [ville] to surrender / *se rendre à la police* to give o.s. up to the police ▸ **rendez-vous !** give yourself up!, surrender! **2.** *(suivi d'un adj)* [devenir] to make o.s. / *rends-toi utile !* make yourself useful! / *ne te rends pas malade pour ça !* it's not worth making yourself ill about ou over it! **3.** [aller] to go ▸ **je me rends à l'école à pied / à vélo / en voiture** I walk / ride (my bike) / drive to school, I go to school on foot / by bike / by car. ◆ **se rendre à** vp + prép [accepter] to yield to / *se rendre à l'avis de ses supérieurs* to bow to the opinion of one's superiors ▸ **se rendre à l'évidence a)** [être lucide] to face facts **b)** [reconnaître les faits] to acknowledge ou to recognize the facts.

rêne [ʀɛn] nf [courroie] rein ; *fig* ▸ **prendre les rênes** to take over the reins ▸ **c'est lui qui tient les rênes (à la direction)** he's the one who's really in charge (up in management).

renfermé, e [ʀɑ̃fɛʀme] adj uncommunicative, withdrawn, silent. ◆ **renfermé** nm : *ça sent le renfermé ici* it smells musty in here.

renfermer [3] [ʀɑ̃fɛʀme] vt to hold, to contain. ◆ **se renfermer** vpi to withdraw (into o.s.).

renflé, e [ʀɑ̃fle] adj [colonne, forme] bulging, bulbous.

renflement [ʀɑ̃fləmɑ̃] nm [d'une colonne, d'un vase] bulge.

renflouer [3] [ʀɑ̃flue] vt **1.** NAUT to refloat **2.** [entreprise, projet] to bail out *(sép)*.

renfoncement [ʀɑ̃fɔ̃smɑ̃] nm [dans un mur] recess, hollow.

renforcer [16] [ʀɑ̃fɔʀse] vt **1.** CONSTR & COUT to reinforce **2.** [grossir - effectif, service d'ordre] to reinforce, to strengthen / *le candidat choisi viendra renforcer notre équipe de chercheurs* the ideal candidate will join our team of researchers **3.** [affermir - conviction] to reinforce, to strengthen, to intensify / *il m'a renforcé dans mon opinion* he confirmed me in my belief. ◆ **se renforcer** vpi [devenir plus fort] to become stronger, to be consolidated.

renfort [ʀɑ̃fɔʀ] nm [aide] reinforcement. **renforts** nmpl MIL [soldats] reinforcements ; [matériel] (fresh) supplies. **à grand renfort de** loc prép with a lot of, with much / *il s'expliquait à grand renfort de gestes* he expressed himself with the help of a great many gestures.

renfrogné, e [ʀɑ̃fʀɔɲe] adj [air, visage] sullen, dour ; [personne] sulky, dour.

rengager [17] [ʀɑ̃gaʒe] **se rengager** vpi MIL to re-enlist, to join up again.

rengaine [ʀɑ̃gɛn] nf **1.** [refrain] (old) tune, (old) song **2.** *fig* : *avec eux, c'est toujours la même rengaine* they never change their tune, with them it's always the same (old) story.

rengainer [4] [ʀɑ̃gene] vt [arme] **rengainer un revolver** to put a revolver back in its holster / *rengainer une épée* to put a sword back in its sheath.

renier [9] [ʀənje] vt [promesse] to break ; [famille, patrie] to disown, to repudiate *sout* ; [religion] to renounce. **se renier** vpi to retract.

renifler [3] [ʀənifle] ◆ vt **1.** [humer] to sniff at *(insép)* **2.** [aspirer par le nez] : *renifler de la cocaïne* to sniff cocaine **3.** *fam & fig* to sniff out *(sép)*. ◆ vi [en pleurant] to sniffle ; [à cause d'un rhume] to snuffle, to sniff.

renne [ʀɛn] nm reindeer.

renom [ʀənɔ̃] nm [notoriété] fame, renown. **de renom** loc adj famous, renowned / *un musicien de (grand) renom* a musician of high renown ou repute.

renommé, e [ʀənɔme] adj [célèbre] famous, renowned, celebrated. **renommée** nf [notoriété] fame, repute / *un musicien de renommée internationale* a world-famous musician, a musician of international repute / *de bonne / fâcheuse renommée* of good / ill repute.

renommer [3] [ʀənɔme] vt **1.** [à un poste] to reappoint, to renominate **2.** INFORM to rename.

renoncement [ʀənɔ̃smɑ̃] nm renunciation.

renoncer [16] [ʀənɔ̃se] vi JEUX to give up ou in. **renoncer à** v + prép [gén] to renounce, to give up ; [projet, métier] to give up, to abandon ; [habitude] to give up ; [pouvoir] to relinquish / *elle ne veut à aucun prix renoncer à son indépendance* nothing would make her give up her independence / *je ne renoncerai jamais* I'll never give up.

renoncule [ʀənɔ̃kyl] nf buttercup, ranunculus *spéc*.

renouer [6] [ʀənwe] ◆ vt **1.** [rattacher - ruban, cravate] to retie, to tie again, to reknot **2.** [reprendre - discussion] to resume, to renew / *renouer une liaison* to rekindle ou to revive an old affair. ◆ vi to get back together again **renouer avec** : *j'ai renoué avec mes vieux amis* I've taken up with my old friends again **renouer avec la tradition** / **l'usage** to revive traditions / customs.

renouveau, x [ʀənuvo] nm [renaissance] revival.

renouvelable [ʀənuvlabl] adj **1.** [offre] repeatable ; [permis, bail, abonnement] renewable / *l'expérience est facilement renouvelable* the experience is easy to repeat **énergie renouvelable** renewable energy **non renouvelable** nonrenewable **2.** ADMIN & POL **mon mandat est renouvelable** I am eligible to stand 🇬🇧 ou run 🇺🇸 (for office) again.

renouveler [24] [ʀənuvle] vt **1.** [prolonger] to renew **2.** [répéter] to renew, to repeat / *renouveler un exploit* / *une tentative* to repeat a feat / an attempt / *j'ai préféré ne pas renouveler l'expérience* I chose not to repeat the experience **3.** [changer] to renew, to change **4.** [réélire - groupe, assemblée] to re-elect. **se renouveler** vpi **1.** [se reproduire] to recur, to occur again and again / *je te promets que cela ne se renouvellera pas* I promise you it

won't happen again **2.** [groupe, assemblée] to be re-elected ou replaced.

🖉 In reformed spelling (see p. 16-18), this verb is conjugated like **peler** : *il renouvèle, elle renouvèlera.*

renouvellement, renouvèlement* [ʀənuvɛlmɑ̃] nm **1.** [reconduction] renewal / *solliciter le renouvellement d'un mandat* to stand 🇬🇧 ou to run 🇺🇸 for re-election **2.** [répétition] repetition, recurrence.

rénovation [ʀenɔvasjɔ̃] nf [d'un meuble, d'un immeuble] renovation ; [d'un quartier] redevelopment, renovation / *la maison est en rénovation* the house is being done up ou is having a complete facelift.

rénové, e [ʀenɔve] adj [quartier, bâtiment] renovated.

rénover [3] [ʀenɔve] vt **1.** [remettre à neuf - meuble] to restore, to renovate ; [- immeuble] to renovate, to do up *(sép)* ; [- quartier] to redevelop, to renovate ; [- salle de bains] to modernize **2.** [transformer en améliorant] : *rénover des méthodes pédagogiques* to update teaching methods / *rénover les institutions politiques* to reform political institutions.

renseignement [ʀɑ̃sɛɲəmɑ̃] nm [information] piece of information, information (U) / *pour avoir de plus amples renseignements, s'adresser à…* for further information ou details, apply to… **demander un renseignement** ou **des renseignements à qqn** to ask sb for information **prendre des renseignements sur** to make enquiries about / *renseignements pris, elle était la seule héritière* after making some enquiries it turned out (that) she was the sole heir **merci pour le renseignement** thanks for letting me know *aussi iron* **aller aux renseignements** to go and (see what one can) find out. **renseignements** nmpl **1.** ADMIN [service] enquiries 🇬🇧 (department), information ; [réception] information ou enquiries 🇬🇧 ou (desk) **2.** [espionnage] **agent / services de renseignements** intelligence agent / services.

 Attention ! Le mot anglais information est indénombrable. Il ne s'emploie jamais ni au pluriel ni avec l'article indéfini an :
Je recherche des renseignements sur l'histoire de cette église. *I'm looking for* (some) *information about the history of the church.*
Ces renseignements me seront très utiles. *This information will be extremely useful.*
Chaque renseignement est payant. *Each piece / item of information has to be paid for.*

🏛 Les renseignements généraux

Created under Vichy, this agency is the intelligence arm of the Ministry of the Interior. It keeps tabs on political parties, lobby groups, and various individuals. In 2008, the RG and the Direction de la surveillance du territoire (DST) were merged to create the Direction centrale du renseignement intérieur (DCRI), although the term **les RG** is still commonly used to refer to the intelligence service.

---

renseigner [4] [ʀɑ̃seɲe] vt [mettre au courant - étranger, journaliste] to give information to, to inform ; [- automobiliste] to give directions to / *elle vous renseignera sur les prix* she'll tell you the prices, she'll give you more information about the prices / *pardon, Monsieur, pouvez-vous* *me renseigner ?* excuse me, Sir, could you help me, please? ▶ **renseigner qqn sur** to tell sb about ▶ **bien renseigné** well-informed ▶ **mal renseigné** misinformed / *je suis mal renseigné sur l'horaire des marées* I don't have much information about the times of the tides. ❖ **se renseigner** vpi to make enquiries ▶ **se renseigner sur qqn / qqch** to find out about sb / sthg / *il aurait fallu se renseigner sur son compte* you should have made (some) enquiries about him / *renseignez-vous auprès de votre agence de voyages* ask your travel agent for further information.

rentabiliser [3] [ʀɑ̃tabilize] vt to make profitable.

rentabilité [ʀɑ̃tabilite] nf profitability ▶ **rentabilité d'un investissement** FIN return on investment.

rentable [ʀɑ̃tabl] adj profitable.

rente [ʀɑ̃t] nf **1.** [revenu] private income / *vivre de ses rentes* to live on ou off one's private income **2.** [pension] pension, annuity, rente *spéc.*

⚠ Rent signifie « loyer » et non rente.

rentier, ère [ʀɑ̃tje, ɛʀ] nm, f person of private means.

rentre-dedans [ʀɑ̃tʀədədɑ̃] nm inv ▶ **faire du rentre-dedans à qqn** *fam* to come on strong with sb.

rentrée [ʀɑ̃tʀe] nf **1.** ENS ▶ **rentrée (scolaire** ou **des classes)** start of the (new) academic year / *la rentrée est fixée au 6 septembre* school starts again ou schools reopen on September 6th **2.** [au Parlement] reopening (of Parliament), new (parliamentary) session ▶ **faire sa rentrée politique a)** [après les vacances] to start the new political season *(after the summer)* **b)** [après une absence] to make one's (political) comeback **3.** [saison artistique] ▶ **la rentrée musicale / théâtrale** the new musical / theatrical season *(after the summer break)* **4.** [retour - des vacances d'été) (beginning of the) autumn 🇬🇧 ou fall 🇺🇸 ; [- de congé ou de week-end] return to work ; TRANSP city-bound traffic **5.** FIN : *j'attends une rentrée pour la fin du mois* I've got some money coming in at the end of the month. ❖ **rentrées** nfpl FIN income, money coming in.

📚 La rentrée

The time of the year when children go back to school has considerable cultural significance in France; coming after the long summer break or **grandes vacances**, it is the time when academic, political, social and commercial activity begins again in earnest.

rentrer [3] [ʀɑ̃tʀe] ◆ vi *(aux être)* **1.** [personne - vue de l'intérieur] to come in ; [- vue de l'extérieur] to go in ; [chose] to go in / *tu es rentré dans Lyon par quelle route ?* which way did you come to Lyon, which road did you take into Lyon? / *la clé ne rentre pas dans la serrure* the key won't go in / *c'est par là que l'eau rentre* that's where the water is coming ou getting in / *fais rentrer le chien* bring the dog back inside ; [s'emboîter] to go ou to fit in ▶ **rentrer dans a)** [poteau] to crash into **b)** [véhicule] to collide with ▶ **rentrer dedans** : *je lui suis rentré dedans* **a)** [en voiture] I drove straight ou right into him **b)** *fam* [verbalement] I laid into him **2.** [faire partie de] to be part of, to be included in / *cela ne rentre pas dans mes attributions* that is not part of my duties **3.** [pour travailler] : *rentrer dans les affaires / la police* to go into business / join the police **4.** [retourner - gén] to return, to come ou to get back ; [revenir chez soi] to come ou to get (back) home ; [aller chez soi] to go ou to return home / *les enfants, rentrez !*

children, get ou come back in! / *je ne rentrerai pas dîner* I won't be home for dinner / *je vous laisse, il faut que je rentre* I'll leave you now, I must go home ou get (back) home **5.** [reprendre ses occupations - lycéen] to go back to school, to start school again ; [- étudiant] to go back, to start the new term **6.** [recouvrer] to come in / *faire rentrer l'argent / les devises* to bring in money / foreign currency **7.** *fam* [explication, idée, connaissances] to sink in / *ça rentre, l'informatique ?* are you getting the hang of computing? / *je le lui ai expliqué dix fois, mais ça n'est toujours pas rentré* I've told him ten times but it hasn't gone ou sunk in yet ▶ **faire rentrer qqch dans la tête de qqn** to get sthg into sb's head, to drum sthg into sb **8.** JEUX & SPORT : *rentrer dans la mêlée* RUGBY to scrum down. ◆ vt *(aux avoir)* **1.** [mettre à l'abri - linge, moisson] to bring ou to get in *(sép)* ; [- bétail] to bring ou to take in *(sép)* ; [- véhicule] to put away *(sép)* ; [- chaise] to carry ou to take in *(sép)* **2.** [mettre - gén] to put in *(sép)* ; [faire disparaître - train d'atterrissage] to raise, to retract ; [- griffes] to draw in *(sép)*, to retract / *rentrer son chemisier dans sa jupe* to tuck one's blouse into one's skirt / *rentre ton ventre / tes fesses !* pull your stomach / bottom in! **3.** [réprimer - colère] to hold back *(sép)*, to suppress **4.** INFORM to input, to key in *(sép)*. ❖ **rentrer dans** v + prép [recouvrer] to recover ▶ **rentrer dans ses frais** to recover one's money / expenses, to get one's money / expenses back ▶ **rentrer dans ses fonds** to recoup (one's) costs. ❖ **se rentrer** vp *(emploi passif)* : *les foins ne se rentrent pas avant juillet* the hay isn't brought in until July. ❖ **se rentrer dedans** vp *(emploi réciproque)* *fam* ▶ **ils se sont rentrés dedans a)** [heurtés] they smashed ou banged into one another **b)** [disputés] they laid into one another, other.

renversant, e [ʀɑ̃vɛʀsɑ̃, ɑ̃t] adj [nouvelle] astounding, amazing, staggering ; [personne] amazing, incredible.

renverse [ʀɑ̃vɛʀs] ❖ **à la renverse** loc adv ▶ **tomber à la renverse** [sur le dos] to fall flat on one's back.

renversé, e [ʀɑ̃vɛʀse] adj **1.** [image] reverse *(modif)*, reversed, inverted ; [objet] upside down, overturned **2.** [stupéfait] ▶ **être renversé** to be staggered.

renversement [ʀɑ̃vɛʀsəmɑ̃] nm **1.** [changement] ▶ **renversement des alliances** reversal ou switch of alliances ▶ **renversement des rôles** role reversal ▶ **renversement de situation** reversal of the situation ▶ **renversement de tendance** shift ou swing (in the opposite direction) **2.** [chute - d'un régime] overthrow.

renverser [3] [ʀɑ̃vɛʀse] vt **1.** [répandre - liquide] to spill ; [faire tomber - bouteille, casserole] to spill, to knock over *(sép)*, to upset ; [- table, voiture] to overturn ; [retourner exprès] to turn upside down **2.** [faire tomber - personne] to knock down *(sép)* / *se faire renverser par une voiture* to get ou be knocked over by a car **3.** [inverser] to reverse / *le Suédois renversa la situation au cours du troisième set* the Swedish player managed to turn the situation round during the third set ▶ **renverser les rôles** to reverse the roles ▶ **renverser la vapeur a)** *pr* to reverse engines **b)** *fig* to change direction **4.** [détruire - obstacle] to overcome ; [- valeurs] to overthrow ; [- régime] to overthrow, to topple / *le président a été renversé* the President was thrown out of ou removed from office ▶ **renverser un gouvernement a)** [par la force] to overthrow ou to topple a government **b)** [par un vote] to bring down ou to topple a government **5.** [incliner en arrière] to tilt ou to tip back *(sép)* **6.** [stupéfier] to amaze, to astound. ❖ **se renverser** vpi **1.** [bouteille] to fall over ; [liquide] to spill ; [véhicule] to overturn ; [bateau] to overturn, to capsize ; [marée] to turn **2.** [personne] to lean over backwards / *se renverser sur sa chaise* to tilt back on one's chair.

renvoi [ʀɑ̃vwa] nm **1.** [d'un colis - gén] return, sending back ; [-par avion] flying back ; [-par bateau] shipping back **2.** SPORT ▸ **renvoi (de la balle)** return **3.** [congédiement - d'un employé] dismissal, sacking 🇬🇧 ; [-d'un élève] expulsion **4.** [ajournement] postponement **5.** [indication] cross-reference ; [note au bas du texte] footnote ▸ **faire un renvoi à** to make a cross-reference to, to cross-refer to **6.** [éructation] belch, burp.

renvoyer [30] [ʀɑ̃vwaje] vt **1.** [colis, formulaire] to send back *(sép)* ; [cadeau] to return, to give back *(sép)* ; [importun] to send away *(sép)* ; [soldat, troupes] to discharge / *on les a renvoyés chez eux* they were sent (back) home ou discharged **2.** [lancer de nouveau - ballon] to send back *(sép)*, to return / *j'étais renvoyé de vendeur en vendeur* I was being passed ou shunted around from one salesman to the next ▸ **renvoyer la balle à qqn a)** FOOT to kick ou to pass the ball back to sb **b)** RUGBY to throw ou to pass the ball back to sb **c)** TENNIS to return to sb **d)** fig to answer sb tit for tat ▸ **renvoyer l'ascenseur à qqn a)** pr to send the lift back to sb **b)** fig to return sb's favour **3.** [congédier] to dismiss **4.** [faire se reporter] to refer / *les numéros renvoient aux notes de fin de chapitre* the numbers refer to notes at the end of each chapter **5.** [refléter] to reflect / *la glace lui renvoyait son image* she saw her reflection in the mirror ; [répercuter] : *la falaise nous renvoyait nos cris* the cliff echoed our cries. **⬦ se renvoyer** vp *(emploi réciproque)* 🄴🄿🄾🅁 **se renvoyer la balle**: *on peut se renvoyer la balle comme ça longtemps !* we could go on forever blaming each other like this!

réorganisation [ʀeɔʀɡanizasjɔ̃] nf reorganization.

réorganiser [3] [ʀeɔʀɡanize] vt to reorganize. **⬦ se réorganiser** vpi to reorganize o.s., to get reorganized.

réorienter [3] [ʀeɔʀjɑ̃te] vt **1.** POL to reorientate, to redirect **2.** ENS to put onto a different course.

réouverture [ʀeuvɛʀtyʀ] nf [d'un magasin, d'un guichet, d'un musée, d'une route, d'un col] reopening.

repaire [ʀəpɛʀ] nm **1.** [d'animaux] den, lair **2.** [d'individus] den, haunt.

répandre [74] [ʀepɑ̃dʀ] vt **1.** [renverser - liquide] to spill ; [verser - sable, sciure] to spread, to sprinkle, to scatter ▸ **répandre des larmes** to shed tears **2.** [propager - rumeur, terreur, usage] to spread **3.** [dégager - odeur] to give off *(insép)* ; [-lumière] to shed, to give out *(insép)* ; [-chaleur, fumée] to give out ou off *(insép)*. **⬦ se répandre** vpi **1.** [eau, vin] to spill **2.** [se propager - nouvelle, mode, coutume] to spread, to become widespread ▸ **se répandre comme une traînée de poudre** to spread like wildfire **3.** [se dégager - odeur] to spread, to be given off. **⬦ se répandre en** vp + prép sout ▸ **se répandre en compliments / en propos blessants** to be full of compliments / hurtful remarks.

répandu, e [ʀepɑ̃dy] adj widespread / *la technique n'est pas encore très répandue ici* the technique isn't widely used here yet.

réparable [ʀepaʀabl] adj **1.** [appareil] repairable / *j'espère que c'est réparable* I hope it can be mended ou repaired, I hope it's not beyond repair **2.** [erreur, perte] reparable.

reparaître, reparaitre* [91] [ʀəpaʀɛtʀ] vi **1.** [journal, revue] to be out again, to be published again **2.** = **réapparaître.**

réparateur, trice [ʀepaʀatœʀ,tʀis] **◆** adj ▸ **un sommeil réparateur** restorative ou refreshing sleep. **◆** nm, f repairer, repairman (repairwoman).

réparation [ʀepaʀasjɔ̃] nf **1.** [processus] repairing, fixing, mending ; [résultat] repair / *pendant les réparations* during (the) repairs **2.** [compensation] redress, compensation ▸ **demander / obtenir réparation** litt to demand / to

obtain redress **3.** DR damages, compensation **4.** [correction - d'une négligence] correction ; [-d'une omission] rectification. **⬦ de réparation** loc adj SPORT penalty *(modif)* ▸ **surface de réparation** penalty area. **⬦ en réparation** loc adj under repair, being repaired.

réparer [3] [ʀepaʀe] vt **1.** [appareil, chaussure] to repair, to mend ; [défaut de construction] to repair, to make good ; [meuble, porcelaine] to restore ▸ **faire réparer qqch** to get sthg repaired ou put right **2.** [compenser] to make up for *(insép)*, to compensate for *(insép)* **3.** [corriger - omission] to rectify, to repair sout ; [-négligence, erreur] to correct, to rectify.

reparler [3] [ʀəpaʀle] vi to speak again ▸ **reparler de**: *il a reparlé de son roman* he talked about his novel again / *retenez bien son nom, c'est un chanteur dont on reparlera* remember this singer's name, you'll be hearing more of him / *je laisse là les Incas, nous allons en reparler* I won't say any more about the Incas now, we'll come back to them later / *il n'en a plus reparlé* he never mentioned it again. **⬦ se reparler** vp *(emploi réciproque)* to get back on speaking terms.

repartie, répartie* [ʀepaʀti] nf [réplique] retort, repartee ▸ **avoir de la repartie** to have a good sense of repartee.

repartir [43] [ʀəpaʀtiʀ] vi *(aux être)* [se remettre en route] to start ou to set off again / *quand repars-tu ?* when are you off ou leaving again? ▸ **l'économie est bien repartie** the economy has picked up again / *c'est reparti, encore une hausse de l'électricité !* here we go again, another rise in the price of electricity!

répartir [32] [ʀepaʀtiʀ] vt **1.** [distribuer - encouragements, sanctions] to give ; [-héritage, travail] to share out *(sép)*, to divide up *(sép)* ; [-soldats, policiers] to deploy, to spread out *(sép)* ; [-chaleur, ventilation] to distribute **2.** [dans le temps] : *répartir des remboursements* to pay back in instalments / *répartir des paiements* to spread out the payments. **⬦ se répartir ◆** vpi [se diviser] to split, to divide (up) / *répartissez-vous en deux équipes* get yourselves ou split into two teams / *les dépenses se répartissent en trois catégories* expenditure falls under three headings. **◆** vpt [partager] ▸ **se répartir le travail / les responsabilités** to share out the work / the responsibility.

répartition [ʀepaʀtisjɔ̃] nf **1.** [partage - de l'impôt, des bénéfices] distribution ; [-d'un butin] sharing out, dividing up ; [-d'allocations, de prestations] allotment, sharing out / *comment se fera la répartition des tâches ?* how will the tasks be shared out ou allocated? **2.** [agencement - dans un appartement] layout **3.** [étalement - dans l'espace] distribution.

repas [ʀəpa] nm [gén] meal ; [d'un nourrisson, d'un animal] feed 🇬🇧, feeding 🇺🇸 ▸ **prendre ses repas à la cantine a)** [de l'école] to have school lunches ou dinners 🇬🇧 **b)** [de l'usine] to eat in the (works) canteen ▸ **à l'heure des repas** at mealtimes ▸ **repas de midi** lunch, midday 🇬🇧 ou noon 🇺🇸 meal ▸ **repas de noces** wedding meal ▸ **repas du soir** dinner, evening meal.

repassage [ʀəpasaʒ] nm [du linge] ironing.

repasser [3] [ʀəpase] **◆** vi [passer à nouveau dans un lieu] to go (back) again ▸ **elle repassera** she'll drop by again / *si tu repasses à Berlin, fais-moi signe* if you're in ou passing through Berlin again, let me know / *il passait et repassait sous l'horloge de la gare* he kept walking up and down under the station clock / *j'ai horreur qu'on repasse derrière moi* I hate to have people go over what I've done ▸ **tu peux toujours repasser !** fam no chance!, nothing doing!, not on your life! **◆** vt **1.** [défriper] to iron **2.** [traverser à nouveau] : *repasser un fleuve* to go back across a river, to cross a river again **3.** [subir à nouveau] ▸ re-

passer un examen to resit an exam UK, to take an exam again **4.** [à nouveau] to pass again / *voulez-vous repasser la salade ?* would you hand ou pass the salad round again? **5.** [remettre] : *repasser un poisson sur le gril* to put a fish back on the grill, to give a fish a bit more time on the grill / *repasse-moi la face A du disque* play me the A-side of the record again **6.** [au téléphone] ▸ **je te repasse Paul** I'll put Paul on again, I'll hand you back to Paul ▸ **repassez-moi le standard** put me through to the switchboard again.

repayer [11] [Rəpeje] vt [payer à nouveau] to pay again ; [payer en plus] to pay more for.

repêchage [Rəpeʃaʒ] nm **1.** [d'un objet] fishing out ; [d'un corps] recovery **2.** ENS letting through.

repêcher [4] [Rəpeʃe] vt **1.** [noyé] to fish out (*sép*), to recover **2.** ENS to let through (*sép*) / *j'ai été repêché à l'oral* I passed on my oral.

repeindre [81] [RəpɛdR] vt to repaint, to paint again.

repenser [3] [Rəpɑse] vt to reconsider, to rethink. ❖ **repenser à** v + prép to think about again ▸ **en y repensant** thinking back on it all.

repentir[1] [Rəpɑtir] nm **1.** [remords] remorse **2.** RELIG repentance.

repentir[2] [37] [Rəpɑtir] ❖ **se repentir** vpi to repent *sout.* ❖ **se repentir de** vp + prép to regret, to be sorry for.

repérage [Rəpera ʒ] nm **1.** MIL location **2.** CINÉ ▸ **être en repérage** to be looking for locations ou choosing settings.

répercussion [Reperkysjɔ̃] nf [conséquence] repercussion, consequence, side-effect.

répercuter [3] [Reperkyte] vt **1.** [renvoyer - son] to echo, to reflect **2.** FIN : *répercuter l'impôt sur le prix de revient* to pass a tax on in the selling price **3.** [transmettre] to pass on ou along (*sép*). ❖ **se répercuter sur** vp + prép to have an effect on ou upon, to affect.

repère [RəpɛR] nm **1.** [gén] line, mark ; [indice - matériel] landmark ; [- qui permet de juger] benchmark, reference mark ▸ **point de repère** landmark **2.** [référence] reference point, landmark / *j'ai l'impression de n'avoir plus aucun (point de) repère* I've lost my bearings.

repérer [18] [Rəpere] vt **1.** [localiser] to locate, to pinpoint **2.** [remarquer] to spot, to pick out (*sép*), to notice / *les ravisseurs se sont fait repérer près de l'hôpital* the kidnappers were spotted near the hospital **3.** [dénicher] to discover. ❖ **se repérer** vpi [déterminer sa position] to find ou to get one's bearings.

📖 In reformed spelling (see p. 16-18), this verb is conjugated like *semer* : *il repèrera, elle repèrerait.*

répertoire [RepɛRtwaR] nm **1.** [liste] index, list **2.** [livre] notebook, book ▸ **répertoire d'adresses** address book ▸ **répertoire des rues** street index **3.** DANSE & MUS repertoire ; THÉÂTRE repertoire, repertory ▸ **jouer une pièce du répertoire a)** [acteur] to be in rep **b)** [théâtre] to put on a play from the repertoire ou a stock play **4.** INFORM directory.

répertorier [9] [RepɛRtɔRje] vt **1.** [inventorier] to index, to list / *répertorier les erreurs* to list ou to pick out the mistakes **2.** [inscrire dans une liste] to list / *répertorié par adresses / professions* listed under addresses / professions.

répéter [18] [Repete] vt **1.** [dire encore] to repeat / *elle ne se l'est pas fait répéter (deux fois)* she didn't need telling twice ; *(en usage absolu)* : *répétez après moi* repeat after me **2.** [révéler par indiscrétion - fait] to repeat ; [- histoire] to retell, to relate / *ne lui répète pas* don't tell her, don't repeat this to her / *ne va pas le répéter (à tout le monde)* don't go telling everybody **3.** [recommencer] to repeat, to do again **4.** [mémoriser - leçon] to go over (*insép*), to practise ; [- morceau de musique] to practise ; [- pièce, film]

to rehearse ; *(en usage absolu)* : *on ne répète pas demain* there's no rehearsal tomorrow **5.** [reproduire - motif] to repeat, to duplicate ; [- refrain] to repeat. ❖ **se répéter** vpi **1.** [redire la même chose] to repeat o.s. / *au risque de me répéter* at the risk of repeating myself **2.** [se reproduire] to recur, to reoccur, to be repeated / *et que ça ne se répète plus !* don't let it happen again! / *l'histoire se répète* history repeats itself.

📖 In reformed spelling (see p. 16-18), this verb is conjugated like *semer* : *il répètera, elle répèterait.*

répétitif, ive [Repetitif, iv] adj repetitive, repetitious.

répétition [Repetisjɔ̃] nf **1.** [d'un mot, d'un geste] repetition **2.** [séance de travail] rehearsal ▸ **être en répétition** to be rehearsing ▸ **répétition générale** dress rehearsal. ❖ **à répétition** loc adj *fam* [renouvelé] : *il fait des bêtises à répétition* he keeps doing stupid things.

repeupler [5] [Rəpœple] vt [secteur] to repopulate ; [étang] to restock ; [forêt] to reafforest UK, to reforest US. ❖ **se repeupler** vpi : *cette région commence à se repeupler* people are starting to move back to the area.

repiquer [3] [Rəpike] vt **1.** [planter - riz, salades] to plant ou to pick ou to bed out **2.** *tfam* [attraper de nouveau] to catch ou to nab again **3.** [enregistrer - sur disque] to transfer ; [- sur cassette] to rerecord, to tape.

répit [Repi] nm respite, rest / *s'accorder quelques minutes de répit* to give o.s. a few minutes' rest. ❖ **sans répit** loc adv [lutter] tirelessly ; [poursuivre, interroger] relentlessly, without respite.

replacer [16] [Rəplase] vt **1.** [remettre] to replace, to put back (*sép*) / *replacer les événements dans leur contexte* to put events into their context **2.** *fam* [réutiliser] to put in (*sép*) again / *elle est bonne, celle-là, je la replacerai* that's a good one, I must remember it ou use it myself sometime! **3.** [trouver un nouvel emploi pour - domestique] to find a new position for ; [- employé] to reassign. ❖ **se replacer** vpi **1.** [domestique] to find (o.s.) a new job **2.** [dans une situation déterminée] to imagine o.s., to visualize o.s.

replanter [3] [Rəplɑte] vt to replant.

repli [Rəpli] nm **1.** [pli - du terrain] fold ; [courbe - d'une rivière] bend, meander **2.** MIL withdrawal, falling back (U) ▸ **solution** ou **stratégie de repli** fallback option **3.** [baisse] fall, drop / *on note un léger repli de la livre sterling* sterling has fallen slightly ou has eased (back) **4.** [introversion] ▸ **repli sur soi** a turning in on o.s.

replier [10] [Rəplije] vt **1.** [plier - journal] to fold up (*sép*) again ; [- couteau] to close again **2.** [ramener - ailes] to fold ; [- jambes] to tuck under (*sép*) **3.** MIL : *replier les unités derrière le fleuve* to withdraw units back to the other side of the river. ❖ **se replier** vpi **1.** MIL to withdraw, to fall back **2.** BOURSE [monnaie] to fall back. ❖ **se replier sur** vp + prép : *se replier sur soi-même* to withdraw into o.s., to turn in on o.s. / *il est trop replié sur lui-même* he's too much of an introvert.

réplique [Replik] nf **1.** [réponse] reply, retort, rejoinder *sout* / *ce gamin a la réplique facile* this kid is always ready with ou is never short of an answer ▸ **argument sans réplique** irrefutable ou unanswerable argument **2.** [dans une pièce, un film] line, cue / *oublier sa réplique* to forget one's lines ▸ **donner la réplique à un acteur a)** [en répétition] to give an actor his cues **b)** [dans une distribution] to play opposite an actor **3.** [reproduction] replica, studio copy **4.** GÉOL aftershock.

répliquer [3] [Replike] vt [répondre] to reply, to retort / *il n'en est pas question, répliqua-t-il* it's out of the question, he replied ou retorted. ❖ **répliquer à** v + prép **1.** [répondre à] to reply to **2.** [contre-attaquer] to respond to.

replonger [17] [RǝplɔƷe] ◆ vt **1.** [plonger à nouveau] to dip back *(sép)* **2.** *fig* [faire sombrer à nouveau] to plunge back *(sép)*, to push back / *le choc la replongea dans la démence* the shock pushed ou tipped her back into madness. ◆ vi **1.** *fig* ▶ **replonger dans l'alcool / la délinquance** to relapse into drinking / delinquency **2.** *arg crime* [retourner en prison] to go back inside. ❖ **se replonger dans** vp + prép to go back to / *se replonger dans son travail* to immerse o.s. in work again, to go back to one's work / *se replonger dans ses recherches* to get involved in one's research again.

répondant [Repɔ̃dɑ̃] nm EXPR⟩ **avoir du répondant** to have money.

répondeur [Repɔ̃dœR] nm ▶ **répondeur (téléphonique)** (telephone) answering machine.

répondre [75] [Repɔ̃dR] ◆ vi **1.** [répliquer] to answer, to reply / *répondez par oui ou par non* answer ou say yes or no / *répondre par un clin d'œil / hochement de tête* to wink / to nod in reply ▶ **répondre à qqn** to answer sb ▶ **répondre à qqch** to answer sthg **2.** [être insolent] to answer back / *répondre à ses parents / professeurs* to answer one's parents / teachers back **3.** [à une lettre] to answer, to reply, to write back ▶ **répondez au questionnaire suivant** answer the following questions, fill in the following questionnaire **4.** [à la porte, au téléphone] to answer ▶ **je vais répondre a)** [à la porte] I'll go **b)** [au téléphone] I'll answer it, I'll get it ▶ **ça ne répond pas** nobody's answering, there's no answer **5.** [réagir - véhicule, personne, cheval] to respond ▶ **répondre à** to respond to / *son organisme ne répond plus au traitement* her body isn't responding to treatment any more / *répondre à une accusation / critique* to counter an accusation / a criticism. ◆ vt **1.** [gén] to answer, to reply ; [après une attaque] to retort ▶ **répondre (que) oui / non** to say yes / no in reply, to answer yes / no / *qu'as-tu répondu ?* what did you say?, what was your answer? / *je n'ai rien trouvé à répondre* I could find no answer ou reply / *elle m'a répondu de le faire moi-même* she told me to do it myself **2.** [par lettre] to answer ou to reply (in writing ou by letter) ▶ **répondre que...** to write (back) that... ❖ **répondre à** v + prép **1.** [satisfaire - besoin, demande] to answer, to meet ; [- attente, espoir] to come ou to live up to, to fulfil ; [correspondre à - norme] to meet ; [- condition] to fulfil ; [- description, signalement] to answer, to fit **2.** [s'harmoniser avec] to match **3.** ▶ **répondre au nom de** [s'appeler] to answer to the name (of). ❖ **répondre de** v + prép **1.** [cautionner - filleul, protégé] to answer for ▶ **répondre de l'exactitude de qqch / de l'intégrité de qqn** to vouch for the accuracy of sthg / sb's integrity / *je ne réponds plus de rien* I am no longer responsible for anything **2.** [expliquer] to answer ou to account for, to be accountable for / *les ministres répondent de leurs actes devant le Parlement* ministers are accountable for their actions before Parliament. ❖ **se répondre** vp *(emploi réciproque)* [instruments de musique] to answer each other ; [sculptures, tableaux] to match each other ; [couleurs, formes, sons] to harmonize.

réponse [Repɔ̃s] nf **1.** [réplique] answer, reply ▶ **avoir (toujours) réponse à tout** : *elle a toujours réponse à tout* **a)** [elle sait tout] she has an answer for everything **b)** [elle a de la repartie] she's never at a loss for ou she's always ready with an answer **2.** [à un courrier] reply, answer, response / *en réponse à votre courrier du 2 mai* in reply ou in response to your letter of May 2nd / *leur lettre est restée sans réponse* their letter remained ou was left unanswered / *leur demande est restée sans réponse* there was no reply ou response to their request **3.** [réaction] response **4.** ÉDUC & UNIV [solution] answer / *la réponse à la question n° 5 est fausse* the answer to number 5 is wrong.

response ou **reply** ?

Response et **reply** peuvent tous deux être employés pour traduire réponse (voir article). Au sens de « réaction », c'est **response** qu'il faut employer.

report [RǝpɔR] nm **1.** [renvoi à plus tard] postponement, deferment **2.** COMPTA carrying forward ou over **3.** [transfert] ▶ **report des voix** transfer of votes.

reportage [RǝpɔRtaƷ] nm [récit, émission] report ▶ **faire un reportage sur qqch** to do a report on sthg.

reporter¹ [RǝpɔRtɛR] nmf (news) reporter ▶ **grand reporter** international reporter.

reporter² [3] [RǝpɔRte] vt **1.** [transcrire - note, insertion] to transfer, to copy out ; COMPTA to carry forward *(sép)* **2.** [retarder - conférence, rendez-vous] to postpone, to put off *(sép)* ; [- annonce, verdict] to put off, to defer ; [- date] to defer, to put back UK ▶ **reporter qqch à une prochaine fois** to put sthg off until another time ; [en arrière dans le temps] to take back *(sép)* **3.** [transférer] to shift, to transfer. ❖ **se reporter à** vp + prép [se référer à] to turn ou to refer to, to see / *reportez-vous à notre dernier numéro* see our last issue.

repos [Rǝpo] nm **1.** [détente] rest / *prendre quelques jours de repos* to take ou to have a few days' rest **2.** [période d'inactivité] rest (period), time off / *trois jours de repos, un repos de trois jours* three days off ▶ **repos hebdomadaire** weekly time off **3.** *litt* [tranquillité - de la nature] peace and quiet ; [- intérieur] peace of mind / *je n'aurai pas de repos tant que...* I won't rest as long as... **4.** *litt* [sommeil] sleep, rest ▶ **repos éternel** eternal rest **5.** MIL ▶ **repos !** at ease! ❖ **au repos** ◆ loc adj [moteur, animal] at rest ; [volcan] dormant, inactive ; [muscle, corps] relaxed. ◆ loc adv MIL : *mettre la troupe au repos* to order the troops to stand at ease. ❖ **de tout repos** loc adj : *le voyage n'était pas de tout repos* it wasn't exactly a restful journey.

reposant, e [Rǝpozɑ̃, ɑ̃t] adj [vacances] relaxing ; [ambiance, lumière, musique] soothing.

reposé, e [Rǝpoze] adj fresh, rested / *on repartira quand tu seras bien reposé* we'll set off again once you've had a good rest.

repose-pieds [Rǝpozpje] nm inv footrest.

repose-poignets [Rǝpozpwaɲɛ] nm inv INFORM wrist rest, wrist pillow, wrist pad.

reposer [3] [Rǝpoze] ◆ vt **1.** [question] to ask again, to repeat ; [problème] to raise again, to bring up *(sép)* again **2.** [objet] to put down (again) ou back down **3.** [personne, corps, esprit] to rest / *reposer ses jambes* to rest one's legs. ◆ vi **1.** *litt* [dormir] to sleep ; [être allongé] to rest, to be lying down ; [être enterré] : *ici reposent les victimes de la guerre* here lie the victims of the war **2.** [être posé] to rest, to lie, to stand / *l'épave reposait par cent mètres de fond* the wreck lay one hundred metres down **3.** [liquide, mélange] ▶ **laissez le vin reposer** leave the wine to settle, let the wine stand ▶ **laissez reposer la pâte / colle** leave the dough to stand / glue to set. ❖ **reposer sur** v + prép **1.** [être posé sur] to rest on, to lie on, to stand on ; CONSTR to be built on ou to rest on **2.** [être fondé - témoignage, conception] to rest on / *sur quelles preuves repose votre affirmation ?* what evidence do you have to support your assertion?, on what evidence do you base your assertion? ❖ **se reposer** vpi [se détendre] to rest / *va te reposer une heure* go and rest ou go take a rest for an hour ▶ **se reposer sur ses lauriers** to rest on one's laurels. ❖ **se**

reposer sur vp + prép [s'en remettre à] to rely on / *le Président se repose trop sur ses conseillers* the President relies ou depends too much on his advisers.

repose-tête [ʀəpoztɛt] (*pl* **repose-tête** *ou* **repose-têtes***) nm headrest.

repositionner [3] [ʀəpozisjɔne] vt [remettre en position] to reposition. ❖ **se repositionner** vpi : *se repositionner sur le marché* to reposition o.s. in the market.

repoussant, e [ʀəpusɑ̃, ɑ̃t] adj repulsive, repellent.

repousser [3] [ʀəpuse] ◆ vt **1.** [faire reculer - manifestants] to push ou to drive back *(sép)* / *repousser une attaque* to drive back ou to repel an attack **2.** [écarter] to push aside ou away *(sép)* ▶ **repousser qqn d'un geste brusque** to push ou to shove sb out of the way roughly ▶ *il repoussa du pied la bouteille vide* a) [violemment] he kicked the empty bottle away b) [doucement] he nudged ou edged the empty bottle out of the way with his foot **3.** [refuser - offre, mesure, demande en mariage] to turn down *(sép)*, to reject ; [- solution, thèse] to reject, to dismiss, to rule out *(sép)* ; [- tentation, idées noires] to resist, to reject, to drive away *(sép)* **4.** [mendiant] to turn away *(sép)* ; [prétendant] to reject **5.** [dégoûter] to repel, to put off *(sép)* **6.** [retarder - conférence, travail] to postpone, to put off *(sép)* ; [- date] to defer, to put back *(sép)* ; [- décision, jugement] to defer / *repoussé au 26 juin* postponed until the 26th of June. ◆ vi [barbe, plante] to grow again ou back.

répréhensible [ʀepʀeɑ̃sibl] adj reprehensible, blameworthy / *un acte répréhensible* a reprehensible ou an objectionable deed / *je ne vois pas ce que ma conduite a de répréhensible* I don't see what's reproachable about my behaviour.

reprendre [79] [ʀəpʀɑ̃dʀ] ◆ vt **1.** [saisir à nouveau - objet] to pick up *(sép)* again, to take again ▶ **reprendre les rênes** a) pr to take in the reins b) fig to resume control **2.** [s'emparer à nouveau de - position, ville] to retake, to recapture ; [- prisonnier] to recapture, to catch again **3.** [suj : maladie, doutes] to take hold of again / *quand la douleur me reprend* when the pain comes back / *ça y est, ça le reprend !* there he goes again! **4.** [aller rechercher - personne] to pick up *(sép)* ; [- objet] to get back *(sép)*, to collect ; [remporter] to take back *(sép)* / *je (te) reprendrai mon écharpe demain* I'll get my scarf back (from you) tomorrow / *vous pouvez (passer) reprendre votre montre demain* you can come (by) and collect ou pick up your watch tomorrow **5.** [réengager - employé] to take ou to have back *(sép)* ; [réadmettre - élève] to take ou to have back **6.** [retrouver - un état antérieur] to go back to / *elle a repris son nom de jeune fille* she went back to her maiden name / *je n'arrivais plus à reprendre ma respiration* I couldn't get my breath back ▶ **reprendre son sang-froid** to calm down ▶ **reprendre courage** to regain ou to recover courage **7.** [à table] ▶ **reprends un biscuit** have another biscuit / *reprends un comprimé dans deux heures* take another tablet in two hours' time ; [chez un commerçant] to have ou to take more (of) **8.** [recommencer, se remettre à - recherche, combat] to take up again ; [- projet] to take up again ; [- enquête] to restart, to reopen ; [- lecture] to go back to, to resume ; [- hostilités] to resume, to reopen ; [- discussion, voyage] to resume, to carry on (with), to continue ▶ **reprendre ses études** to take up one's studies again, to resume one's studies ▶ **reprendre le travail** a) [après des vacances] to go back to work, to start work again b) [après une panne] to get back to work, to start work again c) [après une grève] to go back to work ▶ **reprendre contact avec qqn** to get in touch with sb again ▶ **reprendre la plume** / **la caméra** / **le pinceau** to take up one's pen / movie camera / brush once more ▶ **reprendre la route** ou **son chemin** to set off again, to resume one's journey ▶ **reprendre la mer** a) [marin] to go back to sea b) [navire] to (set) sail

again **9.** [répéter - texte] to read again ; [- argument, passage musical] to repeat ; [- refrain] to take up *(sép)* ▶ **on reprend tout depuis le** ou **au début** [on recommence] let's start (all over) again from the beginning ; TV to repeat ; CINÉ to rerun ; THÉÂTRE to revive, to put on again, to put back on the stage ; [récapituler - faits] to go over *(insép)* again **10.** [dire] to go ou to carry on / *« et lui ? », reprit-elle* "what about him?" she went on **11.** COMM [article refusé] to take back *(sép)* / *les vêtements ne sont ni repris ni échangés* clothes cannot be returned or exchanged / *ils m'ont repris ma voiture pour 3 000 euros* I traded my car in for 3,000 euros ; [prendre à son compte - cabinet, boutique] to take over *(sép)* **12.** [adopter - idée, programme politique] to take up *(sép)* **13.** [modifier - texte] to rework, to go over *(insép)* again ; [- peinture] to touch up *(sép)* ; COUT [gén] to alter ; [rétrécir] to take in ; [en tricot] : *reprendre une maille* to pick up a stitch ; CONSTR to repair ; MÉCAN [pièce] to rework, to machine **14.** [réprimander] to pull up, to reprimand *sout*, to tell off *(sép)* ; [corriger] to correct, to pull up *(sép)* **15.** [surprendre] : *que je ne t'y reprenne plus !* don't let me catch you at it again! / *on ne m'y reprendra plus !* that's the last time you'll catch me doing that! ◆ vi **1.** [s'améliorer - affaires] to improve, to recover, to pick up ; [repousser - plante] to pick up, to recover **2.** [recommencer - lutte] to start (up) again, to resume ; [- pluie, vacarme] to start (up) again ; [- cours, école] to start again, to resume ; [- feu] to rekindle ; [- fièvre, douleur] to return, to start again / *la tempête reprit de plus belle* the storm started again with renewed ferocity **3.** [retourner au travail - employé] to start again. ❖ **se reprendre** vpi **1.** [recouvrer ses esprits] to get a grip on o.s., to pull o.s. together ; [retrouver son calme] to settle down **2.** SPORT [au cours d'un match] to make a recovery, to rally **3.** [se ressaisir - après une erreur] to correct o.s. ❖ **se reprendre à** vp + prép : *elle se reprit à divaguer* she started rambling again ▶ **s'y reprendre** [recommencer] : *je m'y suis reprise à trois fois* I had to start again three times ou to make three attempts.

représailles [ʀəpʀezaj] nfpl reprisals, retaliation *(U)* ▶ **exercer des représailles contre** ou **envers qqn** to take reprisals against sb.

représentant, e [ʀəpʀezɑ̃tɑ̃, ɑ̃t] nm, f **1.** [porte-parole] representative **2.** [délégué] delegate, representative ▶ **représentant syndical** shop steward UK, union representative **3.** COMM ▶ **représentant (de commerce)** (sales) representative, commercial traveller, travelling salesman / *je suis représentant en électroménager* I'm a sales representative for an electrical appliances firm.

représentatif, ive [ʀəpʀezɑ̃tatif, iv] adj representative.

représentation [ʀəpʀezɑ̃tasjɔ̃] nf **1.** [image] representation, illustration **2.** THÉÂTRE performance **3.** [évocation] description, portrayal **4.** ADMIN & POL representation.

représentativité [ʀəpʀezɑ̃tativite] nf representativeness.

représenter [3] [ʀəpʀezɑ̃te] vt **1.** [montrer] to depict, to show, to represent / *la scène représente un intérieur bourgeois* the scene is ou represents a middle-class interior **2.** [incarner] to represent / *elle représentait pour lui l'idéal féminin* she represented ou symbolized ou embodied the feminine ideal for him ; [symboliser] to represent, to stand for *(insép)* **3.** [constituer] to represent, to account for *(insép)* / *les produits de luxe représentent 60 % de nos exportations* luxury items account for ou make up 60% of our exports / *le loyer représente un tiers de mon salaire* the rent amounts ou comes to one third of my salary **4.** THÉÂTRE [faire jouer] to stage, to put on *(sép)* ; [jouer] to play, to perform **5.** [être représentant de] to represent / *le maire s'est fait représenter par son adjoint* the mayor was represented by his deputy, the mayor sent his deputy

---

* In reformed spelling (see p. 16-18).

to represent him **6.** COMM to be a representative of ou for. ❖ **se représenter** ◆ vpi **1.** [à une élection] to stand 🇬🇧 ou to run 🇺🇸 (for election) again ; [à un examen] to sit 🇬🇧 ou to take an examination again, to resit 🇬🇧 **2.** [se manifester à nouveau - problème] to crop ou to come up again / *une occasion qui ne se représentera sans doute jamais* an opportunity which doubtless will never again present itself. ◆ vpt [imaginer] to imagine, to picture / *représentez-vous le scandale que c'était à l'époque !* just imagine ou think how scandalous it was in those days!

répressif, ive [ʀepʀesif, iv] adj repressive.

répression [ʀepʀesjɔ̃] nf **1.** [punition] : *ils exigent une répression plus sévère des actes terroristes* they are demanding a crackdown on terrorist activities **2.** [étouffement - d'une révolte] suppression, repression.

réprimande [ʀepʀimɑ̃d] nf [semonce - amicale] scolding, rebuke ; [- par un supérieur hiérarchique] reprimand ▸ **faire** ou **adresser une réprimande à qqn** to rebuke ou to reprimand sb.

réprimander [3] [ʀepʀimɑ̃de] vt [gronder] to reprimand, to rebuke.

réprimer [3] [ʀepʀime] vt **1.** [étouffer - rébellion] to suppress, to quell, to put down (*sép*) **2.** [punir - délit, vandalisme] to punish **3.** [sourire, colère] to suppress ; [larmes] to hold ou to choke back (*sép*) ; [bâillement] to stifle / *des rires réprimés* repressed ou stifled laughter.

repris, e [ʀepʀi, iz] pp ⟶ **reprendre.** ❖ **repris** nm ▸ **repris de justice** ex-convict. ❖ **reprise** nf **1.** [d'une activité, d'un dialogue] resumption / *reprise des hostilités hier sur le front oriental* hostilities resumed on the eastern front yesterday / *la reprise du travail a été votée à la majorité* the majority voted in favour of going back ou returning to work ▸ **une reprise des affaires** an upturn ou a recovery in business activity ▸ **reprise (économique)** (economic) recovery **2.** RADIO & TV repeat, rerun ; CINÉ rerun, reshowing ; THÉÂTRE revival, reprise ; MUS [d'un passage] repeat, reprise **3.** COMM [action - de reprendre] taking back ; [- d'échanger] trade-in, part exchange 🇬🇧 / *nous ne faisons pas de reprise* goods cannot be returned ou exchanged / *il m'offre une reprise de 1 000 euros pour ma vieille voiture* he'll give me 1,000 euros as a trade-in ou in part exchange 🇬🇧 for my old car **4.** AUTO speeding up, acceleration / *une voiture qui a de bonnes reprises* a car with good acceleration **5.** SPORT [à la boxe] round ; ÉQUIT [leçon] riding lesson ; [cavaliers] riding team ▸ **reprise de volée** TENNIS return volley / *à la reprise, la Corée menait 2 à 0* FOOT Korea was leading 2-0 when the game resumed after halftime ou at the start of the second half **6.** COUT [dans la maille] darn ; [dans le tissu] mend. ❖ **reprises** nfpl ▸ **à maintes reprises** on several ou many occasions / *à trois ou quatre reprises* three or four times, on three or four occasions.

repriser [3] [ʀepʀize] vt [raccommoder - bas, moufle] to darn, to mend ; [- pantalon] to mend.

réprobateur, trice [ʀepʀobatœʀ, tʀis] adj reproving, reproachful ▸ **jeter un regard réprobateur à qqn** to give sb a reproving look, to look at sb reprovingly ou reproachfully.

réprobation [ʀepʀobasjɔ̃] nf [blâme] reprobation *sout*, disapproval.

reproche [ʀəpʀɔʃ] nm **1.** [blâme] reproach ▸ **faire un reproche à qqn** to reproach sb / *je ne vous fais pas reproche de vous être trompé, mais d'avoir menti* what I hold against you is not the fact that you made a mistake, but the fact that you lied **2.** [critique] : *le seul reproche que je ferais à la pièce, c'est sa longueur* the only thing I'd say against the play ou my only criticism of the play is that it's too long. ❖ **sans reproche** loc adj [parfait] above ou beyond reproach, irreproachable ; [qui n'a pas commis d'erreur] blameless.

reprocher [3] [ʀəpʀɔʃe] vt **1.** ▸ **reprocher qqch à qqn** [erreur, faute] to blame ou to reproach sb for sthg / *je lui reproche son manque de ponctualité* what I don't like about her is her lack of punctuality ▸ **reprocher à qqn de faire qqch** to blame sb for doing sthg **2.** : *ce que je reproche à ce beaujolais, c'est sa verdeur* the criticism I would make of this Beaujolais is that it's too young / *je n'ai rien à reprocher à son interprétation* in my view her interpretation is faultless, I can find no fault with her interpretation. ❖ **se reprocher** vpt : *n'avoir rien à se reprocher* to have nothing to feel guilty about.

reproducteur, trice [ʀəpʀodyktœʀ, tʀis] ◆ adj [organe, cellule] reproductive. ◆ nm, f [poule] breeder ; [cheval] stud.

reproduction [ʀəpʀodyksjɔ̃] nf **1.** BIOL & BOT reproduction ; AGR breeding ▸ **cycle / organes de la reproduction** reproductive cycle / organs **2.** [restitution] reproduction, reproducing / *techniques de reproduction des sons* sound reproduction techniques **3.** IMPR [nouvelle publication] reprinting, reissuing ; [technique] reproduction, duplication / '**reproduction interdite**' 'all rights reserved' **4.** [réplique] reproduction, copy.

reproduire [98] [ʀəpʀoduiʀ] vt **1.** [faire un autre exemplaire de] to copy ▸ **reproduire une clé** to cut a key **2.** [renouveler] to repeat **3.** [imiter] to reproduce, to copy **4.** IMPR [republier - texte] to reissue ; [- livre] to reprint ; [photocopier] to photocopy ; [reprographier] to duplicate, to reproduce ; [polycopier] to duplicate. ❖ **se reproduire** vpi **1.** BIOL & BOT to reproduce, to breed **2.** [se renouveler] to recur / *ces tendances se reproduisent de génération en génération* these trends recur ou are repeated with each successive generation / *que cela ne se reproduise plus !* don't let it happen again!

reprogrammer [3] [ʀəpʀogʀame] vt **1.** CINÉ & TV to reschedule **2.** INFORM to reprogram.

reprographie [ʀəpʀogʀafi] nf reprography, repro.

réprouver [3] [ʀepʀuve] vt [attitude, pratique] to condemn, to disapprove of ▸ **des pratiques / tendances que la morale réprouve** morally unacceptable practices / tendencies.

reptile [ʀɛptil] nm reptile.

repu, e [ʀəpy] adj [rassasié] sated *sout*, satiated *sout* ▸ **être repu** to be full (up), to have eaten one's fill / *je suis repu de films policiers* I've had my fill of detective films.

républicain, e [ʀepyblikɛ̃, ɛn] ◆ adj [esprit, système] republican. ◆ nm, f [gén] republican ; [aux États-Unis, en Irlande] Republican.

république [ʀepyblik] nf **1.** [régime politique] republic / *je fais ce que je veux ; on est en république, non ?* fam I'll do as I like, it's a free country, isn't it? **2.** [État] Republic ▸ **la République française** the French Republic ▸ **la République d'Irlande** the Irish Republic, the Republic of Ireland.

répudier [9] [ʀepydje] vt **1.** [renvoyer - épouse] to repudiate, to disown **2.** [renoncer à - nationalité, héritage] to renounce, to relinquish ; [- foi] to renounce.

répugnance [ʀepyɲɑ̃s] nf **1.** [dégoût] repugnance, disgust, loathing ▸ **avoir de la répugnance pour qqch / qqn** to loathe sthg / sb **2.** [mauvaise volonté] reluctance ▸ **éprouver une certaine répugnance à faire qqch** to be somewhat reluctant ou loath to do sthg / *je m'attelai à la tâche avec répugnance* I set about the task reluctantly ou unwillingly.

répugnant, e [ʀepyɲɑ̃, ɑ̃t] adj **1.** [physiquement] repugnant, loathsome, disgusting **2.** [moralement - individu, crime] repugnant ; [- livre, image] disgusting, revolting.

répugner [3] [ʀepyɲe] ❖ **répugner à** v + prép **1.** [être peu disposé à] ▸ **répugner à faire qqch** to be reluctant ou loath to do sthg **2.** [dégoûter] : *tout en cet homme me répugne* everything about that man is repulsive (to me).

répulsion [ʀepylsjɔ̃] nf [dégoût] repulsion, repugnance ▶ **éprouver de la répulsion pour qqch** to feel repulsion for sthg, to find sthg repugnant.

réputation [ʀepytasjɔ̃] nf [renommée] reputation, repute / **se faire une réputation** to make a reputation ou name for o.s. / **un hôtel de bonne / mauvaise réputation** a hotel of good / ill repute / **elle a la réputation de noter sévèrement** she has a reputation ou she's well-known for being a tough marker ▶ **marque de réputation mondiale** ou **internationale** world-famous brand, brand of international repute / **leur réputation n'est plus à faire** their reputation is well-established ▶ **connaître qqn de réputation** to know sb by repute ou reputation.

réputé, e [ʀepyte] adj **1.** [illustre - orchestre, restaurant] famous, renowned / **l'un des musiciens les plus réputés de son temps** one of the most famous musicians of his day / **elle est réputée pour ses colères** she's famous ou renowned for her fits of rage **2.** [considéré comme] reputed / **elle est réputée intelligente** she has a reputation for intelligence, she's reputed to be intelligent.

requérir [39] [ʀəkeʀiʀ] vt **1.** [faire appel à] to call for, to require / **ce travail requiert beaucoup d'attention** the work requires ou demands great concentration ▶ **requérir la force publique** to ask the police to intervene / **requérir de l'aide** to request help **2.** DR to call for, to demand / **le juge a requis une peine de deux ans de prison** the judge recommended a two-year prison sentence.

requête [ʀəkɛt] nf **1.** [demande] request, petition ▶ **à la** ou **sur la requête de qqn** sout at sb's request ou behest **2.** DR petition / **adresser une requête au tribunal** to petition the court, to apply for legal remedy.

requin [ʀəkɛ̃] nm ZOOL shark.

requinquer [3] [ʀəkɛ̃ke] vt fam [redonner des forces à] to pep ou to buck up (sép). ❖ **se requinquer** vpi to recover, to perk up.

requis, e [ʀəki, iz] ◆ pp ⟶ **requérir.** ◆ adj [prescrit] required, requisite / **remplir les conditions requises** to meet the required ou prescribed conditions / **avoir l'âge requis** to meet the age requirements.

réquisition [ʀekizisjɔ̃] nf MIL & fig requisition, requisitioning, commandeering. ❖ **réquisitions** nfpl DR [conclusions] closing speech (for the prosecution) ; [réquisitoire] charge.

réquisitionner [3] [ʀekizisjɔne] vt **1.** [matériel, troupe, employé] to requisition, to commandeer **2.** [faire appel à] ▶ **réquisitionner qqn pour faire qqch** to rope sb into doing sthg.

réquisitoire [ʀekizitwaʀ] nm **1.** DR [dans un procès] prosecutor's arraignment ou speech ou charge **2.** fig : **ces résultats constituent un véritable réquisitoire contre la politique du gouvernement** these results are an indictment of the government's policy.

RER (abr de **Réseau express régional**) nm Paris metropolitan and regional rail system.

rescapé, e [ʀɛskape] ◆ adj surviving. ◆ nm, f [d'un accident] survivor.

rescousse [ʀɛskus] ❖ **à la rescousse** loc adv ▶ **aller / venir à la rescousse de qqn** to go / to come to sb's rescue fig / **nous avons appelé quelques amis à la rescousse** we called on a few friends for help.

réseau, x [ʀezo] nm **1.** TRANSP network / **réseau aérien / ferroviaire / routier** air / rail / road network ▶ **Réseau express régional** = RER **2.** TÉLÉC & TV network ▶ **réseau téléphonique** telephone network **3.** [organisation] network ▶ **développer un réseau commercial** to develop ou to expand a sales network / **réseau de distribution** distribution network ▶ **réseau d'espionnage** spy ring, network of

spies ▶ **réseau de résistance** HIST resistance network ou group ▶ **réseau social** ou **de socialisation** social network **4.** ÉLECTR grid **5.** GÉOGR ▶ **réseau fluvial** river system **6.** INFORM network ▶ **en réseau** networked.

réseautage [ʀezotaʒ] nm : **j'ai fait du réseautage** I've been networking.

réservation [ʀezɛʀvasjɔ̃] nf [d'un billet, d'une chambre, d'une table] reservation, booking ▶ **faire une réservation a)** [à l'hôtel] to make a reservation **b)** [au restaurant] to reserve a table.

réserve [ʀezɛʀv] nf **1.** [stock] reserve, stock / **nous ne disposons pas d'une réserve suffisante d'eau potable** we do not have sufficient reserves of drinking water ▶ **faire des réserves de** to lay in supplies ou provisions of **2.** [réticence] reservation ▶ **faire** ou **émettre des réserves** to express reservations **3.** [modestie, retenue] reserve ▶ **elle est ou demeure** ou **se tient sur la réserve** she's being ou remaining reserved (about it) **4.** ANTHR reservation ; ÉCOL reserve ▶ **réserve de chasse / pêche** hunting / fishing preserve ▶ **réserve naturelle** nature reserve ▶ **réserve ornithologique** ou **d'oiseaux** bird sanctuary **5.** [resserre - dans un magasin] storeroom ; [collections réservées - dans un musée, une bibliothèque] reserve collection **6.** MIL ▶ **la réserve** the reserve. ❖ **de réserve** loc adj **1.** [conservé pour plus tard] reserve (modif) **2.** MIL ▶ **officier de réserve** officer of the reserve. ❖ **en réserve** loc adv **1.** [de côté] in reserve / **avoir de la nourriture en réserve** to have food put by, to have food in reserve / **je tiens en réserve quelques bouteilles pour notre anniversaire** I've put a few bottles aside ou to one side for our anniversary **2.** COMM in stock ▶ **avoir qqch en réserve** to have sthg in stock. ❖ **sans réserve** ◆ loc adj [admiration] unreserved ; [dévotion] unreserved, unstinting ; [approbation] unreserved, unqualified. ◆ loc adv without reservation, unreservedly. ❖ **sous toute réserve** loc adv with all proper reserves / **attention, c'est sous toute réserve !** there's no guarantee as to the accuracy of this! / **la nouvelle a été publiée sous toute réserve** the news was published with no guarantee as to its accuracy.

réservé, e [ʀezɛʀve] adj **1.** [non public] / 'chasse réservée' 'private hunting' **2.** [retenu] reserved, booked UK **3.** [distant] reserved / **une jeune fille très réservée** a very reserved ou demure young girl.

réserver [3] [ʀezɛʀve] vt **1.** [retenir à l'avance] to reserve, to book / **Mesdames, bonsoir, avez-vous réservé ?** good evening, ladies, have you booked UK ou do you have a reservation? **2.** [garder - pour un usage particulier] to save, to keep, to set ou to put aside ; [conserver] to reserve, to keep / **réserver le meilleur pour la fin** to keep ou to save the best till last ▶ **réserver sa réponse** to delay one's answer / **réserver son opinion** to reserve one's opinion **3.** [destiner] to reserve, to have in store ▶ **réserver un accueil glacial / chaleureux à qqn** to reserve an icy / a warm welcome for sb / **que nous réserve l'avenir ?** what does the future have in store for us? ❖ **se réserver** vpi **1.** [par prudence] to hold back **2.** SPORT & fig to save one's strength. ◆ vpt ▶ **se réserver qqch** to reserve ou to keep sthg (for o.s.) ▶ **se réserver le droit de faire qqch** to reserve the right to do sthg.

réservoir [ʀezɛʀvwaʀ] nm **1.** [d'essence, de mazout] tank ; AUTO (petrol) tank UK, (fuel) tank ; [d'eau] (water) tank ; [des W-C] cistern / **réservoir d'eau chaude** hot water tank **2.** BIOL reservoir.

résidant, e [ʀezidɑ̃, ɑ̃t] adj & nm, f resident.

résidence [ʀezidɑ̃s] nf **1.** [domicile] residence ▶ **résidence principale / secondaire** main / second home **2.** [bâtiment] block of (luxury) flats UK, (luxury) apartment block US ▶ **résidence universitaire** UNIV hall of residence UK, dormitory **US 3.** [maison] residential property **4.** DR residence ▸ **être en résidence surveillée** to be under house arrest.

résident, e [ʀezidɑ̃, ɑ̃t] ◆ nm, f resident, (foreign) national. ◆ adj INFORM resident.

résidentiel, elle [ʀezidɑ̃sjɛl] adj residential.

résider [3] [ʀezide] vi **1.** [habiter] ▸ **résider à** to reside sout ou to live in / résider à l'étranger / à Genève to live abroad / in Geneva **2.** fig ▸ **résider dans** to lie in / c'est là que réside tout l'intérêt du film that is where the strength of the film lies.

résidu [ʀezidy] nm **1.** [portion restante] residue **2.** [détritus] residue, remnants.

résignation [ʀeziɲasjɔ̃] nf [acceptation] resignation, resignedness.

résigné, e [ʀeziɲe] adj resigned / prendre un air résigné to look resigned.

résigner [3] [ʀeziɲe] ◆ **se résigner à** vp + prép to resign o.s. to ; (en usage absolu) : il faut se résigner you must resign yourself to it ou accept it.

résiliation [ʀeziljasjɔ̃] nf [d'un bail, d'un contrat, d'un marché - en cours] cancellation, avoidance ; [- arrivant à expiration] termination.

résilier [9] [ʀezilje] vt [bail, contrat, marché - en cours] to cancel ; [- arrivant à expiration] to terminate.

résille [ʀezij] nf [à cheveux] hairnet.

résine [ʀezin] nf BOT & TECHNOL resin.

résineux, euse [ʀezinø, øz] adj **1.** [essence, odeur] resinous **2.** [arbre, bois] resiniferous. ◆ **résineux** nm resiniferous tree.

résistance [ʀezistɑ̃s] nf **1.** [combativité] resistance / elle a opposé une résistance farouche à ses agresseurs she put up a fierce resistance to her attackers **2.** [rébellion] resistance ▸ **la Résistance** HIST the (French) Resistance **3.** [obstacle] resistance / en fermant le tiroir j'ai senti une résistance when I shut the drawer I felt some resistance **4.** [robustesse] resistance, stamina / elle a survécu grâce à sa résistance exceptionnelle she survived thanks to her great powers of resistance **5.** TECHNOL resistance, strength ▸ **résistance aux chocs** resilience / résistance des matériaux strength of materials **6.** ÉLECTR resistance ; [dispositif chauffant] element.

🏛 La Résistance

Calls for resistance following the French-German armistice in 1940, for instance General de Gaulle's radio call from London on 18th June of the same year largely went unheeded. It was not until 1941 that large-scale coordinated action began. The movement won the active support of the French Communist Party after German troops invaded the USSR. In his ambition to impose himself as the leader of a united resistance movement, General de Gaulle integrated all major clandestine groups into the **Conseil national de la Résistance**. In May 1943, he created the French Committee of National Liberation in Algeria, which later became the provisional government for France in 1944.

---

résistant, e [ʀezistɑ̃, ɑ̃t] ◆ adj **1.** [personne] resistant, tough ; [emballage] resistant, strong, solid ; [couleur] fast **2.** ÉLECTR & PHYS resistant ▸ **résistant aux chocs** shockproof ▸ **résistant à la chaleur** heatproof, heat-resistant. ◆ nm, f HIST (French) Resistance fighter.

résister [3] [ʀeziste] ◆ **résister à** v + prép **1.** [agresseur, attaquant] to resist, to hold out against ; [autorité] to resist, to stand up to ; [pression] to resist ; [gendarme, huissier] to put up resistance to / je ne peux pas lui résister, il est si gentil I can't resist him, he's so nice **2.** [fatigue, faim] to withstand, to put up with ; [solitude, douleur] to stand, to withstand ▸ **résister à la tentation** to resist temptation / résister à ses désirs / penchants to fight against one's desires / inclinations **3.** [à l'usure, à l'action des éléments] to withstand, to resist, to be proof against ▸ **qui résiste au feu** fireproof / résister au temps to stand the test of time ; (en usage absolu) : la serrure résiste the lock is sticking **4.** [suj : livre, projet] to stand up / résister à l'analyse / l'examen to stand up to analysis / investigation.

résolu, e [ʀezɔly] ◆ pp ⟶ **résoudre.** ◆ adj [personne] resolute, determined / je suis résolu à ne pas céder I'm determined not to give in.

résolument [ʀezɔlymɑ̃] adv [fermement] resolutely, firmly, determinedly / je m'oppose résolument à cette décision I'm strongly ou firmly opposed to this decision.

résolution [ʀezɔlysjɔ̃] nf **1.** [décision] resolution ▸ **prendre la résolution de faire qqch** to make up one's mind ou to resolve to do sthg **2.** [solution] solution, resolution **3.** POL resolution **4.** [d'un écran] resolution.

résonance [ʀezɔnɑ̃s] nf **1.** PHYS & TÉLÉC resonance ▸ **résonance magnétique** magnetic resonance **2.** litt [écho] connotation, colouring (U).

résonner [ʀezɔne] vi **1.** [sonner] to resonate, to resound **2.** [renvoyer le son] to resound, to be resonant / la pièce résonne sound reverberates ou echoes in the room.

résorber [3] [ʀezɔʀbe] vt **1.** [éliminer - chômage, déficit] to reduce, to bring down (sép), to curb **2.** MÉD to resorb. ◆ **se résorber** vpi **1.** [chômage, inflation] to be reduced **2.** MÉD to be resorbed.

résoudre [88] [ʀezudʀ] vt **1.** [querelle] to settle, to resolve ; [énigme, mystère] to solve ; [difficulté] to resolve, to sort out (sép) ; [problème] to solve, resolve **2.** sout [décider] to decide (on) / je résolus finalement de rentrer chez moi in the end I decided to go back home **3.** sout [entraîner] ▸ **résoudre qqn à faire qqch** to induce ou to move sb to do sthg. ◆ **se résoudre à** vp + prép [accepter de] to reconcile o.s. to / je ne peux m'y résoudre I can't reconcile myself to doing it.

respect [ʀɛspɛ] nm [estime] respect / respect de soi self-respect / élevé dans le respect des traditions brought up to respect traditions ▸ **manquer de respect à qqn** to be disrespectful to sb ▸ **avec (tout)** ou **sauf le respect que je vous dois** with all due respect ▸ **tenir qqn en respect** to keep sb at bay ou at a (respectful) distance. ◆ **respects** nmpl respects, regards ▸ **présenter ses respects à qqn** to present one's respects to sb / mes respects à madame votre mère please give my respects to your mother.

respectabilité [ʀɛspɛktabilite] nf respectability.

respectable [ʀɛspɛktabl] adj [estimable] respectable, deserving of respect ; hum respectable.

respecter [4] [ʀɛspɛkte] vt **1.** [honorer] to respect, to have ou to show respect for / elle sait se faire respecter she commands respect **2.** [se conformer à] to respect, to keep to (insép) / respecter la parole donnée to keep one's word **3.** [ne pas porter atteinte à] to show respect for ▸ **respecter la tranquillité** / **le repos de qqn** to respect sb's need for peace and quiet / rest. ◆ **se respecter** vp (emploi réfléchi) to respect o.s. / une chanteuse qui se respecte ne prend pas de micro no self-respecting singer would use a microphone.

respectif, ive [ʀɛspɛktif, iv] adj respective.

respectivement [ʀɛspɛktivmɑ̃] adv respectively / *Paul et Jean sont âgés respectivement de trois et cinq ans* Paul and John are three and five years old respectively.

respectueusement [ʀɛspɛktɥøzmɑ̃] adv respectfully, with respect.

respectueux, euse [ʀɛspɛktɥø, øz] adj **1.** [personne] respectful ▸ **se montrer respectueux envers qqn** to be respectful to sb ▸ **respectueux de** respectful of / *respectueux des lois* law-abiding **2.** [dans des formules de politesse] : *je vous prie d'agréer mes respectueuses salutations* yours faithfully.

respiration [ʀɛspiʀasjɔ̃] nf PHYSIOL [action] breathing, respiration spéc ; [résultat] breath.

respiratoire [ʀɛspiʀatwaʀ] adj breathing, respiratory spéc.

respirer [3] [ʀɛspiʀe] ◆ vi **1.** PHYSIOL to breathe ▸ **respirer par la bouche / le nez** to breathe through one's mouth / nose / *respirez à fond, expirez !* breathe in, and (breathe) out! **2.** [être rassuré] to breathe again ▸ **ouf, je respire !** phew, thank goodness for that! **3.** [marquer un temps d'arrêt] : *du calme, laissez-moi respirer !* give me a break! ◆ vt **1.** PHYSIOL to breathe (in), to inhale spéc ; [sentir] to smell **2.** [exprimer] to radiate, to exude / *elle respire la santé* she radiates good health / *il respire le bonheur* he's the very picture of happiness.

resplendir [32] [ʀɛsplɑ̃diʀ] vi litt **1.** [étinceler - casque, chaussure] to gleam, to shine **2.** [s'épanouir] : *son visage resplendit de bonheur* her face is shining ou radiant with happiness.

resplendissant, e [ʀɛsplɑ̃disɑ̃, ɑ̃t] adj **1.** [éclatant - meuble, parquet] shining ; [- casserole, émail] gleaming ; [- soleil, temps] glorious **2.** [radieux] radiant, shining, resplendent litt / *tu as une mine resplendissante* you look radiant / *resplendissant de santé* radiant ou blooming with health.

responsabiliser [3] [ʀɛspɔ̃sabilize] vt [rendre conscient de ses responsabilités] ▸ **responsabiliser qqn** to make sb aware of their responsibilities.

responsabilité [ʀɛspɔ̃sabilite] nf **1.** [obligation morale] responsibility ▸ **prends tes responsabilités !** face up to your responsibilities! ▸ **faire porter la responsabilité de qqch à qqn** to hold sb responsible for sthg ▸ **assumer entièrement la responsabilité de qqch** to take on ou to shoulder the entire responsibility for sthg **2.** [charge administrative] function, position / *elle a la responsabilité du département publicité* she's in charge of the advertising department **3.** DR liability, responsibility ; [acte moral] responsibility ▸ **responsabilité civile a)** [d'un individu] civil liability, strict liability **b)** [d'une société] business liability.

responsable [ʀɛspɔ̃sabl] ◆ adj **1.** ▸ **responsable de** [garant de] responsible (for) **2.** DR liable ▸ **responsable civilement** liable in civil law **3.** [réfléchi] responsible / *elle s'est toujours comportée en personne responsable* she has always acted responsibly. ◆ nmf **1.** [coupable] : *le responsable* the person responsible ou to blame **2.** [dirigeant - politique] leader ; [- administratif] person in charge / *réunion avec les responsables syndicaux* meeting with the union representatives.

resquillage [ʀɛskijaʒ] nm fam [sans payer] sneaking in ; TRANSP fare-dodging ; [sans attendre son tour] queue-jumping 🇬🇧, line-jumping 🇺🇸.

resquille [ʀɛskij] nf fam = **resquillage**.

resquiller [3] [ʀɛskije] fam ◆ vi [ne pas payer] to sneak in ; TRANSP to dodge the fare 🇬🇧 ; [ne pas attendre son tour] to push in, to jump the queue 🇬🇧, to cut in the line 🇺🇸. ◆ vt : *resquiller une place pour le concert* to fiddle ou to wangle o.s. a seat for the concert.

resquilleur, euse [ʀɛskijœʀ, øz] nm, f fam [qui ne paie pas] person who sneaks in without paying ; TRANSP fare-dodger 🇬🇧 ; [qui n'attend pas son tour] queue-jumper 🇬🇧, line-jumper 🇺🇸.

ressac [ʀəsak] nm backwash (of a wave).

ressaisir [32] [ʀəseziʀ] ❖ **se ressaisir** vpi [se calmer] to pull o.s. together ▸ **ressaisis-toi !** pull yourself together!, get a hold of ou a grip on yourself! / *il s'est ressaisi et a finalement gagné le deuxième set* he recovered ou rallied and finally won the second set.

ressasser [3] [ʀəsase] vt **1.** [répéter] to go ou harp on about **2.** [repenser à] to turn over in one's mind.

ressayer [ʀeseje] = **réessayer**.

ressemblance [ʀəsɑ̃blɑ̃s] nf **1.** [entre êtres humains] likeness, resemblance / *'toute ressemblance avec des personnages réels ne peut être que fortuite'* 'any resemblance to persons living or dead is purely accidental' **2.** [entre choses] similarity.

ressemblant, e [ʀəsɑ̃blɑ̃, ɑ̃t] adj [photo, portrait] true to life, lifelike.

ressembler [3] [ʀəsɑ̃ble] ❖ **ressembler à** v + prép **1.** [avoir la même apparence que] to resemble, to look like / *elle me ressemble un peu* she looks a bit like me **2.** [avoir la même nature que] to resemble, to be like / *il a toujours cherché à ressembler à son père* he always tried to be like his father **3.** EXPR *ça ne ressemble à rien de ne pas vouloir venir* fam there's no sense in not wanting to come ▸ **cela ne me / te / leur ressemble pas** that's not like me / you / them ▸ **ça lui ressemble bien de... :** *ça lui ressemble bien d'oublier mon anniversaire* it's just like him to forget my birthday. ❖ **se ressembler** vp (emploi réciproque) to look alike, to resemble each other ▸ **se ressembler comme deux gouttes d'eau** to be as alike as two peas (in a pod).

ressemeler [24] [ʀəsəmle] vt to sole, to resole.

✏️ In reformed spelling (see p. 16-18), this verb is conjugated like **acheter** : *il ressemèlera, elle ressemèlerait*.

ressentiment [ʀəsɑ̃timɑ̃] nm sout resentment, ill will ▸ **éprouver du ressentiment à l'égard de qqn** to feel resentment against sb, to feel resentful towards sb.

ressentir [37] [ʀəsɑ̃tiʀ] vt **1.** [éprouver - bienfait, douleur, haine] to feel **2.** MÉTÉOR ▸ **température ressentie** felt air temperature ▸ **froid ressenti** wind chill. ❖ **se ressentir de** vp + prép to feel the effect of / *elle est inquiète et son travail s'en ressent* she's worried and it shows in her work.

resserre [ʀəsɛʀ] nf [à outils] shed, outhouse ; [à produits] storeroom ; [à provisions] store cupboard, larder.

resserrer [4] [ʀəseʀe] vt **1.** [boulon, nœud - serrer de nouveau] to retighten, to tighten again ; [- serrer davantage] to tighten up (sép) **2.** [renforcer - amitié] to strengthen. ❖ **se resserrer** vpi **1.** [devenir plus étroit] to narrow **2.** [se refermer] to tighten **3.** [devenir plus fort] : *nos relations se sont resserrées depuis l'année dernière* we have become closer (to each other) ou our relationship has grown stronger since last year.

resservir [38] [ʀəsɛʀviʀ] ◆ vt **1.** [de nouveau] to serve again **2.** [davantage] to serve (out) some more ou another helping **3.** fam [répéter] : *il nous ressert la même excuse tous les ans* he comes out with ou he trots out the same (old) excuse every year. ◆ vi **1.** [être utile] : *garde-le, ça pourra toujours resservir* keep it, it might come in handy ou useful again (one day) **2.** MIL & TENNIS to serve again. ❖ **se resservir** vp (emploi réfléchi) [reprendre à manger] to help o.s. to some more ou to a second helping / *ressers-toi* help yourself to (some) more. ❖ **se resservir de** vp + prép [réutiliser] to use again.

ressort [ʀəsɔʀ] nm **1.** [mécanisme] spring **2.** [force morale] spirit, drive / *manquer de ressort* to lack drive **3.** [mobile] motivation **4.** [compétence] ▸ **ce n'est pas de mon / son ressort** it is not my / his responsibility. ❖ **à ressort(s)** loc adj spring-loaded ▸ **matelas à ressorts** spring mattress. ❖ **en dernier ressort** loc adv as a last resort.

ressortir [43] [ʀəsɔʀtiʀ] ◆ vt *(aux avoir)* **1.** [vêtement, ustensile] to take out *(sép)* again **2.** [film] to rerelease, to bring out *(sép)* again ; [pièce de théâtre] to rerun **3.** *fam* [répéter] to trot out *(sép)* again / *tu ne vas pas ressortir cette vieille histoire ?* you're not going to come out with that old story again, are you? ◆ vi *(aux être)* **1.** [sortir de nouveau] to go out ou to leave again ; [sortir] to go out, to leave / *il n'est pas encore ressorti de chez le médecin* he hasn't left the doctor's yet **2.** [se détacher] to stand out **3.** [film] to show again, to be re-released. ❖ **ressortir de** v + prép to emerge ou to flow from / *il ressort de tout cela qu'il a menti* the upshot of all this is that he's been lying.

ressortissant, e [ʀəsɔʀtisɑ̃, ɑ̃t] nm, f national.

ressouder [3] [ʀəsude] vt [tuyau] to resolder, to reweld, to weld together *(sép)* again.

ressource [ʀəsuʀs] nf **1.** [secours] recourse, resort / *tu es mon unique ressource* you're the only person who can help me ou my only hope ▸ **en dernière ressource** as a last resort **2.** [endurance, courage] ▸ **avoir de la ressource** to have strength in reserve. ❖ **ressources** nfpl **1.** [fonds] funds, resources, income / *25 ans et sans ressources* 25 years old and no visible means of support ▸ **ressources financières** financial resources **2.** [réserves] resources / *ressources naturelles / minières d'un pays* natural / mineral resources of a country ▸ **ressources humaines** human resources, personnel **3.** [moyens] resources, possibilities / *toutes les ressources de notre langue* all the possibilities ou resources of our language.

ressourcer [16] [ʀəsuʀse] ❖ **se ressourcer** vpi **1.** [retourner aux sources] to go back to one's roots **2.** [reprendre des forces] to recharge one's batteries.

ressurgir [32] [ʀəsyʀʒiʀ] vi [problème] to arise again, to reoccur.

ressusciter [3] [ʀesysite] ◆ vt *(aux avoir)* **1.** RELIG to resurrect, to raise from the dead **2.** [ranimer] to resuscitate ; MÉD to bring back to life, to revive / *ressusciter une mode* to bring back a fashion **3.** *litt* [faire resurgir] to revive, to resurrect ▸ **ressusciter le passé** to summon up ou to revive the past. ◆ vi *(aux être)* RELIG to rise again ou from the dead.

⚠ Le verbe anglais **resuscitate** signifie « ranimer » et non ressusciter.

restant, e [ʀɛstɑ̃, ɑ̃t] adj remaining / *ils se sont partagé les chocolats restants* they shared the chocolates that were left. ❖ **restant** nm [reste] rest, remainder ▸ **pour le restant de mes / ses jours** until my / his dying day.

restaurant [ʀɛstɔʀɑ̃] nm restaurant / *ils vont souvent au restaurant* they often eat out ▸ **restaurant d'entreprise** (staff) canteen 🇬🇧 ou cafeteria 🇺🇸 ▸ **restaurant universitaire** ≃ university cafeteria ou refectory.

restaurateur, trice [ʀɛstɔʀatœʀ, tʀis] nm, f **1.** [d'œuvres d'art] restorer **2.** [qui tient un restaurant] restaurant owner, restaurateur *sout.*

restauration [ʀɛstɔʀasjɔ̃] nf **1.** [d'œuvres d'art] restoration **2.** [rétablissement] restoration **3.** [hôtellerie] catering ▸ **la restauration rapide** the fast-food business.

restaurer [3] [ʀɛstɔʀe] vt **1.** [édifice, œuvre d'art] to restore **2.** *litt* [rétablir] to restore, to reestablish / *restaurer la paix* to restore peace. ❖ **se restaurer** vp *(emploi réfléchi)* to have something to eat.

reste [ʀɛst] nm **1.** [suite, fin] rest / *si vous êtes sages, je vous raconterai le reste demain* if you're good, I'll tell you the rest of the story tomorrow / *pour le reste* ou *quant au reste* for the rest / *et (tout) le reste !* and so on (and so forth)! **2.** [résidu - de nourriture] food left over, leftovers (of food) ; [- de boisson] drink left over ; [- de tissu, de papier] remnant, scrap ; CINÉ out-takes **3.** MATH remainder. ❖ **restes** nmpl **1.** [d'un repas] leftovers / *on mangera les restes ce soir* we'll have the leftovers tonight **2.** [vestiges] remains. ❖ **du reste** loc adv besides, furthermore, moreover / *inutile de discuter, du reste, ça ne dépend pas de moi* there's no point in arguing and, besides, it's not up to me to decide.

rester [3] [ʀɛste] vi **1.** [dans un lieu, une situation] to stay, to remain / *c'est mieux si la voiture reste au garage* it's better if the car stays in the garage / *ceci doit rester entre nous* this is strictly between you and me, this is for our ears only / *restez donc à déjeuner / dîner* do stay for lunch / dinner / *rester debout / assis* to remain standing / seated ▸ **rester paralysé** to be left paralysed ▸ **rester célibataire** to remain single / *elle ne reste pas en place* she never keeps still / *tu veux bien rester tranquille !* will you keep still! / *je n'aime pas rester sur un échec* I don't like to stop at failure ▸ **en rester à**: *nous en sommes restés à la page 160* we left off at ou got as far as page 160 / *nous en resterons à cet accord* we will limit ourselves to ou go no further than this agreement ▸ **restons-en là !** let's leave it at that! ▸ **rester sur le cœur**: *ça m'est resté sur le cœur* it still rankles with ou galls me **2.** [subsister] to be left / *c'est tout ce qui me reste* that's all I have left / *cette mauvaise habitude lui est restée* he still has that bad habit / *restent les deux dernières questions à traiter* the last two questions still have to be dealt with / *reste à savoir qui ira* there still remains the problem of deciding who is to go ; *(tournure impersonnelle)* : *il nous reste un peu de pain et de fromage* we have a little bit of bread and cheese left / *il me reste la moitié à payer* I (still) have half of it to pay / *il nous reste de quoi vivre* we have enough left to live on / *il ne reste plus rien à faire* there's nothing left to be done / *il reste à faire l'ourlet* the hem is all that remains ou that's left to be done / *il reste encore 12 km à faire* there's still 12 km to go / *il n'en reste pas moins que vous avez tort* you are nevertheless wrong **3.** 🇦🇫🇷 & 🇶🇧 [habiter] to live **4.** *euphém* [mourir] to meet one's end ▸ **y rester** *fam* to kick the bucket **5.** [durer] to live on *(insép)*, to endure.

restituer [7] [ʀɛstitɥe] vt **1.** [rendre - bien] to return, to restore ; [- argent] to refund, to return ▸ **restituer qqch à qqn** to return sthg to sb **2.** [reconstituer - œuvre endommagée] to restore, to reconstruct ; [- ambiance] to reconstitute, to render / *restituer fidèlement les sons* to reproduce sounds faithfully.

restitution [ʀɛstitysjɔ̃] nf **1.** [d'un bien] return, restitution ; [d'argent] refund **2.** [d'un son, d'une couleur] reproduction.

resto [ʀɛsto] nm *fam* restaurant ▸ **les Restos du cœur** charity food distribution centres.

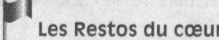 **Les Restos du cœur**

Set up by the comedian Coluche, the **Restos du cœur** (full name, **les Restaurants du cœur**) are run by volunteers who distribute free meals to the poor and homeless, particularly during the winter months.

restreindre [81] [ʀɛstʀɛ̃dʀ] vt [ambition, dépense] to restrict, to limit, to curb ; [budget] to restrict ; [consommation] to cut down *(sép)*. ❖ **se restreindre** vpi **1.** [se rationner] to cut down **2.** [diminuer] : *le champ d'activités de l'entreprise s'est restreint* the company's activities have become more limited / *son cercle d'amis s'est restreint* his circle of friends has got smaller.

restreint, e [ʀɛstʀɛ̃, ɛ̃t] adj [réduit] limited / *l'espace est restreint* there's not much room.

restrictif, ive [ʀɛstʀiktif, iv] adj restrictive.

restriction [ʀɛstʀiksjɔ̃] nf **1.** [réserve] reservation **2.** [limitation] restriction, limitation. ❖ **restrictions** nfpl restrictions. ❖ **sans restriction** loc adv [entièrement] : *je vous approuve sans restriction* you have my unreserved approval.

restructuration [ʀəstʀyktyʀasjɔ̃] nf [d'une société, d'un service] restructuring, reorganization.

restructurer [3] [ʀəstʀyktyʀe] vt [société, organisation] to restructure, to reorganize.

résultat [ʀezylta] nm **1.** [réalisation positive] result ▶ **sans résultat** [action] fruitless **2.** [aboutissement] result, outcome **3.** *fam* [introduisant une conclusion] : *il a voulu trop en faire, résultat, il est malade* he tried to do too much and sure enough he fell ill **4.** MATH result **5.** POL & SPORT result ▶ **le résultat des courses a)** SPORT the racing results **b)** *fig* the outcome (of the situation) **6.** COMPTA profit ▶ **résultat net** net profit. ❖ **résultats** nmpl POL, SPORT & ÉDUC results.

résulter [3] [ʀezylte] ❖ **résulter de** v + prép to result ou to ensue from / *le travail / souci qui en résulte* the ensuing work / worry ; *(tournure impersonnelle)* : *il résulte de l'enquête que...* the result of the investigation shows that...

résumé [ʀezyme] nm **1.** [sommaire] summary, résumé ▶ **résumé des épisodes précédents** the story so far **2.** [bref exposé] summary / *faites-nous le résumé de la situation* sum up ou summarize the situation for us. ❖ **en résumé** loc adv [en conclusion] to sum up ; [en bref] in short, in brief, briefly.

résumer [3] [ʀezyme] vt **1.** [récapituler] to summarize, to sum up *(sép)* **2.** [symboliser] to typify, to symbolize. ❖ **se résumer** vpi [récapituler] to sum up. ❖ **se résumer à** vp + prép to come down to / *cela se résume à peu de chose* it doesn't amount to much.

⚠ Resume signifie « reprendre », « poursuivre » et non résumer.

résurgence [ʀezyʀʒɑ̃s] nf *sout* [réapparition] resurgence, revival.

resurgir [ʀəsyʀʒiʀ] = ressurgir.

résurrection [ʀezyʀɛksjɔ̃] nf **1.** RELIG resurrection **2.** [renaissance] revival.

rétablir [32] [ʀetabliʀ] vt **1.** [établir de nouveau] to restore / *nous prendrons les mesures nécessaires pour rétablir la situation* we'll take the measures required to restore the situation to normal ▶ **rétablir qqn dans son emploi** to reinstate sb / *elle a été rétablie dans tous ses droits* all her rights were restored **2.** [rectifier] to reestablish / *rétablissons les faits* let's reestablish the facts, let's get down to what really happened. ❖ **se rétablir** vpi **1.** [guérir] to recover **2.** [revenir - ordre, calme] to be restored **3.** [reprendre son équilibre] to get one's balance back.

rétablissement [ʀetablismɑ̃] nm **1.** [action] restoration ; [résultat] restoration, reestablishment **2.** [guérison] recovery / *nous vous souhaitons un prompt rétablissement* we wish you a speedy recovery.

rétamé, e [ʀetame] adj *tfam* [épuisé] worn out, knackered 🇬🇧 ; [ivre] pissed 🇬🇧, wrecked ; [démoli] wrecked, smashed up.

rétamer [3] [ʀetame] vt **1.** *tfam* [enivrer] to knock out *(sép)* **2.** *tfam* [fatiguer] to wreck **3.** *tfam* [démolir] to wreck **4.** *tfam* [refuser - candidat] to fail / *ils ont rétamé la moitié des candidats* they failed half the candidates. ❖ **se rétamer** vpi **1.** *fam* [tomber] to come a cropper 🇬🇧, to take a tumble **2.** [échouer] to flunk.

retaper [3] [ʀətape] vt **1.** [lit] to straighten, to make **2.** *fam* [maison] to do up *(sép)* ; [voiture] to fix ou to do up *(sép)* **3.** *fam* [malade] to buck up *(sép)* / *mon séjour à la montagne m'a retapé* my stay in the mountains set me back on my feet again. ❖ **se retaper** *fam* ◆ vp *(emploi réfléchi)* [physiquement] to get back on one's feet again / *elle a grand besoin de se retaper* she badly needs to recharge her batteries. ◆ vpt : *j'ai dû me retaper la lecture du rapport* I had to read through the blasted report again.

retard [ʀətaʀ] ◆ nm **1.** [manque de ponctualité] lateness ▶ **avoir du retard** to be late / *rapportez vos livres sans retard* return your books without delay **2.** [d'une horloge] : *ma montre a plusieurs minutes de retard* my watch is several minutes slow **3.** [d'un élève] backwardness *péj* / *il doit combler son retard en physique* he's got to catch up in physics ▶ **retard scolaire** learning difficulties **4.** [handicap] : *nous avons comblé notre retard industriel en quelques années* we caught up on ou we closed the gap in our industrial development in a few years / *nous avons des années de retard (sur eux)* we're years behind (them) ▶ **retard mental** backwardness. ◆ adj inv delayed(-action), retarded ▶ **insuline / pénicilline retard** slow-release insulin / penicillin. ❖ **en retard** ◆ loc adj ▶ **être en retard** to be late ▶ **elle est très en retard pour son âge a)** PSYCHOL she's rather immature ou slow for her age **b)** ENS she's rather behind for her age ▶ **être en retard dans ses paiements** : *il est en retard dans ses paiements* he's behind ou in arrears with (his) payments ▶ **être en retard sur son époque** ou **son temps** to be behind the times. ◆ loc adv ▶ **arriver en retard** to arrive late / *elle s'est mise en retard* she made herself late.

retardataire [ʀətaʀdatɛʀ] ◆ adj [qui n'est pas à l'heure] late ; [qui a été retardé] delayed. ◆ nmf latecomer.

retardement [ʀətaʀdəmɑ̃] ❖ **à retardement** ◆ loc adj [mécanisme] delayed-action *(modif)*. ◆ loc adv ▶ **comprendre à retardement** to understand after the event.

retarder [3] [ʀətaʀde] ◆ vt **1.** [ralentir - visiteur, passager] to delay, to make late ; [entraver - enquête, progrès, travaux] to delay, to hamper, to slow down *(sép)* / *les problèmes financiers l'ont retardé dans ses études* financial problems slowed him down ou hampered him in his studies **2.** [ajourner] to postpone, to put back *(sép)* **3.** [montre] to put back *(sép)*. ◆ vi [montre] to be slow / *je retarde de quelques minutes* *fam* I'm ou my watch is a few minutes slow.

retenir [40] [ʀətəniʀ] vt **1.** [immobiliser] to hold, to keep / *retiens le chien, il va sauter !* hold the dog back, it's going to jump! ▶ **retenir l'attention de qqn** to hold sb's attention / *votre CV a retenu toute mon attention* I studied your CV with great interest ▶ **retenir qqn à dîner** to invite sb for dinner / *je ne vous retiens pas, je sais que vous êtes pressé* I won't keep you, I know you're in a hurry ▶ **retenir qqn** [le faire rester] to hold back *(sép)* / *je ne sais pas ce qui me retient de l'envoyer promener* *fam* I don't know what's stopping ou keeping me from telling him to go to hell / *retiens-moi ou je fais un malheur* *fam* hold me back or I'll do something desperate **2.** [refouler - émotion, sourire] to curb, to hold in check, to hold back *(sép)* ; [-larmes, sourire] to hold back ; [-cri] to stifle / *retenir son souffle* ou *sa respiration* to hold one's breath **4.** [réserver] to book, to reserve / *retiens la date du 20 juin pour notre réunion* keep June the 20th free for our meeting **5.** [se rappeler] to remember / *et surtout, retiens bien ce qu'on t'a dit* and above all, remember ou don't forget what you've been told ▶ *je te retiens, toi et tes soi-disant bonnes idées !* *fam* I'll remember you and your so-called good ideas! **6.** [candidature, suggestion] to retain, to accept ▶ **retenir une accusation contre qqn** to uphold a charge against sb **7.** [décompter] to deduct, to keep back *(sép)* / *j'ai retenu 60 euros sur votre salaire* I've deducted 60 euros from your salary ▶ **sommes retenues à la base** ou **source** sums deducted at source **8.** [conserver - chaleur] to keep in *(sép)*, to retain, to conserve ; [- eau] to retain ; [- lumière] to reflect **9.** MATH to carry / *je pose 5 et je retiens 4* I put down 5 and carry 4. ❖ **se retenir** ◆ vp *(emploi réfléchi)* **1.** [se contrôler] to restrain o.s. ▶ **se retenir de pleurer** to stop o.s. crying **2.** *fam & euphém* to hold on. ◆ vpi [s'agripper] to hold on.

rétention [ʀetɑ̃sjɔ̃] nf MÉD retention ▶ **faire de la rétention d'urines / d'eau** to suffer from urine / water retention.

retentir [32] [ʀətɑ̃tiʀ] vi **1.** [résonner] to resound, to ring / *de bruyants applaudissements retentirent dans la salle* loud applause burst forth in the hall / *la maison retentit du bruit des ouvriers* the house is filled with the noise of the workers **2.** [avoir des répercussions] ▶ **retentir sur** to have an effect on.

retentissant, e [ʀətɑ̃tisɑ̃, ɑ̃t] adj **1.** [éclatant - cri, bruit, gifle] resounding, ringing ; [- voix] ringing ; [- sonnerie] loud **2.** [remarquable] tremendous ▶ **un succès retentissant** resounding success / *un bide retentissant* *fam* a resounding flop.

retentissement [ʀətɑ̃tismɑ̃] nm **1.** [contrecoup] repercussion **2.** [impact] effect, impact / *le retentissement dans l'opinion publique a été considérable / nul* there was considerable / no effect on public opinion.

retenu, e [ʀətəny] pp → retenir. ❖ **retenue** nf **1.** [déduction] deduction / *opérer une retenue de 9 % sur les salaires* to deduct ou to stop 9% from salaries ▶ **retenue à la source** payment (of income tax) at source ; ≃ PAYE 🇬🇧 **2.** [réserve] reserve, self-control, restraint / *un peu de retenue !* show some restraint!, keep a hold of yourself! **3.** ÉDUC [punition] detention ▶ **mettre qqn en retenue** to keep sb in after school, to put sb in detention.

réticence [ʀetisɑ̃s] nf reluctance, reticence / *parler avec réticence* to speak reticently.

réticent, e [ʀetisɑ̃, ɑ̃t] adj [hésitant] reticent, reluctant, reserved / *se montrer réticent* to seem rather doubtful.

rétine [ʀetin] nf retina.

retiré, e [ʀətiʀe] adj **1.** [isolé] remote, secluded, out-of-the-way / *ils cherchent une maison retirée* they're looking for a secluded house **2.** [solitaire] secluded / *vivre retiré du monde* to live in seclusion **3.** [à la retraite] retired.

retirer [3] [ʀətiʀe] vt **1.** [ôter] to take off ou away *(sép)*, to remove / *il aida l'enfant à retirer son manteau* he helped the child off with his coat **2.** [ramener à soi] : *retire ta main* take your hand away **3.** [faire sortir] to take out *(sép)*, to remove / *elle a été obligée de retirer son fils de l'école* she had to remove her son from the school **4.** [annuler - droit] to take away *(sép)* ; [- plainte, offre] to withdraw ; [- accusation] to take back *(sép)* ▶ **retirer sa candidature** to withdraw one's candidature, to stand down / *la pièce a été retirée de l'affiche après une semaine* the play came off ou closed after a week **5.** [confisquer] : *on lui a retiré la garde des enfants* he lost custody of the children / *on lui a retiré son permis de conduire* he's been banned from driving **6.** [récupérer - argent] to withdraw, to take out *(sép)*, to draw ; [- bagage, ticket] to pick up *(sép)*, to collect / *j'ai*

retiré un peu d'argent de mon compte I drew ou withdrew some money from my bank account **7.** [obtenir] to gain, to get / *retirer un bénéfice important d'une affaire* to make a large profit out of a deal **8.** IMPR to reprint / *retirer une photo* to make a new ou fresh print (from a photo). ❖ **se retirer** vpi **1.** [s'éloigner] to withdraw / *il est tard, je vais me retirer* *sout* it's late, I'm going to retire ou to withdraw ▶ **se retirer de** to withdraw from / *se retirer de la vie active* to retire ▶ **se retirer dans ses appartements** *hum* to retire ou to withdraw to one's room **2.** [s'établir] to retire / *il s'est retiré dans le Midi* he retired to the South of France ; [se cloîtrer] to retire, to withdraw / *se retirer du monde* to cut o.s. off from the world **3.** [mer] to recede, to ebb.

retombées [ʀətɔ̃be] nfpl NUCL fallout ; *fig* [répercussions] repercussions, effects / *les retombées d'une campagne publicitaire* the results of an advertising campaign.

retomber [3] [ʀətɔ̃be] vi *(aux être)* **1.** [bouteille, balai] to fall over again ; [mur, livres empilés] to fall down again ou back down ; [ivrogne, bambin] to fall over ou down again **2.** [atterrir - chat, sauteur, parachutiste, missile] to land ; [- balle] to come (back) down ; [redescendre - couvercle, rideau de fer, clapet] to close ; [- soufflé, mousse] to collapse / *laissez retomber votre main droite* let your right hand come down ou drop down **3.** [devenir moins fort - fièvre, prix] to drop ; [- agitation] to fall, to tail off, to die away ; [- enthousiasme] to fall, to wane **4.** [dans un état, une habitude] to fall back, to lapse *sout* ▶ **retomber en enfance** to go into one's second childhood **5.** MÉTÉOR [vent] to fall (again), to drop, to die down ; [brume] to disappear, to be dispelled ; *(tournure impersonnelle)* : *il retombe de la pluie / neige / grêle* it's raining / snowing / hailing again **6.** [pendre - drapé, guirlande, ourlet] to hang / *les fleurs retombent en lourdes grappes* the flowers are hanging in heavy clusters **7.** [redevenir] ▶ **retomber amoureux** to fall in love again. ❖ **retomber sur** v + prép **1.** [rejaillir] : *la responsabilité retombe sur moi* the blame for it falls on me ▶ **retomber sur le nez de qqn** *fam*: *un de ces jours ça va te retomber sur le nez !* one of these days you'll get your come-uppance ou what's coming to you! **2.** *fam* [rencontrer à nouveau] ▶ **retomber sur qqn** to bump into ou to come across sb again / *je suis retombé sur le même prof / sujet à l'oral* *fam* I got the same examiner / question for the oral exam.

rétorquer [3] [ʀetɔʀke] vt to retort.

rétorsion [ʀetɔʀsjɔ̃] nf [représailles] retaliation ▶ **user de rétorsion envers** to retaliate against.

retouche [ʀətuʃ] nf **1.** [correction] alteration **2.** ART retouching *(U)* **3.** COUT alteration / *faire des retouches à un vêtement* to make alterations to a garment **4.** PHOT touching up *(U)*.

retoucher [3] [ʀətuʃe] vt [modifier - texte, vêtement] to alter ; [- œuvre] to retouch ; [- photo] to retouch, to touch up *(sép)*. ❖ **retoucher à** v + prép [se remettre à] to go back to / *et depuis, tu n'as plus jamais retouché à une cigarette ?* and since then you haven't touched a ou another cigarette?

retour [ʀətuʀ] nm **1.** [chez soi, au point de départ] return ▶ **à ton retour** when you return home ou get back ▶ **sur le chemin** ou **la route du retour** on the way back ▶ **retour à la normale** return to normal ▶ **retour aux sources** return to one's roots ▶ **retour à la terre** return to the land **2.** [nouvelle apparition - d'une célébrité] return, reappearance ; [récurrence - d'une mode, d'un thème] return, recurrence **3.** ▶ **retour arrière** IMPR backspace ▶ **retour de bâton** kickback ▶ **par un juste retour des choses**: *par un juste retour des choses il a été licencié* he was sacked, which seemed fair enough under the circumstances **4.** [réexpédition] return ▶ **retour à l'envoyeur** ou **à l'expé-**

diteur return to sender ▸ **par retour du courrier** by return of post **5.** TENNIS return ▸ **retour de service** return of serve, service return **6.** FIN ▸ **retour sur investissements** return on investments **7.** COMM return **8.** [meuble] ▸ **bureau avec retour** desk with a right-angled extension unit. ◆ adj inv SPORT ▸ **match retour** return match. ❖ **de retour** loc adv back / *je serai de retour demain* I'll be back tomorrow / *de retour chez lui, il réfléchit* (once he was) back home, he thought it over. ❖ **de retour de** loc prép back from / *de retour de Rio, je tentai de la voir* on my return from Rio, I tried to see her. ❖ **en retour** loc adv in return. ❖ **retour d'âge** nm change of life. ❖ **retour de manivelle** nm [choc en retour] backlash ; [conséquence néfaste] backlash, repercussion. ❖ **retour en arrière** nm **1.** CINÉ & LITTÉR flashback **2.** [régression] step backwards *fig*.

retournement [ʀətuʀnəmɑ̃] nm [revirement] ▸ **un retournement de situation** a turnaround ou a reversal (of the situation).

retourner [3] [ʀətuʀne] ◆ vt *(aux avoir)* **1.** [orienter dans le sens contraire] to turn round ou around *(sép)* ▸ **retourner une arme contre** ou **sur qqn** to turn a weapon on sb ; [renverser - situation] to reverse, to turn inside out ou back to front ▸ **je lui ai retourné son** ou **le compliment** I returned the compliment **2.** [renvoyer - colis, lettre] to send back *(sép)* **3.** [mettre à l'envers - literie] to turn round ou around ; [- carte à jouer] to turn up *(sép)* ; [- champ, paille] to turn over *(sép)* ; [- verre] to turn upside down ; [- grillade] to turn over *(sép)* ; [- gant, poche] to turn inside out / *il a retourné la photo contre le mur* he turned the photo against the wall **4.** [fouiller - maison, pièce] to turn upside down **5.** [examiner - pensée] : *tourner et retourner une idée dans sa tête* to mull over an idea (in one's head) **6.** *fam* [émouvoir] : *j'en suis encore tout retourné !* I'm still reeling from the shock! ◆ vi *(aux être)* **1.** [aller à nouveau] to return, to go again ou back / *je n'y étais pas retourné depuis des années* I had not been back there for years **2.** [revenir] to go back, to return / *retourner chez soi* to go (back) home. ◆ v impers : *peut-on savoir de quoi il retourne ?* what is it all about?, what exactly is going on? ❖ **retourner à** v + prép [reprendre, retrouver] to return to, to go back to / *retourner à un stade antérieur* to revert to an earlier stage. ❖ **se retourner** vpi **1.** [tourner la tête] to turn round UK ou around ▸ **partir sans se retourner** to leave without looking back / *tout le monde se retournait sur eux* everybody turned round to look at them **2.** [se mettre sur l'autre face] to turn over / *je me suis retourné dans mon lit toute la nuit* I tossed and turned all night ▸ **se retourner dans sa tombe** : *elle doit se retourner dans sa tombe* she must be turning in her grave **3.** [se renverser - auto, tracteur] to overturn, to turn over **4.** [réagir] to sort things out UK ▸ **ils ne me laissent pas le temps de me retourner** a) [de décider] they won't give me time to make a decision b) [de me reprendre] they won't give me time to sort things out **5.** [situation] to be reversed, to change completely. ❖ **se retourner contre** vp + prép **1.** [agir contre] ▸ **se retourner contre qqn** to turn against sb / *tout cela finira par se retourner contre toi* all this will eventually backfire on you **2.** DR to take (legal) action against.

retracer [16] [ʀətʀase] vt [relater] to relate, to recount *sout*, to tell of *(insép)* *sout*.

rétracter [3] [ʀetʀakte] vt *sout* [aveu, témoignage] to retract, to withdraw. ❖ **se rétracter** vpi [témoin] to recant *sout*, to retract / *il lui a fallu se rétracter* he had to withdraw his statement.

retrait [ʀətʀɛ] nm **1.** [annulation - d'une licence] cancelling ; [- d'un mot d'ordre] calling off ▸ **retrait de permis (de conduire)** DR revocation of driving licence **2.** BANQUE withdrawal / *je veux faire un retrait de 500 euros*

I want to take out ou to withdraw 500 euros **3.** [récupération] ▸ **le retrait des billets / bagages se fera dès 11 h** tickets / luggage may be collected from 11 o'clock onwards. ❖ **en retrait** loc adv set back ▸ **rester en retrait** a) *pr* to stand back b) *fig* to remain in the background. ❖ **en retrait de** loc prép below, beneath.

retraite [ʀətʀɛt] nf **1.** [pension] pension **2.** [cessation d'activité] retirement ▸ **il est à la** ou **en retraite** he has retired ▸ **prendre sa retraite** to retire / *être mis à la retraite* to be retired ▸ **retraite anticipée** early retirement **3.** MIL & RELIG retreat.

retraité, e [ʀətʀete] ◆ adj [qui est à la retraite] retired. ◆ nm, f ADMIN pensioner ; [personne ne travaillant plus] retired person.

retraitement [ʀətʀetmɑ̃] nm reprocessing ▸ **centre** ou **usine de retraitement (des déchets nucléaires)** (nuclear) reprocessing plant.

retranchement [ʀətʀɑ̃ʃmɑ̃] nm MIL retrenchment, entrenchment ; *fig* ▸ **pousser qqn dans ses derniers retranchements** to force sb to the wall.

retrancher [3] [ʀətʀɑ̃ʃe] vt **1.** MATH to subtract **2.** *sout* [enlever] to remove, to excise **3.** [déduire - pour des raisons administratives] to deduct ; [- par sanction] to deduct, to dock. ❖ **se retrancher** vpi **1.** [se protéger] ▸ **se retrancher derrière** a) [se cacher] to hide behind b) [se réfugier] to take refuge behind / *se retrancher sur ses positions* to remain entrenched in one's position **2.** MIL to entrench o.s.

retransmettre [84] [ʀətʀɑ̃smɛtʀ] vt RADIO to broadcast ; TV to broadcast, to screen, to show / *retransmettre une émission en direct / différé* to broadcast a programme live / a recorded programme.

retransmission [ʀətʀɑ̃smisjɔ̃] nf RADIO broadcast ; TV broadcast, screening, showing ▸ **retransmission en direct / différé** live / recorded broadcast.

retravailler [3] [ʀətʀavaje] ◆ vt to work on *(insép)* again. ◆ vi to (start) work again.

rétrécir [32] [ʀetʀesiʀ] ◆ vt TEXT & VÊT to shrink. ◆ vi TEXT & VÊT to shrink / *rétrécir au lavage* to shrink in the wash.

rétrécissement [ʀetʀesismɑ̃] nm **1.** [d'un couloir, d'un diaphragme] narrowing *(U)* ▸ **rétrécissement de la chaussée** bottleneck **2.** TEXT & VÊT shrinkage.

rétribuer [7] [ʀetʀibɥe] vt [employé] to pay, to remunerate ; [travail, service rendu] to pay for *(insép)*.

rétribution [ʀetʀibysjɔ̃] nf **1.** [salaire] remuneration, salary **2.** *sout* [récompense] recompense, reward.

⚠ Le mot anglais **retribution** signifie « punition », « châtiment » et non rétribution.

rétro [ʀetʀo] ◆ adj inv retro ▸ **mode rétro** retro fashion. ◆ nm **1.** *fam abr de* rétroviseur **2.** ▸ **le rétro** retro style.

rétroactif, ive [ʀetʀoaktif, iv] adj retroactive / *avec effet rétroactif au 1er janvier* backdated to January 1st.

rétrograde [ʀetʀoɡʀad] adj **1.** [passéiste - esprit] reactionary, backward ; [- mesure, politique] reactionary, backward-looking, retrograde *sout* **2.** [de recul - mouvement] backward, retrograde *sout*.

rétrograder [3] [ʀetʀoɡʀade] ◆ vt [fonctionnaire] to downgrade, to demote ; [officier] to demote. ◆ vi **1.** AUTO to change down UK, to shift down, to downshift US **2.** [dans une hiérarchie] to move down.

rétroprojecteur [ʀetʀopʀoʒɛktœʀ] nm overhead projector.

rétrospectif, ive [retʀɔspɛktif, iv] adj [étude] retrospective. ❖ **rétrospective** nf ART retrospective ; CINÉ season / *une rétrospective Richard Burton* a Richard Burton season.

rétrospectivement [ʀetʀɔspɛktivmɑ̃] adv in retrospect, retrospectively, looking back.

retroussé, e [ʀətʀuse] adj **1.** [jupe] bunched ou pulled up ; [manches, pantalon] rolled ou turned up **2.** [nez] turned up.

retrousser [3] [ʀətʀuse] vt [jupe] to bunch ou to pull up *(sép)* ; [pantalon] to roll ou to turn up *(sép)* ; [manches] to roll up *(sép)* / *il va falloir retrousser nos manches* pr & fig we'll have to roll our sleeves up.

retrouvailles [ʀətʀuvaj] nfpl [après une querelle] getting back on friendly terms again ; [après une absence] reunion, getting together again.

retrouver [3] [ʀətʀuve] vt **1.** [clés, lunettes] to find (again) ▸ **retrouver un poste** to find a (new) job / *retrouver son chemin* to find one's way (again) ; [après un changement] to find ▸ **retrouver qqn affaibli / changé** to find sb weaker / a different person **2.** [ami, parent] to be reunited with, to meet up with *(insép)* (again) ; [voleur] to catch up with *(insép)* (again), to find ; [revoir par hasard] to come across *(insép)* (again), to run into *(insép)* again ; [rejoindre] to meet up with again / *retrouve-moi en bas* meet me downstairs **3.** [se rappeler] to remember, to recall *sout* / *ça y est, j'ai retrouvé le mot !* that's it, the word's come back to me now! **4.** [jouir à nouveau de] to enjoy again / *retrouver la forme* to get fit again, to be back on form / *retrouver la foi* to find (one's) faith again / *retrouver le sommeil* to go back to sleep / *elle m'a fait retrouver la joie de vivre* she made me feel ou thanks to her I began to feel that life was worth living again **5.** [reconnaître] to recognize, to trace / *on retrouve les mêmes propriétés dans les polymères* the same properties are to be found in polymers. ❖ **se retrouver** ❖ vp *(emploi réciproque)* **1.** [avoir rendez-vous] to meet (one another) **2.** [se réunir] to get together **3.** [se rencontrer à nouveau] to meet again / *on se retrouvera, mon bonhomme !* fam I'll get even with you, chum! ❖ vpi **1.** [être de nouveau] to find o.s. back (again) / *se retrouver dans la même situation (qu'avant)* to find o.s. back in the same situation (as before) **2.** [par hasard] to end up / *à quarante ans, il s'est retrouvé veuf* he (suddenly) found himself a widower at forty / *tu vas te retrouver à l'hôpital* you'll end up in hospital **3.** [se repérer] to find one's way / *je ne m'y retrouve plus dans tous ces formulaires à remplir* I can't make head or tail of all these forms to fill in ▸ **s'y retrouver a)** [résoudre un problème] to sort things out **b)** [faire un bénéfice] to make a profit **4.** [se ressourcer] to find o.s. again, to go back to one's roots.

rétroviseur [ʀetʀɔvizœʀ] nm ▸ **rétroviseur central** (rearview) mirror ▸ **rétroviseur latéral** wing mirror 🇬🇧, side-view mirror 🇺🇸.

réunification [ʀeynifikasjɔ̃] nf reunification.

réunifier [9] [ʀeynifje] vt to reunify, to reunite.

réunion [ʀeynjɔ̃] nf **1.** [rassemblement] gathering, get-together ▸ **réunion de famille** family reunion ou gathering **2.** [congrès] meeting / *dites que je suis en réunion* say that I'm at ou in a meeting ; [séance] session, sitting **3.** [regroupement - de faits, de preuves] bringing together, assembling, gathering ; [- de sociétés] merging ; [- d'États] union **4.** SPORT meeting ▸ **réunion (sportive)** sports meeting, sporting event ▸ **réunion d'athlétisme** athletics meeting ▸ **réunion hippique** horse show.

Réunion (La) [ʀeynjɔ̃] npr f ▸ **(l')île de La Réunion** Réunion / *à La Réunion* in Réunion. ⟶ île

réunionnais, e [ʀeynjɔnɛ, ɛz] adj from Réunion. ❖ **Réunionnais, e** nm, f *inhabitant of Réunion.*

réunir [32] [ʀeyniʀ] vt **1.** [relier - pôles, tuyaux] to join (together) ; [- brins, câbles] to tie together **2.** [mettre ensemble - objets] to collect together *(sép)* ; [- bétail] to round up *(sép)* / *le spectacle réunit ses meilleures chansons* the show is a collection of her best hits ; [province] ▸ **réunir à** to join to **3.** [recueillir - statistiques, propositions] to put ou to collect together ; [- preuves] to put together ; [- fonds] to raise **4.** [rassembler - personnes] to bring together, to reunite. ❖ **se réunir** vpi **1.** [se retrouver ensemble] to meet, to get together **2.** [fusionner] to unite, to join (together).

réussi, e [ʀeysi] adj successful / *comme fête, c'était réussi !* iron call that a party!

réussir [32] [ʀeysiʀ] ❖ vt [manœuvre, œuvre, recette] to make a success of, to carry off *(sép)* ; [exercice] to succeed in doing ; [examen] to pass / *j'ai bien réussi mon coup* fam it worked out (well) for me, I managed to pull it off / *réussir sa vie* to make a success of one's life / *avec ce concert, il réussit un tour de force* his concert is a great achievement. ❖ vi **1.** [dans la vie, à l'école] to do well, to be successful / *il a réussi dans la vie* he's done well in life, he's a successful man ▸ **réussir à un examen** to pass an exam **2.** [affaire, entreprise] to succeed, to be a success / *l'opération n'a pas vraiment réussi* the operation wasn't really a success **3.** [parvenir] ▸ **réussir à faire qqch** to manage to do sthg, to succeed in doing sthg / *j'ai réussi à le réparer / à me couper* I managed to mend it / to cut myself **4.** [convenir] ▸ **réussir à qqn** [climat, nourriture] to agree with sb, to do sb good / *le café lui réussit / ne lui réussit pas* coffee agrees / doesn't agree with him ▸ **rien ne lui réussit** he can't do anything right **5.** AGR & HORT to thrive, to do well.

réussite [ʀeysit] nf **1.** [affaire, entreprise] success ▸ **réussite à un examen** exam pass **2.** JEUX patience 🇬🇧, solitaire 🇺🇸 ▸ **faire une réussite** to have a game of patience.

réutilisable [ʀeytilizabl] adj reusable ▸ **non réutilisable** disposable, throwaway.

réutiliser [3] [ʀeytilize] vt to reuse, to use again.

revaloir [60] [ʀəvalwaʀ] vt ▸ **je te revaudrai ça a)** [en remerciant] I'll repay you some day **b)** [en menaçant] I'll get even with you for that, I'll pay you back for that.

revaloriser [3] [ʀəvalɔʀize] vt **1.** [monnaie] to revaluate **2.** [salaires] to raise, to revalue **3.** [théorie, fonction] to improve the status ou prestige ou standing of, to upgrade.

revanche [ʀəvɑ̃ʃ] nf **1.** [sur un ennemi] revenge ▸ **prendre sa revanche (sur qqn)** to take ou to get one's revenge (on sb) **2.** JEUX & SPORT return game. ❖ **en revanche** loc adv on the other hand.

rêvasser [3] [ʀɛvase] vi to daydream, to dream away, to muse.

rêve [ʀɛv] nm **1.** [d'un dormeur] dream ▸ **faire un rêve** to have a dream / *je l'ai vu en rêve* I saw him in my ou in a dream / *bonne nuit, fais de beaux rêves !* good night, sweet dreams! **2.** [d'un utopiste] dream, fantasy, pipe dream / *mon rêve, ce serait d'aller au Japon* my dream is to go to Japan, I dream of going to Japan **3.** fam : *c'est / ce n'est pas le rêve* it's / it isn't ideal. ❖ **de mes rêves, de ses rêves** loc adj of my / his, etc. dreams / *j'ai le métier de mes rêves* I've got the job I always dreamed of having. ❖ **de rêve** loc adj ideal / *une vie de rêve* a sublime ou an ideal existence.

rêvé, e [ʀɛve] adj perfect, ideal.

revêche [ʀəvɛʃ] adj [personne] surly, cantankerous, tetchy ; [voix, air] surly, grumpy.

réveil [ʀevɛj] nm **1.** [après le sommeil] waking (up), awakening litt / *j'ai des réveils difficiles* ou *le réveil difficile* I find it hard to wake up / *à mon réveil il était là* when I woke up he was there **2.** [prise de conscience] awakening **3.** [de la mémoire, de la nature] reawakening ; [d'une douleur] return, new onset ; [d'un volcan] (new) stirring, fresh eruption **4.** [pendule] alarm (clock) / *j'ai mis le réveil (à 7 h)* I've set the alarm (for 7 o'clock) ▸ **réveil téléphonique** wake-up service.

réveillé, e [ʀeveje] adj awake ▸ **à moitié réveillé** half asleep ▸ **je suis mal réveillée** I'm still half asleep.

réveiller [4] [ʀeveje] vt **1.** [tirer - du sommeil, de l'évanouissement] to wake (up) *(sép)* ; [-d'une réflexion, d'une rêverie] to rouse, to stir / *il faut que l'on se fasse réveiller à 7 heures si on ne veut pas rater l'avion* we need to make sure somebody wakes us up at 7 a.m. if we don't want to miss the plane **2.** [faire renaître - enthousiasme, rancœur, envie] to reawaken, to revive. ⬥ **se réveiller** vpi **1.** [sortir - du sommeil, de l'évanouissement] to wake (up), to awake *litt*, to awaken *litt* ; [-d'une réflexion, de la torpeur] to wake up, to stir ou to rouse o.s. **2.** [se ranimer - passion, souvenir] to revive, to be stirred up ou aroused (again) ; [-volcan] to stir ou to erupt again ; [-maladie, douleur] to start up again, to return.

réveillon [ʀevejɔ̃] nm *family meal eaten on Christmas Eve or New Year's Eve* ▸ **réveillon (de Noël) a)** [fête] Christmas Eve party **b)** [repas] Christmas Eve supper ▸ **réveillon de la Saint-Sylvestre** ou **du Jour de l'An a)** [fête] New Year's Eve party **b)** [repas] New Year's Eve supper.

réveillonner [3] [ʀevejɔne] vi [faire une fête - à Noël] to have a Christmas Eve party ; [-pour la Saint-Sylvestre] to have a New Year's Eve party ; [faire un repas - à Noël] to have a Christmas Eve supper ; [-pour la Saint-Sylvestre] to have a New Year's Eve supper.

révélateur, trice [ʀevelatœʀ, tʀis] adj [détail] revealing, indicative, significant ; [lapsus, sourire] revealing, telltale / *ce sondage est très révélateur de la tendance actuelle* this poll tells us ou reveals a lot about the current trend.

révélation [ʀevelasjɔ̃] nf [information] revelation, disclosure.

révéler [18] [ʀevele] vt **1.** [secret, information, intention] to reveal ; [état de fait] to reveal, to bring to light ; [vérité] to reveal, to tell **2.** [montrer - don, qualité, anomalie] to reveal, to show **3.** [faire connaître] ▸ **révéler qqn** to make sb famous. ⬥ **se révéler** vpi **1.** [s'avérer] ▸ **se révéler coûteux** / **utile** to prove (to be) expensive / useful **2.** [se faire connaître] to be revealed ou discovered, to come to light / *tu t'es révélé sous ton vrai jour* you've showed yourself in your true colours / *elle s'est révélée (au grand public) dans Carmen* she had her first big success in Carmen.

✐ In reformed spelling (see p. 16-18), this verb is conjugated like *semer* : *il révèlera, elle révélerait.*

revenant, e [ʀəvnɑ̃, ɑ̃t] nm, f *fam & hum* ▸ **tiens, un revenant !** hello, stranger!, long time no see! *hum.* ⬥ **revenant** nm [fantôme] ghost, spirit.

revendeur, euse [ʀəvɑ̃dœʀ, øz] nm, f **1.** [détaillant] retailer, dealer **2.** [de billets, de tickets] tout 🇬🇧, scalper 🇺🇸 ; [d'articles d'occasion] (second-hand) dealer ▸ **revendeur de drogue** drug dealer.

revendication [ʀəvɑ̃dikasjɔ̃] nf [réclamation] demand ▸ **journée de revendication** day of action ou of protest ▸ **revendications salariales** wage demands ou claims.

revendiquer [3] [ʀəvɑ̃dike] vt **1.** [réclamer - dû, droit, part d'héritage] to claim ; [-hausse - de salaire] to demand ; *(en usage absolu)* : *le personnel revendique* the staff are making demands ou have put in a claim **2.** [assumer] to lay claim to, to claim ▸ **revendiquer la responsabilité de qqch** to claim responsibility for sthg / *l'attentat n'a pas été revendiqué* nobody has claimed responsibility for the attack / *il n'a jamais revendiqué cette paternité* he never claimed this child as his.

revendre [73] [ʀəvɑ̃dʀ] vt **1.** [vendre - gén] to sell ; [suj : détaillant] to retail / *revends ta voiture, si tu as besoin*

d'argent if you need money sell your car **2.** *fam* EXPR⟩ *elle a du talent* / *de l'ambition à revendre* she's got masses of talent / ambition.

revenir [40] [ʀəvniʀ] vi **1.** [venir à nouveau - gén] to come back ; [-chez soi] to come back, to come (back) home, to return home ; [-au point de départ] to return, to come ou to get back / *passe me voir en revenant du bureau* call in to see me on your way back ou home from the office / *je reviens (tout de suite)* I'll be (right) back / *la lettre m'est revenue* the letter was returned to me ▸ **revenir en arrière a)** [dans le temps] to go back (in time) **b)** [dans l'espace] to retrace one's steps, to go back ▸ **revenir au point de départ a)** to go back to the starting point **b)** *fig* to be back to square one **2.** [se manifester à nouveau - doute, inquiétude] to return, to come back ; [-calme, paix] to return, to be restored ; [-problème] to crop up ou to arise again ; [-occasion] to crop up again ; [-célébration] to come round again ; [-saison] to return, to come back ; [-soleil] to come out again, to reappear / *le temps des fêtes est revenu* the festive season is with us again ou has come round again **3.** SPORT [dans une course] to come back, to catch up **4.** [coûter] ▸ **revenir cher** to be expensive ▸ **revenir à** to cost, to amount to, to come to **5.** CULIN ▸ **faire revenir** to brown. ⬥ **revenir à** v + prép **1.** [équivaloir à] to come down to, to amount to / *ce qui revient à dire que...* which amounts to saying that... / *ça revient au même !* (it) amounts to ou comes to the same thing! **2.** [reprendre - mode, procédé, thème] to go back to, to revert to, to return to / *on revient aux* ou *à la mode des cheveux courts* short hair is coming back ou on its way back ▸ **mais revenons** ou **revenons-en à cette affaire** but let's get ou come back to this matter / *bon, pour (en) revenir à notre histoire...* right, to get back to ou to go on with our story... ▸ **y revenir** : *voilà dix euros, et n'y reviens plus !* here's ten euros, and don't ask me again ! ▸ **revenir à soi** to come to, to come round **3.** [suj : part, récompense] to go ou to fall to, to devolve on ou upon *sout* ; [suj : droit, tâche] to fall to / *avec les honneurs qui lui reviennent* with the honours (which are) due to her / *ses terrains sont revenus à l'État* his lands passed ou went to the State / *tout le mérite t'en revient* the credit is all yours, you get all the credit for it / *la décision nous revient, il nous revient de décider* it's for us ou up to us to decide **4.** [suj : faculté, souvenir] to come back to ▸ **l'appétit lui revient** she's recovering her appetite ou getting her appetite back / *la mémoire lui revient* her memory is coming back / *ça me revient seulement maintenant, ils ont divorcé* I've just remembered, they got divorced ; *(tournure impersonnelle)* ▸ **revenir à qqn** ou **aux oreilles de qqn** to get back to sb, to reach sb's ears **5.** *fam* [plaire à] : *elle a une tête qui ne me revient pas* I don't really like the look of her. ⬥ **revenir de** v + prép **1.** [émotion, étonnement, maladie] to get over, to recover from ; [évanouissement] to come round from, to come to ▸ **en revenir a)** [guérir] to come ou to pull through it, to recover **b)** [échapper à un danger] to come through (it) ▸ **ne pas en revenir** : *je n'en reviens pas !* I can't get over it ! / *je n'en reviens pas qu'il ait dit ça !* it's amazing he should say that!, I can't get over him saying that! **2.** [idée, préjugé] to put ou to cast aside *(sép)*, to throw over *(sép)* ; [illusion] to shake off *(sép)* ; [principe] to give up *(sép)*, to leave behind / *revenir de ses erreurs* to realize ou to recognize one's mistakes. ⬥ **revenir sur** v + prép **1.** [question] to go back over, to hark back to / *elle ne peut s'empêcher de revenir sur cette triste affaire* she can't help going ou mulling over that sad business **2.** [décision, déclaration, promesse] to go back on / *ma décision est prise, je ne reviendrai pas dessus* my mind is made up and I'm not going to change it.

revente [ʀəvɑ̃t] nf resale.

revenu [ʀəvəny] nm **1.** [rétribution - d'une personne] income *(U)* / *elle a de gros / petits revenus* she has a large / small income ▸ **revenu minimum d'insertion** minimum guaranteed income *(now replaced by the "revenu de solidarité active")* ▸ **revenu de solidarité active** minimum guaranteed income **2.** [recettes - de l'État] revenue ▸ **revenus publics** ou **de l'État** public revenue **3.** [intérêt] income, return / *un investissement produisant un revenu de 7 %* an investment with a 7% rate of return ; [dividende] yield / *le revenu d'une action* the yield on a share.

rêver [4] [ʀɛve] ◆ vi **1.** [en dormant] to dream / *c'est ce qu'il m'a dit, je n'ai pas rêvé !* that's what he said, I didn't dream it up ou imagine it! ▸ **on croit rêver !** [ton irrité] is this a joke? **2.** [divaguer] to be imagining things, to be in cloud-cuckoo-land / *(quand on voit) des paysages comme ça, ça fait rêver* scenery like that is just out of this world / *des mots qui font rêver* words that fire the imagination ▸ **faut pas rêver !** let's not get carried away! **3.** [songer] to dream, to daydream ▸ **rêver à** to dream of *(insép)*, to muse over *(insép)* sout. ◆ vt [suj : dormeur] to dream / *rêver que...* to dream that... ❖ **rêver de** v + prép [espérer] to dream of ▸ **rêver de faire qqch** to be longing to do sthg.

réverbère [ʀevɛʀbɛʀ] nm [lampe] street lamp, streetlight.

réverbérer [18] [ʀevɛʀbeʀe] vt [chaleur, lumière] to reflect ; [son] to reverberate, to send back *(sép)*.
📝. In reformed spelling (see p. 16-18), this verb is conjugated like *semer : il réverbèrera, elle réverbèrerait.*

révérence [ʀeveʀɑ̃s] nf [salut] bow, curtsy, curtsey / *elle fit une révérence à Son Altesse* she curtseyed to Her Highness ▸ **tirer sa révérence à qqn** to walk out on sb ▸ **tirer sa révérence à qqch** to bow out of sthg.

révérend, e [ʀeveʀɑ̃, ɑ̃d] adj reverend / *le Révérend Père Thomas* (the) Reverend Father Thomas. ❖ **révérend** nm reverend.

révérer [18] [ʀeveʀe] vt sout to revere, to reverence sout.
📝 In reformed spelling (see p. 16-18), this verb is conjugated like *semer : il révérera, elle révérerait.*

rêverie [ʀɛvʀi] nf [réflexion] daydreaming *(U)*, reverie.

revers [ʀəvɛʀ] nm **1.** [d'une blouse, d'un veston] lapel ; [d'un pantalon] turn-up 🇬🇧, cuff 🇺🇸 ; [d'une manche] (turned-back) cuff ; [d'un uniforme] facing **2.** [d'une feuille, d'un tissu, d'un tableau, de la main] back ; [d'une médaille, d'une pièce] reverse (side) ▸ **c'est le revers de la médaille** that's the other side of the coin, there's the rub **3.** [échec, défaite] setback ▸ **revers de fortune** reverse of fortune, setback (in one's fortunes) **4.** TENNIS backhand (shot) / *faire un revers* to play a backhand shot. ❖ **à revers** loc adv MIL from ou in the rear.

reverser [3] [ʀəvɛʀse] vt **1.** [verser - de nouveau] to pour again, to pour (out) more (of) ; [- dans le récipient d'origine] to pour back *(sép)* **2.** FIN [reporter] to transfer / *la prime d'assurance vous sera intégralement reversée au bout d'un an* the total premium will be paid back to you after one year.

réversible [ʀevɛʀsibl] adj [vêtement] reversible.

revêtement [ʀəvɛtmɑ̃] nm **1.** CONSTR [intérieur - peinture] covering ; [- enduit] coating ; [extérieur - gén] facing ; [- crépi] rendering ▸ **revêtement de sol** flooring *(U)* **2.** TRAV PUB : *refaire le revêtement d'une route* to resurface a road.

revêtir [44] [ʀəvɛtiʀ] vt **1.** sout [habiller] ▸ **revêtir qqn de** to dress ou to array sb in, to clothe sb in ou with **2.** sout [importance, signification] to take on *(insép)*, to assume ; [forme] to appear in, to take on, to assume.

rêveur, euse [ʀɛvœʀ, øz] ◆ adj **1.** [distrait] dreamy **2.** [perplexe] ▸ **ça laisse rêveur !** it makes you wonder! ◆ nm, f dreamer, daydreamer.

revient [ʀəvjɛ̃] nm ⟶ **prix**.

revigorer [3] [ʀəvigɔʀe] vt [stimuler - suj : vent, promenade] to invigorate ; [- suj : bain] to invigorate, to refresh ; [- suj : boisson, aliment] to revive, to refresh.

revirement [ʀəviʀmɑ̃] nm [changement - d'avis] aboutface, change of mind ; [- de situation] turnaround, about-face, sudden turn / *un revirement dans l'opinion publique* a complete swing ou turnaround in public opinion / *un revirement de la tendance sur le marché des valeurs* a sudden reversal of stock market trends.

réviser [3] [ʀevize] vt **1.** ÉDUC & UNIV to revise 🇬🇧, to review 🇺🇸, to go over *(insép)* (again) **2.** [réévaluer - jugement, situation] to review, to reexamine, to reappraise ▸ **réviser à la baisse / hausse** to downgrade / upgrade, to scale down / up **3.** DR ▸ **réviser un procès** to reopen a trial ▸ **réviser un jugement** to review a judgment **4.** [voiture] to service ; [machine] to overhaul / *faire réviser une voiture* to have a car serviced / *faire réviser les freins* to have the brakes checked.

révision [ʀevizjɔ̃] nf **1.** ÉDUC & UNIV revision *(U)* 🇬🇧, review *(sg)* 🇺🇸 **2.** [d'une voiture] service ; [d'une machine] overhaul, overhauling **3.** [fait de réestimer] reevaluation, reappraisal **4.** DR [d'un procès] rehearing ; [d'un jugement] reviewing.

révisionniste [ʀevizjɔnist] adj & nmf revisionist.

revisser [3] [ʀəvise] vt to screw back again.

revitalisant, e [ʀəvitalizɑ̃, ɑ̃t] adj [shampooing, crème] revitalizing.

revivifiant, e [ʀəvivifjɑ̃, ɑ̃t] adj [shampooing, gel douche] revitalizing.

revivre [90] [ʀəvivʀ] ◆ vi **1.** [renaître] to come alive (again) / *quel calme, je me sens revivre !* how quiet it is around here, I feel like a new person! **2.** [nature, campagne] to come alive again **3.** [personne ou animal mort] to come back to life **4.** [redevenir actuel] ▸ **faire revivre qqch : faire revivre la tradition** to restore ou to revive tradition. ◆ vt **1.** [se souvenir de] to relive, to live ou to go through *(insép)* (again) **2.** [vivre à nouveau] to relive.

révocation [ʀevɔkasjɔ̃] nf **1.** ADMIN [d'un fonctionnaire] dismissal ; [d'un dirigeant] removal **2.** DR [d'un acte juridique] repeal, revocation ; [d'un testament] revocation ; [d'un ordre] rescinding.

revoilà [ʀəvwala] prép : *revoilà le printemps !* it looks like spring's here again! / *les revoilà !* there they are again!

revoir¹ [ʀəvwaʀ] nm litt : *le charme du revoir* the delights of meeting again. ❖ **au revoir** ◆ interj goodbye. ◆ nm : *ce n'est qu'un au revoir* we'll meet again.

revoir² [62] [ʀəvwaʀ] vt **1.** [rencontrer à nouveau] to see ou to meet again / *et que je ne te revoie plus ici, compris ?* and don't let me see ou catch you around here again, is that clear? ; [retourner à] to see again, to go back to **2.** [examiner à nouveau - images] to see again, to have another look at ; [- exposition, spectacle] to see again ; [- dossier] to reexamine, to look at *(insép)* again ; [- vidéocassette] to watch again **3.** [modifier - texte] to reexamine, to revise ; [- opinion] to modify, to revise / **'édition revue et corrigée'** 'revised edition' / *revoir à la hausse / baisse* to revise upwards / downwards. ❖ **se revoir** vp *(emploi réciproque)* to meet again.

révoltant, e [ʀevɔltɑ̃, ɑ̃t] adj [violence, lâcheté] appalling, shocking ; [grossièreté] revolting, outrageous, scandalous.

révolte [ʀevɔlt] nf **1.** [sédition] revolt, rebellion **2.** [insoumission] rebellion, revolt ▸ **être en révolte contre qqn** to be in revolt against sb.

révolté, e [ʀevɔlte] ◆ adj **1.** [rebelle] rebellious, rebel *(avant nom)* **2.** [indigné] outraged. ◆ nm, f [gén] rebel.

révolter [3] [ʀevɔlte] vt [scandaliser] to appal, to revolt, to shock / *ça ne te révolte pas, toi ?* don't you think that's disgusting ou revolting ou shocking? ❖ **se révolter** vpi [gén] to revolt / *adolescent, il s'est révolté contre ses parents* he rebelled against his parents when he was a teenager.

révolu, e [ʀevɔly] adj **1.** [fini] past / *l'époque des hippies est révolue* the hippie era is over **2.** ADMIN : *âgé de 18 ans révolus* over 18 (years of age) / *au bout de trois années révolues* after three full years.

révolution [ʀevɔlysjɔ̃] nf **1.** POL revolution ▶ **la Révolution (française)** the French Revolution **2.** [changement] revolution ▶ **faire** ou **causer une révolution dans qqch** to revolutionize sthg **3.** ASTRON & MATH revolution.

🏛 **La Révolution française**

One of the most important events in the history of modern France, from which it emerged as a Republic with an egalitarian constitution. Precipitated by the social and financial abuses of the **Ancien Régime**, it was a turbulent period lasting from the Fall of the Bastille in 1789 until the end of the century. It was marked by the Declaration of Human Rights, the execution of Louis XVI, the Reign of Terror (1793-1794) and war against the other European powers.

---

révolutionnaire [ʀevɔlysjɔnɛʀ] ❖ adj **1.** POL revolutionary **2.** HIST revolutionary **3.** *fig* revolutionary. ❖ nmf **1.** POL revolutionary, revolutionist US **2.** HIST ▶ **un révolutionnaire** a revolutionary.

révolutionner [3] [ʀevɔlysjɔne] vt [système, domaine] to revolutionize ; [vie] to change radically.

revolver, révolver* [ʀevɔlvɛʀ] nm ARM revolver ▶ **un coup de revolver** a gunshot.

révoquer [3] [ʀevɔke] vt **1.** ADMIN [fonctionnaire] to dismiss ; [dirigeant] to remove (from office) **2.** DR [acte juridique] to revoke, to repeal ; [testament] to revoke ; [ordre] to revoke, to rescind.

revue [ʀəvy] nf **1.** [publication - gén] magazine ▶ **revue de mode** fashion magazine ▶ **revue scientifique** science journal **2.** [de music-hall] variety show ; [de chansonniers] revue ▶ **revue à grand spectacle** spectacular **3.** MIL [inspection] inspection, review ; [défilé] review, march-past ▶ **passer en revue a)** [troupes] to hold a review of, to review **b)** [uniformes] to inspect **4.** [inventaire] ▶ **faire la revue de, passer en revue a)** [vêtements, documents] to go ou to look through **b)** [solutions] to go over in one's mind, to review. ❖ **revue de presse** nf review of the press ou of what the papers say.

révulsé, e [ʀevylse] adj [traits, visage] contorted ▶ **les yeux révulsés** with his eyes rolled upwards.

révulser [3] [ʀevylse] vt [dégoûter] to revolt, to fill with loathing, to disgust.

rez-de-chaussée [ʀedʃose] nm inv ground floor US, first floor US ▶ **au rez-de-chaussée** on the ground floor.

rez-de-jardin [ʀedʒaʀdɛ̃] nm inv ground ou garden level ▶ **pièces en rez-de-jardin** ground-level rooms.

RF abr écrite de **République française**.

RFA (abr de **République fédérale d'Allemagne**) npr f FRG, West Germany.

Rh (abr écrite de **Rhésus**) Rh.

rhabiller [3] [ʀabije] vt [habiller à nouveau] to dress again / *rhabille-le* put his clothes back on (for him). ❖ **se rhabiller** vp (emploi réfléchi) **1.** [s'habiller à nouveau] to put one's clothes back on, to dress ou to get dressed again **2.** EXPR **tu peux aller te / il peut aller se rhabiller !** *fam* you've / he's got another think coming!

Rhésus [ʀezys] nm [système sanguin] ▶ **Rhésus positif / négatif** Rhesus positive / negative.

rhétorique [ʀetɔʀik] ❖ adj rhetoric, rhetorical. ❖ nf **1.** [art] rhetoric **2.** dated ÉDUC ≃ year 12 UK ; ≃ sixth grade US.

Rhin [ʀɛ̃] npr m ▶ **le Rhin** the Rhine.

rhinite [ʀinit] nf rhinitis.

rhinocéros [ʀinɔseʀɔs] nm ZOOL rhinoceros, rhino.

rhino-pharyngite [ʀinɔfaʀɛ̃ʒit] (*pl* **rhino-pharyngites**) nf rhinopharyngitis.

Rhodes [ʀɔd] npr Rhodes. ⟶ **île**

rhododendron [ʀɔdɔdɛ̃dʀɔ̃] nm rhododendron.

Rhône [ʀon] npr m [fleuve] ▶ **le Rhône** the (River) Rhône.

rhubarbe [ʀybaʀb] nf rhubarb.

rhum [ʀɔm] nm rum.

rhumatisme [ʀymatism] nm rheumatism (U) / *avoir un rhumatisme* ou *des rhumatismes au genou* to have rheumatism in one's knee.

rhumatologue [ʀymatɔlɔg] nmf rheumatologist.

rhume [ʀym] nm cold / *tu vas attraper un rhume* you're going to catch (a) cold ▶ **rhume des foins** hay fever.

RIB, Rib [ʀib] nm abr de **relevé d'identité bancaire**.

ribambelle [ʀibɑ̃bɛl] nf [quantité] flock, swarm / *suivie d'une ribambelle de gamins* *fam* followed by a long flock of ou a swarm of kids.

ricanement [ʀikanmɑ̃] nm [rire - méchant] sniggering (U), snigger ; [- nerveux] nervous ou jittery laugh ; [- bête] giggle, giggling (U) ▶ **ricanements** sniggering.

ricaner [3] [ʀikane] vi [rire - méchamment] to snigger ; [- nerveusement] to laugh nervously ; [- bêtement] to giggle.

richard, e [ʀiʃaʀ, aʀd] nm, f *fam* & *péj* rich person.

riche [ʀiʃ] ❖ adj **1.** [fortuné - famille, personne] rich, wealthy, well-off ; [- nation] rich, wealthy / *on n'est pas bien riche chez nous* we're not very well-off ▶ **être riche comme Crésus** ou **à millions** to be as rich as Croesus ou Midas **2.** (avant nom) [demeure, décor] lavish, sumptuous, luxurious ; [étoffe, enluminure] magnificent, splendid / *un riche cadre doré* a heavy gilt frame **3.** [végétation] lush, luxuriant, profuse ; [terre] fertile, rich ; [aliment] rich ; [vie] rich / *vous y trouverez une documentation très riche sur Proust* you'll find a wide range of documents on Proust there / *c'est une riche idée que tu as eue là* *fam* ou *iron* that's a wonderful ou great idea you've just had **4.** [complexe] rich / *a un vocabulaire / une langue riche* she has a rich vocabulary / a tremendous command of the language **5.** ▶ **riche en a)** [vitamines, minerais] rich in **b)** [événements] full of ▶ **régime riche en calcium** calcium-rich diet / *la journée fut riche en émotions* the day was packed full of excitement / *leur bibliothèque n'est pas riche en livres d'art* they don't have a very large collection ou choice of art books **6.** ▶ **riche de** [qualités, possibilités] : *un livre riche d'enseignements* a very informative book / *un magazine féminin riche d'idées* a women's magazine packed full of / *son premier roman est riche de promesses* his first novel is full of promise ou shows great promise. ❖ nmf rich person ▶ **les riches** the rich, the wealthy / *voiture de riche* rich man's car.

richement [ʀiʃmɑ̃] adv **1.** [luxueusement] richly, handsomely **2.** [abondamment] lavishly, sumptuously, richly ▶ **richement illustré** lavishly illustrated.

richesse [ʀiʃɛs] nf **1.** [fortune - d'une personne] wealth ; [- d'une région, d'une nation] wealth, affluence, prosperity / *ses livres sont sa seule richesse* his books are all he has **2.** [luxuriance - de la végétation] richness, lushness, profuseness, luxuriance **3.** [complexité - du vocabulaire, de la langue] richness ; [- de l'imagination] creativeness, inventiveness / *la richesse culturelle de notre capitale* the cultural wealth of our capital city. ◆ **richesses** nfpl [biens, capital] riches, wealth (*U*) ; [articles de valeur] treasures, wealth ; [ressources] resources / *richesses minières / naturelles* mining / natural resources.

richissime [ʀiʃisim] adj fantastically wealthy.

ricin [ʀisɛ̃] nm castor-oil plant, ricinus *spéc.*

ricocher [3] [ʀikɔʃe] vi **1.** [caillou] to ricochet, to bounce, to glance / *les enfants font ricocher des pierres sur l'eau* the children are skimming stones across the water ou are playing ducks and drakes **2.** [balle] to ricochet.

ricochet [ʀikɔʃɛ] nm **1.** [d'un caillou] bounce, rebound ▸ **faire des ricochets** to skim pebbles, to play ducks and drakes **2.** [d'une balle] ricochet.

ric-rac, ricrac* [ʀikʀak] adv fam [de justesse] : *avec mon petit salaire, à la fin du mois c'est ric-rac* on my salary, money gets a bit tight at the end of the month.

rictus [ʀiktys] nm grimace, rictus *sout.*

ride [ʀid] nf [d'un visage] line, wrinkle / *le documentaire n'a pas pris une ride* fig the documentary hasn't dated in the slightest.

ridé, e [ʀide] adj [visage] wrinkled, lined ; [pomme] wrinkled.

rideau, x [ʀido] nm [en décoration intérieure] curtain, drape 🇺🇸 ▸ **rideau de douche** shower curtain ▸ **doubles rideaux** thick curtains ▸ **faire grimper qqn au rideaux** fam : *ça risque de le faire grimper aux rideaux* he'll hit the roof. ◆ **rideau de fer** nm **1.** [d'un magasin] (metal) shutter **2.** HIST & POL Iron Curtain.

rider [3] [ʀide] ◆ **se rider** vpi [fruit] to shrivel, to go wrinkly ; [visage] to become wrinkled.

ridicule [ʀidikyl] ◆ adj **1.** [risible - personne] ridiculous, laughable ; [- tenue] ridiculous, ludicrous **2.** [absurde] ridiculous, ludicrous, preposterous. ◆ nm ridicule ▸ **couvrir qqn de ridicule** to heap ridicule on sb ▸ **tourner qqn / qqch en ridicule** to ridicule sb / sthg, to hold sb / sthg up to ridicule / *tomber* ou *donner dans le ridicule* to become ridiculous.

ridiculement [ʀidikylmɑ̃] adv [dérisoirement] ridiculously, ludicrously / *ridiculement petit / bas / grand* ridiculously small / low / big.

ridiculiser [3] [ʀidikylize] vt to ridicule, to hold up to ridicule. ◆ **se ridiculiser** vp (*emploi réfléchi*) to make o.s. (look) ridiculous, to make a fool of o.s.

rien [ʀjɛ̃] ◆ pron indéf **1.** [nulle chose] nothing ▸ **créer qqch à partir de rien** to create something out of nothing ▸ **rien de tel qu'un bon (roman) policier** there's nothing like a good detective story ▸ **rien de cassé / grave, j'espère ?** nothing broken / serious, I hope? ▸ **rien d'autre** nothing else ▸ **rien de plus** nothing else ou more ; [en réponse négative à une question] : *à quoi tu penses ? — à rien !* what are you thinking about? — nothing! ▸ **rien du tout** nothing at all ▸ **de rien:** *je vous remercie — de rien !* thanks — you're welcome ou not at all ou don't mention it ▸ **de rien du tout:** *une affaire de rien du tout* a trifling ou trivial matter / *une égratignure de rien du tout* a little scratch ▸ **rien à déclarer** nothing to declare / *rien à faire, la voiture ne veut pas démarrer* it's no good, the car (just) won't start ▸ **n'en avoir rien à faire** fam ou **à cirer** tfam: *j'en ai rien à faire* ou *à cirer* I don't give a damn ou a toss ▸ **faire semblant de rien** to pretend that nothing happened **2.** [en corrélation avec 'ne'] : *rien n'est plus beau que...* there's nothing more beautiful than... ▸ **plus rien n'a d'importance** nothing matters any more / *ce n'est rien, ça va guérir* it's nothing, it'll get better ▸ *ils se disaient mariés, en fait il n'en est rien* they claimed they were married but they're nothing of the sort / *il n'est (plus) rien pour moi* he's ou he means nothing to me (anymore) / *je ne me souviens de rien* I remember nothing, I don't remember anything / *on ne voit rien avec cette fumée* you can't see anything ou a thing with all this smoke ▸ **cela** ou **ça ne fait rien** it doesn't matter / *ça ne (te) fait rien si je te dépose en dernier ?* would you mind if I dropped you off last?, is it OK with you if I drop you off last? / *ça n'a rien à voir avec toi* it's got nothing to do with you, it doesn't concern you / *je n'ai rien contre lui* I have nothing against him, I don't have anything against him / *ça n'a rien d'un chef-d'œuvre* it's far from being a masterpiece / *il n'y a rien de moins sûr* nothing could be less certain / *pour ne rien vous cacher...* to be completely open with you... / *elle n'avait jamais rien vu de semblable* she had never seen such a thing ou anything like it **3.** [quelque chose] anything / *y a-t-il rien que je puisse faire ?* is there nothing I can do? / *j'ai compris sans qu'il dise rien* I understood without him having to say anything **4.** JEUX ▸ **rien ne va plus** no more va plus **5.** [au tennis] love / *40 à rien* 40 love. ◆ adv tfam really / *ils sont rien riches* they really are rolling in it 🇬🇧, they sure as hell are rich 🇺🇸. ◆ nm **1.** [chose sans importance] ▸ **un rien** the merest trifle ou slightest thing ▸ **un rien l'habille** she looks good in anything ▸ **il se fâche pour un rien** he loses his temper over the slightest little thing / *les petits riens dont la vie est faite* the little things in life **2.** ▸ **un rien de** [très peu de] a touch of / *un rien de frivolité* a touch ou tinge ou hint of frivolity ▸ **en un rien de temps** in (next to) no time. ◆ **en rien** loc adv : *il ne ressemble en rien à son père* he looks nothing like his father. ◆ **pour rien** loc adv : *ne le dérange pas pour rien* don't disturb him for no reason / *il est venu pour rien* he came for nothing / *j'ai acheté ça pour rien chez un brocanteur* I bought it for next to nothing in a second-hand shop ▸ **pour deux / trois fois rien** for next to nothing. ◆ **rien que** loc adv : *rien que cette fois* just this once / *rien qu'une fois* just ou only once / *rien que d'y penser, j'ai des frissons* the mere thought of it ou just thinking about it makes me shiver / *la vérité, rien que la vérité* the truth and nothing but the truth ▸ **rien que ça ?** iron is that all? ◆ **un rien** loc adv a touch, a shade, a tiny bit / *sa robe est un rien trop étroite* her dress is a touch ou a shade ou a tiny bit too tight.

rieur, euse [ʀijœʀ, øz] adj [enfant] cheery, cheerful ; [visage, regard] laughing.

rigide [ʀiʒid] adj **1.** [solide] rigid **2.** [intransigeant] rigid, inflexible, unbending **3.** [austère] rigid, strict.

rigidité [ʀiʒidite] nf **1.** [raideur] rigidity, stiffness **2.** [austérité] strictness, inflexibility.

rigolade [ʀigɔlad] nf fam **1.** [amusement] fun ▸ **prendre qqch à la rigolade** to make a joke of sthg ▸ **c'est de la rigolade !** a) [ce n'est pas sérieux] it's a joke! b) [c'est sans importance] it's nothing! c) [c'est très facile] it's a piece of cake! **2.** [fou rire] fit of laughter / *t'aurais vu la rigolade* it was a right 🇬🇧 ou good laugh!

rigole [ʀigɔl] nf **1.** [fossé] rivulet, rill **2.** CONSTR [d'un mur] ditch ; [d'une fenêtre] drainage groove **3.** HORT [sillon] furrow ; [conduit] trench, channel.

rigoler [3] [ʀigɔle] vi fam **1.** [rire] to laugh / *tu me fais rigoler avec tes remords* you, sorry? don't make me laugh! **2.** [plaisanter] to joke / *il a dit ça pour rigoler* he said that in jest, he meant it as a joke / *tu rigoles !* you're joking ou kidding! **3.** [s'amuser] to have fun / *on a bien rigolé cette année-là* we had some good laughs ou great fun that year.

rigolo, ote [ʀigɔlo, ɔt] *fam* ◆ adj [amusant] funny / *c'est pas rigolo de bosser avec lui* working with him is no joke. ◆ nm, f **1.** [rieur] laugh, scream / *c'est une rigolote* she's a hoot **2.** [incompétent] phoney 🆄🆇, phony 🆄🆂, joker, clown, comedian *péj* / *c'est un (petit) rigolo* he's a real comedian.

rigoureusement [ʀiguʀøzmɑ̃] adv **1.** [scrupuleusement] rigorously **2.** [complètement] ▸ **rigoureusement interdit** strictly forbidden / *les deux portraits sont rigoureusement identiques* the two portraits are exactly the same ou absolutely identical ▸ **c'est rigoureusement vrai** it's perfectly true.

rigoureux, euse [ʀiguʀø, øz] adj **1.** [sévère - personne] severe, rigorous ; [- sanction] harsh, severe ; [- principe] strict **2.** [scrupuleux - analyse, définition, raisonnement] rigorous ; [- contrôle] strict ; [- description] minute, precise ; [- discipline] strict **3.** [rude - climat] harsh.

rigueur [ʀigœʀ] nf **1.** [sévérité] harshness, severity, rigour 🆄🆇, rigor 🆄🆂 ▸ **tenir rigueur à qqn de qqch** to hold sthg against sb **2.** [austérité - d'une gestion] austerity, stringency ; [- d'une morale] rigour 🆄🆇, rigor 🆄🆂, strictness, sternness ▸ **politique de rigueur** austerity (measures) **3.** [âpreté - d'un climat, d'une existence] rigour 🆄🆇, rigor 🆄🆂, harshness, toughness **4.** [précision - d'un calcul] exactness, precision ; [- d'une logique, d'un esprit] rigour 🆄🆇, rigor 🆄🆂. ◆ **rigueurs** nfpl *litt* rigours 🆄🆇, rigors 🆄🆂 / *les rigueurs de l'hiver / de la vie carcérale* the rigours of winter / of prison life. ◆ **à la rigueur** loc adv **1.** [peut-être] : *il a bu deux verres à la rigueur, mais pas plus* he may possibly have had two drinks but no more **2.** [s'il le faut] at a pinch, if need be.

rillettes [ʀijɛt] nfpl rillettes *(potted meat).*

rime [ʀim] nf LITTÉR rhyme.

rimer [3] [ʀime] vi [finir par le même son] to rhyme. ◆ **rimer à** v + prép : *à quoi rime cette scène de jalousie ?* what's the meaning of this jealous outburst? / *tout cela ne rime à rien* none of this makes any sense, there's no sense in any of this.

Rimmel® [ʀimɛl] nm mascara.

rinçage [ʀɛ̃saʒ] nm **1.** [au cours d'une lessive] rinse, rinsing **2.** [pour les cheveux] (colour) rinse.

rince-bouche [ʀɛ̃sbuʃ] nm inv 🇶🇫 mouthwash.

rince-doigts, rince-doigt* [ʀɛ̃sdwa] nm finger bowl.

rincer [16] [ʀɛ̃se] vt [passer à l'eau] to rinse. ◆ **se rincer** vpt : *se rincer la bouche / les mains* to rinse one's mouth (out) / one's hands ▸ **se rincer l'œil** *fam* [regarder] to get an eyeful.

ring [ʀiŋ] nm [estrade] (boxing) ring.

ringard, e [ʀɛ̃gaʀ, aʀd] *fam* ◆ adj *péj* [démodé - gén] corny, naff 🆄🆇 ; [- chanson] corny ; [- décor] naff 🆄🆇, tacky 🆄🆂 / *elle est ringarde* she's such a fuddy-duddy. ◆ nm, f [individu démodé] has-been.

ringuette [ʀɛ̃gɛt] nf 🇶🇫 ringette *(women's sport similar to ice hockey).*

riper [3] [ʀipe] vi [glisser] to slip.

riposte [ʀipɔst] nf **1.** [réplique] retort, riposte **2.** [réaction] reaction **3.** MIL [contre-attaque] counterattack, reprisal.

riposter [3] [ʀipɔste] ◆ vi **1.** [réagir] to respond **2.** [contre-attaquer] to counterattack / *riposter à une agression* to counter an aggression. ◆ vt : *elle riposta que ça ne le regardait pas* she retorted that it was none of his business.

rire¹ [ʀiʀ] nm laugh, laughter *(U)* / *j'adore son rire* I love her laugh ou the way she laughs / *j'entends des rires* I hear laughter ou people laughing ▸ **rires préenregistrés** ou **en boîte** *fam* RADIO & TV prerecorded ou canned laughter.

rire² [95] [ʀiʀ] vi **1.** [de joie] to laugh / *ta lettre nous a beaucoup fait rire* your letter made us all laugh a lot / *ça ne me fait pas rire* that's not funny / *rire de bon cœur* to laugh heartily ▸ **rire bruyamment** to guffaw ▸ **rire de** to laugh ou to scoff at ▸ **c'est à mourir de rire** it's a hoot ou a scream ▸ **il vaut mieux en rire qu'en pleurer** you have to laugh or else you cry ▸ **rire aux éclats** ou **à gorge déployée** to howl with laughter ▸ **rire au nez** ou **à la barbe de qqn** to laugh in sb's face ▸ **tu me fais rire, laisse-moi rire, fais-moi rire !** *iron* don't make me laugh! ▸ **rira bien qui rira le dernier** *prov* he who laughs last laughs longest 🆄🆇 ou best 🆄🆂 *prov* **2.** [plaisanter] ▸ **j'ai dit ça pour rire** ou **pour de rire** *fam* I (only) said it in jest, I was only joking ▸ **tu veux rire !** you must be joking!, you've got to be kidding! ▸ **sans rire, tu comptes y aller ?** joking apart ou aside, do you intend to go?

ris [ʀi] nm CULIN sweetbread / *ris de veau* calf sweetbreads.

risée [ʀize] nf [moquerie] : *être un objet de risée* to be a laughing stock.

risette [ʀizɛt] nf *fam* **1.** [sourire d'enfant] : *allez, fais risette à mamie* come on, give grandma a nice little smile **2.** [flagornerie] ▸ **faire risette** ou **des risettes à qqn** to smarm up 🆄🆇 ou to play up 🆄🆂 to sb.

risible [ʀizibl] adj [ridicule] ridiculous, laughable.

risque [ʀisk] nm **1.** [danger] risk, hazard, danger / *il y a un risque de contagion / d'explosion* there's a risk of contamination / of an explosion / *au risque de te décevoir / de le faire souffrir* at the risk of disappointing you / of hurting him ▸ **zone / population à haut risque** high-risk area / population ▸ **à mes / tes risques et périls** at my / your own risk ▸ **ce sont les risques du métier** it's an occupational hazard **2.** [initiative hasardeuse] risk, chance / *il y a une part de risque* there's an element of risk / *courir* ou *prendre un risque* to run a risk, to take a chance / *avoir le goût du risque, aimer le risque* to enjoy taking chances **3.** [préjudice] risk ▸ **risque d'incendie** fire hazard ou risk ▸ **capitaux à risques** FIN risk ou venture capital.

risqué, e [ʀiske] adj **1.** [dangereux] risky, dangerous **2.** [osé] risqué, racy.

risquer [3] [ʀiske] vt **1.** [engager - fortune, crédibilité] to risk ▸ **risquer sa peau** *fam* ou **sa vie** to risk one's neck ou life ▸ **on risque le coup** ou **la partie ?** shall we have a shot at it?, shall we chance it? ▸ **qui ne risque rien n'a rien** *prov* nothing ventured nothing gained *prov* **2.** [s'exposer à] to risk ▸ **elle risque la mort / la paralysie** she runs the risk of dying / of being left paralysed / *tu peux laisser ça dehors, ça ne risque rien* you can leave it outside, it'll be safe ▸ **qu'est-ce qu'on risque ?** what are the dangers? **3.** [oser] to venture. ◆ **risquer de** v + prép to risk / *il risque de se faire mal* he might hurt himself / *ne m'attends pas, je risque d'être en retard* don't wait for me, I'm likely to be late ou the chances are I'll be late / *je ne risque pas de me remarier !* *hum* (there's) no danger of my getting married again! / *ça ne risque pas de se faire !* there's no chance of that happening! / *ça ne risque pas !* no chance! ◆ **se risquer** vpi ▸ **se risquer à faire qqch** to venture ou to dare to do sthg / *je ne m'y risquerais pas si j'étais toi* I wouldn't take a chance on it if I were you.

rissoler [3] [ʀisɔle] ◆ vt to brown ▸ **pommes rissolées** sauté ou sautéed potatoes. ◆ vi ▸ **faire rissoler** to brown.

ristourne [ʀistuʀn] nf **1.** [réduction] discount, reduction **2.** COMM [versement] bonus.

rite [ʀit] nm **1.** ANTHR & RELIG rite ▸ **rite de passage** rite of passage **2.** [coutume] ritual.

rituel, elle [ʀituɛl] adj **1.** [réglé par un rite] ritual **2.** [habituel] ritual, usual, customary. ◆ **rituel** nm [ensemble de règles] ritual, rite.

rivage [ʀivaʒ] nm [littoral] shore.

rival, e, aux [ʀival, o] ◆ adj [antagonique] rival *(avant nom)*. ◆ nm, f [adversaire] rival, opponent.

rivaliser [3] [ʀivalize] vi ▸ **rivaliser avec** to compete with, to vie with, to rival.

rivalité [ʀivalite] nf [gén] rivalry ; [en affaires] competition.

rive [ʀiv] nf [bord - d'un lac, d'une mer] shore ; [- d'une rivière] bank ▸ **rive droite / gauche** [gén] right / left bank.

▌ **Rive droite, rive gauche**
The Right (north) Bank of the Seine is traditionally associated with business and trade, and has a reputation for being more conservative than the Left Bank. The Left (south) Bank includes districts traditionally favoured by artists, students and intellectuals, and has a reputation for being bohemian and unconventional.

river [3] [ʀive] vt *fig* [fixer] to rivet ▸ **il avait les yeux rivés sur elle / les diamants** he couldn't take his eyes off her / the diamonds ▸ *être rivé à la télévision / à son travail* to be glued to the television / chained to one's work / *rester rivé sur place* to be riveted ou rooted to the spot.

riverain, e [ʀivʀɛ̃, ɛn] nm, f [qui vit au bord - d'un lac] lakeside resident ; [- d'une rivière] riverside resident / **'interdit sauf aux riverains'** 'residents only', 'no entry except for access'.

rivière [ʀivjɛʀ] nf **1.** GÉOGR river **2.** JOAILL ▸ **rivière de diamants** (diamond) rivière.

rixe [ʀiks] nf brawl, scuffle.

Riyad [ʀijad] npr Riyadh.

riz [ʀi] nm rice ▸ **riz pilaf / cantonnais / créole** pilaff / Cantonese / Creole rice ▸ **riz complet** brown rice ▸ **riz au lait** rice pudding ▸ **riz sauvage** wild rice.

rizière [ʀizjɛʀ] nf rice field, paddyfield.

RMI nm abr de **revenu minimum d'insertion**.

RMiste [ɛʀɛmist] nmf *vieilli* person receiving the "RMI".

RN (abr de **route nationale**) nf ≃ A-road ⟦UK⟧ ; ≃ highway ⟦US⟧.

robe [ʀɔb] nf **1.** VÊT dress ▸ **robe de bal** ballgown ▸ **robe de chambre** dressing gown ⟦UK⟧, (bath)robe ⟦US⟧ ▸ **pomme de terre en robe de chambre** jacket potato ▸ **robe-chasuble** pinafore dress ▸ **robe-chemisier** shirtwaister ⟦UK⟧, shirtwaist ⟦US⟧ ▸ **robe de mariée** wedding dress, bridal gown ▸ **robe du soir** evening dress **2.** [tenue - d'un professeur] gown ; [- d'un cardinal, d'un magistrat] robe **3.** [pelage] coat **4.** ŒNOL colour ⟦UK⟧, color ⟦US⟧ *(general aspect of wine in terms of colour and clarity)*.

robinet [ʀɔbinɛ] nm **1.** [à eau, à gaz] tap ⟦UK⟧, faucet ⟦US⟧ ; [de tonneau] spigot ▸ **robinet d'eau chaude / froide** hot / cold water tap **2.** *fam* [sexe masculin] willy ⟦UK⟧, peter ⟦US⟧.

robot [ʀɔbo] nm robot ▸ **robot ménager** ou **de cuisine**, **Robot Marie®** food processor.

robotique [ʀɔbɔtik] nf robotics *(U)*.

robotisation [ʀɔbɔtizasjɔ̃] nf automation, robotization ⟦US⟧.

robotiser [3] [ʀɔbɔtize] vt **1.** [atelier, usine, travail] to automate, to robotize **2.** [personne] to robotize.

robuste [ʀɔbyst] adj **1.** [personne] robust, sturdy, strong **2.** [meuble] sturdy ; [voiture, moteur] rugged, heavy-duty.

robustesse [ʀɔbystɛs] nf [d'une personne] robustness ; [d'un meuble] sturdiness ; [d'un arbre] hardiness.

roc [ʀɔk] nm [pierre] rock.

rocade [ʀɔkad] nf TRAV PUB bypass.

rocaille [ʀɔkaj] nf **1.** [pierraille] loose stones ; [terrain] stony ground **2.** [jardin] rock garden, rockery.

rocailleux, euse [ʀɔkajø, øz] adj **1.** [terrain] rocky, stony **2.** [voix] gravelly.

rocambolesque [ʀɔkɑ̃bɔlɛsk] adj [aventures] fantastic ; [histoire] incredible.

roche [ʀɔʃ] nf GÉOL rock.

rocher [ʀɔʃe] nm GÉOL rock ▸ **le rocher de Gibraltar** the Rock of Gibraltar.

Rocheuses [ʀɔʃøz] npr fpl ▸ **les (montagnes) Rocheuses** the (Great) Rocky Mountains, the Rockies.

rocheux, euse [ʀɔʃø, øz] adj rocky.

rock [ʀɔk] ◆ adj inv MUS rock. ◆ nm MUS rock / *danser le rock* to jive, to rock (and roll) ▸ **rock acrobatique** acrobatic dancing.

rockeur, euse [ʀɔkœʀ, øz] nm, f **1.** [artiste] rock singer ou musician **2.** *fam* [fan] rocker.

rocking-chair [ʀɔkiŋʃɛʀ] (*pl* **rocking-chairs**) nm rocking chair.

rodage [ʀɔdaʒ] nm **1.** [d'un moteur, d'une voiture] running in ⟦UK⟧, breaking in ⟦US⟧ / *tant que la voiture est en rodage* while the car is being run in ⟦UK⟧ ou broken in ⟦US⟧ **2.** *fig* [mise au point] : *le rodage de ce service va prendre plusieurs mois* it'll take several months to get this new service running smoothly.

rodéo [ʀɔdeo] nm [à cheval] rodeo.

roder [3] [ʀɔde] vt **1.** [moteur, voiture] to run in ⟦UK⟧ *(sép)*, to break in ⟦US⟧ *(sép)* **2.** *fig* [mettre au point] ▸ **roder un service / une équipe** to get a department / a team up and running / *il est rodé maintenant* he knows the ropes now.

rôder [3] [ʀode] vi [traîner - sans but] to hang around, to roam ou to loiter about ; [- avec une mauvaise intention] to lurk ou to skulk around / *arrêtez de rôder autour de ma fille* stop hanging round my daughter.

rôdeur, euse [ʀodœʀ, øz] nm, f prowler.

rœsti, rœstis* [ʀøsti] nmpl ⟦SUISSE⟧ rœsti, potato pancake.

rogne [ʀɔɲ] nf *fam* anger ▸ **être / se mettre en rogne (contre qqn)** to be / to get hopping mad (with sb).

rogner [3] [ʀɔɲe] vt **1.** [couper - métal] to pare, to clip ; [- cuir] to pare, to trim ; [- papier] to trim ; [- livre] to guillotine, to trim **2.** [réduire - budget, salaire] to cut (back) ▸ **rogner sur** to cut back ou down on.

rognon [ʀɔɲɔ̃] nm CULIN kidney.

roi [ʀwa] nm **1.** [monarque] king ▸ **les Rois** [Épiphanie] Twelfth Night ▸ **tirer les rois** to eat "galette des rois" **2.** *fig* [personne qui domine] : *le roi des animaux* the king of beasts / *les rois du pétrole* the oil tycoons ou magnates / *c'est vraiment le roi des imbéciles* he's a prize idiot.

roitelet [ʀwatlɛ] nm [oiseau] wren ⟦UK⟧, winter wren ⟦US⟧.

rôle [ʀol] nm **1.** CINÉ, THÉÂTRE & TV role, part ▸ **apprendre son rôle** to learn one's part ou lines / *il joue le rôle d'un espion* he plays (the part of) a spy ▸ **distribuer les rôles** to do the casting, to cast ▸ **rôle de composition** character part ou role ▸ **premier rôle** a) [acteur] leading actor or actress b) [personnage] lead ▸ **jouer les seconds rôles (auprès de qqn)** to play second fiddle (to sb) ▸ **avoir le beau rôle** to have it ou things easy **2.** [fonction] role ▸ **jouer un rôle important dans qqch** to play an important part in sthg / *ce n'est pas mon rôle de m'occuper de ça* it's not my job ou it's not up to me to do it.

rôle-titre [ʀoltitʀ] (*pl* **rôles-titres**) nm title role.

---

* In reformed spelling (see p. 16-18).

roller [ʀɔllœʀ, ʀɔlœʀ] nm [sport] rollerblading, rollerskating ▸ **les rollers** [patins] Rollerblades®, roller-skates ▸ **faire du roller** to go rollerblading, to rollerblade.

rolleur, euse [ʀɔllœʀ, øz] nm, f roller skater.

ROM, Rom [ʀɔm] (abr de **read only memory**) nf ROM, Rom.

romain, e [ʀɔmɛ̃, ɛn] adj Roman. ❖ **Romain, e** nm, f Roman. ❖ **romaine** nf [salade] cos (lettuce) 🇬🇧, romaine (lettuce) 🇺🇸.

roman¹ [ʀɔmɑ̃] nm LITTÉR novel / *sa vie est un vrai roman* you could write a book about his life ▸ **roman d'aventures** / **d'amour** adventure / love story ▸ **roman de cape et d'épée** swashbuckling tale ▸ **roman à clef** roman à clef ▸ **roman d'espionnage** spy story ▸ **roman de gare** péj airport ou 🇺🇸 dime novel ▸ **roman noir** Gothic novel ▸ **roman policier** detective story ou novel.

roman², e [ʀɔmɑ̃, an] adj ARCHIT Romanesque. ❖ **roman** nm ARCHIT ▸ **le roman** the Romanesque.

romancer [16] [ʀɔmɑ̃se] ❖ vt [histoire] to novelize. ❖ vi fig : *tu as tendance à romancer* you have a tendency to embroider the facts.

romancier, ère [ʀɔmɑ̃sje, ɛʀ] nm, f novelist, novel ou fiction writer.

romand, e [ʀɔmɑ̃, ɑ̃d] adj of French-speaking Switzerland. ❖ **Romand, e** nm, f French-speaking Swiss ▸ **les Romands** the French-speaking Swiss.

romanesque [ʀɔmanɛsk] adj **1.** LITTÉR [héros] fiction *(modif)*, fictional ; [technique, style] novelistic **2.** fig [aventure] fabulous, fantastic ; [imagination, amour] romantic.

roman-feuilleton [ʀɔmɑ̃fœjtɔ̃] *(pl* **romans-feuilletons**) nm serialized novel, serial.

roman-fleuve [ʀɔmɑ̃flœv] *(pl* **romans-fleuves**) nm roman-fleuve, saga.

romanichel, elle [ʀɔmaniʃɛl] nm, f péj [Tsigane] Romany, Gipsy.

roman-photo [ʀɔmɑ̃fɔto] *(pl* **romans-photos**) nm photo novel, photo romance.

romantique [ʀɔmɑ̃tik] ❖ adj [sentimental] romantic. ❖ nmf [personne] romantic.

romantisme [ʀɔmɑ̃tism] nm **1.** ART & LITTÉR Romanticism **2.** [sentimentalisme] romanticism.

romarin [ʀɔmaʀɛ̃] nm rosemary.

Rome [ʀɔm] npr Rome ▸ **la Rome antique** Ancient Rome.

rompre [78] [ʀɔ̃pʀ] ❖ vt **1.** [mettre fin à - jeûne, silence, contrat] to break ; [- fiançailles, relations] to break off *(sép)* ; [- marché] to call off *(sép)* ; [- équilibre] to upset / *rompre le charme* to break the spell **2.** [briser] to break **3.** MIL to break ▸ **rompez (les rangs)** ! dismiss!, fall out! ❖ vi **1.** [se séparer] to break up ▸ **rompre avec** to break with **2.** sout [se briser - corde] to break, to snap ; [- digue] to break, to burst.

rompu, e [ʀɔ̃py] adj sout [habitué] ▸ **rompu à** : *rompu aux affaires* / *à la diplomatie* experienced in business / in diplomacy.

romsteck [ʀɔmstɛk] nm [partie du bœuf] rump steak ; [morceau coupé] slice of rump steak.

ronce [ʀɔ̃s] nf **1.** BOT blackberry bush ▸ **les ronces** [buissons] the brambles **2.** [nœud dans le bois] burr, swirl spéc.

ronchon, onne [ʀɔ̃ʃɔ̃, ɔn] fam ❖ adj crotchety, grumpy, grouchy. ❖ nm, f grumbler, grouse, grouch 🇬🇧.

ronchonner [3] [ʀɔ̃ʃɔne] vi fam ▸ **ronchonner (après qqn)** to grouse ou to gripe ou to grouch (at sb).

rond, e [ʀɔ̃, ʀɔ̃d] adj **1.** [circulaire] round, circular ▸ **faire ou ouvrir des yeux ronds** to stare in disbelief **2.** [bien en chair] round, full, plump / *un petit bébé tout rond* a chubby little baby / *de jolies épaules bien rondes* well-rounded

ou well-turned shoulders / *des seins ronds* full breasts **3.** fam [ivre] tight, well-oiled ▸ **rond comme une queue de pelle** three sheets to the wind **4.** [chiffre, somme] round. ❖ **rond** ❖ nm **1.** [cercle] circle, ring / *faire des ronds de fumée* to blow ou to make smoke rings ▸ **faire des ronds dans l'eau** a) pr to make rings in the water b) fig to fritter away one's time **2.** [anneau] ring ▸ **rond de serviette** napkin ring **3.** fam [sou] : *je n'ai plus un rond* I'm flat broke, I'm skint 🇬🇧 / *ils ont des ronds* they're rolling in it, they're loaded **4.** DANSE ▸ **faire des ronds de jambe** fig to bow and scrape. ❖ adv fam EXPR tourner rond to go well, to run smoothly ▸ **ne pas tourner rond** : *qu'est-ce qui ne tourne pas rond ?* what's the matter?, what's the problem? / *ça ne tourne pas rond* things aren't going (very) well / *il ne tourne pas rond* he's got a screw loose ▸ **tout rond** [exactement] exactly. ❖ **en rond** loc adv [se placer, s'asseoir] in a circle ; [danser] in a ring ▸ **tourner en rond** pr & fig to go round (and round) in circles.

ronde [ʀɔ̃d] nf **1.** [inspection - d'un vigile] rounds, round, patrol ; [- d'un soldat] patrol ; [- d'un policier] beat, round, rounds ▸ **faire sa ronde** a) [veilleur] to make one's round ou rounds b) [policier] to be on patrol ou on the beat **2.** MUS semibreve 🇬🇧, whole note 🇺🇸 **3.** [danse] round (dance), ronde ▸ **faire la ronde** to dance round in a circle ou ring. ❖ **à la ronde** loc adv : *il n'y a pas une seule maison à 20 km à la ronde* there's no house within 20 km, there's no house within ou in a 20-km radius.

rondelet, ette [ʀɔ̃dlɛ, ɛt] adj fam **1.** [potelé] chubby, plump, plumpish **2.** [important] ▸ **une somme rondelette** a tidy ou nice little sum.

rondelle [ʀɔ̃dɛl] nf [de salami, de citron] slice ▸ **couper qqch en rondelles** to slice sthg, to cut sthg into slices.

rondement [ʀɔ̃dmɑ̃] adv [promptement] briskly, promptly, quickly and efficiently ▸ **des négociations rondement menées** competently conducting negotiations.

rondeur [ʀɔ̃dœʀ] nf **1.** [forme - d'un visage, d'un bras] roundness, plumpness, chubbiness ; [- d'un sein] fullness ; [- d'une épaule] roundness **2.** [franchise] straightforwardness, directness. ❖ **rondeurs** nfpl euphém curves.

rondin [ʀɔ̃dɛ̃] nm [bois] round billet, log.

rondouillard, e [ʀɔ̃dujaʀ, aʀd] adj fam tubby, podgy 🇬🇧, pudgy 🇺🇸.

rond-point *(pl* ronds-points**), rondpoint*** [ʀɔ̃pwɛ̃] nm roundabout 🇬🇧, traffic circle 🇺🇸.

ronflant, e [ʀɔ̃flɑ̃, ɑ̃t] adj péj [discours] bombastic, highflown ; [promesses] grand ▸ **titre ronflant** grand-sounding title.

ronflement [ʀɔ̃fləmɑ̃] nm [d'un dormeur] snore, snoring *(U)*.

ronfler [3] [ʀɔ̃fle] vi **1.** [en dormant] to snore **2.** fam [dormir] to snooze, to snore away **3.** [vrombir] to roar, to throb ▸ **faire ronfler le moteur** to rev up the engine.

ronger [17] [ʀɔ̃ʒe] vt **1.** [mordiller] to gnaw (away) at (insép), to eat into (insép) / *ronger un os* to gnaw at a bone / *rongé par les vers* / *mites* worm- / moth-eaten ▸ **ronger son frein** pr & fig to champ at the bit **2.** [corroder - suj : mer] to wear away *(sép)* ; [- suj : acide, rouille] to eat into (insép) / *rongé par la rouille* eaten away with rust, rusted away / *être rongé par la maladie* to be wasted by disease. ❖ **se ronger** vpt ▸ **se ronger les ongles** to bite one's nails.

rongeur [ʀɔ̃ʒœʀ] nm rodent.

ronronnement [ʀɔ̃ʀɔnmɑ̃] nm [d'un chat] purr(ing).

ronronner [3] [ʀɔ̃ʀɔne] vi [chat] to purr ; [machine] to drone, to hum.

roquet [ʀɔkɛ] nm [chien] yappy ou noisy dog.

rosace [ʀozas] nf ARCHIT [moulure] (ceiling) rose ; [vitrail] rose window, rosace ; [figure] rosette.

rosâtre [ʀozatʀ] adj pinkish, roseate *litt*.

rosbif [ʀɔzbif] nm **1.** [cru] roasting beef *(U)*, joint ou piece of beef *(for roasting)* ; [cuit] roast beef *(U)*, joint of roast beef **2.** *fam* [Anglais] *pejorative or humorous term used with reference to British people.*

rose [ʀoz] ◆ adj **1.** [gén] pink ; [teint, joue] rosy ▸ **rose bonbon / saumon** candy / salmon pink **2.** [agréable] : *ce n'est pas (tout) rose* it isn't exactly a bed of roses **3.** [érotique] erotic, soft-porn *(modif)* **4.** POL left-wing. ◆ nf BOT rose ▸ **rose trémière** hollyhock 🇬🇧, rose mallow. ◆ nm **1.** [couleur] pink **2.** EXPR *voir la vie* ou *les choses en rose* to see things through rose-tinted spectacles 🇬🇧 ou glasses 🇺🇸. ◆▸ **rose des sables**, **rose du désert** nf gypsum flower. ◆▸ **rose des vents** nf wind rose.

rosé, e [ʀoze] adj **1.** [teinte] pinkish, rosy **2.** [vin] rosé. ◆▸ **rosé** nm rosé (wine).

roseau, x [ʀozo] nm reed.

rosée [ʀoze] nf dew.

rosette [ʀozɛt] nf **1.** [nœud] bow **2.** [cocarde] rose, rosette ▸ **avoir / recevoir la rosette** to be / to be made an officer *(of an order of knighthood or merit).*

rosier [ʀozje] nm rosebush, rose tree.

rossignol [ʀɔsiɲɔl] nm [oiseau] nightingale.

rot [ʀɔt, ʀo] nm [renvoi] belch, burp.

rotation [ʀɔtasjɔ̃] nf **1.** [mouvement] rotation ; [sur un axe] spinning ▸ **mouvement de rotation** rotational *spéc* ou rotary motion ; SPORT turn, turning *(U)* **2.** [renouvellement] turnover ▸ **rotation des stocks / du personnel** inventory / staff turnover.

roter [3] [ʀɔte] vi to belch, to burp.

rôti [ʀoti] nm [viande - crue] joint *(of meat for roasting)* ; [- cuite] joint, roast ▸ **rôti de porc a)** [cru] joint ou piece of pork for roasting **b)** [cuit] piece of roast pork.

rotin [ʀɔtɛ̃] nm rattan / *chaise en rotin* rattan chair.

rôtir [32] [ʀotiʀ] ◆ vt [cuire] to roast / *faire rôtir une viande* to roast a piece of meat. ◆ vi [cuire] to roast. ◆▸ **se rôtir** vp *(emploi réfléchi)* *fam* : *se rôtir au soleil* to bask ou to fry in the sun.

rôtisserie [ʀotisʀi] nf [magasin] rotisserie.

rôtissoire [ʀotiswaʀ] nf [appareil] roaster ; [broche] (roasting) spit, rotisserie.

rotule [ʀɔtyl] nf ANAT kneecap, patella *spéc* ▸ **être sur les rotules** *fam* to be on one's last legs.

rouage [ʀwaʒ] nm **1.** TECHNOL moving part, movement ; [engrenage] cogwheel / *les rouages d'une horloge* the works ou movement of a clock **2.** *fig* cog / *les rouages de la Justice* the wheels of Justice.

roublard, e [ʀublaʀ, aʀd] *fam* ◆ adj [rusé] sly, wily, crafty. ◆ nm, f dodger.

rouble [ʀubl] nm rouble.

roucouler [3] [ʀukule] ◆ vi **1.** [pigeon] to (bill and) coo **2.** *fam* [amoureux] to coo, to whisper sweet nothings **3.** *péj* [chanteur] to croon. ◆ vt [suj : amoureux] to coo.

roue [ʀu] nf **1.** TRANSP wheel / *véhicule à deux / trois roues* two-wheeled / three-wheeled vehicle ▸ **roue motrice** drive ou driving wheel ▸ **roue de secours** spare / wheel **2.** MÉCAN (cog ou gear) wheel ▸ **roue dentée** cogwheel ▸ **roue libre** freewheel / *j'ai descendu la côte en roue libre* I freewheeled down the hill ▸ **être en roue libre** *fig* [personne, addition] to be freewheeling **3.** [objet circulaire] wheel ▸ **la grande roue** the big wheel 🇬🇧, the Ferris wheel 🇺🇸 ▸ **la roue tourne** the wheel of Fortune is turning ▸ **faire la roue a)** [paon] to spread ou to fan its tail **b)** [gymnaste]

to do a cartwheel **c)** [séducteur] to strut about *péj* **4.** NAUT ▸ **roue à aubes** ou **à palettes** paddle wheel.

rouer [6] [ʀwe] vt EXPR **rouer qqn de coups** [le frapper] to pummel sb.

rouge [ʀuʒ] ◆ adj **1.** [gén] red ▸ **être rouge comme un coq** ou **un coquelicot** ou **une écrevisse** ou **un homard** ou **une pivoine** ou **une tomate** to be as red as a beetroot 🇬🇧 ou a lobster **2.** *péj* [communiste] red. ◆ nmf *péj* [communiste] Red. ◆ nm **1.** [couleur] red ▸ **rouge cerise** cherry red **2.** TRANSP : *le feu est passé au rouge* the lights turned to ou went red / *la voiture est passée au rouge* the car went through a red light **3.** *fam* [vin] red wine **4.** [cosmétique] ▸ **rouge (à joues)** blusher, rouge **5.** BANQUE red / *je suis dans le rouge* I'm in the red ou overdrawn. ◆ adv EXPR **voir rouge** to see red. ◆▸ **rouge à lèvres** nm lipstick.

rougeâtre [ʀuʒatʀ] adj reddish, reddy.

rougeaud, e [ʀuʒo, od] adj red-faced, ruddy, ruddy-cheeked.

rouge-gorge [ʀuʒɡɔʀʒ] *(pl* **rouges-gorges)** nm (robin) redbreast, robin.

rougeole [ʀuʒɔl] nf MÉD measles *(sg)* / *avoir la rougeole* to have (the) measles.

rougeoyer [13] [ʀuʒwaje] vi to turn red, to redden, to take on a reddish hue.

rouget [ʀuʒɛ] nm ZOOL ▸ **rouget de roche** surmullet.

rougeur [ʀuʒœʀ] nf MÉD red patch ou blotch.

rougir [32] [ʀuʒiʀ] ◆ vt [colorer en rouge] : *des yeux rougis par les larmes / la poussière* eyes red with weeping / with the dust. ◆ vi **1.** [chose, personne - gén] to go ou to turn red ; [personne - de gêne] to blush ▸ **rougir de plaisir** to flush with pleasure ▸ **rougir de honte** to blush with shame / *je vous aime, dit-il en rougissant* I love you, he said, blushing ou with a blush ▸ **faire rougir qqn** to make sb blush **2.** *fig* ▸ **rougir de** [avoir honte de] to be ashamed of / *tu n'as pas / il n'y a pas à en rougir* there's nothing for you / nothing to be ashamed of **3.** MÉTALL to become red-hot.

rouille [ʀuj] ◆ nf **1.** [corrosion d'un métal] rust **2.** CULIN rouille sauce *(served with fish soup and bouillabaisse).* ◆ adj inv rust, rust-coloured.

rouillé, e [ʀuje] adj **1.** [grille, clef] rusty, rusted **2.** *fig* [muscles] stiff ▸ **être rouillé a)** [physiquement] to feel stiff **b)** [intellectuellement] to feel a bit rusty.

rouiller [3] [ʀuje] ◆ vt [métal] to rust. ◆ vi to rust, to go rusty.

roulade [ʀulad] nf **1.** CULIN rolled meat, roulade **2.** [culbute] roll.

roulant, e [ʀulɑ̃, ɑ̃t] adj **1.** [surface] moving ; [meuble] on wheels **2.** RAIL ▸ **matériel roulant** rolling stock ▸ **personnel roulant** train crews.

roulé, e [ʀule] adj EXPR **être bien roulé** *fam* : *elle est bien roulée* she's got curves in all the right places. ◆▸ **roulé** nm CULIN [gâteau] Swiss roll ; [viande] rolled meat.

rouleau, x [ʀulo] nm **1.** [de papier, de tissu, etc.] roll / *rouleau de parchemin* roll ou scroll of parchment / *rouleau de papier hygiénique* toilet roll 🇬🇧, roll of toilet paper **2.** [outil - de peintre, de jardinier, de relieur] roller ▸ **rouleau à pâtisserie** rolling pin **3.** [bigoudi] roller, curler **4.** CULIN ▸ **rouleau de printemps** spring roll, egg roll 🇺🇸 **5.** SPORT ▸ **rouleau costal** western roll **6.** [vague] roller **7.** TRAV PUB roller ▸ **rouleau compresseur a)** *pr* [à gazole] roadroller **b)** [à vapeur] steamroller **c)** *fig* steamroller.

roulement [ʀulmɑ̃] nm **1.** [grondement] rumble, rumbling *(U)* / *le roulement du tonnerre* the rumble ou roll ou peal of thunder ▸ **roulement de tambour** drum roll

2. [rotation] rotation **3.** MÉCAN [déplacement] rolling ‣ **roulement à billes / à rouleaux / à aiguilles** ball / roller / needle bearings.

rouler [3] [ʀule] ◆ vt **1.** [faire tourner] to roll ‣ **rouler qqn dans la farine** to pull the wool over sb's eyes **2.** [poster, tapis, bas de pantalon] to roll up *(sép)* ; [corde, câble] to roll up, to wind up *(sép)* ; [cigarette] to roll / *rouler un blessé dans une couverture* to wrap an injured person in a blanket **3.** [déplacer - Caddie] to push (along) ; [-balle, tronc, fût] to roll (along) ‣ **avoir roulé sa bosse** : *j'ai roulé ma bosse* I've been around, I've seen it all **4.** *fam* [escroquer - lors d'un paiement] to diddle ; [-dans une affaire] to swindle / *se faire rouler* to be conned ou had **5.** ‣ **rouler des mécaniques a)** *fam* to sway one's shoulders **b)** *fig* to come ou to play the hard guy **6.** [aplatir - gazon, court de tennis] to roll ; CULIN [pâte] to roll out *(sép)*. ◆ vi **1.** [véhicule] to go, to run ; [conducteur] to drive ‣ **une voiture qui a peu / beaucoup roulé** a car with a low / high mileage / *seulement deux heures ? tu as bien roulé !* only two hours? you've made good time! ‣ **rouler au pas** to go at a walking pace, to crawl along / *elle roule en Jaguar* she drives (around in) a Jaguar / *ça roule mal / bien dans Anvers* there's a lot of traffic / there's no traffic through Antwerp ‣ **ça roule !** *fam* everything's going alright! / *salut ! ça roule ?* hi, how's life? **2.** [balle, dé, rocher] to roll ‣ **faire rouler a)** [balle] to roll **b)** [chariot] to wheel (along) **c)** [roue] to roll along / *il a roulé jusqu'en bas du champ* he rolled ou tumbled down to the bottom of the field ‣ **rouler sous la table** to end up (dead drunk) under the table **3.** NAUT to roll **4.** *fam* EXPR ‣ **rouler sur l'or** to be rolling in money ou in it. ❖ **se rouler** vpi [se vautrer] ‣ **se rouler par terre a)** [de colère] to have a fit **b)** [de douleur] to be doubled up with pain **c)** [de rire] to be doubled up with laughter.

roulette [ʀulɛt] nf **1.** [roue - libre] wheel ; [-sur pivot] caster ‣ **à roulettes** on wheels ‣ **marcher** ou **aller comme sur des roulettes a)** *fam* [opération] to go off without a hitch **b)** [organisation, projet] to proceed smoothly, to go like clockwork **2.** [ustensile - de relieur] fillet (wheel) ; [-de graveur] roulette ; COUT tracing wheel ‣ **roulette de dentiste** dentist's drill **3.** JEUX [jeu] roulette ; [roue] roulette wheel ‣ **roulette russe** Russian roulette.

rouli-roulant [ʀuliʀulɑ̃] *(pl* rouli-roulants*)* nm QUÉBEC skateboard.

roulis [ʀuli] nm AÉRON & NAUT roll, rolling / *il y a du roulis* the ship is rolling ‣ **coup de roulis** strong roll.

roulotte, roulote* [ʀulɔt] nf [caravane] caravan UK, mobile home, trailer US.

roumain, e [ʀumɛ̃, ɛn] adj Rumanian, Ro(u)manian. ❖ **Roumain, e** nm, f Rumanian, Ro(u)manian. ❖ **roumain** nm LING Romanian.

Roumanie [ʀumani] npr f ‣ **la Roumanie** Rumania, Ro(u)mania.

round [ʀawnd] nm [à la boxe, dans un débat] round.

roupiller [3] [ʀupije] vi *fam* to have a kip UK, to get some shut-eye US *tfam*.

roupillon [ʀupijɔ̃] nm *fam* ‣ **faire** ou **piquer un roupillon** to have a snooze ou a nap ou a kip UK.

rouquin, e [ʀukɛ̃, in] *fam* ◆ adj [personne] red-haired ; [chevelure] red, ginger *(modif)*, carroty *péj*. ◆ nm, f redhead.

rouspéter [18] [ʀuspete] vi *fam* to grumble, to complain, to make a fuss.

✐ In reformed spelling (see p. 16-18), this verb is conjugated like *semer* : *il rouspètera, elle rouspèterait.*

rousse [ʀus] f ⟶ **roux**.

rousselé, e [ʀusle] QUÉBEC ◆ adj freckled. ◆ nm, f person with freckles.

roussi [ʀusi] nm ‣ **ça sent le roussi a)** *pr* something's burning **b)** *fam & fig* there's trouble ahead ou brewing.

roussir [32] [ʀusiʀ] ◆ vt [brûler] to scorch, to singe. ◆ vi [feuillage, arbre] to turn brown ou russet *sout*.

routard, e [ʀutaʀ, aʀd] nm, f *fam* [auto-stoppeur] hitchhiker ; [marcheur] trekker ; [touriste avec sac à dos] backpacker.

route [ʀut] nf **1.** [voie de circulation] road / *c'est la route de Genève* it's the road to Geneva ‣ **tenir la route** [voiture] to hold the road ‣ **route départementale** secondary road ‣ **route nationale** major road, trunk road UK ; ≃ A road UK ; ≃ highway US **2.** [itinéraire] way / *c'est sur ma route* it's on my way ‣ **faisant route vers a)** [bateau, avion] bound for, heading for, on its way to **b)** [personne] on one's way to, heading for ‣ **route aérienne** air route ‣ **route maritime** shipping ou sea route ‣ **la route de la soie** the silk road ‣ **la Route des vins** tourist trail passing through wine country **3.** [trajet] journey / *j'ai fait la route à pied* I did the journey on foot ‣ **il y a six heures de route a)** [en voiture] it's a six-hour drive ou ride ou journey **b)** [en vélo] it's a six-hour ride ou journey ‣ **(faites) bonne route !** have a good ou safe journey! ‣ **en route** on the way ‣ **prendre la** ou **se mettre en route** to set off, to get going / *reprendre la route, se remettre en route* to set off again, to resume one's journey / *allez, en route !* come on, let's go! **4.** *fig* [voie] road, way, path / *la route est toute tracée pour lui* the path is all laid out for him **5.** ‣ **en route** [en marche]: *mettre en route* **a)** [appareil, véhicule] to start (up) *(sép)* **b)** [projet] to set in motion, to get started ou under way / *se mettre en route* [machine] to start (up).

routier, ère [ʀutje, ɛʀ] ◆ adj road *(modif)*. ◆ nm, f [chauffeur] (long-distance) lorry UK ou truck US driver / *c'est un vieux routier du journalisme* *fig* he's a veteran journalist. ❖ **routier** nm *fam* [restaurant] transport café UK, truck-stop US. ❖ **routière** nf AUTO touring car.

routine [ʀutin] nf [habitude] routine. ❖ **de routine** loc adj [contrôle, visite] routine *(avant nom)* / *une vérification de routine* a routine check.

routinier, ère [ʀutinje, ɛʀ] adj [tâche, corvée] routine *(avant nom)*, humdrum *péj* ; [vérification, méthode] routine *(avant nom)* ; [personne] routine-minded, conventional.

rouvrir [34] [ʀuvʀiʀ] ◆ vt [livre, hôtel, débat, dossier] to reopen. ◆ vi [magasin] to reopen, to open again. ❖ **se rouvrir** vpi [porte, fenêtre] to reopen ; [blessure] to reopen, to open up again.

roux, rousse [ʀu, ʀus] ◆ adj [feuillage, fourrure] reddish-brown, russet ; [chevelure, moustache] red, ginger. ◆ nm, f redhead. ❖ **roux** nm **1.** [teinte - d'un feuillage] reddish-brown (colour), russet ; [-d'une chevelure, d'une moustache] reddish ou gingery colour **2.** CULIN roux.

royal, e, aux [ʀwajal, o] adj **1.** HIST & POL [puissance] royal, regal ; [bijoux, insignes, appartements, palais, académie] royal **2.** [somptueux - cadeau] magnificent, princely ; [-pourboire] lavish ; [-salaire] princely ; [-accueil] royal **3.** [extrême - mépris] total / *il m'a fichu une paix royale* *fam* he left me in total peace.

royalement [ʀwajalmɑ̃] adv **1.** [avec magnificence] royally, regally / *ils nous ont reçus royalement* they treated us like royalty **2.** *fam* [complètement] totally ‣ **je m'en fiche** ou **moque royalement !** I really couldn't care less!, I don't give a damn!

royaliste [ʀwajalist] ◆ adj royalist. ◆ nmf royalist.

royalties* [ʀwajalti] nfpl royalties ‣ **toucher des royalties** to receive royalties.

─────────

***** In reformed spelling (see p. 16-18).

royaume [ʀwajom] nm **1.** HIST & POL kingdom **2.** RELIG
▶ **le royaume céleste** ou **des cieux** the kingdom of Heaven.

Royaume-Uni [ʀwajomyni] npr m ▶ **le Royaume-Uni**
(de Grande-Bretagne et d'Irlande du Nord) the United
Kingdom (of Great Britain and Northern Ireland), the UK.

royauté [ʀwajote] nf **1.** [monarchie] monarchy **2.** [rang]
royalty, kingship.

RP nfpl (abr de relations publiques) PR.

RSA nm abr de revenu de solidarité active.

RSS (abr de really simple syndication) nm ou nf RSS.

RSVP (abr de répondez s'il vous plaît) RSVP.

RTB (abr de Radiotélévision belge) npr f *Belgian*
broadcasting company.

RTT [ɛʀtete] (abr de réduction du temps de travail)
nf (statutory) reduction in working hours.

 RTT

Initially planned as a measure to reduce unemployment, the law on a 35-hour working
week known as **les trente-cinq heures** has
not entirely succeeded but it has generated more leisure time for people in paid
employment in the form of days off known
as **journées (de) RTT.**

RTTiste [ɛʀtetist] nmf *person taking a day off as a result of*
the reduction in working hours.

RU [ʀy] nm **abr de restaurant universitaire.**

ruade [ʀɥad] nf kick / *lancer* ou *décocher une ruade à*
to kick ou to lash out at.

Ruanda [ʀwɑ̃da] npr m ▶ **le Ruanda** Rwanda.

ruban [ʀybɑ̃] nm **1.** [ornement] ribbon ; [liseré] ribbon,
tape ; [bolduc] tape ; [sur chapeau] band ▶ **le ruban rouge**
the ribbon of the Légion d'honneur **2.** [de cassette] tape ;
[de machine à écrire] ribbon ▶ **ruban adhésif** adhesive tape.

rubéole [ʀybeɔl] nf German measles *(U),* rubella *spéc.*

rubis [ʀybi] nm JOAILL ruby.

rubrique [ʀybʀik] nf **1.** [dans la presse] column ▶ **la**
rubrique littéraire the book page ▶ **la rubrique nécrolo-**
gique the obituaries **2.** [catégorie] heading.

ruche [ʀyʃ] nf ENTOM [abri -en bois] beehive ; [-en paille]
beehive, skep *spéc ;* [colonie d'abeilles] hive.

rude [ʀyd] adj **1.** [rugueux -surface, vin] rough ; [-toile]
rough, coarse ; [-peau] rough, coarse ; [-son] rough, harsh ;
[-voix] gruff ; [-manières, personne] uncouth, unrefined ;
[-traits] rugged **2.** [difficile -climat, hiver] harsh, severe ;
[-conditions, concurrent] tough ; [-concurrence] severe,
tough ; [-vie, tâche] hard, tough ; [-côte] hard, stiff ▶ **être**
mis à rude épreuve a) [personne] to be severely tested, to
be put through the mill b) [vêtement, matériel] to get a lot
of wear and tear / *ma patience a été mise à rude épreuve*
it was a severe strain on my patience **3.** [sévère -ton, voix]
rough, harsh, hard ; [-personne] harsh, hard, severe **4.** *fam*
[important, remarquable] : *ça a été un rude coup pour lui* it
was a hard blow for him.

⚠ L'adjectif anglais **rude** signifie « impoli »,
« grossier » et non **rude.**

rudement [ʀydmɑ̃] adv **1.** *fam* [diablement] ▶ **c'est ru-**
dement bon it's really good / *c'est rudement cher* it's incredibly ou awfully expensive / *elle est rudement culottée !*

she's got some cheek **UK** ou gall! **2.** [sans ménagement]
roughly, harshly **3.** [brutalement] hard.

rudesse [ʀydɛs] nf **1.** [rugosité -d'une surface, de la peau]
roughness ; [-d'une toile] roughness, coarseness ; [-d'une
voix, d'un son] roughness, harshness **2.** [rusticité -des ma-
nières] roughness, uncouthness ; [-des traits] ruggedness
3. [sévérité -d'un ton, d'une voix] roughness, harshness,
hardness ; [-d'un maître] severity, harshness / *traiter qqn*
avec rudesse to treat sb brusquely **4.** [dureté -d'un climat,
d'un hiver] hardness, harshness, severity ; [-d'une concurrence, d'une tâche] toughness.

rudimentaire [ʀydimɑ̃tɛʀ] adj [élémentaire] rudimentary, basic.

rudiments [ʀydimɑ̃] nmpl [d'un art, d'une science]
basics, rudiments *sout / tu apprendras vite les rudiments*
you'll soon learn the basics / *je n'ai que des rudiments*
d'informatique I have only a rudimentary knowledge of
computing.

rue [ʀy] nf [voie] street / *de la rue, des rues* street *(modif)*
▶ **rue à sens unique** one-way street ▶ **être à la rue** to be on
the streets ▶ **mettre** ou **jeter qqn à la rue** to turn ou to put
sb out into the street.

 Rue

The names of some Paris streets are used to
refer to the establishments situated there:
la rue de Grenelle the Ministry of Education;
la rue de Valois the Ministry of Culture; **la**
rue d'Ulm the **École normale supérieure.**

ruée [ʀɥe] nf rush / *il y a eu une ruée vers le buffet*
everybody made a mad dash for the buffet ▶ **la ruée vers**
l'or HIST the gold rush.

ruelle [ʀɥɛl] nf [voie] lane, narrow street, alley.

ruer [7] [ʀɥe] vi **1.** [animal] to kick (out) **2.** **EXPR** **ruer**
dans les brancards *fam* a) [verbalement] to kick up a fuss
b) [par ses actions] to kick ou to lash out. ❖ **se ruer** vpi
▶ **se ruer sur qqn** a) [gén] to rush at sb b) [agressivement]
to hurl ou to throw o.s. at sb / *se ruer vers la sortie* to
dash ou to rush towards the exit / *ils se sont tous rués sur*
le buffet they made a mad dash for the buffet.

rugby [ʀygbi] nm rugby (football) ▶ **rugby à quinze**
Rugby Union ▶ **rugby à treize** Rugby League.

rugbyman [ʀygbiman] (pl **rugbymans** ou **rugbymen**
[-mɛn]) nm rugby player.

rugir [32] [ʀyʒiʀ] vi [fauve] to roar.

rugissement [ʀyʒismɑ̃] nm **1.** [d'un lion, d'un moteur]
roar, roaring **2.** *litt* [des flots] roar, roaring ; [du vent, de la
tempête] roar, roaring, howling **3.** [d'une personne] roar.

rugosité [ʀygozite] nf [d'une écorce, d'un plancher, de la
peau] roughness ; [d'une toile] roughness, coarseness.

rugueux, euse [ʀygø, øz] adj [écorce, planche, peau]
rough ; [toile] rough, coarse.

ruine [ʀɥin] nf **1.** [faillite financière] ruin / *courir à la*
ruine to head for ruin **2.** *fam* [dépense exorbitante] ruinous
expense / *30 €, ce n'est pas la ruine !* 30 € won't break ou
ruin you! **3.** [bâtiment délabré] ruin **4.** [destruction -d'une
institution] downfall, ruin ; *fig* ruin / *ce fut la ruine de notre*
mariage it wrecked ou ruined our marriage. ❖ **en ruine**
◆ loc adj ruined. ◆ loc adv in ruins ▶ **tomber en ruine** to
go to ruin.

ruiner [3] [ʀɥine] vt [financièrement] to ruin, to cause the
ruin of, to bring ruin upon *sout / ça ne va pas te ruiner !*

it won't break ou ruin you! ❖ **se ruiner** vpi [perdre sa fortune] to ruin ou to bankrupt o.s. ; [dépenser beaucoup] to spend a fortune.

ruineux, euse [ʀɥinø, øz] adj extravagantly expensive, ruinous.

ruisseau, x [ʀɥiso] nm [ʀu] brook, stream.

ruisselant, e [ʀɥislɑ̃, ɑ̃t] adj [inondé] ▶ **ruisselant (d'eau) a)** [imperméable, personne] dripping (wet) **b)** [paroi] streaming ou running with water / *le visage ruisselant de sueur* her face streaming ou dripping with sweat / *les joues ruisselantes de larmes* his cheeks streaming with tears.

ruisseler [24] [ʀɥisle] vi [couler - eau, sang, sueur] to stream, to drip. ❖ **ruisseler de** vp + prép [être inondé de] : *ruisseler de sang / sueur* to stream with blood / sweat / *les murs ruisselaient d'humidité* the walls were streaming ou oozing with damp.

    📖 In reformed spelling (see p. 16-18), this verb is conjugated like *peler : il ruissèle, elle ruissèlera.*

ruissellement, ruissèlement* [ʀɥisɛlmɑ̃] nm **1.** [écoulement] : *le ruissellement de la pluie sur les vitres* the rain streaming ou running down the window panes **2.** GÉOL ▶ **ruissellement pluvial, eaux de ruissellement** (immediate) runoff.

rumeur [ʀymœʀ] nf **1.** [information] rumour / *selon certaines rumeurs, le réacteur fuirait toujours* rumour has it ou it's rumoured that the reactor is still leaking **2.** [manifestation] ▶ **rumeur de mécontentement** rumblings of discontent **3.** [opinion] ▶ **la rumeur publique**: *la rumeur publique le tient pour coupable* rumour has it that he is guilty.

ruminer [3] [ʀymine] ❖ vi ZOOL to ruminate *spéc*, to chew the cud. ❖ vt **1.** [ressasser - idée] to ponder, to chew over *(sép)* ; [- malheurs] to brood over *(insép)* ; [- vengeance] to ponder **2.** ZOOL to ruminate.

rumsteck [ʀɔmstɛk] = **romsteck.**

rupin, e [ʀypɛ̃, in] *tfam* ❖ adj [quartier] posh ; [intérieur] ritzy, posh ; [famille] well-heeled, posh. ❖ nm, f : *c'est des rupins* they're rolling in money ou rolling in it ▶ **les rupins** the rich.

rupture [ʀyptyʀ] nf **1.** MÉD [dans une membrane] breaking, tearing, splitting ; [dans un vaisseau] bursting ▶ **rupture d'anévrysme** aneurysmal rupture **2.** [cessation - de négociations, de fiançailles] breaking off / *une rupture avec le passé* a break with the past **3.** [dans un couple] break-up **4.** [changement] break ▶ **rupture de cadence** sudden break in rhythm ▶ **rupture de ton** sudden change in ou of tone **5.** COMM ▶ **rupture de stock**: *être en rupture de stock* to be out of stock **6.** DR ▶ **être en rupture de ban avec son milieu / sa famille** *fig* to be at odds with one's environment / one's family ▶ **rupture de contrat** breach of contract **7.** POL ▶ **rupture des relations diplomatiques** breaking off of diplomatic relations.

rural, e, aux [ʀyʀal, o] ❖ adj [droit, population] rural ; [vie, paysage] country *(modif)*, rural. ❖ nm, f country person ▶ **les ruraux** country people, countryfolk. ❖ nm Ⓢⓤⓘⓢⓢⓔ farm building.

ruse [ʀyz] nf **1.** [trait de caractère] cunning, craftiness, slyness ▶ **s'approprier qqch par ruse** to obtain sthg through ou by trickery **2.** [procédé] trick, ruse, wile ▶ **ruse de guerre a)** *pr* tactics, stratagem **b)** *fig* good trick.

rusé, e [ʀyze] ❖ adj [personne] crafty, sly, wily ; [air, regard] sly ▶ **il est rusé comme un renard** he's as sly ou cunning ou wily as a fox. ❖ nm, f : *tu es une petite rusée !* you're a crafty one ou a sly one, my girl!

ruser [3] [ʀyze] vi to use cunning ou trickery ou guile *sout* ▶ **il va falloir ruser** we'll have to be clever!

rush [ʀœʃ] *(pl* rushs ou rushes) nm [ruée] rush, stampede.

russe [ʀys] adj Russian. ❖ **Russe** nmf Russian. ❖ **russe** nm LING Russian.

Russie [ʀysi] npr f ▶ **la Russie** Russia.

Rustine® [ʀystin] nf *pr (bicycle tyre)* rubber repair patch. ❖ **rustine** nf INFORM patch.

rustique [ʀystik] ❖ adj **1.** *sout* [de la campagne - vie] rustic, rural **2.** AGR hardy. ❖ nm ▶ **le rustique a)** [style] rustic style **b)** [mobilier] rustic furniture.

rustre [ʀystʀ] ❖ adj boorish, uncouth. ❖ nmf boor, lout.

rut [ʀyt] nm rut / *être en rut* to (be in) rut.

rutabaga [ʀytabaga] nm swede, rutabaga Ⓤⓢ.

rutilant, e [ʀytilɑ̃, ɑ̃t] adj [propre - carrosserie, armure] sparkling, gleaming.

Rwanda [ʀwɑ̃da] = **Ruanda.**

rythme [ʀitm] nm **1.** MUS rhythm / *avoir le sens du rythme* [personne] to have rhythm ▶ **marquer le rythme** to mark time **2.** CINÉ, THÉÂTRE & LITTÉR rhythm / *le spectacle manque de rythme* the show is a bit slow-moving ou lacks pace **3.** [allure - d'une production] rate ; [- des battements du cœur] rate, speed ; [- de vie] tempo, pace / *travailler à un rythme soutenu* to work at a sustained pace ▶ **à ce rythme-là** at that rate ▶ **suivre le rythme** to keep up (the pace) **4.** ANAT & BIOL ▶ **rythme cardiaque** heartbeat, cardiac rhythm *spéc* ▶ **rythme respiratoire** breathing rate. ❖ **au rythme de** loc prép [au son de] to the rhythm of.

rythmé, e [ʀitme] adj [musique] rhythmic, rhythmical ; [prose] rhythmical / *musique très rythmée* music with a good rhythm ou beat.

rythmer [3] [ʀitme] vt **1.** [mouvements de danse, texte] to put rhythm into, to give rhythm to **2.** *sout* [ponctuer] : *ces événements ont rythmé sa vie* these events gave a certain rhythm to ou punctuated his life.

rythmique [ʀitmik] adj rhythmic, rhythmical.

s, S [ɛs] nm inv (abr de **seconde**) s. **Voir aussi g.**

s' [s] **1.** ⟶ **se 2.** ⟶ **si** (conj).

s/ abr écrite de **sur.**

S (abr écrite de **Sud**) S.

sa [sa] f ⟶ **son.**

SA (abr de **société anonyme**) nf ≃ plc UK ; ≃ Inc US.

sabayon [sabajɔ̃] nm [entremets] zabaglione ; [sauce] sabayon sauce.

sabbatique [sabatik] adj UNIV sabbatical.

sable [sabl] ◆ nm GÉOL sand. ◆ adj inv sand-coloured, sandy. ❖ **sables** nmpl ▸ **sables mouvants** quicksand (U). ❖ **de sable** loc adj [château] sand (modif) ; [dune] sand (modif), sandy ; [fond] sandy.

sablé [sable] nm (shortbread-type) biscuit UK ou cookie US.

sabler [3] [sable] vt **1.** TRAV PUB to grit **2.** CONSTR to sandblast **3.** EXPR **sabler le champagne** to crack a bottle of champagne.

sablier [sablije] nm [gén] hourglass, sand glass ; [de cuisine] egg timer.

saborder [3] [saborde] vt **1.** NAUT to scuttle, to sink **2.** [stopper - entreprise, journal] to scuttle, to sink, to wind up (sép) **3.** [faire échouer - plans, recherche] to scuttle, to put paid to UK, to scupper UK. ❖ **se saborder** vp (emploi réfléchi) **1.** [navire] to go down (by the deliberate actions of the crew) **2.** [entreprise] to fold, to close down ; [parti] to wind (o.s.) up.

sabot [sabo] nm **1.** [soulier] clog, sabot **2.** ZOOL hoof **3.** MÉCAN ▸ **sabot de Denver** wheel clamp UK, Denver boot US.

sabotage [sabotaʒ] nm **1.** [destruction - de matériel] sabotage **2.** [acte organisé] ▸ **un sabotage** an act ou a piece of sabotage **3.** [travail bâclé] botched job.

saboter [3] [sabote] vt **1.** [détruire volontairement] to sabotage **2.** [bâcler] to bungle.

saboteur, euse [sabotœr, øz] nm, f [destructeur] saboteur.

sabre [sabʀ] nm ARM & SPORT sabre UK, saber US.

sabrer [3] [sabʀe] vt **1.** [texte] to make drastic cuts in ; [paragraphe, phrases] to cut, to axe **2.** fam [critiquer - étudiant, copie] to savage, to lay into (insép) ; [-projet] to lay into **3.** fam [renvoyer - employé] to fire, to sack UK, to can US / **se faire sabrer** to get the chop ou sack UK ou boot US **4.** [ouvrir] : **sabrer le champagne** to break open a bottle of champagne (originally, using a sabre).

sac [sak] nm **1.** [contenant - petit, léger] bag ; [-grand, solide] sack ▸ **sac à bandoulière** shoulder bag ▸ **sac de couchage** sleeping bag ▸ **sac à dos** rucksack, knapsack ▸ **sac à main** a) [à poignée] handbag UK, purse US b) [à bandoulière] shoulder bag ▸ **sac de plage** beach bag ▸ **sac (en) plastique** a) [petit] plastic bag b) [solide et grand] plastic carrier (bag) UK, large plastic bag US ▸ **sac de sport** sportsbag ▸ **sac de voyage** overnight ou travelling UK ou traveling US bag **2.** tfam & vieilli [argent] ▸ **dix sacs** a hundred francs **3.** [pillage] sack, pillage ▸ **mettre qqch à sac** to ransack ou to plunder ou to pillage sthg **4.** fam EXPR ▸ **ça y est, l'affaire est** ou **c'est dans le sac !** it's as good as done!, it's in the bag! ▸ **dans le même sac** : ils sont tous à mettre dans le même sac they're all as bad as each other.

saccade [sakad] nf jerk, jolt, (sudden) start. ❖ **par saccades** loc adv jerkingly, joltingly, in fits and starts / la voiture avançait par saccades the car was lurching ou jerking forward.

saccadé, e [sakade] adj [pas] jerky ; [mouvement] disjointed ; [voix] halting.

saccage [sakaʒ] nm (wanton) destruction.

saccager [17] [sakaʒe] vt [maison, parc] to wreck, to wreak havoc in, to devastate ; [matériel, livres] to wreck, to ruin ; [cultures] to lay waste, to devastate ; [ville] to lay waste, to sack / le village a été saccagé par l'inondation / le tourbillon the village was devastated by the flood / hurricane.

SACEM, Sacem [sasɛm] (abr de **Société des auteurs, compositeurs et éditeurs de musique**) npr f body responsible for collecting and distributing royalties in the music industry ; ≃ Performing Rights Society UK ; ≃ Copyright Royalty Tribunal US.

sacerdoce [sasɛʀdɔs] nm **1.** RELIG priesthood **2.** [vie de dévouement] vocation ou calling (requiring the utmost dedication).

sachet [saʃɛ] nm **1.** [petit sac] (small) bag **2.** [dose - de soupe, d'entremets] packet, sachet ; [-d'herbes aromatiques] sachet ▸ **un sachet d'aspirine** a dose of aspirin ▸ **un sachet de thé** a teabag ▸ **du thé en sachets** teabags ▸ **soupe en sachets** packet soup UK, package soup US.

sacoche [sakɔʃ] nf **1.** [de facteur] bag, post bag UK, mail bag **2.** [de vélo] pannier **3.** BELG handbag, purse US.

sac-poubelle [sakpubɛl] (pl **sacs-poubelle**) nm [petit] dustbin UK ou garbage can US liner, binbag ; [grand] rubbish bag UK, garbage bag US.

sacquer [3] [sake] vt tfam **1.** [employé] ▸ **sacquer qqn** to give sb the sack UK ou ax US, to sack UK ou to can US sb ▸ **se faire sacquer** to get the sack UK ou axe US **2.** [étudiant] to fail, to flunk / elle va se faire sacquer à l'examen she'll get slaughtered in the exam.

sacre [sakʀ] nm **1.** [d'un empereur] coronation and anointment ; [d'un évêque] consecration **2.** QUÉBEC [juron] expletive (usually the name of a religious object).

sacré, e [sakʀe] adj **1.** RELIG [édifice] sacred, holy ; [art, textes, musique] sacred, religious ; [animal] sacred **2.** [devoir, promesse] sacred, sacrosanct ; [droit] sacred, hallowed / sa *voiture, c'est sacré !* her car is sacred! **3.** *(avant nom)* fam [en intensif] : *j'ai un sacré boulot en ce moment !* I've got a hell of a lot of work on at the moment! / *sacré farceur !* you old devil! / *t'as eu une sacrée veine !* you were damn lucky! **4.** *(avant nom)* tfam [satané] damned, blasted ▶ **sacré nom de nom !** damn and blast it! ❖ **sacré** nm ▶ **le sacré** the sacred.

sacrement [sakʀəmɑ̃] nm sacrament ▶ **les derniers sacrements** the last rites.

sacrément [sakʀemɑ̃] adv fam & vieilli : *c'est sacrément bon !* it's jolly 🇬🇧 ou damn good!

sacrer [3] [sakʀe] vt **1.** [empereur] to crown and anoint, to sacre arch ; [évêque] to consecrate **2.** [nommer, instituer] to consecrate / *on l'a sacré meilleur acteur du siècle* he was acclaimed ou hailed as the greatest actor of the century.

sacrifice [sakʀifis] nm **1.** RELIG sacrifice, offering **2.** [effort, compromis] sacrifice / *faire des sacrifices* / *un sacrifice* to make sacrifices / a sacrifice.

sacrifié, e [sakʀifje] ❖ adj sacrificed, lost. ❖ nm, f (sacrificial) victim.

sacrifier [9] [sakʀifje] vt **1.** RELIG to sacrifice **2.** [renoncer à - carrière, santé] to sacrifice ; [- loisirs] to give up *(sép)* ▶ **sacrifier sa vie** to make the ultimate sacrifice / *sacrifier ses amis à sa carrière* to sacrifice one's friends to one's career. ❖ **sacrifier à** v + prép sout [se conformer à] to conform to / *sacrifier à la mode* to conform to ou to go along with (the dictates of) fashion. ❖ **se sacrifier** vpi to sacrifice o.s. / *il reste des frites — allez, je me sacrifie !* fam & hum there are some chips left over — oh well, I suppose I'll have to eat them myself!

sacrilège [sakʀilɛʒ] ❖ adj sacrilegious. ❖ nm **1.** RELIG sacrilege, profanation **2.** fig [crime] sacrilege, crime fig / *ce serait un sacrilège de retoucher la photo* it would be criminal ou a sacrilege to touch up the photograph.

sacristie [sakʀisti] nf [d'une église - catholique] sacristy ; [- protestante] vestry.

sacro-saint, e (mpl sacro-saints, fpl sacro-saintes), **sacrosaint***, **e** [sakʀosɛ̃, ɛ̃t] adj vieilli sacrosanct.

sadique [sadik] ❖ adj sadistic. ❖ nmf sadist.

sadisme [sadism] nm sadism.

sadomasochisme [sadomazoʃism] nm sadomasochism.

sadomasochiste [sadomazoʃist] ❖ adj sadomasochistic. ❖ nmf sadomasochist.

safari [safaʀi] nm safari / *faire un safari* to go on (a) safari.

safari-photo [safaʀifoto] (pl safaris-photos) nm photographic ou camera safari.

safran [safʀɑ̃] ❖ nm BOT & CULIN saffron. ❖ adj inv saffron (modif), saffron-yellow.

saga [saga] nf saga.

sagace [sagas] adj sharp, acute, sagacious sout.

sagacité [sagasite] nf sagacity sout, judiciousness, wisdom.

sage [saʒ] ❖ adj **1.** [tranquille, obéissant] good, well-behaved ▶ **sois sage, Paul !** a) [recommandation] be a good boy, Paul b) [remontrance] behave yourself, Paul ▶ **être sage comme une image** to be as good as gold **2.** [sensé, raisonnable - personne] wise, sensible ; [- avis, conduite, décision] wise, sensible, reasonable / *il serait plus sage que tu prennes une assurance* it would be wiser for you to take out insurance. ❖ nmf [personne] wise person.

sage-femme (pl sages-femmes), **sagefemme*** [saʒfam] nf midwife.

sagement [saʒmɑ̃] adv **1.** [tranquillement] quietly, nicely / *attends-moi sagement ici, Marie* wait for me here like a good girl, Marie **2.** [raisonnablement] wisely, sensibly.

sagesse [saʒɛs] nf **1.** [discernement - d'une personne] good sense, insight, wisdom ; [- d'une décision, d'une suggestion] good sense / *elle n'a pas eu la sagesse d'attendre* she wasn't sensible enough ou didn't have the good sense to wait **2.** [obéissance] good behaviour 🇬🇧 ou behavior 🇺🇸.

Sagittaire [saʒitɛʀ] npr m **1.** ASTRON Sagittarius **2.** ASTROL Sagittarius / *elle est Sagittaire* she's Sagittarius ou a Sagittarian.

Sahara [saaʀa] npr m ▶ **le (désert du) Sahara** the Sahara (desert) ▶ **au Sahara** in the Sahara.

saharien, enne [saaʀjɛ̃, ɛn] adj Saharan. ❖ **saharienne** nf VÊT safari jacket.

Sahel [sael] npr m ▶ **le Sahel** the Sahel.

saignant, e [sɛɲɑ̃, ɑ̃t] adj **1.** CULIN [steak] rare **2.** [blessure] bleeding.

saignement [sɛɲmɑ̃] nm bleeding ▶ **saignement de nez** nosebleed.

saigner [4] [sɛɲe] ❖ vi [plaie, blessé] to bleed ▶ **je saigne du nez** my nose is bleeding, I've got a nosebleed. ❖ vt **1.** [malade, animal] to bleed **2.** [faire payer - contribuable] to bleed, to fleece ; [épuiser - pays] to drain the resources of, to drain ou to suck the lifeblood from ▶ **saigner qqn à blanc** to bleed sb dry, to clean sb out. ❖ **se saigner** vp (emploi réfléchi) ▶ **se saigner aux quatre veines pour qqn** to bleed o.s. dry for sb.

saillant, e [sajɑ̃, ɑ̃t] adj **1.** [en relief - veines] prominent ; [- os, tendon, menton] protruding ; [- muscle, yeux] bulging, protruding ; [- rocher] protruding ; [- corniche] projecting ▶ **avoir les pommettes saillantes** to have prominent ou high cheekbones **2.** [remarquable - trait, fait] salient, outstanding.

saillie [saji] nf **1.** [d'un mur, d'une montagne] ledge ; [d'un os] protuberance ▶ **faire saillie, être en saillie** [balcon, roche] to jut out, to project **2.** ZOOL covering, serving.

sain, e [sɛ̃, sɛn] adj **1.** [robuste - enfant] healthy, robust ; [- cheveux, peau] healthy ; [- dent] sound, healthy ▶ **être sain d'esprit** to be sane / *sain de corps et d'esprit* sound in mind and body **2.** [en bon état - charpente, fondations, structure] sound ; [- situation financière, entreprise, gestion] sound, healthy ; [- viande] good **3.** [salutaire - alimentation, mode de vie] wholesome, healthy ; [- air, climat] healthy, invigorating / *tu ne devrais pas rester enfermé toute la journée, ce n'est pas sain* you shouldn't stay in all day long, it's not good for you ou it's unhealthy **4.** [irréprochable - opinion] sane, sound ; [- lectures] wholesome / *son rapport avec sa fille n'a jamais été très sain* her relationship with her daughter was never very healthy. ❖ **sain et sauf, saine et sauve** loc adj safe and sound, unhurt, unharmed / *j'en suis sorti sain et sauf* I escaped unharmed ou without a scratch.

saindoux [sɛ̃du] nm lard.

sainement [sɛnmɑ̃] adv **1.** [hygiéniquement] healthily / *se nourrir sainement* to eat wholesome ou healthy food **2.** [sagement] soundly.

saint, e [sɛ̃, sɛ̃t] ❖ adj **1.** (après le nom) [sacré - lieu, livre, image, guerre] holy ▶ **la semaine sainte** Holy Week **2.** [canonisé] Saint / *saint Pierre / Paul* Saint Peter / Paul **3.** (avant nom) [exemplaire] holy / *ce curé est un saint homme* the priest is a holy man / *sa mère était une sainte femme* his mother was a real saint **4.** [en intensif] : *toute la sainte journée* the whole blessed day / *j'ai une sainte horreur des araignées* I have a real horror of spiders. ❖ nm, f RELIG saint. ❖ **Saint, e** adj RELIG ▶ **la Sainte Vierge** the Blessed Virgin, the Virgin Mary.

* In reformed spelling (see p. 16-18).

saint-bernard [sɛbɛʀnaʀ] nm inv ZOOL Saint Bernard (dog).

sainte-nitouche [sɛtnituʃ] (pl **saintes-nitouches**) nf péj hypocrite / avec ses airs de sainte-nitouche looking as if butter wouldn't melt in her mouth.

Saint-Esprit [sɛtɛspʀi] npr m ▶ **le Saint-Esprit** the Holy Spirit ou Ghost.

sainteté [sɛ̃tte] nf **1.** [d'une personne] saintliness, godliness ; [d'une action, d'une vie] saintliness ; [d'un édifice, des Écritures, de la Vierge] holiness, sanctity ; [du mariage] sanctity **2.** [titre] : Sa / Votre Sainteté His / Your Holiness.

Saint-Jacques [sɛ̃ʒak] npr ▶ **coquille Saint-Jacques** scallop ▶ **noix de Saint-Jacques** scallops.

Saint-Patrick [sɛ̃patʀik] npr ▶ **la Saint-Patrick** Saint Patrick's Day.

Saint-Père [sɛ̃pɛʀ] nm Holy Father.

Saint-Siège [sɛ̃sjɛʒ] npr m ▶ **le Saint-Siège** the Holy See.

Saint-Sylvestre [sɛ̃silvɛstʀ] npr f ▶ **la Saint-Sylvestre** New Year's Eve.

saisir [32] [seziʀ] vt **1.** [avec brusquerie] to grab (hold of), to seize, to grasp ; [pour porter, déplacer] to catch (hold of), to take hold of, to grip ; [pour s'approprier] to snatch ▶ **saisir qqch au vol** to catch sthg in mid-air **2.** [mettre à profit] to seize, to grab ▶ **saisir l'occasion de faire qqch** to seize ou to grasp the opportunity to do sthg / je n'ai pas su saisir ma chance I missed (out on) my chance, I didn't seize the opportunity **3.** [envahir - suj : colère, terreur, dégoût] to take hold of, to seize, to grip / elle a été saisie d'un malaise she suddenly felt faint / elle fut saisie de panique she suddenly panicked / le froid me saisit the cold hit me **4.** [percevoir - bribes de conversation, mot] to catch, to get **5.** [comprendre - explications, sens d'une phrase] to understand, to get, to grasp **6.** DR [débiteur, biens] to seize, to levy distress (upon) ; [articles prohibés] to seize, to confiscate ; [tribunal] to submit ou to refer a case to / la juridiction compétente a été saisie the case was referred to the appropriate jurisdiction **7.** INFORM to capture / saisir des données (sur clavier) to keyboard data **8.** CULIN to seal, to sear. ❖ **se saisir de** vp + prép **1.** [prendre] to grab (hold of), to grip, to seize **2.** sout [étudier] to examine / le conseil doit se saisir du dossier the council will put the file on its agenda.

saisissant, e [sezisɑ̃, ɑ̃t] adj **1.** [vif - froid] biting, piercing **2.** [surprenant - ressemblance] striking, startling ; [- récit, spectacle] gripping ; [- contraste] startling.

saison [sɛzɔ̃] nf **1.** [période de l'année] season ▶ **en cette saison** at this time of (the) year ▶ **en toutes saisons** all year round ▶ **la belle saison** a) [printemps] the spring months b) [été] the summer months ▶ **la mauvaise saison, la saison froide** the winter months ▶ **la saison sèche** the dry season ▶ **la saison des pluies** the rainy season, the rains **2.** [époque pour certains travaux, certains produits] ▶ **la saison des cerises** the cherry season ▶ **la saison des amours** the mating season **3.** [temps d'activité périodique] season / la saison théâtrale the theatre season / la saison touristique the tourist season ; COMM season ▶ **en basse** ou **morte saison** off season ▶ **en haute saison** during the high season ▶ **en pleine saison** at the height of the season. ❖ **de saison** loc adj [adapté à la saison] seasonal / ce n'est pas un temps de saison this weather's unusual for the time of the year ▶ **être de saison** a) [fruit] to be in season b) [vêtement] to be seasonal.

saisonnier, ère [sɛzɔnje, ɛʀ] adj seasonal, seasonable. ❖ **saisonnier** nm [employé] seasonal worker.

salace [salas] adj [histoire, allusion] salacious sout, lewd, lascivious sout ; [individu] salacious, lecherous, lewd.

salade [salad] nf **1.** BOT lettuce **2.** CULIN salad / salade de concombre / haricots cucumber / bean salad ▶ **salade composée** mixed salad ▶ **salade de fruits** fruit salad ▶ **salade niçoise** salade niçoise, niçoise salad **3.** fam [embrouillamini] muddle, tangle. ❖ **salades** nfpl fam [mensonges] tall stories, fibs / dis-moi tout, et ne me raconte pas de salades ! tell me everything and spare me the fairy tales!

saladerie [saladʀi] nf salad bar.

saladier [saladje] nm [récipient] (salad) bowl.

salaire [salɛʀ] nm ÉCON [gén] pay ; [d'un ouvrier] wages, pay ; [d'un cadre] salary ▶ **salaire à la tâche** ou **aux pièces** pay for piece work, piece rate ▶ **salaire de base** basic salary ou pay ▶ **salaire brut** gross pay ▶ **salaire d'embauche** starting salary ▶ **salaire mensuel** monthly pay ▶ **salaire minimum interprofessionnel de croissance = SMIC** ▶ **salaire net** take-home pay, net salary / je n'ai pas droit au salaire unique I'm not entitled to supplementary benefit 🇬🇧 ou to the welfare benefit 🇺🇸 for single-income families ▶ **les gros salaires** high earners.

salami [salami] nm salami.

salant [salɑ̃] nm salt marsh.

salarial, e, aux [salaʀjal, o] adj [politique, revendications] pay (modif), wage (modif), salary (modif).

salariat [salaʀja] nm [personnes] wage earners.

salarié, e [salaʀje] ❖ adj **1.** [au mois] salaried ; [à la semaine] wage-earning **2.** [travail] paid ; [emploi, poste] salaried. ❖ nm, f [au mois] salaried employee ; [à la semaine] wage-earner ▶ **les salariés** the employees.

salaud [salo] tfam ❖ nm bastard, swine / je pars à Tahiti — ben mon salaud ! I'm off to Tahiti — you lucky sod 🇬🇧 ou bastard! ❖ adj m : il est salaud he's a bastard ou a swine.

sale [sal] ❖ adj **1.** [malpropre - visage] dirty, filthy ; [- eau] dirty, murky ; [- mur] dirty, grimy ▶ **blanc sale** dirty white ▶ **être sale comme un cochon** ou **peigne** ou **porc**: il est sale comme un cochon ou peigne ou porc he's filthy dirty **2.** (avant nom) fam [mauvais, désagréable] nasty / c'est une sale affaire it's a nasty business / elle a un sale caractère she has a filthy ou rotten temper ▶ **quel sale temps !** what rotten ou foul weather! / il m'a joué un sale tour he played a dirty trick on me ▶ **avoir une sale tête** ou **gueule** tfam [à faire peur] to look evil, to be nasty-looking. ❖ nm : ton pantalon est au sale your trousers are with the dirty washing.

salé, e [sale] ❖ adj **1.** CULIN [beurre, cacahuètes, gâteaux secs] salted ; [non sucré - mets] savoury 🇬🇧, savory 🇺🇸 ; [- goût] salty ; [conservé dans le sel - morue, porc] salt (modif), salted **2.** [lac] salt (modif) ▶ **eau salée** salt water **3.** fam [exagéré - condamnation] stiff, heavy ; [- addition] steep, stiff **4.** fam [osé - histoire, plaisanterie] spicy, risqué. ❖ **salé** ❖ nm CULIN salt pork ▶ **petit salé** salted (flank end of) belly pork. ❖ adv : je ne mange pas salé I don't like too much salt in my food / je mange salé I like my food well salted.

salement [salmɑ̃] adv **1.** [malproprement] dirtily **2.** tfam [en intensif] : ça m'a fait salement mal it hurt like hell, it was damn ou 🇬🇧 bloody painful.

saler [3] [sale] vt **1.** CULIN [assaisonner] to salt, to add salt to ; [en saumure] to pickle, to salt (down) ; (en usage absolu) : je ne sale presque pas I hardly use any salt **2.** TRAV PUB [chaussée] to salt.

saleté [salte] nf **1.** [manque de propreté] dirtiness / les rues sont d'une saleté incroyable the streets are incredibly dirty ou filthy **2.** [tache, crasse] speck ou piece of dirt / il y a des saletés qui bloquent le tuyau the pipe is blocked up with muck / faire des saletés to make a mess / ne rentre pas avec tes bottes, tu vas faire des saletés don't come in with your boots on, you'll get dirt everywhere **3.** fam [chose de mauvaise qualité] rubbish 🇬🇧, trash 🇺🇸 / à la récréation, *ils ne mangent que des saletés* all they eat at break is junk food **4.** [chose nuisible] foul thing, nuisance / *j'ai attrapé cette saleté à la piscine* I caught this blasted thing at the swimming pool **5.** *tfam* [en injure] : *saleté de chien !* damned dog ! / *quelle saleté de temps !* what foul ou lousy weather! **6.** [calomnie] (piece of) dirt / *tu as encore raconté des saletés sur mon compte* you've been spreading filthy rumours about me again **7.** [acte] dirty ou filthy trick / *il m'a fait une saleté* he played a dirty trick on me. ❖ **saletés** nfpl [grossièretés] dirt, filth, smut / *raconter des saletés* to say dirty things ; *euphém : les chiens font leurs saletés dans les jardins publics* dogs do their business in the parks.

salière [saljɛʀ] nf [petit bol] saltcellar ; [avec trous] salt cellar, salt shaker US ; [à couvercle] salt box, salt pot.

salir [32] [saliʀ] vt **1.** [eau, surface] to (make) dirty ; [vêtements] to (make) dirty, to mess up (*sép*), to soil **2.** [honneur, amitié] to besmirch *litt* ; [réputation] to smear, to besmirch, to sully *litt*. ❖ **se salir** ❖ vp (*emploi réfléchi*) to get dirty, to dirty o.s. ; *fig* to lose one's reputation ▸ **se salir les mains** *pr & fig* to get one's hands dirty. ❖ vpi to get soiled ou dirty / *ne prends pas un manteau beige, ça se salit vite* don't buy a beige coat, it shows the dirt ou it gets dirty very quickly.

salissant, e [salisɑ̃, ɑ̃t] adj **1.** [qui se salit] ▸ **c'est une teinte salissante** this shade shows the dirt **2.** [qui salit - travail] dirty, messy.

salive [saliv] nf **1.** PHYSIOL saliva, spit **2.** *fam* EXPR ▸ **ne gaspillez pas** ou **épargnez votre salive** save ou don't waste your breath ▸ **avaler** ou **ravaler sa salive** [se taire] to keep quiet.

saliver [3] [salive] vi **1.** PHYSIOL to salivate **2.** [avoir l'eau à la bouche] : *le menu me fait saliver* the menu makes my mouth water **3.** *fam* [d'envie] to drool.

salle [sal] nf **1.** [dans une habitation privée] room ▸ **salle de bains a)** [lieu] bathroom **b)** [mobilier] bathroom suite ▸ **salle d'eau** shower room ▸ **salle de jeu a)** [d'une maison] playroom **b)** [d'un casino] gaming room ▸ **salle à manger a)** [lieu] dining room **b)** [mobilier] dining room suite ▸ **salle de séjour** living room **2.** [dans un édifice public] hall, room ; [dans un café] room ; [dans un musée] room, gallery ▸ **salle d'attente** waiting room ▸ **salle d'audience** courtroom ▸ **salle de bal** ballroom ▸ **salle de cinéma** cinema UK, movie theater US ▸ **salle de classe** classroom ▸ **salle des coffres** strongroom ▸ **salle de concert** concert hall, auditorium ▸ **salle de conférences a)** UNIV lecture theatre UK ou hall US **b)** [pour colloques] conference room ▸ **salle de cours** classroom ▸ **salle d'embarquement** departure lounge ▸ **salle d'études** prep room UK, study hall US ▸ **salle des fêtes** village hall ▸ **salle de garde** (hospital) staffroom ▸ **salle d'hôpital, salle commune** *vieilli* hospital ward ▸ **salle de jeu a)** [pour enfants] playroom **b)** [de casino] gaming room ▸ **salle d'opération a)** [à l'hôpital] operating theatre UK ou room US **b)** MIL operations room ▸ **salle paroissiale** church hall ▸ **salle des professeurs a)** ÉDUC (school) staffroom **b)** UNIV senior common room UK, professors' lounge US ▸ **salle de projection** projection room ▸ **salle de rédaction** [d'un journal] newsroom ▸ **salle de restaurant** (restaurant) dining room ▸ **salle de réunion** assembly room ▸ **salle de spectacle** auditorium, theatre UK, theater US ▸ **salle des ventes** auction room UK, auction gallery US **3.** CINÉ & THÉÂTRE [lieu] theatre, auditorium ; [spectateurs] audience ▸ **faire salle comble** to pack the house / *le cinéma a cinq salles* it's a five-screen cinema UK ou movie theater US / *sa dernière production sort en salle en septembre* her latest production will be released ou out in September ▸ **dans les salles obscures** in the cinemas UK ou movie theaters US **4.** SPORT ▸ **athlétisme en salle** indoor athletics.

salon [salɔ̃] nm **1.** [chez un particulier - pièce] living ou sitting room, lounge UK ; [-meubles] living room suite / *salon en cuir* leather suite ▸ **salon de jardin** garden set ▸ **salon de réception** reception room **2.** [dans un hôtel] lounge ; [pour réceptions, fêtes] function room ; [d'un paquebot] saloon, lounge **3.** [boutique] ▸ **salon de beauté** beauty parlour ou salon ▸ **salon de coiffure** hairdressing salon ▸ **salon de thé** tearoom ▸ **salon d'essayage** fitting room, changing room **4.** COMM [exposition] : *Salon de l'automobile* Motor UK ou Car ou Automobile US Show ▸ **Salon du livre** annual book fair in Paris **5.** ART salon **6.** LITTÉR salon.

salopard [salɔpaʀ] nm *tfam* bastard, swine, sod UK.

salope [salɔp] *vulg* nf **1.** [femme de mauvaise vie] slut, slag UK **2.** [femme méprisable] bitch, cow US.

saloper [3] [salɔpe] vt *tfam* **1.** [réparation, travail] to make a mess ou hash of, to cock up UK (*sép*) **2.** [souiller - vêtements, mur] to mess up (*sép*).

saloperie [salɔpʀi] nf *tfam* **1.** [camelote] rubbish UK, trash US / *toutes ces saloperies vous détraquent l'estomac* all this rubbish ou junk food upsets your stomach **2.** [chose désagréable, nuisible] : *depuis que j'ai cette saloperie au poumon...* since I've had this blasted thing on my lung... **3.** [chose sale] : *tu as une saloperie sur ta manche* you've got something dirty on your sleeve **4.** [calomnie] nasty ou catty remark ; [action méprisable] nasty ou dirty trick ▸ **faire une saloperie à qqn** to play a dirty ou nasty trick on sb. ❖ **saloperies** nfpl [grossièretés] filthy language (*U*).

salopette [salɔpɛt] nf [de ville] dungarees UK, overalls US ; [de ski] salopette ; [d'un plombier] overalls.

salsifis [salsifi] nm salsify.

salubre [salybʀ] adj [climat] salubrious, hygienic, wholesome ; [logement] salubrious.

saluer [7] [salɥe] vt **1.** [dire bonjour] to say hello to ▸ **saluer qqn a)** [de la main] to wave to sb **b)** [de la tête] to nod to sb **c)** [en arrivant] to greet sb **d)** [en partant] to take one's leave of sb ▸ **l'acteur salue le public** the actor bows to the audience ou takes his bow / *il m'a demandé de vous saluer* he asked me to give you his regards **2.** MIL to salute **3.** [accueillir] to greet / *son film a été unanimement salué par la presse* her film was unanimously acclaimed by ou met with unanimous acclaim from the press **4.** [rendre hommage à - courage, génie] to salute, to pay homage ou tribute to ; [reconnaître en tant que] to hail ▸ **saluer la mémoire** ou **le souvenir de qqn** to salute sb's memory.

salut [saly] ❖ nm **1.** [marque de politesse] ▸ **faire un salut de la main à qqn** to wave (one's hand) to sb ▸ **faire un salut de la tête à qqn** to nod to sb **2.** MIL salute / *faire le salut* to (give the military) salute **3.** [survie - d'une personne, d'un pays] salvation, safety ; [-d'une entreprise, d'une institution] salvation **4.** RELIG salvation. ❖ interj *fam* [en arrivant] hi ou hello ou hullo (there) ; [en partant] bye, see you, so long US.

salutaire [salytɛʀ] adj **1.** [physiquement - air] healthy ; [-remède] beneficial ; [-exercice, repos] salutary, beneficial / *cette semaine dans les Alpes m'a été salutaire* that week in the Alps did my health a power of good **2.** [moralement - conseil, épreuve] salutary ; [-lecture, effet] beneficial.

salutations [salytasjɔ̃] nfpl greetings, salutation.

Salvador [salvadɔʀ] npr m ▸ **le Salvador** El Salvador.

salvadorien, enne [salvadɔʀjɛ̃, ɛn] adj Salvadorian, Salvadorean. ❖ **Salvadorien, enne** nm, f Salvadorian, Salvadorean.

salve [salv] nf **1.** MIL salvo, volley **2.** *fig* ▸ **salve d'applaudissements** round ou burst of applause.

samaritain, e [samaʀitɛ̃, ɛn] adj Samaritan.
❖ **samaritain** nm Suisse [secouriste] *person qualified to give first aid.* ❖ **Samaritain, e** nm, f Samaritan ▸ **le bon samaritain** the good Samaritan.

samedi [samdi] nm Saturday / *samedi 13 septembre* Saturday 13th September UK, Saturday September 13th US ▸ **samedi en huit** a week on Saturday UK, Saturday week US, a week from Saturday US ▸ **samedi en quinze** two weeks on UK ou from US Saturday ▸ **Samedi saint** Holy ou Easter Saturday. **Voir aussi mardi.**

SAMU, Samu [samy] (abr de Service d'aide médicale d'urgence) npr m *French ambulance and emergency service ;* ≃ ambulance service UK ; ≃ Paramedics US.

 **SAMU**

> The **SAMU** coordinates medical emergency calls within a department and decides how best to deal with a situation. The **SAMU social** deals with the homeless and assists people in need. Its volunteers help those with nowhere to live find emergency housing and help for them.

sanction [sɑ̃ksjɔ̃] nf **1.** [mesure répressive] sanction ▸ **prendre des sanctions contre** to take sanctions against ▸ **sanctions diplomatiques / économiques** diplomatic / economic sanctions **2.** ÉDUC & SPORT punishment, disciplinary action (U) sout / *prendre des sanctions contre un élève* to punish a pupil / *prendre des sanctions contre un sportif* to take disciplinary action against an athlete.

sanctionner [3] [sɑ̃ksjɔne] vt **1.** [punir - délit, élève] to punish ; [-sportif, haut fonctionnaire] to take disciplinary action against ; [-pays] to impose sanctions on **2.** [ratifier - loi] to sanction, to ratify ; [-décision] to sanction, to agree with (insép) / *un cursus de trois années d'études sanctionnée par un diplôme* a three year diploma course.

sanctuaire [sɑ̃ktɥɛʀ] nm RELIG sanctuary.

sandale [sɑ̃dal] nf sandal.

sandwich [sɑ̃dwitʃ] (pl sandwichs ou sandwiches) nm sandwich / *sandwich au fromage* cheese sandwich / *j'étais pris en sandwich entre eux* fam I was sandwiched between them.

sandwicherie [sɑ̃dwitʃʀi] nf sandwich shop ; [avec possibilité de manger sur place] sandwich bar.

sang [sɑ̃] nm **1.** BIOL blood ▸ **à sang froid / chaud** cold- / warm-blooded ▸ **répandre** ou **verser** ou **faire couler le sang** sout to shed ou to spill blood ▸ **en sang** : *être en sang, nager* ou *baigner dans son sang* to be covered in blood ▸ **se mordre les lèvres jusqu'au sang** to bite one's lips until one draws blood ▸ **avoir du sang dans les veines** to have courage ou guts / *il a ça dans le sang* it's in his blood ▸ **mon sang s'est glacé** ou **figé dans mes veines** my blood ran cold ou turned to ice in my veins ▸ **se faire du mauvais sang** ou **un sang d'encre, se manger** ou **se ronger les sangs** to worry o.s. sick, to be worried stiff, to fret **2.** litt [vie] (life) blood ▸ **du sang frais** ou **nouveau** ou **neuf** a) [personnes] new blood b) [argent] new ou fresh money **3.** sout [race, extraction] blood **4.** EXPR **bon sang (de bonsoir) !** fam damn and blast it!

sang-froid [sɑ̃fʀwa] nm inv composure, calm, sang-froid ▸ **garder** ou **conserver son sang-froid** to stay calm, to keep one's cool ▸ **perdre son sang-froid** to lose one's self-control ou cool. ❖ **de sang-froid** loc adv ▸ **tuer qqn de sang-froid** to kill sb in cold blood ou cold-bloodedly / *commis de sang-froid* cold-blooded.

sanglant, e [sɑ̃glɑ̃, ɑ̃t] adj **1.** [blessure, bataille, règne] bloody ; [bras, mains] covered in blood, bloody ; [linge] bloody, blood-soaked ; [spectacle] gory **2.** [blessant - critiques] scathing ; [-affront] cruel.

sangle [sɑ̃gl] nf [lanière - gén] strap ; [-d'un lit, d'une chaise] webbing ; [-d'un cheval] girth.

sangler [3] [sɑ̃gle] vt **1.** [cheval] to girth **2.** [paquet, valise] to strap up (sép) **3.** fig [serrer] : *sanglée dans son corset* tightly corseted.

sanglier [sɑ̃glije] nm ZOOL (wild) boar.

sanglot [sɑ̃glo] nm [hoquet, pleurs] sob / *avec des sanglots dans la voix* with a sob in one's voice.

sangloter [3] [sɑ̃glɔte] vi [pleurer] to sob.

sangsue [sɑ̃sy] nf ZOOL leech.

sanguin, e [sɑ̃gɛ̃, in] adj **1.** [groupe, plasma, transfusion, vaisseau] blood (modif) ; [système] circulatory **2.** [humeur, tempérament] sanguine. ❖ **sanguine** nf **1.** ART [crayon] red chalk, sanguine ; [dessin] red chalk drawing, sanguine **2.** BOT blood orange.

sanguinaire [sɑ̃ginɛʀ] adj **1.** [assoiffé de sang] bloodthirsty **2.** litt [féroce - bataille, conquête] bloody, sanguinary sout.

sanitaire [sanitɛʀ] ◆ adj **1.** ADMIN & MÉD [conditions] sanitary, health (modif) ; [règlement] health ▸ **cordon sanitaire** quarantine line **2.** CONSTR sanitary, plumbing (U) ▸ **l'équipement sanitaire** the plumbing. ◆ nm [installations] plumbing (for bathroom and toilet). ❖ **sanitaires** nmpl (bathroom and) toilet.

sans [sɑ̃] ◆ prép **1.** [indiquant l'absence, la privation, l'exclusion] without / *avec ou sans sucre ?* with or without sugar? / *j'ai trouvé sans problème* I found it without any difficulty ou with no difficulty / *être sans scrupules* to have no scruples, to be unscrupulous ▸ **homme sans cœur / pitié** heartless / pitiless man ▸ **couple sans enfants** childless couple ▸ **sans additif** additive-free / *essence sans plomb* unleaded ou lead-free petrol ▸ **sans commentaire !** no comment! **2.** [exprimant la condition] but for / *sans toi, je ne l'aurais jamais fait* if it hadn't been for you ou but for you, I would never have done it **3.** [avec un infinitif] without ▸ **sans être vu** without being seen / *partons sans plus attendre* come on, let's not wait any more / *tu n'es pas sans savoir qu'il est amoureux d'elle* you must be aware that he's in love with her. ◆ adv without / *il faudra faire sans !* we'll have to go without! / *passe-moi mon manteau, je ne peux pas sortir sans* hand me my coat, I can't go out without it ▸ **c'est un jour sans !** [tout va mal] it's one of those days! ❖ **non sans** loc prép not without / *il l'a persuadé, mais non sans mal* he persuaded her, but not without difficulty, he had quite a job persuading her. ❖ **sans cela, sans ça** loc conj fam otherwise. ❖ **sans que** loc conj : *ils ont réglé le problème sans que nous ayons à intervenir* they dealt with the problem without us having to intervene. ❖ **sans quoi** loc conj : *soyez ponctuels, sans quoi vous ne pourrez pas vous inscrire* be sure to be on time, otherwise you won't be able to register.

> ✐ Notez la différence entre les constructions française et anglaise :
>
> Sans + infinitif
> without + -ing
>
> **Ne partez pas sans me dire au revoir.** *Don't leave without saying goodbye.*
>
> **Elles ont travaillé une semaine entière sans réclamer la moindre récompense.** *They worked for a whole week without asking for anything in return.*
>
> Attention, on ne dit pas without to...

sans-abri [sɑ̃zabʀi] (*pl* sans-abri *ou* sans-abris*) nmf homeless person ▸ **les sans-abri** the homeless.

sans-emploi [sɑ̃zɑ̃plwa] (*pl* sans-emploi *ou* sans-emplois*) nmf unemployed ou jobless person ▸ **les sans-emploi** the unemployed.

sans-fil [sɑ̃fil] (*pl* sans-fil *ou* sans-fils*) ◆ nm cordless telephone. ◆ adj inv INFORM & TÉLÉC wireless.

sans-gêne [sɑ̃ʒɛn] (*pl* sans-gêne *ou* sans-gênes*) ◆ nm lack of consideration, casualness. ◆ nmf ill-mannered person.

sans-logis [sɑ̃lɔʒi] nmf homeless person ▸ **les sans-logis** the homeless.

sans-papiers, sans-papier* [sɑ̃papje] nmf illegal immigrant worker.

sans-plomb [sɑ̃plɔ̃] (*pl* sans-plomb *ou* sans-plombs*) nm unleaded, unleaded petrol 🇬🇧 ou gasoline 🇺🇸, lead-free petrol 🇬🇧 ou gas 🇺🇸.

santal, als [sɑ̃tal] nm BOT sandal ▸ **bois de santal** sandalwood.

santé [sɑ̃te] nf **1.** [de l'esprit, d'une économie, d'une entreprise] health, soundness ; [d'une personne, d'une plante] health / *comment va la santé ?* fam how are you keeping? / *c'est mauvais pour la santé* it's bad for your health ou for you ▸ **en bonne santé a)** [personne] healthy, in good health **b)** [plante] healthy **c)** [économie] healthy, sound **d)** [monnaie] strong ▸ **en mauvaise santé a)** [animal, personne] in bad ou poor health **b)** [plante] unhealthy **c)** [économie, monnaie] weak ▸ **avoir la santé** fam [être infatigable] to be a bundle of energy **2.** ADMIN ▸ **la santé publique** public health ▸ **services de santé** health services. ❖ **à la santé de** loc prép [en portant un toast] : *à votre santé !, à ta santé !* cheers!, your (good) health! / *à la santé de ma femme !* (here's) to my wife!

santiag [sɑ̃tjag] nf cowboy boot.

saoudien, enne [saudjɛ̃, ɛn] adj Saudi (Arabian). ❖ **Saoudien, enne** nm, f Saudi (Arabian).

saoul, e [su, sul] = **soûl.**

saouler [sule] = **soûler.**

sape [sap] nf fig ▸ **travail de sape** (insidious) undermining.

saper [3] [sape] vt **1.** [miner] to sap, to undermine ▸ **saper le moral à qqn** to get sb down **2.** fam [habiller] to dress / *il est toujours bien sapé* he's always really smartly turned out ou dressed. ❖ **se saper** fam vpi : *où est-ce que tu te sapes ?* where do you buy your togs ou gear?

sapeur-pompier [sapœʀpɔ̃pje] (*pl* sapeurs-pompiers) nm fireman.

saphir [safiʀ] nm **1.** JOAILL sapphire **2.** [d'un tourne-disque] needle, stylus.

sapin [sapɛ̃] nm **1.** BOT fir (tree) **2.** MENUIS fir, deal. ❖ **sapin de Noël** nm Christmas tree.

sapinages [sapinaʒ] nmpl 🇶🇧 BOT evergreens.

saquer [sake] tfam = **sacquer.**

SAR (abr écrite de Son Altesse Royale) HRH.

sarbacane [saʀbakan] nf blowpipe.

sarcasme [saʀkasm] nm [remarque] sarcastic remark.

sarcastique [saʀkastik] adj sarcastic.

sarcophage [saʀkɔfaʒ] nm [cercueil] sarcophagus.

Sardaigne [saʀdɛɲ] npr f ▸ **la Sardaigne** Sardinia.

sarde [saʀd] adj Sardinian. ❖ **Sarde** nmf Sardinian. ❖ **sarde** nm LING Sardinian.

sardine [saʀdin] nf [poisson] sardine ▸ **sardines à l'huile** sardines in oil.

SARL, Sarl (abr de société à responsabilité limitée) nf [cotée en Bourse] limited liability company 🇬🇧, public limited company ▸ **Balacor, SARL** ≃ Balacor Ltd 🇬🇧 ; ≃ Balacor plc 🇬🇧 ; ≃ Balacor Inc. 🇺🇸.

sarment [saʀmɑ̃] nm [tige] twining ou climbing stem, bine ▸ **sarment de vigne** vine shoot.

sarrasin [saʀazɛ̃] nm BOT buckwheat.

sas [sas] nm **1.** AÉRON airlock **2.** NAUT [d'écluse] lock (chamber) ; [passage] airlock **3.** [d'une banque] security (double) door.

SAS (abr écrite de Son Altesse Sérénissime) HSH.

Satan [satɑ̃] npr Satan.

satané, e [satane] adj *(avant nom)* fam **1.** [détestable] : *faites donc taire ce satané gosse !* shut that blasted kid up! **2.** [en intensif] : *c'est un satané menteur* he's a downright liar.

satanique [satanik] adj **1.** [de Satan] satanic **2.** [démoniaque, pervers] fiendish, diabolical, satanic.

satellite [satelit] nm ASTRON, ASTRONAUT & TÉLÉC satellite ▸ **transmission par satellite** satellite transmission.

satiété [sasjete] nf satiety ▸ **à satiété, jusqu'à satiété** : *manger à satiété* to eat one's fill.

satin [satɛ̃] nm TEXT satin / *une peau de satin* fig a satin-smooth skin.

satiné, e [satine] adj [étoffe, reflets] satiny, satin *(modif)* ; [papier] calendered ; [peau] satin *(modif)*, satin-smooth ▸ **peinture satinée** silk finish emulsion.

satire [satiʀ] nf [critique] satire, send up 🇬🇧, spoof.

satirique [satiʀik] adj satirical.

satisfaction [satisfaksjɔ̃] nf **1.** [plaisir] satisfaction, gratification ▸ **éprouver de la satisfaction / une grande satisfaction à faire qqch** to feel satisfaction / great satisfaction in doing sth ▸ **donner (entière ou toute) satisfaction à qqn a)** [personne] to give sb (complete) satisfaction **b)** [travail] to fulfil 🇬🇧 ou to fulfill 🇺🇸 sb completely, to give sb a lot of (job) satisfaction / *le problème fut résolu à la satisfaction générale* the problem was solved to everybody's satisfaction **2.** [sujet de contentement] source ou cause for satisfaction / *mon travail m'apporte de nombreuses satisfactions* my job gives me great satisfaction / *mon fils m'apporte de nombreuses satisfactions* my son is a great satisfaction to me **3.** [gain de cause] satisfaction ▸ **accorder ou donner satisfaction à qqn** to give sb satisfaction ▸ **obtenir satisfaction** to obtain satisfaction.

satisfaire [109] [satisfeʀ] vt **1.** [contenter - suj : résultat, travail] to satisfy, to give satisfaction to ; [- suj : explication] to satisfy / *votre rapport ne me satisfait pas du tout* I'm not satisfied at all with your report, I don't find your report at all satisfactory / *j'espère que cet arrangement vous satisfera* I hope (that) you'll find this arrangement satisfactory ou to your satisfaction ; [sexuellement] to satisfy **2.** [répondre à - attente] to come ou to live up to ; [- désir] to satisfy, to fulfil ; [- besoin] to satisfy, to answer ; [- curiosité] to satisfy ; [- demande] to meet, to satisfy, to cope with *(insép)*, to keep up with *(insép)* ; [- faim] to satisfy, to appease ; [- soif] to satisfy, to quench, to slake. ❖ **satisfaire à** v + prép [conditions] to fulfil 🇬🇧, to fulfill 🇺🇸, to meet, to satisfy ; [besoin, exigences] to meet, to fulfil ; [désir] to satisfy, to gratify ; [attente] to live ou to come up to ; [promesse] to fulfil, to keep ; [goût] to satisfy ; [norme] to comply with *(insép)*, to satisfy. ❖ **se satisfaire de** vp + prép to be satisfied ou content with / *tu te satisfais de peu !* you're content with very little!, it doesn't take much to make you happy!

satisfaisant, e [satisfəzɑ̃, ɑ̃t] adj [réponse, travail, devoir scolaire] satisfactory / *de manière satisfaisante* satisfactorily ▸ **peu satisfaisant a)** [résultat, travail] unsatisfactory **b)** ÉDUC poor.

📎 **satisfactory** ou **satisfying** ?

Satisfactory signifie « convenable », « qui donne satisfaction », tandis que **satisfying** se réfère à « ce qui contente, fait plaisir ».

---

satisfait, e [satisfɛ, ɛt] ◆ pp ⟶ **satisfaire.** ◆ adj [air, personne, regard] satisfied, happy ▸ **être satisfait de qqn** to be satisfied ou happy with sb / *être satisfait de soi* ou *de soi-même* to be satisfied with o.s., to be self-satisfied ▸ **être satisfait de a)** [arrangement, résultat] to be satisfied with, to be happy with ou about **b)** [voiture, service] to be satisfied with.

saturation [satyʀasjɔ̃] nf [d'une autoroute, d'un aéroport] saturation, paralysis, gridlocking ; [d'un circuit] saturation, overloading ; [d'un marché] saturation (point) ▸ **arriver** ou **parvenir à saturation a)** [marché, aéroport] to reach saturation point **b)** [marcheur, travailleur] to reach saturation point, to be unable to take anymore.

saturé, e [satyʀe] adj **1.** [imprégné - gén] impregnated ; [- d'un liquide] saturated **2.** [encombré - marché] saturated, glutted **3.** [rassasié, écœuré] : *des enfants saturés de télévision* children who have had too much television **4.** [engorgé - autoroute] saturated, blocked, gridlocked ; [- circuit de communication] saturated.

saturer [3] [satyʀe] vi fam [marché] to become saturated ; [lignes téléphoniques] to overload ; [sonorisation] : *ça sature* we're getting distortion ; [personne] : *deux heures d'informatique et je sature* after two hours of computer science, I can't take anything in any more.

Saturne [satyʀn] npr ASTRON & MYTH Saturn.

satyre [satiʀ] nm **1.** MYTH & ENTOM satyr **2.** [homme lubrique] lecher.

sauce [sos] nf CULIN sauce ; [de salade] salad dressing ; [vinaigrette] French dressing ; [jus de viande] gravy ▸ **sauce béarnaise** / **hollandaise** béarnaise / hollandaise sauce ▸ **sauce madère** / **piquante** Madeira / hot sauce ▸ **pâtes à la sauce tomate** pasta with tomato sauce / *mettre* ou *servir qqch à toutes les sauces* to make sthg fit every occasion.

saucée [sose] nf fam downpour / *prendre* ou *recevoir la saucée* to get drenched ou soaked (to the skin).

saucer [16] [sose] vt **1.** [essuyer] : *saucer son assiette (avec un morceau de pain)* to wipe (off) one's plate (with a piece of bread) **2.** EXPR⟩ *se faire saucer* fam to get soaked (to the skin) ou drenched.

saucette [sosɛt] nf QUÉBEC fam **1.** [petite baignade] quick dip **2.** [courte visite] short visit.

saucière [sosjɛʀ] nf [pour sauce] sauce boat ; [pour jus] gravy boat.

saucisse [sosis] nf CULIN sausage ▸ **saucisse de Francfort** frankfurter ▸ **saucisse de Strasbourg** Strasbourg (pork) sausage, knack-wurst.

saucisson [sosisɔ̃] nm CULIN ▸ **saucisson (sec)** (dry) sausage.

saucissonner [3] [sosisɔne] fam vt [diviser] to chop up / *le film a été saucissonné* the film was divided up into episodes.

sauf¹ [sof] prép **1.** [à part] except, apart from, save *sout* / *il sait tout faire sauf cuisiner* he can do everything except ou but cook / *il s'arrête toujours ici sauf s'il n'a pas le temps* he always stops here except if ou unless he's in a hurry **2.** [à moins de] unless. ◆ **sauf que** loc conj except (for the fact) that, apart from the fact that.

sauf², sauve [sof, sov] adj **1.** [indemne - personne] safe **2.** fig [intact] : *au moins, les apparences sont sauves* at least appearances have been kept up ou saved.

sauf-conduit (pl sauf-conduits), **saufconduit*** [sofkɔ̃dɥi] nm safe-conduct.

sauge [soʒ] nf **1.** BOT salvia **2.** CULIN sage.

saugrenu, e [soɡʀəny] adj peculiar, weird / *en voilà une idée saugrenue !* what a cranky ou daft idea!

saule [sol] nm willow ▸ **saule pleureur** / **blanc** weeping / white willow.

saumâtre [somatʀ] adj **1.** [salé] brackish, briny **2.** fam [désagréable] bitter, nasty / *il l'a trouvée saumâtre !* he wasn't amused!, he was unimpressed! euphém.

saumon [somɔ̃] ◆ nm **1.** ZOOL salmon ▸ **saumon fumé** CULIN smoked salmon 🇬🇧, lox 🇺🇸 **2.** [couleur] salmon-pink. ◆ adj inv salmon (modif), salmon-pink.

saumure [somyʀ] nf brine.

sauna [sona] nm [cabine] sauna (bath) ; [établissement] sauna.

saupoudrer [3] [sopudʀe] vt CULIN to dust, to sprinkle.

saut [so] nm **1.** SPORT jump ▸ **saut en hauteur** / **longueur** high / long jump ▸ **saut de l'ange** swallow 🇬🇧 ou swan 🇺🇸 dive ▸ **saut en ciseaux** scissors jump ▸ **saut à la corde** skipping ▸ **saut à l'élastique** bungee jumping ▸ **saut de haies** hurdling ▸ **saut d'obstacles** show jumping ▸ **saut en parachute a)** [discipline] parachuting, skydiving **b)** [épreuve] parachute jump ▸ **saut à la perche a)** [discipline] pole vaulting **b)** [épreuve] pole vault ▸ **saut périlleux** somersault ▸ **saut à skis a)** [discipline] ski jumping **b)** [épreuve] (ski) jump **2.** [bond] leap ▸ **au saut du lit a)** [en se levant] on ou upon getting up **b)** [tôt] first thing in the morning **3.** [brève visite] flying visit / *elle a fait un saut chez nous hier* she dropped by (our house) yesterday / *fais un saut chez le boucher* pop over ou along ou across to the butcher's **4.** fig leap / *faire un saut dans l'inconnu* to take a leap in the dark ▸ **le grand saut** [la mort] the big sleep ▸ **faire le saut** to take the plunge.

saute [sot] nf fig ▸ **saute d'humeur** mood swing.

sauté [sote] nm sauté ▸ **sauté de veau** sauté of veal.

saute-mouton [sotmutɔ̃] (pl saute-mouton ou saute-moutons*) nm leapfrog ▸ **jouer à saute-mouton** to play leapfrog.

sauter [3] [sote] ◆ vi **1.** [bondir - personne] to jump, to spring up ; [- chat] to jump, to leap ; [- oiseau, insecte] to hop ; [- grenouille, saumon] to leap ; [- balle, curseur] to bounce, to jump ▸ **sauter par la fenêtre** to jump out of the window / *quand je pense que je la faisais sauter sur mes genoux il n'y a pas si longtemps* when I think that not so long ago, I was bouncing ou dandling her on my knee ; fig ▸ **sauter de joie** to jump for joy ▸ **sauter au plafond** fam, **sauter en l'air** fam **a)** [de colère] to hit the roof **b)** [de joie] to be thrilled to bits **2.** JEUX & SPORT ▸ **sauter à la corde** to skip (with a rope) 🇬🇧, to skip ou to jump rope 🇺🇸 ▸ **sauter en parachute** to (parachute) jump, to parachute ▸ **sauter en hauteur** / **longueur** to do the high / long jump ▸ **sauter à la perche** to pole-vault ▸ **sauter en ciseaux** to do a scissors jump **3.** [se ruer] to jump, to pounce / *sauter (à bas) du lit* to jump ou to spring out of bed / *sauter dans un taxi* to jump ou to leap into a taxi ; fig : *sauter sur l'occasion* to jump at the chance ▸ **se faire sauter dessus** to be jumped on ▸ **sauter à la gorge** ou **au collet de qqn** to jump down sb's throat / *va te laver les mains, et que ça saute !* fam go and wash your hands and get a move on ou get your skates on 🇬🇧 ▸ **sauter aux yeux** : *ça saute aux yeux* it's plain for all to see ou as the nose on your face **4.** [exploser] to blow up, to explode, to go off / *faire sauter une mine* to explode a mine / *les plombs ont sauté* ÉLECTR the fuses have blown / *la lampe* / *le circuit a sauté* the lamp / circuit has fused 🇬🇧, the lamp fuse / the circuit has blown 🇺🇸 ; [être projeté] : *faire sauter le bouchon d'une bouteille* to pop a cork ▸ **se faire sauter la cervelle** *fam* ou **le caisson** *fam* to blow one's brains out ▸ **faire sauter la banque** *pr & fig* to break the bank **5.** [changer sans transition] to jump **6.** [cesser de fonctionner - chaîne, courroie] to come off ; [- image de télévision] to flicker ; [- serrure] to snap **7.** *fam* [être renvoyé] to fall / *le gouvernement a sauté* the government has fallen / *faire sauter un directeur* to kick out ou to fire a manager **8.** CULIN : *faire sauter des pommes de terre* to sauté potatoes. ◆ vt **1.** [obstacle] to jump ou to leap over *(insép)* ▸ **sauter le pas** *fig* to take the plunge **2.** [omettre] to skip, to leave out *(sép)* **3.** *vulg* [sexuellement] : *sauter qqn* to lay sb.

sauterelle [sotʀɛl] nf ENTOM grasshopper ; [criquet] locust.

sauteur, euse [sotœʀ, øz] nm, f SPORT jumper. ◆ **sauteuse** nf CULIN high-sided frying pan.

sautiller [3] [sotije] vt [faire de petits sauts] to hop, to skip.

sautoir [sotwaʀ] nm **1.** JOAILL chain ▸ **en sautoir** on a chain ▸ **sautoir de perles** string of pearls **2.** SPORT jumping pit.

sauvage [sovaʒ] ◆ adj **1.** ZOOL [non domestique] wild ; [non apprivoisé] untamed ▸ **il est redevenu sauvage a)** [chat] he's gone feral ou wild **b)** [jeune fauve] he's gone back to the wild **2.** [non cultivé] wild **3.** [peu fréquenté - lieu] wild, remote / *les régions sauvages du nord de l'Écosse* the wilds ou the remote regions of northern Scotland **4.** *vieilli* ou ANTHR savage, uncivilized **5.** [illégal - camping, vente] unauthorized ; [- urbanisme] unplanned. ◆ nmf **1.** *vieilli* ANTHR savage **2.** [personne fruste, grossière] boor, brute **3.** [personne farouche] unsociable person, recluse.

sauvagement [sovaʒmɑ̃] adv savagely, viciously.

sauvageon, onne [sovaʒɔ̃, ɔn] nm, f wild child.

sauvagerie [sovaʒʀi] nf [méchanceté] viciousness, brutality.

sauve [sov] f ⟶ **sauf**.

sauvegarde [sovgaʀd] nf **1.** [protection] safeguard, safeguarding *(U)* / *sauvegarde des ressources naturelles* conservation of natural resources / *sous la sauvegarde de la justice* DR under the protection of the Court **2.** INFORM backup *(U)* ▸ **faire une sauvegarde** to make a backup.

sauvegarder [3] [sovgaʀde] vt **1.** [protéger - bien] to safeguard, to watch over *(insép)* ; [- honneur, réputation] to protect **2.** INFORM to save.

sauve-qui-peut [sovkipø] nm inv panic / *ce fut un sauve-qui-peut général* there was a general stampede.

sauver [3] [sove] vt **1.** [personne - gén] to save, to rescue ; [- dans un accident, une catastrophe] to rescue ▸ **sauver la vie à qqn** to save sb's life ▸ **être sauvé a)** [sain et sauf] to be safe **b)** [par quelqu'un] to have been saved ou rescued / *ils ont atteint la côte, ils sont sauvés !* they've reached the shore, they're safe! ; *fig* : *il y a une banque ouverte, je suis sauvé !* there's a bank open, saved again! ▸ **sauver sa peau** *fam* to save one's skin ou hide **2.** ▸ **sauver les apparences** to keep up appearances **3.** [préserver] to salvage, to save ▸ **sauver qqch de l'oubli** to rescue sthg from oblivion ▸ **sauver les meubles** *fam* to salvage something from the situation. ◆ **se sauver** vpi **1.** [animal] to escape ; [pensionnaire] to run away ; [prisonnier] to escape, to break out *(insép)* ; [matelot] to jump ship / *se sauver à toutes jambes* to take to one's heels (and run) **2.** *fam* [lait] to boil over **3.** *fam* [s'en aller] to leave, to split ▸ **sauve-toi !** run along now! / *bon, je me sauve !* right, I'm off ou on my way! ◆ **sauve qui peut** interj run for your life, every man for himself.

sauvetage [sovtaʒ] nm **1.** [d'un accidenté] rescue / *opérer* ou *effectuer le sauvetage d'un équipage* to rescue a crew / *sauvetage d'une entreprise* *fig* financial rescue of

a company ▸ **sauvetage aérien / en montagne / en mer** air / mountain / sea rescue **2.** NAUT [de l'équipage] life saving, sea rescue ; [de la cargaison] salvage. ◆ **de sauvetage** *loc adj* life *(modif)*.

sauveteur [sovtœʀ] nm rescuer.

sauvette [sovet] ◆ **à la sauvette** ◆ *loc adj* ▸ **marchand** ou **vendeur à la sauvette** (illicit) street peddler ou hawker. ◆ *loc adv* **1.** [illégalement] ▸ **vendre qqch à la sauvette** to hawk ou to peddle sthg (without authorization) **2.** [discrètement] ▸ **faire qqch à la sauvette** to do sthg stealthily.

sauveur [sovœʀ] nm **1.** [bienfaiteur] saviour UK, savior US **2.** RELIG ▸ **le Sauveur** Our Saviour.

sava SMS abr écrite de *ça va*.

savamment [savamɑ̃] adv **1.** [avec érudition] learnedly **2.** [habilement] cleverly, cunningly, skilfully UK, skillfully US.

savane [savan] nf **1.** [dans les pays chauds] bush, savanna, savannah **2.** Québec [marécage] swamp.

savant, e [savɑ̃, ɑ̃t] ◆ adj **1.** [érudit - livre, moine, société] learned ; [- traduction, conversation] scholarly / *c'est trop savant pour lui !* that's (totally) beyond his grasp! **2.** [habile] skilful, clever **3.** [dressé - chien, puce] performing. ◆ nm, f [lettré] scholar. ◆ **savant** nm [scientifique] scientist.

savate [savat] nf [chaussure] worn-out (old) shoe ; [pantoufle] old slipper.

saveur [savœʀ] nf [goût] savour UK, savor US, flavour UK, flavor US.

savoir¹ [savwaʀ] nm knowledge.

savoir² [59] [savwaʀ] ◆ vt **1.** [connaître - donnée, réponse, situation] to know / *que savez-vous de lui ?* what do you know about ou of him? / *tu sais la nouvelle ?* have you heard the news? / *on le savait malade* we knew ou we were aware (that) he was ill **2.** [être informé de] : *que va-t-il arriver à Tintin ? pour le savoir, lisez notre prochain numéro !* what's in store for Tintin? find out in our next issue! / *c'est toujours bon à savoir* it's (always) worth knowing / *c'est sa maîtresse — tu en sais des choses !* she's his mistress — you seem well informed! / *je n'en sais rien du tout* I don't know anything about it, I haven't got a clue / *il est venu ici, mais personne n'en a rien su* he came here, but nobody found out about it ▸ **en savoir long sur qqn / qqch** to know a great deal about sb / sthg / *je sais à quoi m'en tenir sur lui* I know what kind of (a) person he is / *je crois savoir qu'ils ont annulé la conférence* I have reason ou I'm led to believe that they called off the conference / *tout le monde sait que...* it's a well-known fact ou everybody knows that... / *sans (trop) savoir pourquoi* without really knowing why / *je ne sais quel / quelle... some... ou other / *il vendait des tapis, des bracelets et que sais-je encore* he was selling carpets, bracelets and goodness / God knows what else ; *(en usage absolu)* : *oui, oui, je sais !* yes, yes, I'm aware of that ou I know ou I realize! **3.** [être convaincu de] to know, to be certain ou sure / *je savais bien que ça ne marcherait pas !* I knew it wouldn't work! / *je n'en sais trop rien* I'm not too sure, I don't really know ; *(en usage absolu)* : *qui sait ?* who knows? / *on ne sait jamais, sait-on jamais* you never know **4.** [apprendre] : *je l'ai su par son frère* I heard it from her brother ▸ **faire savoir qqch à qqn** to inform sb ou to let sb know of sthg **5.** [se rappeler] to know, to remember / *je ne sais plus la fin de l'histoire* I can't remember the end of the story **6.** [pouvoir] to know how to, to be able to ▸ **savoir faire qqch** to know how to ou to be able to do sthg ▸ **tu sais plonger / conduire ?** can you dive / drive? / *elle ne sait ni lire ni écrire* she can't read or write ▸ **il ne sait pas / sait bien faire la cuisine** he's a bad / good cook / *je ne sais pas mentir* I can't (tell a) lie / *je n'ai pas* su la réconforter I wasn't able to comfort her / **elle ne sait pas se reposer** [elle travaille trop] she doesn't know when to stop / **il a su rester jeune / modeste** he's managed to remain young / modest ▸ **savoir s'y prendre** : *savoir s'y prendre avec les enfants* to know how to handle children, to be good with children ▸ **savoir y faire avec qqn** to know how to handle sb / *il sait y faire avec les filles !* he knows how to get his (own) way with girls! ▸ **on ne saurait être plus aimable / déplaisant** you couldn't be nicer / more unpleasant **7.** [être conscient de] to know, to be aware of ▸ **sachez-le bien** make no ou let there be no mistake about this / *sache qu'en fait, c'était son idée* you should know that in fact, it was his idea ▸ **elle ne sait plus ce qu'elle fait ni ce qu'elle dit a)** [à cause d'un choc, de la vieillesse] she's become confused **b)** [sous l'effet de la colère] she's beside herself (with anger) / *je sais ce que je dis* I know what I'm saying / *tu ne sais pas ce que tu veux / dis* you don't know what you want / what you're talking about ; *(en usage absolu)* ▸ **faudrait savoir !** make up your mind! **8.** [imaginer] ▸ **ne (plus) savoir que** ou **quoi faire** to be at a loss as to what to do, not to know what to do / *je ne savais plus où me mettre* [de honte] I didn't know where to put myself **9.** [pour prendre l'interlocuteur à témoin] : *ce n'est pas toujours facile, tu sais !* it's not always easy, you know! / *tu sais que tu commences à m'énerver ?* fam you're getting on my nerves, you know that ou d'you know that? ◆ adv namely, specifically, i.e. ❖ **se savoir** ◆ vp *(emploi passif)* [nouvelle] to become known / *tout se sait dans le village* news travels fast in the village / *ça finira par se savoir* people are bound to find out. ◆ vpi [personne] : *il se sait malade* he knows he's ill. ❖ **à savoir** loc adv namely, that is, i.e. ❖ **à savoir que** loc conj meaning ou to the effect that *sout.*

savoir-faire [savwaʀfɛʀ] nm inv know-how.

savoir-vivre [savwaʀvivʀ] nm inv good manners, savoir vivre *sout*, breeding / *manquer de savoir-vivre* to have no manners.

savon [savɔ̃] nm soap ▸ **un (morceau de) savon** a bar of soap ▸ **passer un (bon) savon à qqn** *fam* to give sb a (good) telling-off.

 Savon de Marseille

The soap industry has existed in Marseille since the 16th century, and soap from Marseille, usually sold in large square bricks, is renowned for its purity.

---

savonner [3] [savɔne] vt [linge, surface] to soap. ❖ **se savonner** vp *(emploi réfléchi)* to soap o.s. (down) / *se savonner le visage / les mains* to soap (up) one's face / one's hands.

savonneux, euse [savɔnø, øz] adj soapy.

savourer [3] [savuʀe] vt [vin, mets, repas] to enjoy, to savour 🇬🇧 to savor 🇺🇸.

savoureux, euse [savuʀø, øz] adj **1.** [succulent] tasty, flavoursome, full of flavour **2.** *fig* [anecdote, plaisanterie] good, delightful.

savoyard, e [savwajaʀ, aʀd] adj from Savoie. ❖ **Savoyard, e** nm, f inhabitant of or person from Savoie.

saxo [sakso] nm *fam* **1.** [instrument] sax **2.** [musicien] sax (player).

saxophone [saksɔfɔn] nm saxophone.

saxophoniste [saksɔfɔnist] nmf saxophone player, saxophonist.

sbrinz [ʃbʀints] nm hard crumbly Swiss cheese made from cow's milk.

scabreux, euse [skabʀø, øz] adj [indécent] obscene.

scalpel [skalpɛl] nm scalpel.

scalper [3] [skalpe] vt to scalp.

scampi * [skãpi] (pl scampi ou scampis*) nm scampi.

scandale [skãdal] nm **1.** [indignation] scandal ▸ **faire scandale** : *son discours a fait scandale* his speech caused a scandal **2.** [scène] scene, fuss / *il va encore faire un scandale* he's going to make a fuss again **3.** [honte] : *c'est un scandale !* (it's) outrageous!, it's an outrage! / *quel est un scandale !* (it's) outrageous!, it's an outrage! ❖ **à scandale** loc adj [journal, presse] sensationalist.

scandaleusement [skãdaløzmã] adv scandalously, outrageously ▸ **scandaleusement riche** outrageously rich.

scandaleux, euse [skãdalø, øz] adj [attitude, mensonge] disgraceful, outrageous, shocking ; [article, photo] sensational, scandalous ; [prix] outrageous, shocking.

scandaliser [3] [skãdalize] vt to shock, to outrage. ❖ **se scandaliser** vpi ▸ **se scandaliser de qqch** to be shocked ou scandalized by sthg.

scander [3] [skãde] vt [slogan] to chant ; [mots, phrases] to stress.

scandinave [skãdinav] adj Scandinavian. ❖ **Scandinave** nmf [personne] Scandinavian.

Scandinavie [skãdinavi] npr f ▸ **(la) Scandinavie** Scandinavia.

scanner[1] [skanɛʀ] nm **1.** IMPR scanner **2.** MÉD scanner / *passer un scanner* to have a CAT scan.

scanner[2] [3] [skane] vt to scan.

scanneur [skanœʀ] nm = **scanner**.

scaphandre [skafãdʀ] nm **1.** NAUT diving gear, frogman suit ▸ **scaphandre autonome** aqualung **2.** ASTRONAUT spacesuit.

scaphandrier [skafãdʀije] nm NAUT (deep-sea) diver.

scarabée [skaʀabe] nm ENTOM beetle, scarabaeid *spéc.*

scarlatine [skaʀlatin] nf scarlet fever, scarlatina *spéc.*

scarole [skaʀɔl] nf escarole.

scatologique [skatɔlɔʒik] adj [goûts, écrit] scatological ; [humour] lavatorial.

sceau, x [so] nm **1.** [cachet] seal / *sous le sceau du secret* under the seal of secrecy **2.** *litt* [empreinte] mark / *le sceau du génie* the mark ou stamp of genius.

sceller [4] [sele] vt **1.** [officialiser] to seal **2.** [fermer] to put seals on, to seal up *(sép).*

scellés [sele] nmpl seals ▸ **mettre les scellés sur qqch** to seal sthg off. ❖ **sous scellés** loc adv under seal.

scénario [senaʀjo] (pl scénarios ou scenarii [-Rii]) nm **1.** CINÉ [histoire, trame] screenplay, scenario ; [texte] (shooting) script, scenario **2.** THÉÂTRE scenario.

scénariste [senaʀist] nmf scriptwriter.

scène [sɛn] nf **1.** [plateau d'un théâtre, d'un cabaret, etc.] stage ▸ **monter sur scène** to go on the stage / *sortir de scène* to come off stage, to exit ▸ **entrer en scène a)** [art dramatique] to come on stage **b)** *fig* to come ou to step in **2.** [art dramatique] ▸ **la scène** the stage ▸ **mettre « Phèdre » en scène a)** [monter la pièce] to stage "Phèdre" **b)** [diriger les acteurs] to direct "Phèdre" / *la façon dont il met Polonius en scène* the way he presents Polonius / *l'écrivain met en scène deux personnages hauts en couleur* the writer portrays two colourful characters **3.** CINÉ & THÉÂTRE [séquence] scene / *la première scène* the first ou opening scene / *dans la scène d'amour / du balcon* in the love / balcony scene / *la scène se passe à Montréal* the action takes place in ou the scene is set in Montreal **4.** [décor] scene **5.** [moment, événement] scene / *une scène de la* *vie quotidienne* a scene of everyday life **6.** [dispute] scene ▸ **faire une scène (à qqn)** to make a scene ▸ **scène de ménage** row **7.** ART scene ▸ **scène de genre** genre painting **8.** *fig* ▸ **la scène internationale / politique** the international / political scene.

scénique [senik] adj theatrical.

scepticisme [sɛptism] nm scepticism 🇬🇧, skepticism 🇺🇸 ▸ **avec scepticisme** sceptically.

sceptique [sɛptik] ◆ adj [incrédule] sceptical 🇬🇧, skeptical 🇺🇸. ◆ nmf [personne qui doute] sceptic 🇬🇧, skeptic 🇺🇸 ; PHILOS Sceptic 🇬🇧, Skeptic 🇺🇸.

schéma [ʃema] nm **1.** TECHNOL diagram ; [dessin] sketch ▸ **schéma de câblage / montage** wiring / set-up diagram **2.** [aperçu] (broad) outline.

schématique [ʃematik] adj **1.** TECHNOL diagrammatical, schematic **2.** [simplificateur] schematic, simplified.

schématiquement [ʃematikmɑ̃] adv **1.** TECHNOL diagrammatically, schematically **2.** [en simplifiant] : *décrire un projet / une opération schématiquement* to give the basic outline of a project / an operation / *schématiquement, voici comment nous allons nous y prendre* in broad outline, this is how we're planning to handle it.

schématiser [3] [ʃematize] vt **1.** TECHNOL to schematize, to present in diagram form **2.** [simplifier] to simplify.

schisme [ʃism] nm **1.** RELIG schism **2.** *fig* schism, split.

schiste [ʃist] nm MINÉR schist.

schizophrène [skizɔfʀɛn] adj & nmf schizophrenic.

schizophrénie [skizɔfʀeni] nf schizophrenia.

schlinguer [ʃlɛ̃ge] = **chlinguer**.

schnock [ʃnɔk] *tfam* nm [imbécile] blockhead / *espèce de vieux schnock !* you old fogey ou duffer! / *alors, tu viens, du schnock ?* are you coming, dumbo?

schublig [ʃublig] nm SUISSE *type of sausage*.

schuss [ʃus] adv : *descendre (tout) schuss* to schuss down.

sciatique [sjatik] ◆ adj sciatic. ◆ nf sciatica.

scie [si] nf TECHNOL saw ▸ **scie circulaire** circular saw ▸ **scie électrique** power saw ▸ **scie à métaux** hacksaw ▸ **scie sabre** ou **sauteuse** jigsaw, scroll saw.

sciemment [sjamɑ̃] adv **1.** [consciemment] knowingly **2.** [délibérément] deliberately, on purpose.

science [sjɑ̃s] nf **1.** [connaissances] ▸ **la science** science **2.** *(gén au pl)* [domaine spécifique] science ▸ **les sciences appliquées / physiques** the applied / physical sciences ▸ **les sciences de la vie et de la terre** ENS biology ▸ **les sciences économiques** economics ▸ **les sciences exactes** exact sciences ▸ **les sciences humaines a)** [gén] human sciences, the social sciences **b)** UNIV ≃ Arts ▸ **les sciences politiques** politics, political sciences **3.** [érudition] knowledge / *je n'ai pas la science infuse !* I don't know everything! ◆ **sciences** nfpl UNIV [par opposition aux lettres] science, sciences.

science-fiction [sjɑ̃sfiksjɔ̃] *(pl* sciences-fictions*)* nf science fiction / *livre / film de science-fiction* science fiction book / film.

scientifique [sjɑ̃tifik] ◆ adj scientific. ◆ nmf scientist.

scientifiquement [sjɑ̃tifikmɑ̃] adv scientifically.

scier [9] [sje] vt **1.** [couper] to saw / *scier la branche d'un arbre* to saw a branch off a tree / *scier un tronc en rondins* to saw up a tree trunk (into logs) **2.** *fam* [surprendre] ▸ **sa réponse m'a scié** I couldn't believe my ears when I heard his answer.

scierie [siʀi] nf sawmill.

scinder [3] [sɛ̃de] ◆ **se scinder** vpi to split.

scintiller [3] [sɛ̃tije] vi [lumière, bijoux, eau, reflet] to sparkle, to glitter ; [yeux] to sparkle, to twinkle ; [étoile] to twinkle.

scission [sisjɔ̃] nf **1.** POL & RELIG scission, split, rent ▸ **faire scission** to split off *(insép)*, to secede **2.** BIOL & PHYS fission, splitting.

sciure [sjyʀ] nf sawdust.

sclérose [skleʀoz] nf **1.** MÉD sclerosis ▸ **sclérose en plaques** multiple sclerosis **2.** *fig* ossification.

sclérosé, e [skleʀoze] adj **1.** MÉD sclerotic **2.** *fig* antiquated, ossified, creaky (with age).

scléroser [3] [skleʀoze] ◆ **se scléroser** vpi **1.** MÉD to sclerose **2.** *fig* [se figer] to ossify, to become paralyzed.

scolaire [skɔlɛʀ] ◆ adj **1.** [de l'école] school *(modif)* ; [du cursus] school, academic ▸ **en milieu scolaire** in schools **2.** *péj* [écriture, raisonnement] dry, unimaginative / *il a un style très scolaire* his style is very unoriginal. ◆ nmf [enfant] schoolchild.

scolarisation [skɔlaʀizasjɔ̃] nf **1.** [éducation] schooling, (formal) education **2.** ADMIN & DR school attendance, schooling / *la scolarisation est obligatoire à partir de six ans* (attendance at) school ou schooling is compulsory from the age of six.

scolariser [3] [skɔlaʀize] vt **1.** [enfant] to send to school, to provide with formal education **2.** [région, pays] to equip with schools.

scolarité [skɔlaʀite] nf **1.** ADMIN & DR school attendance, schooling **2.** [études] school career ; [période] schooldays / *j'ai eu une scolarité difficile* I had a difficult time at school.

scoliose [skɔljoz] nf scoliosis.

scoop [skup] nm scoop.

scooter, scooteur* [skutœʀ] nm (motor) scooter.

scorbut [skɔʀbyt] nm scurvy.

score [skɔʀ] nm **1.** SPORT score **2.** [résultat] : *faire un bon score aux élections* to get a good result in the election.

scorie [skɔʀi] nf **1.** MÉTALL slag ; [laitier] cinders ; [de fer] (iron) clinker ou dross **2.** *litt* [déchet] : *toutes les scories d'une vie* the waste ou dregs of a lifetime.

scorpion [skɔʀpjɔ̃] nm ZOOL scorpion.

Scorpion [skɔʀpjɔ̃] npr m **1.** ASTRON Scorpio **2.** ASTROL Scorpio ▸ **être Scorpion** to be Scorpio ou a Scorpian.

Scotch® [skɔtʃ] nm adhesive tape, Sellotape® 🇬🇧, Scotchtape® 🇺🇸.

scotch [skɔtʃ] *(pl* scotchs *ou* scotches*)* nm Scotch (whisky).

scotché, e [skɔtʃe] adj : *être scotché devant la télévision* to be glued to the television.

scotcher [3] [skɔtʃe] vt to tape, to sellotape 🇬🇧, to scotchtape 🇺🇸.

scout, e [skut] ◆ adj [relatif au scoutisme] scout *(modif)* ▸ **camp / mouvement scout** scout camp / movement. ◆ nm, f [personne] (Boy) Scout, (Girl) Guide.

scoutisme [skutism] nm **1.** [activité] scouting **2.** [association - pour garçons] Boy Scout movement ; [- pour filles] Girl Guide movement.

Scrabble® [skʀabl] nm Scrabble®.

script [skʀipt] nm CINÉ & RADIO script.

scripte [skʀipt] nmf continuity man (continuity girl ou script girl).

scrupule [skʀypyl] nm [cas de conscience] scruple, qualm (of conscience) / *avoir des scrupules* to have scruples / *n'aie pas de scrupules* don't have any qualms / *elle n'a aucun scrupule* she has no scruples ▸ **avoir scrupule à faire qqch** *sout* to have scruples ou qualms about doing sthg / *n'ayez aucun scrupule à faire appel à moi* don't hesitate to ask for my help. ❖ **sans scrupules** loc adj [individu] unscrupulous, unprincipled, without scruples.

scrupuleusement [skʀypyløzmã] adv scrupulously, punctiliously.

scrupuleux, euse [skʀypylø, øz] adj [honnête] scrupulous, scrupulously honest ▸ **peu scrupuleux** unscrupulous.

scrutateur, trice [skʀytatœʀ, tʀis] ◆ adj searching *(avant nom)*. ◆ nm, f ADMIN scrutineer 🇬🇧, teller 🇺🇸.

scruter [3] [skʀyte] vt **1.** [pour comprendre] to scrutinize, to examine ▸ **scruter qqn du regard** to give sb a searching look **2.** [en parcourant des yeux] to scan, to search / *elles scrutaient l'horizon* they scanned ou searched the horizon.

scrutin [skʀytɛ̃] nm **1.** [façon d'élire] vote, voting *(U)*, ballot / *procéder au scrutin* to take a ballot / *dépouiller le scrutin* to count the votes ▸ **scrutin majoritaire** first past the post election 🇬🇧, election on a majority basis ▸ **scrutin proportionnel** ou **à la proportionnelle** (voting using the system of) proportional representation **2.** [fait de voter] ballot ▸ **par (voie de) scrutin** by ballot **3.** [consultation électorale] election.

sculpter [3] [skylte] vt **1.** ART to sculpt ; [orner de sculptures] to sculpture **2.** [bois] to carve ; [bâton] to scrimshaw.

sculpteur, trice [skyltœʀ, tʀis] nm, f sculptor (sculptress).

sculptural, e, aux [skyltyʀal, o] adj **1.** ART sculptural **2.** [beauté, formes] statuesque.

sculpture [skyltyʀ] nf **1.** ART sculpture *(U)*, sculpting *(U)* ▸ **faire de la sculpture** to sculpt ▸ **sculpture sur bois** woodcarving **2.** [œuvre] sculpture, piece of sculpture.

SDF (abr de **sans domicile fixe**) nmf homeless person ▸ **les SDF** the homeless.

se [sə] *(devant voyelle ou « h » muet s' [s])* pron pers *(emploi réfléchi, 3e pers sg et pl, m et f)* **1.** [avec un verbe pronominal réfléchi] ▸ **se salir** to get dirty ▸ **s'exprimer** to express o.s. / *elle se coiffe* she's doing her hair / *elles s'en sont persuadées* they've convinced themselves of it ; [se substituant à l'adjectif possessif] : *il s'est fracturé deux côtes* he broke two ribs / *se mordre la langue* to bite one's tongue **2.** [avec un verbe pronominal réciproque] : *pour s'aider, ils partagent le travail* to help each other ou one another, they share the work **3.** [avec un verbe pronominal passif] : *ce modèle se vend bien* this model sells well ▸ **ça se mange ?** can you eat it? **4.** [avec un verbe pronominal intransitif] : *ils s'en vont* they're leaving / *il se laisse convaincre trop facilement* he is too easily persuaded / *il s'est fait avoir !* fam he's been had! / *elle se croyait en sécurité* she thought she was safe ▸ **il se dit médecin** he claims to be a doctor **5.** [dans des tournures impersonnelles] ▸ **il se fait tard** it's getting late **6.** fam [emploi expressif] : *il se fait 5 000 euros par mois* he's got 5,000 euros coming in per month.

SE (abr écrite de **Son Excellence**) HE.

séance [seɑ̃s] nf **1.** [réunion] session ▸ **être en séance a)** [comité, Parlement] to be sitting ou in session **b)** [tribunal] to be in session / *la séance est levée !* [au tribunal] the court will adjourn! **2.** BOURSE ▸ **en début / fin de séance, les actions Roman étaient à 130 €** the Roman shares opened / closed at 130 € **3.** [période d'entraînement, de traitement] session ▸ **séance de pose** sitting ▸ **séance de rééducation** (session of) physiotherapy ▸ **séance de spiritisme** seance ▸ **séance de travail** working session **4.** CINÉ showing / *séance à 19 h 10, film à 19 h 30* program 7.10, film starts 7.30 ▸ **la dernière séance** the last showing.

seau, x [so] nm [récipient] bucket, pail ▸ **seau à champagne** Champagne bucket ▸ **seau à glace** ice-bucket 🇬🇧,

ice-pail 🇺🇸. ❖ **à seaux** loc adv fam : *il pleut à seaux, la pluie tombe à seaux* it's pouring ou bucketing 🇬🇧 down.

sébum [sebɔm] nm sebum.

sec, sèche [sɛk, sɛʃ] adj **1.** [air, bois, endroit, vêtement, etc.] dry / *il fait un froid sec* it's cold and dry, there's a crisp cold air ▸ **avoir l'œil sec** ou **les yeux secs a)** MÉD to have dry eyes **b)** fig to be dry-eyed **2.** [légume, fruit] dried ; [alcool] neat **3.** [non gras - cheveux, peau, mine de crayon] dry ; [maigre - personne] lean **4.** [désagréable - ton, voix] harsh, curt, terse ; [- explication, refus, remarque] curt, terse ; [- rire] dry ▸ **un bruit sec** a snap ou crack ▸ **d'un coup sec** smartly, sharply **5.** ART [graphisme, style] dry **6.** ŒNOL [champagne, vin] dry **7.** CARTES ▸ **atout / roi sec** singleton trumps / king. ❖ **sec** ◆ adv [brusquement] hard ▸ **démarrer sec a)** [conducteur] to shoot off at top speed **b)** [course] to get a flying start. ◆ nm AGR dry feed. ❖ **à sec** loc adj **1.** [cours d'eau, source, etc.] dry, dried-up ; [réservoir] empty **2.** fam [sans argent - personne] hard up, broke, cleaned out ; [- caisse] empty. ❖ **au sec** loc adv ▸ **garder** ou **tenir qqch au sec** to keep sthg in a dry place, to keep sthg dry.

sécateur [sekatœʀ] nm ▸ **un sécateur a)** [pour les fleurs] (a pair of) secateurs **b)** [pour les haies] pruning shears.

sécession [sesesjɔ̃] nf secession ▸ **faire sécession** to secede.

sèche [sɛʃ] ◆ f ⟶ **sec**. ◆ nf fam cig, fag 🇬🇧.

sèche-cheveux, sèche-cheveu* [sɛʃʃəvø] nm hair dryer.

sèche-linge [sɛʃlɛ̃ʒ] *(pl* sèche-linge ou sèche-linges*)* nm [à tambour] tumble-drier ; [placard] airing cupboard.

sèche-mains, sèche-main* [sɛʃmɛ̃] nm hand-dryer.

sèchement [sɛʃmã] adv [durement] dryly, curtly, tersely / *ne comptez pas sur moi, répondit-elle sèchement* don't count on me, she snapped back.

sécher [18] [seʃe] ◆ vt **1.** [gén] to dry ; [avec un torchon, une éponge] to wipe dry **2.** arg scol [manquer] ▸ **sécher les cours a)** ÉDUC to play truant 🇬🇧 ou hooky 🇺🇸 **b)** UNIV to cut lectures ou class 🇺🇸. ◆ vi **1.** [surface] to dry (off) ; [linge] to dry ; [éponge] to dry (out) ; [sol, puits] to dry up ; [cours d'eau] to dry up, to run dry **2.** VÊT ▸ **faire sécher du linge** to leave clothes to dry, to let linen dry / *mettre le linge à sécher* to put the washing out to dry / 'faire sécher sans essorer' 'do not spin dry', 'dry flat' / 'faire sécher à plat' 'dry flat' **3.** [plante] to dry up ou out ; [bois] to dry out ; [fruits, viande] to dry **4.** fam [ne pas savoir] : *j'ai séché en physique / sur la deuxième question* I drew a blank in the physics exam / on the second question. ❖ **se sécher** vp *(emploi réfléchi)* to dry o.s. / *se sécher les mains / cheveux* to dry one's hands / hair.

✐ In reformed spelling (see p. 16-18), this verb is conjugated like *semer* : *il sèchera, elle sèchera*.

sécheresse, sècheresse* [sɛʃʀɛs] nf **1.** [d'un climat, d'un terrain, d'un style] dryness ; [d'un trait] dryness, harshness ; [d'une réplique, d'un ton] abruptness **2.** MÉTÉOR drought / *pendant la* ou *les mois de sécheresse* during the dry months.

séchoir [seʃwaʀ] nm [à usage domestique] dryer ▸ **séchoir à linge a)** [à tambour] tumble-drier **b)** [pliant] clotheshorse **c)** [suspendu] ceiling airer.

second, e [səgɔ̃, ɔ̃d] ◆ adj **1.** [dans l'espace, le temps] second / *pour la seconde fois* for the second time ▸ **en second lieu** secondly, in the second place **2.** [dans une hiérarchie] second ; [éclairagiste, maquilleur] assistant *(modif)* ▸ **le second marché** BOURSE the unlisted securities market **3.** [autre - chance, jeunesse, vie] second / *c'est une seconde nature chez lui* it's second nature to him. ◆ nm, f **1.** [dans l'espace, le temps] second **2.** [dans une hiérarchie] second ▸ **arriver le second** [dans une course, une élection] to come

second. ❖ **second** nm **1.** [assistant - d'un directeur] right arm ; [- dans un duel] second ; NAUT first mate ; MIL second in command **2.** [étage] second floor 🇬🇧, third floor 🇺🇸. ❖ **seconde** nf **1.** AUTO second gear / *passe en seconde* change into ou to second gear **2.** TRANSP [classe] second class ; [billet] second-class ticket / *voyager en seconde* to travel second class **3.** ÉDUC ≃ year eleven 🇬🇧 ; ≃ tenth grade 🇺🇸. ❖ **en second** ◆ loc adj ▶ **capitaine en second** first mate. ◆ loc adv second, secondly / *passer en second* to be second.

secondaire [səgɔ̃dɛʀ] ◆ adj [question, personnage, route] secondary ▶ **c'est secondaire** it's of secondary importance ou of minor interest. ◆ nm **1.** ENS secondary 🇬🇧 ou high 🇺🇸 school (U) **2.** ÉCON ▶ **le secondaire** secondary production.

seconde [səgɔ̃d] nf **1.** [division horaire] second **2.** [court instant] ▶ **(attendez) une seconde !** just a second! ▶ **à la seconde** instantly, there and then.

seconder [3] [səgɔ̃de] vt [assister] to assist, to back up (sép).

secouer [6] [səkwe] vt **1.** [arbre, bouteille, personne] to shake ; [tapis] to shake (out) ▶ **secouer la tête a)** [acquiescer] to nod one's head **b)** [refuser] to shake one's head ▶ **secouer qqn comme un prunier** fam to shake sb like a rag doll ▶ **secouer le cocotier** to get rid of the dead wood fig **2.** [poussière, sable, miettes] to shake off (sép) ; fig [paresse, torpeur, etc.] to shake off ▶ **secouer les puces** fam à qqn [le gronder] to tell sb off, to give sb a good ticking-off 🇬🇧 ou chewing out 🇺🇸 **3.** fam [houspiller - personne] to shake up (sép) **4.** [bouleverser - personne] to shake up (sép), to give a jolt ou shock to. ❖ **se secouer** vp (emploi réfléchi) fam to shake o.s. up, to snap out of it / *il serait grand temps de te secouer !* it's high time you pulled yourself together!

secourir [45] [səkuʀiʀ] vt **1.** [blessé] to help ; [personne en danger] to rescue **2.** sout [pauvre, affligé] to aid, to help.

secourisme [səkuʀism] nm first aid.

secouriste [səkuʀist] nmf [d'une organisation] first-aid worker.

secours [səkuʀ] nm **1.** [assistance] help, assistance, aid / *appeler* ou *crier au secours* to call out for help ▶ **au secours !** help! ▶ **porter secours à qqn** to give sb assistance ▶ **venir au secours de qqn** to come to sb's aid ▶ **le Secours catholique** ou **le Secours populaire (français)** charity organizations giving help to the poor **2.** [sauvetage] aid, assistance / *les secours ne sont pas encore arrivés* aid ou help hasn't arrived yet ▶ **le secours en montagne / en mer** sea / mountain rescue **3.** [appui] help ▶ **être d'un grand secours à qqn** to be of great help to sb. ❖ **de secours** loc adj [équipement, porte, sortie] emergency (modif) ; [équipe, poste] rescue (modif).

secousse [səkus] nf **1.** [saccade] jerk, jolt **2.** fig [bouleversement] jolt, shock, upset **3.** GÉOL ▶ **secousse (sismique** ou **tellurique)** (earth) tremor.

secret, ète [səkʀɛ, ɛt] adj **1.** [inconnu - accord, code, document, etc.] secret ▶ **garder** ou **tenir qqch secret** to keep sthg secret **2.** [caché - escalier, passage, tiroir] secret / *une vie secrète* a secret life **3.** [personne] secretive, reserved. ❖ **secret** nm **1.** [confidence] secret / *ce n'est un secret pour personne* it's no secret, everybody knows about it / *elle n'en fait pas un secret* she makes no secret of the fact ▶ **confier un secret à qqn** to let sb into a secret ▶ **être dans le secret** to be in on the secret ▶ **mettre qqn dans le secret** to let sb in on the secret ▶ **ne pas avoir de secrets pour qqn a)** [personne] to have no secrets from sb **b)** [question, machine] to hold no secret for sb ▶ **secret d'État** state secret ▶ **être dans le secret des dieux** to have privileged information ▶ **c'est un secret de Polichinelle** it's an open secret

ou not much of a secret **2.** [recette] secret, recipe ▶ **le secret du bonheur** the secret of ou recipe for happiness / *un soufflé dont lui seul a le secret* a soufflé for which he alone knows the secret ▶ **secret de fabrication** COMM trade secret **3.** [discrétion] secrecy (U) ▶ **secret professionnel** professional confidence **4.** RELIG ▶ **le secret de la confession** the seal of confession. ❖ **au secret** loc adv : *être au secret* to be (detained) in solitary confinement. ❖ **en secret** loc adv **1.** [écrire, économiser] in secret, secretly **2.** [croire, espérer] secretly, privately.

secrétaire [səkʀetɛʀ] ◆ nmf **1.** [dans une entreprise] secretary ▶ **secrétaire du conseil d'administration** secretary to the Board of Directors ▶ **secrétaire de direction** executive secretary, personal assistant ▶ **secrétaire médicale** medical secretary ▶ **secrétaire de rédaction a)** [dans l'édition] desk ou assistant editor **b)** PRESSE subeditor **2.** POL ▶ **secrétaire général a)** [auprès d'un ministre] ≃ permanent secretary 🇬🇧 **b)** [dans un parti] general-secretary ▶ **secrétaire général de l'ONU** Secretary ou Secretary-General of the UN ▶ **secrétaire d'État** ≃ Junior Minister 🇬🇧 ; ≃ State Secretary 🇺🇸 **3.** ADMIN ▶ **secrétaire de mairie** ≃ chief executive 🇬🇧. ◆ nm [meuble] secrétaire sout, writing desk.

secrétariat [səkʀetaʀja] nm **1.** [fonction] secretaryship **2.** [employés] secretarial staff **3.** [bureau] secretariat **4.** [tâches administratives] secretarial work **5.** POL ▶ **secrétariat d'État a)** [fonction] ≃ post of Junior Minister 🇬🇧 ; ≃ post of State Secretary 🇺🇸 **b)** [ministère] ≃ Junior Minister's Office 🇬🇧 ▶ **secrétariat général de l'ONU** UN Secretary-Generalship.

secret(-)défense [səkʀedefɑ̃s] adj inv & nm inv classified, top secret / *ce dossier est classé secret(-)défense* this file is classified / *un document secret(-)défense* a top secret document.

secrètement [səkʀɛtmɑ̃] adv **1.** [en cachette] secretly, in secret **2.** [intérieurement] secretly.

sécréter [18] [sekʀete] vt BOT & PHYSIOL to secrete.
🔖 In reformed spelling (see p. 16-18), this verb is conjugated like *semer : il sécrètera, elle sécrèterait.*

sécrétion [sekʀesjɔ̃] nf secretion.

sectaire [sɛktɛʀ] adj & nmf sectarian.

sectarisme [sɛktaʀism] nm sectarianism.

secte [sɛkt] nf sect.

secteur [sɛktœʀ] nm **1.** ÉCON sector ▶ **secteur d'activité** sector ▶ **secteur primaire** primary sector ou production ▶ **secteur privé** private sector ou enterprise ▶ **secteur public** public sector ▶ **secteur secondaire** manufacturing ou secondary sector ▶ **secteur tertiaire** service ou tertiary sector **2.** [zone d'action - d'un policier] beat ; [- d'un représentant] area, patch ; [- de l'urbanisme] district, area ; MIL & NAUT sector ; ADMIN local area covered by the French health and social services department **3.** fam [quartier] ▶ **se trouver dans le secteur** fam to be somewhere ou someplace 🇺🇸 around / *changer de secteur* to make o.s. scarce **4.** ÉLECTR ▶ **le secteur** the mains (supply) **5.** INFORM sector.

section [sɛksjɔ̃] nf **1.** [d'une autoroute, d'une rivière] section, stretch ; [de ligne de bus, de tramway] fare stage ; [d'un livre] part, section ; [d'une bibliothèque] section ; [d'un service] branch, division, department **2.** ENS department ▶ **section économique / scientifique / littéraire** courses in economics / science / arts **3.** [d'un parti] local branch ▶ **section syndicale a)** local branch of a union **b)** [dans l'industrie de la presse et du livre] (union) chapel **4.** MIL section **5.** POL ▶ **section électorale** ward.

sectionner [3] [sɛksjɔne] vt [tendon, câble, ligne] to sever, to cut ; MÉD to amputate.

sectoriel, elle [sɛktɔʀjɛl] adj sector-based / *application sectorielle d'une mesure* the application of a measure to a certain sector (only).

sectoriser [3] [sɛktɔʀize] vt [gén] to sector, to divide into areas ou sectors ; [services de santé] to divide into areas of health and social services responsibility.

sécu [seky] nf *fam* abr de Sécurité sociale.

séculier, ère [sekylje, ɛʀ] adj secular. ❖ **séculier** nm secular.

secundo [sǝgɔ̃do] adv in the second place, second, secondly.

sécurisant, e [sekyʀizɑ̃, ɑ̃t] adj [qui rassure] reassuring.

sécurisé, e [sekyʀize] adj INFORM [transaction, paiement] secure.

sécuriser [3] [sekyʀize] vt [rassurer] ▶ **sécuriser qqn** to make sb feel secure ou safe, to reassure sb, to give sb a feeling of security.

sécurité [sekyʀite] nf **1.** [protection d'une personne - physique] safety, security ; [- matérielle, affective, etc.] security ▶ **assurer la sécurité de qqn** to ensure the safety of sb ▶ **la sécurité de l'emploi** job security ▶ **sécurité civile** public services dealing with natural disasters, bomb disposal, etc. ▶ **sécurité publique** public safety ▶ **sécurité routière** road safety **2.** [surveillance - de bâtiments, d'installations] security. ❖ **de sécurité** loc adj [dispositif, mesure] safety (modif). ❖ **en sécurité** ◆ loc adj safe / *être / se sentir en sécurité* to be / to feel safe. ◆ loc adv in a safe place ▶ **mettre qqch en sécurité dans un coffre** to keep sthg in a safe. ❖ **en toute sécurité** loc adv in complete safety. ❖ **Sécurité sociale** nf **1.** [système] *French social security system* **2.** [organisme] ≃ DWP ; ≃ Social Security .

🏛 **Sécurité sociale**

The **sécu**, as it is popularly known, created in 1945-1946, provides public health benefits, pensions, maternity leave, etc. These benefits are paid for by obligatory insurance contributions (**cotisations**) made by employers (**cotisations patronales**) and employees (**cotisations salariales**). Many French people have complementary health insurance provided by a **mutuelle**, which guarantees payment of all or part of the expenses not covered by the **Sécurité sociale**.

---

sédatif [sedatif] nm sedative.

sédentaire [sedɑ̃tɛʀ] adj [travail, habitude] sedentary ; [employé] desk-bound.

sédentariser [3] [sedɑ̃taʀize] vt [tribu] to turn into a sedentary population, to settle.

sédiment [sedimɑ̃] nm GÉOL sediment, deposit.

séditieux, euse [sedisjø, øz] adj *sout* **1.** [propos] seditious, rebellious **2.** [troupe, armée] insurrectionary, insurgent.

séducteur, trice [sedyktœʀ, tʀis] nm, f seducer (seductress) / *c'est un grand séducteur* he's a real lady's man / *c'est une grande séductrice* she's a real seductress ou a femme fatale.

séduction [sedyksjɔ̃] nf **1.** [d'une personne] charm ; [d'une musique, d'un tableau] appeal, captivating power / *pouvoir de séduction* powers of seduction **2.** DR ▶ **séduction de mineur** corruption of a minor **3.** [d'une chose] attraction, attractiveness.

séduire [98] [sedɥiʀ] vt **1.** [charmer - suj : personne] to attract, to charm ; [- suj : beauté, gentillesse, sourire] to win

over (sép) ; [- suj : livre, tableau] to appeal to (insép) **2.** [tenter - suj : idée, projet, style de vie] to appeal to (insép), to be tempting to **3.** [sexuellement] to seduce.

séduisant, e [sedɥizɑ̃, ɑ̃t] adj **1.** [charmant - personne] attractive ; [- beauté] seductive, enticing ; [- sourire, parfum, mode, etc.] appealing, seductive **2.** [alléchant - offre, idée, projet] attractive, appealing.

séfarade [sefaʀad] ◆ adj Sephardic. ◆ nmf Sephardi.

segment [sɛgmɑ̃] nm MATH segment.

segmenter [3] [sɛgmɑ̃te] vt [diviser] to segment.

ségrégation [segʀegasjɔ̃] nf [discrimination] segregation.

seiche [sɛʃ] nf ZOOL cuttlefish.

seigle [sɛgl] nm rye.

seigneur [sɛɲœʀ] nm **1.** HIST feudal lord ou overlord **2.** [maître] lord **3.** RELIG ▶ **le Seigneur** the Lord ▶ **Notre Seigneur Jésus-Christ** Our Lord Jesus Christ.

sein [sɛ̃] nm ANAT breast / *elle se promène les seins nus* she walks about topless ▶ **donner le sein à** to breast-feed. ❖ **au sein de** loc prép *sout* within / *au sein de la famille* in the bosom ou midst of the family.

seing [sɛ̃] ❖ **sous seing privé** loc adj ▶ **acte sous seing privé** private agreement, simple contract.

séisme [seism] nm **1.** GÉOL earthquake, seism *spéc* **2.** *fig* [bouleversement] upheaval.

seize [sɛz] dét & nm inv sixteen. **Voir aussi cinq.**

seizième [sɛzjɛm] ◆ adj num sixteenth. ◆ nmf sixteenth. ◆ nm **1.** [arrondissement] ▶ **le seizième** the sixteenth arrondissement (wealthy district of Paris) **2.** [partie] : *le seizième de la somme globale* the sixteenth part of the total sum. **Voir aussi cinquième.** ❖ **seizièmes** nmpl SPORT ▶ **les seizièmes de finale** the first round (of a 4-round knockout competition), the second round (of a 5-round knockout competition).

 Le seizième

This term often refers to the upper class social background, lifestyle, way of dressing, etc., associated with the sixteenth arrondissement in Paris.

---

séjour [seʒuʀ] nm **1.** [durée] stay, sojourn *litt* / *il a fait un séjour de deux mois à la mer* he spent two months at the seaside / *il fait un séjour linguistique aux États-Unis* he is spending some time in the United States learning the language / *je te souhaite un bon séjour à Venise* I hope you have a nice time ou I hope you enjoy your stay in Venice / *il a fait plusieurs séjours en hôpital psychiatrique* he's been in a psychiatric hospital several times **2.** [pièce] ▶ **(salle de) séjour** living ou sitting room, lounge .

séjourner [3] [seʒuʀne] vi [habiter] to stay, to sojourn *litt* / *séjourner à l'hôtel / chez un ami* to stay at a hotel / with a friend.

sel [sɛl] nm **1.** CULIN salt ▶ **sel de cuisine** kitchen salt ▶ **sel de table, sel fin** table salt ▶ **sel de mer** sea salt **2.** GÉOL salt ▶ **sel gemme** rock salt **3.** [piquant] wit (U) / *la situation ne manque pas de sel !* the situation is not without a certain piquancy. ❖ **sels** nmpl PHARM [smelling] salts ▶ **sels d'aluminium** aluminium ou aluminum salts ▶ **sans sels d'aluminium** aluminium-free , aluminum-free ▶ **sels de bain** bath salts. ❖ **sans sel** loc adj [régime, biscotte] salt-free ; [beurre] unsalted.

sélect, e [selɛkt] adj *fam* select, highclass, posh .

sélecteur [selɛktœʀ] nm **1.** RADIO & TÉLÉC selector **2.** MÉCAN gear shift ; [d'une moto] (foot) gearshift control.

sélectif, ive [selɛktif, iv] adj selective.

sélection [selɛksjɔ̃] nf **1.** [fait de choisir] selection / *opérer une sélection parmi 200 candidats* to make a selection ou to choose from 200 candidates ▸ **sélection à l'entrée** UNIV selective entry UK ou admission US **2.** [échantillon] selection, choice **3.** SPORT [équipe] team, squad **4.** BIOL ▸ **sélection naturelle** natural selection.

sélectionné, e [selɛksjɔne] ◆ adj [choisi] selected. ◆ nm, f SPORT squad member, team member.

sélectionner [3] [selɛksjɔne] vt [gén] to select.

sélectionneur, euse [selɛksjɔnœʀ, øz] nm, f SPORT selector.

self [sɛlf] nm *fam* = **self-service.**

self-control [sɛlfkɔ̃tʀɔl] (*pl* **self-controls**) nm self-control, self-command.

self-service [sɛlfsɛʀvis] (*pl* **self-services**) nm [restaurant] self-service (restaurant), cafeteria.

selle [sɛl] nf **1.** [de cheval] saddle ▸ **mettre qqn en selle a)** *pr* to put sb in the saddle **b)** *fig* to give sb a leg up ▸ **se mettre en selle a)** *pr* to get into the saddle, to mount **b)** *fig* to get down to the job ▸ **se remettre en selle** *pr & fig* to get back in ou into the saddle **2.** [de vélo] saddle **3.** MÉD : *allez-vous à la selle régulièrement ?* are you regular? ◆ **selles** nfpl MÉD [excréments] faeces, stools.

seller [4] [sele] vt to saddle (up).

sellerie [sɛlʀi] nf **1.** [équipement] saddlery **2.** [lieu] saddle room, tack-room.

sellette [sɛlɛt] nf HIST [siège] (high) stand ou table ▸ **mettre qqn sur la sellette** to put sb in the hot seat ▸ **être sur la sellette a)** [critiqué] to be in the hot seat, to come under fire **b)** [examiné] to be undergoing reappraisal.

selon [səlɔ̃] prép **1.** [conformément à] in accordance with ▸ **agir selon les vœux de qqn** to act in accordance with sb's wishes **2.** [en fonction de] according to / *dépenser selon ses moyens* to spend according to one's means ▸ **selon le cas** as the case may be / *selon les circonstances / les cas* depending on the circumstances / each individual case ▸ **on se reverra ? — c'est selon !** *fam* shall we see each other again? — it all depends! **3.** [d'après] according to ▸ **selon moi / vous** in my / your opinion, to my / your mind / *selon l'expression consacrée* as the hallowed expression has it. ◆ **selon que** *loc conj* : *selon qu'il fera beau ou qu'il pleuvra* depending on whether it's fine or rainy.

semaine [səmɛn] nf [sept jours] week ▸ **toutes les semaines a)** [nettoyer, recevoir] every ou each week **b)** [publier, payer] weekly, on a weekly basis ▸ **dans une semaine** in a week's time ▸ **la semaine de 35 heures** the 35-hour working week. ◆ **à la semaine** *loc adv* [payer] weekly, on a weekly basis, by the week. ◆ **en semaine** *loc adv* during the week, on weekdays, on a weekday.

sémantique [semɑ̃tik] ◆ adj semantic. ◆ nf semantics (*sg*).

sémaphore [semafɔʀ] nm RAIL semaphore signal.

semblable [sɑ̃blabl] ◆ adj [pareil] similar, alike / *je n'avais jamais rien vu de semblable* I had never seen anything like it ou the like of it ▸ **semblable à** similar to, like. ◆ nmf (*avec possessif*) [être humain] ▸ **vous et vos semblables** you and your kind.

semblant [sɑ̃blɑ̃] nm **1.** [apparence] ▸ **un semblant de** : *un semblant d'intérêt / d'affection* a semblance of interest / affection / *offrir un semblant de résistance* to put on a show of ou to put up a token resistance **2.** ▸ **faire semblant** [feindre] to pretend / *ne fais pas semblant d'avoir oublié* don't pretend to have forgotten ou (that) you've forgotten ▸ **faire semblant d'être malade** to sham illness, to malinger.

sembler [3] [sɑ̃ble] vi to seem, to appear / *elle semble plus âgée que lui* she seems (to be) ou she looks older than him / *ils semblaient bien s'entendre* they seemed

ou appeared to be getting on well / *ça peut sembler drôle à certains* this may seem ou sound funny to some. ◆ **il semble** *v impers* **1.** ▸ **il semble que...** [on dirait que] it seems... / *il semblerait qu'il ait décidé de démissionner* reports claim ou it has been reported that he intends to resign **2.** ▸ **il me / te semble (que)** [je / tu crois que] : *cela ne te semble-t-il pas injuste ?* don't you find this unfair?, doesn't this strike you as being unfair? / *il ne me semblait pas te l'avoir dit* I didn't think I'd told you about it / *il était, me semblait-il, au courant de tout* it seemed ou appeared to me that he was aware of everything / *il me semble qu'on s'est déjà vus* I think we've met before ▸ **comme / quand / qui bon me semble** : *faites comme bon vous semble* do as you think fit ou best, do as you please. ◆ **à ce qu'il semble, semble-t-il** *loc adv* seemingly, apparently / *ils sont blessés, semble-t-il* they seem to be hurt, it seems (as though) they're hurt, apparently, they're hurt.

semelle [səmɛl] nf **1.** [d'une chaussure, d'un ski] sole / *chaussures à semelles compensées* platform shoes ▸ **semelle intérieure** insole, inner sole **2.** *fam* [viande dure] : *c'est de la semelle, ce steak !* this steak is like (shoe) leather ou old boots UK **3.** [d'un fer à repasser] base, sole **4.** EXPR *ne la quitte pas d'une semelle* don't loose track of her, keep on her trail.

semence [səmɑ̃s] nf **1.** [graine] seed **2.** [clou] tack.

semer [19] [səme] vt **1.** AGR & HORT to sow **2.** *fig* [disperser - fleurs, paillettes] to scatter, to strew ▸ **semé de** scattered ou strewn with ▸ **parcours semé d'embûches** course littered with obstacles **3.** [distancer] to lose, to shake off (*sép*) **4.** [propager] to bring / *semer la discorde* to sow the seeds of discord ▸ **semer le doute dans l'esprit de qqn** to sow ou to plant a seed of doubt in sb's mind.

semestre [səmɛstʀ] nm **1.** [dans l'année civile] half-year, six-month period **2.** UNIV half-year, semester.

semestriel, elle [səmɛstʀijɛl] adj **1.** [dans l'année civile] half-yearly **2.** UNIV semestral.

semeur, euse [səmœʀ, øz] nm, f **1.** AGR sower **2.** *fig* [propagateur] ▸ **semeur de trouble** troublemaker.

semi-automatique [səmiotɔmatik] adj semiautomatic.

semi-liberté [səmilibɛʀte] nf temporary release (*from prison*).

séminaire [seminɛʀ] nm **1.** [réunion] seminar, workshop **2.** RELIG seminary.

séminariste [seminaʀist] nm seminarist, seminarian US.

semi-précieux, euse [səmipʀesjø, øz] adj semi-precious.

semi-remorque [səmiʀəmɔʀk] nm articulated lorry UK, trailer truck US, semitrailer US, rig US.

semis [səmi] nm [action] sowing.

sémitique [semitik] adj Semitic.

semonce [səmɔ̃s] nf **1.** *sout* [réprimande] reprimand, rebuke **2.** NAUT ▸ **coup de semonce** warning shot.

semoule [səmul] nf semolina ▸ **semoule de blé dur** durum wheat flour.

sénat [sena] nm [assemblée] senate ▸ **le Sénat** the (French) Senate.

 Le Sénat

The **Sénat** is the upper house of the French Parliament. Its members, the **sénateurs**, are elected in each **département** for a six-year mandate by the deputies of the **Assemblée nationale** and certain other government officials. The president of the Senate may deputise for the president of the Republic.

sénateur, trice [senatœr, tris] nm, f senator.

Sénégal [senegal] npr m ▶ **le Sénégal** Senegal.

sénégalais, e [senegalɛ, ɛz] adj Senegalese.
◈ **Sénégalais, e** nm, f Senegalese.

sénile [senil] adj senile.

sénilité [senilite] nf senility.

senior, sénior [senjɔr] adj & nmf SPORT senior.

sens [sɑ̃s] nm **1.** PHYSIOL sense / *le sens du toucher* the sense of touch ▶ **sixième sens** sixth sense ▶ **reprendre ses sens** a) *pr* to come to b) *fig* to come to one's senses **2.** [instinct] sense ▶ **avoir le sens de l'humour** to have a sense of humour 🇬🇧 ou humor 🇺🇸 ▶ **avoir le sens de l'orientation** to have a good sense of direction ▶ **bon sens** common sense ▶ **plein de bon sens** very sensible ▶ **faire preuve de bon sens** to be sensible ▶ **ça tombe sous le sens** it's obvious, it stands to reason **3.** [opinion] : *à mon sens, c'est impossible* as I see it ou to my mind, it's impossible **4.** [signification - d'un mot, d'une phrase] meaning *(C)*, sense ; [- d'une allégorie, d'un symbole] meaning *(C)* / *ce que tu dis n'a pas de sens* [c'est inintelligible, déraisonnable] what you're saying doesn't make sense ▶ **figuré** in the literal / figurative sense ▶ **au sens strict** strictly speaking **5.** [direction] direction ▶ **dans tous les sens** *pr* in all directions, all over the place ▶ **chercher dans tous les sens** to look everywhere ▶ **arrête de t'agiter dans tous les sens !** keep still for a minute! ▶ **en sens inverse** the other way round ou around ▶ **scier une planche dans le sens de la largeur / longueur** to saw a board widthwise / lengthwise ▶ **fais demi-tour, on va dans le mauvais sens !** turn round, we're going the wrong way ou in the wrong direction! ▶ **la circulation est bloquée dans le sens Paris-province** traffic leaving Paris is at a standstill ▶ **dans le sens de la marche** facing the front *(of a vehicle)* / *dans le sens contraire de la marche* facing the rear *(of a vehicle)* ▶ **dans le sens des aiguilles d'une montre** clockwise ▶ **dans le sens inverse des aiguilles d'une montre** anticlockwise 🇬🇧, counterclockwise 🇺🇸 ▶ **sens giratoire** TRANSP roundabout 🇬🇧, traffic circle 🇺🇸 ▶ **sens interdit** a) [panneau] no-entry sign b) [rue] one-way street ▶ **être** ou **rouler en sens interdit** to be going the wrong way up / down a one-way street ▶ **(rue à) sens unique** one-way street ▶ **à sens unique** a) *fig* [amour] unrequited *sout* b) [décision] unilateral, one-sided **6.** *fig* [orientation] line / *leur politique ne va pas dans le bon sens* their policy's going down the wrong road. ◈ **dans le sens où** *loc conj* in the sense that, in so far as. ◈ **dans un certain sens** *loc adv* in a way, in a sense, as it were. ◈ **en ce sens que** = **dans le sens où**. ◈ **sens dessus dessous** *loc adv* upside down / *la maison était sens dessus dessous* [en désordre] the house was all topsy-turvy.

sensation [sɑ̃sasjɔ̃] nf **1.** [impression] sensation, feeling / *sensation de fraîcheur* feeling of freshness, fresh sensation / *j'avais la sensation qu'on reculait* I had the feeling we were going backwards ▶ **sensations fortes** : *les amateurs de sensations fortes* people who like thrills **2.** [impact] ▶ **faire sensation** to cause a stir ou sensation **3.** PHYSIOL sensation. ◈ **à sensation** *loc adj* sensational.

sensationnel, elle [sɑ̃sasjɔnɛl] adj [spectaculaire - révélation, image] sensational.

sensé, e [sɑ̃se] adj [sage] sensible, well-advised, wise / *dire des choses sensées* to talk sense.

sensibilisation [sɑ̃sibilizasjɔ̃] nf [prise de conscience] awareness / *il y a une grande sensibilisation des jeunes aux dangers du tabagisme* young people are alert to ou aware of the dangers of smoking.

sensibiliser [3] [sɑ̃sibilize] vt [gén] ▶ **sensibiliser qqn à qqch** to make sb conscious ou aware of sthg / *il faudrait*

essayer de sensibiliser l'opinion we'll have to try and make people aware.

sensibilité [sɑ̃sibilite] nf **1.** [physique] sensitiveness, sensitivity ; [intellectuelle] sensibility ; [émotive] sensitivity / *elle est d'une sensibilité maladive* she's painfully ou excruciatingly sensitive / *tu manques totalement de sensibilité* you're utterly insensitive **2.** POL : *toutes sensibilités confondues* all political tendencies.

sensible [sɑ̃sibl] adj **1.** [physiquement, émotivement] sensitive ▶ **sensible à** sensitive to ▶ **sensible à la beauté de qqn** susceptible to sb's beauty / *nous avons été très sensibles à son geste* we really appreciated what (s)he did ▶ **personnes sensibles s'abstenir** not recommended for people of a nervous disposition **2.** [peau, gencive] delicate, sensitive ; [balance, microphone] sensitive, responsive ; [direction de voiture] responsive **3.** [phénomène - perceptible] perceptible ; [- notable] noticeable, marked, sensible *sout* / *hausse / baisse sensible* marked rise / fall **4.** [difficile - quartier, établissement scolaire] problem *(modif)* ; [- dossier] sensisitive **5.** PHOT sensitive.

⚠️ L'adjectif anglais **sensible**, qui signifie avant tout « sensé », « judicieux », ne peut que très rarement être employé pour traduire **sensible**.

sensiblement [sɑ̃siblǝmɑ̃] adv **1.** [beaucoup] appreciably, noticeably, markedly **2.** [à peu près] about, approximately, more or less, roughly / *nos fils sont sensiblement de la même taille* our sons are roughly the same height.

sensiblerie [sɑ̃siblǝri] nf oversensitiveness, squeamishness.

sensualité [sɑ̃sɥalite] nf sensuality.

sensuel, elle [sɑ̃sɥɛl] adj [plaisir, personne] sensual, sybaritic *litt.*

sentence [sɑ̃tɑ̃s] nf [jugement] sentence.

sentencieux, euse [sɑ̃tɑ̃sjø, øz] adj sententious, moralistic, moralizing.

sentier [sɑ̃tje] nm **1.** [allée] path, footpath **2.** *fig & litt* path, way ▶ **sortir des sentiers battus** to get ou to wander off the beaten track.

sentiment [sɑ̃timɑ̃] nm **1.** [émotion] feeling ▶ **prendre qqn par les sentiments** to appeal to sb's feelings **2.** [opinion] feeling, opinion / *si vous voulez savoir mon sentiment* if you want to know what I think ou feel **3.** [conscience] ▶ **avoir le / un sentiment de** to have the / a feeling of. ◈ **sentiments** nmpl [dans la correspondance] : *nos sentiments les meilleurs* kindest regards.

sentimental, e, aux [sɑ̃timɑ̃tal, o] ◆ adj **1.** [affectif] sentimental ▶ **vie sentimentale** love life **2.** *péj* sentimental, mawkish *péj*. ◆ nm, f : *c'est un grand sentimental* he's a sentimentalist, he's very sentimental.

sentinelle [sɑ̃tinɛl] nf MIL sentinel, sentry.

sentir [37] [sɑ̃tir]
◆ vt

A. RESSENTIR, PERCEVOIR **1.** [par l'odorat] to smell ; [par le toucher] to feel ; [par le goût] to taste / *je sens une odeur de gaz* I can smell gas / *je n'ai rien senti !* I didn't feel a thing! / *je sens une lourdeur dans mes jambes* my legs feel heavy / *il sentit les larmes lui monter aux yeux* he could feel tears coming to his eyes ▶ **je n'ai pas senti l'après-midi / les années passer** the afternoon / years just flashed by **2.** [avoir l'intuition de - mépris, présence, réticence] to feel, to sense, to be aware of ; [- danger, menace] to be aware ou conscious of, to sense / *tu ne sens pas ta force* you don't know your own strength / *je le sentais prêt / résolu* I could feel ou tell he was ready / determined / *j'ai senti qu'on me suivait* I felt ou sensed (that) I was being followed ▸ **faire sentir qqch à qqn** to make sb aware of sthg, to show sb sthg / *il m'a fait sentir que j'étais de trop* he made me understand ou he hinted that I was in the way **3.** [apprécier - art, musique] to feel, to have a feeling for **4.** *fam* [être convaincu par] : *je ne la sens pas pour le rôle* my feeling is that she's not right for the part / *je ne le sens pas, ton projet* I'm not convinced by your project **5.** [maîtriser - instrument, outil] to have a feel for ; [- rôle, mouvement à exécuter] to feel at ease with **6.** *fam* [tolérer] : *je ne peux pas sentir ma sœur* I can't bear the sight of ou stand her sister.

B. EXHALER, RENDRE PERCEPTIBLE **1.** [dégager - odeur, parfum] to smell (of), to give off a smell of / *qu'est-ce que ça sent ?* what's that smell? / *sentir le gaz* to smell of gas / *ça sent bon le lilas, ici* there's a nice smell of lilac in here **2.** [annoncer] : *ça sent la pluie / neige* it feels like rain / snow / *ses propositions sentent le traquenard* there's something a bit suspect about his proposals ▸ **se faire sentir** [devenir perceptible] to be felt, to become obvious / *les conséquences de votre décision se feront sentir tôt ou tard* the implications of your decision will be felt sooner or later / *la fatigue se fait sentir chez les coureurs* the runners are showing signs of tiredness **3.** [laisser deviner] to smack of (insép), to savour of (insép) / *son interprétation / style sent un peu trop le travail* her performance / style is rather too constrained / *son accent sentait bon le terroir* he had a wonderfully earthy accent.

◆ vi **1.** [avoir une odeur] to smell ▸ **ça sent bon** a) [fleur, parfum] it smells nice b) [nourriture] it smells good ou nice ▸ **ça sent mauvais** *pr* it doesn't smell very nice **2.** [puer] to smell, to stink, to reek / *il sent des pieds* his feet smell, he's got smelly feet. ◆ **se sentir** ◆ vp *(emploi réciproque) fam* : *ils ne peuvent pas se sentir* they can't stand each other. ◆ vp *(emploi passif)* to show / *il ne l'aime pas — ça se sent* he doesn't like her — you can tell (he doesn't) ou you can sense it. ◆ vpi to feel / *se sentir en sécurité / danger* to feel safe / threatened ▸ **se sentir mal** a) [s'évanouir] to feel faint b) [être indisposé] to feel ill ▸ **se sentir bien** to feel good ou all right / *ne plus se sentir de joie* to be bursting ou beside o.s. with joy. ◆ vpt : *je ne me sens pas le courage / la force de marcher* I don't feel up to walking / have the strength to walk.

séparation [separasjɔ̃] nf **1.** [éloignement] separation, parting **2.** [rupture] break-up, split-up **3.** DR separation (agreement) **4.** POL : *la séparation des pouvoirs* the separation of powers **5.** [cloison] partition, division.

séparatisme [separatism] nm separatism.

séparatiste [separatist] adj & nmf separatist.

séparé, e [separe] adj **1.** [éléments, problèmes, courrier] separate **2.** [époux] separated.

séparément [separemã] adv separately.

séparer [3] [separe] vt **1.** [isoler] to separate / *séparer le blanc et le jaune d'un œuf* to separate the yolk and ou from the white ▸ **séparer qqch de** : *séparer les raisins gâtés des raisins sains* to separate the bad grapes from the good ones, to pick the bad grapes out from amongst the good ones ▸ **séparer le bon grain de l'ivraie** *allusion* BIBLE to separate the wheat from the chaff **2.** [éloigner - gens] to part, to separate, to pull apart *(sép)* / *la guerre a séparé beaucoup de familles* many families were separated ou broken up by the war / *séparez-les, ils vont se tuer !* pull them apart ou they'll kill each other! ▸ **séparer qqn de** : *on les a séparés de leur père* they were separated from ou taken away from their father **3.** [différencier] : *séparer l'amour et l'amitié amoureuse* to distinguish between love and a loving friendship ▸ **tout les sépare** they're worlds apart, they have nothing in common **4.** [diviser] to separate, to

divide / *le Nord est séparé du Sud* ou *le Nord et le Sud sont séparés par un désert* the North is separated from the South by a desert / *deux heures / cinq kilomètres nous séparaient de la frontière* we were two hours / five kilometres away from the border. ◆ **se séparer** ◆ vp *(emploi réciproque)* [se quitter] to break up / *les Beatles se sont séparés en 1970* the Beatles split up ou broke up in 1970 / *on se sépara sur le pas de la porte* we parted on the doorstep. ◆ vpi to divide, to branch (off). ◆ **se séparer de** vp + prép **1.** [se priver de] to part with / *je ne me sépare jamais de mon plan de Paris* I'm never without my Paris street map **2.** [quitter] : *se séparer de son mari* to separate ou to part from one's husband.

sépia [sepja] ◆ nf **1.** ZOOL cuttlefish ink **2.** ART [couleur] sepia ; [dessin] sepia (drawing). ◆ adj inv sepia, sepia-coloured.

sept [sɛt] ◆ dét **1.** seven ▸ **les Sept Merveilles du monde** the Seven Wonders of the World **2.** [dans des séries] seventh ▸ **le tome sept** volume seven **3.** JEUX ▸ **le jeu des sept familles** Happy Families. ◆ nm inv **1.** [numéro] seven **2.** JEUX [carte] seven **3.** TV ▸ **les Sept d'or** annual television awards. **Voir aussi cinq.**

septante [sɛptãt] dét *régional* seventy.

septembre [sɛptãbr] nm September. **Voir aussi mars.**

septennat [sɛptena] nm POL (seven year) term of office / *pendant son premier septennat* during his first term of office.

septentrional, e, aux [sɛptãtrijɔnal, o] adj northern, septentrional *arch*.

septicémie [sɛptisemi] nf blood poisoning, septicaemia UK *spéc*, septicemia US *spéc*.

septième [sɛtjɛm] ◆ adj num seventh ▸ **le septième art** the cinema ▸ **être au septième ciel** to be in seventh heaven. ◆ nmf seventh. ◆ nm **1.** [partie] seventh (part) **2.** [étage] seventh floor UK, sixth story US. ◆ nf ÉDUC year six UK ou fifth grade US (in primary school). **Voir aussi cinquième.**

septièmement [sɛtjɛmmã] adv seventhly, in the seventh place.

septique [sɛptik] adj septic.

septuagénaire [sɛptɥaʒenɛr] ◆ adj seventy-year-old *(avant nom)*, septuagenarian. ◆ nmf septuagenarian, seventy-year-old man / woman.

sépulcre [sepylkr] nm *litt* sepulchre UK, sepulcher US.

sépulture [sepyltyr] nf [lieu] burial place.

séquelle [sekɛl] nf [d'une maladie] aftereffect ; [d'un bombardement, d'une guerre] aftermath, sequel / *sa bronchite n'a pas laissé de séquelles* she suffered no aftereffects from her bronchitis.

séquence [sekãs] nf **1.** CINÉ, GÉOL, MUS & RELIG sequence **2.** INFORM sequence.

séquestration [sekɛstrasjɔ̃] nf DR [d'une personne] illegal confinement ou restraint ; [de biens] sequestration (order).

séquestre [sekɛstr] nm DR [saisie] sequestration ; [personne] sequestrator. ◆ **sous séquestre** loc adj & loc adv ▸ **biens (mis** ou **placés) sous séquestre** sequestrated property.

séquestrer [3] [sekɛstre] vt **1.** [personne] to confine illegally **2.** DR [bien] to sequestrate.

serbe [sɛrb] adj Serbian. ◆ **Serbe** nmf Serb, Serbian. ◆ **serbe** nm LING Serb, Serbian.

Serbie [sɛrbi] npr f ▸ **la Serbie** Serbia.

serbo-croate [sɛrbokrɔat] *(pl* **serbo-croates)** ◆ adj Serbo-Croat, Serbo-Croatian. ◆ nm LING Serbo-Croat, Serbo-Croatian.

séré [sere] nm SUISSE fromage frais.

serein, e [səʀɛ̃, ɛn] adj **1.** [esprit, visage] serene, peaceful **2.** sout [jugement] unbiased, dispassionate ; [réflexion] undisturbed, unclouded.

sereinement [səʀɛnmɑ̃] adv **1.** [tranquillement] serenely, peacefully **2.** sout [impartialement] dispassionately.

sérénade [seʀenad] nf **1.** MUS serenade ; [concert] serenade **2.** fam [scène] row, din.

sérénité [seʀenite] nf [d'une personne] serenity, peacefulness ; [d'un jugement] dispassionateness ; [des pensées] clarity.

sergent [sɛʀʒɑ̃] nm MIL sergeant.

sergent-chef (pl **sergents-chefs**) nm [de l'armée - de terre] staff sergeant ; [- de l'air] flight sergeant 🇬🇧, senior master sergeant 🇺🇸.

série [seʀi] nf **1.** [suite - de questions, d'articles] series (sg) ; [- d'attentats] series, spate, string ; [- d'échecs] series, run, string ; [- de tests] series, battery / il y a eu récemment une série de descentes de police there's been a spate of police raids recently / toute une série de a series of **2.** [ensemble - de clefs, de mouchoirs] set ; [- de poupées russes, de tables gigognes] nest ; COMM & INDUST (production) batch ▶ **série limitée** limited run **3.** [catégorie] class, category **4.** CINÉ ▶ **film de série B** B-movie **5.** TV ▶ **série (télévisée)** television series **6.** SPORT [classement] series ; [épreuve] qualifying heat ou round **7.** GÉOL, MATH, MUS & NUCL series (sg). ❖ **de série** loc adj **1.** COMM [numéro] serial (modif) **2.** AUTO [modèle] production (modif). ❖ **en série** ◆ loc adj **1.** INDUST [fabrication] mass (modif) **2.** ÉLECTR [couplage, enroulement] series (modif). ◆ loc adv **1.** INDUST ▶ **fabriquer qqch en série** to mass-produce sthg **2.** ÉLECTR ▶ **monté en série** connected in series **3.** [à la file] one after the other ▶ **tueur / meurtres en série** serial killer / killings. ❖ **série noire** nf **1.** LITTÉR crime thriller **2.** fig catalogue of disasters.

sérieusement [seʀjøzmɑ̃] adv **1.** [consciencieusement] seriously **2.** [sans plaisanter] seriously, in earnest / je pense me présenter aux élections — sérieusement ? I think I'll stand in the election — really? **3.** [gravement] seriously, gravely ▶ **sérieusement blessé** seriously ou severely injured **4.** [vraiment] : ça commençait à bouchonner sérieusement traffic was really building up.

sérieux, euse [seʀjø, øz] adj **1.** [grave - ton, visage] serious, solemn ; [important - lecture, discussion] serious **2.** [consciencieux - employé] serious, responsible ; [- élève] serious, serious-minded, earnest ; [- travail] conscientious / être sérieux dans son travail to be a conscientious worker, to take one's work seriously / ça ne fait pas très sérieux it doesn't look good **3.** [digne de foi - offre] genuine ; [- candidature, revue] serious ; [- personne] reliable, dependable ; [- analyse, enquête] serious, thorough, in-depth / il me faut quelqu'un de sérieux I need someone reliable **4.** [dangereux - situation, maladie] grave, serious ; [- blessure] severe **5.** [sincère] serious ▶ **'pas sérieux s'abstenir'** 'only genuine inquirers need apply', 'no time-wasters' ; [vrai] : c'est sérieux, tu pars ? it's true that you are leaving? **6.** (avant nom) [important - effort] real ; [- dégâts, difficultés, risques] serious / il a de sérieuses chances de gagner he stands a good chance of winning / on a de sérieuses raisons de le penser we have good reasons to think so / de sérieux progrès techniques considerable technical advances / ils ont une sérieuse avance sur nous they are well ahead of us. ❖ **sérieux** nm **1.** [gravité - d'une personne] seriousness ; [- d'une situation] gravity ▶ **garder son sérieux** to keep a straight face **2.** [application] seriousness, serious-mindedness / elle fait son travail avec sérieux she's serious about her work **3.** [fiabilité - d'une intention] seriousness, earnestness ; [- d'une source de renseignements] reliability, dependability. ❖ **au sérieux** loc adv ▶ **prendre qqch / qqn au sérieux** to take sthg / sb seriously / se prendre (trop) au sérieux to take o.s. (too) seriously.

sérigraphie [seʀigʀafi] nf **1.** [procédé] silk-screen ou screen process printing **2.** [ouvrage] silk-screen print.

serin, e [səʀɛ̃, in] nm, f ZOOL canary.

seriner [3] [səʀine] vt fam [répéter] ▶ **seriner qqch à qqn** to drill ou to drum ou to din sthg into sb.

seringue [səʀɛ̃g] nf MÉD needle, syringe.

serment [sɛʀmɑ̃] nm **1.** [parole solennelle] oath / témoigner sous serment to testify under oath / faire un serment sur l'honneur to pledge one's word of honour ▶ **serment d'Hippocrate** MÉD Hippocratic oath **2.** [promesse] pledge / j'ai fait le serment de ne rien dire I'm pledged ou sworn to secrecy.

sermon [sɛʀmɔ̃] nm RELIG sermon.

sermonner [3] [sɛʀmɔne] vt [morigéner] to lecture, to sermonize, to preach at.

séronégatif, ive [seʀonegatif, iv] ◆ adj [gén] seronegative ; [HIV] HIV negative. ◆ nm, f ▶ **les séronégatifs** HIV negative people.

séropositif, ive [seʀopozitif, iv] ◆ adj [gén] seropositive ; [HIV] HIV positive. ◆ nm, f ▶ **les séropositifs** HIV positive people.

séropositivité [seʀopozitivite] nf [gén] seropositivity ; [HIV] HIV infection.

serpent [sɛʀpɑ̃] nm **1.** ZOOL snake ▶ **serpent à sonnette** rattlesnake **2.** FIN ▶ **le serpent monétaire européen** the (European currency) Snake.

serpenter [3] [sɛʀpɑ̃te] vi to wind along, to meander.

serpentin [sɛʀpɑ̃tɛ̃] nm [de papier] (paper) streamer.

serpillière, serpillère* [sɛʀpijɛʀ] nf floorcloth 🇬🇧, mop 🇺🇸 / il faudrait passer la serpillière dans la cuisine the kitchen floor needs cleaning.

serre [sɛʀ] nf **1.** HORT & AGR [en verre] greenhouse, glasshouse 🇬🇧 ; [en plastique] greenhouse ▶ **légumes poussés en serre** vegetables grown under glass ▶ **serre chaude** hothouse ▶ **effet de serre** greenhouse effect **2.** ORNITH claw, talon.

serré, e [seʀe] adj **1.** [nœud, ceinture] tight **2.** VÊT ▶ **serré à la taille** fitted at the waist, tight-waisted **3.** [contracté] ▶ **les lèvres / dents serrées** with set lips / clenched teeth ▶ **c'est le cœur serré que j'y repense** when I think of it, it gives me a lump in my throat **4.** [dense - style] tight, concise ; [- emploi du temps, planning] tight, busy ; [- réseau] dense ; [- débat] closely-conducted, closely-argued ; [- écriture] cramped **5.** [café] strong **6.** SPORT [arrivée, peloton] close ; [match] tight, close-fought ▶ **jouer** ou **mener un jeu serré** to play a tight game. ❖ **serré** adv ▶ **jouer serré** to play a tight game.

serre-livres, serre-livre* [sɛʀlivʀ] nm bookend.

serrement [sɛʀmɑ̃] nm sout [action] ▶ **serrement de cœur** pang of anguish, tug at the heartstrings ▶ **serrement de main** handshake.

serrer [4] [seʀe] vt **1.** [presser] to hold tight / serre-moi fort dans tes bras hold me tight in your arms ▶ **serrer qqn contre son cœur** to clasp sb to one's bosom ▶ **serrer la main** ou **la pince** fam **à qqn** to shake hands with sb, to shake sb's hand **2.** [suj : vêtement] to be tight / la chaussure droite / le col me serre un peu the right shoe / the collar is a bit tight **3.** [bien fermer - nœud, lacets] to tighten, to pull tight ; [- joint] to clamp ; [- écrou] to tighten (up) ; [- frein à main] to put on tight ▶ **serrer la vis à qqn** fam to crack down hard on sb **4.** [contracter] to clench ▶ **serrer les lèvres** to set ou to tighten one's lips / serrer les dents to clench ou to set ou to grit one's teeth / serrer les mâchoires to clench one's jaws ▶ **en serrant les poings a)** pr clenching one's fists **b)** fig barely containing one's anger / avoir la gorge serrée par l'émotion to be choked with emotion ▶ **serrer les fesses** fam to have the jitters **5.** [rapprocher] ▸ **serrer les rangs** MIL & *fig* to close ranks ▸ **être serrés comme des sardines** ou **des harengs** to be squashed up like sardines **6.** [suivre] : *serrer le trottoir* AUTO to hug the kerb ▸ **serrer qqn de près** to follow close behind sb, to follow sb closely **7.** Québec [ranger] to put away **8.** Québec [enfermer, mettre en lieu sûr] to put in a safe place. ◆ vi AUTO ▸ **serrer à droite / gauche** to keep to the right / left. ◆ **se serrer** ◆ vpi **1.** [se rapprocher] to squeeze up ▸ **se serrer contre qqn a)** [par affection] to cuddle ou to snuggle up to sb **b)** [pour se protéger] to huddle up against sb **2.** [se contracter] to tighten up / *mon cœur se serra en les voyant* my heart sank when I saw them. ◆ vpt ▸ **se serrer la main** to shake hands.

serre-tête [sɛʀtɛt] (*pl* serre-tête ou serre-têtes*) nm **1.** [accessoire] headband, hairband **2.** SPORT [d'athlète] headband ; [de rugbyman] scrum cap.

serrure [seʀyʀ] nf lock.

serrurier [seʀyʀje] nm [qui pose des serrures] locksmith.

sertir [32] [sɛʀtiʀ] vt JOAILL to set / *couronne sertie de diamants* crown set with diamonds.

sérum [seʀɔm] nm **1.** PHYSIOL ▸ **sérum (sanguin)** (blood) serum **2.** PHARM serum ▸ **sérum physiologique** saline ▸ **sérum de vérité** truth drug.

servante [sɛʀvɑ̃t] nf [domestique] servant, maidservant.

serveur [sɛʀvœʀ] nm **1.** [de restaurant] waiter ; [de bar] barman (barmaid) UK, bartender US **2.** SPORT server **3.** INFORM server ▸ **serveur Internet** Internet server ▸ **serveur vocal** voicemail service.

serveuse [sɛʀvøz] nf waitress.

serviable [sɛʀvjabl] adj helpful, obliging, amenable.

service [sɛʀvis] nm **1.** [travail] duty, shift / *mon service commence à 18 h* I go on duty ou I start my shift ou I start work at 6 p.m. / *l'alcool est interdit pendant le service* drinking is forbidden while on duty ▸ **être de service** : *qui est de service ce soir ?* who's on duty tonight? / *il n'est pas de service* he's off-duty ▸ **finir son service** to come off duty ▸ **prendre son service** to go on ou to report for duty ; [pour la collectivité] service, serving ▸ **ses états de service** his service record **2.** [pour un client, un maître] service ▸ **prendre qqn à son service** to take sb into service ▸ **à votre service** at your service / *il a mis son savoir-faire au service de la société* he put his expertise at the disposal of the company ▸ **après dix ans de bons et loyaux services** after ten years of good and faithful service / **'service compris / non compris'** 'service included / not included' ▸ **femme / homme de service** cleaner **3.** [série de repas] sitting / *nous irons au premier / deuxième service* we'll go to the first / second sitting **4.** [département - d'une entreprise, d'un hôpital] department ▸ **service clientèle** customer services ▸ **service de presse a)** [département] press office **b)** [personnes] press officers, press office staff ▸ **service des urgences** casualty (department) UK, emergency room US ; ADMIN ▸ **service postal** postal service ▸ **les services sociaux** the social services **5.** [aide] favour UK, favor US ▸ **rendre un service à qqn** [suj : personne] to do sb a favour, to help sb out / *tu m'as bien rendu service* you were a great help to me / *ton dictionnaire m'a bien rendu service* your dictionary was of great use to me **6.** [assortiment - de linge, de vaisselle] set / *acheter un service de 6 couverts en argent* to buy a 6-place canteen of silver cutlery **7.** TRANSP service ▸ **service d'été / d'hiver** summer / winter timetable **8.** MIL ▸ **service militaire** ou **national** military / national service ▸ **service civil** non-military national service ▸ **en service commandé** on an official assignment **9.** SPORT service, serve ▸ **prendre le service de qqn** to break sb's serve ou service **10.** ÉLECTR duty **11.** FIN servicing **12.** RELIG ▸ **service (divin)** service ▸ **service funèbre** funeral service. ◆ **services** nmpl **1.** [ÉCON services, service

industries, tertiary sector **2.** [collaboration] services ▸ **se passer des services de qqn a)** to do without sb's help **b)** *euphém* [le licencier] to dispense with sb's services ▸ **offrir ses services à qqn** to offer one's services to sb, to offer to help sb out **3.** POL ▸ **services secrets** ou **spéciaux** secret service. ◆ **en service** ◆ loc adj in service, in use. ◆ loc adv : *mettre un appareil en service* to put a machine into service. ◆ **service après-vente** nm **1.** [prestation] after-sales service **2.** [département] after-sales department ; [personnes] after-sales staff. ◆ **service minimum** nm skeleton service / *assurer le service minimum* to provide a skeleton service. ◆ **service d'ordre** nm **1.** [système] policing / *mettre en place un service d'ordre dans un quartier* to establish a strong police presence in an area **2.** [policiers] police (contingent) ; [syndiqués, manifestants] stewards. ◆ **service public** nm public service ou utility / *service public de l'audiovisuel* the publicly-owned channels (*on French television*).

 Service militaire ou national

Until 1996, all French men aged 18 and over were required to do ten months national service unless declared unfit. The system has been phased out and replaced by an obligatory **journée d'appel de préparation à la défense**, one day spent learning about the army and army career opportunities. The **JAPD** is obligatory for men and for women. The object of this reform is to professionalize the army.

serviette [sɛʀvjet] nf **1.** [linge] ▸ **serviette de bain** bath towel ▸ **serviette de plage** beach towel ▸ **serviette de table** table napkin ▸ **serviette de toilette a)** towel **b)** [pour s'essuyer les mains] (hand) towel **2.** [protection] ▸ **serviette hygiénique** ou **périodique** sanitary towel UK ou napkin US **3.** [cartable] briefcase.

serviette-éponge [sɛʀvjetepɔ̃ʒ] (*pl* serviettes-éponges) nf (terry) towel.

servile [sɛʀvil] adj [esprit, attitude] servile, subservient, sycophantic *sout* ; [manières] servile, cringing, fawning.

servir [38] [sɛʀviʀ] ◆ vt **1.** [dans un magasin] to serve / *on vous sert ?* [dans un café, une boutique] are you being attended to *sout* ou served? ▸ **servir qqn de** ou **en qqch** to serve sb with sthg, to serve sthg to sb / *c'est difficile de se faire servir ici* it's difficult to get served here ; [approvisionner] ▸ **servir qqn en** to supply sb with **2.** [donner - boisson, mets] to serve ; [dans le verre] to pour (out) (*sép*) ; [dans l'assiette] to dish out ou up (*sép*), to serve up (*sép*) / *sers le café* pour the coffee / *elle nous a servi un très bon cassoulet* she gave us ou served up some lovely cassoulet / *le dîner est servi !* dinner's ready ou served! ▸ **servir qqch à qqn** to serve sb with ou to help sb to sthg / *sers-moi à boire* give ou pour me a drink ; (*en usage absolu*) : *nous ne servons plus après 23 h* we don't take orders after 11 p.m., last orders are at 11 p.m. **3.** *fam* [raconter] to give / *ils nous servent toujours les mêmes histoires aux informations* they always dish out the same old stories on the news **4.** [travailler pour - famille] to be in service with ; [-communauté, pays, parti] to serve ; [-justice] to be at the service of ; [-patrie, cause] to serve ▸ **servir l'intérêt public a)** [loi, mesure] to be in the public interest **b)** [personne] to serve the public interest ▸ **servir l'État a)** POL to serve the state **b)** [être fonctionnaire] to be employed by the state ▸ **on n'est jamais si bien servi que par soi-même**

prov if you want something doing, do it yourself **5.** [aider -suj : circonstances] to be of service to, to be ou to work to the advantage of ▸ **servir les ambitions de qqn** to serve ou to aid ou to further sb's ambitions / *sa mémoire la sert beaucoup* her memory's a great help to her **6.** [payer -pension, rente] to pay (out) *(sép)* **7.** SPORT to serve **8.** [préparer -arme] to serve **9.** RELIG : *servir la messe* to serve mass **10.** JEUX [cartes] to deal (out) *(sép)* ; [joueur] to serve, to deal to *(sép)* **11.** Suisse [utiliser] to use. ◆ vi **1.** [être utile - outil, vêtement, appareil] to be useful ou of use, to come in handy / *garde la malle, ça peut toujours servir* keep the trunk, you might need it ou it might come in handy one day / *il a servi, ce manteau !* I got a lot of use out of this coat! **2.** [travailler] ▸ **servir dans un café / restaurant a)** [homme] to be a waiter (in a) café / restaurant **b)** [femme] to be a waitress (in a) café / restaurant ; MIL to serve **3.** SPORT to serve / *à toi de servir !* your serve ou service! ◆ **servir à** v + prép **1.** [être destiné à] to be used for **2.** [avoir pour conséquence] ▸ **servir à qqch** : *ça ne sert à rien de lui en parler* it's useless ou of no use to talk about it with him / *ne pleure pas, ça ne sert à rien* don't cry, it won't make any difference / *à quoi servirait-il de lui en parler ?* what would be the good ou point of killing him? **3.** [être utile à] ▸ **servir à qqn** : *merci, ça m'a beaucoup servi* thanks, it was really useful ou a great help / *sa connaissance du russe lui a servi dans son métier* her knowledge of Russian helped her ou was of use to her in her job. ◆ **servir de** v + prép [article, appareil] to be used as ; [personne] to act as, to be / *le coffre me sert aussi de table* I also use the trunk as a table / *je lui ai servi d'interprète* I acted as his interpreter. ◆ **se servir** ◆ vp *(emploi réfléchi)* [à table, dans un magasin] to help o.s. ▸ **servez-vous de** ou **en légumes** help yourself to vegetables / *je me suis servi un verre de lait* I poured myself a glass of milk ▸ **sers-toi !** help yourself! ◆ vp *(emploi passif)* CULIN to be served / *le vin rouge se sert chambré* red wine should be served at room temperature. ◆ **se servir de** vp + prép ▸ **se servir de qqch** to use sthg / *il ne peut plus se servir de son bras droit* he can't use his right arm anymore ▸ **se servir de qqch comme** to use sthg as ▸ **se servir de qqn** to make use of ou to use sb.

serviteur [sɛʀvitœʀ] nm (male) servant / *votre (humble) serviteur !* hum your (humble) servant!, at your service!

ses [se] pl ⟶ **son**.

sésame [sezam] nm **1.** BOT & CULIN sesame / *graine de sésame* sesame seed **2.** EXPR Sésame, ouvre-toi ! open, Sesame! ▸ **le sésame (ouvre-toi) de la réussite** the key to success.

session [sesjɔ̃] nf **1.** [réunion - d'une assemblée] session, sitting **2.** UNIV exam period / *il a été collé à la session de juin* he failed the June exams ▸ **la session de repêchage** the repeat examinations, the resits UK.

set [sɛt] nm **1.** [objet] ▸ **set (de table)** table mat **2.** SPORT set.

setter [setɛʀ] nm ZOOL setter ▸ **setter anglais / irlandais** English / Irish setter.

seuil [sœj] nm **1.** [dalle] doorstep ; [entrée] doorway, threshold **2.** sout [début] threshold, brink / *être au seuil de la mort* to be on the verge of death **3.** [limite] threshold **4.** SCI threshold ▸ **seuil de tolérance** threshold of tolerance **5.** ÉCON ▸ **seuil de rentabilité / saturation** break-even / saturation point ▸ **le seuil de pauvreté** the poverty line.

seul, e [sœl] ◆ adj **1.** [sans compagnie] alone, on one's own / *seul au monde* ou *sur la Terre* (all) alone in the world / *enfin seuls !* alone at last! ▸ **seul à seul** [en privé] in private, privately / *je voudrais te parler seul à seul* I'd like to talk to you in private ▸ **se retrouver seul à seul avec qqn** to find o.s. alone with sb / *elle vit seule avec sa mère*

she lives alone with her mother / *un homme seul a peu de chances de réussir* [sans aucune aide] it's unlikely that anybody could succeed on their own ▸ **tout seul, toute seule** : *elle parle toute seule* she's talking to herself / *il a bâti sa maison tout seul* he built his house all by himself / *le dîner ne se préparera pas tout seul !* dinner isn't going to make itself! **2.** [sans partenaire, non marié] alone, on one's own ▸ **un homme seul a)** [non accompagné] a man on his own **b)** [célibataire] a single man, a bachelor / *elle est seule avec trois enfants* she's bringing up three children on her own / *un club pour personnes seules* a singles club **3.** (avant nom) [unique] only, single, sole / *c'est l'homme d'une seule passion* he's a man with one overriding ou ruling passion / *je n'ai été en retard qu'une seule fois* I was late only once / *pas un seul..., pas une seule...* not one..., not a single... / *un seul et même..., une seule et même...* one and the same... / *un seul et unique..., une seule et unique...* only one (and one only)... / *la seule fois que je l'ai vue* the only ou one time I saw her **4.** [sans autre chose] : *mon salaire seul* ou sout *mon seul salaire ne suffit pas à faire vivre ma famille* my salary alone is not enough to support my family / *le vase seul vaut combien ?* how much is it for just the vase? / *la propriété à elle seule leur donne de quoi vivre* the property alone brings in enough for them to live on **5.** (comme adverbe) only / *seul Pierre a refusé* only Pierre refused, Pierre was the only one to refuse **6.** (avant nom) [simple] mere / *la seule évocation de la scène lui donnait des frissons* the mere mention of ou merely talking about the scene gave him goose pimples. ◆ nm, f **1.** [personne] only one (person) / *je te crois mais je dois être la seule !* I believe you, but thousands wouldn't! **2.** [animal, objet] only one.

 alone ou **lonely** ?
L'adjectif **alone** se réfère à la solitude objective, au fait d'être sans compagnie. L'adjectif **lonely** fait référence au sentiment de solitude, au fait de se sentir seul :
Though I live *alone*, I'm never *lonely*. *Bien que je vive seul, je ne me sens jamais seul.*

seulement [sœlmɑ̃] adv **1.** [uniquement] only / *il y avait seulement deux personnes* there were only two people **2.** [dans le temps] : *il arrive seulement ce soir* he won't arrive before this evening / *je viens seulement de finir* I've only just finished **3.** [même] even / *sais-tu seulement de quoi tu parles ?* do you even know what you're talking about? **4.** [mais] only, but / *je veux y aller, seulement voilà, avec qui ?* I'd love to go, but ou only the problem is who with? ◆ **non seulement..., mais encore** loc corrélative not only... but also.

sève [sɛv] nf BOT sap.

sévère [sevɛʀ] adj **1.** [personne, caractère, règlement] strict, stern, severe **2.** [critique, verdict] severe, harsh / *ne sois pas trop sévère avec lui* don't be too hard on him.

sévèrement [sevɛʀmɑ̃] adv severely, harshly, strictly.

sévérité [severite] nf **1.** [d'un parent, d'un juge] severity, harshness **2.** [d'un verdict, d'un code, d'une éducation] severity, rigidness, strictness **3.** [d'un style] severity, austerity.

sévices [sevis] nmpl : *être victime de sévices* to suffer cruelty, to be ill-treated ▸ **faire subir des sévices à qqn** to ill-treat sb.

sévir [32] [seviʀ] vi **1.** [personne] : *si tu continues à tricher, je vais devoir sévir* if you keep on cheating, I'll have to do something about it / *sévir contre la fraude fiscale* to deal ruthlessly with tax evasion **2.** [fléau, épidémie] to rage, to be rampant ou rife, to reign supreme / *Morin ne sévira pas longtemps comme directeur à la comptabilité* hum Morin won't reign long as head of accounts / *c'est une idée qui sévit encore dans les milieux économiques* unfortunately the idea still has currency among economists.

sevrage [səvʀaʒ] nm **1.** [d'un bébé] weaning **2.** [d'un drogué] coming off (drugs).

sevrer [19] [səvʀe] vt **1.** [bébé] to wean **2.** [drogué] ▶ **sevrer qqn** to get sb off drugs.

sexagénaire [sɛksaʒenɛʀ] ◆ adj sixty-year-old *(avant nom)*, sexagenarian. ◆ nmf sexagenarian, sixty-year-old person.

sex-appeal [sɛksapil] *(pl* **sex-appeals**) nm sex appeal.

sexe [sɛks] nm **1.** [caractéristique] sex ▶ **enfant du sexe masculin / féminin** male / female child ▶ **le sexe fort / faible** the stronger / weaker sex **2.** ANAT sex (organs), genitals **3.** ▶ **le sexe** [sexualité] sex.

sexisme [sɛksism] nm [idéologie] sexism.

sexiste [sɛksist] adj & nmf sexist.

sexologie [sɛksɔlɔʒi] nf sexology.

sexologue [sɛksɔlɔg] nmf sexologist.

sex-symbol [sɛkssɛ̃bɔl] *(pl* **sex-symbols**) nm sex symbol.

sextuple [sɛkstypl] ◆ adj sextuple, sixfold. ◆ nm sextuple.

sextuplés, es [sɛkstyple] nmf pl sextuplets.

sexualité [sɛksɥalite] nf sexuality.

sexué, e [sɛksɥe] adj [animal] sexed ; [reproduction] sexual.

sexuel, elle [sɛksɥɛl] adj [comportement] sexual ; [organes, éducation, hormone] sex *(modif)*.

sexuellement [sɛksɥɛlmɑ̃] adv sexually.

sexy [sɛksi] *(pl* **sexy** ou **sexys***) adj fam sexy.

seyant, e [sɛjɑ̃, ɑ̃t] adj becoming ▶ **peu seyant** unbecoming.

Seychelles [seʃɛl] npr fpl ▶ **les (îles) Seychelles** the Seychelles. ⟶ **île**

SF (abr de **science-fiction**) nf sci-fi ▶ **film de SF** sci-fi movie.

shaker, shakeur* [ʃɛkœʀ] nm (cocktail) shaker.

shampoing, shampooing [ʃɑ̃pwɛ̃] nm **1.** [produit] shampoo ▶ **shampoing colorant** shampoo in-hair colourant 🇬🇧 ou colorant 🇺🇸 ▶ **shampoing pour moquettes** carpet shampoo **2.** [lavage] shampoo ▶ **se faire un shampoing** to shampoo ou to wash one's hair.

shampouineur, euse [ʃɑ̃pwinœʀ, øz] nm, f [personne] shampooer. ◆◆ **shampouineur, shampouineuse** nm & nf [machine] carpet cleaner ou shampooer.

shérif [ʃeʀif] nm **1.** [aux États-Unis] sheriff **2.** [en Grande-Bretagne] sheriff *(representative of the Crown)*.

shetland [ʃɛtlɑ̃d] nm VÊT Shetland jumper.

Shetland [ʃɛtlɑ̃d] npr fpl ▶ **les (îles) Shetland** the Shetland Islands, the Shetlands. ⟶ **île**

shilling [ʃiliŋ] nm shilling.

shit [ʃit] nm arg crime hasch, dope.

shooter [3] [ʃute] vi SPORT to shoot. ◆◆ **se shooter** vpi tfam [drogué] to shoot up, to fix / *se shooter à l'héroïne* to shoot ou to mainline heroin / *il se shoote au café* hum he has to have his fix of coffee.

shopping [ʃɔpiŋ] nm shopping ▶ **faire du shopping** to go shopping / *je fais toujours mon shopping chez eux* I always shop there.

short [ʃɔʀt] nm (pair of) shorts / *être en short* to be in ou wearing shorts.

show-biz [ʃobiz] nm inv fam show biz.

show-business [ʃobiznɛs] nm inv show business.

si¹ [si] nm inv MUS B ; [chanté] si, ti. **Voir aussi fa.**

si² [si] ◆ adv **1.** [tellement -avec un adjectif attribut, un adverbe, un nom] so ; [-avec un adjectif épithète] such / *il est si mignon !* he's (ever) so sweet! / *je la vois si peu* I see so little of her, I see her so rarely / *elle a de si beaux cheveux !* she has such beautiful hair! ; *(en corrélation avec «que»)* ▶ **si... que** so... that / *elle travaille si bien qu'on l'a augmentée* she works so well that she got a rise **2.** [exprimant la concession] however / *si aimable soit-il...* however nice he may be... ; *(en corrélation avec «que»)* : *si dur que ça puisse paraître, je ne céderai pas* however hard it may seem ou hard as it may seem I won't give way **3.** [dans une comparaison] ▶ **si... que** as... as / *il n'est pas si bête qu'il en a l'air* he's not as stupid as he seems **4.** [en réponse affirmative] yes / *ce n'est pas fermé ? — si* isn't it closed? — yes (it is) / *ça n'a pas d'importance — si, ça en a !* it doesn't matter — it DOES ou yes it does! / *je n'y arriverai jamais — mais si !* I'll never manage — of course you will! / *tu ne vas quand même pas lui dire ? — oh que si !* still, you're not going to tell him, are you? — oh yes I am! ◆ conj *(devant « il » ou « ils » s')* **1.** [exprimant une condition] if / *si tu veux, on y va* we'll go if you want / *je ne lui dirai que si tu es d'accord* I'll tell him only if you agree, I won't tell him unless you agree / *avez-vous des enfants ? si oui, remplissez le cadre ci-dessous* do you have any children? if yes, fill in the box below **2.** [exprimant une hypothèse] if / *si tu venais de bonne heure, on pourrait finir avant midi* if you came early we would be able to finish before midday / *s'il m'arrivait quelque chose, prévenez John* should anything happen to me ou if anything should happen to me, call John **3.** [exprimant une éventualité] what if / *et si tu te trompais ?* what if you were wrong? **4.** [exprimant une suggestion] what about / *et si on jouait aux cartes ?* what about playing cards? **5.** [exprimant un souhait, un regret] : *ah, si j'étais plus jeune !* I wish ou if only I were younger! **6.** [dans l'interrogation indirecte] if, whether / *dites-moi si vous venez* tell me if ou whether you're coming **7.** [introduisant une complétive] if, that / *ne sois pas surprise s'il a échoué* don't be surprised that ou if he failed **8.** [introduisant une explication] if / *si quelqu'un a le droit de se plaindre, c'est bien moi !* if anyone has reason to complain, it's me! **9.** [exprimant une concession, l'opposition] : *si son premier roman a été un succès, le second a été éreinté par la critique* though her first novel was a success, the second was slated by the critics **10.** [emploi exclamatif] : *tu penses s'il était déçu / heureux !* you can imagine how disappointed / happy he was! / *si je m'attendais à te voir ici !* well, I (certainly) didn't expect to meet you here ou fancy meeting you here! ◆◆ **si bien que** loc conj de telle sorte que] so / *il ne sait pas lire une carte, si bien qu'on s'est perdus* he can't read a map, and so we got lost. ◆◆ **si ce n'est** loc prép **1.** [pour rectifier] if not / *ça a duré une bonne heure, si ce n'est deux* it lasted at least an hour, if not two **2.** [excepté] apart from, except / *tout vous convient ? — oui, si ce n'est le prix* is everything to your satisfaction? — yes, apart from ou except the price. ◆◆ **si ce n'est que** loc conj apart from the fact that, except (for the fact) that / *il n'a pas de régime, si ce n'est qu'il ne doit pas fumer* he has no special diet, except that he mustn't smoke. ◆◆ **si tant est que** loc conj provided that.

siamois, e [sjamwa, az] adj MÉD Siamese ▶ **frères siamois** (male) Siamese twins ▶ **sœurs siamoises** (female) Siamese twins. ◆◆ **siamois** nm ZOOL Siamese (cat).

Sibérie [sibeʀi] npr f ▶ **(la) Sibérie** Siberia.

sibérien, enne [sibeʀjɛ̃, ɛn] adj Siberian.
❖ **Sibérien, enne** nm, f Siberian.

sibyllin, e [sibilɛ̃, in] adj *litt* [mystérieux] enigmatic, cryptic.

sic [sik] adv sic.

SICAV, Sicav [sikav] (abr de **société d'investissement à capital variable**) nf **1.** [société] open-ended investment trust ; ≃ unit trust 🇬🇧 ; ≃ mutual fund 🇺🇸 ▸ **SICAV monétaire** money market fund **2.** [action] *share in an open-ended investment trust.*

Sicile [sisil] npr f ▸ **(la) Sicile** Sicily.

sicilien, enne [sisiljɛ̃, ɛn] adj Sicilian.
❖ **Sicilien, enne** nm, f Sicilian.

SIDA, Sida [sida] (abr de **syndrome d'immuno-déficience acquise**) nm AIDS, Aids.

side-car [sidkaʀ, sajdkaʀ] (*pl* **side-cars**) nm **1.** [habitacle] sidecar **2.** [moto] motorbike and sidecar.

sidérant, e [sideʀɑ̃, ɑ̃t] adj *fam* staggering, amazing, stunning.

sidérer [18] [sideʀe] vt *fam* [abasourdir] to stagger / *j'étais sidéré d'apprendre cela* I was staggered to hear that, you could have knocked me down with a feather when I heard that.

📝 In reformed spelling (see p. 16-18), this verb is conjugated like *semer* : *il sidèrera, il sidèrerait.*

sidérurgie [sideʀyʀʒi] nf **1.** [technique] (iron and) steel metallurgy **2.** [industrie] (iron and) steel industry.

sidérurgique [sideʀyʀʒik] adj (iron and) steel *(modif).*

siècle [sjɛkl] nm **1.** [100 ans] century / *au début du siècle* at the turn of the century / *au IIᵉ siècle avant / après J.-C* in the 2nd century BC / AD **2.** [époque] age / *vivre avec son siècle* to keep up with the times, to be in tune with one's age / *ça fait des siècles que je ne suis pas allé à la patinoire fam* I haven't been to the ice-rink for ages / *l'affaire du siècle* the bargain of the century ▸ **le siècle des Lumières** the Enlightenment, the Age of Reason.

siège [sjɛʒ] nm **1.** [chaise] seat / *prenez donc un siège* (do) take a seat, do sit down ▸ **siège éjectable** AÉRON ejector 🇬🇧 ou ejection 🇺🇸 seat ▸ **siège auto bébé** baby car seat ▸ **siège auto enfant** child car seat **2.** POL seat ▸ **siège vacant** ou **à pourvoir** vacant seat **3.** [centre - gén] seat ; [-d'un parti] headquarters / *le siège du gouvernement* the seat of government ▸ **siège social** registered ou head office **4.** MIL siege / *faire le siège d'une ville* to lay siege to ou to besiege a town **5.** RELIG ▸ **siège épiscopal** (episcopal) see.

siéger [22] [sjeʒe] vi **1.** [député] to sit / *siéger au Parlement* to have a seat ou to sit in Parliament / *siéger à un comité* to sit on a committee **2.** [organisme] to be based in.

📝 In reformed spelling (see p. 16-18), this verb is conjugated like *semer* : *il siègera, elle siègerait.*

sien, sienne [sjɛ̃, sjɛn] (*mpl* **siens** [sjɛ̃], *fpl* **siennes** [sjɛn]) adj poss : *il a fait sienne cette maxime* sout he made this maxim his own. ❖ **le sien, la sienne** (*mpl* **les siens**, *fpl* **les siennes**) pron poss his *m*, hers *f* ; [en se référant à un objet, un animal] its / *elle est partie avec une valise qui n'était pas la sienne* she left with a suitcase that wasn't hers ou that didn't belong to her ; *(emploi nominal)* ▸ **les siens** one's family and friends ▸ **y mettre du sien a)** [faire un effort] to make an effort **b)** [être compréhensif] to be understanding ▸ **faire des siennes** *fam*: *Jacques a encore fait des siennes* Jacques has (gone and) done it again / *ma voiture ne cesse de faire des siennes !* my car's always playing up!

sieste [sjɛst] nf [repos] (afternoon) nap ou rest / *faire la sieste* to have ou to take a nap (in the afternoon).

sifflant, e [siflɑ̃, ɑ̃t] adj [respiration] hissing, whistling, wheezing. ❖ **sifflante** nf LING sibilant.

sifflement [sifləmɑ̃] nm **1.** [action - gén] whistling *(U)* ; [-d'un serpent] hiss, hissing **2.** [bruit] whistle ▸ **sifflement d'oreilles** ringing in the ears.

siffler [3] [sifle] ❖ vi **1.** [serpent] to hiss ; [oiseau] to whistle **2.** [personne] to whistle ; [gendarme, arbitre] to blow one's whistle **3.** [vent, train, bouilloire] to whistle / *les balles sifflaient de tous côtés* bullets were whistling all around us. ❖ vt **1.** [chanson] to whistle **2.** [chien, personne] to whistle for / *siffler les filles* to whistle at girls **3.** [suj : gendarme] to blow one's whistle at ; [suj : arbitre] to whistle for / *siffler la mi-temps* to blow the half-time whistle, to whistle for half-time **4.** [orateur, pièce] to hiss, to boo, to catcall **5.** *fam* [boire] to swill down *(sép)*, to swig, to knock back *(sép).*

sifflet [siflɛ] nm [instrument] whistle / *donner un coup de sifflet* to (blow the) whistle. ❖ **sifflets** nmpl [huées] hisses, catcalls / *quitter la scène sous les sifflets* to be booed off the stage.

siffloter [3] [siflɔte] ❖ vt ▸ **siffloter qqch a)** [doucement] to whistle sthg to o.s. **b)** [gaiement] to whistle sthg happily. ❖ vi [doucement] to whistle to o.s. ; [gaiement] to whistle away happily.

sigle [sigl] nm acronym, initials.

signal, aux [siɲal, o] nm **1.** [signe] signal ▸ **donner le signal du départ a)** to give the signal for departure **b)** SPORT to give the starting signal ▸ **envoyer un signal de détresse** to send out a distress signal ou an SOS **2.** [dispositif] signal ▸ **signal d'alarme / d'incendie** alarm / fire signal ▸ **actionner le signal d'alarme** to pull the alarm cord ▸ **signal sonore / lumineux** sound / light signal.

signalement [siɲalmɑ̃] nm description, particulars / *donner le signalement de son agresseur* to describe one's attacker.

signaler [3] [siɲale] vt **1.** [faire remarquer - faute, détail] to point out *(sép)*, to indicate, to draw attention to ; [-événement important] to draw attention to ; [-accident, cambriolage] to report ; [-changement d'adresse] to notify / *je l'ai signalé au propriétaire* I told the owner ▸ **rien à signaler** nothing to report / *permettez-moi de vous signaler qu'il est interdit de...* allow me to draw your attention to the fact that ou to point out that it's forbidden to... / *il est déjà 11 h, je te signale !* for your information, it's already 11 o'clock! **2.** [suj : drapeau, sonnerie] to signal ; [suj : panneau indicateur] to signpost, to point to *(insép)* / *il n'a pas signalé qu'il tournait* he didn't signal ou indicate that he was turning **3.** [dénoter] to indicate, to be the sign of / *c'est le symptôme qui nous signale la présence du virus* this symptom tells us that the virus is present. ❖ **se signaler** à vp + prép ▸ **se signaler à l'attention de qqn** to draw sb's attention to o.s. ❖ **se signaler par** vp + prép : *elle se signale surtout par sa bonne volonté* what sets her apart is her willingness to cooperate.

signalétique [siɲaletik] adj [plaque] descriptive, identification *(modif).*

signalisation [siɲalizasjɔ̃] nf **1.** [matériel] ▸ **signalisation aérienne** markings and beacons ▸ **signalisation routière a)** [sur la chaussée] (road) markings **b)** [panneaux] roadsigns **2.** RAIL signals ▸ **signalisation automatique** automatic signalling.

signaliser [3] [siɲalize] vt [route] to provide with roadsigns and markings ; [voie ferrée] to equip with signals ; [piste d'aéroport] to provide with markings and beacons ▸ **c'est bien / mal signalisé** [route] it's been well / badly signposted.

signataire [siɲatɛʀ] ❖ adj signatory. ❖ nmf signatory.

signature [siɲatyʀ] nf **1.** [signe] signature **2.** [marque distinctive] signature / *cet attentat à la bombe porte leur* *signature* this bomb attack bears their mark ou imprint **3.** [acte] signing / *vous serez payé à la signature du contrat* you'll be paid once the contract has been signed.

signe [siɲ] nm **1.** [geste] sign, gesture / *parler par signes* to communicate by sign language ou signs ▶ **faire un signe à qqn** to signal to sb ▶ **faire un signe de tête à qqn a)** [affirmatif] to nod to sb **b)** [négatif] to shake one's head at sb / *agiter la main en signe d'adieu* to wave goodbye ▶ **faire signe à qqn** to signal to sb / *il m'a fait signe d'entrer* he beckoned me in / *fais-lui signe de se taire* signal (to) him to be quiet ▶ **faire signe que oui** to nod (in agreement) ▶ **faire signe que non a)** [de la tête] to shake one's head (in refusal) **b)** [du doigt] to wave one's finger in refusal / *quand vous serez à Paris, faites-moi signe* fig when you're in Paris, let me know ▶ **signe de la croix** RELIG sign of the cross **2.** [indication] sign ▶ *c'est signe de*: *c'est signe de pluie / de beau temps* it's a sign of rain / of good weather ▶ *c'est signe que...* it's a sign that... ▶ *c'est bon signe* it's a good sign, it augurs well *sout* ▶ *c'est mauvais signe* it's a bad sign, it's ominous ▶ *(un) signe de*: *il n'y a aucun signe d'amélioration* there's no sign of (any) improvement ▶ **il n'a pas donné signe de vie depuis janvier** there's been no sign of him since January ▶ **la voiture donne des signes de fatigue** the car is beginning to show its age ▶ **signe annonciateur** ou **avant-coureur** ou **précurseur** forerunner, portent *litt* ▶ **signe prémonitoire** premonitory sign ▶ **signes extérieurs de richesse** DR outward signs of wealth **3.** [marque] mark ▶ **signes particuliers** ou **distinctifs** ADMIN distinguishing marks, special peculiarities / **'signes particuliers : néant'** 'distinguishing marks: none' **4.** LING, MATH, MÉD & MUS sign / *signe d'égalité* ou *d'équivalence* equals sign / *le signe moins / plus* the minus / plus sign **5.** IMPR ▶ **signe de ponctuation** punctuation mark **6.** ASTROL ▶ **signe (du zodiaque)** sign (of the zodiac). ◆ **en signe de** loc prép as a sign ou mark of / *mettre un brassard en signe de deuil* to wear an armband as a sign of mourning.

signer [3] [siɲe] vt **1.** [chèque, formulaire, lettre] to sign ; [pétition] to sign, to put one's name to / **'signer ici'** '(please) sign here' **2.** [laisser sa marque personnelle] to sign, to put one's signature to ▶ *c'est signé* ! it's easy to guess who did that! **3.** [officialiser - contrat, traité] to sign **4.** [être l'auteur de - argenterie] to hallmark ; [- pièce, film] to be the author of ; [- tableau] to sign ; [- ligne de vêtements] to be the creator of / *elle a signé les meilleures chansons de l'époque* she wrote all the best songs of that era. ◆ **se signer** vpi to cross o.s., to make the sign of the cross.

signet [siɲe] nm [d'un livre] bookmark ; INTERNET ▶ **mettre un signet sur** to bookmark.

significatif, ive [siɲifikatif, iv] adj **1.** [riche de sens - remarque, geste, symbole] significant ; [- regard] significant, meaningful / *de façon significative* significantly **2.** [important - écart, différence, changement] significant.

signification [siɲifikasjɔ̃] nf **1.** [sens - d'un terme, d'une phrase, d'un symbole] meaning, signification *sout* ; [- d'une action] meaning **2.** [importance - d'un événement, d'une déclaration] import, significance.

signifier [9] [siɲifje] vt **1.** [avoir tel sens - suj : mot, symbole] to mean, to signify **2.** [indiquer - suj : mimique, geste, acte] to mean / *de telles menaces ne signifient rien de sa part* such threats mean nothing coming from him ; [pour exprimer l'irritation] : *que signifie ceci ?* what's the meaning of this? **3.** [être le signe avant-coureur de] to mean, to betoken *sout* / *cela signifierait sa ruine* that would spell ruin for her **4.** *sout* [notifier] to notify ▶ **signifier ses intentions à qqn** to make one's intentions known ou to state

one's intentions to sb ▶ **signifier son congé à qqn** to give sb notice of dismissal *sout*, to give sb his / her notice **5.** DR [jugement] to notify.

silence [silɑ̃s] nm **1.** [absence de bruit] silence ▶ **un peu de silence, s'il vous plaît !** a) [avant un discours] (be) quiet please! b) [dans une bibliothèque, une salle d'étude] quiet ou silence, please! / *à son arrivée, tout le monde fit silence* there was a hush ou everyone fell silent when she arrived ▶ **garder le silence** to keep silent ou quiet ▶ **faire** ou **obtenir le silence** to make everyone keep quiet ▶ **silence on tourne !** CINÉ quiet on the set! / *il régnait un silence de mort* it was as quiet ou silent as the grave ▶ **silence radio** radio silence **2.** [secret] ▶ **garder le silence sur qqch** to keep quiet about sthg ▶ **imposer le silence à qqn** to shut sb up ▶ **passer qqch sous silence** to pass over sthg in silence, to keep quiet about sthg **3.** [pause] silence ; [dans la conversation] : *son récit était entrecoupé de nombreux silences* his story was interrupted by numerous pauses. ◆ **en silence** loc adv [se regarder] in silence, silently ; [se déplacer] silently, noiselessly ; [souffrir] in silence, uncomplainingly.

silencieusement [silɑ̃sjøzmɑ̃] adv [se regarder] silently, in silence ; [se déplacer] in silence, noiselessly ; [souffrir] in silence, uncomplainingly.

silencieux, euse [silɑ̃sjø, øz] adj **1.** [où règne le calme - trajet, repas, salle] quiet, silent **2.** [qui ne fait pas de bruit - pendule, voiture] quiet, noiseless ; [- mouvement] noiseless **3.** [qui ne parle pas] silent, quiet ; [taciturne] quiet, silent, uncommunicative *péj*. ◆ **silencieux** nm **1.** ARM silencer **2.** AUTO silencer 🇬🇧, muffler 🇺🇸.

silex [silɛks] nm **1.** GÉOL flint, flintstone **2.** ARCHÉOL flint, flint tool.

silhouette [silwɛt] nf **1.** [ligne générale - du corps] figure ; [- d'un véhicule] lines / *elle a une jolie silhouette* she's got a nice ou good figure **2.** [contours] silhouette, outline ; [forme indistincte] (vague) form / *leurs silhouettes se détachaient sur le soleil couchant* they were silhouetted against the sunset.

silice [silis] nf silica.

silicone [silikon] nf silicone.

sillage [sijaʒ] nm **1.** NAUT [trace] wake ; [remous] wash **2.** [d'une personne, d'un véhicule] wake ▶ **marcher dans le sillage de qqn** pr & fig to follow in sb's footsteps ou wake **3.** AÉRON [trace] (vapour) trail ; [remous] wake.

sillon [sijɔ̃] nm **1.** AGR [de gros labours] furrow ; [petite rigole] drill **2.** [d'un disque] groove.

sillonner [3] [sijɔne] vt **1.** [parcourir - suj : canaux, voies] to cross, to criss-cross / *j'ai sillonné la Bretagne* I've visited every corner of ou I've travelled the length and breadth of Brittany / *il sillonnait les mers depuis 20 ans* he'd been ploughing the (ocean) waves for 20 years / *le pays est sillonné de rivières* the country is criss-crossed by rivers **2.** *sout* [marquer] to furrow, to groove / *son visage sillonné de rides* his furrowed ou deeply lined face.

silo [silo] nm AGR silo.

simagrées [simagre] nfpl ▶ **faire des simagrées** [minauder] to put on airs.

similaire [similɛʀ] adj similar.

similarité [similaʀite] nf *sout* similarity, likeness.

simili [simili] ◆ préf ▶ **simili marbre** imitation marble. ◆ nm [imitation] ▶ *c'est du simili* it's artificial ou an imitation.

similicuir [similikɥiʀ] nm imitation leather, Leatherette®.

similitude [similityd] nf [d'idées, de style] similarity, similitude *sout* ; [de personnes] similarity, likeness.

simple [sɛ̃pl] ◆ adj **1.** [facile - exercice, système] straightforward, simple, easy / *c'est très simple à utiliser* it's very easy ou simple to use ▶ **c'est simple comme bonjour** it's as easy as ABC ou as pie **2.** *(avant nom)* [avec une valeur restrictive] mere, simple / *c'est une simple question d'argent* it's simply ou only a matter of money / *pour la simple raison que...* for the simple reason that... / *vous aurez une démonstration gratuite sur simple appel* all you need do is (to) ou simply phone this number for a free demonstration / *ce n'est qu'une simple formalité* it's merely a ou it's a mere formality / *ce n'est qu'un simple employé de bureau* he's just an ordinary office worker **3.** [non raffiné - gens] unaffected, uncomplicated ; [-objets, nourriture, goûts] plain, simple ▶ **elle est apparue dans le plus simple appareil** she appeared in her birthday suit *hum* **4.** [ingénu] simple, simple-minded **5.** [non composé - mot, élément, fleur, fracture] simple ; [-chaînette, nœud] single. ◆ *nm* **1.** [proportion] : *les prix varient du simple au double* prices can double **2.** SPORT singles ▶ **simple messieurs / dames** men's / ladies' singles. ⬩ **simple d'esprit** ◆ *nm* simpleton, halfwit. ◆ *loc adj* : *il est un peu simple d'esprit* he's a bit simple.

simplement [sɛ̃pləmɑ̃] *adv* **1.** [seulement] simply, merely, just **2.** [sans apprêt - parler] simply ; [- s'habiller] simply, plainly / *elle nous a reçus très simplement* she received us simply ou without ceremony **3.** [clairement] : *expliquer qqch simplement* to explain sthg in simple ou straightforward terms.

simplet, ette [sɛ̃plɛ, ɛt] *adj* **1.** [personne - peu intelligente] simple, simple-minded ; [-ingénue] naïve **2.** [sans finesse - jugement, réponse, scénario] simplistic, black-and-white.

simplicité [sɛ̃plisite] *nf* **1.** [facilité] simplicity, straightforwardness / *l'opération est d'une grande simplicité* the operation is very straightforward **2.** [de vêtements, d'un décor, d'un repas] plainness, simplicity ▶ **avec simplicité** simply, plainly / *nous avons dîné en toute simplicité* we had a very simple dinner.

simplification [sɛ̃plifikasjɔ̃] *nf* [d'un système] simplification, simplifying.

simplifier [9] [sɛ̃plifje] *vt* [procédé] to simplify ; [explication] to simplify, to make simpler / *en simplifiant le texte à outrance* ou *à l'excès* by oversimplifying the text / *si tu me disais la vérité, cela simplifierait les choses* it would make things easier if you told me the truth.

simplissime [sɛ̃plisim] *adj* dead easy.

simpliste [sɛ̃plist] *adj* simplistic, oversimple.

simulacre [simylakʀ] *nm* [pour tromper] ▶ **un simulacre de négociations** mock ou sham negotiations / *ce n'était qu'un simulacre de procès* it was a mockery of a trial.

simulateur, trice [simylatœʀ, tʀis] *nm, f* **1.** [imitateur] simulator **2.** [faux malade] malingerer. ⬩ **simulateur** *nm* AÉRON, INFORM & MIL simulator ▶ **simulateur de vol** flight simulator.

simulation [simylasjɔ̃] *nf* **1.** [d'un sentiment] feigning, faking, simulation ; [d'une maladie] malingering **2.** MIL & TECHNOL simulation.

simuler [3] [simyle] *vt* [feindre - douleur, ivresse, folie] to feign ▶ **simuler la maladie a)** [appelé, employé] to malinger **b)** [enfant] to pretend to be ill.

simultané, e [simyltane] *adj* simultaneous.

simultanéité [simyltaneite] *nf* simultaneity, simultaneousness.

simultanément [simyltanemɑ̃] *adv* simultaneously.

sincère [sɛ̃sɛʀ] *adj* **1.** [amitié, chagrin, remords] sincere, genuine, true ; [personne] sincere, genuine ; [réponse] honest, sincere **2.** [dans les formules de politesse] : *nos vœux les plus sincères* our very best wishes / *je vous présente mes*

sincères condoléances please accept my sincere ou heartfelt condolences / *veuillez agréer mes sincères salutations* yours sincerely, yours truly 🇺🇸.

sincèrement [sɛ̃sɛʀmɑ̃] *adv* **1.** [franchement] sincerely, genuinely, truly **2.** *(en tête de phrase)* [réellement] honestly, frankly / *sincèrement, ça ne valait pas le coup* to tell you the truth, it wasn't worth it.

sincérité [sɛ̃seʀite] *nf* [franchise] sincerity / *en toute sincérité* in all sincerity, to be quite honest.

sinécure [sinekyʀ] *nf* sinecure / *ce n'est pas une sinécure fam* it's no picnic.

sine qua non [sinekwanɔn] *loc adj inv* ▶ **condition sine qua non** essential condition.

Singapour [sɛ̃gapuʀ] *npr* Singapore ▶ **à Singapour** in Singapore.

singe [sɛ̃ʒ] *nm* ZOOL [à longue queue] monkey ; [sans queue] ape ▶ **les grands singes** the (great) apes ▶ **faire le singe a)** [faire des grimaces] to make faces **b)** [faire des pitreries] to clown ou to monkey around.

singer [17] [sɛ̃ʒe] *vt* [personne] to ape, to mimic.

singeries [sɛ̃ʒʀi] *nfpl* [tours et grimaces] clowning ; [d'un clown] antics ; [-manières affectées] affectedness, airs and graces ▶ **faire des singeries** to clown ou to monkey around.

singulariser [3] [sɛ̃gylaʀize] ⬩ **se singulariser** *vp (emploi réfléchi)* [se faire remarquer] to make o.s. conspicuous.

singularité [sɛ̃gylaʀite] *nf* **1.** [étrangeté - d'un comportement, d'idées, d'une tenue] oddness, strangeness **2.** [trait distinctif - d'une personne] peculiarity ; [- d'un système] distinctive feature, peculiarity / *la boîte présentait cette singularité de s'ouvrir par l'arrière* the box was unusual in that it opened at the back.

singulier, ère [sɛ̃gylje, ɛʀ] *adj* **1.** [comportement, idées] odd, strange, singular *sout* **2.** [courage, beauté] remarkable, rare, unique **3.** LING singular. ⬩ **singulier** *nm* LING singular.

singulièrement [sɛ̃gyljɛʀmɑ̃] *adv* **1.** [beaucoup] very much **2.** [bizarrement] oddly, in a strange ou peculiar way.

sinistre [sinistʀ] ◆ *adj* **1.** [inquiétant - lieu, bruit] sinister ; [- personnage] sinister, evil-looking **2.** [triste - personne, soirée] dismal **3.** *(avant nom)* [en intensif] : *c'est un sinistre imbécile / une sinistre canaille* he's a total idiot / crook. ◆ *nm* **1.** [incendie] fire, blaze ; [inondation, séisme] disaster **2.** DR [incendie] fire ; [accident de la circulation] accident ▶ **déclarer un sinistre** to put in a claim.

sinistré, e [sinistʀe] ◆ *adj* [bâtiment, village, quartier - gén] damaged, stricken ; [- brûlé] burnt-out ; [- bombardé] bombed-out ; [- inondé] flooded / *la ville est sinistrée* [après un tremblement de terre] the town has been devastated by the earthquake ▶ **les personnes sinistrées a)** [après une catastrophe] the disaster victims **b)** [après des inondations] the flood victims ▶ **région** ou **zone (déclarée) sinistrée** ADMIN disaster area. ◆ *nm, f* disaster victim.

sinon [sinɔ̃] *conj* **1.** [sans cela] otherwise, or else / *je ne peux pas me joindre à vous, sinon je l'aurais fait avec plaisir* I can't join you, otherwise I would have come with pleasure / *j'essaierai d'être à l'heure, sinon partez sans moi* I'll try to be on time, but if I'm not go without me **2.** [si ce n'est] if not / *elle était, sinon jolie, du moins gracieuse* she was, if not pretty, at least graceful **3.** [excepté] except, other than / *que faire, sinon attendre ?* what can we do other than ou except wait?

sinueux, euse [sinɥø, øz] *adj* **1.** [chemin] winding, sinuous ; [fleuve] winding, meandering **2.** [pensée] convoluted, tortuous.

sinuosité [sinyozite] nf **1.** [fait d'être courbé -chemin] winding ; [-rivière] winding, meandering **2.** [courbe -d'un chemin] curve, bend ; [-d'une rivière] meander.

sinus [sinys] nm **1.** ANAT sinus **2.** MATH sine.

sinusite [sinyzit] nf sinusitis.

siphon [sifɔ̃] nm **1.** MÉD, PHYS & ZOOL siphon **2.** [d'appareils sanitaires] trap, U-bend.

siphonné, e [sifɔne] adj *fam* [fou] batty, crackers.

sirène [siʀɛn] nf **1.** [des pompiers] fire siren ; [d'une voiture de police, d'une ambulance, d'une usine] siren ; [d'un navire] siren, (fog) horn **2.** MYTH siren.

sirop [siʀo] nm **1.** CULIN [concentré] syrup, cordial ; [dilué] (fruit) cordial ou drink ▶ **sirop d'érable** maple syrup ▶ **sirop de fraise / de menthe** strawberry / mint cordial ▶ **sirop d'orgeat** barley water **2.** PHARM syrup ▶ **sirop pour** ou **contre la toux** cough mixture.

siroter [3] [siʀɔte] vt to sip, to take sips of.

sisal, als [sizal] nm sisal.

sismique [sismik] adj seismic.

site [sit] nm **1.** [panorama] beauty spot / *il y a plusieurs sites touristiques par ici* there are several tourist spots ou places of interest for tourists round here ▶ **site classé** ADMIN conservation area ; ≃ National Trust area 🇬🇧 ▶ **site historique** historical site **2.** [environnement] setting **3.** [emplacement] site, siting ▶ **site archéologique a)** [gén] archeological site **b)** [en cours d'excavation] archeological dig ▶ **site de lancement** launch area **4.** INTERNET site ▶ **site communautaire** community site ▶ **site de rencontre(s)** dating site ▶ **site Web** ou **Internet** website ▶ **site FTP** FTP site.

sitôt [sito] adv [avec une participiale] : *sitôt levé, je me mettais au travail* no sooner was I up than I'd start work, I'd start work as soon as I was up ▶ **sitôt dit, sitôt fait** no sooner said than done. ◆ **pas de sitôt** loc adv : *on ne se reverra pas de sitôt* we won't be seeing each other again for a while / *je n'y retournerai pas de sitôt !* I won't go back there ou you won't catch me going back there in a hurry!

situation [sityasjɔ̃] nf **1.** [circonstances] situation / *se trouver dans une situation délicate* to find o.s. in an awkward situation ou position / *c'est l'homme de la situation* he's the right man for the job / *étrangers en situation irrégulière* foreign whose papers are not in order ▶ **situation de famille** ADMIN marital status **2.** [emploi rémunéré] job / *elle s'est fait une belle situation* she worked her way up to a very good position **3.** [lieu] situation, position, location. ◆ **en situation de** loc prép ▶ **être en situation de faire qqch** to be in a position to do sthg.

situé, e [sitye] adj : *maison bien / mal située* well- / poorly-situated house.

situer [7] [sitye] vt **1.** [dans l'espace, le temps -gén] to place ; [-roman, film, etc.] to set **2.** [classer] to place, to situate **3.** *fam* [cerner -personne] to define / *on a du mal à la situer* it's difficult to know what makes her tick. ◆ **se situer** ◆ vp *(emploi réfléchi)* ▶ **se situer par rapport à qqn / qqch** to place o.s. in relation to sb / sthg. ◆ vpi [gén] to be situated ou located ; [scène, action] to take place / *où se situe-t-elle dans le mouvement expressionniste ?* where would you place her in the expressionist movement? / *l'augmentation se situera aux alentours de 3 %* the increase will be in the region of 3%.

six [sis] *(devant consonne ou « h » aspiré* [si]*, devant voyelle ou « h » muet* [siz]*)* ◆ dét **1.** six / *le six janvier* (on) the sixth of January 🇬🇧, (on) January sixth 🇺🇸 / *daté du six septembre* dated the sixth of September 🇬🇧 ou September sixth 🇺🇸 **2.** [dans des séries] : *tout le chapitre six* all of chapter six. ◆ nm six. **Voir aussi cinq.**

sixième [sizjem] ◆ adj num sixth. ◆ nmf sixth. ◆ nm **1.** [partie] sixth **2.** [étage] sixth floor 🇬🇧, seventh floor 🇺🇸. ◆ nf ÉDUC year seven 🇬🇧, sixth grade 🇺🇸 / *entrer en sixième* to start attending "collège".

Skaï® [skaj] nm Skaï®, Leatherette®.

skate [skɛt], **skateboard** [skɛtbɔʀd] nm **1.** [activité] skateboarding **2.** [planche] skateboard / *faire du skate* to skateboard.

skater [skɛtœʀ] nm = **skateur**.

skateur, euse [skɛtœʀ, øz] nm, f skateboarder.

sketch [skɛtʃ] *(pl* **sketchs** ou **sketches**) nm CINÉ, THÉÂTRE & TV sketch.

ski [ski] nm **1.** LOISIRS & SPORT [activité] skiing ▶ **faire du ski** to go skiing ▶ **ski alpin / nordique** Alpine / Nordic skiing ▶ **ski acrobatique** hot-dogging ▶ **ski de fond** cross-country skiing ▶ **ski nautique** water-skiing ▶ **ski de randonnée** ski-touring **2.** [matériel] ski. ◆ **de ski** loc adj [chaussures, lunettes] ski *(modif)* ; [vacances, séjour] skiing *(modif)*.

skiable [skjabl] adj skiable / *la station a un grand domaine skiable* the resort has many ski slopes.

skicross [skikʀɔs] nm skicross.

skier [10] [skje] vi to ski.

skieur, euse [skjœʀ, øz] nm, f skier.

skinhead [skinɛd] nm skinhead.

skipper [skipœʀ] nm NAUT skipper.

skippeur, euse [skipœʀ, øz] nm, f = **skipper**.

sky-surfing [skajsœʀfiŋ] *(pl* **sky-surfings**), **sky-surf** *(pl* **sky-surfs**) nm SPORT sky-surfing.

slalom [slalɔm] nm **1.** SPORT [course] slalom ▶ **slalom spécial / géant** special / giant slalom **2.** *fam* [zigzags] zigzagging.

slalomer [3] [slalɔme] vi **1.** SPORT to slalom **2.** *fam* [zigzaguer] ▶ **slalomer entre** to zigzag ou to weave in and out of.

slalomeur, euse [slalɔmœʀ, øz] nm, f slalom skier.

slam [slam] nm [poésie] slam.

slamer [slame] vi to slam.

slameur, euse [slamœʀ, øz] nm, f slammer.

slave [slav] adj Slavonic, Slavic 🇺🇸. ◆ **Slave** nmf Slav ▶ **les Slaves** the Slavs. ◆ **slave** nm LING Slavonic, Slavic.

slim [slim] nm [pantalon] slim-fit ou skinny jeans.

slip [slip] nm **1.** VÊT [d'homme] (pair of) underpants, shorts 🇺🇸 ; [de femme] briefs 🇬🇧, panties, knickers ▶ **slip de bain** [d'homme] bathing ou swimming trunks **2.** NAUT slip, slipway.

sloche, slush [slɔʃ] nf 🇶🇨 slush.

slogan [slɔgã] nm slogan.

slovaque [slɔvak] adj Slovak, Slovakian. ◆ **Slovaque** nmf Slovak, Slovakian.

Slovaquie [slɔvaki] npr f ▶ **la Slovaquie** Slovakia.

slovène [slɔvɛn] adj Slovene, Slovenian. ◆ **Slovène** nmf Slovene, Slovenian. ◆ **slovène** nm LING Slovene.

Slovénie [slɔveni] npr f ▶ **la Slovénie** Slovenia.

slow [slo] nm [gén] slow number ▶ **danser un slow avec qqn** to dance (to) a slow number with sb.

slt SMS abr écrite de **salut**.

smartphone [smaʀtfɔn] nm smartphone.

smash [smaʃ] *(pl* **smashs** ou **smashes**) nm SPORT smash / *faire un smash* to smash / to smash up.

smasher [3] [smaʃe] vi & vt SPORT to smash.

SME (abr de Système monétaire européen) npr m EMS.

SMIC, Smic [smik] (abr de **salaire minimum inter-professionnel de croissance**) nm *index-linked guaranteed minimum wage.*

smicard, e [smikaʀ, aʀd] nm, f *fam* minimum-wage earner.

smoking [smɔkiŋ] nm dinner suit 🇬🇧, tuxedo 🇺🇸 ▸ **veste de smoking** dinner jacket, tuxedo 🇺🇸.

SMS [ɛsɛmɛs] (abr de **short message service**) nm [service] SMS ; [message] text message.

snack [snak] nm = snack-bar.

snack-bar (*pl* **snack-bars**), **snackbar*** [snakbaʀ], **snack** [snak] nm snack bar, self-service restaurant, cafeteria.

SNCB (abr de **Société nationale des chemins de fer belges**) npr f *Belgian railways board.*

SNCF (abr de **Société nationale des chemins de fer français**) npr f *French railways board.*

sniffer [3] [snife] *tfam* vt [cocaïne] to snort.

snob [snɔb] ◆ adj snobbish, snobby. ◆ nmf snob.

snober [3] [snɔbe] vt [personne] to snub ; [chose] to turn one's nose up at.

snobinard, e [snɔbinaʀ, aʀd] *fam* ◆ adj snobbish, hoity-toity. ◆ nm, f snob.

snobisme [snɔbism] nm snobbery, snobbishness.

snowboard [snobɔʀd] nm [planche] snowboard ; [sport] snowboarding ▸ **faire du snowboard** to snowboard.

snowboarder [snobɔʀdœʀ] nm = snowboardeur.

snowboardeur, euse [snobɔʀdœʀ, øz] nm, f snowboarder.

soap opera [sopɔpeʀa] (*pl* **soap operas**), **soap** [sop] (*pl* **soaps**) nm TV soap opera.

sobre [sɔbʀ] adj **1.** [personne - tempérante] abstemious ; [- non ivre] sober **2.** [modéré, discret - architecture, tenue, style] sober, restrained ; [- vêtement] simple.

sobrement [sɔbʀəmɑ̃] adv **1.** [avec modération] temperately, soberly **2.** [avec discrétion, retenue] soberly.

sobriété [sɔbʀijete] nf **1.** [tempérance] soberness, temperance **2.** [discrétion, retenue] soberness **3.** [dépouillement - d'un style, d'un décor] bearness.

sobriquet [sɔbʀikɛ] nm nickname.

sociable [sɔsjabl] adj [individu, tempérament] sociable, gregarious.

social, e, aux [sɔsjal, o] adj **1.** [réformes, problèmes, ordre, politique] social **2.** ADMIN social, welfare *(modif)* ▸ **services sociaux** social services. ◆ **social** nm ▸ **le social** social issues ou matters.

social-démocrate [sɔsjaldemɔkʀat] (*pl* **sociaux-démocrates** [sɔsjodemɔkʀat]) ◆ adj social democratic. ◆ nmf [gén] social democrat ; [adhérent d'un parti] Social Democrat.

socialement [sɔsjalmɑ̃] adv socially.

socialiser [3] [sɔsjalize] vt PSYCHOL to socialize.

socialisme [sɔsjalism] nm socialism ▸ **socialisme d'État** State socialism.

socialiste [sɔsjalist] adj & nmf socialist.

sociétaire [sɔsjetɛʀ] nmf [d'une association] member ▸ **sociétaire de la Comédie-Française** actor co-opted as a *full member of the Comédie-Française.*

société [sɔsjete] nf **1.** SOCIOL ▸ **la société** society / *vivre en société* to live in society ▸ **la société de consommation** the consumer society **2.** [catégorie de gens] society ▸ **cela ne se fait pas dans la bonne société** it's not done in good company ou in the best society ▸ **la haute société** high society **3.** [association - de gens de lettres, de savants]

society ; [- de sportifs] club ▸ **société littéraire / savante** literary / learned society ▸ **société secrète** secret society ▸ **la Société protectrice des animaux** = SPA **4.** COMM, DR & ÉCON company, firm ▸ **société anonyme** (public) limited company ▸ **société à responsabilité limitée** ≃ limited liability company ▸ **Société nationale des chemins de fer français** = SNCF **5.** BANQUE ▸ **société financière / de crédit** finance / credit company.

société-écran [sɔsjeteekʀɑ̃] (*pl* **sociétés-écrans**) nf DR bogus company.

socioculturel, elle [sɔsjokyltyʀɛl] adj sociocultural.

socio-économique (*pl* **socio-économiques**), **socioéconomique*** [sɔsjoekɔnɔmik] adj socioeconomic.

socio-éducatif, ive (*mpl* **socio-éducatifs**, *fpl* **socio-éducatives**), **socioéducatif*, ive** [sɔsjoedykatif, iv] adj socioeducational.

sociologie [sɔsjɔlɔʒi] nf sociology.

sociologique [sɔsjɔlɔʒik] adj sociological.

sociologue [sɔsjɔlɔg] nmf sociologist.

socioprofessionnel, elle [sɔsjɔpʀɔfesjɔnɛl] adj socioprofessional.

socle [sɔkl] nm [d'une statue, d'une colonne] base, plinth ; [d'un objet décoratif, d'une lampe] base.

socquette [sɔkɛt] nf ankle sock, bobby sock 🇺🇸.

soda [sɔda] nm **1.** [boisson gazeuse] fizzy drink, soda 🇺🇸 / *soda à l'orange* orangeade, orange soda 🇺🇸 **2.** [eau de Seltz] soda (water) ▸ **whisky soda** whisky and soda.

sodium [sɔdjɔm] nm sodium.

sœur [sœʀ] nf **1.** [parente] sister ▸ **et ta sœur !** *tfam* mind your own (damn) business! **2.** RELIG sister, nun / *chez les sœurs* with the nuns, in a convent ▸ **sœur Thérèse** Sister Theresa.

sofa [sɔfa] nm sofa.

SOFRES, Sofres [sɔfʀɛs] (abr de **Société française d'enquêtes par sondages**) npr f *French market research company.*

softball [sɔftbol] nm SPORT softball.

software [sɔftwɛʀ] nm software.

soi [swa] pron pers **1.** [représentant un sujet indéterminé] oneself / *être content de soi* to be pleased with oneself / *il ne faut pas penser qu'à soi* one shouldn't think only of oneself / *ne pas regarder derrière soi* not to look back ▸ **prendre sur soi** to get a grip on oneself **2.** [représentant un sujet déterminé] : *on ne pouvait lui reprocher de ne penser qu'à soi* he couldn't be reproached for thinking only of himself **3.** EXPR en soi in itself, per se *sout* ▸ **cela va de soi** that goes without saying.

soi-disant [swadizɑ̃] ◆ adj inv **1.** [qu'on prétend tel - liberté, gratuité] so-called ; [- coupable, responsable] alleged **2.** [qui se prétend tel - aristocrate] self-styled ; [- ami, héritier, génie] so-called. ◆ adv *fam* [à ce qu'on prétend] supposedly / *tu étais soi-disant absent !* you were supposed to be out! / *elle est sortie, soi-disant pour acheter du fromage* she went out, ostensibly to get some cheese ou to get some cheese, she said. ◆ **soi-disant que** loc conj *fam* apparently / *soi-disant qu'il ne nous aurait pas vus !* he didn't see us, or so he said!

soie [swa] nf **1.** TEXT silk ▸ **soie grège / naturelle / sauvage** raw / natural / wild silk **2.** ZOOL [de sanglier, de chenille] bristle ; [de bivalves] byssus.

soierie [swaʀi] nf [étoffe] silk.

soif [swaf] nf **1.** [envie de boire] thirst ▸ **avoir soif** to be thirsty / *ça m'a donné soif* it made me thirsty **2.** fig : *soif de connaissances* thirst for knowledge.

soignant, e [swaɲɑ̃, ɑ̃t] adj caring ⧫ *le personnel soignant est en grève* the nursing staff are on strike.

soigné, e [swaɲe] adj **1.** [propre - apparence, personne] neat, tidy, well-groomed ; [- vêtements] neat ; [- ongles] well kept ; [- mains] well cared for ⧫ **peu soigné a)** [apparence, personne, tenue] untidy **b)** [coiffure] unkempt **2.** [fait avec soin - décoration] carefully done ; [- style] polished ; [- écriture, coiffure] neat, tidy ; [- travail] neat, careful ; [- dîner] carefully prepared ; [- jardin] neat, well-kept ⧫ **peu soigné a)** [jardin] badly kept **b)** [dîner] carelessly put together **c)** [écriture] untidy **d)** [travail] careless, shoddy.

soigner [3] [swaɲe] vt **1.** [malade] to treat, to nurse, to look after *(insép)* ; [maladie] to treat / *il ne veut pas se faire soigner* he refuses (any) treatment / *ils m'ont soigné aux antibiotiques* they treated me with antibiotics / *je n'arrive pas à soigner mon rhume* I can't get rid of my cold / *il a dû aller se faire soigner en Suisse* he had to go to Switzerland for treatment / *il faut te faire soigner !* *fam* you need (to get) your head examined! **2.** [être attentif à - apparence, tenue, présentation, prononciation] to take care ou trouble over ; [- écriture, style] to polish (up) ; [- image de marque] to take good care of, to nurse ; [- repas] to prepare carefully, to take trouble over (the preparation of). ❖ **se soigner** ◆ vp *(emploi réfléchi)* : *il se soigne à l'homéopathie* he relies on homeopathic treatment when he's ill. ◆ vp *(emploi passif)* to be susceptible to treatment / *ça se soigne bien* it can be easily treated.

soigneur [swaɲœR] nm [d'un boxeur] second ; [d'un cycliste] trainer ; [d'une équipe de football, de rugby] physiotherapist 🇬🇧, physical therapist 🇺🇸.

soigneusement [swaɲøzmɑ̃] adv [écrire, plier] neatly, carefully ; [rincer, laver] carefully.

soigneux, euse [swaɲø, øz] adj **1.** [propre et ordonné] tidy / *il n'est pas du tout soigneux dans son travail* he's quite untidy ou messy in his work / *tu n'es pas assez soigneux de tes habits* you're not careful enough with ou you don't take enough care of your clothes **2.** [consciencieux - employé] meticulous ; [- recherches, travail] careful, meticulous / *elle est très soigneuse dans ce qu'elle fait* she's very careful in what she does, she takes great care over her work **3.** ⧫ **soigneux de** [soucieux de] : *soigneux de sa réputation* mindful of his reputation.

soi-même [swamɛm] pron pers oneself.

soin [swɛ̃] nm **1.** [attention] care ⧫ **avoir** ou **prendre soin de qqch** to take care of sthg ⧫ **prendre soin de qqn** to look after ou to take care of sb ⧫ **avoir** ou **prendre soin de faire qqch** to take care to do ou to make a point of doing sthg ⧫ **avec soin** carefully, with care ⧫ **faire qqch sans soin** to do sthg carelessly **2.** [propreté] neatness ⧫ **avec soin** neatly, tidily / *être sans soin* to be untidy **3.** [responsabilité] task / *je te laisse le soin de la convaincre* I leave it (up) to you to convince her ⧫ **confier à qqn le soin de faire qqch** to entrust sb with the task of doing sthg. ❖ **soins** nmpl **1.** [de routine] care ; [médicaments] treatment ⧫ **premiers soins, soins d'urgence** first aid ⧫ **soins de beauté** beauty care ⧫ **soins dentaires** dental treatment ou care ⧫ **soins (médicaux)** medical care ou treatment ⧫ **soins du visage** skin care *(for the face)* **2.** [attention] care, attention ⧫ **confier qqn aux (bons) soins de qqn** to leave sb in the care of sb ⧫ **aux bons soins de** [dans le courrier] care of.

soir [swaR] nm **1.** [fin du jour] evening ; [début de la nuit] night **2.** [dans des expressions de temps] ⧫ **ce soir** tonight, this evening ⧫ **lundi soir** Monday evening ou night ⧫ **hier soir** yesterday evening, last night ⧫ **le 11 au soir** on the 11th in the evening, on the evening of the 11th ⧫ **le soir** in the evening, in the evenings / *tous les soirs, chaque soir* every evening / *vers 6 h du soir* around 6 (o'clock) in the evening, around 6 p.m. / *à 10 h du soir* at 10 (o'clock) at night, at 10 p.m. **3.** PRESSE ⧫ **Le Soir** *Belgian daily newspaper*.

❖ **du soir** loc adj **1.** [journal] evening *(modif)* ; [prière] night *(modif)* **2.** *fam* [personne] ⧫ **il est du soir** he's a night owl.

soirée [swaRe] nf **1.** [fin de la journée] evening ⧫ **bonne soirée !** have a nice evening!, enjoy your evening! **2.** [fête, réunion] party ⧫ **soirée dansante** (evening) dance **3.** CINÉ & THÉÂTRE evening performance.

soit [swa] ◆ conj **1.** [c'est-à-dire] that is to say **2.** [introduisant une hypothèse] ⧫ **soit une droite AB** let AB be a line, given a line AB. ◆ adv ⧫ **soit, j'accepte vos conditions** very well then, I accept your conditions. ❖ **soit que... ou que** loc corrélative either... or. ❖ **soit que..., soit que** loc corrélative either... or. ❖ **soit..., soit** loc corrélative either... or / *c'est soit l'un, soit l'autre* it's (either) one or the other.

soixantaine [swasɑ̃tɛn] nf ⧫ **une soixantaine** about sixty / *avoir la soixantaine* to be about sixty. Voir aussi **cinquantaine**.

soixante [swasɑ̃t] dét & nm inv sixty. Voir aussi **cinquante**.

soixante-dix [swasɑ̃tdis] dét & nm inv seventy. Voir aussi **cinquante**.

soixante-dixième [swasɑ̃tdizjɛm] adj num, nmf & nm seventieth. Voir aussi **cinquième**.

soixante-huitard, e [swasɑ̃tɥitaR, aRd] *fam* ◆ adj [réforme] brought about by the students' revolt of 1968 ; [tendance] anti-establishment. ◆ nm, f veteran of the 1968 students' revolt.

soixantième [swasɑ̃tjɛm] adj num, nmf & nm sixtieth. Voir aussi **cinquième**.

soja [sɔʒa] nm **1.** BOT soya **2.** CULIN ⧫ **graines de soja** soya beans 🇬🇧, soybeans 🇺🇸 ⧫ **germes de soja** bean sprouts.

sol¹ [sɔl] nm inv MUS G ; [chanté] sol, so, soh ; ⟶ **clé**. Voir aussi **fa**.

sol² [sɔl] nm **1.** AGR & HORT [terre] soil **2.** [surface - de la Terre] ground ; [- d'une planète] surface / *l'avion s'est écrasé au sol* the plane crashed **3.** [surface aménagée - à l'intérieur] floor **4.** *litt* [patrie] soil / *sur le sol américain* on American soil **5.** GÉOL soil, solum *spéc*. ❖ **au sol** loc adj **1.** SPORT [exercice] floor *(modif)* **2.** AÉRON [vitesse, ravitaillement] ground *(modif)*.

solage [sɔlaʒ] nm 🇶🇨 ARCHIT foundation.

solaire [sɔlɛR] ◆ adj **1.** [qui a trait au soleil] solar **2.** [qui utilise le soleil - capteur, four] solar ; [- habitat] solar, solar-heated **3.** [qui protège du soleil] sun *(modif)*. ◆ nm ⧫ **le solaire** solar energy.

solarium [sɔlaRjɔm] nm solarium.

soldat [sɔlda] nm **1.** MIL soldier, serviceman ⧫ **simple soldat** ou **soldat de deuxième classe a)** [armée de terre] private **b)** [armée de l'air] aircraftman 🇬🇧, airman basic 🇺🇸 **2.** JEUX ⧫ **(petits) soldats de plomb** tin ou lead ou toy soldiers ⧫ **jouer aux petits soldats** to play with toy soldiers.

solde¹ [sɔld] nf **1.** MIL pay **2.** 🇦🇫 [salaire] salary, wages. ❖ **à la solde de** loc prép *péj* in the pay of.

solde² [sɔld] nm **1.** FIN [d'un compte] (bank) balance ; [à payer] outstanding balance ⧫ **solde créditeur** credit balance, balance in hand ⧫ **solde débiteur** debit balance, balance owed ⧫ **pour solde de tout compte** in (full) settlement **2.** COMM [vente] sale, sales, clearance sale ; [marchandise] sale item ou article ⧫ **acheter** ou **avoir qqch en solde** to buy sthg in the sales 🇬🇧 ou on sale 🇺🇸 ou at sale price / *le bonnet était en solde* the hat was reduced. ❖ **soldes** nmpl sale, sales.

solder [3] [sɔlde] vt **1.** COMM to sell (off) at sale price ou at a reduced price / *toutes nos chemises sont soldées* all our shirts are at a reduced ou at sale price **2.** [dette] to settle **3.** BANQUE [compte] to close. ❖ **se solder par**

vp + prép **1.** [se terminer par] to result in / **se solder par un échec** to result in failure, to come to nothing **2.** COMM, ÉCON & FIN ▶ **se solder par un excédent / un déficit de** to show a surplus / a deficit of.

solderie [sɔldəʀi] nf discount store.

soldeur, euse [sɔldœʀ, øz] nm, f discount trader.

sole [sɔl] nf **1.** CULIN & ZOOL sole ▶ **sole de Douvres** ᴑᴜᴇ́ʙᴇᴄ Dover sole **2.** ᴑᴜᴇ́ʙᴇᴄ [plie] plaice.

soleil [sɔlɛj] nm **1.** [étoile qui éclaire la Terre] ▶ **le Soleil** the Sun ▶ **le soleil levant / couchant** the rising / setting sun **2.** [chaleur] sun, sunshine ; [clarté] sun, sunlight, sunshine ▶ **au soleil** in the sun / **tu es en plein soleil** you're right in the sun **3.** BOT sunflower.

solennel, elle [sɔlanɛl] adj **1.** [obsèques, honneurs, silence] solemn **2.** [déclaration, occasion, personne, ton] solemn, formal.

solennellement [sɔlanɛlmɑ̃] adv **1.** [en grande pompe] formally, ceremoniously **2.** [cérémonieusement] solemnly, in a solemn voice.

Solex® [sɔlɛks] nm ≃ moped.

solfège [sɔlfɛʒ] nm [notation] musical notation ; [déchiffrage] sight-reading.

solidaire [sɔlidɛʀ] adj **1.** [personnes] ▶ **être solidaires a)** [les uns des autres] to stand ou to stick together **b)** [l'un de l'autre] to show solidarity with each other / **nous sommes solidaires de nos camarades** we support ou stand by our comrades **2.** [reliés - processus, pièces mécaniques] interdependent ▶ **être solidaire de** to interact with.

solidarité [sɔlidaʀite] nf [entre personnes] solidarity ▶ **par solidarité avec** out of a fellow-feeling for, in order to show solidarity with.

solide [sɔlid] ◆ adj **1.** [résistant - meubles, matériel] solid, sturdy, strong ; [- papier] tough, strong ; [- vêtements] hard-wearing ; [- bâtiment] solid, strong ; [- verrou, nœud] secure ▶ **peu solide** [chaise, pont] rickety **2.** [établi, stable - formation, culture, technique] sound ; [- entreprise] well-established ; [- institution, argument] solid, sound ; [- professionnalisme, réputation] solid ; [- bases] sound, firm ; [- amitié] firm, enduring ; [- foi] firm, staunch ; [- principes, qualités] staunch, sound, sterling (modif) ; [- monnaie] strong, firm / **elle s'est entourée d'une solide équipe de chercheurs** she's surrounded herself with a reliable ou strong research team **3.** [robuste - personne, membre] sturdy, robust ; [- santé] sound / **avoir une solide constitution** to have an iron constitution **4.** (avant nom) fam [substantiel] substantial, solid / **un solide coup de poing** a mighty punch ▶ **avoir un solide coup de fourchette** to have a hearty appetite. ◆ nm **1.** [ce qui est robuste] : **les voitures suédoises, c'est du solide** Swedish cars are built to last / **son dernier argument, c'est du solide !** fam her last argument is rock solid! **2.** [aliments solides] solids, solid food **3.** MATH & PHYS solid.

solidement [sɔlidmɑ̃] adv **1.** [fortement] securely, firmly **2.** [profondément] firmly / **c'est une croyance solidement ancrée** it's a deeply-rooted ou deep-seated idea.

solidifier [9] [sɔlidifje] ◆ **se solidifier** vpi to solidify, to harden.

solidité [sɔlidite] nf **1.** [d'un meuble] solidity, sturdiness ; [d'un vêtement] sturdiness, durability ; [d'un bâtiment] solidity **2.** [d'une institution, de principes, d'arguments] solidity, soundness ; [d'une équipe] reliability ; [d'une monnaie] strength **3.** [force d'une personne] sturdiness, robustness.

soliloque [sɔlilɔk] nm soliloquy.

soliste [sɔlist] nmf soloist.

solitaire [sɔlitɛʀ] ◆ adj **1.** [personne, existence, activité] solitary, lonely **2.** [isolé - île, quartier, retraite] solitary, lone. ◆ nmf [misanthrope] loner, lone wolf. ◆ nm JEUX

& JOAILL solitaire. ◈ **en solitaire** ◆ loc adj [course, vol] solo (modif) ; [navigation] single-handed. ◆ loc adv [vivre, travailler] on one's own ; [naviguer] single-handed / **il vit en solitaire dans sa vieille maison** he lives on his own in his old house.

solitude [sɔlityd] nf [d'une personne - momentanée] solitude ; [- habituelle] loneliness / **j'aime la solitude** I like to be alone ou on my own ▶ **la solitude à deux** the loneliness of a couple (when the two stop communicating with each other).

solive [sɔliv] nf CONSTR joist.

sollicitation [sɔlisitasjɔ̃] nf **1.** [requête] request, entreaty **2.** [poussée, traction] : **les freins répondent à la moindre sollicitation** the brakes are extremely responsive.

solliciter [3] [sɔlisite] vt **1.** [requérir - entrevue] to request, to solicit, to beg the favour of sout ; [- aide, conseils] to solicit, to seek (urgently) ; [- emploi] to apply for (insép) ▶ **solliciter qqch de qqn** to request sthg from sb **2.** [mettre en éveil - curiosité, attention] to arouse ; [- élève] to spur ou to urge on (sép) **3.** [faire appel à] to approach, to appeal to (insép) ▶ **être très sollicité** to be (very much) in demand **4.** ÉQUIT [cheval] to spur ou to urge on (sép).

sollicitude [sɔlisityd] nf [intérêt - affectueux] (excessive) care, solicitude sout ; [- soucieux] concern, solicitude sout ▶ **être plein de sollicitude envers qqn** to be very attentive to ou towards sb.

solo [sɔlo] (pl **solos** ou **soli** [-li]) nm **1.** MUS solo / **elle joue / chante en solo** she plays / sings solo / **une escalade en solo** fig a solo climb **2.** THÉÂTRE [spectacle] one-man-show.

solstice [sɔlstis] nm solstice.

soluble [sɔlybl] adj CHIM soluble.

solution [sɔlysjɔ̃] nf [résolution, clé] solution, answer / **l'envoyer en prison ne serait pas une solution** sending him to prison wouldn't solve anything ou wouldn't be a solution ▶ **une solution de facilité** an easy way out.

solutionner [3] [sɔlysjɔne] vt to solve, to resolve.

solvabilité [sɔlvabilite] nf [d'une entreprise] solvency ; [d'une personne] creditworthiness.

solvable [sɔlvabl] adj [entreprise] solvent ; [personne] creditworthy.

solvant [sɔlvɑ̃] nm solvent.

somali, e [sɔmali] adj Somalian, Somali. ◈ **Somali, e** nm, f Somali.

Somalie [sɔmali] npr f ▶ **(la) Somalie a)** [république] Somalia **b)** [bassin] Somaliland.

somalien, enne [sɔmaljɛ̃, ɛn] = somali.

somatiser [3] [sɔmatize] vt to somatize.

sombre [sɔ̃bʀ] adj **1.** [pièce, ruelle, couleur, robe] dark / **il fait très sombre** it's very dark **2.** [personne, caractère, humeur, regard] gloomy, melancholy, sombre ; [avenir, perspectives] gloomy / **les jours les plus sombres de notre histoire** the gloomiest ou darkest days of our history **3.** (avant nom) fam [en intensif] : **c'est une sombre crapule** / **un sombre crétin** he's the scum of the earth / a prize idiot / **m'a raconté une sombre histoire de fraude fiscale** he told me some murky story about tax evasion.

sombrer [3] [sɔ̃bʀe] vi **1.** [bateau] to sink, to founder **2.** sout [être anéanti - civilisation] to fall, to decline, to collapse ; [- entreprise] to go bankrupt, to fail, to collapse ; [- projet] to collapse, to fail ; [- espoir] to fade, to be dashed **3.** ▶ **sombrer dans** [s'abandonner à] to sink into / **sombrer dans le sommeil** / **le désespoir** to sink into sleep / despair / **ça l'a fait sombrer dans l'alcool** / **la dépression** it drove him / her to drink / plunged him / her into depression.

sommaire [sɔmɛʀ] ◆ adj **1.** [succinct] brief, succinct **2.** [rudimentaire - réparation] makeshift / **il n'a reçu**

qu'une éducation sommaire his education was rudimentary, to say the least **3.** [superficiel -*analyse*] summary, basic ; [-*examen*] superficial, perfunctory **4.** [expéditif -*procès*] summary. ◆ nm [d'un magazine] summary ; [d'un livre] summary, synopsis / *au sommaire de notre journal ce soir* our main news stories tonight.

sommairement [sɔmɛʁmɑ̃] adv **1.** [brièvement] briefly **2.** [rudimentairement] basically **3.** [expéditivement] summarily.

sommation [sɔmasjɔ̃] nf **1.** MIL [avant de tirer] warning, challenge ▶ *après les sommations d'usage* after the standard warning (had been given) **2.** DR summons **3.** *sout* [requête] demand.

somme¹ [sɔm] nm nap ▶ *faire un (petit) somme* to have a nap.

somme² [sɔm] nf **1.** FIN ▶ *somme (d'argent)* sum ou amount (of money) / *j'ai dépensé des sommes folles* I spent huge amounts of money ▶ *c'est une somme !* that's a lot of money! **2.** MATH sum ▶ *la somme totale* the grand total / *faire la somme de 15 et de 16* to add (up) 15 and 16 **3.** [quantité] : *somme de travail / d'énergie* amount of work / energy / *quand on fait la somme de tout ce que j'ai remué comme archives* when you add up the number of archive documents I've handled. ◆ **en somme** loc adv **1.** [en bref] in short / *en somme, tu refuses* in short, your answer is no **2.** [en définitive] all in all / *c'est assez simple en somme* all in all, it's quite easy. ◆ **somme toute** loc adv all things considered, when all is said and done.

sommeil [sɔmɛj] nm PHYSIOL [repos] sleep / *il cherchait le sommeil* he was trying to sleep ▶ *j'ai le sommeil léger / profond* I'm a light / heavy sleeper / *une nuit sans sommeil* a sleepless night, a night without sleep ▶ *avoir sommeil* to be ou to feel sleepy ▶ *tomber de sommeil* to be ready to drop, to be falling asleep (on one's feet) ▶ *le premier sommeil* the first hours of sleep ▶ *dormir d'un sommeil de plomb* a) [d'habitude] to be a heavy sleeper, to sleep like a log b) [ponctuellement] to be sleeping like a log ou fast asleep. ◆ **en sommeil** loc adv ▶ *rester en sommeil* to remain dormant ou inactive.

sommeiller [4] [sɔmɛje] vi **1.** [personne] to doze **2.** [affaire, passion, volcan] to lie dormant.

sommelier, ère [sɔmǝlje, ɛʁ] nm, f sommelier, wine waiter (waitress). ◆ **sommelière** nf Suisse waitress.

sommer [3] [sɔme] vt **1.** DR ▶ *sommer qqn de faire qqch* to summon sb to do sthg **2.** *sout* [ordonner à] ▶ *sommer qqn de faire qqch* to order sb to do sthg.

sommet [sɔmɛ] nm **1.** [plus haut point -d'un mont] summit, highest point, top ; [-d'un bâtiment, d'un arbre] top **2.** [partie supérieure -d'un arbre, d'une colline] crown ; [-d'une montagne] top, summit ; [-d'une vague] crest ; [-de la tête] crown, vertex *spéc* **3.** [degré suprême -d'une hiérarchie] summit, top ; [-d'une carrière] top, summit, acme *sout* / *une décision prise au sommet* a decision taken from the top **4.** MATH [d'un angle, d'une hyperbole] vertex **5.** POL summit (meeting).

sommier [sɔmje] nm [de lit] (bed) base ▶ *sommier à lattes* slatted base.

sommité [sɔmite] nf authority / *les sommités de la médecine* leading medical experts.

somnambule [sɔmnɑ̃byl] ◆ adj ▶ *être somnambule* to sleepwalk, to be a sleepwalker. ◆ nmf sleepwalker, somnambulist *spéc*.

somnifère [sɔmnifɛʁ] nm [substance] soporific ; [comprimé] sleeping pill ou tablet.

somnolence [sɔmnɔlɑ̃s] nf [d'une personne] drowsiness, sleepiness, somnolence *sout*.

somnolent, e [sɔmnɔlɑ̃, ɑ̃t] adj [personne] drowsy, sleepy, somnolent *sout*.

somnoler [3] [sɔmnɔle] vi **1.** [personne] to doze **2.** [ville] to be sleepy ; [économie] to be lethargic ou in the doldrums ; [faculté intellectuelle] to lie dormant, to slumber.

somptuaire [sɔ̃ptɥɛʁ] adj [dépenses] extravagant.

somptueusement [sɔ̃ptɥøzmɑ̃] adv [décorer, illustrer] sumptuously, lavishly, richly ; [vêtir] sumptuously, magnificently.

somptueux, euse [sɔ̃ptɥø, øz] adj **1.** [luxueux -vêtements, cadeau] sumptuous, splendid ; [-décor, salon, palais] magnificent, splendid **2.** [superbe -banquet] sumptuous, lavish ; [-illustration] lavish.

son¹ [sɔ̃] nm **1.** LING, MUS & PHYS sound / *un son sourd* a thump, a thud / *un son strident* [klaxon, trompette] a blast / *émettre* ou *produire un son* to give out a sound / *le mur rend un son creux* the wall has a hollow sound ▶ *son de cloche: c'est un autre son de cloche* that's (quite) another story / *j'ai entendu plusieurs sons de cloche* I've heard several variants ou versions of that story ▶ *spectacle son et lumière* son et lumière **2.** AUDIO sound, volume / *baisser / monter le son* to turn the sound up / down ▶ *son seul* sound only, wild track / *le son était épouvantable* CINÉ the soundtrack was terrible / *au son, Marcel Blot* sound (engineer), Marcel Blot **3.** AGR bran ▶ *son d'avoine* oat bran / *pain au son* bran loaf. ◆ **au son de** loc prép to the sound of.

son², sa [sɔ̃, sa] (*pl* **ses** [se]) (*devant nf ou adj f commençant par voyelle ou* «*h*» *muet* **son** [sɔn]) dét (*adj poss*) **1.** [d'un homme] his ; [d'une femme] her ; [d'une chose] its ; [d'un bateau, d'une nation] its, her / *son frère et sa sœur, ses frère et sœur* his / her brother and sister / *un de ses amis* a friend of his / hers, one of his / her friends ▶ *donne-lui son biberon* a) [à un petit garçon] give him his bottle b) [à une petite fille] give her her bottle / *dans sa maison à lui* fam in HIS house, in his own house **2.** [d'un sujet indéfini] : *il faut faire ses preuves* ou *montrer ce qu'on vaut* sout, you have to show your mettle / *tout le monde a ses problèmes* everybody has (his ou their) problems **3.** [dans des titres] : *Son Altesse Royale* His / Her Royal Highness **4.** [d'une abstraction] : *dans cette affaire, tout a son importance* in this affair everything is of importance **5.** [emploi expressif] : *ça a son charme* it's got its own charm ou a certain charm / *il fait son intéressant* fam he's trying to draw attention to himself / *il a réussi à avoir son samedi* fam he managed to get Saturday off.

sonar [sɔnaʁ] nm sonar.

sonate [sɔnat] nf sonata.

sondage [sɔ̃daʒ] nm **1.** [enquête] poll, survey / *faire un sondage auprès d'un groupe* to poll a group, to carry out a survey among a group ▶ *sondage d'opinion* opinion poll **2.** MIN & PÉTR [puits] bore hole **3.** NAUT sounding.

sonde [sɔ̃d] nf **1.** ASTRON & MÉTÉOR sonde ▶ *sonde aérienne* balloon sonde ▶ *sonde spatiale* ASTRONAUT (space) probe **2.** MÉD probe, sound ▶ *sonde (creuse)* catheter **3.** PÉTR drill.

sonder [3] [sɔ̃de] vt **1.** [personne -gén] to sound out (*sép*) ; [-dans une enquête] to poll / *je vais tâcher de la sonder là-dessus* I'll try and sound her out on that ▶ *sonder l'opinion* to make a survey of public opinion **2.** NAUT to sound **3.** MÉD [plaie] to probe ; [malade, vessie] to catheterize **4.** PÉTR to bore, to drill.

sondeur, euse [sɔ̃dœʁ, øz] nm, f [pour une enquête] pollster.

songe [sɔ̃ʒ] nm *litt* [rêve] dream ▶ *voir qqch / qqn en songe* to see sthg / sb in one's dreams.

songé, e [sɔ̃ʒe] adj Québec *fam* [réfléchi, intelligent] thoughtful, well thought out.

songer [17] [sɔ̃ʒe] *sout* ◆ vt to muse, to reflect, to think / *comment aurais-je pu songer qu'ils nous trahiraient ?* how could I have imagined that they'd betray us? ◆ vi [rêver] to dream. ◆ **songer à** v + prép *sout* **1.** [penser à] to think about *(insép)* ; [en se souvenant] to muse over *(insép)*, to think back to **2.** [envisager] to contemplate, to think of *(insép)* / *voyons, vous n'y songez pas !* come now, you can't mean it ou be serious! / *il songe sérieusement à se remarier* he's seriously considering ou contemplating remarriage.

songeur, euse [sɔ̃ʒœʀ, øz] adj pensive, thoughtful, reflective ▶ *ça vous laisse songeur* it makes you wonder.

sonné, e [sone] adj **1.** [annoncé par la cloche] gone, past ▶ *il est midi sonné* it's gone UK ou past twelve **2.** *fam* [révolu] : *elle a la cinquantaine bien sonnée* she's on the wrong side of fifty **3.** *fam* [fou] cracked, nuts **4.** *fam* [assommé] groggy, punch-drunk.

sonner [3] [sone] ◆ vi **1.** [téléphone, cloche] to ring ; [minuterie, réveil] to go off ; [carillon, pendule] to chime ; [glas, tocsin] to toll, to sound / *j'ai mis le réveil à sonner pour* ou *à 8 h* I've set the alarm for 8 o'clock **2.** [instrument en cuivre] to sound ; [clefs, pièces métalliques] to jingle, to jangle ; [pièces de monnaie] to jingle, to chink ; [enclume, marteau] to ring, to resound ; [rire] to ring, to peal (out) ; [voix] to resound, to ring ; [personne] ▶ **sonner creux a)** to sound hollow, to give a hollow sound **b)** *fig* to have a hollow ring ▶ **sonner faux** *pr* & *fig* to ring false **3.** [heure] to strike / *4 h ont sonné* it has struck 4 o'clock, 4 o'clock has struck / *attendez que la fin du cours sonne !* wait for the bell!, wait till the bell goes ou rings! **4.** [personne] to ring ▶ **on a sonné** there's someone at the door ▶ **sonner chez qqn** to ring sb's doorbell / *sonner puis entrer* please ring before entering. ◆ vt **1.** [cloche] to ring, to chime ; [glas, tocsin] to sound, to toll ▶ **sonner les cloches à qqn** *fam* to give sb a telling-off ou roasting / *tu vas te faire sonner les cloches !* you'll catch it! **2.** [pour faire venir - infirmière, valet] to ring for / *je ne t'ai pas sonné !* *fam* who asked you? **3.** [pour annoncer - messe, vêpres] to ring (the bells) for ; [MIL - charge, retraite, rassemblement] to sound / *sonner le réveil* MIL to sound the reveille **4.** [suj : horloge] to strike **5.** *fam* [assommer] to knock out *(sép)*, to stun ; [abasourdir] to stun, to stagger, to knock (out) / *ça l'a sonné* he was reeling under the shock! **6.** Belg [appeler] to telephone.

sonnerie [sonʀi] nf TÉLÉC ring / *la sonnerie du téléphone / réveil la fit sursauter* the telephone / alarm clock gave her a start ; [de téléphone mobile] ringtone.

sonnet [sone] nm sonnet.

sonnette [sonet] nf **1.** [avertisseur] bell ▶ **sonnette d'alarme** alarm bell ▶ **tirer la sonnette d'alarme a)** RAIL to pull the communication cord **b)** *fig* to blow the whistle **2.** [son] ▶ **(coup de) sonnette** ring (of the bell).

sono [sono] nf [d'un groupe, d'une discothèque] sound system, sound ; [d'une salle de conférences] public-address system, PA (system).

sonore [sonɔʀ] adj **1.** ACOUST [signal] acoustic, sound *(modif)* ; [onde] sound **2.** [bruyant - rire, voix] loud, ringing, resounding ; [- claque, baiser] loud, resounding **3.** LING [phonème] voiced.

sonorisation [sonɔʀizasjɔ̃] nf [équipement] sound system.

sonoriser [3] [sonɔʀize] vt [discothèque] to fit with a sound system ; [salle de conférences] to fit with a PA system ; [film] to add (the) sound track (to).

sonorité [sonɔʀite] nf [d'un instrument de musique] tone ; [de la voix] sonority *sout*, tone ; [d'une langue] sonority *sout*.

sophistiqué, e [sofistike] adj **1.** [raffiné] sophisticated, refined **2.** [complexe] complex, sophisticated.

sophrologie [sofʀolɔʒi] nf sophrology *(form of autogenic relaxation)*.

soporifique [sopɔʀifik] ◆ adj **1.** PHARM soporific **2.** [ennuyeux] boring, soporific. ◆ nm *vieilli* soporific.

soprane [sopʀan] nf = **soprano (nmf)**.

soprano [sopʀano] *(pl* **sopranos** *ou* **soprani** [-ni]) ◆ nm [voix - de femme] soprano ; [- d'enfant] soprano, treble. ◆ nmf soprano.

sorbet [sɔʀbe] nm sorbet UK, sherbet US.

sorbetière [sɔʀbɔtjɛʀ] nf [de glacier] ice-cream churn ; [de ménage] ice-cream maker.

sorbier [sɔʀbje] nm sorb.

sorcellerie [sɔʀsɛlʀi] nf **1.** [pratique] sorcery, witchcraft **2.** *fam* [effet surprenant] bewitchment, magic / *c'est de la sorcellerie !* it's magic!

sorcier, ère [sɔʀsje, ɛʀ] nm, f [magicien] wizard (witch) / *il ne faut pas être (grand) sorcier pour comprendre cela* *fam* you don't need to be a genius to understand that. ◆ **sorcier** adj m *fam* ▶ *ce n'est pourtant pas sorcier* you don't need to be a genius to understand.

sordide [sɔʀdid] adj **1.** [misérable - taudis, vêtements] wretched, squalid **2.** [vil - égoïsme] petty ; [- crime] foul, vile **3.** [mesquin - motif] squalid, sordid / *de sordides bagarres autour de l'héritage* sordid arguments over the legacy.

Sorlingues [sɔʀlɛ̃g] npr fpl ▶ **les (îles) Sorlingues** the Scilly Isles. ⟶ **île**

sort [sɔʀ] nm **1.** [condition] fate, lot / *être content de son sort* to be happy with one's lot / *tu m'abandonnes à mon triste sort !* you've left me to my fate! ▶ **faire un sort à a)** [plat] to make short work of, to polish off **b)** [bouteille] to polish off, to drink up **2.** [destin] fate, destiny / *toutes les demandes d'emploi subissent le même sort* all letters of application meet with the same fate ou receive the same treatment **3.** ▶ **le mauvais sort** misfortune ▶ **le sort en est jeté** the die is cast **4.** [sortilège - gén] spell ; [- défavorable] curse ▶ **jeter un sort à qqn** to cast a spell on sb.

sortable [sɔʀtabl] adj : *tu n'es vraiment pas sortable* ! I can't take you anywhere!

sortant, e [sɔʀtɑ̃, ɑ̃t] adj **1.** POL outgoing **2.** JEUX ▶ **les numéros sortants** the numbers chosen **3.** INFORM output *(modif)*.

sorte [sɔʀt] nf **1.** [genre] sort, kind, type ▶ **toutes sortes de** all kinds ou sorts ou manner of **2.** [pour exprimer une approximation] ▶ **une sorte de** a sort ou kind of. ◆ **de la sorte** *loc adv* that way / *comment osez-vous me traiter de la sorte ?* how dare you treat me in this way ou like that! ◆ **de (telle) sorte que** *loc conj* **1.** *(suivi du subjonctif)* [de manière à ce que] so that, in such a way that **2.** *(suivi de l'indicatif)* [si bien que] so that. ◆ **en (quelque) sorte** *loc adv* as it were, in a way, somewhat. ◆ **en sorte de** *loc conj* so as to / *fais en sorte d'arriver à l'heure* try to be there on time. ◆ **en sorte que** *litt* = **de (telle) sorte que**.

sortie [sɔʀti] nf **1.** [action] exit ; THÉÂTRE exit / *sa sortie fut très remarquée* her exit ou departure did not go unnoticed / *faire sa sortie* THÉÂTRE to leave the stage, to exit / *faire une fausse sortie* to make as if to leave **2.** [moment] ▶ **à ma sortie de prison / d'hôpital** when I come ou came out of prison / hospital, on my release from prison / discharge from hospital / *les journalistes l'ont assaillie dès sa sortie de l'hôtel* the journalists thronged round her as soon as she stepped ou came out of the hotel ▶ **à la sortie des bureaux / usines,** la circulation est infernale when the offices / factories come out, the traffic is hell / *c'est la sortie de l'école* it's home-time UK, school's out US / *retrouvons-*

nous à la sortie du travail / spectacle let's meet after work / the show / *il s'est retourné à la sortie du virage* he rolled (his car) over just after ou as he came out of the bend **3.** [fin] end / *à la sortie de l'hiver* when winter was (nearly) over / *à ma sortie de l'école* [à la fin de mes études] when I left school **4.** [excursion, promenade] outing ; [soirée en ville] evening ou night out / *on a organisé une petite sortie en famille / à vélo* we've organized a little family outing / cycle ride ▸ **priver qqn de sortie** [adulte] to confine sb to quarters / *mes parents m'ont privé de sortie trois dimanches de suite* my parents grounded me three Sundays in a row ▸ **sortie éducative** ou **scolaire** school outing **5.** AÉRON & MIL sortie / *faire une sortie* to make a sortie / *les pompiers font jusqu'à vingt sorties par semaine* the firemen are called out up to twenty times a week **6.** [porte, issue - d'une école, d'une usine] gates ; [- d'une salle de spectacles] exit, way out / *par ici la sortie !* this way out, please! / *poussé vers la sortie* pushed towards the exit ▸ **attends-moi à la sortie** wait for me outside / *gagner la sortie* to reach the exit / *il gagna la sortie sans encombre* he made his way out unimpeded / *le supermarché se trouve à la sortie de la ville* the supermarket is on the outskirts of the town / **'attention, sortie de garage / véhicules'** 'caution, garage entrance / vehicle exit' ▸ **sortie de secours** emergency exit ▸ **sortie de service** service entrance ▸ **sortie des artistes** stage door **7.** [sur route] exit ▸ **sortie d'autoroute** motorway junction ou exit 🇬🇧, freeway exit 🇺🇸 ▸ **sortie (de route)** turnoff / *à toutes les sorties de Paris* at every major exit from Paris **8.** BANQUE & ÉCON [de produits, de devises] export ; [de capital] outflow ; [sujet de dépense] item of expenditure ; [dépense] outgoing **9.** [d'un disque, d'un film] release ; [d'un roman] publication ; [d'un modèle] launch **10.** INFORM [de données] output, readout ; [option sur programme] exit ▸ **sortie sur imprimante** printout ▸ **sortie papier** output **11.** SPORT [aux jeux de ballon] : *sortie en touche* putting out of play ou into touch ▸ **faire une sortie** [gardien de but] to come out of goal, to leave the goalmouth ; [en gymnastique] exit **12.** [d'un cheval] outing **13.** *fam* [remarque] quip, sally ; [emportement] outburst / *elle a parfois de ces sorties !* she sometimes comes out with the most amazing stuff! **14.** [d'eau, de gaz] outflow, outlet **15.** IMPR [des presses] delivery. ❖ **de sortie** *loc adj* : *c'est son jour de sortie* [d'un domestique] it's his / her day off / *être de sortie* [domestique] to have one's day off / *je suis de sortie demain* *fam* [au restaurant, au spectacle] I'm going out tomorrow.

sortilège [sɔʀtilεʒ] *nm* charm, spell.

sortir¹ [sɔʀtiʀ] *nm litt* [fin] : *dès le sortir de l'enfance, il dut apprendre à se défendre* he was barely out of his childhood when he had to learn to fend for himself. ❖ **au sortir de** *loc prép* **1.** [dans le temps] ▸ **au sortir de l'hiver** as winter draws to a close / *au sortir de la guerre* towards the end of the war **2.** [dans l'espace] : *je vis la cabane au sortir du bois* as I was coming out of the woods, I saw the hut.

sortir² [32] [sɔʀtiʀ] ❖ *vi (aux être)* **1.** [quitter un lieu - vu de l'intérieur] to go out ; [- vu de l'extérieur] to come out / *sortir par la fenêtre* to get out ou to leave by the window ▸ **sors !** get out (of here)! / *fais sortir la guêpe* get the wasp out (of here)! / *Madame, je peux sortir ?* please Miss, may I leave the room? / *une méchante grippe l'empêche de sortir* a bad bout of flu is keeping him indoors ou at home / *elle est sortie déjeuner / se promener* she's gone (out) for lunch / for a walk ▸ **sortir de** : *sortir d'une pièce* to leave a room / *sortir d'une voiture* to get out of a car / *fais sortir ce chien de la voiture* get that dog out of the car / *sortir du lit* to get out of bed ▸ **ça me sort par les yeux** *fam* I'm sick and tired of it, I've had it up to here **2.** [marquant la fin d'une activité, d'une période] ▸ **sortir**

de table to leave the table ▸ **sortir de l'école / du bureau** [finir sa journée] to finish school / work / *sortir de prison* to come out of ou to be released from prison **3.** [pour se distraire] : *je sors très peu* I hardly ever go out ▸ **sortir avec qqn** to go out with sb / *ils sortent ensemble depuis trois ans* *fam* they've been going out together for three years **4.** [apparaître - dent, bouton] to come through ; [- pousse] to come up, to peep through **5.** [se répandre] to come out / *le son sort par là* the sound comes out here **6.** [s'échapper] to get out ▸ **faire sortir qqn / des marchandises d'un pays** to smuggle sb / goods out of a country **7.** [être mis en vente - disque, film] to be released, to come out ; [- livre] to be published, to come out / *ça vient de sortir !* it's just (come) out!, it's (brand) new! **8.** [être révélé au public - sujet d'examen] to come up ; [- numéro à la roulette] to turn ou to come up ; [- tarif, barème] to be out **9.** *fam* [être dit] to come out / *il fallait que ça sorte !* it had to come out ou to be said! **10.** INFORM : *sortir (d'un système)* to exit (from a system) **11.** NAUT & AÉRON ▸ **sortir en mer** to put out to sea **12.** SPORT [balle] to go out ▸ **on a fait sortir le joueur (du terrain)** a) [pour faute] the player was sent off b) [il est blessé] the player had to go off because of injury. ❖ *vt (aux avoir)* **1.** [mener dehors - pour se promener, se divertir] to take out (sép) / *il faut sortir les chiens régulièrement* dogs have to be walked regularly / *viens avec nous au concert, ça te sortira* come with us to the concert, that'll get you out (of the house) **2.** [mettre dehors - vu de l'intérieur] to put out ou outside ; [- vu de l'extérieur] to bring out ou outside (sép) ▸ **sortir la poubelle** to take out the rubbish bin 🇬🇧 ou the trash 🇺🇸 **3.** [présenter - crayon, outil] to take out (sép) ; [- pistolet] to pull out ; [- papiers d'identité] to produce / *on va bientôt pouvoir sortir les vêtements d'été* we'll soon be able to get out our summer clothes **4.** [extraire] ▸ **sortir qqch de** to take ou to get sthg out of ▸ **sortir qqn de** to get ou to pull sb out of ▸ **je vais te sortir d'affaire** ou **d'embarras** ou **de là** I'll get you out of it **5.** *fam* [expulser] to get ou to throw out (sép) **6.** [mettre sur le marché] to launch, to bring out ▸ **sortir un disque / film** a) [auteur] to bring out a record / film b) [distributeur] to release a record / film / *sortir un livre* to bring out ou to publish a book **7.** *fam* [dire] to say, to come out with / *tu sais ce qu'elle m'a sorti ?* you know what she came out with? **8.** [roue, train d'atterrissage] to drop ; [volet] to raise. ❖ **sortir de** *v + prép* **1.** [emplacement, position] to come out of, to come off ▸ **sortir de la piste** a) [voiture] to come off ou to leave the track b) [skieur] to come off the piste ▸ **ça m'était complètement sorti de la tête** ou **de l'esprit** it had gone right out of my head ou mind **2.** [venir récemment de] to have (just) come from / *elle sort de chez moi* she's just left my place / *d'où sors-tu ?* *fam* where have you been? **3.** [venir à bout de] to come out of / *nous avons eu une période difficile mais heureusement nous en sortons* we've had a difficult time but fortunately we're now emerging from it ou we're seeing the end of it now **4.** [se tirer de, se dégager de] : *elle est sortie indemne de l'accident* she came out of the accident unscathed / *qui sortira victorieux de ce match ?* who will win this match? **5.** [se départir de] : *il est sorti de sa réserve après quelques verres de vin* he opened ou loosened up after a few glasses of wine **6.** [s'écarter de] : *attention à ne pas sortir du sujet !* be careful not to get off ou to stray from the subject! ▸ **sortir de l'ordinaire** to be out of the ordinary **7.** [être issu de] : *pour ceux qui sortent des grandes écoles* for those who have studied at ou are the products of the grandes écoles ▸ **mais d'où sors-tu ?** a) [tu es mal élevé] where did you learn such manners?, where were you brought up? b) [tu ne connais rien] where have you been all this time? **8.** [être produit par] to come from. ❖ **se sortir de** *vp + prép* to get out of / *se sortir d'une situation* embarrassante to get (o.s.) out of ou *sout* to extricate o.s. from an embarrassing situation ▶ **s'en sortir** *fam*: *aide-moi à finir, je ne m'en sortirai jamais seul !* give me a hand, I'll never get this finished on my own ▶ **il s'en est finalement sorti a)** [il a survécu] he pulled through in the end **b)** [il a réussi] he won through in the end / *malgré les allocations, on ne s'en sort pas* in spite of the benefit, we're not making ends meet.

SOS (abr de **save our souls**) nm [signal de détresse] SOS ▶ **lancer un SOS** to put ou to send out an SOS.

sosie [sɔzi] nm double, doppelganger / *c'est ton sosie !* he's the spitting image of you!

sot, sotte [so, sɔt] adj [idiot] stupid.

sottement [sɔtmɑ̃] adv foolishly, stupidly.

sottise [sɔtiz] nf **1.** [caractère] stupidity, silliness **2.** [acte] stupid ou foolish action / *je viens de faire une grosse sottise* I've just done something very stupid ou silly **3.** [parole] stupid remark / *ne dis pas de sottises, le soleil se couche à l'ouest* don't be silly ou talk nonsense, the sun sets in the west.

sou [su] nm *fam* [argent] penny, cent 🇺🇸 ▶ **être sans le sou** to be broke ▶ **je suis sans un sou** I haven't got any money (on me). ❖ **sous** nmpl *fam* [argent] cash ▶ *c'est une affaire* ou *une histoire de gros sous* there's a lot of cash involved.

soubassement [subasmɑ̃] nm ARCHIT & CONSTR foundation.

soubresaut [subrəso] nm **1.** [secousse] jerk, jolt **2.** [haut-le-corps] shudder, convulsion.

souche [suʃ] nf **1.** BOT [d'un arbre en terre] stock, bole ; [d'un arbre coupé] stump / [d'une vigne] stock **2.** [d'un carnet] stub, counterfoil 🇬🇧 **3.** [origine] descent, stock ▶ **faire souche** [ancêtre] to found ou to start a line **4.** BIOL strain. ❖ **de souche** loc adj : *ils sont français de souche* they're of French extraction ou origin. ❖ **de vieille souche** loc adj of old stock.

souci [susi] nm **1.** [inquiétude] worry ▶ **se faire du souci** to worry, to fret ▶ **donner du souci à qqn** to worry sb / *mon fils me donne bien du souci !* my son is a great worry to me **2.** [préoccupation] worry / *des soucis d'argent* / *de santé* money / health worries ▶ *c'est le dernier* ou **le cadet de mes soucis !** it's the least of my worries!, I couldn't care less! / *avoir le souci de bien faire* to be concerned ou to care about doing things well **3.** BOT marigold.

soucier [9] [susje] ❖ **se soucier de** vp + prép [s'inquiéter de] to worry about ; [s'intéresser à] to care about.

soucieux, euse [susjø, øz] adj **1.** [préoccupé] worried, preoccupied **2.** ▶ **soucieux de** [attaché à] concerned about, mindful of *litt*.

soucoupe [sukup] nf saucer ▶ **soucoupe volante** flying saucer.

soudain, e [sudɛ̃, ɛn] adj sudden, unexpected. ❖ **soudain** adv all of a sudden, suddenly.

soudainement [sudɛnmɑ̃] adv suddenly, all of a sudden.

Soudan [sudɑ̃] npr m ▶ **le Soudan** the Sudan.

soudanais, e [sudanɛ, ɛz], **soudanien, enne** [sudanjɛ̃, ɛn] adj GÉOGR Sudanese. ❖ **Soudanais, e, Soudanien, enne** nm, f Sudanese (person).

soude [sud] nf CHIM soda ▶ **soude caustique** caustic soda.

soudé, e [sude] adj [équipe] closely-knit.

souder [3] [sude] vt **1.** TECHNOL [par soudure -hétérogène] to solder ; [-autogène] to weld **2.** [unir] to bring ou to bind ou to join together.

soudeur, euse [sudœr, øz] nm, f [par soudure -hétérogène] solderer ; [-autogène] welder.

soudoyer [13] [sudwaje] vt to bribe.

soudure [sudyr] nf [soudage -autogène] welding ; [-hétérogène] soldering.

soufflant, e [suflɑ̃, ɑ̃t] adj [appareil] ▶ **radiateur soufflant** fan heater.

souffle [sufl] nm **1.** [air expiré - par une personne] blow **2.** [respiration] breath ; [rythme respiratoire] breathing ▶ **avoir du souffle** to have a lot of breath / *avoir le souffle court, manquer de souffle* to be short-winded / *être à bout de souffle, n'avoir plus de souffle* [haletant] to be out of breath ▶ **reprendre son souffle** to get one's breath ou wind back ▶ **retenir son souffle** *pr & fig* to hold one's breath ▶ **trouver un deuxième** ou **second souffle a)** *pr* to get ou to find one's second wind **b)** *fig* to get a new lease of life **3.** [courant d'air] ▶ **souffle d'air** ou **de vent** breath of air **4.** *litt* [force] breath, spirit **5.** [d'une explosion] blast **6.** MÉD ▶ **souffle au cœur** heart murmur.

soufflé, e [sufle] adj *fam* [étonné] amazed, staggered, dumbfounded. ❖ **soufflé** nm CULIN soufflé ▶ **soufflé au fromage** cheese soufflé.

souffler [3] [sufle] ❖ vi **1.** [expirer - personne] to breathe out ▶ **soufflez dans le ballon** [Alcootest] blow into the bag / *souffler dans un cor* / *trombone* to blow (into) a horn / trombone **2.** MÉTÉOR [vent] to blow / *le vent soufflait en rafales* ou *bourrasques* there were gusts of wind, the wind was gusting **3.** [respirer avec difficulté] to blow, to puff, to breathe hard **4.** [retrouver sa respiration - personne] to get one's breath back ; [-cheval] to get its breath back / *laisser souffler son cheval* to blow ou to wind one's horse **5.** [se reposer] to have a break. ❖ vt **1.** [bougie] to blow out *(sép)* **2.** [exhaler] : *va souffler ta fumée de cigarette ailleurs* blow your smoke elsewhere ▶ **souffler le chaud et le froid** to blow hot and cold **3.** [murmurer - mot, réponse] to whisper ; THÉÂTRE to prompt / *il a fallu qu'on lui souffle son rôle* she had to have a prompt ; *(en usage absolu)* : *on ne souffle pas !* no whispering!, don't whisper (the answer)! ▶ **ne pas souffler mot (de qqch)** not to breathe a word (about sthg) **4.** [suggérer - idée, conseil] to whisper, to suggest **5.** *fam* [époustoufler - suj : événement, personne] to take aback, to stagger, to knock out *(sép)* / *son insolence m'a vraiment soufflé !* I was quite staggered at her rudeness! **6.** *fam* [dérober] ▶ **souffler qqch à qqn** to pinch sthg from sb / *je me suis fait souffler ma place* someone's pinched my seat **7.** [suj : bombe, explosion] to blow up *(sép)*, to blast away *(sép)* **8.** MÉTALL & TECHNOL to blow.

soufflerie [suflri] nf **1.** INDUST blower ; [d'une forge] bellows **2.** MUS [d'un orgue] bellows.

soufflet [suflɛ] nm **1.** [instrument] (pair of) bellows **2.** [d'un cartable] extendible pocket **3.** COUT [pocket] gusset.

souffleur, euse [suflœr, øz] nm, f **1.** THÉÂTRE prompter **2.** TECHNOL ▶ **souffleur de verre** glassblower.

souffrance [sufrɑ̃s] nf **1.** [fait de souffrir] suffering **2.** [mal -physique] pain ; [-psychologique] pain, torment. ❖ **en souffrance** loc adv ▶ **dossiers en souffrance** files pending.

souffrant, e [sufrɑ̃, ɑ̃t] adj [malade] ▶ **être souffrant** to be unwell.

souffre-douleur [sufrədulœr] (*pl* souffre-douleur *ou* souffre-douleurs*) nmf scapegoat.

souffrir [34] [sufrir] ❖ vt **1.** [endurer - épreuves] to endure, to suffer ▶ **souffrir le martyre** to go through ou to suffer agonies **2.** *litt* [admettre - suj : personne] to allow, to tolerate ; [-suj : règlement] to allow (for), to admit of / *le règlement de son dossier ne peut souffrir aucun délai* the settlement of his case simply cannot be postponed **3.** *fam* [supporter] : *elle ne peut pas la souffrir* she can't stand him. ❖ vi **1.** [avoir mal] to be in pain, to suffer ▶ **faire souffrir** [faire mal] to cause pain to, to hurt / *mon dos* *me fait souffrir ces temps-ci* my back's been hurting (me) lately / *elle l'a fait terriblement souffrir* she's caused him / her a lot of pain **2.** ▶ **souffrir de** [avoir mal à cause de] : *souffrir de la hanche* to have trouble with one's hip ▶ **souffrir de la faim / soif** to suffer from hunger / thirst ▶ **souffrir de la chaleur a)** [être très sensible à] to suffer in the heat **b)** [être atteint par] to suffer from the heat ▶ **souffrir de** *fig* [pâtir de] : *sa renommée a souffert du scandale* his reputation suffered from the scandal ; *(en usage absolu)* : *c'est le sud du pays qui a le plus souffert* the southern part of the country was the worst hit **3.** *fam* [peiner] to toil, to have a hard time (of it).

soufre [sufʀ] nm CHIM sulphur 🇬🇧, sulfur 🇺🇸.

souhait [swɛ] nm wish / *à tes souhaits !, à vos souhaits !* bless you! *(after a sneeze).*

souhaitable [swɛtabl] adj desirable / *ce n'est guère souhaitable* this is not to be desired.

souhaiter [4] [swete] vt **1.** [espérer] to wish ou to hope for *(insép)* / *il ne reviendra plus — souhaitons-le ou c'est à souhaiter !* he won't come back — let's hope not! / *ce n'est pas à souhaiter !* it's not something we would wish for! / *je souhaiterais pouvoir t'aider* I wish I could ou I'd like to be able to help (you) ▶ **souhaiter que** to hope that / *souhaitons que tout aille bien* let's hope everything goes all right **2.** [formuler un vœu de] to wish / *nous vous souhaitons un joyeux Noël* with our best wishes for a happy Christmas / *je te souhaite beaucoup de réussite / d'être heureux* I wish you every success / happiness ▶ **souhaitez-moi bonne chance !** wish me luck! / *je te souhaite bien du plaisir !* *fam, je t'en souhaite !* *iron* best of luck to you!

souiller [3] [suje] vt *litt* **1.** [maculer] to soil **2.** [entacher -réputation] to ruin, to sully *litt*, to tarnish *litt* ; [-innocence] to defile *litt*, to taint *litt*.

souk [suk] nm **1.** [marché] souk **2.** *fam* [désordre] shambles *(sg)* / *c'est le souk ici !* what a mess ou shambles here!

soûl, e, soul*, e [su, sul] adj [ivre] drunk.

soulagement [sulaʒmɑ̃] nm relief, solace *sout* / *à mon grand soulagement, il partit enfin* I was greatly relieved when he left at last.

soulager [17] [sulaʒe] vt **1.** [personne -physiquement] to relieve, to bring relief to / *cela devrait vous soulager de votre mal de tête* this should relieve ou help your headache **2.** [personne -moralement] to relieve, to soothe / *pleure, ça te soulagera* have a good cry, you'll feel better afterwards **3.** [diminuer -misère, souffrances] to relieve ; [-douleur] to relieve, to soothe. **◆ se soulager** vpi *fam & euphém* to relieve o.s.

soûler, souler* [3] [sule] vt **1.** *fam* [rendre ivre] ▶ **soûler qqn** to get sb drunk **2.** [étourdir] to make dizzy ou giddy / *tu me soûles, avec tes questions !* you're making me dizzy with all these questions! **◆ se soûler, se souler*** vpi *fam* [s'enivrer] to get drunk, to booze.

soûlerie, soulerie* [sulʀi] nf *fam* bender, drinking session.

soulèvement [sulɛvmɑ̃] nm [insurrection] uprising.

soulever [19] [sulve] vt **1.** [pour porter, élever -charge] to lift (up) ; [-couvercle, loquet] to lift ; [-capot] to lift, to open ; [-personne allongée] to raise (up) ; [-personne debout] to lift (up) ; [-voile] to lift ; [-chapeau] to raise ; [-voiture] to lift ; [-voiture sur cric] to jack up *(sép)* ; [-avec effort] to heave ▶ **soulever qqn / qqch de terre** to lift sb / sthg off the ground **2.** [remuer -poussière, sable] to raise / *le vent soulevait les feuilles mortes* the wind was stirring up dead leaves **3.** [provoquer -protestations, tollé] to raise ; [-enthousiasme, émotion] to arouse ; [-difficulté] to bring up *(sép)*, to raise **4.** [poser -question, objection] to raise, to bring up *(sép)* **5.** [retourner] ▶ **soulever le cœur** : *ça m'a soulevé*

le cœur it turned my stomach, it made me sick. **◆ se soulever** vpi **1.** [se redresser] to lift ou to raise o.s. up / *il l'aida à se soulever* he helped her to sit up **2.** [peuple] to rise up *(insép)*, to revolt.

soulier [sulje] nm [chaussure] shoe.

souligner [3] [suliɲe] vt **1.** [mettre un trait sous] to underline **2.** [accentuer] to enhance **3.** [faire remarquer] to emphasize, to stress.

soumettre [84] [sumɛtʀ] vt **1.** [se rendre maître de -nation] to subjugate ; [-mutins] to take control of, to subdue, to bring to heel ; [-passion] to control, to tame **2.** [à une épreuve, à un règlement] ▶ **soumettre qqn à** to subject sb to **3.** [présenter -loi, suggestion, texte] to submit / *je voulais d'abord le soumettre à votre approbation* I wanted to submit it for your approval first. **◆ se soumettre 1.** [céder -à l'ennemi] to give in, to submit, to yield ▶ **se soumettre à a)** [se plier à] to submit ou to subject o.s. to **b)** [s'en remettre à] to abide by.

soumis, e [sumi, iz] adj submissive, obedient, dutiful.

soumission [sumisjɔ̃] nf [obéissance -à un pouvoir] submission, submitting ; [-à une autorité] acquiescence, acquiescing.

soupape [supap] nf AUTO & MÉCAN valve ▶ **soupape de sécurité** ou **sûreté** *pr & fig* safety valve.

soupçon [supsɔ̃] nm **1.** [suspicion] suspicion ▶ **avoir des soupçons sur qqn / qqch** to be suspicious of sb / sthg / *être à l'abri* ou *au-dessus de tout soupçon* to be free from ou above all suspicion **2.** [petite quantité] : *un soupçon de maquillage* a hint ou touch of make-up / *un soupçon d'ironie* a touch ou hint of irony / *un soupçon de rhum* a dash ou a (tiny) drop of rum.

soupçonner [3] [supsɔne] vt **1.** [suspecter] to suspect ▶ **soupçonner qqn de meurtre / trahison** to suspect sb of murder / treason **2.** [imaginer] to imagine, to suspect.

soupçonneux, euse [supsɔnø, øz] adj suspicious / *il la regarda d'un air soupçonneux* he looked at her suspiciously.

soupe [sup] nf **1.** CULIN soup ▶ **soupe aux choux / au crabe** cabbage / crab soup ▶ **c'est une soupe au lait, elle est (très) soupe au lait** *fig* she flies off the handle easily **2.** *fam* [repas] grub, nosh ▶ **soupe populaire** soup kitchen **3.** *fam* [neige] slushy snow.

soupente [supɑ̃t] nf [dans un grenier] loft ; [sous un escalier] cupboard ou closet 🇺🇸 *(under the stairs).*

souper¹ [supe] nm **1.** *régional* [dîner] dinner, supper **2.** [après le spectacle] (late) supper.

souper² [3] [supe] vi **1.** *régional* ou *vieilli* [dîner] to have dinner **2.** [après le spectacle] to have a late supper **3.** EXPR **en avoir soupé de** *fam* to be sick of ou fed up with.

soupeser [19] [supəze] vt [en soulevant] to feel the weight of, to weigh in one's hand ou hands.

soupière [supjɛʀ] nf (soup) tureen.

soupir [supiʀ] nm **1.** [expiration] sigh / *soupir de soulagement* sigh of relief / *pousser des soupirs* to sigh / *rendre le dernier soupir* to breathe one's last **2.** MUS crotchet rest 🇬🇧, quarter ou quarter-note rest 🇺🇸.

soupirail, aux [supiʀaj, o] nm [d'une cave] (cellar) ventilator ; [d'une pièce] basement window.

soupirant [supiʀɑ̃] nm suitor.

soupirer [3] [supiʀe] vi [pousser un soupir] to sigh.

souple [supl] adj **1.** [lame] flexible, pliable, supple ; [plastique] non-rigid **2.** [agile -athlète, danseur, corps] supple ; [-démarche] fluid, flowing **3.** [doux -cuir, peau, brosse à dents] soft **4.** [aménageable] flexible, adaptable / *la réglementation / l'horaire est souple* the rules / hours are flexible **5.** [qui sait s'adapter] flexible, adaptable.

souplesse [suplɛs] nf **1.** [d'une personne, d'un félin, d'un corps] suppleness ; [d'une démarche] suppleness, springiness **2.** [malléabilité - d'une matière] flexibility, pliability ; *péj* [servilité] servility **3.** [d'un horaire, d'une méthode] flexibility, adaptability.

souque [suk] nf Québec [jeu] ▸ **souque à la corde** tug of war.

source [suʀs] nf **1.** [point d'eau] spring ▸ **source chaude** hot spring **2.** [origine] spring, source / *où la Seine prend-elle sa source ?* where is the source of the Seine?, where does the Seine originate? **3.** [cause] source / *cette maison n'a été qu'une source d'ennuis* this house has been nothing but trouble ▸ **source de revenus** a source of income, revenue stream ▸ **source de chaleur** source of heat ▸ **source d'énergie** source of energy **4.** PRESSE : *tenir ses renseignements de source sûre* ou *de source bien informée* to have information on good authority ▸ **de source officielle / officieuse, on apprend que...** official / unofficial sources reveal that... **5.** INFORM source **6.** PHYS ▸ **source lumineuse** ou **de lumière** light source.

sourcil [suʀsi] nm eyebrow.

sourciller [3] [suʀsije] vi to frown ▸ **sans sourciller** without batting an eyelid ou turning a hair.

sourd, e [suʀ, suʀd] ◆ adj **1.** [personne] deaf / *sourd de l'oreille gauche* deaf in the left ear ▸ **faire la sourde oreille** to pretend not to hear ▸ **être sourd comme un pot** *fam* to be as deaf as a post **2.** [atténué - son, voix] muffled, muted **3.** [vague - douleur] dull ; [- sentiment] muted, subdued / *j'éprouvais une sourde inquiétude* I felt vaguely worried **4.** LING unvoiced, voiceless. ◆ nm, f deaf person ▸ **les sourds** the deaf.

sourdine [suʀdin] nf MUS [d'une trompette, d'un violon] mute ; [d'un piano] soft pedal ▸ **mettre la sourdine** *fig* to tone it down. ◆ **en sourdine** *loc adv* MUS [jouer] quietly, softly ▸ **mets-la en sourdine !** *fam & fig* shut up!

sourdingue [suʀdɛ̃g] *tfam* adj cloth-eared.

sourd-muet, sourde-muette
[suʀmɥɛ, suʀdmɥɛt] (*mpl* **sourds-muets**, *fpl* **sourdes-muettes**) ◆ adj deaf and dumb. ◆ nm, f deaf-mute, deaf-and-dumb person.

souriant, e [suʀjɑ̃, ɑ̃t] adj [regard, visage] smiling, beaming ; [personne] cheerful.

souricière [suʀisjɛʀ] nf **1.** [ratière] mousetrap **2.** [piège] trap.

sourire¹ [suʀiʀ] nm smile / *il entra, le sourire aux lèvres* he came in with a smile on his lips ou face ▸ **faire un sourire à qqn** to smile at sb / *elle était tout sourire* she was wreathed in ou all smiles ▸ **avoir le sourire** to have a smile on one's face / *il a pris la nouvelle avec le sourire* he took the news cheerfully / *il faut savoir garder le sourire* you have to learn to keep smiling.

sourire² [95] [suʀiʀ] vi to smile / *la remarque peut faire sourire* this remark may bring a smile to your face ou make you smile ▸ **sourire à qqn** to smile at sb, to give sb a smile. ◆ **sourire à** v + prép **1.** [être favorable à] to smile on / *la chance ne te sourira pas toujours !* you won't always be (so) lucky! **2.** [plaire à - suj : idée, perspective] to appeal to.

souris [suʀi] nf **1.** ZOOL mouse ▸ **souris blanche** white mouse **2.** *tfam* [femme] bird UK, chick US **3.** INFORM mouse.

sournois, e [suʀnwa, az] ◆ adj **1.** [personne, regard] cunning, shifty, sly **2.** [attaque, procédé] underhand **3.** [douleur] dull, gnawing. ◆ nm, f sly person.

sous [su] prép **1.** [dans l'espace] under, underneath, beneath ▸ **être sous la douche** to be in the ou having a shower / *se promener sous la pluie* to walk in the rain / *un paysage sous la neige* a snow-covered landscape / *nager sous l'eau* to swim underwater ▸ **sous terre** underground, below ground / *ça s'est passé sous nos yeux* it took place before our very eyes **2.** *fig* [derrière] behind, under, beneath / *sous des dehors taciturnes* behind a stern exterior **3.** [à l'époque de] : *sous Louis XV* during the reign of ou under Louis XV / *sous sa présidence* / *son ministère* under his presidency / ministry **4.** [dans un délai de] within / *sous huitaine* / *quinzaine* within a week / fortnight **5.** [marquant un rapport de dépendance] under / *sous ses ordres* under his command **6.** MÉD : *être sous anesthésie* to be under anaesthetic ▸ **être sous antibiotiques / perfusion** to be on antibiotics / a drip **7.** [marquant la manière] : *emballé sous vide* vacuum-packed / *elle a acheté le billet sous un faux nom* she bought the ticket under an assumed name / *vu sous cet angle* seen from this angle / *parfait sous tous rapports* perfect in every respect **8.** [avec une valeur causale] under / *sous la torture* / *canonnade* under torture / fire / *sous le coup de l'émotion* in the grip of the emotion.

sous-activité [suzaktivite] nf : *être en sous-activité* to be operating below capacity.

sous-alimenté, e [suzalimɑ̃te] adj undernourished, underfed.

sous-bois [subwa] nm undergrowth, underwood / *se promener dans les sous-bois* to walk in the undergrowth.

sous-couche [sukuʃ] nf [de peinture, de vernis] undercoat.

souscripteur [suskriptœr] nm FIN subscriber.

souscription [suskripsjɔ̃] nf **1.** [engagement] subscription, subscribing (U) **2.** [somme] subscription.

souscrire [99] [suskriʀ] vt **1.** DR [signer - acte] to sign, to put one's signature to, to subscribe *sout* ; [- billet, chèque] to draw, to sign **2.** [abonnement, police d'assurance] to take out (*insép*). ◆ **souscrire à** v + prép **1.** [approuver] to approve, to subscribe to, to go along with **2.** BOURSE & ÉCON [emprunt] to subscribe to.

sous-effectif [suzefɛktif] (*pl* sous-effectifs) nm understaffing ▸ **en sous-effectif** understaffed.

sous-employé, e [suzɑ̃plwaje] (*mpl* sous-employés, *fpl* sous-employées) adj underemployed.

sous-employer [13] [suzɑ̃plwaje] vt [travailleur] to underemploy ; [appareil] to underuse.

sous-ensemble [suzɑ̃sɑ̃bl] nm subset.

sous-entendre [73] [suzɑ̃tɑ̃dʀ] vt to imply / *que sous-entendez-vous par là ?* what are you hinting ou driving at?, what are you trying to imply?

sous-entendu [suzɑ̃tɑ̃dy] nm innuendo, hint, insinuation.

sous-équipé, e [suzekipe] adj underequipped.

sous-estimer [3] [suzɛstime] vt [une qualité, un bien] to underestimate, to underrate.

sous-évaluer [7] [suzevalɥe] vt FIN to undervalue.

sous-exploiter [3] [suzɛksplwate] vt to underexploit.

sous-jacent, e [suʒasɑ̃, ɑ̃t] adj [caché] underlying.

sous-louer [6] [sulwe] vt to sublet.

sous-main [sumɛ̃] (*pl* sous-main ou sous-mains*) nm [buvard] desk blotter. ◆ **en sous-main** *loc adv* secretly.

sous-marin, e [sumaʀɛ̃, in] adj [câble, plante] submarine, underwater ; [navigation] submarine ; [courant] submarine, undersea ; [photographie] underwater, undersea. ◆ **sous-marin** nm **1.** NAUT submarine **2.** *fam* [espion] mole **3.** Québec [sandwich] long sandwich, sub US.

sous-marque [sumaʀk] nf sub-brand.

sous-officier [suzɔfisje] nm non-commissioned officer.

sous-payer [11] [supeje] vt to underpay.

sous-produit [supʀɔdɥi] nm INDUST by-product.

sous-pull [supyl] nm thin polo-neck sweater.

sous-qualifié, e [sukalifje] adj underqualified.

sous-répertoire [suʀepɛʀtwaʀ] (pl sous-répertoires) nm INFORM sub-directory.

soussigné, e [susiɲe] ◆ adj undersigned / je soussigné Robert Brand, déclare avoir pris connaissance de l'article 4 l, the undersigned Robert Brand, declare that I have read clause 4. ◆ nm, f : les soussignés déclarent que… the undersigned declare that…

sous-sol [susɔl] nm 1. GÉOL subsoil 2. [d'une maison] cellar ; [d'un magasin] basement, lower ground floor.

sous-titre [sutitʀ] nm 1. PRESSE subtitle, subheading, subhead 2. CINÉ subtitle.

sous-titré, e [sutitʀe] adj subtitled, with subtitles.

sous-titrer [3] [sutitʀe] vt [film] to subtitle.

sous-total [sutɔtal] (pl sous-totaux) nm subtotal.

soustraction [sustʀaksjɔ̃] nf MATH subtraction.

soustraire [112] [sustʀɛʀ] vt 1. MATH to subtract, to take away (sép) 2. [enlever] ▶ soustraire qqn / qqch à to take sb / sthg away from ▶ soustraire qqn à la justice to shield sb from justice, to protect sb from the law. ❖ se soustraire à vp + prép sout : se soustraire à l'impôt / une obligation / un devoir to evade tax / an obligation / a duty / se soustraire à la justice to escape the law.

sous-traitant [sutʀɛtɑ̃] nm subcontractor.

sous-traiter [4] [sutʀete] vt ▶ sous-traiter un travail a) [entrepreneur principal] to subcontract a job, to contract a job out b) [sous-entrepreneur] to contract into ou to subcontract a job.

sous-utiliser [3] [suzytilize] vt to underuse, to underutilize.

sous-verre [suvɛʀ] (pl sous-verres) nm glass mount.

sous-vêtement [suvɛtmɑ̃] nm piece of underwear, undergarment.

soutane [sutan] nf cassock.

soute [sut] nf hold ▶ soute à bagages luggage hold ▶ soute à mazout oil tank.

soutenance [sutnɑ̃s] nf ▶ soutenance (de thèse) oral examination for thesis ; viva 🇬🇧.

soutènement [sutenmɑ̃] nm CONSTR support. ❖ de soutènement loc adj support (modif), supporting.

souteneur [sutnœʀ] nm [proxénète] pimp fam.

soutenir [40] [sutniʀ] vt 1. [maintenir - suj : pilier, poutre] to hold up (sép), to support ; [-suj : attelle, gaine, soutien-gorge] to support 2. [réconforter] to support, to give (moral) support to 3. [être partisan de -candidature, cause, politique, etc.] to support, to back (up), to stand by (insép) / tu soutiens toujours ta fille contre moi ! you always stand up for ou you're always siding with your daughter against me ! / soutenir une équipe to be a fan of ou to support a team 4. [faire valoir - droits] to uphold, to defend ; [-argument, théorie] to uphold, to support 5. [affirmer] to assert, to claim / il soutient que tu mens he keeps saying that you're a liar 6. [résister à -attaque] to withstand ; [-regard] to bear, to support ▶ soutenir la comparaison avec to stand ou to bear comparison with / soutenir un siège MIL to last out ou to withstand a siege 7. [prolonger -attention, discussion, suspense, etc.] to keep up (sép), to sustain ; [-réputation] to maintain, to keep up / il est difficile de soutenir une conversation lorsque les enfants sont présents it's difficult to keep a conversation going ou to keep up a conversation when the children are around 8. UNIV ▶ soutenir sa thèse to defend one's thesis, to take one's viva 🇬🇧. ❖ se soutenir ◆ vp (emploi réciproque) to stand by each other, to stick together. ◆ vpi [se tenir] to hold o.s. up, to support o.s. / le vieillard n'arrivait plus à se soutenir sur ses jambes the old man's legs could no longer support ou carry him.

soutenu, e [sutny] adj 1. [sans faiblesse -couleur] intense, deep ; [-note de musique] sustained ; [-attention, effort] unfailing, sustained, unremitting ; [-rythme] steady, sustained 2. LING formal / en langue soutenue in formal speech.

souterrain, e [suteʀɛ̃, ɛn] adj 1. [sous la terre] underground, subterranean 2. [dissimulé] hidden, secret. ❖ souterrain nm 1. [galerie] underground ou subterranean passage 2. [en ville] subway 🇬🇧, underpass 🇺🇸.

soutien [sutjɛ̃] nm 1. [aide] support ▶ apporter son soutien à qqn to support sb, to back sb up ▶ soutien financier financial backing 2. [défenseur] supporter / c'est l'un des plus sûrs soutiens du gouvernement he's one of the mainstays of the government.

soutien-gorge [sutjɛ̃gɔʀʒ] (pl soutiens-gorge) nm bra, brassiere sout.

soutif [sutif] nm fam bra.

soutirer [3] [sutiʀe] vt [extorquer] ▶ soutirer qqch à qqn to get sthg from ou out of sb ▶ soutirer une promesse à qqn to extract a promise from sb ▶ soutirer des renseignements à qqn to get ou to squeeze some information out of sb / il s'est fait soutirer pas mal d'argent par ses petits enfants his grandchildren managed to squeeze a lot of money out of him.

souvenir¹ [suvniʀ] nm 1. [impression] memory, recollection / je garde un excellent souvenir de ce voyage I have excellent memories of that trip ▶ n'avoir aucun souvenir de to have no remembrance ou recollection of / elle n'en a qu'un vague souvenir she has only a dim ou vague recollection of it / mes souvenirs d'enfance my childhood memories ▶ avoir le souvenir de to have a memory of, to remember 2. [dans des formules de politesse] : mes meilleurs souvenirs à votre sœur (my) kindest regards to your sister ▶ meilleurs souvenirs de Rome greetings from Rome 3. [objet -donné par qqn] keepsake ; [-rappelant une occasion] memento ; [-pour touristes] souvenir 4. (comme adjectif, avec ou sans trait d'union) souvenir (modif) / poser pour la photo-souvenir to pose for a commemorative photograph. ❖ en souvenir de loc prép [afin de se remémorer] : prenez ce livre en souvenir de cet été / de moi take this book as a souvenir of this summer / as something to remember me by.

souvenir² [40] [suvniʀ] ❖ se souvenir de vp + prép [date, événement] to remember, to recollect, to recall ; [personne, lieu] to remember / on se souviendra d'elle comme d'une grande essayiste she'll be remembered as a great essay-writer / je ne me souviens jamais de son adresse I keep forgetting ou I can never remember his address / je ne me souviens pas de l'avoir lu I can't remember ou I don't recall ou I don't recollect having read it.

souvent [suvɑ̃] adv often / on se voit de moins en moins souvent we see less and less of each other / il ne vient pas souvent nous voir he doesn't often come and see us, he seldom comes to see us / le plus souvent c'est elle qui conduit she often drives ou more often than not ou usually, she's the one who does the driving.

📝 Notez les différentes positions possibles de often dans la phrase.

• Avec un verbe autre que be, often s'insère couramment comme suit :

    sujet + [aux/modal] + often + verbe

Il m'arrive souvent de penser à elle. I often think about her.

On peut souvent voir des baleines ici. You can often see whales here. →

→
• **Avec le verbe be, often se place couramment comme suit :**

sujet + be + often

Elle est souvent en retard. *She is often late.*
Les gens sont souvent surpris quand je leur dis ça. *People are often surprised when I tell them that.*

• **Often peut également se rencontrer en début de proposition :**
Souvent les gens qui travaillent devant un ordinateur ont des problèmes de vue. *Often people who work with computers have eye problems.*
Souvent il ne savait pas quoi faire. *Often he didn't know what to do.*

• **Plus rarement, often peut se placer en fin de proposition :**
J'y vais souvent. *I go there often.*
Je pense souvent à toi. *I think of you often.*

souverain, e [suvʀɛ̃, ɛn] ◆ adj **1.** POL [pouvoir, peuple] sovereign **2.** [suprême] supreme ▶ **avoir un souverain mépris pour qqch** to utterly despise sthg **3.** RELIG ▶ **le souverain pontife** the Pope, the Supreme Pontiff ◆ nm, f monarch, sovereign.

souverainement [suvʀɛnmɑ̃] adv [suprêmement] utterly, totally, intensely ▶ **être souverainement indifférent à** to be utterly ou supremely indifferent to.

souveraineté [suvʀɛnte] nf sovereignty.

soviétique [sɔvjetik] adj Soviet.

soyeux, euse [swajø, øz] adj silky.

SPA (abr de **Société protectrice des animaux**) npr f *society for the protection of animals* ; ≃ RSPCA 🇬🇧 ; ≃ SPCA 🇺🇸.

spacieux, euse [spasjø, øz] adj spacious, roomy.

spaghetti [spageti] (*pl* spaghetti *ou* spaghettis) nm : *des spaghettis* spaghetti.

spam [spam] nm INTERNET spam.

sparadrap [spaʀadʀa] nm (sticking) plaster 🇬🇧, band aid, Band aid® 🇺🇸.

spartiate [spaʀsjat] adj [austère] Spartan *fig*, ascetic.

spasme [spasm] nm spasm.

spatial, e, aux [spasjal, o] adj **1.** [de l'espace] spatial **2.** ASTRONAUT, AUDIO & MIL space *(modif)*.

spationaute [spasjɔnot] nmf spaceman (spacewoman).

spatule [spatyl] nf **1.** CULIN spatula **2.** [d'un ski] tip **3.** ART (pallet) knife.

spätzli [ʃpetsli] nmpl 🇨🇭 small dumplings.

speaker, speakerine [spikœʀ, spikʀin] nm, f announcer, link man (woman) 🇬🇧.

spécial, e, aux [spesjal, o] adj **1.** [d'une catégorie particulière] special, particular, specific, distinctive **2.** [exceptionnel - gén] special, extraordinary, exceptional ; [- numéro, édition] special **3.** [bizarre] peculiar, odd / *toi, t'es spécial !* you're a bit weird! ◆ **spéciale** nf **1.** [huître] *type of cultivated oyster* **2.** SPORT (short) off-road rally.

spécialement [spesjalmɑ̃] adv **1.** [à une fin particulière] specially, especially **2.** [très] particularly, specially / *ça n'a pas été spécialement drôle* it wasn't particularly amusing.

spécialisation [spesjalizasjɔ̃] nf specialization, specializing.

spécialisé, e [spesjalize] adj [gén] specialized ; INFORM dedicated, special-purpose.

spécialiser [3] [spesjalize] ◈ **se spécialiser** vpi to specialize.

spécialiste [spesjalist] nmf **1.** [gén & MÉD] specialist **2.** *fam* [habitué] : *c'est un spécialiste des gaffes* he's an expert at putting his foot in it.

spécialité [spesjalite] nf **1.** CULIN speciality 🇬🇧, specialty 🇺🇸 / *spécialités de la région* local specialities ou products **2.** SCI & UNIV field, area, specialism ▶ **spécialité médicale** area of medicine / *le meilleur dans* ou *de sa spécialité* the best in his field **3.** [manie, habitude] : *le vin, c'est sa spécialité* he's the wine expert.

spécification [spesifikasjɔ̃] nf specification.

spécificité [spesifisite] nf specificity.

spécifier [9] [spesifje] vt to specify, to state, to indicate / *spécifier les conditions d'un prêt* to specify ou to indicate the conditions of a loan / *je lui ai bien spécifié l'heure du rendez-vous* I made sure I told him the time of the appointment.

spécifique [spesifik] adj specific.

spécifiquement [spesifikmɑ̃] adv specifically.

spécimen [spesimɛn] nm **1.** [élément typique] specimen, example **2.** IMPR specimen **3.** *fam* [individu bizarre] queer fish 🇬🇧, odd duck 🇺🇸.

spectacle [spektakl] nm **1.** CINÉ, DANSE, MUS & THÉÂTRE show / *aller au spectacle* to go to (see) a show ▶ **le spectacle** show business **2.** [ce qui se présente au regard] sight, scene ▶ **au spectacle de** at the sight of. ◈ **à grand spectacle** loc adj grandiose ▶ **film à grand spectacle** blockbuster. ◈ **en spectacle** loc adv ▶ **se donner** ou **s'offrir en spectacle** to make an exhibition ou a spectacle of o.s.

spectaculaire [spektakylɛʀ] adj [exceptionnel, frappant] spectacular, impressive.

spectateur, trice [spektatœʀ, tʀis] nm, f **1.** CINÉ, DANSE, MUS & THÉÂTRE spectator, member of the audience ▶ **les spectateurs** the audience **2.** [d'un accident, d'un événement] spectator, witness **3.** [simple observateur] onlooker.

spectre [spektʀ] nm **1.** [fantôme] ghost, phantom, spectre 🇬🇧, specter 🇺🇸 **2.** [représentation effrayante] spectre 🇬🇧, specter 🇺🇸 ▶ **le spectre de** the spectre of.

spéculateur, trice [spekylatœʀ, tʀis] nm, f speculator.

spéculation [spekylasjɔ̃] nf speculation.

spéculer [3] [spekyle] vi **1.** BOURSE to speculate / *spéculer sur l'or* to speculate in gold **2.** *litt* [méditer] to speculate.

spéculoos [spekylos] nm 🇧🇪 ginger biscuit.

speech [spitʃ] (*pl* speechs *ou* speeches) nm *fam* (short) speech / *il nous a refait son speech sur l'importance des bonnes manières* he made the same old speech about the importance of good manners.

speed [spid] adj *fam* hyper / *il est complètement speed* he's really hyper.

speedé, e [spide] adj *fam* hyper.

spéléologie [speleɔlɔʒi] nf [science et étude] speleology ; [sport] potholing 🇬🇧, spelunking 🇺🇸.

spéléologue [speleɔlɔg] nmf [savant, chercheur] speleologist ; [sportif] potholer 🇬🇧, spelunker 🇺🇸.

spermatozoïde [spɛʀmatɔzɔid] nm spermatozoid.

sperme [spɛʀm] nm sperm.

sphère [sfɛʀ] nf **1.** ASTRON & GÉOM sphere **2.** [zone] field, area, sphere ▶ **les hautes sphères** the higher realms *litt*.

sphérique [sfeʀik] adj spheric, spherical.

sphinx [sfɛ̃ks] nm ART & MYTH sphinx ▶ **le Sphinx** the Sphinx.

spirale [spiʀal] nf **1.** [circonvolution] spiral, helix / *des spirales de fumée* coils of smoke **2.** [hausse rapide] spiral / *la spirale inflationniste* the inflationary spiral. ❖ **à spirale** loc adj [cahier] spiral, spiralbound. ❖ **en spirale** ◆ loc adj [escalier, descente] spiral. ◆ loc adv in a spiral, spirally / *s'élever / retomber en spirale* to spiral upwards / downwards.

spiritisme [spiʀitism] nm spiritualism, spiritism.

spirituel, elle [spiʀitɥɛl] adj **1.** [non physique] spiritual **2.** [plein d'esprit] witty / *comme c'est spirituel !* how clever! **3.** RELIG spiritual ▸ **concert spirituel** concert of sacred music.

spiritueux [spiʀitɥø] nm spirit.

spleen [splin] nm *litt* spleen *arch*, melancholy.

splendeur [splɑ̃dœʀ] nf **1.** [somptuosité] magnificence, splendour 🇬🇧, splendor 🇺🇸 **2.** [merveille] : *son collier est une splendeur* her necklace is magnificent **3.** [prospérité, gloire] grandeur, splendour / *voilà le macho dans toute sa splendeur hum* that's macho man in all his glory.

splendide [splɑ̃did] adj **1.** [somptueux - décor, fête, étoffe] splendid, magnificent **2.** [beau] magnificent, wonderful, splendid / *elle avait une mine splendide* she was blooming **3.** [rayonnant - soleil] radiant.

spongieux, euse [spɔ̃ʒjø, øz] adj **1.** ANAT spongy **2.** [sol, matière] spongy, sponge-like.

sponsor [spɔ̃sɔʀ] nm (commercial) sponsor.

sponsoring [spɔ̃sɔʀiŋ], **sponsorat** [spɔ̃sɔʀa] nm (commercial) sponsorship.

sponsoriser [3] [spɔ̃sɔʀize] vt to sponsor (commercially).

spontané, e [spɔ̃tane] adj spontaneous.

spontanéité [spɔ̃taneite] nf spontaneity, spontaneousness.

spontanément [spɔ̃tanemɑ̃] adv spontaneously.

sporadique [spɔʀadik] adj [attaque, effort] sporadic, occasional ; [symptôme, crise] sporadic, isolated ; [averse] scattered.

sport [spɔʀ] ◆ adj inv VÊT [pratique, de détente] casual. ◆ nm [ensemble d'activités, exercice physique] sport ; [activité de compétition] (competitive) sport / *faire du sport* to do sport ▸ **sport de combat** combat sport ▸ **sport de compétition** competitive sport ▸ **sport en eau vive** white-water sport ▸ **sport individuel** individual sport ▸ **sports d'équipe** team sports ▸ **sports d'hiver** winter sports ▸ **sports mécaniques** motor sports / *aller aux sports d'hiver* to go skiing, to go on a winter sports holiday 🇬🇧 ou vacation 🇺🇸 ▸ **sports nautiques** water sports. ❖ **de sport** loc adj [terrain, vêtement] sports *(modif)*.

sportif, ive [spɔʀtif, iv] ◆ adj **1.** [association, club, magazine, reportage] sports *(modif)* **2.** [événement, exploit] sporting **3.** [personne] sporty ▸ **elle est très sportive** she does a lot of sport / *je ne suis pas très sportif* I'm not very sporty / *avoir une allure sportive* to look athletic **4.** [loyal - public] sporting, fair ; [- attitude, geste] sporting, sportsmanlike / *avoir l'esprit sportif* to show sportsmanship. ◆ nm, f sportsman (sportswoman).

sportivité [spɔʀtivite] nf [d'une personne] sportsmanship.

spot [spɔt] nm **1.** [projecteur, petite lampe] spotlight **2.** [publicité] ▸ **spot (publicitaire)** commercial.

sprint [spʀint] nm SPORT [course] sprint (race) ; [pointe de vitesse - gén] spurt ; [- en fin de parcours] final spurt ou sprint.

sprinter¹ [spʀintœʀ] nm sprinter.

sprinter² [3] [spʀinte] vi to sprint ; [en fin de parcours] to put on a burst of speed.

sprinteur, euse [spʀintœʀ, øz] nm, f = **sprinter**.

squale [skwal] nm shark.

square [skwaʀ] nm [jardin] (small) public garden ou gardens.

squash [skwaʃ] nm squash / *jouer au squash* to play squash.

squat [skwat] nm [habitation] squat.

squatter¹ [skwatœʀ] nm squatter.

squatter² [skwate], **squattériser** [3] [skwateʀize] vt [bâtiment] to squat in *(insép)*.

squelette [skəlɛt] nm ANAT skeleton.

squelettique [skəletik] adj **1.** [animal, enfant] skeleton-like, skeletal ; [plante] stunted **2.** [troupes] decimated ; [équipe] skeleton *(modif)*.

Sri Lanka [sʀilɑ̃ka] npr m ▸ **le Sri Lanka** Sri Lanka.

sri lankais, e [sʀilɑ̃kɛ, ɛz] adj Sri Lankan.
❖ **Sri Lankais, e** nm, f Sri Lankan.

SS ◆ **1.** (abr écrite de Sécurité sociale) SS ; ≃ DWP 🇬🇧 ; ≃ SSA 🇺🇸 **2.** (abr écrite de Sa Sainteté) HH. ◆ nm (abr de SchutzStaffel) ▸ **un SS** a member of the SS.

St (abr écrite de saint) St., St.

stabiliser [3] [stabilize] vt **1.** [consolider - situation] to stabilize, to normalize **2.** [monnaie, devise, prix] to stabilize. ❖ **se stabiliser** vpi **1.** [situation] to stabilize ; [objet] to steady ; [athlète] to regain one's balance **2.** [personne] to settle down.

stabilité [stabilite] nf [d'un véhicule, d'un échafaudage, d'une monnaie, d'un marché] stability, steadiness.

stable [stabl] adj **1.** [qui ne bouge pas - position, structure] steady, stable **2.** [constant - personne, marché, emploi] stable, steady.

stade [stad] nm **1.** SPORT stadium **2.** [étape, phase] stage / *j'en suis arrivé au stade où…* I've reached the stage where…

stage [staʒ] nm **1.** COMM work placement 🇬🇧, internship 🇺🇸 ; [sur le temps de travail] in-service training ▸ **faire un stage a)** [cours] to go on a training course **b)** [expérience professionnelle] to go on a work placement 🇬🇧, to undergo an internship 🇺🇸 ▸ **stage en entreprise** work experience ou placement ▸ **stage de formation** training course / *stage d'insertion à la vie professionnelle* training scheme for young unemployed people **2.** LOISIRS ▸ **faire un stage de plongée a)** [cours] to have scuba diving lessons **b)** [vacances] to go on a scuba diving holiday 🇬🇧 ou vacation 🇺🇸.

⚠ Le mot anglais **stage** signifie « scène » ou « étape » et non stage.

stagiaire [staʒjɛʀ] nmf [gén] trainee, intern 🇺🇸.

stagnation [stagnasjɔ̃] nf stagnation, stagnating.

stagner [3] [stagne] vi **1.** [liquide] to stagnate **2.** [économie, affaires] to stagnate, to be sluggish.

stalactite [stalaktit] nf stalactite.

stalagmite [stalagmit] nf stalagmite.

stand [stɑ̃d] nm **1.** [de foire] stall, stand **2.** JEUX & MIL ▸ **stand (de tir)** (shooting) range **3.** SPORT ▸ **stand (de ravitaillement)** pit.

standard [stɑ̃daʀ] ◆ adj **1.** [normalisé - modèle, pièce, taille] standard *(modif)* **2.** [non original - discours, goûts] commonplace, unoriginal, standard. ◆ nm TÉLÉC switchboard.

standardiser [3] [stɑ̃daʀdize] vt [normaliser, uniformiser] to standardize.

standardiste [stɑ̃daʀdist] nmf (switchboard) operator.

standing [stɑ̃diŋ] nm **1.** [d'une personne - position sociale] social status ou standing ; [- réputation] (good) reputation, standing **2.** [confort] : *immeuble de grand standing* prestigious block of flats 🇬🇧, luxury apartment building 🇺🇸.

staphylocoque [stafilɔkɔk] nm staphylococcus.

star [staʀ] nf **1.** CINÉ (film) star ; MUS & THÉÂTRE star **2.** [du monde politique, sportif] star.

starisation [staʀizasjɔ̃] nf : *la starisation de la politique / du milieu littéraire* the fact that so many politicians / writers have become media stars.

starlette [staʀlɛt] nf starlet.

starter [staʀtɛʀ] nm **1.** AUTO choke ▸ **mettre le starter** to pull the choke out **2.** SPORT starter.

start-up [staʀtœp] nf inv ÉCON start-up.

station [stasjɔ̃] nf **1.** TRANSP ▸ **station d'autobus** bus stop ▸ **station de métro** underground 🇬🇧 ou subway 🇺🇸 station ▸ **station de taxis** taxi rank 🇬🇧 ou stand 🇺🇸 **2.** [centre] ▸ **station d'épuration** sewerage plant ▸ **station de lavage** carwash **3.** RADIO & TV station ▸ **station de télévision** television station **4.** [lieu de séjour] resort ▸ **station balnéaire** sea ou seaside resort ▸ **station de sports d'hiver** ski resort ▸ **station thermale** (thermal) spa **5.** INFORM ▸ **station de travail** workstation **6.** [position] posture ▸ **station verticale** upright position ▸ **la station debout est déconseillée** standing is not advisable **7.** ASTRONAUT ▸ **station orbitale** orbital station ▸ **station spatiale** space station.

stationnaire [stasjɔnɛʀ] adj MÉD [état] stable.

stationnement [stasjɔnmɑ̃] nm **1.** [arrêt] parking ▸ **stationnement payant** parking fee payable / 'stationnement interdit' 'no parking' **2.** 🇶🇨 car park. ◈ **en stationnement** loc adj [véhicule] parked.

stationner [3] [stasjɔne] vi **1.** [véhicule] to be parked **2.** MIL : *les troupes stationnées en Allemagne* troops stationed in Germany.

station-service [stasjɔ̃sɛʀvis] (*pl* **stations-service**) nf service station, petrol station 🇬🇧, gas station (U) 🇺🇸.

statique [statik] adj [immobile] static.

statisticien, enne [statistisjɛ̃, ɛn] nm, f statistician.

statistique [statistik] ◈ adj statistical. ◈ nf **1.** [étude] statistics (U) **2.** [donnée] statistic, figure.

statistiquement [statistikmɑ̃] adv statistically.

stats [stat] nfpl *fam* stats ▸ **faire des stats** to do stats.

statue [staty] nf ART statue.

statuer [7] [statɥe] vt to rule. ◈ **statuer sur** v + prép ▸ **statuer sur un litige** to rule on a lawsuit.

statuette [statɥɛt] nf statuette.

statu quo (*pl* **statu quo**), **statuquo*** [statykwo] nm [état actuel des choses] status quo.

stature [statyʀ] nf **1.** [carrure] stature **2.** [envergure] stature, calibre.

statut [staty] nm DR & SOCIOL status / *mon statut de femme mariée* my status as a married woman ▸ **statut social** social status. ◈ **statuts** nmpl [règlements] statutes ; ≃ Articles (and Memorandum) of Association.

Ste (abr écrite de sainte) St., St.

Sté (abr écrite de société) Co.

steak [stɛk] nm steak ▸ **steak frites** steak and chips 🇬🇧 ou fries 🇺🇸 ▸ **un steak haché** a beefburger 🇬🇧, a hamburger 🇺🇸 ▸ **steak tartare** steak tartare.

sténodactylo [stenodaktilo] nmf [personne] shorthand typist.

step [stɛp] nm SPORT step.

steppe [stɛp] nf steppe.

stepper, steppeur [stɛpœʀ] nm SPORT [appareil] stepper.

stéréo [steʀeo] ◈ adj inv stereo. ◈ nf [procédé] stereo. ◈ **en stéréo** ◈ loc adj stereo (modif). ◈ loc adv in stereo.

stéréotype [steʀeɔtip] nm [formule banale] stereotype, cliché.

stéréotypé, e [steʀeɔtipe] adj [comportement] stereotyped ; [tournure] clichéd, hackneyed.

stérile [steʀil] adj **1.** [femme] infertile, sterile, barren *litt* ; [homme] sterile ; [sol] barren ; [végétal] sterile **2.** [improductif - artiste] unproductive ; [- imagination] infertile, barren ; [- hypothèse] unproductive, vain ; [- rêve] vain, hopeless ; [- effort] vain, fruitless **3.** MÉD [aseptique] sterile, sterilized.

stérilet [steʀilɛ] nm IUD, coil.

stérilisateur [steʀilizatœʀ] nm sterilizer.

stérilisé, e [steʀilize] adj sterilized.

stériliser [3] [steʀilize] vt **1.** [rendre infécond] to sterilize **2.** [rendre aseptique] to sterilize.

stérilité [steʀilite] nf **1.** [d'une femme] sterility, infertility, barrenness *litt* ; [d'un homme] infertility, sterility ; [d'un sol] barrenness **2.** [de l'esprit] barrenness, unproductiveness.

sterling [stɛʀliŋ] adj inv & nm sterling.

sternum [stɛʀnɔm] nm ANAT breastbone, sternum *spéc*.

stéthoscope [stetɔskɔp] nm stethoscope.

steward [stiwaʀt] nm AÉRON steward.

stick [stik] nm [de fard, de colle] stick. ◈ **en stick** loc adj [déodorant] stick (modif).

sticker [stikœʀ] nm sticker.

stigmate [stigmat] nm **1.** MÉD mark, stigma *spéc* **2.** [marque] : *porter les stigmates de la guerre / débauche* to bear the cruel marks of war / the marks of debauchery **3.** BOT eyespot, stigma **4.** ZOOL (respiratory) stigma. ◈ **stigmates** nmpl RELIG stigmata.

stigmatiser [3] [stigmatize] vt [dénoncer] to stigmatize, to condemn, to pillory *fig*.

stimulant, e [stimylɑ̃, ɑ̃t] adj **1.** [fortifiant - climat] bracing ; [- boisson] stimulant (modif) **2.** [encourageant - résultat, paroles] encouraging. ◈ **stimulant** nm **1.** [remontant, tonique] stimulant **2.** [aiguillon] stimulus, spur.

stimulateur [stimylatœʀ] nm MÉD stimulator ▸ **stimulateur (cardiaque)** pacemaker.

stimulation [stimylasjɔ̃] nf CHIM, PHYSIOL & PSYCHOL stimulation, stimulus.

stimuler [3] [stimyle] vt **1.** [activer - fonction organique] to stimulate **2.** [encourager - personne] to encourage, to motivate **3.** [intensifier - activité] to stimulate.

stipuler [3] [stipyle] vt **1.** DR to stipulate **2.** [spécifier] to stipulate, to specify.

stock [stɔk] nm **1.** COMM stock ; ÉCON stock, supply **2.** [réserve personnelle] stock, collection, supply ▸ **faire des stocks (de)** to stock up (on). ◈ **en stock** loc adv ▸ **avoir qqch en stock** to have sthg in stock.

stockage [stɔkaʒ] nm **1.** [constitution d'un stock] stocking (up) **2.** [conservation - d'énergie, d'informations, de liquides, d'armes] storage.

stocker [3] [stɔke] vt [s'approvisionner en] to stock up on ou with ; [avoir - en réserve] to (keep in) stock ; [- en grande quantité] to stockpile, to hoard.

stoïque [stɔik] adj stoical.

stop [stɔp] ◈ nm **1.** [panneau] stop sign **2.** [lumière] brake light, stoplight **3.** *fam* [auto-stop] hitchhiking ▸ **faire du stop** to hitch, to thumb a lift ou it **4.** [dans un télégramme] stop. ◈ interj stop (it) / *tu me diras stop — stop !* [en versant à boire] say when — when!

stopper [3] [stɔpe] ◈ vt [train, voiture] to stop, to bring to a halt ; [engin, maladie] to stop ; [développement, processus, production] to stop, to halt ; [pratique] to put a stop to, to stop. ◆ vi [marcheur, véhicule, machine, processus, production] to stop, to come to a halt ou standstill.

store [stɔʀ] nm [intérieur] blind ; [extérieur - d'un magasin] awning ▶ **store vénitien** Venetian blind.

⚠ Le mot anglais **store** signifie « magasin » et non **store**.

STP, stp (abr écrite de **s'il te plaît**) pls ; SMS PLZ, PLS.

strabisme [stʀabism] nm squint, strabismus *spéc / elle a un léger strabisme* she has a slight squint.

strangulation [stʀɑ̃gylasjɔ̃] nf strangulation, strangling *(U)*.

strapontin [stʀapɔ̃tɛ̃] nm [siège] jump ou folding seat.

stras [stʀas] = **strass**.

strass [stʀas] nm paste *(U)*, strass.

stratagème [stʀataʒɛm] nm stratagem, ruse.

strate [stʀat] nf **1.** GÉOL stratum **2.** *sout* [niveau] layer / *les strates de la personnalité* the layers ou strata of the personality.

stratège [stʀatɛʒ] nm **1.** MIL strategist **2.** *fig : un fin stratège* a cunning strategist.

stratégie [stʀateʒi] nf **1.** JEUX & MIL strategy **2.** *fig* ▶ **stratégie marketing** marketing strategy.

stratégique [stʀateʒik] adj **1.** MIL strategic, strategical **2.** *fig : un repli stratégique* a strategic retreat.

stratifié, e [stʀatifje] adj stratified. ❖ **stratifié** nm laminate.

stress [stʀɛs] nm stress.

stressant, e [stʀesɑ̃, ɑ̃t] adj stressful, stress-inducing.

stresser [4] [stʀese] vt to put under stress.

Stretch® [stʀɛtʃ] ◆ adj inv stretch *(modif)*, stretchy. ◆ nm inv stretch material.

stretching [stʀɛtʃiŋ] nm stretching / *cours de stretching* stretch class / *faire du stretching* to do stretching exercises.

strict, e [stʀikt] adj **1.** [astreignant, précis - contrôle, ordre, règle, principe] strict, exacting **2.** [minimal] strict ▶ **le strict nécessaire** ou **minimum** the bare minimum ▶ **faire le strict minimum** to do only what is strictly necessary / *les obsèques seront célébrées dans la plus stricte intimité* the funeral will take place strictly in private **3.** [sévère - éducation, personne] strict ; [- discipline] strict, rigorous **4.** [austère - intérieur, vêtement] severe, austere **5.** [rigoureux, absolu] strict, absolute / *c'est ton droit le plus strict* it's your lawful right / *c'est la stricte vérité !* it's absolutely true!

strictement [stʀiktəmɑ̃] adv **1.** [rigoureusement] strictly, scrupulously **2.** [absolument] strictly, absolutely.

strident, e [stʀidɑ̃, ɑ̃t] adj [son, voix] strident, shrill, piercing.

strie [stʀi] nf **1.** [sillon] stria *spéc*, (thin) groove **2.** [ligne de couleur] streak.

strier [10] [stʀije] vt **1.** [creuser] to striate, to groove **2.** [veiner] to streak.

string [stʀiŋ] nm G-string.

strip-tease (*pl* strip-teases), **striptease*** [stʀiptiz] nm striptease act / *faire un strip-tease* to do a striptease.

strip-teaseur, strip-teaseuse (*mpl* strip-teaseurs, *fpl* strip-teaseuses), **stripteaseur*, euse** [stʀiptizœʀ, øz] nm, f stripper, striptease artist.

strophe [stʀɔf] nf [d'un poème] stanza.

structure [stʀyktyʀ] nf **1.** [organisation - d'un service, d'une société, d'un texte] structure **2.** [institution] system, organization **3.** CONSTR building, structure.

structuré, e [stʀyktyʀe] adj structured, organized.

structurel, elle [stʀyktyʀɛl] adj structural.

structurer [3] [stʀyktyʀe] vt to structure, to organize. ❖ **se structurer** vpi to take shape.

stuc [styk] nm stucco. ❖ **en stuc** loc adj stucco *(modif)*.

studette [stydɛt] nf small studio flat 🇬🇧 ou apartment 🇺🇸, bedsitter 🇬🇧.

studieux, euse [stydjø, øz] adj **1.** [appliqué - élève] hard-working, studious **2.** [consacré à l'étude] studious / *une soirée studieuse* an evening of study, a studious evening.

studio [stydjo] nm **1.** [appartement] studio flat 🇬🇧, studio apartment 🇺🇸 **2.** AUDIO, CINÉ & TV studio ▶ **studio d'enregistrement** recording studio **3.** PHOT photography ou photographic studio. ❖ **en studio** loc adv : *tourné en studio* shot in studio.

stupéfaction [stypefaksjɔ̃] nf stupefaction *litt*, astonishment.

stupéfait, e [stypefɛ, ɛt] adj [personne] astounded, stunned, stupefied *litt* / *je suis stupéfait de voir qu'il est revenu* I'm amazed to see he came back.

stupéfiant, e [stypefjɑ̃, ɑ̃t] adj [nouvelle, réaction] astounding, amazing, stupefying *litt*. ❖ **stupéfiant** nm [drogue] drug, narcotic.

stupéfier [9] [stypefje] vt [abasourdir] to astound, to stun.

stupeur [stypœʀ] nf [ahurissement] amazement, astonishment / *je constate avec stupeur que* I am amazed to note that ▶ **à la stupeur générale** to everyone's astonishment.

stupide [stypid] adj **1.** [inintelligent - personne, jeu, initiative, réponse, suggestion] stupid, silly, foolish ; [- raisonnement] stupid **2.** [absurde - accident, mort] stupid.

stupidement [stypidmɑ̃] adv stupidly, absurdly, foolishly.

stupidité [stypidite] nf **1.** [d'une action, d'une personne, d'un propos] stupidity, foolishness **2.** [acte] piece of foolish behaviour **3.** [parole] stupid ou foolish remark.

stups [styp] nmpl *arg crime* ▶ **les stups** the narcotics ou drugs squad.

style [stil] nm **1.** [d'un écrivain, d'un journal] style **2.** [d'un artiste, d'un sportif] style, (characteristic) approach, touch **3.** ART style ▶ **style gothique / Régence** Gothic / Regency style **4.** [genre, ordre d'idée] style / *dis-lui que tu vas réfléchir, ou quelque chose dans ou de ce style* tell him you'll think about it, or something along those lines ou in that vein **5.** *fam* [manière d'agir] style / *tu aurais pu l'avoir dénoncé — ce n'est pas mon style* you could have denounced him — it's not my style ou that's not the sort of thing I'd do ▶ **style de vie** lifestyle **6.** LING ▶ **style direct / indirect** direct / indirect speech. ❖ **de style** loc adj [meuble, objet] period *(modif)*.

styliser [3] [stilize] vt to stylize.

stylisme [stilism] nm fashion design.

styliste [stilist] nmf [de mode, dans l'industrie] designer.

stylistique [stilistik] ◆ adj stylistic. ◆ nf stylistics *(sg)*.

stylo [stilo] nm pen ▶ **stylo (à bille)** ballpoint (pen), Biro® 🇬🇧 ▶ **stylo à encre / cartouche** fountain / cartridge pen.

stylo-feutre [stiloføtʀ] (*pl* stylos-feutres) nm felt-tip pen.

su, e [sy] pp ⟶ **savoir**.

suave [sɥav] adj [manières, ton] suave, sophisticated ; [senteur] sweet ; [teintes] subdued, mellow.

subalterne [sybaltɛʀn] ◆ adj **1.** [position] secondary / *un rôle subalterne* a secondary ou minor role **2.** [personne] subordinate, junior *(modif)*. ◆ nmf subordinate, subaltern, underling *péj*.

subconscient, e [sybkɔ̃sjɑ̃, ɑ̃t] adj subconscious. ❖ **subconscient** nm subconscious.

subdiviser [3] [sybdivize] vt to subdivide / *chapitre subdivisé en deux parties* chapter subdivided into two parts. ❖ **se subdiviser** vpi ▶ **se subdiviser (en)** to subdivide (into).

subdivision [sybdivizjɔ̃] nf [catégorie] subdivision.

subir [32] [sybiʀ] vt **1.** [dommages, pertes] to suffer, to sustain ; [conséquences, défaite] to suffer ; [attaque, humiliation, insultes, sévices] to be subjected to, to suffer / *après tout ce qu'elle m'a fait subir* after all she inflicted on me ou made me go through / *il lui a fait subir les pires humiliations* he made him / her suffer ou endure the most terrible humiliations **2.** [influence] to be under ; [situation, personne] to put up with **3.** [opération, transformation] to undergo.

subit, e [sybi, it] adj sudden.

subitement [sybitmɑ̃] adv suddenly, all of a sudden.

subjectif, ive [sybʒɛktif, iv] adj subjective.

subjectivité [sybʒɛktivite] nf subjectivity, subjectiveness.

subjonctif, ive [sybʒɔ̃ktif, iv] adj subjunctive. ❖ **subjonctif** nm subjunctive.

subjuguer [3] [sybʒyge] vt *sout* [suj : discours, lecture] to enthral, to captivate ; [suj : beauté, charme, regard] to enthral, to beguile ; [suj : éloquence] to enthral.

sublime [syblim] adj **1.** *sout* [noble, grand] sublime, elevated **2.** [exceptionnel, parfait] sublime, wonderful, magnificent / *tu as été sublime* you were magnificent.

sublimer [3] [syblime] vt PSYCHOL to sublimate.

submergé, e [sybmɛʀʒe] adj **1.** [rochers] submerged ; [champs] submerged, flooded **2.** [surchargé, accablé] inundated ▶ **submergé de travail** snowed under with work / *submergé de réclamations* inundated with complaints **3.** [incapable de faire face] swamped, up to one's eyes.

submerger [17] [sybmɛʀʒe] vt **1.** [inonder] to flood, to submerge **2.** [envahir - suj : angoisse, joie] to overcome, to overwhelm ; [- suj : réclamations] to inundate, to swamp ; [- suj : dettes] to overwhelm, to swamp / *notre standard est submergé d'appels* our switchboard's swamped with ou jammed by calls / *je suis submergé de travail* I'm snowed under with work.

submersible [sybmɛʀsibl] nm submersible.

subodorer [3] [sybodɔʀe] vt *hum* [danger] to scent, to smell, to sense.

subordination [sybɔʀdinasjɔ̃] nf **1.** [dans une hiérarchie] subordination, subordinating **2.** LING & LOGIQUE subordination.

subordonné, e [sybɔʀdɔne] ◆ adj **1.** [subalterne] subordinate **2.** LING subordinate, dependent. ◆ nm, f [subalterne] subordinate, subaltern. ❖ **subordonnée** nf LING subordinate ou dependent clause.

subornation [sybɔʀnasjɔ̃] nf subornation ▶ **subornation de témoins** subornation of witnesses.

subside [sypsid] nm [de l'État] grant, subsidy / *il vivait des subsides de ses parents* he lived on the allowance he received from his parents.

subsidiaire [sybzidjɛʀ] adj subsidiary.

subsistance [sybzistɑ̃s] nf [existence matérielle] subsistence ▶ **pourvoir à** ou **assurer la subsistance de qqn** to support ou to maintain ou to keep sb / *elle arrive tout juste à assurer sa subsistance* she just manages to survive, she has just enough to keep body and soul together.

subsister [3] [sybziste] vi **1.** [demeurer - doute, espoir, rancœur, traces] to remain, to subsist ; [- tradition] to live on / *quelques questions subsistent auxquelles on n'a pas répondu* there are still a few questions which remain unanswered **2.** [survivre] to survive / *je n'ai que 50 euros par semaine pour subsister* I only have 50 euros a week to live on.

substance [sypstɑ̃s] nf [matière] substance. ❖ **en substance** loc adv in substance / *c'est, en substance, ce qu'elle m'a raconté* that's the gist of what she told me.

substantiel, elle [sypstɑ̃sjɛl] adj **1.** [nourriture, repas] substantial, filling **2.** [avantage, différence] substantial, significant, important ; [somme] substantial, considerable.

substantif [sypstɑ̃tif] nm substantive.

substituer [7] [sypstitɥe] vt ▶ **substituer qqch à** [remplacer par qqch] to substitute sthg for, to replace by sthg. ❖ **se substituer à** vp + prép [pour aider, représenter] to substitute for, to stand in for, to replace ; [de façon déloyale] to substitute o.s. for.

substitut [sypstity] ◆ nm [produit, personne] ▶ **substitut de** substitute for. ◆ nmf DR deputy ou assistant public prosecutor.

substitution [sypstitysjɔ̃] nf [d'objets, de personnes] substitution / *il y a eu substitution d'enfant* the babies were switched round. ❖ **de substitution** loc adj [réaction] substitution *(modif)* ▶ **produit de substitution** substitute.

subterfuge [syptɛʀfyʒ] nm subterfuge, ruse, trick.

subtil, e [syptil] adj **1.** [argument, esprit, raisonnement, personne] subtle, discerning **2.** [allusion, différence] subtle ; [nuance, distinction] subtle, fine, nice **3.** [arôme, goût, parfum] subtle, delicate.

subtiliser [3] [syptilize] vt [voler] to steal, to spirit away *(sép)* / *ils lui ont subtilisé sa montre* they relieved him of his watch *hum*.

subtilité [syptilite] nf [d'un raisonnement, d'un parfum, d'une nuance] subtlety, subtleness, delicacy.

subvenir [40] [sybvəniʀ] ❖ **subvenir à** v + prép [besoins] to provide for ; [dépenses] to meet.

subvention [sybvɑ̃sjɔ̃] nf subsidy.

subventionner [3] [sybvɑ̃sjɔne] vt [entreprise, théâtre] to subsidize, to grant funds to ; [recherche] to subsidize, to grant funds towards.

subversif, ive [sybvɛʀsif, iv] adj subversive.

subversion [sybvɛʀsjɔ̃] nf subversion, subverting *(U)*.

suc [syk] nm BOT & PHYSIOL juice ▶ **sucs gastriques** gastric juices.

succédané [syksedane] nm [ersatz] substitute.

succéder [18] [syksede] ❖ **succéder à** v + prép **1.** [remplacer dans une fonction] to succeed, to take over from ▶ **succéder à qqn sur le trône** to succeed sb to the throne **2.** [suivre] to follow / *puis les défaites succédèrent aux victoires* after the victories came defeats. ❖ **se succéder** vpi [se suivre] to follow each other ▶ **les crises se succèdent** it's just one crisis after another.

📝 In reformed spelling (see p. 16-18), this verb is conjugated like *semer* : *il succèdera, elle succèderait*.

succès [syksɛ] nm **1.** [heureux résultat, réussite personnelle] success **2.** [exploit, performance] success ; [en amour] conquest / *l'opération est un succès total* the operation is a complete success **3.** [approbation - du public] success, popularity ; [- d'un groupe] success ▶ **avoir du succès**

a) [œuvre, artiste] to be successful b) [suggestion] to be very well received ▸ **avoir du succès auprès de qqn** : *sa pièce a eu beaucoup de succès auprès des critiques mais peu auprès du public* his play was acclaimed by the critics but the public was less than enthusiastic / *il a beaucoup de succès auprès des femmes / jeunes* he's very popular with women / young people **4.** [chanson] hit ; [film, pièce] (box-office) hit ou success ; [livre] success, bestseller ▸ **succès de librairie** bestseller ▸ **un gros succès** a) [film] a big success b) [livre] a best-seller c) [disque] a hit. ❖ **à succès** loc adj [auteur, chanteur] popular. ❖ **avec succès** loc adv successfully, with success. ❖ **sans succès** loc adv [essayer] unsuccessfully, without (any) success.

successeur [syksesœʀ] nm [remplaçant] successor.

successif, ive [syksesif, iv] adj successive.

succession [syksesjɔ̃] nf **1.** DR [héritage] succession, inheritance ; [biens] estate **2.** [remplacement] succession / *prendre la succession d'un directeur* to take over from ou to succeed a manager **3.** [suite] succession, series *(sg).*

successivement [syksesivmɑ̃] adv successively, one after the other.

succinct, e [syksɛ̃, ɛ̃t] adj [bref, concis] succinct, brief, concise.

succomber [3] [sykɔ̃be] vi *sout* **1.** [décéder] to die, to succumb *sout* **2.** [céder - personne] to succumb ▸ **succomber à** a) [désir] to succumb to, to yield to b) [désespoir, émotion] to succumb to *sout*, to give way to c) [fatigue, sommeil] to succumb to *sout* d) [blessures] to die from, to succumb to *sout* / *j'ai succombé à ses charmes* I fell (a) victim ou I succumbed to her charms.

succulent, e [sykylɑ̃, ɑ̃t] adj [savoureux - mets, viande] succulent.

succursale [sykyʀsal] nf COMM branch.

sucer [16] [syse] vt **1.** [liquide] to suck ; [bonbon, glace, sucette] to eat, to suck / *pastilles à sucer* lozenges to be sucked **2.** [doigt, stylo] to suck (on) / *sucer son pouce* to suck one's thumb **3.** *vulg* [comme pratique sexuelle] to suck off *(sép)* / *se faire sucer* to be given a blow job. ❖ **se sucer** vpt ▸ **se sucer la pomme** *tfam* ou **la poire**, *tfam* ou **le museau** *tfam* to neck, to snog UK, to make out US.

sucette [sysɛt] nf [friandise] lollipop, lolly UK.

suçon [sysɔ̃] nm lovebite, hickey US ▸ **faire un suçon à qqn** to give sb a lovebite.

sucre [sykʀ] nm **1.** [produit de consommation] sugar / *confiture sans sucre* sugar-free jam ▸ **sucre de betterave** / **canne** beet / cane sugar ▸ **sucre roux** ou **brun** brown sugar ▸ **sucre candi** candy sugar ▸ **sucre cristallisé** (coarse) granulated sugar ▸ **sucre d'érable** maple sugar ▸ **sucre glace** icing sugar UK, confectioner's ou powdered sugar US ▸ **sucre en morceaux** lump ou cube sugar ▸ **sucre d'orge** a) [produit] barley sugar b) [bâton] stick of barley sugar ▸ **sucre en poudre** (fine) caster sugar ▸ **sucre semoule** (fine) caster sugar ▸ **sucre vanillé** vanilla sugar **2.** [cube] sugar lump ou cube / *tu prends ton café avec un ou deux sucres ?* do you take your coffee with one or two sugars ou lumps? ❖ **au sucre** loc adj [fruits, crêpes] (sprinkled) with sugar.

sucré, e [sykʀe] adj [naturellement] sweet ; [artificiellement] sweetened / *je n'aime pas le café sucré* I don't like sugar in my coffee ▸ **un verre d'eau sucrée** a glass of sugar water ▸ **non sucré** unsweetened. ❖ **sucré** nm ▸ **le sucré** sweet things.

sucrer [3] [sykʀe] vt **1.** [avec du sucre - café, thé] to sugar, to put sugar in ; [-vin] to add sugar to, to chaptalize ; [-fruits] to sprinkle with sugar / *sucrez à volonté* add sugar to taste **2.** *tfam* [supprimer - prime] to stop ; [-réplique, pas-

sage] to do away with *(insép)* / *on lui a sucré son permis de conduire après son accident* his driving licence was revoked after the accident.

sucrerie [sykʀəʀi] nf **1.** [friandise] sweet thing, sweetmeat, sweet UK, candy US / *elle adore les sucreries* she has a sweet tooth ou loves sweet things **2.** QUEBEC [forêt d'érables] maple forest.

Sucrette® [sykʀɛt] nf (artificial) sweetener.

sucrier [sykʀije] nm [pot] sugar basin ou bowl.

sud [syd] ◆ nm inv **1.** [point cardinal] south / *il habite au sud de Paris* he lives to the south of Paris / *aller au ou vers le sud* to go south ou southwards / *la cuisine est plein sud* ou *exposée au sud* the kitchen faces due south ou has a southerly aspect *sout* **2.** [partie d'un pays, d'un continent] south, southern area ou regions / *le sud de l'Italie* Southern Italy. ◆ adj inv **1.** [qui est au sud - façade de maison] south, southfacing ; [-côte, côté, versant] south, southern ; [-portail] south **2.** [dans des noms géographiques] South ▸ **le que sud** the South Pacific.

sud-africain, e [sydafʀikɛ̃, ɛn] (*mpl* sud-africains, *fpl* sud-africaines) adj South African. ❖ **Sud-Africain, e** nm, f South African.

sud-américain, e [sydameʀikɛ̃, ɛn] (*mpl* sud-américains, *fpl* sud-américaines) adj South American. ❖ **Sud-Américain, e** nm, f South American.

sud-coréen, enne [sydkɔʀeɛ̃, ɛn] (*mpl* sud-coréens, *fpl* sud-coréennes) adj South Korean. ❖ **Sud-Coréen, enne** nm, f South Korean.

sud-est [sydɛst] ◆ adj inv southeast. ◆ nm inv [point cardinal] southeast / *au sud-est de Lyon* southeast of Lyon.

sudoku [sydɔky] nm sudoku.

sud-ouest [sydwɛst] ◆ adj inv southwest. ◆ nm inv southwest / *au sud-ouest de Tokyo* southwest of Tokyo.

Sud-Soudan [sydsudɑ̃] nm ▸ **(le) Sud-Soudan** South Sudan ▸ **au Sud-Soudan** in South Sudan.

suède [sɥɛd] nm suede / *des gants en suède* suede ou kid gloves.

Suède [sɥɛd] npr f ▸ **(la) Suède** Sweden.

suédine [syedin] nf suedette.

suédois, e [sɥedwa, az] adj Swedish. ❖ **Suédois, e** nm, f Swede. ❖ **suédois** nm LING Swedish.

suée [sɥe] nf *fam* [transpiration] sweat / *attraper* ou *prendre une (bonne) suée* [en faisant un effort] to work up quite a sweat.

suer [7] [sɥe] ◆ vi **1.** [transpirer - personne] to sweat, to get sweaty / *suer à grosses gouttes* to be streaming with sweat, to be sweating profusely **2.** [bois, plâtres] to ooze, to sweat / *faire suer des oignons* CULIN to sweat onions **3.** *fam* [fournir un gros effort] to slog UK, to slave (away) / *j'en ai sué pour faire démarrer la tondeuse !* I had the devil's own job trying to get the mower started! **4.** *tfam* EXPR **faire suer** [importuner] : *il nous fait suer !* he's a pain in the neck! / *ça me ferait suer de devoir y retourner* I'd hate to have to go back there / *je me suis fait suer toute la journée* I was bored stiff all day long. ◆ vt [sueur] to sweat ▸ **suer sang et eau** [faire de grands efforts] to sweat blood.

sueur [sɥœʀ] nf [transpiration] sweat ▸ **donner des sueurs froides à qqn** to put sb in a cold sweat. ❖ **en sueur** loc adj in a sweat.

Suez [sɥez] npr Suez.

suffire [100] [syfiʀ] vi **1.** [en quantité] to be enough, to be sufficient, to suffice *sout* / *une cuillerée, ça te suffit ?* is one spoonful enough for you? ▸ **suffire à** ou **pour faire qqch**: *deux minutes suffisent pour le cuire* it just takes two minutes to cook / *une heure me suffira pour tout *ranger* one hour will be enough for me to put everything away **2.** [en qualité] to be (good) enough / *des excuses ne me suffisent pas* I'm not satisfied with an apology / *ma parole devrait vous suffire* my word should be good enough for you ▸ **suffire à qqch** : *suffire aux besoins de qqn* to meet sb's needs / *ça suffit à mon bonheur* it's enough to make me happy **3.** *(tournure impersonnelle)* ▸ **il suffit de** *(suivi d'un nom)*: *je n'avais jamais volé — il suffit d'une fois !* I've never stolen before — once is enough! / *il suffit d'une erreur pour que tout soit à recommencer* one single mistake means starting all over again / *il suffirait de peu pour que le régime s'écroule* it wouldn't take much to bring down the regime ▸ **il suffit de** *(suivi de l'infinitif)*: *s'il suffisait de travailler pour réussir !* if only work was enough to guarantee success! / *il te suffit de dire que nous arriverons en retard* just say we'll be late ▸ **il suffit que**: *il suffit qu'on me dise ce que je dois faire* I just have no need to be told what to do / *il suffit que je tourne le dos pour qu'elle fasse des bêtises* I only have to turn my back and she's up to some mischief / *(ça) suffit !* *fam* (that's) enough! ◆ **se suffire** ◆ *vp (emploi réciproque)* : *ils se suffisent l'un à l'autre* they've got each other and that's all they need. ◆ *vpi* ▸ **se suffire à soi-même a)** [matériellement] to be self-sufficient **b)** [moralement] to be quite happy with one's own company.

suffisamment [syfizamɑ̃] *adv* sufficiently, enough / *je t'ai suffisamment prévenu* I've warned you often enough.

suffisance [syfizɑ̃s] *nf* [vanité] self-importance, self-satisfaction.

suffisant, e [syfizɑ̃, ɑ̃t] *adj* **1.** [en quantité] sufficient / *trois bouteilles pour cinq, c'est bien* ou *amplement suffisant* three bottles for five, that's plenty ou that's quite enough **2.** [en qualité] sufficient, good enough / *c'est une raison suffisante pour qu'il accepte* it's a good enough reason ou it's reason enough to make him accept **3.** [arrogant - air, personne] self-important, conceited.

suffixe [syfiks] *nm* suffix.

suffocant, e [syfɔkɑ̃, ɑ̃t] *adj* [atmosphère, chaleur, odeur] suffocating, stifling.

suffoquer [3] [syfɔke] ◆ *vi* [étouffer] to suffocate, to choke / *suffoquer de colère* to be choking with anger / *suffoquer de joie* to be overcome with happiness. ◆ *vt* **1.** [suj : atmosphère, fumée, odeur] to suffocate, to choke **2.** [causer une vive émotion à] to choke / *la colère le suffoquait* he was choking with anger **3.** [choquer - suj : attitude, prix] to stagger, to stun, to confound.

suffrage [syfraʒ] *nm* **1.** POL [système] vote ▸ **être élu au suffrage direct / indirect** to be elected by direct / indirect suffrage ▸ **suffrage universel** universal suffrage **2.** [voix] vote / *obtenir beaucoup / peu de suffrages* to poll heavily / badly **3.** *litt* [approbation] approval, approbation, suffrage *litt* ▸ *sa dernière pièce a enlevé* ou **remporté tous les suffrages** his last play was an unqualified success.

suffragette [syfraʒɛt] *nf* suffragette.

suggérer [18] [sygʒeʀe] *vt* **1.** [conseiller, proposer - acte] to suggest ; [- nom, solution] to suggest, to put forward *(sép)*, to propose / *nous lui avons suggéré de renoncer* we suggested he should give up / *je suggère que nous partions tout de suite* I suggest that we go right away **2.** [évoquer] to suggest, to evoke / *sa peinture suggère plus qu'elle ne représente* his painting is more evocative than figurative.

✎ In reformed spelling (see p. 16-18), this verb is conjugated like *semer* : *il suggèrera, elle suggèrerait*.

📋 Notez que le verbe suggest n'est jamais suivi immédiatement d'un complément d'objet indirect :
Ils nous ont suggéré plusieurs approches possibles. *They suggested several possible approaches [to us].*
Quel type d'améliorations nous suggéreriez-vous ? *What type of improvements would you suggest [to us]?*
Dans l'usage, «to us», «to me», etc., sont le plus souvent omis.

suggestif, ive [sygʒɛstif, iv] *adj* [évocateur] suggestive, evocative.

suggestion [sygʒɛstjɔ̃] *nf* [conseil, proposition] suggestion.

suicidaire [sɥisidɛʀ] *adj* **1.** [instinct, personne, tendance] suicidal **2.** [qui conduit à l'échec] suicidal.

suicide [sɥisid] *nm* [mort] suicide.

suicidé, e [sɥiside] *nm, f* suicide.

suicider [3] [sɥiside] ◆ **se suicider** *vpi* **1.** [se tuer] to commit suicide, to kill o.s. **2.** *fig* [causer soi-même sa perte] to commit suicide.

suie [sɥi] *nf* soot.

suinter [3] [sɥɛte] *vi* **1.** [s'écouler] to ooze, to seep / *l'humidité suinte des murailles* the walls are dripping with moisture **2.** [laisser échapper un liquide - plaie] to weep / *ce mur suinte* this wall is running with moisture.

suisse [sɥis] ◆ *adj* Swiss ▸ **suisse allemand / romand** Swiss German / French. ◆ *nm* **1.** [au Vatican] Swiss guard **2.** [Québec] chipmunk. ◆ **Suisse** *nmf* Swiss (person) ▸ **Suisse allemand / romand** German-speaking / French-speaking Swiss.

Suisse [sɥis] *npr f* ▸ **(la) Suisse** Switzerland ▸ **la Suisse allemande / romande** the German-speaking / French-speaking part of Switzerland.

Suissesse [sɥisɛs] *nf* Swiss woman.

suite [sɥit] *nf* **1.** [prolongation - gén] continuation ; [- d'un film, d'un roman] sequel ; [- d'une émission] follow-up / *la suite au prochain numéro* to be continued (in our next issue) ▸ **suite et fin** final instalment / *je n'ai pas pu entendre la suite* I couldn't hear the rest / *attendons la suite des événements* let's wait to see what happens next ▸ **faire suite à** to follow ▸ **prendre la suite de qqn** to take over from sb, to succeed sb **2.** [série] series, succession **3.** [cortège] suite, retinue **4.** [dans un hôtel] suite **5.** [répercussion] consequence / *la suite logique / naturelle de mon adhésion au parti* the logical / natural consequence of my joining the party ▸ **donner suite à a)** [commande, lettre, réclamation] to follow up *(sép)*, to deal with *(insép)* **b)** [projet] to carry on with / *elle est morte des suites de ses blessures* she died of her wounds **6.** [lien logique] coherence / *tu as de la suite dans les idées !* *hum* you certainly know what you want! **7.** MUS suite. ◆ **à la suite** *loc adv* [en succession] one after the other. ◆ **à la suite de** *loc prép* **1.** [derrière - dans l'espace] behind ; [- dans un écrit] after **2.** [à cause de] following / *à la suite de son discours télévisé, sa cote a remonté* following her speech on TV, her popularity rating went up. ◆ **de suite** *loc adv* **1.** *fam* [immédiatement] straightaway, right away / *il revient de suite* he'll be right back **2.** [à la file] in a row, one after the other, in succession / *on n'a pas eu d'électricité pendant cinq jours de suite* we didn't have any electricity for five whole days ou five days running. ◆ **par la suite** *loc adv* [dans le passé] afterwards, later ; [dans le futur] later. ◆ **par suite de** *loc prép* due to, owing to. ◆ **sans suite** *loc adj* [incohérent] disconnected / *il tenait des propos sans suite* his talk was incoherent. ❖ **suite à** *loc prép* ADMIN ▸ **suite à votre lettre** further to ou in response to ou with reference to your letter / *suite à votre appel téléphonique* further to your phone call.

suivant¹ [sɥivɑ̃] *prép* **1.** [le long de] : *découper suivant le pointillé* cut out following the dotted line **2.** [d'après] according to / *suivant son habitude, elle s'est levée très tôt* as is her habit ou wont *sout*, she got up very early **3.** [en fonction de] according to, depending on / *vous donnerez suivant vos possibilités* you'll give according to your means. ❖ **suivant que** *loc conj* according to whether.

suivant², e [sɥivɑ̃, ɑ̃t] ◆ *adj* **1.** [qui vient après - chapitre, mois, semaine] following, next ; [- échelon, train] next / *quelle est la personne suivante ?* [dans une file d'attente] who's next? **2.** [qui va être précisé] following / *il m'a raconté l'histoire suivante* he told me the following story. ◆ *nm, f* [dans une succession] next one / *(au) suivant, s'il vous plaît* next, please / *pas mardi prochain mais le suivant* not this coming Tuesday but the next one ou the one after. ❖ **suivante** *nf* THÉÂTRE lady's maid.

suivi, e [sɥivi] ◆ *pp* ⟶ **suivre**. ◆ *adj* **1.** [ininterrompu - effort] sustained, consistent ; [- correspondance] regular ; [- qualité] consistent ; [- activité] steady **2.** [logique - propos, raisonnement] coherent ; [- politique] consistent **3.** [qui a la faveur du public] : *mode très suivie* very popular fashion / *conférence peu / très suivie* poorly attended / well-attended conference ▸ **la grève a été peu / très suivie** there was little / a lot of support for the strike. ❖ **suivi** *nm* [d'un cas, d'un dossier] follow-up ▸ **assurer le suivi de** **a)** [cas, dossier] to follow through *(sép)* **b)** [commande] to deal with *(insép)* **c)** COMM [article] to continue to stock / *le travail en petits groupes assure un meilleur suivi* working in small groups means that individual participants can be monitored more successfully.

suivre [89] [sɥivʀ]
◆ *vt*

A. DANS L'ESPACE, LE TEMPS **1.** [pour escorter, espionner, rattraper] to follow / *les enfants suivaient leurs parents en courant* the children were running behind their parents ▸ **suivez le guide** this way (for the guided tour), please / *la police les a suivis sur plusieurs kilomètres* the police chased them for several kilometres / *il l'a fait suivre par un détective privé* he had her followed by a private detective ▸ **suivre qqn de près** **a)** [gén] to follow close behind sb **b)** [pour le protéger] to stick close to sb ▸ **suivre la piste de qqn** to follow sb's trail ▸ **suivre qqn à la trace** to follow sb's tracks ▸ **suivre qqn des yeux** ou **du regard** to follow sb with one's eyes ; *(en usage absolu)* : *marche moins vite, je ne peux pas suivre* slow down, I can't keep up **2.** [se dérouler après] to follow (on from), to come after / *la réunion sera suivie d'une collation* refreshments will be served after the meeting ; *(tournure impersonnelle)* : *il suit de votre déclaration que le témoin ment* it follows from your statement that the witness is lying **3.** [être placé après] to follow, to come after / *votre nom suit le mien sur la liste* your name is right after mine on the list ; *(en usage absolu)* : *dans les pages qui suivent* in the following pages.

B. ADOPTER, OBÉIR À **1.** [emprunter - itinéraire, rue] to follow **2.** [longer - à pied] to walk along ; [- en voiture] to drive along ; [- en bateau] to sail along / *la route suit la rivière sur plusieurs kilomètres* the road runs along ou follows (the course of) the river for several kilometres / *découper en suivant les pointillés* cut along the dotted line **3.** [se soumettre à - traitement] to undergo / *suivre des cours de cuisine* to attend a cookery course ▸ **suivre un régime** to be on a diet **4.** [se conformer à - conseil, personne, instructions] to follow ; [règlement] to comply with *(insép)* / *vous n'avez qu'à*

suivre les panneaux just follow the signs / *son exemple n'est pas à suivre* he's not a good example **5.** CARTES ▸ **je suis** I'm in **6.** COMM [stocker] to stock ; [produire] to produce.

C. OBSERVER, COMPRENDRE **1.** [observer - carrière, progrès, feuilleton] to follow ; [- actualité] to keep up with *(insép)* **2.** [se concentrer sur - exposé, messe] to listen to *(insép)*, to pay attention to / *maintenant, suivez-moi bien* now, listen to me carefully ou pay close attention ; *(en usage absolu)* : *encore un qui ne suivait pas !* [distrait] so, someone else wasn't paying attention! **3.** [comprendre - explications, raisonnement] to follow / *je ne te suis plus* I'm not with you any more **4.** [s'occuper de - dossier, commande] to deal with *(insép)* ; [- élève] to follow the progress of / *je suis suivie par un très bon médecin* I'm with ou under a very good doctor. ◆ *vi* **1.** ÉDUC [assimiler le programme] to keep up / *il a du mal à suivre en physique* he's having difficulty keeping up in physics **2.** [être acheminé après] ▸ **faire suivre son courrier** to have one's mail forwarded **3.** [être ci-après] to follow / *sont reçus les candidats dont les noms suivent* the names of the successful candidates are as follows. ❖ **se suivre** *vpi* **1.** [être l'un derrière l'autre - personnes, lettres] to follow one another / *par temps de brouillard, ne vous suivez pas de trop près* in foggy conditions, keep your distance (from other vehicles) **2.** [être dans l'ordre - pages] to be in the right order, to follow on from one another **3.** [se succéder dans le temps] ▸ **les jours se suivent et ne se ressemblent pas** *prov* who knows what tomorrow holds *phr*, every day is a new beginning ou dawn. ❖ **à suivre** ◆ *loc adj* : *c'est une affaire à suivre* it's something we should keep an eye on. ◆ *loc adv* '**à suivre**' 'to be continued'.

sujet, ette [syʒɛ, ɛt] ◆ *adj* **1.** ▸ **sujet à** [susceptible de] : *sujet à des attaques cardiaques / à des migraines* subject to heart attacks / migraines / *sujet au mal de mer* liable to become seasick, prone to seasickness **2.** ▸ **sujet à** [soumis à] : *sujet à caution* questionable / *leurs informations sont sujettes à caution* their information should be taken warily. ◆ *nm, f* [citoyen] subject. ❖ **sujet** *nm* **1.** [thème - d'une discussion] subject, topic ; [- d'une pièce, d'un roman] subject ; [- d'un exposé, d'une recherche] subject / *le sujet de notre débat de ce soir est...* the question we'll be debating tonight is... / *sujet de conversation* topic (of conversation) / *c'est devenu un sujet de plaisanterie* it has become a standing joke ▸ **sujet d'examen** examination question **2.** [motif] ▸ **sujet de** cause of, ground for, grounds for / *ils ont de nombreux sujets de discorde* they have many reasons to disagree / *leur salaire est leur principal sujet de mécontentement* the main cause of their dissatisfaction is their salary **3.** [figurine] figurine **4.** GRAM [fonction] subject **5.** MÉD, PHILOS & PSYCHOL subject ▸ **sujet d'expérience** experimental subject. ❖ **au sujet de** *loc prép* about, concerning / *c'est au sujet de Martha ?* is it about Martha? / *j'aimerais vous faire remarquer, à ce sujet, que...* concerning this matter, I'd like to point out that... / *je voudrais parler au directeur — c'est à quel sujet ?* I'd like to talk to the manager — what about?

sulfate [sylfat] *nm* sulphate 🇬🇧, sulfate 🇺🇸.

sulfureux, euse [sylfyʀø, øz] *adj* **1.** CHIM sulphurous 🇬🇧, sulfurous 🇺🇸 **2.** [démoniaque] demonic.

sulfurisé, e [sylfyʀize] *adj* sulphurized 🇬🇧, sulfurised 🇺🇸 ▸ **papier sulfurisé** greaseproof paper 🇬🇧, wax paper 🇺🇸.

sultan [syltɑ̃] *nm* sultan.

summum [sɔmɔm] *nm* [d'une carrière] peak, zenith *sout* ; [d'une civilisation] acme ; [de l'élégance, du luxe, de l'arrogance] height / *elle était au summum de son art quand elle peignit ce tableau* her art was at its peak ou height when she painted this picture.

sup [syp] adj inv *fam* [supplémentaire] : *faire des heures sup* to work overtime.

super [sypɛʀ] *fam* ◆ adj inv [personne, idée] great, terrific ; [maison, moto] fantastic, great. ◆ nm [essence] four-star (petrol) 🇬🇧, premium 🇺🇸.

superbe [sypɛʀb] ◆ adj [magnifique - yeux, bijou, ville] superb, beautiful, magnificent ; [- bébé, femme] beautiful, gorgeous, fine-looking ; [- homme] good-looking, handsome ; [- voix] superb, beautiful ; [- journée] glorious, beautiful ; [- temps] wonderful / *tu as une mine superbe aujourd'hui* you look radiant today. ◆ nf *litt* haughtiness / *cela va lui faire perdre de sa superbe* he won't be quite so proud after this.

superbement [sypɛʀbəmɑ̃] adv **1.** [splendidement] superbly, magnificently, beautifully **2.** *litt* [arrogamment] arrogantly, haughtily.

supercarburant [sypɛʀkaʀbyʀɑ̃] nm four-star ou high-octane petrol 🇬🇧, premium 🇺🇸.

supercherie [sypɛʀʃəʀi] nf [tromperie] deception, trick ; [fraude] fraud.

supérette [sypeʀɛt] nf mini-market, superette 🇺🇸.

superficie [sypɛʀfisi] nf [d'un champ] acreage, area ; [d'une maison] surface area, floor space / *l'entrepôt fait 3 000 m² de superficie* ou *a une superficie de 3 000 m²* ; the warehouse has a surface area of 3,000 m²;.

superficiel, elle [sypɛʀfisjɛl] adj **1.** [brûlure] superficial, surface *(modif)* **2.** [connaissances, personne] shallow, insubstantial ; [étude, travail] superficial, perfunctory ; [contrôle] superficial, cursory.

superflu, e [sypɛʀfly] adj **1.** [non nécessaire - biens, excuse, recommandation] superfluous, unnecessary **2.** [trop - détails, exemple] redundant, superfluous / *un grand lessivage ne serait pas superflu* a good scrub wouldn't do any harm ! / *pour vous débarrasser de vos poils superflus* to get rid of unwanted hair ; [kilos] surplus. ❖ **superflu** nm ▸ **le superflu** that which is superfluous.

superforme [sypɛʀfɔʀm] nf *fam* : *être en superforme, tenir la superforme* to be in great form ou on top form ou bursting with health.

super-géant [sypɛʀʒeɑ̃], **super-g** [sypɛʀʒe] nm inv SKI super-giant slalom.

supérieur, e [sypeʀjœʀ] ◆ adj **1.** [plus haut que le reste - étagère, étage] upper, top ; [- ligne] top / *le bord supérieur droit de la page* the top right-hand corner of the page ; [juste au-dessus - étagère, ligne] above / *les jouets sont à l'étage supérieur* toys are on the next floor ou the floor above **2.** [quantitativement - efficacité] higher, greater ; [- prix, rendement, vitesse] higher ; [- volume] bigger, greater ▸ **supérieur en nombre**: *troupes supérieures en nombre* troops superior in number / *taux légèrement supérieur à 8 %* rate slightly over 8% / *il est d'une taille supérieure à la moyenne* he's taller than average **3.** [dans une hiérarchie - échelons] upper, topmost ; [- classes sociales] upper ▸ **enseignement supérieur** higher education ; [juste au-dessus - niveau] next ; [- grade, rang] senior ; [- autorité] higher / *passer dans la classe supérieure* ÉDUC to move up one class / *je lui suis hiérarchiquement supérieur* I'm his superior ou senior **4.** [dans une échelle de valeurs - intelligence, esprit, être] superior ; [- intérêts] higher ▸ **de qualité supérieure** top quality ▸ **supérieur à**: *intelligence supérieure à la moyenne* above-average intelligence / *il est techniquement supérieur au Suédois* SPORT his technique is superior to that of the Swedish player **5.** [hautain - air, ton] superior **6.** MATH superior ▸ **supérieur ou égal à** superior or equal to, greater than or equal to **7.** RELIG : *la Mère supérieure* the mother superior. ◆ nm, f **1.** [dans une hiérarchie] ▸ **supérieur (hiérarchique)** superior **2.** RELIG father (mother) superior. ❖ **supérieur** nm UNIV ▸ **le supérieur** higher education.

supériorité [sypeʀjɔʀite] nf **1.** [en qualité] superiority **2.** [en quantité] superiority.

superlatif, ive [sypɛʀlatif, iv] adj superlative. ❖ **superlatif** nm LING superlative. ❖ **au superlatif** loc adv LING in the superlative.

supermarché [sypɛʀmaʀʃe] nm supermarket.

superpétrolier [sypɛʀpetʀɔlje] nm supertanker.

superposer [3] [sypɛʀpoze] vt [meubles] to stack (up) ; [images, couleurs] to superimpose.

superproduction [sypɛʀpʀɔdyksjɔ̃] nf CINÉ big-budget film 🇬🇧 ou movie 🇺🇸.

superpuissance [sypɛʀpɥisɑ̃s] nf superpower.

supersonique [sypɛʀsɔnik] ◆ adj supersonic. ◆ nm supersonic aircraft.

superstitieux, euse [sypɛʀstisjø, øz] ◆ adj superstitious. ◆ nm, f superstitious person.

superstition [sypɛʀstisjɔ̃] nf superstition.

superviser [3] [sypɛʀvize] vt to supervise, to oversee.

supplanter [3] [syplɑ̃te] vt **1.** [rival] to supplant, to displace, to supersede **2.** [machine, système] to supplant, to take over from *(insép)*.

suppléant, e [sypleɑ̃, ɑ̃t] ◆ adj **1.** ENS [remplaçant] supply 🇬🇧, substitute 🇺🇸 ; [adjoint] assistant **2.** DR & POL deputy. ◆ nm, f **1.** ENS [remplaçant] supply teacher 🇬🇧, substitute teacher 🇺🇸 ; [adjoint] assistant teacher **2.** DR & POL deputy.

suppléer [15] [syplee] ❖ **suppléer à** v + prép **1.** [remédier à - insuffisance] to make up for, to compensate for **2.** [remplacer - suj : personne] to replace.

supplément [syplemɑ̃] nm **1.** [coût] extra ou additional charge ▸ **payer un supplément** to pay extra **2.** [de nourriture] extra portion ; [de crédits] additional facility ▸ **un supplément d'informations** additional ou further information. ❖ **en supplément** loc adv extra / *c'est en supplément* it comes as an extra, it's an extra.

supplémentaire [syplemɑ̃tɛʀ] adj [crédit, dépense] additional, supplementary, extra ▸ **un délai supplémentaire** an extension (of deadline).

suppliant, e [syplijɑ̃, ɑ̃t] adj begging, imploring, beseeching *litt*.

supplice [syplis] nm **1.** HIST torture **2.** [douleur physique] agony, torture ; [douleur morale] torment, agony ▸ **être au supplice** to be in agonies ▸ **mettre qqn au supplice** to torture sb.

supplicié, e [syplisje] nm, f [personne - qui a subi la peine de mort] execution victim ; [- qui a été torturée] torture victim.

supplier [10] [syplije] vt to beg, to implore, to beseech *litt* ▸ **supplier qqn (à genoux) de faire qqch** to beg sb (on bended knee) to do sthg.

support [sypɔʀ] nm **1.** [de colonne, de meuble] base, support ; [de statuette] stand, pedestal ; [pour un échafaudage] support **2.** [de communication] medium ▸ **support pédagogique** teaching aid ▸ **support publicitaire** advertising medium **3.** INFORM medium.

supportable [sypɔʀtabl] adj **1.** [douleur] bearable **2.** [conduite, personne] tolerable.

supporter¹ [sypɔʀtɛʀ] nm SPORT supporter.

supporter² [3] [sypɔʀte] vt **1.** [servir d'assise à] to support, to hold up *(sép)* / *cinq piliers supportent la voûte* the roof is held up by five pillars **2.** [assumer - responsabilité, obligation] to assume ; [prendre en charge - dépense] to bear / *l'acheteur supporte les frais* the fees are borne by the purchaser **3.** [résister à] to stand up to *(insép)*, to withstand / *des plantes qui supportent* / *ne supportent pas le froid* plants that do well / badly in the cold **/ bien supporter une opération** to come through an operation in good shape **/ mal supporter une opération** to have trouble recovering from an operation ▸ **je ne supporte pas l'alcool / la pilule** drink / the pill doesn't agree with me **/ on supporterait bien une petite laine** it's cold enough to wear a pullover **4.** [subir sans faillir - épreuve, privation] to bear, to endure, to put up with (*inség*) ; [- insulte, menace] to bear **/ elle supporte mal la douleur** she can't cope with pain **5.** [tolérer, accepter] to bear, to stand **/ je ne supporte pas de perdre** I can't stand losing ; [personne] to put up with (*inség*), to stand, to bear **/ il faudra le supporter encore deux jours** we'll have to put up with him for two more days **6.** [résister à] to withstand **/ sa théorie ne supportera pas une critique sérieuse** his theory won't stand up to serious criticism **7.** SPORT [encourager] to support. ❖ **se supporter** vp (*emploi réciproque*) to bear ou to stand each other.

supporteur, trice [sypɔʀtœʀ, tʀis] nm, f SPORT supporter.

supposé, e [sypoze] adj **1.** [faux - testament] false, forged ; [- nom] assumed **2.** [présumé - vainqueur] supposed, presumed ; [- père] putative ; [- dimension] estimated **/ l'auteur supposé du pamphlet** the supposed author of the pamphlet.

supposer [3] [sypoze] vt **1.** [conjecturer, imaginer] to suppose, to assume **/ je suppose que tu n'es pas prêt** I take it ou I suppose you're not ready **/ cela laisse supposer que...** this suggests that... **/ en supposant que tu échoues** suppose (that) ou supposing (that) ou let's suppose (that) you fail ▸ **à supposer que** assuming that, supposing **2.** [estimer, penser] : **et tu la supposes assez bête pour se laisser faire ?** so you think she's stupid enough to let it happen? **3.** [impliquer] to imply, to require, to presuppose **/ une mission qui suppose de la discrétion** an assignment where discretion is required ou is a must.

supposition [sypozisjɔ̃] nf [hypothèse] supposition, assumption **/ faire des suppositions** to speculate.

suppositoire [sypozitwaʀ] nm suppository.

suppression [sypʀesjɔ̃] nf **1.** [abrogation] abolition **/ la suppression de la peine de mort** the abolition of the death penalty **2.** [dans un texte] deletion **3.** [élimination] elimination **/ suppression de la douleur par piqûres** elimination of pain by injections **4.** [assassinat] elimination, liquidation.

supprimer [3] [sypʀime] vt **1.** [faire cesser - cause, effet] to do away with (*inség*) ; [- habitude, obstacle] to get rid of (*inség*) ; [- pauvreté, racisme] to put an end to (*inség*), to do away with (*inség*) ; [- douleur] to kill, to stop ; [- fatigue] to eliminate **2.** [démolir - mur, quartier] to knock ou to pull down (*sép*), to demolish **3.** [annuler - loi] to repeal, to annul ; [- projet] to do away with (*inség*) ; [- allocation, prime] to withdraw, to stop **4.** [retirer] ▸ **supprimer des emplois** to lay people off, to make people redundant 🇬🇧 **/ j'ai totalement supprimé le sel** I cut out salt (altogether) **/ ils vont supprimer des trains dans les zones rurales** train services will be cut in rural areas **5.** [enlever - opération, séquence] to cut (out), to take out (*sép*) ; [- mot, passage] to delete ▸ **supprimer les étapes / intermédiaires** to do away with the intermediate stages / the middlemen **6.** [tuer] to eliminate, to do away with (*inség*). ❖ **se supprimer** vp (*emploi réfléchi*) to take one's own life.

suppurer [3] [sypyʀe] vi to suppurate.

suprématie [sypʀemasi] nf supremacy.

suprême [sypʀɛm] ◆ adj **1.** [supérieur] supreme **2.** [extrême - importance, bonheur, plaisir] extreme, supreme ; [- ignorance] utter, blissful, sublime ; [- mépris] sublime **3.** [dernier] supreme, final **/ dans un suprême effort** in a final attempt. ◆ nm CULIN suprême ▸ **suprême de volaille** chicken suprême.

sur¹ [syʀ] prép **1.** [dans l'espace - dessus] on ; [- par-dessus] over ; [- au sommet de] on top of ; [- contre] against **/ sur la table** on the table **/ un visage est dessiné sur le sable** a face has been drawn in the sand **/ elle avait des bleus sur tout le visage** she had bruises all over her face, her face was covered in bruises **/ il a jeté ses affaires sur le lit** he threw his things onto the bed **/ monter sur un manège / un vélo** to get on a roundabout / bicycle **/ ouragan sur la ville** hurricane over the city **/ une chambre avec vue sur la mer** a room with a view of ou over the sea **/ sur la cime de l'arbre** at the top of the tree **/ mettre un doigt sur sa bouche** to put a finger to one's lips **/ sa silhouette se détachait sur le ciel** he was silhouetted against the sky **/ je n'ai pas d'argent sur moi** I haven't got any money on me **/ la clef est sur la porte** the key's in the door **/ je n'ai plus d'argent sur mon compte** I haven't any money left in my account ▸ **sculpture sur bois** ART wood carving **2.** [indiquant la direction] towards, toward 🇺🇸 **/ sur votre gauche, le Panthéon** on ou to your left, the Pantheon **/ en allant sur Rennes** going towards Rennes ▸ **diriger son regard sur qqn** to look in sb's direction ▸ **tirer sur qqn** to shoot at sb **/ le malheur s'est abattu sur cette famille** unhappiness has fallen upon this family **3.** [indiquant une distance] over, for **/ il est le plus rapide sur 400 mètres** he's the fastest over 400 metres 🇬🇧 **/ travaux sur 10 kilomètres** roadworks for 10 kilometres 🇬🇧 ou kilometers 🇺🇸 **4.** [dans le temps - indiquant l'approximation] towards, around **/ sur les quatre heures, quelqu'un a téléphoné** (at) around ou about four, somebody phoned ; [indiquant la proximité] : **sur le moment ou le coup, je me suis étonné** at the time ou at first, I was surprised ▸ **être sur le départ** to be about to leave **5.** [indiquant la durée] : **les versements sont étalés sur plusieurs mois** the instalments are spread over several months **6.** [indiquant la répétition] after, upon **/ je lui ai envoyé lettre sur lettre** I sent him letter after ou upon letter **7.** [indiquant la cause] : **condamné sur faux témoignage** condemned on false evidence ▸ **juger qqn sur ses propos / son apparence** to judge sb by his words / appearance **8.** [indiquant la manière, l'état, la situation] ▸ **avoir un effet sur qqn / qqch** to have an effect on sb / sthg ▸ **être sur ses gardes / la défensive / le qui-vive** to be on one's guard / the defensive / the look-out **/ danser sur un air connu** to dance to a well-known tune ▸ **c'est sur la France Inter** it's on France Inter **9.** [indiquant le moyen] ▸ **vivre sur ses économies / un héritage** to live off one's savings / a legacy **/ je n'aime pas choisir sur catalogue** I don't like choosing from a catalogue **/ ça s'ouvre sur simple pression** you open it by just pressing it **/ le film se termine sur une vue du Lido** the film ends with ou on a view of the Lido **10.** [indiquant le domaine, le sujet] : **on a un dossier sur lui** we've got a file on him **/ je sais peu de choses sur elle** I don't know much about her **/ sur ce point, nous sommes d'accord** we agree on that point ▸ **faire des recherches sur qqch** to do some research into sthg ▸ **s'apitoyer sur soi-même** to feel sorry for oneself **11.** [indiquant une proportion] ▸ [- une mesure] by ▸ **un homme sur deux** one man in two, every second man ▸ **un lundi sur trois** every third Monday **/ tu as une chance sur deux de gagner** you've got a 50-50 chance of winning ▸ **cinq mètres sur trois** five metres by three **/ j'ai eu 12 sur 20** I got 12 out of 20 **12.** [indiquant une relation de supériorité] over **/ régner sur un pays** to rule over a country ▸ **l'emporter sur qqn** to defeat sb.

sur², e [syʀ] adj sour.

sûr, e [syʀ] adj **1.** [certain, convaincu] sure, certain **/ j'en suis tout à fait sûr, j'en suis sûr et certain** I'm absolutely sure, I'm positive **/ c'est sûr et certain** it's 100% sure ▸ **j'en étais sûr !** I knew it! **/ c'est sûr qu'il pleuvra** it's bound to rain **/ c'est sûr qu'ils ne viendront pas** it's certain that they won't come ▸ **une chose est sûre** one thing's for sure **/ tu viendras ? — ce n'est pas sûr** are you coming? —

I don't know for sure ▶ **rien n'est moins sûr** nothing is less certain ▶ **être sûr de** to be sure of / *être sûr de son fait* to be positive / *je suis sûr d'avoir raison* I'm sure I'm right **2.** [fiable - personne, ami] trustworthy, reliable ; [- données, mémoire, raisonnement] reliable, sound ; [- alarme, investissement] safe ; [- main, pied] steady ; [- oreille] keen ; [- goût] reliable / *avoir le coup d'œil / de crayon sûr* to be good at sizing things up / at capturing a likeness *(in drawing)* **3.** [sans danger] safe / *des rues peu sûres* unsafe streets / *le plus sûr est de...* the safest thing is to... ✤ **sûr** adv *fam* ▶ **sûr que**: *sûr qu'il va gagner !* he's bound to win! ▶ **pas sûr**: *il va accepter — pas sûr !* he'll accept — don't count on it! ✤ **à coup sûr** loc adv definitely, no doubt. ✤ **pour sûr** loc adv *fam* for sure.

suraigu, suraiguë *ou* **suraigüe*** [syʀegy] adj [voix, son] very shrill.

surajouter [3] [syʀaʒute] vt to add.

suranné, e [syʀane] adj [style] old-fashioned, outmoded / *une mode surannée* an outdated fashion.

surbooké, e [syʀbuke] adj overbooked.

surbooking [syʀbukiŋ] nm overbooking.

surbrillance [syʀbʀijɑ̃s] nf ▶ **mettre qqch en surbrillance** INFORM to highlight sthg.

surcharge [syʀʃaʀʒ] nf **1.** [excédent de poids] overload, overloading ▶ **surcharge de bagages** excess luggage **2.** [excès] overabundance, surfeit ▶ **surcharge de travail** extra work **3.** ÉLECTR overload **4.** [d'un cheval de course] (weight) handicap. ✤ **en surcharge** loc adj excess *(avant nom)*, extra *(avant nom)*.

surcharger [17] [syʀʃaʀʒe] vt **1.** [véhicule] to overload **2.** [accabler] to overburden ▶ **surchargé de travail** overworked **3.** [raturer] to alter / *un rapport surchargé de ratures* a report containing too many deletions.

surchauffe [syʀʃof] nf **1.** [d'un moteur, d'un appareil] overheating **2.** ÉCON overheating.

surchauffé, e [syʀʃofe] adj **1.** [trop chauffé] overheated **2.** [surexcité] overexcited ▶ **des esprits surchauffés** reckless individuals.

surchemise [syʀʃəmiz] nf overshirt.

surclassement [syʀklasmɑ̃] nm [de voyageur aérien] bumping up *(to business or first class)*.

surclasser [3] [syʀklase] vt **1.** [surpasser] to outclass **2.** TRANSP ▶ **surclasser qqn** to upgrade sb's seat / *ils m'ont surclassé en première* they upgraded my seat to first class, they bumped me up *fam* to first class.

surcoût, surcout* [syʀku] nm [supplément prévu] surcharge, overcharge ; [dépense] overspend, overexpenditure.

surcroît, surcroit* [syʀkʀwa] nm : *un surcroît de travail* extra ou additional work. ✤ **de surcroît, de surcroit*** loc adv moreover, what's more / *il est beau, et intelligent de surcroît* he is handsome, and moreover ou what's more, he's bright. ✤ **par surcroît, par surcroit*** = **de surcroît**.

surdiplômé, e [syʀdiplome] adj overqualified.

surdité [syʀdite] nf deafness.

surdoué, e [syʀdwe] ◆ adj hyperintelligent *spéc*, gifted. ◆ nm, f hyperintelligent *spéc* ou gifted child.

sureau, x [syʀo] nm elder, elderberry tree.

sureffectif [syʀefɛktif] nm overmanning *(U)* ▶ **en sureffectif** [entreprise] overstaffed.

surélever [19] [syʀelve] vt CONSTR [mur] to heighten, to raise.

sûrement, surement* [syʀmɑ̃] adv **1.** [en sécurité] safely **2.** [certainement] certainly, surely / *il sera sûrement en retard* he's bound to ou sure to be late / *ils ont sûre-*

ment été pris dans les embouteillages they must have been caught in the traffic **3.** [oui] : *va-t-elle accepter ?* — *sûrement* will she accept? — she certainly will ou she's bound to / *sûrement pas !* certainly not!

surenchère [syʀɑ̃ʃɛʀ] nf [prix] higher bid, overbid / *faire une surenchère* to overbid.

surenchérir [32] [syʀɑ̃ʃeʀiʀ] vi **1.** [offrir de payer plus] to overbid, to raise one's bid, to make a higher bid **2.** *fig* ▶ **surenchérir sur** to go one better than / *surenchérir sur une offre* to make a better offer.

surendetté, e [syʀɑ̃dete] adj heavily ou deeply indebted.

surendettement [syʀɑ̃dɛtmɑ̃] nm debt burden ; [d'une société] overborrowing.

surestimer [3] [syʀɛstime] vt **1.** [objet] to overvalue **2.** [valeur, personne] to overestimate. ✤ **se surestimer** vp to overestimate one's abilities.

sûreté, sureté* [syʀte] nf **1.** [sécurité] safety ▶ **la sûreté de l'État** state security / *par mesure de sûreté, pour plus de sûreté* as a precaution **2.** [fiabilité - de la mémoire, d'une méthode, d'un diagnostic, des freins] reliability ; [- d'une serrure] security **3.** [système de protection] safety device **4.** DR ▶ **la Sûreté (nationale)** HIST former French criminal investigation department ; ≃ CID 🇬🇧 ; ≃ FBI 🇺🇸. ✤ **en sûreté, en sureté*** loc adv ▶ **mettre qqch en sûreté** to put sthg in a safe place ou away for safekeeping.

surévaluer [7] [syʀevalɥe] vt **1.** [donner une valeur supérieure à] to overvalue / *le conseil municipal a surévalué les terrains* the council overvalued the land **2.** [accorder une importance excessive à] to overestimate. ✤ **se surévaluer** vp to overestimate one's abilities.

surexcité, e [syʀɛksite] adj overexcited.

surexposer [3] [syʀɛkspoze] vt to overexpose.

surf [sœʀf] nm **1.** [planche] surfboard **2.** [sport] surfing / *faire du surf* to go surfing.

surface [syʀfas] nf **1.** [aire] (surface) area ▶ **surface habitable** living space **2.** [espace utilisé] surface / *quelle est la surface de l'entrepôt ?* how big is the warehouse? **3.** [partie extérieure] surface, outside / *la surface de la Terre* the Earth's surface ▶ **refaire surface, revenir à la surface a)** [après évanouissement] to come to ou round **b)** [après anesthésie] to come out of anaesthetic, to come round **c)** [après une dépression] to pull out of it **d)** [après une absence] to reappear **4.** SPORT ▶ **surface de réparation** penalty area. ✤ **grande surface** nf hypermarket 🇬🇧, supermarket 🇺🇸. ✤ **de surface** loc adj **1.** NAUT & PHYS surface *(modif)* **2.** [amabilité, regrets] superficial, outward. ✤ **en surface** loc adv **1.** [à l'extérieur] on the surface **2.** [superficiellement] on the face of things, superficially.

surfacturation [syʀfaktyʀasjɔ̃] nf overbilling.

surfait, e [syʀfɛ, ɛt] adj [auteur, œuvre] overrated ; [réputation] inflated.

surfer [3] [sœʀfe] vi to surf / *surfer sur Internet* to surf the net ou the internet.

surfeur, euse [sœʀfœʀ, øz] nm, f surfer.

surfiler [3] [syʀfile] vt COUT to whip.

surgelé, e [syʀʒəle] adj frozen, deep-frozen. ✤ **surgelé** nm frozen food.

surgir [32] [syʀʒiʀ] vi **1.** [personne, animal, objet] to appear ou to materialize suddenly, to loom up ; [hors du sol et rapidement] to shoot ou to spring up / *des gens, surgis d'on ne sait où* people who had sprung from nowhere **2.** [conflit] to arise ; [difficultés] to crop up, to arise.

surhomme [syʀɔm] nm [gén] superman.

surhumain, e [syʀymɛ̃, ɛn] adj superhuman.

surimi [syʀimi] nm surimi ▸ **bâtonnets de surimi** crab sticks.

surimpression [syʀɛ̃pʀesjɔ̃] nf superimposition.
✦ **en surimpression** loc adj superimposed.

surinfection [syʀɛ̃fɛksjɔ̃] nf secondary infection.

surinformation [syʀɛ̃fɔʀmasjɔ̃] nf information overload.

surinformer [syʀɛ̃fɔʀme] vt to overinform / *le public a tendance à être constamment surinformé* the public tends to be constantly overinformed.

sur-le-champ [syʀləʃɑ̃] loc adv immediately, at once, straightaway.

surlendemain [syʀlɑ̃dmɛ̃] nm : *le surlendemain de la fête* two days after the party / *il m'a appelé le lendemain, et le surlendemain* he called me the next day, and the day after / *et le surlendemain, j'étais à Paris* and two days later, I was in Paris.

surligner [3] [syʀliɲe] vt to highlight *(with a fluorescent pen)*.

surligneur [syʀliɲœʀ] nm highlighter.

surmenage [syʀmənaʒ] nm [nerveux] overstrain, overexertion ; [au travail] overwork, overworking ▸ **surmenage intellectuel** mental strain.

surmené, e [syʀməne] nm, f [nerveusement] person suffering from nervous exhaustion ; [par le travail] overworked person.

surmener [19] [syʀməne] vt [personne - physiquement] to overwork ; [- nerveusement] to overtax. ✦ **se surmener** vp *(emploi réfléchi)* to overtax o.s., to work too hard, to overdo it.

sur-mesure [syʀməzyʀ] nm inv : *c'est du sur-mesure* it's custom made.

surmontable [syʀmɔ̃tabl] adj surmountable, superable *sout*, which can be overcome.

surmonter [3] [syʀmɔ̃te] vt **1.** [être situé sur] to surmount, to top / *un dôme surmonte l'édifice* the building is crowned by a dome **2.** [triompher de - difficulté] to get over, to surmount, to overcome ; [- peur, émotion] to overcome, to get the better of, to master ; [- fatigue] to overcome.

surnager [17] [syʀnaʒe] vi **1.** [flotter] to float **2.** [subsister - ouvrage] to remain ; [- souvenir] to linger on.

surnaturel, elle [syʀnatyʀɛl] adj **1.** [d'un autre monde] supernatural **2.** [fabuleux, prodigieux] uncanny. ✦ **surnaturel** nm ▸ **le surnaturel** the supernatural.

surnom [syʀnɔ̃] nm [appellation] nickname / *Cœur de Lion était le surnom du roi Richard* King Richard was known as the Lionheart.

⚠ **Surname** signifie « nom de famille » et non surnom.

surnombre [syʀnɔ̃bʀ] nm excessive numbers. ✦ **en surnombre** loc adj redundant, excess *(avant nom)* / *nous étions en surnombre* there were too many of us.

surnommer [3] [syʀnɔme] vt to nickname / *dans sa famille, on la surnomme « Rosita »* her family's pet name for her is "Rosita".

surpasser [3] [syʀpase] vt **1.** [surclasser] to surpass, to outdo ▸ **surpasser qqn en habileté** to be more skilful than sb **2.** [aller au-delà de] to surpass, to go beyond / *leur enthousiasme surpasse toutes mes espérances* their enthusiasm is beyond all my expectations, they're far more enthusiastic than I expected. ✦ **se surpasser** vp *(emploi réfléchi)* to excel o.s. / *quel gâteau, tu t'es surpassé !* what a cake, you've really surpassed yourself!

surpayer [11] [syʀpeje] vt **1.** [employé] to overpay **2.** [marchandise] to be overcharged for.

surpêche [syʀpɛʃ] nf overfishing.

surpeuplé, e [syʀpœple] adj overpopulated.

surpiquer [3] [syʀpike] vt to oversew.

surplace [syʀplas] nm ▸ **faire du surplace a)** [à vélo] to go dead slow **b)** [en voiture] to come to a standstill ou a complete stop / *l'économie fait du surplace fig* the economy is marking time ou treading water.

surplomb [syʀplɔ̃] nm overhang. ✦ **en surplomb** loc adj overhanging.

surplomber [3] [syʀplɔ̃be] vt to overhang.

surplus [syʀply] nm **1.** [excédent] surplus, extra / *le surplus de la récolte* the surplus crop **2.** [supplément] supplement ; [- à un prix] surcharge.

surpopulation [syʀpɔpylasjɔ̃] nf overpopulation.

surprenant, e [syʀpʀənɑ̃, ɑ̃t] adj [inattendu, étonnant] surprising, odd.

surprendre [79] [syʀpʀɑ̃dʀ] vt **1.** [dans un acte délictueux] ▸ **surprendre qqn** to catch sb in the act / *on l'a surprise à falsifier la comptabilité* she was caught (in the act of) falsifying the accounts **2.** [prendre au dépourvu] : *ils sont venus nous surprendre à la maison* they paid us a surprise visit at home ▸ **se laisser surprendre par a)** [orage] to get caught in **b)** [marée] to get caught by **c)** [crépuscule] to be overtaken by **3.** [conversation] to overhear / *j'ai surpris leur regard entendu* I happened to see the knowing look they gave each other **4.** [déconcerter] to surprise ▸ **être surpris de qqch** to be surprised at sthg / *cela ne surprendra personne* this will come as a surprise to nobody. ✦ **se surprendre à** vp + prép ▸ **se surprendre à faire** to find ou to catch o.s. doing.

surpris, e [syʀpʀi, iz] ◆ pp ⟶ **surprendre**. ◆ adj **1.** [pris au dépourvu] surprised / *l'ennemi, surpris, n'opposa aucune résistance* caught off their guard, the enemy put up no resistance **2.** [déconcerté] surprised / *je suis surpris de son absence / de ne pas la voir / qu'elle ne réponde pas / de ce qu'elle ne réagisse pas* I'm surprised (that) she's not here / not to see her / (that) she doesn't reply / (that) she hasn't reacted / *être agréablement / désagréablement surpris* to be pleasantly / unpleasantly surprised. ✦ **surprise** nf **1.** [étonnement, stupéfaction] surprise / *à la grande surprise de* to the great surprise of ▸ **à la surprise générale** to everybody's surprise ▸ **regarder qqn avec surprise** to look at sb in surprise **2.** [événement inattendu] surprise ▸ **quelle (bonne) surprise !** what a (nice ou pleasant) surprise! / *tout le monde a eu la surprise d'avoir une prime* everyone was surprised to get a bonus ▸ **visite surprise** surprise ou unexpected visit **3.** [cadeau] surprise ; [pour les enfants] lucky bag. ✦ **par surprise** loc adv MIL : *prendre une ville par surprise* to take a town by surprise. ✦ **sans surprise(s)** loc adj : *ce fut un voyage sans surprise* it was an uneventful trip / *son père est sans surprise* his father is very predictable.

surproduction [syʀpʀɔdyksjɔ̃] nf overproduction.

surprotéger [22] [syʀpʀɔteʒe] vt to overprotect.

surqualifié, e [syʀkalifje] adj overqualified.

surréaliste [syʀrealist] ◆ adj **1.** ART & LITTÉR surrealist **2.** [magique] surreal. ◆ nmf surrealist.

surreprésenté, e [syʀʀəpʀezɑ̃te] adj overrepresented.

surréservation [syʀʀezɛʀvasjɔ̃] nf overbooking.

sursaut [syʀso] nm **1.** [tressaillement] start, jump / *elle eut un sursaut de peur* she jumped in alarm **2.** [regain subit] burst / *un sursaut d'énergie* a burst of energy. ✦ **en sursaut** loc adv [brusquement] with a start / *elle se réveilla en sursaut* she woke up with a start.

sursauter [3] [syʀsote] vi to start, to jump ▶ **faire sursauter qqn** to give sb a start, to make sb start ou jump.

surseoir, sursoir* [66] [syʀswaʀ] ◆ **surseoir à, sursoir à*** v + prép **1.** litt [différer - publication, décision] to postpone, to defer **2.** DR ▶ **surseoir à une exécution** to stay an execution.

sursis, e [syʀsi, iz] pp ⟶ surseoir. ◆ **sursis** nm **1.** [délai] reprieve, extension / ils bénéficient d'un sursis pour payer leurs dettes they've been granted an extension of the time limit for paying their debts **2.** DR reprieve ▶ **bénéficier d'un sursis** to be granted ou given a reprieve **3.** [ajournement] deferment, extension ▶ **sursis d'incorporation** MIL deferment ou deferral of call-up. ◆ **avec sursis** loc adj suspended / il est condamné à (une peine de) cinq ans avec sursis he's been given a five year suspended (prison) sentence. ◆ **en sursis** loc adj **1.** DR in remission **2.** [en attente] : c'est un mort en sursis he's living on borrowed time.

surtaxe [syʀtaks] nf surcharge.

surtitrer [syʀtitʀe] vt **1.** [article] to head **2.** [au théâtre, à l'opéra] to surtitle / la pièce est surtitrée en français the play is surtitled in French.

surtout [syʀtu] adv **1.** [avant tout, par-dessus tout] above all ; [plus particulièrement] particularly, especially / il y avait surtout des touristes dans la salle most of the audience were tourists **2.** [renforçant un conseil, un ordre] : surtout, dis au médecin que tu as de l'asthme be sure to tell the doctor that you've got asthma / surtout, pas de panique ! whatever you do, don't panic! / ne faites surtout pas de bruit don't you make ANY noise / je vais lui dire — surtout pas ! I'll tell her — you'll do nothing of the sort! ◆ **surtout que** loc conj fam especially as.

surveillance [syʀvɛjɑ̃s] nf [contrôle - de travaux] supervision, overseeing ; [- médical] monitoring ▶ **tromper** ou **déjouer la surveillance de qqn** to evade sb sout, to give sb the slip. ◆ **de surveillance** loc adj [service, salle] security (modif) ; [avion, équipe] surveillance (modif) ; [appareil] supervisory ; [caméra] surveillance (modif), closed-circuit (avant nom). ◆ **sans surveillance** loc adj & loc adv unattended, unsupervised. ◆ **sous surveillance** loc adv **1.** [par la police] under surveillance ▶ **mettre** ou **placer qqch sous surveillance** to put sthg under surveillance **2.** MÉD under observation.

surveillant, e [syʀvɛjɑ̃, ɑ̃t] nm, f **1.** [de prison] prison guard ; [d'hôpital] charge nurse UK, sister UK, head nurse US ; [de magasin] store detective ; [de chantier] supervisor, overseer **2.** ENS (paid) monitor ; [d'examen] invigilator UK, proctor US.

surveiller [4] [syʀvɛje] vt **1.** [garder - bébé, bagages] to watch, to keep an eye on ; [- prisonnier] to guard ▶ **surveiller un malade a)** [personne] to watch over a patient **b)** [avec une machine] to monitor a patient **2.** [épier] to watch / on nous surveille we're being watched ; (en usage absolu) to keep watch **3.** [contrôler - travaux, ouvriers] to oversee, to supervise ; [- cuisson] to watch ; [- examen] to invigilate UK, to proctor US / vous devriez surveiller les fréquentations de vos enfants you should keep an eye on the company your children keep **4.** [observer] to watch, to keep watch on ou over ▶ **surveiller qqn de près a)** [gén] to watch sb closely **b)** [police] to keep sb under close surveillance **5.** [prendre soin de - santé, ligne] to watch. ◆ **se surveiller** vp (emploi réfléchi) **1.** [se contrôler] to be careful what one does **2.** [se restreindre] to watch o.s., to keep a watch on o.s. / tu as grossi, tu devrais te surveiller you've put on weight, you should watch yourself.

survenir [40] [syʀvəniʀ] vi **1.** [problème, complication] to arise, to crop up ; [événement, incident] to happen, to occur, to take place **2.** litt [personne] to appear ou to arrive unexpectedly.

survenu, e [syʀvəny] pp ⟶ survenir. ◆ **survenue** nf litt **1.** [d'une personne] unexpected arrival ou appearance **2.** [d'une complication] appearance.

survêt [syʀvɛt] nm fam tracksuit.

survêtement [syʀvɛtmɑ̃] nm SPORT & LOISIRS tracksuit.

survie [syʀvi] nf [continuation de la vie] survival.

survitaminé, e [syʀvitamine] adj fam [animateur, film] supercharged.

survitrage [syʀvitʀaʒ] nm double glazing.

survivant, e [syʀvivɑ̃, ɑ̃t] ◆ adj [conjoint, coutume] surviving (avant nom). ◆ nm, f [rescapé] survivor.

survivre [90] [syʀvivʀ] vi **1.** [réchapper] to survive, to live on **2.** [continuer à exister] to survive / dans le monde des affaires, il faut lutter pour survivre in business, it's a struggle for survival ▶ **survivre à** [accident] to survive ; [personne] to survive, to outlive.

survol [syʀvɔl] nm **1.** AÉRON : l'Espagne a refusé le survol de son territoire Spain refused to allow the aircraft to fly over ou to overfly its territory **2.** [d'un texte] skimming through ; [d'une question] skimming over.

survoler [3] [syʀvɔle] vt **1.** AÉRON to overfly, to fly over **2.** [texte] to skim through ; [question] to skim over.

survolté, e [syʀvɔlte] adj [foule] overexcited ; [ambiance] highly charged.

sus [sy(s)] ◆ **en sus** loc adv sout in addition.

susceptibilité [sysɛptibilite] nf [sensibilité] touchiness, sensitiveness ▶ **ménager la susceptibilité de qqn** to humour sb.

susceptible [sysɛptibl] adj **1.** [sensible] touchy, oversensitive, thinskinned **2.** [exprime la possibilité] ▶ **susceptible de** : ce cheval est susceptible de gagner that horse is capable of winning / votre offre est susceptible de m'intéresser I might be interested in your offer / texte susceptible de plusieurs interprétations text open to a number of interpretations.

susciter [3] [sysite] vt **1.** [envie, jalousie, haine, intérêt, sympathie] to arouse ; [mécontentement, incompréhension, étonnement] to cause, to give rise to (insép) ; [problèmes] to give rise to (insép), to create **2.** [déclencher - révolte] to stir up (sép) ; [- dispute] to provoke ; [- malveillance] to incite.

suspect, e [syspɛ, ɛkt] ◆ adj **1.** [attitude, objet] suspicious, suspect **2.** [suspecté] ▶ **être suspect de qqch** to be suspected ou under suspicion of sthg. ◆ nm, f suspect.

suspecter [4] [syspɛkte] vt [soupçonner] to suspect / on le suspecte d'avoir commis un meurtre he's suspected of murder, he's under suspicion of murder.

suspendre [73] [syspɑ̃dʀ] vt **1.** [accrocher - lustre, vêtement] to hang / suspends ta veste à la patère hang your jacket (up) on the hook **2.** [interrompre - hostilités] to suspend ; [- négociations] to break off (sép) ; [- séance, audience] to adjourn ; [- récit] to interrupt **3.** [différer - décision] to defer, to postpone **4.** [interdire - émission, journal] to ban ; [révoquer - fonctionnaire, prêtre, juge] to suspend. ◆ **se suspendre** à vp + prép to hang from.

suspendu, e [syspɑ̃dy] adj **1.** CONSTR hanging (modif) **2.** TRAV PUB [pont] suspension (modif) **3.** BOT suspended.

suspens [syspɑ̃] ◆ **en suspens** ◆ loc adj [affaire, dossier] pending, unfinished ; [intrigue] unresolved ; [lecteur] uncertain. ◆ loc adv ▶ **tenir qqn en suspens** to keep sb in suspense / laisser une question en suspens to leave a question unanswered ou unresolved.

suspense [syspɛns] nm suspense / *il y a un suspense terrible dans le livre* the book's full of suspense. ❖ **à suspense** loc adj suspense *(modif)* ▶ **roman à suspense** thriller, suspense story.

suspension [syspɑ̃sjɔ̃] nf **1.** DR [interruption] suspension ▶ **suspension d'audience** adjournment (of hearing) ▶ **suspension de séance** adjournment **2.** ADMIN [sanction] suspension **3.** AUTO, CHIM, GÉOGR, MUS & RAIL suspension. ❖ **en suspension** loc adj **1.** [poussière] hanging / *en suspension dans l'air* hanging in the air **2.** CHIM in suspension.

suspicieux, euse [syspisjø, øz] adj *litt* suspicious, suspecting.

suspicion [syspisjɔ̃] nf [défiance] suspicion, suspiciousness.

susurrer [3] [sysyʀe] vt [chuchoter] to whisper ▶ **susurrer des mots doux à l'oreille de qqn** to whisper sweet nothings in sb's ear.

suture [sytyʀ] nf **1.** BOT, GÉOL & ZOOL suture **2.** ANAT & MÉD suture ▶ **point de suture** stitch.

suturer [3] [sytyʀe] vt to stitch up *(sép)*, to suture *spéc*.

SUV (abr de **sport utility vehicle**) nm SUV.

svelte [zvɛlt] adj [membre] slender ; [personne] slender, slim.

sveltesse [zvɛltɛs] nf *litt* svelteness, slenderness, slimness. **SVP** abr de **s'il vous plaît**.

SVT (abr de **sciences de la vie et de la terre**) nfpl ENS biology.

sweat [swit] nm sweatshirt.

sweat-shirt [switʃœrt] *(pl* **sweat-shirts**) nm sweatshirt.

syllabe [silab] nf **1.** LING syllable **2.** [parole] : *elle n'a pas prononcé une syllabe* she never opened her mouth.

sylviculture [silvikyltyʀ] nf forestry, silviculture *spéc*.

symbiose [sɛ̃bjoz] nf BIOL & *fig* symbiosis. ❖ **en symbiose** loc adv in symbiosis, symbiotically.

symbole [sɛ̃bɔl] nm **1.** [signe] symbol **2.** [personnification] symbol, embodiment / *il est le symbole du respect filial* he's the embodiment of filial duty, he's filial duty personified.

symbolique [sɛ̃bɔlik] adj **1.** [fait avec des symboles] symbolic **2.** [sans valeur réelle] token, nominal / *une somme symbolique* a nominal amount.

symboliquement [sɛ̃bɔlikmɑ̃] adv symbolically.

symboliser [3] [sɛ̃bɔlize] vt to symbolize.

symétrie [simetʀi] nf [gén] symmetry.

symétrique [simetʀik] adj [gén] symmetrical.

sympa [sɛ̃pa] adj *fam* [personne, attitude] friendly, nice ; [lieu] nice, pleasant ; [idée, mets] nice / *il n'est vraiment pas sympa* he's not very nice at all.

sympathie [sɛ̃pati] nf **1.** [penchant] liking *(C)* / *je n'ai aucune sympathie pour lui* I don't like him at all, I have no liking for him at all ▶ **inspirer la sympathie** to be likeable **2.** [bienveillance] sympathy *(U)* / *recevoir des témoignages de sympathie* to receive expressions of sympathy **3.** [pour une idée] sympathy / *je n'ai pas beaucoup de sympathie pour ce genre d'attitude* I don't have much time for that kind of attitude. ❖ **sympathies** nfpl [tendances] sympathies / *ses sympathies vont vers les républicains* his sympathies are ou lie with the Republicans.

⚠ Le mot anglais **sympathy** signifie « compassion » et non sympathie.

sympathique [sɛ̃patik] adj **1.** [personne] nice, pleasant, likeable / *elle m'est très sympathique* I like her very much **2.** [visage] friendly ; [idée] good ; [lieu] pleasant, nice ; [mets] appetizing ; [ambiance, réunion, spectacle] pleasant ; [attitude] kind, friendly.

⚠ **Sympathetic** signifie « compatissant » et non sympathique.

sympathisant, e [sɛ̃patizɑ̃, ɑ̃t] nm, f sympathizer.

sympathiser [3] [sɛ̃patize] vi **1.** [s'entendre] ▶ **sympathiser avec** to get on with 🇬🇧, to get along with 🇺🇸 / *nous avons tout de suite sympathisé* we took to ou liked each other right away **2.** POL : *elle sympathise avec les communistes* she's a communist sympathizer.

⚠ To **sympathize** with someone signifie « compatir avec quelqu'un » et non sympathiser avec quelqu'un.

symphonie [sɛ̃fɔni] nf MUS symphony.

symphonique [sɛ̃fɔnik] adj symphonic.

symposium [sɛ̃pozjɔm] nm [colloque] symposium.

symptomatique [sɛ̃ptɔmatik] adj **1.** MÉD symptomatic **2.** [caractéristique] symptomatic, indicative / *c'est symptomatique de leurs relations* it's symptomatic of ou it tells you something about their relationship.

symptôme [sɛ̃ptom] nm **1.** MÉD symptom **2.** [signe] symptom, sign.

synagogue [sinagɔg] nf synagogue.

synchrone [sɛ̃kʀon] adj synchronous.

synchronisation [sɛ̃kʀɔnizasjɔ̃] nf synchronization.

synchroniser [3] [sɛ̃kʀɔnize] vt to synchronize.

syncope [sɛ̃kɔp] nf MÉD syncope faint, fainting / *tomber en syncope, avoir une syncope* to faint.

syndic [sɛ̃dik] nm **1.** ADMIN ▶ **syndic (d'immeuble)** managing agent **2.** 🇨🇭 [président de commune] high-ranking civic official, *similar to a mayor, in certain Swiss cantons*.

 Syndic

A **syndic** is an administrative body which represents the interests of the owners of all the flats in a building, collectively known as the **syndicat de copropriété**. The role of the **syndic** is to ensure the upkeep of the building and to organize meetings during which a vote is taken on any repairs, improvements, etc., that are deemed necessary. The services of the **syndic** are paid for by the owners of the flats.

syndical, e, aux [sɛ̃dikal, o] adj POL (trade) union *(modif)* 🇬🇧, labor union *(modif)* 🇺🇸.

syndicalisme [sɛ̃dikalism] nm **1.** [mouvement] (trade) unionism **2.** [action] (trade) union 🇬🇧 ou labor union 🇺🇸 activity / *faire du syndicalisme* to be active in a union **3.** [doctrine] unionism.

syndicaliste [sɛ̃dikalist] nmf (trade) unionist 🇬🇧, union activist 🇺🇸.

syndicat [sɛ̃dika] nm **1.** POL [travailleurs] (trade) union 🇬🇧, labor union 🇺🇸 / *se former* ou *se regrouper en* *syndicat* to form a trade union ▸ **syndicat ouvrier** trade union ▸ **syndicat patronal** employers' confederation ou association **2.** DR [association] association ▸ **syndicat de communes** association of communes ▸ **syndicat interdépartemental** association of regional administrators ▸ **syndicat de copropriétaires** co-owners' association **3.** FIN ▸ **syndicat d'émission / de garantie** issuing / underwriting syndicate ▸ **syndicat financier** financial syndicate. ⬦ **syndicat d'initiative** nm tourist office, tourist information bureau.

syndiqué, e [sɛ̃dike] adj (belonging to a trade) union / *ouvriers syndiqués / non syndiqués* union / non-union workers.

syndiquer [3] [sɛ̃dike] vt to unionize, to organize. ⬦ **se syndiquer** vp *(emploi réfléchi)* **1.** [personne] to join a (trade) 🇬🇧 ou (labor) 🇺🇸 union **2.** [groupe] to form a (trade) 🇬🇧 ou (labor) 🇺🇸 union.

syndrome [sɛ̃dʀom] nm syndrome.

synergie [sinɛʀʒi] nf ÉCON synergy.

synonyme [sinɔnim] ◆ adj synonymous ▸ **être synonyme de** to be synonymous with. ◆ nm synonym.

synopsis [sinɔpsis] ◆ nf SCI & ÉDUC [bref aperçu] synopsis. ◆ nm CINÉ synopsis.

syntagme [sɛ̃tagm] nm phrase, syntagm *spéc* ▸ **syntagme nominal / verbal / adjectival** noun / verb / adjectival phrase.

syntaxe [sɛ̃taks] nf INFORM & LING syntax.

synthé [sɛ̃te] nm *fam* synthesizer.

synthèse [sɛ̃tɛz] nf **1.** [structuration de connaissances] synthesis **2.** [exposé, ouvrage] summary, résumé / *écrire une synthèse sur l'histoire de l'après-guerre* to write a brief history of the post-war years. ⬦ **de synthèse** loc adj **1.** [non analytique] : *avoir l'esprit de synthèse* to have a systematic mind **2.** [fibre, parole] synthetic.

synthétique [sɛ̃tetik] ◆ adj **1.** [raisonnement, approche] synthetic, synthesizing **2.** CHIM [fibre] synthetic, man-made, artificial. ◆ nm [matière] synthetic ou man-made fibres.

synthétiser [3] [sɛ̃tetize] vt **1.** [idées, résultats, relevés] to synthesize, to bring together **2.** CHIM to synthesize.

synthétiseur [sɛ̃tetizœʀ] nm synthesizer.

syphilis [sifilis] nf syphilis.

Syrie [siʀi] npr f ▸ **(la) Syrie** Syria.

syrien, enne [siʀjɛ̃, ɛn] adj Syrian. ⬦ **Syrien, enne** nm, f Syrian.

systématique [sistematik] adj **1.** [méthodique] methodical, orderly, systematic / *de façon systématique* systematically **2.** [invariable - réaction] automatic, invariable ; [- refus] automatic / *c'est systématique, quand je dis oui, il dit non* when I say yes, he invariably says no.

systématiquement [sistematikmɑ̃] adv systematically.

systématiser [3] [sistematize] vt **1.** [organiser en système] to systemize, to systematize **2.** (en usage absolu) [être de parti pris] to systemize, to systematize / *il ne faut pas systématiser* we mustn't generalize.

système [sistɛm] nm **1.** [structure] system ▸ **système solaire** solar system **2.** [méthode] way, means ▸ **système D** resourcefulness **3.** [appareillage] system / *système de chauffage / d'éclairage* heating / lighting system **4.** ANAT & MÉD system ▸ **système nerveux / digestif** nervous / digestive system **5.** ÉCON ▸ **système monétaire européen** European Monetary System **6.** INFORM system ▸ **système expert** expert system ▸ **système d'exploitation** (operating) system **7.** EXPR ▸ *il me court* ou *porte* ou *tape sur le système fam* he's really getting on my nerves.

t' [t] pron pers **1.** → **te 2.** → **tu.**

T SMS abr écrite de **t'es.**

ta [ta] f → **ton.**

tabac [taba] nm **1.** BOT tobacco plant **2.** [produit] tobacco ▶ **tabac blond / brun** mild / dark tobacco **3.** [magasin] tobacconist's 🇬🇧, tobacco store 🇺🇸 ▶ **un bar tabac, un bar-tabac** a bar with a tobacco counter **4.** MÉTÉOR ▶ **coup de tabac** squall, gale **5.** fam EXPR ▶ **faire un tabac** to be a smash hit ▶ **passer qqn à tabac** to beat sb up, to lay into sb.

tabacologue [tabakɔlɔg] nmf smoking cessation specialist.

tabagie [tabaʒi] nf 🇶 QUÉBEC [magasin] tobacconist's 🇬🇧, tobacco store 🇺🇸.

tabagisme [tabaʒism] nm tobacco addiction, nicotinism spéc.

tabasser [3] [tabase] vt fam to beat up (sép).

table [tabl] nf **1.** [pour les repas] table / **débarrasser** ou **desservir la table** to clear the table / **dresser** ou **mettre la table** to set the table / **qui sera mon voisin de table ?** who will I be sitting next to (for the meal)? / **sortir** ou **se lever de table** to leave the table, to get up from the table ▶ **table d'hôte** table d'hôte **2.** [nourriture] : **aimer la table** to enjoy ou to like good food **3.** [meuble à usages divers] table ▶ **table de chevet** ou **de nuit** bedside table ▶ **table de cuisine / de salle à manger** kitchen / dining-room table ▶ **table basse** coffee table ▶ **table de billard** billiard table ▶ **table de cuisson** hob ▶ **table à dessin** drawing board ▶ **table de jeu** gambling table ▶ **table à langer** baby changing table ▶ **table des négociations** negotiating table ▶ **table d'opération** operating table ▶ **table d'orientation** viewpoint indicator ▶ **table de ping-pong** table-tennis table ▶ **table à rallonges** extension ou draw table ▶ **table à repasser** ironing board ▶ **table ronde** pr & fig round table ▶ **table roulante** trolley 🇬🇧, tea wagon 🇺🇸 ▶ **table de travail** work surface ▶ **tables gigognes** nest of tables **4.** [liste, recueil] table ▶ **table de logarithmes / mortalité / multiplication** log / mortality / multiplication table ▶ **table des matières** (table of) contents ▶ **faire table rase** to wipe the slate clean, to make a fresh start. ❖ **à table** ◆ loc adv at table ▶ **passer à** ou **se mettre à table** to sit down to a meal / **nous serons dix à table** there will be ten of us at table ▶ **se mettre à table** arg crime [parler] to spill the beans. ◆ interj ▶ **à table !** it's ready! ❖ **table d'écoute** nf wiretapping set ou equipment ▶ **mettre qqn sur table d'écoute** to tap sb's phone.

tableau, x [tablo] nm **1.** ÉDUC ▶ **aller au tableau** to go to the front of the classroom (and answer questions or recite a lesson) ▶ **tableau blanc interactif, tableau interactif** interactive whiteboard ▶ **tableau noir** blackboard **2.** [support mural] rack, board **3.** [panneau d'information] board ▶ **tableau d'affichage** notice board 🇬🇧, bulletin board 🇺🇸 ▶ **tableau des arrivées / départs** arrivals / departures board

4. ART painting, picture / **un tableau de Goya** a painting by Goya **5.** [spectacle] scene, picture / **vous voyez d'ici le tableau !** fam you can imagine ou picture the scene! **6.** [description] picture / **vous nous faites un tableau très alarmant de la situation** you've painted an alarming picture of the situation **7.** [diagramme] table **8.** [liste - gén] list, table ; [- d'une profession] roll **9.** INFORM array **10.** MATH table **11.** EXPR ▶ **gagner sur les deux / tous les tableaux** to win on both / all counts. ❖ **tableau de bord** nm **1.** AUTO dashboard **2.** AÉRON & NAUT instrument panel. ❖ **tableau de chasse** nm **1.** CHASSE bag **2.** fam [conquêtes amoureuses] conquests. ❖ **tableau d'honneur** nm ÉDUC roll of honour 🇬🇧, honor roll 🇺🇸.

tablée [table] nf table / **une tablée de jeunes** a tableful ou party of youngsters.

tabler [3] [table] ❖ **tabler sur** v + prép to bank ou to count on / **ne table pas sur une augmentation** don't bank on getting a rise.

tablette [tablet] nf **1.** [petite planche] shelf **2.** CULIN [de chewing-gum] stick ; [de chocolat] bar **3.** INFORM ▶ **tablette (électronique** ou **tactile)** tablet (computer) **4.** EXPR ▶ **mettre qqn sur la tablette** 🇶 QUÉBEC [placardiser] to put sb on the shelf. ❖ **tablettes** nfpl ANTIQ tablets ▶ **je vais l'inscrire** ou **le noter dans mes tablettes** fig I'll make a note of it.

tabletter [4] [tablete] vt 🇶 QUÉBEC **1.** [classer sans donner suite] to forget **2.** fam [placardiser] to put on the shelf.

tableur [tablœr] nm spreadsheet.

tablier [tablije] nm VÊT apron ; [blouse] overall 🇬🇧, work coat 🇺🇸 ; [d'enfant] smock.

tabloïd(e) [tablɔid] adj & nm tabloid.

tabou, e [tabu] adj **1.** ANTHR & RELIG taboo **2.** [à ne pas évoquer] forbidden, taboo. ❖ **tabou** nm ANTHR & RELIG taboo.

taboulé [tabule] nm tabbouleh.

tabouret [taburɛ] nm **1.** [siège] stool **2.** [pour les pieds] foot stool.

tabulateur [tabylatœr] nm tabulator.

tac [tak] interj EXPR ▶ **du tac au tac** tit for tat / **répondre du tac au tac** to answer tit for tat.

tache [taʃ] nf **1.** [marque] stain / **tache de graisse** grease stain ou mark / **je me suis fait une tache** I've stained my clothes ▶ **tache de sang** bloodstain ▶ **tache de vin** wine stain ▶ **faire tache** fam to jar / **le piano moderne fait tache dans le salon** the modern piano looks out of place in the living room ▶ **faire tache d'huile** to spread **2.** [partie colorée] patch, spot **3.** [sur un fruit] mark, blemish **4.** [sur la peau] mark, spot ▶ **tache de rousseur** ou **de son** freckle ▶ **tache de vin** strawberry mark (birthmark) **5.** [souillure morale] blot, stain, blemish **6.** ZOOL patch, spot, mark. ❖ **sans tache** loc adj [réputation] spotless.

tâche [taʃ] nf **1.** [travail] task, job ▸ **tâches ménagères** housework **2.** [mission, rôle] task, mission. ❖ **à la tâche** ◆ loc adj ▸ **travail à la tâche** piecework. ◆ loc adv INDUST : *il est à la tâche* he's a pieceworker / *on n'est pas à la tâche !* fam what's the rush? / *mourir à la tâche* to die in harness.

tacher [3] [taʃe] vt [salir - vêtement, tapis] to stain / *taché de sang* blood-stained. ❖ **se tacher** ◆ vp *(emploi réfléchi)* to get o.s. dirty, to stain one's clothes. ◆ vp *(emploi passif)* [tissu] to soil ; [bois, peinture, moquette] to mark ; [fruit] to become marked / *le blanc se tache facilement* white soils ou gets dirty easily.

tâcher [3] [taʃe] ❖ **tâcher de** v + prép to try to / *tâche d'être à l'heure* try to be on time.

tacheté, e [taʃte] adj spotted.

tachycardie [takikaʀdi] nf tachycardia.

tacite [tasit] adj tacit.

tacitement [tasitmɑ̃] adv tacitly.

taciturne [tasityʀn] adj taciturn, silent, uncommunicative.

tacle [takl] nm tackle.

tacot [tako] nm *fam* banger UK, (old) heap.

tact [takt] nm [délicatesse] tact, delicacy ▸ **avoir du tact** to be tactful ▸ **manquer de tact** to be tactless / *annoncer la nouvelle avec / sans tact* to break the news tactfully / tactlessly.

tactile [taktil] adj tactile.

tactique [taktik] ◆ adj tactical. ◆ nf **1.** MIL tactics *(sg)* **2.** [moyens] tactics *(pl).*

taf [taf] nm *fam* work.

taffe [taf] nf *fam* [de cigarette] drag, puff.

taffetas [tafta] nm TEXT taffeta.

tag [tag] nm tag *(graffiti).*

tagine [taʒin] nm = **tajine.**

tagliatelle, taliatelle* [tagljatɛl] nf tagliatelle *(U).*

taguer [3] [tage] vt to tag *(with graffiti).*

tagueur, euse [tagœʀ, øz] nm, f tagger *(graffitist).*

Tahiti [taiti] npr Tahiti.

tahitien, enne [taisjɛ̃, ɛn] adj Tahitian.
❖ **Tahitien, enne** nm, f Tahitian.

taie [tɛ] nf [enveloppe] ▸ **taie d'oreiller** pillowcase, pillow slip ▸ **taie de traversin** bolster case.

taillader [3] [tajade] vt to gash ou to slash (through).
❖ **se taillader** vpt : *se taillader les poignets* to slash one's wrists.

taille [taj]
nf

A. COUP, COUPE **1.** HORT [d'un arbre - gén] pruning ; [- importante] cutting back ; [- légère] trimming ; [d'une haie] trimming, clipping ; [de la vigne] pruning **2.** ARM [tranchant] edge **3.** ART [du bois, du marbre] carving ; [en gravure] etching **4.** CONSTR [à la carrière] hewing, cutting ; [sur le chantier] dressing **5.** HIST [impôt] taille, tallage **6.** INDUST [d'un engrenage] milling, cutting **7.** JOAILL cutting **8.** MIN longwall, working face **9.** MUS tenor (line).

B. MESURES, AMPLEUR **1.** [d'une personne, d'un animal] height / *une femme de haute taille* a tall woman, a woman of considerable height / *un homme de petite taille* a short man ▸ **de la taille de** as big as, the size of **2.** [d'un endroit, d'un objet] size / *une pièce de taille moyenne* an average-sized room **3.** [importance] size / *une erreur de cette taille est impardonnable* a mistake of this magnitude is unforgivable **4.** VÊT size / *quelle est votre taille ?* what size do you take? / *donnez-moi la taille en dessous / au-dessus* give me one size down / up ▸ **elle a la taille mannequin** she's

got a real model's figure **5.** [partie du corps] waist / *avoir la taille fine* to be slim-waisted ou slender-waisted / *sa robe est serrée / trop serrée à la taille* her dress is fitted / too tight at the waist ▸ **avoir une taille de guêpe** to have an hourglass figure **6.** [partie d'un vêtement] waist / *un jean (à) taille basse* low-waisted ou hipster UK ou hip-hugger US jeans **7.** INFORM ▸ **taille mémoire** storage capacity.
❖ **à la taille de** loc prép in keeping with / *ses moyens ne sont pas à la taille de ses ambitions* his ambitions far exceed his means. ❖ **de taille** loc adj **1.** [énorme] huge, great / *le risque est de taille* the risk is considerable **2.** [capable] ▸ **être de taille** to measure up / *face à un adversaire comme lui, tu n'es pas de taille* you're no match for an opponent like him ▸ **de taille à** capable of, able to.

taillé, e [taje] adj **1.** [bâti] : *un homme bien taillé* a well-built man ▸ **taillé en** ou **comme** : *un gaillard taillé en hercule* a great hulk of a man **2.** [apte à] ▸ **taillé pour** cut out for / *tu n'es pas taillé pour ce métier* you're not cut out for this job **3.** [coupé - arbre] trimmed, pruned ; [- haie] trimmed, clipped ; [- cristal] cut ; [- crayon] sharpened ; [- barbe, moustache] trimmed / *une barbe taillée en pointe* a goatee (beard) / *un costume bien / mal taillé* a well-cut / badly-cut suit.

taille-crayon [tajkʀɛjɔ̃] *(pl* taille-crayon *ou* taille-crayons) nm pencil sharpener.

tailler [3] [taje] ◆ vt **1.** [ciseler - pierre] to cut, to hew *sout* ; [- verre] to engrave ; [- bois, marbre] to carve ; [- diamant] to cut / *la critique l'a taillé en pièces* the reviewers made mincemeat out of him **2.** [barbe, moustache] to trim ; [crayon] to sharpen / *tailler sa barbe en pointe* to trim one's beard into a goatee **3.** COUT [vêtement] to cut (out) ▸ **tailler une bavette** *fam* to have a chat ou a chinwag **4.** HORT [arbre] to prune, to cut back *(sép)* ; [haie] to trim, to clip ; [vigne] to prune. ◆ vi VÊT ▸ **cette robe taille grand / petit** this dress is cut UK ou runs US large / small.
❖ **se tailler** ◆ vpi *tfam* [partir] to scram / *allez, on se taille !* come on, let's clear off! ▸ **taille-toi !** scram!, beat it! ◆ vpt : *se tailler un (beau) succès* to be a great success.

tailleur [tajœʀ] nm **1.** COUT [artisan] tailor ▸ **tailleur pour dames** ladies' tailor **2.** VÊT (lady's) suit.
❖ **en tailleur** loc adv cross-legged.

tailleur-pantalon [tajœʀpɑ̃talɔ̃] *(pl* tailleurs-pantalons) nm trouser suit UK, pantsuit US.

taillis [taji] nm coppice, copse, thicket.

tain [tɛ̃] nm [pour miroir] silvering.

taire [111] [tɛʀ] vt **1.** [passer sous silence - raisons] to conceal, to say nothing about ; [- information] to hush up *(sép)* ; [- plan, projet] to keep secret, to say nothing about, to keep quiet about / *je tairai le nom de cette personne* I won't mention this person's name ▸ **faire taire qqn** to prevent qqn de parler] to silence sb, to force sb to be quiet / *faites taire les enfants* make the children be quiet ▸ **faire taire qqch** to stifle sthg / *fais taire tes scrupules* forget your scruples **2.** *litt* [cacher - sentiment] : *elle sait taire ses émotions* she's able to keep her emotions to herself.
❖ **se taire** vpi **1.** [s'abstenir de parler] to be ou to keep quiet ▸ **tais-toi !** be quiet! / *elle sait se taire et écouter les autres* she knows when to be silent and listen to others **2.** [cesser de s'exprimer] to fall silent / *l'opposition s'est tue* the opposition has gone very quiet **3.** *fam* EXPR *et quand il t'a invitée à danser ? — tais-toi, je ne savais plus où me mettre !* and when he asked you to dance? — don't, I felt so embarrassed!

Taïwan [tajwan] npr Taiwan.

taïwanais, e [tajwanɛ, ɛz] adj Taiwanese.
❖ **Taïwanais, e** nm, f Taiwanese ▸ **les Taïwanais** the Taiwanese.

* In reformed spelling (see p. 16-18).

tajine [taʒin] nm **1.** [mets] *Moroccan lamb (or chicken) stew* **2.** [récipient] tajine.

talc [talk] nm talcum powder, talc.

talent [talɑ̃] nm **1.** [capacité artistique] talent ▸ **avoir du talent** to have talent, to be talented **2.** [don, aptitude particulière] talent, skill, gift / *ses talents de communicateur* his talents as a communicator **3.** [personne] talent / *il est à la recherche de jeunes / nouveaux talents* he's looking for young / new talent. ❖ **de talent** loc adj talented / *un styliste de grand talent* a designer of great talent, a highly talented designer.

talentueux, euse [talɑ̃tɥø, øz] adj *fam* talented, gifted.

taliban [talibɑ̃] adj & nmf Taliban ▸ **les talibans** the Taliban.

talkie-walkie [tɔkiwɔki] (*pl* **talkies-walkies**) nm walkie-talkie.

taloche [talɔʃ] nf *fam* [gifle] cuff, wallop ▸ **filer une taloche à qqn** to clout sb.

talon [talɔ̃] nm **1.** ANAT heel ▸ **talon d'Achille** : *son talon d'Achille* his Achilles' heel ▸ **être** ou **marcher sur les talons de qqn** to follow close on sb's heels **2.** [d'une chaussure] heel ▸ **talons aiguilles** spike ou stiletto 🇬🇧 heels ▸ **porter des talons hauts** ou **des hauts talons** to wear high heels / *chaussures à talons hauts* high-heeled shoes ▸ **porter des talons plats** to wear flat heels **3.** [d'une chaussette] heel **4.** [d'un fromage, d'un jambon] heel **5.** [d'un chèque] stub, counterfoil ; [d'un carnet à souches] counterfoil.

talonner [3] [talɔne] vt **1.** [poursuivre] ▸ **talonner qqn** to follow on sb's heels / *le coureur marocain, talonné par l'Anglais* the Moroccan runner, with the Englishman close on his heels **2.** SPORT to heel, to hook.

talonnette [talɔnɛt] nf [d'une chaussure] heelpiece, heel cap.

talus [taly] nm [d'un chemin] (side) slope.

tamaris [tamaris], **tamarix** [tamariks] nm tamarisk.

tambouille [tɑ̃buj] nf *tfam* grub / *faire la tambouille* to cook (the grub).

tambour [tɑ̃buʀ] nm **1.** MUS [instrument] drum **2.** CONSTR [sas] tambour (door) **3.** TECHNOL [de lave-linge] drum ; [en horlogerie] barrel.

tambourin [tɑ̃buʀɛ̃] nm [de basque] tambourine ; [provençal] tambourin.

tambouriner [3] [tɑ̃buʀine] vi [frapper] to drum (on) / *il est venu tambouriner à notre porte à six heures du matin* he came beating ou hammering on our door at six in the morning.

tamis [tami] nm **1.** [à farine] sieve ; [en fil de soie, de coton] tammy (cloth), tamis ▸ **passer au tamis a)** [farine, sucre] to put through a sieve, to sift, to sieve **b)** [dossier] to go through with a fine-tooth comb **2.** CONSTR [à sable] sifter, riddle *spéc* **3.** SPORT [d'une raquette] strings.

Tamise [tamiz] npr f ▸ **la Tamise** the Thames.

tamiser [3] [tamize] vt **1.** [farine, poudre] to sift, to sieve **2.** [lumière naturelle] to filter ; [éclairage] to subdue **3.** CONSTR [sable] to sift, to riddle *spéc*.

tampon [tɑ̃pɔ̃] ❖ nm **1.** [pour absorber] wad ▸ **tampon périodique** tampon **2.** [pour imprégner] pad ▸ **tampon encreur** ink pad **3.** [pour nettoyer] pad ▸ **tampon Jex®** Brillo pad® ▸ **tampon à récurer** scouring pad, scourer **4.** [pour obturer] plug, bung **5.** [plaque gravée] rubber stamp ; [oblitération] stamp / *le tampon de la poste* the postmark **6.** MÉD swab, tampon. ❖ adj inv POL ▸ **État / zone tampon** buffer state / zone.

tamponner [3] [tɑ̃pɔne] vt **1.** [document, passeport] to stamp ; [lettre timbrée] to postmark **2.** [télescoper] to collide

with *(insép)*, to hit, to bump into *(insép)* ; [violemment] to crash into *(insép)* **3.** [sécher - front, lèvres, yeux] to dab (at). ❖ **se tamponner** ❖ vp *(emploi réciproque)* to collide, to bump into one another. ❖ vp *(emploi réfléchi) tfam* ▸ **je m'en tamponne (le coquillard)** ! I don't give a damn!

tam-tam (*pl* **tam-tams**), **tamtam*** [tamtam] nm MUS [d'Afrique] tom-tom ; [gong] tam-tam.

tandem [tɑ̃dɛm] nm **1.** [vélo] tandem **2.** [couple] pair. ❖ **en tandem** loc adv [agir, travailler] in tandem, as a pair.

tandis que [tɑ̃dikə], **tandis qu'** [tɑ̃dik] loc conj **1.** [pendant que] while, whilst *sout* ; [au même moment que] as **2.** [alors que] whereas.

tangage [tɑ̃gaʒ] nm AÉRON & NAUT pitching / *il y avait du tangage* the boat was pitching.

tangent, e [tɑ̃ʒɑ̃, ɑ̃t] adj **1.** GÉOM & MATH tangent, tangential **2.** *fam* [limite - cas, candidat] borderline / *ses notes sont tangentes* her grades put her on the borderline / *je ne l'ai pas renvoyé, mais c'était tangent* I didn't fire him but I was very close to doing so. ❖ **tangente** nf **1.** GÉOM & MATH tangent **2.** EXPR ▸ **prendre la tangente a)** *fam* [se sauver] to make off **b)** [esquiver une question] to dodge the issue.

tangible [tɑ̃ʒibl] adj **1.** [palpable] tangible, palpable *sout* **2.** [évident] tangible, real.

tango [tɑ̃go] nm tango.

tanguer [3] [tɑ̃ge] vi **1.** NAUT to pitch **2.** *fam* [tituber] to reel, to sway **3.** *fam* [vaciller - décor] to spin.

tanière [tanjɛʀ] nf **1.** [d'un animal] den, lair **2.** [habitation] retreat.

tanin [tanɛ̃] nm tannin.

tank [tɑ̃k] nm INDUST & MIL tank.

tannant, e [tɑ̃nɑ̃, ɑ̃t] adj *fam* [importun] annoying ; [énervant] maddening / *ce que tu peux être tannant avec tes questions* ! you're a real pain with all these questions!

tanner [3] [tane] vt **1.** [traiter - cuir] to tan **2.** [hâler - peau] to tan **3.** *fam* [harceler] to pester, to hassle / *son fils le tanne pour avoir une moto* his son keeps pestering him for a motorbike.

tannin [tanɛ̃] = **tanin**.

tant [tɑ̃] ❖ adv **1.** [avec un verbe] : *il l'aime tant* he loves her so much / *il a tant travaillé sur son projet* he's worked so hard on his project ; [en corrélation avec «que»] : *ils ont tant fait qu'ils ont obtenu tout ce qu'ils voulaient* they worked so hard that they ended up getting everything they wanted ; [avec un participe passé] : *le jour tant attendu arriva enfin* the long-awaited day arrived at last **3.** *sout* [introduisant la cause] : *deux personnes se sont évanouies, tant il faisait chaud* it was so hot (that) two people fainted **4.** [exprimant une quantité imprécise] so much / *il gagne tant de l'heure* he earns so much per hour **5.** [introduisant une comparaison] ▸ **tant... que** : *le spectacle peut plaire tant aux enfants qu'aux parents* the show is aimed at children as well as adults / *pour des raisons tant économiques que politiques* for economic as well as political reasons **6.** EXPR ▸ **vous m'en direz tant** ! *fam, tu m'en diras tant* ! *fam* you don't say! ❖ nm : *vous serez payé le tant de chaque mois* you'll be paid on such and such a date every month. ❖ **en tant que** loc conj **1.** [en qualité de] as **2.** [dans la mesure où] as long as. ❖ **tant bien que mal** loc adv after a fashion / *le moteur est reparti, tant bien que mal, et la voiture* the engine started up again. ❖ **tant de** loc dét **1.** *(suivi d'un nom non comptable)* [tellement de] so much, such ; *(suivi d'un nom comptable)* so many ▸ **tant de gens** so many people ; [en corrélation avec «que»] : *elle a tant de travail qu'elle n'a même plus le temps de faire les courses* she has so much work that she doesn't even have the time to go shopping anymore / *tant d'années ont passé que j'ai oublié* so many years have gone by that I've forgotten **2.** [exprimant une quantité imprécise] : *il y a tant de lignes par page* there are so many lines to a page. **❖ tant et si bien que** loc conj : *tant et si bien que je ne lui parle plus* so much so that we're no longer on speaking terms. **❖ tant il est vrai que** loc conj : *il s'en remettra, tant il est vrai que le temps guérit tout* he'll get over it, for it's true that time is a great healer. **❖ tant mieux** loc adv good, fine, so much the better / *vous n'avez rien à payer — tant mieux !* you don't have anything to pay — good ou fine! / *tant mieux pour lui* good for him. **❖ tant pis** loc adv never mind, too bad / *je reste, tant pis s'il n'est pas content* I'm staying, too bad if he doesn't like it / *tant pis pour lui* too bad (for him). **❖ tant que** loc conj **1.** [autant que] as ou so much as / *manges-en tant que tu veux* have as many ou much as you like **▶ tu l'aimes tant que ça ?** do you love him that much? **▶ elle est jolie — pas tant que ça** she's pretty — not really **2.** [aussi longtemps que] as long as ; [pendant que] while / *tu peux rester tant que tu veux* you can stay as long as you like / *tant que ce n'est pas grave !* fam as long as it's not serious! **▶ tant qu'on y est** while we're at it **▶ pourquoi pas un château avec piscine tant que tu y es !** why not a castle with a swimming pool while you're at it! **❖ tant qu'à** loc conj : *tant qu'à m'expatrier, j'aime mieux que ce soit dans un beau pays* if I have to go and live abroad, I'd rather go somewhere nice **▶ tant qu'à faire** : *tant qu'à faire, je préférerais du poisson* I'd rather have fish if I have the choice / *tant qu'à faire, sortons maintenant* we might as well go out now. **❖ un tant soit peu** loc adv : *si tu étais un tant soit peu observateur* if you were the least bit observant / *si elle avait un tant soit peu de bon sens* if she had the slightest bit of common sense.

tante [tɑ̃t] nf **1.** [dans une famille] aunt **2.** *tfam* [homosexuel] fairy.

tantinet [tɑ̃tinɛ] **❖ un tantinet** loc adv a tiny (little) bit / *un tantinet stupide* a tiny bit stupid.

tantôt [tɑ̃to] adv *fam* [cet après-midi] this afternoon. **❖ tantôt..., tantôt** loc corrélative sometimes..., sometimes.

Tanzanie [tɑ̃zani] npr f **▶ (la) Tanzanie** Tanzania.

tanzanien, enne [tɑ̃zanjɛ̃, ɛn] adj Tanzanian. **❖ Tanzanien, enne** nm, f Tanzanian.

taoïsme [taɔism] nm Taoism.

taon [tɑ̃] nm horsefly.

tapage [tapaʒ] nm **1.** [bruit] din, uproar **▶ faire du tapage** to make a racket **2.** [scandale] scandal, fuss / *ça a fait tout un tapage* there was quite a fuss about it **3.** DR **▶ tapage nocturne** disturbance of the peace at night.

tapant, e [tapɑ̃, ɑ̃t] adj : *je serai là à dix heures tapantes* I'll be there at ten o'clock sharp ou on the dot.

tape [tap] nf **1.** [pour punir] (little) slap, tap **2.** [amicale] pat **▶ donner une petite tape sur le dos / bras de qqn** to pat sb's back / arm.

tape-à-l'œil [tapalœj] adj inv [couleur, bijoux, toilette] flashy, showy.

tapée [tape] nf *fam* [multitude] : *une tapée de dossiers* heaps of files / *il y avait une tapée de photographes* there was a swarm of photographers.

taper [3] [tape] ❖ vt **1.** [personne -gén] to hit ; [-d'un revers de main] to slap **2.** [marteler -doucement] to tap ; [-fort] to hammer, to bang **3.** [heurter] : *taper un coup à une porte* to knock once on a door **4.** [dactylographier] to type / *taper un document à la machine* to type (out) a document **5.** TÉLÉC [code] to dial **6.** *tfam* [demander de l'argent à] : *il m'a tapé de 50 euros* he touched me for

50 euros, he cadged 🇬🇧 ou bummed 🇺🇸 50 euros off me. ❖ vi **1.** [donner un coup à quelque chose] : *elle a tapé du poing sur la table* she banged ou thumped her fist on the table **▶ taper dans une balle a)** [lui donner un coup] to kick a ball **b)** [s'amuser avec] to kick a ball around **2.** [battre, frapper] **▶ taper sur qqn a)** [une fois] to hit sb **b)** [à coups répétés] to beat sb up **▶ se faire taper sur les doigts** to get rapped over the knuckles **▶ la petite veste rose m'avait tapé dans l'œil** *fam* I was really taken with the little pink jacket **▶ elle lui a tapé dans l'œil dès le premier jour** *fam* he fancied her from day one **3.** [dactylographier] **▶ taper (à la machine)** to type / *tape sur cette touche* press this key **4.** *fam* [soleil] to beat down **5.** *fam* [critiquer] **▶ taper sur** [personne, film] to run down (*sép*), to knock / *elle s'est fait taper dessus dans la presse* ou *par les journaux* the newspapers really panned her **6.** *fam* [puiser] **▶ taper dans a)** [réserves, économies] to dig into (*insép*) **b)** [tiroir-caisse] to help o.s. from. **❖ se taper** ❖ vp (emploi réciproque) to hit each other / *ils ont fini par se taper dessus* eventually, they came to blows. ❖ vpt **1.** *fam* [consommer -dîner, petits-fours] to put away (*sép*), to scoff 🇬🇧 ; [-boisson] to knock back (*sép*) **2.** *tfam* [sexuellement] to lay, to have it off with **3.** *fam* [subir -corvée, travail, gêneur] to get landed 🇬🇧 ou lumbered 🇬🇧 ou stuck with / *je me suis tapé les cinq étages à pied* I had to walk up the five floors **4.** EXPR **▶ c'est à se taper la tête contre les murs** *fam* it's enough to drive you stark raving mad. ❖ vpi **▶ je m'en tape** *tfam* I don't give a damn (about it).

tapette [tapɛt] nf **1.** [piège à souris] mousetrap **2.** *tfam & péj* [homosexuel] poof 🇬🇧, fag 🇺🇸 **3.** [contre les mouches] flyswatter ; [pour les tapis] carpet beater.

tapioca [tapjɔka] nm tapioca.

tapir [32] [tapiʀ] ❖ **se tapir** vpi [se baisser] to crouch (down) ; [se dissimuler -par peur] to hide ; [-en embuscade] to lurk.

tapis [tapi] nm **1.** [pièce de tissu -gén] carpet ; [-de taille moyenne] rug ; [-de petite taille] mat **▶ tapis rouge** *pr & fig* red carpet **▶ tapis de selle** saddlecloth **▶ tapis de sol** ground sheet **▶ tapis de souris** INFORM mouse mat ou pad **▶ tapis volant** flying ou magic carpet **2.** *litt* [couche -de feuilles, de neige] carpet **3.** JEUX [de billard, d'une table de jeu] cloth, baize **4.** SPORT [dans une salle de sport] mat ; [à la boxe] canvas **▶ aller au tapis** [boxeur] to be knocked down / *envoyer son adversaire au tapis* to floor one's opponent **5.** TECHNOL **▶ tapis roulant** [pour piétons] moving pavement 🇬🇧 ou sidewalk 🇺🇸, travolator.

tapis-brosse [tapibʀɔs] (*pl* **tapis-brosses**) nm doormat.

tapisser [3] [tapise] vt [mur -avec du papier peint] to wallpaper ; [-de petite taille] to hang with material ; [-avec des tentures] to hang with curtains ou drapes 🇺🇸 ; [fauteuil, étagère] to cover / *tapisser une cloison de posters* to cover a partition with posters.

tapisserie [tapisʀi] nf **1.** [art, panneau] tapestry **▶ faire tapisserie a)** [dans une réunion] to be left out **b)** [au bal] to be a wallflower **2.** [petit ouvrage] tapestry / *faire de la tapisserie* to do tapestry ou tapestry-work **3.** [papier peint] wallpaper (U) **4.** [métier] tapestry-making.

tapissier, ère [tapisje, ɛʀ] nm, f **1.** [fabricant] tapestry-maker **2.** [vendeur] upholsterer **3.** [décorateur] interior decorator.

taponner [3] [tapɔne] 🇨🇦 ❖ vt **1.** [tâter, manipuler] to finger **2.** [attouchements] to grope. ❖ vi **1.** [tâtonner] **▶ taponner avec qqch** to fiddle with sthg **2.** [tergiverser, hésiter] to waver.

tapoter [3] [tapɔte] ❖ vt [dos, joue] to pat ; [surface] to tap. ❖ vi **1.** [tambouriner] to tap / *elle tapotait sur la* *table avec un crayon* she was drumming (on) the table with a pencil **2.** [jouer médiocrement] : *il tapotait sur le vieux piano* he was banging out a tune on the old piano.

taquet [takε] nm **1.** [cale - de meuble] wedge ; [- de porte] wedge, stop **2.** TECHNOL [d'une machine à écrire] tabulator stop.

taquin, e [takε̃, in] adj teasing / *il est un peu taquin par moments* he's a bit of a tease sometimes.

taquiner [3] [takine] vt **1.** [faire enrager] to tease **2.** [être légèrement douloureux] to bother. ❖ **se taquiner** vp *(emploi réciproque)* to tease each other.

taquinerie [takinʀi] nf **1.** [action] teasing **2.** [parole] : *cesse tes taquineries* stop teasing.

tarabiscoté, e [taʀabiskɔte] adj fam **1.** [bijou] overornate **2.** [style, phrases] fussy, affected **3.** [explication, récit] complicated, involved, convoluted.

tarabuster [3] [taʀabyste] vt fam **1.** [houspiller - personne] to pester, to badger / *elle m'a tarabusté jusqu'à ce que j'accepte* she just wouldn't leave me alone until I said yes **2.** [tracasser] to bother.

tarama [taʀama] nm taramasalata.

tard [taʀ] adv **1.** [à la fin de la journée, d'une période] late / *il se fait tard* it's getting late **2.** [après le moment fixé ou opportun] late / *les magasins restent ouverts tard* the shops stay open late ou keep late opening hours ▸ **c'est trop tard** it's too late ▸ **plus tard** later / *nous parlions de lui pas plus tard que ce matin* we were talking about him only ou just this morning. ❖ **au plus tard** loc adv at the latest. ❖ **sur le tard** loc adv late (on) in life.

tarder [3] [taʀde] vi **1.** [être lent à se décider - personne] to delay / *ne pars pas maintenant — j'ai déjà trop tardé* don't go now — I should be gone already **2.** [être long à venir - événement] to be a long time coming, to take a long time to come / *sa décision n'a pas tardé* his decision wasn't long coming / *je t'avais dit qu'on le reverrait, ça n'a pas tardé !* I told you we'd see him again, we didn't have to wait long! / *la réponse tardait à venir* the answer took a long time to come ; [mettre du temps - personne] : *elle devrait être rentrée, elle ne va pas tarder* she should be back by now, she won't be long / *elle n'a pas tardé à se rendre compte que...* it didn't take her long to realize that..., she soon realized that... ❖ **sans (plus) tarder** loc adv without delay.

tardif, ive [taʀdif, iv] adj **1.** [arrivée] late ; [remords] belated *sout*, tardy *litt* / *l'arrivée tardive des secours sur le lieu de l'accident* the late arrival of the emergency services at the scene of the accident **2.** [heure] late, advanced *sout*.

tardivement [taʀdivmã] adv **1.** [à une heure tardive] late **2.** [trop tard] belatedly, tardily *litt*.

tare [taʀ] nf **1.** [défectuosité - physique] (physical) defect ; [- psychique] abnormality **2.** *fig* shortcoming, defect, flaw.

taré, e [taʀe] ❖ adj fam [fou] soft in the head, touched, mad ; [imbécile] stupid. ❖ nm, f fam [fou] loony, nutter ; [imbécile] moron, idiot.

tarentule [taʀɑ̃tyl] nf (European) tarantula.

targette [taʀʒεt] nf small bolt.

targuer [3] [taʀge] ❖ **se targuer de** vp + prép *sout* [se vanter de] to boast about ou of ; [s'enorgueillir de] to pride o.s. on / *il se targue de connaître plusieurs langues* he claims he knows ou to know several languages / *un risque que je me targue d'avoir pris* a risk I'm proud to have taken ou I pride myself on having taken.

tarif [taʀif] nm **1.** [liste de prix] price list ; [barème] rate, rates ▸ **tarif postal** postal ou postage rates ▸ **il est payé au tarif syndical** he's paid the union rate **2.** [prix pratiqué] ▸ **quel est votre tarif ?, quels sont vos tarifs ?** a) [femme de ménage, baby-sitter, mécanicien, professeur particulier]

how much do you charge? b) [conseiller, avocat] what fee do you charge?, what are your fees? ▸ **le tarif étudiant est de 6 €** the price for students is 6 € ▸ **tarif de nuit** night on off-peak rate ▸ **à plein tarif** a) TRANSP full-fare b) LOISIRS full-price ▸ **à tarif réduit** a) TRANSP reduced-fare b) LOISIRS reduced-price ▸ **'tarif réduit pour étudiants'** 'concessions for students' **3.** *fam* [sanction] fine, penalty / *10 jours de prison, c'est le tarif* 10 days in the cooler is what it's usually worth ou what you usually get.

tarification [taʀifikasjɔ̃] nf pricing.

tarir [32] [taʀiʀ] vi **1.** [cesser de couler] to dry up, to run dry **2.** [s'épuiser - conversation] to dry up ; [- enthousiasme, inspiration] to dry up, to run dry ▸ **ne pas tarir d'éloges sur qqn** to be full of praise for sb ▸ **ne pas tarir sur** : *les journaux ne tarissent pas sur la jeune vedette* the papers are full of stories about the young star. ❖ **se tarir** vpi [mare, puits] to dry up ; [rivière] to run dry.

tarot [taʀo] nm **1.** JEUX [carte, jeu] tarot **2.** [cartomancie] Tarot, tarot.

Tartan® [taʀtɑ̃] nm Tartan®.

tartan [taʀtɑ̃] nm tartan.

tarte [taʀt] ❖ nf **1.** CULIN tart, pie 🇺🇸 / *tarte aux pommes* apple tart 🇬🇧 ou pie 🇺🇸 ▸ **tarte à la crème** a) CULIN custard pie ou tart b) [cliché] stock reply, cliché ▸ **tarte Tatin** upside-down apple tart **2.** *tfam* [gifle] clip, clout ▸ **flanquer une tarte à qqn** to give sb a clip round the ear **3.** *fam* EXPR▸ *c'est pas de la tarte* it's easier said than done, it's no picnic. ❖ adj *fam* **1.** [ridicule - personne] plain-looking 🇬🇧, plain 🇬🇧, homely 🇺🇸 ; [- chapeau, robe] naff 🇬🇧, stupid-looking / *ce que tu as l'air tarte !* you look a (real) idiot! **2.** [stupide - personne] dim, dumb 🇺🇸 ; [- film, histoire, roman] daft, dumb 🇺🇸.

tartelette [taʀtəlεt] nf tartlet, little tart.

tartinade [taʀtinad] nf 🇨🇦 CULIN spread.

tartine [taʀtin] nf **1.** CULIN slice of bread ▸ **une tartine de beurre / pâté** a slice of bread and butter / with pâté **2.** *fam & fig* : *c'est juste une carte postale, pas la peine d'en mettre une tartine* ou *des tartines* it's only a postcard, there's no need to write your life story.

tartiner [3] [taʀtine] vt **1.** CULIN to spread / *sors le beurre et tartine les toasts* take the butter out and spread it on the toast **2.** *fam & fig* to churn out / *il a fallu qu'elle tartine des pages et des pages* she had to write page after page.

tartre [taʀtʀ] nm **1.** [dans une bouilloire, une machine à laver] fur, scale **2.** [sur les dents] tartar.

tas [ta] nm [amoncellement - de dossiers, de vêtements] heap, pile ; [- de sable, de cailloux] heap ; [- de planches, de foin] stack / *mettre en tas* [feuilles, objets] to pile ou to heap up / *tas de fumier* dung heap ▸ **tas d'ordures** rubbish 🇬🇧 ou garbage 🇺🇸 heap ▸ **un tas** ou **des tas de** [beaucoup de] a lot of ▸ **tas de paresseux / menteurs !** *fam* you lazy / lying lot! 🇬🇧, you bunch of lazybones / liars! ❖ **dans le tas** loc adv *fam* **1.** [dans un ensemble] : *l'armoire est pleine de vêtements, tu en trouveras bien un ou deux qui t'iront dans le tas* the wardrobe's full of clothes, you're bound to find something there that will fit you **2.** [au hasard] : *la police a tiré / tapé dans le tas* the police fired into the crowd / hit out at random. ❖ **sur le tas** *fam* ❖ loc adj [formation] on-the-job. ❖ loc adv [se former] on the job / *il a appris son métier sur le tas* he learned his trade as he went along.

Taser® [tazœʀ] nm taser.

tasse [tas] nf **1.** [récipient] cup ▸ **tasse à café** coffee cup ▸ **tasse à thé** teacup **2.** [contenu] cup, cupful / *ajouter deux tasses de farine* add two cupfuls of flour / *ce n'est pas ma tasse de thé* it's not my cup of tea.

tassé, e [tase] adj **1.** [serrés - voyageurs] packed ou crammed in **2.** [ratatiné, voûté - personne] wizened. **⟐ bien tassé, e** loc adj *fam* **1.** [café] strong ; [scotch, pastis] stiff ; [verre] full (to the brim), well-filled **2.** [dépassé - âge] : *elle a soixante ans bien tassés* she's sixty if she's a day.

tassement [tasmɑ̃] nm **1.** [récession] slight drop, down-turn / *un tassement des voix de gauche aux dernières élections* a slight fall in the numbers of votes for the left in the last elections **2.** MÉD **⟐ tassement de vertèbres** compression of the vertebrae.

tasser [3] [tase] vt **1.** [neige, terre] to pack ou to tamp down *(sép)* **2.** [entasser] to cram, to squeeze / *tasse les vêtements dans le sac* press the clothes down in the bag. **⟐ se tasser** vpi **1.** [s'effondrer - fondations, terrain] to subside **2.** [se voûter - personne] to shrink **3.** [s'entasser - voyageurs, spectateurs] to cram, to squeeze up / *en se tassant on peut tenir à quatre à l'arrière (de la voiture)* if we squeeze up, four of us can get in the back (of the car) **4.** *fam* [s'arranger - situation] to settle down / *je crois que les choses vont se tasser* I think things will settle down **5.** [ralentir - demande, vente] to fall, to drop ; [- production] to slow down / *le marché des valeurs s'est tassé* the securities market has levelled off.

tata [tata] nf *langage enfantin* [tante] aunty, auntie.

tâter [3] [tate] vt **1.** [fruit, membre, tissu] to feel **2.** *fig* [sonder] **⟐ tâter le terrain** to see how the land lies. **⟐ se tâter ⟐** vp *(emploi réfléchi)* [après un accident] to feel o.s. / *se tâter la jambe | le bras* to feel one's leg / one's arm. **⟐** vpi to be in 🇬🇧 ou of 🇺🇸 two minds / *je ne sais pas si je vais accepter, je me tâte encore* I don't know whether I'll accept, I haven't made up my mind (about it) yet.

tatie [tati] nf *fam* auntie.

tatillon, onne [tatijɔ̃, ɔn] *fam* adj [vétilleux] pernickety.

tâtonnement [tatɔnmɑ̃] nm **⟐ avancer par tâtonnements a)** *pr* to grope one's way along **b)** *fig* to proceed by trial and error / *nous n'en sommes encore qu'aux tâtonnements* we're still trying to find our way.

tâtonner [3] [tatɔne] vi **1.** [pour marcher] to grope ou to feel one's way (along) ; [à la recherche de qqch] to grope about ou around **2.** [hésiter] to grope around ; [expérimenter] to proceed by trial and error.

tâtons [tatɔ̃] **⟐ à tâtons** loc adv [à l'aveuglette] : *avancer à tâtons* to grope ou to feel one's way along / *elle chercha l'interrupteur à tâtons* she felt ou groped around for the switch.

tatou [tatu] nm armadillo.

tatouage [tatwaʒ] nm [dessin] tattoo.

tatouer [6] [tatwe] vt [dessin, personne] to tattoo.

taudis [todi] nm slum, hovel / *c'est un vrai taudis chez lui !* his place is a real slum ou pigsty!

taulard, e [tolaʀ, aʀd] nm, f *arg crime* convict, jailbird.

taule [tol] nf *tfam* [prison] nick 🇬🇧, clink / *elle a fait un an de taule* she did a one year stretch (inside). **⟐ en taule** loc adv *tfam* inside / *je ne veux pas me retrouver en taule* I don't want to wind up inside.

taupe [top] nf **1.** ZOOL [mammifère] mole ; [poisson] por-beagle **2.** *arg scol* second year of a two-year entrance course for the Science sections of the Grandes Écoles **3.** *fam* [agent secret] mole.

taupinière [topinjeʀ], **taupinée** [topine] nf [monti-cule] molehill ; [tunnel] (mole) burrow.

taureau, x [tɔʀo] nm bull **⟐ taureau de combat** fighting bull **⟐ prendre le taureau par les cornes** to take the bull by the horns.

Taureau, x [tɔʀo] npr m **1.** ASTRON Taurus **2.** ASTROL Taurus / *elle est Taureau* she's (a) Taurus ou a Taurean.

tauromachie [tɔʀɔmaʃi] nf bullfighting, tauromachy *spéc.*

taux [to] nm **1.** [tarif] rate **2.** [proportion] rate **⟐ taux de chômage** unemployment rate **⟐ taux d'échec / de réussite** failure / success rate **⟐ taux de mortalité / natalité** death / birth rate **⟐ taux de fréquentation** attendance rate **3. ⟐ taux de change** exchange rate **⟐ taux d'intérêt** interest rate, rate of interest **⟐ taux zéro** zero-rating **4.** MÉD [d'albu-mine, de cholestérol] level.

taverne [tavɛʀn] nf 🇨🇦 [bistrot] tavern.

taxation [taksasjɔ̃] nf FIN taxation, taxing *(U)*.

taxe [taks] nf **1.** FIN tax **⟐ taxe à la valeur ajoutée** value added tax **⟐ taxe intérieure sur les produits pétroliers** domestic tax on petroleum products **2.** ADMIN tax **⟐ taxe d'aéroport** airport tax **⟐ taxe carbone** carbon tax **⟐ taxe foncière** property tax **⟐ taxe d'habitation** *tax paid on resi-dence* ; ≃ council tax 🇬🇧 ; ≃ local tax 🇺🇸 **⟐ taxe de séjour** visitor's ou tourist tax.

taxer [3] [takse] vt **1.** ÉCON & FIN to tax / *taxer les disques à 10 %* to tax records at 10%, to put a 10% tax on records **2.** [accuser] **⟐ taxer qqn de** to accuse sb of, to tax sb with *sout* / *vous m'avez taxé d'hypocrisie* you accused me of being a hypocrite **3.** *fam* [emprunter] to cadge.

taxi [taksi] nm **1.** [voiture] taxi, cab 🇺🇸 **2.** *fam* [conduc-teur] cabby, taxi ou cab driver / *faire le taxi* to be a taxi driver.

Taxiphone® [taksifɔn] nm call shop.

TB, tb (abr écrite de *très bien*) vg.

TBI (abr de *tableau blanc interactif*) nm interactive whiteboard.

Tchad [tʃad] npr m **⟐ le Tchad** Chad.

tchadien, enne [tʃadjɛ̃, ɛn] adj Chadian. **⟐ Tchadien, enne** nm, f Chadian.

tchador [tʃadɔʀ] nm chador, chuddar.

tchao [tʃao] *fam* = **ciao.**

tchatche [tʃatʃ] nf *fam* : *avoir la tchatche* to have the gift of the gab.

tchatcheur, euse [tʃatʃœʀ, øz] nm, f *fam* smooth talker.

tchèque [tʃɛk] adj Czech. **⟐ Tchèque** nmf Czech. **⟐ tchèque** nm LING Czech.

Tchétchénie [tʃetʃeni] npr **⟐ la Tchétchénie** Chechnya.

tchin-tchin, tchintchin* [tʃintʃin] interj *fam* cheers.

TD (abr de *travaux dirigés*) nmpl **1.** ÉDUC *supervised practical work* **2.** UNIV *university class where students do exer-cises set by the teacher.*

te [tə] *(devant voyelle ou «h» muet t')* pron pers *(2ᵉ pers sg)* **1.** [avec un verbe pronominal] **⟐ tu te lèves tard** you get up late / *tu te prends pour qui ?* who do you think you are? / *tu vas te faire mal* you'll hurt yourself **2.** [com-plément] you / *elle t'a envoyé un colis* she's sent you a parcel / *elle t'est devenue indispensable* she has become indispensable to you / *ne te laisse pas faire* don't let your-self be pushed around **3.** *fam* [emploi expressif] : *je te l'ai envoyé balader, celui-là !* I sent 🇭🇮🇲 packing!

technicien, enne [tɛknisjɛ̃, ɛn] nm, f [en entreprise] technician, engineer / *il est technicien en informatique* he's a computer technician.

technico-commercial, e [tɛknikokɔmɛʀsjal, o] *(mpl* **technico-commerciaux,** *fpl* **technico-commerciales)** adj **⟐ agent technico-commercial** sales technician, sales engineer.

Technicolor® [tɛknikɔlɔʀ] nm Technicolor® **⟐ en Tech-nicolor** Technicolor *(modif)*.

technique [tɛknik] ◆ adj **1.** [pratique] technical, practical **2.** [mécanique] technical **3.** [technologique] technical. ◆ nm ENS ▸ **le technique** vocational education. ◆ nf **1.** [méthode] technique **2.** [applications de la science] ▸ **la technique** applied science.

techniquement [tɛknikmɑ̃] adv technically.

techno [tɛkno] adj & nf techno ▸ **la (musique) techno** techno.

technocrate [tɛknɔkʁat] nmf technocrat.

technologie [tɛknɔlɔʒi] nf [technique] technology.

technologique [tɛknɔlɔʒik] adj technological.

technopole [tɛknɔpɔl] nf *large urban centre with teaching and research facilities to support development of hi-tech industries.*

technopôle [tɛknɔpol] nm *area specially designated to accommodate and foster hi-tech industries.*

teck [tɛk] nm teak.

teckel [tekɛl] nm dachshund.

tee [ti] nm SPORT tee / *partir du tee* to tee off.

tee-shirt (*pl* tee-shirts), **teeshirt*** [tiʃœʁt] nm tee-shirt, T-shirt.

Téhéran [teeʁɑ̃] npr Tehran, Teheran.

teigne [tɛɲ] nf **1.** ENTOM tineid **2.** *fam* [homme] louse ; [femme] vixen.

teigneux, euse [tɛɲø, øz] adj *fam* [hargneux] nasty, ornery US.

teindre [81] [tɛ̃dʁ] vt [soumettre à la teinture] to dye. ❖ **se teindre** vp (*emploi réfléchi*) : *se teindre les cheveux / la barbe en roux* to dye one's hair / beard red.

teint [tɛ̃] nm [habituel] complexion ; [momentané] colour, colouring / *avoir le teint pâle / jaune / mat* to have a pale / sallow / matt complexion. ❖ **grand teint** loc adj [couleur] fast ; [tissu] colourfast UK, colorfast US.

teinte [tɛ̃t] nf [couleur franche] colour UK, color US ; [ton] shade, tint, hue.

teinté, e [tɛ̃te] adj **1.** [lunettes] tinted ; [verre] tinted, stained **2.** [bois] stained.

teinter [3] [tɛ̃te] vt [verre] to tint, to stain ; [lunettes, papier] to tint ; [boiseries] to stain.

teinture [tɛ̃tyʁ] nf **1.** [action] dyeing **2.** [produit] dye **3.** PHARM tincture ▸ **teinture d'arnica / d'iode** tincture of arnica / of iodine.

teinturerie [tɛ̃tyʁʁi] nf [boutique] dry cleaner's.

teinturier, ère [tɛ̃tyʁje, ɛʁ] nm, f [qui nettoie] dry cleaner ; [qui colore] dyer.

tek [tɛk] = teck.

tel, telle [tɛl] (*mpl* tels, *fpl* telles) ◆ dét (*adj indéf*)

1. [avec une valeur indéterminée] : *tel jour, tel endroit, à telle heure* on such and such a day, at such and such a place, at such and such a time / *cela peut se produire dans telle ou telle circonstance* it can happen under certain circumstances **2.** [semblable] such / *je n'ai rien dit de tel* I never said such a thing, I said nothing of the sort / *un tel homme peut être dangereux* a man like that can be dangerous / *il n'est pas avare, mais il passe pour tel* he's not mean, but people think he is ▸ **en tant que tel** as such **3.** [ainsi] : *telle avait été sa vie, telle fut sa fin* as had been his / her life, such was his / her death **4.** [introduisant un exemple, une énumération, une comparaison] like / *des métaux tels le cuivre et le fer* metals such as copper and iron / *elle a filé tel l'éclair* she shot off like a bolt of lightning ▸ **tel père, tel fils** *prov* like father, like son *prov* **5.** [en intensif] such / *c'est un tel honneur pour nous...* it is such an honour for us...

1. [introduisant une comparaison] : *il est tel que je l'ai toujours connu* he's just the same as when I knew him / *un homme tel que lui* a man like him / *telle que je la connais, elle va être en retard* knowing her, she's bound to be late ▸ **tu prends le lot tel que** *fam* take the batch as it is **2.** [introduisant un exemple ou une énumération] ▸ **tel que** such as, like **3.** [avec une valeur intensive] : *la douleur fut telle que je faillis m'évanouir* the pain was so bad that I nearly fainted / *il a fait un tel bruit qu'il a réveillé toute la maisonnée* he made such a noise ou so much noise that he woke the whole house up.

◆ pron indéf [désignant des personnes ou des choses non précisées] : *telle ou telle de ses idées aurait pu prévaloir* one or other of his ideas might have prevailed. ❖ **tel quel, telle quelle** loc adj : *tout est resté tel quel depuis son départ* everything is just as he left it.

tél. (abr écrite de **téléphone**) tel.

télé [tele] nf *fam* [poste, émissions] TV / *il n'y a rien ce soir à la télé* there's nothing on TV ou telly tonight.

téléachat [teleaʃa] nm teleshopping.

téléassistance [teleasistɑ̃s] nf remote assistance.

Téléboutique® [telebutik] nf = Taxiphone.

télécabine [telekabin] nf [cabine] cable car.

Télécarte® [telekaʁt] nf phonecard.

téléchargeable [teleʃaʁʒabl] adj downloadable.

téléchargement [teleʃaʁʒəmɑ̃] nm INFORM downloading.

télécharger [17] [teleʃaʁʒe] vt to download.

télécommande [telekɔmɑ̃d] nf AUDIO & TV [procédé, appareil] remote control.

télécommander [3] [telekɔmɑ̃de] vt **1.** [engin, mise à feu, télévision] to operate by remote control **2.** [ordonner de loin] to mastermind, to manipulate / *ces mouvements ont été télécommandés depuis l'Europe* these movements have been masterminded from Europe.

télécommunication [telekɔmynikasjɔ̃] nf telecommunication ▸ **les télécommunications** telecommunications.

téléconférence [telekɔ̃feʁɑ̃s] nf [conférence] teleconference.

téléconseiller, ère [telekɔ̃seje, ɛʁ] nm, f call centre person.

télécopie [telekɔpi] nf fax ▸ **envoyer qqch par télécopie** to fax sthg.

télécopieur [telekɔpjœʁ] nm facsimile machine *spéc*, fax (machine).

télédéclaration [teledeklaʁasjɔ̃] nf online submission ; [de revenus] online tax return.

télédiffusion [teledifyzjɔ̃] nf (television) broadcasting.

télédistribution [teledistʁibysjɔ̃] nf cable television.

téléenseignement, télé-enseignement [teleɑ̃sɛɲmɑ̃] (*pl* téléenseignements ou télé-enseignements) nm distance learning.

téléférique [telefeʁik] = téléphérique.

téléfilm [telefilm] nm film made for television.

télégramme [telegʁam] nm telegram, wire US, cable US.

télégraphique [telegʁafik] adj **1.** TÉLÉC [poteau] telegraph (*modif*) ; [message] telegraphic **2.** *fig* : (en) langage ou style télégraphique (in) telegraphic language ou style.

téléguidage [telegidaʒ] nm radio control.

téléguider [3] [telegide] vt **1.** TECHNOL [maquette] to control by radio **2.** [inspirer] to manipulate.

téléjournal [teleʒuʁnal] nm Québec television news.

télématique [telematik] ◆ adj telematic. ◆ nf data communications, telematics (U).

téléobjectif [teleɔbʒɛktif] nm telephoto (lens).

téléopérateur, trice [teleɔperatœr, tris] nm, f call centre agent.

télépaiement [telepemɑ̃] nm electronic payment.

télépathie [telepati] nf telepathy.

télépéage [telepeaʒ] nm AUTO tele-toll system.

téléphérique [teleferik], **téléférique** nm [cabine] cable-car ; [système] cable-way.

téléphone [telefɔn] nm **1.** [instrument] phone, telephone ▶ **téléphone à carte** cardphone ▶ **téléphone cellulaire** cellphone, cellular phone ▶ **téléphone intelligent** smart phone ▶ **téléphone sans fil / à touches** cordless / pushbutton telephone ▶ **téléphone mobile** mobile phone ▶ **téléphone portable** portable phone ▶ **téléphone public** public telephone, pay-phone ▶ **le téléphone rouge** [entre présidents] the hot line **2.** [installation] phone, telephone ▶ **il a / n'a pas le téléphone** he's / he isn't on the phone 🇬🇧, he has a / has no phone 🇺🇸 **3.** *fam* [numéro] (phone) number. ✧ **au téléphone** loc adv ▶ **je suis au téléphone** I'm on the phone / **je l'ai eu au téléphone** I talked to him on the phone. ✧ **par téléphone** loc adv : *il a réservé par téléphone* he booked over the phone / *faites vos achats par téléphone* do your shopping by phone. ✧ **téléphone arabe** nm grapevine.

téléphoner [3] [telefɔne] ◆ vi to make a phone call / *puis-je téléphoner ?* can I make a phone call?, may I use the phone? / *ne me dérangez pas quand je téléphone* please do not disturb me when I'm on the phone ▶ **téléphoner à qqn** to phone sb, to call sb. ◆ vt to phone / *je te téléphonerai la nouvelle dès que je la connaîtrai* I'll phone and tell you the news as soon as I get it. ✧ **se téléphoner** vp *(emploi réciproque)* to call each other.

téléphonie [telefɔni] nf telephony.

téléphonique [telefɔnik] adj [message, ligne, réseau] telephone *(modif)*, phone *(modif)* ▶ **entretien téléphonique** telephone conversation.

téléprospection [teleprɔspɛksjɔ̃] nf telemarketing.

téléréalité [telerealite] nf reality TV ▶ **émission de téléréalité** reality show.

téléreportage [teleraportaʒ] nm **1.** [émission] television report **2.** [activité] television reporting.

télescope [teleskɔp] nm telescope.

télescoper [3] [teleskɔpe] ✧ **se télescoper** vp *(emploi réciproque)* **1.** [véhicules] to crash into one another **2.** [idées, souvenirs] to intermingle.

télescopique [teleskɔpik] adj [antenne] telescopic.

téléservice [teleservis] nf on-line service.

télésiège [telesjɛʒ] nm chair ou ski lift.

téléski [teleski] nm drag lift, ski tow.

téléspectateur, trice [telespɛktatœr, tris] nm, f television ou TV viewer / *la majorité des téléspectateurs* the majority of viewers ou of the viewing audience.

télésurveillance [telesyrvejɑ̃s] nf (security) telemonitoring.

Télétel® [teletɛl] nm *(French)* public videotex.

télétexte [teletɛkst] nm teletext.

télétravail, aux [teletravaj, o] nm teleworking, telecommuting.

télétravailleur, euse [teletravajœr, øz] nmf teleworker, telecommuter.

téléuniversité [teleyniversite] nf Québec distance learning university.

télévangéliste [televɑ̃ʒelist] nmf televangelist, television ou TV evangelist.

télévendeur, euse [televɑ̃dœr, øz] nm, f telesales operator.

télévente [televɑ̃t] nf telesales.

télévérité [televerite] nf reality TV.

téléviser [3] [televize] vt to broadcast on television, to televise.

téléviseur [televizœr] nm television ou TV set.

télévision [televizjɔ̃] nf **1.** [entreprise, système] television / *il regarde trop la télévision* he watches too much television ▶ **télévision câblée** ou **par câble** cable television ▶ **télévision haute définition** high definition television ▶ **télévision par satellite** satellite television **2.** [appareil] television. ✧ **à la télévision** loc adv on television ou TV / *passer à la télévision* to go on television.

télévision-réalité [televizjɔ̃realite] nf TV reality TV, fly-on-the-wall television ▶ **une émission de télévision-réalité a)** a fly-on-the-wall documentary **b)** [de style feuilleton] a docusoap.

télévisuel, elle [televizɥel] adj televisual.

télex [telɛks] nm telex ▶ **envoyer qqch par télex** to telex sthg.

tellement [tɛlmɑ̃] adv **1.** [avec un adverbe, un adjectif] : *c'est tellement loin* it's so far / *je n'ai pas tellement mal* it doesn't hurt that ou so much / *il est tellement têtu* he's so stubborn **2.** [avec un verbe] : *j'ai tellement pleuré !* I cried so much ! ; [en corrélation avec «que»] : *j'en ai tellement rêvé que j'ai l'impression d'y être déjà allée* I've dreamt about it so much ou so often that I feel I've been there already **3.** [introduisant la cause] : *j'ai mal aux yeux tellement j'ai lu* my eyes hurt from reading so much **4.** EXPR **pas tellement** *fam* not really ▶ **plus tellement** *fam* not really any more / *je n'aime plus tellement ça* I don't really like that any more. ✧ **tellement de** loc dét ▶ **j'ai tellement de travail / de soucis en ce moment** I've got so much work / so many worries at the moment ; [en corrélation avec «que»] : *il y avait tellement de bruit que l'on ne s'entendait plus* there was so much noise that we could no longer hear ourselves speak.

téloche [telɔʃ] nf *fam* telly.

téméraire [temerɛr] adj **1.** [imprudent - personne] foolhardy, rash, reckless **2.** [aventuré - tentative] rash, reckless.

témoignage [temwaɲaʒ] nm **1.** DR [action de témoigner] testimony, evidence ▶ **faux témoignage** perjury, false evidence, false witness **2.** [contenu des déclarations] deposition, (piece of) evidence / *le témoignage du chauffeur de taxi est accablant pour elle* the taxi driver's statement is conclusive evidence against her **3.** [preuve] gesture, expression, token ▶ **recevoir des témoignages de sympathie a)** [après un deuil] to receive messages of sympathy **b)** [pendant une épreuve] to receive messages of support **4.** [récit - d'un participant, d'un observateur] (eyewitness) account / *cette pièce sera un jour considérée comme un témoignage sur la vie des années 80* this play will one day be considered as an authentic account of life in the 80s.

témoigner [3] [temwaɲe] ◆ vi DR to testify, to give evidence / *témoigner en faveur de / contre l'accusé* to give evidence for / against the defendant. ◆ vt DR [certifier] ▶ **témoigner que** to testify that / *il a témoigné avoir passé la soirée avec l'accusé* he testified to spending the evening with the defendant. ✧ **témoigner de** v + prép **1.** DR to testify to **2.** [indiquer - bonté, générosité, intérêt] to show, to indicate ; [prouver] to show, to bear witness ou to testify to, to attest *sout* / *le problème ne fait qu'empirer, comme en témoignent ces statistiques* the problem is only getting worse, witness these statistics ou as these statistics show.

témoin [temwɛ̃] nm **1.** DR [qui fait une déposition] witness / *il a été cité comme témoin* he was called as a witness ‣ **témoin à charge / décharge** witness for the prosecution / defence ‣ **témoin oculaire** eyewitness **2.** [à un mariage, à la signature d'un contrat] witness ; [à un duel] second **3.** [spectateur] witness, eyewitness ‣ **être témoin de qqch** to be witness to ou to witness sthg ‣ **prendre qqn à témoin** to call upon sb as a witness **4.** [preuve] witness / *elle a bien mené sa carrière, témoin sa réussite* she has managed her career well, her success is a testimony to that **5.** RELIG ‣ **Témoin de Jéhovah** Jehovah's Witness **6.** SPORT baton / *passer le témoin* to hand over ou to pass the baton **7.** *(comme adj)* ‣ **appartements témoins** show flats 🇬🇧, model apartments 🇺🇸 ‣ **groupe / sujet témoin** SCI control group / subject.

tempe [tɑ̃p] nf temple / *ses tempes commencent à grisonner* he's going grey at the temples.

tempérament [tɑ̃peramɑ̃] nm **1.** [caractère] temperament, disposition, nature **2.** *fam* [forte personnalité] strong-willed person.

température [tɑ̃peratyʀ] nf **1.** MÉD & PHYSIOL temperature ‣ **avoir** ou **faire de la température** to have a temperature ‣ **prendre la température de** a) [patient] to take the temperature of b) [assemblée, public] to gauge (the feelings of) **2.** MÉTÉOR temperature / *il y eut une brusque chute de la température* ou *des températures* there was a sudden drop in temperature.

tempéré, e [tɑ̃peʀe] adj GÉOGR [climat, région] temperate.

tempérer [18] [tɑ̃peʀe] vt **1.** *litt* [température excessive] to temper *sout*, to ease **2.** [atténuer - colère] to soften, to appease ; [- ardeurs, passion, sévérité] to soften, to temper *sout*.

✐ In reformed spelling (see p. 16-18), this verb is conjugated like *semer : il tempèrera, elle tempèrerait*.

tempête [tɑ̃pɛt] nf **1.** MÉTÉOR storm, tempest *litt* ‣ **tempête de neige** snowstorm ‣ **tempête de sable** sandstorm **2.** [déferlement] wave, tempest, storm / *tempête d'applaudissements / de critiques / de protestations* storm of applause / criticism / protest.

tempêter [4] [tɑ̃pete] vi to rage, to rant (and rave).

temple [tɑ̃pl] nm RELIG [gén] temple ; [chez les protestants] church.

tempo [tɛmpo] nm **1.** MUS tempo **2.** [rythme - d'un film, d'un roman] tempo, pace ; [- de la vie] pace.

temporaire [tɑ̃pɔʀɛʀ] adj temporary.

temporel, elle [tɑ̃pɔʀɛl] adj RELIG [autorité, pouvoir] temporal ; [bonheur] temporal, earthly ; [biens] worldly, temporal.

temporiser [3] [tɑ̃pɔʀize] vi to use delaying tactics, to temporize *sout*.

temps [tɑ̃]
◆ nm

A. CLIMAT weather / *quel temps fait-il à Nîmes ?* what's the weather like in Nîmes? / *avec le temps qu'il fait, par ce temps* in this weather / *il fait un temps gris* it's overcast, the weather's dull 🇬🇧 ou gloomy.

B. DURÉE 1. [écoulement des jours] ‣ **comme le temps passe !, comme** ou **que le temps passe vite !** how time flies! **2.** [durée indéterminée] time *(U)* / *c'est du temps perdu* it's a waste of time ‣ **mettre du temps à faire qqch** to take time to do sthg ‣ **passer son temps à :** *je passe mon temps à lire* I spend (all) my time reading ‣ **pour passer le temps** to while away ou to pass the time ‣ **prendre du temps** to take time ‣ **trouver le temps long** to feel time dragging by **3.** [durée nécessaire] time *(C)* ‣ **le temps que :** *calculer le temps que met la lumière pour aller du Soleil à la Terre* to compute the time that light takes to go from the Sun to the Earth / *va chercher du lait, le temps que je fasse du thé* go and get some milk while I make some tea ‣ **le temps de :** *le temps*

de faire qqch (the) time to do sthg / *le temps d'enfiler un manteau et j'arrive* just let me put on a coat and I'll be with you ‣ **avoir le temps de faire qqch** to have (the) time to do sthg ‣ **prendre son temps** to take one's time ‣ **prendre le temps de faire qqch** to take the time to do sthg ‣ **temps de communication** [sur téléphone portable] airtime ‣ **temps de cuisson / préparation** CULIN cooking / preparation time ‣ **être** ou **travailler à temps partiel** to work part-time ‣ **être** ou **travailler à plein temps** ou **à temps plein** to work full-time ‣ **faire un trois quarts (de) temps** ≃ to work 30 hours per week **4.** [loisir] time *(C)* ‣ **avoir du temps** ou **le temps** to have time ‣ **avoir tout son temps** to have all the time in the world ‣ **avoir du temps devant soi** to have time to spare ou on one's hands ‣ **avoir du temps libre** to have some spare time **5.** [moment favorable] ‣ **il est temps :** *il est (grand) temps !* it's high time!, it's about time! / *la voilà — il était temps !* here she is — it's about time ou and not a minute too soon ou and about time too! ‣ **il est temps de** now's the time for / *il n'est plus temps de discuter, il faut agir* the time for discussion is past ou enough talking, we must act **6.** [époque déterminée] time *(C)* / *le temps n'est plus aux querelles* we should put quarrels behind us, the time for quarrelling is past / *il fut un temps où...* there was a time when... / *être en avance / en retard sur son temps* to be ahead of / behind one's time / *être de son temps* to move with the times / *il y a un temps pour tout* there's a time for everything ‣ **faire son temps** [détenu, soldat] to do ou to serve one's time / *la cafetière / mon manteau a fait son temps fam* the coffee machine's / my coat's seen better days ‣ **en temps normal** ou **ordinaire** usually, in normal circumstances ‣ **en temps utile** in due time ou course ‣ **en son temps** in due course / *chaque chose en son temps* there's a right time for everything **7.** [saison, période de l'année] time *(C)*, season / *le temps des moissons* harvest (time) **8.** [phase - d'une action, d'un mouvement] stage ‣ **dans un premier temps** first ‣ **dans un deuxième temps** secondly **9.** INFORM time ‣ **temps d'accès / d'amorçage** access / start-up time / *traitement en temps réel* real-time processing **10.** LING tense **11.** MÉCAN stroke **12.** MUS beat / *valse à trois temps* waltz in three-four time **13.** RELIG ‣ **le temps de l'avent / du carême** (the season of) Advent / Lent **14.** SPORT [d'une course] time / *elle a fait le meilleur temps aux essais* hers was the best time ou she was the fastest in the trials.

◆ nmpl [époque] times, days / *les temps sont durs* ou *difficiles !* times are hard! ❖ **à temps** loc adv in time / *je n'arriverai / je ne finirai jamais à temps !* I'll never make it / I'll never finish in time! ❖ **au temps de** loc prép in ou at the time of, in the days of. ❖ **au temps où, au temps que** loc conj in the days when, at the time when. ❖ **avec le temps** loc adv with the passing of time. ❖ **ces temps-ci** loc adv these days, lately. ❖ **dans ce temps-là** loc adv in those days, at that time. ❖ **dans le temps** loc adv before, in the old days. ❖ **dans les temps** loc adv on time ‣ **être dans les temps** a) [pour un travail] to be on schedule ou time b) [pour une course] to be within the (time) limit. ❖ **de temps à autre, de temps en temps** loc adv from time to time, occasionally, (every) now and then. ❖ **du temps de** loc prép : *du temps de Louis XIV* in the days of Louis the XIVth / *de mon temps, ça n'existait pas* when I was young ou in my day, there was no such thing. ❖ **en même temps** loc adv at the same time. ❖ **en temps de** loc prép ‣ **en temps de guerre / paix** in wartime / peacetime. ❖ **par les temps qui courent** loc adv *fam* these days, nowadays. ❖ **tout le temps** loc adv all the time, always / *ne me harcèle pas tout le temps !* don't keep on pestering me! ❖ **temps fort** nm

MUS strong beat ; *fig* high point, highlight. ❖ **temps mort** nm **1.** [au basketball, volleyball] time-out **2.** *fig* lull, slack period ; [dans une conversation] lull, pause.

tenable [tənabl] adj [supportable] bearable / *la situation n'est plus tenable, il faut agir* the situation's become untenable ou unbearable, we must take action.

tenace [tənas] adj **1.** [obstiné - travailleur] tenacious, obstinate ; [- chercheur] tenacious, dogged ; [- ennemi] relentless ; [- résistance, volonté] tenacious ; [- refus] dogged ; [- vendeur] tenacious, insistent **2.** [durable - fièvre, grippe, toux] persistent, stubborn ; [- parfum, odeur] persistent, lingering ; [- tache] stubborn ; [- préjugé, impression, superstition] deep-rooted, stubborn, tenacious.

ténacité [tenasite] nf [d'une personne, d'une volonté] tenacity, tenaciousness.

tenaille [tənaj] nf ▶ **tenaille, tenailles a)** [de charpentier, de menuisier] pincers **b)** [de cordonnier] pincers, nippers **c)** [de forgeron] tongs.

tenailler [3] [tənaje] vt *sout* [faim, soif] to gnaw ; [doute, inquiétude, remords] to gnaw (at), to rack, to torment / *être tenaillé par la faim* / *par le remords* to be racked with hunger / tormented by remorse.

tenancier, ère [tənɑ̃sje, ɛʀ] nm, f [d'un café, d'un hôtel, d'une maison de jeu] manager.

tenant, e [tənɑ̃, ɑ̃t] nm, f SPORT ▶ **tenant (du titre)** holder, titleholder. ❖ **tenants** nmpl [d'une terre] adjacent parts ; DR abuttals ▶ **les tenants et les aboutissants** [d'une affaire] the ins and outs, the full details. ❖ **d'un (seul) tenant** loc adj all in one block.

tendance [tɑ̃dɑ̃s] nf **1.** [disposition, propension] tendency ▶ **avoir tendance à** to tend to, to have a tendency to / *tu as un peu trop tendance à croire que tout t'est dû* you're too inclined to think that the world owes you a living **2.** [orientation, évolution - gén] trend ; [- d'un créateur] leanings ; [- d'un livre, d'un discours] drift, tenor / *les nouvelles tendances de l'art* / *la mode* the new trends in art / fashion ; *(comme adj)* ▶ **une coupe très tendance** a very fashionable cut **3.** [position, opinion] allegiance, leaning, sympathy / *un parti de tendance libérale* a party with liberal tendencies **4.** BOURSE & ÉCON trend / *une tendance baissière* ou *à la baisse* a downward trend, a downswing / *une tendance haussière* ou *à la hausse* an upward trend, an upswing **5.** [résultat d'une étude] trend ▶ **tendance générale** (general) trend.

tendancieux, euse [tɑ̃dɑ̃sjø, øz] adj [film, récit, interprétation] tendentious, tendencious ; [question] loaded.

tendeur [tɑ̃dœʀ] nm [pour porte-bagages] luggage strap.

tendinite [tɑ̃dinit] nf tendinitis.

tendon [tɑ̃dɔ̃] nm tendon, sinew ▶ **tendon d'Achille** Achilles' tendon.

tendre[1] [tɑ̃dʀ] ◆ adj **1.** [aimant - personne] loving, gentle, tender ; [- voix] gentle ; [- yeux] gentle, loving ; [affectueux - lettre] loving, affectionate / *elle n'est pas tendre avec lui* she's hard on him / *la presse n'est pas tendre pour elle ce matin* she's been given a rough ride in the papers this morning **2.** [moelleux - viande, légumes] tender **3.** [mou - roche, mine de crayon, métal] soft ▶ **bois tendre** softwood **4.** [doux - teinte] soft, delicate / *un tissu rose* / *vert tendre* a soft pink / green material **5.** [jeune] early / *dès sa plus tendre enfance* since his earliest childhood. ◆ nmf tenderhearted person.

tendre[2] [73] [tɑ̃dʀ] vt **1.** [étirer - câble, corde de raquette] to tighten, to tauten ; [- élastique, ressort] to stretch ; [- corde d'arc] to draw back *(sép)* ; [- arc] to bend ; [- arbalète] to arm ; [- voile] to stretch, to brace ; [- peau d'un tambour] to pull, to stretch **2.** [disposer - hamac, fil à linge, tapisserie] to hang ; [- collet, souricière] to set ▶ **tendre une embus-**

cade ou **un piège à qqn** to set an ambush ou a trap for sb **3.** [allonger - partie du corps] ▶ **tendre le cou** to crane ou to stretch one's neck / *elle tendit son front* / *sa joue à sa mère pour qu'elle l'embrasse* she offered her forehead / her cheek for her mother to kiss ▶ **tendre les bras (vers qqn)** to stretch out one's arms (towards sb) / *vas-y, le poste de directeur te tend les bras* go ahead, the director's job is yours for the taking ▶ **tendre la main** [pour recevoir qqch] to hold out one's hand ▶ **tendre la main à qqn a)** [pour dire bonjour] to hold out one's hand to sb **b)** [pour aider] to offer a helping hand to sb **c)** [pour se réconcilier] to extend a ou the hand of friendship to sb ▶ **tendre l'autre joue** *allusion* BIBLE to turn the other cheek. ❖ **tendre à** v + prép **1.** [avoir tendance à] : *c'est une pratique qui tend à disparaître* it's a custom which is dying out **2.** [contribuer à] : *cela tendrait à prouver que j'ai raison* this would seem to prove that I'm right **3.** [aspirer à] : *tendre à la perfection* to aim at perfection. ❖ **se tendre** vpi **1.** [courroie, câble] to tighten (up), to become taut, to tauten **2.** [atmosphère, relations] to become strained.

tendrement [tɑ̃dʀəmɑ̃] adv [embrasser, regarder, sourire] tenderly, lovingly.

tendresse [tɑ̃dʀɛs] nf [attachement - d'un amant] tenderness ; [- d'un parent] affection, tenderness ▶ **avoir de la tendresse pour qqn** to feel affection for sb.

tendron [tɑ̃dʀɔ̃] nm CULIN ▶ **tendron de veau** middle-cut breast of veal.

tendu, e [tɑ̃dy] ◆ pp ⟶ **tendre**. ◆ adj **1.** [nerveux - de tempérament] tense ; [- dans une situation] tense, strained, fraught ; [- avant un événement, un match] keyed up, tense **2.** [atmosphère] strained ; [rapports] strained, fraught UK ; [situation] tense, fraught UK **3.** [partie du corps, muscle] tensed up **4.** [étiré - corde, courroie] tight, taut ; [- corde d'arc] drawn ; [- arc] drawn, bent ; [- voile, peau de tambour] stretched **5.** [allongé] : *avancer le doigt tendu* / *le poing tendu* / *les bras tendus* to advance with pointed finger / raised fist / outstretched arms.

ténèbres [tenɛbʀ] nfpl [nuit, obscurité] darkness *(U)*, dark *(U)* / *être plongé dans les ténèbres* to be in total darkness.

ténébreux, euse [tenebʀø, øz] ◆ adj *litt* **1.** [forêt, maison, pièce] dark, gloomy, tenebrous *litt* ; [recoin, cachot] dark, murky **2.** [incompréhensible] mysterious, unfathomable ▶ **une ténébreuse affaire** a shady business. ◆ nm, f *hum* ▶ **un beau ténébreux** a tall, dark, handsome stranger.

teneur [tənœʀ] nf **1.** [contenu - d'un document] content ; [- d'un traité] terms / *quelle est exactement la teneur de son article ?* what exactly is her article about? **2.** CHIM content / *teneur en alcool* alcohol content, alcoholic strength / *teneur en matières grasses* fat content **3.** MIN content, grade, tenor / *minerai à forte teneur en plomb* ore with a high lead content.

ténia [tenja] nm tapeworm, taenia *spéc*.

tenir [40] [təniʀ]
◆ vt

A. AVOIR DANS LES MAINS 1. [retenir] to hold (on to) ▶ **tenir la main de qqn** to hold sb's hand **2.** [manier] to hold / *tu tiens mal ta raquette* / *ton arc* you're not holding your racket / your bow properly.

B. CONSERVER 1. [maintenir - dans une position] to hold, to keep ; [- dans un état] to keep / *enlève les vis qui tiennent le panneau* undo the screws which hold the panel in place / *tiens-lui la porte, il est chargé* hold the door open for him, he's got his hands full ▶ **tenir chaud** to keep warm **2.** [garder - note] to hold ▶ **tenir l'accord** to stay in tune **3.** *Belg* [collectionner] to collect.

C. POSSÉDER **1.** [avoir reçu] ▸ **tenir qqch de qqn** [par hérédité] to get sthg from sb / *les propriétés que je tenais de ma mère* [par héritage] the properties I'd inherited from my mother **2.** [avoir capturé] to have caught, to have got hold of ; [avoir à sa merci] to have got / *si je tenais celui qui a défoncé ma portière !* just let me get ou lay my hands on whoever smashed in my car door! **3.** [détenir - indice, information, preuve] to have ; [- contrat] to have, to have won ; [- réponse, solution] to have (found) ou got / *je crois que je tiens un scoop !* I think I've got a scoop! ▸ **tenir qqch de** [l'apprendre] to have (got) sthg from / *nous tenons de source sûre / chinoise que...* we have it on good authority / we hear from Chinese sources that... ▸ **tenir qqch de** [le tirer de] : *je tiens mon autorité de l'État* I derive my power from the state ▸ **elle en tient une couche !** *fam* she's as thick as two short planks ⬚, what a dumb bell! ⬚.

D. OCCUPER, PRONONCER **1.** [avoir prise sur, dominer] to hold / *quand la colère le tient, il peut être dangereux* he can be dangerous when he's angry ; MIL to control ; [avoir de l'autorité sur - classe, élève] to (keep under) control **2.** [diriger, s'occuper de - commerce, maison, hôtel] to run ; [- comptabilité, registre] to keep ▸ **tenir la caisse** to be at the cash desk, to be the cashier / *le soir, il tenait le bar* at night he used to serve behind the bar **3.** [donner - assemblée, conférence, séance] to hold, to have / *le tribunal tiendra audience dans le nouveau bâtiment* the court hearings will be held in the new building **4.** [prononcer - discours] to give ; [- raisonnement] to have ; [- langage] to use ▸ **tenir des propos désobligeants / élogieux** to make offensive / appreciative remarks **5.** ▸ **être tenu à qqch** [astreint à] : *être tenu au secret professionnel* to be bound by professional secrecy / *nous sommes tenus à la discrétion* we're obliged to be very discreet ▸ **être tenu de faire** to have to / *je me sens tenu de la prévenir* I feel morally obliged ou duty-bound to warn her **6.** THÉÂTRE [rôle] to play, to have.

E. EXPRIME UNE MESURE **1.** [occuper] to take up (*sép*), to occupy / *le fauteuil tient trop de place* the armchair takes up too much room ▸ **tenir une place importante** to have ou to hold an important place **2.** [contenir] to hold.

F. ÊTRE CONSTANT DANS **1.** [résister à] (to be able) to take / *il tient l'alcool* he can take ⬚ ou hold his drink ▸ **tenir le coup a)** *fam* [assemblage, vêtements] to hold out **b)** [digue] to hold (out) **c)** [personne] (to be able) to take it ▸ **tenir la route** [véhicule] to have good road-holding ⬚, to hold the road well / *ton raisonnement ne tient pas la route* *fig* your argument doesn't stand up to scrutiny **2.** [respecter] to keep to, to stand by, to uphold ▸ **tenir (sa) parole** to keep one's word / *tenir une promesse* to keep ou to fulfil a promise.

G. CONSIDÉRER *sout* to hold, to consider ▸ **tenir qqn / qqch pour** to consider sb / sthg to be, to look upon sb / sthg as.

◆ *vi* **1.** [rester en position - attache] to hold ; [- chignon] to stay up, to hold ; [- bouton, trombone] to stay on ; [- empilement, tas] to stay up / *tenir en place* to stay in place / *la porte du placard ne tient pas fermée* the cupboard door won't stay shut ▸ **faire tenir qqch avec de la colle / des clous** to glue / to nail sthg into position ▸ **tenir à a)** [être fixé à] to be fixed on ou to **b)** [être contigu à] to be next to ; [personne] : *il ne tient pas encore bien sur sa bicyclette / ses skis / ses jambes* he's not very steady on his bike / his skis / his legs yet / *je ne tiens plus sur mes jambes* [de fatigue] I can hardly stand up any more / *elle ne tient pas en place* she can't sit still **2.** [résister - union] to last, to hold out ; [- chaise, vêtements] to hold ou to last out ; [- digue] to hold out ; [- personne] to hold ou to last out ▸ **tenir bon** ou **ferme a)** [s'agripper] to hold firm ou tight **b)** [ne pas céder] to hold out / *tenez bon, les secours arrivent* hold ou hang on, help's on its way / *il me refusait une augmentation, mais j'ai tenu bon* he wouldn't give me a rise but I held out

ou stood my ground ▸ **ne pas y tenir, ne (pas) pouvoir y tenir** : *n'y tenant plus, je l'appelai au téléphone* unable to stand it any longer, I phoned him **3.** [durer, ne pas s'altérer - fleurs] to keep, to last ; [- tissu] to last (well) ; [- beau temps] to last, to hold out ; [- bronzage] to last ; [- neige] to settle, to stay / *aucun parfum ne tient sur moi* perfumes don't stay on me **4.** [être valable, être d'actualité - offre, pari, rendez-vous] to stand ; [- promesse] to hold / *ça tient toujours pour demain ?* is it still on for tomorrow? ▸ **il n'y a pas de... qui tienne** : *il n'y a pas de congé qui tienne* there's no question of having leave **5.** [pouvoir être logé] to fit / *le compte rendu tient en une page* the report takes up one page / *on tient facilement à cinq dans la barque* the boat sits five in comfort / *on n'arrivera jamais à tout faire tenir dans cette valise* we'll never get everything into this suitcase / *son histoire tient en peu de mots* his story can be summed up in a few words **6.** EXPR **tiens, tenez** [en donnant qqch] here ▸ **tiens, tenez** [pour attirer l'attention, pour insister] : *tiens, le tonnerre gronde* listen, it's thundering / *tiens, rends-toi utile* here, make yourself useful ▸ **tiens, tenez** [exprime la surprise, l'incrédulité] : *tiens, Bruno ! que fais-tu ici ?* (hello) Bruno, what are you doing here? / *tiens, je n'aurais jamais cru ça de lui* well, well, I'd never have expected it of him.

❖ **tenir à** *v + prép* **1.** [être attaché à - personne] to care for, to be very fond of ; [- objet] to be attached to ; [- réputation] to care about ; [- indépendance, liberté] to value **2.** [vouloir] ▸ **tenir à faire qqch** to be eager to do ou to be keen on doing sthg / *je tiens à être présent à la signature du contrat* I insist on being there when the contract is signed ▸ **tenir à ce que** : *je tiens à ce qu'ils aient une bonne éducation* I'm most concerned that they should have a good education / *je voudrais t'aider — je n'y tiens pas* I'd like to help you — I'd rather you didn't **3.** [résulter de] to stem ou to result from, to be due to, to be caused by / *le bonheur tient parfois à peu de chose* sometimes it's the little things that give people the most happiness ▸ **qu'à cela ne tienne** never mind, fear not *hum* **4.** *(tournure impersonnelle)* [être du ressort de] : *il ne tient qu'à toi de mettre fin à ce désordre* it's entirely up to you to sort out this shambles. ❖ **tenir de** *v + prép* **1.** [ressembler à] to take after / *elle est vraiment têtue / douée — elle a de qui tenir !* she's so stubborn / gifted — it runs in the family! **2.** [relever de] : *sa guérison tient du miracle* his recovery is something of a miracle. ❖ **se tenir** ◆ *vp (emploi réciproque)* : *ils marchaient en se tenant la main* they were walking hand in hand / *se tenir par le cou / la taille* to have one's arms round each other's shoulders / waists. ◆ *vp (emploi passif)* [se dérouler - conférence] to be held, to take place ; [- festival, foire] to take place. ◆ *vpt* : *se tenir la tête à deux mains* to hold ou to clutch one's head in one's hands. ◆ *vpi* **1.** [se retenir] to hold on (tight) ▸ **se tenir à a)** to hold on to **b)** [fortement] to cling to, to clutch, to grip **2.** [se trouver - en position debout] to stand, to be standing ; [- en position assise] to sit, to be sitting ou seated / *se tenir debout* to be standing (up) ▸ **se tenir droit a)** [debout] to stand up straight **b)** [assis] to sit up straight / *c'est parce que tu te tiens mal que tu as mal au dos* you get backaches because of bad posture **3.** [se conduire] to behave ▸ **bien se tenir** to behave o.s. ▸ **mal se tenir** to behave o.s. badly **4.** [être cohérent] ▸ **se tenir (bien) a)** [argumentation, intrigue] to hold together, to stand up **b)** [raisonnement] to hold water, to hold together ; [coïncider - indices, événements] to hang together, to be linked **5.** EXPR **s'en tenir à** : *tenez-vous-en aux ordres* confine yourself to carrying out orders ▸ **ne pas se tenir de** [joie, impatience] to be beside o.s. with ▸ **tiens-toi bien, tenez-vous bien** : *ils ont détourné, tiens-toi bien, 4 millions d'euros !* they embezzled, wait for it, 4 million euros! ❖ **se tenir pour** *vp + prép* [se considérer comme] : *je ne me tiens pas encore pour battu* I don't reckon I'm ou I don't consider myself defeated yet.

tennis [tenis] ◆ nm **1.** [activité] tennis ▸ **tennis sur gazon** lawn tennis ▸ **tennis en salle** indoor tennis **2.** [court] (tennis) court. ◆ nmpl ou nfpl [chaussures - pour le tennis] tennis shoes ; [- pour la marche] trainers, sneakers US. ◆ **tennis de table** nm table tennis.

tennisman [tenisman] (*pl* **tennismans** ou **tennismen** [-men]) nm (male) tennis player.

ténor [tenɔʀ] nm **1.** MUS tenor **2.** [vedette] big name.

tension [tɑ̃sjɔ̃] nf **1.** [étirement] tension, tightness **2.** [tension (nerveuse)] tension, strain, nervous stress **3.** [désaccord, conflit, difficulté] tension / *des tensions au sein de la majorité* tension ou strained relationships within the majority **4.** ÉLECTR voltage, tension **5.** MÉD : *avoir* ou *faire fam de la tension* to have high blood pressure ▸ **prendre la tension de qqn** to check sb's blood pressure. ◆ **sous tension** ◆ loc adj ÉLECTR [fil] live. ◆ loc adv : *mettre un appareil sous tension* to switch on an appliance.

tentaculaire [tɑ̃takylɛʀ] adj [ville] sprawling ; [industrie, structure] gigantic.

tentacule [tɑ̃takyl] nm ZOOL tentacle.

tentant, e [tɑ̃tɑ̃, ɑ̃t] adj [nourriture] tempting ; [projet, pari, idée] tempting ; [offre, suggestion] tempting, attractive.

tentation [tɑ̃tasjɔ̃] nf [attrait, désir] temptation / *céder* ou *succomber à la tentation* to yield to temptation.

tentative [tɑ̃tativ] nf [essai] attempt ▸ **tentative d'évasion** escape attempt ▸ **tentative de suicide a)** [gén] suicide attempt **b)** DR attempted suicide ▸ **tentative de meurtre a)** [gén] murder attempt **b)** DR attempted murder.

tente [tɑ̃t] nf [de camping] tent ; [à une garden-party] marquee / *monter une tente* to put up ou to pitch a tent / *passer une semaine sous la tente* to go camping for a week ; [chapiteau de cirque] (circus) tent.

tenter [3] [tɑ̃te] vt **1.** [risquer, essayer] to try, to attempt / *tenter une ascension difficile* to attempt a difficult climb / *je vais tout tenter pour la convaincre* I'll try everything to convince her ▸ **tenter de faire** [chercher à faire] to try ou to attempt ou to endeavour *sout* to do ▸ **tenter le diable** to tempt fate ▸ **tenter (la) fortune** ou **la chance** ou **le sort** to try one's luck **2.** [soumettre à une tentation] to tempt / *le mariage, cela ne te tente pas ?* don't you ever feel like getting married? ▸ **se laisser tenter** to give in to temptation ▸ **être tenté de** to be tempted ou to feel inclined to / *je suis tenté de tout abandonner* I feel like dropping the whole thing.

tente-roulotte [tɑ̃tʀulɔt] (*pl* **tentes-roulottes**) nf Québec tent trailer, camping trailer.

tenture [tɑ̃tyʀ] nf **1.** [tapisserie] hanging ▸ **tenture murale** wall-covering **2.** [rideaux] curtain, drape US.

tenu, e [təny] ◆ pp ⟶ **tenir.** ◆ adj **1.** [soigné, propre] ▸ **bien tenu** tidy, well-kept / *une maison mal tenue* an untidy ou a badly kept house / *des enfants bien / mal tenus* well / poorly turned-out children / *des comptes bien tenus* well-kept accounts **2.** [soumis à une stricte surveillance] : *les élèves sont très tenus* the pupils are kept on a tight rein.

ténu, e [təny] adj **1.** [mince - fil, pointe] fine, slender ; [- voix, air, brume] thin **2.** [subtil - raison, distinction] tenuous.

tenue [təny] nf **1.** [habits - gén] clothes, outfit, dress ; [- de policier, de militaire, de pompier] uniform ▸ **une tenue de sport** sports gear ou kit / 'tenue correcte exigée' 'dress code' ▸ **tenue de soirée** evening dress **2.** [comportement, conduite] behaviour / *voyons, un peu de tenue !* come now, behave yourself! **3.** [attitude corporelle] posture, position **4.** [rigueur intellectuelle] quality / *un magazine d'une haute tenue* a quality magazine **5.** [gestion - d'une maison, d'un établissement] running **6.** AUTO ▸ **tenue de route** road holding **7.** BOURSE [fermeté] firmness ▸ **la bonne / mauvaise tenue des valeurs** the strong / poor performance of the stock market **8.** COMM ▸ **tenue des livres** bookkeeping. ◆ **en petite tenue** loc adj scantily dressed ou clad, in one's underwear / *se promener en petite tenue* to walk around with hardly a stitch on. ◆ **en tenue** loc adj [militaire, policier] uniformed ▸ **ce jour-là, je n'étais pas en tenue a)** [militaire] I was in civilian clothes that day **b)** [policier] I was in plain clothes that day. ◆ **en tenue légère** = **en petite tenue.**

ter [tɛʀ] adv [dans des numéros de rue] b.

TER (abr de **transport express régional**) nm *French regional network of trains and coaches.*

térébenthine [teʀebɑ̃tin] nf turpentine.

tergiverser [3] [tɛʀʒivɛʀse] vi to prevaricate.

termaillage [tɛʀmajaʒ] nm ÉCON leads and lags.

terme [tɛʀm] nm **1.** [dans l'espace] end, term *sout* / *ils arrivèrent enfin au terme de leur voyage* they finally reached the end of their journey **2.** [dans le temps] end, term *sout* / *parvenir à son terme* [aventure, relation] to reach its conclusion ou term *sout* / *la restructuration doit aller jusqu'à son terme* the restructuring must be carried through to its conclusion ▸ **mettre un terme à qqch** to put an end to sthg **3.** [date-butoir] term, deadline / *passé ce terme, vous devrez payer des intérêts* after that date, interest becomes due **4.** [échéance d'un loyer] date for payment of rent ; [montant du loyer] rent **5.** [date d'un accouchement] : *le terme est prévu pour le 16 juin* the baby is due on the 16th June / *elle a dépassé le terme* she is overdue **6.** [mot] term, word / *puis, elle s'exprima en ces termes* then she said this ▸ **en d'autres termes** in other words. ◆ **termes** nmpl **1.** [sens littéral d'un écrit] wording (*U*), terms **2.** [relations] terms ▸ **être en bons / mauvais termes avec qqn** to be on good / bad terms with sb / *nous sommes en très bons termes* we get along splendidly. ◆ **à court terme** ◆ loc adj [prêt, projet] short-term. ◆ loc adv in the short term ou run. ◆ **à long terme** ◆ loc adj [prêt, projet] long-term. ◆ loc adv in the long term ou run. ◆ **à terme** ◆ loc adj **1.** BANQUE ▸ **compte à terme** deposit account requiring notice for withdrawals ; time deposit US **2.** BOURSE ▸ **marché à terme a)** forward market **b)** [change] futures market. ◆ loc adv **1.** [à la fin] to the end, to its conclusion ▸ **arriver à terme a)** [délai] to expire **b)** [travail] to reach completion **c)** [paiement] to fall due / *conduire* ou *mener à terme une entreprise* to bring an undertaking to a successful conclusion, to carry an undertaking through successfully **2.** MÉD at term / *bébé né à terme* baby born at full term. ◆ **aux termes de** loc prép [selon] under the terms of / *aux termes de la loi / du traité* under the terms of the law / of the treaty. ◆ **avant terme** loc adv prematurely / *bébé né avant terme* premature baby / *il est né six semaines avant terme* he was six weeks premature.

terminaison [tɛʀminɛzɔ̃] nf LING ending.

terminal, e, aux [tɛʀminal, o] adj **1.** [qui forme l'extrémité] terminal **2.** MÉD terminal. ◆ **terminal, aux** nm **1.** INFORM terminal **2.** TRANSP terminal. ◆ **terminale** nf ÉDUC final year (*in a lycée*) ; ≃ year thirteen UK ; ≃ senior year US.

terminer [3] [tɛʀmine] vt **1.** [mener à sa fin - repas, tâche, lecture] to finish (off), to end / *c'est terminé, rendez vos copies* time's up, hand in your papers ; *(en usage absolu)* : *j'ai presque terminé* I've nearly finished / *pour terminer, je remercie tous les participants* finally, let me thank all those who took part **2.** [finir - plat, boisson] to finish (off), to eat up *(sép)*. ◆ **(en) terminer avec** v + prép to finish with / *je suis bien soulagé d'en avoir terminé avec cette affaire* I'm really glad to have seen the end of this business. **se terminer** vpi **1.** [arriver à sa fin - durée, période, saison] to draw to a close / *heureusement que ça se termine, j'ai hâte de retrouver ma maison* thank God the end is in sight, I can't wait to get back home **2.** [se conclure] **se terminer bien / mal a)** [film, histoire] to have a happy / an unhappy ending **b)** [équipée, menée] to turn out well / disastrously / *ça s'est terminé en drame* it ended in a tragedy **se terminer par** to end in / *l'histoire se termine par la mort du héros* the story ends with the death of the hero.

📋 Notez la différence entre les constructions française et anglaise :

terminer de + infinitif

finish + -ing

Je vais préparer à manger pendant que tu termines de décharger la voiture. *I'll make us something to eat while you finish unloading the car.*
Avez-vous terminé d'écrire votre rapport ? *Have you finished writing your report?*

---

terminologie [tɛʀminɔlɔʒi] nf terminology.

terminus [tɛʀminys] nm terminus / *terminus ! tout le monde descend !* last stop! all change!

termite [tɛʀmit] nm termite.

termitière [tɛʀmitjɛʀ] nf termite mound, termitarium *spéc.*

ternaire [tɛʀnɛʀ] adj ternary.

terne [tɛʀn] adj **1.** [sans éclat - cheveux, regard] dull; [teint] sallow **2.** [ennuyeux] dull, drab, dreary **3.** [inintéressant] dull.

ternir [32] [tɛʀniʀ] vt **1.** [métal, argenterie] to tarnish; [glace] to dull **2.** [honneur, réputation] to tarnish, to stain, to smear; [souvenir, beauté] to cloud, to dull. **se ternir** vpi **1.** [métal] to tarnish; [miroir] to dull **2.** [honneur, réputation] to become tarnished ou stained; [beauté, nouveauté] to fade; [souvenir] to fade, to grow dim.

terrain [tɛʀɛ̃] nm

A. SOL, TERRE 1. GÉOL soil, ground **terrains calcaires** limestone soil ou areas **2.** AGR soil **3.** [relief] ground, terrain **terrain accidenté** uneven terrain.

B. LIEU À USAGE SPÉCIFIQUE 1. CONSTR piece ou plot of land **terrain à bâtir** development land *(U)*, building plot **2.** AGR land / *terrain cultivé / en friche* cultivated / uncultivated land **3.** LOISIRS & SPORT [lieu du jeu] field, pitch UK; [moitié défendue par une équipe] half ; [installations] ground / *terrain de football / rugby* football / rugby pitch UK ou field / *terrain de golf* golf course ou links **terrain de camping** campsite **terrain de jeu(x)** playground **terrain de sports** sports field ou ground **4.** AÉRON field **terrain (d'aviation)** airfield **5.** MIL ground **terrain d'exercice** ou **militaire** training ground; *(toujours au sg)* [d'une bataille] battleground; [d'une guerre] war ou combat zone / *la prochaine offensive nous permettra de gagner du terrain* the next offensive will enable us to gain ground **6.** [lieu d'un duel] duelling place.

C. SENS ABSTRAIT 1. [lieux d'étude] field **un homme de terrain** a man with practical experience **2.** [domaine de connaissances] : *être sur son terrain* to be on familiar ground fig / *situons la discussion sur le terrain juridique / psychologique* let's discuss this from the legal / psychological angle **3.** [ensemble de circonstances] **sonde le terrain avant d'agir** see how the land lies before making a move **être en terrain neutre / sur un terrain glissant** to be on neutral / on a dangerous ground **trouver un terrain d'entente** to find

common ground **4.** MÉD ground / *quand le virus trouve un terrain favorable* when the virus finds its ideal breeding conditions. **terrain vague** nm piece of waste ground ou land, empty lot US.

terrasse [tɛʀas] nf **1.** [grand balcon] balcony; [entre maison et jardin] terrace, patio; [sur le toit] (roof) terrace **2.** [d'un café, d'un restaurant] : *être assis à la terrasse* to sit outside.

terrassement [tɛʀasmɑ̃] nm TRAV PUB excavation, excavation work, earthworks. **de terrassement** loc adj [travail] excavation *(modif)* ; [engin] earth-moving ; [outil] digging.

terrasser [3] [tɛʀase] vt **1.** [jeter à terre, renverser] to bring ou to strike down *(sép)* **2.** [foudroyer] to strike down *(sép)* / *être terrassé par une crise cardiaque* to be struck down by a heart attack **3.** [atterrer, accabler] to crush, to shatter / *l'annonce de leur mort l'a terrassé* he was shattered by the news of their death.

terre [tɛʀ] nf

A. GLOBE 1. [planète] **la Terre** the Earth **2.** [monde terrestre] earth / *le bonheur existe-t-il sur la terre ?* is there such a thing as happiness on this earth ou in this world?

B. SOL 1. [surface du sol] ground **terre battue a)** [dans une habitation] earth ou hard-earth ou mud floor **b)** [dans une cour] bare ground **c)** [sur un court de tennis] clay (surface) **2.** [élément opposé à la mer] land *(U)* / *on les transporte par voie de terre* they are transported overland ou by land **terre !** NAUT land ahoy! **sur la terre ferme** on dry land, on terra firma **3.** [région du monde] land **les terres arctiques** the Arctic regions / *il reste des terres inexplorées* there are still some unexplored regions **4.** [pays] land, country **terre d'accueil** host country **terre d'exil** place of exile **terre natale** native land ou country **la Terre promise** the Promised Land **5.** [terrain] land *(U)*, estate / *acheter une terre* to buy a piece of land **6.** [symbole de la vie rurale] **la terre** the land, the soil / *homme de la terre* man of the soil **7.** ÉLECTR earth UK, ground US **mettre** ou **relier qqch à la terre** to earth UK ou to ground US sthg.

C. MATIÈRE 1. [substance - gén] earth, soil **mettre** ou **porter qqn en terre** to bury sb ; AGR earth, soil / *terre à vigne / à blé* soil suitable for wine-growing / for wheat **2.** [matière première] clay, earth **terre glaise** (brick) clay, brickearth UK **terre cuite** earthenware / *en terre cuite* earthenware *(modif)* **3.** [pigment] **terre de Sienne** sienna. **terres** nfpl [domaine, propriété] estate, estates. **à terre** loc adv **1.** [sur le sol] on the ground **frapper qqn à terre** to strike sb when he's down **2.** NAUT on land **descendre à terre** to land. **par terre** ◆ loc adj [ruiné, anéanti] spoilt, wrecked. ◆ loc adv [sur le plancher] on the floor ; [sur le sol] on the ground **tomber par terre** to fall down / *j'ai lavé par terre* fam I've washed the floor. **sous terre** loc adv [sous le sol] underground. **sur terre** loc adv **1.** [ici-bas] on (this) earth **2.** EXPR revenir ou redescendre sur terre to come back to earth (with a bump).

terreau, x [tɛʀo] nm compost *(U)*.

terre-neuve [tɛʀnœv] nm inv ZOOL Newfoundland terrier.

terre-plein (*pl* terre-pleins), **terreplein*** [tɛʀplɛ̃] nm [sur route] **terre-plein central** central reservation UK, center divider strip US.

terrer [4] [tɛʀe] **se terrer** vpi **1.** [se mettre à l'abri, se cacher] to go to ground ou to earth, to lie low ; [se retirer du monde] to hide away **2.** [dans un terrier] to go to ground ou to earth, to burrow.

terrestre [tɛʀɛstʀ] adj **1.** [qui appartient à notre planète] earth *(modif)*, earthly, terrestrial ▸ **le globe terrestre** the terrestrial globe **2.** [qui se passe sur la terre] earthly, terrestrial ▸ **durant notre vie terrestre** during our life on earth **3.** [vivant sur la terre ferme] land *(modif)* **4.** [d'ici-bas - joie, plaisir] worldly, earthly.

terreur [tɛʀœʀ] nf [effroi] terror, dread / *vivre dans la terreur de* to live in dread of.

terreux, euse [tɛʀø, øz] adj **1.** [couvert de terre - chaussure, vêtement] muddy ; [-mains] dirty ; [-légume] caked with soil **2.** [brun - couleur, teint] muddy.

terrible [tɛʀibl] adj **1.** [affreux - nouvelle, accident, catastrophe] terrible, dreadful **2.** [insupportable - chaleur, douleur] terrible, unbearable ; [-déception, conditions de vie] terrible / *elle est terrible avec sa façon de bouder sans raison* it's awful the way she sulks for no reason **3.** [en intensif - bruit, vent, orage] terrific, tremendous / *elle a eu une chance terrible* she's been incredibly lucky **4.** [pitoyable] terrible, awful, dreadful / *le plus terrible, c'est de savoir que…* the worst thing ou part of it is knowing that… **5.** *fam* [fantastique] terrific, great / *son concert ? pas terrible !* her concert? it was nothing to write home about!

terriblement [tɛʀibləmɑ̃] adv terribly, dreadfully.

terrien, enne [tɛʀjɛ̃, ɛn] ◆ adj [qui possède des terres] landowning ▸ **propriétaire terrien** landowner. ◆ nm, f [habitant de la Terre] inhabitant of the Earth ; [dans un récit de science-fiction] earthling.

terrier [tɛʀje] nm **1.** [abri - d'un lapin] (rabbit) hole ou burrow ; [-d'un renard] earth, hole, foxhole ; [-d'un blaireau] set **2.** [chien] terrier.

terrifiant, e [tɛʀifjɑ̃, ɑ̃t] adj [effrayant] terrifying.

terrifier [9] [tɛʀifje] vt to terrify.

terril [tɛʀil] nm slag heap.

terrine [tɛʀin] nf CULIN terrine.

territoire [tɛʀitwaʀ] nm **1.** GÉOGR territory **2.** ADMIN area ▸ **territoires d'outre-mer** (French) overseas territories.

territorial, e, aux [tɛʀitɔʀjal, o] adj territorial.

terroir [tɛʀwaʀ] nm **1.** [région agricole] region **2.** [campagne, ruralité] country / *il a gardé l'accent du terroir* he has retained his rural accent.

terroriser [3] [tɛʀɔʀize] vt **1.** [martyriser] to terrorize **2.** [épouvanter] to terrify.

terrorisme [tɛʀɔʀism] nm terrorism.

terroriste [tɛʀɔʀist] adj & nmf terrorist.

tertiaire [tɛʀsjɛʀ] ◆ adj ADMIN & ÉCON ▸ **secteur tertiaire** tertiary sector, service industries. ◆ nm ADMIN & ÉCON ▸ **le tertiaire** the tertiary sector.

tertio [tɛʀsjo] adv third, thirdly.

tes [te] pl ⟶ **ton**.

tesson [tesɔ̃] nm [de verre, de poterie] fragment ▸ **un mur hérissé de tessons de bouteille** a wall with broken glass all along the top.

test [tɛst] nm **1.** [essai, vérification] test ▸ **soumettre qqn à un test, faire passer un test à qqn** to give sb a test ▸ **test d'aptitude** aptitude test **2.** MÉD test ▸ **test de dépistage** screening test / *test de dépistage du SIDA* AIDS test ▸ **test de grossesse** pregnancy test.

testament [tɛstamɑ̃] nm DR will, testament.

tester [3] [tɛste] vt **1.** [déterminer les aptitudes de - élèves] to test **2.** [vérifier le fonctionnement - appareil, produit] to test.

testicule [tɛstikyl] nm testicle, testis *spéc*.

tétaniser [3] [tetanize] vt [paralyser - de peur] to paralyse 🇬🇧, to paralyze 🇺🇸, to petrify ; [-d'étonnement] to stun / *la fureur de leur père les avait tétanisés* they were stunned by their father's anger.

tétanos [tetanos] nm lockjaw, tetanus *spéc*.

têtard [tɛtaʀ] nm ZOOL tadpole.

tête [tɛt]
nf

A. **PARTIE DU CORPS** **1.** ANAT head ▸ **la tête haute** with (one's) head held high ▸ **la tête la première** head first / *de la tête aux pieds* from head to foot ou toe / *avoir mal à la tête* to have a headache / *j'ai la tête qui tourne* [malaise] my head is spinning ▸ **en avoir par-dessus la tête** *fam* to be sick (and tired) of it ▸ **avoir la tête sur les épaules** to have a good head on one's shoulders ▸ **être tombé sur la tête** *fam* to have a screw loose ▸ **il ne réfléchit jamais, il fonce tête baissée** he always charges in ou ahead without thinking ▸ **se cogner** ou **se taper la tête contre les murs** to bang one's head against a (brick) wall **2.** [en référence à la chevelure, à la coiffure] ▸ **se laver la tête** to wash one's hair ▸ **tête nue** bareheaded **3.** [visage, expression] face / *ne fais pas cette tête !* don't pull 🇬🇧 ou make such a long face! / *il a fait une de ces têtes quand je lui ai dit !* you should have seen his face when I told him! ▸ **il a** ou **c'est une tête à claques** *fam* you just want to smack him in the mouth ▸ **tête de nœud** *vulg* dickhead ▸ **faire la tête** to sulk **4.** [mesure] head / *il a une tête de plus que son frère* he's a head taller than his brother **5.** CULIN head ▸ **tête pressée** 🇧🇪 [fromage de tête] pork brawn 🇬🇧, headcheese 🇺🇸 **6.** SPORT header.

B. **SIÈGE DE LA PENSÉE** **1.** [siège des pensées, de l'imagination, de la mémoire] mind, head ▸ **se mettre dans la tête** ou **en tête de faire qqch** to make up one's mind to do sthg ▸ **avoir la grosse tête** *fam* to be big-headed ▸ **avoir toute sa tête** to have all one's faculties ▸ **faire sa mauvaise tête** to dig one's heels in ▸ **monter à la tête de qqn** a) [succès] to go to sb's head b) [chagrin] to unbalance sb ▸ **se monter la tête** to get carried away ▸ **tourner la tête à qqn** to turn sb's head ▸ **il est tête en l'air** he's got his head in the clouds ▸ **il n'a pas de tête** [il est étourdi] he's scatterbrained ou a scatterbrain ▸ **ça m'est sorti de la tête** I forgot, it slipped my mind ▸ **il ne sait plus où donner de la tête** he doesn't know whether he's coming or going ▸ **n'en faire qu'à sa tête** to do exactly as one pleases **2.** [sang-froid, présence d'esprit] head ▸ **avoir** ou **garder la tête froide** to keep a cool head.

C. **PERSONNE, ANIMAL** **1.** [individu] person ▸ **être une tête de lard** ou **de mule** to be as stubborn as a mule, to be pig-headed ▸ **tête de linotte** ou **d'oiseau** ou **sans cervelle** scatterbrain ▸ **forte tête** rebel ▸ **une grosse tête** *fam* a brain **2.** [vie d'une personne] head, neck ▸ **jouer** ou **risquer sa tête** to risk one's skin **3.** [meneur, leader] head, leader ▸ **les têtes pensantes du comité** the brains of the committee **4.** [animal d'un troupeau] head *(inv)*.

D. **PARTIE HAUTE, PARTIE AVANT** **1.** [faîte] top **2.** [partie avant] front end ▸ **tête de lit** bedhead ▸ **prendre la tête** a) [marcher au premier rang] to take the lead b) [commander, diriger] to take over **3.** [début] : *faites ressortir les têtes de chapitres* make the chapter headings stand out **4.** [dans un classement] top, head ▸ **tête d'affiche** top of the bill ▸ **tête de série** SPORT seeded player **5.** [extrémité - d'un objet, d'un organe] head ; [-d'un os] head, caput ▸ **tête d'épingle** pinhead ▸ **gros comme une tête d'épingle** the size of a pinhead **6.** ACOUST head ▸ **tête de lecture** head **7.** IMPR head, top **8.** INFORM head **9.** MIL head ▸ **tête de pont** a) [sur rivière] bridgehead b) [sur plage] beachhead **10.** NUCL head ▸ **tête nucléaire** nuclear warhead. ◆ **à la tête de** loc prép **1.** [en possession de] : *elle s'est trouvée à la tête d'une grosse fortune* she found herself in possession of a great fortune **2.** [au premier rang de] at the head ou front of **3.** [à la direction de] in charge of, at the head of / *être à la tête d'une société* to head a company. ❖ **de tête** ◆ loc adj **1.** [femme, homme] able **2.** [convoi, voiture] front *(avant nom).* ◆ loc adv [calculer] in one's head / *de tête, je dirais que nous étions vingt* at a guess I'd say there were twenty of us. ❖ **en tête** loc adv **1.** [devant] ▶ **être en tête a)** [gén] to be at the front **b)** [dans une course, une compétition] to (be in the) lead **2.** [à l'esprit] ▶ **avoir qqch en tête** to have sthg in mind. ❖ **en tête à tête** loc adv alone together ▶ **dîner en tête à tête avec qqn** to have a quiet dinner (alone) with sb. ❖ **en tête de** loc prép **1.** [au début de] at the beginning ou start of **2.** [à l'avant de] at the head ou front of / *les dirigeants syndicaux marchent en tête du défilé* the union leaders are marching at the head of the procession **3.** [au premier rang de] at the top of ▶ **en tête des sondages** leading the polls. ❖ **par tête** loc adv per head, a head, apiece / *ça coûtera 30 € par tête* it'll cost 30 € a head ou per head ou apiece. ❖ **par tête de pipe** fam = **par tête.** ❖ **sur la tête de** loc prép [en prêtant serment] : *je le jure sur la tête de mes enfants* I swear on my mother's grave. ❖ **tête brûlée** nf hothead. ❖ **tête de mort** nf **1.** [crâne] skull **2.** [emblème] death's head, skull and crossbones. ❖ **tête de Turc** nf whipping boy, scapegoat.

tête-à-queue [tɛtakø] nm inv (180°) spin / *faire un tête-à-queue* to spin round, to spin 180°.

tête-à-tête [tɛtatɛt] nm inv [réunion] tête-à-tête, private talk ▶ **avoir un tête-à-tête avec qqn** to have a tête-à-tête with sb.

tétée [tete] nf [repas] feed 🇬🇧, feeding 🇺🇸.

téter [8] [tete] vt [sein, biberon] to suck (at) / *téter sa mère* to suck (at) one's mother's breast, to feed ou to breast-feed from one's mother.

✐ In reformed spelling (see p. 16-18), this verb is conjugated like *semer : il tètera, elle tèterait.*

tétine [tetin] nf [d'un biberon] teat 🇬🇧, nipple 🇺🇸 ; [sucette] dummy 🇬🇧, pacifier 🇺🇸.

Tétrabrick® [tetrabrik] nm carton.

tétraplégique [tetraplezik] ◆ adj quadriplegic, tetraplegic. ◆ nmf quadriplegic.

têtu, e [tety] adj stubborn, obstinate ▶ **têtu comme une mule** ou **un âne** ou **une bourrique** stubborn as a mule.

teuf [tœf] nf fam party.

teufeur, euse [tœfœr, øz] nm, f fam partygoer.

texte [tɛkst] nm **1.** [écrit] text / *commenter / résumer un texte* to do a commentary on / to do a précis of a text **2.** [œuvre littéraire] text ; [extrait d'une œuvre] passage ▶ **textes choisis** selected passages **3.** MUS [paroles d'une chanson] lyrics ; CINÉ & THÉÂTRE lines **4.** LING [corpus, énoncé] text **5.** LITTÉR text, work / *écrire un court texte d'introduction* to write a short introduction **6.** ÉDUC & UNIV [sujet de devoir] question *(for work in class or homework)* / *je vais vous lire le texte de la dissertation* I'll give you the essay question ▶ **texte libre** free composition. ❖ **dans le texte** loc adv in the original ▶ **en français dans le texte a)** *pr* in French in the original **b)** *fig* to quote the very words used.

textile [tɛkstil] nm **1.** [tissu] fabric, material ▶ **les textiles synthétiques** synthetic ou man-made fibres **2.** [industrie] : *le textile, les textiles* the textile industry.

texto [tɛksto] ◆ adv fam word for word, verbatim. ◆ nm TÉLÉC text-message ▶ **envoyer un texto à qqn** to text sb.

textuel, elle [tɛkstɥɛl] adj **1.** [conforme -à ce qui est écrit] literal, word-for-word ; [-à ce qui a été dit] verbatim **2.** LITTÉR textual ▶ **analyse textuelle** textual analysis.

❖ **textuel** adv fam quote unquote / *elle m'a dit qu'elle s'en fichait, textuel* she told me she didn't care, those were her exact words.

textuellement [tɛkstɥɛlmã] adv word for word.

texture [tɛkstyr] nf [d'un bois, de la peau] texture.

TF1 (abr de Télévision Française 1) npr *French independent television company.*

TGV (abr de train à grande vitesse) nm *French high-speed train.*

thaï, e [taj] adj Thai.

thaïlandais, e [tajlãdɛ, ɛz] adj Thai. ❖ **Thaïlandais, e** nm, f Thai.

Thaïlande [tajlãd] npr f ▶ **(la) Thaïlande** Thailand.

thalassothérapie [talasɔterapi] nf seawater therapy, thalassotherapy spéc.

thé [te] nm **1.** [boisson] tea / *faire du thé* to make (a pot of) tea ▶ **prendre le thé** to have tea ▶ **thé de Chine / Ceylan** China / Ceylon tea ▶ **thé noir / vert** black (leaf) / green tea ▶ **thé citron** lemon tea 🇬🇧, tea with lemon ▶ **thé nature** tea without milk **2.** [réception] tea party ; [repas] (afternoon) tea **3.** BOT tea, tea-plant.

théâtral, e, aux [teatral, o] adj [relatif au théâtre] theatrical, stage (modif), theatre (modif).

théâtre [teatr] nm

A. SPECTACLE 1. [édifice -gén] theatre 🇬🇧, theater 🇺🇸 ; ANTIQ amphitheatre ▶ **aller au théâtre** to go to the theatre ▶ **théâtre d'ombres** shadow theatre ▶ **théâtre de verdure** open-air theatre **2.** [art, profession] drama, theatre 🇬🇧, theater 🇺🇸 / *elle veut faire du théâtre* she wants to go on the stage ou to become an actress ou to act **3.** [genre] drama, theatre 🇬🇧, theater 🇺🇸 / *je préfère le théâtre au cinéma* I prefer theatre ou plays to films ▶ **le théâtre de boulevard** mainstream popular theatre *(as first played in theatres on the Paris boulevards)* ▶ **le théâtre de rue** street theatre. ❖ **de théâtre** loc adj [critique, troupe] drama (modif), theatre (modif) ; [cours] drama (modif) ; [agence] booking ; [jumelles] opera (modif) ; [accessoire, décor] stage (modif) / *une femme de théâtre* a woman of the stage ou theatre.

théière [tejɛr] nf teapot.

thématique [tematik] adj thematic.

thème [tɛm] nm **1.** ART, LITTÉR & MUS theme **2.** [traduction] translation into a foreign language ; ÉDUC prose. ❖ **thème astral** nm ASTROL birth chart.

théologie [teɔlɔʒi] nf theology.

théologien, enne [teɔlɔʒjɛ̃, ɛn] nm, f theologian.

théorème [teɔrɛm] nm theorem.

théoricien, enne [teɔrisjɛ̃, ɛn] nm, f [philosophe, chercheur, etc.] theorist, theoretician.

théorie [teɔri] nf **1.** SCI theory **2.** [connaissance spéculative] theory. ❖ **en théorie** loc adv in theory, theoretically.

théorique [teɔrik] adj theoretical.

théoriquement [teɔrikmã] adv sout [d'un point de vue spéculatif] theoretically, in theory.

thérapeute [terapøt] nmf **1.** [spécialiste des traitements] therapist **2.** [psychothérapeute] therapist.

thérapeutique [terapøtik] adj therapeutic.

thérapie [terapi] nf **1.** [traitement] therapy, treatment **2.** PSYCHOL therapy ▶ **thérapie de groupe** group therapy.

thermal, e, aux [tɛrmal, o] adj [eau] thermal ; [source] thermal, hot.

thermique [tɛrmik] adj [réacteur, équilibre, signature, papier] thermal ; [énergie] thermic.

thermocollant, e [tɛʀmokɔlɑ̃, ɑ̃t] adj [tissu] thermo-adhesive. **❖ thermocollant** nm [tissu] thermo-adhesive.

thermomètre [tɛʀmɔmɛtʀ] nm [appareil] thermometer / *le thermomètre monte / descend* the temperature (on the thermometer) is rising / falling.

Thermos® [tɛʀmos] nf ⟶ **bouteille.**

thermostat [tɛʀmɔsta] nm thermostat.

thésard, e [tezaʀ, aʀd] nm, f *fam* research student, post-grad.

thésauriser [3] [tezɔʀize] **❖** vi to hoard money. **❖** vt to hoard (up).

thèse [tɛz] nf **1.** ENS thesis **▸ thèse de doctorat d'État** ≃ PhD ; ≃ doctoral thesis 🇬🇧 ; ≃ doctoral ou PhD dissertation 🇺🇸 **▸ thèse de troisième cycle a)** [en lettres] ≃ MA 🇬🇧 ; ≃ master's thesis 🇺🇸 **b)** [en sciences] ≃ MSc 🇬🇧 ; ≃ master's thesis 🇺🇸 **2.** [théorie] argument, thesis, theory / *la thèse de l'accident n'est pas écartée* the possibility that it may have been an accident hasn't been ruled out.

thon [tɔ̃] nm tuna (fish), tunny 🇬🇧 **▸ thon à l'huile** tuna in oil **▸ thon au naturel** tuna in brine.

thoracique [tɔʀasik] adj thoracic.

thorax [tɔʀaks] nm thorax.

thune [tyn] nf *tfam* [argent] : *je n'avais pas une thune* I was broke.

thuya [tyja] nm thuja.

thym [tɛ̃] nm thyme.

thyroïde [tiʀɔid] **❖** adj thyroid. **❖** nf thyroid (gland).

Tibet [tibɛ] npr m **▸ le Tibet** Tibet.

tibétain, e [tibetɛ̃, ɛn] adj Tibetan. **❖ Tibétain, e** nm, f Tibetan. **❖ tibétain** nm LING Tibetan.

tibia [tibja] nm ANAT [os] shinbone, tibia *spéc* ; [devant de la jambe] shin.

tic [tik] nm **1.** [manie gestuelle] (nervous) tic, twitch / *il est bourré de tics fam* he's got a lot of nervous tics **2.** [répétition stéréotypée] habit **▸ un tic de langage** a (speech) mannerism.

TIC [tik] **(abr de technologies de l'information et de la communication)** nfpl ICT.

ticket [tikɛ] nm **1.** [de bus, de métro] ticket ; [de vestiaire, de consigne] slip, ticket **▸ ticket de caisse** sales receipt, bill **2.** *fam* EXPR *il a un ticket avec elle* she fancies him 🇬🇧, she's sweet on him 🇺🇸. **❖ ticket modérateur** nm [pour la Sécurité sociale] proportion of medical expenses payable by the patient.

ticket-repas [tikɛʀəpa] (*pl* **tickets-repas**) nm voucher given to employees to cover part of luncheon expenses ; ≃ Luncheon Voucher® 🇬🇧.

Ticket-Restaurant® [tikɛʀɛstɔʀɑ̃] (*pl* **Tickets-Restaurant**) nm voucher given to employees to cover part of luncheon expenses ; ≃ Luncheon Voucher® 🇬🇧.

tic-tac, tictac* [tiktak] nm inv [d'une pendule, d'une bombe] ticking *(U)*, tick-tock **▸ faire tic-tac** to tick (away), to go tick-tock.

tie-break [tajbʀɛk] (*pl* **tie-breaks**) nm tie break.

tiède [tjɛd] **❖** adj **1.** [ni chaud ni froid] lukewarm, warm, tepid ; [pas suffisamment chaud] lukewarm, not hot enough **2.** *fig* [peu enthousiaste - accueil, réaction] lukewarm, unenthusiastic, half-hearted ; [- sentiment] half-hearted / *les syndicalistes sont tièdes* the union members lack conviction ou are apathetic. **❖** adv : *je préfère boire / manger tiède* I don't like drinking / eating very hot things.

tiédir [32] [tjediʀ] vi **1.** [se refroidir - boisson, métal, air] to cool (down) **2.** [se réchauffer] to grow warmer.

tien, tienne [tjɛ̃, tjɛn] (*mpl* **tiens** [tjɛ̃], *fpl* **tiennes** [tjɛn]) adj poss *litt* : *je suis tienne pour toujours* I am

yours forever. **❖ le tien, la tienne** (*mpl* les tiens, *fpl* les tiennes) pron poss yours / *ce parapluie n'est pas le tien* this is not your umbrella, this umbrella is not yours ou doesn't belong to you ; *(emploi nominal)* **▸ les tiens** your family and friends **▸ à la tienne !** *fam* good health!, cheers! **▸ mets-y du tien a)** [fais un effort] make an effort **b)** [sois compréhensif] try to be understanding.

Tiercé® [tjɛʀse] nm **1.** LOISIRS triple forecast / *gagner le tiercé (dans l'ordre / le désordre)* to win on three horses (with the right placings / without the right placings) **2.** [gén - trois gagnants] **▸ le tiercé gagnant a)** *pr* the first three, the three winners **b)** *fig* the winning three ou trio.

tiers [tjɛʀ] nm **1.** [partie d'un tout divisé en trois] third / *elle en a lu un tiers* she's a third of the way through (reading it) / *la maison était brûlée aux deux tiers* two-thirds of the house had been destroyed by fire **2.** *sout* [troisième personne] third person ; [personne étrangère à un groupe] stranger, outsider, third party **3.** DR third party **4.** FIN **▸ tiers provisionnel** thrice-yearly income tax payment based on estimated tax due for the previous year.

tiers-monde [tjɛʀmɔ̃d] (*pl* **tiers-mondes**) nm Third World.

tifs [tif] nmpl *fam* hair.

tige [tiʒ] nf BOT [d'une feuille] stem, stalk ; [de blé, de maïs] stalk ; [d'une fleur] stem.

tignasse [tiɲas] nf *fam* **1.** [chevelure mal peignée] mop ou shock (of hair) **2.** [chevelure] hair.

tigre [tigʀ] nm ZOOL tiger **▸ un tigre royal** ou **du Bengale** a Bengal tiger.

tigré, e [tigʀe] adj [pelage] striped, streaked ; [chat] tabby *(modif)*, tiger *(modif)*.

tigresse [tigʀɛs] nf **1.** ZOOL tigress **2.** *litt* [femme très jalouse] tigress.

tilleul [tijœl] nm **1.** BOT lime (tree) **2.** [feuilles séchées] lime-blossom *(U)* ; [infusion] lime ou lime-blossom tea.

tilsit [tilsit] nm strong firm Swiss cheese with holes in it.

tilt [tilt] nm *fam* EXPR *et soudain, ça a fait tilt* [j'ai compris] and suddenly it clicked ou the penny dropped 🇬🇧.

tilter [3] [tilte] vi *fam* to understand, to twig / *j'ai entendu un bruit en démarrant mais je n'ai pas tout de suite tilté* I heard a noise when I started the engine but I didn't twig what it was.

timbale [tɛ̃bal] nf **1.** [gobelet] (metal) cup **2.** CULIN [moule] timbale mould ; [préparation] timbale **▸ timbale de saumon** salmon timbale **3.** MUS kettledrum / *une paire de timbales* tympani, a set of kettledrums.

timbre [tɛ̃bʀ] nm

▸ **A. MARQUAGE 1.** = timbre-poste **2.** [vignette - au profit d'une œuvre] sticker (given in exchange for a donation to charity) ; [- attestant un paiement] stamp (certifying receipt of payment) **3.** [sceau, marque] stamp **4.** [instrument marqueur] stamp **▸ timbre dateur** date stamp **5.** DR **▸ timbre fiscal** revenue stamp **6.** MÉD **▸ timbre tuberculinique** tuberculosis patch.

▸ **B. SON 1.** ACOUST [qualité sonore - d'un instrument] tone, timbre, colour ; [- d'une voix] tone, resonance / *un beau timbre de voix* beautiful mellow tones, a beautiful rich voice **2.** [sonnette] bell ; [de porte] doorbell **3.** MUS [instrument] (small) bell.

timbré, e [tɛ̃bʀe] adj *fam* [fou] nuts, cracked.

timbre-poste [tɛ̃bʀəpɔst] (*pl* **timbres-poste**) nm (postage) stamp.

timbrer [3] [tɛ̃bʀe] vt [lettre, colis] to stamp, to stick ou to put a stamp on.

timide [timid] ◆ adj **1.** [embarrassé - sourire, air, regard] timid, shy ; [- personne] bashful, diffident / *il est timide avec les femmes* he's shy of ou he shrinks away from women ▸ **faussement timide** coy **2.** [faible] slight, feeble, tiny ▸ **une critique timide** hesitant criticism / *l'auteur de quelques timides réformes* the author of a handful of half-hearted ou feeble reforms. ◆ nmf shy person.

timidement [timidmɑ̃] adv **1.** [avec embarras] timidly, shyly, diffidently ; [gauchement] self-consciously, bashfully **2.** [de façon peu perceptible] slightly, feebly *péj*, faint-heartedly *péj* / *l'euro remonte timidement* the euro is rising slightly.

timidité [timidite] nf **1.** [manque d'assurance] timidity, shyness, diffidence ; [gaucherie] self-consciousness, bashfulness **2.** [d'un projet, d'une réforme] feebleness *péj*, half-heartedness *péj*.

timing [tajmiŋ] nm timing *(of a technical process)*.

Timor [timɔʀ] npr Timor.

timoré, e [timɔʀe] adj timorous, fearful, unadventurous.

Timor-Oriental [timɔʀɔʀjɑ̃tal] npr East Timor.

tintamarre [tɛ̃tamaʀ] nm [vacarme] racket, din.

tinter [3] [tɛ̃te] vi **1.** [sonner lentement] to ring (out), to peal **2.** [produire des sons clairs] to tinkle, to jingle / *tous les verres tintaient sur le plateau* all the glasses were clinking on the tray / *faire tinter des pièces de monnaie* to jingle coins.

tintin [tɛ̃tɛ̃] interj *fam* no go, no way.

TIP [tip] (**abr de titre interbancaire de paiement**) nm *payment slip for bills*.

TIPP (**abr de taxe intérieure sur les produits pétroliers**) nf domestic tax on petroleum products.

tique [tik] nf tick.

tiquer [3] [tike] vi [réagir] to flinch ▸ **tiquer sur qqch** to baulk at sthg.

tir [tiʀ] nm **1.** ARM & MIL [action de lancer au moyen d'une arme] shooting, firing ; [projectiles envoyés] fire ▸ **rectifier le tir a)** *pr* to adjust one's aim **b)** *fig* to change one's approach to a problem **2.** [endroit - pour l'entraînement] rifle ou shooting range ; [- à la foire] shooting gallery **3.** SPORT ▸ **le tir** [discipline olympique] shooting ▸ **tir à la carabine / au pistolet** rifle- / pistol-shooting ▸ **tir à l'arc** archery **4.** FOOT shot ▸ **tir (au but)** shot at goal.

tirade [tiʀad] nf **1.** CINÉ & THÉÂTRE monologue, speech **2.** *péj* [discours] speech, tirade *péj*.

tirage [tiʀaʒ] nm **1.** IMPR [action] printing ; [ensemble d'exemplaires] print run, impression ; [d'une gravure] edition / *un tirage de 50 000 exemplaires* a print run of 50,000 ▸ **tirage limité / numéroté** limited / numbered edition **2.** PRESSE [action] printing, running ; [exemplaires mis en vente] circulation / *un tirage de 50 000* circulation figures ou a circulation of 50,000 **3.** PHOT [action] printing ; [copies] prints **4.** JEUX [d'une carte] taking, picking ; [d'une tombola] draw ▸ **tirage au sort** drawing of lots / *nous t'avons désigné par tirage au sort* we drew lots and your name came up **5.** [d'une cheminée, d'un poêle] draught 🇬🇧, draft 🇺🇸.

tiraillements [tiʀajmɑ̃] nmpl [conflit] struggle, conflict / *il y a des tiraillements dans la famille / le syndicat* there is friction within the family / the union.

tirailler [3] [tiʀaje] vt **1.** [faire souffrir légèrement] to prick / *la faim lui tiraillait l'estomac* he was feeling pangs of hunger **2.** [solliciter] to dog, to plague / *être tiraillé entre l'espoir et l'inquiétude* to be torn between hope and anxiety.

tire [tiʀ] nf **1.** *tfam* [voiture] car **2.** 🇶🇨 [friandise] maple toffee ou taffy.

tiré, e [tiʀe] adj **1.** [fatigué et amaigri - visage] drawn, pinched / *avoir les traits tirés* to look drawn **2.** EXPR **tiré par les cheveux** contrived, far-fetched.

tire-au-flanc [tiʀoflɑ̃] nm inv *fam* skiver, dodger, shirker.

tire-bouchon (*pl* tire-bouchons), **tirebouchon*** [tiʀbuʃɔ̃] nm corkscrew.

tire-d'aile [tiʀdɛl] ◆ **à tire-d'aile** loc adv **1.** [en volant] : *les corbeaux passèrent au-dessus de la maison à tire-d'aile* the crows flew over the house with strong, regular wingbeats **2.** *fig* [à toute vitesse] : *il s'est enfui à tire-d'aile* he took to his heels.

tire-fesses (*pl* tire-fesses), **tire-fesse*** [tiʀfɛs] nm *fam* ski tow.

tirelire [tiʀliʀ] nf [en forme de cochon] piggy bank 🇺🇸 ; [boîte] moneybox 🇬🇧.

tirer [3] [tiʀe]
◆ vt

🅐 **DÉPLACER 1.** [traîner - avec ou sans effort] to pull, to drag ; [- en remorquant] to draw, to tow / *tiré par un cheval* horse-drawn ▸ **tirer qqn par le bras / les cheveux / les pieds** to drag sb by the arm / hair / feet **2.** [amener à soi] to pull ; [étirer - vers le haut] to pull (up) ; [- vers le bas] to pull (down) / *elle me tira doucement par la manche* she tugged ou pulled at my sleeve ▸ **tirer les cheveux à qqn** to pull sb's hair / **tire bien le drap** stretch the sheet (taut) ▸ **tirer la couverture à soi a)** [s'attribuer le mérite] to take all the credit **b)** [s'attribuer le profit] to take the lion's share **3.** [pour actionner - cordon d'appel, élastique] to pull ; [- tiroir] to pull (open ou out) / *tirer les rideaux* to pull ou to draw the curtains ▸ **tirer un verrou a)** [pour ouvrir] to slide a bolt open **b)** [pour fermer] to slide a bolt to, to shoot a bolt ▸ **tirer la chasse d'eau** to flush the toilet **4.** NAUT to draw.

🅑 **EXTRAIRE, OBTENIR 1.** [faire sortir] ▸ **tirer qqch de** to pull ou to draw sthg out of ▸ **tirer qqn de** [le faire sortir de] to get sb out of ▸ **tirer qqn du sommeil** to wake sb up ▸ **tirer qqn de son silence** to draw sb out (of his / her silence) ▸ **tire-moi de là** help me out **2.** [fabriquer] ▸ **tirer qqch de** to derive ou to get ou to make sthg from ▸ **photos tirées d'un film** movie stills **3.** [percevoir - argent] : *elle tire sa fortune de ses terres* she makes her money from her land / *tu ne tireras pas grand-chose de ta vieille montre* you won't get much (money) for your old watch ; [retirer - chèque, argent liquide] to draw **4.** [extraire, dégager] ▸ **tirer la morale / un enseignement de qqch** to learn a lesson from sthg / *ce vers est tiré d'un poème de Villon* this line is (taken) from a poem by Villon ▸ **tirer satisfaction de** to derive satisfaction from **5.** [obtenir, soutirer] ▸ **tirer qqch de** : *tirer de l'argent de qqn* to extract money from sb, to get money out of sb / *la police n'a rien pu tirer de lui* the police couldn't get anything out of him ▸ **tirer des larmes à qqn** to make sb cry / *je n'ai pas pu en tirer davantage* I couldn't get any more out of her **6.** *fam* [voler] : *je me suis fait tirer mon portefeuille au cinéma !* somebody nicked 🇬🇧 ou swiped 🇺🇸 my wallet at the cinema! **7.** JEUX [billet, numéro] to draw, to pick ; [loterie] to draw, to carry out the draw for ; [carte] to draw, to take.

🅒 **PROJETER 1.** ARM [coup de fusil, missile] to fire ; [balle, flèche] to shoot / *tirer un coup de feu* to fire a shot **2.** [feu d'artifice] to set off **3.** CHASSE [lapin, faisan] to shoot **4.** [à la pétanque - boule en main] to throw ; [- boule placée] to knock out (sép) / FOOT to take / *tirer un corner* to take a corner **5.** EXPR **tirer un coup avec qqn** *vulg* to have it off with sb.

🅓 **PASSER** *fam* to spend, to do, to get through (*insép*) / *j'ai encore trois semaines à tirer avant mon congé* I've another three weeks to go before my leave.

🅔 **TRACER, IMPRIMER 1.** [dessiner - ligne] to draw ; [- plan] to draw up (*sép*) / *tirez deux traits sous les verbes* underline the verbs twice **2.** PHOT to print / *je voudrais que* *cette photo soit tirée sur du papier mat* I'd like a matt print of this picture **3.** IMPR [livre] to print ; [estampe, lithographie] to print, to draw ; [tract] to print, to run ; [gravure] to strike, to pull, to print / *ce magazine est tiré à plus de 200 000 exemplaires* this magazine has a print run ou a circulation of 200,000 / **'bon à tirer'** 'passed for press'.

◆ vi **1.** MIL [faire feu] to fire, to shoot / *ne tirez pas, je me rends !* don't shoot, I surrender! / *tirer à balles / à blanc* to fire bullets / blanks ▶ **tirer sur qqn** to take a shot ou to shoot ou to fire at sb / *on m'a tiré dessus* I was fired ou shot at **2.** ARM & SPORT ▶ **tirer à l'arc / l'arbalète a)** [activité sportive] to do archery / crossbow archery **b)** [action ponctuelle] to shoot a bow / crossbow ▶ **tirer à la carabine / au pistolet a)** [activité sportive] to do rifle / pistol shooting **b)** [action ponctuelle] to shoot with a rifle / pistol **3.** FOOT & GOLF to shoot **4.** [exercer une traction] to pull ▶ **tire !** pull!, heave! / *ça tire dans les genoux à la montée* fam going up is tough on the knees / *la moto tire à droite* the motorbike pulls to the right / *ne tire pas sur ton gilet* don't pull your cardigan out of shape **5.** [aspirer - fumeur] : *tirer sur une cigarette* to puff at ou to draw on a cigarette **6.** [avoir un bon tirage - cheminée, poêle] ▶ **tirer (bien)** to draw (well) / *la cheminée / pipe tire mal* the fireplace / pipe doesn't draw properly **7.** [peau] to feel tight ; [points de suture] to pull / *ma peau me tire* fam my skin feels tight **8.** JEUX ▶ **tirer au sort** to draw ou to cast lots **9.** IMPR : *tirer à 50 000 exemplaires* to have a circulation of ou to have a (print) run of 50,000 (copies) **10.** EXPR **ça tire** Belg & Suisse there's a draught. ◆ **tirer à** v + prép **1.** PRESSE ▶ **tirer à la ligne** to pad out an article *(because it is being paid by the line)* **2.** EXPR **tirer à sa fin** to come to an end. ◆ **tirer sur** v + prép [couleur] to verge ou to border on / *ses cheveux tirent sur le roux* his hair is reddish ou almost red. ◆ **se tirer** ◆ vp *(emploi passif)* : *le store se tire avec un cordon* the blind pulls down with a cord. ◆ vpi fam [partir, quitter un endroit] to clear off, to make tracks ; [s'enfuir] to beat it, to clear off ▶ **tire-toi !** [ton menaçant] beat it!, clear ou push off! / *il s'est tiré de chez lui* he's left home. ◆ **se tirer de** vp + prép [se sortir de] to get out of / *il s'est bien / mal tiré de l'entrevue* he did well / badly at the interview ▶ **s'en tirer** fam [s'en sortir] : *avec son culot, elle s'en tirera toujours* with her cheek, she'll always come out on top / *si tu ne m'avais pas aidé à finir la maquette, je ne m'en serais jamais tiré* if you hadn't given me a hand with the model, I'd never have managed / *il y a peu de chances qu'il s'en tire* [qu'il survive] the odds are against him pulling through ▶ **s'en tirer à** ou **avec** ou **pour** [devoir payer] to have to pay / *à quatre, on ne s'en tirera pas à moins de 200 euros le repas* the meal will cost at least 200 euros for the four of us / *il ne s'en tirera pas comme ça* he won't get off so lightly, he won't get away with it.

tiret [tiʀɛ] nm IMPR [de dialogue] dash ; [en fin de ligne] rule.

tireur, euse [tiʀœʀ, øz] nm, f **1.** [criminel, terroriste] gunman ; [de la police] marksman / *bon / mauvais tireur* good / bad shot ▶ **tireur isolé** ou **embusqué** sniper ▶ **tireur d'élite** sharpshooter **2.** ▶ **tireur de cartes, tireuse de cartes** fortune-teller *(who reads cards).*

tiroir [tiʀwaʀ] nm [de meuble] drawer.

tiroir-caisse [tiʀwaʀkɛs] *(pl* **tiroirs-caisses)** nm till.

tisane [tizan] nf [infusion] herb tea, herbal tea.

tissage [tisaʒ] nm [procédé] weaving ; [entrecroisement de fils] weave.

tisser [3] [tise] vt **1.** TEXT [laine, coton, tissu] to weave ▶ **l'habitude tisse des liens** [entre des personnes] the more you get to know someone, the closer you feel to them **2.** [toile d'araignée] to spin **3.** sout [élaborer] to weave, to construct / *l'auteur a subtilement tissé son intrigue* the playwright subtly wove ou constructed the plot.

tisserand, e [tisʀɑ̃, ɑ̃d] nm, f weaver.

tissu [tisy] nm **1.** TEXT fabric, material, cloth ▶ **du tissu d'ameublement** furnishing fabric ou material **2.** fig & sout [enchevêtrement] : *un tissu d'incohérences* a mass of contradictions **3.** SOCIOL fabric, make-up ▶ **le tissu social** the social fabric ▶ **le tissu urbain** the urban infrastructure **4.** BIOL tissue ▶ **tissu musculaire** muscle tissue.

tissu-éponge [tisyepɔ̃ʒ] *(pl* **tissus-éponges)** nm terry, terry-towelling.

titiller [3] [titije] vt **1.** [chatouiller agréablement] to tickle / *le champagne me titillait le palais* the champagne tickled my palate **2.** fig [exciter légèrement] to titillate.

titre [titʀ]
nm

▶ **A. TEXTE EN EXERGUE 1.** [d'un roman, d'un poème] title ; [d'un chapitre] title, heading **2.** PRESSE headline ▶ **les gros titres** the main headlines / *faire les gros titres des quotidiens* to hit ou to make the front page of the daily newspapers.

▶ **B. QUALITÉ, GRADE 1.** [désignation d'un rang, d'une dignité] title / *porter le titre de duc* to have the title of duke ▶ **un titre de noblesse** ou **nobiliaire** a title **2.** [nom de charge, de grade] qualification ▶ **conférer le titre de docteur à qqn** to confer the title of doctor on ou upon sb **3.** SPORT title / *mettre son titre en jeu* to risk one's title.

▶ **C. DOCUMENT 1.** [certificat] credentials ▶ **décliner ses titres universitaires** to list one's academic ou university qualifications / *recruter sur titres* to recruit on the basis of (paper) qualifications ▶ **titre de transport** ticket **2.** BANQUE (transferable) security ▶ **titre interbancaire de paiement** payment slip used to settle bills **3.** BOURSE [certificat] certificate ; [valeur] security ▶ **titre au porteur a)** [action] bearer share **b)** [obligation] floater ou bearer security **4.** DR title ▶ **titre de propriété** title deed, document of title.

▶ **D. COMPOSITION 1.** JOAILL fineness, titre spéc **2.** PHARM titre **3.** TEXT count.

▶ **E. EXPRESSIONS** ▶ **à titre amical** as a friend ▶ **à titre exceptionnel** exceptionally ▶ **à titre officiel / officieux** officially / unofficially ▶ **à titre privé / professionnel** in a private / professional capacity / *décoration attribuée à titre posthume* posthumous award / *à titre provisoire* on a provisional basis ▶ **à titre d'exemple** by way of an example, as an example ▶ **à titre indicatif** for information only ▶ **à quel titre ? a)** [en vertu de quel droit] in what capacity? **b)** [pour quelle raison] on what grounds? ◆ **à aucun titre** loc adv on no account. ◆ **à ce titre** loc adv [pour cette raison] for this reason, on this account. ◆ **à de nombreux titres, à divers titres** loc adv for several reasons, on more than one account. ◆ **à juste titre** loc adv [préférer] understandably, rightly ; [croire] correctly, justly, rightly. ◆ **à plus d'un titre** = **à de nombreux titres.** ◆ **au même titre** loc adv for the same reasons. ◆ **au même titre que** loc conj for the same reasons as. ◆ **en titre** loc adj **1.** ADMIN titular **2.** [officiel - fournisseur, marchand] usual, appointed.

titrer [3] [titʀe] vt PRESSE ▶ **titrer qqch** to run sthg as a headline.

tituber [3] [titybe] vi [ivrogne] to stagger ou to reel ou (along) ; [malade] to stagger (along).

titulaire [titylɛʀ] ◆ adj **1.** [enseignant] tenured ; [évêque] titular ▶ **être titulaire a)** [professeur d'université] to have tenure **b)** [sportif] to be under contract **2.** [détenteur] ▶ **être titulaire de** [permis, document, passeport] to hold / *être titulaire d'un compte en banque* to be an account holder. ◆ nmf **1.** ADMIN incumbent **2.** [détenteur - d'un permis] holder ; [- d'un passeport] bearer, holder.

titulariser [3] [titylaʀize] vt [enseignant] to appoint to a permanent post ; [sportif] to give a contract to ; [professeur d'université] ▶ **être titularisé** to be given ou to be granted tenure.

tjr, tjrs (abr écrite de **toujours**) SMS Alwz.

TNT ◆ nf (abr de **télévision numérique terrestre**) digital television, DTTV. ◆ nm (abr de **trinitrotoluène**) TNT.

toast [tost] nm **1.** [en buvant] toast ▶ **porter un toast à qqn** to drink (a toast) to sb, to toast sb **2.** [pain grillé] piece of toast.

toboggan [tɔbɔgɑ̃] nm **1.** [glissière - sur terre] slide ; [- dans l'eau] chute / **tu veux faire du toboggan ?** do you want to go on the slide? ▶ **toboggan de secours** escape chute **2.** [luge] toboggan / **faire du toboggan** to go tobogganing.

toc [tɔk] ◆ nm fam [imitation sans valeur - d'un matériau] fake, worthless imitation ; [- d'une pierre] rhinestone, paste ; [- d'un bijou] fake ▶ **en toc** fake, imitation / **sa bague, c'est du toc** her ring is fake. ◆ interj **1.** [coups à la porte] ▶ **toc-toc !** knock knock! **2.** fam [après une remarque] ▶ **et toc !** so there!, put that in your pipe and smoke it!

TOC [teose, tɔk] (abr de **trouble obsessionnel compulsif**) nmpl MÉD OCD.

tocsin [tɔksɛ̃] nm alarm bell, tocsin sout / **sonner le tocsin** to ring the alarm, to sound the tocsin sout.

toge [tɔʒ] nf [de magistrat] gown.

Togo [tɔgo] npr m ▶ **le Togo** Togo.

togolais, e [tɔgɔlɛ, ɛz] adj Togolese. ◆ **Togolais, e** nm, f Togolese.

tohu-bohu (pl tohu-bohu), **tohubohu*** (pl tohubohus*) [tɔybɔy] nm **1.** [désordre et confusion] confusion, chaos **2.** [bruit - de voitures, d'enfants] racket, din ; [- d'un marché, d'une gare] hustle and bustle ; [- d'une foule] hubbub ; [- d'une foire] hurly-burly.

toi [twa] pron pers **1.** [sujet] you / **qui va le faire ? — toi** who's going to do it? — you (are) / **qu'est-ce que tu en sais, toi ?** what do you know about it? / **tu t'amuses, toi, au moins** at least you're having fun / **toi seul peux la convaincre** you're the only one who can persuade her **2.** [avec un présentatif] you / **c'est toi ?** is it you? / **c'est toi qui le dit !** that's what you say! **3.** [complément] you / **il vous a invités, Pierre et toi** he's invited you and Pierre ; [après une préposition] : **c'est à toi qu'on l'a demandé** you were the one who was asked, you were asked / **un ami à toi** fam a friend of yours ▶ **c'est à toi ?** is this yours? / **à toi de jouer !** your turn! **4.** [pronom réfléchi] yourself / **alors, tu es content de toi ?** I hope you're pleased with yourself, then!

toile [twal] nf **1.** TEXT [matériau brut] canvas, (plain) fabric ▶ **toile de coton / lin** cotton / linen cloth ▶ **toile de jute** gunny, (jute) hessian ; [tissu grossier] cloth ▶ **toile cirée** waxcloth ▶ **toile émeri** emery cloth ▶ **toile de tente** tent canvas **2.** fam [film] : **se payer une toile** to go to the flicks **3.** ART [vierge] canvas ; [peinte] canvas, painting **4.** COUT cloth **5.** NAUT [ensemble des voiles d'un navire] sails **6.** THÉÂTRE (painted) curtain ▶ **toile de fond** pr & fig backdrop **7.** ZOOL web ▶ **toile d'araignée** cobweb, spider's web. ◆ **de toile, en toile** loc adj [robe, pantalon] cotton (modif) ; [sac] canvas (modif).

toilettage [twalɛtaʒ] nm [d'un chat, d'un chien] grooming.

toilette [twalɛt] nf **1.** [soins de propreté] ▶ **faire sa toilette** to (have) a wash 🇬🇧, to wash up 🇺🇸, to get washed / **faire la toilette d'un mort** to lay out a corpse ▶ **articles** ou **produits de toilette** toiletries **2.** [lustrage du pelage, des plumes] grooming / **le chat fait sa toilette** the cat's washing ou licking itself **3.** sout [tenue vestimentaire] clothes, outfit / **elle est en grande toilette** she is (dressed) in all her finery **4.** [table] dressing table ; [avec vasque] washstand. ◆ **toilettes** nfpl [chez un particulier] toilet(s) 🇬🇧, bathroom 🇺🇸 ; [dans un café] toilet, toilets 🇬🇧, restroom 🇺🇸 ▶ **toilettes (publiques)** (public) toilets 🇬🇧, restroom 🇺🇸 ▶ **aller aux toilettes** to go to the toilet ▶ **je cherche les toilettes a)** [pour dames] I'm looking for the ladies 🇬🇧 ou ladies room 🇺🇸 **b)** [pour hommes] I'm looking for the gents 🇬🇧 ou the men's room 🇺🇸.

toiletter [4] [twalɛte] vt [chien, chat] to groom.

toi-même [twamɛm] pron pers yourself.

toiser [3] [twaze] vt fig ▶ **toiser qqn** to look sb up and down, to eye sb from head to foot.

toison [twazɔ̃] nf **1.** ZOOL fleece **2.** [chevelure] mane **3.** MYTH ▶ **la Toison d'or** the Golden Fleece.

toit [twa] nm **1.** ARCHIT & CONSTR roof ▶ **habiter sous les toits a)** [dans une chambre] to live in an attic room ou in a garret **b)** [dans un appartement] to live in a top-floor flat 🇬🇧 ou top-storey apartment 🇺🇸 with a sloping ceiling ▶ **toit plat / en pente** flat / sloping roof ▶ **toit d'ardoises** slate roof ▶ **toit de chaume** thatched roof ▶ **toit en terrasse** terrace roof **2.** [demeure] roof ▶ **avoir un toit** to have a roof over one's head / **vivre sous le même toit** to live under the same roof **3.** AUTO : **une voiture à toit ouvrant** a car with a sunroof.

toiture [twatyʀ] nf [ensemble des matériaux] roofing ; [couverture] roof.

TOK? SMS abr écrite de **tu es d'accord?**

Tokyo [tɔkjo] npr Tokyo.

tôle [tol] nf **1.** MÉTALL [non découpée] sheet metal ; [morceau] metal sheet ▶ **tôle ondulée** corrugated iron **2.** tfam = **taule**.

tolérable [tɔleʀabl] adj [bruit, chaleur, douleur] bearable, tolerable ; [attitude, entorse à une règle] tolerable, permissible / **son impertinence n'est plus tolérable** her impertinence can no longer be tolerated.

tolérance [tɔleʀɑ̃s] nf [à l'égard d'une personne] tolerance ; [à l'égard d'un règlement] latitude / **ce n'est pas un droit, c'est une simple tolérance** this is not a right, it is merely something which is tolerated / **il y a une tolérance d'un litre d'alcool par personne** each person is allowed to bring in a litre of spirits free of duty ▶ **tolérance orthographique** permitted variation in spelling.

tolérant, e [tɔleʀɑ̃, ɑ̃t] adj **1.** [non sectaire] tolerant, broad-minded **2.** [indulgent] lenient, indulgent, easygoing / **une mère trop tolérante** an overindulgent ou excessively lenient mother.

tolérer [18] [tɔleʀe] vt **1.** [permettre - infraction] to tolerate, to allow / **ils tolèrent le stationnement bilatéral à certaines heures** you're allowed to park on both sides of the street at certain times of the day **2.** [admettre - attitude, personne] to tolerate, to put up with (insép) / **je ne tolérerai pas son insolence** I won't stand for ou put up with ou tolerate his rudeness **3.** [supporter - médicament, traitement] to tolerate / **les femmes enceintes tolèrent bien ce médicament** pregnant women can take this drug without adverse effects.

🖉 In reformed spelling (see p. 16-18), this verb is conjugated like semer : **il tolèrera, elle tolèrerait**.

tollé [tɔle] nm general outcry / **soulever un tollé général** to provoke a general outcry.

TOM [tɔm] (abr de **territoire d'outre-mer**) nm former French overseas territory.

tomate [tɔmat] nf BOT [plante] tomato (plant) ; [fruit] tomato ▶ **tomate cerise** cherry tomato ▶ **tomates farcies** CULIN stuffed tomatoes.

* In reformed spelling (see p. 16-18).

tombal, e, als *ou* **aux** [tɔ̃bal, o] adj funerary, tomb (*modif*), tombstone (*modif*).

tombant, e [tɔ̃bã, ãt] adj [oreille, moustache] floppy ; [seins, fesses] sagging ; [épaules] sloping ; [tentures] hanging.

tombe [tɔ̃b] nf [fosse] grave ; [dalle] tombstone ; [monument] tomb ▶ **aller sur la tombe de qqn** [pour se recueillir] to visit sb's grave ▶ **muet** ou **silencieux comme une tombe** as silent ou quiet as the grave.

tombeau, x [tɔ̃bo] nm [sépulcre] grave, tomb, sepulchre *litt* ▶ **conduire** ou **mettre qqn au tombeau** [causer sa mort] to send sb to his / her grave.

tombée [tɔ̃be] nf : *à la tombée du jour* ou *de la nuit* at nightfall ou dusk.

tomber [3] [tɔ̃be]
◆ vi *(aux être)*

A. ÊTRE ENTRAÎNÉ 1. [personne] to fall (down), to fall over ; [meuble, pile de livres] to fall over, to topple over ; [cloison] to fall down, to collapse ; [avion, bombe, projectile] to fall / *tomber par terre* to fall on the floor, to fall down / *tomber à plat ventre* to fall flat on one's face / *tomber dans l'escalier* to fall down the stairs / *tomber de cheval* to fall off ou from a horse ▶ **tomber de fatigue** to be ready to drop (from exhaustion) ▶ **tomber de sommeil** to be asleep on one's feet ▶ **faire tomber qqn a)** [en lui faisant un croche-pied] to trip sb up **b)** [en le bousculant] to knock ou to push sb over ▶ **faire tomber qqch a)** [en poussant] to push sthg over **b)** [en renversant] to knock sthg over **c)** [en lâchant] to drop sthg **d)** [en donnant un coup de pied] to kick sthg over / *j'ai fait tomber mes lunettes* I've dropped my glasses ▶ **à tomber par terre** *fam* to die for ▶ **tu es tombé bien bas** *fig* you've sunk very low **2.** *sout* [mourir] to fall, to die / *tomber sur le champ de bataille* to fall on the battlefield **3.** [se détacher - feuille, pétale, fruit] to fall ou to drop off ; [- cheveu, dent] to fall ou to come out **4.** [pendre - cheveux, tentures] to hang ; [- moustaches] to droop ; [- seins] to sag, to droop / *ses longs cheveux lui tombaient dans le dos* her long hair hung down her back / *il a les épaules qui tombent* he's got sloping shoulders **5.** [s'abattre, descendre - rayon de soleil, radiations, nuit] to fall ; [- brouillard, gifle, coup] to come down ▶ **la neige / pluie tombait** it was snowing / raining ; *(tournure impersonnelle)* : *il tombe quelques gouttes* it's spitting / *il tombe de grosses gouttes / gros flocons* big drops / flakes are falling / *il tombe de la grêle* it's hailing / *toi, tu as ta paie qui tombe tous les mois* *fam* you have a regular salary coming in (every month) ▶ **tomber sous les yeux de qqn** to come to sb's attention **6.** [déboucher] : *continuez tout droit et vous tomberez sur le marché* keep going straight on and you'll come to the market **7.** [diminuer - prix, température, voix, ton] to fall, to drop ; [- fièvre] to come down, to drop ; [- colère] to die down, to subside ; [- enthousiasme, agitation, intérêt] to fall ou to fade away, to subside ; [- vent] to drop, to fall, to die down ; [- jour] to draw to a close / *la température est tombée de 10 degrés* the temperature has dropped ou fallen (by) 10 degrees / *faire tomber la fièvre* to bring down ou to reduce sb's temperature **8.** [disparaître - obstacle] to disappear, to vanish ; [- objection, soupçon] to vanish, to fade / *ses défenses sont tombées* he dropped his guard **9.** [s'effondrer - cité] to fall ; [- dictature, gouvernement, empire] to fall, to be brought down, to be toppled ; [- record] to be broken ; [- concurrent] to go out, to be defeated ; [- plan, projet] to fall through ▶ **faire tomber a)** [cité] to bring down **b)** [gouvernement] to bring down, to topple **c)** [record] to break **d)** [concurrent] to defeat **10.** [devenir] ▶ **tomber amoureux** to fall in love ▶ **tomber enceinte** to become pregnant ▶ **tomber malade** to become ou to fall ill.

B. SE PRODUIRE, ARRIVER 1. [événement] to fall ou to be on / *mon anniversaire tombe un dimanche* my birthday is ou falls on a Sunday ▶ **tomber juste** [calcul] to work out ex-

actly ▶ **bien tomber** to come at the right moment ou time / *ton bureau l'intéresse — ça tombe bien, je voulais m'en débarrasser* he's interested in your desk — that's good, I wanted to get rid of it ▶ **mal tomber** to come at the wrong moment ou at a bad time ; [personne] ▶ **tomber juste** [deviner] to guess right ▶ **bien tomber a)** [opportunément] to turn up at the right moment **b)** [avoir de la chance] to be lucky ou in luck / *ah, vous tombez bien, je voulais justement vous parler* ah, you've come just at the right moment, I wanted to speak to you ▶ **mal tomber a)** [inopportunément] to turn up at the wrong moment **b)** [ne pas avoir de chance] to be unlucky ou out of luck / *il ne pouvait pas plus mal tomber* he couldn't have picked a worse time ▶ **tu tombes à point !** you've timed it perfectly!, perfect timing! **2.** [nouvelles] to be ou to come out / *à 20 h, la nouvelle est tombée* the news came through at 8 p.m.

◆ vt *(aux avoir)* **1.** [triompher de - candidat, challenger] to defeat **2.** *fam* [séduire] to seduce / *il les tombe toutes* he's got them falling at his feet **3.** EXPR *tomber la veste* *fam* to slip off one's jacket. ◆ **tomber dans** v + prép : se laisser aller à - découragement, désespoir] to sink ou to lapse into (*in-sép*) / *sans tomber dans l'excès inverse* without going to the other extreme / *des traditions qui tombent dans l'oubli* traditions which are falling into oblivion. ◆ **tomber en** v + prép : *tomber en lambeaux* to fall to bits ou pieces ▶ **tomber en ruine** to go to rack and ruin. ◆ **tomber sur** v + prép *fam* **1.** [trouver par hasard - personne] to come across, to run ou to bump into, to meet up with US ; [- objet perdu, trouvaille] to come across ou upon, to stumble across / *je suis tombé sur ton article dans le journal* I came across your article in the newspaper **2.** [avoir affaire à - examinateur, sujet d'examen] to get / *quand j'ai téléphoné, je suis tombé sur sa mère / un répondeur* when I phoned, it was her mother who answered (me) / I got an answering machine **3.** [assaillir - personne] to set about, to go for ▶ **il a fallu que ça tombe sur moi !** it had to be me! **4.** [se porter sur - regard, soupçon] to fall on ; [- conversation] to turn to.

tombeur, euse [tɔ̃bœʀ, øz] nm, f *fam* SPORT : *le tombeur du champion d'Europe* the man who defeated the European champion. ◆ **tombeur** nm *fam* [séducteur] ladykiller.

tombola [tɔ̃bɔla] nf raffle, tombola.

tome [tɔm] nm [section d'un ouvrage] part ; [volume entier] volume.

tomme [tɔm] nf Tomme cheese.

tommette [tɔmɛt] nf red hexagonal floor tile.

ton¹ [tɔ̃] nf [mesure de masse] ton.

ton² [tɔ̃]
nm

A. QUALITÉ SONORE, STYLE 1. [qualité de la voix] tone / *sur un ton monocorde* monotonously **2.** [hauteur de la voix] pitch (of voice) ▶ **ton nasillard** twang **3.** [intonation] tone, intonation / *d'un ton sec* curtly / *hausser le ton* to up the tone / *ne me parle pas sur ce ton !* don't speak to me like that ou in that tone of voice! / *ne le prends pas sur ce ton !* don't take it like that! **4.** [style - d'une lettre, d'une œuvre artistique] tone, tenor **5.** ▶ **le bon ton** good form **6.** LING [en phonétique] tone, pitch.

B. TONALITÉ 1. ACOUST tone **2.** MUS [d'une voix, d'un instrument] tone ; [tube] crook, shank / *baisser / élever le ton en chantant* to lower / to raise the pitch while singing ; [mode musical] key ▶ **le ton majeur / mineur** major / minor key ▶ **donner le ton a)** MUS to give the chord **b)** *fig* to set the tone.

C. NUANCE 1. [couleur] tone, shade / *les verts sont en tons dégradés* the greens are shaded (from dark to light) **2.** ART shade ▶ **les tons chauds / froids** warm / cold tones. ◆ **de bon ton** loc adj in good taste / *il est de bon ton de mépriser l'argent* it's quite the thing ou good form to despise money. ◆ **sur le ton de** loc prép : *sur le ton de la plaisanterie* jokingly, in jest, in a joking tone. ◆ **sur tous les tons** loc adv in every possible way / *on nous répète sur tous les tons que...* we're being told over and over again that..., it's being drummed into us that... ◆ **ton sur ton** loc adj [en camaïeu] in matching tones ou shades.

ton³, ta *(devant nom ou adj commençant par voyelle ou « h » muet ton* [tɔ̃n]) [tɔ̃, ta] *(pl* **tes** [te]) dét *(adj poss)* **1.** [indiquant la possession] your / *ta meilleure amie* your best friend / *ton père et ta mère* your father and mother / *tes frères et sœurs* your brothers and sisters / *un de tes amis* one of your friends, a friend of yours **2.** fam [emploi expressif] : *eh bien regarde-la,* TON *émission !* all right then, watch your (damned) programme! / *arrête de faire ton intéressant !* stop trying to draw attention to yourself! / *alors, tu as réussi à avoir ton lundi ?* so you managed to get Monday off, then? **3.** RELIG Thy.

tonalité [tɔnalite] nf **1.** ART tonality **2.** ACOUST tonality ; [d'une radio] tone **3.** TÉLÉC : *je n'ai pas de tonalité* I'm not getting a ou there's no dialling tone.

tondeuse nf **1.** HORT ▶ **tondeuse (à gazon)** (lawn) mower ▶ **tondeuse électrique / à main** electric / hand mower **2.** [de coiffeur] (pair of) clippers **3.** [pour moutons] (pair of) sheep shears.

tondre [75] [tɔ̃dʀ] vt **1.** [cheveux] to crop ; [laine de mouton] to shear (off) **2.** [mouton] to shear ; [chien] to clip **3.** [pelouse] to mow, to cut ; [haie] to clip **4.** fam [dépouiller, voler] to fleece ; [exploiter] to fleece, to take to the cleaners ▶ **tondre qqn** [au jeu] to clean sb out.

tondu, e [tɔ̃dy] adj [crâne] closely cropped.

toner [tɔnɛʀ] nm TECHNOL toner.

tong [tɔ̃g] nf ▶ **des tongs** (a pair of) flip-flops 🇬🇧 ou thongs 🇺🇸.

tonifiant, e [tɔnifjɑ̃, ɑ̃t] adj [air, climat] bracing, invigorating ; [promenade] invigorating ; [crème, exercice, massage] tonic, toning.

tonifier [9] [tɔnifje] vt [corps, peau] to tone up *(sép)* ; [cheveux] to give new life to ; [esprit] to stimulate.

tonique [tɔnik] ◆ adj **1.** [air, climat] bracing ; [médicament] tonic, fortifying ; [lotion] toning, tonic ; [boisson] tonic ; [activité] stimulating, invigorating **2.** PHYSIOL tonic **3.** LING [syllabe] tonic, stressed. ◆ nm **1.** MÉD tonic **2.** [lotion] toning lotion, skin tonic.

tonitruant, e [tɔnitʀyɑ̃, ɑ̃t] adj thundering, resounding, stentorian litt.

tonnage [tɔnaʒ] nm [d'un bateau] ▶ **tonnage brut / net** gross / net tonnage.

tonne [tɔn] nf **1.** [unité de masse] ton, tonne ▶ **un (camion de) deux tonnes** a two-ton lorry 🇬🇧 ou truck 🇺🇸 **2.** fam : *des tonnes* [beaucoup] tons, heaps, loads / *j'ai des tonnes de choses à vous raconter* I've loads of things to tell you ▶ **en faire des tonnes** [en rajouter] to lay it on (really) thick.

tonneau, x [tɔno] nm **1.** [contenant pour liquide] cask, barrel **2.** [quantité de liquide] caskful, barrelful **3.** [accident] somersault ▶ **faire un tonneau** to roll over, to somersault.

tonnelle [tɔnɛl] nf [abri] bower, arbour.

tonner [3] [tɔne] ◆ vi [artillerie] to thunder, to roar, to boom / *on entendait tonner les canons* you could hear the thunder ou roar of the cannons. ◆ v impers ▶ **il tonne** it's thundering. ◆ **tonner contre** v + prép [suj : personne] to fulminate against.

tonnerre [tɔnɛʀ] nm **1.** [bruit de la foudre] thunder / *le tonnerre gronda dans le lointain* there was a rumble of thunder in the distance ▶ **coup de tonnerre** pr thunderclap **2.** [tumulte soudain] storm, tumult, commotion ▶ **un tonnerre d'applaudissements** thunderous applause. ◆ **du tonnerre (de Dieu)** fam & vieilli ◆ loc adj [voiture, fille] terrific, great ; [repas, spectacle] terrific, fantastic. ◆ loc adv tremendously ou terrifically well / *ça a marché du tonnerre* it went like a dream.

tonsure [tɔ̃syʀ] nf **1.** RELIG [partie rasée] tonsure ; [cérémonie] tonsuring **2.** fam [calvitie] bald patch.

tonte [tɔ̃t] nf **1.** [de moutons -activité] shearing ; [-époque] shearing time **2.** [d'une pelouse] mowing.

tonton [tɔ̃tɔ̃] nm fam [oncle] uncle.

tonus [tɔnys] nm **1.** [dynamisme] dynamism, energy **2.** PHYSIOL tonus ▶ **tonus musculaire** muscle tone.

top [tɔp] nm **1.** [signal sonore] pip, beep / *au quatrième top il sera exactement 1 h* at the fourth stroke, it will be 1 o'clock precisely **2.** [dans une course] ▶ **donner le top de départ** to give the starting signal. ◆ adj fam [excellent] : *c'est top !* that's brilliant!

topaze [tɔpaz] nf topaz.

toper [3] [tɔpe] vi ▶ **tope là !** fam it's a deal!, you're on!

topinambour [tɔpinɑ̃buʀ] nm Jerusalem artichoke.

top modèle (pl top modèles), **top model** (pl top models) [tɔpmɔdɛl] nm top model.

topo [tɔpo] nm fam [discours, exposé] report / *il a fait un long topo sur la situation financière* he gave an extensive report on the financial situation ▶ **c'est toujours le même topo !** it's always the same old story! ▶ **tu vois (d'ici) le topo !** (do) you get the picture?

topographie [tɔpɔgʀafi] nf topography.

toquade [tɔkad] nf **1.** [lubie] fad, whim **2.** [passade] crush ▶ **avoir une toquade pour qqn** to have a crush on sb.

toque [tɔk] nf **1.** [de femme] pill-box hat, toque / *toque de fourrure* (pill-box shaped) fur-hat **2.** [de liftier, de jockey, de magistrat] cap ▶ **toque de cuisinier** chef's hat.

toqué, e [tɔke] fam ◆ adj [cinglé] dotty 🇬🇧, flaky 🇺🇸. ◆ nm, f loony, nutter 🇬🇧, screwball 🇺🇸.

Tora(h) [tɔʀa] npr f ▶ **la Torah** the Torah.

torche [tɔʀʃ] nf **1.** [bâton résineux] torch **2.** ÉLECTR & TECHNOL ▶ **torche électrique** torch 🇬🇧, flashlight 🇺🇸 **3.** AÉRON : *le parachute s'est mis en torche* the parachute didn't open properly.

torcher [3] [tɔʀʃe] vt **1.** tfam [nettoyer -fesses] to wipe **2.** fam [bâcler -lettre, exposé] to botch ; [-réparation] to make a pig's ear of, to botch.

torchis [tɔʀʃi] nm CONSTR cob.

torchon [tɔʀʃɔ̃] nm **1.** [linge de maison] ▶ **torchon (à vaisselle)** tea towel **2.** fam [écrit mal présenté] mess **3.** fam [mauvais journal] rag.

tordant, e [tɔʀdɑ̃, ɑ̃t] adj fam hilarious / *elle est tordante, ta fille* your daughter's a scream ou riot ou hoot.

tordre [76] [tɔʀdʀ] vt **1.** [déformer -en courbant, en pliant] to bend ; [-en vrillant] to twist **2.** [linge mouillé] to wring (out) / *elle tordait nerveusement son mouchoir* she was playing ou toy twiddling her handkerchief nervously **3.** [membre] to twist / *tordre le cou à une volaille* to wring a bird's neck. ◆ **se tordre** ◆ vpi [ver] to twist ; [parechocs] to buckle ▶ **se tordre de douleur** to be doubled up with pain ▶ **se tordre (de rire)** to be doubled ou creased 🇬🇧 up with laughter. ◆ vpt : *se tordre le pied* to sprain ou to twist one's foot.

tordu, e [tɔʀdy] ◆ adj **1.** [déformé -bouche] twisted ; [-doigt] crooked **2.** [plié, recourbé -clef] bent ; [-roue de vélo, pare-chocs] buckled ; [vrillé] twisted **3.** fam [extravagant -idée, logique] twisted, weird ; [-esprit] twisted,

warped / *tu es complètement tordu !* you're off your head!
4. *fam* [vicieux] ▸ **coup tordu** [acte malveillant] mean ou
nasty ou dirty trick. ◆ nm, f *fam* [personne bizarre ou folle]
loony, nutter 🇬🇧, screwball 🇺🇸 / *où il va, l'autre tordu ?*
where's that idiot off to?

torero, ra, **toréro*, ra** [tɔʀeʀo, ʀa] nm, f bullfighter, torero.

tornade [tɔʀnad] nf MÉTÉOR tornado.

torpeur [tɔʀpœʀ] nf torpor.

torpille [tɔʀpij] nf ARM [projectile sous-marin] torpedo.

torpiller [3] [tɔʀpije] vt **1.** MIL to torpedo **2.** [projet] to
torpedo, to scupper.

torréfier [9] [tɔʀefje] vt [café, cacao] to roast ; [tabac] to
toast.

torrent [tɔʀɑ̃] nm **1.** [ruisseau de montagne] torrent,
(fast) mountain stream **2.** [écoulement abondant] torrent, stream ▸ **des torrents d'eau a)** [inondation] a flood
b) [pluie] torrential rain, a torrential downpour / *un torrent
d'injures* a stream ou torrent of abuse. ❖ **à torrents**
loc adv ▸ **il pleut à torrents** it's pouring down.

torrentiel, elle [tɔʀɑ̃sjɛl] adj **1.** [d'un torrent - eau,
allure] torrential **2.** [très abondant] ▸ **des pluies torren-
tielles** torrential rain.

torride [tɔʀid] adj [chaleur, après-midi] torrid, scorching ;
[soleil] scorching ; [région, climat] torrid.

torsade [tɔʀsad] nf **1.** [de cordes] twist / *torsade de
cheveux* twist ou coil of hair **2.** [en tricot] ▸ **(point) torsade** cable stitch. ❖ **à torsades** loc adj **1.** ARCHIT cabled
2. VÊT ▸ **pull à torsades** cablestitch sweater.

torsader [3] [tɔʀsade] vt [fil] to twist ; [cheveux] to twist,
to coil.

torse [tɔʀs] nm **1.** ANAT trunk, torso ▸ **torse nu** : *mettez-
vous torse nu, s'il vous plaît* strip to the waist, please / *il
était torse nu* he was bare-chested **2.** ART torso.

tort [tɔʀ] nm **1.** (*sans article*) ▸ **avoir tort** [se tromper]
to be wrong / *tu as tort de ne pas la prendre au sérieux*
you're making a mistake in not taking her seriously, you're
wrong not to take her seriously / *tu n'avais pas tout à
fait tort / pas tort de te méfier* you weren't entirely wrong /
you were quite right to be suspicious ▸ **donner tort à qqn**
[désapprouver] to disagree with sb / *les faits lui ont donné
tort* events proved her (to be) wrong ou showed that she
was (in the) wrong **2.** [défaut, travers] fault, shortcoming
▸ **je reconnais mes torts** I admit I was wrong / *elle a le
tort d'être trop franche* the trouble ou problem with her
is (that) she's too direct / *tu ne fais pas de sport ? c'est
un tort* don't you do any exercise? you definitely ought to
ou should ▸ **avoir le tort de** to make the mistake of / *il
a eu le tort de lui faire confiance* he made the mistake
of trusting her **3.** [dommage] wrong ▸ **réparer un tort**
to make amends ▸ **faire du tort à qqn** to do harm to sb,
to wrong sb, to harm sb **4.** [part de responsabilité] fault
▸ **avoir tous les torts a)** [gén] to be entirely to blame
b) [dans un accident] to be fully responsible **c)** [dans un
divorce] to be the guilty party ▸ **les torts sont partagés**
both parties are equally to blame / *j'ai des torts envers
eux* I have done them wrong. ❖ **à tort** loc adv **1.** [faus-
sement] wrongly, mistakenly **2.** [injustement] wrongly.
❖ **à tort ou à raison** loc adv right or wrong, rightly or
wrongly. ❖ **à tort et à travers** loc adv : *tu parles à
tort et à travers* you're talking nonsense / *elle dépense son
argent à tort et à travers* money burns a hole in her pocket,
she spends money like water. ❖ **dans mon tort,
dans son tort** loc adv ▸ **être dans son tort** to be in the
wrong. ❖ **en tort** loc adv in the wrong / *dans cet accident, c'est lui qui est en tort* he is to blame for the accident.

torticolis [tɔʀtikɔli] nm stiff neck, torticollis *spéc* / *avoir
un torticolis* to have a stiff neck.

tortiller [3] [tɔʀtije] ◆ vt [mèche, mouchoir, fil, papier]
to twist ; [doigts] to twiddle ; [moustache] to twirl. ◆ vi
1. [onduler] : *tortiller des fesses / hanches* to wiggle one's
bottom / hips **2.** EXPR ▸ **il n'y a pas à tortiller** there's
no getting out of ou away from it. ❖ **se tortiller** vpi
[ver] to wriggle, to squirm ; [personne - par gêne, de douleur]
to squirm ; [- d'impatience] to fidget, to wriggle.

tortionnaire [tɔʀsjɔnɛʀ] nmf torturer.

tortue [tɔʀty] nf **1.** ZOOL tortoise ▸ **tortue marine** turtle
▸ **tortue d'eau douce** terrapin **2.** *fam* [traînard] slowcoach
🇬🇧, slowpoke 🇺🇸 ▸ **avancer comme une tortue** to go at a
snail's pace, to crawl along.

tortueux, euse [tɔʀtɥø, øz] adj **1.** [en lacets - sentier]
winding, tortuous *sout* ; [- ruisseau] meandering, winding,
sinuous *litt* **2.** [compliqué - raisonnement, esprit] tortuous,
devious ; [- moyens] crooked, devious, tortuous ; [- style] convoluted, involved.

torture [tɔʀtyʀ] nf **1.** [supplice infligé] torture **2.** *fig*
[souffrance] torture, torment / *l'attente des résultats fut
pour lui une véritable torture* he suffered agonies waiting
for the results. ❖ **à la torture** loc adv ▸ **mettre qqn à
la torture** to put sb through hell. ❖ **sous la torture**
loc adv under torture.

torturer [3] [tɔʀtyʀe] vt **1.** [supplicier - suj : bourreau]
to torture **2.** [tourmenter - suj : angoisse, faim] to torture, to
torment, to rack ; [- suj : personne] ▸ **torturer qqn** to put sb
through torture / *la jalousie le torturait* he was tortured
by jealousy / *torturé par sa conscience* tormented by his
conscience **3.** [style, texte] to labour. ❖ **se torturer** vp
(*emploi réfléchi*) to torture o.s., to worry o.s. sick / *ne te
torture pas l'esprit !* don't rack your brains (too much)!

torve [tɔʀv] adj : *il m'a lancé un regard torve* he shot
me a murderous sideways look.

Toscane [tɔskan] npr f ▸ **(la) Toscane** Tuscany.

tôt [to] adv **1.** [de bonne heure le matin] early ▸ **se lever
tôt a)** [ponctuellement] to get up early **b)** [habituellement]
to be an early riser ; [de bonne heure le soir] ▸ **se coucher
tôt** to go to bed early ; [au début d'une période] ▸ **tôt dans
l'après-midi** early in the afternoon, in the early afternoon
2. [avant le moment prévu ou habituel] soon / *il est trop tôt
pour le dire* it's too early ou soon to say that / *il fallait
y penser plus tôt* you should have thought about it earlier
ou before / *elle a dû partir plus tôt que prévu* she had to
leave earlier than expected / *ce n'est pas trop tôt !* at last!,
(it's) about time too! **3.** [rapidement] soon ▸ **le plus tôt
possible** as early ou as soon as possible / *le plus tôt sera
le mieux* the sooner, the better. ❖ **au plus tôt** loc adv
1. [rapidement] as soon as possible **2.** [pas avant] at the
earliest / *samedi au plus tôt* on Saturday at the earliest, no
earlier than Saturday. ❖ **tôt ou tard** loc adv sooner or
later.

total, e, aux [tɔtal, o] adj **1.** [entier - liberté] total,
complete / *j'ai une confiance totale en elle* I trust her totally ou implicitly **2.** [généralisé - destruction, échec] total,
utter, complete. ❖ **total** adv *fam* the net result is that /
total, je n'ai plus qu'à recommencer the net result (of all
that) is that I've got to start all over again. ❖ **total, aux**
nm total (amount) ▸ **faire le total** to work out the total.
❖ **totale** nf EXPR ▸ **c'est la totale !** *fam* that's the last
straw! ❖ **au total** loc adv **1.** [addition faite] in total
2. [tout bien considéré] all in all, all things (being) considered,
on the whole.

totalement [tɔtalmɑ̃] adv [ignorant, libre, ruiné] totally,
completely ; [détruit] utterly.

totaliser [3] [tɔtalize] vt **1.** [dépenses, recettes] to add
up (*sép*), to total up (*sép*), to reckon up (*sép*), to totalize

2. [atteindre le total de] to have a total of, to total / *qui totalise le plus grand nombre de points ?* who has the highest score?

totalitaire [tɔtalitɛʀ] adj totalitarian.

totalité [tɔtalite] nf **1.** [ensemble] : *la totalité des marchandises* all the goods / *la presque totalité des tableaux* almost all the paintings **2.** [intégralité] whole / *la totalité de la somme* the whole (of the) sum.

totem [tɔtɛm] nm totem.

touareg, ègue [twaʀɛg] adj Tuareg. **⟷ Touareg, ègue** nm, f Tuareg. **⟷ touareg** nm LING Tuareg.

toubib [tubib] nmf *fam* doctor.

toucan [tukã] nm toucan.

touchant, e [tuʃã, ãt] adj [émouvant] touching, moving / *être touchant de maladresse / sincérité* to be touchingly awkward / earnest.

touche [tuʃ] nf **1.** [gén] key ; [d'un téléviseur] button ; [d'un téléphone] key, button ; [d'un ordinateur, d'une machine à écrire] key / *touche entrée / contrôle* enter / control key **2.** ÉLECTR [plot de contact] contact **3.** MUS [de clavier] key ; [d'instrument à cordes] fingerboard **4.** ESCRIME hit **5.** PÊCHE bite ▸ **avoir une touche avec qqn** *fam* to have something going with sb ▸ **faire une touche** *fam* to score **6.** [coup de pinceau] touch, (brush) stroke ▸ **mettre la touche finale à qqch** to put the finishing touches to sthg **7.** [cachet, style] touch **8.** [trace] note, touch / *une touche de cynisme* a touch ou tinge ou hint of cynicism **9.** [sports de balle - ligne] touchline ; RUGBY [remise en jeu] line-out ; FOOT throw-in ; [- sortie de ballon] : *il y a touche* the ball is in touch ou is out. **⟷ en touche** loc adv into touch / *envoyer le ballon en touche* to kick the ball into touch. **⟷ sur la touche** loc adv SPORT : *rester sur la touche* to stay on the bench ▸ **être** ou **rester sur la touche** *fam & fig* to be left out, to be / remain on the sidelines.

touche-à-tout [tuʃatu] nmf [dilettante] dabbler, Jack-of-all-trades (and master of none).

toucher¹ [tuʃe] nm **1.** [sens] (sense of) touch ; [palpation] touch **2.** [sensation] feel / *le toucher onctueux de l'argile* the smooth feel of clay **3.** [manière de toucher] touch / *avoir un toucher délicat / vigoureux* [gén & MUS] to have a light / energetic touch **4.** MÉD (digital) palpation *spéc*, examination **5.** SPORT touch ▸ **il a un bon toucher de balle** he's got a nice touch. **⟷ au toucher** loc adv : *doux / rude au toucher* soft / rough to the touch / *c'est facile à reconnaître au toucher* it's easy to tell what it is by touching it ou by the feel of it.

toucher² [3] [tuʃe]
◆ vt

A. ÊTRE AU CONTACT DE **1.** [pour caresser, saisir] to touch ; [pour examiner] to feel / *ne me touche pas !* get your hands off me!, don't touch me! / *le parchemin s'effrite dès qu'on le touche* the parchment crumbles at the first touch ▸ **pas touche !** *fam* hands off! **2.** [entrer en contact avec] to touch / *au moment où la navette spatiale touche le sol* when the space shuttle touches down ou lands **3.** *fam* [joindre - suj : personne] to contact, to reach, to get in touch with ; [suj : lettre] to reach **4.** MÉD to palpate *spéc*, to examine **5.** NAUT [port] to put in at, to call at ; [rochers, fonds] to hit, to strike.

B. OBTENIR, ATTEINDRE **1.** [se servir de - accessoire, instrument] to touch **2.** [consommer] to touch / *il n'a même pas touché son repas / la bouteille* he never even touched his meal / the bottle **3.** [blesser] to hit / *touché à l'épaule* hit in the shoulder ▸ **touché!** ESCRIME touché! ▸ **touché, coulé !** JEUX hit, sunk! **4.** [atteindre - suj : mesure] to concern, to affect, to apply to ; [- suj : crise, krach boursier, famine] to affect, to hit ; [- suj : incendie, épidémie] to spread to *(insép)* / *la marée noire a touché tout le littoral* the oil slick spread

all along the coast **5.** [émouvoir - suj : film, geste, gentillesse, spectacle] to move, to touch / *vos compliments me touchent beaucoup* I'm very touched by your kind words ; [affecter - suj : décès] to affect, to shake ; [- suj : critique, propos désobligeants] to affect, to have an effect on / *elle a été très touchée par sa disparition* she was badly shaken by his death **6.** *fam* [s'en prendre à - personne] to touch **7.** [percevoir - allocation, honoraires, pension, salaire] to receive, to get, to draw ; [- indemnité, ration] to receive, to get ; [- chèque] to cash (in) *(sép)* / *elle touche 100 000 euros par an* she earns 100,000 euros a year / *toucher un pourcentage sur les bénéfices* to get a share of the profits ▸ **toucher le chômage** to be on the dole 🇬🇧, to be on welfare 🇺🇸

C. ÊTRE PROCHE DE **1.** [être contigu à] to join onto, to adjoin *sout*, to be adjacent to *sout* **2.** [concerner] : *une affaire qui touche la défense nationale* a matter related to defence, a defence-related matter **3.** [être parent avec] to be related to.

◆ vi **1.** NAUT to touch bottom **2.** PÊCHE to bite **3.** *tfam* [exceller] : *elle touche en informatique !* she's a wizard at ou she knows a thing or two about computers! **4.** EXPR **touchez là !** it's a deal!, (let's) shake on it! **⟷ toucher à** v + prép **1.** [porter la main sur - objet] to touch / *évitez de toucher aux fruits* try not to handle the fruit ; [adversaire, élève] to touch, to lay hands ou a finger on / *si tu touches à un seul cheveu de sa tête...* if you so much as lay a finger on her... ; [porter atteinte à] to interfere with *(insép)*, to harm, to touch **2.** [modifier - appareil, documents, législation] to tamper ou to interfere with **3.** [utiliser - aliment, instrument] to touch ; [- somme d'argent] to touch, to break into / *je n'ai jamais touché à la drogue* I've never been on ou touched drugs ▸ **toucher à tout** a) *pr* to fiddle with ou to touch everything b) *fig* to dabble (in everything) **4.** [être proche de - suj : pays, champ] to adjoin *sout*, to border (upon) ; [- suj : maison, salle] to join on *(insép)* to, to adjoin *sout* ; [confiner à] : *toucher à la perfection* to be close to perfection **5.** [concerner, se rapporter à - activité, sujet] to have to do with, to concern **6.** [aborder - sujet, question] to bring up *(sép)*, to come onto *(insép)*, to broach **7.** *sout* [atteindre - un point dans l'espace, dans le temps] to reach / *le projet touche à son terme* the project is nearing its end. **⟷ se toucher ◆** vp *(emploi réciproque)* [être en contact] to touch, to be in contact ; [jardins, communes] to touch, to be adjacent to (each other), to adjoin each other *sout*. **◆** vp *(emploi réfléchi)* euphém [se masturber] to play with o.s.

touffe [tuf] nf **1.** [de cheveux, de poils] tuft **2.** [d'arbustes] clump, cluster **3.** [de fleurs] clump ▸ **touffe d'herbe** tussock.

touffu, e [tufy] adj [bois, feuillage, haie] thick, dense ; [barbe, sourcils] thick, bushy ; [arbre] thickly-covered, with dense foliage.

touiller [3] [tuje] vt *fam* [sauce] to stir ; [salade] to toss.

toujours [tuʒuʀ] adv **1.** [exprimant la continuité dans le temps] always / *je l'ai toujours dit / cru* I've always said / thought so / *ils n'ont pas toujours été aussi riches* they haven't always been so rich / *ça ne durera pas toujours* it won't last forever ▸ **le ciel toujours bleu** the eternally blue sky / *ils sont toujours plus exigeants* they are more and more demanding **2.** [marquant la fréquence, la répétition] always / *elle est toujours en retard* she is always late / *les erreurs ne sont pas toujours où on les attend* mistakes sometimes occur where we least expect them **3.** [encore] still / *il fait toujours aussi chaud* it is as hot as ever ▸ **toujours pas** still not / *elle n'a toujours pas téléphoné* she hasn't phoned yet, she still hasn't phoned **4.** [dans des emplois expressifs] : *tu peux toujours essayer* you can always try, you might as well try ▸ **ça peut toujours servir** it might come in handy ou useful / *c'est toujours mieux que rien* still, it's better than nothing /

on trouvera toujours un moyen we're sure ou bound to find a way / *c'est toujours ça de pris* that's something (at least). ❖ **comme toujours** loc adv as always, as ever / *il a été charmant, comme toujours* he was charming as always. ❖ **pour toujours** loc adv forever. ❖ **toujours est-il que** loc conj the fact remains that / *j'ignore pourquoi elle a refusé, toujours est-il que le projet tombe à l'eau* I don't know why she refused, but the fact remains that the plan has had to be abandoned.

📋 Notez la position de always dans la phrase.

• Avec un verbe autre que be conjugué, always s'insère comme suit :

sujet + [aux/modal] + always + verbe

Il essaie toujours de me contredire. *He always tries to contradict me.*

J'ai toujours aimé ce qu'il écrivait. *I've always loved what he wrote.*

Vous devriez toujours avoir une pièce d'identité sur vous. *You should always carry ID.*

• Avec le verbe be conjugué, always se place comme suit :

sujet + be + always

Elle est toujours disposée à donner un coup de main. *She's always willing to lend a hand.*

Il est toujours très aimable avec les clients. *He's always very friendly with customers.*

Lorsqu'il signifie « encore », toujours se traduit par still.

• Avec un verbe autre que be conjugué, still s'insère comme suit :

sujet + [aux/modal] + still + verbe

Je ne comprends toujours pas. *I still don't understand.*

Tu travailles toujours dans l'édition ? *Do you still work in publishing?*

• Avec le verbe be conjugué, still se place comme suit :

sujet + be + still

Il est toujours à Marseille ? *Is he still in Marseille?*

---

toupet [tupɛ] nm **1.** *fam* [audace] impudence, nerve, cheek 🇬🇧 / *elle a du toupet* ou *un sacré toupet* she's got some nerve ou 🇬🇧 cheek 🇬🇧. **2.** [de cheveux] tuft of hair, quiff 🇬🇧.

toupie [tupi] nf JEUX (spinning) top.

tour¹ [tuʀ] nf **1.** ARCHIT & CONSTR tower ▶ **la tour de Babel** BIBLE the Tower of Babel ▶ **tour de bureaux** office (tower) block ▶ **tour de contrôle** AÉRON control tower ▶ **la tour Eiffel** the Eiffel tower / *tour de guet* observation tower ▶ **tour d'habitation** tower ou high-rise block ▶ **tour d'ivoire** *fig* ivory tower ▶ **la tour de Londres** the Tower of London ▶ **la tour (penchée) de Pise** the Leaning Tower of Pisa ▶ **immeuble tour** tower block **2.** *fam* [personne grande et corpulente] ▶ **c'est une vraie tour** he's / she's built like the side of a house **3.** JEUX castle, rook **4.** CHIM ▶ **tour de fractionnement** fractionating column **5.** PÉTR ▶ **tour de forage** drilling rig.

tour² [tuʀ]
nm

A. CERCLE 1. [circonférence - d'un fût, d'un arbre] girth ; [- d'un objet, d'une étendue] circumference **2.** [mensuration] ▶ **tour de taille / hanches** waist / hip measurement ▶ **tour de cou** collar size ▶ **tour de poitrine a)** [d'une femme] bust measurement ou size **b)** [d'un homme] chest measurement ou size **3.** [parure] ▶ **tour de cou a)** JOAILL choker **b)** VÊT [en fourrure] fur collar ▶ **tour de lit** (bed) valance **4.** [circuit] tour, circuit ▶ **faire le tour de** *pr* : *faire le tour d'un parc* **a)** to go round a park **b)** [à pied] to walk round a park **c)** [en voiture] to drive round a park ▶ **faire le tour du monde en auto-stop / voilier** to hitch-hike / to sail round the world ▶ **faire le tour de** *fig* : *l'anecdote a fait le tour des bureaux* the story went round the offices ou did the rounds of the offices / *faire le tour d'une question* to consider a problem from all angles ▶ **le Tour de France a)** [cycliste] the Tour de France **b)** [des compagnons] the Tour de France *(carried out by an apprentice to become a journeyman)* ▶ **tour de piste a)** [en athlétisme] lap **b)** ÉQUIT round ▶ **le tour du propriétaire** : *on a fait le tour du propriétaire* we went ou looked round the property ▶ **faire un tour d'horizon** to deal with all aspects of a problem **5.** [promenade - à pied] walk, stroll ; [- en voiture] drive, ride ; [- à vélo, à cheval, en hélicoptère] ride ; [court voyage] trip, outing *(U)* ▶ **faire un tour a)** [à pied] to go for a walk **b)** [en voiture] to go for a drive ou **c)** [à vélo] to go for a ride / *faire un tour en ville* to go into town.

B. PÉRIODE, ÉTAPE 1. [moment dans une succession] turn ; JEUX [gén] turn, go ; [aux échecs] move ▶ **c'est (à) ton tour a)** [gén] it's your turn ou go **b)** [échecs] it's your move ▶ **à qui le tour ?** whose turn is it?, who's next? ▶ **chacun son tour** everyone will have his turn / *attendre son tour* to wait one's turn / *tu parleras à ton tour* you'll have your chance to say something ▶ **tour de garde** [d'un médecin] spell ou turn of duty ▶ **tour de scrutin** ballot ▶ **au premier tour** in the first ballot ou round **2.** SPORT [série de matches] round.

C. ACTION HABILE OU MALICIEUSE 1. [stratagème] trick ▶ **jouer un sale** ou **mauvais tour à qqn** to play a nasty ou dirty trick on sb / *ma mémoire / vue me joue des tours* my memory / sight is playing tricks on me ▶ **et le tour est joué !** and there you have it! ▶ **avoir plus d'un tour dans son sac** to have more than one trick up one's sleeve **2.** [numéro, technique] ▶ **tour de cartes** card trick ▶ **tour de passe-passe** sleight of hand ▶ **tour de prestidigitation** conjuring trick.

D. ASPECT [orientation] turn / *cette affaire prend un très mauvais tour* this business is going very wrong ▶ **tour d'esprit** turn ou cast of mind ▶ **donner le tour a)** 🇨🇭 [maladie] to take a turn for the better **b)** [personne] to wrap up.

E. ROTATION 1. [d'une roue, d'un cylindre] turn, revolution ; [d'un outil] turn ; ASTRON revolution / *faire un tour / trois tours sur soi-même* to spin round once / three times (on o.s.) ▶ **donner deux tours de clef** to give a key two turns, to turn a key twice ▶ **tour de manège** ride on a roundabout 🇬🇧 ou a merry-go-round ▶ **tour de vis** (turn of the) screw **2.** AUTO revolution, rev **3.** MÉD ▶ **tour de reins** : *attraper un tour de reins* to put one's back out, to rick one's back.

F. TECHNOLOGIE lathe ▶ **tour de potier** potter's wheel. ❖ **à tour de bras** loc adv [frapper] with all one's strength ou might. ❖ **à tour de rôle** loc adv in turn / *on peut le faire à tour de rôle si tu veux* we can take (it in) turns if you like. ❖ **tour à tour** loc adv alternately, by turns. ❖ **tour de chant** nm (song) recital. ❖ **tour de force** nm *tour de force*, (amazing) feat. ❖ **tour de main** nm **1.** [savoir-faire] knack / *avoir / prendre le tour de main* to have / to pick up the knack **2.** EXPR *en un tour de main* in no time (at all), in the twinkling of an eye. ❖ **tour de table** nm **1.** ÉCON *a meeting of shareholders or investors to decide a course of action* **2.** [débat] : *faisons un tour de table* I'd like each of you in turn to give his or her comments.

🚩 **Le Tour de France**

The world-famous annual cycle race starts in a different town each year, but the home stretch is always the Champs-Élysées in Paris. The widespread excitement caused by the race, along with the heroic status of many **coureurs cyclistes**, reflects the continuing fondness of the French for cycling in general. In recent years, this positive image has been tarnished by a series of doping scandals.

tourbe [tuʀb] nf [matière] peat, turf.

tourbillon [tuʀbijɔ̃] nm **1.** MÉTÉOR [vent tournoyant] whirlwind, vortex *litt* **2.** [masse d'air, de particules] : *tourbillon de poussière | sable* eddy of dust / sand / *tourbillon de fumée* twist ou coil ou eddy of smoke / *tourbillon de neige* snow flurry **3.** [dans l'eau - important] whirlpool ; [- petit] swirl / *l'eau faisait des tourbillons* the water was eddying ou swirling **4.** *litt* [vertige, griserie] whirl. ❖ **en tourbillons** loc adv : *monter | descendre en tourbillons* to swirl up / down.

tourbillonner [3] [tuʀbijɔne] vi **1.** [eau, rivière] to swirl, to make eddies **2.** [tournoyer - flocons, feuilles, sable] to whirl, to swirl, to flutter ; [- fumée] to whirl, to eddy ; [- danseur] to spin ou to whirl ou to twirl (round).

tourisme [tuʀism] nm **1.** [fait de voyager] touring ▶ **faire du tourisme a)** [dans un pays] to go touring **b)** [dans une ville] to go sightseeing **2.** [commerce] ▶ **le tourisme** tourism, the tourist industry / *notre région vit du tourisme* we are a tourist area ▶ **tourisme culturel** cultural tourism ▶ **tourisme sexuel** sex tourism ▶ **tourisme vert** green tourism, ecotourism.

tourista [tuʀista] nf *fam* traveller's 🇬🇧 ou traveler's 🇺🇸 tummy, t(o)urista 🇺🇸 ▶ **avoir la tourista** to have traveller's tummy.

touriste [tuʀist] nmf **1.** [gén] tourist ; [pour la journée] day-tripper **2.** *fam* [dilettante, amateur] (outside) observer / *vous allez participer au débat ? — non, je suis là en touriste* are you going to take part in the discussion? — no, I'm just watching ou just an observer ou just sitting in.

touristique [tuʀistik] adj **1.** [pour le tourisme - brochure, guide] tourist *(modif)* ▶ **route touristique** scenic route **2.** [qui attire les touristes] tourist *(modif)* / *cette ville est beaucoup trop touristique à mon goût* there are too many tourists in this town for my taste.

tourmente [tuʀmɑ̃t] nf *litt* **1.** [tempête] tempest *litt*, storm **2.** *fig* [bouleversements] turmoil.

tourmenté, e [tuʀmɑ̃te] adj **1.** [angoissé - personne] tormented, troubled, anguished ; [- conscience] tormented, troubled ; [- visage] tormented / *un regard tourmenté* a haunted ou tormented look **3.** [agité - époque] troubled **4.** *sout* [accidenté - paysage, côte] wild, rugged, craggy ; [changeant - ciel] changing, shifting / *un paysage d'orage sous un ciel tourmenté* a stormy landscape under a shifting sky **5.** LITTÉR & ART tortuous **6.** MÉTÉOR & NAUT ▶ **mer tourmentée** rough ou heavy sea.

tourmenter [3] [tuʀmɑ̃te] vt *sout* **1.** [martyriser - animal, personne] to torment, to ill-treat **2.** [suj : faim, soif, douleur] to torment, to plague, to rack ; [suj : incertitude, remords] to torment, to haunt, to rack ; [suj : jalousie] to plague, to torment ; [suj : obsession] to torment, to haunt / *ses rhumatismes le tourmentent* he's plagued by rheumatism. ❖ **se tourmenter** vpi *sout* [s'inquiéter] to worry o.s., to fret, to be anxious / *elle se tourmente pour son fils* she's worried sick about her son.

tournage [tuʀnaʒ] nm CINÉ shooting, filming.

tournant¹ [tuʀnɑ̃] nm **1.** [virage] bend, turn **2.** *fig* turning point, watershed / *elle est à un tournant de sa carrière* she is at a turning point in her career ▶ **attendre qqn au tournant** *fam* to be waiting for a chance to get even with sb, to have it in for sb.

tournant², e [tuʀnɑ̃, ɑ̃t] adj **1.** [dispositif, siège] swivel *(modif)*, swivelling **2.** [scène] revolving ; [escalier, route] winding.

tourné, e [tuʀne] adj **1.** CULIN [altéré - produits laitiers] sour, curdled ; [- vin] sour **2.** EXPR ▶ **bien tourné a)** [taille] neat **b)** [remarque, missive] well-phrased.

tournebroche [tuʀnəbʀɔʃ] nm [gén] roasting jack ou spit ; [d'un four] rotisserie.

tournedos [tuʀnədo] nm tournedos.

tournée [tuʀne] ❖ f ⟶ **tourné**. ❖ nf **1.** [d'un facteur, d'un commerçant] round ▶ **tournée de conférences** lecture tour ▶ **faire une tournée électorale a)** [candidat député] to canvass one's constituency **b)** [dans une élection présidentielle] to go on the campaign trail ▶ **tournée d'inspection** tour of inspection **2.** [d'un artiste, d'une troupe] tour / *être en tournée* to be on tour **3.** [visite] : *faire la tournée des galeries* to do the rounds of ou to go round the art galleries **4.** *fam* [au bar] round ▶ **tournée générale !** drinks all round! / *c'est la tournée du patron* drinks are on the house. ❖ **en tournée** loc adv ▶ **être en tournée a)** [facteur, représentant] to be off on one's rounds **b)** [chanteur] to be on tour.

tournemain [tuʀnəmɛ̃] ❖ **en un tournemain** loc adv in no time at all.

tourner [3] [tuʀne]

❖ vi

A. ⬛ **DÉCRIRE DES CERCLES** **1.** [se mouvoir autour d'un axe - girouette] to turn, to revolve ; [- disque] to revolve, to spin ; [- aiguille de montre, manège] to turn, to go round 🇬🇧 ou around 🇺🇸 ; [- objet suspendu, rouet, toupie] to spin around, to spin (round) ; [- clef, pédale, poignée] to turn ; [- hélice, roue, tour] to spin, to rotate ▶ **tourner sur soi-même a)** to turn round **b)** [vite] to spin (round and round) ▶ **faire tourner a)** [pièce de monnaie, manège, roue] to spin **b)** [clef] to turn / *j'ai la tête qui tourne* my head's spinning ▶ **tourner de l'œil** *fam* to pass out, to faint **2.** [se déplacer en cercle - personne] to go round 🇬🇧 ou around 🇺🇸 ; [- oiseau] to fly ou to wheel round 🇬🇧 ou around, to circle (round) 🇬🇧 ou around ; [- avion] to fly round 🇬🇧 ou around (in circles), to circle ; [- astre, satellite] to revolve, to go round 🇬🇧 ou around / *j'ai tourné 10 minutes avant de trouver à me garer* I drove round for 10 minutes before I found a parking space **3.** *fam* [être en tournée - chanteur] to (be on) tour.

B. ⬛ **CHANGER D'ORIENTATION, D'ÉTAT** **1.** [changer de direction - vent] to turn, to veer, to shift ; [- personne] to turn (off) ; [- véhicule] to turn (off), to make a turn ; [- route] to turn, to bend ▶ **tournez à droite** turn (off to the) right / *tourner au coin de la rue* to turn at the corner (of the street) ▶ **la chance ou la fortune a tourné (pour eux)** their luck has changed **2.** [faire demi-tour] to turn around, to turn (round) 🇬🇧 **3.** *fam* [se succéder - équipes] to rotate **4.** [évoluer] to go, to turn out ▶ **bien tourner** [situation, personne] to turn out well ou satisfactorily ▶ **mal tourner** [initiative, plaisanterie] to turn out badly, to go wrong / *tout ça va mal tourner !* no good will come of it! / *un jeune qui a mal tourné* a youngster who turned out badly ou went off the straight and narrow **5.** [s'altérer - lait] to go off 🇬🇧 ou bad 🇺🇸, to turn (sour) ; [- viande] to go off 🇬🇧 ou bad.

C. ⬛ **MARCHER, RÉUSSIR** **1.** [fonctionner - compteur] to go round 🇬🇧 ou around ; [- taximètre] to tick away ; [- programme informatique] to run / *le moteur tourne* the engine's running ou going ▸ **l'heure** ou **la pendule tourne** time passes / *l'usine tourne à plein (rendement)* the factory's working at full capacity ▸ **faire tourner une entreprise** [directeur] to run a business **2.** [réussir - affaire, entreprise, économie] to be running well.

◆ vt

A. FAIRE CHANGER D'ORIENTATION **1.** [faire pivoter - bouton, clé, poignée, volant] to turn / *tourne le bouton jusqu'au 7* turn the knob to 7 **2.** [mélanger - sauce, café] to (give a) stir ; [- salade] to toss **3.** [diriger - antenne, visage, yeux] to turn / *tourner son regard* ou *les yeux vers* to turn one's eyes ou to look towards **4.** [retourner - carte] to turn over ou up *(sép)* ; [- page] to turn (over) *(sép)* ; [- brochette, grillade] to give a turn, to turn (over) *(sép)* ▸ **tourner et retourner, tourner dans tous les sens a)** [boîte, gadget] to turn over and over **b)** [problème] to turn over and over (in one's mind), to mull over **5.** [contourner - cap] to round ; [- coin de rue] to turn ; [- ennemi] to get round *(insép)* / *tourner la difficulté* / *le règlement* / *la loi* fig to get round the problem / regulations / law.

B. CINÉMA & TÉLÉVISION **1.** ▸ **tourner un film a)** [cinéaste] to shoot ou to make a film 🇬🇧 ou movie 🇺🇸 **b)** [acteur] to make a film 🇬🇧 ou movie 🇺🇸 **2.** ▸ **silence, on tourne !** quiet please, action!

C. METTRE EN FORME **1.** MENUIS & MÉTALL to turn **2.** [formuler - compliment] to turn ; [- critique] to phrase, to express / *il tourne bien ses phrases* he's got a neat turn of phrase **3.** [transformer] : *elle tourne tout au tragique* she always makes a drama out of everything ▸ **tourner qqch / qqn en ridicule** to ridicule sthg / sb, to make fun of sthg / sb.

◆ **tourner à** v + prép ▸ **tourner au burlesque / drame** to take a ludicrous / tragic turn / *tourner à la catastrophe* to take a disastrous turn / *le temps tourne à la pluie* / *neige* it looks like rain / snow. ◆ **tourner autour de** v + prép **1.** [axe] to move ou to turn round / *les planètes qui tournent autour du Soleil* the planets revolving round the Sun **2.** [rôder] ▸ **tourner autour de qqn a)** [gén] to hang ou to hover round sb **b)** [pour le courtiser] to hang round sb **3.** [valoir environ] to be around ou about, to be in the region of / *les réparations devraient tourner autour de 90 €* the repairs should cost around ou should cost about ou should be in the region of 90 € **4.** [concerner - suj : conversation] to revolve round, to centre ou to focus on. ◆ **tourner en** v + prép ▸ **tourner en** ou **to change into.** ◆ **se tourner** vpi **1.** [faire un demi-tour] to turn round / *tourne-toi, je me déshabille* turn round ou turn your back, I'm getting undressed **2.** [changer de position] to turn / *il se tournait et se retournait dans son lit* he was tossing and turning in his bed. ◆ **se tourner contre** vp + prép to turn against. ◆ **se tourner vers** vp + prép **1.** [s'orienter vers] to turn towards ou toward 🇬🇧 ou around 🇺🇸 / *tous les regards se tournèrent vers elle* all eyes turned to look at her **2.** fig ▸ **se tourner vers qqn / Dieu** to turn to sb / God.

tournesol [turnəsɔl] nm BOT sunflower.

tourneur, euse [turnœr, øz] nm, f turner.

tournevis [turnəvis] nm screwdriver.

tourniquet [turnikɛ] nm **1.** [à l'entrée d'un établissement] turnstile **2.** [présentoir] revolving (display) stand **3.** [pour arroser] rotary sprinkler.

tournis [turni] nm **1.** VÉTÉR turnsick, gid, coenuriasis spéc **2.** EXPR avoir le tournis to feel giddy ou dizzy ▸ **donner le tournis à qqn** to make sb (feel) giddy.

tournoi [turnwa] nm JEUX & SPORT tournament ▸ **le tournoi des Six-Nations** the Six Nations Tournament.

tournoyer [13] [turnwaje] vi [feuilles, fumée, flocons] to whirl, to swirl ; [aigle] to wheel ou to circle round ; [danseur] to swirl ou to twirl ou to whirl round / *le radeau*

tournoyait dans les rapides the raft was tossed round (and round) in the rapids ▸ **faire tournoyer qqch** to whirl ou to swing sthg.

tournure [turnyr] nf **1.** [évolution, tendance] trend, tendency / *d'après la tournure que prend la situation* from the way the situation is developing ou going / *attendons de voir quelle tournure prennent les événements* let's wait and see how the situation develops ▸ **prendre tournure** to take shape ▸ **tournure d'esprit** turn ou cast of mind **2.** LING [expression] turn of phrase, expression ; [en syntaxe] form, construction ▸ **tournure impersonnelle / interrogative** impersonal / interrogative form.

tour-opérateur [turɔperatœr] *(pl* **tour-opérateurs)** nm tour operator.

tourte [turt] nf [tarte] pie / *tourte aux poires* / *épinards* pear / spinach pie.

tourteau, x [turto] nm [crabe] ▸ **tourteau (dormeur)** (edible) crab.

tourtereau, x [turtəro] nm ORNITH young turtledove. ◆ **tourtereaux** nmpl hum lovebirds.

tourterelle [turtərɛl] nf turtledove.

tourtière [turtjɛr] nf **1.** [plat] pie dish ou plate **2.** QUÉBEC CULIN meat pie.

tous *(adj* [tu]*, pron* [tus]**)** adj & pron indéf mpl ⟶ **tout.**

Toussaint [tusɛ̃] nf RELIG ▸ **(le) jour de la Toussaint** All Saints' Day.

La Toussaint

All Saints' Day is a public holiday in France. It is the traditional occasion for a visit to the cemetery to lay flowers (usually chrysanthemums) on the graves.

tousser [3] [tuse] vi MÉD to cough.

toussoter [3] [tusɔte] vi **1.** MÉD to have a bit of a cough ou a slight cough **2.** [pour prévenir] to give a little ou discreet cough.

tout [tu] *(devant voyelle ou « h » muet* [tut]**),** **toute** [tut] *(mpl* **tous** *(adj* [tu]*, pron* [tus]**),** *fpl* **toutes** [tut]**)**

◆ adj qualificatif *(au singulier)* **1.** [entier] all (the), the whole (of the) ▸ **toute la nuit** all night / *il se plaint toute la journée* he complains all the time ou the whole day long / *tout le village a participé* the whole village took part / *tout ceci* / *cela* all (of) this / that / *tout ce travail pour rien !* all this work for nothing! ▸ **j'ai tout mon temps** I've plenty of time ou all the time in the world / *ils se sont aimés toute leur vie* they loved each other all their lives ▸ **avec lui, c'est tout l'un ou tout l'autre** with him, it's either (all) black or (all) white **2.** [devant un nom propre] all / *j'ai visité tout Paris en huit jours* I saw all ou the whole of Paris in a week **3.** [devant un nom sans article] : *on a tout intérêt à y aller* it's in our every interest to go ▸ **rouler à toute vitesse** to drive at full ou top speed / *en toute franchise* / *simplicité* in all sincerity / simplicity ▸ **c'est de toute beauté** it's extremely beautiful **4.** [avec une valeur emphatique] : *c'est toute une expédition pour y aller !* getting there involves quite a trek! **5.** *(comme adv)* [entièrement] completely **6.** [unique, seul] only / *c'est tout l'effet que ça te fait ?* is that all it means to you? / *pour toute famille il n'avait qu'une cousine éloignée* one distant cousin was all the family he had **7.** [suivi d'une relative] ▸ **tout ce qu'on dit** everything people say / *tout ce que l'entreprise compte de personnel qualifié* the company's entire qualified workforce ▸ **tout ce qu'il y a de :** *ses enfants sont tout ce qu'il y a de bien élevés* his children are very well-behaved ou are models of good behaviour / *ce projet est tout ce qu'il y a de plus sérieux* this project couldn't be more serious.

◆ **dét** *(adj indéf)*

A. AU SINGULIER [chaque, n'importe quel] any, all, every / *tout citoyen a des droits* every citizen has rights, all citizens have rights / *toute personne ayant vu l'accident* any person who witnessed the accident / *à tout âge* at any age / *à toute heure du jour et de la nuit* at any hour of the day or night ▸ **de tout temps** since time immemorial, from the beginning of time / *tout autre que lui aurait refusé* anyone other than him ou anybody else would have refused.

B. AU PLURIEL 1. [exprimant la totalité] all / *tous les hommes* all men, the whole of mankind / *je veux tous les détails* I want all the details ou the full details / *ça se vend maintenant à tous les coins de rue* it's now sold on every street corner **2.** [devant un nom sans article] : *ils étaient 150 000, toutes disciplines / races confondues* there were 150,000 of them, all disciplines / races together ▸ **champion toutes catégories** overall champion / *il roulait tous feux éteints* he was driving with his lights off **3.** [exprimant la périodicité] every ▸ **tous les jours** every day / *toutes les deux semaines* every other week, every second week, every two weeks / *toutes les fois qu'on s'est rencontrés* every time we've met.

◆ **pron indéf**

A. AU SINGULIER everything, all ; [n'importe quoi] anything / *j'ai tout jeté* I threw everything away ▸ **dis-moi tout** tell me all about it / *t'as tout compris ! fam* that's it!, that's right! / *c'est tout dire* that says it all / *il est prêt à tout* he's ready for anything / *capable de tout* capable of anything ▸ **c'est tout** that's all ▸ **ce sera tout ?** [dans un magasin] will be that all?, anything else? / *ce n'est pas tout* that's not all ▸ **être tout pour qqn** to be everything for sb, to mean everything to sb / *on aura tout vu !* now I've ou we've seen everything! / *avec toi c'est tout ou rien* with you, it's all or nothing ou one extreme or the other / *c'est tout sauf du foie gras* it's anything but foie gras / *tout se passe comme si…* it's as though… / *tout bien considéré, tout bien réfléchi* all things considered / *il a tout de son père* he's every bit like his father.

B. AU PLURIEL 1. [désignant ce dont on a parlé] : *il y a plusieurs points de vue, tous sont intéressants* there are several points of view, they are all interesting / *j'adore les prunes — prends-les toutes* I love plums — take them all ou all of them **2.** [avec une valeur récapitulative] all / *Jean, Pierre, Jacques, tous voulaient la voir* Jean, Pierre, Jacques, they all wanted to see her **3.** [tout le monde] : *vous m'entendez tous ?* can you all hear me? ▸ **des émissions pour tous** programmes suitable for all (audiences) ▸ **tous ensemble** all together. ◆ **tout, toute, toutes** adv *(s'accorde en genre et en nombre devant un adj f commençant par une consonne ou un «h» aspiré)* **1.** [entièrement, tout à fait] quite, very, completely / *ils étaient tout seuls* they were quite ou completely alone ▸ **la ville tout entière** the whole town ▸ **tout neuf** brand new ▸ **tout nu** stark naked ▸ **un tout jeune homme** a very young man / *ses tout premiers mots* his / her very first words / *une robe tout en dentelle* a dress made of lace / *le jardin est tout en longueur* the garden is just one long strip ▸ **toute mouillée** wet ou soaked through, drenched / *tout simplement / autrement* quite simply / differently / *téléphone-moi, tout simplement* just phone me, that's the easiest (way) / *il est toute bonté / générosité* he is goodness / generosity itself / *ça, c'est tout lui !* that's typical of him ou just like him! **2.** [en intensif] ▸ **tout en haut / bas** right at the top / bottom ▸ **c'est tout près** it's very close / *tout contre le mur* right up against the wall / *c'est tout le contraire !* it's quite the opposite! **3.** [déjà] ▸ **tout prêt** ou

préparé ready-made / *tout bébé, elle dansait déjà* even as a baby, she was already dancing **4.** *(avec un gérondif)* [indiquant la simultanéité] : *on mangera tout en marchant* we'll eat while we're walking ; [indiquant la concession] : *tout en avouant son ignorance dans ce domaine, il continuait à me contredire* although he'd confessed his ignorance in that field, he kept on contradicting me. ◆ **tout** nm **1.** [ensemble] whole ▸ **former un tout** to make up a whole **2.** ▸ **le tout** [l'essentiel] the main ou the most important thing / *le tout c'est de ne pas bafouiller* the most important thing is not to stutter ▸ **ce n'est pas le tout, mais je dois partir** *fam* that's all very well, but I've got to go now ▸ **ce n'est pas le tout de critiquer, il faut pouvoir proposer autre chose** it's not enough to criticize, you've got to be able to suggest something else ▸ **tenter le tout pour le tout** to make a (final) desperate attempt ou a last ditch effort ▸ **changer du tout au tout** to change completely. ◆ **du tout** loc adv not at all / *je vous dérange ? — du tout, du tout !* am I disturbing you? — not at all ou not in the least! ◆ **en tout** loc adv **1.** [au total] in total, in all / *cela fait 38 euros en tout* that comes to 38 euros in all ou in total **2.** [exactement] exactly, entirely. ◆ **en tout et pour tout** loc adv (all) in all / *en tout et pour tout, nous avons dépensé 400 euros* all in all, we've spent 400 euros. ◆ **tout à coup** loc adv all of a sudden, suddenly. ◆ **tout à fait** loc adv **1.** [complètement] quite, fully, absolutely / *en es-tu tout à fait conscient ?* are you fully aware of it? / *ce n'est pas tout à fait exact* it's not quite correct **2.** [exactement] exactly / *c'est tout à fait ce que je cherche / le même* it's exactly what I've been looking for / the same **3.** [oui] certainly / *vous faites les retouches ? — tout à fait* do you do alterations? — certainly (we do). ◆ **tout de même** loc adv **1.** [malgré tout] all the same, even so / *j'irai tout de même* all the same, I'll still go **2.** [en intensif] : *tout de même, tu exagères !* steady on!, that's a bit much! ◆ **tout de suite** loc adv **1.** [dans le temps] straight away, right away, at once / *apporte du pain — tout de suite !* bring some bread — right away! **2.** [dans l'espace] immediately / *tournez à gauche tout de suite après le pont* turn left immediately after the bridge. ◆ **tout…** loc conj ▸ **tout directeur qu'il est** ou **qu'il soit,…** he may well be the boss,…

tout-à-l'égout [tutalegu] nm inv main ou mains drainage, main sewer.

toutefois [tutfwa] adv however, nevertheless / *je lui parlerai, si toutefois il veut bien me recevoir* I'll talk to him, that is, if he'll see me.

tout-en-un [tutãnœ̃] nm [livre, appareil] all-in-one.

Tout-le-Monde [tulamɔ̃d] nmf inv ▸ **M., Mme Tout-le-Monde a)** [le citoyen ordinaire] the man (woman) in the street **b)** [n'importe qui] your average Joe Soap UK, John Q. Public US.

toutou [tutu] nm *fam* **1.** [chien] doggie, bow-wow **2.** Québec [peluche] stuffed toy.

tout-petit [tup(ə)ti] *(pl* **tout-petits)** nm [qui ne marche pas] infant ; [qui marche] toddler.

tout-puissant, toute-puissante [tupɥisɑ̃, tutpɥisɑ̃t] *(mpl* **tout-puissants,** *fpl* **toutes-puissantes)** adj [influent] omnipotent, all-powerful.

Tout-Puissant [tupɥisɑ̃] npr m ▸ **le Tout-Puissant** the Almighty.

tout(-)terrain [tutɛʀɛ̃] ◆ adj inv cross-country *(modif.)*. ◆ nm inv dirt-track driving ou riding. ◆ nf inv cross-country car ou vehicle.

toux [tu] nf cough.

toxicodépendance [tɔksikɔdepɑ̃dɑ̃s] nf drug addiction.

toxicodépendant, e [tɔksikɔdepɑ̃dɑ̃, ɑ̃t] ◆ nm, f drug addict. ◆ adj drug-dependent.

toxicomane [tɔksikɔman] ◆ adj drug-addicted. ◆ nmf drug addict.

toxicomanie [tɔksikɔmani] nf drug addiction.

toxine [tɔksin] nf toxin.

toxique [tɔksik] adj toxic, poisonous.

TP nmpl abr de **travaux pratiques**.

TPE [tepeø] ◆ nmpl (abr de **travaux personnels encadrés**) ÉDUC GIS. ◆ nf (abr de **très petite entreprise**) VSB.

trac [tʀak] nm [devant un public] stage fright ou nerves ; [à un examen] exam nerves ▸ **avoir le trac** to have the jitters.

tracas [tʀaka] nmpl [soucis matériels ou financiers] troubles.

tracasser [3] [tʀakase] vt [suj : situation] to worry, to bother ; [suj : enfant] to worry / *son état de santé actuel me tracasse* I'm worried about the current state of his health. ❖ **se tracasser** vpi to worry / *ne te tracasse plus pour cela* don't give it another thought.

tracasserie [tʀakasʀi] nf *(souvent au pl)* petty annoyance / *faire face à des tracasseries administratives* to put up with a lot of frustrating redtape.

trace [tʀas] nf **1.** [empreinte - d'un animal] track, trail, spoor ; [- d'un fugitif] trail ▸ **des traces de pas** footprints, footmarks ▸ **des traces de pneus** tyre ou wheel marks ▸ **suivre la trace** ou **les traces de qqn, marcher sur les traces de qqn** *fig* to follow sb's footsteps **2.** [d'un coup, de brûlures, d'une maladie] mark / *il portait des traces de coups* his body showed signs of having been beaten **3.** [marque, indice] trace, smear / *il y a des traces de doigts sur la vitre* there are fingermarks on the window pane / *sans laisser de traces* without (a) trace / *pas la moindre trace d'effraction* no sign ou evidence ou trace of a break-in / *il n'y a pas trace d'elle* ou *aucune trace d'elle* no sign of her (anywhere) ▸ **ne pas trouver trace de qqch** to find no trace of sthg **4.** [quantité infime] trace / *elle parle sans la moindre trace d'accent* she speaks without the slightest trace ou hint of an accent **5.** [vestige] trace / *on y a retrouvé les traces d'une civilisation très ancienne* traces of a very ancient civilization have been discovered there **6.** [marque psychique] mark **7.** SPORT trail / *faire la trace* to break a trail. ❖ **à la trace** loc adv [d'après les empreintes] ▸ **suivre à la trace** [fuyard, gibier] to track (down). ❖ **sur la trace de** loc prép [à la recherche de] on the trail of ou track of / *ils sont sur la trace du bandit / d'un manuscrit* they are on the bandit's trail / tracking down a manuscript.

tracé [tʀase] nm **1.** [représentation - d'une ville, d'un réseau] layout, plan **2.** [chemin suivi - par un fleuve] course ; [- par une voie] route **3.** [ligne - dans un graphique] line ; [- dans un dessin] stroke, line ; [contour - d'un littoral] outline.

tracer [16] [tʀase] ◆ vt **1.** [trait, cercle, motif] to draw **2.** [inscription, mot] to write **3.** [marquer l'emplacement de - itinéraire] to trace, to plot ; [- chemin, terrain] to mark ou to stake ou to lay out *(sép)* **4.** *fig* [indiquer] to map out *(sép)*, to plot ▸ **tracer le chemin** ou **la route** ou **la voie à qqn** to mark out ou to pave the way for sb. ◆ vi *fam* [aller très vite] to shift UK, to barrel along US / *elle trace, ta bagnole !* your car goes like a bomb!, your car doesn't half shift UK ou barrels right along US.

trachée [tʀaʃe] nf ANAT trachea *spéc*, windpipe.

trachéite [tʀakeit] nf tracheitis.

tract [tʀakt] nm pamphlet, leaflet, tract.

tractations [tʀaktasjɔ̃] nfpl dealings, negotiations.

tracter [3] [tʀakte] vt to tow, to pull.

tracteur [tʀaktœʀ] nm AGR tractor.

traction [tʀaksjɔ̃] nf **1.** [mode de déplacement] traction, haulage **2.** ▸ **traction avant** [système] front-wheel drive **3.** SPORT [sur une barre] pull-up ; [au sol] press-up UK, push-up US.

trader [tʀedœʀ] nm = **tradeur**.

tradeur, euse [tʀedœʀ, øz] nm, f trader.

tradition [tʀadisjɔ̃] nf **1.** [ensemble des coutumes] tradition / *c'est dans la plus pure tradition écossaise* it's in the best Scottish tradition **2.** [usage] tradition, custom. ❖ **de tradition** loc adj traditional / *il est de tradition de / que...* it's a tradition to / that...

traditionnel, elle [tʀadisjɔnɛl] adj **1.** [fondé sur la tradition] traditional **2.** [passé dans les habitudes] usual, traditional.

traditionnellement [tʀadisjɔnɛlmɑ̃] adv **1.** [selon la tradition] traditionally **2.** [comme d'habitude] as usual, as always.

traducteur, trice [tʀadyktœʀ, tʀis] nm, f translator.

traduction [tʀadyksjɔ̃] nf [processus] translating, translation / *traduction de l'espagnol en allemand* translation from Spanish into German ▸ **traduction assistée par ordinateur** computer ou machine (assisted) translation ▸ **traduction automatique** automatic translation ▸ **traduction simultanée** simultaneous translation.

traduire [98] [tʀadɥiʀ] vt **1.** [écrivain, roman, terme] to translate / *livre traduit de l'anglais* book translated from (the) English / *traduire du russe en chinois* to translate from Russian ou out of Russian into Chinese **2.** [exprimer - pensée, sentiment] to express, to reflect, to convey ; [- colère, peur] to reveal, to indicate **3.** DR ▸ **traduire qqn en justice** to bring sb before the courts, to prosecute sb. ❖ **se traduire** vp *(emploi passif)* : *la phrase peut se traduire de différentes façons* the sentence can be translated ou rendered in different ways. ❖ **se traduire par** vp + prép **1.** [avoir pour résultat] : *cela se traduit par des changements climatiques profonds* it results in ou entails radical changes in the climate **2.** [être exprimé par] : *son émotion se traduisit par des larmes* his emotion found expression in tears.

traduisible [tʀadɥizibl] adj translatable / *le proverbe n'est pas traduisible* the proverb cannot be translated.

trafic [tʀafik] nm **1.** [commerce illicite] traffic, trafficking ▸ **trafic d'armes** arms dealing, gunrunning ▸ **le trafic de drogue** ou **de stupéfiants** drug trafficking ▸ **faire du trafic de drogue** a) [gén] to be involved in drug trafficking b) [organisateur] to traffic in drugs c) [revendeur] to deal in ou to push ou to peddle drugs **2.** *fam* [manigance] fishy business **3.** DR ▸ **trafic d'influence** (bribery and) corruption ou corrupt receiving **4.** TRANSP traffic ▸ **trafic aérien** / **ferroviaire** / **maritime** / **portuaire** / **routier** air / rail / sea / port / road traffic.

trafiquant, e [tʀafikɑ̃, ɑ̃t] nm, f dealer, trafficker ▸ **trafiquant de drogue** drug dealer ou trafficker ▸ **trafiquant d'armes** gunrunner, arms dealer.

trafiquer [3] [tʀafike] ◆ vi [faire du commerce illicite] to traffic, to racketeer. ◆ vt *fam* **1.** [falsifier, altérer - comptabilité, résultats électoraux] to doctor ; [- vin] to adulterate ; [- compteur électrique] to tamper with *(insép)* ; [- compteur kilométrique] to rig **2.** *fam* [manigancer] to be up to / *je me demande ce qu'ils trafiquent* I wonder what they're up to.

tragédie [tʀaʒedi] nf **1.** LITTÉR tragedy **2.** [événement funeste] tragedy, disaster, calamity / *l'émeute a tourné à la tragédie* the riot had a tragic outcome.

tragi-comédie *(pl* tragi-comédies*)*, **tragicomédie*** [tʀaʒikɔmedi] nf LITTÉR tragi-comedy.

tragique [tʀaʒik] ◆ adj [dramatique] tragic / *ce n'est pas tragique* it's not the end of the world. ◆ nm **1.** LITTÉR ▸ **le tragique** tragedy, tragic art **2.** fig tragedy / *le tragique de sa situation* the tragic side ou the tragedy of his situation ▸ **prendre qqch au tragique** to make a tragedy out of sthg / *tourner au tragique* to take a tragic turn, to go tragically wrong.

tragiquement [tʀaʒikmɑ̃] adv tragically.

trahir [32] [tʀaiʀ] vt **1.** [son camp] to betray **2.** litt [tromper - ami, amant] ▸ **trahir qqn** to deceive sb, to be unfaithful to sb **3.** [manquer à] to break, to go against / *trahir sa promesse* / *ses engagements* to break one's promise / one's commitments / *trahir la vérité* to distort ou to twist the truth **4.** [dénaturer - pensée] to misinterpret, to distort, to do an injustice to ; [- en traduisant] to give a false rendering of. ◈ **se trahir** vpi **1.** [se révéler] : *l'angoisse se trahissait dans sa voix* her voice betrayed her anxiety **2.** [laisser voir une émotion] to betray o.s., to give o.s. away **3.** [se faire découvrir] to give o.s. away / *il s'est trahi en faisant du bruit* he gave himself away by making a noise.

trahison [tʀaizɔ̃] nf **1.** DR treason **2.** [déloyauté] betrayal, disloyalty.

train [tʀɛ̃]
nm

A. TRANSPORTS & TECHNIQUES **1.** [convoi] train / *le train de 9 h 40* the 9:40 train / *je prends le train à Arpajon* I catch the train at Arpajon ▸ **être dans le train** to be on the train ▸ **train autocouchette** car-sleeper train ▸ **train de banlieue** suburban ou commuter train ▸ **train direct** non-stop ou through train ▸ **train électrique** JEUX train set ▸ **train express** express train ▸ **train à grande vitesse** high-speed train ▸ **train de marchandises** goods UK ou freight train ▸ **train omnibus** slow ou local train ▸ **train postal** mail train ▸ **train rapide** fast train ▸ **train de voyageurs** passenger train ▸ **monter dans** ou **prendre le train en marche** to climb onto ou to jump on the bandwagon **2.** [moyen de transport] ▸ **le train** rail (transport), train ▸ **j'irai par le** ou **en train** I'll go (there) by train **3.** [ensemble, série] set, batch ▸ **train de réformes** set of reforms **4.** AÉRON ▸ **train d'atterrissage** landing gear, undercarriage **5.** AUTO ▸ **train avant** / **arrière** front / rear wheel-axle unit.

B. VITESSE **1.** [allure] pace ▸ **accélérer le train a)** [marcheur, animal] to quicken the pace **b)** [véhicule] to speed up ▸ **au** ou **du train où vont les choses** the way things are going, at this rate ▸ **aller bon train** [en marchant] to walk at a brisk pace / *les négociations ont été menées bon train* the negotiations made good progress **2.** [manière de vivre] ▸ **train de vie** lifestyle, standard of living.

C. PARTIE DU CORPS ZOOL quarters ▸ **train avant** ou de **devant** forequarters ▸ **train arrière** ou **de derrière** hindquarters. ◈ **en train** ◆ loc adj [en cours] ▸ **être en train** [ouvrage, travaux] to be under way / *j'ai un tricot en train* I'm knitting something. ◆ loc adv [en route] : *mettre un roman en train* to start a novel ▸ **se mettre en train** to warm up. ◈ **en train de** loc prép ▸ **être en train de faire qqch** to be (busy) doing sthg / *il est toujours en train de taquiner sa sœur* he's always teasing his sister.

traînailler, traînailler* [tʀenaje] fam = **traînasser**.

traînant, e, traînant*, e [tʀenɑ̃, ɑ̃t] adj **1.** [lent - élocution] drawling, lazy **2.** [qui traîne à terre] trailing.

traînard, e, traînard*, e [tʀenaʀ, aʀd] nm, f fam **1.** [lambin] slowcoach UK, slowpoke US **2.** [dans une marche] straggler.

traînasser, traînasser* [3] [tʀenase] vi fam **1.** [errer paresseusement] to loaf ou to hang about **2.** [lambiner dans son travail] to fall behind **3.** [élocution] to drawl.

traîne, traine* [tʀen] nf **1.** VÊT train **2.** PÊCHE dragnet ▸ **pêche à la traîne** trolling **3.** QUÉBEC ▸ **traîne sauvage** toboggan. ◈ **à la traîne, à la traîne*** loc adj : *être* ou *rester à la traîne* [coureur, pays, élève] to lag ou to drag behind.

traîneau, x, traîneau*, x [tʀeno] nm [véhicule] sleigh, sledge UK, sled US.

traînée, traînée* [tʀene] nf **1.** [trace - au sol, sur un mur] trail, streak ; [- dans le ciel] trail / *une traînée de fumée* a trail of smoke ▸ **se propager** ou **se répandre comme une traînée de poudre** to spread like wildfire **2.** fam & péj [prostituée] tart UK, whore.

traîner, traîner* [4] [tʀene] ◆ vt **1.** [tirer - gén] to pull ; [- avec effort] to drag, to haul ▸ **traîner qqn par les pieds** to drag sb (along) by the feet / *traîner les pieds* to shuffle along, to drag one's feet pr ▸ **traîner la jambe** ou fam **patte** to hobble ou to limp along ▸ **traîner qqn dans la boue** ou **la fange** fig to drag sb's name through the mud **2.** [emmener - personne réticente] to drag along *(sép)* ; [- personne non désirée] to trail, to drag about *(sép)* **3.** [garder avec soi - fétiche, jouet] to drag around *(sép)* **4.** fam [avoir] : *ça fait des semaines que je traîne cette angine* this sore throat has been with ou plaguing me for weeks. ◆ vi **1.** [pendre] : *traîner (par terre)* to drag on the floor ou ground **2.** [ne pas être rangé - documents, vêtements] to lie around, to be scattered around ▸ **laisser traîner qqch** to leave sthg lying around **3.** [s'attarder, flâner] to dawdle ; [rester en arrière] to lag ou to drag behind / *ne traîne pas, Mamie nous attend* stop dawdling ou do hurry up, Grandma's expecting us / *traîner en chemin* ou *en route* to dawdle on the way / *j'aime bien traîner sur les quais* fam I like strolling along the banks of the river ; péj [errer] to hang about ou around / *il traîne dans tous les bistrots* he hangs around in all the bars / *des chiens traînent dans le village* dogs roam around the village **4.** fig & péj [maladie, idée] : *elle attrape toutes les maladies qui traînent* she catches every bug that's going around **5.** fam & péj [s'éterniser - affaire, conversation, procédure] to drag on ; [- superstition, maladie] to linger ou to drag on ▸ **traîner en longueur** [discours, négociations] to drag on / *ça n'a pas traîné !* it didn't take long!, it wasn't long coming! / *faire traîner les pourparlers* / *un procès* to drag out negotiations / a trial. ◈ **se traîner, se traîner*** vpi **1.** [blessé] to crawl / *se traîner par terre* to crawl on the floor ou ground / *je me suis traînée jusque chez le docteur* fig I dragged myself to the doctor's **2.** fam [conducteur, véhicule] to crawl along, to go at a crawl.

traînerie [tʀenʀi] nf QUÉBEC thing left lying around.

training [tʀeniŋ] nm VÊT [chaussure] sports shoe, trainer ; [survêtement] tracksuit.

train-train (pl train-train), **traintrain** (pl traintrain ou traintrains*) [tʀɛ̃tʀɛ̃] nm routine ▸ **le train-train quotidien** the daily grind.

traire [112] [tʀeʀ] vt [vache] to milk ; [lait] to draw / *machine à traire* milking machine.

trait [tʀe] nm **1.** [ligne] line / *tirer* ou *tracer un trait (à la règle)* to draw a line (with a ruler) ▸ **d'un trait de plume** with a stroke of the pen ▸ **tirer un trait sur** : *tirons un trait sur cette dispute* let's forget this argument, let's put this argument behind us / *tirer un trait sur le passé* to turn over a new leaf, to make a complete break with the past **2.** [marque distinctive - d'un système, d'une œuvre, d'un style] characteristic ▸ **trait de caractère** (character) trait **3.** [acte] ▸ **trait d'esprit** witticism, flash of wit ▸ **trait de génie** stroke of genius **4.** EXPR ▸ **avoir trait à** [avoir un rapport avec] to have to do ou to be connected with. ◈ **traits** nmpl [du visage] features / *il a des traits fins* / *grossiers* he has delicate / coarse features ▸ **avoir les**

traits tirés to look drawn. ❖ **à grands traits** loc adv [dessiner, esquisser] roughly, in broad outline. ❖ **de trait** loc adj [bête, cheval] draught. ❖ **d'un (seul) trait** loc adv [avaler] in one gulp, in one go ; [réciter] (all) in one breath ; [dormir] uninterruptedly. ❖ **trait pour trait** loc adv [exactement] exactly / *c'est sa mère trait pour trait* she's the spitting image of her mother. ❖ **trait d'union** nm hyphen ; *fig* link.

traitant, e [tʀɛtɑ̃, ɑ̃t] adj [shampooing] medicated.

traite [tʀɛt] nf **1.** COMM, FIN & DR draft, bill ; [lettre de change] bill of exchange **2.** [commerce, trafic] ▸ **traite des Noirs** slave trade ▸ **traite des Blanches** white slave trade ou traffic **3.** AGR [action] milking *(U)* ; [lait] milk (yield). ❖ **d'une (seule) traite** loc adv [voyager] in one go, without stopping ; [avaler] at one go, in one gulp ; [lire, réciter] in one stretch ou breath ; [dormir] uninterruptedly ; [travailler] without interruption, at a stretch.

traité [tʀete] nm **1.** [accord] treaty ▸ **traité de paix** peace treaty ▸ **le traité de Rome** the Treaty of Rome **2.** [ouvrage] treatise.

traitement [tʀɛtmɑ̃] nm **1.** MÉD & PHARM treatment / *un bon traitement contre les poux* a cure for lice **2.** [d'un fonctionnaire] salary, wage, wages **3.** [façon d'agir envers quelqu'un] treatment ▸ **traitement de choc** shock treatment / *avoir ou* ou *bénéficier d'un traitement de faveur* to enjoy preferential treatment **4.** INFORM processing ▸ **traitement de données** data processing ▸ **traitement de texte a)** word processing **b)** [logiciel] word processing package **5.** INDUST treatment, processing. ❖ **en traitement, sous traitement** loc adj under treatment ▸ *être en* ou *sous traitement* to be being treated ou having treatment ou under treatment.

traiter [4] [tʀete] vt **1.** [se comporter avec] to treat ▸ **traiter qqn durement / complaisamment** to be harsh / accommodating towards sb / *il me traite comme un ami / gamin fam* he treats me like a friend / kid ▸ **bien traiter qqn** to treat sb well ▸ **mal traiter qqn** to treat sb badly, to ill-treat sb ▸ **traiter qqn d'égal à égal** to treat sb as an equal **2.** [soigner - patient, maladie] to treat ▸ **se faire traiter pour** to undergo treatment ou to be treated for **3.** INDUST to treat, to process ; [aliments] to process ; [récoltes - gén] to treat ; [- par avion] to spray ; [lentille] to coat **4.** [qualifier] ▸ **traiter qqn de** : *traiter qqn d'imbécile* to call sb an idiot / *se faire traiter de menteur* to be called a liar ▸ **traiter qqn de tous les noms** to call sb all the names under the sun **5.** COMM [affaire, demande, dossier] to deal with *(insép)*, to handle **6.** [étudier - thème] to treat, to deal with *(insép)* / *vous ne traitez pas le sujet* you're not addressing the question **7.** INFORM [données, texte, images] to process. ❖ **traiter avec** v + prép to negotiate ou to deal / *nous ne traiterons pas avec des terroristes* we won't bargain ou negotiate with terrorists. ❖ **traiter de** v + prép [suj : roman, film, thèse] to deal with *(insép)*, to be about ; [suj : auteur] to deal with. ❖ **se traiter** ❖ vp *(emploi passif)* [maladie] : *ça se traite aux antibiotiques* it can be treated with antibiotics. ❖ vp *(emploi réciproque)* [personne] : *ils se traitaient de menteurs* they were calling each other liars.

traiteur [tʀetœʀ] nm [qui livre] caterer.

traître, esse, **traître*, esse** [tʀetʀ, ɛs] ❖ adj **1.** [déloyal - personne] traitorous, treacherous / *être traître à sa patrie* to be a traitor to ou to betray one's country **2.** [trompeur - visage, sourire] deceptive ; [- paroles] treacherous / *il est traître, ce petit vin de pays ! fam* this little local wine is stronger than you'd think ! **3.** EXPR *elle n'a pas dit un traître mot* she didn't breathe ou say a (single) word. ❖ nm, f [gén & POL] traitor (traitress). ❖ **en traître, en traître*** loc adv ▸ **prendre qqn en traître** to play an underhand trick on sb.

traîtrise, traîtrise* [tʀetʀiz] nf **1.** [caractère] treacherousness, treachery **2.** [acte - perfide] (piece of) treachery ; [- déloyal] betrayal.

trajectoire [tʀaʒɛktwaʀ] nf **1.** [d'une balle, d'un missile] trajectory, path ; [d'une planète, d'un avion] path ▸ **trajectoire de vol** flight path **2.** [carrière professionnelle] career path.

trajet [tʀaʒɛ] nm [chemin parcouru] distance ; [voyage] journey ; [d'un car, d'un autobus] route / *je fais tous les jours le trajet Paris-Egly* I commute everyday between Paris and Egly / *il a fait le trajet en huit heures* he covered the distance in eight hours.

tram [tʀam] nm **1.** [moyen de transport] tram UK, streetcar US **2.** [véhicule] tram UK, tramcar UK, streetcar US.

trame [tʀam] nf **1.** TEXT [base] weft, woof ; [fil] weft, weft thread, pick **2.** [d'un livre, d'un film] thread, basic outline ou framework.

tramer [3] [tʀame] vt [conspiration] to hatch ; [soulèvement] to plot. ❖ **se tramer** vp *(emploi passif)* to be afoot / *il se trame quelque chose* something's afoot.

tramontane [tʀamɔ̃tan] nf tramontane, transmontane.

trampoline [tʀɑ̃polin] nm trampoline / *faire du trampoline* to do trampolining.

tramway [tʀamwe] nm **1.** [moyen de transport] tramway (system) **2.** [véhicule] tramcar UK, streetcar US.

tranchant, e [tʀɑ̃ʃɑ̃, ɑ̃t] adj **1.** [lame] sharp, keen, cutting ; [outil] cutting ; [bord] sharp, cutting **2.** [personne, réponse, ton] curt, sharp. ❖ **tranchant** nm [d'une lame] sharp ou cutting edge ▸ **le tranchant de la main** the edge of the hand.

tranche [tʀɑ̃ʃ] nf **1.** [de pain, de viande, de pastèque] slice ▸ **tranche de bacon** [à frire] rasher (of bacon) ▸ **tranche de saumon a)** [darne] salmon steak **b)** [fumée] slice ou leaf of (smoked) salmon ▸ **une tranche de vie** a slice of life **2.** [subdivision - d'un programme de construction] stage, phase ▸ **tranche horaire** ADMIN period of time ▸ **tranche d'âge** age bracket ▸ **tranche de salaires / de revenus** salary / income bracket ▸ **tranche d'imposition** tax band **3.** RADIO & TV slot **4.** [bord - d'un livre] edge ; [- d'une médaille, d'une pièce] edge, rim. ❖ **en tranche(s)** ◆ loc adj [pain, saucisson] sliced. ◆ loc adv ▸ **débiter** ou **couper qqch en tranches** to slice sthg (up), to cut sthg into slices.

tranché, e [tʀɑ̃ʃe] adj **1.** [sans nuances - couleurs] distinct, clear, sharply contrasted **2.** [distinct - catégories] distinct ; [- caractères] distinct, well-defined, clear-cut **3.** [péremptoire - position] clear-cut, uncompromising, unequivocal. ❖ **tranchée** nf MIL & TRAV PUB trench.

trancher [3] [tʀɑ̃ʃe] ◆ vt **1.** [couper] to cut, to sever *sout*, to slice through ▸ **trancher la gorge de qqn** to cut ou to slit sb's throat **2.** [différend] to settle ; [difficulté] to solve ; [question] to decide. ◆ vi [décider] to make ou to take a decision, to decide. ❖ **trancher avec, trancher sur** v + prép [suj : couleur] to stand out against, to contrast sharply with ; [suj : attitude] to be in sharp contrast ou to contrast strongly with.

tranquille [tʀɑ̃kil] adj **1.** [sans agitation - quartier, rue] quiet ; [- campagne] quiet, peaceful, tranquil *litt* ; [- soirée] calm, quiet, peaceful ; [- sommeil, vie] peaceful, tranquil *litt* ; [- air, eau] still, quiet, tranquil *litt* / *aller* ou *marcher d'un pas tranquille* to stroll unhurriedly **2.** [en paix] : *allons dans mon bureau, nous y serons plus tranquilles pour discuter* let's go into my office, we can talk there without being disturbed ▸ **laisser qqn tranquille** to leave sb alone ou in peace / *laisse-moi tranquille, je suis assez grand pour ouvrir la boîte tout seul !* leave me alone, I'm old enough to open the box on my own ! ▸ **laisser qqch tran-**

quille *fam* [ne pas y toucher] to leave sthg alone **3.** [calme, sage] quiet ▸ **se tenir** ou **rester tranquille a)** to keep quiet ou still **b)** [ne pas se faire remarquer] to keep a low profile **4.** [rassuré] ▸ **être tranquille** to feel ou to be easy in one's mind / *sois tranquille, elle va bien* don't worry ou set your mind at rest, she's all right / *je ne suis pas* ou *ne me sens pas tranquille quand il est sur les routes* I worry when he's on the road / *je serais plus tranquille s'il n'était pas seul* I'd feel easier in my mind knowing that he wasn't on his own **5.** [sûr] : *tu peux être tranquille (que)...* you can rest assured (that)...

tranquillement [trãkilmã] *adv* **1.** [calmement - dormir, jouer] quietly, peacefully ; [- répondre, regarder] calmly, quietly **2.** [sans se presser - marcher, travailler] unhurriedly / *on est allés tranquillement jusqu'à l'église avec grand-mère* we walked slowly to the church with grandma.

tranquillisant, e [trãkilizã, ãt] *adj* [paroles, voix, présence] soothing, reassuring. ❖ **tranquillisant** *nm* PHARM tranquillizer 🇬🇧, tranquilizer 🇺🇸.

tranquilliser [3] [trãkilize] *vt* ▸ **tranquilliser qqn** to set sb's mind at rest, to reassure sb. ❖ **se tranquilliser** *vp* (*emploi réfléchi*) to stop worrying, to be reassured / *tranquillise-toi, je ne rentrerai pas en auto-stop* don't worry, I won't hitch-hike home.

tranquillité [trãkilite] *nf* **1.** [calme - d'un lieu] quietness, peacefulness, tranquillity 🇬🇧, tranquility 🇺🇸 ; [- d'une personne] peace, tranquillity 🇬🇧 *sout*, tranquility 🇺🇸 / *les enfants ne me laissent pas un seul moment de tranquillité* the children don't give me a single moment's peace **2.** [sérénité] ▸ **tranquillité d'esprit** peace of mind. ❖ **en toute tranquillité** *loc adv* [sereinement] with complete peace of mind.

transaction [trãzaksjõ] *nf* BOURSE, COMM & ÉCON transaction, deal.

transat [trãzat] ◆ *nm* deck chair. ◆ *nf* SPORT transatlantic race / *la transat en solitaire* the single-handed transatlantic race.

transatlantique [trãzatlãtik] ◆ *adj* transatlantic. ◆ *nm* NAUT (transatlantic) liner.

transbahuter [3] [trãsbayte] *vt fam* to move, to shift, to cart.

transcendant, e [trãsãdã, ãt] *adj* **1.** *fam* [génial] brilliant / *ce n'est pas transcendant !* [livre, film] it's not exactly brilliant! **2.** MATH & PHILOS transcendental.

transcender [3] [trãsãde] *vt* to transcend. ❖ **se transcender** *vpi* to transcend o.s.

transcoder [3] [trãskode] *vt* to transcode.

transcription [trãskripsjõ] *nf* [fait d'écrire - gén] transcription, transcribing, noting (down) ; [- des notes] copying out (in longhand) ; [- un document officiel] recording.

transcrire [99] [trãskrir] *vt* [conversation] to transcribe, to note ou to take down (*sép*) ; [notes] to copy ou to write out (in longhand) (*sép*) ; [dans un registre] to record.

transe [trãs] *nf* [état d'hypnose] trance. ❖ **en transe(s)** *loc adj* & *loc adv* : *être en transe* to be in a trance ▸ **entrer en transe a)** [médium] to go ou to fall into a trance **b)** *fig & hum* to get all worked up.

transférer [18] [trãsfere] *vt* **1.** [prisonnier, sportif] to transfer ; [diplomate] to transfer, to move ; [évêque] to translate ; [magasin, siège social] to transfer, to move ; [fonds] to transfer ; [reliques] to translate / **'succursale transférée au nº 42'** 'our branch is now at no. 42' **2.** INFORM [information] to transfer **3.** PSYCHOL ▸ **transférer qqch sur qqn** to transfer sthg onto sb.

✍ In reformed spelling (see p. 16-18), this verb is conjugated like *semer : il transfèrera, elle transfèrerait.*

transfert [trãsfɛr] *nm* **1.** [gén & COMM] transfer **2.** INFORM transfer **3.** PSYCHOL transference **4.** TÉLÉC ▸ **transfert d'appel** call forwarding.

transfigurer [3] [trãsfigyre] *vt* to transfigure.

transformateur [trãsfɔrmatœr] *nm* ÉLECTR transformer.

transformation [trãsfɔrmasjõ] *nf* **1.** [d'une personnalité, d'un environnement] transformation ; [d'une matière première, d'énergie] conversion **2.** [résultat d'un changement] transformation, alteration, change **3.** SPORT conversion.

transformer [3] [trãsfɔrme] *vt* **1.** [faire changer - bâtiment, personnalité, institution, paysage] to transform, to change, to alter ; [- matière première] to transform, to convert ; [- vêtement] to make over (*sép*), to alter ▸ **transformer qqch en** [faire devenir] to convert sthg into **2.** SPORT to convert. ❖ **se transformer** *vpi* [quartier, personnalité, paysage, institution] to change / *l'environnement se transforme lentement / rapidement* the environment is changing slowly / rapidly / *ce voyage se transformait en cauchemar* the trip was turning into a nightmare.

transfuge [trãsfyʒ] *nmf* MIL & POL renegade, turncoat ; [qui change de camp] defector.

transfuser [3] [trãsfyze] *vt* MÉD [sang] to transfuse / *elle se fait transfuser régulièrement à cause de sa maladie* she has regular blood transfusions because of her illness.

transfusion [trãsfyzjõ] *nf* ▸ **transfusion sanguine** ou **de sang** blood transfusion ▸ **centre de transfusion sanguine** blood transfusion centre ▸ **faire une transfusion à qqn** to give sb a (blood) transfusion.

transgénérationnel, elle [trãsʒenerasjɔnɛl] *adj* transgenerational.

transgénique [trãsʒenik] *adj* transgenic.

transgresser [4] [trãsgrese] *vt* [loi, règle] to infringe, to contravene, to break ; [ordre] to disobey, to go against / *transgresser les interdits* to break the taboos.

transhumance [trãzymãs] *nf* [de troupeaux] seasonal migration, transhumance *spéc.*

transi, e [trãzi] *adj* : *être transi (de froid)* to be chilled to the bone ou to the marrow.

transiger [17] [trãziʒe] *vi* to (come to a) compromise.

transistor [trãzistɔr] *nm* RADIO transistor (radio).

transit [trãzit] *nm* **1.** COMM [de marchandises, de touristes] transit **2.** PHYSIOL ▸ **transit intestinal** intestinal transit. ❖ **en transit** *loc adj* in transit, transitting.

transiter [3] [trãzite] ◆ *vt* [marchandises] to pass through (*sép*), to transit. ◆ *vi* [voyageurs, marchandises] ▸ **transiter par** to pass through in transit.

transition [trãzisjõ] *nf* [entre deux états] transition. ❖ **de transition** *loc adj* [administration, gouvernement] interim (*modif*) ▸ **période de transition** period of transition, transition ou transitional period. ❖ **sans transition** *loc adv* without transition / *elle passait sans transition de l'enthousiasme à la fureur* her mood used to change ou to switch abruptly from enthusiasm to rage.

translucide [trãslysid] *adj* translucent.

transmetteur [trãsmɛtœr] *nm* TÉLÉC transmitter.

transmettre [84] [trãsmɛtr] *vt* **1.** TÉLÉC to transmit **2.** RADIO & TV [émission] to transmit, to relay, to broadcast **3.** PHYS to transmit ▸ **transmettre un mouvement à qqch** to set sthg in motion **4.** [de la main à la main] to hand (on), to pass on (*sép*) / *l'ailier transmet le ballon à l'avant-centre* the wing-forward passes the ball to the centre-forward ; [de génération en génération] to pass on (*sép*), to hand down (*sép*) **5.** [communiquer - information, ordre, remerciement] to pass on (*sép*), to convey *sout* ; [- pli]

to send on *(sép)*, to forward ; [-secret] to pass on *(sép)*
▪ **transmettez mes amitiés / mes respects à votre frère**
a) [à l'oral] please remember me to / convey my respects
to *sout* your brother b) [dans une lettre] please send my
regards / my respects to your brother / *(en usage absolu)*
écrire au journal, qui transmettra write care of the newspaper 6. [faire partager - goût, émotion] to pass on *(sép)*, to
put over *(sép)* / *il m'a transmis son enthousiasme pour
l'art abstrait* he communicated his enthusiasm for abstract
art to me 7. MÉD to transmit, to pass on *(sép)*.

transmis, e [tʀɑ̃smi, iz] pp ⟶ transmettre.

transmissible [tʀɑ̃smisibl] adj MÉD transmittable, transmissible / *c'est transmissible par contact* / *par la salive* it
can be transmitted by (direct) contact / through saliva.

transmission [tʀɑ̃smisjɔ̃] nf 1. AUTO & MÉCAN [pièces]
▪ **organes de transmission** transmission (system) 2. PHYS
[de chaleur, de son] transmission 3. TÉLÉC transmission ;
RADIO & TV [d'une émission] transmission, relaying, broadcasting 4. INFORM ▪ **transmission à large bande** broadband transmission 5. MÉD passing on, transmission,
transmitting 6. [d'une information, d'un ordre] passing
on, conveying ; [d'un secret] passing on ; [d'une lettre] forwarding, sending on ▪ **transmission de pensée** telepathy,
thought transference 7. [legs - d'un bijou, d'une histoire]
handing down, passing on ; [-d'un état d'esprit] passing on
8. DR [de pouvoirs, de biens] transfer. ❖ **transmissions**
nfpl MIL ▪ **les transmissions** ≃ the Signals Corps.

transparaître, transparaitre* [91] [tʀɑ̃spaʀɛtʀ]
vi [lumière, couleur, sentiment] to show ou to filter
through / *son visage ne laissa rien transparaître* (s)he remained impassive, his / her face showed no emotion.

transparence [tʀɑ̃spaʀɑ̃s] nf 1. [propriété - d'une porcelaine, d'une surface] transparence, transparency ; [-d'une
peau] clearness, transparence, transparency ; [-d'un regard,
d'un liquide] transparency, clearness ▪ **regarder qqch par
transparence** to look at sthg against the light / *on voit son
soutien-gorge par transparence* her bra is showing through
2. [caractère public - de transactions, d'une comptabilité]
public accountability.

transparent, e [tʀɑ̃spaʀɑ̃, ɑ̃t] adj 1. [translucide -
porcelaine, papier, surface] transparent ; [-regard, eau] transparent, limpid ; [-vêtement] transparent, see-through ; [lumi-
neux, clair - peau] transparent, clear 2. [public - comptabilité,
transaction] open. ❖ **transparent** nm [de projection]
transparency.

transpercer [16] [tʀɑ̃spɛʀse] vt 1. [suj : flèche, épée]
to pierce (through), to transfix *litt* ▪ **transpercer qqn d'un
coup d'épée** to run sb through with a sword 2. [pénétrer
- suj : pluie] to get through *(insép)* ▪ **un froid qui trans-
perce** piercing cold.

transpiration [tʀɑ̃spiʀasjɔ̃] nf PHYSIOL [sudation] perspiration ; [sueur] perspiration, sweat.

transpirer [3] [tʀɑ̃spiʀe] vi 1. PHYSIOL to perspire, to
sweat / *transpirer des mains / pieds* to have sweaty hands /
feet / *je transpirais à grosses gouttes* great drops ou beads
of sweat were rolling off my forehead ; *fig* [faire des efforts]
to sweat blood, to be hard at it ▪ **transpirer sur qqch** to
sweat over sthg 2. [être divulgué] to leak out, to come to
light.

transplant [tʀɑ̃splɑ̃] nm [avant l'opération] organ for
transplant ; [après l'opération] transplant, transplanted organ.

transplantation [tʀɑ̃splɑ̃tasjɔ̃] nf 1. MÉD [d'un
organe - méthode] transplantation ; [-opération] transplant
▪ **transplantation cardiaque / rénale / hépatique** heart /
kidney / liver transplant 2. AGR & HORT transplantation, trans-
planting.

transplanter [3] [tʀɑ̃splɑ̃te] vt 1. MÉD [organe] to
transplant ; [embryon] to implant 2. AGR & HORT to transplant.

transport [tʀɑ̃spɔʀ] nm 1. [acheminement - de personnes, de marchandises] transport Ⓤ, transportation Ⓤ ;
[-d'énergie] conveyance, conveying ▪ **transport par air** ou
avion air transport ▪ **transport par mer** shipping ▪ **transport par route** road transport ou haulage ▪ **transport
de troupes** a) MIL [acheminement] troop transportation
b) [navire, avion] (troop) carrier, troop transport 2. [émo-
tion] transport, burst / *transport de joie* transport ou burst
of joy ▪ **transport d'enthousiasme** burst ou gush of enthusiasm ▪ **transports amoureux** *litt* ou *hum* amorous
transports. ❖ **transports** nmpl ADMIN transport network
▪ **transports (publics** ou **en commun)** public transport
(U) / *je passe beaucoup de temps dans les transports
pour aller au travail* I spend a lot of time commuting /
prendre les transports en commun to use public transport / *les transports urbains* the urban transport system.
❖ **de transport** loc adj transport Ⓤ *(modif)*, transportation Ⓤ *(modif)*.

transporter [3] [tʀɑ̃spɔʀte] vt 1. [faire changer d'endroit - cargaison, passager, troupes] to carry, to transport, to
convey *sout* ; [-blessé] to move ▪ **transporter des vivres
par avion / par bateau** to fly / to ship food supplies ▪ **transporter qqch par camion** to send sthg by lorry Ⓤ ou by
truck Ⓤ ▪ **transporter qqch par train** to transport sthg
by rail ▪ **transporter qqn à l'hôpital / d'urgence à l'hôpital** to take / to rush sb to hospital ; *fig* [par l'imaginaire] to
take / *le premier acte nous transporte en Géorgie / au
XVIᵉ siècle* the first act takes us to Georgia / takes us back
to the 16th century 2. *litt* [enthousiasmer] to carry away
(sép), to send into raptures / *être transporté de joie* to be
overjoyed ou in transports of delight. ❖ **se transporter**
vpi 1. [se déplacer] to move 2. *fig* [en imagination] to imagine o.s.

transporteur [tʀɑ̃spɔʀtœʀ] nm [entreprise] haulage
contractor, haulier Ⓤ, hauler Ⓤ ; [en langage juridique] carrier ▪ **transporteur aérien** airline company ▪ **transporteur
routier** road haulage contractor, road haulier Ⓤ ou hauler
Ⓤ.

transposer [3] [tʀɑ̃spoze] vt 1. [intervertir - mots] to
switch (round), to transpose 2. [adapter] : *transposer un
sujet antique à l'époque moderne* to adapt an ancient play
to a contemporary setting.

transsexuel, elle [tʀɑ̃ssɛksɥɛl] adj transexual, transsexual.

transvaser [3] [tʀɑ̃svaze] vt to decant.

transversal, e, aux [tʀɑ̃svɛʀsal, o] adj [qui est en
travers - onde, axe] transverse ▪ **coupe transversale** cross-
section ▪ **rue** ou **voie transversale** cross street.

trapèze [tʀapɛz] nm 1. GÉOM trapezium Ⓤ, trapezoid
Ⓤ 2. ANAT [muscle] trapezius 3. LOISIRS trapeze / *faire du
trapèze* to perform on the trapeze.

trapéziste [tʀapezist] nmf trapezist, trapeze artist.

trappage [tʀapaʒ] nm Ⓠᵁᴱᴮᴱᶜ trapping.

trappe [tʀap] nf 1. [piège] trap ; [sur le sol - porte] trap
door ; [-ouverture] hatch ; [d'une scène de théâtre] trap opening ; [pour parachutiste] exit door ▪ **passer à la trappe** to be
whisked away (without trace).

trapu, e [tʀapy] adj 1. [personne] stocky, thickset 2. [bâ-
timent] squat.

traquenard [tʀaknaʀ] nm [machination] snare, trap /
tomber dans un traquenard to fall into a trap.

---

* In reformed spelling (see p. 16-18).

traquer [3] [tʀake] vt **1.** [criminel, fuyard] to track ou to hunt down *(sép)* ; [vedette] to hound ; [erreur] to hunt down *(sép)* **2.** CHASSE [rechercher] to track down *(sép)* ; [rabattre] to drive ▸ **animal traqué** hunted animal.

trash [tʀaʃ] ◆ adj inv trashy / **un film trash** a (deliberately) trashy film. ◆ nm trash / **elle fait dans le trash** she's pretty trashy.

traumatisant, e [tʀomatizɑ̃, ɑ̃t] adj traumatizing.

traumatiser [3] [tʀomatize] vt to traumatize.

traumatisme [tʀomatism] nm trauma, traumatism ▸ **traumatisme crânien** cranial trauma.

travail, aux [tʀavaj, o] nm

A. ACTION 1. [occupation] ▸ **le travail** work / **je finis le travail à cinq heures** I stop ou finish work at five ▸ **le travail à domicile** outwork ▸ **travail d'intérêt général** DR community service ▸ **le travail au noir a)** [occasionnel] undeclared casual work, moonlighting **b)** [comme pratique généralisée] black economy ▸ **le travail temporaire a)** [gén] temporary work **b)** [dans un bureau] temping **2.** [tâches imposées] work ▸ **donner du travail à qqn** to give sb (some) work to do **3.** [tâche déterminée] job ▸ **c'est un travail de bagnard** ou **forçat** it's back-breaking work ou a back-breaking job ▸ **c'est un travail de fourmi** it's a painstaking task **4.** [efforts] (hard) work / **c'est du travail d'élever cinq enfants !** bringing up five children is a lot of (hard) work ! **5.** [exécution] work / **on lui a confié les peintures et elle a fait du bon / mauvais travail** she was responsible for doing the painting and she made a good / bad job of it ▸ **regarde-moi ce travail !** just look at this mess! ▸ **et voilà le travail !** *fam* and Bob's your uncle! **6.** [façonnage] working **7.** [poste] job, occupation, post ; [responsabilité] job ▸ **chercher du** ou **un travail** to be job-hunting, to be looking for a job ▸ **sans travail** unemployed, jobless, out of work **8.** [dans le système capitaliste] labour **9.** [contrainte exercée - par la chaleur, l'érosion] action **10.** PHYSIOL [accouchement] labour UK, labor US / **le travail n'est pas commencé / est commencé** she has not yet gone / has gone into labour ; [activité] work **11.** MÉCAN & PHYS work **12.** PSYCHOL work, working through.

B. RÉSULTAT, EFFET 1. [écrit] piece **2.** [transformation - gén] work ; [modification interne - dans le bois] warping ; [- dans le vin] working.

C. LIEU D'ACTIVITÉ work, workplace / **aller à son travail** to go to (one's) work. ◆ **travaux** nmpl **1.** [tâches] work, working ▸ **gros travaux** heavy work / **j'ai fait des petits travaux** I did some odd jobs / **ils font des travaux après le pont** there are roadworks after the bridge / 'attention, travaux' 'caution, work in progress' ▸ **travaux domestiques** ou **ménagers** housework ▸ **travaux d'aiguille** COUT needlework ▸ **travaux forcés** hard labour ▸ **travaux manuels a)** [gén] arts and crafts **b)** ÉDUC handicraft ▸ **travaux d'utilité collective** ≃ YTS ▸ **les travaux publics** civil engineering **2.** [d'une commission] work / **nous publierons le résultat de nos travaux** we'll publish our findings. ◆ **au travail** loc adv **1.** [en activité] at work, working / **se mettre au travail** to get down ou to set to work **2.** [sur le lieu d'activité] at work, in the workplace. ◆ **de travail** loc adj **1.** [horaire, séance] working ; [vêtement, camarade, permis] work *(modif)* ▸ **contrat de travail** employment contract **2.** [d'accouchement - période] labour *(modif)* ; [- salle] labour *(modif)*, delivery *(modif)*. ◆ **du travail** loc adj [accident, sociologie, législation] industrial ▸ **droit du travail** employment law. ◆ **en travail** adv PHYSIOL in labour / **entrer en travail** to go into ou to start labour.

✏️ Attention ! Le mot **work** est généralement indénombrable lorsqu'il désigne le travail. Il ne s'emploie ni au pluriel ni avec l'article indéfini a dans ce contexte :
C'est un travail épuisant. *It's exhausting work.*
J'ai un petit travail à faire ce matin. *I've got a little job to do this morning* ou *I've got a bit of work to do this morning.*
Ils font des travaux sur la route. *They're doing some work on the road.*

---

travaillé, e [tʀavaje] adj [élaboré - style] polished, laboured UK, labored US ; [- façade, meuble] finely ou elaborately worked ; [- fer] wrought.

travailler [3] [tʀavaje] ◆ vi **1.** [être actif] to work ▸ **travailler dur** to work hard / **travailler à** ou **sur une chanson** to work at ou on a song **2.** [avoir une profession] to work / **j'ai arrêté de travailler à 55 ans** I stopped work ou retired at 55 ▸ **aller travailler** to go to work / **travailler en usine** to work in a factory **3.** [pratiquer son activité - artiste, athlète] to practise, to train ; [- boxeur] to work out, to train / **faire travailler ses jambes** to make one's legs work, to exercise one's legs **4.** [changer de forme, de nature - armature, poutre] to warp ; [- fondations, vin] to work **5.** [suivi d'une préposition] ▸ **travailler à** [succès] to work ou to strive for. ◆ vt **1.** [façonner - bois, bronze, glaise] to work ; [CULIN - mélange, sauce] to stir ▸ **travailler la pâte a)** CULIN to knead ou to work the dough **b)** [peintre] to work the paste / **travailler la terre** to work ou to till *sout* the land **2.** [perfectionner - discours, style] to work on *(insép)*, to polish up *(sép)*, to hone ; [- matière scolaire] to work at ou on *(insép)*, to go over *(insép)* ; [- concerto, scène] to work on, to rehearse ; [SPORT - mouvement] to practise, to work on ; [- balle] to put (a) spin on **3.** [obséder] to worry / **l'idée de la mort le travaillait** (the idea of) death haunted him / **être travaillé par le remords / l'angoisse** to be tormented by remorse / anxiety.

travailleur, euse [tʀavajœʀ, øz] ◆ adj hardworking, industrious. ◆ nm, f **1.** [exerçant un métier] worker ▸ **travailleur intellectuel** white-collar worker ▸ **travailleur manuel** manual ou US blue-collar worker ▸ **travailleur agricole** agricultural ou farm worker ▸ **travailleur à domicile** outworker, homeworker ▸ **travailleur indépendant** self-employed person, freelance worker **2.** ADMIN ▸ **travailleur social** social worker **3.** [personne laborieuse] hard worker / **c'est un gros travailleur** he's a hard worker ou very hardworking.

travailliste [tʀavajist] ◆ adj Labour *(modif)* ▸ **être travailliste** to be a member of the Labour Party ou party. ◆ nmf member of the Labour Party / **les travaillistes se sont opposés à cette mesure** Labour opposed the move.

travée [tʀave] nf **1.** [rangée de sièges, de personnes assises] row **2.** ARCHIT & CONSTR [d'une voûte, d'une nef] bay ; [solivage] girder ; [d'un pont] span.

traveller's cheque, traveller's check [tʀavlœʀʃek] *(pl* **traveller's cheques** *ou* **traveller's checks)** nm traveller's cheque UK, traveler's check US.

travelling [tʀavliŋ] nm CINÉ [déplacement - gén] tracking ; [- sur plate-forme] dollying ▸ **faire un travelling** [caméra, cameraman] to track, to dolly ▸ **travelling avant / arrière / latéral** tracking ou dollying in / out / sideways.

travelo [tʀavlo] nm *tfam* transvestite, drag queen.

travers [tʀavɛʀ] nm **1.** [viande] ▸ **travers (de porc)** spare rib **2.** *sout* [défaut] fault, shortcoming, failing / **elle tombait dans les mêmes travers que ses prédécesseurs** she displayed the same shortcomings as her predecessors

‣ **un petit travers** a minor fault. ❖ **à travers** loc prép through, across / *à travers la fenêtre* / *le plancher* / *les barreaux* through the window / the floor / the bars ‣ **à travers les âges** throughout the centuries ‣ **prendre** ou **passer à travers champs** to go through the fields ou across country / *passer à travers les mailles du filet* PÊCHE & *fig* to slip through the net. ❖ **au travers de** loc prép [en franchissant] through / *passer au travers des dangers* to escape danger. ❖ **de travers** ❖ loc adj crooked. ◆ loc adv **1.** [en biais - couper] askew, aslant ; [-accrocher] askew / *marcher de travers* [ivrogne] to stagger ou to totter along / *j'ai avalé mon pain de travers* the bread went down the wrong way **2.** [mal] : *elle comprend tout de travers !* she gets everything wrong!, she always gets the wrong end of the stick! ‣ **regarder qqn de travers** to give sb a funny look ‣ **tout va de travers** everything's going wrong / *répondre de travers* to give the wrong answer / *il prend tout ce qu'on lui dit de travers* he takes everything the wrong way. ❖ **en travers** loc adv [en largeur] sideways, across, crosswise / *la remorque du camion s'est mise en travers* the truck jack-knifed. ❖ **en travers de** loc prép [en largeur] across ‣ **s'il se met en travers de mon chemin** ou **de ma route** *fig* if he stands in my way.

traversée [traverse] nf [d'une route, d'un pont, d'une frontière] crossing ; [d'une agglomération, d'un pays] going ou getting through ou across ‣ **faire sa traversée du désert** [politicien] to be in the political wilderness.

traverser [3] [traverse] vt **1.** [parcourir - mer, pièce, route] to go across (*insép*), to cross, to traverse *sout* ; [-pont] to go over ou across (*insép*) ; [-tunnel] to go ou to pass through (*insép*) ‣ **traverser qqch à la nage** / **à cheval** / **en voiture** / **en bateau** / **en avion** to swim / to ride / to drive / to sail / to fly across sthg / *traverser une pièce en courant* / *en sautillant* to run / to skip through a room **2.** [s'étirer d'un côté à l'autre de - suj : voie] to cross, to run ou to go across (*insép*) ; [-suj : pont] to cross, to span ; [-suj : tunnel] to cross, to run ou to go under (*insép*) **3.** [vivre - époque] to live ou to go through (*insép*) ; [-difficultés] to pass ou to go through (*insép*) / *son divorce lui a fait traverser une période difficile* (s)he went through a difficult period because of the divorce **4.** [transpercer - suj : épée] to run through (*insép*), to pierce ; [-suj : balle] to go through (*insép*) ; [-suj : pluie, froid] to come ou to go through (*insép*) / *une image me traversa l'esprit* an image passed ou flashed through my mind.

traversier [traversje] nm ◀Québec▶ ferry.

traversin [traversɛ̃] nm [oreiller] bolster.

travesti, e [travesti] adj **1.** [pour tromper] in disguise, disguised ; [pour s'amuser] dressed up (in fancy dress) **2.** THÉÂTRE [comédien] playing a female part. ❖ **travesti** nm **1.** THÉÂTRE actor playing a female part ; [dans un cabaret] female impersonator, drag artist **2.** [homosexuel] transvestite.

travestir [32] [travestir] vt **1.** [pour une fête] to dress up (*insép*) ; [comédien] to cast in a female part ‣ **travestir qqn en** to dress sb up as **2.** [pensées] to misrepresent ; [vérité] to distort ; [propos] to twist. ❖ **se travestir** vp (*emploi réfléchi*) **1.** [homme] to dress as a woman, to put on drag ; [femme] to dress as a man **2.** [pour une fête] to dress up (in fancy dress), to put fancy dress on.

traviole [travjɔl] ❖ **de traviole** ◆ loc adj *fam* [tableau] aslant, crooked ; [dents] crooked, badly set. ◆ loc adv **1.** [en biais] : *marcher de traviole* [ivrogne] to stagger ou to totter along / *tu as mis ton chapeau de traviole* you've put your hat on crooked ou ◀UK▶ skew-whiff **2.** [mal] : *il fait tout de traviole* he can't do anything right / *tout va de traviole* everything's going wrong / *tu comprends toujours tout de traviole* you always get hold of the wrong end of the stick.

trébucher [3] [trebyʃe] vi [perdre l'équilibre] to stumble, to totter, to stagger ‣ **trébucher contre une marche** to trip over a step ‣ **faire trébucher qqn** to trip sb up.

trèfle [trefl] nm **1.** BOT clover, trefoil ‣ **trèfle à quatre feuilles** four-leaved ◀UK▶ ou four-leaf ◀US▶ clover **2.** JEUX clubs / *la dame de trèfle* the Queen of clubs **3.** [emblème irlandais] shamrock.

tréfonds [trefɔ̃] nm *litt* [partie profonde] : *dans le tréfonds de son âme* in the (innermost) depths of her soul.

treille [trej] nf **1.** [vigne] climbing vine **2.** [tonnelle] arbour.

treillis [treji] nm **1.** TEXT canvas **2.** MIL (usual) outfit **3.** [en lattes] trellis ; [en fer] wire-mesh.

treize [trez] ◆ dét thirteen. ◆ nm inv thirteen. **Voir aussi cinq.**

treizième [trezjɛm] adj num & nmf thirteenth. **Voir aussi cinquième.**

trek [trek], **trekking** [trekiŋ] nm trekking ‣ **faire un trek** to go on a trek ‣ **faire du trekking** to go trekking.

tréma [trema] nm diaeresis ◀UK▶, dieresis ◀US▶.

tremblant, e [trɑ̃blɑ̃, ɑ̃t] adj [flamme] trembling, flickering ; [feuilles] fluttering, quivering ; [main, jambes] shaking, trembling, wobbly ; [voix] tremulous, quavering, shaky / *tremblant de peur* trembling ou shaking ou shuddering with fear / *tremblant de froid* trembling ou shivering with cold.

tremblante [trɑ̃blɑ̃t] nf ‣ **tremblante du mouton** scrapie.

tremble [trɑ̃bl] nm aspen.

tremblement [trɑ̃bləmɑ̃] nm **1.** [d'une personne - de froid] shiver ; [-de peur] tremor, shudder / *son corps était secoué* ou *parcouru de tremblements* his whole body was shaking ou trembling **2.** [de la main] shaking, trembling, tremor ; [de la voix] trembling, quavering, tremor ; [des paupières] twitch, twitching ; [des lèvres] trembling, tremble / *avoir des tremblements* to shake ‣ **et tout le tremblement** and all the rest **3.** [du feuillage] trembling, fluttering ; [d'une lueur, d'une flamme] trembling, flickering ; [d'une cloison, de vitres] shaking, rattling. ❖ **tremblement de terre** nm earthquake.

trembler [3] [trɑ̃ble] vi **1.** [personne] : *trembler de peur* to tremble ou to shake ou to shudder with fear / *trembler de froid* to shiver ou to tremble with cold ‣ **trembler de tout son corps** ou **de tous ses membres** to be shaking ou to be trembling all over, to be all of a tremble **2.** [main, jambes] to shake, to tremble ; [voix] to tremble, to shake, to quaver ; [menton] to tremble, to quiver ; [paupière] to twitch **3.** [feuillage] to tremble, to quiver, to flutter ; [flamme, lueur] to flicker ; [gelée] to wobble ; [cloison, vitre] to shake, to rattle ; [terre] to quake, to shake ‣ **la terre a tremblé** there's been an earthquake ou an earth tremor **4.** [avoir peur] to tremble (with fear) ‣ **trembler devant qqn** / **qqch** to stand in fear of sb / sthg ‣ **trembler à la pensée de** / **que a)** [de crainte] to tremble at the thought of / that **b)** [d'horreur] to shiver at the thought of / that.

trémière [tremjɛr] adj f ⟶ **rose.**

trémolo [tremɔlo] nm **1.** MUS tremolo **2.** [de la voix] : *avec des trémolos dans la voix* with a tremor in his voice.

trémousser [3] [tremuse] ❖ **se trémousser** vpi to wiggle, to wriggle / *elle marchait en se trémoussant* she wiggled her hips as she walked.

trempe [trɑ̃p] nf **1.** [caractère] : *une femme de sa trempe* a woman with such moral fibre **2.** *fam* [punition] hiding, thrashing, belting.

trempé, e [trɑ̃pe] adj **1.** [personne, vêtements] soaked, drenched ; [chaussures, jardin] waterlogged / *trempé de* *sueur* soaked with sweat ▶ **trempé jusqu'aux os** ou **comme une soupe** *fam* soaked to the skin, wet through **2.** MÉTALL quenched **3.** [verre] toughened.

tremper [3] [trɑ̃pe] ◆ vt **1.** [plonger - chiffon] to dip, to soak ; [-sucre, tartine] to dip, to dunk ; [-linge, vaisselle] to soak / *je n'ai fait que tremper les lèvres dans le champagne* I just had a taste ou took a sip of the champagne / *je n'ai fait que me tremper les pieds dans l'eau* I only dipped my feet in the water **2.** [mouiller] : *j'ai trempé ma chemise, tellement je transpirais* I sweated so much (that) my shirt got soaked. ◆ vi [vêtement, vaisselle, lentilles] to soak ▶ **faire tremper qqch** : *j'ai fait tremper les draps* I put the sheets in to soak ▶ **faire tremper des haricots** to soak beans, to leave beans to soak / *attention, tes manches trempent dans la soupe* careful, you've got your sleeves in the soup. ❖ **tremper dans** v + prép [être impliqué dans] to be involved in, to have a hand in. ❖ **se tremper** ◆ vpi to have a quick dip. ◆ vpt : *il s'est trempé les pieds en marchant dans l'eau* he stepped into a puddle and got his feet wet.

trempette [trɑ̃pɛt] nf **1.** *fam* ▶ **faire trempette** to have a (quick) dip **2.** Québec CULIN dip.

tremplin [trɑ̃plɛ̃] nm **1.** SPORT [de gymnastique] springboard ; [de plongeon] diving-board, springboard ▶ **tremplin de ski** ski-jump **2.** [impulsion initiale] springboard, stepping stone, launching pad ▶ **servir de tremplin à qqn** to be a springboard for sb.

trentaine [trɑ̃tɛn] nf : *avoir la trentaine* to be thirtyish ou thirty-something.

trente [trɑ̃t] dét & nm inv thirty ▶ **être sur son trente et un** to be dressed up to the nines ▶ **se mettre sur son trente et un** to get all dressed up. **Voir aussi cinq.**

trente-six *(en fin de phrase* [trɑ̃tsis]*, devant consonne ou «h» aspiré* [trɑ̃tsi]*, devant voyelle ou «h» muet* [trɑ̃tsiz]*)* ◆ dét **1.** [gén] thirty six **2.** *fam* [pour exprimer la multitude] umpteen, dozens of / *il n'y a pas trente-six solutions !* there aren't all that many solutions! / *j'ai trente-six mille choses à faire* I've a hundred and one things to do ▶ **voir trente-six chandelles** to see stars. ◆ nm inv *fam* ▶ **tous les trente-six du mois** once in a blue moon. **Voir aussi cinquante.**

trentième [trɑ̃tjɛm] adj num & nmf thirtieth. **Voir aussi cinquième.**

trépas [trepɑ] nm *litt* ▶ **le trépas** death.

trépidant, e [trepidɑ̃, ɑ̃t] adj [animé - époque] frantic, hectic ; [-vie] hectic ; [-danse, rythme] wild, frenzied.

trépied [trepje] nm tripod.

trépigner [3] [trepiɲe] vi to stamp one's feet / *trépigner de colère* to stamp one's feet in anger ▶ **trépigner d'impatience** to be hopping up and down with impatience.

très [trɛ] adv **1.** [avec un adverbe, un adjectif] very / *une entreprise très compétitive* a highly competitive company / *il est très snob* he's a real snob / *je ne l'ai pas vu depuis très longtemps* I haven't seen him for ages ou for a very long time / *très bien, je m'en vais* all right (then) ou very well (then) ou OK (then), I'm going **2.** [dans des locutions verbales] : *avoir très peur / faim* to be very frightened / hungry / *j'ai très envie de lui dire ses quatre vérités* I very much want to give him a few home truths **3.** [employé seul, en réponse] very / *il y a longtemps qu'il est parti ? — non, pas très* has he been gone long? — no, not very.

trésor [trezɔr] nm **1.** [argent] treasure **2.** [chose précieuse] treasure **3.** *(gén au pl)* [grande quantité] ▶ **des trésors de bienfaits / de patience** a wealth of good / patience **4.** *fam* [terme d'affection] : *mon (petit) trésor* my treasure ou darling ou pet **5.** FIN ▶ **le Trésor (public) a)** [service] the French Treasury **b)** [moyens financiers] state finances **6.** HIST exchequer.

trésorerie [trezɔrri] nf **1.** [argent - gén] treasury, finances ; [-d'une entreprise] liquid assets ; [-d'une personne] budget ▶ **ses problèmes de trésorerie** his cash (flow) problems **2.** [gestion] accounts **3.** [bureaux - gouvernementaux] public revenue office ; [-privés] accounts department.

trésorier, ère [trezɔrje, ɛr] nm, f ADMIN treasurer.

tressaillement [tresajmɑ̃] nm [de joie] thrill ; [de peur] shudder, quiver, quivering.

tressaillir [47] [tresajir] vi [personne, animal - de surprise, de peur] to (give a) start ; [-de douleur] to flinch, to wince.

tresse [trɛs] nf [de cheveux, de fils] plait, braid.

tresser [4] [trese] vt [cheveux, rubans, fils] to plait, to braid ; [corbeille] to weave ; [câble] to twist ; [guirlande] to wreathe ▶ **tresser des couronnes à qqn** *fig* to praise sb to the skies.

tréteau, x [treto] nm trestle.

treuil [trœj] nm winch, windlass.

trêve [trɛv] nf **1.** MIL truce **2.** [repos] rest, break / *elle s'est accordée une trêve dans la rédaction de sa thèse* she took a break from writing her thesis. ❖ **trêve de** loc prép enough / *allez, trêve de plaisanteries, où est la clef ?* come on, stop messing about, where's the key?

tri [tri] nm **1.** [de fiches] sorting out, sorting, classifying ; [de renseignements] sorting out, selecting ; [de candidats] picking out, screening / *il faut faire le tri dans ce qu'il dit* you have to sift out the truth in what he says ▶ **le tri sélectif des ordures ménagères** selective sorting of household waste **2.** [postal] sorting.

triangle [trijɑ̃gl] nm **1.** GÉOM triangle **2.** GÉOGR ▶ **le triangle des Bermudes** the Bermuda Triangle **3.** MUS triangle **4.** AUTO ▶ **triangle de présignalisation** hazard warning triangle ▶ **triangle de sécurité** warning triangle. ❖ **en triangle** loc adv in a triangle.

triangulaire [trijɑ̃gylɛr] adj **1.** [gén & GÉOM] triangular ; [tissu, salle] triangular, triangular-shaped **2.** [à trois éléments] triangular ▶ **élection triangulaire** three-cornered election.

triathlon [trijatlɔ̃] nm triathlon.

tribal, e, aux [tribal, o] adj tribal.

tribord [tribɔr] nm starboard ▶ **à tribord** (to) starboard, on the starboard side.

tribu [triby] nf ANTHR, ANTIQ & INTERNET tribe.

tribulations [tribylasjɔ̃] nfpl (trials and) tribulations *litt*.

tribun [tribœ̃] nm [orateur] eloquent (public) speaker.

tribunal, aux [tribynal, o] nm **1.** DR [édifice] court, courthouse ; [magistrats] court, bench ▶ **porter une affaire devant le tribunal** ou **les tribunaux** to take a matter to court ou before the Courts ▶ **traîner qqn devant les tribunaux** to take sb to court ▶ **tribunal administratif** administrative tribunal ▶ **tribunal de commerce a)** [litiges] commercial court **b)** [liquidations] bankruptcy court ▶ **tribunal correctionnel** ≃ magistrates' court UK ; ≃ county court US ▶ **tribunal pour enfants** juvenile court ▶ **tribunal d'exception** special court ▶ **tribunal d'instance** ≃ magistrates' court UK ; ≃ county court US ▶ **tribunal de police** police court **2.** MIL : *passer devant le tribunal militaire* to be court-martialled.

tribune [tribyn] nf **1.** [places - assises] grandstand ; [-debout] stand ; [-dans un stade de football] terraces, bleachers US **2.** [estrade] rostrum, platform, tribune *sout* **3.** [lieu de discussions] forum **4.** PRESSE ▶ **tribune libre a)** [colonne] opinion column **b)** [page] opinions page.

tribut [triby] nm **1.** *litt* tribute / *la population a payé un lourd tribut à l'épidémie* the epidemic took a heavy toll of the population **2.** HIST tribute.

tributaire [tʀibytɛʀ] adj [dépendant] ▶ **tributaire de** reliant ou dependent on.

tricentenaire [tʀisɑ̃tnɛʀ] ◆ adj three-hundred-year-old. ◆ nm tercentenary.

triceps [tʀisɛps] nm triceps (muscle).

triche [tʀiʃ] nf fam ▶ **c'est de la triche** that's cheating.

tricher [3] [tʀiʃe] vi to cheat ▶ **tricher sur le poids** to give short weight.

tricherie [tʀiʃʀi] nf cheating (U).

tricheur, euse [tʀiʃœʀ, øz] nm, f [au jeu, aux examens] cheat, cheater ; [en affaires] trickster, con man ; [en amour] cheat.

tricolore [tʀikɔlɔʀ] ◆ adj **1.** [aux couleurs françaises] red, white and blue **2.** [français] French ▶ **l'équipe tricolore** the French team **3.** [à trois couleurs] three-coloured UK, three-colored US. ◆ nm French player ▶ **les tricolores** the French (team).

tricot [tʀiko] nm **1.** [technique] knitting / **faire du tricot** to knit, to do some knitting **2.** [étoffe] knitted ou worsted fabric **3.** VÊT [gén] knitted garment ; [pull] jumper UK, pullover, sweater ; [gilet] cardigan ▶ **tricot de corps** ou **de peau** vest UK, undershirt US. ◆ **en tricot** loc adj [cravate, bonnet] knitted.

tricoter [3] [tʀikɔte] ◆ vt [laine, maille] to knit ; [vêtement] to knit (up) ▶ **tricoté (à la) main** hand-knitted. ◆ vi TEXT to knit / **tricoter à la machine** to machine-knit.

tricycle [tʀisikl] nm tricycle.

trier [10] [tʀije] vt **1.** [sortir d'un lot - fruits] to pick (out) ; [- photos, candidats] to select ▶ **ses amis sont triés sur le volet** his friends are hand-picked **2.** [répartir par catégories - lettres] to sort (out) (sép) ; [- œufs] to grade ; [- lentilles] to pick over (sép).

trifouiller [3] [tʀifuje] vt fam [papiers] to mess ou to jumble up (sép). ◆ **trifouiller dans** v + prép fam [fouiller dans - papiers, vêtements] to rummage, to rifle through.

trilingue [tʀilɛ̃g] adj trilingual.

trilogie [tʀilɔʒi] nf ANTIQ & LITTÉR trilogy.

trimaran [tʀimaʀɑ̃] nm trimaran.

trimbal(l)er [3] [tʀɛ̃bale] vt fam **1.** [porter] to lug ou to cart around **2.** [emmener] to take / **le pauvre gosse s'est fait trimballer toute la journée de musée en musée** the poor kid was dragged about from museum to museum all day long **3.** EXPR **qu'est-ce qu'elle trimballe !** tfam she's as thick as two short planks! UK, what a lamebrain! US. ◆ **se trimbal(l)er** vpi fam **1.** [aller et venir] to go about **2.** [se déplacer] to go / **elle se trimballe toujours avec son frère** she drags that brother of hers around with her everywhere.

trimer [3] [tʀime] vi fam to slave away.

trimestre [tʀimɛstʀ] nm **1.** ÉDUC term UK, trimester US, quarter US ▶ **premier trimestre** Autumn term ▶ **deuxième trimestre** Spring term ▶ **troisième trimestre** Summer term **2.** [trois mois] quarter / **payer tous les trimestres** to pay on a quarterly basis.

trimestriel, elle [tʀimɛstʀijɛl] adj **1.** ÉDUC [bulletin] end-of-term ; [réunion] termly **2.** [réunion, magazine, loyer] quarterly.

tringle [tʀɛ̃gl] nf **1.** [pour pendre] rail ▶ **tringle à rideaux** curtain rail **2.** [pour tenir] rod.

trinité [tʀinite] nf **1.** RELIG ▶ **la Trinité** a) the (Holy) Trinity b) [fête] Trinity Sunday **2.** litt [trois éléments] trinity.

trinquer [3] [tʀɛ̃ke] vi **1.** [choquer les verres] to clink glasses ▶ **trinquer à qqch / qqn** to drink (a toast) to sthg / sb **2.** fam [subir un dommage] to get the worst of it, to get it in the neck, to cop it UK / **c'est lui qui va trinquer** he'll be the one who suffers.

trio [tʀijo] nm [trois personnes] trio, threesome.

triomphal, e, aux [tʀijɔ̃fal, o] adj [entrée] triumphant ; [victoire, succès] resounding ; [arc, procession] triumphal.

triomphalisme [tʀijɔ̃falism] nm overconfidence.

triomphe [tʀijɔ̃f] nm **1.** [d'une armée, d'un groupe] triumph, victory ; [d'un artiste, d'une idée] triumph / **l'album est un triomphe** the album is a great success **2.** [ovation] ▶ **faire un triomphe à qqn** to give sb a triumphant welcome.

triompher [3] [tʀijɔ̃fe] vi **1.** [armée] to triumph ; [parti] to win (decisively) **2.** [idée] to triumph, to prevail ; [bêtise, corruption, racisme] to be rife **3.** [artiste] to be a great success **4.** [jubiler] to rejoice, to exult litt, to gloat.

trip [tʀip] nm fam **1.** arg crime trip **2.** EXPR **il est dans son trip écolo** he's going through a green phase at the moment.

tripatouiller [3] [tʀipatuje] fam vt **1.** [truquer - document] to tamper with (insép) ; [- chiffres, résultats] to fiddle UK, to doctor US / **tripatouiller les comptes** to cook the books / **tripatouiller les statistiques** to massage the figures **2.** [modifier - textes] to alter.

tripes [tʀip] nfpl **1.** CULIN : **des tripes** tripe **2.** fam ANAT guts, insides / **la peur m'a pris aux tripes** fig I was petrified with fear.

triple [tʀipl] ◆ adj **1.** [à trois éléments] triple ▶ **en triple exemplaire** in triplicate ▶ **triple saut** triple jump ▶ **triple saut périlleux** triple somersault **2.** [trois fois plus grand] treble, triple **3.** fam [en intensif] : **triple imbécile !** you stupid idiot! ◆ nm : **neuf est le triple de trois** nine is three times three / **on a payé le triple** we paid three times that amount. ◆ **en triple** loc adv [copier, signer] in triplicate.

tripler [3] [tʀiple] ◆ vt **1.** [dépenses, dose] to treble, to triple **2.** ÉDUC : **tripler une classe** to repeat a year UK ou class US for a second time, to do a year UK ou class US for a third time. ◆ vi to treble, to triple.

triplés, ées [tʀiple] nmf pl triplets.

triplex [tʀipleks] nm QUÉBEC [appartement] three-storey flat UK, triplex (apartment) US.

tripoter [3] [tʀipɔte] fam ◆ vt **1.** [toucher distraitement - crayon, cheveux] to twiddle, to play ou to fiddle with **2.** [palper - fruit, objet] to handle, to finger / **ne tripote pas ton bouton** don't keep picking at ou touching your spot **3.** [personne] to fondle, to grope. ◆ vi [fouiller] to rummage ou to root around, to root about. ◆ **se tripoter** vp (emploi réfléchi) fam to play with o.s.

trique [tʀik] nf [bâton] cudgel.

trisomique [tʀizomik] ◆ adj ▶ **enfant trisomique** Down's syndrome child. ◆ nmf Down's syndrome child.

triste [tʀist] adj **1.** [déprimé - personne] sad ; [- sourire, visage] sad, unhappy, sorrowful / **d'un air triste** bleakly ▶ **triste comme la mort** utterly dejected ▶ **faire triste figure** ou **mine** litt to look pitiful **2.** [pénible] sad, unhappy ▶ **son triste sort** his sad ou unhappy fate **3.** [attristant] sad ▶ **c'est pas triste !** fam what a hoot ou laugh! **4.** [terne - couleur] drab, dull ; [morne - rue, saison] bleak ▶ **une ville triste à pleurer** a dreadfully bleak town **5.** (avant nom) [déplorable] deplorable, sorry, sad / **elle était dans un triste état** she was in a sorry state ; [méprisable] ▶ **un triste sire** an unsavoury character.

tristement [tʀistəmɑ̃] adv **1.** [en étant triste] sadly **2.** [de manière pénible] sadly, regrettably ▶ **tristement célèbre** notorious.

tristesse [tʀistɛs] nf [sentiment] sadness.

trithérapie [tʀiteʀapi] nf combination therapy.

triton [tʀitɔ̃] nm ZOOL [amphibien] newt, triton spéc ; [gastropode] triton, Triton's shell.

triturer [3] [tʀityʀe] vt **1.** [pétrir -bras, corps, pâte] to knead **2.** [manipuler -gants, breloque] to fiddle with. ❖ **se triturer** vpt ▸ **se triturer les méninges** ou **la cervelle** fam to rack one's brains.

trivial, e, aux [tʀivjal, o] adj **1.** [grossier] crude, offensive **2.** [banal] trivial, trite / *un détail trivial* a minor detail.

> ⚠ L'adjectif anglais **trivial** signifie « insignifiant », « dérisoire » et non trivial (sauf dans le domaine des mathématiques).

troc [tʀɔk] nm **1.** [système économique] barter ▸ **(économie de) troc** barter economy **2.** [échange] swap.

troène [tʀɔɛn] nm privet.

trognon [tʀɔɲɔ̃] nm [d'une pomme] core ; [d'un chou] stem.

trois [tʀwa] ◆ dét **1.** three **2.** [exprimant une approximation] ▸ **dans trois minutes** in a couple of minutes / *il n'a pas dit trois mots* he hardly said a word. ◆ nm **1.** [chiffre] three **2.** JEUX three. **Voir aussi cinq.**

troisième [tʀwazjem] ◆ adj num third. ◆ nmf third. ◆ nf **1.** ÉDUC year nine 🇬🇧, eighth grade 🇺🇸 **2.** AUTO third gear. **Voir aussi cinquième.**

troisièmement [tʀwazjemmɑ̃] adv thirdly, in the third place.

trois-mâts [tʀwama] nm three-master.

trois-pièces [tʀwapjɛs] nm inv [costume] three-piece suit.

trois-portes [tʀwapɔʀt] nf inv [voiture] two-door hatchback.

trois-quarts [tʀwakaʀ] nm inv **1.** [manteau] three-quarter (length) coat **2.** SPORT three-quarter ▸ **trois-quarts aile / centre** wing / centre (three-quarter).

troll, trole* [tʀɔl] nm MYTH troll.

trombe [tʀɔ̃b] nf MÉTÉOR [sur mer] waterspout ; [sur terre] whirlwind ▸ **trombe d'eau** downpour. ❖ **en trombe** loc adv briskly and noisily ▸ **elle entra en trombe** she burst in / *la voiture passa en trombe* the car shot past / *partir en trombe* to shoot off.

trombine [tʀɔ̃bin] nf tfam [visage] mug ; [physionomie] look / *si tu avais vu sa trombine !* you should have seen his face!

trombone [tʀɔ̃bɔn] nm **1.** MUS [instrument] trombone ; [musicien] trombonist, trombone (player) ▸ **trombone à coulisse / pistons** slide / valve trombone **2.** [agrafe] paper clip.

trompe [tʀɔ̃p] nf **1.** ENTOM & ZOOL [d'éléphant] trunk, proboscis spéc ; [de papillon] proboscis ; [de tapir] snout, proboscis spéc **2.** ANAT ▸ **trompe utérine** ou **de Fallope** Fallopian tube.

trompe-la-mort [tʀɔ̃plamɔʀ] nmf daredevil.

trompe-l'œil [tʀɔ̃plœj] nm inv ART [style] trompe l'œil. ❖ **en trompe-l'œil** loc adj ART ▸ **peinture en trompe-l'œil** trompe l'œil painting.

tromper [3] [tʀɔ̃pe] vt **1.** [conjoint] to be unfaithful to, to deceive sout, to betray sout / *elle le trompe avec Thomas* she's cheating on him with Thomas **2.** [berner, flouer] to dupe, to cheat / *on m'a trompé sur la qualité* I was misinformed as to the quality **3.** [échapper à] ▸ **tromper la vigilance de qqn** to elude sb ▸ **tromper l'ennui** to stave off boredom **4.** [induire en erreur] to mislead ; (en usage absolu) : *c'est un signe qui ne trompe pas* it's a sure sign **5.** litt [décevoir] ▸ **tromper l'espoir de qqn** to disappoint sb **6.** [apaiser -faim] to appease. ❖ **se tromper** vpi **1.** [commettre une erreur] to make a mistake / *je me suis trompé de 3 euros* I was 3 euros out 🇬🇧 ou off 🇺🇸

2. [prendre une chose pour une autre] ▸ **se tromper de jour** to get the day wrong ▸ **se tromper d'adresse** pr to go to the wrong address ▸ **se tromper d'adresse** ou **de porte** fam & fig: *si c'est un complice que tu cherches, tu te trompes d'adresse* if it's an accomplice you want, you've come to the wrong address **3.** [s'illusionner] to make a mistake, to be wrong ▸ **se tromper sur les motifs de qqn** to misunderstand sb's motives / *si je ne me trompe* if I'm not mistaken.

tromperie [tʀɔ̃pʀi] nf [supercherie] deception.

trompette [tʀɔ̃pɛt] nf [instrument] trumpet.

trompette-des-morts [tʀɔ̃pɛtdemɔʀ] (pl trompettes-des-morts), **trompette-de-la-mort** [tʀɔ̃pɛt-dəlamɔʀ] (pl **trompettes-de-la-mort**) nf BOT horn of plenty.

trompettiste [tʀɔ̃petist] nmf trumpet player, trumpet, trumpeter.

trompeur, euse [tʀɔ̃pœʀ, øz] adj [signe, air, apparence] deceptive, misleading.

tronc [tʀɔ̃] nm **1.** BOT trunk **2.** ANAT [d'un être humain] trunk, torso ; [d'un animal] trunk, barrel ; [d'un nerf, d'une artère] trunk, truncus spéc **3.** [boîte pour collectes] offertory box. ❖ **tronc commun** nm [d'une famille] common stock, ancestry ; ENS compulsory subjects, core curriculum.

tronche [tʀɔ̃ʃ] nf fam [visage] face ; [expression] look / *t'aurais vu la tronche qu'il faisait !* you should have seen the look on his face! / *ne fais pas cette tronche !* don't look so miserable!

tronçon [tʀɔ̃sɔ̃] nm **1.** [morceau coupé] segment, section **2.** [d'un texte] part, section.

tronçonner [3] [tʀɔ̃sɔne] vt to cut ou to chop (into sections) / *tronçonner un arbre* to saw a tree (into sections).

tronçonneuse [tʀɔ̃sɔnøz] nf motor saw.

trône [tʀon] nm [siège, pouvoir] throne / *monter sur le trône* to ascend ou to come to the throne.

trôner [3] [tʀone] vi **1.** [personne] to sit enthroned hum ou in state **2.** [bouquet, œuvre d'art] to sit prominently ou imposingly / *son portrait trônait dans le salon* his portrait was displayed in a prominent position in the drawing room.

tronquer [3] [tʀɔ̃ke] vt [phrase, récit] to shorten.

trop [tʀo] adv **1.** [excessivement -devant un adjectif, un adverbe] too ; [-avec un verbe] too much / *de la viande trop cuite* overcooked meat ▸ **elle sort trop peu** she doesn't go out enough / *on a trop chargé la voiture* we've overloaded the car / *tu manges (beaucoup) trop* you eat (far) too much / *ne fais pas trop le difficile* don't be too awkward / *il ne le sait que trop* he knows (it) only too well ; [en corrélation avec 'pour'] : *tu es trop intelligent pour croire cela* you're too intelligent to believe that / *trop beau pour être vrai* too good to be true ▸ **il est trop, lui !** fam he really is too much! **2.** [emploi nominal] : *ne demande pas trop* don't ask for too much / *prends la dernière part — non, c'est trop* have the last slice — no, it's too much ▸ **trop c'est trop !** enough is enough! **3.** [très, beaucoup] so / *ce bébé est trop mignon !* this baby is so cute! ▸ **c'est trop bête !** how stupid! / *vous êtes trop aimable* how very kind of you, you're very ou too kind ; [dans des phrases négatives] : *il n'est pas trop content* he's not very happy ▸ **je ne sais trop** I'm not sure ▸ **sans trop savoir pourquoi** without really knowing why. ❖ **de trop** loc adv : *j'ai payé 1 euro de trop* I paid 1 euro too much / *il y a une assiette de trop* there's one plate too many / *votre remarque était de trop* that remark of yours was uncalled for / *deux jours ne seront pas de trop pour tout terminer* two days should just about be enough to finish everything ▸ **se sentir de trop** to feel that one is in the way. ❖ **en trop** loc adv : *tu as des vêtements en trop à me donner ?*

have you got any spare clothes to give me? / *il y a un verre en trop* there's a ou one glass too many / *se sentir en trop* to feel in the way. ❖ **par trop** loc adv *litt* much too, far too. ❖ **trop de** loc dét **1.** [suivi d'un nom non comptable] too much ; [suivi d'un nom comptable] too many / *ils ont trop d'argent* they've got too much money / *il y a beaucoup trop de monde* there are far too many people ; [en corrélation avec 'pour'] : *j'ai trop de soucis pour me charger des vôtres* I've too many worries of my own to deal with yours ; *(comme nom)* : *le trop d'énergie des enfants* the children's excess ou surplus energy **2.** EXPR **en faire trop a)** [travailler] to overdo things **b)** [pour plaire] to overdo it.

trophée [tʀɔfe] nm trophy.

tropical, e, aux [tʀɔpikal, o] adj tropical.

tropique [tʀɔpik] nm ASTRON & GÉOGR tropic. ❖ **tropiques** nmpl GÉOGR ▶ **les tropiques** the tropics ▶ **sous les tropiques** in the tropics.

trop-perçu [tʀɔpɛʀsy] *(pl* **trop-perçus)** nm overpayment (of taxes), excess payment (of taxes).

trop-plein [tʀɔplɛ̃] *(pl* **trop-pleins)** nm **1.** [de forces, d'émotion] overflow, surplus / *ton trop-plein d'énergie* your surplus energy **2.** [d'eau, de graines] overflow ; [de vin] surplus.

troquer [3] [tʀɔke] vt **1.** [échanger] to exchange, to swop, to swap / *je troquerais bien mon manteau contre le tien* I wouldn't mind swapping coats with you **2.** COMM to barter, to trade / *ils troquent les fruits contre de la soie* they trade fruit for silk.

troquet [tʀɔke] nm *fam* bar.

trot [tʀo] nm ÉQUIT trot, trotting ▶ **trot assis / enlevé** sitting / rising trot. ❖ **au trot** loc adv *fam* [vite] on the double / *allez, et au trot !* come on, jump to it!

trotte [tʀɔt] nf *fam : il y a une bonne trotte d'ici à la plage* it's a fair distance ou it's quite a step from here to the beach.

trotter [3] [tʀɔte] vi **1.** [cheval] to trot **2.** [marcher vite - enfant] to trot ou to run along ; [-souris] to scurry along **3.** *fam* [marcher beaucoup] to do a lot of walking, to cover quite a distance on foot **4.** *fig : une idée qui me trotte dans la tête* an idea which keeps running through my mind.

trotteur, euse [tʀɔtœʀ, øz] nm, f trotter. ❖ **trotteurs** nmpl [chaussures] flat shoes. ❖ **trotteuse** nf [d'une montre] second hand.

trottiner [3] [tʀɔtine] vi **1.** [souris] to scurry (along) ; [cheval] to jog-trot (along) **2.** [personne] to trot along.

trottinette [tʀɔtinɛt] nf [patinette] scooter.

trottoir [tʀɔtwaʀ] nm **1.** [bord de chaussée] pavement 🇬🇧, sidewalk 🇺🇸 ▶ **faire le trottoir** to walk the streets *euphém* **2.** TECHNOL ▶ **trottoir roulant** travelator, travolator, moving walkway.

trou [tʀu] nm **1.** [cavité - gén] hole ; [-sur la route] pothole ▶ **faire un trou dans les économies de qqn** to make a hole in sb's savings / *j'ai eu un trou (de mémoire) en scène* I dried up on stage ▶ **trou noir a)** ASTRON black hole **b)** *fig* depths of despair ▶ **trou normand** glass of Calvados taken between courses ▶ **un trou de souris** a tiny place / *elle a fait son trou dans l'édition* she has made a nice little niche for herself in publishing **2.** [ouverture - dans une clôture, dans les nuages] hole, gap ; [-d'une aiguille] eye ; [-dans du cuir] eyelet / *regarder par le trou de la serrure* to watch through the keyhole **3.** [déchirure] hole, tear, rip / *il a fini par faire un trou à son pull à l'endroit du coude* he finally wore a hole in the elbow of his jumper **4.** [moment] gap ▶ **un trou dans son emploi du temps a)** [élève] a free period **b)** [dans la reconstitution d'un crime] *a period of time during which one's movements cannot be accounted*

for **5.** *fam* [endroit reculé] (little) place, hole *péj*, one-horse-town *hum* / *il n'est jamais sorti de son trou* he's never been away from home **6.** *fam* [prison] ▶ **être au trou** to be inside **7.** *fam* [déficit] deficit / *un trou dans le budget* a budget deficit / *le trou de la Sécurité sociale* the deficit in the French Social Security budget **8.** ANAT hole, foramen *spéc* ▶ **trous de nez** nostrils ▶ **trou du cul** *vulg* ou **de balle** *vulg* arsehole 🇬🇧, asshole 🇺🇸 ▶ **il n'a pas les yeux en face des trous a)** *fam* [il n'est pas observateur] he's pretty unobservant **b)** [il est à moitié endormi] he's still half asleep **9.** AÉRON ▶ **trou d'air** air pocket **10.** GOLF hole / *faire un trou* to get a hole.

troublant, e [tʀublɑ̃, ɑ̃t] adj [événement] disturbing, unsettling, disquieting ; [question, ressemblance] disconcerting.

trouble[1] [tʀubl] ◆ adj **1.** [eau] cloudy, murky ; [vin] cloudy ; [image] blurred ; [photo] blurred, out-of-focus ; [regard, verre] misty, dull **2.** [confus] vague, unclear, imprecise **3.** [équivoque] equivocal, ambiguous ; [peu honnête] dubious. ◆ adv through a blur / *je vois trouble* everything ou my vision is blurred.

trouble[2] [tʀubl] nm **1.** [sentiment - de gêne] confusion, embarrassment ; [-de perplexité] confusion ; [-de peine] distress, turmoil / *la nouvelle sema le trouble dans les esprits* the news sowed confusion in people's minds ou threw people's minds into confusion **2.** MÉD disorder ▶ **trouble caractériel** emotional disorder ▶ **un trouble du comportement** a behaviour problem ▶ **troubles du langage** speech disorders ▶ **troubles de la personnalité a)** personality problems **b)** PSYCHOL personality disorders ▶ **troubles visuels** ou **de la vue** eye trouble **3.** DR disturbance (of rights). ❖ **troubles** nmpl [agitation sociale] unrest, disturbances ▶ **troubles politiques** political unrest ▶ **troubles sociaux** social unrest.

trouble-fête [tʀublǝfɛt] nmf killjoy, spoilsport / *je ne veux pas jouer les trouble-fête, mais…* I don't want to be a spoilsport ou to put a damper on the proceedings but…

troubler [3] [tʀuble] vt **1.** [eau] to cloud **2.** [rendre moins net] to blur, to dim, to cloud ▶ **troubler la vue de qqn** to blur ou to cloud sb's vision **3.** [sommeil] to disturb ; [paix] to disturb, to disrupt ; [silence] to break ; [digestion] to upset **4.** [fête, réunion] to disrupt ; [plan] to upset, to disrupt ▶ **une époque troublée** troubled times ▶ **troubler l'ordre public** to cause a breach of the peace 🇬🇧, to disturb the peace **5.** [déconcerter] to confuse, to disconcert / *un détail nous trouble encore* one detail is still baffling us **6.** [mettre en émoi, impressionner] to disturb / *ce film m'a vraiment troublé* I found the film quite disturbing **7.** [sexuellement] to arouse. ❖ **se troubler** vpi **1.** [eau] to become cloudy ou turbid *litt* ; [vue] to become blurred **2.** [perdre contenance] to get confused / *continuez sans vous troubler* carry on and don't let yourself get ruffled.

troué, e [tʀue] adj : *un vieux châle troué* a tatty 🇬🇧 ou raggedy 🇺🇸 old shawl ▶ **la chaussette est trouée** the sock's got a hole in it.

trouée [tʀue] nf [ouverture] gap.

trouer [3] [tʀue] vt **1.** [percer - carton, tissu] to make a hole in ; [-tôle] to pierce ; [-cloison] to make ou to bore a hole in **2.** *sout* [traverser] to pierce.

trouillard, e [tʀujaʀ, aʀd] *tfam* ◆ adj chicken-livered, chicken-hearted. ◆ nm, f chicken.

trouille [tʀuj] nf *tfam* fear, fright / *ça va lui flanquer* ou *ficher la trouille* it'll scare the living daylights out of her ▶ **j'avais une trouille bleue** I was scared stiff ou to death.

troupe [tʀup] nf **1.** MIL [formation, régiment] troop ▶ **troupes de choc** shock troops **2.** THÉÂTRE company, troupe, theatre 🇬🇧 ou theater 🇺🇸 group.

troupeau, x [tʀupo] nm [de vaches] herd ; [de moutons] flock ; [d'oies] gaggle ; [d'éléphants] herd.

trousse [tʀus] nf [étui] case ; [d'écolier] pencil case ▸ **trousse de maquillage** make-up bag ▸ **trousse de médecin** medical bag ▸ **trousse à outils** tool kit ▸ **trousse de secours** first-aid kit ▸ **trousse de toilette** sponge bag. ❖ **aux trousses de** loc prép ▸ **avoir qqn à ses trousses** to be followed by sb / *il a la police aux trousses* the police are after him.

trousseau, x [tʀuso] nm **1.** [assortiment] ▸ **trousseau (de clés)** bunch of keys **2.** [d'une mariée] trousseau *(including linen)*.

trouvaille [tʀuvaj] nf [objet, lieu] find ; [idée, méthode] brainwave ; [expression] coinage.

trouvé, e [tʀuve] adj **1.** [découvert] ⟶ **enfant 2.** ⟨EXPR⟩ **bien trouvé** [original] well-chosen, apposite / *voilà une réponse bien trouvée !* that's a (pretty) good answer! ▸ **tout trouvé** ready-made.

trouver [3] [tʀuve]
vt

⟨**A. APRÈS UNE RECHERCHE** 1.⟩ [objet perdu, personne, emploi] to find ; [empreintes, trésor] to find, to discover ; [pétrole] to strike, to find / *où pourrais-je la trouver mardi ?* where could I find ou contact her on Tuesday? / *il faut que je trouve 1 000 euros avant demain* I must get hold of ou find 1,000 euros before tomorrow **2.** [détecter] to find, to discover / *ils lui ont trouvé quelque chose au sein* they found a lump in her breast **3.** [acheter] to find, to get / *du safran, on en trouve dans les épiceries fines* you can get ou find saffron in good delicatessens **4.** [rendre visite à] ▸ **aller trouver qqn** to go to sb, to go and see sb.

⟨**B. INVOLONTAIREMENT** 1.⟩ [tomber sur - personne, lettre, trésor] to find / *j'ai trouvé ce livre en faisant du rangement* I found ou came across this book while I was tidying up / *si je m'attendais à te trouver là !* fancy meeting you here! ▸ **trouver qqch par hasard** to chance ou to stumble upon sthg / *on l'a trouvé mort dans la cuisine* he was found dead in the kitchen ▸ **trouver à qui parler** [un confident] to find a friend **2.** [surprendre] to find, to catch / *je l'ai trouvé fouillant* ou *qui fouillait dans mes tiroirs* I found ou I caught him searching through my drawers.

⟨**C. PAR L'ESPRIT, LA VOLONTÉ** 1.⟩ [inventer - prétexte, méthode, etc.] to find / *où as-tu trouvé cette idée ?* where did you get that idea from? ▸ **trouver qqch à répondre** to find an answer **2.** [deviner - solution] to find ; [-réponse, mot de passe] to find (out), to discover ; [-code] to break, to crack / *j'ai trouvé !* I've got it!, I know! **3.** [parvenir à] to find / *ça y est, j'ai trouvé ce que je voulais te dire !* I know what I wanted to tell you! ▸ **je n'arrivais pas à trouver mes mots** I couldn't find the right words, I was lost for words ▸ **trouver à :** *trouver à se loger* to find accommodation ou somewhere to live **4.** [se ménager] to find / *trouver le temps de lire* to find time to read **5.** [ressentir] to find ▸ **trouver du plaisir à (faire) qqch** to take pleasure in (doing) sthg, to enjoy (doing) sthg.

⟨**D. AVOIR COMME OPINION** 1.⟩ [juger, estimer] to find, to think ▸ **trouver qqch remarquable** to find sthg remarkable, to think that sthg is remarkable / *comment me trouves-tu dans cette robe ?* how do you like me in this dress? ▸ **trouver que** to think ou to find that / *il est prétentieux — je ne trouve pas* he's pretentious — I don't think so / *tu trouves ?* do you think so? **2.** [reconnaître] ▸ **trouver qqch à qqn / qqch :** *je lui trouve du charme* I think he's got charm / *mais enfin, qu'est-ce que tu lui trouves, à ce type ?* fam for goodness' sake, what do you see in this guy? ❖ **se trouver**

◆ v impers [le hasard fait que] : *il se trouve que... as it happens... / il se trouve que quelqu'un vous a vu dans mon bureau* as it happens, somebody saw you in my office. ◆ vp *(emploi réfléchi)* [s'estimer] : *je me trouve trop mince* I

think I'm too thin. ◆ vp *(emploi passif)* to be found, to exist / *de bons artisans, cela se trouve difficilement* it's not easy to find ou to get good craftsmen. ◆ vpi **1.** [en un lieu, une circonstance - personne] to be ; [-bâtiment, ville] to be (situated) ou located / *je me trouvais là par hasard* I just happened to be there / *où se trouve la gare ?* where's the station? ▸ **se trouver sur** [figurer] to appear ou to be shown on ; [résider - intérêt, problème] to be, to lie **2.** [dans une situation] to find o.s., to be ▸ **se trouver dans l'impossibilité de faire qqch** to find o.s. ou to be unable to do sthg ▸ **se trouver dans l'obligation de faire qqch** to have no option but to do sthg **3.** [se sentir] to feel / *je me suis trouvé bête d'avoir crié* I felt stupid for having screamed ▸ **se trouver bien / mieux a)** [du point de vue de la santé] to feel good / better **b)** [avec quelqu'un] to feel at ease / more at ease **c)** [dans un vêtement élégant] to feel (that one looks) good / better ▸ **se trouver mal** [s'évanouir] to pass out, to faint **4.** [se réaliser] to find o.s. **5.** [exprime la fortuité d'un événement, d'une situation] to happen ▸ **si ça se trouve** fam maybe.

truand [tʀyɑ̃] nm crook, gangster.

truander [3] [tʀyɑ̃de] fam ◆ vt to con, to swindle / *se faire truander* to be ou get conned. ◆ vi [aux examens] to cheat.

truc [tʀyk] nm fam **1.** [astuce] trick / *j'ai un truc pour rentrer sans payer* I know a way of getting in without paying **2.** CINÉ & THÉÂTRE (special) effect, trick **3.** [chose précise] thing / *je pense à un truc* I've just thought of something / *j'ai plein de trucs à faire* I've got lots to do ; péj thing, business, stuff ▸ **ce n'est pas / c'est mon truc** it's not / it's my cup of tea / *le rock, c'est pas mon truc* rock is not my (kind of) thing, rock doesn't turn me on ▸ **l'écologie, c'est vraiment son truc** he's really into environmental issues **4.** [objet dont on a oublié le nom] thing, thingie ⟨UK⟩, whachamacallit **5.** [personne dont on a oublié le nom] ▸ **Truc** What's-his-name (What's-her-name), Thingie ⟨UK⟩.

trucage [tʀykaʒ] = **truquage**.

truchement [tʀyʃmɑ̃] nm : *par le truchement de son ami* through ou via his friend.

trucider [3] [tʀyside] vt fam to kill / *une heure de retard, on va se faire trucider !* we're an hour late, they'll kill us!

truculent, e [tʀykylɑ̃, ɑ̃t] adj [personne] colourful ⟨UK⟩, colorful ⟨US⟩, larger than life ; [prose] vivid, colourful ⟨UK⟩, colorful ⟨US⟩ ; [plaisanterie] racy.

truelle [tʀyɛl] nf [du maçon] trowel.

truffe [tʀyf] nf **1.** [champignon] truffle **2.** [friandise] (chocolate) truffle **3.** [de chien, de chat] nose.

truffer [3] [tʀyfe] vt **1.** CULIN to garnish with truffles **2.** [emplir] to fill / *truffé de mines* riddled with mines ▸ **truffé d'anecdotes** peppered with anecdotes.

truie [tʀɥi] nf ZOOL sow.

truite [tʀɥit] nf trout ▸ **truite arc-en-ciel / saumonée** rainbow / salmon trout.

truquage [tʀykaʒ] nm CINÉ [action] (use of) special effects ; [résultat] special effect.

truquer [3] [tʀyke] vt [élection, statistiques] to rig ; [entretien] to set up (sép) ; [tableau] to fake.

trust [tʀœst] nm **1.** ÉCON trust **2.** [entreprise] corporation.

tsar [tsaʀ, dzaʀ] nm tsar, czar.

tsé-tsé (pl **tsé-tsé**), **tsétsé*** [tsetse] nf tsetse (fly).

T-shirt [tiʃœʀt] = **tee-shirt**.

tsigane [tsigan] adj Gypsyish. ❖ **Tsigane** nmf (Hungarian) Gypsy.

tsunami [tsynami] nm pr tsunami ; fig upheaval.

TSVP (abr écrite de tournez s'il vous plaît) PTO.

TTC (abr de toutes taxes comprises) *loc adj* inclusive of all tax, including tax.

tu [ty] *pron pers (2e pers sg)* **1.** [sujet d'un verbe] you ; *(élidé en « t » devant voyelle ou « h » muet)* : *t'es bête !* *fam* you're stupid! **2.** RELIG thou ; [en s'adressant à Dieu] ▸ **Tu** Thou **3.** [emploi nominal] ▸ **dire tu à qqn** to use the familiar form ou the "tu" form with ou to sb / *allez, on va se dire tu* ≃ come on, let's not stand on ceremony.

tuant, e [tɥɑ̃, ɑ̃t] *adj fam* **1.** [épuisant] exhausting **2.** [ennuyeux] deadly dull ou boring.

tuba [tyba] *nm* **1.** MUS tuba **2.** SPORT snorkel.

tube [tyb] *nm* **1.** [conduit] tube, pipe **2.** ÉLECTR ▸ **tube cathodique** cathode-ray tube **3.** [contenant] tube ▸ **tube à essai** test tube **4.** ANAT & BOT tube ▸ **tube digestif** digestive tract **5.** *fam* [chanson] (smash) hit, chart-topper / *le tube de l'été* this summer's chart-topper.

tubercule [tybɛʁkyl] *nm* BOT tuber.

tuberculeux, euse [tybɛʁkylø, øz] ◆ *adj* [malade] tuberculous ; [symptôme] tuberculous, tubercular. ◆ *nm, f* tuberculosis sufferer, tubercular.

tuberculose [tybɛʁkyloz] *nf* tuberculosis, TB.

tué, e [tɥe] *nm, f* [dans un accident] : *11 tués et 25 blessés* 11 dead ou 11 people killed and 25 injured.

tuer [7] [tɥe] *vt* **1.** [personne] to kill ▸ **tuer qqn à coups de couteau** to stab sb ou to knife sb to death / *se faire tuer* to be killed / *ta fille me tuera !* [dit par énervement] your daughter will be the death of me! / *ce voyage m'a tué* this trip's worn me out ou killed me ; *(en usage absolu)* : *le tabac tue* tobacco kills ou is a killer **2.** [plante] to kill (off) ; [animal de boucherie] to kill, to slaughter ; [gibier] to shoot ▸ **tuer qqch dans l'œuf** to nip sthg in the bud **3.** [anéantir - tourisme, espoir] to ruin, to spoil, to kill **4.** EXPR **tuer le temps** to kill time. ◆ **se tuer** ◆ *vp (emploi réfléchi)* [volontairement] to kill o.s. ◆ *vpi* [par accident] to die, to be killed. ◆ **se tuer à** *vp + prép* **1.** [s'épuiser à] ▸ **elle se tue à la tâche** ou **à la peine** *litt* ou **au travail** she's working herself to death **2.** [s'évertuer à] : *comme je me tue à te le répéter* as I keep telling you again and again.

tuerie [tyʁi] *nf* slaughter, massacre, bloodbath.

tue-tête [tytɛt] ◆ **à tue-tête** *loc adv* at the top of one's voice / *chantant l'hymne national à tue-tête* bellowing out the national anthem.

tueur, euse [tɥœʁ, øz] *nm, f* [meurtrier] killer ▸ **tueur professionnel** ou **à gages** hired ou professional killer / *tueur en série* serial killer.

tufékoi SMS abr écrite de **tu fais quoi?**

tuile [tɥil] *nf* **1.** CONSTR (roofing) tile **2.** CULIN biscuit 🇬🇧, cookie 🇺🇸 *(in the shape of a curved tile)* **3.** *fam* [événement désagréable] stroke of bad luck, blow / *il nous arrive une (grosse) tuile* we're in big trouble / *on n'a plus de gaz, la tuile !* we're out of gas, what a pain!

tulipe [tylip] *nf* BOT tulip.

tulle [tyl] *nm* TEXT tulle.

tuméfié, e [tymefje] *adj* swollen, tumid *spéc*.

tumeur [tymœʁ] *nf* MÉD tumour 🇬🇧, tumor 🇺🇸 / *tumeur bénigne / maligne / blanche* benign / malignant / white tumour ▸ **tumeur au cerveau** brain tumour.

tumulte [tymylt] *nm* [activité - soudaine] commotion, tumult ; [- incessante] hurly-burly, turmoil.

tumultueux, euse [tymyltɥø, øz] *adj* [discussion] stormy, turbulent, tumultuous ; [foule] boisterous, turbulent ; [vie] stormy, turbulent ; [passion] tumultuous, turbulent ; [flots] turbulent.

tune [tyn] *fam* = **thune**.

tuner [tynœʁ] *nm* RADIO tuner.

tuning [tyniŋ] *nm* AUTO tuning.

tunique [tynik] *nf* VÊT tunic.

Tunisie [tynizi] *npr f* ▸ **la Tunisie** Tunisia.

tunisien, enne [tynizjɛ̃, ɛn] *adj* Tunisian.
◆ **Tunisien, enne** *nm, f* Tunisian.

tunnel [tynɛl] *nm* tunnel ▸ **le tunnel sous la Manche** the Channel Tunnel.

tuque [tyk] *nf* QUÉBEC wool hat, tuque.

turban [tyʁbɑ̃] *nm* [couvre-chef] turban.

turbin [tyʁbɛ̃] *nm* *tfam* work.

turbine [tyʁbin] *nf* turbine.

turbo [tyʁbo] ◆ *adj inv* turbine-driven, turbo *(modif)*. ◆ *nm* AUTO turbo.

turbot [tyʁbo] *nm* turbot.

turbulence [tyʁbylɑ̃s] *nf* **1.** *litt* [d'une foule, d'une fête] rowdiness ; [de l'océan] turbulence *litt* **2.** MÉTÉOR turbulence, turbulency.

turbulent, e [tyʁbylɑ̃, ɑ̃t] *adj* [enfant] boisterous, unruly.

turc, turque [tyʁk] *adj* Turkish. ◆ **Turc, Turque** *nm, f* Turk ▸ **fort comme un Turc** as strong as a horse. ◆ **turc** *nm* LING Turkish. ◆ **à la turque** ◆ *loc adj* [cabinets] seatless, hole-in-the-ground. ◆ *loc adv* [s'asseoir] cross-legged.

turf [tœʁf] *nm* **1.** [activité] horse racing **2.** [terrain] turf, racecourse.

turfiste [tœʁfist] *nmf* racegoer.

turista, tourista [tuʁista] *nf fam* traveller's tummy 🇬🇧, traveler's tummy 🇺🇸.

turlupiner [3] [tyʁlypine] *vt fam* to worry, to bug, to bother / *c'est ce qui me turlupine* that's what's bugging me ou what's on my mind.

turnover [tœʁnɔvœʁ] *nm* turnover.

Turquie [tyʁki] *npr f* ▸ **la Turquie** Turkey.

turquoise [tyʁkwaz] ◆ *nf* turquoise. ◆ *adj inv* turquoise (blue).

tutelle [tytɛl] *nf* **1.** DR guardianship, tutelage ▸ **placer** ou **mettre qqn en** ou **sous tutelle** to put sb into the care of a guardian ▸ **tutelle légale** ou **tutelle d'État** wardship (order) **2.** ADMIN ▸ **tutelle administrative** administrative supervision **3.** POL trusteeship / *territoire sous tutelle* trust territory **4.** [protection] care, protection ; [contrainte] control / *tenir un pays en tutelle* ou *sous sa tutelle* to hold sway over a country.

tuteur, trice [tytœʁ, tʁis] *nm, f* DR guardian.
◆ **tuteur** *nm* HORT prop, support, stake.

tutoiement [tytwamɑ̃] *nm* use of the familiar "tu".

tutoyer [13] [tytwaje] *vt* to use the familiar "tu" with / *elle tutoie son professeur* ≃ she's on first-name terms with her teacher / *je me fais tutoyer par tous mes employés* all my employees call me "tu".

tutu [tyty] *nm* tutu.

tuyau, x [tɥijo] *nm* **1.** [conduit] pipe ▸ **tuyau d'arrosage** (garden) hose, hosepipe ▸ **tuyau d'échappement** exhaust (pipe) **2.** BOT [d'une tige] stalk **3.** *fam* [information] tip / *c'est lui qui m'a filé les tuyaux* I got the info ou gen 🇬🇧 from him.

tuyauter [3] [tɥijote] *vt fam* [informer] to tip off *(sép)*.

tuyauterie [tɥijotʁi] *nf* [canalisations] pipes, piping.

TV (abr de **télévision**) *nf* TV.

TVA (abr de **taxe à la valeur ajoutée**) *nf* VAT.

TVHD (abr de **télévision haute définition**) *nf* HDTV.

twa SMS abr écrite de **toi**.

tweed [twid] *nm* tweed.

tweet [twit] nm INTERNET tweet.

tweeter [3] [twite] vi INTERNET to tweet.

tympan [tɛ̃pɑ̃] nm **1.** ANAT eardrum, tympanum *spéc* / *un bruit à crever* ou *à déchirer les tympans* an earsplitting noise **2.** ARCHIT tympanum.

type [tip] nm **1.** *fam* [homme] man, guy, bloke 🇬🇧 / *quel sale type!* what a nasty piece of work! 🇬🇧, what an SOB! 🇺🇸 / *c'est un chic type* he's a decent sort **2.** [genre] kind, type / *c'est le type d'homme à partir sans payer* he's the type ou sort of man who would leave without paying / *elle a le type indien* she looks Indian / *c'est pas mon type* she's not my type / *c'est le type même du romantique* he's the typical romantic **3.** *(comme adjectif, avec ou sans trait d'union)* typical ▸ **contrat type** model contract ▸ **erreur type** typical ou classic mistake.

typé, e [tipe] adj : *elle est indienne mais pas très typée* she's Indian but doesn't have typical Indian features / *une femme brune très typée* a dark-haired woman with very distinctive looks.

typhoïde [tifɔid] adj & nf typhoid.

typhon [tifɔ̃] nm typhoon.

typhus [tifys] nm MÉD typhus (fever).

typique [tipik] adj [caractéristique] typical, characteristic / *c'est typique d'elle d'être en retard* it's typical of ou just like her to be late.

typiquement [tipikmɑ̃] adv typically.

typographie [tipɔgrafi] nf [présentation] typography.

typographique [tipɔgrafik] adj [procédé] letterpress *(modif)* ; [caractère] typographic.

tyran [tirɑ̃] nm [despote] tyrant.

tyrannie [tirani] nf tyranny.

tyrannique [tiranik] adj tyrannical.

tyranniser [3] [tiranize] vt to tyrannize, to bully / *se faire tyranniser* to be bullied.

tzar [tsar, dzar] = tsar.

tzigane [dzigan] = tsigane.

u, U [y] ❖ **en U** loc adj U-shaped.

ubiquité [ybikɥite] nf ubiquity, ubiquitousness **/** *avoir le don d'ubiquité* hum to be ubiquitous ou everywhere at once.

UE (abr de **Union européenne**) nf EU.

Ukraine [ykʀɛn] npr f Ukraine.

ukrainien, enne [ykʀɛnjɛ̃, ɛn] adj Ukrainian. ❖ **Ukrainien, enne** nm, f Ukrainian.

ulcère [ylsɛʀ] nm ulcer ▶ **ulcère à** ou **de l'estomac** stomach ulcer.

ulcérer [18] [ylseʀe] vt [indigner] to appal, to sicken **/** *ulcéré par tant d'ingratitude* appalled ou sickened by such ungratefulness.

🖉 In reformed spelling (see p. 16-18), this verb is conjugated like *semer* : *il ulcèrera, elle ulcèrerait.*

ULM (abr de **ultraléger motorisé**) nm microlight.

ultérieur, e [ylteʀjœʀ] adj later **/** *à une date ultérieure* at a later date.

ultérieurement [ylteʀjœʀmɑ̃] adv later.

ultimatum [yltimatɔm] nm ultimatum ▶ **adresser un ultimatum à qqn** to present sb with an ultimatum.

ultime [yltim] adj [dernier] ultimate, final.

ultra [yltʀa] ◆ adj extremist, reactionary. ◆ nmf [extrémiste] extremist, reactionary.

ultraconservateur, trice [yltʀakɔ̃sɛʀvatœʀ, tʀis] adj ultraconservative.

ultraléger, ère [yltʀaleʒe, ɛʀ] adj superlight, extralight.

ultralibéral, e, aux [yltʀaliberal, o] ◆ adj [politique] ultra-free market ; [personne] who advocates an ultra-free market. ◆ nm, f ultra-free marketeer.

ultralibéralisme [yltʀaliberalism] nm doctrine of the ultra-free market.

ultramoderne [yltʀamɔdɛʀn] adj ultramodern, state-of-the-art (avant nom).

ultraplat, e [yltʀapla, at] adj ultra slim.

ultrarapide [yltʀaʀapid] adj high-speed.

ultrarésistant, e [yltʀaʀezistɑ̃, ɑ̃t] adj [matériau] ultra-resistant ; [virus] resistant.

ultrasecret, ète [yltʀasəkʀɛ, ɛt] adj top secret.

ultrasensible [yltʀasɑ̃sibl] adj **1.** [instrument] ultrasensitive ; [peau] highly sensitive **2.** PHOT high-speed (avant nom).

ultrason [yltʀasɔ̃] nm ultrasound, ultrasonic sound.

ultraviolet [yltʀavjɔlɛ] nm ultraviolet ray.

un, une [œ̃, yn] (pl **des** [de]) (devant nm commençant par voyelle ou «h» muet [œ̃n], [yn]) ◆ dét (art indéf) **1.** [avec une valeur indéterminée] a, an (devant une voyelle) **/** *un homme a appelé ce matin* a man called this morning **/** *il doit y avoir une erreur* there must be a ou some mistake **/** *il y a des enfants qui jouent dans la rue* there are (some) children playing in the street **2.** [avec une valeur particularisante] a, an (devant une voyelle) **/** *j'irai plutôt un mardi* I'll go on a Tuesday instead **/** *tu es une idiote* you're an idiot **/** *un grand voyage se prépare des mois à l'avance* a ou any long journey needs months of preparation **3.** [avec une valeur emphatique] ▶ **il est d'une bêtise / d'un drôle !** he's so stupid / funny! **/** *j'ai une de ces migraines !* I've got a splitting headache! **/** *j'ai attendu des heures !* I waited for hours! **4.** [avec un nom propre] : *un M. Baloi vous demande au téléphone* there's a Mr Baloi for you (on the phone) **/** *c'est un Apollon* he's a real Adonis ; [désignant une œuvre] : *faire l'acquisition d'un Picasso / d'un Van Gogh* to acquire a Picasso / a Van Gogh. ◆ pron indéf (mpl **uns** [œ̃], fpl **unes** [yn]) **1.** [dans un ensemble] one ; [en corrélation avec «de»] : *un des seuls* one of the few **/** *appelle-le un de ces jours* give him a call one of these days ; [avec l'article défini] : *c'est l'un des concerts les plus réussis de ma carrière* it's one of the most successful concerts of my career **/** *l'un de mes amis* one of my friends, a friend of mine **2.** [en corrélation avec «en»] one **/** *on demanda un médecin, il y en avait un dans la salle* they called for a doctor, there was one in the room **/** *parmi les enfants, il y en a un qui...* one of the children... **3.** (emploi nominal) [quelqu'un] one person, someone **/** *j'en connais une qui va être surprise !* I know someone who's going to get a surprise! ◆ dét (adj num) **1.** one **/** *les enfants de un à sept ans* children (aged) from one to seven **/** *une femme sur cinq* one woman out of in five **/** *je ne resterai pas une minute de plus ici* I won't stay here another minute **/** *une à une, les lumières s'éteignaient* the lights were going out one by one ou one after the other **/** *avale les cachets un par un* swallow the tablets one by one ou one at a time ▶ **il ne faisait qu'un avec sa monture** horse and rider were as one ▶ **et d'un, et de deux !** that's one, and another (one)! **2.** [dans des séries] one **/** *page un* ou *une page one* **/** *il est une heure* it's one o'clock ▶ **une, deux ! une, deux !** left, right! left, right! ▶ **et d'une** firstly, first of all, for a start. ❖ **un** nm inv : *donnez-moi deux chiffres entre un et dix* give me two numbers between one and ten **/** *la clef du un est perdue* the key for number one has been lost.

unanime [ynanim] adj **1.** [commun, général - vote, décision] unanimous **2.** [du même avis] : *la presse unanime a condamné ce geste* the press unanimously condemned this gesture.

unanimement [ynanimmɑ̃] adv unanimously.

unanimité [ynanimite] nf unanimity ▶ **voter à l'unanimité pour qqn** to vote unanimously for sb ▶ **faire l'unanimité** to win unanimous support.

une [yn] ◆ dét (art indéf f) —→ un. ◆ nf PRESSE ▶ **la une** page one, the front page / la naissance de la princesse fait la ou est à la une de tous les quotidiens the birth of the princess is on the front page of all the dailies.

UNESCO, Unesco [ynɛsko] (abr de United Nations Educational, Scientific and Cultural Organization) npr f UNESCO, Unesco.

uni, e [yni] adj **1.** [d'une seule couleur] plain, self-coloured 🇬🇧, self-colored 🇺🇸, solid 🇺🇸 ; [sans motif] plain **2.** [soudé - couple] close ; [- famille, société] close-knit / unis derrière le chef united behind the leader.

unifamilial, e, aux [ynifamiljal, o] adj 🇶🇫 ▶ maison unifamiliale single-family home.

unification [ynifikasjɔ̃] nf [d'un pays] unification, unifying.

unifier [9] [ynifje] vt **1.** [réunir - provinces] to unify, to unite **2.** [uniformiser - tarifs] to standardize, to bring into line with each other.

unifolié [ynifɔlje] nm ▶ l'unifolié the Maple Leaf Flag (of Canada).

uniforme [ynifɔrm] ◆ adj **1.** [régulier - vitesse] uniform, regular, steady ; [- surface] even, smooth, level **2.** [monotone] uniform, unvarying, unchanging / un paysage uniforme an unchanging ou a monotonous landscape. ◆ nm uniform ▶ endosser / quitter l'uniforme [de l'armée] to join / to leave the forces. ❖ en uniforme loc adj in uniform ▶ un policier en uniforme a uniformed policeman.

uniformiser [3] [ynifɔrmize] vt to standardize.

unijambiste [yniʒãbist] nmf one-legged person.

unilatéral, e, aux [ynilateral, o] adj unilateral.

uninominal, e, aux [yninɔminal, o] adj —→ scrutin.

union [ynjɔ̃] nf **1.** [fait de mélanger] union, combination ; [mélange] union, integration **2.** [solidarité] union, unity ▶ l'Union européenne the European union ▶ l'union fait la force prov unity is strength **3.** [liaison entre un homme et une femme] union ▶ union libre free love **4.** [regroupement] union, association / union de consommateurs consumer association ▶ union douanière customs union **5.** HIST ▶ l'Union soviétique ou des républiques socialistes soviétiques the Soviet Union, the Union of Soviet Socialist Republics.

unique [ynik] adj **1.** [seul] (one and) only, one / l'unique explication possible the only possible explanation **2.** [exceptionnel] unique / c'est unique au monde it's unique, there's only one of its kind in the world **3.** fam [étonnant] priceless / il est vraiment unique, lui ! he's priceless, he is! **4.** [dans une famille] ▶ être fils / fille / enfant unique to be an only son / daughter / child.

uniquement [ynikmã] adv only, solely.

unir [32] [ynir] vt [lier] to unite, to bring together (sép). ❖ s'unir vpi **1.** [se regrouper] to unite / s'unir contre un ennemi commun to unite against a common enemy **2.** sout [se marier] to become joined in marriage ou matrimony.

unisexe [ynisɛks] adj unisex.

unisson [ynisɔ̃] ❖ à l'unisson loc adv in unison / nos cœurs battaient à l'unisson our hearts were beating as one ou in unison.

unitaire [yniter] adj COMM ▶ prix unitaire unit price.

unité [ynite] nf **1.** [cohésion] unity ▶ l'unité nationale POL national unity **2.** [étalon] unit, measure ▶ unité de temps unit for measuring time ou time measure **3.** [élément, module] unit, item ▶ unité centrale (de traitement) INFORM central processor unit, mainframe ▶ unité de production INDUST production unit ; LING (distinctive) feature ; UNIV ▶ unité de valeur course credit ou unit **4.** MATH unit

5. MIL unit. ❖ à l'unité ◆ loc adj ▶ prix à l'unité unit price. ◆ loc adv [acheter, vendre] by the unit, singly, individually.

univers [yniver] nm **1.** ASTRON ▶ l'Univers the Universe **2.** [domaine] world, universe.

universel, elle [yniversɛl] adj [mondial] universal.

universellement [yniverselmã] adv universally.

universitaire [yniversiter] ◆ adj [carrière, études] academic, university (modif) ; [année, centre, titre] academic ; [restaurant] university (modif). ◆ nmf **1.** [enseignant] academic, don 🇬🇧 **2.** 🇧🇪 graduate ou post-graduate student.

université [yniversite] nf **1.** [institution, bâtiment] university ▶ université d'été UNIV summer school ▶ université du troisième âge post-retirement ou senior citizens' university **2.** POL : les universités d'été du parti socialiste socialist party summer school (during which party leaders meet younger members).

univoque [ynivɔk] adj **1.** LING unequivocal **2.** [relation, rapport] one-to-one 🇬🇧, one-on-one 🇺🇸.

untel, unetelle, Untelle [œtɛl, yntɛl]nm, f Mr. So-and-so (Mrs. So-and-so) / tu dis «bonjour Mademoiselle Unetelle, puis-je parler au directeur ?» you say "good morning Miss so-and-so ou Miss Whatever-her-name-is, may I speak to the manager?".

upériser [yperize] vt to sterilize at ultrahigh temperature ▶ lait upérisé UHT milk.

uranium [yranjɔm] nm uranium ▶ uranium enrichi / appauvri enriched / depleted uranium.

urbain, e [yrbɛ̃, ɛn] adj [de la ville] urban, city (modif).

urbanisation [yrbanizasjɔ̃] nf urbanization, urbanizing.

urbaniser [3] [yrbanize] vt to urbanize / la côte est très urbanisée the coast is very built-up.

urbanisme [yrbanism] nm town planning 🇬🇧, city planning 🇺🇸.

urgence [yrʒãs] nf **1.** [caractère pressant] urgency / il y a urgence à ce que vous preniez une décision it's urgent for you to come to a decision ▶ il n'y a pas urgence it's not urgent, there's no urgency **2.** [incident] emergency. ❖ urgences nfpl MÉD casualty department 🇬🇧, emergency room 🇺🇸. ❖ d'urgence ◆ loc adj [mesures, soins] emergency. ◆ loc adv as a matter of emergency ▶ opérer d'urgence to perform an emergency operation / on l'a transporté d'urgence à l'hôpital he was rushed (off) to hospital.

urgent, e [yrʒã, ãt] adj urgent / ce n'est pas urgent it's not urgent, there's no (desperate) rush.

urgentissime [yrʒãtisim] adj fam super urgent / elle a un travail urgentissime à finir she has a massively urgent job to finish.

urgentiste [yrʒãtist] nmf MÉD A&E doctor 🇬🇧, ER doctor 🇺🇸.

urinaire [yriner] adj urinary.

urine [yrin] nf urine.

uriner [3] [yrine] vi to urinate, to pass water.

urinoir [yrinwar] nm (public) urinal.

URL (abr de uniform resource locator) nf URL.

urne [yrn] nf **1.** POL ballot box ▶ se rendre aux urnes to go to the polls **2.** [vase] urn ▶ urne funéraire (funeral) urn.

urologue [yrolog] nmf urologist.

URSS [yrs, yɛrɛsɛs] (abr de Union des républiques socialistes soviétiques) npr f ▶ (l')URSS the USSR ▶ l'ex-URSS the former USSR.

URSSAF, Urssaf [yʀsaf] (abr de Unions de recouvrement des cotisations de sécurité sociale et d'allocations familiales) npr f *administrative body responsible for collecting social security payments.*

urticaire [yʀtikɛʀ] nf nettle rash, hives, urticaria *spéc* ▶ *avoir de l'urticaire* to have nettle rash ▶ **donner de l'urticaire** : *les huîtres me donnent de l'urticaire* oysters bring me out in spots ▶ **cette musique, ça me donne de l'urticaire** that music makes my skin crawl.

urticant, e [yʀtikɑ̃, ɑ̃t] adj urticating.

Uruguay [yʀygwɛ] npr m ▶ **l'Uruguay a)** [pays] Uruguay **b)** [fleuve] the Uruguay (River).

uruguayen, enne [yʀygwejɛ̃, ɛn] adj Uruguayan.
❖ **Uruguayen, enne** nm, f Uruguayan.

us [ys] nmpl *litt* customs ▶ **les us et coutumes** habits and customs.

USA (abr de United States of America) npr mpl ▶ **les USA** the USA, the US, the States.

usage [yza3] nm **1.** [utilisation] use ▶ **faire usage de qqch** to use sthg ▶ **faire bon usage de qqch** to put sthg to good use ▶ **faire mauvais usage de qqch** to misuse sthg **2.** [contrôle] use / *perdre l'usage des yeux / d'un bras* to lose the use of one's eyes / an arm **3.** [fonction] use, purpose ▶ **à usage unique** [seringue, produit] use-once-then-throw-away ▶ **à usages multiples** multi-purpose / **'à usage externe'** 'not to be taken internally' **4.** LING (accepted) usage / *le mot est entré dans l'usage* the word is now in common use ▶ **le bon usage** correct usage **5.** [coutume] habit, habitual practice ▶ **l'usage, les usages** accepted ou established custom, (the rules of) etiquette ▶ **c'est l'usage** it's the done thing / *c'est contraire à l'usage* ou *aux usages, c'est contre l'usage* ou *les usages* it's not the done thing, it's contrary to the rules of etiquette. ❖ **à l'usage** loc adv with use / *c'est à l'usage qu'on s'aperçoit des défauts d'une cuisine* you only realize what the shortcomings of a kitchen are after you've used it for a while. ❖ **à l'usage de** loc prép : *un livre de cuisine à l'usage des enfants* a cookery book aimed at ou intended for children. ❖ **d'usage** loc adj [habituel] customary, usual / *finir une lettre avec la formule d'usage* to end a letter in the usual ou accepted manner / *il est d'usage de laisser un pourboire* it is customary to leave a tip.

usagé, e [yza3e] adj **1.** [usé - costume] worn, old ; [- verre] used, old **2.** [d'occasion] used, secondhand.

usager, ère [yza3e, ɛʀ] nm, f [utilisateur] user / *les usagers du téléphone / de la route* telephone / road users.

usant, e [yzɑ̃, ɑ̃t] adj [tâche] gruelling, wearing ; [enfant] wearing, tiresome ▶ **c'est usant** it really wears you down.

USB (abr de universal serial bus) nm INFORM USB ▶ **clé USB** USB key, USB stick 🇬🇧 ▶ **port USB** USB port.

usé, e [yze] adj [vieux - habit] worn, worn-out ; [- pile] worn, old ; [- lame] blunt ; [- pneu] worn.

user [3] [yze] vt **1.** [détériorer - terrain, métal] to wear away *(sép)* ; [- pneu] to wear smooth ; [- veste, couverture] to wear out *(sép)* ▶ **user un jean jusqu'à la corde** ou **trame** to wear out a pair of jeans **2.** [utiliser - eau, poudre] to use ; [- gaz, charbon] to use, to burn ; [- réserves] to use, to go through *(insép)* **3.** [fatiguer] to wear out *(sép)* / *tu m'uses la santé!* fam you'll be the death of me! ❖ **user de** v + prép *sout* [utiliser - autorité, droits] to exercise ; [- mot, tournure] to use ; [- outil] to use ; [- audace, diplomatie] to use, to employ. ❖ **s'user** ❖ vpi **1.** [se détériorer - gén] to wear out ; [- pile] to run down ; [- lame] to go blunt / *les semelles en cuir ne s'usent pas vite* there's a lot of wear in leather soles **2.** [s'affaiblir] : *ma patience commence à* *s'user* my patience is wearing thin. ❖ vpt [se fatiguer] to wear o.s. out ▶ **s'user les yeux** ou **la vue** to strain one's eyes.

usine [yzin] nf INDUST factory, plant, mill ▶ **usine à gaz a)** gasworks **b)** *fig* overly complicated system / *afin d'éviter de monter une usine à gaz, il faudrait faire intervenir les personnes compétentes* to stop things getting unnecessarily complicated, we should bring in people with the right skills.

usiner [3] [yzine] vt to machine.

usité, e [yzite] adj [terme] commonly used.

ustensile [ystɑ̃sil] nm utensil, implement ▶ **ustensiles de cuisine** cooking ou kitchen utensils.

usuel, elle [yzɥɛl] adj [ustensile, vêtement] everyday *(avant nom)* ; [vocabulaire, terme] common, everyday *(avant nom)*.

usure [yzyʀ] nf **1.** [action de s'user] wear (and tear) **2.** ▶ **avoir qqn à l'usure** fam to wear ou to grind sb down (until he gives in).

usurier, ère [yzyʀje, ɛʀ] nm, f usurer.

usurpateur, trice [yzyʀpatœʀ, tʀis] nm, f usurper.

usurpation [yzyʀpasjɔ̃] nf usurpation, usurping.

usurper [3] [yzyʀpe] vt [droit, identité] to usurp / *sa gloire est usurpée* fig her fame isn't rightfully hers.

ut [yt] nm inv MUS C.

utérin, e [yteʀɛ̃, in] adj ANAT uterine.

utérus [yteʀys] nm womb, uterus *spéc.*

utile [ytil] adj **1.** [qui sert beaucoup] useful / *ça peut (toujours) être utile* it might come in handy **2.** [nécessaire] necessary / *il n'est pas utile d'avertir la police* there's no need to notify the police **3.** [serviable] useful / *il cherche toujours à se rendre utile* he always tries to make himself useful / *puis-je t'être utile à quelque chose ?* can I be of any help to you?, can I help you with anything?

utilement [ytilmɑ̃] adv usefully, profitably / *employer son temps utilement* to spend one's time profitably, to make good use of one's time.

utilisable [ytilizabl] adj [objet, appareil] usable / *cet adaptateur est utilisable dans le monde entier* this adapter can be used anywhere in the world.

utilisateur, trice [ytilizatœʀ, tʀis] nm, f [d'un appareil] user ; [d'un service] user, consumer.

utilisation [ytilizasjɔ̃] nf use, utilization ▶ **notice d'utilisation** instructions for use.

utiliser [3] [ytilize] vt [appareil, carte, expression] to use ; [moyens, tactique] to use, to employ.

utilitaire [ytilitɛʀ] ❖ adj utilitarian. ❖ nm INFORM utility (program).

utilité [ytilite] nf [caractère utile] use, usefulness / *chaque ustensile a son utilité* every implement has its specific use / *des objets sans utilité* useless objects / *ça ne t'est plus d'aucune utilité* it's no longer of any use to you, you no longer need it ▶ **reconnu d'utilité publique** officially recognized as beneficial to the public at large.

utopie [ytɔpi] nf **1.** PHILOS utopia, utopian ideal **2.** [chimère] utopian idea ▶ **c'est de l'utopie !** that's all pie in the sky!

utopique [ytɔpik] adj utopian.

utopisme [ytɔpism] nm Utopianism.

utopiste [ytɔpist] nmf **1.** [rêveur] utopian **2.** PHILOS Utopian.

UV ❖ nf abr de unité de valeur. ❖ nm (abr de ultraviolet) UV ▶ **faire des UVs** to go to a solarium.

v, V [ve] ❖ **en V** loc adj V-shaped / *un pull (à col) en V* a V-necked sweater.

V1 SMS abr écrite de *viens*.

vacances [vakɑ̃s] nfpl **1.** [période de loisirs] holidays [UK], vacation [US] ▶ **vacances de neige** skiing holidays ou vacation **2.** [période du calendrier] ▶ **vacances scolaires** school holidays [UK] ou break [US] ▶ **les grandes vacances** the summer holidays [UK], the long vacation [US]. ❖ **en vacances** loc adv on holiday [UK] ou vacation [US] / *partir en vacances* to go (off) on holiday.

vacancier, ère [vakɑ̃sje, ɛʀ] nm, f holidaymaker [UK], vacationist [US], vacationer [US].

vacant, e [vakɑ̃, ɑ̃t] adj [libre -logement] vacant, unoccupied ; [-siège, trône] vacant / *il y a un poste d'ingénieur vacant* there's a vacancy for an engineer.

vacarme [vakaʀm] nm racket, din, row / *les enfants faisaient un vacarme infernal* the children were making a terrible racket ou an awful din.

vacataire [vakatɛʀ] nmf [remplaçant] stand-in, temporary replacement ; UNIV part-time lecturer.

vacation [vakasjɔ̃] nf ÉDUC & UNIV supply work.

vaccin [vaksɛ̃] nm [produit] vaccine.

vaccination [vaksinasjɔ̃] nf vaccination, inoculation.

vacciner [3] [vaksine] vt MÉD to vaccinate / *se faire vacciner contre la rage* to get vaccinated against rabies.

vache [vaʃ] ❖ adj fam rotten, nasty / *allez, ne sois pas vache* come on, don't be rotten, come on, be a sport [UK]. ❖ nf **1.** ZOOL cow ▶ **vache laitière** ou **à lait** milker, dairy cow ▶ **vache à lait** fig cash cow ▶ **période de vaches maigres pour l'économie** lean times for the economy **2.** [cuir] cowhide **3.** fam [homme] swine ; [femme] cow **4.** *(comme interj)* ▶ **(ah) la vache !** a) fam [étonnement] wow!, gosh! b) [indignation, douleur] oh hell! ❖ **en vache** loc adv on the sly ▶ **faire un coup en vache à qqn** to stab sb in the back.

vachement [vaʃmɑ̃] adv tfam really, bloody [UK], dead [UK], real [US] / *elle est vachement belle, ta robe* that's a great dress you're wearing.

vacherie [vaʃʀi] nf fam **1.** [acte] dirty ou rotten trick ▶ **faire une vacherie à qqn** to play a dirty ou rotten trick on sb **2.** [propos] nasty remark.

vaciller [3] [vasije] vi **1.** [tituber -bébé] to totter ; [-ivrogne] to sway, to stagger ▶ **vaciller sur ses jambes** to be unsteady on one's legs **2.** [chaise, pile de livres] to wobble **3.** [flamme] to flicker **4.** [raison, courage] to falter, to waver ; [voix] to falter, to shake ; [mémoire] to be failing, to falter.

vadrouille [vadʀuj] nf [QUÉBEC] [pour laver les sols] mop. ❖ **en vadrouille** loc adv : *partir en vadrouille* to go (off) on a jaunt.

va-et-vient [vaevjɛ̃] nm inv **1.** [circulation] comings and goings, toings and froings **2.** [aller et retour] ▶ **faire le va-et-vient** to go back and forth ou backwards and forwards **3.** ÉLECTR ▶ **(interrupteur de) va-et-vient** two-way switch.

vagabond, e [vagabɔ̃, ɔ̃d] nm, f tramp, vagabond, vagrant.

vagabondage [vagabɔ̃daʒ] nm **1.** [errance] roaming, roving, wandering **2.** DR vagrancy.

vagabonder [3] [vagabɔ̃de] vi to wander, to roam / *ses pensées vagabondent sans parvenir à se fixer* fig her thoughts wander ou drift without any focus.

vagin [vaʒɛ̃] nm vagina.

vaginal, e, aux [vaʒinal, o] adj vaginal.

vagir [32] [vaʒiʀ] vi [crier -bébé] to cry, to wail.

vagissement [vaʒismɑ̃] nm cry.

vague¹ [vag] nf **1.** [dans la mer] wave ▶ **vague de fond** pr & fig groundswell ▶ **faire des vagues** pr & fig to make waves **2.** [mouvement] wave / *vague de protestations* / *grèves* wave of protest / strikes **3.** MÉTÉOR ▶ **vague de chaleur** heatwave ▶ **vague de froid** cold spell.

vague² [vag] ❖ adj **1.** [peu marqué -sourire, détail] vague ; [-souvenir, connaissances] vague, hazy ; [-contour, sensation] vague, indistinct ; [vacant -regard, expression] vacant, abstracted ▶ **esquisser un vague sourire** to smile faintly **2.** *(avant nom)* [non précisé] vague / *un vague cousin à moi* some distant cousin of mine. ❖ nm **1.** [flou] vagueness, indistinctness ; [imprécision] vagueness / *laisser une question dans le vague* to be vague about a matter ▶ **rester dans le vague** to be (as) vague (as possible), to avoid giving any details **2.** [vide] ▶ **regarder dans le vague** to gaze vacantly into space ou the blue. ❖ **vague à l'âme** nm melancholy / *avoir du vague à l'âme* to be melancholy.

vaguelette [vaglɛt] nf wavelet.

vaguement [vagmɑ̃] adv **1.** [de façon imprécise] vaguely / *ils se ressemblent vaguement* they look vaguely alike, there is a vague resemblance between them / *elle est vaguement actrice* péj she's some kind of actress **2.** [un peu] vaguely, mildly.

vaillamment [vajamɑ̃] adv valiantly, bravely, gallantly.

vaillant, e [vajɑ̃, ɑ̃t] adj [courageux -moralement] courageous, brave, stout-hearted ; [-physiquement] valiant.

vain, e [vɛ̃, vɛn] adj **1.** [inutile] vain, fruitless, pointless **2.** *(avant nom)* [serment, espérance] empty, vain ; [promesse] empty, hollow, worthless. ❖ **en vain** loc adv in vain, vainly, fruitlessly.

vaincre [114] [vɛ̃kʀ] vt **1.** [équipe, adversaire] to beat, to defeat ; [armée] to defeat / *nous vaincrons !* we shall overcome! **2.** [peur, douleur, inhibition] to overcome, to conquer, to master ; [mal de tête, maladie] to overcome ; [hostilité, réticences] to overcome, to triumph over *(insép).*

vaincu, e [vɛ̃ky] adj defeated ▸ **s'avouer vaincu** to admit defeat.

vainement [vɛnmɑ̃] adv in vain, vainly.

vainqueur [vɛ̃kœR] ◆ adj m winning, victorious, triumphant, conquering / *sortir vainqueur d'une épreuve* to emerge (as) the winner of a contest. ◆ nm SPORT [gagnant] winner ; MIL victor.

vaisseau, x [vɛso] nm **1.** [navire] ship, vessel *sout* ▸ **vaisseau amiral** flagship **2.** ANAT vessel ▸ **vaisseau capillaire / lymphatique / sanguin** capillary / lymphatic / blood vessel **3.** ASTRONAUT ▸ **vaisseau spatial** spacecraft.

vaisselier [vɛsəlje] nm dresser 🇬🇧, buffet 🇺🇸.

vaisselle [vɛsɛl] nf **1.** [service] crockery **2.** [ustensiles sales] (dirty) dishes ▸ **faire la vaisselle** to do the washing-up 🇬🇧, to do ou to wash the dishes.

val, s ou **vaux** [val, vo] nm [vallée] valley.

valable [valabl] adj **1.** [valide - ticket, acte] valid **2.** [excellent - musicien, athlète] really good.

⚠ **Valuable** signifie « de grande valeur », « précieux » et non valable.

valentin [valɑ̃tɛ̃] nm 🇶🇧 [carte] Valentine card.

valet [valɛ] nm **1.** ▸ **valet de chambre** manservant **2.** JEUX jack, knave ▸ **valet de pique** jack ou knave of spades.

valeur [valœR] nf **1.** [prix] value, worth / *la valeur en a été fixée à 290 euros* its value has been put at 290 euros, it's been valued at 290 euros ▸ **prendre / perdre de la valeur** to increase / to decrease in value ▸ **manuscrit d'une valeur inestimable** invaluable manuscript ▸ **mettre en valeur a)** [terre] to exploit **b)** [capital] to get the best return out of **c)** [connaissances] to put to good use **d)** [taille, minceur] to enhance **e)** [talent, qualités] to bring out, to highlight ▸ **le noir est la couleur qui me met le plus en valeur** black is the colour that suits me best **2.** COMM, ÉCON, FIN & MATH value ▸ **valeur marchande / vénale** market / monetary value ▸ **en valeur absolue** in absolute terms ▸ **valeur ajoutée** *pr & fig* added value **3.** [importance subjective] value ▸ **attacher** ou **accorder une grande valeur à qqch** to prize sthg, to set great value by sthg ▸ **la valeur sentimentale d'un collier** the sentimental value of a necklace **4.** [mérite] worth, merit / *avoir conscience de sa valeur* to know one's own worth **5.** *litt* [personne de mérite] ▸ **valeur sûre**: *une valeur sûre de la sculpture française* one of the top French sculptors. ◆ **valeurs** nfpl **1.** [normes morales] values / *valeurs morales / sociales / familiales* moral / social / family values **2.** BOURSE ▸ **valeurs (mobilières)** stocks and shares, securities. ◆ **de valeur** *loc adj* COMM & FIN [bague, tableau] valuable ▸ **des objets de valeur** valuables, items of value, valuable items.

validation [validasjɔ̃] nf [d'un billet] validation ; [d'un document] authentication ▸ **validation des acquis de l'expérience** system by which people can apply for a paper qualification based on their experience.

valide [valid] adj **1.** [permis, titre de transport] valid **2.** [bien portant] fit, (well and) strong ; [non blessé] ablebodied.

valider [3] [valide] vt [traité] to ratify ; [document] to authenticate ; [testament] to prove, to probate 🇺🇸 ; [billet, passeport] to validate.

validité [validite] nf ADMIN & TRANSP validity / *quelle est la durée de validité du visa ?* how long is the visa valid for?

valise [valiz] nf **1.** [bagage] suitcase, bag ▸ **faire ses valises** *pr* to pack (one's bags) ▸ **faire sa valise** ou **ses valises** [partir] to pack one's bags and go **2.** DR ▸ **la valise diplomatique** the diplomatic bag ou 🇺🇸 pouch.

valisette [valizɛt] nf small case.

vallée [vale] nf GÉOGR valley.

vallon [valɔ̃] nm small valley.

vallonné, e [valɔne] adj undulating, hilly.

valoir [60] [valwaR] ◆ vi **1.** [avoir tel prix] to be worth ; [coûter] to cost ▸ **valoir très cher** to cost a lot, to be very expensive, to be very dear ▸ **ne pas valoir cher** to be cheap ou inexpensive **2.** [avoir telle qualité] to be worth / *que vaut ton jeune élève ?* how good is your young pupil? / *je sais ce que je vaux* I know my worth ou what I'm worth ▸ **ne rien valoir**: *il ne vaut rien, ton marteau* your hammer's no good ou useless / *son idée / projet ne vaut rien* her idea / project is worthless ▸ **ne pas valoir grand-chose**: *mes premières chansons ne valaient pas grand-chose* my early songs weren't particularly good / *l'émission d'hier ne valait pas grand-chose* yesterday's programme wasn't up to much ▸ **valoir mieux que**: *elle vaut mieux que la réputation qu'on lui fait* she's much better than her reputation would suggest / *et il t'a quittée ? tu vaux mieux que ça* and he left you? you deserve better than that **3.** ▸ **valoir par** [tirer sa valeur de]: *ma bague ne vaut que par les souvenirs qu'elle représente* my ring has only sentimental value / *son initiative vaut surtout par son audace* the main merit of his initiative is its boldness **4.** [être valable, applicable] ▸ **valoir pour** to apply to, to hold for / *le règlement vaut pour tout le monde* the rules hold for everyone **5.** EXPR ▸ **faire valoir a)** [argument] to emphasize, to put forward *(sép)* **b)** [opinion, raisons] to put forward *(sép)* **c)** [droit] to assert, to enforce **d)** [qualité] to highlight, to bring out *(sép)* / *faire valoir ses droits à la retraite* to provide evidence for one's entitlement to a pension / *il vaut mieux ne pas répondre* it's best ou better not to answer ▸ **ça vaut mieux**: *appelle le médecin, ça vaut mieux* it would be better ou safer if you called the doctor / *ça vaut mieux ainsi / pour lui* it's better that way / for him. ◆ vt **1.** [procurer] ▸ **valoir qqch à qqn** to earn sb sthg, to bring sthg to sb / *ses efforts lui ont valu une médaille aux jeux Olympiques* his efforts earned him a medal at the Olympic Games / *tous les soucis que m'a valus ce club* all the worries that club cost me ▸ **qu'est-ce qui me vaut l'honneur / le plaisir de ta visite ?** to what do I owe the honour / pleasure of your visit? / *son exploit lui a valu d'être admiré par tous* his achievement earned him widespread admiration **2.** [représenter] to be equivalent to, to be worth / *chaque faute de grammaire vaut quatre points* you lose four points for each grammatical mistake **3.** [mériter] to be worth / *le village vaut le détour / déplacement* the village is worth the detour / journey / *ça vaut le coup d'œil* it's worth seeing ▸ **valoir la peine** ou **le coup** *fam* to be worth it, to be worthwhile / *ça vaut le coup d'essayer* it's worth trying ou a try / *à ce prix-là, ça vaut le coup* at that price, you can't go wrong **4.** [dans une comparaison] to be as good as, to match up (to) / *son idée en vaut une autre* her idea is as good as any other / *ah, rien ne vaut les confitures de grand-mère !* there's nothing like grandma's jam! ◆ **se valoir** vp *(emploi réciproque)* to be equivalent / *vous vous valez bien !* you're both as bad as each other! ◆ **vaille que vaille** *loc adv* somehow (or other).

valorisant, e [valɔRizɑ̃, ɑ̃t] adj **1.** [satisfaisant moralement] : *il fait un travail valorisant* his work brings him a lot of job satisfaction **2.** [donnant du prestige] : *une situation valorisante* a situation which increases one's prestige.

valoriser [3] [valɔRize] vt **1.** ÉCON [région] to develop the economy of **2.** ÉCOL [déchets] to recover **3.** [augmenter le prestige de] : *son succès l'a valorisé aux yeux de ses amis* his success has increased his standing in the eyes of his friends.

valse [vals] nf **1.** DANSE waltz **2.** *fam* [modification] ▶ **la valse des prix** ou **étiquettes** spiralling prices.

valser [3] [valse] vi **1.** [danser] to waltz **2.** *fam* [tomber] to career, to hurtle ▶ **envoyer valser qqch** to send sthg flying ▶ **envoyer valser qqn** to show sb the door.

valve [valv] nf **1.** ANAT, BOT & ZOOL valve **2.** TECHNOL [clapet] valve ; [soupape à clapet] valve.

vampire [vɑ̃piʀ] nm [mort] vampire.

vampiriser [3] [vɑ̃piʀize] vt **1.** [suj : vampire] to suck the blood of **2.** *fam* [dominer] to have under one's sway, to subjugate.

van [vɑ̃] nm [véhicule] horse box 🇬🇧 ou trailer 🇺🇸, horsecar 🇺🇸.

vandale [vɑ̃dal] nm [voyou] vandal.

vandaliser [3] [vɑ̃dalize] vt to vandalize.

vandalisme [vɑ̃dalism] nm vandalism, hooliganism / *commettre des actes de vandalisme* to commit acts of vandalism.

vanille [vanij] nf vanilla. ❖ **à la vanille** loc adj vanilla *(modif)*, vanilla-flavoured.

vanillé, e [vanije] adj vanilla-flavoured.

vanité [vanite] nf [orgueil] vanity, pride, conceit ▶ **tirer vanité de qqch** to pride o.s. on sthg, to take pride in sthg.

vaniteux, euse [vanitø, øz] ❖ adj [orgueilleux] vain, conceited, self-important. ❖ nm, f conceited man (woman).

vanne [van] nf **1.** [d'une écluse] sluicegate ; [d'un moulin] hatch **2.** *fam* [plaisanterie] dig, jibe.

vanné, e [vane] adj *fam* worn out, beat / *je suis vanné !* I've had it!, I'm beat!

vanner [3] [vane] vt **1.** AGR to winnow **2.** *fam* [épuiser] to wear out *(sép)*.

vannerie [vanʀi] nf [tressage] basketwork, basketry / *faire de la vannerie* [paniers] to weave baskets. ❖ **en vannerie** loc adj wicker, wickerwork *(modif)*.

vantard, e [vɑ̃taʀ, aʀd] ❖ adj boastful, boasting, bragging. ❖ nm, f bragger, braggart.

vantardise [vɑ̃taʀdiz] nf **1.** [glorification de soi] boastfulness, bragging **2.** [remarque] boast.

vanter [3] [vɑ̃te] vt [louer, exalter] to praise ; *sout* to extol ▶ **vanter les mérites de qqch** to sing the praises of sthg ▶ **vanter les mérites de qqn** to sing sb's praises ▶ **vanter sa marchandise** *hum* to boast. ❖ **se vanter** vpi to boast, to brag ▶ **se vanter de** : *il s'est vanté de gagner la course* he boasted that he would win the race / *il s'est vanté d'avoir gagné la course* he bragged that he had won the race / *elle l'a fait renvoyer mais elle ne s'en vante pas* she had him fired, but she keeps quiet about it / *il n'y a pas de quoi se vanter* this is nothing to be proud of ou to boast about / *sans (vouloir) me vanter, j'avais déjà compris* I don't wish to boast, but I'd got the idea already.

vapes [vap] nfpl *fam* ▶ **tomber dans les vapes** [s'évanouir] to pass out, to faint.

vapeur [vapœʀ] ❖ nf **1.** [gén] steam ▶ **vapeur (d'eau)** steam, (water) vapour **2.** CHIM & PHYS vapour 🇬🇧, vapor 🇺🇸 ▶ **vapeurs de pétrole** petrol 🇬🇧 ou gas 🇺🇸 fumes. ❖ nm NAUT steamship, steamer. ❖ **à la vapeur** loc adv & adj ▶ **cuit à la vapeur** steam-cooked. ❖ **à vapeur** loc adj steam *(modif)*, steam-driven ▶ **machine à vapeur** steam engine.

vaporisateur [vapɔʀizatœʀ] nm **1.** [pulvérisateur] spray ; [atomiseur] spray, atomizer **2.** TECHNOL [échangeur] vaporizer.

vaporiser [3] [vapɔʀize] vt [pulvériser] to spray.

vaquer [3] [vake] ❖ **vaquer à** v + prép *sout* to attend to, to see to / *vaquer à ses occupations* to attend to ou to go about one's business.

varappe [vaʀap] nf [activités] rock climbing ; [course] rock climb / *faire de la varappe* to go rock-climbing.

varappeur, euse [vaʀapœʀ, øz] nm, f rock climber.

varech [vaʀɛk] nm kelp, varec.

vareuse [vaʀøz] nf COUT loose-fitting jacket.

variable [vaʀjabl] ❖ adj **1.** [changeant - temps] unsettled ; [- taux] variable / *être d'humeur variable* to be moody **2.** [varié - composition, forme] varied, diverse. ❖ nf CHIM, ÉCON, MATH & PHYS variable.

variante [vaʀjɑ̃t] nf [gén & LING] variant.

variation [vaʀjasjɔ̃] nf **1.** [fluctuation] variation, change / *pour vos plantes, attention aux variations de température* your plants do not like changes in temperature ▶ **corrigé des variations saisonnières** seasonally adjusted **2.** MUS variation. ❖ **variations** nfpl [modifications] changes, modifications / *subir des variations* to undergo change ou changes.

varice [vaʀis] nf varicose vein, varix *spéc*.

varicelle [vaʀisɛl] nf chickenpox, varicella *spéc*.

varié, e [vaʀje] adj **1.** [non uniforme - style, répertoire] varied / *une gamme variée de papiers peints* a wide range of wallpapers **2.** *(au pl)* [différents] various, diverse, miscellaneous / *objets divers et variés* various ou miscellaneous objects ▶ **hors-d'œuvre variés** CULIN selection of hors d'œuvres.

varier [9] [vaʀje] ❖ vt [diversifier - cursus, menu, occupations] to vary, to diversify ▶ **pour varier les plaisirs** just for a change. ❖ vi [changer - temps, poids, humeur] to vary, to change / *les produits varient en qualité* products vary in quality / *les prix varient de 90 à 120 euros* prices vary ou range from 90 to 120 euros.

variété [vaʀjete] nf [diversité] variety, diversity. ❖ **variétés** nfpl LITTÉR miscellanies ; MUS easy listening, light music. ❖ **de variétés** loc adj [spectacle, émission] variety ; [musique] light / *disque de variétés* easy listening ou light music record.

variole [vaʀjɔl] nf smallpox, variola *spéc*.

Varsovie [vaʀsɔvi] npr Warsaw / *le pacte de Varsovie* the Warsaw Pact.

vase [vaz] ❖ nf [boue] mud, silt, sludge. ❖ nm **1.** [récipient décoratif] vase **2.** CHIM & PHYS vessel ▶ **vases communicants** connecting vessels. ❖ **en vase clos** loc adv : *nous vivions en vase clos* we led an isolated existence.

vaseux, euse [vazø, øz] adj **1.** [boueux] muddy, silty, sludgy **2.** *fam* [confus - idée, plan] hazy, woolly **3.** *fam* [malade] ▶ **se sentir tout vaseux a)** [affaibli] to feel under the weather, to feel off colour **b)** [étourdi] to feel woozy **4.** *fam* [médiocre] pathetic / *ses blagues vaseuses* his pathetic jokes.

vasistas [vazistas] nm fanlight, transom 🇺🇸.

vasque [vask] nf **1.** [bassin] basin (of fountain) **2.** [coupe] bowl.

vaste [vast] adj [immense - vêtement] enormous, huge ; [- domaine, sujet] vast, far-reaching ; [- palais, gouffre] vast, huge, immense.

Vatican [vatikɑ̃] npr m ▶ **le Vatican** the Vatican.

va-tout *(pl* va-tout), **vatout*** [vatu] nm ▶ **jouer son va-tout** to risk ou to stake one's all.

vaudeville [vodvil] nm vaudeville, light comedy.

vaudou, e [vodu] adj voodoo. ❖ **vaudou** nm voodoo, voodooism.

---

* In reformed spelling (see p. 16-18).

vau-l'eau [volo] ❖ **à vau-l'eau** loc adv ▶ **aller à vau-l'eau a)** (barque) to go with the stream ou current **b)** [affaire, projet] to be going downhill ou to the dogs.

vaurien, enne [voʀjɛ̃, ɛn] nm, f **1.** [voyou] good-for-nothing, scoundrel, rogue **2.** [enfant] : *petit vaurien !* you little devil!

vautour [votuʀ] nm ORNITH vulture.

vautrer [3] [votʀe] ❖ **se vautrer** vpi **1.** [se rouler] to wallow **2.** [s'affaler] to sprawl, to be sprawled / *se vautrer dans un fauteuil* to loll in an armchair.

va-vite [vavit] ❖ **à la va-vite** loc adv in a rush ou hurry / *travail fait à la va-vite* slapdash work.

VDQS (abr de **vin délimité de qualité supérieure**) label indicating quality of wine.

veau, x [vo] nm **1.** ZOOL calf **2.** CULIN veal / *escalope / côtelette de veau* veal escalope / cutlet **3.** [cuir] calf, calfskin.

vecteur [vɛktœʀ] nm MATH vector.

vécu, e [veky] ❖ pp ⟶ **vivre**. ❖ adj [réel] real, real-life, true / *c'est une histoire vécue* it's a true story. ❖ **vécu** nm ▶ **le vécu de qqn** sb's (real-life) experiences.

vedettariat [vədetaʀja] nm stardom.

vedette [vədɛt] nf **1.** [artiste] star ▶ **vedette du petit écran / de cinéma** TV / film star **2.** [célébrité] star, celebrity / *une vedette de la politique / du rugby* a big name in politics / rugby ▶ **présentateur-vedette** star presenter ▶ **produit vedette** leading product **3.** [première place] ▶ **avoir** ou **tenir la vedette a)** THÉÂTRE to top the bill, to have star billing **b)** *fig* to be in the limelight ▶ **ravir** ou **souffler la vedette à qqn** to upstage sb **4.** NAUT launch **5.** MIL sentinel. ❖ **en vedette** loc adv ▶ **mettre qqn / qqch en vedette** to put the spotlight on sb / sthg.

végétal, e, aux [veʒetal, o] adj [fibre] plant ; [huile] vegetable. ❖ **végétal, aux** nm plant, vegetable.

végétalien, enne [veʒetaljɛ̃, ɛn] adj & nm, f vegan.

végétalisé, e [veʒetalize] adj [espace, terrasse] planted ▶ **mur végétalisé** plant wall.

végétaliser [veʒetalize] vt [espace, terrasse] to plant.

végétarien, enne [veʒetaʀjɛ̃, ɛn] adj & nm, f vegetarian.

végétarisme [veʒetaʀism] nm vegetarianism.

végétatif, ive [veʒetatif, iv] adj **1.** ANAT, BOT & MÉD vegetative **2.** [inactif] : *mener une vie végétative* to sit around all day.

végétation [veʒetasjɔ̃] nf BOT vegetation. ❖ **végétations** nfpl MÉD ▶ **végétations (adénoïdes)** adenoids.

végéter [18] [veʒete] vi to vegetate, to stagnate / *le marché végète* trading is slow.

✐ In reformed spelling (see p. 16-18), this verb is conjugated like *semer : il végètera, elle végèterait.*

véhémence [veemɑ̃s] nf vehemence. ❖ **avec véhémence** loc adv vehemently, passionately.

véhément, e [veemɑ̃, ɑ̃t] adj [plaidoyer] vehement, passionate ; [dénégation] vehement, vociferous.

véhicule [veikyl] nm TRANSP vehicle / *véhicule automobile / hippomobile* motor / horse-drawn vehicle ▶ **véhicule utilitaire** commercial vehicle.

véhiculer [3] [veikyle] vt [transmettre -idée], message] to convey, to serve as ou to be a vehicle for.

veille [vɛj] nf **1.** [jour d'avant] : *la veille, je lui avais dit...* the day before, I'd said to him... ▶ **la veille au soir** the night before ▶ **la veille de** the eve of, the day before ▶ **la veille de Noël** Christmas Eve ▶ **la veille de son départ / sa mort** the day before he left / died ▶ **à la veille de**: *à la veille des présidentielles / de la visite du pape*

on the eve of the presidential elections / of the Pope's visit **2.** [éveil] ▶ **état de veille** waking state **3.** [garde] vigil ; MIL night watch. ❖ **en veille** ◆ loc adj [ordinateur] in sleep mode. ◆ loc adv ▶ **mettre en veille** [ordinateur] to put in sleep mode.

veillée [veje] nf **1.** [soir] evening **2.** [réunion] evening gathering **3.** [garde] vigil, watch.

veiller [4] [veje] ◆ vt [un malade] to watch over, to sit up with ; [un mort] to keep watch ou vigil over. ◆ vi **1.** [rester éveillé] to sit ou to stay up (insép) / *ne veille pas trop tard* don't stay up too late **2.** [être sur ses gardes] to be watchful ou vigilant. ❖ **veiller sur** v + prép [surveiller -enfant] to watch (over), to look after, to take care of ; [-santé] to watch, to take care of. ❖ **veiller à** v + prép to see to / *veiller aux intérêts du pays* to attend to ou to see to ou to look after the interests of the country / *je veillerai à ce qu'elle arrive à l'heure* I'll see (to it) ou make sure that she gets there on time.

veilleur [vejœʀ] nm [gardien] ▶ **veilleur de nuit** night watchman.

veilleuse [vejøz] nf [lampe] night-light ; [flamme] pilot light ▶ **mettre en veilleuse a)** [lumière] to dim, to turn down low **b)** *fam & fig* [projet] to put off temporarily, to put on the back burner, to shelve. ❖ **veilleuses** nfpl AUTO sidelights.

veinard, e [vɛnaʀ, aʀd] *fam* nm, f lucky devil ou so-and-so.

veine [vɛn] nf **1.** ANAT vein **2.** [d'un minerai] vein, lode ; [du bois] grain ; [d'une feuille] vein **3.** [inspiration] vein, inspiration / *les deux récits sont de la même veine* the two stories are in the same vein **4.** *fam* [chance] luck ▶ **avoir de la veine** to be lucky ▶ **pas de veine !** hard ou tough luck! **5.** EXPR je suis en veine d'inspiration ce matin I'm feeling inspired this morning.

veineux, euse [vɛnø, øz] adj ANAT venous.

Velcro® [vɛlkʀo] nm Velcro®.

vélin [velɛ̃] nm vellum.

véliplanchiste [veliplɑ̃ʃist] nmf windsurfer.

velléité [veleite] nf vague desire, stray impulse.

vélo [velo] nm [bicyclette] bike, bicycle ▶ **faire du vélo, monter à vélo** to ride a bike ▶ **vélo d'appartement** exercise bike ▶ **vélo de course** racing bike ▶ **vélo tout terrain** mountain bike.

vélocité [velɔsite] nf **1.** *litt* [rapidité] velocity, speed, swiftness **2.** PHYS velocity.

vélodrome [velɔdʀom] nm velodrome.

vélomoteur [velɔmɔtœʀ] nm lightweight motorcycle, moped UK.

velours [vəluʀ] nm TEXT velvet ▶ **velours côtelé, velours à côtes** corduroy.

velouté, e [vəlute] adj [doux -peau] velvet (modif), silky. ❖ **velouté** nm CULIN [potage] cream soup ; [sauce] velouté (sauce) / *velouté de poulet* cream of chicken (soup).

velu, e [vəly] adj [homme, poitrine] hairy.

venaison [vənɛzɔ̃] nf venison.

vénal, e, aux [venal, o] adj **1.** [corrompu] venal, corrupt **2.** [intéressé] venal, mercenary.

vendange [vɑ̃dɑ̃ʒ] nf **1.** [cueillette] grape-picking, grape-harvesting, grape-harvest ▶ **faire la vendange** ou **les vendanges a)** [vigneron] to harvest the grapes **b)** [journalier] to go grape-picking **2.** [quantité récoltée] grape-harvest, grape-yield ; [qualité récoltée] vintage. ❖ **vendanges** nfpl [saison] grape-harvesting time ▶ **vendanges de glace** ice wine harvest.

vendanger [17] [vɑ̃dɑ̃ʒe] ◆ vt to harvest, to pick. ◆ vi to harvest grapes.

vendangeur, euse [vãdãʒœʀ,øz] nm, f grape-picker.
❖ **vendangeuse** nf [machine] grape-picker.

vendeur, euse [vãdœʀ,øz] nm, f **1.** [dans un magasin] salesperson, shop assistant 🇬🇧, (sales) clerk 🇺🇸 **2.** [dans une entreprise] (sales) representative **3.** [marchand] seller ▸ **vendeur de journaux** news ou newspaper man. ❖ **vendeur** nm DR vendor, seller.

vendre [73] [vãdʀ] vt **1.** [céder - propriété, brevet, marchandise] to sell ▸ **vendre qqch à la pièce / à la douzaine / au poids** to sell sthg by unit / by the dozen / by weight ▸ **vendre (qqch) au détail** to retail (sthg) ▸ **vendre qqch à qqn** to sell sb sthg, to sell sthg to sb / **'à vendre'** 'for sale' ▸ **il ne faut jamais vendre la peau de l'ours avant de l'avoir tué** prov don't count your chickens before they are hatched prov **2.** [commercialiser] to sell **3.** [trahir - secret] to sell ; [-associé, confident] to sell down the river ▸ **vendre son âme au diable** to sell one's soul to the devil. ❖ **se vendre** vp (emploi passif) to sell / ça se vend bien / mal actuellement it is / isn't selling well at the moment ▸ **se vendre comme des petits pains** to sell ou to go like hot cakes.

vendredi [vãdʀədi] nm Friday ▸ **le vendredi saint** Good Friday. Voir aussi **mardi**.

vendu, e ◆ pp ⟶ **vendre**. ◆ adj [vénal] corrupt. ◆ nm, f péj turncoat, traitor.

vénéneux, euse [venenø,øz] adj [toxique] poisonous, toxic.

vénérable [venerabl] adj venerable.

vénération [venerasjõ] nf **1.** RELIG reverence **2.** [admiration] veneration, reverence, respect ▸ **avoir de la vénération pour qqn** to revere sb.

vénère [venɛʀ] adj fam pissed off.

vénérer [18] [veneʀe] vt **1.** RELIG to worship, to revere **2.** [admirer] to revere, to worship, to venerate.
✐ In reformed spelling (see p. 16-18), this verb is conjugated like semer : il vénère, elle vénèrerait.

vénerie, vènerie* [venʀi] nf hunting ▸ **la grande vénerie** hunting with hounds ▸ **la petite vénerie** hunting with small dogs.

vénérien, enne [veneʀjɛ̃,ɛn] adj venereal.

Venezuela [venezɥela] npr m ▸ **le Venezuela** Venezuela.

vénézuélien, enne [venezɥeljɛ̃,ɛn] adj Venezuelan. ❖ **Vénézuélien, enne** nm, f Venezuelan.

vengeance [vãʒãs] nf revenge, vengeance / crier ou demander ou réclamer vengeance to cry out for revenge ▸ **soif** ou **désir de vengeance** revengefulness, vengefulness.

venger [17] [vãʒe] vt **1.** [réparer] to avenge **2.** [dédommager] ▸ **venger qqn de qqch** to avenge sb for sthg. ❖ **se venger** vp (emploi réfléchi) [tirer réparation] to revenge ou to avenge o.s., to take vengeance ▸ **je me vengerai !** I'll get my own back! ▸ **se venger de qqn / qqch** to take one's revenge on sb / for sthg.

vengeur, eresse [vãʒœʀ, vãʒʀɛs] adj avenging, revengeful, vengeful.

véniel, elle [venjɛl] adj **1.** [excusable] minor, slight **2.** RELIG venial.

venimeux, euse [vənimø,øz] adj **1.** [toxique] venomous, poisonous **2.** [méchant] venomous, malevolent.

venin [vənɛ̃] nm **1.** [poison] venom **2.** litt [malveillance] ▸ **cracher** ou **jeter son venin** to vent one's spleen.

venir [40] [vəniʀ] ◆ v aux **1.** [se rendre quelque part pour] to come and, to come to / Roger viendra me chercher Roger will come and collect me / je suis venu m'excuser I've come to apologize ▸ **venir voir qqn** to come and see ou to visit sb, to visit with sb 🇺🇸 ▸ **venir voir qqch** to come and see sthg ; (à valeur

d'insistance) : tu l'as bien cherché, alors ne viens pas te plaindre ! you asked for it, so now don't come moaning to me about it! **2.** ▸ **venir de** [avoir fini de] : venir de faire qqch to have just done sthg / je viens de l'avoir au téléphone I was on the phone to her just a few minutes ou a short while ago **3.** sout ▸ **venir à** [exprime un hasard] to happen to / si les vivres venaient à manquer should food supplies run out, if food supplies were to run out.

◆ vi

A. AVEC IDÉE DE MOUVEMENT **1.** [se déplacer, se rendre] to come ▸ **viens plus près** come closer / ils sont venus nombreux they came in droves / comment êtes-vous venus ? how did you get here? / je l'ai rencontrée en venant ici I met her on my way here / alors, tu viens ? are you coming? ▸ **venir de** : d'où viens-tu ? where have you been? / je viens de Paris et je repars à New York I've just been in Paris and now I'm off to New York ▸ **venir sur** [prédateur, véhicule] to move in on, to bear down upon ▸ **venir vers qqn** [s'approcher] to come up to ou towards sb ▸ **venir à qqn** a) [s'adresser à qqn] to come to sb b) [atteindre qqn] to reach sb **2.** ▸ **faire venir** a) [médecin, police, réparateur] to send for, to call b) [parasites, touristes] to attract / faire venir une personne chez soi to have somebody come round / je fais venir mon foie gras directement du Périgord I have my foie gras sent straight from Périgord.

B. SANS IDÉE DE MOUVEMENT ▸ **venir à** ou **jusqu'à** a) [vers le haut] to come up to, to reach (up to) b) [vers le bas] to come down to, to reach (down to) c) [en largeur, en longueur] to come out to, to stretch to, to reach.

C. SURGIR, SE MANIFESTER **1.** [arriver - moment, saison] to come / le moment est venu de the time has come to / quand vient l'hiver when winter comes / puis il vient un âge / moment où... then comes an age / a time when... / alors, elle vient cette bière ? am I getting that beer or not?, how long do I have to wait for my beer? / alors, ça vient ? hurry up! **2.** [apparaître - inspiration, idée, boutons] to come ▸ **prendre la vie comme elle vient** ou **les choses comme elles viennent** ou **les événements comme ils viennent** to take things in one's stride ou as they come, to take life as it comes ▸ **venir à qqn** : l'envie m'est soudain venue d'aller me baigner I suddenly felt like going swimming ou fancied a swim / les mots semblaient lui venir si facilement ! her words seemed to flow so effortlessly! ▸ **venir à l'esprit de qqn** ou **à l'idée de qqn** to come to ou to dawn on sb **3.** [dans une chronologie, un ordre, une hiérarchie] to come / le mois / l'année / la décennie qui vient the coming month / year / decade ▸ **venir après** : fais tes devoirs, la télé viendra après do your homework, we'll see about TV later on **4.** [se développer] to come along ou up (well), to do well / venir à maturité to reach maturity, to ripen.

◆ v impers **1.** [se déplacer] : il vient peu de touristes en hiver few tourists come in winter **2.** ▸ **il me / te, etc. vient** : il me vient une idée I've got an idea / il m'est venu à l'idée de faire I suddenly thought of doing / it dawned on me to do **3.** [exprime un hasard] ▸ **s'il venait à pleuvoir** should it (happen to) rain. ❖ **venir à** v + prép **1.** [choisir] to come to / vous êtes venu tôt à la politique you started your political career early **2.** ▸ **en venir à** a) [thème, problème] to come ou to turn to b) [conclusion] to come to, to reach c) [décision] to come to / en venir au fait ou à l'essentiel to come ou to go straight to the point ▸ **en venir aux mains** ou **coups** to come to blows ▸ **en venir à faire** a) [finir par] to come to b) [en dernière extrémité] to resort ou to be reduced to / j'en viens à me demander si... I'm beginning to wonder whether... ▸ **y venir** [dans une discussion] : et l'argent ? — j'y viens what about the money? — I'm coming to that. ❖ **venir de** v + prép **1.** [être originaire de - suj : personne] to come from, to be from, to be a native of / [- suj : plante,

---
* In reformed spelling (see p. 16-18).

fruit, animal] to come ou to be ou to originate from / *le mot vient du latin* the word comes ou derives from Latin **2.** [provenir de - suj : marchandise] to originate from ; [- suj : bruit, vent] to come from / *ces images nous viennent de Tokyo* these pictures come to you from Tokyo **3.** [être issu de] to come from / *venant d'elle, c'est presque un compliment* coming from her it's almost a compliment **4.** [être dû à - suj : problème] to come ou to stem from, to lie in ou with / *le problème vient de la prise* it's the plug ‣ **c'est de là que vient le mal** / *problème* this is the root of the evil / problem. ❖ **à venir** loc adj : *dans les jours* / *semaines* / *mois à venir* in the days / weeks / months to come / *les générations à venir* future ou coming generations.

Venir faire qqch

Notez l'emploi de come and do sthg qui sert à insister sur l'accomplissement de l'action (avec come to do sthg, on n'est pas certain que l'action est accomplie). En anglais américain, and est souvent omis :

Viens me voir mercredi. *Come and see me on Wednesday* ou *Come see me on Wednesday* US.
Je viendrai te montrer les photos. *I'll come and show you the pictures* ou *I'll come show you the pictures* US.

Au passé, les deux verbes sont au prétérit. Dans ce cas, and ne peut pas être omis :
Il est venu réparer le lave-linge. *He came and fixed the washing machine.*

Notez que la construction come and do sthg relève d'un registre plutôt oral.

Venise [vəniz] npr Venice.

vénitien, enne [venisjɛ̃, ɛn] adj Venetian. ❖ **Vénitien, enne** nm, f Venetian.

vent [vɑ̃] nm **1.** MÉTÉOR wind / *un vent du nord* / *nord-est* a North / North-East wind / *le vent souffle* / *tourne* the wind is blowing / changing ‣ **il y a** ou **il fait du vent** it's windy ou breezy / *un vent de panique a soufflé sur la foule* fig a ripple of panic ran through the crowd **2.** NAUT & AÉRON ‣ **au vent (de)** to windward (of) ‣ **sous le vent (de)** to leeward (of) ‣ **vent arrière** a) AÉRON tail wind b) NAUT rear wind ‣ **vent contraire** adverse wind ‣ **vent debout** head wind ‣ **avoir le vent en poupe** to be up-and-coming, to be going places ‣ **bon vent !** good riddance! ‣ **quel bon vent vous amène ?** to what do we owe the pleasure (of your visit)? / *je le ferai contre vents et marées* I'll do it come hell or high water **3.** MÉD & PHYSIOL : *lâcher des vents* to break wind **4.** CHASSE wind ‣ **avoir vent de qqch** to (get to) hear of sthg. ❖ **dans le vent** loc adj up-to-date. ❖ **en plein vent** loc adj [exposé] exposed (to the wind).

vente [vɑ̃t] nf **1.** [opération] sale **2.** [domaine d'activité] selling ‣ **vente par correspondance** mail-order selling ‣ **vente à domicile** door-to-door selling **3.** DR ‣ **vente (par adjudication) forcée** / **judiciaire** compulsory sale, sale by order of the court **4.** [réunion, braderie] sale ‣ **vente de charité** charity sale ‣ **vente à l'encan** ou **aux enchères** auction (sale) ‣ **vente publique** public sale. ❖ **ventes** nfpl COMM selling, sales / *achats et ventes* buying and selling / *le responsable des ventes* the sales manager. ❖ **en vente** loc adj & loc adv [à vendre] for sale ; [disponible] available, on sale / *en vente en pharmacie* on sale at ou available from the chemist's ‣ **en vente libre** sold with-

out a prescription ‣ **mettre qqch en vente** [commercialiser qqch] to put sthg on the market / *mettre une maison en vente* to put a house up for sale.

venter [3] [vɑ̃te] v impers ‣ **il vente** it's windy, the wind is blowing.

venteux, euse [vɑ̃tø, øz] adj [où le vent souffle] wind-swept, windy.

ventilateur [vɑ̃tilatœʀ] nm [pour rafraîchir] fan.

ventilation [vɑ̃tilasjɔ̃] nf **1.** [appareil] ventilation ; [aération] supply of (fresh) air **2.** [d'une comptabilité] break-down.

ventiler [3] [vɑ̃tile] vt **1.** [aérer] to air, to ventilate ‣ **mal ventilé** stuffy, airless **2.** [diviser - données] to explode, to scatter ; [- élèves, emplois] to distribute, to spread / *ils ont ventilé les postes sur trois régions différentes* they allocated posts in three different areas **3.** FIN to break down *(sép)*.

ventouse [vɑ̃tuz] nf **1.** [en caoutchouc] suction cup **2.** ZOOL sucker **3.** [déboucheur] plunger ‣ **faire ventouse** to adhere ou to hold fast (through suction).

ventre [vɑ̃tʀ] nm **1.** ANAT & ZOOL stomach / *être couché sur le ventre* to be lying down ou flat on one's stomach ‣ **avoir mal au ventre** to have (a) stomachache ‣ **avoir le ventre creux** ou **vide** to have an empty stomach ‣ **avoir le ventre plein** to be full, to have a full stomach / *il s'est sauvé ventre à terre* you couldn't see him for dust ‣ **il n'a rien dans le ventre** fig he's got no guts ‣ **je voudrais bien savoir ce qu'elle a dans le ventre** a) [de manière générale] I'd like to know what makes her tick b) [sur un point précis] I'd like to know what she's up to **2.** [utérus] womb.

ventricule [vɑ̃tʀikyl] nm ventricle.

ventriloque [vɑ̃tʀilɔk] nmf ventriloquist.

ventripotent, e [vɑ̃tʀipɔtɑ̃, ɑ̃t] adj potbellied, rotund euphém.

ventru, e [vɑ̃tʀy] adj **1.** [personne] potbellied, paunchy **2.** [potiche] potbellied.

venu, e [vəny] ◆ pp ⟶ **venir.** ◆ adj **1.** ‣ **bien venu** a) [enfant, plante, animal] strong, sturdy, robust b) [conseil, remarque] timely, apposite c) [attitude] appro-priate d) [roman] mature ‣ **mal venu** a) [enfant, animal] sickly b) [plante] stunted c) [remarque, attitude] uncalled for, unwarranted, ill-advised d) [conseil] untimely, unwelcome **2.** ‣ **être bien venu de** [être bien inspiré de] : *tu serais bien venu de t'excuser* you'd be well-advised to apologize, it would be a good idea for you to apologize ‣ **être mal venu de** [n'être pas qualifié pour] : *tu serais mal venu de te plaindre !* you're hardly in a position to complain! / *il serait mal venu de la critiquer* it wouldn't be appropriate to criticize her. ❖ **venue** nf **1.** [d'une personne] arrival **2.** [d'une saison] approach.

Vénus [venys] ◆ npr Venus. ◆ nf [belle femme] Venus.

vêpres [vɛpʀ] nfpl vespers.

ver [vɛʀ] nm [gén] worm ; [de viande, de fromage, de fruit] maggot ‣ **ver luisant** glowworm ‣ **ver à soie** silkworm ‣ **ver solitaire** tapeworm ‣ **ver de terre** earthworm ‣ **ver de vase** bloodworm ‣ **tirer les vers du nez à qqn** fam to worm sthg out of sb ‣ **le ver est dans le fruit** the rot's set in.

véracité [veʀasite] nf [authenticité] truth / *la véracité de ce témoignage est évidente* this statement is obviously true.

véranda [veʀɑ̃da] nf [galerie] veranda, verandah, porch US.

verbal, e, aux [vɛʀbal, o] adj **1.** [dit de vive voix] ver-bal **2.** LING [adjectif, système] verbal ; [phrase, forme, groupe] verb *(modif)*.

verbalement [vɛʀbalmɑ̃] adv verbally, orally.

verbaliser [3] [vɛʀbalize] ➧ vi to report an offender / *je suis obligé de verbaliser* I'll have to report you. ➧ vt to express verbally, to put into words, to verbalize.

verbe [vɛʀb] nm **1.** GRAM verb **2.** BIBLE ▶ **le Verbe** the Word.

verbeux, euse [vɛʀbø, øz] adj verbose, wordy, long-winded.

verbiage [vɛʀbjaʒ] nm verbiage.

verdâtre [vɛʀdɑtʀ] adj greenish, greeny.

verdict [vɛʀdikt] nm DR verdict ▶ **rendre son verdict** to pass sentence, to return a verdict.

verdir [32] [vɛʀdiʀ] vi **1.** [de peur] to blench **2.** [plante, arbre] to have green shoots.

verdoyant, e [vɛʀdwajɑ̃, ɑ̃t] adj [vert] verdant *litt*, green.

verdure [vɛʀdyʀ] nf **1.** [végétation] greenery, verdure *litt*; [dans un bouquet] greenery, (green) foliage **2.** CULIN salad.

véreux, euse [veʀø, øz] adj **1.** [plein de vers - fruit, viande] wormy, maggoty **2.** [malhonnête - affaire, avocat, architecte, policier] dubious, shady.

verge [vɛʀʒ] nf ANAT penis.

verger [vɛʀʒe] nm (fruit) orchard.

vergetures [vɛʀʒǝtyʀ] nfpl stretchmarks.

verglacé, e [vɛʀglase] adj ▶ **route verglacée** road covered in black ice, icy road.

verglas [vɛʀgla] nm black ice [UK], glare ice [US] / *plaques de verglas* patches of black ice, icy patches.

vergogne [vɛʀgɔɲ] ➧ **sans vergogne** loc adv shamelessly / *mentir sans vergogne* to lie shamelessly ou without compunction.

vergue [vɛʀg] nf NAUT yard.

véridique [veʀidik] adj [conforme à la vérité] genuine, true.

vérificateur, trice [veʀifikatœʀ, tʀis] nm, f inspector, controller. ➧ **vérificateur** nm [contrôleur - de l'altimètre, de filetage] gauge ▶ **vérificateur orthographique** ou **d'orthographe** INFORM spellchecker.

vérification [veʀifikasjɔ̃] nf **1.** [d'identité] check; [d'un témoignage, d'un déplacement] check, verification; [d'un dossier] examination, scrutiny **2.** [d'une hypothèse, d'une preuve] checking, verification **3.** FIN checking ▶ **vérification des comptes** audit **4.** INFORM check, control.

vérifier [9] [veʀifje] vt **1.** [examiner - mécanisme] to check, to verify; [- dossier] to check, to go through **2.** [preuve, témoignage] to check / *vérifie son adresse* check that his address is correct, check his address **3.** [confirmer] to confirm, to bear out *(sép)*. ➧ **se vérifier** vpi [craintes, supposition] to be borne out ou confirmed.

vérin [veʀɛ̃] nm jack.

véritable [veʀitabl] adj **1.** [d'origine] real, true **2.** [authentique - or] real, genuine; [- amitié, sentiment] true **3.** *(avant nom)* [absolu] real / *une véritable ordure* tfam a real bastard.

véritablement [veʀitabləmɑ̃] adv **1.** [réellement] genuinely / *il est véritablement malade* he's genuinely ill **2.** [exactement] really, exactly **3.** [en intensif] truly, really, absolutely.

vérité [veʀite] nf **1.** [ce qui est réel ou exprimé comme réel] ▶ **la vérité** the truth / *c'est la vérité vraie !* fam it's true, honest it is / *la vérité, c'est que ça m'est égal* actually ou the truth is ou in fact I don't care / *dis-moi la vérité* tell me the truth **2.** [chose vraie] ▶ **une vérité** a true fact **3.** [principe] truth / *une vérité première* a basic truth / *les vérités éternelles* undying truths, eternal verities *litt* **4.** [sin-

cérité] truthfulness, candidness / *son récit avait un accent de vérité* her story rang true. ➧ **à la vérité, en vérité** loc adv to tell the truth.

verlan [vɛʀlɑ̃] nm ≃ backslang.

Verlan

This form of slang, popular among young people, involves inverting the syllables of words. The term **verlan** is the word l'envers pronounced back to front. Well-known examples of verlan are **ripou (pourri,** used to refer to corrupt policemen), **laisse béton! (laisse tomber!** – forget it!), and **meuf (femme).** The term **Beur** comes from the **verlan** version of the word **Arabe**.

vermeil, eille [vɛʀmɛj] adj [rouge - pétale, tenture] vermilion; [- teint, joue] ruddy, rosy; [- lèvres] rosy. ➧ **vermeil** nm vermeil, gilded silver.

vermicelle [vɛʀmisɛl] nm ▶ **vermicelle, vermicelles** vermicelli ▶ **vermicelles chinois** Chinese noodles.

vermillon [vɛʀmijɔ̃] ➧ adj inv vermilion, bright red. ➧ nm [couleur] vermilion.

vermine [vɛʀmin] nf **1.** [parasite] vermin **2.** *fig & péj* : *ces gens-là, c'est de la vermine* those people are vermin.

vermoulu, e [vɛʀmuly] adj [piqué des vers] worm-eaten.

verni, e [vɛʀni] adj **1.** [meuble, ongle] varnished; [brique, poterie] enamelled, glazed ▶ **des souliers vernis** patent leather shoes **2.** *fam* [chanceux] lucky.

vernir [32] [vɛʀniʀ] vt [enduire - bois, tableau, ongle] to varnish; [- céramique] to enamel, to glaze.

vernis [vɛʀni] nm **1.** [enduit - sur bois] varnish; [- sur métal] polish; [- sur céramique] enamel **2.** [cosmétique] ▶ **vernis à ongles** nail polish **3.** *fig & péj* ▶ **avoir un vernis de** to have a smattering of / *le vernis d'éducation ne cache pas sa vulgarité* a veneer of good manners does nothing to hide his vulgarity.

vernissage [vɛʀnisaʒ] nm **1.** [d'un tableau, d'un meuble] varnishing; [d'une céramique] glazing; [du métal] enamelling **2.** [d'une exposition] private viewing.

vérolé, e [veʀɔle] adj **1.** *fam* poxy **2.** INFORM infected.

verre [vɛʀ] nm **1.** [matériau] glass ▶ **verre dépoli** frosted ou ground glass ▶ **verre feuilleté** laminated glass ▶ **verre fumé** smoked glass **2.** [récipient] glass ▶ **verre à dents** tooth glass ▶ **verre doseur** measuring glass ▶ **verre gradué** a) [en chimie] graduated vessel b) [pour la cuisine] measuring glass ▶ **verre à pied** stemmed glass ▶ **verre à vin** wineglass **3.** [contenu] : *boire un verre* to have a drink ▶ **verre de** glass of, glassful of ▶ **avoir un verre dans le nez** *fam* to have had one too many. ➧ **verres** nmpl OPT glasses ▶ **verres de contact** contact lenses ▶ **verres correcteurs** correcting lenses ▶ **verres progressifs** multifocal lenses. ➧ **sous verre** loc adv ▶ **mettre qqch sous verre** to put sthg in a clip frame.

verrerie [vɛʀʀi] nf [usine] glassworks.

verrier [vɛʀje] nm **1.** [souffleur de verre] glassblower **2.** [artisan - en verrerie] glassmaker; [- en vitraux] stained-glass maker ou artist. ➧ **verrière** nf **1.** [toit] glass roof **2.** [baie - à hauteur de plafond] glass wall ou partition; [- à mi-hauteur] glass screen **3.** [vitrail] stained-glass window.

verrine [vɛʀin] nf *appetizer ou dessert served in a small glass.*

verr. num [vɛʀnym] (abr de **verrouillage numérique**) nf INFORM num lock.

verroterie [veʀɔtʀi] nf [bibelots] glass trinkets ; [bijoux] glass jewels ; [perles] coloured  ou colored  glass beads.

verrou [veʀu] nm [fermeture] bolt / *mettre* ou *pousser les verrous* to slide the bolts home, to bolt the door. ❖ **sous les verrous** loc adv ▸ **être sous les verrous** to be behind bars.

verrouillage [veʀujaʒ] nm [d'une porte] locking, bolting ; [d'une portière] locking ▸ **verrouillage automatique** ou **central** central locking.

verrouiller [3] [veʀuje] vt **1.** [clore - porte] to lock, to bolt **2.** [empêcher l'accès de] to close off (*sép*) / *la police a verrouillé le quartier* the police have cordoned off ou closed off the area.

verrue [veʀy] nf wart ▸ **verrue plantaire** plantar wart, verruca.

vers[1] [veʀ] ❖ nm LITTÉR **1.** [genre] verse ▸ **vers héroïques** heroic verse ▸ **vers libres** free verse ▸ **vers métriques / syllabiques / rythmiques** quantitative / syllabic / accentual-syllabic verse **2.** [unité] line / *le dernier vers est faux* ou *boiteux* the last line doesn't tally. ❖ nmpl [poème] (lines of) poetry, verse / *écrire* ou *faire des vers* to write poetry ou verse / *vers de circonstance* occasional verse ▸ **des vers de mirliton** doggerel. ❖ **en vers** ❖ loc adj ▸ **conte / lettre en vers** tale told / letter written in verse. ❖ loc adv ▸ **mettre qqch en vers** to put sthg into verse.

vers[2] [veʀ] prép **1.** [dans la direction de] to, towards, toward  / *il regarde vers la mer* he's looking towards the sea / *vers la gauche* to the left / *le village vers lequel nous nous dirigions* the village we were heading for ▸ **il s'est tourné vers moi a)** [pr] he turned to ou towards me **b)** [pour qu'il vous aide] he turned ou came to me / *un pas vers la paix* a step towards peace **2.** [indiquant l'approximation - dans le temps] around ; [- dans l'espace] near ▸ **vers midi** around midday / *vers la fin du mois* towards ou toward  the end of the month / *l'accident a eu lieu vers Ambérieu* the accident happened somewhere near Ambérieu.

Versailles [veʀsaj] npr Versailles.

🏛 **Versailles**

France's greatest palace, by Le Vau and Mansart, with gardens by Le Nôtre. Built at enormous cost by Louis XIV and added to in the 18th century, it was the home of the French court until the Revolution. Numerous treaties were signed there, including the Treaty of Versailles in 1919 marking the end of the First World War.

---

versant [veʀsɑ̃] nm GÉOGR [côté - d'une montagne, d'une vallée] side, slope.

versatile [veʀsatil] adj [esprit, caractère, personne] fickle.

verse [veʀs] ❖ **à verse** loc adv ▸ **il pleut à verse** it's pouring (with rain), it's pouring down.

versé, e [veʀse] adj *sout* versed / *être très / peu versé dans la politique* to be well-versed / not particularly well-versed in politics / *être versé / peu versé dans l'art contemporain* to be conversant with / ignorant of contemporary art.

Verseau [veʀso] nm **1.** ASTRON Aquarius **2.** ASTROL Aquarius / *elle est Verseau* she's Aquarius ou an Aquarian.

versement [veʀsəmɑ̃] nm **1.** [paiement] payment **2.** [paiement partiel] instalment / *effectuer un versement*

to pay an instalment **3.** [dépôt] deposit ▸ **effectuer** ou **faire un versement à la banque** to pay money into a bank account / *versement en espèces* cash deposit.

verser [3] [veʀse] ❖ vt **1.** [répandre - sang, larmes] to shed / *verser des larmes* ou *pleurs* to cry / *sans qu'une goutte de sang n'ait été versée* without a drop of blood being spilt **2.** [servir - liquide] to pour out (*sép*) / *verse-lui-en un peu plus* pour him a bit more, help him to a bit more **3.** [faire basculer - sable, gravier, chargement] to tip / *verse la farine dedans* pour the flour in **4.** [payer] to pay / *on vous versera une retraite* you will receive a pension **5.** [apporter] to add, to append ▸ **verser une pièce au dossier a)** [pr] to add a new item to the file **b)** *fig* to bring further information to bear on the case. ❖ vi to spill, to overturn. ❖ **verser dans** v + prép : *nous versons dans le mélodrame* this is becoming melodramatic.

verset [veʀsɛ] nm [d'un livre sacré, d'un poème] verse.

verseur [veʀsœʀ] adj m ▸ **bec verseur a)** [d'une théière] spout **b)** [d'une casserole, d'une tasse] lip.

versification [veʀsifikasjɔ̃] nf versification, versifying.

version [veʀsjɔ̃] nf **1.** ÉDUC & UNIV translation (*from a foreign language into one's mother tongue*) **2.** [variante - d'une œuvre] version ; [- d'une automobile] model, version ; [- d'un logiciel] version ▸ **en version originale** in the original language **3.** [interprétation] version / *voici ma version des faits* this is my version of the facts, this is how I see what happened.

verso [veʀso] nm [envers] verso, other side. ❖ **au verso** loc adv ▸ **voir au verso** see overleaf.

vert, e [veʀ, veʀt] adj **1.** [couleur] green ▸ **vert de** : *vert de rage* livid ▸ **être vert de peur** to be white with fear **2.** [vin] tart, acid ; [fruit] green, unripe ; *fig* [débutant, apprenti] inexperienced **3.** [bois] green **4.** [vigoureux] sprightly **5.** [agricole, rural] green, agricultural, rural **6.** [écologiste] green **7.** [osé] risqué, raunchy ▸ **en avoir vu des vertes et des pas mûres** to have been through a lot. ❖ **vert** nm **1.** [couleur] green / *peint* ou *teint en vert* painted ou tinted green ▸ **vert bouteille** bottle green ▸ **vert d'eau** sea green ▸ **vert émeraude** emerald green ▸ **vert olive** olive green ▸ **vert pomme** apple green **2.** TRANSP green light ▸ **passer au vert** : *les voitures doivent passer au vert* motorists must wait for the light to turn green / *le feu est passé au vert* the lights have turned (to) green **3.** [EXPR] *se mettre au vert* to go to the countryside. ❖ **Verts** nmpl ▸ **les Verts a)** SPORT the Saint-Étienne football team **b)** POL the Green Party.

vert-de-gris [veʀdəgʀi] adj inv blue-green.

vertébral, e, aux [veʀtebʀal, o] adj vertebral, spinal.

vertèbre [veʀtɛbʀ] nf vertebra / *avoir une vertèbre déplacée* to have a slipped disc.

vertébré, e [veʀtebʀe] adj vertebrate. ❖ **vertébré** nm vertebrate.

vertement [veʀtəmɑ̃] adv harshly, sharply.

vertical, e, aux [veʀtikal, o] adj [droit - position, corps, arbre] vertical, upright ; [- écriture, ligne] vertical. ❖ **verticale** nf vertical line. ❖ **à la verticale** ❖ loc adj vertically. ❖ loc adv vertically.

verticalement [veʀtikalmɑ̃] adv [tout droit] vertically.

vertige [veʀtiʒ] nm **1.** [peur du vide] vertigo / *avoir le vertige* to suffer from vertigo **2.** [malaise] dizzy spell ▸ **avoir un vertige** ou **des vertiges** to feel dizzy ou faint **3.** [égarement] giddiness.

vertigineux, euse [veʀtiʒinø, øz] adj [effrayant - altitude] vertiginous, dizzy, giddy ; [- vitesse] terrifying, breakneck (*avant nom*) / *une baisse vertigineuse des cours* a breathtaking collapse on the stock exchange.

vertu [vɛʀty] nf **1.** *litt* [conduite morale] virtue, virtuousness, righteousness **2.** [propriété] virtue, property, power / *les vertus thérapeutiques des plantes* the healing properties of plants. ❖ **en vertu de** *loc prép* according to / *en vertu de la loi* according to the law, in accordance with the law, under the law.

vertueux, euse [vɛʀtɥø, øz] adj [qui a des qualités morales] virtuous, righteous.

verve [vɛʀv] nf [fougue] verve, gusto ; [esprit] wit. ❖ **en verve** *loc adj* ▸ **être en verve** to be particularly witty.

verveine [vɛʀvɛn] nf **1.** BOT vervain, verbena **2.** [tisane] verbena (tea).

vésicule [vezikyl] nf MÉD [ampoule] blister, vesicle ; [cavité] bladder ▸ **vésicule biliaire / cérébrale** gall / brain bladder.

vessie [vesi] nf ANAT & ZOOL bladder / *il voudrait nous faire prendre des vessies pour des lanternes* he's trying to pull the wool over our eyes.

veste [vɛst] nf jacket ▸ **prendre une veste** to come a cropper ▸ **retourner sa veste** *fam & fig* to change one's colours 🇬🇧 ou colors 🇺🇸.

⚠️ **Vest signifie « maillot de corps » en anglais britannique et « gilet » en anglais américain, et non** veste.

vestiaire [vɛstjɛʀ] nm **1.** [dépôt] cloakroom / *prendre son vestiaire* to collect one's things ou belongings from the cloakroom **2.** [pièce] changing room 🇬🇧, locker room 🇺🇸.

vestibule [vɛstibyl] nm [d'un bâtiment public, d'une maison] (entrance) hall, vestibule ; [d'un hôtel] lobby.

vestige [vɛstiʒ] nm [d'une armée] remnant ; [d'une ville, d'une société] vestige ; [d'une croyance, du passé, d'une coutume] remnant, vestige ; [d'une idée, d'un sentiment] remnant, trace, vestige ▸ **vestiges archéologiques** archeological remains.

vestimentaire [vɛstimãtɛʀ] adj clothing *(modif)* ▸ **dépenses vestimentaires** clothes expenditure, money spent on clothing ▸ **élégance vestimentaire** sartorial elegance *sout.*

veston [vɛstɔ̃] nm jacket.

vêtement [vɛtmã] nm **1.** [habit] piece ou article ou item of clothing, garment *sout* / *il fait froid, mets un vêtement chaud* it's cold, put something warm on / *il portait ses vêtements de tous les jours* he was wearing his everyday clothes ▸ **vêtements de travail** work ou working clothes ▸ **vêtements de sport** sportswear ▸ **vêtements pour homme** menswear ▸ **vêtements pour femme** ladies' wear ▸ **vêtements de ski** skiwear ▸ **vêtements de ville** informal clothes ; [costume distinctif] dress, garb **2.** COMM ▸ **vêtements hommes** menswear ▸ **vêtement dames** ou **femmes** ladies' wear.

vétéran [veteʀã] nm **1.** [soldat] veteran, old campaigner ; [ancien combattant] (war) veteran **2.** [personne expérimentée] veteran, old hand.

vétérinaire [veteʀinɛʀ] ◆ adj veterinary. ◆ nmf vet 🇬🇧, veterinary surgeon 🇬🇧, veterinarian 🇺🇸.

vététiste [vetetist] nmf mountain biker.

vétille [vetij] nf trifle.

vêtir [44] [vetiʀ] vt *sout* [habiller - enfant, malade] to dress. ❖ **se vêtir** vp *(emploi réfléchi) sout* to dress (o.s.).

veto *(pl* veto), **véto*** [veto] nm **1.** POL veto **2.** [interdiction] ▸ **opposer son veto à qqch** to forbid ou to prohibit ou to veto sthg.

vêtu, e [vety] ◆ pp ⟶ **vêtir**. ◆ adj dressed / *être bien / mal vêtu* to be well / badly dressed / *être chaudement vêtu* to be warmly dressed ou clad ▸ **vêtu de** dressed in, wearing / *un enfant vêtu d'un blouson* a child wearing a jacket / *toute de soie vêtue* all dressed in silk.

vétuste [vetyst] adj dilapidated, decrepit.

vétusté [vetyste] nf [d'un bâtiment] dilapidated state ; [d'une loi] obsolescence / *la vétusté de l'installation électrique est en cause* the poor state of the wiring is to blame.

veuf, veuve [vœf, vœv] ◆ adj [personne] ▸ **devenir veuf** to be widowed, to become a widower ▸ **devenir veuve** to be widowed, to become a widow. ◆ nm, f widower (widow).

veule [vøl] adj [personne] spineless, cowardly ; [visage, traits] weak.

veuvage [vœvaʒ] nm [perte d'un mari] widowhood ; [perte d'une femme] widowerhood.

vexant, e [vɛksã, ãt] adj [blessant - personne] hurtful ; [- remarque] cutting, slighting, hurtful.

vexation [vɛksasjɔ̃] nf snub, slight, humiliation.

vexer [4] [vɛkse] vt ▸ **vexer qqn** to hurt sb's feelings ▸ **être vexé** to be hurt ou offended / *il est vexé de n'avoir pas compris* he's cross because he didn't understand. ❖ **se vexer** vpi to be hurt ou offended ou upset, to take offence 🇬🇧 ou offense 🇺🇸 / *se vexer facilement* to be easily offended, to be oversensitive.

VF (abr de **version française**) nf *indicates that a film is dubbed in French.*

VHF (abr de **very high frequency**) nf VHF.

via [vja] prép via, through.

viabiliser [3] [vjabilize] vt to service ▸ **terrain viabilisé** piece of land with water, gas and electricity installed *(for building purposes).*

viabilité [vjabilite] nf [d'un organisme, d'un projet] viability ; [d'un fœtus] survival potential.

viable [vjabl] adj [entreprise, projet] viable, practicable, viable.

viaduc [vjadyk] nm viaduct.

viager, ère [vjaʒe, ɛʀ] adj life *(modif)*. ❖ **viager** nm (life) annuity. ❖ **en viager** *loc adv* ▸ **acheter / vendre une maison en viager** to buy / to sell a house so as to provide the seller with a life annuity.

viande [vjãd] nf CULIN meat ▸ **viande de bœuf** beef ▸ **viande hachée** minced meat, mince 🇬🇧, ground meat 🇺🇸 / **viande de boucherie** fresh meat *(as sold by the butcher)* ▸ **viande froide** dish of cold meat ▸ **viande rouge / blanche** red / white meat.

vibration [vibʀasjɔ̃] nf **1.** [tremblement - d'un moteur, d'une corde] vibration ; [- d'une voix] quaver, tremor, vibration ; [- du sol] vibration **2.** ACOUST & ÉLECTRON vibration.

vibrer [3] [vibʀe] vi **1.** [trembler - diapason, vitre, plancher, voix] to vibrate ▸ **vibrer d'émotion** to quiver ou to quaver with emotion ▸ **faire vibrer qqch** to vibrate sthg **2.** *fig* ▸ **faire vibrer qqn** [l'intéresser] to thrill ou to stir sb.

vibromasseur [vibʀomasœʀ] nm vibrator.

vicaire [vikɛʀ] nm [auxiliaire - d'un curé] curate ; [- d'un évêque, du pape] vicar.

vice [vis] nm **1.** [le mal] vice **2.** [moral] vice / *on ne lui connaît aucun vice* she has no known vice ; *hum* [travers] vice **3.** COMM & DR defect, flaw ▸ **vice caché** hidden ou latent defect ▸ **vice de construction** structural fault ▸ **annulé pour vice de forme** DR annulled because of a mistake in the drafting.

vice-consul, e [viskɔ̃syl] *(mpl* **vice-consuls**, *fpl* **vice-consules**) nm, f vice-consul.

---

vice-présidence [visʀezidɑ̃s] (*pl* **vice-présidences**) nf [d'un État] vice-presidency ; [d'un congrès] vice-chair.

vice-président, e [visʀezidɑ̃, ɑ̃t]
(*mpl* **vice-présidents**, *fpl* **vice-présidentes**) nm, f [d'un État] vice-president ; [d'un meeting] vice-chairman (vice-chairwoman), vice-chairperson.

vice versa [vis(e)vɛʀsa] loc adv vice versa.

vichy [viʃi] nm **1.** TEXT gingham **2.** [eau] Vichy (water) **3.** CULIN vichy ▸ **carottes Vichy** carrots vichy (*glazed with butter and sugar*).

vicié, e [visje] adj [pollué - air, sang] polluted, contaminated.

vicieux, euse [visjø, øz] ◆ adj **1.** [pervers - livre, film] obscene ; [- regard] depraved ; [- personne] lecherous, depraved **2.** [trompeur - coup, balle] nasty ; [- calcul] misleading **3.** [animal] vicious. ◆ nm, f [homme] lecher, pervert / *un vieux vicieux* a dirty old man, an old lecher.

⚠ Lorsque vicieux a le sens de « pervers », il ne se traduit pas par **vicious**, qui signifie « malveillant », « méchant ».

vicinal, e, aux [visinal, o] adj ⟶ **chemin**.

victime [viktim] nf **1.** [d'un accident, d'un meurtre] victim, casualty / *l'accident a fait trois victimes* three people died in the accident **2.** [d'un préjudice] victim / *être la victime d'un escroc* to fall prey to ou to be the victim of a con man.

victimisation [viktimizasjɔ̃] nf victimization.

victoire [viktwaʀ] nf **1.** [fait de gagner - bataille, compétition] victory, winning ; [- dans une entreprise] victory, success *(U)* **2.** [résultat - militaire] victory ; [- sportif] victory, win ; [- dans une entreprise] victory, success.

victorieux, euse [viktɔʀjø, øz] adj SPORT victorious, winning *(avant nom)* ; POL victorious, winning *(avant nom)*, successful ; MIL victorious ; [air] triumphant.

victuailles [viktɥaj] nfpl victuals *sout*, food *(U)*, provisions.

vidange [vidɑ̃ʒ] nf **1.** AUTO oil change / *faire la vidange* to change the oil **2.** BELG [verre consigné] returnable empties.

vidanger [17] [vidɑ̃ʒe] vt **1.** [eaux usées] to empty **2.** AUTO [huile] to change.

vide [vid] ◆ adj **1.** [sans contenu] empty **2.** [sans occupant] empty. ◆ nm **1.** [néant] space / *regarder dans le vide* to stare into space ▸ **parler dans le vide a)** [sans auditoire] to address empty space **b)** [sans contenu] to talk vacuously **2.** PHYS vacuum / *faire le vide* [dans un vase clos] to create a vacuum ; *fig* : *faire le vide autour de soi* to drive all one's friends away / *faire le vide dans son esprit* to make one's mind go blank **3.** [distance qui sépare du sol] (empty) space / *la maison est construite, en partie, au-dessus du vide* part of the house is built over a drop / *avoir peur du vide* to be scared of heights / *tomber dans le vide* to fall into (empty) space **4.** [trou - entre deux choses] space, gap ; [- entre les mots ou les lignes d'un texte] space, blank **5.** [lacune] void, gap, blank / *son départ a laissé un grand vide dans ma vie* she left a gaping void in my life when she went ▸ **vide juridique** DR legal vacuum **6.** [manque d'intérêt] emptiness, void **7.** CONSTR ▸ **vide sanitaire** ventilation space. ◆ **à vide** loc adv : *le moteur tourne à vide* the engine's ticking over ou idling. ◆ **sous vide** ◆ loc adj vacuum *(modif)*. ◆ loc adv ▸ **emballé sous vide** vacuum-packed.

vidéaste [videast] nmf video maker.

vidéo [video] ◆ adj inv video *(modif)* ▸ **système de surveillance vidéo** video surveillance system. ◆ nf video (recording) ▸ **faire de la vidéo** to make videos.

vidéoblog [videoblɔg] nm videoblog.

vidéocassette [videokasɛt] nf videocassette, video.

vidéoclub [videoklœb] nm videoclub.

vidéoconférence [videokɔ̃feʀɑ̃s] nf video conferencing.

vidéodisque [videodisk] nm videodisk US, videodisc UK.

vidéoprojecteur [videopʀɔʒɛktœʀ] nm video projector.

vide-ordures (*pl* **vide-ordures**), **vide-ordure***(*pl* **vide-ordures**) [vidɔʀdyʀ] nm rubbish UK ou garbage US chute.

vidéosphère [videosfɛʀ] nf videosphere.

vidéosurveillance [videosyʀvɛjɑ̃s] nf video surveillance ▸ **caméra / système de vidéosurveillance** video surveillance camera / system.

vidéothèque [videotɛk] nf video library.

vide-poche(s) [vidpɔʃ] (*pl* **vide-poches**) nm [meuble] tidy ; [dans une voiture] glove compartment.

vider [3] [vide] vt **1.** [le contenu de - seau, verre, sac] to empty (out) *(sép)* ; [- poche, valise] to empty (out) *(sép)* ; [- baignoire] to let the water out of, to empty / *vider les ordures* to put out the rubbish UK ou garbage US ▸ **vider de** : *vider une maison de ses meubles* to empty a house of its furniture, to clear the furniture from a house ▸ **vider les lieux** to vacate the premises ▸ **vider son sac** to get things off one's chest, to unburden o.s. **2.** [le milieu de - pomme] to core ; [- volaille] to empty, to clean (out) *(sép)* ; [- poisson] to gut **3.** [boire] to drain / *vider son verre* to drain one's glass **4.** *fam* [épuiser] to do in *(sép)*, to finish off *(sép)* ▸ **être vidé** to be exhausted **5.** *fam* [renvoyer] to throw ou to kick out *(sép)* ▸ **vider qqn a)** [employé] to sack UK ou to fire sb **b)** [client] to throw sb out, to bounce sb US **c)** [élève] to throw ou to chuck sb out **6.** INFORM to dump. ◆ **se vider** vpi **1.** [contenu] to empty ou to drain (out) **2.** [salle, ville] to empty.

videur [vidœʀ] nm [de boîte de nuit] bouncer.

vie [vi] nf **1.** BIOL life ▸ **durée de vie** life span **2.** [existence] life ▸ **laisser la vie sauve à qqn** to spare sb's life / *donner la vie à un enfant* to give birth to a child / *risquer sa vie* to risk one's life ▸ **ôter la vie à qqn** to take sb's life / *revenir à la vie* to come back to life ▸ **sauver la vie de qqn** to save sb's life / *au début de sa vie* at the beginning of his life / *à la fin de sa vie* at the end of his life, late in life ▸ **avoir la vie devant soi a)** [ne pas être pressé] to have all the time in the world **b)** [être jeune] to have one's whole life in front of one / *être entre la vie et la mort* to be hovering between life and death, to be at death's door ▸ **la vie continue** life goes on ▸ **à la vie à la mort** for life (and beyond the grave) **3.** [personne] life / *son rôle est de sauver des vies* his ou her task is to save lives **4.** [entrain] life ▸ **plein de vie a)** [ressemblant] true to life, lifelike **b)** [énergique] lively, full of life **5.** [partie de l'existence] life ▸ **vie privée** private life / *entrer dans la vie active* to start working **6.** [façon de vivre - d'une personne, d'une société] life, lifestyle, way of life ; [- des animaux] life ▸ **faire sa vie avec qqn** to settle down with sb / *rater sa vie* to make a mess of one's life ▸ **refaire sa vie** to start afresh ou all over again / *c'est la vie !* such is ou that's life ! ▸ **mener une vie de bâton de chaise** ou **de patachon** *fam* to lead a riotous life ▸ **une vie de chien** *fam* a dog's life ▸ **ce n'est pas une vie !** I don't call that living ! ▸ **c'est la belle vie** ou **la vie de château !** this is the life ! ▸ **voir la vie en rose** to see life through rose-coloured UK ou rose-colored US spectacles **7.** [biographie] life **8.** [conditions économiques] (cost of) living / *le coût de la vie* the cost of living **9.** RELIG life / *la vie éternelle* everlasting life.

❖ **à vie** loc adj for life, life *(modif)* / *membre à vie* life member. ❖ **en vie** loc adj alive, living. ❖ **sans vie** loc adj [corps] lifeless, inert ; [œuvre] lifeless, dull.

vieil [vjɛj] m ⟶ **vieux**.

vieillard [vjɛjaʀ] nm old man.

vieille [vjɛj] f ⟶ **vieux**.

vieillerie [vjɛjʀi] nf [objet] old thing.

vieillesse [vjɛjɛs] nf [d'une personne] old age / *mourir de vieillesse* to die of old age.

vieilli, e [vjeji] adj [démodé] old-fashioned ; [vieux] : *je l'ai trouvé très vieilli* I thought he'd aged a lot.

vieillir [32] [vjejiʀ] ❖ vi **1.** [prendre de l'âge - personne] to age, to be getting old ; [-vin, fromage] to age, to mature ; [-technique] to become outmoded ▸ **bien vieillir** to grow old gracefully ▸ **il a mal vieilli** he hasn't aged well ▸ **ce film vieillit mal** this film doesn't stand the test of time **2.** [paraître plus vieux] : *il a vieilli de 20 ans* he looks 20 years older / *tu ne vieillis pas* you never seem to look any older. ❖ vt ▸ **vieillir qqn** [suj : vêtement, couleur] to make sb seem older / *vous me vieillissez !* you're making me older than I am! ❖ **se vieillir** vp *(emploi réfléchi)* [en apparence] to make o.s. look older ; [en mentant] to lie about one's age *(by pretending to be older)*.

vieillissement [vjejismɑ̃] nm [naturel] ageing, the ageing process / *les signes qui trahissent le vieillissement* the telltale signs of age ou of the ageing process.

vieillot, otte [vjejo, ɔt] adj old-fashioned.

vielle [vjɛl] nf hurdy-gurdy.

Vienne [vjɛn] npr [en Autriche] Vienna.

viennois, e [vjɛnwa, az] adj [Autriche] Viennese. ❖ **Viennois, e** nm, f [en Autriche] inhabitant of or person from Vienna.

viennoiserie [vjɛnwazʀi] nf *pastry made with sweetened dough (croissant, brioche, etc.)*.

vierge [vjɛʀʒ] ❖ adj **1.** [personne] virgin / *elle / il est encore vierge* she's / he's still a virgin **2.** [vide - cahier, feuille] blank, clean ; [-casier judiciaire] clean ; [-pellicule, film] unexposed ; [-CD, DVD, etc.] blank **3.** [inexploité - sol, terre] virgin / *de la neige vierge* fresh snow. ❖ nf [femme] virgin.

Vierge [vjɛʀʒ] npr f **1.** RELIG ▸ **la Vierge (Marie)** the Virgin (Mary), the Blessed Virgin **2.** ASTROL Virgo **3.** ASTRON Virgo ▸ **être Vierge** to be (a) Virgo ou a Virgoan.

Viêt Nam [vjɛtnam] npr m ▸ **le Viêt Nam** Vietnam / *le Nord / Sud Viêt Nam* North / South Vietnam.

vietnamien, enne [vjɛtnamjɛ̃, ɛn] adj Vietnamese. ❖ **Vietnamien, enne** nm, f Vietnamese ▸ **les Vietnamiens** the Vietnamese. ❖ **vietnamien** nm LING Vietnamese.

vieux, vieille [vjø, vjɛj] *(devant nm commençant par voyelle ou «h» muet* **vieil** [vjɛj]*)* adj **1.** [âgé] old ▸ **les vieilles gens** old people, elderly people, the elderly ▸ **vivre vieux** [personne, animal] to live to be old, to live to a ripe old age ▸ **se faire vieux** to be getting on (in years), to be getting old / *le plus vieux des trois* the eldest ou oldest of the three **2.** *(avant nom)* [de longue date - admirateur, camarade, complicité, passion] old, long-standing ; [-famille, tradition] old, ancient ; [-dicton, recette] old ; [-continent, montagne] old ▸ **le Vieux Monde** the Old World **3.** [désuet - instrument, méthode] old ▸ **une vieille expression a)** [qui n'est plus usitée] an obsolete turn of phrase **b)** [surannée] an old-fashioned turn of phrase ; [usé, fané] old ▸ **recycler les vieux papiers** to recycle waste paper ▸ **un vieux numéro** [de magazine] a back issue **4.** [précédent] old. ❖ **vieux** ❖ nm **1.** *fam & péj* [homme âgé] old man ▸ **un vieux de la vieille a)** [soldat de Napoléon] an old veteran of Na-

poleon's guard **b)** [personne d'expérience] an old hand **2.** *tfam* [père] : *mon / son vieux* my / his old man **3.** *fam* [à valeur affective - entre adultes] ▸ **mon vieux** old chap ou boy 🇬🇧, old buddy 🇺🇸 / *allez, (mon) vieux, ça va s'arranger* come on mate 🇬🇧 ou buddy 🇺🇸, it'll be all right ; [pour exprimer la surprise] : *j'en ai eu pour 800 euros — ben mon vieux !* it cost me 800 euros — good heavens! **4.** *fam* EXPR ▸ **prendre un coup de vieux** : *elle a pris un sacré coup de vieux* she's looking a lot older. ❖ adv ▸ **s'habiller vieux** to wear old-fashioned clothes. ❖ nmpl *péj* **1.** fam [personnes âgées] ▸ **les vieux** old people **2.** *tfam* [parents] : *les* ou *mes vieux* my parents, my folks, my Mum 🇬🇧 ou Mom 🇺🇸 and Dad. ❖ **vieille** nf **1.** *fam & péj* [femme âgée] old woman ou girl **2.** *tfam* [mère] : *la vieille, ma / ta vieille* my / your old lady **3.** *fam* [à valeur affective - entre adultes] : *salut, ma vieille !* hi there! ❖ **de vieux, de vieille** loc adj old-fashioned, antiquated, geriatric *hum* / *tu as des idées de vieux* you're so old-fashioned (in your ideas). ❖ **vieux de, vieille de** loc adj [qui date de] : *une amitié vieille de 20 ans* a friendship that goes back 20 years. ❖ **vieille fille** nf *vieilli* ou *péj* spinster, old maid *péj*. ❖ **vieux garçon** nm *vieilli* ou *péj* bachelor / *des manies de vieux garçon* bachelor ways. ❖ **vieux jeu** loc adj [personne, attitude] old-fashioned ; [vêtements, idées] old-fashioned, outmoded.

vif, vive [vif, viv] adj **1.** [plein d'énergie - personne] lively, vivacious ; [-musique, imagination, style] lively / *avoir le regard vif* to have a lively look in one's eye ▸ **rouler à vive allure** to drive at great speed **2.** [intelligent - élève] sharp ; [-esprit] sharp, quick / *être vif (d'esprit)* to be quick ou quick-witted ou sharp **3.** [emporté - remarque, discussion, reproche] cutting, biting ; [-geste] brusque, brisk **4.** [très intense - froid] biting ; [-couleur] bright, vivid ; [-désir, sentiment] strong ; [-déception, intérêt] keen ; [-félicitations, remerciements] warm ; [-regret, satisfaction] deep, great ; [-douleur] sharp / *porter un vif intérêt à* to be greatly ou keenly interested in / *l'air est vif ce matin* it's chilly this morning **5.** [nu - angle, arête] sharp ; [-joint] dry ; [-pierre] bare **6.** [vivant] ▸ **être brûlé / enterré vif** to be burnt / buried alive. ❖ **vif** nm **1.** ▸ **piquer qqn au vif** to cut sb to the quick **2.** [centre] ▸ **trancher** ou **tailler dans le vif** to go straight to the point / *entrer dans le vif du sujet* to get to the heart of the matter. ❖ **à vif** loc adj [blessure] open. ❖ **de vive voix** loc adv personally / *je le lui dirai de vive voix* I'll tell him personally. ❖ **sur le vif** loc adv [peindre] from life ; [commenter] on the spot / *ces photos ont été prises sur le vif* these photos were unposed.

vif-argent [vifaʀʒɑ̃] *(pl* **vifs-argents)** nm quicksilver.

vigie [viʒi] nf NAUT [balise] danger-buoy ; *vieilli* [guetteur] look-out ; [poste] look-out post ; [panier] crow's nest.

vigilance [viʒilɑ̃s] nf vigilance, watchfulness.

vigilant, e [viʒilɑ̃, ɑ̃t] adj [personne, regard] vigilant, watchful ; [soins] vigilant / *soyez vigilant !* watch out!

vigile [viʒil] nm [d'une communauté privée] ; [veilleur de nuit] night watchman ; [surveillant] guard.

Vigipirate [viʒipiʀat] npr ▸ **le plan Vigipirate** *measures to protect the public from terrorist attacks*.

vigne [viɲ] nf **1.** AGR vine, grapevine ; [vignoble] vineyard **2.** BOT ▸ **vigne vierge** Virginia creeper.

vigneron, onne [viɲəʀɔ̃, ɔn] nm, f wine-grower, wine-producer.

vignette [viɲɛt] nf **1.** COMM (manufacturer's) label ; [sur un médicament] label ou sticker *(for reimbursement within the French Social Security system)* **2.** ADMIN & AUTO ▸ **vignette (auto** ou **automobile)** ≃ (road) tax disc 🇬🇧 ; ≃ (car) registration sticker 🇺🇸 **3.** ART [sur un livre, une gravure] vignette.

vignoble [viɲɔbl] nm vineyard / *le vignoble italien / alsacien* the vineyards of Italy / Alsace.

vigoureusement [viguʀøzmɑ̃] adv [frapper, frictionner] vigorously, energetically ; [se défendre] vigorously ; [protester] forcefully.

vigoureux, euse [viguʀø, øz] adj **1.** [fort - homme] vigorous, sturdy ; [-membres] strong, sturdy ; [-arbre, plante] sturdy ; [-santé] robust ; [-poignée de main, répression] vigorous **2.** [langage, argument] forceful ; [opposition, soutien] strong ; [défense] vigorous, spirited ; [contestation, effort] vigorous, forceful, powerful ; [mesures] energetic.

vigueur [vigœʀ] nf **1.** [d'une personne, d'une plante] strength, vigour 🇬🇧, vigor 🇺🇸 ; [d'un coup] vigour 🇬🇧, vigor 🇺🇸, strength, power ▸ **avec vigueur** vigorously, energetically **2.** [d'un style, d'une contestation] forcefulness, vigour ; [d'un argument] forcefulness / *protester avec vigueur* to object forcefully. ✤ **en vigueur** ◆ loc adj [décret, loi, règlement] in force ; [tarif, usage] current. ◆ loc adv ▸ **entrer en vigueur** [décret, tarif] to come into force ou effect.

VIH (abr de virus d'immunodéficience humaine) nm HIV.

Viking [vikiŋ] nmf Viking ▸ **les Vikings** the Vikings.

vil, e [vil] adj *litt* [acte, personne, sentiment] base, vile, despicable.

vilain, e [vilɛ̃, ɛn] ◆ adj **1.** [laid - figure, personne, etc.] ugly ; [-quartier] ugly, sordid ; [-décoration, bâtiment, habit] ugly, hideous / *ils ne sont pas vilains du tout, tes dessins* your drawings aren't bad at all ▸ **le vilain petit canard** *pr & fig* the ugly duckling **2.** [méchant] naughty / *c'est un vilain monsieur* he's a bad man ▸ **jouer un vilain tour à qqn** to play a rotten ou dirty trick on sb **3.** [sérieux - affaire, blessure, coup, maladie] nasty **4.** [désagréable - odeur] nasty, bad ; [-temps] nasty, awful. ◆ nm, f bad ou naughty boy (girl) / *oh le vilain / la vilaine !* you naughty boy / girl! ✤ **vilain** nm *fam* [situation désagréable] : *il va y avoir du vilain !* there's going to be trouble! / *ça tourne au vilain !* things are getting nasty!

vilebrequin [vilbʀəkɛ̃] nm **1.** TECHNOL (bit) brace **2.** AUTO crankshaft.

vilipender [3] [vilipɑ̃de] vt *litt* to disparage, to revile.

villa [vila] nf **1.** [résidence secondaire] villa **2.** [pavillon] (detached) house.

village [vilaʒ] nm **1.** [agglomération, personnes] village **2.** LOISIRS ▸ **village (de vacances)** holiday 🇬🇧 ou vacation 🇺🇸 village **3.** INTERNET ▸ **village global** ou **planétaire** the global village.

villageois, e [vilaʒwa, az] ◆ adj village *(modif)*, country *(modif)*. ◆ nm, f villager, village resident.

ville [vil] nf **1.** [moyenne] town ; [plus grande] city / *toute la ville en parle* it's the talk of the town / *à la ville comme à la scène* in real life as (well as) on stage ▸ **ville d'eau** spa (town) ▸ **ville nouvelle** new town **2.** [quartier] ▸ **ville haute / basse** upper / lower part of town **3.** ADMIN ▸ **la ville a)** [administration] the local authority **b)** [représentants] the (town) council **4.** [milieu non rural] ▸ **la ville** towns, cities / *les gens de la ville* city-dwellers, townspeople. ✤ **de ville** loc adj VÊT ▸ **chaussures / tenue de ville** shoes / outfit for wearing in town. ✤ **en ville** loc adv ▸ **aller en ville** to go to ou into town 🇬🇧, to go downtown 🇺🇸 / *trouver un studio en ville* to find a flat 🇬🇧 ou studio apartment 🇺🇸 in town.

ville-dortoir [vildɔʀtwaʀ] *(pl* **villes-dortoirs)** nf dormitory town.

villégiature [vileʒjatyʀ] nf holiday 🇬🇧, vacation 🇺🇸 / *être en villégiature* to be on holiday 🇬🇧 ou vacation 🇺🇸 ▸ **lieu de villégiature** holiday resort 🇬🇧, vacation resort 🇺🇸.

vin [vɛ̃] nm ŒNOL [boisson] wine ; [ensemble de récoltes] vintage ▸ **grand vin, vin de grand cru** vintage wine ▸ **vin blanc** white wine ▸ **vin chaud** mulled wine ▸ **vin mousseux** sparkling wine ▸ **vin ordinaire** table wine ▸ **vin rosé** rosé wine ▸ **vin rouge** red wine ▸ **vin de table** table wine. ✤ **vin d'honneur** nm reception *(where wine is served)*.

Le vin

France's strong tradition of vine-growing and winemaking dates back to the Roman Empire. Despite falling domestic consumption and steadily increasing sales of wines from elsewhere in Europe and the New World, wine continues to play a vital role in the country's economy. Wine has a profound influence on local culture in wine-growing areas, where most vineyards are family-run using traditional methods.

The word **terroir** is one of the keys to understanding wine in France. It refers to a wine-growing area (Alsace, Beaujolais, Bordeaux, Bourgogne, Champagne, Val-de-Loire, Vallée du Rhône, Corse, etc.), and it also evokes the characteristics specific to those areas that determine wine type and quality (particularly climate, topography, soil type and local expertise.

Some vineyards that produce wines of exceptional quality are known as **grands crus** (great vineyards), a term which is used by extension to refer to the wines made there. **Premier cru** and **cru bourgeois** wines are also of high quality, though they are slightly less prestigious than **grands crus**. The vital importance of **terroir** explains why French wine is traditionally identified by its geographical origin (area or estate), rather than its varietal (Syrah, Cabernet Sauvignon, Chardonnay, etc.).

The **AOC** (appellation d'origine contrôlée) label guarantees the origin and quality of some 340 wines, and strictly controls the varietals used in their making. The great **appellations** include: "Pomerol", "Pauillac" (Bordeaux), "Sauternes" (Bordeaux), "Mâcon" (Burgundy), "Chablis" (Burgundy), "Pouilly-Fuissé" (Burgundy), "Pouilly-Fumé" (Loire), "Sancerre" (Loire), "Gewurztraminer", "Riesling" (Alsace).

vinaigre [vinɛgʀ] nm **1.** [condiment] vinegar ▸ **vinaigre d'alcool / de cidre / de vin** spirit / cider / wine vinegar **2.** *fam* EXPR **tourner au vinaigre** [vin] to turn sour.

vinaigrer [4] [vinegʀe] vt to add vinegar to / *ce n'est pas assez vinaigré* there's too little vinegar.

vinaigrette [vinegʀɛt] nf vinaigrette, French dressing / *haricots à la* ou *en vinaigrette* beans with vinaigrette ou French dressing.

vinaigrier [vinegʀije] nm [bouteille] vinegar bottle.

vinasse [vinas] nf *fam & péj* [vin] plonk 🇬🇧, jug wine 🇺🇸.

vindicatif, ive [vɛ̃dikatif, iv] adj vindictive.

vindicte [vɛ̃dikt] nf DR ▸ **la vindicte publique** prosecution and punishment ▸ **désigner** ou **livrer qqn à la vindicte populaire** to expose sb to trial by the mob.

vingt [vɛ̃] ◆ dét twenty / *je te l'ai dit vingt fois !* I've told you a hundred times! / *je n'ai plus vingt ans !* I'm not as young as I used to be! / *ah, si j'avais encore mes jambes / mon cœur de vingt ans !* if only I still had the legs / the heart of a twenty year-old! ▸ **vingt dieux !** *fam & vieilli*: *vingt dieux, la belle fille !* strewth 🇬🇧 ou Lord 🇺🇸, what a beauty! / *ne touche pas à ça, vingt dieux !* leave that alone, for God's sake! ◆ nm twenty / *il a joué trois fois le vingt* he played three times on number twenty / *le vingt de chaque mois* the twentieth of the month. **Voir aussi cinq.**

vingtaine [vɛ̃tɛn] nf ▸ **une vingtaine** twenty or so, around twenty.

vingtième [vɛ̃tjɛm] adj num & nmf twentieth. **Voir aussi cinquantième.**

vinicole [vinikɔl] adj [pays] wine-growing ; [industrie, production] wine *(modif).*

vinification [vinifikasjɔ̃] nf [de jus de fruits] vinification ; [pour l'obtention de vin] wine-making process.

viol [vjɔl] nm [d'une personne] rape ▸ **viol collectif** gang rape ; [d'un sanctuaire] violation, desecration.

violacé, e [vjɔlase] adj purplish-blue.

violation [vjɔlasjɔ̃] nf 1. [d'une loi, d'une règle] violation ; [d'un serment] breach ; [d'un accord] violation, breach 2. [d'un sanctuaire, d'une sépulture] violation, desecration / *violation de domicile* forcible entry *(into somebody's home).*

viole [vjɔl] nf viol.

violemment [vjɔlamɑ̃] adv [frapper] violently ; [protester, critiquer] vehemently ; [désirer] passionately.

violence [vjɔlɑ̃s] nf 1. [brutalité - d'un affrontement, d'un coup, d'une personne] violence ; [- d'un sport] roughness, brutality / *répondre à la violence par la violence* to meet violence with violence ; *fig* ▸ **se faire violence** to force o.s. 2. [acte] assault, violent act ▸ **violence à agent** assault on (the person of) a police officer ▸ **violence verbale** verbal violence 3. [intensité - d'un sentiment, d'une sensation] intensity ; [- d'un séisme, du vent, etc.] violence, fierceness.

violent, e [vjɔlɑ̃, ɑ̃t] ◆ adj 1. [brutal - sport, jeu] rough, brutal ; [- attaque, affrontement] fierce, violent, brutal ; [- personne] violent, brutal ; [- tempérament] violent, fiery 2. [intense - pluie] driving ; [- vent, tempête] violent, raging ; [- couleur] harsh, glaring ; [- parfum] pungent, overpowering ; [- effort] huge, strenuous ; [- besoin, envie] intense, uncontrollable, urgent ; [- douleur] violent / *un violent mal de tête* a splitting headache. ◆ nm, f violent person.

violenter [3] [vjɔlɑ̃te] vt [femme] to assault sexually / *elle a été violentée* she was sexually assaulted.

violer [3] [vjɔle] vt 1. [personne] to rape / *se faire violer* to be raped 2. [loi, règle] to violate ; [serment] to break ; [accord, secret professionnel] to violate, to break ; [promesse] to violate ; [secret] to betray 3. [sanctuaire, sépulture] to violate, to desecrate.

violet, ette [vjɔle, ɛt] adj purple, violet. ◆ **violet** nm purple, violet (colour). ◆ **violette** nf violet.

violeur, euse [vjɔlœr, øz] nm, f rapist.

violon [vjɔlɔ̃] nm MUS [instrument - d'orchestre] violin ; [- de violoneux] fiddle ; [artiste] ▸ **premier violon (solo)** first violin ▸ **violon d'Ingres** hobby.

violoncelle [vjɔlɔ̃sɛl] nm cello, violoncello *spéc.*

violoncelliste [vjɔlɔ̃selist] nmf cellist, cello player, violoncellist *spéc.*

violoneux [vjɔlɔnø] nm 🇶🇧 fiddler.

violoniste [vjɔlɔnist] nmf violinist, violin-player.

VIP [viajpi, veipe] (abr de **very important person**) nmf VIP.

vipère [vipɛʀ] nf adder, viper ▸ **c'est une vraie vipère** *fig & péj* she's really vicious.

virage [viʀaʒ] nm 1. [d'une route] bend, curve, turn 🇺🇸 / *prendre un virage* to take a bend, to go round a bend ▸ **virage en épingle à cheveux** hairpin bend 2. [mouvement - d'un véhicule, au ski] turn 3. [changement - d'attitude, d'idéologie] (drastic) change ou shift ▸ **virage à droite / gauche** POL shift to the right / left.

viral, e, aux [viʀal, o] adj *pr & fig* viral.

virée [viʀe] nf *fam* 1. [promenade] ▸ **faire une virée à vélo / en voiture** to go for a bicycle ride / a drive / *si on faisait une virée dans les bars du coin ?* let's hit the local bars 2. [court voyage] trip, tour, jaunt / *on a fait une petite virée en Bretagne* we went for a little jaunt to Brittany.

virement [viʀmɑ̃] nm BANQUE : *faire un virement de 600 euros sur un compte* to transfer 600 euros to an account ▸ **virement bancaire** bank transfer.

virer [3] [viʀe] ◆ vi 1. [voiture] to turn ; [vent] to veer ; [grue] to turn round ; [personne] to turn ou to pivot round ▸ **virer sur l'aile** AÉRON to bank ▸ **virer de bord a)** NAUT [gén] to veer **b)** [voilier] to tack **c)** *fig* to take a new line ou tack 2. MÉD [cuti-réaction] to come up positive. ◆ vt 1. BANQUE to transfer / *virer 50 euros sur un compte* to transfer 50 euros to an account 2. *fam* [jeter - meuble, papiers] to chuck (out), to ditch 3. *fam* [renvoyer - employé] to fire, to sack 🇬🇧 ; [- importun] to kick ou to chuck out *(sép)* ▸ **se faire virer** [employé] to get the sack 🇬🇧 ou the bounce 🇺🇸 4. MÉD ▸ **il a viré sa cuti a)** *pr* his skin test was positive **b)** *fig* he changed radically. ◆ **virer à** v + prép : *virer à l'aigre* [vin] to turn sour / *virer au vert / rouge* to turn green / red.

virevolter [3] [viʀvɔlte] vi 1. [tourner sur soi] to pirouette, to spin round *(insép)* 2. [s'agiter] to dance around.

Virginie [viʀʒini] ◆ nm Virginia (tobacco). ◆ npr f GÉOGR ▸ **(la) Virginie** Virginia ▸ **(la) Virginie-Occidentale** West Virginia.

virginité [viʀʒinite] nf [d'une personne] virginity / *le parti devra se refaire une virginité fig* the party will have to forge itself a new reputation.

virgule [viʀgyl] nf 1. [dans un texte] comma 2. MATH (decimal) point ▸ **4 virgule 9** 4 point 9.

viril, e [viʀil] adj 1. [force, langage] manly, virile 2. [sexuellement] virile.

virilité [viʀilite] nf 1. [gén] virility, manliness 2. [vigueur sexuelle] virility.

virtualité [viʀtɥalite] nf virtuality.

virtuel, elle [viʀtɥɛl] adj 1. [fait, valeur] potential 2. INFORM, OPT & PHYS virtual.

virtuellement [viʀtɥɛlmɑ̃] adv 1. [potentiellement] potentially 2. [très probablement] virtually, to all intents and purposes, practically.

virtuose [viʀtɥoz] nmf MUS virtuoso / *virtuose du violon* violin virtuoso / *c'est une virtuose du tennis / de l'aiguille* she's a brilliant tennis player / needlewoman.

virtuosité [viʀtɥozite] nf virtuosity / *elle a joué la fugue avec une grande virtuosité* she gave a virtuoso rendering of the fugue.

virulence [viʀylɑ̃s] nf [d'un reproche, d'un discours] virulence, viciousness, venom.

virulent, e [viʀylɑ̃, ɑ̃t] adj [critique, discours] virulent, vicious, venomous ; [haine] burning, bitter.

virus [viʀys] nm 1. BIOL virus / *le virus de la grippe* the influenza virus 2. *fig* : *tout le pays était atteint par le virus du loto* the whole country was gripped by lottery fever 3. INFORM virus.

vis [vis] nf TECHNOL screw.

visa [viza] nm **1.** [sur un passeport] visa ▸ **visa de touriste** ou **de visiteur** tourist 🇬🇧 ou non-immigrant 🇺🇸 visa **2.** [sur un document] stamp ▸ **visa de censure** CINÉ (censor's) certificate.

visage [vizaʒ] nm **1.** [d'une personne] face ▸ **à visage découvert a)** [sans masque] unmasked **b)** [sans voile] unveiled **c)** [ouvertement] openly **2.** [aspect] aspect ▸ **l'Afrique aux multiples visages** the many faces of Africa / *enfin une ville à visage humain !* at last a town made for people to live in! / *elle révélait enfin son vrai visage* she was revealing her true self ou nature at last.

visagiste [vizaʒist] nmf hair stylist.

vis-à-vis [vizavi] nm **1.** [personne en face] ▸ **mon vis-à-vis** the person opposite me **2.** [immeuble d'en face] : *nous n'avons pas de vis-à-vis* there are no buildings directly opposite. ❖ **vis-à-vis de** loc prép **1.** [en face de] ▸ **être vis-à-vis de qqn** to be opposite sb **2.** [envers] towards, toward 🇺🇸, vis-à-vis / *quelle position avez-vous vis-à-vis de ce problème ?* what is your position on this problem? ❖ **en vis-à-vis** loc adv ▸ **être en vis-à-vis** to be opposite each other, to be facing each other.

viscéral, e, aux [viseral,o] adj **1.** PHYSIOL visceral **2.** [dégoût] profound ; [peur] deep-rooted, profound ; [jalousie] pathological / *je ne l'aime pas, c'est viscéral* I don't like him, it's a gut feeling.

viscéralement [viseralmã] adv deeply / *il est viscéralement attaché à sa région natale* he is deeply attached to his native region ▸ **être viscéralement opposé à** to be passionately opposed to.

viscères [viser] nmpl viscera.

viscose [viskoz] nf viscose.

visée [vize] nf **1.** (gén au pl) [intention] design, aim ▸ **avoir des visées sur qqn / qqch** to have designs on sb / sthg **2.** ARM aiming, taking aim, sighting.

viser [3] [vize] ❖ vt **1.** ARM [cible] to (take) aim at (insép) ; [jambe, tête] to aim for **2.** [aspirer à - poste] to set one's sights on (insép), to aim for ; [- résultats] to aim at ou for (insép) **3.** [concerner - suj : réforme] to be aimed ou directed at ; [- suj : critique] to be aimed ou directed at, to be meant for / *je ne vise personne !* I don't mean anybody in particular! ▸ **se sentir visé** to feel one is being got at **4.** tfam [regarder] to look at, to check out. ❖ vi **1.** MIL to (take) aim ▸ **viser juste / trop bas** to aim accurately / too low **2.** fig ▸ **viser (trop) haut** to set one's sights ou to aim (too) high. ❖ **viser à** v + prép [suj : politique, personne] to aim at / *mesures visant à faire payer les pollueurs* measures aimed at making the polluters pay.

viseur [vizœr] nm **1.** ARM [gén] sight, sights ; [à lunette] telescopic sight **2.** CINÉ & PHOT viewfinder.

visibilité [vizibilite] nf visibility ▸ **atterrir sans visibilité** to make a blind landing, to land blind ▸ **visibilité nulle** zero visibility.

visible [vizibl] adj **1.** [objet] visible / *visible à l'œil nu* visible to the naked eye **2.** [évident - gêne, intérêt, mépris] obvious, visible ; [- amélioration, différence] visible, perceptible / *il est visible que...* it's obvious ou clear that...

visiblement [vizibləmã] adv [gêné, mécontent] obviously, visibly ; [amélioré] perceptibly, visibly.

visière [vizjer] nf [gén] eyeshade 🇬🇧, vizor 🇺🇸 ; [d'un casque] visor, vizor ; [d'une casquette] peak.

visioconférence [vizjokɔ̃ferɑ̃s] nf videoconference.

vision [vizjɔ̃] nf **1.** [idée] view, outlook / *nous n'avons pas la même vision des choses* we see things differently / *sa vision du monde* her world view **2.** [image] vision ; [hallucination] vision, apparition / *tu as des visions !* fam & hum you're seeing things! **3.** PHYSIOL vision.

visionnaire [vizjɔnɛr] adj & nmf visionary.

visionnement [vizjɔnmã] nm 🇶🇨 screening.

visionner [3] [vizjɔne] vt [film, émission] to view ; [diapositives] to look at.

visionneuse [vizjɔnøz] nf viewer.

visiophone [vizjɔfɔn] nm videophone, viewphone.

visite [vizit] nf **1.** [chez quelqu'un - gén] visit ; [- courte] call ▸ **avoir ou recevoir la visite de qqn** to have a visit from sb ▸ **rendre visite à qqn** to pay sb a visit, to call on sb, to visit sb ▸ **être en visite chez qqn** to be paying sb a visit, to be visiting sb ou with sb 🇺🇸 ▸ **faire une petite visite à qqn** to pop round and see sb ▸ **visite officielle / privée** official / private visit ▸ **visite de politesse** courtesy call ou visit **2.** [à l'hôpital, auprès d'un détenu] visit ▸ **heures de visite** visiting hours **3.** [visiteur] ▸ **avoir de la visite** to have a visitor / *tu attends de la* fam ou *une visite ?* are you expecting a visitor ou somebody? **4.** [exploration - d'un lieu] visit, tour ▸ **visite guidée** guided tour ▸ **visite guidée audio** audio tour **5.** [d'un médecin - chez le patient] visit, call ; [- dans un hôpital] (ward) round ▸ **visite de contrôle** follow-up examination ▸ **visite à domicile** house call ou visit ▸ **passer une visite médicale** to undergo a medical examination, to take a physical examination 🇺🇸.

visiter [3] [vizite] vt **1.** [se promener dans - région, monument] to visit ; [- caves, musée] to go round (insép), to visit ; [- pour acheter] to view ; [- par curiosité] to look round (insép) / *une personne de l'agence vous fera visiter l'appartement* somebody from the agency will show you round ou 🇺🇸 through the flat, 🇬🇧 ou apartment 🇺🇸 **2.** [rendre visite à - détenu] to visit ; [- malade, indigent, client] to visit, to call on (insép) ; 🇶🇨 [rendre visite à] to visit.

visiteur, euse [vizitœr,øz] nm, f **1.** [invité] visitor, caller ; [d'un musée] visitor **2.** [professionnel] ▸ **visiteur de prison** prison visitor.

vison [vizɔ̃] nm **1.** ZOOL mink **2.** [fourrure] mink **3.** VÊT mink (coat).

visqueux, euse [viskø,øz] adj **1.** PHYS [matière] viscous ; [surface] viscid **2.** [peau, personne] slimy.

visser [3] [vise] vt **1.** [fixer - planche, support] to screw on ou to (sép) ; [- couvercle] to screw on ou down (sép) / *le miroir est vissé au mur* the mirror is screwed to the wall ; fig : *être vissé sur son siège* to be glued to one's chair **2.** [en tournant - bouchon, embout] to screw on (sép) ; [- robinet] to turn off (sép).

visseuse [visøz] nf electric screwdriver.

visualisation [vizyalizasjɔ̃] nf **1.** [mentale] visualization, visualizing **2.** INFORM display.

visualiser [3] [vizyalize] vt **1.** [mentalement] to visualize **2.** INFORM to display.

visuel, elle [vizyɛl] adj [mémoire, support] visual ▸ **champ visuel** field of vision, visual field. ❖ **visuel** nm INFORM visual display unit ou terminal, VDU.

visuellement [vizyɛlmã] adv visually.

vital, e, aux [vital,o] adj **1.** BIOL & PHYSIOL vital **2.** [indispensable] vital, essential **3.** [fondamental - problème, question] vital, fundamental.

vitalité [vitalite] nf [d'une personne] vitality, energy ; [d'une économie] dynamism, vitality, buoyancy ; [d'une expression, d'une théorie] vitality / *être plein de vitalité* to be full of energy.

vitamine [vitamin] nf vitamin / *vitamine A / C* vitamin A / C.

vitaminé, e [vitamine] adj with added vitamins, vitaminized.

vite [vit] adv **1.** [rapidement -courir, marcher] fast, quickly ; [-se propager] rapidly, quickly ▶ **roule moins vite** slow down, don't drive so fast ▶ **va plus vite** speed up, go faster / *tout s'est passé si vite que je n'ai pas eu le temps de voir* everything happened so quickly that I didn't see a thing / *comme le temps passe vite !* doesn't time fly! ▶ **elle apprend / travaille vite** she's a quick learner / worker / *ça a été vite réglé* it was settled in no time at all, it was soon settled / *fais vite !* hurry up!, be quick (about it)! / *et plus vite que ça !* and be quick about it! ▶ **vite fait** *fam* quickly / *range-moi ta chambre vite fait !* tidy up your room and be quick about it! ▶ **vite fait, bien fait** *fam*: *on lui a repeint sa grille vite fait, bien fait* we gave her gate a nice new coat of paint in no time / *je vais l'envoyer se faire voir vite fait, bien fait !* *tfam* I'll send him packing once and for all! ▶ **aller plus vite que la musique** ou **les violons** to jump the gun **2.** [à la hâte] quickly, in a hurry ou rush ▶ **manger vite** to bolt one's food (down) ▶ **aller vite** [dans ses conclusions] to be hasty ▶ **ils vont gagner — c'est vite dit !** they're going to win — I wouldn't be so sure! **3.** [sans tarder] quickly, soon / *j'ai vite compris de quoi il s'agissait* I soon realized what it was all about, it didn't take me long to realize what it was all about **4.** [facilement] quickly, easily ▶ **vite fait de**: *méfie-toi, il a vite fait de s'énerver* be careful, he loses his temper easily / *on a vite fait de se brûler avec ça !* it's easy to burn yourself on that thing! **5.** EXPR *vous allez un peu vite en besogne, je ne vous accuse pas !* don't jump to conclusions, I haven't accused you of anything! ❖ **au plus vite** loc adv as soon as possible.

vitesse [vitɛs] nf **1.** [d'un coureur, d'un véhicule] speed / *à la vitesse de 180 km/h* at (a speed of) 180 km/h ▶ **prendre de la vitesse** to pick up speed, to speed up ▶ **gagner / perdre de la vitesse** to gather / to lose speed ▶ **vitesse de croisière** *pr & fig* cruising speed ▶ **vitesse de pointe** top ou maximum speed ▶ **gagner** ou **prendre qqn de vitesse a)** [à pied] to walk faster than sb **b)** [en voiture] to go ou to drive faster than sb **c)** *fig* to beat sb to it, to pip sb at the post , to beat sb by a nose **2.** PHYS [d'un corps] speed, velocity ; [de la lumière] speed ▶ **la vitesse du son** the speed of sound **3.** [rythme -d'une action] speed, quickness, rapidity ; [-d'une transformation] speed, rapidity / *ses cheveux poussent à une vitesse incroyable !* her hair grows so fast! **4.** AUTO & MÉCAN gear ▶ **passer les vitesses a)** to go up through the gears **b)** [en rétrogradant] to go down through the gears ▶ **passer à la vitesse supérieure a)** *pr* to change up *(to next gear)* **b)** *fig* to speed up / *à deux vitesses* *fig* two-tier / *à la vitesse grand V* *fam* at the double, at a rate of knots . ❖ **à toute vitesse** loc adv at full ou top speed, in double-quick time. ❖ **en vitesse** loc adv [rapidement] quickly ; [à la hâte] in a rush ou hurry ▶ **déjeuner / se laver en vitesse** to have a quick lunch / wash / *écrire une lettre en vitesse* to dash off a letter / *on prend un verre en vitesse ?* shall we have a quick drink?

viticole [vitikɔl] adj ▶ **région viticole** wine-growing ou wine-producing region ▶ **entreprise viticole** wine-making company , winery .

viticulteur, trice [vitikyltœʀ,tʀis] nm, f wine-grower, wine-producer, viticulturist *spéc.*

viticulture [vitikyltyʀ] nf vine-growing, viticulture *spéc.*

vitrage [vitʀaʒ] nm **1.** [vitres] windows ; [panneau] glass partition **2.** [verre] window glass.

vitrail, aux [vitʀaj,o] nm [gén] stained-glass window ; [non coloré] leaded glass window.

vitre [vitʀ] nf **1.** [plaque de verre] (window) pane **2.** [fenêtre] window ▶ **vitre arrière** AUTO rear window.

vitré, e [vitʀe] adj [porte -complètement] glass *(modif)* ; [-au milieu] glazed ; [panneau, toit] glass *(modif)*.

vitreux, euse [vitʀø,øz] adj [terne -œil, regard] glassy, glazed.

vitrier [vitʀije] nm glazier.

vitrifier [9] [vitʀifje] vt [parquet] to varnish ; [tuiles] to glaze.

vitrine [vitʀin] nf **1.** [devanture] (shop) window , (store) window , display window ; [vitre] shop window ; [objets exposés] window display / *cet ouvrage est la vitrine de la maison d'édition* this book is the publisher's showcase ▶ **mettre qqch en vitrine** to put sthg (out) on display *(in the window)* **2.** [meuble -de maison] display cabinet ; [-de musée] display cabinet, showcase ; [-de magasin] showcase, display case.

vitriol [vitʀijɔl] nm vitriol / *des propos au vitriol* caustic ou vitriolic remarks.

vitrocéramique [vitʀoseʀamik] adj ▶ **plaque vitro-céramique** ceramic hob.

vitupérer [18] [vitypeʀe] vi *litt* to vituperate *sout* ▶ **vitupérer contre qqn / qqch** to inveigh against sb / sthg.

🖉 In reformed spelling (see p. 16-18), this verb is conjugated like *semer*: *il vitupèrera, elle vitupèrerait.*

vivable [vivabl] adj [situation] bearable ; [habitation] fit for living in ; [personne] ▶ **elle n'est pas vivable** *fam* she's impossible to live with / *ce n'est plus vivable au bureau !* it's unbearable at the office now!

vivace [vivas] adj **1.** BOT hardy **2.** [qui dure -croyance, opinion] deep-rooted ; [-souvenir] abiding ; [-foi] steadfast.

vivacité [vivasite] nf **1.** [promptitude -d'une attaque, d'une démarche, d'un geste] briskness ; [-d'une intelligence] sharpness, acuteness ▶ **vivacité d'esprit** quick-wittedness **2.** [entrain -d'une personne, d'un style] vivaciousness, vivacity, liveliness ; [-d'un marché] liveliness, buoyancy ; [-d'une description] vividness, liveliness ; [-d'un regard] vivacity.

vivant, e [vivɑ̃, ɑ̃t] adj **1.** BIOL [organisme] living ; [personne, animal] alive ▶ **j'en suis sorti vivant** I lived to tell the tale, I survived / *cuire un homard vivant* to cook a live lobster ou a lobster alive **2.** [animé -enfant, conférence, présentation] lively, spirited ; [-bourg, rue] lively, bustling, full of life **3.** [réaliste -description, style] vivid **4.** [incarné, personnifié -preuve, exemple, témoignage] living. ❖ **vivant** nm [période] ▶ **de son vivant a)** [dans le passé] when he was alive **b)** [dans le présent] as long as he lives. ❖ **vivants** nmpl RELIG ▶ **les vivants** the living ▶ **les vivants et les morts a)** [gén] the living and the dead **b)** BIBLE the quick and the dead.

vivat [viva] nm cheer / *s'avancer sous les vivats* to walk forth through a hail of applause.

vive [viv] interj ▸ **vive le Canada / la République !** long live Canada / the Republic! ▸ **vive ou vivent les vacances !** three cheers for holidays!

vivement [vivmã] adv **1.** [exprime un souhait] ▸ **vivement le week-end !** I can't wait for the weekend!, roll on the weekend! 🇬🇧, bring on the weekend! 🇺🇸 / *vivement qu'il s'en aille !* I'll be glad when he's gone! **2.** [extrêmement - ému, troublé] deeply, greatly ; [-intéressé] greatly, keenly ; *je souhaite vivement que…* I sincerely wish that… **3.** [brusquement - interpeller] sharply.

vivier [vivje] nm **1.** PÊCHE [enclos - pour poissons] fishpond ; [-pour homards] crawl ; [-d'un bateau] fish tank ou well **2.** *fig* ▸ **un véritable vivier d'acteurs** a breeding ground for actors.

vivifiant, e [vivifjã, ãt] adj [air] bracing, invigorating ; [expérience] revivifying *sout*, invigorating ; [atmosphère] enlivening, revivifying *sout*.

vivisection [vivisɛksjɔ̃] nf vivisection.

vivoir [vivwaʀ] nm 🇶🇧 living room.

vivoter [3] [vivɔte] vi [personne] to get by ou along (with little money).

vivre [90] [vivʀ] ◆ vi **1.** BIOL [personne, animal] to live, to be alive ; [cellule, plante] to live / *vivre vieux* ou *longtemps* to live to a great age ou ripe old age ▸ **avoir vécu** to have had one's day **2.** [mener une existence] to live / *vivre au jour le jour* to take each day as it comes / *vivre dans le luxe / l'angoisse* to live in luxury / anxiety / *ne vivre que pour la musique / sa famille* to live only for music / one's family / *il fait bon vivre ici* life is good ou it's a good life here ▸ **elle a beaucoup vécu** she's seen life ▸ **on ne vit plus a)** [on est inquiet] we're worried sick **b)** [on est harassé] this isn't a life, this isn't what you can call living **3.** [résider] to live / *vivre au Brésil / dans un château* to live in Brazil / in a castle ▸ **vivre avec qqn a)** [maritalement] to live with sb **b)** [en amis] to share ou to live with sb ▸ **vivre ensemble** [couple non marié] to live together ▸ **être facile à vivre** to be easygoing ou easy to get on with ▸ **être difficile à vivre** to be difficult to get on with **4.** [subsister] to live / *ils ont tout juste de quoi vivre* they've just enough to live on ▸ **faire vivre une famille a)** [personne] to provide a living for ou to support a family **b)** [commerce] to provide a living for a family ▸ **vivre bien / chichement** to have a good / poor standard of living / *ils vivaient de la cueillette et de la chasse* they lived on what they gathered and hunted ou off the land ▸ **vivre de sa plume** to live by one's pen ▸ **vivre de l'air du temps** to live on thin air ▸ **vivre d'amour et d'eau fraîche** to live on love alone **5.** [se perpétuer - croyance, coutume] to be alive / *pour que notre entreprise vive* so that our company may continue to exist. ◆ vt **1.** [passer par - époque, événement] to live through (*insép*) / *vivre des temps difficiles* to live through ou to experience difficult times / *vivre des jours heureux / paisibles* to spend one's days happily / peacefully **2.** [assumer - divorce, grossesse, retraite] to experience ▸ **elle a mal / bien vécu mon départ** she couldn't cope / she coped well after I left **3.** ᴱˣᴾᴿ **vivre sa vie** to live one's own life.

vivres [vivʀ] nmpl food *(U)*, foodstuffs, provisions.

vivrier, ère [vivʀije, ɛʀ] adj ▸ **cultures vivrières** food crops.

vlan, v'lan [vlã] interj [bruit - de porte] bang, wham, slam ; [-de coup] smack, thud, wallop.

VO (abr de version originale) ◆ **en VO** loc adj in the original version / *en VO sous-titrée* in the original version with subtitles.

vocabulaire [vɔkabylɛʀ] nm LING vocabulary.

vocal, e, aux [vɔkal, o] adj vocal.

vocalise [vɔkaliz] nf MUS vocalise *spéc*, singing exercise ▸ **faire des vocalises** to practise scales.

vocation [vɔkasjɔ̃] nf [d'une personne] vocation, calling / *ne pas avoir / avoir la vocation (de)* to feel no / a vocation (for) ▸ **manquer** ou **rater sa vocation** : *j'ai manqué* ou *raté ma vocation, j'aurais dû être architecte* I've missed my vocation, I should have been an architect.

vociférer [18] [vɔsifeʀe] ◆ vi to yell, to shout, to vociferate *sout* ▸ **vociférer contre** to inveigh against *sout*, to berate *sout*. ◆ vt [injures] to scream, to shout.

📖 In reformed spelling (see p. 16-18), this verb is conjugated like *semer* : *il vociférera, elle vociférerait*.

vodka [vɔdka] nf vodka.

vœu, x [vø] nm **1.** [souhait] wish / *faire un vœu* to (make a) wish / *faire le vœu que* to wish ou to pray that ▸ **faire un vœu pieux** to make a vain wish **2.** [serment] vow ▸ **faire (le) vœu de faire qqch** to (make a) vow to do sthg **3.** RELIG / *faire vœu de pauvreté / de chasteté / d'obéissance* to take a vow of poverty / of chastity / of obedience ▸ **prononcer ses vœux** to take one's vows. ◆ **vœux** nmpl [de fin d'année] ▸ **meilleurs vœux** [sur une carte] Season's Greetings / *le président a présenté ses vœux télévisés* the president made his New Year speech ou address on TV ; [dans une grande occasion] wishes / *tous nos vœux pour…* our best wishes for…, with all our wishes for…

vogue [vɔg] nf **1.** [popularité] vogue, popularity **2.** 🇨🇭 [kermesse] village fête. ◆ **en vogue** loc adj fashionable ▸ **être en vogue a)** [vêtement] to be fashionable ou in vogue **b)** [activité, personne] to be fashionable.

voguer [3] [vɔge] vi NAUT to sail.

voici [vwasi] prép **1.** *(suivi d'un singulier)* [désignant ce qui est proche dans l'espace] here is, this is ; *(suivi d'un pluriel)* here are, these are ▸ **voici mes parents a)** here are my parents **b)** [dans des présentations] these are my parents / *les voici !* here they are! ▸ **en voici :** *j'ai perdu mon crayon — en voici un* I've lost my pencil — here's one / *du riz ? en voici !* rice? here you are ou there you are! / *en voici une surprise !* what a surprise! ▸ **nous y voici ! a)** here we are!. **b)** [dans une discussion] now… ▸ **l'homme que voici** this man (here) ; *(tournure elliptique)* : *as-tu un timbre ? — voici !* do you have a stamp? — here (you are)! ; [opposé à 'voilà'] : *voici ma sœur et voilà mon fils* this is my sister and that's my son **2.** [caractérisant un état] : *vous voici rassuré, j'espère* I hope that's reassured you / *me voici prêt* I'm ready now / *nous voici enfin arrivés !* here we are at last! **3.** *(suivi d'un singulier)* [introduisant ce dont on va parler] this ou here is ; *(suivi d'un pluriel)* these are / *voici ce que je pense* this is what I think **4.** [pour conclure] : *voici ce que c'est que de mentir !* this ou that is where lying gets you! **5.** [désignant une action proche dans le temps] : *voici l'heure du départ* it's time to go now ▸ **voici l'orage** here comes the storm / *voici venir le printemps* spring is coming **6.** [exprimant la durée] : *j'y suis allé voici trois mois* I went there three months ago.

voie [vwa] nf **1.** [rue] road ▸ **voie express** ou **rapide** express way ▸ **voie à double sens** two-way road ▸ **voie privée** private road ▸ **la voie publique** ADMIN (public) highway ou thoroughfare ▸ **voie sans issue** no through road, cul-de-sac ▸ **voie à sens unique** one-way road ; TRANSP (traffic) lane ▸ **(route à) trois voies** three-lane road **2.** [moyen d'accès] way ; [itinéraire] route / *par la voie des airs* by air ▸ **par voie de terre** overland, by land ; *fig* ▸ **la voie est libre** the road is clear ▸ **ouvrir la voie à qqn / qqch** to pave the way for sb / sthg, to make way for sb / sthg ▸ **trouver sa voie** to find one's niche in life ▸ **voie fluviale** ou **navigable** (inland) waterway ▸ **voie aérienne**

air route, airway ▸ **voie de communication** communication route ▸ **voie maritime** sea route, seaway **3.** RAIL : *le train 242 est attendu voie 9* train 242 is due to arrive on platform 9 ▸ **voie de garage** ou **de service** ou **de dégagement** siding ▸ **mettre sur une voie de garage a)** *fig* [projet] to shelve, to table **b)** [employé] to push aside, to put on the sidelines ▸ **voie (ferrée)** railway 🇬🇧, railroad 🇺🇸 **4.** [procédure, moyen] ▸ **suivre la voie hiérarchique / diplomatique / normale** to go through the official / diplomatic / usual channels ▸ **par des voies détournées** by devious means, by a circuitous route **5.** CHASSE scent, track ▸ **être sur la bonne voie a)** *pr* to have the scent **b)** *fig* to be on the right track ou lines **6.** PHARM ▸ **par voie orale** ou **buccale** orally **7.** ANAT & PHYSIOL tract, duct ▸ **par les voies naturelles** naturally ▸ **voies respiratoires** airways, respiratory tract ▸ **voies urinaires** urinary tract **8.** INFORM & TÉLÉC [sur bande] track ; [de communication] channel **9.** NAUT ▸ **voie d'eau** leak **10.** ASTRON ▸ **la Voie lactée** the Milky Way. ◆ **voies** nfpl DR ▸ **voies de fait** [coups] assault and battery. ◆ **en bonne voie** loc adj : *être en bonne voie* to be going well / *maintenant, les affaires sont en bonne voie* business is looking up. ◆ **en voie de** loc prép : *espèces en voie de disparition* endangered species / *en voie de guérison* getting better, on the road to recovery. ◆ **par la voie de** loc prép through, via.

voilà [vwala] prép **1.** *(suivi d'un singulier)* [désignant ce qui est éloigné] there ou that is ; *(suivi d'un pluriel)* there ou those are ▸ **le monument que voilà** that monument (there) ; [opposé à 'voici'] : *voici mon lit, voilà le tien* here's ou this is my bed and there's ou that's yours **2.** *(suivi d'un singulier)* [désignant ce qui est proche] here ou this is ; *(suivi d'un pluriel)* here ou these are / *voilà l'homme dont je vous ai parlé* here ou this is the man I spoke to you about / *tiens, les voilà !* look, here ou there they are! ▸ **nous y voilà ! a)** here we are! **b)** [dans une discussion] now... ▸ **l'homme que voilà** this man (here) ▸ **en voilà :** *du riz ? en voilà !* rice? here ou there you are! / *je ne trouve pas de marteau — en voilà un* I can't find a hammer — here's one / *en voilà une surprise / des manières !* what a surprise / way to behave! / *vous vouliez la clef, voilà* you wanted the key, here it is ou here you are / *voilà madame, ce sera tout ?* here you are, madam, will there be anything else? **3.** [caractérisant un état] : *me voilà prêt* I'm ready now / *les voilà enfin partis !* at last they've gone! / *dire que te voilà marié !* to think you're married now! ▸ **me / te / nous, etc. voilà bien !** *fam & iron* now what a mess! **4.** *(suivi d'un singulier)* [introduisant ce dont on va parler] this ou here is ; *(suivi d'un pluriel)* these ou here are / *voilà ce que je lui dirai* this ou here is what I'll say to her / *que veux-tu dire par là ? — eh bien voilà,...* what do you mean by that? — well,... **5.** *(suivi d'un singulier)* [pour conclure] that's ; *(suivi d'un pluriel)* those are / *voilà ce que c'est, la jalousie !* that's jealousy for you! / *voilà ce que c'est que de mentir !* that's where lying gets you! / *on lui paiera les réparations et voilà !* we'll pay for the repairs and that's all (there is to it)! / *et voilà, ça devait arriver !* what did I tell you! / *voilà ! vous avez tout compris* that's it! you've got it ▸ **voilà tout** that's all **6.** [introduisant une objection, une restriction] : *j'en voudrais bien un, seulement voilà, c'est très cher* I'd like one, but the problem is ou but you see, it's very expensive / *voilà, j'hésitais à vous en parler, mais...* well, yes, I wasn't going to mention it, but... **7.** [désignant une action proche dans le temps] ▸ **voilà la pluie a)** [il ne pleut pas encore] here comes the rain **b)** [il pleut] it's raining / *voilà que la nuit tombe* (now) it's getting dark / *voilà Monsieur, je suis à vous dans un instant* yes, sir, I'll be with you in a minute ▸ **ne voilà-t-il pas que** *fam* : *je descends de voiture et ne voilà-t-il pas qu'une contractuelle arrive !* I get out of my car and guess what, a traffic warden turns up! **8.** [exprimant la durée] : *il est ren-*

tré voilà une heure he's been home for an hour, he came home an hour ago / *voilà cinq minutes que je t'appelle !* I've been calling you for five minutes!

voilage [vwala3] nm [rideau] net curtain.

voile¹ [vwal] nm **1.** [d'une toilette, d'un monument] veil / *porter le voile* to wear the veil ▸ **voile de mariée** marriage veil ▸ **prendre le voile** RELIG to take the veil **2.** TEXT [pour rideau] net, (piece of) netting ; [pour chapeau] (piece of) gauze, veil **3.** *fig* veil / *ils ont enfin levé le voile sur ce mystère* they have at last lifted the curtain on this mystery **4.** *litt* [opacité] : *un voile de brume / fumée* a veil of mist / smoke **5.** MÉD ▸ **voile au poumon** shadow on the lung **6.** PHOT fog **7.** ANAT ▸ **voile du palais** velum *spéc*, soft palate.

voile² [vwal] nf **1.** NAUT sail ▸ **faire voile vers** to sail towards ▸ **mettre les voiles** *fam* to clear off **2.** SPORT ▸ **la voile** sailing, yachting ▸ **faire de la voile** to sail, to go yachting. ◆ **à voile** loc adj **1.** NAUT ▸ **bateau à voile a)** sailing boat **b)** HIST clipper **2.** (EXPR) **marcher à voile et à vapeur** *tfam* to be AC/DC ou bisexual. ◆ **toutes voiles dehors** loc adv NAUT in full sail, all sail ou sails set.

voilé, e [vwale] adj **1.** [monument, visage, personne] veiled / *des femmes voilées de noir* women veiled in black **2.** [couvert - lune, soleil] hazy ; [- ciel] overcast ; [- horizon] hazy **3.** [voix] hoarse, husky **4.** [dissimulé - signification] obscure / *sa déception à peine voilée* his thinly-veiled disappointment **5.** PHOT fogged, veiled **6.** [déformé - métal] buckled ; [- bois, plastique] warped.

voiler [3] [vwale] vt **1.** [couvrir] to veil, to hide, to cover **2.** [rendre moins net - contours] to veil ; [- lumière] to dim / *le regard voilé par les larmes* her eyes misty ou blurred with tears ; [enrouer - voix] to make husky **3.** *litt* [dissimuler - fautes] to conceal, to veil ; [- motifs, vérité] to mask, to veil, to disguise **4.** [déformer - métal] to buckle ; [- bois, plastique] to warp. ◆ **se voiler** ◆ vpt : *se voiler le visage* [le couvrir] to wear a veil (over one's face) ▸ **se voiler la face** to bury one's head in the sand, to hide from the truth. ◆ vpi **1.** [lune, soleil] to become hazy ; [ciel - de nuages] to cloud over ; [- de brume] to mist over, to become hazy ou misty ▸ **son regard s'était voilé a)** [mouillé de larmes] her eyes had misted over ou become blurred (with tears) **b)** [terni par la mort] her eyes had become glazed **2.** [métal] to buckle ; [bois, plastique] to become warped.

voilette [vwalɛt] nf (hat) veil.

voilier [vwalje] nm NAUT ▸ **voilier (de plaisance) a)** sailing boat 🇬🇧, sailboat 🇺🇸 **b)** [navire à voiles] sailing ship.

voilure [vwalyʀ] nf NAUT sail, sails.

voir [62] [vwaʀ]
◆ vt

▸ **A. PERCEVOIR AVEC LES YEUX 1.** [distinguer] to see ; PHYSIOL to (be able to) see / *il ne voit rien de l'œil gauche* he can't see anything with his ou he's blind in the left eye / *il faut le voir pour le croire* you have to see it to believe it! / *à la voir si souriante, on ne dirait pas qu'elle souffre* when you see how cheerful she is, you wouldn't think she's in pain / *elle m'a fait voir sa robe de mariée* she showed me her wedding dress / *fais voir !* let me ou show me! ▸ **voir le jour a)** [bébé] to be born **b)** [journal] to come out **c)** [théorie, invention] to appear ▸ **comme je vous vois** : *je les ai vues comme je vous vois* I saw them with my own eyes / *il faut voir comment elle lui répond* you should see the way she speaks to him ▸ **voir venir** : *cela a fait scandale — le gouvernement n'avait rien vu venir* there was a big scandal — the government hadn't seen it coming ou hadn't anticipated that ▸ **je te vois venir, tu veux de l'argent !** *fam* I can see what you're leading up to ou getting at, you want some money! **2.** [assister à - accident, événement] to witness, to see ; [- film, spectacle] to see / *c'est vrai, je l'ai vue le faire* it's true, I saw her do it ▶ **à voir** well worth seeing / *c'est un film à voir absolument* that film is a must / *ici, les terrains ont vu leur prix doubler en cinq ans* land prices here doubled over five years ▶ **tu n'as encore rien vu** you haven't seen anything yet ▶ **on aura tout vu !** that beats everything! ▶ **en voir**: *j'en ai vu, des choses pendant la guerre !* I saw quite a few things in the war! ▶ **j'en ai vu d'autres !** I've seen worse!, I've been through worse! ▶ **il en a vu de toutes les couleurs ou des vertes et des pas mûres** *fam* ou **de belles ou de drôles** he's been through quite a lot ▶ **pour voir**: *mets de l'eau dessus pour voir* pour some water on it, just to see what happens / *répète un peu, pour voir !* (you) DARE say that again! ▶ **vas te faire voir !** *tfam* push off! **3.** [trouver - spécimen] to see, to find, to encounter *sout* ; [- qualité] to see ▶ **un homme galant comme on n'en voit plus** the kind of gentleman they don't make any more **4.** [inspecter - appartement] to see, to view ; [- rapport] to see, to (have a) look at ; [- leçon] to go ou to look over ; [remarquer] to see, to notice **5.** [consulter, recevoir - ami, médecin] to see / *le médecin va vous voir dans quelques instants* the doctor will be with ou see you in a few minutes ▶ **aller voir** to go to / *je dois aller voir le médecin* I've got to go to the doctor's / *je vais aller voir mes amis* I'm going to go and see my friends **6.** [se référer à] ▶ **voir illustration p. 7** see diagram p 7.

B. PENSER, CONCEVOIR 1. [imaginer] to see, to imagine, to picture / *le pull est trop large — je te voyais plus carré que cela* the jumper is too big — I thought you had broader shoulders ▶ **voir d'ici qqn / qqch**: *je vois sa tête / réaction d'ici* I can just imagine his face / reaction **2.** [concevoir - méthode, solution] to see, to think of / *je ne vois pas comment je pourrais t'aider* I can't see how I could help you / *vous voyez quelque chose à ajouter ?* can you think of anything else (which needs adding)? ▶ **voir qqch d'un mauvais œil, ne pas voir qqch d'un bon œil** to be displeased about sthg ; *(en usage absolu)* : *il faut trouver un moyen ! — je ne vois pas* we must find a way! — I can't think of one ou anything **3.** [comprendre - danger, intérêt] to see / *tu vois ce que je veux dire ?* do you see ou understand what I mean? / *je ne vois pas ce qu'il y a de drôle !* I can't see what's so funny!, I don't get the joke! **4.** [constater] to see, to realize ▶ **elle ne nous causera plus d'ennuis — c'est** ou **ça reste à voir** she won't trouble us any more — that remains to be seen ou that's what YOU think! **5.** [considérer, prendre en compte] to see, to consider, to take into account **6.** [examiner] to see, to check / *nous prenons rendez-vous ? — voyez cela avec ma secrétaire* shall we make an appointment? — arrange that with my secretary ▶ **c'est à** ou **il faut voir**: *j'irai peut-être, c'est à voir* I might go, I'll have to see / *les photos seraient mieux en noir et blanc — hum, il faut voir* the pictures would look better in black and white — mm, maybe (maybe not) **7.** [juger] to see ▶ **se faire bien / mal voir**: *se faire bien voir de qqn* to make o.s. popular with sb ▶ **se faire mal voir de qqn** to make o.s. unpopular with sb **8.** EXPR **avoir à voir avec** [avoir un rapport avec] : *vous aurez peu à voir avec les locataires du dessus* you'll have very little to do with the upstairs tenants / *je voudrais vous parler : ça a à voir avec notre discussion d'hier* I would like to speak to you: it's to do with what we were talking about yesterday ▶ **n'avoir rien à voir avec** [n'avoir aucun rapport avec]: *l'instruction n'a rien à voir avec l'intelligence* education has nothing to do with intelligence / *cela n'a rien à voir avec le sujet* that's irrelevant, that's got nothing to do with it ▶ **tu vois, vous voyez**: *tu vois, je préférais ne rien savoir* I preferred to remain in the dark, you see ▶ **attendez voir** *fam* hang on, wait a sec / *dis voir, où est le calendrier ?* *fam* tell me, where's the calendar? / *voyons voir* ou *regardons voir ce que tu as comme note* *fam* let's just have a look and see what mark you got ▶ **voyez-vous cela** ou **ça !**: *une moto à*

14 ans, voyez-vous ça ! a motorbike at 14, whatever next! ▶ **voyons !** come (on) now! / *un peu de courage, voyons !* come on, be brave!

■ vi

A. PERCEVOIR LA RÉALITÉ 1. PHYSIOL to (be able to) see / *il ne voit que d'un œil* he can only see out of one eye / *elle ne ou n'y voit plus* she can't see ou she's blind now ; [exercer sa vue] to see ▶ **voir double** to have double vision **2.** [juger] : *encore une fois, tu as vu juste* you were right, once again.

B. JEUX ▶ **20 euros, pour voir** 20 euros, and I'll see you.

❖ **se voir** ◆ vp *(emploi réfléchi)* **1.** [se contempler] to (be able to) see o.s. ▶ **il s'est vu mourir** *fig* he knew he was dying **2.** [s'imaginer] to see ou to imagine ou to picture o.s. / *elle se voyait déjà championne !* she thought the championship was hers already! ◆ vp *(emploi réciproque)* [se rencontrer] to see each other. ◆ vp *(emploi passif)* **1.** [être visible, évident - défaut] to show, to be visible ; [- émotion, gêne] to be visible, to be obvious, to be apparent / *il porte une perruque, ça se voit bien* you can tell he wears a wig **2.** [se manifester - événement] to happen ; [- attitude, coutume] to be seen ou found. ◆ vpi **1.** [se trouver] ▶ **se voir dans l'impossibilité de faire qqch** to find o.s. unable to do sthg / *se voir dans l'obligation de...* to find o.s. obliged to... **2.** *(suivi d'un infinitif)* : *se voir interdire l'inscription à un club* to be refused membership to a club.

voire [vwaʀ] adv ▶ **voire (même)** (or) even / *certains, voire la majorité* some, or ou perhaps even most ▶ **vexé, voire offensé** upset, not to say offended.

voirie [vwaʀi] nf [entretien des routes] road maintenance ▶ **le service de la voirie** ADMIN road maintenance and cleaning department (of the local council).

voisin, e [vwazɛ̃, in] ◆ adj **1.** [d'à côté] next, adjoining ; [qui est à proximité] neighbouring UK, neighboring US / *il habite la maison voisine* he lives next door / *les pays voisins de l'équateur / de notre territoire* the countries near the equator / bordering on our territory **2.** [similaire - idées, langues] similar ; [- espèces] closely related. ◆ nm, f **1.** [habitant à côté] neighbour UK, neighbor US / *mes voisins du dessus / dessous* the people upstairs / downstairs from me ▶ **voisin de palier** neighbour (across the landing) **2.** [placé à côté] neighbour / *mon voisin de table* the person next to me ou my neighbour at table.

voisinage [vwazinaʒ] nm **1.** [quartier] vicinity, neighbourhood UK, neighborhood US **2.** ▶ **le voisinage de** [les alentours de] : *dans le voisinage de* in the vicinity of / *ils habitent dans le voisinage d'une centrale nucléaire* they live near a nuclear plant **3.** [personnes] neighbours / *tout le voisinage est au courant* the whole neighbourhood knows about it **4.** [rapports] ▶ **être** ou **vivre en bon voisinage avec qqn** to be on neighbourly terms with sb.

voiture [vwatyʀ] nf **1.** [de particulier] car, automobile US / *on y va en voiture ?* shall we go (there) by car?, shall we drive (there)? ▶ **voiture bélier** ramming car / *attaque à la voiture bélier* attack using a ramming car ▶ **voiture de fonction** ou **de service** company car ▶ **voiture de course** racing car ▶ **voiture d'enfant a)** *vieilli* [landau] pram UK, baby carriage US **b)** [poussette] pushchair UK, stroller US ▶ **voiture de location** hire UK ou rental US car ▶ **voiture particulière** private car ▶ **voiture de police** police car ▶ **voiture des pompiers** fire engine ▶ **voiture de série** production car ▶ **voiture de sport** sports car ▶ **voiture de tourisme** private car **2.** RAIL coach, carriage UK, car US ▶ **en voiture !** all aboard! ▶ **voiture de tête / queue** front / rear carriage UK ou car US **3.** [véhicule sans moteur - pour personnes] carriage, coach ; [- pour marchandises] cart.

voiture-bar [vwatyʀbaʀ] *(pl* **voitures-bars)** nf RAIL buffet-car.

voiture-lit [vwatyʀli] (*pl* **voitures-lits**) nf RAIL sleeper 🇬🇧, Pullman 🇺🇸.

voiture-restaurant [vwatyʀʀɛstɔʀɑ̃] (*pl* **voitures-restaurants**) nf RAIL restaurant ou dining car.

voiturette [vwatyʀɛt] nf microcar.

voiturier [vwatyʀje] nm [d'hôtel] porter *(who parks the guests' cars)* ▸ **service de voiturier** valet parking.

voix [vwa] nf **1.** PHYSIOL voice ▸ **voix off** CINÉ voice over ▸ **donner de la voix a)** [chien] to bay **b)** [personne] to shout, to bawl ▸ **de la voix et du geste** with much waving and shouting **2.** MUS [de chanteur] voice ; [partition] part / **avoir de la voix** to have a strong voice ▸ **chanter à plusieurs / cinq voix** to sing in parts / five parts ▸ *fugue à deux / trois voix* fugue for two / three voices ▸ **voix de basse / soprano / ténor** bass / soprano / tenor voice **3.** [personne] voice / *une grande voix de la radio s'éteint* one of the great voices of radio has disappeared **4.** [message] voice / *la voix de la conscience* the voice of one's conscience / *écouter la voix de la raison / de la sagesse / de Dieu* to listen to the voice of reason / of wisdom / of God ▸ **avoir voix au chapitre** to have a ou one's say in the matter **5.** POL vote / *obtenir 1 500 voix* to win ou to get 1,500 votes / *recueillir* ou *remporter 57 % des voix* to win 57% of the vote ou votes ▸ **mettre qqch aux voix** to put sthg to the vote **6.** GRAM voice ▸ **voix active / passive** active / passive voice. ❖ **à voix basse** loc adv in a low voice. ❖ **à haute voix, à voix haute** loc adv **1.** [lire] aloud, out loud **2.** [parler] loud, loudly, in a loud voice / *à haute (et intelligible) voix* loudly and clearly. ❖ **sans voix** loc adj ▸ **être** ou **rester sans voix a)** [d'épouvante] to be speechless, to be struck dumb **b)** [d'émotion, de chagrin] to be speechless.

vol [vɔl] nm **1.** DR theft, robbery ▸ **vol simple / qualifié** common / aggravated theft ▸ **vol à l'arraché** bag snatching ▸ **vol avec effraction** breaking and entering, burglary ▸ **vol à la portière** car mugging ▸ **vol à l'étalage** shoplifting ▸ **vol à main armée** armed robbery ▸ **vol à la roulotte** theft from parked cars ▸ **vol à la tire** pickpocketing ▸ **vol de voiture** car theft **2.** [vente à un prix excessif] : *c'est du vol organisé !* it's a racket! **3.** AÉRON & ASTRONAUT flight / *il y a 40 minutes de vol* it's a 40-minute flight ▸ **vol (en) charter** charter flight ▸ **vol d'essai** test flight ▸ **vol libre** hang-gliding ▸ **pratiquer le** ou **faire du vol libre** to go hang-gliding ▸ **vol régulier** scheduled flight ▸ **vol à voile** gliding **4.** ZOOL flight / *j'ai fait un vol plané !* fam & fig I went flying! ; [groupe - d'oiseaux] flight, flock ; [- d'insectes] swarm / *un vol de perdreaux* flock ou covey of partridges. ❖ **à vol d'oiseau** loc adv as the crow flies. ❖ **au vol** loc adv [en passant] ▸ **saisir au vol** [ballon, clés] to catch in mid-air / *saisir une occasion au vol* to jump at ou to seize an opportunity.

volage [vɔlaʒ] adj fickle.

volaille [vɔlaj] nf CULIN & ZOOL ▸ **une volaille** [oiseau de basse-cour] a fowl / *de la volaille* poultry.

volant[1] [vɔlɑ̃] nm **1.** AUTO steering wheel ▸ **être au volant** to be at the wheel, to be behind the wheel, to be driving ▸ **prendre le** ou **se mettre au volant** to take the wheel, to get behind the wheel **2.** VÊT flounce / *robe à volants* flounced dress.

volant[2]**, e** [vɔlɑ̃, ɑ̃t] adj **1.** AÉRON & ZOOL flying ▸ **personnel volant** AÉRON cabin crew **2.** [mobile - câble, camp, échafaudage, pont, service] flying.

volatil, e [vɔlatil] adj **1.** CHIM volatile **2.** [fluctuant - électorat] fickle ; [- situation] volatile ; [- sentiment] volatile.

volatile [vɔlatil] nm hum [oiseau] bird, (feathered) creature.

volatiliser [3] [vɔlatilize] ❖ **se volatiliser** vpi fam [disparaître] to vanish (into thin air).

vol-au-vent [vɔlovɑ̃] nm inv vol-au-vent.

volcan [vɔlkɑ̃] nm **1.** GÉOGR & GÉOL volcano ▸ **volcan en activité / dormant / éteint** active / dormant / extinct volcano **2.** ▸ **être assis** ou **danser** ou **dormir sur un volcan** to be sitting on a powder keg.

volcanique [vɔlkanik] adj **1.** GÉOGR & GÉOL volcanic **2.** *litt* [passion] fiery, volcanic, blazing.

volcanologie [vɔlkanɔlɔʒi] nf volcanology, vulcanology.

volcanologue [vɔlkanɔlɔg] nmf volcano expert, volcanologist, vulcanologist.

volée [vɔle] nf **1.** [ce qu'on lance] : *volée de flèches* volley ou flight of arrows ▸ **volée de coups** shower of blows **2.** *fam* [défaite] beating, hammering / *je lui ai flanqué sa volée au ping-pong* I licked him at table tennis / *il a pris une sacrée volée en demi-finale* he got trounced ou thrashed in the semi-finals **3.** SPORT volley **4.** ORNITH [formation] flock, flight ; [distance] flight **5.** 🇨🇭 [promotion] : *on était de la même volée* we were in the same year. ❖ **à la volée** loc adv **1.** [en passant] ▸ **attraper** ou **saisir à la volée** [clés, balle] to catch in mid-air **2.** AGR : **semer à la volée** to (sow) broadcast. ❖ **à toute volée** loc adv [frapper, projeter] vigorously, with full force / *claquer une porte à toute volée* to slam ou to bang a door shut ▸ **sonner à toute volée a)** [cloches] to peal (out) **b)** [carillonneur] to peal all the bells.

voler [3] [vɔle] ◆ vi **1.** AÉRON & ORNITH to fly ▸ **voler de ses propres ailes** to stand on one's own two feet, to fend for o.s. **2.** [étincelles, projectile] to fly ▸ **voler en éclats** to be smashed to bits ou to pieces ▸ **ça vole bas !** fam, **ça ne vole pas haut !** fam very funny! iron **3.** sout [se précipiter] ▸ **voler au secours de qqn** to fly to sb's assistance ▸ **voler dans les plumes à qqn** fam to let fly at sb, to have a go at sb. ◆ vt **1.** [objet, idée] to steal ▸ **voler qqch à qqn** to steal sthg from sb / *on m'a volé ma montre* ! my watch has been stolen! / *il volait de l'argent dans la caisse* he used to steal money from the till ▸ **voler un baiser à qqn** litt to steal a kiss from sb ; (en usage absolu) to steal ▸ **n'avoir pas volé :** *je n'ai pas volé mon argent / dîner / week-end* I've certainly earned my money / earned myself some dinner / earned myself a weekend / *tu ne l'as pas volé !* [tu es bien puni] you (certainly) asked for it!, it serves you right! **2.** [personne] to rob / *il s'est fait voler son portefeuille* / *tout son matériel hi-fi* his wallet / all his stereo equipment was stolen ; [léser] to cheat, to swindle / *elle ne t'a pas volé sur le poids de la viande* she gave you a good weight of meat.

volet [vɔle] nm **1.** [d'une maison] shutter **2.** [d'un document - section] section ; ART [d'un polyptyque] wing, volet spéc **3.** [d'une politique, d'un projet de loi] point, part ; [d'une émission] part ▸ **le volet social** [de la construction européenne] the social chapter **4.** AÉRON flap.

voleter [27] [vɔlte] vi [oiseau, papillon] to flutter ou to flit (about).

🖉 In reformed spelling (see p. 16-18), this verb is conjugated like *acheter* : *il volète, elle volètera.*

voleur, euse [vɔlœʀ, øz] ◆ adj ▸ **être voleur a)** [enfant] to be a (bit of a) thief **b)** [marchand] to be a crook ou a cheat. ◆ nm, f [escroc] thief, robber ; [marchand] crook, cheat ▸ **voleur à l'étalage** shoplifter ▸ **au voleur !** stop thief! ▸ **partir** ou **se sauver comme un voleur a)** [en courant] to take to one's heels **b)** [discrètement] to slip away.

volière [vɔljɛʀ] nf [enclos] aviary ; [cage] bird-cage.

volley-ball (*pl* **volley-balls**), **volleyball** * [vɔlebol] nm volleyball.

volleyeur, euse [vɔlejœʀ, øz] nm, f **1.** [au volleyball] volleyball player **2.** TENNIS volleyer.

volontaire [vɔlɔ̃tɛʀ] ◆ adj **1.** [déterminé] self-willed, determined ; [têtu] headstrong, wilful **2.** [voulu - engagement]

---

* In reformed spelling (see p. 16-18).

voluntary ; [-oubli] intentional **3.** [qui agit librement - engagé, travailleur] volunteer *(modif)* ▸ **se porter volontaire pour** to volunteer for. ◆ nmf volunteer.

volontairement [vɔlɔ̃tɛʀmɑ̃] adv **1.** [sans y être obligé] voluntarily, of one's own free will **2.** [intentionnellement] on purpose, intentionally, deliberately / *c'est volontairement que j'ai supprimé ce passage* I deleted this passage on purpose.

volontariat [vɔlɔ̃taʀja] nm ▸ **le volontariat a)** [gén] voluntary work **b)** MIL voluntary service.

volontariste [vɔlɔ̃taʀist] ◆ adj voluntaristic. ◆ nmf voluntarist.

volonté [vɔlɔ̃te] nf **1.** [détermination] will, willpower / *avoir de la volonté* / *beaucoup de volonté* to have willpower / a strong will / *avoir une volonté de fer* to have a will of iron ou an iron will **2.** [désir] will, wish ▸ **faire qqch** / **aller contre la volonté de qqn** to do sthg / go against sb's will / *la volonté de gagner* / *survivre* the will to win / to survive ▸ **montrer sa volonté de faire qqch** to show one's determination to do sthg ▸ **volonté de puissance** PHILOS will-to-power **3.** [disposition] ▸ **bonne volonté** willingness / *faire preuve de bonne volonté* to show willing / *être plein de bonne volonté* to be full of goodwill ▸ **mauvaise volonté** unwillingness / *faire preuve de mauvaise volonté* to be grudging. ❖ **à volonté** ◆ loc adj ▸ **café à volonté** as much coffee as you want, unlimited coffee. ◆ loc adv [arrêter, continuer] at will / *servez-vous à volonté* take as much as you want.

volontiers [vɔlɔ̃tje] adv **1.** [de bon gré] gladly, willingly ; [avec plaisir] with pleasure / *un café ? — très volontiers* a coffee? — yes please ou I'd love one **2.** [souvent] willingly, readily / *on croit volontiers que...* we are apt to think ou ready to believe that...

volt [vɔlt] nm volt.

voltage [vɔltaʒ] nm voltage.

volte-face *(pl* **volte-face)**, **volteface*** [vɔltəfas] nf **1.** [fait de pivoter] about-turn 🇬🇧, about-face 🇺🇸 ▸ **faire volte-face** to turn round **2.** [changement - d'opinion, d'attitude] volteface, U-turn, about-turn 🇬🇧, about-face 🇺🇸 / *le parti a fait une volte-face* the party did a 180 degrees turn ou a U-turn.

voltige [vɔltiʒ] nf **1.** [au trapèze] ▸ **la haute voltige** acrobatics, flying trapeze exercises **2.** ÉQUIT mounted gymnastics, voltige **3.** AÉRON ▸ **voltige (aérienne)** aerobatics **4.** [entreprise difficile] : *la Bourse, c'est de la voltige* speculating on the Stock Exchange is a highly risky business.

voltiger [17] [vɔltiʒe] vi **1.** [libellule, oiseau] to fly about, to flutter (about) ; [abeille, mouche] to buzz about **2.** [flocon, papier] to float around in the air, to flutter (about).

volubile [vɔlybil] adj [qui parle - beaucoup] garrulous, voluble ; [- avec aisance] fluent.

volubilité [vɔlybilite] nf volubility, volubleness, garrulousness.

volume [vɔlym] nm **1.** [tome] volume **2.** ACOUST volume ▸ **augmenter** ou **monter le volume** to turn the sound up ▸ **volume sonore** sound level **3.** [quantité globale] volume, amount / *le volume des exportations* the volume of exports **4.** [poids, épaisseur] volume / *une permanente donnerait du volume à vos cheveux* a perm would give your hair more body ; [cubage] volume.

volumineux, euse [vɔlyminø, øz] adj [sac] bulky, voluminous ; [correspondance] voluminous, massive.

volupté [vɔlypte] nf **1.** [plaisir] sensual ou voluptuous pleasure **2.** [caractère sensuel] voluptuousness.

voluptueux, euse [vɔlyptɥø, øz] adj voluptuous.

volute [vɔlyt] nf [de fumée] coil ; [de lianes] curl, scroll ; [en arts décoratifs] volute.

vomi [vɔmi] nm vomit.

vomir [32] [vɔmiʀ] ◆ vt **1.** PHYSIOL [repas] to bring up *(sép)*, to vomit ; [sang, bile] to bring ou to cough up *(sép)* **2.** fig [fumée] to spew, to vomit ; [foule] to spew forth *(insép)* ; [insultes] to spew out *(insép)* **3.** fig [rejeter avec dégoût] to have no time for, to feel revulsion for. ◆ vi to be sick, to vomit / *une telle hypocrisie me donne envie de vomir* such hypocrisy makes me sick / *ça me fait vomir !* it makes me sick!

vomissement [vɔmismɑ̃] nm [action] vomiting / *si l'enfant est pris de vomissements* if the child starts to vomit.

vorace [vɔʀas] adj [mangeur] voracious ; [appétit] insatiable, voracious ; [lecteur] voracious, avid.

vos [vo] pl → **votre**.

VOST (abr écrite de **version originale sous-titrée**) nf original version with subtitles.

votant, e [vɔtɑ̃, ɑ̃t] nm, f voter.

votation [vɔtasjɔ̃] nf 🇶🇺🇪🇧🇪🇨 & 🇸🇺🇮🇸🇸🇪 voting, election.

vote [vɔt] nm **1.** [voix] vote ▸ **vote défavorable** "no" vote **2.** [élection] vote / *procédons* ou *passons au vote* let's have ou take a vote ▸ **vote à bulletin secret** secret ballot ▸ **vote à main levée** vote by show of hands ▸ **vote par procuration** proxy vote ▸ **le vote utile** tactical voting **3.** [d'une loi] passing ; [de crédits] voting ; [d'un projet de loi] vote.

voter [3] [vɔte] ◆ vi to vote / *voter à droite* / *à gauche* / *au centre* to vote for the right / left / centre ▸ **voter à main levée** to vote by show of hands. ◆ vt [crédits] to vote ; [loi] to pass ; [projet de loi] to vote for *(insép)* / *voter la peine de mort* to pass a vote in favour of capital punishment ; [budget] to approve ▸ **être voté** [projet de loi] to go through.

votre [vɔtʀ] *(pl* **vos** [vo]) dét *(adj poss)* **1.** [indiquant la possession] your ▸ **votre livre et vos crayons a)** [d'une personne] your book and your pencils **b)** [de plusieurs personnes] your books and your pencils / *votre père et votre mère* your father and mother / *un de vos amis* one of your friends, a friend of yours **2.** [dans des titres] ▸ **Votre Majesté** Your Majesty **3.** RELIG Thy.

vôtre [votʀ] dét *(adj poss)* sout yours / *cette maison qui fut vôtre* this house which was yours ou which belonged to you. ❖ **le vôtre, la vôtre** *(pl* **les vôtres)** pron poss : *ma voiture est garée à côté de la vôtre* my car is parked next to yours ; *(emploi nominal)* ▸ **les vôtres** your family and friends / *je ne pourrai pas être des vôtres ce soir* I will not be able to join you tonight ▸ **si au moins vous y mettiez du vôtre !** you could at least make an effort!

vouer [6] [vwe] vt **1.** [dédier - vie, énergie] to devote ; [- admiration, fidélité, haine] to vow **2.** [destiner] ▸ **voué à l'échec** destined for failure, doomed to fail **3.** RELIG [enfant] to dedicate ; [temple] to vow, to dedicate / *voué à la mémoire de...* sacred to the memory of... ❖ **se vouer à** vp + prép to dedicate one's energies ou o.s. to / *se vouer à la cause de* to take up the cause of.

vouloir¹ [vulwaʀ] nm sout ▸ **bon vouloir** goodwill ▸ **mauvais vouloir** ill will.

vouloir² [57] [vulwaʀ] vt

A. AVOIR POUR BUT 1. [être décidé à obtenir] to want / *je le ferai, que tu le veuilles ou non* I'll do it, whether you like it or not ▸ **vouloir absolument (obtenir) qqch** to be set on (getting) sthg / *si tu veux mon avis* if you ask me ▸ **vouloir que:** *je ne veux pas que tu le lui dises* I don't want you to tell him / *je veux absolument que tu ranges ta chambre* I insist (that) you tidy up your bedroom ▸ **vouloir faire qqch**

to want to do sthg / *elle veut récupérer son enfant* / *être reçue par le ministre* she's determined to get her child back / that the Minister should see her / *je ne veux pas entendre parler de ça !* I won't hear of it ou such a thing! / *je ne veux plus en parler* I don't want to talk about it any more ▸ **vouloir qqch de** : *il veut 80 000 euros de son studio* he wants 80,000 euros for his bedsit ▸ **vouloir qqch de qqn** to want sthg from sb / *que veux-tu de moi ?, qu'est-ce que tu me veux ?* what do you want from me? ; *(en usage absolu)* : *il peut vraiment désagréable quand il veut* he can be a real nuisance when he wants to **2.** [prétendre - suj : personne] to claim **3.** [avoir l'intention de] ▸ **vouloir faire qqch** to want ou to intend ou to mean to do sthg / *sans vouloir me mêler de tes affaires* / *te contredire…* I don't want to interfere / to contradict you but… ▸ **vouloir dire** : *j'ai dit «attelle», je voulais dire «appelle»* I said "attelle", I meant "appelle" / *vous voulez dire qu'on l'a tuée ?* do you mean ou are you suggesting (that) she was killed? **4.** [s'attendre à] to expect / *que veux-tu que j'y fasse ?* what do you want me to do about it?, what can I do about it? / *que voulez-vous que je vous dise ?* what can I say?, what do you want me to say?

B. PRÉFÉRER, SOUHAITER **1.** [dans un choix] to want, to wish / *on prend ma voiture ou la tienne ? — c'est comme tu veux* shall we take my car or yours? — as you wish ou please ou like / *je me débrouillerai seule — comme tu voudras !* I'll manage on my own — suit yourself! ▸ **tu l'as ou l'auras voulu !** you asked for it! **2.** [dans une suggestion] to want / *veux-tu de l'aide ?* do you want ou would you like some help? **3.** [dans un souhait] : *je ne veux que ton bonheur* I only want you to be happy / *elle voudrait vous dire quelques mots en privé* she'd like a word with you in private / *je voudrais vous y voir !* I'd like to see how you'd cope with it! **4.** [dans une demande polie] ▸ **veuillez m'excuser un instant** (will you) please excuse me for a moment / *veuillez avoir l'obligeance de…* would you kindly ou please… / *nous voudrions une chambre pour deux personnes* we'd like a double room ▸ **voulez-vous me suivre** please follow me **5.** [dans un rappel à l'ordre] : *veux-tu (bien) me répondre !* will you (please) answer me? / *un peu de respect, tu veux (bien)* a bit less cheek, if you don't mind!

C. SUJ : CHOSE **1.** [se prêter à, être en état de] : *les haricots ne veulent pas cuire* the beans won't cook **2.** [exiger] to require / *comme le veulent les usages* as convention dictates / *les lois le veulent ainsi* that is what the law says ; [prétendre] : *comme le veut une vieille légende* as an old legend has it **3.** [déterminer - suj : destin, hasard, malheur] : *le malheur voulut qu'il fût seul ce soir-là* unfortunately he was alone that night / *le calendrier a voulu que cela tombe un lundi* it fell on a Monday, as it so happened **4.** ▸ **vouloir dire** a) [avoir comme sens propre] to mean b) [avoir comme implication] to mean, to suggest / *je me demande ce que veut dire ce changement d'attitude* I wonder what the meaning of this turn-around is ou what this turn-around means / *cela ne veut rien dire* it doesn't mean anything ▸ **ça veut tout dire !** that says it all! **5.** GRAM to take.

D. LOCUTIONS ▸ **bien vouloir** [consentir] : *bien vouloir faire qqch* to be willing ou to be prepared ou to be quite happy to do sthg / *je veux bien être patient, mais il y a des limites* I can be patient, but there are limits! / *un petit café ? — oui, je veux bien* fancy a coffee? — yes please ▸ **bien vouloir** [admettre] : *je veux bien qu'il y ait des restrictions budgétaires mais…* I understand (that) there are cuts in the budget but… ▸ **moi je veux bien !** (it's) fine by me! / *il a dit nous avoir soutenus, moi je veux bien, mais le résultat est là !* he said he supported us, OK ou and that may be so, but look at the result! ▸ **il t'a cogné ? — je veux !** *fam* : *je veux* did he hit you? — and how ou he sure did!
▸ **que veux-tu, que voulez-vous** : *que veux-tu, j'ai pourtant essayé !* I tried, though! / *c'est ainsi, que voulez-vous !*

that's just the way it is! / *si tu veux, si vous voulez* more or less, if you like. ◈ **vouloir de** v + prép **1.** [être prêt à accepter] ▸ **vouloir de qqn** / **qqch** to want sb / sthg **2.** **EXPR** **en vouloir** *fam* : *elle en veut* a) [elle a de l'ambition] she wants to make it ou to win b) [elle a de l'application] she's dead keen ▸ **en vouloir à qqn** [éprouver de la rancune] to bear ou to have a grudge against sb / *je ne l'ai pas fait exprès, ne m'en veux pas* I didn't do it on purpose, don't be cross with me / *tu ne m'en veux pas ?* no hard feelings? / *elle lui en veut d'avoir refusé* she holds it against him that he said no ▸ **en vouloir à qqn** [le convoiter] : *j'ai l'impression qu'il en veut à ma cadette* I feel he has designs on my youngest daughter / *elle en veut à ma fortune* she's after my money ▸ **en vouloir à qqch** [vouloir le détruire] to seek to damage sthg. ◈ **s'en vouloir** ◆ vp *(emploi réfléchi)* to be angry ou annoyed with o.s. / *je m'en veux de l'avoir laissé partir* I feel bad at having let him go. ◆ vp *(emploi réciproque)* : *elles s'en veulent à mort* they really hate each other. ◈ **en veux-tu en voilà** loc adv *fam* [en abondance] : *il y avait des glaces en veux-tu en voilà* there were ice creams galore. ◈ **si l'on veut** loc adv **1.** [approximativement] if you like **2.** [pour exprimer une réserve] : *il est fidèle… si l'on veut !* he's faithful… after a fashion!

voulu, e [vuly] adj **1.** [requis] required, desired, requisite *sout* / *vous aurez toutes les garanties voulues* you'll have all the required guarantees **2.** [délibéré] deliberate, intentional ▸ **c'est voulu** it's intentional ou (done) on purpose **3.** [décidé d'avance] agreed ▸ **au moment voulu** at the right time ▸ **terminé en temps voulu** completed on schedule.

vous [vu]
◆ pron pers *(2e pers pl)*

A. À UNE SEULE PERSONNE **1.** [sujet ou objet direct] you / *eux m'ont compris, pas vous* they understood me, you didn't / *elle a fait comme vous* she did (the same) as you did ; [en renforcement] : *je vous connais, vous !* I know you! / *vous, vous restez* as for you, you're staying **2.** [objet indirect] ▸ **à vous** [objet] : *c'est à vous* it belongs to you ▸ **à vous !** [dans un magasin, un jeu] it's your turn! / *pensez un peu à vous* think of yourself a bit ▸ **de vous** : *un livre de vous* a book by you / *c'est de vous, cette lettre ?* is this one of your letters? ▸ **chez vous** at your house, in your home **3.** [dans des formes réfléchies] ▸ **taisez-vous !** be quiet! ▸ **regardez-vous** look at yourself.

B. À PLUSIEURS PERSONNES **1.** [sujet ou objet direct] you / *elle vous a accusés tous les trois* she accused all three of you ; [en renforcement] you (people) / *vous, vous restez* as for you (people), you're staying **2.** [après une préposition] ▸ **à vous** [objet] : *c'est à vous* it belongs to you ▸ **à vous** RADIO & TV over to you / *pensez à vous et à vos amis* think of yourselves and of your friends / *à vous trois, vous finirez bien la tarte ?* surely the three of you can finish the tart? **3.** [dans des formes réfléchies] : *taisez-vous tous !* be quiet, all of you! / *regardez-vous* look at yourselves ; [dans des formes réciproques] one another, each other / *battez-vous* fight with each other.

C. POUR TOUS *fam* [valeur intensive] : *elle sait vous séduire une foule* she does know how to captivate a crowd.
◆ nm ▸ **le vous** the "vous" form / *leurs enfants leur disent « vous »* their children use the "vous" form to them.

vous-même [vumɛm] *(pl* **vous-mêmes)** pron pers yourself ▸ **vous-mêmes** yourselves.

voûte, voute* [vut] nf **1.** ARCHIT [construction] vault ; [passage] archway **2.** *litt* vault, canopy ▸ **la voûte céleste** ou **des cieux** the canopy of heaven **3.** ANAT ▸ **voûte plantaire** arch of the foot.

voûté, e, vouté*, e [vute] adj **1.** [homme] stooping, round-shouldered ; [dos] bent **/** *avoir le dos voûté* to stoop, to have a stoop **2.** [galerie] vaulted, arched.

voûter, vouter* [3] [vute] ❖ **se voûter, se vouter*** vpi to stoop, to become round-shouldered.

vouvoiement [vuvwamɑ̃] nm "vous" form of address **/** *ici, le vouvoiement est de rigueur* here people have to address each other as "vous".

vouvoyer [13] [vuvwaje] vt to address as "vous".

voyage [vwajaʒ] nm **1.** [excursion lointaine] journey, trip ; [sur la mer, dans l'espace] voyage ; [circuit] tour, trip **/** *leur voyage en Italie* their trip to Italy **/** *faire un voyage autour du monde* to go round the world ▸ **voyage d'affaires** business trip ▸ **voyage d'agrément** (pleasure) trip ▸ **voyage d'études** field trip ▸ **voyage de noces** honeymoon ▸ **voyage organisé** package tour **2.** [déplacement local] journey ▸ **voyage aller** outward journey ▸ **voyage retour** return ou homeward journey **3.** [allée et venue] trip **/** *on a fait trois voyages pour vider la maison* we made three trips to empty the house.

> 📋 Attention ! Le mot travel est indénombrable sauf dans l'expression idiomatique my / your / his etc. travels. Il ne s'emploie jamais avec l'article indéfini a :
> **Les voyages ouvrent l'esprit.** *Travel broadens the mind.*
> **Je reviens d'un très beau voyage en Chine.** *I've just come back from a wonderful trip to China.*

voyager [17] [vwajaʒe] vi **1.** [faire une excursion] to travel ; [faire un circuit] to tour ▸ **aimer voyager** to like travelling **2.** [se déplacer] to travel ▸ **voyager en bateau / en avion** to travel by sea / by air ▸ **voyager en deuxième classe** to travel second class **3.** [denrées, sacs] to travel **/** *le vin voyage mal* wine doesn't travel well.

voyageur, euse [vwajaʒœr, øz] nm, f **1.** [dans les transports en commun] passenger ; [dans un taxi] fare **2.** [qui explore] traveller **/** *c'est une grande voyageuse* she travels extensively **3.** COMM ▸ **voyageur (de commerce)** commercial traveller.

voyagiste [vwajaʒist] nm tour operator.

voyance [vwajɑ̃s] nf clairvoyance.

voyant, e [vwajɑ̃, ɑ̃t] ❖ adj [couleur] loud, gaudy, garish ; [robe] showy, gaudy, garish. ❖ nm, f **1.** [visionnaire] visionary, seer ; [spirite] ▸ **voyant (extralucide)** clairvoyant **2.** [non aveugle] sighted person. ❖ **voyant** nm ▸ **voyant (lumineux)** indicator ou warning light ; [d'un signal] mark ; [plaque de nivellement] vane levelling shaft.

voyelle [vwajɛl] nf vowel.

voyeur, euse [vwajœr, øz] nm, f voyeur.

voyeurisme [vwajœrism] nm voyeurism.

voyeuriste [vwajœrist] adj péj [émission, reportage] voyeuristic.

voyou, te [vwaju, ut] adj loutish. ❖ **voyou** nm **1.** [jeune délinquant] lout ; [gangster] gangster **2.** [ton affectueux ou amusé] : *petit voyou !* you little rascal !

VPC nf abr de **vente par correspondance.**

vrac [vrak] ❖ **en vrac** loc adj & loc adv **1.** [non rangé] in a jumble **/** *ses idées sont en vrac dans sa dissertation* the ideas are just jumbled together in his essay **2.** [non emballé] loose ; [en gros] in bulk **/** *on invite toute la famille en vrac* fam & fig we're inviting the whole family in one go.

vrai, e [vrɛ] adj **1.** [exact] true **/** *il n'y a pas un mot de vrai dans son témoignage* there's not a word of truth in

her testimony **/** *c'est vrai qu'on n'a pas eu de chance* fam true, we were a bit unlucky ▸ **pas vrai ?** fam: *il l'a bien mérité, pas vrai ?* he deserved it, didn't he ? **/** *on ira tous les deux, pas vrai !* we'll go together, OK ? ▸ **c'est pas vrai ! a)** fam [pour nier] it's ou that's not true! **b)** [ton incrédule] you're joking! **c)** [ton exaspéré] I don't believe this! **d)** [ton horrifié] my God, no! **/** *il est vrai que...* it's true (to say) that... **2.** [authentique - cuir, denrée] genuine, real ; [- or] real ; [- connaisseur] real, true ; [- royaliste, républicain] true **/** *les vraies rousses sont rares* there are few genuine ou real redheads **/** *ce ne sont pas ses vraies dents* they're not her own teeth **/** *c'est un vrai gentleman* he's a real gentleman **/** *ça c'est de la vraie bière, de la vraie de vraie !* that's what I call beer! **3.** [non fictif, non inventé - raison] real ▸ **c'est une histoire vraie** it's a true story **4.** (avant nom) [à valeur intensive] real, complete, utter **/** *c'est un vrai désastre* it's a real ou an utter disaster **/** *elle a été une vraie sœur pour moi* she was a real sister to me **/** *c'est une vraie folle !* she's completely crazy! ❖ **vrai** ❖ adv [conformément à la vérité] ▸ **elle dit vrai a)** [elle dit la vérité] she's telling the truth **b)** [elle a raison] she's right, what she says is right. ❖ nm ▸ **le vrai** [la vérité] the truth ▸ **il y a du** ou **un peu de vrai dans ses critiques** there's some truth ou an element of truth in her criticism. ❖ **à dire (le) vrai = à vrai dire.** ❖ **à vrai dire** loc adv in actual fact, to tell you the truth, to be quite honest. ❖ **pour de vrai** loc adv fam really, truly **/** *cette fois-ci, je pars pour de vrai* this time I'm really leaving.

vraiment [vrɛmɑ̃] adv **1.** [réellement] really **/** *il avait l'air vraiment ému* he seemed really ou genuinely moved **2.** [en intensif] really **/** *il est vraiment bête !* he's really ou so stupid! **/** *tu trouves que j'ai fait des progrès ? — ah oui, vraiment !* do you think I've improved ou made any progress? — oh yes, a lot! **/** *vraiment, il exagère !* he really has got a nerve!

vraisemblable [vrɛsɑ̃blabl] adj [théorie] likely ; [dénouement, excuse] convincing, plausible **/** *une fin peu vraisemblable* a rather implausible ending **/** *il est (très) vraisemblable qu'il ait oublié* he's forgotten, in all likelihood.

vraisemblablement [vrɛsɑ̃blabləmɑ̃] adv in all likelihood ou probability, very likely.

vraisemblance [vrɛsɑ̃blɑ̃s] nf **1.** [d'une œuvre] plausibility, verisimilitude sout **2.** [d'une hypothèse] likelihood. ❖ **selon toute vraisemblance** loc adv in all likelihood.

vrille [vrij] nf **1.** [outil] gimlet **2.** AÉRON spin. ❖ **en vrille** loc adv ▸ **descendre en vrille** to spin downwards.

vriller [3] [vrije] vt to pierce, to bore into.

vrombir [32] [vrɔ̃bir] vi [avion, moteur] to throb, to hum ; [insecte] to buzz, to hum **/** *faire vrombir un moteur* to rev up an engine.

vrombissement [vrɔ̃bismɑ̃] nm [d'un avion, d'un moteur] throbbing sound, humming ; [d'un insecte] buzzing, humming.

VRP (abr de **voyageur représentant placier**) nm rep.

vs (abr écrite de **versus**) prép vs.

VTT (abr de **vélo tout terrain**) nm ATB, mountain bike.

vu¹ [vy] nm inv sout : *au vu et au su de tous* openly.

vu² [vy] prép [en considération de] in view of, considering, given **/** *vu l'article 317 du Code pénal...* DR in view of article 317 of the Penal Code... ❖ **vu que** loc conj [étant donné que] in view of the fact that, seeing that, considering that.

vu³, e [vy] ❖ pp ⟶ **voir.** ❖ adj **1.** ▸ **bien / mal vu** [bien / mal considéré] : *il est bien vu de travailler tard* it's the done thing ou it's good form to work late **/** *fumer,* *c'est assez mal vu ici* smoking is disapproved of here ▸ **être bien vu de qqn** to be well thought-of by sb ▸ **être mal vu de qqn** to be not well thought-of by sb **2**. ▸ **bien / mal vu** [bien / **mal analysé**] : *personnages bien / mal vus* finely observed / poorly-drawn characters ▸ **un problème bien vu** an accurately diagnosed problem **3**. [compris] ▸ **(c'est) vu ?** understood?, get it? / *(c'est) vu !* OK!, got it!

vue [vy] nf **1**. [sens] eyesight, sight / *recouvrer la vue* to get one's sight ou eyesight back / *perdre la vue* to lose one's sight, to go blind / *avoir une bonne vue* to have good eyesight / *avoir une mauvaise vue* to have bad ou poor eyesight ▸ **avoir la vue basse** to have weak eyes **2**. [regard] ▸ **se présenter** ou **s'offrir à la vue de qqn a)** [personne, animal, chose] to appear before sb's eyes **b)** [spectacle, paysage] to unfold before sb's eyes **3**. [fait de voir] sight / *je ne supporte pas la vue du sang* I can't stand the sight of blood **4**. [yeux] eyes / *tu vas t'abîmer la vue* you'll ruin your eyes / *on va leur en mettre plein la vue !* let's really impress them ou knock' em for six! 🇬🇧 **5**. [panorama] view / *d'ici, vous avez une vue magnifique* the view (you get) from here is magnificent ▸ **vue sur la mer** sea view / *une vue imprenable* an unobstructed view / *de ma cuisine, j'ai une vue plongeante sur leur chambre* from my kitchen I can see straight down into their bedroom ▸ **avoir vue sur** to look out on **6**. [image] view ▸ **vue d'ensemble a)** PHOT general view **b)** *fig* overview **7**. [idée, opinion] view, opinion ▸ **avoir des vues bien arrêtées sur qqch** to have firm opinions ou ideas about sthg ; [interprétation] view, understanding, interpretation ▸ **vue de l'esprit** *péj* idle fancy. ❖ **vues** nfpl plans, designs ▸ **avoir des vues sur qqn** to have designs on sb ▸ **avoir des vues sur qqch** to covet sthg. ❖ **à courte vue** loc adj [idée, plan] short-sighted. ❖ **à la vue de** loc prép : *il s'évanouit à la vue du sang* he faints at the sight of blood / *à la vue de tous* in front of everybody, in full view of everybody. ❖ **à vue** ◆ loc adj THÉÂTRE ⟶ **changement**. ◆ loc adv [atterrir] visually ; [tirer] on sight ; [payable] at sight. ❖ **à vue de nez** loc adv *fam* roughly, approximately. ❖ **à vue d'œil** loc adv : *ton cousin grossit à vue d'œil* your cousin is getting noticeably ou visibly fatter / *mes économies disparaissent à vue d'œil* my savings just disappear before my very eyes. ❖ **de vue** loc adv by

sight / *je le connais de vue* I know his face, I know him by sight. ❖ **en vue** ◆ loc adj **1**. [célèbre] prominent ▸ **les gens en vue** people in the public eye ou in the news **2**. [escompté] : *j'ai quelqu'un en vue pour racheter ma voiture* I've got somebody who's interested in buying my car. ◆ loc adv ▸ **mettre qqch (bien) en vue dans son salon** to display sthg prominently in one's lounge. ❖ **en vue de** loc prép **1**. [tout près de] within sight of **2**. [afin de] so as ou in order to / *j'y vais en vue de préparer le terrain* I'm going in order to prepare the ground.

vulcanologie [vylkanɔlɔʒi] = **volcanologie**.

vulcanologue [vylkanɔlɔg] = **volcanologue**.

vulgaire [vylgɛʀ] ◆ adj **1**. [sans goût - meuble, vêtement] vulgar, common, tasteless ; [- couleur] loud, garish ; [- style] crude, coarse, unrefined ; [- personne] uncouth, vulgar **2**. [impoli] crude, coarse **3**. *(avant nom)* [ordinaire] ordinary, common, common-or-garden *hum* / *un vulgaire employé* a common clerk **4**. [non scientifique] ▸ **nom vulgaire** common name ; [non littéraire - langue] vernacular ; [- latin] vulgar. ◆ nm [vulgarité] ▸ **le vulgaire** vulgarity / *la décoration de son appartement est d'un vulgaire !* the way he's decorated his flat is so vulgar!

vulgairement [vylgɛʀmɑ̃] adv **1**. [avec mauvais goût] coarsely, vulgarly, tastelessly **2**. [de façon non scientifique] commonly.

vulgarisateur, trice [vylgaʀizatœʀ, tʀis] adj [ouvrage] popularizing / *l'auteur tente de n'être pas trop vulgarisateur* the author attempts to avoid over-simplification.

vulgarisation [vylgaʀizasjɔ̃] nf popularization ▸ **un ouvrage de vulgarisation** a book for the layman.

vulgariser [3] [vylgaʀize] vt [faire connaître - œuvre, auteur] to popularize, to make accessible to a large audience.

vulgarité [vylgaʀite] nf [caractère vulgaire] vulgarity, coarseness.

vulnérabilité [vylneʀabilite] nf vulnerability, vulnerableness.

vulnérable [vylneʀabl] adj [fragile] vulnerable.

vulve [vylv] nf vulva.

vumètre [vymɛtʀ] nm volume unit meter.

Vve abr écrite de **veuve**.

W (abr écrite de **watt**) W.

wagon [vagɔ̃] nm [voiture] ▸ **wagon (de marchandises)** wagon, truck , freight car, boxcar .

wagon-citerne [vagɔ̃sitɛʀn] (*pl* **wagons-citernes**) nm tank wagon  ou car .

wagon-lit [vagɔ̃li] (*pl* **wagons-lits**) nm sleeper, sleeping car, wagon-lit.

wagon-restaurant [vagɔ̃ʀɛstɔʀɑ̃] (*pl* **wagons-restaurants**) nm dining  ou restaurant  car.

Walkman® [wɔkman] nm Walkman®, personal stereo.

wallaby [walabi] (*pl* **wallabys** ou **wallabies**) nm wallaby.

wallingant, e [walɛ̃gɑ̃, ɑ̃t] nm, f  *péj* Walloon autonomist.

Wallis-et-Futuna [walisefutuna] npr Wallis and Futuna.

wallisien, enne [walizjɛ̃, ɛn] adj Wallisian.
◆ **Wallisien, enne** nm, f Wallisian.

wallon, onne [walɔ̃, ɔn] adj Walloon. ◆ **Wallon, onne** nm, f Walloon. ◆ **wallon** nm LING Walloon.

Wallonie [walɔni] npr f ▸ **(la) Wallonie** Southern Belgium *(where French and Walloon are spoken)*, Wallonia.

WAP [wap] (abr de **Wireless Application Protocol**) nm TÉLÉC WAP ▸ **téléphone WAP** WAP telephone.

warning [waʀniŋ] nm AUTO hazard warning lights , hazard lights .

water-polo (*pl* **water-polos**), **waterpolo*** [watɛʀpɔlo] nm water polo.

waterproof [watɛʀpʀuf] adj inv [montre, mascara] waterproof.

waters [watɛʀ] nmpl *vieilli* toilet.

waterzoï [watɛʀzɔj] nm  *speciality made from fish or meat in cream sauce.*

watt [wat] nm watt.

W-C [vese] (abr de **water closet**) nmpl WC.

Web [wɛb] nm ▸ **le Web** the Web.

webcam [wɛbkam] nf webcam.

webcaméra [wɛbkameʀa] nf  webcam.

weblog [weblɔg] nm blog.

webmaster [wɛbmastɛʀ] nm INFORM Webmaster.

webmestre [wɛbmɛstʀ] nmf INFORM webmaster.

webradio [wɛbʀadjo] nf web radio station.

webtélé [wɛbtele] nf web TV station.

webzine [wɛbzin] nm INFORM webzine.

week-end (*pl* **week-ends**), **weekend*** [wikɛnd] nm weekend **/** *partir en week-end* to go away for the weekend.

western [wɛstɛʀn] nm western.

western-spaghetti [wɛstɛʀnspageti] (*pl* **westerns-spaghettis**) nm spaghetti western.

whisky [wiski] (*pl* **whiskys** ou **whiskies**) nm [écossais] whisky ; [irlandais ou américain] whiskey.

Wi-Fi, wi-fi [wifi] (abr de **Wireless Fidelity**) nm inv Wi-Fi.

Windsurf® [windsœʀf] nm Windsurf® (surfboard).

wishbone [wiʃbon] nm NAUT wishbone.

wok [wɔk] nm wok.

X, X [iks] ◆ nm [lettre] x, X ; MATH x ▸ **l'axe des x** MATH the x axis ▸ **j'ai vu la pièce x fois** I've seen the play umpteen times ▸ **ça fait x temps que je te demande de le faire** I've been asking you to do it for ages ▸ **être né sous X** to be taken into care at birth ▸ **classé X** X-rated ▸ **plainte contre X** DR action against person ou persons unknown. ◆ nf *arg scol* ▸ **l'X** the École Polytechnique. **Voir aussi g.**

xénophobe [gzenɔfɔb] ◆ adj xenophobic. ◆ nmf xenophobe.

xénophobie [gzenɔfɔbi] nf xenophobia.

xérès [gzeʀɛs, kseʀɛs] nm sherry.

XXL (abr de **extra extra large**) adj XXL / *un tee-shirt XXL* an XXL tee-shirt ou T-shirt.

xylographie [ksilɔgʀafi] nf xylography.

xylophone [gsilɔfɔn] nm xylophone.

y [i] pron adv **1.** [représente le lieu] there / *j'y vais souvent* I often go there ▸ **vas-y, entre !** go on in! ▸ **on n'y voit rien** you can't see a thing (here) **2.** [représente une chose] it / *pensez-y, à mon offre* do think about my offer / *n'y comptez pas* don't count ou bank on it ▸ **je n'y manquerai pas** I certainly will **3.** [représente une personne] : *les fantômes, j'y crois* I believe in ghosts **4.** EXPR **il y va de** it's a matter of / *il y va de ma dignité* my dignity's at stake ▸ **y être pour quelque chose** to have something to do with it / *je n'y suis pour rien, moi !* it's (got) nothing to do with me!, it's not my fault! ▸ **laisse-le choisir, il s'y connaît** let him choose, he knows all about it ▸ **avec les petits, il faut savoir s'y prendre** with little children you have to know how to handle them.

Y (abr écrite de **yen**) Y.

ya SMS abr écrite de **il y a**.

yacht [jɔt] nm yacht ▸ **yacht de croisière** cruiser.

ya(c)k [jak] nm yak.

Yalta [jalta] npr Yalta / *la conférence de Yalta* the Yalta Conference.

yaourt [jauʀt] nm yoghurt ▸ **yoghurt à boire** yoghurt drink ▸ **yoghurt aux fruits** fruit yoghurt ▸ **yoghurt maigre** low-fat yoghurt ▸ **yoghurt nature** natural yoghurt.

yaourtière [jauʀtjɛʀ] nf yoghurt maker.

Yémen [jemɛn] npr m ▸ **le Yémen** Yemen ▸ **au Yémen** in Yemen.

yen [jɛn] nm yen.

yeti [jeti] nm yeti.

yeux [jø] pl ⟶ **œil**.

yé-yé [jeje] *fam* adj inv pop *(in the sixties)*.

yiddish, yidiche* [jidiʃ] adj inv & nm inv Yiddish.

ylang-ylang [ilãɡilãɡ] *(pl* **ylangs-ylangs**) nm ylang-ylang, ilang-ilang.

yoga [jɔɡa] nm yoga.

yog(h)ourt [jɔɡuʀt] = **yaourt**.

yogi [jɔɡi] nmf yogi.

Yom Kippour [jɔmkipuʀ] nm inv Yom Kippour.

yougoslave [juɡɔslav] adj Yugoslav, Yugoslavian. ◈ **Yougoslave** nmf Yugoslav, Yugoslavian.

Yougoslavie [juɡɔslavi] npr f ▸ **la Yougoslavie** Yugoslavia ; ▸ **l'ex-Yougoslavie** former Yugoslavia.

youpi [jupi] interj yippee, hooray.

youyou [juju] nm dinghy.

Yo-Yo® [jojo] nm inv yo-yo ▸ **effet yo-yo** *fig* yo-yo effect ▸ **jouer au yo-yo** *fig* to go yo-yo.

yucca [juka] nm yucca.

---

* In reformed spelling (see p. 16-18).

ZAC, Zac [zak] (abr de **zone d'aménagement concerté**) nf area earmarked for local government planning project.

Zambie [zɑ̃bi] npr f ▶ **(la) Zambie** Zambia.

zapper [zape] vi TV to zap (TV channels), to channel-hop.

zapping [zapiŋ] nm ▶ **le zapping** zapping, (constant) channel-hopping.

zazou [zazu] fam ◆ adj [dans les années 40] hep vieilli. ◆ nmf [amateur de jazz] hipster vieilli.

zèbre [zɛbʀ] nm **1.** ZOOL zebra **2.** fam [individu] ▶ **c'est un (drôle de) zèbre, celui-là !** a) [ton dépréciatif] he's a weirdo! b) [ton amusé ou admiratif] he's quite something!

zébrer [18] [zebʀe] vt [de lignes - irrégulières] to streak ; [- régulières] to stripe.

✐ In reformed spelling (see p. 16-18), this verb is conjugated like semer : il zèbrera, elle zèbrerait.

zébrure [zebʀyʀ] nf **1.** [du zèbre, du tigre] stripe **2.** [marque de coup] weal **3.** [d'éclair] streak.

zébu [zeby] nm zebu.

ZEC [zɛk] (abr de **zone d'exploitation contrôlée**) nf Quebec controlled harvesting zone.

zèle [zɛl] nm zeal / elle travaillait avec zèle she worked zealously / fais pas de zèle fam don't do more than you have to!, don't overdo it!

zélé, e [zele] adj zealous.

zen [zɛn] adj inv & nm Zen ▶ **être zen** to be laid back ▶ **rester zen** to keep cool.

zénith [zenit] nm **1.** [sommet] zenith, acme **2.** ASTRON zenith.

ZEP, Zep [zɛp] (abr de **zone d'éducation prioritaire**) nf designated area with special educational needs.

zéro [zeʀo] ◆ nm **1.** MATH zero, nought ; [dans un numéro de téléphone] 0 ; [dans une gradation] zero **2.** PHYS zero (degrees centigrade), freezing (point) **3.** SPORT zero, nil UK / deux buts à zéro two (goals to) nil UK ou zero / zéro partout no score ; TENNIS love all **4.** ÉDUC nought UK, zero ▶ **zéro de conduite** black mark ▶ **zéro pointé** nought UK, zero **5.** fam [incapable] dead loss **6.** (comme adj) [sans intérêt] nil, worthless / au niveau organisation, c'était zéro as far as organisation goes it was useless. ◆ dét ▶ **zéro défaut** zero defect ▶ **zéro faute** no mistakes / zéro heure midnight, zero hour spéc / zéro heure quinze zero hours fifteen / ça te coûtera zéro euro it'll cost you nothing at all. ❖ **à zéro** ◆ loc adj ▶ **avoir le moral** ou **être à zéro** fam to be at an all-time low. ◆ loc adv fam ▶ **recommencer** ou **repartir à zéro** a) [dans sa carrière, dans un raisonnement] to go back to square one ou the drawing board b) [sans argent, sans aide] to start again from scratch.

zeste [zɛst] nm **1.** [d'un agrume] zest ▶ **un zeste de citron** a piece of lemon peel **2.** [petite quantité] pinch / un zeste d'accent a hint ou faint trace of an accent.

zézaiement [zezɛmɑ̃] nm lisp.

zézayer [11] [zezeje] vi to (have a) lisp.

ZI nf abr de **zone industrielle**.

zibeline [ziblin] nf [fourrure, animal] sable.

zieuter [3] [zjøte] vt tfam to eye (up) (sép), to eyeball US.

zigouiller [3] [ziguje] vt tfam to knife (to death), to bump off (sép), to do in (sép) / se faire zigouiller to get done in.

zigzag [zigzag] nm zigzag. ❖ **en zigzag** loc adj zigzagging, winding.

zigzaguer [3] [zigzage] vi to zigzag.

Zimbabwe [zimbabwe] npr m ▶ **le Zimbabwe** Zimbabwe.

zimbabwéen, enne [zimbabweɛ̃, ɛn] adj Zimbabwean. ❖ **Zimbabwéen, enne** nm, f Zimbabwean.

zinc [zɛ̃g] nm **1.** [métal] zinc **2.** fam [comptoir] bar **3.** fam [avion] plane.

zinzin [zɛ̃zɛ̃] fam ◆ adj dotty, batty, nuts. ◆ nm [idiot] nutcase.

Zip® [zip] nm zip UK, zipper US.

zipper [3] [zipe] vt INFORM to zip.

zircon [ziʀkɔ̃] nm zircon.

zizanie [zizani] nf discord / c'est la zizanie entre les frères the brothers are at odds ou loggerheads ▶ **jeter** ou **mettre** ou **semer la zizanie dans un groupe** to stir things up in a group.

zizi [zizi] nm fam [sexe] willy UK, peter US.

zloty [zlɔti] nm [monnaie] zloty.

zob [zɔb] nm vulg cock.

zodiacal, e, aux [zɔdjakal, o] adj [signe] zodiac.

zodiaque [zɔdjak] nm ASTRON & ASTROL zodiac.

zombi(e) [zɔ̃bi] nm zombie.

zona [zona] nm shingles (U), herpes zoster spéc / avoir un zona to suffer from shingles.

zonard [zonaʀ] nm fam dropout.

zone [zon] nf **1.** [domaine] zone, area ▶ **la zone d'activité du directeur commercial** the commercial manager's area ▶ **la zone d'influence de l'Asie** Asia's sphere of influence ▶ **zone de flou** ou **d'incertitude** ou **d'ombre** grey area ▶ **zone de turbulences** (en avion) turbulence zone **2.** ANAT ▶ **zone érogène** erogenous zone **3.** ADMIN [surface délimitée] area, zone ▶ **zone d'activités** business park ▶ **zone d'aménagement concerté** = ZAC ▶ **zone bleue** restricted parking area ▶ **zone franche** free zone ▶ **zone industrielle** industrial estate UK ou park US ▶ **zone inondable**

flood-risk area ▶ **zone interdite** off-limits area / *une zone interdite à la pêche* an area where fishing is prohibited ▶ **zone d'éducation prioritaire** = ZEP ▶ **zone de pêche** fishing ground ▶ **zone piétonnière** ou **piétonne** pedestrian area ou precinct `UK` ou zone `US` ▶ **zone résidentielle** residential area ▶ **zone à urbaniser en priorité** *area earmarked for urgent urban development* ▶ **zone urbaine sensible** = ZUS **4.** HIST ▶ **zone libre / occupée** unoccupied / occupied France **5.** MÉTÉOR ▶ **zone de dépression** ou **zone dépressionnaire** trough of low pressure **6.** GÉOL & MATH zone **7.** FIN ▶ **zone euro** Euroland ▶ **zone monétaire** monetary zone **8.** INFORM ▶ **zone de dialogue** dialogue box **9.** MIL ▶ **zone tampon** buffer zone **10.** ▶ **c'est la zone** **a)** *fam* [quartier pauvre] it's a really rough area **b)** [désordre] it's a real mess ou tip. ❖ **de troisième zone** *loc adj* third-rate.

zoner [3] [zone] ❖ vt to zone. ❖ vi *fam* to doss `UK` ou to bum around.

zoo [zo(o)] nm zoo.

zoologie [zɔɔlɔʒi] nf zoology.

zoologique [zɔɔlɔʒik] adj zoological.

zoologiste [zɔɔlɔʒist] nmf zoologist.

zoom [zum] nm [objet] zoom lens ; [procédé] zoom ▶ **faire un zoom sur** to zoom in on.

zoomer [3] [zume] vi [pour se rapprocher] to zoom in ; [pour s'éloigner] to zoom out.

zou [zu] interj [pour marquer la rapidité] whoosh / *allez, zou les enfants, au lit !* come on, off to bed children! / *on ferme la maison et zou, on part pour l'Italie* we'll shut up the house and whizz off to Italy.

zouave [zwav] nm **1.** MIL Zouave **2.** `EXPR` **faire le zouave** *fam* **a)** [faire le pitre] to clown about **b)** [faire le malin] to show off.

zoulou, e [zulu] adj Zulu. ❖ **Zoulou, e** nm, f Zulu. ❖ **zoulou** nm LING Zulu.

ZUP, Zup [zyp] nf abr de **zone à urbaniser par priorité.**

ZUS (abr de **zone urbaine sensible**) nf *designated urban area with social problems, earmarked for priority assistance or development programmes.*

zut [zyt] interj *fam* drat, blast / *zut alors, y a plus de sucre !* blast (it), there's no sugar left! / *et puis zut, tant pis, je l'achète !* what the hell, I'll buy it!

zwanze [zwãz] nf `BELG` *fam* joke.

zwanzer [3] [zwãze] vi `BELG` *fam* to joke.

zyeuter [zjøte] *tfam* = **zieuter.**

zygomatique [zigɔmatik] adj zygomatic.

Guide de communication
Communication guide

Sommaire
Contents

Correspondance
French and English correspondence

Demandes d'emploi et de stage
Job and internship applications

Vie quotidienne
Daily life

Opening and closing formulas

	OPENING FORMULAS	CLOSING FORMULAS
To a relative or close friend	Cher Cédric,/Mon cher Cédric, Chère Françoise,/Ma chère Françoise, Chère mamie, etc.	Je t'embrasse (très fort)/ À bientôt Bises/Grosses bises Bisous/Gros bisous
To an acquaintance	Cher Monsieur, Chère Madame, Chère Mademoiselle, Cher ami,/Chère amie,	Amicalement Bien amicalement Amitiés
In formal correspondence, when you know the name and sex of the person you are writing to	Monsieur, Madame, Mademoiselle,	Veuillez agréer OR Je vous prie d'agréer, Monsieur, mes salutations distinguées OR l'expression de mes sentiments distingués.
In formal correspondence, when you do not know the name or sex of the person you are writing to	Messieurs, Madame, Monsieur,	Veuillez agréer OR Je vous prie d'agréer, Messieurs,/Madame, Monsieur, mes salutations distinguées OR l'expression de mes sentiments distingués.

Formules d'appel et formules finales

	FORMULES D'APPEL	FORMULES FINALES
À des amis intimes, membres de la famille	Dear David Dear Lily Dear Mum and Dad Dear Uncle Tony	Love With love
		Formules plus affectueuses : Lots of love
		Formules plus neutres : Yours From Best wishes
À des connaissances, des amis	Dear Harriet Dear Sally and Michael Dear Mrs Simpson Dear Mr Brown Dear Mr and Mrs Adams	(With) best wishes (With) kind regards Regards Yours All the best
Dans une lettre d'affaires, lorsqu'on connaît le nom du correspondant	Dear Mr Jones Dear Mrs Clarke Dear Ms Fletcher Dear Dr Illingworth	Yours sincerely *(UK)* Sincerely *(US)* Yours truly (surtout *US*)
Pour s'adresser à quelqu'un dont on ne connaît pas le nom	Dear Sir Dear Madam	Yours faithfully *(UK)* Sincerely yours *(US)*
Pour s'adresser à quelqu'un dont on ne sait si c'est un homme ou une femme, et dont on ignore le nom.	Dear Sir or Madam Dear Sir/Madam Dear Sirs *(UK)* Gentlemen *(US)*	Yours faithfully *(UK)* Sincerely yours *(US)*

guide de communication

Model layout of a letter to a friend or relative

The date is shown in the top right-hand corner and is often preceded by the name of the place where the letter is written. If no place name is given, the date starts with a capital "L" *(Le 2 mars 2013)*.

Note that the opening formula is always followed by a comma.

Grenoble, le 2 mars 2013

Cher Laurent,

J'espère que tu vas bien. Je suis désolée de ne pas avoir répondu à ta lettre plus tôt, mais je suis vraiment débordée en ce moment. Je voulais avant tout te remercier pour le livre que tu m'as envoyé pour mon anniversaire. Je l'ai trouvé passionnant.

Je profite également de cette lettre pour t'annoncer que je vais bientôt me marier... Eh oui, tout arrive ! Tu sais peut-être que j'ai rencontré Pierre il y a un an environ, et que nous vivons ensemble depuis quelque temps. Nous avons l'intention d'officialiser tout ça en mai ou en juin. Si je t'en parle, c'est bien sûr parce que j'aimerais beaucoup que tu viennes. Il faudra que tu réserves tous tes week-ends de mai et juin jusqu'à ce qu'une date précise soit fixée !

J'espère avoir de tes nouvelles bientôt.

Je t'embrasse.

Céline

Présentation type de lettre à un ami, un parent

La présence de la virgule après la formule d'appel n'est pas obligatoire.

Remarquez que, dans les lettres manuscrites, chaque nouveau paragraphe commence en retrait.

Au Royaume-Uni, l'adresse de l'expéditeur figure en haut à droite. Aux États-Unis, dans la correspondance personnelle, les nom et adresse de l'expéditeur n'apparaissent pas.

47 Mulberry Lane,
Oxford
OX4 3LA

19 May 2013

Dear Jane,

Just a few lines to let you have my new address. Sorry I haven't been in touch for so long but we've been very busy trying to organize the move. As always, there were a lot of last-minute complications, but we are now in Oxford and both looking forward to starting our new jobs.

I would have called you but the telephone has not been connected yet and I'm having problems with my mobile! I'll let you have the number as soon as I know it myself.

I must admit that I was a bit sad to leave Paris, but I'm sure it was the right decision. We've already joined the local tennis club in the hope of meeting people and all the neighbours seem really friendly. You'll have to come and see us when we've finished unpacking!

Hope you're well and not working too hard. Drop us a line when you have time. It's always great to hear from you.

Love,

Carol
XXX

Chaque croix figurant au bas de la lettre représente un baiser.

Notez que si la formule d'appel est suivie d'une virgule, la formule finale l'est également.

En anglais britannique, on peut faire figurer « th », « st », « nd » et « rd » après le chiffre : *19th May 2013*. Aux États-Unis, le mois figure le plus souvent avant le jour, qui est séparé de l'année par une virgule : *May 19, 2013*.

Model layout of a formal or business letter

The name and address of the sender are placed at the top left-hand side of the page. These can be followed by the sender's telephone and fax numbers.

It is common to give a brief summary of the contents of the letter above the opening formula.

The name and address of the addressee are placed on the right-hand side, below those of the sender and above the date.
It is customary to insert a comma between the house number and the name of the street, but this is not compulsory.

J.-P. Salvatore
13 Résidence de la Marmande
28, rue de l'Écureuil
80000 Amiens

Monsieur Torrent
Agence Les Sables
5, rue du Marché
85160 Saint-Jean-de-Monts

Amiens, le 3 juin 2013

Objet : réservation de la villa « Marguerite »

Monsieur,

    Suite à notre conversation téléphonique de ce jour, je vous confirme ma réservation de la villa « Marguerite », 10, rue du Rivage, à Saint-Jean-de-Monts, pour la période du 6 au 27 juillet 2013.
    J'ai bien noté que cette villa se trouve à 500 mètres de la mer et près des principaux commerçants. « Marguerite » comporte un salon, une salle à manger, deux chambres et une terrasse, et la cuisine est équipée d'un lave-vaisselle.
    Comme convenu, je vous joins un accompte de 800 euros et vous remettrai le solde à la remise des clés.

    Je vous prie d'agréer, Monsieur, mes salutations distinguées.

J.-P. Salvatore

J.-P. Salvatore

PJ : un chèque de 800 euros, n° 4209374 sur la BNP.

Note that the name of the addressee is never used in the opening formula of a formal or business letter.

Paragraphs can be indented or level with the left-hand margin.

The wording of the opening formula is always repeated in the closing formula.

The sender's name may be written in capitals (for a handwritten letter) or typed below the signature, especially when the signature is not legible.

"PJ" stands for *pièce(s) jointe(s)* and indicates an enclosure. Note that you should mention the document(s) enclosed.

Présentation type de lettre commerciale

Le nom, ou le titre, et l'adresse du destinataire figurent à gauche, au-dessus de la formule d'appel et en dessous d'un numéro de référence éventuel.

Dans le style britannique, la formule d'appel peut être suivie d'une virgule ou non ; elle est suivie de deux points (:) en style américain.

On peut également écrire la date en chiffres. Notez toutefois qu'au Royaume-Uni on donne d'abord le jour, puis le mois et l'année : 2.5.13, et qu'aux États-Unis le mois précède le jour et l'année : 5.2.13.

L'adresse de l'expéditeur figure en haut à droite, sauf s'il s'agit de papier à en-tête, auquel cas elle apparaît en haut au centre de la page.

Harvey & Co
29 Mudeford Road
Manchester
M14 6FR
Tel: 0161 543 7644
E-mail: harvey@uniline.co

The Manager
Lakelands Hotel
Windermere
Cumbria WI6 8YT

2 May 2013

Dear Sir or Madam

Re: Reservation of conference facilities

Following our telephone conversation of this morning, I am writing to confirm the reservation of your conference facilities for the weekend of June 8 and 9.

There will be a total of sixty-eight participants, most of whom will be arriving on the Saturday morning. As I mentioned on the phone, we would like to have a light lunch provided and a four-course meal in the evening. In addition we would appreciate coffee, tea and biscuits mid-morning and mid-afternoon.

If you need to discuss any details, please do not hesitate to contact me. I enclose a list of the participants for your information.

Thanking you in advance.

Yours faithfully

Brian Woods

Mr Brian Woods

Enc.

Il est fréquent de donner, au début de la lettre, un bref résumé de son contenu. Aux États-Unis, ce résumé apparaît avant la formule d'appel.

Les dates ne sont jamais précédées de *of* ou de *the* dans le corps de la lettre. On prononce toutefois *June the eighth* ou *the ninth of June*.

Remarquez que, dans une lettre non manuscrite, les paragraphes ne sont pas en retrait.

Indique qu'il y a des pièces jointes au courrier.

La signature se place sous la formule finale (et non à droite). Dans les lettres commerciales ou officielles, on peut faire figurer le nom dactylographié sous la signature, notamment si celle-ci est peu lisible.

Le style britannique veut qu'il n'y ait pas de ponctuation après la formule finale s'il n'y en a pas après la formule d'appel. Aux États-Unis, en revanche, la formule est suivie d'une virgule.

Addressing an envelope

The name and address are placed in the bottom right-hand corner of the envelope. Each line begins with a capital letter.

The sender's name and address can be placed on the reverse of the envelope at the top. In formal and business correspondence it is usually placed on the front in the top left-hand corner of the envelope.

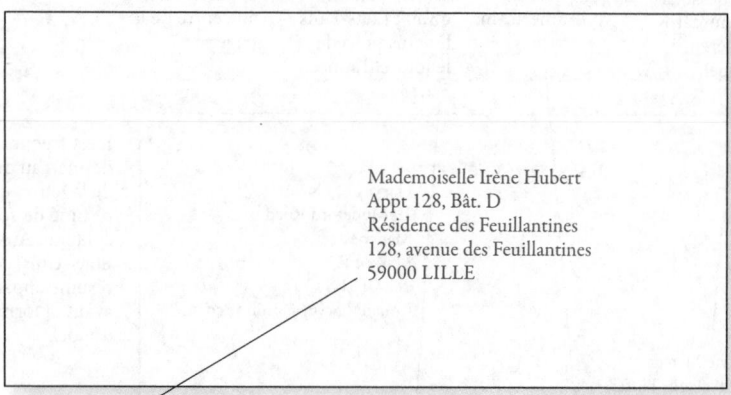

Mademoiselle Irène Hubert
Appt 128, Bât. D
Résidence des Feuillantines
128, avenue des Feuillantines
59000 LILLE

French postcodes consist of five numbers written without any spaces. Of these numbers, the first two indicate the *département*. The postcode is written before the name of the town or village which should be written in capital letters.

In business correspondence abbreviations of titles *(M., Mme, MM., Mmes, Mlle, Mlles)* are possible, although it is preferable to give the title in full *(Monsieur, Madame, Messieurs, Mesdames, Mademoiselle, Mesdemoiselles)*.

Note that the first name is always given in full, even in business correspondence.

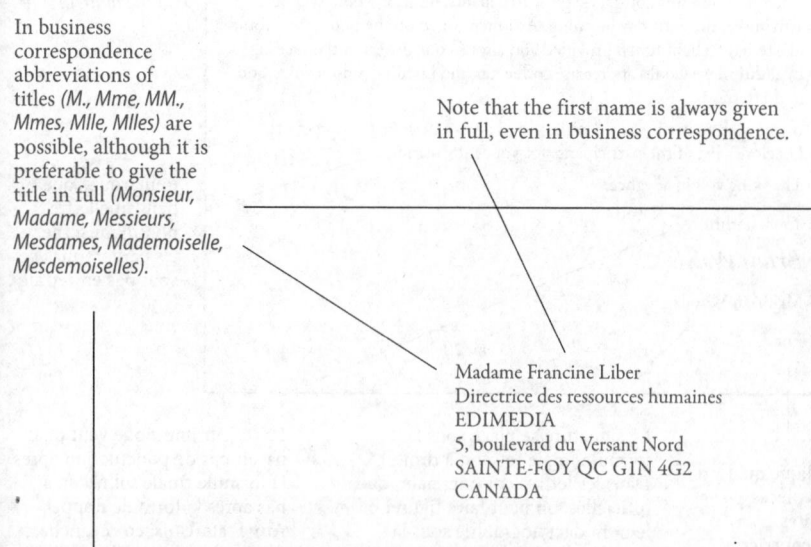

Madame Francine Liber
Directrice des ressources humaines
EDIMEDIA
5, boulevard du Versant Nord
SAINTE-FOY QC G1N 4G2
CANADA

Rédaction de l'enveloppe

• Au Royaume-Uni

L'adresse se place au milieu de l'enveloppe.
L'expéditeur peut éventuellement écrire son adresse au dos de l'enveloppe, en haut.

Dans le style britannique, on donne aujourd'hui couramment les abréviations des titres, les initiales et les adresses sans ponctuation.

Le prénom du destinataire peut être écrit en entier : *Mr John Taylor,* ou seulement avec les initiales : *Mr J P Taylor.*

Le code postal se présente généralement sous la forme de deux groupes de lettres et de chiffres.

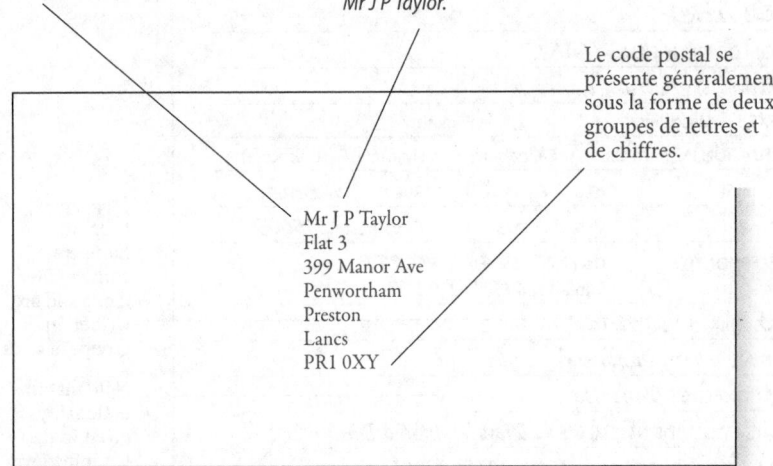

Mr J P Taylor
Flat 3
399 Manor Ave
Penwortham
Preston
Lancs
PR1 0XY

• Aux États-Unis

L'adresse se place au milieu de l'enveloppe.
L'adresse de l'expéditeur figure en haut à gauche du nom et de l'adresse du destinataire.

Aux États-Unis, les abréviations de titres et les initiales s'écrivent avec un point abréviatif. Par ailleurs, les adresses comportent parfois des virgules et un point final.

Le numéro de l'appartement peut être placé avant ou après le numéro et le nom de la rue ou en bas de l'enveloppe à gauche. Il est parfois précédé du signe # signifiant « numéro ».

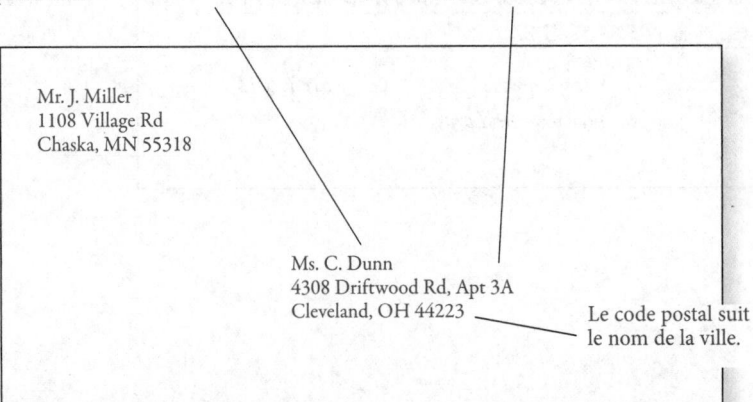

Mr. J. Miller
1108 Village Rd
Chaska, MN 55318

Ms. C. Dunn
4308 Driftwood Rd, Apt 3A
Cleveland, OH 44223

Le code postal suit le nom de la ville.

Filling in a form

Note that *nom*, or the alternative *nom de famille*, means surname.

NOM : *LEROY*

NOM DE JEUNE FILLE : *MANIE*

PRÉNOM(S) : *Patricia Gabrielle*

SEXE : Masculin   (Féminin)

SITUATION DE FAMILLE : Célibataire   (Marié(e))   Divorcé(e)

ADRESSE :   n° : *6*   Rue : *du Béarn*

Ville : *Paris*   Code postal : *75003*

TÉLÉPHONE :   Domicile : *01 49 67 43 22*
Bureau : *01 39 68 92 10*

FAX : *01 39 68 92 11*

E-MAIL : *pleroy@inform.fr*

NATIONALITÉ : *française*

DATE ET LIEU DE NAISSANCE : *28 février 1956 à Dinan*

N° DE SÉCURITÉ SOCIALE : *256022235068041*

PROFESSION : *Photojournaliste*

NOM DE L'EMPLOYEUR : *L'Explorateur*

ADRESSE DE L'EMPLOYEUR : *3, rue de la Liberté
94100 SAINT-MAUR-DES-FOSSÉS*

PERSONNE À CONTACTER EN CAS DE NÉCESSITÉ :

Nom : *Antoine Manie*

Adresse : *22, rue de la Croix Blanche 33000 BORDEAUX*

Téléphone : *05 56 51 83 27*

Fait à   *Paris*   Le *4 avril 2013*
Signature : *P. Leroy*

French telephone numbers consist of ten digits and are written in groups of twos.

Note that the nationality is given in the feminine form to agree with *nationalité*.

It is common in France to ask for the place of birth as well as the date of birth.

communication guide

Remplir un formulaire

TITLE: Mr   Mrs   (Ms)   Miss

SURNAME: *HUTCHINSON*

MAIDEN NAME: *CLARKE*

FIRST NAME(S): *Josephine Ann*

SEX: Male   (Female)

MARITAL STATUS: Single   (Married)   Divorced

ADDRESS: Street number: *13*   Street: *Lexford Drive*

        Town: *Woodbridge* County: *Suffolk*

        Postcode: *IP12 3DG*

TELEPHONE: Home: *01394 412431*

          Office: *01394 430698*

FAX: *01394 430621*

E-MAIL: *jhutchinson@pixie.uk*

NATIONALITY: *British*

DATE OF BIRTH: *19/01/1977*

NATIONAL INSURANCE NUMBER: *NA191487B*

PROFESSION: *Legal secretary*

EMPLOYER: *Brown & Cole*

EMPLOYER'S ADDRESS: *3 Church Road, Woodbridge, Suffolk IP11 4AY*

PERSON TO BE CONTACTED IN CASE OF AN EMERGENCY:

Full name: *Mr James Clarke*

Address: *16 Ecclesall Road, Sheffield S11 8PN*

Telephone: *01142 621637*

Signature: *Josephine Hutchinson*   Date: *4 April 2013*

Il n'est pas courant de demander le lieu de naissance.

Aux États-Unis, on donne le mois avant le jour dans la date de naissance : 01/19/1977.

Aux États-Unis, l'équivalent est le *social security number*.

Par *Full name* on entend le nom et le(s) prénom(s).

Aux États-Unis, on écrirait *April 4, 2013*.

Writing to a friend

Toulouse, le 5 mai 2013

Cher Christophe,

Une fois de plus, j'ai laissé passer plusieurs mois avant de te répondre, je suis impardonnable ! J'ai tout de même des circonstances atténuantes : j'ai changé de service dans ma société, et je suis maintenant beaucoup plus souvent en déplacement.

Tu as l'air de bien t'adapter à ton nouveau cadre de vie ; est-ce que tu t'es fait des amis ? C'est certainement beaucoup plus facile de rencontrer des gens dans une petite ville, surtout quand on est sportif comme toi et qu'on peut s'inscrire à tout un tas de clubs et d'associations.

En tout cas, compte sur moi pour venir te rendre visite très bientôt, puisque tu m'invites si gentiment. J'avais justement l'intention de prendre quelques jours de congé début juillet ; est-ce que la semaine du 1 au 8 te conviendrait ?

J'espère que tu ne seras pas aussi fainéant que moi et que tu répondras vite !

Je t'embrasse.

Christine

Salut, les copains ! Quel temps fait-il à Nancy ? Ici, le soleil brille, la mer est bleue, le sable doré, bref c'est le paradis. Enfin, ça serait vraiment le paradis si Anne ne m'obligeait pas à aller visiter les petits villages de l'intérieur à l'heure de la sieste...

On vous racontera tout plus en détail à notre retour.

Bises.

Sandra

Jérôme et Pascale Hulet

25 bis, rue Georges Clemenceau

54000 Nancy

FRANCE

Écrire à un ami

Tuesday

Hi!
Saw this card and thought of you!
Having a great time exploring Cairo's
markets and museums. Having a few
problems with the language
– but quite a lot of people seem to
understand English. Off to visit the
pyramids tomorrow – and maybe
a camel ride! Wish you were here.

All my love,
Isabelle

Andy and Yvonne Birch
52 Moor Grange View
Wellington Heath
HERTFORDSHIRE
GREAT BRITAIN

24 Lodge Road
Peterborough
PE7 4QZ

15 January 2013

Dear Anne,

Just a quick note to let you know that everything is fine and to
apologize for not having written sooner. As you can see, I have moved
since the last time I wrote - and lost your address in the move!

How are things in Paris? You didn't say much about the course
in your last letter. I hope everything is going well. As you can imagine,
life has been a bit hectic at this end, what with the move and Christmas.
The new house is much larger and closer to work. I now have a spare
bedroom (for visitors!) and a second bathroom. What luxury!

Did Serge write and tell you that he's getting married? I think
the wedding is in August.

Anyway, I must dash. Give my love to Richard and please write
again soon.

Lots of love,

Mary

Arranging a meeting

• Between friends

Meetings between friends are usually arranged by telephone, but also by email or text message. Some useful expressions are given below. Note that despite the informality of the situation the *vous* form may still be used:

> Venez donc prendre un verre à la maison
> Come to my place for a drink
>
> Vous êtes libre ce soir ?
> Are you free this evening?
>
> À quelle heure voulez-vous que je vienne vous chercher ?
> What time do you want me to call for you?

• If you use the *tu* form to each other:

> Tu es libre ce soir ?
> Are you free this evening?
>
> Tu veux passer à la maison après le bureau ?
> Do you want to come to my place after work?
>
> Rendez-vous chez toi ou chez moi ?
> Shall we meet at your place or mine?
>
> On se retrouve à six heures au café de la poste ?
> Shall we meet at six o'clock at the café by the post office?
>
> On se voit ce soir chez Emma
> See you tonight at Emma's
>
> Si on déjeunait ensemble demain ?
> How about having dinner together tomorrow?

A meeting is often suggested in the form of a conditional clause introduced by *si* (if) followed by the imperfect indicative, as in the last example above.

> Salut,
> Ça fait un bail qu'on s'est pas vues ! Et si on se faisait un petit ciné ce soir ? Il y a une rétro de Jarman super intéressante. Ça te dit ?
> Bises
> Anne

Rendez-vous

• Rencontre amicale

Les rendez-vous entre amis se fixent le plus souvent par téléphone mais aussi par e-mail ou en envoyant un SMS sur le portable du destinataire. En plus du jour, de l'heure et du lieu de rendez-vous, vous pouvez suggérer une activité particulière.

What about ten o'clock?
Dix heures, c'est possible ?

How about going to the cinema?
Ça te dit d'aller au cinéma ?

Why don't we eat out tonight?
Et si on allait au resto ce soir ?

Let's have a coffee before we go home.
Prenons un café avant de rentrer.

I suggest we meet up after the show.
Je te propose de nous retrouver après le spectacle.

Shall we just stay in and watch TV?
Et si on se faisait une soirée télé à la maison ?

Hi Jackie!
Long time no see! Shall we meet up for a coffee after college tomorrow? How about 5pm in the City Café? Hope you can make it.
Love,
Shona

Work meetings

Work meetings too are often arranged by email. In this case, the tone of the message will obviously be more formal.

@

De : ....
À : ....
Objet : ....
Date : ....

Bonjour Florence,
Je serai à Marseille au début de la semaine prochaine et j'aimerais faire la connaissance de vos nouveaux collaborateurs. Est-ce que vous pourriez organiser cela et me prévenir rapidement du jour et de l'heure qui conviendraient à tout le monde ?
Merci d'avance.
Cordialement,
Simon

@

De : ....
À : ....
Objet : ....
Date : ....

Cher Marc,
J'ai reçu une proposition intéressante de la société Thomas et Co et j'aimerais en discuter avec vous. Seriez-vous libre lundi après-midi vers 14 heures ? À toutes fins utiles, je retiens la salle de réunion du troisième étage car je viendrai avec l'équipe commerciale.
Dites-moi si cela vous convient.
Bien à vous.
Nicola

Rendez-vous d'affaires

Il est également courant d'organiser ses réunions d'affaires par e-mail. Dans ce cas, le ton du message sera bien sûr plus formel :

From: ....
To: ....
Subject: ....
Date: ....

@

Dear Andrew,
I've been looking at this month's sales figures, and I was wondering if we could meet some time this week to discuss them. I'm free on Wednesday afternoon, from 2pm onwards. Does this suit you? I suggest we meet in the meeting room on the third floor.
Let me know if this is convenient.
George

From: ....
To: ....
Subject: ....
Date: ....

@

Dear Ms Denholm,
Thank you for your application for the post of textile designer. We would be delighted if you could attend an interview on 4 October 2013 at 3pm. Directions to our offices are enclosed. Please let us know if you are able to attend.
We look forward to meeting you on the 4th.
Yours sincerely,
Harry Fielding
Design Director

---

communication guide

Apologies

- **Formal email**

De : John Weber <johnw2@mail.co.uk>
À : Jacques Dumas <dumas@free.fr>
Objet : notre RV mardi à 11h
Date : 16 février 2013

Cher Monsieur Dumas,
Du fait des grèves dans les aéroports, il ne me sera pas possible d'être à Bordeaux mardi.
Je pourrais m'arranger pour prendre le train et arriver jeudi après-midi.
Cependant, ce serait plus facile pour moi de prendre un autre vol et de tout reporter au mardi de la semaine suivante.
Merci de me dire si cela vous convient. Si ce n'est pas le cas, il nous faudra peut-être trouver une autre date.
Cordialement,
John

- **Less formal email**

Cher Jacques,
Je suis désolée mais je ne me sens pas très bien et je ne pourrai pas te retrouver pour déjeuner demain. Tu avais dis que tu resterais quelques jours à Lille, alors peut-être que tu peux passer chez moi à la place ?
A+
Jane

Further example

Cher Michel,
J'espère que tu recevras ce message à temps. J'avais oublié que nous devions nous voir aujourd'hui et je n'ai donc pas annulé la réunion que j'avais cet après-midi.
Est-ce que ça te va si on se voit ce soir ? Si oui, peux-tu passer me prendre au bureau ?
Amitiés,
James

S'excuser

• E-mail formel

From: Jacques Fabry <fabry2@free.fr>
To: Robert Ellis <rellis@mail.co.uk>
Subject: Our meeting Tuesday 11am
Date: 16 Feb 2013

Dear Mr Ellis,
Due to the airport strikes, it will not be possible for me to be in Liverpool on Tuesday.
I could possibly arrange to take the train and be there on Thursday afternoon.
It would be easier for me to take another plane and postpone everything to the following week on Tuesday.
Please let me know if this suits you. If not, maybe we'll have to try to meet some other time.
Yours sincerely,
Jacques

• E-mail moins formel

Dear John,
I'm sorry but I'm not feeling too good and won't be able to meet you for lunch tomorrow. You mentioned you would stay for a couple of days in Lille, so maybe you could come to my place instead.
See you soon,
Martine

Autre exemple

Dear James,
I hope you get this message in time. I had forgotten we were supposed to meet today, and so did not cancel the meeting I have scheduled for this afternoon.
Would it be possible to meet this evening? If that works for you, would you be able to pick me up at the office?
Best wishes,
Michel

Invitations and replies

Traditional format. The name of the grandparents can also be added above those of the parents, in which case the following line of text is replaced by: *ont le plaisir de vous faire part du mariage de leurs petits-enfants et enfants.*

The bride's parents.

The groom's parents.

Monsieur et Madame Pierre Degoulet

Monsieur et Madame André Lebeau

ont le plaisir de vous faire part du mariage de leurs enfants

Sophie et Christophe

et vous prient de leur faire l'honneur d'assister
à la cérémonie religieuse, qui sera célébrée
le samedi 22 juin 2013 à quatorze heures
en l'église Saint-Pierre d'Épernon,
ainsi qu'au dîner organisé à partir de vingt heures
à la Grande Cascade, au Bois de Boulogne.

48, rue des Plantes 75014 Paris

13, rue Beaubourg 75003 Paris

Address of the
bride's parents.

Address of the
groom's parents.

Claire et Jérôme

sont très heureux de vous faire part
de leur mariage, qui aura lieu

le 30 mars 2013

À cette occasion, ils vous invitent à la soirée
qu'ils organisent, à partir de 20 heures,
à la Petite Ferme, 12, rue du Château, 78000 Versailles

Réponse souhaitée avant le 28 février.
23, rue du Montparnasse, 75006 Paris

Perpignan, le 29 avril 2013

Or: *Merci
de répondre avant
le 28 février.*

More modern format.
The invitation comes
from the bride and the
groom themselves. The
address given is theirs.

Chers Pierre et Christine,

Nous vous remercions vivement de votre invitation au
mariage de Sophie et Christophe et nous nous ferons
un plaisir d'assister à la cérémonie religieuse et au dîner,
puisque vous nous proposez si gentiment de nous héberger quelques jours.

Il nous tarde de revoir toute la famille et de féliciter
Sophie en personne!

Nous vous téléphonerons dès que nous aurons réservé un
vol pour Paris.

Amicalement,

Jean-Paul et Marie Dubois

Invitations et réponses

Sur une invitation plus classique, il est parfois fait allusion à la tenue requise : *dress code: formal* en anglais britannique ou *formal attire* en anglais américain, signifient que les hommes doivent porter un costume sombre, et les femmes, une robe de cocktail. *Dress code: black tie* signifie que les hommes doivent porter un smoking, et les femmes, une robe du soir.

Martin and Isabelle
invite you to
Martin's birthday party
on: *Wednesday May 26*
at: *31 Canning Crescent*
from: *8pm*   to: *midnight*
Please bring a bottle

RSVP

L'usage classique veut que l'on ne donne que le prénom du mari. Néanmoins, cette pratique n'est plus considérée comme politiquement correcte, notamment aux États-Unis.

Mr & Mrs Peter Harvey request the pleasure of the company of

Margaret Downey

at the marriage of their daughter
Caroline to Mr Joe Cavanagh
at Oundle Town Hall on Wednesday 18th May 2013

17 Lime Avenue   RSVP
Oundle   17th April 2013
Peterborough PE6 4ED

---

17 Lime Avenue
Oundle
Peterborough
PEG 4ED
25 March 2013

Date à laquelle le destinataire doit avoir répondu à l'invitation.

Dear Mr & Harvey,

Thank you so much for the invitation to Caroline's wedding. I would love to come.

Caroline mentioned that it would be possible to arrange accommodation at The Talbot Inn for the night of the reception. Could you let me have their number so that I can book a room.

Thank you once again for the kind invitation. I look forward to seeing you in May.

Yours sincerely,

Margaret Downey

Greetings cards and congratulations

Other possibilities: *Bonne (et heureuse) année (à vous) ! ; Tous nos vœux pour la nouvelle année.*

In France, Season's greetings are sent in the New Year (throughout January) rather than before Christmas.

Juan-les-Pins, le 6 janvier 2013

Chers Yves et Liliane,

Meilleurs vœux pour la nouvelle année ! Nous espérons que 2013 vous apportera beaucoup de bonnes choses, notamment sur le plan professionnel puisque nous savons que vous envisagez de vous installer à votre compte.

Nous espérons aussi que cette nouvelle année nous donnera l'occasion de vous revoir.

Bien amicalement,

Suzanne et Alain

Other possibility: *que cette nouvelle année vous apporte beaucoup de bonnes choses/ beaucoup de bonheur.*

Les Sables-d'Olonne, le 16 juin 2013

Chère Isabelle,

Toute la famille se joint à moi pour te souhaiter un très très joyeux anniversaire. Nous espérons que tu fêteras ça dignement !

Le contenu du colis devrait te rappeler ton dernier séjour ici. Ne mange pas tout d'un coup !

Tout le monde t'embrasse.

Catherine

Cher Marc,

Bravo ! Je te félicite d'avoir réussi ton bac. Je savais que tu l'aurais sans problème. Tu étais d'ailleurs bien le seul à avoir des doutes là-dessus.

J'ai transmis la nouvelle à tous les copains qui te félicitent aussi. Nous t'attendons de pied ferme en août pour fêter ça !

À bientôt !

Benoît

To be more formal, a card written in the third person can be sent: *Ludovic et Sarah Duval adressent à Claire et Jérôme toutes leurs félicitations et leurs vœux de bonheur à l'occasion de leur mariage.*

Arbois, le 10 mai 2013

Chers Claire et Jérôme,

C'est avec grand plaisir que nous avons appris votre mariage : toutes nos félicitations et tous nos vœux de bonheur !

Nous espérons vous revoir bientôt pour vous féliciter en personne. Comptez-vous passer quelques jours dans le Jura cet été, comme chaque année ?

Très amicalement,

Ludovic et Sarah

Cartes de vœux et félicitations

Wishing you all a Merry Christmas
and a Happy New Year.

Lots of love,

Julie and the family

Ou : *Season's greetings*. Au Royaume-Uni et aux États-Unis, la coutume veut que l'on adresse ses vœux au cours du mois de décembre et non en janvier.

Happy Birthday, Sue!
Have a great day – see you at
the party.
Love, Hubert
X

Ou : *Many happy returns* en anglais britannique.

Good luck with your exams.
We'll all be thinking about you and
keeping our fingers crossed.

Eric, Bridget and the kids

Good luck in your new home.
I hope you'll both be very happy there.

Love,

Pascale

X

Sorry to hear about your accident.
Hope you're feeling better now.

All my love,

Nathalie

X

Ou : *Congratulations on your engagement.*

Congratulations on getting engaged.
I hope you'll be very happy together.
Have you set a date for the wedding yet?

Lots of love,

Stéphanie

X

Ou : *Get well soon.*

Making and cancelling a reservation on-line

Hazel.Brown

De : hazelbrown@easynet.co.uk
À : laroseraie@worldnet.fr
Envoyé : jeudi 6 décembre 2012 18:32
Objet : réservation

Bonjour,

J'ai trouvé votre adresse dans la brochure que m'a envoyée
l'office du tourisme de Villard-de-Lans.

Je voudrais réserver une chambre avec bain pour deux
personnes en demi-pension pour la semaine du 11 au
17 février 2013, de préférence orientation sud et avec balcon.

Salutations,

Hazel Brown

Court Place Barn
23 Lea Road
Bakewell DE45 1AR
ROYAUME-UNI

===============

Hazel.Brown

De : hazelbrown@easynet.co.uk
À : laroseraie@worldnet.fr
Envoyé : vendredi 14 décembre 2012 15:41
Objet : ma réservation pour février

Monsieur,

J'ai bien reçu votre réponse concernant la disponibilité
d'une chambre pour deux. Malheureusement, je viens de me
casser la jambe et dois renoncer à mon séjour en montagne.
J'annule donc notre réservation mais espère bien pouvoir
passer quelques jours à Villard-de-Lans l'année prochaine.

J'espère que cette annulation tardive ne vous causera pas trop
de désagrément et vous adresse mes meilleures salutations.

Hazel Brown

Court Place Barn
23 Lea Road
Bakewell DE45 1AR
ROYAUME-UNI

===============

Faire et annuler une réservation sur Internet

guide de communication

Harry.Catte

From: hcat@hotmail.com
Sent: 7 September 2010 9:12
To: info@hoteljacinta.co.uk

Dear Mr Seymour

I regret to inform you that owing to a change in plans we shall be unable to stay at your hotel between 29 and 31 October 2010.

We hope to choose another date this winter to stay at the Jacinta and consider this unfortunate cancellation a simple postponement. Please accept my apologies for any inconvenience it may have caused.

Yours truly,

Harry Catte

18 Prince Edward Street
EDINBURGH EH10 6AF
0131 423 6561

================

Harry.Catte

From: hcat@hotmail.com
Sent: 14 September 2010 10:44
To: info@hoteljacinta.co.uk

Dear Sir or Madam

Having visited your website at www.hoteljacinta.co.uk, I wish to reserve three nights' bed-and-breakfast accommodation at your hotel from 29-31 October inclusive. I require a double room with en-suite bathroom, and the room should be as quiet as possible. As for dietary requirements, my wife and I are both vegetarians.

Please let me know whether you have a room available for these dates, and also whether your hotel can provide Internet access to guests.

I presume that, at the advertised all-inclusive rate of £37.50 per person per night, the total cost of our stay would be £225. Can you confirm this?

Regards,

Harry Catte
hcat@hotmail.com
18 Prince Edward Street
EDINBURGH EH10 6AF
0131 423 6561

« Best regards »,
n'est employé
que pour
une personne
de connaissance.

Requesting information

Joanna Rice
3 Bramley Court
Farnborough
Hampshire GU14 6GX
ROYAUME-UNI

Université de Provence
Service d'enseignement
du français aux étudiants étrangers
29, avenue Robert Schuman
13621 Aix-en-Provence Cedex 1

Farnborough, le 13 janvier 2013

Madame, Monsieur,

Ayant trouvé votre adresse sur Internet, et ayant consulté votre site, je vous écris pour vous demander de bien vouloir m'envoyer de plus amples renseignements sur vos cours d'été pour étrangers.

J'ai 25 ans et j'ai étudié le français jusqu'au « A-level », l'équivalent du baccalauréat. Après une interruption de plusieurs années, j'aimerais me remettre à niveau, pour des raisons professionnelles notamment.

Pourriez-vous m'indiquer les possibilités d'hébergement pendant la durée du cours, en particulier l'hébergement en famille,

qui serait un bon moyen de compléter l'enseignement fourni à l'université. À défaut, est-il possible de louer une chambre en cité universitaire ?

Dans l'attente de vous lire, je vous prie d'agréer, Madame, Monsieur, l'expression de mes salutations distinguées.

Joanna Rice

Alison Summers
3 Abbey Street
Glastonbury
Somerset BA6 4AC
ROYAUME-UNI

Office du Tourisme
Rond-Point de la Tour Mataguerre
26, place Francheville
24000 Périgueux

Glastonbury, le 25 juin 2013

Madame, Monsieur,

Mon mari et moi-même prévoyons de passer les deux premières semaines d'août dans le Périgord et ses environs. Nous hésitons, pour ce qui est de l'hébergement, entre un séjour à l'hôtel qui nous permettrait de faire un circuit, et une location en gîte qui présenterait l'avantage d'une plus grande autonomie. C'est pourquoi nous souhaiterions recevoir des renseignements (prix, description, emplacement) sur ces deux modes d'hébergement.

Nous aimerions visiter principalement, lors de notre séjour, Bergerac, Périgueux, Sarlat et les grottes de Lascaux. Nous vous serions donc reconnaissants de bien vouloir nous faire parvenir une liste d'hôtels et de gîtes d'où ces sites nous seraient accessibles.

Nous avons l'intention de louer une voiture, de préférence à Périgueux, où nous arriverons par le train. Pourriez-vous nous fournir également une liste d'agences de location de voitures ?

Enfin, si vous disposez d'un calendrier des manifestations culturelles dans la région autour de cette période, je vous remercie de bien vouloir le joindre à la documentation ci-dessus.

Dans l'attente de votre envoi, je vous prie d'agréer, Madame, Monsieur, l'expression de mes salutations distinguées.

Alison Summers

If the person sending the letter is a woman, the word "sentiments" is avoided if the addressee is a man (and vice versa).

communication guide

Demande de renseignements

39, rue de la Moselle
67000 Strasbourg
FRANCE

Bloomsbury School of English
92-96 Gordon Square
OXFORD OX6 5DY

5 March 2013

Dear Sir/Madam

I am writing to ask for more information about the language courses advertised in this month's copy of 'Lingua'.

I am currently studying for a law degree and am particularly interested in obtaining a qualification in business English. The advertisement mentions that your school is recognized by the London Chamber of Commerce and prepares candidates for a number of its exams.

I am hoping to come to England for three or four weeks this summer and would like to know if you will be running Chamber of Commerce exam courses at that time. I have the equivalent of an A-Level in English, although my written language is much better than my spoken English.

I would also be grateful if you could send me further information on accommodation. If possible, I would like to stay with a family but I also understand that the university has rooms that they rent out. Could you let me have some idea of the cost of these two options.

Thanking you in anticipation, I look forward to hearing from you in the near future.

Yours faithfully

Laurent Leblanc

68, rue Borie
74100 Thonon-les-Bains
FRANCE

Tourist Information Centre
49-51 Station Road
GLASGOW G20 9SL

17 May 2013

Dear Sir or Madam,

My wife and I are planning to visit Glasgow in July of this year and would be grateful if you could send us information about the different types of accommodation available. We intend to stay for a period of three weeks and have budgeted around £500 for accommodation. Are we likely to find a reasonable hotel or bed and breakfast for that?

We would also like information on hiring a car. We will be travelling to Glasgow by plane and would ideally like to collect a car at the airport on our arrival.

I have already collected a certain amount of information on places of interest to visit in and around Glasgow. I would, however, be grateful if you could send me details about train services between Glasgow and Edinburgh.

I look forward to hearing from you.

Yours faithfully,

Pascal Mondon

guide de communication

Learning a language abroad

Madame, Monsieur,

Je souhaite avoir des renseignements concernant vos cours de langue.

Je suis actuellement étudiant dans une école de commerce et je souhaiterais vivement suivre une formation diplômante en français des affaires.

Votre site Web indique que votre école est reconnue par la Chambre de commerce et d'industrie de Paris et qu'elle prépare les étudiants à un certain nombre de ses examens.

J'espère pouvoir me rendre en France cet été pour un séjour de trois à quatre semaines et je voudrais savoir si vous proposerez des cours préparant aux examens de la Chambre de commerce pendant cette période.

J'ai étudié le français jusqu'au bac.

Vous remerciant par avance, je vous prie d'agréer, Madame, Monsieur, l'expression de mes sentiments distingués.

Nathaniel Cartwright

Séjours linguistiques

Dear Sir/Madam,

I am writing to ask for more information about your language courses.

I am currently studying in a business school and would be particularly interested in obtaining a qualification in business English.

Your website mentions that your school is recognised by the London Chamber of Commerce and prepares candidates for a number of its exams.

I am hoping to come to England for three or four weeks this summer and would like to know if you will be running Chamber of Commerce exam courses at that time.

I have the equivalent of an A-Level in English.

Thanking you in advance,

Yours faithfully,

Laurent Leblanc

Host family

• **Introducing oneself**

De : Nathaniel White
À : Françoise Denis
Objet : ma famille d'accueil
Date : 4 juin 2013

Chère Madame Denis,

Centerlangs vient de m'envoyer vos coordonnées et je vous
écris pour vous donner quelques informations à mon sujet.
Je m'appelle Nathaniel mais tout le monde m'appelle Nate.
J'habite à New York avec mes parents, mes trois sœurs et notre
chien, Max.
Quand je ne suis pas en classe, j'aime aller au cinéma,
faire de la marche en montagne et lire.
Est-ce que vous avez des animaux ?
Avez-vous toujours habité à Marseille ?
En attendant de vous rencontrer en juillet !

Bien cordialement,
Nate

La famille d'accueil

- ## Se présenter

From: Daniel Coulomb
To: Jennifer Turner
Subject: My host family
Date: 4 June 2013

Dear Mrs Turner,

I have just received your details from Centerlangs, and I am writing to let you know a little about myself.
My name is Daniel, but everyone calls me Danny.
I live in the Massif Central, a range of volcanic mountains in central France.
I live with my parents, my three sisters, and our dog, Max.
When I'm not at school, I enjoy going to the cinema, walking in the mountains and reading.
Do you have any pets?
Have you always lived in Eastbourne?
Looking forward to meeting you all in July!
Yours,
Danny

Host family

• **How to say thank you**

Chère Madame Lazzarelli,

J'ai passé un très agréable séjour à Paris. Je vous remercie pour votre gentillesse, les petits tuyaux touristiques et tout ce que vous avez fait pour moi.

Grâce à vous, j'ai pu constater que ce que les Américains pensent de la cuisine française est tout à fait vrai !

Je voulais également vous remercier à nouveau pour le week-end où vous m'avez emmenée en Bretagne.

Je garde de très bons souvenirs du temps passé avec votre fille à visiter Paris. Si elle vient à Boston un jour, cela me fera vraiment plaisir de la revoir.

J'espère que toute la famille va bien. Transmettez-leur mes amitiés.

Bien cordialement,

Jennifer

communication guide

La famille d'accueil

- **Remerciements**

Dear Mrs Havils,

I had a lovely stay in London. I very much appreciated your kindness, all the tourist tips you gave me and all the generous things you did for me.

Through you, I was able to discover that what French people say about English food is a myth.

I would like to thank you again for having taken me to Brighton with you for the weekend.

I have very fond memories of the time I spent sightseeing with your daugher in London. If she ever comes to Marseille I would be delighted to see her again.

I hope everybody in your family is well. Please give them my regards.

Yours,

Anne

Unsolicited applications

In France, applications should not be more than one page long.

You only use "Cher Monsieur" or "Chère Madame" for a letter addressed to someone you have been introduced to.

John Gardener
28 Cranham Street
Oxford OX3 5GF

A l'attention de Monsieur Dubois
Société Pétrodéveloppements
52, rue du Général Leclerc
78380 Bougival

Oxford, le 3/3/2013

Monsieur,

Votre intervention à la conférence d'Amsterdam m'a fait découvrir de nouveaux aspects de la prospection pétrolière et m'incite à vous écrire pour vous proposer mes services.

J'ai terminé la Royal School of Mines en 1990 et travaillé pendant plusieurs années sur une plate-forme en mer du Nord. J'ai ensuite travaillé dans un bureau d'études à Londres et maintenant j'aimerais de nouveau travailler sur le terrain, dans un environnement à la pointe de la technologie.

Vous avez évoqué un projet sur une plate-forme de forage et mon expérience tant de meneur d'hommes que de spécialiste en forage pourrait vous être très utile. Je peux me libérer rapidement. Je vous joins mon CV où vous trouverez des détails supplémentaires sur ma carrière.

Je reste à votre disposition pour un entretien durant lequel je pourrai vous parler plus en détail de mes motivations.

Dans cette attente, je vous adresse mes salutations les meilleures.

J. Gardener

Applications used to have to be handwritten but this pratice is now less common.

communication guide

Lettres de candidature spontanée

Dans un courrier, l'adresse
du destinataire se place à
gauche.

17, rue Henri Vieuxtemps
4000 Liège
BELGIUM
+32 43 487146

Miss Mary Dodd
Snowdon Mountain Railway
Llanberis
Gwynedd (North Wales)
LL55 4TY
ROYAUME-UNI

6 May 2013

Dear Miss Dodd,

I am writing to inquire about the possibility of gaining work
experience with your company this summer. I am currently
studying for a degree in Tourism at the University of Liège
(Belgium), and hope to gain employment in this field when
I graduate in approximately one year's time.

I hope you will forgive my writing to you speculatively.
I was given your name by a fellow student, Thomas Lenzen, who
did his work experience with you last year. He found it to be an
extremely interesting and useful experience and has very positive
memories of working with you.

I have already gained
considerable experience
of working in the
tourist industry, most
recently at the Musée
Opinel at St-Jean-de-
Maurienne in France,
and at the Boutique
Tintin in Brussels.
References from these
employers are attached
along with my CV. I
have a good command
of English, which forms
part of my degree
course.

I have also spent some time in the UK, including a brief visit to
Wales about eighteen months ago. I found it a beautiful and
fascinating country, to which I am very keen to return. I enjoy
mountaineering, I am something of a railway enthusiast, and I
even have hopes of aquiring a little of the Welsh language!

These are some of the reasons why I believe I would be well
suited to working at the Snowdon Mountain Railway,
whether in the gift shop, the railway exhibition or the café.
I hope you will be able to offer me a position, and look forward
very much to hearing from you.

Yours faithfully,

Paul Lambotte

Le texte doit être
aligné à gauche, non
justifié et
sans alinéa.

La signature est placée en bas
à gauche.

Answering a job advertisement

R & M, société de services spécialisée
dans l'ingénierie documentaire
et la formation technique
recherche un traducteur de langue maternelle
anglaise pour faire la traduction en anglais
de documents techniques français
(domaine des télécoms et de l'informatique).
Ce poste est basé en Rhône-Alpes.
De formation supérieure, bilingue anglais/français,
vous justifiez d'une expérience d'un an minimum
dans la traduction technique.
Envoyez une lettre de candidature et un CV
à drh@ereem.fr

Ian.Butcher

De : ianbutcher@easynet.co.uk
À : drh@ereem.fr
Envoyé : lundi 6 mai 2013 12:11
Objet : traducteur anglophone

Madame, Monsieur,

Votre annonce concernant un poste de traducteur publiée sur le site de
l'APEC m'a vivement intéressé. Je suis en fin de stage dans une société qui
produit du matériel de télécommunications et pour laquelle je viens de
créer un glossaire bilingue français-anglais.

Après des études secondaires à Oxford, j'ai fait des études de langues
(français et allemand) à l'université de Leeds. J'ai ensuite obtenu un master
de traduction à l'université de Paris III-Sorbonne Nouvelle. De langue
maternelle anglaise, je souhaite vivement m'établir en France dans une
région où je pourrai pratiquer le ski.

Je vous envoie mon curriculum vitae en pièce jointe ; il vous fournira une
version plus détaillée de mon parcours professionnel à ce jour.

Je me tiens à votre disposition pour un entretien et vous adresse mes
meilleures salutations.

Ian Butcher
================

You don't usually add your
address and phone numbers.

communication guide

Réponse à une offre d'emploi

Résumé est
l'équivalent
américain
de *CV*.

Quality Control Director

A new director is required for our expanding range
of products.
Applicants should have experience in the dairy industry
and in team management.
Foreign experience would be appreciated.
Applications and résumé to:
Louise Rapple, Human Resources Dept,
Fertnel Cheese Corporation,
1674 Observatory Drive
Madison, WI 53706-1283
USA

guide de communication

132, rue Marcadet
75018 Paris
FRANCE
+33 1 42012645

Louise Rapple
Human Resources Dept
Fertnel Cheese Corporation
1674 Observatory Drive
Madison, WI 53706-1283
USA

May 17, 2013

Re: Post of Quality Control Director

Dear Ms Rapple,

I wish to apply for the post of Quality Control Director advertised in
"Cheese Reporter" of May 13, 2013.

As you will see from the enclosed résumé, I have worked in the dairy products
industry for several years, mostly at the small firm of Fromageries Duval SA here
in Paris, where I am currently Head of Quality Control.

I graduated "avec mention Très Bien" (the French equivalent of Summa Cum
Laude) in Food Science from one of France's most respected universities, and have
acquired a wide knowledge of cheesemaking processes, from traditional artisanal
techniques to high-volume commercial brands.

My experience is principally of traditional French styles, but a period of work
experience with Rivageois Inc. in Canada taught me much about the North
American industry.

I feel I would be an asset to your organization, and would certainly value the
opportunity of working for such a large and prestigious corporation.

Please find attached my résumé. If you require any further details, please do not
hesitate to contact me. I hope to hear from you soon.

Sincerely yours,

Anatole Duplay

Answering a job advertisement on-line

De : joan.taylor@gmail.com
À : jobs@ongcd.org
Date : lundi 14 octobre 2013, 11 h 30
Objet : Candidature – Réf. Chargé(e) financement patrimoine Asie

CV_jtaylor.doc

Madame, Monsieur,

Votre annonce du 6 octobre, postée sur le site européen des ONG de coopération pour la culture, a retenu toute mon attention. Je souhaite poser ma candidature concernant le poste de chargé(e) de recherche de financement pour les ONG de mise en valeur du patrimoine en Asie.

Chargée de développement financier chez Planetwise, une entreprise de soutien aux chantiers de fouilles archéologiques, depuis 5 ans, j'ai pu mettre à profit mes compétences pour identifier puis convaincre les investisseurs potentiels, mais aussi pour suivre le bon usage des fonds et le déroulement des chantiers. Intéressée par la richesse culturelle du continent asiatique, je serais très désireuse de me joindre aux forces vives de la recherche historique en Asie et de contribuer activement à son développement.

De nationalité britannique, je parle couramment le français et le turc. Mon expérience professionnelle comprend 3 postes basés à Lyon et Bruxelles, ainsi qu'à Izmir.
Si ma candidature était retenue, je suis par ailleurs disponible pour l'entretien prévu le 23 novembre.

Cordialement,

Joan Taylor

communication guide

Réponse à une offre d'emploi sur Internet

@

From : danielle.picard@gmail.com
To : jobs@sanford&sanford.com
Date : Mon, Oct 18, 2010 at 11.30 AM
Subject : Application for post of International Communications Manager

 picard_cv.docx

Dear Sir/Madam,

I wish to apply for the post of International Communications Manager, recently advertised on the Guardian website. Business on an international scale is of fundamental importance to a company's success, and I believe I have the skills required to take on this challenging central role in a large and successful company such as Sanford & Sanford.

I have held my current position as Head of International Communications with Worldwide Marketing – a small, independent marketing firm – since 2007. During this time our annual revenue rose by eleven percent, our highest increase since 2001. I worked on a number of projects to ensure the efficacy of our marketing campaigns on the international market, which I believe contributed considerably to our rise in profit. Now I am looking to add to my level of responsibility in a larger organisation, whilst also bringing several years' experience of management and team-leading to your company.

Having already had experience in a number of international posts, I am also keen to make use of my high levels of English , Russian and Arabic, as well as French, which is my mother tongue. I feel this would be essential in a multinational organisation such as yours. Please find my CV attached as a Word document with details of my career history and education. I am available for interview upon request.

Yours faithfully,

Danielle Picard

Internships

• **Cover letter**

Madame,

Je suis étudiante en dernière année d'études commerciales.

J'aimerais savoir s'il serait possible d'effectuer un stage de trois mois dans votre service entre le 1er juillet et le 30 septembre de cette année.

Au cours de mes études, je me suis particulièrement intéressée aux marchés étrangers, à l'import-export ainsi qu'au français des affaires.

C'est pourquoi je pense pouvoir vous être utile pour la réalisation de tâches simples, qui me permettraient par la même occasion de mieux connaître les activités de votre entreprise et de mettre en pratique mes connaissances.

Je suis fiable et ponctuelle et souhaite me familiariser avec le monde du travail.

N'hésitez pas à me contacter si vous désirez de plus amples informations. Je suis disponible pour un entretien les mercredis et vendredis après-midi.

Dans l'attente d'une réponse de votre part, je vous prie d'accepter l'expression de mes meilleurs sentiments,

Brenda Woods

Les stages

- ## Demande de stage

Dear Ms Osborne,

I am a student, currently in my final year of a Business Studies degree.

I would like to inquire as to whether you have any openings for three months' work experience in your department during the period July to September this year.

During my course of study, I have concentrated particularly on overseas markets, imports and exports, and business English, and so I hope that while learning from your business activities, I may also be able to help out with some of the simpler tasks in the office.

I am reliable and punctual, and eager to get an insight into the world of work and put my academic knowledge to use.

Please do not hesitate to contact me if you require any more information.

I am available for an interview on Wednesday and Friday afternoons.

In the meantime, I look forward to hearing from you.

Yours sincerely,

Anne Marceau

communication guide

Accepting an internship, a position

● **Email response**

Cher Monsieur,

Merci pour votre e-mail.

Je suis heureuse de vous confirmer que je suis toujours intéressée par le stage et je suis impatiente de commencer la semaine prochaine.

Pourriez-vous me dire à quelle heure je dois me présenter ?

Bien cordialement,
Marie Martin

● **Further example, more formal**

Madame,

Je vous remercie de votre appel pour me proposer le poste de réceptionniste bilingue, que j'accepte avec plaisir.

Je suis très heureuse d'avoir été sélectionnée pour ce poste et suis impatiente de mettre mes compétences et mon savoir-faire au service de votre entreprise.

Comme convenu, je serai disponible pour commencer à travailler le 1er septembre. N'hésitez pas à me contacter avant cette date si nécessaire.

Je vous prie d'agréer, Madame, mes salutations distinguées.

Lise Fossard

Accepter un stage, un poste

- **Réponse par e-mail**

From: marie_martin@yahoo.fr
To: pstevens@books.com
Re: Internship

Dear Mr Stevens,
Thank you for your email.
I am pleased to confirm that I'm still interested in the internship.
I'm very eager to start next week.
What time should I arrive?
I look forward to meeting you again soon.
Kind regards,
Marie Martin

- **Autre modèle, plus formel**

Dear Ms Bennett,
Thank you for your phone call offering me the position of bilingual receptionist, which I accept with great pleasure.
I am very happy to have been chosen for this job and I'm looking forward to putting my skills and expertise to use for the company.
As agreed, I will be able to start work on 1st September. Please don't hesitate to contact me before this date if necessary.
Yours sincerely,
Lise Fossard

Turning an internship down

• **Negative response as a result of unavailability**

Madame,

Je vous remercie pour votre e-mail.

Je suis désolée de devoir vous informer que j'ai un contretemps concernant les dates du stage.

Malheureusement, déjà engagée auprès d'une autre entreprise, je ne suis plus libre aux dates prévues pour le stage.

Avec mes excuses, je vous prie d'agréer, Madame, l'assurance de mes salutations distinguées.

Julie Lavand

• **Further example**

Monsieur,

J'ai bien reçu votre e-mail et je vous en remercie.

Je ne suis plus disponible pour ce stage aux dates que vous m'indiquez, ayant dû m'engager auprès d'une autre entreprise pour un stage qui débute début juin.

Si cela vous convient, j'enchaînerai avec plaisir avec un stage dans votre société de septembre à novembre.

Bien cordialement,

Laurie Suchet

• **Conflict of internship and studies**

Monsieur,

Je vous écris pour vous informer que, comme je vous l'avais laissé entendre lors de l'entretien et après avoir consulté mes professeurs, il serait en effet déraisonnable pour moi de mener de front mes études et le stage.

Je suis toujours intéressé par la possibilité d'effectuer un stage dans votre entreprise et je vous confirme que je serai pleinement disponible dès le mois de mai.

Bien cordialement,

Daniel Boissier

Décliner une proposition de stage

- **Réponse négative du stagiaire pour cause d'indisponibilité**

Dear Ms Murray,

Thank you for your email.

I am sorry to inform you that I have a problem regarding the proposed dates for the placement.

Unfortunately I am no longer available for the period we had originally agreed as I have accepted a position at another company. Despite this, I would be grateful if you could consider my application for any future opportunities within your organisation.

Please accept my apologies for this late change.

Yours sincerely,

Julie Lavand

- **Autre exemple**

Dear Mr Combes,

Thank you for your email.

Unfortunately, I have already agreed to an internship at another company which starts in early June, rendering me unavailable for the dates you have provided.

If it's all right with you, I would be more than happy to do the two placements back to back and work for you from September to November. Please let me know if this is possible.

Yours sincerely,

Laurie Suchet

- **Impossibilité de mener de front un stage et des études**

@

Dear Mr Brett,

I am writing to inform you that, after consultation with my tutors, and as I had suggested during my interview, I have decided it would be unwise for me to juggle work commitments with my studies.

I am still excited by the prospect of an internship with your company and I can confirm that I will be completely free from May onwards.

Yours sincerely,

Daniel Boissier

French CV

This information is optional. Other marital statuses include: *marié(e), divorcé(e), séparé(e), pacsé(e), veuf (veuve).*

Age can be replaced by date of birth or both can be indicated.

Daniel Peter Lowe

3 Hilda Cottages
Mansfield
Nottinghamshire NG18 7BF
Royaume-Uni
Téléphone : + 44 1623 29385

Célibataire
22 ans
Nationalité britannique

FORMATION

2010-2013	BSc en multimédia (licence), mention très bien Université de Sheffield Projet de dernière année : production d'un CD-ROM utilisant des techniques de vidéo numérique
2009-2010	A-levels (baccalauréat). Options : langue anglaise, mathématiques, informatique, français
2006-2008	GCSEs : langue anglaise, littérature anglaise, mathématiques, physique, chimie, dessin industriel, géographie, français

---

EXPÉRIENCE PROFESSIONNELLE

2012-2013	Animation d'un cybercafé à Mansfield
2011-2012	Participation à la coordination de conférences sur le multimédia (Nottingham, Sheffield, Manchester)
été 2012	Stage d'un mois chez Nova Média, Bruxelles. Travail sur un système de reconnaissance automatique de la parole

---

DIVERS

- Connaissance approfondie de nombreux logiciels :
- Adobe Illustrator, Quark, MS Office, etc.
- Systèmes d'exploitation : Windows (Mac/PC), Linux
- Français lu, écrit, parlé. Nombreux séjours en France.
- Goût pour les voyages, le cinéma, le karaté et la randonnée.

Other possibilities: *notions de japonais, bonne connaissance du japonais, japonais courant.*

guide de communication

CV britannique

L'adresse durant l'année universitaire n'est donnée que si elle est différente de l'adresse permanente.

Selon le statut : *married, divorced, separated.*

Name:	Serge Aubain
Term Address:	46, rue Passerat
	42000 Saint-Etienne
	France
Telephone:	+ 33 5 77 46 98 75
Home Address:	38 avenue Mozart
	86000 Poitiers
	France
Telephone:	+ 33 5 56 43 87 60
Date of Birth:	17.10.90
Nationality:	French
Marital Status:	Single

EDUCATION AND QUALIFICATIONS

2013	École des mines de St-Étienne, 42023 St-Étienne Cedex 2, France
	First year of a Diploma in Civil Engineering.
	Core subjects: Maths, Computing, Physics, Mechanical Engineering, Economics, English. Options: Biotechnology, German.
2011	Lycée Fauriel, 145-149, cours Fauriel, 86000 Poitiers.
	Baccalauréat S (equivalent to A-level). Subjects: Maths, Physics, Chemistry, French, Geography, History, English, German.

WORK EXPERIENCE

July 2013-Sept. 2013	Group leader at a children's holiday camp, La Rochelle. Duties included organizing activities for children aged between 10 and 16 years, teaching tennis and swimming, liaising with other leaders.
2011-2013	Part-time work as a lifeguard at the local swimming pool.

INTERESTS AND OTHER QUALIFICATIONS

Life saving award (gold medallion)
Full clean driving licence
Basic word processing
Tennis (captain of the school tennis team 2005-2007)
Swimming
Theatre

Signifie que le titulaire du permis n'a jamais été pénalisé pour infraction.

REFEREES

Mme Sylvie Pasteur	M. Paul Minoche
(Headmistress)	(Head Lifeguard)
Lycée Fauriel	Piscine de Grouchy
145-149, cours Fauriel	86000 Poitiers
86000 Poitiers	France
France	

En règle générale, si l'on est étudiant, on fournit une référence scolaire ou universitaire et une référence personnelle ou professionnelle.

French CV, English graduate with some experience

Jennifer Susan AXFORD
21 Little Moor Road
Burton-upon-Trent
Staffordshire DE14 5JK
Royaume-Uni
Tél. : + 44 1283 574830

Née le 16 septembre 1989
Nationalité britannique

FORMATION	2012	Licence en gestion Université de St Andrews, Écosse
	2007	A-levels (baccalauréat). Options : français, mathématiques, économie
	2005	GCSEs Options : français, mathématiques, anglais, économie, chimie, allemand, histoire, géographie
EXPÉRIENCE PROFESSIONNELLE	mars 2013	Vendeuse Librairie Waterstone's, Burton-upon-Trent - réassort commandes livres de poche - réception de la marchandise et mise en rayon - accueil et vente
	2012	**Aide vendeuse** à temps partiel Boutique du musée d'art d'Auxerre, France - tenue de caisse - mise en rayon
DIVERS		• Travail bénévole pour une organisation caritative britannique (travail en magasin : tri de vêtements, tenue de caisse ; participation aux campagnes ponctuelles : démarchage, distribution de prospectus, etc.). • Séjour d'un an en France, à Auxerre (janvier - décembre 2010), où j'ai suivi une formation de français pour étrangers, travaillé comme aide vendeuse et donné des cours particuliers d'anglais. • Centres d'intérêt : musique (je joue de la basse dans un groupe), yoga, aromathérapie.

CV américain, diplômé français ayant une première expérience

Remarquez qu'aux États-Unis on n'indique ni la situation de famille ni la date de naissance, car ces informations ne sont plus considérées comme devant être connues de l'employeur.

Anne-Marie Bertheas
20, rue de la Paix
13200 Arles
France
Tél. : 0033 4 46 75 88 09

EMPLOYMENT	2005-	English teacher, Lycée Pothier, 13200 Arles Teaching English to French students aged 13-18 as preparation for the Baccalauréat (equivalent to high school diploma)
	2001-2002	Language assistant, Hutton Comprehensive, Hutton, Lancashire, Great Britain Teaching French to English students aged 11-16 as preparation for the GCSE examination (equivalent to high school diploma)
	1999-2001	Sales assistant, Auchan, Place du Peuple, 13200 Arles Weekend work in the electrical department of a large supermarket.
EDUCATION	1999-2005	University of Lille, Lille, France
	June 2005	CAPES (high school teaching qualification)
	May 2003	Licence d'anglais (equivalent to BA) English Language, Literature and Civilization
	May 2001	Diplôme de Français Langue Étrangère (qualification for teaching French as a foreign language)
LANGUAGES	English	(near-native fluency)
	German	(written and spoken)
	Spanish	(basic knowledge)
OTHER INFORMATION		Word processing (Word, InDesign) Full clean driver's license Secretary of Arles France-Great Britain Society
REFERENCES		Available upon request

Les diplômes américains et britanniques portent parfois des noms différents et il peut être nécessaire de donner un équivalent.

Driving licence en anglais britannique.

French CV, American professional with experience

The CV of somebody with a certain amount of professional experience may begin with a profile summarizing their main skills and/or qualities.

ROSS D. JAGGER

Consultant en gestion d'entreprise

Spécialiste en :
- opérations internationales
- planification stratégique
- investissements

13, rue de Lévy
75017 Paris
Tél. : 01 45 78 93 40
Fax : 01 45 85 03 05
e-mail : djagger@infonie.fr

Date de naissance : 3/6/1965
Double nationalité américaine - française
Marié, 2 enfants

PRINCIPAUX PROJETS

- Planification stratégique, études de concurrence, estimations pour diverses sociétés multinationales.
- Réalisation d'opérations de marketing direct.
- Évaluation de sociétés nouvellement créées. Conseil sur le lancement de nouveaux produits.
- Mise en place d'un système de transactions de devises pour un grand établissement financier.
- Coordination des investissements informatiques pour des sociétés américaines, asiatiques et européennes.
- Travail sur des bases de données client-serveur : bases de vente et de marketing pour divers clients (banque, électronique, agences de publicité).

FORMATION

- **Mastère en Gestion internationale (1993)**
  American Graduate School of International Management, San Diego, Californie, États-Unis
- **Licence d'Économie internationale (1992)**
  Université de l'Illinois

CV britannique, cadre confirmé français

Un candidat ayant déjà une certaine expérience peut commencer son CV par un résumé de ses principales compétences et/ou qualités.

DOMINIQUE PETIT
25, bd St-Denis, 69008 Lyon, France.
Tel. : 0033 4 66 54 11 98
e-mail: dominique.petit@compu.fr

- bilingual editor
- proven organizational and interpersonal skills
- meticulous eye for detail

EMPLOYMENT	2003-	Senior Editor, Larousse Publishing, Lyon, France
		Managing and coordinating reference publishing projects for French and international markets:
		– preparation of schedules and budgets
		– staff recruitment and training
		– administration of Lyon office
		– liaising with freelancers and typesetters
	2000-2003	Editor, Mac Bride, Edinburgh, UK
		Working on a French-English dictionary:
		– compilation and translation of text
		– proofreading
	1998-2000	Translator, Euro Translations, Paris, France
		– commercial and technical translation

EDUCATION	1996-1998	École supérieure d'Interprètes et de Traducteurs (ESIT), Paris, France
	May 1998	Diplôme d'Études supérieures spécialisées (DESS) (postgraduate qualification in translation)
	1991-1996	Université Lumière-Lyon-II, Lyon, France
	June 1996	Maîtrise d'anglais (equivalent to MA)
		Research topic: Accents and Class in British Society
	June 1996	Licence d'anglais (equivalent to BA)
		English
	1984-1991	Lycée Charles-de-Gaulle, Lyon, France
	June 1991	Baccalauréat L (equivalent to A-level)
		Subjects: French, English, German, Spanish, Maths, Geography, History

| OTHER SKILLS | | Word, Excel, Access |
| | | Working knowledge of publishing databases |

PERSONAL DETAILS		Date of Birth:14.01.73
		Marital Status: Married (2 children)
		Nationality: French

| REFEREES | | Available on request |

Requesting a reference letter

• From a teacher

Cher Monsieur,

Lorsque j'ai obtenu mon diplôme en juin l'année dernière, vous m'aviez très gentiment proposé de me recommander de vous si je postulais à un emploi.

J'ai l'intention de poser ma candidature à un poste de traducteur technique chez Astra Oil et souhaiterais faire figurer votre nom parmi les deux références que j'indiquerai dans ma lettre.

La société vous contactera peut-être et j'espère que vous accepterez d'écrire une lettre de recommandation favorable à mon sujet.

Il s'agit d'un travail extrêmement intéressant avec des possibilités d'évolution de carrière.

Je profite de cette occasion pour vous remercier pour votre aide et les excellents conseils que vous m'avez donnés au cours de ma dernière année à Leicester.

Croyez, Cher Monsieur, en mes sentiments respectueux,

Philippe Marchand

• From an employer

Cher Monsieur,

Comme je vous l'avais indiqué lors de notre dernier entretien, je compte poser ma candidature pour un poste de traducteur technique chez Astra Oil.

Ayant effectué, l'année dernière, des traductions techniques pour le compte de votre société, je vous écris pour savoir s'il vous serait possible de rédiger une lettre de recommandation pour moi.

Si vous avez besoin de renseignements complémentaires, n'hésitez pas à me contacter.

Bien cordialement,

Philippe Marchand

communication guide

Demander une lettre de recommandation

Il est d'usage, dans une lettre de candidature, d'indiquer les coordonnées de deux personnes pouvant témoigner de vos qualités et compétences pour l'emploi auquel vous vous présentez.

La personne qui vous recommande est souvent un ancien professeur ou un précédent employeur. La courtoisie veut que l'on demande d'abord à cette personne si elle accepte de vous recommander. Vous pouvez ensuite inscrire son nom, sa profession et son adresse professionnelle à la fin de votre CV sous l'intitulé : *Referees* ou, en anglais américain : *References*.

• À un enseignant

> Dear Dr Linneman,
>
> When I finished my degree in June last year, you very kindly suggested that I might use your name when applying for a job.
>
> I am about to apply for the position of technical translator with Astra Oil, and would like to give your name as one of two referees.
>
> If the company contacts you, would you be happy to write a favourable reference for me.
>
> It is an extremely interesting job with good prospects.
>
> I would like to take this opportunity to thank you for all the help and guidance you offered me during my final year at Leicester.
>
> Yours sincerely,
> Philippe Marchand

• À un professionnel

> James Gleeson
> Northcoast Oil
> 2 Victoria Rd
> Corringham
> Thurrock SS17 0
> UK
>
> Philippe Marchand
> 3, avenue Sadi-Carnot
> 26000 Valence
> France
>
> 3rd March 2012
>
> Dear Mr Gleeson,
>
> As we discussed last time we met, I am about to apply for the position of technical translator for Astra Oil.
>
> Since I did some technical translations for your company last year, I am writing to ask whether it would be possible for you to provide a reference for me?
>
> Please let me know if you need any further information.
>
> Yours sincerely,
> Philippe Marchand

Reference letter

This is a general opening formula used when
there is no one particular contact person.
It is the equivalent of: *To whom it may concern.*

THE WHITE HORSE INN
11 LIME STREET
WADEBRIDGE
CORNWALL PL27 4GG
TEL./FAX: 01208 55694

Wadebridge, le 7 juin 2013

À QUI DE DROIT

Mademoiselle Eileen Mockridge a été employée, de février 2010 à avril 2013,
comme serveuse au White Horse Inn à Wadebridge. En tant que gérant de cet
établissement, j'ai beaucoup apprécié le professionnalisme et la ponctualité
de Eileen Mockridge, dont les rapports avec la clientèle et avec le reste du
personnel étaient excellents.

Je suis persuadé qu'Eileen saura s'intégrer sans difficulté à un nouvel environnement
de travail, et qu'elle donnera entière satisfaction dans un emploi du même type, ou
même à un poste impliquant de plus grandes responsabilités.

Michael J. Clark

Michael J. Clark
Gérant

Lettre de recommandation

La lettre de recommandation ne s'adresse à aucun employeur en particulier. Cette formule générale équivaut à : *À qui de droit.* Aux États-Unis, elle est suivie de deux points (:).

On peut choisir de donner, en début de lettre, l'objet de celle-ci.

LE PETIT PRINCE
PLACE DE L'ÉGLISE
57000 METZ
TÉL. : 0033 3 89 34 57 85

15 September 2013

To whom it may concern

Susan Clarke

This is to certify that Susan Clarke was employed as a receptionist at the above-mentioned establishment from April 15, 2013 to September 15, 2013.

As a receptionist, Susan's duties included taking bookings for the hotel and restaurant, liaising between the two, welcoming guests and generally ensuring the smooth running of the establishment.

I have found Susan to be a pleasant, reliable and hard-working member of staff who has always carried out her duties to the highest possible level. In addition to excellent interpersonal skills, her French has improved to almost native speaker level during her time with us. She has become a highly valued member of our team, popular with both guests and other staff, and will be greatly missed. I have no reservations about recommending her to future employers.

Yours faithfully

Jean-Christophe Pousset

Jean-Christophe Pousset
Manager

Writing an advertisement

There are two kinds of advertisement: those that are asking for goods or services and those that are offering them. These advertisements are found in some newspapers or in shops. There are also free newspapers that specialize in advertisements. These are often available at newsstands, in the underground in big cities, at the entrance to supermarkets, etc. The advertisements are written in a telegraphic style, often with abbreviations, and must give the advertiser's details clearly.

- **Examples of offers of goods or services:**

> Étudiant en médecine garde enfants le soir à partir de 20 heures.

> Jeune fille, maîtrise de maths, donne cours particuliers de la 6e à la terminale.
> <u>Tél.</u> : 06 08 40 00 00 (le soir).

> Vends réfrigérateur bon état, avec compartiment congélation.
> 150 euros, à débattre.
> <u>Tél.</u> : 02 18 53 64 75 (le matin).

- **Examples of requests for goods or services :**

> Mère de famille cherche aide-ménagère 6 heures/semaine.

> Jeune femme à mobilité réduite cherche formation informatique à domicile.
> Pas sérieux s'abstenir.
> <u>Tél.</u> : 02 15 36 57 78 (le matin).

> Étudiant français échangerait heures de conversation en anglais
> contre heures de conversation en français, dans perspective bourse Erasmus
> à Manchester.
> <u>Tél.</u> : 05 45 36 77 88

Écrire une annonce

Une petite annonce se rédige dans un style abrégé. Vous pouvez omettre les articles, les prépositions et certaines formes verbales. Les offres de service se rédigent à la troisième personne. N'oubliez pas d'indiquer un numéro de téléphone afin que l'on puisse vous contacter.

Si vous voulez publier une annonce pour une location, indiquez précisément dans quel quartier se trouve le logement concerné, tous les détails susceptibles de le mettre en valeur et le numéro de téléphone où l'on peut vous joindre. Vous pouvez aussi préciser quel type de locataire vous souhaitez ou ne souhaitez pas : étudiants, fumeurs, etc.

> To let
> Room in friendly shared house in Royan.
> Central heating, access to shared kitchen and living area.
> Rent 220 € per calendar month.
> Call +33 (0)6 87 65 43 21
> Non-smokers only.

> French student reading for MA at Edinburgh offers private French tuition at competitive rates.
> Grammar and spoken language covered in preparation for exams.
> Phone Danièle on 01314 886 798

> Student qualified in teaching French as a foreign language offers help with revision.
> Friendly approach. £12/hour.

> Experienced, mature babysitter seeks 4-5 hours work per week.

communication guide

On the phone

● Calling someone at home

— Allô.

— Oui, allô, est-ce que je suis bien chez monsieur et madame Renouet, s'il vous plaît ?
To check that you have dialled the right number.

— Oui, c'est bien ça.

— Ah, bonjour, madame, excusez-moi de vous déranger, j'aurais voulu parler à Anne-Sophie, s'il vous plaît ?

● The person is out

— Ah non, je regrette, elle n'est pas là pour l'instant. Est-ce que je peux lui transmettre un message ?

— Oui, d'accord. Est-ce que vous pourriez lui dire que Denis a appelé ?

— Bien sûr, je le lui dirai. Je lui demande de vous rappeler ?

— Oui, ça serait bien si elle pouvait me rappeler. Je serai chez moi toute la journée. Merci beaucoup. Au revoir, madame.

— Au revoir, monsieur.

● The person is in

— Oui, je vous la passe. C'est de la part de qui ?

— C'est Denis. C'est au sujet de son séjour en Angleterre.

— D'accord, je vais la chercher.

● Getting the wrong number

— Allô.

— Bonjour, est-ce que je pourrais parler à Éric, s'il vous plaît ?

— Ah non, je regrette, vous avez dû vous tromper de numéro.

— Ah bon ? Ce n'est pas le 05 59 35 67 13 ?
When saying a telephone number the figures are pronounced in pairs, so you would say: *zéro cinq, cinquante-neuf, trente-cinq, soixante-sept, treize.*

— Non, c'est le 05 59 35 67 12.

— Oh pardon, excusez-moi.

— Je vous en prie, au revoir.

— Au revoir.

● Calling a company

— Jutheau S.A., bonjour.

— Bonjour. Pourrais-je avoir le poste 128, s'il vous plaît ?

— Oui, ne quittez pas. Je vous le passe.

— Anne-Marie Béchu, service commercial.

— Bonjour, madame. Pourrais-je parler à monsieur Péri, s'il vous plaît ?

— Oui, c'est de la part de qui ?

— François Lebeau, de chez Lavoisier.

— Je regrette, c'est occupé. Souhaitez-vous patienter ou rappeler plus tard ?

— Je vais attendre un peu.

— Très bien... Je regrette, c'est toujours occupé. Est-ce que je peux prendre un message ?

— Oui, pourriez-vous lui dire de rappeler François Lebeau chez Lavoisier au 01 43 22 77 02 ? C'est au sujet de la réunion du 14 avec les représentants.

— Entendu, monsieur.

— Je vous remercie, madame. Au revoir.

— Au revoir, monsieur.

Au téléphone

• Appeler quelqu'un chez lui

— Hello, 0155 915 3678.

Au Royaume-Uni, certaines personnes annoncent leur numéro de téléphone lorsqu'elles décrochent. Aux États-Unis, cela n'est pas courant.

— Hello, could I speak to Jane, please?

• La personne est absente

— No, I'm sorry, she's not in at the moment. Can I give her a message?

— Yes, please. Could you tell her that Fred rang?

Aux États-Unis, on dirait *called*.

— Yes, of course. Shall I ask her to ring you back?

— Yes, please. I'll be at home all day.

— OK, I'll tell her when she comes in.

— Thank you, goodbye.

— Goodbye.

• La personne est là

— Yes. Who's calling?

— It's Fred. I'm calling about the trip to France.

— OK, one moment, I'll just get her for you.

• Se tromper de numéro

— Hello.

— Hello. Could I speak to Tom, please?

— I'm sorry. I think you must have the wrong number.

— Is that not 742215?

Aux États-Unis, on dit : *Is this 742215?* Notez qu'au Royaume-Uni ainsi qu'aux États-Unis les chiffres sont prononcés séparément. Toutefois, lorsque deux chiffres identiques se suivent, on dira au Royaume-Uni *double 2* alors qu'on prononcera ces chiffres deux fois aux États-Unis.

— No, this is 742216.

— Oh, sorry.

— That's OK.

• Appeler une entreprise

— Good morning, Smith Brothers.

— Good morning. Could I have extension 478, please?

Ou : *Could you put me through to extension 478, please?*

— One moment. I'll put you through.

— Good morning, electrical department. Linda speaking. How may I help you?

— Hello. I'd like to speak to someone about the washing machine I've just bought.

— Hold the line, please. I'll transfer you to our after-sales department. Can I say who's calling?

L'équivalent de cette formule britannique est, aux États-Unis : *Would you mind holding a moment? I'll transfer you...*

— Mrs Jones.

— I'm afraid the line's busy. Would you like to hold?

— Yes, please.

— I'm afraid the line's still busy.

Ou : *the line's engaged* en anglais britannique.

— Would you like to continue holding or would you like to call back later?

— Could I leave a message?

— Certainly.

— Would you ask someone to call me on 01162 476548. It's quite urgent.

Aux États-Unis, on dirait *at* au lieu de *on*.

— I'll make sure someone calls you back within the next ten minutes, Mrs Jones.

— Thank you very much. Goodbye.

— Goodbye. Thank you for calling.

Anglais - Français
English - French

a (pl **a's**), **A** (pl **A's** or **As**) [eɪ] n [in list] : *I'm not going because a) I've no money and b) I've no time* je n'y vais pas parce que primo je n'ai pas d'argent et secundo je n'ai pas le temps. **See also f.**

a (*weak form* [ə], *strong form* [eɪ], *before vowel* **an**, *weak form* [æn], *strong form* [ən]) det **1.** [before countable nouns] un (une) / *a book* un livre / *I can't see a thing* je ne vois rien ; [before professions] : *she's a doctor* elle est médecin / *have you seen a doctor?* as-tu vu un médecin ? **2.** [before numbers] : *a thousand dollars* mille dollars / *a dozen eggs* une douzaine d'œufs / *an hour and a half* une heure et demie ; [per] : *£2 a dozen / a hundred grammes* les cent grammes / *three times a year* trois fois par an **3.** [before terms of quantity, amount] : *a few weeks / months* quelques semaines / mois / *a lot of money* beaucoup d'argent **4.** [before periods of time] : *I'm going for a week / month / year* je pars (pour) une semaine / un mois / un an **5.** [after half, rather, such, what] : *half a glass of wine* un demi-verre de vin / *she's rather an interesting person* c'est quelqu'un d'assez intéressant / *what a lovely dress!* quelle jolie robe ! **6.** [after as, how, so, too + adj] : *that's too big a slice for me* cette tranche est trop grosse pour moi.

a. written abbr of **acre**.

A [eɪ] (pl **A's** or **As**) ◆ n **1.** [letter] A m ▶ **from A to Z** de A à Z **2.** SCH : *to get an A in French* ≃ obtenir plus de 16 sur 20 en français **3.** MUS la m. ◆ adj 🇬🇧 TRANSP ▶ **A road** route f nationale (*en Grande-Bretagne*).

A-1 adj **1.** [first-class, perfect] : *everything's A-1* tout est parfait **2.** [in health] : *to be A-1* être en pleine santé or forme.

A3[1] n [paper size] format m A3.

A3[2] MESSAGING written abbr of **anytime, anywhere, anyplace**.

A4 n [paper size] format m A4.

AA ◆ pr n (abbr of **Automobile Association**) *automobile club britannique et compagnie d'assurances, qui garantit le dépannage de ses adhérents et propose des services touristiques et juridiques* ; ≃ ACF m ; ≃ TCF m. ◆ n 🇺🇸 abbr of **Associate in Arts.**

AAA [ˌtrɪpl'eɪ] (abbr of **American Automobile Association**) pr n *automobile club américain* ; ≃ ACF m ; ≃ TCF m.

AAMOF MESSAGING written abbr of as a matter of fact.

aardvark ['ɑːdvɑːk] n oryctérope m.

AAUP (abbr of **American Association of University Professors**) pr n *syndicat américain des professeurs d'université.*

AB n (abbr of **Bachelor of Arts**) 🇺🇸 UNIV *(titulaire d'une) licence de lettres.*

aback [ə'bæk] adv ▶ **to be taken aback a)** être pris au dépourvu, être interloqué **b)** NAUT être pris bout au vent.

abacus ['æbəkəs] (pl **abacuses** or **abaci** ['æbəsaɪ]) n boulier m.

abandon [ə'bændən] ◆ vt **1.** [leave - person, object] abandonner ; [- post, place] déserter, quitter ▶ **to abandon ship** abandonner or quitter le navire **2.** [give up - search] abandonner, renoncer à ; [- studies, struggle] renoncer à ; [- idea, cause] laisser tomber / *the match was abandoned because of bad weather* on a interrompu le match en raison du mauvais temps. ◆ n [neglect] abandon m.

abandoned [ə'bændənd] adj [person] abandonné, délaissé ; [house] abandonné.

abandonment [ə'bændənmənt] n [of place, person, project] abandon m.

abashed [ə'bæʃt] adj penaud / *to be* or *to feel abashed* avoir honte.

abate [ə'beɪt] vi [storm] s'apaiser ; [pain] diminuer ; [noise] s'atténuer.

abatement [ə'beɪtmənt] n [of noise, strength] diminution f, réduction f.

abattoir ['æbətwɑːr] n abattoirs mpl.

abbey ['æbɪ] n abbaye f.

abbot ['æbət] n abbé m (*dans un monastère*).

abbreviate [ə'briːvɪeɪt] vt [text, title] abréger.

abbreviation [ə,briːvɪ'eɪʃn] n [of expression, title, word] abréviation f.

ABC n [alphabet] alphabet m ▶ **it's as easy as ABC** c'est simple comme bonjour.

abdicate ['æbdɪkeɪt] ◆ vt [right] renoncer à ; [responsibility] abandonner. ◆ vi abdiquer.

abdication [,æbdɪ'keɪʃn] n [of throne] abdication f.

abdomen ['æbdəmen] n abdomen m.

abdominal [æb'dɒmɪnl] adj abdominal ▶ **abdominal muscles** muscles mpl abdominaux, abdominaux mpl.

abduct [ab'dʌkt] vt enlever, kidnapper.

abduction [æb'dʌkʃn] n [of person] rapt m, enlèvement m.

abductor [əb'dʌktər] n [of person] ravisseur m, -euse f.

aberration [,æbə'reɪʃn] n [action, idea] aberration f.

abet [ə'bet] (pt & pp **abetted**, cont **abetting**) vt [aid] aider ; [encourage] encourager.

abeyance [ə'beɪəns] n fml **1.** [disuse] désuétude f / *to fall into abeyance* tomber en désuétude **2.** [suspense] suspens m / *the question was left in abeyance* la question a été laissée en suspens.

abhor [əb'hɔːʳ] (*pt* & *pp* **abhorred**, *cont* **abhorring**) vt *fml* détester, avoir en horreur.

abhorrence [əb'hɒrəns] n *fml* aversion *f*, horreur *f*.

abhorrent [əb'hɒrənt] adj *fml* [detestable - practice, attitude] odieux, exécrable.

abide [ə'baɪd] (*pt* & *pp* **abode** [ə'bəʊd] *or* **abided**) vt supporter / *I can't abide people smoking in restaurants* je ne peux pas supporter les gens qui fument au restaurant / *if there's one thing I can't abide, it's hypocrisy* s'il y a quelque chose que je ne supporte pas, c'est l'hypocrisie. ❖ **abide by** vt insep [decision, law, promise] se conformer à, respecter ; [result] supporter, assumer.

abiding [ə'baɪdɪŋ] adj constant, permanent.

ability [ə'bɪlətɪ] (*pl* **abilities**) n **1.** [mental or physical] capacité *f*, capacités *fpl*, aptitude *f* / *I'll do it to the best of my ability* je le ferai du mieux que je peux, je ferai de mon mieux **2.** [special talent] capacités *fpl*, aptitude *f* ; [artistic or musical] dons *mpl*, capacités *fpl*.

abject ['æbdʒekt] adj [person, deed] abject, vil ; [flattery] servile / *an abject apology* de plates excuses / *they live in abject poverty* ils vivent dans une pauvreté absolue.

abjectly ['æbdʒektlɪ] adv [act, refuse] de manière abjecte ; [apologize] avec servilité, servilement.

ablaze [ə'bleɪz] ❖ adj **1.** [on fire] en flammes **2.** [face] brillant ; [eyes] enflammé, pétillant / *her eyes were ablaze with anger* ses yeux étaient enflammés de colère. ❖ adv ▸ **to set sthg ablaze** embraser qqch.

able ['eɪbl] (*compar* **abler**, *superl* **ablest**) adj **1.** ▸ **to be able to** [to be capable of] : *to be able to do sthg* pouvoir faire qqch / *I wasn't able to see* je ne voyais pas / *I'm not able to tell you* je ne suis pas en mesure de vous le dire / *she's better or more able to explain than I am* elle est mieux à même de vous expliquer que moi **2.** [competent] capable.

able-bodied adj robuste, solide.

ablutions [ə'bluːʃnz] pl n *fml* [washing] ▸ **to do** or **to perform one's ablutions** faire ses ablutions.

ably ['eɪblɪ] adv d'une façon compétente.

ABM (abbr of **anti-ballistic missile**) n ABM *m*.

abnormal [æb'nɔːml] adj anormal.

abnormality [,æbnɔː'mælətɪ] (*pl* **abnormalities**) n **1.** [abnormal state, condition, etc.] anormalité *f*, caractère *m* anormal **2.** [gen & MED & BIOL] anomalie *f* ; [physical deformity] malformation *f*.

abnormally [æb'nɔːməlɪ] adv anormalement.

aboard [ə'bɔːd] ❖ adv à bord ▸ **all aboard!** **a)** NAUT tout le monde à bord ! **b)** RAIL en voiture ! ❖ prep à bord de ▸ **aboard ship** à bord du bateau.

abode [ə'bəʊd] n *fml* demeure *f*.

abolish [ə'bɒlɪʃ] vt [privilege, slavery] abolir ; [right] supprimer ; [law] supprimer, abroger.

abolition [,æbə'lɪʃn] n [of privilege, slavery] abolition *f* ; [of law] suppression *f*, abrogation *f*.

A-bomb (abbr of **atom bomb**) n bombe A *f*.

abominable [ə'bɒmɪnəbl] adj [very bad] abominable, lamentable, affreux.

abominable snowman n ▸ **the abominable snowman** l'abominable homme *m* des neiges.

abominably [ə'bɒmɪnəblɪ] adv [act, behave] abominablement, odieusement.

abomination [ə,bɒmɪ'neɪʃn] n [awful thing] abomination *f*, chose *f* abominable.

aboriginal [,æbə'rɪdʒənl] adj **1.** [culture, legend] aborigène, des aborigènes **2.** BOT & ZOOL aborigène.

aborigine [,æbə'rɪdʒənɪ] n [original inhabitant] aborigène *mf*. ❖ **Aborigine** n [person] aborigène *mf* (d'Australie).

abort [ə'bɔːt] ❖ vi **1.** [mission, plans] avorter, échouer ; [flight] avorter / *the controller gave the order to abort* l'aiguilleur du ciel a donné l'ordre d'abandonner or de suspendre le vol **2.** MED avorter **3.** COMPUT abandonner, interrompre. ❖ vt **1.** [mission, flight] interrompre, mettre un terme à ; [plan] faire échouer **2.** MED avorter.

abortion [ə'bɔːʃn] n **1.** MED avortement *m*, interruption *f* (volontaire) de grossesse ▸ **to have an abortion** se faire avorter ▸ **abortion pill** pilule *f* abortive **2.** [of plans, mission] avortement *m*.

abortive [ə'bɔːtɪv] adj **1.** [attempt] raté, infructueux **2.** [agent, organism, process] abortif.

abound [ə'baʊnd] vi [fish, resources] abonder ; [explanations, ideas] abonder, foisonner.

about [ə'baʊt] ❖ prep **1.** [concerning, on the subject of] à propos de, au sujet de, concernant / *I'm worried about her* je suis inquiet à son sujet / *I'm not happy about her going* ça ne me plaît pas qu'elle y aille / *there's no doubt about it* cela ne fait aucun doute / *what's the book about?* c'est un livre sur quoi ? / *OK, what's this all about?* bon, qu'est-ce qui se passe ? / *I can't do anything about it* je n'y peux rien / *I'd like you to think about my offer* j'aimerais que vous réfléchissiez à ma proposition **2.** [in the character of] : *what I like about her is her generosity* ce que j'aime en or chez elle, c'est sa générosité / *what I don't like about the house is all the stairs* ce qui me déplaît dans cette maison, ce sont tous les escaliers / *there's something about the place that reminds me of Rome* il y a quelque chose ici qui me fait penser à Rome **3.** [busy with] ▸ **while I'm about it** pendant que j'y suis. ❖ adv **1.** [more or less] environ, à peu près / *about £50* 50 livres environ / *about five o'clock* vers cinq heures / *that looks about right* ça a l'air d'être à peu près ça / *I've just about finished* j'ai presque fini ▸ **I've had just about enough!** j'en ai vraiment assez ! / *that's about it for now* c'est à peu près tout pour l'instant **2.** [somewhere near] dans les parages, par ici / *there anyone about?* il y a quelqu'un ? / *there was no one about when I left the building* il n'y avait personne dans les parages quand j'ai quitté l'immeuble / *my keys must be about somewhere* mes clés doivent être quelque part par ici **3.** [in all directions, places] : *there's a lot of flu about* il y a beaucoup de gens qui ont la grippe en ce moment **4.** [in opposite direction] : *to turn about* se retourner. ❖ adj [expressing imminent action] ▸ **to be about to do sthg** être sur le point de faire qqch / *I was just about to leave* j'allais partir, j'étais sur le point de partir.

about-turn UK, **about-face** US n **1.** MIL demi-tour *m* **2.** [change of opinion] volte-face *f inv* / *to do an about-turn* faire volte-face.

above [ə'bʌv] ❖ prep **1.** [in a higher place or position than] au-dessus de / *above ground* en surface / *they live above the shop* ils habitent au-dessus du magasin / *a village on the river above Oxford* un village (situé) en amont d'Oxford **2.** [greater in degree or quantity than] au-dessus de / *it's above my price limit* c'est au-dessus du prix or dépasse le prix que je me suis fixé **3.** [in preference to] plus que / *he values friendship above success* il accorde plus d'importance à l'amitié qu'à la réussite **4.** [beyond] au-delà de / *the discussion was all rather above me* la discussion me dépassait complètement / *above and beyond the call of duty* bien au-delà du strict devoir **5.** [morally or intellectually superior to] : *she's above that sort of thing* elle est au-dessus de ça / *he's not above cheating* il irait jusqu'à tricher ▸ **to get above o.s.** se monter la tête **6.** [in volume, sound] par-dessus / *it's difficult to make oneself heard above all this noise* il est difficile de se faire entendre avec tout ce bruit. ◆ adj *fml* ci-dessus, précité. ◆ adv **1.** [in a higher place or position] au-dessus / *the people in the flat above* les voisins du dessus / *to fall from above* tomber d'en haut **2.** [greater in degree or quantity] : *aged 20 and above* âgé de 20 ans et plus **3.** [a higher rank or authority] en haut / *we've had orders from above* nous avons reçu des ordres d'en haut **4.** [in a previous place] plus haut / *mentioned above* cité plus haut or ci-dessus. ◆ n *fml* ▶ **the above a)** [fact, item] ce qui se trouve ci-dessus **b)** [person] le susnommé (la susnommée) **c)** [persons] les susnommés / *can you explain the above?* pouvez-vous expliquer ce qui précède ? ◆ **above all** adv phr avant tout, surtout.

above-average adj au-dessus de la moyenne.

aboveboard [ə,bʌv'bɔːd] ◆ adj **1.** [person] honnête, régulier **2.** [action, behaviour] franc (franche), honnête. ◆ adv [honestly] honnêtement, de façon régulière.

above-mentioned [-'menʃnd] (*pl* **above-mentioned**) *fml* adj cité plus haut, susmentionné, précité.

above-named (*pl* **above-named**) *fml* adj susnommé.

above-the-line adj FIN [expenses] au-dessus de la ligne.

abracadabra [,æbrəkə'dæbrə] ◆ interj ▶ **abracadabra!** abracadabra ! ◆ n [magical word] formule f magique.

abrasion [ə'breɪʒn] n [graze - on skin] éraflure f, écorchure f.

abrasive [ə'breɪsɪv] adj **1.** TECH abrasif **2.** [character] rêche ; [criticism, wit] corrosif ; [voice] caustique.

abreast [ə'brest] adv [march, ride] côte à côte, de front / *the children were riding three abreast* les enfants faisaient du vélo à trois de front. ◆ **abreast of** prep phr [in touch with] ▶ **to be abreast of sthg** être au courant de qqch / *to keep abreast of recent research* rester informé or au courant des recherches récentes.

abridge [ə'brɪdʒ] vt [book] abréger ; [article, play, speech] écourter, abréger.

abridged [ə'brɪdʒd] adj abrégé.

abroad [ə'brɔːd] adv **1.** [overseas] à l'étranger / *to go abroad* aller à l'étranger / *to live* / *to study abroad* vivre / faire ses études à l'étranger **2.** [over wide area] au loin ; [in all directions] de tous côtés, partout.

abrupt [ə'brʌpt] adj **1.** [sudden - change, drop, movement] brusque, soudain ; [- laugh, question] brusque ; [- departure] brusque, précipité **2.** [behaviour, person] brusque, bourru.

abruptly [ə'brʌptlɪ] adv **1.** [change, move] brusquement, tout à coup ; [ask, laugh] abruptement ; [depart] brusquement, précipitamment **2.** [behave, speak] avec brusquerie, brusquement **3.** [fall, rise] en pente raide, à pic.

abs [æbz] *pl* n *inf* [abdominal muscles] abdos *mpl*.

ABS (abbr of **Antiblockiersystem**) n ABS m.

abscess ['æbsɪs] n abcès m.

abscond [əb'skɒnd] vi *fml* s'enfuir, prendre la fuite.

abseil ['æbseɪl] ◆ vi descendre en rappel. ◆ n (descente f en) rappel m.

abseiling ['æbseɪlɪŋ] n (descente f en) rappel m.

absence ['æbsəns] n **1.** [state of being away] absence f / *in* or *during my absence* pendant mon absence **2.** [lack] manque m, défaut m / *in the absence of adequate information* en l'absence d'informations satisfaisantes, faute de renseignements.

absent ◆ adj ['æbsənt] **1.** [not present] absent / *he was absent from the meeting* il n'a pas participé à la réunion ▶ **to be** or **to go absent without leave** MIL être absent sans permission, être porté manquant **2.** [inattentive - person] distrait ; [- manner] absent, distrait. ◆ vt [æb'sent] ▶ **to absent o.s. (from sthg)** s'absenter (de qqch).

absentee [,æbsən'tiː] ◆ n [someone not present] absent m, -e f ; [habitually] absentéiste mf. ◆ adj absentéiste ▶ **absentee ballot** US vote m par correspondance ▶ **absentee landlord** propriétaire m absentéiste ▶ **absentee voter** électeur m, -trice f votant par correspondance.

absenteeism [,æbsən'tiːɪzm] n absentéisme m.

absent-minded [,æbsənt-] adj [person] distrait ; [manner] absent, distrait.

absent-mindedly [,æbsənt'maɪndɪdlɪ] adv distraitement, d'un air distrait.

absent-mindedness [,æbsənt'maɪndɪdnɪs] n distraction f, absence f.

absolute ['æbsəluːt] ◆ adj **1.** [as intensifier] absolu, total / *what absolute nonsense!* quelles bêtises, vraiment ! / *he's an absolute idiot* c'est un parfait crétin or imbécile / *the whole thing is an absolute mess* c'est un véritable gâchis or un vrai fatras **2.** [entire - secrecy, truth] absolu **3.** [unlimited - power] absolu, souverain ; [- ruler] absolu **4.** [definite, unconditional - decision, refusal] absolu, formel ; [- fact] indiscutable ; [- proof] formel, irréfutable **5.** [independent, not relative] absolu / *in absolute terms* en valeurs absolues. ◆ n absolu m.

absolutely ['æbsəluːtlɪ] adv **1.** [as intensifier] vraiment **2.** [in expressing opinions] absolument / *I absolutely agree* je suis tout à fait d'accord / *do you agree? — absolutely not!* êtes-vous d'accord ? — absolument pas ! **3.** [deny, refuse] absolument, formellement.

absolute majority n majorité f absolue.

absolute zero n zéro m absolu.

absolution [,æbsə'luːʃn] n [forgiveness] absolution f ; RELIG absolution f, remise f des péchés.

absolve [əb'zɒlv] vt **1.** [from blame, sin, etc.] absoudre ; [from obligation] décharger, délier **2.** LAW acquitter.

absorb [əb'sɔːb] vt **1.** *lit & fig* [changes, cost, light, liquid] absorber ; [surplus] absorber, résorber ; [idea, information] absorber, assimiler **2.** [shock, sound] amortir **3.** (*usu passive*) [engross] absorber ▶ **to be absorbed in sthg** être absorbé par qqch.

absorbency [əb'sɔːbənsɪ] n [gen] pouvoir m absorbant ; CHEM & PHYS absorptivité f.

absorbent [əb'sɔːbənt] adj absorbant.

absorbing [əb'sɔːbɪŋ] adj [activity, book] fascinant, passionnant ; [work] absorbant, passionnant.

absorption [əb'sɔːpʃn] n **1.** [of light, liquid, smell] absorption f ; [of surplus] résorption f **2.** [of shock, sound] amortissement m **3.** [fascination] passion f, fascination f ; [concentration] concentration f (d'esprit).

abstain [əb'steɪn] vi [refrain] s'abstenir.

abstainer [əb'steɪnə^r] n **1.** [teetotaller] abstinent m, -e f **2.** [person not voting] abstentionniste mf.

abstemious [æb'stiːmjəs] adj [person] sobre, abstinent ; [diet, meal] frugal.

abstention [əb'stenʃn] n [from action] abstention f ; [from drink, food] abstinence f.

abstinence ['æbstɪnəns] n abstinence f.

abstract ◆ adj ['æbstrækt] abstrait. ◆ n ['æbstrækt] **1.** [idea, term] abstrait m ▶ **in the abstract** dans l'abstrait **2.** [summary] résumé m, abrégé m **3.** ART [painting, sculpture] œuvre f abstraite. ◆ vt [æb'strækt] **1.** [remove] extraire **2.** *euph* [steal] soustraire, dérober.

abstractedly [æb'stræktɪdlɪ] adv distraitement, d'un air distrait.

abstraction [æb'strækʃn] n **1.** [concept] idée f abstraite, abstraction f **2.** [preoccupation] préoccupation f ; [absent-mindedness] distraction f.

absurd [əb'sɜːd] ◆ adj [unreasonable] absurde, insensé ; [ludicrous] absurde, ridicule. ◆ n absurde *m*.

absurdity [əb'sɜːdətɪ] (*pl* **absurdities**) n absurdité *f*.

absurdly [əb'sɜːdlɪ] adv [behave, dress] d'une manière insensée, d'une façon absurde ; [as intensifier] ridiculement.

ABTA ['æbtə] (**abbr of Association of British Travel Agents**) pr n *association des agences de voyage britanniques*.

Abu Dhabi [ˌæbuː'dɑːbɪ] pr n Abou Dhabi.

abundance [ə'bʌndəns] n abondance *f*, profusion *f*.

abundant [ə'bʌndənt] adj [plentiful] abondant.

abundantly [ə'bʌndəntlɪ] adv **1.** [profusely] abondamment ; [eat, serve] abondamment, copieusement ; [grow] à foison **2.** [as intensifier] extrêmement / *she made it abundantly clear that I was not welcome* elle me fit comprendre très clairement que j'étais indésirable.

abuse ◆ n [ə'bjuːs] **1.** [misuse] abus *m* / *such positions are open to abuse* de telles situations incitent aux abus **2.** (*U*) [insults] injures *fpl*, insultes *fpl* ▶ **to heap abuse on sb** accabler qqn d'injures **3.** (*U*) [cruel treatment] mauvais traitements *mpl* **4.** [unjust practice] abus *m*. ◆ vt [ə'bjuːz] **1.** [authority, position] abuser de **2.** [insult] injurier, insulter **3.** [treat cruelly] maltraiter, malmener.

⚠ Be careful when translating the noun or verb abuse, as **abus** and **abuser** are not always the correct equivalents. See the entry for details.

abuse of privilege n POL abus *m* de droit.

abuser [ə'bjuːzər] n **1.** [gen] : *abusers of the system* ceux qui profitent du système **2.** [of child] *personne qui a maltraité un enfant physiquement ou psychologiquement* **3.** [of drugs] ▶ **(drug) abuser** drogué *m*, -e *f*.

abusive [ə'bjuːsɪv] adj **1.** [language] offensant, grossier ; [person] grossier ; [phone call] obscène ▶ **to be abusive to sb** être grossier envers qqn **2.** [behaviour, treatment] brutal.

abusively [ə'bjuːsɪvlɪ] adv **1.** [behave, treat] brutalement **2.** [use] abusivement.

abut [ə'bʌt] (*pt* & *pp* **abutted**, *cont* **abutting**) vi *fml* ▶ **to abut on (to) sthg** être adjacent à qqch.

abysmal [ə'bɪzml] adj [very bad] épouvantable, exécrable.

abysmally [ə'bɪzməlɪ] adv atrocement ; [fail] lamentablement.

abyss [ə'bɪs] n abîme *m*, gouffre *m* ; [in sea] abysse *m* ; *fig* abîme *m*.

Abyssinia [ˌæbɪ'sɪnjə] pr n Abyssinie *f*.

Abyssinian [ˌæbɪ'sɪnjən] ◆ adj abyssinien, abyssin ▶ **the Abyssinian Empire** l'empire *m* d'Éthiopie. ◆ n Abyssinien *m*, -enne *f*.

ac written abbr of **acre**.

a/c (written abbr of **account (current)**) 🇬🇧 cc.

AC n abbr of **alternating current**.

acacia [ə'keɪʃə] n acacia *m*.

academic [ˌækə'demɪk] ◆ adj **1.** [related to formal study - book, institution, job] universitaire, scolaire ; [-failure, system] scolaire ▶ **academic advisor** 🇺🇸 directeur *m*, -trice *f* d'études ▶ **academic year** année *f* universitaire **2.** [intellectual -standard, style, work] intellectuel ; [-person] studieux, intellectuel **3.** [theoretical] théorique, spéculatif ; [not practical] sans intérêt pratique, théorique ▶ **out of academic interest** par simple curiosité. ◆ n universitaire *mf*.

academy [ə'kædəmɪ] (*pl* **academies**) n **1.** [society] académie *f*, société *f* **2.** [school] école *f* ; [private] école *f* privée, collège *m* / *an academy of music* un conservatoire de musique.

Academy Award n oscar *m*.

ACAS ['eɪkæs] (**abbr of Advisory, Conciliation and Arbitration Service**) pr n *organisme britannique de conciliation et d'arbitrage des conflits du travail* ; ≃ conseil *m* de prud'hommes.

accede [æk'siːd] vi *fml* **1.** [agree] agréer, accepter ▶ **to accede to sthg a)** [demand, request] donner suite or accéder à qqch **b)** [plan, suggestion] accepter or agréer qqch **2.** [attain] accéder / *to accede to the throne* monter sur le trône / *to accede to office* entrer en fonction.

acceding country [æk'siːdɪŋ-] n [in EU] pays *m* accédant.

accelerate [ək'seləreɪt] ◆ vt [pace, process, rhythm] accélérer ; [decline, event] précipiter, accélérer ; [work] activer. ◆ vi [move faster] s'accélérer.

acceleration [ək,selə'reɪʃn] n [gen & AUTO] accélération *f*.

accelerator [ək'seləreɪtər] n AUTO & PHYS accélérateur *m*.

accent ['æksent] ◆ n [gen & GRAM & MUS] accent *m*. ◆ vt **1.** [stress -syllable] accentuer, appuyer sur ; [-word] accentuer, mettre l'accent sur ; [put written mark on] mettre un accent sur, accentuer **2.** *fig* [make stand out] mettre en valeur, accentuer.

accentuate [æk'sentjʊeɪt] vt [feature, importance] souligner, accentuer.

accept [ək'sept] vt **1.** [believe as right, true] accepter, admettre / *it is generally accepted that...* il est généralement reconnu que... **2.** [face up to -danger] faire face à, affronter ; [-challenge] accepter, relever ; [-one's fate] se résigner à / *you have to accept the inevitable* il vous faut accepter l'inévitable.

acceptable [ək'septəbl] adj [satisfactory] acceptable, convenable ; [tolerable] acceptable, admissible / *are these conditions acceptable to you?* ces conditions vous conviennent-elles ?

Acceptable Use Policy n COMPUT code de conduite défini par un fournisseur d'accès à l'Internet.

acceptably [ək'septəblɪ] adv [suitably] convenablement ; [tolerably] passablement.

acceptance [ək'septəns] n **1.** [of gift, invitation] acceptation *f* **2.** [assent -to proposal, suggestion] consentement *m* **3.** [approval, favour] approbation *f*, réception *f* favorable / *the idea is gaining acceptance* l'idée fait son chemin.

accepted [ək'septɪd] adj ▶ **accepted ideas** les idées généralement répandues or admises / *it's an accepted fact that too much sun ages the skin* il est généralement reconnu que le soleil à haute dose accélère le vieillissement de la peau.

access ['ækses] ◆ n **1.** [means of entry] entrée *f*, ouverture *f* ; [means of approach] accès *m*, abord *m* ; LAW droit *m* de passage / *the kitchen gives access to the garage* la cuisine donne accès au garage / *'access only'* 'sauf riverains (et livreurs)' **2.** [right to contact, use] accès *m* / *I have access to confidential files* j'ai accès à des dossiers confidentiels / *the father has access to the children at weekends* LAW le père a droit de visite le week-end pour voir ses enfants **3.** COMPUT accès *m* / *to have access to a file* avoir accès à un fichier ▶ **access code** code *m* d'accès. ◆ vt accéder à.

access card n carte *f* d'accès.

accessibility [ək,sesə'bɪlətɪ] n accessibilité *f*.

accessible [ək'sesəbl] adj **1.** [place] accessible, d'accès facile ; [person] d'un abord facile **2.** [available] accessible **3.** [easily understandable] à la portée de tous, accessible.

accession [æk'seʃn] n [to office, position] accession f ; [to fortune] accession f, entrée f en possession / *Queen Victoria's accession (to the throne)* l'accession au trône or l'avènement de la reine Victoria.

accessorize, accessorise [ək'sesəraɪz] vt accessoiriser.

accessory [ək'sesərɪ] (pl **accessories**) ◆ n (usu pl) [supplementary article] accessoire m. ◆ adj [supplementary] accessoire.

access ramp n bretelle f d'accès.

access road n [gen] route f d'accès ; [to motorway] bretelle f d'accès or de raccordement.

access time n temps m d'accès.

accident ['æksɪdənt] ◆ n **1.** [mishap] accident m, malheur m ; [unforeseen event] événement m fortuit, accident m / *her son had a car accident* son fils a eu un accident de voiture ▶ **Accident and Emergency Unit** UK MED (service m des) urgences fpl **2.** [chance] hasard m, chance f / *it was purely by accident that we met* nous nous sommes rencontrés tout à fait par accident. ◆ comp [figures, rate] des accidents ▶ **accident insurance** assurance f (contre les) accidents.

accidental [,æksɪ'dentl] adj [occurring by chance - death, poisoning] accidentel ; [- meeting] fortuit.

accidentally [,æksɪ'dentəlɪ] adv [break, drop] accidentellement ; [meet] par hasard / *he did it accidentally on purpose* hum il l'a fait «exprès sans le vouloir».

accident-prone adj ▶ **to be accident-prone** être prédisposé aux accidents.

acclaim [ə'kleɪm] ◆ vt [praise] acclamer, faire l'éloge de ; [applaud] acclamer, applaudir. ◆ n (U) acclamation f, acclamations fpl / *his play met with great critical acclaim* sa pièce a été très applaudie par la critique.

acclaimed [ə'kleɪmd] adj célèbre.

acclamation [,æklə'meɪʃn] n (U) acclamation f, acclamations fpl.

acclimate ['æklɪmeɪt] vt & vi US = **acclimatize**.

acclimation [,æklɪ'meɪʃn] n US = **acclimatization**.

acclimatization, acclimatisation UK [ə,klaɪmətaɪ'zeɪʃn] n [to climate] acclimatation f ; [to conditions, customs] accoutumance f, acclimatement m.

acclimatize, acclimatise [ə'klaɪmətaɪz], **acclimate** US ['æklɪmeɪt] ◆ vt [animal, plant] acclimater. ◆ vi ▶ **to acclimatize to a)** [climate] s'habituer à, s'accoutumer à **b)** [conditions, customs] s'acclimater à, s'habituer à, s'accoutumer à.

accolade ['ækəleɪd] n [praise] acclamation f, acclamations fpl ; [approval] marque f d'approbation ; [honour] honneur m / *it was the ultimate accolade* c'était la consécration suprême.

accommodate [ə'kɒmədeɪt] vt **1.** [provide lodging for] loger ; [provide with something needed] équiper, pourvoir ; [provide with loan] prêter de l'argent à **2.** [have room for - subj: car] contenir ; [- subj: house, room] contenir, recevoir / *the cottage accommodates up to six people* dans la villa, on peut loger jusqu'à six (personnes).

accommodating [ə'kɒmədeɪtɪŋ] adj [willing to help] obligeant ; [easy to please] accommodant, complaisant.

accommodation [ə,kɒmə'deɪʃn] n (U) [lodging] logement m ; [lodging and services] prestations fpl ▶ **office accommodation** bureaux mpl à louer.
◆ **accommodations** pl n US [lodging, food and services] hébergement m.

accompaniment [ə'kʌmpənɪmənt] n [gen] accompagnement m / *he entered to the accompaniment of wild applause* il entra sous un tonnerre d'applaudissements.

accompanist [ə'kʌmpənɪst] n accompagnateur m, -trice f.

accompany [ə'kʌmpənɪ] (pt & pp **accompanied**) vt [escort] accompagner, escorter / *she was accompanied by her brother* elle était accompagnée de son frère.

accompanying [ə'kʌmpənɪɪŋ] adj : *the accompanying documents* les documents ci-joints / *children will not be allowed in without an accompanying adult* l'entrée est interdite aux enfants non accompagnés ▶ **accompanying letter** lettre f d'accompagnement.

accomplice [ə'kʌmplɪs] n complice mf ▶ **to be an accomplice to** or **in sthg** être complice de qqch.

accomplish [ə'kʌmplɪʃ] vt [manage to do - task, work] accomplir, exécuter ; [- desire, dream] réaliser ; [- distance, trip] effectuer.

accomplished [ə'kʌmplɪʃt] adj [cook, singer] accompli, doué ; [performance] accompli.

accomplishment [ə'kʌmplɪʃmənt] n **1.** [skill] talent m / *speaking fluent French is just one of her many accomplishments* elle parle français couramment, entre autres talents **2.** [feat] exploit m, œuvre f (accomplie) **3.** [completion - of task, trip] accomplissement m ; [- of ambition] réalisation f.

accord [ə'kɔ:d] ◆ n **1.** [consent] accord m, consentement m ▶ **to be in accord with sb** être d'accord avec qqn **2.** [conformity] accord m, conformité f ▶ **to be in accord with sthg** être en accord or en conformité avec qqch **3.** [harmony] accord m, harmonie f **4.** fml [agreement] accord m ; [treaty] traité m. ◆ vt [permission] accorder ; [welcome] réserver ▶ **to accord sb permission** accorder une autorisation or une permission à qqn.
◆ **of one's own accord** adv phr de son plein gré.

accordance [ə'kɔ:dəns] n [conformity] accord m, conformité f. ◆ **in accordance with** prep phr : *in accordance with the law* aux termes de or conformément à la loi.

according [ə'kɔ:dɪŋ] ◆ **according to** prep phr **1.** [on the evidence of] selon, d'après / *according to what you say* d'après ce que vous dites **2.** [in relation to] : *arranged according to height* disposés par ordre de taille **3.** [in accordance with] suivant, conformément à / *everything went according to plan* tout s'est passé comme prévu.

accordingly [ə'kɔ:dɪŋlɪ] adv [appropriately] en conséquence.

accordion [ə'kɔ:djən] n accordéon m.

accordionist [ə'kɔ:djənɪst] n accordéoniste mf.

accost [ə'kɒst] vt [gen] accoster, aborder ; [subj: prostitute] racoler.

account [ə'kaʊnt] n **1.** [report] récit m, compte rendu m / *he gave his account of the accident* il a donné sa version de l'accident **2.** [explanation] compte rendu m, explication f ▶ **to bring** or **to call sb to account** demander des comptes à qqn / *you will be held to account for all damages* il vous faudra rendre des comptes pour tous les dommages causés **3.** [consideration] importance f, valeur f ▶ **to take sthg into account, to take account of sthg** tenir compte de qqch, prendre qqch en compte / *he took little account of her feelings* il ne tenait pas compte or faisait peu de cas de ses sentiments **4.** COMM [in bank, with shop] compte m / *put it on* or *charge it to my account* mettez cela sur mon compte **5.** [detailed record of money] compte m / *his wife keeps the accounts* c'est sa femme qui tient les comptes. ◆ **accounts** pl n [of business] comptabilité f, comptes mpl. ◆ **by all accounts** adv phr aux dires de tous, d'après ce que tout le monde dit.
◆ **on account of** prep phr à cause de / *don't leave on account of me* or *on my account* ne partez pas à cause de moi. ◆ **on no account** adv phr en aucun cas, sous

aucun prétexte. ❖ **account for** vt insep **1.** [explain] expliquer, rendre compte de / *there's no accounting for taste* des goûts et des couleurs, on ne discute pas, chacun ses goûts **2.** [answer for] rendre compte de / *all the children are accounted for* aucun des enfants n'a été oublié / *two hostages have not yet been accounted for* deux otages n'ont toujours pas été retrouvés **3.** [represent] représenter / *wine accounts for 5% of all exports* le vin représente 5 % des exportations totales.

accountability [ə,kaʊntə'bɪlətɪ] n : *the public wants more police accountability* le public souhaite que la police réponde davantage de ses actes ▶ **public accountability** transparence *f*.

accountable [ə'kaʊntəbl] adj [responsible] responsable / *she is not accountable for her actions* elle n'est pas responsable de ses actes.

accountancy [ə'kaʊntənsɪ] n [subject, work] comptabilité *f* ; [profession] profession *f* de comptable.

accountant [ə'kaʊntənt] n comptable *mf*.

account balance n [status] situation *f* de compte.

account charges n frais *mpl* de tenue de compte.

account executive n responsable *mf* grands comptes.

account holder n titulaire *mf*.

accounting [ə'kaʊntɪŋ] n comptabilité *f*.

accounting period n exercice *m* (financier), période *f* comptable.

account manager n = account executive.

account number n numéro *m* de compte.

accoutrements 🇬🇧 [ə'ku:trəmənts], **accouterments** 🇺🇸 [ə'ku:tərmənts] pl n [equipment] attirail *m* ; MIL équipement *m*.

accredit [ə'kredɪt] vt [credit] créditer / *they accredited the discovery to him* on lui a attribué cette découverte / *she is accredited with having discovered radium* on lui attribue la découverte du radium.

accreditation [ə,kredɪ'teɪʃn] n ▶ **to seek accreditation** chercher à se faire accréditer or reconnaître.

accredited [ə'kredɪtɪd] adj **1.** [idea, rumour] admis, accepté **2.** [official, person] accrédité, autorisé.

accrue [ə'kru:] *fml* vi **1.** [increase] s'accroître, s'accumuler ; [interest] courir ▶ **accrued interest** intérêt *m* couru **2.** [benefit, gain] ▶ **to accrue to** revenir à.

accumulate [ə'kju:mjʊleɪt] ❖ vt accumuler. ❖ vi s'accumuler.

accumulation [ə,kju:mjʊ'leɪʃn] n **1.** [process] accumulation *f* **2.** [things collected] amas *m*, tas *m*.

accuracy ['ækjʊrəsɪ] n [of aim, description, report, weapon] précision *f* ; [of figures, watch] exactitude *f* ; [of memory, translation] fidélité *f*, exactitude *f* ; [of prediction] justesse *f*.

accurate ['ækjʊrət] adj [description, report] précis, juste ; [instrument, weapon] précis ; [figures, watch] exact ; [estimate] juste ; [memory, translation] fidèle.

accurately ['ækjʊrətlɪ] adv [count, draw] avec précision ; [tell] exactement ; [judge, estimate] avec justesse ; [remember, translate] fidèlement.

accusation [,ækju:'zeɪʃn] n [gen] accusation *f*.

accuse [ə'kju:z] vt accuser ▶ **to accuse sb of (doing) sthg** accuser qqn de (faire) qqch.

accused [ə'kju:zd] (*pl* **accused**) n ▶ **the accused** l'accusé *m*, -e *f*, l'inculpé *m*, -e *f*.

accuser [ə'kju:zər] n accusateur *m*, -trice *f*.

accusing [ə'kju:zɪŋ] adj accusateur.

accusingly [ə'kju:zɪŋlɪ] adv de façon accusatrice.

accustom [ə'kʌstəm] vt habituer, accoutumer.

accustomed [ə'kʌstəmd] adj [familiar] habitué, accoutumé ▶ **to get** or **to grow accustomed to sthg** s'habituer or s'accoutumer à qqch.

AC/DC written abbr of **alternating current/direct current**.

ace [eɪs] ❖ n **1.** GAMES [on card, dice, dominoes] as *m* / *the ace of spades* l'as de pique ▶ **to have an ace up one's sleeve** or **to have an ace in the hole** avoir un atout en réserve ▶ **to hold all the aces** avoir tous les atouts dans son jeu ▶ **to come within an ace of doing sthg** être à deux doigts de faire qqch **2.** [expert] as *m* **3.** [in tennis] ace *m* **4.** [pilot] as *m*. ❖ adj 🇬🇧 *inf* super, formidable.

acerbic [ə'sɜ:bɪk] adj [taste] acerbe ; [person, tone] acerbe, caustique.

acetate ['æsɪteɪt] n acétate *m*.

acetic acid n acide *m* acétique.

acetone ['æsɪtəʊn] n acétone *f*.

acetylene [ə'setɪli:n] n acétylène *m*.

ache [eɪk] ❖ vi **1.** [feel pain] faire mal, être douloureux / *I ache all over* j'ai mal partout / *my head / tooth aches* j'ai mal à la tête / aux dents **2.** [feel desire] avoir très envie / *she was aching for them to leave* elle mourait d'envie de les voir partir. ❖ n [physical] douleur *f* ; [emotional] peine *f* ▶ **aches and pains** douleurs *fpl*, maux *mpl*.

achieve [ə'tʃi:v] vt [gen] accomplir, faire ; [desire, dream, increase] réaliser ; [level, objective] arriver à, atteindre ; [independence, success] obtenir / *we really achieved something today* on a vraiment bien avancé aujourd'hui.

⚠ **Achever means** to finish, **not** to achieve.

achievement [ə'tʃi:vmənt] n **1.** [deed] exploit *m*, réussite *f* **2.** [successful completion] accomplissement *m*, réalisation *f*.

⚠ **Achèvement means** completion, **not** achievement.

achiever [ə'tʃi:vər] n fonceur *m*, -euse *f*.

Achilles' heel n talon *m* d'Achille.

Achilles' tendon n tendon *m* d'Achille.

aching ['eɪkɪŋ] adj douloureux, endolori.

achingly ['eɪkɪŋlɪ] adv *inf* : *achingly funny* tordant / *achingly hip* [person, bar, clothes] hyper branché.

achy ['eɪkɪ] adj douloureux, endolori.

acid ['æsɪd] ❖ n [gen & CHEM] acide *m*. ❖ adj **1.** [drink, taste] acide **2.** [remark, tone, wit] mordant, acide ; [person] revêche, caustique.

acid house n MUS house music *f*.

acidic [ə'sɪdɪk] adj acide.

acid indigestion n aigreurs *fpl* d'estomac.

acidity [ə'sɪdətɪ] n CHEM & *fig* acidité *f*.

acid jazz [,æsɪd'dʒæz] n (U) MUS acid jazz *m*.

acidly ['æsɪdlɪ] adv [say, reply] d'un ton acide.

acid rain n pluie *f* acide.

acid test n épreuve *f* décisive.

acknowledge [ək'nɒlɪdʒ] vt **1.** [admit truth of] reconnaître, admettre ; [defeat, mistake] reconnaître, avouer **2.** [show recognition of - person] : *she acknowledged him with a nod* elle lui a adressé un signe de la tête / *they acknowledged him as their leader* ils l'ont reconnu comme leur chef **3.** [confirm receipt of - greeting, message] répondre à ; ADMIN [letter, package] accuser réception de.

acknowledged [ək'nɒlɪdʒd] adj [expert, authority] reconnu.

acknowledg(e)ment [ək'nɒlɪdʒmənt] n **1.** [admission] reconnaissance f ; [of mistake] reconnaissance f, aveu m **2.** [letter, receipt] accusé m de réception ; [for payment] quittance f, reçu m. ❧ **acknowledg(e)ments** pl n [in article, book] remerciements mpl.

ACLU (abbr of **American Civil Liberties Union**) pr n ligue américaine des droits du citoyen.

acme ['ækmɪ] n apogée m, point m culminant.

acne ['æknɪ] n acné f.

acorn ['eɪkɔ:n] n gland m.

acoustic [ə'ku:stɪk] adj [feature, phonetics, nerve] acoustique.

acoustics [ə'ku:stɪks] ❧ n (U) [subject] acoustique f. ❧ pl n [of room, theatre] acoustique f / to have bad / good acoustics avoir une mauvaise / bonne acoustique.

ACPO ['ækpəʊ] (abbr of **Association of Chief Police Officers**) n syndicat d'officiers supérieurs de la police britannique.

acquaint [ə'kweɪnt] vt **1.** [inform] aviser, renseigner / I'll acquaint you with the facts je vais vous mettre au courant des faits **2.** [familiarize] ▶ to be acquainted with a) [person, place, subject] connaître b) [fact, situation] être au courant de / we were just getting acquainted on venait juste de faire connaissance.

acquaintance [ə'kweɪntəns] n **1.** [person] connaissance f, relation f **2.** [knowledge] connaissance f / pleased to make your acquaintance enchanté de faire votre connaissance.

acquiesce [ˌækwɪ'es] vi acquiescer, consentir.

acquiescence [ˌækwɪ'esns] n acquiescement m, consentement m.

acquire [ə'kwaɪə*] vt **1.** [advantage, experience, possession, success] acquérir ; [reputation] se faire **2.** [habit] prendre, contracter / I've acquired a taste for champagne j'ai pris goût au champagne.

acquired [ə'kwaɪəd] adj acquis ▶ an acquired taste un goût acquis.

acquired citizenship [ə'kwaɪəd-] n US naturalisation f.

acquisition [ˌækwɪ'zɪʃn] n acquisition f.

acquisitive [ə'kwɪzɪtɪv] adj [for money] âpre au gain ; [greedy] avide.

acquit [ə'kwɪt] (pt & pp **acquitted**, cont **acquitting**) vt **1.** [release - from duty, responsibility] acquitter, décharger ; LAW acquitter, relaxer **2.** [behave] ▶ to acquit o.s. well / badly bien / mal s'en tirer.

acquittal [ə'kwɪtl] n **1.** [of duty] accomplissement m **2.** LAW acquittement m.

acre ['eɪkə*] n ≃ demi-hectare m, acre f / they have acres of room fig ils ont des kilomètres de place.

acreage ['eɪkərɪdʒ] n aire f, superficie f.

acrid ['ækrɪd] adj [smell, taste] âcre.

acrimonious [ˌækrɪ'məʊnjəs] adj [person, remark] acrimonieux, hargneux ; [attack, dispute] virulent.

acrimoniously [ˌækrɪ'məʊnjəslɪ] adv [say] avec amertume.

acrobat ['ækrəbæt] n acrobate mf.

acrobatic [ˌækrə'bætɪk] adj acrobatique.

acrobatics [ˌækrə'bætɪks] pl n acrobatie f.

acronym ['ækrənɪm] n acronyme m.

across [ə'krɒs] ❧ prep **1.** [from one side to the other of] d'un côté à l'autre de ▶ to walk across sthg traverser

qqch / I ran across the street j'ai traversé la rue en courant / they built a bridge across the lake ils ont construit un pont sur le lac / he lay across the bed il était couché or allongé en travers du lit / she felt a pain across her chest une douleur lui a traversé la poitrine **2.** [on or to the other side of] de l'autre côté de / the house across the street la maison d'en face / he sat across the table from me il s'assit en face de moi **3.** [so as to cover] : he leaned across my desk il s'est penché par-dessus mon bureau **4.** [so as to cross] en travers de, à travers / the study of literature across cultures l'étude de la littérature à travers différentes cultures. ❧ adv **1.** [from one side to the other] d'un côté à l'autre / the room is 3 metres across la pièce fait 3 mètres de large / I helped him across je l'ai aidé à traverser **2.** [on or to the other side] de l'autre côté / she walked across to Mary elle s'est dirigée vers Mary. ❧ **across from** prep phr en face de.

across-the-board adj général, systématique.

acrylic [ə'krɪlɪk] ❧ adj acrylique. ❧ n acrylique m.

act [ækt] ❧ vi **1.** [take action] agir / they acted for the best ils ont agi pour le mieux ▶ to act on behalf of sb, to act on sb's behalf agir au nom de qqn **2.** [serve] ▶ to act as servir de, faire office de **3.** [behave] agir, se comporter / you acted like a fool vous vous êtes conduit comme un imbécile / he acts as though he were bored il agit comme s'il s'ennuyait **4.** THEAT jouer **5.** [produce an effect, work] agir. ❧ vt [part] jouer, tenir ; [play] jouer ; fig : stop acting the fool! arrête de faire l'imbécile ! ▶ act your age! sois raisonnable ! ❧ n **1.** [action, deed] acte m ▶ an act of God un acte divin ▶ to be caught in the act être pris sur le fait **2.** [pretence] comédie f, numéro m ▶ to put on an act jouer la comédie **3.** [in circus, show] numéro m ▶ to get one's act together inf se reprendre **4.** THEAT [part of play] acte m **5.** [law] loi f ▶ an act of Congress / Parliament une loi du Congrès / Parlement. ❧ **act on** vt insep [advice, suggestion] suivre ; [order] exécuter. ❧ **act out** vt sep [fantasy] vivre ; [emotions] exprimer (par mime) ; [event, story] mimer. ❧ **act up** vi inf [person] faire l'idiot, déconner ; [child] faire des siennes ; [engine, machine] déconner. ❧ **act upon** vt insep = **act on**.

ACT (abbr of **American College Test**) n examen de fin d'études secondaires aux États-Unis.

acting ['æktɪŋ] ❧ n **1.** [profession] profession f d'acteur, profession f d'actrice / I've done a bit of acting a) [theatre] j'ai fait un peu de théâtre b) [cinema] j'ai fait un peu de cinéma **2.** [performance] interprétation f, jeu m. ❧ adj [temporary] provisoire, par intérim ▶ acting director / president directeur / président par intérim.

action ['ækʃn] ❧ n **1.** [process] action f / it's time for action il est temps d'agir, passons aux actes ▶ to take action prendre des mesures ▶ to put sthg into action a) [idea, policy] mettre qqch en pratique b) [plan] mettre qqch à exécution c) [machine] mettre qqch en marche / the car is out of action UK la voiture est en panne / her accident will put her out of action for four months son accident va la mettre hors de combat pour quatre mois **2.** [deed] acte m, geste m, action f / don't judge her by her actions alone ne la jugez pas seulement sur ses actes ▶ actions speak louder than words les actes en disent plus long que les mots **3.** [activity, events] activité f / he wants to be where the action is il veut être au cœur de l'action ▶ action! CIN silence, on tourne ! ▶ we all want a piece of the action inf nous voulons tous être dans le coup **4.** LAW procès m, action f en justice ▶ to bring an action against sb intenter une action contre qqn **5.** MIL [fighting] combat m, action f ▶ to go into action engager le combat ▶ killed in action tué au combat. ❧ comp [film, photography] d'action. ❧ vt [idea, suggestion] mettre en action or en pratique ; [plan] mettre à exécution.

actionable ['ækʃnəbl] adj [allegations, deed, person] passible de poursuites ; [claim] recevable.

action group n groupe *m* de pression.

action movie ['ækʃənmu:vɪ] n film *m* d'action.

action-packed adj [film] bourré d'action ; [holiday] rempli d'activités, bien rempli.

action replay n 🇬🇧 TV répétition *immédiate d'une séquence*.

action stations ◆ pl n MIL postes *mpl* de combat. ◆ interj ▶ **action stations!** à vos postes !

activate ['æktɪveɪt] vt [gen & CHEM & TECH] activer.

active ['æktɪv] adj **1.** [lively - person] actif, dynamique ; [- imagination] vif, actif **2.** [busy, involved - person] actif, énergique ; [- life, stock market] actif ▶ **to be active in sthg, to take an active part in sthg** prendre une part active à qqch **3.** [keen - encouragement, interest] vif / *you have our active support* vous avez notre soutien total **4.** [in operation - account] actif ; [- case, file] en cours ; [- law, regulation] en vigueur ; [- volcano] en activité **5.** [chemical, ingredient] actif **6.** GRAM actif ▶ **the active voice** la voix active, l'actif *m* **7.** MIL actif ▶ **to be on active service** 🇬🇧 or **duty** 🇺🇸 être en service actif.

active file n COMPUT fichier *m* actif.

actively ['æktɪvlɪ] adv **1.** [involve, participate] activement **2.** [disagree, discourage] vivement, activement.

activewear ['æktɪvweəʳ] n vêtements *mpl* de sport.

active window n COMPUT fenêtre *f* active or activée.

activist ['æktɪvɪst] n militant *m*, -e *f*, activiste *mf*.

activity [æk'tɪvətɪ] (*pl* **activities**) n **1.** [of brain, person] activité *f* ; [of place, bank account] mouvement *m* **2.** [occupation] activité *f* ▶ **leisure activities** des activités de loisir.

activity centre n centre *m* d'activités ; [specifically for children] centre *m* aéré or de loisirs.

activity holiday n 🇬🇧 vacances *fpl* actives.

actor ['æktəʳ] n acteur *m*, comédien *m*.

actress ['æktrɪs] n actrice *f*, comédienne *f*.

actual ['æktʃʊəl] adj **1.** [genuine] réel, véritable ; [existing as a real fact] concret / *what were her actual words?* quels étaient ses mots exacts ? / *to take an actual example* prendre un exemple concret / *the actual result was quite different* le résultat véritable était plutôt différent **2.** [emphatic use] même / *the actual ceremony doesn't start until 10.30* la cérémonie même ne commence pas avant 10 h 30. ◆ **in actual fact** adv phr en fait.

⚠ **Actuel** generally means current, and is hardly ever the correct translation of actual.

actuality [ˌæktʃʊ'ælətɪ] (*pl* **actualities**) n réalité *f* ▶ **in actuality** en réalité.

actually ['æktʃʊəlɪ] adv **1.** [establishing a fact] vraiment / *what did he actually say?* qu'est-ce qu'il a dit vraiment ? **2.** [emphatic use] vraiment / *you mean she actually speaks Latin!* tu veux dire qu'elle parle vraiment le latin ! **3.** [contradicting or qualifying] en fait / *she's actually older than she looks* en fait, elle est plus âgée qu'elle n'en a l'air **4.** [in requests, advice, etc.] en fait / *actually, you could set the table* en fait, tu pourrais mettre la table.

⚠ **Actuellement** means at the moment, not actually.

actuary ['æktjʊərɪ] (*pl* **actuaries**) n actuaire *mf*.

actuate ['æktjʊeɪt] vt **1.** [machine, system] mettre en marche, faire marcher **2.** *fml* [person] faire agir, inciter.

acuity [ə'kju:ətɪ] n [of hearing, sight] acuité *f* ; [of person, thought] perspicacité *f*.

acumen ['ækjʊmen] n perspicacité *f*, flair *m* ▶ **business acumen** sens *m* des affaires.

acupressure ['ækjʊpreʃəʳ] n MED acupressing *m*.

acupuncture ['ækjʊpʌŋktʃəʳ] n acupuncture *f*, acuponcture *f*.

acupuncturist ['ækjʊpʌŋktʃərɪst] n acupuncteur *m*, -trice *f*, acuponcteur *m*, -trice *f*.

acute [ə'kju:t] adj **1.** [hearing, sense] fin / *to have an acute sense of hearing* avoir l'ouïe fine ; [smell] subtil, développé ; [sight] pénétrant, perçant **2.** [perceptive - mind, person] perspicace, pénétrant ; [- intelligence] fin, vif ; [- analysis] fin **3.** [severe - pain] aigu, vif ; [- anxiety, distress] vif ; [- shortage] critique, grave **4.** MED [attack, illness] aigu **5.** [angle] aigu **6.** GRAM [accent] aigu (uë) / *it's spelled with an "e" acute* ça s'écrit avec un « e » accent aigu.

acute-angled adj GEOM à angle(s) aigu(s).

acutely [ə'kju:tlɪ] adv **1.** [intensely - be aware, feel] vivement ; [- suffer] intensément **2.** [extremely - embarrassing, unhappy] très, profondément.

ad [æd] n *inf* [in newspaper] petite annonce *f* ; [on TV] pub *f*.

AD adv (abbr of **Anno Domini**) apr. J.-C.

adage ['ædɪdʒ] n adage *m*.

Adam ['ædəm] pr n Adam ▶ **I don't know him from Adam** je ne le connais ni d'Ève ni d'Adam.

adamant ['ædəmənt] adj résolu, inflexible.

adamantly ['ædəməntlɪ] adv [say, refuse] catégoriquement.

Adam's apple n pomme *f* d'Adam.

adapt [ə'dæpt] ◆ vt **1.** [adjust] adapter, ajuster **2.** [book, play] adapter. ◆ vi s'adapter.

adaptability [əˌdæptə'bɪlətɪ] n [of person] faculté *f* d'adaptation, adaptabilité *f*.

adaptable [ə'dæptəbl] adj adaptable.

adaptation [ˌædæp'teɪʃn] n [of person, work] adaptation *f*.

adapter, adaptor [ə'dæptəʳ] n [device] adaptateur *m* ; [multiple plug] prise *f* multiple.

ADC n (abbr of **analogue-digital converter**) CAN *m*.

add [æd] ◆ vt **1.** [put together] ajouter / *add her name to the list* ajoute son nom à la liste ▶ **to add fuel to the fire** jeter de l'huile sur le feu **2.** [say] ajouter **3.** MATH [figures] additionner ; [column of figures] totaliser. ◆ **add on** vt sep = **add**. ◆ **add to** vt insep ajouter à, accroître. ◆ **add up** ◆ vt sep [find the sum of - figures] additionner ; [- bill, column of figures] totaliser / *we added up the advantages and disadvantages* nous avons fait le total des avantages et des inconvénients. ◆ vi **1.** [figures, results] se recouper / *these figures don't add up* ces chiffres ne font pas le compte ▶ **it just doesn't add up** *fig* il y a quelque chose qui cloche or qui ne marche pas **2.** = **add** (*vi*). ◆ **add up to** vt insep **1.** [subj: figures] s'élever à, se monter à **2.** *fig* [subj: results, situation] signifier, se résumer à.

added ['ædɪd] adj **1.** [gen] supplémentaire **2.** [on food package] ▶ **no added sugar** sans sucre ajouté **3.** COMM & ACCOUNT ▶ **added value** valeur *f* ajoutée.

addendum [ə'dendəm] (*pl* **addenda** [-də]) n addendum *m*, addenda *mpl*.

adder ['ædəʳ] n [snake] vipère *f*.

addict ['ædɪkt] n **1.** MED toxicodépendant *m*, -e *f* **2.** *fig* fanatique *mf*, fana *mf*, mordu *m*, -e *f*.

addicted [ə'dɪktɪd] adj **1.** MED dépendant, toxicodépendant **2.** *fig* ▸ **to be addicted to sthg** s'adonner à qqch, se passionner pour qqch / *she's addicted to exercise / hard work* c'est une mordue d'exercice / de travail.

addiction [ə'dɪkʃn] n MED dépendance *f*; *fig* penchant *m* fort, forte inclination *f* ▸ **addiction therapy** cure *f* de désintoxication.

addictive [ə'dɪktɪv] adj MED qui crée une dépendance / *chocolate is very addictive hum* le chocolat, c'est une vraie drogue, on devient vite accro au chocolat.

Addis Ababa ['ædɪs'æbəbə] pr n Addis-Ababa, Addis-Abeba.

addition [ə'dɪʃn] n **1.** [gen & MATH] addition *f* **2.** [something or someone added] addition *f*, ajout *m* / *they're going to have an addition to the family* leur famille va s'agrandir / *she's a welcome new addition to our staff* nous sommes heureux de la compter au sein du personnel. ❖ **in addition** adv phr de plus, de surcroît.

additional [ə'dɪʃənl] adj additionnel; [supplementary] supplémentaire / *there is an additional charge on certain trains* il y a un supplément à payer pour certains trains.

additionally [ə'dɪʃənəlɪ] adv [moreover] en outre, de plus.

additive ['ædɪtɪv] n additif *m*.

addled ['ædld] adj [person] aux idées confuses, brouillon; [brain] fumeux, brouillon; [ideas] confus.

add-on n COMPUT accessoire *m*.

address [ə'dres] ❖ vt **1.** [envelope, letter, package] adresser, mettre l'adresse sur / *the letter is addressed to you* cette lettre vous est adressée **2.** [direct] adresser / *address all complaints to the manager* adressez vos doléances au directeur **3.** [speak to] s'adresser à; [write to] écrire à / *she stood up and addressed the audience* elle s'est levée et a pris la parole devant l'assistance. ❖ n **1.** [of building, person] adresse *f* / *we've changed our address* nous avons changé d'adresse **2.** [speech] discours *m*, allocution *f*.

> ⚠ When an **address** is a speech, it is not translated by **une adresse** but by **un discours** or **une allocution**. When you are talking about addressing a problem, an issue, etc., use **aborder**, not **adresser**.

address book n carnet *m* d'adresses.

addressee [,ædre'si:] n destinataire *mf*.

Aden ['eɪdn] pr n Aden.

adenoids ['ædɪnɔɪdz] pl n végétations *fpl* (adénoïdes).

adept ❖ adj [ə'dept] habile, adroit ▸ **to be adept at doing sthg** être adroit à faire qqch. ❖ n ['ædept] expert *m*.

adequacy ['ædɪkwəsɪ] n **1.** [of amount, payment, sum] fait *m* d'être suffisant **2.** [of person] compétence *f*, compétences *fpl*, capacité *f*, capacités *fpl*; [of description, expression] justesse *f*.

adequate ['ædɪkwət] adj **1.** [in amount, quantity] suffisant, adéquat **2.** [appropriate] qui convient, adapté / *he proved adequate to the task* il s'est révélé être à la hauteur de la tâche **3.** [just satisfactory] acceptable, satisfaisant.

adequately ['ædɪkwətlɪ] adv **1.** [sufficiently] suffisamment **2.** [satisfactorily] convenablement.

adhere [əd'hɪə] vi **1.** [stick] coller, adhérer **2.** [remain loyal] ▸ **to adhere to a)** [party] adhérer à **b)** [rule] obéir à **c)** [plan] se conformer à **d)** [belief, idea] adhérer à, souscrire à.

adherence [əd'hɪərəns] n adhésion *f*.

adherent [əd'hɪərənt] n [to party] adhérent *m*, -e *f*, partisan *m*, -e *f*; [to agreement] adhérent *m*, -e *f*; [to belief, religion] adepte *mf*.

adhesive [əd'hi:sɪv] ❖ adj adhésif, collant. ❖ n adhésif *m*.

ad hoc [,æd'hɒk] ❖ adj [committee] ad hoc *(inv)*; [decision, solution] adapté aux circonstances, ponctuel. ❖ adv à l'improviste.

ad infinitum [,ædɪnfɪ'naɪtəm] adv à l'infini.

adjacent [ə'dʒeɪsənt] adj [sharing common boundary -house, room] contigu, voisin; [-building] qui jouxte, mitoyen; [-country, territory] limitrophe.

adjective ['ædʒɪktɪv] n adjectif *m*.

adjoin [ə'dʒɔɪn] vt [house, land, room] : *they had rooms adjoining mine* leurs chambres étaient contiguës à la mienne.

adjoining [ə'dʒɔɪnɪŋ] adj contigu, attenant / *at the adjoining table* à la table voisine.

adjourn [ə'dʒɜ:n] ❖ vi [committee, court - break off] suspendre la séance; [-end] lever la séance. ❖ vt [defer] ajourner, remettre, reporter / *let's adjourn this discussion until tomorrow* reportons cette discussion à demain / *the president adjourned the meeting* le président a levé la séance.

adjournment [ə'dʒɜ:nmənt] n [of discussion, meeting] suspension *f*, ajournement *m*; LAW [of trial] remise *f*, renvoi *m*.

adjt. (written abbr of **adjutant**) adjt.

adjudge [ə'dʒʌdʒ] vt *fml* **1.** [pronounce] déclarer **2.** LAW [judge] prononcer, déclarer; [award] adjuger, accorder.

adjudicate [ə'dʒu:dɪkeɪt] vt [claim] décider; [competition] juger.

adjudication [ə,dʒu:dɪ'keɪʃn] n **1.** [process] jugement *m*, arbitrage *f* **2.** [decision] jugement *m*, décision *f*; LAW arrêt *m*.

adjudicator [ə'dʒu:dɪkeɪtə] n [of competition] juge *m*, arbitre *m*; [of dispute] arbitre *m*.

adjunct ['ædʒʌŋkt] n **1.** [addition] accessoire *m* **2.** [subordinate person] adjoint *m*, -e *f*, auxiliaire *mf*.

adjust [ə'dʒʌst] ❖ vt **1.** [regulate - heat, height, speed] ajuster, régler; [-knob, loudness] ajuster; [-brakes, machine, television] régler, mettre au point; [-clock] régler **2.** [alter -plan, programme] ajuster, mettre au point; [-length, size] ajuster; [-salary, wage] rajuster **3.** [correct] rectifier **4.** [position of clothing, hat] rajuster **5.** [adapt] ajuster, adapter. ❖ vi **1.** [adapt] s'adapter **2.** [chair, machine] se régler, s'ajuster.

adjustable [ə'dʒʌstəbl] adj [chair, height, speed] ajustable, réglable; [shape, size] ajustable, adaptable; [hours, rate] flexible ▸ **adjustable spanner** 🇬🇧 or **wrench** 🇺🇸 clé *f* à molette or anglaise.

adjusted [ə'dʒʌstɪd] adj : *well / poorly adjusted children* des enfants bien / mal équilibrés.

adjustment [ə'dʒʌstmənt] n **1.** [to heat, height, speed] ajustement *m*, réglage *m*; [to knob, loudness] ajustement *m*; [to brakes, machine, television] réglage *m*, mise *f* au point; [to clock] réglage *m* **2.** [to plan, programme] ajustement *m*, mise *f* au point; [to length, size] ajustement *m*; [to salary, wage] rajustement *m* **3.** [correction] rectification *f*.

adjutant ['ædʒʊtənt] n MIL adjudant-major *m*.

ad-lib [,æd'lɪb] (*pt & pp* **ad-libbed**, *cont* **ad-libbing**) vi & vt improviser.

adman ['ædmæn] (*pl* **admen** [-men]) n *inf* publicitaire *m*.

admin ['ædmɪn] (**abbr of administration**) n *inf* travail *m* administratif.

administer [ədˈmɪnɪstər] vt **1.** [manage -business, institution] diriger, administrer, gérer ; [-finances, fund] gérer ; [-country, public institution] administrer ; [-estate] régir **2.** *fml* [dispense -blow, medicine, punishment, test, last rites] administrer ; [-law] appliquer ; [-justice] rendre, dispenser.

administrate [ədˈmɪnɪstreɪt] vt = **administer** *(vt)*.

administration [əd,mɪnɪˈstreɪʃn] n **1.** [process -of business, institution] direction *f*, administration *f*, gestion *f* ; [-of finances, fund] gestion *f* ; [-of country, public institution] administration *f* ; [-of estate] curatelle *f* **2.** [people -of business, institution] direction *f*, administration *f* ; [-of country, public institution] administration *f* **3.** POL gouvernement *m*.

administrative [ədˈmɪnɪstrətɪv] adj administratif.

administrative costs pl n frais *mpl* d'administration or de gestion.

administrator [ədˈmɪnɪstreɪtər] n [of business, institution] directeur *m*, -trice *f*, administrateur *m*, -trice *f* ; [of area, public institution] administrateur *m*, -trice *f* ; [of estate] curateur *m*, -trice *f*.

admirable [ˈædmərəbl] adj admirable, excellent.

admirably [ˈædmərəbli] adv admirablement.

admiral [ˈædmərəl] n NAUT amiral *m*.

admiralty [ˈædmərəltɪ] (*pl* **admiralties**) n amirauté *f*.

admiration [,ædməˈreɪʃn] n [feeling] admiration *f*.

admire [ədˈmaɪər] vt admirer.

admirer [ədˈmaɪərər] n admirateur *m*, -trice *f*.

admiring [ədˈmaɪərɪŋ] adj admiratif.

admiringly [ədˈmaɪərɪŋlɪ] adv avec admiration.

admissibility [əd,mɪsəˈbɪlətɪ] n [of behaviour, plan] admissibilité *f* ; LAW recevabilité *f*.

admissible [ədˈmɪsəbl] adj [behaviour, plan] admissible ; [document] valable ; LAW [claim, evidence] recevable.

admission [ədˈmɪʃn] n **1.** [entry] admission *f*, entrée *f* / '**admission £1.50**' 'entrée £1.50' / *to gain admission to a club* être admis dans un club ; SCH & UNIV ▶ **admissions office** service *m* des inscriptions **2.** [fee] droit *m* d'entrée **3.** [statement] déclaration *f* ; [confession] aveu *m* / *an admission of guilt* un aveu.

> ⚠ The French word **admission** is not always the correct translation of the English word admission. See the entry for details.

admit [ədˈmɪt] (*pt & pp* **admitted**, *cont* **admitting**) vt **1.** [concede] admettre, reconnaître, avouer / *I admit I was wrong* je reconnais que j'ai eu tort / *it is generally admitted that women live longer than men* il est généralement admis que les femmes vivent plus longtemps que les hommes **2.** [confess] avouer / *he admitted taking bribes* il a reconnu avoir accepté des pots-de-vin **3.** [allow to enter -person] laisser entrer, faire entrer ; [-air, light] laisser passer, laisser entrer. ❖ **admit to** vt insep [acknowledge] admettre, reconnaître ; [confess] avouer / *she did admit to a feeling of loss* elle a effectivement avoué ressentir un sentiment de perte.

admittance [ədˈmɪtəns] n admission *f*, entrée *f* / '**no admittance**' 'accès interdit au public'.

admittedly [ədˈmɪtɪdlɪ] adv : *admittedly, he's weak on economics, but he's an excellent manager* d'accord, l'économie n'est pas son point fort, mais il fait un excellent gestionnaire / *our members, although admittedly few in number, are very keen* nos membres, peu nombreux il faut le reconnaître, sont très enthousiastes.

admixture [ædˈmɪkstʃər] n *fml* **1.** [mixture] mélange *m* **2.** [ingredient] ingrédient *m*.

admonish [ədˈmɒnɪʃ] vt *fml* [rebuke] réprimander, admonester.

admonition [,ædməˈnɪʃn] n [rebuke] réprimande *f*, remontrance *f*, admonestation *f*.

ad nauseam [,ædˈnɔːzɪæm] adv *lit* jusqu'à la nausée ; *fig* à satiété / *she went on about her holiday ad nauseam* elle nous a raconté ses vacances à n'en plus finir.

ado [əˈduː] n ▶ **without more** or **further ado** sans plus de cérémonie or de manières / '**Much Ado About Nothing**' *Shakespeare* 'Beaucoup de bruit pour rien'.

adolescence [,ædəˈlesns] n adolescence *f*.

adolescent [,ædəˈlesnt] ❖ n adolescent *m*, -e *f*. ❖ adj [boy, girl] adolescent ; *pej* [childish] enfantin, puéril *pej*.

adopt [əˈdɒpt] vt **1.** [child] adopter **2.** [choose -plan, technique] adopter, suivre, choisir ; [-country, name] adopter, choisir ; [-career] choisir, embrasser ; POL [candidate] choisir **3.** [assume -position] prendre ; [-accent, tone] adopter, prendre.

adopted [əˈdɒptɪd] adj [child] adoptif ; [country] d'adoption, adoptif.

adoption [əˈdɒpʃn] n [of child, country, custom] adoption *f*.

adoptive [əˈdɒptɪv] adj [child] adoptif ; [country] d'adoption, adoptif.

adorable [əˈdɔːrəbl] adj adorable.

adoration [,ædəˈreɪʃn] n adoration *f*.

adore [əˈdɔːr] vt **1.** RELIG adorer **2.** *inf* [like] adorer.

adoring [əˈdɔːrɪŋ] adj [look] d'adoration ; [smile] rempli d'adoration ; [mother] dévoué ; [fans] fervent.

adoringly [əˈdɔːrɪŋlɪ] adv avec adoration.

adorn [əˈdɔːn] vt *fml & liter* **1.** [decorate -dress, hair] orner, parer ; [-room, table] orner **2.** [story] embellir.

adornment [əˈdɔːnmənt] n **1.** [act, art] décoration *f* **2.** [of dress, hair] parure *f* ; [of room, table] ornement *m*.

ADP (abbr of **automatic data processing**) n TAI *m*.

adrenalin(e) [əˈdrenəlɪn] n adrénaline *f*.

Adriatic [,eɪdrɪˈætɪk] pr n ▶ **the Adriatic (Sea)** l'Adriatique *f*, la mer Adriatique.

adrift [əˈdrɪft] ❖ adv **1.** [boat] à la dérive / *their boat had been cut adrift* leur bateau avait été détaché **2.** 🇬🇧 [undone] ▶ **to come** or **to go adrift** se détacher, se défaire. ❖ adj [boat] à la dérive ; *fig* abandonné ▶ **to feel adrift** se sentir perdu.

adroit [əˈdrɔɪt] adj adroit, habile.

adroitness [əˈdrɔɪtnɪs] n adresse *f*.

ADSL [,eɪdiːesˈel] (abbr of **Asymmetric Digital Subscriber Line**) n ADSL *m*.

ADT (abbr of **Atlantic Daylight Time**) n heure d'été des Provinces maritimes du Canada et d'une partie des Caraïbes.

aduki bean [əˈduːkɪ-] n haricot *m* adzuki.

adulation [,ædjuˈleɪʃn] n flagornerie *f*.

adult [ˈædʌlt] ❖ n adulte *mf* / '**for adults only**' 'interdit aux moins de 18 ans'. ❖ adj **1.** [fully grown] adulte **2.** [mature] adulte **3.** [book, film, subject] pour adultes.

adult education n enseignement *m* pour adultes.

adulterate [əˈdʌltəreɪt] vt frelater.

adulteration [ə,dʌltəˈreɪʃn] n frelatage *m*.

adulterer [əˈdʌltərər] n adultère *m* (personne).

adulteress [əˈdʌltərɪs] n adultère *f*.

adulterous [əˈdʌltərəs] adj adultère.

adultery [əˈdʌltərɪ] n adultère *m* (acte).

adulthood [ˈædʌlthʊd] n âge *m* adulte.

adult student n 🇺🇸 = mature student.

advance [əd'vɑːns] ◆ vt **1.** [clock, tape, film] faire avancer ; [time, event] avancer / *the date of the meeting was advanced by one week* la réunion a été avancée d'une semaine **2.** [further - project, work] avancer ; [- interest, cause] promouvoir **3.** [suggest - idea, proposition] avancer, mettre en avant ; [- opinion] avancer, émettre ; [- explanation] avancer **4.** [money] avancer, faire une avance de. ◆ vi **1.** [go forward] avancer, s'avancer ▶ **to advance on** or **towards sthg** avancer or s'avancer vers qqch **2.** [make progress] avancer, progresser, faire des progrès. ◆ n **1.** [forward movement] avance f, marche f en avant ; MIL avance f, progression f **2.** [progress] progrès m **3.** [money] avance f / *an advance on his salary* une avance sur son salaire. ◆ comp **1.** [prior] préalable / *advance booking is advisable* il est recommandé de réserver à l'avance ▶ **advance booking office** guichet m de location ▶ **advance notice** préavis m, avertissement m ▶ **advance warning** avertissement m **2.** [preceding] ▶ **advance copy a)** [of book, magazine] exemplaire m de lancement **b)** [of speech] texte m distribué à l'avance. ❖ **advances** pl n avances fpl ▶ **to make advances to sb** faire des avances à qqn. ❖ **in advance** adv phr [beforehand - pay, thank] à l'avance, d'avance ; [- prepare, reserve, write] à l'avance. ❖ **in advance of** prep phr avant.

advanced [əd'vɑːnst] adj [course, education] supérieur ; [child, country, pupil] avancé ; [research, work] poussé ; [equipment, technology] avancé, de pointe ▶ **advanced mathematics** mathématiques fpl supérieures.

advancement [əd'vɑːnsmənt] n **1.** [promotion] avancement m, promotion f **2.** [improvement] progrès m, avancement m.

advancing [əd'vɑːnsɪŋ] adj qui approche, qui avance.

advantage [əd'vɑːntɪdʒ] n [benefit] avantage m / *they have an advantage over us* or *the advantage of us* ils ont un avantage sur nous / *it's to your advantage to learn another language* c'est (dans) ton intérêt d'apprendre une autre langue ▶ **to take advantage of sthg (to do sthg)** profiter de qqch (pour faire qqch) ▶ **to take advantage of sb a)** [make use of] profiter de qqn **b)** [exploit] exploiter qqn **c)** [abuse sexually] abuser de qqn / *this lighting shows the pictures to their best advantage* cet éclairage met les tableaux en valeur.

advantageous [ˌædvən'teɪdʒəs] adj avantageux.

advent ['ædvənt] n avènement m. ❖ **Advent** n RELIG l'Avent m.

Advent calendar n calendrier m de l'Avent.

adventure [əd'ventʃər] ◆ n **1.** [experience] aventure f **2.** [excitement] aventure f. ◆ comp [film, novel] d'aventures.

adventure game n COMPUT jeu m d'aventures.

adventure holiday n voyages organisés avec des activités sportives et de découverte.

adventure playground n 🇬🇧 aire f de jeux.

adventurer [əd'ventʃərər] n aventurier m ; pej aventurier m, intrigant m.

adventurous [əd'ventʃərəs] adj [person, spirit] aventureux, audacieux ; [life, project] aventureux, hasardeux.

adverb ['ædvɜːb] n adverbe m.

adverbial [əd'vɜːbɪəl] adj adverbial.

adversarial [ˌædvə'seərɪəl] adj antagoniste, hostile.

adversary ['ædvəsərɪ] n (pl **adversaries**) n adversaire mf.

adverse ['ædvɜːs] adj [comment, criticism, opinion] défavorable, hostile ; [circumstances, report] défavorable ; [effect] opposé, contraire ; [wind] contraire, debout.

adversely ['ædvɜːslɪ] adv [affect] : *the harvest was adversely affected by frost* la récolte a été très touchée par les gelées.

adversity [əd'vɜːsətɪ] (pl **adversities**) n [distress] adversité f.

advert¹ ['ædvɜːt] n 🇬🇧 inf [advertisement] (petite) annonce f ; COMM annonce f publicitaire, pub f.

advert² [əd'vɜːt] vi fml [refer] se rapporter, se référer.

advertise ['ædvətaɪz] ◆ vt **1.** COMM faire de la publicité pour **2.** [subj: individual, group] mettre une (petite) annonce pour / *we advertised our house in the local paper* nous avons mis or passé une annonce pour vendre notre maison dans le journal local. ◆ vi **1.** COMM faire de la publicité **2.** [make a request] chercher par voie d'annonce / *we advertised for a cook* nous avons mis or fait paraître une annonce pour trouver une cuisinière.

advertisement [🇬🇧 əd'vɜːtɪsmənt 🇺🇸 ˌædvər'taɪzmənt] n **1.** COMM [in all media] annonce f publicitaire, publicité f ; TV spot m publicitaire **2.** [for event, house, sale] (petite) annonce f / *to put an advertisement in the paper* passer une annonce dans le journal / *I got the job through an advertisement* j'ai eu le poste grâce à une annonce.

⚠ **Avertissement** means warning, not advertisement.

advertiser ['ædvəˌtaɪzər] n annonceur m (publicitaire).

advertising ['ædvətaɪzɪŋ] ◆ n (U) **1.** [promotion] publicité f **2.** [advertisements] publicité f **3.** [business] publicité f. ◆ comp [rates, revenues] publicitaire ▶ **advertising agency** agence f de publicité ▶ **advertising campaign** campagne f publicitaire or de publicité.

advertorial [ˌædvə'tɔːrɪəl] n publireportage m.

advice [əd'vaɪs] n (U) [counsel] conseil m / *a piece of advice* un conseil / *let me give you some advice* permettez que je vous donne un conseil or que je vous conseille ▶ **to take** or **follow sb's advice** suivre le conseil de qqn / *to take legal / medical advice* consulter un avocat / un médecin ▶ **advice column a)** [agony column] courrier m du cœur **b)** [for practical advice] rubrique f pratique.

advice slip n [from ATM] reçu m.

advisability [ədˌvaɪzə'bɪlətɪ] n opportunité f, bien-fondé m.

advisable [əd'vaɪzəbl] adj conseillé, recommandé.

advise [əd'vaɪz] vt [give advice to] conseiller, donner des conseils à ; [recommend] recommander ▶ **to advise sb to do sthg** conseiller à qqn de faire qqch / *he advised them against taking legal action* il leur a déconseillé d'intenter une action en justice.

advisedly [əd'vaɪzɪdlɪ] adv délibérément, en connaissance de cause.

adviser 🇬🇧, **advisor** 🇺🇸 [əd'vaɪzər] n conseiller m, -ère f ; SCH & UNIV conseiller m, -ère f pédagogique.

advisory [əd'vaɪzərɪ] adj [role, work] consultatif, de conseil / *he's employed in an advisory capacity* il est employé à titre consultatif.

advocacy ['ædvəkəsɪ] n soutien m appuyé, plaidoyer m.

advocate ◆ vt ['ædvəkeɪt] prôner, préconiser. ◆ n ['ædvəkət] **1.** [supporter] défenseur m, avocat m, -e f / *a strong advocate of free enterprise* un fervent partisan de la libre entreprise **2.** Scot [barrister] avocat m (plaidant), avocate f (plaidante).

advt written abbr of advertisement.

adware ['ædweər] n publiciel m.

adzuki bean [əd'zuːkɪ-] n haricot m adzuki.

A&E [ˌeiənˈdiː] (abbr of accident and emergency) n UK MED service m des urgences, urgences fpl.

Aegean [iːˈdʒiːən] ◆ pr n ▶ **the Aegean** la mer Égée. ◆ adj égéen ▶ **the Aegean Islands** les îles fpl de la mer Égée.

aegis [ˈiːdʒɪs] n MYTH & fig égide f ▶ **under the aegis of** sous l'égide de.

Aeolian Islands pl pr n ▶ **the Aeolian Islands** les îles fpl Éoliennes.

aeon UK, **eon** US [ˈiːɒn] n **1.** [age] période f incommensurable ; GEOL ère f **2.** PHILOS éon m.

aerate [ˈeəreɪt] vt **1.** [liquid] gazéifier ; [blood] oxygéner **2.** [soil] retourner.

aerated [ˈeəreɪtɪd] adj UK inf [angry] énervé.

aerial [ˈeərɪəl] ◆ adj [in the air] aérien. ◆ n UK RADIO & TV antenne f.

aerobatics [ˌeərəʊˈbætɪks] (pl aerobatics) n acrobatie f aérienne, acrobaties fpl aériennes.

aerobic [eəˈrəʊbɪk] adj aérobie.

aerobicized [eəˈrəʊbɪsaɪzd] adj [person] aux muscles tonifiés grâce à l'aérobic.

aerobics [eəˈrəʊbɪks] n (U) aérobic m ▶ **to do aerobics** faire de l'aérobic.

aerodrome [ˈeərədrəʊm] n aérodrome m.

aerodynamic [ˌeərəʊdaɪˈnæmɪk] adj aérodynamique.

aerodynamics [ˌeərəʊdaɪˈnæmɪks] n (U) aérodynamique f.

aerogram [ˈeərəɡræm] n **1.** [letter] aérogramme m **2.** [radiotelegram] radiotélégramme m.

aeromodelling, aeromodeling US [ˈeərəʊˌmɒdlɪŋ] n TECH aéromodélisme m.

aeronautics [ˌeərəˈnɔːtɪks] n (U) aéronautique f.

aeroplane [ˈeərəpleɪn] n UK avion m.

aerosol [ˈeərəsɒl] n **1.** [suspension system] aérosol m **2.** [container] bombe f, aérosol m.

aerospace [ˈeərəʊˌspeɪs] n aérospatiale f.

aesthete, esthete US [ˈiːsθiːt] n esthète mf.

aesthetic, esthetic US [iːsˈθetɪk] adj esthétique.

aesthetically, esthetically US [iːsˈθetɪklɪ] adv esthétiquement ▶ **aesthetically pleasing** agréable à l'œil.

aestheticism [iːsˈθetɪsɪzm] n esthétisme m.

aesthetics, esthetics US [iːsˈθetɪks] n (U) esthétique f.

AFAIK MESSAGING written abbr of as far as I know.

AFAIR MESSAGING written abbr of as far as I remember or recall.

afar [əˈfɑːr] adv liter au loin, à (grande) distance. ◆ **from afar** adv phr de loin.

AFB n abbr of air force base.

affable [ˈæfəbl] adj [person] affable, aimable ; [conversation, interview] chaleureux.

affably [ˈæfəblɪ] adv affablement, avec affabilité.

affair [əˈfeər] n **1.** [event] affaire f **2.** [business, matter] affaire f **3.** [concern] affaire f / whether I go or not is my affair que j'y aille ou non ne regarde que moi **4.** [sexual] liaison f, aventure f / they're having an affair ils couchent ensemble. ◆ **affairs** pl n [business, matters] affaires fpl / I'm not interested in your private affairs je ne m'intéresse pas à votre vie privée / to put one's affairs in order [business] mettre de l'ordre dans ses affaires / given the current state of affairs étant donné la situation actuelle, les choses étant ce qu'elles sont ▶ **affairs of state** affaires d'État.

⚠ Affair is not always translated by **affaire**. See the entry for details.

affect vt [əˈfekt] **1.** [have effect on - person, life] avoir un effet sur, affecter ; [influence - decision, outcome] influer sur, avoir une incidence sur / I don't see how your decision affects her je ne vois pas ce que votre décision change pour elle **2.** [concern, involve] toucher, concerner **3.** [emotionally] affecter, émouvoir, toucher / don't let it affect you ne vous laissez pas abattre par cela **4.** MED [subj: illness, epidemic] atteindre ; [subj: drug] agir sur / it has been proved that smoking affects your health il est prouvé que le tabac est nocif pour la santé / she has had a stroke, but her speech is not affected elle a eu une attaque, mais les fonctions du langage ne sont pas atteintes.

affectation [ˌæfekˈteɪʃn] n [in behaviour, manners] affectation f, manque m de naturel ; [in language, style] manque m de naturel.

affected [əˈfektɪd] adj [person, behaviour] affecté, maniéré ; [accent, dress, language] affecté, recherché.

-affected in comp affecté par ▶ **famine / drought-affected** affecté par la famine / sécheresse.

affectedly [əˈfektɪdlɪ] adv avec affectation, d'une manière affectée.

affection [əˈfekʃn] n **1.** [liking] affection f, tendresse f **2.** (usu pl) affection f ▶ **to gain** or **to win (a place in) sb's affections** gagner l'affection or le cœur de qqn.

affectionate [əˈfekʃənət] adj affectueux, tendre.

affectionately [əˈfekʃənətlɪ] adv affectueusement.

affidavit [ˌæfɪˈdeɪvɪt] n déclaration f sous serment (écrite).

affiliate ◆ vt [əˈfɪlɪeɪt] affilier ▶ **to affiliate o.s. to** or **with** s'affilier à. ◆ n [əˈfɪlɪət] [person] affilié m, -e f ; [organization] groupe m affilié.

affiliated [əˈfɪlɪeɪtɪd] adj [member, organization] affilié / an affiliated company une filiale.

affiliation [əˌfɪlɪˈeɪʃn] n **1.** ADMIN & COMM affiliation f **2.** [connection] attache f.

affinity [əˈfɪnətɪ] (pl affinities) n **1.** [connection, link] lien m, affinité f ; BIOL affinité f, parenté f ; CHEM affinité f / the affinities between the English and German languages la ressemblance or la parenté entre l'anglais et l'allemand **2.** [attraction] affinité f, attraction f / he has little affinity for or with modern art il est peu attiré par l'art moderne / she feels a strong sense of affinity with or for him elle se sent beaucoup d'affinités avec lui **3.** LAW [relation] affinité f.

affinity card [əˈfɪnɪtɪˌkɑːd] n carte f affinitaire.

affirm [əˈfɜːm] vt **1.** [state] affirmer, soutenir **2.** [profess - belief] professer, proclamer ; [- intention] proclamer **3.** [support - person] soutenir.

affirmation [ˌæfəˈmeɪʃn] n affirmation f, assertion f.

affirmative [əˈfɜːmətɪv] ◆ n **1.** GRAM affirmatif m / in the affirmative à l'affirmatif, à la forme affirmative **2.** [in reply] : the answer is in the affirmative la réponse est affirmative. ◆ adj affirmatif.

affirmative action n (U) US mesures fpl d'embauche antidiscriminatoires (en faveur des minorités).

affix vt [əˈfɪks] [seal, signature] apposer ; [stamp] coller ; [poster] afficher, poser.

afflict [əˈflɪkt] vt affecter / to be afflicted with a disease souffrir d'une maladie.

affliction [əˈflɪkʃn] n **1.** [suffering] affliction f ; [distress] détresse f **2.** [misfortune] affliction f, souffrance f.

affluence [ˈæfluəns] n [wealth] richesse f, aisance f.

⚠ In modern French, **affluence** refers to crowds of people arriving somewhere, never to wealth.

affluent ['æfluənt] adj [wealthy] aisé, riche.

afford [ə'fɔːd] vt **1.** [money] avoir les moyens de payer / *she couldn't afford to buy a car* elle n'avait pas les moyens d'acheter or elle ne pouvait pas se permettre d'acheter une voiture **2.** [time, energy] : *the doctor can only afford (to spend) a few minutes with each patient* le médecin ne peut pas se permettre de passer plus de quelques minutes avec chaque patient **3.** [allow o.s.] se permettre / *I can't afford to take any risks* je ne peux pas me permettre de prendre des risques **4.** *liter* [provide] fournir, offrir / *this affords me great pleasure* ceci me procure un grand plaisir.

affordability [ə,fɔːdə'bɪlɪtɪ] n prix m raisonnable.

affordable [ə'fɔːdəbl] adj [commodity] (dont le prix est) abordable.

afforestation [æ,fɒrɪ'steɪʃn] n boisement m.

affray [ə'freɪ] n échauffourée f.

affront [ə'frʌnt] n affront m, insulte f.

Afghan ['æfgæn] ◆ n [person] Afghan m, -e f. ◆ adj afghan.

Afghani [æf'gænɪ] n & adj GEOG & LING = **Afghan.**

Afghanistan [æf'gænɪstæn] pr n Afghanistan m.

aficionado [ə,fɪsjə'naːdəʊ] (pl **aficionados**) n aficionado m, amoureux m.

afield [ə'fiːld] adv : *to go far afield* aller loin / *people came from as far afield as Australia* les gens venaient même d'Australie.

AFL-CIO (abbr of American Federation of Labor and Congress of Industrial Organizations) pr n *la plus grande confédération syndicale américaine.*

afloat [ə'fləʊt] adv [floating] à flot, sur l'eau ▶ **to stay afloat a)** [swimmer] garder la tête hors de l'eau, surnager **b)** [boat] rester à flot ▶ **to keep sthg / sb afloat** maintenir qqch / qqn à flot; *fig* ▶ **to get a business afloat a)** [from start] mettre une entreprise à flot **b)** [from financial difficulties] renflouer une entreprise.

afoot [ə'fʊt] adv [in preparation] : *there is something afoot* il se prépare or il se trame quelque chose.

aforementioned [ə'fɔː,menʃənd] adj *fml* susmentionné, précité.

aforenamed [ə'fɔːneɪmd] adj *fml* susnommé, précité.

aforesaid [ə'fɔːsed] adj *fml* susdit, précité.

afraid [ə'freɪd] adj **1.** [frightened] ▶ **to be afraid** avoir peur ▶ **to make sb afraid** faire peur à qqn / *there's nothing to be afraid of* il n'y a rien à craindre / *he is afraid for his life* il craint pour sa vie **2.** [indicating reluctance, hesitation] : *he isn't afraid of work* il ne travail ne lui fait pas peur **3.** [indicating regret] : *I'm afraid I won't be able to come* je regrette or je suis désolé de ne pouvoir venir ▶ **I'm afraid to say...** j'ai le regret de dire... ▶ **I'm afraid so** j'ai bien peur que oui, j'en ai bien peur ▶ **I'm afraid not** j'ai bien peur que non, j'en ai bien peur.

📋 Note that avoir peur que and craindre que are followed by a verb in the subjunctive, usually preceded by ne:
I'm very much afraid all the money might be lost. *J'ai bien peur que tout cet argent ne soit perdu.*
I'm afraid you're mistaken. *Je crains que vous ne vous trompiez.*

afresh [ə'freʃ] adv de nouveau / *we'll have to start afresh* il va falloir recommencer or reprendre à zéro.

Africa ['æfrɪkə] pr n Afrique f.

African ['æfrɪkən] ◆ n Africain m, -e f. ◆ adj africain.

African American n Noir m américain, Noire f américaine.

African, Caribbean and Pacific Group of States n POL Groupe m des États d'Afrique, des Caraïbes et du Pacifique.

African National Congress n POL Congrès m national africain, ANC m.

African Union n POL Union f africaine.

African violet n saintpaulia m.

Afrikaans [,æfrɪ'kaːns] n afrikaans m.

Afrikaner [,æfrɪ'kaːnər] n Afrikaner mf.

Afro ['æfrəʊ] (pl **Afros**) ◆ adj [hairstyle] afro. ◆ n coiffure f afro.

Afro-American ◆ n Afro-Américain m, -e f. ◆ adj afro-américain.

Afro-Asian ◆ n Afro-Asiatique mf. ◆ adj afro-asiatique.

Afro-Caribbean ◆ n Afro-Antillais m, -e f. ◆ adj afro-antillais.

aft [aːft] ◆ adv NAUT & AERON à or vers l'arrière. ◆ adj [deck] arrière.

AFT (abbr of American Federation of Teachers) pr n *syndicat américain d'enseignants.*

after ['aːftər] ◆ prep **1.** [in time - gen] après; [- period] après, au bout de / *after a while* au bout d'un moment, après un moment / *after dark* après la tombée de la nuit / *it is after six o'clock already* il est déjà six heures passées or plus de six heures / *it's twenty after eight* US il est huit heures vingt / *the day after tomorrow* après-demain m / *after this date* ADMIN passé or après cette date **2.** [in space] après; [in series, priority, etc.] après / *Rothman comes after Richardson* Rothman, vient après Richardson ▶ **after you** [politely] après vous (je vous en prie) **3.** [following consecutively] : *day after day* jour après jour / *(for) mile after mile* sur des kilomètres et des kilomètres / *it's been one crisis after another ever since she arrived* on va de crise en crise depuis son arrivée **4.** [behind] après, derrière / *close the door after you* fermez la porte derrière vous **5.** [in view of] après / *after what you told me* après ce que vous m'avez dit **6.** [in spite of] : *after all the trouble I took, no-one came* après or malgré tout le mal que je me suis donné, personne n'est venu **7.** [in search of] ▶ **to be after sb / sthg** chercher qqn / qqch / *the police are after him* la police est à ses trousses, il est recherché par la police / *what's he after?* **a)** [want] qu'est-ce qu'il veut ? **b)** [looking for] qu'est-ce qu'il cherche ? **c)** [intend] qu'est-ce qu'il a derrière la tête ? ◆ adv après, ensuite / *the day after* le lendemain, le jour suivant / *the week after* la semaine d'après or suivante / *to follow (on) after* suivre. ◆ conj après que / *come and see me after you have spoken to him* venez me voir quand vous lui aurez parlé / *I came after he had left* je suis arrivé après qu'il soit parti / *after saying goodnight to the children* après avoir dit bonsoir aux enfants. ❖ **afters** pl n UK *inf* dessert m / *what's for afters?* qu'est-ce qu'il y a pour le dessert or comme dessert ? ❖ **after all** adv phr **1.** [when all's said and done] après tout **2.** [against expectation] après or malgré tout / *so she was right after all* alors elle avait raison en fait. ❖ **one after another, one after the other** adv phr l'un(e) après l'autre / *he made several mistakes one after the other* il a fait plusieurs fautes d'affilée or à la file.

afterbirth ['aːftəbɜːθ] n placenta m.

aftercare ['aːftəkeər] n MED postcure f.

after-dinner adj [speaker, speech] de fin de dîner or banquet / *an after-dinner drink* ≃ un digestif.

aftereffect ['ɑːftərɪˌfekt] n *(usu pl)* [gen] suite *f* ; MED séquelle *f*.

afterglow ['ɑːftəɡləʊ] n [of sunset] dernières lueurs *fpl*, derniers reflets *mpl* ; *fig* [of pleasure] sensation *f* de bien-être *(après coup)*.

after-hours adj [after closing time] qui suit la fermeture ; [after work] qui suit le travail. ❖ **after hours** adv phr [after closing time] après la fermeture ; [after work] après le travail.

afterlife ['ɑːftəlaɪf] n vie *f* après la mort.

aftermath ['ɑːftəmæθ] n [of event] séquelles *fpl*, suites *fpl* / *in the aftermath of the military coup* à la suite du coup d'État militaire.

afternoon [ˌɑːftə'nuːn] ❖ n après-midi *m inv* / *this afternoon* cet après-midi / *tomorrow* / *yesterday afternoon* demain / hier après-midi / *in the afternoon* a) [in general] l'après-midi b) [of particular day] (dans) l'après-midi / *on Friday afternoons* le vendredi après-midi / *on Friday afternoon* a) [in general] le vendredi après-midi b) [of particular day] vendredi après-midi / *at 2 o'clock in the afternoon* à 2 h de l'après-midi / *on the afternoon of May 16th* (dans) l'après-midi du 16 mai / *good afternoon* a) [hello] bonjour b) [goodbye] au revoir. ❖ comp [class, train] de l'après-midi ; [walk] qui a lieu dans l'après-midi ❱ **afternoon nap** or **rest** sieste *f* ❱ **afternoon performance** CIN & THEAT matinée *f*.

afterpains ['ɑːftəpeɪnz] pl n tranchées *fpl* utérines.

after-party n after *m*.

after-sales adj après-vente *(inv)* ❱ **after-sales service** service *m* après-vente.

after-school adj [activities] extrascolaire.

aftershave ['ɑːftəʃeɪv] n ❱ **aftershave (lotion)** (lotion *f*) après-rasage *m*, (lotion *f*) after-shave *m*.

after-shaving lotion n US = aftershave.

aftershock ['ɑːftəʃɒk] n réplique *f* (d'un séisme).

aftersun ['ɑːftəsʌn] adj ❱ **aftersun cream** crème *f* après-soleil.

aftertaste ['ɑːftəteɪst] n *lit & fig* arrière-goût *m*.

after-tax adj [profits] après impôts, net d'impôt ; [salary] net d'impôt.

afterthought ['ɑːftəθɔːt] n pensée *f* après coup / *the west wing was added as an afterthought* l'aile ouest a été ajoutée après coup.

afterwards US ['ɑːftəwədz], **afterward** US ['æftərwərd] adv après, ensuite / *I only realized afterwards* je n'ai compris qu'après coup or que plus tard.

again [ə'ɡen] adv **1.** [once more] encore une fois, de nouveau / *it's me again!* c'est encore moi !, me revoici ! / *here we are back home again!* nous revoilà chez nous ! / *you'll soon be well again* vous serez bientôt remis ❱ **yet again** encore une fois ; [with negative] ne... plus / *I didn't see them again* je ne les ai plus revus / *not you again!* encore vous ? ❱ **again and again** maintes et maintes fois, à maintes reprises **2.** [indicating forgetfulness] déjà / *what's her name again?* comment s'appelle-t-elle déjà ? **3.** [in quantity] ❱ **as much** / **many again** encore autant / *half as much again* encore la moitié de ça / *half as many pages again* la moitié plus de pages.

against [ə'ɡenst] ❖ prep **1.** [indicating position] contre / *he leant his bike (up) against the wall* il appuya son vélo contre le mur ; [indicating impact] contre / *I banged my knee against the chair* je me suis cogné le genou contre la chaise **2.** [in the opposite direction to - current, stream, grain] contre ; [contrary to - rules, principles] à

l'encontre de / *to go against a trend* s'opposer à une ou aller à l'encontre d'une tendance / *it's against the law to steal* le vol est interdit par la loi / *they sold the farm against my advice* / *wishes* ils ont vendu la ferme sans tenir compte de mes conseils / de ce que je souhaitais **3.** [indicating opposition to - person, proposal, government] contre / *the fight against inflation* / *crime* la lutte contre l'inflation / la criminalité ❱ **to decide against sthg** décider de ne pas faire qqch / *she's against telling him* elle trouve qu'on ne devrait pas le lui dire / *I've nothing against it* je n'ai rien contre **4.** [in competition with] contre ❱ **a race against time** or **the clock** une course contre la montre **5.** [in contrast to] contre, sur / *yellow flowers against a green background* des fleurs jaunes sur un fond vert **6.** [in comparison to, in relation to] en comparaison de, par rapport à / *the dollar fell against the yen* FIN le dollar a baissé par rapport au yen. ❖ adv contre / *are you for or against?* êtes-vous pour ou contre ? / *the odds are 10 to 1 against* a) [gen] il y a une chance sur dix **b)** [in horse racing] la cote est à 10 contre 1.

age [eɪdʒ] ❖ n **1.** [of person, animal, tree, building] âge *m* / *he is 25 years of age* il est âgé de 25 ans / *when I was your age* quand j'avais votre âge / *she's twice my age* elle a le double de mon âge / *I have a son your age* j'ai un fils de votre âge / *she doesn't look her age* elle ne fait pas son âge ❱ **act** or **be your age!** a) [be reasonable] sois raisonnable ! **b)** [don't be silly] ne sois pas stupide ! ❱ **to be of age** US LAW être majeur / *they are below the age of consent* ils tombent sous le coup de la loi sur la protection des mineurs ❱ **to come of age** atteindre sa majorité, devenir majeur **2.** [period - especially historical] époque *f*, âge *m* ; GEOL âge *m* / *through the ages* à travers les âges **3.** *(usu pl)* [long time] éternité *f* ❱ **ages ago** il y a une éternité / *I haven't seen you for* or *in ages!* cela fait une éternité que je ne vous ai (pas) vu ! ❖ vi vieillir, prendre de l'âge / *he's beginning to age* il commence à se faire vieux / *to age well* a) [person] vieillir bien **b)** [wine, cheese] s'améliorer en vieillissant. ❖ vt **1.** [person] vieillir **2.** [wine, cheese] laisser vieillir or mûrir.

age bracket n = age group.

aged ❖ adj **1.** [eɪdʒd] [of the age of] : *a man aged 50* un homme (âgé) de 50 ans **2.** ['eɪdʒɪd] [old] âgé, vieux *(before vowel or silent 'h' vieil, f vieille)*. ❖ pl n ❱ **the aged** les personnes *fpl* âgées.

age group n tranche *f* d'âge.

ageing ['eɪdʒɪŋ] adj [person] vieillissant, qui se fait vieux ; [society] de vieux ; [machinery, car] (qui se fait) vieux.

ageism, agism ['eɪdʒɪzm] n âgisme *m*.

ageist ['eɪdʒɪst] ❖ adj [action, policy] qui relève de l'âgisme. ❖ n personne qui fait preuve d'âgisme.

ageless ['eɪdʒlɪs] adj [person] sans âge, qui n'a pas d'âge ; [work of art] intemporel ; [beauty] toujours jeune.

age limit n limite *f* d'âge.

agency ['eɪdʒənsɪ] *(pl agencies)* n **1.** COMM [for employment] agence *f*, bureau *m* ; [for travel, accommodation] agence *f* **2.** ADMIN service *m*, bureau *m*.

agenda [ə'dʒendə] n **1.** [for meeting] ordre *m* du jour ; [for activities] programme *m* ❱ **to set the agenda** mener le jeu **2.** [set of priorities] ❱ **to have one's own agenda** avoir son propre programme.

> ⚠ The French word **agenda** means a diary or a schedule of events, never the agenda of a meeting.

agenda setting n fait d'influencer la direction d'un débat.

agent ['eɪdʒənt] n **1.** COMM agent m, représentant m, -e f ; [for travel, insurance] agent m ; [for firm] concessionnaire mf ; [for brand] dépositaire mf / where's the nearest Jaguar agent? où est le concessionnaire Jaguar le plus proche ? **2.** [for actor, sportsman, writer] agent m **3.** [spy] agent m.

age-old adj séculaire, antique.

aggravate ['ægrəveɪt] vt **1.** [worsen - illness, conditions] aggraver ; [- situation, problem] aggraver, envenimer ; [- quarrel] envenimer ; LAW ▸ **aggravated assault** coups et blessures **2.** [irritate - person] agacer, ennuyer.

aggravating ['ægreveɪtɪŋ] adj **1.** [worsening - situation, illness, conditions] aggravant **2.** [irritating - person, problem] agaçant, exaspérant.

aggravation [,ægrə'veɪʃn] n **1.** [deterioration - of situation, illness, conditions] aggravation f ; [- of dispute] envenimement m **2.** [irritation] agacement m, exaspération f.

aggregate n ['ægrɪgət] [total] ensemble m, total m ▸ **in the aggregate** or **on aggregate** dans l'ensemble, globalement ▸ **to win on aggregate** SPORT gagner au total des points.

aggression [ə'greʃn] n agression f.

aggressive [ə'gresɪv] adj [gen & PSYCHOL] agressif.

aggressively [ə'gresɪvlɪ] adv [behave] agressivement, avec agressivité ; [campaign] avec dynamisme.

aggressiveness [ə'gresɪvnɪs] n [gen] agressivité f.

aggressor [ə'gresə'] n agresseur m.

aggrieved [ə'griːvd] adj [gen] affligé, chagriné.

aggro ['ægrəʊ] n (U) 🇬🇧 inf **1.** [violence, fighting] grabuge m, bagarre f **2.** [fuss, bother] histoires fpl.

aghast [ə'gɑːst] adj [astounded] interloqué, pantois ; [horrified] horrifié, atterré.

agile [🇬🇧 'ædʒaɪl 🇺🇸 'ædʒəl] adj [person, animal] agile, leste.

agility [ə'dʒɪlətɪ] n [physical] agilité f, souplesse f.

aging ['eɪdʒɪŋ] adj & n = **ageing**.

agism = ageism.

agitate ['ædʒɪteɪt] vt **1.** [liquid] agiter, remuer **2.** [emotionally] agiter, troubler.

agitated ['ædʒɪteɪtɪd] adj agité, troublé / to become or to get agitated se mettre dans tous ses états.

agitation [,ædʒɪ'teɪʃn] n **1.** [emotional] agitation f, émoi m, trouble m / to be in a state of agitation être dans tous ses états **2.** [unrest] agitation f, troubles mpl ; [campaign] campagne f mouvementée.

agitator ['ædʒɪteɪtə'] n POL [person] agitateur m, -trice f.

agitprop ['ædʒɪtprop] n POL agit-prop f inv.

aglow [ə'gləʊ] adj [fire] rougeoyant ; [sky] embrasé.

AGM (abbr of annual general meeting) n 🇬🇧 AGA.

agnostic [æg'nɒstɪk] ◆ n agnostique mf. ◆ adj agnostique.

agnosticism [æg'nɒstɪsɪzm] n agnosticisme m.

ago [ə'gəʊ] adv : they moved here ten years ago ils ont emménagé ici il y a dix ans / how long ago did this happen? cela c'est produit il y a combien de temps ?, il y a combien de temps que cela s'est produit ? / as long ago as 1900 en 1900 déjà, dès 1900.

agog [ə'gɒg] adj en émoi / the children were all agog (with excitement) les enfants étaient tout excités.

agonize, agonise 🇬🇧 ['ægənaɪz] vi se tourmenter / to agonize over or about a decision hésiter longuement avant de prendre une décision / to agonize over how to do sthg se ronger les sangs or se tracasser pour savoir comment faire qqch.

⚠ **Agoniser** means to be dying, not to agonise.

agonized, agonised 🇬🇧 ['ægənaɪzd] adj [behaviour, reaction] angoissé, d'angoisse ; [cry] déchirant.

agonizing, agonising 🇬🇧 ['ægənaɪzɪŋ] adj [situation] angoissant ; [decision] déchirant, angoissant ; [pain] atroce.

agonizingly, agonisingly 🇬🇧 ['ægənaɪzɪŋlɪ] adv atrocement.

agony ['ægənɪ] (pl agonies) n **1.** [physical - pain] douleur f atroce ; [- suffering] souffrance f atroce, souffrances fpl atroces / to be in agony souffrir le martyre **2.** [emotional, mental] supplice m, angoisse f.

⚠ **Agonie** means "death throes" and should not be used to translate other meanings of agony.

agony aunt n 🇬🇧 responsable du courrier du cœur.

agony column n courrier m du cœur.

agoraphobia [,ægərə'fəʊbjə] n agoraphobie f.

agoraphobic [,ægərə'fəʊbɪk] adj agoraphobe.

agrarian [ə'greərɪən] ◆ adj agraire. ◆ n agrarien m, -enne f.

agree [ə'griː] ◆ vi **1.** [share same opinion] être d'accord / I quite agree je suis tout à fait d'accord (avec vous) ▸ **to agree about sthg** être d'accord sur qqch ▸ **to agree with sb** être d'accord avec or être du même avis que qqn **2.** [be in favour] être d'accord / I don't agree with censorship je suis contre or je n'admets pas la censure **3.** [assent] consentir, donner son adhésion / to agree to a proposal donner son adhésion à or accepter une proposition / to agree to sb's request consentir à la requête de qqn **4.** [reach agreement] se mettre d'accord **5.** [correspond - account, estimate] concorder **6.** [be suitable] : the climate here agrees with me le climat d'ici me réussit or me convient très bien / rich food doesn't agree with me la nourriture riche ne me réussit pas **7.** GRAM s'accorder. ◆ vt **1.** [share opinion] ▸ **to agree that...** être d'accord pour dire que... **2.** [consent] ▸ **to agree to do sthg** accepter de or consentir à faire qqch **3.** [admit] admettre, reconnaître / they agreed that they had made a mistake ils ont reconnu or convenu qu'ils avaient fait une faute **4.** [reach agreement on] convenir de ▸ **we agreed to differ** nous sommes restés chacun sur notre position / it was agreed that the money should be invested il a été convenu que l'argent serait investi / to agree a price se mettre d'accord sur un prix ▸ **unless otherwise agreed** LAW sauf accord contraire.

📝 Note that accepter que is followed by a verb in the subjunctive:
They ended up agreeing to let us take the next flight. Ils ont fini par accepter que nous prenions le vol suivant.

agreeable [ə'grɪəbl] adj **1.** [pleasant - situation] plaisant, agréable ; [- person] agréable **2.** [willing] consentant **3.** [acceptable] acceptable, satisfaisant.

agreeably [ə'grɪəblɪ] adv agréablement.

agreed [ə'griːd] ◆ adj **1.** [in agreement] d'accord **2.** [fixed - time, place, price] convenu / as agreed comme convenu. ◆ interj ▸ **agreed!** (c'est) d'accord or entendu !

agreement [ə'griːmənt] n **1.** [gen] accord m ▶ **to be in agreement with sb about sthg** être d'accord avec qqn sur qqch or au sujet de qqch ▶ **to reach agreement** parvenir à un accord **2.** GRAM accord m.

agrichemical [ˌægrɪ'kemɪkəl] ◆ n produit m agrochimique. ◆ adj agrochimique.

agricultural [ˌægrɪ'kʌltʃərəl] adj [produce, machinery, land, society] agricole ; [expert] agronome ; [college] d'agriculture, agricole.

agriculture ['ægrɪkʌltʃər] n agriculture f.

agritourism ['ægrɪtʊərɪzəm] n agritourisme m.

agrochemical [ˌægrəʊ'kemɪkəl] ◆ n produit m agrochimique. ◆ adj agrochimique.

agrochemistry [ˌægrəʊ'kemɪstrɪ] n agrochimie f.

agroclimatology [ˌægrəʊklaɪmə'tɒlədʒɪ] n agroclimatologie f.

agro-industrial ['ægrəʊ-] n agro-industriel.

agro-industry ['ægrəʊ-] n agro-industrie f.

agroterrorism ['ægrəʊterərɪzəm] n agro-terrorisme m.

agroterrorist ['ægrəʊterərɪst] n agro-terroriste mf.

aground [ə'graʊnd] adv ▶ **to run** or **to go aground** s'échouer.

ah [ɑː] interj ▶ **ah!** ah !

aha [ɑː'hɑː] interj ▶ **aha!** ah, ah !, tiens !

ahead [ə'hed] adv **1.** [in space] en avant, devant / the road ahead la route devant nous / eux, etc. / there's a crossroads about half a mile ahead il y a un croisement à environ 800 mètres (d'ici) / go / drive on ahead and I'll catch you up vas-y or pars en avant, je te rattraperai / to push or press ahead with a project poursuivre un projet **2.** [in time] : the years ahead les années à venir / what lies ahead? qu'est-ce qui nous attend ? / looking ahead to the future en pensant à l'avenir / to plan ahead faire des projets / we must think ahead nous devons prévoir **3.** [in competition, race] en avance / three lengths / five points ahead trois longueurs / cinq points d'avance. ❖ **ahead of** prep phr **1.** [in front of] devant **2.** [in time] : he arrived ten minutes ahead of me il est arrivé dix minutes avant moi / to finish ahead of schedule terminer plus tôt que prévu or en avance / the rest of the team are two months ahead of us les autres membres de l'équipe ont deux mois d'avance sur nous ▶ **to be ahead of one's time** fig être en avance sur son époque.

ahem [ə'hem] interj ▶ **ahem!** hum !

a-hole ['eɪhəʊl] n US vulg = **asshole**.

ahoy [ə'hɔɪ] interj ▶ **ahoy!** ohé !, holà ! ▶ **ship ahoy!** ohé du navire !

AI n **1.** (abbr of **artificial intelligence**) IA f **2.** (abbr of **artificial insemination**) IA f.

AICE [eɪs] (abbr of **Advanced International Certificate of Education**) n SCH diplôme international d'études secondaires qui donne accès aux études universitaires, délivré par l'université de Cambridge.

aid [eɪd] ◆ n **1.** [help, assistance] aide f ▶ **to come to sb's aid** venir à l'aide de qqn ▶ **to go to the aid of sb** se porter au secours de or porter secours à qqn **2.** POL aide f ▶ **overseas aid** aide au tiers-monde **3.** [helpful equipment] aide f, support m ▶ **teaching aids** supports or aides pédagogiques ▶ **visual aids** supports visuels **4.** [assistant] aide mf, assistant m, -e f. ◆ vt **1.** [help - person] aider, venir en aide à ; [- financially] aider, secourir ▶ **to aid sb with sthg** aider qqn pour qqch **2.** [give support to - region, industry] aider, soutenir **3.** [encourage - development, understanding] contribuer à **4.** LAW ▶ **to aid and abet sb** être (le) complice de qqn. ❖ **in aid of** prep phr : a collection in aid of the homeless une collecte au profit des sans-abri / what are the cakes in aid of? UK inf les gâteaux sont en l'honneur de quoi ?

AID n (abbr of **artificial insemination by donor**) IAD f.

aide [eɪd] n aide mf, assistant m, -e f.

aids, AIDS [eɪdz] (abbr of **acquired immune deficiency syndrome**) ◆ n sida m. ◆ comp [clinic] pour personnes atteintes du sida ▶ **aids patient** or **sufferer** personne f atteinte du sida ▶ **aids specialist** sidologue mf ▶ **aids test** test m du sida ▶ **the aids virus** le virus du sida.

aids-related adj lié au sida.

aid worker n [voluntary] volontaire mf ; [paid] employé m, -e f d'une organisation humanitaire.

AIH (abbr of **artificial insemination by husband**) n IAC f.

ail [eɪl] vi être souffrant.

ailing ['eɪlɪŋ] adj [person] souffrant, en mauvaise santé ; [economy, industry] malade.

ailment ['eɪlmənt] n mal m, affection f.

aim [eɪm] ◆ n **1.** [intention, purpose] but m ▶ **with the aim of** afin de, dans le but de **2.** [with weapon] ▶ **to take aim (at sthg / sb)** viser (qqch / qqn) / to have a good aim bien viser. ◆ vt **1.** [gun] braquer ; [missile] pointer ; [stone] lancer ; [blow] allonger, décocher ; [kick] donner / he aimed his gun at the man's head il a braqué son pistolet sur la tête de l'homme **2.** fig [criticism, product, programme] destiner / was that remark aimed at me? est-ce que cette remarque m'était destinée ? ◆ vi **1.** [take aim] ▶ **to aim at** or **for sthg** viser qqch **2.** [have as goal] : to aim high viser haut.

aimless ['eɪmlɪs] adj [person] sans but, désœuvré ; [life] sans but ; [occupation, task] sans objet, futile.

aimlessly ['eɪmlɪslɪ] adv [walk around] sans but ; [stand around] sans trop savoir quoi faire.

ain't [eɪnt] inf **1.** abbr of am not **2.** abbr of is not **3.** abbr of are not **4.** abbr of has not **5.** abbr of have not.

air [eər] ◆ n **1.** [gen & PHYS] air m / I went out for a breath of (fresh) air je suis sorti prendre l'air ▶ **to disappear** or **vanish into thin air** se volatiliser, disparaître sans laisser de traces **2.** [sky] air m, ciel m / the smoke rose into the air la fumée s'éleva vers le ciel ▶ **to throw sthg up into the air** lancer qqch en l'air / seen from the air, the fields looked like a chessboard vus d'avion, les champs ressemblaient à un échiquier **3.** AERON : to travel by air voyager par avion **4.** RADIO & TV ▶ **to go on the air** a) [person] passer à l'antenne b) [programme] passer à l'antenne, être diffusé ▶ **to go off the air** a) [person] rendre l'antenne b) [programme] se terminer c) [station] cesser d'émettre **5.** [manner, atmosphere] air m / there is an air of mystery about her elle a un air mystérieux. ◆ comp [piracy, traffic] aérien ; [travel, traveller] par avion. ◆ vt **1.** [linen, bed, room] aérer **2.** [express - opinion, grievance] exprimer, faire connaître ; [- suggestion, idea] exprimer, avancer. ◆ vi US : the movie airs next week le film sera diffusé la semaine prochaine. ❖ **airs** pl n ▶ **to put on** or **to give o.s. airs** donner de grands airs ▶ **airs and graces** UK minauderies fpl. ❖ **in the air** adv phr : there's a rumour in the air that they're going to sell le bruit court qu'ils vont vendre / there's something in the air il se trame quelque chose / the project is still very much (up) in the air le projet n'est encore qu'à l'état d'ébauche or est encore vague.

air ambulance n avion m sanitaire.

airbag ['eəbæg] n AUTO Air Bag® m, coussin m gonflable.

airbase ['eəbeɪs] n base f aérienne.

airbed ['eəbed] n matelas *m* pneumatique.

airborne ['eəbɔːn] adj [plane] en vol / *to become airborne* décoller.

airbrake ['eəbreɪk] n AUTO frein *m* à air comprimé ; AERON aérofrein *m*, frein *m* aérodynamique.

airbrush ['eəbrʌʃ] vt peindre au pistolet.

air bubble n [in wallpaper, liquid] bulle *f* d'air.

Airbus® ['eəbʌs] n Airbus *m*.

air-conditioned adj climatisé.

air-conditioner n climatiseur *m*.

air-conditioning n climatisation *f*.

air-cooled [-kuːld] adj [engine] à refroidissement par air.

aircraft ['eəkrɑːft] (*pl* **aircraft**) n avion *m*.

aircraft carrier n porte-avions *m* inv.

aircrew ['eəkruː] n équipage *m* (d'avion).

air cushion n [gen] coussin *m* pneumatique ; TECH coussin *m* or matelas *m* d'air.

airer ['eərə'] n UK [for clothes] séchoir *m*.

airfare ['eəfeə'] n prix *m* du billet (d'avion), tarif *m* aérien.

airfield ['eəfiːld] n terrain *m* d'aviation, (petit) aérodrome *m*.

air force, airforce n armée *f* de l'air.

Air Force One n *nom de l'avion officiel du président des États-Unis.*

air freight, airfreight ['eəfreɪt] n [cargo] fret *m* aérien ; [transport] transport *m* aérien ▶ **to send sthg by airfreight** expédier qqch par voie aérienne or par avion.

air freighter n avion-cargo *m*.

air freshener [-'freʃənə'] n désodorisant *m* (*pour la maison*).

airgun ['eəgʌn] n [rifle] carabine *f* or fusil *m* à air comprimé ; [pistol] pistolet *m* à air comprimé.

airhead ['eəhed] n *inf* taré *m*, -e *f*.

air hostess ['eə,həʊstɪs] n hôtesse *f* de l'air.

airily ['eərəlɪ] adv avec désinvolture.

airing ['eərɪŋ] n **1.** [of linen, room] aération *f* **2.** fig : *to give an idea an airing* agiter une idée, mettre une idée sur le tapis.

airing cupboard n *placard chauffé faisant office de sèche-linge.*

air-kiss ['eəkɪs] vi s'embrasser (avec affectation).

airlane ['eəleɪn] n couloir *m* aérien or de navigation aérienne.

airless ['eəlɪs] adj **1.** [room] qui manque d'air, qui sent le renfermé **2.** [weather] lourd.

air letter n aérogramme *m*.

airlift ['eəlɪft] ◆ n pont *m* aérien. ◆ vt [passengers, troops - out] évacuer par pont aérien ; [- in] faire entrer par pont aérien ; [supplies, cargo] transporter par pont aérien.

airline ['eəlaɪn] n AERON ligne *f* aérienne.

airliner ['eəlaɪnə'] n avion *m* de ligne.

airlock ['eəlɒk] n **1.** [in spacecraft, submarine] sas *m* **2.** [in pipe] poche *f* or bulle *f* d'air.

airmail ['eəmeɪl] n poste *f* aérienne / **'by airmail'** [on envelope] 'par avion'.

airman ['eəmən] (*pl* **airmen** [-mən]) n **1.** [gen] aviateur *m* **2.** US MIL soldat *m* de première classe (de l'armée de l'air).

air marshal n général *m* de corps aérien.

air mattress n matelas *m* pneumatique.

Air Miles® n *programme de fidélité permettant de bénéficier d'avantages en fonction des distances parcourues en avion.*

airplane ['eəpleɪn] n US avion *m* ▶ **airplane mode** [on mobile phone] mode *m* avion.

airplay ['eəpleɪ] n : *that song is getting a lot of airplay* on entend souvent cette chanson à la radio.

air pocket n [affecting plane] trou *m* d'air ; [in pipe] poche *f* d'air.

air pollution n pollution *f* atmosphérique.

airport ['eəpɔːt] n aéroport *m* ▶ **airport fiction** romans *mpl* de gare ▶ **airport terminal** aérogare *f*.

air pressure n pression *f* atmosphérique.

air raid n attaque *f* aérienne, raid *m* aérien.

air-raid shelter n abri *m* antiaérien.

air rifle n carabine *f* à air comprimé.

air-sea rescue n sauvetage *m* en mer (*par hélicoptère*).

airship ['eəʃɪp] n dirigeable *m*.

airsick ['eəsɪk] adj ▶ **to be** or **to get airsick** avoir le mal de l'air.

airspace ['eəspeɪs] n espace *m* aérien.

airspeed ['eəspiːd] n vitesse *f* relative.

air steward n steward *m*.

air stewardess n *dated* hôtesse *f* de l'air.

airstrike ['eəstraɪk] n raid *m* aérien.

airstrip ['eəstrɪp] n terrain *m* or piste *f* d'atterrissage.

air terminal n aérogare *f*.

airtight ['eətaɪt] adj hermétique, étanche (à l'air).

airtime ['eətaɪm] n **1.** RADIO & TV : *that song is getting a lot of airtime* on entend souvent cette chanson à la radio **2.** [on mobile phone] temps *m* de communication.

air-to-air adj MIL air-air (*inv*), avion-avion (*inv*).

air-to-surface adj MIL air-sol (*inv*).

air-traffic control n contrôle *m* du trafic aérien.

air-traffic controller n contrôleur *m*, -euse *f* du trafic aérien, aiguilleur *m* du ciel.

air travel n déplacement *m* or voyage *m* par avion.

airwaves ['eəweɪvz] pl n ondes *fpl* (hertziennes) ▶ **on the airwaves** sur les ondes, à la radio.

airway ['eəweɪ] n **1.** AERON [route] voie *f* aérienne ; [company] ligne *f* aérienne **2.** MED voies *fpl* respiratoires.

airworthiness ['eə,wɜːðɪnɪs] n AERON tenue *f* en l'air, navigabilité *f* / *certificate of airworthiness* certificat *m* de navigabilité.

airworthy ['eə,wɜːðɪ] adj en état de navigation.

airy ['eərɪ] (*compar* **airier**, *superl* **airiest**) adj **1.** [room] bien aéré, clair **2.** fig [casual - manner] insouciant, désinvolte ; [- ideas, plans, promises] en l'air.

airy-fairy adj UK *inf* [person, notion] farfelu.

aisle [aɪl] n **1.** [in church] bas-côté *m*, nef *f* latérale / *her father led her up the aisle* c'est son père qui l'a menée à l'autel **2.** [in cinema, supermarket, aeroplane] allée *f* ; [on train] couloir *m* (central) ▶ **aisle seat a)** [train] siège *m* côté couloir **b)** [aeroplane] siège *m* au bord d'une) allée.

ajar [ə'dʒɑː'] ◆ adj [door, window] entrouvert, entrebâillé. ◆ adv : *the door stood ajar* la porte est restée entrouverte.

AK written abbr of Alaska.

aka, AKA (abbr of also known as) adv alias, dit.

akimbo [ə'kɪmbəʊ] adv ▶ **with arms akimbo** les mains or poings sur les hanches.

akin [ə'kɪn] adj ▶ **akin to a)** [like] qui ressemble à, qui tient de **b)** [related to] apparenté à.

AL written abbr of Alabama.

Alabama [,ælə'bæmə] pr n Alabama *m*.

alabaster [,ælə'bɑːstə'] n albâtre *m*.

alacrity [ə'lækrətɪ] n *fml* empressement *m*.

Aladdin [ə'lædɪn] pr n Aladin ▸ **Aladdin's cave** *fig* caverne *f* d'Ali Baba.

alarm [ə'lɑːm] ◆ n **1.** [warning] alarme *f*, alerte *f* ▸ **to sound** or **to raise the alarm** donner l'alarme or l'alerte or l'éveil **2.** [anxiety] inquiétude *f*, alarme *f* ▸ *there is no cause for alarm* il n'y a aucune raison de s'alarmer **3.** = **alarm clock.** ◆ comp [signal] d'alarme ▸ **alarm bell** sonnerie *f* d'alarme ▸ *to set (the) alarm bells ringing* *fig* donner l'alerte ▸ **alarm call** [to wake sleeper] réveil *m* téléphonique. ◆ vt **1.** [frighten, worry - person] alarmer, faire peur à ; [- animal] effaroucher, faire peur à **2.** [warn] alerter.

alarm clock n réveil *m*, réveille-matin *m* inv.

alarmed [ə'lɑːmd] adj **1.** [anxious] inquiet / *don't be alarmed* ne vous alarmez or effrayez pas **2.** [vehicle, building] équipé d'une alarme.

alarming [ə'lɑːmɪŋ] adj alarmant.

alarmingly [ə'lɑːmɪŋlɪ] adv d'une manière alarmante.

alarmist [ə'lɑːmɪst] ◆ adj alarmiste. ◆ n alarmiste *mf*.

alas [ə'læs] interj ▸ **alas!** hélas !

Alaska [ə'læskə] pr n Alaska *m*.

Albania [æl'beɪnjə] pr n Albanie *f*.

Albanian [æl'beɪnjən] ◆ n [person] Albanais *m*, -e *f*. ◆ adj albanais.

albatross ['ælbətrɒs] n ZOOL & SPORT albatros *m*.

albeit [ɔːl'biːɪt] conj bien que, encore que, quoique.

Alberta [æl'bɜːtə] pr n Alberta *m*.

Albert Hall ['ælbət-] pr n ▸ **the Albert Hall** *salle de concert à Londres*.

The Albert Hall

Grande salle londonienne accueillant concerts et manifestations diverses; elle porte le nom du prince Albert, époux de la reine Victoria. Réputée pour sa grande capacité, elle est souvent évoquée dans des comparaisons métaphoriques : **enough people to fill the Albert Hall.**

albino [æl'biːnəʊ] n albinos *mf*.

album ['ælbəm] n [book, CD] album *m* ▸ **album cover** pochette *f* de disque.

albumen ['ælbjʊmən] n **1.** [egg white] albumen *m*, blanc *m* de l'œuf **2.** = **albumin.**

albumin ['ælbjʊmɪn] n albumine *f*.

alchemist ['ælkəmɪst] n alchimiste *m*.

alchemy ['ælkəmɪ] n alchimie *f*.

alcohol ['ælkəhɒl] n alcool *m* ▸ **alcohol content** teneur *f* en alcool.

alcohol-free adj sans alcool.

alcoholic [,ælkə'hɒlɪk] ◆ adj [drink] alcoolisé ; [person] alcoolique. ◆ n alcoolique *mf*.

alcoholism ['ælkəhɒlɪzm] n alcoolisme *m*.

alcopop ['ælkəʊpɒp] n prémix *m*.

alcove ['ælkəʊv] n [in room] alcôve *f* ; [in wall] niche *f* ; [in garden] tonnelle *f*.

ale [eɪl] n bière *f* (anglaise), ale *f*. ⟶ **beer**

alert [ə'lɜːt] ◆ n alerte *f* ▸ **to give the alert** donner l'alerte ▸ **to be on the alert a)** [gen] être sur le qui-vive **b)** MIL être en état d'alerte. ◆ adj **1.** [vigilant] vigilant, sur le qui-vive **2.** [lively - child, mind] vif, éveillé. ◆ vt alerter,

donner l'alerte à / *the public should be alerted to these dangers* on devrait attirer l'attention du public sur ces dangers, on devrait sensibiliser l'opinion publique à ces dangers.

alert box n COMPUT message *m* d'alerte.

A-level (abbr of **advanced level**) n 🇬🇧 SCH ▸ **A-levels** or **A-level exams** ≃ baccalauréat *m* / *he teaches A-level physics* ≃ il est professeur de physique en terminale / *to take one's A-levels* ≃ passer son bac.

 **A-level**

Examen sanctionnant la fin du cycle secondaire en Grande-Bretagne. Il se prépare en deux ans après le **GCSE** et donne accès aux études supérieures. Il est beaucoup plus spécialisé que le baccalauréat français, les élèves ne présentent en moyenne que trois matières. Chaque **A-level** est noté séparément et les élèves s'efforcent d'obtenir les meilleurs résultats dans chacune des matières, car le système d'accès à l'Université est très sélectif. En Écosse, l'examen équivalent est le **Higher** ou le **Higher Grade**, qui est moins spécialisé et comprend cinq matières.

alfalfa [æl'fælfə] n luzerne *f*.

alfresco [æl'freskəʊ] adj & adv en plein air.

algae ['ældʒiː] pl n algues *fpl*.

algebra ['ældʒɪbrə] n algèbre *f*.

Algeria [æl'dʒɪərɪə] pr n Algérie *f*.

Algerian [æl'dʒɪərɪən] ◆ n Algérien *m*, -enne *f*. ◆ adj algérien.

Algiers [æl'dʒɪəz] pr n Alger *m*.

algorithm ['ælgərɪðm] n algorithme *m*.

alias ['eɪlɪəs] ◆ adv alias. ◆ n [name] nom *m* d'emprunt, faux nom *m* ; [of author] nom *m* de plume, pseudonyme *m*.

aliasing ['eɪlɪəsɪŋ] n COMPUT aliassage *m*, crénelage *m*.

alibi ['ælɪbaɪ] n LAW alibi *m* ; *fig* alibi *m*, excuse *f*.

Alice band n bandeau *m* (*pour les cheveux*).

alien ['eɪljən] ◆ n **1.** ADMIN [foreigner] étranger *m*, -ère *f* **2.** [in science fiction] extraterrestre *mf*. ◆ adj **1.** [foreign - customs, environment] étranger **2.** [contrary] ▸ **alien to sthg** contraire or opposé à qqch **3.** [in science fiction] extraterrestre.

alienate ['eɪljəneɪt] vt [gen & LAW] aliéner / *this tax will alienate the people* avec cet impôt, ils vont s'aliéner la population.

alienated ['eɪljəneɪtɪd] adj : *many young people feel alienated and alone* beaucoup de jeunes se sentent seuls et rejetés.

alienation [,eɪljə'neɪʃn] n [of support, friends] fait *m* de décourager or d'éloigner.

alight [ə'laɪt] ◆ vi [bird] se poser ; [person - from bus, train] descendre ; [- from bike, horse] descendre, mettre pied à terre. ◆ adj [fire] allumé ; [house] en feu. ◆ adv ▸ **to set sthg alight** mettre le feu à qqch.

align [ə'laɪn] ◆ vt **1.** [place in line - points, objects] aligner, mettre en ligne **2.** FIN & POL aligner ▸ **to align o.s. with sb** s'aligner sur qqn. ◆ vi [points, objects] être aligné ; [persons, countries] s'aligner.

alignment [ə'laɪnmənt] n **1.** [gen & POL] alignement *m* **2.** AUTO parallélisme *m*.

alike [ə'laɪk] ◆ adj semblable / *no two are alike* il n'y en a pas deux pareils. ◆ adv [act, speak, dress] de la même façon or manière / *they look alike* ils se ressemblent / *this affects Peter and his brother alike* cela touche Peter aussi bien que son frère.

alimentary canal n tube *m* digestif.

alimony ['ælɪmənɪ] n pension f alimentaire.

A-line adj [skirt, dress] trapèze *(inv)*.

A-list n **1.** [in Hollywood] *liste des stars les plus en vue du moment* **2.** [for party] *liste d'invités de marque.*

alive [ə'laɪv] adj **1.** [living] vivant, en vie / *while he was alive* de son vivant / *to be burnt alive* être brûlé vif / *to bury sb alive* enterrer qqn vivant / *to keep alive* **a)** [person] maintenir en vie **b)** [hope] garder **c)** [tradition] préserver / *they kept her memory alive* ils sont restés fidèles à sa mémoire / *it's good to be alive* il fait bon vivre **2.** [lively, full of life] plein de vie, vif, actif / *she always comes alive in the evening* elle se réveille toujours le soir **3.** [full, crowded] : *the streets were alive with people* les rues fourmillaient or grouillaient de monde.

alkali ['ælkəlaɪ] n alcali *m*.

alkaline ['ælkəlaɪn] adj alcalin.

all [ɔːl] ◆ det [the whole of] tout (toute), tous (toutes) / *all expenses will be reimbursed* tous les frais seront remboursés / *all day and all night* toute la journée et toute la nuit ; [every one of a particular type] : *all kinds of people* toutes sortes de gens / *for children of all ages* pour les enfants de tous les âges. ◆ predet **1.** [the whole of] tout (toute), tous (toutes) / *all the butter* tout le beurre / *all five women* les cinq femmes **2.** [with comparative adjectives] ▸ **all the better!** tant mieux ! / *you will feel all the better for a rest* un peu de repos vous fera le plus grand bien / *it's all the more unfair since* or *as he promised not to put up the rent* c'est d'autant plus injuste qu'il a promis de ne pas augmenter le loyer. ◆ pron **1.** [everything] tout / *all I want is to rest* tout ce que je veux c'est du repos / *will that be all?* ce sera tout ? / *it was all I could do not to laugh* j'ai eu du mal à m'empêcher de rire / *it's all his fault* c'est sa faute à lui / *you men are all the same!* vous les hommes, vous êtes tous pareils or tous les mêmes ! **2.** [everyone] tous / *don't all speak at once!* ne parlez pas tous en même temps ! **3.** SPORT : *the score is 5 all* le score est de 5 partout / *30 all* [in tennis] 30 partout **4.** [as quantifier] : *all of the butter* / *the cakes* tout le beurre / tous les gâteaux / *all of London* Londres tout entier / *all of it was sold* (le) tout a été vendu / *listen, all of you* écoutez-moi tous / *the book cost me all of £10* le livre ne m'a coûté que 10 livres / *it's all of five minutes' walk away!* hum c'est AU MOINS à cinq minutes à pied ! hum. ◆ adv [as intensifier] tout / *she was all alone* elle était toute seule / *she was all excited* elle était tout excitée / *she was all dressed* or *she was dressed all in black* elle était habillée tout en noir / *the soup went all down my dress* la soupe s'est répandue partout sur ma robe ▸ **to be all for sthg**: *I'm all for it* moi, je suis tout à fait pour. ◆ n tout ▸ **I would give my all to be there** je donnerais tout ce que j'ai pour y être ▸ **the team gave their all** l'équipe a donné son maximum ▸ **to stake one's all** tout miser. ❖ **all along** adv phr depuis le début. ❖ **all but** adv phr presque / *all but finished* presque or pratiquement fini / *I all but missed it* j'ai bien failli le rater, c'est tout juste si je ne l'ai pas raté. ❖ **all in all** adv phr tout compte fait. ❖ **all over** ◆ adj phr [finished] fini / *that's all over and done with now* tout ça c'est bien terminé maintenant. ◆ prep phr partout / *you've got ink all over you!* tu t'es mis de l'encre partout ! / *all over the world* dans le monde entier ▸ **to be all over sb**: *he was all over her* il ne l'a pas laissée tranquille un instant. ◆ adv phr [everywhere] partout / *it was like being a child all over again* c'était comme retomber

en enfance / *that's him all over!* inf ça c'est lui tout craché ! ❖ **all told** adv phr tout compris. ❖ **all too** adv phr : *all too soon* bien trop vite / *the holidays went all too quickly* les vacances ne sont passées que trop vite / *it's all too easy to forget that* c'est tellement facile de l'oublier.

Allah ['ælə] pr n Allah.

all-American adj cent pour cent américain.

all-around adj ᴜꜱ = all-round.

allay [ə'leɪ] vt [fear] apaiser ; [doubt, suspicion] dissiper ; [pain, grief] soulager, apaiser.

all clear ◆ n [signal *m* de) fin f d'alerte / *he received* or *was given the all clear on the project* on lui a donné le feu vert pour le projet. ◆ interj ▸ **all clear!** fin f d'alerte !

all-consuming adj [passion, ambition] dévorant.

all-day adj qui dure toute la journée.

allegation [,ælɪ'ɡeɪʃn] n allégation f.

allege [ə'ledʒ] vt alléguer, prétendre / *he alleges that he was beaten up* il prétend avoir été roué de coups.

alleged [ə'ledʒd] adj [motive, incident, reason] allégué, prétendu ; [thief] présumé.

allegedly [ə'ledʒɪdlɪ] adv prétendument, paraît-il.

allegiance [ə'liːdʒəns] n allégeance f.

alleluia [,ælɪ'luːjə] interj ▸ **alleluia!** alléluia !

all-embracing [-ɪm'breɪsɪŋ] adj exhaustif, complet.

allergen ['ælədʒen] n allergène *m*.

allergenic [ælə'dʒenɪk] adj allergisant.

allergic [ə'lɜːdʒɪk] adj [reaction, person] allergique.

allergy ['ælədʒɪ] *(pl* **allergies)** n allergie f.

alleviate [ə'liːvɪeɪt] vt [pain, suffering] alléger, apaiser, soulager ; [problem, difficulties] limiter, réduire ; [effect] alléger, atténuer ; [boredom] atténuer.

all-expenses-paid adj tous frais payés.

alley cat n chat *m* de gouttière.

alleyway ['ælɪweɪ] n ruelle f, passage *m*.

Allhallows [,ɔːl'hæləʊz] n Toussaint f.

alliance [ə'laɪəns] n alliance f ▸ **to enter into** or **to form an alliance with sb** s'allier ou faire alliance avec qqn.

allied ['ælaɪd] adj **1.** POL [force, nations] allié **2.** [related - subjects] connexe, du même ordre ; ECON & FIN [product, industry] assimilé ; BIOL de la même famille **3.** [connected] allié.

alligator ['ælɪɡeɪtə'] n alligator *m*.

all-important adj de la plus haute importance, d'une importance primordiale ou capitale.

all-in adj ᴜᴷ [price, tariff] net, tout compris, forfaitaire ; [insurance policy] tous risques. ❖ **all in** adv tout compris.

all-inclusive adj [price, tariff] net, tout compris, forfaitaire ; [insurance policy] tous risques.

all-in-one n [garment] combinaison f.

all-in wrestling n lutte f libre, catch *m*.

all-night adj [party, film] qui dure toute la nuit ; [shop, restaurant] de nuit, ouvert la nuit.

all-nighter [-'naɪtə'] n : *the party will be an all-nighter* la fête va durer toute la nuit / *we pulled an all-nighter for the physics exam* ᴜꜱ on a passé la nuit à réviser l'examen de physique.

allocate ['æləkeɪt] vt **1.** [assign - money, duties] allouer, assigner, attribuer / *funds allocated to research* des crédits affectés à la recherche **2.** [share out] répartir, distribuer.

allocation [,ælə'keɪʃn] n **1.** [assignment - of money, duties] allocation f, affectation f ; [- of role, part] attribution f **2.** [sharing out] répartition f **3.** [share - of money] part f ; [- of space] portion f.

allot [ə'lɒt] (*pt* & *pp* **allotted,** *cont* **allotting**) vt
1. [assign - money, duties, time] allouer, assigner, attribuer /
in the allotted time dans le délai imparti **2.** [share out] répartir, distribuer.

allotment [ə'lɒtmənt] n **UK** [land] jardin *m* ouvrier or
familial.

all out adv ▸ **to go all out to do sthg** se donner à fond
pour faire qqch. ◆ **all-out** adj [strike, war] total ; [effort]
maximum.

allow [ə'laʊ] vt **1.** [permit] permettre, autoriser ▸ **to allow
sb to do sthg** permettre à qqn de faire qqch, autoriser qqn
à faire qqch / *the dog is not allowed in the house* on ne
laisse pas le chien entrer dans la maison, l'accès de la maison
est interdit au chien / *'smoking is not allowed'* 'défense
de fumer' / *I won't allow such behaviour!* je ne tolérerai
pas une telle conduite ! **2.** [enable] permettre **3.** [grant
- money, time] accorder, allouer ; [- opportunity] donner ;
[- claim] admettre **4.** [take into account] prévoir, compter /
allow a week for delivery il faut prévoir or compter une
semaine pour la livraison **5.** *liter* [admit] admettre, convenir.
◆ **allow for** vt insep **1.** [take account of] tenir compte
de / *allowing for the bad weather* compte tenu du mauvais temps **2.** [make allowance or provision for] : *remember
to allow for the time difference* n'oublie pas de compter le
décalage horaire / *we hadn't allowed for these extra costs*
nous n'avions pas prévu ces frais supplémentaires.

> ✎ Note that **permettre que** is followed by a
> verb in the subjunctive:
> **The rules allow profits to be paid in full.**
> *Le règlement permet que les bénéfices soient
> versés intégralement.*

allowable [ə'laʊəbl] adj admissible, permis.

allowance [ə'laʊəns] n **1.** ADMIN [grant] allocation *f* ;
[for housing, travel, food] indemnité *f* ; [alimony] pension *f*
alimentaire ; [for student - from state] bourse *f* ; [- from par-
ents] pension *f* alimentaire ; [pension] pension *f* ; [income,
salary] revenu *m*, appointements *mpl* / *his parents give
him a monthly allowance of £100* ses parents lui versent
une mensualité de 100 livres **2.** [discount] rabais *m*, réduction *f* ▸ **tax allowance a)** [deduction] abattement *m* or dégrèvement *m* fiscal **b)** [tax-free part] revenu *m* non imposable
3. **US** [pocket money] argent *m* de poche **4.** **PHR** **to make
allowances for sb** être indulgent avec qqn ▸ **to make allowance** or **allowances for sthg** tenir compte de qqch,
prendre qqch en considération.

alloy ◆ n ['ælɔɪ] alliage *m*. ◆ comp ['ælɔɪ] ▸ **alloy
wheels** AUTO roues *fpl* en alliage léger.

all-party talks n POL *discussions entre tous les partis.*

all-points bulletin n **US** *message radio diffusé par la
police concernant une personne recherchée.*

all-powerful adj tout-puissant.

all-purpose adj [gen] qui répond à tous les besoins,
passe-partout (*inv*) ; [tool, vehicle] polyvalent.

all right, alright [,ɔːl'raɪt] ◆ adj **1.** [adequate]
(assez) bien, pas mal / *the film was all right* le film n'était
pas mal **2.** [in good health] en bonne santé ; [safe] sain et
sauf / *I hope they'll be all right on their own* j'espère
qu'ils sauront se débrouiller tout seuls / *are you all right?*
[not hurt] ça va ? **3.** [indicating agreement, approval] : *is
it all right if they come too?* ça va s'ils viennent aussi ? /
it's all right **a)** [no problem] ça va **b)** [no matter] ça ne fait
rien, peu importe / *is everything all right, Madam?* tout
va bien, Madame ? / *it's all right by me* moi, ça me va
4. [pleasant] bien, agréable ; [nice-looking] chouette **5.** [fi-
nancially] à l'aise, tranquille. ◆ adv **1.** [well, adequately]

bien / *they're doing all right* **a)** [progressing well] ça va
(pour eux) **b)** [succeeding in career, life] ils se débrouillent
bien **2.** [without doubt] : *he was listening all right* ça,
pour écouter, il écoutait. ◆ interj ▸ **all right! a)** [indicating
agreement, understanding] entendu !, d'accord ! **b)** [indicat-
ing approval] c'est ça !, ça va ! **c)** [indicating impatience] ça
va !, ça suffit ! **d)** [indicating change or continuation of activ-
ity] bon ! ◆ **all-right, alright** adj **US** *inf* : *he's an
all-right guy* c'est un type réglo.

all-round **UK**, **all-around** **US** adj [versatile - athlete,
player] complet ; [- ability] complet, polyvalent.

all-rounder [-'raʊndər] n **UK** : *he's a good all-rounder*
a) [gen] il est doué dans tous les domaines, il est bon en
tout **b)** SPORT c'est un sportif complet.

All Saints' Day n (le jour de) la Toussaint.

all-singing all-dancing adj dernier cri.

All Souls' Day n le jour or la fête des Morts.

allspice ['ɔːlspaɪs] n poivre *m* de la Jamaïque, toute-
épice *f*.

all-star adj [show, performance] avec beaucoup de vedettes, à vedettes / *with an all-star cast* avec un plateau
de vedettes.

all-terrain vehicle [ɔːltə,reɪn'viːɪkl] n véhicule *m* tout
terrain, 4x4 *m*.

all-time adj [record] sans précédent.

all told adv en tout.

allude [ə'luːd] vi ▸ **to allude to sb / sthg** faire allusion à
qqn / qqch.

allure [ə'ljʊər] n attrait *m*, charme *m*.

alluring [ə'ljʊərɪŋ] adj séduisant, attrayant.

allusion [ə'luːʒn] n allusion *f*.

allusive [ə'luːsɪv] adj allusif, qui contient une allusion or
des allusions.

all-weather adj [surface] de toute saison, tous temps
▸ **all-weather court** [tennis] (terrain *m* en) quick *m*.

ally ◆ vt [ə'laɪ] allier, unir ▸ **to ally o.s. with sb** s'allier
avec qqn. ◆ n ['ælaɪ] (*pl* **allies**) [gen & POL] allié *m*, -e *f*.

almanac ['ɔːlmənæk] n almanach *m*, agenda *m*.

almighty [ɔːl'maɪtɪ] adj **1.** [omnipotent] tout-puissant,
omnipotent **2.** *inf* [as intensifier - row, racket] formidable,
sacré. ◆ **Almighty** n RELIG ▸ **the Almighty** le Tout-
Puissant.

almond ['ɑːmənd] ◆ n [nut] amande *f*. ◆ comp [icing,
essence] d'amandes ; [cake] aux amandes.

almond paste n pâte *f* d'amande.

almost ['ɔːlməʊst] adv presque / *he is almost 30* il a
presque 30 ans / *I almost cried* j'ai failli pleurer.

alms [ɑːmz] pl n aumône *f*.

aloft [ə'lɒft] adv ▸ **(up) aloft** en haut, en l'air.

alone [ə'ləʊn] ◆ adj **1.** [on one's own] seul / *I'm not
alone in thinking that it's unfair* je ne suis pas le seul à
penser que c'est injuste **2.** [only] seul / *she alone knows
the truth* elle seule connaît la vérité **3.** [lonely] seul. ◆ adv
1. [on one's own] seul / *she managed to open the box
alone* elle a réussi à ouvrir la boîte toute seule ▸ **to go it
alone** faire cavalier seul **2.** [undisturbed] ▸ **to leave** or **to
let sb alone** laisser qqn tranquille / *leave me alone* **a)** [on
my own] laissez-moi seul **b)** [in peace] laissez-moi tranquille,
laissez-moi en paix / *if I were you I would leave well alone*
si j'étais vous, je ne m'en mêlerais pas. ◆ **let alone**
conj phr sans parler de / *she can't even walk, let alone run*
elle ne peut même pas marcher, alors encore moins courir.

along [ə'lɒŋ] ◆ prep [the length of] le long de / *the railway runs along the coast* la voie ferrée longe la côte ; [at
or to a certain point in] : *could you move further along the
row* pourriez-vous vous déplacer vers le bout du rang ? /

the toilets are just along the corridor les toilettes sont juste un peu plus loin dans le couloir. ◆ adv **1.** [indicating progress] : *how far along is the project?* où en est le projet ? / *things are going* or *coming along nicely, thank you* les choses ne se présentent pas trop mal, merci **2.** [indicating imminent arrival] : *I'll be along in a minute* j'arrive tout de suite / *there'll be another bus along shortly* un autre bus va passer bientôt. ◆ **along with** prep phr avec / *my house was flooded along with hundreds of others* ma maison a été inondée avec des centaines d'autres.

alongside [ə,lɒŋ'saɪd] ◆ prep **1.** [along] le long de / *the railway runs alongside the road* la ligne de chemin de fer longe la route **2.** [beside] à côté de / *the car drew up alongside me* la voiture s'est arrêtée à côté de moi **3.** [together with] avec. ◆ adv **1.** NAUT ▸ **to come alongside a)** [two ships] naviguer à couple **b)** [at quayside] accoster **2.** [gen - at side] : *they're going to build a patio with a flower bed alongside* ils vont construire un patio bordé d'un parterre de fleurs.

aloof [ə'luːf] adj distant ▸ **to keep** or **to remain aloof** se tenir à distance.

aloofness [ə'luːfnɪs] n attitude *f* distante, réserve *f*.

aloud [ə'laʊd] adv [read] à haute voix, à voix haute, tout haut ; [think] tout haut.

alpaca [æl'pækə] n alpaga *m*.

alpha ['ælfə] n **1.** [Greek letter] alpha *m* **2.** UK SCH ≃ mention *f* bien ▸ **alpha plus** ≃ mention *f* très bien.

alphabet ['ælfəbet] n alphabet *m*.

alphabetic(al) [,ælfə'betɪk(l)] adj alphabétique / *in alphabetical order* par ordre or dans l'ordre alphabétique.

alphabetically [,ælfə'betɪklɪ] adv alphabétiquement, par ordre alphabétique.

alphabetize, alphabetise ['ælfəbə,taɪz] vt classer par ordre alphabétique.

alpha girl n MARKETING *fille considérée par ses pairs comme très branchée et donnant le ton.*

alpha male n mâle *m* alpha.

alphanumeric [,ælfənjuː'merɪk] adj alphanumérique.

alpine ['ælpaɪn] adj **1.** GEOG des Alpes **2.** [climate, landscape] alpestre ; [club, skiing, troops] alpin.

Alps [ælps] pl pr n ▸ **the Alps** les Alps *fpl*.

al-Qaeda, al-Qaida [,ælkæ'iːdə] pr n Al-Qaida.

already [ɔːl'redɪ] adv déjà.

alright [,ɔːl'raɪt] adj, adv & interj = **all right**.

Alsace [æl'sæs] pr n Alsace *f*.

Alsatian [æl'seɪʃn] n UK [dog] berger *m* allemand.

also ['ɔːlsəʊ] adv **1.** [as well] aussi, également / *she also speaks Italian* elle parle aussi or également l'italien / *he's lazy and also stupid* il est paresseux et en plus il est bête **2.** [furthermore] en outre, de plus, également / *also, it must be pointed out that...* en outre or de plus, il faut signaler que..., il faut également signaler que...

also-ran n **1.** SPORT [gen] concurrent *m* non classé ; [in horse-race] cheval *m* non classé **2.** *fig* [person] perdant *m*, -e *f*.

Alta. written abbr of **Alberta**.

altar ['ɔːltər] n autel *m*.

alter ['ɔːltər] ◆ vt **1.** [change - appearance, plan] changer, modifier / *this alters matters considerably* cela change vraiment tout **2.** SEW faire une retouche or des retouches à, retoucher. ◆ vi changer, se modifier.

⚠ Note that **altérer** usually means not just to change but to spoil, adulterate or distort.

alteration [,ɔːltə'reɪʃn] n **1.** [changing] changement *m*, modification *f* ; [touching up] retouche *f* **2.** [change] changement *m*, modification *f* ; [reorganization] remaniement *m* ; [transformation] transformation *f* ▸ **to make an alteration to sthg** modifier qqch, apporter une modification à qqch **3.** SEW retouche *f* / *to make alterations to a dress* faire des retouches à une robe **4.** CONSTR aménagement *m*, transformation *f* / *they've made major alterations to their house* ils ont fait des transformations importantes dans leur maison.

altercation [,ɔːltə'keɪʃn] n *fml* altercation *f*.

alter ego n alter ego *m*.

alterglobalism [,ɔːltə'gləʊbəlɪzəm] n altermondialisme *m*.

alterglobalist [,ɔːltə'gləʊbəlɪst] n altermondialiste *mf*.

alternate ◆ adj [UK ɔːl'tɜːnət US 'ɔːltərnət] **1.** [by turns] alterné **2.** [every other] tous les deux / *on alternate days* un jour sur deux, tous les deux jours **3.** US [alternative] alternatif. ◆ vi ['ɔːltəneɪt] **1.** [happen by turns] alterner **2.** [vary] alterner / *an economy that alternates between periods of growth and disastrous slumps* une économie où alternent la prospérité et le marasme le plus profond. ◆ vt ['ɔːltəneɪt] (faire) alterner, employer alternativement or tour à tour ; AGR alterner. ◆ n [UK ɔːl'tɜːnət US 'ɔːltərnət] remplaçant *m*, -e *f*, suppléant *m*, -e *f*.

alternately [ɔːl'tɜːnətlɪ] adv alternativement, en alternance, tour à tour.

alternating current n courant *m* alternatif.

alternative [ɔːl'tɜːnətɪv] ◆ n [choice] solution *f*, choix *m* / *he had no alternative but to accept* il n'avait pas d'autre solution que d'accepter / *what's the alternative?* quelle est l'autre solution ? / *there are several alternatives* il y a plusieurs possibilités. ◆ adj **1.** [different, other - solution, government] autre, de rechange / *an alternative proposal* une contre-proposition **2.** [not traditional - lifestyle] peu conventionnel, hors normes ; [- press, theatre] parallèle ▸ **alternative energy** énergies *fpl* de substitution ▸ **alternative technology** technologies *fpl* douces.

alternatively [ɔːl'tɜːnətɪvlɪ] adv comme alternative, sinon.

⚠ **Alternativement** means alternately, not alternatively.

alternator ['ɔːltəneɪtər] n alternateur *m*.

although [ɔːl'ðəʊ] conj **1.** [despite the fact that] bien que, quoique / *although I have never liked him, I do respect him* bien que or quoique je ne l'aie jamais aimé, je le respecte, je ne l'ai jamais aimé, néanmoins je le respecte **2.** [but, however] mais / *I don't think it will work, although it's worth a try* je ne crois pas que ça va marcher, mais ça vaut la peine d'essayer.

📋 Note that bien que, quoique and encore que are followed by verbs in the subjunctive:
Some women choose this profession, although this is less common. *Certaines femmes choisissent ce métier, bien que ce soit plus rare.*
Although it was a long and bitter struggle... *Quoique le combat fût long et acharné...*
... although no one here has ever been convicted of such a crime. *... encore que personne ici n'ait jamais été condamné pour un tel crime.*

altitude ['æltɪtjuːd] n [gen & AERON] altitude *f*; [in mountains] altitude *f*, hauteur *f*.

alt key [ælt-] n touche *f* alt.

alto ['æltəʊ] (*pl* **altos**) ◆ adj [voice - female] de contralto ; [- male] de haute-contre ; [instrument] alto (*inv*). ◆ n **1.** [voice - female] contralto *m* ; [- male] haute-contre *f* **2.** [instrument] alto *m*.

altogether [,ɔːltə'geðər] adv **1.** [entirely] tout à fait, entièrement / *I don't altogether agree with you* je ne suis pas tout à fait or entièrement d'accord avec vous / *that's a different matter altogether* c'est un tout autre problème **2.** [as a whole] en tout / *taken altogether* à tout prendre.

altruism ['æltruːɪzm] n altruisme *m*.

altruist ['æltruːɪst] n altruiste *mf*.

altruistic [,æltruː'ɪstɪk] adj altruiste.

aluminium 🇬🇧 [,ælju'mɪnɪəm], **aluminum** 🇺🇸 [ə'luː-mɪnəm] ◆ n aluminium *m*. ◆ comp [utensil] en aluminium.

alumna [ə'lʌmnə] (*pl* **alumnae** [-niː]) n 🇺🇸 SCH ancienne élève *f* ; UNIV ancienne étudiante *f*.

alumnus [ə'lʌmnəs] (*pl* **alumni** [-naɪ]) n 🇺🇸 SCH ancien élève *m* ; UNIV ancien étudiant *m*.

always ['ɔːlweɪz] adv toujours / *has she always worn glasses?* a-t-elle toujours porté des lunettes ? / *you can always try phoning* vous pouvez toujours essayer de télé-phoner.

always-on [,ɔːlweɪz'ɒn] adj permanent.

Alwz MESSAGING written abbr of **always**.

Alzheimer's (disease) ['ælts,haɪməz-] n maladie *f* d'Alzheimer.

am [æm] vi & aux vb ⟶ **be**.

a.m. (abbr of **ante meridiem**) adv du matin.

AM n (abbr of **amplitude modulation**) AM.

AMA (abbr of **American Medical Association**) pr n ordre américain des médecins.

amalgam [ə'mælgəm] n **1.** [gen & METALL] amalgame *m* **2.** DENT amalgame *m*.

amalgamate [ə'mælgə,meɪt] ◆ vt [firms, businesses] fusionner, unir. ◆ vi [firms] fusionner.

amalgamation [ə,mælgə'meɪʃn] n COMM & ECON fusion *f*.

amass [ə'mæs] vt [fortune, objects, information] amasser, accumuler.

amateur ['æmətər] ◆ n [gen & SPORT] amateur *m*. ◆ adj [sport, photographer] amateur ; [painting, psych-ology] d'amateur.

amateurish [,æmə'tɜːrɪʃ] adj pej d'amateur, de dilet-tante.

amateurism ['æmətərɪzəm] n **1.** SPORT amateurisme *m* **2.** pej [lack of professionalism] amateurisme *m*, dilettan-tisme *m*.

amaze [ə'meɪz] vt stupéfier, ahurir.

amazed [ə'meɪzd] adj [expression, look] de stupéfaction, ahuri, éberlué ; [person] stupéfait, ahuri / *he was amazed to see her there* il était stupéfait de la trouver là.

amazement [ə'meɪzmənt] n stupéfaction *f*, stupeur *f* / *to our amazement* à notre stupéfaction.

amazing [ə'meɪzɪŋ] adj **1.** [astonishing] stupéfiant, ahu-rissant **2.** [brilliant, very good] extraordinaire, sensationnel.

amazingly [ə'meɪzɪŋli] adv incroyablement, extraordi-nairement / *he's amazingly patient* il est d'une patience extraordinaire or étonnante.

Amazon ['æməzn] pr n **1.** [river] ▶ **the Amazon** l'Ama-zone *f* **2.** [region] ▶ **the Amazon (Basin)** l'Amazonie *f* / *the Amazon rain forest* la forêt (tropicale) amazonienne.

Amazonian [,æmə'zəʊnjən] adj amazonien.

ambassador [æm'bæsədər] n POL & fig ambassa-deur *m* / *the Spanish ambassador to Morocco* l'ambassa-deur d'Espagne au Maroc.

amber ['æmbər] ◆ n [colour, resin] ambre *m*. ◆ adj **1.** [necklace, ring] d'ambre **2.** [dress, eyes] ambré ▶ **amber light** feu *m* orange.

ambiance ['æmbɪəns] n = **ambience**.

ambidextrous [,æmbɪ'dekstrəs] adj ambidextre.

ambience, ambiance ['æmbɪəns] n ambiance *f*.

ambient ['æmbɪənt] adj ambiant.

ambiguity [,æmbɪ'gjuːətɪ] (*pl* **ambiguities**) n [uncer-tainty] ambiguïté *f*, équivoque *f* ; [of expression, word] ambi-guïté *f*.

ambiguous [æm'bɪgjuəs] adj ambigu, équivoque.

ambiguously [æm'bɪgjuəslɪ] adv de façon ambiguë.

ambition [æm'bɪʃn] n ambition *f* / *her ambition was to become a physicist* elle avait l'ambition or son ambition était de devenir physicienne.

ambitious [æm'bɪʃəs] adj ambitieux.

ambivalence [æm'bɪvələns] n ambivalence *f*.

ambivalent [æm'bɪvələnt] adj ambivalent ▶ **to be** or **to feel ambivalent about sthg** être or se sentir indécis à pro-pos de qqch.

amble ['æmbl] vi [person] marcher or aller d'un pas tranquille ; [horse] aller l'amble / *we ambled home* nous sommes rentrés lentement or sans nous presser.

ambulance ['æmbjʊləns] ◆ n ambulance *f*. ◆ comp ▶ **ambulance driver** ambulancier *m*, -ère *f*.

ambush ['æmbʊʃ] ◆ vt [attack] attirer dans une embus-cade. ◆ n embuscade *f*, guet-apens *m*.

AMBW MESSAGING written abbr of **all my best wishes**.

ameba [ə'miːbə] (*pl* **amebae** [-biː] or **amebas**) n 🇺🇸 = **amoeba**.

amen [,ɑː'men] interj RELIG ▶ **amen!** amen !

amenable [ə'miːnəbl] adj [cooperative] accommodant, souple ▶ **to be amenable to sthg** être disposé à qqch.

amend [ə'mend] vt **1.** [rectify - mistake, text] rectifier, corriger ; [- behaviour, habits] réformer, amender fml **2.** [law, rule] amender, modifier ; [constitution] amender.

amendment [ə'mendmənt] n **1.** [correction] rectifica-tion *f*, correction *f* ; [modification] modification *f*, révision *f* **2.** [to bill, constitution, law] amendement *m* ; [to contract] avenant *m*.

 Amendments

Les dix premiers amendements à la Consti-tution américaine garantissent des droits fondamentaux et constituent le **Bill of Rights**.

amends [ə'mendz] pl n réparation *f*, compensation *f* ▶ **to make amends for sthg a)** [compensate] faire amende ho-norable, se racheter **b)** [apologize] se faire pardonner.

amenities [ə'miːnətɪz] pl n [features] agréments *mpl* ; [facilities] équipements *mpl* ▶ **urban amenities** équipe-ments *mpl* collectifs.

America [ə'merɪkə] pr n Amérique *f*.

American [ə'merɪkn] ◆ n Américain *m*, -e *f*. ◆ adj américain / *the American embassy* l'ambassade *f* des

États-Unis ▶ **the American Dream** le rêve américain ▶ **American English** (anglais *m*) américain *m*.

American football n 🇬🇧 football *m* américain.

American Indian n Indien *m*, -enne *f* d'Amérique, Amérindien *m*, -enne *f*.

Americanism [ə'merɪkənɪzm] n américanisme *m*.

americanize, americanise [ə'merɪkə,naɪz] vt américaniser.

American plan, AP n 🇺🇸 pension *f* complète.

amethyst ['æmɪθɪst] ◆ n [stone] améthyste *f*. ◆ adj [necklace, ring] d'améthyste.

Amex ['æmeks] pr n (abbr of **American Stock Exchange**) *deuxième place boursière des États-Unis.*

amiable ['eɪmjəbl] adj aimable, gentil.

amiably ['eɪmjəblɪ] adv avec amabilité or gentillesse, aimablement.

amicable ['æmɪkəbl] adj [feeling, relationship] amical, d'amitié ; [agreement, end] à l'amiable.

amicably ['æmɪkəblɪ] adv amicalement.

amid [ə'mɪd], **amidst** [ə'mɪdst] prep au milieu de, parmi / *amid all the noise and confusion, she escaped* dans la confusion générale, elle s'est échappée.

amidst [ə'mɪdst] prep = **amid**.

amino acid [ə'miːnəʊ-] n acide *m* aminé, aminoacide *m*.

amiss [ə'mɪs] ◆ adv **1.** [incorrectly] de travers, mal ▶ **to take sthg amiss** mal prendre qqch **2.** [out of place] mal à propos / *a little tact and diplomacy wouldn't go amiss* un peu de tact et de diplomatie seraient les bienvenus or ne feraient pas de mal. ◆ adj [wrong] : *something seems to be amiss with the engine* on dirait qu'il y a à quelque chose qui ne va pas dans le moteur.

AML MESSAGING written abbr of **all my love**.

ammo ['æməʊ] n (U) inf munitions fpl.

ammonia [ə'məʊnjə] n [gas] ammoniac *m* ; [liquid] ammoniaque *f*.

ammunition [,æmjʊ'nɪʃn] n (U) munitions fpl / *the letter could be used as ammunition against them* la lettre pourrait être tournée contre eux.

ammunition dump n dépôt *m* de munitions.

amnesia [æm'niːzjə] n amnésie *f*.

amnesty ['æmnəstɪ] (*pl* amnesties) n amnistie *f*.

Amnesty International pr n Amnesty International.

amniocentesis [,æmnɪəʊsen'tiːsɪs] (*pl* amniocenteses [-siːz]) n amniocentèse *f*.

amoeba 🇬🇧, **ameba** 🇺🇸 [ə'miːbə] (🇬🇧 *pl* amoebae *or* amoebas ; 🇺🇸 *pl* amebae [-biː] *or* amebas) n amibe *f*.

amoebic dysentery n dysenterie *f* amibienne.

amok [ə'mɒk], **amuck** [ə'mʌk] adv ▶ **to run amok** a) *lit* être pris d'une crise de folie meurtrière or furieuse b) *fig* devenir fou furieux, se déchaîner.

among(st) [ə'mʌŋ(st)] prep **1.** [in the midst of] au milieu de, parmi / *I moved amongst the spectators* je circulais parmi les spectateurs / *she was lost amongst the crowd* elle était perdue dans la foule / *to be amongst friends* être entre amis **2.** [forming part of] parmi / *it is amongst her most important plays* c'est une de ses pièces les plus importantes / *amongst other things* entre autres (choses) **3.** [within a specified group] parmi, entre / *we discussed it amongst ourselves* nous en avons discuté entre nous / *I count her amongst my friends* je la compte parmi or au nombre de mes amis **4.** [to each of] parmi, entre / *share the books amongst you* partagez les livres entre vous, partagez-vous les livres.

amoral [,eɪ'mɒrəl] adj amoral.

amorous ['æmərəs] adj [person] amoureux, porté à l'amour ; [glance] amoureux, ardent ; [letter] d'amour ▶ **amorous advances** des avances.

amorphous [ə'mɔːfəs] adj CHEM amorphe ; [shapeless] amorphe ; *fig* [personality] amorphe, mou *(before vowel or silent 'h' mol, f molle)* ; [ideas] informe, sans forme ; [plans] vague.

amount [ə'maʊnt] n **1.** [quantity] quantité *f* / *in small / large amounts* en petites / grandes quantités / *no amount of talking can bring him back* on peut lui parler tant qu'on veut, ça ne le fera pas revenir / *any amount of* des quantités de, énormément de **2.** [of money] somme *f*. ◆ **amount to** vt insep **1.** [total] se monter à, s'élever à / *after tax it doesn't amount to much* après impôts ça ne représente pas grand-chose / *he'll never amount to much* il ne fera jamais grand-chose **2.** [be equivalent to] : *it amounts to something not far short of stealing* c'est pratiquement du vol / *it amounts to the same thing* cela revient au même.

amp [æmp] n **1.** = **ampere 2.** inf [amplifier] ampli *m*.

amperage ['æmpərɪdʒ] n intensité *f* de courant.

ampere ['æmpeəʳ] n ampère *m*.

ampersand ['æmpəsænd] n esperluette *f*.

amphetamine [æm'fetəmiːn] n amphétamine *f*.

amphibian [æm'fɪbɪən] ◆ n ZOOL amphibie *m*. ◆ adj amphibie.

amphibious [æm'fɪbɪəs] adj amphibie.

amphitheatre 🇬🇧, **amphitheater** 🇺🇸 ['æmfɪ,θɪətər] n amphithéâtre *m*.

ample ['æmpl] adj **1.** [large - clothing] ample ; [- garden, lawn] grand, vaste ; [- helping, stomach] grand **2.** [more than enough - supplies] bien or largement assez de ; [- proof, reason] solide ; [- fortune, means] gros (grosse) / *he was given ample opportunity to refuse* il a eu largement l'occasion or il a eu de nombreuses occasions de refuser.

amplification [,æmplɪfɪ'keɪʃn] n **1.** [of power, sound] amplification *f* **2.** [further explanation] explication *f*, développement *m*.

amplifier ['æmplɪfaɪəʳ] n amplificateur *m*.

amplify ['æmplɪfaɪ] vt **1.** [power, sound] amplifier **2.** [facts, idea, speech] développer.

amplitude ['æmplɪtjuːd] n [breadth, scope] ampleur *f*, envergure *f* ; ASTRON & PHYS amplitude *f*.

amply ['æmplɪ] adv amplement, largement.

amputate ['æmpjʊteɪt] vt amputer.

amputation [,æmpjʊ'teɪʃn] n amputation *f*.

amputee [,æmpjʊ'tiː] n amputé *m*, -e *f*.

Amsterdam [,æmstə'dæm] pr n Amsterdam.

amt written abbr of **amount**.

Amtrak® ['æmtræk] pr n *société nationale de chemins de fer aux États-Unis.*

amuck [ə'mʌk] adv = **amok**.

amulet ['æmjʊlɪt] n amulette *f*, fétiche *m*.

amuse [ə'mjuːz] vt **1.** [occupy] divertir, amuser, distraire / *he amused himself (by) building sandcastles* il s'est amusé à faire des châteaux de sable **2.** [make laugh] amuser, faire rire.

amused [ə'mjuːzd] adj **1.** [occupied] occupé, diverti ▶ **to keep o.s. amused** s'occuper, se distraire **2.** [delighted, entertained] amusé / *I was greatly amused to hear about his adventures* cela m'a beaucoup amusé d'entendre parler de ses aventures ▶ **we are not amused** très drôle ! *iro (expression faisant allusion à une réflexion qu'aurait faite la reine Victoria pour exprimer sa désapprobation).*

amusement [ə'mju:zmənt] n **1.** [enjoyment] amusement m, divertissement m / I listened in amusement amusé, j'ai écouté / much to everyone's amusement au grand amusement de tous **2.** [pastime] distraction f, amusement m **3.** [at a funfair] attraction f.

amusement arcade n arcade f.

amusement park n parc m d'attractions.

amusing [ə'mju:zɪŋ] adj amusant, drôle.

an (stressed [æn], unstressed [ən]) det —→ a.

ANA (abbr of American Nurses Association) pr n syndicat américain d'infirmiers.

anabolic steroid n stéroïde m anabolisant.

anachronism [ə'nækrənɪzm] n anachronisme m.

anachronistic [ə,nækrə'nɪstɪk] adj anachronique.

anaemia 🇬🇧, **anemia** 🇺🇸 [ə'ni:mjə] n MED & fig anémie f.

anaemic 🇬🇧, **anemic** 🇺🇸 [ə'ni:mɪk] adj MED & fig anémique.

anaesthesia 🇬🇧, **anesthesia** 🇺🇸 [,ænɪs'θi:zjə] n anesthésie f.

anaesthetic 🇬🇧, **anesthetic** 🇺🇸 [,ænɪs'θetɪk] ◆ n anesthésique m, anesthésiant m ▶ under anaesthetic sous anesthésie ▶ to give sb an anaesthetic anesthésier qqn. ◆ adj anesthésique, anesthésiant.

anaesthetist 🇬🇧, **anesthetist** 🇺🇸 [æ'ni:sθətɪst] n anesthésiste mf.

anaesthetize, anaesthetise 🇬🇧, **anesthetize** 🇺🇸 [æ'ni:sθətaɪz] vt MED anesthésier ; fig anesthésier, insensibiliser.

anagram ['ænəgræm] n anagramme f.

anal ['eɪnl] adj ANAT anal / anal intercourse or sex sodomie f.

analgesic [,ænæl'dʒi:sɪk] ◆ adj analgésique. ◆ n analgésique m.

analog n & comp 🇺🇸 = **analogue**.

analogous [ə'næləgəs] adj analogue.

analogue 🇬🇧, **analog** 🇺🇸 ['ænəlɒg] comp [clock, watch, computer] analogique.

analogy [ə'nælədʒɪ] (pl analogies) n analogie f ▶ by analogy with sthg par analogie avec qqch.

analyse 🇬🇧, **analyze** 🇺🇸 ['ænəlaɪz] vt **1.** [examine] analyser, faire l'analyse de ; [sentence] analyser, faire l'analyse logique de **2.** PSYCHOL psychanalyser.

analysis [ə'næləsɪs] (pl analyses [-si:z]) n **1.** [examination] analyse f ; [of sentence] analyse f logique / in the final or last or ultimate analysis en dernière analyse, en fin de compte **2.** PSYCHOL psychanalyse f, analyse f ▶ to be in analysis être en analyse, suivre une analyse.

analyst ['ænəlɪst] n [specialist] analyste mf.

analytic(al) [,ænə'lɪtɪk(l)] adj analytique.

analyze vt 🇺🇸 = **analyse**.

anaphylactic [ænəfɪ'læktɪk] adj [shock] anaphylactique.

anarchic [æ'nɑ:kɪk] adj anarchique.

anarchist ['ænəkɪst] n anarchiste mf.

anarchistic [,ænə'kɪstɪk] adj anarchiste.

anarchy ['ænəkɪ] n anarchie f.

anathema [ə'næθəmə] n fml [detested thing] abomination f / such ideas are anathema to the general public le grand public a horreur de ces idées.

anatomical [,ænə'tomɪkl] adj anatomique.

anatomically [,ænə'tomɪklɪ] adv anatomiquement.

anatomy [ə'nætəmɪ] n BIOL [of animal, person] anatomie f ; fig [of situation, society] structure f.

ANC (abbr of African National Congress) pr n ANC m.

ancestor ['ænsestər] n [forefather] ancêtre m, aïeul m.

ancestral [æn'sestrəl] adj ancestral.

ancestry ['ænsestrɪ] (pl ancestries) n **1.** [lineage] ascendance f **2.** [ancestors] ancêtres mpl, aïeux mpl.

anchor ['æŋkər] ◆ n **1.** [for boat] ancre f ▶ to cast or to come to or to drop anchor jeter l'ancre, mouiller **2.** [fastener] attache f **3.** fig [mainstay] soutien m, point m d'ancrage. ◆ vt **1.** [boat] ancrer **2.** [fasten] ancrer, fixer.

anchorage ['æŋkərɪdʒ] n **1.** NAUT [place] mouillage m, ancrage m ; [fee] droits mpl de mouillage or d'ancrage **2.** [fastening] ancrage m, attache f **3.** fig [mainstay] soutien m, point m d'ancrage.

anchorman ['æŋkəmæn] (pl anchormen [-men]) n **1.** TV présentateur m **2.** SPORT pilier m, pivot m.

anchorwoman ['æŋkə,wumən] (pl anchorwomen [-,wɪmɪn]) n TV présentatrice f.

anchovy [🇬🇧 'æntʃəvɪ 🇺🇸 'æntʃəuvɪ] (pl anchovy or anchovies) n anchois m.

ancient ['eɪnʃənt] adj **1.** [custom, ruins] ancien ; [civilization, world] antique ; [relic] historique ▶ ancient Greece la Grèce antique ▶ ancient history lit & fig histoire f ancienne **2.** hum [very old - person] très vieux ; [- thing] antique, antédiluvien.

ancillary [æn'sɪlərɪ] (pl ancillaries) adj **1.** [supplementary] auxiliaire **2.** [subsidiary - reason] subsidiaire ; [- advantage, cost] accessoire.

and (strong form [ænd], weak form [ənd], [ən]) ◆ conj **1.** [in addition to] et / get your hat and coat va chercher ton manteau et ton chapeau / he goes fishing winter and summer (alike) il va à la pêche en hiver comme en été / you can't work for us AND work for our competitors vous ne pouvez pas travailler ET pour nous ET pour nos concurrents / I'm Richard Rogers — and? je suis Richard Rogers — (et) alors ? / there are books and books il y a livres et livres **2.** [then] : he opened the door and went out il a ouvert la porte et est sorti **3.** [with infinitive] : go and look for it va le chercher **4.** [in numbers] : one hundred and three cent trois / three and a half years trois ans et demi / four and two thirds quatre deux tiers **5.** [indicating continuity, repetition] : he cried and cried il n'arrêtait pas de pleurer / for hours and hours pendant des heures (et des heures) ; [with comparative adjectives] : louder and louder de plus en plus fort **6.** [as intensifier] : her room was nice and sunny sa chambre était bien ensoleillée / he's good and mad inf il est fou furieux **7.** [with implied conditional] : one move and you're dead un geste et vous êtes mort. ◆ n : I want no ifs, ands or buts je ne veux pas de discussion. ◆◆ **and all** adv phr **1.** [and everything] et tout (ce qui s'ensuit) / the whole lot went flying, plates, cups, teapot and all tout a volé, les assiettes, les tasses, la théière et tout **2.** 🇬🇧 v inf [as well] aussi / you can wipe that grin off your face and all tu peux aussi arrêter de sourire comme ça. ◆◆ **and so on (and so forth)** adv phr et ainsi de suite.

Andes ['ændi:z] pl pr n ▶ the Andes les Andes fpl.

Andorra [æn'dɔ:rə] pr n Andorre f.

androgynous [æn'drodʒɪnəs] adj BIOL & BOT androgyne.

android ['ændrɔɪd] ◆ adj androïde. ◆ n androïde m.

anecdotal [,ænek'dəutl] adj anecdotique ▶ anecdotal evidence preuve f or témoignage m anecdotique.

anecdote ['ænɪkdəut] n anecdote f.

anemia n 🇺🇸 = **anaemia**.

anemone [ə'nemənɪ] n anémone f.

anesthesia n US = anaesthesia.
anesthesiologist [ænɪsˌθiːzɪˈɒlədʒɪst] n US anesthésiste mf.
aneurism [ˈænjʊərɪzm] n anévrisme m, anévrysme m.
anew [əˈnjuː] adv liter **1.** [again] de nouveau, encore **2.** [in a new way] à nouveau / to start life anew repartir à zéro.
angel [ˈeɪndʒəl] n **1.** RELIG ange m **2.** [person] ange m, amour m / be an angel and fetch me a glass of water sois gentil, va me chercher un verre d'eau.
angel cake n ≃ gâteau m de Savoie.
angel dust n drugs sl PCP f.
Angeleno [ˌændʒəˈliːnəʊ] n habitant de Los Angeles.
angelfish [ˈeɪndʒəlfɪʃ] (pl angelfish or angelfishes) n [fish] scalaire m ; [shark] ange m.
angelic [ænˈdʒelɪk] adj angélique.
angel investor n FIN ange m investisseur.
angelus [ˈændʒələs] n [bell, prayer] angélus m.
anger [ˈæŋgə] ◆ n colère f, fureur f / in a fit or a moment of anger dans un accès or un mouvement de colère. ◆ vt mettre en colère, énerver.
anger management n gestion f de la colère.
angina [ænˈdʒaɪnə] n (U) angine f (de poitrine).
angle [ˈæŋgl] ◆ n **1.** [gen & GEOM] angle m / the roads intersect at an angle of 90° les routes se croisent à angle droit / the car hit us at an angle la voiture nous a heurtés de biais **2.** fig [point of view] angle m, aspect m / seen from this angle vu sous cet angle / what's your angle on the situation? comment voyez-vous la situation ? ◆ vt **1.** [move] orienter / I angled the light towards the workbench j'ai orienté or dirigé la lumière sur l'établi **2.** fig [slant] présenter sous un certain angle. ◆ vi FISHING pêcher à la ligne ▶ to go angling aller à la pêche (à la ligne) ; fig ▶ to angle for sthg chercher (à avoir) qqch.
Angle [ˈæŋgl] n Angle mf.
angle bracket n crochet m.
Anglepoise® [ˈæŋglpɔɪz] n lampe f architecte.
angler [ˈæŋglə] n FISHING pêcheur m, -euse f (à la ligne).
Anglican [ˈæŋglɪkən] ◆ adj anglican. ◆ n anglican m, -e f.
Anglicanism [ˈæŋglɪkənɪzm] n anglicanisme m.
anglicism [ˈæŋglɪsɪzm] n anglicisme m.
anglicize, anglicise [ˈæŋglɪsaɪz] vt angliciser.
angling [ˈæŋglɪŋ] n pêche f à la ligne.
Anglo- in comp anglo-.
Anglo-American ◆ adj anglo-américain. ◆ n Anglo-Américain m, -e f.
Anglo-French adj anglo-français, franco-anglais, franco-britannique.
Anglo-Irish adj anglo-irlandais.
anglophile [ˈæŋgləʊfaɪl] adj anglophile.
anglophobe [ˈæŋgləʊfəʊb] adj anglophobe. ❖ **Anglophobe** n anglophobe mf.
Anglophone [ˈæŋgləʊfəʊn] ◆ n anglophone mf. ◆ adj anglophone.
Anglo-Saxon ◆ n **1.** [person] Anglo-Saxon m, -onne f **2.** LING anglo-saxon m. ◆ adj anglo-saxon.
Anglosphere [ˈæŋgləʊsfɪə] n ▶ the Anglosphere le monde anglophone.
Angola [æŋˈgəʊlə] pr n Angola m.
Angolan [æŋˈgəʊlən] ◆ n Angolais m, -e f. ◆ adj angolais.
angora [æŋˈgɔːrə] ◆ n [cloth, yarn] laine f angora, angora m. ◆ adj [coat, sweater] en angora.

angrily [ˈæŋgrəlɪ] adv [deny, speak] avec colère or emportement ; [leave, stand up] en colère.
angry [ˈæŋgrɪ] (compar angrier, superl angriest) adj **1.** [person - cross] en colère, fâché ; [-furious] furieux ▶ to be angry at or with sb être fâché or en colère contre qqn / she's angry about or at not having been invited elle est en colère parce qu'elle n'a pas été invitée, elle est furieuse de ne pas avoir été invitée ▶ to get angry se mettre en colère, se fâcher / her remarks made me angry ses observations m'ont mis en colère **2.** [look, tone] irrité, furieux ; [outburst, words] violent.
angst [æŋst] n angoisse f.
anguish [ˈæŋgwɪʃ] n [mental] angoisse f ; [physical] supplice m / to be in anguish a) [worried] être angoissé or dans l'angoisse b) [in pain] souffrir le martyre, être au supplice.
anguished [ˈæŋgwɪʃt] adj angoissé.
angular [ˈæŋgjʊlə] adj [features, room] anguleux ; [face] anguleux, osseux ; [body] anguleux, décharné.
animadversion [ˌænɪmædˈvɜːʃən] n fml animadversion f, critique f / to make animadversions on sthg critiquer qqch, se répandre en critiques sur qqch.
animal [ˈænɪml] ◆ n **1.** ZOOL animal m ; [excluding humans] animal m, bête f **2.** pej [brute] brute f. ◆ adj [products, behaviour] animal ▶ animal lover ami m, -e f des animaux or des bêtes ▶ animal rights droits mpl des animaux ▶ animal welfare protection f des animaux.
animate ◆ vt [ˈænɪmeɪt] **1.** [give life to] animer **2.** fig [enliven - face, look, party] animer, égayer ; [-discussion] animer, stimuler **3.** [move to action] motiver, inciter **4.** CIN & TV animer. ◆ adj [ˈænɪmət] vivant, animé.
animated [ˈænɪmeɪtɪd] adj animé / to become animated s'animer.
animated cartoon n dessin m animé.
animation [ˌænɪˈmeɪʃn] n **1.** [of discussion, party] animation f ; [of place, street] activité f, animation f ; [of person] vivacité f, entrain m ; [of face, look] animation f **2.** CIN & TV animation f.
animator [ˈænɪmeɪtə] n animateur m, -trice f.
animatronics [ˌænɪməˈtrɒnɪks] n animatronique f.
anime [ˈænɪmeɪ] n anime m, animé m.
animosity [ˌænɪˈmɒsətɪ] (pl animosities) n animosité f, antipathie f.
aniseed [ˈænɪsiːd] ◆ n graine f d'anis. ◆ comp à l'anis.
ankle [ˈæŋkl] ◆ n cheville f. ◆ comp ▶ ankle boot bottine f ▶ ankle sock socquette f.
anklebone [ˈæŋkəlbəʊn] n astragale m.
ankle-length adj qui descend jusqu'à la cheville.
anklet [ˈæŋklɪt] n **1.** [chain] bracelet m de cheville **2.** US [ankle sock] socquette f.
annals [ˈænlz] pl n annales fpl.
annex ◆ vt [æˈneks] annexer. ◆ n US = annexe.
annexation [ˌænekˈseɪʃn] n [act] annexion f ; [country] pays m annexé ; [document] document m annexe, annexe f.
annexe UK, **annex** US [ˈæneks] n [building, supplement to document] annexe f.
annihilate [əˈnaɪəleɪt] vt [destroy - enemy, race] anéantir, détruire ; [-argument, effort] anéantir, annihiler.
annihilation [əˌnaɪəˈleɪʃn] n [destruction - of argument, enemy, effort] anéantissement m.
anniversary [ˌænɪˈvɜːsərɪ] (pl anniversaries) ◆ n anniversaire m (d'un événement), commémoration f. ◆ comp [celebration, dinner] anniversaire, commémoratif ▶ anniversary card carte f d'anniversaire (de mariage).
annotate [ˈænəteɪt] vt annoter.

annotation [ˌænə'teɪʃn] n [action] annotation f ; [note] annotation f, note f.

announce [ə'naʊns] vt annoncer / *we are pleased to announce the birth / marriage of our son* nous sommes heureux de vous faire part de la naissance / du mariage de notre fils.

announcement [ə'naʊnsmənt] n [public statement] annonce f ; ADMIN avis m ; [notice of birth, marriage] faire-part m.

announcer [ə'naʊnsər] n [gen] annonceur m, -euse f ; RADIO & TV [newscaster] journaliste mf ; [introducing programme] speaker m, speakerine f, annonceur m, -euse f.

annoy [ə'nɔɪ] vt ennuyer, agacer / *he only did it to annoy you* il l'a fait uniquement pour vous ennuyer or contrarier.

annoyance [ə'nɔɪəns] n **1.** [displeasure] contrariété f, mécontentement m / *with a look of annoyance* d'un air contrarié or ennuyé **2.** [source of irritation] ennui m, désagrément m.

annoyed [ə'nɔɪd] adj ▶ **to be / to get annoyed with sb** être / se mettre en colère contre qqn / *she was annoyed* elle était mécontente.

annoying [ə'nɔɪɪŋ] adj [bothersome] gênant, ennuyeux ; [very irritating] énervant, agaçant, fâcheux / *the annoying thing is...* ce qui est énervant dans l'histoire, c'est...

annoyingly [ə'nɔɪɪŋlɪ] adv de manière gênante or agaçante.

annual ['ænjʊəl] ◆ adj annuel / *what's your annual income?* combien gagnez-vous par an ? ◆ n **1.** [publication] publication f annuelle ; [of association, firm] annuaire m ; [for children] album m (de bandes dessinées) **2.** BOT plante f annuelle.

annual earnings pl n **1.** [of company] recette(s) fpl annuelle(s) **2.** [of person] revenu m annuel.

annual general meeting n assemblée f générale annuelle.

annual income n revenu m annuel.

annually ['ænjʊəlɪ] adv annuellement, tous les ans.

annual turnover n chiffre m d'affaires annuel.

annuity [ə'njuːɪtɪ] (pl **annuities**) n [regular income] rente f ▶ **annuity for life** or **life annuity** viager m, rente f viagère ; [investment] viager m, rente f viagère.

annul [ə'nʌl] (pt & pp **annulled**, cont **annulling**) vt [law] abroger, abolir ; [agreement, contract] résilier ; [marriage] annuler ; [judgment] casser, annuler.

annulment [ə'nʌlmənt] n [of law] abrogation f, abolition f ; [of agreement, contract] résiliation f ; [of marriage] annulation f ; [of judgment] cassation f, annulation f.

Annunciation [ə,nʌnsɪ'eɪʃn] n ▶ **the Annunciation** l'Annonciation f.

anode ['ænəʊd] n anode f.

anoint [ə'nɔɪnt] vt [in religious ceremony] oindre, consacrer par l'onction / *they anointed him king* ils l'ont sacré roi.

anomalous [ə'nɒmələs] adj [effect, growth, result] anormal, irrégulier ; GRAM anormal.

anomaly [ə'nɒmlɪ] (pl **anomalies**) n anomalie f.

anon. (written abbr of **anonymous**) anon.

anonymity [ˌænə'nɪmətɪ] n [namelessness] anonymat m.

anonymous [ə'nɒnɪməs] adj anonyme / *to remain anonymous* garder l'anonymat.

anonymously [ə'nɒnɪməslɪ] adv [act, donate] anonymement, en gardant l'anonymat ; [publish] anonymement, sans nom d'auteur.

anorak ['ænəræk] n [coat] anorak m.

anorexia nervosa [-nɜː'vəʊsə] n anorexie f mentale.

anorexic [ˌænə'reksɪk], **anorectic** [ˌænə'rektɪk] ◆ adj anorexique. ◆ n anorexique mf.

another [ə'nʌðər] ◆ det **1.** [additional] un... de plus (une... de plus), encore un (encore une) / *have another chocolate* prenez un autre or reprenez un chocolat / *another 5 miles* encore 5 miles / *another 5 minutes and we'd have missed the train* 5 minutes de plus et on ratait le train / *without another word* sans un mot de plus, sans ajouter un mot **2.** [different] un autre (une autre) / *let's do it another way* faisons-le autrement / *that's another matter entirely!* ça, c'est une tout autre histoire ! ◆ pron **1.** [a similar one] un autre (une autre), encore un (encore une) **2.** [a different one] : *another of the girls* une autre des filles / *bring a dessert of one sort or another* apportez un dessert (, n'importe lequel).

A. N. Other [ˌeɪen'ʌðər] n 🇬🇧 monsieur X, madame X.

ANSI (abbr of **American National Standards Institute**) n association américaine de normalisation.

answer ['ɑːnsər] ◆ vt **1.** [letter, person, telephone, advertisement] répondre à ; [door] aller or venir ouvrir / *I phoned earlier but nobody answered* j'ai téléphoné tout à l'heure mais ça ne répondait pas **2.** [respond correctly to] : *he could only answer two of the questions* il n'a su répondre qu'à deux des questions. ◆ vi répondre, donner une réponse. ◆ n **1.** [reply - to letter, person, request] réponse f ; [- to criticism, objection] réponse f, réfutation f / *I rang the bell but there was no answer* j'ai sonné mais personne n'a répondu or n'a ouvert / *I phoned but there was no answer* j'ai téléphoné mais ça ne répondait pas / *he has an answer for everything* il a réponse à tout / *it's the answer to all my prayers* or *dreams!* c'est ce dont j'ai toujours rêvé ! **2.** [solution] solution f / *the (right) answer* la bonne réponse / *there's no easy answer* lit & fig il n'y a pas de solution facile **3.** [to exam question] réponse f **4.** [equivalent] : *she's England's answer to Edith Piaf* elle est or c'est l'Édith Piaf anglaise. ◆◆ **answer back** ◆ vi répondre (avec insolence). ◆ vt sep répondre (avec insolence) à, répliquer à. ◆◆ **answer for** vt insep [be responsible for] répondre de, être responsable de. ◆◆ **answer to** vt insep **1.** [respond to] : *the cat answers to (the name of) Frankie* le chat répond au nom de Frankie, le chat s'appelle Frankie **2.** [correspond to] répondre à, correspondre à.

answerable ['ɑːnsərəbl] adj [person] responsable, comptable ▶ **to be answerable to sb for sthg** être responsable de qqch devant qqn, être garant de qqch envers qqn.

answering machine ['ɑːnsərɪŋ-] n répondeur m (téléphonique).

answering service n permanence f téléphonique.

answerphone ['ænsəfəʊn] n = **answering machine**.

ant [ænt] n fourmi f.

antacid [ˌænt'æsɪd] ◆ n (médicament m) alcalin m, antiacide m. ◆ adj alcalin, antiacide.

antagonism [æn'tægənɪzm] n antagonisme m, hostilité f.

antagonist [æn'tægənɪst] n antagoniste mf, adversaire mf.

antagonistic [æn,tægə'nɪstɪk] adj [person] opposé, hostile ; [feelings, ideas] antagoniste, antagonique.

antagonize, antagonise [æn'tægənaɪz] vt contrarier, mettre à dos.

Antarctic [ænt'ɑːktɪk] ◆ pr n ▶ **the Antarctic (Ocean)** l'Antarctique m, l'océan m Antarctique. ◆ adj antarctique.

Antarctica [ænt'ɑːktɪkə] pr n Antarctique f, le continent m antarctique.

Antarctic Circle pr n ▶ **the Antarctic Circle** le cercle polaire antarctique.

ante ['ænti] n CARDS mise f ▶ **to up the ante** inf augmenter la mise.

anteater ['ænt,i:tər] n fourmilier m.

antecedent [,ænti'si:dənt] ◆ n GRAM, LOGIC & MATH antécédent. ◆ adj antérieur, précédent.

antediluvian [,æntidi'lu:vjən] adj liter & hum antédiluvien.

antelope ['æntiləup] (pl **antelope** or **antelopes**) n antilope f.

antenatal [,ænti'neitl] UK adj prénatal ▶ **antenatal clinic** service m de consultation prénatale.

antenna [æn'tenə] (pl **antennae** [-ni:] or **antennas**) n US antenne f.

anteroom ['æntirum] n antichambre f, vestibule m.

anthem ['ænθəm] n [song] chant m ; RELIG motet m.

anthill ['ænθil] n fourmilière f.

anthology [æn'θolədʒi] (pl **anthologies**) n anthologie f.

anthrax ['ænθræks] n [disease] charbon m ; [sore] anthrax m.

anthropological [,ænθrəpə'lodʒikl] adj anthropologique.

anthropologist [,ænθrə'polədʒist] n anthropologue mf.

anthropology [,ænθrə'polədʒi] n anthropologie f.

anti- in comp anti-.

antiabortion [,æntiə'bɔ:ʃn] adj : the antiabortion movement le mouvement contre l'avortement.

antiaircraft [,ænti'eəkrɑ:ft] adj [system, weapon] antiaérien.

anti-aliasing [-'eiliəsiŋ] n COMPUT antialiassage m, anticrénelage m.

anti-Americanism n antiaméricanisme m.

antiapartheid [,æntiə'pɑ:theit] adj antiapartheid.

antibacterial [,æntibæk'ti:riəl] adj antibactérien.

antiballistic missile [,æntibə'listik-] n missile m antibalistique.

antibiotic [,æntibai'ɒtik] ◆ adj antibiotique. ◆ n antibiotique m.

antibody ['ænti,bɒdi] (pl **antibodies**) n anticorps m.

anticipate [æn'tisi,peit] vt **1.** [think likely] prévoir, s'attendre à / I didn't anticipate leaving so early je ne m'attendais pas à ce qu'on parte si tôt / as anticipated comme prévu **2.** [be prepared for -attack, decision, event] anticiper, anticiper sur ; [- needs, wishes] devancer, prévenir, aller au devant de.

anticipation [æn,tisi'peiʃn] n **1.** [expectation] attente f **2.** fml [readiness] anticipation f **3.** [eagerness] impatience f, empressement m / fans jostled at the gates in eager anticipation les fans, ne tenant plus d'impatience, se bousculaient aux grilles d'entrée.

anticlimax [,ænti'klaimæks] n [disappointment] déception f / the opening ceremony was a bit of an anticlimax la cérémonie d'ouverture a été quelque peu décevante / what an anticlimax! quelle douche froide !

anticlockwise [,ænti'klokwaiz] UK ◆ adv dans le sens inverse or contraire des aiguilles d'une montre. ◆ adj : turn it in an anticlockwise direction tournez-le dans le sens inverse des aiguilles d'une montre.

anticompetitive [,æntikəm'petitiv] adj ECON anticoncurrentiel.

anticonstitutional ['ænti,konsti'tju:ʃənl] adj POL anticonstitutionnel.

antics ['æntiks] pl n [absurd behaviour] cabrioles fpl, gambades fpl ; [jokes] bouffonnerie f, pitrerie f / they're up to their (old) antics again les voilà repartis avec leurs pitreries.

anticyclone [,ænti'saikləun] n anticyclone m.

antidemocratic ['ænti,deməˈkrætik] adj POL antidémocratique.

antidepressant [,æntidə'presnt] ◆ adj antidépresseur. ◆ n antidépresseur m.

antidote ['æntidəut] n antidote m.

antidumping [,ænti'dʌmpiŋ] adj [law, legislation] antidumping.

anti-Establishment adj POL anticonformiste.

antifascism [,ænti'fæʃizəm] n POL antifascisme m.

antifascist [,ænti'fæʃist] adj & n POL antifasciste.

antifreeze ['æntifri:z] n antigel m.

antiglare ['æntigleər] adj ▶ **antiglare headlights** phares mpl antiéblouissants.

antiglobalization, antiglobalisation [,æntiglaubəlai'zeiʃən] ◆ n POL antimondialisation f. ◆ adj POL antimondialisation.

Antigua [æn'ti:gə] pr n Antigua ▶ **Antigua and Barbuda** Antigua et Barbuda.

antihero ['ænti,hiərəu] (pl **antiheroes**) n antihéros m.

antihistamine [,ænti'histəmin] n antihistaminique m.

anti-inflammatory ◆ adj anti-inflammatoire. ◆ n anti-inflammatoire m.

antimonopoly [,æntimə'nopəli] adj UK ECON [law, legislation] antitrust.

antinuclear [,ænti'nju:kliər] adj antinucléaire.

antioxidant [,ænti'oksidənt] n antioxydant m.

antipathy [æn'tipəθi] (pl **antipathies**) n antipathie f.

antipersonnel ['ænti,pɜ:sə'nel] adj euph antipersonnel (inv).

antiperspirant [,ænti'pɜ:spərənt] ◆ adj antiperspirant ▶ **antiperspirant deodorant** déodorant m antiperspirant. ◆ n antiperspirant m.

antipodean [æn,tipə'diən] adj des antipodes.

Antipodes [æn'tipədi:z] pl pr n ▶ **the Antipodes** l'Australie f et la Nouvelle-Zélande.

antiquarian [,ænti'kweəriən] ◆ adj [collection, shop] d'antiquités ; [bookseller, bookshop] spécialisé dans les livres anciens. ◆ n [collector] collectionneur m, -euse f d'antiquités ; [researcher] archéologue mf ; [merchant] antiquaire mf.

antiquated ['æntikweitid] adj **1.** [outmoded - machine, method] vieillot, obsolète ; [- building, installation] vétuste ; [- idea, manners] vieillot, suranné ; [- person] vieux jeu (inv) **2.** [ancient] très vieux.

antique [æn'ti:k] ◆ adj [very old] ancien ; [dating from Greek or Roman times] antique. ◆ n [furniture] meuble m ancien or d'époque ; [vase] vase m ancien or d'époque ; [work of art] objet m d'art ancien. ◆ comp [lover, shop] d'antiquités ▶ **antique dealer** antiquaire mf.

antiquity [æn'tikwəti] (pl **antiquities**) n **1.** [ancient times] Antiquité f **2.** [building, ruin] monument m ancien, antiquité f ; [coin, statue] objet m ancien ; [work of art] objet d'art m ancien, antiquité f **3.** [oldness] antiquité f.

anti-Semitic adj antisémite.

anti-Semitism n antisémitisme m.

antiseptic [,ænti'septik] ◆ adj antiseptique. ◆ n antiseptique m.

antisocial [,ænti'səuʃl] adj [behaviour, measure] antisocial.

antistatic [,ænti'stætik] adj antistatique.

antitank [ˌæntɪ'tæŋk] adj antichar.

antiterrorist [ˌæntɪ'terərɪst] adj antiterroriste.

antitheft [ˌæntɪ'θeft] adj antivol / *an antitheft device* un antivol, un dispositif contre le vol or antivol.

antithesis [æn'tɪθɪsɪs] (*pl* **antitheses** [-siːz]) n **1.** [exact opposite] contraire *m*, opposé *m* **2.** [contrast, opposition] antithèse *f*, contraste *m*, opposition *f*.

antivirus ['æntɪvaɪrəs] adj antivirus ▶ **antivirus program** COMPUT programme *m* antivirus.

antler ['æntlə'] n corne *f* ▶ **the antlers** les bois *mpl*, la ramure.

antonym ['æntənɪm] n antonyme *m*.

Antwerp ['æntwɜːp] pr n Anvers.

anus ['eɪnəs] n anus *m*.

anvil ['ænvɪl] n enclume *f*.

anxiety [æŋ'zaɪətɪ] (*pl* **anxieties**) n **1.** [feeling of worry] anxiété *f*, appréhension *f* / *a source of deep anxiety* une source d'angoisse profonde **2.** [source of worry] souci *m* **3.** [intense eagerness] grand désir *m*, désir *m* ardent / *in his anxiety to please her, he forgot everything else* il tenait tellement à lui faire plaisir qu'il en oubliait tout le reste.

anxious ['æŋkʃəs] adj **1.** [worried] anxieux, angoissé, inquiet / *she's a very anxious person* c'est une grande angoissée **2.** [worrying] inquiétant, angoissant / *we had one or two anxious moments* nous avons connu quelques moments d'anxiété or d'inquiétude **3.** [eager] anxieux, impatient / *they're anxious to start* ils sont impatients or pressés de commencer / *she's very anxious to please* elle est très désireuse or anxieuse de plaire.

anxiously ['æŋkʃəslɪ] adv **1.** [nervously] avec inquiétude, anxieusement **2.** [eagerly] impatiemment, avec impatience.

anxiousness ['æŋkʃəsnɪs] n = anxiety.

any ['enɪ] ◆ det **1.** [some - in questions] : *have you any money?* avez-vous de l'argent ? / *have any guests arrived?* des invités sont-ils arrivés ? / *were you in any danger?* étiez-vous en danger ? / *any news about the application?* *inf* il y a du neuf pour la candidature ? ; [in conditional clauses] : *if there's any cake left, can I have some?* s'il reste du gâteau, est-ce que je peux en avoir ? / *any nonsense from you and you'll be out!* *inf* tu n'as qu'à bien te tenir, sinon, c'est la porte ! **2.** [in negative phrases] : *he hasn't any change / money / cigarettes* il n'a pas de monnaie / d'argent / de cigarettes / *he can't stand any noise* il ne supporte pas le moindre bruit, il ne supporte aucun bruit / *hardly* or *barely* or *scarcely any* très peu de **3.** [no matter which] n'importe quel (n'importe quelle) / *at any time of day* à n'importe quel moment or à tout moment de la journée / *any one of these paintings is worth a fortune* chacun de ces tableaux vaut une fortune / *any (old) cup will do* n'importe quelle vieille tasse fera l'affaire **4.** [all, every] tout / *give me any money you've got* donne-moi tout l'argent que tu as **5.** [unlimited] : *there are any number of ways of winning* il y a mille façons de gagner. ◆ adv **1.** [with comparative - in questions, conditional statements] : *can you walk any faster?* peux-tu marcher un peu plus vite ? / *if she isn't any better by tomorrow, call the doctor* si elle ne va pas mieux demain, appelez le médecin ; [in negative statements] / *we can't go any further* nous ne pouvons aller plus loin / *it's not getting any easier to find good staff* c'est toujours aussi difficile de trouver de bons employés **2.** *inf* [at all] : *you're not helping me any* tu ne m'aides pas du tout. ◆ pron **1.** [in questions, conditional statements - some, someone] : *did you see any?* en avez-vous vu ? / *did any of them go?* est-ce que certains d'entre eux y sont allés ? / *few, if any, of his supporters remained loyal* aucun ou presque aucun de ses supporters ne lui est

resté fidèle **2.** [in negative statements - even one] : *he won't vote for any of the candidates* il ne votera pour aucun des candidats / *there was hardly any of it left* il n'en restait que très peu / *she's learned two foreign languages, I haven't learned any* elle a étudié deux langues étrangères, je n'en ai étudié aucune **3.** [no matter which one] n'importe lequel (n'importe laquelle) / *study any of her works and you will discover...* étudie n'importe laquelle de ses œuvres et tu découvriras...

anybody ['enɪˌbɒdɪ] pron **1.** *(in questions, conditional statements)* [someone] quelqu'un / *(is) anybody home?* il y a quelqu'un ? / *she'll persuade them, if anybody can* si quelqu'un peut les convaincre, c'est bien elle **2.** *(in negative statements)* [someone] personne / *there was hardly anybody there* il n'y avait presque personne **3.** [no matter who, everyone] : *anybody who wants can join us* tous ceux qui veulent peuvent se joindre à nous / *invite anybody you want* invitez qui vous voulez / *it could happen to anybody* ça pourrait arriver à tout le monde or n'importe qui / *I don't care what anybody thinks* je me fiche de ce que pensent les gens / *she's cleverer than anybody I know* c'est la personne la plus intelligente que je connaisse / *anybody with any sense* or *in their right mind would have...* toute personne un peu sensée aurait... / *anybody would think you'd just lost your best friend* on croirait que tu viens de perdre ton meilleur ami / *he's not just anybody, he's my brother!* ce n'est pas n'importe qui, c'est mon frère !

anyhow ['enɪhaʊ] adv **1.** = **anyway 2.** [in any manner, by any means] : *I had to persuade her somehow, anyhow* il fallait que je trouve un moyen de la convaincre, n'importe lequel **3.** *inf* [haphazardly] n'importe comment.

any more 🇬🇧, **anymore** 🇺🇸 [ˌenɪ'mɔːʳ] adv : *they don't live here any more* ils n'habitent plus ici / *I won't do it any more* je ne le ferai plus (jamais).

ANY1 MESSAGING written abbr of **anyone**.

NE1 MESSAGING written abbr of **anyone**.

anyone ['enɪwʌn] pron = **anybody**.

anyplace ['enɪpleɪs] adv & pron 🇺🇸 *inf* = **anywhere**.

anything ['enɪθɪŋ] pron **1.** [something - in questions] quelque chose / *did you hear anything?* avez-vous entendu quelque chose ? / *can't we do anything?* est-ce qu'il n'y a rien à faire ? ; [in conditional statements] / *if anything should happen, take care of John for me* s'il m'arrivait quelque chose or quoi que ce soit, occupez-vous de John ; [in negative statements] rien / *I didn't say anything* je n'ai rien dit / *I don't know anything about computers* je ne m'y connais pas du tout or je n'y connais rien en informatique **2.** [no matter what] : *just tell him anything* racontez-lui n'importe quoi / *anything you like* tout ce que vous voudrez / *I'd give anything to know the truth* je donnerais n'importe quoi pour savoir la vérité **3.** [all, everything] tout / *her son eats anything* son fils mange de tout / *you can use it to flavour anything from jam to soup* vous pouvez l'utiliser pour parfumer n'importe quoi, de la confiture à la soupe **4.** [in intensifying phrases] : *he isn't anything like his father* il ne ressemble en rien à son père. ◆ **anything but** adv phr tout sauf / *that music is anything but relaxing* cette musique est tout sauf reposante / *is he crazy? — anything but!* est-ce qu'il est fou ? — bien au contraire ! or il est tout sauf ça !

anytime ['enɪtaɪm] adv **1.** [at any time] n'importe quand, à n'importe quel moment **2.** [you're welcome] je t'en prie, je vous en prie.

anyway ['enɪweɪ] adv **1.** [in any case - reinforcing] de toute façon / *what's to stop them anyway?* de toute façon, qu'est-ce qui peut les en empêcher ? ; [summarizing, concluding] en tout cas / *anyway, I have to go* **a)** [I'll be late] bon, il faut que j'y aille **b)** [I don't have any choice] enfin, il faut que j'y aille **2.** [nevertheless, notwithstanding] quand même **/** *thanks anyway* merci quand même **3.** [qualifying] en tout cas **4.** [returning to topic] bref.

anywhere ['eniweə^r], **anyplace** 🇺🇸 ['enipleis] ◆ adv **1.** [in questions] quelque part **/** *have you seen my keys anywhere?* avez-vous vu mes clés (quelque part) **?** / *are you going anywhere at Easter?* vous partez à Pâques ? **2.** [in positive statements - no matter where] n'importe où **/** *just put it down anywhere* posez-le n'importe où **/** *sit anywhere you like* asseyez-vous où vous voulez ; [everywhere] partout **/** *you can find that magazine anywhere* on trouve cette revue partout **3.** [in negative statements - any place] nulle part **/** *I can't find my keys anywhere* je ne trouve mes clés nulle part **/** *look, this isn't getting us anywhere* écoute, tout ça ne nous mène à rien. ◆ pron [any place] : *do they need anywhere to stay?* ont-ils besoin d'un endroit où loger ?

Anzac ['ænzæk] (abbr of **Australia-New Zealand Army Corps**) n *soldat néo-zélandais ou australien* ▸ **Anzac Day** *date anniversaire du débarquement des Alliés australiens et néo-zélandais à Gallipoli, en Turquie, le 25 avril 1915.*

aob, a.o.b., AOB (written abbr of **any other business**) *divers.*

AONB n 🇬🇧 abbr of **area of outstanding natural beauty.**

aorta [eɪ'ɔːtə] (pl **aortas** or **aortae** [-tiː]) n aorte f.

AP n abbr of **American Plan.**

Apache [ə'pætʃi] (pl **Apache** or **Apaches**) ◆ n [person] Apache mf. ◆ adj apache.

apart [ə'pɑːt] adv **1.** [separated - in space] : *the houses were about 10 kilometres apart* les maisons étaient à environ 10 kilomètres l'une de l'autre **/** *he stood with his legs wide apart* il se tenait (debout) les jambes bien écartées **/** *they can't bear to be apart* ils ne supportent pas d'être loin l'un de l'autre or séparés ; [in time] : *the twins were born 3 minutes apart* les jumeaux sont nés à 3 minutes d'intervalle **2.** [in pieces] en pièces, en morceaux ▸ **to break apart** s'émietter **3.** [isolated] à l'écart **/** *she stood apart from the others* elle se tenait à l'écart des autres **4.** [aside] à part ▸ **joking apart** trêve de plaisanterie. ◆ **apart from** prep phr **1.** [except for] à part **/** *it's fine, apart from a few minor mistakes* à part or sauf quelques fautes sans importance, c'est très bien **2.** [as well as] en plus de **/** *she has many interests apart from golf* elle s'intéresse à beaucoup de choses à part le or en plus du golf **/** *quite apart from the fact that it's too big, I don't like the colour* outre (le fait) que c'est trop grand, je n'aime pas la couleur.

apartheid [ə'pɑːtheɪt] n apartheid m.

apartment [ə'pɑːtmənt] n [flat] appartement m, logement m.

apartment building n 🇺🇸 immeuble m (d'habitation).

apathetic [ˌæpə'θetɪk] adj apathique, indifférent.

apathy ['æpəθɪ] n apathie f, indifférence f.

APB (abbr of **all points bulletin**) n 🇺🇸 message radio diffusé par la police concernant une personne recherchée.

APC (abbr of **average propensity to consume**) n ECON PmaC.

ape [eɪp] ◆ n [monkey] grand singe m, anthropoïde m spec. ◆ vt singer.

Apennines ['æpɪnaɪnz] pl pr n ▸ **the Apennines** l'Apennin m, les Apennins mpl.

aperitif [əperə'tiːf] n apéritif m.

aperture ['æpə,tjʊə^r] n **1.** [opening] ouverture f, orifice m ; [gap] brèche f, trouée f **2.** PHOT ouverture f (du diaphragme).

apeshit ['eɪpʃɪt] adj 🇺🇸 vulg ▸ **to go apeshit** être fou de rage, péter les plombs.

apex ['eɪpeks] (pl **apexes** or **apices** ['eɪpɪsiːz]) n [of triangle] sommet m, apex m ; fig point m culminant, sommet m.

APEX ['eɪpeks] (abbr of **advance purchase excursion**) n 🇬🇧 ▸ **APEX fare** tarif m apex.

aphid ['eɪfɪd] n puceron m.

aphrodisiac [ˌæfrə'dɪzɪæk] ◆ adj aphrodisiaque. ◆ n aphrodisiaque m.

apices ['eɪpɪsiːz] pl ⟶ **apex.**

apiece [ə'piːs] adv **1.** [for each item] chacun m, -e f, (la) pièce **2.** [for each person] chacun m, -e f, par personne.

aplenty [ə'plentɪ] adj liter : *she's always had money aplenty* elle a toujours eu beaucoup or énormément d'argent.

aplomb [ə'plɒm] n sang-froid m, aplomb m pej.

APO (abbr of **Army Post Office**) n service postal de l'armée.

Apocalypse [ə'pɒkəlɪps] n Apocalypse f.

apocalyptic [ə,pɒkə'lɪptɪk] adj apocalyptique.

apocryphal [ə'pɒkrɪfl] adj apocryphe.

apolitical [ˌeɪpə'lɪtɪkəl] adj apolitique.

apologetic [ə,pɒlə'dʒetɪk] adj **1.** [person] : *she was very apologetic for being late* elle s'est excusée plusieurs fois d'être arrivée en retard **2.** [letter, look, note, smile] d'excuse.

apologetically [ə,pɒlə'dʒetɪklɪ] adv [say] en s'excusant, pour s'excuser ; [smile] pour s'excuser.

apologize, apologise [ə'pɒlədʒaɪz] vi s'excuser **/** *there's no need to apologize* inutile de vous excuser **/** *I can't apologize enough* je ne sais comment m'excuser.

apology [ə'pɒlədʒɪ] (pl **apologies**) n **1.** [expression of regret] excuses fpl ▸ **to make one's apologies to sb** s'excuser auprès de qqn **/** *the director sends his apologies* le directeur vous prie de l'excuser **2.** 🇬🇧 pej [poor example] : *he's a mere apology for a man* c'est un nul.

⚠ The formal word **apologie** usually means praise; it cannot be used to translate apology when it means saying you are sorry.

apoplectic [ˌæpə'plektɪk] ◆ adj apoplectique ; fig fou de rage. ◆ n apoplectique mf.

apoplexy ['æpəpleksɪ] n apoplexie f.

apostle [ə'pɒsl] n RELIG & fig apôtre m.

apostrophe [ə'pɒstrəfɪ] n apostrophe f.

app [æp] (abbr of **application**) n COMPUT application f, appli f inf.

appal 🇬🇧, **appall** 🇺🇸 [ə'pɔːl] (pt & pp **appalled**, cont **appalling**) vt [scandalize] choquer, scandaliser ; [horrify] écœurer **/** *she was appalled at* or *by the very thought* l'idée même l'écœurait.

Appalachian [ˌæpə'leɪtʃjən] ◆ pr n ▸ **the Appalachians** or **the Appalachian Mountains** les (monts mpl) Appalaches mpl. ◆ adj appalachien.

appall 🇺🇸 vt = **appal.**

appalled [ə'pɔːld] adj écœuré.

appalling [ə'pɔːlɪŋ] adj épouvantable.

appallingly [ə'pɔːlɪŋlɪ] adv **1.** [badly] de façon écœurante **2.** [as intensifier] effroyablement.

apparatus [ˌæpə'rætəs] (pl **apparatus** or **apparatuses**) n **1.** (U) [equipment] équipement m ; [set of instruments] instruments mpl **2.** (U) [in gymnasium] agrès mpl **3.** [machine] appareil m.

apparel [ə'pærəl] (US pt & pp **apparelled**, cont **apparelling** ; US pt & pp **appareled**, cont **appareling**) n US [clothes] habillement m, vêtements mpl ; [industry] confection f.

apparent [ə'pærənt] adj **1.** [obvious] évident, apparent / *for no apparent reason* sans raison apparente **2.** [seeming] apparent, supposé.

apparently [ə'pærəntlɪ] adv **1.** [seemingly] apparemment, en apparence **2.** [according to rumour] à ce qu'il paraît / *apparently, they had a huge row* il paraît qu'ils se sont violemment disputés.

apparition [,æpə'rɪʃn] n apparition f.

appeal [ə'piːl] ◆ n **1.** [request] appel m / *an appeal for help* un appel au secours **2.** LAW appel m, pourvoi m **3.** [attraction] attrait m, charme m / *the idea does have a certain appeal* l'idée est bien séduisante. ◆ vi **1.** [make request] faire un appel ; [publicly] lancer un appel ; [plead] supplier, implorer / *she appealed to me to be patient* elle m'a prié d'être patient / *they're appealing for help for the victims* ils lancent un appel au profit des victimes **2.** [apply] faire appel / *he appealed to them for help* il leur a demandé du secours **3.** LAW interjeter appel, se pourvoir en appel ▸ **to appeal against a sentence** appeler d'un jugement **4.** [please] plaire / *it doesn't really appeal to me* ça ne m'attire pas vraiment, ça ne me dit pas grand-chose.

appeal court n cour f d'appel.

appealing [ə'piːlɪŋ] adj [attractive - dress, person] joli ; [- idea, plan] intéressant.

appear [ə'pɪər] vi **1.** [come into view - person, ghost, stars] apparaître / *the sun appeared from behind a cloud* le soleil est sorti de derrière un nuage **2.** [come into being] apparaître ; [new product] apparaître, être mis sur le marché ; [publication] paraître, sortir, être publié **3.** [be present officially] se présenter, paraître ; [in court] comparaître / *to appear before the court* or *the judge* comparaître devant le tribunal **4.** [actor] jouer / *she appeared as Antigone* elle a joué Antigone / *to appear on TV* passer à la télévision **5.** [seem] paraître, sembler / *she appeared nervous* elle avait l'air nerveuse / *there appears to have been a mistake* il semble qu'il y ait eu erreur / *so it appears* or *so it would appear* c'est ce qu'il semble, on dirait bien / *is she ill? — it appears* so est-elle malade ? — il paraît (que oui).

appearance [ə'pɪərəns] n **1.** [act of appearing] apparition f / *she made a brief appearance at the party* elle a fait une brève apparition à la fête ▸ **to put in an appearance** faire acte de présence **2.** [advent] avènement m ; [of new product] mise f sur le marché ; [of publication] parution f **3.** [in court] comparution f / *to make an appearance before a court* or *a judge* comparaître devant un tribunal **4.** [performance] : *this was her first appearance on the stage* c'était sa première apparition sur scène / *she's made a number of television appearances* elle est passée plusieurs fois à la télévision ▸ **in order of appearance** par ordre d'entrée en scène **5.** [outward aspect] apparence f, aspect m / *to have a good appearance* [person] présenter bien / *don't judge by appearances* ne vous fiez pas aux apparences, il ne faut pas se fier aux apparences / *for appearances' sake* pour la forme.

appease [ə'piːz] vt apaiser, calmer.

appeasement [ə'piːzmənt] n apaisement m ; pej POL conciliation f.

append [ə'pend] vt fml [document, note] joindre ; [signature] apposer.

appendage [ə'pendɪdʒ] n [gen & ZOOL] appendice m.

appendices [ə'pendɪsiːz] pl ⟶ **appendix**.

appendicitis [ə,pendɪ'saɪtɪs] n (U) appendicite f.

appendix [ə'pendɪks] (pl **appendixes** or **appendices** [-siːz]) n **1.** ANAT appendice m ▸ **to have one's appendix out** se faire opérer de l'appendicite **2.** [to book, report] annexe f.

⚠ The word **annexe** is more common than **appendice** when talking about the appendix to a book or document.

appetite ['æpɪtaɪt] n appétit m / *I've lost my appetite* j'ai perdu l'appétit / *they've gone for a swim to work up an appetite* ils sont allés se baigner pour s'ouvrir l'appétit or se mettre en appétit / *I have no appetite for that kind of thing* je n'ai pas de goût pour ce genre de chose.

appetizer, appetiser ['æpɪtaɪzər] n [food] hors-d'œuvre m inv, amuse-gueule m ; [drink] apéritif m.

appetizing, appetising ['æpɪtaɪzɪŋ] adj appétissant.

applaud [ə'plɔːd] ◆ vi applaudir. ◆ vt applaudir, approuver.

applause [ə'plɔːz] n (U) applaudissements mpl, acclamations fpl / *his performance won enthusiastic applause from the audience* son interprétation a été chaleureusement applaudie par le public.

apple ['æpl] ◆ n [fruit] pomme f ; [tree] pommier m ▸ **she's the apple of his eye** il tient à elle comme à la prunelle de ses yeux. ◆ comp ▸ **apple blossom** fleur f de pommier ▸ **apple core** trognon m de pomme ▸ **apple juice** jus m de pomme.

apple butter n US confiture f de pommes.

apple pie n [covered] tourte f aux pommes ; [open] tarte f aux pommes.

applet ['æplət] n COMPUT appelette f, appliquette f.

appliance [ə'plaɪəns] n appareil m ; [small] dispositif m, instrument m ▸ **domestic** or **household appliances** appareils électroménagers ▸ **electrical appliances** appareils électriques.

applicable ['æplɪkəbl] adj applicable.

applicant ['æplɪkənt] n [gen, for patent] demandeur m, -euse f ; [for a position] candidat m, -e f, postulant m, -e f.

application [,æplɪ'keɪʃn] n **1.** [use] application f ; [of lotion, paint] application f **2.** [request] demande f / *a job application* **a)** [spontaneous] une demande d'emploi **b)** [in answer to advertisement] une candidature à un poste / *I submitted my application for a scholarship* j'ai fait ma demande de bourse **3.** COMPUT application f **4.** [diligence] assiduité f.

application form n formulaire m ; [detailed] dossier m de candidature ; UNIV dossier m d'inscription.

application(s) program n programme m d'application.

applicator ['æplɪkeɪtər] n applicateur m.

applied [ə'plaɪd] adj [gen & LING], MATH & SCI appliqué ▸ **applied arts** arts mpl décoratifs.

appliqué [æ'pliːkeɪ] n [decoration] application f ; [decorative work] travail m d'application.

apply [ə'plaɪ] (pt & pp **applied**) ◆ vt **1.** [use] appliquer, mettre en pratique or en application ; [rule, law] appliquer **2.** [pressure] ▸ **to apply pressure to sthg** exercer une pression or appuyer sur qqch / *she applied the brakes* elle a appuyé sur le frein **3.** [paint, lotion, etc.] appliquer, mettre **4.** [devote] ▸ **to apply one's mind to sthg** s'appliquer à qqch. ◆ vi **1.** [make an application] s'adresser, avoir recours à ▸ **'apply within'** s'adresser à l'intérieur or ici ▸ **to apply for a job / scholarship** faire une demande d'emploi / de bourse / *she has decided to apply for the job* elle a décidé de poser sa candidature pour cet emploi **2.** [be relevant] s'appliquer / *this doesn't apply to us* nous ne sommes pas concernés.

appoint [ə'pɔɪnt] vt **1.** [assign] nommer, désigner / *she was appointed to the post of director* elle a été nommée directrice **2.** [date, place] fixer, désigner / *we met on the appointed day* nous nous sommes rencontrés au jour dit or convenu.

appointment [ə'pɔɪntmənt] n **1.** [arrangement] rendez-vous *m* ▶ **to make an appointment with sb** prendre rendez-vous avec qqn / *I made an appointment with the dentist* j'ai pris rendez-vous chez le dentiste / *they made an appointment to have lunch together* ils se sont donné rendez-vous pour déjeuner / *do you have an appointment?* avez-vous (pris) rendez-vous ? **2.** [nomination] nomination *f*, désignation *f* ; [office filled] poste *m* ; [posting] affectation *f*.

⚠ **Appointements** is a formal word for a salary payment; in modern usage **appointement** can never be used to translate appointment.

apportion [ə'pɔːʃn] vt [money] répartir, partager / *to apportion the blame* désigner des coupables.

apposite ['æpəzɪt] adj juste, pertinent.

appositely ['æpəzɪtlɪ] adv de façon pertinente / *appositely named* bien nommé.

appraisal [ə'preɪzl] n appréciation *f*, évaluation *f*.

appraise [ə'preɪz] vt [object] estimer, évaluer (la valeur de) ; [importance, quality] évaluer, apprécier.

appreciable [ə'priːʃəbl] adj sensible, appréciable.

appreciably [ə'priːʃəblɪ] adv sensiblement, de manière appréciable.

appreciate [ə'priːʃɪeɪt] ◆ vt **1.** [value] apprécier ; [art] apprécier, goûter ; [person] apprécier (à sa juste valeur) / *they appreciate good food* ils apprécient la bonne nourriture **2.** [be grateful for] être reconnaissant de, être sensible à / *I would appreciate it if you didn't smoke in the car* je vous serais reconnaissant or je vous saurais gré de ne pas fumer dans la voiture **3.** [realize, understand] se rendre compte de, être conscient de / *he never appreciated its true worth* il ne l'a jamais estimé à sa juste valeur. ◆ vi [increase in value - currency] monter ; [- goods, property] prendre de la valeur.

⚠ **Apprécier** is not always the correct translation of appreciate. See the entry for details.

appreciation [ə,priːʃɪ'eɪʃn] n **1.** [thanks] reconnaissance *f* / *in appreciation of what you have done* en remerciement or pour vous remercier de ce que vous avez fait **2.** [assessment, understanding] évaluation *f*, estimation *f* ; [of art, literature] critique *f* **3.** [increase in value] hausse *f*, augmentation *f*.

appreciative [ə'priːʃjətɪv] adj **1.** [admiring] admiratif **2.** [grateful] reconnaissant / *I am very appreciative of your help* je vous suis très reconnaissant de votre aide.

apprehend [,æprɪ'hend] vt fml **1.** [arrest] arrêter, appréhender **2.** [understand] comprendre, saisir **3.** [fear, dread] redouter, appréhender.

apprehension [,æprɪ'henʃn] n [fear] inquiétude *f*, appréhension *f*.

apprehensive [,æprɪ'hensɪv] adj inquiet, craintif.

apprehensively [,æprɪ'hensɪvlɪ] adv avec appréhension or inquiétude.

apprentice [ə'prentɪs] n apprenti *m*, -e *f* ; [in arts and crafts] élève *mf* / *she's an electrician's apprentice* elle est apprentie électricienne.

apprenticeship [ə'prentɪʃɪp] n apprentissage *m*.

appro ['æprəʊ] (abbr of **approval**) n 🇬🇧 inf ▶ **on appro** à or sous condition, à l'essai.

approach [ə'prəʊtʃ] ◆ vt **1.** lit [person, place] s'approcher de, s'avancer vers / *as we approached Boston* comme nous approchions de Boston ; fig [state, time, quality] approcher de / *we are approaching a time when...* le jour approche où... / *it was approaching Christmas* Noël approchait **2.** [consider] aborder / *that's not the way to approach it* ce n'est pas comme cela qu'il faut s'y prendre **3.** [speak to] parler à / *a salesman approached me* un vendeur m'a abordé / *I approached him about the job* je lui ai parlé du poste. ◆ vi [person, vehicle] s'approcher ; [time, event] approcher, être proche. ◆ n **1.** [of person, vehicle] approche *f*, arrivée *f* / *she heard his approach* elle l'a entendu venir / *the pilot began his approach to Heathrow* le pilote commença sa descente sur or vers Heathrow ; [of time, death] approche *f*, approches *fpl* **2.** [way of tackling] façon *f*, approche *f* / *another approach to the problem* une autre façon d'aborder le problème / *his approach is all wrong* il s'y prend mal **3.** [access] voie *f* d'accès.

approachable [ə'prəʊtʃəbl] adj [place] accessible, approchable ; [person] abordable, approchable.

approaching [ə'prəʊtʃɪŋ] adj [event] prochain, qui est proche ; [vehicle] qui vient en sens inverse.

approbate ['æprə,beɪt] vt 🇺🇸 approuver.

approbation [,æprə'beɪʃn] n approbation *f*, consentement *m* / *a nod / smile of approbation* un signe de tête / un sourire approbateur.

appropriate ◆ adj [ə'prəʊprɪət] [moment, decision] opportun ; [word] bien venu, juste ; [name] bien choisi ; [authority] compétent / *the level of contribution appropriate for* or *to each country* la contribution appropriée à chaque pays / *take the appropriate action* prenez les mesures appropriées / *I am not the appropriate person to ask* ce n'est pas à moi qu'il faut poser la question. ◆ vt [ə'prəʊprɪeɪt] **1.** [take for o.s.] s'approprier, s'emparer de **2.** [set aside] affecter.

appropriately [ə'prəʊprɪətlɪ] adv convenablement ; [speak] avec à-propos, pertinemment ; [decide] à juste titre / *appropriately dressed* habillé comme il faut or pour la circonstance.

appropriation [ə,prəʊprɪ'eɪʃn] n [taking for o.s.] appropriation *f*.

approval [ə'pruːvl] n **1.** [favourable opinion] approbation *f*, accord *m* / *a gesture of approval* un signe approbateur ▶ **to meet with sb's approval** obtenir or recevoir l'approbation de qqn **2.** [sanction] approbation *f*, autorisation *f* / *submit the proposal for his approval* soumettez la proposition à son approbation **3.** COMM ▶ **to buy sthg on approval** acheter qqch à or sous condition / *articles sent on approval* marchandises envoyées à titre d'essai.

approval rating n [of politician] cote *f* de popularité.

approve [ə'pruːv] vt [plan, proposal, etc.] approuver ; [agreement, treaty] ratifier, homologuer. ◆ **approve of** vt insep approuver ; [person] avoir une bonne opinion de / *they don't approve of her going out with that man* ils n'apprécient pas du tout qu'elle sorte avec cet homme.

approved [ə'pruːvd] adj **1.** [method, practice] reconnu, admis **2.** [authorized] autorisé, admis.

approving [ə'pruːvɪŋ] adj approbateur, approbatif.

approvingly [ə'pruːvɪŋlɪ] adv d'une façon approbatrice / *she looked at him approvingly* elle l'a regardé d'un air approbateur.

approx. (written abbr of approximately) adv approx., env.

approximate adj [ə'prɒksɪmət] approximatif.

approximately [ə'prɒksɪmətlɪ] adv à peu près, environ.

approximation [ə,prɒksɪ'meɪʃn] n approximation f.

APR n **1.** (abbr of annualized percentage rate) TEG m **2.** (abbr of annual purchase rate) taux m annuel.

Apr. (written abbr of April) avr.

apricot ['eɪprɪkɒt] n **1.** [fruit] abricot m ; [tree] abricotier m **2.** [colour] abricot m inv.

April ['eɪprəl] n avril m ▶ **April Fools' Day** le premier avril ▶ **an April fool a)** [person] personne à qui l'on a fait un poisson d'avril **b)** [trick] un poisson d'avril ▶ **April showers** giboulées fpl de mars. See also **February**.

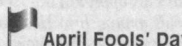

April Fools' Day

En Grande-Bretagne, le premier avril est l'occasion de farces en tout genre ; en revanche, la tradition du « poisson d'avril » n'existe pas.

apron ['eɪprən] n [gen & TECH] tablier m ▶ **he is tied to his mother's apron strings** il est pendu aux jupes de sa mère.

apropos ['æprəpəʊ] ◆ adj opportun, à propos. ◆ adv à propos, opportunément.

APS (abbr of average propensity to save) n ECON PmaE.

apt [æpt] adj **1.** [person] ▶ **to be apt to do sthg** faire qqch facilement, être porté à faire qqch / people are apt to believe the worst les gens croient facilement le pire ▶ **to be apt to do sthg** être susceptible de faire qqch / buttons are apt to get lost les boutons se perdent facilement **2.** [suitable] convenable, approprié ; [remark] juste, qui convient.

apt. (written abbr of apartment) appt.

aptitude ['æptɪtjuːd] n aptitude f, disposition f ▶ **to have an aptitude for sthg** avoir une aptitude à or disposition pour qqch / she shows great aptitude elle promet.

aptitude test n test m d'aptitude.

aptly ['æptlɪ] adv à or avec propos, avec justesse.

aquaculture ['ækwə,kʌltʃər] n aquaculture f.

aqualung ['ækwəlʌŋ] n scaphandre m autonome.

aquamarine [,ækwəmə'riːn] ◆ n [stone] aiguemarine f ; [colour] bleu vert m inv. ◆ adj bleu vert (inv).

aquaplane ['ækwəpleɪn] n aquaplane m.

aquarium [ə'kweərɪəm] (pl aquariums or aquaria [-rɪə]) n aquarium m.

Aquarius [ə'kweərɪəs] ◆ pr n ASTROL & ASTRON Verseau m. ◆ n : he's (an) Aquarius il est (du signe du) Verseau.

aquarobics [,ækwə'rəʊbɪks] n aquagym f.

aquatic [ə'kwætɪk] adj aquatique ; [sport] nautique.

aqueduct ['ækwɪdʌkt] n aqueduc m.

AR written abbr of Arkansas.

ARA (abbr of Associate of the Royal Academy) n membre associé de la RA.

Arab ['ærəb] ◆ n [person] Arabe mf. ◆ adj arabe ▶ **the Arab-Israeli conflict** le conflit israélo-arabe.

Arabia [ə'reɪbjə] pr n Arabie f.

Arabian [ə'reɪbjən] adj arabe, d'Arabie ▶ **the Arabian Desert** le désert d'Arabie ▶ **the Arabian Sea** la mer d'Arabie, la mer d'Oman / **'the Arabian Nights'** or **the Arabian Nights' Entertainment'** 'les Mille et Une Nuits'.

Arabic ['ærəbɪk] ◆ n arabe m. ◆ adj arabe ▶ **Arabic numerals** chiffres mpl arabes.

arable ['ærəbl] adj arable, cultivable ; [crops] cultivable ; [farm] agricole ; [farmer] ▶ **arable farmer** cultivateur ▶ **arable farming** culture f.

ARAM (abbr of Associate of the Royal Academy of Music) n membre associé de la RAM.

arbiter ['ɑːbɪtər] n arbitre m, médiateur m, -trice f / magazines act as arbiters of modern taste les magazines se font les juges ou les arbitres des goûts de notre société.

arbitrary ['ɑːbɪtrərɪ] adj arbitraire.

arbitrate ['ɑːbɪtreɪt] ◆ vt arbitrer, juger. ◆ vi décider en qualité d'arbitre, arbitrer.

arbitration [,ɑːbɪ'treɪʃn] n [gen & INDUST] arbitrage m / they referred the dispute to arbitration ils ont soumis le conflit à l'arbitrage.

arbitrator ['ɑːbɪtreɪtər] n arbitre m, médiateur m, -trice f.

arc [ɑːk] ◆ n arc m. ◆ vi [gen] décrire un arc.

ARC [ɑːk] (abbr of aids-related complex) n ARC m.

arcade [ɑː'keɪd] n [set of arches] arcade f, galerie f ; [shopping] galerie f marchande.

arch [ɑːtʃ] ◆ n **1.** ARCHIT arc m ; [in church] arc m, voûte f **2.** [of eyebrows] courbe f ; [of foot] cambrure f, voûte f plantaire. ◆ vt arquer, cambrer / the cat arched its back le chat fit le gros dos. ◆ adj **1.** [leading] grand, par excellence / my arch rival mon principal adversaire **2.** [mischievous] coquin, espiègle ; [look, smile, tone] malin, espiègle.

arch- [ɑːtʃ] pref grand(e), principal(e).

archaeology n UK = archeology.

archaic [ɑː'keɪɪk] adj archaïque.

archangel ['ɑːk,eɪndʒəl] n archange m.

archbishop [,ɑːtʃ'bɪʃəp] n archevêque m.

Archbishop

L'archevêque de Cantorbéry est le chef spirituel de l'Église anglicane ; l'archevêque de Westminster est le chef spirituel de l'Église catholique en Angleterre et au pays de Galles.

arched [ɑːtʃt] adj **1.** [roof, window] cintré **2.** [back, foot] cambré ; [eyebrows] arqué.

archenemy [,ɑːtʃ'enɪmɪ] (pl archenemies) n pire ennemi m.

archeological [,ɑːkɪə'lɒdʒɪkl] adj archéologique.

archeologist [,ɑːkɪ'ɒlədʒɪst] n archéologue mf.

archeology [,ɑːkɪ'ɒlədʒɪ] n archéologie f.

archer ['ɑːtʃər] n archer m.

archery ['ɑːtʃərɪ] n tir m à l'arc.

archetypal [,ɑːkɪ'taɪpl] adj archétype, archétypique, archétypal.

archetype ['ɑːkɪtaɪp] n archétype m.

archipelago [,ɑːkɪ'pelɪgəʊ] (pl archipelagoes or archipelagos) n archipel m.

architect ['ɑːkɪtekt] n architecte mf ; fig artisan m, créateur m, -trice f.

architectural [,ɑːkɪ'tektʃərəl] adj architectural.

architecturally [ˌɑːkɪˈtektʃərəlɪ] adv au or du point de vue architectural.

architecture [ˈɑːkɪtektʃəʳ] n [gen & COMPUT] architecture f.

archive [ˈɑːkaɪv] ◆ n ▶ **the archives** les archives fpl; [repository] archives fpl, dépôt m. ◆ comp [photo] d'archives. ◆ vt archiver.

archive file n COMPUT fichier m archives.

archive site n COMPUT site m FTP.

archivist [ˈɑːkɪvɪst] n archiviste mf.

archway [ˈɑːtʃweɪ] n porche m; [long] galerie f, arcades fpl.

ARCM (abbr of **Associate of the Royal College of Music**) n membre associé du RCM.

arctic [ˈɑːktɪk] ◆ adj **1.** arctique **2.** fig [cold] glacial. ◆ n US [overshoe] couvre-chaussure m. ❖ **Arctic** [ˈɑːktɪk] pr n ▶ **the Arctic (Ocean)** l'(océan m) Arctique m / **in the Arctic** dans l'Arctique.

Arctic Circle pr n ▶ **the Arctic Circle** le cercle polaire arctique.

ardent [ˈɑːdənt] adj [keen] passionné / an ardent admirer un fervent admirateur.

ardently [ˈɑːdəntlɪ] adv ardemment, passionnément.

ardour US, **ardor** US [ˈɑːdəʳ] n ardeur f, passion f.

arduous [ˈɑːdjʊəs] adj ardu, difficile; [work, task] laborieux, pénible; [path] ardu, raide; [hill] raide, escarpé.

are (vb weak form [əʳ], strong form [ɑːʳ]) vb ⟶ **be**.

area [ˈeərɪə] ◆ n **1.** [surface size] superficie f, aire f **2.** [region] région f; MIL territoire m; [small] secteur m, zone f / a residential / shopping area un quartier résidentiel / commercial **3.** [part, section] partie f; [of room] coin m / living / eating area coin salon / salle à manger **4.** [of study, investigation, experience] domaine m, champ m. ◆ comp [manager, office] régional.

area code n **1.** US code m postal **2.** US TELEC indicatif m de zone.

arena [əˈriːnə] n arène f / when he entered the electoral arena quand il est entré en lice pour les élections.

aren't [ɑːnt] abbr of **are not**.

Argentina [ˌɑːdʒənˈtiːnə] pr n Argentine f.

Argentine [ˈɑːdʒəntaɪn] ◆ n Argentin m, -e f. ◆ adj argentin.

Argentinian [ˌɑːdʒənˈtɪnɪən] ◆ n Argentin m, -e f. ◆ adj argentin.

arguable [ˈɑːgjʊəbl] adj **1.** [questionable] discutable, contestable **2.** [plausible] défendable / it is arguable that... on peut soutenir que...

arguably [ˈɑːgjʊəblɪ] adv possiblement / the Beatles are arguably the most popular group of all time on pourrait dire or on peut soutenir que les Beatles sont le groupe le plus populaire de tous les temps.

argue [ˈɑːgjuː] ◆ vi **1.** [quarrel] se disputer ▶ **to argue (with sb) about sthg** se disputer (avec qqn) au sujet de or à propos de qqch **2.** [reason] argumenter / she argued for / against raising taxes elle a soutenu qu'il fallait / ne fallait pas augmenter les impôts / we argued (about it) all day nous (en) avons discuté toute la journée; LAW témoigner. ◆ vt **1.** [debate] discuter, débattre / a well-argued case une cause bien présentée or défendue / why do you always have to argue the toss inf or point? pourquoi faut-il toujours que tu ergotes or chicanes ? **2.** [person] : he argued me into / out of staying il m'a persuadé / dissuadé de rester **3.** [maintain] soutenir, affirmer.

⚠ The French verb **arguer** is a formal and rare word meaning to argue in the sense of 'to claim' or 'to maintain'; it never means to argue in the sense of 'to quarrel'.

argument [ˈɑːgjʊmənt] n **1.** [quarrel] dispute f / they had an argument about politics ils se sont disputés à propos de politique **2.** [debate] discussion f, débat m ▶ **for the sake of argument** à titre d'exemple / you should listen to both sides of the argument vous devriez écouter les deux versions de l'histoire **3.** [reasoning] argument m / I didn't follow his (line of) argument je n'ai pas suivi son raisonnement / there is a strong argument in favour of the proposal il y a de bonnes raisons pour soutenir or appuyer cette proposition.

⚠ The French word **argument** never means an argument in the sense of a disagreement or dispute.

argumentative [ˌɑːgjʊˈmentətɪv] adj ergoteur, chicaneur.

argy-bargy [ˌɑːdʒɪˈbɑːdʒɪ] n (U) US inf chamailleries fpl.

aria [ˈɑːrɪə] n aria f.

arid [ˈærɪd] adj **1.** lit sec (sèche), desséché **2.** fig [of no interest] aride, ingrat; [fruitless] stérile.

Aries [ˈeəriːz] ◆ pr n ASTROL & ASTRON Bélier m. ◆ n : I'm an Aries je suis (du signe du) Bélier.

arise [əˈraɪz] (pt arose [əˈrəʊz], pp arisen [əˈrɪzn]) vi **1.** [appear, happen] survenir, se présenter / if the need arises en cas de besoin / if the occasion arises si l'occasion se présente **2.** [result] résulter.

aristocracy [ˌærɪˈstɒkrəsɪ] (pl **aristocracies**) n aristocratie f.

aristocrat [US ˈærɪstəkræt US əˈrɪstəkræt] n aristocrate mf.

aristocratic [US ˌærɪstəˈkrætɪk US əˌrɪstəˈkrætɪk] adj aristocratique.

arithmetic n [əˈrɪθmətɪk] arithmétique f.

Arizona [ˌærɪˈzəʊnə] pr n Arizona m.

ark [ɑːk] n arche f / this machine must have come out of the ark hum cet appareil doit remonter au déluge or est vieux comme Hérode.

Arkansas [ˈɑːkənsɔː] pr n Arkansas m.

arm [ɑːm] ◆ n **1.** ANAT bras m ▶ **to hold sb / sthg in one's arms** tenir qqn / qqch dans ses bras / he put his arm round her il a passé son bras autour d'elle / with arms folded les bras croisés ▶ **to welcome sb / sthg with open arms** accueillir qqn / qqch à bras ouverts ▶ **within arm's reach** à portée de la main / we kept him at arm's length nous l'avons tenu à bout de bras / I'd give my right arm for that job je donnerais cher or n'importe quoi pour obtenir cet emploi **2.** [of sea, machinery] bras m; [of clothing] manche f; [of spectacle frames] branche f; [of furniture] bras m, accoudoir m; [of record player] bras m. ◆ vt [person, country] armer. ❖ **arm in arm** adv phr bras dessus bras dessous.

armadillo [ˌɑːməˈdɪləʊ] (pl **armadillos**) n tatou m.

Armageddon [ˌɑːməˈgedn] n Apocalypse f; fig apocalypse f.

armaments [ˈɑːməmənts] pl n armement m.

armband [ˈɑːmbænd] n brassard m; [mourning] brassard m de deuil, crêpe m.

arm candy [ˈɑːmkændɪ] n hum & pej jeune f et jolie compagne.

armchair ['ɑːmtʃeəʳ] n fauteuil *m*.

armed [ɑːmd] adj [with weapons] armé / *they were armed with knives* ils étaient armés de couteaux ▶ **armed robbery** LAW vol *m* or attaque *f* à main armée ▶ **armed to the teeth** armé jusqu'aux dents.

armed forces pl n forces *fpl* armées.

Armenia [ɑːˈmiːnjə] pr n Arménie *f*.

Armenian [ɑːˈmiːnjən] ◆ n [person] Arménien *m*, -enne *f*. ◆ adj arménien.

armful ['ɑːmfʊl] n brassée *f* / *in armfuls* or *by the armful* par pleines brassées, par brassées entières.

armhole ['ɑːmhəʊl] n emmanchure *f*.

armistice ['ɑːmɪstɪs] n armistice *m*.

Armistice Day n l'Armistice *m*.

Armistice Day

L'armistice de la Première Guerre mondiale, **Remembrance Sunday**, est célébré chaque année le dimanche qui précède ou suit le 11 novembre.

armor US n = armour.

armour UK, **armor** US ['ɑːməʳ] n HIST armure *f*.

armoured UK, **armored** US ['ɑːməd] adj MIL blindé.

armoured car n voiture *f* blindée.

armour-plated [-'pleɪtɪd] adj blindé.

armoury UK, **armory** US ['ɑːmərɪ] (UK *pl* **armouries** ; US *pl* **armories**) n arsenal *m*, dépôt *m* d'armes ; fig [resources] arsenal *m* ; US [arms factory] armurerie *f*, fabrique *f* d'armes.

armpit ['ɑːmpɪt] n aisselle *f*.

armrest ['ɑːmrest] n accoudoir *m*.

arms [ɑːmz] ◆ pl n **1.** [weapons] armes *fpl* ▶ **to arms!** aux armes ! ▶ **to be up in arms**: *the villagers are up in arms over the planned motorway* la proposition de construction d'une autoroute a provoqué une levée de boucliers parmi les villageois / *the unions are up in arms over the new legislation* les syndicats s'élèvent ou partent en guerre contre la nouvelle législation **2.** HERALD armes *fpl*, armoiries *fpl*. ◆ comp ▶ **arms control** contrôle *m* des armements ▶ **arms race** course *f* aux armements ▶ **the arms trade** le commerce d'armes.

arm-twisting [-'twɪstɪŋ] n (U) inf pressions *fpl*.

arm-wrestle vi ▶ **to arm-wrestle with sb** faire une partie de bras de fer avec qqn.

arm wrestling n bras *m* de fer.

army ['ɑːmɪ] (*pl* **armies**) ◆ n MIL armée *f* (de terre) ▶ **to go into** or **to join the army** s'engager. ◆ comp [life, nurse, truck, uniform] militaire ; [family] de militaires ▶ **army corps** corps *m* d'armée ▶ **army officer** officier *m* de l'armée de terre.

arnica ['ɑːnɪkə] n BOT & PHARM arnica *f*.

A-road n UK route nationale.

aroma [ə'rəʊmə] n arôme *m*.

aromatherapist [ə,rəʊmə'θerəpɪst] n spécialiste *mf* en aromathérapie, aromathérapeute *mf*.

aromatherapy [ə,rəʊmə'θerəpɪ] n aromathérapie *f*.

aromatic [,ærə'mætɪk] adj aromatique.

arose [ə'rəʊz] pt ⟶ arise.

around [ə'raʊnd] ◆ adv **1.** [in all directions] autour / *the fields all around* les champs tout autour / *for five miles around* sur or dans un rayon de cinq miles

2. [nearby] pas loin / *stay* or *stick around* reste dans les parages / *he's around somewhere* il n'est pas loin, il est dans le coin / *will you be around this afternoon?* tu seras là cet après-midi ? **3.** [in existence] : *that firm has been around for years* cette société existe depuis des années **4.** [here and there] ici et là / *to travel around* voyager / *he's been around* **a)** inf [has travelled widely] il a pas mal roulé sa bosse **b)** [is experienced] il n'est pas né d'hier. ◆ prep **1.** [encircling] autour de / *the area around Berlin* les alentours *mpl* ou les environs *mpl* de Berlin ; fig : *my keys are somewhere around here* mes clés sont quelque part par ici **2.** [through] : *we strolled around town* nous nous sommes promenés en ville **3.** [approximately] autour de / *around five o'clock* vers cinq heures / *around 1920* vers ou aux alentours de 1920 / *he's around your age* il a environ ou à peu près votre âge.

around-the-clock adj ▶ **around-the-clock protection** / **surveillance** protection *f* / surveillance *f* 24 heures sur 24.

arousal [ə'raʊzl] n excitation *f*, stimulation *f*.

arouse [ə'raʊz] vt **1.** [stimulate] stimuler, provoquer ▶ **sexually aroused** excité (sexuellement) **2.** [awaken] réveiller, éveiller.

arrange [ə'reɪndʒ] ◆ vt **1.** [put in order] ranger, mettre en ordre ; [clothing, room] arranger ; [flowers] arranger, disposer **2.** [organize, plan] organiser, arranger / *it has been arranged for us to travel by train* il a été décidé or convenu que nous voyagerions en train / *he has something arranged* or *has arranged something for the weekend* il a quelque chose de prévu pour le week-end **3.** MUS & THEAT adapter / *he arranged the concerto for guitar* il a adapté le concerto pour la guitare. ◆ vi prendre des dispositions, s'arranger / *I've arranged with the boss to leave early tomorrow* je me suis arrangé avec le patron pour partir de bonne heure demain / *he's arranged for the car to be repaired* il a fait le nécessaire pour faire réparer la voiture.

arranged marriage [ə'reɪndʒd-] n mariage *m* arrangé.

arrangement [ə'reɪndʒmənt] n **1.** (usu pl) [plan] disposition *f*, arrangement *m* / *what are the travel arrangements?* comment le voyage est-il organisé ? / *could you make arrangements to change the meeting?* pouvez-vous faire le nécessaire pour changer la date de la réunion ? / *he made arrangements to leave work early* il s'est arrangé pour quitter son travail de bonne heure **2.** [understanding, agreement] arrangement *m* / *he came to an arrangement with the bank* il est parvenu à un accord avec la banque **3.** [layout] arrangement *m*, disposition *f* ; [of room] aménagement *m* ; [of clothing, hair] arrangement *m* **4.** MUS & THEAT adaptation *f*, arrangement *m*.

array [ə'reɪ] n [collection] ensemble *m* impressionnant, collection *f* ; LAW, COMPUT & MATH tableau *m*.

arrears [ə'rɪəz] pl n arriéré *m* / *taxes in arrears* arriéré d'impôts / *I'm worried about getting into arrears* j'ai peur de m'endetter / *we're 6 months in arrears on the loan payments* nous devons 6 mois de traites.

arrest [ə'rest] ◆ vt **1.** [police] arrêter, appréhender **2.** fml [growth, development] arrêter ; [slow down] entraver, retarder. ◆ n [detention] arrestation *f* ▶ **you're under arrest!** vous êtes en état d'arrestation ! / *he was put under arrest* il a été arrêté / *they made several arrests* ils ont procédé à plusieurs arrestations.

arresting [ə'restɪŋ] adj saisissant, frappant.

arrival [ə'raɪvl] n **1.** [of person, train, aeroplane, etc.] arrivée *f* / *on* or *upon arrival* à l'arrivée / *the arrivals board* / *lounge* le tableau / le salon des arrivées **2.** [newcomer] : *late arrivals should report to reception* les retardataires doivent se présenter à la réception / *he's a new ar-*

rival c'est un nouveau venu **/** *the new* or *latest arrival in their family* leur dernier-né or dernière-née.

arrive [ə'raɪv] vi [person, train, aeroplane, etc.] arriver **/** *as soon as you arrive* dès votre arrivée, dès que vous arriverez. **⬥ arrive at** vt insep [decision] arriver or parvenir à ; [perfection] atteindre ; [price] fixer **/** *they finally arrived at a price* ils se sont finalement mis d'accord sur un prix.

arrogance ['ærəgəns] n arrogance *f*, morgue *f*.

arrogant ['ærəgənt] adj arrogant, insolent.

arrogantly ['ærəgəntlɪ] adv de manière arrogante, avec arrogance.

arrow ['ærəʊ] n flèche *f*.

arrow key n COMPUT touche *f* de direction, touche *f* flèche.

arrowroot ['ærəʊruːt] n BOT marante *f* ; CULIN arrowroot *m*.

arse [ɑːs] 🇬🇧 **⬥** n *vulg* cul *m*. **⬥** vt **▶ I can't be arsed** j'ai trop la flemme.

arsehole ['ɑːshəʊl] n 🇬🇧 *vulg* trou *m* du cul.

arsenal ['ɑːsənl] n arsenal *m*.

arsenic ['ɑːsnɪk] n arsenic *m*.

arson ['ɑːsn] n incendie *m* criminel or volontaire.

arsonist ['ɑːsənɪst] n incendiaire *mf* ; [maniac] pyromane *mf*.

art [ɑːt] **⬥** vb arch ⟶ **be.** **⬥** n **1.** [gen] art *m* ; [school subject] dessin *m* **/** *the art of ballet* l'art du ballet **/** *a work of art* une œuvre d'art **▶ arts and crafts** artisanat *m* (d'art) **2.** [skill] art *m*, habileté *f* **/** *the art of survival* l'art de survivre. **⬥** comp [collection, critic, exhibition] d'art **▶ art director** directeur *m*, -trice *f* artistique **▶ art gallery a)** [museum] musée *m* d'art **b)** [shop] galerie *f* d'art **▶ art school** ≃ école *f* des beaux-arts **▶ art student** étudiant *m*, -e *f* en art. **⬥ arts ⬥** pl n UNIV lettres *fpl* **/** *I have an arts degree* j'ai une licence de lettres **▶ Faculty of Arts (and Letters)** faculté *f* des lettres (et sciences humaines). **⬥** comp **▶ arts student** étudiant *m*, -e *f* de or en lettres (et sciences humaines).

Art Deco [-'dekəʊ] n Art *m* déco.

artefact ['ɑːtɪfækt] n = **artifact**.

arterial [ɑː'tɪərɪəl] adj artériel **▶ arterial road** 🇬🇧 route *f* or voie *f* à grande circulation.

arteriosclerosis [ɑːˌtɪərɪəʊsklɪə'rəʊsɪs] n artériosclérose *f*.

artery ['ɑːtərɪ] (*pl* **arteries**) n artère *f* ; [road] artère *f*, route *f* or voie *f* à grande circulation.

art form n moyen *m* d'expression artistique **/** *painting is an art form* la peinture est un art.

artful ['ɑːtfʊl] adj astucieux, habile ; [crafty] rusé, malin **▶ artful dodger** rusé *m*, -e *f* (du nom d'un jeune voleur habile dans le roman de Dickens « Oliver Twist »).

arthouse ['ɑːthaʊs] **⬥** n [cinema] cinéma *m* d'art et d'essai. **⬥** adj [cinema, film] d'art et d'essai.

arthritic [ɑː'θrɪtɪk] **⬥** adj arthritique. **⬥** n arthritique *mf*.

arthritis [ɑː'θraɪtɪs] n arthrite *f*.

artic ['ɑːtɪk] (**abbr of articulated lorry**) n 🇬🇧 *inf* semi-remorque *f*.

artichoke ['ɑːtɪtʃəʊk] n artichaut *m*.

article ['ɑːtɪkl] n **1.** [object] objet *m* **/** *an article of clothing* un vêtement **2.** [in press] article *m* **3.** GRAM article *m*.

articled clerk ['ɑːtɪkld-] n 🇬🇧 clerc *m* d'avoué (lié par un contrat d'apprentissage).

articulate ⬥ adj [ɑː'tɪkjʊlət] **1.** [person] qui s'exprime bien ; [speech] clair, net **2.** [manner of speech] bien articulé, distinct **3.** ANAT & BOT articulé. **⬥** vt [ɑː'tɪkjʊleɪt] **1.** [words, syllables] articuler **2.** *fig* [wishes, thoughts] exprimer clairement. **⬥** vi articuler.

articulated lorry 🇬🇧, **articulated truck** 🇺🇸 [ɑː'tɪkjʊleɪtɪd-] n semi-remorque *f*.

articulately [ɑː'tɪkjʊlətlɪ] adv [speak] distinctement ; [explain] clairement.

articulation [ɑːˌtɪkjʊ'leɪʃn] n ANAT, BOT & LING articulation *f*.

artifact ['ɑːtɪfækt] n objet *m* (fabriqué).

artifice ['ɑːtɪfɪs] n [trick] artifice *m*, ruse *f* ; [scheme] stratagème *m*.

artificial [ˌɑːtɪ'fɪʃl] adj **1.** [man-made] artificiel ; COMM synthétique, artificiel **2.** [affected - person] factice, étudié **/** *an artificial smile* un sourire forcé.

artificial insemination n insémination *f* artificielle.

artificial intelligence n intelligence *f* artificielle.

artificially [ˌɑːtɪ'fɪʃəlɪ] adv artificiellement.

artificial respiration n respiration *f* artificielle.

artillery [ɑː'tɪlərɪ] (*pl* **artilleries**) n artillerie *f*.

artisan [ˌɑːtɪ'zæn] n artisan *m*.

artist ['ɑːtɪst] n [gen & ART] artiste *mf* ; *fig* spécialiste *mf*.

artiste [ɑː'tiːst] n artiste *mf*.

artistic [ɑː'tɪstɪk] adj artistique ; [design, product] de bon goût, décoratif ; [style, temperament] artiste **/** *she is an artistic child* cette enfant a des dons artistiques.

artistically [ɑː'tɪstɪklɪ] adv avec art, artistiquement.

artistry ['ɑːtɪstrɪ] n art *m*, talent *m* artistique.

artless ['ɑːtlɪs] adj [without deceit] naturel, ingénu.

Art Nouveau [ɑːnuː'vəʊ] n Art *m* nouveau, Modern Style *m*.

arts [ɑːts] pl n & comp = **art**.

artsy ['ɑːtzɪ] (*compar* **artsier**, *superl* **artsiest**) adj *inf* = **arty**.

artwork ['ɑːtwɜːk] n [illustration] iconographie *f*, illustration *f*.

arty ['ɑːtɪ] (*compar* **artier**, *superl* **artiest**) adj *inf & pej* [person] qui se veut artiste or bohème ; [clothing] de style bohème ; [object, film, style] prétentieux.

arugula [ə'ruːgələ] n 🇺🇸 roquette *f*.

ARV n **1.** (**abbr of American Revised Version**) *traduction américaine de la Bible* **2.** (**abbr of aids-related virus**) ARV *m* **3.** abbr of **antiretroviral**.

as (*weak form* [əz], *strong form* [æz]) **⬥** conj **1.** [while] alors que **/** *the phone rang as I was coming in* le téléphone s'est mis à sonner alors que or au moment où j'entrais **/** *I listened as she explained the plan to them* je l'ai écoutée leur expliquer le projet **/** *as a student, he worked part-time* lorsqu'il était étudiant, il travaillait à mi-temps ; [when] : *take two aspirins as needed* prenez deux aspirines en cas de douleur **2.** [like] comme, ainsi que **/** *A as in Able* a comme Anatole **/** *as shown by the unemployment rate* comme or ainsi que le montre le taux de chômage **/** *as is often the case* comme c'est souvent le cas **/** *as I told you* comme je vous l'ai dit **/** *leave it as it is* laissez-le tel qu'il est or tel quel **3.** [since] puisque **/** *let her drive, as it's her car* laissez-la conduire, puisque c'est sa voiture **4.** *fml* [concessive use] : *try as they might, they couldn't persuade her* malgré tous leurs efforts, ils n'ont pu la convaincre **5.** [with 'the same', 'such'] : *at the same time as last week* à la même heure que la semaine dernière. **⬥** prep en tant que, comme **/** *as her husband, he cannot testify* étant son mari, il ne peut pas témoigner **/**

he was dressed as a clown il était habillé en clown / *with Vivien Leigh as Scarlett O'Hara* avec Vivien Leigh dans le rôle de Scarlett O'Hara. ◆ adv [in comparisons] : *it's twice as big* c'est deux fois plus grand / *it costs half as much again* ça coûte la moitié plus ▶ **as... as** aussi... que / *as often as possible* aussi souvent que possible / *I worked as much for you as for me* j'ai travaillé autant pour toi que pour moi. ❖ **as for** prep phr quant à / *as for me, I don't intend to go* pour ma part or quant à moi, je n'ai pas l'intention d'y aller. ❖ **as from** prep phr = **as of**. ❖ **as if** conj phr comme si / *he moved as if to strike him* il a fait un mouvement comme pour le frapper / *as if it mattered!* comme si ça avait aucune importance ! ▶ **as if!** *hum* tu parles ! ❖ **as it is** adv phr **1.** [in present circumstances] les choses étant ce qu'elles sont **2.** [already] déjà. ❖ **as it were** adv phr pour ainsi dire. ❖ **as of** prep phr à partir de / *as of yesterday* depuis hier. ❖ **as such** adv phr **1.** [properly speaking] véritablement, à proprement parler / *it's not a contract as such, more a gentleman's agreement* ce n'est pas un véritable contrat or pas un contrat à proprement parler or pas véritablement un contrat, mais plutôt un accord entre hommes de parole **2.** [in itself] même, en soi / *the place as such isn't great* l'endroit même or en soi n'est pas terrible **3.** [in that capacity] à ce titre, en tant que tel / *I'm his father and as such, I insist on knowing* je suis son père et à ce titre j'insiste pour qu'on me mette au courant. ❖ **as though** conj phr = **as if**. ❖ **as to** prep phr **1.** [regarding] : *I'm still uncertain as to the nature of the problem* j'hésite encore sur la nature du problème **2.** = **as for**. ❖ **as well** adv phr [in addition] en plus ; [also] aussi / *he bought the house and the land as well* il a acheté la maison et la propriété aussi / *and then the car broke down as well!* et par-dessus le marché la voiture est tombée en panne ! ❖ **as well as** conj phr [in addition to] en plus de. ❖ **as yet** adv phr encore.

AS ◆ n abbr of Associate in Science. ◆ pr n written abbr of American Samoa.

ASA pr n **1.** (abbr of Advertising Standards Authority) ≃ BVP *m* **2.** (abbr of American Standards Association) ASA *f*.

asafoetida, asafetida US [ˌæsəfəʊˈetɪdə] n ase *f* fétide.

asap, ASAP [ˌeiesei'piː] (abbr of as soon as possible) adv dès que possible, le plus tôt or le plus vite possible, asap.

asbestos [æs'bestəs] n amiante *m*.

asbestosis [ˌæsbes'təʊsɪs] n asbestose *f*.

ASBO ['æzbəʊ] (abbr of anti-social behaviour order) n UK ordonnance civile sanctionnant des comportements antisociaux.

ascend [ə'send] ◆ vi monter ; [in time] remonter. ◆ vt [stairs] monter ; [ladder] monter à ; [mountain] gravir, faire l'ascension de ; [river] remonter ; [throne] monter sur.

ascendancy, ascendency [ə'sendənsɪ] n **1.** [position of power] ascendant *m*, empire *m* **2.** [rise] montée *f*.

ascendant, ascendent [ə'sendənt] n ascendant *m* / *his star is in the ascendant* ASTROL son étoile est à l'ascendant / *his business is in the ascendant* ses affaires prospèrent.

ascending [ə'sendɪŋ] adj **1.** [rising] ascendant **2.** [increasing] ▶ **in ascending order** en ordre croissant.

ascension [ə'senʃn] n ascension *f*.

ascent [ə'sent] n [of mountain] ascension *f*.

ascertain [ˌæsə'teɪn] vt *fml* établir, constater ▶ **to ascertain that sthg is the case** vérifier or s'assurer que qqch est vrai.

ascetic [ə'setɪk] ◆ adj ascétique. ◆ n ascète *mf*.

ASCII ['æskɪ] (abbr of American Standard Code for Information Interchange) n ASCII *m* ▶ **ASCII file** fichier *m* ASCII.

ascorbic acid [ə'skɔːbɪk-] n acide *m* ascorbique.

ascribe [ə'skraɪb] vt attribuer ; [fault, blame] imputer.

ASCU (abbr of Association of State Colleges and Universities) pr n *association des établissements universitaires d'État aux États-Unis*.

ASE (abbr of American Stock Exchange) pr n *deuxième place boursière des États-Unis*.

aseptic [ˌeɪ'septɪk] adj aseptique.

asexual [ˌeɪ'sekʃʊəl] adj asexué.

ash [æʃ] n **1.** [from fire, cigarette] cendre *f* / *the fire reduced the house to ashes* l'incendie a réduit la maison en cendres **2.** [tree, wood] frêne *m*.

ASH [æʃ] (abbr of Action on Smoking and Health) pr n *ligue antitabac britannique*.

ashamed [ə'ʃeɪmd] adj confus, honteux ▶ **to be ashamed (of oneself)** avoir honte / *I'm ashamed of you* j'ai honte de toi, tu me fais honte / *I'm ashamed to say that...* j'avoue à ma grande honte que... / *there is nothing to be ashamed of* il n'y a pas de quoi avoir honte.

> Note that avoir honte que is followed by a verb in the subjunctive:
> **I was ashamed that my brother had found out my secret.** *J'avais honte que mon frère ait découvert mon secret.*

ash can, ashcan n US poubelle *f*.

ashen ['æʃn] adj [ash-coloured] cendré, couleur de cendre ; [face] blême, livide.

ashen-faced adj blême.

ashore [ə'ʃɔːr] adv à terre / *he swam ashore* il a nagé jusqu'à la rive ▶ **to go ashore** débarquer.

ashtray ['æʃtreɪ] n cendrier *m*.

Ash Wednesday n mercredi *m* des Cendres.

Asia [UK 'eɪʃə US 'eɪʒə] pr n Asie *f*.

Asia Minor pr n Asie *f* Mineure.

Asian [UK 'eɪʃn US 'eɪʒn] ◆ n [from Asia] Asiatique *mf*, UK [from Indian subcontinent] *personne originaire du sous-continent indien*. ◆ adj [from Asia] asiatique ; UK [from Indian subcontinent] *originaire du sous-continent indien*.

Asian

Les Britanniques emploient le mot **Asian** pour désigner les habitants de l'Inde et des pays limitrophes ; ainsi, l'expression **the Asian community in Birmingham** fait référence aux personnes d'origine indienne, pakistanaise et bangladaise qui habitent à Birmingham. Pour traduire « Asiatique », il est souvent préférable de choisir l'expression désignant l'habitant du pays en question : **a Chinese person, a Japanese person**, etc.

Asiatic [UK ,eɪʃɪ'ætɪk US ,eɪʒɪ'ætɪk] adj asiatique.

aside [ə'saɪd] ◆ adv de côté, à part / *these problems aside, we have been very successful* à part ces problèmes, ce fut un véritable succès / *we've been putting money aside for the trip* nous avons mis de l'argent de côté pour le voyage. ◆ n aparté *m.* ❖ **aside from** prep phr **1.** [except for] sauf **2.** US [as well as] en plus de.

ask [ɑːsk] ◆ vt **1.** [for opinion, information] ▶ **to ask sb sthg** demander qqch à qqn / *may I ask you a question?* puis-je vous poser une question ? / *but how? I ask you!* inf mais comment ? je vous le demande ! / *don't ask me!* inf est-ce que je sais, moi ? / *no one asked you!* inf on ne t'a rien demandé ! **2.** [request] demander, solliciter / *he asked them a favour* il leur a demandé un service ▶ **to ask sb to do sthg** demander à qqn de faire qqch / *that's asking a lot* c'est beaucoup demander / *that's asking too much of me* tu m'en demandes trop ; COMM ▶ **to ask a price** demander un prix **3.** [invite] inviter / *he asked her to the pictures* il l'a invitée au cinéma. ◆ vi demander / *he was asking about the job* il s'informait or se renseignait sur le poste. ❖ **ask after** vt insep : *she asked after you* elle a demandé de vos nouvelles. ❖ **ask along** vt sep inviter / *we asked them along (with us)* nous leur avons proposé de venir avec nous. ❖ **ask around** vt se renseigner. ❖ **ask back** vt sep [invite again] réinviter ; [for reciprocal visit] inviter / *she asked us back for dinner* elle nous a rendu l'invitation à dîner. ❖ **ask for** vt insep demander / *you're just asking for trouble!* tu cherches des ennuis ! / *he was asking for it!* il l'a cherché ! ❖ **ask in** vt sep inviter à entrer / *he asked us in for a drink* il nous a invités à (entrer) prendre un verre. ❖ **ask out** vt sep inviter à sortir / *they asked us out for dinner / to the theatre* ils nous ont invités au restaurant / au théâtre. ❖ **ask round** vt sep UK inviter (à venir).

askance [ə'skæns] adv du coin de l'œil / *he looked askance at her* il l'a regardée d'un air méfiant.

askew [ə'skjuː] ◆ adv obliquement, de travers. ◆ adj US : *something's askew here* il y a quelque chose qui cloche.

asking price ['ɑːskɪŋ-] n prix *m* de départ, prix *m* demandé.

ASL MESSAGING written abbr of **age, sex, location.**

asleep [ə'sliːp] adj endormi / *she's asleep* elle dort ▶ **to be fast** or **sound asleep** dormir profondément or à poings fermés ▶ **to fall asleep** s'endormir.

ASLEF ['æzlef] (abbr of **Associated Society of Locomotive Engineers and Firemen**) pr n syndicat des cheminots en Grande-Bretagne.

AS-level [eɪ'eslevl] (abbr of **Advanced Subsidiary Level**) n SCH première partie de l'examen A-level.

ASM (abbr of **air-to-surface missile**) n ASM *m.*

as-new adj comme neuf.

asparagus [ə'spærəgəs] n (U) asperge *f* ▶ **asparagus tips** pointes fpl d'asperges.

aspartame [UK ə'spɑːteɪm US 'æspərteɪm] n aspartame *m.*

ASPCA (abbr of **American Society for the Prevention of Cruelty to Animals**) pr n société protectrice des animaux aux États-Unis.

aspect ['æspekt] n **1.** [facet] aspect *m*, côté *m* / *we should examine all aspects of the problem* nous devrions étudier le problème sous tous ses aspects **2.** liter [appearance] air *m*, aspect *m* **3.** [outlook] orientation *f*, exposition *f* / *a house with a northern / southern aspect* une maison exposée au nord / sud.

aspen ['æspən] n tremble *m.*

aspersions [ə'spɜːʃnz] pl n ▶ **to cast aspersions on sb** dénigrer qqn.

asphalt ['æsfælt] ◆ n asphalte *m.* ◆ comp [road, roof] asphalté.

asphyxia [əs'fɪksɪə] n asphyxie *f.*

asphyxiate [əs'fɪksɪeɪt] ◆ vi s'asphyxier. ◆ vt asphyxier.

asphyxiating [əs'fɪksɪeɪtɪŋ] adj asphyxiant.

asphyxiation [əs,fɪksɪ'eɪʃn] n asphyxie *f.*

aspic ['æspɪk] n gelée *f.*

aspirate ◆ vt ['æspəreɪt] aspirer. ◆ adj ['æspərət] aspiré.

aspiration [,æspə'reɪʃn] n [ambition] aspiration *f.*

aspirational [,æspə'reɪʃənl] adj [person] ambitieux ; [brand, product] qui fait chic.

aspire [ə'spaɪər] vi aspirer / *he aspires to political power* il aspire au pouvoir politique / *she aspires to* or *after higher things* elle vise plus haut, ses ambitions vont plus loin.

aspirin ['æsprɪn] n aspirine *f* ; [tablet] (comprimé *m* d')aspirine *f.*

aspiring [ə'spaɪərɪŋ] adj ambitieux ; pej arriviste.

ass [æs] n **1.** [donkey] âne *m* **2.** UK inf [idiot] imbécile *mf* **3.** US vulg [bottom] cul *m.*

assail [ə'seɪl] vt attaquer, assaillir.

assailant [ə'seɪlənt] n fml agresseur *m*, assaillant *m*, -e *f.*

assassin [ə'sæsɪn] n assassin *m.*

assassinate [ə'sæsɪneɪt] vt assassiner.

assassination [ə,sæsɪ'neɪʃn] n assassinat *m.*

assault [ə'sɔːlt] ◆ n **1.** [attack] agression *f* / *he is accused of assault* il est accusé de voie de fait / *a brave assault on widely held beliefs* une attaque courageuse contre des croyances très répandues ▶ **assault and battery** LAW coups mpl et blessures fpl **2.** MIL assaut *m* / *to lead an assault* se lancer à l'assaut. ◆ vt [gen] agresser ; [sexually] violenter.

assault course n parcours *m* du combattant.

assayer [ə'seɪər] n essayeur *m*, -euse *f.*

assemble [ə'sembl] ◆ vt **1.** assembler, amasser ; [people] rassembler, réunir ; [troops] rassembler **2.** [put together] monter, assembler. ◆ vi se rassembler, se réunir.

assembly [ə'semblɪ] (pl **assemblies**) n **1.** [meeting - gen] réunion *f*, assemblée *f* **2.** POL assemblée *f* **3.** SCH réunion de tous les élèves de l'établissement ▶ **assembly hall** hall où les enfants se réunissent le matin avant d'entrer en classe **4.** [building - process] montage *m*, assemblage *m* ; [-end product] assemblage *m.*

assembly language n langage *m* d'assemblage.

assembly line n chaîne *f* de montage.

assemblyman [ə'semblɪmən] (pl **assemblymen** [-mən]) n US POL homme qui siège à une assemblée législative.

assembly point n point *m* de rassemblement.

assemblywoman [ə'semblɪ,wumən] (pl **assemblywomen** [-,wɪmɪn]) n US POL femme qui siège à une assemblée législative.

assent [ə'sent] ◆ vi consentir, acquiescer. ◆ n consentement *m*, assentiment *m.*

assert [ə'sɜːt] vt **1.** [proclaim] affirmer, maintenir ; [innocence] affirmer, protester de **2.** [insist on] défendre, revendiquer / *we must assert our right to speak* nous devons faire valoir notre droit à la parole ; [impose] ▶ **to assert o.s.** se faire respecter, s'imposer.

assertion [ə'sɜːʃn] n affirmation *f*, assertion *f* ; [of rights] revendication *f.*

assertive [əˈsɜːtɪv] adj assuré, autoritaire ; *pej* péremptoire.

assertively [əˈsɜːtɪvlɪ] adv fermement ; *pej* de façon péremptoire.

assertiveness [əˈsɜːtɪvnɪs] n manière f assurée ; *pej* arrogance f.

assertiveness training n stage m d'affirmation de soi.

assess [əˈses] vt **1.** [judge] estimer, évaluer **2.** [value] fixer or déterminer la valeur de **3.** [taxes] évaluer ▶ **assessed income** revenu m imposable.

assessment [əˈsesmənt] n **1.** [judgment] estimation f, évaluation f **2.** ⓊⓀ SCH contrôle m des connaissances ; [on report card] appréciation f des professeurs **3.** [valuation - of amount due] détermination f, évaluation f ; [- of tax] calcul m (de la valeur imposable).

assessor [əˈsesəʳ] n **1.** expert m **2.** LAW (juge m) assesseur m.

asset [ˈæset] n avantage m, atout m. ◆ **assets** pl n [possession] avoir m, capital m ; COMM, FIN & LAW actif m / *assets and liabilities* l'actif m et le passif.

asset-stripper n dépeceur m d'entreprise.

asset-stripping [-ˌstrɪpɪŋ] n *achat d'entreprises pour revente des actifs.*

asshole [ˈæʃəʊl] n ⓊⓈ *vulg* = **arsehole**.

assiduous [əˈsɪdjʊəs] adj assidu.

assiduously [əˈsɪdjʊəslɪ] adv assidûment.

assign [əˈsaɪn] vt **1.** [allot] assigner, attribuer / *I assigned her the task of writing the report* je lui ai chargée de la rédaction du rapport **2.** [appoint] nommer, désigner / *he's been assigned to Moscow* il a été affecté à Moscou **3.** [ascribe] ▶ **to assign a reason for sthg** donner la raison de qqch.

assignable [əˈsaɪnəbl] adj LAW [property] cessible.

assignation [ˌæsɪgˈneɪʃn] n **1.** [meeting] rendez-vous m clandestin **2.** [assignment] attribution f ; [of money] allocation f ; [of person] affectation f.

assignee [ˌæsaɪˈniː] n cessionnaire mf.

assignment [əˈsaɪnmənt] n **1.** tâche f ; [official] mission f ; SCH devoir m **2.** [appointment] attribution f ; [of money] allocation f ; [of person] affectation f.

assimilate [əˈsɪmɪleɪt] ◆ vt **1.** [food, information] assimiler **2.** [immigrants] intégrer. ◆ vi s'assimiler, s'intégrer.

assimilation [əˌsɪmɪˈleɪʃn] n [gen & LING] assimilation f.

assist [əˈsɪst] ◆ vt **1.** [help] aider, assister **2.** [with money] : *assisted by the town hall* avec le concours de la mairie ▶ **assisted passage** billet m subventionné. ◆ vi [help] aider, prêter secours.

assistance [əˈsɪstəns] n aide f, secours m / *may I be of assistance to you?* puis-je vous être utile ? ▶ **to come to sb's assistance** venir au secours de qqn.

assistance dog n chien m guide.

assistant [əˈsɪstənt] ◆ n assistant m, -e f, aide mf ▶ **foreign language assistant a)** SCH assistant m, -e f (en langue étrangère) **b)** UNIV lecteur m, -trice f (en langue étrangère) ▶ **teaching assistant** SCH auxiliaire mf. ◆ comp [director, judge, librarian, secretary] adjoint ▶ **assistant manager** sous-directeur m, directeur m adjoint.

assisted area n ⓊⓀ zone de développement économique prioritaire.

assize [əˈsaɪz] n LAW assises fpl ▶ **assize court** or **court of assizes** cour f d'assises.

ass-kisser n ⓊⓈ *vulg* lèche-cul m.

associate ◆ vt [əˈsəʊʃɪeɪt] associer / *the problems associated with nuclear power* les problèmes relatifs à l'énergie nucléaire / *that kind of behaviour is often associated with an unhappy childhood* ce type de comportement est souvent lié à une enfance malheureuse. ◆ vi [əˈsəʊʃɪeɪt] ▶ **to associate with sb** fréquenter qqn. ◆ n [əˈsəʊʃɪət] **1.** [partner] associé m, -e f ; LAW complice mf **2.** [of club] membre m, associé m, -e f. ◆ adj [əˈsəʊʃɪət] associé, allié / *I'm only an associate member of the organisation* je suis seulement membre associé de l'organisation ▶ **associate editor** rédacteur m associé, rédactrice f associée.

association [əˌsəʊsɪˈeɪʃn] n **1.** [grouping] association f, société f **2.** [involvement] association f, fréquentation f / *through long association with the medical profession* à force de fréquenter la profession médicale **3.** [of ideas] association f / *that trip has many unhappy associations for me* ce voyage me rappelle bien des choses pénibles.

assorted [əˈsɔːtɪd] adj [various] varié, divers / *in assorted sizes* en différentes tailles.

assortment [əˈsɔːtmənt] n assortiment m, collection f ; [of people] mélange m / *there was a good assortment of cakes* il y avait un grand choix ou une bonne sélection de gâteaux.

asst, Asst. written abbr of **assistant**.

assuage [əˈsweɪdʒ] vt *fml* [grief, pain] soulager, apaiser ; [hunger, thirst] assouvir ; [person] apaiser, calmer.

assume [əˈsjuːm] vt **1.** [presume] supposer, présumer / *let's assume that to be the case* mettons ou supposons que ce soit le cas / *he's assumed to be rich* on le suppose riche **2.** [undertake] assumer, endosser **3.** [usurp - power] prendre ; [- right, title] s'approprier, s'arroger **4.** [adopt] assumer, prendre / *she assumed a look of indifference* elle affectait un air d'indifférence.

> ⚠ **Assumer** is not always the correct translation of assume. See the entry for details.

assumed [əˈsjuːmd] adj feint, faux (fausse) ▶ **assumed name** nom m d'emprunt.

assuming [əˈsjuːmɪŋ] conj en admettant or supposant que.

assumption [əˈsʌmpʃn] n **1.** [supposition] supposition f, hypothèse f / *on the assumption that he agrees, we can go ahead* en supposant ou admettant qu'il soit d'accord, nous pouvons aller de l'avant **2.** [of power] appropriation f.

> ⚠ In modern usage, **assomption** is only used to translate assumption in the religious sense. See the entry for appropriate translations.

assurance [əˈʃʊərəns] n **1.** [assertion] affirmation f, assurance f ; [pledge] promesse f, assurance f / *she gave repeated assurances that she would not try to escape* elle a promis à plusieurs reprises qu'elle n'essaierait pas de s'enfuir **2.** [confidence] assurance f, confiance f en soi ; [overconfidence] arrogance f **3.** ⓊⓀ [insurance] assurance f.

assure [əˈʃʊəʳ] vt **1.** [affirm] affirmer, assurer ; [convince] convaincre, assurer ; [guarantee] assurer, certifier **2.** ⓊⓀ [insure] assurer.

assured [əˈʃʊəd] adj **1.** [certain] assuré, certain **2.** [self-confident] assuré, sûr de soi ; [overconfident] arrogant, effronté **3.** ⓊⓀ [insured] assuré.

assuredly [əˈʃʊərɪdlɪ] adv assurément, sûrement, sans aucun doute.

AST (abbr of **Atlantic Standard Time**) n *heure d'hiver des Provinces maritimes du Canada et d'une partie des Caraïbes.*

asterisk ['æstərɪsk] n astérisque m.

astern [ə'stɜːn] ◆ adv à or sur l'arrière, en poupe. ◆ adj à or sur l'arrière.

asteroid ['æstərɔɪd] n astéroïde m.

asthma ['æsmə] n asthme m / she has asthma elle est asthmatique.

asthmatic [æs'mætɪk] ◆ adj asthmatique. ◆ n asthmatique mf.

astigmatism [æ'stɪgmətɪzm] n astigmatisme m.

astonish [ə'stɒnɪʃ] vt [surprise] étonner ; [amaze] stupéfier, ahurir.

astonished [ə'stɒnɪʃt] adj surpris.

astonishing [ə'stɒnɪʃɪŋ] adj [surprising] étonnant ; [amazing] stupéfiant, ahurissant.

astonishingly [ə'stɒnɪʃɪŋlɪ] adv incroyablement / *astonishingly, they both decided to leave* aussi étonnant que cela paraisse, ils ont tous les deux décidé de partir.

astonishment [ə'stɒnɪʃmənt] n [surprise] étonnement m ; [amazement] stupéfaction f, ahurissement m / *they stared in astonishment* ils avaient l'air stupéfait / *a look of astonishment* un regard stupéfait or ahuri.

astound [ə'staʊnd] vt stupéfier, abasourdir.

astounded [ə'staʊndɪd] adj stupéfait.

astounding [ə'staʊndɪŋ] adj stupéfiant, ahurissant.

astoundingly [ə'staʊndɪŋlɪ] adv incroyablement / *astoundingly beautiful* d'une beauté incroyable.

astrakhan [,æstrə'kæn] comp [hat, jacket] d'astrakan.

astral ['æstrəl] adj astral.

astray [ə'streɪ] adv [lost] ▸ **to go astray** s'égarer, se perdre ▸ **to lead sb astray a)** [misinform] mettre or diriger qqn sur une fausse piste **b)** [morally] détourner qqn du droit chemin.

astride [ə'straɪd] prep à califourchon or à cheval sur.

astringent [ə'strɪndʒənt] ◆ adj 1. [remark] acerbe, caustique ; [criticism] dur, sévère 2. [lotion] astringent. ◆ n astringent m.

astrologer [ə'strɒlədʒər] n astrologue mf.

astrological [,æstrə'lɒdʒɪkl] adj astrologique.

astrologist [ə'strɒlədʒɪst] n astrologue mf.

astrology [ə'strɒlədʒɪ] n astrologie f.

astronaut ['æstrənɔːt] n astronaute mf.

astronomer [ə'strɒnəmər] n astronome mf.

astronomic(al) [,æstrə'nɒmɪk(l)] adj ASTRON & fig astronomique.

astronomically [,æstrə'nɒmɪklɪ] adv astronomiquement / *prices have risen astronomically* les prix sont montés en flèche.

astronomy [ə'strɒnəmɪ] n astronomie f.

astrophysics [,æstrəʊ'fɪzɪks] n (U) astrophysique f.

Astroturf® ['æstrəʊ,tɜːf] n gazon m artificiel.

astute [ə'stjuːt] adj [person - shrewd] astucieux, fin, perspicace ; [- crafty] malin, rusé ; [investment, management] astucieux.

astutely [ə'stjuːtlɪ] adv astucieusement, avec finesse or perspicacité.

astuteness [ə'stjuːtnɪs] n finesse f, perspicacité f.

ASV (abbr of **American Standard Version**) n traduction américaine de la Bible.

asylum [ə'saɪləm] n 1. [refuge] asile m, refuge m ▸ **to grant sb political asylum** accorder l'asile politique à qqn 2. [mental hospital] asile m (d'aliénés).

asylum-seeker n demandeur m, -euse f d'asile.

asymmetric(al) [,eɪsɪ'metrɪk(l)] adj asymétrique.

at (weak form [ət], strong form [æt]) prep 1. [indicating point in space] à / *at the door / the bus stop* à la porte / l'arrêt de bus / *at my house / the dentist's* chez moi / le dentiste / *she's at a wedding / committee meeting* [attending] elle est à un mariage / en réunion avec le comité / *where are you at with that report?* US où en êtes-vous avec ce rapport ? ▸ **to be where it's at** inf: *this club is where it's at* cette boîte est super branchée 2. [indicating point in time] à / *at noon / six o'clock* à midi / six heures / *I work at night* je travaille de nuit / *I like to work at night* j'aime travailler la nuit / *I'm busy at the moment* je suis occupé en ce moment ; [indicating age] : *he started working at 15* il a commencé à travailler à (l'âge de) 15 ans 3. [indicating direction] vers, dans la direction de / *look at this!* regarde ça ! / *don't shout at me!* ne me crie pas dessus ! 4. [indicating activity] : *my parents are at work* mes parents sont au travail / *he was at lunch* il était allé déjeuner / *get me some coffee while you're at it* inf prenez-moi du café pendant que vous y êtes / *she's at it again!* inf la voilà qui recommence ! 5. [indicating level, rate] : *the temperature stands at 30°* la température est de 30° / *at 50 mph* à 80 km/h 6. [indicating price] à / *it's a bargain at £5* à 5 livres, c'est une bonne affaire 7. [as adjective complement] en / *he's brilliant / hopeless at maths* il est excellent / nul en maths 8. PHR **to be (on) at sb** inf harceler qqn. ◆ **at all** adv phr : *he's not at all patient* il n'est pas du tout patient / *nothing at all* rien du tout / *if you had any feelings at all* si vous aviez le moindre sentiment.

ATB[1] n (abbr of **all terrain bike**) VTT m.

ATB[2] MESSAGING written abbr of **all the best**.

ATC ◆ n abbr of **air traffic control**. ◆ pr n (abbr of **Air Training Corps**) unité de formation de l'armée de l'air britannique.

8 MESSAGING written abbr of **ate**.

ate [UK et US eɪt] pt ⟶ **eat**.

atheism ['eɪθiɪzm] n athéisme m.

atheist ['eɪθiɪst] ◆ adj athée. ◆ n athée mf.

Athenian [ə'θiːnjən] ◆ n Athénien m, -enne f. ◆ adj athénien.

Athens ['æθɪnz] pr n Athènes.

athlete ['æθliːt] n [gen] sportif m, -ive f ; [track & field competitor] athlète mf.

athlete's foot n (U) mycose f.

athletic [æθ'letɪk] adj [sporty] sportif ; [muscular] athlétique.

athletics [æθ'letɪks] n (U) athlétisme m.

atishoo [ə'tɪʃuː] onomat atchoum !

Atlantic [ət'læntɪk] ◆ adj [coast, community] atlantique ; [wind] de l'Atlantique ▸ **the Atlantic Ocean** l'Atlantique m, l'océan m Atlantique. ◆ pr n ▸ **the Atlantic** l'Atlantique m, l'océan m Atlantique.

Atlantis [ət'læntɪs] pr n Atlantide f.

atlas ['ætləs] n atlas m.

Atlas ['ætləs] pr n 1. GEOG ▸ **the Atlas Mountains** l'Atlas m 2. MYTH Atlas.

atm. (written abbr of **atmosphere**) atm.

ATM[1] (abbr of **automated teller machine**) n distributeur m (de billets), DAB m.

ATM[2] MESSAGING written abbr of **at the moment**.

atmosphere ['ætmə,sfɪər] n 1. [air] atmosphère f 2. [feeling, mood] ambiance f, atmosphère f.

atmospheric [,ætməs'ferɪk] adj 1. [pollution, pressure] atmosphérique 2. [full of atmosphere] : *the film was very atmospheric* il y avait beaucoup d'atmosphère dans ce film.

atoll ['ætɒl] n atoll m.

atom ['ætəm] n **1.** SCI atome m **2.** fig : *there's not an atom of truth in what you say* il n'y a pas une once or un brin de vérité dans ce que tu dis.

atom bomb, atomic bomb n bombe f atomique.

atomic [ə'tɒmɪk] adj [age, bomb, theory] atomique.

atomic energy n énergie f nucléaire or atomique.

atomic number n nombre m or numéro m atomique.

atomizer, atomiser UK ['ætəmaɪzəʳ] n atomiseur m.

atone [ə'təʊn] vi ❯ **to atone for** : *to atone for one's sins* expier ses péchés / *to atone for a mistake* réparer or racheter une faute.

atonement [ə'təʊnmənt] n [of crime, sin] expiation f; [of mistake] réparation f / *to make atonement for one's sins* expier ses péchés.

A to Z n plan m de ville.

ATP (abbr of **Association of Tennis Professionals**) pr n ATP f.

at-risk adj : *an at-risk group* un groupe or une population à risque.

atrocious [ə'trəʊʃəs] adj **1.** [cruel, evil] atroce, horrible **2.** [very bad] affreux, atroce.

atrociously [ə'trəʊʃəslɪ] adv **1.** [cruelly] atrocement, horriblement **2.** [badly] affreusement, atrocement.

atrocity [ə'trɒsətɪ] n (pl **atrocities**) n atrocité f.

atrophy ['ætrəfɪ] (pt & pp **atrophied**) ◆ n atrophie f. ◆ vi s'atrophier. ◆ vt atrophier.

at sign, at-sign n TYPO & COMPUT arobase f.

attach [ə'tætʃ] vt **1.** [connect -handle, label] attacher, fixer ; [-appendix, document] joindre / *the attached letter* la lettre ci-jointe **2.** [associate with] : *he attached himself to a group of walkers* il s'est joint à un groupe de randonneurs **3.** [attribute] attacher, attribuer / *don't attach too much importance to this survey* n'accordez pas trop d'importance à cette enquête.

attaché [ə'tæʃeɪ] n attaché m, -e f.

attaché case n mallette f, attaché-case m.

attached [ə'tætʃt] adj attaché / *he's very attached to his family* il est très attaché or il tient beaucoup à sa famille.

attachment [ə'tætʃmənt] n **1.** [to e-mail] pièce f jointe **2.** [fastening] fixation f **3.** [accessory, part] accessoire m **4.** [affection] attachement m, affection f ; [loyalty] attachement m / *she has a strong attachment to her grandfather* elle est très attachée à son grand-père.

attack [ə'tæk] ◆ vt **1.** [assault -physically] attaquer ; [-verbally] attaquer, s'attaquer à ; MIL attaquer, assaillir **2.** [tackle] s'attaquer à / *a campaign to attack racism* une campagne pour combattre le racisme **3.** [damage] attaquer, ronger / *the disease mainly attacks the very young* la maladie atteint essentiellement les très jeunes enfants. ◆ n **1.** [gen & SPORT] attaque f ; MIL attaque f, assaut m ❯ **to launch an attack on** a) lit donner l'assaut à b) fig [crime] lancer une opération contre c) [problem, policy] s'attaquer à / *the attack on her life failed* l'attentat contre elle a échoué ❯ **to come under attack** être attaqué ❯ **to leave o.s. wide open to attack** prêter le flanc à la critique **2.** [of illness] crise f / *an attack of fever* un accès de fièvre.

attack dog n chien m d'attaque.

attacker [ə'tækəʳ] n [gen] agresseur m, attaquant m, -e f ; SPORT attaquant m.

attagirl ['ætəgɜːrl] excl US bravo !, vas-y ma petite !

attain [ə'teɪn] vt **1.** [achieve -ambition, hopes, objectives] réaliser ; [-happiness] atteindre à ; [-independence, success] obtenir ; [-knowledge] acquérir **2.** [arrive at, reach] atteindre, arriver à.

attainable [ə'teɪnəbl] adj [level, objective, profits] réalisable ; [position] accessible.

attainment [ə'teɪnmənt] n **1.** [of ambition, hopes, objectives] réalisation f ; [of independence, success] obtention f ; [of happiness] conquête f ; [of knowledge] acquisition f **2.** [accomplishment] résultat m (obtenu) ; [knowledge, skill] connaissance f.

attempt [ə'tempt] ◆ n **1.** [effort, try] tentative f, essai m, effort m ❯ **to make an attempt at doing sthg** or **to do sthg** essayer de faire qqch / *she made every attempt to put him at ease* elle a tout fait pour le mettre à l'aise / *he made no attempt to help* il n'a rien fait pour (nous) aider / *he made an attempt on the record* il a essayé de battre le record / *he was shot in an attempt to escape* il fut tué lors d'une tentative d'évasion or en essayant de s'évader **2.** [attack] attentat m / *he survived the attempt on his life* il a survécu à l'attentat perpétré contre lui. ◆ vt [try] tenter, essayer ; [undertake - job, task] entreprendre, s'attaquer à / *he attempted to cross the street* or *he attempted crossing the street* il a essayé de traverser la rue / *he has already attempted suicide once* il a déjà fait une tentative de suicide.

attempted [ə'temptɪd] adj tenté ❯ **attempted murder / suicide** tentative f de meurtre / de suicide.

attend [ə'tend] ◆ vt [go to - conference, meeting] assister à ; [-church, school] aller à / *the concert was well attended* il y avait beaucoup de monde au concert. ◆ vi [be present] être présent / *let us know if you are unable to attend* prévenez-nous si vous ne pouvez pas venir. ❖ **attend to** vt insep **1.** [pay attention to] faire or prêter attention à **2.** [deal with -business, problem] s'occuper de ; [-studies] s'appliquer à ; [-customer] s'occuper de, servir ; [-wound] (faire) soigner.

attendance [ə'tendəns] ◆ n **1.** [number of people present] assistance f / *there was a record attendance of over 500 people* il y avait plus de 500 personnes, ce qui est un record **2.** [presence] présence f / *attendance at classes is obligatory* la présence aux cours est obligatoire / *regular attendance* assiduité f. ◆ comp [record] d'appel ❯ **attendance sheet** feuille f de présence.

attendant [ə'tendənt] ◆ n [in museum, park] gardien m, -enne f ; [in petrol station] pompiste mf ; [servant] domestique mf. ◆ adj fml **1.** [person - accompanying] qui accompagne ; [-on duty] en service **2.** [related] : *he talked about marriage and its attendant problems* il parla du mariage et des problèmes qui l'accompagnent.

attending physician n médecin m traitant.

attention [ə'tenʃn] n **1.** [concentration, thought] attention f / *may I have your attention for a moment?* pourriez-vous m'accorder votre attention un instant ? ❯ **to pay attention** prêter attention / *we paid no attention to the survey* nous n'avons tenu aucun compte de l'enquête ❯ **attention span** capacité f d'attention **2.** [notice] attention f / *the news came to his attention* il a appris la nouvelle / *for the attention of Mr Smith* à l'attention de M. Smith **3.** [care] : *they need medical attention* ils ont besoin de soins médicaux **4.** MIL garde-à-vous m inv ❯ **to stand at** / **to come to attention** se tenir / se mettre au garde-à-vous.

attention-seeking ◆ n : *it's just attention-seeking* il / elle, etc. ne cherche qu'à attirer l'attention sur lui / elle, etc., il / elle, etc. essaie juste de se faire remarquer. ◆ adj : *her attention-seeking behaviour* son besoin constant de se faire remarquer.

attentive [ə'tentɪv] adj **1.** [paying attention] attentif / *attentive to detail* méticuleux **2.** [considerate] attentionné, prévenant / *she was attentive to our every need* elle était attentive à tous nos besoins.

attentively [ə'tentɪvlɪ] adv **1.** [listen, read] attentivement, avec attention **2.** [solicitously] avec beaucoup d'égards.

attenuate vt **1.** [attack, remark] atténuer, modérer ; [pain] apaiser **2.** [form, line] amincir, affiner **3.** [gas] raréfier.

attest [ə'test] fml ◆ vt **1.** [affirm] attester, certifier ; [under oath] affirmer sous serment **2.** [be proof of] démontrer, témoigner de **3.** [bear witness to] témoigner **4.** [put oath to] faire prêter serment à. ◆ vi témoigner, prêter serment / *she attested to the truth of the report* elle a témoigné de la véracité du rapport.

attic ['ætɪk] n [space] grenier m ; [room] mansarde f.

attire [ə'taɪər] fml ◆ n (U) habits mpl, vêtements mpl ; [formal] tenue f. ◆ vt vêtir, habiller, parer.

attitude ['ætɪtjuːd] n **1.** [way of thinking] attitude f, disposition f / *what's your attitude to* or *towards him?* que pensez-vous de lui ? / *attitudes towards homosexuality are changing* les comportements à l'égard de l'homosexualité sont en train de changer **2.** [behaviour, manner] attitude f, manière f / *well, if that's your attitude you can go* eh bien, si c'est comme ça que tu le prends, tu peux t'en aller **3.** fml [posture] attitude f, position f **4.** inf **▸** *to have attitude* **a)** [to be stylish] être stylé **b)** [to be arrogant] être arrogant.

attitudinal [,ætɪ'tjuːdɪnəl] adj relatif aux attitudes **▸** **attitudinal research** enquête f d'attitudes.

attn, ATTN (written abbr of **for the attention of**) attn, à l'attention de.

attorney [ə'tɜːnɪ] (pl **attorneys**) n **1.** [representative] mandataire mf, représentant m, -e f **2.** [solicitor - for documents, sales, etc.] notaire m ; [- for court cases] avocat m, -e f ; [barrister] avocat m, -e f.

Attorney General (pl **Attorneys General** or **Attorney Generals**) n [in England, Wales and Northern Ireland] principal avocat de la Couronne ; [in US] ≃ ministre m de la Justice.

attract [ə'trækt] ◆ vt **1.** [draw, cause to come near] attirer / *to attract criticism* s'attirer des critiques **2.** [be attractive] attirer, séduire, plaire / *she's attracted to men with beards* elle est attirée par les barbus. ◆ vi s'attirer **▸** **opposites attract** les contraires s'attirent.

attraction [ə'trækʃn] n **1.** PHYS [pull] attraction f ; fig attraction f, attirance f / *I don't understand your attraction for* or *to her* je ne comprends pas ce qui te plaît chez or en elle **2.** [appeal - of place, plan] attrait m, fascination f ; [- of person] charme m, charmes mpl **▸** **a tourist attraction** un site touristique.

attractive [ə'træktɪv] adj **1.** [pretty - person, smile] séduisant ; [- dress, picture] attrayant, beau (before vowel or silent 'h' bel, f belle) **2.** [interesting - idea, price] intéressant ; [- offer, opportunity] intéressant, attrayant **3.** PHYS [force] attractif.

attractively [ə'træktɪvlɪ] adv de manière attrayante.

attributable [ə'trɪbjʊtəbl] adj attribuable, imputable, dû.

attribute ◆ vt [ə'trɪbjuːt] [ascribe - accident, failure] attribuer, imputer ; [- invention, painting, quotation] prêter, attribuer ; [- success] attribuer. ◆ n ['ætrɪbjuːt] [feature, quality] attribut m ; [object] attribut m, emblème m.

attribution [,ætrɪ'bjuːʃn] n attribution f.

attrition [ə'trɪʃn] n [wearing down] usure f (par friction) ; INDUST & RELIG attrition f.

attune [ə'tjuːn] vt MUS accorder ; fig accorder, habituer / *her ideas are closely attuned to his* ses idées sont en parfait accord avec les siennes.

Atty. Gen. written abbr of **Attorney General.**

ATV (abbr of **all terrain vehicle**) n VTT m (véhicule tout-terrain).

atypical [,eɪ'tɪpɪkl] adj atypique.

atypically [,eɪ'tɪpɪklɪ] adv pas typiquement.

aubergine ['əʊbəʒiːn] n 🇬🇧 aubergine f.

auburn ['ɔːbən] ◆ adj auburn (inv). ◆ n (couleur f) auburn m.

auction ['ɔːkʃn] ◆ n (vente f aux) enchères fpl **▸** **to put sthg up for auction** mettre qqch en vente aux enchères. ◆ vt **▸** **to auction sthg (off)** vendre qqch aux enchères.

auctioneer [,ɔːkʃə'nɪər] n commissaire-priseur m.

auction room n salle f des ventes.

audacious [ɔː'deɪʃəs] adj **1.** [daring] audacieux, intrépide **2.** [impudent] effronté, impudent.

audacity [ɔː'dæsətɪ] n **1.** [daring] audace f, intrépidité f **2.** [impudence] effronterie f, impudence f.

audible ['ɔːdəbl] adj [sound] audible, perceptible ; [words] intelligible, distinct / *the music was barely audible* on entendait à peine la musique.

audibly ['ɔːdəblɪ] adv distinctement.

audience ['ɔːdjəns] ◆ n **1.** [at film, match, play] spectateurs mpl, public m ; [at concert, lecture] auditoire m, public m ; [of author] lecteurs mpl ; [of artist] public m / *someone in the audience laughed* il y eut un rire dans la salle / *was there a large audience at the play?* y avait-il beaucoup de monde au théâtre ? **2.** RADIO auditeurs mpl, audience f ; TV téléspectateurs mpl, audience f **3.** fml [meeting] audience f **▸** **to grant sb an audience** accorder audience à qqn. ◆ comp [figures] de l'assistance, du public **▸** **audience participation** participation f de l'assistance (à ce qui se passe sur la scène).

audio ['ɔːdɪəʊ] ◆ n son m, acoustique f. ◆ comp **▸** **audio cassette** cassette f audio.

audioblog ['ɔːdɪəʊblɒg] n audioblog m.

audiobook ['ɔːdɪəʊbʊk] n livre m audio.

audio frequency n audiofréquence f.

audiotyping ['ɔːdɪəʊˌtaɪpɪŋ] n audiotypie f.

audiotypist ['ɔːdɪəʊˌtaɪpɪst] n audiotypiste mf.

audiovisual [,ɔːdɪəʊ'vɪzjʊəl] adj audiovisuel **▸** **audiovisual aids** supports mpl audiovisuels **▸** **audiovisual methods** l'audiovisuel, les méthodes audiovisuelles.

audit ['ɔːdɪt] ◆ n vérification f des comptes, audit m. ◆ vt [accounts] vérifier, apurer.

audition [ɔː'dɪʃn] ◆ n **1.** THEAT audition f ; CIN & TV (séance f d')essai m / *the director gave her an audition* **a)** THEAT le metteur en scène l'a auditionnée **b)** CIN & TV le metteur en scène lui a fait faire un essai **2.** [hearing] ouïe f, audition f. ◆ vt THEAT auditionner ; CIN & TV faire un essai à. ◆ vi THEAT [director] auditionner ; [actor] passer une audition ; CIN & TV faire un essai / *I auditioned for "Woyzeck"* **a)** THEAT j'ai passé une audition pour un rôle dans « Woyzeck » **b)** CIN & TV j'ai fait un essai pour un rôle dans « Woyzeck ».

auditor ['ɔːdɪtər] n **1.** [accountant] commissaire m aux comptes, auditeur m, -trice f, audit m **2.** 🇺🇸 [student] auditeur m, -trice f libre.

auditorium [,ɔːdɪ'tɔːrɪəm] (pl **auditoriums** or **auditoria** [-rɪə]) n [of concert hall, theatre] salle f.

au fait [,əʊ'feɪ] adj **▸** **to be au fait with sthg** être au courant de qqch.

Aug. written abbr of **August.**

augment [ɔːg'ment] vt [increase] augmenter, accroître **▸** **augmented reality** réalité f augmentée.

augur [ˈɔːgə] vi : *this weather augurs ill / well for our holiday* ce temps est de mauvais / bon augure pour nos vacances.

August [ˈɔːgəst] n août *m* ▸ **August Bank Holiday** *jour férié tombant le dernier lundi d'août en Angleterre et au pays de Galles, le premier lundi d'août en Écosse.* **See also February.**

auld [ɔːld] adj Scot vieux (vieille) ▸ **the Auld Alliance** HIST *l'ancienne alliance (XIIIᵉ-XIVᵉ siècle) unissant l'Écosse et la France contre l'Angleterre, dont le souvenir est encore souvent évoqué aujourd'hui* ▸ **Auld Lang Syne** MUS *chanson sur l'air de « ce n'est qu'un au revoir » que l'on chante à minuit le soir du 31 décembre.*

aunt [ɑːnt] n tante *f*.

auntie [ˈɑːntɪ] n UK *inf* tantine *f*, tata *f*, tatie *f*.

aunty [ˈɑːntɪ] (*pl* **aunties**) n = **auntie**.

AUP (abbr of Acceptable Use Policy) n COMPUT *code de conduite défini par un fournisseur d'accès à l'Internet.*

au pair [ˌəʊˈpeə] (*pl* **au pairs**) ◆ n (jeune fille *f*) au pair *f*. ◆ vi travailler au pair.

aura [ˈɔːrə] (*pl* **auras** *or* **aurae** [ˈɔːriː]) n [of person] aura *f*, émanation *f* ; [of place] atmosphère *f*, ambiance *f*.

aural [ˈɔːrəl] adj [relating to hearing] auditif, sonore ▸ **aural comprehension** compréhension *f* orale.

aurally [ˈɔːrəlɪ] adv ▸ **aurally handicapped** malentendant.

aurora australis [ɔːˌrɔːrənˈstreɪlɪs] n aurore *f* australe.

aurora borealis [-ˌbɔːrɪˈeɪlɪs] n aurore *f* boréale.

auspices [ˈɔːspɪsɪz] pl n : *under the auspices of the UN* sous les auspices de l'ONU.

auspicious [ɔːˈspɪʃəs] adj [event, start, occasion] propice, favorable ; [sign] de bon augure.

auspiciously [ɔːˈspɪʃəslɪ] adv favorablement, sous d'heureux auspices.

Aussie [ˈɒzɪ] *inf* ◆ n Australien *m*, -enne *f*. ◆ adj australien.

austere [ɒˈstɪə] adj [person] austère, sévère ; [life] austère, sobre, ascétique.

austerity [ɒˈsterətɪ] (*pl* **austerities**) n **1.** [simplicity] austérité *f*, sobriété *f* **2.** [hardship] austérité *f*.

Australasia [ˌɒstrəˈleɪʒə] pr n Australasie *f*.

Australia [ɒˈstreɪljə] pr n Australie *f*.

Australian [ɒˈstreɪljən] ◆ n [person] Australien *m*, -enne *f*. ◆ adj australien.

Austria [ˈɒstrɪə] pr n Autriche *f*.

Austrian [ˈɒstrɪən] ◆ n Autrichien *m*, -enne *f*. ◆ adj autrichien.

autarchy [ˈɔːtɑːkɪ] (*pl* **autarchies**) n = **autocracy**.

authentic [ɔːˈθentɪk] adj [genuine] authentique ; [accurate, reliable] authentique, véridique.

authentically [ɔːˈθentɪklɪ] adv de façon authentique.

authenticate [ɔːˈθentɪkeɪt] vt [painting] établir l'authenticité de ; [signature] légaliser.

authentication [ɔːˌθentɪˈkeɪʃn] n authentification *f*, certification *f*.

authenticity [ˌɔːθenˈtɪsətɪ] n authenticité *f*.

author [ˈɔːθə] n [writer] auteur *m*, écrivain *m*.

authoring [ˈɔːθərɪŋ] n [of DVD] authoring *m (création des menus et du système de navigation).*

authoritarian [ɔːˌθɒrɪˈteərɪən] ◆ adj autoritaire. ◆ n personne *f* autoritaire.

authoritarianism [ɔːˌθɒrɪˈteərɪənɪzm] n autoritarisme *m*.

authoritative [ɔːˈθɒrɪtətɪv] adj **1.** [manner, person] autoritaire **2.** [article, report] qui fait autorité **3.** [official] autorisé, officiel.

authoritatively [ɔːˈθɒrɪtətɪvlɪ] adv avec autorité, de manière autoritaire *pej*.

authority [ɔːˈθɒrətɪ] (*pl* **authorities**) n **1.** [power] autorité *f*, pouvoir *m* / *those in authority in Haiti* ceux qui gouvernent en Haïti **2.** [forcefulness] autorité *f*, assurance *f* / *his opinions carry a lot of authority* ses opinions font autorité **3.** [permission] autorisation *f*, droit *m* / *I decided on my own authority* j'ai décidé de ma propre autorité or de mon propre chef / *without authority* sans autorisation **4.** (*usu pl*) [people in command] autorité *f* ▸ **the authorities** les autorités, l'administration *f* / *the education / housing authority services chargés de l'éducation / du logement* **5.** [expert] autorité *f*, expert *m* ; [article, book] autorité *f* **6.** [testimony] : *we have it on good authority that...* nous tenons de source sûre or de bonne source que...

authorization, authorisation UK [ˌɔːθəraɪˈzeɪʃn] n [act, permission] autorisation *f* ; [official sanction] pouvoir *m*, mandat *m*.

authorize, authorise UK [ˈɔːθəraɪz] vt **1.** [empower] autoriser **2.** [sanction] autoriser, sanctionner.

authorized, authorised UK [ˈɔːθəraɪzd] adj autorisé.

Authorized Version n ▸ **the Authorized Version** *la version anglaise de la Bible de 1611 « autorisée » par le roi Jacques Iᵉʳ d'Angleterre.*

authorship [ˈɔːθəʃɪp] n [of book] auteur *m*, paternité *f* ; [of invention] paternité *f*.

autism [ˈɔːtɪzm] n autisme *m*.

autistic [ɔːˈtɪstɪk] adj autiste.

auto [ˈɔːtəʊ] US n *inf* voiture *f*, auto *f*.

autoantibody [ˈɔːtəʊˌæntɪbɒdɪ] n autoanticorps *m*.

autobiographic(al) [ˈɔːtəˌbaɪəˈgræfɪk(l)] adj autobiographique.

autobiography [ˌɔːtəbaɪˈɒgrəfɪ] (*pl* **autobiographies**) n autobiographie *f*.

autocorrect [ˌɔːtəʊkəˈrekt] vt COMPUT corriger automatiquement.

autocracy [ɔːˈtɒkrəsɪ] (*pl* **autocracies**) n autocratie *f*.

autocrat [ˈɔːtəkræt] n autocrate *m*.

autocratic [ˌɔːtəˈkrætɪk] adj autocratique.

autocross [ˈɔːtəʊkrɒs] n autocross *m*.

Autocue® [ˈɔːtəʊkjuː] n UK téléprompteur *m*.

auto-dial [ˈɔːtəʊˌdaɪəl] n : *a phone with auto-dial* un poste à numérotation automatique.

autofocus [ˈɔːtəʊˌfəʊkəs] n autofocus *m inv*.

autoformat [ˌɔːtəʊˈfɔːmæt] n COMPUT composition *f* automatique.

autograph [ˈɔːtəgrɑːf] ◆ n autographe *m*. ◆ comp [letter] autographe ; [album, hunter] d'autographes. ◆ vt [book, picture] dédicacer ; [letter, object] signer.

automaker [ˈɔːtəʊˌmeɪkə] n US constructeur *m* automobile.

automat [ˈɔːtəmæt] n [machine] distributeur *m* automatique ; US [room] cafétéria *f* équipée de distributeurs automatiques.

automata [ɔːˈtɒmətə] pl ⟶ **automaton**.

automate [ˈɔːtəmeɪt] vt automatiser.

automated [ˈɔːtəmeɪtɪd] adj automatisé.

automatic [,ɔːtə'mætɪk] ◆ adj [machine] automatique ; [answer, smile] automatique, machinal. ◆ n **1.** [weapon] automatique *m* **2.** AUTO voiture *f* à boîte or à transmission automatique.

automatically [,ɔːtə'mætɪklɪ] adv *lit* automatiquement ; *fig* automatiquement, machinalement.

automatic pilot n pilote *m* automatique ▶ **on automatic pilot** en pilotage automatique / *I'm on automatic pilot this morning* je marche au radar ce matin.

automation [,ɔːtə'meɪʃn] n [process of making automatic] automatisation *f* ; [state of being automatic] automation *f*.

automaton [ɔː'tɒmətən] (*pl* **automatons** or **automata** [-tə]) n automate *m*.

automobile ['ɔːtəməbiːl] n US automobile *f*, voiture *f*.

automotive [,ɔːtə'məʊtɪv] adj AUTO [engineering, industry] (de l')automobile.

autonomous [ɔː'tɒnəməs] adj autonome.

autonomy [ɔː'tɒnəmɪ] (*pl* **autonomies**) n [self-government] autonomie *f*.

autopilot [,ɔːtəʊ'paɪlət] n = **automatic pilot.**

autopsy ['ɔːtɒpsɪ] (*pl* **autopsies**) n autopsie *f*.

autosave ['ɔːtəʊ,seɪv] n COMPUT sauvegarde *f* automatique.

autumn ['ɔːtəm] ◆ n automne *m* / *in (the) autumn* en automne. ◆ comp [colours, weather] d'automne, automnal.

autumnal [ɔː'tʌmnəl] adj automnal, d'automne.

auxiliary [ɔːg'zɪljərɪ] (*pl* **auxiliaries**) ◆ adj auxiliaire, supplémentaire. ◆ n **1.** [assistant, subordinate] auxiliaire *mf* ▶ **nursing auxiliary** infirmier *m*, -ère *f* auxiliaire, aide-soignant *m*, -e *f* **2.** GRAM (verbe *m*) auxiliaire *m*.

auxiliary verb n (verbe *m*) auxiliaire *m*.

av. (written abbr of **average**) adj moyen.

AV ◆ n abbr of Authorized Version. ◆ adj abbr of **audiovisual.**

Av. (written abbr of **avenue**) av.

avail [ə'veɪl] ◆ n ▶ **to no avail** sans effet ▶ **to little avail** sans grand effet. ◆ vt ▶ **to avail o.s. of sthg** se servir or profiter de qqch.

availability [ə,veɪlə'bɪlətɪ] (*pl* **availabilities**) n [accessibility] disponibilité *f*.

available [ə'veɪləbl] adj **1.** [accessible, to hand] disponible / *they made the data available to us* ils ont mis les données à notre disposition / *we tried every available means* nous avons essayé (par) tous les moyens possibles / *they're available in three sizes* ils sont disponibles en trois tailles **2.** [free] libre, disponible / *the minister in charge was not available for comment* le ministre responsable s'est refusé à toute déclaration.

available market n marché *m* effectif.

avalanche ['ævəlɑːnʃ] n *lit & fig* avalanche *f*.

avant-garde [,ævɒŋ'gɑːd] ◆ n avant-garde *f*. ◆ adj d'avant-garde, avant-gardiste.

avarice ['ævərɪs] n avarice *f*, pingrerie *f*.

avaricious [,ævə'rɪʃəs] adj avare, pingre.

avatar [,ævə'tɑːr] n RELIG avatar *m* ; *fig* manifestation *f* ; COMPUT [in chatroom] avatar *m*.

avdp. written abbr of avoirdupois.

Ave. (written abbr of **avenue**) av.

avenge [ə'vendʒ] vt venger.

avenger [ə'vendʒər] n vengeur *m*, -eresse *f*.

avenue ['ævənjuː] n **1.** [public] avenue *f*, boulevard *m* ; [private] avenue *f*, allée *f* *(bordée d'arbres)* **2.** *fig* possibi-

lité *f* / *we must explore every avenue* il faut explorer toutes les possibilités.

average ['ævərɪdʒ] ◆ n **1.** [standard amount, quality, etc.] moyenne *f* / *I travelled an average of 100 miles a day* nous avons fait une moyenne de 100 miles par jour or 100 miles par jour en moyenne ▶ **above** / **below average** au-dessus / au-dessous de la moyenne ▶ **on (an)** or **on the average** en moyenne **2.** MATH moyenne *f*. ◆ adj moyen. ◆ vt **1.** MATH établir or faire la moyenne de **2.** [perform typical number of] atteindre la moyenne de / *the factory averages 10 machines a day* l'usine produit en moyenne 10 machines par jour **3.** [divide up] partager. ◆❖ **average out** vi : *factory production averages out at 120 cars a day* l'usine produit en moyenne 120 voitures par jour.

average propensity to consume n ECON propension *f* moyenne à consommer.

average propensity to save n ECON propension *f* moyenne à épargner.

averse [ə'vɜːs] adj : *she's not averse to the occasional glass of wine* elle boit volontiers un verre de vin de temps à autre / *he's not averse to making money out of the crisis* ça ne le gêne pas de profiter de la crise pour se faire de l'argent.

aversion [ə'vɜːʃn] n [dislike] aversion *f* / *she has an aversion to smoking* elle a horreur du tabac.

aversion therapy n thérapie *f* d'aversion.

avert [ə'vɜːt] vt **1.** [prevent] prévenir, éviter **2.** [turn aside - eyes, thoughts] détourner ; [- blow] détourner, parer ; [- suspicion] écarter.

aviary ['eɪvjərɪ] (*pl* **aviaries**) n volière *f*.

aviation [,eɪvɪ'eɪʃn] ◆ n aviation *f*. ◆ comp [design] d'aviation ▶ **aviation fuel** kérosène *m*.

aviator ['eɪvɪeɪtər] n aviateur *m*, -trice *f*, pilote *m*.

avid ['ævɪd] adj avide / *avid to learn* avide d'apprendre.

avidly ['ævɪdlɪ] adv avidement, avec avidité.

avocado [,ævə'kɑːdəʊ] (*pl* **avocados** or **avocadoes**) n [fruit] avocat *m*.

avoid [ə'vɔɪd] vt [object, person] éviter ; [danger, task] éviter, échapper à / *she avoided my eyes* elle évita mon regard / *we can't avoid inviting them* nous ne pouvons pas faire autrement que de les inviter / *don't avoid the issue* n'essaie pas d'éviter or d'éluder la question.

📋 Note that **éviter que** is followed by a verb in the subjunctive:
How can you avoid people using your computer if it's stolen? *Comment éviter qu'on puisse utiliser votre ordinateur en cas de vol ?*

avoidable [ə'vɔɪdəbl] adj évitable.

avoidance [ə'vɔɪdəns] n ▶ **avoidance of duty** manquements *mpl* au devoir ▶ **avoidance of work** le soin que l'on met à éviter le travail ▶ **tax avoidance** évasion *f* fiscale *(par des moyens légaux).*

avowed [ə'vaʊd] adj déclaré.

AVP (abbr of assistant vice-president) n vice-président adjoint.

AWA MESSAGING written abbr of a while ago.

AWACS ['eɪwæks] (abbr of **airborne warning and control system**) n AWACS *m*.

await [ə'weɪt] vt **1.** [wait for] attendre / *a long-awaited holiday* des vacances qui se sont fait attendre **2.** [be in store for] attendre, être réservé à.

awake [ə'weɪk] (*pt* **awoke** [ə'wəʊk], *pp* **awoken** [ə'wəʊkn]) ◆ adj [not sleeping] éveillé, réveillé ▸ **to be awake** être réveillé, ne pas dormir / *the noise kept me awake* le bruit m'a empêché de dormir / *I lay awake all night* je n'ai pas fermé l'œil de la nuit / *he was wide awake* il était bien éveillé. ◆ vi **1.** [emerge from sleep] se réveiller, s'éveiller **2.** [become aware] prendre conscience, se rendre compte. ◆ vt **1.** [person] réveiller, éveiller **2.** *fig* [curiosity, suspicions] éveiller ; [memories] réveiller, faire renaître ; [hope] éveiller, faire naître.

awaken [ə'weɪkn] ◆ vt éveiller. ◆ vi s'éveiller.

awakening [ə'weɪkɪnɪŋ] n *lit* & *fig* [arousal] réveil *m* / *it was a rude awakening* c'était un réveil brutal *or* pénible.

award [ə'wɔːd] ◆ n **1.** [prize] prix *m* ; [medal] médaille *f* **2.** [scholarship] bourse *f*. ◆ vt [give - mark] accorder ; [- medal, prize] décerner, attribuer ; [- scholarship] attribuer, allouer ; LAW [damages] accorder.

award-winner n [person] lauréat *m*, -e *f* ; [film] film *m* primé ; [book] livre *m* primé.

award-winning adj qui a reçu un prix.

aware [ə'weəʳ] adj [cognizant, conscious] conscient ; [informed] au courant, informé ▸ **to be aware of sthg** être conscient de qqch / *I am quite aware of his feelings* je connais *or* je n'ignore pas ses sentiments ▸ **to become aware of sthg** se rendre compte *or* prendre conscience de qqch / *as far as I am aware* autant que je sache / *not that I am aware of* pas que je sache ▸ **politically aware** politisé ▸ **socially aware** au courant des problèmes sociaux.

awareness [ə'weənɪs] n [gen] conscience *f* / *to raise people's awareness* sensibiliser les gens.

awash [ə'wɒʃ] adj *lit* & *fig* [flooded] inondé.

away [ə'weɪ] ◆ adv **1.** [indicating movement] : *he drove away* il s'est éloigné (en voiture) ; [indicating position] : *the village is 10 miles away* le village est à 10 milles ; [in time] : *the holidays are only three weeks away* les vacances sont dans trois semaines seulement **2.** [absent] absent / *the boss is away on business this week* le patron est en déplacement cette semaine / *they're away on holiday / in Madrid* ils sont (partis) en vacances / à Madrid **3.** [continuously] : *she's working away on her novel* elle travaille d'arrache-pied à son roman **4.** SPORT : *the team is (playing) away this Saturday* l'équipe joue à l'extérieur *or* en déplacement samedi. ◆ adj SPORT à l'extérieur / *an away match* un match à l'extérieur / *the away team* l'équipe (qui est) en déplacement. ◆ **away from** prep phr [indicating precise distance] à... de / *two metres away from us* à deux mètres de nous ; [not at, not in] loin de / *somewhere well away from the city* quelque part très loin de la ville.

awayday [ə'weɪdeɪ] n [seminar] séminaire *m* au vert.

AWB MESSAGING written abbr of **a while back**.

awe [ɔː] n effroi *m* mêlé d'admiration et de respect ▸ **to be** *or* **to stand in awe of** être impressionné *or* intimidé par / *I stared at her in awe* je l'ai regardée avec la plus grande admiration.

awe-inspiring adj [impressive] impressionnant, imposant ; [amazing] stupéfiant ; [frightening] terrifiant.

awesome ['ɔːsəm] adj **1.** = **awe-inspiring 2.** *inf* [great] génial.

awe-struck adj [intimidated] intimidé, impressionné ; [amazed] stupéfait ; [frightened] frappé de terreur.

awful ['ɔːfʊl] ◆ adj **1.** [bad] affreux, atroce / *I feel awful* je me sens très mal / *how awful for you!* ça a dû être vraiment terrible (pour vous) ! **2.** [horrific] épouvantable, effroyable **3.** [as intensifier] : *I have an awful lot of work* j'ai énormément de travail. ◆ adv US *inf* = **awfully**.

awfully ['ɔːflɪ] adv [very] très, terriblement / *awfully funny / nice* extrêmement drôle / gentil / *I'm awfully sorry* je suis vraiment *or* sincèrement désolé.

awhile [ə'waɪl] adv *liter* (pendant) un instant *or* un moment.

awkward ['ɔːkwəd] adj **1.** [clumsy - person] maladroit, gauche ; [- gesture] maladroit, peu élégant ; [- style] lourd, gauche ▸ **the awkward age** l'âge ingrat **2.** [embarrassed - person] gêné, ennuyé ; [- silence] gêné, embarrassé / *she felt awkward about going* cela la gênait d'y aller **3.** [difficult - problem, situation] délicat, fâcheux ; [- task] délicat ; [- question] gênant, embarrassant ; [- person] peu commode, difficile / *you've come at an awkward time* vous êtes arrivé au mauvais moment / *they could make things awkward for her* ils pourraient lui mettre des bâtons dans les roues ; [uncooperative] peu coopératif / *he's just being awkward* il essaie seulement de compliquer les choses.

awkwardly ['ɔːkwədlɪ] adv **1.** [clumsily - dance, move] maladroitement, peu élégamment ; [- handle, speak] maladroitement, gauchement **2.** [with embarrassment - behave] d'une façon gênée *or* embarrassée ; [- reply, speak] d'un ton embarrassé *or* gêné, avec gêne.

awkwardness ['ɔːkwədnɪs] n **1.** [clumsiness - of movement, person] maladresse *f*, gaucherie *f* ; [- of style] lourdeur *f*, inélégance *f* **2.** [unease] embarras *m*, gêne *f*.

awning ['ɔːnɪŋ] n **1.** [over window] store *m* ; [on shop display] banne *f*, store *m* ; [at door] marquise *f*, auvent *m* ; NAUT taud *m*, taude *f* **2.** [tent] auvent *m*.

awoke [ə'wəʊk] pt ⟶ **awake**.

awoken [ə'wəʊkn] pp ⟶ **awake**.

AWOL ['eɪwɒl] (abbr of **absent without leave**) adj ▸ **to be / to go AWOL a)** MIL être absent / s'absenter sans permission **b)** *fig* & *hum* disparaître.

awry [ə'raɪ] ◆ adj de travers, de guingois. ◆ adv de travers ▸ **to go awry** mal tourner, aller de travers.

axe UK, **ax** US [æks] (*pl* **axes**) ◆ n hache *f* ▸ **to have an axe to grind a)** [ulterior motive] prêcher pour sa paroisse, être intéressé **b)** [complaint] avoir un compte à régler. ◆ vt **1.** [wood] couper, hacher **2.** *fig* [person] licencier, virer ; [project] annuler, abandonner ; [job, position] supprimer.

axeman ['æksmæn] n *lit* tueur *m* à la hache ; *fig* [in company] cadre chargé des licenciements.

axes ['æksiːz] pl ⟶ **axis**.

axiom ['æksɪəm] n axiome *m*.

axis ['æksɪs] (*pl* **axes** ['æksiːz]) n axe *m*.

axle ['æksl] n [gen] axe *m* ; AUTO essieu *m*.

ayatollah [ˌaɪə'tɒlə] n ayatollah *m*.

aye ◆ interj [aɪ] *arch* & *regional* ▸ **aye!** oui ▸ **aye, aye sir!** NAUT oui, mon commandant ! ◆ n [aɪ] oui *m inv* / *the ayes have it* les oui l'emportent.

AYH (abbr of **American Youth Hostels**) pr n *association américaine des auberges de jeunesse*.

AYP ['eɪwaɪ'piː] (abbr of **Adequate Yearly Progress**) n US SCH *mesure qui permet de déterminer si chaque école publique obtient les résultats escomptés aux tests mis en place par chaque État.*

Ayurvedic [ˌɑːjʊ'veɪdɪk *or* ˌɑːjʊ'viːdɪk] adj ayurvédique.

AZ written abbr of **Arizona**.

azalea [ə'zeɪljə] n azalée *f*.

Azerbaijan [ˌæzəbaɪ'dʒɑːn] pr n Azerbaïdjan *m*.

Azerbaijani [ˌæzəbaɪ'dʒɑːnɪ] ◆ n Azerbaïdjanais *m*, -e *f*. ◆ adj azerbaïdjanais.

Azeri [ə'zerɪ] ◆ n Azéri *mf*. ◆ adj azéri.

AZERTY keyboard [ə'zɜːtɪ-] n clavier *m* AZERTY.

Azores [ə'zɔːz] pl pr n ▸ **the Azores** les Açores *fpl*.

AZT (abbr of **azidothymidine**) n AZT *f*.

b (*pl* b's *or* bs), **B** (*pl* B's *or* Bs) [biː] n [letter] b *m*, B *m* / *B for Bob* B comme Bob / *6B Racine Street* 6 ter, rue Racine. See also **f**.

b 1. written abbr of **billion 2.** written abbr of **born**.

B 1. [indicating secondary importance] ▸ B-movie, B-film, B-picture film *m* de série B ▸ **the B-team** SPORT l'équipe secondaire **2.** SCH & UNIV [mark] bien (= 12 à 14 sur 20) **3.** MUS [note] si *m* **4.** MESSAGING written abbr of **be**.

BA ◆ n (abbr of **Bachelor of Arts**) ≃ (titulaire d'une) licence de lettres. ◆ pr n (abbr of **British Airways**) *compagnie aérienne britannique.*

baa [bɑː] ◆ n bêlement *m*. ◆ vi bêler.

BAA (abbr of **British Airports Authority**) pr n *organisme autonome qui administre les aéroports au Royaume-Uni.*

babble ['bæbl] ◆ vi **1.** [baby] gazouiller, babiller; [person - quickly] bredouiller; [- foolishly] bavarder, babiller **2.** [stream] jaser, gazouiller. ◆ vt [say quickly] bredouiller; [say foolishly] bavarder, babiller. ◆ n **1.** [of voices] rumeur *f*; [of baby] babillage *m*, babil *m*; [of stream] gazouillement *m*, babil *m* **2.** [chatter] bavardage *m*.

babbling ['bæblɪŋ] ◆ n **1.** [of voices] rumeur *f*; [of baby] babillage *m*, babil *m*; [of stream] gazouillement *m*, babil *m* **2.** [chatter] bavardage *m*. ◆ adj babillard.

babe [beɪb] n **1.** *lit* [baby] bébé *m*; *fig* [naive person] innocent *m*, -e *f*, naïf *m*, -ïve *f* **2.** *inf* [young woman] belle gosse *f*, minette *f* **3.** *inf* [term of endearment] chéri *m*, -e *f*.

baboon [bə'buːn] n babouin *m*.

baby ['beɪbɪ] (*pl* babies, pt & pp babied) ◆ n **1.** [infant] bébé *m* / *don't be such a baby!* ne fais pas l'enfant ! ▸ **to leave sb holding the baby**: *they left him holding the baby* il lui ont laissé payer les pots cassés, ils lui ont tout fait retomber dessus **2.** *US inf* [young woman] belle gosse *f*, minette *f* **3.** *US inf* [term of endearment] chéri *m*, -e *f* **4.** *inf* [pet project] bébé *m* ▸ **the new project is his baby** le nouveau projet, c'est son bébé ▸ **it's not my baby** je n'ai rien à voir là-dedans. ◆ comp [care, food, shampoo] pour bébés ▸ **baby's bottle** UK, **baby bottle** biberon *m* ▸ **baby changing area** relais-bébé *m*. ◆ vt dorloter, bichonner. ◆ adj [animal] bébé, petit; [mushroom, tomato] petit ▸ **baby elephant** éléphanteau *m*, bébé *m* éléphant ▸ **baby girl** petite fille *f*.

baby book n livre *m* de bébé.

baby boom n baby boom *m*.

baby boomer [-,buːmə*r*] *n* US enfant *m* du baby boom.

baby buggy n **1.** US = baby carriage **2.** UK [pushchair] ▸ **Baby buggy** poussette *f*.

baby carriage n US voiture *f* d'enfant, landau *m*.

baby doll n poupée *f*. ◆ **baby-doll** adj ▸ **baby-doll pyjamas** or **baby-doll nightdress** baby-doll *m*.

baby face n visage *m* de bébé. ◆ **baby-face** adj au visage de bébé.

baby fat n rondeurs *fpl* (*chez l'enfant*).

baby grand n (piano *m*) demi-queue *m*.

Baby-gro® ['beɪbɪɡrəʊ] n grenouillère *f*.

babyish ['beɪbɪɪʃ] adj *pej* [features, voice] puéril, enfantin; [behaviour] puéril, enfantin, infantile.

baby-minder n nourrice *f*.

baby-sit vi garder des enfants, faire du baby-sitting.

baby-sitter n baby-sitter *mf*.

baby-sitting n garde *f* d'enfants, baby-sitting *m*.

baby sling n porte-bébé *m*, Kangourou® *m*.

baby-snatcher n ravisseur *m*, -euse *f* de bébés.

baby talk n langage *m* enfantin or de bébé.

baby tooth n dent *f* de lait.

baby-walker n trotteur *m*.

babywipe ['beɪbɪwaɪp] n lingette *f*.

baccalaureate [,bækə'lɔːrɪət] n UNIV ≃ licence *f*.

bachelor ['bætʃələr] ◆ n **1.** [man] célibataire *m* **2.** UK UNIV ≃ licencié *m*, -e *f* ▸ **bachelor's degree** ≃ licence *f*. ◆ adj [brother, uncle] célibataire; [life] de célibataire. ◆ **Bachelor of Arts** n UK UNIV [degree] ≃ licence *f* en or ès lettres; [person] ≃ licencié *m*, -e *f* en or ès lettres. ◆ **Bachelor of Law(s)** n UK UNIV [degree] ≃ licence *f* de droit; [person] ≃ licencié *m*, -e *f* en or ès droit. ◆ **Bachelor of Science** n UK UNIV [degree] ≃ licence *f* en or ès sciences; [person] ≃ licencié *m*, -e *f* en or ès sciences.

> ⚠ **Un bachelier** or **une bachelière** means someone who has obtained the baccalauréat. The word never means an unmarried person.

bachelorette party US = hen party.

bachelor flat n garçonnière *f*.

bachelor party n US enterrement *m* de vie de garçon.

back [bæk] ◆ adv **1.** [towards the rear] vers l'arrière, en arrière / *he stepped back* il a reculé d'un pas, il a fait un pas en arrière / *he glanced back* il a regardé derrière lui **2.** [into or in previous place] : *my headache's back* j'ai de nouveau mal à la tête, mon mal de tête a recommencé / *they'll be back on Monday* ils rentrent or ils seront de retour lundi / *I'll be right back* je reviens tout de suite / *is he back at work?* a-t-il repris le travail ? / *he went to his aunt's and back* il a fait un aller et retour chez sa tante **3.** [indicating return to previous state] : *he went back to sleep* il s'est rendormi / *business soon got back to normal* les affaires ont vite repris leur cours normal **4.** [earlier] : *back in the*

17th century au 17ᵉ siècle / *as far back as I can remember* d'aussi loin que je me souvienne / *ten years back* inf il y a dix ans **5.** [in reply, in return] : *you should ask for your money back* vous devriez demander un remboursement or qu'on vous rembourse. ◆ adj **1.** [rear - door, garden] de derrière ; [-wheel] arrière *(inv)* ; [-seat] arrière *(inv)*, de derrière / *the back legs of a horse* les pattes arrière d'un cheval / *the back room is the quietest* la pièce qui donne sur l'arrière est la plus calme **2.** [overdue] arriéré ▶ **back rent /** **taxes** arriéré *m* de loyer / d'impôts. ◆ n **1.** ANAT [of animal, person] dos *m* / *back pain* mal *m* de dos / *my back aches* j'ai mal au dos / *you had your back to me* tu me tournais le dos / *the decision was taken behind my back* la décision a été prise derrière mon dos ▶ **to be flat on one's back** [bedridden] être alité or cloué au lit / *he's always on my back* inf il me critique or harcèle toujours / *get off my back!* inf fiche-moi la paix ! ▶ **to have one's back to the wall** être au pied du mur ▶ **to put sb's back up** énerver qqn ▶ **to put one's back into sthg** mettre toute son énergie à faire qqch / *I'll be glad to see the back of her* je serai content de la voir partir or d'être débarrassé d'elle **2.** [part opposite the front - gen] dos *m*, derrière *m* ; [- of coat, shirt, door] dos *m* ; [- of vehicle, building, head] arrière *m* ; [- of train] queue *f* ; [- of book] fin *f* / *the garden is out* or *round the back* le jardin se trouve derrière la maison **3.** [other side - of hand, spoon, envelope, cheque] dos *m* ; [- of carpet, coin, medal] revers *m* ; [- of page] verso *m* ▶ **to know sthg like the back of one's hand** : *I know this town like the back of my hand* je connais cette ville comme ma poche **4.** [farthest from the front - of cupboard, room, stage] fond *m* / *we'd like a table at the* or *in the very back* nous voudrions une table tout au fond **5.** [of chair] dos *m*, dossier *m* **6.** SPORT arrière *m*. ◆ vt **1.** [move backwards - bicycle, car] reculer ; [-horse] faire reculer ; [-train] refouler / *I backed the car into the garage* j'ai mis la voiture dans le garage en marche arrière **2.** [support financially - company, venture] financer, commanditer ; [-loan] garantir ; [encourage - efforts, person, venture] encourager, appuyer, soutenir ; [-candidate, bill] soutenir **3.** [bet on] parier sur, miser sur ▶ **to back a winner a)** SPORT [horse, team] parier sur un gagnant **b)** FIN [company, stock] bien placer son argent **c)** *fig* jouer la bonne carte. ◆ vi [go in reverse - car, train] faire marche arrière ; [-horse, person] reculer / *the car backed into the driveway* la voiture est entrée en marche arrière dans l'allée. ◈ **back and forth** adv phr ▶ **to go back and forth a)** [person] faire des allées et venues **b)** [machine, piston] faire un mouvement de va-et-vient / *his eyes darted back and forth* il regardait de droite à gauche. ◈ **back to back** adv phr *lit & fig* dos à dos / *they're showing both films back to back* ils montrent deux films l'un après l'autre. ◈ **back to front** adv phr devant derrière. ◈ **in back of** prep phr US derrière. ◈ **back away** vi **1.** [car] faire marche arrière **2.** [person] (se) reculer / *he backed away from her* il a reculé devant lui / *they have backed away from making a decision* ils se sont abstenus de prendre une décision. ◈ **back down** vi [accept defeat] céder. ◈ **back off** vi **1.** [withdraw] reculer **2.** US = **back down**. ◈ **back onto** vt insep [have back facing towards] donner sur (à l'arrière). ◈ **back out** vi **1.** [car] sortir en marche arrière ; [person] sortir à reculons **2.** *fig* [withdraw] se dérober, tirer son épingle du jeu / *to back out of a contract* se rétracter or se retirer d'un contrat. ◈ **back up** vi [car] faire marche arrière. ◆ vt sep **1.** [car, horse] faire reculer ; [train] refouler **2.** [support - claim, story] appuyer, soutenir ; [-person] soutenir, épauler, seconder **3.** COMPUT sauvegarder **4.** TRANSP : *traffic is backed up for 5 miles* il y a un embouteillage sur 8 km.

backache ['bækeɪk] n mal *m* de dos.

backbench ['bækbentʃ] ◆ n banc des membres du Parlement britannique qui n'ont pas de portefeuille. ◆ comp [opinion, support] des «backbenchers».

backbencher [,bæk'bentʃər] n *parlementaire sans fonction ministérielle.*

 Backbencher

Les **backbenchers** sont les députés qui n'occupent pas de poste officiel au gouvernement ou dans le cabinet fantôme. Ils sont assis aux derniers rangs de la Chambre des communes, les premiers rangs étant réservés aux différents ministres.

backbiting ['bækbaɪtɪŋ] n médisance *f*.

backbone ['bækbəʊn] n **1.** ANAT colonne *f* vertébrale ; ZOOL épine *f* dorsale **2.** [of country, organization] pivot *m*, épine *f* dorsale **3.** *fig* [strength of character] fermeté *f*, caractère *m* / *he has no backbone* il n'a rien dans le ventre.

backbreaking ['bæk,breɪkɪŋ] adj éreintant ▶ **backbreaking work** un travail à vous casser les reins.

backchat ['bæktʃæt] n UK *inf* impertinence *f*, insolence *f*.

backcloth ['bækklɒθ], **backdrop** ['bækdrɒp] n THEAT toile *f* de fond ; *fig* toile *f* de fond, fond *m*.

backcomb ['bækkəʊm] vt crêper.

back copy n vieux numéro *m*.

backdate [,bæk'deɪt] vt [cheque, document] antidater.

back door n porte *f* arrière. ◈ **backdoor** adj louche, suspect.

backdoor draft n *enrôlement forcé d'anciennes troupes ou de soldats ayant terminé leur engagement volontaire.*

backdrop ['bækdrɒp] n = **backcloth**.

-backed [bækt] in comp **1.** [chair] à dos, à dossier / *a broad-backed man* un homme qui a le dos large **2.** [supported by] : *US-backed rebels* des rebelles soutenus par les États-Unis.

back end n [of car, bus] arrière *m* ; [of train] queue *f*.

backer ['bækər] n [supporter] partisan *m*, -e *f* ; [financial supporter] commanditaire *mf*, bailleur *m* de fonds.

backfill ['bækfɪl] vt remplir.

backfire [,bæk'faɪər] vi **1.** [car] pétarader **2.** [plan] avoir un effet inattendu / *the plan backfired on him* le projet s'est retourné contre lui or lui est retombé sur le nez.

backflip ['bækflɪp] n [in gymnastics] culbute *f* à l'envers.

backgammon ['bæk,gæmən] n backgammon *m* ▶ **backgammon board** damier *m* ou plateau *m* de backgammon.

background ['bækgraʊnd] ◆ n **1.** [scene, view] fond *m*, arrière-plan *m* ; [sound] fond *m* sonore ; THEAT fond *m* ▶ **in the background** dans le fond, à l'arrière-plan / *his wife remains very much in the background* sa femme est très effacée or reste à l'écart **2.** [of person - history] antécédents *mpl* ; [- family] milieu *m* socioculturel ; [-experience] formation *f*, acquis *m* ; [- education] formation *f*, bagage *m* / *people from a working-class background* gens *mpl* de milieu ouvrier **3.** [of event, situation] contexte *m*, climat *m* / *the talks are taking place against a background of political tensions* les débats ont lieu dans un climat de tension politique / *the report looks at the background to the unrest* le rapport examine l'historique de l'agitation. ◆ adj **1.** [unobtrusive - music, noise] de fond **2.** [facts, material] de base, de fond ▶ **background reading** bibliographie *f*.

backhand ['bækhænd] n revers *m*.

backhanded ['bækhændɪd] adj **1.** [blow, slap] donné avec le revers de la main **2.** [compliment, remark] équivoque.

backhander ['bækhændəʳ] n **1.** [blow, stroke] coup m du revers de la main ; SPORT revers m **2.** 🇬🇧 inf [bribe] pot-de-vin m, dessous-de-table m inv.

backheel ['bækhi:l] n FOOT talonnade f.

backing ['bækɪŋ] n **1.** [support] soutien m, appui m ; [financial support] soutien m financier **2.** [material] renforcement m, support m **3.** MUS [accompaniment] accompagnement m.

backing group n 🇬🇧 musiciens qui accompagnent un chanteur.

back issue n vieux numéro m.

backlash ['bæklæʃ] n contrecoup m / a backlash of violence une réaction de violence.

backless ['bæklɪs] adj [dress] (très) décolleté dans le dos ; [chair] sans dos, sans dossier.

backlist ['bæklɪst] n liste f des ouvrages disponibles.

backlit ['bæklɪt] adj [screen] rétro-éclairé.

backlog ['bæklɒg] n accumulation f, arriéré m / a backlog of orders COMM des commandes inexécutées ou en souffrance.

backlot ['bæklɒt] n 🇺🇸 cour f (derrière un immeuble).

back number n vieux numéro m.

backpack ['bækpæk] n sac m à dos.

backpacker ['bækpækəʳ] n routard m, -e f.

backpacking ['bækpækɪŋ] n ▸ to go backpacking voyager sac au dos.

back passage n **1.** [rectum] rectum m **2.** [alley] ruelle f.

backpedal [,bæk'pedl] (🇬🇧 pt & pp backpedalled, cont backpedalling ; 🇺🇸 pt & pp backpedaled, cont backpedaling) vi **1.** [on bicycle] rétropédaler **2.** [change mind] faire marche arrière fig.

back projection n rétroprojection f.

backrest ['bækrest] n dossier m.

back-scrubber n lave-dos m.

back seat n siège m arrière ▸ to take a back seat fig passer au second plan.

back-seat driver n pej [in car] personne qui donne toujours des conseils au conducteur ; [interfering person] donneur m, -euse f de leçons.

backside [bæk'saɪd] n inf derrière m.

backslash ['bækslæʃ] n barre f oblique inversée, antislash m.

backslide [,bæk'slaɪd] (pt backslid [-'slɪd], pp backslid [-'slɪd] or backslidden [-'slɪdn]) vi retomber, récidiver.

backspace ['bækspeɪs] ◆ vi faire un retour arrière. ◆ vt rappeler. ◆ n espacement m or retour m arrière ▸ backspace key touche f retour (arrière).

backstage [,bæk'steɪdʒ] adv THEAT dans les coulisses or la coulisse, derrière la scène.

backstairs [,bæk'steəz] adj [secret] secret, furtif ; [unfair] déloyal.

back story n récit m enchâssé or secondaire.

backstreet ['bækstri:t] adj [secret] secret, furtif ; [underhanded] louche.

backstroke ['bækstrəʊk] n [in swimming] dos m crawlé.

back talk n 🇺🇸 impertinence f.

back-to-back adj lit & fig dos à dos.

backtrack ['bæktræk] vi lit revenir sur ses pas, rebrousser chemin ; fig faire marche arrière / he's already backtracking from or on his agreement il est déjà en train de revenir sur son accord.

backup ['bækʌp] ◆ n **1.** [support] soutien m, appui m **2.** [reserve] réserve f ; [substitute] remplaçant m **3.** COMPUT sauvegarde f **4.** 🇺🇸 MUS musiciens qui accompagnent un chanteur **5.** 🇺🇸 [traffic jam] embouteillage m. ◆ adj **1.** [furnace] de secours, de réserve ; [plan] de secours ; [supplies] supplémentaire, de réserve ; [team] remplaçant **2.** COMPUT ▸ backup copy copie f de sauvegarde.

backward ['bækwəd] ◆ adj **1.** [directed towards the rear] en arrière, rétrograde / without a backward look sans jeter un regard en arrière **2.** [late in development - country, society, child] arriéré. ◆ adv 🇺🇸 = backwards.

backward-looking adj [ideas] rétrograde.

backwardness ['bækwədnɪs] n [of development - country] sous-développement m ; [-person] retard m mental ; [-of economy] retard m.

backwards ['bækwədz], **backward** 🇺🇸 ['bækwəd] adv **1.** [towards the rear] en arrière / I fell backwards je suis tombé en arrière or à la renverse **2.** [with the back foremost] : to walk backwards marcher à reculons **3.** [in reverse] à l'envers / now say it backwards dis-le à l'envers maintenant **4.** [thoroughly] à fond, sur le bout des doigts. ◆ backwards and forwards adv phr ▸ to go backwards and forwards a) [person] aller et venir b) [machine, piston] faire un mouvement de va-et-vient c) [pendulum] osciller.

backwash ['bækwɒʃ] n sillage m, remous mpl.

backwater ['bæk,wɔːtəʳ] n [of river] bras m mort ; fig [remote spot] coin m tranquille ; pej coin m perdu.

backwoods ['bækwʊdz] adj [remote] isolé ; [backward] peu avancé.

back yard n 🇬🇧 [courtyard] cour f de derrière, arrière-cour f ; 🇺🇸 [garden] jardin m de derrière.

bacn ['beɪkn] n alertes d'e-mail que l'on ne souhaite pas lire tout de suite.

bacon ['beɪkən] n lard m (maigre), bacon m / a slice or rasher of bacon une tranche de lard ▸ bacon and eggs œufs mpl au bacon ou au lard ▸ to bring home the bacon a) inf [be the breadwinner] faire bouillir la marmite b) [succeed] décrocher la timbale or le gros lot.

bacteria [bæk'tɪərɪə] pl n bactéries fpl.

bacterial [bæk'tɪərɪəl] adj bactérien.

bactericidal [bæk,tɪərɪ'saɪdl] adj bactéricide.

bacteriology [bæk,tɪərɪ'ɒlədʒɪ] n bactériologie f.

bad [bæd] (compar worse [wɜːs], superl worst [wɜːst]) ◆ adj **1.** [unpleasant - breath, news, terms, weather] mauvais ; [-smell, taste] mauvais, désagréable / I feel bad about leaving you alone cela m'ennuie de te laisser tout seul / he felt bad about the way he'd treated her il s'en voulait de l'avoir traitée comme ça / he's in a bad mood or bad temper il est de mauvaise humeur / things went from bad to worse les choses se sont gâtées or sont allées de mal en pis **2.** [unfavourable - effect, result] mauvais, malheureux ; [-omen, report] mauvais, défavorable ; [-opinion] mauvais (before noun) / things look bad la situation n'est pas brillante **3.** [severe - accident, mistake] grave ; [-pain] violent, aigu (aiguë) ; [-headache] violent ; [-climate, winter] rude, dur / I have a bad cold j'ai un gros rhume / she has a bad case of flu elle a une mauvaise grippe **4.** [evil, wicked - person] méchant, mauvais ; [-behaviour, habit] mauvais, odieux / you've been a bad girl! tu as été vilaine or méchante ! / bad boy! vilain ! **5.** [harmful] mauvais, néfaste / smoking is bad for your health le tabac est mauvais pour la santé **6.** [unhealthy - leg, arm, person] malade ; [-tooth] malade, carié / how are you? — not so bad comment allez-vous ? — on fait aller or pas trop mal / to have a bad heart être cardiaque **7.** [poor -light, work] mauvais, de mauvaise qualité ; [-actor, pay, performance, road] mauvais /

your painting isn't half bad inf ton tableau n'est pas mal du tout / *he speaks rather bad Spanish* il parle plutôt mal espagnol or un espagnol plutôt mauvais / *I've always been bad at maths* je n'ai jamais été doué pour les maths, j'ai toujours été mauvais en maths **8.** [food] mauvais, pourri ▶ **to go bad a)** [milk] tourner **b)** [meat] pourrir, se gâter. ◆ n US inf [fault] faute f / *my bad, I forgot to turn out the lights* c'est ma faute, c'est moi qui ai oublié d'éteindre les lumières. ◆ adv inf : *he wants it bad* il en meurt d'envie / *she's got it bad for him* elle l'a dans la peau / *he was beaten bad* US il s'est fait méchamment tabasser.

baddie, baddy ['bædɪ] n inf méchant m.

bade [bæd or beɪd] pt ⟶ **bid.**

badge [bædʒ] n [gen] insigne m ; [metal, plastic] badge m ; [fabric] écusson m ; [on lapel] pin's m inv ; [of scout] badge m ; MIL insigne m.

badged [bædʒd] adj [wearing a badge] portant un badge, badgé.

badger ['bædʒər] ◆ n blaireau m. ◆ vt harceler, persécuter / *she badgered us into going* elle nous a harcelés jusqu'à ce que nous y allions.

badly ['bædlɪ] (compar **worse** [wɜːs], superl **worst** [wɜːst]) adv **1.** [poorly] mal / *badly made* or *organized* mal fait / organisé / *things aren't going too badly* ça ne va pas trop mal / *the candidate did* or *came off badly in the exams* le candidat n'a pas bien marché à ses examens / *don't think badly of him for what he did* ne lui en voulez pas de ce qu'il a fait ▶ **to be badly off** être dans la misère **2.** [behave - improperly] mal ; [- cruelly] méchamment, avec cruauté **3.** [severely - burn, damage] gravement, sérieusement ; [- hurt] gravement, grièvement / *she had been badly beaten* elle avait reçu des coups violents / *the army was badly defeated* l'armée a subi une sévère défaite **4.** [very much] énormément / *he badly needs* or *he's badly in need of a holiday* il a grand or sérieusement besoin de (prendre des) vacances / *we badly want to see her* nous avons très envie de la voir.

bad-mannered adj mal élevé.

badminton ['bædmɪntən] n badminton m.

badmouth ['bædmaʊθ] vt inf médire de, dénigrer.

badness ['bædnɪs] n **1.** [wickedness] méchanceté f ; [cruelty] cruauté f **2.** [inferior quality] mauvaise qualité f, mauvais état m.

bad-tempered adj [as character trait] qui a mauvais caractère ; [temporarily] de mauvaise humeur.

baffle ['bæfl] vt [puzzle] déconcerter, dérouter.

baffling ['bæflɪŋ] adj déconcertant, déroutant.

Bafta ['bæftə] (abbr of **British Academy of Film and Television Awards**) n ▶ **Bafta (award)** prix récompensant les meilleurs films et émissions de télévision en Grande-Bretagne.

bag [bæg] (pt & pp **bagged,** cont **bagging**) ◆ n **1.** [container] sac m / *paper / plastic bag* sac en papier / en plastique / *her promotion is in the bag* inf son avancement, c'est dans la poche or dans le sac or du tout cuit **2.** [handbag] sac m (à main) ; [suitcase] valise f ▶ **bags** valises, bagages mpl **3.** [of cloth, skin] poche f ▶ **to have bags under one's eyes** avoir des poches sous les yeux **4.** inf & pej [woman] : *old bag* vieille peau. ◆ vt **1.** [books, groceries] mettre dans un sac **2.** inf [seize] mettre le grappin sur, s'emparer de ; [steal] piquer, faucher / *he bagged the best seat for himself* il s'est réservé la meilleure place. ❖ **bags** inf pl n UK [lots] : *there are bags of things to do* il y a plein de choses à faire.

bagboy ['bægbɔɪ] n US commis m (qui aide à l'emballage des achats).

bagel ['beɪgəl] n petit pain m en couronne (de la cuisine juive).

baggage ['bægɪdʒ] n [luggage] valises fpl, bagages mpl ▶ **baggage check** US [ticket] étiquette f pour bagages ▶ **baggage room** or **checkroom** US consigne f ▶ **baggage handler** bagagiste m ▶ **baggage reclaim** UK or **claim** US retrait m des bagages.

baggy ['bægɪ] (compar **baggier,** superl **baggiest**) adj [clothing - too big] trop ample or grand ; [- loose-fitting] ample.

Baghdad [bæg'dæd] pr n Bagdad.

bag lady n clocharde f.

bagpipes ['bægpaɪps] pl n cornemuse f.

bag-snatcher [-snætʃər] n voleur m, -euse f à l'arraché.

bah [bɑː] interj ▶ **bah!** bah !

Bahamas [bə'hɑːməz] pl pr n Bahamas fpl.

Bahrain, Bahrein [bɑː'reɪn] pr n Bahreïn, Bahrayn ▶ **the Bahrain Islands** les îles fpl Bahreïn.

Bahraini, Bahreini [bɑː'reɪnɪ] ◆ n Bahreïni m, -e f. ◆ adj bahreïni.

Bahrein [bɑː'reɪn] pr n = **Bahrain.**

Bahreini [bɑː'reɪnɪ] n & adj = **Bahraini.**

bail [beɪl] ◆ n **1.** LAW [money] caution f ; [guarantor] caution f, répondant m, -e f ; [release] mise f en liberté provisoire sous caution ▶ **on bail** sous caution / *the judge granted / refused bail* le juge a accordé / refusé la mise en liberté provisoire sous caution ▶ **to stand** or **to go bail for sb** se porter garant de qqn **2.** [in cricket] barrette f. ◆ vt LAW [subj: guarantor] payer la caution pour, se porter garant de ; [subj: judge] mettre en liberté provisoire sous caution. ❖ **bail out** ◆ vt sep **1.** LAW = **bail** (vt) **2.** [help] tirer or sortir d'affaire **3.** [boat] écoper ; [cellar, water] vider. ◆ vi [parachute] sauter en parachute.

bail bondsman n US garant m (d'un condamné en liberté sous caution).

bailiff ['beɪlɪf] n **1.** LAW huissier m **2.** UK [on estate, farm] régisseur m, intendant m.

bail-jump vi US ne pas comparaître au tribunal.

bail-jumper n US accusé m, -e f qui ne comparaît pas au tribunal.

bait [beɪt] ◆ n FISHING & HUNT appât m, amorce f ; fig appât m, leurre m. ◆ vt **1.** [hook, trap] amorcer **2.** [tease] harceler, tourmenter.

baize [beɪz] ◆ n [fabric] feutre m ; [on billiard table] tapis m. ◆ adj [cloth, lining] de feutre.

bake [beɪk] ◆ vt **1.** CULIN faire cuire au four / *she's baking a cake for me* elle me fait un gâteau **2.** [dry, harden] cuire / *the land was baked dry* la terre était desséchée. ◆ vi **1.** [person - cook] : *she got busy baking* **a)** [bread] elle s'est mise à faire du pain **b)** [cake] elle s'est mise à faire de la pâtisserie **2.** [cake, pottery] cuire (au four) **3.** inf [be hot] : *I'm baking!* j'étouffe !, je crève de chaleur !

baked [beɪkt] adj US inf [high on drugs] défoncé.

baked beans ['beɪkt-] pl n haricots mpl blancs à la sauce tomate.

baked potato ['beɪkt-] n pomme f de terre en robe de chambre or en robe des champs.

Bakelite® ['beɪkəlaɪt] n Bakélite® f.

baker ['beɪkər] n boulanger m, -ère f / *I'm going to the baker's (shop)* je vais à la boulangerie ▶ **a baker's dozen** treize à la douzaine.

bakery ['beɪkərɪ] (pl **bakeries**) n boulangerie f.

Bakewell tart ['beɪkwel-] n UK CULIN tarte f à la frangipane et à la confiture de framboises.

baking ['beɪkɪŋ] ◆ n [process] cuisson *f* (au four). ◆ adj **1.** [for cooking] ▶ **baking dish** plat *m* allant au four ▶ **baking tray** plaque *f* de four **2.** [hot - pavement, sun] brûlant ; [- day, weather] torride.

baking powder n levure *f* (chimique).

baking tin n moule *m* à gâteau.

balaclava (helmet) [bælə'klɑːvə-] n passe-montagne *m*.

balance ['bæləns] ◆ n **1.** [of person - physical] équilibre *m*, aplomb *m* ; [- mental] calme *m*, équilibre *m* ▶ **off balance** [physically, mentally] déséquilibré / *he threw me off balance* **a)** *lit* il m'a fait perdre l'équilibre **b)** *fig* il m'a pris par surprise **2.** [of situation] équilibre *m* ; [of painting, sculpture] harmonie *f* / *she tried to strike a balance between the practical and the idealistic* elle a essayé de trouver un juste milieu entre la réalité et l'idéal **3.** [scales] balance *f* / *our future hangs* or *lies in the balance* notre avenir est en jeu **4.** [weight, force] poids *m*, contrepoids *m* **5.** [remainder] solde *m*, reste *m* ; COMM & FIN solde *m* ▶ **balance due** solde débiteur / *I'd like to pay the balance of my account* j'aimerais solder mon compte. ◆ vt **1.** [put in stable position] mettre en équilibre ; [hold in stable position] tenir en équilibre **2.** [act as counterbalance, offset] équilibrer, contrebalancer **3.** [weigh] peser ; *fig* mettre en balance, comparer **4.** [equation, finances] équilibrer / *to balance the books* dresser le bilan, arrêter les comptes. ◆ vi **1.** [remain in stable position] se maintenir en équilibre ; [be in stable position] être en équilibre **2.** [budget, finances] s'équilibrer, être équilibré. ❖ **on balance** adv phr à tout prendre, tout bien considéré. ❖ **balance out** vi : *the advantages and disadvantages balance out* les avantages contrebalancent or compensent les inconvénients.

⚠️ The French word **balance** is not always the appropriate translation for the noun balance, and the verb **balancer** rarely means to balance. See the entry for details.

balanced ['bælənst] adj **1.** [diet, scales, person] équilibré / *a balanced view* une vue impartiale or objective **2.** [programme, report] impartial, objectif.

balance sheet n bilan *m*.

balancing ['bælənsɪŋ] adj **1.** [physical effort] stabilisation *f* ▶ **a balancing act** un numéro d'équilibriste **2.** FIN [account, books - equalizing] balance *f* ; [- settlement] règlement *m*, solde *m*.

balcony ['bælkənɪ] (*pl* **balconies**) n **1.** [of flat, house] balcon *m* **2.** THEAT balcon *m*.

bald [bɔːld] adj **1.** [having no hair] chauve / *he's going bald* il devient chauve, il perd ses cheveux / *a bald patch* **a)** [on person] une calvitie **b)** [on animal] un endroit sans poils **2.** [carpet] usé ; [mountain top] pelé ; [tyre] lisse **3.** [unadorned] brutal / *a bald statement* une simple exposition des faits.

bald eagle n aigle *m* d'Amérique.

 Bald eagle

Cet oiseau est l'emblème des États-Unis. Il figure sur le sceau officiel.

balderdash ['bɔːldədæʃ] n *(U)* dated âneries *fpl*, bêtises *fpl*.

bald-headed adj chauve.

balding ['bɔːldɪŋ] adj qui devient chauve.

baldness ['bɔːldnɪs] n [of person] calvitie *f* ; [of animal] absence *f* de poils.

bald spot n : *to have a bald spot* avoir un début de calvitie.

bale [beɪl] ◆ n [of cloth, hay] balle *f*. ◆ vt = **bail** *(vt)*.

Balearic Islands [,bælɪ'ærɪk-], **Balearics** [,bælɪ-'ærɪks] pl pr n ▶ **the Balearic Islands** les Baléares *fpl*.

baleful ['beɪlfʊl] adj **1.** [menacing] menaçant ; [wicked] sinistre, méchant **2.** [gloomy] lugubre.

Bali ['bɑːlɪ] pr n Bali.

balk, baulk [bɔːk] vi ▶ **to balk at sthg** : *the horse balked at the fence* le cheval a refusé la barrière / *he balked at the idea of murder* il a reculé devant l'idée du meurtre.

Balkan ['bɔːlkən] adj balkanique ▶ **Balkan States** États *mpl* balkaniques, Balkans *mpl*.

Balkans ['bɔːlkənz] pl pr n Balkans *mpl*.

ball [bɔːl] n **1.** [sphere] boule *f* ; [of wool] pelote *f* **2.** SPORT [small] balle *f* ; [large] ballon *m* ; [in snooker] bille *f*, boule *f* ; [in croquet] boule *f* ; [in golf, tennis] balle *f* ; [in rugby] ballon *m* **3.** [dance] bal *m* ; *fig* ▶ **to have a ball** *inf* se marrer comme des fous **4.** PHR the ball *is in his court now* c'est à lui de jouer maintenant, la balle est dans son camp ▶ **to be on the ball a)** [capable] être à la hauteur de la situation **b)** [alert] être sur le qui-vive ▶ **to keep the ball rolling a)** [maintain interest] maintenir l'intérêt **b)** [maintain activity] assurer la continuité **c)** [maintain conversation] alimenter la conversation ▶ **to start** or **to set the ball rolling a)** [in conversation] lancer la conversation **b)** [in deal] faire démarrer l'affaire. ❖ **balls** *vulg* pl n [testicles] couilles *fpl*. ❖ **ball(s) up** UK vt sep *v inf* foutre la merde dans / *he completely balled* or *ballsed up the job* il a complètement salopé le boulot.

 balle, ballon, boule or **bille?**

In general, larger balls such as footballs and beach balls are called **ballons**, and smaller non-inflatable balls such as tennis balls and ping-pong balls are called **balles**. Billiard balls and bowling balls are **boules**. A ball of something, such as clay or snow, is also a **boule**, while very tiny balls are more likely to be called **billes**.

ballad ['bæləd] n [song - narrative] ballade *f* ; [- popular, sentimental] romance *f* ; [musical piece] ballade *f*.

ball-and-socket adj [joint] à rotule.

ballast ['bæləst] n *(U)* **1.** [in balloon, ship] lest *m* **2.** [in road] pierraille *f* ; RAIL ballast *m*.

ball bearing n bille *f* de roulement ▶ **ball bearings** roulement *m* à billes.

ball boy n ramasseur *m* de balles.

ballcock ['bɔːlkɒk] n robinet *m* à flotteur.

ballerina [,bælə'riːnə] n danseuse *f* classique, ballerine *f*.

ballet ['bæleɪ] n ballet *m* ▶ **ballet dancing** danse *f* classique ▶ **ballet shoe** chausson *m* de danse.

ballet dancer n danseur *m*, -euse *f* classique.

ball game n **1.** SPORT [with small ball] jeu *m* de balle ; [with large ball] jeu *m* de ballon **2.** US [baseball] match *m* de base-ball **3.** *inf & fig* [activity] : *it's a whole new ball game* or *it's a different ball game altogether* c'est une tout autre histoire.

ball girl n ramasseuse *f* de balles.

ballistic [bə'lɪstɪk] adj balistique ▸ **to go ballistic** inf péter les plombs.

ballistic missile n missile m balistique.

ballistics [bə'lɪstɪks] n (U) balistique f.

ballocks ['bæləks] vulg pl n, n & interj = **bollocks**.

balloon [bə'luːn] ◆ n **1.** [toy] ballon m **2.** AERON ballon m, aérostat m ▸ to go up in a balloon monter en ballon ▸ **the balloon went up** inf & fig l'affaire a éclaté **3.** [in comic strip] bulle f. ◆ vi **1.** [billow - sail, trousers] gonfler **2.** fig [grow dramatically] augmenter démesurément.

ballooning [bə'luːnɪŋ] n : to go ballooning a) [regularly] pratiquer la montgolfière b) [on one occasion] faire un tour en montgolfière or en ballon.

balloon loan n crédit-ballon m.

balloon mortgage n crédit immobilier dont une part importante du remboursement est due à maturité.

balloon payment n FIN dernier remboursement m (dont le montant est supérieur aux versements précédents).

ballot ['bælət] (pt & pp **ballotted**, cont **ballotting**) ◆ n **1.** [secret vote] scrutin m / to vote by ballot voter à bulletin secret **2.** [voting paper] bulletin m de vote. ◆ vt sonder au moyen d'un vote.

ballot box n [for ballot papers] urne f.

ballot paper n bulletin m de vote.

ball park n **1.** [stadium] stade m de base-ball **2.** inf [approximate range] ordre m de grandeur / his guess was in the right ball park il avait plutôt bien deviné. ◆▸ **ball-park** comp inf ▸ **a ball-park figure** un chiffre approximatif.

ball pit n piscine f à balles.

ballplayer ['bɔːlpleɪər] n US SPORT [baseball] joueur m, -euse f de baseball.

ballpoint ['bɔːlpɔɪnt] ◆ adj à bille ▸ **ballpoint pen** stylo m (à) bille. ◆ n stylo m (à) bille, Bic® m.

ballroom ['bɔːlrʊm] n salle f de bal.

ballroom dancing n danse f de salon.

balls [bɔːlz] pl n & interj ⟶ **ball**.

ballsiness ['bɔːlzɪnɪs] n US v inf culot m.

balls-up UK, **ball-up** US n v inf ▸ **to make a balls-up of sthg** merder qqch.

ballsy ['bɔːlzɪ] adj US v inf culotté.

balm [bɑːm] n lit & fig baume m.

balmy ['bɑːmɪ] adj [weather] doux (douce).

baloney [bə'ləʊnɪ] n **1.** (U) inf [nonsense] idioties fpl, balivernes fpl **2.** US CULIN mortadelle f.

BALPA ['bælpə] (abbr of British Airline Pilots' Association) pr n syndicat britannique des pilotes de ligne.

balsam ['bɔːlsəm] n [balm] baume m.

balsamic [bɔː'sæmɪk] adj ▸ **balsamic vinaigrette** vinaigrette f au vinaigre balsamique.

balsawood ['bɒlsəwʊd] n balsa m.

balti ['bɒltɪ] n curry indien préparé et servi dans une petite poêle.

Baltic ['bɔːltɪk] ◆ pr n ▸ **the Baltic (Sea)** la Baltique. ◆ adj [port, coast] de la Baltique ▸ **the Baltic States** les pays mpl Baltes.

balustrade [,bæləs'treɪd] n balustrade f.

bamboo [bæm'buː] ◆ n bambou m. ◆ comp [screen, table] de or en bambou ▸ **bamboo shoots** pousses fpl de bambou.

bamboozle [bæm'buːzl] vt inf **1.** [cheat] avoir, embobiner **2.** [confuse] déboussoler.

ban [bæn] (pt & pp **banned**, cont **banning**) ◆ n [prohibition] interdiction f, interdit m / they've put a ban on smoking in the office ils ont interdit de fumer dans le bureau. ◆ vt interdire / they are banned from the club ils sont exclus du club.

banal [bə'nɑːl] adj banal.

banality [bə'nælətɪ] n banalité f.

banana [bə'nɑːnə] n [fruit] banane f ; [plant] bananier m. ◆▸ **bananas** adj inf maboul, dingue / to go bananas a) [crazy] devenir dingue b) [angry] piquer une crise.

banana republic n pej république f bananière.

banana skin n peau f de banane, fig gaffe.

banana split n banana split m.

band [bænd] n **1.** [musicians - folk, rock] groupe m ; [- brass, military] fanfare f **2.** [group] bande f, troupe f **3.** [strip - of cloth, metal] bande f ; [- on hat] ruban m ; [- of leather] lanière f **4.** UK [range - in age, price] tranche f. ◆▸ **band together** vi [unite] se grouper ; [gang together] former une bande.

bandage ['bændɪdʒ] ◆ n **1.** [strip of cloth] bande f, bandage m **2.** [prepared dressing] pansement m. ◆ vt [head, limb] bander ; [wound] mettre un bandage sur ; [with prepared dressing] panser.

Band-Aid® ['bændeɪd] n US sparadrap m.

bandan(n)a [bæn'dænə] n bandana m.

B and B, B & B n abbr of bed and breakfast.

bandeau ['bændəʊ] (pl bandeaux [-dəʊz]) n bandeau m (pour retenir les cheveux).

bandit ['bændɪt] n lit & fig bandit m.

bandleader ['bænd,liːdər] n chef m d'orchestre ; MIL chef m de fanfare ; [of pop group] leader m.

bandmaster ['bænd,mɑːstər] n chef m d'orchestre.

band saw n scie f à ruban.

bandsman ['bændzmən] (pl bandsmen [-mən]) n membre m d'un orchestre ; MIL membre m d'une fanfare.

bandstand ['bændstænd] n kiosque m à musique.

bandwagon ['bændwægən] n ▸ **to jump** or **to climb on the bandwagon a)** prendre le train en marche **b)** pej suivre le mouvement.

bandwidth ['bændwɪdθ] n INTERNET bande f passante.

bandy ['bændɪ] (pt & pp **bandied**, compar **bandier**, superl **bandiest**) ◆ vt **1.** [blows] échanger **2.** [ideas, witticisms, insults] échanger / don't bandy words with me ne discute pas avec moi. ◆ adj [person] aux jambes arquées ; [leg - of animal, person] arqué. ◆▸ **bandy about** UK, **bandy around** vt insep [expression, story] faire circuler / his name is often bandied about on parle souvent de lui.

bandy-legged adj : to be bandy-legged avoir les jambes arquées.

bane [beɪn] n [scourge, trial] fléau m / it's / he's the bane of my life ça / il m'empoisonne la vie.

bang [bæŋ] ◆ n **1.** [loud noise - explosion] détonation f ; [- clatter] fracas m ; [- slam] claquement m ; [- supersonic] bang m / she shut the door with a bang elle a claqué la porte ▸ **to go over** or **out with a bang** US, **to go with a bang** inf avoir un succès fou **2.** [bump] coup m violent. ◆ adv **1.** ▸ **to go bang** [explode] éclater / bang go my chances of winning! inf envolées, mes chances de gagner ! **2.** [right] en plein / bang in the middle au beau milieu, en plein milieu / I walked bang into him je suis tombé en plein sur lui. ◆ onomat [gun] pan ! ; [blow, slam] vlan ! ; [explosion] boum ! ◆ vt **1.** [hit - table, window] frapper violemment / he banged his fist on the table il a frappé la table du poing / I banged my head on the ceiling je me suis cogné la tête contre le or au plafond **2.** [slam - door, window] claquer. ◆ vi **1.** [slam] claquer

2. [detonate - gun] détoner. ❖ **bangs** pl n 🇺🇸 frange *f*.
❖ **bang into** vt insep [collide with] se cogner contre,
heurter. ❖ **bang on** vi 🇬🇧 *inf* : *he's always banging
on about his personal problems* il n'arrête pas de casser les
pieds à tout le monde avec ses problèmes personnels.

banger ['bæŋər] n 🇬🇧 *inf* **1.** [sausage] saucisse *f*
▶ **bangers and mash** saucisses-purée *(considérées comme le
plat britannique par excellence)* **2.** [car] tacot *m*, vieux clou *m*
3. [firework] pétard *m*.

Bangkok [,bæŋ'kɒk] pr n Bangkok.

Bangladesh [,bæŋglə'deʃ] pr n Bangladesh *m*.

Bangladeshi [,bæŋglə'deʃi] ◆ n Bangladais *m*, -e *f*,
Bangladeshi *mf*. ◆ adj bangladais, bangladeshi.

bangle ['bæŋgl] n bracelet *m*.

bang-on *inf* ◆ adv 🇬🇧 **1.** [exactly] pile ▶ **to hit sthg
bang-on** frapper qqch en plein dans le mille **2.** [punctually]
à l'heure. ◆ adj : *his answers were bang-on* ses réponses
étaient percutantes.

banish ['bæniʃ] vt [person] exiler ; [thought] bannir, chasser.

banister, bannister ['bænistər] n rampe *f* (de l'escalier).

banjo ['bændʒəu] (🇬🇧 *pl* **banjoes** ; 🇺🇸 *pl* **banjos**) n
banjo *m*.

bank [bæŋk] ◆ n **1.** FIN banque *f* / *I asked the bank
for a loan* j'ai demandé un crédit à ma banque **2.** GAMES
banque *f* ; [in casino] argent qui appartient à la maison de jeu
▶ **to break the bank** faire sauter la banque **3.** [of lake, river]
bord *m*, rive *f* ; [above water] berge *f* ; [of canal] bord *m*,
berge *f* / *the river has overflowed its banks* le fleuve est
sorti de son lit ▶ **the Left Bank** [in Paris] la rive gauche
4. [embankment, mound - of earth, snow] talus *m* ; [- on rail-
way] remblai *m* ; [hill] pente *f* **5.** [row - of levers, switches]
rangée *f*. ◆ vt [cheque, money] déposer à la banque.
◆ vi : *where do you bank?* or *who do you bank with?*
quelle est votre banque ? ❖ **bank on, bank upon**
vt insep [count on] compter sur / *I'm banking on it* je
compte là-dessus.

bankable ['bæŋkəbl] adj bancable, escomptable / *to be
bankable* fig être une valeur sûre.

bank account n compte *m* bancaire.

bank balance n solde *m* bancaire.

bankbook ['bæŋkbʊk] n livret *m* (d'épargne).

bank card n carte *f* bancaire.

bank charges pl n frais *mpl* bancaires.

bank clerk n employé *m*, -e *f* de banque.

bank details n relevé *m* d'identité bancaire, RIB *m*.

bank draft n traite *f* bancaire.

banker ['bæŋkər] n FIN banquier *m*.

banker's card n carte *f* bancaire.

banker's draft n traite *f* bancaire.

banker's order n 🇬🇧 ordre *m* de virement bancaire.

bank holiday n **1.** [in UK] jour *m* férié **2.** [in US]
jour *m* de fermeture des banques.

banking ['bæŋkɪŋ] n (U) FIN [profession] profession *f* de
banquier, la banque ; [activity] opérations *fpl* bancaires.

banking hours pl n heures *fpl* d'ouverture des
banques.

banking house n établissement *m* bancaire.

bank loan n [money lent] prêt *m* bancaire ; [money bor-
rowed] emprunt *m* bancaire.

bank manager n [head of bank] directeur *m*, -trice *f*
d'agence / *my* or *the bank manager* **a)** [head of bank] le
directeur de l'agence où j'ai mon compte **b)** [in charge of
account] le responsable de mon compte.

bank note n billet *m* de banque.

bank rate n taux *m* d'escompte or de l'escompte.

bank robber n cambrioleur *m*, -euse *f* de banque.

bankroll ['bæŋkrəul] 🇺🇸 vt financer.

bankrupt ['bæŋkrʌpt] ◆ adj LAW [insolvent] failli ; fig
[person] ruiné ▶ **to go bankrupt** faire faillite ▶ **to be bankrupt** être en faillite ; fig ▶ **morally bankrupt** sans moralité.
◆ vt [company, person] mettre en faillite ; fig [person] ruiner.

bankruptcy ['bæŋkrəptsɪ] n LAW faillite *f* ; fig [destitu-
tion] ruine *f*.

bank statement n relevé *m* de compte.

bank teller n employé *m*, -e *f* de banque.

banner ['bænər] n [flag] étendard *m* ; COMPUT bandeau *m* ; [placard] bannière *f*.

banner ad n bannière *f* publicitaire.

banner campaign n campagne publicitaire sur Internet
utilisant des bannières publicitaires.

banner headline n PRESS gros titre *m*, manchette *f*.

bannister ['bænistər] n = **banister**.

banns, bans [bænz] pl n bans *mpl*.

banoffee [bə'nɒfiː] n (U) banoffee *m* (dessert au caramel
et à la banane).

banquet ['bæŋkwɪt] n [formal dinner] banquet *m* ; [big
meal] festin *m*.

bantam ['bæntəm] n [hen] poule *f* naine ; [cock] coq *m*
nain.

bantamweight ['bæntəmweɪt] n [boxer] poids coq *m*
inv.

banter ['bæntər] ◆ n (U) badinage *m*, plaisanterie *f*.
◆ vi badiner.

bap [bæp] n 🇬🇧 pain rond que l'on utilise pour faire un sandwich.

baptism ['bæptɪzm] n baptême *m* ▶ **baptism of fire**
baptême du feu.

Baptist ['bæptɪst] ◆ n [member of sect] baptiste *mf*.
◆ adj [sect] ▶ **the Baptist Church** l'Église *f* baptiste.

baptize, baptise [🇬🇧 bæp'taɪz 🇺🇸 'bæptaɪz] vt lit &
fig baptiser.

bar [bɑ:] (pt & pp **barred**, cont **barring**) ◆ n **1.** [pub]
bar *m*, café *m* ; [in hotel, club] bar *m* ; [in station] café *m*,
bar *m* ; [counter] bar *m* **2.** [long piece of metal] barre *f* ; [on
grating, cage] barreau *m* ; [on door] bâcle *f* ; ELEC [element]
barre *f* / *an iron bar* une barre de fer ▶ **to be behind bars**
être sous les verrous or derrière les barreaux ▶ **to set the bar
high** placer la barre haut **3.** [ban] interdiction *f* / *there is
no bar on foreign athletes* les athlètes étrangers sont autorisés à participer aux compétitions **4.** [slab - of chocolate]
tablette *f* ; [- of gold] lingot *m* / *a bar of soap* une savonnette, un pain de savon **5.** MUS mesure *f*. ◆ vt **1.** [put bars
on - window] munir de barreaux / *bar the door* mettez la
barre or la bâcle à la porte / *they barred the door against
intruders* ils ont barré la porte aux intrus **2.** [obstruct] barrer / *he barred her way* or *her path* il lui barra le passage
3. [ban - person] exclure ; [- activity] interdire / *members of
the sect were barred from entering the country* l'entrée
du pays était interdite aux membres de la secte. ◆ prep
excepté, sauf ▶ **bar accidents** sauf accident, sauf imprévu
▶ **bar none** sans exception. ❖ **Bar** n LAW ▶ **the Bar a)**
🇬🇧 le barreau **b)** 🇺🇸 les avocats ▶ **to call sb to the Bar** 🇬🇧,
to admit sb to the Bar 🇺🇸 inscrire qqn au barreau.

Barbadian [bɑ:'beɪdɪən] ◆ n habitant de la Barbade.
◆ adj de la Barbade.

Barbados [bɑ:'beɪdɒs] pr n Barbade *f*.

barbarian [bɑ:'beərɪən] n [boor, savage] barbare *mf*.

barbaric [bɑ:'bærɪk] adj lit & fig barbare.

barbarism ['bɑ:bərɪzm] n **1.** [state] barbarie *f* **2.** [in lan-
guage] barbarisme *m*.

barbarity [bɑːˈbærətɪ] n [brutality] barbarie f, inhumanité f.

barbarous [ˈbɑːbərəs] adj [language, manners, tribe] barbare.

barbecue [ˈbɑːbɪkjuː] (pt & pp **barbecued**, cont **barbecuing**) ◆ n [grill, meal, party] barbecue m / to have a barbecue faire un barbecue. ◆ vt [steak] griller au charbon de bois ; [pig, sheep] rôtir tout entier.

barbed [bɑːbd] adj [arrow, hook] barbelé ; [comment] acéré.

barbed wire, barbwire 🇺🇸 [ˈbɑːˈbwaɪəʳ] n (fil m de fer) barbelé m / a barbed wire fence une haie de barbelés.

barber [ˈbɑːbəʳ] n coiffeur m (pour hommes) / to go to the barber's aller chez le coiffeur (pour hommes).

barbie [ˈbɑːbɪ] n 🇦🇺 inf barbecue m.

barbiturate [bɑːˈbɪtjʊrət] n barbiturique m.

Barbour jacket® [ˈbɑːbəʳ-] n Barbour m (veste en toile cirée à col de velours souvent associée à un style de vie BCBG en Grande-Bretagne).

barbwire [ˈbɑːˈbwaɪəʳ] n 🇺🇸 = barbed wire.

Barcalounger® [ˈbɑːkəlaʊndʒəʳ] n 🇺🇸 fauteuil m réglable.

Barcelona [ˌbɑːsɪˈləʊnə] pr n Barcelone.

bar chart n histogramme m, graphique m à or en barres.

bar code n code-barres m.

bard margin n 🇺🇸 = hard shoulder.

bare [beəʳ] (compar **barer**, superl **barest**) ◆ adj **1.** [naked - body, feet] nu / he killed a tiger with his bare hands il a tué un tigre à mains nues **2.** [unadorned, uncovered] nu ; ELEC [wire] dénudé / his head was bare il était nu-tête / the lawn was just a bare patch of grass la pelouse consistait en un maigre carré d'herbe **3.** [empty] vide / the cupboard was bare le garde-manger était vide **4.** [basic, plain] simple, dépouillé / the bare facts les faits bruts / the bare bones of the story le squelette de l'histoire **5.** [absolute] absolu, strict / the bare necessities of life le minimum vital **6.** [meagre] : a bare 20% of the population is literate à peine 20 % de la population est alphabétisée / they won by a bare majority ils ont gagné de justesse. ◆ vt [part of body] découvrir ; ELEC [wire] dénuder ; [teeth] montrer / to bare one's head se découvrir la tête.

bareback [ˈbeəbæk] adv [ride] à nu, à cru.

barefaced [ˈbeəfeɪst] adj [liar] effronté, éhonté ; [lie] impudent.

barefooted [ˌbeəˈfʊtɪd] ◆ adj aux pieds nus. ◆ adv nu-pieds, (les) pieds nus.

bareheaded [ˌbeəˈhedɪd] ◆ adv nu-tête, (la) tête nue. ◆ adj nu-tête (inv).

barelegged [ˌbeəˈlegd] ◆ adv nu-jambes, (les) jambes nues. ◆ adj aux jambes nues.

barely [ˈbeəlɪ] adv **1.** [only just] à peine, tout juste / I had barely arrived when I heard the news j'étais à peine arrivé que j'ai entendu la nouvelle **2.** [sparsely] très peu ; [poorly] pauvrement.

Barents Sea [ˈbærənts-] pr n ▶ the Barents Sea la mer de Barents.

barf [bɑːf] vi 🇺🇸 v inf dégueuler.

bargain [ˈbɑːgɪn] ◆ n **1.** [deal] marché m, affaire f ▶ to strike or to make a bargain with sb conclure un marché avec qqn **2.** [good buy] occasion f / it's a real bargain! c'est une bonne affaire !, c'est une occasion ! ◆ comp ▶ bargain price prix m avantageux. ◆ vi **1.** [haggle] marchander **2.** [negotiate] négocier / the unions are bargaining with management for an 8% pay rise les syndicats

négocient une hausse de salaire de 8 % avec la direction. ❖ **into the bargain** adv phr par-dessus le marché. ❖ **bargain for** vt insep [anticipate] s'attendre à / they got more than they bargained for ils ne s'attendaient pas à un coup pareil. ❖ **bargain on** vt insep [depend on] compter sur.

bargain basement n [in shop] dans certains grands magasins, sous-sol où sont regroupés les articles en solde et autres bonnes affaires.

bargain-hunter n dénicheur m, -euse f de bonnes affaires.

bargaining [ˈbɑːgɪnɪŋ] n [haggling] marchandage m ; [negotiating] négociations fpl / they have considerable bargaining power ils ont beaucoup de poids dans les négociations / to use sthg as a bargaining chip utiliser qqch comme argument dans une négociation.

barge [bɑːdʒ] ◆ n [on canal] chaland m ; [larger - on river] péniche f. ◆ vi : he barged into the room il fit irruption dans la pièce / she barged past me elle m'a bousculé en passant. ◆ vt : to barge one's way through the crowd foncer à travers la foule. ❖ **barge in** vi [enter] faire irruption ; [meddle] : he keeps barging in on our conversation il n'arrête pas de nous interrompre dans notre conversation. ❖ **barge into** vt insep [bump into - person] rentrer dans ; [- piece of furniture] rentrer dans, se cogner contre.

barge pole n gaffe f ▶ I wouldn't touch it with a barge pole a) 🇬🇧 [disgusting object] je n'y toucherais pas avec des pincettes b) [risky business] je ne m'en mêlerais pour rien au monde.

bar graph n 🇺🇸 histogramme m.

barhop [ˈbɑːhɒp] vi 🇺🇸 faire la tournée des bars.

barista [bəˈriːstə] n [male] barman m ; [female] serveuse f.

baritone, barytone [ˈbærɪtəʊn] ◆ n [singer, voice] baryton m. ◆ adj [part, voice] de baryton.

barium meal n MED bouillie f barytée.

bark [bɑːk] ◆ n **1.** [of dog] aboiement m ; [of fox] glapissement m ; [cough] toux f sèche ▶ his bark is worse than his bite il fait plus de bruit que de mal **2.** [of tree] écorce f. ◆ vi [dog] aboyer ; [fox] glapir ; [cough] tousser ; [speak harshly] crier, aboyer ; [sell] vendre à la criée / the dog barked at the postman le chien a aboyé après le facteur ▶ to be barking up the wrong tree se tromper de cible. ❖ **bark out** vt sep [order] aboyer.

barking [ˈbɑːkɪŋ] ◆ n (U) aboiements m. ◆ adj 🇬🇧 inf ▶ to be barking (mad) être fou à lier.

barking head n 🇺🇸 inf présentateur de radio ou de télévision au style agressif.

barley [ˈbɑːlɪ] n AGR [crop, grain] orge f.

barley sugar n sucre m d'orge.

barley water n 🇬🇧 boisson à base d'orge.

barmaid [ˈbɑːmeɪd] n barmaid f, serveuse f (de bar).

barman [ˈbɑːmən] (pl **barmen** [-mən]) n barman m, serveur m (de bar).

bar mitzvah [ˌbɑːˈmɪtsvə] n [ceremony] bar-mitsva f inv ; [boy] garçon m qui fait sa bar-mitsva.

barmy [ˈbɑːmɪ] (compar **barmier**, superl **barmiest**) adj 🇬🇧 inf maboul, dingue.

barn [bɑːn] n [for hay] grange f ; [for horses] écurie f ; [for cows] étable f.

barnacle [ˈbɑːnəkl] n bernache f (crustacé).

barn dance n bal de campagne où l'on danse des quadrilles.

barn door n fig ▶ it's as big as a barn door c'est gros comme une maison.

barn owl n chouette effraie f.

barnyard ['bɑːnjɑːd] ◆ n cour f de ferme. ◆ adj [animals] de basse-cour ; [humour] rustre.

barometer [bə'rɒmɪtər] n baromètre m.

baron ['bærən] n **1.** [noble] baron m **2.** [magnate] magnat m **/** a press baron un magnat de la presse.

baroness ['bærənɪs] n baronne f.

baronet ['bærənɪt] n baronnet m.

baroque [bə'rɒk] ◆ adj baroque. ◆ n baroque m.

bar phone n téléphone m monobloc.

barque, bark US [bɑːk] n *liter* barque f ; NAUT [3 masts] trois-mâts m inv ; [4 masts] quatre-mâts m inv.

barrack ['bærək] vt [soldiers] caserner. ❖ **barracks** n caserne f.

barracking ['bærəkɪŋ] n chahut m.

barracuda [,bærə'kuːdə] n barracuda m.

barrage ['bærɑːʒ] n **1.** MIL tir m de barrage **2.** *fig* [of punches, questions] pluie f, déluge m ; [of insults, words] déluge m, flot m **3.** [dam] barrage m.

barred [bɑːd] adj [window, opening] à barreaux.

barrel ['bærəl] (US pt & pp **barrelled**, cont **barrelling** ; US pt & pp **barreled**, cont **barreling**) ◆ n **1.** [cask, unit of capacity - of wine] tonneau m, fût m ; [- of cider] fût m ; [- of beer] tonneau m ; [- of oil, tar] baril m ; [- of fish] caque f ▶ **to have sb over a barrel** *inf* tenir qqn à sa merci **2.** [hollow cylinder - of gun, key] canon m ; [- of clock, lock] barillet m ; [- of pen] corps m **3.** *inf* [lot] : *it wasn't exactly a barrel of laughs* c'était très sérieux or déprimant. ◆ vi US *inf* ▶ **to barrel (along)** foncer, aller à toute pompe.

barrel organ n orgue m de Barbarie.

barren ['bærən] adj **1.** [land - infertile] stérile, improductif ; [- bare] désertique **2.** [dry] aride **2.** [sterile - plant, woman] stérile **3.** [dull - film, play] aride ; [- discussion] stérile ; [- writing] aride, sec (sèche).

barrette [bə'ret] n US barrette f (pour cheveux).

barricade [,bærɪ'keɪd] ◆ n barricade f. ◆ vt [door, street] barricader.

barrier ['bærɪər] n **1.** [fence, gate] barrière f ; [at railway station] portillon m **2.** [obstacle] obstacle m ▶ **barrier method** méthode f de contraception locale.

barrier cream n crème f protectrice.

barring ['bɑːrɪŋ] prep excepté, sauf ▶ **barring accidents** sauf accident, sauf imprévu.

barrister ['bærɪstər] n UK ≃ avocat m, -e f.

barroom ['bɑːrʊm] n US bar m ▶ **barroom brawl** bagarre f de bar.

barrow ['bærəʊ] n [wheelbarrow] brouette f ; [fruitseller's] voiture f des quatre saisons ; [for luggage] diable m ; MIN wagonnet m.

bar snack n repas léger pris dans un pub.

bar staff n personnel m de bar.

bar stool n tabouret m de bar.

Bart. n written abbr of baronet.

bartender ['bɑːtendər] n US barman m, barmaid f, serveur m (de bar), serveuse f (de bar).

barter ['bɑːtər] ◆ n (U) échange m, troc m. ◆ vt échanger, troquer. ◆ vi [exchange] faire un échange or un troc ; [haggle] marchander.

base [beɪs] (compar **baser**, superl **basest**) ◆ n **1.** [bottom - gen] partie f inférieure, base f ; [- of tree, column] pied m ; [- of bowl, glass] fond m ; [- of triangle] base f **2.** [of food, paint] base f **3.** [basis of knowledge] base f ; [- of experience] réserve f **4.** [centre of activities] point m de départ ; MIL base f **5.** [in baseball and rounders] base f ▶ **to touch base** : *I just thought I'd touch base* je voulais juste garder le contact. ◆ vt **1.** [found - opinion, project] fon-

der, baser **2.** [locate] baser **/** the job is based in Tokyo le poste est basé à Tokyo. ◆ adj [motive, thoughts, conduct] bas, indigne ; [origins] bas ; [ingratitude, outlook] mesquin ; [coinage] faux (fausse).

⚠ Although the expression **basé sur** is commonly used, it is widely frowned upon and should be avoided in written French; **fondé sur** is considered more correct.

baseball ['beɪsbɔːl] n base-ball m ▶ **baseball cap** casquette f de base-ball.

base camp n camp m de base.

base-jump vi pratiquer le base-jump.

base-jumper n adepte mf de base-jump.

base-jumping n base-jump m (saut en parachute à partir d'une falaise, d'un pont, d'un immeuble, etc.).

Basel ['bɑːzl], **Basle** [bɑːl] pr n Bâle.

baseless ['beɪslɪs] adj [gossip] sans fondement ; [suspicion] injustifié ; [fear, superstition] déraisonnable.

baseline ['beɪslaɪn] n **1.** [in tennis] ligne f de fond ; [in baseball] ligne f des bases **2.** [in surveying] base f ; [in diagram] ligne f zéro ; ART ligne f de fuite **3.** [standard] point m de comparaison.

basement ['beɪsmənt] n sous-sol m **/** in the basement au sous-sol **/** a basement kitchen une cuisine en sous-sol.

base metal n métal m vil.

base rate n FIN taux m de base (utilisé par les banques pour déterminer leur taux de prêt).

bases ['beɪsiːz] pl ⟶ **basis**.

bash [bæʃ] inf ◆ n **1.** [blow] coup m ; [with fist] coup m de poing **2.** [dent - in wood] entaille f ; [- in metal] bosse f, bosselure f **3.** [party] fête f **4.** [attempt] ▶ **to have a bash at sthg, to give sthg a bash** essayer de faire qqch. ◆ vt **1.** [person, one's head] frapper, cogner **2.** [dent - wooden box, table] entailler ; [- car] cabosser, bosseler **3.** *fig* [criticize] critiquer. ❖ **bash in** vt sep inf [door] enfoncer ; [lid] défoncer ; [car, hat] cabosser. ❖ **bash up** vt sep inf [car] bousiller ; [person] tabasser.

bashful ['bæʃfʊl] adj [shy] timide ; [modest] pudique.

-bashing ['bæʃɪŋ] in comp inf ▶ **media-bashing** dénigrement m systématique des médias.

basic ['beɪsɪk] adj **1.** [fundamental - problem, theme] fondamental ; [- aim, belief] principal **2.** [elementary - rule, skill] élémentaire ; [- knowledge, vocabulary] de base **/** basic English anglais m de base **3.** [essential] essentiel **/** the basic necessities of life les besoins mpl vitaux **4.** [primitive] rudimentaire **5.** [as a starting point - hours, salary] de base ▶ **basic wage** salaire m de base. ❖ **basics** pl n ▶ **the basics** l'essentiel m **/** let's get down to basics venons-en à l'essentiel.

⚠ Although the word **basique** is commonly used, many people still consider it incorrect in its non-scientific sense and it should be avoided in written French. See the entry for alternatives.

BASIC ['beɪsɪk] (abbr of beginner's all-purpose symbolic instruction code) n COMPUT basic m.

basically ['beɪsɪklɪ] adv au fond **/** basically I agree with you dans l'ensemble or en gros je suis d'accord avec vous **/** basically, she doesn't know what to think dans le fond, elle ne sait pas quoi penser.

basic commodity n denrée f de base.

basic rate n [UK] taux m de base / *most people are basic rate taxpayers* la plupart des gens sont imposés au taux de base.

basil ['beɪzl] n BOT basilic m.

basilica [bə'zɪlɪkə] n basilique f.

basin ['beɪsn] n **1.** CULIN bol m ; [for cream] jatte f **2.** [for washing] cuvette f ; [plumbed in] lavabo m **3.** GEOG [of river] bassin m ; [of valley] cuvette f **4.** [for fountain] vasque f ; [in harbour] bassin m.

basis ['beɪsɪs] (pl **bases** [-si:z]) n **1.** [foundation] base f / *he can't survive on that basis* il ne peut pas survivre dans ces conditions-là / *on the basis of what I was told* d'après ce qu'on m'a dit **2.** [reason] raison f ; [grounds] motif m / *he did it on the basis that he'd nothing to lose* il l'a fait en partant du principe qu'il n'avait rien à perdre **3.** [system] : *employed on a part-time basis* employé à mi-temps / *paid on a weekly basis* payé à la semaine.

bask [bɑːsk] vi **1.** [lie] : *to bask in the sun* se prélasser au soleil, lézarder **2.** [revel] se réjouir, se délecter.

basket ['bɑːskɪt] n **1.** [container - gen] corbeille f ; [- for wastepaper] corbeille f à papier ; [- for shopping] panier m ; [- for linen] corbeille f or panier m à linge ; [- for baby] couffin m ; [- on donkey] panier m ; [- on someone's back] hotte f **2.** [quantity] panier m **3.** [in basketball - net, point] panier m.

basketball ['bɑːskɪtbɔːl] n basket-ball m, basket m **▸ basketball player** basketteur m, -euse f.

basket case n v inf [nervous wreck] paquet m de nerfs.

basket crane n nacelle f élévatrice.

basket of currencies n ECON & FIN panier m de devises or de monnaies.

basketwork ['bɑːskɪtwɜːk] n (U) [objects] objets mpl en osier ; [skill] vannerie f.

basking shark ['bɑːskɪŋ-] n requin m pèlerin, pèlerin m.

Basle [bɑːl] pr n = Basel.

basmati (rice) [bæz'mɑːtɪ] n (U) CULIN (riz m) basmati m.

basque [bɑːsk] n corsage m très ajusté.

Basque [bɑːsk] ◆ n **1.** [person] Basque mf **2.** LING basque m. ◆ adj basque.

bass¹ [beɪs] ◆ n **1.** [part, singer] basse f **2.** [bass guitar] basse f ; [double bass] contrebasse f. ◆ adj grave, bas.

bass² [bæs] n [freshwater fish] perche f ; [sea fish] bar m, loup m.

bass clef [beɪs-] n clef f de fa.

bass drum [beɪs-] n grosse caisse f.

basset (hound) [bæsɪt-] n basset m (chien).

bass guitar [beɪs-] n guitare f basse.

bassist ['beɪsɪst] n bassiste mf.

bassoon [bə'suːn] n basson m.

bastard ['bɑːstəd] n **1.** liter & pej [child] bâtard m, -e f **2.** v inf & pej [nasty person] salaud m **3.** v inf [affectionate use] : *you lucky bastard!* sacré veinard !

baste [beɪst] vt CULIN arroser.

bastion ['bæstɪən] n lit & fig bastion m.

BASW (abbr of British Association of Social Workers) pr n syndicat britannique des travailleurs sociaux.

bat [bæt] (pt & pp **batted**, cont **batting**) ◆ n **1.** [in baseball and cricket] batte f ; [in table tennis] raquette f **▸ right off the bat** [US] inf sur-le-champ **▸ to do sthg off one's own bat** [UK] inf faire qqch de sa propre initiative **2.** [shot, blow] coup m **3.** ZOOL chauve-souris f. ◆ vi [baseball player, cricketer - play] manier la batte ; [- take one's turn

at playing] être à la batte. ◆ vt **1.** [hit] donner un coup à **2.** [blink] : *she batted her eyelids at him* elle battit des paupières en le regardant / *he didn't bat an eyelid* fig il n'a pas sourcillé or bronché.

batch [bætʃ] n [of letters] paquet m, liasse f ; [of people] groupe m ; [of refugees] convoi m ; [of bread] fournée f ; [of recruits] contingent m ; COMM lot m.

batch file n COMPUT fichier m batch or.bat.

batch processing n COMPUT traitement m par lots.

bated ['beɪtɪd] adj **▸ we waited with bated breath** nous avons attendu en retenant notre souffle.

bath [bɑːθ] (pl **baths** [bɑːðz], pt & pp **bathed**) ◆ n **1.** [wash] bain m ; [tub] baignoire f **▸ to have** [UK] or to **take a bath** prendre un bain / *she's in the bath* elle prend son bain, elle est dans son bain / *a room with bath* une chambre avec salle de bains **2.** [for chemicals, dye] bain m ; PHOT cuvette f. ◆ vt [baby, person] baigner, donner un bain à. ◆ vi [UK] prendre un bain. ◆ **baths** pl n [swimming pool] piscine f ; [public baths] bains-douches mpl ; [at spa] thermes mpl.

bathcap ['bɑːθkæp] n [US] bonnet m de bain.

bath chair n fauteuil m roulant.

bath cube n cube m de sels de bain.

bathe [beɪð] (pt & pp **bathed**) ◆ vi **1.** [UK] [swim] se baigner **2.** [US] [bath] prendre un bain. ◆ vt **1.** [wound] laver ; [eyes, feet] baigner **2.** [covered] : *I was bathed in sweat* j'étais en nage, je ruisselais de sueur / *her face was bathed in tears* son visage était baigné de larmes **3.** [US] [bath] baigner, donner un bain à. ◆ n bain m (dans la mer, dans une rivière).

bather ['beɪðər] n [swimmer] baigneur m, -euse f.

bathing ['beɪðɪŋ] n (U) **1.** [UK] [swimming] baignade f **2.** [washing] bain m.

bathing cap n bonnet m de bain.

bathing costume n maillot m de bain.

bathing suit n = bathing costume.

bathing trunks pl n [UK] maillot m de bain.

bath mat n tapis m de bain.

bath oil n huile f de bain.

bathrobe ['bɑːθrəʊb] n **1.** [for bathroom, swimming pool] peignoir m de bain **2.** [US] [dressing gown] robe f de chambre.

bathroom ['bɑːθrʊm] n salle f de bains.

bath salts pl n sels mpl de bain.

bathtime ['bɑːθtaɪm] n l'heure f du bain.

bath towel n serviette f de bain.

bathtub ['bɑːθtʌb] n baignoire f.

batik [bə'tiːk] n [cloth, technique] batik m.

baton ['bætən] n **1.** [conductor's] baguette f / *under the baton of* sous la baguette de **2.** [policeman's - in traffic] bâton m ; [- in riots] matraque f **3.** SPORT témoin m **▸ to pass the baton to sb** fig passer le relais à qqn.

baton charge n charge f à la matraque.

batsman ['bætsmən] (pl **batsmen** [-mən]) n SPORT batteur m.

battalion [bə'tæljən] n bataillon m.

batten ['bætn] ◆ n [board] latte f, lambourde f ; [in roof] volige f ; [in floor] latte f, lame f de parquet ; NAUT latte f de voile ; THEAT herse f. ◆ vt CONSTR latter ; [floor] planchéier ; [roof] voliger. ◆ **batten down** vt sep **▸ to batten down the hatches a)** lit fermer les écoutilles, condamner les panneaux **b)** fig dresser ses batteries.

batter ['bætər] ◆ vt **1.** [beat - person] battre, maltraiter **2.** [hammer - door, wall] frapper sur **3.** [buffet] : *the ship was battered by the waves* le vaisseau était battu par les vagues. ◆ vi [hammer] : *to batter at* or *on the door* frapper à la porte à coups redoublés. ◆ n **1.** CULIN pâte f *(pour crêpes, beignets, gaufres, clafoutis, etc.)* **2.** [in baseball] batteur m.

battered ['bætəd] adj [damaged -building] délabré ; [-car, hat] cabossé, bosselé ; [-briefcase, suitcase] cabossé ; [face-beaten] meurtri ; [-ravaged] buriné.

battering ['bætərɪŋ] n **1.** [beating] : *he got a bad battering* on l'a rossé sévèrement **2.** [hammering] : *the building took a battering in the war* le bâtiment a été durement éprouvé.

battering ram n bélier m.

battery ['bætərɪ] (pl **batteries**) n **1.** ELEC [in clock, radio] pile f ; [in car] batterie f, accumulateurs mpl **2.** [barrage] tir m de barrage / *a battery of insults* une pluie d'insultes **3.** AGR batterie f.

battery charger n chargeur m.

battery farming n élevage m intensif or en batterie.

battery hen n poule f de batterie.

battery-reared ['rɪəd] adj de batterie.

battle ['bætl] ◆ n **1.** [fight] bataille f / *he was killed in battle* il a été tué au combat ; fig lutte f **2.** [struggle] lutte f / *the battle for freedom* la lutte pour la liberté / *we're fighting the same battle* nous nous battons pour la même cause ▶ **it's half the battle** la partie est presque gagnée. ◆ vi se battre, lutter. ◆ vt US combattre.

battleaxe UK, **battleax** US ['bætəlæks] n **1.** [weapon] hache f d'armes **2.** pej & hum [woman] virago f.

battledress ['bætldres] n tenue f de combat.

battlefield ['bætlfiːld], **battleground** ['bætlgraʊnd] n lit & fig champ m de bataille.

battlement ['bætlmənt] n [crenellation] créneau m. ❖ **battlements** pl n [wall] remparts mpl.

battle-scarred adj [army, landscape] marqué par les combats ; [person] marqué par la vie ; hum [car, table] abîmé.

battleship ['bætlʃɪp] n cuirassé m.

batty ['bætɪ] (compar **battier**, superl **battiest**) adj inf [crazy] cinglé, dingue ; [eccentric] bizarre.

bauble ['bɔːbl] n [trinket] babiole f, colifichet m ; [jester's] marotte f.

baud [bɔːd] n COMPUT & ELEC baud m ▶ **baud rate** vitesse f de transmission (en bauds).

baulk [bɔːk] vi & vt = **balk**.

Bavaria [bə'veərɪə] pr n Bavière f.

Bavarian [bə'veərɪən] ◆ n Bavarois m, -e f. ◆ adj bavarois.

bawdy ['bɔːdɪ] adj paillard.

bawl [bɔːl] ◆ vi **1.** [yell] brailler **2.** [cry] brailler. ◆ vt [slogan, word] brailler, hurler.

bay [beɪ] ◆ n **1.** [on shoreline] baie f ; [smaller] anse f **2.** ARCHIT [recess] travée f ; [window] baie f ; RAIL voie f d'arrêt **3.** BOT & CULIN laurier m **4.** HUNT & fig ▶ **to keep** or **to hold sb at bay** tenir qqn à distance. ◆ vi [bark] aboyer, donner de la voix.

bay leaf n feuille f de laurier.

bayonet ['beɪənɪt] (pt & pp **bayoneted** or **bayonetted**, cont **bayoneting** or **bayonetting**) n baïonnette f.

bay tree n laurier m.

bay window n fenêtre f en saillie.

bazaar [bə'zɑːr] n [in East] bazar m ; [sale for charity] vente f de charité ; [shop] bazar m.

bazooka [bə'zuːkə] n bazooka m.

B2B [ˌbiːtə'biː] (abbr of **business to business**) n B to B.

BB n (abbr of **double black**) sur un crayon à papier, indique une mine grasse.

BBB (abbr of **Better Business Bureau**) pr n organisme dont la vocation est de faire respecter la déontologie professionnelle dans le secteur tertiaire.

BBC (abbr of **British Broadcasting Corporation**) pr n office national britannique de radiodiffusion ▶ **the BBC** la BBC ▶ **BBC English** l'anglais tel qu'il était parlé sur la BBC et qui servait de référence pour la «bonne» prononciation.

BBFN MESSAGING written abbr of **bye bye for now**.

BBL MESSAGING written abbr of **be back later**.

BBQ n written abbr of **barbecue**.

BBS[1] n abbr of **bulletin board system**.

BBS[2] MESSAGING written abbr of **be back soon**.

BC adv (abbr of **before Christ**) av. J.-C.

bcc (written abbr of **blind carbon copy**) CCI.

BCE (abbr of **before the Common Era**) adv av. J.-C.

B cell n MED lymphocyte m B.

BCG (abbr of **bacille Calmette-Guérin**) n BCG m.

BCNU (written abbr of **be seeing you**) MESSAGING @+.

BD (abbr of **Bachelor of Divinity**) n UK (titulaire d'une) licence de théologie.

BDS (abbr of **Bachelor of Dental Surgery**) n UK (titulaire d'une) licence de chirurgie dentaire.

be [biː] (pp **been** [biːn], cont **being** ['biːɪŋ]) (pres; 1st sg **am**, weak form [əm], strong form [æm], pres 2nd sg **are**, weak form [ə], strong form [ɑː], pres 3rd sg **is**, pres pl **are**, weak form [ə], strong form [ɑː], pt 1st sg **was**, weak form [wəz], strong form [wɒz], pt 2nd sg **were**, weak form [wə], strong form [wɜː], pt 3rd sg **was**, weak form [wəz], strong form [wɒz], pt pl **were**, weak form [wə], strong form [wɜː]) ◆ vi **1.** [exist, live] être, exister / *to be or not to be* être ou ne pas être / *God is* Dieu existe / *the greatest scientist that ever was* le plus grand savant qui ait jamais existé or de tous les temps / *that may be, but...* cela se peut, mais..., peut-être, mais... **2.** [used to identify, describe] être / *I'm Bill* je suis or je m'appelle Bill / *she's a doctor / engineer* elle est médecin / ingénieur / *the glasses were crystal* les verres étaient en cristal / *he is American* il est américain, c'est un Américain **3.** [indicating temporary state or condition] : *he was angry / tired* il était fâché / fatigué / *I am hungry / thirsty / afraid* j'ai faim / soif / peur **4.** [indicating health] aller, se porter / *how are you?* comment allez-vous ?, comment ça va ? / *I am fine* ça va **5.** [indicating age] avoir / *how old are you?* quel âge avez-vous ? **6.** [indicating location] être / *the hotel is next to the river* l'hôtel se trouve or est près de la rivière **7.** [indicating measurement] : *the school is two kilometres from here* l'école est à deux kilomètres d'ici **8.** [indicating time, date] être / *it's 5 o'clock* il est 5 h / *yesterday was Monday* hier on était or c'était lundi **9.** [happen, occur] être, avoir lieu / *the concert is on Saturday night* le concert est or a lieu samedi soir **10.** [indicating cost] coûter / *it is expensive* ça coûte or c'est cher **11.** [with 'there'] ▶ **there is, there are** il y a, il est liter / *there is* or *has been no snow* il n'y a pas de neige / *there are six of them* ils sont or il y en a six / *there will be swimming* on nagera **12.** [calling attention to] : *this is my friend John* voici mon ami John / *there are the others* voilà les autres **13.** [with 'it'] : *it was your mother who decided* c'est ta mère qui a décidé **14.** [indicating weather] faire / *it is cold / hot / grey* il fait froid / chaud / gris / *it is windy* il y a du vent **15.** [go] aller, être / *she's been to visit her mother* elle a été or est allée rendre visite à sa mère / *has the plumber been?* le plombier est-il (déjà) passé ? ; [come] être, venir / *she is from Egypt* elle vient d'Égypte **16.** MATH faire / *1 and 1 are 2* 1 et 1 font 2.

◆ aux vb **1.** [forming continuous tenses] : *he is having breakfast* il prend or il est en train de prendre son petit déjeuner / *a problem which is getting worse and worse* un problème qui s'aggrave / *what are you going to do about it?* qu'est-ce que vous allez or comptez faire ? **2.** [forming passive voice] : *she is known as a good negotiator* elle est connue pour ses talents de négociatrice / *what is left to do?* qu'est-ce qui reste à faire ? / *socks are sold by the pair* les chaussettes se vendent par deux / *it is said / thought / assumed that...* on dit / pense / suppose que... / *not to be confused with* à ne pas confondre avec **3.** (with infinitive) [indicating future event] : *the next meeting is to take place on Wednesday* la prochaine réunion aura lieu mercredi ; [indicating expected event] : *they were to have been married in June* ils devaient se marier en juin **4.** (with infinitive) [indicating obligation] : *I'm to be home by 10 o'clock* il faut que je rentre avant 10 h ; [expressing opinion] : *they are to be pitied* ils sont à plaindre ; [requesting information] : *what am I to say to them?* qu'est-ce que je vais leur dire ? **5.** (with passive infinitive) [indicating possibility] : *bargains are to be found even in the West End* on peut faire de bonnes affaires même dans le West End **6.** (with infinitive) [indicating hypothesis] : *if he were* or *were he to die* fml s'il venait à mourir, à supposer qu'il meure **7.** [in tag questions] : *he's always causing trouble, isn't he? — yes, he is* il est toujours en train de créer des problèmes, n'est-ce pas ? — oui, toujours / *you're back, are you?* vous êtes revenu alors ? **8.** [forming perfect tenses] : *we're finished* nous avons terminé / *when I looked again, they were gone* quand j'ai regardé de nouveau, ils étaient partis.

B/E written abbr of **bill of exchange**.

beach [biːtʃ] ◆ n [seaside] plage f ; [shore - sand, shingle] grève f ; [at lake] rivage m. ◆ comp [ball, towel, hut] de plage ▸ **beach umbrella** parasol m.

beach buggy n buggy m.

beach bunny n US inf petite pépée f *(qui passe son temps à la plage).*

beachcomber ['biːtʃ,kəʊməʳ] n [collector] personne qui ramasse des objets sur les plages ; [wave] vague f déferlante.

beachhead ['biːtʃhed] n tête f de pont.

beachwear ['biːtʃweəʳ] n (U) [one outfit] tenue f de plage ; [several outfits] articles mpl de plage.

beacon ['biːkən] n [warning signal] phare m, signal m lumineux ; [lantern] fanal m ; AERON & NAUT balise f.

beacon school n école f pilote.

bead [biːd] n **1.** [of glass, wood] perle f ; [for rosary] grain m / *bead necklace* collier m de perles (artificielles) **2.** [drop - of sweat] goutte f ; [- of water, dew] perle f ; [bubble] bulle f.

beaded ['biːdɪd] adj **1.** [decorated] couvert or orné de perles **2.** [with moisture] couvert de gouttelettes d'eau.

beading ['biːdɪŋ] n SEW [trim] garniture f de perles ; [over cloth] broderie f perlée.

beady ['biːdɪ] (compar **beadier**, superl **beadiest**) adj [eyes, gaze] perçant / *I had to keep a beady eye on the sweets* il fallait que je surveille les bonbons de près.

beady-eyed adj aux yeux perçants.

beagle ['biːgl] n beagle m.

beak [biːk] n [of bird] bec m.

beaker ['biːkəʳ] n gobelet m ; CHEM vase m à bec.

be-all n ▸ **the be-all and end-all** la raison d'être.

beam [biːm] ◆ n **1.** [bar of wood - in house] poutre f ; [- big] madrier m ; [- small] poutrelle f ; [- in gymnastics] poutre f **2.** [ray - of sunlight] rayon m ; [- of searchlight, head-lamp] faisceau m lumineux ; PHYS faisceau m ; AERON & NAUT chenal m de radioguidage **3.** [smile] sourire m radieux. ◆ vi **1.** [smile] : *faces beaming with pleasure* des visages

rayonnants de plaisir / *he beamed when he saw us* il eut un sourire radieux en nous apercevant **2.** [shine - sun] briller, darder ses rayons. ◆ vt RADIO & TV [message] transmettre par émission dirigée / *the pictures were beamed all over the world* les images ont été diffusées dans le monde entier.

beaming ['biːmɪŋ] adj radieux, resplendissant.

bean [biːn] n **1.** BOT & CULIN haricot m **2.** PHR ▸ **to be full of beans** inf péter le feu / *I haven't got a bean* inf je n'ai pas un rond.

beanbag ['biːnbæg] n [in game] balle f lestée ; [seat] sacco m.

bean-counter n inf gratte-papier m.

beanshoot ['biːnʃuːt], **beansprout** ['biːnspraʊt] n germe m de soja.

bear [beəʳ] (pt **bore** [bɔːʳ], pp **borne** [bɔːn]) ◆ vt **1.** [carry - goods, burden] porter ; [- gift, message] apporter ; [- sound] porter, transporter / *they bore him aloft on their shoulders* ils le portèrent en triomphe / *they arrived bearing fruit* ils sont arrivés, chargés de fruits **2.** [sustain - weight] supporter / *the system can only bear a certain amount of pressure* fig le système ne peut supporter qu'une certaine pression **3.** [endure] tolérer, supporter / *the news was more than she could bear* elle n'a pas pu supporter la nouvelle / *I can't bear to see you go* je ne supporte pas que tu t'en ailles / *I can't bear the suspense* ce suspense est insupportable **4.** [accept - responsibility, blame] assumer ; [- costs] supporter **5.** [allow - examination] soutenir, supporter / *it doesn't bear thinking about* je n'ose pas or je préfère ne pas y penser **6.** [show - mark, name, sign, etc.] porter / *I still bear the scars* j'en porte encore les cicatrices **7.** [give birth to] donner naissance à / *she bore him two sons* elle lui donna deux fils **8.** [produce] porter, produire / *the cherry tree bears beautiful blossom in spring* le cerisier donne de belles fleurs au printemps / *his investment bore 8% interest* FIN ses investissements lui ont rapporté 8 % d'intérêt **9.** [feel] porter, avoir en soi ▸ **to bear love / hatred for sb** éprouver de l'amour / de la haine pour qqn. ◆ vi **1.** [move] diriger / *bear (to your) left* prenez sur la gauche or à gauche / **'bear left ahead'** US 'tournez à gauche', 'filez à gauche' **2.** PHR ▸ **to bring pressure to bear on sb** faire pression sur qqn ▸ **to bring one's mind to bear on sthg** s'appliquer à qqch. ◆ n **1.** [animal] ours m, -e f ▸ **he's like a bear with a sore head** UK inf il est d'une humeur de dogue **2.** pej [person] ours m **3.** ST. EX [person] baissier m, -ère f ▸ **bear market** marché m en baisse. ◆◆ **bear down** vi [approach] ▸ **to bear down on** or **upon a)** [ship] venir sur **b)** [person] foncer sur. ◆◆ **bear out** vt sep UK confirmer, corroborer ▸ **to bear sb out** or **bear out what sb says** corroborer ce que qqn dit. ◆◆ **bear up** vi UK tenir le coup, garder le moral / *she's bearing up under the pressure* elle ne se laisse pas décourager par le stress. ◆◆ **bear with** vt insep [be patient with] supporter patiemment / *if you'll just bear with me a minute* je vous demande un peu de patience.

bearable ['beərəbl] adj supportable, tolérable.

bearbaiting ['beə,beɪtɪŋ] n combat m d'ours et de chiens.

beard [bɪəd] n [on person] barbe f ; [goatee] barbiche f / *to have a beard* avoir la barbe / *a man with a beard* un (homme) barbu.

bearded ['bɪədɪd] adj barbu.

beard trimmer n tondeuse f à barbe.

bearer ['beərəʳ] n **1.** [of news, letter] porteur m, -euse f ; [of load, coffin] porteur m ; [servant] serviteur m **2.** [of cheque, title] porteur m, -euse f ; [of passport] titulaire mf.

bear hug n ▸ **to give sb a bear hug** serrer qqn très fort dans ses bras.

bearing ['beərɪŋ] n **1.** [relevance] rapport *m*, relation *f* / *his comments have some* or *a bearing on the present situation* ses remarques ont un certain rapport avec la situation actuelle **2.** [deportment] maintien *m*, port *m* **3.** [direction] position *f* / *to get* or *to find one's bearings* fig se repérer, s'orienter / *to lose one's bearings* fig perdre le nord.

-bearing in comp ▶ **fruit-bearing trees** des arbres fructifères ▶ **rain-bearing clouds** des nuages chargés de pluie.

bearskin ['beəskɪn] n **1.** [piece of fur] peau *f* d'ours **2.** MIL [hat] bonnet *m* à poils.

beast [biːst] n **1.** [animal] bête *f*, animal *m* ▶ **beast of burden** bête de somme **2.** [person - unpleasant] cochon *m* ; [- cruel] brute *f* **3.** [difficult task] : *a beast of a job* un sale boulot.

beastly ['biːstlɪ] **UK** inf adj [person, behaviour] mauvais / *he was beastly to her* il a été infect avec elle.

beat [biːt] (pt **beat**, pp **beaten** ['biːtn]) ◆ vt **1.** [hit - dog, person] frapper, battre ; [- carpet, metal] battre ; CULIN [eggs] battre, fouetter **2.** MUS ▶ **to beat time** battre la mesure / *to beat a drum* battre du tambour **3.** [move - wing] battre / *the bird was beating its wings* l'oiseau battait des ailes **4.** [defeat - at game, sport] battre, vaincre / *she beat him at poker* elle l'a battu au poker / *Liverpool were beaten* Liverpool a perdu / *to beat the world record* battre le record mondial ; fig : *to beat the system* trouver le joint fig / *the problem has me beat* inf or *beaten* le problème me dépasse complètement / *she just beat me to it* elle m'a devancé de peu ; [outdo] : *nothing beats a cup of tea* rien ne vaut une tasse de thé ▶ **that beats the lot!** inf, **that takes some beating!** inf ça, c'est le bouquet ! / *his answer takes some beating!* **a)** inf [critically] c'est le comble ! **b)** [admiringly] on n'aurait pas pu mieux dire ! ▶ **if you can't beat them, join them** si on ne peut pas les battre, alors il faut faire comme eux or entrer dans leur jeu ▶ **to beat sb hollow** or **hands down UK** inf, **to beat the pants off sb** inf battre qqn à plate couture ▶ **(it) beats me** inf cela me dépasse / *it beats me or what beats me is how he gets away with it* inf je ne comprends pas or ça me dépasse qu'il s'en tire à chaque fois ▶ **can you beat it!** inf tu as déjà vu ça, toi ! **5.** [retreat] ▶ **to beat the retreat** MIL battre la retraite / *they beat a hasty retreat when they saw the police arrive* ils ont décampé en vitesse quand ils ont vu arriver la police **6.** **PHR** **beat it!** inf dégage ! ◆ vi **1.** [rain] battre ; [sun] taper ; [wind] souffler en rafales / *to beat on* or *at the door* cogner à la porte / *he doesn't beat about* **UK** or *around* **US** *the bush* il n'y va pas par quatre chemins **2.** [heart, pulse, wing] battre / *with beating heart* le cœur battant / *his heart was beating with terror* son cœur palpitait de terreur. ◆ n **1.** [of heart, pulse, wing] battement *m*, pulsation *f* ; [of drums] battement *m* ; ACOUST battement *m* / *to march to the beat of the drum* marcher au son du tambour **2.** MUS [time] temps *m* ; [in jazz and pop] rythme *m* **3.** [of policeman] ronde *f*, secteur *m* ; [of sentry] ronde *f* / *we need more policemen on the beat* il faudrait qu'il y ait plus de policiers à faire des rondes. ◆ adj inf [exhausted] crevé, vidé. ❖ **beat back** vt sep [enemy, flames] repousser. ❖ **beat down** ◆ vt sep **UK** [seller] faire baisser / *I beat him down to £20* je lui ai fait baisser son prix à 20 livres. ◆ vi [sun] taper ; [rain] tomber à verse or à torrents. ❖ **beat off** vt sep [enemy, attack] repousser. ❖ **beat out** vt sep **1.** [flames] étouffer **2.** [rhythm] marquer **3.** **US** [opponent] battre. ❖ **beat up** vt sep inf [person] tabasser, passer à tabac. ❖ **beat up on** vt insep **US** inf tabasser, passer à tabac.

beatbox ['biːtbɒks] n boîte *f* à rythme(s).

beat-em-up ['biːtəmʌp] n inf [video game] jeu *m* vidéo violent.

beaten ['biːtn] ◆ pp ⟶ **beat**. ◆ adj **1.** [gold] battu, martelé ; [earth, path] battu ; CULIN [eggs, cream, etc.] battu, fouetté ▶ **off the beaten track** fig hors des sentiers battus **2.** [defeated] vaincu, battu **3.** [exhausted] éreinté, épuisé.

beaten-up adj cabossé.

beater ['biːtər] n **1.** CULIN [manual] fouet *m* ; [electric] batteur *m* **2.** HUNT rabatteur *m*.

beating ['biːtɪŋ] n **1.** [thrashing] correction *f* **2.** [defeat] défaite *f* ▶ **to take a beating** [gen & SPORT] se faire battre à plate couture **3.** [of wings, heart] battement *m* **4.** (U) [of metal] batte *f* ; [of drums] battement *m*, roulement *m* ; [of carpet] battage *m*.

beating-up n inf passage *m* à tabac, raclée *f*.

beatnik ['biːtnɪk] ◆ n beatnik *mf*. ◆ adj beatnik.

beat-up adj inf [car] bousillé, déglingué ; **US** [person] amoché.

beautician [bjuː'tɪʃn] n esthéticien *m*, -enne *f*.

beautiful ['bjuːtɪfʊl] adj **1.** [attractive - person, dress] beau *(before vowel or silent 'h'* **bel**, *f* **belle)** **2.** [splendid - weather, meal] magnifique, superbe.

beautifully ['bjuːtəflɪ] adv **1.** [sing, dress] admirablement, à la perfection **2.** [splendidly] : *it was a beautifully played shot* c'était bien joué, c'était une belle balle **3.** [as intensifier - peaceful, warm] merveilleusement.

beautify ['bjuːtɪfaɪ] (pt & pp **beautified**) vt embellir, orner.

beauty ['bjuːtɪ] (pl **beauties**) ◆ n **1.** [loveliness] beauté *f* / *a thing of beauty* un objet d'une rare beauté **2.** [beautiful person] beauté *f* **3.** inf [excellent thing] merveille *f* **4.** [attraction] : *that's the beauty of it* c'est ça qui est formidable. ◆ comp [cream, product, treatment] de beauté.

beauty competition, beauty contest n concours *m* de beauté.

beauty mask n masque *m* de beauté.

beauty parade n défilé *m* d'un concours de beauté.

beauty parlour n institut *m* de beauté.

beauty queen n reine *f* de beauté.

beauty salon n = **beauty parlour**.

beauty sleep n : *I need my beauty sleep* hum j'ai besoin de mon compte de sommeil pour être frais le matin.

beauty spot n **1.** [on skin] grain *m* de beauté ; [artificial] mouche *f* **2.** [scenic place] site *m* touristique.

beaver ['biːvər] n [animal] castor *m* ; [coat] fourrure *f* de castor, castor *m* ; [hat] chapeau *m* de castor, castor *m*. ❖ **beaver away** vi **UK** inf ▶ **to beaver away at sthg** travailler d'arrache-pied à qqch.

bebop ['biːbɒp] n [music, dance] be-bop *m*.

becalm [bɪ'kɑːm] vt (usu passive) ▶ **to be becalmed** être encalminé.

became [bɪ'keɪm] pt ⟶ **become**.

because [bɪ'kɒz] conj parce que / *if she won it was because she deserved to* si elle a gagné, c'est qu'elle le méritait / *it was all the more difficult because he was sick* c'était d'autant plus difficile qu'il était malade. ❖ **because of** prep phr à cause de / *it was all because of a silly misunderstanding* tout ça c'est à cause d'un or tout provenait d'un petit malentendu.

béchamel sauce [,beʃə'mel-] n (sauce *f*) béchamel *f*.

beck [bek] n **PHR** **to be at sb's beck and call** être constamment à la disposition de qqn.

beckon ['bekən] ◆ vi faire signe ▶ **to beckon to sb** faire signe à qqn / *a glittering career beckoned for the young* *singer* la jeune chanteuse avait devant elle une brillante carrière. ◆ vt **1.** [motion] faire signe à / *I beckoned them over to me* je leur ai fait signe d'approcher **2.** [attract, call] attirer.

become [bɪ'kʌm] (*pt* **became** [bɪ'keɪm], *pp* **become**) ◆ vi **1.** [grow] devenir, se faire / *to become weak* s'affaiblir / *we became friends* nous sommes devenus amis **2.** [acquire post of] devenir / *she's become an accountant* elle est devenue comptable. ◆ vt *fml* **1.** [suit - subj: hat, dress] aller à **2.** [befit] convenir à, être digne de / *such behaviour doesn't become him* une telle conduite n'est pas digne de lui. ❖ **become of** vt insep (*only following 'what', 'whatever'*) : *whatever will become of us?* qu'allons-nous devenir ? / *what became of your hat?* où est passé ton chapeau ?

becoming [bɪ'kʌmɪŋ] adj *fml* **1.** [fetching] qui va bien, seyant **2.** [suitable] convenable, bienséant.

BECTU ['bektuː] (*abbr of* **Broadcasting, Entertainment, Cinematograph and Theatre Union**) pr n *syndicat britannique des techniciens du cinéma, du théâtre et de l'audiovisuel.*

bed [bed] (*pt & pp* **bedded**, *cont* **bedding**) ◆ n **1.** [furniture] lit *m* / *they sleep in separate beds* ils font lit à part ▶ **to get out of bed** se lever / *she got* or *put the children to bed* elle a couché les enfants or mis les enfants au lit ▶ **to make the bed** faire le lit / *he's in bed with the flu* il est au lit avec la grippe ▶ **to go to bed with sb** coucher avec qqn ▶ **bed and board** pension *f* complète / **'bed and breakfast'** 'chambres avec petit déjeuner' ▶ **to get out on the wrong side of (the) bed** se lever du pied gauche or du mauvais pied **2.** [plot - of flowers] parterre *m*, platebande *f* ; [- of vegetables] planche *f* ; [- of coral, oysters] banc *m* **3.** [bottom - of river] lit *m* ; [- of lake, sea] fond *m*. ◆ comp ▶ **bed linen** draps *mpl* de lit (et taies *fpl* d'oreiller). ❖ **bed down** vi [go to bed] se coucher ; [spend the night] coucher.

BEd [,biː'ed] (*abbr of* **Bachelor of Education**) n 🇬🇧 (*titulaire d'une*) *licence de sciences de l'éducation.*

bedazzle [bɪ'dæzl] vt [dazzle] éblouir, aveugler ; [fascinate] éblouir.

bed bath n toilette *f* (*d'un malade*).

bedbug ['bedbʌg] n punaise *f* des lits.

bedclothes ['bedkləʊðz] pl n draps *mpl* et couvertures *fpl*.

bedcover ['bed,kʌvər] n dessus-de-lit *m*, couvre-lit *m*.

bedding ['bedɪŋ] ◆ n **1.** [bedclothes] draps *mpl* et couvertures *fpl* ; [including mattress] literie *f* ; MIL matériel *m* de couchage **2.** [for animals] litière *f*. ◆ adj ▶ **bedding plant** plante à repiquer.

bedeck [bɪ'dek] vt *liter* orner, parer.

bedevil [bɪ'devl] (🇬🇧 *pt & pp* **bedevilled**, *cont* **bedevilling** ; 🇺🇸 *pt & pp* **bedeviled**, *cont* **bedeviling**) vt **1.** [plague - plans, project] déranger, gêner ; [- person] harceler, tourmenter / *bedevilled by* or *with problems* assailli par les problèmes **2.** [confuse] embrouiller **3.** [bewitch] ensorceler.

bedfellow ['bed,feləʊ] n [associate] associé *m*, -e *f*, collègue *mf* / *they make strange bedfellows* ils forment une drôle d'association or de paire.

bedlam ['bedləm] n tohu-bohu *m* / *utter bedlam broke out after her speech* un véritable tumulte éclata après son discours.

bedmate ['bedmeɪt] n : *my bedmate* la personne avec qui je dors, mon partenaire / *old computers and new software make terrible bedmates* les vieux ordinateurs et les nouveaux logiciels ne font pas bon ménage.

Bedouin ['beduɪn] (*pl* **Bedouin** *or* **Bedouins**), **Beduin** ['beduɪn] (*pl* **Beduin** *or* **Beduins**) ◆ n Bédouin *m*, -e *f*. ◆ adj bédouin.

bedpan ['bedpæn] n bassin *m* (hygiénique).

bedplate ['bedpleɪt] n TECH semelle *f*.

bedraggled [bɪ'drægld] adj [clothing, person] débraillé ; [hair] ébouriffé, échevelé.

bedridden ['bed,rɪdn] adj alité, cloué au lit.

bedrock ['bedrɒk] n GEOL soubassement *m*, substratum *m* ; *fig* base *f*, fondation *f*.

bedroom ['bedrʊm] ◆ n chambre *f* (à coucher). ◆ comp [scene] d'amour ▶ **bedroom community** 🇺🇸 cité-dortoir *f*.

-bedroomed [,bedrʊmd] in comp ▶ **two-bedroomed flat** trois-pièces *m*.

Beds written abbr of **Bedfordshire**.

bedsettee [,bedse'tiː] n 🇬🇧 canapé-lit *m*.

bedside ['bedsaɪd] ◆ adj [lamp, table] de chevet. ◆ n chevet *m*.

bedsit ['bed,sɪt], **bedsitter** ['bed,sɪtər], **bedsitting room** ['bed'sɪtɪŋ-] n 🇬🇧 chambre *f* meublée, studette *f*.

bedsore ['bedsɔːr] n escarre *f*.

bedspread ['bedspred] n dessus-de-lit *m* inv, couvre-lit *m*.

bedtime ['bedtaɪm] ◆ n heure *f* du coucher / *it's your bedtime* il est l'heure d'aller te coucher. ◆ comp ▶ **bedtime story** histoire *f* (*qu'on lit à l'heure du coucher*) / *I'll read you a bedtime story* je vais te lire une histoire avant que tu t'endormes.

Beduin ['beduɪn] (*pl* **Beduin** *or* **Beduins**) n = **Bedouin**.

bed-wetting [-,wetɪŋ] n incontinence *f* nocturne.

bee [biː] n [insect] abeille *f* ▶ **bee sting** piqûre *f* d'abeille ▶ **to have a bee in one's bonnet (about sthg)** être obsédé (par qqch) ▶ **it's the bee's knees!** *inf* c'est formidable or super !

bee-ach, bee-atch ['biːætʃ] n 🇺🇸 *v inf* = **bitch**.

Beeb [biːb] pr n 🇬🇧 *inf & hum* ▶ **the Beeb** surnom courant de la BBC.

beech [biːtʃ] (*pl* **beech** *or* **beeches**) n [tree] hêtre *m* ; [wood] (bois *m* de) hêtre *m*.

bee-eater n ORNITH guêpier *m*.

beef [biːf] ◆ n **1.** [meat] bœuf *m* ▶ **joint of beef** rôti *m* (de bœuf), rosbif *m* **2.** *inf* [complaint] grief *m* / *what's your beef?* tu as un problème ? ◆ comp [sausage, stew] de bœuf ▶ **beef cattle** bœufs *mpl* de boucherie. ◆ vi *inf* râler. ❖ **beef up** vt sep *inf* [army, campaign] renforcer ; [report, story] étoffer.

beefburger ['biːf,bɜːgər] n hamburger *m*.

beefy ['biːfɪ] (*compar* **beefier**, *superl* **beefiest**) adj **1.** [consistency, taste] de viande, de bœuf **2.** *inf* [brawny] costaud ; [fat] grassouillet.

beehive ['biːhaɪv] n [for bees] ruche *f*.

beekeeper ['biː,kiːpər] n apiculteur *m*, -trice *f*.

beeline ['biːlaɪn] n ligne *f* droite / *he made a beeline for the kitchen* **a)** [headed straight to] il s'est dirigé tout droit vers la cuisine **b)** [rushed to] il s'est précipité or a filé tout droit à la cuisine.

been [biːn] pp ⟶ **be**.

beep [biːp] ◆ n [of car horn] coup *m* de Klaxon® ; [of alarm, timer] signal *m* sonore, bip *m*. ◆ vi [car horn] klaxonner ; [alarm, timer] sonner, faire bip. ◆ vt ▶ **to beep one's horn** klaxonner.

beeper n = **bleeper**.

beer [bɪəʳ] ◆ n bière f. ◆ comp ▶ **beer belly** inf brioche f, bide m ▶ **beer bottle** canette f ▶ **beer garden** jardin d'un pub, où l'on peut prendre des consommations ▶ **beer gut** inf brioche f, bide m.

Beer

Le Royaume-Uni est l'un des pays du monde où l'on consomme le plus de bière, et celle-ci continue de jouer un rôle culturel et social assez important malgré une forte baisse de consommation au profit du vin depuis les années 1970.

La bière traditionnelle, ou **ale**, de fermentation haute, peu gazéifiée et de couleur brune ou ambrée, se décline en plusieurs catégories : la **bitter**, comme son nom l'indique, est plus amère que la **pale ale** et la **mild**. La **stout** est une bière presque noire à la mousse crémeuse. Les bières blondes (**lagers**), de fermentation basse, sont moins traditionnelles.

Les **pubs** sont les lieux privilégiés pour la consommation de la bière, qui reste, en dépit des évolutions sociales, le symbole d'un univers populaire et masculin. Le nom de la brasserie propriétaire du pub figure sur l'enseigne de celui-ci, à moins qu'il ne s'agisse d'une **free house** (pub indépendant). Aux grandes brasseries industrielles s'ajoutent un grand nombre de petites brasseries locales aux méthodes plus ou moins artisanales, dont la production est parfois qualifiée de **real ale**. Il existe enfin de nombreuses microbrasseries (**microbreweries** ou **brewpubs**) qui proposent des bières brassées sur place.

La bière se boit traditionnellement dans deux types de verre, le **straight glass**, légèrement évasé et aux parois lisses, et le **mug**, chope en verre épais souvent ornée d'un motif en creux très caractéristique. Leur contenance est soit d'une pinte (**pint**: environ 0,6 litre), soit d'une demi-pinte (**half pint**). On demandera donc par exemple **a half of bitter, a pint of lager, a half of Brampton's**, etc.

Enfin, le **yard of ale** est une curiosité que l'on trouve accrochée derrière le bar dans certains pubs. Ce verre évasé d'environ un mètre de long fait l'objet de défis que se lancent certains buveurs de bière : il faut en effet une certaine adresse pour boire le **yard of ale** en gardant ses vêtements secs.

beeswax ['biːzwæks] n cire f d'abeille.

beet [biːt] n betterave f (potagère) ▶ **red beet** US betterave f (rouge).

beetle ['biːtl] n [insect] scarabée m, coléoptère m.

beetroot ['biːtruːt] n UK betterave f (potagère or rouge) ▶ **to go (as red as) a beetroot** devenir rouge comme une tomate.

befall [bɪ'fɔːl] (pt **befell** [-'fel], pp **befallen** [-'fɔːlən]) fml & liter vt arriver à, survenir à.

befit [bɪ'fɪt] (pt & pp **befitted**, cont **befitting**) vt fml convenir à, seoir à fml / as befits a woman of her eminence comme il sied à une femme de son rang.

befitting [bɪ'fɪtɪŋ] adj fml convenable, seyant.

B4 MESSAGING written abbr of **before**.

before [bɪ'fɔːʳ] ◆ adv [at a previous time] avant / haven't we met before? est-ce que nous ne nous sommes pas or ne nous sommes-nous pas déjà rencontrés ? / I have never seen this film before c'est la première fois que je vois ce film. ◆ prep **1.** [in time] avant / the day before the meeting la veille de la réunion / the day before yesterday avant-hier / it should have been done before now ça devrait déjà être fait **2.** [in space] devant / on the table before them fml sur la table devant eux / we have a difficult task before us nous avons une tâche difficile devant nous / before my very eyes sous mes propres yeux **3.** [in the presence of] devant, en présence de / to appear before the court / judge comparaître devant le tribunal / juge. ◆ conj [in time] avant de, avant que / she hesitated before answering elle a hésité avant de répondre / may I see you before you leave? puis-je vous voir avant que vous ne partiez or avant votre départ ? ◆ adj d'avant, précédent / the day before la veille / the night before la veille au soir / the week before la semaine d'avant or précédente.

> Note that **avant que** is followed by a verb in the subjunctive, preceded or not by **ne**: **Let's go, before it gets dark!** Allons-y, avant qu'il (ne) fasse nuit !

beforehand [bɪ'fɔːhænd] adv auparavant, à l'avance.

befriend [bɪ'frend] vt [make friends with] prendre en amitié, se prendre d'amitié pour ; [assist] venir en aide à, aider.

befuddle [bɪ'fʌdl] vt [confuse - person] brouiller l'esprit or les idées de, embrouiller ; [- mind] embrouiller.

beg [beg] (pt & pp **begged**, cont **begging**) ◆ vi **1.** [solicit charity] mendier / to beg for food mendier de la nourriture **2.** [ask, plead] supplier / to beg for forgiveness / mercy demander pardon / grâce. ◆ vt **1.** [solicit as charity] mendier ▶ **to beg, borrow or steal** se procurer par tous les moyens **2.** [ask for] demander, solliciter ; [plead with] supplier ▶ **I beg your pardon a)** [excuse me] je vous demande pardon **b)** [I didn't hear you] pardon ? **c)** [indignantly] pardon ! **3.** PHR **to beg the question a)** [evade the issue] éluder la question **b)** [assume something proved] considérer que la question est résolue / that begs the question of whether... cela pose la question de savoir si..., c'est toute la question de savoir si...

began [bɪ'gæn] pt → **begin**.

beggar ['begəʳ] ◆ n **1.** [mendicant] mendiant m, -e f ; [pauper] indigent m, -e f ▶ **beggars can't be choosers** prov faute de merles, mangeons des grives prov, nécessité fait loi prov **2.** UK inf [so-and-so] type m / you lucky beggar! sacré veinard ! ◆ vt [defy] : to beggar (all) description défier toute description / it beggars belief c'est invraisemblable, ça dépasse l'entendement.

begging bowl n sébile f (de mendiant).

begin [bɪ'gɪn] (pt **began** [bɪ'gæn], pp **begun** [-'gʌn], cont **beginning**) ◆ vt **1.** [start] commencer ; [career, term] commencer, débuter ; [task] entreprendre, s'attaquer à ; [work] commencer, se mettre à ▶ **to begin to do** or **doing sthg** commencer à faire qqch, se mettre à faire qqch / she began life as a waitress elle a débuté comme serveuse / the film doesn't begin to compare with the book le film est loin de valoir le livre **2.** [found - institution, club] fonder, inaugurer ; [initiate - business, fashion] lancer ; [- argument, fight, war] déclencher, faire naître ; [- conversation] engager, amorcer ; [- discussion, speech] commencer, ouvrir. ◆ vi **1.** [start - subj: person, career, concert, project, speech] commencer / *the day began badly* / *well* la journée s'annonçait mal / bien / *to begin again* or *afresh* recommencer (à zéro) / *after the film begins* après le début du film / *he began in politics* il a commencé par faire de la politique **2.** [originate - club, country, institution] être fondé ; [- fire, epidemic] commencer ; [- war] éclater, commencer ; [- trouble] commencer ; [- river] prendre sa source ; [- road] commencer ; [- fashion] commencer, débuter. ⬥ **to begin with** adv phr [in the first place] d'abord, pour commencer ; [initially] au départ.

beginner [bɪ'gɪnər] n débutant *m*, -e *f* / *it's beginner's luck!* on a toujours de la chance au début !

beginning [bɪ'gɪnɪŋ] n **1.** [start - of book, career, project] commencement *m*, début *m* / in or *at the beginning* au début, au commencement / *let's start again from the beginning* reprenons depuis le début / *from beginning to end* du début à la fin, d'un bout à l'autre / *it's the beginning of the end* c'est le début de la fin **2.** [early part, stage - of book, career, war] commencement *m*, début *m* ; [- of negotiations] début *m*, ouverture *f* / *since the beginning of time* depuis la nuit des temps **3.** [origin - of event] origine *f*, commencement *m* / *Protestantism had its beginnings in Germany* le protestantisme a pris naissance en Allemagne.

begonia [bɪ'gəʊnjə] n bégonia *m*.

begrudge [bɪ'grʌdʒ] vt **1.** [envy] envier / *she begrudges him his success* elle lui en veut de sa réussite **2.** [give grudgingly] donner or accorder à regret / *he begrudges every minute spent away from his family* il rechigne à passer une seule minute loin de sa famille.

beguile [bɪ'gaɪl] vt **1.** [charm] envoûter, séduire **2.** [delude] enjôler, tromper.

beguiling [bɪ'gaɪlɪŋ] adj charmant, séduisant.

begun [-'gʌn] pp ⟶ **begin.**

behalf [bɪ'hɑːf] ⬥ **on behalf of** 🇬🇧, **in behalf of** 🇺🇸 prep phr ▸ **on behalf of sb a)** [as their representative] de la part de or au nom de qqn **b)** [in their interest] dans l'intérêt de or pour qqn / *she acted on his behalf when he was ill* c'est elle qui l'a représenté quand il était malade / *don't worry on my behalf* ne vous inquiétez pas à mon sujet.

behave [bɪ'heɪv] ◆ vi **1.** [act] se comporter, se conduire / *he behaved badly towards her* il s'est mal conduit envers elle / *she was sorry for the way she'd behaved towards him* elle regrettait la façon dont elle l'avait traité **2.** [act properly] se tenir bien, inf bien se conduire / *will you behave!* sois sage !, tiens-toi bien ! **3.** [function] fonctionner, marcher. ◆ vt ▸ **to behave o.s.** se tenir bien.

behaviour 🇬🇧, **behavior** 🇺🇸 [bɪ'heɪvjər] n [of person] comportement *m*, conduite *f* ; [of animal] comportement *m* / *her behaviour towards her mother was unforgivable* la façon dont elle s'est comportée avec sa mère était impardonnable ▸ **to be on one's best behaviour** se tenir or se conduire de son mieux.

behavioural 🇬🇧, **behavioral** 🇺🇸 [bɪ'heɪvjərəl] adj de comportement, comportemental.

behaviourism 🇬🇧, **behaviorism** 🇺🇸 [bɪ'heɪvjə-rɪzm] n behaviorisme *m*.

behead [bɪ'hed] vt décapiter.

beheld [bɪ'held] pt & pp ⟶ **behold.**

behind [bɪ'haɪnd] ◆ prep **1.** [at the back of] derrière / *she came out from behind the bushes* elle est sortie de derrière les buissons / *lock the door behind you* fermez la porte à clé (derrière vous) **2.** [indicating past time] derrière / *you have to put the incident behind you* il faut que tu ou-

blies cet incident **3.** [indicating deficiency, delay] en retard sur, derrière / *she is behind the other pupils* elle est en retard sur les autres élèves **4.** [responsible for] derrière / *who was behind the plot?* qui était derrière le complot or à l'origine du complot ? / *what's behind all this?* qu'est-ce que ça cache ? ◆ adv **1.** [at, in the back] derrière, en arrière / *he attacked them from behind* il les a attaqués par derrière **2.** [late] en retard / *I'm behind in* or *with my rent* je suis en retard sur mon loyer / *she's too far behind to catch up with the others* elle a pris trop de retard pour pouvoir rattraper les autres. ◆ n euph derrière *m*, postérieur *m*.

behind-the-scenes adj secret / *a behind-the-scenes look at politics* un regard en coulisse sur la politique.

behold [bɪ'həʊld] (*pt & pp* **beheld** [bɪ'held]) vt arch & liter [see] regarder, voir ; [notice] apercevoir / *behold your king* voici votre roi.

BHL8 MESSAGING written abbr of (I'll) be home late.

beige [beɪʒ] ◆ adj beige. ◆ n beige *m*.

Beijing [,beɪ'dʒɪŋ] pr n Beijing.

being [ˈbiːɪŋ] ◆ cont ⟶ **be.** ◆ n **1.** [creature] être *m*, créature *f* ▸ **a human being** un être humain **2.** [essential nature] être *m* / *her whole being rebelled* tout son être se révoltait **3.** [existence] existence *f* ▸ **to bring** or **to call sthg into being** faire naître qqch, susciter qqch.

Beirut, Beyrouth [,beɪ'ruːt] pr n Beyrouth.

Belarus [,belə'ruːs] pr n ▸ **the Republic of Belarus** la république de Biélorussie.

belated [bɪ'leɪtɪd] adj tardif.

belatedly [bɪ'leɪtɪdlɪ] adv tardivement.

belch [beltʃ] ◆ n renvoi *m*, rot *m*. ◆ vi roter. ◆ vt [expel] cracher, vomir.

beleaguered [bɪ'liːgəd] adj **1.** lit assiégé **2.** fig en difficulté.

belfry [ˈbelfrɪ] (*pl* **belfries**) n [of church] beffroi *m*, clocher *m* ; [of tower] beffroi *m*.

Belgian [ˈbeldʒən] ◆ n Belge *mf*. ◆ adj belge.

Belgium [ˈbeldʒəm] pr n Belgique *f*.

Belgrade [,bel'greɪd] pr n Belgrade.

belie [bɪ'laɪ] (*pt & pp* **belied**, *cont* **belying**) vt fml [misrepresent] donner une fausse idée or impression de ; [contradict - hope, impression] démentir, tromper ; [- promise] démentir, donner le démenti à.

belief [bɪ'liːf] n **1.** [feeling of certainty] croyance *f* ▸ *contrary to popular belief* contrairement à ce qu'on croit / *it's beyond belief* c'est incroyable **2.** [conviction, opinion] conviction *f*, certitude *f* / *it's my belief he's lying* je suis certain or convaincu qu'il ment / *in the belief that he would help them* certain or persuadé qu'il allait les aider ▸ **to the best of my belief** autant que je sache **3.** [religious faith] foi *f*, croyance *f* ; [political faith] dogme *m*, doctrine *f* **4.** [confidence, trust] confiance *f*, foi *f*.

believable [bɪ'liːvəbl] adj croyable.

believe [bɪ'liːv] ◆ vt **1.** [consider as real or true] croire / *I don't believe a word of it* je n'en crois rien or pas un mot / *he's getting married! — I don't believe it!* il va se marier ! — c'est pas vrai ! / *he couldn't believe his ears* / *his eyes* il n'en croyait pas ses oreilles / ses yeux / *and, believe it or not, she left* et, crois-le si tu veux, elle est partie **2.** [accept statement or opinion of] croire / *if she is to be believed, she was born a duchess* à l'en croire, elle est duchesse **3.** [hold as opinion, suppose] croire / *it is widely believed that the prisoners have been killed* on pense généralement que les prisonniers ont été tués / *I believe not* je crois que non, je ne crois pas / *I believe so* je crois que oui, je crois. ◆ vi [have religious faith] être croyant, avoir la foi. ⬥ **believe in** vt insep **1.** [be convinced of existence or truth of] : *to believe in miracles / in God* croire aux miracles / en Dieu **2.** [be convinced of value of] : *I believe in free enterprise* je crois à la libre entreprise.

> ✎ Note that when used negatively, croire que is followed by a verb in the subjunctive:
> **I believe it's a begonia.** *Je crois qu'il s'agit (indicative) d'un bégonia.*
> But
> **I don't believe this is the work of terrorists.** *Je ne crois pas qu'il s'agisse d'un acte terroriste.*

believer [bɪ'li:vər] n **1.** [supporter] partisan *m*, adepte *mf* / *he's a great believer in taking exercise* il est convaincu qu'il faut faire de l'exercice **2.** RELIG croyant *m*, -e *f*.

Belisha beacon [bə'li:ʃə-] n 🇬🇧 *globe orange clignotant marquant un passage clouté.*

belittle [bɪ'lɪtl] vt rabaisser, dénigrer.

Belize [be'li:z] pr n Belize *m* / *in Belize* au Belize.

bell [bel] n **1.** [in church] cloche *f* ; [handheld] clochette *f* ; [on bicycle] sonnette *f* ; [for cows] cloche *f*, clarine *f* ; [on boots, toys] grelot *m* ; [sound] glas *m* (de cloche) ▶ **saved by the bell!** sauvé par le gong ! **2.** [electrical device - on door] sonnette *f* **3.** 🇬🇧 *inf* [telephone call] : *I'll give you a bell* je te passe un coup de fil.

bell-bottoms pl n pantalon *m* à pattes d'éléphant.

bellboy ['belbɔɪ] n chasseur *m*, porteur *m*.

belle [bel] n belle *f*, beauté *f* / *the belle of the ball* la reine du bal ▶ **Southern belle** *dame de haut rang dans les États du sud des États-Unis.*

bellhop ['belhɒp] n 🇺🇸 = **bellboy.**

belligerence [bɪ'lɪdʒərəns], **belligerency** [bɪ'lɪdʒərənsɪ] n belligérance *f*.

belligerent [bɪ'lɪdʒərənt] adj belligérant.

bellow ['beləʊ] ◆ vi [bull] beugler, meugler ; [elephant] barrir ; [person] brailler. ◆ vt ▶ **to bellow (out) sthg** brailler qqch. ◆ n [of bull] beuglement *m*, meuglement *m* ; [of elephant] barrissement *m* ; [of person] braillement *m*.

bellows ['beləʊz] pl n [for fire] soufflet *m* ▶ **a pair of bellows** un soufflet.

bell push n bouton *m* de sonnette.

bell-ringer n sonneur *m*, carillonneur *m*.

bell work ['bel,wɜ:k] n 🇺🇸 SCH *travail affiché au tableau que les élèves doivent effectuer dès leur entrée en classe.*

belly ['belɪ] (*pl* bellies, *pt & pp* bellied) n **1.** [stomach] ventre *m* **2.** CULIN ▶ **belly of pork** or **pork belly** poitrine *f* de porc. ❖ **belly up** vi *inf* [fail] tomber à plat, foirer.

bellyache ['belɪeɪk] *inf* ◆ n [pain] mal *m* au or de ventre. ◆ vi râler.

bellyaching ['belɪ,eɪkɪŋ] n (*U*) *inf* ronchonnements *mpl*, rouspétances *fpl*.

belly button n *inf* nombril *m*.

belly dancer n danseuse *f* du ventre or orientale.

belly flop n ▶ **to do a belly flop** faire un plat.

bellyful ['belɪfʊl] n *inf* [of food] ventre *m* plein ; *fig* : *I've had a bellyful of your complaints* j'en ai ras le bol de tes rouspétances.

belly laugh n *inf* gros rire *m*.

belly-up adv *inf* ▶ **to go belly-up a)** [project] tomber à l'eau **b)** [company] faire faillite.

belong [bɪ'lɒŋ] vi **1.** [as property] ▶ **to belong to sb** appartenir à or être à qqn **2.** [as member] : *he belongs to a trade union* il fait partie or il est membre d'un syndicat,

il est syndiqué **3.** [as part, component] appartenir **4.** [be in proper place] être à sa place / *the dishes belong in that cupboard* les assiettes vont dans ce placard / *the two of them belong together* ces deux-là sont faits pour être ensemble / *I don't belong here* je ne suis pas à ma place ici / *he belongs in teaching* sa place est dans l'enseignement.

belongings [bɪ'lɒŋɪŋz] pl n affaires *fpl*, possessions *fpl* ▶ **personal belongings** objets *mpl* or effets *mpl* personnels.

Belorussia [,beləʊ'rʌʃə] pr n = Byelorussia.

Belorussian [,beləʊ'rʌʃn] n & adj = Byelorussian.

beloved [bɪ'lʌvd] ◆ adj chéri, bien-aimé. ◆ n bien-aimé *m*, -e *f*, amour *m*.

below [bɪ'ləʊ] ◆ prep **1.** [at, to a lower position than] au-dessous de, en dessous de ; [under] sous / *the flat below ours* l'appartement au-dessous or en dessous du nôtre / *her skirt came to below her knees* sa jupe lui descendait au-dessous du genou **2.** [inferior to] au-dessous de, inférieur à / *children below the age of five* des enfants de moins de cinq ans **3.** [downstream of] en aval de. ◆ adv **1.** [in lower place, on lower level] en dessous, plus bas / *we looked down onto the town below* nous contemplions la ville à nos pieds / *he could hear two men talking below* il entendait deux hommes parler en bas **2.** [with numbers, quantities] moins / *it was twenty below* *inf* il faisait moins vingt **3.** [in text] plus bas, ci-dessous.

below-average adj en dessous de la moyenne.

below-the-line adj FIN [expenses] au-dessous de la ligne.

below-the-line accounts n comptes *mpl* de résultats exceptionnels.

belt [belt] ◆ n **1.** [gen & SPORT] ceinture *f* ; MIL ceinturon *m*, ceinture *f* / *she now has a doctoral degree under her belt* elle a maintenant un doctorat en poche / *that was a bit below the belt* c'était un peu déloyal comme procédé ▶ **to pull in** or **to tighten one's belt** se serrer la ceinture **2.** [of machine] courroie *f* **3.** [area, zone] région *f*. ◆ vt *inf* [hit] donner or flanquer un coup à. ◆ vi 🇬🇧 *inf* filer / *they went belting along* ils fonçaient. ❖ **belt out** vt sep *inf* : *she belted out the last song* elle s'est donnée à fond dans la dernière chanson. ❖ **belt up** vi **1.** [in car, plane] attacher sa ceinture **2.** 🇬🇧 *inf* [be quiet] la fermer, la boucler.

belt buckle n boucle *f* de ceinture.

belt loop n passant *m* (de ceinture).

beltway ['belt,weɪ] n 🇺🇸 (boulevard *m*) périphérique *m*.

bemoan [bɪ'məʊn] vt pleurer, se lamenter sur.

bemused [bɪ'mju:zd] adj déconcerté, dérouté.

bench [bentʃ] n **1.** [seat] banc *m* ; [caned, padded] banquette *f* ; [in auditorium] gradin *m* ▶ **park bench** banc public ▶ **on the bench** SPORT en réserve 🇬🇧 [in Parliament] banc *m* **3.** [work table] établi *m*, plan *m* de travail **4.** LAW [seat] banc *m* ▶ **the bench** [judge] la cour, le juge ; [judges as group] : *he serves* or *sits on the bench* **a)** [permanent office] il est juge **b)** [for particular case] il siège au tribunal.

benchmark ['bentʃ,mɑ:k] ◆ n *lit* repère *m* ; [in surveying] repère m de nivellement ; *fig* repère *m*, point *m* de référence. ◆ comp ▶ **benchmark test** COMPUT test *m* d'évaluation (de programme).

benchmarking ['bentʃmɑ:kɪŋ] n benchmarking *m*, étalonnage *m* concurrentiel.

benchwarmer ['bentʃwɔ:mər] n 🇺🇸 *inf* SPORT *joueur qui se trouve souvent sur le banc des remplaçants.*

bend [bend] (*pt & pp* bent [bent]) ◆ vt **1.** [arm, finger] plier ; [knee, leg] plier, fléchir ; [back, body] courber ; [head] pencher, baisser / *they bent their heads over their books* ils se penchèrent sur leurs livres ▶ **to bend sb to one's will** plier qqn à sa volonté **2.** [pipe, wire] tordre, courber ;

[branch, tree] courber, faire ployer ; [bow] bander, arquer / *to bend sthg at right angles* plier qqch à angle droit ▸ **to bend the rules** faire une entorse au règlement. ◆ vi **1.** [arm, knee, leg] plier ; [person] se courber, se pencher ; [head] se pencher ; [rod, wire] plier, se courber ; [branch, tree] ployer, plier / *he bent backwards / forwards* il s'est penché en arrière / en avant **2.** [river, road] faire un coude, tourner **3.** [submit] céder. ◆ n [in road] coude *m*, virage *m* ; [in river] méandre *m*, coude *m* ; [in pipe, rod] coude *m* / '**bends for 7 miles**' 'virages sur 10 km' ▸ **to drive sb round the bend** *inf* rendre qqn fou. ◆ **bend down** ◆ vi **1.** [person] se courber, se baisser **2.** [branch, tree] plier, ployer. ◆ vt sep [branch, tree] faire ployer ; [blade, tube] replier, recourber. ◆ **bend over** ◆ vi se pencher ▸ **to bend over backwards to please (sb)** se plier en quatre pour faire plaisir (à qqn). ◆ vt sep replier, recourber.

bender ['bendər] n *inf* [drinking binge] beuverie *f* ▸ **to go on a bender** faire la noce.

bendy ['bendɪ] (*compar* **bendier**, *superl* **bendiest**) adj **1.** [road] sinueux **2.** [flexible] souple, flexible.

bendy bus n UK bus *m* à soufflet.

beneath [bɪ'niːθ] ◆ prep **1.** [under] sous / *the ground beneath my feet* le sol sous mes pieds **2.** [below] : *the valley was spread out beneath us* la vallée s'étalait sous nos pieds **3.** [unworthy of] indigne de / *she thinks the work is beneath her* elle estime que le travail est indigne d'elle **4.** [socially inferior to] inférieur (*socialement*) / *he married beneath him* il a fait une mésalliance *fml*, il n'a pas fait un bon mariage. ◆ adv [underneath] en bas.

benediction [ˌbenɪ'dɪkʃn] n RELIG & *fig* [blessing] bénédiction *f*.

benefactor ['benɪfæktər] n bienfaiteur *m*.

benefactress ['benɪfæktrɪs] n bienfaitrice *f*.

beneficial [ˌbenɪ'fɪʃl] adj [good, useful] avantageux, profitable / *vitamins are beneficial to health* les vitamines sont bonnes pour la santé ▸ **beneficial effects** des effets salutaires.

beneficiary [ˌbenɪ'fɪʃərɪ] (*pl* **beneficiaries**) n [of insurance policy, trust] bénéficiaire *mf* ; [of will] bénéficiaire *mf*, légataire *mf*.

benefit ['benɪfɪt] (*pt & pp* **benefited**, *cont* **benefiting**) ◆ n **1.** [advantage] avantage *m* ▸ **to have the benefit of sthg** bénéficier de qqch / *she is starting to feel the benefits of the treatment* elle commence à ressentir les bienfaits du traitement / *I'm saying this for your benefit* je dis cela pour toi or pour ton bien / *it's to your benefit to watch your diet* il est dans votre intérêt de surveiller ce que vous mangez ▸ **to give sb the benefit of the doubt** laisser or accorder à qqn le bénéfice du doute **2.** [payment] allocation *f*, prestation *f* / *social security benefits* prestations sociales **3.** [performance] spectacle *m* (*au profit d'une association caritative*). ◆ vt [do good to] faire du bien à ; [bring financial profit to] profiter à. ◆ vi : *he will benefit from the experience* l'expérience lui sera bénéfique / *no-one is likely to benefit by* or *from the closures* personne n'a de chance de tirer avantage des fermetures / *you would benefit from a stay in the country* un séjour à la campagne vous ferait du bien.

benefits agency n caisse *f* des allocations sociales.

Benelux ['benɪlʌks] pr n Benelux *m* ▸ **the Benelux countries** les pays du Benelux.

benevolent [bɪ'nevələnt] adj **1.** [kindly] bienveillant **2.** [donor] généreux, charitable ; [organization] de bienfaisance.

BEng [ˌbiː'eŋ] (*abbr of* **Bachelor of Engineering**) n UK (*titulaire d'une*) *licence d'ingénierie*.

Bengal [ˌbeŋ'gɔːl] pr n Bengale *m*.

benign [bɪ'naɪn] adj **1.** [kind - person] affable, aimable ; [- smile] bienveillant ; [- power, system] bienfaisant, salutaire **2.** [harmless] bénin (bénigne) ▸ **benign tumour** tumeur *f* bénigne.

Benin [be'nɪn] pr n Bénin *m*.

bennies ['benɪz] pl n US *inf* [benefits] avantages *mpl* en nature.

bent [bent] ◆ pt & pp ⟶ **bend**. ◆ adj **1.** [curved - tree, tube, wire] tordu, courbé ; [- branch] courbé ; [- back] voûté ; [- person] voûté, tassé **2.** [determined] : *he's bent on becoming an actor* il est décidé à or veut absolument devenir acteur / *to be bent on self-destruction* être porté à l'autodestruction **3.** UK *inf* [dishonest] véreux. ◆ n [liking] penchant *m*, goût *m* ; [aptitude] aptitudes *fpl*, dispositions *fpl* / *she has a natural bent for music* **a)** [liking] elle a un goût naturel pour la musique **b)** [talent] elle a des dispositions naturelles pour la musique.

bento ['bentəu] n (U) bento *m*.

bento box ['bentəu-] n CULIN boîte *f* à bento.

bequeath [bɪ'kwiːð] vt [pass on] transmettre, léguer ; LAW [in will] léguer.

bequest [bɪ'kwest] n legs *m*.

berate [bɪ'reɪt] vt réprimander.

Berber ['bɜːbər] ◆ n [person] Berbère *mf*. ◆ adj berbère.

bereaved [bɪ'riːvd] adj affligé, endeuillé.

bereavement [bɪ'riːvmənt] n [loss] perte *f* ; [grief] deuil *m* / *in his bereavement* dans son deuil.

bereft [-'reft] *fml & liter* ◆ pt & pp ⟶ **bereave**. ◆ adj privé / *bereft of all hope* complètement désespéré.

beret ['bereɪ] n béret *m*.

Bering Sea ['beərɪŋ-] pr n ▸ **the Bering Sea** la mer de Béring.

Bering Strait pr n ▸ **the Bering Strait** le détroit de Béring.

berk [bɜːk] n UK *inf* idiot *m*, -e *f*.

Berks. written abbr of **Berkshire**.

berlin [bə'lɪn] n **1.** ▸ **berlin (wool)** laine *f* à broder **2.** [carriage] berline *f*.

Berlin [bɜː'lɪn] pr n Berlin *m* ▸ **the Berlin Wall** le mur de Berlin.

Berliner [bɜː'lɪnər] n Berlinois *m*, -e *f*.

berm(e) [bɜːm] n US berme *f*.

Bermuda [bə'mjuːdə] pr n Bermudes *fpl*.

Bermudas [bə'mjuːdəz], **Bermuda shorts** pl n bermuda *m*.

Bern [bɜːn] pr n Berne *f*.

berry ['berɪ] (*pl* **berries**, *pt & pp* **berried**) n baie *f*.

berserk [bə'zɜːk] adj fou furieux ▸ **to go berserk a)** [person] devenir fou furieux **b)** [crowd] se déchaîner.

berth [bɜːθ] ◆ n **1.** [bunk] couchette *f* **2.** NAUT [in harbour] mouillage *m*, poste *m* d'amarrage ; [distance] distance *f* **3.** PHR **to give sb a wide berth** UK éviter qqn (à tout prix). ◆ vi [at dock] venir à quai, accoster ; [at anchor] mouiller.

beseech [bɪ'siːtʃ] (*pt & pp* **beseeched** *or* **besought** [-'sɔːt]) vt *fml & liter* **1.** [ask for] solliciter, implorer **2.** [entreat] implorer, supplier ▸ **to beseech sb to do sthg** implorer or supplier qqn de faire qqch.

beset [bɪ'set] (*pt & pp* **beset**, *cont* **besetting**) vt (*usu passive*) **1.** [assail] assaillir, harceler / *I was beset by* or *with doubt* j'étais assailli par le doute / *they are beset with problems* ils sont assaillis de problèmes **2.** [surround] encercler.

beside [bɪ'saɪd] prep **1.** [next to] à côté de, auprès de / *walk beside me* marchez à côté de moi **2.** [in addition to] en plus de, outre ; [apart from] à part, excepté **3.** PHR **to be beside o.s. with rage / excitement / joy** être hors de soi / surexcité / fou de joie.

besides [bɪ'saɪdz] ◆ prep [in addition to] en plus de, outre / *there are three (other) candidates besides yourself* il y a trois (autres) candidats à part vous / *besides which that book is out of print* sans compter que ce livre est épuisé. ◆ adv **1.** [in addition] en plus, en outre / *and more besides* et d'autres encore **2.** [furthermore] en plus / *besides, I don't even like funfairs* d'ailleurs or en plus, je n'aime pas les foires.

besiege [bɪ'siːdʒ] vt **1.** [surround - town] assiéger ; *fig* [person, office] assaillir **2.** [harass] assaillir, harceler / *we've been besieged by requests for help* nous avons été assaillis de demandes d'aide.

besmirch [bɪ'smɜːtʃ] vt *fig* [tarnish] souiller.

besotted [bɪ'sɒtɪd] adj [infatuated] fou *(before vowel or silent 'h' fol, f folle)*, épris ▶ **to be besotted with sb** être fou or follement épris de qqn.

besought [-'sɔːt] pt & pp ⟶ **beseech.**

bespectacled [bɪ'spektəkld] adj qui porte des lunettes, à lunettes.

bespoke [-'spəʊk] ◆ pt & pp ⟶ **bespeak.** ◆ adj [shoemaker, tailor] à façon ; [shoes, suit] fait sur mesure.

best [best] *(pl best)* ◆ adj **1.** *(superl of good)* meilleur / *may the best man win* que le meilleur gagne / *I'm doing what is best for the family* je fais ce qu'il y a de mieux pour la famille / *the best thing (to do) is to keep quiet* le mieux, c'est de ne rien dire / *best of all* le meilleur de tout / *'best before April 2012'* COMM 'à consommer de préférence avant avril 2012' **2.** [reserved for special occasions] plus beau / *she was dressed in her best clothes* elle portait ses plus beaux vêtements **3.** PHR **the best part of** la plus grande partie de / *I waited for the best part of an hour* j'ai attendu près d'une heure or presque une heure. ◆ adv *(superl of well)* mieux / *he does it best* c'est lui qui le fait le mieux / *which film did you like best?* quel est le film que vous avez préféré ? / *I comforted her as best I could* je l'ai consolée de mon mieux or du mieux que j'ai pu / *you had best apologize to her* vous feriez mieux de lui présenter vos excuses. ◆ n **1.** [most outstanding person, thing, part, etc.] le meilleur *m*, la meilleure *f*, les meilleurs *mpl*, les meilleures *fpl* / *it / she is the best there is* c'est le meilleur / la meilleure qui soit / *the best you can say about him is that...* le mieux qu'on puisse dire à son sujet c'est que... ▶ **the best of both worlds** : *she wants the best of both worlds* elle veut tout avoir **2.** [greatest, highest degree] le mieux, le meilleur / *they're the best of friends* ce sont les meilleurs amis du monde / *to the best of my knowledge / recollection* autant que je sache / je me souvienne / *she's not the calmest of people, even at the best of times* ce n'est pas quelqu'un de très calme de toute façon / *it was the best we could do* nous ne pouvions pas faire mieux / *this is Shakespeare at his best* voilà du meilleur Shakespeare ▶ **to do one's best** faire de son mieux or tout son possible ▶ **to get the best out of sb / sthg** tirer un maximum de qqn / qqch ▶ **to look one's best** [gen] être resplendissant / *we'll have to make the best of the situation* il faudra nous accommoder de la situation (du mieux que nous pouvons) **3.** [good wishes] : *(I wish you) all the best* (je vous souhaite) bonne chance. ◆> **at best** adv phr au mieux. ◆> **for the best** adv phr pour le mieux / *it's all for the best* c'est pour le mieux.

best-before date n date *f* limite de consommation.

best-case adj ▶ **this is the best-case scenario** c'est le scénario le plus optimiste.

bestial ['bestjəl] adj bestial.

best man n garçon *m* d'honneur.

Best man

Dans les pays anglo-saxons, le garçon d'honneur est responsable du bon déroulement de la cérémonie du mariage. C'est lui qui présente l'alliance au marié et prononce un discours pendant la réception. La tradition veut que ce discours soit agrémenté de commentaires et de vieilles histoires drôles sur le marié.

bestow [bɪ'stəʊ] vt *fml* [favour, gift, praise] accorder ; [award, honour] conférer, accorder.

best-perceived adj mieux perçu.

best practices pl n bonnes pratiques *fpl*.

best-seller n **1.** [book] best-seller *m*, succès *m* de librairie ; [product] article *m* qui se vend bien **2.** [author] auteur *m* à succès.

best-selling adj [book, item] à fort tirage ; [author] à succès.

bet [bet] *(pt & pp bet or betted, cont betting)* ◆ n pari *m* ▶ **to win / to lose a bet** gagner / perdre un pari / *it's a good* or *safe bet that they'll win* ils vont gagner à coup sûr / *your best bet is to take a taxi* inf tu ferais mieux de prendre un taxi. ◆ vt parier / *I'll bet you anything you want* je te parie tout ce que tu veux / *I bet you won't do it!* inf (t'es pas) chiche ! / *I'll bet my bottom dollar* or *my boots he loses* inf il va perdre, j'en mettrais ma main au feu / *are you going to the party? — you bet!* inf tu vas à la soirée ? — et comment ! or qu'est-ce que tu crois ? ◆ vi parier / *which horse did you bet on?* quel cheval as-tu joué ?, sur quel cheval as-tu misé ? / *to bet 5 to 1* parier or miser à 5 contre 1 / *he said he'd phone me — well, I wouldn't bet on it!* inf il a dit qu'il me téléphonerait — à ta place, je ne me ferais pas trop d'illusions !

beta ['biːtə] n bêta *m inv*.

beta-blocker [-ˌblɒkər] n bêtabloquant *m*.

beta release n COMPUT version *f* bêta.

beta test n test *m* bêta.

beta version = **beta release.**

betcha ['betʃə] excl *inf* ▶ **you betcha!** un peu, oui !

Bethlehem ['beθlɪhem] pr n Bethléem.

betray [bɪ'treɪ] vt **1.** [be disloyal to - friend, principle] trahir ; [-husband, wife] tromper, trahir ; [-country] trahir, être traître à **2.** [denounce] trahir, dénoncer ; [hand over] trahir, livrer **3.** [confidence, hope, trust] trahir, tromper **4.** [disclose - secret, truth] trahir, divulguer ; [-grief, happiness] trahir, laisser voir.

betrayal [bɪ'treɪəl] n **1.** [of person, principle] trahison *f* **2.** [act] (acte *m* de) trahison *f* **3.** [of confidence, trust] abus *m*, trahison *f* **4.** [of secret, truth] trahison *f*, divulgation *f*.

betrayer [bɪ'treɪər] n traître *m*, -esse *f*.

betrothed [bɪ'trəʊðd] *arch* ◆ adj fiancé, promis. ◆ n fiancé *m*, -e *f*, promis *m*, -e *f*.

better ['betər] ◆ adj **1.** *(compar of good)* [superior] meilleur / *that's better!* voilà qui est mieux ! / *I'm better at languages than he is* je suis meilleur or plus fort en langues que lui / *he's a better cook than you are* il cuisine mieux que toi / *I had hoped for better things* j'avais espéré mieux / *it's better if I don't see them* il vaut mieux or il est préférable que je ne les voie pas ▶ **better off** mieux / *they're better off than we are* **a)** [richer] ils ont plus d'argent que nous **b)** [in a more advantageous position] ils sont dans une meilleure position que nous / *he'd have been better off staying where he was* il aurait mieux fait de rester où il était **2.** *(compar of well)* [improved in health] ▶ **to get better** commencer à aller mieux / *now that he's better* maintenant qu'il va mieux. ◆ adv **1.** *(compar of well)* [more proficiently, aptly, etc.] mieux / *he swims better than I do* il nage mieux que moi **2.** [indicating preference] : *I liked his last book better* j'ai préféré son dernier livre ▶ **so much the better** tant mieux ▶ **better late than never** *prov* mieux vaut tard que jamais *prov* **3.** [with adj] mieux, plus / *better looking* plus beau / *she's one of Canada's better-known authors* c'est un des auteurs canadiens les plus or mieux connus **4.** PHR we'd **better be going a)** [must go] il faut que nous partions **b)** [would be preferable] il vaut mieux que nous partions. ◆ n **1.** [superior of two] le meilleur *m*, la meilleure *f* / *there's been a change for the better in his health* son état de santé s'est amélioré ▶ **for better or worse** pour le meilleur ou pour le pire **2.** *(usu pl)* [person] supérieur *m*, -e *f* **3.** PHR to **get the better of sb** : *curiosity got the better of me* ma curiosité l'a emporté / *we got the better of them in the deal* nous l'avons emporté sur eux dans l'affaire. ◆ vt [position, status, situation] améliorer ; [achievement, sales figure] dépasser / *she's eager to better herself* elle a vraiment envie d'améliorer sa situation.

better half n *inf & hum* moitié *f (au sens de mari ou femme)*.

betterment ['betəmənt] n amélioration *f* ; LAW [of property] plus-value *f*.

better-off adj aisé, riche.

betting ['betɪŋ] n [bets] pari *m*, paris *mpl* / *the betting was heavy* les paris allaient bon train / *what's the betting they refuse to go?* je suis prêt à parier qu'ils ne voudront pas y aller.

betting shop n bureau *m* de paris *(appartenant à un bookmaker)*.

Betty Crocker® [ˌbetɪ'krɒkər] pr n *marque américaine de produits alimentaires et de livres de recettes*.

between [bɪ'twiːn] ◆ prep **1.** [in space or time] entre / *the crowd stood between him and the door* la foule le séparait de la porte / *between now and this evening* d'ici ce soir **2.** [in the range that separates] entre / *children between the ages of 5 and 10* les enfants de 5 à 10 ans **3.** [indicating connection, relation] entre / *a bus runs between the airport and the hotel* un bus fait la navette entre l'aéroport et l'hôtel ▶ **between you and me** or **between ourselves** entre nous **4.** [indicating alternatives] entre / *I had to choose between going with them and staying at home* il fallait que je choisisse entre les accompagner et rester à la maison **5.** [added together] : *between us we saved enough money for the trip* à nous deux nous avons économisé assez d'argent pour le voyage **6.** [indicating division] entre / *they shared the cake between them* ils se sont partagé le gâteau. ◆ adv = **in between**. ❖ **in between** ◆ adv phr **1.** [in intermediate position] : *a row of bushes with little clumps of flowers in between* un rang d'arbustes alternant avec des fleurs **2.** [in time] entre-temps, dans l'intervalle. ◆ prep phr entre.

beveled adj US = **bevelled**.

bevelled UK, **beveled** US ['bevld] adj biseauté.

beverage ['bevərɪdʒ] n boisson *f*.

bevvy ['bevi] *(pl* **bevvies)** UK n *regional* [drink] boisson *f* (alcoolisée) ; [drinking bout] beuverie *f*.

bevy ['bevi] *(pl* **bevies)** n [of people] bande *f*, troupeau *m pej* ; [of quails] volée *f* ; [of roe deer] harde *f*.

beware [bɪ'weər] *(infinitive and imperative only)* ◆ vi prendre garde / *beware of married men* méfiez-vous des hommes mariés / **'beware of the dog!'** 'chien méchant !'. ◆ vt prendre garde / *beware what you say to her* prenez garde or faites attention à ce que vous lui dites.

bewilder [bɪ'wɪldər] vt rendre perplexe, dérouter.

bewildered [bɪ'wɪldəd] adj perplexe.

bewildering [bɪ'wɪldərɪŋ] adj déconcertant, déroutant.

bewilderment [bɪ'wɪldəmənt] n confusion *f*, perplexité *f*.

bewitch [bɪ'wɪtʃ] vt **1.** [cast spell over] ensorceler, enchanter **2.** [fascinate] enchanter, charmer.

bewitched [bɪ'wɪtʃt] adj ensorcelé, enchanté.

bewitching [bɪ'wɪtʃɪŋ] adj [smile] enchanteur, charmeur ; [beauty, person] charmant, séduisant.

beyond [bɪ'jɒnd] ◆ prep **1.** [on the further side of] au-delà de, de l'autre côté de / *the museum is a few yards beyond the church* le musée se trouve à quelques mètres après l'église **2.** [outside the range of] au-delà de, au-dessus de / *due to circumstances beyond our control* dû à des circonstances indépendantes de notre volonté / *his guilt has been established beyond (all reasonable) doubt* sa culpabilité a été établie sans aucun or sans le moindre doute ▶ **to be beyond sb** : *economics is completely beyond me* je ne comprends rien à l'économie **3.** [later than] au-delà de, plus de / *the deadline has been extended to beyond 2011* l'échéance a été repoussée au-delà de 2011 **4.** [apart from, other than] sauf, excepté / *I know nothing beyond what I've already told you* je ne sais rien de plus que ce que je vous ai déjà dit. ◆ adv **1.** [on the other side] au-delà, plus loin / *the room beyond was smaller* la pièce suivante était plus petite **2.** [after] au-delà / *major changes are foreseen for next year and beyond* des changements importants sont prévus pour l'année prochaine et au-delà. ◆ n au-delà *m*.

bf (written abbr of **boldface**) TYPO caractères *mpl* gras.

b/f written abbr of **brought forward**.

BF MESSAGING written abbr of **boyfriend**.

BFN, B4N MESSAGING written abbr of **bye for now**.

BG MESSAGING written abbr of **big grin**.

bhangra ['bæŋgrə] n MUS *combinaison de musique traditionnelle du Pendjab et de musique pop occidentale*.

bhp n abbr of **brake horsepower**.

Bhutan [ˌbuː'tɑːn] pr n Bhoutan *m*.

bi- [baɪ] in comp bi-.

biannual [baɪ'ænjʊəl] adj semestriel.

bias ['baɪəs] *(pt & pp* **biased** or **biassed)** ◆ n **1.** [prejudice] préjugé *m* / *there is still considerable bias against women candidates* les femmes qui se présentent sont encore victimes d'un fort préjugé **2.** [tendency] tendance *f*, penchant *m* / *the school has a scientific bias* l'école favorise les sciences **3.** SEW biais *m*. ◆ vt [influence] influencer ; [prejudice] prévenir / *his experience biased him against / towards them* son expérience l'a prévenu contre eux / en leur faveur.

biased, biassed ['baɪəst] adj [partial] partial.

biathlon [baɪ'æθlɒn] n biathlon *m*.

bib [bɪb] n [for child] bavoir *m*, bavette *f*.

bi-band adj bibande.

Bible ['baɪbl] ◆ n Bible *f*. ◆ comp ▶ **the Bible Belt** *États du sud des États-Unis où l'évangélisme est très répandu.* ❖ **bible** n *fig* [manual] bible *f*, évangile *m*.

bible-basher n *inf* = **bible-thumper**.

bible-thumper [-ˌθʌmpər] n *inf & pej* évangéliste *m* de carrefour.

biblical, Biblical ['bɪblɪkl] adj biblique.

bibliography [ˌbɪblɪ'ɒɡrəfɪ] (pl **bibliographies**) n bibliographie f.

bicarbonate [baɪ'kɑːbənət] n bicarbonate m ▸ **bicarbonate of soda** bicarbonate m de soude.

bicentenary [ˌbaɪsen'tiːnərɪ] (pl **bicentenaries**) 🇬🇧 n bicentenaire m.

bicentennial [ˌbaɪsen'tenjəl] adj bicentenaire.

biceps ['baɪseps] (pl **biceps**) n biceps m.

bicker ['bɪkər] vi se chamailler ▸ **to bicker about** or **over sthg** se chamailler à propos de qqch.

bickering ['bɪkərɪŋ] n chamailleries fpl.

bickie ['bɪkɪ] n 🇬🇧 inf [biscuit] petit gâteau m.

bicoastal [baɪ'kəʊstl] adj 🇺🇸 [company] établi sur les deux côtes.

bicultural [ˌbaɪ'kʌltʃərəl] adj biculturel.

bicycle ['baɪsɪkl] ◆ n vélo m, bicyclette f / do you know how to ride a bicycle? sais-tu faire du vélo ? ◆ comp [bell, chain, lamp] de vélo.

bicycle clip n pince f à vélo.

bicycle-friendly adj = bike-friendly.

bicycle path n piste f cyclable.

bicycle pump n pompe f à vélo.

bicycler ['baɪsɪklər] n 🇺🇸 cycliste mf.

bicycle rack n [for parking] râtelier m à bicyclettes or à vélos ; [on car roof] porte-vélos m (inv).

bicycle track n piste f cyclable.

bid [bɪd] ◆ vi (pt & pp bid, cont **bidding**) **1.** [offer to pay] faire une offre, offrir ▸ **to bid for sthg** faire une offre pour qqch / they bid against us ils ont surenchéri sur notre offre **2.** COMM faire une soumission, répondre à un appel d'offres. ◆ vt (pt & pp bid, cont **bidding**) **1.** [offer to pay] faire une offre de, offrir ; [at auction] faire une enchère de **2.** CARDS demander, annoncer **3.** (pt bade [bæd], pp **bidden** ['bɪdn]) liter [say] dire / they bade him farewell ils lui firent leurs adieux / she bade them welcome elle leur souhaita la bienvenue ; liter [order, tell] ordonner, enjoindre ; arch [invite] inviter, convier. ◆ n **1.** [offer to pay] offre f ; [at auction] enchère f / a higher bid une surenchère **2.** COMM [tender] soumission f **3.** CARDS demande f, annonce f **4.** [attempt] tentative f / the prisoners made a bid for freedom les prisonniers ont fait une tentative d'évasion / a rescue bid une tentative de sauvetage.

bidder ['bɪdər] n **1.** [at auction] enchérisseur m, -euse f / sold to the highest bidder vendu au plus offrant **2.** COMM soumissionnaire mf.

bidding ['bɪdɪŋ] n **1.** [at auction] enchères fpl **2.** COMM [tenders] soumissions fpl **3.** CARDS enchères fpl **4.** liter [request] demande f ; [order] ordre m, ordres mpl / at her brother's bidding sur la requête de son frère.

bidding price n 🇺🇸 FIN cours m acheteur.

bide [baɪd] (pt bided or bode [bəʊd], pp bided) vt ▸ **to bide one's time** attendre son heure or le bon moment.

bidet ['biːdeɪ] n bidet m.

bidirectional [baɪdə'rekʃənl] adj bidirectionnel.

bid price n cours m acheteur.

biennial [baɪ'enɪəl] adj **1.** [every two years] biennal, bisannuel **2.** [lasting two years] biennal.

bier [bɪər] n [for corpse] bière f ; [for coffin] brancards mpl.

bifidus ['bɪfɪdəs] n bifidus m.

big [bɪg] (compar **bigger**, superl **biggest**) ◆ adj **1.** [in size - car, hat, majority] grand, gros (grosse) ; [- crowd, field, room] grand ; [- person] grand, fort / the crowd got bigger la foule a grossi / he has a big mouth inf & fig il faut toujours qu'il l'ouvre ▸ **to be too big for one's boots**

or **one's breeches** inf: she's too big for her boots elle ne se prend pas pour n'importe qui **2.** [in height] grand / to get or to grow bigger grandir **3.** [older] aîné, plus grand / my big sister ma grande sœur **4.** [important, significant - decision, problem] grand, important ; [- drop, increase] fort, important / the big day le grand jour / he's big in publishing or he's a big man in publishing c'est quelqu'un d'important dans l'édition **5.** [generous] grand, généreux / he has a big heart il a du cœur or bon cœur / that's big of you! iro quelle générosité ! **6.** inf [popular] à la mode **7.** inf [enthusiastic] ▸ **to be big on sthg** adorer or être fana de qqch / the company is big on research l'entreprise investit beaucoup dans la recherche. ◆ adv **1.** [grandly] : he talks big il se vante, il fanfaronne / to think big voir grand **2.** inf [well] : they made it big in the pop world ce sont maintenant des stars de la musique pop.

bigamist ['bɪgəmɪst] n bigame mf.

bigamy ['bɪgəmɪ] n bigamie f.

Big Apple pr n inf ▸ **the Big Apple** New York (la ville).

big bang theory n la théorie du big-bang or big bang.

Big Ben [-ben] pr n Big Ben.

Big Ben

Nom de la cloche de la tour de l'Horloge du palais de Westminster, souvent donné à tort à la tour elle-même.

big-box store n 🇺🇸 hypermarché m.

big-budget adj à gros budget.

big business n (U) les grandes entreprises fpl.

big cat n fauve m, grand félin m.

Big Crunch pr n ▸ **the Big Crunch** le Big Crunch (contraction et effondrement de l'Univers, envers du Big Bang).

big deal inf ◆ interj ▸ **big deal!** tu parles ! ◆ n : it's no big deal il n'y a pas de quoi en faire un plat !

Big Dipper pr n 🇺🇸 ASTRON ▸ **the Big Dipper** la Grande Ourse. ◆ **big dipper** n 🇬🇧 [in fairground] ▸ **the big dipper** les montagnes fpl russes.

Big Easy pr n 🇺🇸 surnom de La Nouvelle-Orléans.

big end n 🇬🇧 tête f de bielle.

big fish n inf huile f, gros bonnet m.

big game n gros gibier m.

biggie ['bɪgɪ] n inf [success - song] tube m ; [- film, album] succès m.

big gun n inf gros bonnet m.

big hair n 🇺🇸 coiffure volumineuse et apprêtée.

big hand n **1.** [on clock] grande aiguille f **2.** inf [applause] : let's give him a big hand applaudissons-le bien fort.

bighead ['bɪghed] n inf crâneur m, -euse f.

bigheaded [ˌbɪg'hedɪd] adj inf crâneur.

bighearted [ˌbɪg'hɑːtɪd] adj au grand cœur.

Big League n 🇺🇸 = Major League.

big man on campus n 🇺🇸 inf étudiant jouissant d'une certaine popularité grâce à ses exploits sportifs, etc.

big money n inf ▸ **to earn big money** gagner gros.

bigmouth ['bɪgmaʊθ] (pl [-maʊðz]) n inf grande gueule f.

big name n grand nom m.

big noise n 🇬🇧 inf gros bonnet m.

bigot ['bɪgət] n [gen] sectaire mf, intolérant m, -e f ; RELIG bigot m, -e f, sectaire mf.

bigoted ['bɪgətɪd] adj [gen - person] sectaire, intolérant ; [- attitude, opinion] fanatique ; RELIG bigot.

bigotry ['bɪgətrɪ] n [gen] sectarisme *m*, intolérance *f* ; RELIG bigoterie *f*.

big screen n ▸ **the big screen** le grand écran, le cinéma.

big shot n *inf* gros bonnet *m*.

big smoke n UK *inf* ▸ **the big smoke a)** [gen] la grande ville **b)** [London] Londres.

Big Ten pl n US SPORT équipes sportives universitaires du Midwest, réputées de très haut niveau.

big-ticket adj US [expensive] cher / *a big-ticket item* un article haut de gamme.

big time n *inf* ▸ **to hit** or **to make** or **to reach the big time** arriver, réussir. ❖ **big-time** adj *inf* [actor, singer] à succès ; [businessman, politician] de haut vol ; [project] ambitieux, de grande échelle.

big toe n gros orteil *m*.

big top n [tent] grand chapiteau *m* ; [circus] cirque *m*.

big wheel, bigwig ['bɪgwɪg] n *inf* gros bonnet *m*.

bike [baɪk] *inf* ❖ n [bicycle] vélo *m* ; [motorcycle] moto *f*. ❖ vi [bicycle] faire du vélo ; [motorcycle] faire de la moto.

bike-friendly, bicycle-friendly adj [area, city] bien aménagé pour les cyclistes.

bikejack ['baɪkdʒæk] vt : *someone tried to bikejack him* quelqu'un a essayé de lui voler son vélo.

bike lane n piste *f* cyclable.

biker ['baɪkər] n *inf* motard *m*, motocycliste *mf*.

bike shed n cabane *f* or remise *f* à vélos.

bikeway ['baɪkweɪ] n US piste *f* cyclable.

bikini [bɪ'ki:nɪ] n bikini *m*.

bikini line n : *to have one's bikini line done* se faire faire une épilation maillot.

BIL MESSAGING **written abbr of boss is listening.**

bilateral [,baɪ'lætərəl] adj bilatéral.

bilberry ['bɪlbərɪ] (*pl* bilberries) n myrtille *f*.

bile [baɪl] n **1.** ANAT bile *f* **2.** *liter* [irritability] mauvaise humeur *f*, irascibilité *f*.

bilingual [baɪ'lɪŋgwəl] adj bilingue.

bilingualism [baɪ'lɪŋgwəlɪzm] n bilinguisme *m*.

bilious ['bɪljəs] adj MED bilieux ▸ **bilious attack** crise *f* de foie.

bill [bɪl] ❖ n **1.** US [for gas, telephone] facture *f*, note *f* ; [for product] facture *f* ; [in restaurant] addition *f*, note *f* ; [in hotel] note *f* / *may I have the bill please?* l'addition, s'il vous plaît / *put it on my bill* mettez-le sur ma note **2.** [draft of law] projet *m* de loi / *to vote on a bill* mettre un projet de loi au vote **3.** [poster] affiche *f*, placard *m* **4.** THEAT affiche *f* ▸ **to head** or **to top the bill** être en tête d'affiche or en vedette **5.** US [banknote] billet *m* (de banque) **6.** [beak] bec *m*. ❖ vt **1.** [invoice] facturer / *he bills his company for his travel expenses* il se fait rembourser ses frais de voyage par son entreprise **2.** THEAT mettre à l'affiche, annoncer.

billboard ['bɪlbɔ:d] n panneau *m* (d'affichage).

bill collector n agent *m* de recouvrement.

billet ['bɪlɪt] ❖ n [accommodation] cantonnement *m* (chez l'habitant) ; [document] billet *m* de logement. ❖ vt [gen] loger ; MIL cantonner, loger.

billfold ['bɪlfəʊld] n US portefeuille *m*.

billiards ['bɪljədz] n (*U*) (jeu *m* de) billard *m* / *to play (a game of) billiards* jouer au billard.

billing ['bɪlɪŋ] n THEAT : *to get* or *to have top / second billing* être en tête d'affiche / en deuxième place à l'affiche.

billion ['bɪljən] (*pl* billion or billions) n [thousand million] milliard *m* ; UK *dated* [million million] billion *m*.

billionaire [,bɪljə'neər] n milliardaire *mf*.

billionth ['bɪljənθ] ❖ adj milliardième. ❖ n **1.** [ordinal] milliardième *mf* **2.** [fraction] milliardième *m*.

Bill of Rights ❖ n Déclaration *f* des droits. ❖ pr n ▸ **the Bill of Rights** *les dix premiers amendements à la Constitution américaine garantissant, entre autres droits, la liberté d'expression, de religion et de réunion.*

billow ['bɪləʊ] ❖ vi [cloth, flag] onduler ; [sail] se gonfler ; [cloud, smoke] tourbillonner, tournoyer. ❖ n [of smoke] tourbillon *m*, volute *f*.

billy ['bɪlɪ] (*pl* billies) n *inf* [goat] bouc *m*.

billycan ['bɪlɪkæn] n UK & Austr gamelle *f*.

billy goat n bouc *m*.

bimbette [bɪm'bet] n *inf & pej* minette *f*.

bimbo ['bɪmbəʊ] (*pl* bimbos or bimboes) n *inf & pej* bimbo *f*.

bimonthly [,baɪ'mʌnθlɪ] (*pl* bimonthlies) ❖ adj [every two months] bimestriel ; [twice monthly] bimensuel. ❖ adv [every two months] tous les deux mois ; [twice monthly] deux fois par mois.

bin [bɪn] (*pt & pp* binned, *cont* binning) ❖ n **1.** UK [for rubbish] poubelle *f*, boîte *f* à ordures **2.** [for coal, grain] coffre *m* ; [for bread] huche *f*. ❖ vt UK *inf* [discard] flanquer à la poubelle.

binary ['baɪnərɪ] adj [number, system] binaire.

binbag ['bɪnbæg] n sac-poubelle *m*.

bind [baɪnd] (*pt & pp* bound [baʊnd]) ❖ vt **1.** [tie] attacher, lier / *he was bound hand and foot* il avait les pieds et les poings liés **2.** [encircle] entourer, ceindre / *to bind a wound* bander or panser une blessure **3.** [book] relier **4.** [stick together] lier, agglutiner **5.** *fig* [bond, unite] lier, attacher **6.** [oblige] obliger, contraindre / *we are bound to tell the truth* nous sommes obligés or tenus de dire la vérité. ❖ n **1.** [bond] lien *m*, liens *mpl* **2.** *inf* [annoying situation] corvée *f* / *we're in a bit of a bind* nous sommes plutôt dans le pétrin. ❖ **bind over** vt sep UK LAW [order] sommer / *they were bound over to keep the peace* ils ont été sommés de ne pas troubler l'ordre public. ❖ **bind up** vt sep [tie - gen] attacher, lier ; [- wound] bander, panser.

binder ['baɪndər] n **1.** [folder] classeur *m* **2.** [bookbinder] relieur *m*, -euse *f*.

binding ['baɪndɪŋ] ❖ n **1.** [for book] reliure *f* **2.** [for sewing] extrafort *m* **3.** [on skis] fixation *f*. ❖ adj [law] obligatoire ; [contract, promise] qui engage or lie / *the agreement is binding on all parties* l'accord engage chaque partie.

bin-end n fin *f* de série (de vin).

binge [bɪndʒ] *inf* ❖ n **1.** [spree] ▸ **to go on a binge** faire la bringue **2.** [drinking bout] beuverie *f*, bringue *f*. ❖ vi **1.** [overindulge] faire des folies **2.** [overeat] faire des excès (de nourriture).

binge drinking n hyperalcoolisation *f* (*consommation rapide et excessive d'alcool*).

binge eating n hyperphagie *f*, consommation *f* compulsive de nourriture.

bingo ['bɪngəʊ] ❖ n bingo *m* ; ≃ loto *m*. ❖ interj ▸ **bingo!** ça y est !

Bingo

Ce jeu, très populaire au Royaume-Uni et aux États-Unis, consiste à cocher sur une carte des nombres tirés au hasard jusqu'à ce qu'elle soit remplie ; les salles de bingo sont souvent d'anciens cinémas ou des salles municipales.

bingo wings pl n 🇬🇧 inf chair qui pendouille sous les avant-bras.

bin liner n 🇬🇧 sac m (à) poubelle.

binman ['bɪnmæn] (pl **binmen** [-men]) n 🇬🇧 éboueur m.

binner ['bɪnər] n 🇺🇸 personne qui fait les poubelles.

binoculars [bɪ'nɒkjʊlərz] pl n jumelles fpl.

bio ['baɪəʊ] ◆ adj bio (inv). ◆ n (pl **bios**) inf biographie f.

bioavailability [ˌbaɪəʊəveɪlə'bɪlɪti] n biodisponibilité f.

biochemical [ˌbaɪəʊ'kemɪkl] adj biochimique.

biochemistry [ˌbaɪəʊ'kemɪstri] n biochimie f.

biodegradable [ˌbaɪəʊdɪ'greɪdəbl] adj biodégradable.

biodiesel ['baɪəʊdiːzəl] n biodiesel m.

biodiversity [ˌbaɪəʊdaɪ'vɜːsəti] n biodiversité f.

biodynamic [ˌbaɪəʊdaɪ'næmɪk] adj biodynamique.

bioethics [ˌbaɪəʊ'eθɪks] n (U) bioéthique f.

biofuel ['baɪəʊfjuːl] n biocarburant m.

biogeography [baɪəʊdʒɪ'ɒɡrəfɪ] n biogéographie f.

biographer [baɪ'ɒɡrəfər] n biographe mf.

biographical [ˌbaɪə'ɡræfɪkl] adj biographique.

biography [baɪ'ɒɡrəfɪ] n biographie f.

biological [ˌbaɪə'lɒdʒɪkl] adj biologique ▸ **biological washing powder** lessive f aux enzymes.

biological clock n horloge f interne biologique.

biological mother n mère f biologique.

biological weapon n arme f biologique.

biologist [baɪ'ɒlədʒɪst] n biologiste mf.

biology [baɪ'ɒlədʒɪ] n biologie f.

biome ['baɪəʊm] n biome m.

biometric [ˌbaɪəʊ'metrɪk] adj [data, identifier, reader] biométrique.

bionic [baɪ'ɒnɪk] adj bionique.

bionics [baɪ'ɒnɪks] n (U) bionique f.

biopic ['baɪəʊpɪk] n inf film m biographique.

biopiracy ['baɪəʊpaɪrəsɪ] n biopiraterie f, détournement m de ressources génétiques.

bioprivacy [ˌbaɪəʊ'prɪvəsɪ] n protection f de données biométriques.

biopsy ['baɪɒpsɪ] (pl **biopsies**) n biopsie f.

biotechnology [ˌbaɪəʊtek'nɒlədʒɪ] n biotechnologie f.

bioterrorism [ˌbaɪəʊ'terərɪzm] n bioterrorisme m.

bioterrorist ['baɪəʊterərɪst] n bioterroriste mf.

biowarfare [ˌbaɪəʊ'wɔːfeə] n guerre f biologique.

bioweapon ['baɪəʊwepən] n arme f biologique.

bipartite [ˌbaɪ'pɑːtaɪt] adj BIOL & POL biparti, bipartite.

biplane ['baɪpleɪn] n biplan m.

bipolar disorder [baɪ'pəʊlədɪsˌɔː'dər] n MED trouble m bipolaire.

birch [bɜːtʃ] n **1.** [tree] bouleau m ; [wood] (bois m de) bouleau **2.** 🇬🇧 [rod for whipping] verge f.

bird [bɜːd] n **1.** [gen] oiseau m ; CULIN volaille f ▸ **bird of passage** lit & fig oiseau de passage ▸ **bird of prey** oiseau de proie, rapace m ▸ **a little bird told me** mon petit doigt me l'a dit ▸ **the birds and the bees** euph & hum les choses de la vie ▸ **the bird has flown** l'oiseau s'est envolé ▸ **birds of a feather flock together** prov qui se ressemble s'assemble prov ▸ **a bird in the hand is worth two in the bush** prov un tiens vaut mieux que deux tu l'auras prov **2.** 🇬🇧 inf [woman] nana f.

bird box n nichoir m.

bird-brained [-breɪnd] adj inf [person] écervelé, qui a une cervelle d'oiseau ; [idea] insensé.

birdcage ['bɜːdkeɪdʒ] n [small] cage f à oiseaux ; [large] volière f.

bird flu n grippe f aviaire.

birdie ['bɜːdɪ] n **1.** inf [small bird] petit oiseau m, oisillon m **2.** [in golf] birdie m.

birding ['bɜːdɪŋ] n = **bird-watching**.

birdseed ['bɜːdsiːd] n graine f pour les oiseaux.

bird's-eye adj ▸ **a bird's-eye view of sthg** a) lit une vue panoramique de qqch b) fig une vue d'ensemble de qqch.

bird-watcher n ornithologue mf amateur.

bird-watching n ornithologie f ▸ **to go bird-watching** aller observer les oiseaux.

Biro® ['baɪərəʊ] (pl **biros**) n 🇬🇧 stylo m (à) bille ; ≃ Bic® m.

birth [bɜːθ] n **1.** [nativity] naissance f / deaf from birth sourd de naissance **2.** [of child] accouchement m, couches fpl ; [of animal] mise f bas ▸ **to give birth** a) [woman] accoucher b) [animal] mettre bas **3.** fig [origin - of movement, nation] naissance f, origine f ; [- of era, industry] naissance f, commencement m ; [- of product, radio] apparition f **4.** [ancestry, lineage] naissance f, ascendance f / he's Chinese by birth il est chinois de naissance.

birth certificate n acte m or extrait m de naissance.

birth chart n ASTROL thème m astral.

birth control n **1.** [contraception] contraception f **2.** [family planning] contrôle m des naissances.

birthday ['bɜːθdeɪ] ◆ n anniversaire m / her 21st birthday ses 21 ans. ◆ comp [cake, card, present] d'anniversaire ▸ **birthday party** they're giving him a birthday party ils organisent une fête pour son anniversaire.

birthday suit n inf & hum [of man] costume m d'Adam ; [of woman] costume m d'Ève.

birthmark ['bɜːθmɑːk] n tache f de vin.

birth mother n mère f gestationnelle.

birthparent ['bɜːθpeərənt] n parent m biologique.

birthplace ['bɜːθpleɪs] n [town] lieu m de naissance ; [house] maison f natale ; fig berceau m.

birthrate ['bɜːθreɪt] n (taux m de) natalité f.

birthright ['bɜːθraɪt] n droit m (acquis à la naissance).

birth sign n signe m du zodiaque.

birthstone ['bɜːθstəʊn] n pierre f porte-bonheur (selon la date de naissance).

birthweight ['bɜːθweɪt] n poids m à la naissance.

BIS pr n abbr of **Department for Business, Innovation and Skills**.

Biscay ['bɪskeɪ] pr n Biscaye ▸ **the Bay of Biscay** le golfe de Gascogne.

biscuit ['bɪskɪt] n **1.** 🇬🇧 CULIN biscuit m, petit gâteau m ▸ **that really takes the biscuit!** inf ça, c'est vraiment le bouquet ! **2.** 🇺🇸 CULIN petit gâteau que l'on mange avec de la confiture ou avec un plat salé.

bisect [baɪ'sekt] vt [gen] couper en deux ; MATH diviser en deux parties égales.

bisexual [ˌbaɪ'sekʃʊəl] ◆ adj [person, tendency] bisexuel. ◆ n [person] bisexuel m, -elle f.

bisexuality [baɪˌseksjʊ'ælɪtɪ] n bisexualité f.

bishop ['bɪʃəp] n **1.** RELIG évêque m **2.** [in chess] fou m.

bison ['baɪsn] n bison m.

bisque [bɪsk] n [soup] bisque f.

bistro ['biːstrəʊ] (pl **bistros**) n bistro m.

bit¹ [bɪt] n **1.** [piece - of cake, puzzle, wood, land, string] bout m ; [- of food] passage m ; [- of film] séquence f / she picked up her bits and pieces elle a ramassé ses affaires ▸ **to take sthg to bits** démonter qqch ▸ **to fall to bits** [book, clothes] tomber en lambeaux **2.** [unspecified (small) quantity] : *a bit of money* / *time* un peu d'argent / de temps / *there's been a bit of trouble at home* il y a eu quelques problèmes à la maison ▶ **to do one's bit** y mettre du sien, faire un effort **3.** [for horse] mors *m* ▶ **to take the bit between one's teeth** prendre le mors aux dents **4.** [of drill] mèche *f* **5.** COMPUT bit *m*. ❖ **a bit** adv phr **1.** [some time] quelque temps / *let's sit down for a bit* asseyons-nous un instant ou un peu / *he's away quite a bit* il est souvent absent **2.** [slightly] un peu / *she's a good* / *little bit older than he is* elle est beaucoup / un peu plus âgée que lui ; [at all] : *they haven't changed a bit* ils n'ont pas du tout changé / *not a bit of it!* pas le moins du monde ! ▶ *that's a bit much* or **a bit steep!** ça c'est un peu fort ! ❖ **bit by bit** adv phr petit à petit.

bit² [bɪt] pt ⟶ **bite.**

bitch [bɪtʃ] ❖ n **1.** [female canine - gen] femelle *f* ; [dog] chienne *f* ; [fox] renarde *f* ; [wolf] louve *f* **2.** v inf & pej [woman] garce *f* **3.** inf [thing] saloperie *f* / *a bitch of a job* une saloperie de boulot **4.** inf [complaint] motif *m* de râler. ❖ vi inf râler, rouspéter ▶ **to bitch about sb** / **sthg** râler or rouspéter contre qqn / qqch.

bitchy [bɪtʃɪ] (*compar* **bitchier,** *superl* **bitchiest**) adj inf vache / *a bitchy remark* une vacherie.

bite [baɪt] (*pt* **bit** [bɪt], *pp* **bitten** ['bɪtn]) ❖ vt [subj: animal, person] mordre ; [subj: insect, snake] piquer, mordre / *to bite one's nails* se ronger les ongles ▶ **to bite one's tongue a)** *lit* se mordre la langue **b)** *fig* se retenir de dire qqch ▶ **to bite the bullet** serrer les dents ▶ **to bite the dust** mordre la poussière ▶ **to bite the hand that feeds one** montrer de l'ingratitude envers qqn qui vous veut du bien ▶ *once bitten, twice shy* prov c'est échaudé craint l'eau froide *prov.* ❖ vi [animal, person] mordre ; [insect, snake] piquer, mordre ; [fish] mordre (à l'hameçon) / *I bit into the apple* j'ai mordu dans la pomme. ❖ n **1.** [of animal, person] morsure *f* ; [of insect, snake] piqûre *f*, morsure *f* **2.** [piece] bouchée *f* ▶ **to take a bite of sthg a)** [bite into] mordre dans qqch **b)** [taste] goûter (à) qqch **3.** inf [something to eat] : *we stopped for a bite (to eat)* nous nous sommes arrêtés pour manger un morceau **4.** FISHING touche *f* **5.** [sharpness - of mustard, spice] piquant *m* ; [- of speech, wit] mordant *m* ; [- of air, wind] caractère *m* cinglant or mordant. ❖ **bite back** vt sep ▶ **to bite sthg back** se retenir de dire qqch. ❖ **bite off** vt sep arracher d'un coup de dents ▶ **to bite off more than one can chew** avoir les yeux plus grands ou gros que le ventre ▶ **to bite sb's head off** inf enguirlander qqn.

bite-sized [-,saɪzd] adj : *cut the meat into bite-sized pieces* coupez la viande en petits dés.

biting ['baɪtɪŋ] adj **1.** [insect] piqueur, vorace **2.** fig [remark, wit] mordant, cinglant ; [wind] cinglant, mordant ; [cold] mordant, perçant.

bitmap ['bɪtmæp] n mode *m* point, bitmap *m*.

bit part n THEAT petit rôle *m*.

bitrate ['bɪtreɪt] n COMPUT débit *m*, bitrate *m*.

bitten ['bɪtn] pp ⟶ **bite.**

bitter ['bɪtər] ❖ adj **1.** [taste] amer, âpre **2.** [resentful - person] amer ; [- look, tone] amer, plein d'amertume ; [- reproach, tears] amer ▶ **to be bitter about sthg** être amer ou plein d'amertume au sujet de qqch **3.** [unpleasant - disappointment, experience] amer, cruel ; [- argument, struggle] violent ; [- blow] dur / *we fought to the bitter end* nous avons lutté jusqu'au bout **4.** [extreme - enemy] acharné ; [- opposition] violent, acharné ; [- remorse] cuisant **5.** [cold - wind] cinglant, glacial ; [- weather] glacial ; [- winter] rude, dur. ❖ n [beer] *bière pression relativement amère, à forte teneur en houblon.*

bitter lemon n Schweppes® *m* au citron.

bitterly ['bɪtəlɪ] adv **1.** [speak] amèrement, avec amertume ; [criticize] âprement ; [weep] amèrement **2.** [intensely - ashamed, unhappy] profondément ; [- disappointed] cruellement / *it was a bitterly cold day* il faisait un froid de loup.

bitterness ['bɪtənɪs] n **1.** [of disappointment, person, taste] amertume *f* ; [of criticism, remark] âpreté *f* **2.** [of opposition] violence *f.*

bittersweet ['bɪtəswiːt] adj [memory, taste] aigre-doux.

bitty ['bɪtɪ] (*compar* **bittier,** *superl* **bittiest**) adj **1.** 🇬🇧 inf décousu **2.** 🇺🇸 [small] : *a little bitty town* une toute petite ville.

bitumen ['bɪtjumɪn] n bitume *m.*

bivouac ['bɪvuæk] (*pt* & *pp* **bivouacked,** *cont* **bivouacking**) n bivouac *m.*

biweekly [,baɪ'wiːklɪ] (*pl* **biweeklies**) ❖ adj [every two weeks] bimensuel ; [twice weekly] bihebdomadaire. ❖ adv [every two weeks] tous les quinze jours ; [twice weekly] deux fois par semaine.

biyearly [,baɪ'jɪəlɪ] (*pl* **biyearlies**) ❖ adj [every two years] biennal ; [twice yearly] semestriel. ❖ adv [every two years] tous les deux ans ; [twice yearly] deux fois par an.

biz [bɪz] n inf commerce *m* ▶ **the biz** 🇬🇧 [show-business] le monde du spectacle / *he's in the biz* il fait partie du monde du spectacle.

bizarre [bɪ'zɑːr] adj bizarre.

bk written abbr of **book.**

bl written abbr of **bill of lading.**

BL n **1.** (abbr of **Bachelor of Law(s)**) 🇬🇧 ≃ (titulaire d'une) licence de droit **2.** (abbr of **Bachelor of Letters**) 🇬🇧 ≃ (titulaire d'une) licence de lettres.

blab [blæb] (*pt* & *pp* **blabbed,** *cont* **blabbing**) inf vi **1.** [tell secret] vendre la mèche **2.** [prattle] jaser, babiller.

blabber ['blæbər] inf vi jaser, babiller ▶ **to blabber on about sthg** parler de qqch à n'en plus finir.

blabbermouth ['blæbə,mauθ] (*pl* [-mauðz]) n inf pipelette *f.*

black [blæk] ❖ adj **1.** [colour] noir **2.** [race] noir ▶ **black American** Afro-Américain *m,* -e *f* ▶ **black consciousness** négritude *f* ▶ **black man** Noir *m* ▶ **black woman** Noire *f* **3.** [dark] noir, sans lumière **4.** [gloomy - future, mood] noir ; [- despair] sombre / *they painted a black picture of our prospects* ils ont peint un sombre tableau de notre avenir **5.** [angry] furieux, menaçant / *he gave her a black look* il lui a jeté ou lancé un regard noir **6.** [wicked] noir, mauvais / *a black deed* un crime, un forfait. ❖ n **1.** [colour] noir *m* / *to be dressed in black* **a)** [gen] être habillé de ou en noir **b)** [in mourning] porter le deuil **2.** [darkness] obscurité *f*, noir *m* **3.** 🇵🇭🇷 **to be in the black** être créditeur ▶ *it's the new black* inf c'est très tendance. ❖ vt **1.** [make black] noircir ; [shoes] cirer *(avec du cirage noir)* / *he blacked his attacker's eye* il a poché l'œil de son agresseur **2.** 🇬🇧 INDUST boycotter. ❖ **Black** n [person] Noir *m,* -e *f.* ❖ **black out** ❖ vt sep **1.** [extinguish lights] plonger dans l'obscurité ; [in wartime] faire le black-out dans **2.** [memory] effacer (de son esprit), oublier. ❖ vi s'évanouir.

black and blue adj couvert de bleus.

black and white ❖ adj **1.** [photograph, television] noir et blanc **2.** fig [clear-cut] précis, net / *there's no black-and-white solution* le problème n'est pas simple. ❖ n [written down] ▶ **to put sthg down in black and white** écrire qqch noir sur blanc.

blackball ['blækbɔːl] vt blackbouler.

black belt n ceinture *f* noire / *she's a black belt in judo* elle est ceinture noire de judo.

blackberry ['blækbərı] (*pl* **blackberries**) n mûre *f*
▸ **blackberry bush** mûrier *m*.

blackbird ['blækbɜːd] n merle *m* ; [in North America]
étourneau *m*.

blackboard ['blækbɔːd] n tableau *m* (noir).

black box n boîte *f* noire.

black cab n taxi *m* londonien.

blackcurrant [,blæk'kʌrənt] n [bush, fruit] cassis *m*.

blacken ['blækn] ◆ vt **1.** [make black - house, wall] noircir ; [- shoes] cirer *(avec du cirage noir)* **2.** [make dirty] noircir,
salir **3.** *fig* [name, reputation] noircir, ternir. ◆ vi [cloud, sky]
s'assombrir, (se) noircir ; [colour, fruit] (se) noircir, devenir noir.

black eye n œil *m* poché or au beurre noir.

blackhead ['blækhed] n point *m* noir.

black hole n ASTRON trou *m* noir.

black ice n verglas *m*.

blackjack ['blækdʒæk] n [card game] vingt-et-un *m*.

blackleg ['blækleg] (*pt* & *pp* **blacklegged**, *cont*
blacklegging) n 🇬🇧 *pej* jaune *m*, briseur *m* de grève.

blacklist ['blæklɪst] ◆ n liste *f* noire. ◆ vt mettre sur
la liste noire.

black magic n magie *f* noire.

blackmail ['blækmeɪl] ◆ vt faire chanter / *he blackmailed them into meeting his demands* il les a contraints
par le chantage à satisfaire ses exigences. ◆ n chantage *m*.

blackmailer ['blækmeɪlə⁽ʳ⁾] n maître chanteur *m*.

black mark n mauvais point *m* / *it's a black mark
against her* ça joue contre elle.

black market n marché *m* noir / *on the black market*
au marché noir.

black marketeer n vendeur *m*, -euse *f* au marché
noir.

Black Monday n lundi *m* noir.

blackout ['blækaʊt] n **1.** [in wartime] black-out *m inv* ;
[power failure] panne *f* d'électricité **2.** [loss of consciousness]
évanouissement *m*, étourdissement *m* ; [amnesia] trou *m* de
mémoire.

black pepper n poivre *m* gris.

Black Power n POL Black Power *m* (*mouvement séparatiste noir né dans les années 1960 aux États-Unis*).

black pudding n 🇬🇧 boudin *m* (noir).

Black Sea pr n ▸ **the Black Sea** la mer Noire.

black sheep n brebis *f* galeuse.

blacksmith ['blæksmɪθ] n [for horses] maréchal-
ferrant *m* ; [for tools] forgeron *m*.

black spot n 🇬🇧 AUTO & *fig* point *m* noir.

black tie n *nœud papillon noir porté avec une tenue de soirée* / **'black tie'** [on invitation card] 'tenue de soirée exigée'.
◆ **black-tie** adj ▸ *it's black-tie* il faut être en smoking.

bladder ['blædə⁽ʳ⁾] n ANAT vessie *f*.

blade [bleɪd] n **1.** [cutting edge - of knife, razor, tool]
lame *f* ; [- of guillotine] couperet *m* **2.** [of grass] brin *m* ; [of
wheat] pousse *f* ; [of leaf] limbe *m*.

blah [blɑː] *inf* ◆ n [talk] baratin *m*, bla-bla-bla *m inv*.
◆ adj 🇺🇸 [uninteresting] insipide, ennuyeux.

Blairism ['bleərɪzm] n *politique de Tony Blair*.

Blairite ['bleəraɪt] ◆ n partisan *m* de la politique de
Tony Blair. ◆ adj [views, policies] du gouvernement de Tony
Blair.

blame [bleɪm] ◆ n **1.** [responsibility] responsabilité *f*,
faute *f* / *they laid* or *put the blame for the incident on
the secretary* ils ont rejeté la responsabilité de l'incident sur
la secrétaire / *we had to bear* or *to take the blame* nous
avons dû endosser la responsabilité **2.** [reproof] blâme *m*,

réprimande *f*. ◆ vt **1.** [consider as responsible] rejeter la
responsabilité sur / *he is not to blame* ce n'est pas de sa
faute / *you have only yourself to blame* tu ne peux t'en
prendre qu'à toi-même, tu l'as voulu or cherché **2.** [reproach] critiquer, reprocher / *I blame myself for having
left her alone* je m'en veux de l'avoir laissée seule / *I don't
blame you!* (comme) je te comprends !

blameless ['bleɪmlɪs] adj irréprochable, sans reproche.

blameworthy ['bleɪm,wɜːðɪ] adj *fml* [person] fautif,
coupable ; [action] répréhensible.

blanch [blɑːntʃ] vt [gen] décolorer, blanchir ; AGR & CULIN
blanchir ▸ **blanched almonds** amandes *fpl* mondées or
épluchées.

blancmange [blə'mɒndʒ] n *entremets généralement préparé à partir d'une poudre* ; ≃ flan *m* instantané.

bland [blænd] adj **1.** [flavour, food] fade, insipide ; [diet]
fade **2.** [person - dull] insipide, ennuyeux ; [- ingratiating]
mielleux, doucereux.

blandly ['blændlɪ] adv [say - dully] affablement, avec affabilité ; [- ingratiatingly] d'un ton mielleux.

blank [blæŋk] ◆ adj **1.** [paper - with no writing] vierge,
blanc (blanche) ; [- unruled] blanc (blanche) ; [form] vierge,
à remplir / *fill in the blank spaces* remplissez les blancs or
les (espaces) vides / *leave this line blank* n'écrivez rien sur
cette ligne **2.** [empty - screen, wall] vide ; [- cassette] vierge ;
[- cartridge] à blanc ▸ **to go blank a)** [screen] s'éteindre
b) [face] se vider de toute expression / *my mind went
blank* j'ai eu un trou **3.** [face, look - expressionless] vide,
sans expression ; [- confused] déconcerté, dérouté **4.** [absolute - protest, refusal] absolu, net ; [- dismay] absolu, profond.
◆ n **1.** [empty space, void] blanc *m*, (espace *m*) vide *m* /
my mind was a total blank j'ai eu un passage à vide complet ▸ **to draw a blank** avoir un trou or un passage à vide
2. [form] formulaire *m* (vierge or à remplir), imprimé *m*
3. [cartridge] cartouche *f* à blanc. ◆ **blank out** vt sep
[writing] rayer, effacer ; [memory] oublier, effacer de son
esprit.

blank cheque n chèque *m* en blanc ▸ **to write sb a
blank cheque** *fig* donner carte blanche à qqn.

blanket ['blæŋkɪt] ◆ n **1.** [for bed] couverture *f* **2.** *fig*
[of clouds, snow] couche *f* ; [of fog] manteau *m*, nappe *f* ; [of
smoke] voile *m*, nuage *m* ; [of despair, sadness] manteau *m*.
◆ adj général, global.

blanket bath n grande toilette *f* (*d'un malade alité*).

blankly ['blæŋklɪ] adv **1.** [look - without expression] avec
le regard vide ; [- with confusion] d'un air ahuri or interdit
2. [answer, state] carrément ; [refuse] tout net, sans ambages.

blank verse n vers *mpl* blancs or sans rime.

blare [bleə⁽ʳ⁾] ◆ vi [siren, music] beugler ; [voice] brailler.
◆ n [gen] vacarme *m* ; [of car horn, siren] bruit *m* strident ;
[of radio, television] beuglement *m* ; [of trumpet] sonnerie *f*.
◆ **blare out** ◆ vi [radio, television] beugler, brailler ;
[person, voice] brailler, hurler. ◆ vt sep [subj: radio, television] beugler, brailler ; [subj: person] brailler, hurler.

blarney ['blɑːnɪ] *inf* n [smooth talk] baratin *m* ; [flattery]
flatterie *f*.

blasé [🇬🇧 'blɑːzeɪ 🇺🇸 ,blɑː'zeɪ] adj blasé.

blaspheme [blæs'fiːm] ◆ vi blasphémer. ◆ vt blasphémer.

blasphemous ['blæsfəməs] adj [poem, talk] blasphématoire ; [person] blasphémateur.

blasphemy ['blæsfəmɪ] (*pl* **blasphemies**) n blasphème *m*.

blast [blɑːst] ◆ n **1.** [explosion] explosion *f* ; [shock
wave] souffle *m* **2.** [of air] bouffée *f* ; [of steam] jet *m*
3. [sound of car horn, whistle] coup *m* strident ; [- of trumpet] sonnerie *f* ; [- of explosion] détonation *f* ; [- of rocket]

rugissement *m* **4.** PHR **at full blast** : *she had the radio on (at) full blast* elle faisait marcher la radio à fond. ◆ vt **1.** [with explosives] faire sauter / *they blasted a tunnel through the mountain* ils ont creusé un tunnel à travers la montagne avec des explosifs **2.** [with gun] tirer sur. ◆ interj UK *inf* ▶ **blast!** zut ! ◆ **blast off** vi [rocket] décoller. ◆ **blast out** ◆ vt sep [music] beugler. ◆ vi [radio, television] beugler ; [music] retentir.

blasted ['blɑːstɪd] adj *inf* [as intensifier] fichu, sacré / *it's a blasted nuisance! c'est vraiment casse-pieds !

blast furnace n haut-fourneau *m*.

blast-off n lancement *m*, mise *f* à feu *(d'une fusée spatiale).

blatant ['bleɪtənt] adj [discrimination, injustice] évident, flagrant ; [lie] manifeste.

blatantly ['bleɪtəntlɪ] adv [discriminate, disregard] de façon flagrante ; [cheat, lie] de façon éhontée.

blaze [bleɪz] ◆ n **1.** [flame] flamme *f*, flammes *fpl*, feu *m* ; [large fire] incendie *m* **2.** [burst - of colour] éclat *m*, flamboiement *m* ; [- of light] éclat *m* ; [- of eloquence, enthusiasm] élan *m*, transport *m* ; [- of sunlight] torrent *m* / *she married in a blaze of publicity* elle s'est mariée sous les feux des projecteurs / *he finished in a blaze of glory* il a terminé en beauté. ◆ vi **1.** [fire] flamber / *he suddenly blazed with anger* il s'est enflammé de colère **2.** [colour, light, sun] flamboyer ; [gem] resplendir, briller. ◆ vt **1.** [proclaim] proclamer, claironner ; [publish] publier **2.** PHR **to blaze a trail** frayer un chemin.

blazer ['bleɪzər] n blazer *m*.

blazing ['bleɪzɪŋ] adj **1.** [building, town] en flammes, embrasé **2.** [sun] brûlant, ardent ; [heat] torride **3.** [light] éclatant ; [colour] très vif ; [gem] brillant, étincelant ; [eyes] qui jette des éclairs **4.** [argument] violent **5.** [angry] furieux.

bldg written abbr of **building**.

bleach [bliːtʃ] ◆ n [gen] décolorant *m* ▶ **household bleach** eau *f* de Javel. ◆ vt **1.** [gen] blanchir **2.** [hair - chemically] décolorer, oxygéner ; [- with sun] éclaircir / *to bleach one's hair* se décolorer les cheveux / *a bleached blonde* une fausse blonde, une blonde décolorée.

bleachers ['bliːtʃəz] pl n US *dans un stade, places les moins chères car non abritées*.

bleak [bliːk] adj **1.** [place, room] froid, austère ; [landscape] morne, désolé **2.** [weather] morne, maussade ; [winter] rude, rigoureux **3.** [situation] sombre, morne ; [life] morne, monotone / *the future looks bleak* l'avenir se présente plutôt mal.

bleary ['blɪərɪ] *(compar* **blearier***, superl* **bleariest***)* adj [eyes - from fatigue] trouble, voilé ; [- watery] larmoyant ; [vision] trouble.

bleary-eyed [-'aɪd] adj [from sleep] aux yeux troubles ; [watery-eyed] aux yeux vitreux.

bleat [bliːt] ◆ vi **1.** [sheep] bêler ; [goat] bêler, chevroter **2.** [person - speak] bêler, chevroter ; [- whine] geindre, bêler. ◆ n **1.** [of sheep] bêlement *m* ; [of goat] bêlement *m*, chevrotement *m* **2.** [of person - voice] bêlement *m* ; [- complaint] gémissement *m*.

bleed [bliːd] *(pt & pp* **bled** [bled]*)* ◆ vi [lose blood] saigner, perdre du sang / *to bleed to death* saigner à mort / *my heart bleeds for you!* fig & *iro* tu me fends le cœur ! ◆ vt **1.** fig [extort money from] saigner ▶ **to bleed sb dry** or **white** saigner qqn à blanc **2.** [brake, radiator] purger.

bleeding ['bliːdɪŋ] ◆ n [loss of blood] saignement *m* ; [haemorrhage] hémorragie *f* ; [taking of blood] saignée *f*. ◆ adj [wound] saignant, qui saigne ; [person] qui saigne.

bleep [bliːp] ◆ n bip *m*, bip-bip *m*. ◆ vi émettre un bip or un bip-bip. ◆ vt [doctor] appeler (au moyen d'un bip or d'un bip-bip).

bleeper ['bliːpər] n bip *m*, bip-bip *m*.

blemish ['blemɪʃ] ◆ n **1.** [flaw] défaut *m*, imperfection *f* **2.** [on face - pimple] bouton *m* **3.** [on fruit] tache *f* **4.** fig [on name, reputation] tache *f*, souillure *f* liter. ◆ vt **1.** [beauty, landscape] gâter ; [fruit] tacher **2.** fig [reputation] tacher, souiller liter.

blend [blend] ◆ vt **1.** [mix together - gen] mélanger, mêler ; [- cultures, races] fusionner ; [- feelings, qualities] joindre, unir **2.** [colours - mix together] mêler, mélanger ; [- put together] marier. ◆ vi **1.** [mix together - gen] se mélanger, se mêler ; [- cultures, races] fusionner ; [- feelings, sounds] se confondre, se mêler ; [- perfumes] se marier / *the new student blended in well* le nouvel étudiant s'est bien intégré **2.** [colours - form one shade] se fondre ; [- go well together] aller ensemble. ◆ n **1.** [mixture] mélange *m* **2.** fig [of feelings, qualities] alliance *f*, mélange *m*.

blended learning ['blendɪd-] n apprentissage *m* mixte *(en présenciel et à distance).

blender ['blendər] n CULIN mixer *m* ; TECH malaxeur *m*.

bless [bles] *(pt & pp* **blessed***)* vt **1.** [subj: God, priest] bénir / *bless you!* a) [after sneeze] à vos / tes souhaits ! b) [in thanks] merci mille fois ! / *he remembered her birthday, bless his heart!* et il n'a pas oublié son anniversaire, le petit chéri ! ▶ **I'm blessed if I know!** *inf* que le diable m'emporte si je sais ! **2.** *(usu passive)* fml [endow, grant] douer, doter / *she is blessed with excellent health* elle a le bonheur d'avoir une excellente santé.

blessed ◆ pt & pp ⟶ **bless**. ◆ adj ['blesɪd] **1.** [holy] béni, sacré ▶ **the Blessed Virgin** la Sainte Vierge **2.** [favoured by God] bienheureux, heureux **3.** *inf* [as intensifier] sacré, fichu.

blessing ['blesɪŋ] n **1.** [God's favour] grâce *f*, faveur *f* **2.** [prayer] bénédiction *f* ; [before meal] bénédicité *m* **3.** fig [approval] bénédiction *f*, approbation *f* **4.** [advantage] bienfait *m*, avantage *m* ; [godsend] aubaine *f*, bénédiction *f* / *it was a blessing that no one was hurt* c'était une chance que personne ne soit blessé / *it was a blessing in disguise* c'était une bonne chose, en fin de compte.

blest [blest] pt, pp, adj & pl n *arch & liter* = **blessed**.

blew [bluː] pt ⟶ **blow**.

blight [blaɪt] ◆ n **1.** BOT [of flowering plants] rouille *f* ; [of fruit trees] cloque *f* ; [of cereals] rouille, nielle *f* ; [of potato plants] mildiou *m* **2.** [curse] malheur *m*, fléau *m* / *the accident cast a blight on our holiday* l'accident a gâché nos vacances **3.** [condition of decay] ▶ **inner-city blight** la dégradation des quartiers pauvres. ◆ vt **1.** BOT [plants - gen] rouiller ; [cereals] nieller, nouiller **2.** [spoil - happiness, holiday] gâcher ; [- career, life] gâcher, briser ; [- hopes] anéantir, détruire ; [- plans] déjouer.

blighty, Blighty ['blaɪtɪ] n UK *inf & dated* l'Angleterre *f*.

blimey ['blaɪmɪ] interj UK *inf* ▶ **blimey!** ça alors !, mon Dieu !

blind [blaɪnd] ◆ adj **1.** [sightless] aveugle, non voyant ▶ **to go blind** devenir aveugle / *he's blind in one eye* il est aveugle d'un œil or borgne ▶ **to turn a blind eye to sthg** fermer les yeux sur qqch **2.** [unthinking] aveugle / *he flew into a blind rage* il s'est mis dans une colère noire / *she was blind to the consequences* elle ignorait les conséquences, elle ne voyait pas les conséquences **3.** [hidden from sight - corner, turning] sans visibilité **4.** [as intensifier] : *he didn't take a blind bit of notice of what I said* inf il n'a pas fait la moindre attention à ce que j'ai dit / *it doesn't make a blind bit of difference to me* inf cela m'est complètement égal. ◆ vt **1.** [deprive of sight] aveugler, rendre aveugle ; [subj: flash of light] aveugler, éblouir **2.** [deprive of judgment, reason] aveugler / *vanity blinded him to her* *real motives* sa vanité l'empêchait de discerner ses véritables intentions. ◆ n [for window] store *m*, jalousie *f*. ◆ pl n ▶ **the blind** les aveugles *mpl*, les non-voyants *mpl* / *it's a case of the blind leading the blind* c'est l'aveugle qui conduit l'aveugle. ◆ adv **1.** [drive, fly - without visibility] sans visibilité ; [-using only instruments] aux instruments **2.** [purchase] sans avoir vu ; [decide] à l'aveuglette **3.** [as intensifier] : *I would swear blind he was there* j'aurais donné ma tête à couper or j'aurais juré qu'il était là.

blind alley n UK impasse *f*, cul-de-sac *m*.

blind corner n UK AUTO virage *m* sans visibilité.

blind date n rendez-vous *m* or rencontre *f* arrangée *(avec quelqu'un qu'on ne connaît pas)*.

blinders ['blaɪndəz] pl n US œillères *fpl*.

blindfold ['blaɪndfəʊld] ◆ n bandeau *m*. ◆ vt bander les yeux à or de. ◆ adv les yeux bandés / *I could do the job blindfold* je pourrais faire ce travail les yeux bandés or fermés. ◆ adj : *blindfold* or *blindfolded prisoners* prisonniers aux yeux bandés.

blinding ['blaɪndɪŋ] adj [light] aveuglant, éblouissant ; *fig* [speed] éblouissant.

blindly ['blaɪndlɪ] adv [unseeingly] en aveugle, à l'aveuglette ; [without thinking] à l'aveuglette, aveuglément.

blindness ['blaɪndnɪs] n cécité *f* ; *fig* aveuglement *m*.

blind side n AUTO angle *m* mort.

blind spot n **1.** AUTO [in mirror] angle *m* mort ; [in road] endroit *m* sans visibilité **2.** *fig* [weak area] côté *m* faible, faiblesse *f* / *I have a blind spot about mathematics* je ne comprends rien aux mathématiques.

blind test n test *m* aveugle.

blind testing n tests *mpl* aveugles.

bling ['blɪŋ], **bling-bling** ['blɪŋ'blɪŋ] *inf* ◆ adj **1.** [jewellery] clinquant **2.** [approach, attitude] bling-bling / *the bling-bling generation* la génération bling-bling. ◆ n [jewellery] bijoux *mpl* lourds et clinquants.

blini ['blɪni:] pl n blinis *mpl*.

blink [blɪŋk] ◆ vi **1.** [person] cligner or clignoter des yeux ; [eyes] cligner, clignoter **2.** [light] clignoter, vaciller. ◆ vt ▶ **to blink one's eyes** cligner les or des yeux. ◆ n **1.** [of eyelid] clignement *m* (des yeux), battement *m* de paupières ▶ **in the blink of an eye** or **eyelid** en un clin d'œil, en un rien de temps **2.** PHR **on the blink** *inf* en panne.

blinkered ['blɪŋkəd] adj [opinion, view] borné.

blinkers ['blɪŋkəz] pl n [for eyes] œillères *fpl* / *when it comes to her family she wears blinkers* elle a des œillères quand il s'agit de sa famille.

blinking ['blɪŋkɪŋ] *inf* adj UK *euph* sacré, fichu ▶ **blinking idiot!** espèce d'idiot !

blip [blɪp] n **1.** [sound] bip *m*, bip-bip *m* ; [spot of light] spot *m* ; [on graph, screen, etc.] sommet *m* **2.** [temporary problem] mauvais moment *m* (à passer).

bliss [blɪs] n [happiness] bonheur *m* (complet or absolu), contentement *m*, félicité *f liter* / *our holiday was absolute bliss!* on a passé des vacances absolument merveilleuses or divines !

blissful ['blɪsfʊl] adj [happy] bienheureux ; [peaceful] serein / *she remained in blissful ignorance* elle était heureuse dans son ignorance.

blissfully ['blɪsfʊlɪ] adv [agree, smile] d'un air heureux ; [peaceful, quiet] merveilleusement.

blister ['blɪstə*ʳ*] ◆ n [on skin] ampoule *f*, cloque *f*. ◆ vi [skin] se couvrir d'ampoules.

blistering ['blɪstərɪŋ] adj **1.** [sun] brûlant, de plomb ; [heat] torride **2.** [attack, criticism] cinglant, virulent ; [remark] caustique, cinglant.

blisteringly ['blɪstərɪŋlɪ] adv : *it was blisteringly hot* il faisait une chaleur étouffante.

blister pack n UK [for light bulb, pens] emballage *m* bulle, blister (pack) *m* ; [for pills] plaquette *f*.

blithe [blaɪð] adj [cheerful] gai, joyeux ; [carefree] insouciant.

blithely ['blaɪðlɪ] adv [cheerfully] gaiement, joyeusement ; [carelessly] avec insouciance.

blithering ['blɪðərɪŋ] adj *inf* sacré / *a blithering idiot* un crétin fini.

BLitt [,bi:'lɪt] (abbr of **Bachelor of Letters**) n UK *(titulaire d'une licence)* de littérature.

blitz [blɪts] ◆ n [attack] attaque *f* éclair ; [bombing] bombardement *m* / *let's have a blitz and get this work done* attaquons-nous à ce travail pour en finir. ◆ vt [attack] pilonner ; [bomb] bombarder. ◆ **Blitz** n HIST ▶ **the Blitz** le Blitz.

blitzed [blɪtst] adj US *inf* [drunk] bourré.

blizzard ['blɪzəd] n tempête *f* de neige, blizzard *m*.

BLM (abbr of **Bureau of Land Management**) pr n services de l'aménagement du territoire aux États-Unis.

bloated ['bləʊtɪd] adj [gen] gonflé, boursouflé ; [stomach] gonflé, ballonné / *to feel bloated* se sentir ballonné.

bloatware ['bləʊtweə*ʳ*] n logiciels offrant un nombre excessif de fonctionnalités.

blob [blɒb] n [drop] goutte *f* ; [stain] tache *f*.

bloc [blɒk] n bloc *m*.

block [blɒk] ◆ n **1.** [of ice, stone, wood] bloc *m* ; [for butcher, executioner] billot *m* / *the painting was on the (auctioneer's) block* US le tableau était mis aux enchères **2.** [toy] ▶ **(building) blocks** jeu *m* de construction, (jeu de) cubes *mpl* **3.** [of seats] groupe *m* ; [of shares] tranche *f* ; [of tickets] série *f* ; COMPUT bloc *m* **4.** [area of land] pâté *m* de maisons / *the school is five blocks away* US l'école est cinq rues plus loin **5.** UK [building] immeuble *m* ; [of barracks, prison] quartier *m* ; [of hospital] pavillon *m* ▶ **block of flats** immeuble (d'habitation) **6.** [obstruction - in pipe, tube] obstruction *f* ; [-in traffic] embouteillage *m* ; MED & PSYCHOL blocage *m* ▶ **to have a (mental) block about sthg** faire un blocage sur qqch. ◆ comp [booking, vote] groupé. ◆ vt **1.** [obstruct - pipe, tube] boucher ; [-road] bloquer, barrer ; [-view] boucher, cacher ; MED [-artery] obstruer ▶ **to block sb's way** barrer le chemin à qqn **2.** [hinder - traffic] bloquer, gêner ; [-progress] gêner, enrayer ; [-credit, deal, funds] bloquer ; MED [pain] anesthésier ; SPORT [opponent] faire obstruction à. ◆ **block off** vt sep [road] bloquer, barrer ; [door, part of road, window] condamner ; [view] boucher, cacher ; [sun] cacher. ◆ **block out** vt sep **1.** [light, sun] empêcher d'entrer ; [view] cacher, boucher **2.** [ideas] empêcher ; [memory] interdire, censurer. ◆ **block up** vt sep **1.** [pipe, tube] boucher, bloquer ; [sink] boucher **2.** [door, window] condamner.

blockade [blɒ'keɪd] ◆ n MIL blocus *m* / *to lift* or *to raise a blockade* lever un blocus. ◆ vt **1.** MIL faire le blocus de **2.** *fig* [obstruct] bloquer, obstruer.

blockage ['blɒkɪdʒ] n [gen] obstruction *f* ; [in pipe] obstruction *f*, bouchon *m* ; MED [in heart] blocage *m*, obstruction *f* ; [in intestine] occlusion *f* ; PSYCHOL blocage *m*.

blockbuster ['blɒkbʌstə*ʳ*] n *inf* [success - book] bestseller *m*, livre *m* à succès ; [-film] superproduction *f*.

block capital n (caractère *m*) majuscule *f* / *in block capitals* en majuscules.

blockhead ['blɒkhed] n *inf* imbécile *mf*, idiot *m*, -e *f*.

blocking software ['blɒkɪŋ-] n COMPUT logiciel *m* de filtrage.

block letter n (caractère m) majuscule f / in block letters en majuscules (d'imprimerie).

block release n 🇬🇧 INDUST système de stages de formation qui alternent avec une activité professionnelle.

block scheduling ['blɒk,skedʒulɪŋ] n 🇺🇸 SCH journée scolaire organisée en 4 blocs de 90 minutes chacun.

block vote n mode de scrutin utilisé par les syndicats britanniques par opposition au mode de scrutin « OMOV ».

 Block vote

Le **block vote** donne au vote d'un délégué syndical la valeur de toutes les voix de la section qu'il représente.

blog ['blɒg] n COMPUT blog m, blogue m.

blogger ['blɒgə] n COMPUT blogueur m, -euse f.

blogging ['blɒgɪŋ] n COMPUT blogging m, création f de blogs.

blogosphere ['blɒgəusfɪə] n blogosphère m.

blogroll ['blɒgrəul] n blogroll f, liste f de liens vers des blogs.

bloke [bləuk] n 🇬🇧 inf type m.

blokeish ['bləukɪʃ], **blokey** ['bləukɪ] adj inf [behaviour, humour] de mec ; [joke] macho.

blond [blɒnd] ◆ adj blond. ◆ n blond m.

blonde [blɒnd] ◆ adj blond. ◆ n blond m, -e f.

blood [blʌd] n **1.** [fluid] sang m / to donate or to give blood donner son sang / he has blood on his hands fig il a du sang sur les mains ▸ his attitude makes my blood boil son attitude me met hors de moi ▸ it's like getting blood out of a stone ce n'est pas une mince affaire ▸ her blood froze or ran cold at the thought rien qu'à y penser son sang s'est figé dans ses veines ▸ the town's blood is up over these new taxes la ville s'élève or part en guerre contre les nouveaux impôts ▸ travelling is or runs in her blood elle a le voyage dans le sang or dans la peau ▸ new or fresh or young blood : what we need is young blood nous avons besoin de sang neuf **2.** [breeding, kinship] : of noble / Italian blood de sang noble / italien. ❖ **bad blood** n ressentiment m, rancune f / there is bad blood between the two families le torchon brûle entre les deux familles.

blood bank n banque f du sang.

bloodbath ['blʌdbɑːθ] (pl [-bɑːðz]) n massacre m, bain m de sang.

blood brother n frère m de sang.

blood cell n cellule f sanguine, globule m (du sang).

blood count n numération f globulaire.

bloodcurdling ['blʌd,kɜːdlɪŋ] adj terrifiant / a bloodcurdling scream un cri à vous glacer or figer le sang.

blood donor n donneur m, -euse f de sang.

blood group n groupe m sanguin.

bloodhound ['blʌdhaund] n [dog] limier m.

bloodless ['blʌdlɪs] adj **1.** [battle, victory] sans effusion de sang **2.** [cheeks, face] pâle.

bloodletting ['blʌd,letɪŋ] n **1.** [bloodshed] carnage m, massacre m **2.** MED saignée f.

blood money n prix m du sang.

blood orange n (orange f) sanguine f.

blood poisoning n septicémie f.

blood pressure n tension f (artérielle) / the doctor took my blood pressure le médecin m'a pris la tension ▸ to have high / low blood pressure faire de l'hypertension / de l'hypotension.

blood red adj rouge sang (inv).

blood relation, blood relative n parent m, -e f par le sang.

bloodshed ['blʌdʃed] n carnage m, massacre m.

bloodshot ['blʌdʃɒt] adj injecté (de sang).

blood-spattered adj maculé de sang.

blood sport n 🇬🇧 sport m sanguinaire.

bloodstained ['blʌdsteɪnd] adj taché de sang.

bloodstream ['blʌdstriːm] n sang m, système m sanguin.

blood sugar n glycémie f ▸ **blood-sugar level** taux m de glycémie.

blood test n analyse f de sang.

bloodthirsty ['blʌd,θɜːstɪ] (compar bloodthirstier, superl bloodthirstiest) adj [animal, person] assoiffé or avide de sang, sanguinaire liter ; [film] violent, sanguinaire liter.

blood transfusion n transfusion f sanguine or de sang.

blood type n groupe m sanguin.

blood vessel n vaisseau m sanguin.

bloody ['blʌdɪ] (compar bloodier, superl bloodiest) ◆ adj **1.** [wound] sanglant, saignant ; [bandage, clothing, hand] taché or couvert de sang ; [nose] en sang **2.** [battle, fight] sanglant, meurtrier **3.** 🇬🇧 v inf [as intensifier] foutu / you bloody fool! espèce de crétin ! / bloody hell! et merde ! ◆ adv 🇬🇧 v inf vachement / you can bloody well do it yourself! tu n'as qu'à te démerder (tout seul) ! ◆ vt ensanglanter, couvrir de sang.

bloody-minded adj 🇬🇧 inf [person] vache ; [attitude, behaviour] buté, têtu.

bloody-mindedness [-'maɪndɪdnɪs] n 🇬🇧 inf caractère m difficile.

bloom [bluːm] ◆ n **1.** [flower] fleur f **2.** [state] : the roses are just coming into bloom les roses commencent tout juste à fleurir or à s'épanouir / to be in bloom a) [lily, rose] être éclos b) [bush, garden, tree] être en floraison or en fleurs **3.** [of cheeks, face] éclat m. ◆ vi **1.** [flower] éclore ; [bush, tree] fleurir ; [garden] se couvrir de fleurs **2.** fig [person] être en pleine forme ; [arts, industry] prospérer.

bloomer ['bluːmə] n 🇬🇧 CULIN [loaf] pain cranté sur le dessus.

blooming ['bluːmɪŋ] adj **1.** [flower] éclos ; [bush, garden, tree] en fleur, fleuri **2.** [glowing - with health] resplendissant, florissant ; [- with happiness] épanoui, rayonnant **3.** 🇬🇧 inf [as intensifier] sacré, fichu.

blooper ['bluːpə] n 🇺🇸 inf gaffe f, faux pas m.

blossom ['blɒsəm] ◆ n **1.** [flower] fleur f **2.** [state] : to be in blossom être en fleurs. ◆ vi **1.** [flower] éclore ; [bush, tree] fleurir **2.** fig [person] s'épanouir ; [arts, industry] prospérer / she blossomed into a talented writer elle est devenue un écrivain doué.

blot [blɒt] (pt & pp blotted, cont blotting) ◆ n **1.** [spot - gen] tache f ; [- of ink] tache f, pâté m **2.** fig [on character, name] tache f, souillure f ; [on civilization, system] tare f / it's a blot on the landscape ça gâche le paysage. ◆ vt **1.** [dry] sécher **2.** [spot] tacher ; [with ink] tacher, faire des pâtés sur ▸ to blot one's copybook salir sa réputation. ❖ **blot out** vt sep [obscure - light, sun] cacher, masquer ; [- memory, thought] effacer ; [- act, event] éclipser.

blotchy ['blɒtʃɪ] (compar blotchier, superl blotchiest) adj [complexion, skin] marbré, couvert de taches or de marbrures ; [cloth, paper, report] couvert de taches.

blotting paper n (papier m) buvard m.

blouse [blauz] n [for woman] chemisier m, corsage m ; [for farmer, worker] blouse f.

blouson ['bluːzɒn] n 🇬🇧 blouson *m*.

blow [bləʊ] (*pt* blew [bluː], *pp* blown [bləʊn]) ◆ n **1.** [hit] coup *m* ; [with fist] coup *m* de poing ▶ **to come to blows** en venir aux mains **2.** [setback] coup *m*, malheur *m* ; [shock] coup *m*, choc *m* / *to soften* or *to cushion the blow* amortir le choc ▶ **to deal sb / sthg a (serious) blow** porter un coup (terrible) à qqn / qqch / *it was a big blow to her pride* son orgueil en a pris un coup. ◆ vi **1.** [wind] souffler / *it's blowing a gale out there* le vent souffle en tempête là-bas / *let's wait and see which way the wind blows* fig attendons de voir de quel côté or d'où souffle le vent **2.** [person] souffler / *she blew on her hands / on her coffee* elle a soufflé dans ses mains / sur son café / *he blows hot and cold* il souffle le chaud et le froid **3.** [move with wind] : *the window blew open / shut* un coup de vent a ouvert / fermé la fenêtre **4.** [wind instrument] sonner ; [whistle] siffler **5.** [explode - tyre] éclater. ◆ vt **1.** [wind] faire bouger ; [leaves] chasser, faire envoler / *the wind blew the door open / shut* un coup de vent a ouvert / fermé la porte / *the hurricane blew the ship off course* l'ouragan a fait dévier or a dérouté le navire **2.** [subj: person] souffler / *blow your nose !* mouche-toi ! / *he blew the dust off the book* il a soufflé sur le livre pour enlever la poussière ▶ **to blow sb a kiss** envoyer un baiser à qqn **3.** [bubbles, glass] : *to blow bubbles / smoke rings* faire des bulles / ronds de fumée / *to blow glass* souffler le verre **4.** [wind instrument] jouer de ; [whistle] faire retentir / *the referee blew his whistle for time* l'arbitre a sifflé la fin du match ▶ **to blow one's own trumpet** se vanter **5.** [tyre] faire éclater ; [fuse, safe] faire sauter / *the house was blown to pieces* la maison a été entièrement détruite par l'explosion / *their plans were blown sky-high* leurs projets sont tombés à l'eau / *he blew a gasket* 🇬🇧 or *a fuse when he found out* quand il l'a appris, il a piqué une crise **6.** *inf* [squander - money] claquer **7.** [spoil - chance] gâcher / *I blew it!* j'ai tout gâché ! **8.** 🇬🇧 *inf* [disregard] : *blow the expense, we're going out to dinner* au diable l'avarice, on sort dîner ce soir **9.** *inf* 𝗣𝗛𝗥 *the idea blew his mind* l'idée l'a fait flipper ▶ **oh, blow (it)!** 🇬🇧 la barbe !, mince ! ▶ **to blow one's lid** or **stack** or **top** exploser de rage. ❖ **blow away** vt sep **1.** [subj: wind] chasser, disperser **2.** *inf* [astound] sidérer **3.** *inf* [kill] abattre. ❖ **blow down** ◆ vi être abattu par le vent, tomber. ◆ vt sep [subj: wind] faire tomber, renverser ; [subj: person] faire tomber or abattre (en soufflant). ❖ **blow off** ◆ vi [hat, roof] s'envoler. ◆ vt sep **1.** [subj: wind] emporter **2.** [release] laisser échapper, lâcher ▶ **to blow off steam** *inf* dire ce qu'on a sur le cœur **3.** 🇺🇸 *inf* ▶ **to blow sb off a)** [not turn up] poser un lapin à qqn **b)** [ignore] snober qqn **c)** [rebuff] donner un râteau à qqn. ❖ **blow out** ◆ vt sep **1.** [extinguish - candle] souffler ; [- fuse] faire sauter / *to blow one's brains out* se faire sauter or se brûler la cervelle **2.** [subj: storm] : *the hurricane eventually blew itself out* l'ouragan s'est finalement calmé **3.** [cheeks] gonfler. ◆ vi [fuse] sauter ; [candle] s'éteindre ; [tyre] éclater. ❖ **blow over** ◆ vi [storm] se calmer, passer ; *fig* : *the scandal soon blew over* le scandale fut vite oublié. ◆ vt sep [tree] abattre, renverser. ❖ **blow up** ◆ vt sep **1.** [explode - bomb] faire exploser or sauter ; [- building] faire sauter **2.** [inflate] gonfler **3.** [enlarge] agrandir ; [exaggerate] exagérer. ◆ vi **1.** [explode] exploser, sauter / *the plan blew up in their faces* le projet leur a claqué dans les doigts **2.** [begin - wind] se lever ; [- storm] se préparer ; [- crisis] se déclencher **3.** *inf* [lose one's temper] exploser, se mettre en boule.

blow-by-blow adj détaillé / *she gave me a blow-by-blow account* elle m'a tout raconté en détail.

blow-dry ◆ vt faire un brushing à. ◆ n brushing *m*.

blowfly ['bləʊflaɪ] (*pl* **blowflies**) n mouche *f* à viande.

blowgun ['bləʊgʌn] n 🇺🇸 sarbacane *f*.

blow job n *vulg* ▶ **to give sb a blow job** tailler une pipe à qqn.

blowlamp ['bləʊlæmp] n 🇬🇧 lampe *f* à souder, chalumeau *m*.

blown [bləʊn] pp ⟶ **blow**.

blown glass ◆ n verre *m* soufflé. ◆ adj en verre soufflé.

blowout ['bləʊaʊt] n **1.** [of tyre] éclatement *m* / *I had a blowout* j'ai un pneu qui a éclaté **2.** 🇬🇧 *inf* [meal] gueuleton *m*.

blowpipe ['bləʊpaɪp] n **1.** 🇬🇧 [weapon] sarbacane *f* **2.** CHEM & INDUST [tube] chalumeau *m* ; [glassmaking] canne *f* de souffleur, fêle *f*.

blowtorch ['bləʊtɔːtʃ] n lampe *f* à souder, chalumeau *m*.

blowzy ['blaʊzɪ] (*compar* **blowzier**, *superl* **blowziest**) adj 🇬🇧 *pej* [untidy] débraillé ; [sluttish] sale, de souillon.

BLS (abbr of **Bureau of Labor Statistics**) pr n *institut de statistiques du travail aux États-Unis.*

BLT (abbr of **bacon, lettuce and tomato**) n *sandwich avec du bacon, de la laitue et de la tomate.*

blubber ['blʌbər] ◆ n [of whale] blanc *m* de baleine ; *inf & pej* [of person] graisse *f*. ◆ vi pleurer comme un veau or une Madeleine.

bludgeon ['blʌdʒən] vt **1.** [beat] matraquer **2.** [force] contraindre, forcer / *they bludgeoned him into selling the house* ils lui ont forcé la main pour qu'il vende la maison.

blue [bluː] (*cont* **blueing** or **bluing**) ◆ n [colour] bleu *m*, azur *m*. ◆ adj **1.** [colour] bleu / *to be blue with cold* être bleu de froid / *you can argue until you're blue in the face but she still won't give in* vous pouvez vous tuer à discuter, elle ne s'avouera pas vaincue pour autant **2.** [depressed] triste, cafardeux / *to feel blue* avoir le cafard **3.** [obscene - language] obscène, cochon ; [- book, movie] porno **4.** *inf* 𝗣𝗛𝗥 *once in a blue moon* tous les trente-six du mois. ❖ **blues** n **1.** *inf* ▶ **the blues** [depression] le cafard / *to get* or *to have the blues* avoir le cafard **2.** MUS ▶ **the blues** le blues. ❖ **out of the blue** adv phr sans prévenir / *the job offer came out of the blue* la proposition de travail est tombée du ciel.

blue baby n enfant *m* bleu, enfant *f* bleue.

blue badge n 🇬🇧 [for disabled drivers] *carte de conducteur handicapé.*

bluebell ['bluːbel] n jacinthe *f* des bois.

blueberry ['bluːbərɪ] (*pl* **blueberries**) n myrtille *f*.

bluebird ['bluːbɜːd] n oiseau *m* bleu.

blue-black adj bleu tirant sur le noir, bleu-noir.

blue-blooded adj aristocratique, de sang noble.

bluebottle ['bluːˌbɒtl] n [fly] mouche *f* bleue or de la viande.

blue cheese n (fromage *m*) bleu *m*.

blue chip n [stock] valeur *f* de premier ordre ; [property] placement *m* de bon rapport. ❖ **blue-chip** comp [securities, stock] de premier ordre.

blue-collar adj [gen] ouvrier ; [area, background] populaire, ouvrier ▶ **blue-collar worker** col *m* bleu.

blue-eyed adj aux yeux bleus ▶ **the blue-eyed boy** 🇬🇧 *inf* le chouchou.

blue-green adj bleu-vert (*inv*).

blue jeans pl n 🇺🇸 jean *m*.

blue-on-blue adj 🇺🇸 MIL : *we have a blue-on-blue situation* [friendly fire] des soldats ont été tués par des tirs venant de leur propre camp.

blueprint ['bluːprɪnt] n **1.** [of technical drawing] bleu *m* **2.** *fig* [plan] plan *m*, projet *m* ; [prototype] prototype *m*.

blue-sky comp ▶ **blue-sky research** recherches *fpl* sans applications immédiates.

blue state n 🇺🇸 *État qui vote traditionnellement démocrate.*

bluestocking ['bluː₁stɒkɪŋ] 🇺🇰 bas-bleu *m*.

bluetit ['bluːtɪt] n mésange *f* bleue.

Bluetooth ['bluːtuːθ] n TELEC technologie *f* Bluetooth.

bluff [blʌf] ◆ n **1.** [deception] bluff *m* **2.** PHR **to call sb's bluff** défier qqn. ◆ vi bluffer. ◆ vt bluffer / *to bluff one's way through things* marcher au bluff.

blunder ['blʌndər] ◆ n [mistake] bourde *f* ; [remark] gaffe *f*, impair *m* / *I made a terrible blunder* j'ai fait une gaffe or une bévue épouvantable. ◆ vi **1.** [make a mistake] faire une gaffe or un impair **2.** [move clumsily] avancer à l'aveuglette, tâtonner.

blundering ['blʌndərɪŋ] adj [person] maladroit, gaffeur ; [action, remark] maladroit, malavisé.

blunt [blʌnt] ◆ adj **1.** [blade] peu tranchant, émoussé ; [point] émoussé, épointé ; [pencil] mal taillé, épointé ; LAW [instrument] contondant **2.** [frank] brusque, direct / *let me be blunt* permettez que je parle franchement. ◆ vt [blade] émousser ; [pencil, point] épointer ; *fig* [feelings, senses] blaser, lasser.

bluntly ['blʌntlɪ] adv carrément, franchement.

bluntness ['blʌntnɪs] n **1.** [of blade] manque *m* de tranchant, état *m* émoussé **2.** [frankness] franchise *f*, brusquerie *f*.

blur [blɜːr] *(pt & pp* **blurred**, *cont* **blurring)* ◆ n [vague shape] masse *f* confuse, tache *f* floue / *my childhood is all a blur to me now* maintenant mon enfance n'est plus qu'un vague souvenir. ◆ vt **1.** [writing] estomper, effacer ; [outline] estomper **2.** [judgment, memory, sight] troubler, brouiller.

blurb [blɜːb] n notice *f* publicitaire, argumentaire *m* ; [on book] (texte *m* de) présentation *f*.

blurred [blɜːd], **blurry** ['blɜːrɪ] adj flou, indistinct.

blurt [blɜːt] vt lâcher, jeter. ❖ **blurt out** vt sep [secret] laisser échapper.

blush [blʌʃ] ◆ vi [turn red - gen] rougir, devenir rouge ; [- with embarrassment] rougir. ◆ n rougeur *f*.

blusher ['blʌʃər] n fard *m* à joues.

bluster ['blʌstər] ◆ vi **1.** [wind] faire rage, souffler en rafales ; [storm] faire rage, se déchaîner **2.** [speak angrily] fulminer, tempêter **3.** [boast] se vanter, fanfaronner. ◆ vt [person] intimider. ◆ n *(U)* **1.** [boasting] fanfaronnade *f*, fanfaronnades *fpl*, vantardise *f* **2.** [wind] rafale *f*.

blustery ['blʌstərɪ] adj [weather] venteux, à bourrasques ; [wind] qui souffle en rafales, de tempête.

Blvd (written abbr of **boulevard**) bd, boul.

BM n (abbr of **Bachelor of Medicine**) *(titulaire d'une) licence de médecine.*

BMA (abbr of **British Medical Association**) pr n *ordre britannique des médecins.*

BMJ (abbr of **British Medical Journal**) pr n *organe de la BMA.*

BMOC n 🇺🇸 abbr of **big man on campus.**

B-movie n film *m* de série B.

BMus ['biː'mʌz] (abbr of **Bachelor of Music**) n *(titulaire d'une) licence de musique.*

BMX (abbr of **bicycle motorcross**) n **1.** [bicycle] VTT *m* **2.** SPORT cyclo-cross *m inv*.

bn written abbr of **billion.**

BN MESSAGING written abbr of **been.**

BO n (abbr of **body odour**) odeur *f* corporelle / *he's got BO* il sent mauvais.

boa ['bəʊə] n ▶ **boa constrictor** boa constricteur *m*, constrictor *m*.

boar [bɔːr] n [male pig] verrat *m* ; [wild pig] sanglier *m*.

board [bɔːd] ◆ n **1.** [plank] planche *f* ▶ **across the board** : *the policy applies to everybody in the company across the board* cette politique concerne tous les employés de l'entreprise sans exception **2.** [cardboard] carton *m* ; [for games] tableau *m* **3.** ADMIN conseil *m*, commission *f* ▶ **board of directors** conseil d'administration / *who's on the board?* qui siège au conseil d'administration ? ▶ **board of inquiry** commission d'enquête ▶ **the board of health a)** 🇺🇸 le service municipal d'hygiène **b)** MIL le conseil de révision **4.** SCH & UNIV ▶ **board of education** 🇺🇸 ≃ conseil *m* d'administration *(d'un établissement scolaire)* ▶ **board of examiners** jury *m* d'examen **5.** [meals provided] pension *f* ; *arch* [table] table *f* ▶ **board and lodging** (chambre *f* et) pension *f* **6.** AERON & NAUT bord *m* ▶ **to go on board** monter à bord de **7.** PHR **to go by the board** 🇺🇰 être abandonné or oublié ▶ **to take sthg on board a)** [take into account] tenir compte de qqch **b)** [adhere to] adhérer à qqch. ◆ comp [decision, meeting] du conseil d'administration. ◆ vt [plane, ship] monter à bord de ; [bus, train] monter dans ; NAUT [in attack] monter or prendre à l'abordage / *the flight is now boarding at gate 3* embarquement immédiat du vol porte 3. ◆ vi [lodge] être en pension ▶ **to board with sb** être pensionnaire chez qqn. ❖ **board up** vt sep couvrir de planches ; [door, window] boucher, obturer.

boarder ['bɔːdər] n pensionnaire *mf* ; SCH interne *mf*, pensionnaire *mf*.

board game n jeu *m* de société.

boarding card n carte *f* d'embarquement.

boarding house n pension *f* ; SCH internat *m*.

boarding pass n = boarding card.

boarding school n internat *m*, pensionnat *m* ▶ **to go to boarding school** être interne.

Board of Education n 🇺🇸 *commission élue qui statue en matière d'éducation dans chaque comté.*

Board of Trade pr n ▶ **the Board of Trade a)** 🇺🇰 le ministère du Commerce **b)** 🇺🇸 la chambre de commerce.

boardroom ['bɔːdrʊm] n salle *f* de conférence ; *fig* [management] administration *f*.

boardwalk ['bɔːdwɔːk] n 🇺🇸 passage *m* en bois ; [on beach] promenade *f* (en planches).

boast [bəʊst] ◆ n fanfaronnade *f*, fanfaronnades *fpl* / *it's his proud boast that he has never lost a game* il se vante de n'avoir jamais perdu un jeu. ◆ vi se vanter, fanfaronner. ◆ vt [possess] posséder / *the town boasts an excellent symphony orchestra* la ville possède un excellent orchestre symphonique.

boastful ['bəʊstfʊl] adj fanfaron, vantard.

boat [bəʊt] ◆ n [gen] bateau *m* ; [for rowing] barque *f*, canot *m* ; [for sailing] voilier *m* ; [ship] navire *m*, paquebot *m* ▶ **to go by boat** prendre le bateau ▶ **to be in the same boat** : *we're all in the same boat* nous sommes tous logés à la même enseigne. ◆ vi voyager en bateau ▶ **to go boating** aller se promener en bateau.

boater ['bəʊtər] n canotier *m*.

boating ['bəʊtɪŋ] ◆ n canotage *m*. ◆ comp [accident, enthusiast, trip] de canotage.

boatswain ['bəʊsn], **bosun** ['bəʊsn] n maître *m* d'équipage.

boat train n *train qui assure la correspondance avec un bateau.*

bob [bɒb] *(pt & pp* **bobbed**, *cont* **bobbing)* ◆ vi **1.** [cork, buoy] ▶ **to bob up and down** danser sur l'eau **2.** [curtsy] faire une petite révérence. ◆ vt [hair] couper court. ◆ n **1.** [abrupt movement] petit coup *m*, petite secousse *f* ; [of head] hochement *m* or salut *m* de tête ; [curtsy] petite révérence *f* **2.** [hairstyle] (coupe *f* au) carré *m* **3.** (*pl* bob) US dated [shilling] shilling *m* **4.** inf PHR **bits and bobs**: *all my bits and bobs* toutes mes petites affaires / *we'll deal with the bits and bobs later* nous nous occuperons des détails plus tard.

Bob [bɒb] pr n ▶ **Bob's your uncle!** *inf* et voilà le travail !

bobbin ['bɒbɪn] n [gen] bobine *f* ; [for lace] fuseau *m*.

bobble ['bɒbl] n [pompom] pompon *m* ▶ **bobble hat** chapeau *m* à pompon.

bobby ['bɒbɪ] (*pl* **bobbies**) n US inf & dated flic *m*.

bobby pin n US pince *f* à cheveux.

bobby socks, bobby sox pl n US socquettes *fpl* (*de fille*).

bobsled ['bɒbsled], **bobsleigh** ['bɒbsleɪ] n bobsleigh *m*, bob *m*.

bodacious [bəʊ'deɪʃəs] adj US inf [attractive] canon ; [great] génial.

bode [bəʊd] ◆ pt ⟶ **bide**. ◆ vi [presage] augurer, présager / *it bodes well for him* cela est de bon augure pour lui.

bodge [bɒdʒ] vt US inf **1.** [spoil] saboter, bousiller **2.** [mend clumsily] rafistoler.

bodice ['bɒdɪs] n [of dress] corsage *m* ; [corset] corset *m*.

bodily ['bɒdɪlɪ] ◆ adj matériel ▶ **bodily functions** fonctions *fpl* corporelles. ◆ adv [carry, seize] à bras-le-corps.

body ['bɒdɪ] (*pl* **bodies**) ◆ n **1.** [human, animal] corps *m* ▶ **to keep body and soul together** subsister, survivre **2.** [corpse] cadavre *m*, corps *m* **3.** [group] ensemble *m*, corps *m* ; [organization] organisme *m* / *the main body of voters* le gros des électeurs / *a large body of people* une foule énorme ▶ **body politic** corps *m* politique **4.** [mass] masse *f* / *a growing body of evidence* une accumulation de preuves / *the body of public opinion* la majorité de l'opinion publique **5.** [largest part - of document, speech] fond *m*, corps *m* **6.** [of car] carrosserie *f* ; [of plane] fuselage *m* ; [of ship] coque *f* ; [of camera] boîtier *m* ; [of dress] corsage *m* ; [of building] corps *m* **7.** [fullness - wine] corps *m* / *a shampoo that gives your hair body* un shampooing qui donne du volume à vos cheveux. ◆ comp ▶ **body fluids** fluides *mpl* organiques ▶ **body hair** poils *mpl*.

bodybuilder ['bɒdɪbɪldər] n [person] culturiste *mf* ; [machine] extenseur *m* ; [food] aliment *m* énergétique.

body building n culturisme *m*.

body clock n horloge *f* biologique.

body count n pertes *fpl* en vies humaines.

body double n CIN doublure *f* (*pour les scènes d'amour*).

bodyguard ['bɒdɪgɑːd] n garde *m* du corps.

body language n langage *m* du corps.

body lotion n lait *m* corporel.

body odour n odeur *f* corporelle.

body piercing n piercing *m*.

body search n fouille *f* corporelle.

body shampoo n shampooing *m* pour le corps.

body shaper [-'ʃeɪpər] n body *m* minceur.

body shop n atelier *m* de carrosserie.

body stocking n body *m*.

body-surf vi SPORT body-surfer.

body-surfer n SPORT body-surfer *m*, -euse *f*.

body-surfing n SPORT body-surfing *m*.

body warmer [-ˌwɔːmər] n gilet *m* matelassé.

bodywork ['bɒdɪwɜːk] n carrosserie *f*.

B of E n abbr of Bank of England.

boffin ['bɒfɪn] n US inf chercheur *m* scientifique or technique.

bog [bɒg] (*pt & pp* **bogged**, *cont* **bogging**) n **1.** [area] marécage *m*, marais *m* ; [peat] tourbière *f* **2.** US v inf [lavatory] chiottes *fpl*. ◆ **bog down** vt sep empêcher, entraver ; [vehicle] embourber, enliser.

bogey ['bəʊgɪ] n **1.** [monster] démon *m*, fantôme *m* ; [pet worry] bête *f* noire **2.** inf [in nose] crotte *f* de nez.

bogeyman ['bəʊgɪmæn] (*pl* **bogeymen** [-men]) n croque-mitaine *m*, père *m* fouettard.

boggle ['bɒgl] vi [be amazed] être abasourdi / *the mind boggles!* ça laisse perplexe !

boggy ['bɒgɪ] (*compar* **boggier**, *superl* **boggiest**) adj [swampy] marécageux ; [peaty] tourbeux.

bogie ['bəʊgɪ] n RAIL bogie *m* ; [trolley] diable *m*.

bog-standard adj US inf [restaurant, food] ordinaire, médiocre ; [film, book] sans intérêt, médiocre ; [hotel] standard (*inv*), médiocre.

bogus ['bəʊgəs] adj faux (fausse).

Bohemia [bəʊ'hiːmjə] pr n Bohême *f*.

bohemian [bəʊ'hiːmjən] ◆ n bohème *mf*. ◆ adj bohème.

Bohemian [bəʊ'hiːmjən] ◆ n [from Bohemia] Bohémien *m*, -enne *f* ; [gypsy] bohémien *m*, -enne *f*. ◆ adj [of Bohemia] bohémien ; [gypsy] bohémien.

boil [bɔɪl] ◆ n **1.** [on face, body] furoncle *m* **2.** [boiling point] : *bring the sauce to the boil* amenez la sauce à ébullition / *the water's on the boil* US l'eau bout or est bouillante / *the project has gone off the boil* US le projet a été mis en attente. ◆ vt **1.** [liquid] faire bouillir, amener à ébullition **2.** [food] cuire à l'eau, faire bouillir. ◆ vi **1.** [liquid] bouillir / *the kettle's boiling* l'eau bout (dans la bouilloire) **2.** [seethe - ocean] bouillonner ; [-person] bouillir / *I was boiling with anger* je bouillais de rage. ◆ **boil down** vt sep CULIN faire réduire ; fig réduire à l'essentiel. ◆ **boil down to** vt insep revenir à / *it boils down to the same thing* ça revient au même. ◆ **boil over** vi **1.** [overflow] déborder ; [milk] se sauver, déborder **2.** fig [with anger] bouillir / *the unrest boiled over into violence* l'agitation a débouché sur la violence.

boiled ['bɔɪld] adj ▶ **boiled egg** œuf *m* à la coque ▶ **boiled potatoes** pommes de terre *fpl* à l'eau ou bouillies ▶ **boiled sweets** US bonbons *mpl* à sucer.

boiler ['bɔɪlər] n [furnace] chaudière *f* ; [domestic] chaudière *f* ; US [washing machine] lessiveuse *f* ; [pot] casserole *f*.

boiler room n salle *f* des chaudières, chaufferie *f* ; NAUT chaufferie *f*, chambre *f* de chauffe.

boiler suit n US [for work] bleu *m* or bleus *mpl* (de travail) ; [fashion garment] salopette *f*.

boiling ['bɔɪlɪŋ] ◆ adj [very hot] bouillant / *the weather here is boiling* il fait une chaleur infernale ici. ◆ adv : *it's boiling hot today* inf il fait une chaleur à crever aujourd'hui.

boiling point n point *m* d'ébullition ▶ **to reach boiling point a)** lit arriver à ébullition **b)** fig être en ébullition.

boisterous ['bɔɪstərəs] adj [exuberant] tapageur, plein d'entrain.

bok choy [bɒk'tʃɔɪ] n pak choi *m*, chou *m* chinois.

BOL MESSAGING written abbr of best of luck.

bold [bəʊld] ◆ adj **1.** [courageous] intrépide, hardi / *a bold stroke* un coup d'audace **2.** [not shy] assuré ; [brazen] effronté / *may I be so bold as to ask your name?* puis-je me permettre de vous demander qui vous êtes ? ▶ **as bold as brass** US culotté **3.** [colours] vif, éclatant **4.** TYPO : *in bold* en gras. ◆ n caractères *mpl* gras, gras *m*.

boldly ['bəuldlı] adv **1.** [bravely] intrépidement, audacieusement **2.** [impudently] avec impudence, effrontément **3.** [forcefully] avec vigueur, vigoureusement.

boldness ['bəuldnıs] n **1.** [courage] intrépidité f, audace f **2.** [impudence] impudence f, effronterie f **3.** [force] vigueur f, hardiesse f.

Bolivia [bə'lɪvɪə] pr n Bolivie f.

Bolivian [bə'lɪvɪən] ◆ n Bolivien m, -enne f. ◆ adj bolivien.

bollard ['bɒlɑːd] n [on wharf] bollard m ; UK [on road] borne f.

bollocking ['bɒləkɪŋ] n UK v inf engueulade f / he got / she gave him a right bollocking il a reçu / elle lui a passé un sacré savon.

bollocks ['bɒləks], **ballocks** ['bæləks] vulg ◆ pl n UK [testicles] couilles fpl. ◆ interj ▸ **bollocks!** quelles conneries !

Bolshevik ['bɒlʃıvık] ◆ n bolchevik mf. ◆ adj bolchevique.

bolshie, bolshy ['bɒlʃı] inf adj [intractable] ronchon.

bolster ['bəulstər] ◆ vt [strengthen] soutenir. ◆ n [cushion] traversin m. ◈ **bolster up** vt sep soutenir, appuyer.

bolt ['bəult] ◆ vi **1.** [move quickly] se précipiter / a rabbit bolted across the lawn un lapin a traversé la pelouse à toute allure **2.** [escape] déguerpir ; [horse] s'emballer. ◆ vt **1.** [lock] fermer à clé, verrouiller **2.** [food] engloutir. ◆ n **1.** [sliding bar to door, window] verrou m ; [in lock] pêne m **2.** [screw] boulon m **3.** [dash] : we made a bolt for the door nous nous sommes rués sur la porte **4.** [lightning] éclair m ▸ **the news came like a bolt from the blue** UK la nouvelle est arrivée comme un coup de tonnerre. ◆ adv ▸ **bolt upright** droit comme un i.

bolt hole n abri m, refuge m.

bomb [bɒm] ◆ n **1.** [explosive] bombe f ▸ **the bomb** la bombe atomique / the show went like a bomb UK inf le spectacle a eu un succès monstre **2.** UK inf [large sum of money] fortune f / the repairs cost a bomb les réparations ont coûté les yeux de la tête **3.** US inf [failure] fiasco m, bide m. ◆ comp ▸ **bomb scare** alerte f à la bombe. ◆ vt bombarder. ◆ vi inf **1.** [go quickly] filer à toute vitesse **2.** US [fail] être un fiasco or bide. ◈ **bomb out** vt sep détruire par bombardement.

bombard [bɒm'bɑːd] vt bombarder.

bombardment [bɒm'bɑːdmənt] n bombardement m.

bombastic [bɒm'bæstık] adj [style] ampoulé, grandiloquent ; [person] grandiloquent, pompeux.

Bombay mix n mélange apéritif épicé composé de lentilles, de fruits secs et de vermicelles (spécialité indienne).

bomb disposal n déminage m ▸ **bomb disposal expert** démineur m.

bombed-out adj inf **1.** [exhausted] crevé, nase **2.** [drunk] bourré, beurré ; [on drugs] défoncé.

bomber ['bɒmər] n **1.** [aircraft] bombardier m **2.** [terrorist] poseur m, -euse f de bombes.

bomber jacket n blouson m d'aviateur.

bombing ['bɒmıŋ] ◆ n [by aircraft] bombardement m ; [by terrorist] attentat m à la bombe. ◆ comp [mission, raid] de bombardement.

bombproof ['bɒmpruːf] adj blindé.

bombshell ['bɒmʃel] n fig [shock] : her death came as a real bombshell sa mort nous a fait un grand choc or nous a atterrés / their wedding announcement came as a complete bombshell l'annonce de leur mariage a fait l'effet d'une bombe.

bombsight ['bɒmsaıt] n viseur m de bombardement.

bombsite ['bɒmsaıt] n lieu m bombardé.

bona fide [,bəunə'faıdı] adj [genuine] véritable, authentique ; [agreement] sérieux.

bonanza [bə'nænzə] n aubaine f, filon m ; US MIN riche filon m.

bonce [bɒns] n UK inf caboche f.

bond [bɒnd] ◆ n **1.** [link] lien m, liens mpl, attachement m / the marriage bonds les liens conjugaux **2.** [agreement] engagement m, contrat m **3.** FIN [certificate] bon m, titre m. ◆ vt [hold together] lier, unir. ◆ vi **1.** [with adhesive] : the surfaces have bonded les surfaces ont adhéré l'une à l'autre **2.** PSYCHOL former des liens affectifs.

bondage ['bɒndıdʒ] n lit esclavage m ; fig esclavage m, servitude f.

bonded ['bɒndıd] adj FIN titré ; COMM (entreposé) sous douane.

Bondi Beach ['bɒndı-] pr n plage de Sydney, célèbre pour ses surfeurs.

bonding ['bɒndıŋ] n **1.** PSYCHOL liens mpl affectifs **2.** [of two objects] collage m.

bond paper n papier m de qualité supérieure.

bone [bəun] ◆ n **1.** os m ; [of fish] arête f ▸ **chilled** or **frozen to the bone** glacé jusqu'à la moelle (des os) ▸ **to have a bone to pick with sb** : I have a bone to pick with you j'ai un compte à régler avec toi ▸ **to make no bones about sthg** ne pas y aller de main morte or avec le dos de la cuillère ▸ **to be nothing but skin and bone** or **bones, to be nothing but a bag of bones** : he's nothing but a bag of bones il est maigre comme un clou, c'est un sac d'os **2.** [substance] os m ; [in corset] baleine f **3.** [essential] essentiel m / to cut spending (down) to the bone réduire les dépenses au strict minimum. ◆ vt [meat] désosser ; [fish] ôter les arêtes de.

bone china n porcelaine f tendre.

bone-dry adj absolument sec.

bonehead ['bəunhed] n inf crétin m, -e f, imbécile mf.

bone-idle adj UK paresseux comme une couleuvre.

boneless ['bəunlıs] adj [meat] désossé, sans os ; [fish] sans arêtes.

bone marrow n moelle f.

boner ['bəunər] n US **1.** [blunder] gaffe f, bourde f **2.** vulg [erection] ▸ **to have a boner** bander.

bonfire ['bɒn,faıər] n (grand) feu m.

Bonfire Night n UK le 5 novembre (commémoration de la tentative de Guy Fawkes de faire sauter le Parlement en 1605). ⟶ Guy Fawkes' Night

bongo ['bɒŋgəu] (pl bongos or bongoes) n bongo m.

bonhomie ['bɒnəmiː] n bonhomie f.

bonk [bɒŋk] v inf & hum vi s'envoyer en l'air.

bonkers ['bɒŋkəz] adj UK inf fou (before vowel or silent 'h' fol, f folle), cinglé.

Bonn [bɒn] pr n Bonn.

bonnet ['bɒnıt] n **1.** [hat - woman's] bonnet m, chapeau m à brides ; [-child's] béguin m, bonnet m ; Scot [man's] béret m, bonnet m **2.** UK AUTO capot m.

bonny ['bɒnı] (compar bonnier, superl bonniest) adj UK regional [pretty] joli, beau (before vowel or silent 'h' bel, f belle).

bonus ['bəunəs] n [gen & COMM] prime f / the holiday was an added bonus les vacances étaient en prime.

bonus issue n UK ST. EX émission f d'actions gratuites.

bony ['bəunı] (compar bonier, superl boniest) adj **1.** ANAT osseux ; [knees, person] anguleux, décharné **2.** [fish] plein d'arêtes ; [meat] plein d'os.

bonzer ['bɒnzər] adj Austr & NZ v inf vachement bien.

boo [buː] ◆ vt huer, siffler. ◆ vi pousser des huées, siffler. ◆ n huée f. ◆ interj hou ▸ **he wouldn't say boo to a goose** `UK` inf c'est un grand timide.

boob [buːb] inf ◆ n **1.** [mistake] gaffe f **2.** [breast] sein m. ◆ vi gaffer.

boo-boo ['buːbuː] (pl **boo-boos**) n inf [blunder] gaffe f, bourde f.

boob tube n inf **1.** `US` [television set] télé f **2.** `UK` [strapless top] bustier m moulant.

booby prize n prix m de consolation (attribué par plaisanterie au dernier).

booby trap (pt & pp **booby-trapped**, cont **booby-trapping**) n MIL objet m piégé ; [practical joke] farce f.

boogie ['buːgɪ] inf vi [dance] danser ; [party] faire la fête.

boohoo [ˌbuːˈhuː] inf interj hum sniff.

book [bʊk] ◆ n **1.** lit livre m ▸ **to bring sb to book** `UK` obliger qqn à rendre des comptes ▸ **to do things** or **to go by the book** faire qqch selon les règles ▸ **to be in sb's good books** être dans les petits papiers de qqn ▸ **to be in sb's bad books** être mal vu de qqn ▸ **in my book** inf à mon avis / **he can read her like a book** pour lui elle est transparente ▸ **to throw the book at sb** donner le maximum à qqn **2.** [of stamps, tickets] carnet m ; [of matches] pochette f. ◆ vt **1.** [reserve] réserver, retenir ; `US` [tickets] prendre / **have you already booked your trip?** avez-vous déjà fait les réservations pour votre voyage ? / **the tour is fully booked** l'excursion est complète / **the performance is booked up** or **fully booked** on joue à bureaux or guichets fermés **2.** [subj: police] : **he was booked for speeding** il a attrapé une contravention pour excès de vitesse **3.** SPORT prendre le nom de. ◆ vi réserver. ◆ **books** pl n **1.** COMM & FIN [accounts] livre m de comptes ▸ **to keep the books** tenir les comptes or la comptabilité **2.** [of club] registre m / **she's on the association's books** elle est membre de l'association. ◆ **book in** vi `UK` se faire enregistrer ; [at hotel] prendre une chambre. ◆ **book up** vt sep réserver, retenir / **the restaurant is booked up** le restaurant est complet.

bookable ['bʊkəbl] adj **1.** `UK` [seat] qui peut être réservé d'avance **2.** [offence] passible d'une contravention.

bookbag ['bʊkbæg] n `US` cartable m.

bookbinding ['bʊkˌbaɪndɪŋ] n reliure f.

bookcase ['bʊkkeɪs] n bibliothèque f (meuble).

book club n club m du livre, cercle m de lecture.

bookend ['bʊkend] n serre-livres m inv.

Booker Prize ['bʊkə-] pr n ▸ **the Booker Prize** le Booker Prize (prestigieux prix littéraire britannique).

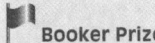

Booker Prize

Le **Booker Prize** est le prix littéraire britannique le plus connu ; créé en 1969, il est accordé chaque année au meilleur roman d'expression anglaise écrit par un citoyen du Commonwealth ou d'Irlande.

book group n club m de lecture.

bookie ['bʊkɪ] n inf bookmaker m.

booking ['bʊkɪŋ] n [reservation] réservation f.

booking clerk n préposé m, -e f aux réservations.

booking office n bureau m de location.

bookish ['bʊkɪʃ] adj [person] qui aime la lecture, studieux ; [style] livresque.

bookkeeper ['bʊkˌkiːpər] n comptable mf.

bookkeeping ['bʊkˌkiːpɪŋ] n comptabilité f.

booklet ['bʊklɪt] n brochure f, plaquette f.

bookmaker ['bʊkˌmeɪkər] n bookmaker m.

bookmark ['bʊkmɑːk] ◆ n signet m, marque-page m ; COMPUT signet m. ◆ vt : **to bookmark a site** mettre un signet à un site.

booksack ['bʊksæk] n `US` = **bookbag**.

bookseller ['bʊkˌselər] n libraire mf.

bookshelf ['bʊkʃelf] (pl **bookshelves** [-ʃelvz]) n étagère f à livres, rayon m (de bibliothèque).

bookshop ['bʊkʃɒp] n `UK` librairie f.

bookstall ['bʊkstɔːl] n étalage m de bouquiniste ; `UK` [in station] kiosque m à journaux.

bookstand ['bʊkstænd] n `US` [furniture] bibliothèque f ; [small shop] étalage m de bouquiniste ; [in station] kiosque m à journaux.

bookstore ['bʊkstɔːr] n `US` librairie f.

book token n `UK` bon d'achat de livres.

bookwork ['bʊkwɜːk] n [accounts] comptabilité f ; [secretarial duties] secrétariat m.

bookworm ['bʊkwɜːm] n fig rat m de bibliothèque.

boom [buːm] ◆ vi **1.** [resonate -gen] retentir, résonner ; [-guns, thunder] tonner, gronder ; [-waves] gronder, mugir ; [-organ] ronfler ; [-voice] tonner, tonitruer **2.** [prosper] prospérer, réussir / **business was booming** les affaires étaient en plein essor / **car sales are booming** les ventes de voitures connaissent une forte progression. ◆ vt [say loudly] tonner. ◆ n **1.** [sound -gen] retentissement m ; [-of guns, thunder] grondement m ; [-of waves] grondement m, mugissement m ; [-of organ] ronflement m ; [-of voice] rugissement m, grondement m **2.** [period of expansion] (vague f de) prospérité f, boom m ; [of trade] forte hausse f or progression f ; [of prices, sales] brusque or très forte hausse, montée f en flèche ; [of product] popularité f, vogue f **3.** NAUT [spar] gui m.

boom and bust (cycle) n ECON cycle m expansion-récession.

boom box n `US` inf radiocassette f.

boomerang ['buːməræŋ] ◆ n boomerang m. ◆ vi faire boomerang.

booming ['buːmɪŋ] adj **1.** [sound] retentissant **2.** [business] prospère, en plein essor.

boom lift n nacelle f élévatrice.

boom operator n CIN perchiste mf.

boom town n ville f en plein essor, ville-champignon f.

boon [buːn] n [blessing] aubaine f, bénédiction f.

boondoggle ['buːndɒgl] `US` ◆ n inf [cushy job] planque f. ◆ vi inf flemmarder, peigner la girafe.

boor [bʊər] n [rough] rustre m ; [uncouth] goujat m, malotru m, -e f.

boorish ['bʊərɪʃ] adj grossier, rustre.

boost [buːst] ◆ vt [sales] faire monter, augmenter ; [productivity] développer, accroître ; [morale, confidence] renforcer ; [economy] relancer. ◆ n **1.** [increase] augmentation f, croissance f ; [improvement] amélioration f **2.** [leg-up] ▸ **to give sb a boost a)** lit faire la courte échelle à qqn **b)** fig donner un coup m de pouce à qqn / **the success gave her morale a boost** le succès lui a remonté le moral.

booster ['buːstər] n **1.** AERON ▸ **booster (rocket)** fusée f de lancement, moteur m auxiliaire **2.** `US` inf [supporter] supporter m **3.** = **booster shot**.

booster cushion, booster seat n rehausseur m.

booster shot n piqûre f de rappel.

boot [buːt] ◆ n **1.** [ankle-length] bottillon m ; [for babies, women] bottine f ; [of soldier, workman] brodequin m ▸ **to give sb the boot** inf flanquer qqn à la porte

▸ **they put the boot in a)** 🇬🇧 *inf & lit* ils lui ont balancé des coups de pied **b)** *fig* ils ont enfoncé méchamment le clou **2.** 🇬🇧 AUTO coffre *m*. ◆ vt **1.** [kick] donner des coups de pied à **2.** COMPUT : *to boot (up) the system* initialiser le système. ◆ **to boot** *adv phr* en plus, par-dessus le marché. ◆ **boot out** vt sep *inf* flanquer à la porte.

boot camp n 🇺🇸 *inf* MIL camp *m* d'entraînement pour nouvelles recrues.

bootcut ['buːtkʌt] adj [trousers, jeans] trompette.

boot disk n COMPUT disque *m* de démarrage.

booth [buːð] n [cubicle - for telephone, language laboratory] cabine *f* ; [- for voting] isoloir *m*.

bootie ['buːtɪ] n 🇺🇸 *vulg* [sex] : *I want some bootie* j'ai envie de baiser / *he came around last night but it was just a bootie call* il est passé hier soir mais c'était juste pour baiser / *she's my bootie call* c'est ma copine de baise.

bootleg ['buːt,leg] (*pt & pp* **bootlegged**, *cont* **bootlegging**) ◆ vt [make] fabriquer illicitement ; [sell] vendre en contrebande. ◆ n [gen] marchandise *f* illicite ; [liquor] alcool *m* de contrebande. ◆ adj de contrebande.

bootlegger ['buːt,legər] n bootlegger *m*.

bootlicker ['buːt,lɪkər] n *inf* lèche-bottes *mf*.

booty ['buːtɪ] n **1.** [spoils] butin *m* **2.** 🇺🇸 *v inf* [buttocks] fesses *fpl* ▸ **shake your booty** remue tes fesses.

booze [buːz] *inf* ◆ n *(U)* alcool *m*, boissons *fpl* alcoolisées / *she's off the booze* elle a arrêté de picoler. ◆ vi picoler.

booze cruise 🇬🇧 *inf* voyage en ferry vers la France ou la Belgique dans le seul but d'y acheter de l'alcool bon marché.

boozer ['buːzər] n *inf* **1.** [drunkard] poivrot *m*, -e *f* **2.** 🇬🇧 [pub] bistro *m*.

booze-up n 🇬🇧 *inf* beuverie *f*, soûlerie *f*.

boozy ['buːzɪ] (*compar* **boozier**, *superl* **booziest**) adj *inf* [person] soûlard ; [party, evening] de soûlographie.

bop [bɒp] (*pt & pp* **bopped**, *cont* **bopping**) ◆ n **1.** [music] bop *m* **2.** *inf* [dance] danse *f*. ◆ vi *inf* [dance] danser le bop.

border ['bɔːdər] ◆ n **1.** [boundary] frontière *f* / *on the border between Norway and Sweden* à la frontière entre la Norvège et la Suède **2.** [edging - of dress, handkerchief] bord *m*, bordure *f* ; [- of plate, notepaper] liséré *m* **3.** [in garden] bordure *f*, plate-bande *f*. ◆ comp [state, post, guard] frontière *(inv)* ; [town, zone] frontière *(inv)*, frontalier ; [search] à la frontière ; [dispute, patrol] frontalier. ◆ vt **1.** [line edges of] border ; [encircle] entourer, encadrer **2.** [be adjacent to] toucher. ◆ **border on**, **border upon** vt insep [verge on] frôler / *his remark borders on slander* sa remarque frise la calomnie.

borderline ['bɔːdəlaɪn] ◆ n limite *f*, ligne *f* de démarcation. ◆ adj limite / *he is a borderline candidate* il est à la limite.

bore [bɔːr] ◆ pt ⟶ **bear**. ◆ vt **1.** [tire] ennuyer / *housework bores me stiff* *inf* or *to tears*, *inf* or *to death* *inf* faire le ménage m'ennuie à mourir **2.** [drill - hole] percer ; [- well] forer, creuser ; [- tunnel] creuser. ◆ n [person] raseur *m*, -euse *f* ; [event, thing] ennui *m*, corvée *f* / *visiting them is such a bore!* quelle barbe de leur rendre visite !

bored [bɔːd] adj [person] qui s'ennuie ; [expression] d'ennui ▸ **to be bored with doing sthg** s'ennuyer à faire qqch ▸ **to be bored stiff** *inf* or **to tears**, *inf* or **to death** *inf* s'ennuyer ferme or à mourir.

boredom ['bɔːdəm] n ennui *m*.

boring ['bɔːrɪŋ] adj [tiresome] ennuyeux ; [uninteresting] sans intérêt.

born [bɔːn] adj **1.** *lit* né ▸ **to be born** naître / *she was born blind* elle est née aveugle / *Victor Hugo was born*

in 1802 Victor Hugo est né en 1802 ▸ **born and bred** né et élevé ; *fig* : *anger born of frustration* une colère née de or due à la frustration ▸ **in all my born days** *inf* de toute ma vie ▸ **I wasn't born yesterday!** *inf* je ne suis pas né d'hier or de la dernière pluie ! **2.** [as intensifier] : *he's a born musician* c'est un musicien-né.

-born in comp originaire de.

born-again adj RELIG & *fig* rené.

borne [bɔːn] pp ⟶ **bear**.

Borneo ['bɔːnɪəʊ] pr n Bornéo.

borough ['bʌrə] n **1.** [British town] *ville représentée à la Chambre des communes par un ou plusieurs députés* **2.** [in London] *une des 32 subdivisions administratives de Londres* **3.** [in New York] *une des 5 subdivisions administratives de New York.*

borrow ['bɒrəʊ] vt [gen & FIN] emprunter ▸ **to borrow sthg from sb** emprunter qqch à qqn ▸ **to live on borrowed time** avoir peu de temps à vivre.

borrower ['bɒrəʊər] n emprunteur *m*, -euse *f*.

borrowing ['bɒrəʊɪŋ] n FIN & LING emprunt *m*.

Bosnia ['bɒznɪə] pr n Bosnie *f*.

Bosnia-Herzegovina [-,heətsəgə'viːnə] pr n Bosnie-Herzégovine *f*.

Bosnian ['bɒznɪən] ◆ n Bosnien *m*, -enne *f*, Bosniaque *mf*. ◆ adj bosnien, bosniaque.

bosom ['bʊzəm] n **1.** [of person] poitrine *f* ; [of woman] seins *mpl* ; *fig & liter* ▸ **a bosom friend** un ami intime **2.** *fig* [centre] sein *m*, fond *m* / *in the bosom of his family* au sein de sa famille.

Bosporus ['bɒspərəs], **Bosphorus** ['bɒsfərəs] pr n Bosphore *m*.

boss [bɒs] ◆ n **1.** *inf* [person in charge] patron *m*, -onne *f*, chef *m* / *I'll show you who's boss!* je vais te montrer qui est le chef ! / *he enjoys being his own boss* il aime être son propre patron **2.** *inf* [of gang] caïd *m* ; 🇺🇸 [politician] manitou *m* (du parti). ◆ vt *inf* [person] commander, donner des ordres à ; [organization] diriger, faire marcher. ◆ **boss about** 🇬🇧, **boss around** vt sep *inf* mener à la baguette.

boss-eyed adj 🇬🇧 *inf* qui louche.

bossy ['bɒsɪ] (*compar* **bossier**, *superl* **bossiest**) adj *inf* autoritaire, dictatorial.

bossy-boots n *inf* : *he / she's a real bossy-boots* il / elle adore donner des ordres / *don't be such a bossy-boots!* arrête de jouer les petits chefs !

Boston Tea Party pr n ▸ **the Boston Tea Party** la « Boston Tea Party ».

 Boston Tea Party

Insurrection menée en 1773 par les Bostoniens, qui jetèrent à la mer des cargaisons de thé pour protester contre les droits de douane imposés par l'Angleterre. Cette **Tea Party** fut suivie d'actes de résistance semblables dans d'autres colonies. Elle durcit les fronts entre **Loyalists** et **Patriots**.

bosun ['bəʊsn] n = **boatswain**.

bot [bɒt] n COMPUT bot *m* informatique, robogiciel *m*.

BOT n abbr of Board of Trade.

botanic(al) [bə'tænɪk(l)] adj botanique ▸ **botanical garden** jardin *m* botanique.

botanist ['bɒtənɪst] n botaniste *mf*.

botany ['bɒtənɪ] n botanique f.

botch [bɒtʃ] inf ◆ vt [spoil] saboter, bâcler ; [repair clumsily] rafistoler ▸ **to make a botched job of sthg** 🇬🇧 bousiller qqch. ◆ n : *those workmen made a real botch* or *botch-up of the job* ces ouvriers ont fait un travail de cochon or ont tout salopé.

both [bəʊθ] ◆ predet les deux, l'un or l'une et l'autre / *both dresses are pretty* les deux robes sont jolies ▸ **you can't have it both ways!** il faut te décider ! ◆ pron tous (les) deux mpl, toutes (les) deux fpl / *both are to blame* c'est leur faute à tous les deux. ❖ **both... and** conj phr : *her job is both interesting and well-paid* son travail est à la fois intéressant et bien payé / *I both read and write Spanish* je sais lire et écrire l'espagnol.

bother ['bɒðər] ◆ vi prendre la peine / *please don't bother getting up!* ne vous donnez pas la peine de vous lever ! / *don't bother about me* ne vous en faites pas or ne vous inquiétez pas pour moi / *let's not bother with the housework* laissons tomber le ménage. ◆ vt **1.** [irritate] ennuyer, embêter ; [pester] harceler ; [disturb] déranger / *would it bother you if I opened the window?* cela vous dérange or ennuie si j'ouvre la fenêtre ? **2.** [worry] tracasser / *it doesn't bother me whether they come or not* cela m'est bien égal qu'ils viennent ou pas **3.** [hurt] faire souffrir / *his leg is bothering him again* sa jambe le fait de nouveau souffrir. ◆ n **1.** [trouble] ennui m ▸ **to be in** or **to have a spot of bother (with sb)** 🇬🇧 avoir des ennuis (avec qqn) / *he doesn't give her any bother* il ne la dérange pas / *the trip isn't worth the bother* le voyage ne vaut pas la peine / *thanks for babysitting — it's no bother!* merci pour le babysitting — de rien ! **2.** [nuisance] ennui m / *homework is such a bother!* quelle corvée, les devoirs ! ◆ interj 🇬🇧 inf flûte, mince.

bothered ['bɒðəd] adj ▸ **to be bothered about sb / sthg** s'inquiéter de qqn / qqch / *he can't be bothered to do his own laundry* il a la flemme de laver son linge lui-même / *I'm not bothered* ça m'est égal ▸ **am I bothered?** 🇬🇧 inf je m'en fous.

bothy ['bɒθɪ] n 🅂🄲🄾🅃 **1.** [mountain shelter] refuge m (de montagne) **2.** [farmworker's dwelling] petite maison très rudimentaire pour les ouvriers agricoles.

botnet ['bɒtnet] n COMPUT botnet m, réseau m de robots IRC.

Botox® ['bəʊtɒks] n (U) MED Botox m.

Botswana [bɒ'tswɑːnə] pr n Botswana m.

bottle ['bɒtl] ◆ n **1.** [container, contents] bouteille f ; [of perfume] flacon m ; [of medicine] flacon m, fiole f ; [jar] bocal m ; [made of stone] cruche f, cruchon m / *a wine bottle* une bouteille à vin ; fig ▸ **to hit the bottle** inf picoler dur **2.** [for baby] biberon m **3.** 🇬🇧 inf [nerve] : *he lost his bottle* il s'est dégonflé / *she's got a lot of bottle* elle a un sacré cran. ◆ vt [wine] mettre en bouteille ; [fruit] mettre en bocal or conserve, conserver. ❖ **bottle up** vt sep [emotions] refouler, ravaler.

bottle bank n conteneur pour la collecte du verre usagé.

bottled ['bɒtld] adj en bouteille or bouteilles.

bottle-fed adj élevé or allaité au biberon.

bottle-feed vt allaiter or nourrir au biberon.

bottleneck ['bɒtlnek] n [in road] rétrécissement m de la chaussée, étranglement m ; [of traffic] embouteillage m, bouchon m ; [in industry] goulet m or goulot m d'étranglement.

bottle opener n ouvre-bouteilles m inv, décapsuleur m.

bottle party n 🇬🇧 soirée où chacun des invités apporte à boire.

bottle-warmer n chauffe-biberon m.

bottom ['bɒtəm] ◆ n **1.** [lowest part - of garment, heap] bas m ; [- of water] fond m ; [- of hill, stairs] bas m, pied m ;

[- of outside of container] bas m ; [- of inside of container] fond m ; [- of chair] siège m, fond m ; [- of ship] carène f / *at the bottom of page one* au bas de la or en bas de page un / *the ship touched (the) bottom* le navire a touché le fond ; fig : *the bottom fell out of the grain market* FIN le marché des grains s'est effondré **2.** [last place] : *he's (at the) bottom of his class* il est le dernier de sa classe / *you're at the bottom of the list* vous êtes en queue de liste **3.** [far end] fond m, bas m **4.** fig [origin, source] base f, origine f / *I'm sure she's at the bottom of all this* je suis sûr que c'est elle qui est à l'origine de cette histoire / *I intend to get to the bottom of this affair* j'entends aller au fin fond de cette affaire or découvrir le pot aux roses **5.** [buttocks] derrière m, fesses fpl. ◆ adj [gen] : *the bottom half of the chart* la partie inférieure du tableau / *the bottom half of the class / list* la deuxième moitié de la classe / liste / *the bottom floor* le rez-de-chaussée / *the bottom end of the table* le bas de la table ▸ **bottom gear** 🇬🇧 AUTO première f (vitesse f). ❖ **at bottom** adv phr au fond. ❖ **bottom out** vi [prices] atteindre son niveau plancher ; [recession] atteindre son plus bas niveau.

Bottom ['bɒtəm] pr n THEAT personnage comique transformé en âne dans «le Songe d'une nuit d'été» de Shakespeare.

bottomless ['bɒtəmlɪs] adj sans fond, insondable ; [unlimited - funds, supply] inépuisable.

bottom line n FIN résultat m net ; fig ▸ **the bottom line** le fond du problème.

bottommost ['bɒtəməʊst] adj le plus bas.

bottom-of-the-range adj bas de gamme.

bottom-up adj [design, approach, democracy] ascendant.

botulism ['bɒtjʊlɪzm] n botulisme m.

bough [baʊ] n liter branche f.

bought [bɔːt] pt & pp ⟶ **buy.**

boulder ['bəʊldər] n rocher m ; [smaller] gros galet m.

boulevard ['buːləvɑːd] n boulevard m.

bounce [baʊns] ◆ n **1.** [rebound] bond m, rebond m **2.** [spring] : *there isn't much bounce in this ball* cette balle ne rebondit pas beaucoup. ◆ vi **1.** [object] rebondir / *the ball bounced down the steps* la balle a rebondi de marche en marche **2.** [person] bondir, sauter **3.** inf [cheque] être refusé pour non-provision. ◆ vt **1.** [cause to spring] faire rebondir / *she bounced the ball against* or *off the wall* elle fit rebondir la balle sur le mur / *he bounced the baby on his knee* il a fait sauter l'enfant sur son genou / *signals are bounced off a satellite* les signaux sont renvoyés or retransmis par satellite / *they bounced ideas off each other* leur échange de vues créait une émulation réciproque **2.** inf [cheque] : *the bank bounced my cheque* la banque a refusé mon chèque. ❖ **bounce back** vi [after illness] se remettre rapidement.

bounce message n [for e-mail] rapport m de non livraison.

bouncer ['baʊnsər] n inf videur m.

bouncy ['baʊnsɪ] (compar **bouncier,** superl **bounciest**) adj **1.** [ball, bed] élastique ; [hair] souple, qui a du volume **2.** [person] plein d'entrain, dynamique.

bound [baʊnd] ◆ pt & pp ⟶ **bind.** ◆ adj **1.** [certain] sûr, certain / *it was bound to happen* c'était à prévoir / *but he's bound to say that* mais il est certain que c'est cela qu'il va dire **2.** [compelled] obligé / *the teacher felt bound to report them* l'enseignant s'est cru obligé de les dénoncer **3.** [heading towards] ▸ **bound for a)** [person] en route pour **b)** [shipment, cargo, etc.] à destination de **c)** [train] à destination or en direction de / *where are you bound (for)?* vous allez dans quelle direction ? **4.** [tied] lié ; LING lié ▸ **bound hand and foot** pieds et poings liés **5.** [book] relié. ◆ n [leap] saut m, bond m. ◆ vi [person] sauter, bondir ; [animal] faire un bond or des bonds, bondir. ◆ vt borner, limiter. ❖ **bounds** pl n limite f, borne f / *her rage knew no bounds* sa colère était sans bornes / *within the bounds of possibility* dans la limite du possible ▶ **out of bounds a)** [gen] dont l'accès est interdit **b)** SPORT hors du jeu.

-bound in comp **1.** [restricted] confiné ▶ **house-bound** confiné à la maison **2.** [heading towards] : *a south-bound train* un train en partance pour le Sud.

boundary ['baʊndərɪ] (pl **boundaries**) n limite f, frontière f ▶ **boundary (line) a)** ligne f frontière **b)** SPORT limites fpl du terrain **c)** [in basketball] ligne f de touche.

boundless ['baʊndlɪs] adj [energy, wealth] illimité ; [ambition, gratitude] sans bornes ; [space] infini.

bounteous ['baʊntɪəs], **bountiful** ['baʊntɪfʊl] adj liter [person] généreux, libéral ; [supply] abondant ; [rain] bienfaisant.

bounty ['baʊntɪ] (pl **bounties**) n **1.** liter [generosity] munificence f **2.** [reward] prime f.

bouquet [buˈkeɪ] n bouquet m.

bourbon ['bɜːbən] n [whisky] bourbon m.

Bourbon ['bʊəbən] ◆ adj Bourbon. ◆ n Bourbon mf.

bourgeois ['bɔːʒwɑː] ◆ n bourgeois m, -e f. ◆ adj bourgeois.

bout [baʊt] n **1.** [period] période f / *a bout of drinking* une soûlerie, une beuverie **2.** [of illness] attaque f ; [of fever] accès m ; [of rheumatism] crise f / *a bout of flu* une grippe **3.** [boxing, wrestling] combat m ; [fencing] assaut m.

boutique [buːˈtiːk] n [shop] boutique f ; [in department store] rayon m.

bovine ['baʊvaɪn] ◆ adj lit & fig bovin. ◆ n bovin m.

Bovril® ['bɒvrɪl] n préparation à base de suc de viande utilisée comme boisson ou comme condiment.

bovver boots pl n 🇬🇧 inf & dated brodequins mpl, rangers mpl.

bovver boy n 🇬🇧 inf & dated loubard m.

bow¹ [baʊ] ◆ vi **1.** [in greeting] incliner la tête, saluer / *I bowed to him* je l'ai salué de la tête **2.** fig [yield] s'incliner / *to bow to the inevitable* s'incliner devant l'inévitable / *I'll bow to your greater knowledge* je m'incline devant tant de savoir or de science. ◆ vt [bend] incliner, courber ; [knee] fléchir ; [head - in shame] baisser ; [- in prayer] incliner ; [- in contemplation] pencher. ◆ n **1.** [gen] salut m ▶ **to take a bow** saluer **2.** [of ship] avant m, proue f / *on the port / starboard bow* par bâbord / tribord avant. ❖ **bow down** vi s'incliner / *he bowed down to her* il s'est incliné devant elle. ❖ **bow out** vi fig tirer sa révérence.

bow² [baʊ] n **1.** [for arrows] arc m **2.** MUS [stick] archet m ; [stroke] coup m d'archet **3.** [in ribbon] nœud m, boucle f.

bowel ['baʊəl] n (usu pl) **1.** ANAT [human] intestin m, intestins mpl ; [animal] boyau m, boyaux mpl, intestins mpl **2.** fig : *the bowels of the earth* les entrailles fpl de la terre.

bowl [baʊl] ◆ n **1.** [receptacle] bol m ; [larger] bassin m, cuvette f ; [shallow] jatte f ; [made of glass] coupe f ; [for washing-up] cuvette f ; [of beggar] sébile f ; [contents] bol m **2.** [rounded part - of spoon] creux m ; [- of pipe] fourneau m ; [- of wine glass] coupe f ; [- of sink, toilet] cuvette f **3.** 🇺🇸 SPORT [arena] amphithéâtre m ; [championship] championnat m, coupe f ; [trophy] coupe f **4.** [ball] boule f ▶ **(game of) bowls** 🇬🇧 (jeu m de) boules fpl. ◆ vi **1.** [play bowls] jouer aux boules ; [play tenpin bowling] jouer au bowling ; [in cricket] lancer (la balle) **2.** [move quickly] filer, aller bon train. ◆ vt **1.** [ball, bowl] lancer, faire rouler ; [hoop] faire rouler **2.** [in cricket] ▶ **to bowl the ball** servir / *he bowled (out) the batsman* il a mis le batteur hors jeu. ❖ **bowl over** vt sep **1.** [knock down] renverser,

faire tomber **2.** inf & fig [amaze] stupéfier, sidérer / *I was bowled over by the news* la nouvelle m'a abasourdi / *he bowled me over with his charm* j'ai été totalement séduit par son charme.

bow-legged [baʊ-] adj à jambes arquées.

bowler ['baʊlər] n **1.** SPORT [in bowls] joueur m, -euse f de boules or pétanque, bouliste mf ; [in tenpin bowling] joueur m, -euse f de bowling ; [in cricket] lanceur m, -euse f **2.** = **bowler hat.**

bowler hat n 🇬🇧 (chapeau m) melon m.

bowlful ['baʊlfʊl] n bol m.

bowling ['baʊlɪŋ] n [bowls] jeu m de boules, pétanque f ; [tenpin] bowling m ; [in cricket] service m.

bowling alley n bowling m.

bowling green n terrain m de boules (sur gazon).

bow tie [baʊ-] n nœud m papillon.

bow window [baʊ-] n 🇬🇧 fenêtre f en saillie, oriel m, bow-window m.

box [bɒks] (pl **boxes**) ◆ n **1.** [container, contents] boîte f ; [with lock] coffret m ; [cardboard box] carton m ; [crate] caisse f ; [for money] caisse f ; [collecting box] tronc m ▶ **to think outside the box** réfléchir de façon créative **2.** [compartment] compartiment m ; THEAT loge f, baignoire f ; LAW [for jury, reporters] banc m ; [for witness] barre f ; [in stable] box m ; [of coachman] siège m (de cocher) **3.** inf [television] télé f **4.** [blow] ▶ **a box on the ears** une gifle, une claque **5.** BOT buis m. ◆ comp [border, hedge] de or en buis. ◆ vi [fight] faire de la boxe, boxer ▶ **to box clever** fig ruser. ◆ vt **1.** [fight] boxer avec, boxer **2.** [put in box] mettre en boîte or caisse **3.** PHR ▶ **to box sb's ears** gifler qqn. ❖ **box in** vt sep [enclose] enfermer, confiner ; [pipes] encastrer / *to feel boxed in* se sentir à l'étroit.

boxed [bɒkst] adj COMM en boîte ▶ **a boxed set** un coffret.

boxer ['bɒksər] n [fighter] boxeur m ; [dog] boxer m.

boxer shorts pl n boxer-short m.

box file n boîte f archive.

boxing ['bɒksɪŋ] n boxe f.

Boxing Day n 🇬🇧 le lendemain de Noël.

boxing glove n gant m de boxe.

boxing ring n ring m.

box junction n 🇬🇧 carrefour m (matérialisé sur la chaussée par des bandes croisées).

box number n [in newspaper] numéro m d'annonce ; [at post office] numéro m de boîte à lettres.

box office n [office] bureau m de location ; [window] guichet m (de location) / *the play was a big success at the box office* la pièce a fait recette. ❖ **box-office** comp : *to be a box-office success* être en tête du box-office.

box of tricks n sac m à malices.

box-pleated adj SEW à plis creux.

boxroom ['bɒksrʊm] n 🇬🇧 débarras m.

boy [bɔɪ] ◆ n **1.** [male child] garçon m, enfant m / *when I was a boy* quand j'étais petit or jeune / *I've known them since they were boys* je les connais depuis leur enfance or depuis qu'ils sont petits / *boys will be boys* un garçon, c'est un garçon ; [son] garçon m, fils m **2.** inf [term of address] : *my dear boy* mon cher ami **3.** [male adult] : *a local boy* un gars du coin / *a night out with the boys* une virée entre copains. ◆ interj inf ▶ **(oh) boy!** 🇺🇸 dis donc !

boy band n boy's band m.

boycott ['bɔɪkɒt] ◆ n boycottage m, boycott m. ◆ vt boycotter.

boyfriend ['bɔɪfrend] n petit ami m.

boyhood ['bɔɪhʊd] n enfance f.

boyish ['bɔɪɪʃ] adj **1.** [youthful] d'enfant, de garçon ; [childish] enfantin, puéril **2.** [tomboyish - girl] garçonnier ; [- behaviour] garçonnier, de garçon.

boy scout n scout m.

boy wonder n petit génie m.

bozo ['bəʊzəʊ] n inf & pej type m.

Bp (written abbr of bishop) Mgr.

bpm written abbr of **beats per minute.**

Br 1. written abbr of **British 2.** (written abbr of **brother**) [preceding name of monk] F.

BR (abbr of **British Rail**) pr n ancienne société des chemins de fer britanniques.

bra [brɑː] n soutien-gorge m.

brace [breɪs] ◆ vt **1.** [strengthen] renforcer, consolider ; [support] soutenir ; CONSTR entretoiser ; [beam] armer **2.** [steady, prepare] : he braced his body / himself for the impact il raidit son corps / s'arc-bouta en préparation du choc **/** he braced himself to try again il a rassemblé ses forces pour une nouvelle tentative. ◆ n **1.** MED appareil m orthopédique ; [for teeth] appareil m dentaire or orthodontique **2.** (pl **brace**) [of game birds, pistols] paire f. ❖ **braces** pl n 🇬🇧 [for trousers] bretelles fpl.

bracelet ['breɪslɪt] n bracelet m.

brace position n [for plane passengers] position f de sécurité.

bracing ['breɪsɪŋ] adj fortifiant, tonifiant.

bracken ['brækn] n (U) fougère f.

bracket ['brækɪt] ◆ n **1.** [L-shaped support] équerre f, support m ; [for shelf] équerre f, tasseau m ; [lamp fixture] fixation f ; ARCHIT console f, corbeau m **2.** [category] groupe m, classe f **/** the high / low income bracket la tranche des gros / petits revenus **3.** MATH & TYPO [parenthesis] parenthèse f ; [square] crochet m **▶** in or between brackets entre parenthèses. ◆ vt fig [categorize] associer, mettre dans la même catégorie.

bracketing ['brækɪtɪŋ] n **1.** [in parentheses] mise f entre parenthèses **;** [in square brackets] mise f entre crochets **2.** [in a vertical list] réunion f par une accolade.

bracket light n applique f.

brackish ['brækɪʃ] adj saumâtre.

brag [bræg] (pt & pp **bragged**, cont **bragging**) ◆ vi se vanter. ◆ n [boasting] vantardise f, fanfaronnades fpl.

braid [breɪd] ◆ n **1.** [trimming] ganse f, soutache f ; [on uniform] galon m **2.** [of hair] tresse f, natte f. ◆ vt [plait] tresser, natter.

braille, Braille [breɪl] ◆ adj braille. ◆ n braille m.

brain [breɪn] ◆ n **1.** ANAT cerveau m ; [mind] cerveau m, tête f ; CULIN cervelle **2.** inf & fig : to blow one's brains out se faire sauter la cervelle **▶** to have sthg on the brain : you've got money on the brain tu es obsédé par l'argent / she's got it on the brain elle ne pense qu'à ça **3.** [intelligence] intelligence f **/** he's got brains il est intelligent. ◆ comp [damage, disease, surgery, tumour] cérébral **▶ brain surgeon** chirurgien m du cerveau. ◆ vt inf [hit] assommer. ❖ **brains** n inf [clever person] cerveau m **/** she's the brains of the family c'est elle le cerveau de la famille.

 cerveau or **cervelle?**

The anatomical term is **cerveau**; **cervelle** is used when brains are being referred to as a food item (**cervelle d'agneau**), or metaphorically to refer to the human mind (**se creuser la cervelle; il n'a rien dans la cervelle**).

brainbox ['breɪnbɒks] n inf [skull] crâne m ; [person] cerveau m.

brainchild ['breɪn,tʃaɪld] (pl **brainchildren** [-,tʃɪldrən]) n inf bébé m **/** the scheme is his brainchild le projet est son bébé.

brain dead adj dans un coma dépassé.

brain death n mort f cérébrale.

brain drain n fuite f or exode m des cerveaux.

brainiac ['breɪnɪæk] n 🇺🇸 inf intello mf.

brainless ['breɪnlɪs] adj [person] écervelé, stupide ; [idea] stupide.

brainpower ['breɪn,paʊə'] n intelligence f.

brainstem ['breɪnstem] n tronc m cérébral.

brainstorm ['breɪnstɔːm] ◆ n **1.** 🇬🇧 inf & fig [mental aberration] idée f insensée or loufoque **2.** 🇺🇸 inf & fig [brilliant idea] idée f géniale. ◆ vi faire du brainstorming. ◆ vt plancher sur.

brainstorming ['breɪn,stɔːmɪŋ] n brainstorming m, remue-méninges m inv.

brainteaser ['breɪn,tiːzə'] n inf problème m difficile, colle f.

brainwash ['breɪnwɒʃ] vt faire un lavage de cerveau à **/** advertisements can brainwash people into believing anything la publicité peut faire croire n'importe quoi aux gens.

brainwashing ['breɪnwɒʃɪŋ] n lavage m de cerveau.

brainwave ['breɪnweɪv] n **1.** MED onde f cérébrale **2.** inf [brilliant idea] inspiration f, idée f or trait m de génie.

brainy ['breɪnɪ] (compar **brainier**, superl **brainiest**) adj inf intelligent, futé.

braise [breɪz] vt braiser.

brake [breɪk] ◆ n [gen & AUTO] frein m **▶ to put on** or **to apply the brakes** freiner. ◆ vi freiner, mettre le frein.

brake horsepower n puissance f au frein.

brake light n feu m de stop.

brake lining n garniture f de frein.

brake shoe n mâchoire f de frein.

bramble ['bræmbl] n **1.** [prickly shrub] roncier m, roncière f **2.** [blackberry bush] ronce f des haies, mûrier m sauvage ; [berry] mûre f sauvage.

Bramley ['bræmlɪ] n **▶ Bramley (apple)** pomme f Bramley (variété de pomme à cuire).

bran [bræn] n son m (de blé), bran m.

branch [brɑːntʃ] ◆ n **1.** [of tree] branche f **2.** COMM [of company] succursale f, filiale f ; [of bank] agence f, succursale f. ◆ vi [tree] se ramifier. ❖ **branch off** vi [road] bifurquer. ❖ **branch out** vi étendre ses activités.

branch line n ligne f secondaire.

brand [brænd] ◆ n **1.** COMM [trademark] marque f (de fabrique) **/** he has his own brand of humour il a un sens de l'humour bien à lui **2.** [identifying mark - on cattle] marque f ; [- on prisoners] flétrissure f. ◆ vt **1.** [cattle] marquer (au fer rouge) **2.** fig [label] étiqueter, stigmatiser **/** she was branded (as) a thief on lui a collé une étiquette de voleuse.

brand building n création f de marque.

brand familiarity n connaissance f de la marque.

brand image n image f de marque.

brandish ['brændɪʃ] vt brandir.

brand-led adj MARKETING conditionné par la marque, piloté par la marque.

brand-loyal adj MARKETING fidèle à la marque.

brand loyalty n fidélité f à la marque.

brand name n marque f (de fabrique).

brand-new adj tout or flambant neuf.

brand recognition n identification f de la marque.

brand-sensitive adj MARKETING sensible aux marques.

brandy ['brændɪ] (pl **brandies**) n [made from grapes] ≃ cognac m ; [made of fruit] eau-de-vie f.

brash [bræʃ] adj [showy] impétueux, casse-cou (inv) ; [impudent] effronté, impertinent.

Brasilia [brə'zɪljə] pr n Brasilia.

brass [brɑːs] ◆ n **1.** [metal] cuivre m (jaune), laiton m **2.** MUS ▸ **the brass** les cuivres mpl. ◆ comp [object, ornament] de or en cuivre ▸ **to get down to brass tacks** en venir au fait or aux choses sérieuses.

brass band n fanfare f, orchestre m de cuivres.

brasserie ['bræsərɪ] n brasserie f.

brassiere [UK 'bræsɪə US brə'zɪr] n soutien-gorge m.

brass knuckles pl n US coup-de-poing m américain.

brat [bræt] n pej morveux m, -euse f, galopin m.

brat pack n [gen] jeunes loups mpl ; CIN terme désignant les jeunes acteurs populaires des années 1980.

bravado [brə'vɑːdəʊ] n bravade f.

brave [breɪv] ◆ adj [courageous] courageux, brave / be brave! sois courageux !, du courage ! ◆ vt [person] braver, défier ; [danger, storm] braver, affronter. ◆ pl n [people] ▸ **the brave** les courageux mpl.

bravely ['breɪvlɪ] adv courageusement, bravement.

bravery ['breɪvərɪ] n courage m, vaillance f ▸ **bravery award** médaille f du courage.

bravo [,brɑː'vəʊ] (pl **bravos**) ◆ interj bravo. ◆ n bravo m.

bravura [brə'vʊərə] n [gen & MUS] bravoure f.

brawl [brɔːl] ◆ n [fight] bagarre f, rixe f. ◆ vi se bagarrer.

brawn [brɔːn] n (U) **1.** [muscle] muscles mpl ; [strength] muscle m / all brawn and no brains tout dans les bras et rien dans la tête **2.** UK CULIN fromage m de tête.

brawny ['brɔːnɪ] (compar **brawnier**, superl **brawniest**) adj [arm] musculeux ; [person] musclé.

bray [breɪ] vi [donkey] braire ; pej [person] brailler ; [trumpet] beugler, retentir.

brazen ['breɪzn] adj [bold] effronté, impudent.

❖ brazen out vt sep : you'll have to brazen it out il va falloir que tu t'en tires par des fanfaronnades.

brazenness ['breɪznnɪs] n effronterie f.

brazier ['breɪzjə'] n [for fire] brasero m.

brazil [brə'zɪl] n ▸ **brazil (nut)** noix f du Brésil.

Brazil [brə'zɪl] pr n Brésil m.

Brazilian [brə'zɪljən] ◆ n Brésilien m, -enne f. ◆ adj brésilien.

BRB MESSAGING written abbr of **be right back**.

breach [briːtʃ] ◆ n **1.** [gap] brèche f, trou m / she stepped into the breach when I fell ill elle m'a remplacé au pied levé quand je suis tombé malade **2.** [violation - of law] violation f ; [- of discipline, order, rules] infraction f ; [- of etiquette, friendship] manquement m ; [- of confidence, trust] abus m ▸ **breach of contract** rupture f de contrat ▸ **breach of the peace** LAW atteinte f à l'ordre public ▸ **breach of promise a)** [gen] manque de parole **b)** [of marriage] violation f de promesse de mariage. ◆ vt **1.** [make gap in] ouvrir une brèche dans, faire un trou dans **2.** [agreement] violer, rompre ; [promise] manquer à.

bread [bred] n (U) [food] pain m / a loaf of bread un pain, une miche / bread and butter du pain beurré ▸ **the bread and wine** RELIG les espèces fpl ▸ **to earn one's daily bread** gagner sa vie or sa croûte / translation is her bread and butter la traduction est son gagne-pain ▸ **to know which side one's bread is buttered (on)** : I know which side my bread is buttered je sais où est mon intérêt.

breadbasket ['bred,bɑːskɪt] n **1.** [basket] corbeille f à pain **2.** GEOG région f céréalière.

bread bin n UK [small] boîte f à pain ; [larger] huche f à pain.

breadboard ['bredbɔːd] n planche f à pain.

bread box US = **bread bin**.

breadcrumb ['bredkrʌm] n miette f de pain. **❖ breadcrumbs** pl n CULIN chapelure f, panure f / fish fried in breadcrumbs du poisson pané.

breaded ['bredɪd] adj enrobé de chapelure.

breadline ['bredlaɪn] n file d'attente pour recevoir des vivres gratuits ▸ **to live** or **to be on the breadline** être sans le sou or indigent.

breadstick ['bredstɪk] n gressin m.

breadth [bredθ] n **1.** [width] largeur f ; [of cloth] lé m / the stage is 60 metres in breadth la scène a 60 mètres de large **2.** [scope - of mind, thought] largeur f ; [- of style] ampleur f ; ART largeur f d'exécution ; MUS jeu m large.

breadwinner ['bred,wɪnə'] n soutien m de famille.

break [breɪk] (pt **broke** [brəʊk], pp **broken** ['brəʊkn]) ◆ vt **1.** [split into pieces - glass, furniture] casser, briser ; [- branch, lace, string] casser ▸ **to break sb's heart** briser le cœur à qqn **2.** [fracture] casser, fracturer / to break one's leg se casser or se fracturer la jambe ; fig : to break one's back inf s'échiner / we've broken the back of the job nous avons fait le plus gros du travail **3.** [render inoperable - appliance, machine] casser **4.** [cut surface of - ground] entamer ; [- skin] écorcher / the seal on the coffee jar was broken le pot de café avait été ouvert ▸ **to break new** or **fresh ground** innover, faire œuvre de pionnier **5.** [violate - law, rule] violer, enfreindre ; [- speed limit] dépasser ; [- agreement, treaty] violer ; [- contract] rompre ; [- promise] manquer à **6.** [put an end to - strike] briser ; [- uprising] mater / he's tried to stop smoking but he can't break the habit il a essayé d'arrêter de fumer mais il n'arrive pas à se débarrasser or se défaire de l'habitude **7.** [wear down, destroy - enemy] détruire ; [- person, will, courage, resistance] briser ; [- witness] réfuter ; [- health] abîmer / this scandal could break them ce scandale pourrait signer leur perte / the experience will either make or break him l'expérience lui sera ou salutaire ou fatale **8.** [bankrupt] ruiner ▸ **to break the bank** [exhaust funds] faire sauter la banque / buying a book won't break the bank! hum acheter un livre ne nous ruinera pas ! **9.** [soften - fall] amortir, adoucir / we planted a row of trees to break the wind nous avons planté une rangée d'arbres pour couper le vent **10.** [reveal, tell] annoncer, révéler / break it to her gently annonce-le lui avec ménagement. ◆ vi **1.** [split into pieces - glass, furniture] se casser, se briser ; [- branch, stick] se casser, se rompre ; [- lace, string] se casser, se briser **2.** [fracture - bone, limb] se fracturer **3.** [become inoperable - lock, tool] casser ; [- machine] tomber en panne **4.** [disperse - clouds] se disperser, se dissiper ; [- troops] rompre les rangs ; [- ranks] se rompre **5.** [escape] ▸ **to break free** se libérer **6.** [fail - health, person, spirit] se détériorer / she or her spirit did not break elle ne s'est pas laissée abattre **7.** [take a break] faire une pause / let's break for coffee arrêtons-nous pour prendre un café **8.** [arise suddenly - day] se lever, poindre ; [- dawn] poindre ; [- news] être annoncé ; [- scandal, war] éclater **9.** [weather] changer ; [storm] éclater **10.** [voice - of boy] muer ; [- with emotion] se briser **11.** [wave] déferler. ◆ n **1.** [in china, glass] cassure f, brisure f ; [in wood] cassure f, rupture f ; [in bone, limb] fracture f ; fig [with friend, group] rupture f ; [in marriage] séparation f / to make a clean break with the past rompre avec le passé **2.** [crack] fissure f, fente f **3.** [gap - in hedge, wall] trouée f, ouverture f ; [- in rock] faille f ; [- in line] interruption f, rupture f / a break in the clouds une éclaircie **4.** [interruption - in conversation] interruption f, pause *f* ; [-in payment] interruption *f*, suspension *f* ; [-in trip] arrêt *m* ; [-in production] suspension *f*, rupture *f* ▪ *a break for commercials* or *a (commercial) break* **a)** RADIO un intermède de publicité **b)** TV un écran publicitaire, une page de publicité **5.** [rest] pause *f* ; [holiday] vacances *fpl* ; ⓊⓀ SCH récréation *f* ▪ *let's take a break* on fait une pause ? ▪ *he drove for three hours without a break* il a conduit trois heures de suite ▪ *give me a break!* inf laisse-moi respirer ! **6.** [escape] évasion *f*, fuite *f* ▪ *to make a break for it* prendre la fuite **7.** inf [opportunity] chance *f* ; [luck] (coup *m* de) veine *f* ▪ *to have a lucky break* avoir de la veine **8.** [change] changement *m* ▪ *a break in the weather* un changement de temps ▪ *the decision signalled a break with tradition* la décision marquait une rupture avec la tradition **9.** liter ▪ *at break of day* au point du jour, à l'aube **10.** SPORT : *to have a service break* or *a break (of serve)* [in tennis] avoir une rupture de service *(de l'adversaire)* ▪ *he made a 70 break* or *a break of 70* [in snooker, pool, etc.] il a fait une série de 70. ❖ **break away** vi **1.** [move away] se détacher ▪ *I broke away from the crowd* je me suis éloigné de la foule **2.** [end association with] rompre **3.** SPORT [in racing, cycling] s'échapper, se détacher du peloton. ❖ **break down** ➡ vi **1.** [vehicle, machine] tomber en panne **2.** [fail - health] se détériorer ; [-authority] disparaître ; [-argument, system] s'effondrer ; [-negotiations, relations, plan] échouer **3.** [lose one's composure] s'effondrer ▪ *to break down in tears* fondre en larmes **4.** [divide] se diviser. ➡ vt sep **1.** [destroy - barrier] démolir, abattre ; [-door] enfoncer ; fig [resistance] briser **2.** [analyse - idea] analyser ; [-reasons] décomposer ; [-accounts] analyser, détailler ; [COMM - costs, figures] ventiler ; [CHEM - substance] décomposer. ❖ **break in** ➡ vt sep **1.** [clothing] porter *(pour user)* ▪ *I want to break these shoes in* je veux que ces chaussures se fassent **2.** [knock down - door] enfoncer. ➡ vi **1.** [burglar] entrer par effraction **2.** [speaker] interrompre. ❖ **break into** vt insep **1.** [subj: burglar] entrer par effraction dans ; [drawer, safe] forcer **2.** [begin suddenly] : *the audience broke into applause* le public s'est mis à applaudir ▪ *the horse broke into a gallop* le cheval a pris le galop **3.** [conversation] interrompre **4.** [start to spend - savings] entamer **5.** COMM percer sur. ❖ **break off** ➡ vi **1.** [separate] se détacher, se casser **2.** [stop] s'arrêter brusquement ▪ *he broke off in mid-sentence* il s'est arrêté au milieu d'une phrase **3.** [end relationship] rompre. ➡ vt sep **1.** [separate] détacher, casser **2.** [end - agreement, relationship] rompre. ❖ **break out** vi **1.** [begin - war, storm] éclater ; [-disease] se déclarer **2.** [become covered] : *to break out in a sweat* se mettre à transpirer **3.** [escape] s'échapper ▪ *to break out from* or *of prison* s'évader (de prison). ❖ **break through** vt insep [sun] percer ▪ *the troops broke through enemy lines* les troupes ont enfoncé les lignes ennemies. ❖ **break up** ➡ vt sep **1.** [divide up - rocks] briser, morceler ; [-property] morceler ; [-soil] ameublir ; [-bread, cake] partager **2.** [destroy - house] démolir ; [-road] défoncer **3.** [end - fight, party] mettre fin à, arrêter ; [-coalition] briser, rompre ; [-organization] dissoudre ; [-empire] démembrer ; [-family] séparer ▪ *his drinking broke up their marriage* le fait qu'il buvait a brisé or détruit leur mariage **4.** [disperse - crowd] disperser. ➡ vi **1.** [split into pieces - road, system] se désagréger ; [-ice] craquer, se fissurer ; [-ship] se disloquer **2.** [come to an end - meeting, party] se terminer, prendre fin ; [-partnership] cesser, prendre fin ▪ *their marriage broke up* leur mariage n'a pas marché **3.** [boyfriend, girlfriend] rompre ▪ *they've broken up* ils se sont séparés **4.** [disperse - clouds] se disperser ; [-group] se disperser ; [-friends] se quitter, se séparer **5.** ⓊⓀ SCH être en vacances ▪ *we break up for Christmas on the 22nd* les vacances de Noël commencent le 22 **6.** ⓊⓈ inf [laugh] se tordre de rire **7.** ⓅⒽⓇ **you're breaking up!** [on phone] je ne te capte plus !

breakable ['breɪkəbl] adj fragile, cassable.
❖ **breakables** pl n : *put away all breakables* rangez tout objet fragile.

breakage ['breɪkɪdʒ] n **1.** [of metal] rupture *f* ; [of glass] casse *f*, bris *m* **2.** [damages] casse *f*.

breakaway ['breɪkəweɪ] adj séparatiste, dissident.

breakdance ['breɪkdɑːns] n smurf *m*. ❖ **break-dance** vi danser le smurf.

break dancing n smurf *m*.

breakdown ['breɪkdaʊn] n **1.** [mechanical] panne *f* **2.** [of communications, negotiations] rupture *f* ; [of railway system] arrêt *m* complet ; [of tradition, state of affairs] détérioration *f*, dégradation *f* **3.** MED [nervous] dépression *f* nerveuse ▪ *to have a breakdown* faire une dépression (nerveuse) ; [physical] effondrement *m* **4.** [analysis] analyse *f* ; [into parts] décomposition *f* ; COMM [of costs, figures] ventilation *f*.

breakdown lorry, breakdown truck n ⓊⓀ dépanneuse *f*.

breaker ['breɪkə*r*] n [wave] brisant *m*.

break-even adj ▪ **break-even point** seuil *m* de rentabilité, point mort *m* ▪ **break-even price** prix *m* d'équilibre.

breakfast ['brekfəst] n petit déjeuner *m* ▪ *to have breakfast* prendre le petit déjeuner.

breakfast cereal n céréales *fpl*.

breakfast room n salle *f* du petit déjeuner.

breakfast television n télévision *f* du matin.

break-in n cambriolage *m*.

breaking ['breɪkɪŋ] n **1.** [shattering] bris *m* ; [of bone] fracture *f* ; LAW [of seal] bris *m* **2.** [violation - of treaty, rule, law] violation *f* **3.** [interruption - of journey] interruption *f* ; [-of silence] rupture *f*.

breaking point n lit point *m* de rupture ; fig : *I've reached breaking point* je suis à bout, je n'en peux plus ▪ *the situation has reached breaking point* la situation est devenue critique.

breakneck ['breɪknek] adj ▪ **at breakneck speed** à une allure folle, à tombeau ouvert.

breakout ['breɪkaʊt] n [from prison] évasion *f* (de prison).

breakthrough ['breɪkθruː] n **1.** [advance, discovery] découverte *f* capitale, percée *f* (technologique) **2.** [in enemy lines] percée *f*.

breakup ['breɪkʌp] n **1.** [disintegration - of association] démembrement *m*, dissolution *f* ; [-of relationship] rupture *f* **2.** [end - of meeting, activity] fin *f*.

breakup value n COMM valeur *f* liquidative.

breakwater ['breɪkˌwɔːtə*r*] n digue *f*, brise-lames *m* inv.

bream [briːm] (pl **bream** or **breams**) n brème *f*.

breast [brest] n **1.** [chest] poitrine *f* ; [of animal] poitrine, poitrail *m* ; CULIN [of chicken] blanc *m* **2.** [bosom - of woman] sein *m*, poitrine *f* ▪ **breast cancer** cancer *m* du sein ; arch [of man] sein *m*.

breastbone ['brestbəʊn] n ANAT sternum *m* ; [of bird] bréchet *m*.

breast-fed adj nourri au sein.

breast-feed ➡ vt allaiter, donner le sein à. ➡ vi allaiter, nourrir au sein.

breast-feeding n allaitement *m* au sein.

breast milk n (U) lait *m* maternel.

breast pocket n poche *f* de poitrine.

breast pump n tire-lait *m*.

breaststroke ['breststrəʊk] n brasse *f*.

breath [breθ] n **1.** [of human, animal] haleine *f*, souffle *m* ▪ *to have bad breath* avoir mauvaise haleine /

he took a deep breath il a respiré à fond **/ let me get my breath back** laissez-moi retrouver mon souffle or reprendre haleine ▸ **to be out of breath** être essoufflé or à bout de souffle ▸ **under one's breath** à voix basse, tout bas **/ he drew his last breath** il a rendu l'âme or le dernier soupir **/ the sight took his breath away** la vue or le spectacle lui a coupé le souffle **2.** [gust] souffle m **/ there isn't a breath of air** il n'y a pas un souffle d'air **/ we went out for a breath of fresh air** nous sommes sortis prendre l'air.

breathable ['briːðəbl] adj respirable.

breathalyse 🇬🇧, **breathalyze** 🇺🇸 ['breθəlaɪz] vt faire passer l'Alcootest® à.

Breathalyser® 🇬🇧, **Breathalyzer®** 🇺🇸 ['breθəlaɪzəʳ] n Alcootest® m.

breathe [briːð] ◆ vi [person] respirer **/ to breathe heavily** or **deeply a)** [after exertion] souffler or respirer bruyamment **b)** [during illness] il respirait péniblement **/ how can I work with you breathing down my neck?** comment veux-tu que je travaille si tu es toujours derrière moi ? ◆ vt **1.** PHYSIOL respirer **/ she breathed a sigh of relief** elle poussa un soupir de soulagement ▸ **to breathe one's last** rendre le dernier soupir or l'âme **/ she breathed new life into the project** elle a insufflé de nouvelles forces au projet **2.** [whisper] murmurer **/ don't breathe a word!** ne soufflez pas mot ! ❖ **breathe in** vi & vt sep inspirer. ❖ **breathe out** vi & vt sep expirer.

breather ['briːðəʳ] n inf moment m de repos or de répit.

breath freshener n purificateur m d'haleine, spray m buccal.

breathing ['briːðɪŋ] n [gen] respiration f, souffle m ; [of musician] respiration f.

breathing space n moment m de répit.

breathless ['breθlɪs] adj **1.** [from exertion] essoufflé, hors d'haleine ; [from illness] oppressé, qui a du mal à respirer **2.** [from emotion] : **his kiss left her breathless** son baiser lui a coupé le souffle.

breathlessness ['breθlɪsnɪs] n essoufflement m.

breathtaking ['breθ,teɪkɪŋ] adj impressionnant **/ a breathtaking view** une vue à (vous) couper le souffle.

breathtakingly ['breθ,teɪkɪŋlɪ] adv de manière impressionnante **/ breathtakingly good** époustouflant **/ breathtakingly stupid** d'une bêtise invraisemblable.

breath test n Alcootest® m.

breathy ['breθɪ] (compar **breathier**, superl **breathiest**) adj qui respire bruyamment ; MUS qui manque d'attaque.

bred [bred] ◆ pt & pp ⟶ **breed**. ◆ adj élevé.

-bred in comp élevé **/ ill / well-bred** mal / bien élevé.

breech [briːtʃ] n [of person] derrière m.

breed [briːd] (pt & pp **bred** [bred]) ◆ n ZOOL [race] race f, espèce f ; [within race] type m ; BOT [of plant] espèce f. ◆ vt **1.** [raise - animals] élever, faire l'élevage de ; [- plants] cultiver ; liter & hum [children] élever **2.** fig [cause] engendrer, faire naître. ◆ vi se reproduire, se multiplier.

breeder ['briːdəʳ] n [farmer] éleveur m, -euse f ; [animal] reproducteur m, -trice f.

breeder reactor n surgénérateur m, surrégénérateur m.

breeding ['briːdɪŋ] n **1.** AGR [raising - of animals] élevage m ; [- of plants] culture f **2.** [upbringing] éducation f.

breeding-ground n **1.** [for wild animals, birds] lieu m de prédilection pour l'accouplement or la ponte **2.** fig : a **breeding-ground for terrorists** une pépinière de terroristes.

breeze [briːz] ◆ n **1.** [wind] brise f **/ a gentle** or **light breeze** une petite or légère brise **/ a stiff breeze** un vent frais **2.** 🇺🇸 inf [easy task] ▸ **that's a breeze** c'est l'enfance

de l'art, c'est du gâteau. ◆ vi **1.** [move quickly] aller vite **2.** [do easily] : **I breezed through the exam** inf j'ai passé l'examen les doigts dans le nez. ❖ **breeze in** vi : **she breezed in a)** [quickly] elle est entrée en coup de vent **b)** [casually] elle est entrée d'un air désinvolte.

breezeblock ['briːzblɒk] n 🇬🇧 parpaing m.

breezy ['briːzɪ] (compar **breezier**, superl **breeziest**) adj **1.** [weather, day] venteux ; [place, spot] éventé **2.** [person - casual] désinvolte ; [- cheerful] jovial, enjoué.

Breton ['bretɒn] ◆ n [person] Breton m, -onne f. ◆ adj breton.

brevity ['brevɪtɪ] n **1.** [shortness] brièveté f **2.** [succinctness] concision f ; [terseness] laconisme m.

brew [bruː] ◆ n **1.** [infusion] infusion f ; [herbal] tisane f **2.** [beer] brassage m ; [amount made] brassin m **3.** inf : **do you want a brew? a)** [tea] tu veux du thé ? **b)** [coffee] tu veux du café ? ◆ vt [make - tea] préparer, faire infuser ; [- beer] brasser. ◆ vi **1.** [tea] infuser ; [beer] fermenter **2.** [make beer] brasser, faire de la bière **3.** fig [storm] couver, se préparer ; [scheme] se tramer, mijoter **/ there's trouble brewing** il y a de l'orage dans l'air.

brewer ['bruːəʳ] n brasseur m.

brewery ['brʊərɪ] (pl **breweries**) n brasserie f (fabrique).

bribe [braɪb] ◆ vt soudoyer, acheter ; [witness] suborner. ◆ n pot-de-vin m **/ to take bribes** se laisser corrompre.

bribery ['braɪbərɪ] n corruption f ; [of witness] subornation f ▸ **bribery and corruption** LAW corruption.

bric-à-brac ['brɪkəbræk] ◆ n bric-à-brac m. ◆ comp ▸ **a bric-à-brac shop / stall** une boutique / un éventaire de brocanteur.

brick [brɪk] ◆ n **1.** [for building] brique f **2.** 🇬🇧 [toy] cube m (de construction). ◆ comp [building] en brique or briques ▸ **it's like talking to a brick wall** autant (vaut) parler à un mur or un sourd.

bricklayer ['brɪk,leɪəʳ] n maçon m, ouvrier-maçon m.

brickwork ['brɪkwɜːk] n [structure] briquetage m, brique f.

bridal ['braɪdl] adj [gown, veil] de mariée ; [chamber, procession] nuptial ; [feast] de noce.

bride [braɪd] n [before wedding] (future) mariée f ; [after wedding] (jeune) mariée f ▸ **the bride and groom** les (jeunes) mariés mpl.

bridegroom ['braɪdgrʊm] n [before wedding] (futur) marié m ; [after wedding] (jeune) marié m.

bridesmaid ['braɪdzmeɪd] n demoiselle f d'honneur.

bride-to-be n future mariée f.

bridge [brɪdʒ] ◆ n **1.** [structure] pont m **2.** fig [link] rapprochement m **3.** [of ship] passerelle f (de commandement) **4.** [of nose] arête f ; [of glasses] arcade f **5.** [dentures] bridge m **6.** [card game] bridge m. ◆ vt [river] construire or jeter un pont sur ; fig : **to bridge the generation gap** combler le fossé entre les générations.

bridging loan n 🇬🇧 prêt-relais m.

bridle ['braɪdl] ◆ n [harness] bride f ; fig [constraint] frein m, contrainte f. ◆ vi [in anger] se rebiffer, prendre la mouche ; [in indignation] redresser la tête.

bridle path, **bridleway** ['braɪdlweɪ] n piste f cavalière.

brief [briːf] ◆ adj **1.** [short in duration] bref, court **2.** [succinct] concis, bref **/ to be brief, I think you're right** en bref, je crois que tu as raison. ◆ vt [bring up to date] mettre au courant ; [give orders to] donner des instructions à. ◆ n **1.** LAW dossier m, affaire f **2.** [instructions] briefing m **/ my brief was to develop sales** la tâche or la mission qui m'a été confiée était de développer les ventes. ❖ **briefs** pl n [underwear] slip m. ❖ **in brief** adv phr en résumé.

briefcase ['bri:fkeɪs] n serviette f, mallette f.

briefing ['bri:fɪŋ] n MIL [meeting] briefing m, instructions fpl.

briefly ['bri:flɪ] adv **1.** [for a short time] un court instant **2.** [succinctly] brièvement ; [tersely] laconiquement / *put briefly, the situation is a mess* en bref, la situation est très embrouillée.

Brig. (written abbr of **brigadier**) n ▸ **Brig. Smith** le général de brigade Smith.

brigade [brɪ'geɪd] n [gen & MIL] brigade f.

brigadier [,brɪgə'dɪə'] n 🇬🇧 général m de brigade.

bright [braɪt] adj **1.** [weather, day] clair, radieux ; [sunshine] éclatant / *the weather will get brighter later* le temps s'améliorera en cours de journée / *cloudy with bright intervals* nuageux avec des éclaircies ▸ **bright and early** tôt le matin, de bon or grand matin ; [room] clair ; [fire, light] vif ; [colour] vif, éclatant **2.** [shining - diamond, star] brillant ; [- metal] poli, luisant ; [- eyes] brillant, vif **3.** [clever] intelligent ; [child] éveillé, vif ▸ **a bright idea** une idée géniale or lumineuse **4.** [cheerful] gai, joyeux ; [lively] animé, vif ▸ **to be bright and breezy** avoir l'air en pleine forme **5.** [promising] brillant / *there are brighter days ahead* des jours meilleurs nous attendent / *the future's looking bright* l'avenir est plein de promesses or s'annonce bien ▸ **to look on the bright side** prendre les choses du bon côté, être optimiste.

brighten ['braɪtn] ◆ vi **1.** [weather] s'améliorer **2.** [person] s'animer ; [face] s'éclairer ; [eyes] s'allumer, s'éclairer **3.** [prospects] s'améliorer. ◆ vt **1.** [decorate - place, person] égayer ; [enliven - conversation] animer, égayer **2.** [prospects] améliorer, faire paraître sous un meilleur jour **3.** [colour] aviver. ❖ **brighten up** vi & vt sep = **brighten**.

brightly ['braɪtlɪ] adv **1.** [shine] avec éclat / *the stars were shining brightly* les étoiles scintillaient / *the fire burned brightly* le feu flambait **2.** [cheerfully] gaiement, joyeusement.

brightly-coloured adj aux couleurs vives.

brightness ['braɪtnɪs] n [of sun] éclat m ; [of light] intensité f ; [of room] clarté f, luminosité f ; [of colour] éclat m.

bright spark n 🇬🇧 inf [clever person] lumière f.

brilliance ['brɪljəns], **brilliancy** ['brɪljənsɪ] n **1.** [of light, smile, career] éclat m, brillant m **2.** [cleverness] intelligence f.

brilliant ['brɪljənt] adj **1.** [light, sunshine] éclatant, intense ; [smile] éclatant, rayonnant ; [colour] vif, éclatant **2.** [outstanding - mind, musician, writer] brillant, exceptionnel ; [- film, novel, piece of work] brillant, exceptionnel ; [- success] éclatant **3.** inf [terrific] sensationnel, super **4.** [intelligent] brillant / *that's a brilliant idea* c'est une idée lumineuse or de génie.

brilliantly ['brɪljəntlɪ] adv **1.** [shine] avec éclat ▸ **brilliantly coloured** d'une couleur vive **2.** [perform, talk] brillamment.

Brillo pad® ['brɪləʊ-] n ≃ tampon m Jex.

brim [brɪm] (pt & pp **brimmed**, cont **brimming**) ◆ n [of hat] bord m ; [of bowl, cup] bord m / *full to the brim* plein à ras bord. ◆ vi déborder / *eyes brimming with tears* des yeux pleins or noyés de larmes. ❖ **brim over** vi déborder.

brimstone ['brɪmstəʊn] n [sulphur] soufre m.

brine [braɪn] n **1.** [salty water] eau f salée ; CULIN saumure f **2.** liter [sea] mer f ; [sea water] eau f de mer.

bring [brɪŋ] (pt & pp **brought** [brɔːt]) vt **1.** [take - animal, person, vehicle] amener / [- object] apporter / *I'll*

bring the books (across) tomorrow j'apporterai les livres demain / *her father's bringing her home today* son père la ramène à la maison aujourd'hui / *he brought his dog with him* il a emmené son chien **2.** [into specified state] entraîner, amener ▸ **to bring sb to his / her senses** ramener qqn à la raison ▸ **to bring sth to an end** or **a close** or **a halt** mettre fin à qqch **3.** [produce] provoquer, causer ▸ **to bring sthg upon sb** attirer qqch sur qqn / *the story brought tears to my eyes* l'histoire m'a fait venir les larmes aux yeux **4.** [force] amener / *she can't bring herself to speak about it* elle n'arrive pas à en parler **5.** LAW ▸ **to bring an action** or **a suit against sb** intenter un procès à or contre qqn ▸ **to bring a charge against sb** porter une accusation contre qqn **6.** [financially] rapporter / *her painting only brings her a few thousand pounds a year* ses peintures ne lui rapportent que quelques milliers de livres par an. ❖ **bring about** vt sep [cause - changes, war] provoquer, amener, entraîner. ❖ **bring along** vt sep [person] amener ; [thing] apporter. ❖ **bring around** = **bring round**. ❖ **bring back** vt sep **1.** [fetch - person] ramener ; [- thing] rapporter **2.** [restore] restaurer **3.** [evoke - memory] rappeler (à la mémoire). ❖ **bring down** vt sep **1.** [reduce - prices, temperature] faire baisser ; [- swelling] réduire **2.** [cause to land - kite] ramener (au sol) ; [- plane] faire atterrir **3.** [cause to fall - prey] descendre ; [- plane, enemy, tree] abattre **4.** [overthrow] faire tomber, renverser. ❖ **bring forward** vt sep **1.** [present - person] faire avancer ; [- witness] produire ; [- evidence] avancer, présenter **2.** [move - date, meeting] avancer. ❖ **bring in** vt sep **1.** [fetch in - person] faire entrer ; [- thing] rentrer **2.** [introduce - laws, system] introduire, présenter ; [- fashion] lancer **3.** [yield, produce] rapporter **4.** LAW [verdict] rendre. ❖ **bring off** vt sep 🇬🇧 inf [trick] réussir ; [plan] réaliser ; [deal] conclure, mener à bien / *did you manage to bring it off?* avez-vous réussi votre coup ? ❖ **bring on** vt sep [induce] provoquer, causer. ❖ **bring out** vt sep **1.** [take out - person] faire sortir ; [- thing] sortir **2.** [commercially - product, style] lancer ; [- music album] sortir ; [- book] publier **3.** [accentuate] souligner / *to bring out the best / worst in sb* faire apparaître qqn sous son meilleur / plus mauvais jour **4.** [encourage - person] encourager. ❖ **bring round**, **bring around** vt sep **1.** [take - person] amener ; [- thing] apporter / *I brought the conversation round to marriage* j'ai amené la conversation sur le mariage **2.** [revive] ranimer **3.** [persuade] convaincre, convertir. ❖ **bring together** vt sep **1.** [people] réunir ; [facts] rassembler **2.** [introduce] mettre en contact, faire se rencontrer **3.** [reconcile] réconcilier. ❖ **bring up** vt sep **1.** [take - person] amener ; [- thing] monter **2.** [child] élever ▸ **to be well / badly brought up** être bien / mal élevé **3.** [mention - fact, problem] signaler, mentionner ; [- question] soulever **4.** [vomit] vomir, rendre.

bring-and-buy n 🇬🇧 ▸ **bring-and-buy (sale)** brocante de particuliers en Grande-Bretagne.

 Bring-and-buy sale
Ces brocantes sont en général destinées à réunir des fonds pour une œuvre de charité. On y vend des objets d'occasion et des produits faits maison.

brink [brɪŋk] n bord m ▸ **to be on the brink of doing sthg** être sur le point de faire qqch.

brisk [brɪsk] adj **1.** [person] vif, alerte ; [manner] brusque **2.** [quick] rapide, vif / *to go for a brisk walk* se promener d'un bon pas / *at a brisk pace* à vive allure **3.** COMM florissant / *business is brisk* les affaires marchent bien.

brisket ['brɪskɪt] n [of animal] poitrine f; CULIN poitrine f de bœuf.

briskly ['brɪsklɪ] adv **1.** [move] vivement; [walk] d'un bon pas; [speak] brusquement; [act] sans délai or tarder **2.** COMM : *cold drinks were selling briskly* les boissons fraîches se vendaient très bien or comme des petits pains.

bristle ['brɪsl] ◆ vi **1.** [hair] se redresser, se hérisser **2.** *fig* [show anger] s'irriter, se hérisser. ◆ n [of beard, brush] poil m; [of boar, pig] soie f; [of plant] poil m, soie f / *a brush with Nylon® / natural bristles* une brosse en nylon / soie.

bristly ['brɪslɪ] (*compar* **bristlier**, *superl* **bristliest**) adj [beard - in appearance] aux poils raides; [-to touch] qui pique; [chin] piquant.

Brit [brɪt] n *inf* Britannique mf.

Britain ['brɪtn] pr n ▶ **(Great) Britain** Grande-Bretagne f.

 The Battle of Britain

Lutte aérienne qui opposa, d'août à octobre 1940, la Luftwaffe à la RAF, l'objectif allemand étant de neutraliser l'espace aérien britannique et d'envahir la Grande-Bretagne. La résistance des forces aériennes britanniques mit un terme au projet des nazis.

Britart ['brɪtɑ:t] pr n *nom qui désigne l'œuvre de certains artistes conceptuels britanniques en vogue depuis le début des années 1990 (Tracey Emin, Damien Hirst, etc.).*

British ['brɪtɪʃ] ◆ adj britannique, anglais ▶ **British English** anglais m britannique. ◆ pl n ▶ **the British** les Britanniques mpl, les Anglais mpl.

British Broadcasting Corporation pr n ▶ **the British Broadcasting Corporation** la BBC.

British Columbia pr n Colombie-Britannique f.

British Council pr n ▶ **the British Council** organisme public chargé de promouvoir la langue et la culture anglaises.

 British Council

La vocation du **British Council** est de promouvoir la langue et la culture anglaises, et de renforcer les liens culturels entre la Grande-Bretagne et les autres pays.

Britisher ['brɪtɪʃər] n US Anglais m, -e f, Britannique mf.

British Isles pl pr n ▶ **the British Isles** les îles fpl Britanniques.

British Library pr n la *bibliothèque nationale britannique.*

 British Library

La bibliothèque nationale britannique héberge plus de 15 millions de volumes, journaux, etc. et reçoit automatiquement un exemplaire de chaque ouvrage qui est publié au Royaume-Uni. Son nouveau siège principal, qui a ouvert ses portes en 1997, se situe entre les gares de **Euston** et **St. Pancras** à Londres. Avant, elle occupait la très pittoresque salle de lecture du **British Museum**.

British Museum pr n British Museum (*grand musée et bibliothèque londoniens*).

British National Party pr n ▶ **the British National Party** *parti d'extrême droite anglais.*

British Rail pr n *ancienne société des chemins de fer britanniques.*

British Summer Time n *heure d'été britannique.*

British Telecom [-'telɪkɒm] pr n *société britannique de télécommunications.*

Briton ['brɪtn] n Britannique mf, Anglais m, -e f; HIST Breton m, -onne f (d'Angleterre).

Britpop ['brɪtpɒp] pr n *nom qui désigne la production de certains groupes pop britanniques du milieu des années 1990 (Blur, Suede, Oasis, etc.).*

Brittany ['brɪtənɪ] pr n Bretagne f.

brittle ['brɪtl] adj **1.** [breakable] cassant, fragile **2.** [person] froid, indifférent; [humour] mordant, caustique; [reply] sec (sèche).

bro [brəʊ] (*abbr of* **brother**) n **1.** *inf* [brother] : *my bro* mon frangin **2.** US [as greeting] : *hey, bro!* salut mon pote !

broach [brəʊtʃ] vt [subject] aborder, entamer.

broad [brɔ:d] ◆ adj **1.** [wide] large / *to be broad in the shoulders* or *to have broad shoulders* être large d'épaules **2.** [extensive] vaste, immense / *a broad syllabus* un programme très divers / *we offer a broad range of products* nous offrons une large or grande gamme de produits ▶ **in broad daylight a)** *lit* au grand jour, en plein jour **b)** *fig* au vu et au su de tout le monde, au grand jour **3.** [general] général / *here is a broad outline* voilà les grandes lignes / *in the broadest sense of the word* au sens le plus large du mot **4.** [not subtle] évident / *a broad hint* une allusion transparente / *he speaks with a broad Scots accent* il a un accent écossais prononcé or un fort accent écossais **5.** [liberal] libéral / *she has very broad tastes in literature* elle a des goûts littéraires très éclectiques **6.** [coarse] grossier, vulgaire. ◆ n **1.** [widest part] : *the broad of the back* le milieu du dos **2.** US *v inf* [woman] gonzesse f.

B-road n UK ≃ route f départementale or secondaire.

broadband ['brɔ:dbænd] ◆ n transmission f à large bande. ◆ adj à larges bandes ▶ **broadband Internet connection** connexion f à haut débit.

broad bean n fève f.

broad-brush adj : *a broad-brush approach* une approche grossière.

broadcast ['brɔ:dkɑ:st] (*pt* & *pp* **broadcast** or **broadcasted**) ◆ n émission f. ◆ vt RADIO diffuser, radiodiffuser, émettre; TV téléviser, émettre. ◆ vi [station] émettre; [actor] participer à une émission; TV paraître à la télévision; [show host] faire une émission.

broadcaster ['brɔ:dkɑ:stər] n personnalité f de la radio or de la télévision.

broadcasting ['brɔ:dkɑ:stɪŋ] n RADIO radiodiffusion f; TV télévision f / *he wants to go into broadcasting* il veut faire une carrière à la radio ou à la télévision.

broaden ['brɔ:dn] ◆ vi s'élargir. ◆ vt élargir.

broad jump n US saut m en longueur.

broadly ['brɔ:dlɪ] adv **1.** [widely] largement / *to smile broadly* faire un grand sourire **2.** [generally] en général ▶ **broadly speaking** d'une façon générale, en gros.

broadly-based adj composé d'éléments variés or divers.

broad-minded adj : *to be broad-minded* avoir les idées larges.

broad-mindedness [-'maɪndɪdnɪs] n largeur f d'esprit.

broadsheet ['brɔ:dʃi:t] n [newspaper] journal m plein format ▶ **the broadsheets** UK PRESS les journaux mpl de qualité.

Broadsheet

Le terme **broadsheet** (Royaume-Uni) ou **broadside** (États-Unis) désigne les journaux de qualité, imprimés sur des feuilles grand format, qui contiennent des informations sérieuses et des rubriques culturelles, sportives et financières de bon niveau. Au Royaume-Uni, les principaux journaux nationaux de qualité sont : **The Guardian** (tendance centre gauche), **The Independent**, **The Daily Telegraph** (tendance conservatrice), **The Times** (tendance centre droit), **The Financial Times**. Cependant, la majorité de ces quotidiens ont aujourd'hui adopté un format réduit, plus pratique pour les usagers des transports en commun, ce qui a eu pour effet d'augmenter considérablement les ventes. Aux États-Unis, les grands journaux nationaux sont **The Christian Science Monitor** et **The Wall Street Journal** ainsi que **The New York Times, The Washington Post** et **The Los Angeles Times** dans leurs éditions nationales.

brocade [brə'keɪd] n brocart *m*.

broccoli ['brɒkəlɪ] n *(U)* brocolis *mpl*.

brochure [🇬🇧 'brəʊʃə 🇺🇸 brəʊ'ʃʊr] n [gen] brochure *f*, dépliant *m* ; SCH & UNIV prospectus *m*.

broil [brɔɪl] 🇺🇸 vt griller, faire cuire sur le gril ; *fig* griller.

broiler ['brɔɪlə'] n [chicken] poulet *m* (à rôtir).

broke [brəʊk] ◆ pt ⟶ **break**. ◆ adj *inf* fauché, à sec ▶ **to go broke** faire faillite ▶ **to go for broke** risquer le tout pour le tout.

broken ['brəʊkn] ◆ pp ⟶ **break**. ◆ adj 1. [damaged -chair, toy, window] cassé, brisé ; [-leg, rib] fracturé, cassé ; [-back] brisé, cassé ; [-biscuits] brisé ; *fig* : *broken heart* cœur brisé / *a broken marriage* un mariage brisé, un ménage désuni 2. [sleep -disturbed] interrompu ; [-restless] agité 3. [speech] mauvais, imparfait / *in broken French* en mauvais français 4. [agreement, promise] rompu, violé ; [appointment] manqué 5. [health] délabré ▶ **he's a broken man since his wife's death** [emotionally] il a le cœur brisé or il est très abattu depuis la mort de sa femme ▶ **the scandal left him a broken man** [financially] le scandale l'a ruiné 6. [uneven -ground] accidenté ; [-coastline] dentelé ; [-line] brisé, discontinu ▶ **broken cloud** *(U)* éclaircie *f*.

broken-down adj [damaged -machine] détraqué ; [-car] en panne.

brokenhearted [ˌbrəʊkn'hɑːtɪd] adj au cœur brisé.

broker ['brəʊkə'] n COMM courtier *m* ; NAUT courtier *m* maritime ; ST. EX ≃ courtier *m* (en Bourse) ; ≃ agent *m* de change.

brokerage ['brəʊkərɪdʒ], **broking** ['brəʊkɪŋ] n courtage *m*.

brolly ['brɒlɪ] *(pl* **brollies**) n 🇬🇧 *inf* pépin *m* (parapluie).

bronchitis [brɒŋ'kaɪtɪs] n *(U)* bronchite *f*.

bronze [brɒnz] ◆ n [alloy] bronze *m*. ◆ comp 1. [lamp, medal, statue] de or en bronze 2. [colour, skin] (couleur *f* de) bronze *(inv)*.

bronzed [brɒnzd] adj bronzé, hâlé.

bronze medal n médaille *f* de bronze.

bronze medallist n : *he's the bronze medallist* il a remporté la médaille de bronze.

brooch [brəʊtʃ] *(pl* **brooches**) n broche *f (bijou)*.

brood [bruːd] ◆ n 1. [of birds] couvée *f*, nichée *f* ; [of animals] nichée *f*, portée *f* 2. *hum* [children] progéniture *f hum*. ◆ vi 1. [bird] couver 2. [danger, storm] couver, menacer 3. [person] ruminer, broyer du noir.

broody ['bruːdɪ] *(compar* **broodier**, *superl* **broodiest**) adj 1. [reflective] pensif ; [gloomy] mélancolique, cafardeux 2. [motherly] ▶ **a broody hen** une (poule) couveuse ▶ **to feel broody** 🇬🇧 *inf & fig* être en mal d'enfant.

brook [brʊk] ◆ vt *(usu neg)* [tolerate] supporter, tolérer ; [answer, delay] admettre, souffrir. ◆ n [stream] ruisseau *m*.

broom [bruːm] n 1. [brush] balai *m* 2. BOT genêt *m*.

broomstick ['bruːmstɪk] n manche *m* à balai.

bros., Bros. [brɒs] *(abbr of* **brothers**) COMM Frères.

broth [brɒθ] n CULIN bouillon *m (de viande et de légumes)*.

brothel ['brɒθl] n maison *f* close or de passe.

brother ['brʌðə'] n 1. [relative] frère *m* / *older* / *younger brother* frère aîné / cadet 2. *(pl* **brethren** ['breðrən]) [fellow member -of trade union] camarade *m* ; [-of professional group] collègue *mf*.

brotherhood ['brʌðəhʊd] n 1. [relationship] fraternité *f*, *fig* [fellowship] fraternité *f*, confraternité *f* ; RELIG confrérie *f* 2. [association] confrérie *f*.

brother-in-law *(pl* **brothers-in-law**) n beau-frère *m*.

brotherly ['brʌðəlɪ] adj fraternel.

brought [brɔːt] pt & pp ⟶ **bring**.

brow [braʊ] n 1. [forehead] front *m* 2. [eyebrow] sourcil *m* 3. [of hill] sommet *m*.

browbeat ['braʊbiːt] *(pt* **browbeat**, *pp* **browbeaten** [-biːtn]) vt intimider, brusquer ▶ **to browbeat sb into doing sthg** forcer qqn à faire qqch en usant d'intimidation.

browbeaten [-biːtn] adj persécuté.

brown [braʊn] ◆ n brun *m*, marron *m*. ◆ adj 1. [gen] brun, marron ; [leather] marron ; [hair] châtain ; [eyes] marron / *the leaves are turning brown* les feuilles commencent à jaunir 2. [tanned] bronzé, bruni ▶ **as brown as a berry** tout bronzé. ◆ vt CULIN faire dorer ; [sauce] faire roussir.

📋 **marron, brun** or **châtain?**

The most commonly used adjective for referring to the colour brown is **marron** (which is invariable):
une robe marron a brown dress.

Another adjective for the same colour, **brun(e)**, is mostly used for describing eyes, hair or skin spots and occasionally for other things:
un ours brun a brown bear.

Some human attributes can be referred to by either adjective:
des yeux marron or *des yeux bruns* brown eyes.

Châtain is an adjective used exclusively to describe brown hair, with an implication of a slightly lighter hue:
de longs cheveux châtains long (chestnut) brown hair.

The nouns **marron** and **brun, e** are used with the same restrictions as the respective adjectives, thus:
Pour peindre les vaches, prends du marron. *To paint the cows use brown.*
La brune que tu as vue hier, c'était ma sœur. *The dark-haired woman you saw yesterday was my sister.*

brown bread n *(U)* pain *m* complet or bis.

brownfield site ['braʊnfi:ld-] n terrain *m* à bâtir *(après démolition de bâtiments préexistants)*.

brown goods pl n COMM *biens de consommation de taille moyenne tels que téléviseur, radio ou magnétoscope*.

brownie ['braʊnɪ] n [cake] brownie *m*. ❖ **Brownie (Guide)** n ≃ jeannette *f*.

brownie point n *inf & hum* bon point *m*.

brownout ['braʊnaʊt] n US [electric failure] baisse *f* de tension.

brown paper n papier *m* d'emballage ▶ **brown paper bag** sac *m* en papier kraft.

brown rat n surmulot *m*.

brown rice n riz *m* complet.

brown sugar n cassonade *f*, sucre *m* roux.

browse [braʊz] ❖ vi **1.** [person] regarder, jeter un œil / *she browsed through the book* elle a feuilleté le livre **2.** COMPUT naviguer. ❖ n [look] : *I popped into the shop to have a browse around* je suis passée au magasin pour jeter un coup d'œil or regarder.

browser ['braʊzər] n COMPUT navigateur *m*, logiciel *m* de navigation, browser *m*.

BRT MESSAGING written abbr of **be right there.**

bruise [bru:z] ❖ n [on person] bleu *m*, contusion *f* ; [on fruit] meurtrissure *f*, talure *f*. ❖ vi [fruit] se taler, s'abîmer / *to bruise easily* [person] se faire facilement des bleus. ❖ vt [person] faire un bleu à, contusionner ; *fig* blesser / *his ego was bruised* son amour-propre en a pris un coup ; [fruit] taler, abîmer ; [lettuce] flétrir.

bruised [bru:zd] adj **1.** [skin, arm] qui a des bleus ; [fruit] talé(e) **2.** *fig* [pride] meurtri(e), blessé(e).

bruiser ['bru:zər] n *inf* [big man] malabar *m* ; [fighter] cogneur *m*.

Brum [brʌm] pr n UK *inf nom familier de Birmingham*.

Brummie ['brʌmi] UK *inf n nom familier désignant un habitant de Birmingham*.

Brummy ['brʌmi] = **Brummie.**

brunch [brʌntʃ] n brunch *m*.

Brunei ['bru:naɪ] pr n Brunei *m*.

brunette [bru:'net] n brune *f*, brunette *f*.

brunt [brʌnt] n : *the village bore the full brunt of the attack* le village a essuyé le plus fort de l'attaque / *she bore the brunt of his anger* c'est sur elle que sa colère a éclaté.

bruschetta [brʊs'ketə] n CULIN bruschetta *f*.

brush [brʌʃ] (pl **brushes**) ❖ n **1.** [gen] brosse *f* ; [paintbrush] pinceau *m*, brosse *f* ; [shaving brush] blaireau *m* ; [scrubbing brush] brosse *f* dure ; [broom] balai *m* ; [shorthandled brush] balayette *f* **2.** [sweep] coup *m* de brosse **3.** [encounter, skirmish] accrochage *m*, escarmouche *f* ; *fig* : *to have a brush with death* frôler la mort / *to have a brush with the law* avoir des démêlés avec la justice **4.** *(U)* [undergrowth] broussailles *fpl* ; [scrubland] brousse *f*. ❖ vt **1.** [clean - teeth] brosser ; [tidy - hair] brosser, donner un coup de brosse à / *she brushed her hair back from her face* elle a brossé ses cheveux en arrière ; [sweep - floor] balayer **2.** [touch lightly] effleurer, frôler ; [surface] raser. ❖ vi effleurer, frôler / *her hair brushed against his cheek* ses cheveux ont effleuré or frôlé sa joue. ❖ **brush aside** vt sep **1.** [move aside] écarter, repousser **2.** [ignore - remark] balayer d'un geste ; [- report] ignorer. ❖ **brush off** vt sep **1.** [remove] enlever *(à la brosse ou à la main)* ; [insect] chasser **2.** [dismiss - remark] balayer or écarter (d'un geste) ; [- person] écarter, repousser. ❖ **brush up** vt sep *inf* [revise] revoir, réviser. ❖ **brush up on** vt insep *inf* réviser.

brushed [brʌʃt] adj gratté ▶ **brushed cotton** pilou *m*, finette *f*.

brush-off n *inf* ▶ **to give sb the brush-off** envoyer promener or balader qqn.

brush-up n **1.** UK [cleanup] coup *m* de brosse **2.** *inf* [revision] révision *f*.

brushwood ['brʌʃwʊd] n *(U)* [undergrowth] broussailles *fpl* ; [cuttings] menu bois *m*, brindilles *fpl*.

brushwork ['brʌʃwɜ:k] n *(U)* [gen] travail *m* au pinceau ; ART touche *f*.

brusque, brusk US [bru:sk] adj [abrupt] brusque ; [curt] brusque, bourru.

brusquely, bruskly US ['bru:sklɪ] adv [abruptly] avec brusquerie ; [curtly] avec brusquerie or rudesse, brutalement.

Brussels ['brʌslz] pr n Bruxelles.

Brussel(s) sprout n chou *m* de Bruxelles.

brutal ['bru:tl] adj [cruel - action, behaviour, person] brutal, cruel ; [uncompromising - honesty] franc (franche), brutal ; [severe - climate, cold] rude, rigoureux.

brutalism ['bru:təlɪzəm] n ARCHIT brutalisme *m*.

brutalist ['bru:təlɪst] adj ARCHIT brutaliste.

brutality [bru:'tælətɪ] (pl **brutalities**) n [cruelty] brutalité *f*, cruauté *f*.

brutalize, brutalise ['bru:təlaɪz] vt [ill-treat] brutaliser.

brutally ['bru:təlɪ] adv [attack, kill, treat] brutalement, sauvagement ; [say] brutalement, franchement ; [cold] extrêmement / *she gave a brutally honest account of events* elle a raconté les événements avec une franchise brutale or un réalisme brutal.

brute [bru:t] ❖ n **1.** [animal] brute *f*, bête *f* **2.** [person - violent] brute *f* ; [- coarse] brute *f* (épaisse), rustre *m*. ❖ adj [purely physical] brutal / *brute force* or *strength* force *f* brutale.

brutish ['bru:tɪʃ] adj [cruel] brutal, violent ; [coarse] grossier.

bs, B/S written abbr of **bill of sale.**

BS n **1.** (abbr of **British Standard/Standards**) UK *indique que le chiffre qui suit renvoie au numéro de la norme fixée par l'Institut britannique de normalisation* **2.** (abbr of **Bachelor of Science**) US UNIV *(titulaire d'une) licence de sciences* **3.** US v *inf* abbr of **bullshit.**

BSA (abbr of **Boy Scouts of America**) pr n *association américaine de scouts*.

BSc (abbr of **Bachelor of Science**) n UK UNIV ≃ *(titulaire d'une) licence de sciences*.

BSC (abbr of **British Steel Corporation**) pr n *entreprise sidérurgique, aujourd'hui privatisée*.

BSE (abbr of **bovine spongiform encephalopathy**) n EBS *f*.

BSI (abbr of **British Standards Institution**) pr n *association britannique de normalisation* ; ≃ AFNOR *f*.

B-side n face *f* B or 2 *(d'un disque)*.

BST n abbr of **British Summer Time.**

BT[1] pr n abbr of **British Telecom.**

BT[2] MESSAGING written abbr of **between.**

Bt. written abbr of **baronet.**

btu (abbr of **British thermal unit**) n *unité de chaleur (1 054,2 joules)*.

BTW (written abbr of **by the way**) adv *inf* à propos.

BTWN MESSAGING written abbr of **between.**

bub [bʌb] US *inf* : **hi, bub! a)** [man] salut, mon vieux ! **b)** [woman] salut, ma vieille !

bubba ['bʌbə] n [US](#) inf = bub.

bubble ['bʌbl] ◆ n **1.** [of foam] bulle f ; [in liquid] bouillon m ; [in champagne] bulle f ; [in glass] bulle f, soufflure f ; [in paint] boursouflure f, cloque f ; [in metal] soufflure f **2.** fig [illusion] ▸ to prick or to burst sb's bubble réduire à néant les illusions de qqn, enlever ses illusions à qqn. ◆ vi **1.** [liquid] bouillonner, faire des bulles ; [champagne] pétiller ; [gas] barboter **2.** [gurgle] gargouiller, glouglouter **3.** [brim] déborder. ❖ **bubble over** vi lit & fig déborder. ❖ **bubble up** vi [liquid] monter en bouillonnant ; fig [feeling] monter.

bubble bath n bain m moussant.

bubble butt n [US](#) inf ▸ to have a bubble butt avoir des petites fesses rondes et fermes.

bubble economy n économie f de bulle.

bubble gum n bubble-gum m.

bubblejet printer ['bʌbldʒet-] n imprimante f à jet d'encre.

bubble pack n [for toy, batteries] emballage m pelliculé ; [for pills] plaquette f.

bubble wrap n papier m bulle.

bubbly ['bʌblɪ] (compar **bubblier**, superl **bubbliest**) ◆ adj **1.** [liquid] pétillant, plein de bulles **2.** [person] pétillant, plein d'entrain. ◆ n inf champ m (champagne).

Bucharest [,bu:kə'rest] pr n Bucarest.

buck [bʌk] ◆ n **1.** [male animal] mâle m **2.** [US](#) inf [dollar] dollar m ▸ to make a fast or quick buck gagner du fric facilement **3.** inf [responsibility] responsabilité f ▸ to pass the buck faire porter le chapeau à qqn ▸ the buck stops here en dernier ressort, c'est moi le responsable **4.** [jump] ruade f. ◆ comp [goat, hare, kangaroo, rabbit] mâle ▸ buck deer daim m, chevreuil m. ◆ vi **1.** [horse] donner une ruade ; [US](#) [car] cahoter, tressauter **2.** [US](#) inf [resist] ▸ to buck against change se rebiffer contre les changements. ◆ vt **1.** [subj: horse] : the horse bucked his rider (off) le cheval a désarçonné or jeté bas son cavalier **2.** [resist] : to buck the system se rebiffer contre le système ▸ to buck the trend résister à la tendance. ❖ **buck up** inf ◆ vt sep **1.** [cheer up] remonter le moral à **2.** [improve] améliorer / you'd better buck up your ideas tu as intérêt à te remuer or à en mettre un coup. ◆ vi **1.** [cheer up] se secouer **2.** [hurry up] se grouiller, se magner.

bucket ['bʌkɪt] ◆ n [container, contents] seau m ▸ to cry or to weep buckets inf pleurer comme une Madeleine or un veau ▸ a bucket and spade un seau et une pelle (symbole, pour un Britannique, de vacances familiales au bord de la mer). ◆ vi [UK](#) inf [rain] pleuvoir à seaux. ❖ **bucket down** vi [UK](#) inf pleuvoir à seaux.

bucket shop n [UK](#) [travel agency] organisme de vente de billets d'avion à prix réduit.

Buckingham Palace ['bʌkɪŋəm-] pr n le palais de Buckingham (résidence officielle du souverain britannique).

buckle ['bʌkl] ◆ n [clasp] boucle f. ◆ vi **1.** [distort -metal] gauchir, se déformer ; [-wheel] se voiler **2.** [give way - knees, legs] se dérober. ◆ vt **1.** [fasten] boucler, attacher **2.** [distort] déformer, fausser ; [metal] gauchir, fausser ; [wheel] voiler. ❖ **buckle down** vi inf s'appliquer / to buckle down to work se mettre au travail.

buckling ['bʌklɪŋ] n METALL [of metal] déformation f, gauchissement m ; AUTO [of wheel] voilure f.

buckraker ['bʌkreɪkə'] n journaliste ou personnage politique qui reçoit une forte rémunération en échange de communications réalisées auprès d'un groupe d'intérêt.

buckraking ['bʌkreɪkɪŋ] n communication fortement rémunérée réalisée par un journaliste ou un personnage politique auprès d'un groupe d'intérêt.

Bucks written abbr of Buckinghamshire.

buck's fizz n [UK](#) cocktail composé de champagne et de jus d'orange.

buckshot ['bʌkʃɒt] n chevrotine f, gros plomb m.

buckskin ['bʌkskɪn] n peau f de daim.

bucktooth ['bʌk,tu:θ] (pl **buckteeth** [-,ti:θ]) n dent f proéminente or qui avance.

buckwheat ['bʌkwi:t] n sarrasin m, blé m noir.

bud [bʌd] (pt & pp **budded**, cont **budding**) ◆ n **1.** [shoot on plant] bourgeon m, il m / the trees are in bud les arbres bourgeonnent ; [for grafting] écusson m **2.** [flower] bouton m **3.** [US](#) inf [term of address] : hey, bud! **a)** [to stranger] eh, vous là-bas ! **b)** [to friend] eh, mon vieux ! ◆ vi BOT [plant] bourgeonner ; [flower] former des boutons.

Budapest [,bju:də'pest] pr n Budapest.

Buddha [[UK](#) 'budə [US](#) bu:də] pr n Bouddha.

Buddhism [[UK](#) 'budɪzm [US](#) bu:dɪzm] n bouddhisme m.

Buddhist [[UK](#) 'budɪst [US](#) budɪst] ◆ n bouddhiste mf. ◆ adj [country, priest] bouddhiste ; [art, philosophy] bouddhique.

budding ['bʌdɪŋ] adj fig [artist, genius] en herbe, prometteur ; [love] naissant.

buddy ['bʌdɪ] (pl **buddies**) n inf [friend] copain m, copine f ; [for Aids patient] compagnon m, compagne f (d'un sidéen).

budge [bʌdʒ] ◆ vi **1.** [move] bouger **2.** fig [yield] céder, changer d'avis. ◆ vt **1.** [move] faire bouger **2.** [convince] convaincre, faire changer d'avis.

budgerigar ['bʌdʒərɪgɑ:'] n [UK](#) perruche f.

budget ['bʌdʒɪt] ◆ n [gen & FIN] budget m / to be on a tight budget disposer d'un budget serré or modeste. ◆ vt budgétiser, inscrire au budget. ◆ vi dresser or préparer un budget. ◆ adj **1.** [inexpensive] économique, pour petits budgets ▸ budget prices prix mpl avantageux or modiques **2.** ECON & FIN budgétaire ▸ budget deficit déficit m budgétaire.

budget account n [with store] compte-crédit m ; [with bank] ≃ compte m permanent.

budgetary ['bʌdʒɪtrɪ] adj budgétaire.

budgie ['bʌdʒɪ] n inf perruche f.

bud vase n soliflore m.

Buenos Aires [,bwenəs'aɪrɪz] pr n Buenos Aires.

buff [bʌf] ◆ n **1.** [colour] (couleur f) chamois m **2.** [enthusiast] : a history buff un mordu d'histoire. ◆ vt polir. ◆ adj [coloured] (couleur) chamois ; [leather] de or en buffle.

buffalo ['bʌfələʊ] (pl **buffalo** or **buffaloes**) n buffle m, bufflesse f, bufflonne f ; [US](#) bison m.

buffalo wings pl n ailes de poulet frites servies avec une sauce relevée.

buffer ['bʌfə'] ◆ n [protection] tampon m ; [US](#) [on car] pare-chocs m inv ; [UK](#) RAIL [on train] tampon m ; [at station] butoir m ; COMPUT mémoire f tampon. ◆ vt tamponner, amortir (le choc).

buffering ['bʌfərɪŋ] n COMPUT [storage] stockage m en mémoire tampon ; [use] utilisation f de mémoire tampon.

buffer state n état m tampon.

buffer zone n région f tampon.

buffet¹ [[UK](#) 'bʊfeɪ [US](#) bə'feɪ] n **1.** [refreshments] buffet m **2.** [sideboard] buffet m **3.** [restaurant] buvette f, cafétéria f ; [in station] buffet m or café m de gare ; [on train] wagon-restaurant m.

buffet² ['bʌfɪt] vt [batter] : buffeted by the waves ballotté par les vagues / the trees were buffeted by the wind les arbres étaient secoués par le vent.

buffet car ['bʊfeɪ-] n wagon-restaurant m.

buffoon [bə'fuːn] n bouffon m, pitre m.

bug [bʌg] (pt & pp **bugged,** cont **bugging**) ◆ n **1.** [insect] insecte m ; [bedbug] punaise f ; fig ▶ **she's been bitten by the film bug** inf c'est une mordue de cinéma **2.** inf [germ] microbe m **3.** COMPUT bug m, bogue m **4.** inf [microphone] micro m (caché). ◆ vt **1.** inf [bother] taper sur les nerfs de ▶ **what's bugging him?** qu'est-ce qu'il a ? **2.** [wiretap - room] poser or installer des appareils d'écoute (clandestins) dans ; [-phone] brancher sur table d'écoute.

bugbear ['bʌgbeə'] n [monster] épouvantail m, croque-mitaine m ; fig [worry] bête noire f, cauchemar m.

bugger ['bʌgə'] ◆ n v inf [unpleasant person] salaud m. ◆ interj 🇬🇧 v inf merde alors ! ◆ vt 🇬🇧 v inf [damn] : oh, bugger it! oh, merde ! ❖ **bugger off** vi 🇬🇧 v inf foutre le camp.

bugger all n 🇬🇧 v inf que dalle.

buggered ['bʌgəd] adj 🇬🇧 v inf **1.** [broken] foutu **2.** [in annoyance] : buggered if I know j'en sais foutre rien.

buggy ['bʌgɪ] (pl **buggies,** compar **buggier,** superl **buggiest**) n [carriage] boghei m ; [for baby] poussette f, poussette-canne f ; 🇺🇸 [pram] voiture f d'enfant.

bugle ['bjuːgl] n clairon m.

bug-ridden adj **1.** [room, hotel] infesté de vermine **2.** [software] plein de bugs or de bogues.

build [bɪld] (pt & pp **built** [bɪlt]) ◆ vt **1.** [dwelling] bâtir, construire ; [temple] bâtir, édifier ; [bridge, machine, ship] construire ; [nest] faire, bâtir / houses are being built des maisons sont en construction / this bed wasn't built for two people ce lit n'a pas été conçu pour deux personnes **2.** [found] bâtir, fonder. ◆ vi **1.** [construct] bâtir **2.** [increase] augmenter, monter. ◆ n **1.** [body type] carrure f, charpente f / of heavy build de forte corpulence or taille / a man of slight build un homme fluet / she's about the same build as I am elle est à peu près de ma taille **2.** [construction] construction f. ❖ **build in** vt sep CONSTR [incorporate] encastrer ; fig [include - special features] intégrer. ❖ **build on** vt sep CONSTR ajouter. ❖ **build up** ◆ vt sep **1.** [develop - business, theory] établir, développer ; [-reputation] établir, bâtir ; [-confidence] donner, redonner ; [-strength] accroître, prendre **2.** [increase - production] accroître, augmenter ; [-excitement] faire monter, accroître ; [-pressure] accumuler **3.** [promote] faire de la publicité pour. ◆ vi **1.** [business] se développer **2.** [excitement] monter, augmenter ; [pressure] s'accumuler.

builder ['bɪldə'] n CONSTR [contractor] entrepreneur m ; [worker] ouvrier m du bâtiment ; [of machines, ships] constructeur m.

building ['bɪldɪŋ] ◆ n **1.** [structure] bâtiment m, construction f ; [monumental] édifice m ; [apartment, office] immeuble m **2.** [work] construction f. ◆ comp [land, plot] à bâtir ; [materials] de construction.

building and loan association n 🇺🇸 = building society.

building block n [toy] cube m ; fig composante f.

building contract n contrat m de construction.

building contractor n entrepreneur m (en bâtiment or construction).

building site n chantier m (de construction).

building society n 🇬🇧 société d'investissement et de crédit immobilier.

 Building societies

Les **building societies** sont des institutions financières mutualistes initialement fondées pour permettre à leurs membres d'acquérir un logement. Autrefois, chaque grande ville anglaise avait sa **building society**, comme en témoignent les noms de la plupart des établissements actuels (**Leeds Building Society, Cambridge Building Society,** etc.). Aujourd'hui, les **building societies** proposent un éventail de services financiers et font directement concurrence aux banques, tout en restant spécialisées dans le prêt immobilier (**mortgage lending**). Certaines **building societies** se sont démutualisées pour devenir des banques. Voir aussi **savings and loan association**.

buildup ['bɪldʌp] n [increase -in pressure] intensification f ; [-in excitement] montée f ; [COMM-in production] accroissement m ; [-in stock] accumulation f ; MIL [in troops] rassemblement m.

built [bɪlt] ◆ pt & pp ⟶ build. ◆ adj [building] bâti, construit ; [person] charpenté / brick-built en or de brique / to be powerfully built être puissamment or solidement charpenté.

built-in adj [beam, wardrobe] encastré ; [device, safeguard] intégré ; fig [feature] inné, ancré ▶ **built-in obsolescence** obsolescence f programmée.

built-up adj [land] bâti ▶ **a built-up area** une agglomération (urbaine).

bulb [bʌlb] n **1.** BOT bulbe m, oignon m **2.** ELEC ampoule f ▶ **a light bulb** une ampoule.

bulbous ['bʌlbəs] adj bulbeux.

Bulgaria [bʌl'geərɪə] pr n Bulgarie f.

Bulgarian [bʌl'geərɪən] ◆ n [person] Bulgare mf. ◆ adj bulgare.

bulge [bʌldʒ] ◆ n **1.** [lump, swelling] renflement m ; [on vase, jug] panse f, ventre m ; 🇬🇧 MIL saillant m **2.** [increase] poussée f. ◆ vi [swell] se gonfler, se renfler / his suitcase was bulging with gifts sa valise était bourrée de cadeaux ; [stick out] faire saillie, saillir.

bulghur, bulghur wheat ['bʌlgə-] n boulgour m.

bulging ['bʌldʒɪŋ] adj [eyes] saillant, globuleux ; [muscles, waist] saillant ; [bag, pockets] gonflé.

bulgur = bulghur.

bulimia [bjuː'lɪmɪə] n boulimie f.

bulimic [bjuː'lɪmɪk] ◆ adj boulimique. ◆ n boulimique mf.

bulk [bʌlk] ◆ n **1.** [mass] masse f ; [stoutness] corpulence f / a man of enormous bulk un homme très corpulent **2.** [main part] ▶ **the bulk** la plus grande partie, la majeure partie / she left the bulk of her fortune to charity elle légua le plus gros de sa fortune aux bonnes œuvres. ◆ comp [order, supplies] en gros. ❖ **in bulk** adv phr par grosses quantités ; COMM en gros ; NAUT en vrac.

bulk buying n (U) achat m par grosses quantités ; COMM achat m en gros.

bulkhead ['bʌlkhed] n cloison f (d'avion, de navire).

bulk mail n (U) envois mpl en nombre.

bulky ['bʌlkɪ] adj **1.** [massive, large] volumineux ; [cumbersome] encombrant **2.** [corpulent, stout] corpulent, gros (grosse) ; [solidly built] massif.

bull [bʊl] ◆ n **1.** [male cow] taureau *m* ▸ **like a bull in a china shop** comme un éléphant dans un magasin de porcelaine ▸ **to take the bull by the horns** prendre le taureau par les cornes **2.** [male of a species] mâle *m* **3.** *v inf* [nonsense] connerie *f*, conneries *fpl*. ◆ comp [elephant, whale] mâle *m*.

bulldog ['bʊldɒg] n ZOOL bouledogue *m*.

bulldog clip n pince *f* à dessin.

bulldoze ['bʊldəʊz] vt **1.** [building] démolir au bulldozer ; [earth, stone] passer au bulldozer **2.** *fig* [push] ▸ **to bulldoze sb into doing sthg** forcer qqn à faire qqch, faire pression sur qqn pour lui faire faire qqch.

bulldozer ['bʊldəʊzə^r] n bulldozer *m*.

bullet ['bʊlɪt] ◆ n balle *f*. ◆ comp [hole] de balle ; [wound] par balle.

bulletin ['bʊlətɪn] n [announcement] bulletin *m*, communiqué *m* ; [newsletter] bulletin *m*.

bulletin board n **1.** US [gen] tableau *m* d'affichage **2.** COMPUT ▸ **bulletin board (system)** panneau *m* d'affichage.

bullet loan n prêt-ballon *m*.

bulletproof ['bʊlɪtpruːf] adj [glass, vest] pare-balles *(inv)* ; [vehicle] blindé.

bullfight ['bʊlfaɪt] n corrida *f*, course *f* de taureaux.

bullfighter ['bʊl,faɪtə^r] n torero *m*, matador *m*.

bullfighting ['bʊl,faɪtɪŋ] n (U) courses *fpl* de taureaux, tauromachie *f*.

bullfinch ['bʊlfɪntʃ] n bouvreuil *m*.

bullhorn ['bʊlhɔːn] n US mégaphone *m*, porte-voix *m inv*.

bullion ['bʊljən] n [gold] or *m* en lingots or en barres ; [silver] argent *m* en lingots or en barres.

bullish ['bʊlɪʃ] adj ST. EX ▸ **the market is bullish** les cours or valeurs sont en hausse.

bull market n marché *m* à la hausse.

bullock ['bʊlək] n [castrated] bœuf *m* ; [young] bouvillon *m*.

bullring ['bʊlrɪŋ] n arène *f (pour la corrida)*.

bull's-eye n [centre of target] mille *m*, centre *m* de la cible ▸ **to hit the bull's-eye** *lit & fig* faire mouche, mettre dans le mille.

bullshit ['bʊlʃɪt] *vulg* n (U) connerie *f*, conneries *fpl*.

bull terrier n bull-terrier *m*.

bully ['bʊlɪ] ◆ n [adult] tyran *m* ; [child] petite brute *f*. ◆ vt [intimidate - spouse, employee] malmener / *she bullies her little sister* elle est tyrannique avec sa petite sœur / *they bullied me into going* on a fait pression sur moi pour que j'y aille. ◆ interj *inf* ▸ **bully for you!** a) chapeau ! b) *iro* quel exploit !, bravo !

bullyboy ['bʊlɪbɔɪ] n UK brute *f*, voyou *m*.

bullying ['bʊlɪŋ] ◆ adj [intimidating] agressif, brutal. ◆ n (U) brimades *fpl*.

bulrush ['bʊlrʌʃ] n jonc *m*, scirpe *m*.

bum [bʌm] (*pt & pp* **bummed**, *cont* **bumming**) *inf* ◆ n **1.** UK [buttocks] fesses *fpl*, pétard *m* **2.** US [tramp] clochard *m*, -e *f*, clodo *m* ; US [lazy person] fainéant *m*, -e *f*, flemmard *m*, -e *f* ; [worthless person] minable *mf*, minus *m*. ◆ adj [worthless] minable, nul ; [injured, disabled] patraque, mal fichu ; [untrue] faux (fausse). ◆ vt US [beg, borrow] ▸ **to bum sthg off sb** emprunter qqch à qqn, taper qqn de qqch. ◆ vt US [be disappointed] être déprimé ; [laze about] traîner. ❖ **bum about** UK, **bum around** vi *inf* **1.** [drift, wander] vagabonder, se balader **2.** [loaf, idle] fainéanter, flemmarder.

bumblebee ['bʌmblbiː] n bourdon *m*.

bumbling ['bʌmblɪŋ] adj [person] empoté, maladroit ; [behaviour] maladroit.

bumf [bʌmf] n UK *inf pej* [useless papers] paperasse *f*.

bummer ['bʌmə^r] n *v inf* [bad experience] poisse *f* / *what a bummer!* les boules !

bump [bʌmp] ◆ n **1.** [lump] bosse *f* **2.** [blow, knock] choc *m*, coup *m* ; [noise from blow] bruit *m* sourd, choc *m* sourd. ◆ vt heurter ; [elbow, head, knee] cogner. ◆ vi **1.** [move with jerks] cahoter **2.** [collide] se heurter. ❖ **bump into** vt insep [object] rentrer dedans, tamponner ; [person] rencontrer par hasard, tomber sur. ❖ **bump off** vt sep *inf* [murder] liquider, supprimer ; [with a gun] descendre. ❖ **bump up** vt sep *inf* [increase] faire grimper ; [prices] gonfler, faire grimper.

bumper ['bʌmpə^r] ◆ n AUTO pare-chocs *m inv*. ◆ adj [crop, harvest] exceptionnel, formidable.

bumper car n auto *f* tamponneuse.

bumper sticker n autocollant *m (pour voiture)*.

bumper-to-bumper adj : *the cars are bumper-to-bumper on the bridge* les voitures roulent pare-chocs contre pare-chocs sur le pont.

bumph n *inf* = **bumf**.

bumpkin ['bʌmpkɪn] n *inf & pej* plouc *m*, péquenaud *m*.

bump start n *démarrage d'un véhicule en le poussant*. ❖ **bump-start** vt démarrer en poussant.

bumptious ['bʌmpʃəs] adj suffisant, prétentieux.

bumpy ['bʌmpɪ] (*compar* **bumpier,** *superl* **bumpiest**) adj [road] cahoteux ; [flight, ride] agité (de secousses) ; [surface, wall] bosselé / *we've got a bumpy ride ahead of us fig* on va traverser une mauvaise passe.

bun [bʌn] n **1.** [bread] petit pain *m* (au lait) **2.** [hair] chignon *m*.

bunch [bʌntʃ] ◆ n **1.** [of flowers, straw] bouquet *m*, botte *f* ; [of grapes] grappe *f* ; [of bananas, dates] régime *m* ; [of feathers, hair] touffe *f* ; [of sticks, twigs] faisceau *m*, poignée *f* ; [of keys] trousseau *m* **2.** *inf* [of people] bande *f* / *he's the best of a bad bunch* c'est le moins mauvais de la bande ; [of things] : *he took out a bunch of papers from the drawer* il sortit un tas de papiers du tiroir **3.** PHR ▸ **thanks a bunch!** *inf & iro* merci beaucoup ! ❖ **bunches** pl n UK couettes *fpl* / *she wears her hair in bunches* elle porte des couettes. ❖ **bunch together** vi [people] se serrer, se presser. ◆ vt sep mettre ensemble ; [flowers] botteler, mettre en bouquets.

bundle ['bʌndl] ◆ n **1.** [of clothes, linen] paquet *m* ; [wrapped in a cloth] paquet *m* ; [of goods] paquet *m*, ballot *m* ; [of sticks, twigs] faisceau *m*, poignée *f* ; [of banknotes, papers] liasse *f* / *he's a bundle of nerves* c'est un paquet de nerfs / *a bundle of firewood* un fagot **2.** COMPUT lot *m* **3.** PHR ▸ **to go a bundle on sthg** UK *inf* s'emballer pour qqch. ◆ vt **1.** [clothes] mettre en paquet ; [for a journey] empaqueter ; [linen] mettre en paquet ; [goods] mettre en paquet ; [banknotes, papers] mettre en liasses ; [sticks, twigs] mettre en faisceaux ; [firewood] mettre en fagots ; [straw] botteler, mettre en bottes **2.** [shove] : *he was bundled into the car* on l'a poussé dans la voiture brusquement or sans ménagement. ❖ **bundle off** vt sep : *the children were bundled off to school* les enfants furent envoyés or expédiés à l'école vite fait. ❖ **bundle up** vt sep **1.** [tie up] mettre en paquet **2.*** [dress warmly] emmitoufler.

bundled ['bʌndld] adj COMPUT ▸ **bundled software** logiciel *m* livré avec le matériel.

bundler ['bʌndlə^r] n POL *leveur de fonds travaillant pour le compte d'un candidat, qui réussit à réunir des sommes importantes sous forme de donations.*

bundling ['bʌndlɪŋ] n [of products] groupage *m*.

bung [bʌŋ] ◆ n **1.** [stopper] bondon *m*, bonde *f* **2.** [hole] bonde *f*. ◆ vt **1.** [hole] boucher **2.** UK *inf* [put carelessly] balancer **3.** *inf* [add] rajouter. ❖ **bung up** vt sep UK *inf* boucher / *my nose is / my eyes are bunged up* j'ai le nez bouché / les yeux gonflés.

bungalow ['bʌngələʊ] n [one storey house] maison f sans étage ; [in India] bungalow m.

bungee ['bʌndʒiː] n [cord] tendeur m ▸ **bungee jumping** saut m à l'élastique.

bungle ['bʌngl] vt gâcher.

bunion ['bʌnjən] n oignon m (cor).

bunk [bʌŋk] n **1.** [berth] couchette f ; [bed] lit m **2.** 🇬🇧 inf ▸ **to do a bunk** se tirer v inf, se faire la malle v inf. ❖ **bunk off** vi 🇬🇧 inf **1.** [scram] décamper, filer **2.** [from school] faire le mur.

bunk bed n lits mpl superposés.

bunker ['bʌŋkə'] n **1.** MIL blockhaus m, bunker m **2.** [for coal] coffre m ; NAUT soute f **3.** GOLF bunker m.

bunkhouse ['bʌŋkhaʊs] (pl [-haʊzɪz]) n 🇺🇸 baraquement m (pour ouvriers).

bunny ['bʌnɪ] n ▸ **bunny (rabbit)** (petit) lapin m, Jeannot lapin m.

bunny hill n 🇺🇸 [in skiing] piste f pour débutants.

Bunsen burner ['bʌnsn-] n (bec m) Bunsen m.

bunting ['bʌntɪŋ] n (U) [flags] fanions mpl, drapeaux mpl.

buoy [🇬🇧 bɔɪ 🇺🇸 'buːɪ] n bouée f, balise f. ❖ **buoy up** vt sep fig [support, sustain] soutenir ; [person] remonter / her son's visit buoyed her up or buoyed up her spirits la visite de son fils l'a remontée or lui a remonté le moral.

buoyancy ['bɔɪənsɪ] n **1.** [ability to float] flottabilité f ; [of gas, liquid] poussée f **2.** fig [resilience] ressort m, force f morale ; [cheerfulness] entrain m, allant m.

buoyant ['bɔɪənt] adj **1.** [floatable] flottable, capable de flotter ; [causing to float] qui fait flotter **2.** fig [cheerful] plein d'allant or d'entrain ; [mood] gai, allègre **3.** FIN [economy, sector] sain, robuste ; ST. EX [market] soutenu.

burble ['bɜːbl] vi [liquid] glouglouter, faire glouglou ; [stream] murmurer.

burbot ['bɜːbət] n lotte f.

burbs [bɜːbz] pl n 🇺🇸 inf ▸ **the burbs** la banlieue.

burden ['bɜːdn] ❖ n **1.** fml [heavy weight, load] fardeau m, charge f **2.** fig [heavy responsibility, strain] fardeau m, charge f ▸ **to be a burden to sb** être un fardeau pour qqn / to increase / to relieve the tax burden augmenter / alléger le fardeau or le poids des impôts ▸ **the burden of proof** LAW la charge de la preuve. ❖ vt [weigh down] charger ▸ **to be burdened with sthg** être chargé de qqch / to burden sb with taxes accabler qqn d'impôts.

bureau ['bjʊərəʊ] (pl bureaus or bureaux [-rəʊz]) n **1.** ADMIN service m, office m ; [in private enterprise] bureau m **2.** 🇬🇧 [desk] secrétaire m, bureau m **3.** 🇺🇸 [chest of drawers] commode f.

bureaucracy [bjʊə'rɒkrəsɪ] n bureaucratie f.

bureaucrat ['bjʊərəkræt] n bureaucrate mf.

bureaucratic [ˌbjʊərə'krætɪk] adj bureaucratique.

burgeoning ['bɜːdʒənɪŋ] adj [industry, population] en expansion, en plein essor / a burgeoning talent un talent en herbe.

burger ['bɜːgə'] n hamburger m.

burglar ['bɜːglə'] n cambrioleur m, -euse f.

burglar alarm n dispositif m d'alarme contre le vol, antivol m.

burglarize ['bɜːgləraɪz] vt 🇺🇸 cambrioler.

burglary ['bɜːglərɪ] (pl burglaries) n cambriolage m.

burgle ['bɜːgl] vt cambrioler.

Burgundy ['bɜːgəndɪ] pr n **1.** [region] Bourgogne f **2.** [wine] bourgogne m.

burial ['berɪəl] ❖ n enterrement m, inhumation f. ❖ comp [place, service] d'inhumation.

burial chamber n caveau m.

burial ground n cimetière m.

burk [bɜːk] n = berk.

Burkina-Faso [bɜːˌkiːnə'fæsəʊ] pr n Burkina m.

burlap ['bɜːlæp] n toile f à sac, gros canevas m.

burlesque [bɜː'lesk] ❖ n **1.** LITER & THEAT burlesque m, parodie f **2.** 🇺🇸 [striptease show] revue f déshabillée, striptease m. ❖ adj burlesque.

burly ['bɜːlɪ] (compar burlier, superl burliest) adj de forte carrure.

Burma ['bɜːmə] pr n Birmanie f.

Burmese [ˌbɜː'miːz] ❖ n [person] Birman m, -e f. ❖ adj birman.

burn [bɜːn] (🇬🇧 pt & pp burned or burnt [bɜːnt] ; 🇺🇸 pt & pp burned) ❖ n [injury] brûlure f. ❖ vi **1.** lit brûler **2.** fig [face, person] : my face was burning with embarrassment] j'avais le visage en feu, j'étais tout rouge / I'm burning a) [from sun] je brûle b) [from fever] je suis brûlant, je brûle / she was burning for adventure elle brûlait du désir d'aventure. ❖ vt **1.** [paper, logs, food] brûler **2.** [car, crop, forest] brûler, incendier / three people were burnt to death trois personnes sont mortes carbonisées or ont été brûlées vives / did you burn yourself? est-ce que tu t'es brûlé ? / the house was burnt to the ground la maison fut réduite en cendres or brûla entièrement ▸ **to burn one's boats** or **bridges** brûler ses vaisseaux or les ponts ▸ **to burn one's fingers** or **to get one's fingers burnt** se brûler les doigts ▸ **to have money to burn** avoir de l'argent à ne pas savoir qu'en faire **3.** COMPUT graver. ❖ **burn down** ❖ vi [be destroyed by fire] brûler complètement. ❖ vt sep [building] détruire par le feu, incendier. ❖ **burn out** ❖ vt sep ELEC [wear out - bulb] griller ; [- fuse] faire sauter ; MECH [engine] griller ▸ **to burn o.s. out** s'épuiser. ❖ vi ELEC [bulb] griller ; [fuse] sauter ; MECH [brakes, engine] griller ; [candle, fire] s'éteindre. ❖ **burn up** vt sep **1.** [destroy by fire] brûler **2.** [consume] : to burn up a lot of calories / energy dépenser or brûler beaucoup de calories / d'énergie.

burned-out ['bɜːnd-] adj = burnt-out.

burner ['bɜːnə'] n [on a stove] brûleur m ; [on a lamp] bec m.

burning ['bɜːnɪŋ] ❖ adj **1.** [on fire] en flammes ; [arrow, fire, torch] ardent **2.** [hot] ardent, brûlant ; fig [intense] ardent, brûlant / he had a burning desire to be a writer il désirait ardemment être écrivain **3.** [crucial, vital] brûlant / a burning issue une question brûlante. ❖ n [sensation, smell] : a smell of burning une odeur de brûlé.

burnish ['bɜːnɪʃ] vt METALL brunir, polir.

burnout ['bɜːnaʊt] n [exhaustion] épuisement m total.

Burns' Night [bɜːnz-] n fête célébrée en l'honneur du poète écossais Robert Burns, le 25 janvier.

burnt [bɜːnt] ❖ pt & pp ⟶ burn. ❖ adj [charred] brûlé, carbonisé.

burnt-out ['bɜːnt-] adj **1.** [destroyed by fire] incendié, brûlé **2.** inf [person] lessivé, vidé.

burp [bɜːp] inf ❖ n rot m. ❖ vi roter.

burqa ['bɜːkə] n burqa f.

burrow ['bʌrəʊ] ❖ n terrier m. ❖ vt **1.** [subj: person] creuser ; [subj: animal, insect] creuser, fouir **2.** fig [nestle] enfouir. ❖ vi **1.** [dig] creuser **2.** [nestle] s'enfouir, s'enfoncer.

bursar ['bɜːsə'] n [treasurer] intendant m, -e f, économe mf.

bursary ['bɜːsərɪ] (pl bursaries) n [grant, scholarship] bourse f (d'études).

burst [bɜːst] (pt & pp burst) ❖ n **1.** [explosion] éclatement m, explosion f ; [puncture] éclatement m, crevai-

son f **2.** [sudden eruption - of laughter] éclat m ; [- of emotion] accès m, explosion f ; [- of ideas] jaillissement m ; [- of thunder] coup m ; [- of flame] jet m, jaillissement m ; [- of applause] salve f / *a burst of gunfire* une rafale / *he had a sudden burst of energy* il a eu un sursaut d'énergie. ◆ vi **1.** [break, explode - balloon] éclater ; [- abscess] crever ; [- tyre] crever, éclater ; [- bottle] éclater, voler en éclats / *his heart felt as if it would burst with joy / grief* il crut que son cœur allait éclater de joie / se briser de chagrin **2.** [enter, move suddenly] : *the front door burst open* la porte d'entrée s'est ouverte brusquement. ◆ vt [balloon, bubble] crever, faire éclater ; [pipe] faire éclater ; [boiler] faire éclater, faire sauter ; [tyre] crever, faire éclater ; [abscess] crever, percer / *the river is about to burst its banks* le fleuve est sur le point de déborder / *to burst a blood vessel* se faire éclater une veine, se rompre un vaisseau sanguin ▶ *don't burst a blood vessel to get it done* ⓊⓀ *inf & hum* ce n'est pas la peine de te crever pour finir, ce n'est pas la peine de te tuer à la tâche. ❖ **burst in** vi [enter violently] faire irruption ; [interrupt] interrompre brutalement la discussion ; [intrude] entrer précipitamment. ❖ **burst out** vt insep [exclaim] s'exclamer, s'écrier / *to burst out laughing* éclater de rire / *they all burst out singing* ils se sont tous mis à chanter d'un coup.

bursting ['bɜːstɪŋ] adj **1.** [full] plein à craquer ▶ *to be bursting at the seams* se défaire aux coutures, se découdre / *the place was bursting at the seams (with people)* l'endroit était plein à craquer / *to be bursting with joy / pride* déborder de joie / d'orgueil **2.** [longing, yearning] ▶ *to be bursting to do sthg* mourir d'envie de faire qqch **3.** inf [desperate to urinate] ▶ *I'm bursting* je ne peux plus attendre, ça presse.

Burundi [bʊ'rʊndɪ] pr n Burundi m.

bury ['berɪ] (*pt & pp* buried) vt **1.** [in the ground] enterrer ; [in water] immerger / *to be buried alive* être enterré vivant / *to be buried at sea* être immergé en haute mer ▶ *to bury the hatchet* enterrer la hache de guerre, faire la paix **2.** [cover completely] ensevelir, enterrer ▶ *to bury one's head in the sand* faire l'autruche **3.** [hide] : *she buried her face in the pillow* elle enfouit or enfonça son visage dans l'oreiller / *he always has his nose buried in a book* il a toujours le nez fourré dans un livre **4.** [occupy] : *to bury o.s. in (one's) work* se plonger dans son travail **5.** [thrust, plunge - knife] enfoncer, plonger.

bus [bʌs] (*pl* buses *or* busses, *pt & pp* bused *or* bussed, *cont* busing *or* bussing) ◆ n **1.** [vehicle] bus m ; ⓊⓈ [coach] car m **2.** COMPUT bus m. ◆ comp [route, service, strike, ticket] d'autobus, de bus. ◆ vt : *the children are bussed to school* les enfants vont à l'école en autobus ; ⓊⓈ SCH [for purposes of racial integration] emmener à l'école en autobus *(pour favoriser l'intégration raciale)*.

busboy ['bʌsbɔɪ] n ⓊⓈ aide-serveur m.

bus conductor n ⓊⓀ receveur m, -euse f d'autobus.

bus driver n conducteur m, -trice f d'autobus.

bush [bʊʃ] n **1.** [shrub] buisson m, arbuste m **2.** [scrubland] ▶ *the bush* la brousse.

bushel ['bʊʃl] (*pt & pp* busheled, *cont* busheling) n [measure] boisseau m.

bushfire ['bʊʃˌfaɪər] n feu m de brousse.

bush league n ⓊⓈ petite équipe locale de baseball.

bushmeat ['bʊʃmiːt] n *(U)* viande f de brousse.

bush taxi n taxi-brousse m.

bushy ['bʊʃɪ] (*compar* bushier, *superl* bushiest) adj **1.** [area] broussailleux **2.** [tree] touffu ; [beard, eyebrows, hair] touffu, fourni.

busily ['bɪzɪlɪ] adv activement ▶ *to be busily engaged in sthg / in doing sthg* être très occupé à qqch / à faire qqch.

business ['bɪznɪs] ◆ n **1.** [firm] entreprise f **2.** (*U*) [trade] affaires fpl / *business is good / bad* les affaires vont bien / mal / *the travel business* les métiers or le secteur du tourisme / *she's in the fashion business* elle est dans la mode / *these high interest rates will put us out of business* ces taux d'intérêt élevés vont nous obliger à fermer ▶ *to go out of business* cesser une activité / *he's got no business sense* il n'a pas le sens des affaires ▶ *to do business with* travailler or traiter avec / *we're not in the business of providing free meals* ce n'est pas notre rôle de fournir des repas gratuits ▶ *let's get down to business* passons aux choses sérieuses ▶ *(now) we're in business!* nous voilà partis ! **3.** [concern] : *it's my (own) business if I decide not to go* c'est mon affaire or cela ne regarde que moi si je décide de ne pas y aller / *it's none of your business* cela ne vous regarde pas / *tell him to mind his own business* dis-lui de se mêler de ses affaires ▶ *to mean business* : *I could see she meant business* je voyais qu'elle ne plaisantait pas **4.** [matter, task] : *any other business* [on agenda] points mpl divers / *she had important business to discuss* elle avait à parler d'affaires importantes / *I'm tired of the whole business* je suis las de toute cette histoire **5.** [rigmarole] : *it was a real business getting tickets for the concert* ça a été toute une affaire pour avoir des billets pour le concert. ◆ comp [lunch, trip] d'affaires ▶ *business expenses* **a)** [for individual] frais mpl professionnels **b)** [for firm] frais mpl généraux ▶ *business hours* **a)** [of office] heures fpl de bureau **b)** [of shop, public service] heures fpl d'ouverture.

business account n compte m professionnel or commercial.

business address n adresse f au lieu de travail.

business card n carte f de visite.

business centre n centre m des affaires.

business class n [on aeroplane] classe f affaires.

business college n ⓊⓀ école f de commerce ; [for management training] école f (supérieure) de gestion.

business cycle n cycle m économique.

Business Expansion Scheme pr n ⓊⓀ système d'aide à la création d'entreprise.

business incubator n incubateur d'entreprises.

business intelligence n veille f économique.

businesslike ['bɪznɪslaɪk] adj **1.** [systematic, methodical] systématique, méthodique **2.** [impersonal, formal] : *her manner was cold and businesslike* son comportement était froid et direct / *our conversation was courteous and businesslike* notre entretien a été courtois et franc.

businessman ['bɪznɪsmæn] (*pl* businessmen [-men]) n homme m d'affaires.

business manager n COMM & INDUST directeur m commercial ; SPORT manager m ; THEAT directeur m.

business model n modèle m économique, business model m.

business park n zone f d'activités.

business partner n associé m, -e f.

business plan n projet m d'entreprise.

business reply card n carte-réponse f.

business reply envelope n enveloppe f préaffranchie.

business school n ⓊⓈ = business college.

business sector n secteur m tertiaire, secteur m d'affaires.

business-to-business adj interentreprises, B to B.

B2C [ˌbiːtəˈsiː] (abbr of business to customer) n B to C.

B2E [biːtuːˈiː] abbr of business to education.

businesswoman ['bɪznɪs,wʊmən]
(*pl* **businesswomen** [-,wɪmɪn]) n femme *f* d'affaires.

busing ['bʌsɪŋ] n 🇺🇸 *système de ramassage scolaire aux États-Unis, qui organise la répartition des enfants noirs et des enfants blancs dans les écoles afin de lutter contre la ségrégation raciale.*

busk [bʌsk] vi 🇺🇰 *jouer de la musique (dans la rue ou le métro).*

busker ['bʌskər] n 🇺🇰 musicien *m*, -enne *f* de rue.

bus lane n voie *f* or couloir *m* d'autobus.

busload ['bʌsləʊd] n : *a busload of workers* un autobus plein d'ouvriers / *the tourists arrived by the busload* or *in busloads* les touristes sont arrivés par cars entiers.

bus pass n 🇺🇰 *carte d'autobus pour le troisième âge* ▸ **I haven't got my bus pass yet!** *fig* ≃ je n'ai pas encore ma carte Vermeil !

bus shelter n Abribus® *m*.

bus station n gare *f* routière.

bus stop n arrêt *m* d'autobus or de bus.

bust [bʌst] (*pt & pp* **busted** or **bust**) ◆ adj *inf*
1. [broken] fichu **2.** [bankrupt] ▸ **to go bust** faire faillite.
◆ n **1.** [breasts] poitrine *f*, buste *m* **2.** ART buste *m*. ◆ vt *inf* **1.** [break] bousiller, abîmer **2.** [arrest, raid] : *he was busted on a drugs charge* il s'est fait choper or embarquer pour une affaire de drogue **3.** 🇺🇸 [catch] découvrir.

busted flush n *inf* grosse déception *f*.

buster ['bʌstər] n *inf* 🇺🇸 [pal] : *thanks, buster* merci, mon (petit) gars.

-buster in comp *inf* ▸ **crime-busters** superflics *mpl*.

bustle ['bʌsl] ◆ vi [hurry] : *he bustled about* or *around the kitchen* il s'affairait dans la cuisine / *the nurse came bustling in* l'infirmière entra d'un air affairé. ◆ n [activity] agitation *f*.

bustling ['bʌslɪŋ] adj [person] affairé ; [place] animé / *the streets were bustling with Christmas shoppers* les rues grouillaient de gens faisant leurs achats de Noël.

bust-up n *inf* **1.** [quarrel] engueulade *f* **2.** [brawl] bagarre *f*.

busty ['bʌstɪ] (*compar* **bustier**, *superl* **bustiest**) adj qui a une forte poitrine.

busy ['bɪzɪ] (*compar* **busier**, *superl* **busiest**, *pt & pp* **busied**) ◆ adj **1.** [person] occupé / *she was busy painting the kitchen* elle était occupée à peindre la cuisine / *he likes to keep (himself) busy* il aime bien s'occuper / *I'm afraid I'm busy tomorrow* malheureusement je suis pris demain **2.** [port, road, street] très fréquenté ; [time, period, schedule] chargé, plein / *I've had a busy day* j'ai eu une journée chargée / *this is our busiest period* [business, shop] c'est la période où nous sommes en pleine activité **3.** 🇺🇸 [telephone line] occupé / *I got the busy signal* ça sonnait occupé. ◆ vt : *he busied himself with household chores* il s'est occupé à des tâches ménagères.

busybody ['bɪzɪ,bɒdɪ] (*pl* **busybodies**) n *inf* fouineur *m*, -euse *f*, fouinard *m*, -e *f*.

but [bʌt] ◆ conj **1.** [to express contrast] mais / *my husband smokes, but I don't* mon mari fume, mais moi non **2.** [except, only] mais / *it tastes like a grapefruit, but sweeter* ça a le goût d'un pamplemousse, mais en plus sucré. ◆ adv [only] ne... que / *I can but try* je ne peux qu'essayer. ◆ prep **1.** [except] sauf, à part / *she wouldn't see anyone but her lawyer* elle ne voulait voir personne sauf or à part son avocat **2.** 🇺🇰 [with numbers] : *I was the last but two to finish* j'étais l'avant-avant-dernier à finir. ◆ n : *you're coming and no buts!* tu viens, et pas de mais !

◈ **but for** prep phr sans / *but for her courage, many more people would have drowned* sans son courage, il y aurait eu beaucoup plus de noyés.

butane ['bju:teɪn] n butane *m* ▸ **butane gas** gaz *m* butane, butane.

butch [bʊtʃ] *inf* adj [woman] hommasse ; [man] macho.

butcher ['bʊtʃər] ◆ n COMM boucher *m* ▸ **butcher's shop** boucherie *f*. ◆ vt **1.** [animal] abattre, tuer **2.** [person] massacrer **3.** *inf* [story, joke] massacrer.

butcher-block adj [kitchen, work surface] en bois massif.

butchery ['bʊtʃərɪ] n *fig* [massacre] boucherie *f*, massacre *m*.

butler ['bʌtlər] n maître *m* d'hôtel ; [in large household] majordome *m*.

butt [bʌt] ◆ n **1.** [end] bout *m* ; [of rifle] crosse *f* ; [of cigarette] mégot *m* **2.** 🇺🇸 *inf* [buttocks] fesses *fpl* **3.** [person] : *he was the butt of all the office jokes* il était la cible de toutes les plaisanteries du bureau **4.** [barrel] tonneau *m*. ◆ vt [subj: animal] donner un coup de corne à ; [subj: person] donner un coup de tête à. ◈ **butt in** vi [interrupt] : *excuse me for butting in* excusez-moi de m'en mêler or de vous interrompre / *she is always butting in on people's conversations* elle s'immisce toujours dans les conversations des autres.

butter ['bʌtər] ◆ n beurre *m* ▸ **butter dish** beurrier *m* ▸ **she looked as if butter wouldn't melt in her mouth** on lui aurait donné le bon Dieu sans confession. ◆ vt beurrer. ◈ **butter up** vt sep *inf* passer de la pommade à.

butter bean n sorte de haricot de Lima.

buttercup ['bʌtəkʌp] n bouton *m* d'or.

buttered ['bʌtəd] adj [bread] beurré ; [vegetables] au beurre.

butterfingers ['bʌtə,fɪŋgəz] n *inf* maladroit *m*, -e *f* (*de ses mains*).

butterfly ['bʌtəflaɪ] (*pl* **butterflies**) n **1.** ENTOM papillon *m* ▸ **she always has** or **gets butterflies (in her stomach) before a performance** elle a toujours le trac avant une représentation **2.** SPORT ▸ **(the) butterfly** la brasse papillon.

buttermilk ['bʌtəmɪlk] n [sour liquid] babeurre *m*.

butterscotch ['bʌtəskɒtʃ] n caramel *m* dur au beurre.

buttery ['bʌtərɪ] (*pl* **butteries**) ◆ adj [smell, taste] de beurre ; [fingers] couvert de beurre ; [biscuits] fait avec beaucoup de beurre ; [wine] aux arômes de beurre frais. ◆ n [storeroom] office *m*.

butthead ['bʌthed] n 🇺🇸 *vulg* connard *m*.

butt naked adj 🇺🇸 *inf* à poil.

buttock ['bʌtək] n fesse *f*.

button ['bʌtn] ◆ n **1.** [on clothing] bouton *m* ; [on device, machine] bouton *m* ; FENCING bouton *m* ▸ **on the button** *inf* exactement **2.** 🇺🇸 [badge] badge *m* ▸ **button it** or **your lip** or **your mouth!** *inf* ferme-la !, boucle-la ! ◆ vi se boutonner. ◈ **button up** ◆ vt sep [piece of clothing] boutonner. ◆ vi [piece of clothing] se boutonner.

buttonhole ['bʌtnhəʊl] ◆ n **1.** [in clothing] boutonnière *f* **2.** 🇺🇰 [flower] : *she was wearing a pink buttonhole* elle portait une fleur rose à la boutonnière. ◆ vt *inf & fig* [detain - person] retenir, coincer.

button mushroom n champignon *m* de couche or de Paris.

buttress ['bʌtrɪs] ◆ n **1.** ARCHIT contrefort *m* **2.** *fig* pilier *m*. ◆ vt ARCHIT étayer ; [cathedral] arc-bouter.

butty ['bʌtɪ] (*pl* **butties**) n 🇺🇰 *inf & regional* **1.** [sandwich] sandwich *m*, casse-croûte *m* **2.** [friend] copain *m*.

buxom ['bʌksəm] adj [plump] plantureux, bien en chair ; [busty] à la poitrine plantureuse.

buy [baɪ] (*pt & pp* **bought** [bɔːt]) ◆ vt **1.** [purchase] acheter ▸ **to buy sthg for sb, to buy sb sthg** acheter qqch à *or* pour qqn / *can I buy you a coffee?* puis-je t'offrir un café ? / *they bought it for £100* ils l'ont payé 100 livres / *£20 won't buy you very much these days* avec 20 livres, on ne va pas très loin de nos jours **2.** [gain, obtain] : *to buy time* gagner du temps **3.** [bribe] acheter **4.** *inf* [believe] : *she'll never buy that story* elle n'avalera *or* ne gobera jamais cette histoire. ◆ n affaire *f* / *this car was a great buy* cette voiture était une très bonne affaire. ❖ **buy in** vt sep **1.** 🇬🇧 [stockpile] stocker **2.** ST. EX acheter, acquérir. ❖ **buy into** vt insep **1.** FIN acheter une participation dans **2.** [believe] ▸ **to buy into sthg** adhérer à qqch. ❖ **buy off, buy over** vt sep [bribe] acheter. ❖ **buy out** vt sep FIN racheter la part de, désintéresser. ❖ **buy up** vt sep acheter en quantité ; FIN [firm, shares, stock] racheter.

buy-back n FIN rachat *m* d'actions.

buyer ['baɪər] n acheteur *m*, -euse *f* ▸ **buyers' market a)** FIN marché *m* demandeur *or* à la hausse **b)** [for house buyers] marché *m* d'offre *or* offreur.

buyout ['baɪaʊt] n rachat *m*.

buy-to-let n investissement *m* locatif.

buzz [bʌz] ◆ n **1.** [of insect] bourdonnement *m*, vrombissement *m* / *there was a buzz of conversation in the room* la pièce résonnait du brouhaha des conversations **2.** *inf* [telephone call] coup *m* de fil **3.** *inf* [strong sensation] : *I get quite a buzz out of being on the stage* je prends vraiment mon pied sur scène. ◆ vi **1.** [insect] bourdonner, vrombir / *the theatre buzzed with excitement* le théâtre était tout bourdonnant d'excitation / *this place is really buzzing* il y a une super ambiance ici **2.** [ears] bourdonner, tinter / *his head was buzzing with ideas* les idées bourdonnaient dans sa tête. ◆ vt **1.** [with buzzer] : *he buzzed the nurse* il appela l'infirmière d'un coup de sonnette **2.** 🇺🇸 *inf* [telephone] passer un coup de fil à **3.** *inf* AERON [building, town, etc.] raser, frôler ; [aircraft] frôler. ❖ **buzz about** *or* **buzz around** vi *inf* s'affairer, s'agiter. ❖ **buzz off** vi *inf* décamper, dégager.

buzzard ['bʌzəd] n 🇬🇧 buse *f* ; 🇺🇸 urubu *m*.

buzzed [bʌzd] adj **1.** 🇺🇸 *inf* [drunk] bourré **2.** [shaved] au corps rasé.

buzzer ['bʌzər] n [for door] sonnette *f* ; [on game show] buzzer *m* ; [on microwave, radio alarm] sonnerie *f*.

buzzing ['bʌzɪŋ] ◆ n [of insects] bourdonnement *m*, vrombissement *m* ; [in ears] bourdonnement, tintement *m*. ◆ adj [insect] bourdonnant, vrombissant.

buzz-kill n 🇺🇸 *inf* rabat-joie *mf*.

buzzword ['bʌzwɜːd] n *inf* mot *m* à la mode.

b/w (**abbr of** black and white) adj NB.

by [baɪ]
◆ adv **1.** [past] : *she drove by without stopping* elle est passée (en voiture) sans s'arrêter **2.** [nearby] : *is there a bank close by?* y a-t-il une banque près d'ici ? **3.** [to, at someone's home] : *I'll stop* or *drop by this evening* je passerai ce soir.
◆ prep
A. IN SPACE 1. [near, beside] près de, à côté de / *come and sit by me* or *my side* viens t'asseoir près *or* auprès de moi **2.** [past] devant / *she walked right by me* elle passa juste devant moi **3.** [through] par / *she left by the back door* elle est partie par la porte de derrière.
B. INDICATING MEANS, CAUSE OR AGENT 1. [indicating means, method] : *by letter* / *phone* par courrier / téléphone / *to go by bus* / *car* / *plane* / *train* aller en autobus / voiture / avion / train **2.** [indicating agent or cause] par / *it was built by the Romans* il fut construit par les Romains / *I was shocked by his reaction* sa réaction m'a choqué / *she had two daughters by him* elle a eu deux filles de lui **3.** [as

a result of] par ; [with present participle] en / *he learned to cook by watching his mother* il a appris à faire la cuisine en regardant sa mère **4.** [indicating authorship] de / *a book by Toni Morrison* un livre de Toni Morrison **5.** [indicating part of person, thing held] par / *she took her by the hand* elle l'a prise par la main.
C. IN TIME 1. [not later than, before] : *she'll be here by tonight* / *five o'clock* elle sera ici avant ce soir / pour cinq heures / *by 1960 most Americans had television sets* en 1960 la plupart des Américains avaient déjà un poste de télévision / *by the time you read this letter I'll be in California* lorsque tu liras cette lettre, je serai en Californie / *he should be in India by now* il devrait être en Inde maintenant **2.** [during] : *he works by night and sleeps by day* il travaille la nuit et dort le jour.
D. ACCORDING TO 1. [according to] d'après / *it's 6:15 by my watch* il est 6 h 15 à *or* d'après ma montre / *you can tell he's lying by the expression on his face* on voit qu'il ment - à l'expression de son visage **2.** [in accordance with] selon, d'après / *to play by the rules* faire les choses dans les règles **3.** [with regard to] de / *he's an actor by trade* or *profession* il est acteur de profession / *it's all right by me* inf moi, je suis d'accord or je n'ai rien contre.
E. INDICATING AMOUNT OR RATE 1. [indicating degree, extent] de / *she won by five points* elle a gagné de cinq points / *his second book is better by far* son deuxième livre est nettement meilleur **2.** [in calculations, measurements] : *multiply* / *divide 12 by 6* multipliez / divisez 12 par 6 / *the room is 6 metres by 3 (metres)* la pièce fait 6 mètres sur 3 (mètres) **3.** [indicating specific amount, duration] : *to be paid by the hour* / *week* / *month* être payé à l'heure / à la semaine / au mois. ❖ **by and by** adv phr *liter* bientôt.

bye-bye interj *inf* au revoir, salut.

B4N = BFN.

byelaw ['baɪlɔː] n = bylaw.

by-election, bye-election n élection *f* (législative) partielle (*en Grande-Bretagne*).

Byelorussia [bɪˌeləʊˈrʌʃə], **Belorussia** [ˌbeləʊˈrʌʃə] pr n Biélorussie *f*.

Byelorussian [bɪˌeləʊˈrʌʃn], **Belorussian** [ˌbeləʊˈrʌʃn] ◆ n Biélorusse *mf*. ◆ adj biélorusse.

bygone ['baɪgɒn] ◆ adj *liter* passé, révolu / *in bygone days* autrefois, jadis. ◆ n PHR **let bygones be bygones** oublions le passé.

BYKT MESSAGING **written abbr of** but you knew that.

bylaw ['baɪlɔː] n **1.** 🇬🇧 ADMIN arrêté *m* municipal **2.** 🇺🇸 [of club, company] statut *m*.

by-line n signature *f* (*en tête d'un article*).

BYOB (**written abbr of** bring your own bottle or booze) «*apportez une bouteille*», inscription que l'on trouve sur un carton d'invitation à une soirée.

bypass ['baɪpɑːs] ◆ n **1.** [road] rocade *f* / *the Oxford bypass* la route qui contourne Oxford **2.** MED pontage *m*, by-pass *m* ▸ **bypass operation** or **bypass surgery** pontage, by-pass. ◆ vt [avoid - town] contourner, éviter ; [- problem, regulation] contourner, éluder ; [- superior] court-circuiter.

by-product n sous-produit *m*, (produit *m*) dérivé *m* ; *fig* conséquence *f* indirecte, effet *m* secondaire.

bystander ['baɪˌstændər] n spectateur *m*, -trice *f*.

byte [baɪt] n octet *m*.

byway ['baɪweɪ] n [road] chemin *m* détourné or écarté.

byword ['baɪwɜːd] n symbole *m*, illustration *f* / *the company has become a byword for inefficiency* le nom de cette entreprise est devenu synonyme d'inefficacité.

c 1. (written abbr of **cent(s)**) ct **2.** (written abbr of **century**) s. **3.** (written abbr of **circa**) vers.

C ◆ n **1.** MUS do m, ut m **2.** SCH & UNIV assez bien. ◆ MESSAGING written abbr of **see**.

c & f (written abbr of **cost and freight**) c et f.

C & G (abbr of **City and Guilds**) n diplôme britannique d'enseignement technique.

C & W n abbr of **country and western (music)**.

ca. (written abbr of **circa**) vers.

c/a 1. written abbr of **capital account 2.** written abbr of **credit account 3.** written abbr of **current account**.

CA written abbr of **California**.

CAA (abbr of **Civil Aviation Authority**) pr n organisme britannique de réglementation de l'aviation civile.

cab [kæb] n **1.** [taxi] taxi m / he's a cab driver il est chauffeur de taxi ▸ **cab rank** station f de taxis **2.** [of lorry, train] cabine f.

CAB pr n UK abbr of **Citizens' Advice Bureau**.

cabala [kə'bɑːlə] n cabale f.

cabalism ['kæbælɪzm] n cabalisme m.

cabaret ['kæbəreɪ] n [nightclub] cabaret m ; [show] spectacle m.

cabbage ['kæbɪdʒ] n chou m.

cabbage patch n ≃ carré m de salades.

cabby, cabbie ['kæbɪ] n inf [taxi-driver] chauffeur m de taxi.

caber ['keɪbər] n SPORT tronc m ▸ **tossing the caber** le lancer de troncs.

cabin ['kæbɪn] n **1.** [hut] cabane f, hutte f **2.** NAUT cabine f **3.** AERON cabine f.

cabin class n deuxième classe f.

cabin crew n équipage m.

cabin cruiser n cruiser m.

cabinet ['kæbɪnɪt] n **1.** [furniture] meuble m (de rangement) ; [for bottles] bar m ; [radio, television] coffret m ; [for precious objects] cabinet m ; [with glass doors] vitrine f **2.** POL cabinet m / they took the decision in cabinet ils ont pris la décision en Conseil des ministres.

cabinet-maker n ébéniste m.

cabinet minister n ministre m siégeant au cabinet.

cable ['keɪbl] ◆ n [rope, wire] câble m. ◆ vt **1.** [lay cables in] câbler **2.** [telegraph] télégraphier à.

cable car n téléphérique m.

cablecast ['keɪblkɑːst] vt US TV transmettre par câble.

cablecasting ['keɪbl,kɑːstɪŋ] n US TV transmission f par câble.

cablegram ['keɪblgræm] n câblogramme m.

cable modem n modem m câble.

cable railway n funiculaire m.

cable television, cable TV n câble m, télévision f par câble.

cabling ['keɪblɪŋ] n câblage m.

caboodle [kə'buːdl] n inf ▸ **the whole (kit and) caboodle** tout le bataclan or bazar.

cache [kæʃ] n [hidden supply] cache f / a cache of weapons or an arms cache une cache d'armes.

cache memory ['kæʃ,memərɪ] n COMPUT mémoire f cache.

cachet ['kæʃeɪ] n lit & fig cachet m.

cack [kæk] UK vulg ◆ n merde f. ◆ vb ▸ **to cack o.s.** chier dans son froc.

cack-handed [kæk-] adj UK inf maladroit, gauche.

cackle ['kækl] ◆ vi **1.** [hen] caqueter **2.** [person - chatter] caqueter, jacasser ; [- laugh] glousser. ◆ n **1.** [of hen] caquet m **2.** [of person - chatter] caquetage m, jacasserie f ; [- laugh] gloussement m.

cacophony [kæ'kɒfənɪ] (pl **cacophonies**) n cacophonie f.

cactus ['kæktəs] (pl **cactuses** or **cacti** [-taɪ]) n cactus m.

cad [kæd] n dated goujat m.

CAD [kæd] (abbr of **computer-aided design**) n CAO f.

cadaverous [kə'dævərəs] adj fml & liter cadavéreux, cadavérique.

CADCAM ['kædkæm] (abbr of **computer-aided design and manufacture**) n CFAO f.

caddie ['kædɪ] n SPORT caddie m.

caddy ['kædɪ] n **1.** UK [container - for tea] boîte f **2.** US [cart] chariot m, Caddie m.

cadence ['keɪdəns] n cadence f.

cadet [kə'det] n MIL élève m officier ; [police] élève m policier ; UK SCH élève qui reçoit une formation militaire.

cadge [kædʒ] inf ◆ vt [food, money] se procurer (en quémandant). ◆ vi : she's always cadging off her friends elle est toujours en train de taper ses amis.

Cadiz [kə'dɪz] pr n Cadix.

Caesar ['siːzər] pr n César.

Caesarean section n césarienne f.

Caesar salad n salade de laitue romaine, de croûtons et de parmesan.

CAF (written abbr of **cost and freight**) C et F.

cafe, café [ˈkæfeɪ] n [in UK] snack m ; [in rest of Europe] café m.

cafeteria [ˌkæfɪˈtɪərɪə] n [self-service restaurant] restaurant m self-service, self m ; US [canteen] cantine f.

cafetiere [kæfəˈtjeər] n cafetière f.

cafetière [kæfˈtjeər] n cafetière f à piston.

caff [kæf] n v inf snack m.

caffeine [ˈkæfiːn] n caféine f.

caffeine-free adj sans caféine.

caftan [ˈkæftæn] n caftan m.

cage [keɪdʒ] ◆ n 1. [with bars] cage f 2. [lift] cabine f ; MIN cage f (d'extraction). ◆ vt mettre en cage, encager.

caged [keɪdʒd] adj en cage.

cagey [ˈkeɪdʒɪ] (compar **cagier**, superl **cagiest**) adj inf [cautious] mesuré, circonspect ; [reticent] réticent.

cagoule [kəˈguːl] n veste f imperméable (à capuche).

cahoots [kəˈhuːts] pl n inf ▶ **to be in cahoots (with sb)** être de mèche (avec qqn).

CAI (abbr of computer-assisted instruction) n EAO m.

cairn [keən] n cairn m.

Cairo [ˈkaɪərəʊ] pr n Le Caire.

cajole [kəˈdʒəʊl] vt enjôler.

cajoling [kəˈdʒəʊlɪŋ] adj cajoleur.

cajolingly [kəˈdʒəʊlɪŋlɪ] adv d'une manière cajoleuse ; [speak] d'un ton cajoleur.

cake [keɪk] ◆ n 1. CULIN [sweet] gâteau m ; [pastry] pâtisserie f ; [savoury] croquette f ▶ **it's a piece of cake** inf ça va être du gâteau 2. [block - of soap, wax] pain m ; [- of chocolate] plaquette f. ◆ comp [dish] à gâteau ▶ **cake pan** US or **tin** UK moule m à gâteau ▶ **cake shop** pâtisserie f. ◆ vt : his boots were caked with mud ses bottes étaient pleines de boue.

cakehole [ˈkeɪkhəʊl] n UK v inf gueule f.

CAL (abbr of computer-assisted learning) n EAO m.

calamine [ˈkæləmaɪn] n calamine f ▶ **calamine lotion** lotion calmante à la calamine.

calamitous [kəˈlæmɪtəs] adj calamiteux.

calamity [kəˈlæmətɪ] (pl **calamities**) n calamité f.

calcified [ˈkælsɪfaɪd] adj CHEM calcifié.

calcium [ˈkælsɪəm] n calcium m.

calculate [ˈkælkjʊleɪt] ◆ vt 1. MATH calculer ; [estimate, evaluate] calculer, évaluer 2. [design, intend] : her remark was calculated to offend the guests sa réflexion était destinée à offenser les invités. ◆ vi MATH calculer, faire des calculs.

calculated [ˈkælkjʊleɪtɪd] adj 1. [considered] calculé, mesuré 2. [deliberate, intentional] délibéré, voulu.

calculating [ˈkælkjʊleɪtɪŋ] adj pej calculateur.

calculatingly [ˈkælkjʊleɪtɪŋlɪ] adv pej de manière calculée.

calculation [ˌkælkjʊˈleɪʃn] n MATH & fig calcul m.

calculator [ˈkælkjʊleɪtər] n [machine] calculateur m ; [small] calculatrice f.

calculus [ˈkælkjʊləs] n calcul m.

calendar [ˈkælɪndər] ◆ n [of dates] calendrier m. ◆ comp [day, month, year] civil, calendaire.

calendar girl n pin-up f.

calf [kɑːf] (pl **calves** [kɑːvz]) n 1. [young cow, bull] veau m 2. [skin] veau m, vachette f 3. ANAT mollet m.

caliber US n = **calibre**.

calibrate [ˈkælɪbreɪt] vt étalonner, calibrer.

calibration [ˌkælɪˈbreɪʃn] n étalonnage m, calibrage m.

calibre UK, **caliber** US [ˈkælɪbər] n 1. [of gun, tube] calibre m 2. [quality] qualité f.

calico [ˈkælɪkəʊ] (pl **calicoes** or **calicos**) n UK TEXT calicot m blanc ; US calicot m imprimé, indienne f.

California [ˌkælɪˈfɔːnjə] pr n Californie f.

Californian [ˌkælɪˈfɔːnjən] ◆ n Californien m, -enne f. ◆ adj californien.

caliper US n = **calliper**.

call [kɔːl] ◆ vi 1. [with one's voice] appeler / to call for help appeler à l'aide ou au secours 2. [on the telephone] appeler / who's calling? qui est à l'appareil ?, c'est de la part de qui ? 3. [animal, bird] pousser un cri 4. UK [visit] passer / I was out when they called je n'étais pas là quand ils sont passés 5. UK [stop] s'arrêter ▶ **to call at** a) [train] s'arrêter à b) [ship] faire escale à. ◆ vt 1. [with one's voice] appeler / can you call the children to the table? pouvez-vous appeler les enfants pour qu'ils viennent à table ? 2. [telephone] appeler / to call the police / fire brigade appeler la police / les pompiers 3. [wake up] réveiller 4. [name or describe as] appeler / he has a cat called Felix UK il a un chat qui s'appelle Félix / what's this called? comment est-ce qu'on appelle ça ?, comment est-ce que ça s'appelle ? / she called him a crook elle l'a traité d'escroc 5. [consider] : (and you) call yourself a Christian! et tu te dis chrétien ! / I don't call that clean ce n'est pas ce que j'appelle propre ▶ **let's call it a day** on arrête là pour aujourd'hui 6. [announce] : to call a meeting convoquer une assemblée 7. [send for, summon] appeler, convoquer fml / she was suddenly called home elle a été rappelée soudainement chez elle. ◆ n 1. [cry, shout] appel m ; [of animal, bird] cri m / a call for help un appel à l'aide ou au secours 2. [on the telephone] appel m / to make a call passer un coup de téléphone / there's a call for you on vous demande au téléphone 3. [visit] visite f ▶ **to make** or **pay a call on sb** UK rendre visite à qqn 4. [demand, need] : there have been renewed calls for a return to capital punishment il y a des gens qui demandent à nouveau le rétablissement de la peine de mort. ◆ **on call** adj phr [doctor, nurse] de garde. ◆ **call away** vt sep : she's often called away on business elle doit souvent partir en déplacement or s'absenter pour affaires. ◆ **call back** ◆ vt sep 1. [on telephone] rappeler 2. [ask to return] rappeler. ◆ vi 1. [on telephone] rappeler 2. [visit again] revenir, repasser. ◆ **call for** vt insep 1. UK [collect] : he called for her at her parents' house il est allé la chercher chez ses parents 2. [put forward as demand] appeler, demander ; [subj: agreement, treaty] prévoir 3. [require] exiger / the situation called for quick thinking la situation demandait or exigeait qu'on réfléchisse vite. ◆ **call in** vt sep 1. [send for] faire venir 2. [recall - defective goods] rappeler. ◆ **call off** vt sep 1. [appointment, meeting, strike] annuler 2. [dog, person] rappeler. ◆ **call on** vt insep UK 1. [request, summon] faire appel à 2. [visit] rendre visite à. ◆ **call out** ◆ vt sep [summon] appeler, faire appel à. ◆ vi [shout] appeler / she called out to a policeman elle appela un agent de police. ◆ **call round** vi UK : can I call round this evening? puis-je passer ce soir ? ◆ **call up** vt sep 1. [telephone] appeler 2. MIL appeler ; [reservists] rappeler. ◆ **call upon** vt insep fml [request, summon] faire appel à.

CALL (abbr of computer-assisted language learning or computer-aided language learning) n enseignement m des langues assisté par ordinateur.

call box n UK cabine f téléphonique.

call centre UK, **call center** US n centre m d'appels.

called-up capital n FIN capital m appelé.

caller [ˈkɔːlər] n 1. [visitor] visiteur m, -euse f 2. TELEC demandeur m, -euse f ▶ **caller identification** identification f d'appel.

caller ID display, caller display n TELEC présentation f du numéro.

call girl n call-girl f.

calligraphy [kə'lɪɡrəfɪ] n calligraphie f.

call-in n US émission f à ligne ouverte.

calling ['kɔ:lɪŋ] n 1. [vocation] appel m intérieur, vocation f 2. fml [profession] métier m, profession f.

calling card n US [visiting card] carte f de visite.

calliper UK, **caliper** US ['kælɪpə'] n 1. MATH ▶ **a pair of calliper compasses** or **callipers** un compas 2. MED ▶ **calliper (splint)** attelle-étrier f.

callisthenics [,kælɪs'θenɪks] n (U) gymnastique f rythmique.

callous ['kæləs] adj [unfeeling] dur, sans cœur ; [behaviour, remark] dur, impitoyable.

calloused ['kæləst] adj [feet, hands] calleux, corné.

callously ['kæləslɪ] adv durement.

callousness ['kæləsnɪs] n dureté f.

callow ['kæləʊ] adj [immature] sans expérience, sans maturité.

call screening n filtrage m d'appels.

call sequence n COMPUT séquence f d'appel.

call-up n UK [conscription] convocation f (au service militaire), ordre m d'incorporation ▶ **call-up papers** ordre m d'incorporation.

callus ['kæləs] n [on feet, hands] cal m, durillon m.

CUB L8R MESSAGING written abbr of **call you back later**.

calm [kɑ:m] ◆ adj calme **/ keep calm!** du calme !, restons calmes ! ▶ **to be calm and collected** être maître de soi, garder son sang-froid. ◆ n calme m ; [after upset, excitement] accalmie f **/ the calm before the storm** le calme qui précède la tempête. ◆ vt calmer ; [fears] apaiser, calmer. ◆ **calm down** ◆ vi se calmer ▶ **calm down!** calmez-vous !, ne vous énervez pas ! ◆ vt sep calmer.

calming ['kɑ:mɪŋ] adj calmant.

calmly ['kɑ:mlɪ] adv calmement.

calmness ['kɑ:mnɪs] n calme m.

Calor gas® ['kælə'-] UK butane m, Butagaz® m.

calorie ['kælərɪ] n calorie f.

calorie-conscious adj : **she's very calorie-conscious** elle fait très attention au nombre de calories qu'elle absorbe.

calorie-controlled adj [diet] hypocalorique, faible en calories.

calorie-free adj sans calories.

calorific [,kælə'rɪfɪk] adj calorifique.

calve [kɑ:v] vi [cow, iceberg] vêler ; [other animals] mettre bas.

calves [kɑ:vz] pl ⟶ **calf**.

Calvinist ['kælvɪnɪst] ◆ adj calviniste. ◆ n calviniste mf.

cam [kæm] n came f.

CAM [kæm] (abbr of **computer-aided manufacturing**) n FAO f.

camaraderie [,kæmə'rɑ:dərɪ] n camaraderie f.

camber ['kæmbə'] n [in road] bombement m.

cambered ['kæmbəd] adj [road] bombé.

Cambodia [kæm'bəʊdjə] pr n Cambodge m.

Cambodian [kæm'bəʊdjən] ◆ n Cambodgien m, -enne f. ◆ adj cambodgien.

Cambridge Certificate n diplôme d'anglais langue étrangère délivré par l'université de Cambridge et comprenant deux niveaux, le First Certificate et le Certificate of Proficiency.

Cambs. written abbr of **Cambridgeshire**.

camcorder ['kæm,kɔ:də'] n Caméscope® m.

came [keɪm] pt ⟶ **come**.

camel ['kæml] ◆ n 1. ZOOL chameau m ; [with one hump] dromadaire m ; [female] chamelle f 2. [colour] fauve m inv. ◆ comp [coat, jacket - of camel hair] en poil de chameau ; [- coloured] fauve (inv).

camellia [kə'mi:ljə] n camélia m.

Camelot ['kæmələt] pr n [in Arthurian legend] Camelot m (château légendaire du roi Arthur).

cameo ['kæmɪəʊ] (pl **cameos**) ◆ n [piece of jewellery] camée m. ◆ comp CIN, THEAT & TV ▶ **a cameo performance** or **role** un petit rôle (joué par un acteur célèbre).

camera ['kæmərə] ◆ n [device - for still photos] appareil m (photographique), appareil photo m ; [- for film, video] caméra f ▶ **to be on camera** être à l'écran. ◆ comp [battery, case] pour appareil photo.

⚠ The word **caméra** only refers to a video or film camera.

cameraman ['kæmərəmæn] (pl **cameramen** [-men]) n cadreur m, cameraman m.

camera phone n téléphone m avec appareil photo.

camera-ready adj prêt à imprimer.

camera-shy adj qui n'aime pas être photographié.

camerawoman ['kæmərə,wʊmən] (pl **camerawomen** [-,wɪmɪn]) n cadreuse f.

camerawork ['kæmərəwɜ:k] n prise f de vue **/ the film has some superb camerawork** certaines scènes sont magnifiquement filmées.

Cameroon [,kæmə'ru:n] pr n Cameroun m.

Cameroonian [,kæmə'ru:nɪən] ◆ n Camerounais m, -e f. ◆ adj camerounais.

camisole ['kæmɪsəʊl], **cami** ['kæmɪ] n caraco m.

camomile ['kæməmaɪl] n camomille f ▶ **camomile tea** infusion f de camomille.

camouflage ['kæməflɑ:ʒ] ◆ n camouflage m. ◆ vt camoufler.

camp [kæmp] ◆ n 1. [place] camp m ; [not permanent] campement m ▶ **to make** or **to pitch** or **to set up camp** établir un camp 2. [group] camp m, parti m ▶ **to be in the same camp** être du même bord. ◆ vi camper. ◆ adj inf 1. [effeminate] efféminé 2. [affected] affecté, maniéré ; [theatrical - person] cabotin ; [- manners] théâtral.

campaign [kæm'peɪn] ◆ n campagne f. ◆ vi mener une campagne, faire campagne ▶ **to campaign against / for sthg** mener une campagne contre / en faveur de qqch.

campaigner [kæm'peɪnə'] n POL & fig militant m, -e f ; MIL vétéran m.

campaign trail n tournée f électorale.

camp bed n lit m de camp.

camp counsellor n moniteur m, -trice f.

camper ['kæmpə'] n 1. [person] campeur m, -euse f 2. [vehicle] ▶ **camper (van)** camping-car m.

campfire ['kæmp,faɪə'] n feu m de camp.

Camp Fire Club pr n organisation américaine de scouts pour garçons et filles.

campground ['kæmpgraʊnd] n US [private] camp m ; [commercial] terrain m de camping, camping m ; [clearing] emplacement m de camping, endroit m où camper.

camphone ['kæmfəʊn] n téléphone m avec appareil photo.

camphor ['kæmfə'] n camphre m.

camping ['kæmpɪŋ] ◆ n camping *m*. ◆ comp [equipment, stove] de camping ▶ **camping gas** butane *m* ▶ **camping ground** or **grounds** or **site** a) [private] camp *m* b) [commercial] terrain *m* de camping, camping *m* c) [clearing] emplacement *m* de camping, endroit *m* où camper.

campsite ['kæmpsaɪt] n [commercial] terrain *m* de camping, camping *m* ; [clearing] emplacement *m* de camping, endroit *m* où camper.

campus ['kæmpəs] (*pl* **campuses**) n UNIV [grounds] campus *m* ; [buildings] campus *m*, complexe *m* universitaire.

camshaft ['kæmʃɑːft] n arbre *m* à cames.

can[1] *(weak form* [kən]*, strong form* [kæn]*; preterite form* **could**, *weak form* [kəd]*, strong form* [kʊd]*, negative forms* **cannot**, *weak form* ['kænət]*, strong form* ['kænɒt]*, frequently shortened to* **can't** [kɑːnt]*, negative not, frequently shortened to* **couldn't** ['kʊdnt]) modal vb **1.** [be able to] pouvoir / *I'll come if I can* je viendrai si je (le) peux / *we'll do everything we can to help* nous ferons tout ce que nous pourrons or tout notre possible pour aider **2.** [with verbs of perception or understanding] : *can you feel it?* tu le sens ? / *we can hear everything our neighbours say* nous entendons tout ce que disent nos voisins **3.** [indicating ability or skill] savoir / *can you drive / sew?* savez-vous conduire / coudre ? / *she can speak three languages* elle parle trois langues **4.** [giving or asking for permission] pouvoir / *can I borrow your sweater? — yes, you can* puis-je emprunter ton pull ? — (mais oui,) bien sûr **5.** [in offers of help] pouvoir / *can I be of any assistance?* puis-je vous aider ? **6.** [expressing opinions] : *you can't blame her for leaving him!* tu ne peux pas lui reprocher de l'avoir quitté ! **7.** [indicating possibility or likelihood] pouvoir / *the contract can still be cancelled* il est toujours possible d'annuler on on peut encore annuler le contrat / *the job can't be finished in one day* il est impossible de finir le travail or le travail ne peut se faire en un jour / *what can I have done with the keys?* qu'est-ce que j'ai bien pu faire des clés ? **8.** [indicating disbelief or doubt] : *you can't be serious!* (ce n'est pas possible !) vous ne parlez pas sérieusement ! / *he can't possibly have finished already!* ce n'est pas possible qu'il ait déjà fini !

can[2] [kæn] ◆ n **1.** [container - for liquid] bidon *m* ; [-for tinned food] boîte *f* (de conserve) ; [-for soft drink] canette *f* ; US [for rubbish] poubelle *f*, boîte *f* à ordures ▶ **a (real) can of worms** un vrai casse-tête ▶ **the film is in the can** CIN le film est dans la boîte ▶ **the deal's in the can** *inf* l'affaire est conclue **2.** US *inf* [prison] taule *f* **3.** US *inf* [toilet] W-C *mpl*, waters *mpl* ; [buttocks] fesses *fpl* **4.** PHR **to carry the can** UK payer les pots cassés. ◆ vt (*pt & pp* **canned**, *cont* **canning**) **1.** [food] mettre en boîte or en conserve, conserver (en boîte) **2.** US *inf* [dismiss from job] virer, renvoyer.

Canada ['kænədə] pr n Canada *m*.

Canadian [kə'neɪdjən] ◆ n Canadien *m*, -enne *f*. ◆ adj [gen] canadien ; [embassy, prime minister] canadien, du Canada ▶ **Canadian English** anglais *m* du Canada.

canal [kə'næl] n [waterway] canal *m* ▶ **canal barge** or **boat** péniche *f*, chaland *m*.

canapé ['kænəpeɪ] n canapé *m* (*petit-four*).

Canaries [kə'neərɪz] pl pr n ▶ **the Canaries** les Canaries *fpl*.

canary [kə'neərɪ] (*pl* **canaries**) n [bird] canari *m*, serin *m*.

Canary Islands pl pr n ▶ **the Canary Islands** les (îles *fpl*) Canaries *fpl*.

cancan ['kænkæn] n cancan *m*, french cancan *m*.

cancel ['kænsl] (UK *pt & pp* **cancelled**, *cont* **cancelling** ; US *pt & pp* **canceled**, *cont* **canceling**) vt **1.** [call off - event, order, reservation, flight] annuler ; [-appointment]

annuler, décommander **2.** [revoke - agreement, contract] résilier, annuler ; [-cheque] faire opposition à. ❖ **cancel out** vt sep [counterbalance] neutraliser, compenser.

cancellation [,kænsə'leɪʃn] n [calling off - of event, reservation] annulation *f* ; [annulment - of agreement, contract] résiliation *f*, annulation *f* ; [-of cheque] opposition *f*.

cancer ['kænsər] ◆ n MED & *fig* cancer *m* / *to die of cancer* mourir (à la suite) d'un cancer / *cigarettes cause cancer* les cigarettes sont cancérigènes or carcinogènes. ◆ comp ▶ **cancer patient** cancéreux *m*, -euse *f* ▶ **cancer research** oncologie *f*, cancérologie *f*.

Cancer ['kænsər] pr n ASTROL & ASTRON Cancer *m* / *he's a Cancer* il est (du signe du) Cancer.

cancer-causing adj cancérigène, carcinogène.

cancerologist [,kænsə'rɒlədʒɪst] n MED cancérologue *mf*.

cancerous ['kænsərəs] adj cancéreux.

candelabra [,kændr'lɑːbrə] (*pl* **candelabra** or **candelabras**), **candelabrum** [,kændr'lɑːbrəm] (*pl* **candelabra** or **candelabrums**) n candélabre *m*.

C and F, C & F (abbr of **cost and freight**) C et F.

candid ['kændɪd] adj [person] franc (franche), sincère ; [smile] franc (franche) ; [account, report] qui ne cache rien.

⚠ **Candide** means innocent or naïve, not candid.

candidacy ['kændɪdəsɪ] n candidature *f*.

candidate ['kændɪdət] n candidat *m*, -e *f*.

candidate country n [EU] pays *m* candidat *(à l'adhésion)*.

candidature ['kændɪdətʃər] n candidature *f*.

candidly ['kændɪdlɪ] adv [speak] franchement ; [smile] candidement, avec candeur.

candidness ['kændɪdnɪs] n franchise *f*.

candied ['kændɪd] adj [piece of fruit, peel] confit ; [whole fruit] confit, glacé.

candle ['kændl] n [of wax - gen] bougie *f*, chandelle *f* ; [-in church] cierge *m*, chandelle *f*.

candlelight ['kændllaɪt] n lueur *f* d'une bougie or d'une chandelle.

candlelit ['kændllɪt] adj éclairé aux bougies or aux chandelles.

candlestick ['kændlstɪk] n [single] bougeoir *m* ; [branched] chandelier *m*.

can-do ['kændu:] adj ▶ **can-do spirit** esprit *m* de battant or de gagneur.

candour UK, **candor** US ['kændər] n candeur *f*, franchise *f*.

candy ['kændɪ] (*pl* **candies**, *pt & pp* **candied**) n US [piece] bonbon *m* ; (U) [sweets in general] bonbons *mpl*, confiserie *f*.

candy apple n US pomme *f* candi.

candy bar n US [chocolate] barre *f* de chocolat ; [muesli] barre *f* de céréales.

candybar phone ['kændɪbɑː-] n téléphone *m* monobloc.

candyfloss ['kændɪflɒs] n UK barbe *f* à papa.

cane [keɪn] ◆ n **1.** [stem of plant] canne *f* ; [in making baskets, furniture] rotin *m*, jonc *m* **2.** [rod - for walking] canne *f* ; [-for punishment] verge *f*, baguette *f* ▶ **to give sb the cane** fouetter qqn **3.** [for supporting plant] tuteur *m*. ◆ comp [furniture] en rotin ; [chair - entirely in cane] en rotin ; [-with cane back, seat] canné. ◆ vt [beat with rod] donner des coups de bâton à, fouetter.

cane sugar n sucre *m* de canne.

canine ['keɪnaɪn] adj **1.** [gen] canin ; ZOOL de la famille des canidés **2.** ANAT ▸ **canine tooth** canine *f*.

canister ['kænɪstər] n **1.** [for flour, sugar] boîte *f* **2.** [for gas, shaving cream] bombe *f*.

canister vacuum cleaner n aspirateur-traîneau *m*.

cannabis ['kænəbɪs] n [plant] chanvre *m* indien ; [drug] cannabis *m*.

canned [kænd] adj **1.** [food] en boîte, en conserve **2.** *pej* [pre-prepared, pre-recorded] ▸ **canned laughter** rires *mpl* préenregistrés.

cannelloni [,kænɪ'ləʊnɪ] n (*U*) cannelloni *mpl*.

cannery ['kænərɪ] (*pl* **canneries**) n conserverie *f*, fabrique *f* de conserves.

cannibal ['kænɪbl] ◆ adj cannibale, anthropophage. ◆ n cannibale *mf*, anthropophage *mf*.

cannibalism ['kænɪbəlɪzm] n cannibalisme *m*, anthropophagie *f*.

cannibalization, cannibalisation n cannibalisation *f*.

cannibalize, cannibalise ['kænɪbəlaɪz] vt [car] cannibaliser, récupérer des pièces détachées de ; [text] récupérer des parties de.

cannily ['kænɪlɪ] adv [assess] avec perspicacité ; [reason] habilement, astucieusement.

cannon ['kænən] (*pl* **cannon** or **cannons**) n [weapon] canon *m*.

cannonball ['kænənbɔ:l] n [ammunition] boulet *m* de canon.

cannot ['kænɒt] vb ⟶ **can**.

canny ['kænɪ] (*compar* **cannier**, *superl* **canniest**) adj [astute] astucieux, habile ; [shrewd] malin (maligne), rusé.

canoe [kə'nu:] (*cont* **canoeing**) ◆ n canoë *m* ; [dug-out] pirogue *f* ; SPORT canoë *m*, canoë-kayak *m*. ◆ vi [gen] faire du canoë ; SPORT faire du canoë or du canoë-kayak.

canoeing [kə'nu:ɪŋ] n SPORT canoë-kayak *m*.

canoeist [kə'nu:ɪst] n canoéiste *mf*.

canola [kə'nəʊlə] n US colza *m*.

canon ['kænən] n RELIG [decree, prayer] canon *m* ; [clergyman] chanoine *m*.

canonize, canonise ['kænənaɪz] vt RELIG & *fig* canoniser.

canoodle [kə'nu:dl] vi US *inf* se faire des mamours.

can opener n ouvre-boîtes *m inv*.

canopy ['kænəpɪ] (*pl* **canopies**) n [over bed] baldaquin *m*, ciel *m* de lit ; [over balcony, passageway] auvent *m*, marquise *f* ; [over throne] dais *m* ; ARCHIT [with columns] baldaquin *m*.

cant [kænt] n (*U*) [insincere talk] paroles *fpl* hypocrites ; [clichés] clichés *mpl*, phrases *fpl* toutes faites.

can't [kɑ:nt] abbr of **cannot**.

Cantab. (written abbr of **Cantabrigiensis**) de l'université de Cambridge.

Cantabrian Mountains [kæn'teɪbrɪən-] pl pr n ▸ **the Cantabrian Mountains** les monts *mpl* Cantabriques.

cantaloup US, **cantaloupe** US ['kæntəlu:p] n cantaloup *m*.

cantankerous [kæn'tæŋkərəs] adj [bad-tempered - habitually] acariâtre, qui a mauvais caractère, grincheux ; [-temporarily] de mauvaise humeur.

canteen [kæn'ti:n] n **1.** [restaurant] cantine *f* **2.** [box for cutlery] coffret *m* ▸ **canteen of cutlery** ménagère *f*.

canter ['kæntər] ◆ n petit galop *m*. ◆ vi aller au petit galop.

Canterbury ['kæntəbrɪ] pr n Cantorbéry.

cantilever ['kæntɪli:vər] n [beam, girder] cantilever *m* ; [projecting beam] corbeau *m*, console *f*.

canton n ['kæntɒn] ADMIN canton *m*.

Canton [kæn'tɒn] pr n Canton.

Cantonese [,kæntə'ni:z] (*pl* **Cantonese**) ◆ n [person] Cantonais *m*, -e *f*. ◆ adj cantonais.

canvas ['kænvəs] (*pl* **canvas** or **canvasses**) ◆ n **1.** [cloth] toile *f* ; [for tapestry] canevas *m* ▸ **under canvas a)** [in tent] sous une tente **b)** NAUT sous voiles **2.** [painting] toile *f*, tableau *m*. ◆ comp [bag, cloth] de or en toile.

canvass ['kænvəs] ◆ vi POL [candidate, campaign worker] solliciter des voix. ◆ vt **1.** [seek opinion of] sonder **2.** POL [person] solliciter la voix de ; [area] faire du démarchage électoral dans **3.** US POL [ballots] pointer.

canvasser ['kænvəsər] n **1.** POL agent *m* électoral (*qui sollicite des voix*) **2.** US [of ballots] scrutateur *m*, -trice *f*.

canvassing ['kænvəsɪŋ] n POL démarchage *m* électoral.

canyon ['kænjən] n canyon *m*, cañon *m*.

canyoning ['kænjənɪŋ] n SPORT canyoning *m*.

cap [kæp] (*pt & pp* **capped**, *cont* **capping**) ◆ n **1.** [hat - with peak] casquette *f* ; [-without peak] bonnet *m* ; [-of jockey, judge] toque *f* ; [-of nurse, traditional costume] coiffe *f* ; [-of soldier] calot *m* ; [-of officer] képi *m* **2.** US SPORT : *he has three England caps* il a été sélectionné trois fois dans l'équipe d'Angleterre **3.** [cover, lid - of bottle, container] capsule *f* ; [-of lens] cache *m* ; [-of tyre valve] bouchon *m* ; [-of pen] capuchon *m* ; [-of mushroom] chapeau *m* ; [-of tooth] couronne *f* ; [-of column, pedestal] chapiteau *m* **4.** [for toy gun] amorce *f* **5.** [contraceptive device] diaphragme *m*. ◆ vt **1.** [tooth] couronner, mettre une couronne à **2.** [outdo] surpasser / *to cap it all* pour couronner le tout, pour comble **3.** [spending] limiter, restreindre **4.** US SPORT sélectionner (dans l'équipe nationale).

CAP [kæp or si:eɪ'pi:] (abbr of **Common Agricultural Policy**) n PAC *f*.

capability [,keɪpə'bɪlətɪ] (*pl* **capabilities**) n [gen] aptitude *f*, capacité *f* / *the work is beyond his capabilities* ce travail est au-dessus de ses capacités.

capable ['keɪpəbl] adj [able] capable / *they are quite capable of looking after themselves* ils sont parfaitement capables de or ils peuvent très bien se débrouiller tout seuls.

capably ['keɪpəblɪ] adv avec compétence, de façon compétente.

capacious [kə'peɪʃəs] adj *fml* [container] de grande capacité or contenance.

capacitor [kə'pæsɪtər] n ELEC condensateur *m*.

capacity [kə'pæsɪtɪ] (*pl* **capacities**) ◆ n **1.** [size of container] contenance *f*, capacité *f* ; [-of room] capacité *f* / *filled to capacity* **a)** [bottle, tank] plein **b)** [ship, theatre] plein, comble **2.** [aptitude] aptitude *f*, capacité *f* **3.** [position] qualité *f*, titre *m* ; LAW [legal competence] pouvoir *m* légal / *they are here in an official capacity* ils sont ici à titre officiel **4.** [of factory, industry] moyens *mpl* de production ; [output] rendement *m* / *the factory is (working) at full capacity* l'usine produit à plein rendement. ◆ comp ▸ **capacity audience** une salle comble ▸ **a capacity crowd** : *they played to a capacity crowd* ils ont joué à guichets fermés.

cape [keɪp] n **1.** [cloak] cape *f*, pèlerine *f* **2.** GEOG [headland] cap *m* ; [promontory] promontoire *m*.

Capes	
Cape Canaveral	cap Canaveral
Cape Cod	cap Cod
the Cape of Good Hope	le cap de Bonne-Espérance
Cape Horn	le cap Horn

capeesh [kə'piːʃ] vi *inf* [understand] comprendre.

caper ['keɪpər] ◆ vi [jump, skip] cabrioler, gambader, faire des cabrioles or des gambades. ◆ n **1.** [practical joke] farce f **2.** CULIN câpre f ; [shrub] câprier m.

Cape Town pr n Le Cap.

Cape Verde [-vɜːd] pr n ▶ **the Cape Verde Islands** les îles fpl du Cap-Vert.

capful ['kæpfʊl] n [of liquid] capsule f (pleine).

capillary ['kæpələrɪ] (pl **capillaries**) ◆ adj capillaire. ◆ n capillaire m.

capita → **per capita.**

capital ['kæpɪtl] ◆ adj **1.** [chief, primary] capital, principal ▸ *it's of capital importance* c'est d'une importance capitale, c'est de la plus haute importance **2.** [upper case] majuscule / *capital D* D majuscule / *he's an idiot with a capital "I"* c'est un imbécile avec un grand «I». ◆ n **1.** [city] capitale f **2.** [letter] majuscule f, capitale f **3.** (U) [funds] capital m, capitaux mpl, fonds mpl ; ECON & FIN [funds and assets] capital m (en espèces et en nature) ▸ **to try and make capital (out) of a situation** essayer de tirer profit or parti d'une situation. ◆ comp de capital ▸ **capital income** revenu m du capital ▸ **capital investment** mise f de fonds.

capital assets pl n actif m immobilisé, immobilisations fpl.

capital expenditure n (U) dépenses fpl d'investissement.

capital gains tax n impôt sur les plus-values.

capital goods pl n biens mpl d'équipement or d'investissement.

capital-intensive adj à forte intensité de capital.

capitalism ['kæpɪtəlɪzm] n capitalisme m.

capitalist ['kæpɪtəlɪst] ◆ adj capitaliste. ◆ n capitaliste mf.

capitalization, capitalisation [ˌkæpɪtəlaɪ'zeɪʃn] n capitalisation f.

capitalize, capitalise ['kæpɪtəlaɪz] vi ▸ **to capitalize on sthg a)** [take advantage of] tirer profit or parti de qqch **b)** [make money on] monnayer qqch.

capital punishment n peine f capitale, peine f de mort.

capital stock n capital m social, fonds mpl propres.

capital transfer tax n impôt m sur le transfert de capitaux.

Capitol ['kæpɪtl] pr n **1.** [in Rome] ▸ **the Capitol** le Capitole **2.** [in US] ▸ **the Capitol a)** [national] le Capitole (siège du Congrès américain) **b)** [state] le Capitole (siège du Congrès de l'État).

Capitol Hill pr n la colline du Capitole, à Washington, où siège le Congrès américain.

> 🏛 **Capitol Hill**
>
> Ce nom désigne, par extension, le Congrès américain : **The proposal will not be welcomed on Capitol Hill.** Le Congrès n'accueillera pas favorablement cette proposition.

capitulate [kə'pɪtjʊleɪt] vi MIL & *fig* capituler.

capitulation [kəˌpɪtjʊ'leɪʃn] n MIL & *fig* capitulation f.

capoeira [ˌkæpəʊ'eɪrə] n capoeira f.

capon ['keɪpən] n chapon m.

cappuccino [ˌkæpʊ'tʃiːnəʊ] (pl **cappuccinos**) n cappuccino m.

capricious [kə'prɪʃəs] adj [person] capricieux, fantasque ; [weather] capricieux, changeant.

Capricorn ['kæprɪkɔːn] pr n ASTROL & ASTRON Capricorne m / *he's a Capricorn* il est (du signe) du Capricorne.

capri pants [kə'priː] n pantacourt m.

caps [kæps] (abbr of **capital letters**) pl n caps ▸ **caps lock** verrouillage m des majuscules.

capsicum ['kæpsɪkəm] n [fruit & plant - sweet] poivron m, piment m doux ; [-hot] piment m.

capsize [kæp'saɪz] ◆ vi [gen] se renverser ; [boat] chavirer. ◆ vt [gen] renverser ; [boat] faire chavirer.

capsule ['kæpsjuːl] n **1.** [gen & AERON], ANAT & BOT capsule f **2.** PHARM capsule f, gélule f.

Capt. (written abbr of **captain**) cap.

captain ['kæptɪn] ◆ n **1.** [of boat] capitaine m ; MIL capitaine m **2.** [of group, team] chef m, capitaine m ; SPORT capitaine m (d'équipe). **3.** US [of police] ≃ commissaire m (de police) de quartier. ◆ vt [gen] diriger ; MIL commander ; SPORT être le capitaine de.

captaincy ['kæptɪnsɪ] n **1.** MIL grade m de capitaine **2.** SPORT poste m de capitaine.

caption ['kæpʃn] n **1.** [under illustration] légende f **2.** [in article, chapter] sous-titre m.

captivate ['kæptɪveɪt] vt captiver, fasciner.

captivating ['kæptɪveɪtɪŋ] adj captivant, fascinant.

captive ['kæptɪv] ◆ n captif m, -ive f, prisonnier m, -ère f ▸ **to take sb captive** faire qqn prisonnier ▸ **to hold sb captive** garder qqn en captivité. ◆ adj [person] captif, prisonnier ; [animal, balloon] captif ▸ **captive audience** public captif.

captivity [kæp'tɪvətɪ] n captivité f ▸ **in captivity** en captivité.

captor ['kæptər] n [gen] personne f qui capture ; [unlawfully] ravisseur m, -euse f.

capture ['kæptʃər] ◆ vt **1.** [take prisoner - animal, criminal, enemy] capturer, prendre ; [-runaway] reprendre ; [-city] prendre, s'emparer de ; GAMES prendre **2.** [gain control of - market] conquérir, s'emparer de ; [-attention, imagination] captiver ; [-admiration, interest] gagner. ◆ n capture f, prise f.

car [kɑːr] ◆ n **1.** [automobile] voiture f, automobile f, auto f **2.** US [of train] wagon m, voiture f ; [in subway] rame f. ◆ comp [engine, tyre, wheel] de voiture, d'automobile ; [journey, trip] en voiture ▸ **car allowance** UK indemnité f de déplacement (en voiture) ▸ **car boot sale** UK marché où chacun vient avec sa voiture (dont le coffre sert de stand) pour vendre des objets de toute sorte ▸ **car chase** course-poursuite f ▸ **car ferry** ferry m ▸ **car radio** autoradio m ▸ **car worker** ouvrier m, -ère f de l'industrie automobile.

Caracas [kə'rækəs] pr n Caracas.

carafe [kə'ræf] n carafe f.

car alarm n alarme f de voiture.

carambola [ˌkærəm'bəʊlə] n carambole f.

caramel ['kærəmel] n caramel m.

caramelize, caramelise ['kærəməlaɪz] ◆ vt caraméliser. ◆ vi se caraméliser.

carat UK, **karat** US ['kærət] n carat m.

caravan ['kærəvæn] (🇬🇧 *pt* & *pp* caravanned, *cont* caravanning ; 🇺🇸 *pt* & *pp* caravanned *or* caravaned, *cont* caravanning *or* caravaning) ◆ n **1.** 🇬🇧 [vehicle] caravane *f* **2.** [of gipsy] roulotte *f*. ◆ vi ▶ **to go caravanning** faire du caravaning *or offic* du caravanage.

caravanning ['kærəvænɪŋ] n caravaning *m*, caravanage *offic*.

caravan site n 🇬🇧 [for campers] camping *m* (pour caravanes) ; [of gipsies] campement *m*.

caraway ['kærəweɪ] n [plant] carvi *m*, cumin *m* des prés ▶ **caraway seeds** (graines *fpl* de) carvi.

carb [kɑːb] n *(gen pl) inf* [carbohydrate] glucide *m* ▶ **a low-carb diet** un régime pauvre en glucides.

carbohydrate [ˌkɑːbəʊ'haɪdreɪt] n **1.** CHEM hydrate *m* de carbone **2.** *(usu pl)* [foodstuff] ▶ **carbohydrates** glucides *mpl*.

car bomb n voiture *f* piégée.

carbon ['kɑːbən] n **1.** CHEM carbone *m* **2.** [copy, paper] carbone *m*.

carbonated ['kɑːbəneɪtɪd] adj carbonaté / *carbonated soft drinks* boissons *fpl* gazeuses.

carbon copy n TYPO carbone *m* ; *fig* réplique *f*.

carbon dating n datation *f* au carbone 14.

carbon dioxide [-daɪ'ɒksaɪd] n gaz *m* carbonique, dioxyde *m* de carbone.

carbon fibre n fibre *f* de carbone.

carbon footprint n empreinte *f* carbone.

carbon monoxide n monoxyde *m* de carbone.

carbon-neutral adj neutre en carbone.

carbon offset n compensation *f* carbone.

carbon paper n TYPO (papier *m*) carbone *m*.

carbon sink n puits *m* de carbone.

carbon tax n taxe *f* sur le carbone or le CO₂, taxe *f* sur les émissions de carbone.

carburettor 🇬🇧, **carburetor** 🇺🇸 [ˌkɑːbə'retər] n carburateur *m*.

carcass, carcase ['kɑːkəs] n [of animal] carcasse *f*, cadavre *m* ; [for food] carcasse *f*.

carcinogen [kɑː'sɪnədʒən] n (agent *m*) carcinogène *m* or cancérogène *m*.

carcinogenic [ˌkɑːsɪnə'dʒenɪk] adj carcinogène, cancérogène.

carcinoma [ˌkɑːsɪ'nəʊmə] *(pl* carcinomas *or* carcinomata [-mətə]) n carcinome *m*.

card [kɑːd] n **1.** GAMES carte *f* / *to play cards* jouer aux cartes / *I still have a couple of cards up my sleeve* j'ai encore quelques atouts dans mon jeu ▶ **to lay** or **to place one's cards on the table** jouer cartes sur table / *it was on the cards* 🇬🇧 or *in the cards* 🇺🇸 *that the project would fail* il était dit or prévisible que le projet échouerait **2.** [with written information -gen] carte *f* ; [-for business] carte *f* (de visite) ; [-for index] fiche *f* ; [-for membership] carte *f* de membre or d'adhérent ; [-for library] carte *f* (d'abonnement) ; [postcard] carte *f* (postale) ; [programme] programme *m* **3.** [cardboard] carton *m*.

cardamom, cardamum ['kɑːdəməm] n cardamome *f*.

cardboard ['kɑːdbɔːd] ◆ n carton *m*. ◆ adj [container, partition] de or en carton ▶ **cardboard box** (boîte *f* en) carton *m* ▶ **cardboard city** quartier où dorment les sans-abri.

card-carrying adj ▶ **card-carrying member** membre *m*, adhérent *m*, -e *f*.

card catalogue n fichier *m* (de bibliothèque).

card game n jeu *m* de cartes.

card holder n [of library] abonné *m*, -e *f* ; [of credit card] titulaire *mf* d'une carte de crédit.

cardiac ['kɑːdɪæk] adj cardiaque.

cardiac arrest n arrêt *m* cardiaque.

cardigan ['kɑːdɪgən] n cardigan *m*.

cardinal ['kɑːdɪnl] ◆ adj [essential] cardinal. ◆ n MATH, ORNITH & RELIG cardinal *m*.

cardinal number n MATH nombre *m* cardinal.

card index n fichier *m*.

cardiogram ['kɑːdɪəgræm] n cardiogramme *m*.

cardiograph ['kɑːdɪəgrɑːf] n cardiographe *m*.

cardiologist [ˌkɑːdɪ'ɒlədʒɪst] n cardiologue *mf*.

cardiology [ˌkɑːdɪ'ɒlədʒɪ] n cardiologie *f*.

cardiovascular [ˌkɑːdɪəʊ'væskjʊlər] adj cardio-vasculaire.

card-operated lock n serrure *f* à carte perforée.

cardphone ['kɑːdfəʊn] n 🇬🇧 téléphone *m* à carte.

cardsharp(er) ['kɑːdˌʃɑːp(ər)] n tricheur *m* (professionnel aux cartes), tricheuse *f* (professionnelle aux cartes).

card table n table *f* de jeu.

card trick n tour *m* de cartes.

card vote n 🇬🇧 vote *m* sur carte *(chaque voix comptant pour le nombre de voix d'adhérents représentés)*.

care [keər] ◆ vi **1.** [feel concern] ▶ **to care about sthg** s'intéresser à or se soucier de qqch / *I don't care what people think* je me moque de ce que pensent les gens ▶ **I couldn't** or **could** 🇺🇸 *inf* **care less if he comes or not** ça m'est complètement égal qu'il vienne ou non / *what do I care?* qu'est-ce que ça peut me faire ? / *who cares?* qu'est-ce que ça peut bien faire ? **2.** [feel affection] ▶ **to care about** or **for sb** aimer qqn **3.** *fml* [like] : *would you care to join us?* voulez-vous vous joindre à nous ? ◆ n **1.** [worry] ennui *m*, souci *m* **2.** *(U)* [treatment -of person] soin *m*, soins *mpl*, traitement *m* ; [-of machine, material] entretien *m* **3.** *(U)* [attention] attention *f*, soin *m* / **'handle with care'** [on package] 'fragile' **4.** [protection, supervision] charge *f*, garde *f* / *I'll take care of the reservations* je me charge des réservations or de faire les réservations, je vais m'occuper des réservations / *I can take care of myself* je peux or je sais me débrouiller (tout seul) / *address the letter to me (in) care of Mrs Dodd* adressez-moi la lettre chez Mme Dodd **5.** 🇬🇧 ADMIN : *the baby was put in care* or *taken into care* on a retiré aux parents la garde de leur bébé. ❖ **care of** prep chez. ❖ **care for** vt insep **1.** [look after -child] s'occuper de ; [-invalid] soigner **2.** [like] aimer / *he still cares for her* **a)** [loves] il l'aime toujours **b)** [has affection for] il est toujours attaché à elle, il tient toujours à elle / *she didn't care for the way he spoke* la façon dont il a parlé lui a déplu / *would you care for a cup of coffee? fml* aimeriez-vous or voudriez-vous une tasse de café ?

CARE [keər] (abbr of **Cooperative for American Relief Everywhere**) pr n *organisation humanitaire américaine*.

care attendant 🇬🇧, **care assistant** 🇺🇸 n aide-soignant *m*, -e *f*.

career [kə'rɪər] ◆ n **1.** [profession] carrière *f*, profession *f* **2.** [life] vie *f*, carrière *f* / *her university career* son parcours universitaire. ◆ comp [diplomat, soldier] de carrière ▶ **career prospects** *good career prospects* de bonnes perspectives de carrière. ◆ vi 🇬🇧 : *to career along* aller à toute vitesse or à toute allure. ❖ **careers** comp SCH & UNIV ▶ **careers advisor** or **adviser** or **officer** conseiller *m*, -ère *f* d'orientation professionnelle ▶ **careers guidance** orientation *f* professionnelle.

career coach n coach *m* carrière.

careerist [kə'rɪərɪst] n *pej* carriériste *mf*.

career-minded adj ambitieux.

career woman n femme qui attache beaucoup d'importance à sa carrière.

carefree ['keəfri:] adj [person] sans souci, insouciant ; [look, smile] insouciant.

careful ['keəfʊl] adj **1.** [cautious] prudent / *be careful!* (faites) attention ! / *be careful not to* or *be careful you don't hurt her feelings* faites attention à or prenez soin de ne pas la froisser / *you can never be too careful* **a)** [gen] on n'est jamais assez prudent **b)** [in double-checking sthg] deux précautions valent mieux qu'une / *to be careful with one's money* **a)** [gen] être parcimonieux **b)** pej être près de ses sous **2.** [thorough - person, work] soigneux, consciencieux ; [- consideration, examination] approfondi / *they showed careful attention to detail* ils se sont montrés très attentifs aux détails.

carefully ['keəflɪ] adv **1.** [cautiously] avec prudence or précaution, prudemment **2.** [thoroughly - work] soigneusement, avec soin ; [- consider, examine] de façon approfondie, à fond ; [- listen, watch] attentivement.

caregiver ['keəgɪvə'] n [family member] aidant m familial, aidante f familiale ; [professional] aide-soignant m, -e f.

careless ['keəlɪs] adj [negligent - person] négligent, peu soigneux ; [- work] peu soigné / *a careless mistake* une faute d'inattention.

carelessly ['keəlɪslɪ] adv [negligently - work, write] sans soin, sans faire attention.

carelessness ['keəlɪsnɪs] n (U) **1.** [negligence] négligence f, manque m de soin or d'attention **2.** [thoughtlessness - of dress] négligence f ; [- of behaviour] désinvolture f ; [- of remark] légèreté f.

carer ['keərə'] n [family member] aidant m familial, aidante f familiale ; [professional] aide-soignant m, -e f.

caress [kə'res] ◆ vt caresser. ◆ n caresse f.

caret ['kærət] n TYPO signe m d'insertion.

caretaker ['keə,teɪkə'] n [of building] concierge mf, gardien m, -enne f.

care worker n aide-soignant m, -e f.

careworn ['keəwɔ:n] adj accablé de soucis, rongé par les soucis.

cargo ['kɑ:gəʊ] (pl cargoes or cargos) n cargaison f, chargement m.

car hire UK, **car rental** US ◆ n location f de voitures. ◆ comp [company, firm] de location de voitures.

Carib ['kærɪb] n **1.** [person] Caraïbe mf **2.** LING caraïbe m.

Caribbean [UK kærɪ'bi:ən US kə'rɪbɪən] ◆ adj des Caraïbes ▶ the Caribbean islands les Antilles fpl. ◆ n ▶ the Caribbean (Sea) la mer des Caraïbes or des Antilles.

caribou ['kærɪbu:] (pl caribou or caribous) n caribou m.

caricature ['kærɪkə,tjʊə'] ◆ n lit & fig caricature f. ◆ vt [depict] caricaturer ; [parody] caricaturer, parodier.

caries ['keəri:z] (pl caries) n carie f.

caring ['keərɪŋ] adj **1.** [loving] aimant ; [kindly] bienveillant **2.** [organization] à vocation sociale.

car jack n cric m.

carjack ['kɑ:,dʒæk] vt : *to be carjacked* se faire voler sa voiture sous la menace d'une arme.

carjacker ['kɑ:,dʒækə'] n auteur d'un vol de voiture sous la menace d'une arme.

carjacking ['kɑ:,dʒækɪŋ] n vol m de voiture sous la menace d'une arme.

car kit n [for phone] kit m auto mains libres.

carload ['kɑ:,ləʊd] n : *a carload of boxes / people* une voiture pleine de cartons / de gens.

carlot [kɑ:lɒt] n US parking m (d'un garage automobile).

carmaker ['kɑ:meɪkə'] n US constructeur m automobile.

carnage ['kɑ:nɪdʒ] n carnage m.

carnal ['kɑ:nl] adj charnel.

carnation [kɑ:'neɪʃn] n œillet m.

carnival ['kɑ:nɪvl] ◆ n **1.** [festival] carnaval m **2.** [fun fair] fête f foraine. ◆ comp [atmosphere, parade] de carnaval.

carnivore ['kɑ:nɪvɔ:'] n carnivore m, carnassier m.

carnivorous [kɑ:'nɪvərəs] adj carnivore, carnassier.

carob ['kærəb] ◆ n [tree] caroubier m ; [pod] caroube f. ◆ comp ▶ **carob bean** caroube f.

carol ['kærəl] (UK pt & pp **carolled**, cont **carolling** ; US pt & pp **caroled**, cont **caroling**) n chant m (joyeux) ▶ **carol singer** personne qui, à l'époque de Noël, va chanter et quêter au profit des bonnes œuvres.

Carol service

Ce service traditionnel a lieu juste avant Noël et se compose de chants de Noël et d'une lecture de passages de la Bible.

carouse [kə'raʊz] vi liter faire ribote arch hum.

carousel [,kærə'sel] n **1.** PHOT [for slides] carrousel m **2.** [for luggage] carrousel m, tapis m roulant (à bagages) **3.** US [merry-go-round] manège m (de chevaux de bois).

carp [kɑ:p] (pl carp or carps) ◆ n [fish] carpe f. ◆ vi inf [complain] se plaindre ; [find fault] critiquer.

carpal tunnel syndrome n syndrome m du canal carpien.

car park n UK parking m, parc m de stationnement.

Carpathian Mountains [kɑ:'peɪθɪən-], **Carpathians** [kɑ:'peɪθɪənz] pl pr n ▶ **the Carpathian Mountains** les Carpates fpl.

carpenter ['kɑ:pəntə'] n [for houses, large-scale works] charpentier m ; [for doors, furniture] menuisier m.

carpentry ['kɑ:pəntrɪ] n [large-scale work] charpenterie f ; [doors, furniture] menuiserie f.

carpet ['kɑ:pɪt] ◆ n [not fitted] tapis m ; [fitted] moquette f. ◆ vt [floor] recouvrir d'un tapis ; [with fitted carpet] recouvrir d'une moquette, moquetter ; [house, room] mettre de la moquette dans, moquetter.

carpet slipper n pantoufle f (recouverte de tapisserie).

carpet sweeper n [mechanical] balai m mécanique ; [electric] aspirateur m.

carphone ['kɑ:,fəʊn] n téléphone m de voiture.

carpool ['kɑ:pu:l] n covoiturage m.

carport ['kɑ:,pɔ:t] n auvent m (pour voiture).

car rental n US = car hire.

carriage ['kærɪdʒ] n **1.** [vehicle - horse-drawn] calèche f, voiture f à cheval ; UK RAIL voiture f, wagon m (de voyageurs) **2.** UK COMM [cost of transportation] transport m, fret m ▶ **carriage paid** (en) port m payé **3.** [bearing, posture] port m, maintien m.

carriage clock n UK horloge f de voyage.

carriage return n retour m chariot.

carriageway ['kærɪdʒweɪ] n UK chaussée f.

carrier ['kærɪə'] n **1.** [device, mechanism] ▶ **luggage carrier** porte-bagages m inv **2.** COMM [transporter - company] entreprise f de transport, transporteur m ; [- aeroplane] appareil m, avion m ; [- ship] navire m **3.** MED [of disease] porteur m, -euse f.

carrier-agnostic adj TELEC tous opérateurs.

carrier bag n 🇬🇧 sac m en plastique.

carrier-based, carrier-borne adj AERON & NAUT embarqué.

carrier pigeon n pigeon m voyageur.

carrion ['kærɪən] n charogne f.

carrot ['kærət] ◆ n 1. [plant & vegetable] carotte f 2. fig [motivation] carotte f ▶ **the carrot and stick approach** la méthode de la carotte et du bâton. ◆ comp ▶ **carrot cake** gâteau m aux carottes.

carry ['kærɪ] (pt & pp carried) ◆ vt 1. [bear - subj: person] porter ; [heavy load] porter, transporter / she carried her baby on her back / in her arms elle portait son enfant sur son dos / dans ses bras / could you carry the groceries into the kitchen? pourrais-tu porter les provisions jusqu'à la cuisine ? 2. [convey, transport - subj: vehicle] transporter ; [- subj: river, wind] porter, emporter ; [- subj: pipe] acheminer, amener ; [- subj: airwaves, telephone wire] transmettre, conduire 3. [be medium for - message, news] porter, transmettre ; MED [disease, virus] porter 4. [have on one's person - identity card, papers] porter, avoir (sur soi) ; [- cash] avoir (sur soi) ; [- gun] porter 5. [comprise, include] porter, comporter / our products carry a 6-month warranty nos produits sont accompagnés d'une garantie de 6 mois ; [have as consequence] entraîner / the crime carries a long sentence ce crime est passible d'une longue peine 6. [subj: magazine, newspaper] rapporter ; [subj: radio, television] transmettre / all the newspapers carried the story l'histoire était dans tous les journaux 7. [bear, hold] porter / to carry o.s. well a) [sit, stand] se tenir droit b) [behave] bien se conduire or se tenir 8. [win] : she carried the audience with her le public était avec elle / the motion was carried la motion a été votée 9. COMM [deal in - stock] vendre, stocker 10. [be pregnant with] attendre / she's carrying their fourth child elle est enceinte de leur quatrième enfant. ◆ vi [ball, sound] porter. ◆❖ **carry away** vt sep 1. [remove] emporter, enlever 2. (usu passive) [excite] : he was carried away by his enthusiasm / imagination il s'est laissé emporter par son enthousiasme / imagination / I got a bit carried away and spent all my money je me suis emballé et j'ai dépensé tout mon argent. ◆❖ **carry off** vt sep 1. [remove forcibly - goods] emporter, enlever ; [- person] enlever 2. [award, prize] remporter 3. [do successfully - aim, plan] réaliser ; [- deal, meeting] mener à bien / she carried it off beautifully elle s'en est très bien tirée 4. euph [kill - subj: disease] emporter. ◆❖ **carry on** vi 1. 🇬🇧 [continue] continuer / I carried on working or with my work j'ai continué à travailler, j'ai continué mon travail 2. inf [make a fuss] faire une histoire or des histoires 3. inf [have affair] ▶ **to carry on with sb** avoir une liaison avec qqn. ◆ vt insep 1. 🇬🇧 [continue - conversation, work] continuer, poursuivre 2. [conduct - work] effectuer, réaliser ; [- negotiations] mener. ◆❖ **carry out** vt sep 1. [take away] emporter 2. [perform - programme, raid] effectuer ; [- idea, plan] réaliser, mettre à exécution ; [- experiment] effectuer, conduire ; [- investigation, research, survey] conduire, mener ; [- instruction, order] exécuter. ◆❖ **carry through** vt sep [accomplish] réaliser, mener à bien or à bonne fin.

carryall ['kærɪɔːl] n 🇺🇸 fourre-tout m inv (sac).

carrycot ['kærɪkɒt] n 🇬🇧 couffin m.

carry-on ◆ n 🇬🇧 inf [fuss] histoires fpl ; [commotion] tapage m, agitation f. ◆ adj ▶ **carry-on items** or **carry-on luggage** bagages mpl à main.

carryout ['kærɪaʊt] 🇺🇸 & 🇸cot n [restaurant] restaurant qui fait des plats à emporter ; [meal] plat m à emporter.

carsick ['kɑː,sɪk] adj : **to be** or **to feel carsick** avoir le mal de la route.

car sickness n mal m de la route.

cart [kɑːt] ◆ n 1. [horse-drawn - for farming] charrette f ; 🇺🇸 [for passengers] charrette f (anglaise), voiture f 2. [hand-cart] charrette f à bras 3. 🇺🇸 [shopping cart] chariot m, Caddie® m. ◆ vt inf & fig [haul] transporter, trimballer. ◆❖ **cart away, cart off** vt sep [rubbish, wood] emporter ; inf [person] emmener.

carte blanche [,kɑːt'blɑːʃ] n carte f blanche ▶ **to give sb carte blanche (to do sthg)** donner carte blanche à qqn (pour faire qqch).

cartel [kɑː'tel] n COMM & POL cartel m.

cartilage ['kɑːtɪlɪdʒ] n cartilage m.

cartographer [kɑː'tɒgrəfər] n cartographe mf.

cartography [kɑː'tɒgrəfɪ] n cartographie f.

carton ['kɑːtn] n [cardboard box] boîte f (en carton), carton m ; [of juice, milk] carton m, brique f ; [of cream, yoghurt] pot m ; [of cigarettes] cartouche f.

cartoon [kɑː'tuːn] n 1. [drawing] dessin m humoristique ; [series of drawings] bande f dessinée ▶ **cartoon strip** bande f dessinée 2. [film] dessin m animé.

cartoonist [kɑː'tuːnɪst] n [of drawings] dessinateur m, -trice f humoristique ; [of series of drawings] dessinateur m, -trice f de bandes dessinées ; [for films] dessinateur m, -trice f de dessins animés, animateur m, -trice f.

cartridge ['kɑːtrɪdʒ] n 1. [for explosive, gun] cartouche f 2. [for pen, tape deck, typewriter, etc.] cartouche f 3. PHOT chargeur m (d'appareil photo).

cartridge paper n papier m à cartouche.

cartwheel ['kɑːtwiːl] n 1. [of cart] roue f de charrette 2. [movement] roue f ▶ **to do** or **to turn a cartwheel** faire la roue.

carve [kɑːv] ◆ vt 1. [stone, wood] tailler ▶ **it's not carved in stone** ce n'est pas gravé dans le marbre 2. CULIN découper. ◆ vi [stone, wood] tailler ; [shape] sculpter, tailler / she carved out a career for herself in the arts fig elle a fait carrière. ◆❖ **carve up** vt sep [cut up - meat] découper ; fig [country, estate] morceler, démembrer.

carvery ['kɑːvərɪ] n (pl carveries) n restaurant où l'on mange de la viande découpée à table.

carving ['kɑːvɪŋ] n [sculpture] sculpture f ; [engraving] gravure f.

carving knife n couteau m à découper.

car wash n [place] portique m de lavage automatique (de voitures) ; [action] lavage m de voitures.

Casablanca [,kæsə'blæŋkə] pr n Casablanca.

cascade [kæ'skeɪd] ◆ n lit cascade f, chute f d'eau ; fig [of hair] flot m. ◆ vi [water] tomber en cascade ; [hair] ruisseler.

case [keɪs]
n

🅰 OBJECT 1. [container] caisse f, boîte f ; [for bottles] caisse f ; [for jewellery] coffret m ; [for camera, guitar] étui m 2. [for display] vitrine f 3. 🇬🇧 [suitcase] valise f.

🅱 SITUATION OR PERSON 1. [instance, situation] cas m, exemple m / it's a clear case of mismanagement c'est un exemple manifeste de mauvaise gestion / in that case dans or en ce cas / in this particular case en l'occurrence / in which case auquel cas / in your case en ce qui vous concerne, dans votre cas / in some cases dans certains cas 2. [actual state of affairs] cas m / as the case or whatever the case may be selon le cas 3. MED [disease] cas m ; [person] malade mf / there have been several cases of meningitis recently il y a eu plusieurs cas de méningite récemment 4. inf [person] cas m / he's a sad case c'est vraiment un pauvre type.

🅲 INVESTIGATION OR ARGUMENT 1. [investigation] affaire f / the case continues affaire à suivre 2. LAW affaire *f*, cause *f*, procès *m* / *her case comes up next week* son procès a lieu la semaine prochaine ▶ **to try a case** juger une affaire **3.** [argument] arguments *mpl* / *there is a good case against / for establishing quotas* il y a beaucoup à dire contre / en faveur de l'établissement de quotas ▶ **to make (out) a case for sthg** présenter des arguments pour or en faveur de qqch. ❖ **in any case** adv phr **1.** [besides] en tout cas **2.** [at least] du moins, en tout cas. ❖ **in case** ◆ adv phr au cas où / *I'll take my umbrella (just) in case* je vais prendre mon parapluie au cas où. ◆ conj phr au cas où. ❖ **in case of** prep phr en cas de.

case-hardened adj METALL cémenté ; *fig* endurci.

case history n antécédents *mpl*.

case-insensitive adj COMPUT qui ne distingue pas les majuscules des minuscules.

case-sensitive adj sensible à la casse.

case study n étude *f* de cas.

casework ['keɪswɜːk] n *travail social personnalisé*.

caseworker ['keɪsˌwɜːkər] n *travailleur social s'occupant de cas individuels et familiaux*.

cash [kæʃ] ◆ n **1.** [coins and banknotes] espèces *fpl*, (argent *m*) liquide *m* / **to pay (in) cash** payer en liquide or en espèces **2.** [money in general] argent *m* / **to be short of cash** être à court (d'argent) **3.** [immediate payment] ▶ **to pay cash (down)** payer comptant ▶ **cash on delivery** paiement *m* à la livraison, (livraison *f*) contre remboursement ▶ **cash with order** payable à la commande. ◆ comp **1.** [problems, worries] d'argent **2.** [price, transaction] (au) comptant ▶ **cash value** valeur *f* de rachat. ◆ vt [cheque] encaisser, toucher / *could you cash this cheque for me?* **a)** [friend] peux-tu me donner de l'argent contre ce chèque ? **b)** [bank] voudriez-vous m'encaisser ce chèque ?

cash and carry n 🇬🇧 libre-service *m* de gros, cash and carry *m inv*.

cashback ['kæʃbæk] n 🇬🇧 [in supermarket] *espèces retirées à la caisse d'un supermarché lors d'un paiement par carte*.

cashbook ['kæʃbʊk] n livre *m* de caisse.

cashbox ['kæʃbɒks] n caisse *f*.

cash card n carte *f* de retrait.

cash cow n vache *f* à lait.

cash crop n culture *f* de rapport or commerciale.

cash desk n caisse *f*.

cash discount n remise *f* au comptant.

cash dispenser n distributeur *m* (de billets).

cashew ['kæʃuː] n [tree] anacardier *m* ▶ **cashew (nut)** (noix *f* de) cajou *m*.

cash flow n marge *f* brute d'autofinancement, cash-flow *m*.

cashier [kæ'ʃɪər] n BANK & COMM caissier *m*, -ère *f*.

cashless ['kæʃlɪs] adj sans argent.

cash machine n distributeur *m* (de billets).

cashmere [kæʃ'mɪər] ◆ n cachemire *m*. ◆ comp [coat, sweater] de or en cachemire.

cashpoint ['kæʃpɔɪnt] n 🇬🇧 distributeur *m* (de billets).

cash price n prix *m* comptant.

cash register n caisse *f* (enregistreuse).

casing ['keɪsɪŋ] n [gen] revêtement *m*, enveloppe *f* ; [for tyre] enveloppe *f* extérieure.

casino [kə'siːnəʊ] (*pl* **casinos**) n casino *m*.

cask [kɑːsk] n [barrel - gen] tonneau *m*, fût *m* ; [-large] barrique *f* ; [-small] baril *m*.

cask-aged adj vieilli en fût.

casket ['kɑːskɪt] n **1.** [small box] coffret *m*, boîte *f* **2.** 🇺🇸 [coffin] cercueil *m*.

Caspian Sea ['kæspɪən-] pr n ▶ **the Caspian Sea** la (mer) Caspienne.

casserole ['kæsərəʊl] ◆ n **1.** [pan] cocotte *f* **2.** [stew] ragoût *m*. ◆ vt (faire) cuire en ragoût.

> ⚠ The French word **casserole** means sauce-pan, not casserole.

cassette [kæ'set] n **1.** [tape] cassette *f* **2.** PHOT [cartridge] chargeur *m*.

cassette deck n lecteur *m* de cassettes.

cassette player n lecteur *m* de cassettes.

cassette recorder n magnétophone *m* à cassettes.

cassock ['kæsək] n soutane *f*.

cast [kɑːst] (*pt & pp* cast) ◆ vt **1.** [throw] jeter, lancer ▶ **to cast one's vote for sb** voter pour qqn **2.** [direct - light, shadow] projeter ; [-look] jeter, diriger / *the accident cast a shadow over their lives* l'accident a jeté une ombre sur leur existence / *could you cast an eye over this report?* voulez-vous jeter un œil sur ce rapport ? / *he cast an eye over the audience* il a promené son regard sur l'auditoire **3.** [film, play] distribuer les rôles de ; [performer] : *the director cast her in the role of the mother* le metteur en scène lui a attribué le rôle de la mère **4.** ART & TECH [form, statue] mouler ; [metal] couler, fondre ; [plaster] couler. ◆ n **1.** CIN & THEAT [actors] distribution *f*, acteurs *mpl* ▶ **cast list a)** CIN & TV générique *m* **b)** THEAT distribution *f* **2.** ART & TECH [act of moulding - metal] coulage *m*, coulée *f* ; [-plaster] moulage *m* ; [-coin, medallion] empreinte *f* ; [mould] moule *m* ; [object moulded] moulage *m* **3.** MED [for broken limb] plâtre *m* / *her arm was in a cast* elle avait un bras dans le plâtre. ❖ **cast about, cast around** vi : *she cast about for an idea / an excuse to leave* elle essaya de trouver une idée / un prétexte pour partir. ❖ **cast aside** vt sep *liter* [book] mettre de côté ; [shirt, shoes] se débarrasser de ; *fig* [person, suggestion] rejeter, écarter. ❖ **cast off** ◆ vt sep **1.** [undo] défaire ; [untie] délier, dénouer ; [in knitting] rabattre ; NAUT [lines, rope] larguer, lâcher ; [boat] larguer or lâcher les amarres de **2.** [rid oneself of - clothing] *liter* enlever, se débarrasser de ; [-bonds] se défaire de, se libérer de ; [-cares, habit, tradition] se défaire de, abandonner. ◆ vi **1.** NAUT larguer les amarres, appareiller **2.** [in knitting] rabattre les mailles. ❖ **cast on** ◆ vi monter les mailles. ◆ vt sep [stitches] monter.

castanets [ˌkæstə'nets] pl n castagnettes *fpl*.

castaway ['kɑːstəweɪ] n NAUT naufragé *m*, -e *f* ; *fig* naufragé *m*, -e *f*, laissé-pour-compte *m*, laissée-pour-compte *f*.

caste [kɑːst] n [gen] caste *f*, classe *f* sociale ; [in Hindu society] caste *f*.

caster ['kɑːstər] n [wheel] roulette *f*.

caster sugar n 🇬🇧 sucre *m* en poudre.

castigate ['kæstɪgeɪt] vt *fml* [criticize - person] critiquer sévèrement, fustiger *fml* ; [-book, play] éreinter.

casting ['kɑːstɪŋ] n CIN & THEAT [selection of actors] attribution *f* des rôles, casting *m*.

casting couch n *inf* : *she denied having got the part on the casting couch* elle a nié avoir couché avec le metteur en scène pour obtenir le rôle.

casting vote n voix *f* prépondérante / *the president has a* or *the casting vote* le président a voix prépondérante.

cast iron n fonte *f*. ❖ **cast-iron** comp **1.** [pot, stove] de or en fonte **2.** *fig* [alibi] inattaquable, en béton.

castle ['kɑːsl] n **1.** [building] château *m* (fort) **2.** [in chess] tour *f*.

castoff ['kɑːstɒf] n (usu pl) [piece of clothing] vieux vêtement m ; fig [person] laissé-pour-compte m, laissée-pour-compte f.

castor ['kɑːstər] n = caster.

castor oil n huile f de ricin.

castrate [kæ'streɪt] vt lit châtrer, castrer ; fig [weaken - person, political movement] émasculer.

castration [kæ'streɪʃn] n lit castration f ; fig [of political movement] émasculation f.

casual ['kæʒʊəl] ◆ adj **1.** [unconcerned] désinvolte, nonchalant ; [natural] simple, naturel / they're very casual about the way they dress ils attachent très peu d'importance à leurs vêtements or à la façon dont ils s'habillent / I tried to appear casual when talking about it j'ai essayé d'en parler avec désinvolture **2.** [informal - dinner] simple, détendu ; [- clothing] sport (inv) **3.** [superficial] superficiel / to make casual conversation parler de choses et d'autres, parler à bâtons rompus / she's just a casual acquaintance of mine c'est quelqu'un que je connais très peu / a casual love affair une aventure ▶ **casual sex** rapports mpl sexuels de rencontre **4.** [occasional - job] intermittent ; [- worker] temporaire. ◆ n [farmworker - for one day] journalier m, -ère f ; [- for harvest, season] (travailleur m) saisonnier m, (travailleuse f) saisonnière f ; [- in construction work] ouvrier m, -ère f temporaire.

casualization [,kæʒʊəlaɪ'zeɪʃən] n précarisation f.

casualize ['kæʒʊəlaɪz] vt précariser.

casually ['kæʒʊəlɪ] adv **1.** [unconcernedly] avec désinvolture, nonchalamment **2.** [informally] simplement / to dress casually s'habiller sport **3.** [glance, remark, suggest] en passant **4.** [by chance] par hasard.

casualty ['kæʒjʊəltɪ] (pl casualties) n **1.** [wounded] blessé m, -e f ; [dead] mort m, -e f **2.** (U) = **casualty department**.

casualty department n MED [emergency ward] service m des urgences ; [accident ward] salle f des accidentés.

cat [kæt] n ZOOL chat m, chatte f ▶ **to let the cat out of the bag** vendre la mèche ▶ he looked like something the cat brought in il était dégoûtant ▶ has the cat got your tongue? tu as perdu ta langue ? ▶ to fight like cat and dog se battre comme des chiffonniers ▶ to put or to set the cat among the pigeons [UK] jeter un pavé dans la mare ▶ to play (a game of) cat and mouse with sb jouer au chat et à la souris avec qqn ▶ when the cat's away the mice will play prov quand le chat n'est pas là les souris dansent prov.

CAT n **1.** (abbr of computer-assisted teaching) [UK] EAO m **2.** [kæt] (abbr of computerized axial tomography) CAT f ▶ **CAT scan** scanographie f.

cataclysmic [,kætə'klɪzmɪk] adj cataclysmique.

catacomb ['kætəkuːm] n (usu pl) catacombe f.

Catalan ['kætə,læn] ◆ n **1.** [person] catalan m, -e f **2.** LING catalan m. ◆ adj catalan.

catalogue [UK], **catalog** [US] ['kætəlɒg] ◆ n catalogue m ; [in library] fichier m ; [US] UNIV guide m de l'étudiant. ◆ vt cataloguer, faire le catalogue de.

Catalonia [,kætə'ləʊnɪə] pr n Catalogne f.

Catalonian [,kætə'ləʊnʃən] ◆ adj catalan. ◆ n [person] catalan m, -e f.

catalyst ['kætəlɪst] n catalyseur m.

catalytic converter n pot m catalytique.

catamaran [,kætəmə'ræn] n catamaran m.

catapult ['kætəpʌlt] ◆ n **1.** [UK] [child's] lance-pierres m inv **2.** AERON & MIL catapulte f. ◆ vt [gen & AERON] catapulter.

cataract ['kætərækt] n **1.** [waterfall] cataracte f, cascade f **2.** MED cataracte f.

catarrh [kə'tɑːr] n catarrhe m.

catastrophe [kə'tæstrəfɪ] n catastrophe f.

catastrophe theory n théorie f des catastrophes.

catastrophic [,kætə'strɒfɪk] adj catastrophique.

catatonic [,kætə'tɒnɪk] adj catatonique.

catbird seat ['kætbɜːd-] n [US] inf ▶ in the catbird seat en position de force.

cat burglar n monte-en-l'air m inv.

catcall ['kætkɔːl] n THEAT sifflet m.

catch [kætʃ] (pt & pp **caught** [kɔːt]) ◆ vt **1.** [ball, thrown object] attraper ▶ **to catch hold of sthg** attraper qqch ; [take hold of] ▶ **to catch sb's arm** saisir or prendre qqn par le bras **2.** [trap - fish, mouse, thief] attraper, prendre / we got caught in a shower / thunderstorm nous avons été surpris par une averse / l'orage ▶ **to catch sb doing sthg** surprendre qqn à faire qqch / you won't catch me doing the washing-up! aucun danger de me surprendre en train de faire la vaisselle ! / don't let me catch you at it again! que je ne t'y reprenne pas ! / you'll catch it when you get home! [UK] inf qu'est-ce que tu vas prendre en rentrant ! **3.** [disease, infection] attraper / to catch a cold attraper un rhume ▶ **to catch cold** attraper or prendre froid **4.** [bus, train] attraper, prendre ; [person] attraper / to catch the last post [UK] arriver à temps pour la dernière levée (du courrier) / I just caught the end of the film j'ai juste vu la fin du film **5.** [on nail, obstacle] : he caught his finger in the door il s'est pris le doigt dans la porte / he caught his coat on the brambles son manteau s'est accroché aux ronces **6.** [hear clearly, understand] saisir, comprendre / I didn't quite catch what you said je n'ai pas bien entendu ce que vous avez dit **7.** [attract] ▶ **to catch sb's attention** or **sb's eye** attirer l'attention de qqn / the idea caught her imagination l'idée a enflammé son imagination. ◆ vi **1.** [ignite - fire, wood] prendre **2.** [on obstacle] : her skirt caught on a nail sa jupe s'est accrochée à un clou / his coat caught in the door son manteau s'est pris dans la porte. ◆ n **1.** [act] prise f ▶ **good catch!** SPORT bien rattrapé ! **2.** [of fish] prise f / he's a good catch hum & fig [man] c'est une belle prise **3.** [snag] piège m / where's or what's the catch? qu'est-ce que ça cache ?, où est le piège ? **4.** [on lock, door] loquet m ; [on window] loqueteau m **5.** [in voice] : with a catch in his voice d'une voix entrecoupée **6.** GAMES jeu m de balle. ◆ **catch on** vi **1.** [fashion, trend, slogan] devenir populaire **2.** inf [understand] piger, saisir, comprendre. ◆ **catch out** vt sep [UK] [by trickery] prendre en défaut ; [in the act] prendre sur le fait. ◆ **catch up** ◆ vi **1.** [as verb of movement] ▶ **to catch up with sb** rattraper qqn / his past will catch up with him one day fig il finira par être rattrapé par son passé **2.** [on lost time] combler son retard ; [on studies] rattraper son retard, se remettre au niveau. ◆ vt sep **1.** [entangle] : the material got caught up in the machinery le tissu s'est pris dans la machine **2.** [absorb, involve] : he was too caught up in the film to notice what was happening il était trop absorbé par le film pour remarquer ce qui se passait / I refuse to get caught up in their private quarrel je refuse de me laisser entraîner dans leurs querelles personnelles.

catch-22 [-twentɪ'tuː] n ▶ **catch-22 situation** situation f sans issue, cercle m vicieux.

catch-all ◆ n fourre-tout m inv. ◆ adj fourre-tout (inv), qui pare à toute éventualité.

catching ['kætʃɪŋ] adj **1.** MED contagieux **2.** fig [enthusiasm] contagieux, communicatif ; [habit] contagieux.

catchment area n ADMIN [for hospital] circonscription hospitalière ; [for school] secteur m de recrutement scolaire.

catchphrase ['kætʃfreɪz] n [in advertising] accroche f ; [set phrase] formule f toute faite ; [of performer] petite phrase f.

catchword ['kætʃwɜːd] n [slogan] slogan m ; POL mot m d'ordre, slogan m.

catchy ['kætʃɪ] (compar **catchier**, superl **catchiest**) adj [tune] qui trotte dans la tête, facile à retenir ; [title] facile à retenir.

catechism ['kætəkɪzm] n catéchisme m.

categorical [ˌkætɪ'gɒrɪkl] adj catégorique.

categorically [ˌkætɪ'gɒrɪklɪ] adv catégoriquement.

categorize, categorise ['kætəgəraɪz] vt catégoriser.

category ['kætəgərɪ] (pl **categories**) n catégorie f.

category leader n chef m de file dans sa catégorie.

cater ['keɪtər] vi s'occuper de la nourriture, fournir des repas. **❖ cater for** vt insep 🇬🇧 **1.** [with food] s'occuper de la nourriture pour **2.** fig [needs] répondre à, pourvoir à ; [tastes] satisfaire.

cater-corner, cater-cornered 🇺🇸 inf **❖** adj diagonal. **❖** adv diagonalement.

caterer ['keɪtərər] n traiteur m.

catering ['keɪtərɪŋ] n restauration f / who did the catering for the wedding? qui a fourni le repas pour le mariage ?

caterpillar ['kætəpɪlər] n ZOOL & TECH chenille f.

caterpillar track n TECH chenille f.

cat-eye adj ▶ **cat-eye glasses** lunettes fpl de star.

catfight ['kætfaɪt] n crêpage m de chignon.

catfighting ['kætfaɪtɪŋ] n crêpage m de chignon.

cat flap n chatière f.

catharsis [kə'θɑːsɪs] (pl **catharses** [-siːz]) n catharsis f.

cathartic [kə'θɑːtɪk] adj cathartique.

cathedral [kə'θiːdrəl] n cathédrale f.

catheter ['kæθɪtər] n cathéter m, sonde f creuse.

cathode ray tube n tube m cathodique.

catholic ['kæθlɪk] adj [broad - tastes] éclectique. **❖ Catholic** **❖** adj RELIG catholique ▶ **the Catholic Church** l'Église f catholique. **❖** n catholique mf.

Catholicism [kə'θɒlɪsɪzm] n catholicisme m.

catkin ['kætkɪn] n BOT chaton m.

cat litter n litière f (pour chats).

catnap ['kætnæp] inf **❖** n (petit) somme m. **❖** vi sommeiller, faire un petit somme.

Catseye®, cat's-eye ['kæts,aɪ] n 🇬🇧 TRANSP catadioptre m (marquant le milieu de la chaussée).

catsuit ['kætsuːt] n combinaison-pantalon f.

catsup ['kætsəp] n 🇺🇸 ketchup m.

cattle ['kætl] pl n (U) bétail m, bestiaux mpl, bovins mpl ▶ **cattle breeder** éleveur m (de bétail) ▶ **cattle shed** étable f ▶ **cattle truck** fourgon m à bestiaux.

cattle grid, cattle guard 🇺🇸 n [sur une route] grille au sol destinée à empêcher le passage du bétail mais non celui des voitures.

catty ['kætɪ] (compar **cattier**, superl **cattiest**) adj inf & pej [person, gossip] méchant, vache / a catty remark une réflexion désagréable.

catwalk ['kætwɔːk] n passerelle f.

Caucasian [kɔː'keɪzjən], **Caucasic** [kɔː'keɪzɪk] **❖** n **1.** [from Caucasia] Caucasien m, -enne f **2.** [white person] Blanc m, Blanche f. **❖** adj **1.** [from Caucasia] caucasien **2.** [race, man] blanc (blanche).

Caucasus ['kɔːkəsəs] pr n ▶ **the Caucasus** le Caucase.

caucus ['kɔːkəs] n 🇺🇸 POL [committee] caucus m.

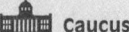

Caucus

Au Canada et aux États-Unis, les **caucus** sont les réunions des dirigeants des partis politiques. Dans certains États américains, il s'agit de réunions de militants lors du processus de désignation du candidat de leur parti à l'élection présidentielle.

caught [kɔːt] pt & pp **⟶** **catch**.

cauldron ['kɔːldrən] n chaudron m.

cauliflower ['kɒlɪˌflaʊər] n chou-fleur m.

causal ['kɔːzl] adj [gen] causal ; GRAM causal, causatif.

cause [kɔːz] **❖** n **1.** [reason] cause f ▶ **to be the cause of sthg** être (la) cause de qqch / the relation of cause and effect la relation de cause à effet **2.** [justification] raison f, motif m / there is cause for anxiety il y a lieu d'être inquiet, il y a de quoi s'inquiéter / with (good) cause à juste titre / without good cause sans cause ou raison valable **3.** [principle] cause f / it's all in a good cause! c'est pour une bonne cause ! **❖** vt causer, provoquer / smoking can cause cancer le tabac peut provoquer des cancers / he has caused us a lot of trouble il nous a créé beaucoup d'ennuis / it will only cause trouble cela ne servira qu'à semer la zizanie.

causeway ['kɔːzweɪ] n GEOG chaussée f.

caustic ['kɔːstɪk] adj CHEM & fig caustique.

caustic soda n soude f caustique.

cauterize, cauterise ['kɔːtəraɪz] vt cautériser.

caution ['kɔːʃn] **❖** n **1.** [care] circonspection f, prudence f / to proceed with caution a) [gen] agir avec circonspection or avec prudence b) [in car] avancer lentement / **'caution!'** 'attention !' **2.** [warning] avertissement m ; [reprimand] réprimande f **3.** LAW avertissement m. **❖** vt **1.** [warn] avertir, mettre en garde ▶ **to caution sb against doing sthg** déconseiller à qqn de faire qqch **2.** LAW ▶ **to caution a prisoner** informer un prisonnier de ses droits.

cautionary ['kɔːʃənərɪ] adj qui sert d'avertissement / a cautionary tale un récit édifiant.

cautious ['kɔːʃəs] adj circonspect, prudent.

cautiously ['kɔːʃəslɪ] adv avec prudence, prudemment.

cautiousness ['kɔːʃəsnɪs] n prudence f, circonspection f.

cavalier [ˌkævə'lɪər] **❖** n [gen & MIL] cavalier m. **❖** adj cavalier, désinvolte. **❖ Cavalier** 🇬🇧 n HIST Cavalier m (partisan de Charles Iᵉʳ d'Angleterre pendant la guerre civile anglaise, de 1642 à 1646).

cavalry ['kævlrɪ] n cavalerie f.

cave¹ [keɪv] **❖** n caverne f, grotte f. **❖** vi ▶ **to go caving** faire de la spéléologie. **❖ cave in** vi **1.** [ceiling, floor] s'écrouler, s'effondrer, s'affaisser ; [wall] s'écrouler, s'effondrer, céder **2.** inf [person] flancher, céder.

⚠ The French word **cave** means a cellar, not a cave.

cave² [keɪv or 'keɪvɪ] 🇬🇧 dated & school sl n ▶ **to keep cave** faire le guet.

caveat ['kævɪæt] n avertissement m ; LAW notification f d'opposition.

cave drawing n = **cave painting**.

cave-dwelling adj cavernicole.

caveman ['keɪvmæn] (pl **cavemen** [-men]) n lit homme m des cavernes ; fig brute f.

cave painting [keɪv-] n peinture f rupestre.

caver ['keɪvər] n spéléologue mf.

cavern ['kævən] n caverne f.

cavernous ['kævənəs] adj fig : a cavernous building un bâtiment très vaste à l'intérieur.

caviar(e) ['kævɪɑːr] n caviar m.

caving ['keɪvɪŋ] n spéléologie f.

cavity ['kævətɪ] (pl **cavities**) n 1. [in rock, wood] cavité f, creux m 2. ANAT cavité f ; [in tooth] cavité f.

cavity wall ◆ n mur m creux or à double paroi. ◆ comp ▶ **cavity wall insulation** isolation f en murs creux.

cavort [kə'vɔːt] vi 1. lit cabrioler, gambader, faire des cabrioles 2. fig : while his wife was off cavorting around Europe pendant que sa femme menait une vie de bâton de chaise en Europe.

cayenne pepper n poivre m de Cayenne.

CB n (abbr of **Citizens' Band**) CB f.

CBC (abbr of **Canadian Broadcasting Corporation**) pr n office national canadien de radiodiffusion.

CBE (abbr of **Commander of (the Order of) the British Empire**) n distinction honorifique britannique.

CBI (abbr of **Confederation of British Industry**) pr n association du patronat britannique ; ≃ MEDEF f.

CBS (abbr of **Columbia Broadcasting System**) pr n chaîne de télévision américaine.

cc n (abbr of **cubic centimetre**) &cm3 ;.

CC written abbr of county council.

CCS n abbr of carbon capture and storage.

CCTV n abbr of closed-circuit television.

CD n (abbr of **compact disc**) CD m.

CD burner n COMPUT graveur m (de CD).

CDI (abbr of **compact disc interactive**) n CDI m.

CDM (abbr of **Clean Development Mechanism**) pr n MDP m.

CD player n lecteur m de CD.

CD-R [,siːdiː'ɑːr] (abbr of **compact disc recordable**) n CD-R m ▶ **CD-R drive** lecteur-graveur m de CD.

Cdr. written abbr of commander.

CD-ROM [,siːdiː'rɒm] (abbr of **compact disc read only memory**) n CD-ROM m, CD-Rom m, cédérom m ▶ **CD-ROM drive** lecteur m de CD-ROM or de disque optique.

CD-RW [,siːdiːɑː'dʌbljuː] (abbr of **compact disc rewriteable**) n CD-RW m.

CDT n abbr of Central Daylight Time.

CD tower n colonne f (de rangement) pour CD.

CDV (abbr of **compact disc video**) n CDV m, CD vidéo m.

CDW n abbr of collision damage waiver.

CD writer n graveur m de CD.

CE n abbr of Church of England.

cease [siːs] ◆ vi fml [activity, noise] cesser, s'arrêter. ◆ vt [activity, efforts, work] cesser, arrêter ▶ **to cease to do** or **to cease doing sthg** cesser de or arrêter de faire qqch. ◆ n ▶ **without cease** fml sans cesse.

ceasefire [,siːs'faɪər] n cessez-le-feu m inv / to agree to a ceasefire accepter un cessez-le-feu.

ceaseless ['siːslɪs] adj incessant, continuel.

ceaselessly ['siːslɪslɪ] adv sans cesse, continuellement.

cedar ['siːdər] n cèdre m.

cede [siːd] vt céder.

cedilla [sɪ'dɪlə] n cédille f.

CEEB (abbr of **College Entry Examination Board**) pr n commission d'admission dans l'enseignement supérieur aux États-Unis.

Ceefax® ['siːfæks] pr n service de télétexte de la BBC.

ceilidh ['keɪlɪ] n soirée de danse et de musique folklorique (en Irlande et en Écosse).

ceiling ['siːlɪŋ] n 1. [of room] plafond m 2. COMM & ECON plafond m / the government has set a 3% ceiling on wage rises le gouvernement a limité à 3 % les augmentations de salaire.

celeb ['sɪleb] n inf célébrité f, star f.

celebrate ['selɪbreɪt] ◆ vt 1. [birthday, Christmas] fêter, célébrer ; [event, victory] célébrer / to celebrate the memory of sthg commémorer qqch 2. RELIG ▶ **to celebrate mass** célébrer la messe. ◆ vi : let's celebrate! a) [gen] il faut fêter ça ! b) [with drinks] il faut arroser ça !

celebrated ['selɪbreɪtɪd] adj célèbre.

celebration [,selɪ'breɪʃn] n 1. [of birthday, Christmas] célébration f ; [of anniversary, past event] commémoration f / in celebration of Christmas pour fêter or célébrer Noël 2. (often pl) [occasion - of birthday, Christmas] fête f, fêtes fpl ; [- of historical event] cérémonies fpl, fête f / this calls for a celebration! il faut fêter ça !, il faut arroser ça !

celebratory [,selə'breɪtərɪ] adj [dinner] de fête ; [marking official occasion] commémoratif ; [atmosphere, mood] de fête, festif / to have a celebratory drink prendre un verre pour fêter l'évènement.

celebrity [sɪ'lebrətɪ] (pl **celebrities**) n [person] vedette f, célébrité f.

celebutante [sɪ'lebjuːtɑ̃nt] n inf jeune célébrité f.

celeriac [sɪ'lerɪæk] n céleri-rave m.

celery ['selərɪ] n céleri (en branches) m.

celestial [sɪ'lestjəl] adj lit & fig céleste.

celibacy ['selɪbəsɪ] n célibat m.

celibate ['selɪbət] adj chaste ; [unmarried] célibataire.

cell [sel] n 1. BIOL & BOT cellule f 2. [in prison, convent] cellule f 3. inf [mobile phone] mobile m.

cellar ['selər] n [for wine] cave f, cellier m ; [for coal, bric-à-brac] cave f ; [for food] cellier m.

cellarman ['seləmən] (pl **cellarmen** [-mən]) n sommelier m.

cellist ['tʃelɪst] n violoncelliste mf.

cello ['tʃeləu] n violoncelle m.

Cellophane® ['seləfeɪn] n Cellophane® f.

cellophane noodles ['seləfeɪn-] pl n CULIN vermicelles mpl chinois.

cellphone ['selfəun] n (téléphone m) portable m, (téléphone m) mobile m.

cellular (tele)phone n téléphone m cellulaire.

cellulite ['seljulaɪt] n cellulite f.

cellulitis [,selju'laɪtɪs] n cellulite f.

Celluloid® ['seljulɔɪd] n Celluloïd® m.

cellulose ['seljuləus] n cellulose f.

Celsius ['selsɪəs] adj Celsius / 25 degrees Celsius 25 degrés Celsius.

Celt [kelt] n Celte mf.

Celtic ['keltɪk] adj celtique, celte.

cement [sɪ'ment] ◆ n CONSTR & fig ciment m. ◆ vt CONSTR & fig cimenter.

cement mixer n bétonnière f.

cemetery ['semɪtrɪ] (pl **cemeteries**) n cimetière m.

cenotaph ['senətɑːf] n cénotaphe m.

censor ['sensər] ◆ n CIN & THEAT censeur m. ◆ vt censurer.

censorship ['sensəʃɪp] n [act, practice] censure f.

censure ['senʃər] vt blâmer, critiquer.

census ['sensəs] n recensement m ▶ **to conduct** or **to take a population census** faire le recensement de la population, recenser la population.

cent [sent] n [coin] cent *m* / *I haven't got a cent* je n'ai pas un sou ▸ **to put one's two cents in** US mettre son grain de sel.

centaur ['sentɔːr] n centaure *m*.

centenarian [ˌsentɪ'neərɪən] ◆ n centenaire *mf*. ◆ adj centenaire.

centenary [sen'tiːnərɪ] (*pl* **centenaries**) UK ◆ n [anniversary] centenaire *m*, centième anniversaire *m*. ◆ comp centenaire ▸ **centenary celebrations** fêtes *fpl* du centenaire.

centennial [sen'tenjəl] US ◆ n centenaire *m*, centième anniversaire *m*. ◆ adj [in age] centenaire, séculaire.

center US = **centre**.

centered ['sentəd] adj US : *he's not very centered* il est un peu paumé.

center strip n US terre-plein *m* central.

centigrade ['sentɪɡreɪd] adj centigrade / *25 degrees centigrade* 25 degrés centigrades.

centigram(me) ['sentɪɡræm] n centigramme *m*.

centilitre UK, **centiliter** US ['sentɪˌliːtər] n centilitre *m*.

centimetre UK, **centimeter** US ['sentɪˌmiːtər] n centimètre *m*.

centipede ['sentɪpiːd] n mille-pattes *m inv*.

central ['sentrəl] adj central / *this concept is central to his theory* ce concept est au centre de sa théorie.

Central African adj centrafricain.

Central African Republic pr n ▸ **the Central African Republic** la République centrafricaine.

Central America pr n Amérique *f* centrale.

Central American adj centraméricain.

Central Asia pr n Asie *f* centrale.

Central Europe pr n Europe *f* centrale.

Central European adj d'Europe centrale.

central government n gouvernement *m* central.

central heating n chauffage *m* central.

centralism ['sentrəlɪzm] n centralisme *m*.

centralization, centralisation [ˌsentrəlaɪ'zeɪʃn] n centralisation *f*.

centralize, centralise ['sentrəlaɪz] vt centraliser.

centralized, centralised ['sentrəlaɪzd] adj centralisé.

central locking n AUTO verrouillage *m* central.

centrally ['sentrəlɪ] adv [located] au centre ; [organized] de façon centralisée ▸ **centrally heated** ayant le chauffage central.

central nervous system n système *m* nerveux central.

central processing unit n COMPUT unité *f* centrale.

central purchasing department n [in company] centrale *f* d'achat(s).

central reservation n UK AUTO [with grass] terre-plein *m* central ; [with barrier] bande *f* médiane.

centre UK, **center** US ['sentər] ◆ n **1.** [gen & GEOM] centre *m* / *in the centre* au centre **2.** [of town] centre *m* **3.** fig [of unrest] foyer *m* ; [of debate] cœur *m*, centre *m* / *the centre of attention* le centre d'attention **4.** [place, building] centre *m* **5.** POL centre *m* ▸ **to be left / right of centre** être du centre gauche / droit. ◆ comp **1.** [central] central **2.** POL du centre. ◆ vt **1.** [place in centre] centrer **2.** fig [attention] concentrer, fixer / *to centre one's hopes on sthg* mettre or fonder tous ses espoirs sur qqch **3.** SPORT ▸ **to centre the ball** centrer. ◆ **centre around** vt insep **centre on** vt insep **centre round** vt insep = **centre around**.

centre-back n arrière *m* central.

centrefold UK, **centerfold** US ['sentəˌfəʊld] n grande photo *f* de pin-up *(au milieu d'un magazine)*.

centre-forward n avant-centre *m*.

centre-half n demi-centre *m*.

centreline UK, **centerline** US ['sentəlaɪn] n axe *m*, ligne *f* médiane.

centrepiece UK, **centerpiece** US ['sentəpiːs] n [outstanding feature] joyau *m* ; [on table] milieu *m* de table ; [of meal] pièce *f* de résistance.

centre-spread n = **centrefold**.

centrifugal [sentrɪ'fjuːɡl] adj centrifuge ▸ **centrifugal force** force *f* centrifuge.

centrist ['sentrɪst] n centriste *mf*.

century ['sentʃʊrɪ] (*pl* **centuries**) n [time] siècle *m* / *in the 20th century* au XXᵉ siècle.

CEO n abbr of chief executive officer.

ceramic [sɪ'ræmɪk] ◆ adj [art] céramique ; [vase] en céramique ▸ **ceramic hob** UK plaque *f* vitrocéramique. ◆ n = **ceramics**.

ceramics [sɪ'ræmɪks] n (U) céramique *f*.

cereal ['sɪərɪəl] n **1.** AGR [plant] céréale *f* ; [grain] grain *m* (de céréale) **2.** CULIN ▸ **(breakfast) cereal** céréales *fpl*.

cereal bowl n assiette *f* creuse, bol *m* à céréales.

cerebral ['serɪbrəl] adj cérébral.

cerebral palsy n paralysie *f* cérébrale.

ceremonial [ˌserɪ'məʊnjəl] adj [rite, visit] cérémoniel ; [robes] de cérémonie.

ceremonious [ˌserɪ'məʊnjəs] adj solennel ; [mock-solemn] cérémonieux.

ceremoniously [ˌserɪ'məʊnjəslɪ] adv solennellement, avec cérémonie ; [mock-solemnly] cérémonieusement.

ceremony [UK 'serɪmənɪ US 'serəməʊnɪ] (*pl* ceremonies) n (U) [formality] cérémonie *f*, cérémonies *fpl* / *we don't stand on ceremony* nous ne faisons pas de cérémonies.

cert [sɜːt] n UK inf certitude *f* / *it's a dead cert that he'll win* il va gagner, ça ne fait pas un pli or c'est couru d'avance.

cert. written abbr of certificate.

certain ['sɜːtn] ◆ adj **1.** [sure] certain, sûr ▸ **to be certain of sthg** être sûr de qqch / *he was certain (that) she was there* il était certain qu'elle était là ▸ **to make certain of sthg a)** [check] vérifier qqch, s'assurer de qqch **b)** [be sure to have] s'assurer qqch **2.** [inevitable - death, failure] certain, inévitable / *the soldiers faced certain death* les soldats allaient à une mort certaine **3.** [definite, infallible - cure] sûr, infaillible. ◆ det **1.** [particular but unspecified] certain / *he has a certain something about him* il a un certain je ne sais quoi **2.** [not known personally] certain / *a certain Mr Roberts* un certain M. Roberts **3.** [some] certain / *to a certain extent* or *degree* dans une certaine mesure. ◆ **for certain** adv phr : *I don't know for certain* je n'en suis pas certain / *I can't say for certain* je ne peux pas l'affirmer / *that's for certain!* c'est sûr et certain !, cela ne fait pas de doute !

Note that when used negatively, être certain que is followed by a verb in the subjunctive.
I'm certain it contains alcohol. Je suis certain que ça contient *(indicative)* de l'alcool.
It's by no means certain that each galaxy contains a black hole. Il n'est pas du tout certain que chaque galaxie contienne un trou noir.

certainly ['sɜːtnlɪ] adv **1.** [without doubt] certainement, assurément / *it will certainly be ready tomorrow* cela sera prêt demain sans faute **2.** [of course] certainement, bien sûr / *can you help me? — certainly!* pouvez-vous m'aider ? — bien sûr or volontiers ! / *certainly not!* bien sûr que non !, certainement pas !

certainty ['sɜːtntɪ] (*pl* **certainties**) n **1.** [conviction] certitude f, conviction f **2.** [fact] certitude f, fait m certain ; [event] certitude f, événement m certain / *their victory is now a certainty* leur victoire est maintenant assurée or ne fait aucun doute.

CertEd [ˌsɜːt'ed] (*abbr of* **Certificate in Education**) n *diplôme universitaire britannique en sciences de l'éducation.*

certifiable [ˌsɜːtɪ'faɪəbl] adj **1.** [gen & LAW] qu'on peut certifier **2.** [insane] bon à enfermer (à l'asile).

certificate [sə'tɪfɪkət] n **1.** [gen & ADMIN] certificat m ▸ **certificate of origin** COMM certificat d'origine **2.** [academic] diplôme m ; [vocational - of apprenticeship] brevet m.

certificate of citizenship n 🇺🇸 certificat m de nationalité.

certificate of deposit n FIN certificat m de dépôt.

certification [ˌsɜːtɪfɪ'keɪʃn] n [act] certification f, authentification f.

certified ['sɜːtɪfaɪd] adj 🇺🇸 SCH ▸ **certified teacher a)** [in state school] professeur m diplômé **b)** [in private school] professeur m habilité.

certified check n 🇺🇸 chèque m de banque.

certified mail n 🇺🇸 envoi m recommandé ▸ **to send sthg by certified mail** envoyer qqch en recommandé avec accusé de réception.

certified public accountant n 🇺🇸 ≃ expert-comptable m.

certify ['sɜːtɪfaɪ] (*pt & pp* **certified**) vt **1.** [gen & ADMIN] certifier, attester ; MED [death] constater **2.** COMM [goods] garantir.

cervical [🇬🇧 sə'vaɪkl 🇺🇸 'sɜːrvɪkl] adj cervical.

cervical smear n frottis m vaginal.

cervix ['sɜːvɪks] (*pl* **cervixes** or **cervices** [-si:z]) n col m de l'utérus.

cessation [se'seɪʃn] n *fml* cessation f, suspension f.

cesspit ['sespɪt] n fosse f d'aisances ; *fig* cloaque m.

cesspool ['sespuːl] n = **cesspit**.

CET n *abbr of* **Central European Time**.

cf. (*written abbr of* **confer**) cf.

c/f *written abbr of* **carried forward**.

CFC (*abbr of* **chlorofluorocarbon**) n CFC m.

CFO ['siːefˈəʊ] (*abbr of* **Chief Financial Officer**) n 🇺🇸 contrôleur m, -euse f de gestion.

cg (*written abbr of* **centigram**) cg.

CG n *abbr of* **coastguard**.

CGA (*abbr of* **colour graphics adapter**) n adaptateur m graphique couleur CGA.

CGI n (*abbr of* **computer-generated images**) COMPUT images fpl créées par ordinateur.

CGT n *abbr of* **capital gains tax**.

ch (*written abbr of* **central heating**) ch. cent.

ch. (*written abbr of* **chapter**) chap.

CH n *abbr of* **Companion of Honour**.

chad [tʃæd] n 🇺🇸 [residue from punched paper] confettis mpl.

Chad [tʃæd] pr n Tchad m.

chafe [tʃeɪf] ◆ vt **1.** [rub] frictionner, frotter **2.** [irritate] frotter contre, irriter. ◆ vi [skin] s'irriter ; *fig* [person] s'irriter, s'impatienter ▸ **to chafe at** or **under sthg** s'irriter de qqch.

chaff [tʃɑːf] n [of grain] balle f ; [hay, straw] menue paille f.

chaffinch ['tʃæfɪntʃ] n pinson m.

chafing dish ['tʃeɪfɪŋ-] n chauffe-plat m.

chagrin ['ʃægrɪn] n *liter* (vif) dépit m, (vive) déception f or contrariété f / *much to my chagrin* à mon grand dépit.

chai [tʃaɪ] n thé indien parfumé aux épices ▸ **chai latte** « chai » au lait.

chain [tʃeɪn] ◆ n **1.** [gen] chaîne f **2.** [of mountains] chaîne f ; [of islands] chapelet m **3.** [of events] série f, suite f ; [of ideas] suite f **4.** COMM [of shops] chaîne f. ◆ vt *lit & fig* enchaîner ; [door] mettre la chaîne à / *the dog was chained to the post* le chien était attaché au poteau (par une chaîne). ❖ **chains** pl n [for prisoner] chaînes fpl, entraves fpl / *a prisoner in chains* un prisonnier enchaîné.

Property chains

Dans le domaine de la vente immobilière en Grande-Bretagne, le mot **chain** fait référence à une situation d'interdépendance où chaque acheteur de la « chaîne » attend de vendre pour pouvoir conclure son achat, tandis que chaque vendeur attend d'acheter un nouveau logement avant de conclure sa vente. Toutes les transactions doivent être conclues le même jour pour que les différents acheteurs et vendeurs puissent déménager, et il suffit qu'une personne retire son offre de vente ou d'achat pour que toutes les transactions échouent (on parle de **broken chain** dans ce cas). Les **chains** sont une source d'anxiété pour toutes les personnes concernées, et la mention **no chain** dans une annonce immobilière est destinée à rassurer les acheteurs potentiels en signalant que la vente ne dépendra pas de l'issue d'autres transactions.

chain guard n cache-chaîne m.

chain letter n lettre f faisant partie d'une chaîne.

chain mail n (U) cotte f de mailles.

chain of custody n chaîne f de détention.

chain reaction n réaction f en chaîne / *to set off a chain reaction* provoquer une réaction en chaîne.

chain saw n tronçonneuse f.

chain-smoke vi fumer cigarette sur cigarette.

chain smoker n fumeur invétéré m, fumeuse invétérée f, gros fumeur m, grosse fumeuse f.

chain store n magasin m à succursales multiples.

chair [tʃeər] ◆ n **1.** [seat] chaise f ; [armchair] fauteuil m / *please take a chair* asseyez-vous, je vous prie **2.** [chairperson] président m, -e f ▸ **to be in the chair** présider. ◆ vt ADMIN [meeting] présider.

chairlift ['tʃeəlɪft] n télésiège m.

chairman ['tʃeəmən] (*pl* **chairmen** [-mən]) n **1.** [at meeting] président m (*d'un comité*) **2.** COMM président-directeur m général, P-DG m.

chairmanship ['tʃeəmənʃɪp] n présidence f (*d'un comité, etc.*).

chairperson [ˈʧeə.pɜːsn] n président *m*, -e *f (d'un comité)*.

chairwoman [ˈʧeə.wʊmən] *(pl* **chairwomen** [-.wɪmɪn]*)* n présidente *f (d'un comité)*.

chaise longue [-ˈlɒŋ] *(pl* **chaises longues***)* n méridienne *f*.

⚠ **Une chaise longue** is a deckchair, not a chaise longue.

chaise lounge *(pl* **chaise lounges***)* n US méridienne *f*.

chalet [ˈʃæleɪ] n chalet *m*.

chalice [ˈʧælɪs] n RELIG calice *m*.

chalk [ʧɔːk] n **1.** [substance] craie *f* / *a piece of chalk* un morceau de craie ▶ **to be as different as chalk and cheese** UK: *they're as different as chalk and cheese* c'est le jour et la nuit **2.** [piece] craie *f* **3.** PHR *by a long chalk* UK de beaucoup, de loin. ✧ **chalk up** vt sep **1.** [credit] ▶ **to chalk sthg up to experience** *fig* mettre qqch au compte de l'expérience **2.** [attain -victory] remporter ; [-profits] encaisser.

chalkboard [ˈʧɔːkbɔːd] n US tableau *m* (noir).

challenge [ˈʧælɪnʤ] ◆ vt **1.** [gen - defy] défier ▶ **to challenge sb to do sthg** défier qqn de faire qqch / *to challenge sb to a game of tennis* inviter qqn à faire une partie de tennis / *to challenge sb to a duel* provoquer qqn en duel **2.** [demand effort from] mettre à l'épreuve **3.** [contest - authority, findings] contester, mettre en cause ▶ **to challenge sb's right to do sthg** contester à qqn le droit de faire qqch **4.** LAW [juror] récuser. ◆ n **1.** [in contest] défi *m* ▶ **to issue a challenge** lancer un défi ▶ **to take up the challenge** relever le défi / *Jackson's challenge for the leadership of the party* la tentative de Jackson pour s'emparer de la direction du parti **2.** [in job, activity] défi *m* **3.** [to right, authority] mise *f* en question, contestation *f*.

challenger [ˈʧælɪnʤər] n [gen] provocateur *m*, -trice *f* ; POL & SPORT challenger *m*.

challenging [ˈʧælɪnʤɪŋ] adj **1.** [defiant] de défi **2.** [demanding -ideas, theory] provocateur, stimulant, exaltant ; [-job, activity] stimulant, qui met à l'épreuve.

chamber [ˈʧeɪmbər] n **1.** [hall, room] chambre *f* ▶ **the upper / lower Chamber** UK POL la Chambre haute / basse **2.** *arch* [lodgings] logement *m*, appartement *m*. ✧ **chambers** pl n [of barrister, judge] cabinet *m* ; [of solicitor] cabinet *m*, étude *f*.

chambermaid [ˈʧeɪmbəmeɪd] n femme *f* de chambre.

chamber music n musique *f* de chambre.

chamber of commerce n chambre *f* de commerce.

chamber orchestra n orchestre *m* de chambre.

chameleon [kəˈmiːljən] n ZOOL & *fig* caméléon *m*.

chamois [ˈʃæmwɑː] *(pl* **chamois***)* n ZOOL chamois *m* ; [hide] peau *f* de chamois ▶ **(a) chamois leather** (une) peau de chamois.

champ [ʧæmp] ◆ vt mâchonner. ◆ vi PHR **to champ at the bit** : *we were all champing at the bit to get started* on rongeait tous notre frein en attendant de commencer.

champagne [.ʃæmˈpeɪn] n [wine] champagne *m* / *a champagne glass* une coupe à champagne.

Champagne [.ʃæmˈpeɪn] pr n Champagne *f*.

champion [ˈʧæmpjən] ◆ n [winner] champion *m*, -onne *f* / *the world chess champion* le champion du monde d'échecs. ◆ vt défendre, soutenir. ◆ adj UK [very good] super.

championship [ˈʧæmpjənʃɪp] n GAMES & SPORT championnat *m*.

chance [ʧɑːns] ◆ n **1.** [possibility, likelihood] : *there was little chance of him finding work* il y avait peu de chances qu'il trouve du travail / *she's got a good* or *strong chance of being accepted* elle a de fortes chances d'être acceptée or reçue ▶ **to be in with a chance** : *he's in with a chance of getting the job* il a une chance d'obtenir le poste **2.** [fortune, luck] hasard *m* / *to leave things to chance* laisser faire les choses / *to leave nothing to chance* ne rien laisser au hasard **3.** [opportunity] : *give her a chance to defend herself* donnez-lui l'occasion de se défendre / *I'm offering you the chance of a lifetime* je vous offre la chance de votre vie / *this is your last chance* c'est votre dernière chance **4.** [risk] risque *m* / *I don't want to take the chance of losing* je ne veux pas prendre le risque de perdre / *he took a chance on a racehorse* il a parié sur un cheval de course. ◆ adj de hasard / *I was a chance witness to the robbery* j'ai été un témoin accidentel du vol. ◆ vt *liter* [risk] hasarder / *he chanced his savings on the venture* il a risqué ses économies dans l'entreprise / *let's chance it* or *our luck* tentons notre chance ▶ **to chance one's arm** risquer le coup. ✧ **chances** pl n [possibility, likelihood] chances *fpl* / *(the) chances are (that) he'll never find out* il y a de fortes or grandes chances qu'il l'apprenne jamais. ✧ **by chance** adv phr par hasard. ✧ **chance on, chance upon** vt insep [person] rencontrer par hasard ; [thing] trouver par hasard.

⚠ Note that **chance** is not always translated by the French word **chance**. See the entry for details.

chancellor [ˈʧɑːnsələr] n **1.** POL chancelier *m* ▶ **the Chancellor of the Exchequer** POL le chancelier de l'Échiquier ; ≃ le ministre des Finances *(en Grande-Bretagne)* **2.** UK UNIV président *m*, -e *f* honoraire ; US président *m*, -e *f* (d'université).

chancy [ˈʧɑːnsɪ] *(compar* **chancier**, *superl* **chanciest***)* adj *inf* risqué.

chandelier [.ʃændəˈlɪər] n lustre *m* (pour éclairer).

change [ʧeɪnʤ] ◆ n **1.** [alteration] changement *m* / *we expect a change in the weather* nous nous attendons à un changement de temps / *a survey showed a radical change in public opinion* un sondage a montré un revirement de l'opinion publique / *a change for the better / worse* un changement en mieux / pire, une amélioration / dégradation / *that makes a change!* voilà qui change ! ▶ **to have a change of heart** changer d'avis **2.** [fresh set or supply] : *a change of clothes* des vêtements de rechange **3.** [money] monnaie *f* / *can you give me change for five pounds?* pouvez-vous me faire la monnaie de cinq livres ? / *I don't have any loose* or *small change* je n'ai pas de petite monnaie. ◆ vt **1.** [substitute, switch] changer, changer de / *to change one's name* changer de nom / *to change one's clothes* changer de vêtements, se changer / *to change trains* changer de train / *to change ends* SPORT changer de camp ▶ **to change one's mind** changer d'avis **2.** [exchange] changer / *if the shoes are too small we'll change them for you* si les chaussures sont trop petites nous vous les changerons ▶ **to change places with sb** changer de place avec qqn / *I wouldn't want to change places with him! fig* je n'aimerais pas être à sa place ! / *I'd like to change my pounds into dollars* FIN j'aimerais changer mes livres contre des or en dollars / *can you change a ten-pound note?* [into coins] pouvez-vous me donner la monnaie d'un billet de dix livres ? **3.** [alter, modify] changer / *he won't change anything in the text* il ne changera rien au texte /

the illness completely changed his personality la maladie a complètement transformé son caractère **4.** [transform] changer, transformer ▸ **to change sthg / sb into sthg** changer qqch / qqn en qqch **5.** [baby, bed] changer. ◆ *vi* **1.** [alter, turn] changer / *to change for the better / worse* changer en mieux / pire / *nothing will make him change* rien ne le changera, il ne changera jamais **2.** [change clothing] se changer / *he changed into a pair of jeans* il s'est changé et a mis un jean **3.** [transportation] changer ▸ **all change!** [announcement] tout le monde descend ! ❖ **change down** *vi* AUTO rétrograder. ❖ **change over** *vi* **1.** UK [switch] : *the country has changed over to nuclear power* le pays est passé au nucléaire **2.** SPORT [change positions] changer de côté. ❖ **change up** *vi* AUTO passer la vitesse supérieure.

changeable ['tʃeɪndʒəbl] *adj* **1.** [variable] variable **2.** [capricious, fickle] changeant, inconstant.

changed [tʃeɪndʒd] *adj* changé, différent / *he's a changed man* c'est un autre homme.

change machine *n* distributeur *m* de monnaie.

change of life *n* ▸ **the change of life** le retour d'âge.

changeover ['tʃeɪndʒ,əʊvər] *n* [switch] changement *m*, passage *m*.

change purse *n* US porte-monnaie *m inv*.

changing ['tʃeɪndʒɪŋ] ◆ *adj* qui change / *we're living in a changing world* nous vivons dans un monde en évolution. ◆ *n* changement *m* ▸ **the Changing of the Guard** la relève de la garde.

changing room *n* UK SPORT vestiaire *m* ; [in shop] cabine *f* d'essayage.

changing table *n* table *f* à langer.

channel ['tʃænl] (UK *pt & pp* **channelled**, *cont* **channelling** ; US *pt & pp* **channeled**, *cont* **channeling**) ◆ *n* **1.** [broad strait] détroit *m*, bras *m* de mer ▸ **the Channel** la Manche ▸ **a Channel** or **cross-Channel ferry** un ferry qui traverse la Manche **2.** [river bed] lit *m* ; NAUT [navigable course] chenal *m*, passe *f* **3.** [passage - for gases, liquids] canal *m*, conduite *f* ; [- for electrical signals] piste *f* **4.** [furrow, groove] sillon *m* ; [on a column] cannelure *f* ; [in a street] caniveau *m* **5.** TV chaîne *f* **6.** *fig* [means] canal *m*, voie *f* / *to go through (the) official channels* suivre la filière officielle. ◆ *vt fig* [direct] canaliser, diriger.

channel-flick, channel-hop *vt* & *vi* TV zapper.

channel-hopper *n* zappeur *m*, -euse *f*.

Channel Islands *pl pr n* ▸ **the Channel Islands** les îles *fpl* Anglo-Normandes.

channel of distribution *n* circuit *m* or canal *m* de distribution.

Channel Tunnel *n* ▸ **the Channel Tunnel** le tunnel sous la Manche.

chant [tʃɑːnt] ◆ *n* **1.** MUS mélopée *f* ; RELIG psalmodie *f* **2.** [slogan, cry] chant *m* scandé. ◆ *vi* **1.** MUS chanter une mélopée ; RELIG psalmodier **2.** [crowd, demonstrators] scander des slogans. ◆ *vt* **1.** MUS chanter ; RELIG psalmodier **2.** [slogans] scander.

chanting ['tʃɑːntɪŋ] ◆ *adj* [voice] monotone, traînant. ◆ *n* MUS mélopée *f* ; RELIG chants *mpl*, psalmodie *f*.

chaos ['keɪɒs] *n* chaos *m*.

chaotic [keɪ'ɒtɪk] *adj* chaotique.

chap [tʃæp] (*pt & pp* **chapped**, *cont* **chapping**) ◆ *n* UK *inf* [man] type *m*. ◆ *vt* gercer, crevasser.

chapat(t)i [tʃə'pætɪ] *n* galette *f* de pain indienne.

chapel ['tʃæpl] *n* [in church, school, etc.] chapelle *f*.

chaperon(e) ['ʃæpərəʊn] ◆ *n* chaperon *m*. ◆ *vt* chaperonner.

chaplain ['tʃæplɪn] *n* aumônier *m* ; [in private chapel] chapelain *m*.

chapped [tʃæpt] *adj* [hands, lips] gercé.

chapter ['tʃæptər] *n* [of book] chapitre *m* / *it's in chapter three* c'est dans le troisième chapitre ▸ **to give** or **quote chapter and verse** : *she can give (you) chapter and verse on the subject* elle peut citer toutes les autorités en la matière.

char [tʃɑːr] (*pt & pp* **charred**, *cont* **charring**) ◆ *vt* **1.** [reduce to charcoal] carboniser, réduire en charbon **2.** [scorch] griller, brûler légèrement. ◆ *vi* [scorch] brûler ; [blacken] noircir.

character ['kærəktər] *n* **1.** [nature, temperament] caractère *m* / *his remark was quite in / out of character* cette remarque lui ressemblait tout à fait / ne lui ressemblait pas du tout **2.** [aspect, quality] caractère *m* **3.** [determination, integrity] caractère *m* **4.** [distinction, originality] caractère *m* / *the house had (great) character* la maison avait beaucoup de caractère **5.** [unusual person] personnage *m* / *he's quite a character!* c'est un phénomène or un sacré numéro ! **6.** *pej* [person] individu *m* **7.** CIN, LITER & THEAT personnage *m* **8.** TYPO caractère *m*.

⚠ Note that **character** is not always translated by **caractère**. See the entry for details.

character actor *n* acteur *m* de genre.

character assassination *n* diffamation *f*.

character-building UK, **character-forming** *adj* qui forme le caractère / *it's character-forming* ça forme le caractère.

characterful ['kærəktəfʊl] *adj* plein de caractère.

characteristic [,kærəktə'rɪstɪk] ◆ *adj* caractéristique / *she refused all honours with characteristic humility* elle refusa tous les honneurs avec l'humilité qui la caractérisait. ◆ *n* caractéristique *f*.

characteristically [,kærəktə'rɪstɪklɪ] *adv* : *he was characteristically generous with his praise* comme on pouvait s'y attendre, il fut prodigue de ses compliments or il ne ménagea pas ses éloges.

characterization [,kærəktəraɪ'zeɪʃn] *n* **1.** *fml* [description] caractérisation *f* **2.** LITER & THEAT représentation *f* or peinture *f* des personnages.

characterize, characterise ['kærəktəraɪz] *vt* caractériser / *his music is characterized by a sense of joy* sa musique se caractérise par une impression de joie / *Shakespeare characterized Henry VI as a weak but pious king* Shakespeare a dépeint Henri VI comme un roi faible mais pieux.

characterless ['kærəktəlɪs] *adj* sans caractère.

character sketch *n* portrait *m* or description *f* rapide.

character witness *n* témoin *m* de moralité.

charade [ʃə'rɑːd] *n* [pretence] feinte *f*. ❖ **charades** *pl n* GAMES charade *f* en action.

char-broil *vt* US CULIN griller au charbon de bois.

char-broiled *adj* US grillé au feu de bois.

charcoal ['tʃɑːkəʊl] ◆ *n* [fuel] charbon *m* de bois. ◆ *comp* **1.** [fuel] à charbon **2.** ART au charbon, au fusain.

chard [tʃɑːd] *n* blette *f*, bette *f*.

charge [tʃɑːdʒ] ◆ *n* **1.** [fee, cost] frais *mpl* / *there's a charge of one pound for use of the locker* il faut payer une livre pour utiliser la consigne automatique / *what's the charge for delivery?* la livraison coûte combien ? / *there's no charge for children* c'est gratuit pour les enfants ▸ **free of charge** gratuitement **2.** LAW [accusation] chef *m* d'accusation, inculpation *f* / *he was arrested on a charge* *of conspiracy* il a été arrêté sous l'inculpation d'association criminelle **/** *you are under arrest — on what charge?* vous êtes en état d'arrestation — pour quel motif ? **/** *he pleaded guilty to the charge of robbery* il a plaidé coupable à l'accusation de vol **3.** [allegation] accusation *f* **/** *the government rejected charges that it was mismanaging the economy* le gouvernement a rejeté l'accusation selon laquelle il gérait mal l'économie **4.** [command, control] : *who's in charge here?* qui est-ce qui commande ici ? **/** *she's in charge of public relations* elle s'occupe des relations publiques **/** *I was put in charge of the investigation* on m'a confié la responsabilité de l'enquête ▸ **to take charge of sthg** prendre en charge qqch, prendre or assumer la direction de qqch **5.** MIL [attack] charge *f* **6.** ELEC & PHYS charge *f*. ◆ vt **1.** [money] faire payer ; [demand payment from] demander, prendre **/** *the doctor charged her $90 for a visit* le médecin lui a fait payer or lui a pris 90 dollars pour une consultation **/** *how much would you charge to take us to the airport?* combien prendriez-vous pour nous emmener à l'aéroport ? **/** *they didn't charge us for the coffee* ils ne nous ont pas fait payer les cafés **2.** [defer payment of] : *I charged all my expenses to the company* j'ai mis tous mes frais sur le compte de la société **3.** [allege] ▸ **to charge that sb has done sthg** accuser qqn d'avoir fait qqch **4.** LAW inculper **/** *I'm charging you with the murder of X* je vous inculpe du meurtre de X **5.** [attack] charger **6.** *fml* [command, entrust] : *I was charged with guarding the prisoner* je fus chargé de la surveillance du prisonnier **7.** ELEC & MIL charger **8.** *fml* [fill] charger. ◆ vi **1.** [demand in payment] demander, prendre **/** *do you charge for delivery?* est-ce que vous faites payer la livraison ? **2.** [rush] se précipiter **/** *the rhino suddenly charged* tout d'un coup le rhinocéros a chargé **/** *suddenly two policemen charged into the room* tout d'un coup deux policiers ont fait irruption dans la pièce **/** *she charged into / out of her office* elle entra dans son / sortit de son bureau au pas de charge **3.** ELEC se charger or recharger.

chargeable ['tʃɑːdʒəbl] adj FIN : *the item is chargeable with duty of £10* l'article est soumis à une taxe de 10 livres **/** *travelling expenses are chargeable to the employer* les frais de déplacement sont à la charge de l'employeur ▸ **chargeable expenses** frais *mpl* facturables.

charge account n 🇺🇸 compte *m* permanent *(dans un magasin)*.

charge card n carte *f* de crédit.

charged ['tʃɑːdʒd] adj **1.** [atmosphere] chargé **/** *a voice charged with emotion* une voix pleine d'émotion **2.** ELEC chargé.

chargé d'affaires [,ʃɑːʒeɪdæˈfeər] (*pl* **chargés d'affaires**) n chargé *m* d'affaires.

charge hand n 🇬🇧 sous-chef *m* d'équipe.

charge nurse n 🇬🇧 infirmier *m*, -ère *f* en chef.

charger ['tʃɑːdʒər] n **1.** ELEC chargeur *m* **2.** *arch & liter* [horse] cheval *m* de bataille.

charge sheet n 🇬🇧 procès-verbal *m*.

charge time n [for electronic device] temps *m* de charge.

char-grill [tʃɑːˈgrɪl] vt 🇬🇧 CULIN griller au charbon de bois.

char-grilled adj 🇬🇧 grillé au feu de bois.

chariot ['tʃærɪət] n char *m*.

charisma [kəˈrɪzmə] n charisme *m*.

charismatic [,kærɪzˈmætɪk] adj charismatique.

charitable ['tʃærɪtəbl] adj **1.** [generous, kind] charitable **2.** [cause, institution] de bienfaisance, de charité.

charitably ['tʃærɪtəblɪ] adv charitablement.

charity ['tʃærətɪ] (*pl* **charities**) n **1.** RELIG charité *f* ; [generosity, kindness] charité **2.** [help to the needy] charité *f* **/** *they raised £10,000 for charity* ils ont collecté 10 000 livres pour les bonnes œuvres **3.** [organization] association *f* caritative, œuvre *f* de bienfaisance ▸ **charity shop** magasin dont les employés sont des bénévoles et dont les bénéfices servent à subventionner une œuvre d'utilité publique.

charlatan ['ʃɑːlətən] n charlatan *m*.

charm [tʃɑːm] ◆ n **1.** [appeal, attraction] charme *m* **2.** [in sorcery] charme *m*, sortilège *m* ▸ **to work like a charm** marcher à merveille or à la perfection **3.** [piece of jewellery] breloque *f*. ◆ vt [please, delight] charmer, séduire **/** *she charmed him into accepting the invitation* elle l'a si bien enjôlé qu'il a accepté l'invitation.

charmer ['tʃɑːmər] n charmeur *m*, -euse *f*.

charming ['tʃɑːmɪŋ] adj charmant **/** *charming!* iro c'est charmant !

charmingly ['tʃɑːmɪŋlɪ] adv de façon charmante.

charmless ['tʃɑːmlɪs] adj sans charme, dépourvu de charme.

charm school n école *f* de bonnes manières **/** *which charm school did you go to?* iro dis-donc, tu en as des manières !

charred [tʃɑːd] adj noirci (par le feu).

chart [tʃɑːt] ◆ n **1.** NAUT carte *f* marine ; ASTRON carte *f* (du ciel) **2.** [table] tableau *m* ; [graph] courbe *f* ; MED courbe *f*. ◆ vt **1.** NAUT [seas, waterway] établir la carte de, faire un levé hydrographique de ; ASTRON [stars] porter sur la carte **2.** [record - on a table, graph] faire la courbe de ; *fig* [progress, development] rendre compte de **3.** *fig* [make a plan of] tracer. ◆ **charts** pl n MUS hit-parade *m* **/** *she's in the charts* elle est au hit-parade.

charter ['tʃɑːtər] ◆ n [statement of rights] charte *f* ; [of a business, organization, university] statuts *mpl*. ◆ vt [hire, rent] affréter.

chartered ['tʃɑːtəd] adj **1.** [hired, rented] affrété **2.** 🇬🇧 [qualified] ▸ **a chartered accountant** un expert-comptable ▸ **a chartered surveyor** un expert immobilier.

charter flight n (vol *m*) charter *m*.

charter member n membre *m* fondateur.

charter plane n (avion *m*) charter *m*.

chart-topping adj 🇬🇧 qui est en tête de hit-parade.

chary ['tʃeərɪ] adj [cautious] précautionneux **/** *he's chary of allowing strangers into his home* il hésite à accueillir des gens qu'il ne connaît pas chez lui.

chase [tʃeɪs] ◆ vt **1.** [pursue] poursuivre **/** *two police cars chased the van* deux voitures de police ont pris la camionnette en chasse **2.** [amorously] courir (après). ◆ n [pursuit] poursuite *f* **/** *the prisoner climbed over the wall and the guards gave chase* le prisonnier escalada le mur et les gardiens se lancèrent à sa poursuite ▸ **cut to the chase!** abrège ! ◆ **chase after** vt insep courir après. ◆ **chase away**, **chase off** vt sep chasser. ◆ **chase up** vt sep 🇬🇧 **1.** [information] rechercher **2.** [organization, person] : *I had to chase him up for the £50 he owed me* j'ai dû lui réclamer les 50 livres qu'il me devait.

chaser ['tʃeɪsər] n [drink] : *they drank scotch with beer chasers* ils ont bu du scotch suivi de la bière.

chasm ['kæzm] n *lit* abîme *m*, gouffre *m* ; *fig* fossé *m*.

chassis ['ʃæsɪ] (*pl* **chassis** ['ʃæsɪ]) n **1.** AUTO châssis *m* ; AERON train *m* d'atterrissage **2.** *inf* [body] châssis *m*.

chaste [tʃeɪst] adj chaste.

chasten ['tʃeɪsn] vt *fml* **1.** [subdue, humble] corriger, maîtriser ; [pride] rabaisser **2.** [punish, reprimand] châtier, punir.

chastened ['tʃeɪsnd] adj abattu.

chastise [ʧæˈstaɪz] vt *fml* [punish, beat] châtier, punir ; [reprimand] fustiger.

chastity [ˈʧæstətɪ] n chasteté f.

chat [ʧæt] (*pt & pp* chatted, *cont* chatting) ◆ vi bavarder, causer. ◆ n [conversation] conversation f / *she came over for a chat* elle est venue bavarder un peu. ❖ **chat up** vt sep UK *inf* baratiner, draguer.

chatline [ˈʧætlaɪn] n [gen] réseau m téléphonique (*payant*) ; [for sexual encounters] téléphone m rose.

chat room, chatroom [ˈʧætruːm] n COMPUT forum m de discussion.

chat show n UK causerie f télévisée, talk-show m.

chatter [ˈʧætər] ◆ vi 1. [person] papoter, bavarder, palabrer ; [bird] jaser, jacasser ; [monkey] babiller 2. [teeth] claquer / *my teeth were chattering from* or *with the cold* j'avais tellement froid que je claquais des dents. ◆ n [of people] bavardage m, papotage m ; [of birds, monkeys] jacassement m.

chatterati [ˌʧætəraːtɪ] pl n UK *inf & pej* ▶ **the chatterati** les intellos mpl.

chatterbox [ˈʧætəbɒks] n *inf* moulin m à paroles.

chatty [ˈʧætɪ] adj [person] bavard ; [letter] plein de bavardages.

chauffeur [ˈʃəʊfər] ◆ n chauffeur m. ◆ vt conduire.

chauffeur-driven adj conduit par un chauffeur.

chauvinism [ˈʃəʊvɪnɪzm] n [nationalism] chauvinisme m ; [sexism] machisme m, phallocratie f.

chauvinist [ˈʃəʊvɪnɪst] n [nationalist] chauvin m, -e f ; [sexist] phallocrate m, machiste m.

> ⚠ The French word **chauvin** refers to nationalistic prejudice or jingoism. When talking about male chauvinism, use **phallocrate** or **machiste**.

chauvinistic [ˈʃəʊvɪˈnɪstɪk] adj [nationalistic] chauvin ; [sexist] machiste, phallocrate.

chav [ʧæv] n UK *inf & pej* racaille f, lascar m.

cheap [ʧiːp] ◆ adj 1. [inexpensive] bon marché / *labour is cheaper in the Far East* la main-d'œuvre est moins chère en Extrême-Orient 2. [poor quality] de mauvaise qualité / *the furniture was cheap and nasty* UK les meubles étaient de très mauvaise qualité 3. [of little value] : *human life is cheap in many countries* il y a beaucoup de pays où la vie humaine a peu de valeur 4. [low, despicable] : *a cheap joke* une plaisanterie de mauvais goût / *he made the girl feel cheap* il fit en sorte que la fille eût honte ▶ **a cheap shot** un coup bas / *alluding to her weight problem was a cheap shot* cette allusion à son problème de poids était un coup bas. ◆ adv [buy, get, sell] bon marché. ❖ **on the cheap** adv phr *inf* : *she furnished the house on the cheap* elle a meublé la maison pour pas cher / *they've got immigrants working for them on the cheap* ils ont des immigrés qui travaillent pour eux au rabais.

cheapen [ˈʧiːpn] vt 1. [lower, debase] abaisser 2. [reduce the price of] baisser le prix de.

cheaply [ˈʧiːplɪ] adv à bon marché.

cheapness [ˈʧiːpnɪs] n 1. [low price] bas prix m 2. [poor quality] mauvaise qualité f.

cheapo [ˈʧiːpəʊ] adj *inf* pas cher.

cheapskate [ˈʧiːpskeɪt] n *inf* radin m, -e f, grippe-sou m.

cheat [ʧiːt] ◆ vt 1. [defraud, swindle] escroquer, léser ▶ **to cheat sb out of sthg** escroquer qqch à qqn / *to feel cheated* se sentir lésé or frustré 2. *fig & liter* [deceive, trick] duper. ◆ vi tricher. ◆ n 1. [dishonest person] tri-

cheur m, -euse f ; [crook, swindler] escroc m, fraudeur m, -euse f 2. [dishonest practice] tricherie f, tromperie f. ❖ **cheat on** vt insep [be unfaithful to] tromper.

cheating [ˈʧiːtɪŋ] ◆ n 1. [at cards, games] tricherie f ; [in exams] copiage m 2. (U) [infidelity] infidélité f, infidélités fpl. ◆ adj [dishonest] malhonnête, trompeur.

cheat sheet n US *inf* antisèche f.

Chechen [ˈʧeʧen] ◆ adj tchétchène. ◆ n Tchétchène mf.

Chechenia [ˌʧeʧenˈjaː], **Chechnya** [ˌʧeʧenˈjaː] pr n Tchétchénie f.

check [ʧek] ◆ vt 1. [inspect, examine] contrôler, vérifier ; [confirm, substantiate] vérifier 2. [contain, limit] enrayer ; [emotions, troops] contenir ; [urge] réprimer ▶ **to check o.s.** se retenir 3. US [coat, hat] mettre au vestiaire ; [luggage] mettre à la consigne 4. US [mark, tick] cocher 5. [in chess] faire échec à. ◆ vi [confirm] vérifier ; [correspond] correspondre, s'accorder. ◆ n 1. [examination, inspection] contrôle m, vérification f 2. [inquiry, investigation] enquête f ▶ **to do** or **to run a check on sb** se renseigner sur qqn 3. [restraint] frein m ▶ **checks and balances** POL aux États-Unis, système d'équilibre des pouvoirs / *he kept* or *held his anger in check* il a contenu or maîtrisé sa colère 4. [in chess] échec m ▶ **in check** en échec ▶ **check!** échec au roi ! 5. US [bill] addition f ; [receipt for coats, luggage] ticket m 6. [square] carreau m 7. US = **cheque**. ◆ adj [pattern, skirt] à carreaux. ❖ **check in** ◆ vi 1. [at airport] se présenter à l'enregistrement 2. [at hotel] se présenter à la réception. ◆ vt sep [at airport] enregistrer. ❖ **check off** vt sep US cocher. ❖ **check on** vt insep 1. [facts] vérifier 2. [person] : *the doctor checked on two patients before leaving* le médecin est allé voir deux patients avant de partir. ❖ **check out** ◆ vi [pay hotel bill] régler sa note ; [leave hotel] quitter l'hôtel. ◆ vt sep 1. [investigate - person] enquêter sur, se renseigner sur ; [- information, machine, place] vérifier 2. *inf* : *check this out* a) [look] vise un peu ça b) [listen] écoute-moi ça. ❖ **check over** vt sep examiner, vérifier. ❖ **check up on** vt insep ▶ **to check up on sb** enquêter or se renseigner sur qqn ▶ **to check up on sthg** vérifier qqch.

 Checks and balances

Ce système de contrôle mutuel, garanti par la Constitution, est l'un des principes fondamentaux du gouvernement américain. Il a été élaboré afin d'assurer l'équilibre entre les pouvoirs législatif, exécutif et judiciaire.

checkbook n US = **chequebook**.

check box n case f (à cocher).

checked [ʧekt] adj [pattern, tablecloth] à carreaux.

checkerboard [ˈʧekəbɔːd] n US [in chess] échiquier m ; [in draughts] damier m.

checkered adj US = **chequered**.

checkers n US = **chequers**.

check guarantee card n US = cheque card.

check-in n enregistrement m.

checking account [ˈʧekɪŋ-] n US compte m chèque or chèques.

checklist [ˈʧeklɪst] n liste f de vérification ; AERON checklist f.

checkmate [ˈʧekmeɪt] n 1. [in chess] échec et mat m 2. *fig* [deadlock, standstill] impasse f ; [defeat] échec m total.

checkout [ˈʧekaʊt] n [in supermarket] caisse f.

checkpoint ['tʃekpɔɪnt] n (poste m de) contrôle m.

checkup ['tʃekʌp] n MED bilan m de santé, check-up m.

Cheddar ['tʃedəʳ] n ▸ **Cheddar (cheese)** cheddar m.

cheek [tʃiːk] n **1.** [of face] joue f ▸ **cheek to cheek** joue contre joue **2.** 🇬🇧 inf [impudence] culot m, toupet m.

cheekbone ['tʃiːkbəʊn] n pommette f.

-cheeked [tʃiːkt] in comp aux joues...

cheekily ['tʃiːkɪlɪ] adv 🇬🇧 avec effronterie or impudence, effrontément.

cheekiness ['tʃiːkɪnɪs] n 🇬🇧 effronterie f, audace f.

cheeky ['tʃiːkɪ] adj 🇬🇧 [person] effronté, impudent ; [attitude, behaviour] impertinent.

cheep [tʃiːp] ◆ n pépiement m. ◆ vi pépier.

cheer [tʃɪəʳ] ◆ n [cry] hourra m, bravo m / I heard a cheer go up j'ai entendu des acclamations / three cheers for the winner! un ban or hourra pour le gagnant ! ◆ vt **1.** [make cheerful - person] remonter le moral à, réconforter **2.** [encourage by shouts] acclamer. ◆ vi pousser des acclamations or des hourras. ❖ **cheer on** vt sep encourager (par des acclamations). ❖ **cheer up** vt sep [person] remonter le moral à, réconforter ; [house, room] égayer. ◆ vi s'égayer, se dérider ▸ **cheer up!** courage !

cheerful ['tʃɪəfʊl] adj [happy - person] de bonne humeur ; [-smile] joyeux, gai ; [-atmosphere, mood] gai, joyeux ; [-colour, wallpaper] gai, riant ; [-news] réjouissant.

cheerfully ['tʃɪəfʊlɪ] adv **1.** [happily] joyeusement, avec entrain **2.** [willingly] de plein gré, avec bonne volonté.

cheerfulness ['tʃɪəfʊlnɪs] n [of person] bonne humeur f ; [of atmosphere, colour] gaieté f ; [of remark, smile] gaieté f, caractère m jovial.

cheerily ['tʃɪərəlɪ] adv joyeusement, avec entrain.

cheering ['tʃɪərɪŋ] ◆ n (U) acclamations fpl, hourras mpl. ◆ adj [remark, thought] encourageant, qui remonte le moral ; [news, sight] encourageant, réconfortant.

cheerio [,tʃɪərɪ'əʊ] interj 🇬🇧 inf [goodbye] salut, tchao.

cheerleader ['tʃɪə,liːdəʳ] n majorette qui stimule l'enthousiasme des supporters des équipes sportives, surtout aux États-Unis.

cheerless ['tʃɪəlɪs] adj morne, triste.

cheers [tʃɪəz] interj 🇬🇧 inf **1.** [toast] à la tienne ! **2.** [goodbye] salut, tchao **3.** [thanks] merci.

cheery ['tʃɪərɪ] (compar **cheerier**, superl **cheeriest**) adj [person] de bonne humeur ; [smile] joyeux, gai.

cheese [tʃiːz] n fromage m ▸ **say cheese!** PHOT souriez ! ◆ comp [omelette, sandwich] au fromage ; [knife] à fromage.

cheeseboard ['tʃiːzbɔːd] n [board] plateau m à fromage or fromages ; [on menu] plateau m de fromages.

cheeseburger ['tʃiːz,bɜːgəʳ] n hamburger m au fromage.

cheesecake ['tʃiːzkeɪk] n [dessert] gâteau m au fromage (blanc).

cheesed off [tʃiːzd-] adj 🇬🇧 inf ▸ **to be cheesed off** en avoir marre.

cheesemonger ['tʃiːzmʌŋgəʳ] n fromager m, -ère f.

cheesy ['tʃiːzɪ] (compar **cheesier**, superl **cheesiest**) adj **1.** [flavour] qui a un goût de fromage, qui sent le fromage ; [smell] qui sent le fromage **2.** 🇺🇸 inf [excuse] nul ; [song, TV programme] ringard ▸ **a cheesy grin** un sourire toutes dents dehors.

cheetah ['tʃiːtə] n guépard m.

chef [ʃef] n CULIN chef m (de cuisine), cuisinier m, -ère f.

chemical ['kemɪkl] ◆ n produit m chimique. ◆ adj chimique ▸ **chemical engineer** ingénieur m chimiste ▸ **chemical engineering** génie m chimique ▸ **chemical warfare** guerre f chimique ▸ **chemical weapons** armes fpl chimiques.

chemically ['kemɪklɪ] adv chimiquement.

chemical toilet n W-C mpl chimiques.

chemist ['kemɪst] n **1.** [scientist] chimiste mf **2.** 🇬🇧 [pharmacist] pharmacien m, -enne f ▸ **chemist's (shop)** pharmacie f.

chemistry ['kemɪstrɪ] ◆ n chimie f / the chemistry is right / wrong l'alchimie fonctionne / ne fonctionne pas. ◆ comp ▸ **chemistry lesson** cours m de chimie.

chemotherapy [,kiːməʊ'θerəpɪ] n chimiothérapie f.

cheque 🇬🇧, **check** 🇺🇸 [tʃek] n chèque m / a cheque for £7 or to the amount of £7 un chèque de 7 livres ▸ **to pay by cheque** payer par chèque.

cheque account n 🇬🇧 compte m chèques.

chequebook 🇬🇧, **checkbook** 🇺🇸 ['tʃekbʊk] n carnet m de chèques, chéquier m.

chequebook holder n porte-chéquier m.

chequebook journalism n dans les milieux de la presse, pratique qui consiste à payer des sommes importantes pour le témoignage d'une personne impliquée dans une affaire.

cheque card n 🇬🇧 carte d'identité bancaire sans laquelle les chèques ne sont pas acceptés en Grande-Bretagne.

chequered 🇬🇧, **checkered** 🇺🇸 ['tʃekəd] adj **1.** [pattern] à carreaux, à damiers **2.** [varied] varié.

chequers 🇬🇧, **checkers** 🇺🇸 ['tʃekəz] n (U) jeu m de dames.

Chequers ['tʃekəz] pr n résidence secondaire officielle du Premier ministre britannique.

cherish ['tʃerɪʃ] vt [person] chérir, aimer ; [ambition, hope] caresser, nourrir ; [experience, memory] chérir ; [right, value] tenir à.

cherry ['tʃerɪ] (pl **cherries**) ◆ n [fruit] cerise f ; [tree] cerisier m. ◆ comp [blossom, wood] de cerisier ; [pie, tart] aux cerises.

cherry-picker n [boom lift] nacelle f élévatrice.

cherub ['tʃerəb] (pl **cherubs** or **cherubim** [-bɪm]) n ART chérubin m ; fig chérubin m, petit ange m.

chervil ['tʃɜːvɪl] n cerfeuil m.

Ches. written abbr of Cheshire.

Cheshire cat n ▸ **to grin like a Cheshire cat** avoir un sourire jusqu'aux oreilles.

chess [tʃes] n (U) échecs mpl.

chessboard ['tʃesbɔːd] n échiquier m.

chessman ['tʃesmæn] (pl **chessmen** [-men]) n pion m, pièce f (de jeu d'échecs).

chest [tʃest] ◆ n **1.** ANAT poitrine f ▸ **to get sthg off one's chest** dire ce qu'on a sur le cœur **2.** [box] coffre m, caisse f. ◆ comp **1.** [cold, measurement, voice, pain] de poitrine ▸ **chest infection** infection f des voies respiratoires **2.** ▸ **chest freezer** congélateur-bahut m.

chesterfield ['tʃestəfiːld] n [sofa] canapé m (dont les accoudoirs sont de la même hauteur que le dossier).

chestnut ['tʃesnʌt] ◆ n [tree] châtaignier m ; [fruit] châtaigne f. ◆ comp **1.** [blossom, wood] de châtaignier ; [stuffing] aux marrons **2.** [colour, hair] châtain ; [horse] alezan ▸ **chestnut brown** châtain (inv).

chest of drawers n commode f.

chesty ['tʃestɪ] (compar **chestier**, superl **chestiest**) adj [cough] de poitrine.

chevron ['ʃevrən] n ARCHIT, HERALD & MIL chevron m.

chew [tʃuː] vt mâcher, mastiquer ▸ **to chew the cud** lit & fig ruminer. ❖ **chew up** vt sep [food] mâchonner, mastiquer.

chewing gum ['tʃuːɪŋ-] n chewing-gum m.

chewy ['tʃuːɪ] (compar **chewier**, superl **chewiest**) adj caoutchouteux.

chic [ʃiːk] ◆ adj chic, élégant. ◆ n chic m, élégance f.

chicanery [ʃɪ'keɪnərɪ] (pl **chicaneries**) n [trickery] ruse f, fourberie f ; [legal trickery] chicane f.

chick [tʃɪk] n **1.** [baby bird - gen] oisillon m ; [- of chicken] poussin m **2.** inf [woman] poupée f.

chicken ['tʃɪkɪn] ◆ n [bird] poulet m ; [young] poussin m **▶ it's a chicken-and-egg situation** inf c'est le problème de l'œuf et de la poule, on ne sait pas lequel est à l'origine de l'autre. ◆ comp [dish, liver, stew] de poulet ; [sandwich] au poulet. ◆ adj inf [cowardly] froussard. ❖ **chicken out** vi inf se dégonfler / **he chickened out of the race** il s'est dégonflé et n'a pas pris part à la course.

chickenfeed ['tʃɪkɪnfiːd] n (U) lit nourriture f pour volaille.

chicken-hearted adj poltron.

chicken-livered [-,lɪvəd] adj = **chicken-hearted**.

chickenpox ['tʃɪkɪnpɒks] n (U) varicelle f.

chicken wire n grillage m.

chick flick n inf film qui cible les jeunes femmes.

chick lit n inf littérature populaire, en général écrite par des femmes, qui cible les jeunes femmes.

chickpea ['tʃɪkpiː] n pois m chiche.

chicory ['tʃɪkərɪ] (pl **chicories**) n [for salad] endive f ; [for coffee] chicorée f.

chide [tʃaɪd] (pt **chided** or **chid** [tʃɪd], pp **chid** [tʃɪd] or **chidden** ['tʃɪdn]) vt fml gronder, réprimander.

chief [tʃiːf] ◆ n **1.** [leader] chef m **▶ chief of police** ≃ préfet m de police **▶ chief of staff a)** MIL chef m d'état-major **b)** US [at White House] secrétaire m général de la Maison Blanche **2.** inf [boss] boss m. ◆ adj **1.** [most important] principal, premier **2.** [head] premier, en chef **▶ Chief Constable** en Grande-Bretagne, chef de la police d'un comté ou d'une région ; ≃ commissaire m divisionnaire **▶ chief executive officer** COMM & INDUST président-directeur général m **▶ chief inspector a)** [gen] inspecteur m principal, inspectrice f principale, inspecteur m, -trice f en chef **b)** UK [of police] ≃ commissaire m de police **c)** US SCH ≃ inspecteur m général ; ≃ inspectrice f générale **▶ chief superintendent** UK [in police] ≃ commissaire m principal.

chiefly ['tʃiːflɪ] adv principalement, surtout.

chief operating officer n directeur m général adjoint, directrice f générale adjointe.

chieftain ['tʃiːftən] n chef m (de tribu).

chieftaincy ['tʃiːftənsɪ] n chefferie f.

chiffon ['ʃɪfɒn] ◆ n mousseline f de soie. ◆ adj [dress, scarf] en mousseline (de soie).

chihuahua [tʃɪ'wɑːwə] n chihuahua m.

chilblain ['tʃɪlbleɪn] n engelure f.

child [tʃaɪld] (pl **children** ['tʃɪldrən]) ◆ n [boy or girl] enfant mf. ◆ comp [psychiatry, psychology] de l'enfant, infantile ; [psychologist] pour enfants **▶ child abuse a)** [sexual] sévices mpl sexuels exercés sur un enfant **b)** [physical] mauvais traitement m infligé à un enfant **▶ child's play** inf : **it's child's play for** or **to him** c'est un jeu d'enfant pour lui **▶ child prodigy** enfant mf prodige.

childbearing ['tʃaɪld,beərɪŋ] ◆ n grossesse f. ◆ adj [complications, problems] de grossesse.

child benefit n (U) allocation f familiale or allocations fpl familiales (pour un enfant) (en Grande-Bretagne).

childbirth ['tʃaɪldbɜːθ] n (U) accouchement m **▶ in childbirth** en couches.

child care n **1.** UK ADMIN protection f de l'enfance **2.** US [day care] **▶ child care center** crèche f, garderie f.

child directory n COMPUT sous-répertoire m.

childfree ['tʃaɪldfriː] adj US [couple, household] sans enfants.

child-friendly adj [area, city] aménagé pour les enfants ; [house, furniture] conçu pour les enfants.

childhood ['tʃaɪldhʊd] ◆ n enfance f. ◆ comp [friend, memories] d'enfance.

childish ['tʃaɪldɪʃ] adj [immature] enfantin, puéril / **don't be so childish** ne fais pas l'enfant.

childishly ['tʃaɪldɪʃlɪ] adv comme un enfant, en enfant.

childless ['tʃaɪldlɪs] adj sans enfants.

childlike ['tʃaɪldlaɪk] adj d'enfant.

child lock n serrure f de sécurité pour enfants.

child maintenance n pension f alimentaire.

childminder ['tʃaɪld,maɪndər] n UK [for very young children] nourrice f ; [for older children] assistante f maternelle.

childminding ['tʃaɪld,maɪndɪŋ] n garde f d'enfants.

childproof ['tʃaɪldpruːf] adj **▶ childproof lock** serrure f de sécurité pour enfants.

children ['tʃɪldrən] pl ⟶ **child**.

children's home n foyer m d'enfants.

child support = **child maintenance**.

Chile ['tʃɪlɪ] pr n Chili m.

Chilean ['tʃɪlɪən] ◆ n Chilien m, -enne f. ◆ adj chilien.

chili ['tʃɪlɪ] n & comp = **chilli**.

chill [tʃɪl] ◆ vt [make cold - food, wine] mettre au frais ; [- champagne] frapper ; [- glass, person] glacer **▶ to be chilled to the bone / to the marrow** être glacé jusqu'aux os / jusqu'à la moelle. ◆ vi **1.** [get colder] se refroidir, rafraîchir **2.** inf [relax] se détendre. ◆ n **1.** [coldness] fraîcheur f, froideur f / **there's a chill in the air** il fait assez frais or un peu froid / **his remark cast a chill over the meeting** fig son observation a jeté un froid dans l'assemblée **2.** [feeling of fear] frisson m / **the story sent chills down her spine** l'histoire lui a fait froid dans le dos **3.** [illness] coup m de froid, refroidissement m **▶ to catch a chill** attraper or prendre froid. ❖ **chill out** vi inf décompresser **▶ chill out!** du calme !

chilli ['tʃɪlɪ] ◆ n [fruit] piment m ; [dish] chili m. ◆ comp **▶ chilli powder** poudre f de piment.

chillin ['tʃɪlɪn] adj US inf génial, cool.

chilling ['tʃɪlɪŋ] adj [wind] frais (fraîche), froid ; fig [look, smile] froid, glacial ; [news, story, thought] qui donne des frissons.

chilly ['tʃɪlɪ] (compar **chillier**, superl **chilliest**) adj [air, room] (très) frais (fraîche), froid.

chime [tʃaɪm] ◆ n [bell] carillon m. ◆ vi [bell, voices] carillonner ; [clock] sonner. ❖ **chime in** vi inf [say] intervenir / **all the children chimed in** tous les enfants ont fait chorus.

chimney ['tʃɪmnɪ] n [in building] cheminée f.

chimneypot ['tʃɪmnɪpɒt] n tuyau m de cheminée.

chimneysweep ['tʃɪmnɪswiːp] n ramoneur m.

chimp [tʃɪmp] inf, **chimpanzee** [,tʃɪmpən'ziː] n chimpanzé m.

chin [tʃɪn] (pt & pp **chinned**, cont **chinning**) n menton m **▶ (keep your) chin up!** courage !

china ['tʃaɪnə] ◆ n [material] porcelaine f / **a piece of china** une porcelaine. ◆ comp [cup, plate] de or en porcelaine ; [shop] de porcelaine.

China ['tʃaɪnə] pr n Chine f.

china clay n kaolin m.

China Sea pr n ▸ **the China Sea** la mer de Chine.

Chinatown ['ʧaɪnətaʊn] n le quartier chinois.

chinchilla [ʧɪn'ʧɪlə] ◆ n chinchilla m. ◆ comp [coat, wrap] de chinchilla.

Chinese [ˌʧaɪ'niːz] (pl **Chinese**) ◆ n **1.** [person] Chinois m, -e f **2.** LING chinois m **3.** 🆄🅺 inf [meal] repas m chinois. ◆ adj chinois.

Chinese cabbage n chou m chinois.

Chinese lantern n lanterne f vénitienne.

chink [ʧɪŋk] ◆ n **1.** [hole] fente f, fissure f; [of light] rayon m / we found a chink in her armour nous avons trouvé son point faible or sensible **2.** [sound] tintement m (de pièces de monnaie, de verres). ◆ vi [jingle] tinter. ◆ vt [jingle] faire tinter.

Chink [ʧɪŋk] n offens terme raciste désignant un Chinois; ≃ Chinetoque mf.

chino ['ʧiːnəʊ] n TEXT chino m / chinos [trousers] chinos mpl.

chintz [ʧɪnts] ◆ n chintz m. ◆ comp [curtain] de chintz; [chair] recouvert de chintz.

chinwag ['ʧɪnwæg] n inf causette f.

chip [ʧɪp] (pt & pp **chipped**, cont **chipping**) ◆ n **1.** [piece] éclat m; [of wood] copeau m, éclat m ▸ **to have a chip on one's shoulder** inf en vouloir à tout le monde **2.** [flaw - in dish, glass] ébréchure f; [- in chair, wardrobe] écornure f **3.** 🆄🅺 CULIN [French fry] (pomme de terre f) frite f; 🆄🆂 [crisp] chips f inv **4.** GAMES [counter] jeton m, fiche f ▸ **when the chips are down** inf dans les moments difficiles **5.** COMPUT puce f. ◆ vt **1.** [dish, glass] ébrécher; [furniture] écorner; [paint] écailler **2.** [in golf, football] ▸ **to chip the ball** cocher. ❖ **chip away at** vt insep ▸ **to chip away at sthg** décaper qqch. ❖ **chip in** inf vi **1.** [contribute] contribuer **2.** [speak] mettre son grain de sel.

chip-and-pin n 🆄🅺 [payment system] paiement m par carte à puce.

chip-based adj COMPUT à puce.

chipboard ['ʧɪpbɔːd] n (U) 🆄🅺 [panneau m d']aggloméré m, panneau m de particules.

chipmunk ['ʧɪpmʌŋk] n tamia m, suisse m 🅲🅰🅽.

chipolata [ˌʧɪpə'lɑːtə] n chipolata f.

chipped [ʧɪpt] adj [dish, glass] ébréché; [furniture] écorné; [paint] écaillé.

chippings ['ʧɪpɪŋz] pl n 🆄🆂 [gen] éclats mpl, fragments mpl; [of wood] copeaux mpl, éclats mpl; [in roadwork] gravillons mpl.

chipset ['ʧɪpset] n COMPUT chipset m.

chip shop n 🆄🅺 boutique où l'on vend du «fish and chips».

chip van n 🆄🅺 friterie f (camionnette).

chiropodist [kɪ'rɒpədɪst] n pédicure mf.

chiropody [kɪ'rɒpədɪ] n (U) [treatment] soins mpl du pied; [science] podologie f.

chiropractor ['kaɪrəˌpræktər] n chiropracteur m, chiropracticien m, -enne f.

chirp [ʧɜːp] ◆ vi [bird] pépier, gazouiller; [insect] chanter, striduler; [person] parler d'une voix flûtée. ◆ n [of bird] pépiement m, gazouillement m; [of insect] chant m, stridulation f ▸ **chirp-chirp** [sound of bird] cri-cri.

chirpily ['ʧɜːpɪlɪ] adv inf gaiement.

chirpiness ['ʧɜːpɪnɪs] n inf humeur f joyeuse, gaieté f.

chirpy ['ʧɜːpɪ] (compar **chirpier**, superl **chirpiest**) adj inf [person] gai, plein d'entrain; [mood, voice] gai, enjoué.

chisel ['ʧɪzl] (🆄🅺 pt & pp **chiselled**, cont **chiselling**; 🆄🆂 pt & pp **chiseled**, cont **chiseling**) ◆ n [gen] ciseau m; [for engraving] burin m. ◆ vt [carve] ciseler.

chit [ʧɪt] n [memo, note] note f; [voucher] bon m; [receipt] reçu m, récépissé m.

chitchat ['ʧɪtʧæt] n (U) bavardage m, papotage m.

chivalrous ['ʃɪvlrəs] adj [courteous] chevaleresque, courtois; [gallant] galant.

chivalry ['ʃɪvlrɪ] n **1.** [courtesy] conduite f chevaleresque, courtoisie f; [gallantry] galanterie f **2.** [knights, system] chevalerie f.

chives [ʧaɪvz] pl n ciboulette f, civette f.

chiv(v)y ['ʧɪvɪ] (pt & pp **chivvied** or **chivied**) vt inf [nag] harceler.

chlamydia [klə'mɪdɪə] n MED chlamydia f.

chloride ['klɔːraɪd] n chlorure m.

chlorinated ['klɔːrɪneɪtɪd] adj [water] chloré.

chlorine ['klɔːriːn] n CHEM chlore m.

chlorofluorocarbon ['klɔːrəˌfluːrəʊ'kɑːbən] n chlorofluorocarbone m.

chloroform ['klɒrəfɔːm] n chloroforme m.

chlorophyll 🆄🅺, **chlorophyl** 🆄🆂 ['klɒrəfɪl] n chlorophylle f.

chocaholic = **chocoholic**.

choccy [ʧɒkɪ] (pl **choccies**) n inf chocolat m.

choc-ice 🆄🅺 ≃ Esquimau® m.

chock [ʧɒk] ◆ n [for door, wheel] cale f; [for barrel] cale f, chantier m; NAUT chantier m, cale f. ◆ vt [barrel, door, wheel] caler; NAUT mettre sur un chantier or sur cales.

chock-a-block, **chock-full** adj inf [room, theatre] plein à craquer; [container] bourré, plein à ras bord.

chocoholic ['ʧɒkəˌhɒlɪk] n inf accro mf du chocolat, fondu m, -e f de chocolat.

chocolate ['ʧɒkələt] ◆ n [drink, sweet] chocolat m. ◆ comp [biscuit, cake] au chocolat, chocolaté ▸ **chocolate chip cookie** cookie m aux pépites de chocolat.

choice [ʧɔɪs] ◆ n **1.** [act of choosing] choix m ▸ **to make a choice** faire un choix / by or from choice de or par préférence **2.** [option] choix m, option f / you have no choice vous n'avez pas le choix **3.** [selection] choix m, assortiment m **4.** [thing, person chosen] choix m / you made the right / wrong choice vous avez fait le bon / mauvais choix. ◆ adj [fruit, meat] de choix, de première qualité.

choir ['kwaɪər] ◆ n [group of singers] chœur m, chorale f; [in church] chœur m, maîtrise f. ◆ comp ▸ **choir practice** répétition f de la chorale.

choirboy ['kwaɪəbɔɪ] n jeune choriste m.

choke [ʧəʊk] ◆ vi étouffer, s'étouffer, s'étrangler ▸ **to choke on sthg** s'étouffer or s'étrangler en avalant qqch de travers / **to choke to death** mourir étouffé. ◆ vt **1.** [asphyxiate] étrangler, étouffer / in a voice choked with emotion d'une voix étranglée par l'émotion **2.** [clog] boucher, obstruer / choked with weeds étouffé par les mauvaises herbes. ◆ n AUTO starter m; TECH [in pipe] buse f. ❖ **choke back**, **choke down** vt sep [anger] refouler, étouffer; [tears] refouler, contenir; [complaint, cry] retenir.

choked [ʧəʊkt] adj [cry, voice] étranglé.

cholera ['kɒlərə] n choléra m.

cholesterol [kə'lestərɒl] n cholestérol m.

chomp [ʧɒmp] inf vi & vt mastiquer bruyamment.

choo-choo [ʧuːʧuː] n baby talk train m.

choose [ʧuːz] (pt **chose** [ʧəʊz], pp **chosen** ['ʧəʊzn]) ◆ vt **1.** [select] choisir, prendre **2.** [elect] élire **3.** [decide] décider, juger bon / I didn't choose to invite her [invited unwillingly] je l'ai invitée contre mon gré. ◆ vi choisir / do as you choose faites comme bon vous semble or comme vous l'entendez or comme vous voulez.

choos(e)y ['tʃuːzɪ] (*compar* **choosier,** *superl* **choosiest**) adj *inf* difficile.

chop [tʃɒp] (*pt & pp* **chopped,** *cont* **chopping**) ◆ vt **1.** [cut -gen] couper ; [-wood] couper ; CULIN hacher **2.** *inf* [reduce -budget, funding] réduire, diminuer ; [-project] mettre au rancart **3.** SPORT [ball] couper. ◆ vi [change direction] varier ▶ **to chop and change** changer constamment d'avis. ◆ n **1.** [blow -with axe] coup *m* de hache ; [-with hand] coup *m* ▶ **to get** or **to be given the chop a)** 🇬🇧 *inf* [employee] être viré **b)** [project] être mis au rancart **2.** CULIN [of meat] côtelette *f*. ◆ **chop down** vt sep abattre. ◆ **chop off** vt sep trancher, couper. ◆ **chop up** vt sep couper en morceaux, hacher.

chopped liver [tʃɒpt-] n foie haché (*spécialité juive*) / *what am I, chopped liver?* 🇺🇸 *inf* et moi, j'existe pas ?

chopper ['tʃɒpər] n **1.** 🇬🇧 [axe] petite hache *f* ; CULIN [cleaver] couperet *m*, hachoir *m* **2.** *inf* [helicopter] hélico *m* **3.** *inf* [motorcycle] chopper *m* ; [bicycle] vélo *m* (*à haut guidon*).

choppiness ['tʃɒpɪnɪs] n [of lake, sea] agitation *f*.

chopping board ['tʃɒpɪŋ-] n planche *f* à découper.

chopping knife n hachoir *m*.

choppy ['tʃɒpɪ] (*compar* **choppier,** *superl* **choppiest**) adj [lake, sea] un peu agité ; [waves] clapotant.

chopstick ['tʃɒpstɪk] n baguette *f* (*pour manger*).

choral ['kɔːrəl] adj choral.

chord [kɔːd] n MUS [group of notes] accord *m*.

chore [tʃɔːr] n [task -routine] travail *m* de routine ; [-unpleasant] corvée *f* ▶ **household chores** travaux *mpl* ménagers / *I have to do the chores* 🇺🇸 il faut que je fasse le ménage.

choreograph ['kɒrɪəɡrɑːf] vt [ballet, dance] chorégraphier, faire la chorégraphie de ; *fig* [meeting, party] organiser.

choreographer [ˌkɒrɪ'ɒɡrəfər] n chorégraphe *mf*.

choreography [ˌkɒrɪ'ɒɡrəfɪ] n chorégraphie *f*.

chorizo [tʃə'riːzəʊ] n chorizo *m*.

chortle ['tʃɔːtl] ◆ vi glousser. ◆ n gloussement *m*, petit rire *m*.

chorus ['kɔːrəs] ◆ n **1.** [choir] chœur *m*, chorale *f* **2.** [refrain] refrain *m* **3.** THEAT [dancers, singers] troupe *f* ; [speakers] chœur *m* **4.** [of complaints, groans] concert *m*. ◆ vt [song] chanter en chœur ; [poem] réciter en chœur ; [approval, discontent] dire or exprimer en chœur.

chorusmaster ['kɔːrəsˌmɑːstər] n THEAT & MUS maître *m* de chant.

chose [tʃəʊz] pt ⟶ **choose.**

chosen ['tʃəʊzn] ◆ pp ⟶ **choose.** ◆ adj choisi.

choux pastry [ʃuː-] n (*U*) pâte *f* à choux.

chow [tʃaʊ] n *inf* [food] bouffe *f*.

chowder ['tʃaʊdər] n soupe crémeuse épaisse contenant des pommes de terre, de l'oignon et du poisson ou des fruits de mer.

Christ [kraɪst] ◆ pr n le Christ, Jésus-Christ *m* ▶ **the Christ child** l'enfant *m* Jésus. ◆ interj ▶ **Christ!** *v inf* Bon Dieu (de Bon Dieu) !

christen ['krɪsn] vt **1.** [gen] appeler, nommer ; [nickname] baptiser, surnommer ; NAUT & RELIG baptiser **2.** *inf* [use for first time] étrenner.

christening ['krɪsnɪŋ] n baptême *m*.

Christian ['krɪstʃən] ◆ n chrétien *m*, -enne *f*. ◆ adj chrétien.

Christianity [ˌkrɪstɪ'ænətɪ] n [religion] christianisme *m*.

Christian name n nom *m* de baptême, prénom *m*.

Christmas ['krɪsməs] ◆ n Noël *m* / *at Christmas* à Noël / *for Christmas* pour Noël ▶ **Merry Christmas!**

joyeux Noël ! ◆ comp [party, present, dinner] de Noël ▶ **Christmas cracker** papillote contenant un pétard et une surprise que l'on ouvre traditionnellement à deux au moment des fêtes de Noël.

Christmas cake n gâteau *m* de Noël (*cake décoré au sucre glace*).

Christmas card n carte *f* de Noël.

Christmas carol n chant *m* de Noël, noël *m* ; RELIG cantique *m* de Noël.

Christmas Day n le jour de Noël.

Christmas Eve n la veille de Noël.

Christmas Island pr n l'île *f* Christmas.

Christmas pudding n 🇬🇧 pudding *m*, plum-pudding *m*.

Christmas stocking n chaussette que les enfants suspendent à la cheminée pour que le père Noël y dépose les cadeaux.

Christmassy ['krɪsməsɪ] adj qui rappelle la fête de Noël / *the town looks so Christmassy* la ville a un tel air de fête.

Christmastime ['krɪsməstaɪm] n la période de Noël or des fêtes (de fin d'année).

Christmas tree n sapin *m* or arbre *m* de Noël.

chrome [krəʊm] ◆ n chrome *m*. ◆ adj [fittings, taps] chromé.

chromium ['krəʊmɪəm] n chrome *m*.

chromosome ['krəʊməsəʊm] n chromosome *m*.

chronic ['krɒnɪk] adj **1.** [long-lasting - illness, unemployment] chronique **2.** [habitual - smoker, gambler] invétéré **3.** 🇬🇧 *inf* [very bad] atroce, affreux.

chronically ['krɒnɪklɪ] adv **1.** [habitually] chroniquement **2.** [severely] gravement, sérieusement.

chronicle ['krɒnɪkl] ◆ n chronique *f* / *their holiday was a chronicle of misadventures* leurs vacances furent une succession de mésaventures. ◆ vt faire la chronique de, raconter.

chronicler ['krɒnɪklər] n chroniqueur *m*, -euse *f*.

chronological [ˌkrɒnə'lɒdʒɪkl] adj chronologique.

chronologically [ˌkrɒnə'lɒdʒɪklɪ] adv chronologiquement, par ordre chronologique.

chronology [krə'nɒlədʒɪ] n chronologie *f*.

chronometer [krə'nɒmɪtər] n chronomètre *m*.

chrysalis ['krɪsəlɪs] (*pl* **chrysalises** [-siːz]) n chrysalide *f*.

chrysanthemum [krɪ'sænθəməm] n chrysanthème *m*.

chubbiness ['tʃʌbɪnɪs] n rondeur *f*.

chubby ['tʃʌbɪ] (*compar* **chubbier,** *superl* **chubbiest**) adj [fingers, person] potelé ; [face] joufflu.

chuck [tʃʌk] vt **1.** *inf* [toss] jeter, lancer **2.** *inf* [give up - activity, job] laisser tomber, lâcher **3.** *inf* [jilt - boyfriend, girlfriend] plaquer. ◆ **chuck away** vt sep *inf* [old clothing, papers] balancer ; [chance, opportunity] laisser passer ; [money] jeter par les fenêtres. ◆ **chuck out** vt sep *inf* [old clothing, papers] balancer ; [person] vider, sortir / *he chucked the troublemakers out* il a flanqué les provocateurs à la porte.

chucking-out time ['tʃʌkɪŋ-] n 🇬🇧 *inf* [in pub] heure *f* de la fermeture.

chuckle ['tʃʌkl] ◆ vi glousser, rire. ◆ n gloussement *m*, petit rire *m*.

chuffed [tʃʌft] adj 🇬🇧 *inf* vachement or super content, ravi.

chug [tʃʌg] vi **1.** [make noise - engine, car, train] s'essouffler, haleter **2.** [move] avancer en soufflant or en haletant.

chum [tʃʌm] n *inf* copain *m*, copine *f*.

chummy ['tʃʌmɪ] (compar **chummier**, superl **chummiest**) adj inf amical.

chump [tʃʌmp] n inf & dated [dolt - boy] ballot m ; [- girl] gourde f.

chunk [tʃʌŋk] n [of meat, wood] gros morceau m ; [of budget, time] grande partie f.

chunky ['tʃʌŋkɪ] (compar **chunkier**, superl **chunkiest**) adj **1.** [person - stocky] trapu ; [- chubby] potelé, enrobé ; [food, stew] avec des morceaux **2.** 🇬🇧 [clothing, sweater] de grosse laine ; [jewellery] gros (grosse).

church [tʃɜːtʃ] ◆ n **1.** [building - gen] église f ; [- Protestant] église f, temple m **2.** [services - Protestant] office m ; [- Catholic] messe f ▶ **to go to church a)** [Protestants] aller au temple or à l'office **b)** [Catholics] aller à la messe or à l'église **3.** (U) [clergy] ▶ **the church** les ordres mpl / **to go into the church** entrer dans les ordres. ◆ comp [bell, roof] d'église. ◆ **Church** n [institution] ▶ **the Church** l'Église f ▶ **Church of England** Église anglicane ▶ **Church of France / of Scotland** Église de France / d'Écosse ▶ **Church of Rome** Église catholique.

 The Church of England

L'Église d'Angleterre (de confession anglicane) est l'Église officielle de la Grande-Bretagne ; son chef laïque est le souverain, son chef spirituel, l'archevêque de Cantorbéry.

churchgoer ['tʃɜːtʃ,gəʊər] n pratiquant m, -e f.

churchgoing ['tʃɜːtʃ,gəʊɪŋ] ◆ adj pratiquant. ◆ n fréquentation f des églises.

church leader n chef m de l'église.

churchman ['tʃɜːtʃmən] (pl **churchmen** [-mən]) n [clergyman] ecclésiastique m ; [churchgoer] pratiquant m.

churchyard ['tʃɜːtʃjɑːd] n [grounds] terrain m autour de l'église ; [graveyard] cimetière m (autour d'une église).

churlish ['tʃɜːlɪʃ] adj [rude] fruste, grossier ; [bad-tempered - person] qui a mauvais caractère, revêche ; [- attitude, behaviour] revêche, désagréable.

churn [tʃɜːn] ◆ vt **1.** [cream] baratter **2.** [mud] remuer ; [water] faire bouillonner. ◆ vi [sea, water] bouillonner / the thought made my stomach churn j'ai eu l'estomac tout retourné à cette idée. ◆ n **1.** [for butter] baratte f **2.** 🇬🇧 [milk can] bidon m. ◆ **churn out** vt sep inf **1.** [produce rapidly - gen] produire rapidement ; [- novels, reports] pondre à la chaîne or en série **2.** [produce mechanically] débiter. ◆ **churn up** vt sep [mud] remuer ; [sea, water] faire bouillonner.

chute [ʃuːt] n **1.** [for parcels] glissière f **2.** [for sledding, in swimming pool] toboggan m.

chutney ['tʃʌtnɪ] n chutney m (condiment à base de fruits).

chutzpah ['hʊtspə] n 🇺🇸 inf culot m.

CI written abbr of **Channel Islands**.

CIA (abbr of **Central Intelligence Agency**) pr n CIA f.

ciabatta [tʃəˈbɑːtə] n ciabatta m.

cicada [sɪˈkɑːdə] (pl **cicadas** or **cicadae** [-diː]) n cigale f.

Cid [sɪd] pr n ▶ **El Cid** le Cid.

CID (abbr of **Criminal Investigation Department**) pr n police judiciaire britannique ; ≃ PJ.

cider ['saɪdər] ◆ n cidre m. ◆ comp ▶ **cider vinegar** vinaigre m de cidre.

cif, CIF (abbr of cost, insurance and freight) adj & adv CAF, C.A.F.

cigar [sɪˈgɑːr] ◆ n cigare m. ◆ comp [box, case, tobacco] à cigares ; [ash, smoke] de cigare ▶ **cigar lighter** allume-cigare m inv.

cigarette [,sɪgəˈret] ◆ n cigarette f. ◆ comp [ash, burn, smoke] de cigarette ; [packet, smoke] de cigarettes ; [paper, tobacco] à cigarettes ▶ **cigarette butt** or **end** mégot m ▶ **cigarette case** étui m à cigarettes, porte-cigarettes m inv ▶ **cigarette lighter** briquet m.

ciggie ['sɪgɪ] n inf clope m ou f, sèche f.

cilantro [sɪˈlæntrəʊ] n 🇺🇸 coriandre f.

C-in-C written abbr of **Commander-in-Chief**.

cinch [sɪntʃ] n inf ▶ **it's a cinch a)** [certainty] c'est du tout cuit **b)** [easy to do] c'est du gâteau.

cinder ['sɪndər] n cendre f.

cinder block n 🇺🇸 parpaing m.

Cinderella [,sɪndəˈrelə] pr n Cendrillon.

cinders ['sɪndəz] n inf Cendrillon f.

cinecamera ['sɪnɪ,kæmərə] n 🇬🇧 caméra f.

cine-film ['sɪnɪ-] n 🇬🇧 film m.

cinema ['sɪnəmə] n 🇬🇧 [building] cinéma m ; [industry] (industrie f du) cinéma m.

cinemagoer ['sɪnɪmə,gəʊər] n personne f qui fréquente les cinémas.

cinematic [,sɪnɪˈmætɪk] adj cinématique.

cinematographic [,sɪnəmætəˈgræfɪk] adj cinématographique.

cinematography [,sɪnəməˈtɒgrəfɪ] n 🇬🇧 cinématographie f.

cinnamon ['sɪnəmən] ◆ n [spice] cannelle f. ◆ adj cannelle (inv).

cipher ['saɪfər] n **1.** [code] chiffre m, code m secret **2.** liter [zero] zéro m / they're mere ciphers fig ce sont des moins que rien.

circa ['sɜːkə] prep circa, vers.

circle ['sɜːkl] ◆ n **1.** [gen & GEOM] cercle m ; [around eyes] cerne m ▶ **to come full circle** revenir au point de départ, boucler la boucle **2.** [group of people] cercle m, groupe m / in artistic / political circles dans les milieux artistiques / politiques **3.** THEAT balcon m. ◆ vt **1.** [draw circle round] entourer (d'un cercle), encercler **2.** [move round] tourner autour de **3.** [surround] encercler, entourer. ◆ vi [bird, plane] faire or décrire des cercles.

circuit ['sɜːkɪt] n **1.** [journey around] circuit m, tour m **2.** ELEC circuit m **3.** SPORT [track] circuit m, parcours m.

circuit board n plaquette f (de circuits imprimés).

circuit breaker n ELEC disjoncteur m.

circuitous [səˈkjuːɪtəs] adj [route] qui fait un détour, détourné ; [journey] compliqué ; fig [reasoning, thinking] contourné, compliqué.

circular ['sɜːkjʊlər] ◆ adj [movement, shape, ticket] circulaire. ◆ n **1.** [letter, memo] circulaire f **2.** [advertisement] prospectus m.

circulate ['sɜːkjʊleɪt] ◆ vt [book, bottle] faire circuler ; [document - from person to person] faire circuler ; [- in mass mailing] diffuser ; [news, rumour] propager. ◆ vi circuler ; [at a party] aller de groupe en groupe.

circulation [,sɜːkjʊˈleɪʃn] n **1.** [gen & FIN] circulation f ▶ **to be in circulation a)** [book, money] être en circulation **b)** [person] être dans le circuit **2.** [of magazine, newspaper] tirage m / the Times has a circulation of 200,000 le Times tire à 200 000 exemplaires **3.** ANAT & BOT circulation f / to have good / poor circulation avoir une bonne / une mauvaise circulation.

circumcise ['sɜːkəmsaɪz] vt circoncire.

circumcised ['sɜːkəmsaɪzd] adj circoncis.

circumcision [ˌsɜːkəm'sɪʒn] n [act] circoncision *f* ; [religious rite] (fête *f* de la) circoncision *f*.

circumference [sə'kʌmfərəns] n circonférence *f*.

circumflex ['sɜːkəmfleks] ◆ n accent *m* circonflexe.
◆ adj circonflexe.

circumnavigate [ˌsɜːkəm'nævɪgeɪt] vt [iceberg, island] contourner *(en bateau)*.

circumscribe ['sɜːkəmskraɪb] vt [restrict] circonscrire, limiter.

circumspect ['sɜːkəmspekt] adj circonspect.

circumstances ['sɜːkəmstənsɪz] pl n [conditions] circonstance *f*, situation *f* / *in* or *under these circumstances* dans les circonstances actuelles, vu la situation actuelle or l'état actuel des choses / *in* or *under normal circumstances* en temps normal / *under no circumstances* en aucun cas / *under similar circumstances* en pareil cas.

circumstantial [ˌsɜːkəm'stænʃl] adj [incidental] accidentel, fortuit ; LAW [evidence] indirect.

circumvent [ˌsɜːkəm'vent] vt [law, rule] tourner, contourner.

circumvention [ˌsɜːkəm'venʃn] n [of law, rule] fait *m* de tourner or contourner.

circus ['sɜːkəs] ◆ n [gen & ANTIQ] cirque *m*. ◆ comp [act, clown, company, tent] de cirque.

cirrhosis [sɪ'rəʊsɪs] n *(U)* cirrhose *f*.

CIS (abbr of **Commonwealth of Independent States**) pr n CEI *f*.

CISC (abbr of **complex instruction set computer**) n CISC *m*.

cissy ['sɪsɪ] n & adj = **sissy**.

cistern ['sɪstən] n [tank] citerne *f* ; [for toilet] réservoir *m* de chasse d'eau.

citadel ['sɪtədəl] n *lit & fig* citadelle *f*.

citation [saɪ'teɪʃn] n citation *f*.

citation file n corpus *m*.

cite [saɪt] vt [quote] citer.

citizen ['sɪtɪzn] n **1.** [of nation, state] citoyen *m*, -enne *f* ; ADMIN [national] ressortissant *m*, -e *f* **2.** [of town] habitant *m*, -e *f*.

Citizens' Advice Bureau pr n *en Grande-Bretagne, bureau où les citoyens peuvent obtenir des conseils d'ordre juridique, social, etc.*

Citizens' Band n *fréquence (de radio) réservée au public* ▶ **Citizens' Band radio** CB *f*.

citizenship ['sɪtɪznʃɪp] n citoyenneté *f*, nationalité *f*.

citric ['sɪtrɪk] adj citrique ▶ **citric acid** acide *m* citrique.

citrus ['sɪtrəs] adj ▶ **citrus fruit** or **fruits** agrumes *mpl*.

city ['sɪtɪ] (*pl* **cities**) ◆ n [town] (grande) ville *f*. ◆ comp [lights, limits, streets] de la ville ; [officers, police, services] municipal ▶ **city life** vie *f* en ville, vie citadine. ◆ **City** pr n [of London] centre d'affaires de Londres ▶ **the City** la City (de Londres) / *he's something in the City* il travaille à la City (de Londres).

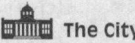

The City

La City, quartier financier de Londres, est une circonscription administrative autonome de la capitale, dont le conseil siège au Guildhall. Elle est dotée de sa propre police et de son propre maire. La City est aussi connue sous son surnom **the Square Mile** (bien qu'elle couvre une superficie plus étendue). Le terme **the City** est souvent employé pour désigner le monde britannique de la finance.

city centre n centre *m* de la ville, centre-ville *m*.

city-dweller n 🇬🇧 citadin *m*, -e *f*.

city hall n **1.** [building] mairie *f*, hôtel *m* de ville **2.** 🇺🇸 [municipal government] administration *f* (municipale).

cityscape ['sɪtɪskeɪp] n paysage *m* urbain.

city technology college n = CTC.

civic ['sɪvɪk] adj [authority, building] municipal ; [duty, right] civique.

civic centre n centre administratif d'une ville, parfois complété par des équipements de loisirs ; ≃ cité administrative.

civics ['sɪvɪks] n *(U)* instruction *f* civique.

civil ['sɪvl] adj **1.** [of community] civil ▶ **civil wedding** or **marriage** mariage *m* civil **2.** [polite] poli, courtois, civil *fml* / *she was very civil to me* elle s'est montrée très aimable avec moi.

civil defence n protection *f* civile.

civil disobedience n résistance *f* passive (à la loi).

civil engineer n ingénieur *m* des travaux publics.

civil engineering n génie *m* civil.

civilian [sɪ'vɪljən] ◆ adj civil *(opposé à militaire)*. ◆ n civil *m*, -e *f* *(opposé à militaire)*.

civility [sɪ'vɪlɪtɪ] (*pl* **civilities**) n [quality] courtoisie *f*, civilité *f*.

civilization, civilisation 🇬🇧 [ˌsɪvɪlaɪ'zeɪʃn] n civilisation *f*.

civilize, civilise ['sɪvɪlaɪz] vt civiliser.

civilized, civilised ['sɪvɪlaɪzd] adj [person, society] civilisé.

civilizing ['sɪvɪlaɪzɪŋ] adj : *the civilizing influence of...* l'influence civilisatrice de...

civil law n droit *m* civil.

civil libertarian n défenseur *m* des droits du citoyen.

civil liberties n libertés *fpl* civiques.

Civil List n liste *f* civile *(allouée à la famille royale britannique)*.

civil partner n conjoint *m*, -e *f* (par union civile).

civil partnership n union *f* civile.

civil rights pl n droits *mpl* civils or civiques ▶ **the civil rights movement** la lutte pour les droits civils or civiques.

The Civil Rights Movement

Même si elle englobe les droits civiques de tout citoyen, l'expression **Civil Rights Movement** fait généralement référence à la lutte pour l'égalité des droits des Noirs américains menée entre les années 1940 et la fin des années 1960.

civil servant n fonctionnaire *mf*.

civil service n fonction *f* publique, administration *f*.

civil union n union *f* civile.

civil war n guerre *f* civile ▶ **the American Civil War** la guerre de Sécession ▶ **the English Civil War** la guerre civile anglaise.

The American Civil War

Déclenchée par l'élection d'Abraham Lincoln, attisée par les différences sociales et économiques, la guerre civile opposa, de 1861 à 1865, le Sud, esclavagiste (les **Confederates**), au Nord, abolitionniste (les **Unionists**). Le conflit, extrêmement meurtrier, se termina par la victoire des fédéraux, dont les troupes étaient supérieures en nombre et en moyens.

🏛 The English Civil War

Guerre entre les partisans du Parlement et les royalistes, qui eut lieu de 1642 à 1646 et généra de nombreuses émeutes de 1646 à 1648. La victoire fut remportée par l'armée de Cromwell, qui fit exécuter le roi Charles Ier en 1649.

CJD (abbr of **Creutzfeldt-Jakob disease**) n MCJ *f*.

cl (written abbr of **centilitre**) cl.

clad [klæd] ◆ pp ⟶ **clothe**. ◆ adj *liter* habillé, vêtu.

cladding ['klædɪŋ] n revêtement *m*, parement *m*.

claim [kleɪm] ◆ vt **1**. [assert, maintain] prétendre, déclarer **2**. [assert one's right to] revendiquer, réclamer ; [responsibility, right] revendiquer / **to claim damages** / **one's due** réclamer des dommages et intérêts / son dû **3**. [apply for - money] demander ; [- expenses] demander le remboursement de **4**. [call for - attention] réclamer, demander ; [- respect, sympathy] solliciter **5**. [take] : *the storm claimed five lives* or *five victims* l'orage a fait cinq victimes. ◆ vi ▶ **to claim for** or **on sthg a)** [insurance] demander le paiement de qqch **b)** [travel expenses] demander le remboursement de qqch. ◆ n **1**. [assertion] affirmation *f*, prétention *f* / *I make no claims to understand why* je ne prétends pas comprendre pourquoi **2**. [right] droit *m*, titre *m* ; [by trade unions] demande *f* d'augmentation, revendication *f* salariale **3**. [demand] demande *f* ▶ **to lay claim to sthg** prétendre à qqch, revendiquer son droit à qqch ▶ **pay claim** demande *f* d'augmentation (de salaire) **4**. [in insurance] demande *f* d'indemnité, déclaration *f* de sinistre ▶ **to put in a claim for sthg** demander une indemnité pour qqch, faire une déclaration de sinistre pour qqch / *the company pays 65% of all claims* la société satisfait 65 % de toutes les demandes de dédommagement ▶ **claim form a)** [for insurance] formulaire *m* de déclaration de sinistre **b)** [for expenses] note *f* de frais.

claimant ['kleɪmənt] n ADMIN demandeur *m*, demanderesse *f* ; LAW demandeur *m*, demanderesse *f*, requérant *m*, -e *f*.

clairvoyant [kleə'vɔɪənt] ◆ n voyant *m*, -e *f*, extralucide *mf*. ◆ adj doué de seconde vue.

clam [klæm] n palourde *f*, clam *m*. ◆ **clam up** vi *inf* refuser de parler.

clamber ['klæmbər] vi grimper (en s'aidant des mains).

clammy ['klæmɪ] (*compar* **clammier**, *superl* **clammiest**) adj [hands, skin] moite (et froid) ; [weather] humide, lourd ; [walls] suintant, humide.

clamor US vi & n = **clamour**.

clamorous ['klæmərəs] adj *fml* [noisy] bruyant.

clamour UK, **clamor** US ['klæmər] ◆ vi vociférer, crier ▶ **to clamour for sthg** demander or réclamer qqch à grands cris or à cor et à cri. ◆ n **1**. [noise] clameur *f*, vociférations *fpl*, cri *m*, cris *mpl* **2**. [demand] revendication *f* bruyante.

clamp [klæmp] ◆ n **1**. [fastener] pince *f* ; MED clamp *m* ; TECH crampon *m* ; [on worktable] valet *m* (d'établi) **2**. AUTO = **wheelclamp**. ◆ vt **1**. [fasten] attacher,

fixer ; TECH serrer, cramponner ▶ **to clamp sthg to sthg** fixer qqch sur qqch (à l'aide d'une pince) **2**. [vehicle] mettre un sabot à. ◆ **clamp down** vi donner un coup de frein ▶ **to clamp down on a)** [expenses, inflation] mettre un frein à **b)** [crime, demonstrations] stopper **c)** [information] censurer **d)** [the press] bâillonner **e)** [person] serrer la vis à.

clampdown ['klæmpdaʊn] n mesures *fpl* répressives, répression *f*.

clamshell ['klæmʃel] n [packaging] coque *f* plastique ; [phone] téléphone *m* à clapet.

clan [klæn] n clan *m*.

clandestine [klæn'destɪn] adj clandestin.

clang [klæŋ] ◆ vi retentir or résonner (d'un bruit métallique). ◆ n bruit *m* métallique.

clanger ['klæŋər] n UK *inf* gaffe *f* ▶ **to drop a clanger** faire une gaffe.

clank [klæŋk] ◆ n cliquetis *m*, bruit *m* sec et métallique. ◆ vi cliqueter, faire un bruit sec.

clap [klæp] (*pt & pp* **clapped**, *cont* **clapping**) ◆ vt **1**. ▶ **to clap one's hands a)** [to get attention, to mark rhythm] frapper dans ses mains, taper des mains **b)** [to applaud] applaudir **2**. [pat] taper, frapper **3**. [put] mettre, poser ▶ **the minute she clapped eyes on him** *inf* dès qu'elle eut posé les yeux sur lui. ◆ vi [in applause] applaudir ; [to get attention, to mark rhythm] frapper dans ses mains. ◆ n [sound - gen] claquement *m* ; [- of hands] battement *m* ; [- of applause] applaudissements *mpl* ▶ **clap of thunder** coup *m* de tonnerre.

clapboard ['klæpbɔːd] n bardeau *m*.

clapped-out [klæpt-] adj UK *inf* [machine] fichu ; [person] crevé.

clapperboard ['klæpəbɔːd] n CIN claquette *f*, claquoir *m*, clap *m*.

clappers ['klæpəz] pl n UK *inf* ▶ **to go** or **to move like the clappers** aller à toute vitesse.

clapping ['klæpɪŋ] n (U) [for attention, to music] battements *mpl* de mains ; [applause] applaudissements *mpl*.

claptrap ['klæptræp] n (U) *inf* [nonsense] âneries *fpl*, bêtises *fpl*.

claret ['klærət] ◆ n UK (vin *m* de) Bordeaux *m* (rouge). ◆ adj bordeaux (*inv*).

clarification [ˌklærɪfɪ'keɪʃn] n [explanation] clarification *f*, éclaircissement *m*.

clarify ['klærɪfaɪ] (*pt & pp* **clarified**) vt [explain] clarifier, éclaircir.

clarinet [ˌklærə'net] n clarinette *f*.

clarity ['klærətɪ] n [of explanation, of text] clarté *f*, précision *f*.

clash [klæʃ] ◆ n **1**. [sound - gen] choc *m* métallique, fracas *m* ; [- of cymbals] retentissement *m* **2**. [between people - fight] affrontement *m*, bagarre *f* ; [- disagreement] dispute *f*, différend *m* **3**. [incompatibility - of ideas, opinions] incompatibilité *f* ; [- of interests] conflit *m* ; [- of colours] discordance *f*. ◆ vi **1**. [metallic objects] s'entrechoquer, se heurter ; [cymbals] résonner **2**. [people - fight] se battre ; [- disagree] se heurter ▶ **to clash with sb over sthg** avoir un différend avec qqn à propos de qqch **3**. [be incompatible - ideas, opinions] se heurter, être incompatible or en contradiction ; [- interests] se heurter, être en conflit ; [- colours] jurer, détonner **4**. [appointments, events] tomber en même temps.

clasp [klɑːsp] ◆ vt [hold] serrer, étreindre ; [grasp] saisir ▶ **to clasp sb** / **sthg in one's arms** serrer qqn / qqch dans ses bras. ◆ n [fastening - of dress, necklace] fermoir *m* ; [- of belt] boucle *f*.

class [klɑːs] ◆ n **1**. [category, division] classe *f*, catégorie *f* / *he's just not in the same class as his brother* il n'arrive pas à la cheville de son frère **/ to be in a class by oneself** or **in a class of one's own** être unique, former une classe à part **2.** SCH & UNIV [group of students] classe *f*; [course] cours *m*, classe *f* **/ the class of 1972** US la promotion de 1972 **3.** UK UNIV [grade] ▶ **first class honours** licence *f* avec mention très bien **4.** inf [elegance] classe *f* **/ to have class** avoir de la classe. ◆ comp ▶ **a class act**: *she's a real class act* elle est vraiment classe. ◆ vt classer, classifier.

class-conscious adj [person -aware] conscient des distinctions sociales ; [-snobbish] snob ; [attitude, manners] snob.

classic ['klæsɪk] ◆ adj *lit & fig* classique. ◆ n [gen] classique *m*.

classical ['klæsɪkl] adj [gen] classique ▶ **classical music** musique *f* classique.

classically ['klæsɪklɪ] adv classiquement, de façon classique **/ a classically trained musician** un musicien de formation classique.

classics ['klæsɪks] n *(U)* ≃ les lettres classiques *fpl*.

classification [,klæsɪfɪ'keɪʃn] n classification *f*.

classified ['klæsɪfaɪd] adj **1.** [arranged] classifié, classé ▶ **classified ad** or **advertisement** petite annonce *f* **2.** [secret] (classé) secret.

classify ['klæsɪfaɪ] vt ranger.

classless ['klɑːslɪs] adj [society] sans classes ; [person, accent] qui n'appartient à aucune classe (sociale).

classmate ['klɑːsmeɪt] n camarade *mf* de classe.

classroom ['klɑːsrʊm] n (salle *f* de) classe *f*.

classroom assistant n SCH aide-éducateur *m*, -trice *f*.

classy ['klɑːsɪ] (*compar* **classier**, *superl* **classiest**) adj *inf* [hotel, restaurant] chic (*inv*), de luxe (*inv*), classe (*inv*) ; [person] chic (*inv*), qui a de la classe, classe (*inv*).

clatter ['klætər] ◆ n [rattle] cliquetis *m* ; [commotion] fracas *m*. ◆ vi [typewriter] cliqueter ; [dishes] s'entrechoquer bruyamment ; [falling object] faire du bruit.

clause [klɔːz] n **1.** GRAM proposition *f* **2.** LAW clause *f*, disposition *f*.

claustrophobia [,klɔːstrə'fəʊbjə] n claustrophobie *f*.

claustrophobic [,klɔːstrə'fəʊbɪk] adj [person] claustrophobe ; [feeling] de claustrophobie ; [place, situation] où l'on se sent claustrophobe.

claw [klɔː] ◆ n [of bird, cat, dog] griffe *f* ; [of bird of prey] serre *f* ; [of crab, lobster] pince *f* ; inf [hand] patte *f* ▶ **to get one's claws into sb** inf mettre le grappin sur qqn. ◆ vt [scratch] griffer ; [grip] agripper or serrer (avec ses griffes) ; [tear] déchirer (avec ses griffes) **/ he clawed his way to the top** *fig* il a travaillé dur pour arriver en haut de l'échelle.

clay [kleɪ] ◆ n [gen] argile *f*, (terre *f*) glaise *f* ; [for pottery] argile *f*. ◆ comp [brick, pot] en argile, en terre ▶ **clay court** SPORT court *m* en terre battue.

clay pigeon n **1.** *lit* pigeon *m* d'argile or de ball-trap ▶ **clay pigeon shooting** ball-trap *m* **2.** US *inf & fig* [sitting duck] cible *f* facile.

clean [kliːn] ◆ adj **1.** [free from dirt -hands, shirt, room] propre, net ; [-animal, person] propre ; [-piece of paper] vierge, blanc (blanche) **/ my hands are clean a)** *lit* j'ai les mains propres, mes mains sont propres **b)** *fig* j'ai la conscience nette or tranquille ▶ **he made a clean breast of it** il a dit tout ce qu'il avait sur la conscience, il a déchargé sa conscience ▶ **to make a clean sweep** faire table rase **2.** [free from impurities -air] pur, frais (fraîche) ; [-water] pur, clair ; [-sound] net, clair **3.** [morally pure -conscience] net, tranquille ; [-joke] qui n'a rien de choquant **4.** [honourable -fight] loyal ; [-reputation] net, sans tache **/ to have a clean record** avoir un casier (judiciaire) vierge **5.** [smooth -curve, line] bien dessiné, net ; [-shape] élégant ; [-cut] franc

(franche) ▶ **to make a clean break** couper net **/ we made a clean break with the past** nous avons rompu avec le passé, nous avons tourné la page **6.** inf ▶ **I'm clean a)** [innocent] je n'ai rien à me reprocher, je n'ai rien fait **b)** [without incriminating material] je n'ai rien sur moi **c)** [unarmed] je n'ai pas d'arme, je ne suis pas armé **d)** [not drinking] je ne bois plus **e)** [not taking drugs] je suis clean, je ne me drogue plus. ◆ vt [room, cooker] nettoyer ; [clothing] laver **/ to clean one's teeth** se laver or se brosser les dents. ◆ vi [person] nettoyer **/ she spends her day cleaning** elle passe sa journée à faire le ménage. ◆ adv inf **1.** [completely] carrément **/ the handle broke clean off** l'anse a cassé net **2.** PHR ▶ **to come clean about sthg** révéler qqch. ◆ n nettoyage *m*. ❖ **clean out** vt sep **1.** [tidy] nettoyer à fond ; [empty] vider **2.** inf [person] nettoyer, plumer ; [house] vider. ❖ **clean up** ◆ vt sep **1.** [make clean] nettoyer à fond **2.** [make orderly -cupboard, room] ranger ; [-affairs, papers] ranger, mettre de l'ordre dans. ◆ vi **1.** [tidy room] nettoyer ; [tidy cupboard, desk] ranger ; [wash oneself] faire un brin de toilette **2.** inf [make profit] gagner gros.

clean-burning adj [fuel] *brûlant sans résidu de combustible*.

clean-cut adj [person] propre (sur soi), soigné.

Clean Development Mechanism pr n ECOL Mécanisme *m* de Développement Propre.

cleaner ['kliːnər] n **1.** [cleaning lady] femme *f* de ménage ; [man] (ouvrier *m*) nettoyeur *m* **2.** [product -gen] produit *m* d'entretien ; [-stain remover] détachant *m* ; [device] appareil *m* de nettoyage **3.** [dry cleaner] teinturier *m*, -ère *f*.

cleaning ['kliːnɪŋ] n [activity -gen] nettoyage *m* ; [-household] ménage *m*.

cleaning fluid n produit *m* nettoyant.

cleaning lady, cleaning woman n femme *f* de ménage.

cleanliness ['klenlɪnɪs] n propreté *f*.

clean-living adj qui mène une vie saine.

cleanly[1] ['kliːnlɪ] adv **1.** [smoothly] net **2.** [fight, play] loyalement.

cleanly[2] ['klenlɪ] (*compar* **cleanlier**, *superl* **cleanliest**) adj propre.

cleanness ['kliːnnɪs] n propreté *f*.

clean room n [in factory, laboratory] salle *f* propre, salle *f* blanche.

cleanse [klenz] vt **1.** [clean -gen] nettoyer ; [-with water] laver ; MED [blood] dépurer ; [wound] nettoyer **2.** *fig* [purify] purifier.

cleanser ['klenzər] n **1.** [detergent] détergent *m*, détersif *m* **2.** [for skin] (lait *m*) démaquillant *m*.

clean-shaven adj [face, man] rasé de près.

cleansing ['klenzɪŋ] ◆ n nettoyage *m*. ◆ adj [lotion] démaquillant ; [power, property] de nettoyage.

cleantech ['kliːntek] n technologies *fpl* propres.

cleanup ['kliːnʌp] n nettoyage *m* à fond.

clear [klɪər] ◆ adj **1.** [transparent -glass, plastic] transparent ; [-water] clair, limpide ; [-river] limpide, transparent ; [-air] pur ▶ **clear honey** miel liquide ▶ **clear soup a)** [plain stock] bouillon *m* **b)** [with meat] consommé *m* **2.** [cloudless -sky] clair, dégagé ; [-weather] clair, beau (*before vowel or silent 'h' bel, f belle*) **/ on a clear day** par temps clair **3.** [not dull -colour] vif ; [-light] éclatant, radieux ; [untainted -complexion, skin] clair, frais (fraîche) **4.** [distinct -outline] net, précis ; [-photograph] net ; [-sound] clair, distinct ; [-voice] clair, argentin **/ make sure your writing is clear** efforcez-vous d'écrire correctement or proprement **5.** [not confused -mind] pénétrant, lucide ; [-thinking, argument, style] clair ; [-explanation, report] clair, intelligible ;

[-instructions] clair, explicite ; [-message] en clair / *he is quite clear about what has to be done* il sait parfaitement ce qu'il y a à faire / *now let's get this clear — I want no nonsense* comprenons-nous bien or soyons clairs — je ne supporterai pas de sottises **6.** [obvious, unmistakable] évident, clair / *it is a clear case of favouritism* c'est manifestement du favoritisme, c'est un cas de favoritisme manifeste / *she made it quite clear to them what she wanted* elle leur a bien fait comprendre ce qu'elle voulait / *it is important to make clear exactly what our aims are* il est important de bien préciser quels sont nos objectifs / *do I make myself clear?* est-ce que je me fais bien comprendre ?, est-ce que c'est bien clair ? **7.** [free from doubt, certain] certain / *I want to be clear in my mind about it* je veux en avoir le cœur net **8.** [unqualified] net, sensible / *they won by a clear majority* ils ont gagné avec une large majorité **9.** [unobstructed, free - floor, path] libre, dégagé ; [-route] sans obstacles, sans danger ; [-view] dégagé / *the roads are clear of snow* les routes sont déblayées or déneigées ▶ *to be clear of sthg* être débarrassé de qqch **10.** [free from guilt] : *is your conscience clear?* as-tu la conscience tranquille ? **11.** [of time] libre / *his schedule is clear* il n'a rien de prévu sur son emploi du temps / *we have four clear days to finish* nous avons quatre jours pleins or entiers pour finir **12.** [net - money, wages] net / *a clear profit* un bénéfice net / *a clear loss* une perte sèche / *clear of taxes* net d'impôts. ◆ adv **1.** [distinctly] distinctement, nettement / *reading you loud and clear* RADIO je te reçois cinq sur cinq **2.** [out of the way] : *we pulled him clear of the wrecked car* / *of the water* nous l'avons sorti de la carcasse de la voiture / de l'eau ▶ **stand clear!** écartez-vous ! **3.** [all the way] entièrement, complètement / *the thieves got clear away* les voleurs ont disparu sans laisser de trace. ◆ n ▶ **to be in the clear a)** [out of danger] être hors de danger **b)** [out of trouble] être tiré d'affaire **c)** [above suspicion] être au-dessus de tout soupçon **d)** [no longer suspected] être blanchi (de tout soupçon). ◆ vt **1.** [remove - object] débarrasser, enlever / *she cleared the plates from the table* elle a débarrassé la table ; [obstacle] écarter **2.** [remove obstruction from - gen] débarrasser ; [-entrance, road] dégager, déblayer ; [-forest, land] défricher ; [-pipe] déboucher / *to clear one's throat* s'éclaircir la gorge or la voix / *clear the room!* évacuez la salle ! / *the police cleared the way for the procession* la police a ouvert un passage au cortège / *the talks cleared the way for a ceasefire* fig les pourparlers ont préparé le terrain or ont ouvert la voie pour un cessez-le-feu **3.** [clarify - skin] purifier ; [-complexion] éclaircir / *his apology cleared the air* fig ses excuses ont détendu l'atmosphère / *I went for a walk to clear my head* **a)** [from hangover] j'ai fait un tour pour m'éclaircir les idées **b)** [from confusion] j'ai fait un tour pour me rafraîchir les idées or pour me remettre les idées en place **4.** [authorize] autoriser, approuver / *you'll have to clear it with the boss* il faut demander l'autorisation or l'accord or le feu vert du patron **5.** [vindicate, find innocent] innocenter, disculper ▶ **to clear sb of a charge** disculper qqn d'une accusation / *give him a chance to clear himself* donnez-lui la possibilité de se justifier or de prouver son innocence **6.** [avoid touching] franchir ; [obstacle] éviter / *the horse cleared the fence with ease* le cheval a sauté sans peine par-dessus or a franchi sans peine la barrière **7.** [settle - account] liquider, solder ; [-cheque] compenser ; [-debt] s'acquitter de ; [-dues] acquitter **8.** [pass through] : *to clear customs* passer la douane **9.** SPORT ▶ **to clear the ball** dégager le ballon. ◆ vi **1.** [weather] s'éclaircir, se lever ; [sky] se dégager ; [fog] se lever, se dissiper **2.** [expression] s'éclairer. ❖ **clear away** ◆ vt sep [remove] enlever, ôter / *we cleared away the dishes* nous avons débarrassé (la table) or desservi. ◆ vi **1.** [tidy up] débarrasser, desservir **2.** [disappear - fog, mist] se dissiper. ❖ **clear off** vi inf

filer ▶ **clear off!** fiche le camp ! ❖ **clear out** ◆ vt sep **1.** [tidy] nettoyer, ranger ; [empty - cupboard] vider ; [- room] débarrasser **2.** [throw out - rubbish, old clothes] jeter / *he cleared everything out of the house* il a fait le vide dans la maison. ◆ vi inf filer / *clear out (of here)!* dégage !, fiche le camp ! ❖ **clear up** ◆ vt sep **1.** [settle - problem] résoudre ; [-mystery] éclaircir, résoudre **2.** [tidy up] ranger, faire du rangement dans. ◆ vi **1.** [weather] s'éclaircir, se lever ; [fog, mist] se dissiper, se lever **2.** [illness] : *his cold is clearing up* son rhume tire à sa fin ; [spots] disparaître.

clearance ['klıərəns] n **1.** [removal - of buildings, litter] enlèvement m ; [- of obstacles] déblaiement m ; [- of people] évacuation f ; COMM [of merchandise] liquidation f **2.** [space] jeu m, dégagement m **3.** [permission] autorisation f, permis m ; [from customs] dédouanement m **4.** BANK [of cheque] compensation f.

clearance sale n liquidation f, soldes mpl.

clear-cut adj [decision, situation] clair ; [difference] clair, net ; [opinion, plan] bien défini, précis.

cleared cheque n chèque m compensé.

clear-headed adj [person] lucide, perspicace ; [decision] lucide, rationnel.

clearing ['klıərıŋ] n **1.** [in forest] clairière f ; [in clouds] éclaircie f **2.** [of land] déblaiement m, défrichement m ; [of passage] dégagement m, déblaiement m ; [of pipe] débouchage m **3.** BANK [of cheque] compensation f ; [of account] liquidation f, solde m **4.** [of debt] acquittement m.

clearing bank n ⅢⅢ banque f de dépôt.

clearing house n **1.** BANK chambre f de compensation **2.** [for information, materials] bureau m central.

clearing-up n nettoyage m.

clearly ['klıəlı] adv **1.** [distinctly - see, understand] clairement, bien ; [-hear, speak] distinctement ; [-describe, explain] clairement, précisément ; [-think] clairement, lucidement **2.** [obviously] manifestement, à l'évidence.

clearout ['klıəraʊt] n ⅢⅢ inf rangement m.

clear-sighted adj fig [person] perspicace, lucide ; [decision, plan] réaliste.

clearway ['klıəweı] n ⅢⅢ AUTO route f à stationnement interdit.

cleavage ['kli:vıdʒ] n **1.** [of woman] décolleté m **2.** BIOL [of cell] division f ; CHEM & GEOL clivage m.

cleaver ['kli:vər] n couperet m.

clef [klef] n MUS clef f, clé f.

cleft [kleft] ◆ pt & pp arch ⟶ **cleave.** ◆ n [opening - gen] fissure f ; [- in rock] fissure f, crevasse f.

cleft palate n palais m fendu.

clematis ['klemətıs] n clématite f.

clemency ['klemənsı] n [mercy] clémence f, magnanimité f.

clement ['klemənt] adj **1.** [person] clément, magnanime **2.** [weather] doux (douce), clément.

clementine ['kleməntaın] n clémentine f.

clench [klentʃ] vt [fist, jaw, buttocks] serrer ; [grasp firmly] empoigner, agripper ; [hold tightly] serrer.

clergy ['klɜ:dʒı] n (membres mpl du) clergé m.

clergyman ['klɜ:dʒımən] (pl **clergymen** [-mən]) n [gen] ecclésiastique m ; [Catholic] curé m, prêtre m ; [Protestant] pasteur m.

clergywoman ['klɜ:dʒı,wʊmən] (pl **clergywomen** [-,wımın]) n (femme f) pasteur m.

cleric ['klerık] n ecclésiastique m.

clerical ['klerıkl] adj [office - staff, work] de bureau ; [-position] de commis / *to do clerical work* travailler dans un bureau.

clerk [UK klɑːk US klɜːrk] n **1.** [in office] employé m, -e f (de bureau), commis m ; [in bank] employé m, -e f de banque **2.** US [sales person] vendeur m, -euse f **3.** US [receptionist] réceptionniste mf.

clever ['klevər] adj **1.** [intelligent] intelligent, astucieux **2.** [skilful - person] adroit, habile ; [- work] bien fait ▸ **to be clever at sthg / at doing sthg** être doué pour qqch / pour faire qqch **3.** [cunning] malin (maligne), astucieux ; pej rusé **4.** [ingenious - book] intelligemment or bien écrit, ingénieux ; [- film] ingénieux, intelligent ; [- idea, plan] ingénieux, astucieux ; [- story] fin, astucieux.

cleverly ['klevəlɪ] adv [intelligently] intelligemment, astucieusement ; [skilfully] adroitement, habilement ; [cunningly] avec ruse ; [ingeniously] ingénieusement.

cleverness ['klevənɪs] n [intelligence] intelligence f, astuce f ; [skilfulness] habileté f, adresse f ; [cunning] ruse f ; [ingenuity] ingéniosité f.

cliché [UK 'kliːʃeɪ US kliːˈʃeɪ] n [idea] cliché m ; [phrase] cliché m, lieu commun m, banalité f.

clichéd [UK 'kliːʃeɪd US kliːˈʃeɪd] adj banal.

click [klɪk] ◆ n **1.** [sound] petit bruit m sec ; [of tongue] claquement m ; LING clic m, click m **2.** COMPUT clic m ▸ **at the click of a mouse** d'un clic de souris. ◆ vi **1.** [make sound] faire un bruit sec **2.** inf [become clear] : it suddenly clicked tout à coup ça a fait « tilt » **3.** inf [be a success] bien marcher ; [get on well] : they clicked from the beginning ils se sont bien entendus dès le début, ça a tout de suite collé entre eux **4.** COMPUT cliquer.

clickable ['klɪkəbl] adj COMPUT cliquable ▸ **clickable image** image f cliquable.

clicking ['klɪkɪŋ] n cliquetis m.

click-through adj ▸ **click-through licence** or **agreement** contrat m de licence en ligne.

clickwrap ['klɪkræp] adj ▸ **clickwrap licence** or **agreement** contrat m de licence en ligne.

client ['klaɪənt] n client m, -e f.

client account n compte m client.

client base n clientèle f.

clientele [ˌkliːənˈtel] n COMM clientèle f ; THEAT clientèle, public m (habituel).

clientelism [klaɪˈentɪlɪzəm] n fml POL clientélisme m.

client-focused adj orienté client.

client-server n COMPUT client-serveur m.

cliff [klɪf] n escarpement m ; [on coast] falaise f ; [in mountaineering] à-pic m inv.

cliffhanger ['klɪfˌhæŋər] n inf [situation in film, story] situation f à suspense ; [moment of suspense] moment m d'angoisse.

climactic [klaɪˈmæktɪk] adj à son apogée, à son point culminant.

climate ['klaɪmɪt] n METEOR climat m ; fig climat m, ambiance f / the climate of opinion (les courants mpl de) l'opinion f.

climate canary n bio-indicateur m du climat.

climate change n changement m climatique.

climate control n US AUTO climatiseur m.

climate refugee n réfugié m, -e f climatique.

climatic [klaɪˈmætɪk] adj climatique.

climatologist [ˌklaɪməˈtɒlədʒɪst] n climatologue mf.

climax ['klaɪmæks] ◆ n **1.** [culmination] apogée m, point m culminant / this brought matters to a climax ceci a porté l'affaire à son point culminant **2.** [sexual] orgasme m. ◆ vi **1.** [film, story] atteindre le or son point culminant **2.** [sexually] atteindre l'orgasme.

climb [klaɪm] ◆ vi **1.** [road, sun] monter ; [plane] monter, prendre de l'altitude ; [prices] monter, augmenter ; [plant] grimper **2.** [person] grimper / to climb over an obstacle escalader un obstacle / to climb to power se hisser au pouvoir **3.** SPORT faire de l'escalade ; [on rocks] varapper. ◆ vt [ascend - stairs, steps] monter, grimper ; [- hill] escalader, grimper ; [- mountain] gravir, faire l'ascension de ; [- cliff, wall] escalader ; [- ladder, tree] monter sur ; [- rope] monter à. ◆ n [of hill, slope] montée f, côte f ; [in mountaineering] ascension f, escalade f. ❖ **climb down** vi **1.** [descend] descendre ; [in mountaineering] descendre, effectuer une descente **2.** [back down] en rabattre, céder.

climbdown ['klaɪmdaʊn] n recul m.

climber ['klaɪmər] n **1.** [person] grimpeur m, -euse f ; [mountaineer] alpiniste mf ; [rock climber] varappeur m, -euse f **2.** [plant] plante f grimpante.

climbing ['klaɪmɪŋ] n **1.** [action] montée f, escalade f **2.** [mountaineering] alpinisme m ; [rock climbing] varappe f, escalade f.

climbing frame n UK cage f à poules (jeu).

climes [klaɪmz] pl n liter régions fpl, contrées fpl.

clinch [klɪntʃ] ◆ vt [settle - deal] conclure ; [- argument] régler, résoudre ; [- agreement] sceller. ◆ n **1.** BOX corps à corps m **2.** inf [embrace] étreinte f, enlacement m.

clincher ['klɪntʃər] n inf argument m irréfutable, argument m massue.

cling [klɪŋ] (pt & pp clung [klʌŋ]) vi **1.** [hold on tightly] s'accrocher, se cramponner / they clung to one another ils se sont enlacés, ils se sont cramponnés l'un à l'autre ; fig : to cling to a hope / to a belief / to the past se raccrocher à un espoir / une croyance / au passé **2.** [stick] adhérer, coller.

clingfilm ['klɪŋfɪlm] n UK film m alimentaire transparent.

clinging ['klɪŋɪŋ] adj [clothing] collant, qui moule le corps ; pej [person] importun.

clingy ['klɪŋɪ] (compar clingier, superl clingiest) adj [clothing] moulant ; pej [person] importun.

clinic ['klɪnɪk] n **1.** [part of hospital] service m **2.** [treatment session] consultation f **3.** UK [private hospital] clinique f **4.** [health centre] centre m médico-social or d'hygiène sociale.

clinical ['klɪnɪkl] adj **1.** MED [lecture, tests] clinique ▸ **clinical trials** tests mpl cliniques **2.** fig [attitude] froid, aseptisé.

clinically ['klɪnɪklɪ] adv **1.** MED cliniquement **2.** fig [act, speak] objectivement, froidement.

clink [klɪŋk] ◆ vt faire tinter or résonner / they clinked (their) glasses (together) ils ont trinqué. ◆ vi tinter, résonner. ◆ n [sound] tintement m (de verres).

clip [klɪp] (pt & pp clipped, cont clipping) ◆ vt **1.** [cut] couper (avec des ciseaux), rogner ; [hedge] tailler ; [animal] tondre / I clipped five seconds off my personal best j'ai amélioré mon record de cinq secondes **2.** UK [ticket] poinçonner **3.** [attach] attacher ; [papers] attacher (avec un trombone) ; [brooch] fixer **4.** inf [hit] frapper, cogner. ◆ n **1.** CIN, RADIO & TV [excerpt] court extrait m **2.** UK [from newspaper] coupure f **2.** [clasp] pince f ; [for paper] trombone m, pince f ; [for pipe] collier m, bague f **3.** [brooch] clip m ; [for hair] barrette f ; [for tie] fixe-cravate m **4.** inf [blow] gifle f, taloche f / he got a clip round the ear il s'est pris une taloche. ❖ **clip on** vt sep [document] attacher (avec un trombone) ; [brooch, earrings] mettre.

clipart n COMPUT clipart m.

clipboard ['klɪpbɔːd] n [writing board] écritoire f à pince, clipboard m.

clip-clop [-klɒp] (pt & pp clip-clopped, cont clip-clopping) ◆ n & onomat clip-clop m. ◆ vi faire clip-clop.

clip-on adj amovible ▶ **clip-on earrings** clips mpl (d'oreilles).

clipped [klɪpt] adj **1.** [speech, style] heurté, saccadé **2.** [hair] bien entretenu.

clippers ['klɪpəz] pl n [for nails] pince f à ongles ; [for hair] tondeuse f ; [for hedge] sécateur m à haie.

clipping ['klɪpɪŋ] n [small piece] petit bout m, rognure f ; [from newspaper] coupure f (de presse).

clique [kliːk] n pej clique f, coterie f.

cliquey ['kliːkɪ], **cliquish** ['kliːkɪʃ] adj pej exclusif, qui a l'esprit de clan.

clitoris ['klɪtərɪs] n clitoris m.

Cllr written abbr of **Councillor**.

cloak [kləʊk] ◆ n [cape] grande cape f. ◆ vt fig masquer, cacher.

cloak-and-dagger adj ▶ **a cloak-and-dagger story** un roman d'espionnage.

cloakroom ['kləʊkrʊm] n **1.** [for coats] vestiaire m ▶ **cloakroom attendant** préposé m, -e f au vestiaire **2.** UK euph [toilet - public] toilettes fpl ; [- in home] cabinets mpl.

clobber ['klɒbə] inf ◆ vt [hit] tabasser ; fig [defeat] battre à plate couture. ◆ n (U) UK effets mpl, barda m.

clock [klɒk] ◆ n **1.** [gen] horloge f ; [small] pendule f ▶ **to put a clock back / forward** retarder / avancer une horloge ; fig : they worked against or to beat the clock ils ont travaillé dur pour finir à temps / we worked round the clock nous avons travaillé 24 heures d'affilée **2.** inf AUTO [mileometer] ≃ compteur m kilométrique / a car with 30,000 miles on the clock une voiture qui a 30 000 miles au compteur. ◆ vt **1.** [measure time] enregistrer ; SPORT [runner] chronométrer / she's clocked five minutes for the mile elle court le mile en cinq minutes **2.** UK v inf [hit] flanquer un marron à. ◆ **clock in** vi [arrive] pointer (à l'arrivée). ◆ **clock off** vi pointer (à la sortie), dépointer. ◆ **clock on** vt insep = **clock in**. ◆ **clock out** vt insep = **clock off**. ◆ **clock up** vt sep [work] effectuer, accomplir ; [victory] remporter / she clocked up 300 miles AUTO elle a fait 300 miles au compteur.

clockface ['klɒkfeɪs] n cadran m.

clock speed n COMPUT vitesse f d'horloge.

clockwise ['klɒkwaɪz] ◆ adv dans le sens des aiguilles d'une montre. ◆ adj : in a clockwise direction dans le sens des aiguilles d'une montre.

clockwork ['klɒkwɜːk] ◆ n [of clock, watch] mouvement m (d'horloge) ; [of toy] mécanisme m, rouages mpl ▶ **to go** or **to run like clockwork** marcher comme sur des roulettes. ◆ adj mécanique.

clod [klɒd] n [of earth] motte f (de terre).

clog [klɒg] (pt & pp **clogged**, cont **clogging**) ◆ vt **1.** [pipe] boucher, encrasser ; [street] boucher, bloquer ; [wheel] bloquer **2.** fig [hinder] entraver, gêner. ◆ n [wooden] sabot m ; [leather] sabot m. ◆ **clog up** vt sep = **clog** (vt).

cloister ['klɔɪstə] n cloître m.

cloistered ['klɔɪstəd] adj fig [life] de reclus.

clone [kləʊn] ◆ n clone m. ◆ vt cloner.

cloning ['kləʊnɪŋ] n clonage m.

close[1] [kləʊs] (compar **closer**, superl **closest**) ◆ adj **1.** [near in space or time] : the library is close to the school la bibliothèque est près de l'école ▶ **in close proximity to sthg** dans le voisinage immédiat de or tout près de qqch / they're very close in age ils ont presque le même âge / we are close to an agreement nous sommes presque arrivés à un accord / to be close to tears être au bord des larmes ▶ **to see sthg at close quarters** voir qqch de près ▶ **to give**

sb a close shave lit raser qqn de près ▶ **that was a close shave** or **thing** or US **call!** inf on l'a échappé belle !, on a eu chaud ! **2.** [in relationship] proche / they're very close (friends) ils sont très proches / a close relative un parent proche / he has close ties with Israel il a des rapports étroits avec Israël / sources close to the royal family des sources proches de la famille royale **3.** [continuous] : they stay in close contact ils restent en contact en permanence **4.** [thorough, careful] attentif, rigoureux / have a close look at these figures examinez ces chiffres de près / upon close examination après un examen détaillé or minutieux / keep a close eye on the kids surveillez les enfants de près **5.** [roughly similar] proche / he bears a close resemblance to his father il ressemble beaucoup à son père **6.** [compact - handwriting, print] serré ; [- grain] dense, compact **7.** UK [stuffy - room] mal aéré, qui manque de ventilation or d'air / it's terribly close today il fait très lourd aujourd'hui. ◆ adv **1.** [near] près / I live close to the river j'habite près de la rivière / did you win? — no, we didn't even come close avez-vous gagné ? — non, loin de là / she lives close by elle habite tout près / I looked at it close to or up je l'ai regardé de près / close together serrés les uns contre les autres / sit closer together! serrez-vous ! **2.** [tight] étroitement, de près / he held me close il m'a serré dans ses bras. ◆ **close to** prep phr [almost, nearly] presque.

close[2] [kləʊz] ◆ vt **1.** [shut - door, window, shop, book] fermer ; fig ▶ **to close one's eyes to sthg** fermer les yeux sur qqch ▶ **to close one's mind to sthg** refuser de penser à qqch / she closed her mind to anything new elle s'est fermée à tout ce qui était neuf **2.** [opening, bottle] fermer, boucher **3.** [conclude] clore, mettre fin à / she closed the conference with a rallying call to the party faithful elle termina la conférence en lançant un appel de solidarité aux fidèles du parti **4.** COMM & FIN [account] arrêter, clore **5.** [move closer together] serrer, rapprocher / the party closed ranks behind their leader fig le parti a serré les rangs derrière le leader. ◆ vi **1.** [shut - gate, window] fermer, se fermer ; [- shop] fermer ; [- cinema, theatre] faire relâche / this window doesn't close properly cette fenêtre ne ferme pas bien or ferme mal **2.** [meeting] se terminer, prendre fin ; [speaker] terminer, finir. ◆ n fin f, conclusion f ; [of day] tombée f / the year drew to a close l'année s'acheva / it's time to draw the meeting to a close il est temps de mettre fin à cette réunion. ◆ **close down** ◆ vi [business, factory] fermer. ◆ vt sep [business, factory] fermer. ◆ **close in** vi **1.** [approach] approcher, se rapprocher ▶ **to close in on** or **upon** se rapprocher de **2.** [evening, night] approcher, descendre ; [day] raccourcir ; [darkness, fog] descendre. ◆ **close off** vt sep isoler, fermer. ◆ **close up** ◆ vt sep fermer ; [wound] refermer, recoudre. ◆ vi [wound] se refermer.

close-cropped [ˌkləʊs'krɒpt] adj [hair] (coupé) ras ; [grass] ras.

closed [kləʊzd] adj [shut - shop, museum, etc.] fermé ; [- eyes] fermé, clos ; [- opening, pipe] obturé, bouché ; [- road] barré ; [- economy, mind] fermé ▶ **to do sthg behind closed doors** faire qqch en cachette ▶ **a closed book** : economics is a closed book to me je ne comprends rien à l'économie.

closed circuit television n télévision f en circuit fermé.

closedown ['kləʊzdaʊn] n [of shop] fermeture f (définitive).

closed shop n **1.** [practice] monopole m d'embauche **2.** [establishment] entreprise dans laquelle le monopole d'embauche est pratiqué.

close-grained ['kləʊs-] adj [wood] à grain fin or serré.

close-knit [kləʊs-] adj fig [community, family] très uni.

closely ['kləʊslɪ] adv **1.** [near] de près ; [tightly] en serrant fort **2.** [carefully - watch] de près ; [-study] minutieusement, de près ; [-listen] attentivement **3.** [directly] : *closely connected with sthg* étroitement lié à qqch **4.** [evenly] : *closely contested elections* élections très serrées or très disputées.

closeness ['kləʊsnɪs] n **1.** [nearness] proximité f **2.** [intimacy - of relationship, friendship, family] intimité f.

closeout ['kləʊzaʊt] n US liquidation f.

close-range [kləʊs-] adj à courte portée.

close-run ['kləʊs-] adj = **close** (adj).

close season [kləʊs-] n UK HUNT fermeture f de la chasse ; FISHING fermeture de la pêche ; FOOT intersaison f.

closet ['klɒzɪt] ◆ n **1.** US [cupboard] placard m, armoire f ; [for hanging clothes] penderie f **2.** fig ▶ **to come out of the closet a)** [gen] sortir de l'anonymat **b)** [homosexual] ne plus cacher son homosexualité, faire son coming out **3.** [small room] cabinet m. ◆ comp secret (secrète) / *she's a closet gambler* elle n'ose pas avouer qu'elle joue. ◆ vt enfermer (*pour discuter*) ▶ **to be closeted with sb** être en tête à tête avec qqn.

closeted ['klɒzɪtɪd] adj [homosexual] dans le placard.

closetful ['klɒzɪt,fʊl] n : *a closetful of dresses* une armoire pleine de robes.

close-up [kləʊs-] ◆ n [photograph] gros plan m ; [programme] portrait m, portrait-interview m. ◆ adj [shot, photograph, picture] en gros plan.

closing ['kləʊzɪŋ] ◆ n [of shop] fermeture f ; [of meeting] clôture f ; ST. EX clôture f. ◆ adj **1.** [concluding] final, dernier ▶ **closing remarks** observations finales ▶ **closing speech** discours m de clôture **2.** [last] de fermeture ▶ **closing date a)** [for applications] date f limite de dépôt **b)** [for project] date f de réalisation (*d'une opération*) **3.** ST. EX ▶ **closing price** cours m à la clôture.

closing-down sale, closing-out sale US n liquidation f.

closing time n heure f de fermeture.

closure ['kləʊʒər] n [gen] fermeture f ; [of factory, shop] fermeture f définitive.

clot [klɒt] (*pt & pp* **clotted**, *cont* **clotting**) ◆ vt cailler, coaguler. ◆ vi (se) cailler, (se) coaguler. ◆ n **1.** [of blood] caillot m ; [of milk] caillot m, grumeau m / *a clot on the lung* / *on the brain* une embolie pulmonaire / cérébrale **2.** UK inf [fool] cruche f.

cloth [klɒθ] ◆ n **1.** [material] tissu m, étoffe f ; NAUT [sail] toile f, voile f ; [for bookbinding] toile f **2.** [for cleaning] chiffon m, linge m ; [tablecloth] nappe f. ◆ comp [clothing] de or en tissu, de or en étoffe.

clothe [kləʊð] (*pt & pp* **clothed** or (*literary*) **clad** [klæd]) vt habiller, vêtir ; *fig* revêtir, couvrir.

cloth-eared adj UK inf dur de la feuille, sourdingue.

clothes [kləʊðz] pl n [garments] vêtements mpl, habits mpl / *to put one's clothes on* s'habiller / *to take one's clothes off* se déshabiller.

clothes basket n panier m à linge.

clothes brush n brosse f à habits.

clothes hanger n cintre m.

clotheshorse ['kləʊðhɔːs] (*pl* [-hɔːsɪz]) n [for laundry] séchoir m à linge.

clothesline ['kləʊðzlaɪn] n corde f à linge.

clothes peg UK, **clothespin** US ['kləʊðzpɪn] n pince f à linge.

clothes rack n US séchoir m.

clothing ['kləʊðɪŋ] n (U) [garments] vêtements mpl, habits mpl / *an article of clothing* un vêtement.

clotted cream ['klɒtɪd-] n crème fraîche très épaisse typique du sud-ouest de l'Angleterre.

cloud [klaʊd] ◆ n METEOR nuage m, nuée f *liter* ▶ **he resigned under a cloud a)** [of suspicion] en butte aux soupçons, il a dû démissionner **b)** [in disgrace] tombé en disgrâce, il a dû démissionner ▶ **to be on cloud nine** être aux anges or au septième ciel ▶ **to have one's head in the clouds** être dans les nuages or la lune ▶ **every cloud has a silver lining** *prov* à quelque chose malheur est bon *prov*. ◆ vt **1.** [make hazy - mirror] embuer ; [-liquid] rendre trouble **2.** [confuse] obscurcir / *don't cloud the issue* ne brouillez pas les cartes **3.** [spoil - career, future] assombrir ; [-reputation] ternir. ◆ vi **1.** [sky] se couvrir (de nuages), s'obscurcir **2.** [face] s'assombrir. ❖ **cloud over** vi = **cloud** (vi).

cloudburst ['klaʊdbɜːst] n grosse averse f.

cloud computing n cloud computing m.

cloud-cuckoo-land n UK inf : *they are living in cloud-cuckoo-land* ils n'ont pas les pieds sur terre.

cloudless ['klaʊdlɪs] adj [sky] sans nuages ; fig [days, future] sans nuages, serein.

cloudy ['klaʊdɪ] (*compar* **cloudier**, *superl* **cloudiest**) adj **1.** METEOR nuageux, couvert **2.** [liquid] trouble ; [mirror] embué ; [gem] taché, nuageux.

clout [klaʊt] inf ◆ n **1.** [blow] coup m ; [with fist] coup m de poing **2.** fig [influence] influence f, poids m ▶ **to have** or **to carry a lot of clout** avoir le bras long. ◆ vt frapper, cogner ; [with fist] donner un coup de poing à, filer une taloche à.

clove [kləʊv] ◆ pt ⟶ **cleave**. ◆ n **1.** [spice] clou m de girofle ; [tree] giroflier m **2.** [of garlic] gousse f.

clover ['kləʊvər] n trèfle m ▶ **to be in clover** fig être comme un coq en pâte.

cloverleaf ['kləʊvəliːf] (*pl* **cloverleaves** [-liːvz]) n BOT feuille f de trèfle.

clown [klaʊn] ◆ n [entertainer] clown m ; fig [fool] pitre m, imbécile mf. ◆ vi [joke] faire le clown ; [act foolishly] faire le pitre or l'imbécile. ❖ **clown about** UK, **clown around** vi = **clown** (vi).

clown fish n poisson-clown m.

cloying ['klɔɪɪŋ] adj écœurant.

cloyingly ['klɔɪɪŋlɪ] adv ▶ **cloyingly sentimental** d'une sentimentalité mièvre.

club [klʌb] (*pt & pp* **clubbed**, *cont* **clubbing**) ◆ n **1.** [association] club m, cercle m ; [nightclub] boîte f de nuit ▶ **a tennis club** un club de tennis ▶ **join the club!** *hum* bienvenue au club !, vous n'êtes pas le seul ! **2.** [weapon] matraque f, massue f **3.** [golf club] club m (de golf) **4.** CARDS trèfle m. ◆ vt matraquer, frapper avec une massue. ❖ **club together** vi [share cost] se cotiser.

Club

Les « clubs » britanniques, aussi appelés **gentlemen's clubs**, sont des lieux de rencontre et de détente très sélectifs, traditionnellement fermés aux femmes ; ils jouaient autrefois un rôle important dans la vie sociale des milieux aisés en Grande-Bretagne.

clubbing ['klʌbɪŋ] n sorties fpl en boîte, clubbing m.

club car n US RAIL wagon-restaurant m.

club class n classe f club.

clubhouse ['klʌbhaʊs] (*pl* [-haʊzɪz]) n club m.

club sandwich n 🇺🇸 sandwich *m* mixte *(à trois étages)*, club-sandwich *m*.

cluck [klʌk] ◆ vi [hen, person] glousser. ◆ n [of hen] gloussement *m* ; [of person - in pleasure] gloussement *m* ; [- in disapproval] claquement *m* de langue.

clue [kluː] n [gen] indice *m*, indication *f* ; [in crosswords] définition *f* ⧸ *give me a clue* mettez-moi sur la piste ⧸ *where's John?* — *I haven't a clue!* où est John ? — je n'en ai pas la moindre idée or je n'en ai aucune idée !

clued-up [kluːd-] adj *inf* informé.

clueless ['kluːlɪs] adj 🇺🇰 *inf* & *pej* qui ne sait rien de rien.

clump [klʌmp] ◆ n [cluster - of bushes] massif *m* ; [- of trees] bouquet *m* ; [- of hair, grass] touffe *f*. ◆ vi [walk] ▸ **to clump (about** or **around)** marcher d'un pas lourd.

clumsily ['klʌmzɪlɪ] adv [awkwardly] maladroitement ; [tactlessly] sans tact.

clumsiness ['klʌmzɪnɪs] n [lack of coordination] maladresse *f*, gaucherie *f*.

clumsy ['klʌmzɪ] adj [uncoordinated - person] maladroit, gauche.

clung [klʌŋ] pt & pp ⟶ **cling**.

clunk [klʌŋk] ◆ n [sound] bruit *m* sourd. ◆ vi faire un bruit sourd.

clunky ['klʌŋkɪ] adj [shoes] gros (grosse) ; [furniture] encombrant ; [user interface] lourd.

cluster ['klʌstər] ◆ n **1.** [of fruit] grappe *f* ; [of dates] régime *m* ; [of flowers] touffe *f* ; [of trees] bouquet *m* ; [of stars] amas *m* ; [of diamonds] entourage *m* **2.** [group - of houses] groupe *m* ; [- of people] rassemblement *m*, groupe *m* ; [- of bees] essaim *m*. ◆ vi [people] se grouper.

cluster bomb n bombe *f* à fragmentation.

clusterfuck ['klʌstəfʌk] n 🇺🇸 *vulg* : *it was a complete clusterfuck* ça a complètement merdé ⧸ *we're in the middle of an economic clusterfuck* on est en plein merdier or bordel sur le plan économique.

cluster headache n migraine *f* ophtalmique.

cluster sampling n échantillonnage *m* aréolaire or par grappes.

clutch [klʌtʃ] ◆ vt **1.** [hold tightly] serrer fortement, étreindre **2.** [seize] empoigner, se saisir de. ◆ vi ▸ **to clutch at sthg a)** *lit* se cramponner à qqch, s'agripper à qqch **b)** *fig* se cramponner à qqch, se raccrocher à qqch. ◆ n **1.** [grasp] étreinte *f*, prise *f* **2.** AUTO [mechanism] embrayage *m* ; [pedal] pédale *f* d'embrayage ▸ **to let in the clutch** embrayer ▸ **to let out the clutch** débrayer **3.** [clutter of eggs] couvée *f* ; *fig* série *f*, ensemble *m*. ⧈ **clutches** pl n *fig* [control] influence *f* ▸ **to fall into sb's clutches** tomber dans les griffes de qqn.

clutch bag n [handbag] pochette *f* (sac à main).

clutter ['klʌtər] ◆ n **1.** [mess] désordre *m* **2.** [disordered objects] désordre *m*, fouillis *m*. ◆ vt ▸ **to clutter (up)** [room] mettre en désordre.

cluttered ['klʌtəd] adj encombré.

cm (written abbr of **centimetre**) cm.

CMI n abbr of **cell-mediated immunity**.

CMi MESSAGING written abbr of **call me**.

CMIIW MESSAGING written abbr of **correct me if I'm wrong**.

CMON MESSAGING written abbr of **come on**.

CND (abbr of **Campaign for Nuclear Disarmament**) pr n *en Grande-Bretagne, mouvement pour le désarmement nucléaire*.

CNG [siːenˈdʒiː] (abbr of **compressed natural gas**) n GNC.

CNS n abbr of **central nervous system**.

co- [kəu] in comp co- ▸ **co-worker** 🇺🇸 collègue *mf*.

c/o (written abbr of **care of**) a/s.

CO written abbr of **Colorado**.

Co. 1. [kəu] (written abbr of **company**) Cie **2.** written abbr of **county**.

coach [kəutʃ] ◆ n **1.** [tutor] répétiteur *m*, -trice *f* ; SPORT [trainer] entraîneur *m*, -euse *f* ; [ski instructor] moniteur *m*, -trice *f* **2.** [bus] car *m*, autocar *m* ; 🇺🇸 RAIL voiture *f*, wagon *m* ; [carriage] carrosse *m*. ◆ comp [driver] de car ; [tour, trip] en car. ◆ vt [tutor] donner des leçons particulières à ; SPORT entraîner.

coaching ['kəutʃɪŋ] n **1.** SCH leçons *fpl* particulières **2.** SPORT entraînement *m*.

coachload ['kəutʃləud] n : *a coachload of tourists* un autocar or car plein de touristes.

coach party n 🇺🇰 excursion *f* en car.

coagulate [kəuˈægjuleɪt] vi (se) coaguler.

coal [kəul] ◆ n [gen] charbon *m*. ◆ comp [bunker, cellar, chute] à charbon ; [depot, fire] de charbon ▸ **coal industry** industrie *f* houillère.

coalesce [ˌkəuəˈles] vi s'unir (en un groupe), se fondre (ensemble).

coalface ['kəulfeɪs] n front *m* de taille.

coalfield ['kəulfiːld] n bassin *m* houiller, gisement *m* de houille.

coal gas n gaz *m* de houille.

coalition [ˌkəuəˈlɪʃn] n coalition *f* ▸ **coalition government** POL gouvernement *m* de coalition.

coalman ['kəulmæn] (*pl* **coalmen** [-men]) n charbonnier *m*, marchand *m* de charbon.

coalmine ['kəulmaɪn] n mine *f* de charbon, houillère *f*.

coalminer ['kəul,maɪnər] n mineur *m*.

coalmining ['kəul,maɪnɪŋ] n charbonnage *m*.

coarse [kɔːs] adj **1.** [rough in texture] gros (grosse), grossier ; [skin] rude ; [hair] épais (épaisse) ; [salt] gros (grosse) **2.** [vulgar - person, behaviour, remark, joke] grossier, vulgaire ; [- laugh] gros (grosse), gras (grasse) ; [- accent] commun, vulgaire.

coarse-featured adj aux traits grossiers or épais.

coarse fishing n pêche *f* à la ligne en eau douce.

coarsely ['kɔːslɪ] adv **1.** [roughly] grossièrement ▸ **coarsely woven** de texture grossière **2.** [uncouthly - speak] vulgairement, grossièrement ; [- laugh] grassement ; [vulgarly] indécemment, crûment.

coarsen ['kɔːsn] ◆ vi **1.** [texture] devenir rude or grossier **2.** [person] devenir grossier or vulgaire ; [features] s'épaissir. ◆ vt **1.** [texture] rendre rude or grossier **2.** [person, speech] rendre grossier or vulgaire ; [features] épaissir.

coast [kəust] ◆ n côte *f* ▸ *the coast is clear* *inf* la voie est libre. ◆ vi [vehicle] avancer en roue libre ; NAUT caboter.

coastal ['kəustl] adj littoral, côtier.

coaster ['kəustər] n [protective mat - for glass] dessous *m* de verre ; [- for bottle] dessous *m* de bouteille ; [stand, tray] présentoir *m* à bouteilles.

coastguard ['kəustgɑːd] n **1.** [organization] ≃ gendarmerie *f* maritime **2.** 🇺🇰 [person] membre *m* de la gendarmerie maritime ; HIST garde-côte *m*.

coastline ['kəustlaɪn] n littoral *m*.

coast-to-coast adj [walk, route, race] d'un bout à l'autre du pays à l'autre ; [TV channel, network] national.

coat [kəut] ◆ n **1.** [overcoat] manteau *m* ; [man's overcoat] manteau *m*, pardessus *m* ; [jacket] veste *f* ;

HERALD ▶ **coat of arms** blason *m*, armoiries *fpl* **2.** [of animal] pelage *m*, poil *m* ; [of horse] robe *f* **3.** [covering - of dust, paint] couche *f*. ◆ vt **1.** [cover] couvrir, revêtir ; [with paint, varnish] enduire / *the shelves were coated with dust* les étagères étaient recouvertes de poussière **2.** CULIN : *to coat sthg with chocolate* enrober qqch de chocolat.

-coated ['kəʊtɪd] in comp ▶ **silver-coated** plaqué argent.

coat hanger n cintre *m*.

coating ['kəʊtɪŋ] n couche *f* ; [on pan] revêtement *m*.

coat tails pl n queue *f* de pie *(costume)* ▶ **to ride on sb's coat tails** profiter de l'influence or de la position de qqn.

coauthor [kəʊ'ɔːθər] n coauteur *m*.

coax [kəʊks] vt cajoler, enjôler.

coaxial [ˌkəʊ'æksɪəl] adj coaxial ▶ **coaxial cable** câble *m* coaxial.

cob [kɒb] n **1.** [horse] cob *m* **2.** [of corn] épi *m*.

cobalt ['kəʊbɔːlt] n cobalt *m*.

cobble ['kɒbl] n [stone] pavé *m*. ❖ **cobble together** vt sep bricoler, concocter.

cobbled ['kɒbld] adj pavé.

cobbler ['kɒblər] n [shoemender] cordonnier *m*. ❖ **cobblers** pl n 🇬🇧 v inf : *that's a load of cobblers!* c'est de la connerie !

cobblestone ['kɒblstəʊn] n pavé *m (rond)*.

COBOL ['kəʊbɒl] (abbr of **common ordinary business oriented language**) n COBOL *m*.

cobra ['kəʊbrə] n cobra *m*.

co-branding n alliance *f* de marques, co-branding *m*.

cobweb ['kɒbweb] n toile *f* d'araignée / *I'm going for a walk to clear away the cobwebs* or *to blow the cobwebs away* je vais faire un tour pour me rafraîchir les idées.

cobweb site n INTERNET site *m* périmé.

Coca-Cola® [ˌkəʊkə'kəʊlə] n Coca-Cola® *m* inv.

cocaine [kəʊ'keɪn] ◆ n cocaïne *f*. ◆ comp ▶ **cocaine addict** or **freak** inf cocaïnomane *mf*.

cock [kɒk] ◆ n **1.** [rooster] coq *m* ; [male bird] (oiseau *m*) mâle *m* **2.** vulg [penis] bite *f*. ◆ vt [raise] : *the dog cocked its ears* le chien a dressé les oreilles. ❖ **cock up** 🇬🇧 v inf vt sep saloper, faire foirer.

cock-a-doodle-doo [ˌkɒkədu:dl'du:] n & onomat cocorico.

cock-a-hoop adj inf fier comme Artaban.

cockamamie [ˌkɒkə'meɪmɪ] adj 🇺🇸 inf [ridiculous, incredible] abracadabrant / *what cockamamie story did he tell you this time?* qu'est-ce qu'il t'a encore raconté comme histoire abracadabrante ?

cock-and-bull story n histoire *f* à dormir debout.

cockatoo [ˌkɒkə'tu:] n cacatoès *m*.

cockerel ['kɒkrəl] n jeune coq *m*.

cocker spaniel ['kɒkə-] n cocker *m*.

cockeyed ['kɒkaɪd] adj inf **1.** [cross-eyed] qui louche **2.** [crooked] de travers **3.** [absurd - idea, plan] absurde ; [- story] qui ne tient pas debout.

cockfight ['kɒkfaɪt] n combat *m* de coqs.

cockiness ['kɒkɪnɪs] n impertinence *f*.

cockle ['kɒkl] n [shellfish] coque *f*.

Cockney ['kɒknɪ] ◆ n [person] cockney *mf (Londonien né dans le «East End»)*. ◆ adj cockney.

cockpit ['kɒkpɪt] n [of plane] cabine *f* de pilotage, cockpit *m* ; [of racing car] poste *m* du pilote ; [of yacht] cockpit *m*.

cockroach ['kɒkrəʊtʃ] n 🇬🇧 cafard *m*, blatte *f*.

cocksure [ˌkɒk'ʃɔːr] adj pej suffisant.

cocktail ['kɒkteɪl] n [mixed drink] cocktail *m (boisson)* ; [gen - mixture of things] mélange *m*, cocktail *m*.

cocktail bar n bar *m (dans un hôtel, un aéroport)*.

cocktail dress n robe *f* de cocktail.

cocktail lounge n bar *m (dans un hôtel, un aéroport)*.

cocktail party n cocktail *m (fête)*.

cocktail shaker n shaker *m*.

cocktail stick n pique *f* à apéritif.

cock-up 🇬🇧 v inf : *it was a cock-up* ça a foiré.

cocky ['kɒkɪ] *(compar* **cockier**, *superl* **cockiest**) adj inf suffisant, qui a du toupet.

cocoa ['kəʊkəʊ] n [powder, drink] cacao *m*.

coconut ['kəʊkənʌt] n noix *f* de coco.

cocoon [kə'ku:n] ◆ n cocon *m* ; fig : *wrapped in a cocoon of blankets* emmitouflé dans des couvertures. ◆ vt [wrap] envelopper avec soin ; [overprotect - child] couver.

cocooned [kə'ku:nd] adj enfermé, cloîtré.

cod [kɒd] *(pl* **cod** or **cods**) n [fish] morue *f* ; CULIN ▶ **cod fillet** filet *m* de cabillaud.

Cod [kɒd] pr n ▶ **Cape Cod** cap *m* Cod.

COD (abbr of **cash on delivery** or **collect on delivery**) adv 🇺🇸 ▶ **to send sthg COD** envoyer qqch contre remboursement.

code [kəʊd] n **1.** [cipher] code *m*, chiffre *m* ; BIOL & COMPUT code *m* **2.** [statement of rules] code *m* ▶ **code of conduct / of honour** code de conduite / de l'honneur ▶ **code of practice a)** [gen] déontologie *f* **b)** [rules] règlements *mpl* et usages *mpl* **3.** [dialling code] code *m*, indicatif *m*.

coded ['kəʊdɪd] adj **1.** [message] codé, chiffré **2.** COMPUT codé.

co-defendant n LAW coaccusé *m*, -e *f* ; [in civil law] codéfendeur *m*, -eresse *f*.

codeine ['kəʊdi:n] n codéine *f*.

code name n nom *m* de code.

codeword ['kəʊdwɜːd] n [password] mot *m* de passe ; [name] mot *m* codé.

cod-liver oil n huile *f* de foie de morue.

codswallop ['kɒdzˌwɒləp] n *(U)* 🇬🇧 inf bêtises *fpl*, âneries *fpl*.

co-ed [-'ed] adj abbr of **coeducational**.

co-edition n coédition *f*.

coeducation [ˌkəʊedʒʊ'keɪʃn] n éducation *f* mixte.

coeducational [ˌkəʊedʒʊ'keɪʃənl] adj mixte.

coefficient [ˌkəʊɪ'fɪʃnt] n coefficient *m*.

coeliac 🇬🇧, **celiac** 🇺🇸 ['si:lɪæk] adj cœliaque.

coerce [kəʊ'ɜːs] vt contraindre, forcer.

coercion [kəʊ'ɜːʃn] n *(U)* coercition *f*, contrainte *f*.

coexist [ˌkəʊɪg'zɪst] vi coexister.

coexistence [ˌkəʊɪg'zɪstəns] n coexistence *f*.

coexistent [ˌkəʊɪg'zɪstənt] adj coexistant.

co-factor n MED [risk factor] facteur *m* prédisposant.

C of C (abbr of **chamber of commerce**) n CCI *f*.

C of E (abbr of **Church of England**) pr n Église *f* anglicane.

coffee ['kɒfɪ] ◆ n [drink] café *m* ▶ **black coffee** café noir ▶ **white coffee** 🇬🇧, **coffee with cream** or **milk** 🇺🇸 **a)** [gen] café au lait **b)** [in café] café crème, crème *m*. ◆ comp [filter, jar, service] à café ; [ice cream, icing] au café ▶ **coffee cake a)** 🇬🇧 moka *m* **b)** 🇺🇸 gâteau *m (que l'on sert avec le café)*.

coffee bar n 🇬🇧 café *m*, cafétéria *f*.

coffee bean n grain *m* de café.

coffee break n pause-café f.

coffee cup n tasse f à café.

coffee grinder n moulin m à café.

coffee machine n [gen] cafetière f ; [in café] percola-teur m.

coffee-maker n cafetière f électrique.

coffee mill n moulin m à café.

coffee morning n 🇬🇧 rencontre amicale autour d'un café, destinée souvent à réunir de l'argent au profit d'œuvres de bienfaisance.

coffeepot ['kɒfɪpɒt] n cafetière f.

coffee shop n ≃ café-restaurant m.

coffee table n table f basse.

coffee-table book n ≃ beau livre m (destiné à être feuilleté plutôt que véritablement lu).

coffers ['kɒfəʳz] pl n [funds - of nation] coffres mpl ; [-of organization] caisses fpl, coffres mpl.

coffin ['kɒfɪn] n [box] cercueil m, bière f.

cog [kɒg] n [gearwheel] roue f dentée ; [tooth] dent f (d'engrenage) ▸ **you're only a (small) cog in the machine** or **the wheel** fig vous n'êtes qu'un simple rouage (dans or de la machine).

cogent ['kəʊdʒənt] adj fml [argument, reasons - convin-cing] convaincant, puissant ; [-pertinent] pertinent ; [-com-pelling] irrésistible.

cogitate ['kɒdʒɪteɪt] vi fml méditer, réfléchir.

cognac ['kɒnjæk] n cognac m.

cognitive ['kɒgnɪtɪv] adj cognitif.

cognoscenti [,kɒnjə'ʃenti:] pl n connaisseurs mpl.

cogwheel ['kɒgwi:l] n roue f dentée.

cohabit [,kəʊ'hæbɪt] vi cohabiter.

cohabitation [,kəʊhæbɪ'teɪʃn] n cohabitation f.

coherence [kəʊ'hɪərəns] n [logical consistency] cohé-rence f.

coherent [kəʊ'hɪərənt] adj [logical - person, structure] cohérent, logique ; [-story, speech] facile à suivre or com-prendre.

coherently [kəʊ'hɪərəntlɪ] adv de façon cohérente.

cohesion [kəʊ'hi:ʒn] n cohésion f.

cohesive [kəʊ'hi:sɪv] adj cohésif.

cohort ['kəʊhɔ:t] n **1.** [group, band] cohorte f **2.** [com-panion] comparse mf, compère m.

co-host ◆ n coprésentateur m, -trice f. ◆ vt coprésen-ter.

COI (abbr of **Central Office of Information**) pr n ser-vice public d'information en Grande-Bretagne.

coil [kɔɪl] ◆ n **1.** [spiral - of rope, wire] rouleau m ; [of hair] rouleau m ; [in bun] chignon m **2.** [single loop - of rope, wire] tour m ; [-of hair] boucle f ; [-of smoke, snake] anneau m **3.** MED [for contraception] stérilet m. ◆ vt [rope] enrouler ; [hair] enrouler, torsader / the snake coiled itself up le serpent s'est lové or enroulé.

coiled [kɔɪld] adj [rope] enroulé, en spirale ; [spring] en spirale ; [snake] lové.

coin [kɔɪn] ◆ n [item of metal currency] pièce f (de mon-naie) / a pound coin une pièce d'une livre. ◆ vt [word] fabriquer, inventer ▸ **to coin a phrase** hum si je puis m'expri-mer ainsi.

coinage ['kɔɪnɪdʒ] n [coins] monnaie f ; [currency system] système m monétaire.

coin-box n 🇬🇧 cabine f téléphonique (à pièces).

coincide [,kəʊɪn'saɪd] vi **1.** [in space, time] coïncider **2.** [correspond] coïncider, s'accorder.

coincidence [kəʊ'ɪnsɪdəns] n [accident] coïncidence f, hasard m.

coincidental [kəʊ,ɪnsɪ'dentl] adj [accidental] de coïnci-dence.

coincidentally [kəʊ,ɪnsɪ'dentəlɪ] adv par hasard.

coin-operated [-'ɒpə,reɪtɪd] adj automatique.

coitus ['kɔɪtəs] n coït m.

Coke® [kəʊk] n [cola] Coca® m.

coke [kəʊk] n **1.** [fuel] coke m **2.** drugs sl [cocaine] co-caïne f, coke f.

cokehead ['kəʊkhed] n inf ▸ **to be a cokehead** être accro à la coke.

Col. (written abbr of **colonel**) Col.

cola ['kəʊlə] n cola m.

COLA ['kəʊlə] comp 🇺🇸 abbr of **cost-of-living adjust-ment**.

colander ['kʌləndəʳ] n passoire f.

cold [kəʊld] ◆ adj **1.** [body, object, food, etc.] froid / she poured cold water on our plans fig sa réaction devant nos projets nous a refroidis ▸ **to get** or **to have cold feet** avoir la trouille **2.** [weather] froid **3.** [unfeeling] froid, indifférent ; [objective] froid, objectif ; [unfriendly] froid, peu aimable ▸ **to be cold towards sb** se montrer froid envers qqn / the play left me cold la pièce ne m'a fait ni chaud ni froid ▸ **in cold blood** de sang-froid **4.** [unconscious] : she was out cold elle était sans connaissance / he knocked him (out) cold il l'a mis KO. ◆ n **1.** METEOR froid m ▸ **to be left out in the cold** : the newcomer was left out in the cold personne ne s'est occupé du nouveau venu **2.** MED rhume m.

 froid or **froideur?**

Le froid is used to talk about cold tem-peratures: **les mois de grand froid** the col-dest months, while la **froideur** refers to the coldness of a person: **elle est d'une froideur glaciale** she's an incredibly cold person. The adjective **froid** refers to both.

cold-blooded adj **1.** [animal] à sang froid **2.** fig [un-feeling] insensible ; [ruthless] sans pitié / a cold-blooded murder un meurtre commis de sang-froid.

cold calling n [on phone] démarchage m téléphonique ; [at home] démarchage m à domicile.

cold cream n crème f de beauté, cold-cream m.

cold cuts pl n 🇺🇸 [gen] viandes fpl froides ; [on menu] assiette f anglaise.

cold-hearted adj sans pitié, insensible.

coldly ['kəʊldlɪ] adv froidement, avec froideur.

coldness ['kəʊldnɪs] n lit & fig froideur f.

cold shoulder n inf ▸ **to give sb the cold shoulder** snober qqn.

cold sore n bouton m de fièvre.

cold storage n conservation f par le froid ▸ **to put sthg into cold storage a)** [food] mettre qqch en chambre froide **b)** [furs] mettre qqch en garde **c)** fig mettre qqch en attente.

cold sweat n sueur f froide.

cold turkey n drugs sl [drugs withdrawal] manque m ▸ **to go cold turkey a)** [stop taking drugs] arrêter de se dro-guer d'un seul coup **b)** [suffer withdrawal symptoms] être en manque.

Cold War n guerre f froide.

coleslaw ['kəʊlslɔ:] n salade f de chou cru.

colic ['kɒlɪk] n *(U)* coliques *fpl.*

collaborate [kə'læbəreɪt] vi collaborer.

collaboration [kə,læbə'reɪʃn] n collaboration *f.*

collaborative [kə'læbərətɪv] adj conjugué, combiné.

collaborator [kə'læbəreɪtər] n collaborateur *m,* -trice *f.*

collage ['kɒlɑ:ʒ] n ART [picture, method] collage *m.*

collagen ['kɒlədʒən] n collagène *m.*

collapse [kə'læps] ◆ vi **1.** [building, roof] s'écrouler, s'effondrer ; [beam] fléchir **2.** *fig* [institution] s'effondrer, s'écrouler ; [government] tomber, chuter ; [plan] s'écrouler ; [market, defence] s'effondrer **3.** [person] s'écrouler, s'effondrer ; [health] se délabrer, se dégrader / *he collapsed and died* il a eu un malaise et il est mort / *to collapse with laughter* se tordre de rire **4.** [fold up] se plier. ◆ n **1.** [of building] écroulement *m,* effondrement *m* ; [of beam] rupture *f* **2.** *fig* [of institution, plan] effondrement *m,* écroulement *m* ; [of government] chute *f* ; [of market, defence] effondrement *m* **3.** [of person] écroulement *m,* effondrement *m* ; [of health] délabrement *m* ; [of lung] collapsus *m.*

collapsible [kə'læpsəbl] adj pliant.

collar ['kɒlər] ◆ n **1.** [on clothing] col *m* ; [detachable - for men] faux col *m* ; [- for women] col *m,* collerette *f* **2.** [for animal] collier *m* ; [neck of animal] collier *m* ; CULIN [beef] collier *m* ; [mutton, veal] collet *m.* ◆ vt *inf* [seize] prendre or saisir au collet, colleter ; [criminal] arrêter ; [detain] intercepter, harponner.

collarbone ['kɒləbəʊn] n clavicule *f.*

collard ['kɒləd] n [greens] chou *m* frisé.

collate [kə'leɪt] vt [information, texts] collationner.

collateral [kɒ'lætərəl] ◆ n FIN [guarantee] nantissement *m.* ◆ adj **1.** [secondary] subsidiaire, accessoire ; FIN subsidiaire ▶ **collateral security** nantissement *m* ; MIL ▶ **collateral damage** dommages *mpl* collatéraux **2.** [parallel] parallèle ; [fact] concomitant ; LAW & MED collatéral.

collateralize [kə'lætərəlaɪz] vt US FIN garantir.

collation [kə'leɪʃn] n [of text] collation *f.*

colleague ['kɒli:g] n [in office, school] collègue *mf* ; [professional, doctor, lawyer] confrère *m.*

collect[1] [kə'lekt] ◆ vt **1.** [gather - objects] ramasser ; [- information, documents] recueillir, rassembler ; [- evidence] rassembler ; [- people] réunir, rassembler ; [- wealth] accumuler, amasser ; *fig* ▶ **to collect o.s. a)** [calm down] se reprendre, se calmer **b)** [reflect] se recueillir / *let me collect my thoughts* laissez-moi réfléchir or me concentrer **2.** [as hobby] collectionner, faire collection de **3.** [money] recueillir ; [taxes, fines, dues] percevoir ; [pension, salary] toucher ; [homework] ramasser, relever **4.** UK [take away] ramasser **5.** [pick up - people] aller chercher, (passer) prendre. ◆ vi **1.** [accumulate - people] se rassembler, se réunir ; [- things] s'accumuler, s'amasser ; [- water, dirt] s'accumuler **2.** [raise money] ▶ **to collect for charity** faire la quête or quêter pour une œuvre de bienfaisance. ◆ adv US ▶ **to call collect** téléphoner en PCV. ◆ adj US ▶ **a collect call** un (appel en) PCV.

collect[2] ['kɒlekt] n [prayer] collecte *f.*

collectable [kə'lektəbl] ◆ adj [desirable to collectors] (très) recherché. ◆ n [collectors' item] objet *m* de collection.

collected [kə'lektɪd] adj [composed] maître de soi, calme.

collecting [kə'lektɪŋ] n collection *f.*

collection [kə'lekʃn] n **1.** *(U)* [collecting - objects] ramassage *m* ; [- information] rassemblement *m* ; [- wealth] accumulation *f* ; [- rent, money] encaissement *m* ; [- debts] recouvrement *m* ; [- taxes] perception *f* **2.** [things collected] collection *f* / *the fashion designers' winter collection* la collection d'hiver des couturiers **3.** [picking up - of rub-

bish] ramassage *m* ; UK [of mail] levée *f* / *your order is ready for collection* votre commande est prête **4.** [sum of money] collecte *f,* quête *f* ▶ **to take** or **to make a collection for** faire une quête or collecte pour ▶ **collection box a)** [gen] caisse *f* **b)** [in church] tronc *m* ▶ **collection plate** [in church] corbeille *f* **5.** [anthology] recueil *m.*

collective [kə'lektɪv] ◆ adj collectif. ◆ n coopérative *f.*

collective bargaining n négociations pour une convention collective.

collectively [kə'lektɪvlɪ] adv collectivement.

collective ownership n propriété *f* collective.

collector [kə'lektər] n [as a hobby] collectionneur *m,* -euse *f* ▶ **collector's item** pièce *f* de collection.

college ['kɒlɪdʒ] n **1.** [institution of higher education] établissement *m* d'enseignement supérieur ; [within university] collège *m* (dans les universités traditionnelles, communauté indépendante d'enseignants et d'étudiants) **2.** [for professional training] école *f* professionnelle, collège *m* technique / *college of art* école des Beaux-Arts / *college of music* conservatoire *m* de musique ▶ **College of Education** UK ≃ IUFM *m* (institut universitaire de formation des maîtres) ▶ **College of Further Education** UK ≃ institut *m* d'éducation permanente **3.** [organization] société *f,* académie *f.*

> ⚠ In the French education system, **un collège** is a secondary school for 11-16 year olds. The word **collège** never means a university.

collide [kə'laɪd] vi [crash] entrer en collision, se heurter ; NAUT aborder.

collie ['kɒlɪ] n colley *m.*

colliery ['kɒljərɪ] *(pl* **collieries)** n houillère *f,* mine *f* (de charbon).

collision [kə'lɪʒn] n [crash] collision *f,* choc *m* ; RAIL collision *f,* tamponnement *m* ; NAUT abordage *m* ▶ **to come into collision with sthg** entrer en collision avec or tamponner qqch.

colloquial [kə'ləʊkwɪəl] adj [language, expression] familier, parlé ; [style] familier.

colloquialism [kə'ləʊkwɪəlɪzm] n expression *f* familière.

collude [kə'lu:d] vi être de connivence or de mèche.

collusion [kə'lu:ʒn] n collusion *f* ▶ **to act in collusion with sb** agir de connivence avec qqn.

Cologne [kə'ləʊn] pr n Cologne.

Colombia [kə'lɒmbɪə] pr n Colombie *f.*

Colombian [kə'lɒmbɪən] ◆ n Colombien *m,* -enne *f.* ◆ adj colombien.

Colombo [kə'lʌmbəʊ] pr n Colombo.

colon ['kəʊlən] n **1.** [in punctuation] deux-points *m* **2.** ANAT côlon *m.*

colonel ['kɜ:nl] n colonel *m* / *Colonel Jones* le colonel Jones.

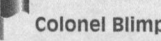

Colonel Blimp

Colonel Blimp est un personnage de vieil officier, réfractaire au changement, créé par le dessinateur britannique David Low ; ce nom, ou simplement **Blimp,** sert à désigner une personne ayant ce type de tempérament.

colonial [kə'ləʊnjəl] ◆ adj [power, life] colonial ; *pej* [attitude] colonialiste. ◆ n colonial *m,* -e *f.*

colonialism [kə'ləʊnjəlɪzm] n colonialisme m.

colonist ['kɒlənɪst] n colon m.

colonize, colonise ['kɒlənaɪz] vt coloniser.

colonnade [,kɒlə'neɪd] n colonnade f.

colony ['kɒlənɪ] (pl **colonies**) n colonie f.

color 🇺🇸 n, vt, vi & comp = **colour**.

Colorado [,kɒlə'rɑːdəʊ] pr n Colorado m.

Colorado beetle n doryphore m.

colossal [kə'lɒsl] adj colossal.

colossus [kə'lɒsəs] (pl **colossuses** or **colossi** [-saɪ]) n colosse m.

colostomy [kə'lɒstəmɪ] (pl **colostomies**) n colostomie f.

colour 🇬🇧, **color** 🇺🇸 ['kʌlə*] ◆ n **1.** [hue] couleur f / what colour are his eyes? de quelle couleur sont ses yeux ? **2.** ART [shade] coloris m, ton m ; [paint] peinture f ; [dye] teinture f, matière f colorante **3.** [complexion] teint m, couleur f (du visage) ▶ **to lose one's colour** pâlir, perdre ses couleurs ▶ **to get one's colour back** reprendre des couleurs ▶ **to have a high colour** avoir le visage rouge **4.** [race] couleur f ▶ **of colour** noir. ◆ comp [photography, picture, slide] en couleur, en couleurs ▶ **colour film a)** [for camera] pellicule f (en) couleur **b)** [movie] film m en couleur ▶ **colour television (set)** téléviseur m couleur. ◆ vt **1.** [give colour to] colorer ; [with paint] peindre ; [with crayons] colorier / he coloured it blue il l'a colorié en bleu **2.** fig [distort - judgment] fausser ; [exaggerate - story, facts] exagérer. ◆ vi [change colour - person] rougir ; [- things] se colorer. ◆ **colours** pl n [of team] élément vestimentaire (écusson, cravate, etc.) décerné aux nouveaux membres d'une équipe sportive ▶ **to get** or **to win one's colours** être sélectionné pour faire partie d'une équipe ▶ **to show one's true colours** se montrer sous son vrai jour.

colour bar n 🇬🇧 discrimination f raciale.

colour barrier 🇬🇧, **color barrier** 🇺🇸 n discrimination f raciale.

colour-blind adj lit daltonien ; fig qui ne fait pas de discrimination raciale.

colour blindness n lit daltonisme m ; fig fait m de ne pas faire de discrimination raciale.

colour chart n nuancier m.

colour code n code m couleur. ◆ **colour-code** vt ▶ **to colour-code sthg** coder qqch avec des couleurs.

colour-coded adj dont la couleur correspond à un code.

coloured 🇬🇧, **colored** 🇺🇸 ['kʌləd] adj **1.** [having colour] coloré ; [drawing] colorié ; [pencils] de couleur **2.** [person - gen] de couleur ; [- in South Africa] métis **3.** fig [distorted - judgment] faussé ; [exaggerated - story] exagéré.

-coloured 🇬🇧, **-colored** 🇺🇸 in comp (de) couleur…

colourfast 🇬🇧, **colorfast** 🇺🇸 ['kʌləfɑːst] adj grand teint, qui ne déteint pas.

colourful 🇬🇧, **colorful** 🇺🇸 ['kʌləfʊl] adj **1.** [brightly coloured] coloré, vif **2.** fig [person] original, pittoresque ; [story] coloré.

colouring 🇬🇧, **coloring** 🇺🇸 ['kʌlərɪŋ] ◆ n **1.** [hue] coloration f, coloris m **2.** [complexion] teint m **3.** [for food] colorant m. ◆ comp ▶ **colouring book** album m à colorier or de coloriages.

colouring-in, coloring-in 🇺🇸 n coloriage m.

colourless 🇬🇧, **colorless** 🇺🇸 ['kʌləlɪs] adj [without colour] incolore, sans couleur.

colour scheme n palette f or combinaison f de couleurs.

colour supplement n 🇬🇧 supplément m illustré.

Colt® [kəʊlt] n [revolver] colt m, pistolet m (automatique).

colt [kəʊlt] n [horse] poulain m.

Columbus [kə'lʌmbəs] pr n ▶ **Christopher Columbus** Christophe Colomb.

column ['kɒləm] n [gen & ARCHIT] colonne f.

column inch n unité de mesure des espaces publicitaires équivalant à une colonne sur un pouce.

columnist ['kɒləmnɪst] n chroniqueur m, -euse f, échotier m, -ère f.

coma ['kəʊmə] n coma m / **in a coma** dans le coma.

comatose ['kəʊmətəʊs] adj comateux.

comb [kəʊm] ◆ n **1.** [for hair] peigne m ; [large-toothed] démêloir m ▶ **to run a comb through one's hair** or **to give one's hair a comb** se donner un coup de peigne, se peigner **2.** [of fowl] crête f ; [on helmet] cimier m. ◆ vt **1.** [hair] peigner / he combed his hair il s'est peigné **2.** fig [search] fouiller, ratisser / the police combed the area for clues la police a passé le quartier au peigne fin or a ratissé le quartier à la recherche d'indices.

combat ['kɒmbæt] (pt & pp **combated**, cont **combating**) ◆ n combat m. ◆ comp [troops, zone] de combat ▶ **combat jacket** veste f de treillis. ◆ vt combattre, lutter contre. ◆ vi combattre, lutter.

combat boots pl n bottes fpl de combat.

combat fatigue n psychose f traumatique, syndrome m commotionnel.

combative ['kɒmbətɪv] adj combatif.

combats, combat trousers pl n pantalon m treillis.

combination [,kɒmbɪ'neɪʃn] n **1.** [gen & CHEM & MATH] combinaison f ; [of circumstances] concours m **2.** [of lock] combinaison f **3.** [association, team] association f, coalition f.

combination lock n serrure f à combinaison.

combination skin n peau f mixte.

combination therapy n MED trithérapie f.

combine ◆ vt [kəm'baɪn] [gen] combiner, joindre ; CHEM combiner / to combine business and or with pleasure joindre l'utile à l'agréable. ◆ vi [kəm'baɪn] [unite] s'unir, s'associer ; [workers] se syndiquer ; POL [parties] fusionner ; CHEM se combiner. ◆ n ['kɒmbaɪn] **1.** [association] association f ; FIN trust m, cartel m ; LAW corporation f **2.** AGR = **combine harvester.**

combined [kəm'baɪnd] adj combiné, conjugué.

combine harvester ['kɒmbaɪn-] n moissonneuse-batteuse f.

combo ['kɒmbəʊ] (pl **combos**) n **1.** MUS combo m **2.** inf [combination] combinaison f **3.** [mixture] mélange m.

combustible [kəm'bʌstəbl] adj combustible.

combustion [kəm'bʌstʃn] n combustion f.

come [kʌm] (pt **came** [keɪm], pp **come** [kʌm]) vi **1.** [move in direction of speaker] venir / coming! j'arrive ! / come here venez ici / come with me a) [accompany] venez avec moi, accompagnez-moi b) [follow] suivez-moi ▶ **to come and go a)** [gen] aller et venir b) fig [pains, cramps, etc.] être intermittent / I don't know whether I'm coming or going inf je ne sais pas où j'en suis / you have come a long way a) lit vous êtes venu de loin b) fig [made progress] vous avez fait du chemin ▶ **to come running** lit & fig arriver en courant / you could see it coming inf on l'a vu venir de loin, c'était prévisible **2.** [as guest, visitor] venir / would you like to come for lunch / dinner? voulez-vous venir déjeuner / dîner ? / I've got people coming a) [short stay] j'ai des invités b) [long stay] il y a des gens qui viennent **3.** [arrive] venir, arriver / to come in time / late arriver à temps / en retard / the time has come to tell the truth le moment est venu de dire la vérité / there will come a point when... il viendra un moment où... **4.** [occupy specific place, position] venir, se trouver / *my birthday comes before yours* mon anniversaire vient avant or précède le tien / *that speech comes in Act 3* / *on page 10* on trouve ce discours dans l'acte 3 / à la page 10 **5.** [occur, happen] arriver, se produire / *such an opportunity only comes once in your life* une telle occasion ne se présente qu'une fois dans la vie / *success was a long time coming* la réussite s'est fait attendre / *take life as it comes* prenez la vie comme elle vient ▸ **come what may** advienne que pourra, quoi qu'il arrive or advienne **6.** [occur to the mind] : *I said the first thing that came into my head* or *that came to mind* j'ai dit la première chose qui m'est venue à l'esprit **7.** [be experienced in a specified way] : *a house doesn't come cheap* une maison coûte or revient cher / *her visit came as a surprise* sa visite nous a beaucoup surpris ▸ *it'll all come right in the end* tout cela va finir par s'arranger **8.** [be available] exister / *this table comes in two sizes* cette table existe or se fait en deux dimensions **9.** [become] devenir / *it was a dream come true* c'était un rêve devenu réalité / *to come unravelled* se défaire **10.** (+ infinitive) [indicating gradual action] en venir à, finir par / *we have come to expect this kind of thing* nous nous attendons à ce genre de chose maintenant ▸ **(now that I) come to think of it** maintenant que j'y songe, réflexion faite **11.** *v inf* [have orgasm] jouir **12.** PHR **how come?** comment ça ? ▸ **come again?** *inf* quoi ? ❖ **come about** vi [occur] arriver, se produire / *how could such a mistake come about?* comment une telle erreur a-t-elle pu se produire ? ❖ **come across** ◆ vi **1.** [walk, travel across - field, street] traverser **2.** [create specified impression] donner l'impression de ; [communicate effectively] : *the author's message comes across well* le message de l'auteur passe bien. ◆ vt insep [person] rencontrer par hasard, tomber sur ; [thing] trouver par hasard, tomber sur. ❖ **come along** vi **1.** [encouraging, urging] : *come along, drink your medicine!* allez, prends or bois ton médicament ! **2.** [accompany] venir, accompagner / *she asked me to come along (with them)* elle m'a invité à aller avec eux or à les accompagner **3.** [progress] avancer, faire des progrès ; [grow] pousser / *the patient is coming along well* le patient se remet bien. ❖ **come apart** vi [object - come to pieces] se démonter ; [- break] se casser ; [project, policy] échouer. ❖ **come around** vt insep = come round. ❖ **come away** vi **1.** [leave] partir, s'en aller / *come away from that door!* écartez-vous de cette porte ! **2.** [separate] partir, se détacher / *the page came away in my hands* la page m'est restée dans les mains. ❖ **come back** vi **1.** [return] revenir / *to come back home* rentrer (à la maison) **2.** [to memory] : *it's all coming back to me* tout cela me revient (à l'esprit or à la mémoire). ❖ **come between** vt insep brouiller, éloigner. ❖ **come by** ◆ vi [stop by] passer, venir. ◆ vt insep [acquire - work, money] obtenir, se procurer ; [- idea] se faire. ❖ **come down** ◆ vt insep [descend - ladder, stairs] descendre ; [- mountain] descendre, faire la descente de. ◆ vi **1.** [descend - plane, person] descendre / *come down from that tree!* descends de cet arbre ! ▸ **to come down in the world** : *he's come down in the world* il a déchu **2.** [fall] tomber / *the ceiling came down* le plafond s'est effondré **3.** [decrease] baisser **4.** [be passed down] être transmis (de père en fils) **5.** [reach a decision] se prononcer / *the majority came down in favour of / against abortion* la majorité s'est prononcée en faveur de / contre l'avortement **6.** [be demolished] être démoli or abattu. ❖ **come down to** vt insep [amount] se réduire à, se résumer à / *it all comes down to the same thing* tout cela revient au même / *that's what his argument comes down to* voici à quoi se réduit son raisonnement. ❖ **come down with** vt insep [become ill] attraper. ❖ **come forward** vi [present oneself] se présenter / *more women are coming forward as candidates* davantage de femmes présentent leur candidature. ❖ **come forward with** vt insep [offer] : *he came forward with a new proposal* il a fait une nouvelle proposition / *to come*

forward with evidence LAW présenter des preuves. ❖ **come from** vt insep venir de / *she comes from China* [Chinese person] elle vient or elle est originaire de Chine / *that's surprising coming from him* c'est étonnant de sa part. ❖ **come in** vi **1.** [enter] entrer / *come in!* entrez ! ; [come inside] rentrer **2.** [in competition] arriver **3.** [be received - money, contributions] rentrer / *how much do you have coming in every week?* combien touchez-vous or encaissez-vous chaque semaine ? ; PRESS [news, report] être reçu / *news is just coming in of a riot in Red Square* on nous annonce à l'instant des émeutes sur la place Rouge **4.** [tide] monter. ❖ **come in for** vt insep [be object of - criticism] être l'objet de, subir ; [- blame] supporter ; [- abuse, reproach] subir. ❖ **come into** vt insep **1.** [inherit] hériter de ; [acquire] entrer en possession de **2.** [play a role in] jouer un rôle. ❖ **come off** ◆ vt insep **1.** [fall off - subj: rider] tomber de ; [- subj: button] se détacher de, se découdre de ; [- subj: handle, label] se détacher de ; [be removed - stain, mark] partir de, s'enlever de **2.** [stop taking - drug, medicine] arrêter de prendre ; [- drink] arrêter de boire **3.** PHR **oh, come off it!** *inf* allez, arrête ton char ! ◆ vi **1.** [rider] tomber ; [handle] se détacher ; [stains] partir, s'enlever ; [tape, wallpaper] se détacher, se décoller ; [button] se détacher, se découdre **2.** [fare, manage] s'en sortir, se tirer de / *you came off well in the competition* tu t'en es bien tiré au concours / *to come off best* gagner **3.** *inf* [happen] avoir lieu, se passer ; [be carried through] se réaliser ; [succeed] réussir. ❖ **come on** vi **1.** (in imperative) [hurry] : *come on!* allez ! / *come on in / up!* entre / monte donc ! **2.** [progress] avancer, faire des progrès ; [grow] pousser, venir bien / *how is your work coming on?* où en est votre travail ? **3.** [begin - illness] se déclarer ; [- storm] survenir, éclater ; [- season] arriver / *as night came on* quand la nuit a commencé à tomber **4.** [start functioning - electricity, gas, heater, lights, radio] s'allumer ; [- motor] se mettre en marche **5.** THEAT [actor] entrer en scène. ◆ vt insep = come upon. ❖ **come on to** vt insep [proceed to consider] aborder, passer à. ❖ **come out** vi **1.** [exit] sortir / *as we came out of the theatre* au moment où nous sommes sortis du théâtre ; [socially] sortir **2.** [make appearance - stars, sun] paraître, se montrer ; [- flowers] sortir, éclore ; [- book] paraître, être publié ; [- film] paraître, sortir ; [- new product] sortir **3.** [be revealed - news, secret] être divulgué or révélé ; [- facts, truth] émerger, se faire jour **4.** [colour - fade] passer, se faner ; [- run] déteindre ; [stain] s'enlever, partir **5.** [declare oneself publicly] se déclarer / *the governor came out against / for abortion* le gouverneur s'est prononcé (ouvertement) contre / pour l'avortement ▸ **to come out (of the closet)** *inf* faire son coming-out. UK [on strike] se mettre en or faire grève **7.** [emerge, finish up] se tirer d'affaire, s'en sortir ; [in competition] se classer / *I came out top in maths* j'étais premier en maths / *to come out on top* gagner **8.** [go into society] faire ses débuts or débuter dans le monde **9.** PHOT : *the pictures came out well / badly* les photos étaient très bonnes / n'ont rien donné. ❖ **come out with** vt insep [say] dire, sortir. ❖ **come over** ◆ vi **1.** [move, travel in direction of speaker] venir / *do you want to come over this evening?* tu veux venir à la maison ce soir ? **2.** [stop by] venir, passer **3.** [change sides] : *he finally came over to their way of thinking* il a fini par se ranger à leur avis **4.** [make specified impression] : *he came over as honest* il a donné l'impression d'être honnête **5.** *inf* [feel] devenir / *he came over all funny* **a)** [felt ill] il s'est senti mal tout d'un coup, il a eu un malaise **b)** [behaved oddly] il est devenu tout bizarre. ◆ vt insep affecter, envahir / *a feeling of fear came over him* il a été saisi de peur, la peur s'est emparée de lui / *what has come over him?* qu'est-ce qui lui prend ? ❖ **come round** vi **1.** [make a detour] faire le détour / *we came round by the factory* nous sommes passés par or nous avons fait le détour par l'usine **2.** [stop by] passer, venir **3.** [occur - regular event] : *the summer holidays will soon be coming round again* bientôt, ce sera de nouveau les grandes vacances **4.** [change mind] changer d'avis **/** *he finally came round to our way of thinking* il a fini par se ranger à notre avis ; [change to better mood] : *don't worry, she'll soon come round* ne t'en fais pas, elle sera bientôt de meilleure humeur **5.** [recover consciousness] reprendre connaissance, revenir à soi ; [get better] se remettre, se rétablir. **❖ come through ◆** vi **1.** [be communicated] : *his sense of conviction came through* on voyait qu'il était convaincu **2.** [be granted, approved] se réaliser **/** *did your visa come through?* avez-vous obtenu votre visa ? **3.** [survive] survivre, s'en tirer **4.** US inf [do what is expected] : *he came through for us* il a fait ce qu'on attendait de lui. **◆** vt insep **1.** [cross] traverser ; *fig* [penetrate] traverser **2.** [survive] : *they came through the accident without a scratch* ils sont sortis de l'accident indemnes. **❖ come to ◆** vi [recover consciousness] reprendre connaissance, revenir à soi. **◆** vt insep **1.** [concern] : *when it comes to physics, she's a genius* pour ce qui est de la physique, c'est un génie **/** *when it comes to paying...* quand il faut payer... **2.** [amount to] s'élever à, se monter à **3.** *fig* [arrive at, reach] : *he got what was coming to him* il n'a eu que ce qu'il méritait **/** *I never thought it would come to this* je ne me doutais pas qu'on en arriverait là. **❖ come under** vt insep **1.** [be subjected to - authority, control] dépendre de ; [- influence] tomber sous, être soumis à **/** *the government is coming under pressure to lower taxes* le gouvernement subit des pressions visant à réduire les impôts **2.** [be classified under] être classé sous. **❖ come up** vi **1.** [move upwards] monter ; [moon, sun] se lever ; [travel in direction of speaker] : *I come up to town every Monday* je viens en ville tous les lundis **2.** [approach] s'approcher **▶ to come up to sb** s'approcher de qqn, venir vers qqn **/** *it's coming up to 5 o'clock* il est presque 5 h **▶ one coffee, coming up!** *inf* et un café, un ! **3.** [plant] sortir, germer **4.** [come under consideration - matter] être soulevé, être mis sur le tapis ; [- question, problem] se poser, être soulevé ; LAW [accused] comparaître ; [case] être entendu **5.** [happen unexpectedly - event] survenir, surgir ; [- opportunity] se présenter **/** *I can't make it, something has come up* je ne peux pas venir, j'ai un empêchement. **❖ come up against** vt insep [be confronted with] rencontrer **/** *they came up against some tough competition* ils se sont heurtés à des concurrents redoutables. **❖ come up to** vt insep **1.** [reach] arriver à **/** *the mud came up to their knees* la boue leur montait or arrivait jusqu'aux genoux **2.** [equal] : *the play didn't come up to our expectations* la pièce nous a déçus. **❖ come up with** vt insep [offer, propose - money, loan] fournir ; [think of - plan, suggestion] suggérer, proposer ; [- answer] trouver ; [- excuse] trouver, inventer. **❖ come upon** vt insep [find unexpectedly - person] rencontrer par hasard, tomber sur ; [- object] trouver par hasard, tomber sur.

comeback ['kʌmbæk] n *inf* **1.** [return] retour *m*, comeback *m* ; THEAT rentrée *f* **2.** [retort] réplique *f*.

comedian [kə'miːdjən] n [comic] comique *m* ; *fig* [funny person] clown *m*, pitre *m*.

comedienne [kə,miːdɪ'en] n [comic] actrice *f* comique.

comedown ['kʌmdaʊn] n *inf* déchéance *f*, dégringolade *f*.

comedy ['kɒmədɪ] (*pl* **comedies**) n [gen] comédie *f* ; THEAT genre *m* comique, comédie *f*.

come-hither adj *inf* aguichant.

comely ['kʌmlɪ] (*compar* **comelier**, *superl* **comeliest**) adj *arch* charmant, beau (*before vowel or silent 'h'* **bel**, f **belle**).

come-on n *inf* attrape-nigaud *m* **▶ to give sb the come-on** faire les yeux doux à qqn.

comet ['kɒmɪt] n comète *f*.

come-uppance [,kʌm'ʌpəns] n *inf* : *you'll get your come-uppance* tu auras ce que tu mérites.

comfort ['kʌmfət] **◆** n **1.** [well-being] confort *m*, bien-être *m* **/** *to live in comfort* vivre dans l'aisance or à l'aise **2.** (*usu pl*) [amenities] aises *fpl*, commodités *fpl* **3.** [consolation] réconfort *m*, consolation *f* **▶ comfort food** nourriture *f* or aliments *mpl* de réconfort **▶ to take comfort in sthg** trouver un réconfort dans qqch **/** *if it's any comfort to you* si cela peut vous consoler. **◆** vt **1.** [console] consoler ; [relieve] soulager **2.** [cheer] réconforter, encourager.

comfortable ['kʌmftəbl] adj **1.** [chair, shoes, bed, room] confortable ; [temperature] agréable ; *fig* [lead, win] confortable **2.** [person] à l'aise **/** *are you comfortable?* êtes-vous bien installé ? **/** *I'm not very comfortable about* or *I don't feel comfortable with the idea* l'idée m'inquiète un peu **3.** [financially secure] aisé, riche ; [easy - job] tranquille **4.** [ample] : *that leaves us a comfortable margin* ça nous laisse une marge confortable.

⚠ **Confortable** is not always the correct translation of comfortable. See the entry for details.

comfortably ['kʌmftəblɪ] adv **1.** [in a relaxed position - sit, sleep] confortablement, agréablement **2.** [in financial comfort] à l'aise **▶ to be comfortably off** être à l'aise **3.** [easily] facilement, à l'aise.

comforter ['kʌmfətə] n **1.** [person] consolateur *m*, -trice *f* **2.** US [quilt] édredon *m* ; [duvet] couette *f*.

comforting ['kʌmfətɪŋ] adj [consoling - remark, thought] consolant, réconfortant, rassurant ; [encouraging] encourageant.

comfort station n US toilettes *fpl* publiques (*sur le bord d'une route*).

comfort zone n : *I like to stay within my comfort zone* j'essaie de ne pas dépasser mes limites or de rester dans ma zone de confort.

comfy ['kʌmfɪ] (*compar* **comfier**, *superl* **comfiest**) adj *inf* [chair] confortable **/** *are you comfy?* vous êtes bien installés ?

comic ['kɒmɪk] **◆** adj comique, humoristique **▶ comic relief** a) THEAT intervalle *m* comique b) *fig* moment *m* de détente (comique) **▶ Comic Relief** association caritative en Grande-Bretagne qui collecte des fonds en organisant chaque année un « téléthon » et en vendant des petits nez rouges en plastique que les gens portent en signe de solidarité. **◆** n **1.** [entertainer] (acteur *m*) comique *m*, actrice *f* comique **2.** [magazine] BD *f*, bande dessinée *f*. **❖ comics** pl n US [in newspaper] bandes *fpl* dessinées.

comical ['kɒmɪkl] adj drôle, comique.

comic book n magazine *m* de bandes dessinées.

comic strip n bande *f* dessinée.

coming ['kʌmɪŋ] **◆** adj **1.** [time, events] à venir, futur ; [in near future] prochain **/** *this coming Tuesday* mardi prochain **2.** *inf* [promising - person] d'avenir, qui promet. **◆** n **1.** [gen] arrivée *f*, venue *f* **▶ coming and going** va-et-vient *m* **▶ comings and goings** allées *fpl* et venues **2.** RELIG avènement *m*.

coming of age n majorité *f*.

🚩 **Coming of age**

À sa majorité (fixée à 18 ans), tout Britannique acquiert le droit de voter, de faire partie d'un jury, de boire de l'alcool dans les pubs et de se marier sans le consentement de ses parents.

coming out n [of homosexual] coming-out *m* ; [of girl] entrée *f* dans le monde (*d'une jeune fille*).

comma ['kɒmə] n GRAM & MUS virgule *f*.

command [kə'mɑːnd] ◆ n **1.** [order] ordre *m* ; MIL ordre *m*, commandement *m* **2.** [authority] commandement *m* ▶ **to be in command of** sthg avoir qqch sous ses ordres, être à la tête de qqch / **he had / took command of the situation** il avait / a pris la situation en main **3.** [control, mastery] maîtrise *f* / **she has a good command of two foreign languages** elle possède bien deux langues étrangères / **her command of Spanish** sa maîtrise de l'espagnol / **all the resources at my command** toutes les ressources à ma disposition or dont je dispose **4.** MIL [group of officers] commandement *m* ; [troops] troupes *fpl* ; [area] région *f* militaire **5.** COMPUT commande *f*. ◆ vt **1.** [order] ordonner, commander / **she commanded that we leave immediately** elle nous a ordonné or nous a donné l'ordre de partir immédiatement **2.** [have control over - army] commander ; [- emotions] maîtriser, dominer **3.** [receive as due] commander, imposer / **to command respect** inspirer le respect, en imposer **4.** [have use of] disposer de **5.** [subj: building, statue - overlook] ▶ **to command a view of** avoir vue sur, donner sur. ◆ vi [order] commander, donner des ordres.

commandant [,kɒmən'dænt] n commandant *m*.

command economy n économie *f* planifiée.

commandeer [,kɒmən'dɪər] vt [officially] réquisitionner ; [usurp] accaparer.

commander [kə'mɑːndər] n [person in charge] chef *m* ; MIL commandant *m* ; NAUT capitaine *m* de frégate.

commander-in-chief n commandant *m* en chef, généralissime *m*.

commanding [kə'mɑːndɪŋ] adj **1.** [in command] qui commande **2.** [overlooking - view] élevé **3.** [tone, voice] impérieux, de commandement ; [look] impérieux ; [air] imposant.

commanding officer n commandant *m*.

commandment [kə'mɑːndmənt] n commandement *m*.

command module n module *m* de commande.

commando [kə'mɑːndəʊ] (*pl* **commandos** or **commandoes**) n commando *m*.

command-orientated adj COMPUT [program] orienté commande.

command performance n représentation (*d'un spectacle*) à la requête d'un chef d'État.

command prompt n COMPUT invite *f* de commande.

commemorate [kə'meməreɪt] vt commémorer.

commemoration [kə,memə'reɪʃn] n commémoration *f* ; RELIG commémoraison *f*.

commemorative [kə'memərətɪv] adj commémoratif.

commence [kə'mens] *fml* ◆ vi commencer. ◆ vt commencer.

commencement [kə'mensmənt] n **1.** *fml* [beginning] commencement *m*, début *m* ; LAW [of law] date *f* d'entrée en vigueur **2.** US UNIV remise *f* des diplômes.

commend [kə'mend] vt **1.** [recommend] recommander, conseiller / **the report has little to commend it** il n'y a pas grand-chose d'intéressant dans ce rapport **2.** [praise] louer, faire l'éloge de.

commendable [kə'mendəbl] adj louable.

commendably [kə'mendəblɪ] adv de façon louable.

commendation [,kɒmen'deɪʃn] n **1.** [praise] éloge *f*, louange *f* **2.** [recommendation] recommandation *f* **3.** [award for bravery] décoration *f*.

commensurate [kə'menʃərət] adj *fml* [proportionate] proportionné.

comment ['kɒment] ◆ n **1.** [remark] commentaire *m*, observation *f* / **she let it pass without comment** elle n'a pas relevé ▶ **no comment!** je n'ai rien à dire ! **2.** (U) [gossip, criticism] : **the decision provoked much comment** la décision a suscité de nombreux commentaires **3.** [note] commentaire *m*, annotation *f* ; [critical] critique *f*. ◆ vi **1.** [remark] faire une remarque or des remarques / **he commented that…** il a fait la remarque que… **2.** [give opinion] : **comment on the text** commentez le texte, faites le commentaire du texte.

commentary ['kɒməntrɪ] (*pl* **commentaries**) n **1.** [remarks] commentaire *m*, observations *fpl* **2.** RADIO & TV commentaire *m*.

commentate ['kɒmənteɪt] vi faire un reportage.

commentator ['kɒmənteɪtər] n **1.** RADIO & TV reporter *m* **2.** [analyst] commentateur *m*, -trice *f*.

commerce ['kɒmɜːs] n (U) [trade] commerce *m*, affaires *fpl*.

commercial [kə'mɜːʃl] ◆ adj **1.** [economic] commercial **2.** [profitable] commercial, marchand **3.** *pej* [profit-seeking - book, pop group] commercial. ◆ n publicité *f*, spot *m* publicitaire.

commercial bank n banque *f* commerciale.

commercial break n page *f* de publicité.

commercial college n école *f* de commerce.

commercialism [kə'mɜːʃəlɪzm] n **1.** [practice of business] (pratique *f* du) commerce *m*, (pratique des) affaires *fpl* **2.** *pej* [profit-seeking] mercantilisme *m*, esprit *m* commercial ; [on large scale] affairisme *m*.

commercialization, commercialisation [kə,mɜːʃəlaɪ'zeɪʃn] n commercialisation *f*.

commercialize, commercialise [kə'mɜːʃəlaɪz] vt commercialiser.

commercial lease n bail *m* commercial.

commercially [kə'mɜːʃəlɪ] adv commercialement.

commercial traveller n *dated* voyageur *m* or représentant *m* de commerce, VRP *m*.

commercial-use adj à usage commercial.

commercial vehicle n véhicule *m* utilitaire, commerciale *f*.

commie ['kɒmɪ] *inf & pej* ◆ adj coco. ◆ n coco *mf*.

commingle [kə'mɪŋgl] vi *fml* se mélanger, se mêler.

commiserate [kə'mɪzəreɪt] vi ▶ **to commiserate with sb a)** [feel sympathy] éprouver de la compassion pour qqn **b)** [show sympathy] témoigner de la sympathie à qqn.

commiseration [kə,mɪzə'reɪʃn] n commisération *f*.

commission [kə'mɪʃn] ◆ n **1.** [authority for special job] commission *f*, mission *f*, ordres *mpl*, instructions *fpl* ; ART commande *f* / **work done on commission** travail fait sur commande **2.** [committee] commission *f*, comité *m* **3.** COMM [fee] commission *f*, courtage *m* / **I get (a) 5% commission** je reçois une commission de 5 %. ◆ vt **1.** [work of art] commander ; [artist] passer commande à / **we commissioned the architect to design a new house** nous avons engagé un architecte pour faire les plans d'une nouvelle maison **2.** [grant authority to] donner pouvoir or mission à, déléguer, charger ▶ **to commission sb to do sthg** charger qqn de faire qqch **3.** MIL [make officer] nommer à un commandement **4.** [make operative] mettre en service ; NAUT [ship] mettre en service, armer. ◆ **out of commission** adj phr [gen] hors service ; [car] en panne ; NAUT [not working] hors service ; [in reserve] en réserve.

commissionaire [kə,mɪʃə'neər] n UK portier *m* (*d'un hôtel, etc.*).

commissioned officer [kə'mɪʃənd-] n officier *m*.

commissioner [kə'mɪʃnər] n 🇬🇧 [of police] ≃ préfet *m* de police ; 🇺🇸 ≃ (commissaire *m*) divisionnaire *m* ; [of government department] haut fonctionnaire.

commit [kə'mɪt] (*pt & pp* **committed,** *cont* **committing**) ◆ vt **1.** [crime] commettre, perpétrer ; [mistake] faire, commettre / *to commit suicide* se suicider **2.** [entrust - thing] confier, remettre ; [- person] confier ▶ **to commit sthg to sb's care** confier qqch aux soins de qqn or à la garde de qqn / *he was committed to a mental hospital* il a été interné / *they committed her to prison* ils l'ont incarcérée **3.** [promise] engager ▶ **to commit o.s. to sthg / to do sthg** s'engager à qqch / à faire qqch. ◆ vi : *he finds it hard to commit* il a du mal à s'engager dans une relation.

commitment [kə'mɪtmənt] n **1.** [promise, loyalty] engagement *m* **2.** [obligation] obligations *fpl*, responsabilités *fpl* ; COMM & FIN engagement *m* financier.

commitment period n période *f* d'engagement.

committal [kə'mɪtl] n [sending - gen] remise *f* ; [- to prison] incarcération *f*, emprisonnement *m* ; [- to mental hospital] internement *m* ; [- to grave] mise *f* en terre.

committed [kə'mɪtɪd] adj [writer, artist] engagé / *a committed Socialist / Christian* un socialiste / chrétien convaincu.

committed costs pl n coûts *mpl* engagés.

committee [kə'mɪtɪ] ◆ n commission *f*, comité *m* ▶ **to be** or **to sit on a committee** faire partie d'une commission or d'un comité ; [in government] commission *f*. ◆ comp [meeting] de commission or comité ; [member] d'une commission, d'un comité.

commode [kə'məʊd] n **1.** [chest of drawers] commode *f* **2.** [for chamber pot] chaise *f* percée.

commodity [kə'mɒdətɪ] (*pl* **commodities**) n **1.** [product] marchandise *f* ; [consumer goods] produit *m*, article *m* ; [food] denrée *f* **2.** ECON [raw material] produit *m* de base, matière *f* première.

common ['kɒmən] ◆ adj **1.** [ordinary] commun, ordinaire ; [plant] commun / *it's quite common* c'est courant or tout à fait banal / *it's a common experience* cela arrive à beaucoup de gens or à tout le monde / *a common occurrence* une chose fréquente or qui arrive souvent / *the common people* le peuple, les gens du commun **2.** [shared, public] commun / *by common consent* d'un commun accord ▶ **the common good** le bien public ▶ **common ground a)** [in interests] intérêt *m* commun **b)** [for discussion] terrain *m* d'entente ▶ **common land** terrain *m* communal or banal **3.** [widespread] général, universel / *it's common knowledge that...* tout le monde sait que..., il est de notoriété publique que... / *it's common practice to thank your host* il est d'usage de remercier son hôte **4.** *pej* [vulgar] commun, vulgaire. ◆ n [land] terrain *m* communal. ❖ **Commons** pl n 🇬🇧 & 🇨🇦 POL ▶ **the Commons** les Communes *fpl*. ❖ **in common** adv phr en commun ▶ **to have sthg in common with sb** avoir qqch en commun avec qqn / *we have nothing in common* nous n'avons rien en commun.

common cold n rhume *m*.

common currency n ECON monnaie *f* commune.

common denominator n MATH & *fig* dénominateur *m* commun.

Common Entrance n 🇬🇧 SCH examen de fin d'études primaires permettant d'entrer dans une « public school ».

commoner ['kɒmənər] n [not noble] roturier *m*, -ère *f*.

common factor n facteur *m* commun.

common gateway interface n COMPUT interface *f* commune de passerelle.

common law n droit *m* coutumier, common law *f*.

 Common law

Ensemble des règles qui constituent la base des systèmes juridiques anglais, gallois, américain et d'autres pays du Commonwealth. À l'inverse des systèmes issus du droit romain, qui s'appuient sur des textes écrits, ces règles ne sont pas écrites et sont établies par la jurisprudence.

commonly ['kɒmənlɪ] adv [usually] généralement, communément / *what is commonly known as...* ce que l'on appelle dans le langage courant...

Common Market n ▶ **the Common Market** le Marché commun.

common-or-garden adj 🇬🇧 *inf* ▶ **the common-or-garden variety** le modèle standard or ordinaire.

commonplace ['kɒmənpleɪs] ◆ adj banal, ordinaire. ◆ n [thing] banalité *f* ; [saying] lieu *m* commun, platitude *f*.

common room n 🇬🇧 SCH & UNIV [for students] salle *f* commune ; [for staff] salle *f* des professeurs.

common sense n bon sens *m*, sens *m* commun.

commonwealth ['kɒmənwelθ] n [country] pays *m* ; [state] État *m* ; [republic] république *f*. ❖ **Commonwealth** ◆ n ▶ **the (British) Commonwealth (of Nations)** le Commonwealth. ◆ comp [games, nations] du Commonwealth.

Commonwealth of Independent States pr n ▶ **the Commonwealth of Independent States** la Communauté des États indépendants.

commotion [kə'məʊʃn] n **1.** [noise] brouhaha *m* **2.** [disturbance] agitation *f*.

communal ['kɒmjʊnl] adj **1.** [shared] commun **2.** [of community] communautaire, collectif.

communally ['kɒmjʊnəlɪ] adv collectivement, en commun.

commune ◆ n ['kɒmjuːn] [group of people] communauté *f* / *to live in a commune* vivre en communauté. ◆ vi [kə'mjuːn] [communicate] communier / *to commune with nature* communier avec la nature.

communicable [kə'mjuːnɪkəbl] adj communicable ; MED [disease] contagieux, transmissible.

communicate [kə'mjuːnɪkeɪt] ◆ vi **1.** [be in touch] communiquer ; [contact] prendre contact, se mettre en contact / *they communicate with each other by phone* ils communiquent par téléphone **2.** [rooms - connect] communiquer. ◆ vt [impart - news] communiquer, transmettre ; [- feelings] communiquer, faire partager.

communicating [kə'mjuːnɪkeɪtɪŋ] adj [room] communicant.

communication [kə,mjuːnɪ'keɪʃn] n [contact] communication *f* / *are you in communication with her?* êtes-vous en contact ou en relation avec elle ? ; [of thoughts, feelings] communication *f* / *to be good at communication* or *to have good communication skills* avoir des talents de communicateur, être un bon communicateur. ❖ **communications** pl n [technology] communications *fpl* ; [roads, telegraph lines, etc.] communications *fpl* ; MIL liaison *f*, communications *fpl*.

communication cord n 🇬🇧 sonnette *f* d'alarme (*dans les trains*).

communications satellite n satellite *m* de télécommunication.

communicative [kə'mjuːnɪkətɪv] adj [talkative] communicatif, expansif.

communicator [kə'mju:nɪkeɪtər] n *personne douée pour la communication.*

communion [kə'mju:njən] n [sharing] communion f. ❖ **Communion** n RELIG [sacrament] communion f ▶ **to give Communion** donner la communion ▶ **to take** or **to receive Communion** recevoir la communion.

communiqué [kə'mju:nɪkeɪ] n communiqué m.

communism, Communism ['kɒmjʊnɪzm] n communisme m.

communist, Communist ['kɒmjʊnɪst] ◆ n communiste mf. ◆ adj communiste.

community [kə'mju:nətɪ] (pl **communities**) n **1.** [group of people, animals] communauté f, groupement m ; RELIG communauté f ; [locality] communauté f / *the business community* le monde des affaires ▶ **community spirit** esprit m de groupe **2.** [sharing] propriété f collective ; LAW communauté f ▶ **community of goods / interests** communauté de biens / d'intérêts. ❖ **Community** n ▶ **the (European) Community** la Communauté (européenne).

⚠ Community cannot always be translated by **communauté**. See the entry for details.

community care n *système britannique d'assistance sociale au niveau local.*

community centre n foyer m municipal, centre m social.

community charge 🇬🇧 fml = poll tax.

community college n 🇺🇸 centre m universitaire (de premier cycle).

community home n 🇬🇧 [for deprived children] assistance f publique.

community service n ≃ travail m d'intérêt général.

commutable [kə'mju:təbl] adj [exchangeable] interchangeable, permutable ; LAW commuable.

commutation ticket n 🇺🇸 carte f d'abonnement.

commute [kə'mju:t] ◆ vi faire un trajet régulier, faire la navette. ◆ vt **1.** [exchange] substituer, échanger **2.** LAW [sentence] commuer.

commuter [kə'mju:tər] ◆ n banliéusard m, -e f *(qui fait un trajet journalier pour se rendre au travail)* ; RAIL abonné m, -e f. ◆ comp [line, train] de banlieue ▶ **the commuter belt** 🇬🇧 la grande banlieue.

commuting [kə'mju:tɪŋ] n (U) trajets mpl réguliers, migrations fpl quotidiennes *(entre le domicile, généralement en banlieue, et le lieu de travail).*

Comoro Islands ['kɒmərəʊ-] pl n ▶ **the Comoro Islands** les îles Comores.

Comoros [kə'mɔ:rɒs] pl pr n Comores fpl.

comp [kɒmp] vt 🇺🇸 [give away] donner.

compact ◆ adj [kəm'pækt] [small] compact, petit ; [dense] dense, serré. ◆ vt [kəm'pækt] [compress] compacter, tasser. ◆ n ['kɒmpækt] **1.** [for powder] poudrier m **2.** 🇺🇸 = compact car.

compact car n 🇺🇸 (voiture f) compacte f, petite voiture f.

compact disc [,kɒmpækt-] ◆ n (disque m) compact m, CD m. ◆ comp ▶ **compact disc player** lecteur m de CD.

companion [kəm'pænjən] n **1.** [friend] compagnon m, compagne f ; [employee] dame f de compagnie / *a travelling companion* un compagnon de voyage / *companions in arms / distress* compagnons d'armes / d'infortune

2. [one of pair] pendant m / *the companion volume* le volume qui va de pair.

companionable [kəm'pænjənəbl] adj [person] sociable, d'une compagnie agréable.

companionship [kəm'pænjənʃɪp] n (U) [fellowship] compagnie f ; [friendship] amitié f, camaraderie f.

company ['kʌmpənɪ] (pl **companies**) ◆ n **1.** [companionship] compagnie f / *she's good company* elle est d'agréable compagnie ▶ **to keep sb company** tenir compagnie à qqn / *here's where we part company* a) *lit* voilà où nos chemins se séparent b) *fig* là, je ne suis plus d'accord avec vous **2.** [companions] compagnie f, fréquentation f / *she has got into* or *she's keeping bad company* elle a de mauvaises fréquentations ▶ **to be in good company** être en bonne compagnie **3.** (U) [guests] invités mpl, compagnie f / *are you expecting company?* attendez-vous de la visite ? **4.** [firm] société f, compagnie f / *Jones & Company* Jones et Compagnie **5.** [group of people] compagnie f, assemblée f ; [of actors] troupe f, compagnie f ; MIL compagnie f ; NAUT [crew] équipage m. ◆ comp [policy] d'entreprise ▶ **company car** voiture f de fonction.

⚠ When talking about a small or medium-sized company, use **une entreprise** or **une société**. Very large companies (such as oil companies and airlines) can be referred to as **compagnies**.

company director n directeur m, -trice f.

company secretary n secrétaire m général, secrétaire f générale *(d'une entreprise).*

comparable ['kɒmprəbl] adj comparable.

comparative [kəm'pærətɪv] ◆ adj **1.** [relative] relatif / *she's a comparative stranger to me* je la connais relativement peu **2.** [study] comparatif ; [field of study] comparé **3.** GRAM comparatif. ◆ n comparatif m.

comparatively [kəm'pærətɪvlɪ] adv **1.** [quite] relativement **2.** [study] comparativement.

comparative testing n essais mpl comparatifs.

compare [kəm'peər] ◆ vt **1.** [contrast] comparer, mettre en comparaison ▶ **compared with** or **to sthg** en comparaison de or par comparaison avec qqch / *compared with the others she's brilliant* elle est brillante par rapport aux autres ▶ **to compare notes** échanger ses impressions **2.** [liken] comparer, assimiler ▶ **to compare sthg to sthg** comparer qqch à qqch. ◆ vi être comparable à ▶ **to compare favourably (with sthg)** soutenir la comparaison (avec qqch) / *how do the two candidates compare?* quelles sont les qualités respectives des deux candidats ? / *how do the brands compare in (terms of) price?* les marques sont-elles comparables du point de vue prix ? / *her cooking doesn't* or *can't compare with yours* il n'y a aucune comparaison entre sa cuisine et la tienne. ◆ n *liter* : *beauty beyond compare* beauté sans pareille.

comparison [kəm'pærɪsn] n [gen] comparaison f / *there's no comparison* il n'y a aucune comparaison (possible) ▶ **to draw** or **to make a comparison between sthg and sthg** faire la comparaison de qqch avec qqch or entre qqch et qqch. ❖ **by comparison** adv phr par comparaison. ❖ **in comparison with** prep phr en comparaison de, par rapport à.

comparison-shop vi faire des achats en comparant les prix.

compartment [kəm'pɑ:tmənt] n compartiment m, subdivision f ; NAUT & RAIL compartiment m.

compartmentalize, compartmentalise [ˌkɒm-paːtˈmentəlaɪz] vt compartimenter.

compass [ˈkʌmpəs] n **1.** [for direction] boussole f; NAUT compas m **2.** GEOM compas m **3.** [limits] étendue f; [range] portée f; MUS étendue f, portée f. **⟨⟩ compasses** pl n GEOM ▸ **(a pair of) compasses** un compas.

⚠️ A ship's compass is **un compas**; a hand-held magnetic compass is **une boussole**.

compassion [kəmˈpæʃn] n compassion f.

compassionate [kəmˈpæʃənət] adj compatissant ▸ **on compassionate grounds** pour des raisons personnelles or familiales.

compassionate leave n [gen & MIL] permission f exceptionnelle *(pour raisons personnelles)*.

compassionately [kəmˈpæʃənətlɪ] adv avec compassion.

compassion fatigue n *lassitude du public à l'égard de la souffrance humaine due à la surenchère d'informations sur le sujet par les médias.*

compatibility [kəmˌpætəˈbɪlətɪ] n compatibilité f.

compatible [kəmˈpætəbl] adj compatible.

compatriot [kəmˈpætrɪət] n compatriote mf.

compel [kəmˈpel] *(pt & pp* **compelled,** *cont* **compelling)** vt **1.** [force] contraindre, obliger **2.** [demand] imposer, forcer.

compelling [kəmˈpelɪŋ] adj **1.** [reason, desire] convaincant, irrésistible **2.** [book, story] envoûtant.

compellingly [kəmˈpelɪŋlɪ] adv irrésistiblement, d'une façon irrésistible.

compendium [kəmˈpendɪəm] *(pl* **compendiums** *or* **compendia** [-dɪə]) n **1.** [summary] abrégé m, précis m **2.** 🇬🇧 [collection] collection f.

compensate [ˈkɒmpenseɪt] ◆ vt [make amends to - person] dédommager, indemniser. ◆ vi [make up] être une or servir de compensation, compenser.

compensation [ˌkɒmpenˈseɪʃn] n **1.** [recompense] indemnité f, dédommagement m; [payment] rémunération f **2.** [adaptation] compensation f; [in weight] contrepoids m; TECH compensation f, neutralisation f.

compere [ˈkɒmpeəʳ] 🇬🇧 ◆ n animateur m, -trice f, présentateur m, -trice f. ◆ vi & vt animer, présenter.

compete [kəmˈpiːt] vi **1.** [vie] rivaliser ▸ **to compete with sb for sthg** rivaliser avec qqn pour qqch, disputer qqch à qqn / *her cooking can't compete with yours* fig sa cuisine n'a rien de commun or ne peut pas rivaliser avec la vôtre **2.** COMM faire concurrence / *we have to compete on an international level* nous devons être à la hauteur de la concurrence sur le plan international **3.** SPORT [take part] participer; [contend] concourir.

competence [ˈkɒmpɪtəns] n [ability] compétence f, aptitude f, capacité f; LING compétence f.

competent [ˈkɒmpɪtənt] adj **1.** [capable] compétent, capable; [qualified] qualifié **2.** [sufficient] suffisant.

competently [ˈkɒmpɪtəntlɪ] adv **1.** [capably] avec compétence **2.** [sufficiently] suffisamment.

competing [kəmˈpiːtɪŋ] adj en concurrence.

competition [ˌkɒmpɪˈtɪʃn] n **1.** [rivalry] compétition f, rivalité f ▸ **to be in competition with sb** être en compétition or concurrence avec qqn; COMM concurrence f **2.** [opposition] concurrence f / *what's the competition doing?* que fait la concurrence ?, que font nos rivaux or concurrents ? **3.** [contest] concours m; SPORT compétition f;

[race] course f / *beauty* / *fishing competition* concours de beauté / de pêche ▸ **to enter a competition** se présenter à un concours.

⚠️ **Compétition** is not always the correct translation of competition. See the entry for details.

competitive [kəmˈpetətɪv] adj **1.** [involving competition] de compétition / *competitive examination* concours m **2.** [person] qui a l'esprit de compétition **3.** [product, price] concurrentiel, compétitif ▸ **competitive advantage** avantage m concurrentiel.

competitively [kəmˈpetətɪvlɪ] adv avec un esprit de compétition.

competitiveness [kəmˈpetətɪvnɪs] n compétitivité f.

competitor [kəmˈpetɪtəʳ] n [gen & COMM & SPORT] concurrent m, -e f; [participant] participant m, -e f.

compilation [ˌkɒmpɪˈleɪʃn] n compilation f.

compile [kəmˈpaɪl] vt **1.** [gather - facts, material] compiler **2.** [compose - list] dresser; [- dictionary] composer *(par compilation)*.

compiler [kəmˈpaɪləʳ] n **1.** [gen] compilateur m, -trice f **2.** [of dictionary] rédacteur m, -trice f **3.** COMPUT compilateur m.

complacence [kəmˈpleɪsns], **complacency** [kəmˈpleɪsnsɪ] n autosatisfaction f.

complacent [kəmˈpleɪsnt] adj satisfait or content de soi, suffisant.

complacently [kəmˈpleɪsntlɪ] adv [act] d'un air suffisant, avec suffisance; [speak] d'un ton suffisant, avec suffisance.

complain [kəmˈpleɪn] vi **1.** [grumble] se plaindre / *he complained of a headache* il s'est plaint d'un mal de tête **2.** [make formal protest] formuler une plainte or une réclamation, se plaindre ▸ **to complain to sb (about sthg)** se plaindre à or auprès de qqn (au sujet de qqch).

complainant [kəmˈpleɪnənt] n demandeur m, demanderesse f.

complaining [kəmˈpleɪnɪŋ] adj [customer] mécontent.

complaint [kəmˈpleɪnt] n **1.** [protest] plainte f, récrimination f ▸ **to make** or **lodge a complaint** se plaindre; COMM réclamation f; LAW plainte f / *complaints department* bureau m or service m des réclamations **2.** [grievance] sujet m or motif m de plainte, grief m **3.** [illness] maladie f, affection f.

complement ◆ n [ˈkɒmplɪmənt] **1.** [gen & MATH & MUS] complément m ▸ **with a full complement** au grand complet **2.** GRAM [of verb] complément m; [of subject] attribut m **3.** [ship's crew, staff] personnel m, effectif m (complet). ◆ vt [ˈkɒmplɪˌment] compléter, être le complément de.

complementary [ˌkɒmplɪˈmentərɪ] adj [gen & MATH] complémentaire.

complementary medicine n médecine f douce.

complete [kəmˈpliːt] ◆ adj **1.** [entire] complet, total / *the complete works of Shakespeare* les œuvres complètes de Shakespeare **2.** [finished] achevé, terminé **3.** [as intensifier] complet, absolu / *he's a complete fool* c'est un crétin fini or un parfait imbécile / *a complete (and utter) failure* un échec total or sur toute la ligne. ◆ vt **1.** [make whole] compléter / *to complete her happiness* pour combler son bonheur / *to complete an order* COMM exécuter une commande **2.** [finish] achever, finir **3.** [form] remplir. **⟨⟩ complete with** prep phr avec, doté or pourvu de / *complete with instructions* comprenant des instructions.

completely [kəm'pliːtlɪ] adv complètement.

completeness [kəm'pliːtnɪs] n état m complet.

completion [kəm'pliːʃn] n [of work] achèvement m / *near completion* près d'être achevé.

complex ['kɒmpleks] ◆ adj [gen & GRAM & MATH] complexe. ◆ n **1.** [system] complexe m, ensemble m ▶ **housing complex** grand ensemble ▶ **shopping / industrial complex** complexe commercial / industriel **2.** PSYCHOL complexe m / *she has a complex about her weight* elle est complexée par son poids.

complexion [kəm'plekʃn] n **1.** [of face] teint m **2.** [aspect] aspect m / *that puts a different complexion on things* voilà qui change la situation.

complexity [kəm'pleksətɪ] n complexité f.

compliance [kəm'plaɪəns] n **1.** [conformity] conformité f **2.** [agreement] acquiescement m ; [submission] complaisance f. ⟿ **in compliance with** prep phr conformément à.

compliancy [kəm'plaɪənsɪ] n = **compliance**.

compliant [kəm'plaɪənt] adj **1.** [accommodating] accommodant, docile **2.** [in keeping] conforme.

complicate ['kɒmplɪkeɪt] vt compliquer, embrouiller.

complicated ['kɒmplɪkeɪtɪd] adj [complex] compliqué, complexe ; [muddled] embrouillé.

complication [,kɒmplɪ'keɪʃn] n [gen & MED] complication f.

complicity [kəm'plɪsətɪ] n complicité f.

compliment ◆ n ['kɒmplɪmənt] [praise] compliment m ▶ **to pay sb a compliment** faire ou adresser un compliment à qqn / *she returned the compliment* iro elle lui a retourné le compliment. ◆ vt ['kɒmplɪment] faire des compliments à, complimenter. ⟿ **compliments** pl n fml [respects] compliments mpl, respects mpl ▶ **to convey** ou **present one's compliments to sb** présenter ses compliments ou hommages à qqn fig / *with the compliments of Mr Smith* avec les hommages ou compliments de M. Smith.

complimentary [,kɒmplɪ'mentərɪ] adj **1.** [approving] flatteur **2.** [given free] gratuit, gracieux ▶ **complimentary copy** exemplaire m offert à titre gracieux.

compliments slip n papillon m *(joint à un envoi)*.

comply [kəm'plaɪ] *(pt & pp* **complied)** vi **1.** [obey] : *to comply with the rules* observer ou respecter les règlements / *I will comply with your wishes* je me conformerai à vos désirs **2.** [machinery] être conforme.

component [kəm'pəʊnənt] n [gen] élément m ; ELEC composant m ; AUTO & TECH pièce f.

comport [kəm'pɔːt] vt fml ▶ **to comport o.s.** se comporter, se conduire.

compose [kəm'pəʊz] vt **1.** [make up] ▶ **to be composed of sthg** se composer ou être composé de qqch **2.** [create, write] composer **3.** [make calm] : *compose yourself!* calmez-vous ! / *I need to compose my thoughts* j'ai besoin de mettre de l'ordre dans mes idées.

composed [kəm'pəʊzd] adj calme, posé.

composer [kəm'pəʊzər] n TYPO & MUS compositeur m, -trice f.

composite ['kɒmpəzɪt] ◆ adj [gen & ARCHIT & PHOT] composite ; BOT & MATH composé. ◆ n [compound] composite m ; ARCHIT (ordre m) composite m ; BOT composée f, composacée f.

composition [,kɒmpə'zɪʃn] n **1.** [gen & ART], LITER & MUS composition f, création f **2.** [thing created] composition f, œuvre f ; SCH [essay] dissertation f **3.** [constitution - parts] composition f, constitution f ; [- mixture] mélange m, composition f ; CONSTR stuc m.

compos mentis [,kɒmpəs'mentɪs] adj sain d'esprit.

compost [UK 'kɒmpɒst US 'kɒmpəʊst] n compost m ▶ **compost heap** tas m de compost.

composure [kəm'pəʊʒər] n calme m, sang-froid m ▶ **to lose one's composure** perdre son calme.

compound ◆ adj ['kɒmpaʊnd] [gen] composé ; CHEM composé, combiné ; MATH complexe ; TECH [engine] compound *(inv).* ◆ n ['kɒmpaʊnd] **1.** [enclosed area] enceinte f, enclos m ; [for prisoners of war] camp m **2.** [mixture] composé m, mélange m ; CHEM composé m ; TECH compound m **3.** GRAM mot m composé. ◆ vt [kəm'paʊnd] [make worse - difficulties, mistake] aggraver.

compound fracture n fracture f multiple.

compound interest n (U) FIN intérêts mpl composés.

comprehend [,kɒmprɪ'hend] ◆ vt [understand] comprendre, saisir. ◆ vi [understand] comprendre, saisir.

comprehensible [,kɒmprɪ'hensəbl] adj compréhensible, intelligible.

comprehension [,kɒmprɪ'henʃn] n **1.** [understanding] compréhension f / *things that are beyond our comprehension* des choses qui nous dépassent **2.** SCH [exercise] exercice m de compréhension.

comprehensive [,kɒmprɪ'hensɪv] ◆ adj **1.** [thorough] complet, exhaustif ; [detailed] détaillé, complet ▶ **comprehensive measures** mesures d'ensemble ▶ **(a) comprehensive insurance (policy)** UK, **comprehensive assurance** US une assurance tous risques **2.** UK SCH ▶ **comprehensive school** établissement secondaire d'enseignement général. ◆ n UK [school] établissement secondaire d'enseignement général.

> ⚠ **Compréhensif** means understanding, not comprehensive.

comprehensively [,kɒmprɪ'hensɪvlɪ] adv [thoroughly] complètement, exhaustivement ; [in detail] en détail.

compress vt [kəm'pres] [squeeze together] comprimer ; fig [condense - ideas, facts, writing] condenser, concentrer.

compression [kəm'preʃn] n compression f ; fig [condensing] réduction f.

comprise [kəm'praɪz] vt **1.** [consist of] comprendre, consister en **2.** [constitute] constituer / *women comprise 60% of the population* les femmes représentent 60 % de la population.

compromise ['kɒmprəmaɪz] ◆ n compromis m / *to reach* ou *arrive at a compromise* aboutir ou parvenir à un compromis. ◆ vi transiger, aboutir à ou accepter un compromis. ◆ vt **1.** [principles, reputation] compromettre / *don't say anything to compromise yourself* ne dites rien qui puisse vous compromettre **2.** [jeopardize] mettre en péril, risquer.

compromising ['kɒmprəmaɪzɪŋ] adj compromettant.

compulsion [kəm'pʌlʃn] n **1.** [force] contrainte f, coercition f / *he is under no compulsion to sell* il n'est nullement obligé de vendre, rien ne l'oblige à vendre **2.** PSYCHOL [impulse] compulsion f.

compulsive [kəm'pʌlsɪv] adj **1.** PSYCHOL [behaviour] compulsif / *he's a compulsive liar* il ne peut pas s'empêcher de mentir, mentir est un besoin chez lui **2.** [reason] coercitif ; fig [absorbing] irrésistible.

compulsively [kəm'pʌlsɪvlɪ] adv **1.** PSYCHOL [drink, steal, smoke] d'une façon compulsive **2.** fig irrésistiblement.

compulsory [kəm'pʌlsərɪ] adj [obligatory] obligatoire.

compulsory purchase n UK expropriation f pour cause d'utilité publique.

compunction [kəm'pʌŋkʃn] n [remorse] remords m ; [misgiving] scrupule m ; RELIG componction f.

computation [ˌkɒmpjuːˈteɪʃn] n **1.** [calculation] calcul m **2.** [reckoning] estimation f.

computational [ˌkɒmpjuːˈteɪʃənl] adj quantitatif, statistique ▸ **computational linguistics** linguistique f computationnelle.

compute [kəmˈpjuːt] vt calculer.

computer [kəmˈpjuːtər] ◆ n [electronic] ordinateur m. ◆ comp ▸ **computer crime** criminalité f informatique ▸ **computer network** réseau m informatique ▸ **computer printout** sortie f papier.

computer-aided, computer-assisted [-əˈsɪstɪd] adj assisté par ordinateur.

computer-aided design n conception f assistée par ordinateur.

computer-aided learning n enseignement m assisté par ordinateur.

computer-aided translation n traduction f assistée par ordinateur.

computer dating n rencontres en ligne.

computer game n jeu m électronique.

computer-generated [kəmˌpjuːtəˈdʒenəreɪtɪd] adj généré par ordinateur.

computer graphics ◆ pl n [function] graphiques mpl. ◆ n [field] infographie® f.

computerization [kəmˌpjuːtəraɪˈzeɪʃn] n [of system, of work] automatisation f, informatisation f.

computerize, computerise [kəmˈpjuːtəraɪz] vt [data - put on computer] saisir sur ordinateur ; [-process by computer] traiter par ordinateur ; [firm] informatiser.

computerized [kəmˈpjuːtəraɪzd] adj informatisé.

computer language n langage m de programmation.

computer literacy n compétence f informatique, compétences fpl informatiques.

computer-literate adj ayant des compétences en informatique.

computer program n programme m informatique.

computer programmer n programmeur m, -euse f.

computer programming n programmation f.

computer science n informatique f.

computer scientist n informaticien m, -enne f.

computer virus n virus m informatique.

computing [kəmˈpjuːtɪŋ] n [use of computers] informatique f ▸ **computing course** stage m d'informatique.

comrade [ˈkɒmreɪd] n [gen & POL] camarade mf.

comradeship [ˈkɒmreɪdʃɪp] n camaraderie f.

comsat [ˈkɒmsæt] n abbr of **communications satellite**.

con [kɒn] (pt & pp conned, cont conning) ◆ vt inf [swindle] arnaquer ; [trick] duper. ◆ n **1.** inf [swindle] arnaque ; [trick] duperie f **2.** inf [convict] taulard m **3.** [disadvantage] contre m.

con artist n inf arnaqueur m.

concave [ˌkɒnˈkeɪv] adj concave.

conceal [kənˈsiːl] vt [hide - object] cacher, dissimuler ; [- emotion, truth] cacher, dissimuler ; [- news] tenir secret ▸ **to conceal sthg from sb** cacher qqch à qqn.

concealed [kənˈsiːld] adj [lighting] indirect ; [driveway, entrance] caché.

concealer [kənˈsiːlər] n [make-up] stick m camouflant.

concealment [kənˈsiːlmənt] n [act of hiding] dissimulation f ; LAW [of criminal] recel m ; [of facts, truth] non-divulgation f.

concede [kənˈsiːd] ◆ vt **1.** [admit] concéder, admettre **2.** [give up] concéder, accorder ; SPORT concéder **3.** [grant - privileges] concéder. ◆ vi céder.

conceit [kənˈsiːt] n [vanity] vanité f, suffisance f.

conceited [kənˈsiːtɪd] adj vaniteux, suffisant.

conceivable [kənˈsiːvəbl] adj concevable, imaginable.

conceivably [kənˈsiːvəblɪ] adv : this might conceivably start a war il est concevable que or il se peut que cela déclenche une guerre.

conceive [kənˈsiːv] ◆ vt **1.** [idea, plan] concevoir **2.** [child] concevoir. ◆ vi **1.** [think] concevoir **2.** [become pregnant] concevoir.

concentrate [ˈkɒnsəntreɪt] ◆ vi **1.** [pay attention] se concentrer, concentrer or fixer son attention ▸ **to concentrate on sthg** se concentrer sur qqch **2.** [gather] se concentrer, converger. ◆ vt **1.** [focus] concentrer **2.** [bring together] concentrer, rassembler ; CHEM concentrer. ◆ n concentré m.

concentrated [ˈkɒnsəntreɪtɪd] adj **1.** [liquid] concentré **2.** [intense] intense.

concentration [ˌkɒnsənˈtreɪʃn] n [gen & CHEM] concentration f.

concentration camp n camp m de concentration.

concentric [kənˈsentrɪk] adj concentrique.

concept [ˈkɒnsept] n concept m.

conception [kənˈsepʃn] n [gen & MED] conception f.

conceptual [kənˈseptʃuəl] adj conceptuel.

conceptualize, conceptualise [kənˈseptʃuəlaɪz] vt concevoir, conceptualiser.

concern [kənˈsɜːn] ◆ n **1.** [worry] inquiétude f, souci m / there's no cause for concern il n'y a pas de raison de s'inquiéter / she showed great concern for their welfare elle s'est montrée très soucieuse de leur bien-être / a look of concern un regard inquiet / this is a matter of great concern c'est un sujet très inquiétant ; [source of worry] souci m, préoccupation f / my main concern is the price ce qui m'inquiète surtout, c'est le prix **2.** [affair, business] affaire f / what concern is it of yours? en quoi est-ce que cela vous regarde ? / it's none of my concern cela ne me regarde pas, ce n'est pas mon affaire **3.** COMM [firm] ▸ **a (business) concern** une affaire, une firme. ◆ vt **1.** [worry] inquiéter / they're concerned about her ils s'inquiètent or se font du souci à son sujet / we were concerned to learn that... nous avons appris avec inquiétude que... / I'm only concerned with the facts je ne m'intéresse qu'aux faits **2.** [involve] concerner / where or as far as the budget is concerned en ce qui concerne le budget ▸ **to concern o.s. in** or **with sthg** s'occuper de or s'intéresser à qqch / this doesn't concern you cela ne vous regarde pas / as far as I'm concerned en ce qui me concerne, quant à moi ▸ **to whom it may concern** à qui de droit **3.** [be important to] intéresser, importer / the outcome concerns us all les résultats nous importent à tous **4.** [subj: book, report] traiter.

concerned [kənˈsɜːnd] adj **1.** [worried] inquiet (inquiète), soucieux **2.** [involved] intéressé.

concerning [kənˈsɜːnɪŋ] prep au sujet de, à propos de.

concert ◆ n [ˈkɒnsət] MUS [performance] concert m. ◆ comp [ˈkɒnsət] [hall, performer, pianist] de concert.

concerted [kənˈsɜːtɪd] adj concerté.

concertina [ˌkɒnsəˈtiːnə] ◆ n concertina m. ◆ vi : the front of the car concertinaed le devant de la voiture a été télescopé.

concerto [kənˈtʃeətəʊ] (pl concertos or concerti [-tiː]) n concerto m.

concession [kən'seʃn] n **1.** [gen & LAW] concession f; COMM [reduction] réduction f ▶ **to make a concession (to sb)** faire une concession (à qqn) **2.** MIN & PETR concession f.

concessionaire [kən,seʃə'neəʳ] n concessionnaire mf.

concessionary [kən'seʃnəri] (pl **concessionaries**) adj [gen & FIN & LAW] concessionnaire; COMM [fare, ticket] à prix réduit.

concierge ['kɒnsierʒ] n ⓊⓈ gérant m, -e f d'hôtel.

conciliation [kən,sili'eiʃn] n **1.** [appeasement] apaisement m **2.** [reconciliation] conciliation f; INDUST médiation f / a conciliation service un service de conciliation.

conciliatory [kən'siliətri] adj [manner, words] conciliant; [person] conciliateur, conciliant; LAW & POL [procedure] conciliatoire.

concise [kən'sais] adj [succinct] concis; [abridged] abrégé.

concisely [kən'saisli] adv avec concision.

conclave ['kɒnkleiv] n [private meeting] assemblée f or réunion f à huis clos; RELIG conclave m.

conclude [kən'klu:d] ◆ vt **1.** [finish] conclure, terminer; [meeting] clore, clôturer **2.** [settle - deal, treaty] conclure **3.** [deduce] conclure, déduire **4.** [decide] décider. ◆ vi **1.** [person] conclure **2.** [event] se terminer, s'achever.

conclusion [kən'klu:ʒn] n **1.** [end] conclusion f, fin f ▶ **to bring sthg to a conclusion** mener qqch à sa conclusion or à terme **2.** [decision, judgment] conclusion f, décision f **3.** [settling - of deal, treaty] conclusion f **4.** PHILOS conclusion f. ❖ **in conclusion** adv phr en conclusion, pour conclure.

conclusive [kən'klu:siv] adj [decisive - proof, argument] concluant, décisif; [final] final.

conclusively [kən'klu:sivli] adv de façon concluante or décisive, définitivement.

concoct [kən'kɒkt] vt **1.** [prepare] composer, confectionner **2.** fig [invent - excuse, scheme] combiner, concocter.

concoction [kən'kɒkʃn] n **1.** [act] confection f, préparation f **2.** [mixture] mélange m, mixture f pej.

concord ['kɒŋkɔ:d] n **1.** fml [harmony] concorde f, harmonie f **2.** GRAM accord m.

concourse ['kɒŋkɔ:s] n [meeting place] lieu m de rassemblement; [in building] hall m; ⓊⓈ [street] boulevard m; [crossroads] carrefour m.

concrete ['kɒŋkri:t] ◆ n CONSTR béton m. ◆ adj **1.** [specific - advantage] concret (concrète), réel; [- example, proposal] concret (concrète) **2.** CONSTR en or de béton. ◆ vt bétonner.

concrete mixer n bétonnière f.

concubine ['kɒŋkjubain] n concubine f.

concur [kən'kɜ:ʳ] (pt & pp **concurred,** cont **concurring**) vi **1.** [agree] être d'accord, s'entendre ▶ **to concur with sb** / **sthg** être d'accord avec qqn / qqch **2.** [occur together] coïncider, arriver en même temps.

concurrent [kən'kʌrənt] adj [simultaneous] concomitant, simultané.

concurrently [kən'kʌrəntli] adv simultanément.

concuss [kən'kʌs] vt **1.** [injure brain] commotionner / to be concussed être commotionné **2.** [shake] ébranler, secouer violemment.

concussion [kən'kʌʃn] n (U) [brain injury] commotion f cérébrale.

condemn [kən'dem] vt **1.** [gen & LAW] condamner / condemned to death condamné à mort **2.** [disapprove of] condamner, censurer **3.** [declare unfit] condamner, déclarer inutilisable; [building] déclarer inhabitable, condamner **4.** ⓊⓈ LAW [property] exproprier pour cause d'utilité publique.

condemnation [,kɒndem'neiʃn] n **1.** [gen & LAW] condamnation f **2.** [criticism] condamnation f, censure f **3.** [of building] condamnation f **4.** ⓊⓈ LAW [of property] expropriation f pour cause d'utilité publique.

condemned [kən'demd] adj condamné.

condensation [,kɒnden'seiʃn] n [gen & CHEM] condensation f; [on glass] buée f, condensation f.

condense [kən'dens] ◆ vt **1.** [make denser] condenser, concentrer; CHEM [gas] condenser; PHYS [beam] concentrer **2.** [report, book] condenser, résumer. ◆ vi [become liquid] se condenser; [become concentrated] se concentrer.

condensed milk n lait m concentré.

condescend [,kɒndi'send] vi **1.** [behave patronizingly] ▶ **to condescend (to sb)** se montrer condescendant (envers qqn or à l'égard de qqn) **2.** [lower o.s.] ▶ **to condescend to do sthg** condescendre à or daigner faire qqch.

condescending [,kɒndi'sendiŋ] adj condescendant.

condescension [,kɒndi'senʃn] n condescendance f.

condiment ['kɒndimənt] n condiment m ▶ **condiment set** service m à condiments.

condition [kən'diʃn] ◆ n **1.** [state - mental, physical] état m **2.** [stipulation] condition f ▶ **to make a condition that** stipuler que **3.** [illness] maladie f, affection f **4.** fml [social status] situation f, position f. ◆ vt [train] conditionner; PSYCHOL provoquer un réflexe conditionné chez, conditionner. ❖ **conditions** pl n [circumstances] conditions fpl, circonstances fpl. ❖ **on condition that** conj phr : I'll tell you on condition that you keep it secret je vais vous le dire à condition que vous gardiez le secret / he'll do it on condition that he's well paid il le fera à condition d'être bien payé.

> 📋 Note that à condition que is followed by a verb in the subjunctive:
> **I'll do it on condition that my friends can come.** Je le ferai à condition que mes amis puissent venir.

conditional [kən'diʃənl] ◆ adj **1.** [dependent on other factors] conditionnel ▶ **to be conditional on** or **upon sthg** dépendre de qqch **2.** GRAM conditionnel. ◆ n conditionnel m / in the conditional au conditionnel.

conditionality [kən,diʃə'næləti] n conditionnalité f.

conditionally [kən'diʃnəli] adv conditionnellement.

conditioned [kən'diʃnd] adj conditionné.

conditioner [kən'diʃnəʳ] n [for hair] baume m démêlant; [for skin] crème f traitante or équilibrante; [for fabric] assouplisseur m.

conditioning [kən'diʃniŋ] ◆ n [gen] conditionnement m; [fitness] mise f en forme. ◆ adj traitant.

condo ['kɒndəu] n ⓊⓈ inf = **condominium.**

condolence [kən'dəuləns] n condoléance f ▶ **to offer one's condolences to sb** présenter ses condoléances à qqn.

condom ['kɒndəm] n préservatif m (masculin).

condominium [,kɒndə'miniəm] n ⓊⓈ [ownership] copropriété f; [building] immeuble m (en copropriété); [flat] appartement m en copropriété.

condone [kən'dəun] vt [overlook] fermer les yeux sur; [forgive] pardonner, excuser.

condor ['kɒndɔ:ʳ] n condor m.

conducive [kən'dju:siv] adj favorable.

conduct ◆ n ['kɒndʌkt] **1.** [behaviour] conduite f, comportement m **2.** [handling - of business, negotiations] conduite f. ◆ vt [kən'dʌkt] **1.** [manage, carry out - campaign] diriger, mener ; [-inquiry] conduire, mener **2.** [guide] conduire, mener **3.** [behave] ▶ **to conduct o.s.** se conduire, se comporter **4.** MUS [musicians, music] diriger **5.** ELEC & PHYS [transmit] conduire, être conducteur de.

conducted tour [kən'dʌktɪd-] n 🇬🇧 [short] visite f guidée ; [longer] voyage m organisé.

conductivity [ˌkɒndʌk'tɪvətɪ] n conductivité f.

conductor [kən'dʌktər] n **1.** MUS chef m d'orchestre **2.** [on bus, train] receveur m ; 🇺🇸 [railway official] chef m de train.

conduit ['kɒnduɪt] n [for fluid] conduit m, canalisation f ; ELEC tube m ; fig [for money] intermédiaire mf.

cone [kəʊn] n **1.** [gen & MATH], OPT & TECH cône m ▶ a **traffic cone** un cône de signalisation **2.** [for ice cream] cornet m **3.** BOT [of pine, fir] pomme f, cône m.

conehead ['kəʊnhed] n 🇺🇸 inf ▶ **you conehead!** imbécile !

cone-shaped [-ʃeɪpt] adj en forme de cône, conique.

confection [kən'fekʃn] n **1.** [act] confection f **2.** CULIN [sweet] sucrerie f, friandise f ; [pastry] pâtisserie f ; [cake] gâteau m.

confectioner [kən'fekʃnər] n [of sweets] confiseur m, -euse f ; [of pastry] pâtissier m, -ère f ▶ a confectioner's (shop) **a)** [for sweets] une confiserie **b)** [for pastry] une pâtisserie ▶ **confectioner's custard** crème f pâtissière ▶ **confectioner's sugar** 🇺🇸 sucre m glace.

confectionery [kən'fekʃnərɪ] (pl **confectioneries**) n [sweets] confiserie f ; [pastry] pâtisserie f.

confederate n [kən'fedərət] [accomplice] complice mf. ❖ **Confederate** ◆ n HIST sudiste mf (pendant la guerre de Sécession américaine) ▶ **the Confederates** les Confédérés. ◆ adj HIST ▶ **the Confederate flag** drapeau des sudistes américains, considéré aujourd'hui comme un symbole raciste ▶ **the Confederate States** les États mpl confédérés (pendant la guerre de Sécession américaine).

confederation [kən,fedə'reɪʃn] n confédération f.

confer [kən'fɜ:r] (pt & pp **conferred**, cont **conferring**) ◆ vi conférer, s'entretenir ▶ **to confer with sb (about sthg)** s'entretenir avec qqn (de qqch). ◆ vt conférer, accorder ▶ **to confer sthg on sb** conférer qqch à qqn.

conference ['kɒnfərəns] n **1.** [meeting] conférence f ; [consultation] conférence f, consultation f **2.** [convention] congrès m, colloque m ; POL congrès m, assemblée f ▶ **conference centre a)** [building] centre de congrès **b)** [town] ville pouvant accueillir des congrès ▶ **conference hall** salle f de conférence **3.** 🇺🇸 SPORT [association] association f, ligue f.

conference call n téléconférence f.

conferencing ['kɒnfərənsɪŋ] n ▶ **audio conferencing** téléconférences fpl, audioconférences fpl ▶ **web conferencing** conférences fpl en ligne, webconférences fpl.

confess [kən'fes] ◆ vt **1.** [admit - fault, crime] avouer, confesser **2.** RELIG [sins] confesser, se confesser de ; [subj : priest] confesser. ◆ vi **1.** [admit] faire des aveux **2.** RELIG se confesser.

confession [kən'feʃn] n **1.** [of guilt] aveu m, confession f **2.** RELIG confession f ; [sect] confession f.

confessional [kən'feʃənl] ◆ n confessionnal m. ◆ adj confessionnel.

confetti [kən'fetɪ] n (U) confettis mpl.

confidant ['kɒnfɪdænt] n confident m.

confidante [ˌkɒnfɪ'dænt] n confidente f.

confide [kən'faɪd] vt **1.** [reveal] avouer en confidence, confier **2.** [entrust] confier. ❖ **confide in** vt insep **1.** [talk freely to] se confier à **2.** [trust] avoir confiance en, se fier à.

confidence ['kɒnfɪdəns] n **1.** [faith] confiance f ▶ **to put one's confidence in sb / sthg** faire confiance à qqn / qqch **2.** [self-assurance] confiance f (en soi), assurance f **3.** [certainty] confiance f, certitude f **4.** [trust] confiance f / I was told in confidence on me l'a dit confidentiellement or en confiance ▶ **to take sb into one's confidence** se confier à qqn, faire des confidences à qqn **5.** [private message] confidence f.

⚠ The French word **confidence** means something said in confidence. For the other meanings of the English word confidence, use **confiance**.

confidence-building adj [exercise, activity] qui vise à stimuler la confiance en soi.

confidence trick n escroquerie f, abus m de confiance.

confident ['kɒnfɪdənt] adj **1.** [self-assured] sûr (de soi), assuré **2.** [certain] assuré, confiant / confident of success sûr de réussir.

confidential [ˌkɒnfɪ'denʃl] adj [private] confidentiel ; [on envelope] confidentiel ▶ **confidential secretary** secrétaire m particulier, secrétaire f particulière.

confidentiality ['kɒnfɪˌdenʃɪ'ælətɪ] n confidentialité f.

confidentiality agreement n accord m de confidentialité.

confidentially [ˌkɒnfɪ'denʃəlɪ] adv confidentiellement.

confidently ['kɒnfɪdəntlɪ] adv **1.** [with certainty] avec confiance **2.** [assuredly] avec assurance.

configuration [kən,fɪɡə'reɪʃn] n [gen & COMPUT] configuration f.

configure [kən'fɪɡə] vt [gen & COMPUT] configurer.

confine [kən'faɪn] vt **1.** [restrict] limiter, borner ▶ **to confine o.s. to sthg** se borner or s'en tenir à qqch **2.** [shut up] confiner, enfermer ; [imprison] incarcérer, enfermer / to confine sb to barracks MIL consigner qqn **3.** [pregnant woman] ▶ **to be confined** accoucher, être en couches.

confined [kən'faɪnd] adj **1.** [area, atmosphere] confiné / in a confined space dans un espace restreint ou réduit **2.** [shut up] renfermé ; [imprisoned] emprisonné, incarcéré / to be confined to barracks MIL être consigné.

confinement [kən'faɪnmənt] n **1.** [detention] détention f, réclusion f ; [imprisonment] emprisonnement m, incarcération f / confinement to barracks MIL consigne f (au quartier) **2.** [in childbirth] couches fpl, accouchement m.

confines ['kɒnfaɪnz] pl n confins mpl, limites fpl.

confirm [kən'fɜ:m] vt **1.** [verify] confirmer, corroborer **2.** [finalize - arrangement, booking] confirmer **3.** [strengthen - position] assurer, consolider ; [- belief, doubts, resolve] fortifier, confirmer, raffermir **4.** [make valid - treaty] ratifier ; [- election] valider ; LAW entériner, homologuer **5.** RELIG confirmer.

confirmation [ˌkɒnfə'meɪʃn] n **1.** [verification] confirmation f **2.** [finalization - of arrangements] confirmation f **3.** [strengthening - of position] consolidation f, raffermissement m **4.** [validation] validation f ; LAW entérinement m, homologation f ; [of treaty] ratification f **5.** RELIG confirmation f.

confirmed [kən'fɜ:md] adj **1.** [long-established] invétéré / he's a confirmed bachelor c'est un célibataire endurci **2.** RELIG confirmé.

confiscate ['kɒnfɪskeɪt] vt confisquer ▶ **to confiscate sthg from sb** confisquer qqch à qqn.

confiscation [ˌkɒnfɪ'skeɪʃn] n confiscation f.

conflagration [ˌkɒnfləˈgreɪʃn] n *fml* incendie *m*, sinistre *m fml*.

conflict ◆ n [ˈkɒnflɪkt] **1.** [clash] conflit *m*, lutte *f* ; MIL conflit *m*, guerre *f* ▶ **conflict of interests** ECON & POL conflit *m* d'intérêts **2.** [disagreement] dispute *f* ; LAW conflit *m* ▶ **to be in conflict (with)** être en conflit (avec) **3.** PSYCHOL [turmoil] conflit *m*. ◆ vi [kənˈflɪkt] [ideas, interests] s'opposer, se heurter.

conflicting [kənˈflɪktɪŋ] adj [opinions] incompatible ; [evidence, reports] contradictoire.

conform [kənˈfɔːm] vi **1.** [comply - person] se conformer, s'adapter ▶ **to conform to** or **with sthg** se conformer or s'adapter à qqch **2.** [action, thing] être en conformité **3.** [correspond] correspondre, répondre **4.** RELIG être conformiste.

conformism [kənˈfɔːmɪzm] n conformisme *m*.

conformist [kənˈfɔːmɪst] ◆ adj conformiste. ◆ n [gen & RELIG] conformiste *mf*.

conformity [kənˈfɔːmətɪ] (*pl* **conformities**) n **1.** [with rules, regulations] conformité *f* **2.** [in behaviour, dress, etc.] conformisme *m* **3.** RELIG conformisme *m*. ◆ **in conformity with** prep phr en accord avec, conformément à.

confound [kənˈfaʊnd] vt **1.** [perplex] déconcerter / *to be confounded* être confondu **2.** *fml* [mix up] confondre.

confounded [kənˈfaʊndɪd] adj *inf & dated* [wretched] maudit.

confront [kənˈfrʌnt] vt **1.** [face] affronter, faire face à ▶ **to be confronted by** or **with sthg** [problem, risk] se trouver en face de qqch **2.** [present] confronter.

confrontation [ˌkɒnfrʌnˈteɪʃn] n **1.** [conflict] conflit *m*, affrontement *m* ; MIL affrontement *m* **2.** [act of confronting] confrontation *f*.

confrontational [ˌkɒnfrʌnˈteɪʃənl] adj [situation] d'affrontement ; [policy] de confrontation ; [person] : *to be confrontational* aimer les conflits.

confuse [kənˈfjuːz] vt **1.** [muddle - person] embrouiller ; [- thoughts] embrouiller, brouiller ; [- memory] brouiller **2.** [perplex] déconcerter, rendre perplexe ; [fluster] troubler ; [embarrass] embarrasser **3.** [mix up] confondre **4.** [disconcert - opponent] confondre.

confused [kənˈfjuːzd] adj **1.** [muddled - person] désorienté ; [- sounds] confus, indistinct ; [- thoughts] confus, embrouillé ; [- memory] confus, vague **2.** [flustered] troublé ; [embarrassed] confus **3.** [disordered] en désordre ; [enemy] confus.

confusing [kənˈfjuːzɪŋ] adj embrouillé, déroutant.

confusingly [kənˈfjuːzɪŋlɪ] adv de façon embrouillée.

confusion [kənˈfjuːʒn] n **1.** [bewilderment] confusion *f* ; [embarrassment] déconfiture *f*, trouble *m*, embarras *m* **2.** [mixing up] confusion *f* **3.** [disorder] désordre *m* ; [of enemy] désordre *m*, désarroi *m*.

conga [ˈkɒŋgə] n conga *f*.

congeal [kənˈdʒiːl] vi [thicken] prendre ; [oil] (se) figer ; [blood] (se) coaguler ; [milk] (se) cailler.

congenial [kənˈdʒiːnjəl] adj [pleasant] sympathique, agréable.

congenital [kənˈdʒenɪtl] adj MED congénital, de naissance.

conger (eel) [ˈkɒŋgə-] n congre *m*, anguille *f* de mer.

congested [kənˈdʒestɪd] adj **1.** [area, town] surpeuplé ; [road] encombré, embouteillé ; [communication lines] encombré **2.** MED [clogged] congestionné.

congestion [kənˈdʒestʃn] n **1.** [of area] surpeuplement *m* ; [of road, traffic] encombrement *m*, embouteillage *m* **2.** MED [blockage] congestion *f*.

congestion charge n UK taxe *f* anti-embouteillages.

conglomerate n [kənˈglɒmərət] [gen & FIN & GEOL] conglomérat *m*.

conglomeration [kənˌglɒməˈreɪʃn] n [mass] groupement *m*, rassemblement *m* ; [of buildings] agglomération *f*.

Congo [ˈkɒŋgəʊ] pr n **1.** [country] ▶ **the Congo** le Congo / *in the Congo* au Congo **2.** [river] ▶ **the Congo** le Congo.

Congolese [ˌkɒŋgəˈliːz] ◆ n Congolais *m*, -e *f*. ◆ adj congolais.

congrats [kənˈgræts] interj *inf* ▶ **congrats!** chapeau !

congratulate [kənˈgrætʃʊleɪt] vt féliciter, complimenter.

congratulations [kənˌgrætʃʊˈleɪʃnz] ◆ interj ▶ **congratulations!** (toutes mes) félicitations !, je vous félicite ! ◆ pl n félicitations *fpl*.

> ⚠ The word **congratulation** exists in French, but it is formal and rarely used. The English word congratulations should be translated by **félicitations**.

congratulatory [kənˈgrætʃʊlətrɪ] adj de félicitations.

congregate [ˈkɒŋgrɪgeɪt] vi se rassembler, se réunir.

congregation [ˌkɒŋgrɪˈgeɪʃn] n [group] assemblée *f*, rassemblement *m* ; RELIG [of worshippers] assemblée *f* (de fidèles), assistance *f* ; [of priests] congrégation *f*.

congress [ˈkɒŋgres] n [association, meeting] congrès *m*. ◆ **Congress** n POL Congrès *m* ; [session] *session du Congrès américain.*

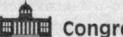 **Congress**

Le Congrès, organe législatif américain, est constitué du Sénat et de la Chambre des représentants ; tout projet de loi doit être approuvé séparément par ces deux chambres.

congressional [kənˈgreʃənl] US adj [gen] d'un congrès. ◆ **Congressional** adj POL du Congrès ▶ **Congressional district** circonscription d'un représentant du Congrès américain ▶ **Congressional Medal of Honor** la plus haute distinction militaire américaine ▶ **Congressional Record** journal officiel du Congrès américain.

congressman [ˈkɒŋgresmən] (*pl* **congressmen** [-mən]) n US POL membre *m* du Congrès américain ▶ **congressman-at-large** représentant du Congrès américain non attaché à une circonscription électorale.

congresswoman [ˈkɒŋgresˌwʊmən] (*pl* **congresswomen** [-ˌwɪmɪn]) n US POL membre *m* (féminin) du Congrès américain.

conic(al) [ˈkɒnɪk(l)] adj en forme de cône, conique.

conifer [ˈkɒnɪfə] n conifère *m*.

coniferous [kəˈnɪfərəs] adj conifère.

conjecture [kənˈdʒektʃə] ◆ n conjecture *f*. ◆ vt conjecturer, présumer. ◆ vi conjecturer, faire des conjectures.

conjoined twins [kənˈdʒɔɪnd-] pl n jumeaux *mpl* conjoints or siamois.

conjugal [ˈkɒndʒʊgl] adj conjugal.

conjugate ◆ vt [ˈkɒndʒʊgeɪt] conjuguer. ◆ vi se conjuguer.

conjugation [ˌkɒndʒʊˈgeɪʃn] n conjugaison *f*.

conjunction [kənˈdʒʌŋkʃn] n **1.** [combination] conjonction f, union f **2.** ASTRON & GRAM conjonction f. ❖ **in conjunction with** prep phr conjointement avec.

conjunctivitis [kənˌdʒʌŋktɪˈvaɪtɪs] n conjonctivite f.

conjure [ˈkʌndʒər] vi faire des tours de passe-passe. ❖ **conjure up** vt sep [object, rabbit] faire apparaître, produire ; [gods, spirits] faire apparaître, invoquer ; [memory] évoquer, rappeler ; [image] évoquer.

conjurer [ˈkʌndʒərər] n [magician] prestidigitateur m, -trice f ; [sorcerer] sorcier m, -ère f.

conjuring [ˈkʌndʒərɪŋ] ❖ n prestidigitation f. ❖ adj ▸ **conjuring trick** tour m de passe-passe or de prestidigitation.

conjuror [ˈkʌndʒərər] = conjurer.

conk [kɒŋk] inf ❖ vt [hit] cogner or frapper (sur la caboche). ❖ n 🇬🇧 [nose] pif m. ❖ **conk out** vi inf tomber en panne.

conker [ˈkɒŋkər] n 🇬🇧 inf marron m. ❖ **conkers** n (U) inf jeu d'enfant qui consiste à tenter de casser un marron tenu au bout d'un fil par son adversaire.

conman [ˈkɒnmæn] (pl **conmen** [-men]) n inf arnaqueur m.

connect [kəˈnekt] ❖ vt **1.** [join - pipes, wires] raccorder ; [- pinions, shafts, wheels] engrener, coupler ▸ **to connect sthg up to sthg** joindre or relier or raccorder qqch à qqch **2.** [join to supply - machine, house, telephone] brancher, raccorder ▸ **to connect sthg to sthg** raccorder qqch à qqch, brancher qqch sur qqch **3.** TELEC mettre en communication, relier ▸ **to connect sb to sb** mettre qqn en communication avec qqn / *I'm trying to connect you* j'essaie d'obtenir votre communication **4.** [link - subj: path, railway, road, airline] relier ▸ **to connect with** or **to relier à 5.** [associate - person, place, event] associer, faire le rapprochement ▸ **to connect sb / sthg with sb / sthg** associer une personne / chose à une autre. ❖ vi **1.** [bus, plane, train] assurer la correspondance ▸ **to connect with** assurer la correspondance avec **2.** [blow, fist, kick] frapper.

connected [kəˈnektɪd] adj **1.** [linked - subjects, species] connexe **2.** [coherent - speech, sentences] cohérent, suivi **3.** [associated] ▸ **to be connected with** avoir un lien or rapport avec **4.** [in family] ▸ **to be connected with** or **to** être parent de.

Connecticut [kəˈnetɪkət] pr n Connecticut m / *in Connecticut* dans le Connecticut.

connecting [kəˈnektɪŋ] adj [cable, wire] de connexion ▸ **connecting flight** correspondance f ▸ **connecting door** porte f de communication.

connection [kəˈnekʃn] n **1.** [link between two things] lien m, rapport m, connexion f ▸ **to make a connection between** or **to** or **with sthg** faire le lien avec qqch **2.** ELEC prise f, raccord m **3.** TELEC communication f, ligne f **4.** [transfer - between buses, planes, trains] correspondance f **5.** [transport] liaison f **6.** [relationship] rapport m, relation f ▸ **family connections** parenté f **7.** [colleague, business contact] relation f (d'affaires). ❖ **in connection with** prep phr à propos de.

connective tissue n tissu m conjonctif.

connectivity [ˌkɒnekˈtɪvɪtɪ] n connectivité f.

connexion [kəˈnekʃn] = connection.

connive [kəˈnaɪv] vi pej [plot] être de connivence.

conniving [kəˈnaɪvɪŋ] adj pej malhonnête, rusé, sournois.

connoisseur [ˌkɒnəˈsɜːr] n connaisseur m, -euse f.

connotation [ˌkɒnəˈteɪʃn] n **1.** [association] connotation f **2.** LING connotation f **3.** LOGIC implication f.

connote [kəˈnəʊt] vt **1.** fml [imply - subj: word, phrase, name] évoquer **2.** LING connoter **3.** LOGIC impliquer.

conquer [ˈkɒŋkər] vt **1.** [defeat - person, enemy] vaincre **2.** [take control of - city, nation] conquérir **3.** [master - feelings, habits] surmonter ; [- disease, disability] vaincre, surmonter **4.** [win over - sb's heart] conquérir ; [- audience, public] conquérir, subjuguer.

conqueror [ˈkɒŋkərər] n conquérant m.

conquest [ˈkɒŋkwest] n [of land, person] conquête f ; [land, person conquered] conquête f.

Cons. written abbr of **Conservative.**

conscience [ˈkɒnʃəns] n **1.** [moral sense] conscience f **2.** (U) [scruples] mauvaise conscience f, remords m, scrupule m ▸ **to have no conscience (about doing sthg)** ne pas avoir de scrupules (à faire qqch).

conscientious [ˌkɒnʃɪˈenʃəs] adj consciencieux.

conscientiously [ˌkɒnʃɪˈenʃəslɪ] adv consciencieusement.

conscientiousness [ˌkɒnʃɪˈenʃəsnɪs] n conscience f.

conscientious objector n objecteur m de conscience.

conscious [ˈkɒnʃəs] ❖ adj **1.** [aware] conscient ▸ **to be conscious of (doing) sthg** être conscient de (faire) qqch ▸ **to become conscious of sthg** prendre conscience de qqch **2.** [awake] conscient / *to become conscious* reprendre connaissance **3.** [deliberate - attempt, effort] conscient ; [- cruelty, rudeness] intentionnel, délibéré **4.** [able to think - being, mind] conscient. ❖ n PSYCHOL ▸ **the conscious** le conscient.

-conscious in comp conscient de ▸ **age-conscious** conscient de son âge ▸ **fashion-conscious** qui suit la mode ▸ **health-conscious** soucieux de sa santé.

consciously [ˈkɒnʃəslɪ] adv consciemment, délibérément.

consciousness [ˈkɒnʃəsnɪs] n **1.** [awareness] conscience f **2.** [mentality] conscience f **3.** [state of being awake] connaissance f.

consciousness raising n sensibilisation f. ❖ **consciousness-raising** comp [campaign, session] de sensibilisation.

conscript ❖ vt [kənˈskrɪpt] [men, troops] enrôler, recruter ; [workers, labourers] recruter. ❖ n [ˈkɒnskrɪpt] conscrit m, appelé m. ❖ adj [ˈkɒnskrɪpt] [army] de conscrits.

conscription [kənˈskrɪpʃn] n conscription f.

consecrate [ˈkɒnsɪkreɪt] vt **1.** [sanctify - church, building, place] consacrer ; [- bread and wine] consacrer **2.** [ordain - bishop] consacrer, sacrer **3.** [dedicate] consacrer, dédier.

consecrated [ˈkɒnsɪkreɪtɪd] adj RELIG consacré.

consecration [ˌkɒnsɪˈkreɪʃn] n **1.** [sanctification] consécration f **2.** [ordination] sacre m **3.** [dedication] consécration f.

consecutive [kənˈsekjʊtɪv] adj **1.** [successive - days, weeks] consécutif **2.** GRAM [clause] consécutif.

consecutively [kənˈsekjʊtɪvlɪ] adv consécutivement.

consensual [kənˈsensjʊəl] adj LAW & MED [contract, agreement] consensuel.

consensus [kənˈsensəs] ❖ n consensus m. ❖ comp [politics] de consensus.

consent [kənˈsent] ❖ vi consentir ▸ **to consent to (do) sthg** consentir à (faire) qqch. ❖ n consentement m, accord m ▸ **the age of consent** âge où les rapports sexuels sont autorisés (16 ans en Grande-Bretagne, 16 ou 18 ans aux États-Unis selon les États).

consenting [kənˈsentɪŋ] adj LAW [adult] consentant / *she is a consenting adult, after all* inf & hum elle est majeure et vaccinée après tout.

consenting adult [kənˈsentɪŋ-] n adulte m consentant.

consequence ['kɒnsɪkwəns] n **1.** [result] conséquence f, suite f ▶ **as a consequence of** à la suite de **2.** [importance] conséquence f, importance f / *it's of no consequence* c'est sans conséquence, cela n'a pas d'importance. ❖ **consequences** pl n conséquences fpl / *to face the consequences* faire face aux conséquences. ❖ **in consequence** adv phr par conséquent.

consequent ['kɒnsɪkwənt] adj *fml* consécutif.

consequential [,kɒnsɪ'kwenʃl] adj *fml* = consequent.

consequently ['kɒnsɪkwəntlɪ] adv par conséquent, donc.

conservation [,kɒnsə'veɪʃn] n **1.** [of works of art] préservation f **2.** [of natural resources] préservation f.

conservation area n zone f protégée.

conservationist [,kɒnsə'veɪʃənɪst] n défenseur m de l'environnement.

conservatism [kən'sɜ:vətɪzm] n **1.** POL = Conservatism **2.** [traditionalism] conservatisme m. ❖ **Conservatism** n [policy of Conservative Party] conservatisme m.

conservative [kən'sɜ:vətɪv] ❖ n [traditionalist] traditionaliste mf, conformiste mf. ❖ adj **1.** [traditionalist - views] conformiste **2.** [conventional - suit, clothes] classique **3.** [modest - estimate] prudent. ❖ **Conservative** ❖ n POL conservateur m, -trice f. ❖ adj POL [policy, government, MP] conservateur.

conservatively [kən'sɜ:vətɪvlɪ] adv [dress] de façon conventionnelle.

Conservative Party pr n ▶ **the Conservative Party** le parti conservateur.

The Conservative Party

Le parti conservateur britannique est né au début du XIXᵉ siècle. Héritier du **Tory Party** fondé au XVIIᵉ siècle, il en conserve le nom dans l'usage courant : **Tory** est synonyme de **Conservative**. La figure la plus emblématique du parti conservateur au XXᵉ siècle fut certainement Margaret Thatcher, Premier ministre de 1979 à 1990, qui incarna une politique de droite intransigeante, voire radicale. Aujourd'hui, le **Conservative Party** a une approche plus modérée et centriste.

conservator [kən'sɜ:vətər] n gardien m, -enne f.

conservatory [kən'sɜ:vətrɪ] (pl **conservatories**) n [greenhouse] jardin m d'hiver.

conserve ❖ vt [kən'sɜ:v] [save - energy, resources, battery] économiser / *to conserve one's strength* ménager ses forces. ❖ n ['kɒnsɜ:v or kən'sɜ:v] confiture f.

consider [kən'sɪdər] ❖ vt **1.** [believe] considérer, estimer, penser **2.** [ponder - problem, offer, possibility] considérer, examiner ; [- issue, question] réfléchir à **3.** [bear in mind - points, facts] prendre en considération ; [- costs, difficulties, dangers] tenir compte de / *all things considered* tout bien considéré **4.** [show regard for - feelings, wishes] tenir compte de **5.** [discuss - report, case] examiner, considérer **6.** [contemplate - picture, scene] examiner, observer. ❖ vi réfléchir.

considerable [kən'sɪdrəbl] adj considérable.

considerably [kən'sɪdrəblɪ] adv considérablement.

considerate [kən'sɪdərət] adj [person] prévenant, plein d'égards, aimable.

considerately [kən'sɪdərətlɪ] adv avec des égards.

consideration [kən,sɪdə'reɪʃn] n **1.** [thought] considération f ▶ **to take sthg into consideration** prendre qqch en considération **2.** [factor] considération f, préoccupation f **3.** [thoughtfulness] égard m ▶ **to show consideration for sb / sb's feelings** ménager qqn / la sensibilité de qqn **4.** [discussion] étude f / *the matter is under consideration* l'affaire est à l'étude **5.** [importance] : *of no consideration* sans importance **6.** *fml* [payment] rémunération f, finance f.

considered [kən'sɪdəd] adj [reasoned - opinion, manner] bien pesé, mûrement réfléchi.

considering [kən'sɪdərɪŋ] ❖ conj étant donné que, vu que. ❖ prep étant donné, vu. ❖ adv *inf* tout compte fait, finalement.

consign [kən'saɪn] vt **1.** [send - goods] envoyer, expédier **2.** [relegate - thing] reléguer **3.** [entrust - person] confier ▶ **to consign sb to sb** confier qqn à or aux soins de qqn.

consignee [,kɒnsaɪ'ni:] n consignataire mf.

consigner [kən'saɪnər] = consignor.

consignment [kən'saɪnmənt] n **1.** [despatch] envoi m, expédition f ▶ **consignment note** bordereau m d'expédition **2.** [batch of goods] arrivage m, lot m.

consignor [kən'saɪnər] n expéditeur m, -trice f.

consist [kən'sɪst] ❖ **consist of** vt insep consister en, se composer de. ❖ **consist in** vt insep *fml* ▶ **to consist in (doing) sthg** consister à faire qqch or dans qqch.

consistence [kən'sɪstəns] (pl **consistences**), **consistency** [kən'sɪstənsɪ] (pl **consistencies**) n **1.** [texture] consistance f **2.** [coherence - of behaviour, argument, etc.] cohérence f, logique f.

consistent [kən'sɪstənt] adj **1.** [constant - opponent, loyalty] constant **2.** [steady - growth, improvement] constant **3.** [idea, argument, account] cohérent.

⚠ The French adjective **consistant** means solid or substantial, not consistent.

consistently [kən'sɪstəntlɪ] adv régulièrement, constamment.

consolation [,kɒnsə'leɪʃn] n consolation f, réconfort m.

consolation prize n *lit & fig* prix m de consolation.

console ❖ vt [kən'səʊl] consoler ▶ **to console sb for sthg (with or by)** consoler qqn de qqch (avec or en). ❖ n ['kɒnsəʊl]. **1.** [control panel] console f, pupitre m **2.** [cabinet] meuble m (pour téléviseur, chaîne hi-fi).

consolidate [kən'sɒlɪdeɪt] vt **1.** [reinforce - forces, power] consolider ; [- knowledge] consolider, renforcer **2.** [combine - companies, states] réunir, fusionner ; [- funds, loans] consolider.

consolidated [kən'sɒlɪdeɪtɪd] adj [annuity, loan, loss] consolidé ; [in name of company] *désigne une société née de la fusion de deux entreprises.*

consolidation [kən,sɒlɪ'deɪʃn] n **1.** [reinforcement - of power] consolidation f ; [- of knowledge] consolidation f, renforcement m **2.** [amalgamation - of companies] fusion f ; [- of funds, loans] consolidation f.

consommé [🇬🇧 kən'sɒmeɪ 🇺🇸 ,kɒnsə'meɪ] n consommé m.

consonant ['kɒnsənənt] ❖ n consonne f. ❖ adj *fml* en accord.

consort ❖ n ['kɒnsɔ:t] [spouse] époux m, épouse f ; [of monarch] consort m. ❖ vi [kən'sɔ:t] ▶ **to consort with sb** fréquenter qqn, frayer avec qqn.

consortium [kən'sɔ:tjəm] (pl **consortiums** or **consortia** [-tjə]) n consortium m.

conspicuous [kən'spɪkjʊəs] adj **1.** [visible -behaviour, hat, person] voyant **▶ to make o.s. conspicuous** se faire remarquer **2.** [obvious -failure, lack] manifeste, évident ; [-bravery, gallantry] insigne **▶ to be conspicuous by one's absence** briller par son absence.

conspicuously [kən'spɪkjʊəslɪ] adv **1.** [visibly -dressed] de façon à se faire remarquer **2.** [obviously -successful] de façon remarquable or évidente.

conspiracy [kən'spɪrəsɪ] (*pl* **conspiracies**) ◆ n [plotting] conspiration *f*, complot *m* ; [plot] complot *m*. ◆ comp **▶ conspiracy theory** thèse *f* du complot.

conspirator [kən'spɪrətər] n conspirateur *m*, -trice *f*, comploteur *m*, -euse *f*, conjuré *m*, -e *f*.

conspiratorial [kən,spɪrə'tɔːrɪəl] adj [smile, whisper, wink] de conspirateur ; [group] de conspirateurs.

conspiratorially [kən,spɪrə'tɔːrɪəlɪ] adv [smile, whisper, wink] d'un air de conspiration.

conspire [kən'spaɪər] vi **1.** [plot] conspirer **▶ to conspire (with sb) to do sthg** comploter or s'entendre (avec qqn) pour faire qqch **▶ to conspire against sb** conspirer contre qqn **2.** [combine -events, the elements] concourir, se conjurer **▶ to conspire to do sthg** concourir à faire qqch **▶ to conspire against sthg** se conjurer contre qqch.

constable ['kʌnstəbl] n agent *m*, gendarme *m*, sergent *m* / *Constable Jenkins* Sergent Jenkins.

constabulary [kən'stæbjʊlərɪ] (*pl* **constabularies**) ◆ n **▶ the constabulary** la police, la gendarmerie. ◆ adj [duties] de policier.

constancy ['kʌnstənsɪ] n **1.** [steadfastness] constance *f* ; [of feelings] constance *f*, fidélité *f* **2.** [stability -of temperature, light] constance *f*.

constant ['kʌnstənt] ◆ adj **1.** [continuous -interruptions, noise, pain] constant, continuel, perpétuel **2.** [unchanging -pressure, temperature] constant **3.** [faithful -affection, friend] fidèle, loyal. ◆ n [gen & MATH] constante *f*.

constantly ['kʌnstəntlɪ] adv constamment, sans cesse.

constellation [,kʌnstə'leɪʃn] n [of stars] constellation *f*.

consternation [,kʌnstə'neɪʃn] n consternation *f*.

constipated ['kʌnstɪpeɪtɪd] adj constipé.

constipation [,kʌnstɪ'peɪʃn] n constipation *f*.

constituency [kən'stɪtjʊənsɪ] (*pl* **constituencies**) ◆ n [area] circonscription *f* électorale ; [people] électeurs *mpl*. ◆ comp [meeting, organization] local.

constituent [kən'stɪtjʊənt] ◆ adj **1.** [component -part, element] constituant, composant **2.** POL [assembly, power] constituant. ◆ n **1.** [voter] électeur *m*, -trice *f* **2.** [element] élément *m* constitutif.

constitute ['kʌnstɪtjuːt] vt **1.** [represent] constituer **2.** [make up] constituer **3.** [set up -committee] constituer.

constitution [,kʌnstɪ'tjuːʃn] n **1.** POL [statute] constitution *f* **2.** [health] constitution *f* **3.** [structure] composition *f*.

 Constitution

La Constitution britannique, à la différence de la Constitution américaine ou française (reposant sur un texte écrit et définitif), n'est pas un document en soi, mais le résultat de la succession des lois dans le temps, fonctionnant sur le principe de la jurisprudence.

constitutional [,kʌnstɪ'tjuːʃənl] adj **1.** POL constitutionnel **2.** [inherent -weakness] constitutionnel.

constitutional law n droit *m* constitutionnel.

constitutionally [,kʌnstɪ'tjuːʃnəlɪ] adv **1.** POL [act] constitutionnellement **2.** [strong, weak] de or par nature.

constrain [kən'streɪn] vt *fml* **1.** [force] contraindre, forcer **▶ to constrain sb to do sthg** contraindre qqn à faire qqch **2.** [limit -feelings, freedom] contraindre, restreindre.

constrained [kən'streɪnd] adj **1.** [inhibited] contraint **▶ to feel constrained to do sthg** se sentir contraint or obligé de faire qqch **2.** [tense -manner, speech] contraint ; [-atmosphere, smile] contraint, gêné.

constraint [kən'streɪnt] n **1.** [restriction] contrainte *f* **2.** [pressure] contrainte *f* **▶ to do sthg under constraint** agir or faire qqch sous la contrainte.

constrict [kən'strɪkt] vt **1.** [make narrower -blood vessels, throat] resserrer, serrer **2.** [hamper -breathing, movement] gêner.

constricting [kən'strɪktɪŋ] adj [clothes] étroit ; *fig* [beliefs, ideology] limité.

constriction [kən'strɪkʃn] n **1.** [in chest, throat] constriction *f* **2.** [restriction] restriction *f*.

construct vt [kən'strʌkt] **1.** [build -bridge, dam, house, road] construire ; [-nest, raft] construire, bâtir **▶ to construct sthg (out) of sthg** construire qqch à partir de qqch **2.** [formulate -sentence, play] construire, composer ; [-system, theory] bâtir.

construction [kən'strʌkʃn] ◆ n **1.** [act of building -road, bridge, house] construction *f* ; [-machine] construction *f*, réalisation *f* ; [-system, theory] construction *f*, élaboration *f* **2.** [structure] construction *f*, édifice *m*, bâtiment *m* **3.** [interpretation] interprétation *f* **4.** GRAM construction *f*. ◆ comp [site, work] de construction ; [worker] du bâtiment **▶ the construction industry** le bâtiment.

constructive [kən'strʌktɪv] adj [criticism, remark] constructif.

constructive dismissal n démission *f* provoquée *(sous la pression de la direction)*.

constructively [kən'strʌktɪvlɪ] adv de manière constructive.

construe [kən'struː] vt [interpret, understand -attitude, statement] interpréter, expliquer ; *dated* [Greek, Latin] expliquer.

consul ['kʌnsəl] n consul *m*.

consular ['kʌnsjʊlər] adj consulaire.

consulate ['kʌnsjʊlət] n consulat *m*.

consult [kən'sʌlt] ◆ vt **1.** [ask -doctor, expert] consulter **▶ to consult sb about sthg** consulter qqn sur or au sujet de qqch **2.** [refer to -book, map, watch] consulter. ◆ vi consulter, être en consultation **▶ to consult with sb** conférer avec qqn.

consultancy [kən'sʌltənsɪ] (*pl* **consultancies**) n **1.** [company] cabinet *m* d'expert-conseil **2.** [advice] assistance *f* technique **▶ consultancy fee** frais *mpl* de consultation **3.** [hospital post] poste *m* de médecin or chirurgien consultant.

consultant [kən'sʌltənt] ◆ n **1.** [doctor -specialist] médecin *m* spécialiste, consultant *m* ; [-in charge of department] consultant *m* **2.** [expert] expert-conseil *m*, consultant *m*. ◆ comp [engineer] conseil *(inv)* ; MED consultant.

consultation [,kʌnsəl'teɪʃn] n **1.** [discussion] consultation *f*, délibération *f* **▶ in consultation with** en consultation or en concertation avec **2.** [reference] consultation *f*.

consultative [kən'sʌltətɪv] adj consultatif.

consulting [kən'sʌltɪŋ] adj [engineer] conseil *(inv)*.

consulting fee n honoraires *mpl* d'expert.

consulting room n cabinet *m* de consultation.

consumable goods n biens *mpl* or produits *mpl* de consommation.

consume [kən'sju:m] vt **1.** [eat or drink] consommer **2.** [use up - energy, fuel] consommer ; [-time] dépenser **3.** [burn up - subj: fire, flames] consumer / *to be consumed with hatred / jealousy* être consumé par la haine / jalousie.

---

consumer or **consommer?**

The verb **consumer** is used when referring to something burning (**une fois la bougie consumée; des objets calcinés mais non entièrement consumés**) and in a metaphorical sense when referring to all-consuming emotions such as love or jealousy (**consumée par la jalousie; la haine me consume**). **Consommer** is used when talking about eating food, using fuel or buying consumer goods (**une voiture qui consomme peu; vous consommez trop de matières grasses; les Français consomment moins**).

---

consumer [kən'sju:mər] ◆ n [purchaser] consommateur m, -trice f. ◆ comp [advice, protection] du consommateur, des consommateurs.

consumerism [kən'sju:mərɪzm] n **1.** [consumer protection] consumérisme m **2.** pej [consumption] consommation f à outrance.

consummate ◆ adj [kən'sʌmət] fml **1.** [very skilful - artist, musician] consommé, accompli **2.** [utter - coward, fool, liar, snob] accompli, parfait, fini. ◆ vt ['kɒnsəmeɪt] [love, marriage] consommer.

consummation [,kɒnsə'meɪʃn] n **1.** [of marriage] consommation f **2.** [culmination - of career, life's work] couronnement m **3.** [achievement - of ambitions, desires] achèvement m.

consumption [kən'sʌmpʃn] n **1.** [eating, drinking] consommation f **2.** [purchasing] consommation f **3.** [using up, amount used - of gas, energy, oil] consommation f, dépense f **4.** dated [tuberculosis] consomption f (pulmonaire), phtisie f.

cont. written abbr of **continued.**

contact ['kɒntækt] ◆ n **1.** [communication] contact m, rapport m ▸ *to be in contact with sb* être en contact or en rapport avec qqn ▸ *to come into contact with sb* entrer or se mettre en contact or en rapport avec qqn ▸ *to make contact with sb* prendre contact avec qqn **2.** [touch] contact m / *always keep one foot in contact with the ground* gardez toujours un pied en contact avec le sol **3.** [person] relation f **4.** ELEC [connector] contact m ; [connection] contact m ▸ *to make / break (the) contact* mettre / couper le contact **5.** inf = **contact lens.** ◆ comp ▸ **contact address / number**: *shall I give you a contact address / number?* voulez-vous que je vous donne l'adresse / le numéro où vous pouvez me joindre or me contacter ? ◆ vt prendre contact avec, contacter.

contactable [kɒn'tæktəbl] adj que l'on peut joindre or contacter, joignable.

contact center n 🇺🇸 centre m d'appels.

contact lens n lentille f de contact.

contact sport n sport m de contact.

contagious [kən'teɪdʒəs] adj lit & fig contagieux.

contain [kən'teɪn] vt **1.** [hold - subj: bag, house, city] contenir **2.** [include - subj: pill, substance] contenir ; [-subj: book, speech] contenir, comporter **3.** [restrain - feelings] contenir, cacher **4.** [curb - enemy, growth, riot] contenir, maîtriser **5.** [hold back - fire] circonscrire ; [-flood waters] contenir, endiguer **6.** [limit - damage] limiter.

contained [kən'teɪnd] adj [person] maître de soi.

container [kən'teɪnər] ◆ n **1.** [bottle, box, tin, etc.] récipient m, boîte f **2.** [for transporting cargo] conteneur m, container m. ◆ comp [port, ship, terminal] porte-conteneurs ; [dock, line, transport] pour porte-conteneurs.

containerize, containerise [kən'teɪnəraɪz] vt [cargo] conteneuriser, transporter par conteneurs ; [port] convertir à la conteneurisation.

containment [kən'teɪnmənt] n POL endiguement m, freinage m, retenue f.

contaminate [kən'tæmɪneɪt] vt **1.** [pollute - food, river, water] contaminer ; fig [corrupt] contaminer, souiller **2.** [irradiate - land, person, soil] contaminer.

contaminated [kən'tæmɪneɪtɪd] adj **1.** [polluted - food, river, water] contaminé ; [-air] contaminé, vicié ; fig [corrupted] contaminé, corrompu **2.** [irradiated - land, person, soil] contaminé.

contamination [kən,tæmɪ'neɪʃn] n **1.** [pollution - of food, river, water] contamination f ; fig contamination f, corruption f **2.** [irradiation - of land, person, soil] contamination f.

cont'd, contd written abbr of **continued.**

contemplate ['kɒntempleɪt] ◆ vt **1.** [ponder] considérer, réfléchir sur **2.** [consider] considérer, envisager ▸ *to contemplate doing sthg* envisager de or songer à faire qqch **3.** [observe] contempler. ◆ vi **1.** [ponder] méditer, se recueillir **2.** [consider] réfléchir.

contemplation [,kɒntem'pleɪʃn] n **1.** [thought] réflexion f **2.** [observation] contemplation f **3.** [meditation] contemplation f, recueillement m, méditation f.

contemplative [kən'templətɪv] adj [look, mood] songeur, pensif ; [life] contemplatif ; RELIG [order, prayer] contemplatif.

contemporary [kən'tempərərɪ] (pl **contemporaries**) ◆ adj **1.** [modern - art, writer] contemporain, d'aujourd'hui ; [-design, style] moderne **2.** [of the same period - account, report] contemporain. ◆ n contemporain m, -e f.

contempt [kən'tempt] n **1.** [scorn] mépris m ▸ *to feel contempt for sb / sthg, to hold sb / sthg in contempt* mépriser qqn / qqch, avoir du mépris pour qqn / qqch ▸ *to be beneath contempt* être tout ce qu'il y a de plus méprisable **2.** LAW outrage m ▸ *to charge sb with contempt (of court)* accuser qqn d'outrage (à magistrat or à la Cour).

contemptible [kən'temptəbl] adj [action, attitude, person] méprisable.

contemptuous [kən'temptʃʊəs] adj fml [look, manner, remark] dédaigneux, méprisant ▸ *to be contemptuous of sb / sthg* dédaigner qqn / qqch, faire peu de cas de qqn / qqch.

contemptuously [kən'temptʃʊəslɪ] adv [laugh, reject, smile] avec mépris, avec dédain.

contend [kən'tend] ◆ vi **1.** [deal] : *this is just one of the difficulties we have to contend with* ce n'est que l'une des difficultés auxquelles nous devons faire face **2.** [compete] combattre, lutter ▸ *to contend with sb for over sthg* disputer or contester qqch à qqn. ◆ vt fml ▸ *to contend that...* soutenir que...

contender [kən'tendər] n [in fight] adversaire mf ; [in race] concurrent m, -e f ; [for title] prétendant m, -e f ; [for political office] candidat m, -e f.

content ◆ n ['kɒntent] **1.** [amount contained] teneur f **2.** [substance - of book, film, speech, website] contenu m ; [meaning] teneur f, fond m **3.** [kən'tent] [satisfaction] contentement m, satisfaction f **4.** LING contenu m. ◆ adj [kən'tent] content, satisfait ▶ **to be content to do sthg** ne pas demander mieux que de faire qqch. ◆ vt [kən'tent] ▶ **to content oneself with (doing) sthg** se contenter de or se borner à (faire) qqch. ◆ **contents** pl n **1.** [of bag, bottle, house, etc.] contenu m **2.** [of book, letter] contenu m / **the contents (list)** or **the list of contents** la table des matières.

contented [kən'tentɪd] adj [person] content, satisfait ; [smile] de contentement, de satisfaction.

contentedly [kən'tentɪdlɪ] adv avec contentement.

content-free adj [website, software] sans contenu.

contention [kən'tenʃn] n **1.** fml [belief] affirmation f / **it is my contention that...** je soutiens que... **2.** [disagreement] dispute f / **his morals are not in contention** sa moralité n'est pas ici mise en doute **3.** PHR **to be in contention for sthg** être en compétition pour qqch.

contentious [kən'tenʃəs] adj **1.** [controversial - issue, subject] contesté, litigieux **2.** [argumentative - family, group, person] querelleur, chicanier.

contentment [kən'tentmənt] n contentement m, satisfaction f.

contest ◆ n ['kɒntest] **1.** [competition] concours m **2.** [struggle] combat m, lutte f ▶ **a contest for / between** un combat pour / entre **3.** SPORT rencontre f ; [boxing] combat m, rencontre f ▶ **a contest with / between** un combat contre / entre. ◆ vt [kən'test] **1.** [dispute - idea, statement] contester, discuter **2.** POL [fight for - election, seat] disputer ; [SPORT - match, title] disputer.

contestant [kən'testənt] n concurrent m, -e f, adversaire mf.

context ['kɒntekst] n contexte m.

context-dependent adj : **to be context-dependent** dépendre du contexte.

context-sensitive adj COMPUT contextuel.

contextual [kɒn'tekstjʊəl] adj [criticism] contextuel.

contextualize, contextualise [kɒn'tekstjʊəlaɪz] vt [events, facts] contextualiser, remettre dans son contexte.

continent ['kɒntɪnənt] ◆ n GEOG continent m. ◆ adj MED continent, qui n'est pas incontinent. ◆ **Continent** n UK ▶ **the Continent** l'Europe f continentale / **on the Continent** en Europe (continentale), outre-Manche.

continental [ˌkɒntɪ'nentl] ◆ adj **1.** [European] d'outre-Manche, européen, d'Europe continentale **2.** GEOG [crust, divide] continental ▶ **continental United States** US désigne les 48 États des États-Unis qui forment un bloc géographique (excluant Hawaii et l'Alaska). ◆ n UK continental m, -e f, habitant m, -e f de l'Europe continentale.

continental breakfast n petit déjeuner m continental.

🚩 **Continental breakfast**

Ce terme désigne un petit déjeuner léger, composé d'un jus de fruits, de café ou de thé et de toasts ou viennoiseries, par opposition au **English breakfast** traditionnel, beaucoup plus copieux et comportant un plat chaud.

continental climate n climat m continental.

continental drift n dérive f des continents.

continental quilt n couette f, duvet m.

continental shelf n plateau m continental, plateforme f continentale.

contingency [kən'tɪndʒənsɪ] (pl **contingencies**) ◆ n fml **1.** [possibility] éventualité f, contingence f

2. [chance] événement m inattendu ; [uncertainty] (cas m) imprévu m, éventualité f. ◆ comp [fund] de prévoyance ; [plan] d'urgence ; [table, coefficient] des imprévus. ◆ **contingencies** pl n FIN frais mpl divers.

contingency fee n LAW aux États-Unis, principe permettant à un avocat de recevoir une part des sommes attribuées à son client si ce dernier gagne son procès.

contingent [kən'tɪndʒənt] ◆ adj fml [dependent] contingent ▶ **to be contingent on** or **upon sthg** dépendre de qqch. ◆ n **1.** MIL contingent m **2.** [representative group] groupe m représentatif.

continual [kən'tɪnjʊəl] adj **1.** [continuous - pain, pleasure, struggle] continuel **2.** [repeated - nagging, warnings] incessant, continuel.

continually [kən'tɪnjʊəlɪ] adv **1.** [continuously - change, evolve] continuellement **2.** [repeatedly - complain, nag, warn] sans cesse.

continuation [kən,tɪnjʊ'eɪʃn] n **1.** [sequel] continuation f, suite f **2.** [resumption] reprise f **3.** [prolongation] prolongement m, suite f.

continue [kən'tɪnjuː] ◆ vi **1.** [carry on] continuer ▶ **to continue to do sthg** or **doing sthg** continuer à faire qqch **2.** [begin again] reprendre. ◆ vt **1.** [carry on - education] poursuivre, continuer ; [- tradition] perpétuer, continuer ; [- treatment] continuer **2.** [resume - conversation, performance, talks] reprendre, continuer.

continuing [kən'tɪnjuːɪŋ] adj continu ; [interest] soutenu ▶ **continuing education** formation f permanente or continue.

continuity [ˌkɒntɪ'njuːətɪ] (pl **continuities**) ◆ n **1.** [cohesion] continuité f **2.** CIN & TV continuité f. ◆ comp [department, studio] pour raccords.

continuity man n scripte m.

continuous [kən'tɪnjʊəs] adj **1.** [uninterrupted - noise, process] continu, ininterrompu ▶ **continuous assessment** contrôle m continu ▶ **continuous performances** CIN spectacle m permanent ▶ **continuous stationery** papier m en continu **2.** [unbroken - line] continu **3.** GRAM [tense] continu.

continuously [kən'tɪnjʊəslɪ] adv continuellement, sans arrêt.

contort [kən'tɔːt] vt [body, features] tordre.

contortion [kən'tɔːʃn] n [of body, features] contorsion f, convulsion f, crispation f.

contortionist [kən'tɔːʃənɪst] n contorsionniste mf, homme m caoutchouc.

contour ['kɒn,tʊər] n **1.** [line] contour m **2.** [shape - of body, car] contour m.

contraband ['kɒntrəbænd] ◆ n (U) [smuggled goods] (marchandises fpl de) contrebande f. ◆ adj [activities, goods] de contrebande.

contraception [ˌkɒntrə'sepʃn] n contraception f.

contraceptive [ˌkɒntrə'septɪv] ◆ n contraceptif m. ◆ adj [device, method] contraceptif.

contract ◆ n ['kɒntrækt] [agreement] contrat m, convention f ; [document] contrat m ▶ **to be under contract** être sous contrat, avoir un contrat. ◆ comp [work] à forfait, contractuel ▶ **contract killer** tueur m à gages. ◆ vt [kən'trækt] **1.** fml [agree] ▶ **to contract (with sb) to do sthg** s'engager par contrat à faire qqch **2.** [acquire - disease, illness, debt] contracter **3.** [make shorter - vowel, word] contracter **4.** [make tense - muscle] contracter. ◆ vi se contracter.

contracting [kən'træktɪŋ] adj ▸ **contracting company a)** [party to a contract] contractant *m* **b)** [sub-contractor] sous-traitant *m* ▸ **contracting parties** COMM & FIN contractants *mpl*.

contraction [kən'trækʃn] n **1.** [shrinkage - of metal] contraction *f* **2.** [short form of word] contraction *f*, forme *f* contractée **3.** [of muscle - esp in childbirth] contraction *f*.

contractor [kən'træktər] n [worker] entrepreneur *m*.

contractual [kən'træktʃʊəl] adj [agreement, obligation] contractuel.

contractually [kən'træktʃʊəlɪ] adv [binding] par contrat.

contradict [,kɒntrə'dɪkt] vt **1.** [challenge - person, statement] contredire **2.** [conflict with - subj: facts, stories] contredire.

contradiction [,kɒntrə'dɪkʃn] n **1.** [inconsistency] contradiction *f* ▸ **in contradiction with** en désaccord avec **2.** [conflicting statement] démenti *m*, contradiction *f* ▸ **a contradiction in terms** une contradiction dans les termes.

contradictory [,kɒntrə'dɪktərɪ] adj [statements, stories] contradictoire, opposé ; [person] qui a l'esprit de contradiction.

contraflow ['kɒntrəfləʊ] 🇬🇧 ◆ n circulation *f* à contre-courant. ◆ comp [system] de circulation *f* à contre-courant.

contralto [kən'træltəʊ] (*pl* **contraltos**) ◆ n [voice] contralto *m* ; [singer] contralto *mf*. ◆ adj [part, voice] de contralto.

contraption [kən'træpʃn] n engin *m*, truc *m*.

contrary ['kɒntrərɪ] adj **1.** [opposed - attitudes, ideas, opinions] contraire, en opposition **2.** [kən'treərɪ] [obstinate - attitude, person] contrariant **3.** *fml* [winds] contraire. ◆❖ **contrary to** prep phr contrairement à. ◆❖ **on the contrary** adv phr au contraire. ◆❖ **to the contrary** adv phr : *the meeting will be at six, unless you hear to the contrary* la réunion sera à six heures, sauf contrordre or avis contraire.

contrast ◆ vt [kən'trɑːst] mettre en contraste ▸ **to contrast sb / sthg with, to contrast sb / sthg to** mettre en contraste qqn / qqch avec. ◆ vi [kən'trɑːst] contraster, trancher ▸ **to contrast with sthg** contraster avec qqch. ◆ n ['kɒntrɑːst] **1.** [difference] contraste *m* ; [person, thing] contraste *m* **2.** ART & TV contraste *m*. ❖ **by contrast, in contrast** adv phr par contraste. ❖ **in contrast with, in contrast to** prep phr par opposition à, par contraste avec.

⚠️ Note that the French verb **contraster** is intransitive. When contrast is transitive, it should not be translated by **contraster**.

contrasting [kən'trɑːstɪŋ], **contrastive** [kən'trɑːstɪv] adj [attitudes, lifestyles, responses] qui fait contraste ; [colours] opposé, contrasté.

contravene [,kɒntrə'viːn] vt [infringe - law, rule] transgresser, enfreindre, violer.

contravention [,kɒntrə'venʃn] n infraction *f*, violation *f*.

contretemps [kɒntrətɑ̃] n contretemps *m*.

contribute [kən'trɪbjuːt] ◆ vt [give - money] donner ; [- article, poem] écrire ; [- ideas] apporter. ◆ vi **1.** [donate money] contribuer **2.** [give] donner **3.** [influence] ▸ **to contribute to sthg** contribuer à qqch **4.** [journalist, author] ▸ **to contribute to** écrire pour.

contributing [kən'trɪbjuːtɪ] adj ▸ **to be a contributing factor in** or **to** contribuer à.

contribution [,kɒntrɪ'bjuːʃn] n **1.** [of money, goods] contribution *f*, cotisation *f* ; [of ideas, enthusiasm] apport *m* **2.** [article] article *m* (*écrit pour un journal*).

contributor [kən'trɪbjʊtər] n **1.** [of money, goods] donateur *m*, -trice *f* **2.** [to magazine] collaborateur *m*, -trice *f* **3.** [factor] facteur *m*.

contributory [kən'trɪbjʊtərɪ] (*pl* **contributories**) adj [cause, factor] contribuant, qui contribue ▸ **contributory pension scheme** régime *m* de retraite (*avec participation de l'assuré*).

contrite ['kɒntraɪt] adj [face, look] contrit, repentant.

contrition [kən'trɪʃn] n contrition *f*, pénitence *f*.

contrivance [kən'traɪvəns] n **1.** [contraption] dispositif *m*, mécanisme *m* **2.** [stratagem] manigance *f*.

contrive [kən'traɪv] ◆ vt **1.** [engineer - meeting] combiner **2.** [invent - device, machine] inventer, imaginer. ◆ vi ▸ **to contrive to do sthg** trouver le moyen de faire qqch.

contrived [kən'traɪvd] adj **1.** [deliberate] délibéré, arrangé **2.** [artificial] forcé, peu naturel, tiré par les cheveux *inf*.

control [kən'trəʊl] ◆ n **1.** [of country, organization] direction *f* ; [of car, machine] contrôle *m* ; [of one's life] maîtrise *f* ; [of oneself] maîtrise *f* (de soi) ; SPORT [of ball] contrôle *m* ▸ **to have control of** or **over sb** avoir de l'autorité sur qqn ▸ **to have control of** or **over sthg** avoir le contrôle de qqch ▸ **to gain control of sthg** prendre le contrôle de qqch ▸ **to be in control of sthg** être maître de qqch ▸ **to lose control of sthg a)** [of car] perdre le contrôle de qqch **b)** [of situation] ne plus être maître de qqch ▸ **under control** : *the situation is under control* nous maîtrisons la situation ▸ **to keep sthg under control** maîtriser qqch ▸ **beyond** or **outside one's control** indépendant de sa volonté ▸ **out of control** : *the fire was out of control* on n'arrivait pas à maîtriser l'incendie **2.** [check] contrôle *m* **3.** [device] ▸ **volume control** (bouton *m* de) réglage *m* du volume ▸ **controls** [on car, aircraft, machine] commandes *fpl* **4.** [in experiment] témoin *m* **5.** [checkpoint - at border] douane *f* ; [- in car rally] contrôle *m* ▸ **passport and custom controls** formalités *fpl* de douane **6.** [restraint] contrôle *m* ▸ **price / wage controls** contrôle des prix / des salaires. ◆ comp [button, knob, switch] de commande, de réglage. ◆ vt **1.** [run - government, organization] diriger **2.** [regulate - machine, system] régler ; [- animal, pupil] tenir, se faire obéir de ; [- crowd] contenir ; [- traffic] régler **3.** [curb - inflation, prices, spending, fire] maîtriser ; [- disease] enrayer, juguler ; [- activities, emotions] maîtriser ; [- imports] limiter / *try to control yourself* essaie de te contrôler or maîtriser.

⚠️ **Contrôle** and **contrôler** are not always the correct translations for the noun and verb control. See the entry for details.

control code n COMPUT code *m* de commande.

control experiment n cas *m* témoin.

control group n groupe *m* témoin.

control key n touche *f* « control ».

controllable [kən'trəʊləbl] adj [animal, person, crowd] discipliné ; [emotions, situation] maîtrisable ; [expenditure, inflation] contrôlable.

controlled [kən'trəʊld] adj **1.** [emotions, voice] contenu ; [person] calme **2.** ECON ▸ **controlled economy** économie *f* dirigée or planifiée **3.** [directed] ▸ **controlled explosion** neutralisation *f* (*d'un explosif*).

controller [kən'trəʊlər] n **1.** [person in charge] responsable *m* **2.** [accountant] contrôleur *m*.

controlling [kən'trəʊlɪŋ] adj [factor] déterminant.

controlling interest n participation f majoritaire.

control panel n tableau m de bord.

control room n salle f des commandes, centre m de contrôle.

control tower n tour f de contrôle.

controversial [ˌkɒntrəˈvɜːʃl] adj [book, film, issue, subject] controversé ; [decision, speech] sujet à controverse ; [person] controversé.

controversy [ˈkɒntrəvɜːsɪ ᵁᴷ kənˈtrɒvəsɪ] n controverse f, polémique f.

conundrum [kəˈnʌndrəm] n **1.** [riddle] devinette f, énigme f **2.** [problem] énigme f.

conurbation [ˌkɒnɜːˈbeɪʃn] n conurbation f.

convalesce [ˌkɒnvəˈles] vi se remettre (d'une maladie).

convalescence [ˌkɒnvəˈlesns] n [return to health] rétablissement m ; [period of recovery] convalescence f.

convalescent [ˌkɒnvəˈlesnt] ◆ n convalescent m, -e f. ◆ adj ▸ **convalescent home** maison f de convalescence or de repos.

convection [kənˈvekʃn] ◆ n GEOL, METEOR & PHYS convection f. ◆ comp [heater, heating] à convection ; [current] de convection.

convector (heater) [kənˈvektər-] n radiateur m à convection, convecteur m.

convene [kənˈviːn] ◆ vt [conference, meeting] convoquer. ◆ vi [board, jury, members] se réunir.

convener [kənˈviːnər] n **1.** ᵁᴷ [in trade union] secrétaire des délégués syndicaux **2.** [of meeting] président m, -e f.

convenience [kənˈviːnjəns] n **1.** [ease of use] commodité f ; [benefit] avantage m ▸ **for convenience** or **for convenience's sake** par commodité ▸ **at your earliest convenience** fml dans les meilleurs délais ▸ **at your convenience** quand cela vous conviendra **2.** [facility] commodités fpl, confort m / the house has every modern convenience la maison a tout le confort moderne **3.** ᵁᴷ fml & euph [lavatory] toilettes fpl ▸ **public conveniences** toilettes publiques.

convenience food n aliment m prêt à consommer, plat m cuisiné.

convenience store n ᵁˢ supérette de quartier qui reste ouverte tard le soir.

convenient [kənˈviːnjənt] adj **1.** [suitable] commode / when would be convenient for you? quand cela vous arrangerait-il ? **2.** [handy] pratique / the house is very convenient for local shops and schools la maison est très bien située pour les magasins et les écoles **3.** [nearby] : I grabbed a convenient chair and sat down j'ai saisi la chaise la plus proche et me suis assis.

conveniently [kənˈviːnjəntlɪ] adv : the cottage is conveniently situated for the beach le cottage est bien situé pour la plage / they very conveniently forgot to enclose the cheque comme par hasard, ils ont oublié de joindre le chèque.

convent [ˈkɒnvənt] ◆ n **1.** RELIG couvent m **2.** [convent school] institution f religieuse. ◆ comp [education, school] religieux / she was convent-educated elle a fait ses études dans une institution religieuse.

convention [kənˈvenʃn] n **1.** (U) [custom] usage m, convenances fpl **2.** [agreement] convention f **3.** [meeting] convention f.

Convention

Aux États-Unis, les **conventions** sont d'immenses rassemblements politiques, au cours desquels les partis nationaux choisissent leurs candidats et définissent leurs objectifs.

conventional [kənˈvenʃənl] adj **1.** [behaviour, ideas] conventionnel ; [person] conformiste ▸ **conventional wisdom** sagesse f populaire **2.** [medicine, methods, art] classique, traditionnel ▸ **conventional oven** four m traditionnel or classique **3.** [non-nuclear] conventionnel.

conventionality [kən,venʃəˈnælətɪ] n conformisme m.

conventionally [kənˈvenʃnəlɪ] adv de façon conventionnelle.

converge [kənˈvɜːdʒ] vi **1.** [merge - paths, lines] converger ; [- groups, ideas, tendencies] converger **2.** [groups, people] se rassembler **3.** MATH converger.

convergence criteria pl n critères mpl de convergence.

conversant [kənˈvɜːsənt] adj fml qui est au courant, qui connaît.

conversation [ˌkɒnvəˈseɪʃn] n conversation f / we had a long conversation about fishing nous avons eu une longue conversation sur la pêche ▸ **to get into conversation with sb** engager la conversation avec qqn ▸ **to make conversation** faire la conversation.

conversational [ˌkɒnvəˈseɪʃənl] adj [tone, voice] de la conversation / conversational Spanish espagnol courant.

conversationalist [ˌkɒnvəˈseɪʃnəlɪst] n causeur m, -euse f / he's a brilliant conversationalist il brille dans la conversation.

conversationally [ˌkɒnvəˈseɪʃnəlɪ] adv [mention, say] sur le ton de la conversation.

conversation piece n [unusual object] curiosité f.

converse ◆ vi [kənˈvɜːs] fml converser ▸ **to converse with sb** s'entretenir avec qqn. ◆ adj [ˈkɒnvɜːs] [opinion, statement] contraire. ◆ n [ˈkɒnvɜːs] **1.** [gen] contraire m, inverse m **2.** MATH & PHILOS inverse m.

conversely [kənˈvɜːslɪ] adv inversement, réciproquement.

conversion [kənˈvɜːʃn] n **1.** [process] conversion f, transformation f **2.** MATH conversion f **3.** [change of beliefs] conversion f **4.** RUGBY transformation f **5.** [converted building] appartement aménagé dans un ancien hôtel particulier, entrepôt, atelier, etc. **6.** LAW conversion f.

conversion rate n [in e-commerce] taux m de conversion.

conversion table n table f de conversion.

convert ◆ vt [kənˈvɜːt] **1.** [building, car] aménager, convertir ; [machine] transformer ▸ **to convert sthg to** or **into sthg** transformer or convertir qqch en qqch **2.** MATH convertir **3.** RELIG convertir ▸ **to convert sb to sthg** convertir qqn à qqch **4.** RUGBY transformer. ◆ vi [kənˈvɜːt] **1.** [vehicle, machine] se convertir **2.** [in rugby] se transformer. ◆ n [ˈkɒnvɜːt] converti m, -e f.

converted [kənˈvɜːtɪd] adj [factory, farmhouse, school] aménagé, transformé.

convertible [kənˈvɜːtəbl] ◆ adj [currency] convertible ; [car, machine, couch] convertible. ◆ n AUTO décapotable f.

convex [kɒnˈveks] adj [lens, surface] convexe.

convey [kənˈveɪ] vt **1.** fml [transport] transporter **2.** [communicate] transmettre **3.** LAW transférer.

conveyancing [kənˈveɪənsɪŋ] n ᵁᴷ LAW procédure f translative (de propriété).

conveyor belt n tapis m roulant.

convict ◆ vt [kən'vɪkt] déclarer or reconnaître coupable ▶ **to convict sb of** or **for sthg** déclarer or reconnaître qqn coupable de qqch. ◆ n ['kɒnvɪkt] détenu m, -e f.

convicted [kən'vɪktɪd] adj [criminal] reconnu coupable.

conviction [kən'vɪkʃn] n **1.** [belief] conviction f **2.** [certainty] certitude f, conviction f **3.** [plausibility] : *the theory carries little conviction* la théorie est peu convaincante **4.** LAW condamnation f.

convince [kən'vɪns] vt convaincre, persuader ▶ **to convince sb of sthg** convaincre or persuader qqn de qqch ▶ **to convince sb to do sthg** convaincre or persuader qqn de faire qqch.

convinced [kən'vɪnst] adj convaincu ▶ **to be convinced of sthg** être convaincu de qqch.

convincing [kən'vɪnsɪŋ] adj [argument, person] convaincant ; [victory, win] décisif, éclatant.

convincingly [kən'vɪnsɪŋlɪ] adv [argue, speak, pretend] de façon convaincante ; [beat, win] de façon éclatante.

convivial [kən'vɪvɪəl] adj [atmosphere, lunch] convivial, joyeux ; [manner, person] joyeux, plein d'entrain.

convocation [,kɒnvə'keɪʃn] n **1.** [summoning] convocation f **2.** [meeting] assemblée f, réunion f ; RELIG synode m.

convoluted ['kɒnvəluːtɪd] adj [shape] convoluté ; [prose, reasoning, sentence] alambiqué.

convoy ['kɒnvɔɪ] ◆ n convoi m ▶ **to travel in convoy** voyager en convoi. ◆ vt convoyer, escorter.

convulse [kən'vʌls] vi [face, lungs, muscle] se convulser, se contracter, se crisper.

convulsion [kən'vʌlʃn] n **1.** MED convulsion f **2.** [revolution, war] bouleversement m ; [earthquake] secousse f.

convulsive [kən'vʌlsɪv] adj convulsif.

coo [kuː] (*pl* **coos**) ◆ n roucoulement m. ◆ vi [pigeon] roucouler ; [baby, person] babiller, gazouiller. ◆ interj *inf* ▶ **coo!** ça alors !

COO n *abbr of* **chief operating officer**.

cook [kʊk] ◆ n cuisinier m, -ère f. ◆ vt **1.** [food, meal] cuisiner, cuire **2.** 🇺🇸 *inf* [fiddle - accounts, books] truquer. ◆ vi [person] cuisiner ; [food] cuire. ◆ **cook up** vt sep *inf* [plan] mijoter ; [excuse, story] inventer.

cookbook ['kʊkbʊk] n livre m de cuisine.

cook-chill adj cuisiné (et réfrigéré).

cooked [kʊkt] adj [food, meat] cuit ▶ **cooked breakfast** 🇬🇧 petit déjeuner m anglais.

cooker ['kʊkər] 🇬🇧 [stove] cuisinière f.

cookery ['kʊkərɪ] n cuisine f ▶ **cookery course** stage m de cuisine ▶ **cookery programme** émission f de cuisine.

cookie ['kʊkɪ] n **1.** 🇺🇸 biscuit m **2.** COMPUT cookie m.

cooking ['kʊkɪŋ] ◆ n [activity] cuisine f ; [food] cuisine f ▶ **cooking time** temps m de cuisson. ◆ comp [oil, sherry] de cuisine ; [apple] à cuire.

cookout ['kʊkaʊt] n 🇺🇸 barbecue m.

cool [kuːl] ◆ adj **1.** [in temperature - breeze, room, weather] frais (fraîche) ; [-drink, water] rafraîchissant, frais (fraîche) ; [-clothes, material] léger **2.** [of colour - blue, green] clair **3.** [calm - person, manner, voice] calme / *keep cool!* inf du calme ! **4.** [unfriendly - response, greeting, welcome] froid **5.** *inf* [of sum of money] coquet, rondelet **6.** *inf* [great] génial, super. ◆ n **1.** [coolness] fraîcheur f **2.** [calm] calme m, sang-froid m. ◆ vt [air, liquid, room] rafraîchir, refroidir ; [brow, feet] rafraîchir ▶ **cool it!** du calme ! ◆ vi [food, liquid] (se) refroidir ; [enthusiasm, passion, temper] s'apaiser, se calmer. ◆ **cool down** ◆ vi **1.** [machine] se refroidir ; *fig*

[situation] se détendre **2.** [person] se calmer. ◆ vt sep [person] calmer ; [situation] calmer, détendre. ◆ **cool off** vi [person - become calmer] se calmer.

coolant ['kuːlənt] n (fluide m) caloporteur m.

coolbox ['kuːlbɒks] n glacière f.

Cool Britannia pr n 🇬🇧 *inf* expression qui évoque l'art, la musique et la mode en Grande-Bretagne de la fin des années 1990.

cooler ['kuːlər] n **1.** [for food] glacière f **2.** *inf* [prison] taule f **3.** [drink] rafraîchissement m ▶ **(wine) cooler** mélange de vin, de jus de fruits et d'eau gazeuse.

cool-headed adj calme, imperturbable.

cooling-off period n **1.** [in dispute] moment m de répit **2.** [after purchase] délai m de réflexion **3.** [contract] délai m de résiliation **4.** SPORT temps m de repos.

cooling tower n refroidisseur m.

coolly ['kuːlɪ] adv **1.** [calmly - react, respond] calmement **2.** [without enthusiasm - greet, welcome] froidement.

coolness ['kuːlnɪs] n **1.** [in temperature - of air, water, weather] fraîcheur f ; [-of clothes] légèreté f **2.** [calmness] calme m, sang-froid m **3.** [lack of enthusiasm] flegme m.

coop [kuːp] n poulailler m. ◆ **coop up** vt sep [animal, person, prisoner] enfermer.

co-op ['kəʊˌɒp] (*abbr of* **co-operative society**) n coopérative f, coop f. ◆ **Co-op** pr n 🇬🇧 ▶ **the Co-op** la Coop.

cooperate [kəʊ'ɒpəreɪt] vi **1.** [work together] collaborer, coopérer ▶ **to cooperate with sb** collaborer avec qqn **2.** [be willing to help] se montrer coopératif.

cooperation [kəʊˌɒpə'reɪʃn] n **1.** [collaboration] coopération f, concours m ▶ **in cooperation with** or **with the cooperation of sb** avec la coopération or le concours de qqn **2.** [willingness to help] coopération f.

cooperative [kəʊ'ɒpərətɪv] ◆ adj **1.** [joint - activity, work] coopératif **2.** [helpful - attitude, person] coopératif. ◆ n coopérative f.

co-opt vt coopter, admettre ▶ **to be co-opted into** or **onto sthg** être coopté à qqch.

coordinate ◆ vt [kəʊˈɔːdɪneɪt] coordonner. ◆ adj [kəʊˈɔːdɪnət] MATH coordonnée f. ◆ adj [kəʊˈɔːdɪnət] GRAM & MATH coordonné ▶ **coordinate clause** proposition f coordonnée ▶ **coordinate geometry** géométrie f analytique. ◆ **coordinates** pl n coordonnés mpl.

coordination [kəʊˌɔːdɪ'neɪʃn] n coordination f.

coordinator [kəʊˈɔːdɪneɪtər] n coordinateur m, coordonnateur m.

cooties ['kuːtɪz] pl n 🇺🇸 baby talk microbes mpl.

co-owner n copropriétaire mf.

co-ownership n copropriété f.

cop [kɒp] (*pt & pp* **copped**, *cont* **copping**) *inf* ◆ n **1.** [policeman] flic m **2.** 🇬🇧 [arrest] arrestation f ▶ **it's a fair cop!** je suis fait ! **3.** PHR ▶ **it's not much cop** 🇬🇧 ça ne vaut pas grand-chose, c'est pas terrible. ◆ vt **1.** [catch] attraper, empoigner / *you'll cop it if he finds out!* qu'est-ce que tu vas prendre s'il s'en rend compte ! **2.** 🇺🇸 *inf* ▶ **to cop an attitude** devenir agressif / *don't cop an attitude with me!* arrête d'être si agressif ! ▶ **to cop a plea** [plead guilty to lesser offence] plaider coupable à une infraction moindre. ◆ **cop out** vi *inf* se défiler ▶ **to cop out of sthg** réussir à échapper à qqch.

copacetic [,kəʊpə'setɪk] adj 🇺🇸 ▶ **everything's copacetic** tout va bien.

co-parenting n coparentalité f.

copartner [,kəʊ'pɑːtnər] n coassocié m, -e f.

cope [kəup] ◆ vi [person] se débrouiller, s'en sortir ; [business, machine, system] supporter. ◆ n RELIG chape f. ◆ vt [provide with coping - wall] chaperonner.

Copenhagen [ˌkəupən'heɪgən] pr n Copenhague.

copier ['kɒpɪər] n photocopieuse f, copieur m.

copilot ['kəuˌpaɪlət] n copilote mf.

copious ['kəupjəs] adj [amount, food] copieux ; [sunshine] abondant ; [notes] abondant.

cop-out n inf dérobade f.

copper ['kɒpər] ◆ n 1. [colour, metal] cuivre m 2. inf [coins] monnaie f 3. inf [policeman] flic m. ◆ comp [coin, kettle, wire] en cuivre. ◆ adj [colour, hair] cuivré.

copperplated [ˌkɒpə'pleɪtɪd] adj cuivré.

coppice ['kɒpɪs] n taillis m.

co-processor n coprocesseur m.

coproduce [ˌkəuprə'dju:s] vt CIN & TV coproduire.

coproduction [ˌkəuprə'dʌkʃn] n CIN & TV coproduction f.

copse [kɒps] n taillis m.

copulate ['kɒpjuleɪt] vi copuler.

copulation [ˌkɒpju'leɪʃn] n copulation f.

copy ['kɒpɪ] (pl **copies**, pt & pp **copied**) ◆ n 1. [duplicate - of painting] copie f, reproduction f ; [- of document, photograph] copie f 2. [of book, magazine, record] exemplaire m 3. (U) [written material] copie f ; [in advertisement] texte m 4. (U) PRESS copie f. ◆ vt 1. [write out - letter, notes] copier ▶ **to copy sthg down** / **out** noter / copier qqch 2. [imitate - person, movements, gestures] copier, imiter ; [- style, system] copier 3. [cheat] copier 4. [photocopy] photocopier 5. TELEC [hear] : **do you copy?** vous me recevez ? ◆ vi [cheat] copier, tricher. ❖ **copy in** vt sep mettre (qqn) en copie ▶ **to copy sb in (on sthg)** mettre qqn en copie (de qqch).

copy and paste ◆ n copier-coller m. ◆ vt copier-coller.

copycat ['kɒpɪkæt] ◆ n inf copieur m, -euse f. ◆ comp [killings, murder] inspiré par un autre.

copy desk n 🇺🇸 PRESS secrétariat m de rédaction.

copy-editing n préparation f de copie.

copy editor n secrétaire mf de rédaction.

copy-protect vt protéger (contre la copie).

copyreader ['kɒpɪˌri:dər] 🇺🇸 = **subeditor**.

copyright ['kɒpɪraɪt] ◆ n copyright m, droit m d'auteur / out of copyright dans le domaine public. ◆ vt obtenir les droits exclusifs ou le copyright. ◆ adj de copyright.

copy typist n dactylographe mf.

copywriter ['kɒpɪˌraɪtər] n rédacteur m, -trice f publicitaire.

coral ['kɒrəl] ◆ n corail m. ◆ comp [earrings, necklace] de corail ; [island] corallien. ◆ adj [pink, red, lipstick] corail ; liter [lips] de corail.

coral reef n récif m de corail.

Coral Sea pr n ▶ **the Coral Sea** la mer de Corail.

cord [kɔ:d] ◆ n 1. [string] cordon m 2. [cable] câble m 3. [corduroy] velours m côtelé. ◆ comp [skirt, trousers] en velours côtelé. ❖ **cords** pl n inf ▶ **(a pair of) cords** un pantalon m en velours côtelé.

cordial ['kɔ:djəl] ◆ adj 1. [warm - greeting, welcome] chaleureux 2. [strong - hatred] cordial. ◆ n [drink] cordial m.

cordially ['kɔ:dɪəlɪ] adv [greet, detest, etc.] cordialement ▶ **cordially yours** 🇺🇸 [at end of letter] salutations amicales.

cordless ['kɔ:dlɪs] adj [telephone, mouse] sans fil.

Cordoba ['kɔ:dəbə] pr n Cordoue.

cordon ['kɔ:dn] ◆ n [barrier] cordon m. ◆ vt = **cordon off**. ❖ **cordon off** vt sep barrer, interdire l'accès à, isoler.

cordon bleu [-blɜ:] adj de cordon bleu / a cordon bleu cook un cordon bleu.

corduroy ['kɔ:dərɔɪ] ◆ n velours m côtelé ▶ **(a pair of) corduroys** (un) pantalon m de or en velours côtelé. ◆ adj de velours côtelé.

core [kɔ:r] ◆ n [of apple, pear] trognon m, cœur m ; [of magnet, earth, organization] noyau m ; [of electric cable] âme f, noyau m ; [of nuclear reactor] cœur m ; [of argument] essentiel m, centre m ; [of computer] mémoire f centrale ▶ **to the core**: to be French / a socialist to the core être français / socialiste jusqu'à la moelle / rotten to the core pourri jusqu'à l'os. ◆ comp ▶ **core business** activité f principale ▶ **core curriculum** SCH tronc m commun ▶ **core market** marché m principal ▶ **core memory** COMPUT mémoire f centrale ▶ **core subject** SCH matière f principale ▶ **core time** [in flexitime] plage f fixe ▶ **core vocabulary** LING vocabulaire m de base. ◆ vt [apple, pear] enlever le trognon de.

CORE [kɔ:r] (abbr of Congress Of Racial Equality) pr n ligue américaine contre le racisme.

corer ['kɔ:rər] n ▶ **apple corer** vide-pomme m inv.

Corfu [kɔ:'fu:] pr n Corfou / in Corfu à Corfou.

corgi ['kɔ:gɪ] n corgi m.

Corgi

Cette race de petit chien roux d'origine galloise est toujours associée à la famille royale britannique car la reine Elisabeth en possède plusieurs.

coriander [ˌkɒrɪ'ændər] n coriandre f.

cork [kɔ:k] ◆ n 1. [substance] liège m 2. [stopper] bouchon m 3. FISHING [float] flotteur m, bouchon m. ◆ comp [tile, bathmat, etc.] de or en liège. ◆ vt [seal - bottle] boucher.

Cork [kɔ:k] pr n Cork.

corkage ['kɔ:kɪdʒ] n (U) droit de débouchage sur un vin qui a été apporté par des consommateurs.

corked [kɔ:kt] adj [wine] bouchonné.

corkscrew ['kɔ:kskru:] ◆ n tire-bouchon m. ◆ comp ▶ **corkscrew curl** tire-bouchon m. ◆ vi [staircase] tourner en vrille ; [plane] vriller.

cormorant ['kɔ:mərənt] n cormoran m.

corn [kɔ:n] ◆ n 1. 🇬🇧 [cereal] blé m ; 🇺🇸 maïs m ▶ **corn on the cob** épi m de maïs 2. (U) inf [banality] banalité f ; [sentimentality] sentimentalité f bébête 3. [on foot] cor m. ◆ comp ▶ **corn plaster** pansement m (pour cors).

Corn written abbr of Cornwall.

corn dog n 🇺🇸 saucisse enrobée de pâte à la farine de maïs et frite à l'huile.

cornea ['kɔ:nɪə] n cornée f.

corned beef [kɔ:nd-] n corned-beef m.

corner ['kɔ:nər] ◆ n 1. [of page, painting, table, etc.] coin m 2. [inside room, house, etc.] coin m 3. [of street] coin m ; [bend in the road] tournant m, virage m ▶ **on** or **at the corner** au coin / it's just around or 🇺🇸 round the corner a) [house, shop, etc.] c'est à deux pas d'ici b) fig [Christmas, economic recovery, etc.] c'est tout proche 4. [of eye] coin m ; [of mouth] coin m, commissure f 5. inf [difficulty] situation f difficile, mauvaise passe f 6. [remote place] coin m 7. FOOT corner m. ◆ comp [cupboard, table, etc.] d'angle. ◆ vt **1.** [animal, prey, etc.] coincer, acculer **2.** COMM accaparer ▶ **to corner the market in sthg** accaparer le marché de qqch. ◆ vi AUTO prendre un virage.

corner flag n SPORT drapeau *m* de corner.

corner kick n FOOT corner *m*.

corner shop n UK magasin *m* du coin.

cornerstone ['kɔːnəstəʊn] n pierre *f* d'angle or angulaire ; *fig* pierre *f* angulaire, fondement *m*.

cornet ['kɔːnɪt] n **1.** MUS [instrument] cornet *m* à pistons **2.** UK ▶ **(ice-cream) cornet** cornet *m* (de glace).

cornfed ['kɔːnfed] adj US *inf* rustre.

cornfield ['kɔːnfiːld] n UK champ *m* de blé ; US champ *m* de maïs.

cornflakes ['kɔːnfleɪks] pl n cornflakes *mpl*, pétales *mpl* or flocons *mpl* de maïs.

cornflour ['kɔːnflaʊər] n UK farine *f* de maïs, Maïzena® *f*.

cornice ['kɔːnɪs] n ARCHIT corniche *f* ; [snow] corniche *f*.

Cornish ['kɔːnɪʃ] ◆ pl n [people] ▶ **the Cornish** les Cornouaillais *mpl*. ◆ n LING cornouaillais *m*. ◆ adj cornouaillais.

Cornishman ['kɔːnɪʃmən] (*pl* **Cornishmen** [-mən]) n Cornouaillais *m*.

Cornishwoman ['kɔːnɪʃ,wʊmən] (*pl* **Cornishwomen** [-,wɪmɪn]) n Cornouaillaise *f*.

corn rows pl n coiffure *f* tressée à l'africaine.

cornstarch ['kɔːnstɑːtʃ] US = **cornflour**.

cornucopia [,kɔːnjuːˈkəʊpjə] n MYTH & *fig* corne *f* d'abondance.

Cornwall ['kɔːnwɔːl] pr n Cornouailles *f* / *in Cornwall* en Cornouailles.

corny ['kɔːnɪ] (*compar* **cornier**, *superl* **corniest**) adj *inf* [trite] bateau, banal ; [sentimental] sentimental, à l'eau de rose.

corollary [kəˈrɒlərɪ] (*pl* **corollaries**) n *fml* corollaire *m*.

coronary ['kɒrənrɪ] ◆ adj MED coronaire. ◆ n MED infarctus *m* du myocarde.

coronary thrombosis n MED infarctus *m* du myocarde, thrombose *f* coronarienne.

coronation [,kɒrəˈneɪʃn] ◆ n [of monarch] couronnement *m*, sacre *m*. ◆ comp [robes, day] du couronnement, du sacre / **'Coronation Street'** feuilleton télévisé britannique.

Coronation Street

Ce feuilleton télévisé, le plus ancien des **soap operas** encore à l'écran, évoque la vie quotidienne de plusieurs familles ouvrières vivant dans une rue d'une ville du nord de l'Angleterre.

coroner ['kɒrənər] n LAW coroner *m*.

Corp. 1. (written abbr of **corporation**) Cie **2.** written abbr of **corporal**.

corpora ['kɔːpərə] pl ⟶ **corpus**.

corporal ['kɔːpərəl] ◆ n MIL caporal-chef *m*. ◆ adj corporel ▶ **corporal punishment** châtiment *m* corporel.

corporate ['kɔːpərət] ◆ adj **1.** LAW ▶ **corporate body** or **institution** personne *f* morale **2.** [of a specific company] d'une société, de la société ; [of companies in general] d'entreprise ; [taxation] sur les sociétés ▶ **corporate America** l'Amérique des entreprises ▶ **corporate law** droit *m* des so-

ciétés or des entreprises **3.** [collective - decision, responsibility] collectif. ◆ n US [corporate headquarters] : *he works at corporate* il travaille au siège.

corporately ['kɔːpərətlɪ] adv **1.** [as a corporation] : *I don't think we should involve ourselves corporately* je ne pense pas que nous devrions nous impliquer en tant que société **2.** [as a group] collectivement.

corporate tax US = **corporation tax**.

corporation [,kɔːpəˈreɪʃn] n **1.** [company] compagnie *f*, société *f* ; LAW personne *f* morale **2.** UK [municipal authorities] municipalité *f*.

corporation tax n UK impôt *m* sur les sociétés.

corporatism ['kɔːpərətɪzm] n corporatisme *m*.

corps [kɔːr] (*pl* **corps**) n **1.** MIL corps *m* ; MIL & ADMIN service *m* ▶ **medical / intelligence corps** service de santé / de renseignements **2.** [trained team of people] corps *m* ▶ **corps de ballet** corps de ballet.

corpse [kɔːps] n cadavre *m*, corps *m*.

corpulent ['kɔːpjʊlənt] adj corpulent.

corpus ['kɔːpəs] (*pl* **corpuses** or **corpora** ['kɔːpərə]) n [collection of writings - by author] recueil *m* ; [- on specific subject] corpus *m*.

corpuscle ['kɔːpʌsl] n PHYSIOL corpuscule *m* ▶ **red / white blood corpuscles** globules *mpl* rouges / blancs.

corral [kɒˈrɑːl] (*pt & pp* **corralled**, *cont* **corralling**) US ◆ n corral *m*. ◆ vt [cattle, horses] enfermer dans un corral ; *fig* encercler.

correct [kəˈrekt] ◆ adj **1.** [right - answer, spelling, etc.] correct / *do you have the correct time?* avez-vous l'heure exacte ? / *that is correct* c'est exact / *to prove (to be) correct* s'avérer juste **2.** [suitable, proper - behaviour, manners, etc.] correct, convenable, bienséant ; [- person] correct, convenable. ◆ vt **1.** [rectify - mistake, spelling, etc.] corriger, rectifier ; [- squint, bad posture, imbalance] corriger ; [- situation] rectifier **2.** [indicate error - to person] corriger, reprendre ; [- in exam, proofs, etc.] corriger ▶ **to correct sb on** or **about sthg** corriger or reprendre qqn sur qqch ▶ **to correct o.s.** se reprendre, se corriger.

correction [kəˈrekʃn] n **1.** [of exam paper, homework, proofs, etc.] correction *f* ; [of error] correction *f*, rectification *f* **2.** [in essay, school work, proofs, etc.] correction *f* ▶ **to make corrections** faire des corrections ▶ **to make corrections to sthg** apporter des corrections à qqch.

correction fluid n liquide *m* correcteur.

correctly [kəˈrektlɪ] adv **1.** [in the right way - answer, pronounce] correctement **2.** [properly - behave, dress, speak] correctement.

correctness [kəˈrektnɪs] n **1.** [of answer, prediction, etc.] exactitude *f*, justesse *f* **2.** [of behaviour, dress, etc.] correction *f*.

correlate ['kɒrəleɪt] ◆ vi ▶ **to correlate (with sthg)** a) [gen] être en corrélation or rapport (avec qqch), correspondre (à qqch) b) [in statistics] être en corrélation (avec qqch). ◆ vt [gen] mettre en corrélation or en rapport, faire correspondre ; [in statistics] corréler ▶ **to correlate sthg with sthg** a) [gen] mettre qqch en corrélation or rapport avec qqch b) [in statistics] corréler qqch avec qqch.

correlation [,kɒrəˈleɪʃn] n corrélation *f*.

correspond [,kɒrɪˈspɒnd] vi **1.** [tally - dates, statements] correspondre ▶ **to correspond with sthg** correspondre à qqch **2.** [be equivalent] correspondre, équivaloir **3.** [exchange letters] correspondre.

correspondence [,kɒrɪˈspɒndəns] ◆ n **1.** [relationship, similarity] correspondance *f*, rapport *m*, relation *f* **2.** [letter-writing] correspondance *f* ▶ **to be in correspondence with sb** être en correspondance avec qqn ▶ **to en-**

ter into (a) correspondence with sb établir une or entrer en correspondance avec qqn **3.** [letters] correspondance *f*, courrier *m*. ◆ comp [course] par correspondance ; [school] d'enseignement par correspondance ▶ **correspondence column** PRESS courrier *m* des lecteurs.

correspondent [ˌkɒrɪ'spɒndənt] n **1.** PRESS, RADIO & TV [reporter] correspondant *m*, -e *f* **2.** [letter-writer] correspondant *m*, -e *f*.

corresponding [ˌkɒrɪ'spɒndɪŋ] adj correspondant.

corridor ['kɒrɪdɔːr] n [in building] corridor *m*, couloir *m* ; [in train] couloir *m* ▶ **the corridors of power a)** *fig* les allées du pouvoir **b)** [behind the scenes] les coulisses du pouvoir.

corroborate [kə'rɒbəreɪt] vt [statement, view, etc.] confirmer, corroborer *liter* / **for lack of corroborating evidence** faute de preuves à l'appui.

corroboration [kəˌrɒbə'reɪʃn] n confirmation *f*, corroboration *f liter* ▶ **to provide corroboration of sthg** confirmer or corroborer qqch.

corroborative [kə'rɒbərətɪv] adj [evidence, statement] à l'appui.

corrode [kə'rəʊd] ◆ vt [subj: acid, rust] corroder, ronger ; *fig* [happiness] entamer, miner. ◆ vi [due to acid, rust] se corroder ; [due to rust] se rouiller.

corrosion [kə'rəʊʒn] n [of metal] corrosion *f*.

corrosion-resistant adj anticorrosion.

corrosive [kə'rəʊsɪv] ◆ adj corrosif. ◆ n corrosif *m*.

corrugated ['kɒrəgeɪtɪd] adj [cardboard, paper] ondulé ▶ **corrugated iron** tôle *f* ondulée.

corrupt [kə'rʌpt] ◆ adj **1.** [dishonest - person, society] corrompu **2.** [depraved, immoral] dépravé, corrompu **3.** [containing alterations - text] altéré **4.** COMPUT [containing errors - disk, file] altéré. ◆ vt **1.** [make dishonest] corrompre **2.** [deprave, debase - person, society] dépraver, corrompre ; [- language] corrompre **3.** [alter - text] altérer, corrompre **4.** COMPUT corrompre.

corruptible [kə'rʌptəbl] adj corruptible.

corruption [kə'rʌpʃn] n **1.** [of official, politician, etc. - action, state] corruption *f* **2.** [depravity, debasement - action, state] dépravation *f*, corruption *f* ▶ **the corruption of minors** LAW le détournement de mineurs **3.** [of text - action] altération *f*, corruption *f* ; [- state] version *f* corrompue ; [of word - action] corruption *f* ; [- state] forme *f* corrompue **4.** COMPUT corruption *f*.

corruptly [kə'rʌptlɪ] adv **1.** [dishonestly] de manière corrompue **2.** [in a depraved way] d'une manière dépravée or corrompue.

corsage [kɔː'sɑːʒ] n [flowers] *petit bouquet de fleurs (à accrocher au corsage ou au poignet)* ; [bodice] corsage *m*.

corset ['kɔːsɪt] n corset *m*.

Corsica ['kɔːsɪkə] pr n Corse *f* / **in Corsica** en Corse.

Corsican ['kɔːsɪkən] ◆ n **1.** [person] Corse *mf* **2.** LING corse *m*. ◆ adj corse.

cortège [kɔː'teɪʒ] n cortège *m*.

cortisone ['kɔːtɪzəʊn] ◆ n cortisone *f*. ◆ comp ▶ **cortisone injection** piqûre *f* de cortisone.

cos¹ [kɒz] ◆ conj *inf* = **because**. ◆ n abbr of co-sine.

cos² [kɒs] n 🇬🇧 ▶ **cos (lettuce)** (laitue *f*) romaine *f*.

COS MESSAGING written abbr of **because**.

C.O.S. (written abbr of **Cash on shipment**) *paiement à l'expédition.*

cosh [kɒʃ] ◆ n gourdin *m*, matraque *f*. ◆ vt assommer, matraquer.

cosign ['kəʊsaɪn] vt cosigner.

cosignatory [ˌkəʊ'sɪgnətrɪ] (pl **cosignatories**) n *fml* cosignataire *mf*.

cosily 🇬🇧, **cozily** 🇺🇸 ['kəʊzɪlɪ] adv [furnished] confortablement.

cosine ['kəʊsaɪn] n MATH cosinus *m*.

cosmetic [kɒz'metɪk] ◆ adj [preparation] cosmétique ; *fig* [superficial - change, measure] superficiel, symbolique ▶ **to have cosmetic surgery** se faire faire de la chirurgie esthétique. ◆ n cosmétique *m*, produit *m* de beauté.

cosmetologist [ˌkɒzmə'tɒlədʒɪst] n cosmétologue *mf*.

cosmetology [ˌkɒzmə'tɒlədʒɪ] n cosmétologie *f*.

cosmic ['kɒzmɪk] adj cosmique.

cosmology [kɒz'mɒlədʒɪ] n cosmologie *f*.

cosmonaut ['kɒzmənɔːt] n cosmonaute *mf*.

cosmopolitan [ˌkɒzmə'pɒlɪtn] ◆ adj [city, person, restaurant, etc.] cosmopolite. ◆ n cosmopolite *mf*.

cosmos ['kɒzmɒs] n cosmos *m* ; *fig* univers *m*.

Cossack ['kɒsæk] n cosaque *m*.

cosset ['kɒsɪt] vt [person] dorloter, choyer, câliner ▶ **to cosset o.s.** se dorloter.

cossie ['kɒzɪ] n 🇬🇧 & 🇦🇺 *inf* maillot *m* de bain.

cost [kɒst] ◆ vt **1.** (*pt & pp* cost) coûter / **how much** or **what does it cost?** combien ça coûte ? / **it cost me £200** cela m'est revenu à or m'a coûté 200 livres / **it cost her a lot of time and effort** cela lui a demandé beaucoup de temps et d'efforts / **it cost him his job** cela lui a coûté son travail, cela lui a fait perdre son travail **2.** (*pt & pp* costed) [work out price of - trip] évaluer le coût de ; [- job, repairs] établir un devis pour. ◆ n **1.** [amount charged or paid] coût *m* ▶ **to buy** / **to sell sthg at cost** [cost price] acheter / vendre qqch au prix coûtant **2.** *fig* prix *m* / **whatever the cost** à tout prix, à n'importe quel prix ▶ **to count the cost of sthg** faire le bilan de qqch. ◆ **costs** pl n LAW frais *mpl* (d'instance) et dépens *mpl*. ◆ **at all costs** adv phr à tout prix. ◆ **at any cost** adv phr en aucun cas.

cost accountant n comptable *m* spécialisé en comptabilité analytique or en comptabilité d'exploitation.

cost analysis n analyse *f* des coûts or du prix de revient.

co-star (*pt & pp* co-starred, *cont* co-starring) ◆ n CIN & TV [of actor, actress] partenaire *mf*. ◆ vi CIN & TV [in film] être l'une des vedettes principales ▶ **to co-star with sb** partager la vedette or l'affiche avec qqn. ◆ vt : *the film co-stars Joe Smith and Mary Brown* le film met en scène Joe Smith et Mary Brown dans les rôles principaux or vedettes / *co-starring...* [in credits] avec...

Costa Rica [ˌkɒstə'riːkə] pr n Costa Rica *m* / **in Costa Rica** au Costa Rica.

Costa Rican [ˌkɒstə'riːkən] ◆ n Costaricien *m*, -enne *f*. ◆ adj costaricien.

cost base n prix *m* de base.

cost-benefit analysis n analyse *f* des coûts et rendements.

cost centre n centre *m* de coût.

cost-conscious adj : *to be cost-conscious* contrôler ses dépenses.

cost-cutting ◆ n compression *f* or réduction *f* des coûts. ◆ adj de compression or de réduction des coûts.

cost-effective adj rentable.

cost-effectiveness n rentabilité *f*.

cost factor n facteur *m* de coût.

costing ['kɒstɪŋ] n [of product] estimation *f* du prix de revient ; [of job, repairs] établissement *m* d'un devis / *based on detailed costings* basé sur des calculs détaillés.

costly ['kɒstlɪ] (*compar* **costlier,** *superl* **costliest**) adj **1.** [expensive] coûteux, cher **2.** [of high quality] somptueux, riche.

cost management n gestion f des coûts.

cost of living ◆ n coût m de la vie. ◆ comp ▶ **cost of living index** indice m du coût de la vie.

cost of sales n coût m des ventes, coût m de revient des produits vendus.

cost-plus adj ▶ **on a cost-plus basis** sur la base du prix de revient majoré.

cost price n prix m coûtant or de revient ▶ **to buy / to sell sthg at cost price** acheter / vendre qqch à prix coûtant.

costume ['kɒstjuːm] ◆ n **1.** CIN, THEAT & TV costume m ▶ **to be (dressed) in costume** porter un costume (de scène) **2.** [fancy dress] costume m, déguisement m ▶ **to be (dressed) in costume** être costumé or déguisé **3.** [traditional dress] ▶ **national costume** costume m national **4.** [for swimming] maillot m de bain. ◆ comp ▶ **costume ball** or **party** bal m costumé ▶ **costume designer** costumier m, -ère f ▶ **costume drama** or **piece** or **play** pièce f en costumes d'époque.

costume jewellery n (U) bijoux mpl fantaisie / *a piece of costume jewellery* un bijou fantaisie.

cosy UK, **cozy** US ['kəʊzɪ] (UK compar **cosier,** superl **cosiest** ; US compar **cozier,** superl **coziest**) ◆ adj **1.** [warm, snug - flat, room, atmosphere] douillet, confortable **2.** [intimate - chat, evening, etc.] intime ; [- novel] à l'atmosphère douce. ◆ n [for tea-pot] couvre-théière m ; [for egg] couvre-œuf m. ❖ **cosy up to** vt insep inf se mettre dans les petits papiers de.

cot [kɒt] n UK [for baby] lit m d'enfant ; US [camp bed] lit m de camp.

cot death n UK mort f subite du nourrisson.

coterie ['kəʊtərɪ] n cercle m, cénacle m ; pej coterie f, clique f.

cottage ['kɒtɪdʒ] n **1.** [in country] petite maison f (à la campagne), cottage m **2.** US [holiday home] maison f de campagne.

cottage cheese n fromage m blanc (égoutté), cottage cheese m.

cottage hospital n UK petit hôpital m de campagne.

cottage industry n industrie f familiale or artisanale.

cottage pie n UK hachis m parmentier.

cotton ['kɒtn] ◆ n **1.** [material, plant] coton m **2.** UK [thread for sewing] fil m **3.** US [cotton wool] coton m hydrophile. ◆ comp [garment] en coton ; [industry, trade] du coton ; [culture, field, grower, plantation] de coton. ❖ **cotton on** vi inf piger ▶ **to cotton on to sthg** piger qqch. ❖ **cotton to** vt insep US inf [like - person] être attiré par ; [- idea, plan, suggestion] approuver.

cotton bud n UK Coton-Tige® m.

cotton candy n US barbe f à papa.

cottonmouth ['kɒtnmaʊθ] n US [dry mouth] ▶ **to have cottonmouth** avoir la bouche pâteuse.

cotton swab n US = cotton bud.

cotton wool UK ◆ n coton m hydrophile, ouate f. ◆ comp ▶ **cotton wool balls** boules fpl de coton.

couch [kaʊtʃ] n [in sofa] canapé m, divan m, sofa m ; [in psychiatrist's office] divan m. ◆ vt formuler.

couchette [kuːˈʃet] n RAIL couchette f.

couch potato n inf & pej : *he's a couch potato* il passe son temps affalé devant la télé.

cougar ['kuːgər] n **1.** [animal] couguar m, cougouar m, puma m **2.** US inf ▶ **she's a cougar** [dates younger men] elle se tape des minets.

cough [kɒf] ◆ n toux f / *to have a cough* tousser. ◆ comp [medicine, sweets] pour or contre la toux, antitussif spec. ◆ vi tousser. ◆ vt [blood] cracher. ❖ **cough up** ◆ vt sep **1.** [blood] cracher (en toussant) **2.** inf [money] cracher, raquer. ◆ vi inf [pay up] banquer, raquer.

cough drop n pastille f contre la toux or antitussive.

coughing ['kɒfɪŋ] n toux f.

cough mixture n sirop m antitussif or contre la toux.

cough sweet = cough drop.

cough syrup = cough mixture.

could [kʊd] modal vb **1.** [be able to] : *I'd come if I could* je viendrais si je (le) pouvais / *she could no longer walk* elle ne pouvait plus marcher / *she could have had the job if she'd wanted it* elle aurait pu obtenir cet emploi si elle l'avait voulu **2.** [with verbs of perception or understanding] : *he could see her talking to her boss* il la voyait qui parlait avec son patron **3.** [indicating ability or skill] : *she could read and write* elle savait lire et écrire / *she could speak three languages* elle parlait trois langues **4.** [in polite requests] : *could I borrow your sweater?* est-ce que je pourrais t'emprunter ton pull ? / *could you help me please?* pourriez-vous or est-ce que vous pourriez m'aider, s'il vous plaît ? **5.** [indicating supposition or speculation] : *they could give up at any time* ils pourraient abandonner n'importe quand / *could he be lying?* se pourrait-il qu'il mente ? / *they could have changed their plans* ils ont peut-être changé leurs plans ; [indicating possibility] : *you could have told me the truth* tu aurais pu me dire la vérité.

> 🗒 Note that il se peut / pourrait que is followed by a verb in the subjunctive:
> **This could be the house we've always dreamed of.** *Il se peut / pourrait que ce soit la maison de nos rêves.*

couldn't ['kʊdnt] abbr of **could not.**

could've ['kʊdəv] abbr of **could have.**

coulis ['kuːlɪ] n coulis m.

council ['kaʊnsl] ◆ n **1.** [group of people] conseil m **2.** UK [elected local body] conseil m municipal ▶ **to be on the council** être élu municipal **3.** [meeting] conseil m ▶ **to hold a council of war** tenir un conseil de guerre. ◆ comp **1.** [meeting] du conseil **2.** UK [election, service, worker] municipal ; [leader, meeting] du conseil municipal ▶ **council estate** cité f ▶ **council flat / house** ≃ logement m social ▶ **council housing** ≃ logements mpl sociaux ▶ **council tenants** locataires de logements sociaux.

councillor UK, **councilor** US ['kaʊnslər] n conseiller m, -ère f / *Councillor (John) Murray* Monsieur le Conseiller Murray ▶ **town / county councillor** conseiller municipal / régional.

councilman ['kaʊnslmæn] (pl **councilmen** [-men]) n US conseiller m.

Council of Europe n Conseil m de l'Europe.

councilor US = councillor.

council tax n (U) impôts mpl locaux (en Grande-Bretagne).

councilwoman ['kaʊnsl,wʊmən] (pl **councilwomen** [-,wɪmɪn]) n US conseillère f.

counsel ['kaʊnsl] (UK pt & pp **counselled,** cont **counselling** ; US pt & pp **counseled,** cont **counseling**) ◆ n **1.** fml [advice] conseil m **2.** LAW avocat m, -e f qui plaide dans une cour. ◆ vt **1.** fml conseiller ▶ **to counsel sb to do sthg** conseiller à qqn de faire qqch **2.** [in therapy] conseiller.

counselling 🆄🇰, **counseling** 🇺🇸 [ˈkaʊnsəlɪŋ] n [psychological] assistance f, conseils mpl / to seek counselling se faire conseiller, prendre conseil.

counsellor 🇬🇧, **counselor** 🇺🇸 [ˈkaʊnsələr] n **1.** [in therapy] conseiller m, -ère f **2.** 🇺🇸 LAW avocat m, -e f.

count [kaʊnt] ◆ n **1.** compte m ; [of ballot papers] décompte m / to have a second count refaire le compte, recompter ▶ **to lose count** perdre le compte / I've lost count of the number of times he's been late je ne compte plus le nombre de fois où il est arrivé en retard ▶ **to keep count (of sthg)** tenir le compte (de qqch) / at the last count a) [gen] la dernière fois qu'on a compté b) ADMIN [of people] au dernier recensement **2.** ▶ **to be out for the count a)** [boxer, person in brawl] être K-O b) [fast asleep] dormir comme une souche **3.** LAW chef m d'accusation / guilty on three counts of murder coupable de meurtre sur trois chefs d'accusation ; fig : the argument is flawed on both counts l'argumentation est défectueuse sur les deux points / I'm annoyed with you on a number of counts je suis fâché contre toi pour un certain nombre de raisons or à plus d'un titre **4.** [nobleman] comte m. ◆ vt **1.** [add up - gen] compter ; [-votes] compter, décompter ▶ **to count sheep** fig [when sleepless] compter les moutons **2.** [include] compter / not counting public holidays sans compter les jours fériés **3.** [consider] considérer, estimer / do you count her as a friend? la considères-tu comme une amie ? / count yourself lucky (that...) estime-toi heureux (que...). ◆ vi **1.** [add up] compter / to count to twenty / fifty / a hundred compter jusqu'à vingt / cinquante / cent / to count on one's fingers compter sur ses doigts **2.** [be considered, qualify] compter / two children count as one adult deux enfants comptent pour un adulte / that / he doesn't count ça / il ne compte pas / his record counted in his favour son casier judiciaire a joué en sa faveur / l'a desservi **3.** [be important] compter / experience counts more than qualifications l'expérience compte davantage que les diplômes / he counts for nothing il n'est pas important, il ne compte pas. ❖ **count in** vt sep [include] compter, inclure ▶ **to count sb in on sthg** inclure or compter qqn dans qqch / count me in compte sur moi, je suis partant. ❖ **count on** vt insep **1.** [rely on] compter sur / we're counting on you nous comptons sur toi **2.** [expect] compter / I wasn't counting on getting here so early je ne comptais pas arriver si tôt. ❖ **count out** vt sep **1.** [money, objects] compter **2.** [exclude] : (you can) count me out ne compte surtout pas sur moi. ❖ **count up** vt sep compter, additionner. ❖ **count upon** vt insep = count on.

countdown [ˈkaʊntdaʊn] n ASTRONAUT compte m à rebours / the countdown to the wedding / Christmas has begun fig la date du mariage / de Noël se rapproche.

countenance [ˈkaʊntɪnəns] ◆ n **1.** fml & liter [face] visage m ; [facial expression] expression f, mine f **2.** fml [support, approval] ▶ **to give** or **to lend countenance to sthg** approuver qqch. ◆ vt fml [support, approve of - terrorism, violence, lying] approuver ; [-idea, proposal] approuver, accepter.

counter [ˈkaʊntər] ◆ n **1.** [in shop] comptoir m / ask at the counter [in bank, post office] demandez au guichet ▶ **it's available over the counter** [medication] on peut l'acheter sans ordonnance **2.** [device] compteur m **3.** [in board game] jeton m **4.** 🇺🇸 [in kitchen] plan m de travail. ◆ comp ▶ **counter staff** [in bank, post office] employés mpl du guichet, guichetiers mpl. ◆ vt [respond to - increase in crime, proposal] contrecarrer ; [-accusation, criticism] contrer ; [-threat] contrer / he countered that the project... il a contré or riposté en disant que le projet... ◆ vi [in box-

ing] contrer. ◆ adv ▶ **to go** or **to run counter to sthg** aller à l'encontre de qqch ▶ **to act counter to sb's advice / wishes** agir à l'encontre des conseils / des souhaits de qqn.

counteract [ˌkaʊntəˈrækt] vt [person] contrebalancer l'influence de ; [influence] contrebalancer ; [effects of drug, taste of sthg] neutraliser ; [rising crime] lutter contre.

counterargument [ˌkaʊntəˈrɑːgjʊmənt] n argument m contraire.

counterattack [ˌkaʊntərəˈtæk] ◆ n MIL & SPORT contre-attaque f, contre-offensive f ; fig [in business, election, etc.] contre-offensive f. ◆ vi MIL & SPORT contre-attaquer ; fig riposter, contrer.

counterbalance [ˌkaʊntəˈbæləns] ◆ n contrepoids m. ◆ vt contrebalancer, faire contrepoids à ; fig contrebalancer, compenser.

counterbid [ˈkaʊntəbɪd] n FIN [during takeover] contre-OPA f inv.

counterblast [ˈkaʊntəblɑːst] n inf riposte f.

counterclaim [ˈkaʊntəkleɪm] n LAW demande f reconventionnelle.

counterclockwise [ˌkaʊntəˈklɒkwaɪz] adj & adv 🇺🇸 dans le sens inverse or contraire des aiguilles d'une montre.

counterculture [ˈkaʊntəˌkʌltʃər] n contre-culture f.

counterespionage [ˌkaʊntərˈespɪənɑːʒ] n contre-espionnage m.

counterfeit [ˈkaʊntəfɪt] ◆ n [banknote, document] faux m, contrefaçon f ; [piece of jewellery] faux m. ◆ adj [banknote, document] faux (fausse) ; [piece of jewellery] contrefait ; fig [sympathy, affection] feint. ◆ vt [banknote, passport, document, piece of jewellery] contrefaire ; fig [sympathy, affection] feindre.

counterfoil [ˈkaʊntəfɔɪl] n 🇬🇧 [of cheque, ticket] talon m.

counterintelligence [ˌkaʊntərɪnˈtelɪdʒəns] n contre-espionnage m ; [information] renseignements mpl (provenant du contre-espionnage).

counterintuitive [ˌkaʊntərɪnˈtjuːɪtɪv] adj qui va contre l'intuition.

countermand [ˌkaʊntəˈmɑːnd] vt [order] annuler.

countermeasure [ˈkaʊntəˌmeʒər] n contre-mesure f.

counteroffensive [ˌkaʊntərəˈfensɪv] n MIL contre-offensive f.

counteroffer [ˌkaʊntərˈɒfər] n offre f ; [higher] surenchère f.

counterpane [ˈkaʊntəpeɪn] n 🇬🇧 dessus-de-lit m inv, couvre-lit m.

counterpart [ˈkaʊntəpɑːt] n homologue mf ; [thing] équivalent m.

counterpoint [ˈkaʊntəpɔɪnt] n MUS contrepoint m.

counterproductive [ˌkaʊntəprəˈdʌktɪv] adj qui va à l'encontre du but recherché, qui a des effets contraires, contre-productif.

counterproposal [ˈkaʊntəprəˌpəʊzl] n contre-proposition f.

counter-revolution n contre-révolution f.

countersank [ˈkaʊntəsæŋk] pt ⟶ **countersink**.

countersign [ˈkaʊntəsaɪn] vt contresigner.

countersink [ˈkaʊntəsɪŋk] (pt **countersank** [ˈkaʊntəsæŋk], pp **countersunk** [-sʌŋk]) vt [screw] noyer ; [hole] fraiser.

countess [ˈkaʊntɪs] n comtesse f.

countless [ˈkaʊntlɪs] adj [deaths, reasons] innombrable ; [difficulties, opportunities] innombrable, sans nombre.

countrified [ˈkʌntrɪfaɪd] adj **1.** *pej* campagnard, provincial **2.** [rural] : *it's quite countrified round here* c'est vraiment la campagne ici.

country [ˈkʌntrɪ] (*pl* **countries**) ◆ n **1.** [land, nation] pays *m* ; [homeland] patrie *f* **2.** [as opposed to the city] campagne *f* / *to live in the country* vivre à la campagne **3.** [area of land, region] région *f* / *this is good farming country* c'est une bonne région agricole **4.** MUS = **country and western.** ◆ comp [house, road, town, bus] de campagne ; [people] de la campagne ; [life] à la campagne ▸ **country music** musique *f* country.

country and western ◆ n MUS musique *f* country. ◆ comp MUS [band, music, singer] country ; [fan] de country.

country club n *club sportif ou de loisirs situé à la campagne.*

country dancing n danse *f* folklorique ▸ **to go country dancing** aller danser des danses folkloriques.

country-dweller n campagnard *m*, -e *f*, habitant *m*, -e *f* de la campagne.

countryfolk [ˈkʌntrɪfəʊk] pl n gens *mpl* de la campagne.

country house n *grande maison de campagne, souvent historique.*

countryman [ˈkʌntrɪmən] (*pl* **countrymen** [-mən]) n **1.** [who lives in the country] campagnard *m*, habitant *m* de la campagne **2.** [compatriot] compatriote *m*.

country park n parc *m* naturel.

countryside [ˈkʌntrɪsaɪd] n campagne *f* ; [scenery] paysage *m* / *in the countryside* à la campagne.

countrywoman [ˈkʌntrɪˌwʊmən] (*pl* **countrywomen** [-ˌwɪmɪn]) n **1.** [who lives in the country] campagnarde *f*, habitante *f* de la campagne **2.** [compatriot] compatriote *f*.

county [ˈkaʊntɪ] (*pl* **counties**) ◆ n comté *m*. ◆ comp [councillor, boundary] de comté ▸ **county cricket** *grands matchs de cricket disputés par les équipes du comté.* ◆ adj *pej* : *the horse sale was full of county types* le marché aux chevaux regorgeait de petits hobereaux.

county council n ≃ conseil *m* général.

county court n [in England, Wales and United States] tribunal *m* d'instance.

county seat n [in US] chef-lieu *m* de comté.

county town n [in England] chef-lieu *m* de comté.

coup [kuː] n **1.** [feat] (beau) coup *m* **2.** [overthrow of government] coup *m* d'État.

coupé [ˈkuːpeɪ] n AUTO coupé *m*.

couple [ˈkʌpl] ◆ n **1.** [pair] couple *m* ▸ **the happy couple** les jeunes mariés **2.** [as quantifier] ▸ **a couple** [a few] quelques-uns, quelques-unes ▸ **a couple of a)** [a few] quelques **b)** [two] deux ▸ **he's a couple years older** il a deux ou trois ans de plus. ◆ vt **1.** [horse] atteler ; RAIL atteler, accrocher **2.** *fig* [studies] associer, suivre en parallèle ▸ **to couple sthg with sthg** associer qqch à qqch.

couplet [ˈkʌplɪt] n distique *m*.

coupling [ˈkʌplɪŋ] n **1.** [mating - of animals, birds, humans] accouplement *m* **2.** [connecting device] accouplement *m* ; RAIL attelage *m*.

coupon [ˈkuːpɒn] n [voucher, form] coupon *m* ▸ **(money-off) coupon** coupon de réduction.

couponing [ˈkuːpənɪŋ] n MARKETING couponing *m*, couponnage *m*.

courage [ˈkʌrɪdʒ] n courage *m* ▸ **to have the courage to do sthg** avoir le courage de faire qqch.

courageous [kəˈreɪdʒəs] adj courageux.

courageously [kəˈreɪdʒəslɪ] adv courageusement.

courgette [kɔːˈʒet] n courgette *f*.

courier [ˈkʊrɪəʳ] n **1.** [messenger] courrier *m*, messager *m* ; [company] messagerie *f* ▸ **to send sthg by courier** envoyer qqch par courrier **2.** [on journey] accompagnateur *m*, -trice *f*.

course [kɔːs] ◆ n **1.** [path, route - of ship, plane] route *f* ; [- of river] cours *m* ▸ **to change course a)** [ship, plane, company] changer de cap or de direction **b)** *fig* [argument, discussion] changer de direction, dévier ▸ **to be on course** [ship, plane] suivre le cap fixé, *fig* être en bonne voie ▸ **to be off course** [ship, plane] dévier de son cap **2.** *fig* [approach] ▸ **course (of action)** ligne *f* (de conduite) **3.** [development, progress - of history, war] cours *m* **4.** SCH & UNIV enseignement *m*, cours *mpl* ▸ **to go on a (training) course** faire un stage / *I'm taking* or *doing a computer course* je suis des cours or un stage d'informatique **5.** MED : *a course of injections* une série de piqûres / *a course of pills* un traitement à base de comprimés / *course of treatment* [for an illness] traitement *m* **6.** [in meal] plat *m* / *first course* entrée *f* **7.** [for golf] terrain *m* ; [for horse-racing] champ *m* de courses **8.** [of bricks] assise *f*. ◆ vi [flow] : *tears coursed down his cheeks* les larmes ruisselaient sur ses joues. ❖ **in the course of** prep phr au cours de. ❖ **of course** adv phr bien sûr / *of course I believe you* / *she loves you* bien sûr que je te crois / qu'elle t'aime / *was there much damage? — of course!* y a-t-il eu beaucoup de dégâts ? — tu parles ! / *of course not!* bien sûr que non !

coursebook [ˈkɔːsbʊk] n livre *m* de classe.

courseware [ˈkɔːsweəʳ] n logiciels *mpl* éducatifs.

coursework [ˈkɔːswɜːk] n travail *m* de l'année *(qui permet d'exercer le contrôle continu)*.

court [kɔːt] ◆ n **1.** LAW [institution] cour *f*, tribunal *m* ; [court room, people in room] cour *f* / *silence in court!* silence dans la salle ! ▸ **to appear in court** [accused, witness] comparaître au tribunal ▸ **to come before a court** comparaître devant un tribunal ▸ **to take sb to court** poursuivre qqn en justice, intenter un procès contre qqn ▸ **to go to court** faire appel à la justice, aller en justice ▸ **to go to court over sthg** faire appel à la justice pour régler qqch ▸ **to settle sthg out of court** régler qqch à l'amiable **2.** [of monarch - people] cour *f* ; [- building] palais *m* **3.** SPORT [tennis, badminton] court *m*, terrain *m* ; [squash] court *m* **4.** [courtyard] cour *f*. ◆ comp LAW ▸ **court reporter** chroniqueur *m* judiciaire ▸ **court usher** huissier *m* de justice. ◆ vt **1.** *lit & dated* faire la cour à, courtiser **2.** *fig* [voters] courtiser, chercher à séduire / *to court popularity* chercher à se rendre populaire. ◆ vi *dated* [one person] fréquenter ; [two people] se fréquenter.

court circular n *rubrique d'un journal indiquant les engagements officiels de la famille royale.*

courteous [ˈkɜːtjəs] adj [person, gesture, treatment] courtois.

courteously [ˈkɜːtjəslɪ] adv [speak, reply, etc.] avec courtoisie, courtoisement.

courtesan [ˌkɔːtɪˈzæn] n courtisane *f*.

courtesy [ˈkɜːtɪsɪ] (*pl* **courtesies**) ◆ n **1.** [politeness] courtoisie *f* **2.** [polite action, remark] politesse *f*. ◆ comp [call, visit] de politesse ▸ **courtesy coach** or **shuttle** [at airport] navette *f* gratuite ▸ **courtesy car** voiture *f* de courtoisie *(mise à la disposition d'un client)* ▸ **courtesy telephone** téléphone *m* de courtoisie. ❖ **(by) courtesy of** prep phr avec l'aimable autorisation de.

courthouse [ˈkɔːthaʊs] (*pl* [-haʊzɪz]) n palais *m* de justice, tribunal *m*.

courtier [ˈkɔːtjəʳ] n courtisan *m*.

court-martial ◆ n (pl **courts-martial**) MIL tribunal m militaire. ◆ vt (UK pt & pp **court-martialled**, cont **court-martialling** ; US pt & pp **court-martialed**, cont **court-martialing**) faire comparaître devant un tribunal militaire.

Court of Appeal pr n cour f d'appel.

court of appeals n US cour f d'appel.

court of inquiry n UK [body of people] commission f d'enquête ; [investigation] enquête f.

court of law n tribunal m, cour f de justice.

court order n ordonnance f du tribunal.

court-ordered adj LAW [sale] judiciaire.

courtroom ['kɔːtrʊm] n salle f d'audience.

courtship ['kɔːtʃɪp] ◆ n **1.** [of couple] : their courtship lasted six years ils se sont fréquentés pendant six ans **2.** [of animals] période f nuptiale, période f des amours. ◆ adj [dance, display, ritual] nuptial.

court shoe n UK escarpin m.

courtyard ['kɔːtjɑːd] n [of building] cour f.

cousin ['kʌzn] n cousin m, -e f.

couture [kuːˈtʊər] n couture f.

cove [kəʊv] n [bay] crique f.

coven ['kʌvən] n ordre m or réunion f de sorcières.

covenant ['kʌvənənt] ◆ n **1.** [promise of money] convention f, engagement m ▶ **(deed of) covenant** contrat m **2.** [agreement] engagement m. ◆ vt [promise payment of] s'engager (par contrat) à payer. ◆ vi ▶ **to covenant for a sum** s'engager (par contrat) à payer une somme.

Covent Garden ['kɒvənt-] pr n Covent Garden.

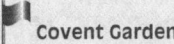

Covent Garden

Halle de l'ancien marché aux fruits, aux légumes et aux fleurs du centre de Londres, **Covent Garden** est aujourd'hui une galerie marchande à la mode ; le terme désigne aussi, par extension, la **Royal Opera House**, située près de l'ancien marché.

Coventry ['kɒvəntrɪ] pr n ▶ **to send sb to Coventry** UK mettre qqn en quarantaine fig.

cover ['kʌvər] ◆ n **1.** [material - for bed] couverture f ; [- for cushion, typewriter] housse f **2.** [lid] couvercle m **3.** [of book, magazine] couverture f ▶ **to read a book (from) cover to cover** lire un livre de la première à la dernière page or d'un bout à l'autre **4.** [shelter, protection] abri m ; [for birds, animals] couvert m ▶ **to take cover** se mettre à l'abri / to take cover from the rain s'abriter de la pluie ▶ **to run for cover** courir se mettre à l'abri ▶ **to keep sthg under cover** garder qqch à l'abri ▶ **to do sthg under cover of darkness** faire qqch à la faveur de la nuit ▶ **to break cover** [animal, person in hiding] sortir à découvert **5.** [in insurance] couverture f ▶ **to have cover against sthg** être couvert or assuré contre qqch / I've taken out cover for medical costs j'ai pris une assurance pour les frais médicaux **6.** [disguise, front - for criminal enterprise] couverture f ; [- for spy] fausse identité f, identité f d'emprunt / your cover has been blown inf vous avez été démasqué **7.** [during a person's absence] remplacement m ▶ **to provide cover for sb** remplacer qqn **8.** MUS [new version of song] reprise f **9.** ▶ **cover letter** US lettre f explicative or de couverture. ◆ vt **1.** [in order to protect] couvrir ; [in order to hide] cacher, dissimuler ; [cushion, chair, settee] recouvrir / to cover sthg with a sheet / blanket recouvrir qqch

d'un drap / d'une couverture / to cover one's eyes / ears se couvrir les yeux / les oreilles **2.** [coat - subj: dust, snow] recouvrir / his face was covered in spots son visage était couvert de boutons / you're covering everything in dust / paint tu mets de la poussière / peinture partout **3.** [extend over, occupy - subj: city, desert, etc.] couvrir une surface de / water covers most of the earth's surface l'eau recouvre la plus grande partie de la surface de la terre / his interests cover a wide field il a des intérêts très variés **4.** [travel over] parcourir, couvrir / we've covered every square inch of the park looking for it nous avons ratissé chaque centimètre carré du parc pour essayer de le retrouver **5.** [deal with] traiter / there's one point we haven't covered il y a un point que nous n'avons pas traité or vu / the law doesn't cover that kind of situation la loi ne prévoit pas ce genre de situation **6.** PRESS, RADIO & TV [report on] couvrir, faire la couverture de **7.** [be enough money for - damage, expenses] couvrir ; [- meal] suffire à payer / £30 should cover it 30 livres devraient suffire ▶ **to cover one's costs** [company] rentrer dans ses frais **8.** [insure] couvrir, garantir ▶ **to be covered against** or **for sthg** être couvert ou assuré contre qqch **9.** [with gun - criminal] couvrir / I've got you covered [to criminal] j'ai mon arme braquée sur toi **10.** SPORT marquer **11.** MUS [song] faire une reprise de. ◆ vi ▶ **to cover for sb** [replace] remplacer qqn. ❖ **cover up** ◆ vt sep **1.** [hide, conceal] cacher, dissimuler ; [in order to protect] recouvrir ; pej [involvement, report, etc.] dissimuler, garder secret ; [affair] étouffer **2.** [in order to keep warm] couvrir. ◆ vi [hide something] ▶ **to cover up for sb** servir de couverture à qqn, couvrir qqn.

coverage ['kʌvərɪdʒ] n **1.** (U) PRESS, RADIO & TV reportage m ▶ **coverage area** [of mobile phone network] zone f de couverture **2.** [in insurance] couverture f.

coveralls ['kʌvərɔːlz] pl n US bleu m or bleus mpl (de travail).

cover charge n [in restaurant] couvert m.

covered ['kʌvəd] adj [walkway, bridge, market] couvert.

cover girl n cover-girl f.

covering ['kʌvərɪŋ] ◆ n [of snow, dust] couche f. ◆ adj ▶ **covering fire** MIL tir m de couverture ▶ **covering letter** UK lettre f explicative or de couverture.

cover note n UK attestation f provisoire.

cover price n [of magazine] prix m.

cover story n article m principal (faisant la couverture).

covert ['kʌvət] ◆ adj [operation, payments, contacts] secret (secrète) ; [threats] voilé ; [glance, look] furtif. ◆ n [hiding place for animals] fourré m, couvert m.

cover-up n : the government has been accused of a cover-up le gouvernement a été accusé d'avoir étouffé l'affaire / it's a cover-up c'est un complot.

cover version n MUS [of song] reprise f.

covet ['kʌvɪt] vt [crave, long for] convoiter ; [wish for] avoir très envie de.

covetous ['kʌvɪtəs] adj [person] avide ; [look] de convoitise.

cow [kaʊ] ◆ n **1.** [farm animal] vache f **2.** [female elephant] éléphant m femelle, éléphante f ; [female seal] phoque m femelle ; [female whale] baleine f femelle **3.** UK v inf & pej [woman] conasse f / you silly cow! espèce d'abrutie ! **4.** PHR ▶ **to have a cow** US inf sauter au plafond. ◆ vt effrayer, intimider.

coward ['kaʊəd] n lâche mf, poltron m, -onne f.

cowardice ['kaʊədɪs] n lâcheté f ▶ **moral cowardice** manque m de force morale.

cowardliness ['kaʊədlɪnɪs] n lâcheté f.

cowardly ['kaʊədlɪ] adj lâche.

cowboy ['kaʊbɔɪ] ◆ n **1.** [in American West] cowboy m **2.** inf & pej petit rigolo m. ◆ comp de cow-boy.

cower ['kaʊər] vi [person] se recroqueviller ; [animal] se tapir.

cowhide ['kaʊhaɪd] n peau f de vache ; [leather] cuir m or peau f de vache.

cowl [kaʊl] n [on sweater, dress] ▶ **cowl neck** or **neckline** col m boule.

co-worker n collègue mf.

cowpat ['kaʊpæt] n bouse f de vache.

cowpoke ['kaʊpəʊk] 🇺🇸 inf cow-boy m.

cowshed ['kaʊʃed] n étable f.

cox [kɒks] ◆ n [of rowing team] barreur m, -euse f. ◆ vt barrer. ◆ vi barrer.

coxswain ['kɒksən] n [of rowing team] barreur m, -euse f ; [of lifeboat] timonier m, homme m de barre.

coy [kɔɪ] adj **1.** [shy -person] qui fait le / la timide ; [-answer, smile] faussement timide **2.** [provocative, playful] coquet **3.** [evasive] évasif.

coyly ['kɔɪlɪ] adv [timidly] avec une timidité affectée or feinte ; [provocatively] coquettement.

coyness ['kɔɪnɪs] n [timidness] timidité f affectée or feinte ; [provocativeness] coquetteries fpl.

coyote [kɔɪ'əʊtɪ] n coyote m ▶ **to be coyote ugly** 🇺🇸 inf être laid or moche comme un pou.

COZ MESSAGING written abbr of **because.**

cozy 🇺🇸 = **cosy.**

cp. (written abbr of **compare**) cf.

c/p (written abbr of **carriage paid**) pp.

CP (abbr of **Communist Party**) pr n PC m.

CPA n 🇺🇸 abbr of **certified public accountant.**

CPI (abbr of **Consumer Price Index**) n IPC m.

Cpl. written abbr of **corporal.**

cpm (written abbr of **copies per minute**) cpm.

CP/M (abbr of **control program for microcomputers**) n CP/M m.

cps (written abbr of **characters per second**) cps.

CPS (abbr of **Crown Prosecution Service**) n ≃ ministère m public.

CPU (abbr of **central processing unit**) n unité f centrale.

cr. 1. written abbr of **credit 2.** written abbr of **creditor.**

crab [kræb] (pt & pp **crabbed**, cont **crabbing**) n **1.** ZOOL crabe m **2.** ASTRON ▶ **the Crab** le Cancer. ◆ **crabs** pl n [pubic lice] morpions mpl.

crab apple n [fruit] pomme f sauvage ▶ **crab apple (tree)** pommier m sauvage.

crabby ['kræbɪ] (compar **crabbier**, superl **crabbiest**) adj inf grognon, ronchon.

crack [kræk] ◆ n **1.** [in cup, glass, egg] fêlure f ; [in ceiling, wall] lézarde f, fissure f ; [in ground] crevasse f ; [in varnish, enamel] craquelure f ; [in skin] gerçure f, crevasse f ; [in bone] fêlure f ; fig [fault - in policy, argument, etc.] fissure f, faiblesse f **2.** [small opening or gap - in floorboards, door, etc.] fente f ; [- in wall] fissure f **3.** [noise] craquement m ; [of thunder] coup m **4.** [blow - on head, knee, etc.] coup m **5.** inf [attempt] tentative f / I'll have a crack (at it) or I'll give it a crack je vais tenter le coup, je vais essayer (un coup) **6.** [joke, witticism] blague f, plaisanterie f **7.** [drug] crack m ▶ **crack baby** bébé né dépendant du crack **8.** PHR ▶ **the crack of dawn** : at the crack of dawn au point du jour / I've been up since the crack of dawn je suis debout or levé depuis l'aube. ◆ adj [regiment, team, etc.] d'élite ▶ **crack shot** tireur m, -euse f d'élite. ◆ vt **1.** [damage - cup, glass, egg] fêler ; [- ice] fendre ; [- ceiling, wall] lézarder, fissurer ; [- ground] crevasser ; [- varnish, enamel] craqueler ; [- skin] gercer, crevasser ; [- bone] fêler **2.** [open - eggs, nuts] casser **3.** [bang, hit - head, knee] ▶ **to crack one's head / knee on sthg** se cogner la tête / le genou contre qqch **4.** [make noise with - whip] faire claquer ; [- knuckles] faire craquer **5.** [solve] ▶ **to crack a code** déchiffrer un code **6.** PHR ▶ **to crack a joke** inf sortir une blague. ◆ vi **1.** [cup, glass, ice] se fissurer, se fêler ; [ceiling, wall] se lézarder, se fissurer ; [ground] se crevasser ; [varnish, enamel] se craqueler ; [skin] se gercer, se crevasser ; [bone] se fêler **2.** [make noise - whip] claquer ; [- twigs] craquer **3.** [give way, collapse - through nervous exhaustion] s'effondrer, craquer ; [- under questioning, surveillance] craquer **4.** inf PHR ▶ **to get cracking a)** [start work] s'y mettre, se mettre au boulot **b)** [get ready, get going] se mettre en route. ◆ **crack down** vi sévir ▶ **to crack down on sthg / sb** sévir contre qqch / qqn. ◆ **crack open** vt sep [eggs, nuts] casser ; inf [bottle] ouvrir, déboucher. ◆ **crack up** ◆ vi **1.** [ice] se fissurer ; [paint, enamel, make-up] se craqueler ; [ground] se crevasser ; [skin] se gercer, se crevasser **2.** inf [through nervous exhaustion] s'effondrer, craquer / I must be cracking up [going mad] je débloque **3.** inf [with laughter] se tordre de rire **4.** 🇺🇸 inf [vehicle] s'écraser. ◆ vt sep **1.** [make laugh] faire se tordre de rire **2.** (always passive) [say good things about] : he's not what he's cracked up to be il n'est pas aussi fantastique qu'on le dit or prétend **3.** 🇺🇸 inf [car, motorbike] bousiller.

crackbrained ['krækbreɪnd] adj inf débile, dingue.

crackdown ['krækdaʊn] n : we're going to have a crackdown on petty theft on va sévir contre les petits larcins / the annual Christmas crackdown on drunk driving les mesures répressives prises tous les ans à Noël contre la conduite en état d'ivresse.

cracked [krækt] adj **1.** [damaged - cup, glass] fêlé ; [- ice] fendu ; [- ceiling, wall] lézardé ; [- ground] crevassé ; [- varnish] craquelé ; [- skin] gercé, crevassé **2.** inf [mad - person] fêlé, taré.

cracker ['krækər] n **1.** [savoury biscuit] biscuit m salé, cracker m **2.** 🇬🇧 [for pulling] papillote contenant un pétard et une surprise, traditionnelle au moment des fêtes de Noël **3.** [firework] pétard m **4.** inf [good-looking person] canon m **5.** inf [something excellent of its kind] : that was a cracker of a goal c'était un but sensass **6.** 🇺🇸 inf & pej [redneck] péquenaud m.

 Cracker

En Grande-Bretagne, les **crackers** sont des petits paquets en forme de papillotes contenant un jouet, une surprise, un chapeau en papier, posés sur les tables à Noël. On se met à deux pour les ouvrir, chacun tirant à une extrémité, jusqu'à ce que le papier se déchire et fasse exploser un petit pétard.

crackerjack ['krækər,dʒæk] adj 🇺🇸 inf extra, génial.

crackers ['krækəz] adj inf cinglé, fêlé, taré ▶ **to drive sb crackers** faire tourner qqn en bourrique.

cracking ['krækɪŋ] ◆ adj **1.** [excellent] génial, épatant **2.** [fast] ▶ **to keep up a cracking pace** aller à fond de train. ◆ adv 🇬🇧 inf & dated ▶ **cracking good** [match, meal] de première.

crackle ['krækl] ◆ vi [paper, dry leaves] craquer ; [fire] crépiter, craquer ; [radio] grésiller. ◆ n [of paper, twigs] craquement *m* ; [of fire] crépitement *m*, craquement *m* ; [of radio] grésillement *m* ; [on telephone] friture *f* ; [of machine-gun fire] crépitement *m*.

crackling ['kræklɪŋ] n **1.** CULIN couenne *f* rôtie **2.** [noise] = **crackle**.

crackpot ['krækpɒt] inf ◆ n [person] tordu *m*, -e *f*, cinglé *m*, -e *f*. ◆ adj [idea, scheme] tordu ; [person] tordu, cinglé.

crack-up n inf **1.** [of person] dépression *f* (nerveuse) **2.** [of country, economy] effondrement *m*.

Cracow ['krækaʊ] pr n Cracovie.

cradle ['kreɪdl] ◆ n **1.** [for baby] berceau *m* ; *fig* berceau *m* **2.** [frame - for painter, window cleaner] pont *m* volant, échafaudage *m* volant ; [- in hospital bed] arceau *m* **3.** TELEC support *m* (du combiné). ◆ vt [hold carefully - baby, kitten] tenir tendrement (dans ses bras) ; [- delicate object] tenir précieusement or délicatement (dans ses bras).

craft [krɑːft] (*pl* **crafts** or **craft**) ◆ n **1.** [of artist, artisan] art *m*, métier *m* **2.** [guile, cunning] ruse *f* **3.** (*pl* **craft**) [boat, ship] bateau *m* ; [aircraft] avion *m* ; [spacecraft] engin *m* or vaisseau *m* spatial. ◆ comp ▶ **craft(s) fair** foire *f* d'artisanat ▶ **craft shop** boutique *f* d'artisanat. ◆ vt (*usu passive*) travailler / *a hand crafted table* une table travaillée à la main.

craftily ['krɑːftɪlɪ] adv astucieusement.

craftiness ['krɑːftɪnɪs] n habileté *f* ; *pej* ruse *f*, roublardise *f*.

craftsman ['krɑːftsmən] (*pl* **craftsmen** [-mən]) n artisan *m*, homme *m* de métier ; [writer, actor] homme *m* de métier.

craftsmanship ['krɑːftsmənʃɪp] n connaissance *f* d'un or du métier.

crafty ['krɑːftɪ] (*compar* **craftier**, *superl* **craftiest**) adj [person, idea, scheme] malin (maligne), astucieux ; *pej* [person] rusé, roublard ; [idea, scheme] rusé.

crag [kræg] n [steep rock] rocher *m* escarpé or à pic.

craggy ['krægɪ] (*compar* **craggier**, *superl* **craggiest**) adj [hill] escarpé, à pic ; *fig* [features] anguleux, taillé à la serpe.

Crakow ['krækaʊ] n Cracovie.

cram [kræm] (*pt & pp* **crammed**, *cont* **cramming**) ◆ vt **1.** [objects] fourrer ; [people] entasser / *to cram sth into a drawer* fourrer qqch dans un tiroir **2.** inf SCH [facts] apprendre à toute vitesse ; [students] faire bachoter. ◆ vi **1.** inf [study hard] bachoter **2.** [into small space] : *we all crammed into his office* nous nous sommes tous entassés dans son bureau.

crammed ['kræmd] adj [full - bus, train, room, suitcase] bourré, bondé ▶ **to be crammed with people** être bondé ▶ **to be crammed with sth** être plein à craquer or bourré de qqch.

cramming ['kræmɪŋ] n inf [intensive learning] bachotage *m* ; [intensive teaching] bourrage *m* de crâne.

cramp [kræmp] ◆ n (*U*) [muscle pain] crampe *f* ▶ **to have cramp** or **US** **a cramp** avoir une crampe ▶ **to have stomach cramp** or **to have cramps** **US** avoir des crampes d'estomac. ◆ vt [hamper - person] gêner ; [- project] entraver, contrarier.

cramped [kræmpt] adj **1.** [room, flat] exigu (exiguë) / *they live in very cramped conditions* ils vivent très à l'étroit **2.** [position] inconfortable **3.** [handwriting] en pattes de mouche, serré.

crampon ['kræmpən] n crampon *m* (à glace).

cram school ['kræm,skuːl] n **US** SCH école privée spécialisée dans le bachotage pour les examens.

cranberry ['krænbərɪ] (*pl* **cranberries**) ◆ n airelle *f*. ◆ comp ▶ **cranberry sauce** sauce *f* aux airelles.

crane [kreɪn] ◆ n **1.** ORNITH grue *f* **2.** TECH & CIN grue *f*. ◆ comp ▶ **crane driver** or **operator** grutier *m*. ◆ vt ▶ **to crane one's neck** tendre le cou. ◆ vi ▶ **to crane (forward)** tendre le cou.

crane fly n tipule *f* des prés or des prairies.

cranium ['kreɪnjəm] (*pl* **craniums** or **crania** ['kreɪnjə]) n [skull - gen] crâne *m* ; [- enclosing brain] boîte *f* crânienne.

crank [kræŋk] ◆ n **1.** inf [eccentric] excentrique *mf* **2.** **US** inf [bad-tempered person] grognon *m*, -onne *f* **3.** MECH ▶ **crank (handle)** manivelle *f*. ◆ vt [engine] démarrer à la manivelle ; [gramophone] remonter à la manivelle. ◆ vi **US** inf [work hard] trimer. ◈ **crank out** vt sep **US** inf [books, plays, etc.] produire en quantités industrielles.

◈ **crank up** vt sep inf **1.** = **crank (vt) 2.** *fig* [increase] augmenter.

crankshaft ['kræŋkʃɑːft] n vilebrequin *m*.

cranky ['kræŋkɪ] (*compar* **crankier**, *superl* **crankiest**) adj inf **1.** [eccentric - person, behaviour, ideas] bizarre **2.** **US** [bad-tempered] grognon **3.** [unreliable - machine] capricieux.

cranny ['krænɪ] (*pl* **crannies**) n fente *f*.

crap [kræp] (*pt & pp* **crapped**, *cont* **crapping**) ◆ n (*U*) **1.** vulg [faeces] merde *f* ▶ **to have a crap** chier **2.** v inf & fig [nonsense] conneries *fpl* **3.** v inf & fig [rubbish] merde *f* **4.** **US** [dice game] jeu de dés similaire au quatre-cent-vingt-et-un et où on parie sur le résultat ▶ **crap game** partie *f* de dés. ◆ vi vulg [defecate] chier. ◆ adj **UK** v inf [of very poor quality] de merde, merdique. ◈ **craps** n **US** ▶ **to shoot craps a)** [play game] jouer aux dés, faire une partie de dés **b)** [throw dice] lancer les dés.

crapper ['kræpə*] n v inf [toilet] chiottes *fpl*, gogues *mpl*.

crappy ['kræpɪ] (*compar* **crappier**, *superl* **crappiest**) adj v inf [programme, book, etc.] de merde, merdique à la con ; [remark, action] dégueulasse.

crash [kræʃ] ◆ n **1.** [accident] accident *m* / *car / plane / train crash* accident de voiture / d'avion / ferroviaire ▶ **to have a crash** avoir un accident **2.** [loud noise] fracas *m* / *a crash of thunder* un coup de tonnerre **3.** FIN [slump] krach *m*, débâcle *f* **4.** COMPUT panne *f*. ◆ comp [diet, programme] intensif ; [of choc] ▶ **crash victim** victime *f* d'un accident de voiture. ◆ adv : *he ran crash into a wall* il est rentré en plein dans le mur / *it went crash* ça a fait boum. ◆ interj boum. ◆ vi **1.** [car, train] avoir un accident ; [plane, pilot] s'écraser, se crasher ; [driver] avoir un accident ▶ **to crash into sth** percuter qqch ▶ **to crash into sb** [subj: person] rentrer dans qqn **2.** [make loud noise - thunder] retentir **3.** [fall, hit with loud noise or violently] / *the tree came crashing down* l'arbre est tombé avec fracas **4.** ST. EX s'effondrer **5.** COMPUT tomber en panne, planter **6.** v inf [sleep] dormir ; [fall asleep] s'endormir. ◆ vt **1.** [vehicle] : *to crash a car* **a)** avoir un accident avec une voiture **b)** [on purpose] démolir une voiture / *to crash a plane* s'écraser en avion **2.** inf [attend without invitation] ▶ **to crash a party** entrer dans une fête sans y être invité. ◈ **crash out** vi v inf [fall asleep] s'endormir ; [spend the night, sleep] roupiller.

crash barrier n glissière *f* de sécurité.

crash course n cours *m* intensif / *a crash course in French* un cours intensif de français.

crash-dive vi [submarine] plonger ; [plane] faire un plongeon.

crash helmet n casque *m* (de protection).

crash-land ◆ vi [aircraft] faire un atterrissage forcé, atterrir en catastrophe. ◆ vt [aircraft] poser or faire atterrir en catastrophe.

crash landing n atterrissage *m* forcé or en catastrophe.

crash pad n v inf piaule f de dépannage.

crash test dummy n mannequin-test m.

crass [kræs] adj [comment, person] lourd ; [behaviour, stupidity] grossier ; [ignorance] grossier, crasse.

crassly ['kræslɪ] adv [behave, comment] lourdement.

crassness ['kræsnɪs] n [of comment, person] lourdeur f, manque m de finesse.

crate [kreɪt] ◆ n 1. [for storage, transport] caisse f ; [for fruit, vegetables] cageot m, cagette f ; [for bottles] caisse f 2. 🇬🇧 inf [old car] caisse f ; [plane] coucou m. ◆ vt [furniture, bottles] mettre dans une caisse or en caisses ; [fruit, vegetables] mettre dans un cageot or en cageots.

crater ['kreɪtər] ◆ n [of volcano, moon, etc.] cratère m ▶ **bomb crater** entonnoir m. ◆ vi [reach lowest ebb] être au plus bas / the movie cratered 🇺🇸 inf le film a été un flop total.

cravat [krə'væt] n 🇬🇧 foulard m (d'homme).

crave [kreɪv] vt 1. [long for - cigarette, drink] avoir terriblement envie de ; [- affection, love] avoir soif or terriblement besoin de ; [- stardom] avoir soif de ; [- luxury, wealth] avoir soif or être avide de ; [in medical, psychological context] éprouver un besoin impérieux de 2. fml [beg] implorer / to crave sb's indulgence faire appel à l'indulgence de qqn.
❖ **crave for** vt insep = **crave** (vt).

craving ['kreɪvɪŋ] n [longing] envie f impérieuse or irrésistible ; [physiological need] besoin m impérieux ▶ **to have a craving for sthg a)** [chocolate, sweets, cigarette] avoir terriblement envie de qqch **b)** [subj: alcoholic, drug addict] avoir un besoin impérieux de qqch.

crawl [krɔːl] ◆ n 1. [person] : it involved a laborious crawl through the undergrowth il a fallu ramper tant bien que mal à travers le sous-bois 2. [vehicle] ralenti m 3. SPORT crawl m. ◆ vi 1. [move on all fours - person] ramper ; [- baby] marcher à quatre pattes 2. [move slowly - traffic, train] avancer au ralenti or au pas ; [- insect, snake] ramper 3. [be infested] ▶ **to be crawling with** être infesté de, grouiller de 4. [come out in goose pimples] ▶ **to make sb's flesh crawl** donner la chair de poule à qqn 5. inf [grovel] ▶ **to crawl to sb** ramper or s'aplatir devant qqn, lécher les bottes de qqn.

crawler ['krɔːlər] n 1. inf & pej [groveller] lèche-bottes mf 2. 🇬🇧 AUTO ▶ **crawler lane** file f or voie f pour véhicules lents 3. COMPUT robot m d'indexation.
❖ **crawlers** pl n [for baby] grenouillère f.

crayfish ['kreɪfɪʃ] (pl **crayfish** or **crayfishes**) n écrevisse f.

crayon ['kreɪɒn] ◆ n [coloured pencil] crayon m de couleur. ◆ vt [draw] dessiner avec des crayons de couleur ; [colour] crayonner (avec des crayons).

craze [kreɪz] ◆ n engouement m, folie f ▶ **a craze for sthg** un engouement pour qqch. ◆ vt [send mad] rendre fou.

crazed [kreɪzd] adj 1. [mad - look, expression] fou (before vowel or silent 'h' **fol**, f **folle**) 2. [ceramics] craquelé.

-crazed in comp rendu fou par / drug-crazed rendu fou par la drogue / power-crazed dictators des dictateurs fous de pouvoir / he was half-crazed with fear il était à moitié fou de peur.

crazily ['kreɪzɪlɪ] adv [behave] comme un fou.

craziness ['kreɪzɪnɪs] n folie f.

crazy ['kreɪzɪ] (compar **crazier**, superl **craziest**) adj 1. [insane - person, dream] fou (before vowel or silent 'h' **fol**, f **folle**) ▶ **to drive** or **to send sb crazy** rendre qqn fou / he went crazy a) [insane] il est devenu fou b) [angry] il est devenu fou (de colère or de rage) ▶ **like crazy** [work, drive, run, spend money] comme un fou 2. inf [very fond] ▶ **to be**

crazy about être fou or dingue de ▶ **to go crazy over sthg** flasher sur qqch 3. [strange, fantastic] bizarre, fou (before vowel or silent 'h' **fol**, f **folle**).

crazy paving n 🇬🇧 dallage irrégulier en pierres plates.

crazy quilt n 🇺🇸 couette f en patchwork.

CRB [ˌsiːɑːˈbiː] (abbr of **Criminal Records Bureau**) n Organisme chargé de vérifier le casier judiciaire de personnels sensibles.

CRE (abbr of **Commission for Racial Equality**) n ▶ **the CRE** commission contre la discrimination raciale.

creak [kriːk] ◆ vi [chair, floorboard, person's joints] craquer ; [door hinge] grincer ; [shoes] crisser. ◆ n [of chair, floorboard, person's joints] craquement m ; [of door hinge] grincement m ; [of shoes] crissement m.

creaky ['kriːkɪ] (compar **creakier**, superl **creakiest**) adj [chair, floorboard, person's joints] qui craque ; [door hinge] grinçant ; [shoes] qui crisse.

cream [kriːm] ◆ n 1. crème f 2. [filling for biscuits, chocolates] crème f 3. [mixture] mélange m crémeux 4. fig [best, pick] crème f / the cream of society la crème or le gratin de la société 5. [for face, shoes, etc.] crème f 6. [colour] crème m. ◆ comp [cake, bun] à la crème ; [jug] à crème ▶ **cream-coloured** crème ▶ **cream sherry** sherry m or xérès m doux. ◆ adj crème. ◆ vt 1. CULIN [beat] écraser, travailler / creamed potatoes purée f de pommes de terre 2. [hands, face] mettre de la crème sur 3. [add cream to - coffee] mettre de la crème dans 4. 🇺🇸 inf [beat up] casser la figure à ; [defeat] battre à plate couture, mettre la pâtée à.
❖ **cream off** vt sep fig : to cream off the best students sélectionner les meilleurs étudiants.

cream cheese n fromage m frais.

cream cracker n 🇬🇧 biscuit m sec.

cream of tartar n crème f de tartre.

cream tea n 🇬🇧 goûter composé de thé et de scones servis avec de la confiture et de la crème.

creamy ['kriːmɪ] (compar **creamier**, superl **creamiest**) adj 1. [containing cream - coffee, sauce] à la crème ; [- milk] qui contient de la crème 2. [smooth - drink, sauce, etc.] crémeux ; [- complexion, voice] velouté 3. [colour] : creamy white blanc cassé.

crease [kriːs] ◆ n 1. [in material, paper - made on purpose] pli m ; [- accidental] faux pli m ; [in skin, on face] pli m 2. [in cricket] limite f du batteur. ◆ vt 1. [on purpose] faire les plis de ; [accidentally] froisser, chiffonner 2. inf [amuse] : this one'll crease you celle-là va te faire mourir de rire. ◆ vi [clothes] se froisser, se chiffonner. ❖ **crease up** ◆ vi inf se tordre de rire. ◆ vt sep faire mourir or se tordre de rire.

creased [kriːst] adj 1. [fabric] froissé 2. [face] plissé.

crease-resistant adj infroissable.

create [kriːˈeɪt] ◆ vt 1. [employment, problem, the world] créer ; [fuss, noise, impression, draught] faire 2. [appoint] : he was created (a) baron il a été fait baron. ◆ vi 🇬🇧 inf [cause a fuss] faire des histoires.

creation [kriːˈeɪʃn] n 1. [process of creating] création f ▶ **the Creation** BIBLE la Création 2. [something created] création f.

creative [kriːˈeɪtɪv] adj [person, mind, skill] créatif ; hum & pej (trop) libre ▶ **creative accounting** latitude comptable laissée aux entreprises pour présenter un résultat plus avantageux ▶ **creative writing** techniques fpl de l'écriture.

creative director n directeur m, -trice artistique.

creatively [kriːˈeɪtɪvlɪ] adv de manière créative.

creativeness [kriːˈeɪtɪvnɪs], **creativity** [ˌkriːeɪˈtɪvətɪ] n créativité f.

creator [kri:'eɪtər] n créateur m, -trice f ▶ **the Creator** le Créateur.

creature ['kri:tʃər] n [person] créature f ; [animal] bête f.

creature comforts pl n confort m matériel.

crèche [kreʃ] n 🇬🇧 crèche f, garderie f.

cred [kred] n : _to have (street) cred_ 🇬🇧 _inf_ [credibility] être branché or dans le coup.

credence ['kri:dns] n croyance f, foi f ▶ **to give** or **to attach credence to sthg** ajouter foi à qqch ▶ **to give** or **to lend credence to sthg** rendre qqch crédible.

credentials [krɪ'denʃlz] pl n **1.** [references] références fpl **2.** [identity papers] papiers mpl d'identité ▶ **to ask to see sb's credentials** demander ses papiers (d'identité) à qqn, demander une pièce d'identité à qqn **3.** [of diplomat] lettres fpl de créance.

credibility [,kredə'bɪlətɪ] ◆ n **1.** [trustworthiness] crédibilité f **2.** [belief] : _it's beyond credibility_ c'est invraisemblable, c'est difficile à croire. ◆ comp ▶ **credibility rating** crédibilité f / _he has a credibility problem_ il manque de crédibilité.

credibility gap n manque m de crédibilité.

credible ['kredəbl] adj [person] crédible ; [evidence, statement] crédible, plausible.

credibly ['kredəblɪ] adv [argue] de manière crédible.

credit ['kredɪt] ◆ n **1.** FIN crédit m ▶ **to be in credit a)** [person] avoir de l'argent sur son compte **b)** [account] être approvisionné / _he has £50 to his credit_ il a 50 livres sur son compte ; [loan] ▶ **to give sb credit** or **to give credit to sb a)** [bank] accorder un découvert à qqn **b)** [shop, pub] faire crédit à qqn ▶ **to sell / to buy / to live on credit** vendre / acheter / vivre à crédit ▶ **interest-free credit** crédit gratuit ▶ **line of credit** 🇺🇸 limite f or plafond m de crédit **2.** [merit, honour] mérite m / _all the credit should go to the team_ tout le mérite doit revenir à l'équipe ▶ **to take the credit for sthg / doing sthg** s'attribuer le mérite de qqch / d'avoir fait qqch ▶ **to give sb the credit for sthg / doing sthg** attribuer à qqn le mérite de qqch / d'avoir fait qqch **3.** [credence] croyance f ▶ **to give credit to sb / sthg** ajouter foi à qqn / qqch / _the theory is gaining credit_ cette théorie est de plus en plus acceptée **4.** UNIV unité f de valeur, UV f. ◆ comp [boom, control] du crédit ; [sales] à crédit ▶ **credit agency** 🇬🇧 or **bureau** 🇺🇸 _établissement chargé de vérifier le passé bancaire de personnes ou d'entreprises sollicitant un crédit_ ▶ **credit agreement** accord m or convention f de crédit ▶ **credit balance** solde m créditeur ▶ **credit broker** courtier m en crédits or en prêts ▶ **credit insurance** assurance-crédit f ▶ **credit side** crédit m, avoir m / _on the credit side, the proposed changes will cut costs_ fig les changements projetés auront l'avantage de réduire les coûts ▶ **credit voucher** chèque m de caisse ▶ **to run a credit check on sb a)** [to ensure enough money in account] vérifier la solvabilité de qqn, vérifier que le compte de qqn est approvisionné **b)** [to ensure no record of bad debts] vérifier le passé bancaire de qqn. ◆ vt **1.** FIN [account] créditer / _to credit an account with £200_ or _to credit £200 to an account_ créditer un compte de 200 livres **2.** [accord] ▶ **to credit sb with intelligence / tact / sense** supposer de l'intelligence / du tact / du bon sens à qqn **3.** [believe] croire / _you wouldn't credit some of the things he's done_ tu n'en reviendrais pas si tu savais les choses qu'il a faites / _I could hardly credit it_ j'avais du mal à le croire. ◆ **credits** pl n CIN & TV générique m.

creditable ['kredɪtəbl] adj honorable, estimable.

credit account n **1.** BANK compte m créditeur **2.** 🇬🇧 [with shop] compte m client.

credit card ◆ n carte f de crédit / _to pay by credit card_ payer avec une or régler par carte de crédit. ◆ comp ▶ **credit card fraud** usage m frauduleux de cartes de crédit

▶ **credit card number** numéro m de carte de crédit ▶ **credit card transactions** transactions fpl effectuées par carte de crédit.

credit control n resserrement m or encadrement m du crédit.

credit crunch n crise f du crédit.

credit facilities pl n 🇬🇧 facilités fpl de crédit.

credit limit n limite f or plafond m de crédit.

credit line n **1.** 🇬🇧 [loan] autorisation f de crédit **2.** 🇺🇸 = **credit limit**.

credit note n 🇬🇧 [in business] facture f or note f d'avoir ; [in shop] avoir m.

creditor ['kredɪtər] n créancier m, -ère f.

credit rating n degré m de solvabilité.

credit report n 🇺🇸 profil m d'emprunteur.

credit score n 🇺🇸 = **credit rating**.

credit squeeze n restriction f or encadrement m du crédit.

credit transfer n virement m, transfert m (de compte à compte).

credit union n 🇺🇸 société f or caisse f de crédit.

creditworthiness ['kredɪt,wɜ:ðɪnɪs] n solvabilité f.

creditworthy ['kredɪt,wɜ:ðɪ] adj solvable.

credulity [krɪ'dju:lətɪ] n crédulité f.

credulous ['kredjuləs] adj crédule, naïf.

creed [kri:d] n [religious] credo m, croyance f ; [political] credo m ▶ **the Creed** RELIG le Credo.

creek [kri:k] n 🇬🇧 [of sea] crique f, anse f ; 🇺🇸 [stream] ruisseau m ; [river] rivière f ▶ **to be up the creek** inf être dans de beaux draps or dans le pétrin ▶ **to be up shit creek (without a paddle)** v inf être dans la merde (jusqu'au cou).

creep [kri:p] (_pt_ & _pp_ **crept** [krept]) ◆ n inf [unpleasant person] sale type m, rat m ; [weak, pathetic person] pauvre type m. ◆ vi **1.** [person, animal] se glisser **2.** [plant - along the ground] ramper ; [-upwards] grimper **3.** 🄿🄷🅁 **to make sb's flesh creep** donner la chair de poule à qqn, faire froid dans le dos à qqn. ◆ **creeps** pl n inf : _he gives me the creeps_ **a)** [is frightening] il me fait froid dans le dos, il me donne la chair de poule **b)** [is unpleasant] il me dégoûte or répugne. ◆ **creep in** vi [person] entrer sans bruit ; fig [mistakes] se glisser ; [doubts, fears] s'insinuer. ◆ **creep out** vi sortir sans bruit. ◆ **creep up** vi **1.** [approach] s'approcher sans bruit ▶ **to creep up to sthg** s'approcher sans bruit de qqch **2.** [increase - water, prices] monter lentement ; [-sales] monter or progresser lentement. ◆ **creep up on** vt insep **1.** [in order to attack, surprise] s'approcher discrètement de, s'approcher à pas de loup de **2.** [catch up with -in competition, business, etc.] rattraper peu à peu.

creeper ['kri:pər] n [plant] plante f grimpante.

creeping ['kri:pɪŋ] adj **1.** [plant - upwards] grimpant ; [-along the ground] rampant **2.** [insect] rampant **3.** 🄿🄷🅁 **creeping inflation** inflation f rampante.

creepy ['kri:pɪ] (_compar_ **creepier**, _superl_ **creepiest**) adj inf qui donne la chair de poule, qui fait froid dans le dos.

creepy-crawly [-'krɔ:lɪ] (_pl_ **creepy-crawlies**) inf n 🇬🇧 petite bestiole f.

cremate [krɪ'meɪt] vt incinérer.

cremation [krɪ'meɪʃn] n incinération f, crémation f.

crematorium [,kremə'tɔ:rɪəm] (_pl_ **crematoria** [-rɪə] or **crematoriums**) n [establishment] crématorium m ; [furnace] four m crématoire.

crematory ['kremətrɪ] (_pl_ **crematories**) 🇺🇸 = **crematorium**.

crème de la crème ['kremdəlæ'krem] n ▸ **the crème de la crème** le gratin, le dessus du panier.

creosote ['krɪəsəʊt] ◆ n créosote f. ◆ vt traiter à la créosote.

crepe [kreɪp] ◆ n **1.** [fabric] crêpe m **2.** = **crepe paper 3.** [pancake] crêpe f. ◆ comp [skirt, blouse, etc.] de or en crêpe.

crepe bandage n bande f Velpeau®.

crepe paper n papier m crépon.

crepe(-soled) shoes [-səʊld-] pl n chaussures fpl à semelles de crêpe.

crept [krept] pt & pp ⟶ **creep.**

Cres. written abbr of Crescent.

crescendo [krɪ'ʃendəʊ] (pl **crescendos** or **crescendoes**) n MUS & fig crescendo m.

crescent ['kresnt] ◆ n **1.** [shape] croissant m **2.** US [street] rue f (en arc de cercle). ◆ adj [shaped] en (forme de) croissant ▸ **crescent moon** croissant m de lune.

cress [kres] n cresson m.

crest [krest] n **1.** [peak - of hill, wave] crête f; [- of ridge] arête f; [- of road] haut m or sommet m de côte **2.** [on bird, lizard] crête f; [on helmet] cimier m **3.** [coat of arms] timbre m; [emblem] armoiries fpl.

crestfallen ['krest,fɔːln] adj découragé, déconfit.

Crete [kriːt] pr n Crète f / **in Crete** en Crète.

cretin ['kretɪn] n **1.** MED crétin m, -e f **2.** inf [idiot] crétin m, -e f, imbécile mf.

cretinous ['kretɪnəs] adj MED & fig crétin.

Creutzfeld-Jacob disease ['krɔɪtsfeld'jækɒb-] n maladie f de Creutzfeld-Jacob.

crevasse [krɪ'væs] n crevasse f.

crevice ['krevɪs] n fissure f, fente f.

crew [kruː] ◆ pt UK ⟶ **crow.** ◆ n **1.** [gen & CIN] équipe f; [on plane, ship] équipage m **2.** inf [crowd, gang] bande f, équipe f. ◆ comp ▸ **crew member** membre mf d'équipage. ◆ vi ▸ **to crew for sb** être l'équipier de qqn. ◆ vt armer (d'un équipage).

crew cut n coupe f de cheveux en brosse.

crewman ['kruːmən] (pl **crewmen** [-mən]) n membre m de l'équipage.

crew neck n col m ras le or du cou, ras-le-cou m.

crib [krɪb] (pt & pp **cribbed**, cont **cribbing**) ◆ n **1.** US [cot] lit m d'enfant **2.** [bin] grenier m (à blé); [stall] stalle f **3.** [manger] mangeoire f, râtelier m; RELIG crèche f **4.** inf [plagiarism] plagiat m; UK SCH [list of answers] antisèche m or f **5.** US inf [house] baraque f; [apartment] appart m. ◆ vt inf [plagiarize] plagier, copier / **he cribbed the answers from his friend** SCH il a copié les réponses sur son ami, il a pompé sur son ami. ◆ vi copier.

cribbage ['krɪbɪdʒ] n (U) jeu de cartes où les points sont marqués sur une planche de bois.

crib death n US mort f subite (du nourrisson).

crick [krɪk] ◆ n ▸ **to have a crick in the neck** avoir un torticolis. ◆ vt : **she cricked her neck** elle a attrapé un torticolis.

cricket ['krɪkɪt] ◆ n **1.** [insect] grillon m **2.** [game] cricket m. ◆ comp [ball, bat, ground, match] de cricket.

cricketer ['krɪkɪtər] n joueur m, -euse f de cricket.

crikey ['kraɪkɪ] interj UK inf & dated mince alors.

crime [kraɪm] n **1.** [serious] crime m; [minor] délit m / **a minor** or **petty crime** un délit mineur ▸ **crimes against humanity** crimes mpl contre l'humanité ▸ **crime prevention** lutte f contre la criminalité ▸ **crime reporter** journaliste mf qui couvre les affaires criminelles ▸ **crime wave** vague f de criminalité ▸ **crime writer** auteur m de romans noirs **2.** MIL manquement m à la discipline, infraction f.

⚠ The French word **crime** has a more restricted meaning than the English word, and refers to serious offences tried at the **"Cour d'assises"**, especially murder. For less serious crimes, use the word **délit.**

Crimea [kraɪ'mɪə] pr n ▸ **the Crimea** la Crimée / **in the Crimea** en Crimée.

criminal ['krɪmɪnl] ◆ n criminel m, -elle f. ◆ adj criminel / **to take criminal proceedings against sb** LAW poursuivre qqn au pénal ▸ **the Criminal Investigation Department** UK = CID ▸ **the Criminal Records Office** UK l'identité f judiciaire.

criminal assault n agression f criminelle, voie f de fait.

criminal court n cour f d'assises.

criminal damage n délit consistant à causer volontairement des dégâts matériels.

criminality [,krɪmɪ'nælətɪ] n criminalité f.

criminalize, criminalise ['krɪmɪnəlaɪz] vt criminaliser.

criminal law n droit m pénal or criminel.

criminal lawyer n avocat m, -e f au criminel, pénaliste mf.

criminal liability n LAW responsabilité f pénale, majorité f pénale.

criminally ['krɪmɪnəlɪ] adv criminellement.

criminal offence n délit m.

criminal record n casier m judiciaire / **she hasn't got a criminal record** son casier judiciaire est vierge, elle n'a pas de casier judiciaire.

Criminal Records Bureau n Organisme chargé de vérifier le casier judiciaire de personnels sensibles.

criminology [,krɪmɪ'nɒlədʒɪ] n criminologie f.

crimp [krɪmp] ◆ vt **1.** [hair] crêper, friser; [pie crust] pincer; [metal] onduler **2.** inf TECH [pinch together] pincer, sertir. ◆ n **1.** [wave in hair] cran m, ondulation f; [fold in metal] ondulation f **2.** TEXT pli m.

crimson ['krɪmzn] ◆ adj cramoisi. ◆ n cramoisi m.

cringe [krɪndʒ] vi **1.** [shrink back] avoir un mouvement de recul, reculer; [cower] se recroqueviller / **to cringe in terror** reculer de peur / **to cringe with embarrassment** être mort de honte / **I cringe at the very thought** j'ai envie de rentrer sous terre rien que d'y penser **2.** [be servile] ramper.

cringeworthy ['krɪndʒ,wɜːðɪ] adj inf hérissant, qui hérisse.

cringing ['krɪndʒɪŋ] adj [fearful] craintif; [servile] servile, obséquieux.

crinkle ['krɪŋkl] ◆ vt froisser, chiffonner. ◆ vi se froisser, se chiffonner. ◆ n [wrinkle] fronce f, pli m; [on face] ride f.

cripple ['krɪpl] ◆ vt **1.** [person] estropier **2.** fig [damage - industry, system] paralyser; [- plane, ship] désemparer. ◆ n **1.** dated & offens [lame person] estropié m, -e f; [invalid] invalide mf; [maimed person] mutilé m, -e f **2.** fig ▸ **an emotional cripple** un caractériel m, une caractérielle f.

crippled ['krɪpld] adj **1.** [person] : **to be crippled with rheumatism** être perclus de rhumatismes **2.** fig [industry, country] paralysé; [plane, ship] accidenté.

crippling ['krɪplɪŋ] adj **1.** [disease] invalidant **2.** fig [strikes] paralysant; [prices, taxes] écrasant.

crisis ['kraısıs] (*pl* **crises** [-si:z]) n crise *f* / *crisis management* gestion *f* des crises / *crisis point* point *m* critique.

crisp [krısp] ◆ adj **1.** [crunchy - vegetable] croquant ; [-cracker] croquant, croustillant ; [-bread] croustillant ; [-snow] craquant **2.** [fresh - clothing] pimpant ; [-linen] apprêté ; [-paper] craquant, raide **3.** [air, weather] vif, tonifiant ; [wine] vif **4.** [concise - style] précis, clair et net **5.** [brusque] tranchant, brusque ; [manner] brusque ; [tone] acerbe. ◆ n ▸ **(potato) crisps** 🇬🇧 (pommes *fpl*) chips *fpl* ▸ **burnt to a crisp** carbonisé. ◆ vt faire chauffer pour rendre croustillant.

crispbread ['krıspbred] n biscuit *m* scandinave.

crispness ['krıspnıs] n **1.** [of food, paper] craquant *m* ; [of clothing, sheets, weather] fraîcheur *f* ; [of wine] caractère *m* vif **2.** [of style] précision *f* **3.** [brusqueness] tranchant *m*, brusquerie *f*.

crispy ['krıspı] (*compar* **crispier**, *superl* **crispiest**) adj [vegetables] croquant ; [biscuits] croquant, croustillant ; [bacon] croustillant.

crisscross ['krıskrɒs] ◆ vt entrecroiser. ◆ vi s'entrecroiser. ◆ adj [lines] entrecroisé ; [in disorder] enchevêtré.

criterion [kraı'tıərıən] (*pl* **criteria** [-rıə]) n critère *m*.

critic ['krıtık] n [reviewer] critique *m* ; [fault-finder] critique *m*, détracteur *m*, -trice *f*.

critical ['krıtıkl] adj **1.** [crucial] critique, crucial ; [situation] critique ; PHYS critique **2.** [analytical] critique ; [disparaging] critique, négatif **3.** ART, LITER & MUS [analysis, edition] critique ; [essay, study] critique, de critique ; [from the critics] des critiques.

critically ['krıtıklı] adj **1.** [analytically] d'un œil critique, en critique ; [disparagingly] sévèrement **2.** [seriously] gravement.

critical path n [gen & COMPUT] chemin *m* critique ▸ **critical path method** méthode *f* du chemin critique.

criticism ['krıtısızm] n critique *f*.

criticize, criticise ['krıtısaız] vt **1.** [find fault with] critiquer, réprouver **2.** [analyse] critiquer, faire la critique de.

critique [krı'ti:k] ◆ n critique *f* (*argumentée, raisonnée*). ◆ vt faire une critique de.

croak [krəʊk] ◆ vi **1.** [frog] coasser ; [crow] croasser **2.** [person] parler d'une voix rauque ; [grumble] ronchonner **3.** *inf* [die] crever. ◆ vt [utter] dire d'une voix rauque or éraillée. ◆ n [of frog] coassement *m* ; [of crow] croassement *m* ; [of person] ton *m* rauque.

croaky ['krəʊkı] adj enroué.

Croat ['krəʊæt] = **Croatian** (*noun*).

Croatia [krəʊ'eıʃə] pr n Croatie *f* / *in Croatia* en Croatie.

Croatian [krəʊ'eıʃn] ◆ n **1.** [person] Croate *mf* **2.** LING croate *m*. ◆ adj croate.

crochet ['krəʊʃeı] ◆ n ▸ **crochet (work)** (travail *m* au) crochet *m*. ◆ vt faire au crochet. ◆ vi faire du crochet.

crockery ['krɒkərı] n [pottery] poterie *f*, faïence *f* ; [plates, cups, bowls, etc.] vaisselle *f*.

crockpot ['krɒkpɒt] n mijoteuse *f*.

crocodile ['krɒkədaıl] n **1.** [reptile] crocodile *m* **2.** 🇬🇧 SCH cortège *m* en rangs (*par deux*).

crocodile tears pl n larmes *fpl* de crocodile.

crocus ['krəʊkəs] n crocus *m*.

croft [krɒft] n 🇬🇧 petite ferme *f*.

croissant n croissant *m*.

crony ['krəʊnı] (*pl* **cronies**) n *inf* pote *m*, copine *f*.

cronyism ['krəʊnıızm] n copinage *f*.

crook [krʊk] ◆ n **1.** *inf* [thief] escroc *m*, filou *m* **2.** [bend - in road] courbe *f*, coude *m* ; [-in river] coude *m*,

détour *m* ; [-in arm] coude *m* ; [-in leg] flexion *f* **3.** [staff - of shepherd] houlette *f* ; [-of bishop] crosse *f*. ◆ vt [finger] courber, recourber ; [arm] plier.

crooked ['krʊkıd] ◆ adj **1.** [not straight, bent - stick] courbé, crochu ; [-path] tortueux ; [-person] courbé / *a crooked smile* un sourire grimaçant **2.** *inf* [dishonest] malhonnête. ◆ adv de travers.

croon [kru:n] ◆ vi & vt **1.** [sing softly] fredonner, chantonner ; [professionally] chanter (*en crooner*) **2.** [speak softly, sentimentally] susurrer. ◆ n fredonnement *m*.

crop [krɒp] (*pt* & *pp* **cropped**, *cont* **cropping**) ◆ n **1.** [produce] produit *m* agricole, culture *f* ; [harvest] récolte *f* ; [of fruit] récolte *f*, cueillette *f* ; [of grain] moisson *f* **2.** *fig* fournée *f* **3.** [of whip] manche *m* ; [riding whip] cravache *f* **4.** [of bird] jabot *m* **5.** [haircut - for man] coupe *f* rase or courte ; [-for woman] coupe courte or à la garçonne. ◆ vt **1.** [cut - hedge] tailler, tondre ; [-hair] tondre ; [-tail] écourter ; PHOT recadrer **2.** [subj: animal] brouter, paître **3.** [farm] cultiver ; [harvest] récolter. ◆ vi [land, vegetables] donner or fournir une récolte. ❖ **crop up** vi *inf* survenir, se présenter.

cropped ['krɒpt] adj ▸ **cropped hair** cheveux coupés ras ▸ **cropped trousers** pantacourt *m*.

cropper ['krɒpə'] n 🇬🇧 *inf* ▸ **to come a cropper a)** [fall] se casser la figure **b)** [fail] se planter.

crop spraying n pulvérisation *f* des cultures.

croquet ['krəʊkeı] ◆ n croquet *m*. ◆ comp [hoop, lawn, mallet] de croquet.

croquette [krɒ'ket] n croquette *f*.

cross [krɒs] ◆ n **1.** [mark, symbol] croix *f* **2.** RELIG croix *f* ▸ **the Cross** la Croix ; *fig* [burden] croix *f* **3.** [hybrid] hybride *m*. ◆ vt **1.** [go across - road, room, sea] traverser ; [-bridge, river] traverser, passer ; [-fence, threshold] franchir **2.** [place one across the other] croiser / *to cross one's arms* / *one's legs* croiser les bras / les jambes **3.** [mark with cross] faire une croix ▸ **to cross o.s.** RELIG faire le signe de (la) croix, se signer ▸ **cross your "t"s** barrez or mettez des barres à vos « t » ▸ **to cross a cheque** 🇬🇧 barrer un chèque **4.** [animals, plants] croiser **5.** [oppose] contrarier, contrecarrer **6.** TELEC : *we've got a crossed line* il y a des interférences sur la ligne. ◆ vi **1.** [go across] traverser / *she crossed (over) to the other side of the road* elle a traversé la route / *they crossed from Dover to Boulogne* ils ont fait la traversée de Douvres à Boulogne **2.** [intersect - lines, paths, roads] se croiser, se rencontrer. ◆ adj **1.** [angry] de mauvaise humeur, en colère / *she's cross with me* elle est fâchée contre moi **2.** [diagonal] diagonal. ❖ **cross off** vt sep [item] barrer, rayer ; [person] radier ▸ **to cross sb off the list** radier qqn. ❖ **cross out** vt sep barrer, rayer.

crossbar ['krɒsbɑ:'] n [on bike] barre *f* ; [on goalposts] barre *f* transversale.

cross-border adj transfrontalier.

crossbow ['krɒsbəʊ] n arbalète *f*.

crossbreed ['krɒsbri:d] (*pt* & *pp* **crossbred** ['krɒsbred]) ◆ vt croiser. ◆ n [animal, plant] hybride *m*, métis *m*, -isse *f* ; *pej* [person] métis *m*, -isse *f*, sang-mêlé *mf*.

cross-Channel adj 🇬🇧 [ferry, route] qui traverse la Manche.

cross-check ◆ vt contrôler (par contre-épreuve or par recoupement). ◆ vi vérifier par recoupement. ◆ n contre-épreuve *f*, recoupement *m*.

cross-country ◆ n cross-country *m*, cross *m*. ◆ adj ▸ **cross-country runner** coureur *m*, -euse *f* de cross ▸ **cross-country skier** fondeur *m*, -euse *f* ▸ **cross-country skiing** ski *m* de fond. ◆ adv à travers champs.

cross-cultural adj interculturel.

cross-curricular adj pluridisciplinaire.

cross-dresser n travesti *m*.

cross-dressing n travestisme *m*, transvestisme *m*.

cross-examination n contre-interrogatoire *m*.

cross-examine vt [gen] soumettre à un interrogatoire serré ; LAW faire subir un contre-interrogatoire à.

cross-eyed adj qui louche.

cross-fertilization n croisement *m* ; *fig* osmose *f*, enrichissement *m* mutuel.

cross-fertilize, cross-fertilise vt croiser.

crossfire ['krɒs,faɪə'] n feux *mpl* croisés ▶ **to be caught in the crossfire** *lit* & *fig* être pris entre deux feux.

crossing ['krɒsɪŋ] n **1.** [intersection] croisement *m* ; [of roads] croisement *m*, carrefour *m* **2.** [sea journey] traversée *f* **3.** [inter-breeding] croisement *m*.

crossing guard n ⓤ employée municipale qui fait traverser les enfants.

cross-legged [krɒs'legɪd] adj en tailleur.

crossly ['krɒslɪ] adv avec mauvaise humeur.

crossover ['krɒs,əʊvə'] ◆ n [of roads] (croisement *m* par) pont *m* routier ; [for pedestrians] passage *m* clouté ; RAIL voie *f* de croisement. ◆ adj MUS [style] hybride.

cross-party adj POL : *cross-party agreement* accord *m* entre partis.

cross-platform adj multiplateforme.

crossply ['krɒsplaɪ] adj [tyre] à carcasse biaise ou croisée.

cross-post vt COMPUT faire un envoi multiple de.

crossposting [krɒs'pəʊstɪŋ] n COMPUT envoi *m* multiple.

cross-purposes pl n ▶ **to be at cross-purposes with sb a)** [misunderstand] comprendre qqn de travers **b)** [oppose] être en désaccord avec qqn / *they were talking at cross-purposes* leur conversation tournait autour d'un quiproquo.

cross-question = cross-examine.

cross-refer ◆ vi ▶ **to cross-refer to sthg** renvoyer à qqch. ◆ vt renvoyer.

cross-reference n renvoi *m*, référence *f*.

crossroads ['krɒsrəʊdz] (*pl* **crossroads**) n croisement *m*, carrefour *m* / *her career is at a crossroads* sa carrière va maintenant prendre un tournant décisif.

cross-section n **1.** [gen & BIOL] coupe *f* transversale **2.** [sample - of population] échantillon *m*.

crosswalk ['krɒswɔːk] n ⓤ passage *m* clouté.

crossways ['krɒsweɪz] (*pl* **crossways**) ◆ n ⓤ = crossroads. ◆ adj & adv = crosswise.

crosswind ['krɒswɪnd] n vent *m* de travers.

crosswise ['krɒswaɪz] adj & adv [shaped like cross] en croix ; [across] en travers ; [diagonally] en travers, en diagonale.

crossword (puzzle) ['krɒswɜːd-] n mots *mpl* croisés.

crotch [krɒtʃ] n [of tree] fourche *f* ; [of trousers] entrejambes *m*.

crotchet ['krɒtʃɪt] n ⓤ noire *f*.

crotchety ['krɒtʃɪtɪ] adj *inf* grognon, bougon.

crouch [kraʊtʃ] ◆ vi ▶ **to crouch (down) a)** [person] s'accroupir, se tapir **b)** [animal] s'accroupir, se ramasser. ◆ n [posture] accroupissement *m* ; [act] action *f* de se ramasser.

croup [kruːp] n **1.** [of animal] croupe *f* **2.** MED croup *m*.

croupier ['kruːpɪə'] n croupier *m*.

crouton ['kruːtɒn] n croûton *m*.

crow [krəʊ] (ⓤ *pt* **crowed** or **crew** [kruː] ; ⓤ *pt* **crowed**) ◆ n **1.** ORNITH corbeau *m* ; [smaller] corneille *f*

2. [sound of cock] chant *m* du coq, cocorico *m*. ◆ vi **1.** [cock] chanter **2.** [boast] se vanter ▶ **to crow over sthg** se vanter de qqch.

crowbar ['krəʊbaː'] n (pince *f* à) levier *m*.

crowd [kraʊd] ◆ n **1.** [throng] foule *f*, masse *f* **2.** *inf* [social group] bande *f* **3.** *fig* & *pej* [people as a whole] ▶ **the crowd** la foule, la masse du peuple. ◆ vi se presser ▶ **to crowd round sb / sthg** se presser autour de qqn / qqch. ◆ vt **1.** [cram] serrer, entasser **2.** *inf* [jostle] bousculer. ❖ **crowd in** vi **1.** [enter] entrer en foule, affluer **2.** *fig* [flood in] ▶ **to crowd in on sb** submerger qqn. ❖ **crowd out** vt sep : *independent traders are being crowded out by bigger stores* les petits commerçants sont étouffés par les grands magasins.

crowded ['kraʊdɪd] adj **1.** [busy - room, building, bus, etc.] bondé, plein ; [- street] plein (de monde) ; [- town] encombré (de monde), surpeuplé **2.** [overpopulated] surpeuplé.

crowdpuller ['kraʊd,pʊlə'] n ⓤ *inf* : *his play is a real crowdpuller* sa pièce attire les foules.

crown [kraʊn] ◆ n **1.** [headdress] couronne *f* **2.** [regal power] couronne *f*, pouvoir *m* royal **3.** [award] prix *m* **4.** [top - of head] sommet *m* de la tête ; [- of hat] fond *m* ; [- of hill, tree] sommet *m*, cime *f* ; [- of roof] faîte *m* ; [- of road] milieu *m* ; [- of tooth] couronne *f* ; [ARCHIT - of arch] clef *f* **5.** [coin] couronne *f* **6.** [outstanding achievement] couronnement *m*. ◆ vt **1.** [confer a title on] couronner, sacrer **2.** [top] couronner / *to crown a tooth* couronner une dent **3.** [in draughts] damer **4.** *inf* [hit] flanquer un coup (sur la tête) à. ❖ **Crown** n ▶ **the Crown** la Couronne, l'État *m* (monarchie) ▶ **counsel for the Crown** ⓤ LAW conseiller *m* juridique de la Couronne ▶ **Crown witness** ⓤ LAW témoin *m* à charge.

crown court n ≃ Cour f d'assises *(en Angleterre et au Pays de Galles)*.

crowning ['kraʊnɪŋ] ◆ n couronnement *m*. ◆ adj *fig* suprême.

crown jewels pl n joyaux *mpl* de la Couronne.

crown prince n prince *m* héritier.

Crown Prosecution Service pr n ▶ **the Crown Prosecution Service** *organisme public qui décide si les affaires doivent être portées devant les tribunaux en Angleterre et au Pays de Galles.*

crow's feet pl n [wrinkles] pattes *fpl* d'oie *(rides)*.

crow's nest n NAUT nid *m* de pie.

CRT (abbr of **cathode-ray tube**) n [in TV set] tube *m* cathodique.

crucial ['kruːʃl] adj **1.** [critical] critique, crucial ; MED & PHILOS crucial **2.** *v inf* [excellent] d'enfer.

crucially ['kruːʃəlɪ] adv fondamentalement.

crucible ['kruːsɪbl] n [vessel] creuset *m* ; *fig* [test] (dure) épreuve *f*.

crucifix ['kruːsɪfɪks] n christ *m*, crucifix *m*.

crucifixion [,kruːsɪ'fɪkʃn] n crucifiement *m*. ❖ **Crucifixion** n ▶ **the Crucifixion** RELIG la crucifixion, la mise en croix.

crucify ['kruːsɪfaɪ] (*pt* & *pp* **crucified**) vt **1.** [execute] crucifier, mettre en croix **2.** *fig* [treat harshly] mettre au pilori.

crude [kruːd] ◆ adj **1.** [vulgar - person, behaviour] vulgaire, grossier ; [- manners] fruste, grossier **2.** [raw] brut ; [sugar] non raffiné **3.** [unsophisticated - tool] grossier, rudimentaire ; [- piece of work] mal fini, sommaire ; [- drawing] grossier **4.** [stark - colour, light] cru, vif. ◆ n = **crude oil**.

crudely ['kru:dlɪ] adv **1.** [vulgarly] grossièrement ; [bluntly] crûment, brutalement **2.** [unsophisticatedly] grossièrement, sommairement.

crude oil n (pétrole m) brut m.

cruel [krʊəl] adj **1.** [unkind] cruel **ı** to be cruel to sb être cruel envers qqn **2.** [painful] douloureux, cruel.

cruelly ['krʊəlɪ] adv cruellement.

cruelty ['krʊəltɪ] (pl **cruelties**) n **1.** [gen] cruauté f **2.** LAW sévices mpl **3.** [cruel act] cruauté f.

cruet ['kru:ɪt] n **1.** [for oil, vinegar] petit flacon m **2.** [set of condiments] service m à condiments.

cruise [kru:z] **◆** n [sea trip] croisière f. **◆** vi **1.** [ship] croiser ; [tourists] être en croisière **2.** [car] rouler ; [plane] voler ; [police car, taxi] marauder, être en maraude **3.** inf [for sexual partner] draguer. **◆** vt **1.** [ocean] croiser dans **2.** inf [sexual partner] draguer.

cruise missile n missile m de croisière.

cruiser ['kru:zə'] n **1.** [warship] croiseur m ; [pleasure boat] yacht m de croisière **2.** 🇺🇸 [police patrol car] voiture f de police (en patrouille).

cruising ['kru:zɪŋ] n [in boat] croisière f, croisières fpl **ı cruising altitude** altitude f de croisière **ı cruising speed** vitesse f de croisière.

crumb [krʌm] n **1.** [of bread] miette f ; [inside loaf] mie f ; fig [small piece] miette f, brin m **2.** 🇺🇸 inf [person] nul m, nulle f.

crumble ['krʌmbl] **◆** vt [bread, stock cube] émietter ; [earth, plaster] effriter. **◆** vi [bread] s'émietter ; [plaster] s'effriter ; [building] tomber en ruines, se désagréger ; [earth, stone] s'ébouler ; fig [hopes, society] s'effondrer, s'écrouler. **◆** n crumble m (dessert composé d'une couche de compote de fruits recouverte de pâte sablée).

crumbly ['krʌmblɪ] (compar **crumblier,** superl **crumbliest**) adj friable.

crummy ['krʌmɪ] (compar **crummier,** superl **crummiest**) adj inf **1.** [bad] minable, nul **2.** [unwell] : I feel crummy je ne me sens pas bien.

crumpet ['krʌmpɪt] n 🇺🇰 **1.** [cake] galette épaisse qu'on mange chaude et beurrée **2.** v inf [women] nanas fpl, pépées fpl.

crumple ['krʌmpl] **◆** vt froisser, friper. **◆** vi **1.** [crease] se froisser, se chiffonner **2.** [collapse] s'effondrer, s'écrouler. **❖ crumple up** vt sep chiffonner.

crumpled ['krʌmpld] adj froissé.

crumple zone n AUTO zone f d'absorption.

crunch [krʌnʃ] **◆** vi **1.** [gravel, snow] craquer, crisser **2.** [chew] croquer **ı** to crunch on sthg croquer qqch. **◆** vt **1.** [chew] croquer **2.** [crush underfoot] faire craquer or crisser, écraser **3.** [process -data, numbers] traiter. **◆** n **1.** [sound -of teeth] coup m de dents ; [-of food] craquement m ; [-of gravel, snow] craquement m, crissement m **2.** inf [critical moment] moment m critique / when it comes to the crunch dans une situation critique, au moment crucial **3.** SPORT [sit-up] redressement m assis. **◆** adj inf critique, décisif. **❖ crunch up** vt sep broyer.

crunchy ['krʌnʃɪ] (compar **crunchier,** superl **crunchiest**) adj [food] croquant ; [snow, gravel] qui craque or crisse.

crunk [krʌŋk] n MUS crunk m (variété de rap).

crusade [kru:'seɪd] **◆** n HIST & fig croisade f. **◆** vi HIST partir en croisade, être à la croisade ; fig faire une croisade **ı** to crusade for / against sthg mener une croisade pour / contre qqch.

crusader [kru:'seɪdə'] n HIST croisé m ; fig champion m, -onne f, militant m, -e f.

crush [krʌʃ] **◆** vt **1.** [smash -gen] écraser, broyer / crushed ice glace f pilée / they were crushed to death ils sont morts écrasés **2.** [crease] froisser, chiffonner **ı crushed velvet** velours m frappé **3.** [defeat -enemy] écraser ; [suppress -revolt] écraser, réprimer ; fig [hopes] écraser **4.** [squash, press] serrer. **◆** vi **1.** [throng] se serrer, s'écraser / we all crushed into the lift nous nous sommes tous entassés dans l'ascenseur **2.** [crease] se froisser. **◆** n **1.** [crowd] foule f, cohue f / in the crush to enter the stadium dans la bousculade pour entrer dans le stade **2.** inf [infatuation] béguin m **ı** to have a crush on sb en pincer pour qqn **3.** 🇺🇰 [drink] jus m de fruit / lemon crush citron m pressé.

crush barrier n barrière f de sécurité.

crushing ['krʌʃɪŋ] adj [defeat] écrasant ; [remark] cinglant, percutant.

crust [krʌst] n **1.** [of bread, pie] croûte f ; [of snow, ice] couche f / the earth's crust GEOL la croûte or l'écorce terrestre **2.** [on wound] croûte f, escarre f **3.** [on wine] dépôt m.

crustacean [krʌ'steɪʃn] **◆** adj crustacé. **◆** n crustacé m.

crusty ['krʌstɪ] (compar **crustier,** superl **crustiest**) **◆** adj **1.** [bread] croustillant **2.** [bad-tempered -person] hargneux, bourru ; [-remark] brusque, sec (sèche). **◆** n 🇺🇰 inf jeune mf crado.

crutch [krʌtʃ] n **1.** [support] support m, soutien m ; [for walking] béquille f ; ARCHIT étançon m ; NAUT support m **2.** fig soutien m **3.** 🇺🇰 = **crotch**.

crux [krʌks] (pl **cruxes** or **cruces** ['kru:si:z]) n [vital point] point m crucial or capital ; [of problem] cœur m / the crux of the matter le nœud de l'affaire.

cry [kraɪ] (pt & pp **cried,** pl **cries**) **◆** vi **1.** [weep] pleurer **2.** [call out] crier, pousser un cri / to cry for help crier au secours **3.** [bird, animal] pousser un cri or des cris ; [hounds] donner de la voix, aboyer. **◆** vt **1.** [weep] pleurer / she cried herself to sleep elle s'est endormie en pleurant / he cried tears of joy il versa des larmes de joie **2.** [shout] crier / "look", she cried « regardez », s'écria-t-elle. **◆** n **1.** [exclamation] cri m **2.** [of birds, animals] cri m ; [of hounds] aboiements mpl, voix f **3.** [weep] **ı** to have a good cry pleurer un bon coup. **❖ cry off** vi [from meeting] se décommander ; [from promise] se rétracter, se dédire. **❖ cry out** vi pousser un cri.

crybaby ['kraɪˌbeɪbɪ] (pl **crybabies**) n inf pleurnichard m, -e f.

crying ['kraɪɪŋ] **◆** adj **1.** [person] qui pleure, pleurant **2.** inf [as intensifier] criant, flagrant / it's a crying shame c'est un scandale. **◆** n (U) **1.** [shouting] cri m, cris mpl **2.** [weeping] pleurs mpl.

cryogenics [ˌkraɪə'dʒenɪks] n (U) [science] cryologie f ; [production] cryogénie f.

cryonics [kraɪ'ɒnɪks] n (U) cryogénisation f.

cryopreservation [ˌkraɪəprezə'veɪʃn] n (U) cryoconservation f.

crypt [krɪpt] n crypte f.

cryptic ['krɪptɪk] adj [secret] secret (secrète) ; [obscure] énigmatique, sibyllin **ı cryptic crossword** mot-croisé dont les définitions sont des énigmes qu'il faut résoudre.

crypto- ['krɪptəʊ] in comp crypto- **ı crypto-fascist** cryptofasciste mf.

crystal ['krɪstl] **◆** n **1.** [gen & MINER] cristal m **2.** [chip] cristal m **3.** 🇺🇸 [of watch] verre m (de montre) **4.** ELECTRON galène f. **◆** adj [vase, glass, water] de cristal.

crystal ball n boule f de cristal.

crystal clear adj clair comme le jour or comme de l'eau de roche ; [voice] cristalline.

crystal-gazing n *(U)* [in ball] (art *m* de la) voyance *f* ; *fig* prédictions *fpl*, prophéties *fpl*.

crystallize, crystallise ['krɪstəlaɪz] ◆ vi *lit & fig* se cristalliser. ◆ vt cristalliser ; [sugar] (faire) candir ▶ **crystallized fruit** fruits *mpl* confits.

CSA pr n **1.** abbr of **Confederate States of America 2.** abbr of **Child Support Agency.**

CSC (abbr of **Civil Service Commission**) pr n *commission de recrutement des fonctionnaires.*

CS gas n 🇬🇧 gaz *m* CS or lacrymogène.

CST n abbr of **Central Standard Time.**

CSU (abbr of **Civil Service Union**) n *syndicat de la fonction publique.*

ct (written abbr of **carat**) ct.

CT ◆ written abbr of **Connecticut.** ◆ n (abbr of **computerized tomography**) ▶ **a CT scan** une scanographie.

CTC (abbr of **city technology college**) n *collège technique britannique, généralement établi dans des quartiers défavorisés.*

CTR n abbr of **click-through rate.**

cu. written abbr of **cubic.**

CU (written abbr of **see you**) MESSAGING @+.

CU@ MESSAGING written abbr of **see you at.**

cub [kʌb] n **1.** [animal] petit *m*, -e *f* **2.** *inf* [youngster] ▶ **young cub** jeune blanc-bec *m* **3.** [scout] louveteau *m* *(scout).*

Cuba ['kju:bə] pr n Cuba **/** *in Cuba* à Cuba.

Cuban ['kju:bən] ◆ n Cubain *m*, -e *f*. ◆ adj cubain ▶ **the Cuban missile crisis** la crise de Cuba *(conflit américano-soviétique dû à la présence de missiles soviétiques à Cuba (1962)).*

cubbyhole ['kʌbɪhəʊl] n **1.** [cupboard] débarras *m*, remise *f* ; [small room] cagibi *m*, réduit *m* **2.** [in desk] case *f* ; AUTO vide-poches *m*.

cube [kju:b] ◆ n **1.** [gen & MATH] cube *m* **2.** (abbr of **cubicle**) poste *m* de travail. ◆ vt **1.** [cut into cubes] couper en cubes or en dés **2.** MATH cuber ; TECH [measure] cuber.

cube farm n *inf* bureau *m* open-space.

cube root n racine *f* cubique.

cubic ['kju:bɪk] adj [shape, volume] cubique ; [measurement] cube ▶ **cubic equation** MATH équation *f* du troisième degré ▶ **cubic metre** mètre *m* cube.

cubicle ['kju:bɪkl] n [in dormitory, hospital ward] alcôve *f*, box *m* ; [in swimming baths, public toilets] cabine *f*.

cubism, Cubism ['kju:bɪzm] n cubisme *m*.

cubist, Cubist ['kju:bɪst] ◆ adj cubiste. ◆ n cubiste *mf*.

cub reporter n jeune journaliste *mf*.

cub scout, Cub Scout n louveteau *m* *(scout).*

cuckoo ['kʊku:] (*pl* **cuckoos**) ◆ n ORNITH [bird, sound] coucou *m*. ◆ adj *inf* [mad] loufoque, toqué.

cuckoo clock n coucou *m* *(pendule).*

cucumber ['kju:kʌmbə'] n concombre *m*.

cud [kʌd] n bol *m* alimentaire *(d'un ruminant).*

cuddle ['kʌdl] ◆ vi se faire un câlin, se câliner. ◆ vt câliner, caresser ; [child] bercer *(dans ses bras)*. ◆ n câlin *m*, caresse *f*, caresses *fpl*. ❖ **cuddle up** vi se blottir, se pelotonner.

cuddly ['kʌdlɪ] (*compar* **cuddlier**, *superl* **cuddliest**) adj [child, animal] câlin.

cuddly toy n peluche *f*.

cudgel ['kʌdʒəl] (🇬🇧 *pt & pp* **cudgelled**, *cont* **cudgelling** ; 🇺🇸 *pt & pp* **cudgeled**, *cont* **cudgeling**) ◆ n gourdin *m*, trique *f*. ◆ vt battre à coups de gourdin.

cue [kju:] n **1.** CIN & THEAT [verbal] réplique *f* ; [action] signal *m* ; MUS signal *m* d'entrée ▶ **to give sb their cue** donner la réplique à qqn **2.** *fig* [signal] signal *m* ▶ **on cue** au bon moment **3.** [for snooker, etc.] queue *f* *(de billard).*

cuff [kʌf] ◆ n **1.** [of sleeve] poignet *m*, manchette *f* ; [of glove] poignet *m* ; [of coat] parement *m* ; 🇺🇸 [of trousers] revers *m* ▶ **off the cuff** à l'improviste **2.** [blow] gifle *f*, claque *f*. ◆ vt **1.** [hit] gifler, donner une gifle or une claque à **2.** *inf* [handcuff] mettre or passer les menottes à **3.** 🇺🇸 [trousers] faire un revers à. ❖ **cuffs** pl n *inf* [handcuffs] menottes *fpl*.

cuff link n bouton *m* de manchette.

cuisine [kwɪ'zi:n] n cuisine *f*.

CUL (written abbr of **see you later**) MESSAGING @+.

cul-de-sac ['kʌldəsæk] n cul-de-sac *m*, impasse *f* **/** '**cul-de-sac**' 'voie sans issue'.

culinary ['kʌlɪnərɪ] adj culinaire.

cull [kʌl] ◆ vt **1.** [sample] sélectionner **2.** [remove from herd] éliminer, supprimer ; [slaughter - seals] abattre, massacrer. ◆ n [slaughter] massacre *m*.

culminate in ['kʌlmɪneɪt] vt insep : *the demonstration culminated in a riot* la manifestation s'est terminée en émeute.

culmination [,kʌlmɪ'neɪʃn] n [climax - of career] apogée *m* ; [- of efforts] maximum *m* ; [- of disagreement] point *m* culminant.

culottes [kju:'lɒts] pl n jupe-culotte *f*.

culpable ['kʌlpəbl] adj *fml* coupable ; LAW ▶ **culpable homicide** homicide *m* volontaire.

culprit ['kʌlprɪt] n coupable *mf*.

cult [kʌlt] ◆ n [sect] secte *m* ; RELIG & *fig* culte *m*. ◆ comp [book, film] culte ▶ **cult figure** idole *f*.

cultivate ['kʌltɪveɪt] vt **1.** [land] cultiver, exploiter ; [crop] cultiver **2.** *fig* [idea, person] cultiver.

cultivated ['kʌltɪveɪtɪd] adj [land] cultivé, exploité ; [person] cultivé ; [voice] distingué.

cultivation [,kʌltɪ'veɪʃn] n **1.** [of land, crops] culture *f* **2.** *fig* [of taste] éducation *f* ; [of relations] entretien *m*.

cultural ['kʌltʃərəl] adj **1.** [events, background] culturel **/** *cultural integration* acculturation *f* **2.** AGR de culture, cultural.

cultural anthropology n culturologie *f*.

culturally ['kʌltʃərəlɪ] adv culturellement.

culture ['kʌltʃə'] ◆ n **1.** [civilization, learning] culture *f* **/** *a man of culture* un homme cultivé or qui a de la culture **2.** AGR [of land, crops] culture *f* ; [of animals] élevage *m* ; [of fowl] aviculture *f* **3.** BIOL culture *f*. ◆ vt [plants] cultiver ; [animals] élever ; [bacteria] faire une culture de.

cultured ['kʌltʃəd] adj **1.** [refined - person] cultivé, lettré **2.** [grown artificially] cultivé ▶ **cultured pearls** perles *fpl* de culture.

culture gap n fossé *m* culturel.

culture shock n choc *m* culturel.

culture vulture n *inf & hum* fana *mf* de culture, culturophage *mf*.

culvert ['kʌlvət] n [for water] caniveau *m* ; [for cable] conduit *m*.

cum [kʌm] prep avec / *a kitchen-cum-dining area* une cuisine *f* avec coin-repas.

cumbersome ['kʌmbəsəm] adj [bulky] encombrant, embarrassant ; *fig* [process, system, style] lourd, pesant.

cumin ['kʌmɪn] n cumin *m*.

cumulative ['kju:mjʊlətɪv] adj cumulatif.

cunning ['kʌnɪŋ] ◆ adj **1.** [shrewd] astucieux, malin (maligne) ; *pej* rusé, fourbe ▶ **he's as cunning as a fox** il est rusé comme un renard **2.** [skilful] habile, astucieux **3.** 🇺🇸 [cute] mignon, charmant. ◆ n **1.** [guile] finesse *f*, astuce *f* ; *pej* ruse *f*, fourberie *f* **2.** [skill] habileté *f*, adresse *f*.

cunningly ['kʌnɪŋlɪ] adv **1.** [shrewdly] astucieusement, finement ; *pej* avec ruse or fourberie **2.** [skilfully] habilement, astucieusement.

cunt [kʌnt] n *vulg* **1.** [vagina] con *m*, chatte *f* **2.** [man] enculé *m* ; [woman] salope *f*.

cup [kʌp] (*pt* & *pp* **cupped**, *cont* **cupping**) ◆ n **1.** [for drinking, cupful] tasse *f* ; RELIG calice *m* / *a cup of coffee* une tasse de café **2.** SPORT [trophy, competition] coupe *f* **3.** 🇺🇸 SPORT [to protect genitals] protège-sexe *m* **4.** [shape -of plant] corolle *f* ; [-of bone] cavité *f* articulaire, glène *f* ; [-of bra] bonnet *m* **5.** [punch] cocktail *m* ▶ **champagne cup** *cocktail au champagne* **6.** TECH godet *m*, cuvette *f* **7.** 🇺🇸 [in golf] trou *m*. ◆ comp **1.** SPORT [winners, holders, match] de coupe **2.** [handle] de tasse ; [rack] pour tasses. ◆ vt [hands] mettre en coupe ; [hold] ▶ **to cup one's hands around sthg** mettre ses mains autour de qqch / *he cupped a hand to his ear* il mit sa main derrière son oreille / *he sat with his chin cupped in his hand* il était assis, le menton dans le creux de sa main.

cupboard ['kʌbəd] n [on wall] placard *m* ; [free-standing -for dishes, pans] buffet *m*, placard *m* ; [-for clothes] placard *m*, armoire *f*.

cupcake n **1.** 🇺🇸 [cake] petit gâteau *m* **2.** [term of affection] mon chou, ma puce.

cup final n finale *f* de la coupe ▶ **the Cup Final** 🇬🇧 la finale de la coupe de football.

cup finalist n finaliste *mf* de la coupe.

Cupid ['kju:pɪd] pr n MYTH Cupidon *m*. ❖ **cupid** n ART [cherub] chérubin *m*, amour *m*.

cupola ['kju:pələ] n ARCHIT [ceiling, roof] coupole *f*, dôme *m* ; [tower] belvédère *m*.

cup tie n match *m* de coupe.

curable ['kjʊərəbl] adj guérissable, curable.

curate ['kjʊərət] n vicaire *m* (*de l'Église anglicane*).

curator [ˌkjʊə'reɪtər] n [of museum] conservateur *m*, -trice *f*.

curb [kɜ:b] ◆ n **1.** [restraint] frein *m* / *a curb on trade* une restriction au commerce **2.** [on harness] ▶ **curb (bit)** mors *m* ▶ **curb (chain)** gourmette *f* **3.** 🇺🇸 = **kerb**. ◆ vt **1.** [restrain -emotion] refréner, maîtriser ; [-expenses] restreindre, mettre un frein à ; [-child] modérer, freiner **2.** 🇺🇸 / 'curb your dog' 'votre chien doit faire ses besoins dans le caniveau'.

curd cheese n fromage *m* blanc battu.

curdle ['kɜ:dl] ◆ vi [milk] cailler ; [sauce] tourner ; [mayonnaise] tomber. ◆ vt [milk] cailler ; [sauce] faire tourner ; [mayonnaise] faire tomber.

cure [kjʊər] ◆ vt **1.** [disease, person] guérir ; *fig* [problem] éliminer, remédier à **2.** [tobacco, meat, fish -gen] traiter ; [-with salt] saler ; [-by smoking] fumer ; [-by drying] sécher. ◆ n **1.** [remedy] remède *m*, cure *f* **2.** [recovery] guérison *f*.

⚠ The French word **cure** means a course of treatment, not a cure in the sense of a remedy.

cure-all n panacée *f*.

curfew ['kɜ:fju:] n couvre-feu *m*.

curio ['kjʊərɪəʊ] (*pl* **curios**) n curiosité *f*, bibelot *m*.

curiosity [ˌkjʊərɪ'ɒsətɪ] (*pl* **curiosities**) n **1.** [interest] curiosité *f* **2.** [novelty -object] curiosité *f* ; [-person] bête *f* curieuse.

curious ['kjʊərɪəs] adj **1.** [inquisitive] curieux **2.** [strange] curieux, singulier.

curiously ['kjʊərɪəslɪ] adv **1.** [inquisitively] avec curiosité **2.** [strangely] curieusement, singulièrement.

curl [kɜ:l] ◆ vi **1.** [hair] friser ; [loosely] boucler **2.** [paper, leaf] se recroqueviller, se racornir ; [lip] se retrousser **3.** [road] serpenter ; [smoke] monter en spirale **4.** SPORT jouer au curling. ◆ vt **1.** [hair] friser ; [loosely] (faire) boucler **2.** [paper] recourber ; [ribbon] faire boucler ; [lip] retrousser. ◆ n **1.** [of hair] boucle *f* (de cheveux) **2.** [spiral] courbe *f* ; [of smoke] spirale *f* ; [of wave] ondulation *f*. ❖ **curl up** ◆ vi **1.** [leaf, paper] s'enrouler, se recroqueviller ; [bread] se racornir **2.** [person] se pelotonner ; [cat] se mettre en boule, se pelotonner ; [dog] se coucher en rond. ◆ vt sep enrouler ▶ **to curl o.s. up a)** [person] se pelotonner **b)** [cat] se mettre en boule, se pelotonner **c)** [dog] se coucher en rond.

curler ['kɜ:lər] n **1.** [for hair] bigoudi *m*, rouleau *m* **2.** SPORT joueur *m*, -euse *f* de curling.

curling ['kɜ:lɪŋ] n SPORT curling *m*.

curling iron n fer *m* à friser.

curling tongs pl n fer *m* à friser.

curly ['kɜ:lɪ] (*compar* **curlier**, *superl* **curliest**) adj [hair -tight] frisé ; [-loose] bouclé.

currant ['kʌrənt] n **1.** BOT [fruit] groseille *f* **2.** [dried grape] raisin de Corinthe.

currency ['kʌrənsɪ] (*pl* **currencies**) n **1.** ECON & FIN monnaie *f*, devise *f* **2.** *fig* [prevalence] cours *m*, circulation *f*.

current ['kʌrənt] ◆ n [gen & ELEC] courant *m* ; *fig* [trend] cours *m*, tendance *f*. ◆ adj **1.** [widespread] courant, commun **2.** [most recent -fashion, trend] actuel ; [-price] courant.

current account n 🇬🇧 compte *m* courant.

current affairs ◆ pl n l'actualité *f*, les questions *fpl* d'actualité. ◆ comp [programme, magazine] d'actualités.

current assets pl n actif *m* de roulement.

current liabilities pl n passif *m* exigible à court terme.

currently ['kʌrəntlɪ] adv actuellement, à présent.

curricular [kə'rɪkjələr] adj au programme.

curriculum [kə'rɪkjələm] (*pl* **curricula** [-lə] *or* **curriculums**) n programme *m* d'enseignement / *the maths curriculum* le programme de maths.

curriculum vitae [-'vi:taɪ] (*pl* **curricula vitae**) n 🇬🇧 curriculum *m* (vitae).

curried ['kʌrɪd] adj au curry or cari / *curried eggs* des œufs au curry or à l'indienne.

curry ['kʌrɪ] (*pl* **curries**, *pt* & *pp* **curried**) ◆ n CULIN curry *m*, cari *m*. ◆ vt **1.** CULIN accommoder au curry **2.** [horse] étriller ; [leather] corroyer.

curry powder n curry *m*, cari *m*.

curse [kɜ:s] ◆ n **1.** [evil spell] malédiction *f* **2.** [swearword] juron *m*, imprécation *f* **3.** *fig* [bane] fléau *m*, calamité *f* **4.** *inf* & *euph* [menstruation] ▶ **the curse**

les règles *fpl*. ◆ vt **1.** [damn] maudire **2.** [swear at] injurier **3.** [afflict] affliger / *he's cursed with a bad temper* il est affligé d'un mauvais caractère. ◆ vi [swear] jurer, blasphémer.

curse word n US juron *m*.

cursor ['kɜːsə^r] n curseur *m*.

cursory ['kɜːsərɪ] adj [superficial] superficiel ; [hasty] hâtif.

curt [kɜːt] adj [person, reply, manner] brusque, sec (sèche).

curtail [kɜː'teɪl] vt **1.** [cut short - story, visit, studies] écourter **2.** [reduce - expenses] réduire, rogner ; [- power, freedom] limiter, réduire.

curtailment [kɜː'teɪlmənt] n **1.** [of studies, visit] raccourcissement *m* **2.** [of expenses] réduction *f* ; [of power, freedom] limitation *f*, réduction *f*.

curtain ['kɜːtn] ◆ n **1.** [gen & THEAT] rideau *m* ; *fig* rideau *m*, voile *m* **2.** THEAT [for actor] rappel *m*. ◆ vt garnir de rideaux. ❖ **curtain off** vt sep séparer par un rideau.

curtain call n rappel *m*.

curtain raiser n THEAT lever *m* de rideau ; *fig* événement *m* avant-coureur, prélude *m*.

curtsey, curtsy ['kɜːtsɪ] (*pl* curtseys *or* curtsies, *pt & pp* curtseyed *or* curtsied) ◆ n révérence *f*. ◆ vi faire une révérence.

curvaceous [kɜː'veɪʃəs] adj *hum* [woman] bien roulée.

curvature ['kɜːvətʃə^r] n [gen] courbure *f* ; MED déviation *f* / *curvature of the spine* [abnormal] déviation de la colonne vertébrale, scoliose *f*.

curve [kɜːv] ◆ n **1.** [gen] courbe *f* ; [in road] tournant *m*, virage *m* ; ARCHIT [of arch] voussure *f* ; [of beam] cambrure *f* **2.** MATH courbe *f* **3.** US SPORT balle *f* coupée. ◆ vi [gen] se courber ; [road] être en courbe, faire une courbe. ◆ vt [gen] courber ; TECH cintrer.

curveball ['kɜːvbɔːl] n US balle *f* coupée ▶ **to throw sb a curveball** *fig* prendre qqn de court.

curved [kɜːvd] adj [gen] courbe ; [edge] arrondi ; [road] en courbe ; [convex] convexe ; TECH cintré.

curve grading ['kɜːv,ɡreɪdɪŋ] n US SCH *système de notation relative tenant compte des performances des élèves de la classe.*

curvy ['kɜːvɪ] (*compar* curvier, *superl* curviest) adj **1.** [road, line] sinueux **2.** *inf* [woman] bien fait.

cushion ['kʊʃn] ◆ n **1.** [pillow] coussin *m* ; *fig* tampon *m* **2.** [in snooker, billiards, etc.] bande *f*. ◆ vt **1.** [sofa] mettre des coussins à ; [seat] rembourrer ; TECH matelasser **2.** *fig* [shock, blow] amortir.

cushy ['kʊʃɪ] (*compar* cushier, *superl* cushiest) adj *inf* peinard, pépère / *a cushy job* une bonne planque.

cuss [kʌs] *inf* ◆ vi jurer, blasphémer. ◆ vt injurier. ◆ n **1.** [oath] juron *m* **2.** [person] type *m* *pej*. ❖ **cuss out** vt sep US *inf* ▶ **to cuss sb out** traiter qqn de tous les noms.

custard ['kʌstəd] n **1.** [sauce] *crème sucrée épaisse servie chaude ou froide* ; ≃ crème *f* anglaise **2.** [dessert] crème *f* renversée, flan *m*.

custard pie n tarte *f* à la crème.

custard powder n ≃ crème *f* anglaise instantanée.

custodial [kʌs'təʊdjəl] adj **1.** LAW de prison **2.** [guarding] ▶ **custodial staff** personnel *m* de surveillance.

custodian [kʌ'stəʊdjən] n **1.** [of building] gardien *m*, -enne *f* ; [of museum] conservateur *m*, -trice *f* ; [of prisoner] gardien *m*, -enne *f*, surveillant *m*, -e *f* **2.** *fig* [of morals, tradition] gardien *m*, -enne *f*, protecteur *m*, -trice *f*.

custody ['kʌstədɪ] (*pl* custodies) n **1.** [care] garde *f* **2.** [detention] garde *f* à vue ; [imprisonment] emprisonnement *m* ; [before trial] détention *f* préventive.

custom ['kʌstəm] ◆ n **1.** [tradition] coutume *f*, usage *m* **2.** COMM [trade] clientèle *f* / *I'll take my custom elsewhere* je vais me fournir ailleurs **3.** LAW coutume *f*, droit *m* coutumier. ◆ adj [custom-made] sur mesure.

customarily [,kʌstə'merəlɪ] adv d'habitude.

customary ['kʌstəmrɪ] adj *fml* **1.** [traditional] coutumier, habituel ; [usual] habituel **2.** LAW coutumier.

custom-built adj (fait) sur commande.

customer ['kʌstəmə^r] n **1.** [client] client *m*, -e *f* **2.** *inf* [character] type *m* *pej*.

customer base n base *f* de clientèle or de consommateurs.

customer care n service *m* client.

customer database n base *f* de données clients.

customer-focused adj orienté client.

customer loyalty n fidélité *f* de la clientèle.

customer profile n profil *m* du client or du consommateur.

customer service n service *m* client.

customizable ['kʌstəmɪzəbəl] adj qui peut être personnalisé.

customization [,kʌstəmaɪ'zeɪʃən] n personnalisation *f*.

customize, customise ['kʌstəmaɪz] vt [make to order] faire or fabriquer or construire sur commande ; [personalize] personnaliser.

custom-made adj [clothing] (fait) sur mesure ; [other articles] (fait) sur commande.

customs ['kʌstəmz] pl n **1.** [authorities, checkpoint] douane *f* ▶ **Customs and Excise** UK ≃ la Régie **2.** [duty] droits *mpl* de douane.

customs duty n droit *m* or droits *mpl* de douane.

customs officer n douanier *m*, -ère *f*.

cut [kʌt] (*pt & pp* cut, *cont* cutting) ◆ vt **1.** [incise, slash, sever] couper / *cut the box open with the knife* ouvrez la boîte avec le couteau / *he fell and cut his knee (open)* il s'est ouvert le genou en tombant / *they cut his throat* ils lui ont coupé la gorge, ils l'ont égorgé / *they cut the prisoners free* or *loose* ils ont détaché les prisonniers **2.** [divide into parts] couper, découper ; [meat] découper ; [slice] découper en tranches / *she cut articles from the paper* elle a coupé des articles dans le journal / *cut the cake in half / in three pieces* coupez le gâteau en deux / en trois **3.** [trim - grass, lawn] tondre ; [- bush, tree] tailler ; [reap - crop] couper, faucher / *I cut my nails / my hair* je me suis coupé les ongles / les cheveux **4.** [shape - dress, suit] couper ; [- diamond, glass, key] tailler ; [- screw] fileter ; [dig - channel, tunnel] creuser, percer ; [engrave] graver ; [sculpt] sculpter **5.** [cross, traverse] couper, croiser **6.** [interrupt] interrompre, couper ▶ **to cut sb short** couper la parole à qqn / *we had to cut our visit short* nous avons dû écourter notre visite ▶ **to cut a long story short,…** : *to cut a long story short, I left* bref or en deux mots, je suis parti **7.** [switch off] couper / *he cut the engine* il a coupé or arrêté le moteur **8.** [reduce] réduire, diminuer / *to cut prices* casser les prix / *the athlete cut 5 seconds off the world record* or *cut the world record by 5 seconds* l'athlète a amélioré le record mondial de 5 secondes **9.** [edit out] faire des coupures dans, réduire **10.** *inf* [absent oneself from - meeting, appointment, etc.] manquer (volontairement), sauter / *I had to cut lunch in order to get there on time* j'ai dû me passer de déjeuner pour arriver à l'heure ▶ **to cut class** or **school** US sécher les cours **11.** [tooth] percer **12.** [record, track] graver, faire **13.** [pack of cards] couper **14.** CIN [film] monter. ◆ vi **1.** [incise, slash] couper, trancher / *she cut into the bread* elle a entamé le pain / *the yacht cut through the waves* *fig* le yacht fendait les vagues ▶ **to cut and run** se sauver, filer ▶ **that argument cuts both** or **two ways** c'est un argument à double tranchant **2.** [cloth, paper] se couper / *the cake will cut into six pieces* ce gâteau peut se couper en six **3.** [hurtfully] faire mal **4.** [take shorter route] couper, passer / *we cut across the fields* nous avons coupé par les champs **5.** [cross] traverser, couper / *this path cuts across or through the swamp* ce sentier traverse or coupe à travers le marécage **6.** [in cards] couper **7.** CIN & TV [stop filming] couper ; [change scenes] : *the film cuts straight from the love scene to the funeral* l'image passe directement de la scène d'amour à l'enterrement. ❖ n **1.** [slit] coupure f ; [deeper] entaille f ; [wound] balafre f ; MED incision f / *she had a nasty cut on her leg from the fall* elle s'était fait une vilaine entaille à la jambe en tombant ▶ **to be a cut above the rest** être nettement mieux que les autres or le reste **2.** [act of cutting] coupure f, entaille f ▶ **to make a cut in sthg** [with knife, scissors, etc.] faire une entaille dans qqch **3.** [blow, stroke] coup m / *a knife / sword cut* un coup de couteau / d'épée **2.** [meat - piece] morceau m ; [- slice] tranche f **5.** [reduction - in price, taxes] réduction f, diminution f ; [- in staff] compression f / *a cut in government spending* une réduction or diminution des dépenses publiques ▶ **the cuts** FIN les compressions fpl budgétaires **6.** [deletion] coupure f / *they made several cuts in the film* ils ont fait plusieurs coupures dans le film **7.** [shape, style - of clothes, hair] coupe f ; [- of jewel] taille f **8.** inf [portion, share] part f / *what's his cut of the profits?* à combien s'élève sa part ? **9.** CIN & TV coupe f. ❖ adj **1.** [hand, flowers] coupé ; [tobacco] découpé **2.** [reduced] réduit ▶ **to sell sthg at cut prices** vendre qqch au rabais **3.** [shaped - clothing] coupé ; [faceted - gem] taillé / *a well-cut suit* un costume bien coupé or de bonne coupe. ❖ **cut across** vt insep **1.** [cross, traverse] traverser, couper à travers **2.** [go beyond] surpasser, transcender **3.** [contradict] contredire, aller à l'encontre de. ❖ **cut back** vt sep **1.** [reduce] réduire, diminuer **2.** [prune, trim] tailler ; [shrub, tree] élaguer, tailler. ❖ **cut back on** vt insep réduire. ❖ **cut down** vt sep **1.** [tree] couper, abattre ; [person - in battle] abattre **2.** [make smaller - article, speech] couper, tronquer ; [- clothing] rendre plus petit ▶ **to cut sb down to size** remettre qqn à sa place **3.** [curtail] réduire, diminuer ; [expenses] réduire, rogner. ❖ **cut down on** vt insep réduire / *I'm going to cut down on drinking / smoking* je vais boire / fumer moins. ❖ **cut in** inf vi **1.** [interrupt] interrompre / *she cut in on their conversation* elle est intervenue dans leur conversation **2.** AUTO faire une queue de poisson. ❖ **cut off** vt sep **1.** [hair, piece of meat, bread] couper ; [arm, leg] amputer, couper / *they cut off the king's head* ils ont décapité le roi ▶ **to cut off one's nose to spite one's face**: *she cut off her nose to spite her face* elle l'a fait par esprit de contradiction **2.** [interrupt - speaker] interrompre, couper **3.** [disconnect, discontinue] couper / *I was cut off* TELEC j'ai été coupé **4.** [separate, isolate] isoler / *the house was cut off by snow drifts* la maison était isolée par des congères / *he cut himself off from his family* il a rompu avec sa famille. ❖ **cut out** ❖ vt sep **1.** [make by cutting - coat, dress] couper, tailler ; [- statue] sculpter, tailler / *I'm not cut out for living abroad* je ne suis pas fait pour vivre à l'étranger ▶ **to have one's work cut out**: *you have your work cut out for you* vous avez du pain sur la planche or de quoi vous occuper **2.** [remove by cutting - article, picture] découper / *advertisements cut out from* or *of the paper* des annonces découpées dans le journal **3.** [eliminate] supprimer ; [stop] arrêter / *he cut out smoking* il a arrêté de fumer ▶ **cut it out!** inf ça suffit !, ça va comme ça ! **4.** inf [rival] supplanter **5.** [deprive] priver / *his father cut him out of his will* son père l'a rayé de son testament. ❖ vi [machine - stop operating] caler ; [- switch off] s'éteindre. ❖ **cut up** ❖ vt sep **1.** [food, wood] couper ; [meat - carve] découper ; [- chop up] hacher **2.** (usu passive) inf [affect deeply] : *she's really cut up about her dog's death* la mort de son chien a été un

coup pour elle. ❖ vi inf UK ▶ **to cut up rough** se mettre en rogne or en boule.

cut-and-dried adj inf : *it's all cut-and-dried* **a)** [prearranged] tout est déjà décidé **b)** [inevitable] il n'y a rien à (y) faire.

cut-and-paste vt & vi couper-coller.

cut and thrust n : *the cut and thrust of parliamentary debate* les joutes oratoires des débats parlementaires.

cutback ['kʌtbæk] n **1.** [reduction - in costs] réduction f, diminution f ; [- in staff] compression f **2.** US CIN retour m en arrière, flash-back m.

cute [kju:t] adj inf **1.** [pretty] mignon ; pej affecté **2.** [clever] malin (maligne).

cutesy ['kju:tsɪ] adj inf & pej mièvre.

cut glass n cristal m taillé. ❖ **cut-glass** adj : *a cut-glass vase* un vase m en cristal taillé / *a cut-glass accent* UK fig un accent distingué.

cuticle ['kju:tɪkl] n [skin] épiderme m ; [on nails] petites peaux fpl, envie f.

cutlery ['kʌtlərɪ] n (U) **1.** [eating utensils] couverts mpl **2.** [knives, trade] coutellerie f.

cutlet ['kʌtlɪt] n **1.** [gen] côtelette f ; [of veal] escalope f **2.** UK [croquette] croquette f.

cutoff (point) ['kʌtɒf-] n [limit] point m de limite.

cutout ['kʌtaʊt] n **1.** [figure] découpage m **2.** ELEC disjoncteur m, coupe-circuit m ; AUTO échappement m libre.

cut-price ❖ adj [articles] à prix réduit, au rabais ; [shop] à prix réduits ; [manufacturer] qui vend à prix réduits. ❖ adv à prix réduit.

cut-rate adj US en promotion, à prix réduit.

cutter ['kʌtər] n **1.** [person - of clothes] coupeur m, -euse f ; [- of jewels] tailleur m ; [- of film] monteur m, -euse f **2.** [tool] coupoir m **3.** [sailing boat] cotre m, cutter m ; [motorboat] vedette f ; [of coastguard] garde-côte m ; [warship] canot m.

cutthroat ['kʌtθrəʊt] ❖ n **1.** [murderer] assassin m **2.** [razor] ▶ **cutthroat (razor)** rasoir m à main. ❖ adj féroce ; [competition] acharné ; [prices] très compétitif.

cutting ['kʌtɪŋ] ❖ n **1.** [act] coupe f ; [of jewel, stone] taille f ; [of film] montage m ; [of trees] coupe f, abattage m **2.** [piece - of cloth] coupon m ; [- from newspaper] coupure f ; AGR [of shrub, vine] marcotte f ; HORT [of plant] bouture f **3.** [for railway, road] tranchée f. ❖ adj **1.** [tool] tranchant, coupant **2.** [wind] glacial, cinglant ; [rain] cinglant **3.** [hurtful - remark] mordant, tranchant ; [- word] cinglant, blessant.

cutting board n US planche f à découper.

cutting-edge adj [technology] de pointe.

cuttlefish ['kʌtlfɪʃ] (pl **cuttlefish**) n seiche f.

CV n **1.** (abbr of **curriculum vitae**) UK CV m **2.** (abbr of **cardio-vascular**) : *a CV workout* une séance de cardio-training.

c.w.o., **CWO** (written abbr of **cash with order**) payable à la commande.

cwt. written abbr of **hundredweight**.

CWU (abbr of **Communication Workers Union**) n *syndicat britannique des communications.*

CYA (written abbr of **see you around** or **see ya**) MESSAGING @+.

cyanide ['saɪənaɪd] n cyanure m.

cyberbanking ['saɪbə,bæŋkɪŋ] n COMPUT transactions fpl bancaires en ligne.

cyberbully ['saɪbəbʊlɪ] n cyberagresseur m.

cyberbullying ['saɪbəbʊlɪŋ] n cyberagression f.

cybercafé ['saɪbə,kæfeɪ] n cybercafé m.

cyberchondria [,saɪbə'kɒndrɪə] n inf comportement hypochondriaque de certains internautes, qui consiste à rechercher des informations médicales sur Internet jusqu'à s'autodiagnostiquer des maladies qu'ils n'ont pas.

cybercrime ['saɪbəkraɪm] n cybercriminalité f.

cyberculture ['saɪbə,kʌltʃə'] n cyberculture f.

cybernaut ['saɪbə,nɔ:t] n cybernaute mf.

cybernetics [,saɪbə'netɪks] n (U) cybernétique f.

cyberpet ['saɪbə,pet] n animal m virtuel.

cyberpunk ['saɪbə,pʌnk] n cyberpunk m.

cybersex ['saɪbə,seks] n cybersexe m.

cyber shop n boutique f en ligne.

cybershopping ['saɪbəʃɒpɪŋ] n achats mpl en ligne, cybershopping m.

cyberspace ['saɪbəspeɪs] n espace m virtuel, cyberespace m.

cybersquatter ['saɪbəskwɒtə'] n cybersquatteur m, -euse f.

cybersquatting ['saɪbəskwɒtɪŋ] n cybersquatting m.

cyberstalking ['saɪbəstɔ:kɪŋ] n harcèlement m en ligne, cyber-harcèlement m.

cyber store = cyber shop.

cybersurfer ['saɪbə,sɜ:fə'] n cybernaute mf.

cyborg ['saɪbɔ:g] n cyborg m.

cyclamen ['sɪkləmən] (pl cyclamen) n cyclamen m.

cycle ['saɪkl] ◆ n **1.** [gen & COMPUT], ELEC & LITER cycle m **2.** [bicycle] vélo m ; [tricycle] tricycle m ; [motorcycle] motocyclette f, moto f. ◆ comp [path, track] cyclable ▶ **cycle lane** piste f cyclable ▶ **cycle rack a)** [on pavement] râtelier m à vélos **b)** [on car] porte-vélos m (inv). ◆ vi faire du vélo.

cycleway ['saɪklweɪ] n 🇬🇧 piste f or bande f cyclable.

cyclic(al) ['saɪklɪk(l)] adj cyclique.

cycling ['saɪklɪŋ] ◆ n cyclisme m. ◆ comp [magazine, shoes, shorts] de cyclisme.

cyclist ['saɪklɪst] n cycliste mf.

cyclone ['saɪkləʊn] n cyclone m.

cygnet ['sɪgnɪt] n jeune cygne m.

cylinder ['sɪlɪndə'] n **1.** AUTO, MATH & TECH cylindre m ▶ **oxygen / gas cylinder** bouteille f d'oxygène / de gaz **2.** [of typewriter] rouleau m ; [of gun] barillet m.

cylinder block n bloc-cylindres m.

cylinder head n culasse f (d'un moteur).

cylinder-head gasket n joint m de culasse.

cylindrical [sɪ'lɪndrɪkl] adj cylindrique.

cymbal ['sɪmbl] n cymbale f.

cynic ['sɪnɪk] ◆ adj [gen & PHILOS] cynique. ◆ n cynique mf.

cynical ['sɪnɪkl] adj [gen & PHILOS] cynique.

cynically ['sɪnɪklɪ] adv cyniquement, avec cynisme.

cynicism ['sɪnɪsɪzm] n [gen & PHILOS] cynisme m.

CYO (abbr of Catholic Youth Organization) pr n association de jeunes catholiques aux États-Unis.

cypher ['saɪfə'] = **cipher.**

cypress ['saɪprəs] n cyprès m.

Cypriot ['sɪprɪət] ◆ n Chypriote mf, Cypriote mf ▶ **Greek Cypriot** Chypriote grec m, Chypriote grecque f ▶ **Turkish Cypriot** Chypriote turc m, Chypriote turque f. ◆ adj chypriote, cypriote.

Cyprus ['saɪprəs] pr n Chypre / in Cyprus à Chypre.

cyst [sɪst] n MED kyste m.

cystic fibrosis ['sɪstɪk-] n mucoviscidose f.

cystitis [sɪs'taɪtɪs] n cystite f.

cytology [saɪ'tɒlədʒɪ] n cytologie f.

CZ pr n abbr of Canal Zone.

czar [zɑ:'] n **1.** [monarch] tsar m **2.** [top person] éminence f grise, ponte m / the government's drug(s) czar haut personnage chargé de mener la lutte contre la drogue.

Czech [tʃek] ◆ n **1.** [person] Tchèque mf **2.** LING tchèque m. ◆ adj tchèque ▶ **the Czech Republic** la République tchèque.

Czechoslovak [,tʃekə'sləʊvæk] = **Czechoslovakian.**

Czechoslovakia [,tʃekəslə'vækɪə] pr n Tchécoslovaquie f / in Czechoslovakia en Tchécoslovaquie.

Czechoslovakian [,tʃekəslə'vækɪən] ◆ n Tchécoslovaque mf. ◆ adj tchécoslovaque.

Czech Republic pr n ▶ **the Czech Republic** la République tchèque.

d (*pl* **d's** *or* **ds**), **D** (*pl* **D's** *or* **Ds**) [di:] n [letter] d *m*,
D *m* / **D for dog** *or* **David** ≃ D comme Désirée / *in 3-D*
en trois dimensions, en 3-D. **See also f.**

d 1. (written abbr of **penny**) *symbole du penny anglais
jusqu'en 1971* **2.** (written abbr of **died**) : *d 1913* mort en
1913.

D ◆ n **1.** MUS ré *m* **2.** SCH & UNIV [grade] *note inférieure à la moyenne (7 sur 20).* ◆ US written abbr of
democrat(ic).

D&T (abbr of **Design and Technology**) n UK SCH technologie *f (matière scolaire)*, techno *f inf.*

DA¹ (abbr of **District Attorney**) n US ≃ procureur *m*
de la République.

DA², da MESSAGING written abbr of **the.**

dab [dæb] (*pt & pp* **dabbed,** *cont* **dabbing**) ◆ n
1. [small amount] ▸ **a dab** un petit peu **2.** [fish] limande *f.*
◆ vt **1.** [touch lightly] tamponner **2.** [daub] : *he dabbed
the canvas with paint* il posait la peinture sur la toile par
petites touches. ◆ **dab on** vt sep appliquer par petites
touches.

dabble ['dæbl] ◆ vt mouiller. ◆ vi *fig* : *he dabbles at
painting* il fait un peu de peinture / *she dabbles in politics*
elle fait un peu de politique / *to dabble on the Stock Market* boursicoter.

dabbler ['dæblər] n dilettante *mf.*

dab hand n UK *inf* ▸ **to be a dab hand at sthg** être doué
en or pour qqch ▸ **to be a dab hand at doing sthg** être
doué pour faire qqch.

dachshund ['dækʃʊnd] n teckel *m.*

dad [dæd] n *inf* [father] papa *m* ; [old man] pépé *m.*

daddy ['dædɪ] (*pl* **daddies**) n *inf* papa *m.*

daddy longlegs [-'lɒŋlegz] n UK [cranefly] tipule *f* ; US
[harvestman] faucheur *m*, faucheux *m.*

daffodil ['dæfədɪl] n jonquille *f.*

Daffodil

La jonquille est un emblème du pays de Galles.

daft [dɑːft] *inf* ◆ adj UK [foolish] idiot, bête / *don't be
daft!* (ne) fais pas l'idiot ! / *he's daft about her* il est fou
d'elle. ◆ adv : *don't talk daft* ne dites pas de bêtises.

dagger ['dægər] n **1.** [weapon] poignard *m* ; [smaller]
dague *f* ▸ **to be at daggers drawn with sb** être à couteaux
tirés avec qqn ▸ **to shoot** US *or* **to look daggers at sb** foudroyer qqn du regard **2.** TYPO croix *f.*

dahlia ['deɪljə] n dahlia *m.*

daily ['deɪlɪ] (*pl* **dailies**) ◆ adj **1.** [routine, task] quotidien, de tous les jours ; [output, wage] journalier / *a daily
paper* un quotidien / *to be paid on a daily basis* être

payé à la journée **2.** PRESS ▸ **the Daily Express** *quotidien
britannique populaire conservateur* ▸ **the Daily Mail** *quotidien britannique populaire du centre droit* ▸ **the Daily Mirror** *quotidien britannique populaire du centre gauche* ▸ **the
Daily Sport** *quotidien britannique à sensation* ▸ **the Daily
Star** *quotidien britannique à sensation de droite* ▸ **the Daily
Telegraph** *quotidien britannique de qualité, de tendance
conservatrice* ⟶ **broadsheet,** ⟶ **tabloid.** ◆ adv
tous les jours, quotidiennement / *twice daily* deux fois par
jour. ◆ n **1.** [newspaper] quotidien *m* **2.** UK *inf* [cleaner]
femme *f* de ménage.

daintily ['deɪntɪlɪ] adv **1.** [eat, hold] délicatement ; [walk]
avec grâce **2.** [dress] coquettement.

dainty ['deɪntɪ] (*compar* **daintier,** *superl* **daintiest,**
pl **dainties**) ◆ adj **1.** [small] menu, petit ; [delicate] délicat **2.** [food] de choix, délicat. ◆ n [food] mets *m* délicat ;
[sweet] friandise *f.*

dairy ['deərɪ] (*pl* **dairies**) ◆ n AGR [building on farm]
laiterie *f* ; [shop] crémerie *f*, laiterie *f.* ◆ comp [cow, farm,
products] laitier ; [butter, cream] fermier ▸ **dairy cattle**
vaches *fpl* laitières ▸ **dairy farmer** producteur *m* de lait or
laitier ▸ **dairy farming** industrie *f* laitière.

daisy ['deɪzɪ] (*pl* **daisies**) n marguerite *f* ; [smaller] pâquerette *f.*

daisy chain n guirlande *f* de pâquerettes.

daisywheel ['deɪzɪwiːl] n marguerite *f* ▸ **daisywheel
printer** imprimante *f* à marguerite.

Dakar ['dækɑː] pr n Dakar.

Dakota [də'kəʊtə] pr n Dakota *m* / *in Dakota* dans le
Dakota.

dal [dɑːl] n lentilles *fpl.*

dale [deɪl] n vallée *f*, vallon *m.*

dally ['dælɪ] (*pt & pp* **dallied**) vi **1.** [dawdle] lanterner
▸ **to dally over sthg** lanterner sur or dans qqch **2.** [toy
- with idea] badiner, caresser ; [- with affections] jouer.

Dalmatian [dæl'meɪʃn] n [dog] dalmatien *m*, -enne *f.*

dam [dæm] (*pt & pp* **dammed,** *cont* **damming**) ◆ n
1. [barrier] barrage *m* (de retenue) **2.** [reservoir] réservoir *m* **3.** [animal] mère *f.* ◆ vt construire un barrage sur.
◆ **dam up** vt sep **1.** *lit* construire un barrage sur **2.** *fig*
[feelings] refouler, ravaler ; [words] endiguer.

damage ['dæmɪdʒ] ◆ n **1.** (*U*) [harm] dommage *m*,
dommages *mpl* ; [visible effects] dégâts *mpl*, dommages *mpl* ; [to ship, shipment] avarie *f*, avaries *fpl* / *damage to property* dégâts *mpl* matériels ▸ **damage limitation**
effort *m* pour limiter les dégâts **2.** *fig* tort *m*, préjudice *m.*
◆ vt [harm - crop, object] endommager, causer des dégâts
à ; [- food] abîmer, gâter ; [- eyes, health] abîmer ; [- ship,
shipment] avarier ; [- reputation] porter atteinte à, nuire à ;
[- cause] faire du tort à, porter préjudice à. ◆ **damages**
pl n LAW dommages *mpl* et intérêts *mpl.*

damaging [ˈdæmɪdʒɪŋ] adj dommageable, nuisible ; LAW préjudiciable.

Damascus [dəˈmæskəs] pr n Damas.

dame [deɪm] n **1.** arch & liter [noble] dame f **▸ (panto-mime) dame** 🇬🇧 THEAT rôle de la vieille dame tenu par un homme, dans la pantomime anglaise **2.** 🇬🇧 [title] **▸ Dame** titre donné à une femme ayant reçu certaines distinctions honorifiques.

dammit [ˈdæmɪt] interj inf mince.

damn [dæm] **◆** interj inf **▸ damn!** mince ! **◆** n inf : I don't give a damn about the money je me fiche pas mal de l'argent / it's not worth a damn ça ne vaut pas un pet de lapin or un clou. **◆** vt **1.** RELIG damner **2.** [condemn] condamner **3.** inf 🅿🅷🆁 damn you! va te faire voir ! v inf / well I'll be damned! ça, c'est le comble ! / I'll be damned if I'll apologize! m'excuser ? plutôt mourir ! v inf. **◆** adj inf fichu, sacré / you damn fool! espèce d'idiot ! / it's a damn nuisance! ce que c'est casse-pieds !, quelle barbe ! / it's one damn thing after another quand ce n'est pas une chose c'est l'autre. **◆** adv inf **1.** [as intensifier] très / he knows damn well what I mean il sait exactement or très bien ce que je veux dire **2.** 🅿🅷🆁 damn all 🇬🇧 que dalle v inf.

damnation [dæmˈneɪʃn] **◆** n damnation f. **◆** interj inf **▸ damnation!** enfer et damnation ! hum.

damned [dæmd] **◆** adj **1.** RELIG damné, maudit **2.** inf = damn. **◆** adv inf rudement, vachement v inf. **◆ ▸** pl n **▸ the damned** RELIG & liter les damnés mpl.

damnedest [ˈdæmdəst] inf **◆** n [utmost] : he did his damnedest to ruin the party il a vraiment fait tout ce qu'il pouvait pour gâcher la soirée. **◆** adj 🇺🇸 incroyable.

damn-fool adj inf crétin, idiot.

damning [ˈdæmɪŋ] adj [evidence, statement] accablant.

Damocles [ˈdæmə.kliːz] pr n Damoclès **▸ the sword of Damocles** l'épée f de Damoclès.

damp [dæmp] **◆** adj [air, clothes, heat] humide ; [skin] moite. **◆** n **1.** [moisture] humidité f **2.** MIN [air] mofette f ; [gas] grisou m. **◆** vt **1.** [wet] humecter **2.** [stifle - sounds] amortir, étouffer ; MUS étouffer ; fig [spirits] décourager, refroidir **3.** [fire] couvrir **4.** TECH amortir. **❖ damp down** vt sep [fire] couvrir ; fig [enthusiasm] refroidir ; [crisis] atténuer, rendre moins violent.

damp course [ˈdæmpkɔːs] n couche f d'étanchéité.

dampen [ˈdæmpən] vt **1.** [wet] humecter **2.** [ardour, courage] refroidir.

damper [ˈdæmpəʳ] n fig douche f froide / the news put a damper on the party / his enthusiasm la nouvelle a jeté un froid sur la fête / a refroidi son enthousiasme.

dampness [ˈdæmpnɪs] n humidité f ; [of skin] moiteur f.

damp-proof adj protégé contre l'humidité, hydrofuge.

damp squib n 🇬🇧 inf déception f.

damson [ˈdæmzn] **◆** n [tree] prunier m de Damas ; [fruit] prune f de Damas. **◆** comp [jam, wine] de prunes (de Damas).

dance [dɑːns] **◆** n **1.** danse f **2.** [piece of music] morceau m (de musique) **3.** [art] danse f **4.** [social occasion] soirée f dansante ; [larger] bal m. **◆** comp [class, school, step, studio] de danse **▸ dance band** orchestre m de bal **▸ dance floor** piste f de danse **▸ dance hall** salle f de bal **▸ dance music** a) musique f dansante **b)** [modern] dance f. **◆** vi [person] danser ; fig [leaves, light, words] danser ; [eyes] scintiller **▸ to dance with sb** danser avec qqn **▸ to ask sb to dance** inviter qqn à danser / it's not the type of music you can dance to ce n'est pas le genre de musique sur lequel on peut danser. **◆** vt [waltz, polka] danser.

dancer [ˈdɑːnsəʳ] n danseur m, -euse f.

dancesport [ˈdɑːnspɔːt] n danse f sportive.

dancing [ˈdɑːnsɪŋ] **◆** n danse f **▸ to go dancing** aller danser. **◆** comp [class, teacher] de danse **▸ dancing part-ner** cavalier m, -ère f. **◆** adj [eyes] scintillant.

D and C (abbr of **dilation and curettage**) n MED (dilation f et) curetage m.

dandelion [ˈdændɪlaɪən] n pissenlit m, dent-de-lion f.

dandruff [ˈdændrʌf] n (U) pellicules fpl **▸ dandruff shampoo** shampooing m antipelliculaire.

dandy [ˈdændɪ] (pl dandies) **◆** n dandy m. **◆** adj 🇺🇸 inf extra, épatant.

Dane [deɪn] n Danois m, -e f.

danger [ˈdeɪndʒəʳ] **◆** n danger m / 'danger, keep out!' 'danger, entrée interdite !' **▸ to be out of / in danger** être hors de / en danger **▸ to be in danger of doing sthg** courir le risque or risquer de faire qqch **▸ to be a danger to sb / sthg** être un danger pour qqn / qqch. **◆** comp **▸ danger area** or **zone** zone f dangereuse **▸ to be on the danger list** MED être dans un état critique **▸ to be off the danger list** être hors de danger **▸ danger money** prime f de risque **▸ danger signal a)** RAIL signal m d'arrêt **b)** fig signal m d'alerte or d'alarme.

dangerous [ˈdeɪndʒərəs] adj [job, sport, criminal, animal] dangereux ; MED [illness] dangereux, grave ; [operation] délicat, périlleux ; [assumption] risqué **▸ to be on dangerous ground** fig être sur un terrain glissant **▸ dangerous driving** conduite f dangereuse.

dangerously [ˈdeɪndʒərəslɪ] adv dangereusement ; [ill] gravement / this firm is dangerously close to collapse / bankruptcy cette entreprise est au bord de l'effondrement / la faillite.

dangle [ˈdæŋgl] **◆** vt [legs, arms, hands] laisser pendre ; [object on chain, string] balancer **▸ to dangle sthg in front of sb a)** balancer qqch devant qqn **b)** fig faire miroiter qqch aux yeux de qqn. **◆** vi [legs, arms, hands] pendre ; [keys, earrings] se balancer.

Danish [ˈdeɪnɪʃ] **◆** n **1.** LING danois m **2.** 🇺🇸 [pastry] = Danish pastry. **◆** pl n **▸ the Danish** les Danois mpl. **◆** adj [person, food, Parliament, countryside] danois ; [king] du Danemark ; [ambassador, embassy, representative] danois, du Danemark ; [dictionary, teacher] de danois / the Danish people les Danois mpl.

Danish blue n [cheese] bleu m du Danemark.

Danish pastry n CULIN sorte de pâtisserie fourrée.

dank [dæŋk] adj humide et froid.

Danube [ˈdænjuːb] pr n **▸ the Danube** le Danube.

dapper [ˈdæpəʳ] adj propre sur soi, soigné.

dappled [ˈdæpld] adj [animal] tacheté.

Dardanelles [ˌdɑːdəˈnelz] pl pr n **▸ the Dardanelles** les Dardanelles fpl.

dare [deəʳ] **◆** modal vb [venture] oser **▸ to dare (to) do sthg** oser faire qqch **▸ don't you dare!** je te le déconseille ! / I dare say you're hungry after your journey je suppose que vous êtes affamés après ce voyage / he was most apologetic — I dare say! il s'est confondu en excuses — j'imagine ! **◆** vt **1.** [challenge] **▸ to dare sb to do sthg** défier qqn de faire qqch / I dare you! chiche ! **2.** liter [death, dishonour] braver, défier ; [displeasure] braver. **◆** n [challenge] défi m **▸ to do sthg for a dare** faire qqch par défi.

daredevil [ˈdeə.devl] **◆** n casse-cou m inv. **◆** adj casse-cou.

daren't [deənt] abbr of dare not.

daring [ˈdeərɪŋ] **◆** n [of person] audace f, hardiesse f ; [of feat] hardiesse f. **◆** adj [audacious] audacieux, hardi ; [provocative] audacieux, provocant.

daringly [ˈdeərɪŋlɪ] adv audacieusement, hardiment / a daringly low neckline un décolleté audacieux or provocant.

dark [dɑːk] ◆ n noir *m* / *to see in the dark* voir dans le noir / *before* / *after dark* avant / après la tombée de la nuit ▸ **to keep sb in the dark about sthg** maintenir qqn dans l'ignorance à propos de qqch ▸ **to be in the dark about sthg** être dans l'ignorance à propos de qqch. ◆ adj **1.** [without light - night, room, street] sombre ; *fig* [thoughts] sombre ; [ideas] noir / *it's very dark in here* il fait très sombre ici / *it's getting dark* il commence à faire nuit, la nuit tombe / *to get dark* [sky] s'assombrir / *it won't be dark for another hour yet* il ne fera pas nuit avant une heure / *it's still dark (outside)* il fait encore nuit / *to look on the dark side* voir tout en noir **2.** [colour] foncé ; [dress, suit] sombre ▸ **dark chocolate** chocolat *m* noir **3.** [hair, eyes] foncé ; [skin, complexion] foncé, brun / *to have dark hair* avoir les cheveux bruns, être brun **4.** [hidden, mysterious] mystérieux, secret (secrète) ; [secret] bien gardé ; [hint] mystérieux, énigmatique ▸ **to keep sthg dark** tenir qqch secret **5.** [sinister] noir.

Dark Ages pl n HIST Haut Moyen Âge *m*.

darken ['dɑːkn] ◆ vt [sky] assombrir ; [colour] foncer. ◆ vi [sky, room] s'assombrir, s'obscurcir ; [hair, wood] foncer ; [face] s'assombrir ; [painting] s'obscurcir.

dark glasses pl n lunettes *fpl* noires.

dark horse n **1.** [secretive person] ▸ **to be a dark horse** être très secret **2.** [competitor, horse] participant *m* inconnu ; 🇺🇸 POL candidat *m* surprise.

darkish ['dɑːkɪʃ] adj [colour, sky, wood] plutôt or assez sombre ; [hair, skin] plutôt brun or foncé ; [person] plutôt brun.

darkly ['dɑːklɪ] adv [hint] énigmatiquement ; [say] sur un ton sinistre.

dark matter n ASTRON matière *f* noire.

darkness ['dɑːknɪs] n **1.** [of night, room, street] obscurité *f* **2.** [of hair, skin] couleur *f* foncée.

darkroom ['dɑːkrum] n PHOT chambre *f* noire.

dark-skinned adj à la peau foncée.

darling ['dɑːlɪŋ] ◆ n **1.** [term of affection] chéri *m*, -e *f* / *yes darling?* oui (mon) chéri ? **2.** [favourite - of teacher, parents] favori *m*, -ite *f*, chouchou *m*, -oute *f* ; [- of media] coqueluche *f*. ◆ adj [beloved] chéri ; [delightful] charmant, adorable.

darn [dɑːn] ◆ n **1.** SEW reprise *f* **2.** PHR **I couldn't** or **I don't give a darn** *inf* je m'en fiche. ◆ vt **1.** SEW repriser, raccommoder **2.** *inf* [damn] : *darn it!* bon sang ! / *darn that cat* / *man!* encore ce chat / bonhomme de malheur ! ◆ interj *inf* bon sang. ◆ adj *inf* de malheur. ◆ adv *inf* vachement.

darning ['dɑːnɪŋ] adj [action] reprise *f*, raccommodage *m* ; [items to be darned] linge *m* à repriser or raccommoder.

darning needle n aiguille *f* à repriser.

dart [dɑːt] ◆ n **1.** SPORT fléchette *f* ; [weapon] flèche *f* / *to play darts* jouer aux fléchettes **2.** SEW pince *f* **3.** [sudden movement] ▸ **to make a dart for the door** / **telephone** se précipiter vers la porte / sur le téléphone ▸ **to make a dart at sb** / **sthg** se précipiter sur qqn / qqch. ◆ vt [glance, look - quickly] lancer, jeter ; [- angrily] darder ; [rays] lancer ; [stronger] darder. ◆ vi ▸ **to dart away** or **off** partir en or comme une flèche ▸ **to dart for the door** / **telephone** se précipiter vers la porte / sur le téléphone ▸ **to dart at sthg** / **sb** se précipiter sur qqch / qqn.

dartboard ['dɑːtbɔːd] n cible *f* (*de jeu de fléchettes*).

dash [dæʃ] ◆ n **1.** [quick movement] mouvement *m* précipité ▸ **to make a dash for it** / [rush] se précipiter ▸ [escape] s'enfuir, s'échapper **2.** 🇺🇸 SPORT sprint *m* **3.** [small amount - of water, soda] goutte *f*, trait *m* ; [- of cream, milk] nuage *m* ; [- of lemon juice, vinegar] filet *m* ; [- of salt, pepper] soupçon *m* ; [- of colour, humour] pointe *f* **4.** [punctuation mark] tiret *m* ; [in Morse code] trait *m* **5.** [style] panache *m*

6. = **dashboard.** ◆ vt **1.** [throw] jeter (avec violence) ▸ **to dash sb's hopes** *fig* réduire les espoirs de qqn à néant **2.** *inf* [damn] : *dash it!* *dated* bon sang ! / *I'll be dashed!* ça alors !, oh, la vache ! ◆ vi **1.** [rush] se précipiter / *I must dash* 🇬🇧 je dois filer **2.** [waves] se jeter. ◆ interj 🇬🇧 *dated* ▸ **dash!** bon sang ! ❖ **dash off** ◆ vi partir en flèche. ◆ vt sep [letter, memo] écrire en vitesse ; [drawing] faire en vitesse.

dashboard ['dæʃbɔːd] n AUTO & COMPUT tableau *m* de bord.

dashing ['dæʃɪŋ] adj pimpant, fringant.

DAT [dæt] (**abbr of digital audio tape**) n DAT *m*.

data ['deɪtə] (*pl of datum, usu with sg vb*) ◆ n informations *fpl*, données *fpl* ; COMPUT données *fpl* / *a piece of data* **a)** une donnée, une information **b)** COMPUT une donnée. ◆ comp COMPUT [entry, retrieval, security, input] de données.

data bank n COMPUT banque *f* de données.

database ['deɪtəbeɪs] ◆ n COMPUT base *f* de données / *database management* gestion *f* de base de données / *database management system* système *m* de gestion de base de données. ◆ vt mettre sous forme de base de données.

data capture n COMPUT saisie *f* de données.

dataglove ['deɪtəglʌv] n gant *m* de données.

data processing ◆ n traitement *m* de l'information. ◆ comp [department, service] de traitement des données or de l'information, informatique.

data protection n protection *f* de l'information.

Data Protection Act n loi *f* sur la protection de l'information (*en Grande-Bretagne*).

data transmission n transmission *f* de données.

date [deɪt] ◆ n **1.** [of letter, day of the week] date *f* / *what's the date today?* or *what's today's date?* quelle est la date aujourd'hui ?, on est le combien aujourd'hui ? / *today's date is the 20th January* nous sommes le 20 janvier / *at a later* or *some future date* plus tard, ultérieurement *fml* ▸ **date of birth** date de naissance **2.** [meeting] rendez-vous *m* ▸ **to go out on a date** sortir en compagnie de quelqu'un **3.** 🇺🇸 [person] ami *m*, -e *f* **4.** [fruit] datte *f*. ◆ vt **1.** [write date on - cheque, letter, memo] dater **2.** [attribute date to - building, settlement, etc.] dater **3.** 🇺🇸 [go out with] sortir avec. ◆ vi **1.** [clothes, style] se démoder ; [novel] vieillir **2.** 🇺🇸 [go out on dates] sortir avec des garçons / filles. ❖ **out of date** adj phr : *to be out of date* **a)** [dress, style, concept, slang] être démodé or dépassé **b)** [magazine, newspaper] être vieux **c)** [dictionary] ne pas être à jour or à la page **d)** [passport, season ticket, etc.] être périmé. ❖ **to date** adv phr à ce jour. ❖ **up to date** adj phr : *to be up to date* **a)** [dress, style, person] être à la mode or à la page **b)** [newspaper, magazine] être du jour / de la semaine, etc. **c)** [dictionary] être à la page or à jour **d)** [passport] être valide or valable **e)** [list] être à jour ▸ **to keep up to date with the news** / **scientific developments** se tenir au courant de l'actualité / des progrès de la science ▸ **to keep sb up to date on sthg** tenir qqn au courant de qqch ▸ **to bring sb up to date on sthg** mettre qqn au courant de qqch. ❖ **date back to, date from** vt insep dater de.

Date

En anglais américain parlé, l'article défini n'est pas utilisé devant les dates. On dira : **December ninth** (américain) ou **the ninth** (britannique). Pour les dates en chiffres, les Américains donnent le mois, le jour, l'année (5.17.07), alors que les Britanniques commencent par le jour, puis le mois et l'année (17.5.07).

datebook ['deɪtbʊk] n 🇺🇸 agenda m.

dated ['deɪtɪd] adj [clothes, style] démodé ; [novel, term, expression, concept] vieilli.

dateline ['deɪt‚laɪn] n **1.** PRESS date f de rédaction **2.** = International Date Line.

date rape n viol commis par une personne connue de la victime.

datestamp ['deɪtstæmp] ◆ n tampon m dateur ; [used for cancelling] oblitérateur m, timbre m à date ; [postmark] cachet m de la poste. ◆ vt [book] tamponner, mettre le cachet de la date sur ; [letter] oblitérer.

dating ['deɪtɪŋ] n [of building, artefact, etc.] datation f.

daub [dɔ:b] ◆ n **1.** [of paint] tache f, barbouillage m ; [done on purpose] barbouillage m **2.** pej [painting] croûte f **3.** [for walls] enduit m. ◆ vt enduire ; [with mud] couvrir. ◆ vi pej [paint badly] peinturlurer, barbouiller.

daubing ['dɔ:bɪŋ] n [painting] peinture f ; [bad painting] croûte f ; [graffiti] graffitis mpl / pro-Nazi daubings des graffitis pro-nazis.

daughter ['dɔ:tər] n fille f.

daughter-in-law n bru f, belle-fille f.

daunt [dɔ:nt] vt intimider.

daunting ['dɔ:ntɪŋ] adj [task, question] intimidant.

dauntless ['dɔ:ntlɪs] adj déterminé.

dawdle ['dɔ:dl] vi pej traîner, lambiner, traînasser ▶ **to dawdle over sthg** traînasser or traîner en faisant qqch.

dawdler ['dɔ:dlər] n lambin m, -e f, traînard m, -e f.

dawdling ['dɔ:dlɪŋ] ◆ n : stop all this dawdling! arrête de traînasser ! ◆ adj traînard.

dawn [dɔ:n] ◆ n **1.** lit aube f / at dawn à l'aube ▶ **at the crack of dawn** au point du jour **2.** fig [of civilization, era] aube f ; [of hope] naissance f, éclosion f. ◆ vi **1.** [day] se lever **2.** fig [new era, hope] naître. ◆ **dawn (up)on** vt insep venir à l'esprit de / the truth dawned on or upon him la vérité lui apparut / it suddenly dawned on her that… il lui est soudain apparu que…

dawn chorus n chant m des oiseaux à l'aube.

dawn raid n descente f à l'aube ; [by police] descente f or rafle f à l'aube ; ST. EX attaque f à l'ouverture.

day [deɪ] ◆ n **1.** [period of twenty-four hours] jour m, journée f / it's a nice or fine day c'est une belle journée, il fait beau aujourd'hui / what day is it (today)? quel jour sommes-nous (aujourd'hui) ? / (on) that day ce jour-là / the day after, (on) the next or following day le lendemain, le jour suivant / the day after tomorrow après-demain / the day before, (on) the previous day la veille, le jour d'avant / the day before yesterday avant-hier / in four days or in four days' time dans quatre jours ; [in greetings] ▶ have a nice day! bonne journée ! ▶ day of reckoning jour de vérité ▶ any day now d'un jour à l'autre ▶ day after day or day in day out jour après jour ▶ for days on end or at a time pendant des jours et des jours ▶ from day to day de jour en jour ▶ to live from day to day vivre au jour le jour ▶ from day one dès le premier jour / she's seventy if she's a day elle a au moins soixante-dix ans ▶ it's been one of those days! tu parles d'une journée ! ▶ let's make a day of it passons-y la journée ▶ that'll be the day! inf [it's highly unlikely] il n'y a pas de danger que ça arrive de sitôt ! **2.** [hours of daylight] jour m, journée f ▶ all day (long) toute la journée / to travel during the or by day voyager pendant la journée or de jour / day and night or night and day jour et nuit, nuit et jour **3.** [working hours] journée f / to work a seven-hour day travailler sept heures par jour, faire des journées de sept heures ▶ day off jour m de congé ▶ it's all in a day's work! ça fait partie du travail ! **4.** (often pl) [lifetime, era] époque f / in the days

of King Arthur or in King Arthur's day du temps du roi Arthur ▶ in days to come à l'avenir ▶ in days gone by par le passé ▶ in the good old days dans le temps / the happiest / worst days of my life les plus beaux / les pires jours de ma vie / during the early days of the strike / my childhood au tout début de la grève / de mon enfance / her day will come son heure viendra / he's had his day il a eu son heure. ◆ comp ▶ day labourer journalier m, -ère f ▶ day pass [for skiing] forfait m journalier ▶ day work travail m de jour. ❖ **in this day and age** adv phr de nos jours, aujourd'hui. ❖ **in those days** adv phr à l'époque. ❖ **one day** adv phr un jour. ❖ **one of these days** adv phr un de ces jours. ❖ **some day** adv phr un jour. ❖ **the other day** adv phr l'autre jour. ❖ **these days** adv phr : what are you up to these days? qu'est-ce que tu fais de beau ces temps-ci ? / honestly, teenagers these days! vraiment, les adolescents d'aujourd'hui ! ❖ **to the day** adv phr jour pour jour. ❖ **to this day** adv phr à ce jour, aujourd'hui encore.

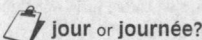

jour or **journée**?

The difference between **jour** and **journée** is less a question of meaning than of conventions of use; indeed in some contexts they are interchangeable: **ce travail m'a pris deux jours** and **ce travail m'a pris deux journées** mean the same.

Most of the time **jour** is an objective, neutral, factual term referring to a day of the week:
Livraison en trois jours maximum. Delivery within three days.
Venez un autre jour. Come another day.
Quel jour sommes-nous ? What day is it?
Il y a vingt ans jour pour jour. Twenty years ago to the day.
Trois fois par jour. Three times a day.

Using **journée** rather than **jour** is more subjective, placing the day in a human perspective and often emphasizing duration:
J'ai de longues journées. I work long hours.
Les travaux prendront quatre bonnes journées. The work will take four full days.
Il n'a pas perdu sa journée ! It's been a good day for him!

Exceptions to the rule of thumb according to which **jour** is more objective and **journée** more subjective occur in set phrases:
Le jour de gloire est arrivé. [from la Marseillaise] The glorious day has dawned.
C'est pas mon jour ! It's not my day!
C'est un jour à marquer d'une pierre blanche ! It's a day to remember!
J'attends les beaux jours pour sortir la table dans le jardin. I'll wait for summer before setting the table up in the garden.

---

day-blind adj héméralope.

daybook ['deɪbʊk] n main f courante, journal m.

dayboy ['deɪbɔɪ] n 🇬🇧 SCH demi-pensionnaire m.

daybreak ['deɪbreɪk] n point m du jour / at daybreak au point du jour.

day care n [for elderly, disabled] service m d'accueil de jour ; [for children] service m de garderie. ❖ **day-care** adj [facilities - for elderly, disabled] d'accueil de jour ; [- for children] de garderie ▸ **day care centre a)** centre d'animation et d'aide sociale **b)** 🇺🇸 [for children] garderie f.

day centre n centre d'animation et d'aide sociale.

day cream n crème f de jour.

daydream ['deɪdriːm] ❖ n rêverie f ; pej rêvasserie f. ❖ vi rêver ; pej rêvasser ▸ **to daydream about sthg** rêver or rêvasser à qqch.

daydreamer ['deɪdriːmə^r] n rêveur m, -euse f.

day for night n CIN nuit f américaine.

daygirl ['deɪɡɜːl] n 🇺🇸 SCH demi-pensionnaire f.

Day-Glo® ['deɪɡləʊ] adj fluorescent.

daylight ['deɪlaɪt] n **1.** [dawn] = daybreak **2.** [light of day] jour m, lumière f du jour.

daylight robbery n inf ▸ **it's daylight robbery** c'est du vol pur et simple.

daylight saving (time) n heure f d'été.

day nursery n garderie f.

day-old adj [chick, baby] d'un jour.

daypack ['deɪpæk] n petit sac à dos m (pour ses affaires de la journée).

day pupil n SCH (élève mf) externe mf.

day release n 🇺🇰 formation f continue en alternance.

day return n 🇺🇰 RAIL aller-retour m valable pour la journée.

day room n salle f commune.

day school n externat m.

day shift n [period worked] service m de jour ; [workers] équipe f de jour / **to work the day shift** travailler de jour, être (dans l'équipe) de jour.

daytime ['deɪtaɪm] ❖ n journée f / **in the daytime** le jour, pendant la journée. ❖ adj de jour ▸ **daytime television** émissions fpl diffusées pendant la journée.

day-to-day adj [life, running of business] quotidien ; [chores, tasks] journalier, quotidien.

day trip n excursion f.

day tripper n excursionniste mf.

daze [deɪz] ❖ n [caused by blow] étourdissement m ; [caused by emotional shock, surprise] ahurissement m ; [caused by medication] abrutissement m ▸ **to be in a daze a)** [because of blow] être étourdi **b)** [because of emotional shock, surprise] être abasourdi or ahuri **c)** [because of medication] être abruti. ❖ vt [subj: blow] étourdir ; [subj: emotional shock, surprise] abasourdir, ahurir ; [subj: medication] abrutir.

dazed [deɪzd] adj [by blow] étourdi ; [by emotional shock, surprise] abasourdi, ahuri ; [by medication] abruti.

dazzle ['dæzl] vt lit & fig éblouir.

dazzling ['dæzlɪŋ] adj éblouissant.

dB (written abbr of decibel) dB.

DBE (abbr of Dame Commander of the Order of the British Empire) n distinction honorifique britannique pour les femmes.

DBS (abbr of direct broadcasting by satellite) n télédiffusion f directe par satellite.

DC n **1.** abbr of direct current **2.** abbr of District of Columbia.

dd. written abbr of delivered.

DD (abbr of Doctor of Divinity) n 🇺🇰 ≃ (titulaire d'un) doctorat en théologie.

D-day n le jour J.

DDS (abbr of Doctor of Dental Surgery) n 🇺🇰 ≃ (titulaire d'un) doctorat en dentisterie.

DDT (abbr of dichlorodiphenyltrichloroethane) n DDT m.

DE written abbr of Delaware.

DEA (abbr of Drug Enforcement Administration) pr n agence américaine de lutte contre la drogue.

deacon ['diːkn] n RELIG diacre m.

deaconess [,diːkə'nes] n RELIG diaconesse f.

deactivate [diː'æktɪ,veɪt] vt désamorcer.

dead [ded] ❖ adj **1.** [not alive - person, animal, plant] mort ; [- flower] fané / dead man mort m / dead woman morte f / the dead woman's husband le mari de la défunte ▸ **to be dead on arrival** être mort or décédé à l'arrivée à l'hôpital / dead or alive mort ou vif / more dead than alive plus mort que vif / dead and buried lit & fig mort et enterré ▸ **to drop (down)** or **to fall down dead** tomber mort ▸ **dead as a doornail** or **a dodo** inf on ne peut plus mort ▸ **over my dead body** inf je ne permettrai pas cela de mon vivant, moi vivant c'est hors de question / I wouldn't be seen dead with him inf plutôt mourir que de me montrer en sa compagnie ▸ **you're dead meat!** tu es un homme mort ! ▸ **dead in the water** mort dans l'œuf **2.** [lacking in sensation - fingers, toes, etc.] engourdi ▸ **to go dead** s'engourdir ▸ **to be dead from the neck up** inf : she's dead from the neck up elle n'a rien dans la tête ▸ **to be dead to the world** inf dormir d'un sommeil de plomb **3.** ELEC [battery] mort, à plat ; TELEC [phone, line] coupé / the line went dead la ligne a été coupée **4.** [complete, exact] : dead silence silence m complet or de mort / on a dead level with sthg exactement au même niveau que qqch / dead cert 🇺🇰 inf [in race, competition] valeur f sûre / to be a dead loss 🇺🇰 inf [person, thing] être complètement nul. ❖ adv **1.** [precisely] : dead ahead tout droit / dead on time 🇺🇰 juste à l'heure / dead on target 🇺🇰 [hit sthg] en plein dans le mille / dead right 🇺🇰 inf tu as entièrement raison **2.** inf [very] super / dead drunk ivre mort **3.** [completely] : the sea was dead calm la mer était parfaitement calme ▸ **to be dead against sthg / sb** être absolument contre qqch / qqn **4.** / **'dead slow'** AUTO 'au pas' **5.** 🅿🅷🆁 to stop dead s'arrêter net ▸ **to stop sb dead** arrêter qqn net. ❖ pl n ▸ **the dead** les morts. ❖ n [depth] : in the dead of winter au cœur de l'hiver / in the or at dead of night au milieu ou au plus profond de la nuit.

dead beat adj inf & fig crevé, mort.

deadbeat ['dedbiːt] n 🇺🇸 inf bon à rien m, bonne à rien f ▸ **a deadbeat dad** un père indigne (qui ne paie pas sa pension alimentaire) ; [tramp] épave f, loque f.

dead duck n inf & fig [plan, proposal - which will fail] désastre m assuré, plan m foireux ; [- which has failed] désastre m, fiasco m / he's a dead duck c'en est fini de lui.

deaden ['dedn] vt [sound] assourdir ; [sense, nerve, hunger pangs] calmer ; [pain] endormir, calmer ; [blow] amortir.

dead end n cul m de sac, voie f sans issue, impasse f / it's a dead end **a)** [job] il n'y a aucune perspective d'avenir **b)** [line of investigation, research] cela ne mènera or conduira à rien / to come to or to reach a dead end fig aboutir à une impasse. ❖ **dead-end** adj [street] sans issue ▸ **a dead-end job** fig un travail qui n'offre aucune perspective d'avenir.

deadening ['dednɪŋ] adj [boredom, task] abrutissant.

deadhead ['dedhed] ❖ n **1.** inf [dull person] nullité f **2.** [person using free ticket - in theatre] spectateur m, -trice f ayant un billet de faveur ; [- on train] voyageur m, -euse f muni(e) d'un billet gratuit **3.** 🇺🇸 [empty vehicle] train, avion, camion, etc. circulant à vide. ❖ vt [flowers] enlever les fleurs fanées de. ❖ vi 🇺🇸 [train] circuler à vide.

dead heat n course dont les vainqueurs sont déclarés ex aequo ; [horse race] dead-heat m.

dead letter n **1.** [letter that cannot be delivered] lettre f non distribuée, (lettre f passée au) rebut m **2.** [law, rule] loi f or règle f caduque ou tombée en désuétude.

deadline ['dedlaɪn] n [day] date f limite ; [hour] heure f limite ▸ **to meet / to miss a deadline** respecter / laisser passer une date limite / I'm working to a deadline j'ai un délai à respecter.

deadlock ['dedlɒk] n impasse f.

deadlocked ['dedlɒkt] adj : to be deadlocked être dans une impasse.

deadly ['dedlɪ] (compar **deadlier,** superl **deadliest**) ◆ adj **1.** [lethal - poison, blow] mortel ; [- snake] au venin mortel ; [- weapon] meurtrier ; fig [hatred] mortel ; [silence, pallor] de mort, mortel / they are deadly enemies fig ce sont des ennemis mortels ▸ **the seven deadly sins** les sept péchés capitaux **2.** [precise] : his aim is deadly il a un tir excellent / with deadly accuracy avec une extrême précision **3.** [extreme] : in deadly earnest [say] avec le plus grand sérieux **4.** inf [boring] mortel, barbant. ◆ adv extrêmement, terriblement.

deadly nightshade n BOT belladone f.

deadpan ['dedpæn] ◆ adj [face, expression] impassible ; [humour] pince-sans-rire (inv). ◆ adv d'un air impassible.

Dead Sea pr n ▸ **the Dead Sea** la mer Morte.

dead tree edition n inf édition f papier, édition f imprimée.

dead weight n lit & fig poids m mort.

dead wood 🇬🇧, **deadwood** 🇺🇸 ['dedwʊd] n [trees, branches] bois m mort ; fig [people] personnel m inutile.

deaf [def] ◆ adj sourd ▸ **to turn a deaf ear to sthg / sb** fig faire la sourde oreille à qqch / qqn / our complaints fell on deaf ears fig nos protestations n'ont pas été entendues ▸ **(as) deaf as a post** sourd comme un pot. ◆ pl n ▸ **the deaf** les sourds mpl.

deaf-and-dumb ◆ adj sourd-muet (attention : le terme « deaf-and-dumb » est considéré comme injurieux). ◆ n sourd-muet m, sourde-muette f.

deafen ['defn] vt lit rendre sourd ; fig casser les oreilles à.

deafening ['defnɪŋ] adj [music, noise, roar] assourdissant ; [applause] retentissant.

deafeningly ['defnɪŋlɪ] adv ▸ **deafeningly loud** assourdissant.

deaf-mute = deaf-and-dumb.

deafness ['defnɪs] n surdité f.

deal [di:l] (pt & pp dealt [delt]) ◆ n **1.** [agreement] affaire f, marché m ; ST. EX opération f, transaction f / business deal affaire, marché, transaction ▸ **to do** or **to make a deal with sb** conclure une affaire ou un marché avec qqn / the deal is off l'affaire est annulée, le marché est rompu / it's a deal! marché conclu ! ▸ **to get a good deal** faire une bonne affaire **2.** CARDS donne f, distribution f / it's my deal c'est à moi de donner **3.** [quantity] : a (good) deal of or a great deal of [money, time, etc.] beaucoup de / he thinks a good / great deal of her il l'estime beaucoup / énormément / I didn't enjoy it a great deal je n'ai pas trop or pas tellement aimé ▸ **big deal!** inf & iro tu parles ! / no big deal inf ça ne fait rien / he made a big deal out of it inf il en a fait tout un plat ou tout un cinéma / what's the big deal? inf et alors ?, et puis quoi ? ◆ vt **1.** CARDS donner, distribuer **2.** [strike] ▸ **to deal sb a blow** assener un coup à qqn ▸ **to deal sthg a blow** or **to deal a blow to sthg** fig porter un coup à qqch **3.** [drugs] revendre. ◆ vi **1.** CARDS distribuer les cartes **2.** COMM négocier, traiter / to deal on the Stock Exchange faire des opérations or des transac-

tions en Bourse / to deal in death / human misery fig être un marchand de mort / de misère humaine **3.** [in drugs] revendre de la drogue. ◆ **deal out** vt sep [cards, gifts] donner, distribuer ; [justice] rendre ; [punishment] distribuer. ◆ **deal with** vt insep **1.** [handle - problem, situation, query, complaint] traiter ; [- customer, member of the public] traiter avec ; [- difficult situation, child] s'occuper de / a difficult child to deal with un enfant difficile / I can't deal with all the work I've got je ne me sors pas de tout le travail que j'ai / the culprits were dealt with severely les coupables ont été sévèrement punis **2.** [do business with] traiter or négocier avec **3.** [be concerned with] traiter de / in my lecture, I shall deal with... dans mon cours, je traiterai de...

dealbreaker ['di:lbreɪkər] n élément m rédhibitoire (pour l'achat d'un produit).

dealer ['di:lər] n **1.** COMM marchand m, -e f, négociant m, -e f ; ST. EX marchand m, -e f de titres ; AUTO concessionnaire mf **2.** [in drugs] dealer m **3.** CARDS donneur m, -euse f.

dealership ['di:ləʃɪp] n AUTO & COMM concession f.

dealing ['di:lɪŋ] n **1.** (U) ST. EX opérations fpl, transactions fpl ; [trading] commerce m **2.** (U) [of cards] donne f, distribution f **3.** ▸ **dealings a)** [business] affaires fpl, transactions fpl **b)** [personal] relations fpl ▸ **to have dealings with sb a)** [in business] traiter avec qqn, avoir affaire à qqn **b)** [personal] avoir affaire à qqn **4.** [in drugs] trafic m de drogue.

dealt [delt] pt & pp ⟶ **deal.**

dean [di:n] n UNIV & RELIG doyen m, -enne f.

Dean's List n 🇺🇸 tableau d'honneur dans les universités américaines.

dear [dɪər] ◆ adj **1.** [loved] cher ; [precious] cher, précieux ; [appealing] adorable, charmant **2.** [in letter] : Dear Sir Monsieur / Dear Sir or Madam Madame, Monsieur / Dear Mrs Baker a) Madame b) [less formal] Chère Madame c) [informal] Chère Madame Baker / Dear Mum and Dad Chers Maman et Papa / My dear Clare Ma chère Clare / Dearest Richard Très cher Richard **3.** [expensive - item, shop] cher ; [- price] haut, élevé. ◆ interj ▸ **dear! dear!** or **dear me!** or **oh dear! a)** [surprise] oh mon Dieu ! **b)** [regret] oh là là ! ◆ n : my dear a) [to child, spouse, lover] mon chéri, ma chérie b) [to friend] mon cher, ma chère. ◆ adv [sell, pay, cost] cher (adv).

dearie ['dɪərɪ] inf ◆ n chéri m, -e f. ◆ interj ▸ **(oh) dearie me!** oh mon Dieu !

dearly ['dɪəlɪ] adv **1.** [very much] beaucoup, énormément **2.** [at high cost] ▸ **to pay dearly for sthg** payer cher qqch.

dearth [dɜ:θ] n pénurie f.

deary ['dɪərɪ] inf = dearie (noun).

death [deθ] n mort f ; LAW décès m / to freeze / to starve to death mourir de froid / de faim / to be beaten to death être battu à mort / to be burnt to death mourir brûlé / to bleed to death perdre tout son sang ▸ **to fight to the death** se battre à mort ▸ **to sentence / to put sb to death** condamner / mettre qqn à mort ▸ **to be sick** or **tired to death of** inf en avoir ras le bol de / to be bored to death inf s'ennuyer à mourir / to be worried / scared to death inf être mort d'inquiétude / de frousse.

deathbed ['deθbed] ◆ n lit m de mort / on one's deathbed sur son lit de mort. ◆ adj [confession] fait à l'article de la mort ; [repentance] exprimé à l'article de la mort.

deathblow ['deθbləʊ] n fig coup m fatal or mortel ▸ **to be the deathblow for sthg** porter un coup fatal or mortel à qqch.

death camp n camp m de la mort.

death cell n cellule f de condamné à mort.

death certificate n acte m or certificat m de décès.

death duty n UK droits mpl de succession.

death knell n glas m ▶ **to sound the death knell for** or **of sthg** fig sonner le glas de qqch.

deathly ['deθlɪ] ◆ adj [silence, pallor] de mort, mortel. ◆ adv : *deathly pale* pâle comme la mort / *deathly cold* glacial.

death penalty n peine f de mort, peine f capitale.

death rate n taux m de mortalité.

death row n US quartier m des condamnés à mort.

death sentence n condamnation f à mort.

death squad n escadron m de la mort.

death tax US = **death duty.**

death throes [-ˌrəʊz] pl n agonie f ; [painful] affres fpl de la mort ; fig agonie f ▶ **to be in one's death throes a)** agoniser, être agonisant **b)** [suffering] connaître les affres de la mort ▶ **to be in its death throes** fig [project, business, etc.] agoniser, être agonisant.

death toll n nombre m de morts.

death trap n véhicule ou endroit extrêmement dangereux.

Death Valley pr n la Vallée de la Mort.

death warrant n ordre m d'exécution ▶ **to sign one's own death warrant** fig signer son propre arrêt de mort.

deathwatch beetle n grande or grosse vrillette f, horloger m de la mort.

death wish n PSYCHOL désir m de mort.

deb [deb] inf = **debutante.**

debacle [deɪ'bɑːkl] n débâcle f.

debar [diː'bɑːr] (pt & pp **debarred,** cont **debarring**) vt interdire à ▶ **to debar sb from sthg / doing sthg** interdire qqch à qqn / à qqn de faire qqch.

debase [dɪ'beɪs] vt [degrade - person, sport] avilir, abaisser ; [- quality of object] dégrader, altérer ; [- currency] altérer ; fig dévaloriser.

debasement [dɪ'beɪsmənt] n [of person, sport] avilisse-ment m, abaissement m ; [of quality of object] dégradation f, altération f ; [of currency] altération f ; fig dévalorisation f.

debatable [dɪ'beɪtəbl] adj discutable, contestable.

debate [dɪ'beɪt] ◆ vt [one person] se demander ; [two or more people] débattre, discuter. ◆ vi discuter ▶ **to debate (with o.s.) whether to do sthg or not** se demander si on doit faire qqch. ◆ n [gen] discussion f ; [organized] débat m ▶ **to have** or **to hold a debate about** or **on sthg** tenir un débat or avoir une discussion sur à propos de qqch.

debating [dɪ'beɪtɪŋ] ◆ n art m du débat. ◆ comp ▶ **debating society** société f de débats contradictoires.

debauched [dɪ'bɔːtʃt] adj débauché.

debauchery [dɪ'bɔːtʃərɪ] n débauche f.

debenture [dɪ'bentʃər] n FIN obligation f.

debilitate [dɪ'bɪlɪteɪt] vt débiliter.

debilitating [dɪ'bɪlɪteɪtɪŋ] adj [illness] débilitant ; [cli-mate] anémiant.

debility [dɪ'bɪlətɪ] n débilité f.

debit ['debɪt] ◆ n FIN débit m / *your account is in debit* UK votre compte est déficitaire or débiteur. ◆ comp FIN ▶ **debit balance** solde m débiteur ▶ **debit entry** écri-ture f au débit ▶ **debit note** note f de débit ▶ **debit side** débit m / *on the debit side, it means we won't see her* fig l'inconvénient, c'est que nous ne la verrons pas. ◆ vt FIN [account] débiter ; [person] porter au débit de qqn / *to debit £50 from sb's account* or *to debit sb's account with £50* débiter 50 livres du compte de qqn, débiter le compte de qqn de 50 livres.

debit card n carte f de paiement à débit immédiat.

debonair [ˌdebə'neər] adj d'une élégance nonchalante.

debrief [ˌdiː'briːf] vt faire faire un compte rendu verbal de mission à, débriefer.

debriefing [ˌdiː'briːfɪŋ] n compte rendu m verbal de mission.

debris ['deɪbriː] n (U) débris mpl.

debt [det] ◆ n [gen] dette f ; ADMIN créance f ▶ **to be in debt** or **to have debts** avoir des dettes, être endetté ▶ **to get** or **to run into debt** s'endetter ▶ **to get out of debt** s'ac-quitter de ses dettes ▶ **to pay one's debts** régler ses dettes ▶ **to be in debt to sb a)** être endetté auprès de qqn **b)** fig avoir une dette envers qqn, être redevable à qqn ▶ **bad debt** mauvaise créance ▶ **outstanding debt** dette or créance à recouvrer. ◆ comp [rescheduling, servicing] de la dette ▶ **debt burden** surendettement m, fardeau m de la dette ▶ **debt collector** agent m de recouvrement.

debtor ['detər] n débiteur m, -trice f.

debug [ˌdiː'bʌg] (pt & pp **debugged,** cont **debugging**) vt **1.** COMPUT [program] déboguer ; [machine] mettre au point **2.** [remove hidden microphones from] débarrasser des micros (cachés) **3.** [remove insects from] débarrasser des insectes, désinsectiser.

debunk [ˌdiː'bʌŋk] vt inf [ridicule] tourner en ridicule ; [show to be false] discréditer.

debut ['deɪbjuː] (pt & pp **debut'd**) ◆ n début m. ◆ vi débuter.

debutante ['debjʊtɑːnt] n débutante f.

Dec. (written abbr of **December**) déc.

decade ['dekeɪd] n **1.** [ten years] décennie f **2.** RELIG dizaine f.

⚠ The word **décade** is rarely used in French, and its most usual meaning is a period of ten days. A decade is **une décennie**.

decadence ['dekədəns] n décadence f.

decadent ['dekədənt] adj décadent.

decaf, decaff ['diːkæf] n inf [coffee] déca m.

decaffeinated [dɪ'kæfɪneɪtɪd] adj décaféiné.

decal ['diːkæl] n US inf décalcomanie f.

decamp [dɪ'kæmp] vi **1.** MIL lever le camp **2.** inf [ab-scond] décamper, ficher le camp.

decant [dɪ'kænt] vt décanter.

decanter [dɪ'kæntər] n carafe f.

decapitate [dɪ'kæpɪteɪt] vt décapiter.

decathlete [dɪ'kæθliːt] n décathlonien m, -enne f.

decathlon [dɪ'kæθlɒn] n décathlon m.

decay [dɪ'keɪ] ◆ vi **1.** [rot - food, wood, flowers] pourrir ; [- meat] s'avarier, pourrir ; [- corpse] se décomposer ; [- tooth] se carier ; [- building] se délabrer ; [- stone] s'effriter, se désa-gréger ; fig [beauty, civilization, faculties] décliner **2.** PHYS dépérir, se dégrader, se désintégrer. ◆ vt [wood] pourrir ; [stone] désagréger ; [tooth] carier. ◆ n **1.** [of food, wood, flowers] pourrissement m ; [of corpse] décomposition f ; [of building] délabrement m ; [of stone] effritement m, désa-grégation f ; fig [of beauty, faculties] délabrement m ; [of civilization] déclin m ▶ **to fall into decay** lit & fig se déla-brer / moral decay déchéance f morale ▶ **tooth decay** (U) caries fpl **2.** PHYS désintégration f, dégradation f.

deceased [dɪ'siːst] (pl **deceased**) ◆ adj décédé, dé-funt. ◆ n ▶ **the deceased** le défunt, la défunte.

deceit [dɪ'siːt] n **1.** [quality] duplicité f **2.** [trick] super-cherie f, tromperie f **3.** LAW fraude f / *by deceit* fraudu-leusement.

deceitful [dɪ'si:tfʊl] adj trompeur ; [behaviour] trompeur, sournois.

deceitfully [dɪ'si:tfʊlɪ] adv trompeusement, avec duplicité.

deceive [dɪ'si:v] vt tromper ▸ **to deceive sb into doing sthg** amener qqn à faire qqch en le trompant ▸ **to deceive o.s.** se mentir à soi-même.

> ⚠ **Décevoir** means to disappoint, not to deceive.

decelerate [,di:'seləreɪt] vi & vt ralentir.

December [dɪ'sembər] n décembre. See also **February**.

decency ['di:snsɪ] (pl **decencies**) n décence f ▸ **to have the (common) decency to do sthg** avoir la décence de faire qqch.

decent ['di:snt] adj **1.** [proper, morally correct] décent, convenable **2.** [satisfactory, reasonable - housing, wage] décent, convenable ; [- price] convenable, raisonnable **3.** inf [kind, good] bien, sympa.

decently ['di:sntlɪ] adv **1.** [properly] décemment, convenablement **2.** [reasonably] : *the job pays decently* le travail paie raisonnablement bien.

decentralization [di:,sentrəlaɪ'zeɪʃn] n décentralisation f.

decentralize [,di:'sentrəlaɪz] vt décentraliser.

decent-sized adj [house, room] de bonnes dimensions.

deception [dɪ'sepʃn] n **1.** [act of deceiving] tromperie f, duperie f / *by deception* LAW en usant de tromperie **2.** [trick] subterfuge m, tromperie f **3.** [state of being deceived] duperie f.

> ⚠ **Déception** means disappointment, not deception.

deceptive [dɪ'septɪv] adj trompeur.

deceptively [dɪ'septɪvlɪ] adv : *it looks deceptively easy / near* cela donne l'illusion d'être facile / tout près, on a l'impression que c'est facile / tout près.

decibel ['desɪbel] n décibel m.

decide [dɪ'saɪd] ◆ vt **1.** [resolve] décider ▸ **to decide to do sthg** décider de faire qqch **2.** [determine - outcome, sb's fate, career] décider de, déterminer ; [- person] décider **3.** [settle - debate, war] décider de l'issue de. ◆ vi **1.** [make up one's mind] décider, se décider / *you decide* c'est toi qui décides ▸ **to decide against / in favour of doing sthg** décider de ne pas / de faire qqch ▸ **to decide in favour of sb / sthg** LAW décider en faveur de qqn / qqch ▸ **to decide against sb / sthg** LAW décider contre qqn / qqch **2.** [determine] : *but circumstances decided otherwise* mais les circonstances en ont décidé autrement. ◆ **decide (up)on** vt insep décider de, se décider pour.

decided [dɪ'saɪdɪd] adj **1.** [distinct - improvement, difference] net, incontestable ; [- success] éclatant **2.** [resolute - person, look] décidé, résolu ; [- opinion, stance] ferme ; [- effort] résolu ; [- refusal] ferme, catégorique.

decidedly [dɪ'saɪdɪdlɪ] adv **1.** [distinctly - better, different] vraiment **2.** [resolutely] résolument, fermement.

decider [dɪ'saɪdər] n [goal] but m décisif ; [point] point m décisif ; [match] match m décisif, rencontre f décisive ; [factor] facteur m décisif.

deciding [dɪ'saɪdɪŋ] adj décisif, déterminant / *the chairperson has the deciding vote* la voix du président est prépondérante.

deciduous [dɪ'sɪdjʊəs] adj [tree] à feuilles caduques ; [leaves, antlers] caduc.

decilitre 🇬🇧, **deciliter** 🇺🇸 ['desɪ,li:tər] n décilitre m.

decimal ['desɪml] ◆ adj décimal. ◆ n chiffre m décimal.

decimal point n virgule f.

decimate ['desɪmeɪt] vt décimer.

decipher [dɪ'saɪfər] vt [code, handwriting] déchiffrer.

decision [dɪ'sɪʒn] n **1.** décision f ▸ **to make** or **to take a decision a)** prendre une décision, se décider **b)** LAW & ADMIN prendre une décision ▸ **to come to** or **to arrive at** or **to reach a decision** parvenir à une décision / *it's your decision* c'est toi qui décides **2.** fml [decisiveness] décision f, résolution f, fermeté f.

decision-maker n décideur m, -euse f, décisionnaire mf.

decision-making n prise f de décision.

decisive [dɪ'saɪsɪv] adj **1.** [manner, person] décidé, résolu **2.** [factor, argument] décisif, déterminant.

decisively [dɪ'saɪsɪvlɪ] adv **1.** [resolutely] résolument, sans hésitation **2.** [conclusively] de manière décisive.

decisiveness [dɪ'saɪsɪvnɪs] n **1.** [of person] décision f **2.** [of battle] caractère m décisif or déterminant.

deck [dek] ◆ n **1.** NAUT pont m ▸ **on deck** sur le pont ▸ **below deck** or **decks** sous le pont **2.** [of plane, bus] étage m ▸ **top** or **upper deck** [of bus] impériale f **3.** 🇺🇸 CARDS jeu m de cartes **4.** [in hi-fi system] platine f **5.** 🇺🇸 [of house] ponton m. ◆ comp NAUT [officer, cabin, crane] de pont. ◆ vt = **deck out**. ◆ **deck out** vt sep parer, orner / *to deck o.s. out in one's best clothes* se mettre sur son trente et un.

deckchair ['dektʃeər] n chaise f longue, transat m ▸ **deckchair attendant a)** [male] garçon m de plage **b)** [female] fille f de plage.

-decker ['dekər] suffix : *double-decker bus* bus m à impériale / *double-decker sandwich* sandwich m double.

deckhand ['dekhænd] n matelot m.

decking ['dekɪŋ] n terrasse f en bois ; [duckboards] caillebotis m.

declaim [dɪ'kleɪm] ◆ vi déclamer ▸ **to declaim against sthg** récriminer or se récrier contre qqch. ◆ vt déclamer.

declamatory [dɪ'klæmətrɪ] adj [style] déclamatoire.

declaration [,deklə'reɪʃn] n **1.** [gen] déclaration f **2.** CARDS annonce f.

Declaration of Independence n ▸ **the Declaration of Independence** 🇺🇸 HIST la Déclaration d'indépendance (américaine).

> **The Declaration of Independence**
>
> Document rédigé par Thomas Jefferson et proclamant, le 4 juillet 1776, l'indépendance des 13 colonies de la Nouvelle-Angleterre. Cette déclaration est considérée comme l'acte de naissance des États-Unis d'Amérique.

declare [dɪ'kleər] ◆ vt **1.** [proclaim - independence, war, etc.] déclarer / *have you anything to declare?* [at customs] avez-vous quelque chose à déclarer ? **2.** [announce] déclarer ▸ **to declare o.s. a)** [proclaim one's love] se déclarer **b)** POL se présenter, présenter sa candidature **3.** CARDS ▸ **to declare one's hand** annoncer son jeu. ◆ vi **1.** ▸ **to declare for / against** faire une déclaration en faveur de / contre **2.** CARDS faire l'annonce, annoncer ; [in cricket] déclarer la tournée terminée *(avant sa fin normale)*.

declared [dɪ'kleəd] adj [intention, opponent] déclaré, ouvert.

declassify [ˌdiː'klæsɪfaɪ] (pt & pp **declassified**) vt [information] déclasser.

declension [dɪ'klenʃn] n GRAM déclinaison f.

decline [dɪ'klaɪn] ◆ n [decrease - in prices, standards, crime, profits] baisse f; fig [of civilization] déclin m ▶ **to be in decline** être en déclin ▶ **to be on the decline a)** [prices, sales] être en baisse **b)** [civilization, influence] être sur le déclin. ◆ vt **1.** [refuse - invitation, honour, offer of help] décliner, refuser; [- food, drink] refuser; [- responsibility] décliner ▶ **to decline to do sthg** refuser de faire qqch **2.** GRAM décliner. ◆ vi **1.** [decrease, diminish - empire, health] décliner; [- prices, sales, population] baisser, être en baisse, diminuer; [- influence, enthusiasm, fame] baisser, diminuer / to decline in importance / value / significance perdre de son importance / de sa valeur / de sa signification **2.** [refuse] refuser **3.** [slope downwards] être en pente, descendre **4.** GRAM se décliner.

declining [dɪ'klaɪnɪŋ] adj [health, industry, market] sur le déclin.

declutch [ˌdiː'klʌtʃ] vi AUTO débrayer.

declutter [diː'klʌtər] vt [room, computer, one's life] désencombrer.

decode [ˌdiː'kəʊd] vt décoder, déchiffrer; COMPUT & TV décoder.

decoder [ˌdiː'kəʊdər] n décodeur m.

decommission [ˌdiːkə'mɪʃn] vt **1.** [shut down - nuclear power station] déclasser **2.** MIL [remove from active service - warship, aircraft, weapon] mettre hors service.

decompose [ˌdiːkəm'pəʊz] ◆ vi se décomposer. ◆ vt CHEM & PHYS décomposer.

decomposition [ˌdiːkɒmpə'zɪʃn] n [gen & CHEM] & PHYS décomposition f.

decompress [ˌdiːkəm'pres] vt [gas, air] décomprimer; [diver] faire passer en chambre de décompression.

decompression [ˌdiːkəm'preʃn] n décompression f.

decompression chamber n chambre f de décompression.

decompression sickness n maladie f des caissons.

decongestant [ˌdiːkən'dʒestənt] ◆ n MED décongestif m. ◆ adj MED décongestif.

deconstruct [ˌdiːkən'strʌkt] vt déconstruire.

deconstruction [ˌdiːkən'strʌkʃn] n déconstruction f.

decontaminate [ˌdiːkən'tæmɪneɪt] vt décontaminer.

decontamination ['diːkənˌtæmɪ'neɪʃn] n décontamination f.

decontrol [ˌdiːkən'trəʊl] ◆ vt lever le contrôle gouvernemental sur ▶ **to decontrol prices** libérer les prix. ◆ n [of prices] libération f.

decor ['deɪkɔːr] n décor m.

decorate ['dekəreɪt] ◆ vt **1.** [house, room - paint] peindre; [- wallpaper] tapisser, décorer **2.** [dress, hat] garnir, orner; [cake, tree, street] décorer **3.** [give medal to] décorer, médailler. ◆ vi [paint] peindre; [wallpaper] tapisser.

decorating ['dekəreɪtɪŋ] n [of house, room] décoration f ▶ **painting and decorating** 🇬🇧 peinture f et décoration.

decoration [ˌdekə'reɪʃn] n **1.** [action - of house, street, cake, tree] décoration f; [- of dress, hat] ornementation f **2.** [ornament - for house, street, cake, tree] décoration f; [- for dress, hat] garniture f, ornements mpl ▶ **Christmas decorations** décorations de Noël **3.** [medal] décoration f, médaille f.

decorative ['dekərətɪv] adj décoratif, ornemental.

decorator ['dekəreɪtər] n décorateur m, -trice f.

decorous ['dekərəs] adj fml [behaviour] bienséant, séant, convenable; [person] convenable, comme il faut.

decorum [dɪ'kɔːrəm] n bienséance f, décorum m.

decoy n ['diːkɔɪ] **1.** [for catching birds - live bird] appeau m, chanterelle f; [- artificial device] leurre m **2.** fig [person] appât m; [message, tactic] piège m.

decrease ◆ vi [dɪ'kriːs] [number, enthusiasm, population, speed] décroître, diminuer; [value, price] diminuer, baisser; [in knitting] diminuer, faire des diminutions. ◆ vt [dɪ'kriːs] réduire, diminuer. ◆ n ['diːkriːs] [in size] réduction f, diminution f; [in popularity] baisse f; [in price] réduction f, baisse f / a decrease in numbers une baisse des effectifs ▶ **to be on the decrease** être en diminution or en baisse.

decreasing [diː'kriːsɪŋ] adj [amount, energy, population] décroissant; [price, value, popularity] en baisse.

decreasingly [diː'kriːsɪŋli] adv de moins en moins.

decree [dɪ'kriː] ◆ n POL décret m, arrêté m; RELIG décret m; 🇺🇸 LAW jugement m, arrêt m / by royal decree par décret du roi / de la reine. ◆ vt décréter; POL décréter, arrêter; RELIG décréter; LAW ordonner (par jugement).

decrepit [dɪ'krepɪt] adj [building, furniture] délabré; [person, animal] décrépit.

decrepitude [dɪ'krepɪtjuːd] n décrépitude f.

decriminalize [diː'krɪmɪnəˌlaɪz] vt dépénaliser.

decrypt [diː'krɪpt] vt décrypter.

dedicate ['dedɪkeɪt] vt **1.** [devote] consacrer ▶ **to dedicate o.s. to sb / sthg** se consacrer à qqn / qqch **2.** [book, song, etc.] dédier **3.** [consecrate - church, shrine] consacrer **4.** 🇺🇸 [open for public use] inaugurer.

dedicated ['dedɪkeɪtɪd] adj **1.** [devoted] dévoué / to be dedicated to one's work être dévoué à son travail / he is dedicated il se donne à fond **2.** COMPUT dédié.

dedication [ˌdedɪ'keɪʃn] n **1.** [devotion] dévouement m **2.** [in book, on photograph, etc.] dédicace f **3.** [of church, shrine] consécration f.

deduce [dɪ'djuːs] vt déduire ▶ **to deduce sthg from sthg** déduire qqch de qqch.

deduct [dɪ'dʌkt] vt déduire, retrancher; [tax] prélever / to deduct £10 from the price déduire or retrancher 10 livres du prix.

deductible [dɪ'dʌktəbl] adj déductible.

deduction [dɪ'dʌkʃn] n **1.** [inference] déduction f / by (a process of) deduction par déduction **2.** [subtraction] déduction f ▶ **tax deductions** prélèvements mpl fiscaux.

deductive [dɪ'dʌktɪv] adj déductif.

deed [diːd] ◆ n **1.** [action] action f / to do one's good deed for the day faire sa bonne action or sa BA de la journée **2.** LAW acte m notarié. ◆ vt 🇺🇸 LAW transférer par acte notarié.

deed poll n LAW contrat m unilatéral / to change one's name by deed poll LAW changer de nom par contrat unilatéral, changer de nom officiellement.

deejay ['diːdʒeɪ] n inf DJ mf.

deem [diːm] vt fml juger, considérer, estimer.

de-emphasize [diː'emfəsaɪz] vt [need, claim, feature] moins insister sur, se montrer moins insistant sur.

deep [diːp] ◆ adj **1.** [going far down - water, hole, wound, etc.] profond / the water / hole is five metres deep l'eau / le trou a cinq mètres de profondeur / to be in a deep sleep être profondément endormi ▶ **the deep end** [of swimming pool] le grand bain ▶ **to be thrown in at the deep end** fig être mis dans le bain tout de suite **2.** [going far back - forest, cupboard, serve] profond / deep in the forest au (fin) fond de la forêt ▶ **deep space** profondeurs fpl de l'espace **3.** [strong - feelings] profond **4.** [profound - thinker] profond **5.** [mysterious, difficult to understand - book] profond **6.** [dark - colour] profond **7.** [low - sound, note] grave ; [- voice] grave, profond. ◆ adv profondément / *they went deep into the forest* ils se sont enfoncés dans la forêt / *he looked deep into her eyes* **a)** [romantically] il a plongé ses yeux dans les siens **b)** [probingly] il l'a regardée intensément dans les yeux / *deep down she knew she was right* au fond or dans son for intérieur elle savait qu'elle avait raison / *he thrust his hands deep into his pockets* il plongea les mains au fond de ses poches. ◆ n *liter* **1.** [ocean] ▸ **the deep** l'océan *m* **2.** [depth] : *in the deep of winter* au plus profond or au cœur de l'hiver.

-deep in comp : *she was knee / waist-deep in water* elle avait de l'eau jusqu'aux genoux / jusqu'à la taille / *the water is only ankle-deep* l'eau ne monte or n'arrive qu'aux chevilles.

deep-dish pie n US CULIN tourte f.

deepen ['di:pn] ◆ vt [hole, river bed, knowledge] approfondir ; [mystery] épaissir ; [love, friendship] faire grandir, intensifier ; [sound, voice] rendre plus grave ; [colour] rendre plus profond, intensifier. ◆ vi [sea, river] devenir plus profond ; [silence, mystery] s'épaissir ; [crisis] s'aggraver, s'intensifier ; [knowledge] s'approfondir ; [love, friendship] s'intensifier, grandir ; [colour] devenir plus profond, s'intensifier ; [sound] devenir plus grave.

deepening ['di:pnɪŋ] ◆ adj [silence, shadows, emotion] de plus en plus profond ; [crisis] qui s'aggrave or s'intensifie ; [love, friendship] de plus en plus profond. ◆ n [of hole, channel] approfondissement *m* ; [of silence, love] intensification *f*.

deep-fat fryer n friteuse f.

deep-fat frying n cuisson f en bain de friture.

deep freeze n [in home, shop] congélateur *m* ; [industrial] surgélateur *m*. ◆◆ **deep-freeze** vt [at home] congeler ; [industrially] surgeler.

deep-fried adj frit.

deep-fry vt faire frire.

deep-fryer = deep-fat fryer.

deep-heat treatment n MED thermothérapie f.

deeply ['di:plɪ] adv **1.** [dig, breathe, sleep, admire, regret, think] profondément ; [drink] à grands traits **2.** [offended, relieved, grateful, religious] profondément, extrêmement.

deepness ['di:pnɪs] n [of ocean, voice, writer, remark] profondeur f ; [of note, sound] gravité f.

deep-pan pizza n CULIN pizza f à pâte épaisse.

deep-rooted adj [tree] dont les racines sont profondes ; *fig* [ideas, belief, prejudice] profondément ancré or enraciné ; [feeling] profond.

deep-sea adj [creatures, exploration] des grands fonds ▸ **deep-sea diver** plongeur *m* sous-marin, plongeuse f sous-marine ▸ **deep-sea diving** plongée f sous-marine ▸ **deep-sea fisherman** pêcheur *m* hauturier or en haute mer ▸ **deep-sea fishing** pêche f hauturière or en haute mer.

deep-seated [-'si:tɪd] adj [sorrow, dislike] profond ; [idea, belief, complex, prejudice] profondément ancré or enraciné.

deep-set adj enfoncé.

deep-six vt US *inf* [throw away] balancer.

Deep South pr n ▸ **the Deep South** [in the US] l'extrême Sud conservateur (Alabama, Floride, Géorgie, Louisiane, Mississippi, Caroline du Sud, partie orientale du Texas).

deep throat n informateur *m*, indicateur *m*.

deep vein thrombosis n thrombose f veineuse profonde.

deep web n INTERNET web *m* caché.

deer [dɪər] (*pl* deer) ◆ n cerf *m*, biche f. ◆ comp [hunter, park] de cerf or cerfs.

deerstalker ['dɪə,stɔːkər] n **1.** [hunter] chasseur *m*, -euse f de cerf **2.** [hat] chapeau *m* à la Sherlock Holmes.

de-escalate [,di:'eskəleɪt] ◆ vt [crisis] désamorcer ; [tension] faire baisser. ◆ vi [crisis] se désamorcer ; [tension] baisser.

deface [dɪ'feɪs] vt [statue, painting - with paint, aerosol spray] barbouiller ; [- by writing slogans] dégrader par des inscriptions ; [book] abîmer or endommager par des gribouillages or des inscriptions.

defamation [,defə'meɪʃn] n diffamation f.

defamatory [dɪ'fæmətrɪ] adj diffamatoire.

default [dɪ'fɔːlt] ◆ n **1.** LAW [non-appearance - in civil court] défaut *m*, non-comparution f ; [- in criminal court] contumace f **2.** *fml* [absence] ▸ **in default of** à défaut de **3.** COMPUT sélection f par défaut **4.** FIN défaut *m* de paiement, manquement *m* à payer. ◆ comp COMPUT [drive, font, value] par défaut. ◆ vi **1.** LAW manquer à comparaître, faire défaut **2.** FIN manquer or faillir à ses engagements / *to default on a payment* ne pas honorer un paiement **3.** SPORT [win, lose] déclarer forfait **4.** COMPUT prendre une sélection par défaut. ◆◆ **by default** adv phr **1.** SPORT par forfait **2.** COMPUT par défaut.

defeat [dɪ'fiːt] ◆ n [of army, opposition] défaite f ; [of project, bill] échec *m* ▸ **to suffer a defeat** connaître une défaite, échouer ▸ **to admit defeat** s'avouer vaincu. ◆ vt [army, adversary] vaincre ; [team, government] battre ; [attempts, project, bill] faire échouer / *that defeats the object* ça n'avance à rien.

defeatism [dɪ'fiːtɪzm] n défaitisme m.

defeatist [dɪ'fiːtɪst] ◆ adj défaitiste. ◆ n défaitiste mf.

defecate ['defəkeɪt] vi déféquer.

defect ◆ n ['di:fekt] défaut *m* ▸ **physical defect** malformation f ▸ **hearing / speech defect** défaut de l'ouïe / de prononciation. ◆ vi [dɪ'fekt] POL [to another country] passer à l'étranger ; [to another party] quitter son parti pour un autre / *to defect to the West* passer à l'Ouest.

defection [dɪ'fekʃn] n [to another country] passage *m* à un pays ennemi ; [to another party] passage *m* à un parti adverse.

defective [dɪ'fektɪv] adj [machine, reasoning] défectueux ; [hearing, sight, organ] déficient.

defector [dɪ'fektər] n POL & *fig* transfuge mf.

defence UK, **defense** US [dɪ'fens] ◆ n **1.** [protection] défense f ▸ **Ministry of Defence** UK, **Department of Defense** US ≃ ministère *m* de la Défense ▸ **Secretary of State for Defence** UK, **Secretary of Defense** US ≃ ministre *m* de la Défense **2.** [thing providing protection] protection f, défense f ; [argument] défense f ▸ **defences a)** [weapons] moyens *mpl* de défense **b)** [fortifications] défenses, fortifications *fpl* **3.** LAW défense f ▸ **the defence** [lawyers] la défense **4.** SPORT défense f. ◆ comp **1.** MIL [forces] de défense ; [cuts, minister, spending] de la défense **2.** LAW [lawyer] de la défense ; [witness] à décharge.

defenceless UK, **defenseless** US [dɪ'fenslɪs] adj sans défense, vulnérable.

defence mechanism n mécanisme *m* de défense.

defend [dɪ'fend] vt **1.** [protect] défendre ; [justify] justifier ▸ **to defend sthg / sb from** or **against attack** défendre qqch / qqn contre une attaque ▸ **to defend o.s.** se défendre **2.** SPORT [goalmouth, title] défendre **3.** LAW défendre.

defendant [dɪ'fendənt] n LAW [in civil court] défendeur *m*, -eresse f ; [in criminal court] inculpé *m*, -e f ; [accused of serious crimes] accusé *m*, -e f.

defender [dɪˈfendəʳ] n **1.** [of a cause, rights, etc.] défenseur m, avocat m, -e f **2.** SPORT [player] défenseur m ; [of title, record] détenteur m, -trice f.

defending [dɪˈfendɪŋ] adj SPORT [champion] en titre.

defense US = defence.

defensible [dɪˈfensəbl] adj [idea, opinion, etc.] défendable.

defensive [dɪˈfensɪv] ◆ adj [strategy, weapon, game, etc.] défensif / *she's very defensive about it* elle est très susceptible quand on parle de cela. ◆ n MIL & *fig* défensive f ▸ **to be on the defensive** être or se tenir sur la défensive ▸ **to go on the defensive** se mettre sur la défensive.

defensively [dɪˈfensɪvlɪ] adv : *they played very defensively* SPORT ils ont eu un jeu très défensif / *"it's not my fault", she said, defensively* « ce n'est pas de ma faute », dit-elle, sur la défensive.

defer [dɪˈfɜːʳ] (*pt & pp* deferred, *cont* deferring) ◆ vt [decision, meeting] remettre, reporter ; [payment, business, judgment] différer, retarder. ◆ vi [give way] ▸ **to defer to sb** s'en remettre à qqn.

deference [ˈdefərəns] n déférence f, égard m, considération f.

deferential [ˌdefəˈrenʃl] adj déférent, révérencieux ▸ **to be deferential to sb** faire montre de déférence or d'égards envers qqn.

deferred [dɪˈfɜːd] adj [gen] ajourné, retardé ; [payment, shares] différé ; [annuity] à paiement différé, à jouissance différée.

defiance [dɪˈfaɪəns] n défi m. ❖ **in defiance of** prep phr ▸ **in defiance of sb / sthg** au mépris de qqn / qqch.

defiant [dɪˈfaɪənt] adj [gesture, remark, look] de défi ; [person, reply] provocateur.

defiantly [dɪˈfaɪəntlɪ] adv [act] avec une attitude de défi ; [reply, look at] d'un air de défi.

defibrillator [diːˈfɪbrɪleɪtəʳ] n MED défibrillateur m.

deficiency [dɪˈfɪʃnsɪ] (*pl* deficiencies) n **1.** MED [shortage] carence f / *a deficiency in* or *of calcium, a calcium deficiency* une carence en calcium ▸ **mental deficiency** déficience f mentale **2.** [flaw - in character, system] défaut m.

deficient [dɪˈfɪʃnt] adj **1.** [insufficient] insuffisant ▸ **to be deficient in sthg** manquer de qqch **2.** [defective] défectueux.

deficit [ˈdefɪsɪt] n FIN & COMM déficit m.

defile ◆ vt [dɪˈfaɪl] [grave, memory] profaner. ◆ vi [dɪˈfaɪl] MIL défiler. ◆ n [ˈdiːfaɪl] [valley, passage] défilé m.

define [dɪˈfaɪn] vt **1.** [term, word] définir ; [boundary, role, subject] définir, délimiter ; [concept, idea, feeling] définir, préciser **2.** [object, shape] définir.

defining [dɪˈfaɪnɪŋ] adj [moment, lesson, event] décisif.

definite [ˈdefɪnɪt] adj **1.** [precise, clear] précis ; [advantage, improvement, opinion] net ; [answer] définitif ; [orders, proof] formel ; [price] fixe **2.** [certain] certain, sûr.

definite article n article m défini.

definitely [ˈdefɪnɪtlɪ] adv certainement, sans aucun doute / *that's definitely not the man I saw* je suis sûr que ce n'est pas l'homme que j'ai vu / *are you going to the show? — definitely!* est-ce que tu vas au spectacle ? — absolument !

definition [defɪˈnɪʃn] n **1.** [of term, word] définition f ; [of duties, territory] définition, délimitation f ▸ **by definition** par définition **2.** [of photograph, sound] netteté f ; TV définition f.

definitive [dɪˈfɪnɪtɪv] adj **1.** [conclusive] définitif ; [battle, victory] définitif, décisif ; [result] définitif, qui fait autorité **2.** [authoritative] : *the definitive book on the subject* le livre qui fait autorité or décisif en la matière.

definitively [dɪˈfɪnɪtɪvlɪ] adv définitivement.

deflate [dɪˈfleɪt] ◆ vt **1.** [balloon, tyre] dégonfler ; *fig* [person] démonter **2.** ECON [prices] faire baisser, faire tomber. ◆ vi [balloon, tyre] se dégonfler.

deflation [dɪˈfleɪʃn] n ECON & GEOG déflation f.

deflationary [dɪˈfleɪʃnərɪ], **deflationist** [dɪˈfleɪʃənɪst] adj déflationniste.

deflect [dɪˈflekt] vt faire dévier ; *fig* [attention, criticism] détourner.

deflection [dɪˈflekʃn] n déviation f.

defog [ˌdiːˈfɒg] vt US AUTO désembuer.

defogger [ˌdiːˈfɒgəʳ] n US AUTO dispositif m anti-buée *(inv)*.

deforest [ˌdiːˈfɒrɪst] vt déboiser.

deforestation [diːˌfɒrɪˈsteɪʃn] n déboisement m, déforestation f.

deform [diˈfɔːm] vt déformer ; *fig* [distort, ruin] défigurer.

deformed [dɪˈfɔːmd] adj difforme.

deformity [dɪˈfɔːmətɪ] n difformité f.

Defra [ˈdefrə] (abbr of **Department for Environment, Food & Rural Affairs**) n UK ADMIN ministère m de l'Agriculture.

defrag [diːˈfræg] vt inf = defragment.

defragment [ˌdiːfrægˈment] vt COMPUT défragmenter.

defraud [dɪˈfrɔːd] vt [the state] frauder ; [company, person] escroquer, frustrer *spec*.

defray [dɪˈfreɪ] vt *fml* rembourser, prendre en charge.

defrost [ˌdiːˈfrɒst] ◆ vt **1.** [food] décongeler ; [refrigerator] dégivrer **2.** US [demist] désembuer ; [de-ice] dégivrer. ◆ vi [food] se décongeler ; [refrigerator] se dégivrer.

deft [deft] adj adroit, habile ; [fingers] habile.

deftly [ˈdeftlɪ] adv adroitement, habilement.

defunct [dɪˈfʌŋkt] adj défunt.

defuse [ˌdiːˈfjuːz] vt *lit & fig* désamorcer.

defy [dɪˈfaɪ] (*pt & pp* defied) vt **1.** [disobey] s'opposer à ; [law, rule] braver **2.** [challenge, dare] défier **3.** *fig* [make impossible] défier.

degenerate ◆ vi [dɪˈdʒenəreɪt] dégénérer. ◆ adj [dɪˈdʒenərət] *liter* dégénéré ; [person] dépravé. ◆ n [dɪˈdʒenərət] *liter* [person] dépravé m, -e f.

degenerative [dɪˈdʒenərətɪv] adj dégénératif.

degradation [ˌdegrəˈdeɪʃn] n **1.** [deterioration] dégradation f ; ECOL dégradation f **2.** [corruption, debasement] avilissement m, dégradation f ; [poverty] misère f abjecte.

degrade [dɪˈgreɪd] vt **1.** [deteriorate] dégrader **2.** [debase] avilir, dégrader.

degrading [dɪˈgreɪdɪŋ] adj avilissant, dégradant.

degree [dɪˈgriː] n **1.** [unit of measurement] degré m **2.** [extent, amount] : *there was a certain degree of mistrust between them* il y avait un certain degré de méfiance entre eux **3.** [stage, step] degré m **4.** [academic qualification] diplôme m universitaire / *she has a degree in economics* elle est diplômée en sciences économiques / *he's taking or doing a degree in biology* il fait une licence de biologie ▸ **degree ceremony** cérémonie f de remise des diplômes **5.** GRAM & MUS degré m **6.** US LAW : *murder in the first degree* homicide m volontaire. ❖ **by degrees** adv phr par degrés, au fur et à mesure. ❖ **to a degree** adv phr [to an extent] jusqu'à un certain point.

-degree in comp ▸ **first / second / third-degree burns** brûlures fpl au premier / deuxième / troisième degré ▸ **first-degree murder** US LAW ≃ homicide m volontaire.

dehire [ˌdiːˈhaɪəʳ] vt US *euph* [dismiss] remercier.

dehumanize, dehumanise [diːˈhjuːmənaɪz] vt déshumaniser.

dehumidify [ˌdiːhjuːˈmɪdɪfaɪ] vt déshumidifier.

dehydrate [ˌdiːhaɪˈdreɪt] vt déshydrater.

dehydrated [ˌdiːhaɪˈdreɪtɪd] adj déshydraté(e).

dehydration [ˌdiːhaɪˈdreɪʃn] n déshydratation f.

de-ice [diːˈaɪs] vt dégivrer.

de-icer [diːˈaɪsər] n dégivreur m.

deign [deɪn] vt daigner / *he didn't deign to reply* fml & hum il n'a pas daigné répondre.

deity [ˈdiːɪtɪ] (pl **deities**) n **1.** MYTH dieu m, déesse f, divinité f **2.** RELIG ▶ **the Deity** Dieu m, la Divinité.

déjà vu [ˌdeʒɑːˈvuː] n déjà-vu m inv.

dejected [dɪˈdʒektɪd] adj abattu, découragé.

dejectedly [dɪˈdʒektɪdlɪ] adv [speak] d'un ton abattu ; [look] d'un air abattu.

dejection [dɪˈdʒekʃn] n abattement m, découragement m.

Del (written abbr of **delete**) [on keyboard] Suppr.

Delaware [ˈdeləweər] pr n Delaware m / *in Delaware* dans le Delaware.

delay [dɪˈleɪ] ◆ vt **1.** [cause to be late] retarder ; [person] retarder, retenir **2.** [postpone, defer] reporter, remettre. ◆ vi tarder. ◆ n **1.** [lateness] retard m / *there are long delays on the M25* UK la circulation est très ralentie or est très perturbée sur la M25 **2.** [waiting period] : *without delay* sans tarder or délai.

> ⚠ The word **délai** usually means the time it takes to perform a task, make a delivery, etc. It does not imply lateness and is rarely used to translate the word delay.

delayed [dɪˈleɪd] adj ▶ **to be delayed** [person, train] être retardé(e).

delayed-action [dɪˈleɪd-] adj [fuse, shutter] à retardement.

delaying [dɪˈleɪɪŋ] adj dilatoire.

delectable [dɪˈlektəbl] adj délectable.

delegate ◆ n [ˈdelɪɡət] délégué m, -e f. ◆ vt [ˈdelɪɡeɪt] déléguer. ◆ vi [ˈdelɪɡeɪt] déléguer.

delegation [ˌdelɪˈɡeɪʃn] n **1.** [group of delegates] délégation f **2.** [of duties, power] délégation f.

delete [dɪˈliːt] vt supprimer ; [erase] effacer ; [cross out] barrer, biffer.

delete key n COMPUT touche f effacer.

deletion [dɪˈliːʃn] n suppression f.

Delhi [ˈdelɪ] pr n Delhi ▶ **Delhi belly** inf & hum turista f, tourista f.

deli [ˈdelɪ] n inf abbr of **delicatessen**.

deliberate ◆ adj [dɪˈlɪbərət] **1.** [intentional] délibéré, volontaire, voulu **2.** [unhurried, careful] mesuré, posé. ◆ vi [dɪˈlɪbəreɪt] délibérer ▶ **to deliberate on** or **upon sthg** délibérer sur qqch. ◆ vt [dɪˈlɪbəreɪt] délibérer sur.

deliberately [dɪˈlɪbərətlɪ] adv **1.** [intentionally] volontairement / *I didn't hurt him deliberately* je n'ai pas fait exprès de le blesser **2.** [carefully] de façon mesurée, avec mesure ; [walk] d'un pas ferme.

deliberation [dɪˌlɪbəˈreɪʃn] n **1.** [consideration, reflection] délibération f, réflexion f **2.** [care, caution] attention f, soin m. ❖ **deliberations** pl n délibérations fpl.

delicacy [ˈdelɪkəsɪ] (pl **delicacies**) n **1.** [refinement] délicatesse f, finesse f ; [fragility, frailty] délicatesse f, fragilité f ; [difficulty] délicatesse f ; [tact] délicatesse f **2.** [fine food] mets m délicat.

delicate [ˈdelɪkət] adj **1.** [fingers, lace, china] délicat, fin **2.** [child, health] délicat, fragile **3.** [situation, question]

délicat, difficile **4.** [smell, colour] délicat **5.** [instrument] sensible.

delicately [ˈdelɪkətlɪ] adv délicatement, avec délicatesse.

delicatessen [ˌdelɪkəˈtesn] n **1.** UK [fine foods shop] épicerie fine f **2.** US [food shop] ≃ traiteur m ; [restaurant] ≃ restaurant m.

delicious [dɪˈlɪʃəs] adj délicieux.

deliciously [dɪˈlɪʃəslɪ] adv délicieusement.

delight [dɪˈlaɪt] ◆ vi : *she delights in irritating people* elle prend plaisir or se complaît à énerver les gens. ◆ vt ravir, réjouir. ◆ n [pleasure] joie f, (grand) plaisir m.

delighted [dɪˈlaɪtɪd] adj ravi / *I'm delighted to see you again* je suis ravi de vous revoir ▶ **to be delighted with sthg** être ravi de qqch.

> 📋 Note that être content / heureux / ravi que and se réjouir que are followed by a verb in the subjunctive:
> **I'm delighted you're here.** Je suis ravi que vous soyez là.

delightful [dɪˈlaɪtful] adj [person, place] charmant ; [book, experience, film] merveilleux.

delightfully [dɪˈlaɪtfulɪ] adv [dance, perform, sing] merveilleusement, à ravir.

delimit [diːˈlɪmɪt] vt fml délimiter.

delineate [dɪˈlɪnɪeɪt] vt fml **1.** [outline, sketch] tracer **2.** fig [define, describe] définir, décrire.

delinquency [dɪˈlɪŋkwənsɪ] (pl **delinquencies**) n **1.** [criminal behaviour] délinquance f **2.** [negligence] faute f.

delinquent [dɪˈlɪŋkwənt] ◆ adj **1.** [law-breaking] délinquant ; [negligent] fautif **2.** FIN [overdue] impayé. ◆ n **1.** [law-breaker] délinquant m, -e f **2.** [bad debtor] mauvais payeur m.

delirious [dɪˈlɪrɪəs] adj **1.** MED en délire / *to become delirious* se mettre à délirer, être pris de délire **2.** fig [excited, wild] délirant, en délire.

deliriously [dɪˈlɪrɪəslɪ] adv de façon délirante, frénétiquement / *deliriously happy* follement heureux.

delirium [dɪˈlɪrɪəm] n **1.** MED délire m **2.** fig [state of excitement] délire m.

delist [diːˈlɪst] vt COMM & MARKETING [product] déréférencer.

deliver [dɪˈlɪvər] ◆ vt **1.** [carry, transport] remettre ; COMM livrer ▶ **to deliver the goods** inf: *can he deliver the goods?* est-ce qu'il peut tenir parole ? **2.** fml & liter [save, rescue] délivrer **3.** MED ▶ **to deliver a baby** faire un accouchement **4.** [pronounce, utter] ▶ **to deliver a sermon / speech** prononcer un sermon / discours / *the jury delivered a verdict of not guilty* LAW le jury a rendu un verdict de non-culpabilité **5.** US POL : *can he deliver the Black vote?* est-ce qu'il peut nous assurer les voix des Noirs ? **6.** [strike] ▶ **to deliver a blow (to the head / stomach)** porter or liter asséner un coup (à la tête / à l'estomac). ◆ vi **1.** [make delivery] livrer **2.** inf [do as promised] tenir parole, tenir bon. ❖ **deliver up** vt sep [fugitive, town] livrer.

deliverance [dɪˈlɪvərəns] n fml & liter [release, rescue] délivrance f.

delivery [dɪˈlɪvərɪ] (pl **deliveries**) ◆ n **1.** COMM livraison f **2.** [transfer, handing over] remise f **3.** MED accouchement m **4.** [manner of speaking] débit m, élocution f **5.** fml & liter [release, rescue] délivrance f. ◆ comp **1.** COMM [note, truck, van, service] de livraison ▶ **delivery man** livreur *m* ▸ **delivery charges** frais *mpl* de livraison **2.** MED ▸ **the delivery room** la salle de travail or d'accouchement.

delouse [ˌdiːˈlaʊs] vt [animal, person] épouiller ; [clothing, furniture] enlever les poux de.

delta ['deltə] ◆ n delta *m*. ◆ comp en delta.

delts [delts] pl n *inf* [deltoid muscles] muscles *mpl* deltoïdes.

delude [dɪˈluːd] vt tromper, duper.

deluded [dɪˈluːdɪd] adj **1.** [mistaken, foolish] : *a poor deluded young man* un pauvre jeune homme qu'on a trompé or induit en erreur **2.** PSYCHOL sujet à des délires.

deluge ['deljuːdʒ] ◆ n *lit & fig* déluge *m*. ◆ vt inonder.

delusion [dɪˈluːʒn] n **1.** [illusion, mistaken idea] illusion *f* **2.** PSYCHOL délire *m*.

deluxe [dəˈlʌks] adj de luxe.

delve [delv] vi **1.** [investigate] fouiller **2.** [search] : *he delved into the bag* il a fouillé dans le sac **3.** [dig, burrow] creuser ; [animal] fouiller.

Dem. written abbr of **Democrat(ic).**

demagog ['deməgɒg] US = demagogue.

demagogue ['deməgɒg] n démagogue *mf*.

demagogy ['deməgɒgɪ] n démagogie *f*.

demand [dɪˈmɑːnd] ◆ vt **1.** [ask forcefully] exiger ; [money] réclamer / *the terrorists demanded to be flown to Tehran* les terroristes exigeaient d'être emmenés en avion à Téhéran **2.** [require, necessitate] exiger, réclamer. ◆ n **1.** [obligation, requirement] exigence *f* ▸ **to make demands on sb** exiger beaucoup de qqn **2.** [firm request] ▸ **wage demands** revendications *fpl* salariales **3.** ECON & COMM demande *f* ▸ **to be in (great) demand** être (très) demandé or recherché. ◆ **on demand** adv phr sur demande.

> ⚠ **Demander** simply means to ask, and does not imply insistence. It is rarely the correct translation for to demand.

> 🗒 Note that exiger que is followed by a verb in the subjunctive:
> **They demand that we (should) be present in the main European markets.** *Ils exigent que nous soyons présents dans les principaux marchés européens.*

demanding [dɪˈmɑːndɪŋ] adj [person] exigeant ; [job, profession] difficile, astreignant / *the work is not physically demanding* ce travail ne demande pas beaucoup de force physique / *intellectually demanding* intellectuellement exigeant / *emotionally demanding* très éprouvant sur le plan émotionnel.

demand-led adj ECON tiré par la demande.

demarcate ['diːmɑːkeɪt] vt *fml* délimiter.

demarcation [ˌdiːmɑːˈkeɪʃn] n [boundary, border] démarcation *f*.

dematerialize, dematerialise [diːməˈtɪərɪəlaɪz] vi se volatiliser.

demean [dɪˈmiːn] vt *fml* avilir, rabaisser.

demeaning [dɪˈmiːnɪŋ] adj avilissant, déshonorant.

demeanour UK, **demeanor** US [dɪˈmiːnər] n *fml* [behaviour] comportement *m* ; [manner] allure *f*, maintien *m*.

demented [dɪˈmentɪd] adj MED dément ; *fig* fou *(before vowel or silent 'h'* **fol, f folle)**.

dementia [dɪˈmenʃə] n démence *f*.

demerara [ˌdeməˈreərə] n ▸ **demerara sugar** cassonade *f*.

demerger [ˌdiːˈmɜːdʒər] n scission *f*.

demerit [diːˈmerɪt] n **1.** *fml* [flaw] démérite *m*, faute *f* **2.** US SCH & MIL blâme *m*.

demijohn ['demɪdʒɒn] n dame-jeanne *f*, bonbonne *f*.

demilitarize, demilitarise [ˌdiːˈmɪlɪtəraɪz] vt démilitariser / *a demilitarized zone* une zone démilitarisée.

demise [dɪˈmaɪz] n *arch & liter* [death] mort *f*, disparition *f* ; [end] fin *f*, mort *f*.

demist [ˌdiːˈmɪst] vt UK désembuer.

demister [ˌdiːˈmɪstər] n UK dispositif *m* antibuée.

demo ['deməʊ] (*pl* demos) (abbr of demonstration) ◆ n **1.** *inf* manif *f* **2.** MUS démo *f* **3.** COMPUT version *f* de démonstration or d'évaluation. ◆ vt faire une démo de.

demob [ˌdiːˈmɒb] (*pt & pp* demobbed, *cont* demobbing) UK *inf* ◆ vt démobiliser. ◆ n [demobilization] démobilisation *f*. ◆ comp ▸ **demob suit** ≃ tenue *f* civile.

demobilization [diːˌməʊbɪlaɪˈzeɪʃn] n démobilisation *f*.

demobilize, demobilise [ˌdiːˈməʊbɪlaɪz] vt démobiliser.

democracy [dɪˈmɒkrəsɪ] (*pl* democracies) n démocratie *f*.

democrat ['deməkræt] n démocrate *mf*. ◆ **Democrat** n [in US] démocrate *mf*.

democratic [ˌdeməˈkrætɪk] adj [country, organization, principle] démocratique ; [person] démocrate ▸ **the Democratic Party** le parti démocrate (américain).

democratically [ˌdeməˈkrætɪklɪ] adv démocratiquement.

Democratic Republic of Congo n République *f* démocratique du Congo.

democratize, democratise [dɪˈmɒkrətaɪz] ◆ vt démocratiser. ◆ vi se démocratiser.

demographic [ˌdeməˈɡræfɪk] adj démographique.

demography [dɪˈmɒɡrəfɪ] n démographie *f*.

demolish [dɪˈmɒlɪʃ] vt **1.** *lit & fig* [destroy] démolir **2.** *inf* [devour] dévorer.

demolition [ˌdeməˈlɪʃn] n *lit & fig* démolition *f* ▸ **demolition gang** équipe *f* de démolition. ◆ **demolitions** pl n MIL explosifs *mpl* ▸ **a demolitions expert** UK un expert en explosifs.

demon ['diːmən] n **1.** [devil, evil spirit] démon *m* **2.** *fig* diable *m* / *he's a demon tennis player* il joue au tennis comme un dieu.

demonic [diːˈmɒnɪk] adj diabolique.

demonize, demonise ['diːmənaɪz] vt diaboliser.

demonstrable [dɪˈmɒnstrəbl] adj démontrable.

demonstrably [dɪˈmɒnstrəblɪ] adv manifestement.

demonstrate ['demənstreɪt] ◆ vt **1.** [prove, establish] démontrer **2.** [appliance, machine] faire une démonstration de **3.** [ability, quality] faire preuve de. ◆ vi POL manifester ▸ **to demonstrate against sthg** manifester contre qqch.

demonstration [ˌdemənˈstreɪʃn] ◆ n **1.** [proof] démonstration *f* **2.** COMM & INDUST démonstration *f* **3.** POL [protest] manifestation *f* / *to hold a demonstration* faire une manifestation **4.** [of emotion] démonstration *f*, manifestation *f* **5.** MIL démonstration *f*. ◆ comp [car, copy, lesson, model] de démonstration.

> ⚠ The French word **démonstration** never means a demonstration in the sense of a protest. For this meaning, use **une manifestation**.

demonstrative [dɪ'mɒnstrətɪv] ◆ adj démonstratif. ◆ n démonstratif *m*.

demonstrator ['demənstreɪtər] n **1.** COMM & INDUST [person] démonstrateur *m*, -trice *f* **2.** POL [protester] manifestant *m*, -e *f* **3.** 🇬🇧 UNIV ≃ préparateur *m*, -trice *f* **4.** 🇺🇸 COMM [appliance, machine] modèle *m* de démonstration.

demoralization [dɪ,mɒrəlaɪ'zeɪʃn] n démoralisation *f*.

demoralize, demoralise [dɪ'mɒrəlaɪz] vt démoraliser.

demoralized [dɪ'mɒrəlaɪzd] adj démoralisé / *to become demoralized* perdre courage ou le moral.

demoralizing [dɪ'mɒrəlaɪzɪŋ] adj démoralisant.

demote [,diː'məʊt] vt rétrograder.

demotion [,diː'məʊʃn] n rétrogradation *f*.

demotivate [,diː'məʊtɪveɪt] vt démotiver.

demo version n COMPUT version *f* de démonstration ou d'évaluation.

demure [dɪ'mjʊər] adj **1.** [modest] modeste, pudique ; [well-behaved] sage ; [reserved] retenu **2.** *pej* [coy] d'une modestie affectée.

demutualize, demutualise [diː'mjuːtuːəlaɪz] vi FIN se démutualiser.

demystify [,diː'mɪstɪfaɪ] (*pt & pp* **demystified**) vt démystifier.

den [den] n **1.** ZOOL repaire *m*, tanière *f* ; *fig* [hideout] repaire *m*, nid *m* / *a den of thieves* un nid de brigands / *a den of iniquity* un lieu de perdition **2.** [room, study] ≃ bureau *m* ; ≃ cabinet *m* de travail.

denationalize, denationalise [,diː'næʃnəlaɪz] vt dénationaliser.

deniable [dɪ'naɪəbl] adj niable.

denial [dɪ'naɪəl] n **1.** [of story, rumour] démenti *m* ; [of wrongdoing] dénégation *f* ; [of request, right] refus *m* ▸ **denial of justice** LAW déni *m* de justice **2.** [abstinence] abnégation *f* **3.** PSYCHOL dénégation *f*.

denier ['denɪər ou də'nɪər] n 🇬🇧 [measure] denier *m*.

denigrate ['denɪgreɪt] vt dénigrer.

denim ['denɪm] ◆ n TEXT (toile *f* de) jean *m*, denim *m*. ◆ comp [jacket] en jean. ❖ **denims** pl n blue-jean *m*, jean *m*.

Denmark ['denmɑːk] pr n Danemark *m* / *in Denmark* au Danemark.

den mother n 🇺🇸 [in scout group] cheftaine *f*.

denomination [dɪ,nɒmɪ'neɪʃn] n **1.** FIN valeur *f* / *small / large denomination notes* petites / grosses coupures **2.** RELIG confession *f*, culte *m* **3.** *fml* [designation, specification] dénomination *f*.

denominational [dɪ,nɒmɪ'neɪʃənl] adj : *a denominational school* une école confessionnelle.

denominator [dɪ'nɒmɪneɪtər] n dénominateur *m*.

denote [dɪ'nəʊt] vt [indicate] dénoter ; [represent] signifier.

denounce [dɪ'naʊns] vt dénoncer.

dense [dens] adj **1.** [thick] dense ; [fog, smoke] épais (épaisse) ; [undergrowth, vegetation] dense, dru *liter* ; PHOT opaque **2.** [prose] dense, ramassé **3.** *inf* [stupid] bouché, obtus.

densely ['densli] adv : *a densely populated area* une région très peuplée ou à forte densité de population / *a densely wooded valley* une vallée très boisée.

density ['densətɪ] n densité *f*.

dent [dent] ◆ n **1.** [in metal] bosse *f* ; [in bed, pillow] creux *m* **2.** *fig* [reduction] : *to make a dent in one's savings* faire un trou dans ses économies. ◆ vt [metal] cabosser, bosseler ; *fig* [pride] froisser ; [confidence] entamer.

dental ['dentl] ◆ adj **1.** MED dentaire **2.** LING dental. ◆ n dentale *f*.

dental floss n fil *m* dentaire.

dental hygienist n assistant *m*, -e *f* de dentiste (*qui s'occupe du détartrage, etc.*).

dental nurse n assistant *m*, -e dentaire.

dental plate n dentier *m*.

dental surgeon n 🇬🇧 chirurgien-dentiste *m*.

dental surgery n 🇬🇧 [office] cabinet *m* dentaire.

dental treatment n traitement *m* dentaire.

dented ['dentɪd] adj [metal] cabossé.

dentist ['dentɪst] n dentiste *mf* ▸ **dentist's chair** fauteuil *m* de dentiste ▸ **the dentist's surgery** 🇬🇧 or **office** 🇺🇸 le cabinet dentaire ▸ **to go to the dentist's** aller chez le dentiste.

dentistry ['dentɪstrɪ] n dentisterie *f*.

dentures ['dentʃəz] pl n dentier *m*.

denude [dɪ'njuːd] vt dénuder.

denunciation [dɪ,nʌnsɪ'eɪʃn] n dénonciation *f*.

Denver boot ['denvə-] n *inf* AUTO sabot *m* de Denver.

deny [dɪ'naɪ] (*pt & pp* **denied**) vt **1.** [declare untrue] nier ; [report, rumour] démentir / *there's no denying that we have a problem* il est indéniable que nous avons un problème **2.** [refuse] refuser, dénier *liter* **3.** [deprive] priver.

deodorant [diː'əʊdərənt] n déodorant *m*.

deodorizer [diː'əʊdəraɪzər] n [for home] désodorisant *m*.

depart [dɪ'pɑːt] ◆ vi *fml* **1.** [leave] partir **2.** [deviate, vary] s'écarter. ◆ vt quitter.

departed [dɪ'pɑːtɪd] *euph & fml* ◆ adj [dead] défunt, disparu. ◆ n ▸ **the departed** le défunt, la défunte, le disparu, la disparue.

department [dɪ'pɑːtmənt] n **1.** ADMIN [division] département *m* ; [ministry] ministère *m* ▸ **Department of Motor Vehicles** aux États-Unis, agence d'État qui gère les permis de conduire et l'immatriculation des véhicules ▸ **the Department of State** 🇺🇸 le Département d'État ; ≃ le ministère des Affaires étrangères ▸ **Department of Trade** 🇺🇸 ministère du Commerce **2.** INDUST service *m* / *the sales / personnel department* le service commercial / du personnel **3.** [field, responsibility] domaine *m* / *recruiting staff is not my department* le recrutement n'est pas mon domaine ou de mon ressort / *cooking's not really my department* *fig* la cuisine n'est pas vraiment mon domaine ou ma spécialité **4.** COMM rayon *m* / *the toy department* le rayon des jouets **5.** SCH département *m*, section *f* ; UNIV département, UFR *f* **6.** GEOG département *m*.

departmental [,diːpɑː'mentl] adj **1.** ADMIN du département ; INDUST du service ; COMM du rayon **2.** GEOG du département, départemental.

department store n grand magasin *m*.

departure [dɪ'pɑːtʃər] ◆ n **1.** [leaving] départ *m* **2.** [variation, deviation] modification *f* **3.** [orientation] orientation *f*. ◆ comp [gate] d'embarquement ; [time] de départ ▸ **departure lounge** salle *f* d'embarquement.

depend [dɪ'pend] ❖ **depend on, depend upon** vt insep **1.** [be determined by] dépendre de / *are we going out? — it (all) depends* est-ce qu'on sort ? — ça dépend **2.** [rely on] dépendre de **3.** [trust, be sure of] compter sur. ❖ **depending on** prep phr selon.

dependable [dɪ'pendəbl] adj [machine] fiable ; [person] fiable, sérieux ; [organization, shop] sérieux.

dependant [dɪ'pendənt] n ADMIN personne *f* à charge.

dependence [dɪ'pendəns] n dépendance *f* / *the government hopes to reduce our dependence on oil* le gouvernement espère diminuer notre dépendance vis-à-vis du pétrole.

dependency [dɪ'pendənsɪ] (pl **dependencies**) n dépendance f.

dependency culture n ECON situation d'une société dont les membres ont une mentalité d'assistés.

dependent [dɪ'pendənt] adj **1.** [person] dépendant / she's financially dependent on her parents elle dépend financièrement or elle est à la charge de ses parents / he has two dependent children ADMIN il a deux enfants à charge **2.** [contingent] : the prosperity of his business was dependent on the continuation of the war la prospérité de son entreprise dépendait or était tributaire de la poursuite de la guerre.

depersonalize, depersonalise [ˌdiː'pɜːsnəlaɪz] vt dépersonnaliser.

depict [dɪ'pɪkt] vt **1.** [describe] dépeindre **2.** [paint, draw] représenter.

depiction [dɪ'pɪkʃn] n **1.** [description] description f **2.** [picture] représentation f.

depilatory [dɪ'pɪlətrɪ] (pl **depilatories**) ◆ adj épilatoire, dépilatoire. ◆ n épilatoire m, dépilatoire m.

deplete [dɪ'pliːt] vt **1.** [reduce] diminuer, réduire **2.** [impoverish, exhaust] épuiser.

depletion [dɪ'pliːʃn] n **1.** [reduction] diminution f, réduction f **2.** [exhaustion] épuisement m ; [of soil] appauvrissement m.

deplorable [dɪ'plɔːrəbl] adj déplorable, lamentable.

deplore [dɪ'plɔːr] vt **1.** [regret] déplorer, regretter **2.** [condemn, disapprove of] désapprouver, condamner.

deploy [dɪ'plɔɪ] ◆ vt déployer. ◆ vi se déployer.

deployment [dɪ'plɔɪmənt] n déploiement m.

depoliticize, depoliticise [ˌdiː'pɒlɪtɪsaɪz] vt dépolitiser.

depopulate [ˌdiː'pɒpjʊleɪt] vt dépeupler.

depopulated [ˌdiː'pɒpjʊleɪtɪd] adj dépeuplé.

depopulation [diːˌpɒpjʊ'leɪʃn] n dépeuplement m.

deport [dɪ'pɔːt] vt [expel] expulser ; HIST [to colonies, camp] déporter.

deportable alien [dɪ'pɔːtəbl-] n US immigré m, -e f susceptible d'être reconduit(e) à la frontière.

deportation [ˌdiːpɔː'teɪʃn] n expulsion f ; HIST [to colonies, camp] déportation f ▶ **deportation order** arrêt m d'expulsion.

deportee [ˌdiːpɔː'tiː] n expulsé m, -e f ; HIST [prisoner] déporté m, -e f.

deportment [dɪ'pɔːtmənt] n fml & dated [behaviour] comportement m ; [carriage, posture] maintien m.

depose [dɪ'pəʊz] ◆ vt **1.** [remove] destituer ; [sovereign] déposer, destituer **2.** LAW déposer. ◆ vi faire une déposition.

deposit [dɪ'pɒzɪt] ◆ vt **1.** [leave, place] déposer **2.** [subj: liquid, river] déposer **3.** BANK déposer, remettre **4.** [pay] verser **5.** US [insert] mettre. ◆ n **1.** BANK dépôt m / to make a deposit of £200 faire un versement de 200 livres **2.** FIN & COMM [down payment] acompte m, arrhes fpl **3.** [guarantee against loss or damage] caution f ; [on a bottle] consigne f **4.** UK POL cautionnement m **5.** MINER gisement m **6.** [sediment, silt] dépôt m ; [in wine] dépôt m.

deposit account n UK compte m sur livret.

deposition [ˌdepə'zɪʃn] n **1.** LAW déposition f **2.** MINER dépôt m **3.** [removal of leader] déposition f.

depositor [də'pɒzɪtər] n déposant m, -e f.

depot n ['depəʊ] **1.** [warehouse] dépôt m ; US [garage] dépôt m, garage m **2.** US MIL ≃ caserne f **3.** ['diːpəʊ] US [station] gare f ▶ **bus depot** gare routière.

depravation [ˌdeprə'veɪʃn] n dépravation f.

depraved [dɪ'preɪvd] adj dépravé, perverti.

depravity [dɪ'prævətɪ] (pl **depravities**) n dépravation f, corruption f.

deprecating ['deprɪkeɪtɪŋ] = **deprecatory**.

deprecatory ['deprɪkətrɪ] adj **1.** [disapproving] désapprobateur ; [derogatory] dénigrant **2.** [apologetic] navré.

depreciate [dɪ'priːʃɪeɪt] ◆ vt **1.** FIN [devalue] déprécier, dévaloriser **2.** [denigrate] dénigrer, déprécier. ◆ vi se déprécier, se dévaloriser.

depreciation [dɪˌpriːʃɪ'eɪʃn] n **1.** FIN dépréciation f, dévalorisation f **2.** [disparagement] dénigrement m, dépréciation f.

depress [dɪ'pres] vt **1.** [deject, sadden] déprimer **2.** ECON [reduce] (faire) baisser **3.** fml [push down on] appuyer sur.

depressed [dɪ'prest] adj **1.** [melancholy] déprimé, abattu ; MED déprimé **2.** ECON [area, industry] en déclin, touché par la crise, déprimé ; [prices, profits, wages] en baisse **3.** [sunken, hollow] creux.

depressing [dɪ'presɪŋ] adj déprimant ; [idea, place] triste, sinistre.

depressingly [dɪ'presɪŋlɪ] adv [say, speak] d'un ton abattu / unemployment is depressingly high le taux de chômage est déprimant.

depression [dɪ'preʃn] n **1.** [melancholy] dépression f ; MED dépression f (nerveuse) / she suffers from depression elle fait de la dépression / he's in a state of depression il est dans un état dépressif **2.** ECON [slump] dépression f, crise f économique / the country's economy is in a state of depression l'économie du pays est en crise ▶ **the Great Depression** US HIST la grande dépression **3.** [hollow, indentation] creux m ; GEOG dépression f **4.** METEOR dépression f.

 The Great Depression

On appelle ainsi la plus grave crise économique qui ébranla les États-Unis au XXᵉ siècle. Elle dura de 1929 (date du krach de Wall Street) au début des années 1940 et plongea le pays dans le chômage et la misère.

depressive [dɪ'presɪv] ◆ adj dépressif. ◆ n dépressif m, -ive f.

depressurization [diːˌpreʃəraɪ'zeɪʃn] n dépressurisation f.

deprivation [ˌdeprɪ'veɪʃn] n (U) privation f.

deprive [dɪ'praɪv] vt priver ▶ **to deprive sb of sthg** priver qqn de qqch.

deprived [dɪ'praɪvd] adj [area, child] défavorisé.

deprogram [diːˈprəʊgræm] vt déprogrammer.

dept. written abbr of **department**.

depth [depθ] n **1.** [distance downwards] profondeur f **2.** [in deep water] : she swam too far and got out of her depth elle a nagé trop loin et a perdu pied ▶ **to be out of one's depth a)** lit ne plus avoir pied **b)** fig perdre pied **3.** PHOT ▶ **depth of field / focus** profondeur f de champ / foyer **4.** [of a voice, sound] registre m grave **5.** [extent, intensity] profondeur f ; [of colour] intensité f / we must study the proposal in depth nous devons étudier à fond or en profondeur cette proposition. ◆ **depths** pl n : the ocean depths les grands fonds mpl / the depths of the *earth* les profondeurs *fpl* or entrailles *fpl* de la terre ; *fig* : *she's in the depths of despair* elle touche le fond du désespoir / *in the depths of winter* au cœur de l'hiver.

deputation [ˌdepjʊ'teɪʃn] n députation *f*, délégation *f*.

deputize, deputise ['depjʊtaɪz] ◆ vt députer. ◆ vi ▶ **to deputize for sb** représenter qqn.

deputy ['depjʊtɪ] (*pl* **deputies**) ◆ n **1.** [assistant] adjoint *m*, -e *f* **2.** [substitute] remplaçant *m*, -e *f* **3.** POL [elected representative] député *m* **4.** US [law enforcement agent] shérif *m* adjoint. ◆ comp ▶ **deputy chairman** vice-président *m* ▶ **deputy head teacher** or **deputy head** *inf* directeur *m* adjoint, directrice *f* adjointe ▶ **deputy manager** directeur *m* adjoint ▶ **deputy mayor** adjoint *m*, -e *f* au maire.

derail [dɪ'reɪl] ◆ vt faire dérailler. ◆ vi dérailler.

derailment [dɪ'reɪlmənt] n déraillement *m*.

deranged [dɪ'reɪndʒd] adj dérangé, déséquilibré.

derby [UK 'dɑːbɪ US 'dɜːbɪ] n **1.** [match] ▶ **a local derby** un derby **2.** US [race] derby *m*. ❖ **Derby** pr n ▶ **the Derby** grande course annuelle de chevaux à Epsom, en Grande-Bretagne.

deregulate [ˌdiː'regjʊleɪt] vt **1.** ECON [prices, wages] libérer, déréguler **2.** [relax restrictions on] assouplir les règlements de, déréglementer.

deregulation [ˌdiːregjʊ'leɪʃn] n **1.** ECON [of prices, wages] libération *f*, dérégulation *f* **2.** [relaxation of restrictions] assouplissement *m* des règlements, déréglementation *f*.

derelict ['derəlɪkt] ◆ adj **1.** [abandoned] abandonné, délaissé **2.** [negligent, neglectful] négligent. ◆ n **1.** [vagrant] clochard *m*, -e *f*, vagabond *m*, -e *f* **2.** NAUT navire *m* abandonné.

dereliction [ˌderə'lɪkʃn] n **1.** [abandonment] abandon *m* **2.** US [negligence] négligence *f* ▶ **dereliction of duty** manquement *m* au devoir.

deride [dɪ'raɪd] vt tourner en dérision, railler.

derision [dɪ'rɪʒn] n dérision *f*.

derisive [dɪ'raɪsɪv] adj moqueur.

derisively [dɪ'raɪsɪvlɪ] adv avec dérision ; [say, speak] d'un ton moqueur.

derisory [də'raɪzərɪ] adj **1.** [ridiculous] dérisoire **2.** [mocking, scornful] moqueur.

derivation [ˌderɪ'veɪʃn] n dérivation *f*.

derivative [dɪ'rɪvətɪv] ◆ adj **1.** [gen] dérivé **2.** *pej* peu original, banal. ◆ n [gen] dérivé *m* ; MATH dérivée *f*.

derive [dɪ'raɪv] ◆ vt **1.** [gain, obtain] : *she derives great pleasure from her garden* elle tire beaucoup de plaisir de son jardin **2.** [deduce] dériver de. ◆ vi ▶ **to derive from** provenir de.

dermatitis [ˌdɜːmə'taɪtɪs] n (U) dermite *f*, dermatite *f*.

dermatologist [ˌdɜːmə'tɒlədʒɪst] n dermatologiste *mf*, dermatologue *mf*.

dermatology [ˌdɜːmə'tɒlədʒɪ] n dermatologie *f*.

derogatory [dɪ'rɒgətrɪ] adj [comment, remark] désobligeant, critique ; [word] péjoratif.

> ⚠ **Dérogatoire** is a technical word meaning dispensatory, **not** derogatory.

derrick ['derɪk] n UK [crane] mât *m* de charge ; PETR derrick *m*.

derv [dɜːv] n UK gas-oil *m*.

desalination [diːˌsælɪ'neɪʃn] ◆ n dessalement *m*. ◆ comp [plant] de dessalement.

descend [dɪ'send] vi **1.** *fml* [go, move down] descendre **2.** [fall] tomber, s'abattre **3.** [pass on by ancestry] descendre ; [pass on by inheritance] revenir / *dogs and wolves probably descend from a common ancestor* les chiens et les loups descendent probablement d'un ancêtre commun / *Lord Grey's title descended to his grandson* le titre de Lord Grey est revenu à son petit-fils **4.** [attack, invade] ▶ **to descend on sb a)** [attack] se jeter sur qqn **b)** [intrude on] faire irruption chez qqn **5.** [sink, stoop] s'abaisser, descendre / *you don't want to descend to their level* tu ne vas quand même pas te rabaisser à leur niveau.

descendant [dɪ'sendənt] n descendant *m*, -e *f*.

descended [dɪ'sendɪd] adj : *she is descended from the Russian aristocracy* elle descend or est issue de l'aristocratie russe.

descending [dɪ'sendɪŋ] adj descendant.

descent [dɪ'sent] n **1.** [move downward] descente *f* **2.** *fig & liter* [decline] chute *f* **3.** [origin] origine *f* / *of Irish descent* d'origine irlandaise **4.** [succession, transmission] transmission *f* **5.** [invasion] descente *f*.

describe [dɪ'skraɪb] vt **1.** [recount, represent] décrire **2.** [characterize] définir, qualifier **3.** [outline, draw] décrire.

description [dɪ'skrɪpʃn] n **1.** [account, representation] description *f* ; [physical] portrait *m* ; ADMIN signalement *m* / *can you give us a description of the man?* pouvez-vous nous faire un portrait de l'homme ? / *a man answering the police description* un homme correspondant au signalement donné par la police **2.** [kind] sorte *f*, genre *m*.

descriptive [dɪ'skrɪptɪv] adj descriptif.

desecrate ['desɪkreɪt] vt profaner.

desecration [ˌdesɪ'kreɪʃn] n profanation *f*.

deseed [ˌdiː'siːd] vt [fruit] épépiner.

desegregate [ˌdiː'segrɪgeɪt] vt abolir la ségrégation raciale dans.

deselect [ˌdiːsɪ'lekt] vt UK POL ne pas réinvestir (*un candidat*).

desensitize, desensitise [ˌdiː'sensɪtaɪz] vt désensibiliser.

desert[1] ['dezət] ◆ n [wilderness] désert *m*. ◆ comp [area, plant, sand] désertique.

desert[2] [dɪ'zɜːt] ◆ vt [person] abandonner, délaisser *liter* ; [place] abandonner, déserter ; [organization, principle] déserter. ◆ vi MIL déserter.

deserted [dɪ'zɜːtɪd] adj désert.

deserter [dɪ'zɜːtəʳ] n déserteur *m*.

desertion [dɪ'zɜːʃn] n MIL désertion *f* ; LAW [of spouse] abandon *m* (du domicile conjugal) ; [of cause, organization] défection *f*, désertion *f*.

desert island ['dezət-] n île *f* déserte.

deserts [dɪ'zɜːts] pl n [reward] ▶ **to get one's just deserts** avoir ce que l'on mérite.

deserve [dɪ'zɜːv] vt mériter / *I think he got what he deserved* je pense qu'il a eu ce qu'il méritait.

deserved [dɪ'zɜːvd] adj mérité(e).

deservedly [dɪ'zɜːvɪdlɪ] adv à juste titre, à bon droit.

deserving [dɪ'zɜːvɪŋ] adj [person] méritant ; [cause, organization] méritoire.

desiccated ['desɪkeɪtɪd] adj **1.** [dehydrated] ▶ **desiccated coconut** noix *f* de coco séchée **2.** [dull - style] aride ; [- person] desséché.

design [dɪ'zaɪn] ◆ n **1.** [drawing, sketch] dessin *m* ; INDUST dessin *m*, plan *m* ; ARCHIT plan *m*, projet *m* ; TEXT modèle *m* ; [of book] maquette *f* **2.** INDUST [composition, structure - of car, computer, etc.] conception *f* **3.** [subject for study] design *m* ▶ **book design** conception *f* graphique

❱ **fashion design** stylisme *m* **4.** [pattern] motif *m* **5.** [purpose, intent] dessein *m* ❱ **to do sthg by design** faire qqch à dessein or exprès ❱ **to have designs on sb / sthg** avoir des vues sur qqn / qqch. ◆ comp [course] de dessin ❱ **design award** prix *m* du meilleur design ❱ **design department** bureau *m* d'études ❱ **design engineer** ingénieur *m* d'études ❱ **design fault** défaut *m* de conception ❱ **design studio** cabinet *m* de design. ◆ vt [plan] concevoir ; [on paper] dessiner ; ARCHIT faire les plans de ; TEXT concevoir, créer / *to be designed for sb* [aimed at] s'adresser à qqn.

Design and Technology *n* 🇬🇧 SCH technologie *f* *(matière scolaire)*, techno *f inf.*

designate ◆ vt ['dezɪgneɪt] *fml* **1.** [appoint, name] désigner, nommer / *this area has been designated a no-smoking zone* cette zone est destinée aux non-fumeurs ❱ **designated driver** personne qui s'engage à ne pas boire pour pouvoir reconduire d'autres personnes en voiture **2.** [indicate, signify] indiquer, montrer. ◆ adj ['dezɪgnət] désigné.

designation [,dezɪg'neɪʃn] *n* désignation *f.*

designer [dɪ'zaɪnə*ʳ*] ◆ *n* ART & INDUST dessinateur *m*, -trice *f* ; TEXT modéliste *mf*, styliste *mf* ; CIN & THEAT décorateur *m*, -trice *f* ; [of high fashion clothes] couturier *m*, -ère *f* ; [of books, magazines] maquettiste *mf* ; [of furniture] designer *m*. ◆ comp [jeans] haute couture ; [glasses, handbag] de marque ; [furniture] design.

designer stubble *n hum* barbe *f* de deux jours.

desirability [dɪ,zaɪərə'bɪlətɪ] *n (U)* **1.** [benefits] intérêt *m*, avantage *m*, opportunité *f* **2.** [attractiveness] charmes *mpl*, attraits *mpl.*

desirable [dɪ'zaɪərəbl] adj **1.** [advisable] souhaitable, désirable *fml* **2.** [attractive] à désirer, tentant **3.** [sexually appealing] désirable, séduisant.

desire [dɪ'zaɪə*ʳ*] ◆ *n* **1.** [wish] désir *m*, envie *f* / *she had no desire to go back* elle n'avait aucune envie d'y retourner **2.** [sexual attraction] désir *m*. ◆ vt **1.** [want, wish] désirer / *the agreement left much* or *a great deal or a lot to be desired* l'accord laissait beaucoup à désirer / *his words had the desired effect* ses paroles eurent l'effet désiré or escompté **2.** [want sexually] désirer.

desist [dɪ'zɪst] vi *fml* cesser.

desk [desk] ◆ *n* **1.** [in home, office] bureau *m* ; [with folding top] secrétaire *m* ; SCH [for pupil] pupitre *m* ; [for teacher] bureau *m* **2.** [reception counter] réception *f* ; [cashier] caisse *f* **3.** PRESS [section] service *m* / *the sports desk* le service des informations sportives. ◆ comp [diary, job, lamp] de bureau ❱ **desk tidy** porte-crayon *m.*

deskbound ['deskbaund] adj sédentaire.

desk clerk *n* 🇺🇸 réceptionniste *mf.*

desk editor *n* rédacteur *m*, -trice *f.*

deskill [,di:'skɪl] vt déqualifier.

desktop ['desktɒp] *n* [computer interface] bureau *m*. ◆ adj [computer, model] de bureau.

desktop publishing *n* publication *f* assistée par ordinateur, PAO *f*, microédition *f.*

desolate ◆ adj ['desələt] **1.** [area, place - empty] désert ; [- barren, lifeless] désolé ; *fig* [gloomy, bleak] morne, sombre **2.** [person - sorrowful] consterné, abattu ; [- friendless] délaissé. ◆ vt ['desəleɪt] **1.** [area, place - devastate] dévaster, saccager ; [- depopulate] dépeupler **2.** [person] désoler, navrer.

desolation [,desə'leɪʃn] *n* **1.** [barrenness, emptiness] caractère *m* désert, désolation *f* ; [devastation, ruin] dévastation *f*, ravages *mpl* **2.** [despair, sorrow] désolation *f*, consternation *f* ; [loneliness] solitude *f.*

despair [dɪ'speə*ʳ*] ◆ *n* **1.** [hopelessness] désespoir *m* / *in despair, she took her own life* de désespoir elle a mis fin à ses jours / *their son drove them to despair* leur fils les

désespérait or les réduisait au désespoir **2.** [cause of distress] désespoir *m* / *William was the despair of his teachers* William faisait or était le désespoir de tous ses professeurs. ◆ vi désespérer / *she began to despair of ever finding her brother alive* elle commençait à désespérer de retrouver un jour son frère vivant.

despairing [dɪ'speərɪŋ] adj [cry, look] de désespoir, désespéré ; [person] abattu, consterné.

despairingly [dɪ'speərɪŋlɪ] adv [look, speak] avec désespoir.

despatch [dɪ'spætʃ] = **dispatch**.

desperate ['desprət] adj **1.** [hopeless, serious] désespéré / *the refugees are in desperate need of help* les réfugiés ont désespérément besoin d'assistance **2.** [reckless] désespéré / *he died in a desperate attempt to escape* il est mort en essayant désespérément de s'évader / *a desperate criminal / man* un criminel / homme prêt à tout **3.** [intent, eager] : *to be desperate for money* avoir un besoin urgent d'argent / *she was desperate to leave home* elle voulait à tout prix partir de chez elle.

desperately ['desprətlɪ] adv **1.** [hopelessly, seriously] désespérément ❱ **desperately ill** gravement malade **2.** [recklessly] désespérément.

desperation [,despə'reɪʃn] *n* désespoir *m* / *he agreed in desperation* en désespoir de cause, il a accepté.

despicable [dɪ'spɪkəbl] adj [person] méprisable, détestable ; [action, behaviour] méprisable, ignoble.

despicably [dɪ'spɪkəblɪ] adv [behave] bassement, d'une façon indigne.

despise [dɪ'spaɪz] vt [feel contempt for] mépriser.

despite [dɪ'spaɪt] prep malgré, en dépit de / *despite the fact that* malgré le fait que.

📋 Note that malgré que is followed by a verb in the subjunctive:
I was happy despite my parents' not being able to attend. *J'étais content malgré que mes parents n'aient pas pu venir.*

---

despondent [dɪ'spɒndənt] adj abattu, consterné.

despondently [dɪ'spɒndəntlɪ] adv d'un air consterné ; [say, speak] d'un ton consterné.

despot ['despɒt] *n* despote *m.*

despotic [de'spɒtɪk] adj despotique.

dessert [dɪ'zɜːt] ◆ *n* dessert *m*. ◆ comp [dish, plate] à dessert ❱ **a dessert apple** une pomme à couteau ❱ **a dessert wine** un vin de dessert.

dessertspoon [dɪ'zɜːtspuːn] *n* cuiller *f* à dessert.

destabilization [di:,steɪbɪlaɪ'zeɪʃn] *n* déstabilisation *f.*

destabilize, destabilise [,di:'steɪbɪlaɪz] vt déstabiliser.

destination [,destɪ'neɪʃn] *n* destination *f.*

destined ['destɪnd] adj **1.** [intended] : *she felt she was destined for an acting career* elle sentait qu'elle était destinée à une carrière d'actrice / *their plan was destined to fail* or *for failure* leur projet était voué à l'échec **2.** [bound] : *the flight was destined for Sydney* le vol était à destination de Sydney.

destiny ['destɪnɪ] *n* [fate] destin *m* ; [personal fate] destinée *f*, destin *m.*

destitute ['destɪtjuːt] ◆ adj [extremely poor] dans la misère, sans ressources. ◆ pl *n* ❱ **the destitute** les indigents *mpl* or démunis *mpl.*

destitution [,destɪ'tjuːʃn] *n* misère *f*, indigence *f.*

de-stress [diː'stres] n déstresser *inf*.

destroy [dɪ'strɔɪ] vt **1.** [demolish, wreck] détruire **2.** [ruin, spoil - efforts, hope, love] anéantir, briser ; [- career, friendship, marriage] briser ; [- health] ruiner **3.** [kill - farm animal] abattre ; [- pet] supprimer, (faire) piquer.

destroyer [dɪ'strɔɪər] n MIL destroyer *m*, contre-torpilleur *m*.

destruction [dɪ'strʌkʃn] n **1.** [demolition, devastation] destruction *f* **2.** [elimination - of evidence] suppression *f* ; [- of life, hope] anéantissement *m* **3.** *fig* [ruin] ruine *f*.

destructive [dɪ'strʌktɪv] adj destructeur.

destructively [dɪ'strʌktɪvlɪ] adv de façon destructrice.

destructiveness [dɪ'strʌktɪvnɪs] n [of bomb, weapon] capacité *f* destructrice ; [of criticism] caractère *m* destructeur ; [of person] penchant *m* destructeur.

desultory ['desəltrɪ] adj *fml* [conversation] décousu, sans suite ; [attempt] peu suivi, peu soutenu, sans suite.

Det. written abbr of **detective**.

detach [dɪ'tætʃ] vt **1.** [handle, hood] détacher **2.** [person] ▸ **to detach o.s.** se détacher, prendre du recul **3.** MIL [troops] envoyer en détachement.

detachable [dɪ'tætʃəbl] adj [collar, lining] amovible.

detached [dɪ'tætʃt] adj **1.** [separate] détaché, séparé ▸ **detached house** 🇬🇧 maison *f* individuelle, pavillon *m* **2.** [objective] objectif ; [unemotional] détaché.

detachment [dɪ'tætʃmənt] n [indifference] détachement *m* ; [objectivity] objectivité *f*.

detail [🇬🇧 'diːteɪl 🇺🇸 dɪ'teɪl] ◆ n [item, element] détail *m* / **there's no need to go into detail** or **details** ça ne sert à rien d'entrer dans les détails / **the author recounts his childhood in great detail** l'auteur raconte son enfance dans les moindres détails / **attention to detail is important** il faut être minutieux or méticuleux. ◆ vt **1.** [enumerate, specify] raconter en détail, détailler, énumérer **2.** MIL détacher, affecter. ◆ **details** pl n [particulars] renseignements *mpl*, précisions *fpl* ; [name, address, etc.] coordonnées *fpl*.

detailed [🇬🇧 'diːteɪld 🇺🇸 dɪ'teɪld] adj détaillé.

detailing ['diːteɪlɪŋ] n 🇺🇸 [thorough cleaning] nettoyage *m* complet.

detain [dɪ'teɪn] vt **1.** *fml* [delay] retenir **2.** LAW [keep in custody] retenir, garder à vue.

detainee [ˌdiːteɪ'niː] n détenu *m*, -e *f*.

detect [dɪ'tekt] vt déceler, discerner, distinguer, découvrir ; MIL & MIN détecter ; MED dépister.

detectable [dɪ'tektəbl] adj MIL & MIN détectable ; [illness] que l'on peut dépister.

detection [dɪ'tekʃn] ◆ n **1.** [discovery] découverte *f* ; MIL & MIN détection *f* ; MED dépistage *m* **2.** [investigation] recherche *f* / **crime detection** la recherche des criminels. ◆ adj [device] de détection ; MED de dépistage.

detective [dɪ'tektɪv] ◆ n [on a police force] ≃ inspecteur *m*, -trice *f* de police ; [private] détective *m*. ◆ comp [film, novel, story] policier ▸ **detective agency** agence *f* de détectives privés ▸ **detective work** investigations *fpl*.

detector [dɪ'tektər] n détecteur *m*.

detector van n 🇬🇧 voiture-radar utilisée pour la détection des postes de télévision non déclarés.

detention [dɪ'tenʃn] n **1.** [captivity] détention *f* / **in detention a)** [gen] en détention **b)** MIL aux arrêts **2.** SCH retenue *f*, consigne *f* ▸ **to put sb in detention** consigner qqn, mettre qqn en retenue.

deter [dɪ'tɜːr] (*pt* & *pp* **deterred**, *cont* **deterring**) vt **1.** [discourage - person] dissuader ▸ **to deter sb from doing sthg** dissuader qqn de faire qqch **2.** [prevent - attack] prévenir.

detergent [dɪ'tɜːdʒənt] ◆ n détergent *m*, détersif *m* ; 🇺🇸 [washing powder] lessive *f*. ◆ adj détersif, détergent.

deteriorate [dɪ'tɪərɪəreɪt] vi se détériorer.

deterioration [dɪˌtɪərɪə'reɪʃn] n détérioration *f* ; [in health, relations] dégradation *f*, détérioration *f*.

determination [dɪˌtɜːmɪ'neɪʃn] n **1.** [resolve] détermination *f*, résolution *f* **2.** [establishment, fixing - of prices, wages, etc.] détermination *f*, fixation *f* ; [- of boundaries] délimitation *f*, établissement *m*.

determine [dɪ'tɜːmɪn] vt **1.** [control, govern] déterminer, décider de **2.** [establish, find out] déterminer, établir **3.** [settle - date, price] déterminer, fixer ; [- boundary] délimiter, établir **4.** *liter* [resolve] : **she determined to prove her innocence** elle a décidé de or s'est résolue à prouver son innocence.

determined [dɪ'tɜːmɪnd] adj **1.** [decided, resolved] déterminé, décidé ▸ **to be determined to do sthg** être déterminé or résolu à faire qqch **2.** [resolute] : **they made determined efforts to find all survivors** ils ont fait tout ce qu'ils ont pu pour retrouver tous les survivants.

determining [dɪ'tɜːmɪnɪŋ] adj déterminant.

deterrent [dɪ'terənt] ◆ n **1.** [gen] agent *m* de dissuasion **2.** MIL arme *f* de dissuasion. ◆ adj dissuasif, de dissuasion.

detest [dɪ'test] vt détester / **she detests having to make small talk** elle a horreur de or elle déteste papoter.

detestable [dɪ'testəbl] adj détestable, exécrable.

detonate ['detəneɪt] ◆ vt faire détoner or exploser. ◆ vi détoner, exploser.

detonation [ˌdetə'neɪʃn] n détonation *f*, explosion *f*.

detonator ['detəneɪtər] n détonateur *m*, amorce *f* ; RAIL pétard *m*.

detour ['diːˌtʊər] n [in road, stream] détour *m* ; [for traffic] déviation *f*.

detox ['diːtɒks] n *inf* désintoxication *f* ▸ **detox centre** centre *m* de désintoxication.

detoxification [diːˌtɒksɪfɪ'keɪʃn] n [of person] désintoxication *f* ▸ **detoxification programme** cure *f* de désintoxication.

detract [dɪ'trækt] vi ▸ **to detract from sthg** diminuer qqch.

detractor [dɪ'træktər] n détracteur *m*, -trice *f*.

detriment ['detrɪmənt] n : **to his detriment** à son détriment or préjudice / **to the detriment of his work** aux dépens de son travail.

detrimental [ˌdetrɪ'mentl] adj ▸ **detrimental to** [health, reputation] nuisible à, préjudiciable à ▸ **detrimental to** [interests] qui nuit à, qui cause un préjudice à.

Deutschmark ['dɔɪtʃˌmɑːk] n mark *m* allemand.

devaluation [ˌdiːvæljʊ'eɪʃn] n dévaluation *f*.

devalue [ˌdiː'væljuː] vt dévaluer.

devastate ['devəsteɪt] vt **1.** [country, town] dévaster, ravager ; [enemy] anéantir **2.** [overwhelm] foudroyer, accabler, anéantir / **he was devastated by his mother's death** la mort de sa mère l'a complètement anéanti.

devastated ['devəsteɪtɪd] adj **1.** [area, city] dévasté **2.** [person] accablé.

devastating ['devəsteɪtɪŋ] adj **1.** [disastrous - passion, storm] dévastateur, ravageur ; [- news] accablant ; [- argument, effect] accablant, écrasant **2.** [highly effective - person, charm] irrésistible.

devastatingly ['devəsteɪtɪŋlɪ] adv de manière dévastatrice ; [as intensifier] : **devastatingly beautiful** d'une beauté irrésistible.

devastation [ˌdevə'steɪʃn] n [disaster] dévastation *f*.

develop [dɪ'veləp] ◆ vi **1.** [evolve - country, person] se développer, évoluer ; [- feeling] se former, grandir ; [- plot] se développer, se dérouler ▸ **to develop into sthg** devenir qqch **2.** [become apparent - disease] se manifester, se déclarer ; [- talent, trend] se manifester ; [- event] se produire **3.** PHOT se développer. ◆ vt **1.** [form - body, mind] développer, former ; [- story] développer ; [- feeling] former **2.** [expand - business, market] développer ; [- idea, argument] développer, expliquer (en détail), exposer (en détail) **3.** [improve - skill] développer, travailler ; [- machine, process] mettre au point **4.** [acquire - disease] contracter ; [- cold, tic] attraper ; [- symptoms] présenter **5.** [land, resources] exploiter, mettre en valeur, aménager **6.** MATH, MUS & PHOT développer.

developed [dɪ'veləpt] adj [film] développé ; [land] mis en valeur, aménagé ; [country] développé.

developer [dɪ'veləpər] n **1.** [of land] promoteur m (de construction) **2.** [person] ▸ **to be a late developer** se développer sur le tard **3.** PHOT révélateur m, développateur m.

developing country, developing nation n pays m or nation f en voie de développement.

development [dɪ'veləpmənt] n **1.** [of body, person, mind] développement m, formation f ; [of ideas, language] développement m, évolution f ; [of argument, theme] développement m, exposé m ; [of plot, situation] déroulement m, développement m ; [of business] développement m, expansion f ; [of invention, process] mise f au point ; [of region] mise f en valeur, exploitation f ▸ **development grant** subvention f pour le développement **2.** [incident] fait m nouveau **3.** [tract of land] ▸ **industrial development** zone f industrielle ▸ **housing development a)** [of houses] lotissement m **b)** [of blocks of flats] cité f **4.** MATH, MUS & PHOT développement m.

developmental [dɪ,veləp'mentl] adj de développement ▸ **developmental disorder** trouble m du développement.

development area n zone économiquement sinistrée bénéficiant d'aides publiques en vue de sa reconversion.

deviance ['diːvjəns], **deviancy** ['diːvjənsɪ] n [gen & PSYCHOL] déviance f.

deviant ['diːvjənt] ◆ adj **1.** [behaviour] déviant, qui s'écarte de la norme ; [growth] anormal ▸ **sexually deviant** perverti **2.** LING déviant. ◆ n déviant m, -e f ▸ **sexual deviant** pervers m, -e f.

deviate ['diːvɪeɪt] vi **1.** [differ] dévier, s'écarter **2.** [plane, ship] dévier, dériver ; [missile] dévier.

deviation [,diːvɪ'eɪʃn] n **1.** [from custom, principle] déviation f ; [from social norm] déviance f **2.** [in statistics] écart m **3.** [of plane, ship] déviation f, dérive f ; [of missile] déviation f, dérivation f **4.** MATH, MED & PHILOS déviation f.

device [dɪ'vaɪs] n **1.** [gadget] appareil m, engin m, mécanisme m ▸ **safety device** dispositif m de sécurité **2.** [scheme] ruse f, stratagème m ▸ **to leave sb to their own devices** laisser qqn se débrouiller (tout seul).

devil ['devl] (UK pt & pp **devilled**, cont **devilling** ; US pt & pp **deviled**, cont **deviling**) ◆ n **1.** [demon] diable m, démon m ▸ **the Devil** RELIG le Diable, Satan m ▸ **to play devil's advocate** se faire l'avocat du diable **2.** inf & fig [person] : you little devil! petit monstre ! / you lucky devil! veinard ! / poor devil! pauvre diable ! **3.** inf [as intensifier] : what the devil are you doing? mais enfin, qu'est-ce que tu fabriques ? / how the devil should I know? comment voulez-vous que je sache ? ▸ **to have the luck of the devil** or **the devil's own luck** avoir une veine de pendu or de cocu ▸ **speak** or **talk of the devil (and he appears)!** quand on parle du loup (on en voit la queue) ! ◆ vt **1.** CULIN accommoder à la moutarde et au poivre ▸ **devilled egg** œuf m à la diable **2.** US inf [harass] harceler.

devilish ['devlɪʃ] adj [fiendish] diabolique, infernal ; [mischievous] espiègle.

devil-may-care adj [careless] insouciant ; [reckless] casse-cou.

devious ['diːvjəs] adj **1.** [cunning - person] retors, sournois ; [- means, method] détourné ; [- mind] tortueux **2.** [winding - route] sinueux.

deviously ['diːvjəslɪ] adv sournoisement.

deviousness ['diːvjəsnɪs] n [of person] sournoiserie f ; [of plan] complexité f.

devise [dɪ'vaɪz] vt **1.** [plan] imaginer, inventer, concevoir, élaborer ; [plot] combiner, manigancer **2.** LAW [property] léguer.

deviser [dɪ'vaɪzər] n [of plan] inventeur m, -trice f ; [of scheme] auteur m.

devoid [dɪ'vɔɪd] adj ▸ **devoid of** dépourvu de, dénué de.

devolution [,diːvə'luːʃn] n **1.** [of duty, power] délégation f ; LAW [of property] transmission f, dévolution f **2.** POL décentralisation f.

devolve [dɪ'vɒlv] ◆ vi [duty, job] incomber ; [by chance] incomber, échoir / the responsibility devolves on or upon him la responsabilité lui incombe or lui échoit. ◆ vt déléguer ▸ **to devolve sthg on** or **upon** or **to sb** déléguer qqch à qqn, charger qqn de qqch.

devote [dɪ'vəʊt] vt consacrer ▸ **to devote o.s. to a)** [study, work] se consacrer or s'adonner à **b)** [a cause] se vouer or se consacrer à **c)** [pleasure] se livrer à.

devoted [dɪ'vəʊtɪd] adj [friend, servant, service] dévoué, fidèle ; [admirer] fervent.

devotee [,devə'tiː] n [of opera, sport, etc.] passionné m, -e f ; [of doctrine] adepte mf, partisan m, -e f ; [of religion] adepte mf.

devotion [dɪ'vəʊʃn] n **1.** [to person] dévouement m, attachement m ; [to cause] dévouement m **2.** RELIG dévotion f, piété f. ◆ **devotions** pl n dévotions fpl, prières fpl.

 dévotion or **dévouement?**

Dévotion usually refers to religious devotion or fervour, whereas **dévouement** is used in more general contexts to refer to devotion to a cause or to other people.

devour [dɪ'vaʊər] vt **1.** [food] dévorer, engloutir ; fig [book] dévorer **2.** [subj: fire] dévorer, consumer.

devout [dɪ'vaʊt] adj [person] pieux, dévot ; [hope, prayer] fervent.

dew [djuː] n rosée f.

dexterity [dek'sterətɪ] n adresse f, dextérité f.

dexterous ['dekstrəs] adj [person] adroit, habile ; [movement] adroit, habile, agile.

dextrose ['dekstrəʊs] n dextrose m.

DfE (abbr of **Department for Education**) n ministère britannique de l'éducation nationale.

DfT (abbr of **Department for Transport**) n ministère britannique du transport.

DG (abbr of **director-general**) n DG m.

dhal [dɑːl] n CULIN plat indien à base de lentilles et d'épices.

DHTML [,diːeɪtʃtiːem'el] (abbr of **Dynamic Hypertext Markup Language**) n COMPUT DHTML m.

diabetes [,daɪə'biːtiːz] n diabète m.

diabetic [,daɪə'betɪk] ◆ adj diabétique. ◆ n diabétique mf. ◆ comp [jam, biscuits] pour diabétiques.

diabolical [ˌdaɪə'bɒlɪkl] adj inf [terrible] atroce, épouvantable, infernal.

diagnose ['daɪəgnəʊz] vt [illness] diagnostiquer ; fig [fault, problem] déceler, discerner.

diagnosis [ˌdaɪəg'nəʊsɪs] (pl diagnoses [-si:z]) n MED & fig diagnostic m ; BIOL & BOT diagnose f.

diagnostic [ˌdaɪəg'nɒstɪk] adj diagnostique.

diagonal [daɪ'ægənl] ◆ adj diagonal. ◆ n diagonale f.

diagonally [daɪ'ægənəlɪ] adv en diagonale, diagonalement, obliquement.

diagram ['daɪəgræm] (🇬🇧 pt & pp **diagrammed**, cont **diagramming** ; 🇺🇸 pt & pp **diagramed** or **diagramming**, cont **diagraming** or **diagramming**) n [gen] diagramme m, schéma m ; MATH diagramme m, figure f.

dial ['daɪəl] (🇬🇧 pt & pp **dialled**, cont **dialling** ; 🇺🇸 pt & pp **dialed**, cont **dialing**) ◆ n [of clock, telephone] cadran m ; [of radio, TV] bouton m (de réglage). ◆ vt [number] faire, composer.

Dial-a-...

Ce préfixe introduit le nom de certains services téléphoniques aux États-Unis et au Royaume-Uni: **dial-a-wake-up** (réveil), **dial-a-date** (rencontres), **dial-a-prayer** (prières préenregistrées), etc.

dialect ['daɪəlekt] n [regional] dialecte m, parler m ; [local, rural] patois m.

dialling code ['daɪəlɪŋ-] n 🇬🇧 indicatif m.

dialling tone 🇬🇧 ['daɪəlɪŋ-], **dial tone** 🇺🇸 n tonalité f.

dialogue 🇬🇧, **dialog** 🇺🇸 ['daɪəlɒg] n dialogue m.

dialogue box 🇬🇧, **dialog box** 🇺🇸 n COMPUT boîte f de dialogue.

dial tone 🇺🇸 = dialling tone.

dial-up n ▸ **dial-up connection** connexion f par téléphone ▸ **dial-up modem** modem m téléphonique.

dialysis [daɪ'ælɪsɪs] (pl dialyses [-si:z]) n dialyse f ▸ **dialysis machine** dialyseur m.

diameter [daɪ'æmɪtər] n [gen & GEOM] diamètre m.

diametrically [ˌdaɪə'metrɪklɪ] adv GEOM diamétralement.

diamond ['daɪəmənd] ◆ n **1.** [gem] diamant m ▸ **he's a diamond in the rough** il a un cœur d'or sous ses dehors frustes **2.** [shape] losange m **3.** CARDS carreau m **4.** [in baseball] terrain m (de base-ball). ◆ comp **1.** [brooch, ring, etc.] de diamant or diamants ▸ **diamond necklace** collier m or rivière f de diamants **2.** [mine] de diamant or diamants ▸ **diamond drill** foreuse f à pointe de diamant ▸ **diamond merchant** diamantaire m.

diamond wedding n noces fpl de diamant.

diaper ['daɪəpər] n 🇺🇸 [nappy] couche f (de bébé).

diaphanous [daɪ'æfənəs] adj diaphane.

diaphragm ['daɪəfræm] n diaphragme m.

diarrhoea 🇬🇧, **diarrhea** 🇺🇸 [ˌdaɪə'rɪə] n diarrhée f / **to have diarrhoea** avoir la diarrhée.

diary ['daɪərɪ] (pl diaries) n **1.** [personal] journal m (intime) ▸ **to keep a diary** tenir un journal **2.** 🇬🇧 [for business] agenda m.

diatribe ['daɪətraɪb] n diatribe f.

dice [daɪs] (pl dice) ◆ n **1.** [game] dé m / **to play dice** jouer aux dés **2.** CULIN dé m, cube m. ◆ vt CULIN couper en dés or en cubes. ◆ vi jouer aux dés.

dicey ['daɪsɪ] (compar **dicier**, superl **diciest**) adj inf risqué, dangereux, délicat.

dichotomy [daɪ'kɒtəmɪ] (pl **dichotomies**) n dichotomie f.

dick [dɪk] n **1.** vulg [penis] queue f **2.** 🇬🇧 v inf [idiot] con m.

dickens ['dɪkɪnz] n inf : **what the dickens are you doing?** mais qu'est-ce que tu fabriques ?

dickhead ['dɪkhed] n v inf con m.

Dictaphone® ['dɪktəfəʊn] n Dictaphone® m, machine f à dicter.

dictate ◆ vt [dɪk'teɪt] **1.** [letter] dicter ▸ **to dictate sthg to sb** dicter qqch à qqn **2.** [determine - terms, conditions] dicter, imposer / **he dictates how we run the business** c'est lui qui décide de la marche de l'entreprise / **our budget will dictate the type of computer we buy** le type d'ordinateur que nous achèterons dépendra de notre budget. ◆ vi [dɪk'teɪt] [give dictation] dicter. ◆ n ['dɪkteɪt] **1.** [order] ordre m **2.** (usu pl) [principle] précepte m / **the dictates of conscience / reason** la voix de la conscience / raison. ◆❖ **dictate to** vt insep donner des ordres à / **I won't be dictated to** je n'ai pas d'ordres à recevoir !

dictation [dɪk'teɪʃn] n [of letter, story] dictée f.

dictator [dɪk'teɪtər] n dictateur m.

dictatorial [ˌdɪktə'tɔːrɪəl] adj dictatorial.

dictatorship [dɪk'teɪtəʃɪp] n dictature f.

diction ['dɪkʃn] n **1.** [pronunciation] diction f, élocution f **2.** [phrasing] style m, langage m.

dictionary ['dɪkʃənrɪ] (pl **dictionaries**) n dictionnaire m.

dictum ['dɪktəm] (pl **dicta** ['dɪktə] or **dictums**) n fml **1.** [statement] affirmation f **2.** [maxim] dicton m, maxime f.

did [dɪd] pt ⟶ do.

didactic [dɪ'dæktɪk] adj didactique.

diddle ['dɪdl] vt 🇬🇧 inf duper, rouler ▸ **to diddle sb out of sthg** carotter qqch à qqn.

diddly-squat ['dɪdlɪ-] n 🇺🇸 inf que dalle.

didn't ['dɪdnt] abbr of did not.

die [daɪ] ◆ vi **1.** [person] mourir, décéder / **she's dying** elle est mourante or à l'agonie / **she died of cancer** elle est morte du or d'un cancer ; fig ▸ **to die laughing** inf mourir de rire ▸ **I nearly died** inf, **I could have died** inf **a)** [from fear] j'étais mort de trouille **b)** [from embarrassment] j'aurais voulu rentrer sous terre, je ne savais plus où me mettre **2.** [animal, plant] mourir **3.** [engine] caler, s'arrêter **4.** [fire, love, memory] s'éteindre, mourir ; [tradition] s'éteindre, disparaître, mourir ; [smile] disparaître, s'évanouir **5.** inf [want very much] ▸ **to be dying for sthg** avoir une envie folle de qqch ▸ **to be dying to do sthg** mourir d'envie de faire qqch. ◆ vt ▸ **to die a natural / violent death** mourir de sa belle mort / de mort violente. ◆ n **1.** (pl **dice** [daɪs] GAMES dé m (à jouer) **2.** (pl **dies**) ARCHIT [dado] dé m (d'un piédestal) ; TECH [stamp] matrice f ; [in minting] coin m. ◆❖ **die away** vi s'affaiblir, s'éteindre, mourir. ◆❖ **die back** vi [plant] dépérir. ◆❖ **die down** vi **1.** [wind] tomber, se calmer ; [fire - in chimney] baisser ; [- in building, forest] s'apaiser, diminuer ; [noise] diminuer ; [anger, protest] se calmer, s'apaiser **2.** [plant] se flétrir, perdre ses feuilles et sa tige. ◆❖ **die off** vi mourir les uns après les autres. ◆❖ **die out** vi [family, tribe, tradition] disparaître, s'éteindre ; [fire] s'éteindre.

diehard ['daɪhɑːd] ◆ n conservateur m, -trice f, réactionnaire mf. ◆ adj intransigeant ; POL réactionnaire.

diesel ['diːzl] n [vehicle] diesel m ; [fuel] gas-oil m, gazole m.

diesel engine n AUTO moteur m diesel ; RAIL motrice f.

diesel fuel, diesel oil n gas-oil m, gazole m.

diet ['daɪət] ◆ n **1.** [regular food] alimentation f, nourriture f / *they live on a diet of rice and fish* ils se nourrissent de riz et de poisson **2.** [restricted or special food] régime m ▶ **to be on a diet** être au régime ▶ **to go on a diet** faire ou suivre un régime **3.** [assembly] diète f. ◆ comp [drink, food] de régime, basses calories ▶ **diet Coke®** Coca® light ▶ **diet pill** coupe-faim m inv. ◆ vi suivre un régime.

dietary ['daɪətrɪ] (pl **dietaries**) adj [supplement] alimentaire ; [of special food] de régime, diététique ▶ **dietary fibre** cellulose f végétale.

diet-conscious adj : *she is very diet-conscious* elle fait très attention à ce qu'elle mange.

dieter ['daɪətər] n personne f qui suit un régime.

dietician [,daɪə'tɪʃn] n diététicien m, -enne f.

differ ['dɪfər] vi **1.** [vary] différer, être différent **2.** [disagree] être en désaccord, ne pas être d'accord.

difference ['dɪfrəns] n **1.** [dissimilarity] différence f ; [in age, size, weight] écart m, différence f / *I can't tell the difference between the two* je ne vois pas la différence entre les deux / *it makes no difference* ou *it doesn't make the slightest difference* ça n'a aucune importance, ça revient au même, ça ne change absolument rien / *that makes all the difference* voilà qui change tout **2.** [disagreement] différend m / *a difference of opinion* une différence ou divergence d'opinion **3.** [in numbers, quantity] différence f.

different ['dɪfrənt] adj **1.** [not identical] différent, autre ▶ **different from** ou **to** ou US **than** différent de / *that's quite a different matter* ça, c'est une autre affaire ou histoire **2.** [various] divers, différents, plusieurs **3.** [unusual] singulier.

differential [,dɪfə'renʃl] ◆ adj **1.** MATH différentiel **2.** AUTO différentiel m. ◆ n [in salary] écart m salarial.

differentiate [,dɪfə'renʃɪeɪt] ◆ vt **1.** [distinguish] différencier, distinguer **2.** MATH différencier, calculer la différentielle de. ◆ vi faire la différence ou distinction.

differently ['dɪfrəntlɪ] adv différemment, autrement / *I do it differently from* ou US *than you* je le fais différemment de ou autrement que vous, je ne fais pas ça comme vous.

differently abled [-eɪbld] adj [in politically correct language] handicapé.

difficult ['dɪfɪkəlt] adj **1.** [problem, task] difficile, dur, ardu ; [book, question] difficile **2.** [awkward] difficile, peu commode.

difficulty ['dɪfɪkəltɪ] (pl **difficulties**) n **1.** (U) [trouble] difficulté f, difficultés fpl ▶ **to have** ou **experience difficulty (in) doing sthg** avoir du mal ou de la peine ou des difficultés à faire qqch **2.** [obstacle, problem] difficulté f, problème m ; [predicament] difficulté f, embarras m ▶ **to get into difficulties** être ou se trouver en difficulté ▶ **to be in financial difficulties** avoir des ennuis d'argent, être dans l'embarras.

diffidence ['dɪfɪdəns] n manque m d'assurance ou de confiance en soi, timidité f.

diffident ['dɪfɪdənt] adj [person] qui manque de confiance en soi ou d'assurance ; [remark, smile] timide ; [tone] hésitant.

diffuse ◆ vt [dɪ'fju:z] diffuser, répandre. ◆ vi [dɪ'fju:z] se diffuser, se répandre.

diffused [dɪ'fju:zd] adj diffus.

dig [dɪg] (pt & pp **dug** [dʌg], cont **digging**) ◆ vt **1.** [in ground - hole] creuser ; [- tunnel] creuser, percer ; [with spade] bêcher **2.** [jab] enfoncer / *she dug me in the ribs (with her elbow)* elle m'a donné un coup de coude dans les côtes **3.** v inf & dated [understand] piger ; [appreciate, like] aimer ; [look at] viser. ◆ vi **1.** [person] creuser ; [animal] fouil-

ler, fouir **2.** v inf & dated [understand] piger. ◆ n **1.** [in ground] coup m de bêche **2.** ARCHEOL fouilles fpl ▶ **to go on a dig** faire des fouilles **3.** [jab] coup m ▶ **to give sb a dig in the ribs** donner un coup de coude dans les côtes de qqn **4.** inf [snide remark] coup m de patte / *that was a dig at you* c'était une pierre dans votre jardin. ◆ **dig in** ◆ vi **1.** MIL [dig trenches] se retrancher ; fig tenir bon **2.** inf [eat] commencer à manger / *dig in!* allez-y, mangez, attaquez ! ◆ vt sep **1.** [mix with ground] enterrer **2.** [jab] enfoncer **3.** PHR **to dig in one's heels** se braquer, se buter ▶ **to dig o.s. in** a) lit se retrancher b) fig camper sur ses positions. ◆ **dig into** vt insep **1.** [delve into] fouiller dans / *don't dig into your savings* fig n'entame pas tes économies, ne pioche pas dans tes économies **2.** [jab] : *your elbow is digging into me* ton coude me rentre dans les côtes. ◆ **dig out** vt sep **1.** [remove] extraire ; [from ground] déterrer / *they had to dig the car out of the snow* il a fallu qu'ils dégagent la voiture de la neige (à la pelle) **2.** [find] dénicher. ◆ **dig up** vt sep **1.** [ground - gen] retourner ; [- with spade] bêcher **2.** [plant] arracher **3.** [unearth] déterrer ; inf & fig [find] dénicher.

digest ◆ vt [dɪ'dʒest] **1.** [food] digérer **2.** [idea] assimiler, digérer ; [information] assimiler, comprendre **3.** [classify] classer ; [sum up] résumer. ◆ vi [dɪ'dʒest] digérer.

digestible [dɪ'dʒestəbl] adj lit & fig digeste, facile à digérer.

digestion [dɪ'dʒestʃn] n digestion f.

digestive [dɪ'dʒestɪv] ◆ adj digestif ▶ **digestive biscuit** UK sorte de sablé ▶ **digestive system** système m digestif. ◆ n [drink] digestif m ; UK [biscuit] sorte de sablé.

digger ['dɪgər] n [machine] excavatrice f, pelleteuse f.

digibox ['dɪdʒɪbɒks] n UK [TV] décodeur m numérique.

digicam ['dɪdʒɪkæm] n caméra f numérique.

digit ['dɪdʒɪt] n **1.** [number] chiffre m / *three-digit number* nombre à trois chiffres **2.** [finger] doigt m ; [toe] orteil m.

digital ['dɪdʒɪtl] adj **1.** ANAT digital **2.** [clock, watch] à affichage numérique ; [display] numérique.

digital audio tape = DAT.

digital broadcasting n diffusion f numérique.

digital camera n appareil photo m numérique.

digital display n affichage m numérique.

digital gap n fracture f numérique.

digitally remastered adj remixé en numérique.

digital radio n radio f numérique.

digital recording n enregistrement m numérique.

digital rights management n gestion f de droits numériques.

digital signature n signature f électronique ou numérique.

digital television, digital TV n télévision f numérique.

digitize, digitise ['dɪdʒɪtaɪz] vt numériser.

dignified ['dɪgnɪfaɪd] adj [person] plein de dignité, digne ; [silence] digne.

dignitary ['dɪgnɪtrɪ] (pl **dignitaries**) n dignitaire m.

dignity ['dɪgnətɪ] (pl **dignities**) n [importance, poise] dignité f / *she considered it beneath her dignity* elle s'estimait au-dessus de ça.

digress [daɪ'gres] vi s'éloigner, s'écarter.

digression [daɪ'greʃn] n digression f.

digs [dɪgz] pl n inf piaule f.

dike [daɪk] = **dyke**.

diktat ['dɪktæt] n **1.** POL [decree] diktat m **2.** [statement] affirmation f catégorique.

dilapidated [dɪˈlæpɪdeɪtɪd] adj [house] délabré ; [car] déglingué.

dilate [daɪˈleɪt] ◆ vi [physically] se dilater. ◆ vt dilater.

dilemma [dɪˈlemə] n dilemme *m* ▶ **to be in a dilemma** être pris dans un dilemme.

diligence [ˈdɪlɪdʒəns] n [effort] assiduité *f*, application *f*, zèle *m*.

diligent [ˈdɪlɪdʒənt] adj [person] assidu, appliqué ; [work] appliqué, diligent.

dill [dɪl] n aneth *m*.

dilly-dally [ˈdɪlɪdælɪ] (*pt & pp* **dilly-dallied**) vi *inf* [dawdle] lanterner, lambiner ; [hesitate] hésiter, tergiverser.

dilute [daɪˈluːt] ◆ vt **1.** [liquid] diluer, étendre ; [milk, wine] mouiller, couper d'eau ; [sauce] délayer, allonger ; [colour] délayer **2.** PHARM diluer **3.** *fig* [weaken] diluer, édulcorer. ◆ adj [liquid] dilué, coupé or étendu (d'eau) ; [colour] délayé, adouci ; *fig* dilué, édulcoré.

dilution [daɪˈluːʃn] n [act, product] dilution *f* ; [of milk, wine] coupage *m*, mouillage *m* ; *fig* édulcoration *f*.

dim [dɪm] (*pt & pp* **dimmed**, *cont* **dimming**) ◆ adj **1.** [light] faible, pâle ; [lamp] faible ; [room] sombre ; [colour] terne, sans éclat ▶ **to grow dim a)** [light] baisser **b)** [room] devenir sombre **c)** [colour] devenir terne **2.** [indistinct -shape] vague, imprécis ; [-sight] faible, trouble ; [-sound] vague, indistinct / *she has only a dim memory of it* elle n'en a qu'un vague souvenir **3.** [gloomy] sombre, morne ▶ **to take a dim view of sthg** ne pas beaucoup apprécier qqch, voir qqch d'un mauvais œil **4.** *inf* [stupid] gourde. ◆ vt **1.** [light] baisser / *dim your headlights* US AUTO mettez-vous en codes **2.** [beauty, colour, hope, metal] ternir ; [memory] estomper, effacer ; [mind, senses] affaiblir, troubler ; [sound] affaiblir ; [sight] baisser, troubler. ◆ vi [light] baisser, s'affaiblir ; [beauty, glory, hope] se ternir ; [colour] devenir terne or mat ; [memory] s'estomper, s'effacer ; [sound] s'affaiblir ; [sight] baisser, se troubler. ❖ **dim out** vt sep US plonger dans un black-out partiel.

dime [daɪm] n US pièce *f* de dix cents.

dimension [daɪˈmenʃn] n **1.** [measurement, size] dimension *f* ; ARCHIT & GEOM dimension *f*, cote *f* ; MATH & PHYS dimension *f* **2.** *fig* [scope] étendue *f* ; [aspect] dimension *f*. ❖ **dimensions** pl n TECH [of bulky object] encombrement *m*.

-dimensional [dɪˈmenʃənl] in comp ▶ **two / four-dimensional** à deux / quatre dimensions.

dime store n US supérette *f* de quartier.

diminish [dɪˈmɪnɪʃ] ◆ vt **1.** [number] diminuer, réduire ; [effect, power] diminuer, amoindrir ; [value] réduire **2.** [person] déprécier, rabaisser. ◆ vi diminuer, se réduire.

diminished [dɪˈmɪnɪʃt] adj [number, power, speed] diminué, amoindri ; [reputation] diminué, terni ; [value] réduit ▶ **diminished responsibility** LAW responsabilité *f* atténuée.

diminishing [dɪˈmɪnɪʃɪŋ] adj [influence, number, speed] décroissant, qui va en diminuant ; [price, quality] qui baisse, en baisse.

diminutive [dɪˈmɪnjʊtɪv] ◆ adj [tiny] minuscule, tout petit ; LING diminutif. ◆ n diminutif *m*.

dimly [ˈdɪmlɪ] adv [shine] faiblement, sans éclat ; [see] indistinctement, à peine ; [remember] vaguement, à peine.

dimmer switch n variateur *m* (de lumière).

dimple [ˈdɪmpl] ◆ n [in cheek, chin] fossette *f* ; [in surface of ground, water] ride *f*, ondulation *f*. ◆ vi [cheek] former or creuser des fossettes ; [surface of ground] onduler, former des rides ; [surface of water] rider, se rider.

dim sum [dɪmˈsʌm] n CULIN dim sum *m*.

dimwit [ˈdɪmwɪt] n *inf* crétin *m*, -e *f*.

dim-witted adj *inf* crétin, gourde.

din [dɪn] (*pt & pp* **dinned**, *cont* **dinning**) ◆ n [of people] tapage *m*, tumulte *m* ; [in classroom] chahut *m* ; [of industry, traffic] vacarme *m*. ◆ vt ▶ **to din sthg into sb** *inf* faire (bien) comprendre qqch à qqn, faire entrer qqch dans la tête de qqn.

dine [daɪn] vi dîner ▶ **to dine off** or **on sthg** dîner de qqch. ❖ **dine out** vi dîner dehors or en ville.

diner [ˈdaɪnər] n **1.** [person] dîneur *m*, -euse *f* **2.** RAIL wagon-restaurant *m* ; US petit restaurant *m* sans façon.

dingbat [ˈdɪŋbæt] n *inf* **1.** US [thing] truc *m*, machin *m* **2.** [fool] crétin *m*, -e *f*, gourde *f*.

dingdong [ˌdɪŋˈdɒŋ] n **1.** [sound] ding dong *m* **2.** UK [quarrel] dispute *f* ; [fight] bagarre *f*.

dinghy [ˈdɪŋgɪ] n (*pl* **dinghies**) n [rowing boat] petit canot *m*, youyou *m* ; [sailboat] dériveur *m* ; [rubber] canot *m* pneumatique, dinghy *m*.

dingy [ˈdɪndʒɪ] (*compar* **dingier**, *superl* **dingiest**) adj [shabby] miteux ; [dirty] douteux ; [colour] terne.

dining car [ˈdaɪnɪŋ-] n wagon-restaurant *m*.

dining club n club-restaurant *m* pour étudiants.

dining hall [ˈdaɪnɪŋ-] n SCH & UNIV réfectoire *m*.

dining room [ˈdaɪnɪŋ-] ◆ n salle *f* à manger. ◆ comp [curtains, furniture] de (la) salle à manger.

dining table [ˈdaɪnɪŋ-] n table *f* de salle à manger.

dinkie [ˈdɪŋkɪ] (abbr of **double income no kids**) n *inf* personne mariée aisée et sans enfants.

dinkum [ˈdɪŋkəm] Austr *inf* ◆ adj [person] franc (franche), sincère ; [thing] authentique / *fair dinkum* régulier, vrai de vrai. ◆ adv franchement, vraiment.

dinner [ˈdɪnər] n **1.** [evening meal - early] dîner *m* ; [-very late] souper *m* ; *regional* [lunch] déjeuner *m* / *to be at dinner* être en train de dîner / *they went out to dinner* **a)** [in restaurant] ils ont dîné au restaurant or en ville **b)** [at friends] ils ont dîné chez des amis. ◆ comp [fork, knife] de table ▶ **dinner bell** : *she rang the dinner bell* elle a sonné pour annoncer le dîner ▶ **dinner duty** SCH service *m* de réfectoire ▶ **dinner hour a)** [at work] heure *f* du déjeuner **b)** [at school] pause *f* de midi ▶ **dinner plate** (grande) assiette *f*.

dinner dance n dîner *m* dansant.

dinner jacket n UK smoking *m*.

dinner lady n UK employée d'une cantine scolaire.

dinner party n dîner *m* (*sur invitation*).

dinner service n service *m* de table.

dinner table n table *f* de salle à manger / *at* or *over the dinner table* pendant le dîner, au dîner.

dinnertime [ˈdɪnətaɪm] n heure *f* du dîner.

dinosaur [ˈdaɪnəsɔːr] n dinosaure *m*.

dint [dɪnt] = **dent**. ❖ **by dint of** prep phr à force de.

diocese [ˈdaɪəsɪs] n diocèse *m*.

dioxin [daɪˈɒksɪn] n dioxine *f*.

dip [dɪp] (*pt & pp* **dipped**, *cont* **dipping**) ◆ vi **1.** [incline -ground] descendre, s'incliner ; [-road] descendre, plonger ; [-head] pencher, amoindrir **2.** [drop -sun] baisser, descendre à l'horizon ; [-price] diminuer, baisser ; [-temperature] baisser ; [-plane] piquer ; [-boat] tanguer, piquer **3.** [during dance] se renverser. ◆ vt **1.** [immerse] tremper, plonger ; TECH tremper ; [clean] décaper ; [dye] teindre ; [sheep] laver **2.** [plunge] plonger **3.** UK AUTO ▶ **to dip one's headlights** se mettre en codes ▶ **dipped headlights** codes *mpl*, feux *mpl* de croisement. ◆ n **1.** *inf* [swim] baignade *f*, bain *m* (*en mer, en piscine*) ▶ **to go for a dip** aller se baigner, aller faire trempette **2.** [liquid] bain *m* ; [for sheep] bain *m* parasiticide **3.** [slope -in ground] déclivité *f* ; [-in road] descente *f* ; GEOL pendage *m* **4**. [bob] inclinaison *f* ; [of head] hochement *m* **5**. [drop - in temperature] baisse *f* ; [- in price] fléchissement *m*, baisse *f* **6**. CULIN *pâte ou mousse (à tartiner) servie avec du pain ou des biscuits salés* ▶ **avocado dip** mousse *f* à l'avocat **7**. [in dance] tombé *m*. ❖ **dip into** vt insep **1**. [dabble] : *I've only really dipped into Shakespeare* j'ai seulement survolé or feuilleté Shakespeare **2**. [draw upon] puiser dans.

Dip. written abbr of **diploma.**

diphtheria [dɪf'θɪərɪə] n diphtérie *f*.

diphthong ['dɪfθɒŋ] n diphtongue *f*.

diploma [dɪ'pləʊmə] n diplôme *m*.

diplomacy [dɪ'pləʊməsɪ] n POL & *fig* diplomatie *f*.

diplomat ['dɪpləmæt] n POL & *fig* diplomate *mf*.

diplomatic [ˌdɪplə'mætɪk] adj **1**. POL diplomatique **2**. *fig* [person] diplomate ; [action, remark] diplomatique.

diplomatically [ˌdɪplə'mætɪklɪ] adv POL diplomatiquement ; *fig* avec diplomatie, diplomatiquement.

diplomatic bag 🇬🇧, **diplomatic pouch** 🇺🇸 n valise *f* diplomatique.

diplomatic corps n corps *m* diplomatique.

diplomatic immunity n immunité *f* diplomatique.

diplomatic relations pl n relations *fpl* diplomatiques.

dippy ['dɪpɪ] (*compar* **dippier**, *superl* **dippiest**) adj *inf* écervelé.

dipstick ['dɪpstɪk] n **1**. AUTO jauge *f* (de niveau d'huile) **2**. *inf* [idiot] empoté *m*, -e *f*.

dipswitch ['dɪpswɪtʃ] n 🇬🇧 basculeur *m* (des phares).

dire ['daɪər] adj **1**. [fearful] affreux, terrible ; [ominous] sinistre **2**. [very bad] : *the film was pretty dire* le film était vraiment mauvais **3**. [extreme] extrême ▶ **to be in dire straits** être dans une mauvaise passe or aux abois.

direct [dɪ'rekt] ❖ vt **1**. [supervise - business] diriger, gérer, mener ; [- office, work] diriger ; [- movements] guider ; [- traffic] régler **2**. CIN, RADIO & TV [film, programme] réaliser ; [actors] diriger ; THEAT [play] mettre en scène **3**. [address] adresser / *the accusation was directed at him* l'accusation le visait / *he directed my attention to the map* il a attiré mon attention sur la carte **4**. [point] diriger / *can you direct me to the train station?* pourriez-vous m'indiquer le chemin de la gare ? **5**. [instruct] ordonner **6**. LAW ▶ **to direct the jury** instruire le jury ▶ **directed verdict** 🇺🇸 *verdict rendu par le jury sur la recommandation du juge* **7**. 🇺🇸 MUS diriger. ❖ vi **1**. [command] diriger, commander **2**. 🇺🇸 MUS diriger **3**. THEAT mettre en scène. ❖ adj **1**. [straight] direct / *direct flight* / *route* vol *m* / chemin *m* direct ▶ **direct memory access** COMPUT accès *m* direct à la mémoire ▶ **direct tax** impôt *m* direct ▶ **direct taxation** imposition *f* directe **2**. MIL ▶ **direct hit** coup *m* au but **3**. [immediate - cause, effect] direct, immédiat ▶ **direct marketing** marketing *m* direct ▶ **direct selling** vente *f* directe **4**. [frank] franc (franche), direct ; [denial, refusal] catégorique, absolu **5**. [exact] exact, précis **6**. ASTRON, GRAM & LOGIC direct ▶ **direct question** GRAM question *f* au style direct. ❖ adv directement.

direct access n accès *m* direct.

direct action n action *f* directe.

direct costs n coûts *mpl* directs.

direct current n courant *m* continu.

direct debit n prélèvement *m* automatique.

direct dialling n automatique *m*.

direct discourse 🇺🇸 = **direct speech.**

direction [dɪ'rekʃn] n **1**. [way] direction *f*, sens *m* / *in every direction* dans toutes les directions, en tous sens, dans tous les sens / *in the direction of Chicago* dans la or en

direction de Chicago **2**. [control] direction *f* **3**. CIN, RADIO & TV réalisation *f* ; THEAT mise *f* en scène. ❖ **directions** pl n indications *fpl*, instructions *fpl*, mode *m* d'emploi ▶ **to give sb directions** indiquer son chemin à qqn / *I asked for directions to the station* j'ai demandé le chemin de la gare ▶ **stage directions** THEAT indications scéniques.

directive [dɪ'rektɪv] ❖ n directive *f*, instruction *f*. ❖ adj directeur.

directly [dɪ'rektlɪ] ❖ adv **1**. [straight] directement **2**. [promptly] immédiatement / *directly after lunch* tout de suite après le déjeuner / *directly before the film* juste avant le film / *I'll be there directly* j'arrive tout de suite **3**. [frankly] franchement **4**. [exactly] exactement / *directly opposite the station* juste en face de la gare. ❖ conj 🇬🇧 aussitôt que, dès que.

direct mail n publipostage *m*.

directness [dɪ'rektnɪs] n **1**. [of person, reply] franchise *f* ; [of remark] absence *f* d'ambiguïté **2**. [of attack] caractère *m* direct.

direct object n complément *m* (d'objet) direct.

director [dɪ'rektər] n **1**. [person - of business] directeur *m*, -trice *f*, chef *m* ; [- of organization] directeur *m*, -trice *f* ▶ **Director of Education** 🇬🇧 ≃ recteur *m* d'académie ▶ **Director of Public Prosecutions** 🇬🇧 LAW ≃ procureur *m* de la République ▶ **director of studies** UNIV directeur *m*, -trice *f* d'études or de travaux **2**. 🇺🇸 MUS chef *m* d'orchestre **3**. CIN, RADIO & TV réalisateur *m*, -trice *f* ; THEAT metteur *m* en scène ▶ **director of programmes** directeur *m*, -trice *f* des programmes.

directorate [dɪ'rektərət] n **1**. [board] conseil *m* d'administration **2**. [position] direction *f*, poste *m* de directeur.

director-general n directeur *m* général.

directorial [ˌdaɪrek'tɔːrɪəl] adj de mise en scène.

director's chair n régisseur *m*.

directorship [dɪ'rektəʃɪp] n direction *f*, poste *m* or fonctions *fpl* de directeur.

directory [dɪ'rektərɪ] (*pl* **directories**) n **1**. [of addresses] répertoire *m* (d'adresses) ; TELEC annuaire *m* (des téléphones), bottin *m* ; COMPUT répertoire *m* ▶ **street directory** répertoire des rues ▶ **commercial directory** annuaire du commerce **2**. [of instructions] mode *m* d'emploi.

directory enquiries 🇬🇧, **directory assistance** 🇺🇸 n (service m des) renseignements *mpl* téléphoniques.

direct speech n 🇬🇧 discours *m* or style *m* direct.

dirt [dɜːt] n (*U*) **1**. [grime] saleté *f*, crasse *f* ; [mud] boue *f* ; [excrement] crotte *f*, ordure *f* **2**. [soil] terre *f* **3**. [obscenity] obscénité *f* **4**. *inf* [scandal] ragots *mpl*, cancans *mpl* **5**. INDUST [in material, solution] impuretés *fpl*, corps *mpl* étrangers ; [in machine] encrassement *m*.

dirt bike n moto *f* tout-terrain.

dirt-cheap *inf* ❖ adv pour rien. ❖ adj très bon marché.

dirt road n chemin *m* de terre.

dirt track n [gen] piste *f* ; SPORT (piste) cendrée *f*.

dirty ['dɜːtɪ] (*compar* **dirtier**, *superl* **dirtiest**, *pt & pp* **dirtied**) ❖ adj **1**. [not clean - clothes, hands, person] sale, malpropre, crasseux ; [- machine] encrassé ; [- wound] infecté ; [muddy] plein de boue, crotté / *don't get dirty!* ne vous salissez pas ! / *he got his shirt dirty* il a sali sa chemise / *this rug gets dirty easily* ce tapis est salissant **2**. [colour] sale **3**. [nasty] sale / *politics is a dirty business* il est difficile de garder les mains propres quand on fait de la politique / *a dirty campaign* une campagne sordide / *that's a dirty lie* ce n'est absolument pas vrai / *dirty money* argent sale or mal acquis / *he's a dirty fighter* il se bat en traître ▶ **to give sb a dirty look** regarder qqn de travers or d'un sale œil

4. [weather] sale, vilain **5.** [obscene] grossier, obscène **/** *to have a dirty mind* avoir l'esprit mal tourné ▸ **dirty magazines** revues *fpl* pornographiques ▸ **a dirty old man** *inf* un vieux cochon or vicelard ▸ **a dirty joke / story** une blague / histoire cochonne ▸ **a dirty word** une grossièreté, un gros mot **6.** *inf* [sexy] ▸ **a dirty weekend** un week-end coquin. ◆ adv *inf* **1.** [fight, play] déloyalement ; [talk] grossièrement **2.** 🇬🇧 [as intensifier] vachement **/** *a dirty great skyscraper* un gratte-ciel énorme. ◆ vt [soil] salir ; [machine] encrasser ▸ **to dirty one's hands** *lit & fig* se salir les mains. ◆ n 🇺🇸 ▸ **to do the dirty on sb** *inf* jouer un sale tour or faire une vacherie à qqn.

dirty bomb n bombe *f* sale.

dirty trick n [malicious act] sale tour *m* ▸ **to play a dirty trick on sb** jouer un sale tour or un tour de cochon à qqn. ❖ **dirty tricks** pl n : *they've been up to their dirty tricks again* ils ont encore fait des leurs ▸ **dirty tricks campaign** POL *manœuvres déloyales visant à discréditer un adversaire politique.*

dis [dɪs] vt 🇺🇸 *inf* = **diss.**

disability [ˌdɪsə'bɪlətɪ] (*pl* **disabilities**) n **1.** [state - physical] incapacité *f*, invalidité *f* **2.** [handicap] infirmité *f* ; ADMIN handicap *m* ▸ **disability benefit** allocation *f* d'invalidité ▸ **disability pension** pension *f* d'invalidité.

disable [dɪs'eɪbl] vt **1.** [accident, illness] rendre infirme ; [maim] mutiler, estropier **2.** [machine] mettre hors service ; [ship] faire subir une avarie à, désemparer ; [gun, tank] mettre hors d'action ; [army, battalion] mettre hors de combat.

disabled [dɪs'eɪbld] ◆ adj [handicapped] infirme ; ADMIN handicapé ; [maimed] mutilé, estropié **/** *disabled ex-servicemen* invalides *mpl* or mutilés *mpl* de guerre ▸ **severely disabled** souffrant d'un handicap sévère. ◆ pl n ▸ **the disabled a)** [handicapped] les handicapés *mpl* **b)** [maimed] les mutilés *mpl* or estropiés *mpl*.

disabuse [ˌdɪsə'bjuːz] vt détromper, ôter ses illusions à.

disadvantage [ˌdɪsəd'vɑːntɪdʒ] ◆ n [condition] désavantage *m*, inconvénient *m* ▸ **to be at a disadvantage** être désavantagé or dans une position désavantageuse. ◆ vt désavantager, défavoriser.

disadvantaged [ˌdɪsəd'vɑːntɪdʒd] ◆ adj [gen] défavorisé ; [economically] déshérité. ◆ pl n ▸ **the disadvantaged** les défavorisés *mpl*.

disadvantageous [ˌdɪsædvɑːn'teɪdʒəs] adj désavantageux, défavorable ▸ **to be disadvantageous to sb** être désavantageux or défavorable à qqn.

disaffected [ˌdɪsə'fektɪd] adj [discontented] hostile, mécontent ; [disloyal] rebelle.

disaffection [ˌdɪsə'fekʃn] n désaffection *f*, détachement *m*.

disagree [ˌdɪsə'griː] vi **1.** [person, people] ne pas être d'accord, être en désaccord ▸ **to disagree with sb about** or **on sthg** ne pas être d'accord avec or ne pas être du même avis que qqn sur qqch **2.** [figures, records] ne pas concorder **3.** [food, weather] ne pas convenir.

disagreeable [ˌdɪsə'grɪəbl] adj [person, remark] désagréable, désobligeant ; [experience, job] désagréable, pénible ; [smell] désagréable, déplaisant.

disagreement [ˌdɪsə'griːmənt] n **1.** [of opinions, records] désaccord *m*, conflit *m* **2.** [quarrel] différend *m*, querelle *f*.

disallow [ˌdɪsə'laʊ] vt [argument, opinion] rejeter ; SPORT refuser ; LAW débouter, rejeter.

disappear [ˌdɪsə'pɪər] vi **1.** [vanish - person, snow] disparaître ; [- object] disparaître, s'égarer ; LING s'amuïr **2.** [cease

to exist - pain, tribe] disparaître ; [- problem] disparaître, s'aplanir ; [- memory] s'effacer, s'estomper ; [- tradition] disparaître, tomber en désuétude.

disappearance [ˌdɪsə'pɪərəns] n [gen] disparition *f*.

disappoint [ˌdɪsə'pɔɪnt] vt **1.** [person] décevoir, désappointer **2.** [hope] décevoir ; [plan] contrarier, contrecarrer.

disappointed [ˌdɪsə'pɔɪntɪd] adj **1.** [person] déçu, désappointé **/** *I'm very disappointed in him* il m'a beaucoup déçu **/** *I was disappointed to hear you won't be coming* j'ai été déçu d'apprendre que vous ne viendrez pas **/** *are you disappointed at* or *with the results?* les résultats vous ont-ils déçu ?, avez-vous été déçu par les résultats ? **2.** [ambition, hope] déçu ; [plan] contrarié, contrecarré.

> 📋 Note that **être déçu que** is followed by a verb in the subjunctive:
> **I'm disappointed my husband isn't here.** *Je suis déçue que mon mari ne soit pas là.*

disappointing [ˌdɪsə'pɔɪntɪŋ] adj décevant.

disappointingly [ˌdɪsə'pɔɪntɪŋlɪ] adv : *disappointingly low grades* des notes d'une faiblesse décourageante or décevante.

disappointment [ˌdɪsə'pɔɪntmənt] n **1.** [state] déception *f*, désappointement *m*, déconvenue *f* **2.** [letdown] déception *f*, désillusion *f*.

disapproval [ˌdɪsə'pruːvl] n désapprobation *f* ; [strong] réprobation *f*.

disapprove [ˌdɪsə'pruːv] ◆ vi désapprouver ▸ **to disapprove of sthg** désapprouver qqch. ◆ vt désapprouver.

disapproving [ˌdɪsə'pruːvɪŋ] adj désapprobateur, de désapprobation.

disapprovingly [ˌdɪsə'pruːvɪŋlɪ] adv [look] d'un air désapprobateur ; [speak] d'un ton désapprobateur, avec désapprobation.

disarm [dɪs'ɑːm] ◆ vt **1.** [country, enemy, critic] désarmer **2.** [charm] désarmer, toucher. ◆ vi désarmer.

disarmament [dɪs'ɑːməmənt] ◆ n désarmement *m*. ◆ comp [conference, negotiations, talks] sur le désarmement.

disarming [dɪs'ɑːmɪŋ] ◆ adj désarmant, touchant. ◆ n désarmement *m*.

disarmingly [dɪs'ɑːmɪŋlɪ] adv de façon désarmante.

disarray [ˌdɪsə'reɪ] n [of person] confusion *f*, désordre *m* ; [of clothing] désordre *m*.

disassociate [ˌdɪsə'səʊʃɪeɪt] = **dissociate.**

disaster [dɪ'zɑːstər] ◆ n **1.** [misfortune] désastre *m*, catastrophe *f* ; [natural] catastrophe *f*, sinistre *m* **2.** *fig* : *as a manager, he's a disaster!* en tant que directeur, ce n'est pas une réussite ! ◆ comp [fund] d'aide aux sinistrés ; [area] sinistré ▸ **disaster movie** film *m* catastrophe.

disaster area n *lit* région *f* sinistrée ; *fig* champ *m* de bataille.

disastrous [dɪ'zɑːstrəs] adj désastreux, catastrophique.

disband [dɪs'bænd] ◆ vt [army, club] disperser ; [organization] disperser, dissoudre. ◆ vi [army] se disperser ; [organization] se dissoudre.

disbelief [ˌdɪsbɪ'liːf] n incrédulité *f*.

disbelieve [ˌdɪsbɪ'liːv] ◆ vt [person] ne pas croire ; [news, story] ne pas croire à. ◆ vi RELIG ne pas croire.

disc [dɪsk] n **1.** [flat circular object] disque *m* **2.** [record] disque *m* **3.** ANAT disque *m* (intervertébral) **4.** [identity tag] plaque *f* d'identité ▸ **parking disc** AUTO disque *m* de stationnement ▸ **disc parking** stationnement *m* avec disque.

disc. written abbr of discount.

discard vt [dɪˈskɑːd] [get rid of] se débarrasser de, mettre au rebut ; [idea, system] renoncer, abandonner.

discarded [dɪˈskɑːdɪd] adj [small object] jeté ; [larger] abandonné.

disc brake 🇬🇧, **disk brake** 🇺🇸 n frein m à disque.

discern [dɪˈsɜːn] vt [see] discerner, distinguer ; [understand] discerner.

discernible [dɪˈsɜːnəbl] adj [visible] visible ; [detectable] discernable, perceptible.

discerning [dɪˈsɜːnɪŋ] adj [person] judicieux, sagace ; [taste] fin, délicat ; [look] perspicace.

discernment [dɪˈsɜːnmənt] n discernement m, perspicacité f.

discharge ◆ vt [ˈdɪstʃɑːdʒ] **1.** [release - patient] laisser sortir, libérer ; [- prisoner] libérer, mettre en liberté **2.** [dismiss - employee] renvoyer, congédier ; [- official] destituer ; MIL [from service] renvoyer à la vie civile ; [from active duty] démobiliser ; [for lack of fitness] réformer **3.** [unload - cargo] décharger ; [- passengers] débarquer **4.** [emit - liquid] dégorger, déverser ; [- gas] dégager, émettre ; ELEC décharger **5.** [perform - duty] remplir, s'acquitter de ; [- function] remplir. ◆ n [dɪsˈtʃɑːdʒ] **1.** [release - of patient] sortie f ; [of prisoner] libération f, mise f en liberté **2.** [dismissal - of employee] renvoi m ; [- of soldier] libération f ; [after active duty] démobilisation f **3.** [emission] émission f ; [of liquid] écoulement m.

disciple [dɪˈsaɪpl] n [gen & RELIG] disciple m.

disciplinarian [ˌdɪsɪplɪˈneərɪən] ◆ n partisan m de la manière forte. ◆ adj disciplinaire.

disciplinary [ˈdɪsɪplɪnərɪ] adj **1.** [corrective - measure] disciplinaire ; [committee] de discipline **2.** [relating to field] relatif à une discipline.

discipline [ˈdɪsɪplɪn] ◆ n **1.** [training, control] discipline f **2.** [area of study] discipline f, matière f. ◆ vt **1.** [train - person] discipliner ; [- mind] discipliner, former **2.** [punish] punir.

disciplined [ˈdɪsɪplɪnd] adj discipliné.

disc jockey n animateur m, -trice f (de radio ou de discothèque), disc-jockey m.

disclaim [dɪsˈkleɪm] vt [deny - responsibility] rejeter, décliner ; [- knowledge] nier ; [- news, remark] démentir ; [- paternity] désavouer.

disclaimer [dɪsˈkleɪmər] n **1.** [denial] démenti m, désaveu m **2.** LAW désistement m, renonciation f.

disclose [dɪsˈkləʊz] vt [reveal - secret] divulguer, dévoiler ; [- news] divulguer ; [- feelings] révéler **2.** [uncover] exposer, montrer.

disclosure [dɪsˈkləʊʒər] n **1.** [revelation] divulgation f, révélation f **2.** [fact revealed] révélation f.

disco [ˈdɪskəʊ] (pl discos) ◆ n discothèque f, boîte f. ◆ comp [dancing, music] disco.

discolor 🇺🇸 = discolour.

discolour 🇬🇧, **discolor** 🇺🇸 [dɪsˈkʌlər] ◆ vt [change colour of, fade] décolorer ; [turn yellow] jaunir. ◆ vi [change colour, fade] se décolorer ; [turn yellow] jaunir.

discoloured 🇬🇧, **discolored** 🇺🇸 [dɪsˈkʌləd] adj [faded] décoloré ; [yellowed] jauni.

discomfort [dɪsˈkʌmfət] ◆ n **1.** [pain] malaise m ; [unease] gêne f **2.** [cause of pain, unease] incommodité f, inconfort m. ◆ vt incommoder, gêner.

disconcert [ˌdɪskənˈsɜːt] vt **1.** [fluster] déconcerter, dérouter **2.** [upset] troubler, gêner.

disconcerting [ˌdɪskənˈsɜːtɪŋ] adj **1.** [unnerving] déconcertant, déroutant **2.** [upsetting] gênant.

disconnect [ˌdɪskəˈnekt] vt **1.** [detach] détacher, séparer ; [plug, pipe, radio, TV] débrancher ; RAIL [carriages] décrocher **2.** [gas, electricity, telephone, water] couper.

disconnected [ˌdɪskəˈnektɪd] adj **1.** [remarks, thoughts] décousu, sans suite ; [facts] sans rapport **2.** [detached - wire, plug, etc.] détaché ; [- telephone] déconnecté.

disconsolate [dɪsˈkɒnsələt] adj triste, inconsolable.

discontent [ˌdɪskənˈtent] ◆ n **1.** [dissatisfaction] mécontentement m **2.** [person] mécontent m, -e f. ◆ adj mécontent. ◆ vt mécontenter.

discontented [ˌdɪskənˈtentɪd] adj mécontent.

discontinue [ˌdɪskənˈtɪnjuː] vt [gen] cesser, interrompre ; COMM & INDUST [production] abandonner ; [product] interrompre ; [publication] interrompre la publication de.

discord [ˈdɪskɔːd] n (U) [conflict] désaccord m, discorde f.

discordant [dɪsˈkɔːdənt] adj [opinions] incompatible, opposé ; [colours, sounds] discordant.

discotheque [ˈdɪskəʊtek] n discothèque f (pour danser).

discount ◆ n [ˈdɪskaʊnt] **1.** COMM [price reduction] remise f, rabais m / she gave a discount on lui a fait une remise / the store is currently offering a 5% discount on radios le magasin fait (une réduction de) 5 % sur les radios en ce moment **2.** FIN [deduction] escompte m. ◆ vt [dɪsˈkaʊnt] **1.** [disregard] ne pas tenir compte de **2.** COMM [article] faire une remise ou un rabais sur **3.** FIN [sum of money] faire une remise de, escompter.

discount house n 🇺🇸 [shop] solderie f, magasin m de vente au rabais.

discount store n solderie f.

discourage [dɪsˈkʌrɪdʒ] vt **1.** [dishearten] décourager / to become discouraged se laisser décourager **2.** [dissuade] décourager, dissuader ▸ **to discourage sb from doing sthg** dissuader qqn de faire qqch.

discouraged [dɪsˈkʌrɪdʒd] adj découragé.

discouragement [dɪsˈkʌrɪdʒmənt] n **1.** [attempt to discourage] : I met with discouragement on all sides tout le monde a essayé de me décourager **2.** [deterrent] : the metal shutters act as a discouragement to vandals les rideaux métalliques servent à décourager les vandales.

discouraging [dɪsˈkʌrɪdʒɪŋ] adj décourageant.

discourse n [ˈdɪskɔːs] **1.** fml [sermon] discours m ; [dissertation] discours m, traité m **2.** LING discours m.

discourteous [dɪsˈkɜːtjəs] adj discourtois, impoli / to be discourteous to or towards sb être discourtois ou impoli avec ou envers qqn.

discover [dɪsˈkʌvər] vt **1.** [country, answer, reason] découvrir **2.** [realize] se rendre compte **3.** [actor, singer, etc.] découvrir.

discoverer [dɪsˈkʌvərər] n découvreur m.

discovery [dɪsˈkʌvərɪ] (pl discoveries) n **1.** [act, event] découverte f **2.** [actor, singer, place, thing] découverte f.

discredit [dɪsˈkredɪt] ◆ vt **1.** [person] discréditer **2.** [report, theory - cast doubt on] discréditer, mettre en doute ; [- show to be false] montrer l'inexactitude de. ◆ n [loss of good reputation] discrédit m ▸ **to bring discredit on** or **upon** jeter le discrédit sur.

discreet [dɪsˈkriːt] adj discret (discrète).

discreetly [dɪsˈkriːtlɪ] adv discrètement, de manière discrète.

discrepancy [dɪsˈkrepənsɪ] (pl discrepancies) n [in figures] contradiction f ; [in statements] contradiction f, désaccord m, divergence f.

discrete [dɪsˈkriːt] adj [gen & TECH] & MATH discret (discrète).

discretion [dɪ'skreʃn] n **1.** [tact, prudence] discrétion f **2.** [judgment, taste] jugement m / I'll leave it to your discretion je laisse cela à votre discrétion or jugement / use your own discretion jugez par vous-même.

discretionary [dɪ'skreʃnərɪ] adj discrétionnaire.

discriminate [dɪ'skrɪmɪneɪt] ◆ vi **1.** [on grounds of race, sex, etc.] ▶ **to discriminate in favour of** favoriser / she was discriminated against elle faisait l'objet or était victime de discriminations **2.** [distinguish] établir or faire une distinction, faire une différence. ◆ vt distinguer.

discriminating [dɪ'skrɪmɪneɪtɪŋ] adj [showing discernment] judicieux ; [in matters of taste] qui a un goût sûr ; [audience, eye] averti ; [judgment] perspicace.

discrimination [dɪ,skrɪmɪ'neɪʃn] n **1.** [on grounds of race, sex, etc.] discrimination f **2.** [good judgment] discernement m ; [in matters of taste] goût m **3.** [ability to distinguish] ▶ **powers of discrimination** capacités fpl de distinction, discernement m.

discriminatory [dɪ'skrɪmɪnətrɪ] adj [treatment, proposals] discriminatoire.

discus ['dɪskəs] (pl discuses or disci [-kaɪ]) n SPORT disque m.

discuss [dɪ'skʌs] vt [talk about - problem, price, subject, etc.] discuter de, parler de ; [- person] parler de ; [debate] discuter de ; [examine - subj: author, book, report, etc.] examiner, parler de, traiter de / I'll discuss it with him j'en parlerai or discuterai avec lui / I don't want to discuss it je ne veux pas en parler.

discussion [dɪ'skʌʃn] n [talk] discussion f ; [debate] débat m ; [examination - by author in report] traitement m ; [- of report] examen m / it is still under discussion c'est encore en cours de discussion.

discussion forum n INTERNET forum m de discussion.

discussion group n groupe m de discussion.

discussion list n INTERNET liste f de discussion.

discussion thread n INTERNET fil m de discussion.

disdain [dɪs'deɪn] ◆ vt fml dédaigner. ◆ n dédain m, mépris m / with or in disdain avec dédain, dédaigneusement.

disdainful [dɪs'deɪnfʊl] adj dédaigneux ▶ **to be disdainful of sb / sthg** se montrer dédaigneux envers qqn / qqch, dédaigner qqn / qqch.

disease [dɪ'ziːz] n **1.** BOT, MED & VET maladie f **2.** fig mal m, maladie f.

diseased [dɪ'ziːzd] adj BOT, MED & VET malade ; fig [mind] malade, dérangé ; [imagination] malade.

disembark [,dɪsɪm'bɑːk] ◆ vi débarquer. ◆ vt [passengers, cargo] débarquer.

disembodied [,dɪsɪm'bɒdɪd] adj [voice, spirit] désincarné.

disembowel [,dɪsɪm'baʊəl] (UK pt disembowelled, cont disembowelling ; US pt disemboweled, cont disemboweling) vt éviscérer, éventrer.

disenchanted [,dɪsɪn'tʃɑːntɪd] adj désillusionné ▶ **to be disenchanted with sb / sthg** avoir perdu ses illusions sur qqn / qqch, être désillusionné par qqn / qqch.

disenchantment [,dɪsɪn'tʃɑːntmənt] n désillusion f.

disenfranchise [,dɪsɪn'fræntʃaɪz] vt priver du droit de vote.

disengage [,dɪsɪn'geɪdʒ] vt **1.** MECH désenclencher ; [lever, catch] dégager ; AUTO [handbrake] desserrer ▶ **to disengage the clutch** AUTO débrayer **2.** [release] dégager.

disengagement [,dɪsɪn'geɪdʒmənt] n [from political group, organization] désengagement m.

disentangle [,dɪsɪn'tæŋgl] vt [string, plot, mystery] démêler / I tried to disentangle myself from the net j'ai essayé de me dépêtrer du filet.

disfavour UK, **disfavor** US [dɪs'feɪvər] n désapprobation f, défaveur f.

disfigure [dɪs'fɪgər] vt défigurer.

disfigured [dɪs'fɪgəd] adj défiguré.

disfigurement [dɪs'fɪgəmənt] n défigurement m.

disfranchise [,dɪs'fræntʃaɪz] = **disenfranchise**.

disgorge [dɪs'gɔːdʒ] ◆ vt **1.** [food] régurgiter, rendre ; fig [contents, passengers, pollutants] déverser **2.** [give unwillingly - information] donner avec répugnance or à contrecœur. ◆ vi [river] se jeter, se dégorger.

disgrace [dɪs'greɪs] ◆ n **1.** [dishonour] disgrâce f **2.** [disapproval] ▶ **to be in disgrace (with sb)** être en disgrâce (auprès de qqn) **3.** [shameful example or thing] honte f. ◆ vt **1.** [bring shame on] faire honte à, couvrir de honte, déshonorer ▶ **to disgrace o.s.** se couvrir de honte **2.** (usu passive) [discredit] disgracier.

disgraceful [dɪs'greɪsfʊl] adj [behaviour] honteux, scandaleux ; inf [hat, jacket, etc.] miteux.

disgracefully [dɪs'greɪsfʊlɪ] adv honteusement.

disgruntled [dɪs'grʌntld] adj mécontent.

disguise [dɪs'gaɪz] ◆ n déguisement m ▶ **in disguise** déguisé. ◆ vt **1.** [voice, handwriting, person] déguiser ▶ **to be disguised as sb / sthg** être déguisé en qqn / qqch **2.** [feelings, disappointment, etc.] dissimuler, masquer ; [truth, facts] dissimuler, cacher ; [unsightly feature] cacher ; [bad taste of food, cough mixture, etc.] couvrir.

disgust [dɪs'gʌst] ◆ n [sick feeling] dégoût m, aversion f, répugnance f ; [displeasure] écœurement m, dégoût m. ◆ vt [sicken] dégoûter ; [displease] écœurer.

disgusted [dɪs'gʌstɪd] adj [displeased] écœuré ; [sick] écœuré, dégoûté.

disgusting [dɪs'gʌstɪŋ] adj [sickening - person, behaviour, smell] écœurant, dégoûtant ; [- habit, language] dégoûtant ; [very bad] écœurant, déplorable.

disgustingly [dɪs'gʌstɪŋlɪ] adv : a disgustingly bad meal un repas épouvantable.

dish [dɪʃ] ◆ n **1.** [plate] assiette f ▶ **to wash** or **to do the dishes** faire la vaisselle **2.** [food] plat m **3.** [amount of food] plat m **4.** inf [good-looking man or woman] canon m **5.** [of telescope] miroir m concave (de télescope). ◆ vt inf **1.** UK [chances, hopes] ruiner **2.** PHR **to dish the dirt** [gossip] faire des commérages. ◆ vi US inf ▶ **to dish on sb** cafarder qqn / I shouldn't dish on her, but she's cheating on her husband je ne devrais pas la cafarder mais elle trompe son mari. ◆ **dish out** ◆ vt sep **1.** [food] servir **2.** inf & fig [money, leaflets, etc.] distribuer ; [advice] prodiguer. ◆ vi [serve food] faire le service. ◆ **dish up** ◆ vt sep [food] servir or verser or mettre dans un plat ; inf [arguments, excuses, etc.] ressortir. ◆ vi [serve food] servir.

dish aerial UK, **dish antenna** US n TV antenne f parabolique.

disharmony [,dɪs'hɑːmənɪ] n manque m d'harmonie.

dishcloth ['dɪʃklɒθ] n torchon m (à vaisselle).

dishearten [dɪs'hɑːtn] vt décourager, abattre, démoraliser.

disheartened [dɪs'hɑːtnd] adj découragé.

disheartening [dɪs'hɑːtnɪŋ] adj décourageant.

dishevelled UK, **disheveled** US [dɪ'ʃevld] adj [hair] ébouriffé, dépeigné ; [clothes] débraillé, en désordre ; [person, appearance] débraillé.

dishonest [dɪs'ɒnɪst] adj malhonnête.

dishonesty [dɪs'ɒnɪstɪ] n malhonnêteté f.

dishonour UK, **dishonor** US [dɪsˈɒnəʳ] ◆ n déshonneur *m* ▶ **to bring dishonour on sb / one's country** déshonorer qqn / son pays. ◆ vt **1.** [family, country, profession, etc.] déshonorer **2.** FIN [cheque] refuser d'honorer.

dishonourable UK, **dishonorable** US [dɪsˈɒnrəbl] adj [conduct] déshonorant / *he was given a dishonourable discharge* MIL il a été renvoyé pour manquement à l'honneur.

dish rack n égouttoir *m* (à vaisselle).

dishtowel [ˈdɪʃtaʊəl] US = **tea towel.**

dishwasher [ˈdɪʃˌwɒʃəʳ] n [machine] lave-vaisselle *m* ; [person] plongeur *m*, -euse *f*.

dishwashing liquid n US liquide *m* vaisselle.

dish(washing) soap n US liquide *m* vaisselle.

dishwater [ˈdɪʃˌwɔːtəʳ] n eau *f* de vaisselle.

dishy [ˈdɪʃɪ] (*compar* **dishier**, *superl* **dishiest**) adj UK *inf* séduisant, sexy.

disillusion [ˌdɪsɪˈluːʒn] ◆ vt faire perdre ses illusions à, désillusionner. ◆ n = **disillusionment.**

disillusioned [ˌdɪsɪˈluːʒnd] adj désillusionné, désabusé ▶ **to be disillusioned with sb / sthg** avoir perdu ses illusions sur qqn / qqch.

disillusionment [ˌdɪsɪˈluːʒnmənt] n désillusion *f*, désabusement *m*.

disincentive [ˌdɪsɪnˈsentɪv] n : *taxes are a disincentive to expansion* les impôts découragent l'expansion.

disinclination [ˌdɪsɪnklɪˈneɪʃn] n [of person] peu *m* d'inclination.

disinclined [ˌdɪsɪnˈklaɪnd] adj ▶ **to be disinclined to do sthg** être peu disposé ou enclin à faire qqch.

disinfect [ˌdɪsɪnˈfekt] vt désinfecter.

disinfectant [ˌdɪsɪnˈfektənt] n désinfectant *m*.

disinfection [ˌdɪsɪnˈfekʃn] n désinfection *f*.

disinformation [ˌdɪsɪnfəˈmeɪʃn] n désinformation *f*.

disingenuous [ˌdɪsɪnˈdʒenjʊəs] adj peu sincère.

disinherit [ˌdɪsɪnˈherɪt] vt déshériter.

disintegrate [dɪsˈɪntɪgreɪt] vi [stone, wet paper] se désagréger ; [plane, rocket] se désintégrer ; *fig* [coalition, the family] se désagréger.

disintegration [dɪsˌɪntɪˈgreɪʃn] n [of stone, wet paper] désagrégation *f* ; [of plane, rocket] désintégration *f* ; *fig* [of coalition, the family] désagrégation *f*.

disinterest [ˌdɪsˈɪntərest] n [lack of interest] manque *m* d'intérêt.

disinterested [ˌdɪsˈɪntrəstɪd] adj **1.** [objective] désintéressé **2.** *inf* [uninterested] indifférent.

disinvestment [ˌdɪsɪnˈvestmənt] n désinvestissement *m*.

disjointed [dɪsˈdʒɔɪntɪd] adj [conversation, film, speech] décousu, incohérent.

disk [dɪsk] n **1.** COMPUT [hard] disque *m* ; [soft] disquette *f* ▶ **on disk** sur disque, sur disquette ▶ **to write sthg to disk** sauvegarder qqch sur disque or disquette **2.** US = **disc.**

disk crash n COMPUT atterrissage *m* de tête.

disk drive n COMPUT lecteur *m* de disquettes.

diskette [dɪsˈket] n COMPUT disquette *f*.

disk operating system n COMPUT système *m* d'exploitation de disques.

disk space n COMPUT espace *m* disque.

dislike [dɪsˈlaɪk] ◆ vt ne pas aimer. ◆ n [for sb] aversion *f*, antipathie *f* ; [for sthg] aversion *f* ▶ **to have a dislike for** or **of sthg** détester qqch ▶ **to take a dislike to sb / sthg** prendre qqn / qqch en grippe.

dislocate [ˈdɪsləkeɪt] vt [shoulder, knee, etc. - subj: person] se démettre, se déboîter, se luxer ; [- subj: accident, fall] démettre, déboîter, luxer.

dislocation [ˌdɪsləˈkeɪʃn] n **1.** [of shoulder, knee, etc.] luxation *f*, déboîtement *m* **2.** [disruption - of plans] perturbation *f*.

dislodge [dɪsˈlɒdʒ] vt [fish bone, piece of apple, etc.] dégager ; [large rock] déplacer ; *fig* [enemy, prey] déloger ; [leader, title holder] prendre la place de.

disloyal [ˌdɪsˈlɔɪəl] adj déloyal ▶ **to be disloyal to sb / sthg** être déloyal envers qqn / qqch.

dismal [ˈdɪzml] adj [day, weather] horrible ; [streets, countryside] lugubre ; [song] mélancolique, triste ; *fig* [result, performance] lamentable ; [future, prospect] sombre.

dismantle [dɪsˈmæntl] ◆ vt [object, scenery, exhibition] démonter ; *fig* [system, arrangement] démanteler. ◆ vi se démonter.

dismantling [dɪsˈmæntlɪŋ] n [of object, scenery] démontage *m* ; *fig* [of system, reforms] démantèlement *m*.

dismay [dɪsˈmeɪ] ◆ n consternation *f* ; [stronger] désarroi *m*. ◆ vt consterner ; [stronger] emplir de désarroi, effondrer.

dismayed [dɪsˈmeɪd] adj consterné, effondré.

dismember [dɪsˈmembəʳ] vt démembrer.

dismiss [dɪsˈmɪs] vt **1.** [from job - employee] licencier, congédier, renvoyer ; [- magistrate, official] destituer, révoquer, relever de ses fonctions **2.** [not take seriously - proposal] rejeter ; [- objection, warning] ne pas tenir compte de, ne pas prendre au sérieux ; [- problem] écarter, refuser de considérer **3.** [send away] congédier ; *fig* [thought, possibility] écarter ; [memory] effacer ; [suggestion, idea] rejeter ; SCH [class] laisser partir **4.** LAW [hung jury] dissoudre ▶ **to dismiss a charge** [judge] rendre une ordonnance de non-lieu.

dismissal [dɪsˈmɪsl] n **1.** [from work - of employee] licenciement *m*, renvoi *m* ; [- of magistrate, official] destitution *f*, révocation *f* **2.** [of proposal] rejet *m* **3.** LAW : *the dismissal of the charges against you* le non-lieu qui a été prononcé en votre faveur.

dismissive [dɪsˈmɪsɪv] adj [tone of voice, gesture] dédaigneux ▶ **to be dismissive of sb / sthg** ne faire aucun cas de qqn / qqch.

dismissively [dɪsˈmɪsɪvlɪ] adv [offhandedly] d'un ton dédaigneux ; [in final tone of voice] d'un ton sans appel.

dismount [ˌdɪsˈmaʊnt] vi descendre.

disobedience [ˌdɪsəˈbiːdjəns] n désobéissance *f*.

disobedient [ˌdɪsəˈbiːdjənt] adj désobéissant.

disobey [ˌdɪsəˈbeɪ] vt désobéir à.

disorder [dɪsˈɔːdəʳ] ◆ n **1.** [untidiness - of house, room, desk] désordre *m* **2.** [unrest] trouble *m* **3.** MED trouble *m*, troubles *mpl*. ◆ vt [make untidy - files, papers] mettre en désordre.

disordered [dɪsˈɔːdəd] adj [room] en désordre.

disorderly [dɪsˈɔːdəlɪ] adj **1.** [untidy - room, house] en désordre, désordonné **2.** [unruly - crowd, mob] désordonné, agité ; [- conduct] désordonné ; [- meeting, demonstration] désordonné, confus.

disorganization [dɪsˌɔːgənaɪˈzeɪʃn] n désorganisation *f*.

disorganized [dɪsˈɔːgənaɪzd] adj désorganisé.

disorient [dɪsˈɔːrɪənt], **disorientate** UK [dɪsˈɔːrɪənteɪt] vt désorienter.

disoriented [dɪsˈɔːrɪəntɪd], **disorientated** UK [dɪsˈɔːrɪənteɪtɪd] adj désorienté(e).

disorienting [dɪsˈɔːrɪəntɪŋ] adj déroutant.

disown [dɪs'əʊn] vt [child, opinion, statement] renier, désavouer ; [country] renier.

disparaging [dɪ'spærɪdʒɪŋ] adj [person, newspaper report - about person] désobligeant, malveillant ; [- about proposals, ideas] critique.

disparagingly [dɪ'spærɪdʒɪŋlɪ] adv [say, look at] d'un air désobligeant.

disparate ['dɪspərət] adj *fml* disparate.

disparity [dɪ'spærətɪ] *(pl* **disparities**) n [in ages] disparité *f* ; [in report, statement] contradiction *f*.

dispassionate [dɪ'spæʃnət] adj [objective - person, report, analysis, etc.] impartial, objectif / *to be dispassionate* rester objectif or impartial.

dispassionately [dɪ'spæʃnətlɪ] adv [unemotionally] sans émotion, calmement ; [objectively] objectivement, impartialement.

dispatch [dɪ'spætʃ] ◆ vt **1.** [send - letter, merchandise, telegram] envoyer, expédier ; [- messenger] envoyer, dépêcher ; [- troops, envoy] envoyer **2.** [complete - task, work] expédier, en finir avec **3.** *euph* [kill - person] tuer **4.** *inf* [food] s'envoyer. ◆ n **1.** [of letter, merchandise, telegram] envoi *m*, expédition *f* ; [of messenger, troops, envoy] envoi *m* **2.** MIL & PRESS [report] dépêche *f*. ◆ comp ▶ **dispatch clerk** expéditionnaire *mf*.

dispatch box n **1.** [for documents] boîte *f* à documents **2.** UK POL ▶ **the dispatch box** tribune d'où parlent les membres du gouvernement et leurs homologues du cabinet fantôme.

dispatch rider n estafette *f*.

dispel [dɪ'spel] *(pt & pp* **dispelled,** *cont* **dispelling)** vt [clouds, mist - subj: sun] dissiper ; [- subj: wind] chasser ; [doubts, fears, anxiety] dissiper.

dispensable [dɪ'spensəbl] adj dont on peut se passer, superflu.

dispensary [dɪ'spensərɪ] *(pl* **dispensaries**) n pharmacie *f* ; [for free distribution of medicine] dispensaire *m*.

dispensation [ˌdɪspen'seɪʃn] n ADMIN, LAW & RELIG [exemption] dispense *f*.

dispense [dɪ'spens] vt **1.** [subj: person, machine] distribuer **2.** [administer - justice, charity] exercer **3.** PHARM préparer. ◆ **dispense with** vt insep [do without] se passer de ; [get rid of] se débarrasser de.

dispenser [dɪ'spensər] n [machine] distributeur *m*.

dispensing [dɪ'spensɪŋ] adj UK : *dispensing chemist* **a)** [person] préparateur *m*, -trice *f* en pharmacie **b)** [establishment] pharmacie *f* / *dispensing optician* opticien *m*.

dispersal [dɪ'spɜːsl] n [of crowd, seeds] dispersion *f* ; [of gas - disappearance] dissipation *f* ; [- spread] dispersion *f* ; [of light - by prism] dispersion *f*, décomposition *f*.

disperse [dɪ'spɜːs] ◆ vt [crowd, seeds] disperser ; [clouds, mist - subj: sun] dissiper ; [- subj: wind] chasser ; [gas, chemical - cause to spread] propager ; [- cause to vanish] disperser. ◆ vi [crowds, seeds] se disperser ; [clouds, mist, smoke - with sun] se dissiper ; [- with wind] être chassé ; [gas, chemicals - spread] se propager ; [- vanish] se dissiper ; [light - with prism] se décomposer.

dispirited [dɪ'spɪrɪtɪd] adj abattu.

dispiritedly [dɪ'spɪrɪtɪdlɪ] adv [say] d'un ton découragé or abattu ; [look] d'un air découragé or abattu ; [play, do something] sans enthousiasme.

dispiriting [dɪ'spɪrɪtɪŋ] adj décourageant.

displace [dɪs'pleɪs] vt **1.** [refugees, population] déplacer **2.** CHEM & PHYS [water, air, etc.] déplacer.

displaced [dɪs'pleɪst] adj ▶ **displaced person** ADMIN & POL personne *f* déplacée.

displacement [dɪs'pleɪsmənt] n [of people, bone] déplacement *m*.

display [dɪ'spleɪ] ◆ vt **1.** [gifts, medals, ornaments, etc.] exposer ; *pej* exhiber ; [items in exhibition] mettre en exposition, exposer ; COMM [goods for sale] mettre en étalage, exposer **2.** [notice, poster, exam results] afficher **3.** [courage, determination, skill] faire preuve de, montrer ; [anger, affection, friendship, interest] manifester **4.** PRESS & TYPO mettre en vedette **5.** COMPUT [subj: screen] afficher ; [subj: user] visualiser. ◆ vi [birds, fish, etc.] faire la parade. ◆ n **1.** [of gifts, medals, ornaments] exposition *f* ; COMM [of goods, merchandise] mise *f* en étalage ; [goods, merchandise] étalage *m*, exposition *f* ▶ **to be on display** être exposé ▶ **to put sthg on display** exposer qqch **2.** [of poster, notice, etc.] affichage *m* **3.** [of affection, friendship, interest, anger] manifestation *f* ; [of courage, determination, ignorance, etc.] démonstration *f* / *a fireworks display* un feu d'artifice **4.** COMPUT [screen, device] écran *m* ; [visual information] affichage *m*, visualisation *f* ; [of calculator] viseur *m* **5.** [by birds, fish] parade *f*. ◆ comp ▶ **display advertisement** placard *m* publicitaire ▶ **display cabinet** or **case a)** [in shop] étalage *m*, vitrine *f* **b)** [in home] vitrine *f* ▶ **display copy** [of book] exemplaire *m* de démonstration ▶ **display rack** or **unit** présentoir *m*.

displease [dɪs'pliːz] vt mécontenter.

displeased [dɪs'pliːzd] adj mécontent ▶ **to be displeased with** or **at** être mécontent de.

displeasure [dɪs'pleʒər] n mécontentement *m*.

disposable [dɪ'spəʊzəbl] ◆ adj **1.** [throwaway - lighter, nappy, cup] jetable ; [- bottle] non consigné ; [- wrapping] perdu **2.** [available - money] disponible ▶ **disposable income** FIN revenus *mpl* disponibles (après impôts). ◆ n **1.** [nappy] couche *f* jetable **2.** [lighter] briquet *m* jetable.

disposable camera n appareil *m* photo jetable.

disposal [dɪ'spəʊzl] n **1.** [taking away] enlèvement *m* ; [of rubbish, by authority] enlèvement *m*, ramassage *m* ; [sale] vente *f* ; LAW [of property] cession *f* **2.** [resolution - of problem, question] résolution *f* ; [- of business] exécution *f*, expédition *f* **3.** US [disposal unit] broyeur *m* d'ordures (dans un évier) **4.** [availability] ▶ **to be at sb's disposal** être à la disposition de qqn ▶ **to have sthg at one's disposal** avoir qqch à sa disposition ▶ **to put sthg / sb at sb's disposal** mettre qqch / qqn à la disposition de qqn **5.** *fml* [arrangement] disposition *f*, arrangement *m* ; [of troops] déploiement *m*.

dispose [dɪ'spəʊz] vt [incline] : *his moving testimonial disposed the jury to leniency* son témoignage émouvant a disposé le jury à l'indulgence. ◆ **dispose of** vt insep **1.** [get rid of - waste, rubbish, problem] se débarrasser de ; [by taking away - refuse] enlever, ramasser ; [by selling] vendre ; [by throwing away] jeter ; [workers] congédier, renvoyer **2.** [deal with - problem, question] résoudre, régler ; [- task, matter under discussion] expédier, régler ; [- food] s'envoyer **3.** [have at one's disposal] disposer de, avoir à sa disposition **4.** *inf* [kill - person, animal] liquider ; *fig* [team, competitor] se débarrasser de.

disposed [dɪ'spəʊzd] adj ▶ **to be disposed to do sthg** être disposé à faire qqch ▶ **to be well / ill disposed towards sb** être bien / mal disposé envers qqn.

disposition [ˌdɪspə'zɪʃn] n **1.** [temperament, nature] naturel *m* **2.** *fml* [arrangement - of troops, buildings] disposition *f* ; [- of ornaments] disposition *f*, arrangement *m* **3.** [inclination, tendency] disposition *f*.

dispossess [ˌdɪspəˈzes] vt déposséder.

disproportion [ˌdɪsprəˈpɔːʃn] n disproportion f.

disproportionate [ˌdɪsprəˈpɔːʃnət] adj [excessive] disproportionné ▸ **to be disproportionate to sthg** être disproportionné à or avec qqch.

disprove [ˌdɪsˈpruːv] (pp **disproved** or **disproven** [-ˈpruːvn]) vt [theory] prouver la fausseté de.

disputable [dɪˈspjuːtəbl] adj discutable, contestable.

dispute [dɪˈspjuːt] ◆ vt **1.** [question - claim, theory, statement, etc.] contester, mettre en doute ; LAW [will] contester **2.** [debate - subject, motion] discuter, débattre **3.** [fight for - territory, championship, title] disputer. ◆ n **1.** [debate] discussion f, débat m / **the matter is beyond (all) dispute** la question est tout à fait incontestable / **open to dispute** contestable **2.** [argument - between individuals] dispute f, différend m ; [- between management and workers] conflit m ; LAW litige m ▸ **to be in dispute with sb over sthg** être en conflit avec qqn sur qqch ▸ **to be in dispute** [proposals, territory, ownership] faire l'objet d'un conflit.

> ⚠ The French word **dispute** means a quarrel or an argument, and should not be used to translate other senses of the English word dispute.

disputed [dɪˈspjuːtɪd] adj **1.** [decision, fact, claim] contesté **2.** [fought over] : **this is a much disputed territory** ce territoire fait l'objet de beaucoup de conflits.

disqualification [dɪsˌkwɒlɪfɪˈkeɪʃn] n [from standing for election] exclusion f ; [from sporting event] disqualification f ; [from exam] exclusion f / **your disqualification from driving will last for four years** vous aurez un retrait de permis (de conduire) de quatre ans.

disqualify [ˌdɪsˈkwɒlɪfaɪ] (pt & pp **disqualified**) vt exclure ; SPORT disqualifier ; SCH exclure ▸ **to disqualify sb from driving** retirer son permis (de conduire) or infliger un retrait de permis (de conduire) à qqn.

disquiet [dɪsˈkwaɪət] fml ◆ n inquiétude f. ◆ vt inquiéter, troubler ▸ **to be disquieted by sthg** être inquiet or s'inquiéter de qqch.

disquieting [dɪsˈkwaɪətɪŋ] adj fml inquiétant, troublant.

disregard [ˌdɪsrɪˈgɑːd] ◆ vt [person, order, law, rules] ne tenir aucun compte de ; [sb's feelings, instructions, remark, warning] ne tenir aucun compte de, négliger ; [danger] ne tenir aucun compte de, ignorer. ◆ n [for person, feelings] manque m de considération ; [of order, warning, danger, etc.] mépris m.

disrepair [ˌdɪsrɪˈpeər] n [of building] mauvais état m, délabrement m ; [of road] mauvais état m ▸ **to fall into disrepair a)** [building] se délabrer **b)** [road] se dégrader, s'abîmer.

disreputable [dɪsˈrepjʊtəbl] adj [dishonourable - behaviour] honteux ; [not respectable - person] de mauvaise réputation, louche ; [- area, club] mal famé, de mauvaise réputation ; hum [clothing] miteux.

disrepute [ˌdɪsrɪˈpjuːt] n discrédit m ▸ **to bring sthg into disrepute** discréditer qqch.

disrespect [ˌdɪsrɪˈspekt] n irrespect m, irrévérence f ▸ **to show disrespect towards sb / sthg** manquer de respect à qqn / qqch ▸ **to treat sb / sthg with disrespect** traiter qqn / qqch irrespectueusement.

disrespectful [ˌdɪsrɪˈspektful] adj irrespectueux, irrévérencieux ▸ **to be disrespectful to sb** manquer de respect à qqn.

disrupt [dɪsˈrʌpt] vt [lesson, meeting, train service] perturber ; [conversation] interrompre ; [plans] déranger, perturber.

disruption [dɪsˈrʌpʃn] n [of lesson, meeting, train service, plans] perturbation f ; [of conversation] interruption f.

disruptive [dɪsˈrʌptɪv] adj [factor, person, behaviour] perturbateur.

diss [dɪs] vt 🇺🇸 inf faire semblant de ne pas voir, ignorer.

dissatisfaction [ˈdɪsˌsætɪsˈfækʃn] n mécontentement m.

dissatisfied [ˌdɪsˈsætɪsfaɪd] adj mécontent ▸ **to be dissatisfied with sb / sthg** être mécontent de qqn / qqch.

dissect [dɪˈsekt] vt [animal, plant] disséquer ; fig [argument, theory] disséquer ; [book, report] éplucher.

disseminate [dɪˈsemɪneɪt] vt [knowledge, ideas] disséminer, propager ; [information, news] diffuser, propager.

dissension [dɪˈsenʃn] n dissension f, discorde f.

dissent [dɪˈsent] ◆ vi [person] différer ; [opinion] diverger. ◆ n (U) [gen] opinion f divergente.

dissenter [dɪˈsentər] n [gen] dissident m, -e f.

dissenting [dɪˈsentɪŋ] adj [opinion] divergent.

dissertation [ˌdɪsəˈteɪʃn] n 🇬🇧 UNIV mémoire m ; 🇺🇸 thèse f.

disservice [ˌdɪsˈsɜːvɪs] n mauvais service m ▸ **to do sb a disservice** faire du tort à qqn, rendre un mauvais service à qqn.

dissident [ˈdɪsɪdənt] ◆ n dissident m, -e f. ◆ adj dissident.

dissimilar [ˌdɪˈsɪmɪlər] adj différent.

dissimilarity [ˌdɪsɪmɪˈlærətɪ] (pl **dissimilarities**) n différence f.

dissipate [ˈdɪsɪpeɪt] ◆ vt [disperse - cloud, fears] dissiper ; [waste - fortune] dilapider, gaspiller ; [- energies] disperser, gaspiller ; PHYS [heat, energy] dissiper. ◆ vi [cloud, crowd] se disperser ; [fears, hopes] s'évanouir ; PHYS [energy] se dissiper.

dissipated [ˈdɪsɪpeɪtɪd] adj [person] débauché ; [habit, life] de débauche ; [society] décadent.

dissociate [dɪˈsəʊʃɪeɪt] vt **1.** [gen] dissocier, séparer ▸ **to dissociate o.s. from sthg** se dissocier or désolidariser de qqch **2.** CHEM dissocier.

dissolute [ˈdɪsəluːt] adj [person] débauché ; [life] de débauche, dissolu liter.

dissolution [ˌdɪsəˈluːʃn] n **1.** [gen] dissolution f **2.** 🇺🇸 LAW [divorce] divorce m.

dissolve [dɪˈzɒlv] ◆ vt **1.** [salt, sugar] dissoudre **2.** [empire, marriage, Parliament] dissoudre. ◆ vi **1.** [salt, sugar] se dissoudre ; fig [fear, hopes] s'évanouir, s'envoler **2.** [marriage, Parliament] être dissout ; [empire] se dissoudre.

dissonance [ˈdɪsənəns] n MUS dissonance f ; fig discordance f.

dissonant [ˈdɪsənənt] adj MUS dissonant ; fig [colours, opinions] discordant.

dissuade [dɪˈsweɪd] vt [person] dissuader ▸ **to dissuade sb from doing sthg** dissuader qqn de faire qqch ▸ **to dissuade sb from sthg** détourner qqn de qqch.

distance [ˈdɪstəns] ◆ n **1.** [between two places] distance f **2.** [distant point, place] ▸ **to see / to hear sthg in the distance** voir / entendre qqch au loin ▸ **to see sthg from a distance** voir qqch de loin **3.** [separation in time] : **at a distance of 200 years, it's very difficult to know** 200 ans plus tard, il est très difficile de savoir **4.** fig [gap] : **there's a great distance between us** il y a un grand fossé entre nous **5.** [aloofness, reserve] froideur f. ◆ comp ▸ **distance learning** télé-enseignement m ▸ **distance race** SPORT épreuve f de fond ▸ **distance runner** SPORT coureur m, -euse f de fond. ◆ vt distancer ▸ **to distance o.s. (from sb / sthg)** fig prendre ses distances (par rapport à qqn / qqch).

distant ['dɪstənt] ◆ adj **1.** [faraway - country, galaxy, place] lointain, éloigné **2.** [in past - times] lointain, reculé ; [- memory] lointain / *in the (dim and) distant past* il y a bien or très longtemps, dans le temps **3.** [in future - prospect] lointain / *in the not too distant future* dans un avenir proche, prochainement **4.** [relation] éloigné ; [resemblance] vague **5.** [remote - person, look] distant ; [aloof] froid. ◆ adv : *three miles distant from here* à trois miles d'ici / *not far distant* pas très loin.

distantly ['dɪstəntlɪ] adv [resemble] vaguement / *to be distantly related* **a)** [people] avoir un lien de parenté éloigné **b)** [ideas, concepts, etc.] avoir un rapport éloigné.

distaste [dɪs'teɪst] n dégoût *m*, répugnance *f*.

distasteful [dɪs'teɪstfʊl] adj [unpleasant - task] désagréable ; [in bad taste - joke, remark, etc.] de mauvais goût ▸ **to be distasteful to sb** déplaire à qqn.

distastefully [dɪs'teɪstfʊlɪ] adv [with repugnance - look] d'un air dégoûté ; [with bad taste - presented, portrayed] avec mauvais goût.

Dist. Atty written abbr of district attorney.

distend [dɪ'stend] ◆ vt gonfler. ◆ vi [stomach] se ballonner, se gonfler ; [sails] se gonfler.

distended [dɪ'stendɪd] adj gonflé ; [stomach] gonflé, ballonné.

distil 🇬🇧, **distill** 🇺🇸 [dɪ'stɪl] (*pt & pp* distilled, cont distilling) ◆ vt *lit & fig* distiller. ◆ vi se distiller.

distiller [dɪ'stɪlər] n distillateur *m*.

distillery [dɪ'stɪlərɪ] (*pl* distilleries) n distillerie *f*.

distinct [dɪ'stɪŋkt] adj **1.** [different] distinct ▸ **to be distinct from** se distinguer de **2.** [clear - memory] clair, net ; [- voice, announcement] distinct **3.** [decided, evident - accent] prononcé ; [- preference] marqué ; [- lack of respect, interest] évident ; [- likeness] clair, net, prononcé ; [- advantage, improvement] net. ❖ **as distinct from** prep phr par opposition à.

distinction [dɪ'stɪŋkʃn] n **1.** [difference] distinction *f* **2.** [excellence] distinction *f* **3.** SCH & UNIV [mark] mention *f* **4.** [honour, award] honneur *m*.

distinctive [dɪ'stɪŋktɪv] adj [colour, feature] distinctif.

distinctively [dɪ'stɪŋktɪvlɪ] adv [coloured] de manière distinctive.

distinctly [dɪ'stɪŋktlɪ] adv **1.** [clearly - speak, hear] distinctement, clairement ; [remember] clairement **2.** [very] vraiment, franchement.

distinguish [dɪ'stɪŋgwɪʃ] ◆ vt **1.** [set apart] distinguer ▸ **to distinguish o.s.** se distinguer ▸ **to distinguish sthg from sthg** distinguer qqch de qqch **2.** [tell apart] distinguer **3.** [discern] distinguer. ◆ vi faire or établir une distinction ▸ **to distinguish between two things / people** faire la distinction entre deux choses / personnes.

distinguishable [dɪ'stɪŋgwɪʃəbl] adj **1.** [visible] visible **2.** [recognizable] reconnaissable.

distinguished [dɪ'stɪŋgwɪʃt] adj **1.** [eminent] distingué **2.** [refined - manners, voice] distingué.

distinguishing [dɪ'stɪŋgwɪʃɪŋ] adj [feature, mark, characteristic, etc.] distinctif ▸ **distinguishing features** [on passport] signes *mpl* particuliers.

distort [dɪ'stɔːt] ◆ vt **1.** [face, image, structure, etc.] déformer ; *fig* [facts, truth] déformer, dénaturer ; [judgment] fausser **2.** ELECTRON, RADIO & TV déformer. ◆ vi [face, structure, sound] se déformer.

distorted [dɪ'stɔːtɪd] adj [face, limbs] déformé ; *fig* [facts, truth, account] déformé, dénaturé ; [view of life] déformé, faussé ; [judgment] faussé.

distortion [dɪ'stɔːʃn] n **1.** *lit & fig* déformation *f* **2.** ELECTRON & RADIO distorsion *f* ; TV déformation *f*.

distract [dɪ'strækt] vt **1.** [break concentration of] distraire ; [disturb] déranger **2.** [amuse] distraire.

distracted [dɪ'stræktɪd] adj **1.** [with thoughts elsewhere] distrait **2.** [upset] affolé, bouleversé.

distracting [dɪ'stræktɪŋ] adj **1.** [disruptive] gênant **2.** [amusing] distrayant.

distraction [dɪ'strækʃn] n **1.** [interruption - of attention, from objective] distraction *f* **2.** [amusement] distraction *f* **3.** [anxiety] affolement *m* ; [absent-mindedness] distraction *f* **4.** [madness] affolement *m* ▸ **to drive sb to distraction** rendre qqn fou.

distraught [dɪ'strɔːt] adj [with worry] angoissé, fou d'angoisse ; [after death] fou or éperdu de douleur, désespéré.

distress [dɪ'stres] ◆ n [suffering - mental] angoisse *f* ; [- physical] souffrance *f* ; [hardship] détresse *f* ▸ **to be in distress a)** [horse, athlete] souffrir **b)** [mentally] être angoissé **c)** [ship] être en détresse or perdition **d)** [aircraft] être en détresse. ◆ vt [upset] faire de la peine à, tourmenter.

distressed [dɪ'strest] adj **1.** [mentally] tourmenté ; [very sorry] affligé ; [physically] souffrant ; [financially] dans le besoin ▸ **to be distressed by** or **about sthg** être affligé par qqch **2.** [furniture, leather, clothing] vieilli.

distressing [dɪ'stresɪŋ] adj pénible.

distress signal n signal *m* de détresse.

distribute [dɪ'strɪbjuːt] vt **1.** [hand out - money, leaflets, gifts, etc.] distribuer **2.** [share out, allocate - wealth, weight] répartir ; [- paint] répandre **3.** CIN & COMM [supply] distribuer.

distribution [ˌdɪstrɪ'bjuːʃn] ◆ n **1.** [of leaflets, money, etc.] distribution *f* **2.** CIN & COMM [delivery, supply] distribution *f* ; [of books] diffusion *f* **3.** [of wealth] répartition *f*, distribution *f* ; [of load] répartition *f*. ◆ comp COMM [agreement, network] de distribution.

distribution list n [for e-mail] liste *f* de distribution.

distributor [dɪ'strɪbjʊtər] n **1.** CIN & COMM distributeur *m* **2.** AUTO distributeur *m* ▸ **distributor cap** tête *f* de Delco or d'allumeur.

district ['dɪstrɪkt] ◆ n [of country] région *f* ; [of town] quartier *m* ; [administrative area - of country] district *m* ; [- of city] arrondissement *m* ; [surrounding area] région *f* ▸ **the District of Columbia** le district fédéral de Columbia. ◆ comp ▸ **district manager** COMM directeur *m* régional, directrice *f* régionale.

district attorney n [in US] procureur *m* de la République.

district council n [in UK] conseil *m* municipal.

district court n [in US] ≈ tribunal *m* d'instance (fédéral).

district nurse n 🇬🇧 infirmière *f* visiteuse.

distrust [dɪs'trʌst] ◆ vt se méfier de. ◆ n méfiance *f*.

distrustful [dɪs'trʌstfʊl] adj méfiant ▸ **to be deeply distrustful of** éprouver une extrême méfiance pour or à l'égard de.

disturb [dɪ'stɜːb] vt **1.** [interrupt - person] déranger ; [- silence, sleep] troubler **2.** [distress, upset] troubler, perturber ; [alarm] inquiéter **3.** [alter condition of - water] troubler ; [- mud, sediment] agiter, remuer ; [- papers] déranger.

disturbance [dɪ'stɜːbəns] n **1.** [interruption, disruption] dérangement *m* **2.** POL ▸ **disturbances** [unrest] troubles *mpl*, émeute *f* **3.** [noise] bruit *m*, vacarme *m* **4.** [distress, alarm] trouble *m*, perturbation *f*.

disturbed [dɪ'stɜːbd] adj **1.** [distressed, upset] troublé, perturbé ; [alarmed] inquiet (inquiète) ▸ **to be disturbed at**

or **by** sthg être troublé par or perturbé par or inquiet de qqch / *mentally disturbed* mentalement dérangé **2.** [interrupted -sleep] troublé.

disturbing [dɪˈstɜːbɪŋ] adj [alarming] inquiétant ; [distressing, upsetting] troublant, perturbant.

disturbingly [dɪˈstɜːbɪŋlɪ] adv : *the level of pollution is disturbingly high* la pollution a atteint un niveau inquiétant.

disunity [ˌdɪsˈjuːnətɪ] n désunion f.

disuse [ˌdɪsˈjuːs] n ▸ **to fall into disuse** [word, custom, law] tomber en désuétude.

disused [ˌdɪsˈjuːzd] adj [building, mine] abandonné, désaffecté.

ditch [dɪtʃ] ◆ n [by roadside] fossé *m* ; [for irrigation, drainage] rigole f. ◆ vt **1.** *inf* [abandon -car] abandonner ; [-plan, idea] abandonner, laisser tomber ; [-boyfriend, girlfriend] plaquer, laisser tomber ; [throw out] se débarrasser de **2.** AERON ▸ **to ditch a plane** faire un amerrissage forcé. ◆ vi **1.** AERON faire un amerrissage forcé **2.** AGR creuser un fossé.

dither [ˈdɪðə^r] *inf* ◆ vi [be indecisive] hésiter, se tâter. ◆ n ▸ **to be in a dither** hésiter, se tâter.

ditherer [ˈdɪðərə^r] n *inf* : *he's such a terrible ditherer* il est toujours à hésiter sur tout.

dithering [ˈdɪðərɪŋ] n COMPUT tramage *m*.

ditsy [ˈdɪtsɪ] (*compar* **ditsier**, *superl* **ditsiest**) adj 🇺🇸 *inf* écervelé.

ditto [ˈdɪtəʊ] ◆ adv *inf* : *I feel like a drink — ditto* j'ai bien envie de prendre un verre — idem / *I don't like her — ditto* je ne l'aime pas — moi non plus. ◆ comp ▸ **ditto mark** guillemets *mpl* itératifs, signes *mpl* d'itération.

diuretic [ˌdaɪjʊˈretɪk] ◆ adj diurétique. ◆ n diurétique *m*.

diva [ˈdiːvə] n diva f.

divan [dɪˈvæn] n [couch] divan *m* ▸ **divan (bed)** divan-lit *m*.

dive [daɪv] (🇬🇧 *pt* & *pp* **dived** ; 🇺🇸 *pt* **dove** [dəʊv] or **dived**, *pp* **dived**) ◆ vi **1.** [person, bird, submarine] plonger ; [aircraft] plonger, piquer, descendre en piqué **2.** [as sport] faire de la plongée **3.** *inf* [rush] : *they dived for the exit* ils se sont précipités or ils ont foncé vers la sortie / *to dive under the table* plonger or se jeter sous la table. ◆ n **1.** [of swimmer, bird, submarine] plongeon *m* ; [by aircraft] piqué *m* **2.** *inf* [sudden movement] : *to make a dive for the exit* se précipiter vers la sortie **3.** *inf* & *pej* [bar, café, etc.] bouge *m*. ❖ **dive in** vi **1.** [swimmer] plonger **2.** *inf* : *dive in!* [eat] attaquez !

dive-bomb vt [subj: plane] bombarder or attaquer en piqué ; [subj: bird] attaquer en piqué.

diver [ˈdaɪvə^r] n **1.** [from diving board, underwater] plongeur *m*, -euse f ; [deep-sea] scaphandrier *m* **2.** [bird] plongeur *m*.

diverge [daɪˈvɜːdʒ] vi [paths] se séparer, diverger ; *fig* [opinions] diverger.

divergence [daɪˈvɜːdʒəns] n [of paths] séparation f, divergence f ; *fig* [of opinions] divergence f.

divergent [daɪˈvɜːdʒənt] adj [opinions] divergent.

diverse [daɪˈvɜːs] adj divers.

diversification [daɪˌvɜːsɪfɪˈkeɪʃn] n diversification f.

diversify [daɪˈvɜːsɪfaɪ] (*pt* & *pp* **diversified**) ◆ vi [company] se diversifier. ◆ vt diversifier.

diversion [daɪˈvɜːʃn] n **1.** [of traffic] déviation f ; [of river] dérivation f, détournement *m* **2.** [distraction] diversion f / *to create a diversion* **a)** [distract attention] faire (une) diversion **b)** MIL opérer une diversion **3.** [amusement] distraction f.

diversionary [daɪˈvɜːʃnrɪ] adj [remark, proposal] destiné à faire diversion ▸ **diversionary tactics** tactique f de diversion.

diversity [daɪˈvɜːsətɪ] n diversité f.

divert [daɪˈvɜːt] vt **1.** [reroute -traffic] dévier ; [-train, plane, ship] dévier (la route de) ; [-river, attention, conversation, blow] détourner **2.** [money] transférer ; [illegally] détourner **3.** [amuse] distraire.

divest [daɪˈvest] vt *fml* **1.** [take away from] priver ▸ **to divest sb of sthg** priver qqn de qqch **2.** [rid] ▸ **to divest o.s. of a)** [opinion, belief] se défaire de **b)** [coat] enlever **c)** [luggage] se débarrasser de.

divide [dɪˈvaɪd] ◆ vt **1.** [split up -territory, property, work] diviser ; [share out] partager, répartir ▸ **to divide sthg in** or **into two** couper or diviser qqch en deux **2.** [separate] séparer **3.** MATH diviser **4.** [disunite -family, party] diviser. ◆ vi **1.** [cells, group of people, novel] se diviser **2.** [river, road] se séparer **3.** MATH diviser. ◆ n [gap] fossé *m*. ❖ **divide off** vt sep séparer ▸ **to divide sthg off from sthg** séparer qqch de qqch. ❖ **divide out** vt sep partager, répartir ▸ **to divide sthg out between** or **among people** partager qqch entre des gens. ❖ **divide up** ◆ vi = **divide** (*vi*). ◆ vt sep = **divide** (*vt*).

divided [dɪˈvaɪdɪd] adj **1.** [property, territory] divisé ; BOT découpé ▸ **divided highway** 🇺🇸 route f à quatre voies ▸ **divided skirt** jupe-culotte f **2.** [disunited -family, party] divisé / *opinion is divided on the matter* les avis sont partagés sur ce problème ▸ **to have divided loyalties** être déchiré.

dividend [ˈdɪvɪdend] n FIN & MATH dividende *m*.

divider [dɪˈvaɪdə^r] n **1.** [in room] meuble *m* de séparation **2.** [for files] intercalaire *m*.

dividing [dɪˈvaɪdɪŋ] adj [fence, wall] de séparation ▸ **dividing line a)** *lit* limite f **b)** *fig* distinction f.

divine [dɪˈvaɪn] adj **1.** RELIG divin **2.** *inf* [delightful] divin.

diving [ˈdaɪvɪŋ] n [underwater] plongée f sous-marine ; [from board] plongeon *m*.

diving board n plongeoir *m*.

diving suit n scaphandre *m*.

divinity [dɪˈvɪnətɪ] (*pl* **divinities**) ◆ n **1.** [god, goddess] divinité f **2.** [theology] théologie f ; SCH instruction f religieuse ▸ **Faculty / Doctor of Divinity** faculté f de / docteur *m* en théologie. ◆ comp ▸ **divinity school** 🇺🇸 faculté f (libre) de théologie ▸ **divinity student** étudiant *m*, -e f en théologie.

divisible [dɪˈvɪzəbl] adj divisible ▸ **divisible by** divisible par.

division [dɪˈvɪʒn] n **1.** [act, state] division f ; [sharing out] partage *m* **2.** [section -of company, organization] division f ; [-of scale, thermometer] graduation f ; [compartment -in box, bag] compartiment *m* **3.** BIOL, MIL & SPORT division f **4.** MATH division f **5.** [that which separates] division f ; [dividing line] division f, scission f ; [in room] cloison f **6.** [dissension] division f.

division sign n MATH symbole *m* de division.

divisive [dɪˈvaɪsɪv] adj [policy, issue] qui crée des divisions.

divisiveness [dɪˈvaɪsɪvnɪs] n : *the divisiveness of this policy is evident to everyone* il apparaît clairement à tout le monde que cette politique crée des or est source de divisions.

divorce [dɪˈvɔːs] ◆ n **1.** LAW divorce *m* **2.** *fig* séparation f, divorce *m*. ◆ comp [case, proceedings] de divorce ▸ **divorce court** chambre spécialisée dans les affaires familiales au tribunal de grande instance ▸ **divorce lawyer** avocat *m* spécialisé dans les affaires or cas de divorce. ◆ vt **1.** LAW [subj: husband, wife] divorcer d'avec ; [subj: judge] prononcer le divorce de **2.** *fig* séparer ▸ **to divorce sthg from sthg** séparer qqch de qqch. ◆ vi divorcer.

divorced [dɪ'vɔ:st] adj **1.** LAW divorcé **2.** *fig : to be divorced from reality* **a)** [person] être coupé de la réalité, ne pas avoir les pieds sur terre **b)** [suggestion, plan] être irréaliste.

divorcee [dɪ,vɔ:'si:] n divorcé *m*, -e *f*.

divulge [daɪ'vʌldʒ] vt divulguer, révéler.

Dixie ['dɪksɪ] pr n [US] *inf* le Sud *(terme désignant le sud-est des États-Unis, particulièrement les anciens États esclavagistes).*

DIY n & comp **abbr of do-it-yourself.**

dizzily ['dɪzɪlɪ] adv **1.** [walk] avec une sensation de vertige **2.** [behave] étourdiment.

dizziness ['dɪzɪnɪs] n (U) vertiges *mpl*.

dizzy ['dɪzɪ] (*compar* **dizzier**, *superl* **dizziest**) adj **1.** [giddy] *: to feel dizzy* avoir le vertige, avoir la tête qui tourne ▸ *it makes me (feel) dizzy* cela me donne le vertige ▸ **dizzy spell** or **turn** éblouissement *m* **2.** [height, speed] vertigineux **3.** *inf* [scatterbrained] étourdi.

DJ n **1.** (abbr of disk jockey) DJ *m* **2.** (abbr of dinner jacket) smoking *m*.

Djakarta [dʒə'kɑ:tə] = **Jakarta.**

Djibouti [dʒɪ'bu:tɪ] pr n (République *f* de) Djibouti / *in Djibouti* à Djibouti.

Dk, DK MESSAGING written abbr of **don't know.**

dl (written abbr of **decilitre**) dl.

DLit(t) [di:'lɪt] n **1.** (abbr of Doctor of Literature) docteur *m* ès lettres **2.** (abbr of Doctor of Letters) docteur *m* ès lettres.

DLO (abbr of dead-letter office) n *centre de recherche du courrier.*

dm (written abbr of **decimetre**) dm.

DM (written abbr of **Deutsche Mark**) DM.

DMA n abbr of **direct memory access.**

DMus n [,di:'mju:z] (abbr of Doctor of Music) n [UK] docteur *m* en musique.

DMZ n abbr of **demilitarized zone.**

DNA n (abbr of **deoxyribonucleic acid**) n ADN *m* ▸ **DNA test** test *m* ADN.

D-notice n [UK] *censure imposée à la presse pour sécurité d'État.*

DNS [,di:en'es] (abbr of Domain Name System) n COMPUT DNS.

do[1] [du:] (*pres (3rd sing)* **does** [dʌz], *pt* **did** [dɪd], *pp* **done** [dʌn]) (*negative forms* **do not** *frequently shortened to* **don't** [dəʊnt], **does not** *frequently shortened to* **doesn't** [dʌznt], **did not** *frequently shortened to* **didn't** [dɪdnt], *cont* **doing** [du:ɪŋ]) ◆ aux vb **1.** [in questions] *: do you know her?* est-ce que tu la connais ?, la connais-tu ? **2.** [in tag questions] *: he takes you out a lot, doesn't he?* il t'emmène souvent dîner dehors, n'est-ce pas ou hein ? / *so you want to be an actress, do you?* alors tu veux devenir actrice ? **3.** [with the negative] *: I don't believe you* je ne te crois pas **4.** [for emphasis] *: do you mind if I smoke?* — *yes I* DO *mind* cela vous dérange-t-il que je fume ? — justement, oui, ça me dérange / DO *sit down* asseyez-vous donc **5.** [elliptically] *: so do I / does she* moi / elle aussi / *neither do I / does she* moi / elle non plus / *I may come to Paris next month — let me know if you do* il se peut que je vienne à Paris le mois prochain — préviens-moi si tu viens / *I liked her — you didn't!* [surprised] elle m'a plu — non ! vraiment ? **6.** [in sentences beginning with adverbial phrase] *: not only did you lie...* non seulement

tu as menti... ◆ vt **1.** [be busy or occupied with] faire / *what are you doing?* qu'est-ce que tu fais ?, que fais-tu ?, qu'es-tu en train de faire ? / *what do you do for a living?* qu'est-ce que vous faites dans la vie ? ; [carry out - task, work] faire / *he did a good job* il a fait du bon travail ▸ **to do sthg about sthg** / **sb** *: what are you going to do about the noise?* qu'est-ce que tu vas faire au sujet du bruit ? ▸ **to do sthg for sb** / **sthg** *: what can I do for you?* que puis-je (faire) pour vous ? ▸ **to do sthg to sb** / **sthg** *: who did this to you?* qui est-ce qui t'a fait ça ? ▸ **that does it!** cette fois c'en est trop ! **2.** [produce, provide - copy, report] faire / *I don't do portraits* je ne fais pas les portraits **3.** [work on, attend to] s'occuper de / *to do the garden* s'occuper du jardin **4.** [clean, tidy - room, cupboard] faire ; [arrange - flowers] arranger / *to do one's teeth* se brosser les dents **5.** SCH & UNIV [subject] étudier ; [UK] [course] suivre / *to do medicine* / *law* étudier la médecine / le droit, faire sa médecine / son droit **6.** AUTO & TRANSP [speed, distance] faire / *the car will do over 100* la voiture peut faire du 160 **7.** CULIN [cook] faire ; [prepare - vegetables, salad] préparer / *how would you like your steak done?* comment voulez-vous votre steak ? **8.** [be enough or suitable for] suffire / *will £10 do you?* 10 livres, ça te suffira ? **9.** [finish] *: well that's that done, thank goodness* bon, voilà qui est fait, dieu merci **10.** [imitate] imiter, faire **11.** *inf* [cheat] rouler, avoir / *you've been done* tu t'es fait rouler or avoir **12.** *v inf* [take] ▸ **to do drugs** se camer. ◆ vi **1.** [perform - in exam, competition, etc.] s'en tirer, s'en sortir / *try to do better in future* essaie de mieux faire à l'avenir ▸ **well done!** bien joué !, bravo ! **2.** [referring to health] *: how is she doing, doctor?* comment va-t-elle, docteur ? ▸ **how do you do?** [on being introduced] enchanté, ravi **3.** [act, behave] faire / *do as you're told!* fais ce qu'on te dit ! / *you would do well to listen to your mother* tu ferais bien d'écouter ta mère **4.** [be enough] suffire / *will £20 do?* 20 livres, ça ira or suffira ? **5.** [be suitable] aller / *that will do (nicely)* ça ira or conviendra parfaitement, cela fera très bien l'affaire / *this won't do* ça ne peut pas continuer comme ça **6.** (*always in perfect tense*) [finish] *: have you done?* tu as fini ? **7.** [be connected with] *: that's got nothing to do with it!* [is irrelevant] cela n'a rien à voir ! / *I want nothing to do with it* / *you* je ne veux rien avoir à faire là-dedans / avec toi / *it's nothing to do with me* je n'y suis pour rien / *what I said to him has got nothing to do with you* **a)** [it's none of your business] ce que je lui ai dit ne te regarde pas **b)** [it's not about you] ce que je lui ai dit n'a rien à voir avec toi / *that has a lot to do with it* cela joue un rôle très important. ◆ n **1.** [tip] *: the do's and don'ts of car maintenance* les choses à faire et à ne pas faire dans l'entretien des voitures **2.** *inf* [party, celebration] fête *f*. ◆ **do away with** vt insep **1.** [abolish - institution, rule, restriction] abolir ; [get rid of - object] se débarrasser de **2.** [kill] se débarrasser de, faire disparaître. ◆ **do down** vt sep [UK] *inf* [criticize, disparage] rabaisser, médire sur, dire du mal de ▸ **to do o.s. down** se rabaisser. ◆ **do for** vt insep *v inf* **1.** [UK] [murder] zigouiller ; [cause death of] tuer **2.** [ruin - object, engine] bousiller ; [cause failure of - plan] ruiner ; [- company] couler / *I'm done for* je suis cuit **3.** [UK] [exhaust] tuer, crever / *shopping always does for me* je suis toujours crevé après les courses. ◆ **do in** vt sep *v inf* **1.** [murder, kill] zigouiller, buter, butter **2.** [exhaust] = **do for 3.** [injure] ▸ **to do one's back** / **one's knee in** se bousiller le dos / le genou. ◆ **do out of** vt sep *inf* [money, job] faire perdre. ◆ **do over** vt sep **1.** [room] refaire **2.** [US] [do again] refaire **3.** *inf* [beat up] casser la gueule or la tête à **4.** [UK] [burgle, rob - house, bank, etc.] cambrioler. ◆ **do up** ◆ vt sep **1.** [fasten - dress, jacket] fermer ; [- zip] fermer, remonter ; [- buttons] boutonner ; [- shoelaces] attacher **2.** [wrap, bundle up] emballer **3.** *inf* [renovate - house, cottage, etc.] refaire, retaper ; [old dress, hat] arranger ; [make more glamorous]

▶ **to do o.s. up** se faire beau / belle. ◆ vi [skirt, dress] se fermer ; [zip] se fermer, se remonter ; [buttons] se fermer, se boutonner. ❖ **do with** vt insep **1.** *(after 'could')* 🇬🇧 *inf* [need, want] avoir besoin de / *I could do with a drink* je prendrais bien un verre, j'ai bien envie de prendre un verre **2.** *(after 'can't')* 🇬🇧 *inf* [tolerate] supporter / *I can't do or be doing with all this noise* je ne supporte pas ce vacarme **3.** *(after 'what')* [act with regard to] faire de / *what do you want me to do with this?* que veux-tu que je fasse de ça ? **4.** *(always with pp)* [finish with] finir avec / *can I borrow the ashtray if you've done with it?* puis-je emprunter le cendrier si tu n'en as plus besoin ? ❖ **do without** ◆ vi faire sans. ◆ vt insep se passer de / *I could have done without this long wait* j'aurais bien pu me passer de cette longue attente.

do² [dəʊ] n MUS do *m*.

DOA adj abbr of **dead on arrival**.

doable ['duːəbl] adj *inf* faisable.

d.o.b., DOB written abbr of **date of birth**.

Doberman (pinscher) ['dəʊbəmən('pɪnʃə')] n doberman *m*.

doc [dɒk] n *inf* [doctor] toubib *m* / *morning, doc* bonjour docteur.

docile [🇬🇧 'dəʊsaɪl 🇺🇸 'dɒsəl] adj docile.

docility [də'sɪlətɪ] n docilité *f*.

dock [dɒk] ◆ vi [ship] se mettre à quai ; [spacecraft] s'amarrer. ◆ vt **1.** [ship] mettre à quai ; [spacecraft] amarrer **2.** [money] ▶ **to dock sb's pay / pocket money** faire une retenue sur la paie / réduire l'argent de poche de qqn **3.** [animal's tail] couper. ◆ n **1.** NAUT dock *m*, docks *mpl* **2.** LAW banc *m* des accusés **3.** [for electronic device] station *f* d'accueil. ◆ comp [manager] des docks ▶ **dock worker** 🇬🇧 docker *m* ▶ **dock strike** grève *f* des dockers.

docker ['dɒkə'] n 🇬🇧 docker *m*.

docking station n [for electronic device] station *f* d'accueil.

dockyard ['dɒkjɑːd] n chantier *m* naval or de constructions navales ▶ **naval dockyard** arsenal *m* maritime or de la marine.

doctor ['dɒktə'] ◆ n **1.** MED docteur *m*, médecin *m* / *dear Doctor Cameron* [in letter] docteur / *I've an appointment with Doctor Cameron* j'ai rendez-vous avec le docteur Cameron / *thank you, doctor* merci, docteur ▶ **to go to the doctor** or **doctor's** aller chez le docteur or médecin **2.** UNIV docteur *m*. ◆ vt **1.** [tamper with - results, figures] falsifier, trafiquer ; [- wine] frelater **2.** [drug - drink, food] mettre de la drogue dans ; [- racehorse] doper **3.** 🇬🇧 [castrate, sterilize - cat, dog] châtrer **4.** [treat] soigner.

doctoral ['dɒktərəl] adj [thesis, degree] de doctorat.

doctorate ['dɒktərət] n doctorat *m* ▶ **to have / to do a doctorate in sthg** avoir / faire un doctorat en qqch.

doctrine ['dɒktrɪn] n doctrine *f*.

docudrama [,dɒkjʊ'drɑːmə] n TV docudrame *m*.

document ◆ n ['dɒkjʊmənt] document *m* ; LAW acte *m*. ◆ vt ['dɒkjʊment] **1.** [write about in detail] décrire (de façon détaillée) ; [record on film - subj: film] montrer (en détail), présenter (de façon détaillée) ; [- subj: photographer] faire un reportage sur **2.** [support - with evidence or proof] fournir des preuves à l'appui de, attester ; [- with citations, references] documenter.

documentary [,dɒkjʊ'mentərɪ] *(pl* **documentaries)** ◆ adj [factual - film, programme] documentaire. ◆ n CIN & TV documentaire *m*.

documentation [,dɒkjʊmen'teɪʃn] n documentation *f*.

document case n porte-documents *m inv*.

docusoap ['dɒkjuːsəʊp] n docudrame *m (sous forme de feuilleton)*.

DOD pr n 🇺🇸 abbr of **Department of Defense**.

doddering ['dɒdərɪŋ] adj *inf* [walk] hésitant, chancelant ; *pej* [elderly person] gâteux.

doddery ['dɒdərɪ] adj *inf* [walk] hésitant / *I still feel a bit doddery* [after illness] je me sens encore un peu faible or flagada.

doddle ['dɒdl] n 🇬🇧 *inf* ▶ **it's a doddle** c'est simple comme bonjour, c'est du gâteau.

Dodecanese [,dəʊdɪkə'niːz] pl pr n ▶ **the Dodecanese** le Dodécanèse / *in the Dodecanese* dans le Dodécanèse.

dodge [dɒdʒ] ◆ n **1.** [evasive movement] écart *m* ; [by footballer, boxer] esquive *f* **2.** 🇬🇧 *inf* [trick] truc *m*, combine *f*. ◆ vi [make evasive movement] s'écarter vivement ; [footballer, boxer] faire une esquive. ◆ vt [blow] esquiver ; [falling rock, ball] éviter ; [bullets] passer entre, éviter ; [pursuer, police] échapper à ; [creditor, landlord, etc.] éviter ; [question] éluder.

Dodgem® ['dɒdʒəm] n 🇬🇧 auto *f* tamponneuse.

dodgy ['dɒdʒɪ] *(compar* **dodgier,** *superl* **dodgiest)** adj 🇬🇧 *inf* **1.** [risky, dangerous - plan, idea] risqué **2.** [dishonest - person] roublard, combinard ; [- scheme] douteux, suspect.

dodo ['dəʊdəʊ] *(pl* **dodos** or **dodoes)** n **1.** [extinct bird] dronte *m*, dodo *m* **2.** *inf* [fool] andouille *f*.

doe [dəʊ] n [deer] biche *f* ; [rabbit] lapine *f* ; [hare] hase *f* ; [rat] rate *f*, ratte *f*.

DOE (abbr of **Department of Energy**) pr n *ministère américain de l'Énergie*.

doer ['duːə'] n : *she is more (of) a doer than a talker* elle préfère l'action à la parole.

does [dʌz] ⟶ **do** *(vb)*.

doesn't ['dʌznt] abbr of **does not**.

dog [dɒg] *(pt & pp* **dogged,** *cont* **dogging)** ◆ n **1.** chien *m* **2.** [male fox, wolf, etc.] mâle *m* **3.** *inf* [person] : *you lucky dog!* sacré veinard ! / *dirty dog* sale type *m* **4.** *v inf & pej* [ugly woman] cageot *m*, boudin *m* **5.** 🇺🇸 *inf* [hopeless thing] : *it's a dog* c'est nul **6.** 🇬🇧 [hot dog] hot dog *m*. ◆ comp [breeder, breeding] de chiens ; [bowl, basket, food] pour chien ▶ **dog fox** renard *m* mâle ▶ **dog racing** courses *fpl* de lévriers ▶ **dog track** cynodrome *m*. ◆ vt **1.** [follow closely] suivre de près **2.** [plague] ▶ **to be dogged by bad health / problems** ne pas arrêter d'avoir des ennuis de santé / des problèmes.

dog and pony show n 🇺🇸 *inf* **1.** [exaggerated show] ▶ **to put on a dog and pony show** faire tout un cinéma **2.** [presentation] : *I have to do a dog and pony show for the sales force* il faut que je fasse une présentation pour les commerciaux.

dog biscuit n biscuit *m* pour chien.

dog collar n [for dog] collier *m* pour or de chien ; *hum* [of clergyman] col *m* d'ecclésiastique.

dog dirt n 🇬🇧 crottes *fpl* de chien.

dog-eared adj [page] corné ; [book] aux pages cornées.

dog-end n *inf* [of cigarette] mégot *m*.

dogfight ['dɒgfaɪt] n [between dogs] combat *m* de chiens ; MIL [between aircraft] combat *m* rapproché.

dogfish ['dɒgfɪʃ] n roussette *f*, chien *m* de mer.

dog food n nourriture *f* pour chiens.

dogged ['dɒgɪd] adj [courage, perseverance] tenace ; [person, character] tenace, déterminé, persévérant ; [refusal] obstiné.

doggedly ['dɒgɪdlɪ] adv [fight, persist] avec ténacité or persévérance ; [refuse] obstinément.

doggie ['dɒgɪ] = **doggy**.

doggie doo [ˈdɒgɪduː] n US inf crottes fpl de chien.

doggone [ˈdɑːgɑːn] US inf interj ▸ **doggone (it)!** zut !, nom d'une pipe !

doggy [ˈdɒgɪ] (pl **doggies**) inf ◆ n baby talk toutou m. ◆ adj [smell] de chien ▸ **he's a doggy person** il adore les chiens.

doggy bag n sachet (ou boîte) que l'on propose aux clients dans les restaurants pour qu'ils emportent ce qu'ils n'ont pas consommé.

doggy paddle ◆ n nage f du petit chien. ◆ vi faire la nage du petit chien.

dog handler n maître-chien m.

doghouse [ˈdɒghaʊs] (pl [-haʊzɪz]) n **1.** US [kennel] chenil m, niche f **2.** PHR **to be in the doghouse (with sb)** inf ne pas être en odeur de sainteté or être en disgrâce (auprès de qqn).

dog licence n UK permis de posséder un chien.

dogma [ˈdɒgmə] n dogme m.

dogmatic [dɒgˈmætɪk] adj dogmatique ▸ **to be dogmatic about sthg** être dogmatique au sujet de qqch.

dogmatism [ˈdɒgmətɪzm] n dogmatisme m.

dog mess n UK crottes fpl de chien ; [referred to in official notices] déjections fpl canines.

do-gooder [-ˈgʊdə] n pej âme f charitable, bonne âme f.

dog paddle = **doggy paddle**.

dogsbody [ˈdɒgzˌbɒdɪ] (pl **dogsbodies**) n UK inf bonne f à tout faire.

dog tag n US MIL plaque f d'identification.

dog-tired adj inf épuisé.

doh [dəʊ] n MUS do m.

doily [ˈdɔɪlɪ] (pl **doilies**) n napperon m.

doing [ˈduːɪŋ] n [work, activity] : **it's all your doing** tout cela, c'est de ta faute / **it's none of my doing** je n'y suis pour rien / **that'll take some doing** cela ne va pas être facile.

doings [ˈduːɪŋz] n UK inf [thing] machin m, truc m.

do-it-yourself ◆ n bricolage m. ◆ comp [manual, shop] de bricolage ▸ **a do-it-yourself enthusiast** un bricoleur.

dojo [ˈdəʊdʒəʊ] n SPORT dojo m.

doldrums [ˈdɒldrəmz] pl n **1.** GEOG [zone] zones fpl des calmes équatoriaux, pot au noir m ; [weather] calme m équatorial **2.** PHR **to be in the doldrums a)** [person] avoir le cafard, broyer du noir **b)** [activity, trade] être en plein marasme.

dole [dəʊl] n (U) UK inf ▸ **dole (money)** (indemnités fpl de) chômage m ▸ **to be / to go on the dole** être / s'inscrire au chômage / **the dole queues are getting longer** de plus en plus de gens pointent au chômage. ❖ **dole out** vt sep [distribute] distribuer ; [in small amounts] distribuer au compte-gouttes.

doleful [ˈdəʊlfʊl] adj [mournful - look, voice] malheureux ; [- person, song] triste.

doll [dɒl] n **1.** [for child] poupée f ; [for ventriloquist] marionnette f de ventriloque ▸ **doll's house** UK, **doll house** US lit fig maison f de poupée **2.** inf [girl] nana f, souris f ; [attractive girl] poupée f **3.** inf [dear person] amour m **4.** US inf [nice person] : **he's a real doll** il est vraiment adorable. ❖ **doll up** vt sep ▸ **to get dolled up** or **to doll o.s. up** se faire beau / belle, se pomponner.

dollar [ˈdɒlə] ◆ n [currency] dollar m. ◆ comp ▸ **dollar bill** billet m d'un dollar ▸ **dollar diplomacy** diplomatie f du dollar ▸ **dollar sign** (signe m du) dollar m.

dollarization [dɒləraɪˈzeɪʃn] n dollarisation f inf.

dollop [ˈdɒləp] inf ◆ n [of mashed potatoes, cream, etc.] (bonne) cuillerée f ; [of mud, plaster, clay] (petit) tas m ; [of butter, margarine] (gros or bon) morceau m. ◆ vt : **to dollop food out onto plates** balancer de la nourriture dans des assiettes.

dolly [ˈdɒlɪ] (pl **dollies**, pt & pp **dollied**) n **1.** inf [for child] = **doll 2.** CIN & TV [for camera] chariot m.

dolphin [ˈdɒlfɪn] n dauphin m ▸ **dolphin-friendly** [tuna] pêché sans dommages pour les dauphins.

domain [dəˈmeɪn] n **1.** [territory, sphere of interest] domaine m **2.** MATH & SCI domaine m.

domain name n COMPUT nom m de domaine.

Domain Name System n COMPUT système m de nom de domaine.

dome [dəʊm] n **1.** ARCHIT dôme m, coupole f **2.** [of head] calotte f ; [of hill] dôme m ; [of heavens, sky] voûte f.

domestic [dəˈmestɪk] ◆ adj **1.** [household - duty, chore] ménager / **domestic staff** employés mpl de maison, domestiques mpl / **domestic appliance** / **product** appareil m / produit m ménager **2.** [of the family - duties, problems] familial ; [- life] familial, de famille ▸ **domestic violence** violence f familiale or domestique **3.** [not foreign - affairs, flight, trade, policy] intérieur ; [- currency, economy, news, produce] national **4.** [not wild - animal] domestique. ◆ n UK fml domestique mf ; US femme f de ménage.

domestically [dəˈmestɪklɪ] adv ECON & POL ▸ **to be produced domestically** être produit à l'intérieur du pays or au niveau national.

domesticate [dəˈmestɪkeɪt] vt [animal] domestiquer, apprivoiser ; hum [person] habituer aux tâches ménagères.

domesticated [dəˈmestɪkeɪtɪd] adj [animal] domestiqué, apprivoisé.

domestication [dəˌmestɪˈkeɪʃn] n [of animal] domestication f, apprivoisement m.

domesticity [ˌdəʊmeˈstɪsətɪ] n [home life] vie f de famille.

domicile [ˈdɒmɪsaɪl] ◆ n ADMIN, FIN & LAW domicile m. ◆ vt ADMIN, FIN & LAW domicilier ▸ **domiciled at** domicilié à.

domiciliary [ˌdɒmɪˈsɪljərɪ] adj ADMIN [visit] domiciliaire ; [care, services] à domicile.

dominance [ˈdɒmɪnəns] n **1.** [ascendancy - of race, person, football team, etc.] prédominance f ; [- of animal, gene] dominance f **2.** [importance] importance f.

dominant [ˈdɒmɪnənt] ◆ adj **1.** dominant ; [nation, political party, team, etc.] prédominant ; [person, personality] dominateur ; [building, geographical feature - most elevated] dominant ; [- most striking] le plus frappant **2.** MUS de dominante. ◆ n MUS dominante f ; SCI dominance f.

dominate [ˈdɒmɪneɪt] ◆ vt dominer ▸ **to be dominated by sb** être dominé par qqn. ◆ vi dominer.

dominating [ˈdɒmɪneɪtɪŋ] adj dominateur.

domination [ˌdɒmɪˈneɪʃn] n domination f ; [of organization] contrôle m ; [of conversation] monopolisation f.

domineering [ˌdɒmɪˈnɪərɪŋ] adj autoritaire.

Dominica [dəˈmɪnɪkə] pr n Dominique f / **in Dominica** à la Dominique.

Dominican Republic pr n ▸ **the Dominican Republic** la République dominicaine / **in the Dominican Republic** en République dominicaine.

dominion [dəˈmɪnjən] n **1.** [rule, authority] domination f, empire m **2.** [territory] territoire m ; [in British Commonwealth] dominion m.

domino [ˈdɒmɪnəʊ] (pl **dominoes**) ◆ n domino m. ◆ comp ▸ **domino effect** effet m d'entraînement ▸ **domino theory** théorie f des dominos.

don [dɒn] (*pt & pp* **donned**, *cont* **donning**) ◆ vt *fml* [put on] mettre. ◆ n **1.** UK UNIV *professeur d'université (en particulier à Oxford et Cambridge)* **2.** US chef *m* de la Mafia.

doN MESSAGING written abbr of **doing**.

Don [dɒn] pr n ▸ **the (River) Don** le Don.

donate [dəˈneɪt] ◆ vt [money, goods] faire un don de ; [specific amount] faire (un) don de / *to donate blood* donner son or du sang. ◆ vi [give money, goods] faire un don, faire des dons.

donation [dəˈneɪʃn] n [action] don *m*, donation *f* ; [money, goods or blood given] don *m* / *to make a donation to a charity* faire un don or une donation à une œuvre (de charité).

done [dʌn] ◆ pp ⟶ **do**. ◆ adj **1.** [finished] fini / *are you done yet?* tu as enfin fini ? ▸ **to get sthg done** [completed] finir qqch **2.** [cooked - food] cuit **3.** *inf* [exhausted] crevé, claqué **4.** *inf* [used up] : *that's the milk done* il n'y a plus de lait **5.** [fitting] ▸ **it's not the done thing** or **it's not done** ça ne se fait pas.

donkey [ˈdɒŋkɪ] n âne *m*, ânesse *f*.

donkey jacket n UK *veste longue en tissu épais, généralement bleu foncé.*

donkeywork [ˈdɒŋkɪwɜːk] n (U) *inf* ▸ **to do the donkeywork a)** [drudgery] faire le sale boulot **b)** [difficult part] faire le gros du travail.

donor [ˈdəʊnəʳ] n **1.** [gen & LAW] donateur *m*, -trice *f* **2.** MED [of blood, organ] donneur *m*, -euse *f*.

donor card n carte *f* de don d'organe.

don't [dəʊnt] ◆ vb abbr of **do not**. ◆ n (*usu pl*) chose *f* à ne pas faire.

don't know n [on survey] sans opinion *mf* ; [voter] indécis *m*, -e *f*.

donut [ˈdəʊnʌt] US = **doughnut**.

doodah [ˈduːdɑː] n *inf* truc *m*, bidule *m*.

doodle [ˈduːdl] ◆ vi & vt gribouiller, griffonner. ◆ n gribouillage *m*, griffonnage *m*.

doom [duːm] ◆ n (U) [terrible fate] destin *m* (malheureux), sort *m* (tragique) ; [ruin] perte *f*, ruine *f* ; [death] mort *f*. ◆ vt condamner.

doomed [duːmd] adj condamné / *to be doomed (to failure)* être voué à l'échec.

Doomsday [ˈduːmzdeɪ] n jour *m* du Jugement dernier ▸ **till Doomsday** *inf* jusqu'à la fin du monde or des temps.

door [dɔːʳ] n **1.** [of building, room] porte *f* / *he lives two doors down* il habite deux portes plus loin ▸ **out of doors** dehors, en plein air ▸ **to go from door to door** aller de porte en porte / *can someone answer the door?* est-ce que quelqu'un peut aller ouvrir ? ▸ **the agreement leaves the door open for further discussion** l'accord laisse la porte ouverte à des discussions ultérieures ▸ **the discovery opens the door to medical advances** la découverte ouvre la voie à des progrès médicaux ▸ **having a famous name certainly helps to open doors** avoir un nom célèbre ouvre sans doute bien des portes ▸ **to lay sthg at sb's door** imputer qqch à qqn, reprocher qqch à qqn ▸ **she closed** or **shut the door on any further negotiations** elle a rendu toute nouvelle négociation impossible ▸ **to show sb the door** *lit & fig* montrer la porte à qqn **2.** [of car] porte *f*, portière *f* ; [of train] portière *f*.

doorbell [ˈdɔːbel] n sonnette *f* / *the doorbell rang* on sonna à la porte.

door chain n chaînette *f* de sûreté.

do-or-die adj [chance, effort] désespéré, ultime ; [attitude, person] jusqu'au-boutiste.

door handle n poignée *f* de porte ; AUTO poignée *f* de portière.

doorknob [ˈdɔːnɒb] n poignée *f* de porte.

doorknocker [ˈdɔːˌnɒkəʳ] n heurtoir *m*, marteau *m* (*de porte*).

doorman [ˈdɔːmən] (*pl* **doormen** [-mən]) n [at hotel] portier *m* ; [at apartment building] concierge *m*.

doormat [ˈdɔːmæt] n *lit* paillasson *m*, essuie-pieds *m* (*inv*) ; *fig* [person] chiffe *f* molle.

doorstep [ˈdɔːstep] ◆ n **1.** [step] pas *m* de la porte, seuil *m* de porte **2.** UK *hum* [piece of bread] grosse tranche *f* de pain. ◆ adj UK ▸ **doorstep salesman** vendeur *m* à domicile, démarcheur *m* ▸ **doorstep selling** vente *f* à domicile, porte-à-porte *m inv*, démarchage *m*.

doorstepping [ˈdɔːstepɪŋ] UK ◆ n [by politician] démarchage *m* électoral ; [by journalists] *pratique journalistique qui consiste à harceler les gens jusque chez eux.* ◆ adj [politician] *qui fait du démarchage électoral* ; [journalist] *qui harcèle les gens jusque chez eux.*

doorstop [ˈdɔːstɒp] n butoir *m* de porte.

door-to-door ◆ adj ▸ **door-to-door enquiries** enquête *f* de voisinage ▸ **door-to-door salesman** vendeur *m* à domicile, démarcheur *m* ▸ **door-to-door selling** vente *f* à domicile, porte-à-porte *m inv*. ◆ adv : *a 2-hour trip door-to-door* un trajet de 2 heures de porte à porte.

doorway [ˈdɔːweɪ] n porte *f* / *standing in the doorway* debout dans l'embrasure de la porte.

doozy [ˈduːzɪ] n US *inf* : *wow, that bruise is a real doozy!* eh ben, il est énorme ce bleu !

dope [dəʊp] ◆ n **1.** (U) *inf* [illegal drug] drogue *f*, dope *f* **2.** [for athlete, horse] dopant *m* **3.** *inf* [idiot] crétin *m*, -e *f*, andouille *f*. ◆ comp [drugs] ▸ **dope addict** toxicomane *mf* drogué *m*, -e *f* ▸ **dope dealer** or **pusher** dealer *m* ▸ **dope test** test *m* antidoping. ◆ vt [drug - horse, person] doper ; [- drink, food] mettre une drogue ou un dopant dans.

dopey [ˈdəʊpɪ] (*compar* **dopier**, *superl* **dopiest**) = **dopy**.

doppelgänger [ˈdɒplˌɡæŋəʳ] n double *m* (*d'une personne vivante*), sosie *m*.

dopy [ˈdəʊpɪ] (*compar* **dopier**, *superl* **dopiest**) adj **1.** [drugged] drogué, dopé ; [sleepy] (à moitié) endormi **2.** *inf* [silly] idiot, abruti.

dork [dɔːk] n US *inf* [idiot] niais *m*, -e *f* ; [studious person] binoclard *m*, -e *f*.

dorky [ˈdɔːkɪ] adj US *inf* débile.

dorm [dɔːm] n *inf* abbr of **dormitory**.

dormant [ˈdɔːmənt] adj **1.** [idea, passion] qui sommeille ; [energy, reserves] inexploité ; [disease] à l'état latent ; [law] inappliqué ▸ **to lie dormant** sommeiller **2.** [animal] endormi ; [plant] dormant **3.** [volcano] en repos, en sommeil.

dormer [ˈdɔːməʳ] n ▸ **dormer (window)** lucarne *f*.

dormice [ˈdɔːmaɪs] pl ⟶ **dormouse**.

dormitory [ˈdɔːmətrɪ] (*pl* **dormitories**) ◆ n [room] dortoir *m* ; US UNIV résidence *f* universitaire. ◆ comp UK ▸ **dormitory town** ville-dortoir *f*.

Dormobile® [ˈdɔːməˌbiːl] n UK camping-car *m*.

dormouse [ˈdɔːmaʊs] (*pl* **dormice** [ˈdɔːmaɪs]) n loir *m*.

Dors written abbr of **Dorset**.

DOS [dɒs] (abbr of **disk operating system**) n DOS *m*.

dosage [ˈdəʊsɪdʒ] n [giving of dose] dosage *m* ; [amount] dose *f* ; [directions on bottle] posologie *f*.

dose [dəʊs] ◆ n **1.** [amount] dose *f* / *in small / large doses* à faible / haute dose **2.** [of illness] attaque *f* / *a bad dose of flu* une mauvaise grippe. ◆ vt **1.** [subj: pharmacist] doser **2.** [person] administrer un médicament à.

dosh [dɒʃ] n UK *inf* fric *m*.

doss [dɒs] 🇬🇧 *v inf* ◆ n **1.** [bed] lit *m*, pieu *m* **2.** [nap] somme *m*, roupillon *m* **3.** [easy thing] ▶ **it was a real doss** c'était fastoche. ◆ vi coucher, roupiller. ❖ **doss around** vi *v inf* glander. ❖ **doss down** vi *v inf* coucher, crécher.

dosser ['dɒsə˞] n 🇬🇧 *v inf* [person] sans-abri *mf*, clochard *m*, -e *f* ; [house] foyer *m* de sans-abri.

dosshouse ['dɒshaʊs] (*pl* [-haʊzɪz]) n 🇬🇧 *inf* foyer *m* de sans-abri.

dossier ['dɒsɪeɪ] n dossier *m*, documents *mpl*.

dot [dɒt] (*pt & pp* **dotted**, *cont* **dotting**) ◆ n [gen & MUS] point *m* ; [on material] pois *m* ▶ **dot, dot, dot** [in punctuation] points de suspension ▶ **dots and dashes** [Morse code] points et traits *mpl*. ◆ vt **1.** [mark] marquer avec des points, pointiller ; [an 'i'] mettre un point sur **2.** [spot] parsemer. ❖ **on the dot** adv phr : *at 3 o'clock on the dot* à 3 h pile or tapantes.

DOT (*abbr of* **Department of Transportation**) pr n *ministère américain des Transports.*

dotage ['dəʊtɪdʒ] n gâtisme *m* ▶ **to be in one's dotage** être gâteux, être retombé en enfance.

dotcom ['dɒtkɒm] n dot com *f*, point com *f*.

dote [dəʊt] vi ▶ **to dote (up)on sb** être fou de qqn, aimer qqn à la folie.

doting ['dəʊtɪŋ] adj : *he has a doting mother* sa mère l'aime à la folie.

dot-matrix printer n imprimante *f* matricielle.

dotted ['dɒtɪd] adj **1.** [shirt, tie] à pois **2.** ▶ **dotted line a)** ligne *f* en pointillés **b)** AUTO ligne *f* discontinue / *tear along the dotted line* détachez suivant le pointillé.

dotty ['dɒtɪ] (*compar* **dottier**, *superl* **dottiest**) adj 🇬🇧 *inf* [crazy] fou (*before vowel or silent 'h' fol*, *f* **folle**), dingue / *he's absolutely dotty about her* il est fou d'elle.

double ['dʌbl] ◆ adj **1.** [twice as large - quantity, portion] double **2.** [line, row] double / *double doors* or *a double door* une porte à deux battants ; [with figures, letters] deux fois / *double five two one* **a)** [figure] deux fois cinq deux un **b)** [phone number] cinquante-cinq, vingt et un / *"letter" is spelt with a double "t"* « lettre » s'écrit avec deux « t » ▶ **to throw a double six / three** faire un double six / trois ▶ **to be in double figures** [inflation, unemployment] dépasser la barre or le seuil des 10 % ▶ **to be into double figures** dépasser la dizaine **3.** [folded in two] en double, replié ▶ **double thickness** double épaisseur **4.** [for two people] pour or à deux personnes **5.** [dual - purpose, advantage] double ; [ambiguous] double, ambigu (ambiguë). ◆ predet [twice] deux fois plus. ◆ n **1.** [twice the amount] double *m* ; [of alcohol] double *m* / *he charged us double* il nous a fait payer le double **2.** [duplicate] double *m*, réplique *f* ; [of person] double *m*, sosie *m* ; CIN & TV [stand-in] doublure *f* ; THEAT acteur (with two parts) acteur *m*, -trice *f* qui tient deux rôles **3.** [turn] demi-tour *m*. ◆ adv [in two] en deux ; [two of the same] ▶ **to see double** voir double. ◆ vt **1.** [increase] doubler **2.** [fold] plier en deux, replier **3.** CIN & TV doubler. ◆ vi **1.** [increase] doubler **2.** [turn] tourner, faire un crochet **3.** [serve two purposes] : *the dining room doubles as a study* la salle à manger sert également de bureau. ❖ **double back** ◆ vi [animal, person, road] tourner brusquement. ◆ vt sep [sheet] mettre en double. ❖ **double for** vt insep CIN & THEAT doubler. ❖ **double over** = **double up** (*vi*). ❖ **double up** ◆ vi **1.** [bend over] se plier, se courber / *he doubled up in pain* il se plia en deux de douleur / *to double up with laughter* se tordre de rire **2.** [share] partager. ◆ vt sep plier en deux, replier.

double act n duo *m* comique.

double agent n agent *m* double.

double-barrelled 🇬🇧, **double-barreled** 🇺🇸 [-'bærəld] adj **1.** [gun] à deux coups ; *fig* [question, remark] équivoque **2.** 🇬🇧 [name] ≃ à particule.

double bass [-beɪs] n contrebasse *f*.

double bed n grand lit *m*, lit *m* à deux places.

double bill n double programme *m*.

double-blind adj [experiment, test] en double aveugle ; [method] à double insu, à double anonymat.

double-breasted [-'brestɪd] adj croisé.

double-check vi & vt revérifier. ❖ **double check** n revérification *f*.

double chin n double menton *m*.

double click n COMPUT double-clic *m*. ❖ **double click** ◆ vi faire un double-clic, cliquer deux fois. ◆ vt double-cliquer ▶ **to double-click on sthg** double-cliquer sur qqch.

double cream n 🇬🇧 crème *f* fraîche épaisse.

double-cross vt trahir, doubler. ❖ **double cross** n trahison *f*, traîtrise *f*.

double-crosser [-'krɒsə˞] n traître *m*, -esse *f*, faux jeton *m*.

double date n 🇺🇸 sortie *f* à quatre (*deux couples*). ❖ **double-date** vi 🇺🇸 sortir à quatre (*deux couples*).

double-dealer n fourbe *m*.

double-dealing ◆ n (U) fourberie *f*, double jeu *m*. ◆ adj fourbe, faux comme un jeton.

double-decker [-'dekə˞] n **1.** 🇬🇧 [bus] autobus *m* à impériale **2.** *inf* [sandwich] club sandwich *m*.

double-declutch vi 🇬🇧 faire un double débrayage.

double-density adj [disk] double densité.

double-digit adj à deux chiffres.

double digits 🇺🇸 = **double figures**.

double Dutch n 🇬🇧 *inf* charabia *m*, baragouin *m*.

double-edged [-'edʒd] adj *lit & fig* à double tranchant.

double entendre [,duːblɑː'tɑːdr] n mot *m* or expression *f* à double sens.

double fault n double faute *f*.

double figures pl n 🇬🇧 ▶ **to be in(to) double figures** être au-dessus de dix, dépasser la dizaine.

double first n 🇬🇧 ≃ mention *f* très bien (*dans deux disciplines à la fois*).

double-glazing 🇬🇧 ◆ n (U) double vitrage *m*. ◆ comp [salesman] de double vitrage.

double indemnity n 🇺🇸 indemnité *f* double.

double-jointed adj désarticulé.

double-lock vt fermer à double tour.

double-page spread n PRESS & TYPO double page *f*.

double-park ◆ vi stationner en double file. ◆ vt garer en double file.

double parking n stationnement *m* en double file.

double-quick adj très rapide / *in double-quick time* **a)** [move] au pas de course or de gymnastique **b)** [finish, work] en vitesse, en moins de rien.

double room n chambre *f* pour deux personnes.

doubles ['dʌblz] (*pl* **doubles**) n double *m* / *to play doubles* jouer un double / *a doubles player* un joueur de double / *ladies' / men's doubles* double dames / messieurs.

double-side adj ▶ **double-side tape** bande *f* adhésive double face.

double-sided adj [disk] double face.

double spacing n double interligne *m* / *in double spacing* à double interligne.

double standard n ‣ **to have double standards** faire deux poids, deux mesures.

double take n *inf* ‣ **to do a double take** marquer un temps d'arrêt *(par surprise)*.

double-talk n *(U)* *inf* [ambiguous] *propos ambigus et contournés* ; [gibberish] charabia *m*.

double taxation n double imposition *f*.

doublethink ['dʌbl,θɪŋk] n *(U)* raisonnement de mauvaise foi qui contient des contradictions flagrantes.

double time n **1.** [pay] salaire *m* double **2.** MIL pas *m* redoublé **3.** MUS mesure *f* double.

double vision n double vision *f*.

double whammy [-'wæmɪ] n *inf* double malédiction *f*.

double yellow line n 🇬🇧 ‣ **to be parked on a double yellow line** être en stationnement interdit.

doubly ['dʌblɪ] adv [twice as much] doublement, deux fois plus ; [in two ways] doublement.

doubt [daʊt] ◆ n **1.** [uncertainty -about fact] doute *m*, incertitude *f* ‣ **to cast doubt on sthg** mettre en doute or jeter le doute sur qqch / *there is no doubt about it* cela ne fait pas de doute / *no doubt* sans doute / *without (any) doubt* sans aucun or le moindre doute **2.** [feeling of distrust] doute *m* / *I have my doubts about him* j'ai des doutes sur lui or à son sujet. ◆ vt **1.** [consider unlikely] : *I doubt (whether) she'll be there* je doute qu'elle soit là / *she'll be there — I don't doubt it* elle sera là — je n'en doute pas or j'en suis certain / *I doubt it* j'en doute **2.** [distrust] douter de. ◆ vi douter, avoir des doutes.

> 📝 Note that douter que is followed by a verb in the subjunctive:
> **I doubt if we're representative of the French population**. *Je doute que nous soyons représentatifs de la population française.*

doubtful ['daʊtfʊl] adj **1.** [unlikely] improbable, douteux **2.** [uncertain -person] incertain, indécis **3.** [questionable -answer, results] douteux, discutable **4.** [dubious -person] louche, suspect ; [-affair] douteux, louche.

doubtfully ['daʊtfʊlɪ] adv [uncertainly] avec doute, d'un air de doute ; [indecisively] avec hésitation, de façon indécise.

doubtless ['daʊtlɪs] adv [certainly] sans aucun or le moindre doute ; [probably] (très) probablement.

douche bag n 🇺🇸 **1.** [bag] poche *m* à lavement **2.** *v inf* [despicable person] pauvre con *m*, pauvre conne *f*.

dough [dəʊ] n **1.** CULIN pâte *f* **2.** *inf* [money] blé *m*.

doughnut ['dəʊnʌt] 🇺🇸 n beignet *m*.

dour [dʊəʳ] adj [sullen] renfrogné ; [stern] austère, dur ; [stubborn] buté.

douse [daʊs] vt **1.** [fire] éteindre **2.** [drench] tremper, inonder.

dove¹ [dʌv] n ORNITH & POL colombe *f*.

dove² [dəʊv] pt 🇺🇸 ⟶ **dive**.

dovecot(e) ['dʌvkɒt] n colombier *m*, pigeonnier *m*.

Dover ['dəʊvəʳ] pr n Douvres ‣ **the Strait of Dover** le pas de Calais.

Dover sole n sole *f*.

dovetail ['dʌvteɪl] vi **1.** TECH se raccorder **2.** [combine] bien cadrer, concorder.

dowager ['daʊədʒəʳ] n douairière *f* / *the dowager duchess* la duchesse douairière.

dowdy ['daʊdɪ] (*compar* **dowdier**, *superl* **dowdiest**, *pl* **dowdies**) adj [person] sans chic, inélégant ; [dress] peu flatteur, sans chic.

Dow Jones [,daʊ'dʒəʊnz] pr n ‣ **the Dow Jones (average** or **index)** l'indice *m* Dow Jones.

down¹ [daʊn] ◆ prep **1.** [towards lower level of] : *a line down the middle of the page* une ligne verticale au milieu de la page / *to go down the steps* / *the escalator* / *the mountain* descendre l'escalier / l'escalier mécanique / la montagne **2.** [at lower level of] en bas de / *it's down the stairs* c'est en bas de l'escalier / *they live down the street* ils habitent plus loin or plus bas dans la rue **3.** [along] le long de / *he walked down the street* il a descendu la rue **4.** [through] à travers **5.** 🇬🇧 *inf* [to] à / *they went down the shops* ils sont partis faire des courses. ◆ adv **1.** [downwards] vers le bas, en bas ‣ **down!** [to dog] couché !, bas les pattes ! **2.** [reduced, lower] : *prices are down* les prix ont baissé / *the pound is down two cents against the dollar* FIN la livre a baissé de deux cents par rapport au dollar ; [below expected, desired level] : *the tyres are down* a) [underinflated] les pneus sont dégonflés b) [flat] les pneus sont à plat / *the cashier is £10 down* il manque 10 livres au caissier **3.** [on paper] : *get it down in writing* or *on paper* mettez-le par écrit / *it's down in my diary* / *on the calendar* c'est dans mon agenda / sur le calendrier / *he's down to speak at the conference* il est inscrit en tant qu'intervenant à la conférence **4.** [from city, the north] : *we're going down south* nous descendons vers le sud / 🇬🇧 UNIV : *she came down from Oxford* a) [on vacation] elle est descendue d'Oxford b) [graduated] elle est sortie d'Oxford **5.** [out of action -machine, computer] en panne / *the wires are down* les lignes sont coupées **6.** 🅿🅷🆁 *down with the system!* à bas le système ! ◆ adj [depressed] déprimé, malheureux / *to feel down* avoir le cafard. ◆ vt **1.** [knock down -opponent] mettre à terre / [-object, target] faire tomber / *the pilot downed two enemy aircraft* le pilote a descendu deux avions ennemis **2.** [drink] descendre ; [eat] avaler. ◆ **down to** prep phr [indicating responsibility] : *it's down to you now* c'est à toi de jouer maintenant *fig*.

down² [daʊn] n **1.** [on bird, person, plant, fruit] duvet *m* **2.** [hill] colline *f* dénudée ; [sand dune] dune *f*.

down-and-out ◆ adj indigent, sans ressources. ◆ n clochard *m*, -e *f* ‣ **the down-and-out** or **down-and-outs** les sans-abri *mpl*.

down-at-heel adj [shabby] miteux ; [shoe] éculé.

downbeat ['daʊnbiːt] ◆ n MUS temps *m* frappé. ◆ adj *inf* **1.** [gloomy -person] abattu, triste ; [-story] pessimiste **2.** [relaxed -person] décontracté, flegmatique ; [-situation] décontracté.

downcast ['daʊnkɑːst] adj **1.** [dejected] abattu, démoralisé **2.** [eyes, look] baissé.

downer ['daʊnəʳ] n **1.** *inf* [experience] expérience *f* déprimante ‣ **to be on a downer** faire de la déprime, être déprimé **2.** *v inf* [drug] tranquillisant *m*, sédatif *m*.

downfall ['daʊnfɔːl] n **1.** [of person, institution] chute *f*, ruine *f* ; [of dream, hopes] effondrement *m* **2.** [of rain, snow] chute *f*.

downgrade ['daʊngreɪd] vt **1.** [job] dévaloriser, déclasser ; [person] rétrograder ; [hotel] déclasser **2.** [belittle] rabaisser.

downhearted [,daʊn'hɑːtɪd] adj abattu, découragé.

downhill [,daʊn'hɪl] ◆ adv ‣ **to go downhill** a) [car, road] descendre, aller en descendant b) [business] péricliter c) *fig* se dégrader. ◆ adj **1.** [road] en pente, incliné ; [walk] en descente ; *fig* : *it should all be downhill from now on* maintenant ça devrait aller comme sur des roulettes **2.** [in skiing] ‣ **downhill skiing** ski *m* alpin ‣ **downhill race** descente *f* ‣ **downhill racer** or **skier** descendeur *m*, -euse *f*. ◆ n [of road] descente *f* ; [in skiing] descente *f*.

Downing Street ['daʊnɪŋ-] pr n Downing Street *(rue de Londres où se trouve la résidence officielle du Premier ministre britannique)*.

 Downing Street

C'est à **Downing Street**, à Londres, que se trouvent les résidences officielles du Premier ministre (au n° 10) et du chancelier de l'Échiquier (au n° 11). Tony Blair a été le premier chef de gouvernement à avoir choisi de résider au n° 11 pour des raisons de confort familial. Par extension, le nom de la rue est employé pour désigner le Premier ministre et ses fonctions.

down-in-the-mouth adj : *to be down-in-the-mouth* être abattu.

downlink ['daʊnlɪŋk] n liaison f satellite-terre.

download [ˌdaʊn'ləʊd] vt COMPUT télécharger.

downloadable [ˌdaʊn'ləʊdəbl] adj COMPUT téléchargeable.

downloading [ˌdaʊn'ləʊdɪŋ] n COMPUT téléchargement m.

down-market adj [product] bas de gamme ; [book] grande diffusion *(inv)*.

down payment n acompte m ▶ **to make a down payment on sthg** verser un acompte pour qqch.

downplay ['daʊnpleɪ] vt [event, person] minimiser l'importance de ; [situation] dédramatiser.

downpour ['daʊnpɔːr] n averse f, déluge m.

downright ['daʊnraɪt] ◆ adj **1.** [lie] effronté, flagrant ; [refusal] catégorique **2.** [of person, speech] franc (franche), direct. ◆ adv [as intensifier] franchement, carrément.

downs [daʊnz] pl n UK ▶ **the downs** les Downs fpl.

downscale [ˌdaʊn'skeɪl] US adj = **down-market**.

downshift [ˌdaʊn'ʃɪft] vi US rétrograder.

downside ['daʊnsaɪd] n **1.** [underside] dessous m ▶ **downside up** US sens dessous dessus **2.** [trend] : *prices have tended to be on the downside* la tendance des prix est plutôt à la baisse **3.** [disadvantage] inconvénient m.

downsize ['daʊnsaɪz] vt **1.** [company] réduire les effectifs de **2.** COMPUT [application] réduire l'échelle de.

downsizing ['daʊnsaɪzɪŋ] n INDUST réduction f des effectifs ; COMPUT réduction f d'échelle.

Down's syndrome [daʊnz-] n trisomie 21 f ▶ **Down's syndrome baby** bébé m trisomique.

downstairs [ˌdaʊn'steəz] ◆ adv **1.** [gen] en bas (de l'escalier) ▶ **to come** or **to go downstairs** descendre (les escaliers) **2.** [on lower floor] à l'étage en dessous or inférieur ; [on ground floor] au rez-de-chaussée / *the family downstairs* la famille du dessous. ◆ adj **1.** [gen] en bas **2.** [of lower floor] de l'étage au-dessous or inférieur ; [of ground floor] du rez-de-chaussée. ◆ n rez-de-chaussée m inv.

downstream [ˌdaʊn'striːm] ◆ adv **1.** [live] en aval ; [move] vers l'aval / *the boat drifted downstream* la barque dérivait au fil de l'eau **2.** ECON en aval. ◆ adj **1.** [gen] (situé) en aval **2.** ECON en aval.

downswing ['daʊnswɪŋ] n **1.** [trend] tendance f à la baisse, baisse f **2.** GOLF mouvement m descendant.

downtime ['daʊntaɪm] n (U) **1.** lit période f de non-fonctionnement *(d'une machine, d'une usine)* **2.** US fig [time for relaxing] : *on the weekends I need some downtime* j'ai besoin de faire une pause le week-end.

down-to-earth adj terre à terre *(inv)*, réaliste.

downtown [ˌdaʊn'taʊn] US ◆ n centre-ville m. ◆ adj : *downtown New York* le centre or centre-ville de New York. ◆ adv en ville.

downtrodden ['daʊnˌtrɒdn] adj **1.** [person] opprimé **2.** [grass] piétiné.

downturn ['daʊntɜːn] n baisse f.

down under adv UK inf ▶ **to go** / **to live down under** a) [to Australia] aller / vivre en Australie b) [to New Zealand] aller / vivre en Nouvelle-Zélande c) [gen] aller / vivre aux antipodes.

downward ['daʊnwəd] ◆ adj [movement] vers le bas. ◆ adv US = **downwards**.

downward-compatible adj COMPUT compatible vers le bas.

downward mobility n ECON régression f sociale.

downwards ['daʊnwədz] adv vers le bas, de haut en bas / *she put the letter face downwards* elle a posé la lettre à l'envers / *the road drops sharply downwards* la route descend brusquement.

downwind [ˌdaʊn'wɪnd] adj & adv sous le vent ▶ **to be downwind of sthg** être sous le vent de qqch.

downy ['daʊnɪ] (*compar* **downier**, *superl* **downiest**) adj **1.** [leaf, skin] couvert de duvet, duveté ; [fruit] duveté, velouté **2.** [fluffy] duveteux **3.** [filled with down] garni de duvet.

dowry ['daʊərɪ] (*pl* **dowries**) n dot f.

doz. (written abbr of **dozen**) douz.

doze [dəʊz] ◆ vi sommeiller. ◆ n somme m. ❖ **doze off** vi s'assoupir.

dozen ['dʌzn] n douzaine f / *a dozen eggs* une douzaine d'œufs / *half a dozen* une demi-douzaine / *have some more, there are dozens of them* reprenez-en, il y en a beaucoup or des tas.

dozy ['dəʊzɪ] (*compar* **dozier**, *superl* **doziest**) adj **1.** [drowsy] à moitié endormi, assoupi **2.** inf [stupid] lent, engourdi.

DP n **1.** abbr of **data processing 2.** abbr of **disabled person**.

DPh (written abbr of **Doctor of Philosophy**) = PhD.

DPH (abbr of **Diploma in Public Health**) n UK diplôme m de santé publique.

DPhil [ˌdiːˈfɪl] = PhD.

dpi abbr of **dots per inch**.

DPP pr n UK abbr of **Director of Public Prosecutions**.

DPT (abbr of **diphtheria, pertussis, tetanus**) n DCT.

Dr 1. (written abbr of **Doctor**) : *Dr Jones* [on envelope] Dr Jones / *Dear Dr Jones* **a)** [in letter] Monsieur, Madame **b)** [less formal] Cher Monsieur, Chère Madame **c)** [if acquainted] Cher Docteur **2.** written abbr of **drive**.

drab [dræb] (*compar* **drabber**, *superl* **drabbest**) adj **1.** [colour] terne, fade ; [surroundings] morne, triste **2.** [shabby] miteux.

drabness ['dræbnɪs] n [of colour] caractère m or aspect m terne, fadeur f ; [of surroundings] caractère m or aspect m morne, tristesse f, grisaille f.

draconian [drə'kəʊnjən] adj draconien.

draft [drɑːft] ◆ n **1.** [of letter] brouillon m ; [of novel, speech] premier jet m, ébauche f ; [of plan] avant-projet m **2.** COMM & FIN traite f, effet m **3.** MIL [detachment] détachement m **4.** US MIL conscription f / *he left in order to avoid the draft* il est parti pour éviter de faire son service **5.** US [beer] pression f. ◆ vt **1.** [draw up - first version] faire le brouillon de, rédiger ; [- diagram] dresser ; [- plan]

esquisser, dresser ; LAW [contract, will] rédiger, dresser ; [bill] préparer **2.** [gen & MIL] détacher, désigner ❯ **to draft sb to sthg / to do sthg** détacher qqn à qqch / pour faire qqch **3.** US MIL [enlist] appeler (sous les drapeaux), incorporer. ◆ comp [version] préliminaire ❯ **draft letter a)** [gen] brouillon de lettre **b)** [formal] projet *m* de lettre ❯ **draft treaty** projet *m* de convention.

draft beer n US = **draught beer**.

draft dodger n US MIL réfractaire *m*.

draft dodging n insoumission *f*.

draftee [,drɑː'tiː] n US recrue *f*.

draftsman (*pl* **draftsmen**) US = **draughtsman**.

drafty (*compar* **draftier**, *superl* **draftiest**) US = **draughty**.

drag [dræg] (*pt & pp* **dragged**, *cont* **dragging**) ◆ vt **1.** [pull] traîner, tirer ❯ **to drag sthg on** or **along the ground** traîner qqch par terre / *don't drag me into this!* ne me mêlez pas à vos histoires ! **2.** [search] draguer. ◆ vi **1.** [trail] traîner (par terre) ; [anchor] chasser **2.** [hang behind] traîner, rester à l'arrière **3.** [search] draguer **4.** [go on and on] traîner, s'éterniser **5.** AUTO [brakes] frotter, gripper, se gripper. ◆ n **1.** [pull] tirage *m* ; AERON, AUTO & NAUT résistance *f*, traînée *f* **2.** [dredge] drague *f* ; [sledge] traîneau *m* ; AGR [harrow] herse *f* ; NAUT araignée *f* **3.** [brake] sabot *m* or patin *m* de frein **4.** [handicap] entrave *f*, frein *m* **5.** *inf* [bore] : *he's a real drag!* c'est un vrai casse-pieds ! / *what a drag!* quelle barbe !, c'est la barbe ! **6.** *inf* [puff on cigarette] bouffée *f*, taffe *f* **7.** *inf* [women's clothing] ❯ **in drag** en travesti **8.** US *inf* [street] ❯ **the main drag** la rue principale. ◆ comp *inf* [disco, show] de travestis ❯ **drag artist** transformiste *m*. ❖ **drag along** vt sep [chair, toy] tirer, traîner ; [person] traîner, entraîner ❯ **to drag o.s. along** se traîner. ❖ **drag apart** vt sep séparer de force. ❖ **drag away** vt sep emmener de force. ❖ **drag down** vt sep **1.** [lower] entraîner (en bas) **2.** [weaken] affaiblir ; [depress] déprimer, décourager. ❖ **drag in** vt sep apporter (de force). ❖ **drag on** ◆ vi se prolonger, s'éterniser. ◆ vt insep ❯ **to drag on a cigarette** tirer sur une cigarette. ❖ **drag out** vt sep [prolong] faire traîner. ❖ **drag up** vt sep **1.** [affair, story] remettre sur le tapis, ressortir **2.** US *inf* [child] élever à la diable or tant bien que mal.

drag and drop ◆ vi & vt COMPUT glisser-déposer, glisser-lâcher. ◆ n COMPUT glisser-déposer *m*, glisser-lâcher *m*.

dragnet ['drægnet] n **1.** [for fish] seine *f*, drège *f* **2.** [for criminals] rafle *f*.

dragon ['drægən] n MYTH & ZOOL & *fig* dragon *m*.

dragonfly ['drægənflaɪ] (*pl* **dragonflies**) n libellule *f*.

dragoon [drə'guːn] ◆ n dragon *m*. ◆ vt [force] contraindre, forcer / *he dragooned us into going* il nous a contraints à y aller.

drag queen n *inf* travelo *v inf m*.

drag racing n course *f* de dragsters.

dragster ['drægstər] n voiture *f* à moteur gonflé, dragster *m*.

drain [dreɪn] ◆ n **1.** [in house] canalisation *f* or tuyau *m* d'évacuation ; [of dishwasher] tuyau *m* de vidange ; [outside house] puisard *m* ; [sewer] égout *m* ; [grid in street] bouche *f* d'égout **2.** AGR & MED drain *m* **3.** [depletion] perte *f*, épuisement *m*. ◆ vt **1.** [dry - dishes, vegetables] égoutter ; [- land] drainer, assécher ; [- reservoir] vider, mettre à sec ; [- mine] drainer ; [- oil tank] vider, vidanger ; AGR & MED drainer **2.** [deplete] épuiser. ◆ vi **1.** [colour] disparaître ; [blood] s'écouler ; [dishes, vegetables] s'égoutter. ❖ **drain away** ◆ vi [liquid] s'écouler ; [hope, strength]

s'épuiser. ◆ vt sep faire écouler. ❖ **drain off** ◆ vt sep **1.** [liquid] faire écouler ; [dishes, vegetables] égoutter **2.** AGR & MED drainer. ◆ vi s'écouler.

drainage ['dreɪnɪdʒ] n (U) **1.** [process] drainage *m*, assèchement *m* **2.** [system - in house] système *m* d'évacuation des eaux ; [- in town] système *m* d'égouts ; [- of land] système *m* de drainage ; GEOL système *m* hydrographique **3.** [sewage] eaux *fpl* usées, vidanges *fpl*.

drainboard ['dreɪnbɔːrd] US = **draining board**.

drained [dreɪnd] adj épuisé, éreinté.

drainer ['dreɪnər] = **draining board**.

draining board, draining rack n égouttoir *m*.

drainpipe ['dreɪnpaɪp] n [from roof] (tuyau *m* de) descente *f* ; [from sink] tuyau *m* d'écoulement ; AGR [on land] drain *m*.

drainpipe trousers pl n UK pantalon-cigarette *m*.

drake [dreɪk] n canard *m* (mâle).

dram [dræm] n *inf* [drop] goutte *f*.

drama ['drɑːmə] n **1.** [theatre] théâtre *m* ❯ **drama critic** critique *mf* de théâtre ❯ **drama school** école *f* de théâtre **2.** [play] pièce *f* (de théâtre), drame *m* **3.** [situation] drame *m* **4.** [excitement] drame *m*.

drama queen n *inf* : *he's a real drama queen* il en fait des tonnes / *don't be such a drama queen* arrête ton cinéma.

dramatic [drə'mætɪk] adj **1.** LITER, MUS & THEAT dramatique **2.** [effect, entry] théâtral, dramatique ; [change] remarquable, spectaculaire ; [rise in prices] spectaculaire, vertigineux ; [scenery] spectaculaire, grandiose.

⚠ When dramatic means spectacular or striking, it cannot be translated by **dramatique**.

dramatically [drə'mætɪklɪ] adv **1.** LITER, MUS & THEAT du point de vue théâtral **2.** [act, speak] de manière dramatique, dramatiquement ; [change] de manière remarquable or spectaculaire.

dramatics [drə'mætɪks] ◆ n (U) THEAT art *m* dramatique, dramaturgie *f*. ◆ pl n *fig* [behaviour] comédie *f*, cirque *m*.

dramatist ['dræmətɪst] n auteur *m* dramatique, dramaturge *m*.

dramatization [,dræmətaɪ'zeɪʃn] n **1.** [for theatre] adaptation *f* pour la scène ; [for film] adaptation *f* pour l'écran ; [for television] adaptation *f* pour la télévision **2.** [exaggeration] dramatisation *f*.

dramatize, dramatise ['dræmətaɪz] ◆ vt **1.** [for theatre] adapter pour la scène ; [for film] adapter pour l'écran ; [for television] adapter pour la télévision **2.** [exaggerate] faire un drame de, dramatiser ; [make dramatic] rendre dramatique.

dramedy ['drɑːmədɪ] n comédie *f* dramatique.

drank [dræŋk] pt ⟶ **drink**.

drape [dreɪp] ◆ n [way something hangs] drapé *m*. ◆ vt **1.** [adorn - person, window] draper ; [- altar, room] tendre **2.** [hang] étendre. ❖ **drapes** pl n US [drapery] tentures *fpl* ; [curtains] rideaux *mpl*.

draper ['dreɪpər] n UK marchand *m*, -e *f* de tissus.

drapery ['dreɪpərɪ] (*pl* **draperies**) n **1.** (U) [material] étoffes *fpl* ; [arrangement of material] draperie *f* **2.** (*usu pl*) [hangings] tentures *fpl* ; [curtains] rideaux *mpl*.

drastic ['dræstɪk] adj [measures] sévère, draconien ; [change, effect] radical ; [remedy] énergique.

drastically ['dræstɪklɪ] adv radicalement ; [cut, reduce] radicalement, sévèrement.

drat [dræt] interj *inf* ▸ **drat!** diable !, bon sang !

dratted ['drætɪd] adj *inf* sacré.

draught UK, **draft** US [drɑːft] ◆ n **1.** [breeze] courant *m* d'air **2.** [in fireplace] tirage *m* **3.** [drink - swallow] trait *m*, gorgée *f* **4.** [medicine] potion *f*, breuvage *m* **5.** ▸ **on draught** [beer] à la pression **6.** GAMES dame *f* **7.** [pulling] traction *f*, tirage *m* ; NAUT [of ship] tirant *m* (d'eau). ◆ adj [horse] de trait.

draught beer UK, **draft beer** US n bière *f* pression.

draughtboard ['drɑːftbɔːd] n UK GAMES damier *m*.

draught excluder [-ɪk'skluːdə'] n UK bourrelet *m* (de porte).

draught-proof ◆ vt calfeutrer. ◆ adj calfeutré.

draught-proofing [-ˌpruːfɪŋ] n calfeutrage *m*.

draughts [drɑːfts] n UK GAMES (jeu *m* de) dames *fpl*.

draughtsman UK, **draftsman** US ['drɑːftsmən] (UK *pl* **draughtsmen** [-mən] ; US *pl* **draftsmen** [-mən]) n [artist] dessinateur *m*, -trice *f* ; ARCHIT & INDUST dessinateur *m* industriel, dessinatrice *f* industrielle.

draughtsmanship UK, **draftsmanship** US ['drɑːftsmənʃɪp] n [of artist] talent *m* de dessinateur, coup *m* de crayon ; [of work] art *m* du dessin.

draughty UK, **drafty** US ['drɑːftɪ] (UK *compar* **draughtier**, *superl* **draughtiest** ; US *compar* **draftier**, *superl* **draftiest**) adj [house, room] plein de courants d'air ; [street, corner] exposé à tous les vents ou aux quatre vents.

draw [drɔː] (*pt* **drew** [druː], *pp* **drawn** [drɔːn]) ◆ vt **1.** [pull] tirer ▸ **to draw the curtains** a) [open] tirer ou ouvrir les rideaux b) [shut] tirer ou fermer les rideaux / *I drew my coat closer around me* je me suis enveloppé dans mon manteau **2.** [haul, pull behind - car] tirer, traîner, remorquer ; [- trailer] remorquer **3.** [take out] tirer, retirer ; [remove] retirer, enlever ; [tooth] arracher, extraire / *he drew his knife from* ou *out of his pocket* il a tiré son couteau de sa poche / *the thief drew a gun on us* le voleur a sorti un pistolet et l'a braqué sur nous / *to draw a sword* dégainer une épée **4.** [lead] conduire, entraîner ; *fig* : *I was drawn into the controversy* j'ai été mêlé à ou entraîné dans la dispute / *to draw a meeting to a close* mettre fin à une réunion **5.** [attract, elicit] attirer ▸ **to be drawn to sb** être attiré par qqn ▸ **to draw sb's attention to sthg** faire remarquer qqch à qqn **6.** [take from source] tirer, puiser / *to draw water from a well* puiser de l'eau dans un puits / *to draw (out) money from the bank* retirer de l'argent à la banque / *his confession drew tears from his mother* son aveu a arraché des larmes à sa mère / *I draw comfort from the fact that he didn't suffer* je me console en me disant qu'il n'a pas souffert **7.** [breathe in] : *we barely had time to draw (a) breath* nous avons à peine eu le temps de souffler **8.** [choose at random] tirer ▸ **to draw lots** tirer au sort **9.** [earn - amount, salary] gagner, toucher ; [- pension] toucher ; [FIN - interest] rapporter **10.** [sketch] dessiner ; [line, triangle] tracer ; [map] faire / *to draw a picture of sb* faire le portrait de qqn ▸ **to draw the line at sthg** ne pas admettre qqch, se refuser à qqch / *you have to draw the line somewhere* il faut fixer des limites, il y a des limites **11.** [formulate - comparison, parallel, distinction] établir, faire ; [- conclusion] tirer. ◆ vi **1.** [move] : *the crowd drew to one side* la foule s'est rangée sur le côté ou s'est écartée / *the bus drew into the coach station* l'autocar est arrivé ou entré dans la gare routière ▸ **to draw ahead of sb** prendre de l'avance sur qqn / *they drew level with* ou *alongside the window* ils sont arrivés à la hauteur de la fenêtre / *they drew nearer to us* ils se sont approchés un peu plus de nous ▸ **to draw to an end** ou **to a close** tirer ou toucher à sa fin **2.** [sketch] dessiner **3.** [be equal - two competitors] être ex aequo (*inv*) ; [- two teams] faire match nul / *Italy drew against Spain* l'Italie et l'Espagne ont fait match nul / *the two contestants drew for third prize* les

deux concurrents ont remporté le troisième prix ex aequo ou sont arrivés troisièmes ex aequo. ◆ n **1.** [act of pulling] ▸ **to be quick on the draw** a) *lit* dégainer vite, avoir la détente rapide b) *fig* avoir de la repartie **2.** [card] carte *f* tirée / *it's your draw* c'est à vous de tirer une carte **3.** [raffle, lottery] loterie *f*, tombola *f* **4.** [attraction] attraction *f* **5.** GAMES partie *f* nulle ; SPORT match *m* nul / *the chess tournament ended in a draw* le tournoi d'échecs s'est terminé par une partie nulle. ◆ **draw apart** ◆ vi se séparer. ◆ vt sep prendre à l'écart. ◆ **draw aside** ◆ vi s'écarter, se ranger. ◆ vt sep [person] prendre ou tirer à l'écart ; [thing] écarter. ◆ **draw away** ◆ vi **1.** [move away - person] s'éloigner, s'écarter ; [- vehicle] s'éloigner, démarrer **2.** [move ahead] prendre de l'avance. ◆ **draw back** ◆ vi **1.** [move backwards] reculer, se reculer, avoir un mouvement de recul **2.** [avoid commitment] se retirer. ◆ vt sep [person] faire reculer ; [one's hand, thing] retirer. ◆ **draw in** ◆ vi **1.** [move] : *the train drew in* le train est entré en gare / *the bus drew in to the kerb* a) [pulled over] le bus s'est rapproché du trottoir b) [stopped] le bus s'est arrêté le long du trottoir **2.** [day, evening] diminuer, raccourcir / *the nights are drawing in* les nuits raccourcissent ou diminuent. ◆ vt sep **1.** [pull in] rentrer / *to draw in the reins* tirer sur les rênes, serrer la bride **2.** [involve] impliquer, mêler **3.** [attract] attirer **4.** [air] aspirer, respirer. ◆ **draw into** vt sep ▸ **to draw sb into sthg** mêler qqn à qqch / *he drew me into the conversation* il m'a mêlé à la conversation. ◆ **draw on** ◆ vt insep [as source] faire appel à / *I drew on my own experiences for the novel* je me suis inspiré ou servi de mes propres expériences pour mon roman / *I had to draw on my savings* j'ai dû prendre ou tirer sur mes économies. ◆ vi [time - come near] approcher ; [- get late] avancer. ◆ **draw out** ◆ vt sep **1.** [remove] sortir, retirer, tirer ; [money] retirer **2.** [extend - sound, visit] prolonger ; [- meeting, speech] prolonger, faire traîner ; [TECH - metal] étirer ; [- wire] tréfiler **3.** [cause to speak freely] faire parler **4.** [information, secret] soutirer ▸ **to draw sthg out of sb** soutirer qqch de qqn. ◆ vi [vehicle] sortir, s'éloigner. ◆ **draw up** ◆ vt sep **1.** UK [pull up] tirer / *she drew herself up (to her full height)* elle s'est redressée (de toute sa hauteur) **2.** UK [move closer - chair] approcher ; [MIL - troops] aligner, ranger **3.** [formulate - document] dresser, rédiger ; [- bill, list] dresser, établir ; [- plan] préparer, établir. ◆ vi UK **1.** [move] se diriger **2.** [stop - vehicle] s'arrêter, stopper ; [- person] s'arrêter. ◆ **draw upon** vt insep : *they had to draw upon their emergency funds* ils ont dû tirer sur ou prendre sur leur caisse de réserve / *you have to draw upon your previous experience* il faut faire appel à votre expérience antérieure.

drawback ['drɔːbæk] n inconvénient *m*, désavantage *m* / *there are drawbacks to the scheme* ce projet présente des inconvénients.

drawbridge ['drɔːbrɪdʒ] n pont-levis *m*, pont *m* basculant ou à bascule.

drawer n **1.** [drɔːr] [in chest, desk] tiroir *m* **2.** ['drɔːə'] [of cheque] tireur *m*.

drawing ['drɔːɪŋ] ◆ n ART dessin *m*. ◆ comp [paper, table] à dessin ; [lesson, teacher] de dessin.

drawing board n planche *f* à dessin ▸ **it's back to the drawing board** il faudra tout recommencer.

drawing pin n UK punaise *f* (à papier).

drawing room n **1.** [living room] salon *m* ; [reception room] salle *f* ou salon *m* de réception **2.** US RAIL compartiment *m* privé.

drawl [drɔːl] ◆ n débit *m* traînant, voix *f* traînante. ◆ vi parler d'une voix traînante. ◆ vt dire d'une voix traînante.

drawn [drɔːn] ◆ pp ⟶ draw. ◆ adj **1.** [blind, curtain] fermé, tiré **2.** [face, features] tiré / *he looked tired and drawn* il avait l'air fatigué et avait les traits tirés **3.** [game] nul.

drawn-out adj prolongé, qui traîne / *a long drawn-out dispute* un conflit qui traîne en longueur or qui n'en finit pas.

drawstring ['drɔːstrɪŋ] n cordon *m*.

dread [dred] ◆ n terreur *f*, effroi *m*. ◆ vt craindre, redouter / *she's dreading the journey* elle redoute or elle appréhende le voyage / *I dread to think of what might happen* je n'ose pas imaginer ce qui pourrait arriver.

dreaded ['dredɪd] adj redoutable, terrible *also hum*.

dreadful ['dredfʊl] adj **1.** [terrible - crime, pain] affreux, épouvantable ; [- enemy, weapon] redoutable **2.** [unpleasant] atroce, affreux **3.** [as intensifier] : *he's a dreadful bore!* c'est un casse-pieds insupportable !, c'est un horrible casse-pieds ! / *what a dreadful waste!* quel affreux gaspillage !

dreadfully ['dredfʊlɪ] adv **1.** [very] terriblement **2.** [badly] affreusement.

dreadlocks ['dredlɒks] pl n dreadlocks *fpl*, locks *fpl*.

dreads [dredz] pl n = dreadlocks.

dream [driːm] (*pt & pp* dreamt [dremt] *or* dreamed) ◆ vi **1.** [in sleep] rêver ▸ **to dream about sb** rêver de qqn **2.** [daydream] rêvasser, rêver / *for years she'd dreamt of having a cottage in the country* elle a, durant des années, rêvé d'avoir un cottage à la campagne ▸ **dream on!** inf on peut toujours rêver ! **3.** [imagine] ▸ **to dream of doing sthg** songer à faire qqch / *nobody dreamt of suspecting her* personne n'a songé à or il n'est venu à l'idée de personne de la soupçonner / *don't tell anyone — I wouldn't dream of it!* ne le dis à personne — jamais je ne songerais à faire une chose pareille ! ◆ vt **1.** [in sleep] rêver / *he dreamt a dream* il a fait un rêve / *she dreamt we were in Spain* elle a rêvé que nous étions en Espagne / *you must have dreamt it* vous avez dû le rêver **2.** [daydream] rêvasser **3.** [imagine] songer, imaginer / *I never dreamt that he would actually accept the offer!* j'étais à mille lieues de supposer qu'il accepterait effectivement la proposition ! ◆ n **1.** [during sleep] rêve *m* / *I had a dream about my mother last night* j'ai rêvé de ma mère la nuit dernière ▸ **to see sthg in a dream** voir qqch en rêve / *the child had a bad dream* l'enfant a fait un mauvais rêve or un cauchemar / *the meeting was like a bad dream* la réunion était un cauchemar **2.** [wish, fantasy] rêve *m*, désir *m* / *the woman of his dreams* la femme de ses rêves / *even in her wildest dreams she never thought she'd win first prize* même dans ses rêves les plus fous, elle n'avait jamais pensé remporter le premier prix / *the holiday was like a dream come true* les vacances étaient comme un rêve devenu réalité **3.** [marvel] merveille *f* / *my interview went like a dream* mon entretien s'est passé à merveille / *she's a real dream* inf c'est un amour, elle est vraiment adorable **4.** [daydream] rêverie *f*, rêve *m* / *he's always in a dream* il est toujours dans les nuages or en train de rêver. ◆ comp [car, person, house] de rêve / *his dream house* la maison de ses rêves / *she lives in a dream world* elle vit dans les nuages. ❖ **dream up** vt sep imaginer, inventer, concocter.

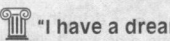
dreamer ['driːmər] n *lit* rêveur *m*, -euse *f* ; [idealist] rêveur *m*, -euse *f*, utopiste *mf* ; *pej* songe-creux *m inv*.

dreamily ['driːmɪlɪ] adv [act] d'un air rêveur or songeur ; [speak] d'un ton rêveur or songeur ; [absent-mindedly] d'un air absent.

dreamlike ['driːmlaɪk] adj irréel, onirique.

dreamt [dremt] pt & pp ⟶ **dream**.

dreamy ['driːmɪ] (*compar* dreamier, *superl* dreamiest) adj **1.** [vague - person] rêveur, songeur ; [- expression] rêveur ; [absent-minded] rêveur, distrait **2.** [impractical - person] utopique, rêveur ; [- idea] chimérique, utopique **3.** [music, voice] langoureux **4.** inf [wonderful] magnifique, ravissant.

dreary ['drɪərɪ] (*compar* drearier, *superl* dreariest) adj [surroundings] morne, triste ; [life] morne, monotone ; [work, job] monotone, ennuyeux ; [person] ennuyeux (comme la pluie) ; [weather] maussade, morne.

dredge [dredʒ] ◆ vt **1.** [river] draguer **2.** CULIN [with flour, sugar] saupoudrer ; [with breadcrumbs] paner. ◆ n NAUT drague *f*. ❖ **dredge up** vt sep *lit* draguer ; *fig* [scandal, unpleasant news] déterrer, ressortir.

dredger ['dredʒər] n **1.** NAUT [ship] dragueur *m* ; [machine] drague *f* **2.** CULIN saupoudreuse *f*, saupoudroir *m*.

dregs [dregz] pl n *lit & fig* lie *f* / *the dregs of society* la lie or les bas-fonds de la société.

drench [drentʃ] vt [soak] tremper, mouiller.

drenching ['drentʃɪŋ] ◆ n trempage *m*. ◆ adj ▸ **drenching rain** pluie *f* battante or diluvienne.

Dresden ['drezdən] ◆ pr n [city] Dresde. ◆ n [china] porcelaine *f* de Saxe, saxe *m*.

dress [dres] ◆ n **1.** [frock] robe *f* **2.** [clothing] habillement *m*, tenue *f* **3.** [style of dress] tenue *f*, toilette *f* / *formal / informal dress* tenue de cérémonie / de ville. ◆ vt **1.** [clothe] habiller / *she dressed herself* or *got dressed* elle s'est habillée **2.** [arrange] orner, parer ; [groom - horse] panser ; [- hair] coiffer ; [- shop window] faire la vitrine de ; [- ship] pavoiser **3.** [wound] panser **4.** CULIN [salad] assaisonner, garnir ; [meat, fish] parer. ◆ vi [get dressed, wear clothes] s'habiller / *to dress for dinner* a) [gen] se mettre en tenue de soirée b) [men] se mettre en smoking c) [women] se mettre en robe du soir. ❖ **dress down** ⟨UK⟩ ◆ vi s'habiller simplement. ◆ vt sep inf [scold] passer un savon à. ❖ **dress up** ◆ vi **1.** [put on best clothes] s'habiller, se mettre sur son trente et un / *he was all dressed up* il était tout endimanché **2.** [put on disguise] se déguiser, se costumer / *she dressed up as a clown* elle s'est déguisée en clown. ◆ vt sep **1.** [put on best clothes] habiller **2.** [disguise] déguiser **3.** [smarten] rendre plus habillé **4.** [embellish] orner.

dress circle n premier balcon *m*, corbeille *f*.

dress code n tenue *f* (vestimentaire) de rigueur.

dress designer n modéliste *mf*, dessinateur *m*, -trice *f* de mode ; [famous] couturier *m*.

dressed [drest] adj habillé / *a well-dressed / smartly-dressed man* un homme bien habillé / élégant / *dressed in blue chiffon* vêtu de mousseline de soie bleue / *she was dressed as a man* elle était habillée en homme.

dresser ['dresər] n **1.** [person] : *he's a smart / sloppy dresser* il s'habille avec beaucoup de goût / avec négligence **2.** THEAT habilleur *m*, -euse *f* **3.** [for dishes] buffet *m*, dressoir *m* **4.** ⟨US⟩ [for clothing] commode *f*.

dressing ['dresɪŋ] n **1.** [act of getting dressed] habillement *m*, habillage *m* **2.** CULIN [sauce] sauce *f*, assaisonnement *m* ; ⟨US⟩ [stuffing] farce *f* / *an oil and vinegar dressing* une vinaigrette **3.** [for wound] pansement *m*.

dressing-down n ⟨UK⟩ inf réprimande *f*, semonce *f*.

dressing gown n robe *f* de chambre, peignoir *m*.

dressing room n [at home] dressing-room m, dressing m, vestiaire m ; [at gymnasium, sports ground] vestiaire m ; THEAT loge f (d'acteur) ; 🇺🇸 [in shop] cabine f d'essayage.

dressing table n coiffeuse f, (table f de) toilette f.

dressing-up n [children's game] déguisement m.

dressmaker ['dres,meɪkər] n couturière f ; [famous] couturier m.

dressmaking ['dres,meɪkɪŋ] n couture f, confection f des robes.

dress rehearsal n THEAT (répétition f) générale f ; fig [practice] répétition f générale.

dress sense n ▶ to have good dress sense savoir s'habiller.

dress shirt n chemise f de soirée.

dressy ['dresɪ] (compar dressier, superl dressiest) adj [clothes] (qui fait) habillé, élégant ; [person] élégant, chic ; [event] habillé.

drew [dru:] pt ⟶ draw.

drib [drɪb] n ▶ in dribs and drabs petit à petit.

dribble ['drɪbl] ◆ vi 1. [trickle] couler lentement, tomber goutte à goutte 2. [baby] baver 3. SPORT dribbler. ◆ vt 1. [trickle] laisser couler ou tomber lentement 2. SPORT [ball, puck] dribbler. ◆ n 1. [trickle] filet m 2. fig [small amount] ▶ a dribble of un petit peu de 3. SPORT dribble m.

dried [draɪd] adj [fruit] sec (sèche) ; [meat] séché ; [milk, eggs] déshydraté.

dried-up adj [apple, person] ratatiné, desséché ; [talent, well] tari ; [beauty, love] fané.

drier ['draɪər] ◆ compar ⟶ dry. ◆ n [for clothes] séchoir m (à linge) ; [for hair - hand-held] séchoir m (à cheveux), sèche-cheveux m inv ; [-helmet] casque m (sèche-cheveux).

drift [drɪft] ◆ vi 1. [float - on water] dériver, aller à la dérive ; [-in current, wind] être emporté 2. [sand, snow] s'amonceler, s'entasser 3. [move aimlessly] marcher nonchalamment / people began to drift away / in / out les gens commençaient à s'en aller / entrer / sortir d'un pas nonchalant ; fig : the conversation drifted from one topic to another la conversation passait d'un sujet à un autre / he just drifts along il flâne simplement / to drift apart a) [friends] se perdre de vue b) [couple] se séparer petit à petit. ◆ vt 1. [subj: current] entraîner, charrier ; [subj: wind] emporter, pousser 2. [sand, snow] amonceler, entasser. ◆ n 1. [flow] mouvement m, force f ; [of air, water] poussée f 2. [of leaves, sand] amoncellement m, entassement m ; [of fallen snow] amoncellement m, congère f ; [of falling snow] rafale f, bourrasque f ; [of clouds] traînée f ; [of dust, mist] nuage m ; GEOL [deposits] apports mpl 3. [trend] tendance f 4. [meaning] sens m, portée f / do you get my drift? voyez-vous où je veux en venir ? ❖ **drift off** vi [fall asleep] s'assoupir.

drifter ['drɪftər] n 1. [person] personne qui n'a pas de but dans la vie 2. [boat] drifter m, dériveur m.

driftwood ['drɪftwʊd] n (U) bois mpl flottants.

drill [drɪl] ◆ n 1. [manual] porte-foret m ; [electric] perceuse f ; [of dentist] fraise f (de dentiste), roulette f ; [for oil well] trépan m ; [pneumatic] marteau m piqueur ; MIN perforatrice f 2. [bit] ▶ drill (bit) foret m, mèche f 3. [exercise] exercice m ; MIL manœuvre f, drill m. ◆ vt 1. [metal, wood] forer, percer ; [hole] percer ; [dentist] fraiser / to drill an oil well forer un puits de pétrole 2. inf SPORT [ball] : he drilled the ball into the back of the net il envoya la balle droit au fond du filet 3. [train] faire faire des exercices à ; MIL faire faire l'exercice à. ◆ vi 1. [bore] forer 2. [train]

faire de l'exercice, s'entraîner ; MIL être à l'exercice, manœuvrer. ❖ **drill into** vt sep faire comprendre, enfoncer dans la tête.

drilling ['drɪlɪŋ] n (U) [in metal, wood] forage m, perçage m ; [by dentist] fraisage m.

drilling platform n plate-forme f (de forage).

drilling rig n 1. [on land] derrick m, tour f de forage 2. [at sea] = drilling platform.

drily ['draɪlɪ] adv [wryly] d'un air pince-sans-rire ; [coldly] sèchement, d'un ton sec.

drink [drɪŋk] (pt drank [dræŋk], pp drunk [drʌŋk]) ◆ vt boire, prendre / would you like something to drink? voulez-vous boire quelque chose ? / I never drink coffee je ne prends jamais de café / the water is not fit to drink l'eau n'est pas potable / red Burgundy is best drunk at room temperature le bourgogne rouge est meilleur bu chambré. ◆ vi boire / I don't drink je ne bois pas / 'don't drink and drive' 'boire ou conduire, il faut choisir'. ◆ n 1. [nonalcoholic] boisson f / may I have a drink? puis-je boire quelque chose ? / a drink of water un verre d'eau / give the children a drink donnez à boire aux enfants / there's plenty of food and drink il y a tout ce qu'on veut à boire et à manger 2. [alcoholic] verre m ; [before dinner] apéritif m ; [after dinner] digestif m / we invited them in for a drink nous les avons invités à prendre un verre / I need a drink! vite, donnez-moi à boire ! 3. [mouthful] gorgée f 4. [alcohol] la boisson, l'alcool m / to be the worse for drink être en état d'ébriété / to drive under the influence of drink conduire en état d'ivresse ou d'ébriété / to smell of drink sentir l'alcool. ◆ comp : he has a drink problem il boit. ❖ **drink away** vt sep [troubles] noyer ; [fortune] boire. ❖ **drink down** vt sep avaler ou boire d'un trait. ❖ **drink in** vt sep [story, words] boire ; [atmosphere, surroundings] s'imprégner de. ❖ **drink to** vt insep boire à, porter un toast à / we drank to their success nous avons bu ou porté un toast à leur succès. ❖ **drink up** vt sep boire (jusqu'à la dernière goutte), finir. ◆ vi vider son verre.

drinkable ['drɪŋkəbl] adj [safe to drink] potable ; [tasty] buvable.

drink-driver n 🇬🇧 conducteur m, -trice f ivre.

drink-driving n 🇬🇧 conduite f en état d'ivresse.

drinker ['drɪŋkər] n buveur m, -euse f.

drinking ['drɪŋkɪŋ] ◆ n fait m de boire. ◆ comp [man] qui boit ; [habits] de buveur ; [bout, companion, session] de beuverie.

drinking chocolate n chocolat m à boire ; [powder] chocolat m en poudre ; [hot drink] chocolat m chaud.

drinking fountain n [in street] fontaine f publique ; [in building] fontaine f d'eau potable.

drinking-up time n 🇬🇧 moment où les clients doivent finir leur verre avant la fermeture du bar.

drinking water n eau f potable.

drinks machine, drink machine n 🇺🇸 distributeur m de boissons.

drip [drɪp] (pt & pp dripped, cont dripping) ◆ vi 1. [liquid] tomber goutte à goutte, dégoutter 2. [tap] fuir, goutter ; [nose] couler ; [washing] s'égoutter ; [walls] suinter ; [hair, trees] dégoutter, ruisseler. ◆ vt laisser tomber goutte à goutte. ◆ n 1. [falling drops - from tap, gutter, ceiling] égouttement m, dégoulinement m 2. [sound - from trees, roofs] bruit m de l'eau qui goutte ; [-from tap] bruit d'un robinet qui fuit ou goutte 3. [drop] goutte f 4. inf & pej [person] nouille f, lavette f 5. MED [device] goutte-à-goutte m inv ; [solution] perfusion f ▶ she's on a drip elle est sous perfusion.

drip-dry ◆ adj qui ne nécessite aucun repassage. ◆ vi s'égoutter. ◆ vt (faire) égoutter.

drip-feed ◆ n [device] goutte-à-goutte *m inv* ; [solution] perfusion *f*. ◆ vt alimenter par perfusion.

dripping ['drɪpɪŋ] ◆ n **1.** CULIN [of meat] graisse *f (de rôti)* **2.** [of liquid] égouttement *m*, égouttage *m*. ◆ adj **1.** [tap] qui fuit or goutte **2.** [very wet] trempé.

drippy ['drɪpɪ] *(compar* **drippier,** *superl* **drippiest)** adj **1.** *inf & pej* [person] mou *(before vowel or silent 'h' mol, f molle)* **2.** [tap] qui fuit or goutte.

drive [draɪv] *(pt* **drove** [drəʊv], *pp* **driven** ['drɪvn]) ◆ vt **1.** [bus, car, train] conduire ; [racing car] piloter / *I drive a Volvo* j'ai une Volvo / *he drives a taxi / lorry* il est chauffeur de taxi / camionneur / *she drives racing cars* elle est pilote de course / *he drove her into town* il l'a conduite or emmenée en voiture en ville / *she drove the car into a tree* elle a heurté un arbre avec la voiture **2.** [chase] chasser, pousser ▶ **to drive sb out of the house / of the country** chasser qqn de la maison / du pays / *we drove the cattle back into the shed* nous avons fait rentrer le bétail dans l'étable / *the strong winds had driven the ship off course* les vents forts avaient dévié le navire de sa route ; *fig* : *her words drove all worries from his mind* ses paroles lui ont fait complètement oublier ses soucis **3.** [work] : *it doesn't pay to drive your workers too hard* on ne gagne rien à surmener ses employés **4.** [force] pousser, inciter / *he was driven to it* on lui a forcé la main / *the situation is driving me to despair / distraction* la situation me pousse au désespoir / me rend fou ▶ **to drive sb crazy** or **mad** or **up the wall** *inf* rendre qqn fou **5.** [hammer] ▶ **to drive a nail home** enfoncer un clou ; *fig* ▶ **to drive a point home** faire admettre son point de vue **6.** [operate - machine] faire fonctionner ; MECH entraîner / *driven by electricity* marchant à l'électricité **7.** SPORT ▶ **to drive a ball a)** exécuter un drive **b)** [in golf] driver. ◆ vi **1.** [operate a vehicle] conduire ; [travel in vehicle] aller en voiture / *do you* or *can you drive?* savez-vous conduire ? / *I was driving at 100 mph* je roulais à 160 km/h / *we drove home / to the coast* nous sommes rentrés / descendus sur la côte en voiture / *they drove all night* ils ont roulé toute la nuit / *drive on the right* roulez à droite, tenez votre droite **2.** [car] rouler. ◆ n **1.** AUTO [trip] promenade *f* or trajet *m* (en voiture) / *we went for a drive* nous avons fait une promenade or un tour en voiture / *it's an hour's drive from here* c'est à une heure d'ici en voiture **2.** [road - public] avenue *f*, rue *f* ; [- private] voie *f* privée *(menant à une habitation)* ; [in street names] allée *f* **3.** [energy] dynamisme *m*, énergie *f* / *we need someone with drive* il nous faut quelqu'un de dynamique or d'entreprenant **4.** [urge] besoin *m*, instinct *m* **5.** [campaign] campagne *f / the company is having a sales drive* la compagnie fait une campagne de vente **6.** SPORT [in cricket, tennis] coup *m* droit ; [in golf] drive *m* ; [in football] tir *m*, shoot *m* **7.** COMPUT [for disk] unité *f* or lecteur *m* de disquettes ; [for tape] dérouleur *m*. ◆◆ **drive along** vi [car] rouler, circuler ; [person] rouler, conduire. ◆◆ **drive at** vt insep vouloir dire / *she didn't understand what he was driving at* elle ne comprenait pas où il voulait en venir. ◆◆ **drive away** ◆ vi [person] s'en aller or partir (en voiture) ; [car] démarrer. ◆ vt sep [car] démarrer ; *lit* [person] emmener en voiture ; *fig* repousser, écarter ; [animal] chasser, éloigner. ◆◆ **drive back** ◆ vi [person] rentrer en voiture ; [car] retourner. ◆ vt sep **1.** [person] ramener or reconduire en voiture ; [car] reculer **2.** [repel] repousser, refouler / *fear drove them back* la peur leur a fait rebrousser chemin. ◆◆ **drive down** vt sep [person] descendre (en voiture) ; [car] descendre ; ECON [prices, inflation] faire baisser. ◆◆ **drive in** ◆ vi [person] entrer (en voiture) ; [car] entrer. ◆ vt sep [nail, stake] enfoncer ; [screw] visser ; [rivet] poser. ◆◆ **drive off** ◆ vi [leave

- person] s'en aller or s'éloigner en voiture ; [- car] démarrer. ◆ vt sep [frighten away] éloigner, chasser. ◆◆ **drive on** ◆ vi [continue trip] poursuivre sa route ; [after stopping] reprendre la route. ◆ vt sep [push] pousser, inciter. ◆◆ **drive out** ◆ vi [person] sortir (en voiture) ; [car] sortir. ◆ vt sep [person] chasser, faire sortir ; [thought] chasser. ◆◆ **drive over** ◆ vi venir or aller en voiture. ◆ vt insep [crush] écraser. ◆ vt sep conduire or emmener en voiture. ◆◆ **drive up** vi [person] arriver (en voiture) ; [car] arriver ; ECON [prices, inflation] faire monter.

drive-by shooting n fusillade exécutée d'un véhicule *en marche*.

drive-in US ◆ n [cinema] drive-in *m inv* ; [restaurant, bank, etc.] désigne tout commerce où l'on est servi dans sa voiture. ◆ adj où l'on reste dans sa voiture.

drivel ['drɪvl] *(UK pt & pp* **drivelled,** *cont* **drivelling** ; *US pt & pp* **driveled,** *cont* **driveling)** ◆ n *(U)* **1.** [nonsense] bêtises *fpl*, radotage *m* **2.** [saliva] bave *f*. ◆ vi **1.** [speak foolishly] dire des bêtises, radoter **2.** [dribble] baver.

driven ['drɪvn] pp ──▶ **drive.**

-driven in comp **1.** MECH (fonctionnant) à ▶ **electricity / steam-driven engine** machine électrique / à vapeur **2.** *fig* déterminé par ▶ **market / consumer-driven** déterminé par les contraintes du marché / les exigences du consommateur **3.** COMPUT contrôlé par ▶ **menu-driven** contrôlé par menu.

driver ['draɪvə*] n **1.** [of car] conducteur *m*, -trice *f* ; [of bus, taxi, lorry] chauffeur *m*, conducteur *m*, -trice *f* ; [of racing car] pilote *m* ; [of train] mécanicien *m*, conducteur *m*, -trice *f* ; [of cart] charretier *m*, -ère *f* ; SPORT [of horse-drawn vehicle] driver *m* **2.** [of animals] conducteur *m*, -trice *f* **3.** [golf club] driver *m*, driveur *m* **4.** COMPUT [software] driver *m*, pilote *m* ; [hardware] unité *f* de contrôle.

driver's license n US permis *m* de conduire.

drive-through ◆ adj où l'on reste dans sa voiture. ◆ n drive-in *m inv*.

driveway ['draɪvweɪ] n voie *f* privée *(menant à une habitation)*.

driving ['draɪvɪŋ] ◆ adj **1.** [rain] battant **2.** [powerful] fort ; [ambition] ferme. ◆ n conduite *f*.

driving force n MECH force *f* motrice / *she's the driving force behind the project* c'est elle le moteur du projet.

driving instructor n moniteur *m*, -trice *f* de conduite or d'auto-école.

driving lesson n leçon *f* de conduite.

driving licence n UK permis *m* de conduire.

driving mirror n rétroviseur *m*.

driving school n auto-école *f*.

driving seat n place *f* du conducteur / *she's in the driving seat fig* c'est elle qui mène l'affaire or qui tient les rênes.

driving test n examen *m* du permis de conduire.

drizzle ['drɪzl] ◆ n bruine *f*, crachin *m*. ◆ vi bruiner, crachiner.

drizzly ['drɪzlɪ] adj de bruine or crachin, bruineux.

DRM (abbr of **digital rights management**) n GDN *f*.

droll [drəʊl] adj [comical] drôle, comique ; [odd] curieux, drôle.

dromedary ['drɒmədərɪ] *(pl* **dromedaries)** n dromadaire *m*.

drone [drəʊn] ◆ n **1.** [sound - of bee] bourdonnement *m* ; [- of engine] ronronnement *m* ; [louder] vrombissement *m* **2.** [male bee] abeille *f* mâle, faux-bourdon *m* ; *pej* [person] fainéant *m*, -e *f* **3.** MUS bourdon *m* **4.** [plane]

avion *m* téléguidé, drone *m*. ◆ vi [bee] bourdonner ; [engine] ronronner ; [loudly] vrombir ▸ **to drone on** [person] parler d'un ton monotone.

drool [dru:l] vi baver ▸ **to drool over sthg** *fig* baver d'admiration or s'extasier devant qqch.

droop [dru:p] ◆ vi [head] pencher ; [eyelids] s'abaisser ; [body] s'affaisser ; [shoulders] tomber ; [flowers] commencer à baisser la tête or à se faner. ◆ n [of eyelids] abaissement *m* ; [of head] attitude *f* penchée ; [of body, shoulders] affaissement *m* ; [of spirits] langueur *f*, abattement *m*.

droopy ['dru:pɪ] (*compar* **droopier**, *superl* **droopiest**) adj [moustache, shoulders] qui tombe ; [flowers] qui commence à se faner.

drop [drɒp] (*pt & pp* **dropped**, *cont* **dropping**) ◆ vt **1.** [let fall - accidentally] laisser tomber ; [-liquid] laisser tomber goutte à goutte ; [-trousers] laisser tomber ; [-bomb] lancer, lâcher ; [-stitch] sauter, laisser tomber ; [release] lâcher / *drop it!* [to dog] lâche ça ! / *they dropped soldiers / supplies by parachute* ils ont parachuté des soldats / du ravitaillement **2.** [lower - voice] baisser ; [-speed] réduire ; [-hem] ressortir **3.** [deliver] déposer / *could you drop me at the corner please?* pouvez-vous me déposer au coin s'il vous plaît ? **4.** [abandon - friend] laisser tomber, lâcher ; [-discussion, work] abandonner, laisser tomber / *let's drop the subject* ne parlons plus de cela, parlons d'autre chose / *just drop it!* laissez tomber !, assez ! **5.** [utter - remark] laisser échapper ▸ **to drop a hint about sthg** faire allusion à qqch / *he dropped me a hint that she wanted to come* il m'a fait comprendre qu'elle voulait venir **6.** [send - letter, note] écrire, envoyer / *I'll drop you a line next week* je t'enverrai un petit mot la semaine prochaine / *I'll drop it in the post* or *mail* je le mettrai à la poste **7.** [omit - when speaking] ne pas prononcer ; [-when writing] omettre ; [-intentionally] supprimer / *he drops his h's* il n'aspire pas les h / *to drop a player from a team* SPORT écarter un joueur d'une équipe. ◆ vi **1.** [fall - object] tomber, retomber ; [-liquid] tomber goutte à goutte ; [-ground] s'abaisser / *the road drops into the valley* la route plonge vers la vallée **2.** [sink down - person] se laisser tomber, tomber ; [collapse] s'écrouler, s'affaisser / *she dropped to her knees* elle est tombée à genoux / *I'm ready to drop* **a)** [from fatigue] je tombe de fatigue, je ne tiens plus sur mes jambes **b)** [from sleepiness] je tombe de sommeil / *drop dead!* *inf* va te faire voir ! **3.** [decrease - price, speed] baisser, diminuer ; [-temperature] baisser ; [-wind] se calmer, tomber ; [-voice] baisser **4.** [end] cesser / *there the matter dropped* l'affaire en est restée là. ◆ n **1.** [of liquid] goutte *f* / *drop by drop* goutte à goutte / *he's had a drop too much (to drink)* *inf* il a bu un verre de trop **2.** [decrease - in price] baisse *f*, chute *f* ; [-in temperature] baisse *f* ; [-in voltage] chute *f* **3.** [fall] chute *f* ; [in parachuting] saut *m* (en parachute) / *it was a long drop from the top of the wall* ça faisait haut depuis le haut du mur **4.** [vertical distance] hauteur *f* de chute ; [slope] descente *f* brusque ; [abyss] à-pic *m inv*, précipice *m* ; [in climbing] vide *m* / *a sudden drop in the ground level* une soudaine dénivellation. ◆ **drops** pl n MED gouttes *fpl*. ◆ **drop back** vi retourner en arrière, se laisser devancer or distancer. ◆ **drop by** vi passer. ◆ **drop down** vi [person] tomber (par terre) ; [table leaf] se rabattre. ◆ **drop in** ◆ vi passer ▸ **to drop in on sb** passer voir qqn. ◆ vt [deliver] déposer. ◆ **drop off** ◆ vt sep [person] déposer ; [package, thing] déposer, laisser. ◆ vi **1.** [fall asleep] s'endormir ; [have a nap] faire un (petit) somme **2.** [decrease] diminuer, baisser **3.** [fall off] tomber. ◆ **drop out** vi **1.** [fall out] tomber **2.** [withdraw] renoncer / *she dropped out of the race* elle s'est retirée de la course / *he dropped out of school* il a abandonné

ses études ; [from society] vivre en marge de la société. ◆ **drop round** UK ◆ vi = **drop in**. ◆ vt sep [deliver] déposer.

drop- adj COMPUT [menu] déroulant.

Drop Add ['drɒp,æd] n US *période en début de trimestre pendant laquelle les élèves peuvent modifier leur choix de cours*.

drop-dead adv *inf* vachement.

drop goal n drop-goal *m*, drop *m*.

drop-in centre n UK centre *m* d'assistance sociale (*où l'on peut aller sans rendez-vous*).

drop kick n coup *m* de pied tombé.

droplet ['drɒplɪt] n gouttelette *f*.

drop-off n **1.** [decrease] baisse *f*, diminution *f* **2.** US [descent] à-pic *m inv*.

dropout ['drɒpaʊt] n *inf* [from society] marginal *m*, -e *f* ; [from studies] étudiant *m*, -e *f* qui abandonne ses études.

dropper ['drɒpə'] n compte-gouttes *m inv*.

droppings ['drɒpɪŋz] pl n [of animal] crottes *fpl* ; [of bird] fiente *f*.

drop shot n amorti *m*.

dross [drɒs] n (U) [waste] déchets *mpl*, impuretés *fpl* / *it's total dross* ça ne vaut rien.

drought [draʊt] n **1.** [no rain] sécheresse *f* **2.** [shortage] disette *f*, manque *m*.

drove [drəʊv] ◆ pt ⟶ **drive**. ◆ n [of animals] troupeau *m* en marche ; [of people] foule *f*, multitude *f* / *every summer the tourists come in droves* chaque été les touristes arrivent en foule.

drown [draʊn] ◆ vt **1.** [person, animal] noyer ▸ **to be drowned** **a)** se noyer **b)** [in battle, disaster, etc.] mourir noyé ▸ **to drown o.s.** se noyer **2.** [field, village] noyer **3.** [make inaudible] noyer, couvrir. ◆ vi se noyer ; [in battle, disaster, etc.] mourir noyé. ◆ **drown out** vt sep = **drown**.

drowse [draʊz] vi somnoler. ◆ **drowse off** vi s'assoupir.

drowsily ['draʊzɪlɪ] adv d'un air somnolent.

drowsiness ['draʊzɪnɪs] n (U) somnolence *f*.

drowsy ['draʊzɪ] (*compar* **drowsier**, *superl* **drowsiest**) adj [person, voice] somnolent, engourdi ; [place] endormi.

drudge [drʌdʒ] ◆ n **1.** [person] bête *f* de somme **2.** [work] besogne *f*. ◆ vi besogner, peiner.

drudgery ['drʌdʒərɪ] n (U) travail *m* de bête de somme.

drug [drʌg] (*pt & pp* **drugged**, *cont* **drugging**) ◆ n **1.** [medication] médicament *m* ▸ **to be on drugs** prendre des médicaments **2.** [illegal substance] drogue *f* ; LAW stupéfiant *m* ▸ **to be on drugs** se droguer ▸ **to take drugs** **a)** se droguer **b)** [athlete] se doper. ◆ comp [abuse, dealing, trafficking] de drogue ▸ **Drug Squad** [police] brigade *f* des stupéfiants ▸ **drugs test** [of athlete, horse] contrôle *m* antidopage ▸ **drug user** drogué *m*, -e *f*. ◆ vt droguer ; [athlete, horse] doper.

⚠ **Une drogue** is usually a narcotic substance, not a form of medication. When a drug is a medicine, use **un médicament**.

drug abuse n usage *m* de stupéfiants.

drug addict n drogué *m*, -e *f*, toxicomane *mf*.

drug addiction n toxicomanie *f*.

druggie ['drʌgɪ] n *inf* [addict] toxico *mf*.

druggist ['drʌgɪst] n US [person] pharmacien *m*, -enne *f* ; [shop] ▸ **druggist** or **druggist's** pharmacie *f*.

drug-peddler, drug-pusher n dealer *m*.

drugstore ['drʌgstɔːʳ] n US pharmacie f *(où l'on trouve également des produits tels que des cosmétiques, des journaux, etc.).*

druid ['druːɪd] n druide m, -esse f.

drum [drʌm] *(pt & pp* **drummed,** *cont* **drumming)** ◆ n **1.** [instrument - gen] tambour m ; [- African] tam-tam m / **to play (the) drums** jouer de la batterie **2.** [for fuel] fût m, bidon m ; [for rope] cylindre m ; COMPUT [cylinder] tambour m **3.** [noise - of rain, fingers] tambourinement m. ◆ vi **1.** MUS [on drum kit] jouer de la batterie ; [on one drum] jouer du tambour **2.** [rain, fingers] tambouriner. ◆ vt [on instrument] tambouriner / **to drum one's fingers on the table** tambouriner de ses doigts sur la table. ❖ **drum in** vt sep insister lourdement sur. ❖ **drum into** vt sep ▶ **to drum sthg into sb** enfoncer qqch dans la tête de qqn. ❖ **drum out** vt sep expulser / *he was drummed out of the club / the army* il a été expulsé du club / de l'armée. ❖ **drum up** vt insep [customers, support] attirer, rechercher ; [supporters] battre le rappel de ; [enthusiasm] chercher à susciter.

drumbeat ['drʌmbiːt] n battement m de tambour.

drum brake n AUTO frein m à tambour.

drum kit n batterie f.

drummer ['drʌməʳ] n [in band] batteur m ; [tribal] joueur m de tambour ; MIL tambour m.

drum roll n roulement m de tambour.

drumstick ['drʌmstɪk] n **1.** MUS baguette f **2.** CULIN pilon m.

drunk [drʌŋk] ◆ pp ⟶ **drink.** ◆ adj **1.** *lit* soûl, saoul, ivre ▶ **to get sb drunk** soûler qqn ▶ **drunk and disorderly** LAW en état d'ivresse publique **2.** *fig* : *drunk with power / success* ivre de pouvoir / succès. ◆ n [habitual] ivrogne mf ; [on one occasion] homme m soûl or ivre, femme f soûle or ivre.

drunkard ['drʌŋkəd] n ivrogne mf.

drunken ['drʌŋkn] adj [person] ivre ; [laughter, sleep] d'ivrogne ; [evening, party] très arrosé.

drunk(en)-driving US = drink-driving.

drunkenness ['drʌŋkənnɪs] n [state] ivresse f ; [habit] ivrognerie f.

druthers ['drʌðəz] pl n US *inf* ▶ **if I had my druthers** si j'avais le choix.

dry [draɪ] *(compar* **drier,** *superl* **driest,** *pt & pp* **dried)** ◆ adj **1.** [climate, season, clothing, skin] sec (sèche) ▶ **to go** or **to run dry** [well, river] s'assécher, se tarir ▶ **to keep sthg dry** garder qqch au sec ▶ **to be dry a)** [be thirsty] mourir de soif *fig*, avoir soif **b)** [cow] être tarie or sèche **2.** [vermouth, wine] sec (sèche) ; [champagne] brut ▶ **medium dry** [wine] demi-sec **3.** [where alcohol is banned] où l'alcool est prohibé ; [where alcohol is not sold] où on ne vend pas d'alcool ; [person] : *he's been dry for two years* ça fait deux ans qu'il ne boit plus ▶ **dry state** US État ayant adopté les lois de la prohibition **4.** [boring - book, lecture] aride **5.** [wit, sense of humour] caustique, mordant **6.** US *inf* POL [hardline] ultra-conservateur. ◆ n **1.** [with towel, cloth] ▶ **to give sthg a dry** essuyer qqch **2.** [dry place] : *come into the dry* viens te mettre au sec. ◆ vt [hair, clothes, fruit, leaves] (faire) sécher ; [dishes] essuyer / *to dry one's eyes* se sécher les yeux, sécher ses yeux. ◆ vi [clothes, hair, fruit, leaves] sécher / *you wash, I'll dry* tu laves et moi j'essuie. ❖ **dry off** ◆ vi [clothes, person] = dry out. ◆ vt sep sécher ▶ **to dry o.s. off** se sécher. ❖ **dry out** ◆ vi **1.** [clothes] sécher ; [person] se sécher **2.** [alcoholic] se désintoxiquer. ◆ vt sep [alcoholic] désintoxiquer. ❖ **dry up** vi **1.** [well, river] s'assécher, se tarir ; [puddle, street] sécher ; [inspiration] se tarir ; [cow] se tarir **2.** [dry the dishes] essuyer la vaisselle **3.** *inf* [be lost for words - actor, speaker] sécher.

dry battery = dry cell.

dry-clean vt nettoyer à sec.

dry cleaner n [person] teinturier m, -ère f ▶ **dry cleaner's** [shop] teinturerie f.

dry-cleaning n *(U)* **1.** [action] nettoyage m à sec **2.** [clothes - being cleaned] vêtements mpl laissés au nettoyage (à sec) or chez le teinturier or à la teinturerie ; [- to be cleaned] vêtements à emmener au nettoyage (à sec) or chez le teinturier or à la teinturerie.

dry dock n cale f sèche / *in dry dock* en cale sèche.

dryer ['draɪəʳ] = drier.

dry ginger n boisson gazeuse au gingembre.

dry goods pl n **1.** US tissus et articles de bonneterie mpl **2.** UK [tobacco, coffee, etc.] denrées fpl non périssables.

dry ice n neige f carbonique / *dry ice machine* machine f à neige carbonique.

drying-out clinic n *inf* centre m de désintoxication pour alcooliques.

drying rack n séchoir m.

dry land n terre f ferme.

dryly ['draɪlɪ] = drily.

dryness ['draɪnɪs] n **1.** [of region, weather, skin] sécheresse f **2.** [of wit, humour] mordant m, causticité f.

dry-roasted adj [peanuts] grillé à sec.

dry rot n *(U)* [in wood] moisissure f sèche ; [in potatoes] pourriture f sèche.

dry run n **1.** [trial, practice] coup m d'essai, test m **2.** MIL entraînement m avec tir à blanc.

dry ski slope n piste f de ski artificielle.

dry-stone adj [wall] en pierres sèches.

drysuit ['draɪsuːt] n combinaison f de plongée.

DSc (abbr of **Doctor of Science**) n UK *(titulaire d'un)* doctorat en sciences.

DST n abbr of **daylight saving time.**

DT n abbr of **data transmission.**

DTP (abbr of **desktop publishing**) n PAO f.

DT's [,diː'tiːz] (abbr of **delirium tremens**) pl n *inf* ▶ **to have the DT's** avoir une crise de delirium tremens.

DTV (abbr of **digital television**) n DTV f.

dual ['djuːəl] adj [purpose, nationality] double / *to have a dual personality* souffrir d'un dédoublement de la personnalité ▶ **dual controls** AERON & AUTO double commande f.

dual-branded adj à double marque.

dual carriageway n UK AUTO route f à quatre voies.

dual-control adj [car, plane] à double commande.

dual-core processor n processeur m à double cœur.

dual-currency adj [system] bi-monétaire.

dual economy n économie f duale.

dual enrollment ['djuːəlɪn'rəʊlmənt] n US programme qui permet aux lycéens de suivre également des cours à l'université.

dual-heritage adj métis.

dual-purpose adj à double fonction.

dub [dʌb] *(pt & pp* **dubbed,** *cont* **dubbing)** vt **1.** [nickname] surnommer **2.** CIN & TV [add soundtrack, voice] sonoriser ; [in foreign language] doubler.

Dubai [,duː'baɪ] pr n Dubai / *in Dubai* à Dubai.

dubbing ['dʌbɪŋ] n CIN & TV [addition of soundtrack] sonorisation f ; [in a foreign language] doublage m.

dubious ['djuːbjəs] adj **1.** [unsure - reply, voice] dubitatif ; [- expression] dubitatif, d'incertitude ; [- outcome, value] incertain **2.** [suspect - person, nature, reputation, decision] douteux.

dubiously ['dju:bjəslı] adv **1.** [doubtfully] d'un air de doute **2.** [in suspect manner] d'une manière douteuse.

Dublin ['dʌblɪn] pr n Dublin.

Dubliner ['dʌblɪnə'] n Dublinois m, -e f.

duchess ['dʌtʃɪs] n duchesse f.

duchy ['dʌtʃɪ] (pl duchies) n duché m.

duck [dʌk] ◆ n **1.** [bird] canard m **2.** [in cricket] score m nul **3.** [material] coutil m. ◆ vt **1.** [dodge - blow] esquiver ▶ **to duck one's head (out of the way)** baisser vivement la tête **2.** [submerge in water] faire boire la tasse à **3.** [evade - responsibility, question] se dérober à, esquiver. ◆ vi [drop quickly] se baisser vivement ; [in boxing] esquiver un coup. ◆ **duck out** vi inf **1.** [move quickly] : to duck out of a room s'esquiver d'une pièce **2.** [avoid] se défiler ▶ **to duck out of doing sthg** se défiler pour ne pas faire qqch ▶ **to duck out (of sthg)** se soustraire (à qqch).

ducking ['dʌkɪŋ] n : he got a ducking on lui a fait boire la tasse ▶ **ducking and diving** UK inf dérobades fpl.

duckling ['dʌklɪŋ] n caneton m ; [female] canette f ; [older] canardeau m.

duckpond ['dʌkpɒnd] n mare f aux canards.

duct [dʌkt] n [for gas, liquid, electricity] conduite f, canalisation f ; ANAT conduit m, canal m ; BOT vaisseau m.

duct tape n US ruban m adhésif industriel.

dud [dʌd] inf ◆ adj [false - coin, note] faux (fausse) ; [useless - drill, video] qui ne marche pas ; [- shell, bomb] qui a raté ; [- idea] débile. ◆ n [person] nullité f, tache f ; [cheque] chèque m en bois ; [coin] fausse pièce f de monnaie ; [note] faux billet m ; [shell] obus m qui a raté or qui n'a pas explosé.

dude [dju:d] n US inf [man] type m, mec m.

dude ranch n US ranch qui propose des activités touristiques.

due [dju:] ◆ n [what one deserves] ▶ **but then, to give him his due,...** mais pour lui rendre justice... ◆ adj **1.** [owed, payable - amount, balance, money] dû / when's the next instalment due? quand le prochain versement doit-il être fait ? ▶ **to be due an apology** avoir droit à des excuses **2.** [expected] : we're due round there at 7.30 on nous attend à 7 h 30, nous devons y être à 7 h 30 ▶ **to be due to do sthg** devoir faire qqch **3.** [proper] ▶ **to give sthg due consideration** accorder mûre réflexion à qqch ▶ **in due course** or **time a)** [at the proper time] en temps voulu **b)** [in the natural course of events] à un certain moment **c)** [at a later stage, eventually] plus tard ▶ **with (all) due respect...** avec tout le respect que je vous dois..., sauf votre respect... ◆ adv [east, west, etc.] plein. ◆ **dues** pl n droits mpl. ◆ **due to** prep phr **1.** [owing to] à cause de, en raison de **2.** [because of] grâce à.

duel ['dju:əl] (UK pt & pp **duelled**, cont **duelling** ; US pt & pp **dueled**, cont **dueling**) ◆ n duel m. ◆ vi se battre en duel.

duet [dju:'et] n duo m / to sing / to play a duet chanter / jouer en duo.

duff [dʌf] ◆ adj UK inf [useless] qui ne marche pas ; [idea] débile. ◆ n **1.** CULIN variante du plum-pudding **2.** US inf [buttocks] fesses fpl **3.** UK inf ▶ **to be up the duff** être en cloque. ◆ **duff up** vt sep UK inf [beat up] tabasser, démolir.

duffel bag n sac m marin.

duffel coat n duffel-coat m, duffle-coat m.

duffer ['dʌfə'] n UK inf [useless person] gourde f ; SCH nullité f, cancre m ▶ **to be a duffer at sthg** être nul en qqch.

dug [dʌg] ◆ pt & pp ⟶ **dig**. ◆ n mamelle f ; [of cow, goat] pis m.

dugout ['dʌgaut] n **1.** MIL tranchée-abri f ; SPORT banc m abri de touche **2.** [canoe] canoë m creusé dans un tronc.

DUI abbr of **driving under the influence**.

duke [dju:k] n duc m.

Duke of Edinburgh's Award Scheme pr n ▶ **the Duke of Edinburgh's Award Scheme** ≃ la bourse du duc d'Édimbourg.

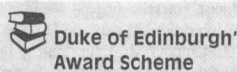

Duke of Edinburgh's Award Scheme

Cette bourse récompense des projets d'intérêt collectif ou personnel réalisés par des jeunes de 14 à 23 ans. Réputés pour leur grande difficulté, ces projets font parfois l'objet de comparaisons humoristiques : I should get a Duke of Edinburgh award for sitting through that film!

dull [dʌl] ◆ adj **1.** [slow-witted - person] peu intelligent ; [- reflexes] ralenti **2.** [boring - book, person, lecture] ennuyeux, assommant **3.** [not bright - colour] terne, fade ; [- light, eyes] terne ; [- weather, sky] sombre, maussade **4.** [not sharp - blade] émoussé ; [- pain] sourd ; [- sound] sourd, étouffé **5.** [listless - person] abattu. ◆ vt [sound] assourdir ; [colour, metal] ternir ; [blade, pleasure, senses, impression] émousser ; [grief] endormir. ◆ vi [colour] se ternir, perdre son éclat ; [pleasure] s'émousser ; [pain] s'atténuer ; [eyes] s'assombrir, perdre son éclat ; [mind] s'affaiblir, décliner.

dullness ['dʌlnɪs] n **1.** [slow-wittedness] lenteur f or lourdeur f d'esprit **2.** [tedium - of book, speech] caractère m ennuyeux **3.** [dimness - of light] faiblesse f ; [- of weather] caractère m maussade **4.** [of sound, pain] caractère m sourd ; [of blade] manque m de tranchant **5.** [listlessness] apathie f.

duly ['dju:lɪ] adv **1.** [properly] comme il convient ; [in accordance with the rules] dans les règles, dûment **2.** [as expected - arrive, call] comme prévu.

dumb [dʌm] adj **1.** [unable or unwilling to speak] muet **2.** inf [stupid] bête. ◆ **dumb down** vt insep [society, television programme] niveler par le bas.

dumbass ['dʌmæs] US v inf ◆ n taré m, -e f, débile mf. ◆ adj débile.

dumbbell ['dʌmbel] n SPORT haltère m.

dumbfound [dʌm'faund] vt abasourdir, interloquer.

dumbfounded [dʌm'faundɪd] adj [person] muet de stupeur, abasourdi, interloqué ; [silence] stupéfait ▶ **to be dumbfounded at** or **by sthg** être abasourdi or interloqué par qqch.

dumbing down ['dʌmɪŋ-] n nivellement m par le bas.

dumbstruck ['dʌmstrʌk] = **dumbfounded**.

dumb waiter n UK [lift] monte-plats m inv ; [trolley] table f roulante ; [revolving tray] plateau m tournant.

dumdum ['dʌmdʌm] n **1.** MIL [bullet] balle f dum-dum **2.** inf [fool] imbécile mf.

dummy ['dʌmɪ] (pl dummies) ◆ n **1.** [in shop window, for dressmaking] mannequin m ; [of ventriloquist] marionnette f ; FIN [representative] prête-nom m, homme m de paille **2.** [fake object] objet m factice ; [book, model for display] maquette f **3.** UK [for baby] tétine f **4.** inf [fool] imbécile mf **5.** SPORT feinte f. ◆ adj [fake] factice. ◆ **dummy up** vi US inf [remain quiet] : he decided to dummy up il a décidé de la boucler.

dummy issue n numéro m zéro.

dummy run n [trial] essai m ; AERON & MIL attaque f simulée or d'entraînement.

dump [dʌmp] ◆ vt **1.** [rubbish, waste] déverser, déposer ; [sand, gravel] déverser ; [car, corpse] abandonner ; [oil - subj: ship] vidanger **2.** [get rid of - boyfriend, girlfriend] plaquer ; [- member of government, board] se débarrasser de ▶ **to dump sb / sthg on sb** *inf* laisser qqn / qqch sur les bras de qqn **3.** [set - bags, shopping, suitcase] poser **4.** COMM vendre en dumping **5.** COMPUT [memory] vider. ◆ vi *inf* ▶ **to dump on sb** [criticize] débiner qqn. ◆ n **1.** [rubbish heap] tas m d'ordures ; [place] décharge f, dépôt m d'ordures **2.** MIL dépôt m **3.** *inf & pej* [town, village] trou m ; [messy room, flat] dépotoir m **4.** COMPUT [of memory] vidage m.

dumper truck ['dʌmpə-] 🇬🇧 dumper m, tombereau m.

dumping ['dʌmpɪŋ] n **1.** [of rubbish, waste] dépôt m or décharge f d'ordures or de déchets ; [of toxic or nuclear waste - at sea] déversement m or immersion f de déchets ; [- underground] entreposage m sous terre de déchets ; [of oil from ship] vidange f **2.** COMM dumping m **3.** COMPUT [of memory] vidage m.

dumping ground n [for rubbish] décharge f, dépôt m d'ordures ; *fig* [for inferior goods] dépotoir m.

dumpling ['dʌmplɪŋ] n **1.** CULIN [savoury] boulette f de pâte ; 🇬🇧 [sweet] variante du plum-pudding **2.** *inf* [plump person] boulot m, -otte f.

dumps [dʌmps] pl n *inf* ▶ **to be in the dumps** avoir le cafard or bourdon.

dump truck n 🇺🇸 = dumper truck.

dumpy ['dʌmpɪ] adj *inf* [person] courtaud ; [bottle] pansu.

dunce [dʌns] n âne m, cancre m.

dune [djuːn] n dune f.

dung [dʌŋ] n (U) crotte f ; [of cow] bouse f ; [of horse] crottin m ; [of wild animal] fumées fpl ; [manure] fumier m.

dungarees [ˌdʌŋɡə'riːz] pl n 🇬🇧 salopette f ; 🇺🇸 [overalls] bleu m de travail ▶ **a pair of dungarees a)** 🇬🇧 une salopette **b)** 🇺🇸 un bleu de travail.

dungeon ['dʌndʒən] n [underground] cachot m souterrain ; [tower] donjon m.

dunk [dʌŋk] vt [dip] tremper.

Dunkirk [dʌn'kɜːk] pr n GEOG Dunkerque.

dunno [də'nəʊ] *inf abbr of* I don't know.

dunny ['dʌnɪ] n 🇦🇺 *inf* [toilet] chiottes mpl.

duo ['djuːəʊ] n MUS & THEAT duo m ; [couple] couple m.

dupe [djuːp] ◆ vt duper, leurrer ▶ **to dupe sb into doing sthg** duper or leurrer qqn pour qu'il / elle fasse qqch. ◆ n dupe f.

duplex ['djuːpleks] ◆ adj **1.** [double, twofold] double ▶ **duplex apartment** (appartement m en) duplex m **2.** ELEC & TELEC duplex. ◆ n [apartment] (appartement m en) duplex m ; 🇺🇸 [house] maison convertie en deux appartements.

duplicate ◆ vt ['djuːplɪkeɪt] **1.** [document] dupliquer, faire un double or des doubles de ; [key] faire un double or des doubles de **2.** [repeat - work] refaire ; [- feat] reproduire. ◆ n ['djuːplɪkət] [of document, key] double m ; ADMIN & LAW duplicata m, copie f conforme ▶ **in duplicate** en double, en deux exemplaires. ◆ adj ['djuːplɪkət] [key, document] en double ; [receipt, certificate] en duplicata.

duplication [ˌdjuːplɪ'keɪʃn] n **1.** [on machine] reproduction f ; [result] double m **2.** [repetition - of work, efforts] répétition f.

duplicity [djuː'plɪsətɪ] n fausseté f, duplicité f.

Dur written abbr of Durham.

durability [ˌdjʊərə'bɪlətɪ] n [of construction, relationship, peace] caractère m durable, durabilité f ; [of fabric] résistance f ; [of politician, athlete] longévité f.

durable ['djʊərəbl] adj [construction, friendship, peace] durable ; [fabric, metal] résistant ; [politician, athlete] qui jouit d'une grande longévité ; COMM ▶ **durable goods** biens mpl durables or non périssables. ◆ **durables** pl n biens mpl durables or non périssables.

duration [djuː'reɪʃn] n durée f ▶ **for the duration of the summer holiday** pendant toute la durée des grandes vacances.

duress [djuː'res] n contrainte f ▶ **under duress** sous la contrainte.

Durex® ['djʊəreks] n **1.** 🇬🇧 [condom] préservatif m **2.** 🇦🇺 Scotch® m (ruban adhésif).

during ['djʊərɪŋ] prep pendant ; [in the course of] au cours de.

dusk [dʌsk] n crépuscule m ▶ **at dusk** au crépuscule.

dusky ['dʌskɪ] (compar duskier, superl duskiest) adj **1.** [light] crépusculaire ; [colour] sombre, foncé ; [room] sombre **2.** [skin] mat.

dust [dʌst] ◆ n **1.** (U) [on furniture, of gold, coal] poussière f **2.** [action] ▶ **to give sthg a dust** épousseter qqch **3.** [earthly remains] poussière f. ◆ vt **1.** [furniture, room] épousseter **2.** [with powder, flour] saupoudrer **3.** PHR **it's done and dusted a)** [the work is finished] c'est complètement terminé **b)** [the file is closed] l'affaire est classée. ◆ **dust down** vt sep [with brush] brosser ; [with hand] épousseter. ◆ **dust off** vt sep [dust, crumbs, dandruff] nettoyer, enlever ; *fig* [skill] se remettre à ; [speech, lecture notes] ressortir.

dust bag n [for vacuum cleaner] sac m à poussière.

dustbin ['dʌstbɪn] n 🇬🇧 poubelle f ▶ **dustbin lid** couvercle m de poubelle ▶ **dustbin liner** sac-poubelle m.

dustbin man 🇬🇧 = dustman.

dust bowl n GEOG zone f semi-désertique ; [in US] ▶ **the Dust Bowl** le Dust Bowl.

🚩 **The Dust Bowl**

Nom d'une région des Grandes Plaines aux États-Unis où sévissaient, dans les années 1930, de redoutables tempêtes de poussière provoquées par la sécheresse et l'érosion. Le changement climatique, ajouté à la dépression des années 1930, poussa des milliers de paysans à émigrer vers la Californie. C'est ce thème qu'on retrouve dans le roman de J. Steinbeck *les Raisins de la colère (The Grapes of Wrath)*.

dustcart ['dʌstkɑːt] n 🇬🇧 camion m des éboueurs.

dust cover n **1.** = dust jacket **2.** [for machine] housse f de rangement ; [for furniture] housse f de protection.

duster ['dʌstər] n **1.** [cloth] chiffon m (à poussière) ; [for blackboard] tampon m effaceur **2.** 🇺🇸 [garment - for doing housework] blouse f, tablier m ; [- for driving] cache-poussière m inv **3.** [lightweight coat] manteau m léger **4.** AGR poudreuse f ; [aircraft] avion servant à répandre de l'insecticide sur les champs.

dusting ['dʌstɪŋ] n **1.** [of room, furniture] époussetage m, dépoussiérage m ▶ **to do the dusting** épousseter, enlever or faire la poussière **2.** [with sugar, insecticide] saupoudrage m.

dust jacket n [for book] jaquette f.

dustman ['dʌstmən] (pl dustmen [-mən]) n 🇬🇧 éboueur m.

dustpan ['dʌstpæn] n pelle f à poussière.

dustproof ['dʌstpruːf] adj imperméable or étanche à la poussière.

dust sheet n UK housse f de protection.

dust storm n tempête f de poussière.

dust-up n inf accrochage m, prise f de bec.

dusty ['dʌstɪ] (compar dustier, superl dustiest) adj 1. [room, furniture, road] poussiéreux 2. [colour] cendré.

Dutch [dʌtʃ] ◆ pl n ▶ the Dutch les Hollandais mpl, les Néerlandais mpl. ◆ n LING néerlandais m. ◆ adj [cheese] de Hollande ; [bulbs, city] hollandais ; [embassy, government, etc.] néerlandais ; [dictionary, teacher] de néerlandais. ◆ adv ▶ to go Dutch (with sb) inf [share cost equally] partager les frais (avec qqn).

Dutch auction n vente f à la baisse.

Dutch barn n UK hangar m à armature métallique.

Dutch cap n diaphragme m (contraceptif).

Dutch courage n inf courage trouvé dans la boisson.

Dutchman ['dʌtʃmən] (pl Dutchmen [-mən]) n Hollandais m, Néerlandais m ▶ (then) I'm a Dutchman! fig je mange mon chapeau !

Dutchwoman ['dʌtʃ,wʊmən] (pl Dutchwomen [-,wɪmɪn]) n Hollandaise f, Néerlandaise f.

dutiable ['djuːtjəbl] adj taxable.

dutiful ['djuːtɪfʊl] adj [child] obéissant, respectueux ; [husband, wife] qui remplit ses devoirs conjugaux ; [worker, employee] consciencieux.

dutifully ['djuːtɪflɪ] adv consciencieusement.

duty ['djuːtɪ] n 1. [moral or legal obligation] devoir m ▶ to do one's duty (by sb) faire son devoir (envers qqn) 2. (usu pl) [responsibility] fonction f 3. [tax] taxe f, droit m 4. PHR [on duty] a) [soldier, doctor] de garde b) [policeman] de service ▶ to go on / off duty a) [soldier] prendre / laisser la garde b) [doctor] prendre la / cesser d'être de garde c) [policeman] prendre / quitter son service.

duty-bound adj tenu (par son devoir).

duty-free ◆ adj [goods] hors taxe, en franchise ; [shop] hors taxe. ◆ adv hors taxe, en franchise. ◆ n marchandises fpl hors taxe or en franchise.

duty officer n officier m de service.

duvet ['duːveɪ] n couette f ▶ duvet cover housse f de couette.

DVD (abbr of digital versatile or video disc) n DVD m.

DVD burner n graveur m de DVD.

DVD player n lecteur m de DVD.

DVD-ROM (abbr of digital versatile or video disc read only memory) n DVD-ROM m.

DVI (abbr of digital video interface) n DVI f.

DVLA (abbr of Driver and Vehicle Licensing Agency) pr n service des immatriculations et des permis de conduire en Grande-Bretagne.

DVM (abbr of Doctor of Veterinary Medicine) n UK docteur vétérinaire.

DVR (abbr of digital video recorder) n DVR m.

DVT n abbr of deep vein thrombosis.

dwarf [dwɔːf] (pl dwarfs or dwarves [dwɔːvz]) ◆ n 1. [person] nain m, -e f 2. [tree] arbre m nain 3. MYTH nain m, -e f. ◆ adj [plant, animal] nain. ◆ vt fig [in size] écraser ; [in ability] éclipser.

dweeb [dwiːb] n US inf pauvre mec m.

dwell [dwel] (pt & pp dwelt [dwelt] or dwelled) vi liter résider, demeurer. ◆ dwell on, dwell upon vt insep [the past - think about] penser sans cesse à ; [- talk about] parler sans cesse de ; [problem, fact, detail] s'attarder sur.

dwelling ['dwelɪŋ] n hum & liter résidence f.

dwelt [dwelt] pt & pp ⟶ dwell.

DWI (abbr of driving while intoxicated) n US [drunk driver] conducteur m, -trice f en état d'ébriété.

dwindle ['dwɪndl] vi [popularity, light] baisser ; [hopes, savings, population] se réduire, diminuer.

dwindling ['dwɪndlɪŋ] adj [population, audience] en baisse, décroissant ; [savings, hopes, popularity] décroissant.

DWP (abbr of Department of Work and Pensions) ministère britannique de la Sécurité sociale.

dye [daɪ] ◆ n [substance] teinture f ; [colour] teinte f, couleur f. ◆ vt [fabric, hair] teindre. ◆ vi [fabric] se teindre.

dyed [daɪd] adj teint(e).

dyed-in-the-wool [daɪd-] adj bon teint (inv).

dying ['daɪɪŋ] ◆ adj 1. [person, animal] mourant ; liter agonisant ; [tree, forest] mourant ; [species] en voie de disparition 2. fig [art, craft] en train de disparaître ; [industry] agonisant, en train de disparaître. ◆ n [death] mort f. ◆ pl n ▶ the dying les mourants mpl, les agonisants mpl.

dyke [daɪk] n 1. [against flooding] digue f ; [for carrying water away] fossé m ; Scot [wall] mur m 2. v inf [lesbian] gouine f.

dynamic [daɪˈnæmɪk] ◆ adj 1. [person] dynamique 2. TECH dynamique. ◆ n dynamique f.

dynamics [daɪˈnæmɪks] ◆ pl n [of a situation, group] dynamique f. ◆ n (U) TECH dynamique f.

dynamism ['daɪnəmɪzm] n [of person] dynamisme m.

dynamite ['daɪnəmaɪt] ◆ n [explosive] dynamite f ▶ this story is dynamite! fig cette histoire, c'est de la dynamite ! ▶ this band is dynamite! fig ce groupe est génial ! ◆ vt [blow up] dynamiter.

dynamo ['daɪnəməʊ] n TECH dynamo f.

dynasty [UK 'dɪnəstɪ US 'daɪnəstɪ] n dynastie f.

dysentery ['dɪsntrɪ] n (U) MED dysenterie f.

dysfunction [dɪsˈfʌŋkʃn] n MED dysfonction f, dysfonctionnement m.

dysfunctional [dɪsˈfʌŋkʃənl] adj dysfonctionnel.

dyslexia [dɪsˈleksɪə] n dyslexie f.

dyslexic [dɪsˈleksɪk] ◆ adj dyslexique. ◆ n dyslexique mf.

dyspepsia [dɪsˈpepsɪə] n (U) MED dyspepsie f.

E ◆ n **1.** MUS mi m ∕ **in E flat** en mi bémol **2.** (abbr of **ecstasy**) drugs sl [drug] ecstasy m ; [pill] comprimé m d'ecstasy. ◆ (written abbr of **East**) E.

ea. (written abbr of **each**) : *£3.00 ea.* 3 livres pièce.

e-account n compte m en banque en ligne.

each [iːʧ] ◆ det chaque ∕ *each day* chaque jour, tous les jours ∕ *each (and every) one of us ∕ you ∕ them* chacun ∕ chacune d'entre nous ∕ vous ∕ eux (sans exception). ◆ pron [every one] chacun, chacune ∕ *each of his six children* chacun de ses six enfants ∕ *a number of suggestions, each more crazy than the last* un certain nombre de suggestions toutes plus folles les unes que les autres ∕ *or would you like some of each?* ou bien voudriez-vous un peu de chaque ? ◆ adv [apiece] : *we have a book ∕ a room each* nous avons chacun un livre ∕ une pièce ∕ *the tickets cost £20 each* les billets coûtent 20 livres chacun. ◆ **each other** pron phr : *to hate each other* **a)** se détester (l'un l'autre) **b)** [more than two people] se détester (les uns les autres) ∕ *do you two know each other?* est-ce que vous vous connaissez ? ∕ *the two sisters wear each other's clothes* les deux sœurs échangent leurs vêtements.

eager [ˈiːgər] adj [impatient, keen] impatient ; [learner, helper] enthousiaste, fervent ; [crowd, face, look] passionné, enfiévré ▸ **to be eager to do sthg a)** [impatient] avoir hâte de faire qqch **b)** [very willing] faire preuve d'enthousiasme or de ferveur pour faire qqch.

eager beaver n inf travailleur m acharné, travailleuse f acharnée, mordu m, -e f du travail.

eagerly [ˈiːgəlɪ] adv [wait] impatiemment ; [help] avec empressement ; [say, look at] avec passion or enthousiasme.

eagerness [ˈiːgənɪs] n [to know, see, find out] impatience f ; [to help] empressement m ; [in eyes, voice] excitation f, enthousiasme m.

eagle [ˈiːgl] n **1.** [bird] aigle m **2.** [standard, seal] aigle f **3.** [lectern] aigle m **4.** GOLF eagle m.

eagle-eyed ◆ adj aux yeux de lynx. ◆ adv [watch] avec une grande attention.

eaglet [ˈiːglɪt] n aiglon m, -onne f.

E and OE (written abbr of **errors and omissions excepted**) UK s e & o.

ear [ɪər] n **1.** [of person, animal] oreille f **2.** [of grain] épi m.

earache [ˈɪəreɪk] n mal m d'oreille ∕ *to have earache* UK or *an earache* avoir mal à l'oreille.

earbashing [ˈɪəbæʃɪŋ] n UK inf : *to give sb an earbashing* passer un savon à qqn, souffler dans les bronches à qqn.

ear buds pl n oreillettes fpl.

eardrum [ˈɪədrʌm] n tympan m.

-eared [ɪəd] in comp ▸ **long ∕ short-eared** à oreilles fpl longues ∕ courtes ▸ **pointy-eared** inf aux oreilles en pointe.

earful [ˈɪəfʊl] n ▸ **to give sb an earful** inf [tell off] passer un savon à qqn ▸ **to give sb an earful about sthg** US [say a lot to] raconter qqch à qqn en long, en large et en travers.

earl [ɜːl] n comte m.

earlier [ˈɜːlɪə] comparl → **early**.

earliest [ˈɜːlɪəst] superl → **early**.

earlobe [ˈɪələʊb] n lobe m de l'oreille.

early [ˈɜːlɪ] (compar **earlier**, superl **earliest**) ◆ adj **1.** [morning] matinal ∕ *I had an early breakfast* j'ai déjeuné de bonne heure ▸ **to get off to an early start** partir de bonne heure ∕ *it's too early to get up* il est trop tôt pour se lever ▸ **to be an early riser** être matinal or un lève-tôt **2.** [belonging to the beginning of a period of time - machine, film, poem] premier ; [- Edwardian, Victorian, etc.] du début de l'époque ∕ *in the early afternoon ∕ spring ∕ fifties* au début de l'après-midi ∕ du printemps ∕ des années cinquante ∕ *I need an early night* je dois me coucher de bonne heure ∕ *it's too early to tell* il est trop tôt pour se prononcer, on ne peut encore rien dire ∕ *the early Roman Empire* l'Empire romain naissant ∕ *an early Picasso* une des premières œuvres de Picasso ∕ *he's in his early twenties* il a une vingtaine d'années ∕ *from an early age* dès l'enfance ∕ *in the early stages of the project* dans une phase initiale du projet **3.** [ahead of time] ▸ **to be early** [person, train, flight, winter] être en avance ∕ *let's have an early lunch* déjeunons de bonne heure ∕ *you're too early* vous arrivez trop tôt, vous êtes en avance ∕ *Easter is early this year* Pâques est de bonne heure cette année **4.** [relating to the future - reply] prochain ∕ *at your earliest convenience* COMM dans les meilleurs délais. ◆ adv **1.** [in the morning - rise, leave] tôt, de bonne heure ∕ *let's set off as early as we can* mettons-nous en route le plus tôt possible **2.** [at the beginning of a period of time] : *early in the evening ∕ in the afternoon* tôt le soir ∕ (dans) l'après-midi ∕ *early in the year ∕ winter* au début de l'année ∕ de l'hiver ∕ *I can't make it earlier than 2.30* je ne peux pas avant 14 h 30 ▸ **early on** tôt ▸ **earlier on** plus tôt **3.** [ahead of schedule] en avance ; [earlier than usual] de bonne heure.

early bird n ▸ **to be an early bird** inf être matinal.

early closing n UK COMM jour où l'on ferme tôt.

early retirement n retraite f anticipée.

early-warning adj ▸ **early-warning system** système m de pré-alerte.

earmark [ˈɪəmɑːk] ◆ vt réserver ; [money] affecter, assigner. ◆ n **1.** [mark in ear] marque f à l'oreille **2.** US POL fonds fédéraux alloués à des projets spécifiques.

earmuffs [ˈɪəmʌfs] pl n protège-oreille m.

earn [ɜːn] ◆ vt **1.** [money] gagner ; [interest] rapporter **2.** [respect, punishment - subj: activities] valoir ; [- subj: person] mériter. ◆ vi [person] gagner de l'argent ; [investment] rapporter ▸ **earning capacity a)** [of person] potentiel *m* de revenu **b)** [of firm] rentabilité *f*.

earned income credit n 🇺🇸 aide aux foyers à faible revenu, prélevée sur les salaires.

earner ['ɜːnər] n **1.** [person] salarié *m*, -e *f* **2.** 🇬🇧 inf [source of income] : *it's a nice little earner* [business, shop, etc.] c'est une bonne petite affaire.

earnest ['ɜːnɪst] adj **1.** [person, expression, tone] sérieux **2.** [hope, request] ardent, fervent ; [endeavour] fervent ; [desire] profond. ❖ **in earnest** ◆ adv phr [seriously] sérieusement, sincèrement ; [in a determined way] sérieusement. ◆ adj phr ▸ **to be in earnest** être sérieux.

earnestly ['ɜːnɪstlɪ] adv [behave] sérieusement ; [study, work] sérieusement, avec ardeur ; [speak, nod, look at] gravement.

earnestness ['ɜːnɪstnɪs] n sérieux *m*, gravité *f*.

earnings ['ɜːnɪŋz] pl n [of person, business] revenus *mpl*.

earnings-related adj proportionnel au revenu.

earphones ['ɪəfəʊnz] pl n écouteurs *mpl*, casque *m*.

earpiece ['ɪəpiːs] n [of telephone receiver, personal stereo] écouteur *m*.

earplugs ['ɪəplʌgz] pl n [for sleeping] boules *fpl* Quiès ; [for protection against water, noise] protège-tympans *mpl*.

earring ['ɪərɪŋ] n boucle *f* d'oreille.

earshot ['ɪəʃɒt] n ▸ **out of / within earshot** hors de / à portée de voix.

ear-splitting adj [noise] assourdissant.

earth [ɜːθ] ◆ n **1.** [the world, the planet] terre *f* ▸ **the planet Earth** la planète Terre / *on earth* sur terre ▸ **why / how / who on earth?** pourquoi / comment / qui diable ? **2.** [ground] terre *f* / *to fall to earth* tomber par terre **3.** [soil] terre *f* **4.** 🇬🇧 ELEC [connection, terminal] terre *f* **5.** [of fox] terrier *m*, tanière *f*. ◆ vt 🇬🇧 ELEC relier à la terre.

earthed [ɜːθt] adj 🇬🇧 ELEC mis à la terre.

earthenware ['ɜːθnweər] ◆ n [pottery] poterie *f* ; [glazed] faïence *f*. ◆ adj en or de terre (cuite), en or de faïence.

Earth-friendly adj écologique, qui respecte l'environnement.

earthling ['ɜːθlɪŋ] n terrien *m*, -enne *f*.

earthly ['ɜːθlɪ] ◆ adj **1.** [worldly] terrestre **2.** inf [possible] : *there's no earthly reason why I should believe you* je n'ai absolument aucune raison de te croire. ◆ n 🇬🇧 inf [chance] : *he doesn't have an earthly of passing the exam* il n'a aucune chance de réussir à l'examen.

earth mother n **1.** MYTH déesse *f* de la Terre **2.** inf & fig mère *f* nourricière.

earthquake ['ɜːθkweɪk] n tremblement *m* de terre.

earth sciences pl n sciences *fpl* de la Terre.

earth-shaking [-ˌʃeɪkɪŋ], **earth-shattering** adj inf fracassant, extraordinaire.

earth tremor n secousse *f* sismique.

earthwards ['ɜːθwədz] adv en direction de la Terre.

earthwork(s) ['ɜːθwɜːk(s)] pl n CONSTR terrassement *m* ; ARCHEOL & MIL fortification *f* en terre.

earthworm ['ɜːθwɜːm] n ver *m* de terre, lombric *m*.

earthy ['ɜːθɪ] adj **1.** [taste, smell] de terre **2.** [humour] truculent ; [person, character] direct **3.** [wine] aux arômes de terre.

E2EG MESSAGING written abbr of **ear to ear grin**.

earwax ['ɪəwæks] n cire *f* (sécrétée par les oreilles), cérumen *m*.

earwig ['ɪəwɪg] n perce-oreille *m*.

earworm ['ɪəwɜːm] n inf air accrocheur qu'on n'arrive pas à se sortir de la tête.

ease [iːz] ◆ n **1.** [comfort] aise *f* ▸ **to be** or **to feel at ease** être ou se sentir à l'aise **2.** [facility] facilité *f* ; [of movements] aisance *f* ▸ **to do sthg with ease** faire qqch facilement or aisément **3.** [affluence] ▸ **to live a life of ease** avoir la belle vie, mener une vie facile. ◆ vt **1.** [alleviate - anxiety, worry] calmer ; [- pain] calmer, soulager ; [- pressure, tension] relâcher ; [- traffic flow] rendre plus fluide ; [- sb's workload] alléger **2.** [move gently] ▸ **to ease sthg out** faire sortir qqch délicatement ▸ **to ease sb out** [from position, job] pousser qqn vers la sortie fig. ◆ vi [pain] se calmer, s'adoucir ; [situation, tension, rain] se calmer. ❖ **ease back** vt sep [throttle, lever] tirer doucement. ❖ **ease off** ◆ vt sep [lid, bandage] enlever délicatement. ◆ vi [rain] se calmer ; [business] ralentir ; [traffic] diminuer ; [tension] se relâcher. ❖ **ease up** vi [slow - in car] ralentir ; [rain] se calmer ; [business, work] ralentir ; [traffic] diminuer ▸ **to ease up on sb / sthg** y aller doucement avec qqn / qqch.

easel ['iːzl] n chevalet *m*.

easement ['iːzmənt] n LAW servitude *f*.

easily ['iːzɪlɪ] adv **1.** [without difficulty] facilement **2.** [undoubtedly] sans aucun doute **3.** [very possibly] : *he could easily change his mind* il pourrait bien changer d'avis **4.** [in a relaxed manner - talk] de manière décontractée ; [- smile, answer] d'un air décontracté.

easiness ['iːzɪnɪs] n **1.** [lack of difficulty] facilité *f* **2.** [relaxed nature] décontraction *f*.

east [iːst] ◆ n est *m* ▸ **the East a)** [the Orient] l'Orient *m* **b)** [Eastern Europe] l'Est *m* **c)** [in US] l'Est *m* (États situés à l'est du Mississippi) ▸ **East-West relations** relations *fpl* Est-Ouest / *on the east of the island* à l'est de l'île / *to the east of the mainland* à l'est ou au large de la côte est du continent / *the wind is (coming) from the east* le vent vient de l'est. ◆ adj [coast, shore, face of mountain] est, oriental ; [wind] d'est. ◆ adv [go, look, travel] en direction de l'est, vers l'est ; [sail] cap vers l'est / *further east* plus à l'est / *east of* à l'est de ▸ **back east** 🇺🇸 inf dans l'est (des États-Unis).

eastbound ['iːstbaʊnd] adj [traffic, train] en direction de l'est.

East End n [of city] quartiers *mpl* est ▸ **the East End** quartier industriel de Londres, connu pour ses docks et, autrefois, pour sa pauvreté.

Easter ['iːstər] ◆ n Pâques *fpl*. ◆ comp [holiday, Sunday, weekend] de Pâques ; [week] de Pâques, pascal ; [celebrations] pascal ▸ **Easter Day** (jour *m* de) Pâques.

Easter basket n 🇺🇸 panier de friandises présenté aux enfants comme étant un cadeau de l'Easter bunny.

Easter bunny n [gen] lapin *m* de Pâques ; [in the US] personnage imaginaire qui distribue des friandises aux enfants.

Easter egg n **1.** [egg] œuf *m* de Pâques **2.** COMPUT fonction *f* cachée, Easter egg *m*.

Easter Island pr n l'île *f* de Pâques / *in* or *on Easter Island* dans l'île de Pâques.

easterly ['iːstəlɪ] ◆ adj [in the east] situé à l'est ; [from the east] d'est ; [to the east] vers l'est, en direction de l'est. ◆ n vent *m* d'est.

eastern ['iːstən] adj [Europe] de l'Est ; [France, Scotland, etc.] de l'Est ; [region, seaboard] est, oriental ; [culture, philosophy] oriental ▸ **eastern hemisphere** hémisphère *m* oriental ▸ **the Eastern Bloc** le bloc de l'Est ▸ **the Eastern Establishment** 🇺🇸 l'élite *f* de la côte Est.

Easterner ['iːstənər] n **1.** [in US] personne qui vient de l'est des États-Unis **2.** [oriental] Oriental *m*, -e *f*.

East German ◆ adj est-allemand, d'Allemagne de l'Est. ◆ n Allemand *m*, -e *f* de l'Est.

East Germany pr n ▶ **(former) East Germany** (l'ex-) Allemagne *f* de l'Est ✲ *in East Germany* en Allemagne de l'Est.

east-northeast ◆ n est-nord-est *m*. ◆ adj [direction] est-nord-est ; [wind] d'est-nord-est. ◆ adv en direction de l'est-nord-est ; [blow] d'est-nord-est.

east-southeast ◆ n est-sud-est *m*. ◆ adj [direction] est-sud-est ; [wind] d'est-sud-est. ◆ adv en direction de l'est-sud-est ; [blow] d'est-sud-est.

eastward ['iːstwəd] ◆ adj est. ◆ adv = **eastwards**.

eastwards ['iːstwədz] adv en direction de l'est, vers l'est.

easy ['iːzɪ] (*compar* easier, *superl* easiest) ◆ adj **1.** [not difficult] facile ✲ *it's easy to see why* / *that…* on voit bien pourquoi / que… ✲ *it's easy to say that…* c'est facile de dire que… **2.** [at peace] ▶ **to feel easy in one's mind** être tranquille, avoir l'esprit tranquille **3.** [easygoing -person, atmosphere] décontracté ; [- disposition, nature] facile ; [- manner] décontracté, naturel ; [- style] coulant, facile ✲ *I'm easy inf* [I don't mind] ça m'est égal **4.** [sexually] : *she's an easy lay* v *inf* & *pej* elle couche avec tout le monde, c'est une Marie-couche-toi-là **5.** [pleasant] ▶ **to be easy on the eye a)** [film, painting] être agréable à regarder **b)** [person] être un plaisir pour les yeux. ◆ adv [in a relaxed or sparing way] doucement ▶ **to go easy on** or **with sb** y aller doucement avec qqn ▶ **to go easy on** or **with sthg** y aller doucement avec or sur qqch ▶ **he's got it easy** *inf* [has an easy life] il se la coule douce, il a la belle vie ▶ **take it easy! a)** [gen] doucement ! **b)** 🇺🇸 [on parting] bon courage ! ▶ **to take things** or **it** or **life easy** [relax] se reposer.

easy-care adj d'entretien facile.

easy chair n fauteuil *m*.

easygoing [iːzɪgəʊɪŋ] adj [person] décontracté, facile à vivre ; [lifestyle] décontracté.

easy listening n MUS variété *f*.

easy-peasy n fastoche *inf*, facile.

eat [iːt] (*pt* ate [et or eɪt], *pp* eaten ['iːtn]) ◆ vt manger ✲ *to eat (one's) breakfast* / *lunch* / *dinner* prendre son petit déjeuner / déjeuner / dîner ✲ *would you like something to eat?* voulez-vous manger quelque chose ? ◆ vi manger ✲ *let's eat* à table. ✲ **eats** *pl* n *inf* bouffe *f*. ✲ **eat away** ◆ vt sep [subj: waves] ronger ; [subj: mice] ronger ; [subj: acid, rust] ronger, corroder ; *fig* [confidence] miner ; [support, capital, resources] entamer. ◆ vi [person] manger. ✲ **eat away at** vt insep = **eat away** (*vt sep*). ✲ **eat in** vt manger chez soi or à la maison. ✲ **eat into** vt insep **1.** [destroy] attaquer **2.** [use up -savings] entamer ; [- time] empiéter sur. ✲ **eat out** ◆ vi sortir déjeuner or dîner, aller au restaurant. ◆ vt sep ▶ **to eat one's heart out** se morfondre. ✲ **eat up** ◆ vi manger. ◆ vt sep [food] terminer, finir ; *fig* [electricity, gas, petrol] consommer beaucoup de ▶ **to be eaten up with** [jealousy, hate, ambition] être rongé or dévoré par.

eatable ['iːtəbl] adj [fit to eat] mangeable ; [edible] comestible.

eaten ['iːtn] pp —→ **eat**.

eater ['iːtər] n **1.** [person] mangeur *m*, -euse *f* **2.** 🇬🇧 *inf* [apple] pomme *f* à couteau.

eatery ['iːtərɪ] n restaurant *m*.

eating ['iːtɪŋ] ◆ n : *eating is one of his favourite pastimes* manger constitue un de ses passe-temps favoris. ◆ adj **1.** [for eating] ▶ **eating apple** / **pear** pomme *f* / poire *f* à couteau ▶ **eating place** or **house** restaurant *m* **2.** [of eating] ▶ **eating habits** habitudes *fpl* alimentaires ▶ **eating disorder** trouble *m* du comportement alimentaire.

eau de Cologne [ˌəʊdəkə'ləʊn] n eau *f* de Cologne.

eaves ['iːvz] pl n avant-toit *m*, corniche *f*.

eavesdrop ['iːvzdrɒp] (*pt & pp* eavesdropped, *cont* eavesdropping) vi écouter de manière indiscrète, espionner.

e-banking n services *mpl* bancaires en ligne.

ebb [eb] ◆ n [of tide] reflux *m* ; [of public opinion] variations *fpl*. ◆ vi **1.** [tide] baisser, descendre **2.** *fig* = **ebb away**. ✲ **ebb away** vi [confidence, enthusiasm, strength, etc.] baisser peu à peu ; [completely] disparaître.

ebb tide n marée *f* descendante.

Ebola [ɪ'bələ] n MED (virus *m*) Ebola *m*.

Ebonics n *argot des Noirs américains dans les quartiers défavorisés.*

ebony ['ebənɪ] ◆ n [tree] ébénier *m* ; [wood] ébène *m*. ◆ adj [chair, table, etc.] en ébène ; *fig* [eyes, hair] d'ébène.

e-book n livre *m* électronique, e-book *m*.

e-broker n FIN courtier *m*, -ère *f* en ligne.

ebullient [ɪ'bʊljənt] adj exubérant.

e-business n (U) commerce *m* en ligne, e-business *m*.

EBV (abbr of Epstein-Barr Virus) n EBV *m*.

EC (abbr of European Community) ◆ n CE *f*. ◆ comp [ruling, states, membership] de la CE.

e-card n COMPUT carte *f* électronique.

e-cash n monnaie *f* électronique.

ECB (abbr of European Central Bank) n BCE *f*.

eccentric [ɪk'sentrɪk] ◆ adj **1.** [person, clothes, behaviour] excentrique **2.** ASTRON, MATH & TECH excentré. ◆ n [person] excentrique *mf*.

eccentrically [ɪk'sentrɪklɪ] adv **1.** [dress, talk] de manière excentrique **2.** ASTRON, MATH & TECH excentriquement.

eccentricity [ˌeksen'trɪsətɪ] (*pl* eccentricities) n excentricité *f*.

ecclesiastical [ɪˌkliːzɪ'æstɪkl] adj [robes, traditions, calendar] ecclésiastique ; [history] de l'Église ; [music] d'église.

ECG n **1.** (abbr of electrocardiogram) ECG *m* **2.** (abbr of electrocardiograph) ECG *m*.

echelon ['eʃəlɒn] n **1.** [level] échelon *m* **2.** MIL échelon *m*.

echo ['ekəʊ] (*pl* echoes) ◆ n écho *m*. ◆ vt [sound] répéter ; *fig* [colour, theme] reprendre, rappeler ; [architecture, style] rappeler, évoquer. ◆ vi [noise, voice, music] résonner ; [place] faire écho, résonner.

echocardiogram [ˌekəʊ'kɑːdɪəʊgræm] n échocardiogramme *m*.

éclair [eɪ'kleər] n CULIN éclair *m*.

eclectic [ɪ'klektɪk] ◆ n éclectique *mf*. ◆ adj éclectique.

eclipse [ɪ'klɪps] ◆ n ASTRON & *fig* éclipse *f*. ◆ vt ASTRON & *fig* éclipser.

eclogue ['eklɒg] n LITER églogue *f*.

eco- ['iːkəʊ] (abbr of ecology or ecological) pref éco-.

ecofreak ['iːkəʊfriːk] n *inf* écologiste enragé *m*, écologiste enragée *f*.

eco-friendly [ˌiːkəʊ-] adj qui respecte l'environnement.

eco-hazard n substance *f* toxique.

eco-house n maison *f* écologique.

eco-label n écolabel *m*.

eco-labelling n 🇬🇧 attribution *f* d'écolabels.

E-coli [ˌiː'kəʊlaɪ] n MED E-coli *m*, bactérie *f* Escherichia coli.

ecological [ˌiːkə'lɒʤɪkl] adj écologique.

ecologically [ˌiːkə'lɒʤɪklɪ] adv écologiquement.

ecologist [ɪ'kɒləʤɪst] n **1.** [expert] écologue *mf* **2.** [supporter] écologiste *mf*.

ecology [ɪ'kɒləʤɪ] n écologie *f*.

e-commerce [ˌiː-] n commerce *m* électronique, cyber-commerce *m*.

economic [ˌiːkə'nɒmɪk] adj **1.** ECON [climate, growth, system, indicator] économique **2.** [profitable] rentable.

economical [ˌiːkə'nɒmɪkl] adj [person] économe ; [machine, method, approach] économique ▶ **to be economical with sthg** économiser qqch.

economically [ˌiːkə'nɒmɪklɪ] adv **1.** ECON économiquement **2.** [live] de manière économe ; [write] avec sobriété ; [use] de manière économe, avec parcimonie.

Economic and Monetary Union n Union *f* économique et monétaire.

economics [ˌiːkə'nɒmɪks] ◆ n *(U)* [science] économie *f* (politique), sciences *fpl* économiques. ◆ pl n [financial aspects] aspect *m* économique.

economist [ɪ'kɒnəmɪst] n économiste *mf* ▶ **the Economist** PRESS hebdomadaire britannique politique, économique et financier.

economize [ɪ'kɒnəmaɪz] vi économiser, faire des économies ▶ **to economize on sthg** économiser sur qqch.

economy [ɪ'kɒnəmɪ] *(pl* **economies)** ◆ n **1.** [system] économie *f* **2.** [saving] économie *f* ▶ **economies of scale** économies d'échelle ▶ **false economy** fausse économie. ◆ comp [pack] économique ▶ **economy car** aux États-Unis, voiture de taille moyenne, consommant peu par rapport aux «grosses américaines» ▶ **economy class** classe *f* touriste. ◆ adv [fly, travel] en classe touriste.

economy-class syndrome n syndrome *m* de la classe économique.

economy-size(d) adj [pack, jar] taille économique *(inv)*.

ecopolitics ['iːkəʊ,pɒlɪtɪks] n *(U)* politique *f* et environnement *m (sujet d'étude)*.

ecosystem ['iːkəʊ,sɪstəm] n écosystème *m*.

ecotax ['iːkəʊtæks] n écotaxe *f*.

ecoterrorism n écoterrorisme *m*.

ecoterrorist ['iːkəʊ,terərɪst] n écoterroriste *mf*.

eco-tourism ['iːkəʊ-] n écotourisme *m*, tourisme *m* vert.

eco-warrior ['iːkəʊ-] n éco-guerrier *m*, -ère *f*.

ecstasy ['ekstəsɪ] *(pl* **ecstasies)** n **1.** extase *f*, ravissement *m* **2.** [drug] ecstasy *f*.

ecstatic [ek'stætɪk] adj ravi ▶ **to be ecstatic about sthg / sb a)** [in admiration] être en extase devant qqch / qqn **b)** [with joy] être ravi de qqch / qqn.

ecstatically [ek'stætɪklɪ] adv avec extase.

ECT n abbr of electroconvulsive therapy.

ectoplasm ['ektəplæzm] n ectoplasme *m*.

Ecuador ['ekwədɔːr] pr n Équateur *m / in Ecuador* en Équateur.

Ecuadoran [ˌekwə'dɔːrən], **Ecuadorian** [ˌekwə'dɔːrɪən] ◆ n Équatorien *m*, -enne *f*. ◆ adj équatorien.

ecumenical [iːkjuː'menɪkl] adj œcuménique.

eczema [ɪg'ziːmə] n MED eczéma *m*.

ed. ◆ **1.** (written abbr of edited) sous la dir. de, coll. **2.** (written abbr of edition) éd., édit. ◆ n (abbr of editor) éd., édit.

Edam ['iːdæm] n édam *m*.

eddy ['edɪ] *(pl* **eddies)** ◆ n tourbillon *m*. ◆ vi tourbillonner.

edema US = **oedema**.

Eden ['iːdn] pr n BIBLE Éden *m* ; *fig* éden *m*.

edge [edʒ] ◆ n **1.** [of blade] fil *m*, tranchant *m* **2.** [outer limit - of table, cliff, road] bord *m* ; [- of page] bord *m*, marge *f* ; [- of forest] lisière *f*, orée *f* ; [- of coin, book] tranche *f* ; [- of ski] carre *f*. ◆ vt **1.** [give a border to] border ▶ **to edge sthg with sthg** border qqch de qqch **2.** [sharpen] aiguiser, affiler, affûter **3.** [move gradually] ▶ **to edge one's way** avancer or progresser lentement. ◆ vi avancer or progresser lentement. ◈ **on edge** adj & adv phr : *to be on edge* être énervé or sur les nerfs. ◈ **edge out** ◆ vt sep ▶ **to edge sb out of a job** pousser qqn vers la sortie en douceur. ◆ vi sortir lentement. ◈ **edge up** ◆ vt sep ▶ **to edge prices up** faire monter les prix doucement. ◆ vi **1.** [prices] monter doucement **2.** [approach slowly] ▶ **to edge up to sb / sthg** s'avancer lentement vers qqn / qqch.

-edged [edʒd] in comp ▶ **double-edged a)** [blade, knife, sword] à double tranchant, à deux tranchants **b)** *fig* [compliment, remark] à double tranchant ▶ **sharp-edged** bien affilé or aiguisé.

edger ['edʒər] n [gardening tool] taille-bordures *m*.

edgeways UK ['edʒweɪz], **edgewise** US ['edʒwaɪz] adv de côté.

edgily ['edʒɪlɪ] adv nerveusement.

edginess ['edʒɪnɪs] n **1.** [nervousness] nervosité *f* **2.** [modernity] caractère *m* ultra-contemporain.

edging ['edʒɪŋ] n [border - on dress, of flowers, etc.] bordure *f*.

edgy ['edʒɪ] *(compar* edgier, *superl* edgiest*)* adj **1.** [nervous] nerveux, sur les nerfs **2.** [contemporary] ultra-contemporain.

edible ['edɪbl] adj [mushroom, berry] comestible.

edict ['iːdɪkt] n POL décret *m* ; *fig* ordre *m*.

edifice ['edɪfɪs] n *lit & fig* édifice *m*.

edify ['edɪfaɪ] *(pt & pp* edified*)* vt *fml* édifier.

edifying ['edɪfaɪɪŋ] adj *fml* édifiant.

Edinburgh ['edɪnbrə] pr n Édimbourg ▶ **the Edinburgh Festival** le Festival d'Édimbourg.

🚩 **Edinburgh Festival**

Le Festival international d'Édimbourg, créé en 1947, est aujourd'hui l'un des plus grands festivals de théâtre et de musique du monde; il a lieu chaque année d'août à septembre. Le festival « off » **(Fringe)** est une grande rencontre du théâtre expérimental.

---

edit ['edɪt] ◆ n [of text] révision *f*, correction *f*. ◆ vt **1.** [correct - article, book] corriger, réviser ; [COMPUT - file] éditer ; [prepare for release - book, article] éditer, préparer pour la publication ; [- film, TV programme, tape] monter **2.** [be in charge of - review, newspaper] diriger la rédaction de. ◈ **edit out** vt sep couper, supprimer.

editing ['edɪtɪŋ] n [of newspaper, magazine] rédaction *f* ; [initial corrections] révision *f*, correction *f* ; [in preparation for publication] édition *f*, préparation *f* à la publication ; [of film, tape] montage *m* ; COMPUT [of file] édition *f*.

edition [ɪ'dɪʃn] n [of book, newspaper] édition *f*.

editor ['edɪtər] n **1.** [of newspaper, review] rédacteur *m*, -trice *f* en chef ; [of author] éditeur *m*, -trice *f* ; [of dictionary] rédacteur *m*, -trice *f* ; [of book, article - who makes corrections] correcteur *m*, -trice *f* ; [- who writes] rédacteur *m*, -trice *f* ; [of film] monteur *m*, -euse *f* **2.** COMPUT éditeur *m*.

editorial [ˌedɪ'tɔːrɪəl] ◆ adj PRESS [decision, comment] de la rédaction ; [job, problems, skills] de rédaction, rédactionnel ▶ **editorial freedom** liberté *f* éditoriale. ◆ n PRESS éditorial *m*.

editor-in-chief n rédacteur *m*, -trice *f* en chef.

EDP n abbr of **electronic data processing**.

EDT n abbr of **Eastern Daylight Time**.

educate ['edʒʊkeɪt] vt [pupil] instruire, donner une éducation à ; [mind, tastes, palate] éduquer, former ; [customers, public] éduquer.

educated ['edʒʊkeɪtɪd] adj [person] instruit ; [voice] distingué.

education [,edʒʊ'keɪʃn] ◆ n **1.** éducation *f* ; [teaching] enseignement *m* **2.** PHR adult or **continuing education** formation *f* continue ▸ **higher** or **university education** enseignement *m* supérieur or universitaire ▸ **Minister of** or **Secretary of State for Education** UK ministre *m* de l'Éducation ▸ **primary / secondary education** (enseignement *m*) primaire *m* / secondaire *m*. ◆ comp [costs, budget] de l'éducation ▸ **the education system** le système éducatif ▸ **(local) education authority** UK ≃ académie *f* régionale.

educational [,edʒʊ'keɪʃənl] adj [programme, system] éducatif ; [establishment] d'éducation, d'enseignement ; [books, publisher] scolaire ; [method, film, visit, TV] éducatif, pédagogique ▸ **educational qualifications** qualifications *fpl*, diplômes *mpl*.

educationalist [,edʒʊ'keɪʃnəlɪst] n pédagogue *mf*.

educationally [,edʒʊ'keɪʃnəlɪ] adv d'un point de vue éducatif.

educative ['edʒʊkətɪv] adj éducatif.

educator ['edʒʊkeɪtər] n US éducateur *m*, -trice *f*.

edutainment ◆ n [games] jeux *mpl* éducatifs ; [TV programmes] émissions *fpl* éducatives pour les enfants ; [software] logiciels *mpl* ludo-éducatifs. ◆ adj ludo-éducatif.

Edwardian [ed'wɔ:dɪən] adj [architecture, design] édouardien, de style Édouard VII, (des années) 1900 ; [society, gentleman] de l'époque d'Édouard VII, des années 1900 ▸ **Edwardian style** style *m* Édouard VII.

EEA (abbr of **European Economic Area**) n EEE *m*.

e-economy n économie *f* en ligne.

EEG n **1.** (abbr of **electroencephalogram**) EEG *m* **2.** (abbr of **electroencephalograph**) EEG *m*.

eejit ['i:dʒɪt] n IR & Scot inf idiot *m*, -e *f*, andouille *f*.

eek [i:k] interj inf hi.

eel [i:l] n anguille *f*.

EEPROM ['i:prɒm] (abbr of **electrically erasable programmable ROM**) n COMPUT EEPROM *f*.

eerie ['ɪərɪ] (*compar* eerier, *superl* eeriest) adj [house, silence, sound] inquiétant, sinistre.

eerily ['ɪərəlɪ] adv sinistrement, d'une manière sinistre.

eery ['ɪərɪ] (*compar* eerier, *superl* eeriest) = eerie.

EET n abbr of **Eastern European Time**.

eew [i:w] excl US beurk inf.

efface [ɪ'feɪs] vt lit & fig effacer ▸ **to efface o.s.** s'effacer.

effect [ɪ'fekt] ◆ n **1.** [of action, law] effet *m* ; [of chemical, drug, weather] effet *m*, action *f* ▸ **to have an effect on** avoir or produire un effet sur ▸ **to take effect** [drug] (commencer à) faire effet **2.** [meaning] sens *m* ▸ **to this** or **that effect** dans ce sens **3.** [impression] effet *m* **4.** THEAT ▸ **stage effects** effets *mpl* de scène. ◆ vt fml [reform] effectuer ; [sale, purchase] réaliser, effectuer ; [improvement] apporter ; [cure, rescue, reconciliation] mener à bien. ◆ **effects** pl n fml ▸ **household effects** articles *mpl* ménagers ▸ **personal effects** effets *mpl* personnels. ◆ **in effect** ◆ adj phr [law, system] en vigueur. ◆ adv phr [in fact] en fait, en réalité.

effective [ɪ'fektɪv] adj **1.** [which works well - measure, treatment, advertising, etc.] efficace ; [- worker, manager] efficace ; [- argument] qui porte ; [- service, system] qui fonc-

tionne bien ; [- disguise] réussi **2.** ADMIN & FIN : *effective as from January 1st* [law] en vigueur or applicable à compter du 1ᵉʳ janvier / *to become effective* entrer en vigueur **3.** [actual] véritable **4.** [creating effect - colour, illustration] qui fait de l'effet.

effectively [ɪ'fektɪvlɪ] adv **1.** [efficiently - work, run, manage] efficacement **2.** [successfully] avec succès **3.** [in fact] en réalité, en fait **4.** [impressively] d'une manière impressionnante.

effectiveness [ɪ'fektɪvnɪs] n **1.** [efficiency - of treatment, advertising] efficacité *f* ; [- of undertaking, attempt] succès *m* **2.** [effect - of entrance, gesture, colour] effet *m*.

effeminate [ɪ'femɪnət] adj [man, voice] efféminé.

effervesce [,efə'ves] vi [liquid] être en effervescence ; [wine] pétiller ; [gas] s'échapper (d'un liquide) par effervescence ; fig [person] déborder de vie.

effervescence [,efə'vesns] n [of liquid] effervescence *f* ; [of wine] pétillement *m* ; fig [of person] vitalité *f*, pétulance *f* ; [of personality] pétulance *f*.

effervescent [,efə'vesənt] adj [liquid] effervescent ; [wine] pétillant ; fig [person] débordant de vie, pétulant ; [personality] pétulant.

effete [ɪ'fi:t] adj fml [weak - person] mou *(before vowel or silent 'h' mol, f molle)* ; [- civilization, society] affaibli ; [decadent] décadent.

efficacious [efɪ'keɪʃəs] adj fml efficace.

efficacy ['efɪkəsɪ] n fml efficacité *f*.

efficiency [ɪ'fɪʃənsɪ] n [of person, company, method] efficacité *f* ; [of machine - in operation] fonctionnement *m* ; [- in output] rendement *m*.

efficient [ɪ'fɪʃənt] adj [person, staff, method, company] efficace ; [piece of work] bien fait ; [machine - in operation] qui fonctionne bien ; [- in output] qui a un bon rendement.

efficiently [ɪ'fɪʃəntlɪ] adv [work - person] efficacement.

effigy ['efɪdʒɪ] (*pl* effigies) n effigie *f*.

effing ['efɪŋ] UK v inf ◆ adj de merde. ◆ adv foutrement. ◆ n : *there was a lot of effing and blinding* on a eu droit à un chapelet de jurons.

efflorescent [,eflə'resənt] adj efflorescent.

effluent ['efluənt] n [waste] effluent *m*.

effort ['efət] n **1.** [physical or mental exertion] effort *m* **2.** [attempt] essai *m*, tentative *f*.

effortless ['efətlɪs] adj [win] facile ; [style, movement] aisé.

effortlessly ['efətlɪslɪ] adv facilement, sans effort or peine.

effrontery [ɪ'frʌntərɪ] n effronterie *f*.

effusive [ɪ'fju:sɪv] adj [person] expansif ; [welcome, thanks] chaleureux ; pej exagéré.

effusively [ɪ'fju:sɪvlɪ] adv avec effusion ; pej avec une effusion exagérée.

E-fit® ['i:fɪt] n portrait-robot *m* électronique.

EFL (abbr of **English as a foreign language**) n anglais langue étrangère.

EFT [eft] (abbr of **electronic funds transfer**) n COMPUT TEF *m*.

EFTA ['eftə] (abbr of **European Free Trade Association**) pr n AELE *f*, AEL-E *f*.

EFTPOS ['eftpɒs] (abbr of **electronic funds transfer at point of sale**) n COMPUT TEF/TPV *m*.

EFTS [efts] (abbr of **electronic funds transfer system**) n *système électronique de transfert de fonds*.

e.g. (abbr of **exempli gratia**) adv par exemple.

EGA (abbr of **enhanced graphics adapter**) n adaptateur *m* graphique couleur EGA.

egalitarian [ɪˌgælɪˈteərɪən] ◆ n égalitariste *mf*. ◆ adj égalitaire.

egalitarianism [ɪˌgælɪˈteərɪənɪzm] n égalitarisme *m*.

egg [eg] n **1.** CULIN œuf *m* ▶ **fried egg** œuf sur le plat ▶ **hard-boiled egg** œuf dur ▶ **soft-boiled egg** œuf à la coque ▶ **egg white / yolk** blanc *m* / jaune *m* d'œuf **2.** [of bird, insect, fish] œuf *m*; [of woman] ovule *m*. ❖ **egg on** vt sep encourager, inciter ▶ **to egg sb on to do sthg** encourager or inciter qqn à faire qqch.

eggcup [ˈegkʌp] n coquetier *m*.

egghead [ˈeghed] n *inf* intello *mf*.

egg-laying ◆ adj ovipare. ◆ n ponte *f*.

eggplant [ˈegplɑːnt] n US aubergine *f*.

eggshell [ˈegʃel] ◆ n **1.** coquille *f* d'œuf **2.** [colour] coquille *f* d'œuf **3.** PHR **to be walking on eggshells** US *inf* marcher sur des œufs. ◆ adj [finish, paint] coquille d'œuf *(inv)*.

eggslice [ˈegslaɪs] n spatule *f*.

egg timer n sablier *m*.

egg wash n CULIN badigeon *m* à l'œuf battu.

egg whisk n CULIN fouet *m*.

eggy [ˈegɪ] adj *inf* [stained] taché or souillé de jaune d'œuf.

EGM (abbr of **extraordinary general meeting**) n AGE *f*.

ego [ˈiːgəʊ] n [self-esteem] amour-propre *m*; PSYCHOL ego *m inv*, moi *m inv*.

egocentric [ˌiːgəʊˈsentrɪk] adj égocentrique.

egocentricity [ˌiːgəʊsenˈtrɪsətɪ], **egocentrism** [ˌiːgəʊˈsentrɪzm] n égocentrisme *m*.

egoism [ˈiːgəʊɪzm] n [selfishness] égoïsme *m*.

egoist [ˈiːgəʊɪst] n égoïste *mf*.

egoistic [ˌiːgəʊˈɪstɪk] adj égoïste.

egoistically [ˌiːgəʊˈɪstɪklɪ] adv égoïstement.

ego-surfing n *recherche de son propre nom sur Internet*.

egotism [ˈiːgətɪzm] n égocentrisme *m*, égotisme *m*.

egotist [ˈiːgətɪst] n égocentrique *mf*, égotiste *mf*.

egotistic(al) [ˌiːgəˈtɪstɪk(l)] adj égocentrique, égotiste.

egotistically [ˌiːgəˈtɪstɪklɪ] adv de manière égocentrique or égotiste.

ego trip n *inf*: **she's just on an ego trip** c'est par vanité qu'elle le fait. ❖ **ego-trip** vi *inf*: **you're just ego-tripping** tu fais ça par vanité.

Egypt [ˈiːdʒɪpt] pr n Égypte *f* / **in Egypt** en Égypte.

Egyptian [ɪˈdʒɪpʃn] ◆ n **1.** [person] Égyptien *m*, -enne *f* **2.** LING égyptien *m*. ◆ adj égyptien.

eh [eɪ] interj **1.** [what did you say?] ▶ **eh?** hein ? **2.** [seeking agreement] ▶ **eh?** hein ? **3.** [in astonishment] ▶ **eh?** quoi ? **4.** [in doubt, hesitation] heu.

EHRC (abbr of **Equality and Human Rights Commission**) n Commission pour l'égalité et les droits de l'Homme.

eiderdown [ˈaɪdədaʊn] n **1.** [feathers] duvet *m* d'eider **2.** [for bed] édredon *m*.

eight [eɪt] ◆ n **1.** [number, numeral] huit *m* **2.** [in rowing] huit *m*. ◆ adj huit. ◆ pron huit. See also **five**.

eighteen [ˌeɪˈtiːn] ◆ pron dix-huit. ◆ adj dix-huit. ◆ n dix-huit *m*. See also **fifteen**.

eighteenth [ˌeɪˈtiːnθ] ◆ adj dix-huitième. ◆ n [in series] dix-huitième *mf*; [fraction] dix-huitième *m*. See also **fifteenth**.

eighth [eɪtθ] ◆ adj huitième. ◆ n [in series] huitième *mf*; [fraction] huitième *m*. ◆ adv **1.** [in contest] en huitième position, à la huitième place **2.** [on list] huitièmement. See also **fifth**.

eighth grade n US SCH *classe de l'enseignement secondaire correspondant à la quatrième (13-14 ans)*.

eightieth [ˈeɪtɪɪθ] ◆ adj quatre-vingtième. ◆ n [in series] quatre-vingtième *mf*; [fraction] quatre-vingtième *m*. See also **fiftieth**.

eighty [ˈeɪtɪ] ◆ pron quatre-vingt. ◆ adj quatre-vingts. ◆ n quatre-vingt *m*. See also **fifty**.

Eire [ˈeərə] pr n Eire *f*.

either [UK ˈaɪðər US ˈiːðər] ◆ det **1.** [one or the other] l'un ou l'autre (l'une ou l'autre) / **you can take either route** tu peux prendre l'un ou l'autre de ces chemins / **either bus will get you there** les deux bus y vont **2.** [each] chaque / **there were candles at either end of the table** il y avait des bougies aux deux bouts or à chaque bout de la table. ◆ pron [one or the other] l'un ou l'autre (l'une ou l'autre) / **I don't like either of them** je ne les aime ni l'un ni l'autre / **which would you like? — either** lequel voudriez-vous ? — n'importe lequel. ◆ adv non plus / **we can't hear anything either** nous n'entendons rien non plus. ❖ **either... or** conj phr ou... ou, soit... soit ; [with negative] ni... ni / **either you stop complaining or I go home!** ou tu arrêtes de te plaindre, ou je rentre chez moi / **they're either very rich or very stupid** ils sont soit très riches soit très bêtes / **I've not met either him or his brother** je n'ai rencontré ni lui ni son frère. ❖ **either way** adv phr [in either case] dans les deux cas / **either way I lose** dans les deux cas je suis perdant.

ejaculate [ɪˈdʒækjʊleɪt] ◆ vi **1.** PHYSIOL éjaculer **2.** *fml* [call out] s'écrier, s'exclamer. ◆ vt **1.** PHYSIOL éjaculer **2.** *fml* [utter] lancer, pousser.

ejaculation [ɪˌdʒækjʊˈleɪʃn] n **1.** PHYSIOL éjaculation *f* **2.** *fml* [exclamation] exclamation *f*.

eject [ɪˈdʒekt] ◆ vt **1.** [troublemaker] expulser **2.** [cartridge, pilot] éjecter ; [lava] projeter. ◆ vi [pilot] s'éjecter.

ejection [ɪˈdʒekʃn] n **1.** [of troublemaker] expulsion *f* **2.** [of cartridge, pilot] éjection *f* ; [of lava] projection *f*.

ejection seat US = **ejector seat**.

ejector seat [ɪ] UK n siège *m* éjectable.

eke [iːk] ❖ **eke out** vt sep **1.** [make last] faire durer **2.** [scrape] ▶ **to eke out a living** gagner tout juste sa vie **3.** [by adding something] augmenter.

EKG (abbr of **electrocardiogram**) n US ECG *m*.

El [el] (abbr of **elevated railroad**) n US *inf* métro *m* aérien (à Chicago).

elaborate ◆ adj [ɪˈlæbrət] [system, preparations] élaboré ; [style, costume] recherché, travaillé ; [pattern] compliqué ; [details] minutieux ; [map, plans] détaillé. ◆ vt [ɪˈlæbəreɪt] [work out in detail - plan, scheme, etc.] élaborer ; [describe in detail] décrire en détail. ◆ vi [ɪˈlæbəreɪt] [go into detail] donner des détails. ❖ **elaborate on** vt insep [idea, statement] développer.

elaborately [ɪˈlæbərətlɪ] adv [decorated, designed, etc.] minutieusement, avec recherche ; [planned] minutieusement ; [packaged] de manière élaborée.

elaboration [ɪˌlæbəˈreɪʃn] n [working out - of scheme, plan] élaboration *f* ; [details] exposé *m* minutieux.

élan [eɪˈlæn] n vigueur *f*, énergie *f*.

elapse [ɪˈlæps] vi s'écouler, passer.

elastic [ɪˈlæstɪk] ◆ adj **1.** [material] élastique ▶ **elastic stockings** bas *mpl* anti-varices **2.** *fig* [timetable, arrangements, concept] souple ; [word, moral principles] élastique, souple ; [working hours] élastique. ◆ n **1.** [material] élastique m **2.** ⓊⓈ [rubber band] élastique m, caoutchouc m.

elasticated ⓊⓀ [ɪˈlæstɪkeɪtɪd], **elasticized** ⓊⓈ [ɪˈlæstɪsaɪzd] adj [stockings, waist] élastique.

elastic band n ⓊⓀ élastique m.

elasticity [ˌelæˈstɪsətɪ] n élasticité f.

elastin [ɪˈlæstɪn] n élastine f.

Elastoplast® [ɪˈlæstəplɑːst] n ⓊⓀ pansement m adhésif.

elated [ɪˈleɪtɪd] adj fou de joie, euphorique.

elation [ɪˈleɪʃn] n allégresse f, exultation f, euphorie f.

elbow [ˈelbəʊ] ◆ n **1.** [of arm, jacket, pipe, river] coude m **2.** ⓅⒽⓇ **to give sb the elbow** ⓊⓀ inf [employee] virer qqn **b)** [boyfriend, girlfriend] larguer qqn **c)** [tenant] mettre qqn à la porte. ◆ vt [hit] donner un coup de coude à ; [push] pousser du coude. ❖ **elbow out** vt sep [from job] se débarrasser de.

elbow grease n inf huile f de coude.

elbow pad n coudière f.

elbow-rest n accoudoir m.

elbowroom [ˈelbəʊrʊm] n : I don't have enough elbowroom **a)** je n'ai pas assez de place (pour me retourner) **b)** fig je n'ai pas suffisamment de liberté d'action.

elder [ˈeldər] ◆ adj [brother, sister] aîné. ◆ n **1.** [of two children] aîné m, -e f **2.** [of tribe, the Church] ancien m **3.** [senior] : you should respect your elders (and betters) vous devez le respect à vos aînés **4.** BOT sureau m.

elderberry [ˈeldəˌberɪ] n baie f de sureau ▶ **elderberry wine** vin m de sureau.

elderflower [ˈeldəˌflaʊər] n fleur f de sureau.

elderly [ˈeldəlɪ] ◆ adj âgé. ◆ pl n ▶ **the elderly** les personnes fpl âgées.

elder statesman n [gen] vétéran m ; [politician] vétéran m de la politique.

eldest [ˈeldɪst] ◆ adj aîné. ◆ n aîné m, -e f.

Eldorado, El Dorado [ˌeldɒˈrɑːdəʊ] pr n l'Eldorado m.

elect [ɪˈlekt] ◆ vt **1.** [by voting] élire **2.** fml [choose] choisir ▶ **to elect to do sthg** choisir de faire qqch. ◆ adj ▶ **the President elect** le futur président. ◆ pl n RELIG ▶ **the elect** les élus mpl.

elected [ɪˈlektɪd] adj élu.

election [ɪˈlekʃn] ◆ n élection f. ◆ comp [day, results] des élections ; [agent, campaign, promise, speech] électoral.

🏛️ **Mid-term elections**

Les élections de mi-mandat aux États-Unis ont lieu exactement deux ans après la présidentielle, le mardi suivant le premier lundi de novembre. Sont en jeu tous les sièges de la Chambre des représentants, un tiers de ceux du Sénat, et la plupart des postes de gouverneur dans les États. Les électeurs en profitent souvent pour faire un pied de nez au président en exercice ; si son parti perd la majorité au Congrès, le président peut devenir un **lame duck** (canard boiteux) qui n'arrive pas à faire adopter ses projets de loi.

---

electioneering [ɪˌlekʃəˈnɪərɪŋ] ◆ n campagne f électorale ; pej propagande f électorale. ◆ adj [speech, campaign] électoral ; pej propagandiste.

elective [ɪˈlektɪv] ◆ adj **1.** [with power to elect - assembly] électoral **2.** [chosen - official, post] électif **3.** [optional - course, subject] optionnel, facultatif ▶ **elective surgery** chirurgie f de confort. ◆ n ⓊⓈ SCH & UNIV [subject] cours m optionnel ou facultatif.

elector [ɪˈlektər] n électeur m, -trice f.

electoral [ɪˈlektərəl] adj électoral ▶ **electoral college** collège m électoral (qui élit le président des États-Unis) ▶ **on the electoral roll** or **register** ⓊⓀ sur la liste électorale.

electorate [ɪˈlektərət] n électorat m.

electric [ɪˈlektrɪk] ◆ adj [cooker, cable, current, motor, musical instrument] électrique ; fig [atmosphere] chargé d'électricité ; [effect] électrisant ▶ **electric blanket** couverture f chauffante ▶ **electric fire** or **heater** appareil m de chauffage électrique ▶ **electric light a)** [individual appliance] lumière f électrique **b)** [lighting] éclairage m or lumière f électrique. ◆ n ⓊⓀ inf électricité f. ❖ **electrics** pl n ⓊⓀ installation f électrique.

electrical [ɪˈlektrɪkl] adj [appliance] électrique ; [failure, fault] au niveau de l'installation électrique ▶ **electrical engineer** ingénieur m électricien ▶ **electrical engineering** électrotechnique f.

electrically [ɪˈlektrɪklɪ] adv électriquement.

electrical shock ⓊⓈ = electric shock.

electric blue ◆ n bleu m électrique. ◆ adj bleu électrique.

electric chair n chaise f électrique.

electric eel n anguille f électrique.

electric fence n clôture f électrique.

electrician [ˌɪlekˈtrɪʃn] n électricien m, -enne f.

electricity [ˌɪlekˈtrɪsətɪ] ◆ n électricité f. ◆ comp ▶ **electricity bill** note f d'électricité ▶ **electricity supply** alimentation f en électricité.

electric ray n ZOOL torpille f.

electric shock, electrical shock ⓊⓈ n décharge f électrique ▶ **electric shock treatment** traitement m par électrochocs.

electric storm n orage m.

electrification [ɪˌlektrɪfɪˈkeɪʃn] n électrification f.

electrify [ɪˈlektrɪfaɪ] vt [railway line] électrifier ; fig [audience] électriser.

electrifying [ɪˈlektrɪfaɪŋ] adj fig électrisant.

electrocardiogram [ɪˌlektrəʊˈkɑːdɪəgræm] n électrocardiogramme m.

electrocardiograph [ɪˌlektrəʊˈkɑːdɪəgrɑːf] n électrocardiographe m.

electrochemical [ɪˌlektrəʊˈkemɪkl] adj électrochimique.

electrochemistry [ɪˌlektrəʊˈkemɪstrɪ] n électrochimie f.

electroconvulsive therapy [ɪˌlektrəʊkənˈvʌlsɪv-] n MED thérapie f par électrochocs.

electrocute [ɪˈlektrəkjuːt] vt électrocuter.

electrocution [ɪˌlektrəˈkjuːʃn] n électrocution f.

electrode [ɪˈlektrəʊd] n électrode f.

electrodynamic [ɪˌlektrəʊdaɪˈnæmɪk] adj électrodynamique f.

electroencephalogram [ɪˌlektrəʊenˈsefələgræm] n électroencéphalogramme m.

electroencephalograph [ɪˌlektrəʊenˈsefələgrɑːf] n électroencéphalographe m.

electrolysis [ˌɪlekˈtrɒləsɪs] n électrolyse f.

electrolyte [ɪˈlektrəʊlaɪt] n électrolyte m.

electromagnet [ɪˌlektrəʊˈmægnɪt] n électro-aimant m.

electromagnetic [ɪ,lektrəʊmæg'netɪk] adj électromagnétique.

electron [ɪ'lektrɒn] n électron m.

electronic [,ɪlek'trɒnɪk] adj électronique ▸ **electronic data processing** traitement m électronique de données ▸ **electronic funds transfer** transfert m de fonds électronique ▸ **electronic news gathering** journalisme m électronique ▸ **electronic tag** bracelet m électronique. ❖ **electronics** ◆ n (U) électronique f. ◆ pl n composants mpl électroniques. ◆ comp ▸ **electronics engineer** ingénieur m électronicien, électronicien m, -enne f ▸ **electronics industry** industrie f électronique.

electronically [,ɪlek'trɒnɪklɪ] adv électroniquement ; [operated] par voie électronique.

electron microscope n microscope m électronique.

electroplate [ɪ'lektrəʊpleɪt] ◆ vt plaquer par galvanoplastie ; [with gold] dorer par galvanoplastie ; [with silver] argenter par galvanoplastie. ◆ n (U) articles mpl plaqués (par galvanoplastie) ; [with silver] articles mpl argentés.

electroplated [ɪ'lektrəʊpleɪtɪd] adj métallisé(e) par galvanoplastie.

electroshock [ɪ'lektrəʊʃɒk] n électrochoc m ▸ **electroshock therapy** thérapie f par électrochocs.

elegance ['elɪgəns] n élégance f.

elegant ['elɪgənt] adj [person, style, solution] élégant ; [building, furniture] aux lignes élégantes.

elegantly ['elɪgəntlɪ] adv élégamment.

elegiac [elɪ'dʒaɪək] ◆ adj élégiaque. ◆ n élégie f.

elegy ['elɪdʒɪ] (pl **elegies**) n élégie f.

element ['elɪmənt] n **1.** [water, air, etc.] élément m **2.** [in kettle, electric heater] résistance f **3.** [small amount - of danger, truth, the unknown] part f **4.** (usu pl) [rudiment] rudiment m **5.** [in society, group] élément m.

elemental [,elɪ'mentl] adj [basic] fondamental, de base.

elementary [,elɪ'mentərɪ] adj élémentaire ▸ **elementary particle** particule f élémentaire ▸ **elementary school / education** US école f / enseignement m primaire.

elephant ['elɪfənt] n éléphant m.

elevate ['elɪveɪt] vt [raise - in height, rank, etc.] élever.

elevated ['elɪveɪtɪd] adj **1.** [height, position, rank] haut, élevé ; [thoughts] noble, élevé ; [style] élevé, soutenu **2.** [raised - road] surélevé / elevated railway or railroad US métro m aérien.

elevation [,elɪ'veɪʃn] n **1.** [of roof, in rank] élévation f ; RELIG [of host] élévation f ; [of style, language] caractère m élevé or soutenu **2.** [height] : elevation above sea-level élévation f par rapport au niveau de la mer **3.** [hill] élévation f, hauteur f **4.** ARCHIT élévation f.

elevator ['elɪveɪtər] n **1.** US [lift] ascenseur m **2.** [for grain] élévateur m.

eleven [ɪ'levn] ◆ pron onze. ◆ adj onze. ◆ n onze m ; SPORT équipe f ; FOOT onze m, équipe f. See also **five**.

elevenses [ɪ'levnzɪz] n UK inf boisson ou en-cas pour la pause de onze heures.

eleventh [ɪ'levnθ] ◆ adj onzième. ◆ n [in series] onze mf ; [fraction] onzième m. See also **fifth**.

eleventh grade n US SCH classe de l'enseignement secondaire correspondant à la première (16-17 ans).

eleventh grader [ɪ'levnθ,greɪdər] n US SCH lycéen m, -enne f (en troisième année).

eleventh hour n ▸ **at the eleventh hour** à la dernière minute. ❖ **eleventh-hour** adj de dernière minute.

elf [elf] (pl **elves** [elvz]) n elfe m.

elfin ['elfɪn] adj fig [face, features] délicat.

elicit [ɪ'lɪsɪt] vt [information, explanation, response] obtenir ; [facts, truth] découvrir, mettre au jour ▸ **to elicit sthg from sb** tirer qqch de qqn.

elide [ɪ'laɪd] vt élider.

eligibility [,elɪdʒə'bɪlətɪ] n [to vote] éligibilité f ; [for a job] admissibilité f.

eligible ['elɪdʒəbl] adj [to vote] éligible ; [for a job] admissible ; [for promotion] pouvant bénéficier d'une promotion ; [for marriage] mariable / an eligible bachelor un bon or beau parti.

eliminate [ɪ'lɪmɪneɪt] vt [competitor, alternative] éliminer ; [stain, mark] enlever, faire disparaître ; [item from diet] supprimer, éliminer ; [possibility] écarter, éliminer ; [kill] éliminer, supprimer ; MATH & PHYSIOL éliminer.

elimination [ɪ,lɪmɪ'neɪʃn] n élimination f.

elimination competition US n = knockout competition.

elision [ɪ'lɪʒn] n élision f.

elite [ɪ'liːt], **élite** [eɪ'liːt] ◆ n élite f. ◆ adj d'élite.

elitism [ɪ'liːtɪzm] n élitisme m.

elitist [ɪ'liːtɪst] ◆ n élitiste mf. ◆ adj élitiste.

elixir [ɪ'lɪksər] n élixir m.

Elizabethan [ɪ,lɪzə'biːθn] ◆ adj élisabéthain. ◆ n Élisabéthain m, -e f.

elk [elk] (pl **elk** or **elks**) n élan m.

ellipse [ɪ'lɪps] n MATH ellipse f.

ellipsis [ɪ'lɪpsɪs] (pl **ellipses** [-siːz]) n GRAM ellipse f.

elliptic [ɪ'lɪptɪk] adj elliptique.

elliptical [ɪ'lɪptɪkl] adj **1.** [in shape] en ellipse **2.** fml [indirect, cryptic] elliptique.

elm [elm] n orme m.

elocution [,elə'kjuːʃn] n élocution f, diction f.

elongate ['iːlɒŋgeɪt] ◆ vt allonger ; [line] prolonger. ◆ vi s'allonger, s'étendre.

elongated ['iːlɒŋgeɪtɪd] adj [in space] allongé ; [in time] prolongé.

elope [ɪ'ləʊp] vi s'enfuir pour se marier ▸ **to elope with sb** s'enfuir avec qqn pour l'épouser.

elopement [ɪ'ləʊpmənt] n fugue f amoureuse (en vue d'un mariage).

eloquence ['eləkwəns] n éloquence f.

eloquent ['eləkwənt] adj éloquent.

eloquently ['eləkwəntlɪ] adv éloquemment, avec éloquence.

El Salvador [el'sælvədɔːr] pr n Salvador m / in El Salvador au Salvador.

else [els] adv **1.** [after indefinite pronoun] d'autre / anybody or anyone else a) [at all] n'importe qui d'autre b) [in addition] quelqu'un d'autre / he's no cleverer than anybody else il n'est pas plus intelligent qu'un autre / anything else a) [at all] n'importe quoi d'autre b) [in addition] quelque chose d'autre / would you like or will there be anything else? a) [in shop] vous fallait-il autre chose ? b) [in restaurant] désirez-vous autre chose ? / I couldn't do anything else but or except apologize je ne pouvais (rien faire d'autre) que m'excuser / anywhere else ailleurs / everything else tout le reste / everywhere else partout ailleurs / nobody or no one else personne d'autre / we're alive, nothing else matters nous sommes vivants, c'est tout ce qui compte / there's nothing else for it il n'y a rien d'autre à faire / somebody or someone else quelqu'un d'autre / something else autre chose, quelque chose d'autre / somewhere or US someplace else ailleurs, autre part ▸ **if all else fails** en dernier recours ▸ **if nothing else**: it'll teach him a lesson, if nothing else au moins, ça lui servira de leçon ▶ **he's / she's / it's something else!** *inf* il est / elle est / c'est incroyable ! **2.** *(after interrogative pronoun)* [in addition] d'autre / **what / who else?** quoi / qui d'autre ? ; [otherwise] autrement / **how / why else would I do it?** comment / pourquoi le ferais-je sinon ? / **where else would he be?** où peut-il être à part là ?

elsewhere [els'weər] adv ailleurs.

ELT (abbr of **English language teaching**) n *enseignement de l'anglais.*

elucidate [ɪ'luːsɪdeɪt] ◆ vt [point, question] élucider, expliciter ; [reasons] expliquer. ◆ vi expliquer, être plus clair.

elude [ɪ'luːd] vt [enemy, pursuers] échapper à ; [question] éluder ; [blow] esquiver ; [sb's gaze] éviter, fuir ; [obligation, responsibility] se dérober à, se soustraire à ; [justice] se soustraire à.

elusive [ɪ'luːsɪv] adj [enemy, prey, happiness, thought] insaisissable ; [word, concept] difficile à définir ; [answer] élusif, évasif.

elusively [ɪ'luːsɪvlɪ] adv [answer] de manière élusive ; [move] de manière insaisissable.

elves [elvz] pl ⟶ **elf.**

elvish ['elvɪʃ] adj **1.** *fig* [face, features] délicat **2.** [music, dance] féerique **3.** [mischievous] espiègle.

'em [əm] *inf* = **them.**

emaciated [ɪ'meɪʃɪeɪtɪd] adj émacié, décharné.

e-mail ['iːmeɪl] (abbr of **electronic mail**) ◆ n courrier *m* électronique, e-mail *m*. ◆ vt [message] envoyer par courrier électronique or e-mail ; [person] envoyer un courrier électronique or e-mail à. ◆ comp ▶ **e-mail account** compte *m* de courrier électronique ▶ **e-mail address** adresse *f* électronique.

emanate ['emǝneɪt] ◆ vi ▶ **to emanate from** émaner de. ◆ vt [love, affection] exsuder, rayonner de ; [concern] respirer.

emancipate [ɪ'mænsɪpeɪt] vt [women] émanciper ; [slaves] affranchir.

emancipated [ɪ'mænsɪpeɪtɪd] adj émancipé.

emancipation [ɪ,mænsɪ'peɪʃn] n émancipation *f* ▶ **the Emancipation Proclamation** US HIST la proclamation d'émancipation.

🏛 **The Emancipation Proclamation**

Discours du président Abraham Lincoln, en 1863, déclarant les esclaves de la Confédération (États sudistes) libres. Bien qu'elle soit restée sans effet pratique (ces États échappaient au contrôle fédéral), cette proclamation représente, pour les Américains, l'officialisation de l'émancipation des esclaves.

---

e-marketing n marketing *m* électronique.

emasculate [ɪ'mæskjʊleɪt] vt [castrate] émasculer ; *fig* émasculer, affaiblir.

emasculation [ɪ,mæskjʊ'leɪʃn] n [castration] émasculation *f* ; *fig* émasculation *f*, affaiblissement *m*.

embalm [ɪm'bɑːm] vt embaumer.

embalmer [ɪm'bɑːmər] n embaumeur *m*, thanatopracteur *m*.

embankment [ɪm'bæŋkmənt] n [of concrete] quai *m* ; [of earth] berge *f* ; [to contain river] digue *f* ; [along railway, road] talus *m*.

embargo [em'bɑːgəʊ] *(pl* embargoes*)* ◆ n **1.** COMM & POL embargo *m* ▶ **to put** or **to place** or **to lay an embargo on sthg** mettre l'embargo sur qqch ▶ **to lift / to break an embargo** lever / enfreindre un embargo **2.** *fig* [on spending] interdiction *f* ▶ **to put an embargo on sthg** interdire or bannir qqch. ◆ vt COMM & POL mettre l'embargo sur ; *fig* interdire.

embark [ɪm'bɑːk] ◆ vt [passengers, cargo] embarquer. ◆ vi embarquer, monter à bord. ◆ **embark on, embark upon** vt insep [journey, career] commencer, entreprendre ; [explanation, venture] se lancer dans.

embarkation [,embɑː'keɪʃn], **embarkment** [ɪm'bɑːkmənt] n [of passengers, cargo] embarquement *m*.

embarrass [ɪm'bærəs] vt embarrasser, gêner.

embarrassed [ɪm'bærəst] adj embarrassé ▶ **to feel embarrassed (about sthg)** être embarrassé or se sentir gêné (à propos de qqch).

embarrassing [ɪm'bærəsɪŋ] adj [experience, person] embarrassant, gênant ; [situation] embarrassant, délicat.

embarrassingly [ɪm'bærəsɪŋlɪ] adv de manière embarrassante.

embarrassment [ɪm'bærəsmənt] n embarras *m*, gêne *f* ▶ **to be an embarrassment** or **a source of embarrassment to sb** être une source d'embarras pour qqn, faire honte à qqn.

embassy ['embəsɪ] *(pl* embassies*)* n ambassade *f*.

embattled [ɪm'bætld] adj [army] engagé dans la bataille ; [town] ravagé par les combats ; *fig* en difficulté, aux prises avec des difficultés.

embed [ɪm'bed] *(pt & pp* embedded, *cont* embedding*)* vt [in wood] enfoncer ; [in rock] sceller ; [in cement] sceller, noyer ; [jewels] enchâsser, incruster.

embedded [ɪm'bedɪd] adj **1.** [in wood] enfoncé ; [in rock] scellé ; [in cement] scellé, noyé ; [jewels] enchâssé, incrusté **2.** [journalist] embarqué *(avec les forces armées).*

embellish [ɪm'belɪʃ] vt [garment, building] embellir, décorer, orner ; [account, story, etc.] enjoliver, embellir.

embellishment [ɪm'belɪʃmənt] n [of building] embellissement *m* ; [of garment] décoration *f* ; [of account, story, etc.] enjolivement *m*, embellissement *m* ; [in handwriting] fioritures *fpl*.

ember ['embər] n charbon *m* ardent, morceau *m* de braise ▶ **embers** braise *f*.

embezzle [ɪm'bezl] ◆ vt [money] détourner, escroquer ▶ **to embezzle money from sb** escroquer de l'argent à qqn. ◆ vi ▶ **to embezzle from a company** détourner les fonds d'une société.

embezzlement [ɪm'bezlmənt] n [of funds] détournement *m*.

embezzler [ɪm'bezlər] n escroc *m*, fraudeur *m*, -euse *f*.

embitter [ɪm'bɪtər] vt [person] remplir d'amertume, aigrir ; [relations] altérer, détériorer.

embittered [ɪm'bɪtəd] adj aigri.

emblazon [ɪm'bleɪzn] vt : *the shield is emblazoned with dragons* le bouclier porte des dragons / *he had the word "revolution" emblazoned across his jacket* sa veste arborait fièrement le mot « révolution ».

emblazoned [ɪm'bleɪznd] adj **1.** [design, emblem] ▶ **emblazoned (on)** blasonné(e) (sur) **2.** [flag, garment] ▶ **to be emblazoned with** arborer l'insigne or le blason de.

emblem ['embləm] n emblème *m*.

emblematic [,emblə'mætɪk] adj emblématique.

embodiment [ɪm'bɒdɪmənt] n **1.** [epitome] incarnation *f*, personnification *f* **2.** [inclusion] intégration *f*, incorporation *f*.

embody [ɪm'bɒdɪ] (*pt & pp* embodied) vt **1.** [epitomize - subj: person] incarner ; [- subj: action] exprimer **2.** [include] inclure, intégrer.

embolden [ɪm'bəʊldən] vt *fml* enhardir, donner du courage à ▶ **to feel emboldened to do sthg** se sentir le courage de faire qqch.

embolism ['embəlɪzm] n MED embolie *f*.

emboss [ɪm'bɒs] vt [metal] repousser, estamper ; [leather] estamper, gaufrer ; [cloth, paper] gaufrer.

embossed [ɪm'bɒst] adj [metal] repoussé ; [leather] gaufré ; [cloth, wallpaper] gaufré, à motifs en relief.

embrace [ɪm'breɪs] ◆ vt **1.** [friend, child] étreindre ; [lover] étreindre, enlacer ; [official, visitor, statesman] donner l'accolade à **2.** [include] regrouper, comprendre, embrasser **3.** [adopt - religion, cause] embrasser ; [- opportunity] saisir. ◆ vi [friends] s'étreindre ; [lovers] s'étreindre, s'enlacer ; [statesmen] se donner l'accolade. ◆ n [of friend, child] étreinte *f* ; [of lover] étreinte *f*, enlacement *m* ; [of official visitor, statesman] accolade *f*.

embrocation [,embrə'keɪʃn] n embrocation *f*.

embroider [ɪm'brɔɪdə] ◆ vt [garment, cloth] broder ; *fig* [story, truth] embellir, enjoliver. ◆ vi [with needle] broder ; *fig* [embellish] broder, enjoliver.

embroidered [ɪm'brɔɪdəd] adj [garment, cloth] brodé.

embroidery [ɪm'brɔɪdərɪ] (*pl* embroideries) ◆ n [on garment, cloth] broderie *f* ; *fig* [of story, truth] enjolivement *m*, embellissement *m*. ◆ comp [frame, silk, thread] à broder.

embroil [ɪm'brɔɪl] vt mêler, impliquer ▶ **to get embroiled in sthg** se retrouver mêlé à qqch.

embryo ['embrɪəʊ] (*pl* embryos) n BIOL & *fig* embryon *m* ▶ **in embryo** [foetus, idea] à l'état embryonnaire.

embryonic [,embrɪ'ɒnɪk] adj BIOL embryonnaire ; *fig* à l'état embryonnaire.

emcee [,em'si:] *inf* ◆ n abbr of master of ceremonies. ◆ vt animer.

EMD ['i:'em'di:] (abbr of Emergency Make-Up Day) n US SCH journée de rattrapage si l'école a été fermée précédemment en raison d'une catastrophe naturelle.

emend [i:'mend] vt corriger.

emerald ['emərəld] ◆ n **1.** [gem stone] émeraude *f* **2.** [colour] ▶ **emerald (green)** (vert *m*) émeraude *m*. ◆ comp [brooch, ring] en émeraude.

emerge [ɪ'mɜːdʒ] vi [person, animal] sortir ; [sun] sortir, émerger ; [truth, difficulty] émerger, apparaître.

emergence [ɪ'mɜːdʒəns] n émergence *f*.

emergency [ɪ'mɜːdʒənsɪ] (*pl* emergencies) ◆ n **1.** (cas *m* d')urgence *f* ▶ **in case of emergency** or **in an emergency** en cas d'urgence **2.** MED [department] (service *m* des) urgences *fpl*. ◆ comp [measures, procedure, meeting] d'urgence ▶ **emergency brake a)** frein *m* de secours **b)** US frein *m* à main / **'emergency exit'** 'sortie *f* de secours' ▶ **emergency landing** AERON atterrissage *m* forcé ▶ **emergency powers** pouvoirs *mpl* extraordinaires ▶ **emergency room** US salle *f* des urgences ▶ **emergency services** services *mpl* d'urgence ▶ **emergency stop** UK AUTO arrêt *m* d'urgence ▶ **emergency ward** UK MED salle *f* des urgences.

emergent [ɪ'mɜːdʒənt] adj [theory, nation] naissant.

emerging market n ECON marché *m* émergent.

emery board n lime *f* à ongles.

emetic [ɪ'metɪk] ◆ adj émétique. ◆ n émétique *m*, vomitif *m*.

emigrant ['emɪgrənt] ◆ n émigrant *m*, -e *f* ; [when established abroad] émigré *m*, -e *f*. ◆ comp [worker, population] émigré.

emigrate ['emɪgreɪt] vi émigrer.

emigration [,emɪ'greɪʃn] n émigration *f*.

émigré ['emɪgreɪ] n émigré *m*.

eminence ['emɪnəns] n **1.** [prominence] rang *m* éminent **2.** [high ground] éminence *f*, hauteur *f*. ◆ **Eminence** n RELIG [title] Éminence *f*.

eminent ['emɪnənt] adj [distinguished] éminent.

eminently ['emɪnəntlɪ] adv éminemment.

emir [e'mɪə] n émir *m*.

emirate ['emərət] n émirat *m*.

emissary ['emɪsərɪ] (*pl* emissaries) n émissaire *m*.

emission [ɪ'mɪʃn] n [gen & ECOL] émission *f*.

emissions cap n ECOL plafonnement *m* des émissions.

emissions target n ECOL cible *f* de réduction des émissions.

emissions trading n ECOL échange *m* de quotas d'émissions.

emit [ɪ'mɪt] (*pt & pp* emitted, *cont* emitting) vt [sound, radiation, light] émettre ; [heat] dégager, émettre ; [gas] dégager ; [sparks, cry] lancer.

Emmental, Emmenthal ['emən,tɑːl] n Emmental *m*.

emollient [ɪ'mɒlɪənt] ◆ adj émollient ; *fig* adoucissant, calmant. ◆ n émollient *m*.

emolument [ɪ'mɒljʊmənt] n (*usu pl*) *fml* ▶ **emoluments** émoluments *mpl*, rémunération *f*.

e-money n argent *m* électronique, argent *m* virtuel.

emoticon [ɪ'məʊtɪkɒn] n émoticon *m*, smiley *m*.

emotion [ɪ'məʊʃn] n [particular feeling] sentiment *m* ; [faculty] émotion *f*.

emotional [ɪ'məʊʃənl] adj **1.** [stress] émotionnel ; [life, problems] affectif **2.** [person - easily moved] sensible, qui s'émeut facilement ; [- stronger] émotif ; [appealing to the emotions - plea, speech, music] émouvant ; [charged with emotion - issue] passionné, brûlant ; [- reunion, scene] chargé d'émotion ; [governed by emotions - person] passionné, ardent ; [- reaction, state] émotionnel.

emotional intelligence adj intelligence *f* émotionnelle.

emotionally [ɪ'məʊʃnəlɪ] adv [react, speak] avec émotion.

emotionless [ɪ'məʊʃnlɪs] adj [person, face, eyes] impassible ; [style] froid.

emotive [ɪ'məʊtɪv] adj [issue] sensible ; [word, phrase] à forte teneur émotionnelle.

empathize ['empəθaɪz] vi ▶ **to empathize with sb** s'identifier à qqn.

empathy ['empəθɪ] n [affinity - gen] affinité *f*, affinités *fpl*, sympathie *f* ; PHILOS & PSYCHOL empathie *f* ; [power, ability] capacité *f* à s'identifier à autrui.

emperor ['empərə] n empereur *m*.

emphasis ['emfəsɪs] (*pl* emphases [-si:z]) n **1.** [importance] accent *m* ▶ **to place** or **to lay** or **to put emphasis on sthg** mettre l'accent sur qqch **2.** LING [stress] accent *m*.

> ⚠ **Emphase** is a formal word meaning pomposity, **not** emphasis.

emphasize ['emfəsaɪz] vt **1.** [detail, need, importance] insister sur **2.** [physical feature] accentuer **3.** LING [syllable] accentuer ; [word] accentuer, appuyer sur.

emphatic [ɪm'fætɪk] adj [refusal] catégorique ; [gesture] appuyé ; [speaker, manner] énergique, vigoureux, LING emphatique.

⚠ **Emphatique** only means emphatic in the field of linguistics. In other contexts it means pompous or bombastic.

emphatically [ɪm'fætɪklɪ] adv **1.** [speak, reply] énergiquement ; [deny] catégoriquement **2.** [definitely] clairement.
emphysema [ˌemfɪ'siːmə] n emphysème m.
empire ['empaɪə'] n empire m. ❖ **Empire** comp [costume, furniture, style] Empire.
empire-building n : *there's too much empire-building going on* on joue trop les bâtisseurs d'empires.
empirical [ɪm'pɪrɪkl] adj empirique.
empirically [ɪm'pɪrɪklɪ] adv empiriquement.
empiricism [ɪm'pɪrɪsɪzm] n empirisme m.
employ [ɪm'plɔɪ] ❖ vt **1.** [give work to] employer **2.** [use - means, method, word] employer, utiliser ; [- skill, diplomacy] faire usage de, employer ; [- force] employer, avoir recours à **3.** [occupy] ▸ **to employ oneself / to be employed in doing sthg** s'occuper / être occupé à faire qqch. ❖ n fml service m ▸ **to be in sb's employ** travailler pour qqn, être au service de qqn.
employable [ɪm'plɔɪəbl] adj [person] susceptible d'être employé ; [method] utilisable.
employed [ɪm'plɔɪd] ❖ adj employé. ❖ pl n personnes fpl qui ont un emploi.
employee [ɪm'plɔɪiː] n employé m, -e f, salarié m, -e f.
employer [ɪm'plɔɪə'] n employeur m, patron m ; ADMIN employeur m ▸ **employers** [as a body] patronat m.
employment [ɪm'plɔɪmənt] n **1.** [work] emploi m ▸ **to be in employment** avoir un emploi ou du travail / *full employment* plein emploi / *employment contract* contrat m d'emploi ▸ **Secretary (of State) for** or **Minister of Employment** UK, **Secretary for Employment** US ≃ ministre m du Travail **2.** [recruitment] embauche f ; [providing work] emploi m ; [use - of method, word] emploi m ; [- of force, skill] usage m, emploi m.
Employment Act n UK POL loi sur l'égalité des chances pour l'emploi.
employment agency, employment bureau n agence f or bureau m de placement.
employment tribunal n LAW conseil m de prud'hommes.
emporium [em'pɔːrɪəm] (pl **emporiums** or **emporia** [-rɪə]) n grand magasin m.
empower [ɪm'paʊə'] vt fml habiliter, autoriser ▸ **to empower sb to do sthg** habiliter or autoriser qqn à faire qqch.
empowering [ɪm'paʊərɪŋ] adj qui donne un sentiment de pouvoir.
empowerment [ɪm'paʊəmənt] n : *the empowerment of women / of ethnic minorities* la plus grande autonomie des femmes / des minorités ethniques.
empress ['emprɪs] n impératrice f.
emptiness ['emptɪnɪs] n vide m.
empty ['emptɪ] (pl **empties**, compar **emptier**, superl **emptiest**) ❖ adj [glass, room, box, etc.] vide ; [city, street] désert ; [cinema] désert, vide ; [job, post] vacant, à pourvoir ; fig [words, talk] creux ; [promise] en l'air, vain ; [gesture] dénué de sens ; [threat] en l'air. ❖ n inf [bottle] bouteille f vide ; [glass] verre m vide. ❖ vt [glass, pocket, room] vider ; [car, lorry] décharger. ❖ vi [building, street, container] se vider ; [water] s'écouler. ❖ **empty out** ❖ vt sep vider. ❖ vi [tank, container] se vider ; [water, liquid] s'écouler.
empty-handed [-'hændɪd] adj les mains vides, bredouille.
empty-headed adj écervelé, sans cervelle.

EMT (abbr of **emergency medical technician**) n technicien médical des services d'urgence.
emu ['iːmjuː] n émeu m.
EMU (abbr of **Economic and Monetary Union**) n UEM f.
emulate ['emjʊleɪt] vt [person, action] imiter ; COMPUT émuler.
emulsify [ɪ'mʌlsɪfaɪ] vt émulsionner, émulsifier.
emulsion [ɪ'mʌlʃn] n **1.** CHEM & PHOT émulsion f **2.** [paint] (peinture f) émulsion f.
emulsion paint = **emulsion** (noun).
enable [ɪ'neɪbl] vt ▸ **to enable sb to do sthg a)** permettre à qqn de faire qqch **b)** LAW habiliter or autoriser qqn à faire qqch.
enabled [ɪ'neɪbld] adj COMPUT [option] activé.
enabler [ɪ'neɪblə'] n **1.** [social worker] travailleur m social, travailleuse f sociale **2.** [personal assistant] assistant m, -e f **3.** US PSYCHOL personne qui encourage implicitement des comportements dysfonctionnels chez un proche / *if you put up with his abuse, you're his enabler* supporter sa violence, c'est l'encourager / *she became obese, and I realise now I was her enabler* elle est devenue obèse, et je me rends compte aujourd'hui que j'en suis en grande partie responsable.
enact [ɪ'nækt] vt **1.** LAW [bill, law] promulguer **2.** [scene, play] jouer ▸ **to be enacted** fig se dérouler.
enactment [ɪ'næktmənt] n **1.** LAW [of bill, law, etc.] promulgation f **2.** [of play] représentation f.
enamel [ɪ'næml] (UK pt & pp **enamelled**, cont **enamelling** ; US pt & pp **enameled**, cont **enameling**) ❖ n **1.** ART [on clay, glass, etc.] émail m **2.** [paint] peinture f laquée or vernie **3.** [on teeth] émail m. ❖ comp [mug, saucepan] en émail, émaillé. ❖ vt émailler.
enamelled UK, **enameled** US [ɪ'næmld] adj [mug, saucepan] émaillé, en émail.
enamoured UK, **enamored** US [ɪ'næməd] adj ▸ **to be enamoured of a)** liter [person] être amoureux or épris de **b)** [job, flat] être enchanté or ravi de.
en bloc [ɑ̃'blɒk] adv en bloc.
enc. 1. (written abbr of **enclosure**) PJ **2.** written abbr of **enclosed**.
encamp [ɪn'kæmp] ❖ vi camper. ❖ vt faire camper ▸ **to be encamped** camper.
encampment [ɪn'kæmpmənt] n campement m.
encapsulate [ɪn'kæpsjʊleɪt] vt PHARM mettre en capsule ; fig résumer.
encase [ɪn'keɪs] vt recouvrir, entourer.
encash [ɪn'kæʃ] vt UK encaisser.
encephalomyelitis [en,sefələʊmaɪə'laɪtɪs] n encéphalomyélite f.
encephalopathy [en,sefə'lɒpəθɪ] n encéphalopathie f.
enchant [ɪn'tʃɑːnt] vt **1.** [delight] enchanter, ravir **2.** [put spell on] enchanter, ensorceler.
enchanted [ɪn'tʃɑːntɪd] adj enchanté.
enchanting [ɪn'tʃɑːntɪŋ] adj charmant.
enchantingly [ɪn'tʃɑːntɪŋlɪ] adv [sing, play] merveilleusement bien.
enchantment [ɪn'tʃɑːntmənt] n **1.** [delight] enchantement m, ravissement m **2.** [casting of spell] enchantement m, ensorcellement m.
enchilada [enʧɪ'lɑːdə] n plat mexicain consistant en une galette de maïs frite, farcie à la viande et servie avec une sauce piquante ▸ **the big enchilada** US inf le patron, le big boss.

encircle [ɪnˈsɜːkl] vt entourer ; MIL & HUNT encercler, cerner.

encl. = **enc.**

enclave [ˈenkleɪv] n enclave f.

enclose [ɪnˈkləʊz] vt **1.** [surround - with wall] entourer, ceinturer ; [- with fence] clôturer **2.** [in letter] joindre **▶ to enclose sthg with a letter** joindre qqch à une lettre.

enclosed [ɪnˈkləʊzd] adj **1.** [area] clos **2.** COMM [cheque] ci-joint, ci-inclus **/ please find enclosed my CV** veuillez trouver ci-joint or ci-inclus mon CV.

enclosure [ɪnˈkləʊʒər] n **1.** [enclosed area] enclos m, enceinte f **2.** [with letter] pièce f jointe or annexée or incluse **3.** [action] action f de clôturer.

encode [enˈkəʊd] vt coder, chiffrer ; COMPUT encoder.

encoding [enˈkəʊdɪŋ] n codage m ; COMPUT encodage m.

encompass [ɪnˈkʌmpəs] vt **1.** [include] englober, comprendre, regrouper **2.** fml [surround] entourer, encercler.

encore [ˈɒŋkɔːr] **◆** interj **▶ encore!, encore!** bis !, bis ! **◆** n bis m. **◆** vt [singer, performer] rappeler, bisser ; [song] bisser.

encounter [ɪnˈkaʊntər] **◆** vt [person, enemy] rencontrer ; [difficulty, resistance, danger] rencontrer, se heurter à. **◆** n [gen & MIL] rencontre f.

encourage [ɪnˈkʌrɪdʒ] vt [person] encourager, inciter ; [project, research, attitude] encourager **▶ to encourage sb to do sthg** encourager or inciter qqn à faire qqch.

encouragement [ɪnˈkʌrɪdʒmənt] n encouragement m.

encouraging [ɪnˈkʌrɪdʒɪŋ] adj encourageant ; [smile, words] d'encouragement.

encroach [ɪnˈkrəʊtʃ] **◆ encroach on, encroach upon** vi : the sea is gradually encroaching on the land la mer gagne progressivement du terrain.

encrust [ɪnˈkrʌst] vt [with jewels] incruster ; [with mud, snow, ice] couvrir **▶ to be encrusted with sthg** être incrusté or couvert or recouvert de qqch.

encrypt [enˈkrɪpt] vt coder, chiffrer ; COMPUT crypter.

encryption [enˈkrɪpʃn] n COMPUT cryptage m, cryptologie f.

encumber [ɪnˈkʌmbər] vt fml [person, room] encombrer, embarrasser.

encyclopaedia [ɪnˌsaɪkləˈpiːdjə] = **encyclopedia**.

encyclopedia [ɪnˌsaɪkləˈpiːdjə] n encyclopédie f.

encyclopedic [ɪnˌsaɪkləˈpiːdɪk] adj encyclopédique.

end [end] **◆** n **1.** [furthermost part, tip, edge] bout m **/ at the end of the garden** au bout or fond du jardin **▶ to change ends** SPORT changer de côté ; [area, aspect] côté m **/ the marketing / manufacturing end of the operation** le côté marketing / fabrication de l'opération, tout ce qui est marketing / fabrication **▶ this is the end of the road** or **line** c'est fini **▶ to go to the ends of the earth** aller jusqu'au bout du monde **▶ to keep one's end up** tenir bon **▶ to make (both) ends meet** [financially] joindre les deux bouts **2.** [conclusion, finish] fin f **/ from beginning to end** du début à la fin, de bout en bout **▶ to be at an end** être terminé or fini **▶ to bring sthg to an end a)** [meeting] clore qqch **b)** [situation] mettre fin à qqch **c)** [speech] achever qqch **▶ to come to an end** s'achever, prendre fin **▶ to put an end to sthg** mettre fin à qqch **/ we want an end to the war** nous voulons que cette guerre cesse or prenne fin **/ and that was the end of it** et ça s'est terminé comme ça **▶ it's not the end of the world** inf ce n'est pas la fin du monde **/ we'll never hear the end of it** on n'a pas fini d'en entendre parler **/ is there no end to his talents?** a-t-il donc tous les talents ?, n'y a-t-il pas de limite à ses talents ? **3.** [aim] but m, fin f **▶ to achieve** or **to attain one's end** atteindre son but **/ with this end in view** or **mind, to this end** dans ce but, à cette fin **▶ an end in itself** une fin en soi **▶ the end justifies the means** la fin justifie les moyens **4.** [remnant - of cloth, rope] bout m ; [- of loaf] croûton m. **◆** vt [speech, novel] terminer, conclure ; [meeting, discussion] clore ; [day] terminer, finir ; [war, speculation, relationship] mettre fin or un terme à ; [work] terminer, finir, achever **/ he decided to end it all** [life, relationship] il décida d'en finir. **◆** vi [story, film] finir, se terminer, s'achever ; [path, road, etc.] se terminer, s'arrêter ; [season, holiday] se terminer, toucher à sa fin **/ how** or **where will it all end?** comment tout cela finira-t-il or se terminera-t-il ? **/ the discussion ended in an argument** la discussion s'est terminée en dispute **/ to end in failure / divorce** se solder par un échec / un divorce **/ the word ends in -ed** le mot se termine par or en -ed. **◆ in the end** adv phr finalement **/ we got there in the end** finalement nous y sommes arrivés, nous avons fini par y arriver. **◆ no end** adv phr inf : it upset her / cheered her up no end ça l'a bouleversée / ravie à un point (inimaginable). **◆ no end of** det phr inf : it'll do you no end of good cela vous fera un bien fou **/ to have no end of trouble doing sthg** avoir énormément de mal or un mal fou or un mal de chien à faire qqch. **◆ on end** adv phr **1.** [upright] debout **/ her hair was standing on end** elle avait les cheveux dressés sur la tête **2.** [in succession] entier **/ for hours / days on end** pendant des heures entières / des jours entiers. **◆ end off** vt sep terminer. **◆ end up** vi finir **/ they ended up in Manchester** ils se sont retrouvés à Manchester **/ to end up in hospital / in prison** finir à l'hôpital / en prison **▶ to end up doing sthg** finir par faire qqch.

endanger [ɪnˈdeɪndʒər] vt [life, country] mettre en danger ; [health, reputation, future, chances] compromettre.

endangered species [ɪnˈdeɪndʒəd-] n espèce f en voie de disparition.

end-consumer n COMM utilisateur m final ; [of foodstuffs] consommateur m final, utilisateur m final.

endear [ɪnˈdɪər] vt faire aimer **▶ to endear o.s. to sb** faire aimer de qqn.

endearing [ɪnˈdɪərɪŋ] adj [personality, person] attachant ; [smile] engageant.

endearingly [ɪnˈdɪərɪŋlɪ] adv de manière attachante ; [smile] de manière engageante.

endearment [ɪnˈdɪəmənt] n **▶ endearments** or **words of endearment** mots mpl tendres **▶ term of endearment** terme m affectueux.

endeavour UK, **endeavor** US [ɪnˈdevər] fml **◆** n effort m. **◆** vi **▶ to endeavour to do sthg** s'efforcer or essayer de faire qqch.

endemic [enˈdemɪk] **◆** adj MED endémique. **◆** n MED endémie f.

endgame [ˈendɡeɪm] n **1.** objectif m **2.** CHESS fin f de partie.

ending [ˈendɪŋ] n **1.** [of story, book] fin f **2.** LING terminaison f.

endive [ˈendaɪv] n **1.** [curly-leaved] (chicorée f) frisée f **2.** US [chicory] endive f.

endless [ˈendlɪs] adj **1.** [speech, road, job] interminable, sans fin ; [patience] sans bornes, infini ; [resources] inépuisable, infini **2.** TECH [belt, screw] sans fin.

endlessly [ˈendlɪslɪ] adv [speak] continuellement, sans cesse ; [extend] à perte de vue, interminablement.

endnote [ˈendnəʊt] n COMPUT note f de fin de document.

endocranium [ˌendəˈkreɪnɪəm] (pl endocrania [ˌendəʊˈkreɪnɪə]) n endocrâne m.

endocrinology [ˌendəʊkraɪˈnɒlədʒɪ] n MED endocrinologie f.

end-of-month adj de fin de mois.

end-of-year adj **1.** [gen] de fin d'année **2.** FIN de fin d'exercice.

endometriosis [ˌendəʊmiːˈtrɪˈəʊsɪs] n endométriose f.

endorphin [enˈdɔːfɪn] n MED endorphine f.

endorse [ɪnˈdɔːs] vt **1.** [cheque] endosser ; [document - sign] apposer sa signature sur ; [- annotate] apposer une remarque sur **2.** [UK] LAW ▶ **to endorse a driving licence** faire état d'une infraction sur un permis de conduire **3.** [approve - action, decision] approuver ; [- opinion] soutenir, adhérer à ; [- appeal, candidature] appuyer.

endorsement [ɪnˈdɔːsmənt] n **1.** [of cheque] endossement m ; [of document - signature] signature f ; [- annotation] remarque f **2.** [UK] LAW [on driving licence] *infraction dont il est fait état sur le permis de conduire* **3.** [approval - of action, decision] approbation f ; [- of claim, candidature] appui m.

endoscope [ˈendəskəʊp] n MED endoscope m.

endow [ɪnˈdaʊ] vt **1.** [institution] doter ; [university chair, hospital ward] fonder **2.** *(usu passive)* ▶ **to be endowed with sthg** être doté de qqch.

endowment [ɪnˈdaʊmənt] n **1.** [action, money] dotation f **2.** *(usu pl)* *fml* [talent, gift] don m, talent m.

endowment assurance, endowment insurance n [UK] assurance f à capital différé.

endowment mortgage n [UK] *hypothèque garantie par une assurance-vie.*

endowment policy n assurance f mixte.

end product n INDUST & COMM produit m final ; *fig* résultat m.

end result n résultat m final.

end table n bout m de canapé.

endurable [ɪnˈdjʊərəbl] adj supportable, endurable.

endurance [ɪnˈdjʊərəns] ◆ n endurance f. ◆ comp ▶ **endurance test** épreuve f d'endurance.

endure [ɪnˈdjʊə] ◆ vt [bear - hardship] endurer, subir ; [- pain] endurer ; [- person, stupidity, laziness] supporter, souffrir. ◆ vi *fml* [relationship, ceasefire, fame] durer ; [memory] rester.

enduring [ɪnˈdjʊərɪŋ] adj [friendship, fame, peace] durable ; [democracy, dictatorship] qui dure ; [epidemic, suffering] tenace ; [actor, politician] qui jouit d'une grande longévité *(en tant qu'acteur, homme politique, etc.).*

end user n [gen & COMPUT] utilisateur m final, utilisatrice f finale.

endways [ˈendweɪz] adv ▶ **put it endways on** mets-le en long.

endwise [ˈendwaɪz] [US] = endways.

enema [ˈenɪmə] n [act] lavement m ; [liquid] produit m à lavement.

enemy [ˈenɪmɪ] *(pl* enemies*)* ◆ n **1.** ennemi m, -e f **2.** MIL : *the enemy was* or *were advancing* l'ennemi avançait. ◆ comp [forces, attack, missile, country] ennemi ; [advance, strategy] de l'ennemi ▶ **enemy fire** feu m de l'ennemi.

enemy-occupied adj [territory] occupé par l'ennemi.

energetic [ˌenəˈdʒetɪk] adj [person, measures] énergique ; [music] vif, rapide ; [campaigner, supporter] enthousiaste.

energetically [ˌenəˈdʒetɪklɪ] adv énergiquement.

energize [ˈenədʒaɪz] vt [person] donner de l'énergie à, stimuler ; ELEC exciter, envoyer de l'électricité dans.

energy [ˈenədʒɪ] *(pl* energies*)* ◆ n **1.** [vitality] énergie f **2.** [effort] énergie f **3.** PHYS énergie f **4.** [power] éner-

gie f ▶ **Minister of** or **Secretary (of State) for Energy** ministre m de l'Énergie. ◆ comp [conservation, consumption] d'énergie ; [supplies, programme, level] énergétique.

energy-saving adj [device] pour économiser l'énergie.

enervate [ˈenəveɪt] vt amollir, débiliter.

enervating [ˈenəveɪtɪŋ] adj amollissant, débilitant.

enfold [ɪnˈfəʊld] vt [embrace] étreindre ▶ **to enfold sb in one's arms** étreindre qqn, entourer qqn de ses bras.

enforce [ɪnˈfɔːs] vt [policy, decision] mettre en œuvre, appliquer ; [law] mettre en vigueur ; [subj: police] faire exécuter ; [one's rights] faire valoir ; [one's will, discipline] faire respecter ; [contract] faire exécuter.

enforceable [ɪnˈfɔːsəbl] adj exécutoire.

enforced [ɪnˈfɔːst] adj forcé.

enforcement [ɪnˈfɔːsmənt] n [of law] application f ; [of contract] exécution f.

enforcer [ɪnˈfɔːsə] n [US] agent m de police.

enfranchise [ɪnˈfræntʃaɪz] vt [give vote to - women, workers] accorder le droit de vote à ; [emancipate - slaves] affranchir.

ENG (abbr of **electronic news gathering**) n journalisme m électronique.

engage [ɪnˈgeɪdʒ] ◆ vt **1.** [occupy, involve] ▶ **to engage sb in conversation a)** [talk to] discuter avec qqn **b)** [begin talking to] engager la conversation avec qqn **2.** *fml* [employ - staff] engager ; [- lawyer] engager les services de **3.** *fml* [attract, draw - interest, attention] attirer ; [- sympathy] susciter **4.** AUTO & TECH engager **5.** MIL [the enemy] engager (le combat avec) l'ennemi. ◆ vi **1.** [take part] ▶ **to engage in** prendre part à **2.** ▶ **to engage with** [communicate with] communiquer avec **3.** MIL ▶ **to engage in battle with the enemy** engager le combat avec l'ennemi **4.** AUTO & TECH s'engager ; [cogs] s'engrener ; [machine part] s'enclencher **5.** *fml* [promise] ▶ **to engage to do sthg** s'engager à faire qqch.

engaged [ɪnˈgeɪdʒd] adj **1.** [of couple] fiancé ▶ **to get engaged** se fiancer **2.** [busy, occupied] occupé **3.** [UK] [telephone] occupé **4.** [toilet] occupé.

engaged tone n [UK] tonalité f « occupé ».

engagement [ɪnˈgeɪdʒmənt] n **1.** [betrothal] fiançailles fpl **2.** [appointment] rendez-vous m **3.** MIL engagement m **4.** AUTO & TECH engagement m **5.** [recruitment] engagement m, embauche f **6.** *fml* [promise, duty] obligation f, engagement m **7.** [for actor, performer] engagement m, contrat m.

engagement ring n bague f de fiançailles.

engaging [ɪnˈgeɪdʒɪŋ] adj [smile, manner, tone] engageant ; [person, personality] aimable, attachant.

engender [ɪnˈdʒendə] vt engendrer, créer ▶ **to engender sthg in sb** engendrer qqch chez qqn.

engine [ˈendʒɪn] n **1.** [in car, plane] moteur m ; [in ship] machine f ▶ **(railway) engine** [UK] locomotive f. ◆ comp [failure, trouble] de moteur or machine ▶ **engine block** AUTO bloc-moteur m ▶ **engine oil** AUTO huile f à or de moteur.

engine driver n [UK] RAIL mécanicien m, conducteur m.

engineer [ˌendʒɪˈnɪə] ◆ n **1.** [for roads, machines, bridges] ingénieur m ; [repairer] dépanneur m, réparateur m ; [technician] technicien m, -enne f ; MIL soldat m du génie ; NAUT mécanicien m ▶ **aircraft engineer** AERON mécanicien m de piste or d'avion ▶ **flight engineer** AERON ingénieur m de vol, mécanicien m navigant *(d'avion)* ▶ **the Royal Engineers** MIL le génie *(britannique)* **2.** [US] RAIL = **engine driver 3.** *fig* [of plot, scheme, etc.] instigateur m,

-trice *f*, artisan *m*. ◆ ◆ vt **1.** [road, bridge, car] concevoir **2.** *pej* [bring about - event, situation] manigancer **3.** [work - goal, victory] amener.

> ⚠ **Un ingénieur** is an engineer with high-level academic qualifications. For people who do repairs, use **technicien** or **dépanneur**.

engineering [ˌendʒɪ'nɪərɪŋ] ◆ n ingénierie *f*, engineering *m*. ◆ comp ▶ **engineering firm** entreprise *f* de construction mécanique ▶ **engineering work** [on railway line] travail *m* d'ingénierie.

engine room n NAUT salle *f* des machines.

England ['ɪŋɡlənd] pr n Angleterre *f*.

English ['ɪŋɡlɪʃ] ◆ adj anglais ; [history, embassy] d'Angleterre ; [dictionary, teacher] d'anglais. ◆ n LING anglais *m* ▶ **in plain** or **simple English** clairement ▶ **English as a Foreign Language** anglais langue étrangère ▶ **English Language Teaching** enseignement *m* de l'anglais ▶ **English as a Second Language** anglais deuxième langue. ◆ pl n ▶ **the English** les Anglais *mpl*.

English breakfast n petit déjeuner *m* anglais or à l'anglaise, breakfast *m*.

 English breakfast

Le petit déjeuner traditionnel anglais se compose d'un plat chaud (œufs au bacon, saucisses, etc.), de céréales ou de porridge, et de toasts, le tout accompagné de café ou de thé ; il est aujourd'hui souvent remplacé par une collation plus légère.

Englishman ['ɪŋɡlɪʃmən] (*pl* **Englishmen** [-mən]) n Anglais *m*.

English muffin n 🇺🇸 = crumpet.

English sheepdog n 🇺🇸 bobtail *m*.

English-speaking adj [as native language] anglophone ; [as learned language] parlant anglais.

Englishwoman ['ɪŋɡlɪʃˌwʊmən] (*pl* **Englishwomen** [-ˌwɪmɪn]) n Anglaise *f*.

engrave [ɪn'ɡreɪv] vt graver.

engraver [ɪn'ɡreɪvər] n graveur *m*.

engraving [ɪn'ɡreɪvɪŋ] n gravure *f*.

engrossed [ɪn'ɡrəʊst] adj ▶ **to be engrossed in sthg** être absorbé par qqch.

engrossing [ɪn'ɡrəʊsɪŋ] adj absorbant.

engulf [ɪn'ɡʌlf] vt engloutir.

enhance [ɪn'hɑːns] vt [quality, reputation, performance] améliorer ; [value, chances, prestige] augmenter, accroître ; [taste, beauty] rehausser, mettre en valeur.

enhanced [ɪn'hɑːnst] adj [reputation quality, performance] amélioré, meilleur ; [prestige value, chances] augmenté, accru ; [taste, beauty] rehaussé, mis en valeur.

-enhanced in comp ▶ **computer-enhanced** [graphics] optimisé par ordinateur.

enhancement [ɪn'hɑːnsmənt] n [of quality, reputation, performance] amélioration *f* ; [of value, chances, prestige] augmentation *f*, accroissement *m* ; [of taste, beauty] rehaussement *m*, mise *f* en valeur.

enigma [ɪ'nɪɡmə] n énigme *f*.

enigmatic [ˌenɪɡ'mætɪk] adj énigmatique.

enigmatically [ˌenɪɡ'mætɪklɪ] adv [smile, speak] d'un air énigmatique ; [worded] énigmatiquement, d'une manière énigmatique.

enjoy [ɪn'dʒɔɪ] ◆ vt **1.** [like - in general] aimer ; [- on particular occasion] apprécier ▶ **to enjoy sthg / doing sthg** aimer qqch / faire qqch / *enjoy your meal!* bon appétit ! ▶ **to enjoy o.s.** s'amuser **2.** [possess - rights, respect, privilege, income, good health] jouir de ; [profits] bénéficier de. ◆ vi ▶ **enjoy!** a) 🇺🇸 [enjoy yourself] amusez-vous bien ! b) [in restaurant] bon appétit !

enjoyable [ɪn'dʒɔɪəbl] adj [book, film, day] agréable ; [match, contest] beau *(before vowel or silent 'h' bel, f belle)* ; [meal] excellent.

enjoyably [ɪn'dʒɔɪəblɪ] adv de manière agréable.

enjoyment [ɪn'dʒɔɪmənt] n **1.** [pleasure] plaisir *m* ▶ **to get enjoyment from sthg / doing sthg** tirer du plaisir de qqch / à faire qqch **2.** [of privileges, rights, etc.] jouissance *f*.

enlarge [ɪn'lɑːdʒ] ◆ vt **1.** [expand - territory, house, business] agrandir ; [- field of knowledge, group of friends] étendre, élargir ; [- hole] agrandir, élargir ; [- pores] dilater ; [MED - organ] hypertrophier **2.** PHOT agrandir. ◆ vi [gen] s'agrandir, se développer ; [pores] se dilater ; MED [organ] s'hypertrophier. ◆ **enlarge on, enlarge upon** vt insep [elaborate on] s'étendre sur, donner des détails sur.

enlarged [ɪn'lɑːdʒd] adj [majority] accru ; [photograph] agrandi ; MED [tonsil, liver] hypertrophié.

enlargement [ɪn'lɑːdʒmənt] n **1.** [of territory, house, business] agrandissement *m* ; [of group of friends, field of knowledge] élargissement *m* ; [of hole] agrandissement *m*, élargissement *m* ; [of pore] dilatation *f* ; MED [of organ] hypertrophie *f* **2.** PHOT agrandissement *m*.

enlighten [ɪn'laɪtn] vt éclairer ▶ **to enlighten sb about sthg / as to why...** éclairer qqn sur qqch / sur la raison pour laquelle...

enlightened [ɪn'laɪtnd] adj [person, view, policy] éclairé.

enlightening [ɪn'laɪtnɪŋ] adj [book, experience] instructif.

enlightenment [ɪn'laɪtnmənt] n [explanation, information] éclaircissements *mpl* ; [state] édification *f*, instruction *f*. ◆ **Enlightenment** n HIST ▶ **the (Age of) Enlightenment** le Siècle des lumières.

enlist [ɪn'lɪst] vt **1.** MIL enrôler **2.** [help, support, etc.] mobiliser, faire appel à.

enlisted [ɪn'lɪstɪd] adj 🇺🇸 ▶ **enlisted man** (simple) soldat *m*.

enliven [ɪn'laɪvn] vt [conversation, party] animer.

en masse [ɑ̃'mæs] adv en masse, massivement.

enmesh [ɪn'meʃ] vt *lit* prendre dans un filet ; *fig* mêler ▶ **to become** or **get enmeshed in sthg** s'empêtrer dans qqch.

enmity ['enmɪtɪ] (*pl* **enmities**) n *fml* inimitié *f*, hostilité *f* ▶ **enmity for / towards sb** inimitié pour / envers qqn.

ennoble [ɪ'nəʊbl] vt [confer title upon] anoblir ; *fig* [exalt, dignify] ennoblir, grandir.

enormity [ɪ'nɔːmətɪ] (*pl* **enormities**) n **1.** [of action, crime] énormité *f* **2.** *fml* [atrocity] atrocité *f* ; [crime] crime *m* très grave **3.** [great size] énormité *f*.

enormous [ɪ'nɔːməs] adj **1.** [very large - thing] énorme ; [- amount, number] énorme, colossal **2.** [as intensifier] énorme, grand.

enormously [ɪ'nɔːməslɪ] adv énormément, extrêmement.

enough [ɪ'nʌf] ◆ det assez de / *enough money* assez or suffisamment d'argent / *you've had more than enough wine* tu as bu plus qu'assez de vin / *she's not fool enough to believe that!* elle n'est pas assez bête pour le croire !

◆ pron : *do you need some money? — I've got enough* avez-vous besoin d'argent ? — j'en ai assez or suffisamment ▶ **enough is enough!** ça suffit comme ça !, trop c'est trop ! ▶ **enough said!** *inf* je vois ! ▶ **that's enough!** ça suffit ! / *it's enough to drive you mad* c'est à vous rendre fou ▶ **to have had enough (of sthg)** en avoir assez de qqch. ◆ adv **1.** [sufficiently] assez, suffisamment / *he's old enough to understand* il est assez grand pour comprendre / *it's a good enough reason* c'est une raison suffisante **2.** [fairly] assez / *she's honest enough* elle est assez honnête **3.** [with adverb] ▶ **oddly** or **strangely enough, nobody knows her** chose curieuse, personne ne la connaît.

en passant [ɑ̃'pæsɑ̃] adv en passant.

enquire [ɪn'kwaɪər] = inquire.

enquiry [ɪn'kwaɪrɪ] (*pl* **enquiries**) n **1.** [request for information] demande f (de renseignements) ▶ **to make enquiries about sthg** se renseigner sur qqch **2.** [investigation] enquête f. ❖ **enquiries** pl n [information desk, department] renseignements *mpl*.

enquiry desk, enquiry office n accueil m.

enrage [ɪn'reɪdʒ] vt rendre furieux, mettre en rage.

enraged [ɪn'reɪdʒd] adj [person] furieux ; [animal] enragé / *he was enraged to discover that...* il enrageait de découvrir que...

enrapture [ɪn'ræptʃər] vt enchanter, ravir / *we were enraptured by the beauty of the island* nous étions en extase devant la beauté de l'île.

enrich [ɪn'rɪtʃ] vt [mind, person, life] enrichir ; [soil] fertiliser, amender ; PHYS enrichir.

enriching [ɪn'rɪtʃɪŋ] adj enrichissant.

enrol 🇬🇧, **enroll** 🇺🇸 [ɪn'rəʊl] (*pt & pp* **enrolled**, *cont* **enrolling**) ◆ vt **1.** [student] inscrire, immatriculer ; [member] inscrire ; MIL [recruit] enrôler, recruter **2.** 🇺🇸 POL [prepare] dresser, rédiger ; [register] enregistrer ▶ **enroled bill** projet m de loi enregistré. ◆ vi [student] s'inscrire ; MIL s'engager, s'enrôler ▶ **to enrol on** or **for a course** s'inscrire à un cours.

enrolment 🇬🇧, **enrollment** 🇺🇸 [ɪn'rəʊlmənt] n [registration - of members] inscription f ; [- of students] inscription f, immatriculation f ; [- of workers] embauche f ; MIL enrôlement m, recrutement m.

ensconce [ɪn'skɒns] vt *fml & hum* installer / *she ensconced herself* / *was ensconced in the armchair* elle se cala / était bien calée dans le fauteuil.

ensconced [ɪn'skɒnst] adj *liter* ▶ **ensconced (in)** bien installé(e) (dans).

ensemble [ɒn'sɒmbl] n [gen & MUS] ensemble m.

enshrine [ɪn'fraɪn] vt *lit* enchâsser ; *fig* [cherish] conserver pieusement or religieusement.

ensign [ˈensaɪn] n **1.** [flag] drapeau m, enseigne f ; NAUT pavillon m **2.** [symbol] insigne m, emblème m **3.** 🇺🇸 MIL (officier m) porte-étendard m **4.** 🇺🇸 NAUT enseigne m de vaisseau de deuxième classe.

enslave [ɪn'sleɪv] vt *lit* réduire en esclavage, asservir ; *fig* asservir.

enslavement [ɪn'sleɪvmənt] n *lit* asservissement m, assujettissement m ; *fig* sujétion f, asservissement m, assujettissement m.

ensue [ɪn'sju:] vi s'ensuivre, résulter.

ensuing [ɪn'sju:ɪŋ] adj [action, event] qui s'ensuit ; [month, year] suivant.

en suite [ˌɒn'swi:t] adj & adv : *with en suite bathroom* or *with bathroom en suite* avec salle de bain particulière.

ensure [ɪn'ʃʊər] vt **1.** [guarantee] assurer, garantir **2.** [protect] protéger, assurer.

ENT (abbr of **ear, nose & throat**) ◆ n ORL f. ◆ adj ORL.

entail [ɪn'teɪl] vt **1.** [imply - consequence, expense] entraîner ; [- difficulty, risk] comporter ; [- delay, expense] occasionner ; LOGIC entraîner **2.** LAW ▶ **to entail an estate** substituer un héritage ▶ **an entailed estate** un bien grevé.

entangle [ɪn'tæŋgl] vt **1.** [ensnare] empêtrer, enchevêtrer ▶ **to become** or **get entangled in sthg** s'empêtrer dans qqch **2.** [snarl - hair] emmêler ; [- threads] emmêler, embrouiller **3.** *fig* [involve] entraîner, impliquer ; *fig* [with person] ▶ **to be entangled with** avoir une liaison avec.

entanglement [ɪn'tæŋglmənt] n **1.** [in net, undergrowth] enchevêtrement m **2.** [of hair, thread] emmêlement m **3.** *fig* [involvement] implication f.

entente [ɒn'tɒnt] n entente f. ❖ **entente cordiale** n entente f cordiale.

enter [ˈentər] ◆ vt **1.** [go into - room] entrer dans ; [- building] entrer dans, pénétrer dans **2.** [join - university] s'inscrire à, se faire inscrire à ; [- profession] entrer dans ; [- army] s'engager or entrer dans ; [- politics] se lancer dans **3.** [register] inscrire **4.** [record - on list] inscrire ; [- in book] noter ; COMPUT [data, name, password] entrer, saisir **5.** [submit] présenter. ◆ vi **1.** [come in] entrer **2.** [register] s'inscrire. ❖ **enter into** vt insep **1.** [begin - explanation] se lancer dans ; [- conversation, relations] entrer en ; [- negotiations] entamer **2.** [become involved in] : *to enter into an agreement with sb* conclure un accord avec qqn **3.** [affect] entrer dans / *my feelings don't enter into my decision* mes sentiments n'ont rien à voir avec or ne sont pour rien dans ma décision. ❖ **enter upon** vt insep [career] débuter or entrer dans ; [negotiations] entamer ; [policy] commencer.

enteritis [ˌentəˈraɪtɪs] n *(U)* entérite f.

enter key n COMPUT (touche f) entrée f or retour m.

enterprise [ˈentəpraɪz] n **1.** [business, project] entreprise f **2.** [initiative] initiative f, esprit m entreprenant or d'initiative.

enterprise culture n esprit m d'entreprise.

enterprise zone n 🇬🇧 zone d'encouragement à l'implantation d'entreprises dans les régions économiquement défavorisées.

enterprising [ˈentəpraɪzɪŋ] adj [person] entreprenant, plein d'initiative ; [project] audacieux, hardi.

entertain [ˌentəˈteɪn] ◆ vt **1.** [amuse] amuser, divertir **2.** [show hospitality towards] recevoir **3.** [idea] considérer, penser à ; [hope] caresser, nourrir ; [doubt] entretenir ; [suggestion] admettre. ◆ vi recevoir.

entertainer [ˌentəˈteɪnər] n [comedian] comique m, amuseur m, -euse f ; [in music hall] artiste mf (de music-hall), fantaisiste mf.

entertaining [ˌentəˈteɪnɪŋ] ◆ n : *she enjoys entertaining* elle aime bien recevoir. ◆ adj amusant, divertissant.

entertainment [ˌentəˈteɪnmənt] n **1.** [amusement] amusement m, divertissement m / *entertainment center* or *system* 🇺🇸 système m audio-vidéo ▶ **entertainment allowance** frais *mpl* de représentation **2.** [performance] spectacle m, attraction f.

enthral 🇬🇧, **enthrall** 🇺🇸 [ɪn'θrɔ:l] (*pt & pp* **enthralled**, *cont* **enthralling**) vt [fascinate] captiver, passionner.

enthralling [ɪn'θrɔ:lɪŋ] adj [book, film] captivant, passionnant ; [beauty, charm] séduisant.

enthrallingly [ɪn'θrɔ:lɪŋlɪ] adv d'une manière captivante.

enthrone [ɪn'θrəʊn] vt [monarch] mettre sur le trône, introniser ; [bishop] introniser.

enthuse [ɪn'θjuːz] ◆ vi s'enthousiasmer. ◆ vt enthousiasmer, emballer.

enthusiasm [ɪn'θjuːzɪæzm] n **1.** [interest] enthousiasme m **2.** [hobby] passion f.

enthusiast [ɪn'θjuːzɪæst] n enthousiaste mf, fervent m, -e f.

enthusiastic [ɪnˌθjuːzɪ'æstɪk] adj [person, response] enthousiaste ; [shout, applause] enthousiaste, d'enthousiasme.

enthusiastically [ɪnˌθjuːzɪ'æstɪklɪ] adv [receive] avec enthousiasme ; [speak, support] avec enthousiasme or ferveur ; [work] avec zèle.

entice [ɪn'taɪs] vt attirer, séduire **▶ to entice sb away from sthg** éloigner qqn de qqch.

enticing [ɪn'taɪsɪŋ] adj [offer] attrayant, séduisant ; [person] séduisant ; [food] alléchant, appétissant.

enticingly [ɪn'taɪsɪŋlɪ] adv de façon séduisante.

entire [ɪn'taɪə] adj **1.** [whole] entier, tout **2.** [total] entier, complet (complète) ; [absolute] total, absolu **3.** [intact] entier, intact.

entirely [ɪn'taɪəlɪ] adv entièrement, totalement.

entirety [ɪn'taɪrətɪ] (pl entireties) n **1.** [completeness] intégralité f **▶ in its entirety** en (son) entier, intégralement **2.** [total] totalité f.

entitle [ɪn'taɪtl] vt **1.** [give right to] autoriser **▶ to be entitled to do sthg a)** [by status] avoir qualité pour or être habilité à faire qqch **b)** [by rules] avoir le droit or être en droit de faire qqch ; LAW habiliter **2.** [film, painting, etc.] intituler **3.** [bestow title on] donner un titre à.

entitlement [ɪn'taɪtlmənt] n droit m.

entity ['entətɪ] (pl entities) n entité f.

entomology [ˌentə'mɒlədʒɪ] n entomologie f.

entourage [ˌɒntʊ'rɑːʒ] n entourage m.

entrails ['entreɪlz] pl n lit & fig entrailles fpl.

entrance¹ ['entrəns] ◆ n **1.** [means of entry] entrée f ; [large] portail m ; [foyer] entrée f, vestibule m **2.** [arrival] entrée f **3.** [admission] admission f **4.** [access] accès m, admission f. ◆ comp [card, ticket] d'entrée, d'admission **▶ entrance examination a)** [for school] examen m d'entrée **b)** [for job] concours m de recrutement **▶ entrance requirements** qualifications fpl exigées à l'entrée.

entrance² [ɪn'trɑːns] vt **1.** [hypnotize] hypnotiser, faire entrer en transe **2.** fig [delight] ravir, enchanter.

entrance fee ['entrəns-] n [to exhibition, fair, etc.] droit m d'entrée ; UK [to club, organization, etc.] droit m or frais mpl d'inscription.

entrance hall ['entrəns-] n [in house] vestibule m ; [in hotel] hall m.

entrancing [ɪn'trɑːnsɪŋ] adj enchanteur, ravissant.

entrant ['entrənt] n **1.** [in exam] candidat m, -e f ; [in race] concurrent m, -e f, participant m, -e f **2.** [to profession, society] débutant m, -e f.

entrapment [ɪn'træpmənt] n incitation au délit par un policier afin de justifier une arrestation.

entreat [ɪn'triːt] vt fml implorer, supplier **▶ to entreat sb to do sthg** supplier qqn de faire qqch.

entreaty [ɪn'triːtɪ] (pl entreaties) n fml supplication f, prière f.

entrée ['ɒntreɪ] n [course preceding main dish] entrée f ; US [main dish] plat m principal or de résistance.

entrenched [ɪn'trentʃt] adj **1.** MIL retranché **2.** fig [person] inflexible, inébranlable ; [idea] arrêté ; [power, tradition] implanté.

entrepreneur [ˌɒntrəprə'nɜːʳ] n entrepreneur m (homme d'affaires).

entrepreneurial [ˌɒntrəprə'nɜːrɪəl] adj [spirit, attitude] d'entrepreneur ; [society, person] qui a l'esprit d'entreprise ; [skills] d'entrepreneur.

entrust [ɪn'trʌst] vt confier **▶ to entrust sthg to sb** confier qqch à qqn **▶ to entrust sb with a job** charger qqn d'une tâche, confier une tâche à qqn.

entry ['entrɪ] (pl entries) ◆ n **1.** [way in] entrée f ; [larger] portail m **2.** [act] entrée f **3.** [admission] entrée f, accès m / 'no entry' **a)** [on door] 'défense d'entrer', 'entrée interdite' **b)** [in street] 'sens interdit' **4.** [in dictionary] entrée f ; [in diary] notation f ; [in encyclopedia] article m ; [on list] inscription f ; COMPUT [of data] entrée (des données) ; [in account book, ledger] écriture f **5.** [competitor] inscription f ; [item submitted for competition] participant m, -e f, concurrent m, -e f **6.** (U) [number of entrants] taux m de participation. ◆ comp [fee, form] d'inscription.

entry-level adj [bottom-of-the-range] bas de gamme, d'entrée de gamme.

Entryphone® ['entrɪˌfəʊn] n Interphone® m.

entry visa n visa m d'entrée.

entryway ['entrɪˌweɪ] n US entrée f ; [larger] portail m ; [foyer] foyer m, vestibule m.

entwine [ɪn'twaɪn] vt entrelacer.

enuf MESSAGING written abbr of **enough**.

E number n UK inf additif m code E.

enumerate [ɪ'njuːməreɪt] vt énumérer, dénombrer.

enunciate [ɪ'nʌnsɪeɪt] ◆ vt **1.** [articulate] articuler, prononcer **2.** fml [formulate - idea, theory, policy] énoncer, exprimer. ◆ vi articuler.

envelop [ɪn'veləp] vt envelopper.

envelope ['envələʊp] n [for letter] enveloppe f.

enviable ['envɪəbl] adj enviable.

enviably ['envɪəblɪ] adv d'une manière enviable.

envious ['envɪəs] adj [person] envieux, jaloux ; [look, tone] envieux, d'envie.

enviously ['envɪəslɪ] adv avec envie.

environment [ɪn'vaɪərənmənt] n **1.** ECOL & POL [nature] environnement m **▶ the Secretary of State for the Environment** ≃ le ministre de l'Environnement **2.** [surroundings - physical] cadre m, milieu m ; [- social] milieu m, environnement m ; [- psychological] milieu m, ambiance f ; BIOL, BOT & GEOG milieu m ; LING & COMPUT environnement m.

environment agency n agence f pour la protection de l'environnement.

environmental [ɪnˌvaɪərən'mentl] adj **1.** ECOL & POL écologique **▶ Environmental Protection Agency** US Agence f pour la protection de l'environnement **2.** [of surroundings] du milieu.

Environmental Health Officer n UK inspecteur m sanitaire.

environmentalist [ɪnˌvaɪərən'mentəlɪst] n **1.** ECOL écologiste mf **2.** PSYCHOL environnementaliste mf.

environmentally [ɪnˌvaɪərən'mentəlɪ] adv ECOL écologiquement.

environment-friendly, environmentally friendly adj [policy, product] écologique.

environs [ɪn'vaɪərənz] pl n fml environs mpl, alentours mpl.

envisage [ɪn'vɪzɪdʒ] vt [imagine] envisager ; [predict] prévoir.

envision [ɪn'vɪʒn] US = **envisage**.

envoy ['envɔɪ] n [emissary] envoyé m, -e f, représentant m, -e f.

envy ['envɪ] (*pl* envies, *pt & pp* envied) ◆ n **1.** [jealousy] envie *f*, jalousie *f* / out of envy par envie or jalousie **2.** [object of jealousy] objet *m* d'envie. ◆ vt envier.

enzyme ['enzaɪm] n enzyme *f*.

EOD MESSAGING written abbr of end of discussion.

EOL n MESSAGING written abbr of end of lecture.

eon ['iːɒn] = aeon.

EP n **1.** (abbr of extended play) super 45 tours *m*, EP *m* **2.** abbr of European Plan **3.** (abbr of European Parliament) Parlement *m* européen.

EPA pr n abbr of Environmental Protection Agency.

epaulette 🇬🇧, **epaulet** 🇺🇸 [,epə'let] n épaulette *f*.

ephemeral [ɪ'femərəl] adj [short-lived] éphémère, fugitif ; ZOOL éphémère.

epic ['epɪk] ◆ adj **1.** [impressive] héroïque, épique ; hum épique, homérique **2.** LITER épique. ◆ n **1.** LITER épopée *f*, poème *m* or récit *m* épique **2.** [film] film *m* à grand spectacle.

epicentre 🇬🇧, **epicenter** 🇺🇸 ['epɪsentər] n épicentre *m*.

epidemic [,epɪ'demɪk] lit & fig ◆ n épidémie *f*. ◆ adj épidémique.

epidural [,epɪ'djʊərəl] ◆ adj épidural. ◆ n anesthésie *f* épidurale, péridurale *f*.

epigram ['epɪgræm] n épigramme *f*.

epigraph ['epɪgrɑːf] n épigraphe *f*.

epilepsy ['epɪlepsɪ] n épilepsie *f*.

epileptic [,epɪ'leptɪk] ◆ adj épileptique ▸ an epileptic fit une crise d'épilepsie. ◆ n épileptique mf.

epilog 🇺🇸, **epilogue** ['epɪlɒg] n épilogue *m*.

Epiphany [ɪ'pɪfənɪ] n Épiphanie *f*, fête *f* des rois.

episcopal [ɪ'pɪskəpl] adj épiscopal.

episode ['epɪsəʊd] n épisode *m*.

episodic [,epɪ'sɒdɪk] adj épisodique.

epistle [ɪ'pɪsl] n **1.** fml & hum [letter] lettre *f*, épître *f* hum ; ADMIN courrier *m* **2.** LITER épître *f*. ✦ **Epistle** n BIBLE ▸ the Epistle to the Romans l'Épître *f* aux Romains.

epitaph ['epɪtɑːf] n épitaphe *f*.

epithet ['epɪθet] n épithète *f*.

epitome [ɪ'pɪtəmɪ] n [typical example] modèle *m*, type *m* or exemple *m* même.

epitomize, epitomise [ɪ'pɪtəmaɪz] vt [typify] personnifier, incarner.

epoch ['iːpɒk] n époque *f*.

epoch-making adj qui fait époque, qui fait date.

eponymous [ɪ'pɒnɪməs] adj du même nom, éponyme.

EPOS ['iːpɒs] (abbr of electronic point of sale) n point de vente électronique.

EQ [iː'kjuː] (abbr of emotional intelligence quotient) n QE *m*, quotient *m* émotionnel.

equable ['ekwəbl] adj [character, person] égal, placide ; [climate] égal, constant.

equably ['ekwəblɪ] adv tranquillement, placidement.

equal ['iːkwəl] (🇬🇧 pt & pp equalled, cont equalling ; 🇺🇸 pt & pp equaled, cont equaling) ◆ adj **1.** [of same size, amount, degree, type] égal ▸ to be equal to sthg égaler qqch ▸ equal ops inf or equal opportunities chances fpl égales, égalité *f* des chances ▸ equal opportunity employer entreprise s'engageant à respecter la législation sur la non-discrimination dans l'emploi ▸ equal rights égalité des droits ▸ Equal Rights Amendment = ERA **2.** [adequate] ▸ equal to: he proved equal to the task il s'est montré à la

hauteur de la tâche ▸ to feel equal to doing sthg se sentir le courage de faire qqch. ◆ n égal *m*, -e *f*, pair *m*. ◆ vt **1.** [gen & MATH] égaler **2.** [match] égaler.

equality [iː'kwɒlətɪ] (pl equalities) n égalité *f* / equality of opportunity égalité des chances.

equalize, equalise ['iːkwəlaɪz] ◆ vt [chances] égaliser ; [taxes, wealth] faire la péréquation de. ◆ vi SPORT égaliser.

equalizer ['iːkwəlaɪzər] n **1.** SPORT but *m* or point *m* égalisateur **2.** ELECTRON égaliseur *m* **3.** 🇺🇸 inf [gun] flingue *f*.

equally ['iːkwəlɪ] adv **1.** [evenly] également **2.** [to same degree] également, aussi **3.** [by the same token] : efficiency is important, but equally we must consider the welfare of the staff l'efficacité, c'est important, mais nous devons tout autant considérer le bien-être du personnel.

equal sign, equals sign n signe *m* d'égalité or d'équivalence.

equanimity [,ekwə'nɪmətɪ] n fml sérénité *f*, équanimité *f* liter.

equate [ɪ'kweɪt] vt **1.** [regard as equivalent] assimiler, mettre sur le même pied **2.** [make equal] égaler, égaliser ▸ to equate sthg to sthg MATH mettre qqch en équation avec qqch.

equation [ɪ'kweɪʒn] n **1.** fml [association] assimilation *f* **2.** fml [equalization] égalisation *f* **3.** CHEM & MATH équation *f*.

equator [ɪ'kweɪtər] n équateur *m* / at or on the equator sous or à l'équateur.

equatorial [,ekwə'tɔːrɪəl] adj équatorial.

Equatorial Guinea pr n Guinée-Équatoriale *f* / in Equatorial Guinea en Guinée-Équatoriale.

equestrian [ɪ'kwestrɪən] ◆ adj [event] hippique ; [skills] équestre ; [statue] équestre ; [equipment, clothing] d'équitation. ◆ n [rider] cavalier *m*, -ère *f* ; MIL [in circus] écuyer *m*, -ère *f*.

equidistant [,iːkwɪ'dɪstənt] adj équidistant, à distance égale.

equilateral [,iːkwɪ'lætərəl] adj équilatéral.

equilibrium [,iːkwɪ'lɪbrɪəm] n équilibre *m* ▸ in equilibrium en équilibre.

equine ['ekwaɪn] adj [disease, family] équin ; [profile] chevalin ▸ equine distemper gourme *f*.

equinox ['iːkwɪnɒks] n équinoxe *m*.

equip [ɪ'kwɪp] (pt & pp equipped, cont equipping) vt **1.** [fit out - factory] équiper, outiller ; [- laboratory, kitchen] installer, équiper ; [- army, ship] équiper **2.** fig [prepare] ▸ to be well-equipped to do sthg avoir tout ce qu'il faut pour faire qqch **3.** [supply - person] équiper, pourvoir ; [- army, machine, factory] équiper, munir.

equipment [ɪ'kwɪpmənt] n (U) **1.** [gen] équipement *m* ; [in laboratory, office, school] matériel *m* ; MIL & SPORT équipement *m*, matériel *m* **2.** [act] équipement *m*.

equitable ['ekwɪtəbl] adj équitable, juste.

equitably ['ekwɪtəblɪ] adv équitablement, avec justice.

equity ['ekwɪtɪ] (pl equities) n **1.** [fairness] équité *f* **2.** LAW [system] équité *f* ; [right] droit *m* équitable **3.** FIN [market value] fonds mpl or capitaux mpl propres ; [share] action *f* ordinaire. ✦ **Equity** pr n principal syndicat britannique des travailleurs du spectacle.

equivalence [ɪ'kwɪvələns] n équivalence *f*.

equivalent [ɪ'kwɪvələnt] ◆ adj équivalent ▸ to be equivalent to sthg être équivalent à qqch, équivaloir à qqch. ◆ n équivalent *m* / the French equivalent for or of "pound" l'équivalent français du mot « pound ».

equivocal [ɪˈkwɪvəkl] adj **1.** [ambiguous - words, attitude] ambigu (ambiguë), équivoque **2.** [dubious - behaviour, person] suspect, douteux ; [- outcome] incertain, douteux.

equivocally [ɪˈkwɪvəklɪ] adv **1.** [ambiguously] de manière équivoque or ambiguë **2.** [dubiously] de manière douteuse.

equivocate [ɪˈkwɪvəkeɪt] vi fml user d'équivoques or de faux-fuyants, équivoquer liter.

equivocation [ɪˌkwɪvəˈkeɪʃn] n (U) fml [words] paroles fpl équivoques ; [prevarication] tergiversation f.

er [ɜːr] interj heu.

ER 1. (written abbr of **Elizabeth Regina**) emblème de la reine Élisabeth **2.** (abbr of **Emergency Room**) US urgences fpl.

era [ˈɪərə] n [gen] époque f ; GEOL & HIST ère f.

ERA [ˈɪərə] (abbr of **Equal Rights Amendment**) n projet de loi américain rejeté en 1982 qui posait comme principe l'égalité des individus quels que soient leur sexe, leur religion ou leur race.

eradicate [ɪˈrædɪkeɪt] vt [disease] éradiquer, faire disparaître ; [poverty, problem] faire disparaître, supprimer ; [abuse, crime] extirper, supprimer ; [practice] bannir, mettre fin à ; [weeds] détruire, déraciner.

eradication [ɪˌrædɪˈkeɪʃn] n [of disease] éradication f ; [of poverty, problem] suppression f ; [of abuse, crime] extirpation f, suppression f ; [of practice] fin f ; [of weeds] destruction f, déracinement m.

erasable [ɪˈreɪzəbl] adj effaçable.

erase [ɪˈreɪz] ◆ vt [writing] effacer, gratter ; [with rubber] gommer ; COMPUT & fig effacer. ◆ vi s'effacer.

eraser [ɪˈreɪzər] n gomme f.

erect [ɪˈrekt] ◆ adj **1.** [upright] droit ; [standing] debout **2.** PHYSIOL [penis, nipples] dur. ◆ vt **1.** [build - building, wall] bâtir, construire ; [- statue, temple] ériger, élever ; [- equipment] installer ; [- roadblock, tent] dresser **2.** fig [system] édifier ; [obstacle] élever.

erection [ɪˈrekʃn] n **1.** [of building, wall] construction f ; [of statue, temple] érection f ; [of equipment] installation f ; [of roadblock, tent] dressage m ; fig [of system, obstacle] édification f **2.** [building] bâtiment m, construction f **3.** PHYSIOL érection f.

ergonomic [ˌɜːgəʊˈnɒmɪk] adj ergonomique.

ergonomically [ˌɜːgəʊˈnɒmɪkəlɪ] adv du point de vue ergonomique.

ergonomics [ˌɜːgəˈnɒmɪks] n (U) ergonomie f.

ERISA [əˈriːsə] (abbr of **Employee Retirement Income Security Act**) n loi américaine sur les pensions de retraite.

Eritrea [ˌerɪˈtreɪə] pr n Érythrée f / in Eritrea en Érythrée.

Eritrean [ˌerɪˈtreɪən] ◆ n Érythréen m, -enne f. ◆ adj érythréen.

ERM (abbr of **exchange rate mechanism**) n mécanisme m de change (du SME).

ermine [ˈɜːmɪn] n [fur, robe, stoat] hermine f.

Ernie [ˈɜːnɪ] (abbr of **Electronic Random Number Indicator Equipment**) n en Grande-Bretagne, ordinateur qui sert au tirage des numéros gagnants des bons à lots.

erode [ɪˈrəʊd] ◆ vt [subj: water, wind] éroder, ronger ; [subj: acid, rust] ronger, corroder ; fig [courage, power] ronger, miner. ◆ vi [rock, soil] s'éroder.

erogenous [ɪˈrɒdʒɪnəs] adj érogène.

erosion [ɪˈrəʊʒn] n [of soil, rock] érosion f ; [of metal] corrosion f ; fig [of courage, power] érosion f, corrosion f.

erotic [ɪˈrɒtɪk] adj érotique.

erotica [ɪˈrɒtɪkə] pl n ART art m érotique ; LITER littérature f érotique.

erotically [ɪˈrɒtɪklɪ] adv érotiquement.

eroticism [ɪˈrɒtɪsɪzm] n érotisme m.

err [ɜːr] vi fml **1.** [make mistake] se tromper **2.** [sin] pécher, commettre une faute.

errand [ˈerənd] n commission f, course f.

errata [eˈrɑːtə] ◆ pl ⟶ **erratum**. ◆ pl n [list] errata m inv ▶ **errata slip** liste f des errata.

erratic [ɪˈrætɪk] adj **1.** [irregular - results] irrégulier ; [- performance] irrégulier, inégal ; [- person] fantasque, excentrique ; [- mood] changeant ; [- movement, course] mal assuré **2.** GEOL & MED erratique.

erratically [ɪˈrætɪklɪ] adv [act, behave] de manière fantasque or capricieuse ; [move, work] irrégulièrement, par à-coups.

erratum [eˈrɑːtəm] (pl **errata** [eˈrɑːtə]) n erratum m.

erroneous [ɪˈrəʊnjəs] adj erroné, inexact.

erroneously [ɪˈrəʊnjəslɪ] adv erronément, à tort.

error [ˈerər] n **1.** [mistake] erreur f, faute f ▶ **errors and omissions excepted** COMM sauf erreur ou omission **2.** MATH [mistake] faute f ; [deviation] écart m **3.** [mistakenness] erreur f.

error message n message m d'erreur.

erstwhile [ˈɜːstwaɪl] liter & hum ◆ adj d'autrefois. ◆ adv autrefois, jadis.

erudite [ˈeruːdaɪt] adj [book, person] érudit, savant ; [word] savant.

erudition [ˌeruːˈdɪʃn] n érudition f.

erupt [ɪˈrʌpt] vi **1.** [volcano - start] entrer en éruption ; [- continue] faire éruption **2.** [pimples] sortir, apparaître ; [tooth] percer **3.** fig [fire, laughter, war] éclater ; [anger] exploser.

eruption [ɪˈrʌpʃn] n **1.** [of volcano] éruption f **2.** [of pimples] éruption f, poussée f ; [of teeth] percée f **3.** fig [of laughter] éclat m, éruption f ; [of anger] accès m, éruption f ; [of violence] explosion f, accès m.

ESA (abbr of **European Space Agency**) pr n ESA f, ASE f.

escalate [ˈeskəleɪt] ◆ vi [fighting, war] s'intensifier ; [prices] monter en flèche. ◆ vt [fighting] intensifier ; [problem] aggraver ; [prices] faire grimper.

escalation [ˌeskəˈleɪʃn] n [of fighting, war] escalade f, intensification f ; [of prices] escalade f, montée f en flèche.

escalator [ˈeskəleɪtər] n escalier m roulant or mécanique, escalator m.

escalator clause n clause f d'indexation or de révision.

escalope [ˈeskəlɒp] n escalope f.

escapade [ˌeskəˈpeɪd] n [adventure] équipée f ; [scrape] fredaine f, escapade f ; [prank] frasque f.

escape [ɪˈskeɪp] ◆ vi **1.** [get away - person, animal] échapper, s'échapper ; [- prisoner] s'évader **2.** [gas, liquid, steam] s'échapper, fuir **3.** [survive, avoid injury] s'en tirer, en réchapper. ◆ vt **1.** [avoid] échapper à ▶ **to escape doing sthg** éviter de faire qqch **2.** [elude notice, memory of] échapper à. ◆ n **1.** [of person] fuite f, évasion f ; [of prisoner] évasion f **2.** [diversion] évasion f **3.** [of gas, liquid] fuite f ; [of exhaust fumes, steam] échappement m. ◆ comp [plot, route] d'évasion ; [device] de sortie, de secours ▶ **escape key** COMPUT touche f d'échappement.

escape artist US = **escapologist**.

escape clause n clause f échappatoire.

escaped [ɪ'skeɪpt] adj échappé / *an escaped prisoner* un évadé.

escapee [ɪ,skeɪ'piː] n évadé *m*, -e *f*.

escape lane n voie *f* de détresse.

escape route n **1.** [from prison] moyen *m* d'évasion **2.** [from fire] itinéraire d'évacuation en cas d'incendie.

escapism [ɪ'skeɪpɪzm] n évasion *f* hors de la réalité, fuite *f* devant la réalité.

escapist [ɪ'skeɪpɪst] ◆ n personne *f* cherchant à s'évader du réel. ◆ adj d'évasion.

escapologist [,eskə'pɒlədʒɪst] n *virtuose de l'évasion dans les spectacles de magie.*

escarpment [ɪ'skɑːpmənt] n escarpement *m*.

eschew [ɪs'tʃuː] vt *fml* [duty, work, activity] éviter ; [alcohol] s'abstenir de ; [publicity, temptation, involvement] fuir.

escort ◆ n ['eskɔːt] **1.** [guard] escorte *f*, cortège *m* ; MIL & NAUT escorte *f* ▸ **under the escort of** sous l'escorte de **2.** [consort - male] cavalier *m* ; [- female] hôtesse *f* **3.** [male prostitute] prostitué *m*, escort (boy) *m* ; [female prostitute] prostituée *f*, escort (girl) *f*. ◆ comp ['eskɔːt] d'escorte. ◆ vt [ɪ'skɔːt] *fml* accompagner, escorter ; MIL [police] escorter / *they escorted him in / out* ils l'ont fait entrer / sortir sous escorte.

escort agency n service *m* or bureau *m* d'hôtesses.

ESF [iːes'ef] (abbr of European Social Fund) n FSE *m*.

e-shopping n achats *mpl* en ligne.

e-signature n signature *f* électronique.

Eskimo ['eskɪməʊ] (pl Eskimo or Eskimos) ◆ n **1.** [person] Esquimau *m*, Esquimaude *f* **2.** LING esquimau *m*. ◆ adj esquimau.

Eskimo

Aux États-Unis et au Canada, le terme **Eskimo**, créé par des non-Inuits, est souvent considéré comme péjoratif ; on lui préfère **Inuit**.

Eskimo roll n esquimautage *m*.

ESL (abbr of English as a Second Language) n *anglais seconde langue.*

ESOL ['iːsɒl] (abbr of English for Speakers of Other Languages) n US SCH anglais *m* langue seconde.

esophagus [iː'sɒfəgəs] (pl esophagi [-gaɪ]) US = oesophagus.

esoteric [,esə'terɪk] adj [obscure] ésotérique ; [private] secret (secrète).

esp. written abbr of especially.

ESP n **1.** (abbr of extrasensory perception) perception *f* extrasensorielle **2.** (abbr of English for specific purposes) *anglais spécialisé.*

espadrille [,espə'drɪl] n espadrille *f*.

especial [ɪ'speʃl] adj *fml* [notable] particulier, exceptionnel ; [specific] particulier.

especially [ɪ'speʃəlɪ] adv **1.** [to a particular degree] particulièrement, spécialement ; [particularly] en particulier, surtout **2.** [for a particular purpose] exprès.

Esperanto [,espə'ræntəʊ] ◆ n espéranto *m*. ◆ adj en espéranto.

espionage ['espɪə,nɑːʒ] n espionnage *m*.

esplanade [,esplə'neɪd] n esplanade *f*.

espouse [ɪ'spaʊz] vt *fml* [belief, cause] épouser, adopter.

espresso [e'spresəʊ] (pl espressos) n (café *m*) express *m* ▸ **espresso machine** machine *f* à express.

Esq. (written abbr of esquire) : *James Roberts, Esq.* M. James Roberts.

esquire [ɪ'skwaɪər] n UK **1.** = Esq **2.** HIST écuyer *m*.

essay ◆ n ['eseɪ] **1.** LITER essai *m* ; SCH composition *f*, dissertation *f* ; UNIV dissertation *f* **2.** *fml* [attempt] essai *m*, tentative *f*. ◆ vt [e'seɪ] *fml* **1.** [try] essayer, tenter **2.** [test] mettre à l'épreuve.

⚠️ An essay written by a student is **une dissertation**, not **un essai**.

essayist ['eseɪɪst] n essayiste *mf*.

essence ['esns] n **1.** [gen] essence *f*, essentiel *m* **2.** PHILOS essence *f*, nature *f* ; RELIG essence *f* **3.** CHEM essence *f* **4.** CULIN extrait *m*. ◆◇ **in essence** adv phr essentiellement, surtout.

essential [ɪ'senʃl] ◆ adj **1.** [vital - action, equipment, services] essentiel, indispensable ; [- point, role] essentiel, capital ; [- question] essentiel, fondamental / *it is essential that...* il est indispensable que... *(+ subjunctive)* / *it is essential to know whether...* il est essentiel or il importe de savoir si... **2.** [basic] essentiel, fondamental ▸ **essential oils** huiles *fpl* essentielles. ◆ n objet *m* indispensable ▸ **the essentials** l'essentiel.

📋 Note that **il est essentiel que** is followed by a verb in the subjunctive: **It's essential that you be represented by a lawyer.** *Il est essentiel que vous vous fassiez représenter par un avocat.*

essentially [ɪ'senʃəlɪ] adv [fundamentally] essentiellement, fondamentalement ; [mainly] essentiellement, principalement.

Essex girl ['esɪks-] n UK inf & pej *stéréotype de jeune fille bête et vulgaire.*

Essex man ['esɪks-] n UK inf *stéréotype du réactionnaire bête et vulgaire.*

est [est] n (abbr of Erhard Seminars Training) *méthode de formation psychologique créée par Werner Erhard.*

est. 1. written abbr of established **2.** written abbr of estimated.

EST n abbr of Eastern Standard Time.

establish [ɪ'stæblɪʃ] vt **1.** [create, set up - business] fonder, créer ; [- government] constituer, établir ; [- society, system] constituer ; [- factory] établir, monter ; [- contact] établir ; [- relations] établir, nouer ; [- custom, law] instaurer ; [- precedent] créer ; [- order, peace] faire régner **2.** [confirm - authority, power] affirmer ; [- reputation] établir **3.** [prove - identity, truth] établir ; [- cause, nature] déterminer, établir ; [- guilt, need] établir, prouver ; [- innocence] établir, démontrer.

established [ɪ'stæblɪʃt] adj **1.** [existing, solid - order, system] établi ; [- government] établi, au pouvoir ; [- business] établi, solide ; [- law] établi, en vigueur ; [- tradition] établi, enraciné ; [- reputation] établi, bien assis ▸ **the established Church** l'Église *f* officielle **2.** [proven - fact] acquis, reconnu ; [- truth] établi, démontré.

establishment [ɪ'stæblɪʃmənt] n **1.** [of business] fondation *f*, création *f* ; [of government] constitution *f* ; [of society, system] constitution *f*, création *f* ; [of law] instauration *f* **2.** [institution] établissement *m* / *a business establishment* un établissement commercial, une firme **3.** [staff]

personnel *m* ; MIL & NAUT effectif *m*. ❖ **Establishment** n [ruling powers] ▶ **the Establishment** les pouvoirs *mpl* établis, l'ordre *m* établi, l'establishment *m* / *the financial Establishment* ceux qui comptent dans le monde financier.

estate [ɪ'steɪt] n **1.** [land] propriété *f*, domaine *m* / *her country estate* ses terres *fpl* **2.** [UK] [development - housing] lotissement *m*, cité *f* ; [- trading] zone *f* commerciale **3.** LAW [property] biens *mpl*, fortune *f* ; [of deceased] succession *f* **4.** *fml* [state, position] état *m*, rang *m*.

estate agency n [UK] agence *f* immobilière.

estate agent n [UK] [salesperson] agent *m* immobilier.

estate-bottled adj [wine] mis en bouteille à la propriété.

estate car n [UK] break *m*.

estd., est'd. written abbr of **established**.

esteem [ɪ'stiːm] ❖ vt **1.** [respect - person] avoir de l'estime pour, estimer ; [- quality] estimer, apprécier **2.** *fml* [consider] estimer, considérer. ❖ n estime *f*, considération *f*.

esthete ['iːsθiːt] [US] = **aesthete**.

estimate ❖ n ['estɪmət] **1.** [evaluation] évaluation *f*, estimation *f* **2.** COMM [quote] devis *m*. ❖ vt ['estɪmeɪt] **1.** [calculate - cost, number] estimer, évaluer ; [- distance, speed] estimer, apprécier **2.** [judge] estimer, juger.

estimated ['estɪmeɪtɪd] adj estimé ▶ **estimated time of arrival / of departure** heure d'arrivée / de départ estimée.

estimation [ˌestɪ'meɪʃn] n **1.** [calculation] estimation *f*, évaluation *f* **2.** [judgment] jugement *m*, opinion *f* / *in my estimation* à mon avis, selon moi **3.** [esteem] estime *f*, considération *f*.

Estonia [e'stəʊnjə] pr n Estonie *f* / *in Estonia* en Estonie.

Estonian [e'stəʊnjən] ❖ n **1.** [person] Estonien *m*, -enne *f* **2.** LING estonien *m*. ❖ adj estonien.

estranged [ɪ'streɪndʒd] adj [couple] séparé ▶ **to become estranged from sb** se brouiller avec or se détacher de qqn.

estrogen [US] = **oestrogen**.

estuary ['estjʊərɪ] (*pl* **estuaries**) n estuaire *m*.

ETA (abbr of **estimated time of arrival**) n HPA.

e-tailer n vendeur *m*, -euse *f* en ligne.

et al. [ˌet'æl] (abbr of **et alii**) adv phr et al.

etc. (written abbr of **et cetera**) etc.

et cetera [ɪt'setərə] adv et cetera, et cætera.

etch [etʃ] vi & vt graver ; ART & TYPO graver à l'eau-forte.

etching ['etʃɪŋ] n **1.** [print] (gravure *f* à l')eau-forte *f* **2.** [technique] gravure *f* à l'eau-forte.

ETD (abbr of **estimated time of departure**) n HPD *f*.

eternal [ɪ'tɜːnl] ❖ adj **1.** [gen & PHILOS & RELIG] éternel ▶ **the Eternal city** la Ville éternelle, Rome **2.** [perpetual] continuel, perpétuel ; [arguments, problems] éternel ; [discussion, wrangling] continuel, sempiternel *pej*. ❖ n ▶ **the Eternal** l'Éternel *m*.

eternally [ɪ'tɜːnəlɪ] adv **1.** [forever] éternellement **2.** *pej* [perpetually] perpétuellement, continuellement.

eternity [ɪ'tɜːnətɪ] (*pl* **eternities**) n *lit & fig* éternité *f*.

eternity ring n bague *f* de fidélité.

ether ['iːθər] n **1.** CHEM & PHYS éther *m* **2.** MYTH & *liter* [sky] ▶ **the ether** l'éther *m*, la voûte céleste.

ethereal [ɪ'θɪərɪəl] adj [fragile] éthéré, délicat ; [spiritual] éthéré, noble.

Ethernet n Ethernet ▶ **Ethernet cable** câble *m* Ethernet.

ethic ['eθɪk] ❖ n éthique *f*, morale *f*. ❖ adj moral, éthique *fml*.

ethical ['eθɪkl] adj moral, éthique *fml*.

ethics ['eθɪks] ❖ n (U) [study] éthique *f*, morale *f*. ❖ pl n [principles] morale *f* ; [morality] moralité *f* ▶ **medical ethics** code *m* déontologique or de déontologie.

Ethiopia [ˌiːθɪ'əʊpjə] pr n Éthiopie *f* / *in Ethiopia* en Éthiopie.

Ethiopian [ˌiːθɪ'əʊpjən] ❖ n **1.** [person] Éthiopien *m*, -enne *f* **2.** LING éthiopien *m*. ❖ adj éthiopien.

ethnic ['eθnɪk] ❖ adj **1.** [of race] ethnique ▶ **ethnic cleansing** purification *f* ethnique ▶ **ethnic group** ethnie *f* **2.** [traditional] folklorique, traditionnel. ❖ n [of race] ethnique ▶ membre *m* d'une minorité ethnique.

ethnicity ['eθnɪsɪtɪ] n appartenance *f* ethnique.

ethnic minority n minorité *f* ethnique.

ethnocentric [ˌeθnəʊ'sentrɪk] adj ethnocentrique.

ethnology [eθ'nɒlədʒɪ] n ethnologie *f*.

ethos ['iːθɒs] n éthos *m*.

e-ticket n e-billet *m*, billet *m* électronique.

etiquette ['etɪket] n (U) [code of practice] étiquette *f* ; [customs] bon usage *m*, convenances *fpl*.

Eton ['iːtn] pr n ▶ **Eton (College)** l'école d'Eton.

Eton

Eton, l'une des plus anciennes et des plus célèbres **public schools**, est fréquentée essentiellement par les enfants de la grande bourgeoisie et de l'aristocratie britanniques. Plusieurs anciens Premiers ministres et membres de la famille royale y ont fait leurs études.

e-trade n (U) commerce *m* en ligne.

ETV (abbr of **Educational Television**) n [US] chaîne *f* de télévision éducative et culturelle.

etymological [ˌetɪmə'lɒdʒɪkl] adj étymologique.

etymologist [ˌetɪ'mɒlədʒɪst] n étymologiste *mf*.

etymology [ˌetɪ'mɒlədʒɪ] n étymologie *f*.

EU pr n abbr of **European Union**.

eucalyptus [ˌjuːkə'lɪptəs] (*pl* **eucalyptuses** or **eucalypti** [-taɪ]) n eucalyptus *m*.

Eucharist ['juːkərɪst] n Eucharistie *f*.

eugenics [juː'dʒenɪks] n (U) eugénique *f*, eugénisme *m*.

eulogize, eulogise ['juːlədʒaɪz] vt faire l'éloge or le panégyrique de.

eulogy ['juːlədʒɪ] (*pl* **eulogies**) n **1.** [commendation] panégyrique *m* **2.** [funeral oration] oraison *f* or éloge *m* funèbre.

eunuch ['juːnək] n eunuque *m*.

euphemism ['juːfəmɪzm] n euphémisme *m*.

euphemistic [ˌjuːfə'mɪstɪk] adj euphémique.

euphemistically [ˌjuːfə'mɪstɪklɪ] adv par euphémisme, euphémiquement *fml*.

euphoria [juː'fɔːrɪə] n euphorie *f*.

euphoric [juː'fɒrɪk] adj euphorique.

Eurasia [jʊə'reɪʒə] pr n Eurasie *f*.

Eurasian [jʊə'reɪʒən] ❖ n Eurasien *m*, -enne *f*. ❖ adj [person] eurasien ; [continent] eurasiatique.

eureka [jʊə'riːkə] interj ▶ **eureka!** eurêka !

euro ['jʊərəʊ] n [currency] euro *m*.

Euro- in comp euro-.

euro area n zone *f* euro.

euro cent n centime *m*, (euro) cent *m* *offic*.

Eurocentric [ˈjʊərəʊˌsentrɪk] adj eurocentrique, européocentrique.

Eurocheque [ˈjʊərəʊˌtʃek] n eurochèque m.

Eurocrat [ˈjʊərəʊˌkræt] n eurocrate mf.

Eurocurrency [ˈjʊərəʊˌkʌrənsɪ] n eurodevise f, euromonnaie f.

Eurodollar [ˈjʊərəʊˌdɒləʳ] n eurodollar m.

Euroland [ˈjʊərəʊlænd] n POL euroland m.

Euro-MP [ˈjʊərəʊ-] (abbr of European Member of Parliament) n député m or parlementaire m européen, eurodéputé m.

Europe [ˈjʊərəp] pr n Europe f / in Europe en Europe.

European [ˌjʊərəˈpiːən] ◆ n [inhabitant of Europe] Européen m, -enne f; [pro-Europe] partisan m de l'Europe unie, Européen m, -enne f. ◆ adj européen ▶ **the Single European Market** le Marché unique (européen) ▶ **European plan** 🇺🇸 [in hotel] chambre f sans pension.

European Central Bank pr n Banque f centrale européenne.

European Commission pr n Commission f des communautés européennes.

European Community pr n Communauté f européenne.

European Court of Human Rights pr n ▶ **the European Court of Human Rights** la Cour européenne des droits de l'homme.

European Court of Justice pr n ▶ **the European Court of Justice** la Cour européenne de justice.

European Currency Unit n unité f monétaire européenne.

European Economic Community pr n HIST Communauté f économique européenne.

Europeanism [ˌjʊərəˈpiːənɪzm] n européanisme m.

Europeanize, Europeanise [ˌjʊərəˈpiːənaɪz] vt européaniser.

European Monetary System pr n ▶ **the European Monetary System** le système monétaire européen.

European Parliament pr n Parlement m européen.

European Single Market n Marché m unique européen.

European Social Fund n Fonds m social européen.

European Standards Commission n Comité m européen de normalisation.

European Union pr n Union f européenne.

Europhile [ˈjʊərəʊˌfaɪl] n partisan m de l'Europe unie.

Euro-rebel n POL anti-Européen m, -enne f.

Eurosceptic [ˈjʊərəʊˌskeptɪk] n eurosceptique mf.

Eurostar® [ˈjʊərəʊstɑːʳ] n Eurostar® m.

Eurotunnel® [ˈjʊərəʊˌtʌnl] n Eurotunnel m.

Eurovision® [ˈjʊərəʊˌvɪʒn] n Eurovision® f ▶ **the Eurovision Song Contest** le concours Eurovision de la chanson.

euro-zone n zone f euro.

Eustachian tube [juːˈsteɪʃən-] n trompe f d'Eustache.

euthanasia [ˌjuːθəˈneɪzjə] n euthanasie f.

evacuate [ɪˈvækjʊeɪt] vt [gen & PHYSIOL] évacuer.

evacuation [ɪˌvækjʊˈeɪʃn] n [gen & PHYSIOL] évacuation f.

evacuee [ɪˌvækjuːˈiː] n évacué m, -e f.

evade [ɪˈveɪd] vt 1. [escape from - pursuers] échapper à; [- punishment] échapper à, se soustraire à 2. [avoid - responsibility] éviter, esquiver; [- question] esquiver, éluder; [- eyes, glance] éviter.

⚠ **s'évader** means to escape, **not** to evade something.

evaluate [ɪˈvæljʊeɪt] vt 1. [value] évaluer, déterminer le montant de 2. [assess - situation, success, work] évaluer, former un jugement sur la valeur de; [- evidence, reasons] peser, évaluer.

evaluation [ɪˌvæljuˈeɪʃn] n 1. [of damages, worth] évaluation f 2. [of situation, work] évaluation f, jugement m; [of evidence, reasons] évaluation f.

evangelical [ˌiːvænˈdʒelɪkl] ◆ adj évangélique. ◆ n évangélique m.

evangelism [ɪˈvændʒəlɪzm] n évangélisme m.

evangelist [ɪˈvændʒəlɪst] n 1. BIBLE ▶ **Evangelist** évangéliste m 2. [preacher] évangélisateur m, -trice f 3. fig [zealous advocate] prêcheur m, -euse f.

evangelize, evangelise [ɪˈvændʒəlaɪz] ◆ vt évangéliser, prêcher l'Évangile à. ◆ vi RELIG prêcher l'Évangile.

evaporate [ɪˈvæpəreɪt] ◆ vi [liquid] s'évaporer; fig [hopes, doubts] s'envoler, se volatiliser. ◆ vt faire évaporer.

evaporated milk [ɪˈvæpəreɪtɪd-] n lait m condensé.

evaporation [ɪˌvæpəˈreɪʃn] n évaporation f.

evasion [ɪˈveɪʒn] n 1. [avoidance] fuite f, évasion f; [of duty] dérobade f 2. [deception, trickery] détour m, fauxfuyant m, échappatoire f.

⚠ **Évasion** means escape, **not** evasion.

evasive [ɪˈveɪsɪv] adj évasif.

evasively [ɪˈveɪsɪvlɪ] adv évasivement.

evasiveness [ɪˈveɪsɪvnɪs] n caractère m évasif.

eve [iːv] n veille f; RELIG vigile f.

Eve [iːv] pr n Ève.

even¹ [ˈiːvn] ◆ adj 1. [level] plat, plan; [smooth] uni 2. [steady - breathing, temperature] égal; [- rate, rhythm] régulier 3. [equal - distribution, spread] égal / the score is or the scores are even ils sont à égalité / it's an even game la partie est égale / now we're even nous voilà quittes, nous sommes quittes maintenant / there's an even chance he'll lose il y a une chance sur deux qu'il perde ▶ **to bet even money a)** [gen] donner chances égales **b)** [in betting] parier le même enjeu ▶ **to get even with sb** se venger de qqn 4. [calm - temper] égal; [- voice] égal, calme 5. [number] pair. ◆ adv 1. [indicating surprise] même / he even works on Sundays il travaille même le dimanche 2. (with comparative) [still] encore / even better encore mieux / even less encore moins. ❖ **even as** conj phr fml [at the very moment that] au moment même où / even as we speak au moment même où nous parlons. ❖ **even if** conj phr même si. ❖ **even so** adv phr [nevertheless] quand même, pourtant / yes, but even so oui, mais quand même. ❖ **even then** adv phr 1. [in that case also] quand même 2. [at that time also] même à ce moment-là. ❖ **even though** conj phr : even though she explained it in detail bien qu'elle l'ait expliqué en détail. ❖ **even out** vt sep [surface] égaliser, aplanir; [prices] égaliser; [supply] répartir or distribuer plus également. ❖ **even up** vt sep égaliser / to even things up rétablir l'équilibre.

even² [ˈiːvn] n arch & liter [evening] soir m.

even-handed adj équitable, impartial.

evening [ˈiːvnɪŋ] ◆ n 1. [part of day] soir m ▶ **(good) evening!** bonsoir! / in the evening le soir / it is 8 o'clock in the evening il est 8 h du soir / this evening ce soir / that evening ce soir-là / tomorrow evening demain soir /

on the evening of the fifteenth le quinze au soir / *every Friday evening* tous les vendredis soir or soirs / *I work evenings* je travaille le soir **2.** [length of time] soirée *f* **3.** [entertainment] soirée *f.* ◆ comp [newspaper, train] du soir ▸ **evening fixture** rencontre *f* sportive en nocturne ▸ **an evening match** SPORT une nocturne ▸ **the Evening Standard** PRESS *quotidien populaire londonien de tendance conservatrice.* ⟶ **tabloid** ❖ **evenings** adv US le soir.

 soir or **soirée?**

The word **soir** refers to the evening as a subdivision of the day and is used to situate events in time (**hier soir, ce soir, tous les soirs**). The word **soirée** refers to the evening as a stretch of time during which activities take place (**ça m'a pris une soirée entière; on a terminé la soirée en boîte; toute la soirée**) and is also used to refer to the evening in progress (**la soirée vient de commencer**).

 bonsoir or **bonne soirée?**

Bonsoir ! is a greeting that you would exchange with someone you met from approximately nightfall in the winter, or from 6ish or 7ish p.m. in the summer. This is very variable and the best strategy is to listen to what people say and let yourself be guided by them. In some parts of France, the greeting **bonsoir** may in fact be used at any time of the day, including in the morning!

Bonne soirée !, in keeping with the meaning explained above, is a greeting that you would use to express your hope that the person's evening activities will turn out pleasurable to them.

evening class n cours *m* du soir.
evening dress n [for men] tenue *f* de soirée, habit *m* ; [for women] robe *f* du soir / *in evening dress* a) [man] en tenue de soirée b) [woman] en robe du soir, en toilette de soirée.
evening star n étoile *f* du berger.
evening wear n *(U)* = **evening dress**.
evenly ['iːvnlɪ] adv **1.** [breathe, move] régulièrement ; [talk] calmement, posément **2.** [equally - divide] également, de façon égale ; [- spread] de façon égale, régulièrement.
evenness ['iːvnnɪs] n **1.** [of surface] égalité *f*, caractère *m* lisse **2.** [of competition, movement] régularité *f.*
evensong ['iːvnsɒŋ] n [Anglican] office *m* du soir ; [Roman Catholic] vêpres *fpl.*
even Stevens [-'stiːvənz] adj ▸ **to be even Stevens** être quitte.
event [ɪ'vent] n **1.** [happening] événement *m* ▸ **the course of events** la suite des événements, le déroulement des faits / *in the course of events* par la suite, au cours des événements / *in the normal course of events* normalement / *I realized after the event* j'ai réalisé après coup / *the party was quite an event* la soirée était un véritable

événement **2.** [organized activity] manifestation *f* / *the society organizes a number of social events* l'association organise un certain nombre de soirées or de rencontres ▸ **events management** événementiel *m* / *I work in events* je travaille dans l'événementiel *m* **3.** SPORT [meeting] manifestation *f* ; [competition] épreuve *f* ; [in horseracing] course *f* ▸ **field events** épreuves d'athlétisme ▸ **track events** épreuves sur piste. ❖ **at all events, in any event** adv phr en tout cas, de toute façon. ❖ **in either event** adv phr dans l'un ou l'autre cas. ❖ **in the event** adv phr en fait, en l'occurrence. ❖ **in the event of** prep phr : *in the event of rain* en cas de pluie / *in the event of her refusing* au cas où or dans le cas où elle refuserait. ❖ **in the event that** conj phr au cas où / *in the unlikely event that he comes* au cas or dans le cas fort improbable où il viendrait.
eventful [ɪ'ventful] adj **1.** [busy - day, holiday, life] mouvementé, fertile en événements **2.** [important] mémorable, très important.
event horizon n ASTRON horizon *m* des événements.
eventide ['iːvntaɪd] n *liter* soir *m*, tombée *f* du jour.
eventing [ɪ'ventɪŋ] n *participation à toutes les épreuves d'un concours hippique.*
eventual [ɪ'ventʃʊəl] adj [final] final, ultime ; [resulting] qui s'ensuit.

 Éventuel means possible, not eventual.

eventuality [ɪ,ventʃʊ'ælətɪ] *(pl* **eventualities)** n éventualité *f.*
eventually [ɪ'ventʃʊəlɪ] adv finalement, en fin de compte / *I'll get around to it eventually* je le ferai un jour ou l'autre / *eventually, I decided to give up* pour finir or en fin de compte, j'ai décidé d'abandonner, j'ai finalement décidé d'abandonner.

⚠ **Éventuellement** means possibly, not eventually.

ever ['evə'] adv **1.** [always] toujours / *yours ever* or *ever yours* [in letter] amicalement vôtre **2.** [at any time] jamais / *do you ever meet him?* est-ce qu'il vous arrive (jamais) de le rencontrer ? / *all they ever do is work* ils ne font que travailler / *he hardly* or *scarcely ever smokes* il ne fume presque jamais ; [with comparatives] : *lovelier / more slowly than ever* plus joli / plus lentement que jamais / *he's as sarcastic as ever* il est toujours aussi sarcastique ; [with superlatives] : *the first / biggest ever* le tout premier / plus grand qu'on ait jamais vu **3.** [in questions] : *why ever not?* mais enfin, pourquoi pas ? ❖ **ever after** adv phr pour toujours / *they lived happily ever after* ils vécurent heureux jusqu'à la fin de leurs jours. ❖ **ever so** adv phr *inf* [extremely] vraiment / *she's ever so clever* elle est vraiment intelligente / *ever so slightly off-centre* un tout petit peu décentré / *thanks ever so much* merci vraiment. ❖ **ever such** det phr *inf* vraiment / *they've got ever such pretty curtains in the shop* ils ont vraiment de jolis rideaux dans ce magasin.
Everest ['evərɪst] pr n ▸ **(Mount) Everest** le mont Everest, l'Everest *m.*
Everglades ['evə,ɡleɪdz] pl pr n ▸ **the Everglades** les Everglades *mpl* ▸ **the Everglades National Park** le parc national des Everglades.
evergreen ['evəɡriːn] ◆ n **1.** [tree] arbre *m* à feuilles persistantes ; [conifer] conifère *m* ; [bush] arbuste *m* à feuilles

persistantes **2.** *fig* [song, story] chanson *f* or histoire *f* qui ne vieillit jamais. ◆ adj **1.** [bush, tree] à feuilles persistantes **2.** *fig* [song, story] qui ne vieillit pas.

everlasting [ˌevəˈlɑːstɪŋ] adj **1.** [eternal - hope, mercy] éternel, infini ; [- fame] éternel, immortel ; [- God, life] éternel **2.** [incessant] perpétuel, éternel.

evermore [ˌevəˈmɔːr] adv toujours ▸ **for evermore** pour toujours, à jamais.

eversion [ɪˈvɜːʃən] n éversion *f*.

every [ˈevrɪ] det **1.** [each] tout, chaque / *every room has a view of the sea* les chambres ont toutes vue or toutes les chambres ont vue sur la mer / *not every room is as big as this* toutes les chambres ne sont pas aussi grandes que celle-ci / *every one of these apples* chacune de or toutes ces pommes / *every one of them arrived late* ils sont tous arrivés en retard / *every (single) one of these pencils is broken* tous ces crayons (sans exception) sont cassés / *every day* tous les jours, chaque jour / *every time I go out* chaque fois que je sors / *of every age / every sort / every colour* de tout âge / toute sorte / toutes les couleurs ▸ **every little helps** *prov* les petits ruisseaux font les grandes rivières *prov* **2.** [with units of time, measurement, etc.] tout / *every two days* or *every second day* or *every other day* tous les deux jours, un jour sur deux / *once every month* une fois par mois / *every third man* un homme sur trois / *three women out of* or *in every ten, three out of every ten women* trois femmes sur dix ▸ **every other** : *every other Sunday* un dimanche sur deux **3.** [indicating confidence, optimism] tout / *I have every confidence that...* je ne doute pas un instant que... / *you have every reason to be happy* vous avez toutes les raisons or tout lieu d'être heureux / *we wish you every success* nous vous souhaitons très bonne chance **4.** [with possessive adj] chacun, moindre / *his every action bears witness to it* chacun de ses gestes or tout ce qu'il fait en témoigne / *her every wish* son moindre désir, tous ses désirs. ◆ **every now and again, every now and then, every once in a while, every so often** adv phr de temps en temps, de temps à autre.

everybody [ˈevrɪˌbɒdɪ] = **everyone**.

everyday [ˈevrɪdeɪ] adj **1.** [daily] de tous les jours, quotidien **2.** [ordinary] banal, ordinaire.

EVRY1 MESSAGING written abbr of **everyone**.

everyone [ˈevrɪwʌn] pron tout le monde, chacun / *as everyone knows* comme chacun or tout le monde le sait / *everyone else* tous les autres ▸ **everyone who was anyone was there** tous les gens qui comptent étaient là.

everyplace [ˈevrɪˌpleɪs] adv 🇺🇸 *inf* = **everywhere**.

everything [ˈevrɪθɪŋ] pron **1.** [all things] tout / *everything he says* tout ce qu'il dit / *they sell everything* ils vendent de tout **2.** [the most important thing] l'essentiel *m* / *winning is everything* l'essentiel, c'est de gagner / *money isn't everything* il n'y a pas que l'argent qui compte.

everywhere [ˈevrɪweər] adv partout / *everywhere she went* partout où elle allait.

evict [ɪˈvɪkt] vt **1.** [person] expulser, chasser **2.** [property] récupérer par moyens juridiques.

eviction [ɪˈvɪkʃn] n expulsion *f* / *an eviction notice* un mandat d'expulsion / *eviction order* ordre *m* d'expulsion.

evidence [ˈevɪdəns] ◆ n **1.** [proof] preuve *f* ; [testimony] témoignage *m* ▸ **against all the evidence** contre toute évidence **2.** LAW [proof] preuve *f* ; [testimony] témoignage *m* ▸ **to give evidence against / for sb** témoigner contre / en faveur de qqn **3.** [indication] signe *m*, marque *f*

▸ **to be in evidence** [person] : *his daughter was nowhere in evidence* sa fille n'était pas là or n'était pas présente. ◆ vt *fml* manifester, montrer.

⚠ **Except in the expression** against all the evidence, **the word** evidence **is never translated by** évidence.

evident [ˈevɪdənt] adj évident, manifeste / *it is quite evident that he's not interested* on voit bien qu'il ne s'y intéresse pas, il ne s'y intéresse pas, c'est évident.

evidently [ˈevɪdəntlɪ] adv **1.** [apparently] apparemment / *did he refuse? — evidently not* a-t-il refusé ? — non apparemment or à ce qu'il paraît **2.** [clearly] de toute évidence, manifestement / *he was evidently in pain* il était évident or clair qu'il souffrait.

evil [ˈiːvl] (🇬🇧 *compar* **eviller,** *superl* **evillest** ; 🇺🇸 *compar* **eviler,** *superl* **evilest**) ◆ adj **1.** [wicked - person] malveillant, méchant ; [- deed, plan, reputation] mauvais ; [- influence] néfaste ; [- doctrine, spell, spirit] malfaisant **2.** [smell, taste] infect, infâme. ◆ n mal *m*.

evil eye n ▸ **the evil eye** le mauvais œil ▸ **to give sb the evil eye** jeter le mauvais œil à qqn.

evil-minded adj malveillant, mal intentionné.

evince [ɪˈvɪns] vt *fml* [show - interest, surprise] manifester, montrer ; [- quality] faire preuve de, manifester.

⚠ Évincer **means** to supplant, **not** to evince.

evocation [ˌevəʊˈkeɪʃn] n évocation *f*.

evocative [ɪˈvɒkətɪv] adj **1.** [picture, scent] évocateur **2.** [magic] évocatoire.

evoke [ɪˈvəʊk] vt **1.** [summon up - memory, spirit] évoquer **2.** [elicit - admiration] susciter ; [- response, smile] susciter, provoquer.

evolution [ˌiːvəˈluːʃn] n **1.** [of language, situation] évolution *f* ; [of art, society, technology] développement *m*, évolution *f* ; [of events] développement *m*, déroulement *m* **2.** BIOL, BOT & ZOOL évolution *f*.

evolutionary [ˌiːvəˈluːʃnərɪ] adj évolutionniste.

evolve [ɪˈvɒlv] ◆ vi évoluer, se développer ; BIOL, BOT & ZOOL évoluer ▸ **to evolve from sthg** se développer à partir de qqch. ◆ vt [system, theory] développer, élaborer.

e-wallet n portefeuille *m* électronique.

ewe [juː] n brebis *f* ▸ **a ewe lamb** une agnelle.

ex [eks] ◆ prep **1.** COMM départ, sortie / *price ex works* prix *m* départ or sortie usine **2.** FIN sans. ◆ n *inf* [gen] ex *mf* ; [husband] ex-mari *m* ; [wife] ex-femme *f* / *my ex* **a)** [girlfriend] mon ancienne petite amie **b)** [boyfriend] mon ancien petit ami.

ex- in comp ex-, ancien / *his ex-wife* son ex-femme / *the ex-president* l'ancien président, l'ex-président.

exacerbate [ɪɡˈzæsəbeɪt] vt *fml* **1.** [make worse] exacerber, aggraver **2.** [annoy] énerver, exaspérer.

exact [ɪɡˈzækt] ◆ adj **1.** [accurate, correct] exact, juste **2.** [precise - amount, idea, value] exact, précis ; [- directions, place, time] précis **3.** [meticulous - work] rigoureux, précis ; [- mind] rigoureux ; [- science] exact ; [- instrument] de précision. ◆ vt **1.** [demand - money] extorquer **2.** [insist upon] exiger.

exacting [ɪɡˈzæktɪŋ] adj [person] exigeant ; [activity, job] astreignant, exigeant.

exactitude [ɪɡˈzæktɪtjuːd] n exactitude *f*.

exactly [ɪɡˈzæktlɪ] adv **1.** [accurately] précisément, avec précision **2.** [entirely, precisely] exactement, justement / *I* *don't remember exactly* je ne me rappelle pas au juste / *it's exactly the same thing* c'est exactement la même chose / *it's exactly 5 o'clock* il est 5 h juste.

exaggerate [ɪg'zædʒəreɪt] ◆ vi exagérer. ◆ vt **1.** [overstate - quality, situation, size] exagérer ; [- facts] amplifier ; [- importance] s'exagérer **2.** [emphasize] accentuer.

exaggerated [ɪg'zædʒəreɪtɪd] adj **1.** [number, story] exagéré ; [fashion, style] outré **2.** MED exagéré.

exaggeratedly [ɪg'zædʒəreɪtɪdlɪ] adv d'une manière exagérée, exagérément.

exaggeration [ɪg,zædʒə'reɪʃn] n exagération f.

exalt [ɪg'zɔːlt] vt **1.** [praise highly] exalter, chanter les louanges de **2.** [in rank] élever (à un rang plus important).

exaltation [,egzɔːl'teɪʃn] n (U) **1.** [praise] louange f, louanges fpl, exaltation f **2.** [elation] exultation f, exaltation f.

exalted [ɪg'zɔːltɪd] adj **1.** [prominent - person] de haut rang, haut placé ; [- position, rank] élevé **2.** [elated] exalté.

exam [ɪg'zæm] **(abbr of examination)** ◆ n ▶ **to sit** or **to take an exam** passer un examen ▶ **to pass / to fail an exam** réussir à / échouer à un examen. ◆ comp d'examen ▶ **exam board** commission f d'examen ▶ **exam nerves** trac m des examens ▶ **exam paper a)** [set of questions] sujet m d'examen **b)** [written answer] copie f (d'examen) ▶ **exam room** 🇺🇸 = consulting room.

examination [ɪg,zæmɪ'neɪʃn] ◆ n **1.** [of records, proposal, etc.] examen m ; [of building - by official] inspection f ; [- by potential buyer] visite f ▶ **on examination** après examen / *the proposal is still under examination* la proposition est encore à l'étude **2.** MED examen m médical ; [at school, work] visite f médicale ; [regular] bilan m de santé **3.** fml SCH & UNIV examen m **4.** LAW [of witness] audition f ; [of suspect] interrogatoire m. ◆ comp [question, results] d'examen ▶ **examination board** commission f d'examen ▶ **examination paper a)** [set of questions] sujet m d'examen **b)** [written answer] copie f (d'examen).

examine [ɪg'zæmɪn] vt **1.** [records, proposal, etc.] examiner, étudier ; [building] inspecter **2.** MED examiner **3.** SCH & UNIV faire passer un examen à **4.** LAW [witness] entendre ; [suspect] interroger.

examiner [ɪg'zæmɪnər] n [in school, driving test] examinateur m, -trice f ▶ **the examiners** SCH & UNIV les examinateurs, le jury.

examining body [ɪg'zæmɪnɪŋ-] n jury m d'examen.

example [ɪg'zɑːmpl] n **1.** [illustration] exemple m **2.** [person or action to be imitated] exemple m, modèle m / *you're an example to us all* vous êtes un modèle pour nous tous ▶ **to follow sb's example** suivre l'exemple de qqn / *to set a good / bad example* montrer le bon / mauvais exemple **3.** [sample, specimen] exemple m, spécimen m ; [of work] échantillon m **4.** [warning] exemple m / *let this be an example to you* que ça te serve d'exemple ▶ **to make an example of sb** faire un exemple du cas de qqn. ❖ **for example** adv phr par exemple.

exasperate [ɪg'zæspəreɪt] vt [irritate] exaspérer.

exasperating [ɪg'zæspəreɪtɪŋ] adj exaspérant.

exasperatingly [ɪg'zæspəreɪtɪŋlɪ] adv : *the service is exasperatingly slow in this restaurant* le service est d'une lenteur exaspérante or désespérante dans ce restaurant.

exasperation [ɪg,zæspə'reɪʃn] n [irritation, frustration] exaspération f / *to look at sb in exasperation* regarder qqn avec exaspération or un air exaspéré.

excavate ['ekskəveɪt] vt **1.** [hole, trench] creuser, excaver **2.** ARCHEOL [temple, building] mettre au jour.

excavation [,ekskə'veɪʃn] n **1.** [of hole, trench] excavation f, creusement m **2.** ARCHEOL [of temple, building] mise f au jour.

excavator ['ekskə,veɪtər] n **1.** [machine] excavateur m, excavatrice f **2.** [archaeologist] personne qui conduit des fouilles.

exceed [ɪk'siːd] vt **1.** [be more than] dépasser, excéder **2.** [go beyond - expectations, fears] dépasser ; [- budget] excéder, déborder / *to exceed one's authority* outrepasser ses pouvoirs / *to exceed the speed limit* dépasser la limite de vitesse, faire un excès de vitesse / '*do not exceed the stated dose*' 'ne pas dépasser la dose prescrite'.

exceedingly [ɪk'siːdɪŋlɪ] adv [extremely] extrêmement.

excel [ɪk'sel] (pt & pp **excelled**) ◆ vi exceller / *to excel at* or *in music* exceller en musique. ◆ vt surpasser ▶ **to excel o.s.** lit & iro se surpasser.

excellence ['eksələns] n [high quality] qualité f excellente ; [commercially] excellence f ▶ **centre of excellence** centre m d'excellence.

Excellency ['eksələnsɪ] (pl **Excellencies**) n Excellence f ▶ **Your / His Excellency** Votre / Son Excellence.

excellent ['eksələnt] adj excellent ; [weather] magnifique / *excellent!* formidable !, parfait !

except [ɪk'sept] ◆ prep [apart from] à part, excepté, sauf / *except weekends* à part or excepté or sauf le weekend. ◆ conj **1.** [apart from] : *I'll do anything except sell the car* je ferai tout sauf vendre la voiture / *except if* sauf or à part si **2.** [only] seulement, mais / *we would stay longer except (that) we have no more money* nous resterions bien plus longtemps, mais or seulement nous n'avons plus d'argent. ◆ vt [exclude] excepter, exclure / *present company excepted* à l'exception des personnes présentes, les personnes présentes exceptées. ❖ **except for** prep phr sauf, à part.

excepting [ɪk'septɪŋ] prep à part, excepté, sauf / *not excepting… …* y compris.

exception [ɪk'sepʃn] n **1.** [deviation, exemption] exception f **2.** PHR **to take exception to sthg** s'offenser or s'offusquer de qqch, être outré par qqch.

exceptionable [ɪk'sepʃnəbl] adj [objectionable] offensant, outrageant.

exceptional [ɪk'sepʃənl] adj exceptionnel / *in exceptional circumstances* dans des circonstances exceptionnelles.

exceptionally [ɪk'sepʃnəlɪ] adv exceptionnellement / *that's exceptionally kind of you* c'est extrêmement gentil de votre part / *she's an exceptionally bright child* c'est une enfant d'une intelligence exceptionnelle.

excerpt ['eksɜːpt] n [extract] extrait m ▶ **an excerpt from sthg** un extrait de qqch.

excess ◆ n [ɪk'ses] **1.** [unreasonable amount] excès m / *an excess of salt / fat in the diet* un excès de sel / de graisses dans l'alimentation **2.** [difference between two amounts] supplément m, surplus m ; [in insurance] franchise f **3.** [over-indulgence] excès m / *a life of excess* une vie d'excès **4.** (usu pl) [unacceptable action] excès m, abus m / *the excesses of the occupying troops* les excès or abus commis par les soldats pendant l'occupation. ◆ adj ['ekses] [extra] en trop, excédentaire ▶ **excess profit** superbénéfice m. ❖ **in excess of** prep phr [a stated percentage, weight] au-dessus de / *she earns in excess of £25,000 a year* elle gagne plus de 25 000 livres par an. ❖ **to excess** adv phr ▶ **to carry sthg to excess** pousser qqch trop loin / *he does* or *carries it to excess* il exagère, il dépasse les bornes / *to eat / to drink to excess* manger / boire à l'excès.

excess baggage ['ekses-] n (U) [on plane] excédent m de bagages.

excess fare ['ekses-] n [UK] supplément *m* de prix.

excessive [ɪk'sesɪv] adj [unreasonable] excessif ; [demand] excessif, démesuré.

excessively [ɪk'sesɪvlɪ] adv excessivement.

excess luggage = excess baggage.

exchange [ɪks'tʃeɪndʒ] ◆ vt **1.** [give and receive - gifts, letters, blows] échanger / *shots were exchanged* il y a eu un échange de coups de feu ▸ **to exchange sthg with sb** échanger qqch avec qqn ▸ **to exchange places with sb** changer de place avec qqn / *we exchanged addresses* nous avons échangé nos adresses **2.** [give in return for sthg else] échanger ▸ **to exchange sthg for sthg** échanger qqch contre qqch. ◆ n **1.** [of prisoners, ideas] échange *m* ▸ **exchange of contracts** échange *m* de contrats à la signature **2.** [discussion] échange *m* / *a heated exchange* un échange enflammé **3.** [cultural, educational] échange *m* / *as part of an exchange* dans le cadre d'un échange ▸ **exchange student** *étudiant qui prend part à un échange avec l'étranger* ▸ **exchange visit** : *the Spanish students are here on an exchange visit* les étudiants espagnols sont en visite ici dans le cadre d'un échange **4.** TELEC central *m* téléphonique **5.** FIN change *m* ▸ **exchange control** contrôle *m* des changes **6.** = stock exchange. ❖ **in exchange** adv phr en échange. ❖ **in exchange for** prep phr en échange de.

exchangeable [ɪks'tʃeɪndʒəbl] adj échangeable, qui peut être échangé.

exchange broker n cambiste *mf*.

exchange rate n taux *m* de change.

Exchange Rate Mechanism pr n mécanisme *m* (des taux) de change (du SME).

exchange value n contre-valeur *f*.

exchequer [ɪks'tʃekər] n [finances] finances *fpl*. ❖ **Exchequer** n POL [department] ▸ **the exchequer** le ministère des Finances *(en Grande-Bretagne)*.

excise¹ ['eksaɪz] n **1.** [tax] taxe *f*, contribution *f* indirecte **2.** [UK] [government office] régie *f*, service *m* des contributions indirectes.

excise² [ek'saɪz] vt **1.** *fml* [remove from a text] retrancher **2.** MED exciser.

excise duty ['eksaɪz-] n [taxation] contribution *f* indirecte. ❖ **excise duties** pl n droits *mpl* de régie.

excitable [ɪk'saɪtəbl] adj excitable, nerveux.

excite [ɪk'saɪt] vt **1.** [agitate] exciter, énerver **2.** [fill with enthusiasm] enthousiasmer **3.** [sexually] exciter **4.** [arouse - interest, curiosity] exciter, soulever, éveiller **5.** PHYSIOL exciter.

excited [ɪk'saɪtɪd] adj **1.** [enthusiastic, eager] excité ▸ **to be excited about** or **at sthg** être excité par qqch **2.** [agitated] : *don't go getting excited* or *don't get excited* ne va pas t'énerver **3.** [sexually] excité **4.** PHYS excité.

excitedly [ɪk'saɪtɪdlɪ] adv [behave, watch] avec agitation ; [say] sur un ton animé ; [wait] fébrilement.

excitement [ɪk'saɪtmənt] n **1.** [enthusiasm] excitation *f*, animation *f*, enthousiasme *m* **2.** [agitation] excitation *f*, agitation *f* **3.** [sexual] excitation *f* **4.** [exciting events] animation *f*.

exciting [ɪk'saɪtɪŋ] adj **1.** [day, life, events, match] passionnant, palpitant ; [prospect] palpitant ; [person, novel, restaurant] formidable ; [news] sensationnel **2.** [sexually] excitant.

excl. (written abbr of **excluding**) ▸ **excl. taxes** HT.

exclaim [ɪk'skleɪm] ◆ vi s'exclamer. ◆ vt : *"but why?", he exclaimed* « mais pourquoi ? » s'exclama-t-il.

exclamation [,eksklə'meɪʃn] n exclamation *f*.

exclamation mark [UK], **exclamation point** [US] n point *m* d'exclamation.

exclamatory [ɪk'sklæmətrɪ] adj exclamatif.

exclude [ɪk'sklu:d] vt **1.** [bar] exclure ▸ **to exclude sb from sthg** exclure qqn de qqch **2.** [not take into consideration] exclure ▸ **to exclude sthg / sb from sthg** exclure qqch / qqn de qqch.

excluding [ɪk'sklu:dɪŋ] prep à l'exclusion or l'exception de, sauf, à part / *not excluding... ...* y compris.

exclusion [ɪk'sklu:ʒn] n **1.** [barring] exclusion *f* ▸ **the exclusion of sb from a society / conversation** l'exclusion de qqn d'une société / conversation **2.** [omission] exclusion *f* ▸ **the exclusion of sthg / sb from sthg** l'exclusion de qqch / qqn de qqch.

exclusion clause n clause *f* d'exclusion.

exclusive [ɪk'sklu:sɪv] ◆ adj **1.** [select - restaurant, neighbourhood] chic ; [- club] fermé **2.** [deal] exclusif / *to have an exclusive contract with a company* avoir un contrat exclusif avec une société ▸ **exclusive to** réservé (exclusivement) à **3.** [excluding taxes, charges, etc.] : *exclusive of VAT* TVA non comprise **4.** [excluding time] : *from the 14th to the 19th October, exclusive* du 14 au 19 octobre exclu **5.** [incompatible] exclusif / *they are mutually exclusive* [propositions] l'une exclut l'autre, elles sont incompatibles **6.** [sole] unique / *their exclusive concern* leur seul souci / *the exclusive use of gold* l'emploi exclusif d'or. ◆ n PRESS exclusivité *f* ; [interview] interview *f* exclusive. ❖ **exclusive of** prep ▸ **exclusive of interest** intérêts non compris.

exclusive licence n licence *f* exclusive.

exclusively [ɪk'sklu:sɪvlɪ] adv [only] exclusivement / *published exclusively in the "Times"* publié en exclusivité dans le «Times».

exclusiveness [ɪk'sklu:sɪvnɪs], **exclusivity** [ˌeksklu:-'sɪvətɪ] n **1.** [of restaurant, address, district] chic m **2.** [of contract] nature f exclusive.

exclusive rights n droits mpl exclusifs, exclusivité f.

excommunicate [ˌekskə'mju:nɪkeɪt] vt RELIG excommunier.

excommunication ['ekskə,mju:nɪ'keɪʃn] n RELIG excommunication f.

ex-con n inf ancien taulard m, ancienne taularde f.

excrement ['ekskrɪmənt] n (U) fml excréments mpl.

excrete [ɪk'skri:t] vt excréter.

excruciating [ɪk'skru:ʃɪeɪtɪŋ] adj **1.** [extremely painful] extrêmement douloureux, atroce **2.** inf [extremely bad] atroce, abominable.

excruciatingly [ɪk'skru:ʃɪeɪtɪŋlɪ] adv [painful, boring] atrocement, affreusement.

excursion [ɪk'skɜ:ʃn] n **1.** [organized trip] excursion f **2.** [short local journey] expédition f **3.** [into a different field] incursion f.

excusable [ɪk'skju:zəbl] adj excusable, pardonnable.

excuse ◆ n [ɪk'skju:s] **1.** [explanation, justification] excuse f / *that's no excuse* ce n'est pas une excuse or une raison / *there's no excuse for that kind of behaviour* ce genre de comportement est sans excuse or inexcusable ▸ **to make one's excuses** s'excuser, présenter ses excuses **2.** [example] : *a poor excuse for a father* un père lamentable **3.** [pretext] excuse f, prétexte m ▸ **an excuse to do** or **for doing sthg** une excuse or un prétexte pour faire qqch. ◆ vt [ɪk'skju:z] **1.** [justify - bad behaviour] excuser / *he tried to excuse himself by saying that...* il a essayé de se justifier en disant que... **2.** [forgive - bad behaviour, person] excuser, pardonner ▸ **excuse me a)** [to get past] pardon **b)** [as interruption, to attract sb's attention] pardon, excusez-moi **c)** 🇺🇸 [as apology] pardon, excusez-moi ▸ **to excuse o.s.** s'excuser **3.** [exempt] dispenser ▸ **to excuse sb from sthg** dispenser qqn de qqch ▸ **to excuse sb from doing sthg** dispenser qqn de faire qqch **4.** [allow to go] excuser / *please may I be excused?* **a)** [to go to lavatory] puis-je sortir, s'il vous plaît ? **b)** [from table] puis-je sortir de table, s'il vous plaît ?

ex-directory 🇬🇧 ◆ adj sur la liste rouge. ◆ adv ▸ **to go ex-directory** se mettre sur la liste rouge.

exec. [ɪg'zek] n abbr of executive.

execrable ['eksɪkrəbl] adj fml exécrable.

executable ◆ adj COMPUT exécutable. ◆ n COMPUT fichier m exécutable.

execute ['eksɪkju:t] vt **1.** [put to death] exécuter **2.** fml [carry out] exécuter **3.** LAW [will, sentence, law] exécuter **4.** COMPUT exécuter.

execution [ˌeksɪ'kju:ʃn] n **1.** [of person] exécution f **2.** fml [of order, plan, drawing] exécution f ▸ **to put sthg into execution** mettre qqch à exécution **3.** LAW [of will, sentence, law] exécution f **4.** COMPUT exécution f.

executioner [ˌeksɪ'kju:ʃnə] n bourreau m.

executive [ɪg'zekjʊtɪv] ◆ n **1.** [person] cadre m / *a business executive* un cadre commercial **2.** [body] corps m exécutif ; POL [branch of government] exécutif m. ◆ adj **1.** [dining room, washroom, etc.] des cadres, de la direction ; [suite, chair] de cadre, spécial cadre **2.** [function, role] exécutif / *an executive officer in the civil service* un cadre de l'administration ▸ **executive director** cadre m supérieur

▸ **executive producer** producteur m délégué ▸ **executive privilege** droit dont bénéficie le président des États-Unis de ne pas divulguer certaines informations au Congrès.

executor [ɪg'zekjʊtə] n LAW [of will] exécuteur m, -trice f testamentaire.

exemplary [ɪg'zemplərɪ] adj **1.** [very good - behaviour, pupil] exemplaire **2.** [serving as a warning] exemplaire.

exemplify [ɪg'zemplɪfaɪ] vt **1.** [give example of] illustrer, exemplifier **2.** [be example of] illustrer.

exempt [ɪg'zempt] ◆ adj exempt ▸ **to be exempt from sthg** être exempt de qqch. ◆ vt [gen] exempter ; [from tax] exonérer ▸ **to exempt sb / sthg from sthg** exempter qqn / qqch de qqch.

exemption [ɪg'zempʃn] n [action, state] exemption f ▸ **tax exemption** exonération f fiscale.

exercise ['eksəsaɪz] ◆ n **1.** [physical] exercice m / *exercise is good for you* l'exercice est bon pour la santé / *it's good exercise* c'est un bon exercice / *the doctor has told him to take more exercise* le docteur lui a dit de faire plus d'exercice **2.** [mental, in education] exercice m / *piano exercises* exercices de piano **3.** [use] exercice m / *in the exercise of one's duties* dans l'exercice de ses fonctions **4.** MIL exercice m / *they're on exercises* ils sont à l'exercice **5.** [activity, operation] : *it was an interesting exercise* cela a été une expérience intéressante / *it was a pointless exercise* cela n'a servi absolument à rien **6.** 🇺🇸 [ceremony] cérémonie f ▸ **graduation exercises** cérémonie de remise des diplômes. ◆ vt **1.** [body, muscle] exercer, faire travailler ; [dog, horse] donner de l'exercice à **2.** [troops] entraîner **3.** [use, put into practice - right, option, authority] exercer **4.** fml [preoccupy] préoccuper. ◆ vi **1.** [take exercise] faire de l'exercice **2.** [train] s'exercer, s'entraîner.

exercise bike n vélo m d'appartement.

exercise book n **1.** [for writing in] cahier m d'exercices **2.** [containing exercises] livre m d'exercices.

exercise yard n [in prison] cour f, préau m.

exert [ɪg'zɜ:t] vt **1.** [pressure, force] exercer **2.** ▸ **to exert o.s.** [make effort] se donner de la peine or du mal.

exertion [ɪg'zɜ:ʃn] n **1.** [of force] exercice m **2.** [effort] effort m.

exes ['eksɪz] pl n inf [expenses] ▸ **to put sthg on exes** faire passer qqch en note de frais.

exfoliant [eks'fəʊlɪənt] n exfoliant m.

exfoliate [eks'fəʊlɪeɪt] ◆ vi s'exfolier. ◆ vt exfolier.

exfoliating [eks'fəʊlɪeɪtɪŋ] adj BIOL & GEOL exfoliant ▸ **exfoliating cream** crème f exfoliante ▸ **exfoliating scrub** crème f exfoliante, gommage m exfoliant.

ex gratia [eks'greɪʃə] adj ▸ **ex gratia payment** paiement m à titre gracieux.

exhale [eks'heɪl] ◆ vt [air] expirer ; [gas, fumes] exhaler. ◆ vi [breathe out] expirer.

exhaust [ɪg'zɔ:st] ◆ n **1.** [on vehicle - system] échappement m ; [- pipe] pot m or tuyau m d'échappement **2.** (U) [fumes] gaz mpl d'échappement. ◆ vt **1.** [use up - supplies, possibilities] épuiser **2.** [tire out] épuiser, exténuer.

exhausted [ɪg'zɔ:stɪd] adj **1.** [person, smile] épuisé, exténué **2.** [used up - mine, land] épuisé.

exhausting [ɪg'zɔ:stɪŋ] adj [job, climb, climate] épuisant, exténuant, éreintant ; [person] fatigant, excédant.

exhaustion [ɪg'zɔ:stʃn] n **1.** [tiredness] épuisement m, éreintement m, grande fatigue f **2.** [of supplies, topic] épuisement m.

exhaustive [ɪg'zɔ:stɪv] adj [analysis, treatment] exhaustif ; [investigation, enquiry] approfondi, poussé.

exhaustively [ɪg'zɔ:stɪvlɪ] adv exhaustivement.

exhaust pipe n 🇬🇧 pot m or tuyau m d'échappement.

exhaust valve n soupape f d'échappement.

exhibit [ɪɡ'zɪbɪt] ◆ vt **1.** [subj: artist] exposer; [subj: companies] présenter **2.** [show, display - ID card, passport] montrer **3.** [manifest - courage, self-control] montrer, manifester. ◆ vi [painter, company] exposer. ◆ n **1.** [in an exhibition] objet m (exposé) **2.** LAW pièce f à conviction **3.** US [exhibition] exposition f.

exhibition [ˌeksɪ'bɪʃn] n **1.** [of paintings, products] exposition f; [of film] présentation f ▶ **exhibition centre** centre m d'exposition **2.** [of bad manners, ingenuity] démonstration f ▶ **to make an exhibition of o.s.** se donner en spectacle **3.** UK UNIV bourse f d'études.

exhibitionism [ˌeksɪ'bɪʃnɪzm] n **1.** [gen] besoin m or volonté f de se faire remarquer **2.** PSYCHOL exhibitionnisme m.

exhibitionist [ˌeksɪ'bɪʃnɪst] n **1.** [gen] personne qui cherche toujours à se faire remarquer **2.** PSYCHOL exhibitionniste mf.

exhibitor [ɪɡ'zɪbɪtər] n [at gallery, trade fair] exposant m.

exhilarate [ɪɡ'zɪləreɪt] vt exalter, griser.

exhilarated [ɪɡ'zɪləreɪtɪd] adj [mood, laugh] exalté.

exhilarating [ɪɡ'zɪləreɪtɪŋ] adj exaltant, grisant.

exhilaration [ɪɡˌzɪlə'reɪʃn] n exaltation f, griserie f.

exhort [ɪɡ'zɔːt] vt fml exhorter ▶ **to exhort sb to do sthg** exhorter qqn à faire qqch.

exhume [eks'hjuːm] vt fml exhumer.

ex-husband n ex-mari m.

exile ['eksaɪl] ◆ n **1.** [banishment] exil m ▶ **to live in exile** vivre en exil ▶ **to go into exile** partir en exil **2.** [person] exilé m, -e f. ◆ vt exiler, expatrier.

exiled ['eksaɪld] adj exilé / the exiled government le gouvernement en exil.

exist [ɪɡ'zɪst] vi exister / he earns enough to exist on il gagne suffisamment pour vivre.

existence [ɪɡ'zɪstəns] n **1.** [being] existence f ▶ **to come into existence a)** [species] apparaître **b)** [the earth] se former **c)** [law, institution] naître, être créé ▶ **to go out of existence** cesser d'exister **2.** [life] existence f.

existential [ˌeɡzɪ'stenʃl] adj existentiel.

existentialism [ˌeɡzɪ'stenʃəlɪzm] n existentialisme m.

existentialist [ˌeɡzɪ'stenʃəlɪst] ◆ n existentialiste mf. ◆ adj existentialiste.

existing [ɪɡ'zɪstɪŋ] adj actuel.

exit ['eksɪt] ◆ n **1.** [way out - from room, motorway] sortie f ▶ **exit ramp** bretelle f de sortie / 'exit only' 'réservé à la sortie' **2.** THEAT sortie f, exit m inv; [act of going out - from a room] sortie f **3.** COMPUT sortie f. ◆ vi **1.** THEAT sortir **2.** [go out, leave] sortir; [bullet] ressortir **3.** COMPUT sortir. ◆ vt COMPUT sortir de; [leave] quitter, sortir de.

exit charge(s) n frais mpl de sortie.

exit interview n entretien entre un employeur et son employé lors du départ de ce dernier.

exit poll UK, **exit survey** US [-'sɜːveɪ] n sondage réalisé auprès des votants à la sortie du bureau de vote.

exit strategy n stratégie f de sortie.

exit visa n visa m de sortie.

exodus ['eksədəs] n exode m. ◆ **Exodus** n **1.** [book] ▶ **(the Book of) Exodus** (l')Exode **2.** [journey] exode m.

ex officio [eksə'fɪʃɪəʊ] ◆ adj [member] de droit. ◆ adv [act, decide, etc.] de droit.

exonerate [ɪɡ'zɒnəreɪt] vt disculper, innocenter.

exorbitant [ɪɡ'zɔːbɪtənt] adj [price, demands, claims] exorbitant, démesuré, excessif.

exorbitantly [ɪɡ'zɔːbɪtəntlɪ] adv [priced] excessivement, démesurément.

exorcism ['eksɔːsɪzm] n exorcisme m ▶ **to carry out** or **to perform an exorcism** pratiquer un exorcisme.

exorcist ['eksɔːsɪst] n exorciste mf.

exorcize, exorcise ['eksɔːsaɪz] vt [evil spirits, place] exorciser.

exothermia [ˌeksəʊ'θɜːmɪə] n exothermie f.

exotic [ɪɡ'zɒtɪk] adj exotique / an exotic-sounding name un nom à consonance exotique.

exotically [ɪɡ'zɒtɪklɪ] adv [dressed, decorated] avec exotisme / exotically perfumed **a)** [flower] aux senteurs exotiques **b)** [person] au parfum exotique.

expand [ɪk'spænd] ◆ vt **1.** [empire, army, staff] agrandir; [company, business] agrandir, développer; [chest, muscles, ideas] développer; [knowledge, influence] élargir, étendre; COMPUT [memory] étendre; [gas, metal] dilater **2.** MATH [equation] développer. ◆ vi **1.** [empire, army, staff] s'agrandir; [company, business] s'agrandir, se développer; [chest, muscles, market] se développer; [knowledge, influence] s'étendre, s'élargir; [gas, metal] se dilater; [volume of traffic] augmenter; [in business] se développer, s'agrandir **2.** [on an idea] s'étendre. ◆ **expand (up)on** vt insep développer.

expandable [ɪk'spændɪbl] adj [gas, material] expansible; [idea, theory] qui peut être développé; [basic set] qui peut être complété; COMPUT [memory] extensible.

expanding [ɪk'spændɪŋ] adj **1.** [company, empire, gas, metal] en expansion; [influence] grandissant; [industry, market] en expansion, qui se développe **2.** [extendable] : expanding suitcase / briefcase valise / serviette extensible.

expanse [ɪk'spæns] n étendue f.

expansion [ɪk'spænʃn] n [of empire] expansion f, élargissement m; [of army, staff] augmentation f, accroissement m; [of chest, muscles, ideas] développement m; [of knowledge, influence] élargissement m; [of gas, metal] expansion f, dilatation f; COMPUT [of memory] extension f; [of business] développement m, agrandissement m, extension f.

expansion card n COMPUT carte f d'extension.

expansionism [ɪk'spænʃənɪzm] n expansionnisme m.

expansionist [ɪk'spænʃənɪst] ◆ adj expansionniste. ◆ n expansionniste mf.

expansion slot n COMPUT emplacement m or logement m pour carte d'extension.

expansive [ɪk'spænsɪv] adj **1.** [person, mood, gesture] expansif **2.** PHYS [gas] expansible, dilatable.

expansively [ɪk'spænsɪvlɪ] adv [talk, gesture] de manière expansive.

expat [ˌeks'pæt] **(abbr of expatriate)** inf ◆ n expat mf. ◆ adj [person] expatrié; [bar, community] des expatriés.

expatriate ◆ n [eks'pætrɪət] expatrié m, -e f. ◆ adj [eks'pætrɪət] [Briton, American, etc.] expatrié; [bar, community] des expatriés.

expect [ɪk'spekt] ◆ vt **1.** [anticipate] s'attendre à / we expected that it would be much bigger nous nous attendions à ce qu'il soit beaucoup plus gros, nous pensions qu'il allait être beaucoup plus gros ▶ **to expect sb to do sthg** s'attendre à ce que qqn fasse qqch / she is as well as can be expected elle va aussi bien que sa condition le permet / what can you expect from a government like that? que voulez-vous, avec un gouvernement pareil ! / as might have been expected or as was to be expected comme on pouvait s'y attendre **2.** [count on] : we're expecting you to help us nous comptons sur votre aide / don't expect me to be there! ne t'attends pas à ce que j'y sois ! **3.** [demand]

▸ **to expect sb to do sthg** demander à qqn de faire qqch **4.** [suppose, imagine] imaginer, penser, supposer / *I expect so* je pense, j'imagine / *I don't expect so* je ne pense pas, j'imagine que non / *I expect you're right* tu dois avoir raison / *I expect you'll be wanting something to drink* **a)** vous boirez bien quelque chose **b)** [grudgingly] j'imagine que vous voulez quelque chose à boire **5.** [baby] attendre **6.** [await] attendre / *I'm expecting friends for dinner* j'attends des amis à dîner. ◆ vi ▸ **to be expecting** [be pregnant] être enceinte, attendre un enfant.

📋 Note that *s'attendre à ce que* is followed by a verb in the subjunctive:
Don't expect them to be experts. *Ne vous attendez pas à ce qu'ils soient des experts.*

expectancy [ɪk'spektənsɪ], **expectance** [ɪk'spektəns] n [anticipation] : *the look of expectancy on his face* l'attente qui se lisait sur son visage / *in a tone of eager expectancy* sur un ton plein d'espérance or d'espoir.

expectant [ɪk'spektənt] adj **1.** [anticipating] : *with an expectant look in his eye* avec dans son regard l'air d'attendre quelque chose / *in an expectant tone of voice* la voix chargée d'espoir **2.** [pregnant] ▸ **expectant mother** future maman f.

expectantly [ɪk'spektəntlɪ] adv [enquire, glance] avec l'air d'attendre quelque chose ; [wait] impatiemment.

expectation [ˌekspek'teɪʃn] n **1.** (U) [anticipation] ▸ **in expectation of** dans l'attente de **2.** *(usu pl)* [sthg expected] attente f ▸ **to exceed sb's expectations** dépasser l'attente or les espérances de qqn.

expected [ɪk'spektɪd] adj attendu / *please state expected salary* indiquez vos prétentions.

expectorant [ɪk'spektərənt] n expectorant m.

expedient [ɪk'spi:djənt] ◆ adj [advisable] indiqué, convenable, opportun ; [involving self-interest] commode. ◆ n expédient m.

expedite ['ekspɪdaɪt] vt *fml* [work, legal process] hâter, activer, accélérer ; [completion of contract, deal] hâter / *to expedite matters* accélérer or activer les choses.

expedition [ˌekspɪ'dɪʃn] n [scientific, of explorers, to shops, etc.] expédition f ▸ **to go on an expedition** aller or partir en expédition, aller faire une expédition.

expeditionary [ˌekspɪ'dɪʃnərɪ] adj MIL ▸ **expeditionary mission** mission f d'expédition ▸ **expeditionary force** force f expéditionnaire.

expel [ɪk'spel] vt **1.** [from school] renvoyer ; [from country, club] expulser **2.** [gas, liquid] expulser.

expend [ɪk'spend] vt **1.** [time, energy] consacrer ; [resources] utiliser, employer ▸ **to expend time / energy on sthg** consacrer du temps / de l'énergie à qqch **2.** [use up] épuiser.

expendability [ɪk,spendə'bɪlətɪ] n caractère m superflu or négligeable.

expendable [ɪk'spendəbl] adj [person, workforce, object] superflu ; [troops, spies] qui peut être sacrifié.

expenditure [ɪk'spendɪtʃə'] n **1.** [act of spending] dépense f **2.** (U) [money spent] dépenses fpl ▸ **expenditure on sthg** dépenses en qqch / *arms / defence expenditure* dépenses en armes / liées à la défense.

expense [ɪk'spens] n **1.** [cost] coût m **2.** [expensiveness] cherté f, coût m élevé **3.** *fig* ▸ **at the expense of sthg** aux dépens de qqch. ◆ **expenses** pl n frais mpl ▸ **to put**

sthg **on expenses** mettre qqch dans les notes de frais / *travelling expenses* frais de déplacement / *all expenses paid* tous frais payés.

expense account ◆ n indemnité f or allocation f pour frais professionnels ▸ **to put sthg on the expense account** mettre qqch dans les (notes de) frais. ◆ comp ▸ **an expense account dinner** un dîner passé dans les notes de frais.

expenses-paid adj [trip, holiday] tous frais payés.

expensive [ɪk'spensɪv] adj cher / *to have expensive tastes* avoir des goûts de luxe / *it's an expensive place to live* la vie y est chère / *that could be an expensive mistake* *lit & fig* c'est une erreur qui pourrait coûter cher.

expensively [ɪk'pensɪvlɪ] adv à grands frais.

experience [ɪk'spɪərɪəns] ◆ n **1.** [in life, in a subject] expérience f **2.** [event] expérience f. ◆ vt **1.** [undergo -hunger, hardship, recession] connaître **2.** [feel -thrill, emotion, despair] sentir, ressentir **3.** [have personal knowledge of] : *come and experience Manhattan* venez découvrir Manhattan / *to experience a real Scottish New Year* assister à un vrai réveillon écossais.

experienced [ɪk'spɪərɪənst] adj expérimenté / *we're looking for someone a bit more experienced* nous recherchons quelqu'un qui ait un peu plus d'expérience ▸ **to be experienced in sthg** avoir l'expérience de qqch ▸ **to be experienced at doing sthg** avoir l'habitude de faire qqch.

experiment [ɪk'sperɪmənt] ◆ n *lit & fig* expérience f ▸ **to carry out** or **to conduct an experiment** réaliser or effectuer une expérience ▸ **an experiment in sthg** une expérience de qqch / *as an* or *by way of experiment* à titre d'expérience. ◆ vi faire une expérience or des expériences / *to experiment with a new technique* expérimenter une nouvelle technique / *to experiment on animals* faire des expériences sur les animaux.

experimental [ɪk,sperɪ'mentl] adj expérimental.

experimentally [ɪk,sperɪ'mentəlɪ] adv [by experimenting] expérimentalement ; [as an experiment] à titre expérimental.

experimentation [ɪk,sperɪmen'teɪʃn] n expérimentation f.

expert ['eksp3:t] ◆ n expert m, spécialiste mf / *to be an expert on one's subject* / *in one's field* être un expert dans sa matière / dans son domaine. ◆ adj [person] expert ; [advice, opinion] autorisé, d'expert ▸ **to be expert at doing sthg** être expert à faire qqch ▸ **to be expert at sthg** être expert en qqch ▸ **expert testimony** LAW témoignage m d'expert.

expertise [ˌeksp3:'ti:z] n compétence f d'expert, savoir-faire m ▸ **to do sthg with great expertise** faire qqch avec beaucoup de compétence.

expertly ['eksp3:tlɪ] adv d'une manière experte, expertement.

expert system n COMPUT système m expert.

expiate ['ekspɪeɪt] vt *fml* expier.

expiration [ˌekspɪ'reɪʃn] n **1.** *fml* [expiry] expiration f **2.** *fml* [exhalation] expiration f **3.** *arch & liter* [death] mort f.

expiration date US = expiry date.

expire [ɪk'spaɪə'] vi **1.** [contract, lease, visa, etc.] expirer, arriver à terme **2.** [exhale] expirer **3.** *arch & liter* [die] expirer.

expiry [ɪk'spaɪərɪ] n [of contract, lease, visa, etc.] expiration f, échéance f.

expiry date n [of contract, lease, visa, etc.] date f d'expiration or d'échéance.

explain [ɪk'spleɪn] ◆ vt **1.** [clarify] expliquer **2.** [account for] expliquer ▶ **to explain o.s.** s'expliquer. ◆ vi [clarify] expliquer. ◇ **explain away** vt sep [justify, excuse] justifier.

explanation [ˌeksplə'neɪʃn] n **1.** [clarification] explication *f* ▶ **to give** or **to offer an explanation for sthg** donner une explication à qqch ▶ **to find an explanation for sthg** trouver une explication à qqch **2.** [justification] explication *f* / *you'd better have a good explanation!* j'espère que tu as une bonne excuse or une explication valable !

explanatory [ɪk'splænətrɪ] adj explicatif.

expletive [ɪk'spliːtɪv] ◆ n **1.** [swearword] juron *m* **2.** GRAM explétif *m*. ◆ adj GRAM explétif.

explicable [ɪk'splɪkəbl] adj explicable.

explicit [ɪk'splɪsɪt] adj [denial, meaning, support] explicite / *explicit sex and violence on the television* le sexe et la violence montrés ouvertement à la télévision / *sexually explicit scenes* certaines scènes du film peuvent choquer / *the film has some explicit scenes* certaines scènes du film peuvent choquer / *it contains explicit language* cela comporte des mots qui peuvent choquer.

⚠ **Explicite** means explicit, but it does not mean 'likely to cause offence'. See the entry for details.

explicitly [ɪk'splɪsɪtlɪ] adv explicitement.
explode [ɪk'spləʊd] ◆ vt [detonate] faire exploser or sauter ; *fig* [theory, myth, etc.] détruire, anéantir. ◆ vi [bomb, mine, etc.] exploser, sauter ; *fig* : *to explode with laughter* éclater de rire / *to explode with anger* exploser de colère.

exploit ◆ n ['eksplɔɪt] exploit *m*. ◆ vt [ɪk'splɔɪt] **1.** [workers] exploiter **2.** [natural resources] exploiter.

exploitation [ˌeksplɔɪ'teɪʃn] n [of workers, of natural resources] exploitation *f*.

exploitative [ɪk'splɔɪtətɪv] adj [practices] relevant de l'exploitation / *the company's exploitative attitude towards the workforce* la manière dont l'entreprise exploite la main-d'œuvre.

exploration [ˌeksplə'reɪʃn] n **1.** [of place, problem] exploration *f* **2.** MED exploration *f*.

exploratory [ɪk'splɒrətrɪ] adj [journey] d'exploration ; [talks, discussions] exploratoire ▶ **exploratory drilling** forage *m* d'exploration ▶ **exploratory surgery** chirurgie *f* exploratrice.

explore [ɪk'splɔːr] ◆ vt **1.** [country] explorer ; [town] découvrir **2.** [issue, possibility, problem] explorer, examiner **3.** MED explorer, sonder. ◆ vi faire une exploration.

explorer [ɪk'splɔːrər] n **1.** [person] explorateur *m*, -trice *f* **2.** [instrument] sonde *f*.

explosion [ɪk'spləʊʒn] n **1.** [of bomb, gas] explosion *f* **2.** [act of exploding] explosion *f*.

explosive [ɪk'spləʊsɪv] ◆ adj **1.** explosif ; [gas] explosible **2.** LING explosif. ◆ n **1.** [in bomb] explosif *m* ▶ **high explosive** explosif puissant ▶ **explosives expert** expert *m*, -e *f* en explosifs **2.** LING explosive *f*.

explosive belt n ceinture *f* explosive.

expo ['ekspəʊ] (*pl* **expos**) n [exhibition] expo *f*.

exponent [ɪk'spəʊnənt] n **1.** [of idea, theory] apôtre *m*, avocat *m*, -e *f* ; [of skill] représentant *m*, -e *f* / *he is a leading exponent of this theory* il est l'un des plus fervents apôtres de cette théorie **2.** MATH exposant *m*.

exponential [ˌekspə'nenʃl] adj exponentiel.

export ◆ n ['ekspɔːt] **1.** [action] exportation *f* **2.** [product] exportation *f*. ◆ comp [duty, licence, trade] d'exportation ▶ **export agent** commissionnaire *m* exportateur ▶ **export ban** interdiction *f* d'exporter. ◆ vt [ɪk'spɔːt] **1.** *lit & fig* exporter **2.** COMPUT exporter. ◆ vi [ɪk'spɔːt] exporter.

exportable [ɪk'spɔːtəbl] adj exportable.

exportation [ˌekspɔː'teɪʃn] n *fml* exportation *f*.

exporter [ek'spɔːtər] n exportateur *m*, -trice *f*.

expose [ɪk'spəʊz] vt **1.** [uncover] découvrir ; PHOT exposer ▶ **to expose sb / sthg to sthg** exposer qqn / qqch à qqch ▶ **to expose o.s.** [exhibitionist] s'exhiber ▶ **to expose o.s. to sthg** [to criticism, ridicule, risk] s'exposer à qqch **2.** [reveal, unmask - plot] découvrir ; [- spy] découvrir, démasquer.

exposé [eks'pəʊzeɪ] n PRESS révélations *fpl*.

exposed [ɪk'spəʊzd] adj [location, house, position, etc.] exposé ; TECH [parts, gears] apparent, à découvert ; ARCHIT [beam] apparent.

exposition [ˌekspə'zɪʃn] n **1.** [explanation] exposé *m* **2.** [exhibition] exposition *f*.

exposure [ɪk'spəʊʒər] n **1.** [to harm, radiation] exposition *f* **2.** [to cold] : *to suffer from (the effects of) exposure* souffrir des effets d'une exposition au froid **3.** [unmasking, revealing - of crime, scandal] révélation *f*, divulgation *f* **4.** PHOT pose *f* ▶ **exposure time** temps *m* de pose **5.** [position of house] exposition *f* **6.** [media coverage] couverture *f*.

exposure meter n exposimètre *m*, posemètre *m*.

expound [ɪk'spaʊnd] vt exposer.

express [ɪk'spres] ◆ n **1.** [train] express *m* / *to travel by express* voyager en express **2.** [system of delivery] exprès *m* ▶ **the Express** PRESS *nom abrégé du* «*Daily Express*». ◆ adj **1.** [clear - instructions, purpose] clair / *with the express intention of...* avec la claire intention de... **2.** [fast - delivery, messenger] express ▶ **express company** entreprise *f* de livraison exprès ▶ **express train** train *m* express, express *m*. ◆ adv [send] en exprès. ◆ vt **1.** [voice, convey] exprimer / *to express an interest in (doing) sthg* manifester de l'intérêt pour (faire) qqch / *she expresses her feelings by painting* elle exprime ses sentiments par or à travers la peinture ▶ **to express o.s.** s'exprimer ▶ **to express o.s. through sthg** s'exprimer par or à travers qqch **2.** [render in a different form] exprimer / *to express sthg as a fraction* MATH exprimer qqch sous la forme d'une fraction **3.** *fml* [juice] extraire, exprimer ; [milk] tirer **4.** [send] envoyer en exprès.

expression [ɪk'spreʃn] n **1.** [of feelings, thoughts, friendship] expression *f* **2.** [feeling - in art, music] expression *f* **3.** [phrase] expression *f* ▶ **set** or **fixed expression** LING expression or locution *f* figée or toute faite **4.** [facial] expression *f*.

expressionism [ɪk'spreʃənɪzm] n ART expressionnisme *m*.

expressionist [ɪk'spreʃənɪst] ◆ adj ART expressionniste. ◆ n ART expressionniste *mf*.

expressionistic [ɪkˌspreʃə'nɪstɪk] adj ART expressionniste.

expressionless [ɪk'spreʃənlɪs] adj [face, person] inexpressif, sans expression ; [voice] inexpressif, éteint, terne.

expressive [ɪk'spresɪv] adj [face, gesture, smile] expressif ▶ **to be expressive of sthg** être indicatif de qqch.

expressively [ɪk'spresɪvlɪ] adv [gesture, smile] avec expression.

expressiveness [ɪk'spresɪvnɪs] n [of face, gesture, smile] expressivité *f*.

expressly [ɪk'spreslɪ] adv expressément / *I expressly forbid you to leave* je vous interdis formellement de partir.

expresso n expresso *m*.

expresso maker n machine f à expresso.

expressway [ɪk'spresweɪ] n US autoroute f.

expropriate [eks'prəʊprɪeɪt] vt exproprier.

expropriation [eks,prəʊprɪ'eɪʃn] n expropriation f.

expulsion [ɪk'spʌlʃn] n **1.** [from party, country] expulsion f ; [from school] renvoi m **2.** [of breath] expulsion f.

exquisite [ɪk'skwɪzɪt] adj **1.** [food, beauty, manners] exquis ; [jewellery, craftsmanship] raffiné **2.** [intense - pleasure, pain, thrill] intense.

exquisitely [ɪk'skwɪzɪtlɪ] adv **1.** [superbly] de façon exquise **2.** [intensely] intensément.

ex-serviceman (pl **ex-servicemen**) n retraité m de l'armée.

ex-servicewoman (pl **ex-servicewomen**) n retraitée f de l'armée.

ext. (written abbr of **extension**) : ext. 4174 p. 4174.

extant [ek'stænt] adj fml encore existant.

extemporize [ɪk'stempəraɪz] ◆ vt [speech, piece of music] improviser. ◆ vi [speaker, musician] improviser.

extend [ɪk'stend] ◆ vt **1.** [stretch out - arm, leg] étendre, allonger ; [-wings] ouvrir, déployer ; [-aerial] déplier, déployer **2.** [in length, duration - guarantee, visa, news programme] prolonger ; [-road, runway] prolonger, allonger **3.** [make larger, widen - frontiers, law, enquiry, search] étendre ; [-building] agrandir ; [-vocabulary] enrichir, élargir **4.** [offer - friendship, hospitality] offrir ; [-thanks, condolences, congratulations] présenter ; [-credit] accorder **5.** [stretch - horse, person] pousser au bout de ses capacités or à son maximum. ◆ vi **1.** [protrude - wall, cliff] avancer, former une avancée **2.** [stretch - country, forest, hills, etc.] s'étendre.

extendable [ɪk'stendəbl] adj **1.** [in space] ◆ **extendable aerial** antenne f télescopique ◆ **extendable ladder** échelle f à coulisse **2.** [in time - contract, visa] renouvelable.

extended [ɪk'stendɪd] adj [in time - contract, visit] prolongé / to be on extended leave être en arrêt prolongé / owing to the extended news bulletin en raison de la prolongation du bulletin d'informations ◆ **extended coverage** [on radio, TV] informations détaillées sur un événement.

extended family n ◆ **the extended family** la famille élargie.

extended-play [ɪk'stendɪd-] adj [record] double-durée.

extension [ɪk'stenʃn] n **1.** [of arm, legislation, frontiers] extension f **2.** [of house, building] ◆ **to build an extension onto** agrandir **3.** [of motorway] prolongement m **4.** [of contract, visa, time period] prolongation f **5.** [telephone - in office building] poste m ; [-in house] poste m supplémentaire **6.** ELEC prolongateur m, rallonge f. ◆ **by extension** adv phr par extension.

extension cable n rallonge f.

extension cord US n = extension lead.

extension lead n UK prolongateur m, rallonge f.

extensive [ɪk'stensɪv] adj [desert, powers, knowledge] étendu ; [damage] important, considérable ; [tests, research, investigation] approfondi ; AGR extensif / the issue has been given extensive coverage in the media ce problème a été largement traité dans les médias / to make extensive use of sthg beaucoup utiliser qqch, faire un usage considérable de qqch.

⚠ Extensive should only be translated by extensif in the agricultural sense.

extensively [ɪk'stensɪvlɪ] adv [damaged, altered, revised] considérablement ; [quote] abondamment ; [travel, read]

beaucoup ; [discuss] en profondeur / to use sthg extensively beaucoup utiliser qqch, faire un usage considérable de qqch.

extent [ɪk'stent] n **1.** [size, range - of ground, damage, knowledge] étendue f ; [-of debts] importance f **2.** [degree] mesure f, degré m / to what extent? dans quelle mesure ? ◆ **to that extent** sur ce point, à cet égard ◆ **to the extent that...** or **to such an extent that...** à tel point que... ◆ **to a large extent**, **to agreat extent** dans une large mesure, en grande partie. ◆ **to an extent, to some extent**, **to a certain extent** adv phr dans une certaine mesure, jusqu'à un certain point or degré.

extenuating [ɪk'stenjueɪtɪŋ] adj ◆ **extenuating circumstances** circonstances fpl atténuantes.

exterior [ɪk'stɪərɪər] ◆ adj extérieur ◆ **exterior angle** MATH angle externe ◆ **exterior to** extérieur à. ◆ n [of house, building] extérieur m ; [of person] apparence f, dehors m.

exterminate [ɪk'stɜːmɪneɪt] vt [pests] exterminer ; [race, people] exterminer, anéantir.

extermination [ɪk,stɜːmɪ'neɪʃn] n [of pests] extermination f ; [of race, people] extermination f, anéantissement m.

exterminator [ɪk'stɜːmɪneɪtər] n [person - gen] exterminateur m, -trice f ; [-of rats, mice] dératiseur m ; [poison] mort-aux-rats f inv.

external [ɪk'stɜːnl] ◆ adj [events, relations, trade, wall] extérieur ◆ **external degree** UK diplôme délivré par une université à des étudiants libres ◆ **external device** COMPUT dispositif m externe, périphérique m ◆ **external examiner** UNIV examinateur m, -trice f venant de l'extérieur ◆ **'for external use only'** PHARM 'à usage externe uniquement'. ◆ n (usu pl) : he judges people by externals il juge les gens sur leur apparence.

externalize, externalise [ɪk'stɜːnəlaɪz] vt extérioriser.

externally [ɪk'stɜːnəlɪ] adv à l'extérieur / 'to be used externally' PHARM 'à usage externe'.

extinct [ɪk'stɪŋkt] adj [species, race] disparu / extinct volcano volcan m éteint / to become extinct a) [species, tradition] s'éteindre b) [method] disparaître.

extinction [ɪk'stɪŋkʃn] n [of race, species] extinction f, disparition f ; [of fire] extinction f / to hunt an animal to extinction chasser un animal jusqu'à extinction de l'espèce.

extinguish [ɪk'stɪŋgwɪʃ] vt [fire, candle, etc.] éteindre ; fig [memory] effacer.

extinguisher [ɪk'stɪŋgwɪʃər] n extincteur m.

extn. = ext.

extol, extoll US [ɪk'stəʊl] (pt & pp **extolled**, cont **extolling**) vt fml [person] chanter les louanges de ; [system, virtues, merits] vanter.

extort [ɪk'stɔːt] vt [money] extorquer, soutirer ; [confession, promise] extorquer, arracher ◆ **to extort money from sb** extorquer or soutirer de l'argent à qqn.

extortion [ɪk'stɔːʃn] n [of money, promise, confession] extorsion f.

extortionate [ɪk'stɔːʃnət] adj [price, demand] exorbitant, démesuré / that's extortionate! [very expensive] c'est exorbitant or du vol !

extortionately [ɪk'stɔːʃnətlɪ] adv démesurément, excessivement.

extortioner [ɪk'stɔːʃnər], **extortionist** [ɪk'stɔːʃnɪst] n extorqueur m, -euse f.

extra ['ekstrə] ◆ adj **1.** [additional] supplémentaire / I put an extra jumper on j'ai mis un pull en plus / he made an extra effort to get there on time il a redoublé d'efforts pour y arriver à l'heure / *as an extra precaution* pour plus de précaution / *an extra helping of cake* une autre part de gâteau / *no extra charge / cost* aucun supplément de prix / frais supplémentaire / *service / VAT is extra* le service / la TVA est en supplément / *extra pay* supplément de salaire / *she asked for an extra £2* elle a demandé 2 livres de plus / *at no extra charge* sans supplément de prix ▸ **extra time** a) [to pay, finish, etc.] délai *m* b) SPORT prolongations *fpl* / *the game has gone into extra time* les joueurs sont en train de jouer les prolongations 2. [spare] en plus. ◆ adv 1. [extremely - polite, kind] extrêmement ; [- strong, white] super- / *to work extra hard* travailler d'arrache-pied / *extra dry* a) [wine] très sec b) [champagne, vermouth] extra-dry *(inv)* / *extra fine* [flour, sugar] extrafin, surfin 2. [in addition] plus, davantage / *to pay extra for a double room* payer plus or un supplément pour une chambre double. ◆ *n* 1. [addition] supplément *m* / *the paper comes with a business extra* le journal est vendu avec un supplément affaires / *a car with many extras* une voiture avec de nombreux accessoires en option 2. [in film] figurant *m*, -e *f* 3. [additional charge] supplément *m* 4. [luxury] ▸ **little extras** petits extras *mpl* or luxes *mpl*.

extra- in comp extra- ▸ **extra-large** grande taille ▸ **extra-special** ultra-spécial.

extract ◆ vt [ɪkˈstrækt] 1. [take out - juice, oil, bullet] extraire ; [- tooth] arracher, extraire ; [- cork] ôter, enlever 2. [obtain - information] soutirer, arracher ; [- money] soutirer. ◆ *n* [ˈekstrækt] 1. [from book, piece of music] extrait *m* 2. [substance] extrait *m* ; PHARM extrait *m*, essence *f*.

extraction [ɪkˈstrækʃn] *n* 1. [removal - of juice, oil, bullet] extraction *f* ; [- of tooth] extraction *f*, arrachage *m* 2. [descent] extraction *f* / *he is of Scottish extraction* il est d'origine écossaise.

extractor [ɪkˈstræktər] *n* [machine, tool] extracteur *m* ; [fan] ventilateur *m*, aérateur *m*.

extracurricular [ˌekstrəkəˈrɪkjʊlər] adj SCH hors programme, extrascolaire ; UNIV hors programme ▸ **extracurricular activities** activités *fpl* extrascolaires.

extradite [ˈekstrədaɪt] vt [send back] extrader ; [procure extradition of] obtenir l'extradition de.

extradition [ˌekstrəˈdɪʃn] ◆ *n* extradition *f*. ◆ comp [order, treaty] d'extradition.

extramarital [ˌekstrəˈmærɪtl] adj extraconjugal ▸ **extramarital sex** rapports *mpl* extraconjugaux.

extramural [ˌekstrəˈmjʊərəl] adj 1. UNIV [course, studies, activities] ▸ **Department of Extramural Studies** ≈ Institut *m* d'éducation permanente 2. [district] extramuros.

extraneous [ɪkˈstreɪnjəs] adj 1. [irrelevant - idea, point, consideration, issue] étranger, extérieur ▸ **to be extraneous to sthg** a) [idea, point, issue] être étranger à qqch b) [detail] être sans rapport avec qqch 2. [from outside - noise, force] extérieur.

extranet *n* extranet *m*.

extraordinarily [ɪkˈstrɔːdnrəlɪ] adv 1. [as intensifier] extraordinairement, incroyablement 2. [unusually] extraordinairement, d'une manière inhabituelle.

extraordinary [ɪkˈstrɔːdnrɪ] adj 1. [remarkable] extraordinaire 2. [surprising, unusual - story] inouï, invraisemblable ; [- house] curieux, singulier ; [- appearance, outfit] insolite, singulier ; [- event] invraisemblable ; [- behaviour, speech] étonnant, surprenant 3. [additional - meeting, session] extraordinaire.

extraordinary general meeting *n* 🇬🇧 assemblée *f* générale extraordinaire.

extrapolate [ɪkˈstræpəleɪt] ◆ vt [infer from facts] déduire par extrapolation ; MATH établir par extrapolation. ◆ vi extrapoler ▸ **to extrapolate from sthg** extrapoler à partir de qqch.

extrapolation [ɪkˌstræpəˈleɪʃn] *n* extrapolation *f*.

extrasensory [ˌekstrəˈsensərɪ] adj extrasensoriel ▸ **extrasensory perception** perception *f* extrasensorielle.

extra-special adj : *you'll have to take extra-special care over it* il faudra que tu y fasses particulièrement attention.

extraterrestrial [ˌekstrətəˈrestrɪəl] ◆ adj extraterrestre. ◆ *n* extraterrestre *mf*.

extravagance [ɪkˈstrævəgəns] *n* 1. [wasteful spending] dépenses *fpl* extravagantes 2. [extravagant purchase] folie *f*.

extravagant [ɪkˈstrævəgənt] adj 1. [wasteful, profligate - person] dépensier, prodigue ; [- tastes] coûteux, de luxe / *to be extravagant with one's money* être gaspilleur or dépensier, gaspiller son argent 2. [exaggerated - idea, opinion] extravagant ; [- claim, behaviour, prices] extravagant, excessif.

extravagantly [ɪkˈstrævəgəntlɪ] adv 1. [wastefully] : *to live extravagantly* vivre sur un grand pied 2. [exaggeratedly - behave, act, talk] de manière extravagante ; [- praise] avec excès.

extravaganza [ɪkˌstrævəˈgænzə] *n* [lavish performance] œuvre *f* à grand spectacle.

extra-virgin adj [olive oil] extra vierge.

extreme [ɪkˈstriːm] ◆ adj 1. [heat, pain, views, measures] extrême ▸ **extreme sports** sports *mpl* extrêmes 2. [furthest away] extrême. ◆ *n* extrême *m*. ◆ **in the extreme** adv phr à l'extrême.

extremely [ɪkˈstriːmlɪ] adv [as intensifier] extrêmement.

extreme sport *n* sport *m* extrême.

extremism [ɪkˈstriːmɪzm] *n* POL extrémisme *m*.

extremist [ɪkˈstriːmɪst] ◆ adj extrémiste. ◆ *n* extrémiste *mf*.

extremity [ɪkˈstremətɪ] (*pl* **extremities**) *n* 1. [furthermost tip] extrémité *f* 2. (*usu pl*) [hand, foot] ▸ **the extremities** les extrémités *fpl* 3. [extreme nature - of belief, view, etc.] extrémité *f* 4. [adversity, danger] extrémité *f* 5. (*usu pl*) [extreme measure] extrémité *f* / *to drive sb to extremities* pousser or conduire qqn à des extrêmes.

extricate [ˈekstrɪkeɪt] vt [thing] extirper, dégager ; [person] dégager / *to extricate o.s. from a tricky situation* se sortir or se tirer d'une situation délicate.

extrovert [ˈekstrəvɜːt] ◆ adj PSYCHOL extraverti, extroverti. ◆ *n* PSYCHOL extraverti *m*, -e *f*, extroverti *m*, -e *f*.

extruded [ɪkˈstruːdɪd] adj extrudé.

exuberance [ɪgˈzjuːbərəns] *n* 1. [of person, writing] exubérance *f* 2. [of vegetation] exubérance *f*.

exuberant [ɪgˈzjuːbərənt] adj 1. [person, mood, style] exubérant 2. [vegetation] exubérant.

exuberantly [ɪgˈzjuːbərəntlɪ] adv avec exubérance.

exude [ɪgˈzjuːd] ◆ vi [liquid, sap, blood, etc.] exsuder. ◆ vt [blood, sap] exsuder ; *fig* [confidence, love] déborder de.

exult [ɪgˈzʌlt] vi [rejoice] exulter, jubiler ; [triumph] exulter / *to exult at* or *in one's success* [rejoice] se réjouir de son succès / *to exult over defeated opponents* [triumph] exulter de la défaite de ses adversaires.

exultant [ɪgˈzʌltənt] adj [feeling, shout, look] d'exultation ; [mood, crowd] jubilant / *to be* or *to feel exultant* exulter.

exultation [ˌegzʌlˈteɪʃn] *n* exultation *f*.

ex-wife *n* ex-femme *f*.

eye [aɪ] (cont **eyeing** or **eying**) ◆ n **1.** [organ] œil m / to have green eyes avoir les yeux verts / a girl with green eyes une fille aux yeux verts / before your very eyes! sous vos yeux ! / look me in the eye and say that regarde-moi bien dans les yeux et dis-le-moi / I saw it with my own eyes je l'ai vu de mes yeux vu or de mes propres yeux / with one's eyes closed / open les yeux fermés / ouverts / she can't keep her eyes open fig elle dort debout / I could do it with my eyes closed je pourrais le faire les yeux fermés / he went into it with his eyes open il s'y est lancé en toute connaissance de cause **2.** [gaze] regard m / the film looks at the world through the eyes of a child dans ce film, on voit le monde à travers les yeux d'un enfant / with a critical eye d'un œil critique / I couldn't believe my eyes je n'en croyais pas mes yeux / he couldn't take his eyes off her il ne pouvait pas la quitter des yeux **3.** SEW [of needle] chas m, œil m ; [eyelet] œillet m **4.** [of potato, twig] œil m **5.** [of storm] œil m, centre m **6.** [photocell] œil m électrique **7.** PHR to close or shut one's eyes to sthg: we can't close or shut our eyes to the problem on ne peut pas fermer les yeux sur ce problème / they can't close their eyes to the fact that the company's at fault ils sont bien obligés d'admettre que la société est en faute ▶ for your eyes only ultra-confidentiel ▶ to have an eye or a good eye for sthg: she has a good eye for detail elle a l'œil pour ce qui est des détails / he only has eyes for her il n'a d'yeux que pour elle / she has her eye on the mayor's position elle vise la mairie / in my / her eyes à mes / ses yeux / in the eyes of the law aux yeux or au regard de la loi ▶ to run or to cast one's eye over sthg jeter un coup d'œil à qqch ▶ to try to catch sb's eye essayer d'attirer le regard de qqn / could you keep your eye on the children / the house? pourriez-vous surveiller les enfants / la maison ? / keep an eye on the situation suivez de près la situation ▶ to keep one's eye open for sthg être attentif à qqch ▶ an eye for an eye (and a tooth for a tooth) œil pour œil (dent pour dent) / his eyes are too big for his stomach il a les yeux plus grands que le ventre ▶ to give sb the eye a) inf [flirt] faire de l'œil à qqn b) [give signal] faire signe à qqn (d'un clin d'œil) ▶ to have eyes in the back of one's head: he has eyes in the back of his head il a des yeux derrière la tête / I've never clapped inf or set or laid eyes on her je ne l'ai jamais vue de ma vie ▶ to keep one's eyes skinned or peeled for sthg / sb inf: keep your eyes peeled for trouble restez vigilant ▶ to make eyes at sb faire de l'œil à qqn ▶ to see eye to eye with sb (about sthg): she and I don't see eye to eye a) [disagree] elle ne voit pas les choses du même œil que moi, elle n'est pas de mon avis b) [dislike one another] elle et moi, nous ne nous entendons pas / that's one in the eye for him! inf ça lui fera les pieds ! ▶ to be up to one's eyes in it: we're up to our eyes in it a) [overworked] on a du travail jusque là ! b) [in deep trouble] on est dans les ennuis jusqu'au cou ! ◆ vt regarder, mesurer du regard / the child eyed the man warily l'enfant dévisagea l'homme avec circonspection. ◆ with an eye to prep phr ▶ with an eye to sthg / to doing sthg en vue de qqch / de faire qqch / with an eye to the future en vue or en prévision de l'avenir. ◆ **eye up** vt sep v inf reluquer.

eyeball ['aɪbɔːl] ◆ n globe m oculaire. ◆ vt inf regarder fixement, reluquer.

eyebath ['aɪbɑːθ] n UK MED œillère f.

eyebolt ['aɪbɒlt] n tire-fond m.

eyebrow ['aɪbraʊ] n sourcil m ▶ to raise one's eyebrows lever les sourcils.

eyebrow pencil n crayon m à sourcils.

eye candy n (U) inf tape m à l'œil hum pej.

eye-catcher n tire-l'œil mf.

eye-catching adj [colour, dress] qui attire l'œil ; [poster, title] accrocheur, tapageur.

eye contact n contact m visuel / to establish eye contact (with sb) croiser le regard (de qqn) / to maintain eye contact (with sb) regarder (qqn) dans les yeux.

-eyed [aɪd] in comp aux yeux... / she stared at him, wide-eyed elle le regardait, les yeux écarquillés.

eye drops pl n gouttes fpl (pour les yeux).

eyeful ['aɪfʊl] n **1.** [of dirt, dust] : I got an eyeful of sand j'ai reçu du sable plein les yeux **2.** inf [look] regard m ▶ get an eyeful of that! visez un peu ça ! **3.** inf [woman] belle fille f.

eyelash ['aɪlæʃ] n cil m.

eyelet ['aɪlɪt] n **1.** [gen & SEW] œillet m **2.** [peephole - in mask] trou m pour les yeux ; [- in door, wall] judas m.

eye level n ▶ at eye level au niveau des yeux.

eyelid ['aɪlɪd] n paupière f.

eyeliner ['aɪˌlaɪnər] n eye-liner m.

eye-opener n inf **1.** [surprise] révélation f, surprise f **2.** US [drink] petit verre pris au réveil.

eye-opening adj inf qui ouvre les yeux, révélateur.

eyepatch ['aɪpætʃ] n [after operation] cache m, pansement m (sur l'œil) ; [permanent] bandeau m.

eye-popper n : US inf to be an eye-popper valoir vraiment le coup d'œil.

eye-popping adj US inf sensationnel.

eye shadow n fard m à paupières.

eyesight ['aɪsaɪt] n vue f.

eyesore ['aɪsɔːr] n abomination f, horreur f.

eyestrain ['aɪstreɪn] n fatigue f des yeux.

eyetooth ['aɪtuːθ] (pl eyeteeth [-tiːθ]) n canine f supérieure ▶ I'd give my eyeteeth for a bike like that UK inf je donnerais n'importe quoi pour avoir un vélo comme ça.

eyewash ['aɪwɒʃ] n MED collyre m.

eyewear ['aɪweər] n (U) lunettes fpl.

eyewitness ['aɪwɪtnɪs] ◆ n témoin m oculaire. ◆ comp [account, description] d'un témoin oculaire.

eyrie ['ɪərɪ] n aire f (d'aigle).

EZ MESSAGING written abbr of easy.

e-zine ['iːziːn] n magazine m électronique.

EZY MESSAGING written abbr of easy.

f (*pl* f's *or* fs), **F** (*pl* F's *or* Fs) [ef] ◆ *n* [letter] f *m*, F *m* ⫽ *f for Freddie* ≃ F comme François ▶ **the F word** 🇬🇧 *euph* le mot «*fuck*». ◆ **1.** written abbr of **fathom** **2.** written abbr of **female 3.** (written abbr of **feminine**) f, fém.

f 1. (written abbr of **function of**) MATH f de **2.** (written abbr of **forte**) MUS f.

F ◆ *n* **1.** MUS fa *m* **2.** SCH [grade] ▶ **to get an F** échouer. ◆ **1.** (written abbr of **Fahrenheit**) F **2.** (written abbr of franc) F.

fa [fɑː] = **fah.**

f.a., FA (abbr of **fanny adams**) *n* 🇬🇧 *inf* ▶ **sweet f.a.** que dalle.

FA (abbr of **Football Association**) *pr n* ▶ **the FA** *la* Fédération britannique de football ▶ **the FA cup** championnat de football dont la finale se joue à Wembley.

FAA (abbr of **Federal Aviation Administration**) *pr n* direction fédérale de l'aviation civile américaine.

fab [fæb] *adj* 🇬🇧 *inf* super.

fable ['feɪbl] *n* **1.** [legend] fable *f*, légende *f* ; LITER fable **2.** [false account] fable *f*.

fabled ['feɪbld] *adj* **1.** [famous] légendaire, célèbre ; [fictitious] légendaire, fabuleux.

fabric ['fæbrɪk] *n* **1.** [cloth] tissu *m*, étoffe *f* **2.** [framework, structure] structure *f* ⫽ *the fabric of society fig* la structure de la société.

fabricate ['fæbrɪkeɪt] *vt* **1.** [make] fabriquer **2.** [story] inventer, fabriquer ; [document] faire un faux, contrefaire.

fabrication [ˌfæbrɪ'keɪʃn] *n* **1.** *fml* [manufacture] fabrication *f*, production *f* **2.** [falsehood] fabrication *f*.

fabric conditioner, fabric softener *n* assouplissant *m* (textile).

fabulous ['fæbjʊləs] *adj* **1.** [astounding] fabuleux, incroyable **2.** *inf* [good] génial, super **3.** [fictitious] fabuleux, légendaire.

fabulously ['fæbjʊləslɪ] *adv* fabuleusement.

facade, façade [fə'sɑːd] *n* ARCHIT & *fig* façade *f*.

face [feɪs] ◆ *n* **1.** ANAT visage *m*, figure *f* ⫽ *I know that face* je connais cette tête-là, cette tête me dit quelque chose ▶ *she was lying face down* or *downwards* elle était étendue à plat ventre or face contre terre ▶ *she was lying face up* or *upwards* elle était étendue sur le dos ⫽ *he told her to her face what he thought of her* il lui a dit en face or sans ambages ce qu'il pensait d'elle ▶ *to look sb in the face lit* regarder qqn en face or dans les yeux ⫽ *I'll never be able to look him in the face again fig* je n'oserai plus jamais le regarder en face **2.** [expression] mine *f*, expression *f* ▶ *to make* or *to pull a face at sb* faire une grimace à qqn ▶ *to put on a brave* or *bold face* : *she put on*

a brave face elle a fait bonne contenance **3.** [appearance] apparence *f*, aspect *m* ⫽ *it changed the face of the town* cela a changé la physionomie de la ville ⫽ *this is the ugly face of capitalism* voici l'autre visage or le mauvais côté du capitalisme **4.** [front - of building] façade *f*, devant *m* ; [- of cliff] paroi *f* ; [of mountain] face *f* **5.** [of clock] cadran *m* ; [of coin] face *f* ; [of page] recto *m* ; [of playing card] face *f*, dessous *m* ; [of the earth] surface *f* ▶ *it fell face down* / *up* **a)** [gen] c'est tombé du mauvais / bon côté **b)** [card, coin] c'est tombé face en dessous / en dessus ▶ *to vanish off the face of the earth* disparaître de la circulation or de la surface de la Terre **6.** PHR *to lose* / *to save face* perdre / sauver la face ⫽ *he won't show his face here again!* il ne risque pas de remettre les pieds ici ! ⫽ *her plans blew up in her face* tous ses projets se sont retournés contre elle ⫽ *get out of my face, will you?* ne me fais pas chier ! ◆ *comp* [cream] pour le visage. ◆ *vt* **1.** [turn towards] faire face à ⫽ *face the wall* tournez-vous vers le mur **2.** [be turned towards] faire face à, être en face de ⫽ *he faced the blackboard* il était face au or faisait face au tableau ⫽ *she was facing him* elle était en face de lui ⫽ *facing one another* l'un en face de l'autre, en vis-à-vis ⫽ *a room facing the courtyard* une chambre sur cour or donnant sur la cour ⫽ *the house faces south* la maison est orientée or exposée au sud **3.** [confront] faire face or front à, affronter ▶ *to be faced with sthg* être obligé de faire face à or être confronté à qqch ⫽ *faced with the evidence* devant l'évidence, confronté à l'évidence ▶ *to face the music inf*: *we'll just have to face the music* il va falloir affronter la tempête or faire front **4.** [deal with] faire face à ⫽ *I can't face telling her* je n'ai pas le courage de le lui dire ⫽ *we must face facts* il faut voir les choses comme elles sont **5.** [risk - disaster] être menacé de ; [- defeat, fine, prison] encourir, risquer ⫽ *faced with eviction, he paid his rent* face à or devant la perspective d'une expulsion, il a payé son loyer **6.** [subj: problem, situation] se présenter à ⫽ *the problem facing us* le problème qui se pose (à nous) or devant lequel on se trouve. ◆ *vi* **1.** [turn] se tourner ; [be turned] être tourné ⫽ *she was facing towards the camera* elle était tournée vers or elle faisait face à l'appareil photo **2.** [house, window] être orienté ; [look over] faire face à, donner sur ⫽ *the terrace faces towards the mountain* la terrasse donne sur la montagne. ❖ **in the face of** *prep phr* : *in the face of adversity* face à l'adversité. ❖ **on the face of it** *adv phr* à première vue. ❖ **face up to** *vt insep* faire face à, affronter ⫽ *he won't face up to the fact that he's getting older* il ne veut pas admettre qu'il vieillit.

facecloth ['feɪsklɒθ] 🇬🇧 = **face flannel.**

-faced [feɪst] *in comp* au visage... ▶ **white-faced** blême, au visage pâle.

face flannel *n* 🇬🇧 ≃ gant *m* de toilette.

faceless ['feɪslɪs] *adj* anonyme.

face-lift n **1.** [surgery] lifting *m* / *to have a face-lift* se faire faire un lifting **2.** *inf* [renovation] restauration *f*.

face mask n [cosmetic] masque *m* de beauté ; SPORT masque *m*.

face-off n SPORT remise *f* en jeu ; *fig* confrontation *f*.

face pack n masque *m* de beauté.

face powder n poudre *f* de riz.

face-saving adj qui sauve la face.

facet ['fæsɪt] n facette *f*.

facetious [fə'si:ʃəs] adj [person] facétieux, moqueur ; [remark] facétieux, comique.

facetiously [fə'si:ʃəslɪ] adv de manière facétieuse, facétieusement.

F2F, FTF MESSAGING written abbr of **face to face**.

face value n FIN valeur *f* nominale / *I took her remark at face value fig* j'ai pris sa remarque au pied de la lettre or pour argent comptant.

facial ['feɪʃl] ◆ adj facial ▶ **facial hair** poils *mpl* du visage ▶ **facial mask** masque *f* pour le visage ▶ **facial scrub** lotion *f* exfoliante pour le visage. ◆ n soin *m* du visage / *to have a facial* se faire faire un soin du visage.

facile [UK 'fæsaɪl US 'fæsl] adj **1.** [easy - solution, victory] facile **2.** *pej* [superficial - person] superficiel, complaisant ; [- remark] facile, creux.

facilitate [fə'sɪlɪteɪt] vt faciliter.

facilitator [fə'sɪlɪteɪtəʳ] n SOCIOL animateur *m*, -trice *f* de groupe.

facility [fə'sɪlətɪ] (*pl* **facilities**) n **1.** [ease] facilité *f* **2.** [skill] facilité *f*, aptitude *f* / *to have a facility for* or *with languages* avoir beaucoup de facilité pour les langues **3.** (*usu pl*) [equipment] équipement *m* ; [means] moyen *m* ▶ **the facilities** *euph* les toilettes *fpl* **4.** [building] installation *f* **5.** [device] mécanisme *m* ; COMPUT fonction *f* **6.** [service] service *m*.

facing ['feɪsɪŋ] n CONSTR revêtement *m* ; SEW revers *m*.

facsimile [fæk'sɪmɪlɪ] n fac-similé *m*.

fact [fækt] n **1.** [true item of data] fait *m* ; [known circumstance] : *the fact that he left is in itself incriminating* le fait qu'il soit parti est compromettant en soi ▶ **to know for a fact that**: *I know for a fact that they're friends* je sais pertinemment qu'ils sont amis ▶ **to know sthg for a fact**: *I know it for a fact* je le sais de source sûre, c'est un fait certain ▶ **that's a fact**: *there's something strange going on, (and) that's a fact* il se passe quelque chose de bizarre, c'est sûr ▶ **is that a fact?** vraiment ? **2.** (U) [reality] faits *mpl*, réalité *f* / *based on fact* **a)** [argument] basé sur des faits **b)** [book, film] basé sur des faits réels / *fact and fiction* le réel et l'imaginaire / *the fact (of the matter) is that I forgot all about it* la vérité, c'est que j'ai complètement oublié / *the fact remains he's my brother* il n'en est pas moins mon frère. ❖ **fact of life** n fait *m*, réalité *f* ▶ **the facts of life** *euph* les choses *fpl* de la vie. ❖ **in fact** adv phr **1.** [giving extra information] : *he asked us, in fact ordered us, to be quiet* il nous a demandé, ou plutôt ordonné, de nous taire **2.** [correcting] en fait **3.** [emphasizing, reinforcing] : *did she in fact say when she was going to arrive?* est-ce qu'elle a dit quand elle arriverait en fait ?

> 📋 Note that **le fait que** can be followed by a verb in the indicative or the subjunctive:
> **The fact that they didn't understand.** *Le fait qu'ils n'ont pas compris* or *Le fait qu'ils n'aient pas compris.*

fact-finding adj d'information.

faction ['fækʃn] n **1.** [group] faction *f* **2.** [strife] dissension *f*, discorde *f* **3.** [book, programme] docudrame *m*.

factional ['fækʃənl] adj de faction.

factoid ['fæktɔɪd] n *inf* **1.** [falsehood stated as fact] fausse information *f* **2.** [piece of trivial news] fait *m* divers.

factor ['fæktəʳ] n **1.** [element] facteur *m*, élément *m* / *factor 6* [in suntan cream] indice *m* 6 **2.** BIOL & MATH facteur *m* **3.** [agent] agent *m*. ❖ **factor in** vt sep [add to calculation] inclure.

factoring ['fæktərɪŋ] n FIN affacturage *m*.

factorize, factorise ['fæktəraɪz] vt mettre en facteurs.

factory ['fæktərɪ] (*pl* **factories**) ◆ n usine *f* ; [smaller] fabrique *f*. ◆ comp [chimney, worker] d'usine ▶ **factory price** prix *m* usine or sortie usine ▶ **factory floor** : *on the factory floor* dans les ateliers, parmi les ouvriers.

factory farming n élevage *m* industriel.

factory ship n navire-usine *m*.

factotum [fæk'təʊtəm] n factotum *m*.

fact sheet n prospectus *m*, brochure *f*.

factual ['fæktʃʊəl] adj [account, speech] factuel, basé sur les or des faits ; [event] réel.

faculty ['fækltɪ] (*pl* **faculties**) ◆ n **1.** [mental] faculté *f* / *his critical faculties* son sens critique **2.** UNIV [section] faculté *f* ; US [staff] corps *m* enseignant. ◆ comp [member, staff] de faculté.

fad [fæd] n *inf* [craze] mode *f*, vogue *f* ; [personal] lubie *f*, (petite) manie *f*.

faddy ['fædɪ] (*compar* **faddier**, *superl* **faddiest**) adj UK *inf* [idea, taste] capricieux ; [person] maniaque, capricieux.

fade [feɪd] ◆ vi **1.** [colour] pâlir, passer ; [material] se décolorer, passer ; [light] baisser, diminuer **2.** [wither - flower] se faner, se flétrir ; *fig* [beauty] se faner **3.** [disappear - figure] disparaître ; [- memory, sight] baisser ; [- thing remembered, writing] s'effacer ; [- sound] baisser, s'éteindre ; [- anger, interest] diminuer ; [- hope, smile] s'éteindre **4.** *liter* [die] dépérir, s'éteindre. ◆ vt **1.** [discolour - material] décolorer ; [- colour] faner **2.** [reduce] baisser ; CIN & TV faire disparaître en fondu. ❖ **fade away** vi [gen] disparaître ; [memory, sight] baisser ; [thing remembered, writing] s'effacer ; [sound] s'éteindre ; [anger, interest] diminuer ; [hope, smile] s'éteindre. ❖ **fade out** vi [sound] disparaître, s'éteindre ; *fig* [interest] diminuer, tomber ; [fashion] passer.

faded ['feɪdɪd] adj [material] décoloré, déteint ; [jeans] délavé ; [flower] fané, flétri ; [beauty] défraîchi, fané.

faeces UK, **feces** US ['fi:si:z] pl n fèces *fpl*.

Faeroe, Faroe ['feərəʊ] n ▶ **the Faeroe Islands, the Faeroes** les îles *fpl* Féroé ▶ **in the Faeroe Islands** aux îles Féroé.

faff [fæf] UK *inf* ◆ vi faire la mouche du coche / *stop faffing (about* or *around)!* arrêtez de tourner en rond ! ◆ n [panic] panique *f* ; [effort] : *it's too much of a faff* c'est trop compliqué.

fag [fæg] (*pt* & *pp* **fagged**, *cont* **fagging**) ◆ n **1.** UK *inf* [cigarette] clope *m* ou *f* **2.** US *v inf* & *pej* [homosexual] pédé *m* **3.** UK *inf* [task] corvée *f*, barbe *f* **4.** UK [at school] jeune élève d'une «*public school*» qui exécute des corvées pour un élève de dernière année. ◆ vi UK [at school] ▶ **to fag for sb** faire les corvées de qqn.

fag end n UK *inf* [remainder] reste *m* ; [of cloth] bout *m* ; [of conversation] dernières bribes *fpl* ; [cigarette] mégot *m*.

fagged [fægd] adj UK *inf* **1.** [exhausted] crevé, claqué **2.** [bothered] : *I can't be fagged* j'ai trop la flemme.

faggot ['fægət] n **1.** UK [of sticks] fagot *m* **2.** UK CULIN boulette *f* de viande **3.** US *v inf* & *pej* [homosexual] pédé *m*, tapette *f*.

fah [fɑː] n fa *m*.

Fahrenheit ['færənhaɪt] adj Fahrenheit *(inv)* / *it's 6 ° centigrade — what's that in Fahrenheit?* il fait 6 ° centigrade — ça fait combien en Fahrenheit ?

fail [feɪl] ◆ vi **1.** [not succeed - attempt, plan] échouer, ne pas réussir ; [- negotiations] échouer, ne pas aboutir ; [- person] échouer / *he failed (in his efforts) to convince us* il n'a pas réussi or il n'est pas arrivé à nous convaincre **2.** SCH & UNIV échouer, être recalé / *I failed in maths* j'ai été collé or recalé en maths **3.** [stop working] tomber en panne, céder ; [brakes] lâcher **4.** [grow weak - eyesight, health, memory] baisser, faiblir ; [- person, voice] s'affaiblir ; [- light] baisser **5.** [be insufficient] manquer, faire défaut **6.** [go bankrupt] faire faillite. ◆ vt **1.** [not succeed in] échouer à, ne pas réussir à ; SCH & UNIV [exam] échouer à, être recalé à ; [candidate] refuser, recaler **2.** [let down] décevoir, laisser tomber **3.** [neglect] manquer, négliger / *they never fail to call* ils ne manquent jamais d'appeler. ◆ n SCH & UNIV échec *m*. ❖ **without fail** adv phr [for certain] sans faute, à coup sûr ; [always] inévitablement, immanquablement.

failed [feɪld] adj qui n'a pas réussi, raté.

failing ['feɪlɪŋ] ◆ n défaut *m*. ◆ prep à défaut de ▸ **failing this** à défaut ▸ **failing which** faute or à défaut de quoi. ◆ adj [health] défaillant ; [business] qui fait faillite ; [marriage] qui va à la dérive ; [US] [student] faible, mauvais.

fail-safe adj [device, machine] à sûreté intégrée ; [plan] infaillible.

failure ['feɪljər] n **1.** [lack of success] échec *m*, insuccès *m* **2.** SCH & UNIV échec *m* / *failure in an exam* / *in maths* échec à un examen / en maths **3.** [fiasco] échec *m*, fiasco *m* ; [of plan] échec *m*, avortement *m* **4.** [person] raté *m*, -e *f* **5.** [breakdown] panne *f* **6.** [lack] manque *m* ▸ **crop failure** perte *f* des récoltes **7.** [non-performance] manquement *m*, défaut *m* **8.** [bankruptcy] faillite *f*.

faint [feɪnt] ◆ adj **1.** [slight - breeze, feeling, sound, smell] faible, léger ; [- idea] flou, vague ; [- breathing, light] faible ; [- voice] faible, éteint / *he hasn't the faintest chance of winning* il n'a pas la moindre chance de gagner / *I haven't the faintest idea* je n'en ai pas la moindre idée **2.** [colour] pâle, délavé **3.** [half-hearted] faible, sans conviction **4.** [dizzy] prêt à s'évanouir, défaillant / *to feel faint* se sentir mal, être pris d'un malaise / *he was faint with exhaustion* la tête lui tournait de fatigue. ◆ vi s'évanouir / *he fainted from the pain* il s'est évanoui de douleur ▸ **a fainting fit** un évanouissement / *to be fainting from* or *with hunger* défaillir de faim. ◆ n évanouissement *m*, syncope *f*.

faint-hearted ◆ adj [person] timoré, pusillanime ; [attempt] timide, sans conviction. ◆ pl n : *not for the faint-hearted* à déconseiller à ceux qui ont le cœur mal accroché.

faint-heartedness [-'hɑːtɪdnɪs] n pusillanimité *f*.

faintly ['feɪntlɪ] adv **1.** [breathe, shine] faiblement ; [mark, write] légèrement ; [say, speak] d'une voix éteinte, faiblement **2.** [slightly] légèrement, vaguement.

faintness ['feɪntnɪs] n **1.** [of light, sound, voice] faiblesse *f* ; [of image, writing] manque *m* de clarté **2.** [dizziness] malaise *m*, défaillance *f*.

fair [feər] ◆ adj **1.** [just - person, decision] juste, équitable ; [- contest, match, player] loyal, correct ; [- deal, exchange] équitable, honnête ; [- price] correct, convenable ; [- criticism, profit] justifié, mérité / *it's not fair to the others* ce n'est pas juste or honnête vis-à-vis des autres / *it's only fair to let him speak* ce n'est que justice de le laisser parler ▸ **fair enough!** très bien !, d'accord ! **2.** [light - hair] blond ; [- skin] clair, blanc (blanche) **3.** *liter* [lovely] beau *(before vowel or silent 'h' bel, f belle)* **4.** [weather] beau *(before vowel or silent 'h' bel, f belle)* ; [tide, wind] favorable, propice **5.** [adequate] passable, assez bon **6.** [substantial] considérable **7.** [US] *inf* [real] véritable. ◆ adv [act] équi-

tablement, loyalement ▸ **to play fair** jouer franc jeu. ◆ n **1.** [entertainment] foire *f*, fête *f* foraine ; [for charity] kermesse *f*, fête *f* **2.** COMM foire *f* / *the Book Fair* a) la Foire du livre b) [in Paris] le Salon du livre.

fair copy n [UK] copie *f* au propre or au net.

fair game n proie *f* idéale.

fairground ['feəgraʊnd] n champ *m* de foire ▸ **fairground attraction** or **ride** attraction *f* (de fête foraine).

fair-haired adj [blond] blond, aux cheveux blonds.

fairly ['feəlɪ] adv **1.** [justly - treat] équitablement, avec justice ; [- compare, judge] impartialement, avec impartialité **2.** [honestly] honnêtement, loyalement **3.** [moderately] assez, passablement **4.** [UK] [positively] absolument, vraiment.

fair-minded adj équitable, impartial.

fair-mindedness [-'maɪndɪdnɪs] n impartialité *f*.

fairness ['feənɪs] n **1.** [justice] justice *f*, honnêteté *f* ▸ **in all fairness** en toute justice ▸ **in fairness** or **out of fairness to you** pour être juste envers or avec vous **2.** [of hair] blondeur *f*, blond *m* ; [of skin] blancheur *f*.

fair play n fair-play *m inv*, franc-jeu *m offic*.

fair sex n ▸ **the fair sex** le beau sexe.

fair-sized adj assez grand.

fair-skinned adj blanc (blanche), de peau.

fair trade n commerce *m* équitable.

fairway ['feəweɪ] n **1.** [in golf] fairway *m* **2.** NAUT chenal *m*, passe *f*.

fair-weather adj [clothing, vessel] qui convient seulement au beau temps ▸ **a fair-weather friend** un ami des beaux or bons jours.

fairy ['feərɪ] *(pl* fairies*)* ◆ n **1.** [sprite] fée *f* **2.** *v inf & pej* [homosexual] pédé *m*, tapette *f*. ◆ adj [enchanted] magique ; [fairylike] féerique, de fée.

fairy godmother n bonne fée *f*.

fairy lights pl n guirlande *f* électrique.

fairy story n LITER conte *m* de fées ; [untruth] histoire *f* à dormir debout.

fairy tale n LITER conte *m* de fées ; [untruth] histoire *f* invraisemblable or à dormir debout. ❖ **fairy-tale** adj : *a fairy-tale ending* une fin digne d'un conte de fées.

fait accompli [ˌfeɪtə'kɒmplɪ] n fait *m* accompli.

faith [feɪθ] n **1.** [trust] confiance *f* / *I have faith in him* je lui fais confiance ▸ **to put one's faith in sthg** mettre ses espoirs dans qqch **2.** RELIG [belief] foi *f* / *faith in God* foi en Dieu **3.** [particular religion] foi *f*, religion *f* **4.** [honesty] *he did it in good faith* il l'a fait en toute bonne foi / *he acted in bad faith* il a agi de mauvaise foi **5.** [loyalty] fidélité *f*.

faithful ['feɪθfʊl] ◆ adj **1.** [believer, friend, lover] fidèle ▸ **faithful to sb / sthg** fidèle à qqn / qqch **2.** [reliable] sûr, solide **3.** [accurate - account, translation] fidèle, exact ; [- copy] conforme. ◆ pl n ▸ **the faithful** a) [supporters] les fidèles *mpl* b) RELIG les fidèles or croyants *mpl*.

faithfully ['feɪθfʊlɪ] adv **1.** [loyally] fidèlement, loyalement ▸ **yours faithfully** [in letter] veuillez agréer mes salutations distinguées **2.** [accurately] exactement, fidèlement.

faithfulness ['feɪθfʊlnɪs] n **1.** [loyalty] fidélité *f*, loyauté *f* **2.** [of report, translation] fidélité *f*, exactitude *f* ; [of copy] conformité *f*.

faith healer n guérisseur *m*, -euse *f*.

faithless ['feɪθlɪs] adj **1.** [dishonest, unreliable] déloyal, perfide **2.** RELIG infidèle, non-croyant.

faith school n [UK] SCH école *f* confessionnelle.

fake [feɪk] ◆ vt **1.** [make - document, painting] faire un faux de, contrefaire ; [- style, furniture] imiter **2.** [alter - document] falsifier, maquiller ; [- account] falsifier ; [- election, interview, photograph] truquer **3.** [simulate] feindre ▸ **to fake it a)** faire semblant **b)** [simulate orgasm] simuler l'orgasme **4.** [ad-lib] improviser. ◆ vi faire semblant ; SPORT feinter. ◆ n **1.** [thing] article *m* or objet *m* truqué ; [antique, painting] faux *m* **2.** [person] imposteur *m*. ◆ adj [antique, painting] faux (fausse) ; [account, document] falsifié, faux (fausse) ; [elections, interview, photograph] truqué.

falafel = felafel.

falcon ['fɔːlkən] n faucon *m*.

falconry ['fɔːlkənrɪ] n fauconnerie *f*.

Falkland ['fɔːlklənd] pr n ▸ **the Falkland Islands** or **the Falklands** les (îles *fpl*) Falkland *fpl*, les (îles *fpl*) Malouines *fpl* / **in the Falkland Islands** aux îles Falkland, aux Malouines ▸ **the Falklands War** la guerre des Malouines.

> 🏛 **The Falklands War**
>
> Conflit armé qui opposa, en 1982, l'Argentine au Royaume-Uni, à la suite de l'attaque par la junte militaire argentine d'une colonie britannique, les îles Malouines. L'armée argentine se rendit deux mois plus tard. Cette victoire, très populaire en Angleterre, renforça, à l'époque, de manière significative la cote de popularité du Premier ministre, Margaret Thatcher.

fall [fɔːl] (*pt* fell [fel], *pp* fallen ['fɔːln]) ◆ vi **1.** [barrier, cup, napkin, person] tomber / *she fell off the stool* / *out of the window* elle est tombée du tabouret / par la fenêtre / *the crowd fell on* or *to their knees* la foule est tombée à genoux ▸ **to fall on one's feet** *lit & fig* retomber sur ses pieds ▸ **to fall short**: *the job fell short of her expectations* le poste ne répondait pas à ses attentes **2.** [move deliberately] se laisser tomber / *I fell into the armchair* je me suis laissé tomber dans le fauteuil **3.** [bridge, building] s'écrouler, s'effondrer **4.** [ground] descendre, aller en pente **5.** [darkness, light, night, rain, snow] tomber / *as night fell* à la tombée de la nuit **6.** [land - eyes, blow, weapon] tomber / *my eyes fell on the letter* mon regard est tombé sur la lettre **7.** [face, spirits] s'assombrir / *my spirits fell* tout d'un coup, j'ai perdu le moral **8.** [hang down] tomber, descendre / *the curtains fall right to the floor* les rideaux tombent or descendent jusqu'au sol **9.** [decrease in level, value - price, temperature] baisser, tomber **10.** [occur] tomber / *May Day falls on a Tuesday this year* le Premier Mai tombe un mardi cette année **11.** [become] : *to fall asleep* s'endormir / *to fall ill* or *sick* tomber malade / *to fall in love (with sb)* tomber amoureux (de qqn) / *to fall silent* se taire **12.** [be classified] : *the athletes fall into two categories* les sportifs se divisent en deux catégories / *that falls outside my area of responsibility* cela ne relève pas de ma responsabilité. ◆ n **1.** [tumble] chute *f* / *a fall from a horse* une chute de cheval ▸ **to be heading** or **riding for a fall** courir à l'échec **2.** [of rain, snow] chute *f* / *there was a heavy fall of snow overnight* il y a eu de fortes chutes de neige dans la nuit **3.** [collapse - of building, wall] chute *f*, effondrement *m* ; [- of dirt, rock] éboulement *m*, chute *f* ; [- of city, country] chute *f*, capitulation *f* ; [- of regime] chute *f*, renversement *m* **4.** [decrease - in price, temperature] baisse *f* ; [- in currency] dépréciation *f*, baisse *f* ; [more marked] chute *f* **5.** US [autumn] automne *m* / *in the fall* en automne. ❖ **falls** pl n [waterfall] cascade *f*, chute *f* d'eau ▸ **Niagara Falls** les chutes du Niagara. ❖ **fall about** vi UK *inf* se tordre de rire / *they fell about (laughing)* ils se tordaient de rire. ❖ **fall apart** vi **1.** [book, furniture] tomber en morceaux ; *fig* [nation] se désagréger ; [conference] échouer ;

[system] s'écrouler, s'effondrer / *her plans fell apart at the seams* ses projets sont tombés à l'eau **2.** [person] s'effondrer / *he more or less fell apart after his wife's death* il a plus ou moins craqué après la mort de sa femme. ❖ **fall back** vi **1.** [retreat, recede] reculer, se retirer ; MIL se replier, battre en retraite **2.** [lag, trail] se laisser distancer, être à la traîne. ❖ **fall back on** vt insep ▸ **to fall back on sthg** avoir recours à qqch. ❖ **fall behind** ◆ vi se laisser distancer, être à la traîne ; [in cycling] décrocher / *we can't fall behind in* or *with the rent* nous ne pouvons pas être en retard pour le loyer. ◆ vt insep prendre du retard sur. ❖ **fall down** vi [book, person, picture] tomber (par terre) ; [bridge, building] s'effondrer, s'écrouler ; [argument, comparison] s'écrouler, s'effondrer. ❖ **fall down on** vt insep ▸ **to fall down on sthg** échouer à qqch / *he's been falling down on the job lately* il n'était pas or ne s'est pas montré à la hauteur dernièrement. ❖ **fall for** vt insep *inf* **1.** [become infatuated with] tomber amoureux de **2.** [be deceived by] se laisser prendre par / *they actually fell for it!* ils ont vraiment mordu !, se sont vraiment fait avoir ! ❖ **fall in** vi **1.** [tumble] tomber / *you'll fall in!* tu vas tomber dedans ! **2.** [line up] se mettre en rang, s'aligner ; MIL [troops] former les rangs ; [one soldier] rentrer dans les rangs. ❖ **fall in with** vt insep [frequent] ▸ **to fall in with sb** se mettre à fréquenter qqn. ❖ **fall into** vt insep [tumble into] tomber dans / *to fall into sb's clutches* or *sb's hands* tomber dans les griffes de qqn, tomber entre les mains de qqn / *the pieces began to fall into place* *fig* les éléments ont commencé à se mettre en place. ❖ **fall off** vi **1.** [drop off] tomber ; [in mountain climbing] dévisser **2.** [diminish - attendance, exports, numbers, sales] diminuer, baisser ; [- enthusiasm, production] baisser, tomber ; [- population, rate] baisser, décroître ; [- interest, zeal] se relâcher. ❖ **fall on** vt insep **1.** [drop on] tomber sur **2.** [meet with] tomber sur, trouver / *they fell on hard times* ils sont tombés dans la misère, ils ont subi des revers de fortune **3.** [responsibility] revenir à, incomber à. ❖ **fall out** vi **1.** [drop out] tomber **2.** [quarrel] se brouiller, se disputer. ❖ **fall over** vi [lose balance] tomber (par terre). ❖ **fall through** vi échouer / *the deal fell through* l'affaire n'a pas abouti.

fallacious [fəˈleɪʃəs] adj [statement] fallacieux, faux (fausse) ; [hope] faux (fausse), illusoire.

fallacy [ˈfæləsɪ] (*pl* **fallacies**) n [misconception] erreur *f*, idée *f* fausse ; [false reasoning] mauvais raisonnement *m*, sophisme *m* ; LOGIC sophisme *m*.

fallback [ˈfɔːlbæk] n **1.** [retreat] retraite *f*, recul *m* **2.** [reserve] réserve *f* / *what's our fallback position?* sur quoi est-ce qu'on peut se rabattre ?

fallen [ˈfɔːln] ◆ pp ⟶ **fall**. ◆ adj **1.** [gen] tombé ; [hero, soldier] tombé, mort ; [leaf] mort **2.** [immoral] perdu ; [angel, woman] déchu. ◆ pl n ▸ **the fallen** ceux qui sont morts à la guerre.

faller [ˈfɔːlə] n ST. EX valeur *f* à la baisse.

fall guy n *inf* [dupe] pigeon *m* ; US [scapegoat] bouc *m* émissaire.

fallible [ˈfæləbl] adj faillible.

falling [ˈfɔːlɪŋ] adj [gen] qui tombe ; [population] décroissant ; [prices, value] en baisse.

falling-off n réduction *f*, diminution *f*, baisse *f*.

Fallopian tube [fəˈləʊpɪən-] n trompe *f* utérine or de Fallope.

fallout [ˈfɔːlaʊt] n (U) [radioactive] retombées *fpl* (radioactives) ; *inf & fig* [consequences] retombées *fpl*, répercussions *fpl* ▸ **fallout shelter** abri *m* antiatomique.

fallow [ˈfæləʊ] adj AGR [field, land] en jachère, en friche ▸ **to lie fallow** être en jachère ; *fig* [period] non productif.

false [fɔːls] adj **1.** [wrong] faux (fausse) ; [untrue] erroné, inexact ▸ **false move** : *don't make any false moves* ne faites pas de faux pas ▸ **false start** faux départ m **2.** [fake] faux (fausse) ; [artificial] artificiel ▸ **a false bottom** un double fond ▸ **false eyelashes** faux cils mpl **3.** [deceptive] faux (fausse), mensonger ; LAW ▸ **under false pretences** par des moyens frauduleux **4.** [insincere] perfide, fourbe ; [disloyal] déloyal ▸ **a false friend a)** un ami déloyal **b)** LING un faux ami ▸ **false modesty** fausse modestie f.

false alarm n fausse alerte f.

falsehood [ˈfɔːlshʊd] n fml **1.** [lie] mensonge m **2.** [lying] faux m **3.** [falseness] fausseté f.

falsely [ˈfɔːlslɪ] adv [claim, state] faussement ; [accuse, judge] à tort, injustement ; [interpret] mal ; [act] déloyalement.

false memory syndrome n syndrome m des faux souvenirs.

falseness [ˈfɔːlsnɪs] n **1.** [of belief, statement] fausseté f **2.** [of friend, lover] infidélité f **3.** [insincerity] fausseté f, manque m de sincérité.

false teeth pl n dentier m.

falsetto [fɔːlˈsetəʊ] (pl **falsettos**) ◆ n fausset m. ◆ adj de fausset, de tête.

falsifiable [ˌfɔːlsɪˈfaɪəbəl] adj PHILOS falsifiable.

falsification [ˌfɔːlsɪfɪˈkeɪʃn] n falsification f.

falsify [ˈfɔːlsɪfaɪ] (pt & pp **falsified**) vt **1.** [document] falsifier ; [evidence] maquiller ; [accounts, figures] truquer **2.** [misrepresent] déformer, dénaturer **3.** [disprove] réfuter.

falter [ˈfɔːltə] ◆ vi **1.** [waver] vaciller, chanceler ; [courage, memory] faiblir **2.** [stumble] chanceler, tituber **3.** [in speech] hésiter, parler d'une voix mal assurée. ◆ vt balbutier, bredouiller.

faltering [ˈfɔːltərɪŋ] adj [attempt] timide, hésitant ; [voice] hésitant ; [steps] chancelant, mal assuré ; [courage, memory] défaillant.

fame [feɪm] n célébrité f, renommée f.

famed [feɪmd] adj célèbre, renommé / *famed for his generosity* connu or célèbre pour sa générosité.

familiar [fəˈmɪljə] ◆ adj **1.** [well-known] familier **2.** [acquainted] ▸ **to be familiar with sthg** bien connaître qqch ▸ **to become familiar with sthg** se familiariser avec qqch **3.** [informal] familier, intime **4.** pej [presumptuous - socially] familier ; [- sexually] trop entreprenant. ◆ n [spirit] démon m familier.

familiarity [fəˌmɪlɪˈærətɪ] (pl **familiarities**) n **1.** [of face, place] caractère m familier **2.** [with book, rules, language] connaissance f / *her familiarity with his work* sa connaissance de ses œuvres **3.** [intimacy] familiarité f, intimité f **4.** (usu pl) pej [undue intimacy] familiarité f, privauté f.

familiarization [fəˌmɪljəraɪˈzeɪʃn] n familiarisation f.

familiarize, familiarise [fəˈmɪljəraɪz] vt **1.** [inform] familiariser ▸ **to familiarize o.s. with sthg** se familiariser avec qqch **2.** [make widely known] répandre, vulgariser.

family [ˈfæmlɪ] (pl **families**) ◆ n [gen & BIOL], BOT & LING famille f / *have you any family?* **a)** [relatives] avez-vous de la famille ? **b)** [children] avez-vous des enfants ? / *a large family* une famille nombreuse ▸ **to start a family** avoir un (premier) enfant. ◆ comp [life] familial, de famille ; [car, friend] de la famille ; [dinner, likeness, quarrel] de famille ; [business, programme] familial ▸ **a family business** une entreprise familiale ▸ **family room** [in hotel] chambre f familiale ▸ **family circle** cercle m de (la) famille ▸ **family doctor** docteur m de famille ▸ **family law** droit m de la famille ▸ **family practice** US médecine f générale ▸ **family practitioner** US médecin m de famille, (médecin) généraliste m.

family credit n prestation complémentaire pour familles à faibles revenus ayant au moins un enfant.

family-friendly adj [pub, hotel, campsite] qui accueille volontiers les familles ; [policy, proposal] qui favorise la famille ; [show, entertainment] pour toute la famille.

family leave n congé m parental.

family man n ▸ **he's a family man** il aime la vie de famille, c'est un bon père de famille.

family name n nom m de famille.

family planning n planning m familial ▸ **a family planning clinic** un centre de planning familial.

family-run adj [hotel, restaurant] géré en famille, familial.

family-size(d) adj [jar, packet] familial.

family tree n arbre m généalogique.

famine [ˈfæmɪn] n famine f.

famished [ˈfæmɪʃt] adj affamé.

famous [ˈfeɪməs] adj **1.** [renowned] célèbre, renommé / *the stately home is famous for its gardens* le château est connu or célèbre pour ses jardins **2.** dated [first-rate] fameux, formidable.

famously [ˈfeɪməslɪ] adv **1.** inf fameusement (bien), rudement bien / *they get on famously* ils s'entendent à merveille or comme larrons en foire **2.** [notedly] : *her famously long legs* ses longues jambes si célèbres / *Eisenhower famously referred to the "military-industrial complex"* dans une phrase devenue célèbre, Eisenhower a parlé du « complexe militaro-industriel ».

fan [fæn] (pt & pp **fanned**, cont **fanning**) ◆ n **1.** [supporter] enthousiaste mf, passionné m, -e f ; [of celebrity] fan mf ; SPORT supporteur m, -trice f **2.** [ventilator - mechanical] ventilateur m ; [- hand-held] éventail m **3.** AGR [machine] tarare m ; [basket] van m. ◆ vt **1.** [face, person] éventer ▸ **to fan o.s.** s'éventer **2.** [fire] attiser, souffler sur. ◆ vi s'étaler (en éventail). ◆ **fan out** ◆ vi [spread out] s'étaler (en éventail) ; [army, search party] se déployer. ◆ vt sep étaler (en éventail).

fan-assisted oven n four m à chaleur tournante.

fanatic [fəˈnætɪk] ◆ adj fanatique. ◆ n fanatique mf.

fanatical [fəˈnætɪkl] adj fanatique.

fanatically [fəˈnætɪkəlɪ] adv fanatiquement.

fanaticism [fəˈnætɪsɪzm] n fanatisme m.

fan belt n courroie f de ventilateur.

fanciable [ˈfænsɪəbl] adj US inf plutôt bien, pas mal du tout.

fanciful [ˈfænsɪfʊl] adj **1.** [imaginary] imaginaire **2.** [imaginative] imaginatif, plein d'imagination **3.** [whimsical - person] capricieux, fantaisiste ; [- notion] fantasque, excentrique ; [- clothing] extravagant.

fancily [ˈfænsɪlɪ] adv d'une façon recherchée or raffinée.

fan club n cercle m or club m de fans.

fan-cooled [-kuːld] adj refroidi par ventilateur.

fancy [ˈfænsɪ] (compar **fancier**, superl **fanciest**, pl **fancies**, pt & pp **fancied**) ◆ adj **1.** [elaborate - clothes] recherché, raffiné ; [- style] recherché, travaillé ; [- excuse] recherché, compliqué / *fancy cakes* pâtisseries fpl **2.** [high-quality] de qualité supérieure, de luxe **3.** pej [overrated - price] exorbitant ; [- talk, words] extravagant. ◆ n **1.** [whim] caprice m, fantaisie f **2.** US [liking] goût m, penchant m ▸ **to take a fancy to sb** se prendre d'affection pour qqn **3.** [imagination] imagination f, fantaisie f **4.** [notion] idée f fantasque, fantasme m. ◆ vt **1.** US inf [want] avoir envie de ; [like] aimer / *do you fancy a cup of tea?* ça te dirait une tasse de thé ? ▸ **to fancy sb** s'enticher de qqn **2.** inf [imagine] imaginer, s'imaginer / *she fancies herself as* *an intellectual* elle se prend pour une intellectuelle ▸ **fancy that!** tiens ! voyez-vous cela ! **3.** *liter* [believe] croire, se figurer.

fancy dress n ⓊⓀ déguisement *m*, costume *m* / *in fancy dress* déguisé ▸ **a fancy dress ball** un bal masqué or costumé ▸ **fancy dress party** fête *f* déguisée.

fancy-free adj sans souci.

fancy goods pl n nouveautés *fpl*, articles *mpl* de fantaisie.

fancy-pants ['fænsɪpænts] adj ⓊⓈ *inf* [restaurant, hotel, neighbourhood] classe ; [person] frimeur.

fanfare ['fænfeəʳ] n MUS fanfare *f* ; *fig* [ostentation] : *with much fanfare* avec des roulements de tambour, avec éclat.

fang [fæŋ] n [of snake] crochet *m* ; [of wolf, vampire] croc *m*, canine *f*.

fan heater n radiateur *m* soufflant.

fanlight ['fænlaɪt] n imposte *f* (semi-circulaire).

fan mail n courrier *m* des admirateurs.

Fannie Mae ['fænɪmeɪ] pr n *organisme de crédit américain*.

fanny ['fænɪ] (*pl* **fannies**) n **1.** ⓊⓀ *vulg* [female genitals] chatte *f* **2.** ⓊⓈ *inf* [buttocks] fesses *fpl*.

fanny pack n ⓊⓈ banane *f* (sac).

fan-shaped adj en éventail.

fantabulous [fæn'tæbjələs] adj ⓊⓈ *inf* génial.

fantasize, fantasise ['fæntəsaɪz] vi fantasmer, se livrer à des fantasmes.

fantastic [fæn'tæstɪk] adj **1.** *inf* [wonderful] fantastique, sensationnel **2.** *inf* [very great -success] inouï, fabuleux ; [-amount, rate] phénoménal, faramineux **3.** [preposterous, strange -idea, plan, story] fantastique, bizarre.

fantastically [fæn'tæstɪklɪ] adv fantastiquement, extraordinairement.

fantasy ['fæntəsɪ] (*pl* **fantasies**) n **1.** [dream] fantasme *m* ; PSYCHOL fantasme *m* ; [notion] idée *f* fantasque / *sexual fantasy* fantasme *m* **2.** [imagination] imagination *f* **3.** LITER & MUS fantaisie *f*.

⚠ **Fantaisie** is only used in literary or musical contexts. See the entry for alternative translations.

fantasy football n jeu *où chaque participant se constitue une équipe virtuelle avec les noms de footballeurs réels, chaque but marqué par ceux-ci dans la réalité valant un point dans le jeu.*

fanzine ['fænziːn] n revue *f* spécialisée, fanzine *m*.

fao (written abbr of **for the attention of**) à l'attention de.

FAO (abbr of **Food and Agriculture Organization**) pr n FAO *f*.

FAQ ⬥ adv (written abbr of **free alongside quay**) ⓊⓀ FLQ. ⬥ n [fak or ɜːfeɪ'kjuː] (abbr of **frequently asked questions**) COMPUT FAQ *f*.

far [fɑːʳ] (*compar* **farther** ['fɑːðəʳ] or **further** ['fɜːðəʳ], *superl* **farthest** ['fɑːðɪst] or **furthest** ['fɜːðɪst]) ⬥ adv **1.** [distant in space] loin / *how far is it to town?* combien y a-t-il jusqu'à la ville ? / *how far is he going?* jusqu'où va-t-il ? / *have you come far?* êtes-vous venu de loin ? / *far away* or *off in the distance* au loin, dans le lointain / *far beyond* bien au-delà / *far out at sea* en pleine mer ; *fig* : *his work is far above the others'* son travail est de loin supérieur à celui des autres / *how far have you got with*

the translation? où en es-tu de la traduction ? ▸ **far and wide** de tous côtés / *far be it from me to interfere!* loin de moi l'idée d'intervenir ! / *he's not far off* or *wrong* il n'a pas tout à fait tort **2.** [distant in time] loin / *as far back as 1800* déjà en 1800, dès 1800 / *as far back as I can remember* d'aussi loin que je me souvienne / *he's not far off sixty* il n'a pas loin de la soixantaine **3.** (with compar) [much] beaucoup, bien / *she is far more intelligent than I am* elle est bien or beaucoup plus intelligente que moi **4.** ⟨PHR⟩ **to go far a)** [person, idea] aller loin, faire son chemin / *this has gone far enough* trop, c'est trop, c'est allé trop loin / *his policy doesn't go far enough* sa politique ne va pas assez loin / *I would even go so far as to say...* j'irais même jusqu'à dire..., je dirais même... **b)** [make progress] *she's gone too far to back out* elle s'est trop engagée pour reculer **c)** [money] *£5 doesn't go far nowadays* on ne va pas loin avec 5 livres de nos jours ▸ **to go too far** [exaggerate] dépasser les bornes, exagérer / *you're going too far!* vous exagérez ! ⬥ adj **1.** [distant] lointain, éloigné ; [remote] éloigné ▸ **it's a far cry from what she expected** ce n'est pas du tout or c'est loin de ce qu'elle attendait **2.** [more distant] autre, plus éloigné / *on the far side* de l'autre côté / *the far end* de l'autre bout de, l'extrémité de **3.** [extreme] extrême / *the far left* / *right* POL l'extrême gauche *f* / droite *f*. ⬥ **as far as** ⬥ prep phr jusqu'à / *I'll walk with you as far as the end of the lane* je vais vous accompagner jusqu'au bout du chemin. ⬥ conj phr **1.** [distance] : *as far as the eye can see* à perte de vue **2.** [to the extent that] autant que / *as far as possible* autant que possible, dans la mesure du possible / *as far as she's* / *I'm concerned* en ce qui la / me concerne, pour sa / ma part. ⬥ **by far** adv phr de loin, de beaucoup / *she's by far the cleverest* or *the cleverest by far* c'est de loin or de beaucoup la plus intelligente. ⬥ **far from** adv phr [not at all] loin de / *I'm far from approving all he does* je suis loin d'approuver tout ce qu'il fait ▸ **far from it** : *he's not rich, far from it* il n'est pas riche, loin de là or tant s'en faut. ⬥ **so far** adv phr jusqu'ici, jusqu'à présent / *so far this month* depuis le début du mois ▸ **so far so good** jusqu'ici ça va. ⬥ **so far as** conj phr = **as far as**.

faraway ['fɑːrəweɪ] adj [distant] lointain, éloigné ; [isolated] éloigné ; [sound, voice] lointain ; [look] absent.

farce [fɑːs] n THEAT & *fig* farce *f* / *this law is a farce* cette loi est grotesque or dérisoire.

farcical ['fɑːsɪkl] adj risible, ridicule.

fare [feəʳ] ⬥ n **1.** [charge -for bus, underground] prix *m* du billet or ticket ; [-for boat, plane, train] prix *m* du billet ; [-in taxi] prix *m* de la course **2.** [passenger] voyageur *m*, -euse *f* ; [in taxi] client *m*, -e *f* **3.** [food] nourriture *f*, chère *f*. ⬥ comp ▸ **fare dodger** resquilleur *m*, -euse *f*. ⬥ vi : *how did you fare at the booking office?* comment ça s'est passé au bureau de réservation ?

Far East pr n ▸ **the Far East** l'Extrême-Orient *m*.

Far Eastern adj extrême-oriental.

fare stage n ⓊⓀ [of bus] section *f*.

farewell [ˌfeə'wel] ⬥ n adieu *m* ▸ **to bid sb farewell** dire adieu à qqn. ⬥ comp [dinner, party] d'adieu.

far-fetched [-'fetʃt] adj bizarre, farfelu.

far-flung adj [widespread] étendu, vaste ; [far] lointain.

farm [fɑːm] ⬥ n ferme *f*, exploitation *f* (agricole). ⬥ comp [equipment] agricole ▸ **farm labourer** or **worker** ouvrier *m*, -ère *f* agricole ▸ **farm produce** produits *mpl* agricoles or de ferme ▸ **farm shop** magasin *qui vend des produits de la ferme*. ⬥ vt [land] cultiver, exploiter ; [animals] élever. ⬥ vi être fermier, être cultivateur. ⬥ **farm out** vt sep **1.** [shop] mettre en gérance ; [work] donner or confier à un sous-traitant **2.** [child] : *she farms her children out on an aunt* elle confie (la garde de) ses enfants à une tante.

farmable ['fɑːməbl] adj [land] cultivable.

farmer ['fɑːməʳ] n [of land] fermier m, -ère f, agriculteur m, -trice f ; [of animals] éleveur m, -euse f.

farmers' market n marché m de producteurs.

farmhand ['fɑːmhænd] n ouvrier m, -ère f agricole.

farmhouse ['fɑːmhaʊs] (pl [-haʊzɪz]) n (maison f de) ferme f ▸ **farmhouse Cheddar** cheddar m fermier.

farming ['fɑːmɪŋ] ◆ n agriculture f ▸ **fish / mink farming** élevage m de poisson / vison ▸ **fruit / vegetable farming** culture f fruitière / maraîchère. ◆ comp [methods] de culture, cultural ; [equipment, machines] agricole ; [community, region] rural.

farmland ['fɑːmlænd] n (U) terre f arable, terres fpl arables.

farmstead ['fɑːmsted] n 🇺🇸 ferme f (et ses dépendances).

farmyard ['fɑːmjɑːd] n cour f de ferme ▸ **farmyard animal** animal m de (la) ferme.

Faroese ◆ adj féroïen. ◆ n **1.** GEOG Féroïen m, -enne f **2.** LING féroïen m.

Faroes Isles, Faroes pl n îles fpl Féroé.

far-off adj [place, time] lointain, éloigné.

far-reaching [-'riːʃɪŋ] adj d'une grande portée.

farrier ['færɪəʳ] n 🇬🇧 [blacksmith] maréchal-ferrant m ; [vet] vétérinaire mf.

farsighted [,fɑː'saɪtɪd] adj **1.** [shrewd -person] prévoyant, perspicace ; [-action] prévoyant ; [decision] pris avec clairvoyance **2.** 🇺🇸 MED hypermétrope.

far-sightedly [-'saɪtɪdlɪ] adv d'une manière prévoyante.

farsightedness [,fɑː'saɪtɪdnɪs] n **1.** [of person] prévoyance f, perspicacité f ; [of act, decision] clairvoyance f **2.** 🇺🇸 MED hypermétropie f, presbytie f.

fart [fɑːt] v inf ◆ n **1.** [gas] pet m **2.** [person] birbe m / *he's a boring old fart* il est rasoir, c'est un raseur. ◆ vi péter. ❖ **fart about** 🇬🇧, **fart around** vi v inf gaspiller or perdre son temps, glander.

farther ['fɑːðəʳ] (compar of far) ◆ adv **1.** [more distant] plus loin / *how much farther is it?* c'est encore à combien ? / *have we much farther to go?* avons-nous encore beaucoup de chemin à faire ? / *farther ahead* loin devant / *farther along the corridor* plus loin dans le couloir / *farther away* or *farther off* plus loin / *to move farther and farther away* s'éloigner de plus en plus / *farther back* plus (loin) en arrière / *move farther back* reculez(-vous) / *farther back than 1900* avant 1900 / *farther down / up* plus bas / haut / *farther on* or *forward* plus loin **2.** [in addition] en plus, de plus. ◆ adj plus éloigné, plus lointain / *the farther end of the tunnel* l'autre bout du tunnel.

farthest ['fɑːðɪst] (superl of far) ◆ adj le plus lointain, le plus éloigné. ◆ adv le plus loin / *it's 3 km at the farthest* il y a 3 km au plus or au maximum / *the farthest removed* le plus éloigné.

fas, FAS (abbr of free alongside ship) adj & adv 🇬🇧 FLB.

fascia (pl fasciae [-ʃiː]) n ['feɪʃə] **1.** [on building] panneau m **2.** 🇬🇧 [dashboard] tableau m de bord **3.** ['fæʃɪə] ANAT fascia m.

fascinate ['fæsɪneɪt] vt **1.** [delight] fasciner, captiver / *she was fascinated by* or *with his story* elle était fascinée par son histoire **2.** [prey] fasciner.

fascinating ['fæsɪneɪtɪŋ] adj [country, idea, person] fascinant, captivant ; [book, speaker, speech] fascinant, passionnant.

fascinatingly ['fæsɪneɪtɪŋlɪ] adv d'une façon fascinante or passionnante.

fascination [,fæsɪ'neɪʃn] n fascination f, attrait m / *her fascination with the Orient* la fascination qu'exerce sur elle l'Orient.

fascism ['fæʃɪzm] n fascisme m.

fascist ['fæʃɪst] ◆ adj fasciste. ◆ n fasciste mf.

fashion ['fæʃn] ◆ n **1.** [current style] mode f ▸ **in fashion** à la mode, en vogue ▸ **to come back into fashion** revenir à la mode ▸ **out of fashion** démodé, passé de mode ▸ **to go out of fashion** se démoder **2.** [manner] façon f, manière f ▸ **after a fashion** tant bien que mal. ◆ comp [editor, magazine, photographer] de mode ; [industry] de la mode ▸ **fashion designer** modéliste mf / *the great fashion designers* les grands couturiers ▸ **fashion house** maison f de (haute) couture ▸ **fashion model** mannequin m ▸ **fashion show** présentation f des modèles or des collections, défilé m de mode. ◆ vt [gen] fabriquer, modeler ; [carving, sculpture] façonner ; [dress] confectionner ; fig [character, person] former, façonner ▸ **to fashion sthg out of clay** façonner qqch en argile.

fashionable ['fæʃnəbl] adj [clothing] à la mode ; [café, neighbourhood] chic, à la mode ; [subject, writer] à la mode, en vogue / *a café fashionable with writers* un café fréquenté par des écrivains / *it is no longer fashionable to eat red meat* cela ne se fait plus de manger de la viande rouge.

fashionably ['fæʃnəblɪ] adv élégamment, à la mode / *we were fashionably late* on était un peu en retard, comme le veut l'étiquette.

fashionista [fæʃə'nɪstə] n inf fashionista mf.

fashion victim n hum victime f de la mode.

fast [fɑːst] ◆ adj **1.** [quick] rapide ▸ **fast bowler** [in cricket] lanceur m rapide ▸ **fast train** rapide m **2.** [clock] en avance / *my watch is (three minutes) fast* ma montre avance (de trois minutes) **3.** [secure -knot, rope] solide ; [-door, window] bien fermé ; [-grip] ferme, solide ; [-friend] sûr, fidèle / *to make a boat fast* amarrer un bateau **4.** [colour] bon teint (inv), grand teint (inv). ◆ adv **1.** [quickly] vite, rapidement **2.** [ahead of correct time] en avance / *my watch is running fast* ma montre avance **3.** [securely] ferme, solidement **4.** [soundly] profondément ▸ **to be fast asleep** dormir à poings fermés or profondément. ◆ n jeûne m / *a fast day* RELIG un jour maigre or de jeûne. ◆ vi [gen] jeûner, rester à jeun ; RELIG jeûner, faire maigre.

fastball ['fæstbɔːl] n [in baseball] balle f rapide (lancée vers le batteur).

fast breeder reactor n surrégénérateur m, surgénérateur m.

fasten ['fɑːsn] ◆ vt **1.** [attach] attacher ; [close] fermer ▸ **to fasten sthg with glue / nails / string to sthg** coller / clouer / lier qqch à qqch / *fasten your seatbelts* attachez votre ceinture **2.** [attention, eyes] fixer / *he fastened his eyes on the door* il a fixé la porte des yeux or a fixé son regard sur la porte **3.** [ascribe -guilt, responsibility] attribuer ; [-crime] imputer ▸ **to fasten sthg on sb** attribuer qqch à qqn. ◆ vi [bra, dress] s'attacher ; [bag, door, window] se fermer. ❖ **fasten down** vt sep [flap, shutter] fermer ; [envelope, sticker] coller. ❖ **fasten on** vt sep [belt, holster] fixer. ❖ **fasten onto** vt insep **1.** [seize upon] saisir **2.** [grip] se cramponner à, s'accrocher à. ❖ **fasten up** vt sep fermer, attacher. ❖ **fasten upon** vt insep **1.** [gaze at] fixer / *her eyes fastened upon the letter* elle fixait la lettre du regard or des yeux **2.** [seize upon] saisir.

fastener ['fɑːsnəʳ], **fastening** ['fɑːsnɪŋ] n [gen] attache f ; [on box, door] fermeture f ; [on bag, necklace] fermoir m ; [on clothing] fermeture f ; [button] bouton m ; [hook] agrafe f ; [press stud] pression f, bouton-pression m ; [zip] fermeture f Éclair.

fast food n fast-food m, prêt-à-manger m offic.
◆ **fast-food** comp [chain, place, restaurant] de restauration rapide, de fast-food ▸ **fast-food restaurants** des fast-foods mpl.

fast-forward ◆ vi se dérouler en avance rapide. ◆ vt : to fast-forward a tape faire avancer or défiler une cassette. ◆ comp ▸ **fast-forward button** touche f d'avance rapide.

fastidious [fə'stɪdɪəs] adj **1.** [fussy about details] tatillon, pointilleux ; [meticulous - person] méticuleux, minutieux ; [-work] minutieux **2.** [fussy about cleanliness] méticuleux, maniaque.

⚠ **Fastidieux** means boring, not fastidious.

fast lane n [in the UK] voie f de droite ; [on the continent, in the US, etc.] voie f de gauche.

fast-moving adj [film] plein d'action ▸ **fast-moving events** des évènements rapides.

fast-paced [-'peɪst] adj [novel, film, TV show] au rythme trépidant ; [game, sport] rapide.

fast-track adj ▸ **fast-track executives** des cadres qui gravissent rapidement les échelons.

fat [fæt] (compar **fatter**, superl **fattest**, pt & pp **fatted**, cont **fatting**) ◆ adj **1.** [heavy, overweight - person] gros (grosse), gras (grasse) ; [-cheeks, limb] gros (grosse) ; [-face] joufflu ▸ **to get** or **to grow fat** grossir, engraisser **2.** [meat] gras (grasse) **3.** [thick, hefty] gros (grosse) **4.** [productive - year] gras (grasse), prospère ; [-land, soil] fertile, riche **5.** inf PHR **get this into your fat head** mets-toi ça dans la tête une fois pour toutes / I reckon you'll get it back — fat chance! je pense qu'on te le rendra — tu parles ! / a fat lot of good it did him! ça l'a bien avancé !, le voilà bien avancé ! ◆ n **1.** [gen & ANAT] graisse f **2.** CULIN [on raw meat] graisse f, gras m ; [on cooked meat] gras m ; [as cooking medium] matière f grasse ; [as part of controlled diet] lipide m.

fatal ['feɪtl] adj **1.** [deadly - disease, injury] mortel ; [-blow] fatal, mortel ; [-result] fatal **2.** [ruinous - action, consequences] désastreux, catastrophique ; [-influence] néfaste, pernicieux ; [-mistake] fatal, grave **3.** [crucial] fatal, fatidique.

fatalism ['feɪtəlɪzm] n fatalisme m.

fatalist ['feɪtəlɪst] ◆ adj fataliste. ◆ n fataliste mf.

fatalistic [ˌfeɪtə'lɪstɪk] adj fataliste.

fatality [fə'tælətɪ] (pl **fatalities**) n **1.** [accident] accident m mortel ; [person killed] mort m, -e f **2.** fml [destiny] fatalité f.

fatally ['feɪtəlɪ] adv [wounded] mortellement / fatally ill condamné, perdu / the plan was fatally flawed le projet était voué à l'échec.

⚠ **Fatalement** means inevitably, not fatally.

fat-assed [-æst] adj US v inf gros.

fat city n US inf ▸ **to be in fat city** être plein aux as.

fate [feɪt] n **1.** [destiny] destin m, sort m **2.** [of person, thing] sort m. ◆ **Fates** pl pr n ▸ **the Fates** les Parques fpl.

fated ['feɪtɪd] adj [destined] destiné / they seem fated to be unhappy ils semblent destinés or condamnés à être malheureux.

fateful ['feɪtfʊl] adj [decisive - day, decision] fatal, décisif ; [disastrous] désastreux, catastrophique.

fat-free adj sans matières grasses, sans corps gras.

fathead ['fæthed] n inf & dated imbécile mf.

father ['fɑːðər] ◆ n **1.** [male parent] père m / he's like a father to me il est comme un père pour moi / on my father's side du côté de mon père **2.** (usu pl) [ancestor] ancêtre m, père m **3.** [founder, leader] père m, fondateur m. ◆ vt **1.** [child] engendrer ; fig [idea, science] concevoir, inventer **2.** [impose] attribuer ▸ **to father sthg on sb** attribuer qqch à qqn. ◆ **Father** n RELIG **1.** [priest] père m / Father Brown le (révérend) père Brown / yes, Father oui, mon père **2.** [God] : the Father, the Son and the Holy Ghost le Père, le Fils et le Saint-Esprit / Our Father who art in Heaven Notre Père qui êtes aux cieux **3.** POL ▸ **the Father of the House** titre traditionnel donné au doyen (par l'ancienneté) des parlementaires britanniques.

Father Christmas pr n UK le Père Noël.

father figure n personne f qui joue le rôle du père.

fatherhood ['fɑːðəhʊd] n paternité f.

father-in-law n beau-père m.

fatherlike ['fɑːðəˌlaɪk], **fatherly** ['fɑːðəlɪ] adj paternel.

Father's Day n fête f des pères.

fathom ['fæðəm] (pl **fathom** or **fathoms**) ◆ n brasse f (mesure). ◆ vt **1.** [measure depth of] sonder **2.** inf [understand] sonder, pénétrer.

fatigue [fə'tiːg] ◆ n **1.** [exhaustion] fatigue f, épuisement m **2.** TECH [in material] fatigue f ▸ **metal fatigue** fatigue du métal **3.** MIL [chore] corvée f / I'm on fatigues je suis de corvée. ◆ comp **1.** MIL [shirt, trousers] de corvée ▸ **fatigue duty** corvée f **2.** TECH [limit] de fatigue. ◆ vt **1.** fml [person] fatiguer, épuiser **2.** TECH [material] fatiguer. ◆ **fatigues** pl n MIL [clothing] treillis m, tenue f de corvée.

fatless ['fætlɪs] adj sans matières grasses.

fatness ['fætnɪs] n **1.** [of person] embonpoint m, corpulence f **2.** [of meat] teneur f en graisse.

fatten ['fætn] ◆ vt [animal, person] engraisser ; [ducks, geese] gaver. ◆ vi [animals] engraisser ; [person] engraisser, prendre de l'embonpoint. ◆ **fatten up** vt sep [person] engraisser, faire grossir ; AGR [animal] mettre à l'engrais.

fattening ['fætnɪŋ] ◆ adj qui fait grossir. ◆ n [of animals] engraissement m ; [of ducks, geese] gavage m.

fatty ['fætɪ] (compar **fattier**, superl **fattiest**, pl **fatties**) ◆ adj **1.** [food] gras (grasse) **2.** [tissue] adipeux. ◆ n inf & pej gros m (bonhomme m), grosse f (bonne femme f).

fatuous ['fætjʊəs] adj [person, remark] sot (sotte), niais ; [look, smile] niais, béat.

fatuously ['fætjʊəslɪ] adv [say] sottement, niaisement ; [smile] niaisement, béatement.

fatwa ['fætwə] n RELIG fatwa f.

faucet ['fɔːsɪt] n US robinet m.

fault ['fɔːlt] ◆ n **1.** (U) [blame, responsibility] faute f / it's not my fault ce n'est pas de ma faute / whose fault is it? à qui la faute ?, qui est fautif ? / it's nobody's fault but your own vous n'avez à vous en prendre qu'à vous-même ▸ **to be at fault** être fautif or coupable **2.** [mistake] erreur f / a fault in the addition une erreur d'addition **3.** [flaw - in person] défaut m ; [- in machine] défaut m, anomalie f ▸ **to find fault with sthg** trouver à redire à qqch, critiquer qqch ▸ **to find fault with sb** critiquer qqn **4.** GEOL faille f **5.** TENNIS faute f. ◆ vt critiquer ▸ **to fault sthg / sb** trouver des défauts à qqch / chez qqn.

faultless ['fɔːltlɪs] adj [performance, work] impeccable, irréprochable ; [behaviour, person] irréprochable ; [logic, reasoning] sans faille.

fault-tolerant adj COMPUT quasi insensible aux défaillances, qui tolère les pannes.

faulty ['fɔ:ltɪ] (*compar* **faultier**, *superl* **faultiest**) adj [machine] défectueux ; [work] défectueux, mal fait ; [reasoning] défectueux, erroné.

fauna ['fɔ:nə] (*pl* **faunas** *or* **faunae** [-ni:]) n faune f.

faux pas [ˌfəʊ'pɑ:] (*pl* **faux pas** [ˌfəʊ'pɑ:]) n bévue f, gaffe f.

fava bean ['fɑ:və-] n US fève f.

fave [feɪv] adj *inf* préféré.

favor US = favour.

favorite US = favourite.

favour UK, **favor** US ['feɪvər] ◆ n 1. [approval] faveur f, approbation f ▶ **to be in favour a)** [person] être bien en cour, être bien vu **b)** [artist, fashion] être à la mode or en vogue ▶ **to be out of favour a)** [person] être mal en cour, ne pas être bien vu **b)** [artist, book] ne pas être à la mode or en vo gue **c)** [fashion] être démodé or dépassé ▶ **to fall out of favour with sb** perdre les bonnes grâces de qqn ▶ **to find favour with sb** trouver grâce aux yeux de qqn, gagner l'approbation de qqn ▶ **to be in favour of sthg** être partisan de qqch, être pour qqch ▶ **to be in favour of doing sthg** être d'avis de or être pour faire qqch **2.** [act of goodwill] service m, faveur f / *will you do me a favour* or *do a favour for me?* voulez-vous me rendre (un) service ? / *may I ask a favour of you* or *ask you a favour?* puis-je vous demander un service ? **3.** [advantage] : *everything is in our favour* tout joue en notre faveur, nous avons tout pour nous / *the odds are in his favour* il est (donné) favori / *the magistrates decided in his favour* les juges lui ont donné raison or gain de cause / *he dropped the idea in favour of our suggestion* il a laissé tomber l'idée au profit de notre suggestion **4.** [partiality] faveur f, partialité f **5.** *liter* : *a woman's favours* les faveurs d'une femme **6.** [gift] petit cadeau m (offert aux invités lors d'une fête). ◆ vt **1.** [prefer] préférer ; [show preference for] montrer une préférence pour **2.** [support -suggestion, team] être partisan de, être pour ; [-candidate, project] favoriser, appuyer ; [-theory] soutenir **3.** [benefit] favoriser, faciliter **4.** [honour] favoriser, gratifier / *she favoured him with a smile* elle l'a gratifié d'un sourire / *he favoured us with his company* il nous a fait l'honneur de se joindre à nous **5.** [resemble] ressembler à.

favourable UK, **favorable** US ['feɪvrəbl] adj [answer, comparison, impression] favorable ; [time, terms] bon, avantageux ; [weather, wind] propice / *to be favourable to an idea* approuver une idée.

favourably UK, **favorably** US ['feɪvrəblɪ] adv [compare, react] favorablement ; [consider] d'un bon œil ▶ **to be favourably disposed to** or **towards sthg** voir qqch d'un bon œil ▶ **to be favourably disposed to** or **towards sb** être bien disposé envers qqn.

favoured UK, **favored** US ['feɪvəd] adj favorisé / *the favoured few* les privilégiés mpl.

favourite UK, **favorite** US ['feɪvrɪt] ◆ adj favori, préféré. ◆ n **1.** [gen] favori m, -ite f, préféré m, -e f **2.** SPORT favori m. ❖ **favorites** pl n COMPUT favoris mpl, signets mpl.

favouritism UK, **favoritism** US ['feɪvrɪtɪzm] n favoritisme m.

fawn [fɔ:n] ◆ n **1.** [animal] faon m **2.** [colour] fauve m. ◆ adj (de couleur) fauve. ◆ vi ▶ **to fawn on sb a)** [person] ramper devant qqn, passer de la pommade à qqn **b)** [dog] faire la fête à qqn.

fax [fæks] ◆ n [machine] fax m, télécopieur m ; [document] fax m, télécopie f / *by fax* par télécopie. ◆ vt faxer, envoyer par télécopie or par télécopieur.

fax machine n fax m, télécopieur m.

fax modem n modem m fax.

fax number n numéro m de fax.

faze [feɪz] vt *inf* déconcerter, dérouter.

FBI (abbr of **Federal Bureau of Investigation**) pr n ▶ **the FBI** le FBI.

FC 1. SPORT written abbr of **Football Club 2.** MESSAGING written abbr of **fingers crossed**.

FCC (abbr of **Federal Communications Commission**) pr n *conseil fédéral de l'audiovisuel aux États-Unis* ≃ CSA m.

FCO pr n abbr of **Foreign and Commonwealth Office**.

FD ◆ (written abbr of **Fidei Defensor**) UK *Défenseur de la foi.* ◆ n US abbr of **Fire Department**.

FDA pr n abbr of **Food and Drug Administration**.

FDD [ˌefdi:'di:] (abbr of **floppy disk drive**) n COMPUT lecteur m de disquettes.

FDR pr n abbr of **Franklin Delano Roosevelt**.

FE n UK & Austr abbr of **Further Education**.

fear [fɪər] ◆ n **1.** [dread] crainte f, peur f / *for fear that she might find out* de peur qu'elle ne l'apprenne **2.** [awe] crainte f, respect m **3.** [risk] risque m, danger m / *there is no fear of her leaving* elle ne risque pas de partir, il est peu probable qu'elle parte ▶ **no fear!** *inf*: *will you tell him? — no fear!* lui direz-vous ? — pas de danger or pas question ! ◆ vt **1.** [be afraid of] craindre, avoir peur de / *to fear the worst* craindre le pire / *I fear he's in danger* je crains or j'ai peur qu'il ne soit en danger **2.** *fml* [be sorry] regretter / *I fear it's too late* je crois bien qu'il est trop tard **3.** [revere -God] révérer, craindre. ◆ vi : *he fears for his life* il craint pour sa vie.

> Note that **de peur que** and **de crainte que** are followed by a verb in the subjunctive preceded by **ne** :
> **I locked him in for fear that he might do something stupid.** *Je l'ai enfermé de peur qu'il ne fasse une bêtise.*

fearful ['fɪəful] adj **1.** [very bad] épouvantable, affreux **2.** *inf & dated* [as intensifier] affreux **3.** [afraid] peureux, craintif / *she is fearful of angering him* elle craint de le mettre en colère.

fearfully ['fɪəfulɪ] adv **1.** [look, say] peureusement, craintivement **2.** *inf & dated* [as intensifier] affreusement, horriblement.

fearless ['fɪəlɪs] adj intrépide, sans peur.

fearlessly ['fɪəlɪslɪ] adv avec intrépidité.

fearlessness ['fɪəlɪsnɪs] n audace f, absence f de peur.

fearsome ['fɪəsəm] adj **1.** [frightening] redoutable, effroyable **2.** *liter* [afraid] peureux, craintif ; [timid] extrêmement timide.

feasibility [ˌfi:zə'bɪlətɪ] n ▶ **the feasibility of doing sthg** la possibilité de faire qqch.

feasibility study n étude f de faisabilité.

feasible ['fi:zəbl] adj [plan, suggestion] faisable, réalisable.

feast [fi:st] ◆ n **1.** [large meal] festin m **2.** RELIG fête f. ◆ comp ▶ **feast day** (jour m de) fête f. ◆ vi festoyer ▶ **to feast on** or **off sthg** se régaler de qqch. ◆ vt *fig* ▶ **to feast o.s. on sthg** se régaler de qqch ▶ **to feast one's eyes on sthg** repaître ses yeux de qqch *liter*, se délecter à la vue de qqch.

feat [fi:t] n exploit m, prouesse f.

feather ['feðə] ◆ n [of bird] plume f; [on tail, wing] penne f; [of arrow] penne f. ◆ comp [mattress] de plume; [headdress] de plumes.

feather bed n lit m de plumes.

featherbed ['feðəbed] (pt & pp **featherbedded**, cont **featherbedding**) vt pej [industry, business] protéger (excessivement).

featherbedding ['feðəbedɪŋ] n pej [of industry, business] protection f excessive.

featherbrained ['feðəbreɪnd] adj inf étourdi, tête en l'air.

feather duster n plumeau m.

feathered ['feðəd] adj [headdress] de plumes ▸ our feathered friends hum nos amis les oiseaux.

featherweight ['feðəweɪt] ◆ n 1. [boxer, category] poids plume m inv 2. fig [person of little importance] poids plume m inv. ◆ adj [contest, championship] poids plume; [champion] de la catégorie or des poids plume.

feathery ['feðərɪ] adj fig [light and soft - snowflake] doux et léger comme la plume.

feature ['fiːtʃə] ◆ n 1. [facial] trait m 2. [characteristic - of style, landscape, play, etc.] caractéristique f, particularité f; [-of personality] trait m, caractéristique f; [-of car, machine, house, room] caractéristique f 3. RADIO & TV reportage m; PRESS [special] article m de fond; [regular] chronique f 4. CIN film m, long métrage m. ◆ vt 1. CIN [star - actor, actress] avoir pour vedette / also featuring Mark Williams avec Mark Williams 2. PRESS [display prominently] : the story / the picture is featured on the front page le récit / la photo est en première page 3. COMM [promote] promouvoir, mettre en promotion 4. [subj: car, appliance] comporter, être équipé or doté de; [subj: house, room] comporter. ◆ vi 1. CIN figurer, jouer 2. [appear, figure] figurer.

feature creep n COMPUT excès de fonctionnalités dans un logiciel.

feature film n CIN long métrage m.

feature-length adj CIN : a feature-length film un long métrage / a feature-length cartoon un film d'animation.

featureless ['fiːtʃəlɪs] adj [desert, city, etc.] sans traits distinctifs or marquants.

feature writer n PRESS journaliste mf.

Feb. (written abbr of **February**) févr.

February ['februərɪ] ◆ n février m / I don't like February je n'aime pas le mois de février / this has been the wettest February on record cela a été le mois de février le plus pluvieux qu'on ait jamais vu / in February en février, au mois de février / in the month of February au mois de février / February first / ninth US, the first / ninth of February, February the first / ninth le premier / neuf février / during (the month of) February pendant le mois de février / last / next February en février dernier / prochain / at the beginning / end of February au début / à la fin février / in the middle of February au milieu du mois de février, à la mi-février / early / late in February or in early / late February au début / à la fin du mois de février / every or each February tous les ans en février. ◆ comp [weather] de février, du mois de février.

feces US = faeces.

feckless ['feklɪs] adj [ineffectual] incapable, qui manque d'efficacité; [irresponsible] irresponsable.

fecklessness ['feklɪsnɪs] n [ineffectuality] manque m d'efficacité; [irresponsibility] irresponsabilité f.

fed [fed] ◆ pt & pp ⟶ **feed**. ◆ n US inf agent m (du bureau) fédéral or du FBI.

fed. abbr of **federal**, abbr of **federation**.

Fed [fed] ◆ pr n 1. abbr of **Federal Reserve Board** 2. abbr of **Federal Reserve System**. ◆ 1. written abbr of **federal** 2. written abbr of **federation** 3. abbr of **Federal Agent**.

federal ['fedrəl] ◆ adj 1. [republic, system] fédéral ▸ the **Federal Bureau of Investigation** = FBI ▸ the **Federal Deposit Insurance Corporation** organisme américain garantissant la sécurité des dépôts dans les banques qui en sont membres ▸ the **Federal Republic of Germany** la République fédérale d'Allemagne ▸ the **Federal Reserve Board** organe de contrôle de la banque centrale américaine ▸ the **Federal Reserve System** système bancaire fédéral américain ▸ the **Federal Trade Commission** l'une des deux autorités fédérales chargées du respect de la loi antitrust aux États-Unis 2. [responsibility, funding] du gouvernement fédéral; [taxes] fédéral. ◆ n US HIST nordiste m, fédéral m.

Federal Agent n US agent m fédéral, agente f fédérale.

federalism ['fedrəlɪzm] n fédéralisme m.

federalist ['fedrəlɪst] ◆ adj fédéraliste. ◆ n fédéraliste mf.

federalize ['fedrəlaɪz] ◆ vt fédéraliser. ◆ vi se fédéraliser.

federally ['fedrəlɪ] adv : to be federally funded être financé par le gouvernement fédéral.

Federal Reserve n US Réserve f fédérale.

federation [,fedə'reɪʃn] n fédération f.

fedora [fɪ'dɔːrə] n [hat] chapeau m mou.

fed up adj inf : to be fed up en avoir marre, en avoir ras le bol / she's fed up with him elle en a marre de lui.

fee [fiː] n 1. [for doctor, lawyer] honoraires mpl 2. [for speaker, performer] cachet m; [retainer - for company director] jetons mpl de présence (d'un administrateur); [for private tutor] appointements mpl; [for translator] tarif m; [for agency] commission f.

feeble ['fiːbəl] adj 1. [lacking strength] faible 2. [lacking conviction, force - attempt, excuse] piètre; [-argument] léger; [-smile] timide 3. [silly - joke] qui manque de finesse, bête.

feeble-minded adj faible d'esprit.

feeble-mindedness [-'maɪndɪdnɪs] n faiblesse f d'esprit.

feebleness ['fiːblnɪs] n faiblesse f.

feebly ['fiːblɪ] adv [say, shine] faiblement; [smile] timidement; [suggest] sans (grande) conviction.

feed [fiːd] (pt & pp fed [fed]) ◆ vt 1. [provide food for - person, family] nourrir; [-country] approvisionner; [-army] ravitailler 2. [give food to - person, animal] donner à manger à; [subj: bird] donner la becquée à; [breastfeed] allaiter; [bottlefeed] donner le biberon à; [fertilize - plant, soil, lawn, etc.] nourrir ▸ to feed sthg to sb, to feed sb sthg donner qqch à manger à qqn 3. fig [supply - fire, furnace] alimenter; [-lake, river] se jeter dans; [-imagination, hope, rumour] alimenter, nourrir 4. [transmit] : to feed information to sb or to feed sb information a) donner des informations à qqn b) [in order to mislead] donner de fausses informations à qqn (afin de le tromper) 5. TECH [introduce - liquid] faire passer; [-solid] faire avancer; [insert - paper, wire, etc.] introduire / to feed data into a computer entrer des données dans un ordinateur 6. THEAT [give cue to] donner la réplique à 7. SPORT passer la balle à, servir. ◆ vi [person, animal] manger; [baby - gen] manger; [-breastfeed] téter. ◆ n 1. [foodstuff for animal] nourriture f; [hay, oats, etc.] fourrage m 2. [meal for baby - breast milk] tétée f; [-bottled milk] biberon m 3. inf [meal] repas m 4. TECH [introduction - of liquid] alimentation f; [-of solid] avancement m; [device] dispositif m d'alimentation or d'avancement 5. inf THEAT [cue] réplique f; [comedian's partner] faire-valoir m.

❖ **feed back** vt sep [information, results] renvoyer.
❖ **feed in** vt sep [paper, wire] introduire ; COMPUT [data] entrer. ❖ **feed on** vt insep se nourrir de ; *fig* se repaître de. ❖ **feed up** vt sep [animal] engraisser ; [goose] gaver.

feedback ['fiːdbæk] n **1.** ELECTRON rétroaction *f* ; [in microphone] effet *m* Larsen ; COMPUT réaction *f*, rétroaction *f*, retour *m* or remontée *f* de l'information **2.** *(U)* [information] réactions *fpl*, échos *mpl*.

feedbag ['fiːdbæg] n **1.** [container] sac *m* à nourriture ; [containing food] sac *m* de nourriture **2.** 🇺🇸 [for horse] = **nosebag**.

feeder ['fiːdər] ◆ n **1.** [person] mangeur *m* **2.** [child's bottle] biberon *m* **3.** [feeding device - for cattle] nourrisseur *m*, mangeoire *f* automatique ; [- for poultry] mangeoire *f* automatique ; [- for machine] chargeur *m* **4.** [river] affluent *m* ; [road] voie *f* or bretelle *f* de raccordement ; [air route] ligne *f* régionale de rabattement *(regroupant les passagers vers un aéroport principal)* **5.** ELEC câble *m* or ligne *f* d'alimentation. ◆ comp ▶ **feeder primary school** école primaire fournissant des élèves à un collège ▶ **feeder road** voie *f* or bretelle *f* de raccordement ▶ **feeder route** [in air transport] ligne *f* régionale de rabattement *(regroupant les passagers vers un aéroport principal)*.

feed hopper n trémie *f*.

feeding ['fiːdɪŋ] ◆ n [of person, baby, animal, machine] alimentation *f*. ◆ comp ▶ **feeding bottle** biberon *m* ▶ **feeding ground** or **grounds** lieux où viennent se nourrir des animaux ▶ **feeding time** [for child, animal] heure *f* des repas.

feel [fiːl] *(pt & pp* **felt** [felt]) ◆ vi *(with complement)* **1.** [physically] : *to feel hot / cold / hungry / thirsty* avoir chaud / froid / faim / soif / *to feel good / old / full of energy* se sentir bien / vieux / plein d'énergie / *I felt really bad about it* j'étais dans mes petits souliers ▶ **to feel as though** or **as if** or **like** croire que, avoir l'impression que / *he's not feeling himself today* il n'est pas en forme aujourd'hui **2.** [emotionally] : *to feel glad / sad / undecided* être heureux / triste / indécis / *I know how you feel* je sais ce que tu ressens / *if that's how you feel...* si c'est comme ça que tu vois les choses... / *how do you feel about him / the plan?* qu'est-ce que tu penses de lui / ce projet ?, comment le trouves-tu / trouves-tu ce projet ? **3.** [in impersonal constructions] : *it feels good to be alive / home* c'est bon d'être en vie / chez soi / *it feels strange to be back* ça fait drôle d'être de retour / *does that feel better?* est-ce que c'est mieux comme ça ? **4.** [give specified sensation] : *to feel hard / soft / smooth / rough* être dur / doux / lisse / rêche (au toucher) / *the room felt hot / stuffy* il faisait chaud / l'atmosphère était étouffante dans la pièce **5.** [be capable of sensation] sentir **6.** [grope] = **feel about 7.** 🔤 **to feel like** [want, have wish for] avoir envie de / *do you feel like going out tonight?* ça te dit de sortir ce soir ? ◆ vt **1.** [touch] toucher ; [explore] tâter, palper / *feel the quality of this cloth* apprécie la qualité de ce tissu ▶ **to feel one's way** **a)** avancer à tâtons **b)** [in new job, difficult situation, etc.] avancer avec précaution / *I'm still feeling my way* je suis en train de m'habituer tout doucement **2.** [be aware of - wind, sunshine, atmosphere, tension] sentir ; [- pain] sentir, ressentir ; [be sensitive to - cold, beauty] être sensible à / *I could feel myself blushing* je me sentais rougir / *he felt the full force of the blow* il a reçu le coup de plein fouet **3.** [experience - sadness, happiness, joy, relief] ressentir, éprouver ; [to be affected by - sb's absence, death] être affecté par / *to feel fear / regret* avoir peur / des regrets / *to feel the effects of sthg* ressentir les effets de qqch **4.** [think] penser, estimer / *I feel it is my duty to tell you* j'estime qu'il est de mon devoir de te le dire / *she feels very strongly that...* elle est tout à fait convaincue que... / *I can't help feeling that...* je ne peux pas m'empêcher de penser que... ◆ n **1.** [tactile quality, sensation] : *this garment has a really nice feel*

to it ce vêtement est vraiment agréable au toucher **2.** [act of feeling, touching] ▶ **to have a feel of sthg** toucher qqch **3.** [knack] ▶ **to get the feel of sthg** s'habituer à qqch / *to have a real feel for translation / music* avoir la traduction / la musique dans la peau **4.** [atmosphere] atmosphère *f* / *the room has a nice homely feel (to it)* on se sent vraiment bien dans cette pièce / *his music has a really Latin feel (to it)* il y a vraiment une influence latine dans sa musique. ❖ **feel about** vi [in drawer, pocket] fouiller / *to feel about in the dark for sthg* chercher qqch à tâtons dans le noir, tâtonner dans le noir pour trouver qqch. ❖ **feel for** vt insep [sympathize with] : *I feel for you* **a)** je compatis **b)** *hum* comme je te plains ! ❖ **feel up to** vt insep ▶ **to feel up to (doing) sthg a)** [feel like] se sentir le courage de faire qqch **b)** [feel physically strong enough] se sentir la force de faire qqch **c)** [feel qualified, competent] se sentir capable or à même de faire qqch / *I don't really feel up to it* **a)** [feel strong enough] je ne m'en sens pas la force **b)** [feel competent enough] je ne me sens pas à la hauteur.

feeler ['fiːlər] n [of insect] antenne *f* ; [of snail] corne *f* ; [of octopus] tentacule *m*.

feelgood ['fiːlgʊd] adj *inf* : *it's a real feelgood film* c'est un film qui donne la pêche ▶ **the feelgood factor** l'optimisme *m* ambiant.

feeling ['fiːlɪŋ] ◆ n **1.** [sensation] sensation *f* **2.** [opinion] avis *m*, opinion *f* / *what is your feeling about...* que pensez-vous de... **3.** [awareness - relating to the future] pressentiment *m* ; [- caused by external factors] impression *f* / *I had a feeling he would write* j'avais le pressentiment qu'il allait écrire / *I had a feeling you'd say that* j'étais sûr que tu allais dire ça **4.** [sensitivity, understanding] émotion *f*, sensibilité *f* **5.** *(often pl)* [emotion] sentiment *m* ▶ **to hurt sb's feelings** blesser qqn ▶ **to show one's feelings** extérioriser ses émotions ▶ **bad** or **ill feeling** hostilité *f* / *I know the feeling* je sais ce que c'est / *the feeling is mutual* c'est réciproque ▶ **to say sthg with feeling** dire qqch avec émotion ▶ **no hard feelings?** sans rancune ? ◆ adj [person, look] sympathique.

fee-paying adj [school] privé ▶ **fee-paying students** étudiants qui paient tous les droits d'inscription.

feet [fiːt] pl ⟶ **foot**.

feign [feɪn] vt [surprise, innocence] feindre ; [madness, death] simuler.

feigned [feɪnd] adj [surprise, innocence] feint ; [illness, madness, death] simulé.

feint [feɪnt] ◆ n MIL & SPORT feinte *f*. ◆ vi MIL & SPORT faire une feinte.

feisty ['faɪstɪ] *(compar* **feistier**, *superl* **feistiest**) adj *inf* [lively] plein d'entrain ; [combative] qui a du cran.

felafel [fə'læfəl] n CULIN falafel *m*.

felicitous [fɪ'lɪsɪtəs] adj *fml* **1.** [happy] heureux **2.** [word] bien trouvé, heureux ; [colour combination] heureux.

feline ['fiːlaɪn] ◆ adj [grace] félin ; [characteristic] du chat. ◆ n félin *m*.

fell [fel] ◆ pt ⟶ **fall**. ◆ vt [tree] abattre, couper ; *fig* [opponent] abattre, terrasser. ◆ n 🇬🇧 GEOG montagne *f*, colline *f* ▶ **the fells** [high moorland] les landes *fpl* des plateaux. ◆ comp ▶ **fell walking** randonnée *f* en basse montagne. ◆ adj 🔤 **in** or **at one fell swoop** d'un seul coup.

fella ['felə] n *inf* [man] mec *m*, type *m*.

feller ['felər] 🇬🇧 *inf* = **fellow** *(noun)*.

fellow ['feləʊ] ◆ n **1.** *inf & dated* [man] gars *m*, type *m* / *an old fellow* un vieux bonhomme / *the poor fellow's just lost his job* le pauvre vient juste de perdre son travail / *my dear fellow* mon cher ami **2.** *liter* [comrade] ami *m*, -e *f*, camarade *mf* ; [other human being] semblable *mf*; [person in same profession] confrère *m*, consœur *f* **3.** UNIV [professor] professeur *m* (faisant également partie du conseil d'administration); [postgraduate student] étudiant *m*, -e *f* de troisième cycle (souvent chargé de cours) ▶ **research fellow** chercheur *m*, -euse *f* dans une université **4.** [of society] membre *m*. ◆ adj : *fellow prisoner* / *student* camarade *mf* de prison / d'études / *fellow passenger* / *sufferer* / *soldier* compagnon *m* de voyage / d'infortune / d'armes / *fellow being* or *creature* semblable *mf*, pareil *m*, -eille *f* / *one's fellow man* son semblable / *fellow worker* **a)** [in office] collègue *mf* (de travail) **b)** [in factory] camarade *mf* (de travail), compagnon *m* de travail / *fellow citizen* concitoyen *m*, -enne *f* / *fellow countryman* / *countrywoman* compatriote *mf* / *fellow traveller* **a)** [companion on journey] compagnon *m* de voyage or de route **b)** POL communisant *m*, -e *f*.

fellowship ['feləʊʃɪp] n **1.** [friendship] camaraderie *f*; [company] compagnie *f* **2.** [organization] association *f*, société *f*; RELIG confrérie *f* **3.** UNIV [scholarship] bourse *f* d'études de l'enseignement supérieur; [position] poste *m* de chercheur.

felon ['felən] n LAW criminel *m*, -elle *f*.

felony ['feləni] n 🇺🇸 LAW crime *m*.

felt [felt] ◆ pt & pp ⟶ **feel**. ◆ n TEXT feutre *m*. ◆ comp de or en feutre ▶ **felt pen** feutre *m*.

felt-tip (pen) n (stylo *m*) feutre *m*.

female ['fiːmeɪl] ◆ adj **1.** [animal, plant, egg] femelle; [sex, quality, voice, employee] féminin; [vote] des femmes; [equality] de la femme, des femmes / *female doctor* femme médecin / *female company* la compagnie féminine or des femmes / *male and female clients* des clients et des clientes **2.** TECH femelle. ◆ n **1.** [animal, plant] femelle *f* **2.** offens gonzesse *f*.

⚠ The adjective **femelle** is normally used to refer to animals, not humans.

female genital mutilation n excision *f*.

feminine ['femɪnɪn] ◆ adj **1.** [dress, woman, hands, etc.] féminin **2.** GRAM [ending, form] féminin. ◆ n GRAM féminin *m* / *in the feminine* au féminin.

femininity [,femɪ'nɪnətɪ] n féminité *f*.

feminism ['femɪnɪzm] n féminisme *m*.

feminist ['femɪnɪst] ◆ adj féministe. ◆ n féministe *mf*.

fen [fen] n marais *m*, marécage *m* ▶ **the Fens** région de plaines anciennement marécageuses dans le sud-est de l'Angleterre.

fence [fens] ◆ n **1.** [gen] barrière *f*; [completely enclosing] barrière *f*, clôture *f*; [high and wooden] palissade *f* **2.** [in show-jumping] obstacle *m* **3.** v inf [of stolen goods] receleur *m*, -euse *f* **4.** TECH protection *f*. ◆ comp ▶ **fence post** piquet *m* de clôture. ◆ vt **1.** [land] clôturer **2.** v inf [stolen goods] receler. ◆ vi **1.** SPORT faire de l'escrime **2.** [evade question] se dérober; [joust verbally] s'affronter verbalement **3.** v inf [handle stolen goods] faire du recel. ❖ **fence in** vt sep **1.** [garden] clôturer **2.** fig [restrict - person] enfermer, étouffer. ❖ **fence off** vt sep séparer à l'aide d'une clôture.

fence-mending n fig reprise *f* des relations.

fencing ['fensɪŋ] ◆ n **1.** SPORT escrime *f* **2.** [fences] clôture *f*, barrière *f*; [material] matériaux *mpl* pour clôture **3.** v inf [handling stolen goods] recel *m*. ◆ comp [lesson, match] d'escrime.

fend [fend] vi ▶ **to fend for o.s. a)** se débrouiller tout seul **b)** [financially] s'assumer, subvenir à ses besoins.

❖ **fend off** vt sep [blow] parer; [attack, attacker] repousser; fig [question] éluder, se dérober à; [person at door, on telephone] éconduire.

fender ['fendər] n **1.** [for fireplace] garde-feu *m* inv **2.** NAUT défense *f* **3.** 🇺🇸 [on car] aile *f*; [on bicycle] garde-boue *m* inv; [on train, tram - shock absorber] pare-chocs *m* inv; [- for clearing track] chasse-pierres *m* inv.

fennel ['fenl] n fenouil *m*.

fenugreek ['fenjʊ,griːk] n fenugrec *m*.

feral ['fɪərəl] adj [cat, goat, sheep] devenu sauvage.

ferment ◆ vt [fə'ment] faire fermenter ▶ **to ferment trouble** fig fomenter des troubles. ◆ vi [fə'ment] fermenter. ◆ n ['fɜːment] **1.** [agent] ferment *m*; [fermentation] fermentation *f* **2.** fig [unrest] agitation *f*.

fermentation [,fɜːmən'teɪʃn] n fermentation *f*.

fermented [fə'mentɪd] adj fermenté.

fern [fɜːn] n fougère *f*.

ferocious [fə'rəʊʃəs] adj [animal, appetite, criticism, fighting] féroce; [weapon] meurtrier; [competition] acharné; [heat] terrible, intense; [climate] rude.

ferociously [fə'rəʊʃəslɪ] adv [bark, criticize, attack] avec férocité, férocement; [look at sb] d'un œil féroce.

ferociousness [fə'rəʊʃəsnɪs], **ferocity** [fə'rɒsətɪ] n [of person, animal, attack, criticism] férocité *f*; [of climate] rudesse *f*; [of heat] intensité *f*, caractère *m* torride.

ferret ['ferɪt] ◆ n furet *m*. ◆ vi **1.** [hunt with ferrets] chasser au furet ▶ **to go ferreting** aller à la chasse au furet **2.** fig = **ferret about**, **ferret around**. ❖ **ferret about** 🇬🇧, **ferret around** vi [in pocket, drawer] fouiller; [in room] fouiller, fureter / to ferret about for information fureter dans le but de trouver des renseignements. ❖ **ferret out** vt sep [information, truth] dénicher.

Ferris wheel ['ferɪs-] n grande roue *f*.

ferry ['ferɪ] (pl ferries, pt & pp ferried) ◆ n [large] ferry *m*; [small] bac *m* / to take the ferry prendre le ferry or le bac ▶ **a ferry crossing** une traversée en ferry or bac ▶ **ferry service** ligne *f* de ferry ▶ **ferry terminal** gare *f* maritime ▶ **car ferry** ferry(-boat) *m* ▶ **passenger ferry** ferry *m* pour passagers piétons. ◆ vt **1.** [by large boat - subj: company] transporter en ferry; [by small boat - subj: company] faire traverser en bac; [- subj: boat] transporter **2.** fig [by vehicle - goods] transporter; [- people] conduire.

ferryboat ['ferɪbəʊt] n ferry *m*.

ferryman ['ferɪmən] (pl ferrymen [-mən]) n passeur *m*.

fertile ['fɜːtaɪl] adj [land, soil] fertile; [person, couple, animal] fécond; fig [imagination] fertile, fécond.

fertility [fɜː'tɪlətɪ] ◆ n [of land, soil] fertilité *f*; [of person, animal] fécondité *f*; fig [of imagination] fertilité *f*, fécondité *f*. ◆ comp [rate] de fécondité; [rite, symbol] de fertilité ▶ **fertility clinic** centre *m* de traitement de la stérilité ▶ **fertility drug** médicament *m* pour le traitement de la stérilité.

fertilization [,fɜːtɪlaɪ'zeɪʃn] n **1.** BIOL [of egg] fécondation *f* **2.** AGR [of soil] fertilisation *f*.

fertilize, fertilise ['fɜːtɪlaɪz] vt **1.** BIOL [animal, plant, egg] féconder **2.** AGR [land, soil] fertiliser.

fertilizer ['fɜːtɪlaɪzər] n AGR engrais *m*.

fervent ['fɜːvənt] adj [desire, supporter, etc.] fervent, ardent.

fervently ['fɜːvəntlɪ] adv [beg, desire, speak, etc.] avec ferveur; [believe] ardemment.

fervour 🇬🇧, **fervor** 🇺🇸 ['fɜːvər] n ferveur *f*.

fess up [fes-] vi inf cracher le morceau.

fester ['festər] vi **1.** [wound] suppurer; fig [memory, resentment] s'aigrir **2.** 🇬🇧 inf [do nothing] buller.

festering ['festrɪŋ] adj [wound] suppurant ; [hatred, crisis, unrest, rebellion, resentment] qui couve.

festival ['festəvl] n [of music, film, etc.] festival *m* ; RELIG fête *f*.

festive ['festɪv] adj [atmosphere] de fête / *the festive season* la période des fêtes.

festivity [fes'tɪvətɪ] (*pl* **festivities**) n [merriness] fête *f*. ❖ **festivities** pl n festivités *fpl* / *the Christmas festivities* les fêtes *fpl* de Noël.

festoon [fe'stuːn] ◆ n feston *m*, guirlande *f*. ◆ vt orner de festons, festonner ▶ **to be festooned in sthg** *fig* [draped with] être couvert de qqch.

feta ['fetə] n ▶ **feta (cheese)** feta *f*.

fetal US = **foetal**.

fetch [feʧ] ◆ vt **1.** [go to get] aller chercher ; [come to get] venir chercher ▶ **to fetch sb from the station / from school** aller chercher qqn à la gare / à l'école **2.** [generate - response, laugh] susciter **3.** [be sold for - money] rapporter ; [- price] atteindre **4.** *fml* [utter - sigh, groan] pousser **5.** *inf* [deal - blow] : *he fetched him one with his right fist* il lui a flanqué *or* envoyé un droit. ◆ vi aller chercher ▶ **fetch!** [to dog] va chercher ! ❖ **fetch up** *inf* ◆ vi **1.** [end up] se retrouver / *to fetch up in hospital / in a ditch* se retrouver à l'hôpital / dans un fossé **2.** [vomit] rendre. ◆ vt sep [vomit] rendre.

fetching ['feʧɪŋ] adj [smile, person, look] séduisant ; [hat, dress] seyant.

fetchingly ['feʧɪŋlɪ] adv [smile] d'un air séduisant.

fête [feɪt] ◆ n fête *f*, kermesse *f* ▶ **village fête** fête de village. ◆ vt fêter.

🚩 **Fête**

En Grande-Bretagne, les **village fêtes** sont des fêtes de village, avec des ventes de produits artisanaux, des manifestations sportives et des jeux pour enfants ; elles sont souvent destinées à réunir des fonds pour des œuvres de charité.

fetid ['fetɪd] adj fétide.

fetish ['fetɪʃ] n PSYCHOL & RELIG fétiche *m* ▶ **to have a fetish for sthg** être un fétichiste de qqch ▶ **to have a fetish for** *or* **to make a fetish of sthg** être obsédé par qqch, être un maniaque de qqch.

fetishism ['fetɪʃɪzm] n PSYCHOL & RELIG fétichisme *m*.

fetishistic [ˌfetɪ'ʃɪstɪk] adj PSYCHOL fétichiste.

fetlock ['fetlɒk] n [of horse - part of leg] partie *f* postérieure du pied ; [- joint] boulet *m* ; [- hair] fanon *m*.

fetter ['fetər] vt [slave, prisoner] enchaîner ; [horse] entraver ; *fig* entraver. ❖ **fetters** pl n [of prisoner] fers *mpl*, chaînes *fpl* ; [of horse] entraves *fpl* ; *fig* [of marriage, job] chaînes *fpl*, sujétions *fpl* / *in fetters* a) [prisoner] enchaîné b) *fig* entravé ▶ **to put sb in fetters** a) mettre qqn aux fers b) *fig* entraver qqn.

fettle ['fetl] n *inf* ▶ **to be in fine** *or* **good fettle** aller bien.

fetus US = **foetus**.

feud [fjuːd] ◆ n [between people, families] querelle *f* ; [more aggressive - between families] vendetta *f* ▶ **to have a feud with sb** être à couteaux tirés avec qqn. ◆ vi se quereller, se disputer ▶ **to feud with sb (over sthg)** se quereller *or* se disputer avec qqn (pour qqch).

feudal ['fjuːdl] adj [society, system] féodal ; *pej* [extremely old-fashioned] moyenâgeux ▶ **feudal lord** seigneur *m*.

feudalism ['fjuːdəlɪzm] n féodalisme *m*.

feuding ['fjuːdɪŋ] n (*U*) querelle *f*, querelles *fpl* ; [more aggressive] vendetta *f*.

fever ['fiːvər] n **1.** MED [illness] fièvre *f* / *to have a fever* [high temperature] avoir de la température *or* de la fièvre **2.** *fig* excitation *f* fébrile ▶ **to be in a fever about sthg** [nervous, excited] être tout excité à cause de qqch.

fevered ['fiːvəd] adj [brow] fiévreux ; *fig* [imagination] enfiévré.

feverish ['fiːvərɪʃ] adj MED fiévreux ; *fig* [activity, atmosphere] fébrile.

fever pitch n *fig* : *things are at fever pitch here* l'excitation ici est à son comble / *excitement is rising to fever pitch* l'excitation est de plus en plus fébrile.

few [fjuː] pron [not many] : *I didn't realize how few there were* je ne m'étais pas rendu compte qu'ils étaient aussi peu nombreux / *the few who knew her* les quelques personnes qui la connaissaient. ❖ **a few** ◆ det phr quelques / *he has a few more friends than I have* il a un peu plus d'amis que moi / *a few more days / months / years* quelques jours / mois / années de plus. ◆ pron phr quelques-uns (quelques-unes) / *we need a few more / less* il nous en faut un peu plus / moins / *a few of you* quelques-uns d'entre vous / *he's had a few (too many)* *inf* [drinks] il a bu un coup (de trop). ❖ **a good few, quite a few** det phr un assez grand nombre de / *there were a good few* *or* *quite a few mistakes in it* il y avait un assez grand nombre de *or* pas mal de fautes dedans.

fewer ['fjuːər] (*compar of* **few**) ◆ det moins de / *there have been fewer accidents than last year* il y a eu moins d'accidents que l'an dernier / *the fewer people turn up the better* moins il y aura de monde et mieux ce sera ▶ **no fewer than** pas moins de. ◆ pron moins / *there are fewer of you than I thought* vous êtes moins nombreux que je ne le pensais.

fewest ['fjuːɪst] (*superl of* **few**) ◆ adj le moins de / *the fewest mistakes possible* le moins d'erreurs possible. ◆ pron : *I had the fewest* c'est moi qui en ai eu le moins.

fez [fez] n fez *m*.

Fez [fez] pr n Fès.

FH UK written abbr of **fire hydrant**.

FHA (abbr of **Federal Housing Administration**) pr n organisme de gestion des logements sociaux aux États-Unis.

fiancé [fɪ'ɒnseɪ] n fiancé *m*.

fiancée [fɪ'ɒnseɪ] n fiancée *f*.

fiasco [fɪ'æskəʊ] (UK *pl* **fiascos** ; US *pl* **fiascoes**) n fiasco *m*.

fiat money n US monnaie *f* fiduciaire.

fib [fɪb] *inf* ◆ n petit mensonge *m*. ◆ vi raconter des histoires.

fibber ['fɪbər] n *inf* menteur *m*, -euse *f*.

fibre UK, **fiber** US ['faɪbər] n **1.** [of cloth, wood] fibre *f* **2.** (*U*) [in diet] fibres *fpl*.

fibreboard UK, **fiberboard** US ['faɪbəbɔːd] n panneau *m* de fibres.

fibreglass UK, **fiberglass** US ['faɪbəglɑːs] ◆ n fibre *f* de verre. ◆ comp [boat, hull, etc.] en fibre de verre.

fibre optic ◆ n ▶ **fibre optics** fibre *f* optique, fibres *fpl* optiques. ◆ adj [cable] en fibres optiques.

fibre-tip pen n feutre *m* pointe fibre.

fibroid ['faɪbrɔɪd] ◆ adj [tissue] fibreux ▶ **fibroid tumour** fibrome *m*. ◆ n [tumour] fibrome *m*.

fibrositis [ˌfaɪbrə'saɪtɪs] n (*U*) fibrosite *f*.

fibrous ['faɪbrəs] adj fibreux.

FICA (abbr of Federal Insurance Contributions Act) pr n *loi américaine régissant les cotisations sociales.*

fickle ['fɪkl] adj [friend, fan] inconstant ; [weather] changeant, incertain ; [lover] inconstant, volage.

fiction ['fɪkʃn] ◆ n **1.** *(U)* LITER ouvrages *mpl* or œuvres *fpl* de fiction / *a work* or *piece of fiction* un ouvrage or une œuvre de fiction **2.** [invention] fiction *f.* ◆ comp ▪ **fiction writer** auteur *m* d'ouvrages de fiction.

fictional ['fɪkʃənl] adj fictif.

fictionalize ['fɪkʃənəlaɪz] vt romancer.

fictitious [fɪk'tɪʃəs] adj [imaginary, invented] fictif.

fiddle ['fɪdl] ◆ n **1.** MUS [instrument] violon *m* ▪ **to play second fiddle to sb** jouer les seconds violons or rôles auprès de qqn **2.** *inf* [swindle] truc *m*, combine *f* ▪ **to be on the fiddle** traficoter. ◆ vi **1.** [be restless] ▪ **stop fiddling!** tiens-toi tranquille !, arrête de remuer ! ▪ **to fiddle with sthg a)** [aimlessly, nervously] jouer avec qqch **b)** [interfere with] jouer avec or tripoter qqch **2.** [tinker] bricoler **3.** MUS jouer du violon **4.** *inf* [cheat] trafiquer. ◆ vt **1.** *inf* [falsify - results, financial accounts] truquer, falsifier ; [- election] truquer / *he fiddled it so that he got the results he wanted* il a trafiqué pour obtenir les résultats qu'il voulait **2.** *inf* [gain dishonestly - money, time off] carotter **3.** [play - tune] jouer au violon. ❖ **fiddle about** 🇬🇧, **fiddle around** vi **1.** [fidget] jouer **2.** *inf* [mess about] bricoler ; [loaf about, waste time] traînasser.

fiddler ['fɪdlər] n *inf* **1.** MUS joueur *m*, -euse *f* de violon, violoniste *mf* **2.** [swindler] arnaqueur *m*, -euse *f.*

fiddly ['fɪdlɪ] adj *inf* [awkward - job, task] délicat, minutieux ; [- small object] difficile à manier, difficile à tenir entre les doigts.

fidelity [fɪ'delətɪ] n **1.** [of people] fidélité *f* **2.** [of translation] fidélité *f* **3.** ELECTRON fidélité *f.*

fidget ['fɪdʒɪt] *inf* ◆ vi [be restless] avoir la bougeotte, gigoter ▪ **to fidget with sthg** jouer avec qqch, tripoter qqch. ◆ n [restless person] : *she's such a fidget* elle ne tient pas en place, elle gigote tout le temps.

fidgety ['fɪdʒɪtɪ] adj *inf* qui ne tient pas en place.

fiduciary [fɪ'duːʃjərɪ] ◆ adj LAW & FIN fiduciaire. ◆ n LAW & FIN fiduciaire *m.*

field [fiːld] ◆ n **1.** AGR champ *m* **2.** SPORT [pitch] terrain *m* ▪ **the field** [in baseball] les défenseurs *mpl* ▪ **to take the field** entrer sur le terrain ▪ **to lead the field a)** [in race] mener la course, être en tête **b)** *fig* [in sales, area of study] être en tête **c)** [subj: theory] faire autorité **3.** [of oil, minerals etc.] gisement *m* **4.** MIL ▪ **field (of battle)** champ *m* de bataille / *bravery in the field* bravoure sur le champ de bataille **5.** [sphere of activity, knowledge] domaine *m* **6.** [practice rather than theory] terrain *m* / *to work / to study in the field* travailler / étudier sur le terrain **7.** PHYS & OPT champ *m* ▪ **field of vision** champ visuel or de vision ; MIL ▪ **field of fire** champ *m* de tir **8.** COMPUT champ *m* **9.** HERALD [on coat of arms, coin] champ *m* ; [on flag] fond *m.* ◆ vt **1.** [team] présenter ; [player] faire jouer ; MIL [men, hardware] réunir ; POL [candidate] présenter **2.** [in cricket, baseball - ball] arrêter (et renvoyer) / *to field a question* *fig* savoir répondre à une question. ◆ vi [in cricket, baseball] être en défense, tenir le champ.

field day n SCH journée *f* en plein air ; MIL jour *m* des grandes manœuvres ▪ **to have a field day a)** *inf & fig* s'en donner à cœur joie **b)** [do good business] faire recette.

fielder ['fiːldər] n [in cricket, baseball] joueur *m* de l'équipe défendante or champ.

field event n compétition *f* d'athlétisme *(hormis la course).*

field glasses pl n jumelles *fpl.*

field hockey n 🇺🇸 hockey *m* (sur gazon).

field hospital n MIL antenne *f* chirurgicale, hôpital *m* de campagne.

field label n [in dictionary] rubrique *f*, indicateur *m* de domaine.

field marshal n 🇬🇧 MIL maréchal *m.*

fieldmouse ['fiːldmaʊs] *(pl* **fieldmice** [-maɪs]*)* n mulot *m.*

field office n bureau *m* local, succursale *f.*

field searching n COMPUT recherche *f* thématique.

field study n étude *f* sur le terrain.

field trip n SCH & UNIV voyage *m* d'études ; [of one afternoon, one day] sortie *f* d'études.

fieldwork ['fiːldwɜːk] n *(U)* travaux *mpl* sur le terrain ; [research] recherches *fpl* sur le terrain.

field worker n [social worker] travailleur *m* social, travailleuse *f* sociale ; [researcher] chercheur *m*, -euse *f* de terrain.

fiend [fiːnd] n **1.** [demon] démon *m*, diable *m* ; [evil person] monstre *m* **2.** *inf* [fanatic, freak] mordu *m*, -e *f*, fana *mf.*

fiendish ['fiːndɪʃ] adj **1.** [fierce - cruelty, look] diabolique, démoniaque **2.** *inf* [plan, cunning] diabolique ; [very difficult - problem] abominable, atroce.

fiendishly ['fiːndɪʃlɪ] adv **1.** [cruelly] diaboliquement **2.** *inf* [extremely] : *fiendishly difficult* abominablement or atrocement difficile.

fierce [fɪəs] adj **1.** [animal, person, look, words] féroce **2.** [heat, sun] torride ; [competition, fighting, loyalty, resistance] acharné ; [battle, criticism, desire, hatred, temper] féroce.

fiercely ['fɪəslɪ] adv **1.** *lit* férocement **2.** *fig* [argue, attack, criticize, fight] violemment ; [resist] avec acharnement ; [independent] farouchement.

fierceness ['fɪəsnɪs] n **1.** [of animal, look, person] férocité *f* **2.** [of desire] violence *f* ; [of sun] ardeur *f* ; [of resistance] acharnement *m* ; [of criticism] férocité *f.*

fierily ['faɪərɪlɪ] adv [speak] avec fougue.

fiery ['faɪərɪ] adj [heat, sun, coals] ardent ; [speech] violent, fougueux ; [sky, sunset] embrasé ; [curry] très épicé ▪ **the fiery cross** 🇺🇸 la croix en flammes *(symbole du Ku Klux Klan).*

fiesta [fɪ'estə] n fiesta *f.*

FIFA ['fiːfə] (abbr of Fédération Internationale de Football Association) pr n FIFA *f.*

FIFO (abbr of first in first out) n PEPS *m.*

fifteen [fɪf'tiːn] ◆ det quinze / *about fifteen people* une quinzaine de personnes / *to be fifteen* avoir quinze ans. ◆ n **1.** [numeral] quinze *m inv* / *about fifteen* une quinzaine **2.** [in rugby] quinze *m* / *the opposing fifteen* l'équipe rivale. ◆ pron quinze / *fifteen is not enough* quinze, ce n'est pas assez.

fifteenth [fɪf'tiːnθ] ◆ det quinzième / *Louis the Fifteenth* Louis Quinze or XV. ◆ n [fraction] quinzième *m* ; [in series] quinzième *mf.*

fifth [fɪfθ] ◆ det cinquième / *a fifth part* un cinquième / *on the fifth day of the month* le cinq du mois / *in fifth place* à la cinquième place / *fifth from the end* right cinquième en partant de la fin / droite / *on the fifth floor* a) 🇬🇧 au cinquième étage b) 🇺🇸 au quatrième étage ▪ **fifth gear** AUTO cinquième vitesse ▪ **fifth form** 🇬🇧 SCH classe de l'enseignement secondaire correspondant à la seconde ▪ **Fifth Amendment** Cinquième Amendement *m (de la Constitution des États-Unis, permettant à un accusé de ne pas répondre à une question risquant de jouer en sa défaveur)* ▪ **Fifth Avenue** la Cinquième Avenue ▪ **the Fifth Republic** la Cinquième or Vᵉ République ▪ **George the Fifth** Georges Cinq or V. ◆ n **1.** [day of month] cinq *m inv* / *the fifth,* *on the fifth* le cinq / *July fifth* US, *the fifth of July, July the fifth* le cinq juillet ; [fraction] cinquième *m* ; [in series] cinquième *mf* ▸ **the fifth of November** *jour anniversaire de la Conspiration des poudres aussi appelé Guy Fawkes' Day* **2.** MUS quinte *f* **3.** US [Fifth Amendment] ▸ **I'll take the Fifth** US *expression utilisée par une personne appréhendée pour invoquer le Cinquième Amendement.*

fifth column n cinquième colonne *f*.

fifth grade n US SCH *classe de l'enseignement primaire correspondant au CM2 (9-10 ans).*

fiftieth ['fɪftɪəθ] ◆ adj cinquantième. ◆ n [fraction] cinquantième *m* ; [in series] cinquantième *mf*.

fifty ['fɪftɪ] ◆ det cinquante / *about fifty people* une cinquantaine de personnes. ◆ n **1.** [numeral] cinquante *m inv* / *about fifty* une cinquantaine / *to be fifty* avoir cinquante ans / *the fifties* les années cinquante / *in the early / late fifties* au début / à la fin des années cinquante / *she is in her fifties* elle a dans les cinquante ans / *to be in one's early / late fifties* avoir une petite cinquantaine / la cinquantaine bien sonnée / *he must be close to* or *getting on for fifty* il doit approcher de la cinquantaine / *to do fifty* AUTO ≃ faire du quatre-vingts **2.** US [money] billet *m* de cinquante (dollars). ◆ comp ▸ **fifty-one** cinquante et un ▸ **fifty-two** / **-three** cinquante-deux / **-trois** ▸ **fifty-first** cinquante et unième ▸ **fifty-second** cinquante-deuxième ▸ **fifty-odd** : *there were fifty-odd people at the party* il y avait une cinquantaine de personnes à la soirée. ◆ pron cinquante / *there are fifty (of them)* il y en a cinquante.

fifty-fifty ◆ adj : *on a fifty-fifty basis* moitié-moitié, fifty-fifty / *his chances of winning / surviving are fifty-fifty* il a une chance sur deux de gagner / de s'en tirer. ◆ adv moitié-moitié, fifty-fifty ▸ **to go fifty-fifty (with sb on sthg)** faire moitié-moitié or fifty-fifty (avec qqn pour qqch).

fig [fɪg] n [fruit] figue *f* ▸ **fig (tree)** figuier *m*.

fight [faɪt] (*pt & pp* **fought** [fɔːt]) ◆ n **1.** [physical] bagarre *f* ; [verbal] dispute *f* ; [of army, boxer] combat *m*, affrontement *m* ; [against disease, poverty, etc.] lutte *f*, combat *m* ▸ **to have** or **to get into a fight with sb** a) [physical] se battre avec qqn b) [verbal] se disputer avec qqn ▸ **to pick a fight (with sb)** chercher la bagarre (avec qqn) **2.** [fighting spirit] combativité *f*. ◆ vi [physically - person, soldier] se battre ; [-boxer] combattre ; [-two boxers] s'affronter ; [verbally] se disputer ; [against disease, injustice, etc.] lutter / *he fought in the war* il a fait la guerre / *they were always fighting over* or *about money* ils se disputaient toujours pour des problèmes d'argent. ◆ vt [person, animal] se battre contre ; [boxer] combattre (contre), se battre contre ; [disease, terrorism, fire, etc.] lutter contre, combattre ▸ **to fight a battle** livrer (une) bataille ▸ **to fight a court case** a) [subj: lawyer] défendre une cause b) [subj: plaintiff, defendant] être en procès ▸ **to fight an election** [politician] se présenter à une élection. ❖ **fight back** ◆ vi [in physical or verbal dispute] se défendre, riposter ; [in boxing, football match] se reprendre ; [in race] revenir. ◆ vt sep [tears] refouler ; [despair, fear, laughter] réprimer. ❖ **fight off** vt sep [attack, enemy, advances] repousser ; [sleep] combattre ; [disease] résister à. ❖ **fight on** vi continuer le combat. ❖ **fight out** vt sep : *just leave them to fight it out* laisse-les se bagarrer et régler cela entre eux.

fightback ['faɪtbæk] n reprise *f*.

fighter ['faɪtər] ◆ n **1.** [person who fights] combattant *m*, -e *f* ; [boxer] boxeur *m* / *he's a fighter* fig c'est un battant **2.** [plane] avion *m* de chasse, chasseur *m*. ◆ comp [pilot] de chasseur, d'avion de chasse ; [squadron] de chasseurs, d'avions de chasse ; [plane] de chasse.

fighter-bomber n MIL chasseur *m* bombardier.

fighting ['faɪtɪŋ] ◆ n (*U*) [physical] bagarre *f*, bagarres *fpl* ; [verbal] dispute *f*, disputes *fpl*, bagarre *f*, bagarres *fpl* ; MIL combat *m*, combats *mpl*. ◆ comp [forces, unit] de combat ▸ **fighting cock** coq *m* de combat ▸ **fighting men** MIL combattants *mpl* ▸ **fighting spirit** esprit *m* combatif.

fig leaf n BOT feuille *f* de figuier ; [on statue, in painting] feuille *f* de vigne ; *fig* camouflage *m*.

figment ['fɪgmənt] n ▸ **a figment of the imagination** un produit or une création de l'imagination.

figurative ['fɪgərətɪv] adj **1.** [language, meaning] figuré **2.** ART figuratif.

figuratively ['fɪgərətɪvlɪ] adv au (sens) figuré.

figure [UK 'fɪgər US 'fɪgjər] ◆ n **1.** [number, symbol] chiffre *m* ; [amount] somme *f* / *six-figure number* nombre de six chiffres ▸ **to put a figure on sthg** [give cost] évaluer le coût de or chiffrer qqch **2.** [human shape] ligne *f* / *she has a good figure* elle a une jolie silhouette, elle est bien faite / *to look after one's figure* faire attention à sa ligne / *to keep / to lose one's figure* garder / perdre la ligne **3.** [human outline] silhouette *f* **4.** [character in novel, film, etc.] personnage *m* **5.** [in geometry, skating, dancing] figure *f* ▸ **figure of eight** UK, **figure eight** US huit *m* **6.** [illustration, diagram] figure *f* **7.** [rhetorical] ▸ **figure of speech** figure *f* de rhétorique **8.** [statuette] figurine *f*. ◆ vi **1.** [appear] figurer, apparaître **2.** *inf* [make sense] sembler logique or normal / *that figures!* a) [I'm not surprised] ça m'étonnes ! b) [that makes sense] c'est logique ▸ **go figure!** inf va comprendre ! ◆ vt **1.** *inf* [reckon] penser **2.** US *inf* = **figure out**. ❖ **figure on** vt insep *inf* [plan on] compter. ❖ **figure out** vt sep **1.** [understand -person] arriver à comprendre **2.** [work out -sum, cost, etc.] calculer.

figurehead ['fɪgəhed] n NAUT figure *f* de proue ; *fig* [of organization, society] représentant *m* nominal, représentante *f* nominale ; *pej* homme *m* de paille.

figure-hugging [-ˌhʌgɪŋ] adj [dress] moulant.

figure skating ◆ n patinage *m* artistique. ◆ comp [champion, championship] de patinage artistique.

figurine [UK 'fɪgəriːn US 'fɪgjəˈriːn] n figurine *f*.

Fiji ['fiːdʒiː] pr n Fidji / *in Fiji* à Fidji ▸ **the Fiji Islands** les îles *fpl* Fidji / *in the Fiji Islands* aux îles Fidji.

Fijian [ˌfiːˈdʒiːən] ◆ n [person] Fidjien *m*, -enne *f*. ◆ adj fidjien.

filament ['fɪləmənt] n BOT & ELEC filament *m*.

filch [fɪltʃ] vt *inf* [steal] piquer.

file [faɪl] ◆ n **1.** [folder] chemise *f* ; [box] classeur *m* **2.** [dossier, documents] dossier *m* ; [series or system of files] fichier *m* ▸ **to have** / **to keep sthg on file** avoir / garder qqch dans ses dossiers / *it's on file* c'est dans les dossiers, c'est classé ▸ **to have** / **to keep a file on** avoir / garder un dossier sur ▸ **to open** / **to close a file on** ouvrir / fermer un dossier sur **3.** COMPUT fichier *m* / *data on file* données *fpl* sur fichier ▸ **data file** fichier de données **4.** [row, line] file *f* ▸ **in single** or **Indian file** en or à la file indienne **5.** [for metal, fingernails] lime *f*. ◆ comp ▸ **file copy** copie *f* à classer ▸ **file extension** extension *f* de fichier ▸ **file format** format *m* de fichier ▸ **file name** nom *m* de fichier. ◆ vt **1.** [documents, information] classer / *to be filed under a letter / subject* être classé sous une lettre / dans une catégorie **2.** LAW ▸ **to file a suit against sb** intenter un procès à qqn / *to file a claim* déposer une demande **3.** [metal] limer / *to file one's fingernails* se limer les ongles / *to file through sthg* limer qqch. ◆ vi **1.** [classify documents, information] faire du classement **2.** [walk one behind the other] : *the troops filed past the general* les troupes ont défilé devant le général / *they all filed in / out* ils sont tous entrés / sortis à la file. ❖ **file away** vt sep **1.** [documents] classer **2.** [rough edges] polir à la lime ; [excess material] enlever à la lime. ❖ **file down** vt sep [metal, fingernails, rough surface] polir à la lime. ❖ **file for** vt insep : *to file for divorce* demander le divorce / *to file for bankrupcy* déposer son bilan.

file clerk n 🇺🇸 documentaliste *mf*.

file footage n 🇺🇸 images *fpl* d'archives.

file management n COMPUT gestion *f* de fichiers.

file manager n COMPUT gestionnaire *m* de fichiers.

filename n nom *m* de fichier.

file-sharing n partage *m* de fichiers.

filet 🇺🇸 = fillet.

filibuster ['fɪlɪbʌstər] ❖ n POL obstruction *f* (parlementaire). ❖ vi POL faire de l'obstruction. ❖ vt POL [legislation] faire obstruction à.

filigree ['fɪlɪgriː] ❖ n filigrane *m*. ❖ adj en or de filigrane.

filing ['faɪlɪŋ] n **1.** [of documents] classement *m* **2.** LAW [of complaint, claim] dépôt *m*.

filing cabinet n classeur *m*.

filing clerk n documentaliste *mf*.

Filipino [,fɪlɪ'piːnəʊ] (*pl* Filipinos) ❖ n [person] Philippin *m*. ❖ adj philippin.

fill [fɪl] ❖ n ▸ **to eat one's fill** manger à sa faim, se rassasier ▸ **to drink one's fill** boire tout son soûl ▸ **to have had one's fill of sb / sthg** inf : *I've had my fill of it / her* j'en ai assez / assez d'elle. ❖ vt **1.** [cup, glass, bottle] remplir ; [room, streets - subj: people, smoke, laughter] envahir ; [chocolates] fourrer ; [cake, pie] garnir ; [vegetables] farcir ; [pipe] bourrer / *to be filled with people* [room, street] être plein or rempli de gens / *to be filled with horror / admiration* être rempli d'horreur / d'admiration **2.** [plug - hole] boucher ; [- tooth] plomber / *to have a tooth filled* se faire plomber une dent **3.** [position, vacancy - subj: employee] occuper ; [- subj: employer] pourvoir **4.** [occupy - time] occuper **5.** [meet - requirement] répondre à **6.** [supply] : *to fill an order* **a)** [in bar, restaurant] apporter ce qui a été commandé **b)** [for stationery, equipment, etc.] livrer une commande. ❖ vi [room, bath, bus] se remplir ; [sail] se gonfler / *her eyes filled with tears* ses yeux se sont remplis de larmes. ❖ **fill in** ❖ vi faire un remplacement ▸ **to fill in for sb** remplacer qqn. ❖ vt sep **1.** [hole, window, door] boucher **2.** [complete - form, questionnaire] compléter, remplir ; [insert - name, missing word] insérer **3.** [bring up to date] mettre au courant ▸ **to fill sb in on sthg** mettre qqn au courant de qqch **4.** [use - time] occuper. ❖ **fill out** ❖ vi **1.** [cheeks] se remplir ; [person] s'étoffer **2.** [sails] se gonfler. ❖ vt sep **1.** [complete - form] remplir **2.** [pad out - essay, speech] étoffer. ❖ **fill up** ❖ vi se remplir / *to fill up with petrol* faire le plein d'essence / *don't fill up on biscuits, you two!* ne vous gavez pas de biscuits, vous deux ! ❖ vt sep **1.** [make full] remplir ; [person with food] rassasier / *he filled the car up* il a fait le plein (d'essence) **2.** [use - day, time] occuper.

filled [fɪld] adj **1.** [roll] garni(e) **2.** [with emotion] ▸ **filled (with)** plein(e) (de).

filler ['fɪlər] n **1.** [for holes, cracks] mastic *m* ; [for cavity, open space] matière *f* de remplissage **2.** [funnel] entonnoir *m* **3.** [in quilt, bean bag, etc.] matière *f* de rembourrage ; [in cigar] tripe *f* **4.** PRESS & TV bouche-trou *m* **5.** LING ▸ **filler (word)** mot *m* de remplissage.

filler cap n bouchon *m* du réservoir d'essence.

fillet ['fɪlɪt] ❖ n CULIN filet *m* / *fillet steak is expensive* le filet de bœuf est cher. ❖ vt [meat, fish - prepare] préparer ; [cut into fillets - fish] faire des filets dans, lever les filets de ; [- meat] faire des steaks dans ▸ **filleted sole** filets *mpl* de sole.

fill-in n inf [person] remplaçant *m*, -e *f*.

filling ['fɪlɪŋ] ❖ adj [foodstuff] bourratif. ❖ n **1.** [in tooth] plombage *m* **2.** CULIN [for cake, pie - sweet] garniture *f* ; [for vegetables, poultry - savoury] farce *f*.

filling station n station-service *f*, station *f* d'essence.

fillip ['fɪlɪp] n coup *m* de fouet ▸ **to give sb / sthg a fillip** donner un coup de fouet à qqn / qqch.

filly ['fɪlɪ] (*pl* fillies) n **1.** [horse] pouliche *f* **2.** inf & dated [girl] fille *f*.

film [fɪlm] ❖ n **1.** [thin layer - of oil, mist, dust] film *m*, pellicule *f* **2.** PHOT pellicule *f* ▸ **a roll of film** une pellicule **3.** CIN film *m* ▸ **to shoot** or **to make a film (about sthg)** tourner or faire un film (sur qqch) ▸ **to be in films** faire du cinéma. ❖ comp [critic, star, producer] de cinéma ; [clip, premiere] d'un film ; [sequence] de film ; [archives, award, rights] cinématographique ▸ **film buff** inf cinéphile *mf* ▸ **film director** metteur *m* en scène ▸ **film festival** festival *m* de cinéma ▸ **the film industry** l'industrie *f* cinématographique or du cinéma ▸ **film maker** cinéaste *mf* ▸ **film rights** droits *mpl* cinématographiques ▸ **film set** plateau *m* de tournage ▸ **film speed** PHOT sensibilité *f* d'une pellicule. ❖ vt [event, people] filmer ; CIN [scene] filmer, tourner. ❖ vi [record] filmer ; CIN tourner. ❖ **film over** vi s'embuer, se voiler.

filmgoer ['fɪlm,gəʊər] n amateur *m* de cinéma, cinéphile *mf*.

filming ['fɪlmɪŋ] n CIN tournage *m*.

film noir n CIN film *m* noir.

filmy ['fɪlmɪ] adj [material] léger, vaporeux, aérien.

filo ['fiːləʊ] n CULIN ▸ **filo (pastry)** pâte feuilletée très fine.

Filofax® ['faɪləʊfæks] n Filofax® *m*.

filter ['fɪltər] ❖ n **1.** CHEM, MECH & PHOT filtre *m* **2.** 🇬🇧 AUTO flèche *f* lumineuse (*autorisant le dégagement des voitures à droite ou à gauche*). ❖ comp ▸ **filter coffee** café *m* filtre ▸ **filter lane** 🇬🇧 AUTO voie *f* de dégagement ▸ **filter paper** papier *m* filtre. ❖ vt [coffee, oil, water, etc.] filtrer. ❖ vi **1.** [liquid, light] filtrer **2.** 🇬🇧 AUTO suivre la voie de dégagement. ❖ **filter in** vi [light, sound, information, news] filtrer ; [people] entrer petit à petit. ❖ **filter out** ❖ vt sep [sediment, impurities] éliminer par filtrage or filtration. ❖ vi [people] sortir petit à petit. ❖ **filter through** vi lit & fig filtrer.

filter-tipped adj [cigarette] (bout) filtre.

filth [fɪlθ] n (*U*) **1.** [on skin, clothes] crasse *f* ; [in street] saleté *f* **2.** [obscene books, films, etc.] ordures *fpl*, obscénités *fpl* ; [obscene words, jokes] grossièretés *fpl*, obscénités *fpl* **3.** 🇬🇧 v inf ▸ **the filth** [police] les flics *mpl*.

filthy ['fɪlθɪ] (*compar* filthier, *superl* filthiest) ❖ adj **1.** [dirty] dégoûtant, crasseux **2.** [obscene, smutty - language, talk, jokes] grossier, obscène, ordurier ; [- person] grossier, dégoûtant ; [- film, book, photograph] obscène, dégoûtant ; [- habit] dégoûtant **3.** inf [nasty - temper, day] atroce, abominable ; [- trick] vicieux, méchant ; [- look] méchant ; [- weather] sale. ❖ adv ▸ **to be filthy rich** inf être plein aux as.

filtration [fɪl'treɪʃn] n filtrage *m*, filtration *f*.

filtration plant n station *f* d'épuration.

Fimbra ['fɪmbrə] (**abbr of Financial Intermediaries, Managers and Brokers Regulatory Association**) pr n *organisme britannique contrôlant les activités des courtiers d'assurances.*

fin [fɪn] n **1.** [of fish] nageoire *f* ; [of shark] aileron *m* ; [of boat] dérive *f* **2.** [of aircraft, spacecraft] empennage *m* ; [of rocket, bomb] ailette *f* **3.** AUTO [of radiator] ailette *f*.

finagle [fɪ'neɪgəl] vt 🇺🇸 inf [obtain, through cleverness] se débrouiller pour avoir ; [through devious means] obtenir par subterfuge, carotter.

final ['faɪnl] ◆ adj **1.** [last] dernier ▶ **a final-year student** UNIV un étudiant en or de dernière année **2.** [definitive] définitif ; [score] final **3.** PHILOS [cause] final ; GRAM [clause] de but, final. ◆ n **1.** SPORT finale f / **to get to the final** or **finals** arriver en finale **2.** PRESS dernière édition f ▶ **late final** dernière édition du soir. ❖ **finals** pl n UNIV examens mpl de dernière année.

final cut n CIN final cut m, montage m définitif.

finale [fɪ'nɑːlɪ] n MUS finale m ; fig final m, finale m.

finalist ['faɪnəlɪst] n [in competition] finaliste mf.

finality [faɪ'nælətɪ] n [of decision, death] irrévocabilité f, caractère m définitif / **there was a note of finality in his voice** il y avait quelque chose d'irrévocable dans sa voix.

finalization [,faɪnəlaɪ'zeɪʃn] n [of details, plans, arrangements] mise f au point ; [of deal, agreement] conclusion f.

finalize, finalise ['faɪnəlaɪz] vt [details, plans] mettre au point ; [deal, decision, agreement] mener à bonne fin ; [preparations] mettre la dernière main or touche à, mettre la touche finale à ; [date] arrêter / **nothing has been finalized yet** rien n'a encore été décidé or arrêté.

finally ['faɪnəlɪ] adv **1.** [eventually] finalement, enfin **2.** [lastly] enfin **3.** [irrevocably] définitivement.

finance ◆ n ['faɪnæns] (U) [money management] finance f ; [financing] financement m. ◆ vt [faɪ'næns] financer ; [project, enterprise] financer, trouver les fonds pour. ❖ **finances** pl n finances fpl, fonds mpl.

finance company n établissement m de crédit.

financial [faɪ'nænʃl] adj financier / **but does it make financial sense?** mais est-ce que c'est avantageux or intéressant du point de vue financier ? ▶ **financial administrator** administrateur m financier, administratrice f financière ▶ **financial adviser** conseiller m financier ▶ **financial backer** bailleur m de fonds ▶ **financial controller** contrôleur m financier ▶ **financial director** directeur m financier ▶ **financial services** services mpl financiers.

financial bubble n bulle f financière.

financially [faɪ'nænʃəlɪ] adv financièrement / **are they financially sound?** est-ce qu'ils ont une bonne assise financière ?

financial year n [gen] année f fiscale ; [of company] exercice m financier ; ADMIN année f budgétaire.

 Financial year

En Grande-Bretagne, pour les impôts sur le revenu, l'année fiscale commence le 6 avril pour les particuliers et le 1ᵉʳ avril pour les organismes publics.

---

financier [fɪ'nænsɪə] n financier m.

finch [fɪntʃ] n fringillidé m spec ; [goldfinch] chardonneret m ; [chaffinch] pinson m ; [bullfinch] bouvreuil m.

find [faɪnd] (pt & pp **found** [faʊnd]) ◆ vt **1.** [by searching] trouver ; [lost thing, person] retrouver / **I can't find my place** [in book] je ne sais plus où j'en suis / **my wallet / he was nowhere to be found** mon portefeuille / il était introuvable ; [look for, fetch] chercher / **go and find me a pair of scissors** va me chercher une paire de ciseaux ▶ **to find one's feet** [in new job, situation] prendre ses repères / **she couldn't find it in her heart** or **herself to say no** elle n'a pas eu le cœur de dire non ▶ **to find one's way** trouver son chemin / **I'll find my own way out** je trouverai la sortie tout seul **2.** [come across by chance] trouver / **we left everything as we found it** nous avons tout laissé dans l'état où nous l'avions trouvé / **I found her waiting outside** je l'ai trouvée qui attendait dehors **3.** [expressing an opinion,

personal view] trouver / **I find her very pretty** je la trouve très jolie / **she finds it very difficult / impossible to talk about it** il lui est très difficile / impossible d'en parler **4.** [discover, learn] constater / **they came back to find the house had been burgled** à leur retour, ils ont constaté que la maison avait été cambriolée / **I think you'll find I'm right** je pense que tu t'apercevras que j'ai raison **5.** LAW ▶ **to find sb guilty / innocent** déclarer qqn coupable / non coupable / **how do you find the accused?** déclarez-vous l'accusé coupable ou non coupable ? **6.** [reflexive use] ▶ **to find o.s.** : **I woke up to find myself on a ship** je me suis réveillé sur un bateau / **I find / found myself in an impossible situation** je me trouve / me suis retrouvé dans une situation impossible. ◆ vi LAW ▶ **to find for / against the plaintiff** prononcer en faveur de l'accusation / de la défense. ◆ n [object] trouvaille f ; [person] merveille f. ❖ **find out** ◆ vi **1.** [investigate, make enquiries] se renseigner ▶ **to find out about sthg** se renseigner sur qqch **2.** [learn, discover] : **his wife / his boss found out** sa femme / son chef a tout découvert / **I didn't find out about it in time** je ne l'ai pas su à temps. ◆ vt sep **1.** [learn, discover - truth, real identity] découvrir ; [- answer, phone number] trouver ; [- by making enquiries, reading instructions] se renseigner sur / **what have you found out about him / it?** qu'est-ce que tu as découvert sur lui / là-dessus ? **2.** [catch being dishonest] prendre ; [show to be a fraud] prendre en défaut / **you've been found out** tu as été découvert.

finding ['faɪndɪŋ] n **1.** [discovery, conclusion] ▶ **findings** conclusions fpl, résultats mpl **2.** LAW verdict m.

fine [faɪn] (compar **finer**, superl **finest**) ◆ adj **1.** [of high quality - meal, speech, view] excellent ; [beautiful and elegant - clothes, house] beau (before vowel or silent 'h' **bel**, f **belle**) ; [- fabric] précieux **2.** [very thin - hair, nib, thread] fin **3.** [not coarse - powder, grain, drizzle] fin ; [- features, skin] fin, délicat **4.** [good, OK] : **how are you?** — **fine, thanks** comment ça va ? — bien, merci / **more coffee?** — **no thanks, I'm fine** encore du café ? — non, ça va, merci / **I'll be back in about an hour or so** — **fine** je serai de retour d'ici environ une heure — d'accord or entendu or très bien ▶ **(that's) fine** très bien, parfait / **that's fine by** or **with me** ça me va **5.** [well] : **that looks fine to me** cela m'a l'air d'aller / **he looks fine now** [in health] il a l'air de bien aller maintenant / **that sounds fine a)** [suggestion, idea] très bien, parfait **b)** [way of playing music] cela rend très bien m **6.** [weather] beau **7.** [subtle - distinction, language] subtil ; [precise - calculations] minutieux, précis **8.** inf & iro [awful, terrible] : **you picked a fine time to leave me / tell me!** tu as bien choisi ton moment pour me quitter / me le dire ! / **you're a fine one to talk!** ça te va bien de dire ça !, tu peux parler ! ◆ adv [well] bien. ◆ n [punishment] amende f, contravention f ▶ **to impose a fine on sb** infliger une amende à qqn. ◆ vt [order to pay] condamner à une amende, donner une contravention à / **she was fined for speeding** elle a reçu une contravention pour excès de vitesse.

fine art n (U) beaux-arts mpl / **he's got it down to a fine art** inf il est expert en la matière.

finely ['faɪnlɪ] adv **1.** [grated, ground, sliced] finement **2.** [delicately, subtly - tuned] avec précision **3.** [carved, sewn, etc.] délicatement.

fineness ['faɪnnɪs] n **1.** [of clothes, manners] raffinement m ; [of work of art, features, handwriting] finesse f **2.** [of sand, sugar, etc.] finesse f **3.** [purity - of metal] pureté f **4.** [thinness - of thread, hair, nib] finesse f ; fig [of detail, distinction] subtilité f.

finery ['faɪnərɪ] n (U) parure f / **the princess in all her finery** la princesse dans or parée de ses plus beaux atours / **to be dressed in all one's finery** porter sa tenue d'apparat.

finesse [fɪ'nes] ◆ n **1.** [skill] finesse f **2.** CARDS impasse f. ◆ vi CARDS ▸ **to finesse against a card** faire l'impasse à une carte. ◆ vt CARDS ▸ **to finesse a card** faire l'impasse en jouant une carte.

fine-tooth(ed) comb n peigne m fin ▸ **to go through sthg with a fine-toothed comb** fig passer qqch au peigne fin.

fine-tune vt [machine, engine, radio] régler avec précision ; fig [plan] peaufiner ; [economy] gérer grâce à des mesures fiscales et monétaires.

fine-tuning [-'tju:nɪŋ] n [of machine, engine, radio] réglage m fin ; fig [of plan] peaufinage m ; [of economy] réglage obtenu par des mesures fiscales et monétaires.

finger ['fɪŋgə'] ◆ n **1.** ANAT doigt m / to wear a ring on one's finger porter une bague au doigt ▸ **to have a finger in every pie** jouer sur tous les tableaux ▸ **to keep one's fingers crossed** croiser les doigts (pour souhaiter bonne chance) ▸ **to point the finger (of suspicion) at sb** diriger les soupçons sur qqn ▸ **to have one's finger on the pulse a)** [person] être très au fait de ce qui se passe **b)** [magazine, TV programme] être à la pointe de l'actualité ▸ **to work one's fingers to the bone** s'épuiser à la tâche / you never lift or raise a finger to help tu ne lèves jamais le petit doigt pour aider **2.** [of glove] doigt m **3.** [of alcohol] doigt m ; [of land] bande f. ◆ comp ▸ **finger exercises** MUS exercices mpl de doigté ▸ **finger puppet** marionnette f à doigts. ◆ vt **1.** [feel] tâter du doigt ; pej tripoter **2.** MUS doigter, indiquer le doigté de **3.** v inf [inform on] balancer, donner.

finger bowl n rince-doigts m inv.

finger buffet n buffet où sont servis des petits sandwichs, des petits-fours et des légumes crus.

finger food n [savoury] amuse-gueules mpl ; [sweet] petits-fours mpl.

fingering ['fɪŋgərɪŋ] n **1.** MUS [technique, numerals] doigté m **2.** pej [touching] tripotage m.

fingerless glove ['fɪŋgələs-] n mitaine f.

fingermark ['fɪŋgəmɑ:k] n trace f ou marque f de doigt.

fingernail ['fɪŋgəneɪl] n ongle m (de la main).

finger paint n peinture f pour peindre avec les doigts.

finger painting n peinture f avec les doigts / children love finger painting les enfants adorent peindre avec leurs doigts.

fingerprint ['fɪŋgəprɪnt] ◆ n empreinte f digitale ▸ **genetic fingerprint** empreinte or code m génétique. ◆ comp ▸ **fingerprint expert** spécialiste mf en empreintes digitales or en dactyloscopie. ◆ vt [person] prendre les empreintes digitales de ; [object, weapon] relever les empreintes digitales sur.

fingertip ['fɪŋgətɪp] ◆ n bout m du doigt ▸ **to have information at one's fingertips a)** [be conversant with] connaître des informations sur le bout des doigts **b)** [readily available] avoir des informations à portée de main. ◆ comp ▸ **fingertip controls** commandes fpl à touches ▸ **fingertip search** passage m au peigne fin, examen m minutieux.

finial ['fɪnɪəl] n ARCHIT fleuron m.

finicky ['fɪnɪkɪ] adj **1.** [person] pointilleux, tatillon pej ; [habit] tatillon ▸ **to be finicky about sthg** être pointilleux or pej tatillon sur qqch **2.** [job, task] minutieux.

finish ['fɪnɪʃ] ◆ n **1.** [end, closing stage - of life, game, etc.] fin f ; [- of race] arrivée f **2.** [created with paint, varnish, veneer] finitions fpl **3.** [quality of workmanship, presentation, etc.] finition f **4.** SPORT [of athlete] finish m **5.** [shot at goal] but m **6.** [of wine] longueur f en bouche. ◆ vt **1.** [end, complete - work, meal, school] finir, terminer, achever ; [- race] finir, terminer ; [consume - supplies, food, drink] finir, terminer ▸ **to finish doing sthg** finir or terminer de faire qqch **2.** [ruin - sb's career] mettre un terme à ; [- sb's chances] détruire, anéantir **3.** [exhaust] achever, tuer **4.** [put finish on - wood, garment] finir, mettre les finitions à. ◆ vi [come to an end - concert, film, etc.] (se) finir, se terminer, s'achever ; [complete activity - person] finir, terminer ▸ **to finish by doing sthg** finir or terminer en faisant qqch / to finish first / third [in race] arriver premier / troisième. ❖ **finish off** ◆ vi [speech, meal] finir, terminer. ◆ vt sep **1.** [complete - work, letter] finir, terminer, achever ; [- passing move in sport] terminer, finir, conclure **2.** [consume - drink] finir, terminer **3.** [kill - person, wounded animal] achever ; fig [exhaust - person] achever, tuer. ❖ **finish up** ◆ vi [end up] finir. ◆ vt sep [meal, food, drink] finir, terminer. ❖ **finish with** vt insep **1.** [have no further use for] ne plus avoir besoin de **2.** [want no more contact with] en finir avec **3.** [end relationship] rompre avec.

finished ['fɪnɪʃt] adj **1.** fini ; fig [performance] parfaitement exécuté ; [appearance] raffiné **2.** inf [exhausted] mort, crevé **3.** [ruined - career] fini, terminé **4.** [completed - work, job] fini, terminé, achevé ; [consumed - wine, cake] fini **5.** [over] fini.

finishing line ['fɪnɪʃɪŋ-] n UK SPORT ligne f d'arrivée.

finishing school n école privée de jeunes filles surtout axée sur l'enseignement des bonnes manières.

finish line US = finishing line.

finite ['faɪnaɪt] adj limité ; PHILOS & MATH [number, universe] fini ; GRAM [verb] à aspect fini.

Finland ['fɪnlənd] pr n Finlande f / in Finland en Finlande.

Finn [fɪn] n **1.** [inhabitant of Finland] Finlandais m, -e f **2.** HIST Finnois m, -e f.

Finnish ['fɪnɪʃ] ◆ n LING finnois m. ◆ adj **1.** [gen] finlandais **2.** HIST finnois.

fiord [fjɔ:d] n fjord m.

fir [fɜ:'] ◆ n [tree, wood] sapin m. ◆ comp ▸ **fir cone** UK pomme f de pin ▸ **fir tree** sapin m.

fire ['faɪə'] ◆ n **1.** [destructive] incendie m ▸ **fire!** au feu ! ▸ **to set fire to sthg** or **to set sthg on fire** mettre le feu à qqch ▸ **to cause** or **to start a fire** [person, faulty wiring] provoquer un incendie ▸ **on fire** en feu ▸ **forest fire** incendie or feu m de forêt **2.** [in hearth, campsite] feu m ▸ **to light** or **to make a fire** allumer un feu, faire du feu ▸ **open fire** feu de cheminée **3.** [element] feu m **4.** MIL feu m ▸ **to open** / **to cease fire** ouvrir / cesser le feu **5.** UK [heater] appareil m de chauffage **6.** [passion, ardour] flamme f. ◆ comp ▸ **fire appliance** UK camion m de pompiers ▸ **fire prevention** mesures fpl de sécurité contre l'incendie ▸ **fire regulations** consignes fpl en cas d'incendie. ◆ vt **1.** [shot, bullet] tirer ; [gun, cannon, torpedo] décharger ; [arrow] décocher **2.** [inspire - person, an audience, supporters, the imagination] enflammer **3.** [in kiln] cuire **4.** [power, fuel - furnace] chauffer **5.** inf [dismiss] virer. ◆ vi **1.** [shoot - person] tirer, faire feu ▸ **fire!** MIL feu ! ▸ **to fire at** or **on sb** tirer sur qqn **2.** [engine] tourner ; [spark plug] s'allumer ; [pin on print head] se déclencher. ❖ **fire away** vi inf [go ahead] ▸ **fire away!** allez-y ! ❖ **fire off** vt sep [round of ammunition] tirer ; fig [facts, figures] balancer.

fire alarm n alarme f d'incendie.

firearm ['faɪərɑ:m] n arme f à feu.

fireball ['faɪəbɔ:l] n boule f de feu.

firebomb ['faɪəbɒm] ◆ n bombe f incendiaire. ◆ vt [building] attaquer à la bombe incendiaire.

firebrand ['faɪəbrænd] n fig exalté m, -e f.

firebreak ['faɪəbreɪk] n [in forest] coupe-feu m inv.

fire brigade n brigade f des pompiers or sapeurs-pompiers.

fire chief n US capitaine m des pompiers or sapeurs-pompiers.

firecracker ['faɪə,krækər] n pétard m.

-fired ['faɪəd] in comp chauffé à ▶ **oil-fired / gas-fired central heating** chauffage central au mazout / gaz.

fire-damaged adj endommagé par le feu.

fire department US = **fire brigade**.

fire door n porte f coupe-feu.

fire drill n exercice m de sécurité (en cas d'incendie).

fire-eater n [in circus] cracheur m de feu ; fig personne f belliqueuse, bagarreur m, -euse f.

fire engine n voiture f de pompiers.

fire escape n escalier m de secours or d'incendie.

fire exit n sortie f de secours.

fire extinguisher n extincteur m.

firefight ['faɪəfaɪt] n bataille f armée.

fire fighter n pompier m, sapeur-pompier m (volontaire).

fire fighting ◆ n lutte f contre les incendies. ◆ comp [equipment, techniques] de lutte contre les incendies.

firefly ['faɪəflaɪ] (pl **fireflies**) n luciole f.

fireguard ['faɪəgɑːd] n [for open fire] pare-feu m, garde-feu m.

fire hazard n : all those empty boxes are a fire hazard toutes ces boîtes vides constituent or représentent un risque d'incendie.

firehouse ['faɪəhaʊs] n US caserne f de pompiers.

fire hydrant n bouche f d'incendie.

firelight ['faɪəlaɪt] n lueur f or lumière f du feu.

firelighter ['faɪəlaɪtər] n allume-feu m.

fireman ['faɪəmən] (pl **firemen** [-mən]) n **1.** pompier m, sapeur-pompier m **2.** RAIL chauffeur m de locomotive.

fire master UK, **fire chief** US n capitaine m des pompiers.

fireplace ['faɪəpleɪs] n cheminée f.

fire plug n US [fire hydrant] bouche f d'incendie.

firepower ['faɪə,paʊər] n puissance f de feu.

fireproof ['faɪəpruːf] ◆ adj [door, safe] à l'épreuve du feu ; [clothing, toys] ininflammable ; [dish] allant au feu. ◆ vt ignifuger, rendre ininflammable.

fire-raiser n pyromane mf, incendiaire mf.

fire-retardant adj ignifuge.

fire service = **fire brigade**.

fireside ['faɪəsaɪd] n coin m du feu.

fire station n caserne f de pompiers.

firestorm ['faɪəstɔːm] n tempête f de feu.

fire truck n US voiture f de pompiers.

firewall ['faɪəwɔːl] n COMPUT pare-feu m.

fire warden n [in forest] guetteur m d'incendie.

firewood ['faɪəwʊd] n bois m à brûler ; [for use in home] bois m de chauffage.

firework ['faɪəwɜːk] n pièce f d'artifice ▶ **firework** or **fireworks display** feu m d'artifice.

firing ['faɪərɪŋ] ◆ n **1.** (U) MIL tir m **2.** [of piece of pottery] cuisson f, cuite f **3.** inf [dismissal] renvoi m **4.** AUTO [of engine, sparkplug] allumage m. ◆ comp ▶ **firing order** or **sequence** AUTO [of engine] ordre m d'allumage ▶ **firing pin** percuteur m ▶ **firing practice** exercice m de tir ▶ **firing range** champ m de tir.

firing line n MIL ligne f de tir ▶ **to be in the firing line** fig être dans la ligne de tir.

firing squad n peloton m d'exécution.

firm [fɜːm] ◆ n [company] entreprise f ; [of solicitors] étude f ; [of lawyers, barristers, consultants] cabinet m. ◆ adj **1.** [solid, hard - flesh, fruit, mattress, etc.] ferme **2.** [stable, secure - basis] solide ; [- foundations] stable ; COMM & FIN [currency, market, etc.] stable **3.** [strong - handshake, grip, leadership] ferme **4.** [unshakeable, definite - belief, evidence, friendship] solide ; [- view, opinion] déterminé, arrêté ; [- intention, voice, agreement, offer] ferme ; [- date] définitif. ◆ adv ▶ **to stand firm on sthg** ne pas céder sur qqch. ◆ vt ▶ **to firm the soil** tasser le sol. ◆ vi = **firm up** (vi). ❖ **firm up** ◆ vt sep [make firm - muscles, prices] raffermir. ◆ vi [muscles, prices] se raffermir.

firmly ['fɜːmlɪ] adv **1.** [securely - hold, grasp sthg] fermement ; [- closed, secured] bien **2.** [say, deny, refuse, deal with] fermement, avec fermeté.

firmness ['fɜːmnɪs] n **1.** [hardness - of flesh, fruit, mattress] fermeté f **2.** [stability - of basis] solidité f ; [- of foundations] stabilité f ; COMM & FIN [of currency, market, prices] stabilité f **3.** [strength - of grip, character, belief] fermeté f **4.** [of voice, denial, refusal] fermeté f.

firmware ['fɜːmweər] n micrologiciels mpl / a piece of firmware un micrologiciel.

first [fɜːst] ◆ det **1.** [in series] premier / the first six months les six premiers mois / Louis the First Louis Premier or Iᵉʳ / I'm first je suis or c'est moi le premier / I don't know the first thing about cars je n'y connais absolument rien en voitures / I'll pick you up first thing (in the morning) je passerai te chercher demain matin à la première heure / there's a first time for everything il y a un début à tout **2.** [immediately] tout de suite / first thing after lunch tout de suite après le déjeuner **3.** [most important - duty, concern] premier / the first priority la priorité des priorités / first things first! prenons les choses dans l'ordre ! ◆ adv **1.** [before the others - arrive, leave, speak] le premier, la première, en premier / you go first vas-y en premier / women and children first les femmes et les enfants d'abord ▶ **to come first a)** [in race] arriver premier **b)** [in exam] avoir la première place, être premier / her career comes first sa carrière passe d'abord or avant tout ▶ **to put one's family first** faire passer sa famille d'abord or avant tout **2.** [firstly, before anything else] d'abord / first, I want to say thank you tout d'abord, je voudrais vous remercier, je voudrais d'abord vous remercier / what should I do first? qu'est-ce que je dois faire en premier ? / I'm a mother first and a wife second je suis une mère avant d'être une épouse **3.** [for the first time] pour la première fois ; [initially] au début **4.** [sooner, rather] : I'd die first plutôt mourir. ◆ n **1.** [before all others] ▶ **the first** le premier (la première) / he was among the first to realise il a été parmi les premiers à s'en rendre compte **2.** [achievement] première f / that's a notable first for France c'est une grande première pour la France **3.** [first time] : the first we heard / knew of it was when... nous en avons entendu parler pour la première fois / l'avons appris quand... **4.** UK UNIV : he got a first in economics ≃ il a eu mention très bien en économie **5.** AUTO première f. ❖ **at first** adv phr au début. ❖ **first and foremost** adv phr d'abord et surtout. ❖ **first of all** adv phr tout d'abord, pour commencer. ❖ **in the first place** adv phr [referring to a past action] d'abord / why did you do it in the first place? et puis d'abord, pourquoi tu as fait ça ? See also **fifth**.

first aid ◆ n (U) [technique] secourisme m ; [attention] premiers soins mpl. ◆ comp [class, manual] de secourisme ▶ **first aid kit** or **box** trousse f à pharmacie.

first-aider [-'eɪdər] n secouriste mf.

First Amendment n  ▶ **the First Amendment** le Premier Amendement *(de la Constitution des États-Unis, garantissant les libertés individuelles du citoyen américain, notamment la liberté d'expression).*

first-born ◆ adj premier-né. ◆ n premier-né *m*, première-née *f*.

first class n **1.** [on train, plane] première classe *f* **2.** [for letter, parcel] tarif *m* normal. ❖ **first-class** ◆ adj **1.** [seat] en première classe ; [compartment, ticket] de première classe **2.** [letter, stamp] au tarif normal **3.** ⬛ UNIV ▶ **to graduate with first-class honours** obtenir son diplôme avec mention très bien **4.** [excellent] = **first-rate**. ◆ adv [travel] en première classe ; [send letter] au tarif normal.

first cousin n cousin *m* germain, cousine *f* germaine.

first-day cover n [for stamp collector] émission *f* premier jour.

first-degree adj **1.** MED [burn] au premier degré **2.** LAW [in US] ▶ **first-degree murder** meurtre *m* avec préméditation.

first-generation adj de première génération.

first grade n ⬛ SCH *classe de l'école primaire correspondant au CP (5-6 ans).*

firsthand [fɜːstˈhænd] ◆ adj [knowledge, information, news] de première main. ◆ adv [hear of sthg] de première main.

first lady n [in US] *femme du président des États-Unis.*

first language n langue *f* maternelle.

first lieutenant n NAUT lieutenant *m* de vaisseau ; ⬛ MIL & AERON lieutenant *m*.

firstly [ˈfɜːstlɪ] adv premièrement.

first mate n NAUT second *m*.

First Minister n ⬛ POL *leader d'un des gouvernements régionaux du Royaume-Uni (Northern Ireland Assembly, Scottish Parliament, Welsh Assembly).*

first name n prénom *m* ▶ **to be on first name terms with sb** appeler qqn par son prénom.

first night ◆ n THEAT première *f*. ◆ comp THEAT ▶ **first night nerves** trac *m (du soir de la première).*

first offender n délinquant *m*, -e *f* primaire.

first officer = **first mate**.

first-past-the-post adj ⬛ POL [system] majoritaire à un tour.

first-rate adj [excellent - wine, meal, restaurant] de première qualité, excellent ; [- idea, performance, student] excellent.

first refusal n préférence *f*.

first school n ⬛ école *f* primaire.

First Secretary n [in Welsh Assembly] président *m* de l'Assemblée galloise.

first-time adj : *first-time (house) buyer* primo-accédant *f* / *first-time visitors to the country* les personnes visitant le pays pour la première fois.

First World War n ▶ **the First World War** la Première Guerre Mondiale.

FIS n abbr of Family Income Supplement.

fiscal [ˈfɪskl] adj [measures, policy, etc.] fiscal ▶ **fiscal year a)** ⬛ [gen] année *f* fiscale **b)** [of company] exercice *m* financier **c)** ADMIN année *f* budgétaire.

fish [fɪʃ] *(pl* fish *or* fishes) ◆ n poisson *m* ▶ **fish and chips** poisson frit avec des frites. ◆ comp [course, restaurant] de poisson. ◆ vi **1.** SPORT pêcher ▶ **to go fishing** aller à la pêche **2.** [search, seek] ▶ **to fish for information** essayer de soutirer des informations ▶ **to fish for compliments** rechercher les compliments. ◆ vt [river, lake, etc.] pêcher dans. ❖ **fish out** vt sep [from water] repêcher. ❖ **fish up** vt sep [from water] repêcher.

fish-and-chip shop n ⬛ *magasin vendant du poisson frit et des frites.*

fishbowl [ˈfɪʃbəʊl] n bocal *m* à poissons.

fishcake [ˈfɪʃkeɪk] n CULIN croquette *f* de poisson.

fisherman [ˈfɪʃəmən] *(pl* fishermen [-mən]) n pêcheur *m*.

fishery [ˈfɪʃərɪ] *(pl* fisheries) n [fishing ground] pêcherie *f* ; [fishing industry] industrie *f* de la pêche.

fish-eye lens n PHOT fish-eye *m*.

fish factory n usine *f* piscicole.

fish farm n établissement *m* piscicole.

fish farming n pisciculture *f*.

fish finger n CULIN bâtonnet *m* de poisson pané.

fish hook n hameçon *m*.

fishing [ˈfɪʃɪŋ] ◆ n pêche *f* / 'no fishing' 'pêche interdite'. ◆ comp [vessel, permit, port, tackle] de pêche ; [season] de la pêche ; [village, party] de pêcheurs.

fishing boat n bateau *m* de pêche.

fishing ground n zone *f* de pêche.

fishing line n ligne *f* de pêche.

fishing rod n canne *f* à pêche, gaule *f*.

fishmonger [ˈfɪʃˌmʌŋgəʳ] n ⬛ poissonnier *m*, -ère *f* / **to go to the fishmonger's** aller à la poissonnerie or chez le poissonnier.

fishnet [ˈfɪʃnet] ◆ n ⬛ [for catching fish] filet *m* (de pêche). ◆ adj ▶ **fishnet stockings / tights** bas *mpl* / collants *mpl* résille. ❖ **fishnets** pl n = **fishnet stockings / tights**.

fish sauce n sauce *f* de poisson, nam pla *m*.

fish slice n pelle *f* à poisson.

fish stick ⬛ = **fish finger**.

fish tank n [in house] aquarium *m* ; [on fish farm] vivier *m*.

fishwife [ˈfɪʃwaɪf] *(pl* fishwives [-waɪvz]) n poissonnière *f*, marchande *f* de poisson.

fishwrap, fish wrapper n ⬛ inf [bad newspaper] torchon *m*.

fishy [ˈfɪʃɪ] *(compar* fishier, *superl* fishiest) adj **1.** [smell] de poisson **2.** inf [suspicious] louche.

fission [ˈfɪʃn] n PHYS fission *f* ; BIOL scissiparité *f*.

fissure [ˈfɪʃəʳ] ◆ n [crevice, crack] fissure *f* ; *fig* fissure *f*, brèche *f*. ◆ vi se fissurer, se fendre.

fist [fɪst] n poing *m*.

fistfight [ˈfɪstfaɪt] n bagarre *f* aux poings ▶ **to have a fistfight with sb** se battre aux poings contre qqn.

fisticuffs [ˈfɪstɪkʌfs] n (U) hum bagarre *f*.

fit [fɪt] ◆ adj *(compar* fitter, *superl* fittest) **1.** [suitable] convenable / *that dress isn't fit to wear* cette robe n'est pas mettable / *fit to eat* **a)** [edible] mangeable

b) [not poisonous] comestible / *fit to drink* [water] potable / *a meal fit for a king* un repas digne d'un roi / *she's not a fit mother* c'est une mère indigne / *that's all he's fit for* c'est tout ce qu'il mérite ▸ **to think** or **to see fit to do sthg** trouver or juger bon de faire qqch / *do as you see* or *think fit* fais comme tu penses or juges bon **2.** *inf* [ready] : *to be fit to drop* être mort de fatigue / *I feel fit to burst* je me sens prêt à éclater ▸ **to be fit to be tied** US [extremely angry] : *I was fit to be tied* j'étais furieux **3.** [healthy] en forme ▸ **to get fit** UK retrouver la forme / *the patient is not fit enough to be discharged* le patient n'est pas en état de quitter l'hôpital ▸ **to be as fit as a fiddle** se porter comme un charme. ◆ n **1.** [size] : *it's a perfect fit* **a)** [item of clothing] cela me / vous, etc. va à merveille **b)** [fridge, stove, piece of furniture] cela s'adapte parfaitement **c)** [two interlocking pieces] cela s'emboîte bien **2.** MED [of apoplexy, epilepsy, hysterics] crise *f* / *fit of coughing* or *coughing fit* quinte *f* de toux ▸ **to have a fit** MED avoir une crise / *she'll have a fit when she finds out* *fig* elle va faire une crise quand elle le saura ▸ **to throw a fit** *inf* piquer une crise **3.** [outburst - of anger] mouvement *m*, accès *m*, moment *m* ; [- of depression] crise *f* ; [- of pique, generosity] moment *m* / *he did it in a fit of rage* il a fait cela dans un mouvement de rage / *he had us all in fits* il nous a fait hurler or mourir de rire / *to get a fit of the giggles* être pris d'un or piquer un fou rire. ◆ vt (UK *pt & pp* fitted ; US *pt & pp* fit, *cont* fitting) **1.** [be of the correct size for] : *those trousers fit you better than the other ones* ce pantalon te va mieux que l'autre / *none of the keys fitted the lock* aucune des clés n'entrait dans la serrure / *the nut doesn't fit the bolt* l'écrou n'est pas de la même taille que le boulon **2.** [correspond to, match - description] correspondre à / *to make the punishment fit the crime* adapter le châtiment au crime ▸ **to fit the bill** faire l'affaire **3.** [make suitable for] : *what do you think fits you for the job?* en quoi estimez-vous correspondre au profil de l'emploi ? **4.** [install - lock, door, window, etc.] installer ; [- carpet] poser / *to fit a key in a lock* engager or mettre une clé dans une serrure **5.** [attach, fix on] fixer **6.** [equip] équiper ▸ **to fit sthg with sthg** équiper qqch de qqch. ◆ vi (UK *pt & pp* fitted ; US *pt & pp* fit, *cont* fitting) **1.** [be of the correct size] : *the dress doesn't fit* la robe ne lui / me, etc. va pas / *this lid / key doesn't fit* ce couvercle / cette clé n'est pas le bon / la bonne / *we won't all fit round one table* nous ne tiendrons pas tous autour d'une table **2.** [correspond, match - description] correspondre / *it all fits* tout concorde ▸ **to fit with sthg** correspondre à qqch. ❖ **fit in** ◆ vi **1.** [go in space available] tenir / *we won't all fit in* nous ne tiendrons pas tous **2.** [in company, group, etc.] s'intégrer / *I feel that I don't fit in* j'ai l'impression de ne pas être à ma place ▸ **to fit in with a)** [statement] correspondre à **b)** [plans, arrangements] cadrer avec **c)** [colour scheme] s'accorder avec. ◆ vt sep **1.** [install] installer **2.** [find room for - clothes in suitcase] faire entrer / *how on earth are you going to fit everyone in?* [in room, car, etc.] comment diable vas-tu réussir à faire tenir tout le monde ? **3.** [find time for - patient] prendre ; [- friend] trouver du temps pour. ❖ **fit into** ◆ vt insep [furniture into room, clothes into suitcase, etc.] entrer dans, tenir dans ; [people into room, car] tenir dans ; [piece into another] s'emboîter dans. ❖ vt sep ▸ **to fit sthg into sthg** faire entrer or tenir qqch dans qqch.

FITB MESSAGING written abbr of **fill in the blank**.

fitful ['fɪtfʊl] adj [sleep] intermittent / *attendance has been fitful* les gens ne sont pas venus régulièrement.

fitfully ['fɪtfʊlɪ] adv [work] par à-coups ; [attend] irrégulièrement ; [sleep] de manière intermittente.

fitment ['fɪtmənt] n UK [in bathroom, kitchen, etc.] élément *m* démontable.

fitness ['fɪtnɪs] ◆ n **1.** [health] forme *f* physique **2.** [suitability - of person for job] aptitude *f*. ◆ comp ▸ **fitness centre** UK club *m* de mise en forme ▸ **fitness freak** *inf* fana *mf* d'exercice physique ▸ **fitness training** entraînement *m* physique.

fitted ['fɪtɪd] adj **1.** [jacket] ajusté **2.** UK [made to measure] : *the house has fitted carpets in every room* il y a de la moquette dans toutes les pièces de la maison ▸ **fitted sheet** drap-housse *m* **3.** UK [built-in - cupboard] encastré ▸ **fitted kitchen** cuisine *f* encastrée **4.** [suited] ▸ **to be fitted for sthg / doing sthg** être apte à qqch / à faire qqch.

fitter ['fɪtə] n **1.** [of machine] monteur *m*, -euse *f* ; [of carpet] poseur *m*, -euse *f* **2.** [of clothes] essayeur *m*, -euse *f*.

fitting ['fɪtɪŋ] ◆ adj [suitable - conclusion, remark] approprié ; [- tribute] adéquat ; [socially correct] convenable. ◆ n **1.** [trying on - of clothes] essayage *m* **2.** UK [of shoe] : *have you got it in a wider / narrower fitting?* l'avez-vous en plus large / plus étroit ? ◆ comp ▸ **fitting room** **a)** salon *m* d'essayage **b)** [cubicle] cabine *f* d'essayage. ❖ **fittings** pl n UK ▸ **bathroom fittings** éléments *mpl* de salle de bains ▸ **electrical fittings** appareillage *m* électrique.

-fitting in comp ▸ **close-fitting** or **tight-fitting a)** [item of clothing] moulant **b)** [screwtop lid] qui ferme bien **c)** [lid of saucepan] adapté ▸ **loose-fitting** [item of clothing] ample, large.

fittingly ['fɪtɪŋlɪ] adv [dressed] convenablement.

fit-up n UK *crime sl* coup *m* monté.

five [faɪv] ◆ n [number, numeral, playing card] cinq *m* / *five times table* table *f* des cinq / *I'm waiting for a number five* (bus) j'attends le (bus numéro) cinq / *he's five* [image] avoir cinq ans / *it's five to / past five* il est cinq heures moins cinq / cinq heures cinq / *to get five out of ten* avoir cinq sur dix / *a table for five* une table pour cinq (personnes). ◆ det cinq / *trains leave at five minutes to the hour* le train part toutes les heures à moins cinq / *to be five years old* avoir cinq ans. ◆ pron cinq / *there are five (of them)* **a)** [people] ils sont cinq **b)** [objects] il y en a cinq.

five and dime, five and ten n US bazar *m*, supérette *f*.

five-a-side UK ◆ n SPORT football *m* à dix. ◆ comp SPORT ▸ **five-a-side football** football *m* à dix.

five-day week n semaine *f* de cinq jours.

fivefold ['faɪvfəʊld] ◆ adj [increase] au quintuple. ◆ adv par cinq, au quintuple.

five-o'clock shadow n barbe *f* d'un jour, barbe *f* naissante.

fiver ['faɪvə] n *inf* [five pounds] billet *m* de cinq livres ; [five dollars] billet *m* de cinq dollars.

five-spice powder n cinq-épices *m*.

five-star adj [hotel] cinq étoiles.

five-year adj [plan] quinquennal.

fix [fɪks] ◆ vt **1.** [fasten in position - mirror, sign] fixer ; [attention, gaze] fixer ; [sthg in mind] inscrire, graver **2.** [set - date, price, rate, limit] fixer ; [- meeting place] convenir de **3.** [arrange, sort out] s'occuper de **4.** *inf* [settle a score with] s'occuper de, régler son compte à **5.** US *inf* [prepare - meal, drink] préparer **6.** *inf* [adjust - make-up, tie] arranger **7.** [mend, repair - car, puncture, etc.] réparer **8.** *inf* [race, fight, election, result] truquer ; [interview] arranger ; [jury, official, security guard, etc. - bribe] acheter **9.** AERON & NAUT [position] déterminer **10.** ART & PHOT [drawing, photo] fixer. ◆ n **1.** *inf* [tight spot, predicament] pétrin *m* ▸ **to be in a fix** être dans une mauvaise passe **2.** *drugs sl* dose *f*, fix *m* **3.** AERON & NAUT ▸ **to get a fix on a)** [ship] déterminer la position de **b)** *fig* [get clear idea of] se faire une idée de **4.** *inf* [unfair arrangement] : *the result was a fix* le résultat avait été truqué. ❖ **fix on** ◆ vt sep [attach] fixer. ◆ vt insep [decide on - date, candidate] choisir. ❖ **fix up** ◆ vt sep **1.** [install, erect] mettre en place, installer **2.** inf [arrange - date, meeting] fixer ; [- deal, holiday] organiser, mettre au point **3.** [room] refaire ; [flat, house] refaire, retaper. ◆ vi s'arranger pour que.

fixated [fɪk'seɪtɪd] adj fixé ▶ **to be fixated on sthg** être fixé sur qqch.

fixation [fɪk'seɪʃn] n **1.** PSYCHOL fixation f ▶ **to have a fixation about sthg** faire une fixation sur qqch **2.** CHEM fixation f.

fixed [fɪkst] adj **1.** [immovable - glare] fixe ; [- idea] arrêté ; [- smile] figé / the seats are fixed to the floor les sièges sont fixés au sol **2.** [set, unchangeable - price, rate, plans] fixe ▶ **of no fixed abode** LAW sans domicile fixe ▶ **fixed assets** FIN immobilisations fpl ▶ **fixed capital** FIN capitaux mpl immobilisés ▶ **fixed costs** FIN coûts mpl fixes ▶ **fixed disk** COMPUT disque m non amovible ▶ **fixed-rate mortgage** crédit m immobilier à taux fixe **3.** inf [placed] : how are you fixed for time / money? **a)** [how much] combien de temps / d'argent as-tu ? **b)** [is it sufficient] as-tu suffisamment de temps / d'argent ?

fixedly ['fɪksɪdlɪ] adv [stare] fixement.

fixed-price menu n menu m à prix fixe.

fixer ['fɪksər] n **1.** inf [person] combinard m, -e f **2.** PHOT fixateur m **3.** [adhesive] adhésif m.

fixture ['fɪkstʃər] ◆ n **1.** [in building] installation f fixe ▶ **bathroom fixtures** installations fpl sanitaires / 'fixtures and fittings £2000' 'reprise 2 000 livres' **2.** SPORT rencontre f. ◆ comp ▶ **fixture list** SPORT calendrier m.

fizz [fɪz] ◆ vi [drink] pétiller ; [firework] crépiter. ◆ n **1.** [of drink] pétillement m **2.** [sound] sifflement m **3.** inf [soft drink] boisson f gazeuse ; 🇬🇧 [champagne] champagne m.

fizziness ['fɪzɪnɪs] n [of drink] pétillement m.

fizzle ['fɪzl] ◆ vi [drink] pétiller ; [fire, firework] crépiter. ❖ **fizzle out** vi fig [interest, enthusiasm] tomber ; [plan, project] tomber à l'eau ; [book, film, party, strike, etc.] tourner or partir en eau de boudin ; [career] tourner court.

fizzy ['fɪzɪ] (compar **fizzier**, superl **fizziest**) adj [soft drink] gazeux ; [wine] pétillant, mousseux.

fjord [fjɔːd] = **fiord**.

FL written abbr of Florida.

flab [flæb] n inf [of person] graisse f, lard m ; [in text] délayage m, verbiage m.

flabbergasted ['flæbəɡɑːstɪd] adj inf sidéré.

flabby ['flæbɪ] (compar **flabbier**, superl **flabbiest**) adj inf [arms, stomach] flasque, mou (before vowel or silent 'h' mol, f molle) ; [person] empâté ; fig [argument, speech] qui manque de concision.

flaccid ['flæsɪd] adj flasque.

flag [flæɡ] (pt & pp **flagged**, cont **flagging**) ◆ n **1.** [emblem of country, signal] drapeau m ; [for celebration] banderole f, fanion m ; NAUT pavillon m ▶ **flag of convenience** NAUT pavillon de complaisance **2.** [for charity] badge ou autocollant que l'on obtient lorsque l'on verse de l'argent à une œuvre de charité **3.** [in taxi] : the flag was down / up le taxi était pris / libre **4.** COMPUT drapeau m, fanion m **5.** [paving stone] dalle f **6.** BOT iris m. ◆ vt **1.** [put marker on - page of book] marquer / to flag an error COMPUT indiquer or signaler une erreur par un drapeau or un fanion **2.** [floor] daller. ◆ vi [strength] faiblir ; [energy, enthusiasm, interest, spirits] faiblir, tomber ; [efforts] se relâcher ; [conversation] tomber, s'épuiser. ❖ **flag down** vt sep [taxi, bus, motorist, etc.] faire signe de s'arrêter à. ❖ **flag up** vt sep [identify] marquer.

flag day n **1.** [in UK] jour de quête d'une œuvre de charité **2.** [in US] ▶ **Flag Day** le 14 juin (commémore l'adoption du drapeau américain).

Flag day

En Grande-Bretagne, les **flag days** ont lieu en général le samedi. On fait appel à la générosité des particuliers qui, en contrepartie de leurs dons pour des œuvres de bienfaisance, reçoivent un insigne ou un badge. Aux États-Unis, **Flag Day** commémore l'adoption le 14 juin 1777 de **Stars and Stripes**, l'actuel drapeau américain.

flagged [flæɡd] adj dallé.

flagging ['flæɡɪŋ] adj [enthusiasm, spirits] qui baisse ; [conversation] qui tombe or s'épuise.

flagon ['flæɡən] n [jug] cruche f ; [bottle] bouteille f.

flagpole ['flæɡpəʊl] n mât m.

flagrant ['fleɪɡrənt] adj [injustice, lie, abuse] flagrant.

flagrantly ['fleɪɡrəntlɪ] adv [abuse, disregard, defy, etc.] d'une manière flagrante.

flagship ['flæɡʃɪp] ◆ n NAUT vaisseau m or bâtiment m amiral ; fig [product] tête f de gamme. ◆ comp ▶ **flagship restaurant** restaurant m principal ▶ **flagship store** magasin m phare.

flagstaff ['flæɡstɑːf] = **flagpole**.

flagstone ['flæɡstəʊn] = **flag** (noun).

flag-waving n (U) inf & fig discours mpl cocardiers.

flail [fleɪl] ◆ n AGR fléau m. ◆ vt AGR battre au fléau ; [arms] agiter. ◆ vi [person, limbs] s'agiter violemment. ❖ **flail about** ◆ vi [person, limbs] s'agiter dans tous les sens. ◆ vt sep [arms, legs] battre.

flair [fleər] n **1.** [stylishness] style m **2.** [gift] don m ▶ **to have a flair for sthg** avoir un don pour qqch.

flak [flæk] ◆ n **1.** [gunfire] tir m antiaérien or de DCA **2.** (U) inf & fig [criticism] critiques fpl. ◆ comp ▶ **flak jacket** gilet m pare-balles.

flake [fleɪk] ◆ n **1.** [of snow] flocon m ; [of metal] paillette f ; [of skin] peau f morte ; [of paint] écaille f **2.** 🇺🇸 inf [person] barjo mf. ◆ vi **1.** [plaster] s'effriter, s'écailler ; [paint] s'écailler ; [skin] peler ; [fish] s'émietter **2.** 🇺🇸 inf : she flaked on the meeting elle a raté la réunion. ◆ vt CULIN [fish] émietter ▶ **flaked almonds** amandes fpl effilées. ❖ **flake off** vi = **flake** (vi). ❖ **flake out** vi inf s'écrouler ; [fall asleep] s'endormir.

flaky ['fleɪkɪ] (compar **flakier**, superl **flakiest**) adj **1.** [paint, rock] effrité ▶ **flaky pastry** CULIN pâte f feuilletée **2.** 🇺🇸 inf [person] barjo ; [idea] loufoque.

flambé ['flɑːbe] (pt & pp **flambéed**, cont **flambéing**) ◆ vt flamber. ◆ adj flambé.

flamboyance [flæm'bɔɪəns] n [of style, dress, behaviour, etc.] extravagance f.

flamboyant [flæm'bɔɪənt] adj [behaviour, lifestyle, personality] extravagant ; [colour] éclatant ; [clothes] aux couleurs éclatantes ; pej voyant ; ARCHIT flamboyant.

flamboyantly [flæm'bɔɪəntlɪ] adv de manière extravagante.

flame [fleɪm] ◆ n **1.** [of fire, candle] flamme f ▶ **to be in flames** [building, car] être en flammes **2.** liter [of passion, desire] flamme f. ◆ vi fig [face, cheeks] s'empourprer ; [passion, anger] brûler. ◆ vt **1.** CULIN flamber **2.** [via e-mail] descendre, injurier. ◆ **flame up** vi [fire] s'embraser ; *fig* [person] s'enflammer.

flame-coloured adj ponceau *(inv)*, couleur de feu *(inv)*.

flame-grilled adj CULIN grillé au feu de bois.

flamenco [flə'meŋkəʊ] ◆ n flamenco *m*. ◆ comp [dancer] de flamenco ▶ **flamenco music** flamenco *m*.

flameout ['fleɪmaʊt] n panne *f* de moteur *(d'avion)*.

flameproof ['fleɪmpruːf] adj [clothing] ininflammable, à l'épreuve des flammes ; [dish] allant au feu.

flamethrower ['fleɪmθrəʊə] n lance-flammes *m inv*.

flame war n COMPUT échange *m* d'insultes.

flaming ['fleɪmɪŋ] ◆ n [via e-mail] échange *m* or envoi *m* de propos injurieux. ◆ adj **1.** [sun, sky] embrasé ; [fire] flamboyant **2.** UK *inf* [extremely angry] : *to be in a flaming temper* être d'une humeur massacrante, être furax / *we had a flaming row about it* nous avons eu une belle engueulade là-dessus **3.** *inf* [as intensifier] fichu **4.** *inf & pej* [effeminate] : *a flaming queen* un homo efféminé, une folle. ◆ adv UK *inf* [as intensifier] fichtrement.

flamingo [flə'mɪŋgəʊ] n flamant *m* rose.

flammable ['flæməbl] adj [material, substance] inflammable.

flan [flæn] ◆ n CULIN tarte *f* ; [savoury] quiche *f*. ◆ comp CULIN ▶ **flan case** fond *m* de tarte.

Flanders ['flɑːndəz] n Flandre *f*, Flandres *fpl* / *in Flanders* dans les Flandres, en Flandre.

flange [flændʒ] n [on pipe] bride *f*, collerette *f* ; RAIL [on rail] patin *m*.

flank [flæŋk] ◆ n flanc *m*. ◆ vt **1.** [be on either side of] encadrer **2.** MIL flanquer.

flannel ['flænl] (UK *pt* & *pp* **flannelled**, *cont* **flannelling** ; US *pt* & *pp* **flanneled**, *cont* **flanneling**) ◆ n **1.** TEXT flanelle *f* **2.** UK [for washing] ≃ gant *m* de toilette **3.** (U) UK *inf* [empty words] baratin *m*, blabla *m*, blablabla *m*. ◆ comp TEXT [nightgown, sheet, trousers, suit] en or de flanelle. ◆ vi UK *inf* [use empty words] faire du baratin or du blabla or du blablabla. ◆ **flannels** pl n pantalon *m* en or de flanelle.

flannelette [flænə'let] ◆ n TEXT pilou *m*. ◆ comp TEXT [nightgown, sheet] en or de pilou.

flap [flæp] (*pt* & *pp* **flapped**, *cont* **flapping**) ◆ n **1.** [of sails] claquement *m* ; [of wings] battement *m* **2.** [of counter, desk - hinged] abattant *m* ; [- sliding] rallonge *f* ; [of pocket, tent, envelope] rabat *m* ; [in floor, door] trappe *f* ; [of aircraft] volet *m* (hypersustentateur) **3.** *inf* [panic] panique *f* ▶ **to be in a flap** être dans tous ses états, être paniqué. ◆ vi **1.** [wings] battre ; [sails, shutters, washing, curtains] claquer **2.** *inf* [panic] paniquer, s'affoler. ◆ vt : *the bird flapped its wings* l'oiseau a battu des ailes.

flapjack ['flæpdʒæk] n CULIN [in UK] biscuit *m* à l'avoine ; [in US] *petite crêpe épaisse*.

flare [fleə] ◆ n **1.** [bright flame - of fire, match] flamboiement *m* **2.** [signal] signal *m* lumineux ; [rocket] fusée *f* éclairante **3.** [in clothes] évasement *m*. ◆ vi **1.** [flame, match] flamboyer **2.** [tempers] s'échauffer **3.** [nostrils] frémir **4.** [clothes] s'évaser. ◆ vt [clothes] évaser. ◆ **flares** pl n ▶ **(a pair of) flares** un pantalon à pattes d'éléphant. ◆ **flare up** vi [fire] s'embraser ; *fig* [dispute, quarrel, violence] éclater ; [disease, epidemic, crisis] apparaître, se déclarer ; [person] s'emporter.

flared [fleəd] adj [trousers] à pattes d'éléphant ; [dress] évasé ; [skirt] évasé, à godets.

flare gun n pistolet *m* de détresse, lance-fusées *m inv*.

flash [flæʃ] ◆ n **1.** [of light, diamond] éclat *m* ; [of metal] reflet *m*, éclat *m* ▶ **in a flash** [very quickly] en un éclair, en un clin d'œil **2.** [of news] flash *m* (d'information) **3.** MIL [on uniform] écusson *m* **4.** [of colour] tache *f* **5.** PHOT flash *m* **6.** US *inf* [flashlight] torche *f*. ◆ vi **1.** [light, torch, sign] clignoter ; [diamond] briller, lancer des éclats ▶ **to flash at sb** AUTO faire un appel de phares à qqn **2.** [move fast] filer comme l'éclair, aller à la vitesse de l'éclair / *to flash past* or *by* [time] passer à toute vitesse **3.** UK *inf* [expose o.s.] s'exhiber **4.** US *inf* ▶ **to flash on sth** être inspiré par qqch. ◆ vt **1.** [torch - turn on and off] faire clignoter **2.** [give brief glimpse of - passport, photograph, etc.] montrer rapidement **3.** [news, information] diffuser. ◆ adj *inf* **1.** *pej* = **flashy** **2.** [expensive - looking] chic. ◆ **flash back** vi [in novel, film, etc.] ▶ **to flash back to sth** revenir en arrière sur or faire un flash-back sur qqch.

flashback ['flæʃbæk] n [in novel, film, etc.] flash-back *m inv*, retour *m* en arrière.

flashbulb ['flæʃbʌlb] n PHOT ampoule *f* de flash.

flash card n SCH *carte portant un mot, une image, etc. utilisée dans l'enseignement comme aide à l'apprentissage.*

flashcube ['flæʃkjuːb] n PHOT cube *m* de flash.

flash drive n COMPUT clé *f* USB.

flasher ['flæʃə] n **1.** AUTO [indicator] clignotant *m* **2.** *inf* [person] exhibitionniste *mf*.

flash flood n crue *f* subite.

flash gun n PHOT flash *m*.

flashily ['flæʃɪlɪ] adv *inf & pej* d'une manière tapageuse or tape-à-l'œil, tapageusement.

flashlight ['flæʃlaɪt] n **1.** PHOT ampoule *f* de flash **2.** US [torch] torche *f* électrique, lampe *f* électrique or de poche **3.** [flashing signal] fanal *m*.

flash photography n photographie *f* au flash.

flashpoint ['flæʃpɔɪnt] n **1.** CHEM point *m* d'éclair **2.** *fig* [trouble spot] poudrière *f*.

flashy ['flæʃɪ] adj *inf & pej* [person, car, clothes, taste] tapageur, tape-à-l'œil *(inv)* ; [colour] voyant, criard.

flask [flɑːsk] n PHARM fiole *f* ; CHEM ballon *m* ; [for water, wine] gourde *f*.

flat [flæt] ◆ adj **1.** [countryside, feet, stomach] plat ; [surface] plan ; [roof] plat, en terrasse ; [nose] épaté, camus ; [tyre - deflated] à plat, dégonflé ; [- punctured] crevé ; [ball, balloon] dégonflé **2.** [soft drink, beer, champagne] éventé ▶ **to go flat** [beer, soft drink] s'éventer, perdre ses bulles ; *fig* [monotonous - style, voice] monotone, terne ; [without emotion - voice] éteint ; [stock market, business] au point mort ; [social life] peu animé **3.** [battery] à plat **4.** MUS en dessous du ton ▶ **to be flat a)** [singer] chanter en dessous du ton **b)** [instrumentalist] jouer en dessous du ton / *E flat* mi bémol **5.** [categorical - refusal, denial] catégorique **6.** COMM [rate, fare, fee] fixe. ◆ adv **1.** [categorically] catégoriquement **2.** [exactly] : *in thirty seconds flat* en trente secondes pile **3.** MUS en dessous du ton **4.** PHR **flat broke** *inf* complètement fauché. ◆ n **1.** UK [in house] appartement *m* ▶ **(block of) flats** immeuble *m* (d'habitation) **2.** [of hand, blade] plat *m* **3.** [in horse racing] ▶ **the flat a)** [races] le plat **b)** [season] la saison des courses de plat **4.** MUS bémol *m* **5.** US *inf* [puncture] crevaison *f* ; [punctured tyre] pneu *m* crevé ; [deflated tyre] pneu *m* à plat. ◆ **flats** pl n GEOG ▶ **salt flats** marais *mpl* salants. ◆ **flat out** adv phr : *to work flat out* travailler d'arrache-pied / *to be going flat out* **a)** [car] être à sa vitesse maximale **b)** [driver, runner, horse] être au maximum or à fond.

flat-bed lorry n UK semi-remorque *m* à plateau.

flat-bed scanner n scanner *m* à plat.

flat-bed truck n US = **flat-bed lorry**.

flat cap n casquette f.

flat-chested [-'tʃestɪd] adj : *to be flat-chested* **a)** ne pas avoir de poitrine **b)** *pej* être plat comme une planche à pain or une limande.

flatfish ['flætfɪʃ] n poisson m plat.

flat-footed adj **1.** MED aux pieds plats **2.** *inf* [clumsy] empoté ; [tactless] maladroit, lourdaud **3.** [off guard] ▶ **to catch sb flat-footed** *inf* prendre qqn par surprise.

flat-hunt vi *(usu in progressive)* 🇬🇧 chercher un appartement.

flat-leaf parsley n BOT & CULIN persil m plat.

flatlet ['flætlɪt] n 🇬🇧 studio m.

flatline ['flætlaɪn] vi 🇺🇸 *inf* [die] mourir.

flatly ['flætlɪ] adv **1.** [categorically - deny, refuse] catégoriquement **2.** [without emotion - say, speak] d'une voix éteinte ; [monotonously] avec monotonie.

flatmate ['flætmeɪt] n 🇬🇧 *personne avec qui on partage un appartement.*

flat-pack ◆ n meuble m en kit. ◆ adj ▶ **flat-pack furniture** meubles *mpl* en kit.

flat-packed adj [furniture] en kit.

flat racing n [in horse racing - races] plat m ; [- season] saison f des courses de plat.

flat-screen adj TV & COMPUT à écran plat.

flatten ['flætn] ◆ vt **1.** [path, road, ground] aplanir ; [dough, metal] aplatir ; [animal, person - subj: vehicle] écraser ; [house, village - subj: bulldozer, earthquake] raser ; [crop - subj: wind, storm] écraser, aplatir ; [piece of paper] étaler **2.** *inf* [defeat thoroughly] écraser, battre à plate couture **3.** *inf* [knock to the ground] démolir **4.** *inf* [subdue - person] clouer le bec à **5.** MUS [note] baisser d'un demi-ton, bémoliser. ◆ vi **= flatten out.** ❖ **flatten out** vi **1.** [countryside, hills] s'aplanir **2.** AERON [plane] se redresser ; [pilot] redresser l'appareil. ◆ vt sep [piece of paper] étaler à plat ; [bump, path, road] aplanir.

flatter ['flætər] ◆ vt [subj: person] flatter ; [subj: dress, photo, colour] avantager / *don't flatter yourself!* or *you flatter yourself!* non mais tu rêves ! ◆ vi flatter.

flatterer ['flætərər] n flatteur m, -euse f.

flattering ['flætərɪŋ] adj [remark, person, offer] flatteur ; [picture, colour] avantageux, flatteur ; [dress] seyant.

flattery ['flætərɪ] n *(U)* flatterie f.

flatulence ['flætjʊləns] n flatulence f.

flatulent ['flætjʊlənt] adj flatulent.

flatware ['flætweər] n *(U)* 🇺🇸 [cutlery] couverts *mpl* ; [serving dishes] plats *mpl* ; [plates] assiettes *fpl.*

flaunt [flɔːnt] vt [wealth, beauty] étaler, faire étalage de ; [car, jewellery] faire parade de, exhiber ▶ **to flaunt o.s.** s'afficher.

flautist ['flɔːtɪst] n 🇬🇧 MUS flûtiste mf.

flavonoid n flavonoïde m.

flavor 🇺🇸 = **flavour.**

flavour 🇬🇧, **flavor** 🇺🇸 ['fleɪvər] ◆ n [of food, drink] goût m ; [of ice-cream, tea] parfum m / *chocolate / coffee flavour ice-cream* glace au chocolat / au café. ◆ comp ▶ **flavour enhancers** agents *mpl* de sapidité. ◆ vt [with spices, herbs] assaisonner ; [with fruit, alcohol] parfumer.

-flavoured ['fleɪvəd] in comp ▶ **chocolate-flavoured** au chocolat ▶ **vanilla-flavoured** à la vanille.

flavouring 🇬🇧, **flavoring** 🇺🇸 ['fleɪvərɪŋ] n CULIN [savoury] assaisonnement m ; [sweet] parfum m, arôme m.

flavourless 🇬🇧, **flavorless** 🇺🇸 ['fleɪvələs] adj sans goût, insipide.

flavoursome 🇬🇧, **flavorsome** 🇺🇸 ['fleɪvəsəm] adj [food] savoureux.

flaw [flɔː] ◆ n [in material, plan, character] défaut m ; LAW vice m de forme. ◆ vt [object] endommager ; [sb's character, beauty] altérer.

flawed [flɔːd] adj imparfait.

flawless ['flɔːlɪs] adj parfait.

flax [flæks] n lin m.

flaxen ['flæksn] adj [hair] blond pâle or filasse.

flay [fleɪ] vt [animal] dépouiller, écorcher ; [person] fouetter ; *fig* [criticize] éreinter ▶ **to flay sb alive** faire la peau à qqn.

flea [fliː] ◆ n puce f / *to have fleas* avoir des puces ▶ **to send sb off with a flea in his / her ear a)** *inf* [dismiss] envoyer balader qqn **b)** [scold] passer un savon à qqn. ◆ comp ▶ **flea circus** cirque m de puces savantes ▶ **flea powder** poudre f antipuce.

fleabite ['fliːbaɪt] n piqûre f or morsure f de puce ; *fig* [trifle] broutille f.

flea-bitten adj couvert de puces ; *fig* [shabby] miteux.

flea collar n collier m antipuces.

flea market n marché m aux puces.

fleapit ['fliːpɪt] n *inf* cinéma m or théâtre m miteux.

fleck [flek] ◆ n [of colour] moucheture f, tacheture f ; [of sunlight] moucheture f ; [of dust] particule f. ◆ vt [with colour] moucheter, tacheter ; [with sunlight] moucheter / *hair flecked with grey* cheveux *mpl* grisonnants.

fled [fled] pt & pp ⟶ **flee.**

fledgeling ['fledʒlɪŋ] ◆ n **1.** [young bird] oisillon m **2.** *fig* novice mf, débutant m, -e f. ◆ comp [company, industry, political party, etc.] naissant.

flee [fliː] *(pt & pp fled [fled])* ◆ vi s'enfuir, fuir ▶ **to flee from sb / sthg** fuir qqn / qqch. ◆ vt [person, danger, temptation] fuir ; [country, town] s'enfuir de.

fleece [fliːs] ◆ n **1.** [of sheep] toison f **2.** [sheepskin] peau f de mouton **3.** [polar fleece] (laine f) polaire m **4.** [jacket] veste f en (laine) polaire ; [sweat] sweat m en (laine) polaire. ◆ comp **1.** [sheepskin] en peau de mouton **2.** [polar fleece] en laine polaire. ◆ vt *inf* [cheat] escroquer.

fleece-lined adj [with sheepskin] doublé en peau de mouton ; [with polar fleece] doublé en laine polaire.

fleecy ['fliːsɪ] adj [material] laineux ; [clouds] cotonneux.

fleet [fliːt] ◆ n **1.** NAUT flotte f ; [smaller] flottille f **2.** [of buses, taxis] parc m. ◆ adj *liter* rapide ▶ **fleet of foot** aux pieds ailés.

fleet-footed adj *liter* au pied léger.

fleeting ['fliːtɪŋ] adj [memory] fugace ; [beauty, pleasure] passager.

fleetingly ['fliːtɪŋlɪ] adv [glimpse] rapidement.

Fleet Street [fliːt-] pr n *rue de Londres, dont le nom sert à désigner les grands journaux britanniques.*

Fleet Street

Cette rue de la City est traditionnellement associée à la presse. Même si, aujourd'hui, de nombreux journaux se sont établis dans d'autres quartiers de Londres, notamment les Docklands, **Fleet Street** continue à désigner le monde du journalisme.

Fleming ['flemɪŋ] n Flamand m, -e f.

Flemish ['flemɪʃ] ◆ n LING flamand *m*. ◆ pl n ▶ **the Flemish** les Flamands *mpl*. ◆ adj flamand.

flesh [fleʃ] n **1.** [of person, animal, fruit] chair *f* **2.** RELIG chair *f* **3.** [colour] couleur *f* chair. ◆◆ **flesh out** ◆ vt sep [essay, report, etc.] étoffer. ◆ vi [person] s'étoffer, prendre de la carrure.

flesh-coloured adj [tights] couleur chair.

flesh wound n blessure *f* superficielle ou légère.

fleshy ['fleʃɪ] (*compar* **fleshier,** *superl* **fleshiest**) adj [person] bien en chair ; [part of the body, fruit, leaf] charnu.

flew [fluː] pt —→ **fly.**

flex [fleks] ◆ vt [one's arms, knees] fléchir ▶ **to flex one's muscles a)** *lit* bander or faire jouer ses muscles **b)** *fig* faire étalage de sa force. ◆ n [wire] fil *m* ; [heavy-duty] câble *m*.

flexibility [ˌfleksə'bɪlətɪ] n [of object] flexibilité *f*, souplesse *f* ; *fig* [of plan, approach] flexibilité *f* ; [of person's character] souplesse *f*.

flexible ['fleksəbl] adj flexible, souple ; *fig* [approach, plans, timetable, etc.] flexible ; [person's character] souple ; [as regards timing, arrangements] arrangeant / *flexible working hours* horaires *mpl* variables ▶ **flexible response** MIL riposte *f* graduée.

flexitime ['fleksɪtaɪm] n *(U)* horaires *m* à la carte or flexibles ▶ **to be on** or **to work flexitime** avoir des horaires à la carte.

flextime ['flekstaɪm] = **flexitime.**

flick [flɪk] ◆ n **1.** [with finger] chiquenaude *f* ; [with wrist] petit or léger mouvement *m* ; [with tail, whip, duster] petit or léger coup *m* **2.** US *inf* [film] film *m*. ◆ vt [switch] appuyer sur. ◆◆ **flicks** pl n *inf & dated* ▶ **the flicks** le ciné, le cinoche. ◆◆ **flick over** vt sep [pages of book, newspaper, etc.] tourner rapidement. ◆◆ **flick through** vt insep [book, newspaper] feuilleter.

flicker ['flɪkər] ◆ vi [flame, light] vaciller, trembler ; [eyelids, TV screen] trembler. ◆ n [of flame, light] vacillement *m*, tremblement *m* ; [of eyelids, TV screen] tremblement *m*.

flicker-free adj [screen] anti-scintillements *(inv)*.

flick knife n (couteau *m* à) cran *m* d'arrêt.

flier ['flaɪər] n **1.** AERON [pilot] aviateur *m*, -trice *f* **2.** ORNITH : *the heron is an ungainly flier* le héron a un vol peu élégant **3.** *inf* SPORT [start to race] départ *m* lancé ; [false start] faux départ *m* ▶ **to get a flier** [good start] partir comme un boulet de canon **4.** *inf* [fall] vol *m* plané **5.** [leaflet] prospectus *m*.

flies [flaɪz] pl n **1.** = **fly 2.** THEAT dessus *mpl*, cintres *mpl*.

flight [flaɪt] n **1.** [flying] vol *m* ▶ **to be in flight** être en vol **2.** [journey - of bird, spacecraft, plane, missile] vol *m* **3.** AERON [journey in plane - by passenger] voyage *m* ; [- by pilot] vol *m* ; [plane itself] vol *m* **4.** [group of birds] vol *m*, volée *f* ; [group of aircraft] flotte *f* aérienne **5.** [fleeing] fuite *f* **6.** [of stairs] ▶ **flight (of) stairs** or **steps** escalier *m* **7.** *fig* : *a flight of the imagination* une envolée de l'imagination / *it was just a flight of fancy* ce n'était qu'une idée folle **8.** [on arrow, dart] penne *f*, empennage *m* **9.** PHR ▶ **to be in the first** or **top flight** faire partie de l'élite.

flight attendant n [male] steward *m* ; [female] hôtesse *f* de l'air.

flight crew n équipage *m* (d'un avion).

flight deck n [of aircraft] poste *m* or cabine *f* de pilotage, habitacle *m* ; [of aircraft carrier] pont *m* d'envol.

flight path n trajectoire *f* de vol.

flight recorder n enregistreur *m* de vol.

flight simulator n simulateur *m* de vol.

flighty ['flaɪtɪ] (*compar* **flightier,** *superl* **flightiest**) adj inconstant ; [in romantic relationships] volage, inconstant.

flimflam ['flɪmflæm] US *inf* ◆ n [nonsense] foutaises *fpl* ; [deceitful talk] blabla *m*, baratin *m*. ◆ vt rouler, escroquer.

flimsily ['flɪmzɪlɪ] adv [built, constructed] d'une manière peu solide, peu solidement.

flimsy ['flɪmzɪ] (*compar* **flimsier,** *superl* **flimsiest**) ◆ adj **1.** [material] fin, léger ; [clothes, shoes] léger ; [sthg built] peu solide ; [paper] peu résistant, fragile ; [toys, books] fragile **2.** [argument, case, excuse, etc.] léger. ◆ n [paper] papier *m* pelure ; [with typing on it] double *m* sur pelure.

flinch [flɪntʃ] vi **1.** [wince, with pain] tressaillir **2.** [shy away] : *to flinch from one's duty / obligations* reculer devant son devoir / ses obligations.

fling [flɪŋ] (*pt & pp* **flung** [flʌŋ]) ◆ vt lancer, jeter. ◆ n **1.** *inf* [attempt, try] ▶ **to have a fling at sthg** essayer de faire qqch **2.** [wild behaviour] ▶ **to have a fling with sb** *inf* [affair] avoir une aventure avec qqn **3.** [dance] *danse traditionnelle écossaise*. ◆◆ **fling about** vt sep [objects] lancer. ◆◆ **fling away** vt sep [discard] jeter (de côté). ◆◆ **fling back** vt sep [ball] renvoyer ; [curtains] ouvrir brusquement. ◆◆ **fling off** vt sep [coat, dress] jeter. ◆◆ **fling out** vt sep [object] jeter, balancer ; [person] mettre à la porte, jeter dehors. ◆◆ **fling up** vt sep [throw - in air] jeter en l'air ; [- to sb in higher position] lancer, envoyer.

flint [flɪnt] ◆ n [substance] silex *m* ; [for cigarette lighter] pierre *f* à briquet. ◆ comp [tools, axe] en silex.

flinty ['flɪntɪ] (*compar* **flintier,** *superl* **flintiest**) adj [rocks, soil] siliceux ; [wine] minéral ; *fig* [heart] de pierre.

flip [flɪp] (*pt & pp* **flipped,** *cont* **flipping**) ◆ n **1.** [little push, flick] petit coup *m* **2.** [turning movement] demi-tour *m (sur soi-même)* ; [somersault - in diving] saut *m* périlleux ; [- in gymnastics] flip-flap *m* **3.** ▶ **to have a (quick) flip through a magazine** feuilleter un magazine **4.** [drink] *boisson alcoolisée à l'œuf* **5.** US *inf* [attitude] petite boucle *f*. ◆ vt **1.** [move with a flick] donner un petit coup sec à **2.** [throw] envoyer, balancer **3.** PHR ▶ **to flip one's lid** *inf* = **flip (vi).** ◆ vi *inf* **1.** [become ecstatic] être emballé, flasher ▶ **to flip over sthg** être emballé par qqch, flasher sur qqch **2.** [get angry] exploser, piquer une crise ; [go mad] devenir dingue, perdre la boule ; [under effects of stress] craquer. ◆ adj *inf* [flippant] désinvolte. ◆ interj *inf* mince, zut. ◆◆ **flip out** vi *inf* [get angry] exploser, piquer une crise ; [become ecstatic] être emballé, flasher. ◆◆ **flip over** vt sep [turn over - stone, person] retourner ; [- page] tourner. ◆ vi [turn over - plane, boat, fish] se retourner ; [- page] tourner tout seul. ◆◆ **flip through** vt insep [magazine] feuilleter.

flip chart n tableau *m* à feuilles.

flip-flop ◆ n **1.** [sandal] tong *f* **2.** ELECTRON bascule *f* **3.** US *inf* [in attitude, policy] volte-face *f inv*, revirement *m*. ◆ vi US *inf* faire volte-face, retourner sa veste.

flip-flopper ['flɪpflɒp] n homme ou femme politique qui change d'opinions politiques.

flippant ['flɪpənt] adj désinvolte.

flippantly ['flɪpəntlɪ] adv avec désinvolture.

flipper ['flɪpər] n **1.** [for swimming] palme *f* **2.** [of seal, penguin] nageoire *f*.

flip phone n téléphone *m* à clapet.

flipping ['flɪpɪŋ] UK *inf* ◆ adj [as intensifier] fichu. ◆ adv [as intensifier] fichtrement.

flip side n *inf* [of record] face *f* B ; *fig* [disadvantage] inconvénient *m*.

flip top ◆ n [of packet] couvercle *m* à rabat. ◆ adj [mobile phone] à clapet.

flirt [flɜːt] ◆ vi **1.** [sexually] flirter **/** *he flirts with everybody* il flirte avec tout le monde **2.** *fig* : *to flirt with danger / death* frayer avec le danger / la mort. ◆ n **1.** [person] charmeur *m*, -euse *f* **2.** [act] badinage *m* amoureux.

flirtation [flɜːˈteɪʃn] n badinage *m* amoureux.

flirtatious [flɜːˈteɪʃəs] adj charmeur.

flit [flɪt] (*pt & pp* **flitted**, *cont* **flitting**) ◆ vi **1.** [bird, bat, etc.] voleter **2.** 🇬🇧 *regional* [move house] déménager. ◆ n 🇬🇧 *regional* déménagement *m*.

float [fləʊt] ◆ n **1.** [for fishing line] bouchon *m*, flotteur *m* ; [on raft, seaplane, fishing net, in carburettor, toilet cistern] flotteur *m* ; [for swimming] planche *f* **2.** [vehicle -in parade, carnival] char *m* ; [-for milk delivery] voiture *f* du livreur de lait **3.** [cash advance] avance *f* ; [business loan] prêt *m* de lancement ; [money in cash register] encaisse *f* **4.** [drink] *soda avec une boule de glace.* ◆ vi **1.** [on water] flotter ; [be afloat -boat] flotter, être à flot **2.** [in the air -balloon, piece of paper] voltiger ; [-mist, clouds] flotter ; [-ghost, apparition] flotter, planer **3.** [currency] flotter. ◆ vt **1.** [put on water -ship, raft, platform] mettre à flot ; [-paper ship, toy] faire flotter **2.** [launch -company] lancer, créer ; FIN [bonds, share issue] émettre **3.** FIN [currency] faire flotter **4.** *fig* [idea] lancer, proposer ; [plan] proposer. ◈ **float about** 🇬🇧, **float around** vi *inf* [rumours] courir ; [unoccupied person] traîner. ◈ **float off** vt sep [free -boat] remettre à flot. ◆ vi **1.** [be carried away -log, ship, etc.] partir or être emporté au fil de l'eau ; [in the air -balloon, piece of paper] s'envoler **2.** *fig* [person] s'envoler, disparaître.

floater [ˈfləʊtər] n 🇺🇸 [floating voter] (électeur *m*) indécis *m*, électrice *f* indécise.

float glass n verre *m* flotté.

floating [ˈfləʊtɪŋ] ◆ adj **1.** [on water] flottant **▸ floating crane** ponton-grue *m* **2.** **▸ floating voters** (électeurs *mpl*) indécis *mpl* **3.** FIN [currency, exchange rate] flottant ; [capital] disponible **4.** COMPUT [accent] flottant **▸ floating point** virgule *f* flottante. ◆ n **1.** [putting on the water] mise *f* à flot ; [getting afloat again] remise *f* à flot **2.** [of new company] lancement *m*, création *f* **3.** [of currency] flottement *m* **4.** [of new idea, plan] proposition *f*.

floating floor n parquet *m* flottant.

flock [flɒk] ◆ n **1.** [of sheep] troupeau *m* ; [of birds] vol *m*, volée *f* ; *inf* [of people] foule *f* ; RELIG ouailles *fpl* ; TEXT bourre *f* **▸ flock wallpaper** papier *m* tontisse. ◆ vi aller or venir en foule or en masse, affluer. ◈ **flock together** vi [sheep] se regrouper, s'attrouper.

floe [fləʊ] n = **ice floe**.

flog [flɒg] (*pt & pp* **flogged**, *cont* **flogging**) vt **1.** [beat] fouetter **2.** *inf* [sell] vendre. ◈ **flog off** vt sep 🇬🇧 *inf* [sell off] bazarder.

flogging [ˈflɒgɪŋ] n [beating] flagellation *f* ; LAW supplice *m* du fouet or de la flagellation.

flood [flʌd] ◆ n **1.** *lit* inondation *f* **▸ the Flood** le Déluge **▸ to be in flood** [river] être en crue **▸ flood warning** avis *m* de crue **2.** *fig* [of applications, letters, offers] déluge *m* ; [of light] flot *m* **▸ to be in floods of tears** pleurer à chaudes larmes **3.** = **flood tide 4.** = **floodlight**. ◆ vt **1.** [unintentionally] inonder ; [deliberately] inonder, noyer **2.** AUTO [carburettor] noyer **3.** [river - subj: rain] faire déborder **4.** (*usu passive*) *fig* [person - with letters, replies] inonder, submerger **/** *to be flooded with applications / letters* être submergé de demandes / lettres **/** *to be flooded in light* [room, valley] être inondé de lumière **5.** COMM **▸ to flood the market** inonder le marché. ◆ vi **1.** [river] être en crue, déborder **2.** [land, area] être inondé **3.** *fig* [move in large quantities] : *refugees are still flooding across the border* les réfugiés continuent à passer la frontière en foule or en masse **/** *light was flooding through the window* la lumière

entrait à flots par la fenêtre. ◈ **flood back** vi [people] revenir en foule or en masse ; [strength, memories] revenir à flots, affluer. ◈ **flood in** vi [people] entrer en foule or en masse, affluer ; [applications, letters] affluer ; [light, sunshine] entrer à flots. ◈ **flood out** ◆ vt sep inonder **/** *hundreds of families have been flooded out* [from homes] l'inondation a forcé des centaines de familles à quitter leurs maisons. ◆ vi [people] sortir en foule or en masse ; [words] sortir à flots ; [ideas] se bousculer, affluer.

flood-damaged adj abîmé or endommagé par les eaux.

floodgate [ˈflʌdgeɪt] n vanne *f*, porte *f* d'écluse **▸ to open the floodgates** *fig*: *the new law will open the floodgates to all kinds of fraudulent practices* cette nouvelle loi est la porte ouverte à toutes sortes de pratiques frauduleuses.

flooding [ˈflʌdɪŋ] n (*U*) inondation *f* ; [of submarine's tanks] remplissage *m*.

floodlight [ˈflʌdlaɪt] (*pt & pp* **floodlit** [-lɪt] or **floodlighted**) ◆ n [lamp] projecteur *m* ; [light] lumière *f* des projecteurs. ◆ vt [football pitch, stage] éclairer (aux projecteurs) ; [building] illuminer *f*.

floodlit [ˈflʌdlɪt] adj [match, stage] éclairé (aux projecteurs) ; [building] illuminé.

flood tide n marée *f* montante.

floor [flɔːr] ◆ n **1.** [ground -gen] sol *m* ; [-wooden] plancher *m*, parquet *m* ; [-tiled] carrelage *m* **/** *to put sthg / to sit on the floor* poser qqch / s'asseoir par terre **2.** [bottom part -of lift, cage] plancher *m* ; [-of sea, ocean] fond *m* **3.** [storey] étage *m* **/** *on the second floor* **a)** 🇬🇧 au deuxième étage **b)** 🇺🇸 au premier étage **4.** [for dancing] piste *f* (de danse) **5.** [in parliament, assembly, etc.] enceinte *f* ; [of stock exchange] parquet *m*. ◆ vt **1.** [building, house] faire le sol de ; [with linoleum] poser le revêtement de sol dans ; [with parquet] poser le parquet or plancher dans, parqueter ; [with tiles] poser le carrelage dans, carreler **2.** *inf* [opponent] terrasser **3.** *inf* [puzzle, baffle] dérouter ; [surprise, amaze] abasourdir.

floor area n [of room, office] surface *f*.

floorboard [ˈflɔːbɔːd] n lame *f* (de parquet).

floor cleaner n (produit *m*) nettoyant *m* pour sols.

floor cloth n serpillière *f* ; [old rag] chiffon *m*.

floor covering n [linoleum, fitted carpet] revêtement *m* de sol ; [rug] tapis *m*.

flooring [ˈflɔːrɪŋ] n (*U*) **1.** [act] : *the flooring has still to be done* il reste encore le plancher à faire **2.** [material] revêtement *m* de sol.

floor lamp n 🇺🇸 lampadaire *m*.

floor model n modèle *m* d'exposition.

floor plan n plan *m*.

floor sample n 🇺🇸 modèle *m* d'exposition.

floor show n spectacle *m* de cabaret.

floorspace [ˈflɔːspeɪs] n espace *m*.

floorwalker [ˈflɔːˌwɔːkər] n ≃ chef *m* de rayon.

floozie, floozy [ˈfluːzɪ] (*pl* **floozies**) n *inf* traînée *f*.

flop [flɒp] (*pt & pp* **flopped**, *cont* **flopping**) ◆ vi **1.** [fall slackly - head, arm, etc.] tomber ; [- person] s'affaler, s'effondrer **2.** *inf* [attempt, idea, recipe] louper ; [fail - play, film] faire un four or un bide ; [- actor] faire un bide. ◆ n *inf* [failure] fiasco *m*, bide *m*.

floppy [ˈflɒpɪ] (*compar* **floppier**, *superl* **floppiest**) ◆ adj [ears, tail, plant] pendant ; [collar, brim of hat] mou (*before vowel or silent 'h'* **mol**, *f* **molle**) ; [trousers, sweater] flottant, large. ◆ n COMPUT disquette *f*.

floppy disk n COMPUT disquette *f*.

flora [ˈflɔːrə] *pl* n flore *f*. ◈ **Flora** pr n MYTH Flore.

floral ['flɔːrəl] adj [arrangement, display] floral ; [pattern, fabric, dress] à fleurs, fleuri.

Florence ['flɒrəns] pr n Florence.

floret ['flɔːrɪt] n fleuron m.

florid ['flɒrɪd] adj. **1.** [complexion] coloré **2.** [style, architecture] chargé ; [music] qui comporte trop de fioritures.

Florida ['flɒrɪdə] pr n Floride f **/ in Florida** en Floride.

florist ['flɒrɪst] n fleuriste mf **▶ florist's (shop)** fleuriste m.

floss [flɒs] ◆ n **1.** [for embroidery] fil m de schappe or de bourrette **2.** [for teeth] fil m or soie f dentaire. ◆ vt [teeth] nettoyer au fil or à la soie dentaire.

flossy ['flɒsɪ] adj **1.** [resembling floss] cotonneux **2.** US inf [showy] tape-à-l'œil.

flotation [fləʊ'teɪʃn] n **1.** [of ship - putting into water] mise f à flot ; [-off sandbank] remise f à flot ; [of logs] flottage m **▶ flotation rings** flotteurs mpl **▶ flotation tank** caisson m étanche **▶ flotation vest** gilet m de sauvetage **2.** [of new company] lancement m, création f ; FIN [of loan by means of share issues] émission f d'actions (permettant de financer la création d'une entreprise).

flotilla [flə'tɪlə] n flottille f.

flotsam ['flɒtsəm] n (U) morceaux mpl d'épave **▶ flotsam and jetsam** morceaux d'épave et détritus mpl.

flounce [flaʊns] ◆ n [in garment] volant m. ◆ vi : **to flounce into / out of a room** entrer dans une / sortir d'une pièce de façon très théâtrale.

flounced [flaʊnst] adj [skirt] à volants.

flouncy ['flaʊnsɪ] adj [dress, skirt] froufroutant.

flounder ['flaʊndə] ◆ vi **1.** [in water, mud] patauger péniblement **2.** [in speech, lecture, etc.] perdre pied, s'empêtrer. ◆ n [fish] flet m.

flour ['flaʊə] ◆ n farine f. ◆ vt saupoudrer de farine, fariner.

flourish ['flʌrɪʃ] ◆ vi [business, economy, plant] prospérer ; [arts, literature, etc.] fleurir, s'épanouir ; [in health] être en pleine forme or santé. ◆ vt [wave, brandish - sword, diploma] brandir. ◆ n **1.** [in lettering, design] ornement m, fioriture f ; [in signature] paraphe m, parafe m **2.** [wave] grand geste m de la main **3.** [in musical or written style] fioriture f.

flourishing ['flʌrɪʃɪŋ] adj [business, trade] florissant, prospère ; [trader] prospère ; [in health] en pleine forme or santé ; [plant] qui prospère.

floury ['flaʊərɪ] adj **1.** [covered in flour - hands] enfariné ; [- clothes] couvert de farine **2.** [potatoes] farineux.

flout [flaʊt] vt [orders, instructions] passer outre à ; [tradition, convention] se moquer de ; [laws of physics] défier.

flow [fləʊ] ◆ vi **1.** [liquid] couler ; [electric current, air] circuler **2.** [traffic, crowd] circuler, s'écouler **3.** [hair, dress] flotter **4.** [prose, style, novel] couler ; [work, project] avancer, progresser **5.** [appear in abundance] : the whisky flowed freely le whisky a coulé à flots **6.** [tide] monter **7.** [emanate] provenir. ◆ n **1.** [of liquid] circulation f ; [of river] écoulement m ; [of lava] coulée f ; [of tears] ruissellement m **2.** [amount - of traffic, people, information, work] flux m ; [movement - of work] acheminement m ; [- of information] circulation f **3.** [of dress, cape] drapé m **4.** [of prose, novel, piece of music] flot m **▶ to be in full flow** [orator] être en plein discours **5.** [of the tide] flux m. ◆ **flow in** vi [water, liquid] entrer, s'écouler ; [contributions, messages of sympathy, people] affluer. ◆ **flow out** vi [water, liquid] sortir, s'écouler ; [people, crowds] s'écouler.

flowchart ['fləʊtʃɑːt] n organigramme m, graphique m d'évolution.

flow diagram = **flowchart**.

flower ['flaʊə] ◆ n **1.** BOT fleur f **/ flower market** marché m aux fleurs **▶ to be in flower** être en fleur or fleurs **2.** fig : the flower of the youth of Athens / of the army liter la fine fleur de la jeunesse athénienne / de l'armée. ◆ vi **1.** [plant, tree] fleurir **2.** liter [artistic movement, genre] fleurir, s'épanouir.

flowerbed ['flaʊəbed] n parterre m de fleurs.

flowered ['flaʊəd] adj [dress, pattern] fleuri, à fleurs.

flower girl n **1.** [selling flowers] marchande f de fleurs **2.** US & Scot [at wedding] petite fille qui porte des fleurs dans un mariage ; ≃ demoiselle f d'honneur.

floweriness ['flaʊərɪnɪs] n [of language, speech, compliments] style m fleuri.

flowering ['flaʊərɪŋ] ◆ n **1.** [of plant, tree] floraison f **2.** [of artistic movement, talents] épanouissement m. ◆ adj [plant, tree - which flowers] à fleurs ; [- which is in flower] en fleurs.

flowerpot ['flaʊəpɒt] n pot m de fleurs.

flower-seller n vendeur m, -euse f de fleurs.

flowery ['flaʊərɪ] adj **1.** [fields, perfume] fleuri ; [smell] de fleurs ; [pattern, dress, carpet] à fleurs **2.** [language, compliments] fleuri.

flowing ['fləʊɪŋ] adj [style, prose] fluide ; [beard, hair, robes] flottant ; [movement] fluide, coulant.

flown [fləʊn] pp ⟶ **fly**.

fl. oz. written abbr of **fluid ounce**.

flu [fluː] n grippe f **/ to have flu** UK, **to have the flu** avoir la grippe, être grippé.

fluctuate ['flʌktʃʊeɪt] vi [rate, temperature, results, etc.] fluctuer ; [interest, enthusiasm, support] être fluctuant or variable ; [person - in enthusiasm, opinions, etc.] être fluctuant or changeant.

fluctuating ['flʌktʃʊeɪtɪŋ] adj [rate, figures, prices, etc.] fluctuant ; [enthusiasm, support, etc.] fluctuant, variable ; [needs, opinions, etc.] fluctuant, changeant.

fluctuation [ˌflʌktʃʊ'eɪʃn] n fluctuation f.

flue [fluː] n [chimney] conduit m ; [for stove, boiler] tuyau m ; MUS [of organ] tuyau m.

fluency ['fluːənsɪ] n **1.** [in speaking, writing] facilité f, aisance f **2.** [in a foreign language] : fluency in French is desirable la connaissance du français parlé est souhaitable **3.** SPORT [of play, strokes] facilité f, aisance f.

fluent ['fluːənt] adj **1.** [prose, style] fluide **2.** [in a foreign language] : to be fluent in French or to speak fluent French parler couramment (le) français **3.** SPORT [play, strokes] facile, aisé.

fluently ['fluːəntlɪ] adv **1.** [speak, write] avec facilité or aisance **2.** [speak a foreign language] couramment **3.** SPORT [play] avec facilité or aisance.

fluff [flʌf] ◆ n (U) [on baby animal, baby's head] duvet m ; [from pillow, material, etc.] peluches fpl ; [collected dust] moutons mpl. ◆ vt UK inf [lines, entrance] rater, louper. ◆ **fluff up** vt sep [feathers] hérisser, ébouriffer ; [pillows, cushions] secouer.

fluffy ['flʌfɪ] (compar **fluffier**, superl **fluffiest**) adj **1.** [material, sweater] pelucheux ; [chick, kitten, hair] duveteux ; [mousse, sponge] léger ; [clouds] cotonneux **▶ fluffy toy** UK (jouet m en) peluche f **2.** [covered in fluff, dust] couvert de moutons.

fluid ['fluːɪd] ◆ adj **1.** [substance] fluide, liquide **2.** [flowing - style, play, match] fluide **3.** [liable to change - situation] indécis, indéterminé ; [- plans] indéterminé. ◆ n fluide m, liquide m **▶ body fluids** sécrétions fpl corporelles **▶ to be on fluids** [patient] ne prendre que des liquides.

fluidity [flu:ˈɪdətɪ] n **1.** [of substance] fluidité f **2.** [of style, play] fluidité f **3.** [liability to change - of situation, plans] indétermination f.

fluid ounce n 🇬🇧 ≃ 0,028 litre ; 🇺🇸 ≃ 0,03 litre.

fluke [flu:k] ◆ n *inf* [piece of good luck] coup m de bol or pot ; [coincidence] hasard m ▸ **by (a) sheer fluke** [coincidence] par un pur hasard. ◆ comp [shot, discovery] heureux.

fluky [ˈfluːkɪ] adj *inf* **1.** [lucky - shot, guess] heureux **2.** 🇺🇸 [strange] bizarre.

flummox [ˈflʌməks] vt déconcerter, dérouter.

flummoxed [ˈflʌməkst] adj : *I was completely flummoxed* ça m'a complètement démonté.

flung [flʌŋ] pt & pp ⟶ **fling**.

flunk [flʌŋk] 🇺🇸 *inf* ◆ vi [in exam, course] se planter. ◆ vt [subj: student - French, maths] se planter en ; [-exam] se planter à. ◆ **flunk out** 🇺🇸 *inf* vi [from college, university] se faire virer (*à cause de la médiocrité de ses résultats*).

fluorescent [fluəˈresənt] adj [lighting, paint] fluorescent.

fluoridate [ˈfluərɪdeɪt] vt [water] enrichir en fluor.

fluoride [ˈfluəraɪd] n fluorure m ▸ **fluoride toothpaste** dentifrice m au fluor.

fluorine [ˈfluəriːn] n fluor m.

flurry [ˈflʌrɪ] *(pl* **flurries**, *pt & pp* **flurried**, *cont* **flurrying)** ◆ n **1.** [of snow, wind] rafale f **2.** *fig* : *a flurry of activity* un branle-bas de combat / *to be in a flurry of excitement* être tout excité. ◆ vt *(usu passive)* agiter, troubler.

flush [flʌʃ] ◆ n **1.** [facial redness] rougeur f **2.** [of beauty, youth] éclat m **3.** [on toilet - device] chasse f (d'eau) **4.** [in card games] flush m. ◆ vi **1.** [face, person] rougir **2.** [toilet] : *it's not flushing properly* la chasse d'eau ne marche pas bien. ◆ vt **1.** [cheeks, face] empourprer **2.** [with water] ▸ **to flush the toilet** tirer la chasse (d'eau) ▸ **to flush sthg down the toilet / sink** jeter qqch dans les toilettes / l'évier **3.** HUNT lever, faire sortir. ◆ adj **1.** [level] au même niveau / *flush with the side of the cupboard* dans l'alignement du placard / *flush with the ground* au niveau du sol, à ras de terre **2.** *inf* [with money] en fonds **3.** TYPO justifié. ◆ adv **1.** [fit, be positioned] : *this piece has to fit flush into the frame* ce morceau doit être de niveau au niveau de la charpente **2.** TYPO ▸ **set flush left / right** justifié à gauche / droite. ◆ **flush away** vt sep [in toilet] jeter dans les toilettes ; [in sink] jeter dans l'évier. ◆ **flush out** vt sep **1.** [clean out - container, sink, etc.] nettoyer à grande eau ; [-dirt, waste] faire partir **2.** HUNT [animal] faire sortir, lever ; *fig* [person] faire sortir ; [truth] faire éclater.

flushed [flʌʃt] adj **1.** [person] rouge ; [cheeks] rouge, en feu **2.** *fig* : *flushed with success* enivré or grisé par le succès.

fluster [ˈflʌstər] ◆ vt [make agitated, nervous] troubler, rendre nerveux. ◆ n ▸ **to be in a fluster** être troublé or nerveux ▸ **to get into a fluster** se troubler, devenir nerveux.

flustered [ˈflʌstəd] adj troublé ▸ *to get flustered* se troubler, devenir nerveux.

flute [fluːt] n **1.** MUS flûte f **2.** ARCHIT [groove on column] cannelure f **3.** [glass] flûte f.

fluted [ˈfluːtɪd] adj ARCHIT cannelé.

flutist [ˈfluːtɪst] 🇺🇸 = **flautist**.

flutter [ˈflʌtər] ◆ vi **1.** [wings] battre ; [flag] flotter ; [washing] flotter, voler ; [heart] palpiter ; [pulse] battre irrégulièrement **2.** [butterfly, bird] voleter, voltiger ; [leaf, paper] voltiger. ◆ vt [fan, piece of paper] agiter ; [wings] battre ▸ **to flutter one's eyelashes at sb** aguicher qqn en battant des cils. ◆ n **1.** [of heart] battement m irrégulier, pulsation f

irrégulière ; [of pulse] battement m irrégulier ; MED palpitation f ; [of wings] battement m **2.** *inf* [nervous state] ▸ **to be all in** or **of a flutter** être dans tous ses états **3.** AERON oscillation f **4.** 🇬🇧 *inf* [gamble] pari m.

flux [flʌks] n (U) **1.** [constant change] : *to be in a state of constant flux* **a)** [universe] être en perpétuel changement **b)** [government, private life, etc.] être en proie à des changements permanents **2.** MED flux m **3.** METALL fondant m.

fly [flaɪ] *(pl* **flies**, *pt* **flew** [fluː], *pp* **flown** [fləʊn])* ◆ n **1.** ENTOM & FISHING mouche f **2.** *(often pl)* [on trousers] braguette f **3.** [entrance to tent] rabat m **4.** = **flysheet 5.** = **flywheel 6.** PHR ▸ **on the fly a)** 🇬🇧 *inf* [secretly] *he did it on the fly* il l'a fait en douce **b)** [on the spot] *to make decisions on the fly* prendre des décisions sur-le-champ **c)** [as you go] *create audio playlists on the fly* créez des listes de lecture audio de façon autonome. ◆ vi **1.** [bird, insect, plane, pilot] voler ; [passenger] prendre l'avion ; [arrow, bullet, missile] voler, filer **2.** [move quickly - person] filer ; [-time] passer à toute vitesse ; [shoot into air - sparks, dust, shavings] voler ▸ **to knock** or **to send sb flying** envoyer qqn rouler à terre ▸ **to knock** or **to send sth flying** envoyer qqch voler **3.** [kite] voler ; [flag] être déployé ; [in wind - flag, coat] flotter ; [-hair] voler **4.** [be successful] cartonner **5.** PHR ▸ **to let fly a)** [physically] envoyer or décocher un coup **b)** [verbally] s'emporter ▸ **to (let) fly at sb a)** [physically] sauter or se jeter sur qqn **b)** [verbally] s'en prendre violemment à qqn. ◆ vt **1.** [plane, helicopter - subj: pilot] piloter **2.** [passengers, people, goods] transporter en avion ; [route - subj: pilot, passenger] emprunter ; [airline] voyager avec ; [distance - subj: passenger, pilot, plane] parcourir ; [combat mission] effectuer / *to fly the Atlantic* **a)** [pilot, passenger] traverser l'Atlantique en avion **b)** [plane] traverser l'Atlantique **3.** [flag - subj: ship] arborer ; [kite] faire voler. ◆ adj **1.** 🇬🇧 *inf & dated* [sharp] malin (maligne), rusé **2.** 🇺🇸 *inf* [stylish] stylé, cool. ◆ **fly about** vi [bird, insect] voleter, voltiger ; [plane, pilot] voler dans les parages, survoler les parages. ◆ **fly away** vi [bird, insect, plane] s'envoler. ◆ **fly back** ◆ vi [bird, insect] revenir ; [plane] revenir ; [passenger] rentrer en avion. ◆ vt sep [person, passengers - to an area] emmener en avion ; [-from an area] ramener en avion ; [-to own country] rapatrier en avion. ◆ **fly by** vi [time] passer à toute vitesse. ◆ **fly in** ◆ vi **1.** [person] arriver en avion ; [plane] arriver **2.** [bird, insect] entrer. ◆ vt sep [troops, reinforcements, food] envoyer en avion ; [subj: pilot - to an area] emmener ; [-from an area] amener. ◆ **fly off** ◆ vi **1.** [bird, insect] s'envoler ; [plane] décoller ; [person] partir en avion **2.** [hat, lid] s'envoler ; [button] sauter. ◆ vt sep **1.** [from oil rig, island] évacuer en avion or hélicoptère **2.** [transport by plane - to an area] emmener en avion ; [-from an area] amener en avion. ◆ **fly out** ◆ vi **1.** [person] partir (en avion), prendre l'avion ; [plane] s'envoler **2.** [come out suddenly - from box, pocket] s'échapper. ◆ vt sep [person, supplies - to an area] envoyer par avion ; [-from an area] évacuer par avion. ◆ **fly past** vi **1.** [plane, bird] passer ; [plane - as part of display, ceremony] défiler **2.** [time, days] passer à toute vitesse.

flyaway [ˈflaɪəweɪ] adj [hair] fin, difficile.

fly ball n [in baseball] chandelle f.

flyblown [ˈflaɪbləʊn] adj *lit* couvert or plein de chiures de mouches ; [meat] avarié ; *fig* très défraîchi.

flyby [ˈflaɪbaɪ] *(pl* **flybys)** n **1.** [of spacecraft] *passage d'un avion ou d'un engin spatial à proximité d'un objectif* **2.** 🇺🇸 = **flypast**.

fly-by-night *inf* ◆ adj **1.** [unreliable] peu fiable, sur qui on ne peut pas compter ; [firm, operation] véreux, louche

2. [passing] éphémère. ◆ n [person - irresponsible] écervelé m, -e f ; [-in debt] débiteur m, -trice f qui décampe en douce.

flyer ['flaɪə^r] = **flier.**

fly-fishing n pêche f à la mouche.

fly half n RUGBY demi m d'ouverture.

flying ['flaɪɪŋ] ◆ n [piloting plane] pilotage m ; [travelling by plane] voyage m en avion / to be afraid of flying avoir peur de prendre l'avion. ◆ adj **1.** [animal, insect] volant **2.** [school] d'aviation ; [staff] navigant ▶ **flying lessons** leçons fpl de pilotage (aérien) **3.** [fast] rapide.

flying colours pl n ▶ **to pass with flying colours** réussir brillamment.

flying doctor n médecin m volant.

flying fish n poisson m volant, exocet m.

flying officer n lieutenant m de l'armée de l'air.

flying picket n piquet m de grève volant.

flying saucer n soucoupe f volante.

Flying Squad pr n ▶ **the Flying Squad** brigade de détectives britanniques spécialisés dans la grande criminalité.

flying start n SPORT départ m lancé.

flying visit n visite f éclair.

flyleaf ['flaɪliːf] (pl **flyleaves** [-liːvz]) n page f de garde.

fly-on-the-wall adj [documentary] pris sur le vif.

flyover ['flaɪˌəʊvə^r] n **1.** 🇬🇧 AUTO pont m routier **2.** 🇺🇸 = **flypast.**

flypast ['flaɪˌpɑːst] n 🇬🇧 défilé m aérien.

flysheet ['flaɪʃiːt] n **1.** [on tent] auvent m **2.** [circular] feuille f volante ; [instructions] mode m d'emploi.

fly spray n bombe f insecticide.

fly-tipping n dépôt m d'ordures illégal.

flyweight ['flaɪweɪt] ◆ n poids m mouche. ◆ adj de poids mouche.

flywheel ['flaɪwiːl] n TECH volant m.

FM n **1.** (abbr of **frequency modulation**) FM f **2.** abbr of **field marshal.**

FMCS (abbr of **Federal Mediation and Conciliation Service**) pr n organisme américain de conciliation des conflits du travail.

FO n **1.** abbr of **field office 2.** 🇬🇧 abbr of **Foreign Office.**

foal [fəʊl] ◆ n [of horse] poulain m ; [of donkey] ânon m / the mare is in foal la jument est pleine. ◆ vi mettre bas, pouliner.

foam [fəʊm] ◆ n [gen] mousse f ; [of mouth, sea] écume f ; [in fire-fighting] mousse f (carbonique) ▶ **foam bath** bain m moussant. ◆ vi [soapy water] mousser, faire de la mousse ; [sea] écumer, moutonner ▶ **to foam at the mouth a)** [animal] baver, écumer **b)** [person] baver, avoir l'écume aux lèvres.

foaming ['fəʊmɪŋ] = **foamy.**

foam rubber n caoutchouc m Mousse.

foamy ['fəʊmɪ] (compar **foamier, superl foamiest**) adj [liquid] mousseux ; [sea] écumeux.

fob¹ [fɒb] (pt & pp **fobbed,** cont **fobbing**) n [pocket] gousset m ; [chain] chaîne f (de gousset). ◆ **fob off** vt sep se débarrasser de.

fob², FOB (abbr of **free on board**) adj & adv FOB.

FOB, f.o.b. (abbr of **free on board**) FOB, F.o.b.

fob watch n montre f de gousset.

foc (abbr of **free of charge**) Fco.

focaccia [ˌfəˈkætʃə] n fougasse f.

focal ['fəʊkl] adj focal.

focal length n distance f focale, focale f.

focal point n OPT foyer m ; fig [of room] point m de convergence.

foci ['fəʊsaɪ] pl ⟶ **focus.**

focus ['fəʊkəs] (pl **focuses** or **foci** ['fəʊsaɪ], pt & pp **focussed,** cont **focussing**) ◆ n **1.** OPT foyer m / the picture is in / out of focus l'image est nette / floue, l'image est / n'est pas au point **2.** [centre - of interest] point m central ; [- of trouble] foyer m, siège m **3.** MED siège m, foyer m. ◆ vt **1.** OPT mettre au point ▶ **to focus a camera (on sthg)** faire la mise au point d'un appareil photo (sur qqch) **2.** [eyes] fixer **3.** [direct - heat, light] faire converger ; [- beam, ray] diriger ; fig [attention] concentrer. ◆ vi **1.** OPT mettre au point **2.** [eyes] se fixer, accommoder spec ▶ **to focus on sthg a)** [eyes] se fixer sur qqch **b)** [person] fixer le regard sur qqch **3.** [converge - light, rays] converger ; fig [attention] se concentrer.

focus group n **1.** POL & TV groupe m de discussion **2.** MARKETING groupe-témoin m, focus group m.

fodder ['fɒdə^r] n (U) [feed] fourrage m ; fig & pej [material] substance f, matière f.

foe [fəʊ] n liter & fml ennemi m, -e f, adversaire mf.

FOE pr n **1.** (abbr of **Friends of the Earth**) AT mpl **2.** (abbr of **Fraternal Order of Eagles**) organisation caritative américaine.

foetal 🇬🇧, **fetal** 🇺🇸 ['fiːtl] adj fœtal.

foetus 🇬🇧, **fetus** 🇺🇸 ['fiːtəs] n fœtus m.

fog [fɒg] (pt & pp **fogged,** cont **fogging**) ◆ n **1.** [mist] brouillard m, brume f **2.** fig [mental] brouillard m, confusion f **3.** PHOT voile f. ◆ vt **1.** [glass, mirror] embuer ; PHOT [film] voiler **2.** [confuse] embrouiller. ◆ vi ▶ **to fog (over** or **up) a)** [glass, mirror] s'embuer **b)** PHOT [film] se voiler.

fogbound ['fɒgbaʊnd] adj pris dans le brouillard or la brume.

fogey ['fəʊgɪ] n inf schnock m.

foggiest ['fɒgɪəst] ◆ n inf ▶ **I haven't the foggiest** je n'ai aucune idée, je n'en ai pas la moindre idée. ◆ adj ⟶ **foggy.**

foggy ['fɒgɪ] (compar **foggier,** superl **foggiest**) adj **1.** [misty] brumeux / it's foggy il y a du brouillard or de la brume **2.** PHOT [film] voilé **3.** 🇵🇭🇷 ▶ **I haven't the foggiest idea** or **notion** je n'ai aucune idée, je n'en ai pas la moindre idée.

foghorn ['fɒghɔːn] n corne f or sirène f de brume ▶ **a voice like a foghorn** une voix tonitruante or de stentor.

fog lamp 🇬🇧, **fog light** 🇺🇸 n feu m de brouillard.

fogy ['fəʊgɪ] (pl **fogies**) = **fogey.**

foible ['fɔɪbl] n [quirk] marotte f, manie f ; [weakness] faiblesse f.

foil [fɔɪl] ◆ n **1.** [metal sheet] feuille f or lame f de métal **2.** [complement] repoussoir m ; [person] faire-valoir m inv **3.** [sword] fleuret m **4.** [in jewellery] paillon m. ◆ vt [thwart - attempt] déjouer ; [- plan, plot] contrecarrer.

foist [fɔɪst] ◆ **foist on** vt sep **1.** [pass on] : you're not foisting (off) your old rubbish on or onto me il n'est pas question que j'hérite de ta vieille camelote **2.** [impose on] : she foisted her ideas on us elle nous a imposé ses idées.

fold [fəʊld] ◆ vt [bend] plier / he folded his arms il s'est croisé les bras. ◆ vi **1.** [bed, chair] se plier, se replier **2.** inf [fail - business] faire faillite, fermer (ses portes) ; [- newspaper] disparaître, cesser de paraître ; [- play] être retiré de l'affiche. ◆ n **1.** [crease] pli m **2.** [enclosure] parc m à moutons ; [flock] troupeau m **3.** fig [group] ▶ **to return to the fold**

rentrer au bercail. ❖ **fold away** ◆ vt sep plier et ranger. ◆ vi se plier, se replier. ❖ **fold down** ◆ vt sep [sheet] replier, rabattre ; [chair, table] plier / *he folded down a corner of the page* il a corné la page. ◆ vi se rabattre, se replier. ❖ **fold in** vt sep CULIN incorporer. ❖ **fold over** ◆ vt sep [newspaper] plier, replier ; [sheet] replier, rabattre. ◆ vi se rabattre, se replier. ❖ **fold up** ◆ vt sep plier, replier. ◆ vi **1.** [chair, table] se plier, se replier **2.** = **fold** *(vi)*.

-fold in comp : *a ten-fold increase* une multiplication par dix / *your investment should multiply six-fold* votre investissement devrait vous rapporter six fois plus.

foldaway ['fəʊldə,weɪ] adj pliant.

folder ['fəʊldər] n **1.** [cover] chemise *f* ; [binder] classeur *m* ; [for drawings] carton *m* ; COMPUT répertoire *m* **2.** [circular] dépliant *m*, brochure *f*.

folding ['fəʊldɪŋ] adj pliant ▸ **folding chair a)** [without arms] chaise *f* pliante **b)** [with arms] fauteuil *m* pliant ▸ **folding door** porte *f* (en) accordéon ▸ **folding seat** or **stool a)** [gen] pliant *m* **b)** AUTO & THEAT strapontin *m*.

foldout ['fəʊldaʊt] n encart *m*.

foley ['fəʊli] n CIN bruitage *m* ▸ **foley artist** bruiteur *m*, -euse *f*.

foliage ['fəʊlɪdʒ] n feuillage *m*.

folic acid ['fəʊlɪk-] n acide *m* folique.

folk [fəʊk] ◆ pl n **1.** [people] gens *mpl* **2.** [race, tribe] race *f*, peuple *m*. ◆ n MUS [traditional] musique *f* folklorique ; [contemporary] musique *f* folk, folk *m*. ◆ adj : *folk dance* or *dancing* danse *f* folklorique / *folk wisdom* la sagesse populaire. ❖ **folks** pl n inf **1.** US [family] famille *f*, parents *mpl* **2.** [people] : *the old folks* les vieux *mpl*.

folklore ['fəʊklɔːr] n folklore *m*.

folk music n [traditional] musique *f* folklorique ; [contemporary] musique *f* folk, folk *m*.

folk singer n [traditional] chanteur *m*, -euse *f* de chansons folkloriques ; [contemporary] chanteur *m*, -euse *f* folk.

folk song n [traditional] chanson *f* or chant *m* folklorique ; [contemporary] chanson *f* folk.

folksy ['fəʊksi] (compar **folksier**, superl **folksiest**) adj inf **1.** US [friendly] sympa **2.** [casual - person] sans façon ; [-speech] populaire **3.** [dress, manners, town] typique ; [story] populaire.

follicle ['fɒlɪkl] n follicule *m*.

follow ['fɒləʊ] ◆ vt **1.** [come after] suivre ; [in procession] aller or venir à la suite de, suivre / *to follow sb in / out* entrer / sortir à la suite de qqn **2.** [pursue] suivre, poursuivre ; [suspect] filer **3.** [go along] suivre, longer **4.** [conform to - diet, instructions, rules] suivre ; [-orders] exécuter ; [-fashion] suivre, se conformer à ; [-sb's advice, example] suivre **5.** [understand] suivre, comprendre **6.** [watch] suivre or regarder attentivement ; [listen] suivre or écouter attentivement **7.** [take an interest in] suivre, se tenir au courant de **8.** [accept - ideas] suivre ; [-leader] appuyer, être partisan de ; [-cause, party] être partisan de, être pour **9.** [practice - profession] exercer, suivre ; [-career] poursuivre ; [-religion] pratiquer ; [-method] employer, suivre. ◆ vi **1.** [come after] suivre / *he answered as follows* il a répondu comme suit **2.** [ensue] s'ensuivre, résulter **3.** [understand] suivre, comprendre **4.** [imitate] suivre, faire de même. ❖ **follow on** vi **1.** [come after] suivre **2.** [in cricket] *reprendre la garde du guichet au début de la seconde partie faute d'avoir marqué le nombre de points requis.* ❖ **follow through** ◆ vt sep [idea, plan] poursuivre jusqu'au bout or jusqu'à sa conclusion. ◆ vi [in ball games] accompagner son coup or sa balle ; [in billiards] faire or jouer un coulé. ❖ **follow up** ◆ vt sep **1.** [pursue - advantage, success] exploiter, tirer parti de ; [-offer] donner suite à **2.** [maintain contact] suivre ;

[subj: doctor] suivre, surveiller **3.** [continue, supplement] faire suivre, compléter. ◆ vi exploiter un avantage, tirer parti d'un avantage.

follower ['fɒləʊər] n **1.** [disciple] disciple *m*, partisan *m*, -e *f* / *a follower of fashion* quelqu'un qui suit la mode **2.** [supporter] partisan *m*, fan *mf* **3.** [attendant] domestique *mf* / *the king and his followers* le roi et sa suite.

following ['fɒləʊɪŋ] ◆ adj **1.** [next] suivant **2.** [wind] arrière *(inv)*. ◆ prep après, suite à. ◆ n **1.** [supporters] partisans *mpl*, disciples *mpl* ; [entourage] suite *f* **2.** [about to be mentioned] : *he said the following* il a dit ceci / *her reasons are the following* ses raisons sont les suivantes.

follow-my-leader n UK *jeu où tout le monde doit imiter tous les mouvements d'un joueur désigné.*

follow-the-leader US = **follow-my-leader.**

follow-through n **1.** [plan] suite *f*, continuation *f* **2.** [in ball games] accompagnement *m* (d'un coup) ; [in billiards] coulé *m*.

follow-up ◆ n **1.** [to event, programme] suite *f* ; [on case, file] suivi *m* ; MED [appointment] visite *f* or examen *m* de contrôle **2.** [bill, letter] rappel *m*. ◆ adj [action, survey, work] complémentaire / *a follow-up visit* une visite de contrôle / *a follow-up letter* / *phone call* une lettre / un coup de téléphone de rappel or de relance ▸ **follow-up care** MED soins *mpl* post-hospitaliers.

folly ['fɒli] (pl **follies**) n **1.** (U) fml [foolishness] folie *f*, sottise *f* **2.** ARCHIT [building] folie *f*. ❖ **follies** pl n THEAT folies *fpl*.

FOMCL (written abbr of **fell off my chair laughing**) MESSAGING MDR.

foment [fəʊ'ment] vt MED & fig fomenter.

fond [fɒnd] adj **1.** ▸ **to be fond of sb** aimer beaucoup qqn, avoir de l'affection pour qqn ▸ **to be fond of sthg** aimer beaucoup qqch, être amateur de qqch / *he's fond of reading* il aime lire ; [loving - friend, wife] affectueux, tendre ; [-parent] indulgent, bon ; [-look] tendre / *with fondest love* affectueusement **2.** [hope] fervent ; [ambition, wish] cher **3.** liter [foolish] naïf.

fondant ['fɒndənt] n fondant *m*.

fondle ['fɒndl] vt caresser.

fondly ['fɒndli] adv **1.** [lovingly] tendrement, affectueusement **2.** [foolishly] naïvement.

fondness ['fɒndnɪs] n [for person] affection *f*, tendresse *f* ; [for things] prédilection *f*, penchant *m* ▸ **fondness for sb** affection pour or envers qqn.

fondue ['fɒnduː] n fondue *f* ▸ **fondue set** service *m* à fondue.

font [fɒnt] n **1.** RELIG fonts *mpl* baptismaux **2.** TYPO fonte *f* ; COMPUT police *f*.

food [fuːd] n **1.** (U) [nourishment] nourriture *f*, vivres *mpl* / *is there any food?* y a-t-il de quoi manger ? **2.** fig [material] matière *f* / *the accident gave her much food for thought* l'accident l'a fait beaucoup réfléchir **3.** HORT engrais *m*. ◆ comp [industry, product] alimentaire ; [crop] vivrier ▸ **food hall** [in shop] rayon *m* d'alimentation ▸ **food stamp** US bon *m* alimentaire *(accordé aux personnes sans ressources)* ▸ **Food and Agriculture Organization** Organisation *f* des Nations Unies pour l'alimentation et l'agriculture ▸ **Food and Drug Administration** US *organisme officiel chargé de contrôler la qualité des aliments et de délivrer les autorisations de mise sur le marché pour les produits pharmaceutiques.*

food chain n chaîne *f* alimentaire.

food court n *partie d'un centre commercial où se trouvent les restaurants.*

foodie ['fuːdi] n inf fin gourmet *m*.

food miles pl n kilomètres *mpl* alimentaires.

food mixer n mixeur *m*.

food poisoning n intoxication f alimentaire.

food processor n robot *m* ménager or de cuisine.

food safety n sécurité f alimentaire.

foodstore ['fu:dstɔ:ʳ] n magasin *m* d'alimentation.

foodstuff ['fu:dstʌf] n aliment *m*.

food technology n technologie f alimentaire.

fool [fu:l] ◆ n **1.** [idiot] idiot *m*, -e f, imbécile *mf* ▶ **to make a fool of sb** a) [ridicule] ridiculiser qqn, se payer la tête de qqn b) [trick] duper qqn **2.** [jester] bouffon *m*, fou *m* **3.** CULIN *sorte de mousse aux fruits.* ◆ vt [deceive] duper, berner. ◆ vi **1.** [joke] faire l'imbécile or le pitre **2.** [mess with] ▶ **to fool with** a) [drugs] toucher à b) [machine] tripoter / *you'd better not fool with him* on ne plaisante pas avec lui. ◆ adj US *inf* idiot, sot. ◆ **fool about** US, **fool around** vi **1.** [joke] faire l'imbécile or le pitre **2.** [waste time] perdre du temps **3.** [mess with] ▶ **to fool around with** [drugs] toucher à **4.** *inf* [have sex] avoir or se payer des aventures.

foolhardy ['fu:l,hɑ:dɪ] adj [act, person] téméraire, imprudent ; [remark] imprudent.

foolish ['fu:lɪʃ] adj **1.** [unwise] insensé, imprudent / *it would be foolish to leave now* ce serait de la folie de partir maintenant **2.** [ridiculous] ridicule, bête.

foolishly ['fu:lɪʃlɪ] adv [stupidly] bêtement, sottement ; [unwisely] imprudemment.

foolishness ['fu:lɪʃnɪs] n bêtise f, sottise f.

foolproof ['fu:lpru:f] adj [machine] indéréglable ; [plan] infaillible, à toute épreuve.

foolscap ['fu:lzkæp] ◆ n ≃ papier *m* ministre. ◆ comp [paper, size] ministre (inv).

foot [fut] (*pl* **feet** [fi:t]) ◆ n **1.** [of person, cow, horse, pig] pied *m* ; [of bird, cat, dog] patte f / *I came on foot* je suis venu à pied ▶ **to be on one's feet** a) [standing] être or se tenir debout b) [after illness] être sur pied or rétabli or remis / *put your feet up* reposez-vous un peu / *I've never set foot in her house* je n'ai jamais mis les pieds dans sa maison / *we got the project back on its feet* fig on a relancé le projet / *the children are always under my feet* les enfants sont toujours dans mes jambes **2.** [of chair, glass, lamp] pied *m* **3.** [lower end - of bed, stocking] pied *m* ; [- of table] bout *m* ; [- of cliff, mountain, hill] pied *m* ; [- of page, stairs] bas *m* / *at the foot of the stairs* en bas de l'escalier **4.** [measurement] pied *m* (anglais) **5.** PHR **to run** or **to rush sb off their feet** accabler qqn de travail, ne pas laisser à qqn le temps de souffler ▶ **my foot!** *inf: he claims he's divorced — divorced, my foot!* il prétend être divorcé — divorcé, mon œil ! ▶ **to fall** or **to land on one's feet** retomber sur ses pieds ▶ **to find one's feet** s'adapter ▶ **to get a foot in the door** poser des jalons, établir le contact ▶ **to have one's** or **both feet (firmly) on the ground** avoir les pieds sur terre ▶ **to have two left feet** *inf* être pataud or empoté ▶ **to put one's foot down** a) faire acte d'autorité b) AUTO accélérer ▶ **to put one's foot in it** US *inf* or **in one's mouth** *inf* mettre les pieds dans le plat ▶ **to put a foot right/wrong** US: *I never seem able to put a foot right* j'ai l'impression que je ne peux jamais rien faire comme il faut / *she didn't put a foot wrong* elle n'a pas commis la moindre erreur ▶ **to get** or **to start off on the right/wrong foot** être bien/mal parti. ◆ vt [pay] ▶ **to foot the bill** *inf* payer (l'addition) / *who's going to foot the bill?* qui va régler la douloureuse ?

footage ['fotɪdʒ] n (U) **1.** [length] longueur f en pieds **2.** CIN [length] métrage *m* ; [material filmed] séquences *fpl*.

foot-and-mouth disease n fièvre f aphteuse.

football ['futbɔ:l] ◆ n **1.** UK football *m* ; US football américain **2.** [ball] ballon *m* (de football), balle f. ◆ comp [match, team] de football ; [season] du football ▶ **football club** UK club *m* de football ▶ **football field** US, **football pitch** UK terrain *m* de football ▶ **football game** US match *m* de football américain ▶ **football ground** UK terrain *m* de football ▶ **football hooligans** hooligans *mpl* ▶ **football fan** fan *mf* de foot ▶ **the Football League** *association réunissant les clubs de football professionnels en Angleterre, sauf ceux qui jouent en première division* ▶ **football supporter** supporter *m* (de football).

footballer ['futbɔ:ləʳ] n UK joueur *m*, -euse f de football, footballeur *m*, -euse f ; US joueur *m*, -euse f de football américain.

football player = **footballer.**

football pools pl n UK pronostics *mpl* (sur les matchs de football) ▶ **to do the football pools** parier sur les matchs de football.

footbath ['futbɑ:θ] (*pl* [-bɑ:ðz]) n bain *m* de pieds.

footbrake ['futbreɪk] n frein *m* à pied.

footbridge ['futbrɪdʒ] n passerelle f.

footer ['futəʳ] n COMPUT titre *m* en bas de page.

-footer in comp : *the boat is a 15-footer* le bateau mesure 15 pieds or environ 4,50 mètres.

footfall ['futfɔ:l] n **1.** [sound of footsteps] bruit *m* de pas **2.** [customers, visitors] fréquentation f.

foot fault n TENNIS faute f de pied.

foothills ['futhɪlz] pl n contreforts *mpl*.

foothold ['futhəʊld] n *lit* prise f de pied ; *fig* position f avantageuse.

footie ['futɪ] n UK & Austr *inf* [football] foot *m*.

footing ['futɪŋ] n **1.** [balance] prise f de pied ▶ **to get one's footing** prendre pied ▶ **to keep/to lose one's footing** garder/perdre l'équilibre **2.** [position] : *to be on an equal footing* être sur un pied d'égalité / *let's try to keep things on a friendly footing* essayons de rester en bons termes.

footlights ['futlaɪts] pl n *lit* rampe ; *fig* [the stage] le théâtre, les planches *fpl*.

footling ['fu:tlɪŋ] adj *inf* [trivial] insignifiant, futile.

footloose ['futlu:s] adj ▶ **footloose and fancy-free** libre comme l'air.

footman ['futmən] (*pl* **footmen** [-mən]) n valet *m* de pied.

footmark ['futmɑ:k] n UK empreinte f (de pied).

footnote ['futnəʊt] ◆ n [on page] note f en bas de page ; [in speech] remarque f supplémentaire. ◆ vt annoter, mettre des notes de bas de page.

footpath ['futpɑ:θ] (*pl* [-pɑ:ðz]) n [path] sentier *m* ; [paved] trottoir *m*.

footprint ['futprɪnt] n **1.** [of foot] empreinte f (de pied) **2.** ▶ **carbon footprint** empreinte f carbone.

footrest ['futrest] n [gen] repose-pieds *m* ; [stool] tabouret *m*.

footsie ['futsɪ] n *inf* ▶ **to play footsie with sb** a) UK faire du pied à qqn b) US être le complice de qqn.

Footsie ['futsɪ] pr n *inf nom familier de l'indice boursier du Financial Times.*

footslogger ['fut,slɒgəʳ] n *inf* MIL pousse-caillou *m inv*, biffin *m*.

foot soldier n fantassin *m*.

footsore ['futsɔ:ʳ] adj : *I was tired and footsore* j'étais fatigué et j'avais mal aux pieds.

footstep ['futstep] n [action] pas *m* ; [sound] bruit *m* de pas.

footstool ['futstu:l] n tabouret m.

footwear ['futweər] n *(U)* chaussures *fpl*.

footwork ['futwɜ:k] n SPORT jeu m de jambes.

footy = footie.

fop [fɒp] n dandy m.

foppish ['fɒpɪʃ] adj [man] dandy ; [dress] de dandy ; [manner] de dandy.

4 (written abbr of for) MESSAGING pr.

for [fɔː']
prep

A. PURPOSE, RECIPIENT OR DESTINATION **1.** [expressing purpose or function] pour / *we were in Vienna for a holiday* / *for work* nous étions à Vienne en vacances / pour le travail / *what for?* pourquoi ? / *what's this knob for?* à quoi sert ce bouton ? **2.** [indicating recipient or beneficiary] pour, à l'intention de / *these flowers are for her* ces fleurs sont pour elle / *he left a note for them* il leur a laissé un mot, il a laissé un mot à leur intention / *see for yourself!* voyez par vous-même ! **3.** [indicating direction, destination] pour, dans la direction de / *they left for Spain* ils sont partis pour l'Espagne / *the ship made for port* le navire a mis le cap sur le port.

B. TIME, DISTANCE OR AMOUNT **1.** [indicating span of time - past, future] pour, pendant ; [- action uncompleted] depuis / *they're going away for the weekend* ils partent pour le week-end / *I lived there for one month* j'y ai vécu pendant un mois / *I've lived here for two years* j'habite ici depuis deux ans / *you haven't been here for a long time* il y a or voilà or ça fait longtemps que vous n'êtes pas venu **2.** [indicating amount] : *it's £2 for a ticket* c'est 2 livres le billet / *he's selling it for £200* il le vend 200 livres.

C. EQUIVALENCE, CAUSE OR COMPARISON **1.** [indicating exchange, equivalence] : *he exchanged the bike for another model* il a échangé le vélo contre or pour un autre modèle / *what's the Spanish for "good"?* comment dit-on « bon » en espagnol ? / *F for François* F comme François **2.** [on behalf of] pour / *I'm speaking for all parents* je parle pour or au nom de tous les parents / *I'll go to the meeting for you* j'irai à la réunion à votre place **3.** [in favour of] pour / *for* or *against* pour ou contre **4.** [because of] pour, en raison de / *candidates were selected for their ability* les candidats ont été retenus en raison de leurs compétences / *he couldn't speak for laughing* il ne pouvait pas parler tellement il riait **5.** [indicating cause, reason] de / *the reason for his leaving* la raison de son départ / *she apologized for being late* elle s'est excusée d'être en retard.

D. FOLLOWED BY INFINITIVE [in phrase with infinitive verbs] : *it's not for him to decide* il ne lui appartient pas or ce n'est pas à lui de décider / *it was difficult for her to apologize* il lui était difficile de s'excuser / *for us to arrive on time we'd better leave now* si nous voulons être à l'heure, il vaut mieux partir maintenant. **for all** prep phr malgré / *for all their efforts* malgré tous leurs efforts.

FOR adj & adv abbr of free on rail.

forage ['fɒrɪdʒ] n **1.** [search] fouille f ; [food] fourrage m **2.** MIL [raid] raid m, incursion f. vi **1.** [search] fourrager, fouiller **to forage for sthg** fouiller pour trouver qqch **2.** MIL [raid] faire un raid or une incursion. vt **1.** [obtain] trouver en fourrageant **2.** [feed] donner du fourrage à, donner à manger à.

forage harvester n fourragère f.

foray ['fɒreɪ] n MIL [raid] raid m, incursion f ; [excursion] incursion f. vi faire une raid or une incursion.

forbad(e) [fə'bæd] pt forbid.

forbearance [fɔː'beərəns] n **1.** [patience] patience f, tolérance f **2.** [restraint] abstention f.

forbearing [fɔː'beərɪŋ] adj patient.

forbid [fə'bɪd] (*pt* forbad *or* forbade [fə'bæd], *pp* forbidden [-'bɪdn]) vt **1.** [not allow] interdire, défendre **to forbid sb to do sthg** défendre or interdire à qqn de faire qqch **2.** [prevent] empêcher **God forbid!** pourvu que non !

forbidden [-'bɪdn] pp forbid. adj interdit, défendu.

forbidding [fə'bɪdɪŋ] adj [building, look, sky] menaçant ; [person] sévère, menaçant.

forbiddingly [fə'bɪdɪŋlɪ] adv : *the castle towered forbiddingly over the town* le château, menaçant, dominait la ville.

force [fɔːs] vt **1.** [compel] forcer, obliger **to force sb to do sthg** contraindre or forcer qqn à faire qqch **to force sb's hand** forcer la main à qqn **2.** [wrest] arracher, extorquer **3.** [impose] imposer **to force sthg on** or **upon sb** imposer qqch à qqn **to force o.s. on sb** imposer sa présence à qqn **4.** [push] : *to force one's way into a building* entrer or pénétrer de force dans un immeuble / *I forced my way through the crowd* je me suis frayé un chemin or passage à travers la foule / *the car forced us off the road* la voiture nous a forcés à quitter la route **5.** [break open] forcer / *to force open a door* / *lock* forcer une porte / une serrure. n **1.** [power] force f, puissance f / *France is a force to be reckoned with* la France est une puissance or force avec laquelle il faut compter **2.** [strength] force f ; [violence] force f, violence f / *they used force to control the crowd* ils ont employé la force pour contrôler la foule **3.** [of argument, word] force f, poids m **4.** PHYS force f / *the force of gravity* la pesanteur **5.** [of people] force f / *the allied forces* les armées *fpl* alliées, les alliés *mpl* **6.** PHR force of circumstances force f des choses **by sheer force** de vive force / *she managed it through sheer force of will* elle y est arrivée uniquement à force de volonté / *the law comes into force this year* la loi entre en vigueur cette année. **by force of** prep à force de **by** or **from force of habit** par la force de l'habitude. **in force** adv phr en force / *the students were there in force* les étudiants étaient venus en force or en grand nombre. **in(to) force** adv phr en application, en vigueur / *the rules now in force* les règlements *mpl* en vigueur. **force down** vt sep **1.** [push down] faire descendre (de force) **2.** [food] se forcer à manger or à avaler.

forced [fɔːst] adj **1.** [compulsory] forcé **2.** [smile] forcé, artificiel **3.** [plant] forcé.

force-feed vt nourrir de force ; [livestock] gaver.

forceful ['fɔːsful] adj [person] énergique, fort ; [argument, style] puissant ; [impression] puissant.

forcefully ['fɔːsfulɪ] adv avec force, avec vigueur.

forcemeat ['fɔːsmiːt] n farce f.

forceps ['fɔːseps] pl n **(a pair of) forceps** un forceps.

forcible ['fɔːsəbl] adj **1.** [by force] de or par force **forcible entry** LAW effraction f **2.** [powerful - argument, style] puissant ; [- personality] puissant, fort ; [- speaker] puissant **3.** [emphatic - opinion] catégorique ; [- wish] vif.

forcibly ['fɔːsəblɪ] adv **1.** [by force] de force, par la force / *they were forcibly removed from the house* on les a fait sortir de force de la maison **2.** [argue, speak] énergiquement, avec vigueur or force **3.** [recommend, remind] fortement.

ford [fɔːd] n gué m. vt passer or traverser à gué.

fore [fɔː'] adj **1.** [front] à l'avant, antérieur / *the fore and hind legs* les pattes de devant et de derrière **2.** NAUT à l'avant. n NAUT avant m, devant m ; *fig* **to come to the fore** a) [person] percer, commencer à être connu

b) [courage] se manifester, se révéler. ◆ adv NAUT à l'avant / *fore and aft* de l'avant à l'arrière. ◆ interj [in golf] ▶ **fore!** attention !, gare !

forearm ◆ n ['fɔːr,ɑːm] avant-bras *m*. ◆ vt [fɔːr'ɑːm] prémunir.

forebear ['fɔːbeə^r] n ancêtre *m*.

foreboding [fɔː'bəʊdɪŋ] n [feeling] pressentiment *m*, prémonition *f* ; [omen] présage *m*, augure *m*.

forecast ['fɔːkɑːst] (*pt & pp* forecast *or* forecasted) ◆ vt [gen & METEOR] prévoir ; [in betting] pronostiquer. ◆ n **1.** [gen & METEOR] prévision *f* / *economic forecast* prévisions économiques ▶ **the weather forecast** le bulletin météorologique, la météo **2.** [in betting] pronostic *m*.

forecaster ['fɔːkɑːstə^r] n pronostiqueur *m*, -euse *f* ▶ **weather forecaster** météorologiste *mf*, météorologue *mf*.

foreclose [fɔː'kləʊz] ◆ vt [mortgage] saisir. ◆ vi saisir le bien hypothéqué ▶ **to foreclose on sb** saisir les biens de qqn ▶ **to foreclose on a mortgage** saisir un bien hypothéqué.

foreclosure [fɔː'kləʊʒə^r] n forclusion *f*.

forecourt ['fɔːkɔːt] n avant-cour *f*, cour *f* de devant ; [of petrol station] devant *m*.

forefather ['fɔː,fɑːðə^r] n ancêtre *m*.

forefinger ['fɔː,fɪŋgə^r] n index *m*.

forefront ['fɔːfrʌnt] n premier rang *m* ▶ **to be at** *or* **in the forefront of sthg a)** [country, firm] être au premier rang de qqch **b)** [person] être une sommité dans qqch.

forego [fɔː'gəʊ] (*pt* forewent [-'went], *pp* foregone [-'gɒn]) = **forgo**.

foregoing [fɔː'gəʊɪŋ] ◆ adj précédent, susdit. ◆ n précédent *m*, -e *f* / *if we are to believe the foregoing* si nous devons croire ce qui précède.

foregone conclusion ['fɔːgɒn-] n issue *f* certaine ou prévisible.

foreground ['fɔːgraʊnd] ◆ n [gen & ART & PHOT] premier plan / *in the foreground* au premier plan. ◆ vt privilégier.

forehand ['fɔːhænd] ◆ n SPORT coup *m* droit. ◆ adj ▶ **forehand volley** volée *f* de face.

forehead ['fɔːhed] n front *m*.

foreign ['fɒrən] adj **1.** [country, language, person] étranger ; [aid, visit - to country] à l'étranger ; [-from country] de l'étranger ; [products] de l'étranger ; [trade] extérieur ▶ **foreign affairs** affaires *fpl* étrangères ▶ **foreign correspondent** correspondant *m*, -e *f* à l'étranger ▶ **foreign minister** ministre *m* des Affaires étrangères ▶ **foreign policy** politique *f* étrangère *or* extérieure **2.** [alien] étranger / *such thinking is foreign to them* un tel raisonnement leur est étranger / *a foreign body, foreign matter* un corps étranger.

foreigner ['fɒrənə^r] n étranger *m*, -ère *f*.

foreignness ['fɒrɪnnɪs] n air *m* étranger ; [of place] caractère *m* étranger ; [exotic nature] exotisme *m*.

Foreign Office n ▶ **the Foreign (and Commonwealth) Office** le ministère britannique des Affaires étrangères.

Foreign Secretary, **Foreign and Commonwealth Secretary** n ▶ **the Foreign Secretary** le ministre britannique des Affaires étrangères.

foreleg ['fɔːleg] n [of horse] jambe *f* de devant *or* antérieure ; [of dog, cat] patte *f* de devant *or* antérieure.

foreman ['fɔːmən] (*pl* foremen [-mən]) n INDUST contremaître *m*, chef *m* d'équipe ; LAW président *m*, -e *f*.

foremost ['fɔːməʊst] ◆ adj [first - in position] le plus en avant ; [- in importance] principal, le plus important. ◆ adv en avant.

forename ['fɔːneɪm] n 🇬🇧 prénom *m*.

forensic [fə'rensɪk] adj **1.** [chemistry] légal ; [expert] légiste / *forensic evidence* expertise médico-légale / *forensic medicine* or *science* médecine *f* légale / *forensic scientist* médecin *m* légiste **2.** [skill, term] du barreau.

foreplay ['fɔːpleɪ] n *(U)* préliminaires *mpl*.

forerunner ['fɔː,rʌnə^r] n [precursor] précurseur *m* ; [omen] présage *m*, signe *m* avant-coureur.

foresee [fɔː'siː] (*pt* foresaw [-'sɔː], *pp* foreseen [-'siːn]) vt prévoir, présager.

foreseeable [fɔː'siːəbl] adj prévisible.

foreseen [-'siːn] pp —→ foresee.

foreshadow [fɔː'ʃædəʊ] vt présager, annoncer.

foreshortened [fɔː'ʃɔːtnd] adj réduit.

foresight ['fɔːsaɪt] n prévoyance *f*.

foresighted [fɔː,saɪtɪd] adj [person] prévoyant.

foreskin ['fɔːskɪn] n prépuce *m*.

forest ['fɒrɪst] n forêt *f*.

forestall [fɔː'stɔːl] vt **1.** [prevent] empêcher, retenir **2.** [anticipate - desire, possibility] anticiper, prévenir ; [- person] devancer, prendre les devants sur.

forestry ['fɒrɪstrɪ] n sylviculture *f* ▶ **the Forestry Commission** organisme britannique de gestion des forêts domaniales ; ≃ les Eaux et Forêts *fpl*.

foretaste ['fɔːteɪst] n avant-goût *m*.

foretell [fɔː'tel] (*pt & pp* foretold [-'təʊld]) vt prédire.

forethought ['fɔːθɔːt] n [premeditation] préméditation *f* ; [foresight] prévoyance *f*.

foretold [-'təʊld] pt & pp —→ foretell.

4eva (written abbr of **for ever**), **4E** MESSAGING pr tjr.

forever [fə'revə^r] adv **1.** [eternally] (pour) toujours, éternellement / *Europe forever!* vive l'Europe ! **2.** [incessantly] toujours, sans cesse **3.** [for good] pour toujours ! **4.** inf [a long time] très longtemps / *it'll take forever!* ça va prendre des lustres !

forewarn [fɔː'wɔːn] vt prévenir, avertir.

forewarning [,fɔː'wɔːnɪŋ] n avertissement *m*.

foreword ['fɔːwɜːd] n avant-propos *m*, préface *f*.

forfeit ['fɔːfɪt] ◆ vt **1.** [lose] perdre ; [give up] renoncer à, abandonner **2.** LAW [lose] perdre (par confiscation) ; [confiscate] confisquer. ◆ n **1.** [penalty] prix *m*, peine *f* ; COMM [sum] amende *f*, dédit *m* **2.** LAW [loss] perte *f* (par confiscation) **3.** [game] ▶ **to play forfeits** jouer aux gages ▶ **to pay a forfeit** avoir un gage. ◆ adj *fml* [subject to confiscation] susceptible d'être confisqué ; [confiscated] confisqué.

forfeiture ['fɔːfɪtʃə^r] n **1.** LAW [loss] perte *f* par confiscation ; *fig* [surrender] renonciation *f* **2.** [penalty] prix *m*, peine *f* ; COMM [sum] amende *f*, dédit *m*.

forgave [fə'geɪv] pt —→ forgive.

forge [fɔːdʒ] ◆ vt **1.** [metal, sword] forger / *to forge an alliance* / *a friendship* sceller une alliance / une amitié **2.** [counterfeit - money, signature] contrefaire ; [- picture] faire un faux de, contrefaire ; [- document] faire un faux de / *a forged passport* un faux passeport. ◆ vi [go forward] avancer / *to forge into the lead* prendre la tête. ◆ n [machine, place] forge *f*. ❖ **forge ahead** vi prendre de l'avance ; *fig* faire son chemin, réussir, prospérer.

forger ['fɔːdʒə^r] n [gen] faussaire *mf* ; [of money] faux-monnayeur *m*, faussaire *mf*.

forgery ['fɔːdʒərɪ] (pl **forgeries**) n **1.** [of money, picture, signature] contrefaçon f ; [of document] falsification f ▸ **to prosecute sb for forgery** poursuivre qqn pour faux (et usage de faux) **2.** [object] faux m.

forget [fə'get] (pt **forgot** [-'gɒt], pp **forgotten** [-'gɒtn]) ◆ vt **1.** [be unable to recall] oublier / I'll never forget seeing him play Lear je ne l'oublierai jamais or je le reverrai toujours dans le rôle de Lear / I forgot (that) you had a sister j'avais oublié que tu avais une sœur ; [not think about] oublier / to forget o.s. s'oublier **2.** [neglect, overlook] oublier, omettre / she forgot to mention that she was married elle a oublié or a omis de dire qu'elle était mariée / forget it! a) inf [in reply to thanks] il n'y a pas de quoi ! b) [in reply to apology] ce n'est pas grave !, ne vous en faites pas ! c) [in irritation] laissez tomber ! d) [in reply to question] cela n'a aucune importance !, peu importe ! **3.** [leave behind] oublier, laisser **4.** [give up -idea, plan] abandonner, renoncer à. ◆ vi ▸ **to forget about sb / sthg** oublier qqn / qqch.

forgetful [fə'getful] adj [absent-minded] distrait ; [careless] négligent, étourdi ▸ **to be forgetful of sthg** fml être oublieux de qqch.

forgetfulness [fə'getfulnɪs] n [absent-mindedness] manque m de mémoire ; [carelessness] négligence f, étourderie f.

forget-me-not n myosotis m.

forgettable [fə'getəbl] adj qui ne présente pas d'intérêt.

forgivable [fə'gɪvəbl] adj pardonnable.

forgivably [fə'gɪvəblɪ] adv : she was, quite forgivably, rather annoyed with him! elle était plutôt en colère contre lui, et on la comprend !

4gv MESSAGING written abbr of **forgive**.

forgive [fə'gɪv] (pt **forgave** [fə'geɪv], pp **forgiven** [-'gɪvn]) vt **1.** [pardon] pardonner ▸ **to forgive sb (for) sthg** pardonner qqch à qqn **2.** [debt, payment] ▸ **to forgive (sb) a debt** faire grâce (à qqn) d'une dette.

4gvn MESSAGING written abbr of **forgiven**.

forgiveness [fə'gɪvnɪs] n **1.** [pardon] pardon m **2.** [tolerance] indulgence f, clémence f.

forgiving [fə'gɪvɪŋ] adj indulgent, clément.

forgo [fɔː'gəʊ] (pt **forwent** [-'went], pp **forgone** [-'gɒn]) vt renoncer à, se priver de.

forgot [-'gɒt] pt ⟶ **forget**.

forgotten [-'gɒtn] pp ⟶ **forget**.

fork [fɔːk] ◆ n **1.** [for eating] fourchette f **2.** AGR fourche f **3.** [junction -in road, railway] bifurcation f, embranchement m **4.** [on bicycle, motorbike] fourche f. ◆ vt **1.** AGR fourcher **2.** [food] prendre avec une fourchette. ◆ vi **1.** [river, road] bifurquer, fourcher **2.** [car, person] bifurquer, tourner. ◆◆ **fork out** inf ◆ vt sep [money] allonger, cracher. ◆ vi casquer v inf.

forked [fɔːkt] adj [tongue] fourchu ; [river, road] à bifurcation.

forked lightning n éclair m en zigzag.

forkful ['fɔːkfʊl] n **1.** [of food] fourchetée f **2.** [of hay] fourchée f.

forklift ['fɔːklɪft] n ▸ **forklift (truck)** chariot m élévateur.

forlorn [fə'lɔːn] adj **1.** [wretched] triste, malheureux **2.** [lonely -person] abandonné, délaissé ; [-place] désolé, désert **3.** [desperate] désespéré.

forlornly [fə'lɔːnlɪ] adv **1.** [wretchedly] tristement **2.** [desperately] désespérément.

form [fɔːm] ◆ n **1.** [shape] forme f / in the form of a heart en forme de cœur **2.** [body, figure] forme f, silhouette f **3.** [aspect, mode] forme f / it's written in the form of a letter c'est écrit sous forme de lettre / her anxiety showed itself in the form of anger son inquiétude se manifesta par de la colère **4.** [kind, type] forme f, sorte f / we studied three different forms of government nous avons examiné trois systèmes de gouvernement or trois régimes différents **5.** [document] formulaire m ; [for bank, telegram] formule f / to fill in or out a form remplir un formulaire **6.** [condition] forme f, condition f / John was on or in good form at lunch John était en forme or plein d'entrain pendant le déjeuner / he's off form or out of form il n'est pas en forme ▸ **to study the form** [in horse racing] examiner la tenue des performances des chevaux **7.** [formula] forme f, formule f / form of address formule de politesse / the correct form of address for a senator la manière correcte de s'adresser à un sénateur **8.** UK SCH [class] classe f / she's in the first form ≃ elle est en sixième. ◆ vt **1.** [shape] former, construire ; [character, mind] former, façonner ; [sentence] construire **2.** [take the shape of] former, faire / form a queue UK or line US please faites la queue s'il vous plaît **3.** [develop -opinion] se former, se faire ; [-plan] concevoir, élaborer ; [-habit] contracter / to form an impression avoir une impression **4.** [organize -association, club] créer, fonder ; [-committee, government] former ; [COMM -company] fonder, créer **5.** [constitute] composer, former / to form a part of sthg faire partie de qqch. ◆ vi **1.** [materialize] se former, prendre forme **2.** [take shape] se former.

formal ['fɔːml] ◆ adj **1.** [conventional -function] officiel, solennel ; [-greeting] solennel, cérémonieux ▸ **formal dress a)** [for ceremony] tenue f de cérémonie **b)** [for evening] tenue f de soirée **2.** [official -announcement, approval] officiel ; [-order] formel, explicite / she had no formal education elle n'a jamais fait d'études **3.** [correct -person] solennel ; [-behaviour, style] soigné, solennel, guindé pej **4.** [ceremonial] formaliste, méthodique **5.** GRAM & LING formaliste, formel **6.** PHILOS formel. ◆ n US **1.** [dance] bal m **2.** [suit] habit m de soirée.

formality [fɔː'mælətɪ] (pl **formalities**) n **1.** [ceremoniousness] cérémonie f ; [solemnity] solennité f, gravité f ; [stiffness] froideur f, raideur f ; [convention] formalité f, étiquette f **2.** [procedure] formalité f.

formalize, formalise ['fɔːməlaɪz] vt formaliser.

formally ['fɔːmlɪ] adv **1.** [conventionally] solennellement, cérémonieusement / formally dressed **a)** [for ceremony] en tenue de cérémonie **b)** [for evening] en tenue de soirée **2.** [officially] officiellement, dans les règles / an agreement was formally drawn up un accord a été rédigé en bonne et due forme **3.** [speak] de façon soignée ; [behave] de façon solennelle or guindée pej **4.** [study, research] de façon méthodique ; [arrange] de façon régulière **5.** [nominally] pour la forme.

format ['fɔːmæt] (cont **formatting**, pt & pp **formatted**) ◆ n **1.** [size] format m **2.** [layout] présentation f **3.** COMPUT format m. ◆ vt **1.** [layout] composer la présentation de **2.** COMPUT formater.

formation [fɔː'meɪʃn] n **1.** [establishment -of club] création f, fondation f ; [-of committee, company] formation f, fondation f ; [-of government] formation f **2.** [development -of character, person] formation f ; [-of idea] développement m, élaboration f ; [-of plan] élaboration f, mise f en place **3.** BOT, GEOL & MED formation f **4.** [arrangement] formation f, disposition f ; MIL [unit] formation f, dispositif m.

formative ['fɔːmətɪv] adj formateur.

formatting ['fɔːmætɪŋ] n COMPUT formatage m.

forme UK, **form** US [fɔːm] n PRINT forme f.

former ['fɔːmər] ◆ adj **1.** [time] passé / in former times or days autrefois, dans le passé **2.** [earlier, previous] ancien, précédent / *my former wife* mon ex-femme **3.** [first] premier. ◆ n [first] premier *m*, -ère *f*, celui-là *m*, celle-là *f*.

formerly ['fɔːməlɪ] adv autrefois, jadis.

form feed n COMPUT avancement *m* du papier.

form-filling n : *there was a lot of form-filling* il y avait beaucoup de papiers à remplir.

Formica® [fɔː'maɪkə] n Formica *m*, plastique *m* laminé.

formidable ['fɔːmɪdəbl] adj **1.** [inspiring fear] redoutable, terrible ; [inspiring respect] remarquable **2.** [difficult] ardu.

formidably ['fɔːmɪdəblɪ] adv redoutablement, terriblement.

formless ['fɔːmlɪs] adj [shape] informe ; [fear, idea] vague.

Formosa [fɔː'məʊsə] pr n Formose / *in Formosa* à Formose.

formula ['fɔːmjʊlə] n **1.** (*pl* formulas *or* formulae [-liː]) [gen & CHEM & MATH] formule *f* / *a formula for happiness* une recette qui assure le bonheur **2.** (*pl* formulas) [expression] formule *f* **3.** (*pl* formulas) AUTO formule *f* ▸ **formula 1 (racing)** la formule 1 **4.** (*pl* formula) [for baby] ≃ bouillie *f* (*pour bébé*).

formulaic [,fɔːmjʊ'leɪɪk] adj stéréotypé.

formulate ['fɔːmjʊleɪt] vt **1.** [express] formuler **2.** [plan] élaborer.

formulation [,fɔːmjʊ'leɪʃn] n **1.** [of idea] formulation *f*, expression *f* **2.** [of plan] élaboration *f*.

fornicate ['fɔːnɪkeɪt] vi *fml* forniquer.

fornication [,fɔːnɪ'keɪʃn] n *fml* fornication *f*.

forsake [fə'seɪk] (*pt* forsook [-'sʊk], *pp* forsaken [-'seɪkn]) vt *fml* **1.** [abandon - family, spouse] abandonner ; [- friend] délaisser ; [- place] quitter **2.** [give up] renoncer à.

forsaken [-'seɪkn] ◆ pp —→ forsake. ◆ adj *liter* [person] abandonné ; [place] abandonné, désert.

forsook [-'sʊk] pt —→ forsake.

forsythia [fɔː'saɪθɪə] n forsythia *m*.

fort [fɔːt] n fort *m* ; [smaller] fortin *m*.

forte[1] ['fɔːteɪ] n [strong point] fort *m*.

forte[2] ['fɔːtɪ] ◆ adj & adv MUS forte. ◆ n forte *m*.

forth [fɔːθ] adv *liter* **1.** [out, forward] en avant / *to go or to set forth* se mettre en route / *to bring forth* produire / *to send forth* envoyer **2.** [forwards in time] : *from this moment forth* dorénavant, désormais / *from this day forth* à partir d'aujourd'hui or de ce jour.

forthcoming [fɔːθ'kʌmɪŋ] adj **1.** [imminent - event] à venir ; [- book] à paraître ; [- film] qui va sortir prochainement **2.** [made available] : *no answer was forthcoming* il n'y a eu aucune réponse / *the funds were not forthcoming* les fonds n'ont pas été débloqués **3.** [verbally] : *he wasn't very forthcoming* il n'a pas été très bavard.

forthright ['fɔːθraɪt] adj [person, remark] franc (franche), direct.

forthwith [,fɔːθ'wɪθ] adv *fml* incontinent *liter*, sur-le-champ.

fortieth ['fɔːtɪɪθ] ◆ n **1.** [ordinal] quarantième *m* **2.** [fraction] quarantième *m*. ◆ det quarantième. See also fifth.

fortification [,fɔːtɪfɪ'keɪʃn] n fortification *f*.

fortified wine n 🇬🇧 vin *m* de liqueur, vin *m* doux naturel.

fortify ['fɔːtɪfaɪ] (*pt & pp* fortified) vt **1.** [place] fortifier, armer ; *fig* [person] réconforter, remonter **2.** [wine] augmenter la teneur en alcool, alcooliser ; [food] renforcer en vitamines.

fortitude ['fɔːtɪtjuːd] n courage *m*, force *f* morale.

fortnight ['fɔːtnaɪt] n 🇬🇧 quinzaine *f*, quinze jours *mpl*.

fortnightly ['fɔːt,naɪtlɪ] (*pl* fortnightlies) 🇬🇧 ◆ adj bimensuel. ◆ adv tous les quinze jours. ◆ n bimensuel *m*.

fortress ['fɔːtrɪs] n [fort] fort *m* ; [prison] forteresse *f* ; [castle] château *m* fort ; [place, town] place *f* forte.

fortuitous [fɔː'tjuːɪtəs] adj fortuit, imprévu.

fortunate ['fɔːtʃnət] ◆ adj [person] heureux, chanceux ; [choice, meeting] heureux, propice. ◆ pl n : *the less fortunate* les déshérités *mpl*.

fortunately ['fɔːtʃnətlɪ] adv heureusement, par bonheur.

fortune ['fɔːtʃuːn] n **1.** [wealth] fortune *f* **2.** [future] destin *m* ▸ **to tell sb's fortune** dire la bonne aventure à qqn **3.** [chance, fate] sort *m*, fortune *f* **4.** [luck] fortune *f*, chance *f* / *by good fortune* par chance, par bonheur.

fortune cookie n 🇺🇸 biscuit chinois dans lequel est caché un horoscope.

fortune-teller n [gen] diseur *m*, -euse *f* de bonne aventure ; [with cards] tireur *m*, -euse *f* de cartes, cartomancien *m*, -enne *f*.

fortune-telling n [gen] fait de dire la bonne aventure ; [with cards] cartomancie *f*.

forty ['fɔːtɪ] (*pl* forties) ◆ det quarante (*inv*). ◆ n quarante *m* ▸ **the lower forty-eight** 🇺🇸 les quarante-huit États américains (*à part l'Alaska et Hawai*). See also fifty.

forty winks pl n *inf* petit somme *m*.

forum ['fɔːrəm] (*pl* forums *or* fora ['fɔːrə]) n *fig* [gen] forum *m*, tribune *f* ; HIST forum *m* ; INTERNET forum *m*.

forward ['fɔːwəd] ◆ adj **1.** [towards front - movement] en avant, vers l'avant ; [- position] avant / *the seat is too far forward* le siège est trop avancé or en avant **2.** [advanced] : *the project is no further forward* le projet n'a pas avancé ▸ **forward planning** planification *f* à long terme **3.** [brash] effronté, impertinent **4.** [buying, delivery] à terme. ◆ adv [in space] en avant ; : *to move forward* avancer / *he reached forward* il a tendu le bras en avant / *three witnesses came forward* *fig* trois témoins se sont présentés / *clocks go forward one hour at midnight* il faut avancer les pendules d'une heure à minuit. ◆ vt **1.** [send on] faire suivre ; COMM expédier, envoyer **2.** [advance, promote] avancer, favoriser. ◆ n SPORT avant *m*.

forwarding address ['fɔːwədɪŋ-] n adresse *f* pour faire suivre le courrier ; COMM adresse *f* pour l'expédition.

forward-looking adj [person] tourné vers or ouvert sur l'avenir ; [plans] tourné vers l'avenir or le progrès ; [company, policy] qui va de l'avant, dynamique, entreprenant.

forwardness ['fɔːwədnɪs] n **1.** [presumption] effronterie *f*, impertinence *f* ; [eagerness] empressement *m* **2.** 🇬🇧 [of child, season] précocité *f* ; [of project] état *m* avancé.

forward roll n cabriole *f*, culbute *f*.

forwards ['fɔːwədz] adv = forward.

forward slash n COMPUT barre *f* oblique.

forwent [-'went] pt —→ forgo.

4yeo MESSAGING written abbr of for your eyes only.

fossil ['fɒsl] ◆ n fossile *m*. ◆ adj fossilisé.

fossil fuel n combustible *m* fossile.

fossilized ['fɒsɪlaɪzd] adj **1.** *lit* fossilisé **2.** *fig* fossilisé, figé ; LING figé.

foster ['fɒstər] ◆ vt **1.** 🇬🇧 LAW [subj: family, person] accueillir ; [subj: authorities, court] placer **2.** [idea, hope] nourrir, entretenir **3.** [promote] favoriser, encourager. ◆ adj ▸ **foster child** enfant *m* placé dans une famille d'accueil ▸ **foster home** or **parents** famille *f* d'accueil ▸ **foster mother / father** mère *f* / père *m* de la famille d'accueil.

fought [fɔːt] pt & pp —→ fight.

foul [faʊl] ◆ adj **1.** [food, taste] infect ; [smell] infect, fétide ; [breath] fétide **2.** [filthy - linen] sale, souillé ; [- place] immonde, crasseux ; [- air] vicié, pollué ; [- water] croupi **3.** inf [horrible - weather] pourri ; [- person] infect, ignoble **4.** [language] grossier, ordurier **5.** liter [vile] vil ; [unfair] déloyal **6.** [clogged] obstrué, encrassé **7.** PHR **to fall** or **to run foul of sb** se brouiller avec qqn. ◆ n SPORT [in boxing] coup m bas ; [in football, baseball, etc.] faute f. ◆ vt **1.** [dirty] salir, souiller ; [air, water] polluer, infecter ; [subj : dog] salir **2.** [clog] obstruer, encrasser ; [entangle] embrouiller, emmêler ; [nets] se prendre dans **3.** [collide with] entrer en collision avec **4.** SPORT commettre une faute contre **5.** fig [reputation] salir. ◆ vi **1.** [tangle] s'emmêler, s'embrouiller **2.** SPORT commettre une faute. ◆ **foul up** vt sep **1.** [contaminate] polluer ; [clog] obstruer, encrasser **2.** inf [bungle] ficher en l'air, flanquer par terre.

foul-mouthed adj au langage grossier.

foul play n SPORT jeu m irrégulier or déloyal ; [in cards, games] tricherie f / the police suspect foul play fig la police croit qu'il y a eu meurtre or croit au meurtre.

foul-smelling [-'smelɪŋ] adj puant, fétide.

foul-up n inf [mix-up] cafouillage m ; [mechanical difficulty] problème m or difficulté f mécanique.

found [faʊnd] ◆ pt & pp ⟶ **find.** ◆ vt **1.** [establish - organization, town] fonder, créer ; [- business] fonder, établir **2.** [base] fonder, baser ▶ **to be founded on** être fondé sur **3.** [cast] fondre.

foundation [faʊn'deɪʃn] n **1.** [of business, town] fondation f, création f **2.** [institution] fondation f, institution f dotée ; [endowment] dotation f, fondation f **3.** [basis] base f, fondement m **4.** [make-up] fond m de teint **5.** UK [of building] fondations fpl. ◆ **foundations** pl n CONSTR fondations fpl.

foundation course n cours m introductif.

foundation hospital n UK hôpital faisant partie du système de sécurité sociale britannique, mais géré par une équipe privée.

foundation stage n UK SCH programme destiné aux jeunes enfants (de 3 à 4 ans) avant leur scolarisation à 5 ans.

foundation stone n pierre f commémorative.

founder ['faʊndər] ◆ n fondateur m, -trice f ▶ **founder member** UK membre m fondateur. ◆ vi **1.** [ship] sombrer, chavirer **2.** fig [fail] s'effondrer, s'écrouler **3.** [horse - in mud] s'embourber ; [- go lame] se mettre à boiter.

founding ['faʊndɪŋ] ◆ n [of business, organization, town] fondation f, création f. ◆ adj fondateur.

founding father n père m fondateur.

foundling ['faʊndlɪŋ] n fml enfant mf trouvé.

foundry ['faʊndrɪ] (pl **foundries**) n [place] fonderie f ; [of articles] fonderie f, fonte f ; [articles] fonte f.

fount [faʊnt] n **1.** UK TYPO fonte f **2.** liter [spring] source f.

fountain ['faʊntɪn] n [natural] fontaine f, source f ; [man-made] fontaine f, jet m d'eau.

fountain pen n stylo m à encre.

four [fɔːr] ◆ n **1.** [number] quatre m **2.** [in rowing] quatre m. ◆ det quatre. **See also five.**

four-by-four n AUTO 4 x 4 m.

four-door adj à quatre portes.

four-eyes n inf binoclard m, -e f.

Four-F n personne inapte (physiquement) au service militaire.

four-leaf clover, four-leaved clover n trèfle m à quatre feuilles.

four-legged [-'legɪd] adj quadrupède, à quatre pattes ▶ **our four-legged friends** hum nos compagnons à quatre pattes.

four-letter word n gros mot m, obscénité f.

four-ply adj [wool] à quatre fils ; [wood] contreplaqué (à quatre plis).

four-poster (bed) n lit m à baldaquin or à colonnes.

foursome ['fɔːsəm] n **1.** [people] groupe m de quatre personnes ; [two couples] deux couples mpl **2.** [game] partie f à quatre.

four-star adj [gen & MIL] à quatre étoiles ▶ **four-star hotel** hôtel m quatre étoiles or de première catégorie.

fourteen [,fɔː'tiːn] ◆ det quatorze. ◆ n quatorze m. **See also five.**

fourteenth [,fɔː'tiːnθ] ◆ n **1.** [ordinal] quatorzième mf **2.** [fraction] quatorzième m. ◆ det quatorzième ▶ **Louis the Fourteenth** Louis Quatorze or XIV. ◆ adv quatorzièmement. **See also fifth.**

fourth [fɔːθ] ◆ n **1.** [ordinal] quatrième mf ▶ **the Fourth of July** le 4 Juillet (fête nationale de l'Indépendance aux États-Unis) **2.** [fraction] quart m **3.** MUS quarte f. ◆ det quatrième / **fourth-class mail** US paquet-poste m ordinaire / **the fourth finger** l'annulaire m / **to go** or **to change into fourth (gear)** AUTO passer en quatrième. ◆ adv quatrièmement. **See also fifth.**

fourth estate n ▶ **the fourth estate** le quatrième pouvoir, la presse.

fourth grade n US SCH classe de l'école primaire correspondant au CM1 (8-9 ans).

fourthly ['fɔːθlɪ] adv quatrièmement, en quatrième lieu.

Fourth World pr n ▶ **the Fourth World** le quartmonde.

four-way stop n US carrefour m à quatre stops.

four-wheel drive n propulsion f à quatre roues motrices ; [car] voiture f à quatre roues motrices, quatre-quatre m inv / **with four-wheel drive** à quatre roues motrices.

fowl [faʊl] (pl **fowl** or **fowls**) n [for eating - collectively] volaille f ; [- one bird] volaille f, volatile m.

fox [fɒks] (pl **fox** or **foxes**) ◆ n [animal, fur] renard m ▶ **fox cub** renardeau m. ◆ vt **1.** [outwit] duper, berner **2.** [baffle] souffler.

foxed [fɒkst] adj [paper] marqué or taché de rousseurs.

foxglove ['fɒksɡlʌv] n digitale f (pourprée).

foxhole ['fɒkshəʊl] n **1.** [of fox] terrier m de renard, renardière f **2.** MIL gourbi m.

foxhound ['fɒkshaʊnd] n fox-hound m, chien m courant.

foxhunt ['fɒkshʌnt] n chasse f au renard.

foxhunting ['fɒks,hʌntɪŋ] n chasse f au renard.

foxy ['fɒksɪ] (compar **foxier**, superl **foxiest**) adj **1.** [wily] rusé, malin (maligne) **2.** US inf & dated [sexy] sexy (inv).

foyer ['fɔɪeɪ] n **1.** [of cinema, hotel] hall m, vestibule m ; [of theatre] foyer m **2.** US [of house] entrée f, vestibule m.

FP n **1.** abbr of former pupil **2.** US abbr of fire-plug.

FPA (abbr of Family Planning Association) pr n association pour le planning familial.

Fr. 1. (written abbr of **father**) P **2.** (written abbr of **friar**) F.

fracas [UK 'fræka: US 'freɪkæs] (UK pl **fracas** [-ka:z] US pl **fracases** [-kəsɪz]) n [brawl] rixe f, bagarre f ; [noise] fracas m.

fraction ['frækʃn] n **1.** MATH fraction f **2.** fig [bit] fraction f, petite partie f.

fractionally ['frækʃnəlɪ] adv **1.** [slightly] un tout petit peu **2.** CHEM par fractionnement.

fractious ['frækʃəs] adj *fml* **1.** [unruly] indiscipliné, turbulent **2.** [irritable - child] grognon, pleurnicheur ; [- adult] irascible, revêche.

fracture ['fræktʃər] ◆ n fracture f. ◆ vt [break] fracturer. ◆ vi [break] se fracturer.

fragile [🇬🇧 'frædʒaɪl 🇺🇸 'frædʒl] adj **1.** [china, glass] fragile ; *fig* [peace, happiness] précaire, fragile **2.** [person] fragile, frêle.

fragility [frə'dʒɪlətɪ] n fragilité f.

fragment ◆ n ['frægmənt] [of china, text] fragment m, morceau m ; [of bomb] éclat m ; *fig* [of conversation] bribe f. ◆ vt [fræg'ment] [break] fragmenter, briser ; [divide] fragmenter, morceler. ◆ vi [fræg'ment] se fragmenter.

fragmentary ['frægməntrɪ] adj fragmentaire.

fragmentation [,frægmen'teɪʃn] n [breaking] fragmentation f ; [division] fragmentation f, morcellement m ▶ **fragmentation bomb** bombe f à fragmentation ▶ **fragmentation grenade** grenade f offensive.

fragmented [fræg'mentɪd] adj fragmenté, morcelé.

fragrance ['freɪɡrəns] n parfum m.

fragrance-free adj non parfumé.

fragrant ['freɪɡrənt] adj parfumé.

fragrant rice n riz m parfumé.

frail [freɪl] adj **1.** [object] fragile ; [person] fragile, frêle ; [health] délicat, fragile **2.** [happiness, hope] fragile, éphémère.

frailty ['freɪltɪ] (*pl* **frailties**) n [of health, hope, person] fragilité f ; [of character] faiblesse f.

frame [freɪm] ◆ n **1.** [border - gen] cadre m ; [- of canvas, picture, etc.] cadre m, encadrement m ; [- of window] cadre m, châssis m ; [- of door] encadrement m ; [- for spectacles] monture f **2.** [support, structure - gen] cadre m ; [- of bicycle] cadre m ; [- of car] châssis m ; [- of lampshade, racket, tent] armature f ; [- of machine] bâti m ; [- for walking] déambulateur m ; CONSTR charpente f ; TEXT métier m **3.** [in snooker, pool, etc.] triangle m **4.** [body] charpente f **5.** [setting, background] cadre m ; [area, scope] cadre m **6.** PHOT image f ; CIN image f, photogramme m ; TV trame f. ◆ vt **1.** [enclose, encase] encadrer **2.** *fml* [design, draft] élaborer ; [formulate, express] formuler **3.** *inf* [incriminate falsely] ▶ **to frame sb** monter un (mauvais) coup contre qqn.

frame of mind n état m d'esprit.

framework ['freɪmwɜːk] n **1.** [structure] cadre m, structure f ; CONSTR charpente f ; TECH bâti m **2.** *fig* cadre m.

franc [fræŋk] n franc m.

France [frɑːns] pr n France f / *in France* en France.

franchise ['fræntʃaɪz] ◆ n **1.** POL suffrage m, droit m de vote **2.** COMM & LAW franchise f. ◆ vt accorder une franchise à.

franchisee [,fræntʃaɪ'ziː] n COMM franchisé m.

franchiser ['fræntʃaɪzər] n COMM franchiseur m.

Francophile ['fræŋkəfaɪl] ◆ adj francophile. ◆ n francophile mf.

Francophobe ['fræŋkəfəʊb] ◆ adj francophobe. ◆ n francophobe mf.

Francophone ['fræŋkəfəʊn] ◆ adj francophone. ◆ n francophone mf.

Franglais ['frɒŋɡleɪ] n franglais m.

frank [fræŋk] ◆ adj franc (franche). ◆ vt 🇬🇧 affranchir. ◆ n 🇬🇧 **1.** [on letter] affranchissement m **2.** 🇺🇸 *inf* [sausage] saucisse f (de Francfort) ; [hot dog] hot-dog m.

Frank [fræŋk] n HIST Franc m, Franque f.

Frankfurt ['fræŋkfət] pr n ▶ **Frankfurt (am Main)** Francfort(-sur-le-Main).

frankfurter ['fræŋkfɜːtər] n saucisse f de Francfort.

frankincense ['fræŋkɪnsens] n encens m.

franking machine ['fræŋkɪŋ-] n machine f à affranchir.

frankly ['fræŋklɪ] adv franchement, sincèrement.

frankness ['fræŋknɪs] n franchise f.

frantic ['fræntɪk] adj **1.** [distraught, wild] éperdu, affolé / *she was frantic with worry* elle était folle d'inquiétude **2.** [very busy] : *a scene of frantic activity* une scène d'activité frénétique.

frantically ['fræntɪklɪ] adv désespérément.

frappe [🇬🇧 'fræpeɪ 🇺🇸 fræ'peɪ] n [drink] milk-shake m (épais).

frat [fræt] n 🇺🇸 abbr of **fraternity**.

fraternal [frə'tɜːnl] adj fraternel ▶ **fraternal twins** des faux jumeaux.

fraternally [frə'tɜːnəlɪ] adv fraternellement.

fraternity [frə'tɜːnətɪ] n (*pl* **fraternities**) **1.** [friendship] fraternité f **2.** [association] confrérie f **3.** 🇺🇸 UNIV *association d'étudiants très sélective*.

fraternize, fraternise ['frætənaɪz] vi fraterniser.

fraud [frɔːd] n **1.** LAW fraude f ; FIN escroquerie f **2.** [dishonest person] imposteur m **3.** [product, work] supercherie f.

fraudster ['frɔːdstər] n 🇬🇧 fraudeur m, -euse f.

fraudulence ['frɔːdjʊləns] n caractère m frauduleux.

fraudulent ['frɔːdjʊlənt] adj frauduleux ; LAW fraudatoire.

fraudulently ['frɔːdjʊləntlɪ] adv frauduleusement.

fraught [frɔːt] adj **1.** [filled] chargé, lourd / *fraught with danger* rempli de dangers **2.** 🇬🇧 *inf* [tense] tendu.

fray [freɪ] ◆ vt (*usu passive*) **1.** [clothing, fabric, rope] effilocher **2.** [nerves] mettre à vif. ◆ vi **1.** [clothing, fabric, rope] s'effilocher **2.** *fig* : *tempers began to fray* les gens commençaient à s'énerver or perdre patience. ◆ n ▶ **the fray** la mêlée.

frayed [freɪd] adj **1.** [garment] élimé **2.** *fig* : *tempers were increasingly frayed* les gens étaient de plus en plus irritables.

frazzled ['fræzld] adj *inf* [exhausted] crevé.

FRB (abbr of **Federal Reserve Board**) pr n *organe de contrôle de la Banque centrale américaine.*

FRCP (abbr of **Fellow of the Royal College of Physicians**) n *membre du RCP.*

FRCS (abbr of **Fellow of the Royal College of Surgeons**) n *membre du RCS.*

freak [friːk] ◆ n **1.** [abnormal event] caprice m de la nature ; [abnormal person] phénomène m de foire ; [eccentric person] phénomène m, farfelu m, -e f **2.** *inf* [fanatic] fana mf ; [addict] accro mf **3.** *liter* [caprice] foucade f. ◆ adj [accident, storm] insolite, anormal. ◆ vi *v inf* = **freak out (vi).** ❖ **freak out** *v inf* ◆ vi **1.** [on drugs] flipper **2.** [lose control of one's emotions] perdre les pédales. ◆ vt sep **1.** [cause to hallucinate] faire flipper **2.** [upset emotionally] déboussoler.

freaking, freakin' 🇺🇸 *v inf* ◆ adj : *that freaking car* cette voiture à la con. ◆ adv : *I don't freaking well know!* je ne sais pas, bordel ! / *it's freakin' cold* il fait vachement froid.

freakish ['friːkɪʃ] adj **1.** [abnormal, strange] étrange, insolite **2.** *liter* [capricious, changeable] changeant.

freaky ['friːkɪ] adj *inf* bizarre, insolite.

freckle ['frekl] ◆ n tache f de rousseur or son. ◆ vt marquer de taches de rousseur. ◆ vi se couvrir de taches de rousseur.

freckled ['frekld] adj taché de son, marqué de taches de rousseur.

free [fri:] ◆ adj **1.** [unconfined, unrestricted - person, animal, passage, way] libre / *the hostage managed to get free* l'otage a réussi à se libérer ▸ **to cut sb free** délivrer qqn en coupant ses liens ▸ **to let sb go free** relâcher qqn, remettre qqn en liberté ▸ **to set free a)** [prisoner, animal] remettre en liberté **b)** [slave] affranchir **c)** [hostage] libérer / *you are free to leave* vous êtes libre de partir / *feel free to visit us any time* ne vous gênez pas pour nous rendre visite quand vous voulez / *can I use the phone? — yes, feel free* puis-je téléphoner ? — mais certainement **2.** [unattached] libre, sans attaches **3.** [democratic] libre / *it's a free country!* on est en démocratie ! **4.** [at no cost] gratuit / *free admission* entrée f gratuite or libre ▸ **there's no such thing as a free lunch** les gens sont tous intéressés **5.** [not in use, unoccupied] libre / *could you let us know when you're free?* pourriez-vous nous faire savoir quand vous êtes libre or disponible ? / *she has very little free time* elle a peu de temps libre **6.** [unhampered] : *to be free from pain* ne pas souffrir / *I just want to be free of him!* je veux être débarrassé de lui ! **7.** [generous] : *she's very free with her criticism* elle ne ménage pas ses critiques. ◆ adv **1.** [at no cost] gratuitement **2.** [without restraint] librement. ◆ vt **1.** [release - gen] libérer ; [-prisoner] libérer, relâcher ; [-tied-up animal] détacher ; [-caged animal] libérer ; [-slave] affranchir ; COMM [prices, trade] libérer ; [funds] débloquer **2.** [disengage, disentangle] dégager / *she tried to free herself from his grasp* elle essaya de se libérer or dégager de son étreinte.

-free in comp ▸ **additive-free** sans additifs ▸ **salt-free** sans sel.

free agent n personne f libre or indépendante / *I'm a free agent* je ne dépends de personne.

freebie, freebee inf ['fri:bɪ] n cadeau m.

free climbing n SPORT escalade f libre.

freedom ['fri:dəm] n liberté f ▸ **freedom of speech / association** liberté d'expression / de réunion ▸ **freedom of information** liberté d'information ▸ **freedom of worship** liberté du culte.

freedom fighter n combattant m, -e f de la liberté.

free enterprise n libre entreprise f.

free-fall n chute f libre.

Freefone® ['fri:fəʊn] n UK appel gratuit, ≃ numéro m vert.

free-for-all n mêlée f générale.

free-form adj de forme libre.

freegan n personne qui se nourrit d'aliments encore consommables trouvés dans les poubelles, récupérés après la fermeture de marchés, etc.

free gift n COMM cadeau.

freehold ['fri:həʊld] ◆ n ≃ propriété f foncière inaliénable. ◆ adv ▸ **to buy / to sell sthg freehold** acheter / vendre qqch en propriété inaliénable. ◆ adj ▸ **freehold property** propriété f inaliénable.

freeholder ['fri:həʊldər] n ≃ propriétaire m foncier ; ≃ propriétaire f foncière (à perpétuité).

free house n UK pub libre de ses approvisionnements (et non lié à une brasserie particulière).

free jazz n free jazz m.

free kick n coup m franc.

freelance ['fri:lɑ:ns] ◆ n travailleur m indépendant, travailleuse f indépendante, free-lance mf ; [journalist, writer]

pigiste mf. ◆ adj indépendant, free-lance. ◆ adv en free-lance, en indépendant. ◆ vi travailler en free-lance or indépendant.

freelancer ['fri:lɑ:nsər] n travailleur m indépendant, travailleuse f indépendante, free-lance mf.

freeloader ['fri:ləʊdər] n inf pique-assiette mf, parasite mf.

freely ['fri:lɪ] adv **1.** [without constraint] librement **2.** [liberally - spend] largement ; [-perspire, weep] abondamment.

freeman ['fri:mən] (pl freemen [-mən]) n HIST homme m libre ; [citizen] citoyen m / *he's a freeman of the city* il est citoyen d'honneur de la ville.

free-market adj ▸ **free-market economy** économie f de marché.

freemason, Freemason ['fri:,meɪsn] n franc-maçon m.

freemasonry, Freemasonry ['fri:,meɪsnrɪ] n franc-maçonnerie f.

free paper n UK journal m gratuit.

Freepost® ['fri:pəʊst] n UK port m payé.

free-range adj [chicken] fermier ▸ **free-range eggs** œufs mpl de poules élevées en plein air.

freesia ['fri:zjə] n freesia m.

free speech n liberté f de parole or d'expression.

free spirit n non-conformiste mf.

free-standing adj isolé ; GRAM indépendant.

freestyle ['fri:staɪl] n [in swimming] nage f libre ; [in skiing] ski m artistique or acrobatique ; [in wrestling] lutte f libre.

freethinker [,fri:'θɪŋkər] n libre-penseur m.

F2T MESSAGING written abbr of free to talk.

Freetown ['fri:taʊn] pr n Freetown.

free trade n libre-échange m.

free-trade agreement n accord m de libre-échange.

freeware ['fri:weər] n COMPUT gratuiciels mpl.

freeway ['fri:weɪ] n US autoroute f.

freewheel [,fri:'wi:l] ◆ n [on bicycle] roue f libre. ◆ vi **1.** [cyclist] être en roue libre **2.** [motorist] rouler au point mort.

freewheeling [,fri:'wi:lɪŋ] adj inf désinvolte, sans-gêne (inv).

free will n libre arbitre m.

freeze [fri:z] (pt froze [frəʊz], pp frozen ['frəʊzn]) ◆ vi **1.** [earth, pipes, water] geler ; [food] se congeler / *to freeze to death* mourir de froid **2.** fig [stop moving] : (everybody) freeze! que personne ne bouge ! ◆ vt **1.** [water] geler, congeler ; [food] congeler ; [at very low temperatures] surgeler ; MED [blood, human tissue] congeler **2.** ECON & FIN [assets] geler ; [prices, wages] bloquer **3.** CIN ▸ **freeze it!** arrêtez l'image ! ◆ n METEOR gel m ; ECON & FIN gel m, blocage m ▸ **pay freeze** gel or blocage des salaires. ❖ **freeze out** vt sep inf exclure. ❖ **freeze over** vi geler. ❖ **freeze up** vi **1.** [turn to ice] geler **2.** inf [become immobilized] rester pétrifié.

freeze-dried adj lyophilisé.

freeze-dry vt lyophiliser.

freeze-drying n lyophilisation f.

freeze-frame n arrêt m sur image.

freezer ['fri:zər] n congélateur m ; [in refrigerator] freezer m ▸ **freezer compartment** compartiment m congélateur (d'un réfrigérateur).

freezing ['fri:zɪŋ] ◆ adj METEOR glacial ; [person] gelé, glacé / *it's freezing in this room!* on gèle dans cette pièce !

◆ n : *it's two degrees above / below freezing* il fait deux degrés au-dessus / au-dessous de zéro. ◆ adv : *a freezing cold day* une journée glaciale.

freezing point n point *m* de congélation.

freight [freɪt] ◆ n **1.** [goods] fret *m* **2.** [transport] ▶ **to send goods by freight** envoyer des marchandises en régime ordinaire. ◆ comp [transport] de fret ▶ **freight charges** frais *mpl* de port. ◆ vt transporter.

freight train n US train *m* de marchandises.

freight yard n US dépôt *m* de marchandises.

French [frentʃ] ◆ pl n [people] ▶ **the French** les Français. ◆ n LING français *m*. ◆ adj [person, cooking, customs] français ; [ambassador, embassy, king] de France.

French bean n haricot *m* vert.

French bread n baguette *f*.

French Canadian ◆ adj canadien français. ◆ n **1.** [person] Canadien *m* français, Canadienne *f* française **2.** LING français *m* canadien.

French chalk n craie *f* de tailleur.

French dip n US sauce *f* (*pour tremper les aliments*).

French door = French window.

French dressing n [in UK] vinaigrette *f* ; [in US] *sauce de salade à base de mayonnaise et de ketchup.*

french fries pl n frites *fpl*.

French horn n cor *m* d'harmonie.

French kiss ◆ n baiser *m* profond. ◆ vt embrasser sur la bouche (*avec la langue*). ◆ vi s'embrasser sur la bouche (*avec la langue*).

Frenchman ['frentʃmən] (*pl* **Frenchmen** [-mən]) n Français *m*.

French polish n UK vernis *m* (à l'alcool). ◆ **French-polish** vt UK vernir (à l'alcool).

French stick n UK baguette *f*.

French toast n [in UK] *pain grillé d'un seul côté* ; [in US] pain *m* perdu.

French window n UK porte-fenêtre *f*.

Frenchwoman ['frentʃ,wʊmən] (*pl* **Frenchwomen** [-,wɪmɪn]) n Française *f*.

frenemy ['frenəmɪ] n *ennemi qui se fait passer pour un ami.*

frenetic [frə'netɪk] adj frénétique.

frenetically [frə'netɪklɪ] adv frénétiquement.

frenzied ['frenzɪd] adj [activity] frénétique, forcené ; [crowd] déchaîné ; [person] forcené, déchaîné.

frenzy ['frenzɪ] n **1.** [fury, passion] frénésie *f* **2.** [fit, outburst] accès *m*, crise *f*.

frequency ['fri:kwənsɪ] n fréquence *f*.

frequency modulation n modulation *f* de fréquence.

frequent ◆ adj ['fri:kwənt] fréquent. ◆ vt [frɪ'kwent] *liter* fréquenter.

frequently ['fri:kwəntlɪ] adv fréquemment, souvent.

frequent user card n carte *f* de fidélité.

fresco ['freskəʊ] (*pl* **frescoes** *or* **frescos**) n fresque *f*.

fresh [freʃ] ◆ adj **1.** [recently made or produced] frais (fraîche) **2.** [idea, problem] nouveau (*before vowel or silent 'h' nouvel, f nouvelle*), original ; [news, paint] frais (fraîche) ; [impression] frais (fraîche) **3.** [not salt - water] doux (douce) **4.** [rested] frais (fraîche) **5.** [clean] frais (fraîche), pur **6.** [bright] ▶ **fresh colours** des couleurs fraîches **7.** METEOR [gen] frais (fraîche) ; [on Beaufort scale] ▶ **fresh breeze** bonne brise *f* ▶ **fresh gale** coup *m* de vent **8.** [refreshing - taste] rafraîchissant **9.** US *inf* [impudent] insolent ; [child] mal élevé

10. US *inf* [sexually forward] effronté. ◆ adv fraîchement ▶ **to be fresh out of sthg** *inf* être à court de or manquer de qqch.

freshen ['freʃn] ◆ vt rafraîchir. ◆ vi NAUT [wind] fraîchir. ◆ **freshen up** ◆ vi faire un brin de toilette. ◆ vt sep **1.** [person] faire un brin de toilette à **2.** [house, room] donner un petit coup de peinture à **3.** [drink] : *let me freshen up your drink* laisse-moi te resservir à boire.

fresher ['freʃər] n *inf* UNIV bizut *m*, bizuth *m*, étudiant *m*, -e *f* de première année.

fresh-faced adj [person] au teint frais.

freshly ['freʃlɪ] adv récemment.

freshman ['freʃmən] (*pl* **freshmen** [-mən]) US = fresher.

freshness ['freʃnɪs] n fraîcheur *f*.

freshwater ['freʃ,wɔ:tər] adj ▶ **freshwater fish** poisson *m* d'eau douce.

fret [fret] (*pt & pp* **fretted**, *cont* **fretting**) ◆ vi [worry] tracasser ▶ **to fret about** or **over sb** se faire du souci pour qqn. ◆ vt [worry] : *to fret one's life away* passer sa vie à se tourmenter or à se faire du mauvais sang. ◆ n [on a guitar] touchette *f*, frette *f*.

fretful ['fretfʊl] adj [anxious] soucieux ; [irritable, complaining] grincheux, maussade.

fretfully ['fretfʊlɪ] adv [anxiously - ask, say] avec inquiétude.

fretsaw ['fretsɔ:] n scie *f* à chantourner.

Freudian slip n lapsus *m*.

FRG (abbr of **Federal Republic of Germany**) pr n RFA *f*.

Fri. (written abbr of **Friday**) ven.

friar ['fraɪər] n frère *m*, moine *m*.

fricassee ['frɪkəsi:] ◆ n fricassée *f*. ◆ vt fricasser.

frickin' ['frɪkɪn], **fricking** ['frɪkɪŋ] adj US *vulg* = freakin(g).

friction ['frɪkʃn] n **1.** PHYS friction *f* **2.** [discord] friction *f*, conflit *m*.

friction tape n US chatterton *m*.

Friday ['fraɪdeɪ] n vendredi *m* / *it's Friday today* nous sommes or on est vendredi aujourd'hui / *he leaves on Friday, he leaves Friday* US il part vendredi / *the cleaning woman comes on Fridays* la femme de ménage vient le vendredi / *I work Fridays* je travaille le vendredi / *there's a market each Friday* or *every Friday* il y a un marché tous les vendredis or chaque vendredi / *the following Friday* le vendredi suivant / *she saw the doctor last Friday* elle a vu le médecin vendredi dernier / *I have an appointment next Friday* j'ai un rendez-vous vendredi prochain / *a week from Friday, a week on Friday* UK, *Friday week* UK vendredi en huit / *Friday morning* vendredi matin.

fridge [frɪdʒ] n UK réfrigérateur *m*.

fridge-freezer n réfrigérateur-congélateur *m*.

fried [fraɪd] adj frit ▶ **fried eggs** œufs *mpl* poêlés or sur le plat ▶ **fried food** friture *f* ▶ **fried potatoes** pommes *fpl* frites ▶ **(special) fried rice** riz *m* cantonais.

friend [frend] ◆ n **1.** [gen] ami *m*, -e *f* ▶ **to make friends** se faire des amis ▶ **Friends of the Earth** les Amis de la Terre ▶ **the (Society of) Friends** RELIG la Société des Amis, les Quakers **2.** [addressing someone] : *listen, friend* écoute, mon pote **3.** [colleague] collègue *mf* **4.** [patron] mécène *m*, ami *m*, -e *f*. ◆ vt US [on networking site] marquer comme ami.

friendless ['frendlɪs] adj sans amis.

friendliness ['frendlɪnɪs] n gentillesse *f*.

friendly ['frendlɪ] (*compar* **friendlier**, *superl* **friendliest**) ◆ adj **1.** [person] aimable, gentil ; [animal] gentil ; [advice, game, smile] amical ▸ **to be friendly to** or **towards sb** être gentil or aimable avec qqn **2.** [close, intimate] ami ; [allied] ami ▸ **friendly fire** MIL feu *m* allié. ◆ n [match] match *m* amical.

friendly society n ⬛ société *f* mutuelle or de secours mutuels.

friendly takeover bid n OPA *f* amicale.

F? MESSAGING written abbr of **friends?**

friendship ['frendʃɪp] n amitié *f.*

Friesian ['friːʒən] n ▸ **Friesian (cow)** frisonne *f.*

frieze [friːz] n **1.** ARCHIT frise *f* **2.** TEXT ratine *f.*

frigate ['frɪgət] n frégate *f.*

frigate bird n ORNITH frégate *f.*

frigging ['frɪgɪŋ] adj *v inf* : *move your frigging car!* enlève-moi cette foutue bagnole !

fright [fraɪt] n **1.** [sudden fear] frayeur *f*, peur *f* ▸ **to take fright at sthg** avoir peur de qqch ▸ **to give sb a fright** faire une frayeur à qqn **2.** *inf* [mess] : *you look an absolute fright* tu fais vraiment peur à voir.

frighten ['fraɪtn] vt effrayer, faire peur à ▸ **to frighten sb out of doing sthg** dissuader qqn de faire qqch en lui faisant peur ▸ **to frighten sb into doing sthg** obliger qqn à faire qqch en lui faisant peur. ◈ **frighten away** vt sep faire fuir (par la peur) ; [animal] effaroucher. ◈ **frighten off** vt sep **1.** [cause to flee] faire fuir ; [animal] effaroucher **2.** [intimidate] chasser, faire peur à, faire fuir.

frightened ['fraɪtnd] adj effrayé ▸ **to be frightened of sthg** avoir peur de qqch.

> 🗒 Note that **avoir peur que** and **craindre que** are followed by a verb in the subjunctive, usually preceded by ne:
> **I was frightened they might want to kill me.**
> *J'avais peur* / *Je craignais qu'ils ne veuillent me tuer.*

frightening ['fraɪtnɪŋ] adj effrayant.

frighteningly ['fraɪtnɪŋlɪ] adv à faire peur.

frightful ['fraɪtfʊl] adj **1.** [horrible] affreux, horrible **2.** ⬛ *inf* [unpleasant] : *we had a frightful time parking the car* on a eu un mal fou à garer la voiture / *he's a frightful bore* [as intensifier] il est horriblement or affreusement casse-pieds.

frightfully ['fraɪtfʊlɪ] adv ⬛ *inf & dated* : *I'm frightfully sorry* je suis absolument désolé.

frigid ['frɪdʒɪd] adj **1.** [very cold] glacial, glacé ; GEOG & METEOR glacial **2.** [sexually] frigide.

frigidity [frɪ'dʒɪdətɪ] n **1.** [coldness] froideur *f* **2.** PSYCHOL frigidité *f.*

frill [frɪl] n TEXT ruche *f*, volant *m* ; CULIN papillote *f* ; ORNITH collerette *f.* ◈ **frills** pl n [ornamentation, luxuries] : *without frills* sans façon.

frilly ['frɪlɪ] adj **1.** TEXT orné de fanfreluches **2.** [style] affecté, apprêté.

fringe [frɪndʒ] ◆ n **1.** [decorative edge] frange *f* **2.** [of hair] frange *f* **3.** [periphery] périphérie *f*, frange *f* ▸ **on the fringe** or **fringes of a)** *lit* en bordure de **b)** *fig* en marge de **4.** THEAT ▸ **the Fringe (festival)** ⬛ le festival off. ◆ vt franger.

fringe benefit n avantage *m* annexe or en nature.

fringe theatre n ⬛ théâtre *m* d'avant-garde or expérimental.

Frisbee® ['frɪzbɪ] n Frisbee *m inv.*

Frisian Islands pl pr n ▸ **the Frisian Islands** l'archipel *m* frison.

frisk [frɪsk] ◆ vi [play] gambader. ◆ vt [search] fouiller. ◆ n [search] fouille *f.*

frisky ['frɪskɪ] (*compar* **friskier**, *superl* **friskiest**) adj [animal] fringant ; [person] gaillard.

fritter ['frɪtə*] ◆ n CULIN beignet *m.* ◆ vt = **fritter away.** ◈ **fritter away** vt sep gaspiller.

fritz [frɪts] n ⬛ *inf* ▸ **to be on the fritz** être en panne.

frivolity [frɪ'vɒlətɪ] (*pl* **frivolities**) n frivolité *f.*

frivolous ['frɪvələs] adj frivole.

frivolously ['frɪvələslɪ] adv de manière frivole.

frizz [frɪz] ◆ n : *she had a frizz of blond hair* elle avait des cheveux blonds tout frisés. ◆ vt faire friser. ◆ vi friser.

frizzly ['frɪzlɪ] (*compar* **frizzlier**, *superl* **frizzliest**), **frizzy** ['frɪzɪ] (*compar* **frizzier**, *superl* **frizziest**) adj crépu.

fro [frəʊ] ⟶ to and fro.

frock [frɒk] n [dress] robe *f* ; RELIG froc *m.*

frog [frɒg] n **1.** ZOOL grenouille *f* ▸ **frog's legs** CULIN cuisses *fpl* de grenouille **2.** [on uniform] brandebourg *m* ; [on women's clothing] soutache *f.* ◈ **Frog** n ⬛ *v inf* [French person] *terme injurieux désignant un Français.*

frogman ['frɒgmən] (*pl* **frogmen** [-mən]) n homme-grenouille *m.*

frogmarch ['frɒgmɑːtʃ] vt ⬛ *porter par les bras et les jambes, le visage vers le sol.*

frogspawn ['frɒgspɔːn] n frai *m* de grenouilles.

frolic ['frɒlɪk] (*pt & pp* **frolicked**, *cont* **frolicking**) ◆ vi s'ébattre, gambader. ◆ n [run] gambades *fpl* ; [game] jeu *m.*

from (*weak form* [frəm], *strong form* [frɒm]) prep **1.** [indicating starting point - in space] de ; [- in time] de, à partir de, depuis ; [- in price, quantity] à partir de / *where's your friend from?* d'où est or vient votre ami ? / *I've just come back from there* j'en reviens / *from now on* désormais, dorénavant / *from the age of four* à partir de quatre ans / *knives from £2 each* des couteaux à partir de 2 livres la pièce / *6 from 14 is 8* 6 ôté de 14 donne 8 **2.** [indicating origin, source] de / *who's the letter from?* de qui est la lettre ? / *I bought my piano from a neighbour* j'ai acheté mon piano à un voisin / *you mustn't borrow money from them* vous ne devez pas leur emprunter de l'argent / *he translates from English into French* il traduit d'anglais en français **3.** [off, out of] : *she took a book from the shelf* elle a pris un livre sur l'étagère / *he took a beer from the fridge* il a pris une bière dans le frigo **4.** [indicating cause, reason] : *you can get sick from drinking the water* vous pouvez tomber malade en buvant l'eau / *he died from grief* il est mort de chagrin **5.** [using] : *Calvados is made from apples* le calvados est fait avec des pommes / *she played the piece from memory* elle joua le morceau de mémoire **6.** [judging by] d'après / *from what I gather...* d'après ce que j'ai cru comprendre... **7.** [indicating prevention, protection] de / *we sheltered from the rain in a cave* nous nous sommes abrités de la pluie dans une caverne.

frond [frɒnd] n fronde *f* ; [on palm tree] feuille *f.*

front [frʌnt] ◆ n **1.** [forward part] devant *m* ; [of vehicle] avant *m* ; [of queue] début *m* ; [of stage] devant *m* ; [of building] façade *f* / *I'll be at the front of the train* je serai en tête de or à l'avant du train / *our seats were at the front of the theatre* nous avions des places aux premiers rangs (du théâtre) / *she wrote her name on the front of the envelope* elle écrivit son nom sur le devant de l'enveloppe **2.** [seashore] bord *m* de mer, front *m* de mer / *the hotel is on the front* l'hôtel est au bord de la or sur le front de mer **3.** MIL front *m* **/** *on the Eastern* **/** *Western* front sur le front est **/** ouest ; *fig* : *the Prime Minister is being attacked on all fronts* on s'en prend au Premier ministre de tous côtés **4.** [appearance] façade *f* ▶ **to put on a bold** or **brave front** faire preuve de courage. ◆ adj **1.** [in a forward position] de devant **/** *front seat* **/** *wheel* AUTO siège *m* **/** roue *f* avant **/** *the front page* PRESS la première page **/** *his name is on the front cover* son nom est en couverture **/** *a front view* une vue de face. **2.** LING ▶ **a front vowel** une voyelle avant or antérieure. ◆ vi 🇬🇧 [face] : *the hotel fronts onto the beach* l'hôtel donne sur la plage. ◆ vt [lead] être à la tête de, diriger ; TV [present] présenter. ❖ **in front** adv phr [in theatre, vehicle] à l'avant ; [ahead, leading] en avant **/** *there was a very tall man in the row in front* il y avait un très grand homme assis devant moi ▶ **to be in front** être en tête or premier. ❖ **in front of** prep phr devant **/** *he was right in front of me* il était juste devant moi.

frontage ['frʌntɪdʒ] n **1.** [wall] façade *f* ; [shopfront] devanture *f* **2.** [land] terrain *m* en bordure.

frontal ['frʌntl] ◆ adj MIL [assault, attack] de front ; ANAT & MED frontal ▶ **frontal system** METEOR système *m* de fronts. ◆ n RELIG parement *m*.

frontbench [,frʌnt'bentʃ] n 🇬🇧 POL [members of the government] ministres *mpl* ; [members of the opposition] ministres *mpl* du cabinet fantôme ▶ **the frontbenches** [in Parliament] *à la Chambre des communes, bancs situés à droite et à gauche du président et occupés respectivement par les ministres du gouvernement en exercice et ceux du gouvernement fantôme.*

frontbencher [,frʌnt'bentʃə^r] n 🇬🇧 POL [member of the government] ministre *m* ; [member of the opposition] membre *m* du cabinet fantôme.

front desk n réception *f.*

front door n [of house] porte *f* d'entrée ; [of vehicle] portière *f* avant.

frontier [🇬🇧 'frʌn,tɪə 🇺🇸 frʌn'tɪər] ◆ n **1.** *lit & fig* [border] frontière *f* **2.** 🇺🇸 ▶ **the frontier** la Frontière *(nom donné à la limite des terres habitées par les colons pendant la colonisation de l'Amérique du Nord).* ◆ comp **1.** [dispute] de frontière ; [post] frontière **2.** 🇺🇸 [spirit] de pionnier ▶ **a frontier town** une bourgade d'une région limitrophe du pays.

frontispiece ['frʌntɪspiːs] n frontispice *m.*

front line n ▶ **the front line** MIL la première ligne. ❖ **front-line** adj **1.** MIL [soldiers, troops] en première ligne ; [ambulance] de zone de combat **2.** POL ▶ **the front line states** les États *mpl* limitrophes **3.** 🇺🇸 SPORT ▶ **front line player** avant *m.*

front-loader n [washing machine] machine *f* à laver à chargement frontal.

front-loading adj [washing machine] à chargement frontal.

front lot n 🇺🇸 cour *f (devant un immeuble).*

front man n **1.** [representative, spokesman] porte-parole *m inv*, représentant *m* **2.** *pej* [figurehead] prête-nom *m* **3.** TV [presenter] présentateur *m.*

frontman ['frʌntmæn] n [lead singer] chanteur *m.*

front of house n THEAT *partie d'un théâtre où peuvent circuler les spectateurs.*

front-page, front page adj [article, story] de première page.

front-rank adj : *a front-rank question* une question de premier ordre or plan.

front room n [at front of house] *pièce qui donne sur le devant de la maison* ; [sitting room] salon *m.*

front-runner n favori *m*, -e *f.*

front-wheel drive n traction *f* avant.

front yard n 🇺🇸 jardin *m (devant une maison).*

frost [frɒst] ◆ n **1.** [freezing weather] gel *m*, gelée *f* **2.** [frozen dew] givre *m*, gelée *f* blanche **3.** *inf* [cold manner] froideur *f.* ◆ vt **1.** [freeze] geler ; [cover with frost] givrer **2.** 🇺🇸 [cake] glacer **3.** TECH [glass pane] dépolir. ◆ vi [freeze] geler ; [become covered with frost] se givrer. ❖ **frost over, frost up** ◆ vi se givrer. ◆ vt sep givrer.

frostbite ['frɒstbaɪt] n *(U)* gelure *f.*

frostbitten ['frɒst,bɪtn] adj [hands, nose] gelé ; [plant] gelé, grillé par le gel.

frosted ['frɒstɪd] adj **1.** [frozen] gelé ; [covered with frost] givré **2.** [pane of glass] dépoli **3.** 🇺🇸 [cake] glacé **4.** [lipstick, nail varnish] nacré.

frost-free adj [refrigerator, freezer] à dégivrage automatique.

frostily ['frɒstɪlɪ] adv de manière glaciale, froidement.

frosting ['frɒstɪŋ] n 🇺🇸 glaçage *m*, glace *f.*

frostproof ['frɒstpruːf] adj résistant à la gelée.

frosty ['frɒstɪ] (*compar* **frostier**, *superl* **frostiest**) adj **1.** [weather, air] glacial **2.** [ground, window] couvert de givre **3.** [answer, manner] glacial, froid.

froth [frɒθ] ◆ n *(U)* **1.** [foam] écume *f*, mousse *f* ; [on beer] mousse *f* ; [on lips] écume *f* **2.** [trivialities, empty talk] futilités *fpl.* ◆ vi [liquid] écumer, mousser ; [beer, soap] mousser ▶ **to froth at the mouth** écumer, baver. ◆ vt faire mousser.

frothy ['frɒθɪ] (*compar* **frothier**, *superl* **frothiest**) adj **1.** [liquid] mousseux, écumeux ; [beer] mousseux ; [sea] écumeux **2.** [entertainment, literature] creux **3.** [dress, lace] léger, vaporeux.

frown [fraʊn] ◆ vi froncer les sourcils, se renfrogner ▶ **to frown at sb** regarder qqn de travers, faire les gros yeux à qqn. ◆ n froncement *m* de sourcils. ◆ comp ▶ **frown lines** rides *fpl* inter-sourcilières. ❖ **frown on, frown upon** vt insep désapprouver.

froze [frəʊz] pt ⟶ **freeze.**

frozen ['frəʊzn] ◆ pp ⟶ **freeze.** ◆ adj **1.** [ground, lake, pipes] gelé ; [person] gelé, glacé ▶ **frozen food a)** [in refrigerator] aliments *mpl* congelés **b)** [industrially frozen] surgelés *mpl* ▶ **frozen food compartment** congélateur *m* ▶ **frozen peas** petits pois *mpl* surgelés **2.** [prices, salaries] bloqué ; FIN [assets, credit] gelé, bloqué **3.** MED ▶ **frozen shoulder** épaule *f* ankylosée.

FRS ◆ n (abbr of **Fellow of the Royal Society**) ≃ membre *m* de l'Académie des sciences. ◆ pr n **abbr of Federal Reserve System.**

fructose ['frʌktəʊs] n fructose *m.*

frugal ['fruːgl] adj **1.** [person] économe, frugal ; [life] frugal, simple **2.** [meal] frugal.

frugally ['fruːgəlɪ] adv [live] simplement, frugalement ; [distribute, give] parcimonieusement.

fruit [fruːt] ◆ n *(pl* **fruit**) *lit* fruit *m* **/** *to eat fruit* manger des fruits **/** *a piece of fruit* un fruit ; *fig* fruit *m* **2.** 🇺🇸 *v inf & pej* [homosexual] pédé *m*, tante *f.* ◆ comp [basket, knife] à fruits ; [diet, farm, stall] fruitier ▶ **fruit farmer** arboriculteur *m* (fruitier) ▶ **fruit juice / salad** jus *m* / salade *f* de fruits ▶ **fruit tree** arbre *m* fruitier. ◆ vi BOT donner.

fruit-bearing adj [tree, etc.] frugifère, fructifère.

fruit bowl n compotier *m.*

fruit cake n **1.** [cake] cake *m* **2.** *inf* [lunatic] cinglé *m*, -e *f.*

fruit cocktail n macédoine *f* de fruits.

fruit-eating adj [animal] frugivore.

fruiterer ['fru:tərə'] n 🇬🇧 marchand *m*, -e *f* de fruits, fruitier *m*, -ère *f*.

fruit fly n mouche *f* du vinaigre, drosophile *f*.

fruitful ['fru:tful] adj **1.** [discussion, suggestion] fructueux, utile ; [attempt, collaboration] fructueux **2.** [soil] fertile, fécond ; [plant, tree] fécond, productif.

fruitfully ['fru:tfulɪ] adv fructueusement.

fruition [fru:'ɪʃn] n *fml* réalisation *f* ▸ **to come to fruition** se réaliser.

fruitless ['fru:tlɪs] adj **1.** [discussion, effort] vain, sans résultat **2.** [plant, tree] stérile, infécond ; [soil] stérile.

fruitlessly ['fru:tlɪslɪ] adv en vain, vainement.

fruit machine n 🇬🇧 machine *f* à sous.

fruity ['fru:tɪ] (*compar* **fruitier**, *superl* **fruitiest**) adj **1.** [flavour, sauce] fruité, de fruit ; [perfume, wine] fruité **2.** [voice] étoffé, timbré **3.** *inf* [joke, story] corsé, salé **4.** *inf* [effeminate] efféminé.

frump [frʌmp] n femme *f* mal habillée.

frumpily ['frʌmpɪlɪ] adv : **frumpily dressed** mal fagoté.

frumpish ['frʌmpɪʃ], **frumpy** ['frʌmpɪ] adj mal habillé.

frumpishly ['frʌmpɪʃlɪ] adv : **frumpishly dressed** mal fagoté.

frustrate [frʌ'streɪt] vt [person] frustrer, agacer, contrarier ; [efforts, plans] contrecarrer, faire échouer, contrarier ; [plot] déjouer, faire échouer.

frustrated [frʌ'streɪtɪd] adj **1.** [annoyed] frustré, agacé ; [disappointed] frustré, déçu ; [sexually] frustré **2.** [attempt, effort] vain.

frustrating [frʌ'streɪtɪŋ] adj agaçant, frustrant, pénible.

frustration [frʌ'streɪʃn] n [gen & PSYCHOL] frustration *f*.

fry [fraɪ] (*pt & pp* **fried**, *pl* **fries**) ◆ vt CULIN faire frire, frire. ◆ vi [food] frire ; *fig* [person] griller. ◆ n *(U)* ZOOL [fish] fretin *m* ; [frogs] têtards *mpl*. ❖ **fries** pl n 🇺🇸 = **french fries**. ❖ **fry up** vt sep faire frire, frire.

fryer ['fraɪə'] n **1.** [pan] poêle *f* (à frire) ; [for deep-fat frying] friteuse *f* **2.** [chicken] poulet *m* à frire.

frying pan 🇬🇧, **fry pan** 🇺🇸 n poêle *f* (à frire).

fry-up n 🇬🇧 *inf* plat constitué de plusieurs aliments frits ensemble.

FSA (abbr of **Food Standards Agency**) n *agence pour la sécurité alimentaire.*

ft 1. written abbr of **foot 2.** written abbr of **fort**.

FT pr n abbr of **Financial Times**.

FTC pr n abbr of **Federal Trade Commission**.

FTP (abbr of **file transfer protocol**) n FTP *m*.

FTSE ['futsi] (abbr of **Financial Times Stock Exchange**) pr n ▸ **the FTSE 100 index** l'index FTSE 100.

fuchsia ['fju:ʃə] n [colour] fuchsia *m* ; BOT fuchsia *m*.

fuck [fʌk] *vulg* ◆ vt baiser ▸ **fuck you!** or **go fuck yourself!** va te faire foutre or enculer ! ▸ **fuck it!** putain de merde ! ◆ vi baiser ▸ **don't fuck with me!** *fig* essaie pas de te foutre de ma gueule ! ◆ n **1.** [act] baise *f* **2.** [sexual partner] : **he's a good fuck** il baise bien **3.** 🇺🇸 [idiot] : **you stupid fuck!** espèce de connard ! **4.** [as intensifier] : **what the fuck do you expect?** mais qu'est-ce que tu veux, putain de merde ? **5.** 🅿🅷🆁 **I don't give a fuck** j'en ai rien à branler. ◆ interj putain de merde ! ❖ **fuck about** 🇬🇧, **fuck around** *vulg* ◆ vi déconner. ◆ vt sep faire chier. ❖ **fuck off** vi *vulg* foutre le camp / **fuck off!** va te faire enculer or foutre ! ❖ **fuck up** *vulg* ◆ vt sep [plan, project] foutre la merde dans ; [person] foutre dans la merde. ◆ vi merder. ❖ **fuck with** vt insep : **don't fuck with me** ne me me fais pas chier.

fuck all n *vulg* que dalle.

fucker ['fʌkə'] n *vulg* : **you stupid fucker!** mais qu'est-ce que tu peux être con !

fucking ['fʌkɪŋ] *vulg* ◆ adj : **I'm fed up with this fucking car!** j'en ai plein le cul de cette putain de bagnole ! / **you fucking idiot!** pauvre con ! ▸ **fucking hell!** putain de merde ! ◆ adv : **he's fucking stupid!** tu parles d'un con ! / **it was a fucking awful day!** tu parles d'une putain de journée !

fuck-me adj *vulg* : **a fuck-me dress** une robe *f* de pute / **fuck-me shoes** chaussures *fpl* de pute.

fuckwit n 🇺🇸 *vulg* pauvre con *m*, pauvre conne *f*.

fuddled ['fʌdld] adj [ideas, mind] embrouillé, confus ; [person - confused] confus ; [- tipsy] gris, éméché.

fuddy-duddy ['fʌdɪˌdʌdɪ] (*pl* **fuddy-duddies**) n *inf* vieux schnock *m*, vieille schnoque *f*.

fudge [fʌdʒ] ◆ n **1.** *(U)* [sweet] caramel *m* **2.** *(U)* [dodging] faux-fuyant *m*, échappatoire *f*. ◆ vi [evade, hedge] esquiver le problème. ◆ vt **1.** [make up - excuse] inventer ; [- story] monter ; [- figures, results] truquer **2.** [avoid, dodge] esquiver **3.** 🇺🇸 [ruin] : **I fudged it** je l'ai complètement raté.

fuel [fjʊəl] (🇬🇧 *pt & pp* **fuelled**, *cont* **fuelling** ; 🇺🇸 *pt & pp* **fueled**, *cont* **fueling**) ◆ n **1.** [gen & AERON] combustible *m* ; [coal] charbon *m* ; [oil] mazout *m*, fuel *m*, fioul *m* ; [wood] bois *m* ; AUTO carburant *m* **2.** *fig* ▸ **to add fuel to the flames** jeter de l'huile sur le feu. ◆ comp [bill, costs] de chauffage ▸ **fuel gauge** jauge *f* à essence ▸ **fuel injector** injecteur *m* de carburant ▸ **fuel tank a)** [in home] cuve *f* à mazout **b)** [in car] réservoir *m* de carburant or d'essence **c)** [in ship] soute *f* à mazout or à fuel. ◆ vt **1.** [furnace] alimenter (en combustible) ; [car, plane, ship] approvisionner en carburant **2.** *fig* [controversy] aviver.

fuel-efficient adj économique, qui ne consomme pas beaucoup.

fuel pump n pompe *f* d'alimentation.

fug [fʌg] n 🇬🇧 renfermé *m*.

fugitive ['fju:dʒɪtɪv] ◆ n [escapee] fugitif *m*, -ive *f*, évadé *m*, -e *f* ; [refugee] réfugié *m*, -e *f*. ◆ adj **1.** [debtor, slave] fugitif **2.** *liter* [beauty, happiness] éphémère, passager ; [impression, thought, vision] fugitif, passager.

fugue [fju:g] n MUS & PSYCHOL fugue *f*.

fulcrum ['fulkrəm] (*pl* **fulcrums** *or* **fulcra** [-krə]) n [pivot] pivot *m*, point *m* d'appui ; *fig* [prop, support] point *m* d'appui.

fulfil 🇬🇧, **fulfill** 🇺🇸 [ful'fɪl] (*pt & pp* **fulfilled**, *cont* **fulfilling**) vt **1.** [carry out - ambition, dream, plan] réaliser ; [- prophecy, task] accomplir, réaliser ; [- promise] tenir ; [- duty, obligation] remplir, s'acquitter de **2.** [satisfy - condition] remplir ; [- norm, regulation] répondre à, obéir à ; [- desire, need] satisfaire, répondre à ; [- prayer, wish] exaucer **3.** COMM [order] exécuter ; [contract] remplir, respecter.

fulfilled [ful'fɪld] adj [life] épanoui, heureux ; [person] épanoui, comblé.

fulfilling [ful'fɪlɪŋ] adj extrêmement satisfaisant.

fulfilment 🇬🇧, **fulfillment** 🇺🇸 [ful'fɪlmənt] n **1.** [of ambition, dream, wish] réalisation *f* ; [of desire] satisfaction *f* ; [of plan, condition, contract] exécution *f* ; [of duty, prophecy] accomplissement *m* ; [of prayer] exaucement *m* **2.** [satisfaction] (sentiment *m* de) contentement *m* or satisfaction *f* **3.** COMM [of order] exécution *f*.

full [ful] ◆ adj **1.** [completely filled] plein, rempli / **don't talk with your mouth full** ne parle pas la bouche pleine / **I've got a full week ahead of me** j'ai une semaine chargée devant moi **2.** *fig* ▸ **(to be) full of** [filled with] (être) plein de / **the children were full of excitement** les enfants étaient très excités / **her parents were full of hope** ses parents étaient remplis d'espoir ▶ **to be full of o.s.** être plein de soi-même or imbu de sa personne / *he's full of his own importance* il est pénétré de sa propre importance **3.** [crowded -room, theatre] comble, plein ; [-hotel, restaurant, train] complet (complète) / *the hotel was full (up)* l'hôtel était complet **4.** [satiated] rassasié, repu / *I'm full (up)!* 🇬🇧 je n'en peux plus ! **5.** [complete, whole] tout, complet (complète) / *she listened to him for three full hours* elle l'a écouté pendant trois heures entières / *the house is a full 10 miles from town* la maison est à 15 bons kilomètres or est au moins à 15 kilomètres de la ville / *full fare* **a)** [for adult] plein tarif **b)** [for child] une place entière / *he leads a very full life* il a une vie bien remplie **6.** [maximum] plein / *they had the music on full volume* ils avaient mis la musique à fond / *full employment* ECON plein emploi *m* / *she caught the full force of the blow* elle a reçu le coup de plein fouet **7.** [detailed] détaillé / *I didn't get the full story* je n'ai pas entendu tous les détails de l'histoire **8.** [plump -face] plein, rond ; [-figure] rondelet, replet (replète) ; [-lips] charnu / *dresses designed to flatter the fuller figure* des robes qui mettent en valeur les silhouettes épanouies. ◆ adv **1.** [entirely, completely] complètement, entièrement / *I turned the heat full on* 🇬🇧 or *on full* j'ai mis le chauffage à fond / *he put the radio full on* 🇬🇧 il a mis la radio à fond **2.** [directly, exactly] carrément / *the blow caught her full in the face* elle a reçu le coup en pleine figure **3.** 🄿🄷🄰 *you know full well I'm right* tu sais très bien or parfaitement que j'ai raison. ❖ **in full** adv phr intégralement / *write out your name in full* écrivez votre nom en toutes lettres / *they published the book in full* ils ont publié le texte intégral or dans son intégralité. ❖ **to the full** adv phr au plus haut degré, au plus haut point.

fullback ['fʊlbæk] n arrière *m*.

full-blooded [-'blʌdɪd] adj **1.** [hearty -person] vigoureux, robuste ; [-effort] vigoureux, puissant ; [-argument] violent **2.** [purebred] de race pur, pur sang.

full-blown adj **1.** [flower] épanoui **2.** *fig* [complete] à part entière **3.** MED ▶ **full-blown AIDS** 🇬🇧 sida *m* avéré.

full-bodied [-'bɒdɪd] adj [wine] qui a du corps, corsé.

full-court press n [basketball] zone-presse *f*.

full cream milk n 🇬🇧 lait *m* entier.

full dress n [evening clothes] tenue *f* de soirée ; [uniform] grande tenue *f*. ❖ **full-dress** adj ▶ **full-dress uniform** tenue *f* de cérémonie, grande tenue *f*.

full-face(d) adj **1.** [person] au visage rond **2.** [photograph] de face.

full-fashioned 🇺🇸 = fully-fashioned.

full-fat adj entier.

full-flavoured adj **1.** [tobacco] qui a du corps ; [wine] généreux **2.** [story, joke, etc.] épicé, corsé.

full-fledged 🇺🇸 = fully-fledged.

full-grown adj adulte.

full house n **1.** CARDS full *m* **2.** THEAT salle *f* comble.

full-length ◆ adj [mirror, portrait] en pied ; [curtain, dress] long (longue) / *a full-length film* un long métrage. ◆ adv : *he was stretched out full-length on the floor* il était étendu de tout son long par terre.

full monty [-'mɒntɪ] n *inf* ▶ **the full monty** la totale.

full moon n pleine lune *f*.

fullness ['fʊlnɪs] n **1.** [state] état *m* plein, plénitude *f* ; MED [of stomach] plénitude *f* **2.** [of details, information] abondance *f* **3.** [of face, figure] rondeur *f* **4.** [of skirt, sound, voice] ampleur *f*.

full-on adj *inf* [documentary, film -hard-hitting] dur ; [-sexually explicit] cru / *he's full-on* **a)** [gen] il en fait trop **b)** [making sexual advances] il est entreprenant.

full-page adj pleine page.

full-scale adj **1.** [model, plan] grandeur nature *(inv)* **2.** [all-out -strike, war] total ; [-attack, investigation] de grande envergure.

full-screen menu n COMPUT menu *m* plein écran.

full-size(d) adj [animal, plant] adulte ; [drawing, model] grandeur nature *(inv)* ▶ **full-sized car** 🇬🇧 grosse voiture *f*.

full stop n 🇬🇧 **1.** [pause] arrêt *m* complet **2.** GRAM point *m*.

full time n [of working week] temps *m* complet ; SPORT fin *f* de match. ❖ **full-time** ◆ adj **1.** [job] à plein temps **2.** SPORT ▶ **full-time score** score *m* final. ◆ adv à plein temps, à temps plein.

fully ['fʊlɪ] adv **1.** [totally -automatic, dressed, satisfied, trained] complètement, entièrement **2.** [thoroughly -answer, examine, explain] à fond, dans le détail **3.** [at least] au moins, bien.

fully-fashioned 🇬🇧, **full-fashioned** 🇺🇸 [-'fæʃnd] adj moulant.

fully-fitted adj [kitchen] intégré.

fully-fledged 🇬🇧, **full-fledged** 🇺🇸 adj **1.** [bird] qui a toutes ses plumes **2.** *fig* à part entière.

fulness ['fʊlnɪs] = fullness.

fulsome ['fʊlsəm] adj [apology, thanks] excessif, exagéré ; [welcome] plein d'effusions ; [compliments, praise] dithyrambique.

fumble ['fʌmbl] ◆ vi [grope -in the dark] tâtonner ; [-in pocket, purse] fouiller. ◆ vt **1.** [handle awkwardly] manier gauchement or maladroitement **2.** SPORT [miss -catch] attraper or arrêter maladroitement. ◆ n **1.** [grope] tâtonnements *mpl* **2.** SPORT [bad catch] prise *f* de balle maladroite.

fume [fju:m] ◆ n *(usu pl)* ▶ **fumes a)** [gen] exhalaisons *fpl*, émanations *fpl* **b)** [of gas, liquid] vapeurs *fpl*. ◆ vi **1.** [gas] émettre or exhaler des vapeurs ; [liquid] fumer **2.** [person] rager. ◆ vt **1.** [treat with fumes] fumer, fumiger **2.** [rage] : *"this is your fault", she fumed* « c'est de ta faute », dit-elle d'un ton rageur.

fumigate ['fju:mɪgeɪt] vi & vt désinfecter par fumigation, fumiger *fml*.

fumigation [ˌfju:mɪgeɪʃn] n fumigation *f*.

fun [fʌn] ◆ n **1.** [amusement] amusement *m* ; [pleasure] plaisir *m* ▶ **to have fun** s'amuser ▶ **to make fun of** or **to poke fun at sb** se moquer de qqn **2.** [playfulness] enjouement *m*, gaieté *f*. ◆ adj *inf* rigolo, marrant.

function ['fʌŋkʃn] ◆ vi fonctionner, marcher. ◆ n **1.** [role -of machine, organ] fonction *f* ; [-of person] fonction *f*, charge *f* **2.** [working] fonctionnement *m* **3.** [ceremony] cérémonie *f* ; [reception] réception *f* ; [meeting] réunion *f* **4.** [gen & LING & MATH] fonction *f* **5.** COMPUT fonction *f*.

functional ['fʌŋkʃnəl] adj **1.** [gen & MATH & PSYCHOL] fonctionnel ▶ **functional illiterate** *personne qui, sans être tout à fait analphabète, est incapable de faire face à la vie de tous les jours dans une société industrialisée* **2.** [in working order] : *the machine is no longer functional* la machine ne marche plus or ne fonctionne plus.

functional food n aliment *m* fonctionnel.

functionality [fʌŋkʃˈnælətɪ] n fonctionnalité *f*.

functionary ['fʌŋkʃnərɪ] *(pl* **functionaries***)* n [employee] employé *m*, -e *f (dans une administration)* ; [civil servant] fonctionnaire *mf*.

function key n COMPUT touche *f* de fonction.

function room n salle *f* de réception.

fund [fʌnd] ◆ n **1.** [reserve of money] fonds *m*, caisse *f* **2.** *fig* fond *m*, réserve *f*. ◆ vt **1.** [provide money for] financer **2.** FIN [debt] consolider. ❖ **funds** pl n [cash resources] fonds *mpl*.

fundamental [ˌfʌndə'mentl] ◆ adj **1.** [basic - concept, rule, principle] fondamental, de base ; [- difference, quality] fondamental, essentiel ; [- change, mistake] fondamental **2.** [central] fondamental, principal **3.** MUS fondamental. ◆ n **1.** *(usu pl)* : *the fundamentals of chemistry* les principes *mpl* de base de la chimie **2.** MUS fondamentale *f*.

fundamentalism [ˌfʌndə'mentəlɪzm] n [gen & RELIG] fondamentalisme *m* ; [Muslim] intégrisme *m*.

fundamentalist [ˌfʌndə'mentəlɪst] ◆ adj [gen & RELIG] fondamentaliste ; [Muslim] intégriste. ◆ n [gen & RELIG] fondamentaliste *mf* ; [Muslim] intégriste *mf*.

fundamentally [ˌfʌndə'mentəlɪ] adv **1.** [at bottom] fondamentalement, essentiellement **2.** [completely] : *I disagree fundamentally with his policies* je suis radicalement or fondamentalement opposé à sa politique.

fundholder ['fʌndhəʊldər] n *cabinet médical ayant obtenu le droit de gérer son propre budget auprès du système de sécurité sociale britannique.*

funding ['fʌndɪŋ] n *(U)* fonds *mpl*, financement *m*.

funding gap n écart *m* de financement.

fund management n gestion *f* de fonds.

fundraiser ['fʌndˌreɪzər] n [person] collecteur *m*, -trice *f* de fonds ; [event] *projet organisé pour collecter des fonds.*

fund-raising [-ˌreɪzɪŋ] ◆ n collecte *f* de fonds. ◆ adj [dinner, project, sale] organisé pour collecter des fonds.

funeral ['fju:nərəl] ◆ n **1.** [service] enterrement *m*, obsèques *fpl* ; [more formal] funérailles *fpl* ; [in announcement] obsèques *fpl* ; [burial] enterrement *m* **2.** [procession - on foot] cortège *m* funèbre ; [- in cars] convoi *m* mortuaire. ◆ adj funèbre.

funeral director n entrepreneur *m* de pompes funèbres.

funeral home US = **funeral parlour**.

funeral march n marche *f* funèbre.

funeral parlour n entreprise *f* de pompes funèbres.

funeral pyre n bûcher *m* (funéraire).

funeral service n service *m* or office *m* funèbre.

funereal [fju:'nɪərɪəl] adj [atmosphere, expression] funèbre, lugubre ; [voice] sépulcral, lugubre ; [pace] lent, mesuré.

funfair ['fʌnfeər] n fête *f* foraine.

fun-filled adj divertissant.

fungal ['fʌŋgl] adj fongique.

fungi ['fʌŋgaɪ] pl ⟶ **fungus**.

fungicidal [ˌfʌndʒɪ'saɪdl] adj antifongique, fongicide.

fungicide ['fʌndʒɪsaɪd] n fongicide *m*.

fungus ['fʌŋgəs] *(pl* fungi ['fʌŋgaɪ]) ◆ n BOT champignon *m* ; [mould] moisissure *f* ; MED fongus *m*. ◆ comp ▸ **fungus infection** fongus *m*.

funk [fʌŋk] ◆ n **1.** MUS musique *f* funk, funk *m inv* **2.** *inf & dated* [fear] trouille *f*, frousse *f* ; [depression] découragement *m*. ◆ vt [be afraid of] ne pas avoir le courage de. ◆ adj funky (*inv*).

funky ['fʌŋkɪ] (*compar* funkier, *superl* funkiest) adj *inf* **1.** US [excellent] génial, super ; [fashionable] branché, dans le vent **2.** MUS funky (*inv*).

fun-loving adj qui aime s'amuser or rire.

funnel ['fʌnl] (US *pt & pp* funnelled, *cont* funnelling ; US *pt & pp* funneled, *cont* funneling) ◆ n **1.** [utensil] entonnoir *m* **2.** [smokestack] cheminée *f*. ◆ vt [liquid] (faire) passer dans un entonnoir ; [crowd, funds] canaliser. ◆ vi : *the crowd funnelled out of the gates* la foule s'est écoulée par les grilles.

funnel cloud n tornade *f*.

funnily ['fʌnɪlɪ] adv **1.** [oddly] curieusement, bizarrement **2.** [in a funny manner] drôlement, comiquement.

funny ['fʌnɪ] (*pl* funnies) ◆ adj **1.** [amusing] amusant, drôle, comique **2.** [odd] bizarre, curieux, drôle **3.** [dubious, suspicious] louche **4.** UK *inf* [mad] fou (*before vowel or silent 'h'* fol, f folle). ◆ adv *inf* [walk, talk] bizarrement.

funny bone n *inf* ANAT petit juif *m*.

funny farm n US *inf & euph* maison *f* de fous.

funny papers pl n US supplément *m* bandes dessinées.

fun-packed adj divertissant.

fun run n course *f* à pied pour amateurs (*pour collecter des fonds*).

fur [fɜ:r] (*pt & pp* furred, *cont* furring) ◆ n **1.** [on animal] poil *m*, pelage *m*, fourrure *f* **2.** [coat, pelt] fourrure *f* **3.** [in kettle, pipe] incrustation *f*, [dépôt de] tartre *m* **4.** MED [on tongue] enduit *m*. ◆ vt **1.** [kettle, pipe] entartrer, incruster **2.** MED [tongue] empâter. ◆ vi ▸ **to fur (up)** [kettle, pipe] s'entartrer, s'incruster.

fur coat n [manteau *m* de] fourrure *f*.

furious ['fjʊərɪəs] adj **1.** [angry] furieux / *she was furious with me for being late* elle m'en voulait de mon retard **2.** [raging, violent - sea, storm] déchaîné ; [- effort, struggle] acharné ; [- pace, speed] fou (*before vowel or silent 'h'* fol, f folle).

furiously ['fjʊərɪəslɪ] adv **1.** [answer, look] furieusement **2.** [fight, work] avec acharnement ; [drive, run] à une allure folle.

furled [fɜ:ld] adj [umbrella, flag] roulé ; [sail] serré.

furlong ['fɜ:lɒŋ] n furlong *m* (= 201,17 mètres).

furnace ['fɜ:nɪs] n [for central heating] chaudière *f* ; INDUST fourneau *m*, four *m*.

furnish ['fɜ:nɪʃ] vt **1.** [supply - food, provisions] fournir ; [- information, reason] fournir, donner **2.** [house, room] meubler.

furnished ['fɜ:nɪʃt] adj [room, apartment] meublé.

furnishings ['fɜ:nɪʃɪŋz] pl n **1.** [furniture] meubles *mpl*, mobilier *m*, ameublement *m* **2.** US [clothing] habits *mpl*, vêtements *mpl* ; [accessories] accessoires *mpl*.

furniture ['fɜ:nɪtʃər] ◆ n *(U)* **1.** [for house] meubles *mpl*, mobilier *m*, ameublement *m* / *a piece of furniture* un meuble **2.** NAUT & TYPO garniture *f* **3.** [accessories] ▸ **street furniture** mobilier *m* urbain ▸ **door furniture** éléments décoratifs pour portes d'entrée. ◆ comp [shop, store] d'ameublement, de meubles ▸ **furniture polish** encaustique *f*, cire *f* ▸ **furniture showroom** magasin *m* de meubles.

furore UK [fjʊ'rɔ:rɪ], **furor** US ['fjʊrɔr] n scandale *m*, tumulte *m*.

furrier ['fʌrɪər] n fourreur *m*.

furrow ['fʌrəʊ] ◆ n [in field] sillon *m* ; [in garden] rayon *m*, sillon *m* ; [on forehead] ride *f*, sillon *m* ; [on sea] sillage *m*. ◆ vt **1.** [soil, surface] sillonner **2.** [brow] rider. ◆ vi se plisser.

furrowed ['fʌrəʊd] adj ridé, sillonné de rides.

furry ['fɜ:rɪ] (*compar* furrier, *superl* furriest) adj **1.** [animal] à poils ; [fabric] qui ressemble à de la fourrure ; [toy] en peluche **2.** [kettle, pipe] entartré ; [tongue] pâteux, chargé.

further ['fɜ:ðər] ◆ adv (*compar of far*) **1.** [at a greater distance in space, time] plus loin / *further to the south* plus au sud / *she's never been further north than Leicester* elle n'est jamais allée plus au nord que Leicester / *how much* *further is it?* c'est encore loin ? / *he got further and further away from the shore* il a continué à s'éloigner de la rive / *she moved further back* elle a reculé encore plus / *further back than 1960* avant 1960 / *further forward, further on* plus en avant, plus loin **2.** [more] plus, davantage / *I have nothing further to say* je n'ai rien à ajouter, je n'ai rien d'autre or rien de plus à dire / *until you hear further* jusqu'à nouvel avis **3.** [to a greater degree] : *her arrival only complicated things further* son arrivée n'a fait que compliquer les choses **4.** *fml* [moreover] de plus, en outre **5.** PHR *I would go even further and say he's a genius* j'irais même jusqu'à dire que c'est un génie / *this information must go no further* cette information doit rester entre nous or ne doit pas être divulguée. ◆ adj *(compar of far)* **1.** [more distant] plus éloigné, plus lointain **2.** [additional - comments, negotiations] additionnel, autre ; [- information, news] supplémentaire, complémentaire / *until further notice* jusqu'à nouvel ordre ▶ **without further ado** sans plus de cérémonie. ◆ vt [cause, one's interests] avancer, servir, favoriser ; [career] servir, favoriser ; [chances] augmenter. ❖ **further to** prep phr *fml* suite à.

further education ◆ n UK enseignement *m* post-scolaire. ◆ comp [class, college] d'éducation permanente.

furthermore [ˌfɜːðəˈmɔːr] adv en outre, par ailleurs.

furthermost [ˈfɜːðəməʊst] adj *liter* le plus éloigné, le plus lointain.

furthest [ˈfɜːðɪst] *(superl of far)* ◆ adv le plus loin. ◆ adj le plus lointain, le plus éloigné.

furtive [ˈfɜːtɪv] adj [behaviour, look] furtif ; [person] sournois.

furtively [ˈfɜːtɪvlɪ] adv furtivement, en douce.

fury [ˈfjʊərɪ] *(pl furies)* n **1.** [anger] fureur *f*, furie *f* ▶ **to be in a fury** être dans une colère noire or en furie **2.** [violence - of storm, wind] violence *f* ; [- of fight, struggle] acharnement *m* **3.** [frenzy] frénésie *f*. ❖ **Furies** pl n MYTH ▶ **the Furies** les Furies *fpl*, les Érinyes *fpl*.

fuse [fjuːz] ◆ vi **1.** [melt] fondre ; [melt together] fusionner **2.** [join] s'unifier, fusionner **3.** UK ELEC : *the lights / the appliance fused* les plombs ont sauté. ◆ vt **1.** [melt] fondre ; [melt together] fondre, mettre en fusion **2.** [unite] fusionner, unifier, amalgamer **3.** UK ELEC ▶ **to fuse the lights** faire sauter les plombs **4.** [explosive] amorcer. ◆ n **1.** ELEC plomb *m*, fusible *m* **2.** [of explosive] amorce *f*, détonateur *m* ; MIN cordeau *m*.

fuse box n boîte *f* à fusibles, coupe-circuit *m inv* ; AUTO porte-fusible *m*.

fused [fjuːzd] adj [kettle, plug] avec fusible incorporé.

fuselage [ˈfjuːzəlɑːʒ] n fuselage *m*.

fuse wire n fusible *m*.

fusillade [ˌfjuːzəˈleɪd] n fusillade *f*.

fusion [ˈfjuːʒn] n METALL fonte *f*, fusion *f* ; PHYS fusion *f* ; *fig* [of ideas, parties] fusion *f*, fusionnement *m*.

fusion food n cuisine *f* fusion.

fuss [fʌs] ◆ n **1.** (U) [bother] histoires *fpl* **2.** PHR ▶ **to kick up** *inf* or ▶ **to make a fuss about** or **over sthg** faire des histoires or tout un plat au sujet de qqch ▶ **to make a fuss of** or **over sb** être aux petits soins pour qqn. ◆ vi [become agitated] s'agiter ; [worry] s'inquiéter, se tracasser ; [rush around] s'affairer ▶ **to fuss over sb** être aux petits soins pour qqn. ◆ vt **1.** UK agacer, embêter **2.** US *inf* PHR *do you want meat or fish? — I'm not fussed* veux-tu de la viande ou du poisson ? — ça m'est égal.

fussbudget [ˈfʌsˌbʌdʒət] US = **fusspot**.

fussily [ˈfʌsɪlɪ] adv **1.** [fastidiously] de façon méticuleuse or tatillonne ; [nervously] avec anxiété **2.** [over-ornate] de façon tarabiscotée.

fussiness [ˈfʌsɪnɪs] n **1.** [fastidiousness] côté *m* tatillon **2.** [ornateness - of decoration] tarabiscotage *m*.

fusspot [ˈfʌspɒt] n *inf* **1.** [worrier] anxieux *m*, -euse *f* **2.** [fastidious person] tatillon *m*, -onne *f*.

fussy [ˈfʌsɪ] *(compar fussier, superl fussiest)* adj **1.** [fastidious] tatillon, pointilleux / *he's fussy about his food / about what he wears* il fait très attention à ce qu'il mange / à ce qu'il porte / *where shall we go? — I'm not fussy* où est-ce qu'on va ? — ça m'est égal **2.** [over-ornate - decoration] trop chargé, tarabiscoté ; [- style] ampoulé, qui manque de simplicité.

fusty [ˈfʌstɪ] *(compar fustier, superl fustiest)* adj [room] qui sent le renfermé ; [smell] de renfermé, de moisi ; *fig* [idea, outlook] vieux jeu.

futile [UK ˈfjuːtaɪl US ˈfuːtl] adj [action, effort] vain ; [remark, question] futile, vain ; [idea] futile, creux.

futility [fjuːˈtɪlətɪ] *(pl futilities)* n [of action, effort] futilité *f*, inutilité *f* ; [of remark, question] inanité *f* ; [of gesture] futilité *f*.

futon [ˈfuːtɒn] n futon *m*.

future [ˈfjuːtʃər] ◆ n **1.** [time ahead] avenir *m* / *in (the) future* à l'avenir / *in the distant future* dans un avenir lointain **2.** [in science fiction] futur *m* **3.** GRAM futur *m*. ◆ adj **1.** futur **2.** COMM [delivery, estate] à terme. ❖ **in future** adv phr à l'avenir.

⚠️ Except in the contexts of grammar and science fiction, it is preferable to use **avenir**, not **futur**, to translate the noun future.

future perfect n futur *m* antérieur.

future-proof ◆ adj COMPUT évolutif. ◆ vt COMPUT rendre évolutif.

futures [ˈfjuːtʃəz] pl n ST. EX marchandises *fpl* achetées à terme / *the futures market* le marché à terme.

future tense n future *m*.

futuristic [ˌfjuːtʃəˈrɪstɪk] adj futuriste.

fuze [fjuːz] US = **fuse** *(noun)*.

fuzz [fʌz] ◆ n *(U)* **1.** [down - on peach] duvet *m* ; [- on body] duvet *m*, poils *mpl* fins ; [- on head] duvet *m*, cheveux *mpl* fins **2.** [frizzy hair] cheveux *mpl* crépus or frisottants **3.** [on blanket, sweater] peluches *fpl* **4.** *v inf* [police] ▶ **the fuzz** les flics *mpl* **5.** US [lint] peluches *fpl*. ◆ vt **1.** [hair] frisotter **2.** [image, sight] rendre flou. ◆ vi **1.** [hair] frisotter **2.** [image, sight] devenir flou **3.** [blanket, sweater] pelucher.

fuzzy [ˈfʌzɪ] *(compar fuzzier, superl fuzziest)* adj **1.** [cloth, garment] peluché, pelucheux **2.** [image, picture] flou **3.** [confused - ideas] confus **4.** [hair] crépu, frisottant.

fuzzy matching n COMPUT recherche *f* floue.

fwd. written abbr of **forward**.

FWIW n MESSAGING written abbr of **for what it's worth**.

f-word n ▶ **the f-word** le mot « fuck ».

fwy written abbr of **freeway**.

FY n written abbr of **fiscal year**.

FYA MESSAGING written abbr of **for your amusement**.

FYEO MESSAGING written abbr of **for your eyes only**.

FYI (written abbr of **for your information**) adv pour information, pour info.

g [dʒiː] (*pl* g's *or* gs), **G** (*pl* G's *or* Gs) n [letter] g *m*, G *m*. See also f.

g 1. (written abbr of **gram**) g **2.** (written abbr of **gravity**) g.

G ◆ n **1.** MUS [note] sol *m* **2.** (abbr of **grand**) UK *inf* mille livres *fpl*, US mille dollars *mpl*. ◆ **1.** (written abbr of **good**) B **2.** (written abbr of **general (audience)**) US CIN *tous publics*.

G7 n ECON & POL le G7, le groupe des 7.

G8 n ECON & POL le G8, le groupe des 8.

GA written abbr of **Georgia**.

gab [gæb] (*pt & pp* **gabbed**, *cont* **gabbing**) *inf* ◆ n (U) [chatter] parlotte *f*, parlote *f*. ◆ vi papoter.

gabardine [ˌgæbəˈdiːn] = **gaberdine**.

gabble [ˈgæbl] ◆ vi **1.** [idly] faire la parlote, papoter **2.** [inarticulately] bredouiller, balbutier. ◆ vt bredouiller, bafouiller. ◆ n baragouin *m*, flot *m* de paroles.

gaberdine [ˌgæbəˈdiːn] ◆ n gabardine *f*. ◆ comp ▶ **gaberdine raincoat** gabardine *f*.

gable [ˈgeɪbl] n [wall] pignon *m* ; [over arch, door, etc.] gâble *m*, gable *m*.

Gabon [gæˈbɒn] pr n Gabon *m* / in Gabon au Gabon.

Gabonese [ˌgæbəˈniːz] ◆ n Gabonais *m*, -e *f*. ◆ pl n ▶ **the Gabonese** les Gabonais. ◆ adj gabonais.

gad [gæd] (*pt & pp* **gadded**, *cont* **gadding**) vi ▶ **to gad about** vadrouiller.

Gad [gæd] interj *arch & hum* ▶ **(by) Gad!** sapristi !, sacrebleu !

gadabout [ˈgædəbaʊt] n UK *inf* vadrouilleur *m*, -euse *f*.

gadget [ˈgædʒɪt] n gadget *m*.

gadgetry [ˈgædʒɪtrɪ] n (U) gadgets *mpl*.

Gaelic [ˈgeɪlɪk] ◆ adj gaélique. ◆ n LING gaélique *m*.

gaffe [gæf] n [blunder] bévue *f* / a social gaffe un faux pas, un impair.

gaffer [ˈgæfər] n *inf* **1.** UK [boss] ▶ **the gaffer** le patron, le chef **2.** [old man] vieux *m*.

gag [gæg] (*pt & pp* **gagged**, *cont* **gagging**) ◆ n **1.** [over mouth] bâillon *m* **2.** *inf* [joke] gag *m* **3.** MED ouvrebouche *m*. ◆ vt [silence] bâillonner ; *fig* bâillonner, museler. ◆ vi [retch] avoir un haut-le-cœur.

gaga [ˈgɑːgɑː] adj *inf* [senile, crazy] gaga / he's absolutely gaga about her il est complètement fou d'elle.

gage [geɪdʒ] n US = **gauge**.

gaggle [ˈgægl] ◆ n *lit & fig* troupeau *m*. ◆ vi cacarder.

gaiety [ˈgeɪətɪ] (*pl* **gaieties**) n gaieté *f*.

gaily [ˈgeɪlɪ] adv **1.** [brightly] gaiement **2.** [casually] tranquillement.

gain [geɪn] ◆ n **1.** [profit] gain *m*, profit *m*, bénéfice *m* ; *fig* avantage *m* **2.** [acquisition] gain *m* **3.** [increase] augmentation *f* **4.** ELECTRON gain *m*. ◆ vt **1.** [earn, win, obtain] gagner **2.** [increase] gagner **3.** [obtain more] gagner, obtenir **4.** [subj: clock, watch] avancer de **5.** *liter* [reach] atteindre, gagner. ◆ vi **1.** [profit] profiter, gagner **2.** [clock] avancer. ◆ **gain on** vt insep [catch up] rattraper.

gainful [ˈgeɪnfʊl] adj *fml* **1.** [profitable] profitable, rémunérateur **2.** [paid] rémunéré.

gainfully [ˈgeɪnfʊlɪ] adv *fml* de façon profitable, avantageusement ▶ **to be gainfully employed** avoir un emploi rémunéré.

gainsay [ˌgeɪnˈseɪ] (*pt & pp* **gainsaid** [-ˈsed]) vt *fml* [deny] nier ; [contradict] contredire.

gait [geɪt] n démarche *f*, allure *f*.

gaiters [ˈgeɪtəz] pl n guêtres *fpl*.

gal [gæl] n *inf* [girl] fille *f*.

gal. written abbr of **gallon**.

GAL MESSAGING written abbr of **get a life**.

gala [ˈgɑːlə] ◆ n **1.** [festivity] gala *m* **2.** UK SPORT réunion *f* sportive ▶ **swimming gala** concours *m* de natation. ◆ comp [dress, day, evening] de gala ▶ **a gala occasion** une grande occasion.

galactic [gəˈlæktɪk] adj galactique.

galangal n galangal *m*.

Galapagos Islands [gəˈlæpəgəs-] pl pr n ▶ **the Galapagos Islands** les (îles *fpl*) Galápagos *fpl*.

galaxy [ˈgæləksɪ] (*pl* **galaxies**) n **1.** ASTRON galaxie *f* ▶ **the Galaxy** la Voie lactée **2.** [gathering] constellation *f*, pléiade *f*.

gale [geɪl] n **1.** [wind] coup *m* de vent, grand vent *m* / a force 9 gale un vent de force 9 ▶ **gale warning** avis *m* de coup de vent **2.** [outburst] éclat *m*.

Galicia [gəˈlɪʃɪə] pr n **1.** [Central Europe] Galicie *f* **2.** [Spain] Galice *f*.

gall [gɔːl] ◆ n **1.** ANAT [human] bile *f* ; [animal] fiel *m* **2.** [bitterness] fiel *m*, amertume *f* **3.** [nerve] culot *m* **4.** BOT galle *f* **5.** MED & VET écorchure *f*, excoriation *f*. ◆ comp ▶ **gall duct** ANAT voie *f* biliaire. ◆ vt [annoy] énerver.

gall. written abbr of **gallon**.

gallant [ˈgælənt] ◆ adj **1.** [brave] courageux, vaillant **2.** (*also* [gəˈlænt]) [chivalrous] galant **3.** *liter* [noble] noble ; [splendid] superbe, splendide. ◆ n *liter* galant *m*.

gallantly [ˈgæləntlɪ] adv **1.** [bravely] courageusement, vaillamment **2.** [chivalrously] galamment.

gallantry [ˈgæləntrɪ] (*pl* **gallantries**) n **1.** [bravery] courage *m*, vaillance *f* **2.** [brave deed] prouesse *f*, action *f* d'éclat **3.** [chivalry, amorousness] galanterie *f*.

gall bladder n vésicule *f* biliaire.

galleon ['gælɪən] n galion m.

gallery ['gælərɪ] (pl **galleries**) ◆ n **1.** [of art] musée m (des beaux-arts) / private gallery galerie f **2.** [balcony] galerie f ; [for spectators] tribune f / the press gallery la tribune de la presse **3.** [covered passageway] galerie f **4.** THEAT [upper balcony] dernier balcon m ; [audience] galerie f **5.** [tunnel] galerie f **6.** GOLF [spectators] public m. ◆ comp ▶ **gallery owner** galeriste mf.

galley ['gælɪ] ◆ n **1.** [ship] galère f ; [ship's kitchen] cambuse f ; [aircraft kitchen] office m ou f **2.** TYPO [container] galée f ; [proof] placard m. ◆ comp ▶ **galley kitchen** kitchenette f, cuisinette f offic.

gallic ['gælɪk] adj CHEM gallique.

Gallic ['gælɪk] adj **1.** [French] français / Gallic charm charme m latin **2.** [of Gaul] gaulois.

galling ['gɔːlɪŋ] adj [annoying] irritant ; [humiliating] humiliant, vexant.

gallivant [,gælɪ'vænt] vi hum ▶ **to gallivant about** or **around** se balader.

gallon ['gælən] n gallon m.

gallop ['gæləp] ◆ vi galoper / to gallop away or off partir au galop. ◆ vt faire galoper. ◆ n galop m. ❖ **gallop through** vt insep faire à toute vitesse.

galloping ['gæləpɪŋ] adj [horse] au galop ; fig galopant.

gallows ['gæləʊz] (pl **gallows**) n potence f, gibet m.

gallstone ['gɔːlstəʊn] n calcul m biliaire.

Gallup Poll ['gæləp-] n sondage m (d'opinion) (réalisé par l'institut Gallup).

galoshes [gə'lɒʃɪz] pl n caoutchoucs mpl (pour protéger les chaussures).

galvanize, galvanise ['gælvənaɪz] vt lit & fig galvaniser.

Gambia ['gæmbɪə] pr n ▶ **(the) Gambia** (la) Gambie / in (the) Gambia en Gambie.

Gambian ['gæmbɪən] ◆ n Gambien m, -enne f. ◆ adj gambien.

gambit ['gæmbɪt] n [chess] gambit m.

gamble ['gæmbl] ◆ vi jouer. ◆ vt parier, miser. ◆ n **1.** [wager] pari m **2.** [risk] coup m de poker. ❖ **gamble away** vt sep perdre au jeu. ❖ **gamble on** vt insep miser or tabler or compter sur.

gambler ['gæmblər] n joueur m, -euse f.

gambling ['gæmblɪŋ] ◆ n (U) jeu m, jeux mpl d'argent. ◆ adj joueur.

gambol ['gæmbl] (UK pt & pp **gambolled**, cont **gambolling** ; US pt & pp **gamboled**, cont **gamboling**) ◆ vi gambader, cabrioler. ◆ n gambade f, cabriole f.

gambrel roof ['gæmbrəl-] n toit m mansardé.

game [geɪm] ◆ n **1.** [gen] jeu m **2.** [contest] partie f ; [esp professional] match m **3.** [division of match - in tennis, bridge] jeu m **4.** [playing equipment, set] jeu m **5.** inf [scheme, trick] ruse f, stratagème m **6.** inf [undertaking, operation] : at this stage in the game à ce stade des opérations **7.** [activity] travail m **8.** CULIN & HUNT gibier m **9.** [PHR] **to be on the game** UK v inf faire le tapin. ◆ comp de chasse. ◆ adj **1.** [plucky] courageux, brave **2.** [willing] prêt, partant **3.** UK [lame] estropié. ◆ vi fml [gamble] jouer (de l'argent). ❖ **games** pl n [international] jeux mpl ; UK SCH sport m.

gamebag ['geɪmbæg] n gibecière f.

gamekeeper ['geɪm,kiːpər] n garde-chasse m.

gamely ['geɪmlɪ] adv courageusement, vaillamment.

game plan n stratégie f, plan m d'attaque.

gamer ['geɪmər] n **1.** [who plays computer games] amateur de jeux vidéo **2.** US [athlete, sportsperson] sportif très compétitif.

game reserve n réserve f (pour animaux sauvages).

games console n console f de jeu.

game show n jeu m télévisé.

gamesmanship ['geɪmzmənʃɪp] n art de gagner (aux jeux) en déconcertant son adversaire.

game theory n théorie f des jeux.

gameware ['geɪmweər] n COMPUT ludiciel m.

gamey [geɪmɪ] (compar **gamier**, superl **gamiest**) = gamy.

gaming ['geɪmɪŋ] **1.** [video games] jeux mpl vidéo **2.** fml = gambling (noun).

gamma ['gæmə] n gamma m.

gamma ray n rayon m gamma.

gammon ['gæmən] n UK [cut] jambon m ; [meat] jambon m fumé.

gammy ['gæmɪ] (compar **gammier**, superl **gammiest**) adj UK inf estropié.

gamut ['gæmət] n MUS & fig gamme f ▶ **to run the (whole) gamut of sthg** passer par toute la gamme de qqch.

gamy ['geɪmɪ] (compar **gamier**, superl **gamiest**) adj [meat] faisandé.

gander ['gændər] n **1.** [goose] jars m **2.** UK inf [look] ▶ **to have** or **to take a gander at sthg** jeter un coup d'œil sur qqch.

gang [gæŋ] n **1.** [gen] bande f ; [of criminals] gang m **2.** [of workmen] équipe f ; [of convicts] convoi m **3.** TECH [of tools] série f. ❖ **gang up** vi se mettre à plusieurs ▶ **to gang up against** or **on sb** se liguer contre qqn.

gang-bang n vulg viol m collectif.

gangbuster ['gæŋbʌstər] n US inf **1.** [police officer] ≃ flic m de la brigade antigang **2.** fig : the campaign is progressing like gangbusters la campagne marche très fort.

Ganges ['gændʒiːz] pr n ▶ **the (River) Ganges** le Gange.

gangland ['gæŋlænd] ◆ n le milieu. ◆ comp ▶ **a gangland killing** un règlement de comptes (dans le milieu).

gangling ['gæŋglɪŋ] adj dégingandé.

ganglion ['gæŋglɪən] (pl **ganglia** ['gæŋglɪə]) n ANAT ganglion m.

gangly ['gæŋlɪ] = gangling.

gangplank ['gæŋplæŋk] n passerelle f (d'embarquement).

gang-rape vt commettre un viol collectif sur.

gangrene ['gæŋgriːn] ◆ n MED & fig gangrène f. ◆ vi se gangrener.

gangrenous ['gæŋgrɪnəs] adj gangreneux.

gangsta ['gæŋstə] n **1.** [music] : gangsta (rap) gangsta rap m **2.** [rapper] rappeur m, -euse f gangsta **3.** US [gang member] membre d'un gang.

gangster ['gæŋstər] ◆ n gangster m. ◆ comp [film, story] de gangsters.

gangway ['gæŋweɪ] ◆ n **1.** NAUT = gangplank **2.** [passage] passage m ; UK [in theatre] allée f. ◆ interj ▶ **gangway!** dégagez le passage !

gannet ['gænɪt] n **1.** ORNITH fou m de Bassan **2.** UK inf [greedy person] glouton m, -onne f.

gantry ['gæntrɪ] (pl **gantries**) n [for crane] portique m.

GAO (abbr of **General Accountability Office**) pr n Cour des comptes américaine.

gaol [dʒeɪl] UK = jail.

gap [gæp] n **1.** [hole, breach] trou m, brèche f **2.** [space between objects] espace m ; [narrower] interstice m, jour m **3.** [blank] blanc m **4.** [in time] intervalle m **5.** [lack] vide m **6.** [omission] lacune f **7.** [silence] pause f, silence m **8.** [disparity] écart m, inégalité f **9.** [mountain pass] col m.

gape [geɪp] ◆ vi **1.** [stare] regarder la bouche bée / *what are you gaping at?* qu'est-ce que tu regardes avec cet air bête ? **2.** [open one's mouth wide] ouvrir la bouche toute grande **3.** [be open] être béant, béer *liter.* ◆ n [stare] regard m ébahi.

gaping ['geɪpɪŋ] adj **1.** [staring] bouche bée *(inv)* **2.** [wide open] béant.

gappy ['gæpɪ] *(compar* **gappier**, *superl* **gappiest)** adj **1.** [account, knowledge] plein de lacunes **2.** ▶ **gappy teeth** des dents écartées.

gap year n SCH & UNIV *année d'interruption volontaire des études, avant l'entrée à l'université.*

garage ◆ n [UK] 'gæra:ʒ or 'gærɪdʒ, [US] gə'ra:ʒ] **1.** [shelter for car] garage m / *garage door* porte f de garage **2.** [UK] [filling station] station-service f ; [for selling cars] concessionnaire m automobile **3.** MUS garage m. ◆ vt [[UK] 'gæra:ʒ, [US] gə'ra:ʒ] mettre au garage.

garage sale n *vente d'occasion chez un particulier ;* ≃ vide-grenier m.

garam masala n garam masala m *(mélange d'épices employé dans la cuisine indienne).*

garb [gɑ:b] *liter.* ◆ n costume m, mise f. ◆ vt vêtir.

garbage ['gɑ:bɪdʒ] n *(U)* **1.** [US] [waste matter] ordures fpl, détritus mpl **2.** inf [nonsense] bêtises fpl, âneries fpl **3.** COMPUT données fpl erronées.

garbage bag n [US] sac-poubelle m.

garbage can n [US] poubelle f.

garbage chute n [US] vide-ordures m inv.

garbage collector n [US] éboueur m.

garbage disposal unit n [US] broyeur m d'ordures.

garbage man [US] = **garbage collector.**

garbage truck n [US] camion m des éboueurs.

garble ['gɑ:bl] vt [involuntarily - story, message] embrouiller ; [- quotation] déformer ; [deliberately - facts] dénaturer, déformer.

garbled ['gɑ:bld] adj [story, message, explanation - involuntarily] embrouillé, confus ; [- deliberately] dénaturé, déformé.

garden ['gɑ:dn] ◆ n jardin m ▶ **to do the garden** jardiner, faire du jardinage ▶ **the Garden of Eden** le jardin m d'Éden, l'Éden m ▶ **the Garden of England** surnom du comté de Kent, célèbre pour ses vergers et ses champs de houblon. ◆ comp ▶ **garden chair** chaise f de jardin ▶ **garden path** allée f *(dans un jardin)* ▶ **garden shears** cisaille f or cisailles fpl de jardin ▶ **garden shed** resserre f ▶ **garden tools** outils mpl de jardinage ▶ **garden wedding** [US] mariage m en plein air. ◆ vi jardiner, faire du jardinage. ◆⁺ **gardens** pl n [park] jardin m public.

garden centre n jardinerie f.

garden city n cité-jardin f.

gardener ['gɑ:dnə⁰] n jardinier m, -ère f.

garden flat n rez-de-jardin m inv.

garden gnome n gnome m (décoratif).

gardenia [gɑ:'di:njə] n gardénia m.

gardening ['gɑ:dnɪŋ] ◆ n jardinage m. ◆ comp [book, programme] de or sur le jardinage ; [gloves] de jardinage.

garden party n [UK] garden-party f.

garden snail n petit-gris m.

garden-variety adj [US] ordinaire.

gargantuan [gɑ:'gæntjʊən] adj gargantuesque.

gargle ['gɑ:gl] ◆ vi se gargariser, faire des gargarismes. ◆ n gargarisme m.

gargoyle ['gɑ:gɔɪl] n gargouille f.

garish ['geərɪʃ] adj [colour] voyant, criard ; [clothes] voyant, tapageur ; [light] cru, aveuglant.

garishly ['geərɪʃlɪ] adv : *garishly dressed* vêtu de manière tapageuse.

garishness ['geərɪʃnɪs] n [of appearance] tape-à-l'œil m inv ; [of colour] crudité f, violence f.

garland ['gɑ:lənd] ◆ n [on head] couronne f de fleurs ; [round neck] guirlande f or collier m de fleurs ; [hung on wall] guirlande f. ◆ vt [decorate] décorer avec des guirlandes, enguirlander ; [crown] couronner de fleurs.

garlic ['gɑ:lɪk] n ail m ▶ **garlic bread** pain beurré frotté d'ail et servi chaud ▶ **garlic butter** beurre m d'ail ▶ **garlic mushrooms** champignons mpl à l'ail ▶ **garlic salt** sel m d'ail ▶ **garlic sausage** saucisson m à l'ail.

garlicky ['gɑ:lɪkɪ] adj [taste] d'ail ; [breath] qui sent l'ail.

garment ['gɑ:mənt] n vêtement m / *the garment industry* la confection.

garner ['gɑ:nə⁰] vt [grain] rentrer, engranger ; fig [information] glaner, grappiller ; [compliments] recueillir. ◆⁺ **garner in, garner up** vt sep engranger.

garnet ['gɑ:nɪt] ◆ n [stone, colour] grenat m. ◆ adj **1.** [in colour] grenat *(inv)* **2.** [jewellery] de or en grenat.

garnish ['gɑ:nɪʃ] ◆ vt **1.** CULIN garnir ; [decorate] embellir / *garnished with parsley* garni de persil **2.** [US] LAW faire pratiquer une saisie-arrêt à. ◆ n garniture f.

garret ['gærət] n [room] mansarde f.

garrison ['gærɪsn] ◆ n garnison f. ◆ vt **1.** [troops] mettre en garnison **2.** [town] placer une garnison dans.

garrulous ['gærələs] adj **1.** [person] loquace, bavard **2.** [style] prolixe, verbeux.

garter ['gɑ:tə⁰] n **1.** [for stockings] jarretière f ; [for socks] fixe-chaussette m ▶ **Knight of the Garter** chevalier m de l'ordre de la Jarretière **2.** [US] [suspender] jarretelle f.

garter belt n [US] porte-jarretelles m inv.

gas [gæs] *(pl* **gasses)** ◆ n **1.** [domestic] gaz m **2.** CHEM gaz m **3.** MIN grisou m **4.** MED gaz m anesthésique or anesthésiant **5.** [US] AUTO essence f **6.** [US] inf [amusement] : *the party was a real gas* on s'est bien marrés or on a bien rigolé à la soirée **7.** [UK] inf [chatter] bavardage m **8.** *(U)* [US] [in stomach] gaz mpl. ◆ vt **1.** [poison] asphyxier or intoxiquer au gaz ▶ **to gas o.s.** a) [poison] s'asphyxier au gaz b) [suicide] se suicider au gaz **2.** MIL gazer. ◆ vi inf [chatter] bavarder, jacasser. ◆ comp [company, industry] du gaz ; [engine, boiler] à gaz ▶ **gas central heating** chauffage m central au gaz ▶ **gas pedal** [US] accélérateur m. ◆⁺ **gas up** [US] ◆ vt sep ▶ **to gas the automobile up** faire le plein d'essence. ◆ vi faire le plein d'essence.

gasbag ['gæsbæg] n [UK] inf & pej moulin m à paroles, pie f.

gas chamber n chambre f à gaz.

Gascony ['gæskənɪ] pr n Gascogne f.

gas cooker n [UK] cuisinière f à gaz, gazinière f.

gaseous ['gæsjəs or 'gæɪzjəs] adj PHYS gazeux.

gas fire n [UK] (appareil m de) chauffage m au gaz.

gas-fired adj [UK] ▶ **gas-fired central heating** chauffage m central au gaz.

gas fitter n installateur m d'appareils à gaz.

gas guzzler n inf AUTO voiture f qui consomme beaucoup.

gash [gæʃ] ◆ vt **1.** [knee, hand] entailler ; [face] balafrer, taillader **2.** [material] déchirer, lacérer. ◆ n **1.** [on knee, hand] entaille f ; [on face] balafre f, estafilade f **2.** [in material] (grande) déchirure f, déchiqueture f.

gas heater n [radiator] radiateur *m* à gaz ; [for water] chauffe-eau *m* *inv* à gaz.

gas jet n brûleur *m*.

gasket ['gæskɪt] n MECH joint *m* (d'étanchéité) ▶ **(cylinder) head gasket** AUTO joint *m* de culasse.

gas lighter n [for cooker] allume-gaz *m* ; [for cigarettes] briquet *m* à gaz.

gas main n conduite *f* de gaz.

gasman ['gæsmæn] (*pl* **gasmen** [-men]) n employé *m* du gaz.

gas mask n masque *m* à gaz.

gas meter n compteur *m* à gaz.

gasoline, gasolene ['gæsəli:n] US AUTO essence *f*.

gasometer [gæ'sɒmɪtə'] n gazomètre *m*.

gas oven n [domestic] four *m* à gaz ; [cremation chamber] four *m* crématoire.

gasp [gɑ:sp] ◆ vi **1.** [be short of breath] haleter, souffler **2.** [in shock, surprise] avoir le souffle coupé **3.** US *inf* & *fig* : *I'm gasping (for a drink)* je meurs de soif. ◆ vt : *"what?" he gasped* « quoi ? », dit-il d'une voix pantelante. ◆ n halètement *m*.

gas-permeable adj : *gas-permeable (contact) lenses* lentilles *fpl* perméables au gaz.

gas ring n [part of cooker] brûleur *m* ; [small cooker] réchaud *m* à gaz.

gassed up [gæst-] adj US *inf* [drunk] bourré.

gas station n US poste *m* d'essence, station-service *f* / *gas station attendant* employé *m*, -e *f* de station-service, pompiste *mf*.

gas stove n UK [in kitchen] cuisinière *f* à gaz, gazinière *f* ; [for camping] réchaud *m* à gaz.

gassy ['gæsɪ] (*compar* **gassier**, *superl* **gassiest**) adj **1.** CHEM gazeux **2.** [drink] gazeux **3.** *inf* [chatty] bavard **4.** [bloated] ballonné **5.** [causing wind] qui provoque des ballonnements **6.** MIN grisouteux.

gas tank n **1.** [domestic] cuve *f* à gaz **2.** US AUTO réservoir *m* à essence.

gas tap n [on cooker] bouton *m* de cuisinière à gaz ; [at mains] robinet *m* de gaz.

gastric ['gæstrɪk] adj gastrique.

gastric bypass n dérivation *f* gastrique.

gastric flu n (U) grippe *f* intestinale or gastro-intestinale.

gastric juice n suc *m* gastrique.

gastric ulcer n ulcère *m* de l'estomac, gastrite *f* ulcéreuse.

gastritis [gæs'traɪtɪs] n (U) gastrite *f*.

gastroenteritis [,gæstrəʊ,entə'raɪtɪs] n (U) gastroentérite *f*.

gastro-intestinal ['gæstrəʊ-] adj gastro-intestinal.

gastronomic [,gæstrə'nɒmɪk] adj gastronomique.

gastronomy [gæs'trɒnəmɪ] n gastronomie *f*.

gastropub ['gæstrəʊpʌb] n UK pub *m* gastronomique.

gastroscopy [gæs'trɒskəpɪ] n gastroscopie *f*, fibroscopie *f* gastrique.

gasworks ['gæswɜ:ks] pl n usine *f* à gaz.

gate [geɪt] ◆ n **1.** [into garden] porte *f* ; [into driveway, field] barrière *f* ; [bigger - of mansion] portail *m* ; [- into courtyard] porte *f* cochère ; [low] portillon *m* ; [wrought iron] grille *f* **2.** [at airport] porte *f* **3.** [on ski slope] porte *f* **4.** [on canal] ▶ **lock gates** écluse *f*, portes *fpl* d'écluse **5.** SPORT [spectators] nombre *m* de spectateurs (admis) ; [money] recette *f*, entrées *fpl* **6.** ELECTRON gâchette *f* **7.** PHOT fenêtre *f* **8.** [in horse racing] starting-gate *f*. ◆ vt UK SCH consigner, mettre en retenue.

gateau ['gætəʊ] (*pl* **gateaux** [-təʊz]) n gros gâteau *m* (*décoré et fourré à la crème*).

gatecrash ['geɪtkræʃ] *inf* ◆ vi [at party] s'inviter, jouer les pique-assiette ; [at paying event] resquiller. ◆ vt : *to gatecrash a party* aller à une fête sans invitation.

gatecrasher ['geɪtkræʃə'] n *inf* [at party] pique-assiette *mf* ; [at paying event] resquilleur *m*, -euse *f*.

gatehouse ['geɪthaʊs] (*pl* [-haʊzɪz]) n [of estate] loge *f* du portier ; [of castle] corps *m* de garde.

gatekeeper ['geɪt,ki:pə'] n **1.** portier *m*, -ère *f* **2.** RAIL garde-barrière *mf*.

gatepost ['geɪtpəʊst] n montant *m* de barrière or de porte ▶ **between you, me and the gatepost** UK *inf* soit dit entre nous.

gateway ['geɪtweɪ] n porte *f*, entrée *f* ; COMPUT portail *m* ; *fig* porte *f* / *this is a gateway drug* c'est une porte vers les drogues dures.

gather ['gæðə'] ◆ vt **1.** [pick, collect - mushrooms, wood] ramasser ; [- flowers, fruit] cueillir **2.** [bring together - information] recueillir ; [- taxes] percevoir, recouvrer ; [- belongings] ramasser **3.** [gain] prendre **4.** [prepare] : *to gather one's thoughts* se concentrer **5.** [embrace] serrer **6.** [clothes] ramasser **7.** [deduce] déduire, comprendre **8.** SEW froncer **9.** PHR **to gather dust** ramasser la poussière. ◆ vi **1.** [people] se regrouper, se rassembler ; [crowd] se former ; [troops] se masser **2.** [clouds] s'amonceler ; [darkness] s'épaissir ; [storm] menacer, se préparer. ❖ **gathers** pl n SEW fronces *fpl*. ❖ **gather in** vt sep **1.** [harvest] rentrer ; [wheat] récolter ; [money, taxes] recouvrer ; [books, exam papers] ramasser **2.** SEW : *gathered in at the waist* froncé à la taille. ❖ **gather round** vi se regrouper, se rassembler. ❖ **gather together** ◆ vi se regrouper, se rassembler. ◆ vt sep [people] rassembler, réunir ; [books, belongings] rassembler, ramasser. ❖ **gather up** vt sep **1.** [objects, belongings] ramasser **2.** [skirts] ramasser, retrousser ; [hair] ramasser, relever.

gathering ['gæðərɪŋ] ◆ n **1.** [group] assemblée *f*, réunion *f* / *a social gathering* une fête **2.** [accumulation] accumulation *f* ; [of clouds] amoncellement *m* **3.** [bringing together - of people] rassemblement *m* ; [- of objects] accumulation *f*, amoncellement *m* **4.** [harvesting] récolte *f* ; [picking] cueillette *f* **5.** [increase - in speed, force] accroissement *m* **6.** (U) SEW froncis *m*, fronces *fpl*. ◆ adj *liter* : *the gathering storm* l'orage qui se prépare or qui menace.

gator ['geɪtə'] n US *inf* alligator *m*.

GATT [gæt] (**abbr of General Agreement on Tariffs and Trade**) pr n GATT *m*.

gauche [gəʊʃ] adj gauche, maladroit.

gaudy ['gɔ:dɪ] (*compar* **gaudier**, *superl* **gaudiest**) adj [dress] voyant ; [colour] voyant, criard, tape-à-l'œil (*inv*) ; [display] tapageur.

gauge UK, **gage** US [geɪdʒ] ◆ n **1.** [instrument] jauge *f*, indicateur *m* **2.** [standard measurement] calibre *m*, gabarit *m* ; [diameter - of wire, cylinder, gun] calibre *m* **3.** RAIL [of track] écartement *m* ; AUTO [of wheels] écartement *m* **4.** TECH [of steel] jauge *f* **5.** CIN [of film] pas *m* **6.** *fig* : *the survey provides a gauge of current trends* le sondage permet d'évaluer les tendances actuelles. ◆ vt **1.** [measure, calculate] mesurer, jauger **2.** [predict] prévoir **3.** [standardize] normaliser.

Gaul [gɔ:l] ◆ pr n GEOG Gaule *f*. ◆ n [person] Gaulois *m*, -e *f*.

gaunt [gɔ:nt] adj **1.** [emaciated - face] creux, émacié ; [- body] décharné, émacié **2.** [desolate - landscape] morne, lugubre, désolé ; [- building] lugubre, désert.

gauntlet ['gɔ:ntlɪt] n [medieval glove] gantelet *m* ; [for motorcyclist, fencer] gant *m* (à crispin or à manchette) ▶ **to throw down / to take up the gauntlet** jeter / relever le gant.

gauze [gɔ:z] n gaze *f*.

gave [geɪv] pt ⟶ **give.**

gawk [gɔːk] *inf* vi être or rester bouche bée ▸ **to gawk at sb** regarder qqn bouche bée.

gawky ['gɔːkɪ] (*compar* **gawkier**, *superl* **gawkiest**) adj *inf* gauche, emprunté.

gawp [gɔːp] vi 🇬🇧 *inf* rester bouche bée.

gay [geɪ] ◆ adj **1.** [homosexual] gay, homosexuel **2.** *inf* [rubbish] : *that's so gay* c'est nul **3.** *dated* [cheerful, lively -appearance, party, atmosphere] gai, joyeux ; [-laughter] enjoué, joyeux ; [-music, rhythm] gai, entraînant, allègre **4.** *dated* [bright -colours, lights] gai, vif, éclatant. ◆ n homosexuel m, -elle f, gay m / **gay rights** les droits mpl des homosexuels.

gay-affirmative adj 🇺🇸 ▸ **to be gay-affirmative** avoir une attitude positive à l'égard des homosexuels.

gay-bashing [-bæʃɪŋ] n *inf* agressions fpl homophobes.

gaydar ['geɪdɑːʳ] n *inf* capacité d'un homosexuel à reconnaître d'autres homosexuels.

Gaza Strip ['gɑːzə] pr n ▸ **the Gaza Strip** la bande de Gaza.

gaze [geɪz] ◆ vi ▸ **to gaze at sthg** regarder qqch fixement or longuement. ◆ n regard m fixe. ❖ **gaze about** 🇺🇸, **gaze around** vi regarder autour de soi.

gazebo [gə'ziːbəʊ] (*pl* **gazebos**) n belvédère m.

gazelle [gə'zel] (*pl* **gazelle** or **gazelles**) n gazelle f.

gazette [gə'zet] ◆ n [newspaper] journal m ; [official publication] journal m officiel. ◆ vt 🇬🇧 publier or faire paraître au journal officiel.

gazetteer [,gæzɪ'tɪəʳ] n index m or nomenclature f géographique.

gazillion [gə'zɪljən] n 🇺🇸 *inf* ▸ **gazillions of...** des tonnes de...

gazump [gə'zʌmp] 🇬🇧 *inf* vt augmenter le prix d'un bien immobilier après une promesse de vente orale.

gazunder vi 🇬🇧 *inf* proposer un prix d'achat inférieur pour un bien immobilier à la dernière minute.

GB, Gb [dʒiː'biː] (abbr of **gigabyte**) n gigaoctet m.

GB (abbr of **Great Britain**) pr n G-B f.

GBH n abbr of **grievous bodily harm**.

GC (abbr of **George Cross**) n *distinction honorifique britannique.*

GCH 🇬🇧 written abbr of **gas central heating**.

GCHQ (abbr of **Government Communications Headquarters**) pr n *centre d'interception des télécommunications étrangères en Grande-Bretagne.*

GCSE (abbr of **General Certificate of Secondary Education**) n *premier examen de fin de scolarité en Grande-Bretagne.*

 GCSE

Examen sanctionnant la fin de la première partie de l'enseignement secondaire. Chaque élève présente les matières de son choix (généralement entre 5 et 10) selon un système d'unités de valeur. Le nombre d'unités et les notes obtenues déterminent le passage dans la classe supérieure. Après cet examen, les élèves peuvent choisir d'arrêter leurs études ou de préparer les **A-levels**.

GD, gd MESSAGING written abbr of **good.**

g'day [gə'deɪ] interj 🇦🇺 salut.

Gdns. written abbr of **Gardens.**

GDP (abbr of **gross domestic product**) n 🇬🇧 PIB m.

GDR (abbr of **German Democratic Republic**) pr n RDA f.

gear [gɪəʳ] ◆ n **1.** (U) [accessories, equipment -for photography, camping] équipement m, matériel m ; [-for manual work] outils mpl, matériel m ; [-for household] ustensiles mpl **2.** (U) [personal belongings] effets mpl personnels, affaires fpl ; [luggage] bagages mpl **3.** (U) [clothes] vêtements mpl, tenue f **4.** (U) 🇬🇧 *inf* [fashionable clothes] fringues fpl **5.** (U) [apparatus] mécanisme m, dispositif m **6.** [in car, on bicycle] vitesse f / **to change gear** changer de vitesse / **to be in first / second gear** être en première / seconde. ◆ vt [adapt] adapter. ❖ **gear up** vt sep [prepare] ▸ **to be geared up** être paré or fin prêt.

gearbox ['gɪəbɒks] n boîte f de vitesses.

gearing ['gɪərɪŋ] n **1.** MECH engrenage m **2.** 🇬🇧 FIN effet m de levier.

gearknob ['gɪənɒb] n AUTO poignée f du levier de vitesse.

gear lever 🇬🇧, **gear shift** 🇺🇸 n levier m de vitesse.

gear shift 🇺🇸 = **gear lever.**

gear stick n levier m de changement de vitesse.

gear wheel n roue f dentée, pignon m.

gee [dʒiː] interj ▸ 🇺🇸 *inf* ▸ **gee!** ça alors ! ▸ **gee whiz!** super !, génial !

geek [giːk] n *inf* débile mf ▸ **computer geek** fada mf or dingue mf d'informatique.

geeky adj *inf* caractéristique de jeunes hommes obsédés par l'informatique ou les sciences et socialement inaptes.

geese [giːs] pl ⟶ **goose.**

gee up ◆ interj hue ! ◆ vt sep 🇬🇧 *inf* faire avancer.

geezer ['giːzəʳ] n 🇬🇧 *inf* bonhomme m, coco m.

Geiger counter ['gaɪgəʳ-] n compteur m Geiger.

geisha (girl) ['geɪʃə-] n geisha f.

gel[1] [dʒel] (*pt & pp* **gelled**, *cont* **gelling**) ◆ n **1.** CHEM [gen] gel m **2.** THEAT filtre m coloré. ◆ vi **1.** [idea, plan -take shape] prendre forme or tournure, se cristalliser **2.** [jellify] se gélifier.

gel[2] [gel] 🇬🇧 *hum* = **girl.**

gelatin ['dʒelətɪn], **gelatine** [,dʒelə'tiːn] n **1.** [substance] gélatine f **2.** THEAT filtre m coloré.

gelatinous [dʒə'lætɪnəs] adj gélatineux.

gelding ['geldɪŋ] n (cheval m) hongre m.

gelignite ['dʒelɪgnaɪt] n gélignite f.

gem [dʒem] ◆ n **1.** [precious stone] gemme f, pierre f précieuse ; [semiprecious stone] gemme f, pierre f fine **2.** [masterpiece] joyau m, bijou m, merveille f **3.** [person] : *you're a gem!* tu es un ange ! ◆ vt orner, parer.

Gemini ['dʒemɪnaɪ] pr n ASTROL & ASTRON Gémeaux mpl / *he's a Gemini* il est Gémeaux.

gemstone ['dʒemstəʊn] n [precious] gemme f, pierre f précieuse ; [semiprecious] gemme f, pierre f fine.

gen [dʒen] (*pt & pp* **genned**, *cont* **genning**) n (U) 🇬🇧 *inf* tuyaux mpl, renseignements mpl. ❖ **gen up** 🇬🇧 *inf* ◆ vi se rencarder ▸ **to gen up on** se rencarder sur. ◆ vt sep rencarder, mettre au parfum.

gen. (written abbr of **general**, **generally**) gén.

Gen. (written abbr of **general**) Gal.

gender ['dʒendəʳ] n **1.** GRAM genre m **2.** [sex] sexe m ▸ **gender studies** champ de recherche sur les différences entre les hommes et les femmes d'un point de vue sociologique.

gender reassignment n changement *m* de sexe.

gender-specific adj propre à l'un des deux sexes.

gene [dʒi:n] n gène *m*.

genealogical [,dʒi:njə'lɒdʒɪkl] adj généalogique.

genealogist [,dʒi:nɪ'ælədʒɪst] n généalogiste *mf*.

genealogy [,dʒi:nɪ'ælədʒɪ] n généalogie *f*.

genera ['dʒenərə] pl ⟶ **genus**.

general ['dʒenərəl] ◆ adj **1.** [common] général **2.** [approximate] général **3.** [widespread] général, répandu **4.** [overall - outline, plan, impression] d'ensemble **5.** [ordinary] ▶ **the general public** le grand public *m*. ◆ n **1.** [in reasoning] ▶ **to go from the general to the particular** aller du général au particulier **2.** MIL général *m*. ❖ **in general** adv phr en général.

general anaesthetic, general anesthetic 🇺🇸 n anesthésie *f* générale.

general assembly n assemblée *f* générale.

general delivery n 🇺🇸 poste *f* restante.

general election n élections *fpl* législatives.

general headquarters n (grand) quartier *m* général.

general hospital n centre *m* hospitalier.

generalist ['dʒenərəlɪst] n non-spécialiste *mf*, généraliste *mf*.

generality [,dʒenə'rælətɪ] (*pl* **generalities**) n **1.** [generalization] généralité *f* **2.** *fml* [majority] plupart *f*.

generalization [,dʒenərəlaɪ'zeɪʃn] n **1.** [general comment] généralisation *f* **2.** [spread] généralisation *f*.

generalize, generalise ['dʒenərəlaɪz] ◆ vt généraliser. ◆ vi **1.** [person] généraliser **2.** MED [disease] se généraliser.

generalized ['dʒenərəlaɪzd] adj **1.** [involving many] généralisé **2.** [non-specific] général.

general knowledge n culture *f* générale.

generally ['dʒenərəlɪ] adv **1.** [usually] en général, d'habitude **2.** [in a general way] en général, de façon générale **3.** [by most] dans l'ensemble.

general manager n directeur *m* général, directrice *f* générale.

general meeting n assemblée *f* générale.

general practice n médecine *f* générale.

general practitioner n médecin *m* généraliste, omnipraticien *m*, -enne *f*.

general-purpose adj polyvalent.

general strike n grève *f* générale ▶ **the General Strike** *la grève de mai 1926 en Grande-Bretagne, lancée par les syndicats par solidarité avec les mineurs*.

generate ['dʒenəreɪt] vt **1.** [produce - electricity, power] produire, générer ; *fig* [emotion] susciter, donner naissance à **2.** LING & COMPUT générer.

generation [,dʒenə'reɪʃn] n **1.** [age group] génération *f* **2.** [by birth] : *she is second generation Irish* elle est née de parents irlandais **3.** [period of time] génération *f* **4.** [model - of machine] génération *f* **5.** (U) [of electricity] génération *f*, production *f* ; LING génération *f*.

generation gap n écart *m* entre les générations ; [conflict] conflit *m* des générations.

generator ['dʒenəreɪtər] n **1.** [electric] générateur *m*, groupe *m* électrogène ; [of steam] générateur *m*, chaudière *f* (à vapeur) ; [of gas] gazogène *m* **2.** [person] générateur *m*, -trice *f*.

generic [dʒɪ'nerɪk] adj générique.

generosity [,dʒenə'rɒsətɪ] n générosité *f*.

generous ['dʒenərəs] adj **1.** [with money, gifts] généreux **2.** [in value - gift] généreux ; [in quantity - sum, salary] généreux, élevé **3.** [copious] copieux, abondant ; [large] bon, abondant **4.** [physically - size] généreux, ample.

generously ['dʒenərəslɪ] adv **1.** [unsparingly] généreusement, avec générosité **2.** [with magnanimity - agree, offer] généreusement ; [- forgive] généreusement, avec magnanimité **3.** [copiously] : *the soup was rather generously salted* [oversalted] la soupe était très généreusement salée **4.** [in size] amplement.

genesis ['dʒenəsɪs] (*pl* **geneses** [-si:z]) n genèse *f*, origine *f*. ❖ **Genesis** in BIBLE la Genèse.

genetic [dʒɪ'netɪk] adj génétique.

genetically [dʒɪ'netɪklɪ] adv génétiquement ▶ **genetically modified** génétiquement modifié ▶ **genetically modified organism** organisme *m* génétiquement modifié.

genetic code n code *m* génétique.

genetic engineering n génie *m* génétique.

genetic fingerprinting n empreinte *f* génétique.

geneticist [dʒɪ'netɪsɪst] n généticien *m*, -enne *f*.

genetic pool n pool *m* génétique.

genetics [dʒɪ'netɪks] n (U) génétique *f*.

Geneva [dʒɪ'ni:və] pr n Genève ▶ **Lake Geneva** le lac Léman.

Geneva Convention pr n ▶ **the Geneva Convention** la Convention de Genève.

genial ['dʒi:njəl] adj [friendly - person] aimable, affable ; [- expression, voice] cordial, chaleureux ; [- face] jovial.

geniality [,dʒi:nɪ'ælətɪ] n [of person, expression] cordialité *f*, amabilité *f*.

genially ['dʒi:njəlɪ] adv affablement, cordialement, chaleureusement.

genie ['dʒi:nɪ] (*pl* **genii** [-nɪaɪ]) n génie *m*, djinn *m*.

genital ['dʒenɪtl] adj génital. ❖ **genitals** pl n organes *mpl* génitaux.

genitalia [,dʒenɪ'teɪlɪə] pl n organes *mpl* génitaux, parties *fpl* génitales.

genitive ['dʒenɪtɪv] ◆ n génitif *m* / *in the genitive* au génitif. ◆ adj du génitif / *the genitive case* le génitif.

G9 MESSAGING written abbr of **genius**.

genius ['dʒi:njəs] n (*pl* **geniuses**) **1.** [person] génie *m* **2.** [special ability] génie *m* / *a work* / *writer of genius* une œuvre / un écrivain de génie ▶ **to have a genius for sthg** avoir le génie de qqch **3.** [special character - of system, idea] génie *m* (particulier), esprit *m* **4.** (*pl* **genii** [-nɪaɪ]) [spirit, demon] génie *m*.

genoa ['dʒenəʊə] n NAUT génois *m*.

Genoa ['dʒenəʊə] pr n Gênes.

genocide ['dʒenəsaɪd] n génocide *m*.

genome ['dʒi:nəʊm] n génome *m*.

genomics [dʒɪ'nəʊmɪks] n (sg) génomique.

genre ['ʒɑrə] ◆ n genre *m*. ◆ comp ▶ **genre painting** peinture *f* de genre.

gent [dʒent] (abbr of **gentleman**) n 🇬🇧 *inf* monsieur *m*. ❖ **gents** n *inf* ▶ **the gents** les toilettes *fpl* (pour hommes).

genteel [dʒen'ti:l] adj **1.** [refined] comme il faut, distingué **2.** [affected - speech] maniéré, affecté ; [- manner] affecté ; [- language] précieux.

gentility [dʒen'tɪlətɪ] n **1.** [good breeding] distinction *f* **2.** [gentry] petite noblesse *f* **3.** (U) [affected politeness] manières *fpl* affectées.

gentle ['dʒentl] adj **1.** [mild - person, smile, voice] doux (douce) ; [- landscape] agréable **2.** [light - knock, push, breeze] léger ; [- rain] fin, léger ; [- exercise] modéré **3.** [discreet - rebuke, reminder] discret (discrète) **4.** [gradual - slope, climb] doux (douce).

⚠ **Gentil** means **nice** or **kind**, not **gentle**.

gentleman ['dʒentlmən] (*pl* **gentlemen** [-mən]) n **1.** [man] monsieur *m* **2.** [well-bred man] homme *m* du monde, gentleman *m* **3.** [man of substance] rentier *m* ; [at court] gentilhomme *m*.

gentlemanly ['dʒentlmənlɪ] adj [person] bien élevé ; [appearance, behaviour] distingué ; [status] noble.

gentlemen [-mən] pl ⟶ **gentleman**.

gentlemen's agreement n gentleman's agreement *m*, accord *m* reposant sur l'honneur.

gentleness ['dʒentlnɪs] n douceur *f*, légèreté *f*.

gentlewoman ['dʒentl,wʊmən] (*pl* **gentlewomen** [-,wɪmɪn]) n **1.** [of noble birth] dame *f* **2.** [refined] femme *f* du monde **3.** [lady-in-waiting] dame *f* d'honneur or de compagnie.

gently ['dʒentlɪ] adv **1.** [mildly - speak, smile] avec douceur **2.** [discreetly - remind, reprimand, suggest] discrètement **3.** [lightly] : *the rain was falling gently* la pluie tombait doucement **4.** [gradually] doucement, progressivement **5.** [slowly - move, heat] doucement.

gentrification [,dʒentrɪfɪ'keɪʃn] n embourgeoisement *m*.

gentrified ['dʒentrɪfaɪd] adj 🇬🇧 [area, street] qui s'est embourgeoisé.

gentry ['dʒentrɪ] (*pl* **gentries**) n petite noblesse *f*.

genuflect ['dʒenjuːflekt] vi faire une génuflexion.

genuine ['dʒenjuːn] adj **1.** [authentic - antique] authentique ; [- gold, mahogany] véritable, vrai **2.** [sincere - person] naturel, franc (franche) ; [- emotion] sincère, vrai ; [- smile, laugh] vrai, franc (franche) **3.** [real - mistake] fait de bonne foi **4.** [not impersonated - repairman, official] vrai, véritable **5.** [serious - buyer] sérieux.

genuinely ['dʒenjuːnlɪ] adv [truly] authentiquement ; [sincerely] sincèrement, véritablement.

genus ['dʒiːnəs] (*pl* **genera** ['dʒenərə]) n BIOL genre *m*.

geochemical [,dʒiːəʊ'kemɪkl] adj géochimique.

geochemist [,dʒiːəʊ'kemɪst] n géochimiste *mf*.

geodynamics [,dʒiːəʊdaɪ'næmɪks] n *(U)* géodynamique *f*.

geographer [dʒɪ'ɒgrəfər] n géographe *mf*.

geographical [dʒɪə'græfɪkl] adj géographique.

geography [dʒɪ'ɒgrəfɪ] n **1.** [science] géographie *f* / *geography lesson* cours *m* de géographie **2.** [layout] : *I don't know the geography of the building* je ne connais pas le plan du bâtiment.

geological [,dʒɪə'lɒdʒɪkl] adj géologique.

geologist [dʒɪ'ɒlədʒɪst] n géologue *mf*.

geology [dʒɪ'ɒlədʒɪ] n géologie *f*.

geometrical [,dʒɪə'metrɪkl] adj géométrique.

geometrically [,dʒɪə'metrɪklɪ] adv géométriquement.

geometry [dʒɪ'ɒmətrɪ] n géométrie *f*.

geophysics [,dʒiːəʊ'fɪzɪks] n *(U)* géophysique *f*.

Geordie ['dʒɔːdɪ] 🇬🇧 *inf* n **1.** [person] surnom des habitants de Tyneside, dans le nord-est de l'Angleterre **2.** [dialect] dialecte parlé par les habitants de Tyneside.

George Cross n décoration britannique décernée aux civils pour des actes de bravoure.

Georgia ['dʒɔːdʒə] pr n [in US, CIS] Géorgie *f* / *in Georgia* en Géorgie.

Georgian ['dʒɔːdʒən] ◆ n [inhabitant of Georgia] Géorgien *m*, -enne *f*. ◆ adj **1.** [of Georgia] géorgien **2.** HIST géorgien *(du règne des rois George I-IV 1714-1830)* **3.** LITER ▶ **Georgian poetry** poésie *f* géorgienne *(poésie britannique des années 1912-1922)*.

geostrategy [,dʒiː'əʊ'strætədʒɪ] n géostratégie *f*.

geothermal [,dʒiː:əʊ'θɜːml], **geothermic** [,dʒiː:əʊ'θɜːmɪk] adj géothermique.

geothermics [,dʒiː:əʊ'θɜːmɪks] n *(U)* géothermie *f*.

geotropical [,dʒiː:əʊ'trɒpɪkl] adj géotropique.

geranium [dʒɪ'reɪnjəm] ◆ n géranium *m*. ◆ adj rouge géranium *(inv)*, incarnat.

gerbil ['dʒɜːbɪl] n gerbille *f*.

geriatric [,dʒerɪ'ætrɪk] ◆ adj MED gériatrique ▶ **geriatric hospital** hospice *m* ▶ **geriatric medicine** gériatrie *f* ▶ **geriatric nurse** infirmier *m* (spécialisé en gériatrie), infirmière *f* (spécialisée) en gériatrie ▶ **geriatric ward** service *m* de gériatrie. ◆ n **1.** [patient] malade *mf* en gériatrie **2.** *pej* vieux *m*, vieille *f*.

geriatrics [,dʒerɪ'ætrɪks] n *(U)* gériatrie *f*.

germ [dʒɜːm] n **1.** [microbe] microbe *m*, germe *m* **2.** BIOL germe *m* **3.** *fig* germe *m*, ferment *m*.

german ['dʒɜːmən] n 🇺🇸 [dance] allemande *f*.

German ['dʒɜːmən] ◆ n **1.** [person] Allemand *m*, -e *f* **2.** LING allemand *m*. ◆ adj allemand.

Germanic [dʒɜː'mænɪk] ◆ adj germanique. ◆ n LING germanique *m*.

German measles n *(U)* rubéole *f*.

German shepherd (dog) n berger *m* allemand.

Germany ['dʒɜːmənɪ] pr n Allemagne *f* / *in Germany* en Allemagne.

germ-free adj stérilisé, aseptisé.

germicide ['dʒɜːmɪsaɪd] n bactéricide *m*.

germinate ['dʒɜːmɪneɪt] ◆ vi **1.** BIOL germer **2.** *fig* [originate] germer, prendre naissance. ◆ vt **1.** BIOL faire germer **2.** *fig* faire germer, donner naissance à.

germination [,dʒɜːmɪ'neɪʃn] n germination *f*.

germproof ['dʒɜːmpruːf] adj résistant aux microbes.

germ warfare n guerre *f* bactériologique.

gerontology [,dʒerɒn'tɒlədʒɪ] n gérontologie *f*.

gerrymandering ['dʒerɪmændərɪŋ] n *pej* charcutage *m* électoral.

gerund ['dʒerənd] n gérondif *m*.

gestation [dʒe'steɪʃn] n gestation *f*.

gesticulate [dʒe'stɪkjʊleɪt] ◆ vi gesticuler. ◆ vt [answer, meaning] mimer.

gesticulation [dʒe,stɪkjʊ'leɪʃn] n gesticulation *f*.

gesture ['dʒestʃər] ◆ n **1.** [expressive movement] geste *m* **2.** [sign, token] geste *m*. ◆ vi : *to gesture with one's hands / head* faire un signe de la main / de la tête.

get [get] (🇬🇧 *pt & pp* got [gɒt], *cont* getting [getɪŋ] ; 🇺🇸 *pt* got [gɒt], *pp* gotten [gɒtn], *cont* getting [getɪŋ]) ◆ vt

A. RECEIVE, OBTAIN OR CATCH 1. [receive - gift, letter, phone call] recevoir, avoir ; [- benefits, pension] recevoir, toucher ; [MED - treatment] suivre / *the living room gets a lot of sun* le salon est très ensoleillé / *he got 5 years for smuggling* il a écopé de or il a pris 5 ans (de prison) pour contrebande / *you're really going to get it!* *inf* qu'est-ce que tu vas prendre or écoper ! **2.** [obtain - gen] avoir, trouver, obtenir ; [- through effort] se procurer, obtenir ; [- licence, loan, permission] obtenir ; [- diploma, grades] avoir, obtenir / *they got him a job* ils lui ont trouvé du travail / *the town gets its water from the reservoir* la ville reçoit son eau du réservoir / *I'm going to get something to drink / eat* **a)** [fetch] je vais chercher quelque chose à boire / manger **b)** [consume] je vais boire / manger quelque chose / *get plenty of sleep* dormez beaucoup / *I got a lot from* or *out of my trip to China* mon voyage en Chine m'a beaucoup apporté / *he didn't get a chance to introduce himself* il n'a pas eu l'occasion de se présenter **3.** [obtain in exchange] recevoir / *they got a lot of money for their flat* la vente de leur appartement leur a rapporté beaucoup d'argent **4.** [offer as gift] offrir, donner **5.** [buy] acheter, prendre **6.** [learn - information, news] recevoir, apprendre **7.** [reach by calculation or experimentation - answer, solution] trouver ; [- result] obtenir **8.** [earn, win - salary] recevoir, gagner, toucher ; [- prize] gagner ; [- reputation] se faire / *someone's trying to get your attention* **a)** [calling] quelqu'un vous appelle **b)** [waving] quelqu'un vous fait signe **9.** [bring, fetch] (aller) chercher / *get me my coat* va me chercher or apporte-moi mon manteau / *we had to get a doctor* nous avons dû faire venir un médecin / *what can I get you to drink?* qu'est-ce que je vous sers à boire ? **10.** [catch - ball] attraper ; [- bus, train] prendre, attraper **11.** [capture] attraper, prendre ; [seize] prendre, saisir **12.** [answer - door, telephone] répondre / *the doorbell's ringing — I'll get it!* quelqu'un sonne à la porte — j'y vais !

B. EXPERIENCE OR ENCOUNTER 1. [become ill with] attraper / *he got a chill* il a pris or attrapé froid **2.** [experience, feel - shock] recevoir, ressentir, avoir ; [- fun, pain, surprise] avoir / *I get the impression he doesn't like me* j'ai l'impression que je ne lui plais pas.

C. CAUSE 1. *(with adj or pp)* [cause to be] : *she managed to get the window closed / open* elle a réussi à fermer / ouvrir la fenêtre / *get the suitcases ready* préparez les bagages / *to get things under control* prendre les choses en main **2.** *(with infinitive)* [cause to do or carry out] : *we couldn't get her to leave* on n'a pas pu la faire partir / *get him to move the car* demande-lui de déplacer la voiture / *I got it to work* or *working* j'ai réussi à le faire marcher **3.** *(with past participle)* [cause to be done or carried out] ▶ **to get sthg done / repaired** faire faire / réparer qqch / *to get one's hair cut* se faire couper les cheveux / *it's impossible to get anything done around here* **a)** [by oneself] il est impossible de faire quoi que ce soit ici **b)** [by someone else] il est impossible d'obtenir quoi que ce soit ici **4.** [cause to come, go, move] : *how are you going to get this package to them?* comment allez-vous leur faire parvenir ce paquet ? / *they eventually got all the boxes downstairs / upstairs* ils ont fini par descendre / monter toutes leurs boîtes / *his friends managed to get him home* ses amis ont réussi à le ramener (à la maison).

D. CONTACT OR ABSORB 1. [hear correctly] entendre, saisir / *I didn't get his name* je n'ai pas saisi son nom **2.** [establish telephone contact with] : *I got her father on the phone* j'ai parlé à son père or j'ai eu son père au téléphone **3.** *inf* [understand] comprendre, saisir / *I don't get it, I don't get the point* je ne comprends or ne saisis pas, je n'y suis pas du tout / *don't get me wrong* comprenez-moi bien / *I don't get the joke* je ne vois pas ce qui est (si) drôle / *(I've) got it!* ça y est !, j'y suis ! **4.** [take note of] remarquer.

E. HARM or AFFECT 1. *inf* [hit] atteindre ; [hit and kill] tuer **2.** *inf* [harm, punish] : *everyone's out to get me* tout le monde est après moi **3.** *inf* [take vengeance on] se venger de / *we'll get you for this!* on te revaudra ça ! **4.** *inf* [baffle, puzzle] : *you've got me there* alors là, aucune idée.
◆ **vi**

A. BECOME OR START DOING 1. [become] devenir / *I'm getting hungry / thirsty* je commence à avoir faim / soif / *get dressed!* habille-toi ! / *to get married* se marier / *how did that vase get broken?* comment se fait-il que ce vase soit cassé ? / *to get used to (doing) sthg* s'habituer à (faire) qqch **2.** [used to form passive] : *to get elected* se faire élire, être élu / *I'm always getting invited to parties* on m'invite toujours à des soirées **3.** *(with present participle)* [start]

commencer à, se mettre à / *let's get going* or *moving!* **a)** [let's leave] allons-y ! **b)** [let's hurry] dépêchons(-nous) !, grouillons-nous ! **c)** [let's start to work] au travail ! / *I'll get going on that right away* je m'y mets tout de suite.

B. MOVEMENT 1. [go] aller, se rendre ; [arrive] arriver / *when did you get home?* quand es-tu rentré ? / *how do you get to the museum?* comment est-ce qu'on fait pour aller au musée ? / *now you're getting somewhere!* enfin tu avances ! / *I'm not getting anywhere* or *I'm getting nowhere (fast)* *inf* with this project je fais du surplace avec ce projet **2.** [move in specified direction] : *to get into bed* se coucher / *get over here!* viens ici !

C. FOLLOWED BY INFINITIVE 1. [start] commencer à, se mettre à / *to get to know sb* apprendre à connaître qqn / *you'll get to like it in the end* ça finira par te plaire / *they got to talking about the past* ils en sont venus or se sont mis à parler du passé **2.** [become] devenir / *it's getting to be impossible to find a flat* ça devient impossible de trouver un appartement **3.** [manage] réussir à **4.** *inf* [be allowed to] : *I never get to drive* on ne me laisse jamais conduire.
❖ **get about** vi **1.** [be up and about, move around] se déplacer / *she gets about on crutches / in a wheelchair* elle se déplace avec des béquilles / en chaise roulante **2.** [travel] voyager **3.** [story, rumour] se répandre, circuler. ❖ **get across** ◆ vi pénétrer, passer / *the river was flooded but we managed to get across* la rivière était en crue mais nous avons réussi à traverser. ◆ vt sep communiquer / *I can't seem to get the idea across to them* je n'arrive pas à leur faire comprendre ça. ❖ **get ahead** vi [succeed] réussir, arriver. ❖ **get along** vi **1.** [fare, manage] aller / *how are you getting along?* comment vas-tu ?, comment ça va ? / *she's getting along well in her new job* elle se débrouille bien dans son nouveau travail **2.** [advance, progress] avancer, progresser **3.** [be on good terms] s'entendre / *she's easy to get along with* elle est facile à vivre **4.** [move away] s'en aller, partir ; [go] aller, se rendre. ❖ **get around** ◆ vt insep [obstacle, problem] contourner ; [law, rule] tourner. ◆ vi = **get about.** ❖ **get around to** vt insep : *she won't get around to reading it before tomorrow* elle n'arrivera pas à (trouver le temps de) le lire avant demain / *he finally got around to fixing the radiator* il a fini par or il est finalement arrivé à réparer le radiateur. ❖ **get at** vt insep **1.** [reach - object, shelf] atteindre ; [- place] parvenir à, atteindre / *I've put the pills where the children can't get at them* j'ai mis les pilules là où les enfants ne peuvent pas les atteindre **2.** [discover] trouver / *to get at the truth* connaître la vérité **3.** [mean, intend] entendre / *I see what you're getting at* je vois où vous voulez en venir **4.** *inf* [criticize] s'en prendre à, s'attaquer à **5.** *inf* [bribe, influence] acheter, suborner. ❖ **get away** vi **1.** [leave] s'en aller, partir / *she has to get away from home* / *her parents* il faut qu'elle parte de chez elle / s'éloigne de ses parents / *to get away from the daily grind* échapper au train-train quotidien **2.** [move away] s'éloigner / *get away from me!* fichez-moi le camp ! **3.** [escape] s'échapper, se sauver / *the thief got away with all the jewels* le voleur est parti or s'est sauvé avec tous les bijoux / *you can't get away from it* or *there's no getting away from it* c'est comme ça, on n'y peut rien ▶ **get away (with you)!** *UK* inf à d'autres ! ❖ **get away with** vt insep : *he got away with cheating on his taxes* personne ne s'est aperçu qu'il avait fraudé le fisc / *I can't believe you got away with it!* je n'arrive pas à croire que personne ne t'ait rien dit ! ❖ **get back** ◆ vi **1.** [move backwards] reculer **2.** [return] revenir, retourner / *I can't wait to get back home* je suis impatient de rentrer (à la maison) / *to get back to sleep* se rendormir / *to get back to work* **a)** [after break] se remettre au travail **b)** [after holiday, illness] reprendre le travail / *getting* or *to get back to the point* pour en revenir au sujet

qui nous préoccupe / *I'll get back to you on that* **a)** [call back] je vous rappelle pour vous dire ce qu'il en est **b)** [discuss again] nous reparlerons de cela plus tard. ◆ vt sep **1.** [recover - something lost or lent] récupérer ; [-force, strength] reprendre, récupérer ; [-health, motivation] retrouver / *he got his job back* il a été repris / *you'll have to get your money back from the shop* il faut que vous vous fassiez rembourser par le magasin **2.** [return] rendre **3.** [return to original place] remettre, replacer. ❖ **get back at** vt insep se venger de. ❖ **get by** vi **1.** [pass] passer **2.** [manage, survive] se débrouiller, s'en sortir / *how do you get by on that salary?* comment tu te débrouilles or tu t'en sors avec un salaire comme ça ? ❖ **get down** ◆ vi descendre / *get down off that chair!* descends de cette chaise ! / *they got down on their knees* ils se sont mis à genoux / *get down!* **a)** [hide] couchez-vous ! **b)** [to dog] bas les pattes ! ◆ vt sep **1.** [write down] noter **2.** [depress] déprimer, démoraliser / *don't let it get you down* ne te laisse pas abattre **3.** [swallow] avaler, faire descendre. ❖ **get down to** vt insep se mettre à / *it's not so difficult once you get down to it* ce n'est pas si difficile une fois qu'on s'y met / *it's hard getting down to work after the weekend* c'est difficile de reprendre le travail après le week-end. ❖ **get in** ◆ vi **1.** [into building] entrer **2.** [return home] rentrer **3.** [arrive] arriver **4.** [be admitted - to club] se faire admettre ; [-to school, university] entrer, être admis or reçu / *he applied to Oxford but he didn't get in* il voulait entrer à Oxford mais il n'a pas pu **5.** [be elected - person] être élu ; [-party] accéder au pouvoir **6.** [interject] glisser. ◆ vt sep **1.** [fit in] : *I hope to get in a bit of reading on holiday* j'espère pouvoir lire ou que je trouverai le temps de lire pendant mes vacances **2.** [collect, gather - crops] rentrer, engranger ; [-debts] recouvrer ; [-taxes] percevoir **3.** [lay in] : *to get in supplies* s'approvisionner **4.** [hand in, submit] rendre, remettre. ◆ vt insep [building] entrer dans ; [vehicle] monter dans / *he had just got in the door when the phone rang* il venait juste d'arriver or d'entrer quand le téléphone a sonné. ❖ **get into** ◆ vt insep **1.** [arrive in] arriver à **2.** [put on - dress, shirt, shoes] mettre ; [-trousers, stockings] enfiler, mettre ; [-coat] endosser / *can you still get into your jeans?* est-ce que tu rentres encore dans ton jean ? **3.** [be admitted to - club, school, university] entrer dans / *to get into office* être élu **4.** [become involved in] : *he wants to get into politics* il veut se lancer dans la politique **5.** [become accustomed to] : *he soon got into her way of doing things* il s'est vite fait or s'est vite mis à sa façon de faire les choses **6.** [experience a specified condition or state] : *to get into debt* s'endetter / *she got into trouble with the teacher* elle a eu des ennuis avec le professeur **7.** [cause to act strangely] prendre / *what's got into you?* qu'est-ce qui te prend ?, quelle mouche te pique ? ◆ vt sep **1.** [cause to be admitted to - club] faire entrer à ; [-school, university] faire entrer dans / *the president got his son into Harvard* le président a fait entrer or accepter or admettre son fils à Harvard **2.** [cause to be in a specified condition or state] mettre / *she got herself into a terrible state* elle s'est mis dans tous ses états **3.** [involve in] impliquer dans, entraîner dans **4.** *inf* [make interested in] faire découvrir ; [accustom to] habituer à, faire prendre l'habitude de. ❖ **get in with** vt insep s'insinuer dans les bonnes grâces de, se faire bien voir de. ❖ **get off** ◆ vi **1.** [leave bus, train, etc.] descendre ▸ **to tell sb where to get off** *inf* : *I told him where to get off!* je l'ai envoyé sur les roses !, je l'ai envoyé promener ! **2.** [depart - person] s'en aller, partir ; [-car] démarrer ; [-plane] décoller ; [-letter, parcel] partir / *the project got off to a bad / good start* *fig* le projet a pris un mauvais / bon départ **3.** [leave work] finir, s'en aller ; [take time off] se libérer / *can you get off early tomorrow?* peux-tu quitter le travail de bonne heure demain ? **4.** [escape punishment] s'en sortir, s'en tirer, en être quitte / *the students got off with a fine / warning* les étudiants en ont été quittes pour une amende / un avertissement **5.** [go to sleep] s'endormir. ◆ vt insep **1.** [leave - bus, train, etc.] descendre de / *he got off his horse*

il est descendu de cheval / *if only the boss would get off my back* si seulement le patron me fichait la paix **2.** [depart from] partir de, décamper de **3.** [escape from] se libérer de ; [avoid] échapper à. ◆ vt sep **1.** [cause to leave, climb down] faire descendre **2.** [send] envoyer, faire partir **3.** [remove - clothing, lid] enlever, ôter ; [-stains] faire partir or disparaître, enlever **4.** [free from punishment] tirer d'affaire ; [in court] faire acquitter / *he'll need a good lawyer to get him off* il lui faudra un bon avocat pour se tirer d'affaire **5.** [put to sleep] endormir. ❖ **get off with** vt insep **UK** *inf* sortir avec. ❖ **get on** ◆ vi **1.** [bus, plane, train] monter ; [ship] monter à bord **2.** [fare, manage] : *how's your husband getting on?* comment va votre mari ? / *how did he get on at the interview?* comment s'est passé son entretien ?, comment ça a marché pour son entretien ? **3.** [make progress] avancer, progresser **4.** [succeed] réussir, arriver / *to get on in life* or *in the world* faire son chemin or réussir dans la vie **5.** [continue] continuer / *we must be getting on* il faut que nous partions / *they got on with the job* ils se sont remis au travail **6.** [be on good terms] s'entendre / *my mother and I get on well* je m'entends bien avec ma mère / *to be difficult / easy to get on with* être difficile / facile à vivre **7.** [grow old - person] se faire vieux / *she's getting on (in years)* elle commence à se faire vieille **8.** **PHR** **get on with it!** **a)** [continue speaking] continuez ! **b)** [continue working] allez ! au travail ! **c)** [hurry up] mais dépêchez-vous enfin ! ◆ vt insep [bus, train] monter dans ; [plane] monter dans, monter à bord de ; [ship] monter à bord de ; [bed, horse, table, bike] monter sur / *get on your feet* levez-vous, mettez-vous debout. ◆ vt sep **1.** [help onto - bus, train] faire monter dans ; [-bed, bike, horse, table] faire monter sur **2.** [coat, gloves, shoes] mettre, enfiler ; [lid] mettre. ❖ **get on for** vt insep : *the president is getting on for sixty* le président approche la soixantaine or a presque soixante ans / *it's getting on for midnight* il est presque minuit, il n'est pas loin de minuit / *there were getting on for ten thousand demonstrators* il n'y avait pas loin or il y avait près de dix mille manifestants. ❖ **get onto** vt insep **1.** = **get on** (*vt insep*) **2.** [turn attention to] ▸ **to get onto a subject** or **onto a topic** aborder un sujet / *I'll get right onto it!* je vais m'y mettre tout de suite ! **3.** [contact] prendre contact avec, se mettre en rapport avec ; [speak to] parler à ; [call] téléphoner à, donner un coup de fil à **4.** *inf* [become aware of] découvrir. ❖ **get out** ◆ vi **1.** [leave - of building, room] sortir ; [-of car, train] descendre ; [-organization, team] quitter / *you'd better get out of here* tu ferais bien de partir or sortir ▸ **get out of here!** **a)** [leave] sortez d'ici ! **b)** **US** *inf* [I don't believe it] mon œil ! **2.** [go out] sortir **3.** [information, news] se répandre, s'ébruiter / *the secret got out* le secret a été éventé **4.** [escape] s'échapper / *he was lucky to get out alive* il a eu de la chance de s'en sortir vivant. ◆ vt sep **1.** [champagne, furniture] sortir ; [person] (faire) sortir **2.** [produce, make - book] publier, sortir ; [-list] établir, dresser **3.** [speak with difficulty] prononcer, sortir. ❖ **get out of** ◆ vt insep **1.** [avoid] éviter, échapper à ; [obligation] se dérober or se soustraire à / *he tried to get out of helping me* il a essayé de se défausser pour ne pas devoir m'aider / *we have to go, there's no getting out of it* il faut qu'on y aille, il n'y a rien à faire or il n'y a pas moyen d'y échapper **2.** [escape from] : *to get out of trouble* se tirer d'affaire. ◆ vt sep **1.** [take out of] sortir de **2.** [help to avoid] : *the phone call got her out of having to talk to me* *fig* le coup de fil lui a évité d'avoir à me parler / *he'll never get himself out of this one!* il ne s'en sortira jamais ! **3.** [extract - cork] sortir de ; [-nail, splinter] enlever de ; [-stain] faire partir de, enlever de **4.** [gain from] gagner, retirer ▸ **to get a lot out of sthg** tirer (un) grand profit de qqch. ❖ **get over** ◆ vt insep **1.** [cross - river, street] traverser, franchir ; [-fence, wall] franchir, passer par-dessus **2.** [recover from - illness] se remettre de, guérir de ; [-accident] se remettre de ; [-loss] se remettre de, se consoler de / *I'll never get over her* je ne l'oublierai jamais / *I can't get over it!* je n'en reviens pas ! / *he'll get over it!* il n'en mourra pas !

3. [master, overcome - obstacle] surmonter ; [- difficulty] surmonter, venir à bout de. ◆ vt sep **1.** [cause to cross] faire traverser, faire passer **2.** [communicate - idea, message] faire passer. ◆ vi **1.** [cross] traverser **2.** [idea, message] passer. ◆ **get over with** vt insep [finish with] en finir avec / *let's get it over (with)* finissons-en. ◆ **get round** ◆ vt insep = get around. ◆ vt sep = get around. ◆ vi = get about. ◆ **get round to** = get around to. ◆ **get through** ◆ vi **1.** [reach destination] parvenir / *the message didn't get through* le message n'est pas arrivé / *despite the crowds, I managed to get through* malgré la foule, j'ai réussi à passer **2.** [candidate, student - succeed] réussir ; [- in exam] être reçu, réussir **3.** [bill, motion] passer, être adopté ou voté **4.** [make oneself understood] se faire comprendre **5.** [contact] contacter ; TELEC obtenir la communication / *I can't get through to his office* je n'arrive pas à avoir son bureau. ◆ vt insep **1.** [come through - hole, window] passer par ; [- crowd] se frayer un chemin à travers ou dans ; [- military lines] percer, franchir **2.** [survive - storm, winter] survivre à ; [- difficulty] se sortir de, se tirer de **3.** [complete, finish - book] finir, terminer ; [- job, project] achever, venir à bout de / *I got through an enormous amount of work* j'ai abattu beaucoup de travail **4.** [consume, use up] consommer, utiliser / *they got through their monthly salary in one week* en une semaine ils avaient dépensé tout leur salaire du mois. ◆ vt sep **1.** [transmit - message] faire passer, transmettre, faire parvenir **2.** [make understood] : *when will you get it through your thick head that I don't want to go?* inf quand est-ce que tu vas enfin comprendre que je ne veux pas y aller ? **3.** [bill, motion] faire adopter, faire passer / *the party got the bill through the Senate* le parti a fait voter ou adopter le projet de loi par le Sénat. ◆ **get to** vt insep **1.** [reach] arriver à / *where have you got to in the book?* où en es-tu dans le livre ? / *it got to the point where he couldn't walk another step* il en est arrivé au point de ne plus pouvoir faire un pas **2.** [deal with] s'occuper de **3.** inf [have an effect on] : *don't let it get to you!* ne t'énerve pas pour ça ! ◆ **get together** ◆ vi **1.** [meet] se réunir, se rassembler / *can we get together after the meeting?* on peut se retrouver après la réunion ? **2.** [reach an agreement] se mettre d'accord. ◆ vt sep [people] réunir, rassembler ; [things] rassembler, ramasser ; [thoughts] rassembler ▶ **to get one's act together** inf se secouer. ◆ **get up** ◆ vi **1.** [arise from bed] se lever / *get up!* sors du lit !, debout !, lève-toi ! **2.** [rise to one's feet] se lever, se mettre debout / *to get up from the table* se lever ou sortir de table **3.** [climb up] monter **4.** [subj: wind] se lever. ◆ vt insep [stairs] monter ; [ladder, tree] monter à ; [hill] gravir. ◆ vt sep **1.** [cause to rise to feet] faire lever ; [awaken] réveiller **2.** [generate, work up] : *to get up speed* gagner de la vitesse. ◆ **get up to** vt insep faire / *he gets up to all kinds of mischief* il fait des tas de bêtises.

getaway ['getəweɪ] ◆ n **1.** [escape] fuite f **2.** AUTO [start] démarrage m ; [in racing] départ m. ◆ adj : *a getaway car / vehicle* une voiture / un véhicule de fuyard.

get-go n ⓤⓢ inf ▶ **from the get-go** dès le début.

get-rich-quick adj inf ▶ **a get-rich-quick scheme** un projet pour faire fortune rapidement.

get-there n ⓤⓢ inf pêche f, allant m.

get-together n [meeting] (petite) réunion f ; [party] (petite) fête f.

getup ['getʌp] n inf [outfit] accoutrement m ; [disguise] déguisement m.

get-up-and-go n inf allant m, dynamisme m.

get-well card n carte de vœux pour un bon rétablissement.

geyser [ⓤⓚ 'giːzə^r ⓤⓢ 'gaɪzər] n **1.** GEOL geyser m **2.** ⓤⓚ [domestic] chauffe-eau m inv (à gaz).

GF MESSAGING written abbr of **girlfriend**.

G-force n pesanteur f.

GG MESSAGING written abbr of good game.

Ghana ['gɑːnə] pr n Ghana m / *in Ghana* au Ghana.

Ghanaian [gɑːˈneɪən], **Ghanian** ['gɑːnɪən] ◆ n Ghanéen m, -enne f. ◆ adj ghanéen.

ghastly ['gɑːstlɪ] (compar ghastlier, superl ghastliest) adj **1.** inf [very bad] affreux, épouvantable, atroce **2.** [frightening, unnatural] horrible, effrayant.

ghee n ghee m, beurre m clarifié.

gherkin ['gɜːkɪn] n cornichon m.

ghetto ['getəʊ] (pl ghettos or ghettoes) n ghetto m.

ghetto blaster [-ˌblɑːstər] n inf grand radiocassette portatif.

ghettoization [getəʊaɪ'zeɪʃn] n ghettoïsation f.

ghost [gəʊst] ◆ n **1.** [phantom] revenant m, fantôme m, spectre m **2.** [shadow, hint] ombre f **3.** TV image f secondaire or résiduelle **4.** [writer] nègre m **5.** ⓟⓗⓡ **to give up the ghost** rendre l'âme. ◆ vt ▶ **to ghost a book for an author** servir de nègre à l'auteur d'un livre. ◆ adj [story, film] de revenants, de fantômes.

ghosting ['gəʊstɪŋ] n TV image f fantôme, fantôme m.

ghostlike ['gəʊst,laɪk] ◆ adj spectral, de spectre. ◆ adv comme un spectre.

ghostly ['gəʊstlɪ] (compar ghostlier, superl ghostliest) adj spectral, fantomatique.

ghost town n ville f fantôme.

ghostwrite ['gəʊstraɪt] (pt ghostwrote [-rəʊt], pp ghostwritten [-,rɪtn]) ◆ vt écrire or rédiger (comme nègre). ◆ vi ▶ **to ghostwrite for sb** servir de nègre à qqn.

ghostwriter ['gəʊst,raɪtər] n nègre m.

ghostwritten [-,rɪtn] pp ⟶ ghostwrite.

ghostwrote [-rəʊt] pt ⟶ ghostwrite.

ghoul [guːl] n **1.** [evil spirit] goule f **2.** [macabre person] amateur mf de macabre.

ghoulish ['guːlɪʃ] adj **1.** [ghostly] de goule, vampirique **2.** [person, humour] morbide, macabre.

GHQ (abbr of general headquarters) n GQG m.

GHz (abbr of gigahertz) n GHz m.

GI (abbr of Government Issue) n [soldier] GI m, soldat m américain.

giant ['dʒaɪənt] ◆ n **1.** [in size] géant m, -e f **2.** fig : *a literary giant* un géant de la littérature. ◆ adj géant, gigantesque.

giantess ['dʒaɪəntes] n géante f.

giantkiller ['dʒaɪənt,kɪlər] n SPORT petite équipe victorieuse d'une équipe plus forte.

giantkilling ['dʒaɪənt,kɪlɪŋ] ⓤⓚ SPORT victoire surprise d'un concurrent peu coté.

giant panda n panda m géant.

giant-size(d) adj [pack] géant.

gibber ['dʒɪbər] vi [person] bredouiller, bafouiller / *to gibber with fear* bafouiller de peur.

gibbering ['dʒɪbərɪŋ] adj : *I was a gibbering wreck!* j'étais dans un de ces états ! / *he's a gibbering idiot* inf c'est un sacré imbécile.

gibberish ['dʒɪbərɪʃ] n baragouin m, charabia m.

gibbon ['gɪbən] n gibbon m.

gibe [dʒaɪb] ◆ vi ▶ **to gibe at sb** railler qqn, se moquer de qqn. ◆ n [remark] raillerie f, moquerie f.

giblets ['dʒɪblɪts] pl n abats mpl de volaille.

Gibraltar [dʒɪˈbrɔːltər] pr n Gibraltar / *in Gibraltar* à Gibraltar ▶ **the Strait of Gibraltar** le détroit de Gibraltar.

Gibraltarian [ˌdʒɪbrɔːlˈteərɪən] ◆ adj & n gibraltarien. ◆ n Gibraltarien *m*, -ne *f*.

giddily ['gɪdɪlɪ] adv **1.** [dizzily] vertigineusement **2.** [frivolously] à la légère, avec insouciance.

giddiness ['gɪdɪnɪs] n *(U)* **1.** [dizziness] vertiges *mpl*, étourdissements *mpl* **2.** [frivolousness] légèreté *f*, étourderie *f*.

giddy ['gɪdɪ] (*compar* giddier, *superl* giddiest) adj **1.** [dizzy - person] : to be or to feel giddy **a)** [afraid of height] avoir le vertige, être pris de vertige **b)** [unwell] avoir un étourdissement **2.** [lofty] vertigineux, qui donne le vertige **3.** [frivolous - person, behaviour] frivole, écervelé.

giddy up interj [to horse] ❱ giddy up! hue !

gift [gɪft] ◆ n **1.** [present - personal] cadeau *m* ; [- official] don *m* **2.** [talent] don *m* **3.** *inf* [bargain] affaire *f* **4.** *inf* [easy thing] : *that exam question was a gift* ce sujet d'examen, c'était du gâteau **5.** [donation] don *m*, donation *f* **6.** RELIG : *the gift of tongues* le don des langues. ◆ vt 🇺🇸 *fml* donner, faire don de.

GIFT [gɪft] (abbr of gamete intrafallopian transfer) n FIVETE *f*.

gift certificate 🇺🇸 = gift token.

gift coupon n bon *m* de réduction, point-cadeau *m*.

gifted ['gɪftɪd] adj [person] doué ; [performance] talentueux.

gift horse n ❱ don't or never look a gift horse in the mouth *prov* à cheval donné on ne regarde pas la bouche *prov*.

gift shop n boutique *f* de cadeaux.

gift token n bon *m* d'achat.

gift voucher 🇬🇧 **1.** = gift token **2.** = gift coupon.

gift-wrap vt faire un paquet cadeau de.

gift-wrapped ['gɪftræpt] adj [article] sous paquet-cadeau.

gig [gɪg] n **1.** [carriage] cabriolet *m* **2.** [boat] yole *f*, guigue *f* **3.** *inf* [concert] concert *m* (*de rock, de jazz*).

gigabyte ['gɪgəbaɪt] n gigaoctet *m*.

gigahertz ['gɪgəhɜːts] n gigahertz *m*.

gigantic [dʒaɪˈgæntɪk] adj géant, gigantesque.

giggle ['gɪgl] ◆ vi [stupidly] rire bêtement, ricaner ; [nervously] rire nerveusement. ◆ n [uncontrollable] fou rire *m* ; [nervous] petit rire *m* nerveux ; [stupid] ricanement *m*.

giggly ['gɪglɪ] adj qui rit bêtement.

GIGO ['gaɪgəʊ] n abbr of garbage in, garbage out.

gigolo ['ʒɪgələʊ] (*pl* gigolos) n gigolo *m*.

gigot ['dʒɪgət] n gigot *m*.

gild [gɪld] (*pt* gilded, *pp* gilded or gilt [gɪlt]) ◆ n = guild. ◆ vt dorer.

gilded ['gɪldɪd] adj doré.

gill[1] [dʒɪl] n [measure] quart *m* de pinte.

gill[2] [gɪl] n [of mushroom] lamelle *f*. ◆❖ gills pl n [of fish] ouïes *fpl*, branchies *fpl*.

gilt [gɪlt] ◆ pp ⟶ gild. ◆ adj doré. ◆ n **1.** [gilding] dorure *f* **2.** [security] valeur *f* de tout repos.

gilt-edged [-edʒd] adj **1.** ST. EX [securities] de père de famille, sans risque **2.** [page] doré sur tranche.

gimme ['gɪmɪ] *inf* abbr of give me.

gimmick ['gɪmɪk] n **1.** [sales trick] truc *m*, astuce *f* ; [in politics] astuce *f*, gadget *m* **2.** [gadget, device] gadget *m*.

gimmicky ['gɪmɪkɪ] adj *inf* qui relève du procédé.

gimp [gɪmp] n 🇺🇸 *inf pej* [person] gogol *v inf mf*.

gin [dʒɪn] (*pt & pp* ginned, *cont* ginning) n **1.** [drink] gin *m* **2.** [trap] piège *m* **3.** INDUST [machine] égreneuse *f* (de coton).

ginger ['dʒɪndʒə'] ◆ n **1.** [spice] gingembre *m* **2.** [colour] brun roux *m*. ◆ adj [hair] roux (rousse), rouquin ; [cat] roux (rousse). ◆❖ Ginger pr n *inf* [nickname] Poil de Carotte. ◆❖ ginger up vt sep [activity, group, meeting] animer ; [speech, story] relever, pimenter, égayer.

ginger ale n boisson gazeuse aux extraits de gingembre.

ginger beer n boisson légèrement alcoolisée obtenue par la fermentation de gingembre.

gingerbread ['dʒɪndʒəbred] n pain *m* d'épices.

ginger group n dans une organisation politique ou autre, faction dynamique cherchant à faire bouger les choses en incitant à l'action.

ginger-haired adj roux (rousse).

gingerly ['dʒɪndʒəlɪ] ◆ adv [cautiously] avec circonspection, précautionneusement ; [delicately] délicatement. ◆ adj [cautious] circonspect, prudent ; [delicate] délicat.

ginger nut n biscuit *m* au gingembre.

ginger snap = ginger nut.

gingham ['gɪŋəm] n (tissu *m*) vichy *m*.

gingivitis [ˌdʒɪndʒɪˈvaɪtɪs] n *(U)* MED gingivite *f*.

ginormous [ˌdʒaɪˈnɔːməs] adj *inf* gigantesque.

ginseng ['dʒɪnseŋ] n ginseng *m*.

gipsy ['dʒɪpsɪ] (*pl* gipsies) ◆ n Gitan *m*, -e *f*, bohémien *m*, -enne *f* ; *fig* [wanderer] vagabond *m*, -e *f*. ◆ adj [camp] de Gitans ; [dance, music] gitan.

giraffe [dʒɪˈrɑːf] n girafe *f*.

girder ['gɜːdə'] n poutre *f* (métallique), fer *m* profilé ; [light] poutrelle *f*.

girdle ['gɜːdl] ◆ n **1.** [corset] gaine *f* **2.** *liter* [belt] ceinture *f*. ◆ vt *liter* ❱ to girdle sthg with sthg ceindre qqch de qqch.

girl [gɜːl] n **1.** [child] (petite) fille *f* **2.** [daughter] fille *f* **3.** [young woman] (jeune) fille *f* **4.** *inf* [girlfriend] (petite) amie *f*, copine *f* **5.** SCH [pupil] élève *f* **6.** [employee] (jeune) employée *f* ; [maid] bonne *f* ; [in shop] vendeuse *f* ; [in factory] ouvrière *f*.

girl Friday n employée de bureau affectée à des tâches diverses.

girlfriend ['gɜːlfrend] n [of boy] copine *f*, (petite) amie *f* ; 🇺🇸 [of girl] copine *f*, amie *f*.

Girl Guide 🇬🇧, **Girl Scout** 🇺🇸 n éclaireuse *f*.

girlhood ['gɜːlhʊd] n [as child] enfance *f* ; [as adolescent] adolescence *f*.

girlie ['gɜːlɪ] adj *inf* ❱ girlie magazine magazine *m* masculin, revue *f* érotique.

girlish ['gɜːlɪʃ] adj [appearance, smile, voice] de fillette, de petite fille ; *pej* [boy] efféminé.

Girl Scout 🇺🇸 = Girl Guide.

giro ['dʒaɪrəʊ] n **1.** [system] système de virement interbancaire introduit par la Poste britannique ❱ (bank) giro virement *m* bancaire ❱ giro cheque chèque *m* postal ❱ National Giro ≃ Comptes Chèques Postaux **2.** *inf* [for unemployed] chèque *m* d'allocation de chômage.

girth [gɜːθ] ◆ n **1.** [circumference] circonférence *f*, tour *m* **2.** [stoutness] corpulence *f*, embonpoint *m* **3.** [of saddle] sangle *f*. ◆ vt [horse] sangler.

gist [dʒɪst] n essentiel *m*.

git [gɪt] n 🇬🇧 *v inf* connard *m*, connasse *f*.

give [gɪv] (*pt* gave [geɪv], *pp* given ['gɪvn]) ◆ vt

A. OFFER OR GRANT 1. [hand over] donner ; [as gift] donner, offrir / *I gave him the book* or *I gave the book to him* je lui ai donné le livre / *I gave him my coat to hold* je lui ai confié mon manteau / *she gave them her trust* elle leur a fait confiance, elle leur a donné sa confiance ▸ **to give as good as one gets** rendre coup pour coup ▸ **give it all you've got!** *inf* mets-y le paquet ! / *I'll give you something to cry about!* *inf* je vais te donner une bonne raison de pleurer, moi ! **2.** [grant - right, permission, importance, etc.] donner / *give the matter your full attention* prêtez une attention toute particulière à cette affaire / *she hasn't given her approval yet* elle n'a pas encore donné son consentement **3.** [admit, concede] reconnaître, accorder / *she's certainly intelligent, I'll give you that* elle est très intelligente, ça, je te l'accorde **4.** [provide with - drink, food] donner, offrir ; [- lessons, classes, advice] donner ; [- help] prêter / *to give sb / sthg one's support* soutenir qqn / qqch / *give me time to think* donnez-moi or laissez-moi le temps de réfléchir / *just give me time!* sois patient ! **5.** [confer - award] conférer **6.** [dedicate] donner, consacrer / *he gave his life to save the child* il est mort or il a donné sa vie pour sauver l'enfant **7.** [in exchange] donner ; [pay] payer **8.** [transmit] donner, passer / *I hope I don't give you my cold* j'espère que je ne vais pas te passer mon rhume.

B. CAUSE, INFLICT OR COMMUNICATE 1. [cause] donner, causer ; [headache] donner ; [pleasure, surprise, shock] faire **2.** [impose - task] imposer ; [- punishment] infliger / *he was given (a sentence of) 15 years* LAW il a été condamné à 15 ans de prison **3.** [communicate - impression, order, signal] donner ; [- address, information] donner, fournir ; [- news, decision] annoncer / *to give sb a message* communiquer un message à qqn **4.** [suggest, propose - explanation, reason] donner, avancer ; [- hint] donner / *don't give me that (rubbish)!* *inf* ne me raconte pas d'histoires !

C. UTTER SOUND OR PERFORM ACTION 1. [utter - sound] rendre, émettre ; [- answer] donner, faire ; [- cry, sigh] pousser / *he gave a laugh* il a laissé échapper un rire **2.** [make - action, gesture] faire / *she gave them an odd look* elle leur a jeté or lancé un regard curieux **3.** [perform in public - concert] donner ; [- lecture, speech] faire ; [- interview] accorder **4.** [hold - lunch, party, supper] donner, organiser.

D. OTHER SENSES 1. [estimate the duration of] donner, estimer / *I give him one week at most* je lui donne une semaine (au) maximum **2.** PHR **to give way a)** [ground] s'affaisser **b)** [bridge, building, ceiling] s'effondrer, s'affaisser **c)** [ladder, rope] céder, (se) casser / *her legs gave way (beneath her)* ses jambes se sont dérobées sous elle / *it's easier to give way to his demands than to argue* il est plus commode de céder à ses exigences que de lui résister / *his joy gave way to sorrow* sa joie a fait place à la peine / '**give way to pedestrians**' 'priorité aux piétons' / '**give way**' 'cédez le passage'.

◆ vi **1.** [contribute] donner / *please give generously* nous nous en remettons à votre générosité **2.** [collapse, yield - ground, wall] s'affaisser / *something's got to give* quelque chose va lâcher ; [cloth, elastic] se relâcher ; [person] céder **3.** US *inf* ▸ **what gives?** qu'est-ce qui se passe ?

◆ n [of metal, wood] élasticité f, souplesse f / *there's not enough give in this sweater* ce pull n'est pas assez ample. ⬥ **give or take** prep phr à… près / *give or take a few days* à quelques jours près. ⬥ **give away** vt sep **1.** [hand over] donner ; [as gift] donner, faire cadeau de ; [prize] distribuer / *it's so cheap they're practically giving it away* c'est tellement bon marché, c'est comme s'ils en faisaient cadeau **2.** [bride] conduire à l'autel **3.** [throw away - chance, opportunity] gâcher, gaspiller **4.** [reveal - information] révéler ; [- secret] révéler, trahir / *he didn't give anything away* il n'a rien dit **5.** [betray] trahir / *her accent gave her away* son accent l'a trahie. ⬥ **give back** vt sep [return] rendre ; [property, stolen object] restituer. ⬥ **give in** ◆ vi [relent, yield] céder ▸ **to give in to sthg / sb** céder à qqch / qqn. ◆ vt sep [hand in - book, exam paper] rendre ; [- found object, parcel]

remettre ; [- application, name] donner. ⬥ **give off** vt sep [emit, produce - gas, smell] émettre. ⬥ **give out** ◆ vt sep **1.** [hand out] distribuer **2.** [emit] émettre, faire entendre **3.** [make known] annoncer, faire savoir. ◆ vi **1.** [fail - machine] tomber en panne ; [- brakes] lâcher ; [- heart] flancher **2.** [run out] s'épuiser, manquer / *her strength was giving out* elle était à bout de forces, elle n'en pouvait plus. ⬥ **give up** ◆ vt sep **1.** [renounce - habit] renoncer à, abandonner ; [- friend] abandonner, délaisser ; [- chair, place] céder ; [- activity] cesser / *she'll never give him up* elle ne renoncera jamais à lui / *he's given up smoking* il a arrêté de fumer **2.** [resign from - job] quitter ; [- position] démissionner de **3.** [hand over - keys] rendre, remettre ; [- prisoner] livrer ; [- responsibility] se démettre de / *the murderer gave himself up (to the police)* le meurtrier s'est rendu or livré (à la police). ◆ vi : *I give up* **a)** [in game, project] je renonce **b)** [in guessing game] je donne ma langue au chat / *we can't give up now!* on ne va pas laisser tomber maintenant. ⬥ **give up on** vt insep ▸ **to give up on sb a)** [stop waiting for] renoncer à attendre qqn **b)** [stop expecting sthg from] ne plus rien attendre de qqn / *I give up on him, he won't even try* j'abandonne, il ne fait pas le moindre effort.

give-and-take n **1.** [compromise] concessions *fpl* (mutuelles) **2.** [in conversation] échange.

giveaway ['gɪvə,weɪ] ◆ n **1.** [free gift] cadeau m ; COMM prime f, cadeau m publicitaire **2.** US RADIO & TV jeu m (doté de prix) **3.** [revelation] révélation f (involontaire). ◆ adj **1.** [free] gratuit ; [price] dérisoire **2.** US **giveaway program a)** RADIO jeu m radiophonique **b)** TV jeu m télévisé **3.** *inf* [revealing] révélateur.

giveback ['gɪvbæk] n US [cut in pay] réduction f de salaire ; [reduced bonus] réduction f de prime.

given ['gɪvn] ◆ pp ⟶ **give.** ◆ adj **1.** [specified] donné ; [precise] déterminé **2.** [prone] ▸ **to be given to sthg** avoir une tendance à qqch ▸ **to be given to doing sthg** être enclin à faire qqch. ◆ prep **1.** [considering] étant donné **2.** PHR **given the chance** or **opportunity** si l'occasion se présentait. ◆ n [sure fact] fait m acquis. ⬥ **given that** conj étant donné que.

given name n US prénom m.

giver ['gɪvər] n donateur m, -trice f.

gizmo ['gɪzməʊ] (*pl* **gizmos**) n US *inf* gadget m, truc m.

gizzard ['gɪzəd] n gésier m.

glacé ['glæseɪ] adj **1.** [cherries] glacé, confit ▸ **glacé icing** glaçage m (d'un gâteau) **2.** [leather, silk] glacé.

glacial ['gleɪʃəl] adj **1.** [weather, wind] glacial **2.** [politeness, atmosphere] glacial **3.** GEOL glaciaire.

glaciated ['gleɪsɪeɪtɪd] adj glaciaire.

glacier ['glæsjər] n glacier m.

glad [glæd] ◆ adj **1.** [person] heureux, content / *(I'm) glad you came* (je suis) heureux or bien content que tu sois venu / *he's decided not to go — I'm glad about that* il a décidé de ne pas partir — tant mieux / *I was glad to hear the news* j'étais ravi d'apprendre la nouvelle **2.** *liter* [news, occasion] joyeux, heureux ; [laughter] de bonheur ; [shout] joyeux. ◆ n *inf* = **gladiolus.**

> 🗒 Note that **être content / heureux / ravi que** and **se réjouir que** are followed by a verb in the subjunctive:
> **I'm really glad my children are with me.** *Je suis très content que mes enfants soient auprès de moi.*

gladden ['glædn] vt [person] rendre heureux, réjouir ; [heart] réjouir.

glade [gleɪd] n *liter* clairière f.

glad hand n *inf* ▶ **to give sb the glad hand** accueillir qqn chaleureusement or à bras ouverts.

glad-hand ['glædhænd] vt *inf & pej* accueillir avec de grandes démonstrations d'amitié.

gladiator ['glædɪeɪtər] n gladiateur m.

gladiolus [,glædɪ'əʊləs] (*pl* **gladioli** [-laɪ] *or* **gladioluses**) n glaïeul m.

gladly ['glædlɪ] adv avec plaisir, avec joie, de bon cœur.

glad rags pl n *inf* vêtements mpl chic ▶ **to put on one's glad rags** se mettre sur son trente et un, se saper.

glam [glæm] (*pt & pp* **glammed**, *cont* **glamming**) 🇬🇧 *inf* ◆ adj = **glamorous**. ◆ n = **glamour**. ❖ **glam up** vt sep *inf* **1.** [person] ▶ **to get glammed up a)** [with clothes] mettre ses belles fringues, se saper **b)** [with make-up] se faire une beauté, se faire toute belle **2.** [building] retaper ; [town] embellir.

glamor 🇺🇸 = **glamour**.

glamorize, glamorise ['glæməraɪz] vt idéaliser, montrer or présenter sous un jour séduisant.

glamorous ['glæmərəs] adj **1.** [alluring -person] séduisant, éblouissant **2.** [exciting -lifestyle] brillant ; [-career] brillant, prestigieux ; [-show] splendide ; [-place] chic.

glamorously ['glæmərəslɪ] adv brillamment, de manière éblouissante.

glamour 🇬🇧, **glamor** 🇺🇸 ['glæmər] n **1.** [allure -of person] charme m, fascination f ; [-of appearance, dress] élégance f, chic m **2.** [excitement -of lifestyle, show] éclat m, prestige m.

glance [glɑːns] ◆ vi **1.** [look] ▶ **to glance at sb** or **sthg** jeter un coup d'œil (rapide) à qqn or sur qqch **2.** [read quickly] : *she glanced through* or *over the letter* elle parcourut rapidement la lettre **3.** [look in given direction] : *he glanced back* or *behind* il a jeté un coup d'œil en arrière **4.** [gleam] étinceler. ◆ n **1.** [look] coup m d'œil, regard m **2.** [gleam] lueur f, éclat m ; [in water] reflet m. ❖ **glance away** vi détourner les yeux. ❖ **glance off** ◆ vi [arrow, bullet] ricocher, faire ricochet ; [sword, spear] être dévié, ricocher. ◆ vt insep ▶ **to glance off sthg a)** [subj: arrow, bullet] ricocher sur qqch **b)** [subj: sword, spear] dévier sur qqch. ❖ **glance up** vi **1.** [look upwards] regarder en l'air or vers le haut **2.** [from book] lever les yeux.

glancing ['glɑːnsɪŋ] adj **1.** [blow] : *he struck me a glancing blow* il m'asséna un coup oblique **2.** [gleaming -sunlight] étincelant **3.** [indirect -allusion] indirect, fortuit.

gland [glænd] n PHYSIOL glande f.

glandular ['glændjʊlər] adj glandulaire, glanduleux.

glandular fever n (U) mononucléose f (infectieuse).

glare [gleər] ◆ vi **1.** [sun, light] briller d'un éclat éblouissant **2.** [person] ▶ **to glare at sb** regarder qqn avec colère. ◆ n **1.** [light] lumière f éblouissante or aveuglante ; [of sun] éclat m **2.** [of publicity] feux mpl **3.** [of anger] regard m furieux ; [of contempt] regard m méprisant.

glaring ['gleərɪŋ] adj **1.** [dazzling -light] éblouissant, éclatant ; [-car headlights] éblouissant ; [-sun] aveuglant **2.** [bright -colour] vif ; *pej* criard, voyant **3.** [angry] furieux **4.** [obvious -error] qui saute aux yeux, qui crève les yeux, patent ; [-injustice, lie] flagrant, criant.

glaringly ['gleərɪŋlɪ] adv : *it's glaringly obvious* ça crève les yeux.

glasnost ['glæznɒst] n glasnost f.

glass [glɑːs] ◆ n **1.** [substance] verre m **2.** [vessel, contents] verre m **3.** [in shop, museum] vitrine f **4.** [glassware]

verrerie f **5.** [telescope] longue-vue f **6.** [barometer] baromètre m. ◆ comp [ornament, bottle] en verre ; [door] vitré ; [industry] du verre. ◆ vt [bookcase, porch] vitrer ; [photograph] mettre sous verre. ❖ **glasses** pl n **1.** [spectacles] lunettes fpl **2.** [binoculars] jumelles fpl.

glassblower ['glɑːs,bləʊər] n souffleur m (de verre).

glassblowing ['glɑːs,bləʊɪŋ] n soufflage m (du verre).

glass ceiling n plafond m de verre (*frontière invisible qui empêche la progression dans la hiérarchie*).

glass fibre ◆ n fibre m de verre. ◆ adj en fibre de verre.

glasshouse ['glɑːshaʊs] (*pl* [-haʊzɪz]) n **1.** 🇬🇧 [greenhouse] serre f **2.** 🇬🇧 *mil sl* [prison] prison f militaire, trou m.

glassware ['glɑːsweər] n [glass objects] verrerie f ; [tumblers] verrerie f, gobeleterie f.

glassy ['glɑːsɪ] (*compar* **glassier**, *superl* **glassiest**) adj **1.** [eye, expression] vitreux, terne **2.** [smooth -surface] uni, lisse.

glassy-eyed adj à l'œil terne or vitreux.

Glaswegian [glæz'wiːdʒən] ◆ n [inhabitant] habitant m, -e f de Glasgow ; [by birth] natif m, -ive f de Glasgow ; [dialect] dialecte m de Glasgow. ◆ adj de Glasgow.

glaucoma [glɔː'kəʊmə] n (U) glaucome m.

glaze [gleɪz] ◆ vt **1.** [floor, tiles] vitrifier ; [pottery, china] vernisser ; [leather, silk] glacer **2.** [photo, painting] glacer **3.** CULIN glacer **4.** [window] vitrer. ◆ n **1.** [on pottery] vernis m ; [on floor, tiles] vernis m, enduit m vitrifié ; [on cotton, silk] glacé m **2.** [on painting, on paper, photo] glacé m, glacis m **3.** CULIN glace f **4.** 🇺🇸 [ice] verglas m. ❖ **glaze over** vi : *his eyes glazed over* ses yeux sont devenus vitreux.

glazed [gleɪzd] adj **1.** [floor, tiles] vitrifié ; [pottery] vernissé, émaillé ; [leather, silk] glacé **2.** [photo, painting] glacé **3.** CULIN glacé **4.** [window] vitré ; [picture] sous verre **5.** [eyes] vitreux, terne.

glazier ['gleɪzjər] n vitrier m.

glazing ['gleɪzɪŋ] n **1.** [of pottery] vernissage m ; [of floor, tiles] vitrification f ; [of leather, silk] glaçage m **2.** CULIN [process] glaçage m ; [substance] glace f.

gleam [gliːm] ◆ vi **1.** [metal, polished surface] luire, reluire ; [stronger] briller ; [cat's eyes] luire ; [water] miroiter **2.** *fig* : *her eyes gleamed with anticipation / mischief* ses yeux brillaient d'espoir / de malice. ◆ n **1.** [on surface] lueur f, miroitement m **2.** *fig* lueur f.

gleaming ['gliːmɪŋ] adj [metal] luisant, brillant ; [furniture] reluisant ; [kitchen] étincelant.

glean [gliːn] vt **1.** [collect -information, news] glaner **2.** AGR glaner.

glee [gliː] n **1.** [joy] joie f, allégresse f **2.** MUS chant m a capella (*à plusieurs voix*).

gleeful ['gliːfʊl] adj joyeux, radieux.

gleefully ['gliːfʊlɪ] adv joyeusement, avec allégresse or joie.

glen [glen] n vallon m, vallée f étroite et encaissée (*en Écosse ou en Irlande*).

glib [glɪb] adj [answer, excuse] (trop) facile, désinvolte ; [lie] éhonté, désinvolte.

glibly ['glɪblɪ] adv [talk, argue, reply] avec aisance, facilement ; [lie] avec désinvolture, sans sourciller.

glide [glaɪd] ◆ vi **1.** [gen] glisser **2.** *fig* [time, weeks] ▶ **to glide by** s'écouler **3.** AERON planer ▶ **to go gliding** du vol à voile **4.** [in skating, skiing] glisser. ◆ vt (faire) glisser. ◆ n **1.** [gen] glissement m **2.** DANCE glissade f **3.** MUS port m de voix **4.** AERON vol m plané **5.** LING [in diphthong] glissement m ; [between two vowels] semi-voyelle f de transition.

glider ['glaɪdə'] n **1.** AERON planeur m **2.** US [swing] balançoire f.

gliding ['glaɪdɪŋ] n AERON vol m à voile.

glimmer ['glɪmə'] ◆ vi [moonlight, candle] jeter une faible lueur, luire faiblement. ◆ n **1.** [of light] (faible) lueur f **2.** fig : a glimmer of hope / interest une (faible) lueur d'espoir / d'intérêt.

glimpse [glɪmps] ◆ vt entrevoir, entrapercevoir. ◆ n ▶ to catch a glimpse of sthg entrevoir or entrapercevoir qqch.

glint [glɪnt] ◆ vi **1.** [knife] étinceler, miroiter ; [water] miroiter **2.** fig [eyes] étinceler. ◆ n **1.** [of light] reflet m, miroitement m **2.** fig : there was a strange glint in his eye il y avait une lueur étrange dans son regard.

glisten ['glɪsn] vi [wet or damp surface] luire, miroiter.

glistening ['glɪsnɪŋ] adj luisant.

glitch [glɪtʃ] n inf [in plan] pépin m ; [in machine] signal indiquant une baisse de tension du courant.

glitter ['glɪtə'] ◆ vi **1.** [bright object] étinceler, scintiller, miroiter ; [jewel] chatoyer, étinceler ; [metal] reluire **2.** [eyes] briller. ◆ n **1.** [of object] scintillement m **2.** [of glamour] éclat m, splendeur f **3.** [decoration, make-up] paillettes fpl.

glitterati [ˌglɪtə'rɑːtiː] pl n inf ▶ the glitterati hum le beau monde m inv.

glitterball ['glɪtəbɔːl] n boule f à facettes.

glittering ['glɪtərɪŋ] adj **1.** [jewels] scintillant, étincelant, brillant **2.** [glamorous] éclatant, resplendissant.

glittery ['glɪtərɪ] adj **1.** [light] scintillant, brillant **2.** pej [jewellery] clinquant ; [make-up, décor] voyant, tape-à-l'œil.

glitz [glɪts] n inf tape-à-l'œil m, clinquant m.

glitzy ['glɪtsɪ] (compar glitzier, superl glitziest) adj inf tape-à-l'œil (inv).

gloat [gləʊt] ◆ vi exulter, se délecter, jubiler ▶ to gloat over sthg se réjouir de qqch. ◆ n exultation f, jubilation f.

global ['gləʊbl] adj **1.** [world-wide] mondial, planétaire ▶ global warming réchauffement m de la planète **2.** [overall - system, view] global.

globalism ['gləʊbəlɪzm] n mondialisme m.

globalist ['gləʊbəlɪst] n mondialiste mf.

globalization, globalisation [ˌgləʊbəlaɪ'zeɪʃn] n mondialisation f.

globalize, globalise ['gləʊbəlaɪz] vt **1.** [make world-wide] mondialiser **2.** [generalize] globaliser.

globally ['gləʊbəlɪ] adv **1.** [world-wide] mondialement, à l'échelle planétaire **2.** [generally] globalement.

global market n marché m mondial or international.

global marketplace n COMM marché m mondial or international.

global strategy n stratégie f globale.

global village n village m planétaire.

globe [gləʊb] n **1.** GEOG globe m (terrestre), terre f **2.** [model] globe m, mappemonde f **3.** [spherical object] globe m, sphère f ; [as lampshade] globe ; [as goldfish bowl] bocal m ; [of eye] globe.

globe artichoke n artichaut m.

globefish ['gləʊbfɪʃ] n poisson-globe m.

globetrotter ['gləʊbˌtrɒtə'] n globe-trotter m.

globetrotting ['gləʊbˌtrɒtɪŋ] n (U) voyages mpl aux quatre coins du monde.

globule ['glɒbjuːl] n globule m.

glom [glɒm] vi US inf : he glommed on to her ideas il s'est approprié ses idées / he's glommed on to her and they're always together il s'est collé à elle et ils sont toujours ensemble.

gloom [gluːm] n (U) **1.** [darkness] obscurité f, ténèbres fpl **2.** [despondency] tristesse f, mélancolie f.

gloomily ['gluːmɪlɪ] adv sombrement, mélancoliquement, tristement.

gloomy ['gluːmɪ] (compar gloomier, superl gloomiest) adj **1.** [person - depressed] triste, mélancolique ; [- morose] sombre, lugubre **2.** [pessimistic - outlook] sombre ; [- news] triste **3.** [sky] obscur, sombre ; [weather] morne, triste **4.** [place, landscape] morne, lugubre.

glorification [ˌglɔːrɪfɪ'keɪʃn] n glorification f.

glorified ['glɔːrɪfaɪd] adj : he's called an engineer but he's really just a glorified mechanic on a beau l'appeler ingénieur, il n'est que mécanicien, il n'a d'ingénieur que le nom, en réalité c'est un mécanicien.

glorify ['glɔːrɪfaɪ] (pt & pp glorified) vt **1.** RELIG glorifier, rendre gloire à **2.** [praise - hero, writer] exalter.

glorious ['glɔːrɪəs] adj **1.** [illustrious - reign, saint, victory] glorieux ; [- hero] glorieux, illustre ; [- deed] glorieux, éclatant ▶ the Glorious Twelfth a) [in Ireland] célébration de la victoire des Protestants sur les Catholiques (le 12 juillet 1690) en Irlande b) [in UK] date d'ouverture de la chasse à la grouse (le 12 août) **2.** [wonderful - view, place] merveilleux, splendide ; [- weather, day] splendide, superbe, magnifique ; [- colours] superbe ; [- holiday, party] merveilleux, sensationnel.

gloriously ['glɔːrɪəslɪ] adv glorieusement.

glory ['glɔːrɪ] (pl glories, pt & pp gloried) n **1.** [honour, fame] gloire f ; [magnificence] magnificence f, éclat m **2.** [splendour] gloire f, splendeur f **3.** [masterpiece] gloire f, joyau m **4.** RELIG ▶ to give glory to God rendre gloire à Dieu. ◆ glory in vt insep ▶ to glory in (doing) sthg se glorifier de or s'enorgueillir de (faire) qqch.

Glos written abbr of Gloucestershire.

gloss [glɒs] ◆ n **1.** [sheen] lustre m, brillant m, éclat m ; [on paper, photo] glacé m, brillant m ; [on furniture] vernis m **2.** [appearance] apparence f, vernis m **3.** [charm] charme m, attrait m **4.** [annotation, paraphrase] glose f, commentaire m **5.** = gloss paint. ◆ vt **1.** [paper] satiner, glacer ; [metal] faire briller, lustrer **2.** [explain, paraphrase] gloser. ◆ gloss over vt insep **1.** [minimize - failure, fault, mistake] glisser sur, passer sur, atténuer **2.** [hide - truth, facts] dissimuler, passer sous silence.

glossary ['glɒsərɪ] (pl glossaries) n glossaire m.

gloss paint n peinture f brillante.

glossy ['glɒsɪ] (compar glossier, superl glossiest, pl glossies) ◆ adj **1.** [shiny - fur] lustré, luisant ; [- hair] brillant ; [- leather, satin] lustré, luisant, glacé ; [- leaves] luisant ; [surface - polished] brillant, poli ; [- painted] brillant, laqué **2.** fig [display, presentation, spectacle] brillant, scintillant, clinquant pej **3.** [photo] glacé, sur papier glacé ; [paper] glacé. ◆ n inf = glossy magazine.

glossy magazine n magazine m (sur papier glacé).

glove [glʌv] ◆ n gant m. ◆ comp à gants, de gants.

glove box n AUTO & NUCL boîte f à gants.

glove compartment n AUTO boîte f à gants.

glove puppet n marionnette f (à gaine).

glow [gləʊ] ◆ vi **1.** [embers, heated metal] rougeoyer ; [sky, sunset] s'embraser, flamboyer ; [jewel] briller, rutiler **2.** [person] rayonner ; [eyes] briller, flamboyer. ◆ n **1.** [of fire, embers] rougeoiement m ; [of heated metal] lueur f ; [of sky, sunset] embrasement m, flamboiement m ; [of sun] feux mpl ; [of colours, jewel] éclat m **2.** [of health, beauty] éclat m **3.** [pleasure] plaisir m.

glower ['glaʊə'] vi avoir l'air furieux, lancer des regards furieux ▶ to glower at sb a) [angrily] lancer à qqn un regard noir b) [threateningly] jeter à qqn un regard menaçant.

glowing ['gləʊɪŋ] adj **1.** [fire, embers] rougeoyant ; [heated metal] incandescent ; [sky, sunset] radieux, flamboyant ; [jewel] brillant **2.** [complexion] éclatant ; [eyes] brillant, flamboyant **3.** [laudatory] élogieux, dithyrambique.

glowingly ['gləʊɪŋlɪ] adv ▶ **to speak glowingly of sb / sthg** parler de qqn / qqch en termes enthousiastes or chaleureux.

glow-worm n ver m luisant.

glucose ['glu:kəʊs] n glucose m.

glue [glu:] ◆ vt **1.** [stick] coller ▶ **to glue sthg to / onto sthg** coller qqch à / sur qqch **2.** fig coller / **to be glued to the spot** être or rester cloué sur place. ◆ n colle f.

glue-sniffer [-,snɪfər] n : **to be a glue-sniffer** inhaler or sniffer (de la colle).

glue-sniffing [-,snɪfɪŋ] n inhalation f de colle.

glug [glʌg] (pt & pp **glugged**, cont **glugging**) inf ◆ n : **glug (glug)** glouglou m / **he took a long glug of lemonade** il prit une longue goulée de limonade. ◆ vi faire glouglou.

glum [glʌm] adj triste, morose.

glumly ['glʌmlɪ] adv tristement, avec morosité.

glut [glʌt] (pt & pp **glutted**, cont **glutting**) ◆ vt **1.** [with food] ▶ **to glut o.s. with** or **on sthg** se gorger or se gaver de qqch **2.** [saturate - market] saturer, inonder, surcharger. ◆ n excès m, surabondance f, surplus m.

gluten ['glu:tən] n gluten m.

gluten-free adj sans gluten.

glutes [glu:ts] pl n inf muscles mpl fessiers.

gluteus ['glu:tɪəs] n ANAT (muscle) fessier m ▶ **gluteus maximus** grand fessier m.

glutinous ['glu:tɪnəs] adj glutineux.

glutton ['glʌtn] n glouton m, -onne f, goulu m, -e f.

gluttonous ['glʌtənəs] adj glouton, goulu.

gluttony ['glʌtənɪ] n gloutonnerie f, goinfrerie f.

glycerin ['glɪsərɪn], **glycerine** ['glɪsəri:n] n glycérine f.

gm (written abbr of gram) g.

GM (dʒi:'em) (abbr of genetically modified) adj génétiquement modifié.

G-man [US] agent m du FBI.

GMAT (abbr of Graduate Management Admissions Test) n test en langue anglaise qui permet d'évaluer l'aptitude des candidats au MBA.

GMB (abbr of General, Municipal, Boilermakers and Allied Trades Union) pr n important syndicat britannique.

GMO (abbr of genetically modified organism) n OGM m.

GMT (abbr of Greenwich Mean Time) n GMT m.

GMTA MESSAGING written abbr of great minds think alike.

gnarled [nɑ:ld] adj [tree, fingers] noueux.

gnash [næʃ] ◆ vt ▶ **to gnash one's teeth** grincer des dents. ◆ n grincement m (de dents).

gnat [næt] n moustique m.

gnaw [nɔ:] ◆ vt [bone] ronger. ◆ vi ▶ **to gnaw (away) at sthg** ronger qqch ▶ **to gnaw through sthg** ronger qqch jusqu'à le percer. ◆ **gnaw away** vt sep **1.** [animal] ronger **2.** [erode] ronger, miner. ◆ **gnaw off** vt sep ▶ **to gnaw sthg off** ronger qqch jusqu'à le détacher.

gnawing ['nɔ:ɪŋ] adj **1.** [pain] lancinant, tenaillant ; [hunger] tenaillant **2.** [anxiety, doubt] tenaillant, torturant.

gnome [nəʊm] n **1.** MYTH gnome m **2.** [aphorism] aphorisme m.

GNP (abbr of gross national product) n PNB m.

gnu [nu:] n gnou m.

GNVQ (abbr of general national vocational qualification) n [UK] diplôme sanctionnant deux années d'études professionnelles à la fin du secondaire ; ≃ baccalauréat m professionnel.

go¹ [gəʊ] n [game] go m.

go² [gəʊ] (pres (3rd pers sg) **goes** [gəʊz], pt **went** [went], pp **gone** [gɒn], pl **goes** [gəʊz]) ◆ vi

A. TRAVEL OR PROCEED **1.** [move, travel - person] aller ; [- vehicle] aller, rouler / **I want to go home** je veux rentrer / **the truck was going at 150 kilometres an hour** le camion roulait à or faisait 150 kilomètres à l'heure / **to go to the doctor** aller voir or aller chez le médecin / **to go to sb for advice** aller demander conseil à qqn / **I'll go next** c'est à moi après / **here we go!** le voilà ! / **there he goes!** ça y est, ça recommence ! / **there he goes again!** a) [there he is again] le revoilà ! b) [he's doing it again] ça y est, il est reparti ! **2.** [engage in a specified activity] aller / **to go shopping** aller faire des courses / **let's go for a walk / bike ride / swim** allons nous promener / faire un tour à vélo / nous baigner / **don't go and tell him!** or **don't go telling him!** ne va pas le lui dire !, ne le lui dis pas ! **3.** [proceed to specified limit] aller / **he'll go as high as £300** il ira jusqu'à 300 livres / **now you've gone too far!** là tu as dépassé les bornes ! **4.** [depart, leave] s'en aller, partir / **I must be going** il faut que je m'en aille or que je parte ▶ **get going!** inf vas-y !, file ! **5.** [indicating regular attendance] aller, assister / **to go to church / school** aller à l'église / l'école / **to go to work** [to one's place of work] aller au travail **6.** [indicating direction or route] aller, mener.

B. WITH STATE OR SITUATION **1.** [be or remain in specified state] être / **to go barefoot / naked** se promener pieds nus / tout nu **2.** [become] devenir / **my father is going grey** mon père grisonne / **she went white with rage** elle a blêmi de colère / **have you gone mad?** tu es devenu fou ? **3.** [stop working - engine] tomber en panne ; [- fuse] sauter ; [- bulb, lamp] sauter, griller / **the battery's going** la pile commence à être usée **4.** [wear out] s'user ; [split] craquer **5.** [deteriorate, fail - health] se détériorer ; [- hearing, sight] baisser / **his voice is going** il devient aphone / **her mind has started to go** elle n'a plus toute sa tête or toutes ses facultés.

C. FUTURE, INTENTION OR FUNCTION **1.** [begin an activity] commencer / **what are we waiting for? let's go!** qu'est-ce qu'on attend ? allons-y ! ▶ **here goes!** inf, **here we go!** allez ! on y va ! ▶ **go!** partez ! / **you'd better get going on** or **with that report!** tu ferais bien de te mettre à or de t'attaquer à ce rapport ! **2.** [expressing intention] ▶ **to be going to do sthg** a) [be about to] aller faire qqch, être sur le point de faire qqch b) [intend to] avoir l'intention de faire qqch / **I was going to visit her yesterday but her mother arrived** j'avais l'intention de or j'allais lui rendre visite hier mais sa mère est arrivée **3.** [expressing future] : **are you going to be at home tonight?** est-ce que vous serez chez vous ce soir ? / **she's going to be a doctor** elle va être médecin **4.** [function - clock, machine] marcher, fonctionner ; [start functioning] démarrer / **the car won't go** la voiture ne veut pas démarrer / **the washing machine is still going** la machine à laver tourne encore, la lessive n'est pas terminée ▶ **to get sthg going** a) [car, machine] mettre qqch en marche b) [business, project] lancer qqch **5.** [sound - alarm clock, bell] sonner ; [- alarm, siren] retentir **6.** [make movement] : **she went like this with her eyebrows** elle a fait comme ça avec ses sourcils.

D. DISAPPEAR **1.** [disappear] disparaître / **all the sugar's gone** il n'y a plus de sucre / **all our money has gone**

a) [spent] nous avons dépensé tout notre argent **b)** [lost] nous avons perdu tout notre argent **c)** [stolen] on a volé tout notre argent **2.** [be eliminated] : *the last paragraph must go* il faut supprimer le dernier paragraphe / *I've decided that car has to go* j'ai décidé de me débarrasser de cette voiture. **E. EXTEND OR DEVELOP 1.** [extend, reach] aller, s'étendre / *the path goes right down to the beach* le chemin descend jusqu'à la mer. [develop, turn out] se passer / *I'll see how things go* je vais voir comment ça se passe / *everything went wrong* ça a mal tourné / *how's it going? inf, how are things going?* (comment) ça va ? **3.** [time - elapse] s'écouler, passer ; [- last] durer / *the journey went quickly* je n'ai pas vu le temps passer pendant le voyage.
F. VALIDITY, CONTENT OR WORTH 1. [be accepted] : *whatever the boss says goes* c'est le patron qui fait la loi **2.** [be valid, hold true] s'appliquer / *that goes for us too* **a)** [that applies to us] ça s'applique à nous aussi **b)** [we agree with that] nous sommes aussi de cet avis **3.** [be expressed, run - report, story] : *the story* or *rumour goes that she left him* le bruit court qu'elle l'a quitté **4.** [be identified as] ▸ **to go by** or **under the name of** répondre au nom de **5.** [be sold] se vendre / *the necklace went for £350* le collier s'est vendu 350 livres ▸ **going, going, gone!** une fois, deux fois, adjugé !
G. WITH RECIPIENT OR RESULT 1. [be given - award, prize] aller, être donné ; [- inheritance, property] passer **2.** [be spent] : *a small portion of the budget went on education* une petite part du budget a été consacrée or est allée à l'éducation **3.** [contribute] contribuer, servir / *all that just goes to prove my point* tout ça confirme bien ce que j'ai dit / *it has all the qualities that go to make a good film* ça a toutes les qualités d'un bon film.
H. OTHER SENSES AND PHRASES 1. [be compatible - colours, flavours] aller ensemble / *orange and mauve don't really go* l'orange et le mauve ne vont pas vraiment ensemble **2.** [be available] : *let me know if you hear of any jobs going* faites-moi savoir si vous entendez parler d'un emploi / *are there any flats going for rent in this building?* y a-t-il des appartements à louer dans cet immeuble ? **3.** [belong] aller, se mettre, se ranger **4.** [be contained in, fit] aller / *the piano barely goes through the door* le piano entre or passe de justesse par la porte **5.** [endure] supporter, tenir le coup **6.** **PHR** *she isn't bad, as teachers go* elle n'est pas mal comme enseignante / *as houses go, it's pretty cheap* ce n'est pas cher pour une maison / *there goes my chance of winning a prize* je peux abandonner tout espoir de gagner un prix ▸ **there you go! a)** [here you are] tiens ! **b)** [I told you so] voilà !
◆ vt **1.** [follow, proceed along] aller, suivre / *if we go this way, we'll get there much more quickly* si nous passons par là, nous arriverons bien plus vite **2.** [travel] faire, voyager / *we've only gone 5 kilometres* nous n'avons fait que 5 kilomètres **3.** [say] faire ; [make specified noise] faire / *the gun went bang* et pan ! le coup est parti / *then he goes "hand it over"* inf puis il fait « donne-le-moi ».
◆ n **1.** [attempt, try] coup m, essai m ▸ **to have a go at sthg / doing sthg** essayer qqch / de faire qqch / *he had another go* il a fait une nouvelle tentative, il a ressayé / *let's have a go!* essayons ! / *have another go!* encore un coup ! **2.** **UK** GAMES [turn] tour m / *it's your go* c'est ton tour or c'est à toi (de jouer) **3.** inf [success] succès m, réussite f / *he's made a go of the business* il a réussi à faire marcher l'affaire / *I tried to persuade her but it was no go* j'ai essayé de la convaincre mais il n'y avait rien à faire **4.** inf **PHR** **to have a go at sb a)** [physically] rentrer dans qqn **b)** [verbally] passer un savon à qqn / *they had a real go at one another!* qu'est-ce qu'ils se sont mis ! ▸ **it's all go** ça n'arrête pas !
❖ **going on** adv phr : *he must be going on fifty* il doit approcher la or aller sur la cinquantaine. ❖ **on the go** adj phr inf **1.** [busy] : *I've been on the go all day* je n'ai pas

arrêté de toute la journée **2.** [in hand] : *I have several projects on the go at present* j'ai plusieurs projets en route en ce moment. ❖ **to go** ◆ adv phr à faire / *there are only three weeks / five miles to go* il ne reste plus que trois semaines / cinq miles / *five done, three to go* cinq de faits, trois à faire. ◆ adj phr **US** : *two hamburgers to go* deux hamburgers à emporter ! ❖ **go about** vt insep **1.** [get on with] s'occuper de / *to go about one's business* vaquer à ses occupations **2.** [set about] se mettre à / *she showed me how to go about it* elle m'a montré comment faire or comment m'y prendre. ❖ **go across** ◆ vt insep traverser. ◆ vi traverser / *your brother has just gone across to the shop* ton frère est allé faire un saut au magasin en face. ❖ **go after** vt insep **1.** [follow] suivre **2.** [pursue, seek - criminal] poursuivre ; [- prey] chasser ; [- job, prize] essayer d'obtenir. ❖ **go against** vt insep **1.** [disregard] aller contre, aller à l'encontre de / *she went against my advice* elle n'a pas suivi mon conseil **2.** [conflict with] contredire / *the decision went against public opinion* la décision est allée à l'encontre de or a heurté l'opinion publique / *it goes against my principles* c'est contre mes principes **3.** [be unfavourable to - subj: luck, situation] être contraire à ; [- subj: opinion] être défavorable à ; [- subj: behaviour, evidence] nuire à, être préjudiciable à / *the verdict went against the defendant* le verdict a été défavorable à l'accusé or a été prononcé contre l'accusé.
❖ **go ahead** vi **1.** [precede] passer devant **2.** [proceed] aller de l'avant / *go ahead! tell me!* vas-y ! dis-le-moi ! / *the mayor allowed the demonstrations to go ahead* le maire a permis aux manifestations d'avoir lieu **3.** [advance, progress] progresser, faire des progrès. ❖ **go along** vi **1.** [move from one place to another] aller, avancer / *we can talk it over as we go along* nous pouvons en discuter en chemin or en cours de route / *I just make it up as I go along* j'invente au fur et à mesure **2.** [progress] se dérouler, se passer. ❖ **go along with** vt insep [decision, order] accepter, s'incliner devant ; [rule] observer, respecter / *I can't go along with you on that* je ne suis pas d'accord avec vous là-dessus. ❖ **go around** vi **1.** [habitually] passer son temps à **2.** [document, illness] circuler ; [gossip, rumour] courir, circuler ▸ **what goes around comes around** on finit toujours par payer. ❖ **go away** vi partir, s'en aller / *go away!* va-t-en ! / *I'm going away for a few days* je pars pour quelques jours. ❖ **go back** vi **1.** [return] revenir, retourner / *she went back to bed* elle est retournée au lit, elle s'est recouchée / *they went back home* ils sont rentrés (chez eux or à la maison) / *to go back to work* **a)** [continue task] se remettre au travail **b)** [return to place of work] retourner travailler **c)** [return to employment] reprendre le travail / *to go back on one's steps* rebrousser chemin, revenir sur ses pas / *we went back to the beginning* nous avons recommencé **2.** [retreat] reculer **3.** [revert] revenir / *we went back to the old system* nous sommes revenus à l'ancien système / *he went back to his old habits* il a repris ses anciennes habitudes **4.** [in time] remonter / *our records go back to 1850* nos archives remontent à 1850 / *we go back a long way, Sam and me* inf ça remonte à loin, Sam et moi **5.** [extend, reach] s'étendre / *the garden goes back 150 metres* le jardin s'étend sur 150 mètres. ❖ **go back on** vt insep [fail to keep - agreement] rompre, violer ; [- promise] manquer à, revenir sur. ❖ **go before** ◆ vi [precede] passer devant ; [happen before] précéder / *the election was like nothing that had gone before* l'élection ne ressemblait en rien aux précédentes. ◆ vt insep **1.** [precede] précéder **2.** [appear before] : *to go before a judge / jury* passer devant un juge / un jury / *the matter went before the court* l'affaire est allée devant les tribunaux. ❖ **go by** ◆ vi [pass - car, person] passer ; [- time] passer, s'écouler / *as the years go by* avec les années, à mesure que les années passent. ◆ vt insep **1.** [act in accordance with, be guided by] suivre, se baser sur / *don't go by*

the map ne vous fiez pas à la carte **2.** [judge by] juger d'après / *going by her accent, I'd say she's from New York* si j'en juge d'après son accent, je dirais qu'elle vient de New York. **go down** ◆ vi **1.** [descend, move to lower level] descendre **2.** [proceed, travel] aller **3.** [set -moon, sun] se coucher, tomber **4.** [sink -ship] couler, sombrer ; [-person] couler, disparaître (sous l'eau) **5.** [decrease, decline -level, price, quality] baisser ; [-amount, numbers] diminuer ; [-rate, temperature] baisser, s'abaisser ; [-fever] baisser, tomber ; [-tide] descendre / *the dollar is going down in value* le dollar perd de sa valeur, le dollar baisse / *he's gone down in my estimation* il a baissé dans mon estime **6.** [become less swollen -swelling] désenfler, dégonfler ; [-balloon, tyre] se dégonfler **7.** [produce specified reaction] être reçu / *a cup of coffee would go down nicely* une tasse de café serait la bienvenue / *his speech went down badly / well* son discours a été mal / bien reçu / *how will the proposal go down with the students?* comment les étudiants vont-ils prendre la proposition ? **8.** [be noted, recorded] être noté ; [in writing] être pris or couché par écrit / *this day will go down in history* ce jour restera une date historique / *she will go down in history as a woman of great courage* elle entrera dans l'histoire grâce à son grand courage **9.** [reach as far as] descendre, s'étendre / *this path goes down to the beach* ce sentier va or descend à la plage **10.** [continue as far as] aller, continuer. ◆ vt insep descendre de / *my food went down the wrong way* j'ai avalé de travers. **go down with** vt insep tomber malade de / *he went down with pneumonia* il a attrapé une pneumonie. **go for** vt insep **1.** [fetch] aller chercher **2.** [try to obtain] essayer d'obtenir, viser / *go for it!* inf vas-y ! / *she was really going for it* elle donnait vraiment son maximum **3.** [attack -physically] tomber sur, s'élancer sur ; [-verbally] s'en prendre à / *dogs usually go for the throat* en général, les chiens attaquent à la gorge **4.** inf [like] aimer, adorer / *I don't really go for that idea* l'idée ne me dit pas grand-chose **5.** [choose, prefer] choisir, préférer **6.** [apply to, concern] concerner, s'appliquer à **7.** [be to the advantage of] : *she has a lot going for her* elle a beaucoup d'atouts / *that idea hasn't got much going for it frankly* cette idée n'est franchement pas très convaincante. **go in** vi **1.** [enter] entrer, rentrer **2.** [disappear -moon, sun] se cacher. **go in for** vt insep **1.** [engage in -activity, hobby, sport] pratiquer, faire ; [-occupation] se consacrer à ; [-politics] s'occuper de, faire / *she went in for company law* elle s'est lancée dans le droit commercial **2.** inf [be interested in] s'intéresser à ; [like] aimer / *I don't go in much for opera* je n'aime pas trop l'opéra, l'opéra ne me dit rien **3.** [take part in -competition, race] prendre part à ; [-examination] se présenter à **4.** [apply for -job, position] poser sa candidature à, postuler. **go into** vt insep **1.** [enter -building, house] entrer dans ; [-activity, profession] entrer or dans ; [-politics, business] se lancer dans / *to go into the army* **a)** [as profession] devenir militaire de carrière **b)** [as conscript] partir au service **2.** [be invested -subj: effort, money, time] : *two months of research went into our report* nous avons mis or investi deux mois de recherche dans notre rapport **3.** [embark on -action] commencer à ; [-explanation, speech] se lancer or s'embarquer dans, (se mettre à) donner ; [-problem] aborder **4.** [examine, investigate] examiner, étudier **5.** [explain in depth] entrer dans / *I won't go into details* je ne vais pas entrer dans les détails / *let's not go into that* ne parlons pas de ça. **go off** ◆ vi **1.** [leave] partir, s'en aller / *she went off to work* elle est partie travailler **2.** [stop operating -light, radio] s'éteindre ; [-heating] s'éteindre, s'arrêter ; [-pain] partir, s'arrêter **3.** [become activated -bomb] exploser ; [-gun] partir ; [-alarm] sonner **4.** [have specified outcome] se passer / *the interview went off badly / well* l'entretien s'est mal / bien passé **5.** [U] [deteriorate -food] s'avarier, se gâter ; [-milk] tourner ; [-butter] rancir. ◆ vt insep [U] inf [stop lik-

ing] perdre le goût de / *he's gone off jazz / smoking* il n'aime plus le jazz / fumer, le jazz / fumer ne l'intéresse plus. **go off with** vt insep **1.** [leave with] partir avec **2.** [make off with] partir avec / *someone has gone off with his keys* quelqu'un est parti avec ses clés. **go on** ◆ vi **1.** [move, proceed] aller ; [without stopping] poursuivre son chemin ; [after stopping] repartir, se remettre en route / *you go on, I'll catch up* allez-y, je vous rattraperai (en chemin) **2.** [continue action] continuer / *she went on (with her) reading* elle a continué à or de lire / *go on, ask her* vas-y, demande-lui / *the party went on into the small hours* la soirée s'est prolongée jusqu'à très tôt le matin ▶ **go on (with you)!** [U] inf allons, arrête de me faire marcher ! ▶ **to be going on with** : *they have enough (work) to be going on with* ils ont du pain sur la planche or de quoi faire pour le moment / *here's £25 to be going on with* voilà 25 livres pour te dépanner **3.** [proceed to another action] : *he went on to explain why* il a ensuite expliqué pourquoi **4.** [be placed, fit] aller **5.** [happen, take place] se passer / *what's going on here?* qu'est-ce qui se passe ici ? / *several conversations were going on at once* il y avait plusieurs conversations à la fois / *while the war was going on* pendant la guerre **6.** [elapse] passer, s'écouler / *as time goes on* avec le temps, à mesure que le temps passe **7.** inf [chatter, talk] parler, jacasser ▶ **to go on about sthg** : *he goes on and on about politics* il parle politique sans cesse / *don't go on about it!* ça va, on a compris ! **8.** inf [act, behave] se conduire, se comporter / *what a way to go on!* en voilà des manières ! ◆ vt insep [be guided by] se laisser guider par, se fonder or se baser sur / *the detective didn't have much to go on* le détective n'avait pas grand-chose sur quoi s'appuyer or qui puisse le guider. **go on at** vt insep inf [criticize] critiquer ; [nag] s'en prendre à / *he's always going on at his wife about money* il est toujours sur le dos de sa femme avec les questions d'argent / *don't go on at me!* laisse-moi tranquille ! **go out** vi **1.** [leave] sortir / *to go out to dinner* sortir dîner / *she goes out to work* elle travaille en dehors de la maison or hors de chez elle **2.** [travel] partir ; [emigrate] émigrer / *they went out to Africa* **a)** [travelled] ils sont partis en Afrique **b)** [emigrated] ils sont partis vivre or ils ont émigré en Afrique **3.** [date] sortir ▶ **to go out with sb** sortir avec qqn **4.** [fire, light] s'éteindre **5.** [tide] descendre, se retirer **6.** [be published -brochure, pamphlet] être distribué ; [be broadcast -radio or television programme] être diffusé **7.** [feelings, sympathies] aller / *our thoughts go out to all those who suffer* nos pensées vont vers tous ceux qui souffrent. **go over** ◆ vi **1.** [move overhead] passer **2.** [move in particular direction] aller ; [cross] traverser / *I went over to see her* je suis allé la voir ; [capsize -boat] chavirer, capoter **3.** [change, switch] changer / *when will we go over to the metric system?* quand est-ce qu'on va passer au système métrique ? **4.** [change allegiance] passer, se joindre **5.** [be received] passer. ◆ vt insep **1.** [move, travel over] passer par-dessus **2.** [examine -argument, problem] examiner, considérer ; [-accounts, report] examiner, vérifier **3.** [repeat] répéter ; [review -notes, speech] réviser, revoir ; [-facts] récapituler, revoir ; SCH réviser / *let's go over it again* reprenons, récapitulons. **go round** vi **1.** [be enough] : *is there enough cake to go round?* est-ce qu'il y a assez de gâteau pour tout le monde ? **2.** [visit] aller / *we went round to his house* nous sommes allés chez lui **3.** [be continuously present -idea, tune] : *that song keeps going round in my head* j'ai cette chanson dans la tête **4.** [spin -wheel] tourner / *my head's going round* fig j'ai la tête qui tourne. **go through** ◆ vt insep **1.** [crowd, tunnel] traverser / *a shiver went through her* fig un frisson l'a parcourue or traversée **2.** [endure, experience] subir, souffrir / *we all have to go through it sometime* on doit tous y passer un jour ou l'autre / *we've gone through a lot together* nous avons vécu beaucoup de choses ensemble **3.** [consume, use up - supplies] épuiser ; [- money] dépenser ; [wear out] user **4.** [examine - accounts, document] examiner, vérifier ; [- list, proposal] éplucher ; [- mail] dépouiller ; [- drawer, pockets] fouiller (dans) ; [- files] chercher dans ; [sort] trier **5.** [carry out, perform - movement, work] faire ; [- formalities] remplir, accomplir. ◆ vi [offer, proposal] être accepté ; [business deal] être conclu, se faire ; [bill, law] passer, être voté / *the adoption finally went through* l'adoption s'est faite finalement. ❖ **go through** vt insep ▶ **to go through with sthg** aller jusqu'au bout de qqch, exécuter qqch / *they went through with their threat* ils ont exécuté leur menace. ❖ **go together** vi [colours, flavours] aller bien ensemble ; [characteristics, ideas] aller de pair. ❖ **go under** vi **1.** [go down - ship] couler, sombrer ; [- person] couler, disparaître (sous l'eau) **2.** *fig* [fail - business] couler, faire faillite ; [- project] couler, échouer ; [- person] échouer, sombrer. ❖ **go up** ◆ vi **1.** [ascend, climb - person] monter, aller en haut ; [- lift] monter / *I'm going up to bed* je monte me coucher **2.** [reach as far as] aller, s'étendre / *the road goes up to the house* la route mène or va à la maison **3.** [increase - amount, numbers] augmenter, croître ; [- price] monter, augmenter ; [- temperature] monter, s'élever / *rents are going up* les loyers sont en hausse **4.** [sudden noise] s'élever **5.** [appear - notices, posters] apparaître ; [be built] être construit **6.** THEAT [curtain] se lever / *before the curtain goes up* avant le lever du rideau. ◆ vt insep monter / *to go up a hill* l *ladder* monter une colline l *sur une* échelle. ❖ **go with** vt insep **1.** [accompany, escort] accompagner, aller avec ; *fig* : *to go with the crowd* suivre la foule or le mouvement **2.** [be compatible - colours, flavours] aller avec / *that hat doesn't go with your suit* ce chapeau ne va pas avec ton ensemble **3.** [be part of] aller avec / *the sense of satisfaction that goes with having done a good job* le sentiment de satisfaction qu'apporte le travail bien fait. ❖ **go without** ◆ vt insep se passer de, se priver de. ◆ vi s'en passer / *we'll just have to go without* il faudra s'en passer, c'est tout !

goad [gəʊd] ◆ n aiguillon *m*. ◆ vt **1.** [cattle] aiguillonner, piquer **2.** [person] harceler, provoquer ▶ **to goad sb into doing sthg** pousser qqn à faire qqch, harceler qqn jusqu'à ce qu'il fasse qqch. ❖ **goad on** vt sep aiguillonner.

go-ahead ◆ n feu *m* vert. ◆ adj [dynamic - person] dynamique, entreprenant, qui va de l'avant ; [- attitude, business] dynamique.

goal [gəʊl] ◆ n **1.** [aim] but *m*, objectif *m* **2.** SPORT but *m*. ◆ comp de but.

goal difference n différence *f* de buts.

goal-driven adj volontariste.

goalie ['gəʊlɪ] n *inf* SPORT goal *m*, gardien *m* (de but).

goalkeeper ['gəʊlˌkiːpə*r*] n gardien *m* (de but), goal *m*.

goalkeeping ['gəʊlˌkiːpɪŋ] n jeu *m* du gardien de but.

goal kick n coup *m* de pied de but, dégagement *m* aux six mètres.

goalless ['gəʊllɪs] adj ▶ **a goalless draw** un match sans but marqué or zéro à zéro.

goal line n ligne *f* de but.

goalmouth ['gəʊlˌmaʊθ] *(pl* [-maʊðz]) n : *in the goal-mouth* directement devant le but.

goalpost ['gəʊlpəʊst] n poteau *m* (de but).

goaltender ['gəʊlˌtendə*r*] n US [in ice hockey] gardien *m* de but.

goat [gəʊt] n **1.** ZOOL chèvre *f* **2.** *inf* [lecher] ▶ **old goat** vieux satyre *m* **3.** *inf & dated* [foolish person] andouille *f* **4.** PHR **to get sb's goat** *inf* taper sur les nerfs or le système à qqn.

goatee [gəʊ'tiː] n barbiche *f*, bouc *m*.

gob [gɒb] *(pt & pp* **gobbed,** *cont* **gobbing)** ◆ n **1.** UK v *inf* [mouth] gueule *f* **2.** *inf* [lump - of mud, clay] motte *f* ; [- of spittle] crachat *m*, mollard *m*. ◆ vi v *inf* [spit] mollarder.

gobble ['gɒbl] ◆ vi [turkey] glouglouter. ◆ vt *inf* [eat greedily] enfourner, engloutir. ❖ n glouglou *m*.

gobbledegook, gobbledygook ['gɒbldɪguːk] n *inf* charabia *m*.

gobby ['gɒbɪ] adj UK *inf* : *to be gobby* être une grande gueule.

go-between n intermédiaire *mf*.

Gobi ['gəʊbɪ] pr n ▶ **the Gobi Desert** le désert de Gobi.

goblet ['gɒblɪt] n coupe *f*, verre *m* à pied ; HIST gobelet *m*.

goblin ['gɒblɪn] n esprit *m* maléfique, lutin *m*.

gobshite ['gɒbʃaɪt] n UK v *inf* [man] trouduc *m* ; [woman] connasse *f*.

gobsmacked ['gɒbsmækt] adj *inf* : *I was gobsmacked* j'en suis resté baba.

go-cart n **1.** = **go-kart 2.** US [toy wagon] chariot *m*.

god [gɒd] n dieu *m*. ❖ **God** n **1.** RELIG Dieu *m* **2.** [in interjections and expressions] ▶ **thank God! a)** *inf* heureusement ! **b)** *liter* grâce à Dieu !, Dieu soit loué ! ▶ **(my** or **by) God!** *inf* mon Dieu ! ▶ **for God's sake** *inf* : *for God's sake, don't tell him!* surtout ne lui dis rien. ❖ **gods** pl n UK *inf* THEAT ▶ **the gods** le poulailler.

god-awful adj v *inf* atroce, affreux.

godchild ['gɒdtʃaɪld] *(pl* **godchildren** [-ˌtʃɪldrən]) n filleul *m*, -e *f*.

goddammit [ˌgɒd'dæmɪt] excl v *inf* bordel !

goddam(n) ['gɒdæm] US v *inf* ◆ interj ▶ **goddamn!** zut ! ◆ n : *he doesn't care* or *give a goddamn* il s'en fout. ◆ adj sacré, fichu. ◆ adv vachement.

goddamned ['gɒdæmd] US v *inf* = **goddam(n)** *(adj, adv)*.

goddaughter ['gɒdˌdɔːtə*r*] n filleule *f*.

goddess ['gɒdɪs] n déesse *f*.

godfather ['gɒdˌfɑːðə*r*] n parrain *m*.

god-fearing adj croyant, pieux.

godforsaken ['gɒdfəˌseɪkn] adj *inf* paumé.

godless ['gɒdlɪs] adj irréligieux, impie.

godlike ['gɒdlaɪk] adj divin, céleste.

godmother ['gɒdˌmʌðə*r*] n marraine *f*.

godparent ['gɒdˌpeərənt] n parrain *m*, marraine *f*.

godsend ['gɒdsend] n aubaine *f*, bénédiction *f*.

godson ['gɒdsʌn] n filleul *m*.

goer ['gəʊə*r*] n UK *inf* **1.** [fast person, vehicle, animal] fonceur *m*, -euse *f* **2.** [sexually active person] : *he's l she's a real goer* il l elle n'y va pas par quatre chemins *(pour séduire qqn)*.

goes [gəʊz] ⟶ **go** *(vb)*.

gofer ['gəʊfə*r*] n *inf* [office employee] employé(e) de bureau.

go-getter [-'getə*r*] n *inf* fonceur *m*, -euse *f*, battant *m*, -e *f*.

go-getting [-'getɪŋ] adj *inf* [person] plein d'allant, entreprenant ; [approach] dynamique.

goggle ['gɒgl] vi ouvrir de grands yeux or des yeux ronds ▶ **to goggle at sb / sthg** regarder qqn / qqch avec des yeux ronds. ❖ **goggles** pl n **1.** [protective] lunettes *fpl* (de protection) ; [for motorcyclist] lunettes *fpl* (de motocycliste) ; [for diver] lunettes *fpl* de plongée ; [for swimmer] lunettes *fpl* **2.** *inf* [glasses] bésicles *fpl*.

go-go dancer n danseur *m* de go-go.

going ['gəʊɪŋ] ◆ n **1.** [leaving] départ *m* **2.** [progress] progrès *m* **3.** [condition of ground] état *m* du terrain. ◆ adj **1.** [profitable] ▸ **going concern**: *her company is a going concern* son entreprise est en pleine activité **2.** [current] actuel.

going-away adj [party, present] d'adieu.

going-over (*pl* **goings-over**) n *inf* **1.** [checkup] révision *f*, vérification *f* ; [cleanup] nettoyage *m* **2.** *fig* ▸ **to give sb a (good) going-over a)** [scolding] passer un savon à qqn **b)** [beating] passer qqn à tabac.

goings-on pl n *inf* **1.** *pej* [behaviour] conduite *f*, activités *fpl* **2.** [events] événements *mpl*.

go-kart n kart *m*.

Golan Heights ['gəʊˌlæn-] pl pr n ▸ **the Golan Heights** le plateau du Golan.

gold [gəʊld] ◆ n **1.** [metal, colour] or *m* **2.** [gold medal] médaille *f* d'or. ◆ adj **1.** [made of gold - coin, ingot, medal] d'or ; [- tooth, watch] en or **2.** [gold-coloured] or *(inv)*, doré.

gold card n carte *f* de crédit illimité.

gold-digger n chercheur *m* d'or ; *fig* aventurier *m*, -ère *f*.

gold dust n poudre *f* d'or.

golden ['gəʊldən] adj **1.** *lit & fig* [made of gold] en or, d'or ; [opinion] favorable **2.** [colour] doré, (couleur) d'or **3.** *inf* [very successful] ▸ **golden boy / girl** enfant *mf* prodige.

Golden Age n ▸ **the Golden Age** l'âge *m* d'or.

golden eagle n aigle *m* royal.

golden handcuffs pl n *inf* primes *fpl* (*versées à un cadre à intervalles réguliers pour le dissuader de partir*).

golden handshake n *inf* gratification *f* de fin de service.

golden hello n *inf* gratification *f* de début de service.

golden jubilee n (fête *f* du) cinquantième anniversaire *m*.

golden oldie n *inf* vieux tube *m*.

golden retriever n golden retriever *m*.

golden rule n règle *f* d'or.

golden syrup n 🇬🇧 mélasse *f* raffinée.

golden wedding n noces *fpl* d'or.

goldfinch ['gəʊldfɪntʃ] n chardonneret *m*.

goldfish ['gəʊldfɪʃ] n **1.** [as pet] poisson *m* rouge **2.** ZOOL cyprin *m* doré.

goldfish bowl n bocal *m* (à poissons rouges).

gold leaf n feuille *f* d'or.

goldmine ['gəʊldmaɪn] n *lit & fig* mine *f* d'or.

gold plate n **1.** [utensils] orfèvrerie *f*, vaisselle *f* d'or **2.** [plating] plaque *f* d'or.

gold-plated adj plaqué or.

gold-rimmed adj : *gold-rimmed spectacles* lunettes *fpl* à montures en or.

gold rush n ruée *f* vers l'or ▸ **the Gold Rush** 🇺🇸 HIST la ruée vers l'or.

 The Gold Rush

Mouvement de migration de grande ampleur qui, en 1848, à la suite de la découverte de gisements d'or en Californie, déplaça des centaines de milliers d'Américains vers la côte ouest. Un an plus tard, seuls 80 000 d'entre eux avaient atteint leur but, après avoir échappé à la maladie et aux dangers du voyage.

goldsmith ['gəʊldsmɪθ] n orfèvre *m*.

gold standard n étalon-or *m*.

golf [gɒlf] ◆ n golf *m*. ◆ comp ▸ **golf bag** sac *m* de golf ▸ **golf cart** caddie *m* (de golf). ◆ vi jouer au golf.

golf ball n **1.** SPORT balle *f* de golf **2.** [for typewriter] boule *f*.

golf club n **1.** [stick] club *m* or crosse *f* or canne *f* de golf **2.** [building, association] club *m* de golf.

golf course n (terrain *m* de) golf *m*.

golfer ['gɒlfər] n joueur *m*, -euse *f* de golf, golfeur *m*, -euse *f*.

golly ['gɒlɪ] (*pl* **gollies**) *inf* interj *dated* ▸ **(good) golly!** ciel !, mince (alors) !, flûte !

gondola ['gɒndələ] n **1.** [boat] gondole *f* **2.** [on airship or balloon, for window cleaner] nacelle *f* **3.** [in supermarket] gondole *f* **4.** [ski lift] cabine *f* (de téléphérique).

gondolier [ˌgɒndə'lɪər] n gondolier *m*.

gone [gɒn] ◆ pp ⟶ **go**. ◆ adj **1.** [past] passé, révolu **2.** [away] : *be gone with you!* disparaissez de ma vue ! **3.** *inf* [pregnant] : *she is 4 months gone* elle est enceinte de 4 mois **4.** *inf* [infatuated] ▸ **to be gone on sb / sthg** être (complètement) toqué de qqn / qqch **5.** *euph* [dead] mort **6.** 🅿🅷🆁 **to be far gone a)** *inf* [weak] être bien faible **b)** [drunk] être bien parti. ◆ prep 🇬🇧 : *it's gone 11* il est 11 h passées or plus de 11 h.

goner ['gɒnər] n *inf* ▸ **to be a goner** être fichu or cuit.

gong [gɒŋ] n **1.** [instrument] gong *m* **2.** 🇬🇧 *inf & hum* [medal] médaille *f*.

gonna ['gɒnə] 🇺🇸 *inf* abbr of going to.

gonorrhoea 🇬🇧, **gonorrhea** 🇺🇸 [ˌgɒnə'rɪə] n blennorragie *f*.

gonzo ['gɒnzəʊ] adj 🇺🇸 *inf* [style] particulier, bizarre ; [person] barge.

goo [guː] n *inf* [sticky stuff] matière *f* poisseuse.

good [gʊd] (*compar* **better** ['betər], *superl* **best** [best]) ◆ adj

A. AGREEABLE [enjoyable, pleasant - book, feeling, holiday] bon, agréable ; [- weather] beau (*before vowel or silent 'h' bel, f belle*) / *we're good friends* nous sommes très amis / *they had a good time* ils se sont bien amusés / *it's good to be home* ça fait du bien or ça fait plaisir de rentrer chez soi / *it's good to be alive* il fait bon vivre ; [agreeable] bon / *wait until he's in a good mood* attendez qu'il soit de bonne humeur / *to feel good* être en forme ▸ **it's too good to be true** c'est trop beau pour être vrai or pour y croire / *have a good day!* bonne journée ! ▸ **good to see you** 🇺🇸 *inf* content de te voir.

B. HIGH QUALITY OR COMPETENT 1. [high quality - clothing, dishes] bon, de bonne qualité ; [- painting, film] bon ; [- food] bon / *he speaks good English* il parle bien anglais / *this work isn't good enough* ce travail laisse beaucoup à désirer **2.** [competent, skilful] bon, compétent / *she's a good listener* c'est quelqu'un qui sait écouter ▸ **to be good at sthg** être doué pour or bon en qqch / *he's good with children* il sait s'y prendre avec les enfants / *to be good with one's hands* être habile or adroit de ses mains **3.** [useful] bon ▸ **to be good for nothing** être bon à rien.

C. MORALLY 1. [kind] bon, gentil ; [loyal, true] bon, véritable ; [moral, virtuous] bon / *she's a good person* c'est quelqu'un de bien / *he's a good sort* c'est un brave type / *you're too good for him* tu mérites mieux que lui / *it's good of you to come* c'est aimable or gentil à vous d'être venu **2.** [well-behaved] sage / *be good!* sois sage !

D. DESIRABLE OR CONVENIENT 1. [desirable, positive] bon, souhaitable ; [cause] bon / *she had the good fortune to arrive just then* elle a eu la chance d'arriver juste à ce moment-là / *it's a good job* or *good thing he decided not to go* c'est une chance qu'il ait décidé de or heureusement qu'il a décidé de ne pas y aller / *all good wishes for the New Year* tous nos meilleurs vœux pour le nouvel an **2.** [favourable - contract, deal] avantageux, favorable ; [- opportunity, sign] bon, favorable / *she's in a good position to help us* elle est bien placée pour nous aider **3.** [convenient, suitable - place, time] bon, propice ; [- choice] bon, convenable / *this is as good a time as any* autant le faire maintenant **4.** [acceptable] bon, convenable / *we made the trip in good time* le voyage n'a pas été trop long / *that's all very good* or *all well and good but…* c'est bien joli or bien beau tout ça mais… **5.** [beneficial] bon, bienfaisant / *it's good for him to spend time outdoors* ça lui fait du bien or c'est bon pour lui de passer du temps dehors / *if you know what's good for you, you'll listen* fig si tu as le moindre bon sens, tu m'écouteras.

E. ATTRACTIVE OR SOUND 1. [sound, strong] bon, valide / *my eyesight / hearing is good* j'ai une bonne vue / l'ouïe fine **2.** [attractive - appearance] bon, beau *(before vowel or silent 'h' bel, f belle)* ; [- features, legs] beau *(before vowel or silent 'h' bel, f belle)*, joli / *you're looking good!* a) [healthy] tu as bonne mine ! b) [well-dressed] tu es très bien ! / *that colour looks good on him* cette couleur lui va bien / *he has a good figure* il est bien fait **3.** [valid, well-founded] bon, valable / *she had a good excuse / reason for not going* elle avait une bonne excuse pour / une bonne raison de ne pas y aller **4.** [reliable, trustworthy - brand, car] bon, sûr ; [COMM & FIN - cheque] bon ; [- investment, securities] sûr ; [- debt] bon, certain / *this coat is good for another year* ce manteau fera encore un an **5.** [honourable, reputable] bon, estimé.

F. INTENSIFYING 1. [ample, considerable] bon, considérable / *a good amount* or *deal of money* beaucoup d'argent / *a good-sized room* une assez grande pièce / *take good care of your mother* prends bien soin de ta mère / *the trip will take you a good two hours* il vous faudra deux bonnes heures pour faire le voyage **2.** [proper, thorough] bon, grand / *I gave the house a good cleaning* j'ai fait le ménage à fond / *have a good cry* pleure un bon coup / *we had a good laugh* on a bien ri.

G. INDICATING APPROVAL bon, très bien / *she left him — good!* elle l'a quitté — tant mieux ! ▸ **that's a good one!** a) inf [joke] elle est (bien) bonne, celle-là ! b) iro [far-fetched story] à d'autres ! ▸ **good on you!** inf or **for you** bravo !, très bien !
◆ adv **1.** [as intensifier] bien, bon / *the two friends had a good long chat* les deux amis ont longuement bavardé / *we took a good long walk* nous avons fait une bonne or une grande promenade **2.** PHR **to make good a)** [succeed] réussir **b)** [reform] changer de conduite, se refaire une vie / *they made good their promise* ils ont tenu parole or ont respecté leur promesse ▸ **to make sthg good a)** [mistake] remédier à qqch **b)** [damages, injustice] réparer qqch **c)** [losses] compenser qqch **d)** [deficit] combler qqch **e)** [wall, surface] apporter des finitions à qqch ▸ **to make good on sthg** US honorer qqch.
◆ n **1.** [morality, virtue] bien m / *she recognized the good in him* elle a vu ce qu'il y avait de bon en lui ▸ **to be up to no good** préparer un mauvais coup **2.** [use] : *this book isn't much good to me* ce livre ne me sert pas à grand-chose / *I was never any good at mathematics* je n'ai jamais été doué pour les maths, je n'ai jamais été bon or fort en maths / *he'd be no good as a teacher* il ne ferait pas un bon professeur / *what's the good?* à quoi bon ? / *it's no good, I give up* ça ne sert à rien, j'abandonne **3.** [benefit, welfare] bien m / *a holiday will do her good* des vacances lui feront du bien ▸ **the common good** l'intérêt m commun. ❖ **as good as** adv phr pour ainsi dire, à peu de chose près / *he's as good as dead* c'est comme s'il était mort / *it's as good as new* c'est comme neuf / *they as good as called us cowards* ils

n'ont pas dit qu'on était des lâches mais c'était tout comme. ❖ **for good** adv phr pour de bon / *they finally settled down for good* ils se sont enfin fixés définitivement ▸ **for good and all** une (bonne) fois pour toutes, pour de bon.

goodbye [,gʊd'baɪ] ◆ interj ▸ **goodbye!** au revoir ! ◆ n adieu m, au revoir m ▸ **to say goodbye to sb** dire au revoir or faire ses adieux à qqn, prendre congé de qqn.

good-for-nothing ◆ adj bon or propre à rien. ◆ n vaurien m, -enne f, propre-à-rien mf.

Good Friday n le Vendredi saint.

good-hearted adj [person] bon, généreux ; [action] fait avec les meilleures intentions.

good-humoured adj [person] qui a bon caractère ; [generally] bon enfant *(inv)* ; [on one occasion] de bonne humeur ; [discussion] amical ; [joke, remark] sans malice.

goodie ['gʊdɪ] inf = **goody**.

goodish ['gʊdɪʃ] adj inf **1.** [quite good] assez bon, passable **2.** [number, quantity, amount] assez grand.

good-looker n inf [man] bel homme m ; [younger] beau garçon m ; [woman] belle femme f ; [younger] belle fille f.

good-looking adj [person] beau *(before vowel or silent 'h' bel, f belle)*.

good looks pl n [attractive appearance] beauté f.

good-natured adj [person] facile à vivre, qui a un bon naturel ; [face, smile] bon enfant *(inv)* ; [remark] sans malice.

goodness ['gʊdnɪs] n **1.** [of person] bonté f, bienveillance f, bienfaisance f ; [of thing] (bonne) qualité f, excellence f, perfection f **2.** [nourishment] valeur f nutritive **3.** inf [in interjections] ▸ **(my) goodness!** mon Dieu ! ▸ **for goodness' sake** pour l'amour de Dieu, par pitié ▸ **goodness knows!** Dieu seul le sait !

good night interj ▸ **good night!** a) [when leaving] bonsoir ! b) [when going to bed] bonne nuit !

goods [gʊdz] pl n **1.** [possessions] biens mpl ▸ **goods and chattels** biens et effets mpl **2.** COMM marchandises fpl, articles mpl **3.** US inf [information] renseignements mpl.

good Samaritan n bon Samaritain m, bonne Samaritaine f. ❖ **Good Samaritan** n BIBLE ▸ **the Good Samaritan** le bon Samaritain.

good-sized adj de bonne taille.

goods train n train m de marchandises.

good-tempered adj [person] qui a bon caractère, d'humeur égale.

goodwill [,gʊd'wɪl] ◆ n **1.** [benevolence] bienveillance f ▸ **to show goodwill towards sb** faire preuve de bienveillance à l'égard de qqn **2.** [willingness] bonne volonté f **3.** COMM clientèle f, (biens mpl) incorporels mpl. ◆ comp d'amitié, de bienveillance.

goody ['gʊdɪ] *(pl* **goodies***)* inf ◆ interj ▸ **goody!** génial !, chouette !, chic ! ◆ n *(usu pl)* **1.** [good thing] bonne chose f ; [sweet] bonbon m, friandise f **2.** [good person] bon m.

gooey ['gu:ɪ] adj inf **1.** [substance] gluant, visqueux, poisseux ; [sweets] qui colle aux dents **2.** [sentimental] sentimental.

goof [gu:f] inf ◆ n **1.** [fool] imbécile mf, andouille f **2.** US [blunder] gaffe f. ◆ vi [blunder] faire une gaffe. ❖ **goof around** vi US inf déconner. ❖ **goof off** vi US inf [waste time] flemmarder ; [malinger] tirer au flanc.

goofy ['gu:fɪ] *(compar* **goofier***, superl* **goofiest***)* adj inf **1.** [stupid] dingo **2.** UK [teeth] en avant.

Google® ['gu:gl] vt [look up using Google] rechercher avec Google®.

goo-goo ◆ adj US inf ▸ **to go goo-goo** [baby] faire areu. ◆ interj baby talk areu areu.

goolies ['gu:lɪ] pl n v inf roupettes fpl.

goon [gu:n] n inf **1.** [fool] abruti m, -e f **2.** US [hired thug] casseur m (au service de quelqu'un) ▶ **goon squad** [strike-breakers] milice f patronale.

goose [gu:s] (pl **geese** [gi:s]) ◆ n **1.** [bird] oie f ▶ **goose egg** US zéro m **2.** inf [fool] : *don't be such a goose!* ne sois pas si bête ! ◆ vt US inf [prod] ▶ **to goose sb** donner un petit coup sur les fesses de quelqu'un pour le faire sursauter.

gooseberry ['guzbəri] n **1.** BOT groseille f à maquereau **2.** [unwanted person] ▶ **to play gooseberry** tenir la chandelle.

goose bumps US inf = goose pimples.

gooseflesh ['gu:sfleʃ] n (U) = goose pimples.

goose pimples pl n UK la chair de poule.

goosestep ['gu:s,step] (pt & pp **goosestepped**, cont **goosestepping**) ◆ n pas m de l'oie. ◆ vi faire le pas de l'oie.

GOP (abbr of **Grand Old Party**) pr n le parti républicain aux États-Unis.

gopher ['gəufər] n **1.** COMPUT gopher m **2.** [rodent] gaufre m, gauphre m **3.** inf = gofer.

gore [gɔ:ʳ] ◆ n [blood] sang m (coagulé). ◆ vt [wound] blesser à coups de cornes, encorner.

gorge [gɔ:dʒ] ◆ n GEOG défilé m, gorge f. ◆ vt ▶ **to gorge o.s. (on sthg)** se gaver or se gorger or se bourrer (de qqch).

gorgeous ['gɔ:dʒəs] adj **1.** inf [wonderful - person, weather] magnifique, splendide, superbe ; [-flat, clothing] magnifique, très beau ; [-food, meal] délicieux **2.** [magnificent - fabric, clothing] somptueux.

gorilla [gə'rɪlə] n **1.** ZOOL gorille m **2.** inf [thug] voyou m ; [bodyguard] gorille m.

gormless ['gɔ:mlɪs] adj UK inf [person, expression] stupide, abruti.

gorse [gɔ:s] n (U) ajoncs mpl.

gory ['gɔ:rɪ] (compar **gorier**, superl **goriest**) adj [battle, scene, sight, death] sanglant.

gosh [gɒʃ] interj inf ▶ **gosh!** oh dis donc !, ça alors !, hé ben !

gosling ['gɒzlɪŋ] n oison m.

go-slow n UK grève f du zèle, grève f perlée.

gospel ['gɒspl] ◆ n **1.** fig ▶ **to take sthg as gospel** prendre qqch pour parole d'évangile **2.** MUS gospel m. ◆ comp **1.** fig ▶ **the gospel truth** la vérité vraie **2.** MUS ▶ **gospel music** gospel m. ❖ **Gospel** n BIBLE ▶ **the Gospel** l'Évangile m.

gossamer ['gɒsəmər] ◆ n (U) [cobweb] fils mpl de la Vierge, filandres fpl ; [gauze] gaze f ; [light cloth] étoffe f transparente. ◆ comp arachnéen, très léger, très fin.

gossip ['gɒsɪp] ◆ n **1.** (U) [casual chat] bavardage m, papotage m ; pej [rumour] commérage m, ragots mpl, racontars mpl ; [in newspaper] potins mpl **2.** pej [person] bavard m, -e f, pie f, commère f. ◆ vi bavarder, papoter ; [maliciously] faire des commérages, dire du mal des gens.

gossip column n échos mpl.

gossip columnist n échotier m, -ère f.

gossipy ['gɒsɪpɪ] adj inf [person] bavard ; [letter] plein de bavardages ; pej cancanier ; [style] anecdotique.

got [gɒt] pt & pp ⟶ get.

gotcha ['gɒtʃə] interj inf **1.** [I understand] ▶ **gotcha!** pigé ! **2.** [cry of success] ▶ **gotcha!** a) ça y est (je l'ai) ! b) [cry when catching sb] je te tiens !

goth [gɒθ] n [member of fashion movement] goth mf.

Goth [gɒθ] n ▶ **the Goths** les Goths mpl.

Gothic ['gɒθɪk] ◆ adj [gen & ARCHIT] & PRINT gothique ▶ **Gothic novel** roman m gothique. ◆ n [gen & ARCHIT] gothique m ; LING gotique m, gothique m.

Gothic novel

Genre littéraire, en vogue en Grande-Bretagne dans la seconde moitié du XVIIIe siècle, caractérisé par des ambiances fantastiques, des événements mystérieux et violents, des atmosphères de ruine et de déclin.

go-to adj US inf : *he's your go-to guy* c'est votre interlocuteur or c'est à lui qu'il faut s'adresser en cas de problème.

gotta ['gɒtə] US inf **1.** abbr of have got a **2.** abbr of have got to.

gotten ['gɒtn] pp US & Scot ⟶ get.

G2G = GTG.

gouge [gaudʒ] ◆ n gouge f. ◆ vt [with gouge] gouger. ❖ **gouge out** vt sep [with gouge] gouger, creuser (à la gouge) ; [with thumb] évider, creuser.

goulash ['gu:læʃ] n goulache m, goulasch m.

gourd [guəd] n [plant] gourde f, cucurbitacée f ; [fruit] gourde f, calebasse f ; [container] gourde f, calebasse f.

gourmand ['guəmənd] n [glutton] gourmand m, -e f ; [gourmet] gourmet m.

gourmet ['guəmeɪ] ◆ n gourmet m, gastronome mf. ◆ comp [meal, restaurant] gastronomique.

gout [gaut] n (U) MED goutte f.

govern ['gʌvən] ◆ vt **1.** [country] gouverner, régner sur ; [city, region, bank, etc.] gouverner ; [affairs] administrer, gérer ; [company, organization] diriger, gérer **2.** [determine - behaviour, choice, events, speed] déterminer **3.** [restrain - passions] maîtriser, dominer **4.** GRAM [case, mood] gouverner, régir **5.** TECH régler. ◆ vi COMM & POL gouverner, commander, diriger.

governable ['gʌvnəbl] adj gouvernable.

governess ['gʌvənɪs] n gouvernante f.

governing ['gʌvənɪŋ] adj **1.** COMM & POL gouvernant, dirigeant ▶ **governing body** conseil m d'administration **2.** [factor] dominant / *the governing principle* le principe directeur.

government ['gʌvnmənt] ◆ n **1.** [process of governing - country] gouvernement m, direction f ; [-company] administration f, gestion f ; [-affairs] conduite f **2.** POL [governing authority] gouvernement m ; [type of authority] gouvernement m, régime m ; [the State] gouvernement m, État m. ◆ comp [measure, policy] gouvernemental, du gouvernement ; [borrowing, expenditure] de l'État, public ; [minister, department] du gouvernement ▶ **government bonds** obligations fpl d'État, bons mpl du Trésor ▶ **government subsidy** subvention f d'État.

governmental [,gʌvn'mentl] adj gouvernemental, du gouvernement.

government-funded adj subventionné par l'État.

government-sponsored adj parrainé par le gouvernement.

governor ['gʌvənər] n **1.** [of bank, country] gouverneur m ; UK [of prison] directeur m, -trice f ; UK [of school] membre m du conseil d'établissement ▶ **State governor** US gouverneur m d'État **2.** UK inf [employer] patron m, boss m **3.** TECH régulateur m.

governor-general (pl **governor-generals**), **Governor-General** n gouverneur m général.

governorship ['gʌvənəʃɪp] n fonctions fpl de gouverneur.

govt (written abbr of **government**) gvt.

gown [gaun] n **1.** [gen] robe f **2.** SCH & UNIV toge f.

GP (abbr of **general practitioner**) n (médecin m) généraliste m.

GPA n US abbr of **grade point average**.

GPO pr n [in US] (abbr of **Government Printing Office**) ▶ **the GPO** ≃ l'imprimerie f nationale.

GPS [ˌdʒiːpiːˈes] (abbr of **Global Positioning System**) n GPS m.

gr. written abbr of **gross**.

grab [græb] (pt & pp **grabbed,** cont **grabbing**) ◆ vt **1.** [object] saisir, s'emparer de ; [person] attraper **2.** fig [opportunity] saisir ; [attention] retenir ; [power] prendre ; [land] s'emparer de ; [quick meal] avaler, prendre (en vitesse) ; [taxi] prendre **3.** inf PHR how does that grab you? qu'est-ce que tu en dis ? ◆ vi ▶ **to grab at sb** / **sthg** essayer d'agripper qqn / qqch. ◆ n **1.** [movement] mouvement m vif ; [sudden theft] vol m (à l'arraché) **2.** UK TECH benne f preneuse.

grace [greɪs] ◆ n **1.** [physical] grâce f ; [decency, politeness, tact] tact m **2.** RELIG grâce f **3.** [amnesty] grâce f ; [respite] grâce f, répit m **4.** [prayer] ▶ **to say grace a)** [before meals] dire le bénédicité **b)** [after meals] dire les grâces. ◆ vt **1.** [honour] honorer **2.** fml & liter [adorn] orner, embellir. ❖ **Grace** n [term of address] : Your Grace **a)** [to Archbishop] Monseigneur ou (Votre) Excellence (l'archevêque) **b)** [to Duke] Monsieur le duc **c)** [to Duchess] Madame la duchesse. ❖ **Graces** pl n MYTH ▶ **the three Graces** les trois Grâces fpl.

graceful [ˈgreɪsfʊl] adj [person, movement] gracieux ; [language, style, apology] élégant.

gracefully [ˈgreɪsfʊlɪ] adv [dance, move] avec grâce, gracieusement ; [apologize] avec élégance.

graceless [ˈgreɪslɪs] adj [behaviour, person, movement] gauche.

gracious [ˈgreɪʃəs] ◆ adj **1.** [generous, kind - gesture, smile] gracieux, bienveillant ; [- action] généreux / to be gracious to or towards sb faire preuve de bienveillance envers qqn **2.** [luxurious] ▶ **gracious living** la vie facile. ◆ interj ▶ **(good** or **goodness) gracious (me)!** mon Dieu !

graciously [ˈgreɪʃəslɪ] adv [smile] gracieusement ; [accept, agree, allow] avec bonne grâce ; fml gracieusement ; RELIG miséricordieusement.

graciousness [ˈgreɪʃəsnɪs] n [of person] bienveillance f, générosité f, gentillesse f ; [of action] grâce f, élégance f ; [of lifestyle, surroundings] élégance f, raffinement m ; RELIG miséricorde f, clémence f.

gradable [ˈgreɪdəbl] adj **1.** [capable of being graded] qui peut être classé **2.** LING comparatif.

gradation [grəˈdeɪʃn] n gradation f, progression f, échelonnement m ; [stage] gradation f, degré m, palier m ; LING alternance f (vocalique), apophonie f.

grade [greɪd] ◆ n **1.** [level] degré m, niveau m ; [on scale] échelon m, grade m ; [on salary scale] indice m **2.** MIL grade m, rang m, échelon m ; [in hierarchy] échelon m, catégorie f **3.** [quality - of product] qualité f, catégorie f ; [- of petrol] grade m ; [size of products] calibre m **4.** US SCH [mark] note f ; [year] année f, classe f / a grade A student un excellent élève / he's in fifth grade ≃ il est en CM2 **5.** US = **grade school 6.** MATH grade m **7.** US [gradient] déclivité f, pente f ; RAIL rampe f **8.** PHR **to make the grade** être à la hauteur. ◆ vt **1.** [classify - by quality] classer ; [- by size] calibrer ; [arrange in order] classer **2.** SCH [mark] noter.

grade crossing n US RAIL passage m à niveau.

grade point average n US SCH moyenne f.

grade school n US école f primaire.

gradient [ˈgreɪdjənt] n **1.** UK [road] déclivité f, pente f, inclinaison f ; RAIL rampe f, pente f, inclinaison f **2.** METEOR & PHYS gradient m.

grading [ˈgreɪdɪŋ] n [classification] classification f ; [by size] calibration f ; SCH notation f.

gradual [ˈgrædʒʊəl] ◆ adj [change, improvement] graduel, progressif ; [slope] doux (douce). ◆ n RELIG graduel m.

gradually [ˈgrædʒʊəlɪ] adv progressivement, petit à petit, peu à peu.

graduate ◆ n [ˈgrædʒʊət] **1.** UNIV licencié m, -e f, diplômé m, -e f ; US SCH bachelier m, -ère f **2.** US [container] récipient m gradué. ◆ adj UNIV diplômé, licencié ▶ **graduate school** US école où l'on poursuit ses études après avoir obtenu un bachelor's degree ▶ **graduate student** étudiant de deuxième / troisième cycle. ◆ vi [ˈgrædʒʊeɪt] **1.** UNIV ≃ obtenir son diplôme ; US SCH obtenir son diplôme de fin de Senior High School ; ≃ obtenir le or être reçu au baccalauréat **2.** [gain promotion] être promu, passer. ◆ vt [ˈgrædʒʊeɪt] **1.** [calibrate] graduer **2.** US SCH & UNIV conférer or accorder un diplôme à.

graduated [ˈgrædʒʊeɪtɪd] adj [tax] progressif ; [measuring container, exercise, thermometer] gradué ; [colours] dégradé.

graduation [ˌgrædʒʊˈeɪʃn] ◆ n **1.** [gen] graduation f **2.** US UNIV & SCH [ceremony] (cérémonie f de) remise f des diplômes. ◆ comp ▶ **graduation day** jour m de la remise des diplômes.

graffiti [grəˈfiːtɪ] n (U) graffitis mpl.

graft [grɑːft] ◆ n **1.** HORT greffe f, greffon m ; MED greffe f **2.** (U) US inf [corruption] magouilles fpl **3.** (U) UK inf [hard work] travail m pénible. ◆ vt HORT & MED greffer. ◆ vi **1.** [be involved in bribery] donner or recevoir des pots-de-vin **2.** HORT & MED : pears graft fairly easily les poires se greffent assez facilement **3.** UK inf [work hard] bosser dur.

graham cracker [ˈgreɪəm-] n US biscuit rond légèrement sucré.

grain [greɪn] n **1.** (U) [seeds of rice, wheat] grain m ; [cereal] céréales fpl ; US blé m / a cargo of grain une cargaison de céréales **2.** [single] grain m / grains of rice / wheat grains mpl de riz / de blé ; [particle] grain m / a grain of salt / sand un grain de sel / de sable **3.** fig [of madness, sense, truth, etc.] grain m, brin m **4.** [in leather, stone, wood, etc.] grain m ; PHOT grain m ▶ **to go against the grain** : I'll help you, but it goes against the grain je vous aiderai, mais ce n'est pas de bon cœur / it goes against the grain for him to accept that they are right ce n'est pas dans sa nature d'admettre qu'ils aient raison **5.** UK [weight] ≃ grain m (poids).

graininess [ˈgreɪnɪnɪs] n [of image] grain m.

grainy [ˈgreɪnɪ] (compar **grainier,** superl **grainiest**) adj [surface, texture - of wood] veineux ; [- of stone] grenu, granuleux ; [- of leather, paper] grenu, grené ; PHOT qui a du grain.

gram [græm] n **1.** [metric unit] gramme m **2.** BOT [plant] pois m ; [seed] pois m, graine f de pois.

grammar [ˈgræmə(r)] n **1.** LING grammaire f **2.** [book] grammaire f.

grammar checker n COMPUT vérificateur m grammatical.

grammar school n [in UK] type d'école secondaire ; [in US] école primaire.

 Grammar school

En Grande-Bretagne, ces écoles secondaires peuvent recevoir le soutien de l'État, mais elles demeurent indépendantes. On y entre sur concours ou sur dossier. L'enseignement qui y est dispensé est de haut niveau, traditionnel, et prépare aux études supérieures. Les élèves des **grammar schools** représentent une infime minorité de l'ensemble des élèves britanniques.

grammatical [grə'mætɪkl] adj grammatical.

grammatically [grə'mætɪklɪ] adv grammaticalement, du point de vue grammatical.

gramme [græm] = gram.

gramophone ['græməfəʊn] UK dated ◆ n gramophone m, phonographe m. ◆ comp ▶ **gramophone needle** aiguille f de phonographe or de gramophone ▶ **gramophone record** dated disque m.

gran [græn] n UK inf mamie f, mémé f.

Granada [grə'nɑ:də] pr n Grenade.

granary ['grænərɪ] ◆ n grenier m à blé, silo m (à céréales). ◆ comp ▶ **granary bread, granary loaf** pain m aux céréales.

grand [grænd] ◆ adj **1.** [impressive - house] magnifique ; [- style] grand, noble ; [- music, occasion] grand ; [pretentious, self-important] suffisant, prétentieux ; [dignified, majestic] majestueux, digne **2.** UK dated or regional [wonderful] super **3.** PHR that comes to a grand total of £536 ça fait en tout 536 livres. ◆ n UK inf mille livres fpl ; US mille dollars mpl.

grandad ['grændæd] n inf pépé m, papy m.

Grand Canyon pr n ▶ **the Grand Canyon** le Grand Canyon.

grandchild ['grændtʃaɪld] (pl grandchildren [-,tʃɪldrən]) n petit-fils m, petite-fille f.

granddad ['grændæd] inf = grandad.

granddaughter ['græn,dɔ:tər] n petite-fille f.

grand duke n grand-duc m.

grandeur ['grændʒər] n [of person] grandeur f, noblesse f ; [of building, scenery] splendeur f, magnificence f.

grandfather ['grænd,fɑ:ðər] n grand-père m.

grandfather clock n horloge f (de parquet).

grand finale n apothéose f.

grandiloquence [græn'dɪləkwəns] n fml grandiloquence f.

grandiloquent [græn'dɪləkwənt] adj fml grandiloquent.

grandiose ['grændɪəʊz] adj pej [building, style, plan] grandiose.

grand jury n [in US] jury m d'accusation.

grand larceny n US vol m qualifié.

grandly ['grændlɪ] adv [behave, say] avec grandeur ; [live] avec faste ; [dress] avec panache.

grandma ['grænmɑ:] n inf grand-mère f, mémé f, mamie f.

Grand Master n [of masonic lodge] Grand Maître m.

grandmother ['græn,mʌðər] n grand-mère f.

Grand National pr n ▶ **the Grand National** la plus importante course d'obstacles de Grande-Bretagne, qui se déroule à Aintree, dans la banlieue de Liverpool.

grandness ['grændnɪs] n [of behaviour] grandeur f, noblesse f ; [of lifestyle] faste m ; [of appearance] panache m.

grandpa ['grænpɑ:] inf = grandad.

grandparent ['græn,peərənt] n : my grandparents mes grands-parents mpl.

grand piano n piano m à queue.

grand prix [,grɒn'pri:] (pl grands prix [,grɒn'pri:]) ◆ n grand prix m. ◆ comp ▶ **grand prix racing** course f de grand prix.

grand slam n grand chelem m.

grandson ['grænsʌn] n petit-fils m.

grandstand ['grændstænd] ◆ n tribune f. ◆ vi US faire l'intéressant.

grandstanding ['grændstændɪŋ] n [in politics] démagogie f.

grand total n somme f globale, total m général.

granita [grə'ni:tə] n granité m.

granite ['grænɪt] ◆ n granit m, granite m. ◆ comp de granit or granite.

granny, grannie ['grænɪ] n inf mamie f, mémé f.

granny flat n UK appartement m indépendant (dans une maison).

granola [grə'nəʊlə] n US muesli m.

grant [grɑ:nt] ◆ vt **1.** [permission, wish] accorder ; [request] accorder, accéder à ; SPORT [goal, point] accorder ; [credit, loan, pension] accorder ; [charter, favour, privilege, right] accorder, octroyer, concéder ; [property] céder / to grant sb permission to do sthg accorder à qqn l'autorisation de faire qqch **2.** [accept as true] accorder, admettre, concéder / I grant you I made an error of judgement je vous accorde que j'ai fait une erreur de jugement / I'll grant you that point je vous concède ce point / granted, he's not very intelligent, but... d'accord, il n'est pas très intelligent, mais... / granted! d'accord !, soit ! **3.** PHR to take sthg for granted considérer que qqch va de soi, tenir qqch pour certain or établi ▶ **to take sb for granted** ne plus faire cas de qqn / he takes her for granted il la traite comme si elle n'existait pas / you take me too much for granted vous ne vous rendez pas compte de tout ce que je fais pour vous. ◆ n **1.** [money given] subvention f, allocation f ; [to student] bourse f **2.** [transfer - of property] cession f ; [- of land] concession f ; [permission] octroi m.

grant-aided adj [student] boursier ; [industry] subventionné ; [school] qui reçoit une subvention.

grant-maintained adj subventionné (par l'État).

granular ['grænjʊlər] adj [surface] granuleux, granulaire ; [structure] grenu.

granulated sugar ['grænjʊleɪtɪd-] n sucre m semoule.

granule ['grænju:l] n granule m.

grape [greɪp] n [fruit] grain m de raisin.

grapefruit ['greɪpfru:t] n pamplemousse m f.

grapevine ['greɪpvaɪn] n vigne f.

graph [grɑ:f] n **1.** [diagram] graphique m, courbe f **2.** LING graphie f.

graphic ['græfɪk] adj **1.** MATH graphique **2.** [vivid] imagé. ⬥ **graphics** ◆ n (U) [drawing] art m graphique. ◆ pl n MATH (utilisation f des) graphiques mpl ; [drawings] représentations fpl graphiques ; COMPUT infographie f.

graphically ['græfɪklɪ] adv **1.** MATH graphiquement **2.** [vividly] de façon très imagée.

graphical user interface n interface f graphique.

graphic artist n graphiste mf.

graphic arts pl n arts mpl graphiques.

graphic design n conception f graphique.

graphic designer n graphiste mf, maquettiste mf.

graphic equalizer n égaliseur m graphique.

graphic novel n bande f dessinée.

graphics card ['græfɪks-] n COMPUT carte f graphique.

graphite ['græfaɪt] ◆ n graphite m, plombagine f, mine f de plomb. ◆ adj en graphite.

graphology [græ'fɒlədʒɪ] n graphologie f.

graph paper n papier m quadrillé ; [in millimetres] papier m millimétré.

grapple ['græpl] ◆ n TECH grappin m. ◆ vt **1.** TECH saisir avec un grappin **2.** US [person] ▶ **to grapple sb** saisir qqn contre soi. ◆ vi **1.** [physically] ▶ **to grapple with sb** en venir aux mains avec qqn **2.** fig : to grapple with a problem être aux prises avec un problème.

grappling hook, grappling iron ['græplɪŋ-] n NAUT grappin m, crochet m ; [of balloon] ancre f.

grasp [grɑːsp] ◆ vt **1.** [physically] saisir ; [opportunity] saisir ; [power] se saisir de, s'emparer de **2.** [understand] saisir, comprendre. ◆ n **1.** [grip] (forte) poigne f ; [action of holding] prise f, étreinte f **2.** fig [reach] portée f **3.** [understanding] compréhension f **4.** [handle] poignée f. ❖ **grasp at** vt insep [attempt to seize] chercher à saisir, essayer de saisir ; [accept eagerly] saisir.

grasping ['grɑːspɪŋ] adj avare, avide.

grass [grɑːs] ◆ n **1.** [gen] herbe f ; [lawn] pelouse f, gazon m **2.** BOT ▶ **grasses** graminées fpl **3.** v inf [marijuana] herbe f **4.** 🇬🇧 v inf [informer] mouchard m, indic m. ◆ vt **1.** ▶ **to grass (over)** a) [field] enherber, mettre en pré b) [garden] gazonner, engazonner **2.** 🇺🇸 [animals] mettre au vert. ◆ vi 🇬🇧 v inf cafarder ▶ **to grass on sb** donner or vendre qqn.

grasshopper ['grɑːs,hɒpər] n sauterelle f, grillon m.

grassland ['grɑːslænd] n prairie f, pré m.

grass roots ◆ pl n POL ▶ **the grass roots** la base. ◆ comp POL ▶ **at (the) grass roots level** au niveau de la base.

grass snake n couleuvre f.

grassy ['grɑːsɪ] adj herbu, herbeux.

grate [greɪt] ◆ n [fireplace] foyer m, âtre m ; [for holding coal] grille f de foyer. ◆ vt **1.** CULIN râper **2.** [chalk, metal] faire grincer. ◆ vi **1.** [machine, metal] grincer **2.** fig : the baby's crying began to grate (on him) les pleurs du bébé ont commencé à l'agacer / his behaviour grates after a while son comportement est agaçant au bout d'un moment.

grateful ['greɪtful] adj reconnaissant ▶ **to be grateful towards** or **to sb for sthg** être reconnaissant envers qqn de qqch.

gratefully ['greɪtfulɪ] adv avec reconnaissance or gratitude.

grater ['greɪtər] n râpe f.

gratification [,grætɪfɪ'keɪʃn] n [state or action] satisfaction f, plaisir m ; PSYCHOL gratification f.

gratify ['grætɪfaɪ] vt **1.** [person] faire plaisir à, être agréable à **2.** [whim, wish] satisfaire.

gratifying ['grætɪfaɪɪŋ] adj [pleasant] agréable, plaisant ; [rewarding] gratifiant.

gratin n gratin m.

grating ['greɪtɪŋ] ◆ n grille f, grillage m. ◆ adj [irritating] agaçant, irritant, énervant ; [sound] grinçant, discordant ; [voice] discordant.

gratis ['grætɪs] ◆ adj gratuit. ◆ adv gratuitement.

gratitude ['grætɪtjuːd] n gratitude f, reconnaissance f.

gratuitous [grə'tjuːɪtəs] adj [unjustified] gratuit, sans motif, injustifié.

gratuitously [grə'tjuːɪtəslɪ] adv [without good reason] gratuitement, sans motif.

gratuity [grə'tjuːətɪ] n **1.** fml [tip] gratification f, pourboire m **2.** 🇬🇧 [payment to employee] prime f ; MIL prime f de démobilisation.

gravadlax ['grævədlæks] n CULIN saumon séché et mariné dans un mélange d'épices, de sel et de sucre.

grave[1] [greɪv] ◆ n [hole] fosse f ; [burial place] tombe f. ◆ adj [illness, situation] grave, sérieux.

grave[2] [grɑːv] ◆ n LING ▶ **grave (accent)** accent m grave. ◆ adj LING grave.

gravedigger ['greɪv,dɪgər] n fossoyeur m.

gravel ['grævl] (🇬🇧 pt & pp **gravelled**, cont **gravelling** ; 🇺🇸 pt & pp **graveled**, cont **graveling**) ◆ n gra-

vier m ; [finer] gravillon m ; MED gravelle f. ◆ comp ▶ **gravel path** chemin m de gravier. ◆ vt gravillonner, répandre du gravier sur.

gravelled 🇬🇧, **graveled** 🇺🇸 ['grævld] adj couvert de gravier.

gravelly ['grævəlɪ] adj **1.** [like or containing gravel] graveleux ; [road] de gravier ; [riverbed] caillouteux **2.** [voice] rauque, râpeux.

gravely ['greɪvlɪ] adv **1.** [speak] gravement, sérieusement **2.** [as intensifier - ill] gravement ; [- wounded] grièvement.

gravestone ['greɪvstəun] n pierre f tombale.

graveyard ['greɪvjɑːd] n lit & fig cimetière m.

gravitas ['grævɪtæs] n sérieux m.

gravitate ['grævɪteɪt] vi graviter.

gravitational [,grævɪ'teɪʃənl] adj gravitationnel, de gravitation.

gravity ['grævɪtɪ] n **1.** [seriousness] gravité f **2.** PHYS [force] pesanteur f ; [phenomenon] gravitation f.

gravy ['greɪvɪ] n **1.** CULIN sauce f (au jus de viande) **2.** 🇺🇸 v inf [easy money] bénef m.

gravy boat n saucière f.

gravy train n inf assiette f au beurre.

gray 🇺🇸 = **grey**.

graze [greɪz] ◆ vi [animals] brouter, paître, pâturer ; [humans] grignoter. ◆ vt **1.** [touch lightly] frôler, effleurer, raser **2.** [skin] érafler, écorcher **3.** [animals] faire paître ; [grass] brouter, paître ; [field] pâturer. ◆ n écorchure f, éraflure f.

grease [griːs] ◆ n [gen] graisse f ; AUTO [lubricant] graisse f, lubrifiant m ; [used lubricant] cambouis m ; [dirt] crasse f. ◆ vt [gen] graisser ; AUTO graisser, lubrifier.

greased lightning ['griːst-] n : like greased lightning inf à tout berzingue, à fond la caisse.

grease gun n (pistolet m) graisseur m, pompe f à graisse.

greasepaint ['griːspeɪnt] n THEAT fard m (gras).

greaseproof ['griːspruːf] adj 🇬🇧 imperméable à la graisse ▶ **greaseproof paper** CULIN papier m sulfurisé.

greasy ['griːsɪ] adj **1.** [food, substance] graisseux, gras (grasse) ; [tools] graisseux ; [cosmetics, hair, hands] gras (grasse) **2.** [pavement, road] gras (grasse), glissant **3.** [clothes - dirty] crasseux, poisseux ; [- covered in grease marks] taché de graisse, plein de graisse **4.** [obsequious] obséquieux.

greasy spoon n inf gargote f.

GR8 MESSAGING written abbr of **great**.

great [greɪt] (compar **greater**, superl **greatest**) ◆ adj **1.** [in size, scale] grand / he made a great effort to be nice il a fait un gros effort pour être agréable **2.** [in degree] : a great friend un grand ami / with great pleasure avec grand plaisir / to be in great pain souffrir (beaucoup) **3.** [in quantity] : a great number of un grand nombre de / a great crowd une grande or grosse foule, une foule nombreuse **4.** [important - person, event] grand / a great occasion une grande occasion **5.** [main] : the great hall la grande salle, la salle principale **6.** inf [term of approval] : she has a great voice elle a une voix magnifique / she's great! [nice person] elle est super !, je l'adore ! / what's that film like? — great! comment est ce film ? — génial ! / you look great tonight! [appearance] tu es magnifique ce soir ! **7.** [keen] : she's a great reader elle adore lire, elle lit beaucoup **8.** inf [good at or expert on] : he's great at languages il est très doué pour les langues. ◆ n : it's one of the all-time greats c'est un des plus grands classiques. ◆ adv [as intensifier] : a great big fish un énorme poisson.

great-aunt n grand-tante f.

Great Barrier Reef pr n ▶ **the Great Barrier Reef** la Grande Barrière.

Great Bear pr n ▶ **the Great Bear** la Grande Ourse.

Great Britain pr n Grande-Bretagne *f* / *in Great Britain* en Grande-Bretagne.

greatcoat ['greɪtkəʊt] n pardessus *m*, manteau *m* ; MIL manteau *m*, capote *f*.

Great Dane n danois *m*.

greater ['greɪtər] compar —→ **great**.

Greater London pr n le Grand Londres.

greater-than sign n signe *m* «plus grand que», signe *m* «supérieur à».

great-grandchild n arrière-petit-fils *m*, arrière-petite-fille *f*.

great-granddaughter n arrière-petite-fille *f*.

great-grandfather n arrière-grand-père *m*.

great-grandmother n arrière-grand-mère *f*.

great-grandparents pl n arrière-grands-parents *mpl*.

great-grandson n arrière-petit-fils *m*.

Great Lakes pl pr n ▶ **the Great Lakes** les Grands Lacs *mpl*.

greatly ['greɪtlɪ] adv très, beaucoup, fortement.

great-nephew n petit-neveu *m*.

greatness ['greɪtnɪs] n **1.** [size] grandeur *f*, énormité *f*, immensité *f* ; [intensity] intensité *f* **2.** [eminence] grandeur *f*, importance *f*.

great-niece n petite-nièce *f*.

great-uncle n grand-oncle *m*.

Great Wall of China pr n ▶ **the Great Wall of China** la Grande Muraille (de Chine).

Great War n ▶ **the Great War** la Grande Guerre, la guerre de 14 or de 14-18.

Grecian ['griːʃn] adj grec (grecque).

Greece [griːs] pr n Grèce *f* / *in Greece* en Grèce.

greed [griːd] n [for fame, power, wealth] avidité *f* ; [for food] gloutonnerie *f*.

greedily ['griːdɪlɪ] adv [gen] avidement ; [consume food] gloutonnement, voracement.

greediness ['griːdɪnɪs] = **greed**.

greedy ['griːdɪ] adj [for food] glouton, gourmand ; [for fame, power, wealth] avide.

Greek [griːk] ◆ n **1.** [person] Grec *m*, Grecque *f* **2.** LING grec *m*. ◆ adj grec (grecque) ▶ **the Greek Islands** les îles *fpl* grecques.

Greek salad n salade *f* grecque (*composée de tomates, concombre, oignons, feta et olives noires*).

green [griːn] ◆ adj **1.** [colour] vert ; [field, valley] vert, verdoyant ▶ **to go** or **to turn green a)** [tree] devenir vert, verdir **b)** [traffic light] passer au vert **c)** [person] devenir blême, blêmir ▶ **to be** or **to go green with envy** être vert de jalousie **2.** [unripe fruit] vert, pas mûr ; [undried timber] vert ; [meat] frais (fraîche) ; [bacon] non fumé **3.** [naive] naïf ; [inexperienced] inexpérimenté **4.** [ecological] écologique, vert. ◆ n **1.** [colour] vert *m* **2.** [grassy patch] pelouse *f*, gazon *m* **3.** GOLF green *m*. ◆ **Green** adj UK ECON & POL vert / *the Green party* le parti écologiste, les Verts *mpl*. ◆ **greens** pl n **1.** [vegetables] légumes *mpl* verts **2.** US [foliage] feuillage *m* (*dans un bouquet*). ◆ **Greens** pl n UK POL ▶ **the Greens** les Verts *mpl*, les écologistes *mpl*.

green audit n audit *m* vert.

greenback ['griːnbæk] n US inf dollar *m*.

green bean n haricot *m* vert.

green belt n ceinture *f* verte.

Green Beret n US inf marine *m* ▶ **the Green Berets** les bérets *mpl* verts.

green card n **1.** [insurance] carte *f* verte (*prouvant qu'un véhicule est assuré pour un voyage à l'étranger*) **2.** US [work permit] carte *f* de séjour.

greenery ['griːnərɪ] n verdure *f*.

greenfield site ['griːnfiːld-] n terrain non construit à l'extérieur d'une ville.

greenfinch ['griːnfɪntʃ] n verdier *m*.

green-fingered [-'fɪŋɡəd] adj UK qui a la main verte.

green fingers pl n UK ▶ **to have green fingers** avoir le pouce vert, avoir la main verte.

greenfly ['griːnflaɪ] (*pl* **greenfly** or **greenflies**) n puceron *m* (vert).

greengage ['griːnɡeɪdʒ] n reine-claude *f*.

greengrocer ['griːnˌɡrəʊsər] n UK marchand *m* de fruits et légumes.

greenhorn ['griːnhɔːn] n US inf blanc-bec *m*.

greenhouse ['griːnhaʊs] (*pl* [-haʊzɪz]) ◆ n serre *f*. ◆ comp ▶ **greenhouse plants** plantes *fpl* de serre ▶ **greenhouse gases** gaz *mpl* à effet de serre.

greenhouse effect n ▶ **the greenhouse effect** l'effet *m* de serre.

greening ['griːnɪŋ] n prise *f* de conscience écologique.

greenish ['griːnɪʃ] adj tirant sur le vert ; *pej* verdâtre.

greenkeeper ['griːnˌkiːpər] n *personne qui entretient les pelouses des terrains de sport*.

Greenland ['griːnlənd] pr n Groenland *m* / *in Greenland* au Groenland.

Greenlander ['griːnləndər] n Groenlandais *m*, -e *f*.

green light n *lit & fig* feu *m* vert.

green onion n US ciboule *f*, cive *f*.

green paper n POL document formulant des propositions destinées à orienter la politique gouvernementale.

green peas pl n petits pois *mpl*.

green pepper n poivron *m* vert.

green pound n ECON livre *f* verte.

green salad n salade *f* (verte).

green shoots pl n ECON [signs of recovery] premiers signes *mpl* de reprise.

greenskeeper ['griːnzˌkiːpər] n US *personne chargée de l'entretien d'un terrain de golf ou de bowling*.

green tax n taxe *f* verte.

green tea n thé *m* vert.

green thumb US = **green fingers**.

green-thumbed [-'θʌmd] US = **green-fingered**.

Greenwich Mean Time ['grenɪdʒ-] n heure *f* (du méridien) de Greenwich.

greet [griːt] vt [meet, welcome] saluer, accueillir.

greeter ['griːtər] n [male] employé qui accueille les clients ; [female] hôtesse *f*.

greeting ['griːtɪŋ] n salut *m*, salutation *f* ; [welcome] accueil *m*. ◆ **greetings** pl n [good wishes] compliments *mpl*, salutations *fpl*.

greetings card UK, **greeting card** US n carte *f* de vœux.

gregarious [grɪ'ɡeərɪəs] adj [animal, bird] grégaire ; [person] sociable.

gremlin ['gremlɪn] n inf & hum diablotin malfaisant que l'on dit responsable de défauts mécaniques ou d'erreurs typographiques.

Grenada [grə'neɪdə] pr n Grenade *f* / *in Grenada* à la Grenade.

grenade [grə'neɪd] n MIL grenade f ▶ **grenade launcher** lance-grenades m.

Grenadian [grə'neɪdɪən] ◆ n Grenadin m, -e f. ◆ adj grenadin.

grenadier [,grenə'dɪər] n [soldier] grenadier m.

grenadine ['grenədi:n] n grenadine f.

grew [gru:] pt —→ **grow**.

grey 🇬🇧, **gray** 🇺🇸 [greɪ] ◆ adj **1.** [colour, weather] gris **2.** [hair] gris, grisonnant ▶ **to go grey** grisonner **3.** [complexion] gris, blême **4.** [life, situation] morne. ◆ n **1.** [colour] gris m **2.** [horse] (cheval m) gris m. ◆ vi [hair] grisonner, devenir gris.

grey area n zone f d'incertitude or de flou.

grey cell n ANAT cellule f grise.

grey-haired adj aux cheveux gris, grisonnant.

Greyhound® pr n ▶ **Greyhound buses** réseau d'autocars couvrant tous les États-Unis.

greyhound ['greɪhaʊnd] n lévrier m, levrette f / **greyhound racing** course f de lévriers / **a greyhound (racing) track** un cynodrome.

greying 🇬🇧, **graying** 🇺🇸 ['greɪɪŋ] adj grisonnant.

grey matter n matière f grise.

greyscale 🇬🇧, **grayscale** 🇺🇸 ['greɪskeɪl] n COMPUT niveau m de gris.

grey squirrel n écureuil m gris, petit-gris m.

grid [grɪd] ◆ n **1.** [grating] grille f, grillage m **2.** [electrode] grille f ; ELEC réseau m **3.** [on chart, map] grille f ; [lines on map] quadrillage m **4.** 🇺🇸 AUTO zone quadrillée **5.** 🇺🇸 SPORT = **gridiron**. ◆ comp ▶ **grid pattern** : the city was built on a grid pattern la ville était construite en quadrillé or en damier.

griddle ['grɪdl] ◆ n [iron plate] plaque f en fonte ; [on top of stove] plaque f chauffante. ◆ vt cuire sur une plaque (à galette).

gridiron ['grɪd,aɪən] n **1.** CULIN gril m **2.** THEAT gril m **3.** 🇺🇸 [game] football m américain ; [pitch] terrain m de football.

gridline ['grɪdlaɪn] n COMPUT quadrillage m.

gridlock ['grɪdlɒk] n 🇺🇸 [traffic jam] embouteillage m ; fig blocage m.

gridlocked ['grɪdlɒkt] adj [roads] bloqué ; fig [situation, negotiations] bloqué.

grief [gri:f] n **1.** [sorrow] chagrin m, peine f, (grande) tristesse f **2.** [as interjection] ▶ **good grief!** mon Dieu !, ciel ! **3.** PHR **to come to grief a)** [person] avoir de graves ennuis **b)** [project, venture] échouer, tomber à l'eau.

grief-stricken adj accablé(e) de douleur.

grievance ['gri:vns] n **1.** [cause for complaint] grief m, sujet m de plainte ; [complaint] réclamation f, revendication f ▶ **grievance procedure** procédure permettant aux salariés de faire part de leurs revendications **2.** [grudge] ▶ **to nurse a grievance** entretenir or nourrir une rancune or un ressentiment **3.** [injustice] injustice f, tort m **4.** [discontent] mécontentement m.

grieve [gri:v] ◆ vt peiner, chagriner. ◆ vi [feel grief] avoir de la peine or du chagrin, être peiné ▶ **to grieve at** or **over** or **about sthg** avoir de la peine à cause de qqch ; [express grief] pleurer.

grieving ['gri:vɪŋ] ◆ adj [person] en deuil. ◆ n deuil m.

grievous ['gri:vəs] adj **1.** fml [causing pain] affreux, cruel, atroce **2.** liter [grave, serious] grave, sérieux **3.** LAW ▶ **grievous bodily harm** coups mpl et blessures fpl.

grievously ['gri:vəslɪ] adv fml gravement, sérieusement.

griffin ['grɪfɪn] n MYTH griffon m.

grill [grɪl] ◆ vt **1.** CULIN (faire) griller **2.** inf [interrogate] cuisiner. ◆ vi CULIN griller. ◆ n **1.** CULIN [device] gril m ; [dish] grillade f **2.** [grating] grille f, grillage m **3.** AUTO = **grille**.

grille [grɪl] n **1.** [grating] grille f, grillage m **2.** AUTO calandre f.

grilling ['grɪlɪŋ] n **1.** 🇺🇸 [of food] cuisson f sur le or au gril **2.** inf [interrogation] : **to give sb a grilling** cuisiner qqn.

grim [grɪm] adj **1.** [hard, stern] sévère ; [reality, necessity, truth] dur **2.** [gloomy] sinistre, lugubre **3.** [unpleasant] : his new film is pretty grim son nouveau film n'est pas terrible ; [unwell] patraque ; [depressed] déprimé, abattu.

grimace [grɪ'meɪs] ◆ n grimace f. ◆ vi [in disgust, pain] grimacer, faire la grimace ; [to amuse] faire des grimaces.

grime [graɪm] n (U) crasse f, saleté f.

grimly ['grɪmlɪ] adv **1.** [threateningly] d'un air menaçant ; [unhappily] d'un air mécontent **2.** [defend, struggle] avec acharnement ; [hold on] inflexiblement, fermement ; [with determination] d'un air résolu, fermement.

grimness ['grɪmnɪs] n **1.** [sternness] sévérité f, gravité f **2.** [of story] côté m sinistre or macabre ; [of prospects, situation] côté m difficile.

grimy ['graɪmɪ] adj sale, crasseux.

grin [grɪn] ◆ n grand sourire m. ◆ vi sourire.

grind [graɪnd] (pt & pp **ground** [graʊnd]) ◆ n **1.** [monotonous work] corvée f / the daily grind le train-train quotidien **2.** 🇺🇸 inf [hard worker] bûcheur m, -euse f, bosseur m, -euse f. ◆ vt **1.** [coffee, corn, pepper] moudre ; [stones] concasser ; 🇺🇸 [meat] hacher ; [into powder] pulvériser, réduire en poudre ; [crush] broyer, écraser **2.** [rub together] écraser l'un contre l'autre ▶ **to grind one's teeth** grincer des dents **3.** [polish - lenses] polir ; [- stones] polir, égriser ; [sharpen - knife] aiguiser or affûter (à la meule) **4.** [turn handle] tourner. ◆ vi **1.** [crush] : this pepper mill doesn't grind very well ce moulin à poivre ne moud pas très bien **2.** [noisily] grincer ▶ **to grind to a halt** / **to a standstill a)** [machine, vehicle] s'arrêter / s'immobiliser en grinçant **b)** [company, economy, production] s'immobiliser peu à peu, s'arrêter progressivement **3.** 🇺🇸 inf [work hard] bûcher or bosser (dur). ◆ **grind down** vt sep **1.** lit pulvériser, réduire en poudre ; [lens] meuler **2.** fig [oppress] opprimer, écraser. ◆ **grind out** vt sep **1.** [extinguish by grinding] : she ground out her cigarette in the ashtray elle a écrasé sa cigarette dans le cendrier **2.** fig [produce slowly] : he was grinding out a tune on the barrel-organ il jouait un air sur l'orgue de Barbarie. ◆ **grind up** vt sep pulvériser.

grinder ['graɪndər] n **1.** [tooth] molaire f **2.** [person - of minerals] broyeur m, -euse f ; [- of knives, blades, etc.] rémouleur m **3.** [machine - for crushing] moulin m, broyeur m ; [- for sharpening] affûteuse f, machine f à aiguiser.

grinding ['graɪndɪŋ] ◆ n [sound] grincement m. ◆ adj **1.** [sound] : a grinding noise un bruit grinçant **2.** [oppressive] : grinding poverty misère f écrasante ▶ **to come to a grinding halt a)** [machine] s'arrêter en grinçant **b)** [production, negotiations] s'enrayer brusquement.

grindingly ['graɪndɪŋlɪ] adv : grindingly boring d'un ennui mortel / grindingly slow d'une lenteur insupportable.

grindstone ['graɪndstəʊn] n meule f.

grinning ['grɪnɪŋ] adj [face, person] souriant.

grip [grɪp] (pt & pp **gripped**, cont **gripping**) ◆ n **1.** [strong hold] prise f, étreinte f ; [on racket] tenue f ; [of tyres on road] adhérence f **2.** [handclasp] poigne f **3.** inf [self-control] : he's losing his grip il perd les pédales / **get a grip (of** or **on yourself)!** secoue-toi un peu ! **4.** [understanding] : he has a good grip of the subject il connaît or domine bien son sujet **5.** [handle] poignée f **6.** CIN & THEAT machiniste mf **7.** dated [bag] sac m de voyage **8.** PHR **to come** or **to get to grips with a problem** s'attaquer à un problème ▸ **to come** or **to get to grips with the enemy** être confronté à l'ennemi, être aux prises avec l'ennemi. ◆ vt **1.** [grasp - rope, rail] empoigner, saisir **2.** [hold tightly] serrer, tenir serré **3.** [subj: tyres] adhérer / to grip the road [car] coller à la route **4.** [hold interest] passionner. ◆ vi [tyres] adhérer.

gripe [graɪp] ◆ n **1.** inf [complaint] ronchonnements mpl **2.** MED = **gripes.** ◆ vi inf [complain] ronchonner, rouspéter. ◈ **gripes** pl n MED coliques fpl.

griping ['graɪpɪŋ] n (U) inf ronchonnements mpl, rouspétance f.

gripping ['grɪpɪŋ] adj [story, play] captivant, passionnant, palpitant.

grisly ['grɪzlɪ] adj épouvantable, macabre, sinistre.

grist [grɪst] n blé m (à moudre).

gristle ['grɪsl] n (U) [cartilage] cartilage m, tendons mpl ; [in meat] nerfs mpl.

gristly ['grɪslɪ] adj pej nerveux, tendineux.

grit [grɪt] (pt & pp **gritted,** cont **gritting**) ◆ n **1.** [gravel] gravillon m **2.** [sand] sable m **3.** [for fowl] gravier m **4.** [dust] poussière f **5.** inf [courage] cran m. ◆ vt **1.** [road, steps] gravillonner, répandre du gravillon sur **2.** PHR **to grit one's teeth** serrer les dents. ◈ **grits** pl n US gruau m de maïs.

gritter ['grɪtər] n camion m de sablage.

gritty ['grɪtɪ] (compar **grittier,** superl **grittiest**) adj **1.** [road] couvert de gravier **2.** inf [person] qui a du cran **3.** [play, film] naturaliste.

grizzle ['grɪzl] vi UK inf [cry fretfully] pleurnicher, geindre.

grizzled ['grɪzld] adj [person, beard] grisonnant.

grizzly ['grɪzlɪ] (compar **grizzlier,** superl **grizzliest**) ◆ adj [greyish] grisâtre ; [hair] grisonnant. ◆ n = **grizzly bear.**

grizzly bear n grizzli m, grizzly m, ours m brun (des montagnes Rocheuses).

groan [grəʊn] ◆ n **1.** [of pain] gémissement m, plainte f **2.** [of disapproval] grognement m **3.** [complaint] ronchonnement m. ◆ vi **1.** [in pain] gémir **2.** [in disapproval] grogner **3.** [be weighed down by] gémir **4.** [complaint] ronchonner.

grocer ['grəʊsər] n UK épicier m / at the grocer's (shop) à l'épicerie, chez l'épicier.

grocery ['grəʊsərɪ] (pl **groceries**) n [shop] épicerie f. ◈ **groceries** pl n [provisions] épicerie f (U), provisions fpl.

grody ['grəʊdɪ] adj US inf dégueulasse.

groggily ['grɒgɪlɪ] adv inf **1.** [weakly] faiblement **2.** [unsteadily - from exhaustion, from blows] de manière chancelante or groggy.

groggy ['grɒgɪ] (compar **groggier,** superl **groggiest**) adj inf **1.** [weak] faible, affaibli **2.** [unsteady - from exhaustion] groggy (inv), vacillant, chancelant ; [- from blows] groggy (inv), sonné.

groin [grɔɪn] n **1.** ANAT aine f **2.** UK euph [testicles] bourses fpl **3.** ARCHIT arête f **4.** US = **groyne.**

groom [gruːm] ◆ n **1.** [for horses] palefrenier m, -ère f, valet m d'écurie **2.** = **bridegroom.** ◆ vt **1.** [clean - horse] panser ; [- dog] toiletter ; [- subj: monkeys, cats] / cats groom themselves les chats font leur toilette **2.** [prepare - candidate] préparer, former **3.** ▸ **to groom a child** [paedophile] manipuler un mineur à des fins sexuelles sur Internet.

grooming ['gruːmɪŋ] n **1.** [of person] toilette f ; [neat appearance] présentation f **2.** [of horse] pansage m ; [of dog] toilettage m **3.** [by paedophile] manipulation de mineurs à des fins sexuelles sur Internet.

groove [gruːv] ◆ n **1.** [for pulley, in column] cannelure f, gorge f ; [in folding knife] onglet m ; [in piston] gorge f ; [for sliding door] rainure f ; [on record] sillon m **2.** inf [rut] ▸ **to get into** or **to be stuck in a groove** s'encroûter **3.** MUS groove m **4.** ▸ **to be in the groove** [be up-to-date] être branché, être dans le coup. ◆ vt [make a groove] canneler, rainurer, rainer. ◆ vi **1.** US [enjoy oneself] s'éclater **2.** [dance] danser.

grooved [gruːvd] adj cannelé, rainé.

groovy ['gruːvɪ] (compar **groovier,** superl **grooviest**) inf adj **1.** [excellent] sensationnel, sensass, super **2.** [trendy] dans le vent.

grope [grəʊp] ◆ vi [seek - by touch] tâtonner, aller à l'aveuglette ; [- for answer] chercher ▸ **to grope (about** or **around) for sthg** chercher qqch à tâtons or à l'aveuglette. ◆ vt inf [sexually] tripoter, peloter.

gross [grəʊs] ◆ adj **1.** [vulgar, loutish - person] grossier, fruste ; [- joke] cru, grossier **2.** [flagrant - inefficiency] flagrant **3.** [fat] obèse, énorme **4.** [overall total] brut ▸ **gross income** [in accounts] produit m or revenu m brut ▸ **gross margin** marge f brute ▸ **gross profits** bénéfices mpl bruts **5.** inf [disgusting] dégueulasse. ◆ n **1.** (pl **grosses**) [whole amount] ▸ **the gross** le gros **2.** [twelve dozen] grosse f, douze douzaines fpl. ◆ vt COMM faire or obtenir une recette brute de. ◈ **gross out** vt sep US inf dégoûter, débecter v inf.

gross domestic product n produit m intérieur brut.

grossly ['grəʊslɪ] adv **1.** [coarsely] grossièrement **2.** [as intensifier] outre mesure, excessivement.

gross national product n produit m national brut.

grotesque [grəʊ'tesk] ◆ adj grotesque. ◆ n grotesque m.

grotesquely [grəʊ'tesklɪ] adv grotesquement, absurdement.

grotto ['grɒtəʊ] (pl **grottos** or **grottoes**) n grotte f.

grotty ['grɒtɪ] (compar **grottier,** superl **grottiest**) adj UK inf **1.** [unattractive] moche ; [unsatisfactory] nul **2.** [unwell] : to feel grotty ne pas se sentir bien, être mal fichu.

grouch [graʊtʃ] inf ◆ vi rouspéter, ronchonner, grogner ▸ **to grouch about sthg** rouspéter or ronchonner après qqch, grogner contre qqch. ◆ n rouspéteur m, -euse f.

grouchy ['graʊtʃɪ] (compar **grouchier,** superl **grouchiest**) adj inf grincheux, ronchon, grognon.

ground [graʊnd] ◆ pt & pp ⟶ **grind.** ◆ n **1.** [earth] terre f ; [surface] sol m / at ground level au niveau du sol / the children sat on the ground les enfants se sont assis par terre / above ground en surface / below ground sous terre / to burn sthg to the ground réduire qqch en cendres / to fall to the ground tomber par or à terre ▸ **to get off the ground** a) lit [aeroplane] décoller b) fig [project] démarrer ▸ **to suit sb down to the ground** : it suits him down to the ground ça lui va à merveille, ça lui convient parfaitement ▸ **to run a company into the ground** faire couler une entreprise **2.** (U) [land] terrain m ; [region] région f, coin m **3.** UK [piece of land] terrain m ; [stadium] stade m **4.** [area used for specific purpose] ▸ **training ground** terrain m d'entraînement or d'exercice **5.** MIL terrain m ▸ **to give** / **to lose ground** céder / perdre du terrain ▸ **to stand** or **to hold one's ground** tenir bon ▸ **to gain ground** a) [in battle] gagner du terrain b) [idea, concept] faire son chemin, progresser c) [news] se répandre **6.** (U) [area of reference] domaine m, champ m / his article covers a lot of ground dans son article, il aborde beaucoup de domaines **7.** [subject] terrain *m*, sujet *m* / *you're on dangerous ground* vous êtes sur un terrain glissant **8.** [background] fond *m* **9.** [of sea] fond *m* **10.** US ELEC terre *f*, masse *f*. ◆ comp au sol ▶ **ground crew** personnel *m* au sol ▶ **ground frost** gelée *f* blanche ▶ **ground staff** *personnel qui s'occupe de l'entretien d'un terrain de sport.* ◆ vt **1.** [base] fonder, baser / *my fears proved well grounded* mes craintes se sont révélées fondées, il s'est avéré que mes craintes étaient fondées **2.** [train] former / *the students are well grounded in computer sciences* les étudiants ont une bonne formation or de bonnes bases en informatique **3.** [plane, pilot] ▶ **to be grounded** être interdit de vol **4.** [ship] échouer **5.** US ELEC relier à la terre or à la masse **6.** *inf* [child] priver de sortie. ❖ **grounds** pl n **1.** [around house] parc *m*, domaine *m*; [around block of flats, hospital] terrain *m*; [more extensive] parc *m* **2.** [reason] motif *m*, raison *f*; [cause] cause *f*, raison *f*; [basis] base *f*, raison *f*; [pretext] raison *f*, prétexte *m* / *there are grounds for suspecting arson* il y a lieu de penser qu'il s'agit d'un incendie criminel / *he was excused on the grounds of poor health* il a été exempté en raison de sa mauvaise santé; LAW : *grounds for complaint* grief *m* / *grounds for divorce* motif *m* de divorce **3.** [of coffee] marc *m*.

> **Ground zero**
>
> Depuis les attentats du 11 septembre 2001, cette expression est venue s'appliquer au site de l'ancien **World Trade Center** sur l'île de Manhattan à New York. Elle tire son origine du jargon militaire, dans lequel elle désigne le point d'impact sur terre d'une éventuelle frappe nucléaire.

ground beef n US steak *m* haché.

ground-breaking adj révolutionnaire.

ground control n AERON contrôle *m* au sol.

ground cover n végétation *f* basse ▶ **ground cover plant** (plante *f*) couvre-sol *m inv.*

grounded ['graʊndɪd] adj ▶ **to be grounded** [emotionally stable] avoir les pieds sur terre.

ground floor n rez-de-chaussée *m*.

ground hog n marmotte *f* d'Amérique ▶ **Ground Hog Day** US le 2 février, jour où les marmottes sont censées avoir fini leur hibernation.

ground-in adj [dirt] incrusté.

grounding ['graʊndɪŋ] n **1.** [training] formation *f*; [knowledge] connaissances *fpl*, bases *fpl* **2.** [of plane] interdiction *f* de vol.

groundless ['graʊndlɪs] adj sans fondement, sans motif.

ground level n **1.** [ground floor] rez-de-chaussée *m* **2.** [lowest level in organization] base *f*.

groundnut ['graʊndnʌt] = **peanut.**

ground plan n **1.** [plan of ground floor] plan *m* au sol **2.** [plan of action] plan *m* d'action.

ground rent n redevance *f* foncière.

ground rule n procédure *f*, règle *f*.

groundsheet ['graʊndʃiːt] n tapis *m* de sol.

groundskeeper ['graʊnzkiːpər] n US préposé *m* à l'entretien d'un terrain de sport.

groundsman ['graʊndzmən] (*pl* **groundsmen** [-mən]) n gardien *m* de stade.

groundspeed ['graʊndspiːd] n AERON vitesse *f* au sol.

groundswell ['graʊndswel] n lame *f* de fond.

ground-to-air adj MIL [missile] sol-air *(inv).*

ground-to-ground adj MIL [missile] sol-sol *(inv).*

groundwork ['graʊndwɜːk] n *(U)* travail *m* préparatoire, canevas *m*.

group [gruːp] ◆ n **1.** [of people] groupe *m*; POL [party] groupement *m*; [literary] groupe *m*, cercle *m* **2.** [of objects] groupe *m*, ensemble *m*; [of mountains] massif *m* **3.** [in business] groupe *m* **4.** [blood] groupe *m* **5.** MUS groupe *m* **6.** LING groupe *m*, syntagme *m* **7.** MIL groupe *m*. ◆ comp [work] de groupe; [action, decision] collectif. ◆ vt **1.** [bring together] grouper, réunir; [put in groups] disposer en groupes **2.** [combine] combiner. ◆ vi se grouper, se regrouper.

group captain n colonel *m* de l'armée de l'air / *Group Captain Ross* le colonel Ross.

groupie ['gruːpɪ] n *inf* groupie *f*.

grouping ['gruːpɪŋ] n groupement *m*.

group leader n [on package tour] accompagnateur *m*, -trice *f*; [for group of children] moniteur *m*, -trice *f*.

group practice n MED cabinet *m* médical.

group therapy n thérapie *f* de groupe.

groupware ['gruːpweər] n COMPUT logiciel *m* de groupe, synergiciel *m*.

grouse [graʊs] ◆ n **1.** [bird] grouse *f*, lagopède *m* d'Écosse **2.** *inf* [grumble] rouspétance *f*; [complaint] grief *m* ▶ **to have a grouse about sthg** rouspéter contre qqch. ◆ comp ▶ **grouse moor** chasse *f* réservée (à la chasse à la grouse) ▶ **grouse shooting** chasse *f* à la grouse. ◆ vi *inf* rouspéter, râler.

grout [graʊt] ◆ n coulis *m* au ciment. ◆ vt jointoyer.

grove [grəʊv] n bosquet *m*.

grovel ['grɒvl] (UK *pt & pp* **grovelled**, *cont* **grovelling**; US *pt & pp* **groveled**, *cont* **groveling**) vi **1.** [act humbly] ramper, s'aplatir ▶ **to grovel to sb (for sthg)** s'aplatir devant qqn (pour obtenir qqch) **2.** [crawl on floor] se vautrer par terre.

grow [grəʊ] (*pt* **grew** [gruː], *pp* **grown** [grəʊn]) ◆ vi **1.** [plants] croître, pousser; [hair] pousser; [seeds] germer **2.** [person - in age, height] grandir **3.** [originate] : *this custom grew from* or *out of a pagan ceremony* cette coutume est née d'une or a pour origine une cérémonie païenne **4.** [increase] s'accroître, augmenter **5.** [become] devenir / *to grow old* devenir vieux, vieillir **6.** (with infinitive) [come gradually] : *I've grown to respect him* j'ai appris à le respecter / *to grow to like* / *to dislike* finir par aimer / détester. ◆ vt **1.** [crops, plants] cultiver **2.** [beard, hair] laisser pousser **3.** FIN [company] agrandir. ❖ **grow apart** vi [couple] s'éloigner l'un de l'autre. ❖ **grow away** vi : *they began to grow away from each other* ils ont commencé à s'éloigner l'un de l'autre *fig.* ❖ **grow back** vi [hair, nail] repousser. ❖ **grow into** vt insep **1.** [become] devenir (en grandissant) **2.** [clothes] : *he'll soon grow into those shoes* il pourra bientôt mettre ces chaussures, bientôt ces chaussures lui iront **3.** [become used to] : *to grow into a job* s'habituer à or s'adapter à un travail. ❖ **grow on** vt insep plaire de plus en plus à. ❖ **grow out** vi [perm, dye] disparaître. ❖ **grow out of** vt insep **1.** [clothes] : *he's grown out of most of his clothes* la plupart de ses vêtements ne lui vont plus, il ne rentre plus dans la plupart de ses vêtements **2.** [habit] perdre (avec le temps). ❖ **grow up** vi **1.** [person] grandir, devenir adulte **2.** [emotions, friendship] naître, se développer.

grow bag n *sac plastique rempli de terreau dans lequel on fait pousser une plante.*

grower ['grəʊəʳ] n **1.** [producer] producteur m, -trice f; [professional] cultivateur m, -trice f; [amateur gardener] amateur m de jardinage **2.** [plant, tree] : a slow grower une plante qui pousse lentement.

growing ['grəʊɪŋ] ◆ adj **1.** [plant] croissant, qui pousse; [child] grandissant, en cours de croissance **2.** [increasing - debt] qui augmente; [- amount, number] grandissant, qui augmente; [- friendship, impatience] grandissant. ◆ comp ▶ **wheat / potato growing region** région qui produit du blé / de la pomme de terre, région à blé / pommes de terre. ◆ n [of agricultural products] culture f.

growing pains pl n **1.** [of children] douleurs fpl de croissance **2.** [of business, project] difficultés fpl de croissance, problèmes mpl de départ.

growl [graʊl] ◆ vi [animal] grogner, gronder; [person] grogner, grommeler; [thunder] tonner, gronder; [stomach] gargouiller ▶ **to growl at sb** grogner contre qqn. ◆ vt [answer, instructions] grommeler, grogner. ◆ n grognement m, grondement m; [in stomach] gargouillement m, gargouillis m.

grown [grəʊn] ◆ pp ⟶ **grow.** ◆ adj **1.** [person] adulte **2.** [garden] : the garden is all grown over le jardin est tout envahi par les mauvaises herbes.

grown-up ◆ n adulte mf, grande personne f. ◆ adj adulte.

growth [grəʊθ] n **1.** (U) [development - of child, plant] croissance f; [- of friendship] développement m, croissance f; [- of organization] développement m **2.** (U) [increase - in numbers, amount] augmentation f, croissance f; [- of market, industry] croissance f, expansion f; [- of influence, knowledge] développement m, croissance f **3.** [of beard, hair, weeds] pousse f **4.** MED excroissance f, tumeur f, grosseur f.

growth area n secteur m en expansion or en croissance.

growth industry n industrie f en plein essor or de pointe.

growth market n marché m porteur or en croissance.

growth rate n taux m de croissance.

groyne 🇬🇧, **groin** 🇺🇸 [grɔɪn] n brise-lames m inv.

GRSM (abbr of Graduate of the Royal Schools of Music) n diplômé du conservatoire de musique britannique.

grub [grʌb] ◆ vi **1.** [animal] fouir **2.** [rummage] fouiller. ◆ n **1.** [insect] asticot m **2.** inf [food] bouffe f. ❖ **grub up** vt sep [bone] déterrer; [root] extirper; [plant] déraciner; [insects] déloger.

grubby ['grʌbɪ] adj sale, crasseux, malpropre.

grudge [grʌdʒ] ◆ n rancune f ▶ **to bear** or **to hold a grudge against sb** en vouloir à qqn, avoir de la rancune contre qqn. ◆ vt = begrudge.

grudging ['grʌdʒɪŋ] adj [compliment, praise] fait or donné à contrecœur; [agreement] réticent.

grudgingly ['grʌdʒɪŋlɪ] adv à contrecœur, avec réticence.

gruel [grʊəl] n bouillie f d'avoine.

gruelling 🇬🇧, **grueling** 🇺🇸 ['grʊəlɪŋ] adj [race] éreintant, épuisant; [punishment] sévère; [experience] très difficile, très dur.

gruesome ['gruːsəm] adj [sight] horrible; [discovery] macabre.

gruff [grʌf] adj **1.** [manner] brusque **2.** [speech, voice] bourru.

gruffly ['grʌflɪ] adv **1.** [of manner] avec brusquerie **2.** [of speech, voice] : to speak gruffly parler d'un ton bourru.

gruffness ['grʌfnɪs] n **1.** [of manner] brusquerie f **2.** [of speech, voice] ton m bourru.

grumble ['grʌmbl] ◆ vi **1.** [complain] grogner, grommeler / he's always grumbling about something il rouspète constamment contre quelque chose **2.** [thunder, artillery] gronder / my stomach kept grumbling loudly mon estomac n'arrêtait pas de gargouiller bruyamment. ◆ n **1.** [complaint] ronchonnement m, sujet m de plainte **2.** [of thunder, artillery] grondement m.

grumbling ['grʌmblɪŋ] ◆ adj grincheux, grognon / a grumbling stomach un estomac qui gargouille ▶ **grumbling appendix** MED appendicite f chronique. ◆ n (U) plaintes fpl, protestations fpl.

grump [grʌmp] n inf bougon m, -onne f, ronchon m, -onne f ▶ **to have the grumps** être de mauvais poil.

grumpily ['grʌmpɪlɪ] adv inf en ronchonnant, d'un ton or air ronchon.

grumpiness ['grʌmpɪnɪs] n inf mauvaise humeur f, maussaderie f, caractère m désagréable.

grumpy ['grʌmpɪ] adj inf ronchon, bougon.

grunge [grʌndʒ] n inf **1.** 🇺🇸 [dirt] crasse f **2.** [music, fashion] grunge m.

grungy ['grʌndʒɪ] adj inf **1.** 🇺🇸 [dirty] crasseux **2.** [style, fashion] grunge (inv).

grunt [grʌnt] ◆ vi grogner, pousser un grognement. ◆ vt [reply] grommeler, grogner. ◆ n [sound] grognement m.

grunt work n inf travail m fastidieux.

GSM (abbr of global system for mobile communication) n TELEC GSM m.

GSOH MESSAGING **1.** written abbr of good salary, own home **2.** written abbr of good sense of humour.

G-string n **1.** MUS (corde f de) sol m **2.** [item of clothing] string m.

GTG, G2G MESSAGING written abbr of got to go.

GTSY MESSAGING written abbr of glad to see you.

GU written abbr of Guam.

guac(h)amole [ˌgwɑːkəˈməʊlɪ] n (U) guacamole m, purée f d'avocat.

Guadeloupe [ˌgwɑːdəˈluːp] pr n Guadeloupe f / in Guadeloupe à la or en Guadeloupe.

Guam [gwɑːm] pr n Guam / in Guam à Guam.

guarantee [ˌgærənˈtiː] ◆ n **1.** COMM garantie f ▶ **to be under guarantee** être sous garantie **2.** LAW [pledge] caution f, garantie f, gage m **3.** [person] garant m, -e f ▶ **to act as guarantee** se porter garant **4.** [firm promise] garantie f. ◆ comp ▶ **guarantee agreement** garantie f. ◆ vt **1.** [goods] garantir **2.** [loan, cheque] garantir, cautionner **3.** [assure] certifier, assurer.

guarantor [ˌgærənˈtɔːʳ] n garant m, -e f, caution f ▶ **to stand guarantor for sb** se porter garant pour qqn.

guard [gɑːd] ◆ n **1.** [person] gardien m, garde m; [group] garde f ▶ **guard of honour** garde f d'honneur **2.** [watch] garde f ▶ **to be on guard (duty)** être de garde ▶ **to stand guard** monter la garde **3.** [supervision] garde f, surveillance f ▶ **to put a guard on sb / sthg** faire surveiller qqn / qqch **4.** [attention] garde f ▶ **on guard!** [in fencing] en garde! ▶ **to be on one's guard** être sur ses gardes **5.** 🇬🇧 RAIL chef m de train **6.** [protective device - on machine] dispositif m de sûreté or de protection; [- personal] protection f. ◆ vt **1.** [watch over - prisoner] garder **2.** [defend - fort, town] garder, défendre **3.** [protect - life, reputation] protéger **4.** GAMES garder. ❖ **Guards** pl n MIL [regiment] Garde f royale (britannique). ❖ **guard against** vt insep se protéger contre or de, se prémunir contre ▶ **to guard against doing sthg** se garder de faire qqch.

guard dog n chien m de garde.

guarded ['gɑːdɪd] adj prudent, circonspect, réservé.

guardedly ['gɑːdɪdlɪ] adv avec réserve, prudemment.

guardian ['gɑːdjən] n **1.** [gen] gardien m, -enne f ; [of museum] conservateur m, -trice f ▶ **the Guardian** PRESS *quotidien britannique de qualité, plutôt de gauche* **2.** LAW [of minor] tuteur m, -trice f. ⟶ **broadsheet**

guardian angel n ange m gardien.

guardianship ['gɑːdjənʃɪp] n **1.** [gen] garde f **2.** LAW tutelle f.

guardrail ['gɑːdreɪl] n **1.** [on ship] bastingage m, garde-corps m inv **2.** RAIL contre-rail m **3.** US [on road] barrière f de sécurité.

guardroom ['gɑːdrʊm] n **1.** MIL [for guards] corps m de garde **2.** [for prisoners] salle f de garde.

guardsman ['gɑːdzmən] (pl [-mən]) n UK MIL soldat m de la garde royale ; US soldat m de la garde nationale.

guard's van n UK fourgon m du chef de train.

Guatemala [,gwɑːtə'mɑːlə] pr n Guatemala m / **in Guatemala** au Guatemala.

Guatemalan [,gwɑːtə'mɑːlən] ◆ n Guatémaltèque mf. ◆ adj guatémaltèque.

guava ['gwɑːvə] n [tree] goyavier m ; [fruit] goyave f.

gubernatorial [,guːbənə'tɔːrɪəl] adj US de or du gouverneur ▶ **gubernatorial elections** élections des gouverneurs.

GUDLUK MESSAGING **written abbr of good luck.**

Guernsey ['gɜːnzɪ] ◆ pr n [island] Guernesey f / **in Guernsey** à Guernesey. ◆ n **1.** [cow] vache f de Guernesey **2.** [sweater] jersey m, tricot m.

guer(r)illa [gə'rɪlə] ◆ n guérillero m. ◆ comp ▶ **guerrilla band** or **group** guérila f, groupe m de guérilleros ▶ **guerrilla warfare** guérila f (combat).

guess [ges] ◆ n **1.** [at facts, figures] ▶ **to have** UK or **to take** US **a guess at sthg** (essayer de) deviner qqch **2.** [hypothesis] supposition f, conjecture f. ◆ vt **1.** [attempt to answer] deviner **2.** [imagine] croire, penser, supposer. ◆ vi deviner ▶ **to guess at sthg** deviner qqch.

guesstimate ['gestɪmət] n inf calcul m au pifomètre.

guesswork ['geswɜːk] n (U) conjecture f, hypothèse f ▶ **to do sthg by guesswork** faire qqch au hasard.

guest [gest] ◆ n **1.** [visitor - at home] invité m, -e f, hôte mf ; [at table] invité m, -e f, convive mf ▶ **guest of honour** invité d'honneur, invitée d'honneur **2.** [in hotel] client m, -e f ; [in boarding-house] pensionnaire mf. ◆ vi [appear as guest] être reçu comme invité.

guest book n livre m d'or.

guesthouse ['gesthaʊs] (pl [-haʊzɪz]) n pension f de famille.

guest list n liste f des invités.

guestroom ['gestrʊm] n chambre f d'amis.

guest speaker n conférencier m, -ère f (invité à parler par une organisation, une association).

guest star n invité-vedette m, invitée-vedette f.

guest worker n travailleur immigré m, travailleuse immigrée f.

guff [gʌf] n (U) inf bêtises fpl, idioties fpl.

guffaw [gʌ'fɔː] ◆ n gros éclat m de rire. ◆ vi rire bruyamment, s'esclaffer. ◆ vt : "of course!" he guffawed « bien sûr ! », s'esclaffa-t-il.

GUI (abbr of graphical user interface) n COMPUT interface f utilisateur graphique.

Guiana [gɪ'ɑːnə] pr n Guyane f ▶ **the Guianas** les Guyanes / **in Guiana** en Guyane ▶ **Dutch Guiana** Guyane hollandaise ▶ **French Guiana** Guyane française.

guidance ['gaɪdəns] n **1.** [advice] conseils mpl **2.** [instruction] direction f, conduite f ; [supervision] direction f, supervision f **3.** [information] information f **4.** AERON guidage m.

guidance counselor n US conseiller m, -ère f d'orientation.

guide [gaɪd] ◆ n **1.** [for tourists] guide mf **2.** [influence, direction] guide m, indication f **3.** [indication] indication f, idée f **4.** [manual] guide m, manuel m pratique **5.** UK [girl scout] ▶ **(Girl) Guide** éclaireuse f / she's **in the Guides** elle est éclaireuse **6.** [machine part] guide m. ◆ vt **1.** [show the way] guider, conduire / **to guide sb in / out** conduire qqn jusqu'à l'entrée / la sortie **2.** [instruct] diriger, conduire **3.** [advise] conseiller, guider, orienter **4.** AERON guider.

guidebook ['gaɪdbʊk] n guide m touristique (manuel).

guided missile n missile m téléguidé.

guide dog n chien m d'aveugle.

guided tour n visite f guidée.

guideline ['gaɪdlaɪn] n **1.** [for writing] ligne f **2.** [hint, principle] ligne f directrice, directives fpl.

guiding ['gaɪdɪŋ] ◆ adj [principle] directeur. ◆ n guidage m, conduite f.

guild [gɪld] n **1.** [professional] guilde f, corporation f **2.** [association] confrérie f, association f, club m ▶ **women's / church guild** cercle m féminin / paroissial.

guildhall ['gɪldhɔːl] n palais m des corporations ▶ **The Guildhall** l'hôtel de ville de la City de Londres.

guile [gaɪl] n (U) fml [trickery] fourberie f, tromperie f ; [cunning] ruse f, astuce f.

guileless ['gaɪllɪs] adj fml candide, ingénu.

guillemot ['gɪlɪmɒt] (pl **guillemot** or **guillemots**) n guillemot m.

guillotine ['gɪlə,tiːn] ◆ n **1.** [for executions] guillotine f **2.** [for paper] massicot m **3.** POL procédure parlementaire consistant à fixer des délais stricts pour l'examen de chaque partie d'un projet de loi. ◆ vt **1.** [person] guillotiner **2.** [paper] massicoter **3.** [discussion] clôturer.

guilt [gɪlt] n culpabilité f.

guilt-free adj non culpabilisant / guilt-free desserts des desserts que l'on peut manger sans se sentir coupable.

guiltily ['gɪltɪlɪ] adv d'un air coupable.

guilty ['gɪltɪ] (compar **guiltier**, super **guiltiest**) adj **1.** LAW coupable / guilty of murder coupable de meurtre ▶ **to plead guilty / not guilty** plaider coupable / non coupable **2.** fig coupable ▶ **to have a guilty conscience** avoir mauvaise conscience.

guinea ['gɪnɪ] n [money] guinée f (ancienne monnaie britannique).

Guinea ['gɪnɪ] pr n Guinée f / **in Guinea** en Guinée.

Guinea-Bissau [-bɪ'saʊ] pr n Guinée-Bissau f / **in Guinea-Bissau** en Guinée-Bissau.

guinea fowl (pl guinea fowl) n pintade f.

guinea pig n cochon m d'Inde, cobaye m ; [used in experiments] cobaye m.

guise [gaɪz] n [appearance] apparence f, aspect m ▶ **under** or **in the guise of** sous l'apparence de.

guitar [gɪ'tɑːr] n guitare f ▶ **guitar player** guitariste mf.

guitarist [gɪ'tɑːrɪst] n guitariste mf.

gulag ['guːlæg] n goulag m.

gulch [gʌltʃ] n US ravin m.

gulf [gʌlf] ◆ n **1.** [bay] golfe m ▶ **the Gulf of Mexico** le golfe du Mexique **2.** [chasm] gouffre m, abîme m **3.** GEOG ▶ **the Gulf** le golfe Persique. ◆ comp [country, oil] du Golfe ▶ **the Gulf War** la guerre du Golfe ▶ **Gulf War Syndrome** MED syndrome m de la guerre du Golfe.

Gulf States pl pr n ▸ **the Gulf States a)** [in US] les États du golfe du Mexique **b)** [round Persian Gulf] les États du Golfe.

Gulf Stream pr n ▸ **the Gulf Stream** le Gulf Stream.

gull [gʌl] n [bird] mouette f, goéland m.

gullet ['gʌlɪt] n [œsophagus] œsophage m ; [throat] gosier m.

gulley ['gʌlɪ] (pl gulleys) = **gully**.

gullibility [ˌgʌlə'bɪlətɪ] n crédulité f, naïveté f.

gullible ['gʌləbl] adj crédule, naïf.

gullibly ['gʌləblɪ] adv naïvement.

gully ['gʌlɪ] (pl gullies) n **1.** [valley] ravin m **2.** [drain] caniveau m, rigole f.

gulp [gʌlp] ◆ vt ▸ **to gulp (down) a)** [food] engloutir **b)** [drink] avaler à pleine gorge **c)** [air] avaler. ◆ vi [with emotion] avoir un serrement de gorge. ◆ n [act of gulping] : she swallowed it in one gulp elle l'a avalé d'un seul coup ; [with emotion] serrement m de gorge. ❖ **gulp back** vt sep avaler.

gum [gʌm] (pt & pp **gummed**, cont **gumming**) ◆ n **1.** ANAT gencive f **2.** [chewing gum] chewing-gum m **3.** [adhesive] gomme f, colle f **4.** BOT [substance] gomme f **5.** 🇺🇸 = **gumdrop**. ◆ vt **1.** [cover with gum] gommer **2.** [stick] coller. ◆ interj 🇺🇸 inf & dated ▸ **by gum!** nom d'un chien !, mince alors ! ❖ **gum up** vt sep inf [mechanism] bousiller ; [plan] ficher en l'air.

GUM (abbr of **genito-urinary medicine**) n médecine f génito-urinaire.

gumball ['gʌmbɔːl] n 🇺🇸 boule f de chewing-gum.

gumboil ['gʌmbɔɪl] n parulie f, abcès m gingival.

gumboot ['gʌmbuːt] n 🇺🇰 botte f de caoutchouc.

gumdrop ['gʌmdrɒp] n boule f de gomme.

gumption ['gʌmpʃn] n (U) inf **1.** 🇺🇰 [common sense] jugeote f **2.** [initiative] initiative f.

gumshield ['gʌmʃiːld] n protège-dents m inv.

gumshoe ['gʌmʃuː] 🇺🇸 v inf & dated n [detective] privé m.

gun [gʌn] (pt & pp **gunned**, cont **gunning**) ◆ n **1.** arme f à feu ; [pistol] pistolet m ; [revolver] revolver m ; [rifle] fusil m ; [cannon] canon m **2.** [hunter] fusil m **3.** inf [gunman] gangster m ▸ **hired gun** tueur m à gages **4.** [dispenser] pistolet m ▸ **paint gun** pistolet m à peinture. ◆ comp ▸ **gun law** loi f réglementant le port d'armes ▸ **gun lobby** lobby m favorable au port d'armes. ◆ vt AUTO ▸ **to gun the engine** accélérer. ❖ **gun down** vt sep abattre. ❖ **gun for** vt insep **1.** [look for] chercher **2.** [try hard for] faire des pieds et des mains pour obtenir.

gunboat ['gʌnbəʊt] n canonnière f.

gundog ['gʌndɒg] n chien m de chasse.

gunfight ['gʌnfaɪt] n fusillade f.

gunfire ['gʌnfaɪə] n (U) coups mpl de feu, fusillade f ; [of cannon] tir m d'artillerie.

gunge [gʌndʒ] n (U) inf substance f collante, amas m visqueux.

gung-ho [ˌgʌŋ'həʊ] adj tout feu tout flamme, enthousiaste.

gunk [gʌŋk] n (U) inf substance f visqueuse, amas m répugnant.

gun licence n permis m de port d'armes.

gunman ['gʌnmən] (pl gunmen [-mən]) n gangster m (armé) ; [terrorist] terroriste m (armé).

gunner ['gʌnə] n artilleur m, canonnier m.

gunpoint ['gʌnpɔɪnt] n ▸ **to have** or **to hold sb at gunpoint** menacer qqn d'un pistolet or d'un revolver or d'un fusil.

gunpowder ['gʌnˌpaʊdə] n poudre f à canon.

Gunpowder Plot n ▸ **the Gunpowder Plot** 🇺🇰 HIST la Conspiration des poudres.

🏛 **The Gunpowder Plot**

Complot catholique, conduit par Guy Fawkes, le 5 novembre 1605, pour faire sauter le Parlement britannique et tuer le roi protestant Jacques Iᵉʳ qui avait refusé d'instaurer la liberté de culte. Le complot fut déjoué et son instigateur exécuté. Cet événement est commémoré tous les ans par la **Guy Fawkes' Night**.

---

gunrunning ['gʌnˌrʌnɪŋ] n (U) trafic m d'armes.

gunshot ['gʌnʃɒt] n [shot] coup m de feu / a gunshot wound une blessure de or par balle.

gunsmith ['gʌnsmɪθ] n armurier m.

gurgle ['gɜːgl] ◆ vi [liquid] glouglouter, gargouiller ; [stream] murmurer ; [person - with delight] glousser, roucouler ; [baby] gazouiller. ◆ n [of liquid] glouglou m, gargouillis m ; [of stream] murmure m, gazouillement m ; [of laughter] gloussement m, roucoulement m ; [of baby] gazouillis.

gurney ['gɜːnɪ] n 🇺🇸 chariot m d'hôpital.

guru ['gʊruː] n gourou m.

gush [gʌʃ] ◆ vi **1.** [flow] jaillir **2.** [talk effusively] parler avec animation. ◆ n **1.** [of liquid, gas] jet m, flot m **2.** [of emotion] vague f, effusion f.

gushing ['gʌʃɪŋ] adj **1.** [liquid] jaillissant, bouillonnant **2.** [person] trop exubérant.

gusset ['gʌsɪt] n **1.** SEW soufflet m **2.** CONSTR gousset m.

gust [gʌst] ◆ n : a gust (of wind) un coup de vent, une rafale. ◆ vi [wind] souffler en bourrasques ; [rain] faire des bourrasques.

gusto ['gʌstəʊ] n délectation f, enthousiasme m.

gusty ['gʌstɪ] (compar gustier, superl gustiest) adj : a gusty wind un vent qui souffle en rafales, des rafales de vent.

gut [gʌt] ◆ n **1.** (usu pl) ANAT boyau m, intestin m ▸ **guts** intestins mpl, boyaux mpl, entrailles fpl ▸ **gut feeling** pressentiment m ▸ **gut reaction** réaction f instinctive or viscérale **2.** (usu pl) inf [of machine] intérieur m **3.** (U) [thread - for violins] corde f de boyau ; [-for rackets] boyau m. ◆ vt **1.** [fish, poultry, etc.] étriper, vider **2.** [building] ne laisser que les quatre murs de. ❖ **guts** ◆ n inf [glutton] morfal m, -e f. ◆ pl n ▸ **to have guts** avoir du cran or du cœur au ventre ▸ **to hate sb's guts** ne pas pouvoir blairer qqn.

gut-churning adj inf déchirant.

gut course n 🇺🇸 UNIV matière f lourde or difficile.

gutrot ['gʌtrɒt] n 🇺🇰 inf **1.** [drink] tord-boyaux m inv **2.** [stomach upset] mal m de bide.

gutsy ['gʌtsɪ] (compar gutsier, superl gutsiest) adj inf **1.** [courageous] qui a du cran **2.** [powerful - film, language, novel] qui a du punch, musclé.

gutted ['gʌtɪd] adj 🇺🇰 v inf ▸ **to be** or **to feel gutted** en être malade.

gutter ['gʌtə] ◆ n [on roof] gouttière f ; [in street] caniveau m, ruisseau m. ◆ vi [candle flame] vaciller, trembler.

guttering ['gʌtərɪŋ] n (U) [of roof] gouttières fpl.

gutter press n *pej* presse *f* de bas étage, presse *f* à scandale.

guttural ['gʌtərəl] ◆ adj guttural. ◆ n LING gutturale *f*.

gut-wrenching adj *inf* déchirant.

guv [gʌv], **guvnor** ['gʌvnər] n UK *inf* ▸ **the guv a)** [boss] le chef, le boss **b)** *dated* [father] le pater, le paternel.

guy [gaɪ] n **1.** *inf* [man] gars *m*, type *m* / *are you guys ready?* **a)** vous êtes prêts, les gars ? **b)** US [to both men and women] tout le monde est prêt ? **2.** UK [for bonfire] *effigie de Guy Fawkes* **3.** [for tent] corde *f* de tente.

Guyana [gaɪˈænə] pr n Guyana *m* / *in Guyana* au Guyana.

Guy Fawkes' Night [-ˈfɔːks-] pr n *fête célébrée le 5 novembre en commémoration de la Conspiration des poudres.*

🚩 **Guy Fawkes' Night**

Cette fête populaire a lieu chaque année le 5 novembre autour d'un feu de joie où brûle l'effigie (**the Guy**) de Guy Fawkes, instigateur de la Conspiration des poudres. Des feux d'artifice sont tirés.

guyline US ['gaɪlaɪn], **guy rope** n corde *f* de tente.

guzzle ['gʌzl] *inf* ◆ vt [food] bouffer, bâfrer ; [drink] siffler. ◆ vi [eat] s'empiffrer, se goinfrer ; [drink] boire trop vite.

GWP (abbr of global warming potential) n PRG *m*.

gym [dʒɪm] n [hall, building] gymnase *m* ; [activity] gymnastique *f*, gym *f*.

gymkhana [dʒɪmˈkɑːnə] n gymkhana *m*.

gymnasium [dʒɪmˈneɪzjəm] (*pl* **gymnasiums** *or* **gymnasia** [-zɪə]) n gymnase *m*.

gymnast ['dʒɪmnæst] n gymnaste *mf*.

gymnastic [dʒɪmˈnæstɪk] adj [exercises] de gymnastique ; [ability] de gymnaste.

gymnastics [dʒɪmˈnæstɪks] n *(U)* gymnastique *f*.

gym shoe n chaussure *f* de gymnastique or gym.

gymslip ['dʒɪmˌslɪp], **gym tunic** n [part of uniform] blouse *f* d'écolière.

gynaecology [ˌgaɪnəˈkɒlədʒɪ] UK = **gynecology**.

gynecological [ˌgaɪnəkəˈlɒdʒɪkl] adj gynécologique.

gynecologist [ˌgaɪnəˈkɒlədʒɪst] n gynécologue *mf*.

gynecology [ˌgaɪnəˈkɒlədʒɪ] n gynécologie *f*.

gyp [dʒɪp] (*pt & pp* **gypped**, *cont* **gypping**) *inf* n **1.** UK : *my knee's been giving me gyp* j'ai mal au genou **2.** US *inf* [cheat] ▸ *what a gyp!* quelle arnaque !

gypsophila [dʒɪpˈsɒfɪlə] n gypsophile *f*.

gypsum ['dʒɪpsəm] n gypse *m*.

gypsy ['dʒɪpsɪ] (*pl* **gypsies**) = **gipsy**.

gyrate [dʒaɪˈreɪt] vi tournoyer.

gyration [dʒaɪˈreɪʃn] n giration *f*.

gyroscope ['dʒaɪrəskəʊp] n gyroscope *m*.

h [eɪtʃ] (*pl* h's *or* hs), **H** (*pl* H's *or* Hs) n [letter] h *m*, H *m* ▶ **to drop one's h's** avaler ses h *(et révéler par là ses origines populaires)*. See also **f**.

h & c written abbr of **hot and cold (water)**.

ha [hɑː] interj [in triumph, sudden comprehension] ha !, ah ! ; [in contempt] peuh !

habeas corpus [ˌheɪbjəsˈkɔːpəs] n LAW habeas corpus *m* ▶ **to issue a writ of habeas corpus** délivrer un (acte d')habeas corpus.

🏛 The Habeas Corpus Act

Ordre écrit, datant de 1679, autorisant tout individu arrêté à demander à un juge ou à un tribunal d'examiner le caractère légal de son arrestation. Complété ultérieurement par d'autres lois (en 1816 et en 1960), cet ordre est toujours en vigueur en Grande-Bretagne et dans tous les pays soumis à la **Common Law** (Écosse exceptée). Il a également été intégré à la Constitution américaine.

---

haberdashery [ˈhæbədæʃərɪ] n **1.** UK [draper's] mercerie *f* **2.** US [shirtmaker's] marchand *m*, -e *f* de vêtements d'hommes *(en particulier de gants et de chapeaux)*.

habit [ˈhæbɪt] n **1.** [custom] habitude *f* ▶ **to be in / to get into the habit of doing sthg** avoir / prendre l'habitude de faire qqch ▶ **to make a habit of sthg / of doing sthg** prendre l'habitude de qqch / de faire qqch **2.** inf [drug dependency] ▶ **to have a habit** être accro *v inf* ▶ **to kick the habit** [drugs, tobacco] décrocher **3.** [dress - of monk, nun] habit *m* ; [- for riding] tenue *f* de cheval.

habitable [ˈhæbɪtəbl] adj habitable.

habitat [ˈhæbɪtæt] n habitat *m*.

habitation [ˌhæbɪˈteɪʃn] n **1.** [occupation] habitation *f* **2.** [place] habitation *f*, résidence *f*, demeure *f*.

habit-forming [-ˌfɔːmɪŋ] adj [drug] qui crée une accoutumance ou une dépendance.

habitual [həˈbɪtʃʊəl] adj [customary - generosity, lateness, good humour] habituel, accoutumé ; [- liar, drinker] invétéré ▶ **habitual offender** LAW récidiviste *mf*.

habitually [həˈbɪtʃʊəlɪ] adv habituellement, ordinairement.

habituate [həˈbɪtʃʊeɪt] vt *fml* ▶ **to habituate o.s. / sb to sthg** s'habituer / habituer qqn à qqch.

hack [hæk] ◆ n **1.** [sharp blow] coup *m* violent ; [kick] coup *m* de pied **2.** [cut] entaille *f* **3.** *pej* [writer] écrivaillon *m* ; [politician] politicard *m* **4.** [horse for riding] cheval *m* de selle ; [horse for hire] cheval *m* de louage ; [old horse, nag] rosse *f*, carne *f* **5.** [ride] ▶ **to go for a hack** aller faire une promenade à cheval **6.** [cough] toux *f* sèche. ◆ comp ▶ **hack writer** écrivaillon *m*, écrivain *m* médiocre ▶ **hack writing** travail *m* d'écrivaillon. ◆ vt **1.** [cut] taillader, tailler **2.** [kick - ball] donner un coup de pied sec dans **3.** COMPUT ▶ **to hack one's way into a system** entrer dans un système par effraction **4.** inf *I can't hack it* [can't cope] je n'en peux plus, je craque. ◆ vi **1.** [cut] donner des coups de couteau *(de hache, etc.)* ▶ **to hack (away) at sthg** taillader qqch **2.** [kick] ▶ **to hack at sb's shins** donner des coups de pied dans les tibias à qqn **3.** COMPUT ▶ **to hack into a system** entrer dans un système par effraction **4.** [on horseback] aller à cheval ▶ **to go hacking** aller faire une promenade à cheval. ◆ **hack down** vt sep [tree] abattre à coups de hache ; [person] massacrer à coups de couteau *(de hache, etc.)*. ◆ **hack off** vt sep [branch, sb's head] couper. ◆ **hack through** vt insep ▶ **to hack through sthg** se frayer un chemin dans qqch à coups de hache. ◆ **hack up** vt sep [meat, wood] tailler *or* couper en menus morceaux ; [body, victim] mettre en pièces, découper en morceaux.

hacker [ˈhækə] n COMPUT [enthusiast] mordu *m*, -e *f* de l'informatique ; [pirate] pirate *m* informatique.

hackie [ˈhækɪ] US inf chauffeur *m* de taxi.

hacking [ˈhækɪŋ] ◆ n *(U)* **1.** [in football, rugby, etc.] coups *mpl* de pied dans les tibias **2.** COMPUT piratage *m (informatique)*. ◆ adj ▶ **hacking cough** toux *f* sèche.

hacking jacket n veste *f* de cheval.

hackles [ˈhæklz] pl n [of dog] poils *mpl* du cou.

hackney carriage [ˈhæknɪ-] n **1.** [horse-drawn] fiacre *m* **2.** *fml* [taxi] taxi officiellement agréé.

hackneyed [ˈhæknɪd] adj [subject] réchauffé, rebattu ; [turn of phrase] banal, commun.

hacksaw [ˈhæksɔː] n scie *f* à métaux.

had (weak form [həd], strong form [hæd]) pt & pp — **have**.

haddock [ˈhædək] n aiglefin *m*, églefin *m* ; [smoked] haddock *m*.

hadn't [ˈhædnt] abbr of **had not**.

haematite UK, **hematite** US [ˈhiːmətaɪt] n hématite *f*.

haematology UK, **hematology** US [ˌhiːməˈtɒlədʒɪ] n hématologie *f*.

haemoglobin UK, **hemoglobin** US [ˌhiːməˈɡləʊbɪn] n hémoglobine *f*.

haemophilia UK, **hemophilia** US [ˌhiːməˈfɪlɪə] n hémophilie *f*.

haemophiliac UK, **hemophiliac** US [ˌhiːməˈfɪlɪæk] n hémophile *mf*.

haemorrhage 🇬🇧, **hemorrhage** 🇺🇸 ['hemərɪdʒ] ◆ n hémorragie f. ◆ vi faire une hémorragie.

haemorrhoids 🇬🇧, **hemorrhoids** 🇺🇸 ['hemərɔɪdz] pl n hémorroïdes fpl.

hag [hæg] n [witch] sorcière f ; pej [old woman] vieille sorcière f, vieille chouette f ; [unpleasant woman] harpie f.

haggard ['hægəd] adj ▶ **to be** or **look haggard** avoir les traits tirés.

haggis ['hægɪs] n plat typique écossais fait d'une panse de brebis farcie.

haggle ['hægl] ◆ vi **1.** [bargain] marchander ▶ **to haggle over the price** marchander sur le prix **2.** [argue over details] chicaner, chipoter ▶ **to haggle over** or **about sthg** chicaner or chipoter sur qqch. ◆ n : after a long haggle over the price après un long marchandage sur le prix.

haggling ['hæglɪŋ] n (U) **1.** [over price] marchandage m **2.** [about details, wording] chicanerie f, chipotage m.

HAGN MESSAGING written abbr of **have a good night**.

Hague [heɪg] pr n ▶ **The Hague** La Haye.

hail [heɪl] ◆ n METEOR grêle f ; fig [of stones] grêle f, pluie f ; [of abuse] avalanche f, déluge m ; [of blows] grêle f. ◆ vi METEOR grêler. ◆ vt **1.** [call to - taxi, ship, person] héler **2.** [greet - person] acclamer, saluer **3.** [acclaim - person, new product, invention, etc.] acclamer, saluer. ◆ interj arch salut à vous or toi. ◆ **hail down** vi [blows, stones, etc.] pleuvoir. ◆ **hail from** vt insep [ship] être en provenance de ; [person] venir de, être originaire de.

Hail Mary n RELIG [prayer] Je vous salue Marie m inv, Ave (Maria) m inv.

hailstone ['heɪlstəʊn] n grêlon m.

hailstorm ['heɪlstɔːm] n averse f de grêle.

hair [heər] ◆ n **1.** (U) [on person's head] cheveux mpl ▶ **to get** or **to have one's hair cut** se faire couper les cheveux ▶ **to get one's hair done** se faire coiffer **2.** [single hair - on person's head] cheveu m ; [- on person's or animal's face or body] poil m **3.** (U) [on body, face] poils mpl ; [on animal] poils mpl ▶ **hair removal** dépilation f. ◆ comp **1.** [cream, conditioner, lotion] capillaire, pour les cheveux **2.** [colour] de cheveux **3.** [mattress] de crin.

hairball ['heəbɔːl] n **1.** [of cat's fur] boule f de poils **2.** 🇺🇸 fig [messy situation] ▶ **it's a hairball** c'est vraiment un sac de nœuds.

hairband ['heəbænd] n bandeau m.

hairbrush ['heəbrʌʃ] n brosse f à cheveux.

haircare ['heəkeər] n soin m du cheveu ▶ **haircare products** produits mpl de soin pour les cheveux.

hairclip ['heəklɪp] n barrette f.

hair conditioner n après-shampooing m.

haircut ['heəkʌt] n coupe f (de cheveux).

hairdo ['heəduː] n inf coiffure f.

hairdresser ['heə,dresər] n [shop] salon m de coiffure / to go to the hairdresser's aller chez le coiffeur.

hairdressing ['heə,dresɪŋ] n [skill] coiffure f ▶ **hairdressing salon** salon m de coiffure.

hair drier, hair dryer n [hand-held] sèche-cheveux m inv, séchoir m ; [over the head] casque m.

-haired [heəd] in comp ▶ **long / short-haired a)** [person] aux cheveux longs / courts **b)** [animal] à poil(s) long(s) / court(s) ▶ **wire-haired** [dog] à poils durs.

hair gel n gel m pour les cheveux.

hairgrip ['heəgrɪp] n 🇬🇧 pince f à cheveux.

hair lacquer n laque f (pour les cheveux).

hairless ['heəlɪs] adj [head] chauve, sans cheveux ; [face] glabre ; [body] peu poilu ; [animal] sans poils ; [leaf] glabre.

hairline ['heəlaɪn] ◆ n [of the hair] naissance f des cheveux. ◆ comp ▶ **hairline crack** fêlure f ▶ **hairline fracture** MED fêlure f.

hairnet ['heənet] n résille f, filet m à cheveux.

hairpiece ['heəpiːs] n [toupee] perruque f (pour hommes) ; [extra hair] postiche m.

hairpin ['heəpɪn] n **1.** [for hair] épingle f à cheveux **2.** ▶ **hairpin (bend)(turn)** virage m en épingle à cheveux.

hair-raising [-,reɪzɪŋ] adj inf [adventure, experience, story, account] à faire dresser les cheveux sur la tête, effrayant, terrifiant ; [prices, expenses] affolant, exorbitant.

hair remover n crème f dépilatoire.

hair restorer n produit m pour la repousse des cheveux.

hair's breadth n : we came within a hair's breadth of going bankrupt / of winning first prize nous avons été à deux doigts de la faillite / de gagner le premier prix.

hair slide n 🇬🇧 barrette f.

hairsplitting ['heə,splɪtɪŋ] ◆ adj : that's a hairsplitting argument or distinction c'est de la chicanerie, c'est couper les cheveux en quatre. ◆ n (U) chicanerie f, pinaillage m.

hair spray n laque f or spray m (pour les cheveux).

hairstyle ['heəstaɪl] n coiffure f.

hairstylist ['heə,staɪlɪst] n styliste mf en coiffure.

hair wax n cire f pour les cheveux.

hairy ['heərɪ] (compar hairier, superl hairiest) adj **1.** [arms, chest] poilu, velu ; [person, animal] poilu ; [stalk of plant] velu **2.** inf [frightening] à faire dresser les cheveux sur la tête ; [difficult, daunting] qui craint.

Haiti ['heɪtɪ] pr n Haïti / in Haiti à Haïti.

Haitian ['heɪʃn] ◆ adj haïtien. ◆ n Haïtien m, -enne f.

HAK (written abbr of **hugs and kisses**) MESSAGING biz.

hake [heɪk] n merlu m, colin m.

halal [həˈlɑːl] ◆ n [meat] viande f halal. ◆ adj halal.

halcyon ['hælsɪən] adj ▶ **those halcyon days** liter ces temps heureux.

hale [heɪl] adj ▶ **hale and hearty** en pleine santé.

half [🇬🇧 hɑːf 🇺🇸 hæf] (pl **halves** [🇬🇧 hɑːvz 🇺🇸 hævz]) ◆ n **1.** moitié f ; [of standard measured amount] demi m, -e f ; [of ticket, coupon] souche f ▶ **to cut / to break sthg in half** couper / casser qqch en deux / it cuts the journey time in half cela réduit de moitié la durée du voyage / three and a half pieces / years trois morceaux / ans et demi / bigger by half 🇬🇧 plus grand de moitié, moitié plus grand / two halves make a whole deux moitiés or demis font un tout ▶ **to go halves with sb** partager avec qqn / they don't do things by halves ils ne font pas les choses à moitié / he always was too clever by half 🇬🇧 il a toujours été un peu trop malin / that was a walk and a half! inf c'était une sacrée promenade ! ▶ **and that's not the half of it** inf et ce n'est que le début ▶ **my better** or **other half** hum ma (chère) moitié ▶ **to see how the other half lives** voir comment on vit de l'autre côté de la barrière, voir comment vivent les autres **2.** [period of sports match] mi-temps f inv **3.** 🇬🇧 [half pint of beer] demi m (de bière). ◆ pron : leave half of it for me laisse-m'en la moitié / half of us were students la moitié d'entre nous étaient des étudiants. ◆ adj : a half chicken un demi-poulet / at half speed au ralenti / to travel half fare voyager à demi-tarif. ◆ predet : half the time he seems to be asleep on a l'impression qu'il est endormi la moitié du temps / half a minute! inf une (petite) minute ! / he's not half the man he used to be il n'est plus que l'ombre de lui-même ▶ **to have half a mind to do sthg** inf avoir bien envie de faire qqch. ◆ adv **1.** [finished, asleep, dressed] à moitié ; [full, empty, blind] à moitié, à demi / *to be half full of sthg* être à moitié rempli de qqch / *to be half English and half French* être moitié anglais moitié français / *I half think that...* je suis tenté de penser que... **2.** 🇬🇧 *inf* [as intensifier] : *it's not half cold today!* il fait rudement *or* sacrément froid aujourd'hui ! / *he didn't half yell* il a hurlé comme un fou / *did you complain? — I didn't half!* *or* *not half!* est-ce que vous vous êtes plaint ? — et comment ! *or* pas qu'un peu ! **3.** [time] : *it's half past two* 🇬🇧, *it's half two* il est deux heures et demie **4. to earn half as much as sb** gagner moitié moins que qqn ▸ **to be half as big again (as sb / sthg)** être moitié plus grand (que qqn / qqch).

halfback ['hɑːfbæk] n SPORT demi *m*.

half-baked [-'beɪkt] adj *inf & fig* [scheme, proposal] qui ne tient pas debout ; [person] niais.

half board 🇬🇧 ◆ n demi-pension *f*. ◆ adv en demi-pension.

half-bottle n demi-bouteille *f*.

half-breed ◆ n **1.** [animal] hybride *m* ; [horse] cheval *m* demi-sang **2.** *dated & offens* [person] métis *m*, -isse *f*. ◆ adj **1.** [animal] hybride ; [horse] demi-sang **2.** *dated & offens* [person] métis.

half-brother n demi-frère *m*.

half-caste *dated & offens* ◆ n [person] métis *m*, -isse *f*. ◆ adj métis.

half cock n ▸ **to go off at half cock** [plan] avorter.

half-cut adj 🇬🇧 *inf* [drunk] bourré, pété, fait.

half-day ◆ n [at school, work] demi-journée *f*. ◆ adj : *a half-day holiday* une demi-journée de congé ▸ **half-day closing** demi-journée *f* de fermeture.

half-dozen n demi-douzaine *f* / *a half-dozen eggs* une demi-douzaine d'œufs.

half-eaten adj à moitié mangé.

half-full adj à moitié *or* à demi plein.

half-hearted adj [attempt, attitude] qui manque d'enthousiasme *or* de conviction, timide, hésitant ; [acceptance] tiède, qui manque d'enthousiasme / *he was very half-hearted about it* il était vraiment peu enthousiaste à ce propos.

half-heartedly [-'hɑːtɪdlɪ] adv [accept, agree, say] sans enthousiasme *or* conviction, du bout des lèvres.

half-hour ◆ n [period] demi-heure *f* / *on the half-hour* à la demie. ◆ comp : *at half-hour intervals* toutes les demi-heures.

half-hourly adj & adv toutes les demi-heures.

half-joking adj mi-figue, mi-raisin.

half-jokingly adv d'un air mi-figue, mi-raisin.

half-length adj [portrait] en buste.

half-light n demi-jour *m*.

half-marathon n semi-marathon *m*.

half-mast n ▸ **at half-mast** *hum* a) [flag] en berne b) [trousers] arrivant à mi-mollet.

half measure n demi-mesure *f*.

half-moon n demi-lune *f* ; [on fingernail] lunule *f*.

half-naked adj à moitié nu.

half-note n 🇺🇸 [minim] blanche *f*.

half-open ◆ adj [eyes, door, window] entrouvert. ◆ vt [eyes, door, window] entrouvrir.

halfpenny ['heɪpnɪ] (*pl* **halfpennies**) 🇬🇧 *dated* ◆ n demi-penny *m*. ◆ comp d'un demi-penny.

half-pint ◆ n [measurement] ≃ quart *m* de litre / *I'll just have a half-pint* [of beer] je prendrai juste un demi. ◆ comp ▸ **a half-pint glass** ≃ un verre de 25 cl.

half-price ◆ n demi-tarif *m* / *these goods are going at half-price* ces produits sont vendus à moitié prix. ◆ adj

[goods] à moitié prix ; [ticket] (à) demi-tarif. ◆ adv : *children get in half-price* les enfants payent demi-tarif / *I got it half-price* [purchase] je l'ai eu à moitié prix.

half-shut adj [eyes, door, window] mi-clos, à moitié fermé.

half-sister n demi-sœur *f*.

half step n 🇺🇸 MUS demi-ton *m*.

half term n 🇬🇧 SCH congé scolaire en milieu de trimestre. ⬥ **half-term** adj ▸ **half-term holiday** petites vacances *fpl*.

half-time ◆ n **1.** SPORT mi-temps *f inv* **2.** [in work] mi-temps *m*. ◆ comp SPORT [whistle] de la mi-temps ; [score] à la mi-temps.

half-truth n demi-vérité *f*.

halfway [hɑːf'weɪ] ◆ adv **1.** [between two places] à mi-chemin / *it's halfway between Rennes and Cherbourg* c'est à mi-chemin entre Rennes et Cherbourg / *we had got halfway to Manchester* nous étions arrivés à mi-chemin de Manchester / *we had climbed halfway up the mountain* nous avions escaladé la moitié de la montagne / *halfway through the programme / film* à la moitié de l'émission / du film / *we're almost halfway there* a) [in travelling, walking, etc.] nous sommes presque à mi-chemin, nous avons fait presque la moitié du chemin b) [in work, negotiations] nous sommes presque à mi-chemin **2.** *inf* [more or less] : *a halfway decent salary* un salaire à peu près décent. ◆ comp ▸ **halfway stage** : *work has reached the halfway stage* le travail est à mi-chemin ▸ **halfway point** : *at the halfway point of his career* au milieu de sa carrière ▸ **halfway mark** [in race] : *they're at the halfway mark* ils sont à mi-course ▸ **halfway line** SPORT ligne *f* médiane.

halfway house n **1.** [on journey] (auberge *f*) relais *m* **2.** [for rehabilitation] centre *m* de réadaptation *(pour anciens détenus, malades mentaux, drogués, etc.)* **3.** *fig* [halfway stage] (stade *m* de) transition *f* ; [compromise] compromis *m*.

half-wit n *inf* imbécile.

half-yearly ◆ adj semestriel. ◆ adv tous les six mois.

halibut ['hælɪbət] n flétan *m*.

halitosis [,hælɪ'təʊsɪs] n *(U)* mauvaise haleine *f* ; MED halitose *f*.

hall [hɔːl] n **1.** [of house] entrée *f*, vestibule *m* ; [of hotel, very large house] hall *m* ; [corridor] couloir *m* **2.** [large room] salle *f* **3.** [building] ▸ **hall of residence** 🇬🇧 UNIV résidence *f* universitaire / *I'm living in hall* 🇬🇧 UNIV je loge à l'université ▸ **hall of fame** *fig* panthéon *m* **4.** [mansion, large country house] château *m*, manoir *m*.

hallal [hə'lɑːl] = **halal**.

halleluja(h) [,hælɪ'luːjə] ◆ interj alléluia. ◆ n alléluia *m*.

hallmark ['hɔːlmɑːk] ◆ n **1.** *lit* poinçon *m* **2.** *fig* marque *f*. ◆ vt [precious metals] poinçonner.

hallo [hə'ləʊ] interj = **hello**.

halloumi [hæ'luːmɪ] n CULIN halloumi *m*, haloumi *m*.

hallowed ['hæləʊd] adj saint, béni.

Halloween, Hallowe'en [,hæləʊ'iːn] pr n Halloween *f*.

hallstand ['hɔːlstænd] n portemanteau *m*.

hallucinate [hə'luːsɪneɪt] vi avoir des hallucinations.

hallucination [,həluːsɪ'neɪʃn] n hallucination *f*.

hallucinatory [hə'luːsɪnətrɪ] adj hallucinatoire.

hallucinogenic [hə,luːsɪnə'dʒenɪk] adj hallucinogène.

hallway ['hɔːlweɪ] n [of house] vestibule *m*, entrée *f* ; [corridor] couloir *m*.

halo ['heɪləʊ] (*pl* **halos** *or* **haloes**) n [of saint] auréole *f*, nimbe *m* ; ASTRON halo *m* ; *fig* auréole *f*.

halo effect n effet *m* de halo.

halogen ['hælədʒen] n CHEM halogène m.

halt [hɔːlt] ◆ n **1.** [stop] halte f ▸ **to bring to a halt a)** [vehicle] arrêter, immobiliser **b)** [horse] arrêter **c)** [production, project] interrompre ▸ **to call a halt to sthg** mettre fin à qqch ▸ **to come to a halt** [vehicle, horse] s'arrêter, s'immobiliser **2.** UK [small railway station] halte f. ◆ vi [stop] s'arrêter ▸ **halt!** (**, who goes there?**) MIL halte ! (, qui va là ?). ◆ vt arrêter ; [troops] faire faire halte à, stopper ; [production - temporarily] interrompre, arrêter ; [- for good] arrêter définitivement.

halter ['hɔːltər] n **1.** [for horse] licou m, collier m **2.** [on women's clothing] = **halter neck**.

halter neck n : *a dress with a halter neck* une robe dos nu or bain de soleil. ❖ **halter-neck** comp [dress] dos nu, bain de soleil.

halter top n bain m de soleil.

halting ['hɔːltɪŋ] adj [verse, style] boiteux, heurté ; [voice, step, progress] hésitant ; [growth] discontinu.

haltingly ['hɔːltɪŋlɪ] adv [say, speak] de façon hésitante.

halva, halwa ['hælvə] n (U) halva m.

halve [UK hɑːv US hæv] vt **1.** [separate in two] couper or diviser or partager en deux **2.** [reduce by half] réduire or diminuer de moitié.

halves [UK hɑːvz US hævz] pl ⟶ **half**.

ham [hæm] (pt & pp **hammed**, cont **hamming**) ◆ n **1.** [meat] jambon m / *ham and eggs* œufs mpl au jambon **2.** [radio operator] radioamateur m **3.** [actor] cabot m, cabotin m, -e f **4.** [of leg] cuisse f. ◆ comp ▸ **ham acting** cabotinage m. ◆ vi = **ham up**. ❖ **ham up** vt sep ▸ **to ham it up** inf en faire trop.

Hamburg ['hæmbɜːg] pr n Hambourg.

hamburger ['hæmbɜːgər] n **1.** [beefburger] hamburger m **2.** US [minced beef] viande f hachée.

ham-fisted [-'fɪstɪd], **ham-handed** [-'hændɪd] adj [person] empoté, maladroit ; [behaviour] maladroit.

hamlet ['hæmlɪt] n [small village] hameau m.

hammer ['hæmər] ◆ n **1.** [tool] marteau m **2.** [of piano] marteau m ; [of firearm] chien m **3.** [in ear] marteau m. ◆ vt **1.** [nail, spike, etc.] enfoncer au marteau ; [metal] marteler ▸ **to hammer a nail into sthg** enfoncer un clou dans qqch ▸ **to hammer sthg flat / straight** aplatir / redresser qqch à coups de marteau **2.** inf [defeat] battre à plate couture ; [criticize] descendre en flammes. ◆ vi frapper or taper au marteau ; fig [heart] battre fort ▸ **to hammer on the table** [with fist] taper du poing sur la table / *to hammer at the door* tambouriner à la porte. ❖ **hammer away** vi [with hammer] donner des coups de marteau ▸ **to hammer away at sthg a)** taper sur qqch avec un marteau, donner des coups de marteau sur qqch **b)** fig [at agreement, contract] travailler avec acharnement à la mise au point de qqch **c)** [problem] travailler avec acharnement à la solution de qqch. ❖ **hammer down** vt sep [nail, spike] enfoncer (au marteau) ; [door] défoncer. ❖ **hammer in** vt sep [nail, spike] enfoncer (au marteau). ❖ **hammer into** vt sep fig ▸ **to hammer sthg into sb** faire entrer qqch dans la tête de qqn. ❖ **hammer out** vt sep [dent] aplatir au marteau ; fig [solution, agreement] mettre au point, élaborer ; [tune, rhythm] marteler.

hammock ['hæmək] n hamac m.

hammy ['hæmɪ] (compar **hammier**, superl **hammiest**) adj inf affecté, exagéré.

hamper ['hæmpər] ◆ vt [impede - work, movements, person] gêner ; [- project] gêner la réalisation de, entraver. ◆ n [for picnic] panier m ; US [for laundry] panier m à linge sale.

hamster ['hæmstər] n hamster m.

hamstring ['hæmstrɪŋ] (pt & pp **hamstrung** [-strʌŋ]) ◆ n tendon m du jarret. ◆ vt [cripple - animal, person] couper les tendons à ; fig handicaper.

hancock ['hænkɒk] n US [signature] signature f.

hand [hænd] ◆ n **1.** [of person] main f ▸ **to hold sb's hand** tenir la main de qqn ▸ **to hold hands** se tenir par la main ▸ **to take sb's hand, to take sb by the hand** prendre qqn par la main, prendre la main de qqn ▸ **to have one's hands full** fig avoir beaucoup à faire, avoir du pain sur la planche ▸ **to get** or **to lay one's hands on sthg** [obtain] dénicher qqch / *just wait till I get* or *lay my hands on her!* fig attends un peu que je l'attrape ! ▸ **hands off!** bas les pattes !, pas touche ! ▸ **(put your) hands up!** les mains en l'air !, haut les mains ! / *hands up anyone who knows the answer* SCH que ceux qui connaissent la réponse lèvent le doigt or la main / *my hands are tied* fig j'ai les mains liées ▸ **to sit on one's hands a)** [applaud half-heartedly] applaudir sans enthousiasme **b)** [do nothing] ne rien faire ▸ **to ask for sb's hand in marriage** demander la main de qqn, demander qqn en mariage ▸ **at hand, near** or **close at hand a)** [about to happen] proche **b)** [nearby] à proximité ▸ **hand in hand** la main dans la main ▸ **to go hand in hand (with sthg)** fig aller de pair (avec qqch) ▸ **to make money hand over fist** gagner de l'argent par millions / *I could do it with one hand tied behind my back* je pourrais le faire sans aucun effort or les doigts dans le nez ▸ **on the one hand... but on the other hand...** [used in the same sentence] d'un côté... mais de l'autre... ▸ **on the other hand** [when beginning new sentence] d'un autre côté **2.** [assistance] ▸ **to give sb a hand (with sthg)** donner un coup de main à qqn / *do you need a hand (with that)?* as-tu besoin d'un coup de main ? **3.** [control, management] ▸ **to need a firm hand** avoir besoin d'être sérieusement pris en main ▸ **to rule with a firm hand** diriger avec de la poigne ▸ **to take sb / sthg in hand** prendre qqn / qqch en main ▸ **to get out of hand a)** [dog, child] devenir indocile **b)** [meeting, situation] échapper à tout contrôle / *it's out of my hands* cela ne m'appartient plus, ce n'est plus ma responsabilité or de mon ressort ▸ **to have sb on one's hands** avoir qqch / qqn sur les bras / *now that that's off my hands* à présent que je suis débarrassé de cela / *to fall into the wrong hands* [information, secret, etc.] tomber en de mauvaises mains ▸ **to take matters into one's own hands** prendre les choses en main ▸ **hands down** sans conteste / *she's the best dancer hands down* c'est sans conteste la meilleure danseuse **4.** [applause] ▸ **to give sb a (big) hand** applaudir qqn (bien fort) **5.** [influence, involvement] ▸ **to have a hand in sthg** avoir quelque chose à voir dans qqch / *I had no hand in it* je n'avais rien à voir là-dedans, je n'y étais pour rien **6.** ▸ **to turn one's hand to sthg** : *she can turn her hand to anything* elle peut tout faire ▸ **to keep one's hand in** garder la main ▸ **to try one's hand at sthg** s'essayer à qqch **7.** [in cards - cards held] main f, jeu m ; [- round, game] partie f ▸ **to show** or **to reveal one's hand** fig dévoiler son jeu ▸ **to throw in one's hand** fig jeter l'éponge **8.** [of clock] aiguille f **9.** [handwriting] écriture f **10.** [worker] ouvrier m, -ère f ; [on ship] homme m, membre m de l'équipage / *she was lost with all hands* [ship] il a coulé avec tous les hommes à bord or tout l'équipage. ◆ vt passer, donner ▸ **to hand sthg to sb** passer or donner qqch à qqn / *you have to hand it to her, she IS a good mother* fig c'est une bonne mère, il faut lui accorder cela. ❖ **by hand** adv phr [written] à la main ; [made, knitted, sewn] (à la) main / *to wash sthg by hand* laver qqch à la main / *to send sthg by hand* faire porter qqch. ❖ **in hand** adv phr **1.** [available - money] disponible ; [time] devant soi **2.** [being dealt with] en cours / *the matter is in hand* on s'occupe de l'affaire / *I have the situation well in hand* j'ai la situation bien en main. ❖ **on hand** adj phr [person] disponible. ❖ **out of hand** adv phr [immediately] sur-le-champ.

to hand adv phr [letter, information, etc.] sous la main / *he took the first one that came to hand* il a pris le premier qui lui est tombé sous la main. **hand back** vt sep [return] rapporter, rendre. **hand down** vt sep **1.** [pass, give from high place] passer, donner **2.** [heirloom, story] transmettre / *the necklace / property has been handed down from mother to daughter for six generations* le collier est transmis / la propriété est transmise de mère en fille depuis six générations. **hand in** vt sep [return, surrender - book] rendre ; [- ticket] remettre ; [- exam paper] rendre, remettre ; [something found - to authorities, police, etc.] déposer, remettre / *to hand in one's resignation* remettre sa démission. **hand on** vt sep **1.** [give to someone else] passer ▶ **to hand sthg on to sb** passer qqch à qqn **2.** = **hand down**. **hand out** vt sep [distribute] distribuer / *he's very good at handing out advice* il est très fort pour ce qui est de distribuer des conseils. **hand over** ◆ vt sep **1.** [pass, give - object] passer, donner / *we now hand you over to the weather man / Bill Smith in Moscow* RADIO & TV nous passons maintenant l'antenne à notre météorologue / Bill Smith à Moscou **2.** [surrender - weapons, hostage] remettre ; [- criminal] livrer ; [- power, authority] transmettre / *hand it over!* donne ! ◆ vi ▶ **to hand over to** a) [government minister, chairman, etc.] passer le pouvoir à b) [in meeting] donner la parole à ; TELEC passer or donner le combiné à. **hand round** vt sep [distribute] distribuer.

HAND MESSAGING written abbr of **have a nice day**.

hand- in comp (à la) main ▶ **hand-knitted** tricoté (à la) main ▶ **hand-stitched** cousu main.

handbag ['hændbæg] ◆ n 🇺🇸 sac m à main. ◆ vt 🇺🇸 inf [attack verbally] : *she handbagged him* elle l'a violemment attaqué.

handball n **1.** ['hændbɔːl] [game] handball m **2.** [hænd-'bɔːl] FOOT main f.

handbill ['hændbɪl] n 🇺🇸 prospectus m.

handbook ['hændbʊk] n [for car, machine] guide m, manuel m ; [for tourist's use] guide m.

handbrake ['hændbreɪk] n 🇺🇸 frein m à main.

handclap ['hændklæp] n ▶ **to give sb the slow handclap** 🇺🇸 siffler qqn.

handcrafted ['hænd,krɑːftɪd] adj fabriqué or fait à la main.

hand cream n crème f pour les mains.

handcuff ['hændkʌf] vt passer les menottes à ▶ **to handcuff sb to sthg** attacher qqn à qqch avec des menottes.

handcuffs ['hændkʌfs] pl n menottes fpl ▶ **to be in handcuffs** avoir les menottes (aux mains).

hand-drier n sèche-mains m inv.

handful ['hændfʊl] n **1.** [amount] poignée f ▶ **a handful of** fig [a few] quelques **2.** inf [uncontrollable person] ▶ **to be a handful** être difficile.

hand grenade n grenade f à main.

handgun ['hændgʌn] n 🇺🇸 revolver m, pistolet m.

hand-held adj [appliance] à main ; [camera] portatif ▶ **hand-held computer** ordinateur m de poche.

handicap ['hændɪkæp] (pt & pp handicapped) ◆ n **1.** [physical, mental] handicap m ; fig [disadvantage] handicap m, désavantage m. SPORT handicap m. ◆ vt **1.** fig handicaper, désavantager **2.** SPORT handicaper.

handicapped ['hændɪkæpt] ◆ adj handicapé / *to be mentally / physically handicapped* être handicapé mental / physique. ◆ pl n ▶ **the handicapped** les handicapés mpl.

handicraft ['hændɪkrɑːft] n **1.** [items] objets mpl artisanaux, artisanat m **2.** [skill] artisanat m.

handiwork ['hændɪwɜːk] n (U) [work] travail m manuel ; [result] œuvre f.

handkerchief ['hæŋkətʃɪf] (pl handkerchiefs or handkerchieves [-tʃiːvz]) n mouchoir m.

handle ['hændl] ◆ n **1.** [of broom, knife, screwdriver] manche m ; [of suitcase, box, drawer] poignée f ; [of cup] anse f ; [of saucepan] queue f ; [of stretcher] bras m **2.** [name of Internet user] pseudo m **3.** inf [name - of citizens' band user] nom m de code ; [- which sounds impressive] titre m de noblesse **4.** inf ▶ **to get a handle on sthg** piger qqch. ◆ vt **1.** [touch] toucher à, manipuler / **'handle with care'** 'fragile' **2.** [operate - ship] manœuvrer, gouverner ; [- car] conduire ; [- gun] se servir de, manier ; [- words, numbers] manier **3.** [cope with - crisis, problem] traiter ; [- situation] faire face à ; [- crowd, traffic, death] supporter **4.** [manage, process] s'occuper de ; [address - topic, subject] aborder, traiter / *to handle stolen goods* receler des objets volés. ◆ vi [car, ship] répondre.

handlebars ['hændlbɑːz] pl n guidon m.

handler ['hændlə'] n **1.** [of dogs] maître-chien m **2.** [of baggage] bagagiste m **3.** 🇺🇸 [PR person] attaché m, -e de presse.

handling ['hændlɪŋ] ◆ n **1.** [of pesticides, chemicals] manipulation f / *handling of stolen goods* recel m d'objets volés **2.** [of tool, weapon] maniement m **3.** [of situation, operation] : *my handling of the problem* la façon dont j'ai traité le problème **4.** [of order, contract] traitement m, exécution f ; [of goods, baggage] manutention f. ◆ comp ▶ **handling charges** a) [frais de traitement] frais mpl de traitement b) [for physically shifting goods] frais mpl de manutention.

hand lotion n lotion f pour les mains.

hand luggage n (U) bagages mpl à main.

handmade [,hænd'meɪd] adj fabriqué or fait (à la) main.

hand-me-down inf ◆ n vêtement m de seconde main. ◆ adj [clothes] de seconde main ; fig [ideas] reçu.

handout ['hændaʊt] n **1.** [donation] aide f, don m **2.** [printed sheet or sheets] polycopié m **3.** [leaflet] prospectus m.

handover ['hændəʊvə'] n [of power] passation f, transmission f, transfert m ; [of territory] transfert m ; [of hostage, prisoner] remise f ; [of baton] transmission f, passage m.

handpick [hænd'pɪk] vt **1.** [fruit, vegetables] cueillir à la main **2.** fig [people] sélectionner avec soin, trier sur le volet.

handpicked [,hænd'pɪkt] adj [people] trié sur le volet.

hand puppet n 🇺🇸 marionnette f (à gaine).

handrail ['hændreɪl] n [on bridge] rambarde f, garde-fou m ; NAUT rambarde f ; [of stairway - gen] rampe f ; [- against wall] main f courante.

handset ['hændset] n TELEC combiné m.

handsewn [,hænd'səʊn] adj cousu main, cousu à la main.

hands-free [hændz-] adj TELEC mains libres.

hands-free kit n kit m mains libres.

handshake ['hændʃeɪk] n **1.** poignée f de main **2.** COMPUT établissement m de liaison, poignée f de main.

hands-off [hændz'ɒf] adj [policy] non interventionniste, de non-intervention ; [manager] non interventionniste.

handsome ['hænsəm] adj **1.** [good-looking - person, face, room] beau (before vowel or silent 'h' bel, f belle) ; [- building, furniture] élégant **2.** [generous - reward, compliment] beau (before vowel or silent 'h' bel, f belle) ; [- conduct, treatment] généreux ; [- apology] sincère **3.** [substantial - profit, price] bon ; [- fortune] joli.

handsomely ['hænsəmlɪ] adv **1.** [beautifully] avec élégance, élégamment **2.** [generously] généreusement, avec générosité ; [sincerely] sincèrement **3.** [substantially] : *to win handsomely* gagner haut la main.

hands-on [hændz'ɒn] adj [training, experience] pratique ; [exhibition] *où le public peut toucher les objets exposés.*

handstand ['hændstænd] n appui *m* renversé, équilibre *m* sur les mains.

hand-to-hand adj & adv au corps à corps.

hand-to-mouth ◆ adj ▸ **to lead** or **to have a hand-to-mouth existence** tirer le diable par la queue. ◆ adv ▸ **to live hand-to-mouth** tirer le diable par la queue.

hand towel n serviette *f*, essuie-mains *m inv.*

handwash ['hændwɒʃ] ◆ vt laver à la main. ◆ n : *to do a handwash* faire une lessive à la main.

handwriting ['hænd,raɪtɪŋ] n écriture *f* ▸ **handwriting expert** graphologue *mf.*

handwritten ['hænd,rɪtn] adj manuscrit, écrit à la main.

handy ['hændɪ] (*compar* **handier**, *superl* **handiest**) adj *inf* **1.** [near at hand] proche **2.** [person - good with one's hands] adroit de ses mains **3.** [convenient, useful] commode, pratique ▸ **to come in handy** être utile.

handyman ['hændɪmæn] (*pl* **handymen** [-men]) n [employee] homme *m* à tout faire ; [odd job expert] bricoleur *m.*

hang [hæŋ] ◆ vt (*pt & pp* **hung**) **1.** [suspend - curtains, coat, decoration, picture] accrocher, suspendre ; [-door] fixer, monter ; [-art exhibition] mettre en place ; [-wallpaper] coller, poser ; [CULIN - game, meat] faisander ▸ **to hang sthg from** or **on sthg** accrocher qqch à qqch ▸ **to hang one's head (in shame)** baisser la tête (de honte) **2.** (*usu passive*) [adorn] décorer / *a tree hung with lights* un arbre décoré or orné de lumières **3.** (*pt & pp* **hanged**) [criminal] pendre ▸ **to hang o.s.** se pendre ▸ **(you) might as well be hanged for a sheep as a lamb** UK quitte à être puni, autant l'être pour quelque chose qui en vaille la peine. ◆ vi (*pt & pp* **hung**) **1.** [be suspended - rope, painting, light] être accroché, être suspendu ; [-clothes on clothes line] être étendu, pendre ▸ **to hang from sthg** être accroché or suspendu à qqch / *her pictures are now hanging in several art galleries* ses tableaux sont maintenant exposés dans plusieurs galeries d'art / *his suit hangs well* son costume tombe bien / *time hangs heavy (on) my / his hands* le temps me / lui semble long **2.** [float - mist, smoke, etc.] flotter, être suspendu **3.** (*pt & pp* **hanged**) [criminal] être pendu / *she can go hang* UK *inf* elle peut aller se faire voir. ◆ n *inf* [knack, idea] ▸ **to get the hang of doing sthg** prendre le coup pour faire qqch ▸ **to get the hang of sthg** [understand] piger qqch / *are you getting the hang of your new job?* est-ce que tu te fais à ton nouveau travail ? / *you'll soon get the hang of it* tu vas bientôt t'y faire. ❧ **hang about** UK, **hang around** *inf* ◆ vi **1.** [wait] attendre / *he kept me hanging about* or *around for half an hour* il m'a fait poireauter pendant une demi-heure / *hang about, that's not what I mean!* attends or doucement, ce n'est pas ce que je veux dire ! **2.** [be idle, waste time] traîner (à ne rien faire) / *we can't afford to hang about if we want that contract* nous ne pouvons pas nous permettre de traîner si nous voulons obtenir ce contrat **3.** [be an unwanted presence] : *that kid's been hanging around for the past hour* ça fait une heure que ce gamin traîne dans les parages. ◆ vt insep ▸ **to hang about** or **around a place** traîner dans un endroit. ❧ **hang back** vi [wait behind] rester un peu plus longtemps ; [not go forward] se tenir or rester en arrière / *he hung back from saying what he really thought* UK *fig* il s'est retenu de dire ce qu'il pensait vraiment. ❧ **hang down** vi [light] pendre ; [hair] descendre, tomber. ❧ **hang in** vi *inf* ▸ **hang in**

there! tiens bon !, accroche-toi ! ❧ **hang on** ◆ vi **1.** [hold tight] se tenir, s'accrocher / *hang on tight* tiens-toi or accroche-toi bien **2.** *inf* [wait] attendre ▸ **hang on!** a) [wait] attends ! b) [indicating astonishment, disagreement, etc.] une minute ! / *hang on and I'll get him for you* [on phone] ne quitte pas, je te le passe **3.** [hold out, survive] résister, tenir (bon) ▸ **hang on in there!** *inf* [don't give up] tiens bon !, tiens le coup ! ◆ vt insep **1.** [listen to] : *she hung on his every word* elle buvait ses paroles, elle était suspendue à ses lèvres **2.** [depend on] dépendre de. ❧ **hang onto** vt insep **1.** [cling to] s'accrocher à **2.** *inf* [keep] garder, conserver. ❧ **hang out** ◆ vi **1.** [protrude] pendre / *his shirt tails were hanging out* sa chemise pendait ▸ **to let it all hang out** a) *inf* [person] se relâcher complètement, se laisser aller b) [speak without restraint] se défouler **2.** *inf* [frequent] traîner / *where does she hang out?* quels sont les endroits qu'elle fréquente ? ◆ vt sep [washing] étendre ; [flags] déployer. ❧ **hang together** vi [be consistent - alibi, argument, plot, etc.] tenir ; [- different alibis, statements] concorder. ❧ **hang up** ◆ vt sep [coat, hat, etc.] accrocher. ◆ vi TELEC raccrocher ▸ **to hang up on sb** raccrocher au nez de qqn.

hangar ['hæŋər] n AERON hangar *m.*

hangdog ['hæŋdɒg] adj ▸ **to have a hangdog look** or **expression** avoir un air penaud or de chien battu.

hanger ['hæŋər] n [hook] portemanteau *m* ; [coat hanger] portemanteau *m*, cintre *m* ; [loop on garment] cordon *m* or ganse *f* d'accrochage (*à l'intérieur d'un vêtement*).

hanger-on (*pl* **hangers-on**) n *pej* parasite *m.*

hang-glider n [aircraft] deltaplane *m* ; [person] libériste *mf*, adepte *mf* du deltaplane.

hang-gliding n deltaplane *m.*

hanging ['hæŋɪŋ] ◆ adj **1.** [suspended] suspendu **2.** LAW ▸ **hanging judge** juge *m* à la main lourde ▸ **hanging offence** crime *m* passible de pendaison. ◆ n **1.** [death penalty] pendaison *f* **2.** [of wallpaper] pose *f* ; [of decorations, pictures] accrochage *m*, mise *f* en place **3.** [tapestry] ▸ **wall hangings** tentures *fpl* (murales).

hangman ['hæŋmən] (*pl* **hangmen** [-mən]) n [executioner] bourreau *m.*

hangover ['hæŋ,əʊvər] n **1.** [from alcohol] gueule *f* de bois **2.** [relic] reste *m*, vestige *m*, survivance *f.*

hang time n SPORT temps *m* de suspension (*du ballon en l'air*).

hang-up n **1.** *inf* [complex] complexe *m*, blocage *m* **2.** COMPUT blocage *m*, interruption *f.*

hank [hæŋk] n pelote *f.*

hanker ['hæŋkər] vi ▸ **to hanker after** or **for sthg** rêver de qqch, avoir énormément envie de qqch.

hankering ['hæŋkərɪŋ] n rêve *m*, envie *f* ▸ **to have a hankering after** or **for sthg** rêver de qqch, avoir énormément envie de qqch.

hankie, hanky ['hæŋkɪ] (*pl* **hankies**) n *inf abbr of* **handkerchief.**

hanky-panky [-'pæŋkɪ] n (*U*) *inf* **1.** [sexual activity] galipettes *fpl* **2.** [mischief] entourloupettes *fpl*, blagues *fpl.*

Hanoi [hæ'nɔɪ] pr n Hanoi.

Hansard ['hænsɑ:d] pr n UK POL *compte rendu quotidien des débats de la Chambre des communes.*

Hants written abbr of **Hampshire.**

Hanukkah ['hɑ:nəkə] n RELIG Hanoukka.

haphazard [,hæp'hæzəd] adj mal organisé.

haphazardly [,hæp'hæzədlɪ] adv sans organisation, n'importe comment.

hapless ['hæplɪs] adj *liter* malchanceux.

happen ['hæpən] vi **1.** [occur] arriver, se passer, se produire **2.** [chance] : *do you happen to have his address?* auriez-vous son adresse, par hasard ? ❖ **happen along, happen by** vi *inf* passer par hasard. ❖ **happen on, happen upon** vt insep : *I happened on an old friend / a good pub* je suis tombé sur un vieil ami / un bon pub.

happening ['hæpənɪŋ] ❖ n [occurrence] événement *m* ; THEAT happening *m*. ❖ adj *inf* branché.

happily ['hæpɪlɪ] adv **1.** [contentedly - say, smile] d'un air heureux ; [-play, chat] tranquillement ▶ **they lived happily ever after** ≃ ils vécurent heureux et eurent beaucoup d'enfants / *to be happily married* a) [man] être un mari comblé b) [woman] être une épouse comblée **2.** [gladly] volontiers **3.** [luckily] heureusement **4.** [appropriately] heureusement, avec bonheur.

happiness ['hæpɪnɪs] n bonheur *m*.

happy ['hæpɪ] (*compar* **happier**, *superl* **happiest**) adj **1.** [content] heureux / *to make sb happy* rendre qqn heureux / *I'm not at all happy about your decision* je ne suis pas du tout content de votre décision / *happy ending* [in book, film] fin *f* heureuse, dénouement *m* heureux ▶ **happy birthday** or **anniversary!** joyeux anniversaire ! ▶ **Happy Christmas!** Joyeux Noël ! ▶ **Happy New Year!** Bonne Année ! **2.** [willing] : *I'm only too happy to help* je suis ravi de rendre service / *I would be happy to do it* je le ferais volontiers **3.** [lucky, fortunate - coincidence] heureux **4.** [apt, appropriate - turn of phrase, choice of words] heureux **5.** *inf* [drunk] gris, pompette.

> 🏷️ Note that être content / heureux / ravi que and se réjouir que are followed by a verb in the subjunctive:
> **I'm really happy you've been able to make the journey.** Je suis très heureux que vous ayez pu faire le voyage.

happy-clappy [-'klæpɪ] (*pl* **happy-clappies**) 🇬🇧 *inf & pej* ❖ adj [service, meeting, Christian] exubérant. ❖ n chrétien *m*, -enne *f* évangélique *(agaçant de par sa joie exubérante)*.

happy event n [birth] heureux événement *m*.

happy-go-lucky adj décontracté ; *pej* insouciant.

happy hour n [in pub, bar] happy hour *f (heure, généralement en début de soirée, pendant laquelle les boissons sont moins chères)*.

happy medium n équilibre *m*, juste milieu *m*.

harangue [hə'ræŋ] ❖ vt [person, crowd, etc.] haranguer ▶ **to harangue sb about sthg** haranguer qqn au sujet de qqch. ❖ n harangue *f*.

Harare [hə'rɑːrɪ] pr n Harare.

harass ['hærəs] vt [torment] tourmenter ; [with questions, demands] harceler ; MIL harceler / *to sexually harass an employee* harceler une employée sexuellement.

> ⚠️ Harasser means to exhaust, not to harass.

harassed ['hærəst] adj stressé ▶ **to be sexually harassed** être victime de harcèlement sexuel.

harassment ['hærəsmənt] n [tormenting] tracasserie *f* ; [with questions, demands] harcèlement *m* ; [stress] stress *m* ; MIL harcèlement *m* ▶ **police / sexual harassment** harcèlement policier / sexuel.

harbinger ['hɑːbɪndʒə*r*] n *liter* signe *m* avant-coureur / *a harbinger of doom* a) [event, incident, etc.] un mauvais présage b) [person] un oiseau de malheur.

harbour 🇬🇧, **harbor** 🇺🇸 ['hɑːbə*r*] ❖ n [for boats] port *m* ; *fig* havre *m*. ❖ comp ▶ **the harbour lights** les lumières *fpl* du port ▶ **harbour master** capitaine *m* de port. ❖ vt **1.** [person] abriter, héberger ; [criminal] donner asile à, receler **2.** [grudge, suspicion] nourrir, entretenir en soi **3.** [conceal - dirt, germs] renfermer, receler.

hard [hɑːd] ❖ adj **1.** [not soft - substance, light, colour] dur ; LING [consonant] dur / *to get* or *to become hard* durcir ▶ **(as) hard as nails** : *she is (as) hard as nails* a) [emotionally] elle est dure, elle n'a pas de cœur b) [physically] c'est une dure à cuire ▶ **rock hard, (as) hard as rock** dur comme la pierre **2.** [concrete - facts] concret (concrète), tangible ; [-evidence] tangible **3.** [difficult - question, problem, etc.] difficile, dur / *I find it hard to understand / believe that...* je n'arrive pas à comprendre / croire que... / *it's hard to say* c'est difficile à dire / *he's hard to get on with* il n'est pas facile à vivre / *it's hard to beat* [value for money] pour le prix, c'est imbattable / *life is hard* c'est dur, la vie ▶ **to fall on hard times** a) [financially] connaître des temps difficiles or une période de vaches maigres b) [have difficult times] connaître des temps difficiles, en voir de dures ▶ **to give sb a hard time** en faire voir de dures à qqn ▶ **to learn sthg the hard way** a) [involving personal loss, suffering, etc.] apprendre qqch à ses dépens b) [in a difficult way] faire la rude apprentissage de qqch / *some people always have to do things the hard way* il y a des gens qui choisissent toujours la difficulté ▶ **to play hard to get** [flirt] jouer les insaisissables **4.** [severe - voice, face, eyes] dur, froid ; [-climate, winter] rigoureux, rude ; [-frost] fort, rude ▶ **to be hard on sb** être dur avec qqn ▶ **hard cheese!** 🇬🇧 *dated inf*, **hard lines!** 🇬🇧 *inf*, **hard luck!** pas de chance !, pas de veine !, pas de bol ! **5.** [strenuous] : *it's hard work* c'est dur / *it's been a long hard day* la journée a été longue / *she's a hard worker* c'est un bourreau de travail / *he's a hard drinker* c'est un gros buveur, il boit beaucoup / *it's hard going making conversation with him* c'est difficile de discuter avec lui. ❖ adv **1.** [strenuously - pull, push, hit, breathe] fort ; [-work] dur ; [-run] à toutes jambes ; [-listen] attentivement ▶ **to work hard at sthg** beaucoup travailler qqch ▶ **to try hard to do sthg** essayer de son mieux de faire qqch ▶ **to think hard** beaucoup réfléchir ▶ **to look hard at sb** regarder qqn bien en face ▶ **to look hard at sthg** examiner qqch / *as hard as possible* or *as hard as one can* a) [work, try] le plus possible b) [push, hit, squeeze] de toutes ses forces ▶ **to be hard at it** : *they're hard at it* a) 🇬🇧 [working] ils sont plongés dans leur travail b) *inf* [engaged in sex] ils sont en train de s'envoyer en l'air **2.** [with difficulty] difficilement ▶ **to be hard put (to it) to do sthg** avoir du mal à faire qqch **3.** [harshly, severely - treat sb] durement, sévèrement ▶ **to feel hard done by** : *he's feeling hard done by* il a l'impression d'avoir été injustement traité ; [heavily, strongly - rain] à verse ; [-freeze, snow] fort **4.** [solid] : *the ground was frozen hard* le gel avait complètement durci la terre / *to set hard* [concrete, mortar] prendre.

hard-and-fast adj [rule] strict, absolu ; [information] correct, vrai.

hardass ['hɑːdæs] n 🇺🇸 *v inf* [unpleasant person] enfoiré *m*, -e *f*.

hardback ['hɑːbæk] ❖ n [book] livre *m* cartonné. ❖ adj cartonné.

hardball ['hɑːdbɔːl] n ▶ **to play hardball** *inf & fig* employer les grands moyens.

hard-bitten [-'bɪtən] adj endurci.

hardboard ['hɑːdbɔːd] n panneau *m* de fibres.

hard-boiled [-'bɔɪld] adj **1.** [egg] dur **2.** *inf* [person] dur.

hard cash n [argent *m*] liquide *m*.

hard copy n COMPUT sortie f papier, tirage m.

hard core n **1.** [nucleus] noyau m dur **2.** MUS hard rock m, hard m **3.** [pornography] porno m hard.
◆ **hard-core** adj [belief in political system] dur ; [believer] endurci ; [support] ferme ; [pornography, rock music] hard.

hard court n 🇬🇧 [for tennis] court m en dur.

hardcover ['hɑːd,kʌvər] = **hardback**.

hard currency n monnaie f or devise f forte.

hard disk n COMPUT disque m dur.

hard-disk drive n COMPUT unité f de disque dur.

hard-earned [-'ɜːnt] adj [money] durement gagné ; [victory] durement or difficilement remporté ; [reputation] durement acquis ; [holiday, reward] bien mérité.

harden ['hɑːdn] ◆ vt [person - physically, emotionally] endurcir ; [steel] tremper ; LING [consonant] durcir ; MED [arteries] durcir, scléroser ▸ **to harden o.s. to sthg** s'endurcir à qqch. ◆ vi **1.** [snow, skin, steel] durcir ; [concrete, mortar] prendre ; MED [arteries] durcir, se scléroser ; [person - emotionally] s'endurcir, se durcir ; [- physically] s'endurcir ; [attitude] se durcir **2.** FIN [prices, market] s'affermir.

hardened ['hɑːdnd] adj [snow, skin] durci ; [steel] trempé, durci ; [arteries] sclérosé / a hardened criminal un criminel endurci or invétéré ▸ **to become hardened to sthg** se blinder contre qqch.

hardening ['hɑːdnɪŋ] n [of snow, skin, attitudes] durcissement m ; [of steel] trempe f ; [of person - physical] endurcissement m ; [- emotional] durcissement m ; FIN [of prices] affermissement m ▸ **hardening of the arteries** MED durcissement or sclérose f des artères.

hard-faced [-'feɪst] adj au visage dur.

hard-fought [-'fɔːt] adj [game, battle] rudement disputé.

hard hat n **1.** inf [of construction worker] casque m **2.** 🇺🇸 inf [construction worker] ouvrier m du bâtiment.
◆ **hard-hat** adj 🇺🇸 caractéristique des attitudes conservatrices des ouvriers du bâtiment.

hard-headed [-'hedɪd] adj **1.** [tough, shrewd - person] à la tête froide ; [- realism] froid, brut ; [- bargaining] dur ; [- decision] froid **2.** 🇺🇸 [stubborn - person] qui a la tête dure ; [- attitude] entêté.

hard-hearted adj [person] insensible, dur, au cœur de pierre ; [attitude] dur.

hard-hit adj gravement atteint or touché.

hard-hitting [-'hɪtɪŋ] adj **1.** [verbal attack] rude ; [speech, report] implacable, sans indulgence **2.** [boxer] qui frappe dur.

hardiness ['hɑːdɪnɪs] n [of person] résistance f, robustesse f ; [of plant, tree] résistance f.

hard labour n (U) travaux mpl forcés.

hard line n ligne f de conduite dure ▸ **to take a hard line on sb / sthg** adopter une ligne de conduite dure avec qqn / sur qqch. ◆ **hard-line** adj [policy, doctrine] dur ; [politician] intransigeant, endurci, intraitable. ◆ **hard lines** pl n 🇬🇧 inf ▸ **hard lines!** pas de chance !

hardliner [,hɑːd'laɪnər] n partisan m, -e f de la manière forte.

hardly ['hɑːdlɪ] adv **1.** [barely] à peine, ne... guère / he can hardly read il sait à peine or tout juste lire / you can hardly move in here for furniture c'est à peine si on peut bouger ici tellement il y a de meubles / I can hardly believe it j'ai du mal à le croire / hardly anyone presque personne / you've hardly touched your food tu n'as presque rien mangé / I can hardly wait to see her je suis très impatient de la voir / hardly a week goes by without a telephone call from her il se passe rarement une semaine sans qu'elle téléphone / I need hardly say that... ai-je besoin de vous dire que..., je n'ai pas besoin de vous dire que...

2. [expressing negative opinion] : it's hardly surprising, is it? ça n'a rien de surprenant, ce n'est guère surprenant / he'd hardly have said that cela m'étonnerait qu'il ait dit cela.

hardness ['hɑːdnɪs] n **1.** [of snow, skin, water] dureté f ; [of steel] trempe f, dureté f **2.** [difficulty] difficulté f ▸ **hardness of hearing** MED surdité f partielle **3.** [severeness - of personality] dureté f ; [- of heart] dureté f, froideur f **4.** [strenuousness] difficulté f **5.** FIN affermissement m.

hard-nosed [-'nəʊzd] inf = **hard-headed**.

hard of hearing ◆ pl n ▸ **the hard of hearing** les malentendants mpl. ◆ adj ▸ **to be hard of hearing** être dur d'oreille.

hard-pressed [-'prest], **hard-pushed** [-'pʊʃt] adj : to be hard-pressed for time manquer de temps ▸ **to be hard-pressed to do sthg** avoir du mal à faire qqch.

hardscape ['hɑːdskeɪp] n hardscape m (éléments en dur dans l'aménagement paysager).

hard sell ◆ n vente f agressive. ◆ comp ▸ **hard sell approach** or **tactics** méthode f de vente agressive.

hardship ['hɑːdʃɪp] ◆ n épreuves fpl. ◆ comp ▸ **hardship allowance** [for student] aide accordée à un étudiant en cas de graves problèmes financiers.

hard shoulder n 🇬🇧 AUTO bande f d'arrêt d'urgence.

hard up adj inf [short of money] fauché, à sec.

hardware ['hɑːdweər] ◆ n (U) **1.** COMM quincaillerie f **2.** COMPUT matériel m, hardware m **3.** MIL matériel m de guerre, armement m **4.** inf [guns] armes fpl. ◆ comp COMPUT [company, manufacturer] de matériel informatique ; [problem] de matériel or hardware.

hardware shop, hardware store n quincaillerie f.

hardwearing [,hɑːd'weərɪŋ] adj robuste, résistant.

hard-wired [-'waɪəd] adj COMPUT câblé.

hard-won [-'wʌn] adj [victory, trophy, independence] durement gagné ; [reputation] durement acquis.

hardwood ['hɑːdwʊd] ◆ n [wood] bois m dur ; [tree] arbre m à feuilles caduques. ◆ comp [floor] en bois dur.

hardworking [,hɑːd'wɜːkɪŋ] adj travailleur ; [engine, machine, printer] robuste.

hardy ['hɑːdɪ] (compar **hardier**, superl **hardiest**) adj **1.** [strong - person, animal] robuste, résistant ; [- plant] résistant ▸ **hardy annual** BOT plante f annuelle ▸ **hardy perennial** a) BOT plante f vivace b) fig serpent m de mer **2.** [intrepid - explorer, pioneer] intrépide, courageux.

hardy har har [-hɑːhɑː] interj 🇺🇸 ha ! ha ! très drôle.

hare [heər] (pl **hare** or **hares**) ◆ n **1.** CULIN & ZOOL lièvre m **2.** SPORT [at dog race] lièvre m **3.** 🇬🇧 GAMES ▸ **hare and hounds** jeu m de piste. ◆ vi 🇬🇧 inf ▸ **to hare off** filer à toutes jambes.

harebrained ['heəbreɪnd] adj [reckless, mad - person] écervelé ; [- scheme] insensé, fou (before vowel or silent 'h' fol, f folle).

harelip [,heə'lɪp] n bec-de-lièvre m.

harem [🇬🇧 hɑː'riːm 🇺🇸 'hærəm] n lit & fig harem m ▸ **harem pants** pantalon m bouffant.

haricot (bean) ['hærɪkəʊ-] n haricot m blanc.

harissa [hæ'riːsə] n CULIN harissa f.

hark [hɑːk] vi liter [recall] prêter l'oreille, ouïr. ◆ **hark back to** vt insep [recall] revenir à ▸ **to hark back to sthg** revenir (tout le temps) à qqch.

Harlequin ['hɑːlɪkwɪn] pr n Arlequin. ◆ **harlequin** adj [costume] bigarré ; [dog's coat] tacheté.

Harley Street ['hɑːlɪ-] pr n rue du centre de Londres célèbre pour ses spécialistes en médecine.

harlot ['hɑːlət] n arch prostituée f.

harm [hɑːm] ◆ n (U) [physical] mal *m* ; [psychological] tort *m*, mal *m* ▶ **to do sb harm** faire du mal à qqn. ◆ vt **1.** [person - physically] faire du mal à ; [- psychologically] faire du tort à, nuire à **2.** [surface] abîmer, endommager ; [crops] endommager **3.** [cause, interests] causer du tort à, être préjudiciable à ; [reputation] salir.

harmful ['hɑːmfʊl] adj **1.** [person, influence] nuisible, malfaisant **2.** [chemicals] nocif ; [effects] nuisible.

harmless ['hɑːmlɪs] adj **1.** [person] inoffensif, qui n'est pas méchant ; [animal] inoffensif **2.** [joke] sans malice, anodin ; [pastime] innocent.

harmlessly ['hɑːmlɪslɪ] adv sans faire de mal, sans dommage or dommages.

harmonic [hɑːˈmɒnɪk] ◆ n MATH & MUS harmonique *m*. ◆ adj [gen & MATH & MUS] harmonique.

harmonica [hɑːˈmɒnɪkə] n harmonica *m*.

harmonics [hɑːˈmɒnɪks] n (U) harmoniques *mpl*.

harmonious [hɑːˈməʊnjəs] adj harmonieux.

harmoniously [hɑːˈməʊnjəslɪ] adv harmonieusement.

harmonium [hɑːˈməʊnjəm] n harmonium *m*.

harmonize, harmonise ['hɑːmənaɪz] ◆ vt **1.** MUS [instrument, melody] harmoniser **2.** [colours] harmoniser, assortir **3.** [views, statements] harmoniser, faire concorder ; [people] concilier, amener à un accord. ◆ vi **1.** MUS [sing in harmony] chanter en harmonie ; [be harmonious] être harmonieux or en harmonie ; [write harmony] harmoniser, faire des harmonies **2.** [colours] aller (bien) ensemble, se marier (bien).

harmony ['hɑːmənɪ] (*pl* **harmonies**) n **1.** MUS harmonie *f* **2.** [agreement - of colours] harmonie *f* ; [- of temperaments] harmonie *f*, accord *m*.

harness ['hɑːnɪs] ◆ n **1.** [for horse, oxen] harnais *m*, harnachement *m* ; [for parachute, car seat] harnais *m* ; [for child] harnais *m* **2. to get** or **to be back in harness** reprendre le collier. ◆ vt **1.** [horse] harnacher, mettre le harnais à ; [oxen, dogs] atteler **2.** *fig* [resources] exploiter, maîtriser.

harp [hɑːp] n MUS harpe *f*. ❖ **harp on** *inf* ◆ vi chanter (toujours) le même refrain or la même rengaine ▶ **to harp on about sthg** rabâcher qqch, revenir sans cesse sur qqch ▶ **to harp on at sb about sthg** rebattre les oreilles à qqn au sujet de qqch. ◆ vt insep ▶ **to harp on sthg** revenir sans cesse sur qqch, rabâcher qqch.

harpist ['hɑːpɪst] n harpiste *mf*.

harpoon [hɑːˈpuːn] ◆ n harpon *m*. ◆ vt harponner.

harpsichord ['hɑːpsɪkɔːd] n clavecin *m*.

harpy ['hɑːpɪ] (*pl* **harpies**) n *fig* harpie *f*, mégère *f*. ❖ **Harpy** n MYTH ▶ **the Harpies** les Harpyes *fpl* or Harpies *fpl*.

harridan ['hærɪdn] n harpie *f*, vieille sorcière *f*.

harrowing ['hærəʊɪŋ] ◆ adj [story] poignant, navrant, angoissant ; [cry] déchirant ; [experience] pénible, angoissant. ◆ n hersage *m*.

harry ['hærɪ] (*pt* & *pp* **harried**) vt **1.** [harass - person] harceler, tourmenter **2.** [pillage - village] dévaster, mettre à sac **3.** MIL [enemy, troops] harceler.

harsh [hɑːʃ] adj **1.** [cruel, severe - person] dur, sévère, cruel ; [- punishment, treatment] dur, sévère ; [- fate] cruel ; [- criticism, judgment, words] dur, sévère ▶ **to be harsh with sb** être dur envers or avec qqn **2.** [conditions, weather] rude, rigoureux **3.** [bitter - struggle] âpre, acharné **4.** [cry, voice] criard, strident ; [tone] dur **5.** [colour, contrast] choquant ; [light] cru **6.** [bleak - landscape, desert] dur, austère.

harshly ['hɑːʃlɪ] adv **1.** [treat, punish] sévèrement, avec rigueur **2.** [answer, speak] avec rudesse or dureté ; [judge] sévèrement, durement **3.** [cry, shout] d'un ton strident.

harshness ['hɑːʃnɪs] n **1.** [of person] dureté *f*, sévérité *f* ; [of punishment, treatment] sévérité *f* ; [of judgement] dureté *f*, sévérité *f* ; [of statement, words, tone] dureté *f* **2.** [of climate] rigueur *f*, rudesse *f* **3.** [of cry, voice] discordance *f* **4.** [of light, contrast] dureté *f*.

harvest ['hɑːvɪst] ◆ n **1.** [gathering - of cereal, crops] moisson *f* ; [- of fruit, mushrooms] récolte *f*, cueillette *f* ; [- of grapes] vendange *f*, vendanges *fpl* **2.** [yield] récolte *f* **3.** *fig* [from experience, research] moisson *f*. ◆ vt **1.** AGR [cereal, crops] moissonner ; [fruit, mushrooms] cueillir, récolter ; [grapes] vendanger **2.** *fig* [benefits] moissonner ; [consequences] récolter. ◆ vi [for cereal, crops] moissonner, faire la moisson ; [for fruit] faire les récoltes ; [for grapes] vendanger.

harvest festival n fête *f* des moissons.

has (weak form [həz], strong form [hæz]) ⟶ **have**.

has-been ['hæzbiːn] n *inf* has been *m inv*.

hash [hæʃ] ◆ n **1.** 🇬🇧 *inf* [muddle, mix-up] pagaille *f*, embrouillamini *m* ; [mess, botch] gâchis *m* ▶ **to make a hash of sthg** bousiller qqch, ficher qqch en l'air **2.** CULIN hachis *m* **3.** *inf* [marijuana] hasch *m*. ◆ vt CULIN hacher. ❖ **hash up** vt sep **1.** 🇬🇧 *inf* [mess up] bâcler, bousiller / *I'm afraid I completely hashed up the interview* j'ai bien peur d'avoir complètement merdé à l'entretien **2.** CULIN hacher.

hash browns pl n 🇺🇸 pommes de terre râpées et sautées (présentées parfois sous forme de galette).

hashish ['hæʃiːʃ] n haschisch *m*.

hash key n touche *f* dièse.

hash mark n dièse *m*.

Hasid ['hæsɪd] n juif *m*, -ive *f* hassidique.

Hasidic [həˈsɪdɪk] adj hassidique.

hasn't ['hæznt] abbr of **has not**.

Hassid, Hassidic 1. = **Hasid 2.** = **Hasidic**.

hassle ['hæsl] *inf* ◆ n **1.** [difficulty, irritation] embêtement *m*, emmerdement *m* **2.** [quarrel] dispute *f*, chamaillerie *f*. ◆ vt [annoy, nag] embêter, harceler. ◆ vi [argue] se quereller, se chamailler.

haste [heɪst] n [speed] hâte *f* ; [rush] précipitation *f* ▶ **to do sthg in haste** faire qqch à la hâte, se dépêcher de faire qqch ▶ **to make haste** se hâter, se dépêcher.

hasten ['heɪsn] ◆ vt **1.** [speed up - event, decline] précipiter, hâter **2.** [urge on - person] presser **3.** [say quickly] : *it wasn't me, I hastened to add* ce n'était pas moi, m'empressai-je d'ajouter. ◆ vi *liter* [verb of movement] : *to hasten away* partir à la hâte, se hâter de partir.

hastily ['heɪstɪlɪ] adv **1.** [hurriedly] précipitamment, avec précipitation, à la hâte **2.** [impetuously, rashly] hâtivement, sans réfléchir.

hasty ['heɪstɪ] adj **1.** [quick, hurried] précipité, à la hâte **2.** [rash] irréfléchi, hâtif.

hat [hæt] n **1.** chapeau *m* **2.** *fig* [role] rôle *m*, casquette *f*.

hatbox ['hætbɒks] n boîte *f* à chapeau.

hatch [hætʃ] ◆ vt **1.** ZOOL [eggs] faire éclore **2.** *fig* [plan, plot] tramer, manigancer **3.** ART hachurer. ◆ vi [eggs] éclore ; [chicks] sortir de l'œuf. ◆ n **1.** [hatching of egg] éclosion *f* **2.** [brood] couvée *f* **3.** NAUT écoutille *f* **4.** [trapdoor] trappe *f* ; [for inspection, access] trappe, panneau *m* ; [in aircraft, spaceship] sas *m* ; [in dam, dike] vanne *f* (d'écluse) **5.** [hatchway - for service] passe-plat *m*.

hatchback ['hætʃbæk] n **1.** [door] hayon *m* **2.** [model] voiture *f* à hayon, cinq portes *f*.

hatcheck clerk ['hætʃek-] n préposé *m*, -e *f* au vestiaire.

hatchet ['hætʃɪt] n hachette *f*, hache *f* (à main).

hatchet-faced adj au visage en lame de couteau.

hatchet job n inf ‣ **to do a hatchet job on sb / sthg** démolir qqn / qqch.

hatchway ['hætʃ,weɪ] n NAUT écoutille *f* ; [gen] trappe *f*.

H8 MESSAGING written abbr of hate.

hate [heɪt] ◆ vt *(no cont)* [gen] détester, avoir horreur de ; [intensely] haïr, abhorrer / *I hate getting up early* j'ai horreur de me lever tôt / *she hates having to wear school uniform* elle a horreur d'avoir à porter un uniforme scolaire / *I hate her for what she has done* je lui en veux vraiment pour ce qu'elle a fait / *I hate myself for letting them down* je m'en veux beaucoup de les avoir laissés tomber ‣ **to hate it when sb does sthg** détester que qqn fasse qqch ; [polite use] : *I would hate you to think I was avoiding you* je ne voudrais surtout pas vous donner l'impression que je cherchais à vous éviter / *I hate to mention it, but you still owe me £5* je suis désolé d'avoir à vous le faire remarquer, mais vous me devez toujours 5 livres / *I hate to bother you, but could I use your phone?* je ne voudrais surtout pas vous déranger, mais puis-je utiliser votre téléphone ? ◆ n **1.** [emotion] haine *f* **2.** [person hated] personne *f* que l'on déteste ; [thing hated] chose *f* que l'on déteste.

> 🖊 Note that **détester que** is followed by a verb in the subjunctive:
> **I hate it when he drinks like that.** *Je déteste qu'il boive comme ça.*

hate campaign n campagne *f* de dénigrement.

hate crime n délit *m* de haine.

hated ['heɪtɪd] adj détesté.

hateful ['heɪtfʊl] adj odieux, détestable, abominable.

hate mail n lettres *fpl* d'injures.

hater ['heɪtə˞] n ennemi *m*, -e *f* / *to be an animal hater* détester les animaux.

hatred ['heɪtrɪd] n haine *f* ‣ **to feel hatred for sb** avoir de la haine pour qqn, haïr qqn.

hat trick n 🇬🇧 [three goals] hat-trick *m* ; [three wins] trois victoires *fpl* consécutives.

haughtily ['hɔːtɪlɪ] adv avec arrogance, de manière hautaine.

haughtiness ['hɔːtɪnɪs] n arrogance *f*, caractère *m* hautain.

haughty ['hɔːtɪ] (compar **haughtier**, superl **haughtiest**) adj hautain, arrogant.

haul [hɔːl] ◆ vt **1.** [pull] tirer, traîner ; [tow] tirer, remorquer / *they were hauled in front of* or *before a judge* on les traîna devant un tribunal **2.** [transport] transporter ; [by truck] camionner, transporter **3.** [move with effort] hisser **4. to haul ass** 🇺🇸 v inf se magner. ◆ vi **1.** [pull] tirer **2.** NAUT [boat] lofer. ◆ n **1.** [catch, takings - of fisherman, customs] prise *f*, coup *m* de filet ; [- of robbers] butin *m* **2.** [pull] ‣ **to give a haul on a rope / fishing net** tirer sur une corde / un filet de pêche **3.** [distance] parcours *m*, trajet *m* **4.** [in time] : *training to be a doctor is a long haul* les études de médecine sont très longues. ◆❖ **haul in** vt sep [catch, net, rope] tirer, amener / *Tom was hauled in on a drink-driving charge* Tom a été épinglé pour conduite en état d'ivresse. ◆ **haul off** ◆ vt sep [take away] conduire, amener. ◆ vi 🇺🇸 inf lever le bras or le poing. ◆❖ **haul up** vt sep [pull up] tirer, hisser / *to haul sb up before a judge* traîner qqn devant le tribunal or le juge.

haulage ['hɔːlɪdʒ] ◆ n *(U)* **1.** [as business] transports *mpl*, transport *m* (routier) **2.** [act] transport *m* **3.** [cost] (frais *mpl* de) transport *m*. ◆ comp [company] de transport routier, de transports routiers ‣ **haulage contractor** entrepreneur *m* de transports routiers ‣ **haulage firm** transporteur *m*.

haulier 🇬🇧 ['hɔːljə˞], **hauler** 🇺🇸 ['hɔːlə˞] n **1.** [business] entreprise *f* de transports routiers **2.** [owner] entrepreneur *m* de transports routiers **3.** [driver] routier *m*, camionneur *m*.

haunch [hɔːntʃ] n **1.** CULIN [of venison] cuissot *m* ; [of beef] quartier *m* **2.** [of human] hanche *f* **3.** [of animal] ‣ **haunches** arrière-train *m*, derrière *m*.

haunt [hɔːnt] ◆ vt **1.** [subj: ghost, spirit] hanter **2.** [subj: problems] hanter, tourmenter **3.** inf [frequent - bar] hanter, fréquenter ; [- streets] hanter, traîner dans. ◆ n **1.** [place] lieu *m* que l'on fréquente beaucoup, lieu *m* de prédilection **2.** [refuge - for animals, criminals] repaire *m*.

haunted ['hɔːntɪd] adj **1.** [house, castle] hanté **2.** [look] hagard, égaré.

haunting ['hɔːntɪŋ] adj [memory, sound] obsédant ; [tune] qui vous trotte dans la tête.

hauntingly ['hɔːntɪŋlɪ] adv : *hauntingly beautiful* d'une beauté obsédante.

Havana [hə'vænə] ◆ pr n [city] La Havane. ◆ n [cigar, tobacco] havane *m*. ◆ comp [tobacco, cigar] de Havane.

have [hæv] (pres **has** (3rd pers sg, weak form [həz], strong form [hæz]), pt & pp **had** [hæd])
◆ aux vb **1.** [used to form perfect tenses] avoir, être / *to have finished* avoir fini / *to have left* être parti / *to have sat down* s'être assis / *you were silly not to have accepted* tu es bête de ne pas avoir accepté / *after* or *when you have finished, you may leave* quand vous aurez fini, vous pourrez partir / *she was ashamed of having lied* elle avait honte d'avoir menti / *I have been thinking* j'ai réfléchi / *I have known her for three years* / *since childhood* je la connais depuis trois ans / depuis mon enfance / *she claimed she hadn't heard the news* elle a prétendu ne pas avoir entendu la nouvelle / *we had gone to bed early* nous nous étions couchés de bonne heure ‣ **to have had it** : *he's had it* a) inf [is in trouble] il est fichu or foutu b) [is worn out] il est à bout **2.** [elliptical uses] : *have you ever had the measles?* — *yes, I have* / *no, I haven't* avez-vous eu la rougeole ? — oui / non / *she hasn't finished* — *yes, she has!* elle n'a pas fini — (mais) si ! / *you've forgotten his birthday* — *no, I haven't!* tu as oublié son anniversaire — mais non ! **3.** [in tag questions] : *you've read "Hamlet", haven't you?* vous avez lu « Hamlet », n'est-ce pas ? / *he hasn't arrived, has he?* il n'est pas arrivé, si ?

◆ vt

A. POSSESS 1. [be in possession of, own] avoir, posséder / *do you have* or *have you got a car?* avez-vous une voiture ? / *he has (got) £10 left* il lui reste 10 livres / *do we have any milk in the house?* est-ce qu'on a du lait or est-ce qu'il y a du lait à la maison ? / *she has a baker's shop* / *bookshop* elle tient une boulangerie / librairie / *I've got it!* ça y est, j'ai trouvé or j'y suis ! **2.** [enjoy the use of] avoir, disposer de / *we had a couple of hours to do our errands* nous disposions de or nous avions quelques heures pour faire nos courses **3.** [possess as quality or attribute] avoir / *she has (got) red hair* elle a les cheveux roux, elle est rousse / *she has what it takes* or *she has it in her to succeed* elle a ce qu'il faut pour réussir **4.** [possess knowledge or understanding of] : *do you have any experience of teaching?* avez-vous déjà enseigné ?

B. EXPERIENCE OR SHOW 1. [indicating experience of a specified situation] : *to have a dream* / *nightmare* faire un rêve / cauchemar / *I've had my appendix taken out* je me suis fait opérer de l'appendicite **2.** [be infected with, suffer from] avoir / *do you have* or *have you got a headache?* avez-vous mal à la tête ? **3.** (delexicalized use) [perform, take part in - bath, lesson] prendre ; [- meeting] avoir / *I'll* *have no part in it* je refuse de m'en mêler / *to have a party* a) [organize] organiser une fête b) [celebrate] faire la fête **4.** [pass, spend] passer, avoir / *I had a horrible day at work* j'ai passé une journée atroce au travail / *have a nice day!* bonne journée ! / *to have a good time* s'amuser **5.** [exhibit, show] avoir, montrer / *he had the nerve to refuse* il a eu le culot de refuser.

C. RECEIVE OR ACCEPT 1. [obtain, receive] avoir, recevoir / *I'd like him to have this picture* j'aimerais lui donner cette photo / *we had a phone call from the mayor* nous avons reçu or eu un coup de fil du maire / *I have it on good authority* je le tiens de bonne source / *she let them have the wardrobe for £300* elle leur a laissé or cédé l'armoire pour 300 livres ▶ **to let sb have it** : *I let him have it* a) *inf* [attacked him] je lui ai réglé son compte b) [told him off] je lui ai passé un savon **2.** [invite] recevoir, avoir / *she's having some people (over) for* or *to dinner* elle reçoit or elle a du monde à dîner **3.** [accept, take] vouloir / *do what you want, I'm having nothing more to do with your schemes* fais ce que tu veux je ne veux plus être mêlé à tes combines **4.** *(in negative)* [allow, permit] : *I will not have him in my house!* il ne mettra pas les pieds chez moi ! / *I won't have it!* ça ne va pas se passer comme ça ! / *we can't have you sleeping on the floor* nous ne pouvons pas vous laisser dormir par terre.

D. HOLD OR GAIN ADVANTAGE OVER 1. [clutch] tenir / *he had (got) his assailant by the throat* il tenait son agresseur à la gorge **2.** *fig* [gain control or advantage over] : *I have (got) you right where I want you now!* je vous tiens ! **3.** *(in passive) inf* [cheat, outwit] avoir / *you've been had!* tu t'es fait avoir !

E. CAUSE 1. [cause to be] : *the news had me worried* la nouvelle m'a inquiété / *we'll have everything ready* tout sera prêt **2.** *(with past participle)* [cause to be done] ▶ **to have sthg done** faire faire qqch / *I had my hair cut* je me suis fait couper les cheveux **3.** *(with infinitive)* [cause to do] ▶ **to have sb do sthg** faire faire qqch à qqn / *she had him invite all the neighbours round* elle lui a fait inviter tous les voisins **4.** *(with 'will' or 'would')* [wish for] vouloir / *what would you have me do?* que voudriez-vous que je fasse ? / *I'll have you know I have a degree in French* je vous fais remarquer que j'ai une licence de français.

F. CONSUME [food, meal] avoir, prendre / *to have breakfast in bed* prendre le petit déjeuner au lit / *would you like to have coffee?* voulez-vous (prendre) un café ? / *what will you have? — I'll have the lamb* [in restaurant] qu'est-ce que vous prenez ? — je vais prendre de l'agneau.

G. GIVE BIRTH TO : *she's had a baby* elle a eu un bébé / *our dog has just had puppies* notre chien vient d'avoir des petits.

H. WITH LOCATION OR POSITION placer, mettre / *I had my back to the window* je tournais le dos à la fenêtre / *he had his head down* il avait la tête baissée.

I. OBLIGATION OR NECESSITY 1. [indicating obligation] ▶ **to have (got) to do sthg** devoir faire qqch, être obligé de faire qqch / *don't you have to* or *haven't you got to phone the office?* est-ce que tu ne dois pas appeler le bureau ? / *you don't have to* or *you haven't got to go* tu n'es pas obligé d'y aller / *I hate having to get up early* j'ai horreur de devoir me lever tôt / *(expressing disbelief, dismay, etc.)* : *you've got to be joking!* vous plaisantez !, c'est une plaisanterie ! **2.** [indicating necessity] devoir / *I'll have to think about it* il va falloir que j'y réfléchisse / *the plumbing has to be redone* la plomberie a besoin d'être refaite / *do you have to turn the music up so loud?* vous ne pourriez pas baisser un peu la musique ? **3.** [feel obligation or necessity in regard to] : *I have (got) a lot of work to finish* j'ai beaucoup de travail à finir **4.** **to have to do with sthg** : *the book has to do with archaeology* ce livre traite de l'archéologie / *their argument had to do with money* ils se disputaient à propos d'argent ▶ **to have noth-**

ing to do with sb or sthg : *this has nothing to do with you* ça ne te concerne or regarde pas / *I'll have nothing more to do with her* je ne veux plus avoir affaire à elle / *they had nothing to do with her being fired* ils n'avaient rien à voir avec son licenciement. ◆ **haves** pl n ▶ **the haves** les riches *mpl*, les nantis *mpl* / *the haves and the have-nots* les riches et les pauvres, les nantis et les démunis. ◆ **have in** vt sep **1.** [cause to enter] faire entrer / *she had him in for a chat* elle l'a fait entrer pour discuter **2.** [doctor, plumber] faire venir **3.** **to have it in for sb** *inf* avoir une dent contre qqn. ◆ **have off** vt sep ▶ **to have it off with sb** UK *v inf* coucher avec qqn. ◆ **have on** vt sep **1.** [wear] porter / *what does she have on?* qu'est-ce qu'elle porte ?, comment est-elle habillée ? **2.** [radio, television] : *he has the radio / television on all night* sa radio / sa télévision est allumée toute la nuit **3.** [commitment, engagement] : *we have a lot on today* nous avons beaucoup à faire aujourd'hui **4.** UK *inf* [tease, trick] faire marcher **5.** *they have nothing on me* ils n'ont aucune preuve contre moi. ◆ **have out** vt sep **1.** [tooth] se faire arracher **2.** [settle] ▶ **to have it out with sb** s'expliquer avec qqn. ◆ **have over** vt sep [invite] inviter ▶ **to have one over on sb** avoir le dessus sur qqn. ◆ **have up** vt sep *inf* [bring before the authorities] : *they were had up by the police for vandalism* ils ont été arrêtés pour vandalisme / *he was had up (before the court) for breaking and entering* il a comparu (devant le tribunal) pour effraction.

have-a-go hero n UK *inf* membre du public, auteur d'un acte héroïque.

haven ['heɪvn] n [refuge] abri *m*, refuge *m*.

have-nots pl n ▶ **the have-nots** les démunis *mpl*, les défavorisés *mpl*.

haven't ['hævnt] abbr of **have not**.

haversack ['hævəsæk] n havresac *m*.

havoc ['hævək] n *(U)* ravages *mpl*, chaos *m* ▶ **to wreak havoc on sthg** ravager qqch.

Hawaii [hə'waɪɪ] pr n Hawaii / *in Hawaii* à Hawaii.

Hawaiian [hə'waɪən] ◆ n **1.** [person] Hawaïen *m*, -enne *f* **2.** LING hawaïen *m*. ◆ adj hawaïen.

hawk [hɔːk] ◆ n **1.** [bird] faucon *m* **2.** POL faucon *m*. ◆ vi **1.** HUNT chasser au faucon **2.** [clear throat] se racler la gorge. ◆ vt **1.** [sell - from door to door] colporter ; [- in market, street] vendre à la criée **2.** *fig* [news, gossip] colporter **3.** [cough up] cracher.

hawker ['hɔːkər] n [street vendor] marchand *m* ambulant ; [door-to-door] démarcheur *m*, colporteur *m*.

hawk-eyed adj **1.** [keen-sighted] au regard d'aigle **2.** *fig* [vigilant] qui a l'œil partout.

hawkish ['hɔːkɪʃ] adj POL dur.

hawknosed ['hɔːknəʊzd] adj [person] au nez aquilin.

hawthorn ['hɔːθɔːn] ◆ n aubépine *f*. ◆ comp [hedge, berry] d'aubépine.

hay [heɪ] n foin *m*.

hay fever n rhume *m* des foins.

haymaking ['heɪˌmeɪkɪŋ] n *(U)* fenaison *f*, foins *mpl*.

hayride ['heɪraɪd] n US *lit* promenade dans un chariot rempli de paille ; *fig* ▶ **it was no hayride** ça n'a pas été une partie de plaisir.

haystack ['heɪˌstæk] n meule *f* de foin.

haywire ['heɪˌwaɪər] adj *inf* [system, person] détraqué ▶ **to go haywire** a) [machine] déblocquer, se détraquer b) [plans] mal tourner.

hazard ['hæzəd] ◆ n **1.** [danger, risk] risque *m*, danger *m* **2.** [in golf] obstacle *m*. ◆ vt **1.** [risk - life] risquer, hasarder ; [- reputation] risquer **2.** [venture - statement, advice, suggestion] hasarder, se risquer à faire ▶ **to hazard**

a guess: *would you care to hazard a guess as to the weight?* voulez-vous essayer de deviner combien ça pèse ? **3.** [stake, bet -fortune] risquer, miser. **hazards** pl n AUTO feux *mpl* de détresse.

⚠ **Hasard means** chance, **not** danger.

hazardous ['hæzədəs] adj **1.** [dangerous] dangereux, risqué / *hazardous waste* déchets *mpl* dangereux **2.** [uncertain] hasardeux, incertain.

hazard warning ◆ n AUTO signal *m* de danger. ◆ comp AUTO ▸ **hazard warning triangle** triangle *m* de présignalisation ▸ **hazard warning lights** feux *mpl* de détresse.

Hazchem ['hæzkem] 🇬🇧 abbr of **hazardous chemicals**.

haze [heɪz] ◆ n **1.** METEOR brume *f* / *a heat haze* une brume de chaleur **2.** (*U*) [steam] vapeur *f*, vapeurs *fpl* ; [smoke] nuage *m* **3.** [confusion] brouillard *m* ▸ **to be in a haze** être dans le brouillard. ◆ vt 🇺🇸 **1.** [harass] harceler **2.** MIL faire subir des brimades à ; SCH bizuter.

hazel ['heɪzl] ◆ n noisetier *m*. ◆ adj [colour] noisette (*inv*).

hazelnut ['heɪzl.nʌt] ◆ n [nut] noisette *f* ; [tree] noisetier *m*. ◆ comp [flavour] de noisette ; [ice cream, yoghurt] à la noisette.

haziness ['heɪzɪnɪs] n **1.** [of sky, weather] état *m* brumeux **2.** [of memory, thinking] flou *m*, imprécision *f* **3.** PHOT flou *m*.

Hazmat ['hæzmæt] n 🇺🇸 abbr of **hazardous material**.

hazy ['heɪzɪ] (*compar* **hazier**, *superl* **haziest**) adj **1.** [weather, sky] brumeux **2.** [memory] flou, vague ; [thinking, ideas] flou, embrouillé / *she's rather hazy about the details of what happened* elle n'a qu'un vague souvenir de ce qui s'est passé **3.** PHOT flou **4.** [colour] pâle.

H-bomb (abbr of **hydrogen bomb**) n bombe *f* H.

HD adj **1.** (abbr of **high density**) COMPUT HD **2.** (abbr of **high definition**) HD.

HDD (abbr of **hard disk drive**) n COMPUT disque *m* dur.

HDMI (abbr of **high definition multimedia interface**) n HDMI *m*.

HD-ready adj prêt pour la TVHD.

HDTV (abbr of **high-definition television**) n TVHD *f*.

HDV (abbr of **high definition video**) n HDV *m*.

he [hi:] ◆ pron il / *he works in London* il travaille à Londres / *he and I* lui et moi / *there he is!* le voilà ! / *she is older than he is* fml elle est plus âgée que lui / *that's what HE thinks!* c'est ce qu'il croit ! ◆ n [animal] mâle *m* ; [boy] garçon *m*.

HE 1. written abbr of **high explosive 2.** (written abbr of **His/Her Excellency**) S. Exc., SE.

head [hed] (*pl* **heads**) ◆ n **1.** [of human, animal] tête *f* / *she has a lovely head of hair* elle a de très beaux cheveux or une très belle chevelure / *he's already a head taller than his mother* il dépasse déjà sa mère d'une tête ▸ **from head to toe** or **foot** de la tête aux pieds / *she was dressed in black from head to foot* elle était tout en noir or entièrement vêtue de noir ▸ **a head** or **per head** par tête, par personne ▸ **to fall head over heels in love with sb** tomber éperdument amoureux de qqn ▸ **to have one's head in the clouds** avoir la tête dans les nuages / *wine always goes to my head* le vin me monte toujours à la tête / *all this praise has gone to his head* toutes ces

louanges lui ont tourné la tête / *I could do it standing on my head* c'est simple comme bonjour ▸ **to have one's head screwed on (the right way)** : *she's got her head screwed on* elle a la tête sur les épaules / *she's head and shoulders above the rest* les autres ne lui arrivent pas à la cheville ▸ **to laugh one's head off** rire à gorge déployée ▸ **to shout** or **to scream one's head off** crier à tue-tête **2.** [mind, thoughts] tête *f* ▸ **to take it into one's head to do sthg** se mettre en tête de faire qqch / *the idea never entered my head* ça ne m'est jamais venu à l'esprit / *don't put silly ideas into his head* ne lui mettez pas des idées stupides en tête / *I can't get these dates into my head* je n'arrive pas à retenir ces dates / *the answer has gone right out of my head* j'ai complètement oublié la réponse ▸ **it's doing my head in!** inf ça me tape sur le système ! / *I just can't get my head round the idea that she's gone* inf je n'arrive vraiment pas à me faire à l'idée qu'elle est partie **3.** [aptitude] : *in my job, you need a good head for figures* pour faire mon métier, il faut savoir manier les chiffres / *she has no head for business* elle n'a pas le sens des affaires / *I've no head for heights* j'ai le vertige **4.** [clear thinking, common sense] : *keep your head!* gardez votre calme !, ne perdez pas la tête ! ▸ **to keep a cool head** garder la tête froide ▸ **he's off his head!** 🇬🇧 inf il est malade !, il est pas bien ! **5.** [intelligence, ability] tête *f* / *we'll have to put our heads together and find a solution* nous devrons nous y mettre ensemble pour trouver une solution ▸ **off the top of my head** : *off the top of my head, I'd say it would cost about £1,500* à vue de nez je dirais que ça coûte dans les 1 500 livres / *her lecture was completely over my head* sa conférence m'a complètement dépassé ▸ **to talk over sb's head** s'exprimer de manière trop compliquée pour qqn ▸ **two heads are better than one** *prov* deux avis valent mieux qu'un **6.** inf [headache] mal *m* de tête **7.** [chief, boss -of police, government] chef *m* ; [-of school, of company] directeur *m*, -trice *f* **8.** [authority, responsibility] : *she went over my head to the president* elle est allée voir le président sans me consulter ▸ **on your (own) head be it!** c'est toi qui en prends la responsabilité !, à tes risques et périls ! **9.** [top, upper end, extremity -of racquet, pin, hammer] tête *f* ; [-of staircase] haut *m*, tête *f* ; [-of bed] chevet *m*, tête *f* ; [-of arrow] pointe *f* ; [-of page] tête *f* ; [-of letter] en-tête *m* ; [-of cane] pommeau *m* ; [-of valley] tête *f* ; [-of river] source *f* / *at the head of the procession* / *queue* en tête de (la) procession / de (la) queue / *sitting at the head of the table* assis au bout de la or en tête de table **10.** BOT & CULIN [of corn] épi *m* ; [of garlic] tête *f*, gousse *f* ; [of celery] pied *m* ; [of asparagus] pointe *f* **11.** [of coin] côté *m* pile / *heads or tails?* pile ou face ? / *I can't make head nor tail of this* pour moi ça n'a ni queue ni tête **12.** (*pl* head) [of livestock] tête *f* / *50 head of cattle* 50 têtes de bétail **13.** MED [of abscess, spot] tête *f* ▸ **to come to a head a)** [abscess, spot] mûrir **b)** fig [problem] arriver au point critique / *his resignation brought things to a head* sa démission a précipité les choses. ◆ comp **1.** ANAT ▸ **head injuries** blessures *fpl* à la tête **2.** [chief -gardener, nurse, buyer] en chef ▸ **head porter** chef-portier *m*. ◆ vt **1.** [command -group, organization] être à la tête de ; [-project, revolt] diriger, être à la tête de ; [chair -discussion] mener ; [-commission] présider **2.** [be first] être or venir en tête de **3.** [steer -vehicle] diriger ; [-person] guider, diriger **4.** [provide title for] intituler ; [be title of] être en tête de **5.** FOOT : *he headed the ball into the goal* il a marqué de la tête. ◆ vi [car, crowd, person] aller, se diriger. **head for** vt insep [car, person] se diriger vers ; [trouble] mettre le cap sur / *she headed for home* elle rentra (à la maison) / *he's heading for trouble* il va (tout droit) à la catastrophe. **head off** ◆ vt sep **1.** [divert -animal, vehicle, person] détourner de son chemin ; [-enemy] forcer à reculer / *she headed off all questions about her private life* fig elle a éludé toute question sur sa vie privée

2. [crisis, disaster] prévenir, éviter ; [rebellion, revolt, unrest] éviter. ◆ vi partir. ❖ **head up** vt sep [be leader of] diriger.

headache ['hedeɪk] n **1.** [pain] mal m de tête ; [migraine] migraine f / **to have a headache** [gen] avoir mal à la tête, avoir la migraine **2.** fig [problem] problème m.

headachy ['hedeɪkɪ] adj inf : I'm feeling a bit headachy j'ai un peu mal à la tête.

headband ['hedbænd] n bandeau m.

headbang ['hedbæŋ] vi inf secouer violemment la tête en rythme (sur du heavy metal).

headbanger ['hedbæŋə'] n inf **1.** [heavy metal fan] fan mf de heavy metal **2.** 🇬🇧 [mad person] cinglé m, -e f, toqué m, -e f.

headboard ['hed,bɔːd] n tête f de lit.

head boy n 🇬🇧 élève chargé d'un certain nombre de responsabilités et qui représente son école aux cérémonies publiques.

headbutt ['hedbʌt] ◆ n coup m de tête, coup m de boule. ◆ vt donner un coup de tête or de boule à.

head case n inf dingue mf.

head cold n rhume m de cerveau.

head count n vérification f du nombre de personnes présentes.

headdress ['hed,dres] n [gen] coiffure f ; [belonging to regional costume] coiffe f.

-headed ['hedɪd] in comp à tête... ❱ **a silver-headed cane** une canne à pommeau d'argent ❱ **a three-headed dragon** un dragon à trois têtes.

headed notepaper ['hedɪd-] n 🇬🇧 papier m à en-tête.

header ['hedə'] n **1.** [fall] chute f (la tête la première) ; [dive] plongeon m (la tête la première) **2.** FOOT (coup m de) tête f **3.** COMPUT en-tête m ❱ **header block** en-tête ❱ **header card** carte f en-tête **4.** CONSTR (pierre f en) boutisse f.

head first [,hed'fɜːst] adv **1.** [dive, fall, jump] la tête la première **2.** [rashly] sans réfléchir, imprudemment.

headgear ['hed,gɪə'] n (U) coiffure f.

head girl n 🇬🇧 élève chargée d'un certain nombre de responsabilités et qui représente son école aux cérémonies publiques.

headhunt ['hedhʌnt] ◆ vi recruter des cadres (pour une entreprise). ◆ vt ❱ **to be headhunted** être recruté par un chasseur de têtes.

headhunter ['hed,hʌntə'] n ANTHR & fig chasseur m de têtes.

heading ['hedɪŋ] n **1.** [title - of article, book] titre m ; [-of chapter] titre m, intitulé m **2.** [subject] rubrique f **3.** [letterhead] en-tête m **4.** AERON & NAUT [direction] cap m.

headlamp ['hedlæmp] n **1.** 🇬🇧 = **headlight 2.** MIN lampe-chapeau f.

headland ['hedlənd] n promontoire m, cap m.

headless ['hedlɪs] adj **1.** [arrow, body, screw] sans tête **2.** [company, commission] sans chef.

headlight ['hedlaɪt] n [on car] phare m ; [on train] fanal m, feu m avant.

headline ['hedlaɪn] ◆ n **1.** [in newspaper] (gros) titre m, manchette f **2.** RADIO & TV [news summary] grand titre m. ◆ vt **1.** PRESS mettre en manchette **2.** [provide headline for] intituler **3.** 🇺🇸 [have top billing in] avoir le rôle principal dans. ◆ vi 🇺🇸 [have top billing] avoir le rôle principal.

headliner ['hedlaɪnə'] n 🇺🇸 vedette f.

headlock ['hedlɒk] n cravate f.

headlong ['hedlɒŋ] ◆ adv **1.** [dive, fall] la tête la première **2.** [rush - head down] tête baissée ; [-at great speed]

à toute allure or vitesse **3.** [rashly] sans réflexion, imprudemment. ◆ adj **1.** [dive, fall] la tête la première **2.** [impetuous - action] imprudent, impétueux.

headmaster [,hed'mɑːstə'] n SCH proviseur m, directeur m, chef m d'établissement.

headmistress [,hed'mɪstrɪs] n SCH directrice f, chef m d'établissement.

head office n siège m social, bureau m central.

head-on ◆ adv **1.** [collide, hit] de front, de plein fouet **2.** [confront, meet] de front. ◆ adj **1.** [collision - of car, plane] de front, de plein fouet ; [-of ships] par l'avant **2.** [confrontation, disagreement] violent.

headphone jack n prise f casque.

headphones ['hedfəʊnz] pl n casque m (à écouteurs).

headquarter [hed'kwɔːtə'] vt ❱ **to be headquartered in** avoir son siège à.

headquarters [,hed'kwɔːtəz] pl n **1.** [of bank, office] siège m social, bureau m central ; [of army, police] quartier m général **2.** MIL [commanding officers] quartier m général.

headrest ['hedrest] n appuie-tête m, repose-tête m.

headroom ['hedrʊm] n place f, hauteur f.

headscarf ['hedskɑːf] (pl **headscarves** [-skɑːvz]) n foulard m.

headset ['hedset] n [with microphone] casque m (à écouteurs et à micro) ; 🇺🇸 [headphones] casque m (à écouteurs).

headship ['hedʃɪp] n SCH poste m de directeur or de directrice.

headstand ['hedstænd] n : **to do a headstand** faire le poirier.

head start n **1.** [lead] avance f **2.** [advantage] avantage m.

headstone ['hedstəʊn] n **1.** [of grave] pierre f tombale **2.** ARCHIT [keystone] clef f de voûte.

headstrong ['hedstrɒŋ] adj **1.** [wilful] têtu, entêté **2.** [rash] impétueux, imprudent.

head teacher n [man] proviseur m, directeur m, chef m d'établissement ; [woman] directrice f, chef m d'établissement.

head-up adj [in aeroplane, car] ❱ **head-up display** affichage m tête-haute.

head waiter n maître m d'hôtel.

headway ['hedweɪ] n **1.** [progress] ❱ **to make headway** a) [gen] avancer, faire des progrès b) NAUT faire route **2.** [headroom] place f, hauteur f.

headwind ['hedwɪnd] n [gen & AERON] vent m contraire ; NAUT vent m debout.

heady ['hedɪ] (compar **headier**, superl **headiest**) adj **1.** [intoxicating - wine] capiteux, qui monte à la tête ; [-perfume] capiteux **2.** [exciting - experience, time] excitant, passionnant ; [-atmosphere] excitant, enivrant.

heal [hiːl] ◆ vt **1.** [make healthy - person] guérir ; [-wound] guérir, cicatriser **2.** [damage, division] remédier à, réparer ; [disagreement] régler. ◆ vi [person] guérir ; [wound] se cicatriser, se refermer ; [fracture] se consolider. ❖ **heal up** vi [wound] se cicatriser, guérir ; [burn] guérir ; [fracture] se consolider.

healer ['hiːlə'] n guérisseur m, -euse f.

healing ['hiːlɪŋ] ◆ n [of person] guérison f ; [of wound] cicatrisation f, guérison f ; [of fracture] consolidation f. ◆ adj **1.** [remedy, treatment] curatif m ; [ointment] cicatrisant **2.** [soothing - influence] apaisant.

health [helθ] n **1.** [general condition] santé f ❱ **to be in good / poor health** être en bonne / mauvaise santé / health problems problèmes mpl de santé ❱ **Department**

of Health ≃ ministère de la Santé ▸ **the health minister** le ministre de la Santé **2.** [good condition] (bonne) santé *f* **3.** [in toast] ▸ **(to your) good health!** à votre santé !

Health and Safety Committee n *comité d'hygiène, de sécurité et des conditions de travail* ; ≃ CHSCT *m*.

Health and Safety Executive pr n 🇬🇧 inspection *f* du travail.

health care n services *mpl* médicaux.

health centre n centre *m* médico-social.

health club n club *m* de remise en forme.

health farm n centre *m* de remise en forme.

health food n aliments *mpl* diététiques or biologiques ▸ **health food shop** magasin *m* de produits diététiques.

health hazard n risque *m* pour la santé.

healthily ['helθɪlɪ] adv [eat, live] sainement.

health insurance n assurance *f* maladie.

health risk n risque *m* pour la santé.

health service n = National Health Service.

health visitor n 🇬🇧 infirmière visiteuse qui s'occupe surtout des enfants en bas âge, des personnes âgées, etc.

healthy ['helθɪ] (compar **healthier**, superl **healthiest**) adj **1.** [in good health - person] sain, en bonne santé ; [- animal, plant] en bonne santé **2.** [showing good health - colour, skin] sain ; [appetite] robuste, bon **3.** [beneficial - air, climate] salubre ; [- diet, food] sain ; [- exercise] bon pour la santé, salutaire **4.** [thriving - economy] sain ; [- business] prospère, bien assis **5.** [substantial - profits] considérable ; [- sum] considérable, important ; [- difference] appréciable **6.** [sensible - attitude] sain ; [- respect] salutaire.

heap [hi:p] ◆ n **1.** [pile] tas *m*, amas *m* **2.** inf [large quantity] tas *m*, masse *f* / *you've got heaps of time* tu as largement le temps or tout ton temps **3.** inf [old car] vieux clou *m*. ◆ vt **1.** [collect into a pile] entasser, empiler **2.** fig [lavish] ▸ **to heap sthg on sb** couvrir qqn de qqch. ◆ **heap up** vt sep [pile - books, furniture] entasser, empiler ; [- money, riches] amasser.

heaped 🇬🇧 [hi:pt], **heaping** 🇺🇸 ['hi:pɪŋ] adj gros (grosse) / *a heaped teaspoonful* une cuiller à café bombée or pleine.

heaps [hi:ps] adv inf & dated drôlement.

hear [hɪəʳ] (pt & pp **heard** [hɜ:d]) ◆ vt **1.** [perceive with sense of hearing] entendre / *can you hear me?* m'entendez-vous (bien) ? / *we can't hear you* nous ne vous entendons pas, nous n'entendons pas ce que vous dites / *he was heard to observe* or *remark that he was against censorship* fml on l'a entendu dire qu'il était opposé à la censure / *I've heard it said that…* j'ai entendu dire que… / *to hear my sister talk you'd think we were poor* à entendre ma sœur, vous pourriez croire que nous sommes pauvres / *don't believe everything you hear* n'écoutez pas tous les bruits qui courent, ne croyez pas tout ce qu'on raconte / *you're hearing things* tu t'imagines des choses / *I can hardly hear myself think* je n'arrive pas à me concentrer (tant il y a de bruit) / *let's hear it for the Johnson sisters!* un grand bravo pour les sœurs Johnson !, et on applaudit bien fort les sœurs Johnson ! **2.** [listen to - music, person] écouter ; [- concert, lecture, mass] assister à, écouter **3.** [subj: authority, official] : *the court will hear the first witness today* LAW la cour entendra le premier témoin aujourd'hui / *the case will be heard in March* l'affaire se plaidera au mois de mars **4.** [understand, be told] entendre, apprendre / *I hear you're leaving* j'ai appris or j'ai entendu (dire) que tu partais / *have you heard the latest?* connaissez-vous la dernière ? / *have you heard anything more about the accident?* avez-vous eu d'autres nouvelles de l'accident ? **5.** *have you heard the one about the Scotsman and the Irishman?* connaissez-vous l'histoire de l'Écossais et de

l'Irlandais ? / *I've heard good things about that school* j'ai eu des échos favorables de cette école. ◆ vi **1.** [able to perceive sound] entendre **2.** [be aware of] être au courant / *haven't you heard? he's dead* vous n'êtes pas au courant ? il est mort **3.** **hear, hear!** bravo ! ◆ **hear about** vt insep **1.** [learn] entendre / *have you heard about the accident?* êtes-vous au courant pour or de l'accident ? / *I've heard so much about you* j'ai tellement entendu parler de vous **2.** [have news of] avoir or recevoir des nouvelles de / *I hear about her through her sister* j'ai de ses nouvelles par sa sœur. ◆ **hear from** vt insep **1.** [receive news of] avoir or recevoir des nouvelles de / *they'd be delighted to hear from you* ils seraient ravis d'avoir de tes nouvelles / *(I am) looking forward to hearing from you* [in letters] dans l'attente de vous lire **2.** [listen to] écouter. ◆ **hear of** vt insep **1.** [know of] entendre parler de, connaître / *I've never heard of her* je ne la connais pas **2.** [receive news of] entendre parler de / *the whole town had heard of his success* la ville entière était au courant de son succès or sa réussite / *who ever heard of eating pizza for breakfast!* quelle (drôle d')idée de manger de la pizza au petit déjeuner ! **3.** *(usu neg)* [accept, allow] : *her father won't hear of it* son père ne veut pas en entendre parler or ne veut rien savoir / *may I pay for dinner? — I wouldn't hear of it!* puis-je payer or vous offrir le dîner ? — (il n'en est) pas question ! ◆ **hear out** vt sep écouter jusqu'au bout / *at least hear me out before you refuse my offer* au moins écoutez-moi jusqu'au bout avant de refuser ma proposition.

hearing ['hɪərɪŋ] ◆ adj [person] qui entend bien. ◆ n **1.** [sense of] ouïe *f* / *to have good / bad hearing* entendre bien / mal **2.** [earshot] ▸ **within hearing** à portée de voix **3.** [act of listening] audition *f* **4.** [chance to be heard] ▸ **to give sb a fair hearing** laisser parler qqn, écouter ce que qqn a à dire **5.** LAW audition *f* **6.** [official meeting] séance *f*.

hearing aid n appareil *m* acoustique, audiophone *m*.

hearing impaired pl n ▸ **the hearing impaired** les malentendants *mpl*.

hearsay ['hɪəseɪ] n ouï-dire *m inv*, rumeur *f*.

hearse [hɜ:s] n corbillard *m*, fourgon *m* mortuaire.

heart [hɑ:t] ◆ n **1.** ANAT [organ] cœur *m* / *he has a weak heart* il est cardiaque, il a le cœur malade ; fig : *her heart leapt* son cœur bondit / *her heart sank* elle eut un serrement de cœur / *she waited, her heart in her mouth* elle attendait, son cœur battant la chamade **2.** [bosom] poitrine *f* **3.** [seat of feelings, love] cœur *m* / *he has a heart of gold* / *of stone* il a un cœur d'or / de pierre / *the letter was written straight from the heart* la lettre était écrite du fond du cœur ▸ **to have one's heart set on sthg** s'être mis qqch dans la tête / *they have your welfare at heart* ils ne pensent qu'à ton bien, c'est pour ton bien qu'ils font cela / *my heart's desire is to see Rome again* liter mon plus cher désir est or ce que je désire le plus au monde c'est de revoir Rome **4.** [innermost thoughts] fond *m* / *in his heart of hearts* au fond de lui-même or de son cœur, en son for intérieur / *there's a woman / a man after my own heart* voilà une femme / un homme selon mon cœur / *I thank you from the bottom of my heart* or *with all my heart* je vous remercie du fond du cœur or de tout mon cœur ▸ **to take sthg to heart** prendre qqch à cœur **5.** [disposition, humour] ▸ **to have a change of heart** changer d'avis **6.** [interest, enthusiasm] : *I worked hard but my heart wasn't in it* j'ai beaucoup travaillé mais je n'avais pas le cœur à l'ouvrage or le cœur n'y était pas / *she read to her heart's content* elle a lu tout son soûl / *a subject close to one's heart* un sujet qui tient à cœur / *she puts her heart* or *she throws herself heart and soul into her work* elle se donne à son travail corps et âme **7.** [courage] ▸ **to lose**

heart perdre courage, se décourager ▸ **take heart!** courage ! **8.** [compassion] cœur *m* / *he has no heart* il n'a pas de cœur, il manque de cœur / *she didn't have the heart to refuse* or *she couldn't find it in her heart to refuse* elle n'a pas eu le courage or le cœur de refuser / *her heart's in the right place* elle a bon cœur ▸ **have a heart!** pitié ! **9.** [core, vital part - of matter, topic] fond *m*, vif *m* ; [- of city, place] centre *m*, cœur *m* / *the heart of the matter* le fond du problème **10.** [of cabbage, celery, lettuce] cœur *m* ; [of artichoke] cœur *m*, fond *m* **11.** CARDS cœur *m* / *hearts are trumps* atout cœur **12.** [shape] cœur *m*. ◆ comp ▸ **heart disease** maladie cardiovasculaire ▸ **heart surgery** chirurgie *f* du cœur ▸ **heart trouble** (U) maladie *f* du cœur, troubles *mpl* cardiaques / *to have* or *to suffer from heart trouble* souffrir du cœur, être cardiaque. ◆◇ **at heart** adv phr au fond / *at heart she was a good person* elle avait un bon fond / *my sister's a gypsy at heart* ma sœur est une bohémienne dans l'âme. ◆◇ **by heart** adv phr par cœur ▸ **to learn / to know sthg by heart** apprendre / savoir qqch par cœur.

heartache ['hɑːteɪk] n chagrin *m*, peine *f*.

heart attack n MED crise *f* cardiaque.

heartbeat ['hɑːtbiːt] n battement *m* de cœur, pulsation *f*.

heartbreak ['hɑːtbreɪk] n [grief - gen] (immense) chagrin *m*, déchirement *m* ; [- in love] chagrin *m* d'amour.

heartbreaking ['hɑːtbreɪkɪŋ] adj déchirant, navrant.

heartbroken ['hɑːtbrəʊkn] adj [person - gen] qui a un immense chagrin ; [- stronger] qui a le cœur brisé.

heartburn ['hɑːtbɜːn] n (U) brûlures *fpl* d'estomac.

heart condition n : *to have a heart condition* souffrir du cœur, être cardiaque.

hearten ['hɑːtn] vt encourager, donner du courage à.

heartening ['hɑːtnɪŋ] adj encourageant, réconfortant.

heart failure n [condition] défaillance *f* cardiaque ; [cessation of heartbeat] arrêt *m* du cœur.

heartfelt ['hɑːtfelt] adj [apology, thanks] sincère.

hearth [hɑːθ] n **1.** [of fireplace] foyer *m*, âtre *m* **2.** [home] foyer *m*.

hearthrug ['hɑːθrʌg] n devant *m* de foyer.

heartily ['hɑːtɪlɪ] adv **1.** [enthusiastically - joke, laugh] de tout son cœur ; [- say, thank, welcome] chaleureusement, de tout cœur ; [- eat] de bon appétit **2.** [thoroughly] : *I heartily recommend it* je vous le conseille vivement.

heartiness ['hɑːtɪnɪs] n **1.** [of thanks, welcome] cordialité *f*, chaleur *f* ; [of agreement] sincérité *f* ; [of appetite] vigueur *f* ; [of dislike] ardeur *f* **2.** [enthusiasm] zèle *m*, empressement *m*.

heartland ['hɑːtlænd] n cœur *m*, centre *m*.

heartless ['hɑːtlɪs] adj [person] sans cœur, impitoyable ; [laughter, treatment] cruel.

heartlessly ['hɑːtlɪslɪ] adv sans pitié.

heartlessness ['hɑːtlɪsnɪs] n [of person] manque *m* de cœur, caractère *m* impitoyable.

heartrending ['hɑːtrendɪŋ] adj déchirant, qui fend le cœur.

heart-searching [-ˌsɜːʃɪŋ] n examen *m* de conscience.

heart-stopping adj terrifiant.

heartstrings ['hɑːtstrɪŋz] pl n ▸ **to play on** or **to pull on** or **to tug at sb's heartstrings** faire vibrer or toucher la corde sensible de qqn.

heartthrob ['hɑːtθrɒb] n coqueluche *f*, idole *f*.

heart-to-heart ◆ adj & adv à cœur ouvert *fig*. ◆ n conversation *f* intime or à cœur ouvert.

heart transplant n greffe *f* du cœur.

heartwarming ['hɑːtˌwɔːmɪŋ] adj réconfortant, qui réchauffe le cœur.

hearty ['hɑːtɪ] (*pl* **hearties**, *compar* **heartier**, *superl* **heartiest**) adj **1.** [congratulations, welcome] cordial, chaleureux ; [thanks] sincère ; [approval, recommendation] sans réserves ; [laugh] gros (grosse), franc (franche) ; [knock, slap] vigoureux **2.** [person - robust] vigoureux, robuste, solide ; [- cheerful] jovial **3.** [meal] copieux, abondant **4.** [thorough] absolu.

heat [hiːt] ◆ n **1.** [gen & PHYSIOL] chaleur *f* ; [of fire, sun] ardeur *f*, chaleur *f* / *the heat of summer* le plus fort de l'été / *in the heat of the day* au (moment le) plus chaud de la journée **2.** [temperature] température *f*, chaleur *f* ▸ **body heat** chaleur *f* animale ; CULIN : *turn up the heat* mettre le feu plus fort / *reduce the heat* réduire le feu or la chaleur **3.** [heating] chauffage *m* **4.** [intensity of feeling, fervour] feu *m*, passion *f* **5.** [high point of activity] fièvre *f*, feu *m* / *in the heat of argument* dans le feu de la discussion / *in the heat of the moment* dans l'agitation or l'excitation du moment **6.** *inf* [coercion, pressure] : *the mafia turned the heat on the mayor* la mafia a fait pression sur le maire / *I'm lying low until the heat is off* je me tiens à carreau jusqu'à ce que les choses se calment **7.** SPORT [round of contest] manche *f* ; [preliminary round] (épreuve *f*) éliminatoire *f* **8.** ZOOL chaleur *f*, rut *m* ▸ **on heat** 🇬🇧, **in heat** en chaleur, en rut. ◆ vi [food, liquid] chauffer ; [air, house, room] se réchauffer. ◆ vt [gen & PHYSIOL] chauffer ; [overheat] échauffer. ◆◇ **heat up** ◆ vt sep réchauffer. ◆ vi [food, liquid] chauffer ; [air, house, room] se réchauffer.

heat bump n bouton *m* de chaleur.

heated ['hiːtɪd] adj **1.** [room, swimming pool] chauffé **2.** [argument, discussion] passionné ; [words] vif ; [person] échauffé.

heatedly ['hiːtɪdlɪ] adv [debate, talk] avec passion ; [argue, deny, refuse] avec passion or emportement, farouchement.

heater ['hiːtər] n **1.** [for room] appareil *m* de chauffage ; [for water] chauffe-eau *m inv* ; [for car] (appareil de) chauffage *m* **2.** 🇺🇸 v inf [gun] flingue *m*.

heat exhaustion n épuisement *m* dû à la chaleur.

heath [hiːθ] n **1.** [moor] lande *f* **2.** [plant] bruyère *f*.

heathen ['hiːðn] (*pl* **heathen** or **heathens**) ◆ n [pagan] païen *m*, -enne *f* ; [barbaric person] barbare *mf*. ◆ adj [pagan] païen ; [barbaric] barbare.

heather ['heðər] n bruyère *f*.

heating ['hiːtɪŋ] ◆ n chauffage *m*. ◆ comp [apparatus, appliance, system] de chauffage.

heat loss n perte *f* or déperdition *f* de chaleur.

heatproof ['hiːtpruːf] adj [gen] résistant à la chaleur ; [dish] qui va au four.

heat rash n irritation *f* or inflammation *f* due à la chaleur.

heat-resistant adj [gen] résistant à la chaleur, thermorésistant *spec* ; [dish] qui va au four.

heat-seeking [-ˌsiːkɪŋ] adj [missile] autoguidé par infrarouge.

heat sink n COMPUT dissipateur *m* de chaleur.

heatstroke ['hiːtstrəʊk] n (U) coup *m* de chaleur.

heat wave n vague *f* de chaleur, canicule *f*.

heave [hiːv] (*pt* & *pp* **heaved** ['həʊv], *cont* **heaving**) ◆ vt **1.** [lift] lever or soulever avec effort ; [pull] tirer fort ; [drag] traîner avec effort **2.** [throw] jeter, lancer **3.** *fig* ▸ **to heave a sigh of relief** pousser un soupir de soulagement. ◆ vi **1.** (*pt* & *pp* **heaved** or **hove**) [rise and fall - sea, waves, chest] se soulever ; [- ship] tanguer **2.** [lift] lever, soulever ; [pull] tirer ▸ **heave!** ho ! hisse ! **3.** [retch] avoir des haut-le-cœur ; [vomit] vomir **4.** NAUT aller, se déplacer **▶ to heave into sight** or **into view** NAUT & *fig* paraître or poindre *liter* à l'horizon. **◆** n **1.** [attempt to move] : *one more heave and we're there* encore un coup or un petit effort et ça y est **2.** [retching] haut-le-cœur *m inv*, nausée *f* ; [vomiting] vomissement *m*. **❖ heaves** pl n VET pousse *f*. **❖ heave to ◆** vi se mettre en panne. **◆** vt sep mettre en panne.

heaven ['hevn] n **1.** RELIG ciel *m*, paradis *m* **▶ to go to heaven** aller au ciel, aller au or en paradis / *in heaven* au ciel, au or en paradis / *Our Father, who art in Heaven* Notre Père, qui êtes aux cieux **2.** *fig* : *this is sheer heaven!* c'est divin or merveilleux !, c'est le paradis ! ; [emphatic uses] **▶ heaven forbid!** pourvu que non !, j'espère bien que non ! / *heaven help us if they catch us* que le ciel nous vienne en aide s'ils nous attrapent **▶ good heavens!** ciel !, mon Dieu ! **▶ for heaven's sake! a)** [in annoyance] mince ! **b)** [in pleading] pour l'amour du ciel ! **3.** *she's in heaven when she's with him* elle est au septième ciel or aux anges quand elle est avec lui **▶ to move heaven and earth to do sthg** remuer ciel et terre pour faire qqch. **❖ heavens** pl n [sky] **▶ the heavens** *liter* le ciel, le firmament *liter* / *the heavens opened* il s'est mis à pleuvoir à torrents.

heavenly ['hevnlı] adj **1.** [of space] céleste, du ciel ; [holy] divin **2.** [wonderful] divin, merveilleux.

heaven-sent adj providentiel.

heavily ['hevılı] adv **1.** [fall, land] lourdement, pesamment ; [walk] d'un pas lourd or pesant, lourdement **2.** [laboriously -move] avec difficulté, péniblement ; [-breathe] péniblement, bruyamment **3.** [deeply -sleep] profondément **4.** [as intensifier -bet, drink, smoke] beaucoup ; [-fine, load, tax] lourdement ; [-stress] fortement, lourdement / *it was raining heavily* il pleuvait des cordes.

heavily-built adj solidement bâti.

heaviness ['hevınıs] n **1.** [weight -of object, physique] lourdeur *f*, pesanteur *f*, poids *m* ; [-of movement, step] lourdeur, pesanteur **2.** [depression] abattement *m*, découragement *m* ; [sadness] tristesse *f* **3.** [of weather] lourdeur *f* **4.** [of humour] manque *m* de subtilité ; [of style] lourdeur *f* **5.** [of food] caractère *m* indigeste.

heavy ['hevı] (*compar* **heavier**, *superl* **heaviest**, *pl* **heavies**) **◆** adj **1.** [in weight] lourd ; [box, parcel] lourd, pesant / *how heavy is he?* combien pèse-t-il ? / *it's too heavy for me to lift* je ne peux pas le soulever, c'est or ça pèse trop lourd **▶ heavy goods vehicle** UK poids *m* lourd **2.** [burdened, laden] chargé, lourd / *her eyes were heavy with sleep* elle avait les yeux lourds de sommeil **3.** [in quantity -expenses, payments] important, considérable ; [-fine, losses] gros (grosse), lourd ; [-taxes] lourd ; [-casualties, damages] énorme, important ; [-crop] abondant, gros (grosse) ; [-dew] abondant / *she has a heavy cold* elle a un gros rhume, elle est fortement enrhumée / *heavy rain* forte pluie / *heavy seas* grosse mer / *to be a heavy sleeper* avoir le sommeil profond or lourd / *heavy traffic* circulation dense, grosse circulation **4.** [using large quantities] : *he's a heavy drinker / smoker* il boit / fume beaucoup, c'est un grand buveur / fumeur **5.** [ponderous -movement] lourd ; [-step] pesant, lourd ; [-sigh] gros (grosse), profond ; [-thud] gros (grosse) / *he was dealt a heavy blow* **a)** [hit] il a reçu un coup violent **b)** [from fate] ça a été un rude coup or un gros choc pour lui **6.** [thick -coat, sweater] gros (grosse) ; [-soil] lourd, gras (grasse) **7.** [person -fat] gros (grosse), corpulent ; [-solid] costaud, fortement charpenté / *a man of heavy build* un homme solidement bâti **8.** [coarse, solid -line, lips] gros (grosse), épais (épaisse) ; [thick -beard] gros (grosse), fort **9.** [grave, serious -news] grave ; [-responsibility] lourd ; [-defeat] lourd, grave **10.** [depressed -mood, spirits] abattu, déprimé / *with a heavy heart* or *heavy at heart* le cœur

gros **11.** [tiring -task] lourd, pénible ; [-work] pénible ; [-day, schedule, week] chargé, difficile **▶ heavy going** *fig* : *they found it heavy going* ils ont trouvé cela pénible or difficile / *I found his last novel very heavy going* j'ai trouvé son dernier roman très indigeste **12.** [difficult to understand -not superficial] profond, compliqué, sérieux ; [-tedious] indigeste **13.** [clumsy -humour, irony] peu subtil, lourd ; [-style] lourd **14.** [food, meal] lourd, indigeste ; [wine] corsé, lourd **15.** [ominous, oppressive -air, cloud, weather] lourd ; [-sky] couvert, chargé, lourd ; [-silence] lourd, pesant, profond ; [-smell, perfume] lourd, fort. **◆** adv **1.** [lie, weigh] lourd, lourdement / *the lie weighed heavy on her conscience* le mensonge pesait lourd sur sa conscience **2.** [harshly] **▶ to come on heavy with sb** être dur avec qqn.

heavy cream n US crème *f* à fouetter.

heavy-duty adj **1.** [clothing, furniture] résistant ; [cleanser, equipment] à usage industriel **2.** *inf* [serious] sérieux.

heavy-handed adj **1.** [clumsy -person] maladroit ; [-style, writing] lourd **2.** [tactless -remark] qui manque de tact ; [-joke] lourd, qui manque de subtilité ; [-compliment] lourd, (trop) appuyé **3.** [harsh -person] dur, sévère ; [-action, policy] arbitraire.

heavyhearted [,hevı'hɑ:tıd] adj abattu, découragé.

heavy hitter n US **1.** [baseball] *joueur qui frappe fort et marque beaucoup de points* **2.** *fig* personne *f* influente, gros bonnet *m*.

heavy industry n industrie *f* lourde.

heavy metal n **1.** PHYS métal *m* lourd **2.** MUS heavy metal *m*.

heavyweight ['hevıweıt] **◆** n **1.** [large person, thing] colosse *m* ; *inf & fig* [important person] personne *f* de poids or d'envergure, ponte *m* **2.** SPORT poids *m* lourd. **◆** adj **1.** [cloth, wool] lourd ; [coat, sweater] gros (grosse) **2.** *inf & fig* [important] important **3.** SPORT [championship, fight] poids lourd / *heavyweight champion* champion *m* poids lourd or dans la catégorie poids lourd(s).

Hebrew ['hi:bru:] **◆** n **1.** [person] Hébreu *m*, Israélite *mf* **▶ the Hebrews** les Hébreux *mpl* **2.** LING hébreu *m*. **◆** adj hébreu (*m only*), hébraïque.

Hebrides ['hebrıdi:z] pl pr n **▶ the Hebrides** les (îles *fpl*) Hébrides / *in the Hebrides* aux Hébrides.

heck [hek] *inf* **◆** n : *that's a heck of a lot of money!* c'est une sacrée somme d'argent ! / *how the heck should I know?* mais enfin, comment veux-tu que je sache ? **◆** interj zut, flûte.

heckle ['hekl] **◆** vt [interrupt] interrompre bruyamment ; [shout at] interpeller, harceler. **◆** vi crier (*pour gêner un orateur*).

heckler ['heklər] n chahuteur *m*, -euse *f*.

heckling ['heklıŋ] **◆** n (U) harcèlement *m*, interpellations *fpl*. **◆** adj qui fait du harcèlement, qui interpelle.

hectare ['hekteər] n hectare *m*.

hectic ['hektık] adj **1.** [turbulent] agité, bousculé ; [eventful] mouvementé **2.** [flushed] fiévreux ; MED [fever, flush] hectique.

hector ['hektər] **◆** vt harceler, tyranniser. **◆** vi être tyrannique, être une brute. **❖ Hector** pr n Hector.

hectoring ['hektərıŋ] **◆** n (U) harcèlement *m*, torture *f*. **◆** adj [behaviour] tyrannique ; [tone, voice] impérieux, autoritaire.

he'd [hi:d] **1.** abbr of **he had 2.** abbr of **he would**.

hedge [hedʒ] **◆** n **1.** [shrubs] haie *f* **2.** *fig* [protection] sauvegarde *f* / *a hedge against inflation* une sauvegarde or une couverture contre l'inflation **3.** [statement] déclaration *f* évasive. **◆** comp [clippers, saw] à haie.

◆ vt **1.** [enclose] entourer d'une haie, enclore **2.** [guard against losing] couvrir ▶ **to hedge one's bets** se couvrir. ◆ vi **1.** [plant] planter une haie ; [trim] tailler une haie **2.** [in action] essayer de gagner du temps, atermoyer ; [in answering] éviter de répondre, répondre à côté ; [in explaining] expliquer avec des détours **3.** [protect] se protéger. ❖ **hedge about** 🇬🇧, **hedge around** vt sep entourer / *the offer was hedged about with conditions* fig l'offre était assortie de conditions. ❖ **hedge in** vt sep entourer d'une haie, enclore / *hedged in by restrictions* fig assorti de restrictions.

hedgehog ['heʤhɒg] n hérisson m.

hedgerow ['heʤrəʊ] n haies fpl.

hedge trimmer n taille-haie m.

hedonism ['hi:dənɪzm] n hédonisme m.

hedonist ['hi:dənɪst] n hédoniste mf.

hedonistic [ˌhi:də'nɪstɪk] adj hédoniste.

heebie-jeebies [ˌhi:bɪ'ʤi:bɪz] pl n inf ▶ **to have the heebie-jeebies** avoir la frousse ou les chocottes / *he gives me the heebie-jeebies* il me met mal à l'aise.

heed [hi:d] ◆ n ▶ **to take heed of sthg, to pay** or **to give heed to sthg** tenir bien compte de qqch. ◆ vt **1.** [warning, words] faire bien attention à, tenir compte de, prendre garde à **2.** [person - listen to] bien écouter ; [-obey] obéir à.

heedless ['hi:dlɪs] adj ▶ **heedless of:** *heedless of the danger* sans se soucier du danger.

heedlessly ['hi:dlɪslɪ] adv **1.** [without thinking] sans faire attention, à la légère **2.** [inconsiderately] avec insouciance, négligemment.

heel [hi:l] ◆ n **1.** ANAT talon m **2.** [of shoe] talon m **3.** [of glove, golf club, hand, knife, sock, tool] talon m **4.** [of bread] talon m, croûton m ; [of cheese] talon m, croûte f **5.** v inf & dated [contemptible man] salaud m **6.** NAUT [of keel] talon m ; [of mast] caisse f **7.** [incline - of ship] bande f ; [-of vehicle, tower] inclinaison f. ◆ vt **1.** [boot, shoe] refaire le talon de **2.** SPORT [ball] talonner. ◆ vi **1.** [to dog] ▶ **heel!** au pied ! **2.** [ship] gîter, donner de la bande ; [vehicle, tower] s'incliner, se pencher. ❖ **heel over** vi [ship] gîter, donner de la bande ; [vehicle, tower] s'incliner, se pencher ; [cyclist] se pencher.

heel bar n talon-minute m, réparations-minute fpl.

heels [hi:lz] = **high heels**.

hefty ['heftɪ] (*compar* **heftier,** *superl* **heftiest**) adj inf **1.** [package - heavy] lourd ; [-bulky] encombrant, volumineux ; [book] épais (épaisse), gros (grosse) ; [person] costaud **2.** [part, profit] gros (grosse) **3.** [blow, slap] puissant.

heifer ['hefər] n génisse f.

height [haɪt] n **1.** [tallness - of person] taille f, grandeur f ; [-of building, tree] hauteur f / *what height are you?* combien mesurez-vous ? **2.** [distance above ground - of mountain, plane] altitude f ; [-of ceiling, river, stars] hauteur f / *to be at a height of three metres above the ground* être à trois mètres au-dessus du sol **3.** [high position] hauteur f / *I'm afraid of heights* j'ai le vertige **4.** fig [peak - of career, success] point m culminant ; [-of fortune, fame] apogée m ; [-of arrogance, stupidity] comble m / *at the height of the battle / storm* au plus fort de la bataille / de l'orage / *it's the height of fashion* c'est le dernier cri.

height-adjustable adj réglable en hauteur.

heighten ['haɪtn] ◆ vt **1.** [make higher - building, ceiling, shelf] relever, rehausser **2.** [increase - effect, fear, pleasure] augmenter, intensifier ; [-flavour] relever ; MED [fever] faire monter, aggraver. ◆ vi [fear, pleasure] augmenter, monter.

heightened ['haɪtnd] adj **1.** [building, ceiling, shelf] relevé, rehaussé **2.** [fear, pleasure] intensifié ; [colour] plus vif.

heinous ['heɪnəs] adj liter & fml odieux, atroce.

heir [eər] n [gen] héritier m ; LAW héritier m, légataire mf / *the heir to the throne* l'héritier du trône or de la couronne.

heiress ['eərɪs] n héritière f.

heirless ['eəlɪs] adj sans héritier.

heirloom ['eəlu:m] n [family property] ▶ **(family) heirloom** objet m de famille.

heist [haɪst] 🇺🇸 inf ◆ n [robbery] vol m ; [in bank] braquage m ; [stolen objects] butin m. ◆ vt [steal] voler ; [commit armed robbery] braquer.

held [held] pt & pp ⟶ **hold**.

helices ['helɪsi:z] pl ⟶ **helix**.

helicopter ['helɪkɒptər] ◆ n hélicoptère m. ◆ comp [patrol, rescue] en hélicoptère ; [pilot] d'hélicoptère ▶ **helicopter transfer** or **transport** héliportage m. ◆ vt transporter en hélicoptère.

helipad ['helɪpæd] n héliport m.

heliport ['helɪpɔ:t] n héliport m.

helium ['hi:lɪəm] n hélium m.

helix ['hi:lɪks] (*pl* **helices** ['helɪsi:z] or **helixes**) n **1.** ARCHIT & GEOM [spiral] hélice f **2.** ANAT & ZOOL hélix m.

hell [hel] n **1.** RELIG enfer m ; MYTH [underworld] les Enfers ▶ **to go to hell a)** [Christianity] aller en enfer **b)** MYTH descendre aux Enfers ▶ **go to hell!** inf va te faire voir ! ▶ **to give sb hell** inf passer un savon or faire sa fête à qqn **2.** [torture] enfer m **3.** inf [used as emphasis] : *he's as happy / tired as hell* il est vachement heureux / fatigué / *a hell of a lot of books* tout un tas or un paquet de livres / *they had a hell of a time getting the car started* ils en ont bavé pour faire démarrer la voiture / *to run / to shout like hell* courir / crier comme un fou / *what the hell are you doing?* qu'est-ce que tu fous ? / *who the hell do you think you are?* mais tu te prends pour qui ? ❖ **Hell** = **hell**.

he'll [hi:l] abbr of **he will**.

hell-bent adj inf acharné.

Hellenistic [ˌhelɪ'nɪstɪk] adj [language, period] hellénistique.

hellhole ['helhəʊl] n inf bouge m.

hellish ['helɪʃ] ◆ adj **1.** [cruel - action, person] diabolique **2.** inf [dreadful] infernal. ◆ adv inf = **hellishly.**

hellishly ['helɪʃlɪ] adv 🇬🇧 inf atrocement, épouvantablement.

hello [hə'ləʊ] (*pl* **hellos**) ◆ interj **1.** [greeting] bonjour, salut ; [in the evening] bonsoir ; [on answering telephone] allô **2.** [to attract attention] hé, ohé **3.** [in surprise] tiens. ◆ n [greeting] bonjour m, salutation f.

hell-raiser n inf fouteur m, -euse f de merde.

Hell's Angels pl pr n Hell's Angels mpl (nom d'un groupe de motards au comportement souvent considéré comme violent).

helluva ['heləvə] adj inf : *he's a helluva guy* c'est un type vachement bien / *I had a helluva time* **a)** [awful] je me suis emmerdé **b)** [wonderful] je me suis vachement marré.

helm [helm] ◆ n **1.** NAUT barre f, gouvernail m ▶ **to be at the helm a)** lit tenir la barre or le gouvernail **b)** fig tenir la barre or les rênes ▶ **to take the helm** lit & fig prendre la barre, prendre la direction des opérations **2.** arch [helmet] casque m. ◆ vt NAUT gouverner, barrer ; fig diriger.

helmet ['helmɪt] n [gen] casque m ; [medieval] heaume m.

helmsman ['helmzmən] (*pl* **helmsmen** [-mən]) n timonier m, homme m de barre.

help [help] ◆ vt **1.** [assist, aid - gen] aider, venir en aide à ; [-elderly, poor, wounded] secourir, venir en aide à / *can I help you with the dishes?* puis-je t'aider à faire la vaisselle ? / *they help one another take care of the children* ils s'entraident pour s'occuper des enfants / *he helped me on* / *off with my coat* il m'a aidé à mettre / enlever mon manteau ▸ **so help me God! a)** [I swear] je le jure devant Dieu ! **b)** [praying for help] que Dieu me vienne en aide ! / *I'll get you for this, so help me* inf j'aurai ta peau, je le jure ! **2.** [contribute to] contribuer à ; [encourage] encourager, favoriser **3.** [remedy - situation] améliorer ; [- pain] soulager / *it helped to ease my headache* cela a soulagé mon mal de tête / *crying won't help anyone* cela ne sert à rien or n'arrange rien de pleurer **4.** [serve] servir / *I helped myself to the cheese* je me suis servi en fromage / *help yourself!* servez-vous ! **5.** (with 'can', usu neg) [avoid, refrain from] : *I can't help thinking that we could have done more* je ne peux pas m'empêcher de penser qu'on aurait pu faire plus / *we couldn't help laughing* or *but laugh* nous ne pouvions pas nous empêcher de rire **6.** (with 'can', usu neg) [control] : *he can't help it if she doesn't like it* il n'y est pour rien or ce n'est pas de sa faute si cela ne lui plaît pas / *I can't help it* je n'y peux rien, ce n'est pas de ma faute / *it can't be helped* tant pis ! on n'y peut rien or on ne peut pas faire autrement. ◆ vi être utile / *she helps a lot around the house* elle se rend très utile à la maison, elle rend souvent service à la maison / *is there anything I can do to help?* puis-je être utile ? / *every little bit helps* les petits ruisseaux font les grandes rivières prov. ◆ n **1.** [gen] aide f, assistance f ; [to drowning or wounded person] secours m, assistance f / *can I be of any help?* puis-je faire quelque chose pour vous ?, puis-je vous rendre service ? / *he went to get help* il est allé chercher du secours / *he opened the window with the help of a crowbar* il a ouvert la fenêtre à l'aide d'un levier / *she did it without any help* elle l'a fait toute seule / *the situation is now beyond help* la situation est désespérée or irrémédiable maintenant **2.** [something that assists] aide f, secours m / *you've been a great help* vous m'avez été d'un grand secours, vous m'avez beaucoup aidé **3.** (U) **US** [employees] personnel m, employés mpl **4.** [domestic aid] femme f de ménage. ❖ **help along** vt sep [person] aider à marcher or avancer ; [plan, project] faire avancer. ❖ **help out** ◆ vt sep [gen] aider, venir en aide à ; [with supplies, money] dépanner. ◆ vi aider, donner un coup de main.

help button n COMPUT case f d'aide.

help desk n COMPUT service m d'assistance, support m.

helper ['helpər] n **1.** [gen] aide mf, assistant m, -e f ; [professional] auxiliaire mf **2.** **US** [home help] femme f de ménage **3.** MED ▸ **helper T-cell** lymphocyte m T « helper » (T4).

helpful ['helpfʊl] adj **1.** [person] obligeant, serviable **2.** [advice, suggestion] utile ; [gadget, information, map] utile ; [medication] efficace, salutaire.

helpfully ['helpfʊlɪ] adv avec obligeance, obligeamment.

helpfulness ['helpfʊlnɪs] n **1.** [of person] obligeance f, serviabilité f **2.** [of gadget, map, etc.] utilité f.

helping ['helpɪŋ] n portion f.

helping hand n main f secourable.

helpless ['helplɪs] adj **1.** [vulnerable] désarmé, sans défense **2.** [physically] faible, impotent ; [mentally] impuissant **3.** [powerless - person] impuissant, sans ressource ; [- anger, feeling] impuissant ; [- situation] sans recours, désespéré / *he was helpless to stop her leaving* il était incapable de l'empêcher de partir / *they were helpless with laughter* ils n'en pouvaient plus de rire, ils étaient morts de rire.

helplessly ['helplɪslɪ] adv **1.** [without protection] sans défense, sans ressource **2.** [unable to react] sans pouvoir réagir ; [argue, struggle, try] en vain.

helplessness ['helplɪsnɪs] n **1.** [defencelessness] incapacité f de se défendre, vulnérabilité f **2.** [physical] incapa-

cité f, impotence f ; [mental] incapacité f **3.** [powerlessness - of person] impuissance f, manque m de moyens ; [- of anger, feeling] impuissance f.

helpline ['helplaɪn] n service m d'assistance téléphonique.

help menu n COMPUT menu m d'aide.

Helsinki ['helsɪŋkɪ] pr n Helsinki.

helter-skelter [,heltə'skeltər] ◆ adv [run, rush] en désordre, à la débandade ; [organize, throw] pêle-mêle, en vrac. ◆ adj [rush] à la débandade ; [account, story] désordonné. ◆ n **UK** [ride in fairground] toboggan m.

hem [hem] (pt & pp **hemmed**, cont **hemming**) ◆ n **1.** [of trousers, skirt] ourlet m ; [of handkerchief, sheet] bord m, ourlet m **2.** [hemline] (bas m de l')ourlet m. ◆ vt ourler, faire l'ourlet de. ◆ interj ▸ **hem!** a) [to call attention] hem ! **b)** [to indicate hesitation, pause] euh ! ◆ vi faire hem ▸ **to hem and haw** bafouiller. ❖ **hem in** vt sep [house, people] entourer, encercler ; [enemy] cerner / *he felt hemmed in* a) [in room] il faisait de la claustrophobie, il se sentait oppressé **b)** [in relationship] il se sentait prisonnier or pris au piège / *hemmed in by rules* fig entravé par des règles or règlements.

he-man ['hi:mæn] n inf homme m viril.

hematology **US** = haematology.

hemisphere ['hemɪ,sfɪər] n hémisphère m.

hemline ['hemlaɪn] n (bas m de l')ourlet m.

hemlock ['hemlɒk] n BOT [poison] ciguë f.

hemoglobin **US** = haemoglobin.

hemophilia **US** = haemophilia.

hemorrhage **US** = haemorrhage.

hemorrhoids **US** = haemorrhoids.

hemp [hemp] n **1.** [fibre, plant] chanvre m **2.** [marijuana] marijuana f ; [hash] haschisch m, hachisch m.

hen [hen] n **1.** [chicken] poule f **2.** [female] femelle f ▸ **hen bird** oiseau m femelle **3.** inf [woman] mémère f.

hence [hens] adv **1.** [therefore] donc, d'où **2.** fml [from this time] d'ici **3.** fml [from here] d'ici.

henceforward [,hens'fɔ:wəd], **henceforth** [,hens-'fɔ:θ] adv dorénavant, désormais.

henchman ['hentʃmən] (pl **henchmen** [-mən]) n [follower] partisan m, adepte m pej ; [right-hand man] homme m de main, suppôt m pej.

Henley ['henlɪ] pr n ville dans l'Oxfordshire ▸ **Henley Regatta** importante épreuve internationale d'aviron.

Henley Regatta

Cette épreuve internationale d'aviron a lieu tous les ans sur la Tamise, au mois de juillet. C'est une manifestation autant mondaine que sportive.

henna ['henə] ◆ n henné m. ◆ vt teindre au henné.

hen night, hen party n inf [gen] soirée entre copines ; [before wedding] : *she's having her hen night* elle enterre sa vie de jeune fille.

henpecked ['henpekt] adj dominé.

hepatitis [,hepə'taɪtɪs] n (U) hépatite f.

her [hɜːr] ◆ det son m, sa f, ses mf / *her book* son livre / *her glasses* ses lunettes / *her university* son université. ◆ pron **1.** [direct object - unstressed] la, l' (before vowel or silent 'h') ; [- stressed] elle / *I recognize her* je la reconnais / *why did you have to choose HER?* pourquoi l'as-tu choisie elle ? **2.** [indirect object - unstressed] lui ; [-stressed] à elle **/** *give her the money* donne-lui l'argent **3.** [after preposition] elle **/** *I was in front of her* j'étais devant elle **4.** [with 'to be'] : *it's her* c'est elle.

herald ['herəld] **◆** vt **1.** [announce] annoncer, proclamer **2.** [hail] acclamer. **◆** n **1.** [medieval messenger] héraut *m* **2.** [forerunner] héraut *m*, avant-coureur *m*.

heraldic [he'rældık] adj héraldique.

heraldry ['herəldrı] n **1.** [system, study] héraldique *f* **2.** [coat of arms] blason *m* **3.** [pageantry] faste *m*, pompe *f* (héraldique).

herb [hɜːb US ɜːrb] n **1.** BOT herbe *f* **▶ herbs** CULIN fines herbes, herbes aromatiques **2.** *inf* [marijuana] herbe *f*.

herbaceous [hɜː'beıʃəs US ɜːr'beıʃəs] adj [plant, stem] herbacé.

herbaceous border n bordure *f* de plantes herbacées.

herbal ['hɜːbl US 'ɜːrbl] **◆** adj aux herbes **/** *herbal medicine* a) [practice] phytothérapie *f* b) [medication] médicament *m* à base de plantes **/** *herbal tea* tisane *f*. **◆** n traité *m* sur les plantes, herbier *m* arch.

herbalist ['hɜːbəlıst US 'ɜːrbəlıst] n herboriste *mf*.

herbicide ['hɜːbısaıd US 'ɜːrbısaıd] n herbicide *m*.

herbivore ['hɜːbıvɔːʳ US 'ɜːrbıvɔːʳ] n herbivore *m*.

herbivorous ['hɜːbıvərəs US ɜːr'bıvərəs] adj herbivore.

herd [hɜːd] **◆** n **1.** [of cattle, goats, sheep] troupeau *m* ; [of wild animals] troupe *f* ; [of horses] troupe *f*, bande *f* ; [of deer] harde *f* **2.** *inf* [of people] troupeau *m* *pej*, foule *f*. **◆** vt **1.** [bring together] rassembler (en troupeau) ; [look after] garder **2.** [drive] mener, conduire. **◆ herd together ◆** vi s'assembler en troupeau, s'attrouper. **◆** vt sep rassembler en troupeau.

herder ['hɜːdəʳ US] [gen] gardien *m*, -enne *f* de troupeau ; [of cattle] vacher *m*, -ère *f*, bouvier *m*, -ère *f* ; [of sheep] berger *m*, -ère *f*.

herdsman ['hɜːdzmən] (*pl* **herdsmen** [-mən]) n [gen] gardien *m* de troupeau ; [of cattle] vacher *m*, bouvier *m* ; [of sheep] berger *m*.

here [hıəʳ] **◆** adv **1.** [at, in this place] : *she left here yesterday* elle est partie d'ici hier **/** *is Susan here?* est-ce que Susan est là ? **/** *he won't be here next week* il ne sera pas là la semaine prochaine **/** *they're here* a) [I've found them] ils sont ici b) [they've arrived] ils sont arrivés **/** *winter is here* c'est l'hiver, l'hiver est arrivé ; *(after preposition)* : *around here* par ici **/** *I'm in here* je suis là or ici **/** *where are you? — over here!* où êtes-vous ? — (par) ici ! **2.** [drawing attention to sthg] voici, voilà **/** *here's the key!* voilà or voici la clef ! **/** *here they come!* les voilà ! or voici ! **▶ here goes** *inf*, **here goes nothing** US *inf* allons-y ! **/** *here we go again!* ça y est, c'est reparti pour un tour ! **3.** [emphasizing specified object, person, etc.] : *ask the lady here* demandez à cette dame ici **/** *it's this one here that I want* c'est celui-ci que je veux **4.** [at this point] maintenant ; [at that point] alors, à ce moment-là **/** *here I would like to remind you...* maintenant je voudrais vous rappeler... **5.** *here's to* [in toasts] à **/** *here's to us!* à nous !, à nos amours ! **◆** interj **1.** [giving, taking, etc.] **▶ here!** tiens !, tenez ! **2.** [protesting] : *here! what do you think you're doing?* hé ! qu'est-ce que tu fais ? **◆ here and now** adv phr sur-le-champ. **◆ here and there** adv phr ici et là. **◆ here, there and everywhere** adv phr *hum* un peu partout.

hereabouts UK ['hıərə,bauts], **hereabout** US ['hıərə,baut] adv par ici, près d'ici, dans les environs.

hereafter [,hıər'ɑːftəʳ] **◆** n [life after death] au-delà *m* *inv* **/** *in the hereafter* dans l'autre monde. **◆** adv **1.** *fml* LAW [in document] ci-après **2.** *liter* [after death] dans l'au-delà.

hereby [,hıə'baı] adv *fml* LAW [in statement] par la présente (déclaration) ; [in document] par le présent (document) ; [in letter] par la présente ; [in act] par le présent acte, par ce geste ; [in will] par le présent testament.

hereditary [hı'redıtrı] adj héréditaire.

heredity [hı'redətı] n hérédité *f*.

herein [,hıər'ın] adv *fml* **1.** [in this respect] en ceci, en cela **2.** LAW [in this document] ci-inclus.

heresy ['herəsı] (*pl* **heresies**) n hérésie *f*.

heretic ['herətık] n hérétique *mf*.

herewith [,hıə'wıð] adv *fml* **1.** [enclosed] ci-joint, ci-inclus **2.** = **hereby**.

heritage ['herıtıdʒ] n héritage *m*, patrimoine *m*.

heritage centre n site *m* touristique *(faisant partie du patrimoine historique national)*.

hermaphrodite [hɜː'mæfrədaıt] **◆** adj hermaphrodite. **◆** n hermaphrodite *m*.

hermetic [hɜː'metık] adj hermétique.

hermetically [hɜː'metıklı] adv hermétiquement.

hermit ['hɜːmıt] n [gen] ermite *m*, solitaire *m* ; RELIG ermite *m*.

hermitage ['hɜːmıtıdʒ] n ermitage *m*.

hermit crab n bernard-l'ermite *m* *inv*, pagure *m*.

hernia ['hɜːnıə] (*pl* **hernias** or **herniae** [-nıiː]) n hernie *f*.

hero ['hıərəu] (*pl* **heroes**) n **1.** [person] héros *m* **2.** US [sandwich] sorte de gros sandwich.

heroic [hı'rəuık] adj **1.** [act, behaviour, person] héroïque **2.** *liter* épique, héroïque.

heroically [hı'rəuıklı] adv héroïquement.

heroics [hı'rəuıks] pl n [language] emphase *f*, déclamation *f* ; [behaviour] affectation *f*, emphase *f*.

heroin ['herəuın] **◆** n héroïne *f*. **◆** comp **▶ heroin addict** or **user** héroïnomane *mf* **▶ heroin addiction** héroïnomanie *f*.

heroine ['herəuın] n héroïne *f (femme)*.

heroism ['herəuızm] n héroïsme *m*.

heron ['herən] (*pl* **heron** or **herons**) n héron *m*.

hero worship n [admiration] adulation *f*, culte *m* (du héros) ; ANTIQ culte *m* des héros. **◆ hero-worship** vt aduler, idolâtrer.

herpes ['hɜːpiːz] n (U) herpès *m*.

herpetologist [,hɜːpı'tɒlədʒıst] n erpétologiste *mf*.

herring ['herıŋ] (*pl* **herring** or **herrings**) n hareng *m*.

herringbone ['herıŋbəun] **◆** n **1.** [bone] arête *f* de hareng **2.** TEXT [pattern] (dessin *m* à) chevrons *mpl* ; [fabric] tissu *m* à chevrons **3.** [in skiing] montée *f* en ciseaux or en pas de canard. **◆** comp **▶ herringbone tweed** tweed *m* à chevrons.

hers [hɜːz] pron **1.** [gen] le sien *m*, la sienne *f*, les siens *mpl*, les siennes **/** *this car is hers* cette voiture lui appartient or est à elle **/** *hers was the best photograph* sa photographie était la meilleure **2.** [after preposition] : *she took his hand in hers* elle a pris sa main dans la sienne **/** *he's an old friend of hers* c'est un vieil ami à elle, c'est un de ses vieux amis **3.** [indicating authorship] d'elle.

herself [hɜː'self] pron **1.** [reflexive form] se, s' *(before vowel or silent 'h')* **/** *she bought herself a car* elle s'est acheté une voiture **/** *she considers herself lucky* elle considère qu'elle a de la chance **2.** [emphatic form] elle-même **/**

she built the shelves herself elle a monté les étagères elle-même **3.** [with preposition] elle */ the old woman was talking to herself* la vieille femme parlait toute seule */ she did it all by herself* elle l'a fait toute seule.

Herts written abbr of **Hertfordshire**.

hertz [hɜːts] (*pl* **hertz**) n hertz *m*.

he's [hiːz] **1.** abbr of **he is 2.** abbr of **he has**.

hesitance ['hezɪtəns], **hesitancy** ['hezɪtənsɪ] n hésitation *f*, indécision *f*.

hesitant ['hezɪtənt] adj **1.** [person - uncertain] hésitant, indécis ; [- cautious] réticent **2.** [attempt, speech, voice] hésitant.

hesitantly ['hezɪtəntlɪ] adv [act, try] avec hésitation, timidement ; [answer, speak] d'une voix hésitante.

hesitate ['hezɪteɪt] vi hésiter */ don't hesitate to call me* n'hésitez pas à m'appeler.

hesitation [,hezɪ'teɪʃn] n hésitation *f*.

hessian ['hesɪən] ◆ n (toile *f* de) jute *m*. ◆ comp [fabric, sack] de jute.

heterogeneous [,hetərə'dʒiːnjəs] adj hétérogène.

heterosexism [,hetərə'seksɪzm] n hétérosexisme *m*.

heterosexual [,hetərə'sekʃʊəl] ◆ adj hétérosexuel. ◆ n hétérosexuel *m*, -elle *f*.

heterosexuality ['hetərə,sekʃʊ'ælətɪ] n hétérosexualité *f*.

het up adj inf [angry] énervé ; [excited] excité, agité ▶ **to get all het up (about sthg)** se mettre dans tous ses états or s'énerver (pour qqch).

hew [hjuː] (*pt* **hewed**, *pp* **hewed** *or* **hewn** [hjuːn]) vt [wood] couper ; [stone] tailler ; [coal] abattre.

HEW (abbr of **Department of) Health, Education and Welfare**) pr n *ancien ministère américain de l'Éducation et de la Santé publique.*

hex [heks] **US** ◆ n **1.** [spell] sort *m*, sortilège *m* **2.** [witch] sorcière *f*. ◆ vt jeter un sort à.

hexagon ['heksəgən] n hexagone *m*.

hexagonal [hek'sægənl] adj hexagonal.

hey [heɪ] interj ▶ **hey!** a) [to draw attention] hé !, ohé ! b) [to show surprise] tiens ! ▶ **hey (there)!** **US** [as greeting] salut !

heyday ['heɪdeɪ] n [of cinema, movement] âge *m* d'or, beaux jours *mpl* ; [of nation, organization] zénith *m*, apogée *m* / in her heyday a) [youth] quand elle était dans la force de l'âge b) [success] à l'apogée de sa gloire, au temps de sa splendeur.

HF (abbr of **high frequency**) HF.

HGV (abbr of **heavy goods vehicle**) n **UK** PL *m*.

hi [haɪ] interj inf **1.** [hello] salut **2.** [hey] hé, ohé.

HI written abbr of **Hawaii**.

hiatal hernia [haɪ'eɪtl-] = **hiatus hernia**.

hiatus [haɪ'eɪtəs] (*pl* **hiatus** *or* **hiatuses**) n ANAT, LING & LITER hiatus *m* ; [in manuscript] lacune *f* ; [break, interruption] pause *f*, interruption *f*.

hiatus hernia n hernie *f* hiatale.

hibachi [hɪ'bɑːtʃɪ] n *petit barbecue de table.*

hibernate ['haɪbəneɪt] vi hiberner.

hibernation [,haɪbə'neɪʃn] n hibernation *f*.

hiccough ['hɪkʌp], **hiccup** ['hɪkʌp] ◆ n **1.** [sound] hoquet *m* / to have (the) hiccoughs avoir le hoquet **2.** [problem] contretemps *m*. ◆ vi hoqueter.

hick [hɪk] **US** inf ◆ n péquenaud *m*, -e *f*, plouc *mf*. ◆ adj de péquenaud.

hickey ['hɪkɪ] n **US** inf **1.** [gadget] bidule *m* **2.** [lovebite] suçon *m*.

hickory ['hɪkərɪ] (*pl* **hickories**) ◆ n [tree] hickory *m*, noyer *m* blanc d'Amérique ; [wood] (bois *m* de) hickory *m*. ◆ comp en (bois de) hickory ▶ **hickory nut** fruit *m* du hickory, noix *f* d'Amérique.

hid [hɪd] pt ⟶ **hide**.

hidden ['hɪdn] ◆ pp ⟶ **hide**. ◆ adj caché */ hidden from sight* à l'abri des regards indiscrets, caché */ a village hidden away in the mountains* un village caché or niché dans les montagnes */ a hidden agenda* un plan secret ▶ **hidden tax** impôt *m* indirect or déguisé.

hide [haɪd] (*pt* **hid** [hɪd], *pp* **hidden** ['hɪdn]) ◆ vt **1.** [conceal - person, thing] cacher ; [- disappointment, dismay, fright] dissimuler ▶ **to hide sthg from sb** a) [ball, letter] cacher qqch à qqn b) [emotion] dissimuler qqch à qqn **2.** [keep secret] taire, dissimuler */ to hide the truth (from sb)* taire or dissimuler la vérité (à qqn). ◆ vi se cacher ▶ **to hide from sb** se cacher de qqn. ◆ n **1.** **UK** cachette *f* ; [in hunting] affût *m* **2.** [animal skin - raw] peau *f* ; [- tanned] cuir *m* **3.** inf & fig [of person] peau *f*. ◆ adj de or en cuir.
❖ hide away ◆ vi se cacher ▶ **to hide away (from sb / sthg)** se cacher (de qqn / qqch). ◆ vt sep cacher.
❖ hide out vi se tenir caché */ he's hiding out from the police* il se cache de la police.

hide-and-seek n cache-cache *m* / to play (at) hide-and-seek jouer à cache-cache.

hideaway ['haɪdəweɪ] n cachette *f*.

hidebound ['haɪdbaʊnd] adj [person] obtus, borné ; [attitude, view] borné, rigide.

hideous ['hɪdɪəs] adj **1.** [physically ugly] hideux, affreux **2.** [ghastly - conditions, situation] atroce, abominable.

hideously ['hɪdɪəslɪ] adv **1.** [deformed, wounded] hideusement, atrocement, affreusement **2.** fig [as intensifier] terriblement, horriblement.

hideout ['haɪdaʊt] n cachette *f*.

hidey-hole ['haɪdɪhəʊl] n inf planque *f*.

hiding ['haɪdɪŋ] n **1.** [concealment] ▶ **to be in hiding** se tenir caché ▶ **to go into hiding** a) [criminal] se cacher, se planquer b) [spy, terrorist] entrer dans la clandestinité **2.** inf [thrashing] rossée *f* ▶ **to give sb a good hiding** donner une bonne raclée à qqn **3.** [defeat] raclée *f*, dérouillée *f*.

hiding place n cachette *f*.

hierarchical [,haɪə'rɑːkɪkl] adj hiérarchique.

hierarchically [,haɪə'rɑːkɪklɪ] adv hiérarchiquement.

hierarchy ['haɪərɑːkɪ] (*pl* **hierarchies**) n **1.** [organization into grades] hiérarchie *f* ; [of animals, plants] classification *f*, classement *m* **2.** [upper levels of authority] dirigeants *mpl*, autorités *fpl*.

hieroglyphics [,haɪərə'glɪfɪks] pl n écriture *f* hiéroglyphique.

hi-fi ['haɪfaɪ] (abbr of **high fidelity**) inf ◆ n **1.** (U) hi-fi *f* inv **2.** [stereo system] chaîne *f* (hi-fi) ; [radio] radio *f* (hi-fi). ◆ comp [equipment, recording, system] hi-fi (inv).

higgledy-piggledy [,hɪgldɪ'pɪgldɪ] inf ◆ adv pêle-mêle, en désordre. ◆ adj en désordre, pêle-mêle.

high [haɪ] ◆ adj **1.** [tall] haut */ how high is that building?* quelle est la hauteur de ce bâtiment ? */ the walls are three metres high* les murs ont or font trois mètres de haut, les murs sont hauts de trois mètres */ the building is eight storeys high* c'est un immeuble de or à huit étages */ when I was only so high* quand je n'étais pas plus grand que ça **2.** [above ground level - river, tide] haut ; [- altitude, shelf] haut, élevé **3.** [above average - number] grand, élevé ; [- speed, value] grand ; [- cost, price, rate] élevé ; [- salary] élevé, gros (grosse) ; [- pressure] élevé, haut ; [- polish] brillant */ she suffers from high blood pressure* elle a de la tension / *built to withstand high temperatures* conçu pour résister à des températures élevées / *he has a high temperature* il a beaucoup de température or fièvre / *areas of high unemployment* des régions à fort taux de chômage / *milk is high in calcium* le lait contient beaucoup de calcium **4.** [better than average - quality] grand, haut ; [-standard] haut, élevé ; [-mark, score] élevé, bon ; [-reputation] bon / *high-quality goods* articles de qualité supérieure or de première qualité / *to have a high opinion of sb* avoir une bonne or haute opinion de qqn **5.** [honourable - ideal, thought] noble, élevé ; [-character] noble **6.** [of great importance or rank] haut, important **7.** [sound, voice] aigu (aiguë) **8.** [prominent - cheekbones] saillant **9.** 🇺🇰 [meat] avancé, faisandé ; [butter, cheese] rance **10.** [cheerful] plein d'entrain, enjoué / *spirits are high amongst the staff* la bonne humeur règne parmi le personnel **11.** *inf* [drunk] parti, éméché ▶ **to feel (as) high as a kite** : *they were feeling as high as kites* **a)** [drunk] ils étaient bien partis **b)** [drugged] ils planaient **c)** [happy] ils étaient au septième ciel. ◆ *adv* **1.** [at, to a height] haut, en haut ; [at a great altitude] à haute altitude, à une altitude élevée ▶ **up high** en haut ▶ **higher up** plus haut / *higher and higher* de plus en plus haut / *she threw the ball high into the air* elle a lancé le ballon très haut / *the shelf was high above her head* l'étagère était bien au-dessus de sa tête ; *fig* ▶ **to look high and low for sthg** or **sb** : *we looked high and low for him* nous l'avons cherché partout ▶ **to set one's sights high** or **to aim high** viser haut ▶ **to hold one's head high** *lit & fig* porter la tête haute **2.** [at, to a greater degree than normal] haut / *they set the price / standards too high* ils ont fixé un prix / niveau trop élevé / *I turned the heating up high* j'ai mis le chauffage à fond / *salaries can go as high as £30,000* les salaires peuvent monter jusqu'à or atteindre 30 000 livres ▶ **to run high a)** [river] être en crue **b)** [sea] être houleuse or grosse / *feelings were running high* les esprits se sont échauffés. ◆ *n* **1.** [height] haut *m* ▶ **on high a)** [at a height] en haut **b)** *fig* [in heaven] au ciel / *the decision came from on high hum* la décision fut prononcée en haut lieu **2.** [great degree or level] haut *m* / *to reach a new high* atteindre un nouveau record / *prices are at an all-time high* les prix ont atteint leur maximum **3.** AUTO [fourth gear] quatrième *f* ; [fifth gear] cinquième *f* **4.** METEOR [anti-cyclone] anticyclone *m* **5.** *inf* [state of excitement] : *she's been on a permanent high since he came back* elle voit tout en rose depuis son retour ▶ **to be on a high a)** [drunk] être (complètement) parti **b)** [on drugs] planer.

-high in comp à la hauteur de... ▶ **shoulder-high** à la hauteur de l'épaule.

high-and-mighty adj arrogant, impérieux ▶ **to be high-and-mighty** se donner de grands airs.

high-angle shot n CIN plan *m* en plongée.

highball ['hɑɪˌbɔːl] 🇺🇸 n boisson à base d'un alcool avec de l'eau et des glaçons.

highbrow ['hɑɪbraʊ] ◆ adj [literature, film] pour intellectuels ; [taste] intellectuel. ◆ n intellectuel *m*, -elle *f*, grosse tête *f*.

high-cal adj 🇺🇸 *inf* : *I avoid high-cal food* j'évite tout ce qui est calorique.

high chair n chaise *f* haute (pour enfants).

high-class adj [person] de la haute société, du grand monde ; [flat, neighbourhood] de grand standing ; [job, service] de premier ordre ; [car, hotel, restaurant] de luxe / *a high-class prostitute* une prostituée de luxe.

high command n haut commandement *m*.

high commissioner n [gen & ADMIN] haut commissaire *m*.

High Court ◆ n ▶ **the High Court (of Justice)** ≃ le tribunal de grande instance (*principal tribunal civil en Angle-*

terre et au pays de Galles) ▶ **the High Court of Judiciary** *la plus haute instance de justice en Écosse.* ◆ comp ▶ **High Court judge** ≃ juge *m* du tribunal de grande instance.

high-definition adj à haute définition.

high-density adj **1.** [housing] à grande densité de population **2.** COMPUT haute densité.

high-diving n plongeon *m* de haut vol, haut vol *m*.

high-end adj [top-of-the-range] haut de gamme.

higher ['hɑɪə̯r] ◆ adj **1.** [at greater height] plus haut **2.** [advanced] supérieur. ◆ adv plus haut. ◆ n 🇸 = Higher Grade.

higher education n enseignement *m* supérieur ▶ **to go on to higher education** faire des études supérieures.

Higher Grade n 🇸 diplôme *m* de fin d'études secondaires ; ≃ baccalauréat *m*.

high explosive n explosif *m* puissant.

highfalutin [ˌhɑɪfəˈluːtɪn] adj *inf* affecté, prétentieux.

high-fibre adj [food, diet] riche en fibres.

high-five n *inf* geste que font deux personnes pour se féliciter ou se dire bonjour et qui consiste à se taper dans la main.

high-flier n [ambitious person] ambitieux *m*, -euse *f*, jeune loup *m* ; [talented person] cerveau *m*, grosse tête *f*, crack *m*.

high-flyer = high-flier.

high-flying adj **1.** [aircraft] qui vole à haute altitude ; [bird] qui vole haut **2.** [person] ambitieux ; [behaviour, goal] extravagant.

high frequency n haute fréquence *f*. ◆ **high-frequency** adj à or de haute fréquence.

high gear n AUTO [fourth] quatrième *f* (vitesse *f*) ; [fifth] cinquième *f* (vitesse *f*).

high-handed adj [overbearing] autoritaire, despotique ; [inconsiderate] cavalier.

high-handedness [-'hændɪdnɪs] n [overbearing attitude - of person] caractère *m* autoritaire, despotisme *m* ; [-of behaviour] caractère *m* arbitraire ; [lack of consideration] caractère *m* cavalier.

high-heeled [-'hiːld] adj à talons hauts, à hauts talons.

high heels pl n hauts talons *mpl*.

high horse n *inf* ▶ **to get on one's high horse** monter sur ses grands chevaux.

high-income adj à revenus élevés.

high jinks pl n *inf* chahut *m*.

high jump n SPORT saut *m* en hauteur.

high jumper n sauteur *m* (*qui fait du saut en hauteur*).

highland ['hɑɪlənd] ◆ n région *f* montagneuse. ◆ adj des montagnes. ◆ **Highland** adj [air, scenery] des Highlands ; [holiday] dans les Highlands ▶ **Highland dress** costume écossais pour les hommes. ◆ **Highlands** pl n GEOG ▶ **the Highlands** [of Scotland] les Highlands *fpl*.

highlander ['hɑɪləndə̯r] n [mountain dweller] montagnard *m*, -e *f*. ◆ **Highlander** n habitant *m*, -e *f* des Highlands, Highlander *m*.

Highland fling n danse des Highlands traditionnellement exécutée en solo.

Highland games pl n jeux *mpl* écossais.

 Highland games

En Écosse, fête de plein air où se déroulent simultanément des concours (danse, cornemuse) et des épreuves sportives (courses, lancer du marteau, lancer de troncs, tir à la corde, ces deux derniers étant typiquement écossais).

high-level adj **1.** [discussion, meeting] à un haut niveau ; [diplomat, official] de haut niveau, de rang élevé / *high-level officers* **a)** [of company] cadres supérieurs **b)** MIL officiers supérieurs **2.** COMPUT ▸ **high-level language** langage *m* évolué or de haut niveau.

high life n ▸ **the high life** la grande vie / *she has a taste for the high life* elle a des goûts de luxe.

highlight ['haɪlaɪt] ◆ vt **1.** [emphasize] souligner, mettre en relief **2.** [with pen] surligner ; COMPUT mettre en surbrillance **3.** ART & PHOT rehausser **4.** [hair] faire des mèches dans. ◆ n **1.** [major event - of news] événement *m* le plus marquant ; [- of evening, holiday] point *m* culminant, grand moment *m* **2.** [in hair - natural] reflet *m* ; [- bleached] mèche *f* **3.** ART & PHOT rehaut *m*.

highlighter (pen) ['haɪlaɪtər] n surligneur *m*.

highly ['haɪlɪ] adv **1.** [very] très, extrêmement **2.** [very well] très bien **3.** [favourably] : *to speak / think highly of sb* dire / penser beaucoup de bien de qqn / *I highly recommend it* je vous le conseille vivement or chaudement **4.** [at an important level] haut / *a highly placed source* une source haut placée / *a highly placed official* **a)** [gen] un officiel de haut rang **b)** ADMIN un haut fonctionnaire.

highly-strung adj nerveux, tendu.

high mass, High Mass n grand-messe *f*.

high-minded adj de caractère noble, qui a des principes (élevés).

highness ['haɪnɪs] n [of building, wall] hauteur *f*. ◈ **Highness** n [title] ▸ **His / Her Highness** son Altesse *f*.

high-octane adj *lit* à haut degré d'octane / *high-octane petrol* **a)** supercarburant *m*, super *m* **b)** *fig* explosif.

high-performance adj performant.

high-pitched adj **1.** [sound, voice] aigu (uë) ; MUS [note] haut **2.** [roof] à forte pente.

high point n [major event - of news] événement *m* le plus marquant ; [- of evening, holiday] point *m* culminant, grand moment *m* ; [- of film, novel] point *m* culminant / *the high point of the party* le clou de la soirée.

high-powered [-'pauəd] adj **1.** [engine, rifle] puissant, de forte puissance ; [microscope] à fort grossissement **2.** [dynamic - person] dynamique, entreprenant ; [- advertising, course, method] dynamique **3.** [important] très important.

high-pressure ◆ adj **1.** [cylinder, gas] à haute pression ▸ **high-pressure area** METEOR anticyclone *m*, zone *f* de hautes pressions (atmosphériques) **2.** *fig* [methods, selling] agressif ; [job, profession] stressant. ◆ vt US *inf* forcer la main à.

high priest n grand prêtre *m*.

high-principled adj aux principes élevés.

high profile n ▸ **to have a high profile** être très en vue. ◈ **high-profile** adj [job, position] qui est très en vue ; [campaign] qui fait beaucoup de bruit.

high-rent adj **1.** [housing] à loyer élevé **2.** US [high-quality] haut de gamme *(inv)*.

high-res [haɪrez] adj *inf abbr of* **high-resolution**.

high-resolution adj à haute résolution.

high-rise adj [flat] qui est dans une tour ; [skyline] composé de tours. ◈ **high rise** n tour *f (immeuble)*.

high-risk adj à haut risque, à hauts risques.

high school ◆ n [in US] ≃ lycée *m* ; [in UK] établissement *m* d'enseignement secondaire. ◆ comp [diploma] de fin d'études secondaires ; [teacher] de lycée.

high seas pl n : *on the high seas* en haute or pleine mer.

high season n haute or pleine saison *f*. ◈ **high-season** comp [prices] de haute saison.

high society n haute société *f*, grand monde *m*.

high-speed adj ultra-rapide / *high-speed train* train *m* à grande vitesse, TGV *m*.

high-spirited adj **1.** [person] plein d'entrain or de vivacité ; [activity, fun] plein d'entrain **2.** [horse] fougueux, nerveux.

high spirits pl n pétulance *f*, vitalité *f*, entrain *m* ▸ **to be in high spirits** avoir de l'entrain, être plein d'entrain.

high spot n **1.** = **high point 2.** US [place] endroit *m* intéressant.

high street n UK ▸ **the high street** la grand-rue, la rue principale. ◈ **high-street** comp UK ▸ **the high-street banks** les grandes banques *(britanniques)* ▸ **high-street shops** le petit commerce ▸ **high-street fashion** prêt-à-porter *m*.

high-strung = **highly-strung.**

hightail ['haɪteɪl] vt US *inf* filer.

high tea n *repas léger pris en début de soirée et accompagné de thé.*

high tech n **1.** [technology] technologie *f* avancée or de pointe **2.** [style] high-tech *m*. ◈ **high-tech** comp **1.** [industry, sector] de pointe ; [equipment] de haute technicité **2.** [furniture, style] high-tech *(inv)*.

high-tension adj à haute tension.

high tide n **1.** [of ocean, sea] marée *f* haute / *at high tide* à marée haute **2.** *fig* [of success] point *m* culminant.

high treason n haute trahison *f*.

high water n [of ocean, sea] marée *f* haute ; [of river] crue *f*.

highway ['haɪweɪ] n [road] route *f* ; US [main road] grande route, route nationale ; US [public road] voie *f* publique ; US [interstate] autoroute *f*.

Highway Code n UK ▸ **the Highway Code** le code de la route.

high wire n corde *f* raide or de funambule.

hijack ['haɪdʒæk] ◆ vt **1.** [plane] détourner ; [car, train] s'emparer de, détourner **2.** [rob] voler. ◆ n détournement *m*.

hijacker ['haɪdʒækər] n **1.** [of plane] pirate *m* (de l'air) ; [of car, train] gangster *m* **2.** [robber] voleur *m*.

hijacking ['haɪdʒækɪŋ] n **1.** [of car, plane, train] détournement *m* **2.** [robbery] vol *m*.

hike [haɪk] ◆ vi faire de la marche à pied. ◆ vt **1.** [walk] faire à pied, marcher **2.** [price] augmenter (brusquement). ◆ n **1.** [gen & MIL] marche *f* à pied ; [long walk] randonnée *f* à pied, marche *f* à pied ; [short walk] promenade *f* **2.** US [increase] hausse *f*, augmentation *f*. ◈ **hike up** vt sep **1.** [hitch up - skirt] relever ; [- trousers] remonter **2.** [price, rent] augmenter (brusquement).

hiker ['haɪkər] n [gen & MIL] marcheur *m*, -euse *f* ; [in mountains, woods] randonneur *m*, -euse *f*, promeneur *m*, -euse *f*.

hiking ['haɪkɪŋ] n (U) [gen & MIL] marche *f* à pied ; [in mountains, woods] randonnée *f*, trekking *m* ▸ **hiking boots** chaussures fpl de marche.

hilarious [hɪ'leərɪəs] adj [funny - person, joke, story] hilarant.

hilariously [hɪ'leərɪəslɪ] adv joyeusement, gaiement.

hilarity [hɪ'lærətɪ] n hilarité *f*.

hill [hɪl] n **1.** colline *f*, coteau *m* **2.** [slope] côte *f*, pente *f* **3.** [mound - of earth] levée *f* de terre, remblai *m* ; [- of things] tas *m*, monceau *m*.

hillbilly ['hɪl,bɪlɪ] *(pl* **hillbillies)** US ◆ n montagnard *m*, -e *f* des Appalaches ; *pej* péquenaud *m*, -e *f*, plouc *mf*. ◆ adj des Appalaches.

hillock ['hɪlək] n [small hill] mamelon m, butte f ; [artificial hill] monticule m, amoncellement m.

hillside ['hɪl,saɪd] n (flanc m de) coteau m.

hill start n démarrage m en côte.

hilltop ['hɪl,tɒp] ◆ n sommet m de la colline / *on the hilltop* au sommet or en haut de la colline. ◆ adj [village] au sommet or en haut de la colline.

hillwalker ['hɪl,wɔːkəʳ] n UK randonneur m, -euse f *(en terrain vallonné).*

hillwalking ['hɪl,wɔːkɪŋ] n (U) UK randonnée f *(en terrain vallonné).*

hilly ['hɪlɪ] (*compar* hillier, *superl* hilliest) adj [country, land] vallonné ; [road] accidenté, à fortes côtes.

hilt [hɪlt] n [of dagger, knife] manche m ; [of sword] poignée f, garde f ; [of gun] crosse f.

him [hɪm] pron **1.** [direct object - unstressed] le, l' *(before vowel or silent 'h')* ; [-stressed] lui / *I recognize him* je le reconnais / *why did you have to choose HIM?* pourquoi l'as-tu choisi lui ? **2.** [indirect object - unstressed] lui ; [-stressed] à lui / *give him the money* donne-lui l'argent **3.** [after preposition] lui / *I was in front of him* j'étais devant lui **4.** [with 'to be'] : *it's him* c'est lui / *if I were him* si j'étais lui, si j'étais à sa place.

Himalayan [,hɪmə'leɪən] adj himalayen.

Himalayas [,hɪmə'leɪəz] pl pr n ◗ *the Himalayas* l'Himalaya m / *in the Himalayas* dans l'Himalaya.

himbo ['hɪmbəʊ] n US *inf* [male bimbo] *homme séduisant mais superficiel.*

himself [hɪm'self] pron **1.** [reflexive form] se, s' *(before vowel or silent 'h')* / *he bought himself a car* il s'est acheté une voiture / *he considers himself lucky* il considère qu'il a de la chance **2.** [emphatic form] lui-même / *he built the shelves himself* il a monté les étagères lui-même / *I spoke with the teacher himself* j'ai parlé au professeur en personne **3.** [with preposition] lui / *the old man was talking to himself* le vieil homme parlait tout seul / *he did it all by himself* il l'a fait tout seul **4.** [his usual self] : *he isn't quite himself* il n'est pas dans son état habituel / *he's feeling more himself now* il va mieux maintenant.

hind [haɪnd] ◆ n [deer] biche f. ◆ adj de derrière.

hinder ['hɪndəʳ] vt [person] gêner ; [progress] entraver, gêner ◗ *to hinder sb from doing sthg* empêcher qqn de faire qqch.

Hindi ['hɪndɪ] ◆ n LING hindi m. ◆ adj hindi.

hindmost ['haɪndməʊst] adj dernier, du bout.

hindquarters ['haɪndkwɔː,təz] pl n arrière-train m.

hindrance ['hɪndrəns] n **1.** [person, thing] obstacle m, entrave f **2.** (U) [action] : *without any hindrance from the authorities* **a)** [referring to person] sans être gêné par les autorités **b)** [referring to project] sans être entravé par les autorités.

hindsight ['haɪndsaɪt] n sagesse f acquise après coup / *with the benefit* or *wisdom of hindsight* avec du recul, après coup.

Hindu ['hɪnduː] ◆ n Hindou m, -e f. ◆ adj hindou.

Hinduism ['hɪnduːɪzm] n hindouisme m.

hinge [hɪndʒ] ◆ n [of door] gond m, charnière f ; [of box] charnière f. ◆ vt [door] munir de gonds or charnières ; [box] munir de charnières. ◆ **hinge on, hinge upon** vt insep dépendre de.

hinged [hɪndʒd] adj à charnière or charnières ◗ **hinged flap** [of counter] abattant m.

hinky ['hɪŋkɪ] adj US *inf* bizarre, louche.

hint [hɪnt] ◆ n **1.** [indirect suggestion] allusion f ; [clue] indice m ◗ **to drop a hint (about sthg)** faire une allusion (à qqch) **2.** [helpful suggestion, tip] conseil m, truc m

3. [small amount, trace - of emotion] note f ; [-of colour] touche f ; [-of flavouring] soupçon m. ◆ vt insinuer. ◆ vi ◗ **to hint at sthg** faire allusion à qqch.

hinterland ['hɪntəlænd] n arrière-pays m.

hip [hɪp] ◆ n **1.** [part of body] hanche f **2.** [berry] fruit m de l'églantier / du rosier, cynorhodon m, gratte-cul m. ◆ comp ◗ **hip measurement** or **size** tour m de hanches. ◆ interj ◗ **hiphip, hooray!** hip hip hip, hourra ! ◆ adj *inf* [fashionable] branché.

hip bath n bain m de siège.

hipbone ['hɪpbəʊn] n os m iliaque.

hip flask n flasque f.

hip-hop n [music] hip-hop m.

hippie ['hɪpɪ] ◆ n hippie mf, hippy mf. ◆ adj hippie, hippy.

hippo ['hɪpəʊ] n *inf* hippopotame m.

hippocampus [,hɪpəʊ'kæmpəs] n ANAT, MYTH & ZOOL hippocampe m.

hippodrome ['hɪpədrəʊm] n hippodrome m ; [not for racing] arène f.

hippopotamus [,hɪpə'pɒtəməs] (*pl* hippopotamuses or hippopotami [-maɪ]) n hippopotame m.

hippy ['hɪpɪ] (*pl* hippies) = hippie.

hip replacement n [operation] remplacement m de la hanche par une prothèse ; [prosthesis] prothèse f de la hanche.

hipsters ['hɪpstəz] pl n UK [trousers] pantalon m (à) taille basse.

hire ['haɪəʳ] ◆ n **1.** UK [of car, room, suit, etc.] location f / **'for hire' a)** 'à louer' **b)** [taxi] 'libre' **2.** [cost - of car, boat, etc.] (prix m de) location f ; [-of worker] paie f **3.** US [employee] employé m, -e f. ◆ comp ◗ **hire charges** (frais mpl or prix m de) location f. ◆ vt **1.** UK [car, room, suit, etc.] louer ◗ **to hire sthg from sb** louer qqch à qqn **2.** [staff] engager ; [labourer] embaucher, engager ◗ **hired killer** or **assassin** tueur m à gages. ◆ vi engager du personnel, embaucher (des ouvriers). ◆ **hire out** vt sep UK [car, room, suit, etc.] louer ◗ **to hire o.s. out a)** se faire engager **b)** [labourer] se faire engager or embaucher.

hire car n UK voiture f de location.

hired help n [for housework] aide f ménagère.

hire purchase n UK location-vente f, vente f à tempérament ◗ **to buy** or **to get sthg on hire purchase** acheter qqch en location-vente / **hire purchase agreement** contrat m de location.

hi-res ['haɪrez] (*abbr of* high-resolution) adj *inf* COMPUT (à) haute résolution.

hiring ['haɪərɪŋ] n **1.** [of car] location f **2.** [of employee] embauche f.

Hiroshima [hɪ'rɒʃɪmə] pr n Hiroshima.

his [hɪz] ◆ det son m, sa f, ses mf pl / *his table* sa table / *his glasses* ses lunettes / *his university* son université / *he has broken his arm* il s'est cassé le bras. ◆ pron **1.** [gen] le sien m, la sienne f, les siens mpl, les siennes / *it's his* c'est à lui, c'est le sien / *the responsibility is his* c'est lui qui est responsable, la responsabilité lui revient **2.** [after preposition] : *a friend of his* un de ses amis / *that dog of his is a nuisance* son sacré chien est vraiment embêtant.

his and hers adj : *his and hers towels* des serviettes brodées « lui » et « elle ».

Hispanic [hɪ'spænɪk] ◆ n US Hispano-Américain m, -e f. ◆ adj hispanique.

hiss [hɪs] ◆ n [of gas, steam] sifflement m, chuintement m ; [of person, snake] sifflement m ; [of cat] crachement *m*. ◆ vt [say quietly] souffler ; [bad performer, speaker, etc.] siffler. ◆ vi [gas, steam] siffler, chuinter ; [snake] siffler ; [cat] cracher ; [person - speak quietly] souffler ; [- in disapproval, anger] siffler.

hissy fit ['hɪsɪ] n *inf* ▶ **to have a hissy fit** piquer une crise.

histogram ['hɪstəgræm] n histogramme *m*.

historian [hɪ'stɔːrɪən] n historien *m*, -enne *f*.

historic [hɪ'stɒrɪk] adj **1.** [memorable - day, occasion, meeting, etc.] historique **2.** [of time past] révolu, passé ; [fear] ancestral ▶ **historic building** monument *m* historique.

historical [hɪ'stɒrɪkəl] adj historique ▶ **historical present** GRAM présent *m* historique.

historically [hɪ'stɒrɪklɪ] adv historiquement ; [traditionally] traditionnellement.

history ['hɪstərɪ] (*pl* **histories**) ◆ n **1.** (U) [the past] histoire *f* ▶ **to make history** entrer dans l'histoire **2.** (U) [development, lifespan] histoire *f* **3.** [account] histoire *f* **4.** (U) [record] : *employment history* expérience *f* professionnelle / *medical history* antécédents *mpl* médicaux. ◆ comp [book, teacher, lesson] d'histoire.

histrionics [ˌhɪstrɪ'ɒnɪks] pl n *pej* comédie *f*, simagrées *fpl*.

hit [hɪt] (*pt* & *pp* **hit**, *cont* **hitting**) ◆ n **1.** [blow] coup *m* / *that was a hit at me* fig ça m'était destiné, c'est moi qui étais visé **2.** SPORT [in ball game] coup *m* ; [in shooting] tir *m* réussi ; [in fencing] touche *f* ▶ **to score a hit a)** [in shooting] faire mouche, toucher la cible **b)** [in fencing] faire or marquer une touche / *we sent the mailshot to fifty companies and got thirteen hits* fig nous avons contacté cinquante entreprises par publipostage et avons eu treize réponses favorables **3.** [success - album, play, book] succès *m* ; [- song] succès *m*, hit *m*, tube *m* / *a hit with the public* / *the critics* un succès auprès du public / des critiques ▶ **to make a hit with sb** [person] conquérir qqn / *she's a hit with everyone* elle a conquis tout le monde **4.** COMPUT visite *f*. ◆ comp ▶ **hit record** (disque *m* à) succès *m* ▶ **hit single** or **song** succès, hit *m*, tube *m*. ◆ vt **1.** [strike with hand, fist, stick, etc. - person] frapper ; [- ball] frapper or taper dans ; [- nail] taper sur ▶ **to hit sb in the face** / **on the head** frapper qqn au visage / sur la tête / *to hit sb where it hurts most* fig toucher qqn là où ça fait mal ▶ **to hit the nail on the head** mettre le doigt dessus **2.** [come or bring forcefully into contact with - subj: ball, stone] heurter ; [- subj: bullet, arrow] atteindre, toucher / *the bullet hit him in the shoulder* la balle l'a atteint or touché à l'épaule / *the windscreen was hit by a stone* une pierre a heurté le parebrise ▶ **to hit one's head** / **knee (against sthg)** se cogner la tête / le genou (contre qqch) / *it suddenly hit me that...* fig il m'est soudain venu à l'esprit que... **3.** [attack - enemy] attaquer **4.** [affect] toucher / *the region worst hit by the earthquake* la région la plus sévèrement touchée par le tremblement de terre / *the child's death has hit them all very hard* la mort de l'enfant les a tous durement touchés or frappés **5.** *inf* [reach] arriver à **6.** SPORT [score - runs] marquer ; [in fencing] toucher **7.** *v inf* [kill] descendre, liquider **8.** US *inf* [borrow money from] taper / *to hit sb for $10* taper qqn de 10 dollars **9.** PHR ▶ **to hit the bottle a)** *inf* [drink] picoler **b)** [start to drink] se mettre à picoler ▶ **to hit the ceiling** or **roof** *inf* sortir de ses gonds, piquer une colère folle ▶ **to hit the deck** *inf* [lie down] se mettre à terre ▶ **to hit the hay** or **the sack** *inf* aller se mettre au pieu, aller se pieuter ▶ **to hit home** [remark, criticism] faire mouche ▶ **to hit the road** se mettre en route ▶ **that really hits the spot** [food, drink] c'est juste ce dont j'avais besoin. ◆ vi **1.** frapper, taper **2.** [inflation, recession, etc.] se faire sentir. ❖ **hit back** ◆ vi [reply forcefully, retaliate] riposter, rendre la pareille / *he hit back with accusations that they*

were giving bribes il a riposté en les accusant de verser des pots-de-vin ▶ **to hit back at sb** / **sthg** [in speech] répondre à qqn / qqch. ◆ vt sep : *to hit the ball back* renvoyer le ballon / *he hit me back* il m'a rendu mon coup. ❖ **hit off** vt sep PHR ▶ **to hit it off** [get on well] bien s'entendre ▶ **to hit it off with sb** bien s'entendre avec qqn / *we hit it off immediately* le courant est tout de suite passé entre nous. ❖ **hit on** vt insep **1.** [find - solution, plan, etc.] trouver **2.** US *inf* [try to pick up] draguer. ❖ **hit out** vi **1.** [physically - once] envoyer un coup ; [- repeatedly] envoyer des coups / *he started hitting out at me* il s'est mis à envoyer des coups dans ma direction **2.** [in speech, writing] ▶ **to hit out at** or **against** s'en prendre à, attaquer. ❖ **hit upon** vt insep = **hit on**.

hit-and-miss = **hit-or-miss**.

hit-and-run n accident *m* avec délit de fuite ▶ **hit-and-run driver** conducteur *m*, -trice *f* coupable de délit de fuite.

hitch [hɪtʃ] ◆ vt **1.** *inf* ▶ **to hitch a lift a)** [gen] se faire emmener en voiture **b)** [hitchhiker] se faire prendre en stop **2.** [railway carriage] attacher, atteler ; [horse - to fence] attacher ; [- to carriage] atteler ; [rope] attacher, nouer **3.** PHR ▶ **to get hitched** *inf* **a)** [one person] se caser **b)** [couple] passer devant Monsieur le Maire. ◆ vi = **hitchhike**. ◆ n **1.** [difficulty] problème *m*, anicroche *f* **2.** US *inf* MIL : *he's doing a five year hitch in the navy* il s'est engagé pour cinq ans dans la marine **3.** [knot] nœud *m* **4.** [pull] ▶ **to give sthg a hitch (up)** remonter or retrousser qqch **5.** US [towbar] barre *f* de remorquage. ❖ **hitch up** vt sep **1.** [trousers, skirt, etc.] remonter, retrousser **2.** [horse, oxen, etc.] atteler.

hitchhike ['hɪtʃhaɪk] ◆ vi faire du stop or de l'autostop / *to hitchhike to London* aller à Londres en stop. ◆ vt : *to hitchhike one's way round Europe* faire l'Europe en auto-stop.

hitchhiker ['hɪtʃhaɪkər] n auto-stoppeur *m*, -euse *f*, stoppeur *m*, -euse *f*.

hitchhiking ['hɪtʃhaɪkɪŋ], **hitching** ['hɪtʃɪŋ] n autostop *m*, stop *m*.

hi-tech, hitech ['haɪˌtek] ◆ n **1.** [in industry] technologie *f* de pointe **2.** [style of interior design] high-tech *m*. ◆ adj **1.** [equipment, industry] de pointe **2.** [design, furniture] high-tech.

hither ['hɪðər] adv *arch* ici ▶ **hither and thither** *liter* & *hum* çà et là, de ci de là.

hitherto [ˌhɪðə'tuː] adv *fml* jusqu'ici, jusqu'à présent.

hit list n *inf* liste *f* noire.

hit man n *inf* tueur *m* à gages.

hit-or-miss adj *inf* [method, approach] basé sur le hasard ; [work] fait n'importe comment or à la va-comme-je-te-pousse.

hit parade n *dated* hit-parade *m*.

hit squad n *inf* commando *m* de tueurs.

HIV (abbr of **human immunodeficiency virus**) n VIH *m*, HIV *m* ▶ **to be HIV negative** être séronégatif ▶ **to be HIV positive** être séropositif.

hive [haɪv] ◆ n [for bees] ruche *f* ; [group of bees] essaim *m*. ◆ vt mettre en ruche. ◆ vi entrer dans une ruche. ❖ **hive off** vt sep transférer.

hiya ['haɪjə] interj *inf* salut.

hl (written abbr of **hectolitre**) hl.

HM (abbr of **His/Her Majesty**) SM.

HMG (abbr of **His/Her Majesty's Government**) n *expression utilisée sur des documents officiels en Grande-Bretagne.*

HMI (abbr of His/Her Majesty's Inspector) n *inspecteur de l'Éducation nationale en Grande-Bretagne.*

HMO (abbr of Health Maintenance Organization) n *aux États-Unis, système de couverture médicale privilégiant la médecine préventive auquel certains contrats d'assurance donnent droit.*

HMS (abbr of His/Her Majesty's Ship) *dénomination officielle précédant le nom de tous les bâtiments de guerre de la marine britannique.*

HMSO (abbr of His/Her Majesty's Stationery Office) pr n *maison d'édition publiant les ouvrages ou documents approuvés par le Parlement, les ministères et autres organismes officiels* ; ≃ *l'Imprimerie nationale.*

HNC n abbr of Higher National Certificate.

HND n abbr of Higher National Diploma.

hoard [hɔːd] ◆ n [of goods] réserve *f*, provisions *fpl* ; [of money] trésor *m*, magot *m*. ◆ vt [goods] faire provision or des réserves de, stocker ; [money] accumuler, thésauriser. ◆ vi faire des réserves, stocker.

hoarder ['hɔːdə] n [gen] *personne ou animal qui fait des réserves* ; [of money] thésauriseur *m*, -euse *f*.

hoarding ['hɔːdɪŋ] n 1. (U) [of goods] mise *f* en réserve or en stock ; [of money] thésaurisation *f*, accumulation *f* 2. UK [fence] palissade *f* 3. UK [billboard] panneau *m* publicitaire or d'affichage.

hoarfrost ['hɔː,frɒst] n givre *m*.

hoarse [hɔːs] adj [person] enroué ; [voice] rauque, enroué.

hoarsely ['hɔːslɪ] adv d'une voix rauque or enrouée.

hoax [həʊks] ◆ n canular *m* ▸ to play a hoax on sb jouer un tour à qqn, monter un canular à qqn ▸ (bomb) hoax fausse alerte *f* à la bombe. ◆ comp ▸ hoax (telephone) call canular *m* téléphonique. ◆ vt jouer un tour à, monter un canular à.

hoaxer ['həʊksər] n mauvais plaisant *m*.

hob [hɒb] n [on stove top] plaque *f* (chauffante) ; [by open fire] plaque *f*.

hobble ['hɒbl] ◆ vi boitiller. ◆ vt [horse] entraver. ◆ n 1. [limp] boitillement *m* 2. [for horse] entrave *f*. ◆ comp ▸ hobble skirt jupe *f* entravée.

hobby ['hɒbɪ] n (pl hobbies) n passe-temps *m*, hobby *m*.

hobbyhorse ['hɒbɪhɔːs] n 1. [toy] cheval *m* de bois (composé d'une tête sur un manche) 2. [favourite topic] sujet *m* favori, dada *m*.

hobnob ['hɒbnɒb] (pt & pp hobnobbed, cont hobnobbing) vi ▸ to hobnob with sb frayer avec qqn, fréquenter qqn.

hobo ['həʊbəʊ] (pl hobos or hoboes) n US inf 1. [tramp] clochard *m*, -e *f*, vagabond *m*, -e *f* 2. [itinerant labourer] saisonnier *m*, -ère *f*.

Ho Chi Minh City pr n Hô Chi Minh-Ville.

hock [hɒk] ◆ n 1. [joint] jarret *m* 2. [wine] vin *m* du Rhin 3. inf PHR in hock a) [in pawn] au clou b) [in debt] endetté. ◆ vt [pawn] mettre au clou.

hockey ['hɒkɪ] ◆ n 1. UK hockey *m* sur gazon 2. US hockey *m* sur glace. ◆ comp UK [ball, match, pitch, team] de hockey ; US de hockey sur glace ▸ hockey player a) UK joueur *m*, -euse *f* de hockey, hockeyeur *m*, -euse *f* b) US joueur *m*, -euse *f* de hockey sur glace ▸ hockey stick a) UK crosse *f* de hockey b) US crosse *f* de hockey sur glace.

hocus-pocus [,həʊkəs'pəʊkəs] n 1. [of magician] tours mpl de passe-passe 2. [trickery] tricherie *f*, supercherie *f* ; [deceptive talk] paroles *fpl* trompeuses ; [deceptive action] trucage *m*, supercherie *f*.

hod [hɒd] ◆ n [for bricks] *outil utilisé par les maçons pour porter les briques* ; [for mortar] auge *f*, oiseau *m* ; [for coal] seau *m* à charbon. ◆ comp ▸ hod carrier apprenti *m* or aide *m* maçon.

hodgepodge ['hɒdʒpɒdʒ] US = hotchpotch.

Hodgkin's disease ['hɒdʒkɪnz-] n MED maladie *f* de Hodgkin.

hoe [həʊ] ◆ n houe *f*, binette *f*. ◆ vt biner, sarcler.

hog [hɒg] (pt & pp hogged, cont hogging) ◆ n [castrated pig] cochon *m* or porc *m* châtré ; US [pig] cochon *m*, porc *m* ; fig [greedy person] goinfre *mf* ; [dirty person] porc *m*. ◆ vt inf monopoliser.

hog heaven n US inf ▸ to be in hog heaven être comme un coq en pâte.

Hogmanay ['hɒgməneɪ] n Scot *les fêtes de la Saint-Sylvestre en Écosse.*

hog-wild adj US inf : *she won the lottery and went hog-wild après avoir gagné à la loterie elle s'est autorisé toutes les extravagances.*

ho-hum [həʊ'hʌm] adj US inf 1. [mediocre] médiocre 2. [unenthusiastic] peu enthousiaste / *I was pretty ho-hum about it* ça ne m'a pas emballé.

hoi polloi [,hɔɪpə'lɔɪ] pl n pej ▸ the hoi polloi la populace.

hoist [hɔɪst] ◆ vt [sails, flag] hisser ; [load, person] lever, hisser. ◆ n 1. [elevator] monte-charge *m* ; [block and tackle] palan *m* 2. [upward push, pull] ▸ to give sb a hoist up a) [lift] soulever qqn b) [pull] tirer qqn.

hoity-toity [,hɔɪtɪ'tɔɪtɪ] adj inf & pej prétentieux, péteux.

hokum ['həʊkəm] n (U) US inf [nonsense] fadaises *fpl*, foutaises *fpl* ; [sentimentality in play, film, etc.] niaiseries *fpl*, sentimentalisme *m*.

hold [həʊld] (pt & pp held [held])
◆ vt

A. IN ONE'S HAND(S) [clasp, grasp] tenir ▸ to hold sthg in one's hand a) [book, clothing, guitar] avoir qqch à la main b) [key, money] tenir qqch dans la main ▸ to hold sb's hand *lit & fig* tenir la main à qqn ▸ to hold hands se donner la main, se tenir (par) la main ▸ to hold sb in one's arms tenir qqn dans ses bras ▸ to hold sb close or tight serrer qqn contre soi.

B. SUSTAIN, POSSESS OR CONTAIN 1. [keep, sustain] ▸ to hold sb's attention retenir l'attention de qqn ▸ to hold one's serve [in tennis] défendre son service ▸ to hold one's own tenir bon or ferme / *she is well able to hold her own* elle sait se défendre 2. [continue without deviation] tenir 3. TELEC : *will you hold (the line)?* voulez-vous patienter ? / *hold the line!* ne quittez pas ! 4. [have, possess - degree, permit, ticket] avoir, posséder ; [- job, position] avoir, occuper 5. [contain] contenir, tenir / *the hall holds a maximum of 250 people* la salle peut accueillir or recevoir 250 personnes au maximum, il y a de la place pour 250 personnes au maximum dans cette salle ▸ to hold one's drink bien supporter l'alcool 6. [have, exercise] exercer 7. [have in store] réserver / *who knows what the future may hold?* qui sait ce que nous réserve l'avenir ? 8. AUTO : *the new car holds the road well* la nouvelle voiture tient bien la route.

C. KEEP IN PLACE 1. [maintain in position] tenir, maintenir / *her hair was held in place with hairpins* des épingles (à cheveux) retenaient or maintenaient ses cheveux / *hold the picture a bit higher* tenez le tableau un peu plus haut 2. [carry] tenir ▸ to hold o.s. upright or erect se tenir droit.

D. KEEP BACK OR CONTROL 1. [confine, detain] détenir / *the police are holding him for questioning* la police l'a gardé à vue pour l'interroger 2. [keep back, retain] retenir /

once she starts talking politics there's no holding her! fig dès qu'elle commence à parler politique, rien ne peut l'arrêter ! **3.** [reserve, set aside] retenir, réserver **4.** [keep in check] : *inflation has been held at the same level for several months* le taux d'inflation est maintenu au même niveau depuis plusieurs mois **5.** [keep control or authority over] : *the guerrillas held the bridge for several hours* MIL les guérilleros ont tenu le pont plusieurs heures durant ▶ **hold it!** or **hold everything!** a) [stop and wait] attendez ! b) [stay still] arrêtez !, ne bougez plus !

E. BELIEVE OR CONSIDER 1. [assert, claim] maintenir, soutenir ; [believe] croire, considérer / *she holds strong views on the subject* elle a une opinion bien arrêtée sur le sujet **2.** [consider, regard] tenir, considérer ▶ **to hold sb responsible for sthg** tenir qqn pour responsable de qqch ▶ **to hold sb in high esteem** avoir beaucoup d'estime pour qqn, tenir qqn en haute estime.

F. ORGANISE OR PUT ON [carry on, engage in - conversation, meeting] tenir ; [- party] donner ; [organize] organiser / *the book fair is held in Frankfurt* la foire du livre se tient or a lieu à Francfort.

◆ vi **1.** [cling - person] se tenir, s'accrocher / *hold fast!* or *hold tight!* accrochez-vous bien ! / *their resolve held fast* or *firm in the face of fierce opposition* fig ils ont tenu bon face à une opposition acharnée ; [remain in place - nail, fastening] tenir bon **2.** [last - luck] durer ; [- weather] durer, se maintenir **3.** [remain valid - invitation, offer] tenir ; [- argument, theory] valoir, être valable **4.** [stay, remain] ▶ **hold still!** inf ne bougez pas !

◆ n **1.** [grasp, grip] prise f ; [in wrestling] prise f ▶ **to catch** or **to grab** or **to seize** or **to take hold of sthg** se saisir de or saisir qqch / *grab (a) hold of that towel* tiens ! prends cette serviette / *there was nothing for me to grab hold of* il n'y avait rien à quoi m'accrocher or me cramponner / *I still had hold of his hand* je le tenais toujours par la main ▶ **to get hold of sthg** [find] se procurer or trouver qqch / *where did you get hold of that idea?* où est-ce que tu es allé chercher cette idée ? ▶ **to get hold of sb** trouver qqn / *just wait till the newspapers get hold of the story* attendez un peu que les journaux s'emparent de la nouvelle ▶ *get a hold on yourself* ressaisis-toi, ne te laisse pas aller ▶ **to take hold** a) [fire] prendre b) [idea] se répandre ▶ **no holds barred** SPORT & fig tous les coups sont permis **2.** [controlling force or influence] prise f, influence f ▶ **to have a hold over sb** avoir de l'influence sur qqn **3.** [delay, pause] pause f, arrêt m / *the company has put a hold on all new orders* l'entreprise a suspendu or gelé toutes les nouvelles commandes **4.** [store - in plane] soute f ; [- in ship] cale f. ❖ **on hold** adv phr [gen & TELEC] en attente / *we've put the project on hold* nous avons mis le projet en attente. ❖ **hold against** vt sep ▶ **to hold sthg against sb** en vouloir à qqn de qqch. ❖ **hold back** ◆ vt sep **1.** [control, restrain - animal, person] retenir, tenir ; [- crowd, enemy forces] contenir ; [- anger, laughter, tears] retenir, réprimer ; [- inflation] contenir **2.** [keep - money, supplies] retenir ; fig [information, truth] cacher, taire / *she's holding something back from me* elle me cache quelque chose **3.** US SCH : *they held her back a year* ils lui ont fait redoubler une classe, ils l'ont fait redoubler **4.** [prevent progress of] empêcher de progresser. ◆ vi fig [refrain] se retenir / *he has held back from making a commitment* il s'est abstenu de s'engager. ❖ **hold down** vt sep **1.** [keep in place - paper, carpet] maintenir en place ; [- person] forcer à rester par terre, maintenir au sol ; [- keyboard key] maintenir appuyé **2.** [keep to limit] restreindre, limiter / *they're holding unemployment down to 4%* ils maintiennent le taux de chômage à 4 % / *to hold prices down* empêcher les prix de monter, empêcher la montée des prix **3.** [employee] ▶ **to hold down a job** garder un emploi / *he's never managed to*

hold down a job il n'a jamais pu garder un emploi bien long-temps. ❖ **hold forth** vi pérorer, disserter. ❖ **hold in** vt sep **1.** [stomach] rentrer **2.** [emotion] retenir ; [anger] contenir. ❖ **hold off** ◆ vt sep **1.** [keep at distance] tenir à distance or éloigné / *I can't hold the reporters off any longer* je ne peux plus faire attendre or patienter les journalistes **2.** [delay, put off] remettre à plus tard / *he held off going to see the doctor until May* il a attendu le mois de mai pour aller voir le médecin. ◆ vi **1.** [rain] : *at least the rain held off* au moins il n'a pas plu **2.** [abstain] s'abstenir. ❖ **hold on** vi **1.** [grasp, grip] tenir bien, s'accrocher ▶ **to hold on to sthg** bien tenir qqch, s'accrocher à qqch, se cramponner à qqch **2.** [keep possession of] garder / *hold on to this contract for me* [keep it] garde-moi ce contrat **3.** [continue, persevere] tenir, tenir le coup **4.** [wait] attendre ; [stop] arrêter ; TELEC : *hold on please!* ne quittez pas ! ◆ vt sep [maintain in place] tenir or maintenir en place. ❖ **hold out** ◆ vi **1.** [last - supplies, stocks] durer / *will the car hold out till we get home?* la voiture tiendra-t-elle (le coup) jusqu'à ce qu'on rentre ? **2.** [refuse to yield] tenir bon, tenir le coup / *the management held out against any suggested changes* la direction a refusé tous les changements proposés. ◆ vt sep [extend, offer] tendre ▶ **to hold out one's hand to sb** lit & fig tendre la main à qqn. ◆ vt insep [offer] offrir / *I can't hold out any promise of improvement* je ne peux promettre aucune amélioration / *the doctors hold out little hope for him* les médecins ont peu d'espoir pour lui. ❖ **hold out for** vt insep exiger / *the workers held out for a shorter working week* les ouvriers réclamaient une semaine de travail plus courte. ❖ **hold out on** vt insep inf : *you're holding out on me!* tu me caches quelque chose ! ❖ **hold over** vt sep **1.** [position] tenir au-dessus de / *they hold the threat of redundancy over their workers* fig ils maintiennent la menace de licenciement sur leurs ouvriers **2.** [postpone] remettre, reporter / *we'll hold these items over until the next meeting* on va remettre ces questions à la prochaine réunion. ❖ **hold to** ◆ vt insep [promise, tradition] s'en tenir à, rester fidèle à ; [decision] maintenir, s'en tenir à. ◆ vt sep : *we held him to his promise* nous lui avons fait tenir parole / *if I win, I'll buy you lunch — I'll hold you to that!* si je gagne, je t'invite à déjeuner — je te prends au mot ! ❖ **hold together** vt sep [book, car] maintenir ; [community, family] maintenir l'union de. ❖ **hold up** ◆ vt sep **1.** [lift, raise] lever, élever / *I held up my hand* j'ai levé la main / *she felt she would never be able to hold her head up again* fig elle pensait qu'elle ne pourrait plus jamais marcher la tête haute **2.** [support] soutenir / *my trousers were held up with safety pins* mon pantalon était maintenu par des épingles de sûreté **3.** [delay] retarder ; [stop] arrêter / *the accident held up traffic for an hour* l'accident a bloqué la circulation pendant une heure / *I was held up* j'ai été retenu **4.** [rob] faire une attaque à main armée. ◆ vi [clothing, equipment] tenir ; [supplies] tenir, durer ; [weather] se maintenir / *the car held up well during the trip* la voiture a bien tenu le coup pendant le voyage. ❖ **hold with** vt insep UK [agree with] être d'accord avec ; [approve of] approuver.

holdall ['həʊldɔːl] n UK (sac m) fourre-tout m inv.

holder ['həʊldə'] n **1.** [for lamp, plastic cup, etc.] support m **2.** [person - of ticket] détenteur m, -trice f ; [- of passport, post, diploma] titulaire mf ; [SPORT - of record, cup] détenteur m, -trice f ; [- of title] détenteur m, -trice f, tenant m, -e f ; [FIN - of stock] porteur m, -euse f, détenteur m, -trice f.

holding ['həʊldɪŋ] ◆ n **1.** [of meeting] tenue f **2.** [in boxing] : *holding is against the rules* il est contraire au règlement de tenir son adversaire **3.** [land] propriété f **4.** FIN participation f ▶ **holdings** a) [lands] propriétés fpl, terres fpl b) [stocks] participation f, portefeuille m. ◆ comp ▶ **holding company** FIN (société f en) holding m

▶ **holding operation** opération f de maintien ▶ **holding pattern** AERON : *we were in a holding pattern over Heathrow for two hours* nous avons eu une attente de deux heures au-dessus de Heathrow.

hold-up n 1. [robbery] hold-up m, vol m à main armée 2. [delay - on road, railway track, etc.] ralentissement m ; [- in production, departure, etc.] retard m. ❖ **hold-ups** pl n [stockings] bas mpl auto-fixants.

hole [həʊl] ❖ n 1. [in the ground] trou m ; [in wall, roof, etc.] trou m ; [in clouds] éclaircie f ▶ **to wear a hole in sthg** faire un trou à qqch 2. inf & pej [boring place] trou m 3. inf [tricky situation] pétrin m ▶ **to be in a hole** être dans le pétrin 4. SPORT [in golf] trou m ▶ **to get a hole in one** faire un trou en un / *an 18-hole (golf) course* un parcours de 18 trous. ❖ vt 1. [make hole in] trouer 2. [in golf] ▶ **to hole the ball** faire le trou. ❖ vi 1. [sock, stocking] se trouer 2. [in golf] faire le trou. ❖ **hole up** ❖ vi 1. [animal] se terrer 2. inf [hide] se planquer. ❖ vt sep *(usu passive)* : *they're holed up in a hotel* ils se planquent or ils sont planqués dans un hôtel.

holiday ['hɒlɪdeɪ] ❖ n 1. UK [period without work] vacances fpl ▶ **on holiday** en vacances ▶ **to go on holiday** aller or partir en vacances 2. [day off] jour m de congé. ❖ comp [mood, feeling, destination] de vacances ; [pay] versé pendant les vacances. ❖ vi UK passer les vacances.

holiday camp n UK centre de vacances familial *(avec animations et activités diverses).*

holiday home n UK maison f de vacances, résidence f secondaire.

holiday let n location f saisonnière.

holidaymaker ['hɒlɪdeɪ,meɪkə'] n UK vacancier m, -ère f.

holiday resort n UK lieu m de vacances or de séjour.

holiday season n UK saison f des vacances.

holier-than-thou ['həʊlɪəðən'ðaʊ] adj pej [attitude, tone, person] moralisateur.

holiness ['həʊlɪnɪs] n sainteté f.

holistic [həʊ'lɪstɪk] adj MED & PHILOS holistique.

holland ['hɒlənd] n TEXT hollande f.

Holland ['hɒlənd] pr n [country] Hollande f, Pays-Bas mpl / *in Holland* en Hollande, aux Pays-Bas.

hollandaise (sauce) [,hɒlən'deɪz-] n CULIN sauce f hollandaise.

holler ['hɒlr] inf ❖ vi brailler, beugler. ❖ vt brailler. ❖ n braillement m. ❖ **holler out** vi & vt sep inf = holler.

hollow ['hɒləʊ] ❖ adj 1. [not solid - tree, container] creux 2. [sunken - eyes, cheeks] creux, cave 3. [empty - sound] creux, caverneux ; [- laugh, laughter] faux (fausse), forcé 4. [worthless - promise, words] vain. ❖ adv ▶ **to sound hollow** a) [tree, wall] sonner creux b) [laughter, excuse, promise] sonner faux. ❖ n 1. [in tree] creux m, cavité f 2. [in ground] enfoncement m, dénivellation f 3. [in hand, back] creux m. ❖ vt creuser. ❖ **hollow out** vt sep creuser.

hollow-eyed adj aux yeux caves or enfoncés.

holly ['hɒlɪ] ❖ n [tree, leaves] houx m. ❖ comp ▶ **holly berry** baie f de houx, cenelle f ▶ **holly tree** houx m.

Hollywood ['hɒlɪwʊd] ❖ pr n Hollywood ▶ **the Hollywood Bowl** *salle de concerts semi-couverte à Hollywood.* ❖ adj hollywoodien.

holocaust ['hɒləkɔːst] n holocauste m ▶ **the Holocaust** l'Holocauste.

hologram ['hɒləgræm] n hologramme m.

hols [hɒlz] pl n UK inf SCH vacances fpl.

Holstein ['hɒlstaɪn] n US [cow] frisonne f.

holster ['həʊlstə'] n [for gun - on waist, shoulder] étui m de revolver ; [- on saddle] fonte f ; [for piece of equipment] étui m.

holy ['həʊlɪ] (*compar* holier, *superl* holiest) ❖ adj 1. [sacred - bread, water] bénit ; [- place, ground, day] saint 2. [devout] saint 3. inf [as intensifier] : *that child is a holy terror* [mischievous] cet enfant est un vrai démon 4. PHR **holy smoke!** or **holy mackerel!** or **holy cow!** mince alors !, ça alors ! ▶ **holy shit!** US vulg merde alors ! ❖ n ▶ **the Holy of Holies a)** RELIG le saint des saints **b)** hum & fig [inner sanctum] sanctuaire m, antre m sacré **c)** [special place] lieu m saint.

Holy Bible n ▶ **the Holy Bible** la Sainte Bible.

Holy Communion n la Sainte Communion.

Holy Ghost n ▶ **the Holy Ghost** le Saint-Esprit, l'Esprit saint.

Holy Grail n ▶ **the Holy Grail** le (Saint) Graal.

Holy Land n ▶ **the Holy Land** la Terre sainte.

holy orders pl n ordres mpl.

holy roller n US pej : *he's a real holy roller* il fait vraiment du prêchi-prêcha.

Holy Spirit = Holy Ghost.

Holy Trinity n ▶ **the Holy Trinity** la Sainte Trinité.

holy war n guerre f sainte.

homage ['hɒmɪdʒ] n hommage m ▶ **to pay** or **to do homage to sb, to do sb homage** rendre hommage à qqn.

hombre ['ɒmbreɪ] n US inf mec m.

home [həʊm] ❖ n 1. [one's house] maison f ; [more subjectively] chez-soi m inv / *I left home at 16* j'ai quitté la maison à 16 ans / *his home is in Nice* il habite Nice ▶ **at home** chez soi, à la maison 2. [family unit] foyer m ; ADMIN habitation f, logement m 3. [native land] patrie f, pays m natal 4. BOT & ZOOL habitat m 5. [mental hospital] maison f de repos ; [old people's home] maison f de retraite ; [children's home] foyer m pour enfants 6. GAMES & SPORT [finishing line] arrivée f ; [on board game] case f départ ; [goal] but m ▶ **to be at home** to recevoir. ❖ adv 1. [to or at one's house] chez soi, à la maison ▶ **to go** or **to get home** rentrer (chez soi or à la maison) ▶ **to see sb home** raccompagner qqn jusque chez lui / elle 2. [from abroad] au pays natal, au pays ▶ **to send sb home** rapatrier qqn 3. [all the way] à fond / *to drive a nail home* enfoncer un clou jusqu'au bout. ❖ adj 1. [concerning family, household - life] de famille, familial ; [- for family consumption] familial, à usage familial ▶ **home comforts** confort m du foyer 2. [to, for house] à or pour la maison / *home visit / delivery* visite f / livraison f à domicile / *home decorating* décoration f intérieure 3. [national - gen] national, du pays ; [- market, policy] intérieur ▶ **home sales** ventes fpl sur le marché intérieur 4. SPORT [team - national] national ; [- local] local / *the home team today is...* l'équipe qui reçoit aujourd'hui est... / *home game* match m à domicile. ❖ vi [person, animal] revenir or rentrer chez soi ; [pigeon] revenir au colombier. ❖ **home in on** vt insep 1. [subj: missile] se diriger (automatiquement) sur or vers ; [proceed towards - goal] se diriger vers ; fig mettre le cap sur 2. [direct attention to - problem, solution] mettre l'accent sur ; [- difficulty, question] viser, cerner. ❖ **home on to** = home in on.

home address n [on form] domicile m (permanent) ; [not business address] adresse f personnelle.

home banking n la banque à domicile.

homeboy ['həʊmbɔɪ] n US : *he's a homeboy* a) [from our town] c'est un gars de chez nous b) [in our gang] c'est un des nôtres.

home brew n [beer] bière f faite à la maison ; [wine] vin m fait à la maison.

home-brewed adj [beer] fait maison.

homecoming ['həʊm,kʌmɪŋ] n [to family] retour *m* au foyer or à la maison ; [to country] retour *m* au pays. ❖ **Homecoming** n US SCH & UNIV fête donnée en l'honneur de l'équipe de football d'une université ou d'une école et à laquelle sont invités les anciens élèves.

home computer n ordinateur *m* personnel, micro-ordinateur *m*.

home cooking n cuisine *f* familiale.

Home Counties pl pr n ▶ **the Home Counties** l'ensemble des comtés limitrophes de Londres.

home economics, home ec US inf n (U) économie *f* domestique.

home fries pl n US CULIN pommes de terre *fpl* sautées.

home ground n **1.** ▶ **to be on home ground a)** [near home] être en pays de connaissance **b)** *fig* [familiar subject] être sur son terrain **2.** SPORT : *our home ground* notre terrain.

homegrown [,həʊm'grəʊn] adj [not foreign] du pays ; [from own garden] du jardin.

home help n UK aide *f* ménagère.

homeland ['həʊmlænd] n **1.** [native country] patrie *f* **2.** [South African political territory] homeland *m*.

homeless ['həʊmlɪs] ❖ adj sans foyer ; [pet] abandonné, sans foyer. ❖ pl n ▶ **the homeless** les sans-abri *mpl*.

homelessness ['həʊmlɪsnɪs] n : *the problem of homelessness* le problème des sans-abri.

home life n vie *f* de famille.

home loan n prêt *m* immobilier.

home-loving adj casanier.

homely ['həʊmlɪ] (*compar* homelier, *superl* homeliest) adj **1.** [unpretentious] simple, modeste **2.** US [plain, unattractive - person] peu attrayant.

homemade [,həʊm'meɪd] adj **1.** [made at home] fait à la maison *(inv)* / *a homemade bomb* une bombe de fabrication artisanale **2.** [made on premises] maison *(inv)*, fait maison.

homemaker ['həʊm,meɪkə] n femme *f* au foyer.

home movie n film *m* d'amateur.

Home Office n ▶ **the Home Office** le ministère britannique de l'Intérieur.

homeopath ['həʊmɪəʊpæθ] n homéopathe *mf*.

homeopathic [,həʊmɪəʊ'pæθɪk] adj homéopathique.

homeopathy [,həʊmɪ'ɒpəθɪ] n homéopathie *f*.

homeostatic [,həʊmɪəʊ'stætɪk] adj homéostatique.

homeowner ['həʊm,əʊnə] n propriétaire *mf*.

home page n COMPUT page *f* d'accueil.

homer ['həʊmə] n US abbr of home run.

Homer ['həʊmə] pr n Homère.

homeroom ['həʊm,ruːm] n US **1.** [place] salle où l'on fait l'appel **2.** [group] élèves rassemblés pour l'appel.

home rule n autonomie *f*. ❖ **Home Rule** n mouvement pour l'autonomie de l'Irlande.

Home Rule

Régime d'autonomie revendiqué par l'Irlande entre 1870 et 1914. Le projet de loi fut refusé à plusieurs reprises par les Communes mais, finalement, une loi sur l'autonomie fut votée en 1914, proposant la création d'un Parlement composé de deux chambres chargées des affaires locales. La mise en vigueur de

cette loi, déjà compromise par l'opposition des protestants unionistes de l'Ulster, fut reportée lorsque la Première Guerre mondiale éclata. À la suite de l'insurrection nationaliste de 1916, les partisans du Home Rule revendiquèrent l'autonomie totale. Après deux ans de guerre civile, l'Irlande obtint son autonomie en 1921 et devint l'État libre d'Irlande, le nord-est du pays restant lié à la Grande-Bretagne.

home run n **1.** [in baseball] *coup de batte qui permet au batteur de marquer un point en faisant un tour complet en une seule fois* **2.** [last leg of trip] dernière étape *f* du circuit.

homeschooling ['həʊm,skuːlɪŋ] n US SCH instruction *f* à la maison.

Home Secretary n ministre *m* de l'Intérieur en Grande-Bretagne.

home shopping n [by telephone, computer] télé-achat *m* ; [by post] achat *m* par correspondance.

homesick ['həʊmsɪk] adj nostalgique ▶ **to be homesick** avoir le mal du pays ▶ **to be homesick for sb** s'ennuyer de qqn ▶ **to be homesick for sthg** avoir la nostalgie de qqch.

homesickness ['həʊm,sɪknɪs] n mal *m* du pays.

homesite ['həʊmsaɪt] n US terrain *m* à bâtir.

homespun ['həʊmspʌn] ❖ adj **1.** [wool] filé à la maison, de fabrication domestique ; [cloth] de homespun **2.** [simple] simple, sans recherche. ❖ n homespun *m*.

homestead ['həʊmsted] ❖ n **1.** US HIST *terre dont la propriété est attribuée à un colon sous réserve qu'il y réside et l'exploite* **2.** [buildings and land] propriété *f* ; [farm] ferme *f*. ❖ vt US [acquire] acquérir ; [settle] s'installer à, coloniser.

home straight, home stretch n SPORT & *fig* dernière ligne *f* droite.

home town n **1.** [of birth] ville *f* natale **2.** [of upbringing] : *his home town* la ville où il a grandi.

home truth n vérité *f* désagréable ▶ **to tell sb a few home truths** dire ses (quatre) vérités à qqn.

homeward ['həʊmwəd] ❖ adj du retour. ❖ adv = homewards.

homewards ['həʊmwədz] adv **1.** [to house] vers la maison **2.** [to homeland] vers la patrie / *to be homewards bound* prendre le chemin du retour / *the plane flew homewards* l'avion faisait route vers sa base.

homework ['həʊmwɜːk] ❖ n (U) SCH devoirs *mpl* (à la maison) ; [research] travail *m* préparatoire. ❖ comp ▶ **a homework exercise** un devoir (à la maison).

homeworker ['həʊm,wɜːkə] n travailleur *m*, -euse *f* à domicile.

homeworking ['həʊm,wɜːkɪŋ] n travail *m* à domicile.

homey ['həʊmɪ] (*pl* homies, *compar* homier, *superl* homiest) inf n US [friend] pote *m*.

homicidal ['hɒmɪsaɪdl] adj LAW homicide.

homicide ['hɒmɪsaɪd] n LAW **1.** [act] homicide *m* **2.** [person] homicide *mf*.

homily ['hɒmɪlɪ] (*pl* homilies) n **1.** RELIG homélie *f* **2.** *pej* sermon *m*, homélie *f*.

homing ['həʊmɪŋ] adj [pre-programmed] autoguidé ; [heat-seeking] à tête chercheuse ▶ **homing device** mécanisme *m* d'autoguidage.

homing pigeon n pigeon *m* voyageur.

homo ['həʊməʊ] v inf & pej ❖ n pédé *m*, homo *mf*. ❖ adj pédé, homo.

homoeopath ['həʊmɪəʊpæθ] = homeopath.

homoerotic [ˌhəʊməʊɪˈrɒtɪk] adj homoérotique.

homogeneous [ˌhɒməˈdʒiːnjəs] adj homogène.

homogenize, homogenise [həˈmɒdʒənaɪz] vt homogénéiser, homogénéifier.

homonym [ˈhɒmənɪm] n homonyme m.

homophobia [ˌhəʊməʊˈfəʊbjə] n homophobie f.

homophobic [ˌhəʊməʊˈfəʊbɪk] adj homophobe.

homosexual [ˌhɒməˈsekʃʊəl] ◆ n homosexuel m, -elle f. ◆ adj homosexuel.

homosexuality [ˌhɒmə,sekʃʊˈælətɪ] n homosexualité f.

homy [ˈhəʊmɪ] (compar homier, superl homiest) adj inf US [comfortable] accueillant, confortable.

hon [hʌn] n US inf chéri m, -e f.

hon. written abbr of honorary.

Hon. written abbr of honourable.

honcho [ˈhɒntʃəʊ] n US inf [boss] chef m.

Honduran [hɒnˈdjʊərən] ◆ n Hondurien m, -enne f. ◆ adj hondurien.

Honduras [hɒnˈdjʊərəs] pr n Honduras m.

hone [həʊn] ◆ vt 1. [sharpen] aiguiser, affûter, affiler; [re-sharpen] repasser 2. [refine - analysis, thought] affiner. ◆ n pierre f à aiguiser. ◆ **hone down** vt sep [reduce] tailler; [make slim] faire maigrir.

honest [ˈɒnɪst] ◆ adj 1. [not deceitful] honnête, probe; [trustworthy] intègre / the honest truth la pure vérité 2. [decent, upright] droit; [virtuous] honnête 3. [not fraudulent] honnête 4. [frank - face] franc (franche), sincère. ◆ adv inf : I didn't mean it, honest! je plaisantais, je te le jure !

honestly [ˈɒnɪstlɪ] adv honnêtement.

honesty [ˈɒnɪstɪ] n 1. [truthfulness - of person] honnêteté f; [- of text, words] véracité f, exactitude f 2. [incorruptibility] intégrité f 3. [upright conduct] droiture f 4. [sincerity] sincérité f, franchise f 5. BOT monnaie-du-pape f. ◆ **in all honesty** adv phr en toute sincérité.

honey [ˈhʌnɪ] (pl honies) ◆ n 1. miel m; fig miel m, douceur f 2. US inf [sweetheart] chou m; [addressing man] mon chéri; [addressing woman] ma chérie. ◆ adj miellé.

honeybee [ˈhʌnɪbiː] n abeille f.

honeycomb [ˈhʌnɪkəʊm] ◆ n 1. [in wax] rayon m or gâteau m de miel 2. [material] structure f alvéolaire 3. [pattern] nid m d'abeille; TEXT nid m d'abeille. ◆ vt 1. [surface] cribler 2. [interior] miner.

honeyed [ˈhʌnɪd] adj fig mielleux.

honeymoon [ˈhʌnɪmuːn] ◆ n 1. [period] lune f de miel; [trip] voyage m de noces / they're on their honeymoon ils sont en voyage de noces 2. fig état m de grâce. ◆ comp [couple, suite] de voyage de noces ▶ **honeymoon period** [of prime minister, president] lune f de miel, état m de grâce. ◆ vi passer sa lune de miel.

honeymooner [ˈhʌnɪmuːnər] n jeune marié m, jeune mariée f.

honeysuckle [ˈhʌnɪ,sʌkl] n chèvrefeuille m.

honeytrap [ˈhʌnɪ,træp] n piège tendu à une personnalité par la presse à sensation afin d'en tirer des confidences.

Hong Kong [ˌhɒŋˈkɒŋ] pr n Hong Kong, Hongkong / in Hong Kong à Hongkong.

honk [hɒŋk] ◆ vi 1. [car] klaxonner 2. [goose] cacarder. ◆ vt ▶ **to honk one's horn** donner un coup de Klaxon. ◆ n 1. [of car horn] coup m de Klaxon ▶ honk, honk! tut-tut ! 2. [of geese] cri m ▶ honk, honk! couin-couin !

honker [ˈhɒŋkər] n US inf 1. [nose] blaire m, tarin m 2. [breast] nichon m.

honkie, honky [ˈhɒŋkɪ] (pl honkies) n US v inf terme injurieux désignant un Blanc.

honking [ˈhɒŋkɪŋ] adj inf 1. [huge] énorme 2. [brilliant] génial.

Honolulu [ˌhɒnəˈluːluː] pr n Honolulu.

honor US = honour.

honorary [UK ˈɒnərərɪ US ɒnəˈreərɪ] adj [titular position] honoraire; [in name only] à titre honorifique, honoraire; [unpaid position] à titre gracieux / honorary degree grade honoris causa / honorary secretary secrétaire honoraire.

honor roll n US tableau m d'honneur.

honors program [ˈɒnəz,prəʊgræm] n US enseignement réservé aux meilleurs élèves.

honour UK, **honor** US [ˈɒnər] ◆ n 1. [personal integrity] honneur m 2. [public, social regard] honneur m 3. fml [pleasure] : it is a great honour to introduce Mr Reed c'est un grand honneur pour moi de vous présenter Monsieur Reed 4. [credit] honneur m, crédit m 5. [mark of respect] honneur m ▶ Your Honour a) Votre Honneur b) LAW ≃ Monsieur le Juge c) ≃ Monsieur le président 6. GAMES [face card] honneur m. ◆ vt 1. [person] honorer, faire honneur à 2. [fulfil the terms of] honorer; [observe - boycott, rule] respecter 3. [pay - debt] honorer. ◆ **honours** pl n UK UNIV [degree] ≃ licence f ▶ first- / second-class honours : she got first- / second-class honours elle a eu sa licence avec mention très bien / mention bien. ◆ **in honour of** prep phr en honneur de.

honourable UK, **honorable** US [ˈɒnrəbl] adj 1. honorable ▶ honourable discharge : he got an honourable discharge il a été rendu à la vie civile 2. [title] ▶ the (Right) Honourable le (très) honorable / my honourable friend the member for Calderdale mon collègue l'honorable député du Calderdale.

⌂ Honourable

Cette appellation est utilisée devant le nom de certains membres de l'aristocratie britannique : the Honourable James Porter ou the Hon. James Porter. Elle est également employée à la Chambre des communes lorsqu'un député parle d'un autre député : the honourable member for Oxford. Lorsqu'un député désigne un collègue du même parti, il emploie l'expression my honourable friend ; lorsque son interlocuteur appartient au parti opposé, le terme consacré est the honourable gentleman ou lady.

honourably UK, **honorably** US [ˈɒnərəblɪ] adv honorablement.

honour bound adj ▶ to be honour bound (to) être tenu par l'honneur (à).

honour killing n crime m d'honneur.

honours list n UK liste de distinctions honorifiques conférées par le monarque deux fois par an.

Hons. written abbr of honours degree.

hooch [huːtʃ] n US v inf [drink] gnôle f.

hood [hʊd] ◆ n 1. [garment] capuchon m; [with collar] capuche f; [with eye-holes] cagoule f; UNIV épitoge f ▶ a rain hood une capuche 2. UK AUTO [cover] capote f; US AUTO capot m; [of pram] capote f; [for fumes, smoke] hotte f ▶ hood ornament US calicot m 3. [of animals, plants] capuchon m; [for falcons] chaperon m, capuchon m 4. US crime sl [gangster] gangster m, truand m 5. US inf [neighbourhood] ▸ **the hood** le quartier **6.** *inf* = **hoodlum.** ◆ vt mettre le capuchon ; [falcon] chaperonner, enchaperonner.

hooded ['hʊdɪd] adj [clothing] à capuchon ; [person] encapuchonné ▸ **hooded eyes** *fig* yeux *mpl* tombants.

hoodie ['hʊdɪ] n *inf* **1.** [top] sweat-shirt *m* à capuche **2.** 🇬🇧 [person] *jeune qui porte un sweat-shirt à capuche.*

hoodlum ['hu:dləm] n *inf* voyou *m*.

hoodwink ['hʊdwɪŋk] vt tromper, avoir / *he hoodwinked me into coming* par un tour de passe-passe il m'a fait venir.

hooey ['hu:ɪ] n *inf* foutaise *f*.

hoof [hu:f or hʊf] (*pl* **hoofs** or **hooves** [hu:vz]) ◆ n sabot *m* (*d'animal*). ◆ vt ▸ **to hoof it a)** *inf* [go on foot] aller à pinces **b)** [flee] se cavaler **c)** [dance] guincher.

hoo-ha ['hu:,ha:] n *inf* **1.** [noise] boucan *m*, potin *m* ; [chaos] pagaille *f*, tohu-bohu *m* ; [fuss] bruit *m*, histoires *fpl* **2.** 🇺🇸 [party] fête *f* charivarique.

hook [hʊk] ◆ n **1.** [gen] crochet *m* ; [for coats] patère *f* ; [on clothes] agrafe *f* ; NAUT gaffe *f* **2.** [fishing] hameçon *m* **3.** [in advertising] accroche *f* **4.** [in golf] hook *m* ; [in cricket] coup *m* tourné ▸ **a right / left hook** [in boxing] un crochet (du) droit / gauche **5.** *inf* PHR **to get sb off the hook** tirer qqn d'affaire ▸ **to let** or **to get sb off the hook** [obligation] libérer qqn de sa responsabilité. ◆ vt **1.** [snag] accrocher ; [seize - person, prey] attraper ; [- floating object] gaffer, crocher **2.** [loop] : *hook the rope around the tree* passez la corde autour de l'arbre / *she hooked one leg round the leg of the chair* elle passa or enroula une jambe autour du pied de la chaise **3.** FISHING [fish] prendre ; TECH hameçonner **4.** [in golf] faire un hook ; [in boxing] donner un crochet à ; [in rugby] talonner *(le ballon)* ; [in cricket] renvoyer d'un coup tourné **5.** *inf & fam* [marry] passer la corde au cou à. ◆ vi **1.** [fasten] s'agrafer **2.** GOLF hooker. ◆ **hook on** ◆ vi s'accrocher. ◆ vt sep accrocher. ◆ **hook up** ◆ vt sep **1.** [trailer] accrocher ; [dress] agrafer ; [boat] amarrer **2.** *inf* [install] installer ; [plug in] brancher **3.** RADIO & TV faire un duplex entre **4.** = **hitch up**. ◆ vi **1.** [dress] s'agrafer **2.** 🇺🇸 *inf* [meet] se rencontrer, se donner rendez-vous ; [work together] faire équipe **3.** 🇺🇸 *inf* [be in relationship] ▸ **to hook up with sb** sortir avec qqn **4.** RADIO & TV ▸ **to hook up with** faire une émission en duplex avec.

hooked [hʊkt] adj **1.** [hook-shaped] recourbé **2.** [having hooks] muni de crochets ; [fishing line] muni d'un hameçon **3.** *inf & fig* [addicted] : *he got hooked on hard drugs* il est devenu accro aux drogues dures.

hooker ['hʊkə-] n **1.** RUGBY talonneur *m* **2.** 🇺🇸 *v inf* [prostitute] pute *f*.

hookey, hooky ['hʊkɪ] n 🇺🇸, 🇦🇺 & 🇳🇿 *inf* ▸ **to play hookey** sécher les cours, faire l'école buissonnière.

hook-nosed adj au nez recourbé or crochu.

hooligan ['hu:lɪgən] n hooligan *m*, vandale *m*.

hooliganism ['hu:lɪgənɪzm] n vandalisme *m*.

hoop [hu:p] ◆ n **1.** [ring] cerceau *m* **2.** 🇺🇸 *inf* [basketball] ▸ **hoop(s)** basket *m*. ◆ comp ▸ **hoop earrings** (anneaux *mpl*) créoles *fpl*.

hoopla ['hu:plɑ:] n **1.** 🇬🇧 [funfair game] jeu *m* d'anneaux *(dans les foires)* **2.** 🇺🇸 *inf* = **hoo-ha 3.** 🇺🇸 *inf* [advertising] publicité *f* tapageuse.

hooray [hʊ'reɪ] interj hourra, hurrah.

hoot [hu:t] ◆ n **1.** [shout - of delight, pain] cri *m* ; [jeer] huée *f* / *hoots of laughter* éclats *mpl* de rire **2.** [of owl] hululement *m* **3.** AUTO coup *m* de Klaxon ; [of train] sifflement *m* ; [of siren] mugissement *m* **4.** *inf* [least bit] : *I don't give* or *care a hoot* or *two hoots* je m'en fiche, mais alors complètement, je m'en contrefiche **5.** *inf* [amusing event] :

bonne partie *f* de rigolade / *he's a real hoot!* c'est un sacré rigolo !, il est tordant ! ◆ vi **1.** *inf* [person] : *to hoot with laughter* s'esclaffer **2.** [owl] hululer **3.** AUTO klaxonner ; [train] siffler ; [siren] mugir. ◆ **hoot down** vt sep *inf* [person, show] huer, conspuer.

hootch [hu:tʃ] *v inf* = **hooch**.

hooter ['hu:tə-] n 🇬🇧 **1.** [car horn] Klaxon® *m* ; [in factory, ship] sirène *f* **2.** [party toy] mirliton *m* **3.** *inf* [nose] pif *m* **4.** 🇺🇸 *inf* [breast] néné *m*, nichon *m*.

Hoover® ['hu:və-] n aspirateur *m*. ◆ **hoover** vt 🇬🇧 : *to hoover a carpet* passer l'aspirateur sur un tapis.

hooves [hu:vz] *pl* → **hoof**.

hop [hɒp] (*pt & pp* **hopped**, *cont* **hopping**) ◆ n **1.** [jump] saut *m* à cloche-pied ; [in rapid series] sautillement *m* **2.** AERON étape *f* **3.** BOT houblon *m*. ◆ vt *inf* **1.** 🇺🇸 [bus, subway, etc. -legally] sauter dans ; [-illegally] prendre en resquillant **2.** PHR **hop it!** allez, dégage ! ◆ vi **1.** [jump] sauter ; [in rapid series] sautiller **2.** [jump on one leg] sauter à cloche-pied **3.** *inf* [travel by plane] : *we hopped across to Paris for the weekend* nous sommes allés à Paris en avion pour le week-end. ◆ **hop off** vi *inf* [leave] décamper.

hope [həʊp] ◆ n **1.** [desire, expectation] espoir *m* ; *fml* espérance *f* ▸ **to give up hope (of)** perdre l'espoir (de) ▸ **to raise sb's hopes a)** [for first time] susciter or faire naître l'espoir de qqn or chez qqn **b)** [anew] faire renaître l'espoir de qqn **c)** [increase] renforcer l'espoir de qqn **2.** [chance] espoir *m*, chance *f* **3.** RELIG espérance *f*. ◆ vi espérer ▸ **to hope for sthg** espérer qqch. ◆ vt espérer / *hoping* or *I hope to hear from you soon* j'espère avoir de tes nouvelles bientôt / *I really hope so!* je l'espère bien ! / *I hope not* j'espère que non.

hope chest n 🇺🇸 *lit* coffre *m* à trousseau ; *fig* trousseau *m*.

hopeful ['həʊpfʊl] ◆ adj **1.** [full of hope] plein d'espoir **2.** [inspiring hope] encourageant, prometteur. ◆ n aspirant *m*, candidat *m*.

hopefully ['həʊpfəlɪ] adv **1.** [smile, speak, work] avec espoir, avec optimisme **2.** [with luck] on espère que… / *will you get it finished today? — hopefully!* est-ce que tu l'auras terminé pour aujourd'hui ? — je l'espère ! or oui, avec un peu de chance !

hopeless ['həʊplɪs] adj **1.** [desperate - person] désespéré ; [- situation] désespéré, sans espoir **2.** [incurable - addiction, ill person] incurable **3.** [inveterate - drunk, liar] invétéré, incorrigible **4.** *inf* [incompetent - person] nul ; [- at job] incompétent **5.** [pointless] : *it's hopeless trying to explain to him* il est inutile d'essayer de lui expliquer.

hopelessly ['həʊplɪslɪ] adv **1.** [speak] avec désespoir **2.** [irremediably] : *they are hopelessly in debt / in love* ils sont complètement endettés / éperdument amoureux / *by this time we were hopelessly late / lost* nous étions maintenant vraiment en retard / complètement perdus.

h2cus MESSAGING written abbr of **hope to see you soon**.

hopper ['hɒpə-] n [feeder bin] trémie *f* ▸ **hopper car** RAIL wagon-trémie *m*.

hopping ['hɒpɪŋ] adv *inf* [as intensifier] : *he was hopping mad* il était fou furieux.

hopscotch ['hɒpskɒtʃ] n marelle *f*.

horde [hɔ:d] n **1.** [nomadic] horde *f* **2.** *fig* [crowd] essaim *m*, horde *f* ; [of agitators] horde *f*.

horizon [hə'raɪzn] n horizon *m* / *we saw a boat on the horizon* nous vîmes un bateau à l'horizon. ◆ **horizons** *pl* n [perspectives] horizons *mpl* / *to broaden one's horizons* élargir ses horizons.

horizontal [ˌhɒrɪ'zɒntl] ◆ adj **1.** horizontal **2.** ADMIN & COMM [communication, integration] horizontal. ◆ n horizontale f.

horizontally [ˌhɒrɪ'zɒntəlɪ] adv horizontalement.

hormonal [hɔː'məʊnl] adj hormonal.

hormone ['hɔːməʊn] n hormone f ▸ **hormone deficiency** insuffisance f hormonale ▸ **hormone replacement therapy** traitement m hormonal substitutif.

horn [hɔːn] ◆ n **1.** [gen] corne f ; [pommel] pommeau m **2.** MUS cor m **3.** AUTO klaxon m ; [manual] corne f **4.** NAUT sirène f **5.** HUNT corne f, cor m, trompe f **6.** 🇺🇸 CULIN cornet m **7.** 🇺🇸 inf téléphone m. ◆ adj [handle, bibelot] en corne. ❖ **horn in** vi inf [on conversation] mettre son grain de sel ; [on a deal] s'immiscer.

hornet ['hɔːnɪt] n frelon m.

hornpipe ['hɔːnpaɪp] n matelote f *(danse)*.

horn-rimmed adj à monture d'écaille.

horny ['hɔːnɪ] adj **1.** [calloused - nail, skin] calleux ; VET encorné **2.** v inf [randy] excité (sexuellement) **3.** v inf [having sex appeal] sexy.

horoscope ['hɒrəskəʊp] n horoscope m.

horrendous [hɒ'rendəs] adj **1.** lit terrible **2.** fig [very bad] affreux, horrible.

horrendously [hɒ'rendəslɪ] adv horriblement.

horrible ['hɒrəbl] adj **1.** [horrific] horrible, affreux ; [morally repulsive] abominable **2.** [dismaying] horrible, effroyable **3.** [very unpleasant] horrible, atroce ; [food] infect.

horribly ['hɒrəblɪ] adv **1.** [nastily] horriblement, atrocement, affreusement **2.** [as intensifier] affreusement.

horrid ['hɒrɪd] adj **1.** [unkind] méchant ; [ugly] vilain / *he was horrid to me* il a été méchant avec moi **2.** = **horrible**.

horridly ['hɒrɪdlɪ] adv [as intensifier] atrocement, affreusement.

horrific [hɒ'rɪfɪk] adj **1.** lit horrible, terrifiant ; liter horrifique **2.** fig [very unpleasant] horrible.

horrifically [hɒ'rɪfɪklɪ] adv **1.** [gruesomely] atrocement **2.** [as intensifier] : *horrifically expensive* affreusement cher.

horrified ['hɒrɪfaɪd] adj horrifié.

horrify ['hɒrɪfaɪ] *(pt & pp* **horrified)** vt **1.** [terrify] horrifier **2.** [weaker use] horrifier, scandaliser.

horrifying ['hɒrɪfaɪɪŋ] adj **1.** [terrifying] horrifiant, terrifiant **2.** [weaker use] scandaleux.

horror ['hɒrəʳ] n **1.** [feeling] horreur f **2.** [unpleasantness] horreur f **3.** inf [person, thing] horreur f.

horror film, horror movie n film m d'épouvante.

horror-stricken, horror-struck adj glacé or frappé d'horreur.

hors d'œuvre [ɔː'dɜːvr] n hors-d'œuvre m inv ; [cocktail snack] amuse-gueule m.

horse [hɔːs] ◆ n **1.** [animal] cheval m / *to ride a horse* monter à cheval **2.** [trestle] tréteau m ; SPORT cheval m d'arçons. ◆ comp ▸ **horse manure a)** crottin m de cheval **b)** [as fertilizer] fumier m de cheval. ◆ pl n MIL cavalière f. ❖ **horse about** 🇬🇧, **horse around** vi inf [noisily] chahuter.

horseback ['hɔːsbæk] n ▸ **on horseback** à cheval.

horsebox ['hɔːsbɒks] n 🇬🇧 [trailer] van m ; [stall] box m.

horsecar ['hɔːskɑːʳ] n 🇺🇸 fourgon m à chevaux.

horse chestnut n [tree] marronnier m (d'Inde) ; [nut] marron m (d'Inde).

horse-drawn adj tiré par des chevaux, à chevaux.

horsefly ['hɔːsflaɪ] *(pl* **horseflies)** n taon m.

horsehair ['hɔːsheəʳ] ◆ n crin m (de cheval). ◆ adj de crin (de cheval).

horseman ['hɔːsmən] *(pl* **horsemen** [-mən]) n **1.** [rider] cavalier m, écuyer m **2.** [breeder] éleveur m de chevaux.

horsemanship ['hɔːsmənʃɪp] n **1.** [activity] équitation f **2.** [skill] talent m de cavalier.

horsemeat ['hɔːsmiːt] n viande f de cheval.

horse opera n 🇺🇸 inf & hum western m.

horseplay ['hɔːspleɪ] n (U) chahut m brutal, jeux mpl tapageurs or brutaux.

horsepower ['hɔːsˌpaʊəʳ] n [unit] cheval-vapeur m, cheval m / *a 10-horsepower motor* un moteur de 10 chevaux / *it's a 4-horsepower car* c'est une 4 chevaux.

horse racing n (U) courses fpl (de chevaux).

horseradish ['hɔːsˌrædɪʃ] n BOT raifort m, radis m noir. ◆ comp ▸ **horseradish sauce** sauce f au raifort.

horserider ['hɔːsraɪdəʳ] n 🇺🇸 cavalier m, -ère f.

horse riding n 🇬🇧 équitation f.

horseshoe ['hɔːsʃuː] n fer m à cheval.

horse show n = **horse trials**.

horse trader n **1.** lit maquignon m **2.** 🇺🇸 inf [hard bargainer] négociateur m, -trice f redoutable.

horse-trading n 🇬🇧 inf négociation f dure ; pej maquignonnage m.

horsetrailer ['hɔːstreɪləʳ] n 🇺🇸 = **horsebox**.

horse trials pl n concours m hippique.

horsewhip ['hɔːswɪp] *(pt & pp* **horsewhipped,** cont **horsewhipping)** ◆ n cravache f. ◆ vt cravacher.

horsewoman ['hɔːsˌwʊmən] *(pl* **horsewomen** [-ˌwɪmɪn]) n cavalière f, écuyère f ; [sidesaddled] amazone f.

horsey, horsy ['hɔːsɪ] adj inf **1.** [horse-like] chevalin **2.** [fond of horses] féru de cheval.

horticultural [ˌhɔːtɪ'kʌltʃərəl] adj horticole / *horticultural show* exposition f horticole or d'horticulture.

horticulture ['hɔːtɪkʌltʃəʳ] n horticulture f.

hosanna [həʊ'zænə] ◆ n hosanna m. ◆ interj ▸ **hosanna!** hosanna !

hose [həʊz] ◆ n **1.** [tube] tuyau m ; AUTO Durit® f **2.** (U) [stockings] bas mpl ; [tights] collant m, collants mpl ; COMM articles mpl chaussants *(de bonneterie)* ; HIST chausses fpl ; [knee breeches] haut-de-chausse m, haut-de-chausses m, culotte f courte. ◆ vt [lawn] arroser au jet ; [fire] arroser à la lance. ❖ **hose down** vt sep **1.** [wash] laver au jet **2.** [with fire hose] arroser à la lance.

hosepipe ['həʊzpaɪp] ◆ n tuyau m. ◆ comp ▸ **a hosepipe ban** une interdiction d'arroser.

hosiery ['həʊziərɪ] n (U) **1.** [trade] bonneterie f **2.** [stockings] bas mpl ; [socks] chaussettes fpl ; COMM articles mpl chaussants *(de bonneterie)* / *the (women's) hosiery department* le rayon des bas.

hospice ['hɒspɪs] n [for the terminally ill] hôpital pour grands malades en phase terminale.

hospitable [hɒ'spɪtəbl] adj hospitalier.

hospital ['hɒspɪtl] ◆ n hôpital m / *in hospital* à l'hôpital / *to hospital* 🇬🇧, *to the hospital* 🇺🇸 à l'hôpital / *to go into hospital* aller à l'hôpital. ◆ comp [centre, service, staff, treatment] hospitalier ; [bed, ward] d'hôpital ▸ **a hospital case** un patient hospitalisé.

hospitality [ˌhɒspɪ'tælətɪ] ◆ n hospitalité f. ◆ comp ▸ **hospitality room** or **suite** salon m de réception *(où sont offerts des rafraîchissements lors d'une conférence, d'un événement sportif, etc.).*

hospitalize, hospitalise ['hɒspɪtəlaɪz] vt hospitaliser.

host [həʊst] ◆ n **1.** [person] hôte m (qui reçoit); TV animateur m, -trice f; [innkeeper] aubergiste mf **2.** BIOL & ZOOL hôte m **3.** [large number] foule f **4.** RELIG & liter armée f. ◆ adj [cell] hôte; [team] qui reçoit / *the host city for the Olympic Games* la ville organisatrice des jeux Olympiques ▶ **host computer a)** ordinateur m principal **b)** [in network] serveur m / *host country* pays m d'accueil. ◆ vt [TV show] animer; [event] organiser; COMPUT héberger. ❖ **Host** n RELIG ▶ **the Host** l'hostie f.

hostage ['hɒstɪdʒ] n otage m.

hostage-taking n prise f d'otages.

hostel ['hɒstl] n [residence] foyer m.

hostelry ['hɒstəlrɪ] n hôtellerie f; arch hostellerie f.

hostess ['həʊstes] n **1.** [at home] hôtesse f **2.** [in night-club] entraîneuse f **3.** = **air hostess.**

host family n famille f d'accueil.

hostile [UK 'hɒstaɪl US 'hɒstl] ◆ adj hostile ▶ **to be hostile to sthg** être hostile à qqch. ◆ n US inf ennemi m.

hostile takeover bid n OPA f hostile.

hostility [hɒ'stɪlətɪ] (pl **hostilities**) n hostilité f ▶ **to show hostility to** or **towards sb** manifester de l'hostilité or faire preuve d'hostilité envers qqn.

hosting n COMPUT [of web site] hébergement m.

host name n COMPUT nom m d'hôte.

hot [hɒt] (compar **hotter**, superl **hottest**, pt & pp **hotted**, cont **hotting**) ◆ adj **1.** [high in temperature] chaud / *to be hot* avoir (très or trop) chaud **2.** METEOR: *it's hot* il fait très chaud / *in (the) hot weather* pendant les chaleurs **3.** [clothing] qui tient chaud **4.** [colour] chaud, vif **5.** [pungent, spicy - food] épicé, piquant, relevé; [- spice] fort **6.** [fresh, recent] tout frais (toute fraîche) **7.** [close, following closely] ▶ **to be hot on the trail** être sur la bonne piste **8.** [fiery, vehement] violent **9.** [intense - anger, shame] intense, profond **10.** [keen] enthousiaste, passionné / *he's hot on my sister* US inf il en pince pour ma sœur **11.** inf [exciting] chaud **12.** inf [difficult, unpleasant] chaud, difficile **13.** UK inf [severe, stringent] sévère, dur / *the police are really hot on drunk driving* la police ne badine vraiment pas avec la conduite en état d'ivresse **14.** inf [very good] génial, terrible; [skilful] fort, calé / *I don't feel so hot* je ne suis pas dans mon assiette / *I'm not so hot at maths* je ne suis pas très calé en maths **15.** inf [in demand, popular] très recherché **16.** inf MUS ▶ **hot jazz** (jazz m) hot m **17.** inf [sexually attractive] ▶ **to be hot (stuff)** être sexy (inv) **18.** inf [stolen] volé **19.** inf [sought by police] recherché par la police **20.** ELEC [wire] sous tension **21.** NUCL [atom] chaud; inf [radioactive] chaud, radioactif. ◆ adv ▶ **to go hot and cold at the thought of sthg** avoir des sueurs froides à l'idée de qqch. ❖ **hots** pl n inf ▶ **to have the hots for sb** craquer pour qqn. ❖ **hot up** UK inf ◆ vt sep [intensify - argument, contest] échauffer; [- bombing, fighting] intensifier; [- party] mettre de l'animation dans; [- music] faire balancer, faire chauffer. ◆ vi [intensify - discussion] s'échauffer; [- fighting, situation] chauffer, s'intensifier.

hot air n inf : *he's full of hot air* c'est une grande gueule v inf.

hot-air balloon n montgolfière f.

hotbed ['hɒtbed] n HORT couche f chaude, forcerie f; fig pépinière f, foyer m.

hot-blooded adj [person - passionate] fougueux, au sang chaud.

hotchpotch ['hɒtʃpɒtʃ] n UK **1.** [jumble] fatras m, salmigondis m **2.** CULIN ≃ hochepot m; ≃ salmigondis m.

hot-cross bun n petit pain brioché aux raisins secs et marqué d'une croix que l'on vend traditionnellement à Pâques.

hot-desking n partage m de bureaux.

hot dog ◆ n **1.** [sausage] hot dog m **2.** [in skiing] ski m acrobatique; [in surfing] surf m acrobatique **3.** US inf [show-off] m'as-tu-vu mf. ◆ vi **1.** [in skiing] faire du ski acrobatique; [in surfing] faire du surf acrobatique **2.** US inf [show off] crâner, poser (pour la galerie). ◆ interj US inf ▶ **hot dog!** génial !, super !

hot-dogger [-dɒgər] n **1.** SPORT skieur m, -euse f acrobatique; [in surfing] personne qui fait du surf acrobatique **2.** US inf [show-off] frimeur m, -euse f, crâneur m, -euse f.

hot-dogging [-dɒgɪŋ] n **1.** SPORT ski m acrobatique; [in surfing] acrobatique surf m **2.** US inf [showing off] frime f.

hotel [həʊ'tel] ◆ n hôtel m. ◆ comp [prices, reservation, room] d'hôtel ▶ **hotel accommodation** hébergement m en hôtel ▶ **the hotel business** l'hôtellerie f ▶ **the hotel industry** or **trade** l'industrie f hôtelière.

hotelier [həʊ'telɪər] n hôtelier m, -ère f.

hotelkeeper [həʊ'tel,ki:pər] n hôtelier m, -ère f.

hot flush UK, **hot flash** US n bouffée f de chaleur.

hotfoot ['hɒt,fʊt] inf ◆ adv à toute vitesse. ◆ vt ▶ **to hotfoot it** galoper à toute vitesse.

Ht4U (written abbr of **hot for you**) MESSAGING tu me plais.

hothead ['hɒthed] n tête f brûlée, exalté m, -e f.

hotheaded [,hɒt'hedɪd] adj [person] impétueux, exalté; [attitude] impétueux.

hothouse ['hɒthaʊs] (pl [-haʊzɪz]) ◆ n **1.** HORT serre f (chaude) **2.** fig [hotbed] foyer m. ◆ adj de serre (chaude).

hot key n COMPUT raccourci m clavier.

hot line n TELEC ligne directe ouverte vingt-quatre heures sur vingt-quatre; POL téléphone m rouge.

hotlist ['hɒtlɪst] n COMPUT hotlist f.

hotly ['hɒtlɪ] adv [dispute] vivement; [pursue] avec acharnement; [say] avec flamme.

hot pad n US dessous-de-plat m.

hot pants pl n mini-short m (très court et moulant).

hotplate ['hɒtpleɪt] n [on stove] plaque f chauffante; [portable] chauffe-plats m inv.

hotpot ['hɒtpɒt] n UK ragoût de viande et de pommes de terre.

hot potato n lit pomme de terre f chaude; inf & fig sujet m brûlant et délicat.

hot rod n inf AUTO voiture f gonflée.

hot seat n inf **1.** [difficult situation] ▶ **to be in the hot seat** être sur la sellette **2.** US [electric chair] chaise f électrique.

hotshot ['hɒtʃɒt] inf ◆ n [expert] as m, crack m; [VIP] gros bonnet m. ◆ adj super.

hotspot n **1.** [dangerous area] point m chaud or névralgique **2.** inf [night club] boîte f de nuit **3.** TECH point m chaud.

hot-tempered adj colérique, emporté.

hot ticket n inf ▶ **to be a hot ticket** être très en demande.

hottie ['hɒtɪ] n US inf [man] mec m canon; [woman] fille f canon.

hot tub n sorte de Jacuzzi qu'on installe dehors.

hot water n lit eau f chaude; fig : *their latest prank got them into* or *landed them in hot water* leur dernière farce leur a attiré des ennuis.

hot-water bottle n bouillotte f.

hot-wire vt inf ▸ **to hot-wire a car** faire démarrer une voiture en bricolant les fils de contact.

houmous, houmus ['humʊs] = hummus.

hound [haʊnd] ◆ n [dog - gen] chien m ; [- for hunting] chien m courant, chien m de meute / **the hounds** or **a pack of hounds** HUNT la meute. ◆ vt **1.** [give chase] traquer, pourchasser **2.** [harass] s'acharner sur, harceler. ◈ **hound down** vt sep prendre dans des rets, coincer ; HUNT forcer. ◈ **hound out** vt sep chasser de / **he was hounded out of town** il a été chassé de la ville.

hour ['aʊəʳ] n **1.** [unit of time] heure f / **a quarter of an hour** un quart d'heure / **half an hour** or **a half hour** une demi-heure / **an hour and three-quarters** une heure trois quarts / **at 60 km an** or **per hour** à 60 km à l'heure / **it's a two-hour drive / walk from here** c'est à deux heures de voiture / de marche d'ici / **he gets £10 an hour** il touche 10 livres (de) l'heure / **a 35-hour week** une semaine de 35 heures / **the shop is open 24 hours a day** le magasin est ouvert 24 heures sur 24 / **he was an hour late** il était en retard d'une heure / **we arrived with hours to spare** nous sommes arrivés avec plusieurs heures devant nous or en avance de plusieurs heures / **we waited for hours and hours** on a attendu des heures **2.** [time of day] heure f ▸ **on the hour** : it chimes on the hour ça sonne à l'heure juste / **every hour on the hour** toutes les heures justes ▸ **in the early** or **small hours (of the morning)** au petit matin, au petit jour **3.** fig [specific moment] heure f, moment m. ◈ **hours** pl n heures fpl / **opening hours** heures d'ouverture / **do you work long hours?** as-tu de longues journées de travail ? / **he keeps late hours** c'est un couche-tard, il veille tard / **to keep regular hours** avoir une vie réglée ▸ **until all hours** : he was out until all hours il est rentré à une heure indue.

hourglass ['aʊɡlɑːs] ◆ n sablier m. ◆ adj en forme d'amphore ▸ **an hourglass figure** une taille de guêpe.

hour hand n petite aiguille f.

hourly ['aʊəlɪ] ◆ adj **1.** [each hour - flights, trains] : hourly departures départs toutes les heures ; COMM & TECH [earnings, rate] horaire **2.** [continual - anticipation] constant, perpétuel. ◆ adv **1.** [each hour] une fois par heure, chaque heure, toutes les heures ▸ **to be paid hourly** être payé à l'heure **2.** [repeatedly] sans cesse ; [at any time] à tout moment.

house ◆ n [haʊs] (pl houses ['haʊzɪz]) **1.** maison f / **at** or **to his house** chez lui ▸ **to keep house (for sb)** tenir la maison or le ménage (de qqn) ▸ **to set up house** monter son ménage, s'installer / **they set up house together** ils se sont mis en ménage ▸ **to get on** or **along like a house on fire** : we got on like a house on fire nous nous entendions à merveille or comme larrons en foire ▸ **to set** or **to put one's house in order** mettre de l'ordre dans ses affaires **2.** COMM [establishment] maison f (de commerce), compagnie f ; RELIG maison f religieuse ; 🇬🇧 SCH au sein d'une école, répartition des élèves en groupes concurrents ▸ **a bottle of house red (wine)** une bouteille de (vin) rouge de la maison or de l'établissement ▸ **drinks are on the house!** la tournée est aux frais de la maison ! **3.** [family line] maison f / **the House of York** la maison de York **4.** THEAT salle f, auditoire m / **to have a full house** jouer à guichets fermés or à bureaux fermés **5.** ▸ **the House a)** 🇬🇧 POL la Chambre **b)** 🇺🇸 POL la Chambre des représentants **c)** ST. EX la Bourse **6.** [in debate] ▸ **this house believes...** la motion à débattre est la suivante... **7.** MUS = house music. ◆ vt [haʊz] [accommodate - subj: organization, person] héberger, loger ; [- subj: building] recevoir. ◆ interj [in bingo] ▸ **house!** ≃ carton !

House

Dans certaines écoles en Grande-Bretagne (particulièrement dans les **grammar schools** et les **public schools**), les élèves sont répartis en groupes, qui portent chacun un nom et une couleur et développent entre eux un véritable esprit de compétition.

house arrest n assignation f à domicile or à résidence ▸ **to put sb under house arrest** assigner qqn à domicile or à résidence.

houseboat ['haʊsbəʊt] n house-boat m, péniche f (aménagée).

housebound ['haʊsbaʊnd] adj qui ne peut quitter la maison.

housebreaking ['haʊs,breɪkɪŋ] n cambriolage m.

housebroken ['haʊs,brəʊkn] adj 🇺🇸 [pet] propre.

housebuilder ['haʊsbɪldəʳ] n entrepreneur m en bâtiment.

housebuilding ['haʊsbɪldɪŋ] n construction f de logements.

housecoat ['haʊskəʊt] n robe f d'intérieur.

houseful ['haʊsfʊl] n : **a houseful of guests** une pleine maisonnée d'invités.

houseguest ['haʊsgest] n invité m, -e f.

household ['haʊshəʊld] ◆ n ménage m, (gens mpl de la) maison f, maisonnée f ; ADMIN & ECON ménage / **the head of the household** le chef de famille. ◆ adj [products, expenses] de ménage ; ADMIN & ECON des ménages ▸ **household appliance** appareil m ménager.

householder ['haʊs,həʊldəʳ] n [occupant] occupant m, -e f ; [owner] propriétaire mf ; [tenant] locataire mf.

household name n : **we want to make our brand a household name** nous voulons que notre marque soit connue de tous / **she's a household name** tout le monde la connaît or sait qui elle est.

house-hunt vi chercher un or être à la recherche d'un logement.

househunting ['haʊs,hʌntɪŋ] n recherche f d'un logement.

house husband n père m au foyer.

housekeeper ['haʊs,kiːpəʳ] n [institutional] économe f, intendante f ; [private] gouvernante f / **she's a good / bad housekeeper** c'est une bonne / mauvaise maîtresse de maison.

housekeeping ['haʊs,kiːpɪŋ] n (U) **1.** [of household - skill] économie f domestique ; [- work] ménage m **2.** [of organization] services mpl généraux **3.** COMPUT opérations fpl de nettoyage et d'entretien.

houseleek n joubarbe f.

houseman ['haʊsmən] (pl housemen [-mən]) n 🇬🇧 MED ≃ interne m.

house martin n hirondelle f de fenêtre.

housemaster ['haʊs,mɑːstəʳ] n 🇬🇧 SCH professeur responsable d'une « house ».

housemen [-mən] pl ⟶ houseman.

housemistress ['haʊs,mɪstrɪs] n 🇬🇧 SCH professeure responsable d'une « house ».

house music n house f (music).

House of Commons pr n ▸ **the House of Commons** la Chambre des communes.

House of Commons

La Chambre des communes, chambre basse du Parlement britannique, est composée de 646 députés (**MPs**) élus au suffrage universel pour cinq ans, qui siègent environ 175 jours par an.

House of Lords pr n ▶ **the House of Lords** la Chambre des lords.

 House of Lords

La Chambre des lords, chambre haute du Parlement britannique, est composée de **lords** spirituels (hommes d'Église) et de **lords** temporels (nobles), dont la plupart sont nommés par le gouvernement. C'est la plus haute cour au Royaume-Uni (Écosse non comprise). Elle peut amender des projets de loi votés par la Chambre des communes, qui, à son tour, peut rejeter des décisions prises par la Chambre des lords.

House of Representatives pr n ▶ **the House of Representatives** la Chambre des représentants (aux États-Unis).

 House of Representatives

La Chambre des représentants constitue, avec le Sénat, l'organe législatif américain; ses membres sont élus par le peuple, proportionnellement à la population de chaque État.

house-owner n propriétaire mf.

houseplant ['haʊsplɑːnt] n plante f d'intérieur.

house-proud adj : he's very house-proud il attache beaucoup d'importance à l'aspect intérieur de sa maison, tout est toujours impeccable chez lui.

houseroom ['haʊsrʊm] n 🇬🇧 place f (pour loger qqn ou qqch) / I wouldn't give that table houseroom! je ne voudrais pas de cette table chez moi !

house rule n règle f de la maison ; GAMES règle f du jeu particulière.

house-sit vi ▶ **to house-sit for sb** s'occuper de la maison de qqn pendant son absence.

house-sitter n personne qui garde une maison en l'absence de ses occupants.

Houses of Parliament pl pr n ▶ **the Houses of Parliament** le Parlement m (britannique).

house-to-house adj [enquiry] de porte en porte ▶ **to make a house-to-house search for sb / sthg** aller de porte en porte à la recherche de qqn / qqch, fouiller chaque maison à la recherche de qqn / qqch.

house-train vt dresser à la propreté.

housewarming ['haʊsˌwɔːmɪŋ] n pendaison f de crémaillère ▶ **to give** or **to have a housewarming (party)** pendre la crémaillère.

housewife ['haʊswaɪf] (pl **housewives** [-waɪvz]) n ménagère f ; [not career woman] femme f au foyer.

housewifely ['haʊsˌwaɪflɪ] adj de ménagère.

house wine n cuvée f du patron.

housework ['haʊswɜːk] n (travaux mpl de) ménage m / to do the housework faire le ménage.

housing ['haʊzɪŋ] ◆ n **1.** [accommodation] logement m **2.** TECH [of mechanism] carter m ; PHOT boîtier m ▶ **wheel housing** boîte f de roue ▶ **watch housing** boîtier de montre **3.** CONSTR encastrement m. ◆ comp ▶ **housing shortage** crise f du logement.

housing association n association britannique à but non lucratif qui construit ou rénove des logements pour les louer à ses membres.

housing benefit n 🇬🇧 allocation de logement versée par l'État aux individus justifiant de revenus faibles.

housing development n **1.** [estate] lotissement m **2.** [activity] construction f de logements.

housing estate n 🇬🇧 [of houses] lotissement m ; [of flats] cité f.

housing project n **1.** 🇺🇸 = housing estate **2.** [plan] plan m d'aménagement immobilier.

HOV (abbr of High Occupancy Vehicle) n 🇺🇸 ▶ **HOV lane** voie d'autoroute réservée aux automobiles occupées par au moins deux passagers.

hovel ['hɒvl] n taudis m, masure f.

hover ['hɒvər] ◆ vi **1.** [in air - smoke] stagner ; [- balloon, scent] flotter ; [- insects] voltiger ; [- helicopter, hummingbird] faire du surplace **2.** [linger - person] rôder ; [- smile] flotter ; [- danger] planer **3.** [hesitate] hésiter. ◆ n = hover-craft.

hovercraft ['hɒvəkrɑːft] n aéroglisseur m.

hoverport ['hɒvəpɔːt] n hoverport m.

how [haʊ] ◆ adv **1.** [in what way] comment / how could you be so careless? comment as-tu pu être aussi étourdi ? ▶ **how is it that...** comment se fait-il que... ▶ **how so?, how can that be?** comment cela (se fait-il) ? ▶ **how's that (again)?** comment ? **2.** [in greetings, friendly enquiries, etc.] comment / how are you? comment allez-vous ? / how are things? ça marche ? / how did you like or how was the film? comment as-tu trouvé le film ? ▶ **how do you do?** bonjour ! **3.** [in exclamations] que, comme / how incredible! c'est incroyable ! / how cool is that! inf trop cool ! / how stupid was that? c'était particulièrement stupide ! **4.** (with adj, adv) [referring to measurement, rate, degree] : how tall are you? combien mesures-tu ? / how old is she? quel âge a-t-elle ? ; [referring to time, distance, quantity] : how much does this bag cost? combien coûte ce sac ? ◆ conj **1.** [in what way] comment / he's learning how to read il apprend à lire **2.** [the fact that] : I remember how he always used to turn up late je me souviens qu'il était toujours en retard **3.** inf [however] comme / did you like it? — and how! ça t'a plu ? — et comment ! ◆ **how about** adv phr inf : how about a beer? et si on prenait une bière ? / how about you? what do you think? et toi, qu'est-ce que tu en penses ? ◆ **how come** adv phr inf ▶ **how come?** comment ça se fait ? / how come you left? comment ça se fait que tu sois parti ?

howdy ['haʊdɪ] interj 🇺🇸 inf ▶ **howdy!** salut !

however [haʊ'evər] ◆ adv **1.** [indicating contrast or contradiction] cependant, pourtant, toutefois **2.** (with adj or adv) [no matter how] si... que, quelque... que / however nice he tries to be... si gentil qu'il essaie d'être... **3.** (in questions) [emphatic use] comment. ◆ conj [in whatever way] de quelque manière que, comme.

howl [haʊl] ◆ n **1.** [of person, animal] hurlement m ; [of child] braillement m, hurlement m ; [of wind] mugissement m **2.** ELECTRON effet m Larsen. ◆ vi **1.** [person, animal] hurler ; [child] brailler ; [wind] mugir / to howl with laughter hurler de rire / to howl in or with rage hurler de rage **2.** *inf* [cry] chialer ; [complain] gueuler. ❖ vt crier, hurler. ❖ **howl down** vt sep [speaker] : *they howled him down* ils l'ont réduit au silence par leurs huées.

howler ['haʊlə⁻] n *inf* [blunder] gaffe f, bourde f.

howling ['haʊlɪŋ] ❖ n [of person, animal] hurlement m, hurlements mpl ; [of child] braillement m, braillements mpl ; [of wind] mugissement m, mugissements mpl. ❖ adj *inf* [error] énorme ; [success] fou.

how-to US ❖ n : *he gave me the how-to* il m'a expliqué comment il fallait faire. ❖ adj : *he loves those how-to cookery programmes* il adore ces émissions où l'on explique des recettes de cuisine / *how-to books* livres mpl pratiques.

hp, HP ❖ n (abbr of hire purchase) ▶ **to buy sthg on hp** acheter qqch à crédit. ❖ (written abbr of horsepower) CV.

HQ (abbr of headquarters) n QG m.

HR n abbr of human resources.

HRH (written abbr of His/Her Royal Highness) SAR.

HRT n abbr of hormone replacement therapy.

HRU MESSAGING written abbr of how are you.

HS US written abbr of high school.

HST n **1.** (abbr of high speed train) ≃ TGV m **2.** abbr of Hawaiian Standard Time.

ht written abbr of height.

HT (written abbr of high tension) HT.

HTH MESSAGING written abbr of hope that helps.

HTML (abbr of Hypertext Markup Language) n COMPUT HTML m.

hub [hʌb] n [of wheel] moyeu m ; *fig* centre m.

hub airport n US hub m.

hubbub ['hʌbʌb] n [of voices] brouhaha m ; [uproar] vacarme m, tapage m.

hubcap ['hʌbkæp] n AUTO enjoliveur m (de roue).

huckleberry ['hʌklbərɪ] (*pl* huckleberries) n airelle f, myrtille f.

HUD [hʌd] (abbr of Department of Housing and Urban Development) pr n *ministère américain de l'Urbanisme et du Logement.*

huddle ['hʌdl] ❖ n **1.** [of people] petit groupe m (serré) ; [of objects] tas m, amas m ; [of roofs] enchevêtrement m ▶ **to go into a huddle** *inf* se réunir en petit comité **2.** SPORT concentration f (d'une équipe). ❖ vi **1.** [crowd together] se blottir **2.** [crouch] se recroqueviller, se blottir. ❖ **huddle together** vi se serrer or se blottir les uns contre les autres ; [for talk] se mettre en petit groupe or cercle serré. ❖ **huddle up** vi = huddle (vi).

hue [hjuː] n **1.** [colour] teinte f, nuance f **2.** PHR a **hue and cry** US une clameur (de haro) ▶ **to raise a hue and a cry against sb / sthg** crier haro sur qqn / qqch.

huff [hʌf] ❖ vi ▶ **to huff and puff a)** [with exertion] haleter **b)** [with annoyance] maugréer. ❖ n *inf* ▶ **to be in a huff** être froissé or fâché ▶ **to take the huff** US prendre la mouche, s'offusquer.

huffily ['hʌfɪlɪ] adv [reply] d'un ton vexé or fâché ; [behave] avec (mauvaise) humeur.

huffy ['hʌfɪ] adj [piqued] froissé, vexé ; [touchy] susceptible.

hug [hʌg] (*pt & pp* hugged, *cont* hugging) ❖ vt **1.** [in arms] serrer dans ses bras, étreindre **2.** *fig* [idea] tenir à, chérir **3.** [keep close to] serrer. ❖ n étreinte f ▶ **to give sb a hug** serrer qqn dans ses bras, étreindre qqn.

huge [hjuːdʒ] adj **1.** [in size, degree] énorme, immense ; [in extent] vaste, immense ; [in volume] énorme, gigantesque **2.** *inf* [wonderful] énorme, génial.

hugely ['hjuːdʒlɪ] adv [increase] énormément ; [as intensifier] énormément, extrêmement.

huggable ['hʌgəbl] adj trognon.

H&K (written abbr of hugs and kisses) MESSAGING biz.

huh [hʌ] interj [surprise] ▶ **huh?** hein ? ; [scepticism] ▶ **huh!** hum !

hulk [hʌlk] n **1.** [ship] épave f ; *pej* vieux rafiot m ; [used as prison, storehouse] ponton m **2.** [person, thing] mastodonte m.

hulking ['hʌlkɪŋ] adj [person] balourd, massif ; [thing] gros (grosse), imposant.

hull [hʌl] ❖ n **1.** [of ship] coque f ; MIL [of tank] caisse f **2.** [of peas, beans] cosse f, gousse f ; [of nut] écale f ; [of strawberry] pédoncule m. ❖ vt **1.** [peas] écosser ; [nuts] écaler, décortiquer ; [grains] décortiquer ; [strawberries] équeuter **2.** [ship] percer la coque de.

hullabaloo [ˌhʌləbə'luː] n *inf* raffut m, chambard m, barouf m.

hullo [hə'ləʊ] interj UK **1.** ▶ **hullo!** a) [on meeting] salut ! b) [on phone] allô ! **2.** [for attention] ▶ **hullo!** ohé !, holà ! ▶ **hullo there!** holà, vous ! **3.** [in surprise] ▶ **hullo!** tiens !

hum [hʌm] (*pt & pp* hummed, *cont* humming) ❖ vi **1.** [audience, bee, wires] bourdonner ; [person] fredonner, chantonner ; [top, fire] ronfler ; ELECTRON ronfler ; [air conditioner] ronronner **2.** [be lively] grouiller **3.** UK *inf* [stink] cocotter **4.** PHR **to hum and haw a)** *lit* bafouiller **b)** *fig* tergiverser, tourner autour du pot. ❖ vt [tune] fredonner, chantonner. ❖ n **1.** [of bees, voices] bourdonnement m ; [of vehicle] vrombissement m ; [of fire, top] ronflement m ; ELECTRON ronflement m ; [of machine] ronronnement m **2.** UK *inf* [stench] puanteur f, mauvaise odeur f. ❖ interj ▶ **hum!** hem !, hum !

human ['hjuːmən] ❖ adj humain / *the human race* le genre humain, l'espèce humaine. ❖ n (être m) humain m.

humane [hjuː'meɪn] adj [compassionate - action, person] humain, plein d'humanité ; [- treatment] humain.

humanely [hjuː'meɪnlɪ] adv humainement.

Human Genome Project n projet m génome humain ▶ **the Human Genome Project** le projet génome humain.

human interest n PRESS dimension f humaine ▶ **a human interest story** un reportage à caractère social.

humanism ['hjuːmənɪzm] n humanisme m.

humanist ['hjuːmənɪst] ❖ n humaniste m. ❖ adj humaniste.

humanitarian [hjuːˌmænɪ'teərɪən] ❖ n humanitaire mf. ❖ adj humanitaire.

humanity [hjuː'mænətɪ] n **1.** [mankind] humanité f **2.** [compassion] humanité f. ❖ **humanities** pl n [arts] lettres fpl ; [classical culture] lettres fpl classiques.

humanize, humanise ['hjuːmənaɪz] vt humaniser.

humankind [ˌhjuːmən'kaɪnd] n l'humanité f, le genre humain.

humanly ['hjuːmənlɪ] adv humainement.

human nature n nature f humaine.

human resources pl n ressources fpl humaines.

human rights pl n droits mpl de l'homme.

human shield n bouclier m humain.

human trafficking n trafic m or traite f d'êtres humains.

humble ['hʌmbl] ◆ adj **1.** [meek] humble **2.** [modest] modeste. ◆ vt humilier, mortifier ▶ **to humble o.s. before sb** s'humilier devant qqn.

humbling ['hʌmblɪŋ] adj [experience] qui rend humble.

humbly ['hʌmblɪ] adv **1.** [speak, ask] humblement, avec humilité **2.** [live] modestement.

humbug ['hʌmbʌg] (pt & pp **humbugged**, cont **humbugging**) ◆ n **1.** [person] charlatan m, fumiste mf; (U) [deception] charlatanisme m **2.** (U) [nonsense] balivernes fpl **3.** UK [sweet] berlingot m. ◆ vt tromper.

humdinger [,hʌm'dɪŋər] n inf **1.** [person] : she's a real humdinger! elle est vraiment extra or sensass or terrible ! **2.** [thing] : that was a humdinger of a game! quel match extraordinaire ! / they had a real humdinger of a row! ils se sont engueulés, quelque chose de bien !

humdrum ['hʌmdrʌm] ◆ adj [person, story] banal; [task, life] monotone, banal, routinier. ◆ n monotonie f, banalité f.

humid ['hju:mɪd] adj humide.

humidifier [hju:'mɪdɪfaɪər] n humidificateur m.

humidity [hju:'mɪdətɪ] n humidité f.

humiliate [hju:'mɪlɪeɪt] vt humilier.

humiliating [hju:'mɪlɪeɪtɪŋ] adj humiliant.

humiliation [hju:,mɪlɪ'eɪʃn] n humiliation f.

humility [hju:'mɪlətɪ] n humilité f.

hummingbird ['hʌmɪŋbɜ:d] n oiseau-mouche m, colibri m.

hummus ['humʊs] n houmous m.

humongous [hju:'mʌŋgəs] adj US inf énorme.

humor US = humour.

humorist ['hju:mərɪst] n humoriste mf.

humorous ['hju:mərəs] adj [witty -remark] plein d'humour, amusant ; [-person] plein d'humour, drôle.

humour UK, **humor** US ['hju:mər] ◆ n **1.** [wit, fun] humour m ▶ **sense of humour** sens m de l'humour **2.** fml [mood] humeur f, disposition f **3.** arch MED humeur f. ◆ vt [person -indulge, gratify] faire plaisir à ; [-treat tactfully] ménager ; [whim, fantasy] se prêter à.

humourless UK, **humorless** US ['hju:mələs] adj [person] qui manque d'humour ; [book, situation, speech] sans humour.

hump [hʌmp] ◆ n **1.** [on back of animal or person] bosse f; [hillock] bosse f, mamelon m ; [bump] tas m **2.** UK inf PHR ▶ **to get the hump** avoir le cafard or le bourdon. ◆ vt **1.** [back] arrondir, arquer **2.** UK inf [carry] trimbaler, trimballer **3.** v inf [have sex with] baiser. ◆ vi v inf [have sex] baiser.

humpback(ed) bridge n pont m en dos d'âne.

humpback whale n baleine f à bosse.

humungous [hju:'mʌŋgəs] adj inf [huge] énorme ; [great] super, génial.

humus ['hju:məs] n humus m.

hunch [hʌntʃ] ◆ n [inkling] pressentiment m, intuition f ▶ **to act on a hunch** suivre son instinct. ◆ vt [back] arrondir ; [shoulders] voûter.

hunchback ['hʌntʃbæk] n **1.** [person] bossu m, -e f **2.** ANAT bosse f.

hunchbacked ['hʌntʃbækt] adj bossu.

hunched [hʌntʃt] adj voûté.

hundred ['hʌndrəd] ◆ det cent / a hundred guests cent invités / six hundred pages six cents pages / about a hundred metres une centaine de mètres / one or a hundred per cent cent pour cent / if I've told you once, I've told you a hundred times! je te l'ai dit cent fois ! ◆ n cent m / he has a hundred (of them) il en a cent / one

hundred and one cent un / two hundred deux cents / two hundred and one deux cent un / about a hundred or a hundred odd une centaine / in nineteen hundred en dix-neuf cents / in nineteen hundred and ten en dix-neuf cent dix / hundreds of des centaines de.

hundreds and thousands pl n paillettes de sucre colorées servant à décorer les gâteaux.

hundredth ['hʌndrətθ] n centième mf ; [fraction] centième m.

hundredweight ['hʌndrədweɪt] n UK (poids m de) cent douze livres (50,8 kg); US (poids m de) cent livres (45,4 kg).

hung [hʌŋ] ◆ pt & pp → **hang**. ◆ adj [situation] bloqué ▶ **a hung parliament / jury** un parlement / un jury sans majorité.

Hungarian [hʌŋ'geərɪən] ◆ n **1.** [person] Hongrois m, -e f **2.** LING hongrois m. ◆ adj hongrois.

Hungary ['hʌŋgərɪ] pr n Hongrie f / in Hungary en Hongrie.

hunger ['hʌŋgər] ◆ n faim f. ◆ vi fig ▶ **to hunger after** or **for sthg** avoir faim or soif de qqch.

hunger strike n grève f de la faim ▶ **to go on (a) hunger strike** faire la grève de la faim.

hung over adj inf : to be hung over avoir une or la gueule de bois.

hungrily ['hʌŋgrəlɪ] adv [eat] voracement, avidement ; fig [read, listen] avidement.

hungry ['hʌŋgrɪ] (compar **hungrier**, superl **hungriest**) adj **1.** [for food] ▶ **to be hungry** avoir faim **2.** fig [desirous] avide / hungry for affection avide d'affection.

hung up adj inf coincé ▶ **to be hung up on sb / sthg** faire une fixation sur qqn / qqch ▶ **to be hung up about sthg a)** [personal problem] être complexé par qqch **b)** [sexual matters] être coincé quand il s'agit de qqch.

hunk [hʌŋk] n **1.** [piece] gros morceau m **2.** inf [man] beau mec m or mâle m.

hunky ['hʌŋkɪ] adj inf : he's really hunky c'est un beau mec.

hunky-dory [,hʌŋkɪ'dɔ:rɪ] adj inf ▶ **to be hunky-dory** être au poil.

hunt [hʌnt] ◆ vt **1.** [for food, sport -subj: person] chasser, faire la chasse à ; [-subj: animal] chasser **2.** UK SPORT [area] chasser dans **3.** [pursue] pourchasser, poursuivre **4.** [search] fouiller **5.** [drive out] chasser. ◆ vi **1.** [for food, sport] chasser / to go hunting aller à la chasse ▶ **to hunt for sthg a)** [person] chasser or faire la chasse à qqch **b)** [animal] chasser qqch **2.** [search] chercher (partout). ◆ n **1.** SPORT [activity] chasse f; [hunters] chasse f, chasseurs mpl ; [area] chasse f; [fox-hunt] chasse f au renard ▶ **a tiger / bear hunt** une chasse au tigre / à l'ours **2.** [search] chasse f, recherche f / the hunt is on for the terrorists la chasse aux terroristes est en cours. ❖ **hunt down** vt sep [animal] forcer, traquer ; [person] traquer ; [thing, facts] dénicher ; [abuses, errors] faire la chasse à ; [truth] débusquer. ❖ **hunt out** vt sep UK dénicher, découvrir.

hunter ['hʌntər] n **1.** SPORT [person] chasseur m ; [horse] cheval m de chasse, hunter m ; [dog] chien m courant or de chasse **2.** [gen] chasseur m ; [pursuer] poursuivant m **3.** [watch] (montre f à) savonnette f.

hunter-gatherer n chasseur-cueilleur m.

hunting ['hʌntɪŋ] ◆ n **1.** SPORT chasse f; UK [fox-hunting] chasse f au renard ; HIST [mounted deer-hunt] chasse f à courre ; HIST [as an art] vénerie f **2.** [pursuit] chasse f, poursuite f. ◆ adj [boots, gun, knife, licence] de chasse.

hunting ground n SPORT & fig terrain m de chasse.

huntsman ['hʌntsmən] (pl **huntsmen** [-mən]) n **1.** [hunter] chasseur m **2.** [master of hounds] veneur m.

hurdle ['hɜːdl] ◆ n **1.** SPORT haie f / the 400 metre hurdles le 400 mètres haies **2.** fig obstacle m **3.** [for fences] claie f. ◆ vt [jump] sauter, franchir ; [overcome] franchir. ◆ vi SPORT faire de la course de haies.

hurdler ['hɜːdlə*] n coureur m, -euse f (qui fait des courses de haies).

hurl [hɜːl] ◆ vt **1.** [throw] lancer, jeter (avec violence) ▸ to hurl o.s. at sb / sthg se ruer sur qqn / qqch **2.** [yell] lancer, jeter / to hurl abuse at sb lancer des injures à qqn, accabler qqn d'injures. ◆ vi US inf [vomit] dégueuler, gerber.

hurling ['hɜːlɪŋ] n SPORT jeu irlandais voisin du hockey sur gazon.

hurly-burly ['hɜːlɪ,bɜːlɪ] UK ◆ n tohu-bohu m. ◆ adj turbulent.

hurrah UK [hʊ'rɑː], **hurray** [hʊ'reɪ] ◆ n hourra m. ◆ interj ▸ hurrah! hourra !

hurricane ['hʌrɪkən] n ouragan m ; [in Caribbean] hurricane m.

hurried ['hʌrɪd] adj [meeting, reply, gesture, trip] rapide ; [departure, steps] précipité ; [judgment, decision] hâtif ; [work] fait à la hâte.

hurriedly ['hʌrɪdlɪ] adv [examine] à la hâte ; [leave] précipitamment.

hurry ['hʌrɪ] (pl **hurries**, pt & pp **hurried**) ◆ n **1.** [rush] hâte f, précipitation f ▸ to be in a hurry to do sthg avoir hâte de faire qqch **2.** [eagerness] empressement m / he's in no hurry to see her again il n'est pas pressé or il n'a aucune hâte de la revoir. ◆ vi se dépêcher, se presser, se hâter / he hurried into / out of the room il est entré dans / sorti de la pièce en toute hâte or précipitamment. ◆ vt **1.** [chivvy along] faire se dépêcher, presser, bousculer **2.** [preparations, work] activer, presser, hâter **3.** [transport hastily] emmener d'urgence. ◆ **hurry along** ◆ vi marcher d'un pas pressé. ◆ vt sep [person] faire presser le pas à, faire se dépêcher or s'activer ; [work] activer, accélérer. ◆ **hurry on** vi se dépêcher, continuer à la hâte or en hâte. ◆ **hurry up** ◆ vi se dépêcher, se presser. ◆ vt sep [person] faire se dépêcher ; [production, work] activer, pousser.

hurt [hɜːt] (pt & pp **hurt**) ◆ vt **1.** [cause physical pain to] faire mal à ▸ to hurt o.s. se faire mal / I hurt my elbow on the door je me suis fait mal au coude contre la porte **2.** [injure] blesser **3.** [upset] blesser, faire de la peine à **4.** [disadvantage] nuire à **5.** [damage - crops, machine] abîmer, endommager ; [- eyesight] abîmer. ◆ vi faire mal / my head hurts ma tête me fait mal. ◆ n **1.** [physical pain] mal m ; [wound] blessure f **2.** [mental pain] peine f **3.** [damage] tort m. ◆ adj **1.** [physically] blessé **2.** [offended] froissé, blessé **3.** US [damaged] ▸ hurt books livres endommagés.

hurtful ['hɜːtfʊl] adj [event] préjudiciable, nuisible ; [memory] pénible ; [remark] blessant, offensant.

hurtle ['hɜːtl] vi : to hurtle along avancer à toute vitesse or allure / he went hurtling down the stairs il dévala les escaliers / the motorbike came hurtling towards him la moto fonça sur lui à toute vitesse.

husband ['hʌzbənd] ◆ n mari m, époux m. ◆ vt [resources, strength] ménager, économiser.

husbandry ['hʌzbəndrɪ] n **1.** AGR agriculture f ; [as science] agronomie f **2.** fml [thrift] économie f.

hush [hʌʃ] ◆ n silence m, calme m. ◆ interj ▸ hush! a) [gen] silence ! b) [stop talking] chut ! ◆ vt **1.** [silence] faire taire **2.** [appease] apaiser, calmer. ◆ vi se taire. ◆ **hush up** vt sep **1.** [affair] étouffer ; [witness] faire taire, empêcher de parler **2.** [noisy person] faire taire.

hushed [hʌʃt] adj [whisper, voice] étouffé ; [silence] profond, grand.

hush-hush adj inf secret (secrète), archi-secret.

hush money n (U) inf pot-de-vin m (pour acheter le silence) ▸ to pay sb hush money acheter le silence de qqn.

husk [hʌsk] ◆ n [of wheat, oats] balle f ; [of maize, rice] enveloppe f ; [of nut] écale f. ◆ vt [oats, barley] monder ; [maize] éplucher ; [rice] décortiquer ; [wheat] vanner ; [nuts] écaler.

huskily ['hʌskɪlɪ] adv [speak] d'une voix rauque ; [sing] d'une voix voilée.

husky ['hʌskɪ] (compar **huskier**, superl **huskiest**, pl **huskies**) ◆ adj **1.** [of voice - hoarse] rauque, enroué ; [- breathy] voilé **2.** inf [burly] costaud. ◆ n [dog] chien m esquimau or de traîneau.

hussy ['hʌsɪ] (pl **hussies**) n arch & hum [shameless woman] garce f, gourgandine f dated.

hustings ['hʌstɪŋz] pl n UK **1.** [campaign] campagne f électorale ▸ to go / to be out on the hustings partir / être en campagne électorale **2.** [occasion for speeches] ≃ débat m public (pendant la campagne électorale).

hustle ['hʌsl] ◆ vt **1.** [cause to move - quickly] presser ; [- roughly] bousculer, pousser ▸ to hustle sb in / out faire entrer / sortir qqn énergiquement **2.** inf [obtain - resourcefully] faire tout pour avoir ; [- underhandedly] magouiller pour avoir **3.** US inf [swindle] rouler, arnaquer / he hustled me out of $100 il m'a roulé or arnaqué de 100 dollars ; [pressure] ▸ to hustle sb into doing sthg forcer la main à qqn pour qu'il fasse qqch **4.** US inf [steal] piquer **5.** US v inf [subj: prostitute] racoler. ◆ vi **1.** UK inf [shove] bousculer **2.** = hurry **3.** US inf [work hard] se bagarrer (pour réussir) **4.** US v inf [engage in suspect activity] monter des coups, trafiquer ; [politically] magouiller **5.** US v inf [prostitute] faire le tapin, tapiner. ◆ n **1.** [crush] bousculade f **2.** inf [bustle] grande activité f / the hustle and bustle of the big city le tourbillon d'activité des grandes villes **3.** US v inf [swindle] arnaque f. ◆ **hustle up** US inf ◆ vt sep [prepare quickly] préparer en cinq sec. ◆ vi & vt sep = **hurry up**.

hustler ['hʌslə*] n **1.** inf [dynamic person] type m dynamique, débrouillard m, -e f, magouilleur m, -euse f **2.** inf [swindler] arnaqueur m, -euse f **3.** US v inf [female prostitute] pute f ; [male prostitute] prostitué m.

hut [hʌt] n [primitive dwelling] hutte f ; [shed] cabane f, baraque f ; [alpine] refuge m, chalet-refuge m ; MIL baraquement m.

hutch [hʌtʃ] n **1.** [cage] cage f ; [for rabbits] clapier m **2.** US [Welsh dresser] vaisselier m.

hyacinth ['haɪəsɪnθ] n **1.** BOT jacinthe f **2.** [colour] bleu jacinthe (inv), bleu violet (inv).

hybrid ['haɪbrɪd] ◆ n [gen] hybride m ; [bicycle] VTC m. ◆ adj hybride ▸ hybrid car voiture f hybride.

hybridization [,haɪbrɪdaɪ'zeɪʃn] n hybridation f.

hydrangea [haɪ'dreɪndʒə] n hortensia m.

hydrant ['haɪdrənt] n prise f d'eau.

hydrate ['haɪdreɪt] ◆ n hydrate m. ◆ vt hydrater. ◆ vi s'hydrater.

hydraulic [haɪ'drɔːlɪk] adj hydraulique ▸ hydraulic engineer ingénieur m hydraulicien, hydraulicien m, -enne f.

hydraulically [haɪ'drɔːlɪklɪ] adv hydrauliquement.

hydraulics [haɪ'drɔːlɪks] n (U) hydraulique f.

hydrocarbon [,haɪdrə'kɑːbən] n hydrocarbure m.

hydrochloric [,haɪdrə'klɒrɪk] adj chlorhydrique ▸ hydrochloric acid acide m chlorhydrique.

hydroelectric [,haɪdrəʊɪ'lektrɪk] adj hydro-électrique ▸ hydroelectric power énergie f hydro-électrique.

hydroelectricity [ˌhaɪdrəʊɪlek'trɪsəti] n hydro-électricité f.

hydrofluorocarbon [ˌhaɪdrəʊ'fluərəʊkɑːbən] n hydrofluorocarbone m.

hydrofoil ['haɪdrəfɔɪl] n hydrofoil m, hydroptère m.

hydrogen ['haɪdrədʒən] n hydrogène m.

hydrogenated [haɪ'drɒdʒɪneɪtɪd] adj CHEM hydrogéné.

hydrogenation [haɪdrɒdʒɪ'neɪʃən] n CHEM hydrogénation f.

hydrogen bomb n bombe f à hydrogène.

hydrogen peroxide n eau f oxygénée.

hydrophobia [ˌhaɪdrə'fəʊbjə] n hydrophobie f.

hydroplane ['haɪdrəpleɪn] vi se dresser comme un hydroglisseur.

hydrotherapy [ˌhaɪdrə'θerəpɪ] n hydrothérapie f.

hyena [haɪ'iːnə] n hyène f.

hygiene ['haɪdʒiːn] n hygiène f ▸ **personal hygiene** hygiène personnelle or corporelle.

hygienic [haɪ'dʒiːnɪk] adj hygiénique.

hygienically [haɪ'dʒiːnɪklɪ] adv de façon hygiénique.

hygienist [haɪ'dʒiːnɪst] n ≃ assistant m or assistante f dentaire.

hymn [hɪm] ◆ n **1.** RELIG hymne f, cantique m **2.** [gen - song of praise] hymne m. ◆ vt liter chanter un hymne à la gloire de.

hymn book n livre m de cantiques.

hype [haɪp] ◆ n (U) inf [publicity] battage m publicitaire. ◆ vt inf **1.** [falsify] baratiner **2.** [publicize] monter un gros coup de pub autour de.

hyped up [haɪpt-] adj inf speed (inv), speedé.

hyper ['haɪpə] adj inf = **hyperactive.**

hyperactive [ˌhaɪpər'æktɪv] adj hyperactif.

hyperactivity [ˌhaɪpəræk'tɪvəti] n hyperactivité f.

hyperbola [haɪ'pɜːbələ] n MATH hyperbole f.

hyperbole [haɪ'pɜːbəli] n hyperbole f.

hypercritical [ˌhaɪpə'krɪtɪkl] adj hypercritique.

hyperinflation [ˌhaɪpərɪn'fleɪʃn] n hyperinflation f.

hyperlink ['haɪpəlɪŋk] n COMPUT lien m hypertexte, hyperlien m ▸ **hypertext link** lien m hypertexte.

hypermarket [ˌhaɪpə'mɑːkɪt] n 🇬🇧 hypermarché m.

hypermedia ['haɪpəmiːdɪə] pl n hypermédia mpl.

hypersensitive [ˌhaɪpə'sensɪtɪv] adj hypersensible.

hypersensitivity ['haɪpəˌsensɪ'tɪvəti] n hypersensibilité f.

hypertension [ˌhaɪpə'tenʃn] n hypertension f.

hypertext ['haɪpətekst] n COMPUT & LITER hypertexte m.

hyperventilate [ˌhaɪpə'ventɪleɪt] vi faire de l'hyperventilation or de l'hyperpnée.

hyphen ['haɪfn] ◆ n trait m d'union. ◆ vt = **hyphenate.**

hyphenate ['haɪfəneɪt] vt mettre un trait d'union à ▸ **a hyphenated word** un mot qui s'écrit avec un trait d'union.

hypnosis [hɪp'nəʊsɪs] n hypnose f ▸ **to be under hypnosis** être en état hypnotique or d'hypnose.

hypnotherapist [ˌhɪpnəʊ'θerəpɪst] n PSYCHOL hypnothérapeute mf, médecin m hypnotiseur.

hypnotherapy [ˌhɪpnəʊ'θerəpɪ] n hypnothérapie f.

hypnotic [hɪp'nɒtɪk] ◆ adj hypnotique. ◆ n [drug] hypnotique m ; [person] hypnotique mf.

hypnotism ['hɪpnətɪzm] n hypnotisme m.

hypnotist ['hɪpnətɪst] n hypnotiseur m, -euse f.

hypnotize, hypnotise ['hɪpnətaɪz] vt hypnotiser.

hypoallergenic ['haɪpəʊˌælə'dʒenɪk] adj hypoallergique.

hypochondria [ˌhaɪpə'kɒndrɪə] n hypocondrie f.

hypochondriac [ˌhaɪpə'kɒndrɪæk] ◆ adj hypocondriaque. ◆ n hypocondriaque mf, malade mf imaginaire.

hypocrisy [hɪ'pɒkrəsɪ] (pl **hypocrisies**) n hypocrisie f.

hypocrite ['hɪpəkrɪt] n hypocrite mf.

hypocritical [ˌhɪpə'krɪtɪkl] adj hypocrite / it would be hypocritical of me to get married in church ce serait hypocrite de ma part de me marier à l'église.

hypodermic [ˌhaɪpə'dɜːmɪk] ◆ adj hypodermique. ◆ n **1.** [syringe] seringue f hypodermique **2.** [injection] injection f hypodermique.

hyponym ['haɪpənɪm] n hyponyme m.

hypothalamus [ˌhaɪpəʊ'θæləməs] n hypothalamus m.

hypothermia [ˌhaɪpəʊ'θɜːmɪə] n hypothermie f.

hypothesis [haɪ'pɒθɪsɪs] (pl **hypotheses** [-siːz]) n hypothèse f / to put forward or to advance a hypothesis émettre or énoncer une hypothèse / this confirms my hypothesis that… cela confirme mon hypothèse selon or d'après laquelle…

hypothesize, hypothesise [haɪ'pɒθɪsaɪz] ◆ vt supposer. ◆ vi faire des hypothèses or des suppositions.

hypothetical [ˌhaɪpə'θetɪkl] adj hypothétique / it's purely hypothetical c'est purement hypothétique.

hypothetically [ˌhaɪpə'θetɪklɪ] adv hypothétiquement.

hysterectomy [ˌhɪstə'rektəmɪ] (pl **hysterectomies**) n hystérectomie f.

hysteria [hɪs'tɪərɪə] n **1.** PSYCHOL hystérie f **2.** [hysterical behaviour] crise f de nerfs.

hysterical [hɪs'terɪkl] adj **1.** PSYCHOL hystérique **2.** [sobs, voice] hystérique ; [laugh] hystérique, nerveux / he was hysterical with grief il était fou de chagrin **3.** [overexcited] : it's nothing to get hysterical about! ce n'est pas la peine de faire une crise (de nerfs) ! **4.** inf [very funny] tordant, hilarant.

hysterically [hɪs'terɪklɪ] adv hystériquement / to laugh hysterically être plié en deux de rire / it was hysterically funny! c'était à mourir de rire !

hysterical pregnancy n 🇺🇸 grossesse f nerveuse.

hysterics [hɪs'terɪks] pl n **1.** = **hysteria 2.** [fit] (violente) crise f de nerfs ▸ **to go into** or **to have hysterics** avoir une (violente) crise de nerfs **3.** inf [laughter] crise f de rire ▸ **to go into** or **to have hysterics** attraper un or avoir le fou rire.

Hz (written abbr of **hertz**) Hz.

I (*pl* **I's** *or* **Is**), **I** (*pl* **I's** *or* **Is**) [aɪ] n [letter] i *m*, I *m* / *I as in Ivor* ≃ I comme Irma. **See also f.**

I [aɪ] pron [gen] je, j' *(before vowel or silent 'h')* ; [emphatic] moi / *I like skiing* j'aime skier / *Ann and I have known each other for years* Ann et moi nous connaissons depuis des années / *I found it, not you* c'est moi qui l'ai trouvé, pas vous.

IA written abbr of **Iowa.**

IAC MESSAGING written abbr of **in any case.**

IAE MESSAGING written abbr of **in any event.**

IAEA (abbr of **International Atomic Energy Agency**) pr n AIEA *f*.

IM4U MESSAGING written abbr of **I am for you.**

IAP (abbr of **Internet Access Provider**) n fournisseur *m* d'accès à l'Internet.

ib = **ibid.**

IB [ˈaɪˈbiː] (abbr of **International Baccalaureate**) n SCH Baccalauréat *m* international.

Iberian [aɪˈbɪərɪən] ◆ n **1.** [person] Ibère *mf* **2.** LING ibère *m*. ◆ adj ibérique.

Iberian Peninsula pr n ▶ **the Iberian Peninsula** la péninsule Ibérique.

ibex [ˈaɪbeks] (*pl* **ibex** *or* **ibexes**) n bouquetin *m*.

ibid (written abbr of **ibidem**) ibid.

i/c written abbr of **in charge.**

IC¹ (abbr of **integrated circuit**) n CI *m*.

IC² MESSAGING written abbr of **I see.**

ICA pr n **1.** (abbr of **Institute of Contemporary Arts**) centre d'art moderne à Londres **2.** UK abbr of **Institute of Chartered Accountants 3.** abbr of **International Cooperation Administration.**

ICBM (abbr of **intercontinental ballistic missile**) n ICBM *m*.

ICC pr n (abbr of **International Chamber of Commerce**) CCI *f*.

ice [aɪs] ◆ n **1.** (U) [frozen water] glace *f* ; [ice cube] glaçon *m*, glaçons *mpl* **2.** [on road] verglas *m* **3.** [in ice rink] glace *f* **4.** [ice-cream] glace *f* **5.** (U) US *v inf* [diamonds] diams *mpl*, cailloux *mpl*. ◆ vt **1.** [chill -drink] rafraîchir ; [-with ice cubes] mettre des glaçons dans **2.** [cake] glacer. ◆ vi (se) givrer. ❖ **ice over** ◆ vi [lake, river, etc.] geler ; [window, propellers] (se) givrer. ◆ vt sep ▶ **to be iced over a)** [lake, river, etc.] être gelé **b)** [window, propellers] être givré. ❖ **ice up** ◆ vi **1.** [lock, windscreen, propellers] (se) givrer, se couvrir de givre **2.** [road] se couvrir de verglas. ◆ vt sep ▶ **to be iced up a)** [lock, windscreen, propellers] être givré **b)** [road] être verglacé.

ICE MESSAGING written abbr of **in case of emergency.**

ice age n période *f* glaciaire. ❖ **ice-age** adj (datant) de la période glaciaire.

iceberg [ˈaɪsbɜːg] n **1.** iceberg *m* **2.** inf [cold person] glaçon *m*.

iceberg lettuce n laitue *f* iceberg.

icebox [ˈaɪsbɒks] n **1.** UK [freezer compartment] freezer *m* **2.** [coolbox] glacière *f* **3.** fig glacière *f*.

icebreaker [ˈaɪsˌbreɪkər] n **1.** [vessel] brise-glace *m inv* **2.** [at party] façon *f* de briser la glace.

ice bucket n seau *m* à glace.

ice cap n calotte *f* glaciaire.

ice-climbing n escalade *f* de murs de glace.

ice-cold adj [hands, drink] glacé ; [house, manners] glacial.

ice cream n glace *f* / *chocolate / strawberry ice cream* glace au chocolat / à la fraise.

ice cream bar n barre *f* glacée.

ice-cream cone, ice-cream cornet n cornet *m* de glace.

ice-cream soda n soda *m* avec de la glace.

ice-cream truck US, **ice-cream van** UK n camionnette *f* de vendeur de glaces.

ice cube n glaçon *m*.

iced [aɪst] adj **1.** [chilled -drink] glacé **2.** [decorated -cake, biscuit] glacé.

ice dancing n danse *f* sur glace.

ice floe n glace *f* flottante.

ice hockey n hockey *m* sur glace.

Iceland [ˈaɪslənd] pr n Islande *f* / *in Iceland* en Islande.

Icelander [ˈaɪsləndər] n Islandais *m*, -e *f*.

Icelandic [aɪsˈlændɪk] ◆ n islandais *m*. ◆ adj islandais.

ice lolly (*pl* **ice lollies**) n UK ≃ bâton *m* glacé.

ice maiden n : *she's an ice maiden* c'est un glaçon.

ice pack n **1.** [pack ice] banquise *f* **2.** [ice bag] sac *m* à glaçons ; MED poche *f* à glace.

ice pick n pic *m* à glace.

ice rink n patinoire *f*.

ice skate n patin *m* (à glace). ❖ **ice-skate** vi patiner ; [professionally] faire du patinage (sur glace) ; [for pleasure] faire du patin (à glace).

ice-skater n patineur *m*, -euse *f*.

ice-skating n patinage *m* (sur glace) / *to go ice-skating* faire du patin (à glace).

ice storm n tempête *f* de pluie verglaçante.

ice-tray n bac *m* à glace *or* à glaçons.

icicle [ˈaɪsɪkl] n glaçon *m* (*qui pend d'une gouttière, etc.*).

icily ['aɪsɪlɪ] adv d'une manière glaciale / *to answer icily* répondre d'un ton or sur un ton glacial.

icing ['aɪsɪŋ] n **1.** CULIN glaçage *m* **2.** [on aeroplane - process] givrage *m* ; [- ice] givre *m*.

icing sugar n 🇬🇧 sucre *m* glace.

ICJ (abbr of **International Court of Justice**) pr n CIJ *f*.

icon ['aɪkɒn] n icône *f*.

iconoclast [aɪ'kɒnəklæst] n iconoclaste *mf*.

iconoclastic [aɪ,kɒnə'klæstɪk] adj iconoclaste.

ICQ MESSAGING written abbr of **I seek you.**

ICR (abbr of **Institute of Cancer Research**) pr n *institut américain de recherche sur le cancer.*

ICT n (abbr of **Information and Communications Technology**) TIC *f*.

ICU [,aɪsiːˈjuː] (abbr of **intensive care unit**) n MED unité *f* de soins intensifs, service *m* de réanimation.

icy ['aɪsɪ] (*compar* **icier**, *superl* **iciest**) adj **1.** [weather] glacial ; [hands] glacé ; [ground] gelé **2.** [covered in ice - road] verglacé ; [- window, propeller] givré, couvert de givre **3.** *fig* [reception, stare] glacial.

ID ◆ n **(abbr of identification)** *(U)* papiers *mpl* / *do you have any ID?* vous avez une pièce d'identité ? ◆ **written abbr of Idaho.**

I'd [aɪd] **1.** abbr of **I had 2.** abbr of **I would.**

Idaho ['aɪdəhəʊ] pr n Idaho *m* / *in Idaho* dans l'Idaho.

ID card n carte *f* d'identité.

IDD (abbr of **international direct dialling**) n indicatif *m* du pays.

idea [aɪˈdɪə] n **1.** [plan, suggestion, inspiration] idée *f* / *what a good idea!* quelle bonne idée ! / *I've had an idea* j'ai une idée / *it wasn't MY idea!* l'idée n'était pas de moi ! ▶ **that's the idea!** c'est ça ! ▶ **what's the idea?** [showing disapproval] qu'est-ce que ça veut dire or signifie ? **2.** [notion] idée *f* / *our ideas about the universe* notre conception de l'univers / *sorry, but this is not my idea of fun* désolé, mais je ne trouve pas ça drôle or ça ne m'amuse pas / *don't put ideas into his head* ne va pas lui fourrer or lui mettre des idées dans la tête / *you've no idea how difficult it was* tu n'imagines pas à quel point c'était difficile / *has anyone any idea how the accident occurred?* est-ce qu'on a une idée de la façon dont l'accident est arrivé ? / *I have a rough idea of what happened* je m'imagine assez bien ce qui est arrivé / *no idea!* aucune idée ! / *I haven't the slightest idea* je n'en ai pas la moindre idée / *I've no idea where it came from* je ne sais vraiment pas d'où ça vient / *what gave him the idea that it would be easy?* qu'est-ce qui lui a laissé croire que ce serait facile ? **3.** [estimate] indication *f*, idée *f* / *can you give me an idea of how much it will cost?* est-ce que vous pouvez m'indiquer à peu près combien ça va coûter ? **4.** [suspicion] soupçon *m*, idée *f* / *she had an idea that something was going to happen* elle se doutait que quelque chose allait arriver **5.** [objective, intention] but *m*.

ideal [aɪˈdɪəl] ◆ adj idéal ▶ **the Ideal Home Exhibition** ≃ le salon de l'habitat. ◆ n idéal *m*.

idealism [aɪˈdɪəlɪzm] n idéalisme *m*.

idealist [aɪˈdɪəlɪst] ◆ n idéaliste *mf*. ◆ adj idéaliste.

idealistic [aɪ,dɪəˈlɪstɪk] adj idéaliste.

idealize, idealise [aɪˈdɪəlaɪz] vt idéaliser.

ideally [aɪˈdɪəlɪ] adv **1.** [perfectly] parfaitement / *the shop is ideally situated* l'emplacement du magasin est idéal **2.** [in a perfect world] dans l'idéal / *ideally, I would like to work in advertising* mon rêve ce serait de travailler dans la publicité.

identical [aɪˈdentɪkl] adj identique ▶ **identical to** or **with** identique à / *they were wearing identical dresses* elles portaient la même robe.

identically [aɪˈdentɪklɪ] adv identiquement / *to be identically dressed* être habillé exactement de la même façon.

identical twins pl n vrais jumeaux *mpl*, vraies jumelles *fpl*.

identifiable [aɪˈdentɪfaɪəbl] adj identifiable.

identification [aɪ,dentɪfɪˈkeɪʃn] n **1.** [gen] identification *f* **2.** (U) [identity papers] papiers *mpl*.

identification parade n 🇬🇧 séance *f* d'identification (au cours de laquelle on demande à un témoin de reconnaître une personne).

identify [aɪˈdentɪfaɪ] (*pt & pp* **identified**) ◆ vt **1.** [recognize, name] identifier **2.** [distinguish - subj: physical feature, badge, etc.] : *she wore a red rose to identify herself* elle portait une rose rouge pour se faire reconnaître or pour qu'on la reconnaisse **3.** [acknowledge - difficulty, issue, etc.] définir **4.** [associate - people, ideas, etc.] : *he has long been identified with right-wing groups* il y a longtemps qu'il est assimilé or identifié aux groupuscules de droite ▶ **to identify o.s. with** s'identifier avec. ◆ vi ▶ **to identify with** s'identifier à or avec.

Identikit® [aɪˈdentɪkɪt] n ▶ **Identikit (picture)** portrait-robot *m*.

identity [aɪˈdentətɪ] (*pl* **identities**) ◆ n **1.** [name, set of characteristics] identité *f* / *it was a case of mistaken identity* il y a eu erreur sur la personne **2.** [sense of belonging] identité *f*. ◆ comp [bracelet, papers] d'identité.

identity card n carte *f* d'identité.

identity fraud n fraude *f* identitaire.

identity parade = **identification parade.**

identity theft n vol *m* d'identité.

ideological [,aɪdɪəˈlɒdʒɪkl] adj idéologique.

ideologically [,aɪdɪəˈlɒdʒɪklɪ] adv du point de vue idéologique, idéologiquement / *ideologically sound* **a)** [idea] défendable sur le plan idéologique **b)** [person] dont les idées sont défendables sur le plan idéologique.

ideology [,aɪdɪˈɒlədʒɪ] (*pl* **ideologies**) n idéologie *f*.

idiocy ['ɪdɪəsɪ] n [stupidity] stupidité *f*, idiotie *f*.

idiom ['ɪdɪəm] n **1.** [expression] locution *f*, expression *f* idiomatique **2.** [language] idiome *m* **3.** [style - of music, writing, etc.] style *m*.

idiomatic [,ɪdɪəˈmætɪk] adj idiomatique / *his Italian is fluent and idiomatic* il parle un italien tout à fait idiomatique.

idiosyncrasy [,ɪdɪəˈsɪŋkrəsɪ] (*pl* **idiosyncrasies**) n [peculiarity] particularité *f* ; [foible] manie *f*.

idiosyncratic [,ɪdɪəsɪŋˈkrætɪk] adj [style, behaviour] caractéristique.

idiot ['ɪdɪət] n [fool] idiot *m*, -e *f*, imbécile *mf*.

idiot box n *inf & pej* télé *f*.

idiotic [,ɪdɪˈɒtɪk] adj idiot.

idiot light n [on dashboard] voyant *m* lumineux.

idiot-proof *inf* ◆ adj COMPUT à l'épreuve de toute fausse manœuvre. ◆ vt rendre infaillible.

IDK MESSAGING written abbr of **I don't know.**

idle ['aɪdl] ◆ adj **1.** [person - inactive] inoccupé, désœuvré ; [- lazy] oisif, paresseux **2.** [not in use - factory, equipment] arrêté, à l'arrêt ▶ **to stand idle** [machine] être arrêté or au repos ▶ **to lie idle a)** [factory] chômer **b)** [money] dormir, être improductif **3.** [futile, pointless] inutile, vain ; [empty - threat, promise, etc.] vain, en l'air ; [- rumour] sans fondement. ◆ vi [engine] tourner au ralenti.

◆ vt US [make unemployed -permanently] mettre au chômage ; [-temporarily] mettre en chômage technique. ❖ **idle away** vt sep ▶ **to idle away one's time** tuer le temps.

idleness ['aɪdlnɪs] n 1. [laziness] oisiveté f, paresse f ; [inactivity] désœuvrement m 2. [futility] futilité f.

idler ['aɪdlə'] n [lazy person] paresseux m, -euse f, fainéant m, -e f.

idly ['aɪdlɪ] adv 1. [lazily] paresseusement 2. [casually] négligemment 3. [unresponsively] sans réagir.

idol ['aɪdl] n idole f.

idolatry [aɪ'dɒlətrɪ] n idolâtrie f.

idolize, idolise ['aɪdəlaɪz] vt idolâtrer.

idyll ['ɪdɪl] n idylle f.

idyllic [ɪ'dɪlɪk] adj idyllique.

i.e. (abbr of **id est**) adv c'est-à-dire, à savoir.

IED (abbr of **Improvised Explosive Device**) EEI m.

IEP ['aɪ'i:'pi:] (abbr of **Individualized Education Program**) n US SCH programme m d'aide individualisée (document qui fixe des objectifs et accorde des aides (tiers-temps, utilisation de l'ordinateur) aux élèves ayant des besoins spécifiques).

if [ɪf] ◆ conj 1. [supposing that] si / if he comes, we'll ask him s'il vient, on lui demandera / if possible si (c'est) possible / if so si c'est le cas 2. [whenever] si / if you ever come or if ever you come to London, do visit us si jamais tu passes à Londres, viens nous voir 3. [whether] : to ask / to know / to wonder if demander / savoir / se demander si / it doesn't matter if he comes or not peu importe qu'il vienne ou (qu'il ne vienne) pas 4. [with verbs or adjectives expressing emotion] : I'm sorry if I upset you je suis désolé si je t'ai fait de la peine. ◆ n si m / if you get the job — and it's a big if — you'll have to move to London si tu obtiens cet emploi, et je dis bien si, tu devras aller t'installer à Londres / no ifs and buts, we're going il n'y a pas de « mais » qui tienne or pas de discussions, on y va. ❖ **if anything** adv phr plutôt / he doesn't look any slimmer, if anything, he's put on weight il n'a pas l'air plus mince, il a même plutôt grossi. ❖ **if I were you** adv phr à ta place, si j'étais toi, à votre place, si j'étais vous / if I were you I'd accept the offer si j'étais toi or à ta place, j'accepterais la proposition. ❖ **if not** conj phr sinon / did you finish on time? and if not, why not? avez-vous terminé à temps ? sinon, pourquoi ? / hundreds, if not thousands des centaines, voire des milliers. ❖ **if only** conj phr 1. [providing a reason] au moins / I think I should come along too, if only to make sure you don't get into mischief je crois que je devrais venir aussi, ne serait-ce que pour m'assurer que vous ne faites pas de bêtises 2. [expressing a wish] si seulement / if only I could drive si seulement je savais conduire.

iffy ['ɪfɪ] (compar **iffier**, superl **iffiest**) adj inf [situation] incertain ; [result] tangent.

igloo ['ɪglu:] n igloo m, iglou m.

ignite [ɪg'naɪt] ◆ vt [set fire to] mettre le feu à, enflammer ; [light] allumer ; [interest] susciter ; [conflict] déclencher. ◆ vi [catch fire] prendre feu, s'enflammer ; [be lit] s'allumer ; [conflict] se déclencher.

ignition [ɪg'nɪʃn] n 1. AUTO allumage m ▶ **to turn on / off the ignition** mettre / couper le contact 2. PHYS & CHEM ignition f.

ignition key n clef f de contact.

ignominy ['ɪgnəmɪnɪ] n ignominie f.

ignoramus [ˌɪgnə'reɪməs] (pl **ignoramuses**) n ignare mf.

ignorance ['ɪgnərəns] n 1. [lack of knowledge, awareness] ignorance f / out of or through sheer ignorance par pure ignorance 2. pej [bad manners] grossièreté f.

ignorant ['ɪgnərənt] adj 1. [uneducated] ignorant 2. [unaware] ignorant 3. pej [bad-mannered] mal élevé, grossier.

ignore [ɪg'nɔ:'] vt 1. [pay no attention to -person, remark] ne pas prêter attention à, ignorer 2. [take no account of -warning, request, etc.] ne pas tenir compte de 3. [overlook] : they can no longer ignore what is going on here il ne leur est plus possible d'ignorer or de fermer les yeux sur ce qui se passe ici.

iguana [ɪ'gwɑ:nə] n iguane m.

IIRC MESSAGING written abbr of **if I recall correctly**.

IKBS (abbr of **intelligent knowledge-based system**) n système m expert.

ikon ['aɪkɒn] = **icon**.

IL written abbr of **Illinois**.

ilk [ɪlk] n [type] : people of that ilk ce genre de personnes / books of that ilk des livres de ce genre.

ill [ɪl] ◆ adj 1. [sick, unwell] malade ▶ **to fall** or **to be taken ill** tomber malade 2. UK [injured] : he is critically ill with stab wounds il est dans un état critique après avoir reçu de nombreux coups de couteau 3. liter [bad] mauvais, néfaste. ◆ n 1. liter [evil] mal m ▶ **to think / speak ill of sb** penser / dire du mal de qqn ▶ **for good or ill** [whatever happens] quoi qu'il arrive 2. [difficulty, trouble] malheur m. ◆ adv 1. [hardly] à peine, difficilement 2. fml [badly] mal ▶ **to augur** or **to bode ill** être de mauvais augure.

ill. (written abbr of **illustration**) ill.

I'll [aɪl] 1. abbr of **I shall** 2. abbr of **I will**.

ill-advised adj [remark, comment] peu judicieux, hors de propos, déplacé ; [action] peu judicieux, déplacé.

ill-at-ease adj gêné, mal à l'aise.

ill-behaved adj qui se conduit or se tient mal.

ill-bred adj mal élevé.

ill-conceived [-kən'si:vd] adj mal pensé.

ill-considered adj [hasty] hâtif ; [thoughtless] irréfléchi.

ill-disposed [-dɪs'pəʊzd] adj mal disposé ▶ **to be ill-disposed towards sb** être mal disposé envers qqn ▶ **to be ill-disposed to do sthg** être peu enclin à faire qqch.

illegal [ɪ'li:gl] adj 1. LAW illégal ▶ **illegal entry** violation f de domicile ▶ **illegal immigrant** immigré m clandestin, immigrée f clandestine 2. COMPUT [character] interdit ; [instruction] erroné.

illegality [ˌɪli:'gælətɪ] (pl **illegalities**) n illégalité f.

illegally [ɪ'li:gəlɪ] adv illégalement, d'une manière illégale.

illegible [ɪ'ledʒəbl] adj illisible.

illegitimate [ˌɪlɪ'dʒɪtɪmət] adj 1. [child] naturel ; LAW illégitime 2. [activity] illégitime, interdit 3. [argument] illogique.

ill-equipped adj 1. [lacking equipment] mal équipé, mal préparé 2. [lacking qualities -for job, situation] ▶ **to be ill-equipped (for)** ne pas être à la hauteur (de), être mal armé (pour).

ill-fated adj [action] malheureux, funeste ; [person] qui joue de malheur, malheureux ; [day] néfaste, de malchance ; [journey] funeste, fatal.

ill feeling n ressentiment m, animosité f.

ill-fitting adj [garment, lid, window] mal ajusté.

ill-founded [-'faʊndɪd] adj [hopes, confidence] mal fondé ; [suspicions] sans fondement.

ill-gotten adj ▶ **ill-gotten gains** biens mpl mal acquis.

ill health n mauvaise santé f.

ill-humoured, ill-humored US adj caractériel.

illicit [ɪ'lɪsɪt] adj illicite.

ill-informed adj [person] mal renseigné ; [remark] inexact, faux (fausse).

Illinois [ˌɪlɪˈnɔɪ] pr n Illinois m / **in Illinois** dans l'Illinois.

ill-intentioned [-ɪnˈtenʃənd] adj malintentionné (towards envers).

illiteracy [ɪˈlɪtərəsɪ] n illettrisme m, analphabétisme m.

illiterate [ɪˈlɪtərət] ◆ adj **1.** [unable to read] analphabète, illettré **2.** [uneducated] ignorant, sans éducation. ◆ n analphabète mf.

ill-mannered adj [person] mal élevé, impoli ; [behaviour] grossier, impoli.

ill-matched adj mal assorti.

illness [ˈɪlnɪs] n maladie f.

illogical [ɪˈlɒdʒɪkl] adj illogique.

ill-prepared adj mal préparé.

ill-qualified adj ▶ **ill-qualified to do sthg a)** [unqualified for] peu qualifié pour faire qqch **b)** [unfit for] peu apte à faire qqch.

ill-suited adj mal assorti ▶ **to be ill-suited for** or **to sthg** être inapte à qqch.

ill-tempered adj [by nature] grincheux, qui a mauvais caractère ; [temporarily] de mauvaise humeur ; [remark, outburst, etc.] plein de mauvaise humeur.

ill-timed [-ˈtaɪmd] adj [arrival, visit] inopportun, intempestif, qui tombe mal ; [remark, question] déplacé, mal à propos (inv).

ill-treat vt maltraiter.

ill-treatment n mauvais traitement m.

illuminate [ɪˈluːmɪneɪt] ◆ vt **1.** [light up] illuminer, éclairer **2.** [make clearer] éclairer **3.** [manuscript] enluminer. ◆ vi s'illuminer.

illuminated [ɪˈluːmɪneɪtɪd] adj **1.** [lit up - sign, notice] lumineux **2.** [decorated - manuscript] enluminé.

illuminating [ɪˈluːmɪneɪtɪŋ] adj [book, speech] éclairant.

illumination [ɪˌluːmɪˈneɪʃn] n **1.** [light] éclairage m ; [of building] illumination f **2.** [of manuscript] enluminure f. ❖ **illuminations** pl n [coloured lights] illuminations fpl.

illusion [ɪˈluːʒn] n **1.** [false impression] illusion f / mirrors give an illusion of space les miroirs donnent une illusion d'espace **2.** [false belief] illusion f ▶ **to be under an illusion** se faire une illusion / she has no illusions or is under no illusions about her chances of success elle ne se fait aucune illusion sur ses chances de succès or de réussir **3.** [magic trick] illusion f.

illusionist [ɪˈluːʒənɪst] n [conjurer, magician] illusionniste mf.

illusory [ɪˈluːsərɪ] adj illusoire.

illustrate [ˈɪləstreɪt] vt **1.** [with pictures] illustrer **2.** [demonstrate] illustrer.

illustration [ˌɪləˈstreɪʃn] n **1.** [picture] illustration f **2.** [demonstration] illustration f / by way of illustration à titre d'exemple.

illustrative [ˈɪləstrətɪv] adj [picture, diagram] qui illustre, explicatif ; [action, event, fact] qui démontre, qui illustre.

illustrator [ˈɪləstreɪtər] n illustrateur m, -trice f.

illustrious [ɪˈlʌstrɪəs] adj illustre.

ill will n malveillance f / I bear them no ill will je ne leur garde pas rancune, je ne leur en veux pas.

ILO (abbr of **International Labour Organization**) pr n OIT f.

ILU (written abbr of **I love you**) MESSAGING je t'm.

ILU2 MESSAGING written abbr of **I love you too**.

ILUA MESSAGING written abbr of **I love you a lot**.

ILWU (abbr of **International Longshoremen's and Warehousemen's Union**) pr n syndicat international de dockers et de magasiniers.

I'm [aɪm] abbr of **I am**.

image [ˈɪmɪdʒ] n **1.** [mental picture] image f / many people have the wrong image of her / of life in New York beaucoup de gens se font une fausse idée d'elle / de la vie à New York **2.** [public appearance] ▶ **(public) image** image f de marque **3.** [likeness] image f **4.** [in art] image f **5.** OPT & PHOT image f.

image-conscious adj soucieux de son image.

imagery [ˈɪmɪdʒrɪ] n (U) **1.** [in literature] images fpl **2.** [visual images] imagerie f.

imaginable [ɪˈmædʒɪnəbl] adj imaginable.

imaginary [ɪˈmædʒɪnrɪ] adj **1.** [in one's imagination - sickness, danger] imaginaire **2.** [fictional - character] fictif.

imagination [ɪˌmædʒɪˈneɪʃn] n [creativity] imagination f.

imaginative [ɪˈmædʒɪnətɪv] adj [person] imaginatif ; [writing, idea, plan] original.

imagine [ɪˈmædʒɪn] vt **1.** [picture - scene, person] imaginer, s'imaginer, se représenter / I'd imagined him to be a much smaller man je l'imaginais plus petit / I can't imagine (myself) getting the job je n'arrive pas à imaginer que je puisse être embauché / you can't imagine how awful it was vous ne pouvez pas (vous) imaginer or vous figurer combien c'était horrible / (you can) imagine his delight! vous pensez s'il était ravi ! / just imagine! tu t'imagines ! / you're imagining things tu te fais des idées **2.** [suppose, think] supposer, imaginer.

imaginings [ɪˈmædʒɪnɪŋz] pl n [fears, dreams] : never in my worst imaginings did I think it would come to this je n'aurais jamais pensé que les choses en arriveraient là.

imam [ɪˈmɑːm] n imam m.

imbalance [ˌɪmˈbæləns] ◆ n déséquilibre m. ◆ vt déséquilibrer.

imbecile [ˈɪmbɪsiːl] ◆ n **1.** [idiot] imbécile mf, idiot m, -e f **2.** PSYCHOL imbécile mf. ◆ adj imbécile, idiot.

imbue [ɪmˈbjuː] vt : her parents had imbued her with high ideals ses parents lui avaient inculqué de nobles idéaux / his words were imbued with resentment ses paroles étaient pleines de ressentiment.

IMCO MESSAGING written abbr of **in my considered opinion**.

IMF (abbr of **International Monetary Fund**) pr n FMI m.

IMHO MESSAGING written abbr of **in my honest (or humble) opinion**.

IMI MESSAGING written abbr of **I mean it**.

imitate [ˈɪmɪteɪt] vt imiter.

imitation [ˌɪmɪˈteɪʃn] ◆ n **1.** [copy] imitation f **2.** [act of imitating] imitation f. ◆ comp faux (fausse) ▶ **imitation fur** fourrure f synthétique ▶ **imitation jewellery** bijoux mpl (de) fantaisie ▶ **imitation leather** imitation f cuir, simili-cuir m.

immaculate [ɪˈmækjʊlət] adj **1.** [clean - house, clothes] impeccable, d'une propreté irréprochable **2.** [faultless - work, behaviour, etc.] parfait, impeccable **3.** [morally pure] irréprochable.

immaculately [ɪˈmækjʊlətlɪ] adv **1.** [spotlessly - clean, tidy] impeccablement **2.** [faultlessly - behave, perform, etc.] d'une manière irréprochable, impeccablement.

immaterial [ˌɪməˈtɪərɪəl] adj **1.** [unimportant] sans importance **2.** PHILOS immatériel.

immature [ˌɪməˈtjʊər] adj **1.** [childish] immature **2.** BOT & ZOOL immature, jeune.

immaturity [ˌɪmə'tjʊərətɪ] n **1.** [of person] manque *m* de maturité, immaturité *f* **2.** PSYCHOL, BOT & ZOOL immaturité *f*.

immeasurable [ɪ'meʒrəbl] adj *lit* incommensurable.

immediacy [ɪ'miːdjəsɪ] n impact *m* immédiat.

immediate [ɪ'miːdjət] adj **1.** [instant] immédiat, urgent ; [close in time] immédiat **2.** [nearest] immédiat, proche **3.** [direct - cause, influence] immédiat, direct.

immediately [ɪ'miːdjətlɪ] ◆ adv **1.** [at once] tout de suite, immédiatement **2.** [directly] directement **3.** [just] juste. ◆ conj UK dès que.

immemorial [ˌɪmɪ'mɔːrɪəl] adj immémorial ▸ **since** or **from time immemorial** de temps immémorial.

immense [ɪ'mens] adj immense, considérable.

immensely [ɪ'menslɪ] adv immensément, extrêmement.

immensity [ɪ'mensətɪ] n immensité *f*.

immerse [ɪ'mɜːs] vt **1.** [in liquid] immerger, plonger **2.** fig : *I immersed myself in my work* je me suis plongé dans mon travail.

immersion [ɪ'mɜːʃn] n **1.** [in liquid] immersion *f* **2.** fig [in reading, work] absorption *f* ▸ **immersion course** stage *m* intensif **3.** ASTRON & RELIG immersion *f*.

immersion heater n chauffe-eau *m inv* électrique.

immigrant ['ɪmɪgrənt] ◆ n immigré *m*, -e *f*. ◆ adj immigré ▸ **immigrant children** enfants d'immigrés.

immigrate ['ɪmɪgreɪt] vi immigrer.

immigration [ˌɪmɪ'greɪʃn] ◆ n **1.** [act of immigrating] immigration *f* ▸ **the Immigration and Naturalization Service** services américains de contrôle de l'immigration ▸ **the Immigration Control Act** loi de 1986 permettant aux immigrés illégaux résidant aux États-Unis depuis 1982 de recevoir un visa **2.** [control section] ▸ **immigration (control)** services mpl de l'immigration. ◆ comp de l'immigration.

imminent ['ɪmɪnənt] adj imminent.

immobile [ɪ'məʊbaɪl] adj immobile.

immobility [ˌɪmə'bɪlətɪ] n immobilité *f*.

immobilize, immobilise [ɪ'məʊbɪlaɪz] vt [gen & FIN] immobiliser.

immobilizer, immobiliser [ɪ'məʊbɪlaɪzəʳ] n AUTO système *m* antidémarrage.

immoderate [ɪ'mɒdərət] adj immodéré, excessif.

immodest [ɪ'mɒdɪst] adj **1.** [indecent] impudique **2.** [vain] prétentieux.

immoral [ɪ'mɒrəl] adj immoral.

immorality [ˌɪmə'rælətɪ] n immoralité *f*.

immortal [ɪ'mɔːtl] ◆ adj immortel. ◆ n immortel *m*, -elle *f*.

immortality [ˌɪmɔː'tælətɪ] n immortalité *f*.

immortalize, immortalise [ɪ'mɔːtəlaɪz] vt immortaliser.

immov(e)able [ɪ'muːvəbl] adj **1.** [fixed] fixe ; [impossible to move] impossible à déplacer **2.** [determined - person] inébranlable.

immune [ɪ'mjuːn] adj **1.** MED immunisé / *immune to measles* immunisé contre la rougeole **2.** fig ▸ **immune to** [unaffected by] à l'abri de, immunisé contre ; [exempt] ▸ **immune from** exempt de, exonéré de.

immune system n système *m* immunitaire.

immunity [ɪ'mjuːnətɪ] n **1.** MED immunité *f*, résistance *f* / *immunity to* or *against measles* immunité contre la rougeole **2.** [exemption] ▸ **immunity from** exonération *f* de, exemption *f* de **3.** [diplomatic, parliamentary] immunité *f* / *immunity from prosecution* immunité, inviolabilité *f*.

immunization, immunisation [ˌɪmjuːnaɪ'zeɪʃn] n immunisation *f*.

immunize, immunise ['ɪmjuːnaɪz] vt immuniser, vacciner.

immunodeficiency [ˌɪmjuːnəʊdɪ'fɪʃənsɪ] n immunodéficience *f*.

immutable [ɪ'mjuːtəbl] adj immuable.

IMNSHO MESSAGING written abbr of **in my not so humble opinion.**

IMO MESSAGING written abbr of **in my opinion.**

imp [ɪmp] n [devil] lutin *m* ; [child] coquin *m*, -e *f*.

impact n ['ɪmpækt] **1.** *lit* impact *m* ▸ **on impact** au moment de l'impact **2.** fig impact *m*, impression *f* / *the scandal had little impact on the election results* le scandale a eu peu de répercussions or d'incidence sur les résultats de l'élection / *you made* or *had quite an impact on him* vous avez fait une forte impression sur lui **3.** [marketing] impact *m*.

impair [ɪm'peəʳ] vt **1.** [weaken] diminuer, affaiblir **2.** [damage] détériorer, endommager.

impaired [ɪm'peəd] adj **1.** [weakened] affaibli, diminué **2.** [damaged] détérioré, endommagé ▸ **impaired hearing / vision** ouïe *f* / vue *f* affaiblie.

impairment [ɪm'peəmənt] n **1.** [weakening] affaiblissement *m*, diminution *f* **2.** [damage] détérioration *f*.

impale [ɪm'peɪl] vt empaler ▸ **to impale o.s. on sthg** s'empaler sur qqch.

impart [ɪm'pɑːt] vt **1.** [communicate - news, truth] apprendre **2.** [transmit - knowledge, wisdom] transmettre **3.** [give - quality, flavour] donner.

impartial [ɪm'pɑːʃl] adj impartial.

impartiality [ɪmˌpɑːʃɪ'ælətɪ] n impartialité *f*.

impassable [ɪm'pɑːsəbl] adj [road] impraticable ; [stream, frontier] infranchissable.

impasse [æm'pɑːs] n impasse *f*.

impassioned [ɪm'pæʃnd] adj passionné ; [plea] fervent.

impassive [ɪm'pæsɪv] adj impassible.

impassively [ɪm'pæsɪvlɪ] adv impassiblement.

impatience [ɪm'peɪʃns] n **1.** [lack of patience] impatience *f* **2.** [irritation] irritation *f* **3.** [intolerance] intolérance *f*.

impatient [ɪm'peɪʃnt] adj **1.** [eager, anxious] impatient / *I'm impatient to see her again* je suis impatient de la revoir **2.** [easily irritated] : *she's impatient with her children* elle n'a aucune patience avec ses enfants **3.** [intolerant] intolérant.

impatiently [ɪm'peɪʃntlɪ] adv impatiemment, avec impatience.

impeach [ɪm'piːtʃ] vt **1.** [accuse] accuser, inculper **2.** ADMIN & POL [in US] entamer une procédure d'impeachment contre.

impeachment [ɪm'piːtʃmənt] n LAW [accusation] mise *f* en accusation ; [in US] mise en accusation d'un élu devant le Congrès.

impeccable [ɪm'pekəbl] adj impeccable, irréprochable.

impeccably [ɪm'pekəblɪ] adv impeccablement.

impede [ɪm'piːd] vt **1.** [obstruct - traffic, player] gêner **2.** [hinder - progress] ralentir ; [- plan] faire obstacle à ; [- person] gêner.

impediment [ɪm'pedɪmənt] n **1.** [obstacle] obstacle *m* **2.** [handicap] défaut *m* (physique).

impel [ɪm'pel] (pt & pp **impelled**, cont **impelling**) vt **1.** [urge, incite] inciter ; [compel] obliger, contraindre / *I felt impelled to intervene* je me sentais obligé d'intervenir **2.** [propel] pousser.

impending [ɪm'pendɪŋ] adj (before noun) imminent.

impenetrable [ɪm'penɪtrəbl] adj **1.** [wall, forest, fog] impénétrable ; *fig* [mystery] insondable, impénétrable **2.** [incomprehensible - jargon, system, etc.] incompréhensible.

imperative [ɪm'perətɪv] ◆ adj **1.** [essential] (absolument) essentiel, impératif **2.** [categorical - orders, voice] impérieux, impératif **3.** GRAM impératif. ◆ n impératif *m* / *in the imperative* à l'impératif.

imperceptible [,ɪmpə'septəbl] adj imperceptible.

imperceptibly [,ɪmpə'septəblɪ] adv imperceptiblement.

imperfect [ɪm'pɜːfɪkt] ◆ adj **1.** [flawed - work, argument] imparfait ; [faulty - machine] défectueux ; [-goods] de second choix **2.** [incomplete] incomplet (incomplète), inachevé **3.** GRAM imparfait **4.** LAW inapplicable (pour vice de forme). ◆ n GRAM imparfait *m* / *in the imperfect* à l'imparfait.

imperfection [,ɪmpə'fekʃn] n [imperfect state] imperfection *f* ; [fault] imperfection *f*, défaut *m*.

imperial [ɪm'pɪərɪəl] adj **1.** [in titles] impérial **2.** [majestic] majestueux, auguste **3.** [imperious] impérieux **4.** [size - of clothes] grande taille *(inv)* ; [-of paper] grand format *(inv)* (*UK* = 762 mm x 559 mm, *US* = 787 mm x 584 mm) **5.** UK [measure] ▶ **imperial pint** pinte *f* (britannique).

imperialism [ɪm'pɪərɪəlɪzm] n impérialisme *m*.

imperialist [ɪm'pɪərɪəlɪst] ◆ adj impérialiste. ◆ n impérialiste *mf*.

imperious [ɪm'pɪərɪəs] adj [authoritative] impérieux, autoritaire.

imperiously [ɪm'pɪərɪəslɪ] adv [authoritatively] impérieusement, autoritairement.

impermeable [ɪm'pɜːmɪəbl] adj [soil, cell, wall] imperméable ; [container] étanche.

impersonal [ɪm'pɜːsnl] adj **1.** [objective] objectif **2.** [cold] froid, impersonnel **3.** GRAM impersonnel.

impersonally [ɪm'pɜːsnəlɪ] adv **1.** [objectively] de façon impersonnelle.

impersonate [ɪm'pɜːsəneɪt] vt **1.** [imitate] imiter **2.** [pretend to be] se faire passer pour.

impersonation [ɪm,pɜːsə'neɪʃn] n **1.** [imitation] imitation *f* **2.** [pretence of being] imposture *f*.

impersonator [ɪm'pɜːsəneɪtər] n **1.** [mimic] imitateur *m*, -trice *f* **2.** [impostor] imposteur *m*.

impertinence [ɪm'pɜːtɪnəns] n impertinence *f*.

impertinent [ɪm'pɜːtɪnənt] adj **1.** [rude] impertinent, insolent ▶ **to be impertinent to sb** être impertinent envers qqn **2.** [irrelevant] hors de propos, non pertinent.

impertinently [ɪm'pɜːtɪnəntlɪ] adv avec impertinence.

imperturbable [,ɪmpə'tɜːbəbl] adj imperturbable.

impervious [ɪm'pɜːvjəs] adj **1.** [unreceptive, untouched - person] imperméable, fermé / *impervious to criticism* imperméable à la critique **2.** [resistant - material] : *impervious to heat* résistant à la chaleur / *impervious to water* imperméable.

impetuous [ɪm'petʃʊəs] adj impétueux.

impetus ['ɪmpɪtəs] n **1.** [force] force *f* d'impulsion ; [speed] élan *m* ; [weight] poids *m* **2.** *fig* [incentive, drive] impulsion *f*, élan *m*.

impinge [ɪm'pɪndʒ] vi **1.** [affect] ▶ **to impinge on** or **upon** affecter **2.** [encroach] ▶ **to impinge on** or **upon** empiéter sur.

impish ['ɪmpɪʃ] adj espiègle, taquin, malicieux.

impishness ['ɪmpɪʃnɪs] n espièglerie *f*.

implacable [ɪm'plækəbl] adj implacable.

implant ◆ vt [ɪm'plɑːnt] n **1.** [instil - idea, feeling] inculquer **2.** MED [graft] greffer ; [place under skin] implanter. ◆ n ['ɪmplɑːnt] [under skin] implant *m* ; [graft] greffe *f*.

implausible [ɪm'plɔːzəbl] adj invraisemblable.

implement ◆ n ['ɪmplɪmənt] **1.** [tool] outil *m* / *agricultural implements* matériel *m* agricole **2.** *fig* [means] instrument *m*. ◆ vt ['ɪmplɪment] [plan, orders] exécuter ; [ideas, policies] appliquer, mettre en œuvre.

implementation [,ɪmplɪmen'teɪʃn] n [of ideas, policies] application *f*, mise *f* en œuvre ; [of plan, orders] exécution *f*.

implicate ['ɪmplɪkeɪt] vt impliquer ▶ **to be implicated in sthg** être impliqué dans qqch.

implication [,ɪmplɪ'keɪʃn] n **1.** [possible repercussion] implication *f* / *I don't think you understand the implications of what you are saying* je ne suis pas sûr que vous mesuriez la portée de vos propos / *the full implications of the report are not yet clear* il est encore trop tôt pour mesurer pleinement les implications de ce rapport **2.** [suggestion] suggestion *f* ; [insinuation] insinuation *f* ; [hidden meaning] sous-entendu *m* ▶ **by implication** par voie de conséquence **3.** [involvement] implication *f*.

> ⚠ When translating the word implication in the sense of a suggestion or insinuation, do not use the French word **implication**, as it does not have this meaning.

implicit [ɪm'plɪsɪt] adj **1.** [implied] implicite **2.** [total - confidence, obedience] total, absolu.

implicitly [ɪm'plɪsɪtlɪ] adv **1.** [by implication] implicitement **2.** [totally] absolument.

implied [ɪm'plaɪd] adj implicite, sous-entendu.

implode [ɪm'pləʊd] vi imploser.

implore [ɪm'plɔːr] vt supplier.

imploring [ɪm'plɔːrɪŋ] adj suppliant.

imploringly [ɪm'plɔːrɪŋlɪ] adv : *he looked at me imploringly* il me suppliait du regard.

imply [ɪm'plaɪ] (*pt & pp* implied) vt **1.** [insinuate] insinuer ; [give impression] laisser entendre or supposer **2.** [presuppose] impliquer ; [involve] comporter.

impolite [,ɪmpə'laɪt] adj impoli ▶ **to be impolite to sb** être or se montrer impoli envers qqn.

impolitely [,ɪmpə'laɪtlɪ] adv impoliment.

import ◆ n ['ɪmpɔːt] **1.** COMM importation *f* **2.** [imported article] importation *f*, article *m* importé **3.** *fml* [meaning] signification *f* ; [content] teneur *f* **4.** *fml* [importance] importance *f*. ◆ comp [ban, licence, surcharge] d'importation ; [duty] de douane, sur les importations ; [trade] des importations. ◆ vt [ɪm'pɔːt] **1.** COMM importer **2.** [imply] signifier.

importance [ɪm'pɔːtns] n importance *f* ▶ **to be of importance** avoir de l'importance ▶ **to give importance to sthg** attacher de l'importance à qqch.

important [ɪm'pɔːtnt] adj **1.** [essential] important / *it is important that you (should) get the job* il est important que vous obteniez cet emploi / *it is important for her to know the truth* il est important pour elle de connaître or il est important qu'elle connaisse la vérité / *my job is important to me* mon travail compte beaucoup pour moi **2.** [influential] : *an important book / writer* un livre-clé / grand écrivain.

> 📋 Note that il est important que is followed by a verb in the subjunctive:
> **It's really important that they should know this.** Il est très important qu'ils le sachent.

importantly [ɪm'pɔːtntlɪ] adv d'un air important / *and, more importantly...* et, ce qui est plus important...

importation [ˌɪmpɔː'teɪʃn] n importation f.

importer [ɪm'pɔːtər] n **1.** [person] importateur m, -trice f **2.** [country] pays m importateur.

import-export n import-export m.

impose [ɪm'pəʊz] ◆ vt [price, tax, attitude, belief] imposer ; [fine, penalty] infliger ▸ **to impose o.s. on sb** imposer sa présence à qqn. ◆ vi s'imposer ▸ **to impose on sb** abuser de la gentillesse de qqn.

imposing [ɪm'pəʊzɪŋ] adj [person, building] impressionnant.

imposition [ˌɪmpə'zɪʃn] n **1.** [of tax, sanction] imposition f **2.** [burden] charge f, fardeau m **3.** TYPO imposition f.

⚠ Be careful when using the French word **imposition**, as it is more restricted in meaning than the English word (see the entry for details).

impossibility [ɪmˌpɒsə'bɪlətɪ] (pl **impossibilities**) n impossibilité f.

impossible [ɪm'pɒsəbl] ◆ adj **1.** [not possible] impossible / *it's impossible for me to leave work before 6 p.m.* il m'est impossible de quitter mon travail avant 18 h **2.** [difficult to believe] impossible, invraisemblable / *it is impossible that he should be lying* il est impossible qu'il mente **3.** [unbearable] impossible, insupportable. ◆ n impossible m.

📝 Note that **être impossible que** is followed by a verb in the subjunctive:
It was impossible for them to know that. *Il était impossible qu'ils le sachent.*

impossibly [ɪm'pɒsəblɪ] adv **1.** [extremely] extrêmement **2.** [unbearably] insupportablement.

impostor, imposter [ɪm'pɒstər] n imposteur m.

impotence ['ɪmpətəns] n [gen & MED] impuissance f.

impotent ['ɪmpətənt] adj **1.** [powerless] faible, impuissant **2.** [sexually] impuissant.

impound [ɪm'paʊnd] vt [gen] saisir ; [car] mettre en fourrière.

impoverish [ɪm'pɒvərɪʃ] vt appauvrir.

impoverished [ɪm'pɒvərɪʃt] adj appauvri, très pauvre.

impoverishment [ɪm'pɒvərɪʃmənt] n appauvrissement m.

impracticable [ɪm'præktɪkəbl] adj [not feasible] irréalisable, impraticable.

impractical [ɪm'præktɪkl] adj [plan] irréaliste ; [person] qui manque d'esprit pratique.

imprecise [ɪmprɪ'saɪs] adj imprécis.

imprecision [ˌɪmprɪ'sɪʒn] n imprécision f.

impregnable [ɪm'pregnəbl] adj **1.** [fortress] imprenable **2.** fig [argument] irréfutable.

impregnate ['ɪmpregneɪt] vt [fill] imprégner ▸ **impregnated with** imprégné de.

impresario [ˌɪmprɪ'sɑːrɪəʊ] (pl **impresarios**) n impresario m.

impress ◆ vt [ɪm'pres] **1.** [influence, affect - mind, person] faire impression sur, impressionner **2.** ▸ **to impress sthg on sb** [make understand] faire comprendre qqch à qqn **3.** [print] imprimer, marquer. ◆ n ['ɪmpres] empreinte f.

impression [ɪm'preʃn] n **1.** [impact - on person, mind, feelings] impression f / *he made a strong impression on them* il leur a fait une forte impression **2.** [idea, thought] impression f / *I was under the impression that you were unable to come* j'étais persuadé que vous ne pouviez pas venir **3.** [mark, imprint] marque f, empreinte f **4.** [printing] impression f ; [edition] tirage m **5.** [impersonation] imitation f ▸ **to do impressions** faire des imitations.

impressionable [ɪm'preʃnəbl] adj impressionnable.

impressionism [ɪm'preʃənɪzm] n ART & LITER impressionnisme m.

impressionist [ɪm'preʃənɪst] n [entertainer] imitateur m, -trice f ; ART & LITER impressionniste. ❖ **Impressionist** ◆ n impressionniste mf. ◆ adj impressionniste.

impressive [ɪm'presɪv] adj impressionnant.

impressively [ɪm'presɪvlɪ] adv remarquablement.

imprint ◆ n ['ɪmprɪnt] [mark] empreinte f, marque f. ◆ vt [ɪm'prɪnt] **1.** [print] imprimer **2.** [in sand, clay, mud] imprimer ▸ **to be imprinted in** être imprimé dans **3.** fig [fix] implanter, graver.

imprison [ɪm'prɪzn] vt **1.** [put in prison] mettre en prison, incarcérer **2.** [sentence] condamner.

imprisonment [ɪm'prɪznmənt] n emprisonnement m.

improbability [ɪmˌprɒbə'bɪlətɪ] (pl **improbabilities**) n **1.** [of event] improbabilité f **2.** [of story] invraisemblance f.

improbable [ɪm'prɒbəbl] adj **1.** [unlikely] improbable **2.** [hard to believe] invraisemblable.

improbably [ɪm'prɒbəblɪ] adv invraisemblablement.

impromptu [ɪm'prɒmptjuː] ◆ adj impromptu, improvisé. ◆ adv impromptu. ◆ n impromptu m.

improper [ɪm'prɒpər] adj **1.** [rude, shocking - words, action] déplacé **2.** [unsuitable] peu convenable **3.** [dishonest] malhonnête **4.** [incorrect - method, equipment] inadapté, inadéquat.

improperly [ɪm'prɒpəlɪ] adv **1.** [indecently] de manière déplacée **2.** [unsuitably] : *he was improperly dressed* il n'était pas habillé comme il faut **3.** [dishonestly] malhonnêtement **4.** [incorrectly] incorrectement, de manière incorrecte.

impropriety [ɪmprə'praɪətɪ] (pl **improprieties**) n **1.** [of behaviour] inconvenance f **2.** [of language] impropriété f.

improve [ɪm'pruːv] ◆ vt **1.** [make better - work, facilities, result] améliorer **2.** [increase - knowledge, productivity] accroître, augmenter **3.** [cultivate] : *to improve one's mind* se cultiver l'esprit. ◆ vi [get better] s'améliorer ; [increase] augmenter ; [make progress] s'améliorer, faire des progrès. ❖ **improve on, improve upon** vt insep **1.** [result, work] améliorer **2.** [offer] ▸ **to improve on sb's offer** enchérir sur qqn.

improved [ɪm'pruːvd] adj [gen] amélioré ; [services] amélioré, meilleur ; [offer, performance] meilleur.

improvement [ɪm'pruːvmənt] n **1.** amélioration f ; [in person's work, performance] progrès m **2.** [in building, road, etc.] rénovation f, aménagement m ▸ **(home) improvements** travaux mpl de rénovation.

improvisation [ˌɪmprəvaɪ'zeɪʃn] n improvisation f.

improvise ['ɪmprəvaɪz] vt & vi improviser.

impudence ['ɪmpjʊdəns] n effronterie f, impudence f.

impudent ['ɪmpjʊdənt] adj effronté, impudent.

impulse ['ɪmpʌls] n **1.** [desire, instinct] impulsion f, besoin m, envie f ▸ **to act on impulse** agir par impulsion **2.** ELEC & PHYSIOL impulsion f.

impulse buy n achat m d'impulsion or spontané.

impulse buyer n acheteur m impulsif, acheteuse f impulsive.

impulse buying n *(U)* achats *mpl* d'impulsion.

impulsive [ɪm'pʌlsɪv] adj **1.** [instinctive, spontaneous] impulsif ; [thoughtless] irréfléchi **2.** [force] impulsif.

impulsively [ɪm'pʌlsɪvlɪ] adv par or sur impulsion, impulsivement.

impunity [ɪm'pjuːnətɪ] n *fml* impunité *f* ▶ **to act with impunity** agir en toute impunité or impunément.

impure [ɪm'pjʊəʳ] adj **1.** [unclean - air, milk] impur **2.** *liter* [sinful - thought] impur, mauvais ; [- motive] bas.

impurity [ɪm'pjʊərətɪ] *(pl* **impurities)** n impureté *f*.

IMS (abbr of **International Monetary System**) n ECON SMI *m*.

IMTNG MESSAGING written abbr of **I am in a meeting**.

in [ɪn]
◆ prep
A. IN SPACE 1. [within a defined area or space] dans / *in a box* dans une boîte / *in the house* dans la maison / *in Catherine's house* chez Catherine **2.** [indicating movement] dans / *throw the letter in the bin* jette la lettre à la poubelle / *we headed in the direction of the port* nous nous sommes dirigés vers le port **3.** [contained by a part of the body] dans / *he had a knife in his hand* il avait un couteau dans or à la main / *with tears in his eyes* les larmes aux yeux **4.** [on or behind a surface] dans **5.** [in a specified institution] : *she's in hospital / in prison* elle est à l'hôpital / en prison / *he teaches in a language school* il enseigne dans une école de langues ; US [in school] à l'école **6.** [with geographical names] : *in Paris* à Paris / *in France* en France / *in the States* aux États-Unis / *in Portugal* au Portugal / *in the Third World* dans les pays du tiers-monde.
B. IN TIME 1. [during a specified period of time] en / *in 1992* en 1992 / *in March* en mars, au mois de mars / *in (the) summer / autumn / winter* en été / automne / hiver / *in (the) spring* au printemps / *at 5 o'clock in the afternoon / morning* à 5 h de l'après-midi / du matin **2.** [after a specified period of time] dans / *I'll be back in five minutes* je reviens dans cinq minutes, j'en ai pour cinq minutes.
C. SHAPE, STATE OR FORM 1. [indicating form, method] : *in English / French* en anglais / français **2.** [indicating state of mind] : *to be in love* être amoureux **3.** [indicating state, situation] dans, en / *in the present circumstances* dans les circonstances actuelles / *in this weather* par or avec ce temps / *in the rain / snow* sous la pluie / neige / *in danger / silence* en danger / silence / *in my presence* en ma présence **4.** [wearing] en / *he was in a suit* il était en costume / *who's that woman in the hat?* qui est la femme avec le or au chapeau ? **5.** [among] chez / *a disease common in five-year-olds* une maladie très répandue chez les enfants de cinq ans.
D. FIELD OF ACTIVITY [indicating specified field, sphere of activity] dans / *to be in the army / navy* être dans l'armée / la marine / *a degree in Italian* un diplôme d'italien.
E. RATIOS OR AMOUNTS 1. [indicating approximate number, amount] : *they came in their thousands* ils sont venus par milliers / *he's in his forties* il a la quarantaine **2.** [in ratios] sur / *one child in three* un enfant sur trois.
◆ adv **1.** [into an enclosed space] à l'intérieur, dedans / *he jumped in* il sauta dedans **2.** [at home or place of work] : *is your wife / the boss in?* est-ce que votre femme / le patron est là ? / *it's nice to spend an evening in* c'est agréable de passer une soirée chez soi **3.** [indicating entry] : *to go in* entrer / *come in!* entrez ! / *in we go!* on y va ! **4.** [indicating transmission] : *entries must be in by May 1st* les bulletins doivent nous parvenir avant le 1ᵉʳ mai **5.** PHR **to be in for** sthg : *you're in for a bit of a disappointment* tu vas être déçu / *he's in for a surprise / shock* il va avoir une surprise / un choc ▶ **to be in for it** : *now he's really in for it* cette fois-

ci, il va y avoir droit ▶ **to be in on sthg** : *he's in on the secret* il est dans le secret / *he's in on it* il est dans le coup ▶ **to be in with sb** *inf* être en bons termes avec qqn.
◆ adj *inf* **1.** [fashionable] à la mode, branché ▶ **to be the in thing** être à la mode **2.** [for a select few] ▶ **an in joke** : *it's an in joke* c'est une plaisanterie or une blague entre nous / eux, etc., c'est un(e) private joke. ◈ **ins** pl n : *the ins and outs (of a situation)* les tenants et les aboutissants (d'une situation). ◈ **in all** adv phr en tout / *there are 30 in all* il y en a 30 en tout. ◈ **in between** ◆ adv phr **1.** [in intermediate position] : *a row of bushes with little clumps of flowers in between* un rang d'arbustes alternant avec des fleurs / *she either plays very well or very badly, never in between* elle joue très bien ou très mal, jamais entre les deux **2.** [in time] entre-temps, dans l'intervalle. ◆ prep *in* entre. ◈ **in that** conj phr puisque / *I'm not badly off in that I have a job and a flat but...* je ne peux pas me plaindre puisque j'ai un emploi et un appartement mais…

in. written abbr of **inch(es)**.

IN written abbr of **Indiana**.

inability [ˌɪnə'bɪlətɪ] n incapacité *f* / *our inability to help them* notre incapacité à les aider.

inaccessibility ['ɪnək,sesɪ'bɪlətɪ] n inaccessibilité *f*.

inaccessible [ˌɪnək'sesəbl] adj **1.** [impossible to reach] inaccessible **2.** [unavailable - person] inaccessible, inabordable ; [- information] inaccessible **3.** [obscure - film, book, music] inaccessible, incompréhensible.

inaccuracy [ɪn'ækjʊrəsɪ] *(pl* **inaccuracies)** n [of translation, calculation, information] inexactitude *f* ; [of word, expression] inexactitude *f*, impropriété *f*.

inaccurate [ɪn'ækjʊrət] adj [incorrect - figures] inexact ; [- term] impropre ; [- result] erroné ; [- description] inexact.

inaction [ɪn'ækʃn] n inaction *f*.

inactive [ɪn'æktɪv] adj **1.** [person, animal - resting] inactif, peu actif ; [- not working] inactif **2.** [lazy] paresseux, oisif **3.** [inoperative - machine] au repos, à l'arrêt **4.** [dormant - volcano] qui n'est pas en activité ; [- disease, virus] inactif **5.** CHEM & PHYS inerte.

inactivity [ˌɪnæk'tɪvətɪ] n inactivité *f*, inaction *f*.

inadequacy [ɪn'ædɪkwəsɪ] *(pl* **inadequacies)** n **1.** [insufficiency - of resources, facilities] insuffisance *f* **2.** [social] incapacité *f*, inadaptation *f* ; [sexual] impuissance *f*, incapacité *f* **3.** [failing] défaut *m*, faiblesse *f*.

inadequate [ɪn'ædɪkwət] adj **1.** [insufficient] insuffisant **2.** [unsatisfactory] médiocre **3.** [unsuitable - equipment] inadéquat **4.** [incapable] incapable ; [sexually] impuissant.

inadequately [ɪn'ædɪkwətlɪ] adv de manière inadéquate ; [fund, invest] insuffisamment.

inadmissible [ˌɪnəd'mɪsəbl] adj inacceptable ▶ **inadmissible evidence** LAW témoignage *m* irrecevable.

inadvertent [ˌɪnəd'vɜːtnt] adj **1.** [not deliberate] accidentel, involontaire **2.** [careless] : *an inadvertent error* une erreur commise par inadvertance.

inadvertently [ˌɪnəd'vɜːtəntlɪ] adv par mégarde or inadvertance.

inadvisability ['ɪnəd,vaɪzə'bɪlətɪ] n inopportunité *f*.

inadvisable [ˌɪnəd'vaɪzəbl] adj déconseillé.

inalienable [ɪn'eɪljənəbl] adj inaliénable.

inane [ɪ'neɪn] adj [person] idiot, imbécile ; [behaviour] stupide, inepte ; [remark] idiot, stupide, inepte.

inanely [ɪ'neɪnlɪ] adv de façon idiote or stupide or inepte.

inanimate [ɪn'ænɪmət] adj inanimé.

inanity [ɪ'nænətɪ] *(pl* **inanities)** n **1.** [stupidity] stupidité *f* **2.** [stupid remark] ineptie *f*, bêtise *f*.

inapplicable [ˌɪnə'plɪkəbl] adj inapplicable.

inappropriate [ˌɪnəˈprəʊprɪət] adj [unsuitable - action, remark] inopportun, mal à propos ; [- time, moment] inopportun ; [- clothing, equipment] peu approprié, inadéquat ; [- name] mal choisi.

inappropriately [ˌɪnəˈprəʊprɪətlɪ] adv de manière peu convenable or appropriée.

inarticulate [ˌɪnɑːˈtɪkjʊlət] adj **1.** [person] qui bredouille **2.** [words, sounds] indistinct.

inasmuch [ˌɪnəzˈmʌtʃ] ❖ **inasmuch as** conj *fml* attendu que.

inasmuch as [ˌɪnəzˈmʌtʃ-] conj *fml* [given that] étant donné que, vu que ; [insofar as] dans la mesure où.

inattention [ˌɪnəˈtenʃn] n manque *m* d'attention, inattention *f* / *your essay shows inattention to detail* il y a beaucoup d'erreurs de détail dans votre travail.

inattentive [ˌɪnəˈtentɪv] adj **1.** [paying no attention] inattentif **2.** [neglectful] peu attentionné, négligent.

inattentively [ˌɪnəˈtentɪvlɪ] adv sans prêter or faire attention.

inaudible [ɪˈnɔːdɪbl] adj inaudible.

inaudibly [ɪˈnɔːdɪblɪ] adv indistinctement.

inaugural [ɪˈnɔːgjʊrəl] ❖ adj inaugural, d'inauguration ▶ **inaugural address** or **speech** US POL discours *m* inaugural. ❖ n US discours *m* inaugural (*d'un président des États-Unis*).

inaugurate [ɪˈnɔːgjʊreɪt] vt **1.** [open ceremoniously] inaugurer **2.** [commence formally] inaugurer **3.** [herald - era] inaugurer **4.** [instate - official] installer (dans ses fonctions), investir ; [- king, bishop] introniser.

inauguration [ɪˌnɔːgjʊˈreɪʃn] n **1.** [of building] inauguration *f*, cérémonie *f* d'ouverture ; [of policy, era, etc.] inauguration *f* **2.** [of official] investiture *f*.

inauspicious [ˌɪnɔːˈspɪʃəs] adj défavorable, peu propice.

in-basket US = in-tray.

in-between adj intermédiaire.

inboard [ˈɪnbɔːd] adj NAUT ▶ **inboard motor** in-bord *m inv*.

inborn [ˌɪnˈbɔːn] adj [characteristic, quality] inné ; MED congénital, héréditaire.

inbound [ˈɪnbaʊnd] adj [flight, passenger, etc.] à l'arrivée.

inbox [ˈɪnbɒks] n COMPUT boîte *f* de réception.

in-box US = in-tray.

inbred [ˌɪnˈbred] adj **1.** [characteristic, quality] inné **2.** BIOL [trait] acquis par sélection génétique ; [strain] produit par le croisement d'individus consanguins ; [person] de parents consanguins ; [family, group] consanguin.

inbreeding [ˌɪnˈbriːdɪŋ] n [of animals] croisement *m*.

inbuilt [ˈɪnbɪlt] adj **1.** [device] incorporé, intégré **2.** [quality, defect] inhérent.

inc. (written abbr of **inclusive**) : *12-15 April inc.* du 12 au 15 avril inclus.

inc. (written abbr of **incorporated**) US ≃ SARL.

incalculable [ɪnˈkælkjʊləbl] adj incalculable.

in camera [ˌɪnˈkæmərə] adj & adv *fml* à huis clos.

incandescent [ˌɪnkænˈdesnt] adj incandescent.

incantation [ˌɪnkænˈteɪʃn] n incantation *f*.

incapable [ɪnˈkeɪpəbl] adj **1.** [unable] incapable ▶ **to be incapable of doing sthg** être incapable de faire qqch **2.** [incompetent] incapable.

incapacitate [ˌɪnkəˈpæsɪteɪt] vt **1.** [cripple] rendre infirme or invalide **2.** LAW frapper d'incapacité légale.

incapacitated [ˌɪnkəˈpæsɪteɪtɪd] adj inapte physiquement ▶ **incapacitated for work** mis dans l'incapacité de travailler.

incapacity [ˌɪnkəˈpæsətɪ] (*pl* **incapacities**) n [gen & LAW] incapacité *f* / *his incapacity for work* son incapacité à travailler / *her incapacity to adapt* son incapacité à s'adapter.

in-car adj [computer, applications] embarqué.

incarcerate [ɪnˈkɑːsəreɪt] vt incarcérer.

incarceration [ɪnˌkɑːsəˈreɪʃn] n incarcération *f*.

incarnate [ɪnˈkɑːneɪt] *liter* ❖ adj incarné. ❖ vt incarner.

incarnation [ˌɪnkɑːˈneɪʃn] n incarnation *f* / *I must have known her in a previous incarnation* hum j'ai dû la connaître dans une vie antérieure.

incendiary [ɪnˈsendjərɪ] (*pl* **incendiaries**) ❖ n **1.** [arsonist] incendiaire *mf* **2.** [bomb] bombe *f* incendiaire **3.** *fig* [agitator] fauteur *m* de troubles. ❖ adj **1.** [causing fires] incendiaire ▶ **incendiary bomb / device** bombe *f* / dispositif *m* incendiaire **2.** [combustible] inflammable **3.** *fig* [speech, statement] incendiaire, séditieux.

incense ❖ n [ˈɪnsens] encens *m*. ❖ vt [ɪnˈsens] [anger] rendre furieux, excéder / *I was absolutely incensed* j'étais hors de moi.

incentive [ɪnˈsentɪv] ❖ n **1.** [motivation] motivation *f* ▶ **to give sb the incentive to do sthg** motiver qqn à faire qqch **2.** FIN & INDUST incitation *f*, encouragement *m*. ❖ comp incitateur, incitatif ▶ **incentive scheme** UK programme *m* d'encouragement.

incentive-based adj reposant sur l'incitation.

incentivize, incentivise [ɪnˈsentɪvaɪz] vt motiver.

inception [ɪnˈsepʃn] n création *f*.

incessant [ɪnˈsesnt] adj incessant.

incessantly [ɪnˈsesntlɪ] adv continuellement, sans cesse.

incest [ˈɪnsest] n inceste *m*.

incestuous [ɪnˈsestjʊəs] adj incestueux.

inch [ɪntʃ] ❖ n **1.** pouce *m* / *it's about 6 inches wide* cela fait à peu près 15 centimètres de large **2.** PHR **inch by inch** petit à petit, peu à peu ▶ **to be within an inch of doing sthg** être à deux doigts de faire qqch. ❖ vt : *to inch one's way in / out* entrer / sortir petit à petit. ❖ vi : *to inch in / out* entrer / sortir petit à petit.

incidence [ˈɪnsɪdəns] n **1.** [rate] taux *m* **2.** GEOM & PHYS incidence *f* ▶ **angle / point of incidence** angle *m* / point *m* d'incidence.

incident [ˈɪnsɪdənt] n incident *m*.

incidental [ˌɪnsɪˈdentl] ❖ adj **1.** [minor] secondaire, accessoire ; [additional] accessoire ▶ **incidental expenses** faux frais *mpl* **2.** [related] ▶ **incidental to** en rapport avec, occasionné par. ❖ n [chance happening] événement *m* fortuit ; [minor detail] détail *m* secondaire. ❖ **incidentals** pl n [expenses] faux frais *mpl*.

incidentally [ˌɪnsɪˈdentəlɪ] adv **1.** [by chance] incidemment, accessoirement **2.** [by the way] à propos.

incidental music n musique *f* d'accompagnement.

incident room n UK [in police station] salle *f* des opérations.

incinerate [ɪnˈsɪnəreɪt] vt incinérer.

incinerator [ɪnˈsɪnəreɪtər] n incinérateur *m*.

incipient [ɪnˈsɪpɪənt] adj naissant.

incision [ɪnˈsɪʒn] n incision *f*.

incisive [ɪnˈsaɪsɪv] adj [mind] perspicace, pénétrant ; [wit, remark] incisif.

incisively [ɪnˈsaɪsɪvlɪ] adv [think] de façon incisive ; [ask, remark] de manière perspicace or pénétrante.

incisor [ɪnˈsaɪzər] n incisive *f*.

incite [ɪnˈsaɪt] vt ▶ **to incite sb to do sthg** inciter qqn à faire qqch / *to incite sb to violence* inciter qqn à la violence.

incitement [ɪnˈsaɪtmənt] n incitation f.

incl. (written abbr of **including**) ▸ **incl. VAT** TTC.

inclement [ɪnˈklemənt] adj liter [weather] inclément.

inclination [ˌɪnklɪˈneɪʃn] n **1.** [tendency] disposition f, prédisposition f, tendance f **2.** [liking] penchant m, inclination f **3.** [slant, lean] inclinaison f ; [of body] inclination f.

incline ◆ vt [ɪnˈklaɪn] **1.** [dispose] disposer, pousser **2.** [lean, bend] incliner. ◆ vi [ɪnˈklaɪn] **1.** [tend] tendre, avoir tendance **2.** [lean, bend] s'incliner. ◆ n [ˈɪnklaɪn] inclinaison f ; [slope] pente f, déclivité f ; RAIL rampe f.

inclined [ɪnˈklaɪnd] adj **1.** [tending, disposed] avoir tendance à / I'm inclined to agree j'aurais tendance à être d'accord ▸ to be well inclined towards sb être bien disposé envers qqn **2.** [slanting, leaning] incliné.

include [ɪnˈkluːd] vt comprendre, inclure / does that remark include me? cette remarque vaut-elle aussi pour moi ? / don't forget to include the cheque n'oubliez pas de joindre le chèque.

included [ɪnˈkluːdɪd] adj : myself included y compris moi / **'service not included'** 'service non compris'.

including [ɪnˈkluːdɪŋ] prep (y) compris / 14 guests including the children 14 invités y compris les enfants / 14 guests not including the children 14 invités sans compter les enfants / up to and including page 40 jusqu'à la page 40 incluse.

inclusion [ɪnˈkluːʒn] n [gen & GEOL & MATH] inclusion f.

inclusive [ɪnˈkluːsɪv] adj **1.** inclus, compris / inclusive of tax taxes fpl comprises / from July to September inclusive de juillet à septembre inclus **2.** [list] exhaustif ; [survey] complet (complète), poussé.

inclusively [ɪnˈkluːsɪvlɪ] adv inclusivement.

inclusivity [ˌɪnkluːˈsɪvɪtɪ] n inclusion f, politique f d'inclusion.

incognito [ˌɪnkɒɡˈniːtəʊ] (pl **incognitos**) ◆ adv incognito / to remain incognito **a)** [witness] garder l'anonymat **b)** [star, politician] garder l'incognito. ◆ n incognito m.

incoherence [ˌɪnkəʊˈhɪərəns] n incohérence f.

incoherent [ˌɪnkəʊˈhɪərənt] adj [person, argument] incohérent ; [thought] incohérent, décousu.

incoherently [ˌɪnkəʊˈhɪərəntlɪ] adv de manière incohérente.

income [ˈɪnkʌm] n revenu m.

income bracket, **income group** n tranche f de revenus.

incomes policy n UK politique f des revenus.

income support n prestation complémentaire en faveur des personnes justifiant de faibles revenus.

income tax n impôt m sur le revenu (des personnes physiques) ▸ **income tax inspector** inspecteur m des contributions directes or des impôts ▸ **income tax return** déclaration f de revenus, feuille f d'impôts.

incoming [ˈɪnˌkʌmɪŋ] adj **1.** [in direction] : incoming train / flight train m / vol m à l'arrivée / incoming passengers passagers mpl à l'arrivée / incoming mail courrier m (du jour) / incoming calls appels mpl téléphoniques (reçus) / the incoming tide la marée montante **2.** [cash, interest] qui rentre **3.** [official, administration, tenant] nouveau (before vowel or silent 'h' **nouvel**, f **nouvelle**). ◆ **incomings** pl n [revenue] rentrée f, rentrées fpl, recettes fpl.

incommunicado [ˌɪnkəmjuːnɪˈkɑːdəʊ] adj & adv sans communication avec le monde extérieur.

incomparable [ɪnˈkɒmpərəbl] adj incomparable.

incomparably [ɪnˈkɒmpərəblɪ] adv incomparablement, infiniment.

incompatibility [ˈɪnkəmˌpætəˈbɪlətɪ] n incompatibilité f ; [grounds for divorce] incompatibilité f d'humeur.

incompatible [ˌɪnkəmˈpætɪbl] adj incompatible.

incompetence [ɪnˈkɒmpɪtəns], **incompetency** [ɪnˈkɒmpɪtənsɪ] n incompétence f.

incompetent [ɪnˈkɒmpɪtənt] ◆ adj incompétent. ◆ n incompétent m, -e f, incapable mf.

incomplete [ˌɪnkəmˈpliːt] adj **1.** [unfinished] inachevé **2.** [lacking something] incomplet (incomplète).

incomprehensible [ˌɪnkɒmprɪˈhensəbl] adj incompréhensible.

inconceivable [ˌɪnkənˈsiːvəbl] adj inconcevable, inimaginable.

inconclusive [ˌɪnkənˈkluːsɪv] adj peu concluant.

incongruity [ˌɪnkɒŋˈɡruːətɪ] (pl **incongruities**) n **1.** [strangeness, discordancy] incongruité f **2.** [disparity] disparité f.

incongruous [ɪnˈkɒŋɡruəs] adj [strange, discordant] incongru ; [disparate] incohérent.

incongruously [ɪnˈkɒŋɡruəslɪ] adv : the incongruously named Palace Hotel le Palace Hôtel, au nom incongru.

inconsequential [ˌɪnkɒnsɪˈkwenʃl] adj sans importance.

inconsiderable [ˌɪnkənˈsɪdərəbl] adj insignifiant, négligeable.

inconsiderate [ˌɪnkənˈsɪdərət] adj [person] qui manque de prévenance ; [action, remark] irréfléchi.

inconsiderately [ˌɪnkənˈsɪdərətlɪ] adv sans aucune considération.

inconsistency [ˌɪnkənˈsɪstənsɪ] (pl **inconsistencies**) n **1.** [incoherence] manque m de cohérence, incohérence f **2.** [contradiction] contradiction f.

inconsistent [ˌɪnkənˈsɪstənt] adj **1.** [person] incohérent (dans ses comportements) **2.** [performance] inégal **3.** [reasoning] incohérent **4.** [incompatible] incompatible ▸ **inconsistent with** incompatible avec.

> ⚠ **Inconsistant** means flimsy, runny or weak, **not** inconsistent.

inconsolable [ˌɪnkənˈsəʊləbl] adj inconsolable.

inconsolably [ˌɪnkənˈsəʊləblɪ] adv de façon inconsolable.

inconspicuous [ˌɪnkənˈspɪkjʊəs] adj [difficult to see] à peine visible, qui passe inaperçu ; [discreet] peu voyant, discret (discrète).

incontinence [ɪnˈkɒntɪnəns] n incontinence f.

incontinent [ɪnˈkɒntɪnənt] adj incontinent.

incontrovertible [ˌɪnkɒntrəˈvɜːtəbl] adj indiscutable / incontrovertible evidence une preuve irréfutable.

inconvenience [ˌɪnkənˈviːnjəns] ◆ n **1.** [disadvantage] inconvénient m **2.** [trouble] : to cause inconvenience déranger, gêner / I hope it's not putting you to too much inconvenience j'espère que cela ne vous dérange pas trop ; [disadvantages] incommodité f, inconvénients mpl. ◆ vt déranger, incommoder.

inconvenient [ˌɪnkənˈviːnjənt] adj **1.** [inopportune, awkward] inopportun / if it's not inconvenient si cela ne vous dérange pas **2.** [impractical - tool, kitchen] peu pratique.

inconveniently [ˌɪnkənˈviːnjəntlɪ] adv **1.** [happen, arrive] au mauvais moment, inopportunément **2.** [be situated] de façon malcommode, mal.

incorporate [ɪnˈkɔːpəreɪt] vt incorporer.

incorporated [ɪn'kɔːpəreɪtɪd] adj constitué en société commerciale / *Bradley & Jones Incorporated* ≃ Bradley & Jones SARL.

incorrect [ˌɪnkə'rekt] adj **1.** [wrong - answer, result] erroné, faux (fausse) ; [-sum, statement] inexact, incorrect **2.** [improper] incorrect.

incorrectly [ˌɪnkə'rektlɪ] adv **1.** [wrongly] : *I was incorrectly quoted* j'ai été cité de façon incorrecte / *the illness was incorrectly diagnosed* il y a eu erreur de diagnostic **2.** [improperly] incorrectement.

incorrigible [ɪn'kɒrɪdʒəbl] adj incorrigible.

incorruptible [ˌɪnkə'rʌptəbl] adj incorruptible.

increase ◆ vi [ɪn'kriːs] augmenter, croître / *to increase by 10%* augmenter de 10 % / *to increase in size* grandir / *to increase in intensity* s'intensifier. ◆ vt [ɪn'kriːs] augmenter. ◆ n ['ɪnkriːs] augmentation f / *an increase in population* un accroissement de la population. ❖ **on the increase** adj phr : *crime is on the increase* la criminalité est en hausse.

increased [ɪn'kriːst] adj accru.

increasing [ɪn'kriːsɪŋ] adj croissant, grandissant.

increasingly [ɪn'kriːsɪŋlɪ] adv de plus en plus.

incredible [ɪn'kredəbl] adj **1.** [unbelievable] incroyable, invraisemblable **2.** *inf* [fantastic, amazing] fantastique, incroyable.

> 📋 Note that incroyable que is followed by a verb in the subjunctive:
> **I find it incredible that you eventually told him.** *Je trouve incroyable que tu aies fini par lui dire.*

incredibly [ɪn'kredəblɪ] adv **1.** [amazingly] : *incredibly, we were on time* aussi incroyable que cela puisse paraître, nous étions à l'heure **2.** [extremely] incroyablement.

incredulity [ˌɪnkrɪ'djuːlətɪ] n incrédulité f.

incredulous [ɪn'kredjʊləs] adj incrédule.

incredulously [ɪn'kredjʊləslɪ] adv avec incrédulité.

increment ['ɪnkrɪmənt] ◆ n **1.** [increase] augmentation f **2.** COMPUT incrément m **3.** MATH accroissement m. ◆ vt COMPUT incrémenter.

incremental [ˌɪnkrɪ'mentl] adj **1.** [increasing] croissant **2.** COMPUT incrémentiel, incrémental.

incriminate [ɪn'krɪmɪneɪt] vt incriminer, mettre en cause ▶ **to incriminate o.s.** se compromettre.

incriminating [ɪn'krɪmɪneɪtɪŋ] adj accusateur, compromettant ▶ **incriminating evidence** pièce f or pièces fpl à conviction.

in-crowd n *inf* coterie f ▶ **to be in with the in-crowd** être branché.

incrust [ɪn'krʌst] = **encrust**.

incubate ['ɪnkjʊbeɪt] ◆ vt **1.** BIOL [eggs - subj: bird] couver ; [- subj: fish] incuber **2.** *fig* [in incubator] incuber **2.** *fig* [plot, idea] couver. ◆ vi **1.** BIOL [egg] être en incubation **2.** MED [virus] incuber **3.** *fig* [plan, idea] couver.

incubation [ˌɪnkjʊ'beɪʃn] n [of egg, virus, disease] incubation f ▶ **incubation period** (période f d')incubation.

incubator ['ɪnkjʊbeɪtə'] n [for premature baby] couveuse f, incubateur m ; [for eggs, bacteria] incubateur m.

inculcate ['ɪnkʌlkeɪt] vt inculquer ▶ **to inculcate sb with an idea** or **to inculcate an idea in sb** inculquer une idée à qqn.

incumbent [ɪn'kʌmbənt] ◆ adj fml **1.** [obligatory] : *it is incumbent on* or *upon the manager to check the tak-*

ings il incombe or il appartient au directeur de vérifier la recette **2.** [in office] en fonction, en exercice. ◆ n [office holder] titulaire mf.

incur [ɪn'kɜː'] (pt & pp **incurred**, cont **incurring**) vt [blame, loss, penalty] s'exposer à, encourir ; [debt] contracter ; [losses] subir.

incurable [ɪn'kjʊərəbl] adj [illness] incurable, inguérissable ; *fig* [optimist] inguérissable, infatigable.

incurably [ɪn'kjʊərəblɪ] adv : *to be incurably ill* avoir une maladie incurable / *to be incurably lazy* *fig* être irrémédiablement paresseux.

incursion [UK ɪn'kɜːʃn US ɪn'kɜːʒn] n incursion f.

indebted [ɪn'detɪd] adj **1.** [for help] redevable ▶ **to be indebted to sb for sthg** : *I am greatly indebted to you for doing me this favour* je vous suis extrêmement reconnaissant de m'avoir rendu ce service **2.** [owing money] endetté.

indecency [ɪn'diːsnsɪ] (pl **indecencies**) n [gen] indécence f ; LAW attentat m à la pudeur ▶ **gross indecency** outrage m à la pudeur.

indecent [ɪn'diːsnt] adj **1.** [obscene] indécent **2.** [unseemly] indécent, inconvenant, déplacé.

indecent assault n attentat m à la pudeur.

indecent exposure n outrage m public à la pudeur.

indecently [ɪn'diːsntlɪ] adv indécemment.

indecipherable [ˌɪndɪ'saɪfərəbl] adj indéchiffrable.

indecision [ˌɪndɪ'sɪʒn] n indécision f.

indecisive [ˌɪndɪ'saɪsɪv] adj **1.** [hesitating - person] indécis, irrésolu **2.** [inconclusive] peu concluant.

indecisively [ˌɪndɪ'saɪsɪvlɪ] adv **1.** [hesitatingly] de manière indécise, avec hésitation **2.** [inconclusively] de manière peu convaincante or concluante.

indeed [ɪn'diːd] adv **1.** [used to confirm] effectivement, en effet / *we are aware of the problem; indeed, we are already investigating it* nous sommes conscients du problème ; en fait, nous sommes déjà en train de l'étudier **2.** [used to qualify] : *the problem, if indeed there is one, is theirs* c'est leur problème, si problème il y a **3.** [used as intensifier] vraiment / *thank you very much indeed* merci beaucoup / *that's praise indeed!* ça, c'est un compliment !, voilà ce qui s'appelle un compliment ! **4.** [as surprised, ironic response] : *he asked us for a pay rise — indeed!* il nous a demandé une augmentation — eh bien ! or vraiment ?

indefatigable [ˌɪndɪ'fætɪgəbl] adj infatigable.

indefatigably [ˌɪndɪ'fætɪgəblɪ] adv infatigablement, sans se fatiguer, inlassablement.

indefensible [ˌɪndɪ'fensəbl] adj **1.** [conduct] injustifiable, inexcusable ; [argument] insoutenable, indéfendable **2.** MIL indéfendable.

indefinable [ˌɪndɪ'faɪnəbl] adj indéfinissable.

indefinite [ɪn'defɪnɪt] adj [indeterminate] indéterminé, illimité / *for an indefinite period* pour une période indéterminée ; [vague, imprecise] flou, peu précis.

indefinite article n article m indéfini.

indefinitely [ɪn'defɪnətlɪ] adv **1.** [without limit] indéfiniment **2.** [imprecisely] vaguement.

indelible [ɪn'deləbl] adj [ink, stain] indélébile ▶ [memory] impérissable.

indelibly [ɪn'deləblɪ] adv de manière indélébile.

indelicate [ɪn'delɪkət] adj [action] déplacé, indélicat ; [person, remark] indélicat, qui manque de tact.

indemnify [ɪn'demnɪfaɪ] (pt & pp **indemnified**) vt **1.** [compensate] indemniser, dédommager ▶ **to be indem-**

nified for sthg être indemnisé or dédommagé de qqch **2.** [insure] assurer, garantir ▸ **to be indemnified for** or **against sthg** être assuré contre qqch.

indemnity [ın'demnətı] (*pl* **indemnities**) n **1.** [compensation] indemnité *f*, dédommagement *m* **2.** [insurance] assurance *f* **3.** [exemption - from prosecution] immunité *f*.

indent ◆ vt [ın'dent] **1.** [line of text] mettre en retrait **2.** [edge] denteler, découper ; [more deeply] échancrer **3.** [surface] marquer, faire une empreinte dans **4.** 🇬🇧 COMM [goods] commander. ◆ vi [ın'dent] [at start of paragraph] faire un alinéa.

indentation [ˌınden'teıʃn] n **1.** [in line of text] renfoncement *m* **2.** [in edge] dentelure *f* ; [deeper] échancrure *f* ; [in coastline] découpure *f* **3.** [on surface] empreinte *f*.

independence [ˌındı'pendəns] n [gen & POL] indépendance *f* ▸ **the (American) War of Independence** la guerre d'Indépendance (américaine).

🏛 **The American War of Independence**

Guerre d'indépendance des 13 colonies de la Nouvelle-Angleterre, en réaction à la dureté de l'administration britannique qui leur imposait de lourdes taxes. Marqué par la Déclaration d'indépendance du 4 juillet 1776, le conflit dura sept ans; la République fédérée des États-Unis fut reconnue en 1783 au traité de Paris.

Independence Day n fête *f* nationale de l'Indépendance *(aux États-Unis)*.

independent [ˌındı'pendənt] ◆ adj **1.** indépendant **2.** GRAM, PHILOS & MATH indépendant. ◆ n **1.** [gen] indépendant *m*, -e *f* ▸ **The Independent** PRESS quotidien britannique de qualité sans affiliation politique particulière — **broadsheet 2.** POL indépendant *m*, -e *f*, non-inscrit *m*, -e *f*.

independently [ˌındı'pendəntlı] adv de manière indépendante, de manière autonome ▸ **independently of** indépendamment de.

independent school n 🇬🇧 école *f* privée.

in-depth adj en profondeur.

indescribable [ˌındı'skraıbəbl] adj indescriptible.

indescribably [ˌındı'skraıbəblı] adv incroyablement.

indestructible [ˌındı'strʌktəbl] adj indestructible.

indeterminate [ˌındı'tɜːmınət] adj **1.** [undetermined, indefinite] indéterminé / *indeterminate sentence* peine *f* (de prison) de durée indéterminée **2.** [vague, imprecise] flou, vague **3.** LING, MATH & PHILOS indéterminé.

index ['ındeks] (*pl* **indexes** or **indices** [-dısı:z]) ◆ n **1.** (*pl* **indexes**) [in book, database] index *m* **2.** (*pl* **indexes**) [in library] catalogue *m*, répertoire *m* ; [on index cards] fichier *m* **3.** (*pl* **indexes**) [finger] index *m* **4.** (*pl* **indices** [-dısı:z]) ECON & PHYS indice *m* **5.** (*pl* **indices** [-dısı:z]) MATH [subscript] indice *m* ; [superscript] exposant *m*. ◆ vt **1.** [word, book, database] indexer **2.** ECON indexer ▸ **indexed to** indexé sur.

index card n fiche *f*.

index finger n index *m*.

index-linked adj 🇬🇧 indexé.

index page n index *m*, page *f* d'accueil.

India ['ındjə] pr n Inde *f* / *in India* en Inde.

India ink 🇺🇸 = **Indian ink.**

Indian ['ındjən] ◆ n [person - in America, Asia] Indien *m*, -enne *f*. ◆ adj [American or Asian] indien.

Indiana [ˌındı'ænə] pr n Indiana *m* / *in Indiana* dans l'Indiana.

Indian ink n 🇬🇧 encre *f* de Chine.

Indian Ocean pr n ▸ **the Indian Ocean** l'océan *m* Indien.

Indian summer n été *m* de la Saint-Martin, été *m* indien ; *fig* vieillesse *f* heureuse.

India rubber n 🇬🇧 [substance] caoutchouc *m* ; [eraser] gomme *f*.

indicate ['ındıkeıt] ◆ vt **1.** [show, point to] indiquer **2.** [make clear] signaler / *as I have already indicated* comme je l'ai déjà signalé or fait remarquer / *she indicated that the interview was over* elle a fait comprendre que l'entretien était terminé **3.** 🇬🇧 AUTO ▸ **to indicate (that one is turning) left** / **right** mettre son clignotant à gauche / à droite (pour tourner) **4.** [recommend, require] indiquer. ◆ vi 🇬🇧 AUTO mettre son clignotant.

indication [ˌındı'keıʃn] n **1.** [sign] indication *f* / *she gave no indication that she had seen me* rien ne pouvait laisser supposer qu'elle m'avait vu **2.** [act of indicating] indication *f*.

indicative [ın'dıkətıv] ◆ adj **1.** [symptomatic] indicatif ▸ **indicative of** : *his handwriting is indicative of his mental state* son écriture est révélatrice de son état mental **2.** GRAM indicatif ▸ **the indicative mood** le mode indicatif, l'indicatif *m*. ◆ n GRAM indicatif *m* / *in the indicative* à l'indicatif.

indicator ['ındıkeıtə^r] n **1.** [instrument] indicateur *m* ; [warning lamp] voyant *m* **2.** AUTO clignotant *m* **3.** [at station, in airport] ▸ **arrivals** / **departures indicator** panneau *m* des arrivées / des départs **4.** *fig* indicateur *m*.

indices [-dısı:z] pl —→ **index.**

indict [ın'daıt] vt LAW inculper, mettre en examen *spec.*

indictable [ın'daıtəbl] adj LAW **1.** [person] passible de poursuites **2.** [crime] passible des tribunaux.

indictment [ın'daıtmənt] n **1.** LAW inculpation *f*, mise *f* en examen *spec* **2.** *fig* : *a damning indictment of government policy* un témoignage accablant contre la politique gouvernementale.

indie ['ındı] adj *inf* [band, charts] indépendant *(dont les disques sont produits par des maisons indépendantes).*

indifference [ın'dıfrəns] n **1.** [unconcern] indifférence *f* ▸ **indifference towards** manque *m* d'intérêt pour **2.** [mediocrity] médiocrité *f* **3.** [unimportance] insignifiance *f* **4.** PHILOS indifférence *f*.

indifferent [ın'dıfrənt] adj **1.** [unconcerned, cold] indifférent **2.** [unimportant] indifférent / *it's indifferent to me whether they go or stay* qu'ils partent ou qu'ils restent, cela m'est égal or indifférent **3.** [mediocre] médiocre, quelconque.

indigenous [ın'dıdʒınəs] adj [animal, plant, custom] indigène ; [population] autochtone.

indigestible [ˌındı'dʒestəbl] adj indigeste.

indigestion [ˌındı'dʒestʃn] n (U) indigestion *f*.

indignant [ın'dıgnənt] adj indigné, outré / *he was indignant at her attitude* il était indigné par son attitude.

indignantly [ın'dıgnəntlı] adv avec indignation.

indignation [ˌındıg'neıʃn] n indignation *f*.

indignity [ın'dıgnətı] (*pl* **indignities**) n indignité *f*.

indigo ['ındıgəʊ] (*pl* **indigos** or **indigoes**) ◆ n **1.** [dye, colour] indigo *m* **2.** [plant] indigotier *m*. ◆ adj indigo *(inv)*.

indirect [ˌındı'rekt] adj indirect.

indirect costs pl n coûts *mpl* indirects.

indirect discourse 🇺🇸, **indirect speech** 🇬🇧 n discours *m* indirect.

indirect lighting n éclairage *m* indirect.

indirectly [ˌɪndɪˈrektlɪ] adv indirectement.

indirect object n objet *m* indirect.

indirect speech n discours *m* indirect.

indirect tax n impôts *mpl* indirects.

indirect taxation n fiscalité *f* indirecte.

indiscernible [ˌɪndɪˈsɜːnəbl] adj indiscernable, imperceptible.

indiscreet [ˌɪndɪˈskriːt] adj indiscret (indiscrète).

indiscreetly [ˌɪndɪˈskriːtlɪ] adv indiscrètement.

indiscretion [ˌɪndɪˈskreʃn] n indiscrétion *f*.

indiscriminate [ˌɪndɪˈskrɪmɪnət] adj : *it was indiscriminate slaughter* ce fut un massacre aveugle / *children are indiscriminate in their television viewing* les enfants regardent la télévision sans discernement.

indiscriminately [ˌɪndɪˈskrɪmɪnətlɪ] adv : *he reads indiscriminately* il lit tout ce qui lui tombe sous la main.

indispensable [ˌɪndɪˈspensəbl] adj indispensable ▶ **indispensable to** indispensable à or pour.

indisposed [ˌɪndɪˈspəʊzd] adj *fml* **1.** *euph* [sick] indisposé, souffrant **2.** [unwilling] peu enclin, peu disposé ▶ **to be indisposed to do sthg** être peu enclin or peu disposé à faire qqch.

indisputable [ˌɪndɪˈspjuːtəbl] adj incontestable, indiscutable.

indisputably [ˌɪndɪˈspjuːtəblɪ] adv incontestablement, indiscutablement.

indistinct [ˌɪndɪˈstɪŋkt] adj indistinct.

indistinctly [ˌɪndɪˈstɪŋktlɪ] adv indistinctement.

indistinguishable [ˌɪndɪˈstɪŋgwɪʃəbl] adj **1.** [alike] impossible à distinguer **2.** [imperceptible] imperceptible.

individual [ˌɪndɪˈvɪdʒʊəl] ◆ adj **1.** [for one person] individuel **2.** [single, separate] particulier **3.** [distinctive] personnel, particulier. ◆ n [gen & BIOL & LOGIC] individu *m*.

individualism [ˌɪndɪˈvɪdʒʊəlɪzm] n [gen & PHILOS & POL] individualisme *m*.

individualist [ˌɪndɪˈvɪdʒʊəlɪst] n individualiste *mf*.

individualistic [ˈɪndɪˌvɪdʒʊəˈlɪstɪk] adj individualiste.

individuality [ˈɪndɪˌvɪdʒʊˈælətɪ] (*pl* **individualities**) n individualité *f*.

individually [ˌɪndɪˈvɪdʒʊəlɪ] adv **1.** [separately] individuellement **2.** [distinctively] de façon distinctive.

indivisible [ˌɪndɪˈvɪzəbl] adj indivisible.

Indochina [ˌɪndəʊˈtʃaɪnə] pr n Indochine *f* / *in Indochina* en Indochine.

indoctrinate [ɪnˈdɒktrɪneɪt] vt endoctriner.

indoctrination [ɪnˌdɒktrɪˈneɪʃn] n endoctrinement *m*.

indolence [ˈɪndələns] n [laziness] paresse *f*, indolence *f*.

indolent [ˈɪndələnt] adj [lazy] paresseux, indolent.

indomitable [ɪnˈdɒmɪtəbl] adj indomptable, irréductible.

Indonesia [ˌɪndəˈniːzjə] pr n Indonésie *f* / *in Indonesia* en Indonésie.

Indonesian [ˌɪndəˈniːzjən] ◆ n **1.** [person] Indonésien *m*, -enne *f* **2.** LING indonésien *m*. ◆ adj indonésien.

indoor [ˈɪndɔːr] adj [toilet] à l'intérieur ; [clothing] d'intérieur ; [swimming pool, tennis court] couvert ; [sport] pratiqué en salle.

indoors [ˌɪnˈdɔːz] adv à l'intérieur / *I don't like being indoors all day* je n'aime pas rester enfermée toute la journée.

indubitably [ɪnˈdjuːbɪtəblɪ] adv assurément, indubitablement.

induce [ɪnˈdjuːs] vt **1.** [cause] entraîner, provoquer **2.** [persuade] persuader, décider / *nothing will induce me to change my mind* rien ne me décidera à or ne me fera changer d'avis **3.** MED [labour] déclencher (artificiellement) / *she was induced* son accouchement a été provoqué.

-induced [ɪnˈdjuːst] in comp ▶ **work-induced injury** accident *m* du travail ▶ **drug-induced sleep** sommeil *m* provoqué par des médicaments.

inducement [ɪnˈdjuːsmənt] n **1.** [encouragement] persuasion *f* **2.** [reward] incitation *f*, récompense *f* ; [bribe] pot-de-vin *m*.

induction [ɪnˈdʌkʃn] n **1.** [into office, post] installation *f* ; [into mystery, new field] initiation *f* **2.** [causing] provocation *f*, déclenchement *m* **3.** MED [of labour] déclenchement *m* (artificiel) **4.** PHILOS induction *f* **5.** 🇺🇸 MIL conscription *f*, appel *m* sous les drapeaux **6.** BIOL, ELEC & TECH induction *f*.

induction course n stage *m* préparatoire or de formation.

induction hob n plaque *f* de cuisson à induction.

indulge [ɪnˈdʌldʒ] ◆ vi ▶ **to indulge in** se livrer à. ◆ vt **1.** [person] gâter ▶ **to indulge o.s.** se faire plaisir **2.** [desire, vice] assouvir / *he indulges her every whim* il se prête à or il lui passe tous ses caprices.

indulgence [ɪnˈdʌldʒəns] n **1.** [tolerance, kindness] indulgence *f* **2.** [gratification] assouvissement *m* **3.** [privilege] privilège *m* ; [treat] gâterie *f*.

indulgent [ɪnˈdʌldʒənt] adj [liberal, kind] indulgent, complaisant.

industrial [ɪnˈdʌstrɪəl] adj [gen] industriel ; [unrest] social ▶ **industrial accident** accident *m* du travail ▶ **industrial diamond** diamant *m* industriel or de nature ▶ **industrial dispute** conflit *m* social ▶ **industrial espionage** espionnage *m* industriel ▶ **industrial injury** accident *m* du travail ▶ **the Industrial Revolution** la révolution industrielle.

🏛 **The Industrial Revolution**

Processus d'industrialisation qui, au XVIIIᵉ siècle, apporta de profonds changements dans la société britannique en bouleversant ses structures et son fonctionnement traditionnel. Si la richesse nationale augmenta rapidement, apportant à la Grande-Bretagne un rayonnement économique mondial, elle fut synonyme de misère pour la classe ouvrière jusqu'au XXᵉ siècle.

industrial action 🇬🇧, **job action** 🇺🇸 n (U) grève *f*, grèves *fpl* ▶ **to take industrial action** 🇬🇧 se mettre en grève.

industrial estate n 🇬🇧 zone *f* industrielle.

industrialist [ɪnˈdʌstrɪəlɪst] n industriel *m*.

industrialization, industrialisation [ɪnˌdʌstrɪəlaɪˈzeɪʃn] n industrialisation *f*.

industrialize, industrialise [ɪnˈdʌstrɪəlaɪz] ◆ vt industrialiser. ◆ vi s'industrialiser.

industrialized, industrialised [ɪnˈdʌstrɪəlaɪzd] adj industrialisé.

industrial park 🇺🇸 = industrial estate.

industrial relations pl n relations *fpl* entre le patronat et les travailleurs.

industrial-strength adj [adhesive, bleach, etc.] à usage industriel ; *hum* [coffee] hyper-costaud.

industrial tribunal n ≃ conseil *m* de prud'hommes.

industrious [ɪnˈdʌstrɪəs] adj travailleur.

industriously [ɪnˈdʌstrɪəslɪ] adv avec application, industrieusement *liter*.

industry [ˈɪndʌstrɪ] (*pl* **industries**) n **1.** [business] industrie *f* **2.** application *f*, diligence *f*.

industry-standard adj normalisé.

inebriated [ɪˈniːbrɪeɪtɪd] adj *fml* ivre.

inedible [ɪnˈedɪbl] adj **1.** [unsafe to eat] non comestible **2.** [unpleasant to eat] immangeable.

ineffective [ˌɪnɪˈfektɪv] adj **1.** [person] inefficace, incapable, incompétent **2.** [action] inefficace, sans effet.

ineffectual [ˌɪnɪˈfektʃʊəl] adj incompétent.

inefficiency [ˌɪnɪˈfɪʃnsɪ] (*pl* **inefficiencies**) n inefficacité *f*, manque *m* d'efficacité.

inefficient [ˌɪnɪˈfɪʃnt] adj inefficace.

inefficiently [ˌɪnɪˈfɪʃntlɪ] adv inefficacement.

inelegant [ɪnˈelɪgənt] adj inélégant.

inelegantly [ɪnˈelɪgəntlɪ] adv de façon peu élégante.

ineligibility [ɪnˌelɪdʒəˈbɪlətɪ] n **1.** [gen] : *his ineligibility for unemployment benefit* le fait qu'il n'ait pas droit aux allocations de chômage **2.** [for election] inéligibilité *f*.

ineligible [ɪnˈelɪdʒəbl] adj **1.** [unqualified] non qualifié / *to be ineligible for military service* être inapte au service militaire / *they are ineligible to vote* ils n'ont pas le droit de voter **2.** [for election] inéligible.

inept [ɪˈnept] adj inepte.

ineptitude [ɪˈneptɪtjuːd] n ineptie *f*.

inequality [ˌɪnɪˈkwɒlətɪ] (*pl* **inequalities**) n inégalité *f*.

inequitable [ɪnˈekwɪtəbl] adj inéquitable.

inert [ɪˈnɜːt] adj inerte.

inertia [ɪˈnɜːʃə] n inertie *f*.

inertia-reel seat belt n ceinture *f* de sécurité à enrouleur.

inertia selling n *(U)* 🇬🇧 vente *f* forcée.

inescapable [ˌɪnɪˈskeɪpəbl] adj [outcome] inévitable, inéluctable ; [fact] indéniable.

inessential [ˌɪnɪˈsenʃl] adj non essentiel.

inestimable [ɪnˈestɪməbl] adj inestimable, incalculable.

inevitability [ɪnˌevɪtəˈbɪlətɪ] n inévitabilité *f*.

inevitable [ɪnˈevɪtəbl] ◆ adj [outcome, consequence] inévitable, inéluctable ; [end] inévitable, fatal / *it's inevitable that someone will feel left out* il est inévitable ou on ne pourra empêcher que quelqu'un se sente exclu. ◆ n inévitable *m*.

> 📋 Note that **inévitable que** is followed by a verb in the subjunctive:
> **It's inevitable that he'll hold it against you.**
> *Il est inévitable qu'il t'en tienne rigueur.*

inevitably [ɪnˈevɪtəblɪ] adv inévitablement, fatalement.

inexact [ˌɪnɪgˈzækt] adj [imprecise] imprécis ; [wrong] inexact, erroné.

inexcusable [ˌɪnɪkˈskjuːzəbl] adj inexcusable, impardonnable.

inexhaustible [ˌɪnɪgˈzɔːstəbl] adj **1.** [source, energy, patience] inépuisable, illimité **2.** [person] infatigable.

inexorable [ɪnˈeksərəbl] adj inexorable.

inexorably [ɪnˈeksərəblɪ] adv inexorablement.

inexpensive [ˌɪnɪkˈspensɪv] adj bon marché *(inv)*, peu cher.

inexpensively [ˌɪnɪkˈspensɪvlɪ] adv [sell] (à) bon marché, à bas prix ; [live] à peu de frais.

inexperience [ˌɪnɪkˈspɪərɪəns] n inexpérience *f*, manque *m* d'expérience.

inexperienced [ˌɪnɪkˈspɪərɪənst] adj inexpérimenté.

inexplicable [ˌɪnɪkˈsplɪkəbl] adj inexplicable.

inexplicably [ˌɪnɪkˈsplɪkəblɪ] adv inexplicablement.

inexpressible [ˌɪnɪkˈspresəbl] adj inexprimable, indicible.

inextricably [ˌɪnɪkˈstrɪkəblɪ] adv inextricablement.

infallibility [ɪnˌfæləˈbɪlətɪ] n infaillibilité *f*.

infallible [ɪnˈfæləbl] adj infaillible.

infamous [ˈɪnfəməs] adj **1.** [notorious] tristement célèbre, notoire **2.** [shocking - conduct] déshonorant, infamant.

infancy [ˈɪnfənsɪ] (*pl* **infancies**) n **1.** [early childhood] petite enfance *f* **2.** *fig* débuts *mpl*, enfance *f* / *when electronics was still in its infancy* quand l'électronique n'en était qu'à ses balbutiements.

infant [ˈɪnfənt] ◆ n **1.** [young child] petit enfant *m*, petite enfant *f*, enfant *mf* en bas âge ; [baby] bébé *m* ; [newborn] nouveau-né *m* **2.** 🇬🇧 SCH élève *dans les premières années d'école primaire*. ◆ comp **1.** [food] pour bébés ; [disease] infantile ▸ **infant mortality rate** taux *m* de mortalité infantile **2.** 🇬🇧 [teacher, teaching] des premières années d'école primaire.

infanticide [ɪnˈfæntɪsaɪd] n **1.** [act] infanticide *m* **2.** [person] infanticide *mf*.

infantile [ˈɪnfəntaɪl] adj **1.** *pej* [childish] infantile, puéril **2.** [of, for infants] infantile.

infantry [ˈɪnfəntrɪ] ◆ n infanterie *f*. ◆ adj de l'infanterie.

infant school n 🇬🇧 école *f* maternelle *(5-7 ans)*.

infatuate [ɪnˈfætjʊeɪt] vt : *he was infatuated with her* il s'était entiché d'elle.

infatuation [ɪnˌfætjʊˈeɪʃn] n engouement *m* / *his infatuation for* or *with her* son engouement pour elle.

infect [ɪnˈfekt] vt **1.** MED [wound, organ, person, animal] infecter ▸ **to infect sb with sthg** transmettre qqch à qqn **2.** [food, water] contaminer.

infected [ɪnˈfektɪd] adj [wound] infecté ; [area] contaminé.

infection [ɪnˈfekʃn] n **1.** MED infection *f* / *a throat infection* une infection de la gorge, une angine **2.** *fig* contagion *f*, contamination *f*.

infectious [ɪnˈfekʃəs] adj **1.** MED [disease] infectieux ; [person] contagieux **2.** *fig* contagieux, communicatif.

infer [ɪnˈfɜːr] (*pt & pp* **inferred**, *cont* **inferring**) vt **1.** [deduce] conclure, inférer, déduire **2.** [imply] suggérer, laisser supposer.

inference [ˈɪnfrəns] n déduction *f*.

inferior [ɪnˈfɪərɪər] ◆ adj **1.** [quality, worth, social status] inférieur **2.** [in rank] subalterne **3.** ANAT & SCI [in space, position] inférieur. ◆ n [in social status] inférieur *m*, -e *f* ; [in rank, hierarchy] subalterne *mf*, subordonné *m*, -e *f*.

inferiority [ɪnˌfɪərɪˈɒrətɪ] (*pl* **inferiorities**) n infériorité *f*.

inferiority complex n complexe *m* d'infériorité.

infernal [ɪnˈfɜːnl] adj **1.** *inf* [awful] infernal **2.** [of hell] infernal ; [diabolical] infernal, diabolique.

inferno [ɪnˈfɜːnəʊ] (*pl* **infernos**) n **1.** [fire] brasier *m* **2.** [hell] enfer *m*.

infertile [ɪnˈfɜːtaɪl] adj [person, animal] stérile ; [land, soil] stérile, infertile *liter*.

infertility [ˌɪnfə'tɪlətɪ] n stérilité f, infertilité f liter.

infest [ɪn'fest] vt infester ▸ **infested with** infesté de.

infestation [ˌɪnfe'steɪʃn] n infestation f.

infidelity [ˌɪnfɪ'delətɪ] (pl **infidelities**) n [betrayal] infidélité f.

infighting ['ɪnˌfaɪtɪŋ] n (U) **1.** 🇬🇧 [within group] conflits mpl internes, luttes fpl intestines **2.** [in boxing] corps à corps m.

infiltrate ['ɪnfɪltreɪt] ◆ vt **1.** [organization] infiltrer, noyauter **2.** [subj: liquid] s'infiltrer dans. ◆ vi s'infiltrer.

infiltration [ˌɪnfɪl'treɪʃn] n **1.** [of group] infiltration f, noyautage m **2.** [by liquid] infiltration f.

infiltrator ['ɪnfɪltreɪtər] n agent m infiltré.

infinite ['ɪnfɪnət] ◆ adj **1.** [not finite] infini **2.** fig [very great] infini, incalculable / he showed infinite patience il a fait preuve d'une patience infinie / the government, in its infinite wisdom, has decided to close the factory iro le gouvernement, dans son infinie sagesse, a décidé de fermer l'usine. ◆ n infini m.

infinitely ['ɪnfɪnətlɪ] adv infiniment.

infinitesimal [ˌɪnfɪnɪ'tesɪml] adj **1.** MATH infinitésimal **2.** [tiny] infinitésimal, infime.

infinitive [ɪn'fɪnɪtɪv] ◆ n infinitif m. ◆ adj infinitif.

infinity [ɪn'fɪnətɪ] (pl **infinities**) n **1.** infinité f, infini m **2.** MATH & PHOT infini m.

infinity pool n piscine f à débordement.

infirm [ɪn'fɜːm] ◆ adj [in health, body] invalide, infirme. ◆ pl n ▸ **the infirm** les infirmes mpl.

infirmary [ɪn'fɜːmərɪ] (pl **infirmaries**) n [hospital] hôpital m, dispensaire m ; [sickroom] infirmerie f.

infirmity [ɪn'fɜːmətɪ] (pl **infirmities**) n **1.** [physical] infirmité f **2.** [moral] défaut m, faiblesse f.

inflamed [ɪn'fleɪmd] adj **1.** MED [eyes, throat, tendon] enflammé, irrité **2.** fig [passions, hatred] enflammé, ardent.

inflammable [ɪn'flæməbl] adj inflammable.

inflammation [ˌɪnflə'meɪʃn] n inflammation f.

inflammatory [ɪn'flæmətrɪ] adj **1.** [speech, propaganda] incendiaire **2.** MED inflammatoire.

inflatable [ɪn'fleɪtəbl] ◆ adj [toy] gonflable ; [mattress, boat] pneumatique. ◆ n structure f gonflable.

inflate [ɪn'fleɪt] ◆ vt **1.** [tyre, balloon, boat] gonfler ; [lungs] emplir d'air ; [chest] gonfler, bomber **2.** [opinion, importance] gonfler, exagérer **3.** ECON [prices] faire monter, augmenter ; [economy] provoquer l'inflation de. ◆ vi **1.** [tyre] se gonfler ; [lungs] s'emplir d'air ; [chest] se gonfler, se bomber **2.** ECON [prices, money] subir une inflation.

inflated [ɪn'fleɪtɪd] adj **1.** [tyre] gonflé **2.** [opinion, importance] exagéré ; [style] emphatique, pompier **3.** [price] exagéré.

inflation [ɪn'fleɪʃn] n **1.** ECON inflation f **2.** [of tyre, balloon, boat] gonflement m ; [of idea, importance] grossissement m, exagération f.

inflationary [ɪn'fleɪʃnrɪ] adj inflationniste.

inflation-proof adj protégé contre les effets de l'inflation.

inflation rate n taux m d'inflation.

inflect [ɪn'flekt] ◆ vt **1.** LING [verb] conjuguer ; [noun, pronoun, adjective] décliner ▸ **inflected form** forme f fléchie **2.** [tone, voice] moduler **3.** [curve] infléchir. ◆ vi LING : adjectives do not inflect in English les adjectifs ne prennent pas de désinence en anglais.

inflection [ɪn'flekʃn] n **1.** [of tone, voice] inflexion f, modulation f **2.** LING désinence f, flexion f **3.** [curve] flexion f, inflexion f, courbure f **4.** MATH inflexion f.

inflexibility [ɪnˌfleksə'bɪlətɪ] n inflexibilité f, rigidité f.

inflexible [ɪn'fleksəbl] adj inflexible, rigide.

inflict [ɪn'flɪkt] vt infliger.

infliction [ɪn'flɪkʃən] n [action] action f d'infliger.

in-flight adj en vol ▸ **in-flight meal** plateau-repas m.

inflow ['ɪnfləʊ] n [of water, gas] arrivée f, afflux m.

influence ['ɪnfluəns] ◆ n influence f ▸ **to bring one's influence to bear on sthg** exercer son influence sur qqch / he is a man of influence c'est un homme influent / he is a bad influence on them il a une mauvaise influence sur eux / they acted under his influence ils ont agi sous son influence / she was under the influence of drink / drugs elle était sous l'emprise de l'alcool / de la drogue ▸ **to be under the influence** inf [drunk] être soûl. ◆ vt influencer, influer sur / don't let yourself be influenced by them ne te laisse pas influencer par eux / he is easily influenced il se laisse facilement influencer, il est très influençable.

influential [ˌɪnflu'enʃl] adj influent, puissant ; [newspaper, TV programme] influent, qui a de l'influence.

influenza [ˌɪnflu'enzə] n (U) fml grippe f.

influx ['ɪnflʌks] n **1.** [inflow] afflux m **2.** [of river] embouchure f.

info ['ɪnfəʊ] n (U) inf tuyaux mpl.

infomercial [ˌɪnfəʊ'mɜːʃl] n 🇺🇸 publicité télévisée sous forme de débat sur l'annonceur et son produit.

inform [ɪn'fɔːm] ◆ vt **1.** [give information to] informer **2.** [influence] influencer. ◆ vi ▸ **to inform on** or **against sb** dénoncer qqn.

informal [ɪn'fɔːml] adj **1.** [discussion, meeting] informel ; [dinner] décontracté **2.** [clothes] : his dress was informal il était habillé simplement **3.** [unofficial - arrangement, agreement] officieux ; [- visit, talks] non officiel **4.** [colloquial] familier.

⚠️ The French word **informel** is much more restricted in meaning than the English word informal, as the entry shows.

informality [ˌɪnfɔː'mælətɪ] (pl **informalities**) n **1.** [of gathering, meal] simplicité f ; [of discussion, interview] absence f de formalité ; [of manners] naturel m **2.** [of expression, language] familiarité f, liberté f.

informally [ɪn'fɔːməlɪ] adv **1.** [casually - entertain, discuss] sans cérémonie ; [- behave] simplement, avec naturel ; [- dress] simplement **2.** [unofficially] officieusement **3.** [colloquially] familièrement, avec familiarité.

informant [ɪn'fɔːmənt] n [gen & SOCIOL & LING] informateur m, -trice f.

information [ˌɪnfə'meɪʃn] n **1.** (U) [facts] renseignements mpl, informations fpl / a piece or bit of information un renseignement, une information / do you have any information on or about the new model? avez-vous des renseignements concernant or sur le nouveau modèle ? **2.** [communication] information f **3.** (U) [knowledge] connaissances fpl / for your information, please find enclosed... ADMIN à titre d'information, vous trouverez ci-joint... **4.** COMPUT & SCI information f **5.** (U) [service, department] (service m des) renseignements mpl / to call information 🇺🇸 appeler les renseignements.

information bureau 🇬🇧, **information office** n bureau m or service m des renseignements.

information highway, information superhighway n autoroute f de l'information.

information retrieval n recherche f documentaire ; COMPUT recherche f d'information.

information scientist n informaticien m, -enne f.

information superhighway = information highway.

information system n système m d'information.

information technology n technologie f de l'information, informatique f.

informative [ɪnˈfɔːmətɪv] adj [lecture, book, TV programme] instructif ; [person] : *he wasn't very informative about his future plans* il ne nous a pas dit grand-chose de ses projets.

informed [ɪnˈfɔːmd] adj **1.** [having information] informé, renseigné / *according to informed sources* selon des sources bien informées **2.** [based on information] : *an informed choice* un choix fait en toute connaissance de cause / *he made an informed guess* il a essayé de deviner en s'aidant de ce qu'il sait.

informer [ɪnˈfɔːməʳ] n [denouncer] informateur m ▶ **police informer** indicateur m (de police).

infotainment [ˈɪnfəʊteɪnmənt] n info-divertissement m.

infrared [ˌɪnfrəˈred] ◆ adj infrarouge. ◆ n infrarouge m.

infrastructure [ˈɪnfrəˌstrʌktʃəʳ] n infrastructure f.

infrequent [ɪnˈfriːkwənt] adj [event] peu fréquent, rare ; [visitor] épisodique.

infrequently [ɪnˈfriːkwəntlɪ] adv rarement, peu souvent.

infringe [ɪnˈfrɪndʒ] ◆ vt [agreement, rights] violer, enfreindre ; [law] enfreindre, contrevenir à ; [patent] contrefaire. ◆ vi ▶ **to infringe on** or **upon** empiéter sur.

infringement [ɪnˈfrɪndʒmənt] n [violation] infraction f, atteinte f ; [encroachment] empiètement m.

infuriate [ɪnˈfjʊərɪeɪt] vt [enrage] rendre furieux ; [exasperate] exaspérer.

infuriating [ɪnˈfjʊərɪeɪtɪŋ] adj agaçant, exaspérant.

infuriatingly [ɪnˈfjʊərɪeɪtɪŋlɪ] adv : *infuriatingly stubborn* d'un entêtement exaspérant.

infuse [ɪnˈfjuːz] ◆ vt **1.** [inspire] inspirer, insuffler, infuser *liter* ▶ **to infuse sb with sthg, to infuse sthg into sb** inspirer or insuffler qqch à qqn **2.** CULIN (faire) infuser. ◆ vi CULIN infuser.

infusion [ɪnˈfjuːʒn] n infusion f.

ingenious [ɪnˈdʒiːnjəs] adj [person, idea, device] ingénieux, astucieux.

ingeniously [ɪnˈdʒiːnjəslɪ] adv ingénieusement.

ingenuity [ˌɪndʒɪˈnjuːətɪ] (pl **ingenuities**) n ingéniosité f.

ingenuous [ɪnˈdʒenjʊəs] adj [naive] ingénu ; [frank] candide.

ingest [ɪnˈdʒest] vt [food, liquid] ingérer.

ingot [ˈɪŋgət] n lingot m.

ingrained [ˌɪnˈgreɪnd] adj [attitude, fear, prejudice] enraciné, inébranlable ; [habit] invétéré, tenace ; [belief] inébranlable ▶ **ingrained dirt** crasse f.

ingratiate [ɪnˈgreɪʃɪeɪt] vt ▶ **to ingratiate o.s. with sb** s'insinuer dans les bonnes grâces de qqn.

ingratiating [ɪnˈgreɪʃɪeɪtɪŋ] adj [manners, person] insinuant ; [smile] mielleux.

ingratitude [ɪnˈgrætɪtjuːd] n ingratitude f.

ingredient [ɪnˈgriːdjənt] n **1.** CULIN ingrédient m **2.** [element] élément m, ingrédient m liter.

ingrowing toenail [ˈɪnˌgrəʊɪŋ-] n 🇬🇧 ongle m incarné.

ingrown [ˈɪnˌgrəʊn] adj **1.** [toenail] incarné **2.** [ingrained -habit] enraciné, tenace.

inhabit [ɪnˈhæbɪt] vt habiter.

inhabitant [ɪnˈhæbɪtənt] n habitant m, -e f.

inhalation [ˌɪnhəˈleɪʃn] n **1.** [of air] inspiration f **2.** [of gas, glue] inhalation f.

inhalator [ˈɪnhəleɪtəʳ] n inhalateur m.

inhale [ɪnˈheɪl] ◆ vt [fumes, gas] inhaler ; [fresh air, scent] respirer ; [smoke] avaler. ◆ vi [smoker] avaler la fumée ; [breathe in] aspirer.

inhaler [ɪnˈheɪləʳ] = **inhalator**.

inherent [ɪnˈhɪərənt or ɪnˈherənt] adj inhérent ▶ **inherent in** or **to** inhérent à.

inherently [ɪnˈhɪərəntlɪ or ɪnˈherəntlɪ] adv intrinsèquement, par nature.

inherit [ɪnˈherɪt] ◆ vt **1.** [property, right] hériter (de) ; [title, peerage] accéder à **2.** [situation, tradition, attitude] hériter ; [characteristic, feature] hériter (de). ◆ vi hériter.

inheritance [ɪnˈherɪtəns] n **1.** [legacy] héritage m **2.** [succession] succession f **3.** SCI hérédité f / *genetic inheritance does not explain this phenomenon* ce phénomène ne peut s'expliquer par l'héritage génétique **4.** [heritage] héritage m, patrimoine m / *our cultural inheritance* notre héritage culturel.

inherited [ɪnˈherɪtɪd] adj [disease, defect] héréditaire ; [gene] hérité.

inhibit [ɪnˈhɪbɪt] vt **1.** [hinder -person, freedom] gêner, entraver **2.** [check -growth, development] freiner, entraver **3.** [suppress -desires, emotions] inhiber, refouler ; PSYCHOL inhiber **4.** CHEM inhiber.

inhibited [ɪnˈhɪbɪtɪd] adj inhibé.

inhibiting [ɪnˈhɪbɪtɪŋ] adj inhibant.

inhibition [ˌɪnhɪˈbɪʃn] n [gen] inhibition f.

inhospitable [ˌɪnhɒˈspɪtəbl] adj **1.** [person] peu accueillant **2.** [weather] rude, rigoureux.

in-house ◆ adj interne (à une entreprise) ; [training] maison (inv). ◆ adv sur place.

inhuman [ɪnˈhjuːmən] adj [behaviour] inhumain, barbare ; [person, place, process] inhumain.

inhumane [ˌɪnhjuːˈmeɪn] adj cruel.

inhumanity [ˌɪnhjuːˈmænətɪ] (pl **inhumanities**) n **1.** [quality] inhumanité f, barbarie f, cruauté f **2.** [act] atrocité f, brutalité f.

inimitable [ɪˈnɪmɪtəbl] adj inimitable.

initial [ɪˈnɪʃl] (🇬🇧 pt & pp **initialled**, cont **initialling** ; 🇺🇸 pt & pp **initialed**, cont **initialing**) ◆ adj initial / *the project is still in its initial stages* le projet en est encore à ses débuts ▶ **initial letter** initiale f. ◆ n [letter] initiale f. ◆ vt [memo, page] parapher, parafer, signer de ses initiales.

initialize, initialise [ɪˈnɪʃəlaɪz] vt COMPUT initialiser.

initially [ɪˈnɪʃəlɪ] adv initialement, à l'origine.

initiate ◆ vt [ɪˈnɪʃɪeɪt] **1.** [talks, debate] amorcer, engager ; [policy] lancer ; [quarrel, reaction] provoquer, déclencher **2.** [person] initier ▶ **to initiate sb into sthg** initier qqn à qqch. ◆ n [ɪˈnɪʃɪət] initié m, -e f.

initiation [ɪˌnɪʃɪˈeɪʃn] ◆ n **1.** [start] commencement m, début m **2.** [of person] initiation f. ◆ comp ▶ **initiation ceremony** cérémonie f d'initiation.

initiative [ɪˈnɪʃətɪv] n **1.** [drive] initiative f ▶ **to act on one's own initiative** agir de sa propre initiative / *you'll have to use your initiative* vous devrez prendre des initiatives **2.** [first step] initiative f ▶ **to take the initiative** prendre l'initiative **3.** [lead] initiative f.

initiator [ɪˈnɪʃɪeɪtəʳ] n initiateur m, -trice f, instigateur m, -trice f.

inject [ɪnˈdʒekt] vt **1.** MED faire une piqûre de, injecter / *to inject sb with penicillin* faire une piqûre de pénicilline à qqn **2.** *fig* injecter / *they've injected billions of dollars into the economy* ils ont injecté des milliards de dollars dans l'économie.

injection [ɪn'dʒekʃn] n MED & *fig* injection f ▸ **to give sb an injection** MED faire une injection *or* une piqûre à qqn.

injunction [ɪn'dʒʌŋkʃn] n **1.** LAW ordonnance f ▸ **to take out an injunction against sb** mettre qqn en demeure **2.** [warning] injonction f, recommandation f formelle.

injure ['ɪndʒər] vt **1.** [physically] blesser / *he injured his knee skiing* il s'est blessé au genou en faisant du ski **2.** [damage - relationship, interests] nuire à **3.** [offend] blesser, offenser **4.** [wrong] faire du tort à.

injured ['ɪndʒəd] ◆ adj **1.** [physically] blessé **2.** [offended - person] offensé. ◆ pl n ▸ **the injured** les blessés *mpl.*

injurious [ɪn'dʒʊərɪəs] adj *fml* **1.** [detrimental] nuisible, préjudiciable ▸ **injurious to** préjudiciable à **2.** [insulting] offensant, injurieux.

injury ['ɪndʒərɪ] (*pl* **injuries**) n **1.** [physical] blessure f / *be careful, you'll do yourself an injury!* [UK] fais attention, tu vas te blesser ! **2.** *fml* & *liter* [wrong] tort m, préjudice m.

injury time n *(U)* SPORT arrêts *mpl* de jeu.

injustice [ɪn'dʒʌstɪs] n injustice f.

ink [ɪŋk] ◆ n **1.** encre f / *in ink* à l'encre **2.** [of squid, octopus, etc.] encre f, noir m ▸ **ink sac** sac m *or* poche f à encre. ◆ vt encrer. ◆ **ink in** vt sep [drawing] repasser à l'encre.

inkblot ['ɪŋkblɒt] n tache f d'encre, pâté m.

inkjet printer ['ɪŋkdʒet-] n imprimante f à jet d'encre.

inkling ['ɪŋklɪŋ] n vague *or* petite idée f.

inkpad ['ɪŋkpæd] n tampon m (encreur).

inkstain ['ɪŋksteɪn] n tache f d'encre.

inky ['ɪŋkɪ] (*compar* **inkier**, *superl* **inkiest**) adj **1.** [ink-stained] taché d'encre **2.** [dark] noir comme l'encre.

inlaid [,ɪn'leɪd] adj incrusté ; [wood] marqueté, incrusté.

inland ◆ adj ['ɪnlənd] **1.** [not coastal - town, sea] intérieur **2.** [UK] [not foreign] intérieur. ◆ adv [ɪn'lænd] [travelling] vers l'intérieur ; [located] à l'intérieur.

Inland Revenue n [UK] ▸ **the Inland Revenue** ≃ le fisc.

in-laws pl n *inf* [gen] belle-famille f ; [parents-in-law] beaux-parents *mpl.*

inlet ['ɪnlet] ◆ n **1.** [in coastline] anse f, crique f ; [between offshore islands] bras m de mer **2.** TECH [intake] arrivée f, admission f ; [opening] (orifice m d')entrée f ; [for air] prise f (d'air). ◆ comp d'arrivée ▸ **inlet pipe** tuyau m d'arrivée ▸ **inlet valve** soupape f d'admission.

in-line skates pl n patins *mpl* en ligne, rollers *mpl.*

in-line skating n SPORT roller m.

inmate ['ɪnmeɪt] n [of prison] détenu m, -e f ; [of mental institution] interné m, -e f ; [of hospital] malade *mf* ; [of house] occupant m, -e f, résident m, -e f.

inmost ['ɪnməʊst] = **innermost**.

inn [ɪn] n [pub, small hotel] auberge f.

innards ['ɪnədz] pl n *inf* entrailles *fpl.*

innate [ɪ'neɪt] adj [inborn] inné, naturel.

innately [ɪ'neɪtlɪ] adv naturellement.

inner ['ɪnər] adj **1.** [interior - courtyard, pocket, walls, lane] intérieur ; [- structure, workings] interne ▸ **Inner London** *partie centrale de l'agglomération londonienne* **2.** [inward - feeling, conviction] intime ; [- life, voice, struggle, warmth] intérieur **3.** [privileged] : *in the inner circles of power* dans les milieux proches du pouvoir / *her inner circle of advisers / friends* le cercle de ses conseillers / amis les plus proches.

inner city (*pl* **inner cities**) n *quartier défavorisé dans le centre d'une grande ville.*

innermost ['ɪnəməʊst] adj **1.** [feeling, belief] intime **2.** [central - place, room] le plus au centre.

inner tube n [of tyre] chambre f à air.

innings ['ɪnɪŋz] (*pl* **innings**) n [in cricket] tour m de batte / *he's had a good innings* [UK] *fig* il a bien profité de la vie.

innkeeper ['ɪn,kiːpər] n aubergiste *mf.*

innocence ['ɪnəsəns] n innocence f.

innocent ['ɪnəsənt] ◆ adj **1.** [not guilty] innocent ▸ **to be innocent of a crime** être innocent d'un crime **2.** [naïve] innocent, naïf **3.** *fml* [devoid] ▸ **innocent of** dépourvu de, sans. ◆ n innocent m, -e f.

innocently ['ɪnəsəntlɪ] adv innocemment.

innocuous [ɪ'nɒkjʊəs] adj inoffensif.

innovate ['ɪnəveɪt] vi & vt innover.

innovation [,ɪnə'veɪʃn] n innovation f.

innovative ['ɪnəvətɪv] adj innovateur, novateur.

innovator ['ɪnəveɪtər] n innovateur m, -trice f, novateur m, -trice f.

innuendo [,ɪnju:'endəʊ] (*pl* **innuendos** *or* **innuendoes**) n [insinuation] insinuation f, sous-entendu m.

innumerable [ɪ'nju:mərəbl] adj innombrable.

innumerate [ɪ'nju:mərət] adj qui ne sait pas compter.

inoculate [ɪ'nɒkjʊleɪt] vt MED [person, animal] vacciner ▸ **to inoculate sb against sthg** vacciner qqn contre qqch.

inoculation [ɪ,nɒkjʊ'leɪʃn] n inoculation f.

inoffensive [,ɪnə'fensɪv] adj inoffensif.

inoperable [ɪn'ɒprəbl] adj **1.** MED inopérable **2.** [unworkable] impraticable.

inoperative [ɪn'ɒprətɪv] adj inopérant.

inopportune [ɪn'ɒpətju:n] adj [moment] déplacé, mal à propos ; [time] mal choisi, inopportun ; [behaviour] inconvenant, déplacé.

inordinate [ɪn'ɔ:dɪnət] adj [immense - size] démesuré ; [- pleasure, relief] incroyable ; [- amount of money] exorbitant.

inordinately [ɪn'ɔ:dɪnətlɪ] adv démesurément, excessivement.

inorganic [,ɪnɔ:'gænɪk] adj inorganique.

in-patient n hospitalisé m, -e f, malade *mf.*

input ['ɪnpʊt] (*pt* & *pp* **input**, *cont* **inputting**) ◆ n *(U)* **1.** [during meeting, discussion] contribution f **2.** COMPUT [data] données *fpl* (en entrée) ; [entering] entrée f (de données). ◆ comp [device, file, program] d'entrée. ◆ vt [gen] (faire) entrer, introduire ; COMPUT saisir.

input/output n COMPUT entrée-sortie f.

inquest ['ɪnkwest] n LAW enquête f ; [into death] *enquête menée pour établir les causes des morts violentes, non naturelles ou mystérieuses.*

inquire [ɪn'kwaɪər] ◆ vt [ask] demander. ◆ vi [seek information] se renseigner, demander ▸ **to inquire about sthg** demander des renseignements *or* se renseigner sur qqch. ◆ **inquire after** vt insep [UK] demander des nouvelles de. ◆ **inquire into** vt insep se renseigner sur ; [investigate] faire des recherches sur ; ADMIN & LAW enquêter sur.

inquiring [ɪn'kwaɪərɪŋ] adj [voice, look] interrogateur ; [mind] curieux.

inquiringly [ɪn'kwaɪərɪŋlɪ] adv d'un air interrogateur.

inquiry [[UK] ɪn'kwaɪərɪ [US] ɪnkwərɪ] (*pl* **inquiries**) n **1.** [request for information] demande f (de renseignements) ▸ **to make inquiries (about sb / sthg)** se renseigner (sur qqn / qqch) **2.** [investigation] enquête f ▸ **to hold** *or* **to conduct an inquiry into sthg** faire une enquête sur qqch / *the police are making inquiries* la police enquête, une enquête (policière) est en cours **3.** [questioning] : *a look / tone of inquiry* un regard / ton interrogateur.

inquiry desk n [UK] bureau m de renseignements.

inquisition [ˌɪnkwɪ'zɪʃn] n **1.** *pej* [gen] inquisition *f*
2. HIST ▸ **the Inquisition** l'Inquisition *f* **3.** LAW enquête *f*.
inquisitive [ɪn'kwɪzətɪv] adj [curious] curieux ; *pej*
[nosy] indiscret (indiscrète).
inquisitively [ɪn'kwɪzətɪvlɪ] adv [curiously] avec curiosité ; *pej* [nosily] de manière indiscrète.
inquisitiveness [ɪn'kwɪzətɪvnɪs] n [curiosity] curiosité *f* ; *pej* [nosiness] indiscrétion *f*.
inroads ['ɪnrəʊdz] pl n *fig* ▸ **to make inroads in** or **into**
or **on a)** [supplies, funds] entamer **b)** [spare time, somebody's rights] empiéter sur / *they have made significant
inroads into our market share* ils ont considérablement
mordu sur notre part du marché.
insane [ɪn'seɪn] ◆ adj **1.** [mentally disordered] fou *(before vowel or silent 'h' fol, f folle)* ▸ **to go insane** perdre
la raison **2.** *fig* [person] fou *(before vowel or silent 'h'
fol, f folle)* / *it's driving me insane!* ça me rend fou ! ;
[scheme, price] démentiel. ◆ pl n ▸ **the insane** les malades *mpl* mentaux.
insanely [ɪn'seɪnlɪ] adv **1.** [crazily - laugh, behave, talk]
comme un fou **2.** [as intensifier - funny, rich] follement.
insanitary [ɪn'sænɪtrɪ] adj insalubre, malsain.
insanity [ɪn'sænɪtɪ] n folie *f*, démence *f*.
insatiable [ɪn'seɪʃəbl] adj insatiable.
inscribe [ɪn'skraɪb] vt **1.** [on list] inscrire ; [on plaque,
tomb, etc.] graver, inscrire **2.** [dedicate] dédicacer **3.** GEOM
inscrire.
inscription [ɪn'skrɪpʃn] n [on plaque, tomb] inscription *f* ; [in book] dédicace *f*.
inscrutable [ɪn'skru:təbl] adj [person] énigmatique,
impénétrable ; [remark] énigmatique.
insect ['ɪnsekt] n insecte *m* ▸ **insect repellent** produit *m*
insectifuge.
insecticide [ɪn'sektɪsaɪd] n insecticide *m*.
insecure [ˌɪnsɪ'kjʊər] adj **1.** [person - temporarily] inquiet
(inquiète) ; [- generally] pas sûr de soi, qui manque d'assurance **2.** [chair, nail, scaffolding, etc.] peu solide **3.** [place]
peu sûr **4.** [future, market] incertain ; [peace, job, relation-
ship] précaire.
insecurely [ˌɪnsɪ'kjʊəlɪ] adv : *insecurely balanced* en
équilibre instable / *insecurely closed / bolted / attached* mal
fermé / verrouillé / attaché.
insecurity [ˌɪnsɪ'kjʊərətɪ] (pl **insecurities**) n **1.** [lack
of confidence] manque *m* d'assurance ; [uncertainty] incertitude *f* ▸ **job insecurity** précarité *f* de l'emploi **2.** [lack of
safety] insécurité *f*.
insemination [ɪnˌsemɪ'neɪʃn] n insémination *f*.
insensible [ɪn'sensəbl] adj *fml* **1.** [unconscious] inconscient, sans connaissance ; [numb] insensible / *her body was
insensible to any pain* son corps était insensible à toute
douleur **2.** [cold, indifferent] : *insensible to the suffering of
others* insensible or indifférent à la souffrance d'autrui.
insensitive [ɪn'sensətɪv] adj **1.** [cold-hearted] insensible,
dur **2.** [physically] insensible / *insensitive to pain* insensible
à la douleur.
insensitively [ɪn'sensətɪvlɪ] adj avec un grand manque
de tact.
insensitivity [ɪnˌsensə'tɪvətɪ], **insensitiveness** [ɪn-
'sensətɪvnɪs] n insensibilité *f*.
inseparable [ɪn'seprəbl] adj inséparable.
insert ◆ vt [ɪn's3:t] introduire, insérer. ◆ n ['ɪns3:t]
1. [gen] insertion *f* ; [extra text] encart *m* **2.** SEW pièce *f* rapportée ; [decorative] incrustation *f*.
insertion [ɪn's3:ʃn] n **1.** [act] insertion *f* **2.** [thing in-
serted] = **insert**.
in-service adj ▸ **in-service training** formation *f* permanente or continue.

inset ['ɪnset] (*pt & pp* inset, *cont* insetting) n **1.** [in
map, text] encadré *m* ; [on video, TV screen] incrustation *f*
2. [in newspaper, magazine - extra pages] encart *m*.
inshore ◆ adj ['ɪnʃɔ:r] [near shore] côtier ▸ **inshore
fishing** pêche *f* côtière. ◆ adv [ɪn'ʃɔ:r] [near shore] près de
la côte ; [towards shore] vers la côte.
inside [ɪn'saɪd] ◆ adv **1.** [within enclosed space] dedans,
à l'intérieur **2.** [indoors] à l'intérieur / *bring the chairs inside* rentre les chaises **3.** *inf* [in prison] en taule. ◆ prep
1. [within] à l'intérieur de, dans / *inside the house* à l'intérieur de la maison **2.** [in less than] en moins de / *I'll have
it finished inside 6 days* je l'aurai terminé en moins de
6 jours. ◆ n **1.** [inner part] intérieur *m* / *she has a scar
on the inside of her wrist* elle a une cicatrice à l'intérieur
du poignet **2.** [of pavement, road] : *walk on the inside*
marchez loin du bord. ◆ adj **1.** [door, wall] intérieur /
inside leg measurement hauteur *f* de l'entrejambe / *the
inside pages* [of newspaper] les pages intérieures ▸ **the inside lane a)** [in athletics] la corde **b)** [driving on left] la voie
de gauche **c)** [driving on right] la voie de droite **2.** *fig* : *he
has inside information* il a quelqu'un dans la place / *find
out the inside story* essaie de découvrir les dessous de
l'histoire / *it looks like an inside job* on dirait que c'est
quelqu'un de la maison qui a fait le coup. ◆ **insides**
pl n *inf* [stomach] estomac *m* ; [intestines] intestins *mpl*,
tripes *fpl*. ◆ **inside out** adv phr **1.** [with inner part out-
wards] : *your socks are on inside out* tu as mis tes chaussettes à l'envers / *they turned the room inside out* *fig* ils
ont mis la pièce sens dessus dessous **2.** [thoroughly] : *she
knows her job inside out* elle connaît parfaitement son travail.
insider [ˌɪn'saɪdər] n initié *m*, -e *f*.
insider dealing, **insider trading** n (U) ST. EX
délit *m* d'initiés.
insidious [ɪn'sɪdɪəs] adj insidieux.
insight ['ɪnsaɪt] n **1.** [stomach] perspicacité *f* **2.** [idea,
glimpse] aperçu *m*, idée *f* / *his book offers us new insights
into human behaviour* son livre nous propose un nouveau
regard sur le comportement humain.
insignia [ɪn'sɪgnɪə] (pl **insignia** or **insignias**) n insigne *m*, insignes *mpl*.
insignificance [ˌɪnsɪg'nɪfɪkəns] n insignifiance *f*.
insignificant [ˌɪnsɪg'nɪfɪkənt] adj **1.** [unimportant] insignifiant, sans importance **2.** [negligible] insignifiant, négligeable.
insincere [ˌɪnsɪn'sɪər] adj peu sincère.
insincerity [ˌɪnsɪn'serətɪ] n manque *m* de sincérité.
insinuate [ɪn'sɪnjʊeɪt] vt **1.** [imply] insinuer, laisser entendre **2.** [introduce] insinuer.
insinuation [ɪnˌsɪnjʊ'eɪʃn] n **1.** [hint] insinuation *f*, allusion *f* **2.** [act, practice] insinuation *f*.
insipid [ɪn'sɪpɪd] adj insipide, fade.
insist [ɪn'sɪst] ◆ vi **1.** [demand] insister ▸ **to insist
on sthg / doing sthg**: *he insisted on a new contract* il a
exigé un nouveau contrat / *I insist on seeing the manager* j'exige de voir le directeur **2.** [maintain] ▸ **to insist
on** maintenir **3.** [stress] ▸ **to insist on** insister sur. ◆ vt
1. [demand] insister / *you should insist that you be paid*
vous devriez exiger qu'on vous paye **2.** [maintain] maintenir,
soutenir.

> 📝 Note that **exiger que** is followed by a
> verb in the subjunctive:
> **He insisted I (should) write to my family.** *Il
> a exigé que j'écrive à ma famille.*

insistence [ɪn'sɪstəns] n : *their insistence on secrecy has hindered negotiations* en exigeant le secret, ils ont entravé les négociations / *at* or *on my insistence* sur mon insistance.

insistent [ɪn'sɪstənt] adj [person] insistant ; [demand] pressant ; [denial, refusal] obstiné / *she was most insistent* elle a beaucoup insisté.

insistently [ɪn'sɪstəntlɪ] adv [stare, knock] avec insistance ; [ask, urge] avec insistance, instamment.

insofar as [,ɪnsəʊ'fɑːʳ-] conj phr dans la mesure où / *insofar as it's possible* dans la limite or mesure du possible.

insole ['ɪnsəʊl] n semelle f intérieure.

insolence ['ɪnsələns] n insolence f.

insolent ['ɪnsələnt] adj insolent.

insolently ['ɪnsələntlɪ] adv insolemment, avec insolence.

insoluble [ɪn'sɒljʊbl] adj [problem, substance] insoluble.

insolvency [ɪn'sɒlvənsɪ] n insolvabilité f.

insolvent [ɪn'sɒlvənt] adj insolvable.

insomnia [ɪn'sɒmnɪə] n *(U)* insomnie f.

insomniac [ɪn'sɒmnɪæk] ◆ adj insomniaque. ◆ n insomniaque mf.

insomuch as [,ɪnsəʊ'mʌtʃ-] = inasmuch as.

inspect [ɪn'spekt] ◆ vt 1. [scrutinize] examiner, inspecter 2. [check officially - school, product, prison] inspecter ; [- ticket] contrôler ; [- accounts] contrôler 3. MIL [troops] passer en revue. ◆ vi faire une inspection.

inspection [ɪn'spekʃn] n 1. [of object] examen m (minutieux) ; [of place] inspection f / *on closer inspection* en regardant de plus près 2. [official check] inspection f ; [of ticket, passport] contrôle m ; [of school, prison] (visite f d')inspection f 3. MIL [of troops] revue f, inspection f.

inspector [ɪn'spektəʳ] n 1. [gen] inspecteur m, -trice f ; [on public transport] contrôleur m, -euse f 2. Ⓤ SCH inspecteur m, -trice f 3. [in police force] ▶ **(police) inspector** ≃ inspecteur m, -trice f (de police).

inspiration [,ɪnspə'reɪʃn] n 1. [source of ideas] inspiration f ▶ **to draw one's inspiration from** s'inspirer de ▶ **to be an inspiration to sb** être une source d'inspiration pour qqn 2. [bright idea] inspiration f.

inspirational [,ɪnspə'reɪʃənl] adj 1. [inspiring] inspirant 2. [inspired] inspiré.

inspire [ɪn'spaɪəʳ] vt 1. [person, work of art] inspirer ▶ **to inspire sb to do sthg** inciter or pousser qqn à faire qqch 2. [arouse - feeling] inspirer / *to inspire courage in sb* insuffler du courage à qqn.

inspired [ɪn'spaɪəd] adj [artist, poem] inspiré ; [moment] d'inspiration ; [performance] extraordinaire ; [choice, decision] bien inspiré, heureux.

inspiring [ɪn'spaɪərɪŋ] adj [speech, book] stimulant ; [music] exaltant.

inst. **(written abbr of instant)** COMM courant / *of the 9th inst.* du 9 courant or de ce mois.

instability [,ɪnstə'bɪlətɪ] *(pl* **instabilities)** n instabilité f.

install [ɪn'stɔːl] vt 1. [machinery, equipment, software] installer 2. [settle - person] installer / *she installed herself in an armchair* elle s'installa dans un fauteuil 3. [appoint - manager, president] nommer.

installation [,ɪnstə'leɪʃn] n [gen & MIL] installation f.

installer [ɪn'stɔːləʳ] n COMPUT [program] programme m d'installation.

installment plan n Ⓤ *système de paiement à tempérament* ▶ **to buy sthg on an installment plan** acheter qqch à crédit.

instalment Ⓤ, **installment** Ⓤ [ɪn'stɔːlmənt] n 1. [payment] acompte m, versement m partiel ▶ **monthly instalments** mensualités fpl ▶ **to pay in** or **by instalments** payer par versements échelonnés 2. [of serial, story] épisode m ; [of book] fascicule m ; [of TV documentary] volet m, partie f / *published in instalments* publié par fascicules.

instance ['ɪnstəns] n 1. [example] exemple m ▶ **as an instance of** comme exemple de ; [case] occasion f, circonstance f 2. [stage] : *in the first / second instance* en premier / second lieu. ❖ **for instance** adv phr par exemple.

instant ['ɪnstənt] ◆ adj 1. [immediate] immédiat ▶ **instant replay** TV ralenti m 2. CULIN [coffee] instantané, soluble ; [soup, sauce] instantané, en sachet ; [milk] en poudre ; [mashed potato] en flocons ; [dessert] à préparation rapide. ◆ n instant m, moment m.

instant-access adj [bank account] à accès immédiat.

instantaneous [,ɪnstən'teɪnjəs] adj instantané.

instantaneously [,ɪnstən'teɪnjəslɪ] adv instantanément.

instantly ['ɪnstəntlɪ] adv [immediately] immédiatement, instantanément.

instant messaging n messagerie f instantanée.

instead [ɪn'sted] adv : *he didn't go to the office, he went home instead* au lieu d'aller au bureau, il est rentré chez lui / *I don't like sweet things, I'll have cheese instead* je n'aime pas les sucreries, je prendrai plutôt du fromage / *since I'll be away, why not send Mary instead?* puisque je ne serai pas là, pourquoi ne pas envoyer Mary à ma place ? ❖ **instead of** prep phr au lieu de / *instead of reading a book* au lieu de lire un livre / *her son came instead of her* son fils est venu à sa place / *I had an apple instead of lunch* j'ai pris une pomme en guise de déjeuner.

instep ['ɪnstep] n 1. ANAT cou-de-pied m 2. [of shoe] cambrure f.

instigate ['ɪnstɪgeɪt] vt 1. [initiate - gen] être à l'origine de ; [- project] promouvoir ; [- strike, revolt] provoquer ; [- plot] ourdir 2. [urge] inciter, pousser ▶ **to instigate sb to do sthg** pousser or inciter qqn à faire qqch.

instigation [,ɪnstɪ'geɪʃn] n [urging] instigation f, incitation f / *at her instigation* à son instigation.

instigator ['ɪnstɪgeɪtəʳ] n instigateur m, -trice f.

instil Ⓤ, **instill** Ⓤ [ɪn'stɪl] vt [principles, ideals] inculquer ; [loyalty, courage, fear] insuffler ; [idea] faire comprendre.

instinct ['ɪnstɪŋkt] n instinct m ▶ **by instinct** d'instinct.

instinctive [ɪn'stɪŋktɪv] adj instinctif.

instinctively [ɪn'stɪŋktɪvlɪ] adv instinctivement.

institute ['ɪnstɪtjuːt] ◆ vt 1. [establish - system, guidelines] instituer, établir ; [- change] introduire, apporter ; [- committee] créer, constituer ; [- award, organization] fonder, créer 2. [take up - proceedings] engager, entamer ; [- inquiry] ouvrir. ◆ n institut m.

institute of education n Ⓤ *école formant des enseignants.*

institution [,ɪnstɪ'tjuːʃn] n 1. [organization] organisme m, établissement m ; [governmental] institution f ; [educational, penal, religious] établissement m ; [private school] institution f ; [hospital] hôpital m, établissement m hospitalier ; *euph* [mental hospital] établissement m psychiatrique 2. [custom, political or social structure] institution f 3. *hum* [person] institution f.

institutional [,ɪnstɪ'tjuːʃənl] adj [hospital, prison, school, etc.] institutionnel.

institutionalize, institutionalise [ˌɪnstɪˈtjuːʃən-ˌlaɪz] vt **1.** [establish] institutionnaliser ▶ **to become institutionalized** s'institutionnaliser **2.** [place in a hospital, home] placer dans un établissement *(médical ou médico-social)* ▶ **to be institutionalized** être interné ▶ **to become institutionalized** ne plus être capable de se prendre en charge *(après des années passées dans des établissements spécialisés).*

institutional racism, institutionalized racism n racisme *m* institutionnel.

in-store adj [bakery, childcare facilities, etc.] dans le magasin, sur place ▶ **in-store promotion** promotion *f* sur le lieu de vente.

instruct [ɪnˈstrʌkt] vt **1.** [command, direct] charger / *we have been instructed to accompany you* nous sommes chargés de or nous avons mission de vous accompagner **2.** [teach] former ▶ **to instruct sb in sthg** enseigner or apprendre qqch à qqn **3.** [inform] informer **4.** LAW [jury, solicitor] donner des instructions à.

instruction [ɪnˈstrʌkʃn] n **1.** [order] instruction *f* ▶ **instructions (for use)** mode *m* d'emploi **2.** *(U)* [teaching] leçons *fpl* ; MIL instruction *f.*

instruction manual n COMM & TECH manuel *m* (d'utilisation et d'entretien).

instructive [ɪnˈstrʌktɪv] adj instructif.

instructor [ɪnˈstrʌktər] n **1.** [gen] professeur *m* ; MIL instructeur *m* ▶ **sailing instructor** moniteur *m*, -trice *f* de voile **2.** US UNIV ≃ assistant *m*, -e *f.*

instructress [ɪnˈstrʌktrɪs] n instructrice *f*, monitrice *f.*

instrument [ˈɪnstrʊmənt] n **1.** MED, MUS & TECH instrument *m* **2.** *fig* [means] instrument *m*, outil *m.*

instrumental [ˌɪnstrʊˈmentl] adj **1.** [significant] : *her work was instrumental in bringing about the reforms* elle a largement contribué à faire passer les réformes / *an instrumental role* un rôle déterminant **2.** MUS instrumental.

instrumentalist [ˌɪnstrʊˈmentəlɪst] n MUS instrumentiste *mf.*

instrument panel, instrument board n AERON & AUTO tableau *m* de bord ; TECH tableau *m* de contrôle.

insubordinate [ˌɪnsəˈbɔːdɪnət] adj insubordonné.

insubordination [ˈɪnsəˌbɔːdɪˈneɪʃn] n insubordination *f.*

insubstantial [ˌɪnsəbˈstænʃl] adj **1.** [structure] peu solide ; [book] facile, peu substantiel ; [garment, snack, mist] léger ; [claim] sans fondement ; [reasoning] faible, sans substance **2.** [imaginary] imaginaire, chimérique.

insufferable [ɪnˈsʌfərəbl] adj insupportable, intolérable.

insufficient [ˌɪnsəˈfɪʃnt] adj insuffisant.

insufficiently [ˌɪnsəˈfɪʃntlɪ] adv insuffisamment.

insular [ˈɪnsjʊlər] adj **1.** [island - tradition, authorities] insulaire ; [isolated] isolé **2.** *fig & pej* [mentality] isolé, borné.

insulate [ˈɪnsjʊleɪt] vt **1.** [against cold, heat, radiation] isoler ; [hot water pipes, tank] calorifuger ; [soundproof] insonoriser **2.** ELEC isoler **3.** *fig* [protect] protéger.

insulating tape [ˈɪnsjʊleɪtɪŋ-] n chatterton *m.*

insulation [ˌɪnsjʊˈleɪʃn] n **1.** [against cold] isolation *f* (calorifuge), calorifugeage *m* ; [sound-proofing] insonorisation *f*, isolation *f* **2.** ELEC isolation *f* **3.** [feathers, foam, etc.] isolant *m* **4.** *fig* [protection] protection *f.*

insulin [ˈɪnsjʊlɪn] n insuline *f.*

insult ◆ vt [ɪnˈsʌlt] [abuse] insulter, injurier ; [offend] faire (un) affront à, offenser ◆ n [ˈɪnsʌlt] insulte *f*, injure *f*, affront *m* ▶ **to add insult to injury** pour couronner le tout.

insulting [ɪnˈsʌltɪŋ] adj [language] insultant, injurieux ; [attitude] insultant, offensant ; [behaviour] grossier.

insultingly [ɪnˈsʌltɪŋlɪ] adv [speak] d'un ton insultant or injurieux ; [act] d'une manière insultante.

insurance [ɪnˈʃɔːrəns] ◆ n **1.** *(U)* [against fire, theft, accident] assurance *f* ; [cover] garantie *f* (d'assurance), couverture *f* ; [premium] prime *f* (d'assurance) ▶ **to take out insurance (against sthg)** prendre or contracter une assurance, s'assurer (contre qqch) **2.** *fig* [means of protection] garantie *f*, moyen *m* de protection. ◆ comp [premium, scheme] d'assurance ; [company] d'assurances.

insurance broker n courtier *m* or agent *m* d'assurance(s).

insurance policy n police *f* d'assurance, contrat *m* d'assurance.

insure [ɪnˈʃɔːr] vt **1.** [car, building, person] assurer / *he insured himself* or *his life* il a pris or contracté une assurance-vie ▶ **insured against** assuré contre **2.** *fig* [protect] : *what strategy can insure (us) against failure?* quelle stratégie peut nous prévenir contre l'échec or nous garantir que nous n'échouerons pas ?

insured [ɪnˈʃɔːd] *(pl* **insured)** ◆ adj assuré. ◆ n assuré *m*, -e *f.*

insurer [ɪnˈʃɔːrər] n assureur *m.*

insurgent [ɪnˈsɜːdʒənt] ◆ n insurgé *m*, -e *f.* ◆ adj insurgé.

insurmountable [ˌɪnsəˈmaʊntəbl] adj insurmontable.

insurrection [ˌɪnsəˈrekʃn] n insurrection *f.*

intact [ɪnˈtækt] adj intact.

intake [ˈɪnteɪk] n **1.** SCH & UNIV admission *f*, inscription *f* ; MIL recrutement *m* **2.** [of food] consommation *f.*

intangible [ɪnˈtændʒəbl] adj [quality, reality] intangible, impalpable ; [idea, difficulty] indéfinissable, difficile à cerner.

integral [ˈɪntɪɡrəl] adj **1.** [essential - part, element] intégrant, constitutif / *it's an integral part of your job* cela fait partie intégrante de votre travail **2.** [entire] intégral, complet (complète).

integrate [ˈɪntɪɡreɪt] ◆ vt **1.** [combine] : *the two systems have been integrated* on a combiné les deux systèmes **2.** [include in a larger unit] intégrer ▶ **to integrate sb in a group** intégrer qqn dans un groupe. ◆ vi [fit in] s'intégrer ▶ **to integrate into** s'intégrer dans.

integrated [ˈɪntɪɡreɪtɪd] adj [gen] intégré ▶ **integrated neighborhood** US quartier *m* multiracial ▶ **integrated school** US école où se pratique l'intégration (raciale) ▶ **integrated studies** SCH études *fpl* interdisciplinaires.

integrated circuit n circuit *m* intégré.

integration [ˌɪntɪˈɡreɪʃn] n intégration *f* ▶ **racial integration** déségrégation *f.*

integrity [ɪnˈteɡrətɪ] n **1.** [uprightness] intégrité *f*, probité *f* **2.** [wholeness] totalité *f.*

intel [ˈɪntel] n US [military intelligence] service *m* de renseignements de l'armée.

intellect [ˈɪntəlekt] n **1.** [intelligence] intelligence *f* **2.** [mind, person] esprit *m.*

intellectual [ˌɪntəˈlektjʊəl] ◆ adj [mental] intellectuel ; [attitude, image] d'intellectuel / *intellectual property* propriété *f* intellectuelle. ◆ n intellectuel *m*, -elle *f.*

intellectualize, intellectualise [ˌɪntəˈlektjʊəlaɪz] ◆ vt intellectualiser. ◆ vi tenir des discours intellectuels.

intellectually [ˌɪntəˈlektjʊəlɪ] adv intellectuellement.

intelligence [ɪnˈtelɪdʒəns] n *(U)* **1.** [mental ability] intelligence *f* ▶ **to have the intelligence to do sthg** avoir l'intelligence de faire qqch **2.** [information] renseignements *mpl*, information *f*, informations *fpl* / *he used to work in intelligence* il travaillait pour les services secrets or de renseignement **3.** [intelligent being] intelligence *f.*

intelligence quotient n quotient *m* intellectuel.

intelligence service n POL service m de renseignements.

intelligence test n test m d'aptitude intellectuelle.

intelligent [ɪn'telɪdʒənt] adj intelligent.

intelligent card n 🇬🇧 carte f à mémoire or à puce.

intelligent design n dessein m intelligent.

intelligently [ɪn'telɪdʒəntlɪ] adv intelligemment.

intelligentsia [ɪn,telɪ'dʒentsɪə] n intelligentsia f.

intelligible [ɪn'telɪdʒəbl] adj intelligible.

intend [ɪn'tend] vt **1.** [plan, have in mind] ▶ **to intend to do sthg, to intend doing** or 🇺🇸 **on doing sthg** avoir l'intention de or projeter de faire qqch **2.** [destine] destiner / *a book intended for the general public* un livre destiné or qui s'adresse au grand public.

intended [ɪn'tendɪd] adj **1.** [planned - event, trip] prévu ; [- result, reaction] voulu ; [- market, public] visé **2.** [deliberate] intentionnel, délibéré.

intense [ɪn'tens] adj **1.** [gen] intense ; [battle, debate] acharné ; [hatred] violent, profond ; [pleasure] vif **2.** [person] : *he's so intense* **a)** [serious] il prend tout très au sérieux **b)** [emotional] il prend tout très à cœur **3.** 🇺🇸 inf [very good] génial.

intensely [ɪn'tenslɪ] adv **1.** [with intensity - work, stare] intensément, avec intensité ; [- love] profondément, passionnément **2.** [extremely - hot, painful, curious] extrêmement ; [- moving, affected, bored] profondément.

intensifier [ɪn'tensɪfaɪər] n **1.** LING intensif m **2.** PHOT renforçateur m.

intensify [ɪn'tensɪfaɪ] (*pt & pp* **intensified**) ◆ vt [feeling, impression, colour] renforcer ; [sound] intensifier. ◆ vi s'intensifier, devenir plus intense.

intensity [ɪn'tensətɪ] (*pl* **intensities**) n intensité f.

intensive [ɪn'tensɪv] adj intensif.

-intensive in comp qui utilise beaucoup de... ▶ **energy-intensive** [appliance, industry] grand consommateur d'énergie ▶ **labour-intensive** qui nécessite une main-d'œuvre importante.

intensive care n (U) MED soins mpl intensifs / *in intensive care* en réanimation.

intensive care unit n unité f de soins intensifs.

intensively [ɪn'tensɪvlɪ] adv intensivement.

intent [ɪn'tent] ◆ n intention f, but m. ◆ adj **1.** [concentrated] attentif, absorbé **2.** [determined] résolu, déterminé ▶ **to be intent on doing sthg** être déterminé or résolu à faire qqch. ❖ **to all intents and purposes** adv phr en fait.

intention [ɪn'tenʃn] n intention f / *I have absolutely no intention of spending my life here* je n'ai aucune intention de passer ma vie ici / *I have every intention of calling her!* j'ai bien l'intention de l'appeler !

intentional [ɪn'tenʃənl] adj intentionnel, voulu.

intentionally [ɪn'tenʃənəlɪ] adv intentionnellement.

intently [ɪn'tentlɪ] adv [alertly - listen, watch] attentivement ; [thoroughly - question, examine] minutieusement.

inter [ɪn'tɜːr] (*pt & pp* **interred,** *cont* **interring**) vt fml enterrer, inhumer.

interact [,ɪntər'ækt] vi **1.** [person] : *they interact very well together* le courant passe bien (entre eux), ils s'entendent très bien **2.** [forces] interagir ; [substances] avoir une action réciproque **3.** COMPUT dialoguer.

interaction [,ɪntər'ækʃn] n interaction f.

interactive [,ɪntər'æktɪv] adj interactif.

interactive whiteboard n tableau m blanc interactif.

interactivity [,ɪntəræk'tɪvɪtɪ] n interactivité f.

interbreed [,ɪntə'briːd] (*pt & pp* **interbred** [-bred]) ◆ vt [crossbreed - animals] croiser ; [- races] métisser. ◆ vi **1.** [crossbreed - animals] se croiser ; [- races] se métisser **2.** [within family, community] contracter des mariages consanguins.

intercede [,ɪntə'siːd] vi intercéder.

intercept ◆ vt [,ɪntə'sept] intercepter. ◆ n ['ɪntəsept] interception f.

interception [,ɪntə'sepʃn] n interception f.

interchange ◆ vt [,ɪntə'tʃeɪndʒ] **1.** [exchange - opinions, information] échanger **2.** [switch round] intervertir, permuter. ◆ n ['ɪntətʃeɪndʒ] **1.** [exchange] échange m **2.** [road junction] échangeur m.

interchangeable [,ɪntə'tʃeɪndʒəbl] adj interchangeable.

intercity [,ɪntə'sɪtɪ] (*pl* **intercities**) adj [travel] d'une ville à l'autre, interurbain ▶ **intercity train** 🇬🇧 (train m) rapide m.

intercom ['ɪntəkɒm] n Interphone® m.

intercommunicate [,ɪntəkə'mjuːnɪkeɪt] vi communiquer.

interconnect [,ɪntəkə'nekt] ◆ vt [gen] connecter. ◆ vi [rooms, buildings] communiquer ; [circuits] être connecté.

intercourse ['ɪntəkɔːs] n **1.** [sexual intercourse] rapports mpl (sexuels) ▶ **to have intercourse (with sb)** avoir des rapports sexuels (avec qqn) **2.** fml [communication] relations fpl, rapports mpl ▶ **social intercourse** communication f.

interdenominational ['ɪntədɪ,nɒmɪ'neɪʃənl] adj interconfessionnel.

interdepartmental ['ɪntə,diːpɑːt'mentl] adj [in company, hospital] entre services ; [in university, ministry] interdépartemental.

interdependence [,ɪntədɪ'pendəns] n interdépendance f.

interdependent [,ɪntədɪ'pendənt] adj interdépendant.

interest ['ɪntrəst] ◆ n **1.** [curiosity, attention] intérêt m / *she takes a great / an active interest in politics* elle s'intéresse beaucoup / activement à la politique ▶ **to show (an) interest in sthg** manifester de l'intérêt pour qqch **2.** [appeal] intérêt m / *of no interest* sans intérêt ▶ **to be of interest to sb** intéresser qqn **3.** [pursuit, hobby] centre d'intérêt m **4.** [advantage, benefit] intérêt m **5.** [group with common aim] intérêt m ▶ **interest group** groupe m d'intérêt **6.** [share, stake] intérêts mpl / *he has an interest in a sawmill* il a des intérêts dans une scierie **7.** FIN intérêts mpl. ◆ vt intéresser / *can I interest you in our new model?* puis-je attirer votre attention sur notre nouveau modèle ?

interested ['ɪntrestɪd] adj **1.** [showing interest] intéressé ▶ **to be interested in sthg** s'intéresser à qqch / *would you be interested in meeting him?* ça t'intéresserait de le rencontrer ? / *we'd be interested to know* nous aimerions or voudrions savoir **2.** [involved, concerned] intéressé ▶ **interested party** partie f intéressée.

interest-free adj FIN sans intérêt ▶ **interest-free credit** crédit m gratuit.

interesting ['ɪntrəstɪŋ] adj intéressant.

interestingly ['ɪntrəstɪŋlɪ] adv de façon intéressante / *interestingly enough, they were out* chose intéressante, ils étaient sortis.

interest rate n taux m d'intérêt.

interface ◆ n ['ɪntəfeɪs] [gen & COMPUT] interface f. ◆ vi [,ɪntə'feɪs] COMPUT & TECH faire interface ▶ **to interface with** faire interface avec, s'interfacer à.

interfere [,ɪntə'fɪər] vi **1.** [intrude] s'immiscer, s'ingérer **2.** [clash, conflict] ▶ **to interfere with** entraver **3.** [meddle]

▸ **to interfere with** toucher (à) / *to interfere with a child* *euph* se livrer à des attouchements sur un enfant **4.** RADIO : *local radio sometimes interferes with police transmissions* la radio locale brouille or perturbe parfois les transmissions de la police.

interference [ˌɪntəˈfɪərəns] n **1.** [gen] ingérence *f*, intervention *f* / *she won't tolerate interference in* or *with her plans* elle ne supportera pas qu'on s'immisce dans ses projets **2.** *(U)* RADIO parasites *mpl*, interférence *f*.

interfering [ˌɪntəˈfɪərɪŋ] adj [person] importun / *she's an interfering busybody* elle fourre son nez partout.

intergenerational [ˌɪntədʒenəˈreɪʃənl] adj intergénérationnel.

interim [ˈɪntərɪm] ◆ n intérim *m*. ◆ adj [government, measure, report] provisoire ; [post, function] intérimaire. ❖ **in the interim** adv phr entre-temps.

interior [ɪnˈtɪərɪə] ◆ adj intérieur. ◆ n **1.** [gen] intérieur *m* ▸ **Secretary / Department of the Interior** ministre / ministère chargé de l'administration des domaines et des parcs nationaux aux États-Unis **2.** ART (tableau *m* d')intérieur *m*.

interior decorator n décorateur *m*, -trice *f* (d'intérieur).

interior design n architecture *f* d'intérieur.

interior designer n architecte *mf* d'intérieur.

interject [ˌɪntəˈdʒekt] vt [question, comment] placer.

interlinked [ˌɪntəˈlɪŋkt] adj : *the problems are interlinked* les problèmes sont liés.

interlock ◆ vt [ˌɪntəˈlɒk] **1.** TECH enclencher **2.** [entwine] entrelacer. ◆ vi [ˌɪntəˈlɒk] **1.** TECH [mechanism] s'enclencher ; [cogwheels] s'engrener **2.** [groups, issues] s'imbriquer. ◆ n [ˈɪntəlɒk] **1.** TECH enclenchement *m* **2.** TEXT interlock *m*.

interloper [ˈɪntələupə] n intrus *m*, -e *f*.

interlude [ˈɪntəluːd] n **1.** [period of time] intervalle *m* **2.** THEAT intermède *m* ; MUS & TV interlude *m*.

intermarriage [ˌɪntəˈmærɪdʒ] n **1.** [within family, clan] endogamie *f* **2.** [between different groups] mariage *m* mixte.

intermarry [ˌɪntəˈmærɪ] (*pt & pp* intermarried) vi **1.** [within family, clan] pratiquer l'endogamie **2.** [between different groups] : *members of different religions intermarried freely* les mariages mixtes se pratiquaient librement.

intermediary [ˌɪntəˈmiːdjərɪ] (*pl* intermediaries) ◆ adj intermédiaire. ◆ n intermédiaire *mf*.

intermediate [ˌɪntəˈmiːdjət] adj **1.** [gen] intermédiaire **2.** SCH [class] moyen.

intermediate technology n technologie *f* intermédiaire.

interminable [ɪnˈtɜːmɪnəbl] adj interminable.

interminably [ɪnˈtɜːmɪnəblɪ] adv interminablement.

intermingle [ˌɪntəˈmɪŋgl] vi se mêler.

intermission [ˌɪntəˈmɪʃn] n **1.** [break] pause *f*, trêve *f* ; [in illness, fever] intermission *f* / *without intermission* sans relâche **2.** CIN & THEAT entracte *m*.

intermittent [ˌɪntəˈmɪtənt] adj intermittent.

intermittently [ˌɪntəˈmɪtəntlɪ] adv par intervalles, par intermittence.

intern ◆ vt [ɪnˈtɜːn] POL interner. ◆ vi [ɪnˈtɜːn] US MED faire son internat ; SCH faire son stage pédagogique ; [with firm] faire un stage en entreprise. ◆ n [ˈɪntɜːn] **1.** MED interne *mf* ; US SCH (professeur *m*) stagiaire *mf* ; US [in firm] stagiaire *mf* **2.** [internee] interné *m*, -e *f* (politique).

internal [ɪnˈtɜːnl] adj **1.** [gen] interne, intérieur **2.** [inside country] intérieur ▸ **internal affairs** POL affaires *fpl* inté-

rieures **3.** [inside organization, institution] interne ▸ **internal examiner** SCH examinateur *m*, -trice *f* d'un établissement scolaire.

internal-combustion engine n moteur *m* à explosion or à combustion interne.

internalize, internalise [ɪnˈtɜːnəlaɪz] vt [values, behaviour] intérioriser.

internally [ɪnˈtɜːnəlɪ] adv intérieurement.

Internal Revenue Service pr n US fisc *m*.

international [ˌɪntəˈnæʃənl] ◆ adj international. ◆ n **1.** SPORT [match] match *m* international ; [player] international *m*, -e *f* **2.** POL ▸ **the International** l'Internationale *f*.

International Court of Justice pr n Cour *f* internationale de justice.

International Date Line pr n ligne *f* de changement de date.

internationalize, internationalise [ˌɪntəˈnæʃnəlaɪz] vt internationaliser.

internationally [ˌɪntəˈnæʃnəlɪ] adv internationalement.

International Monetary Fund pr n Fonds *m* monétaire international.

International Standards Organization n Organisation *f* internationale de normalisation.

International Trade Administration n ▸ **the International Trade Administration** l'Administration *f* du commerce international.

internee [ˌɪntɜːˈniː] n interné *m*, -e *f* (politique).

Internet [ˈɪntənet] ◆ pr n Internet *m*. ◆ comp ▸ **Internet café** cybercafé *m* ▸ **Internet company** cyberentreprise *f*.

Internet access n *(U)* accès *m* à l'Internet.

Internet Access Provider n fournisseur *m* d'accès à l'Internet.

Internet address n adresse *f* Internet.

Internet banking n banque *f* en ligne.

Internet connection n connexion *f* Internet.

Internet Presence Provider n fournisseur d'accès à Internet proposant l'hébergement de sites Web.

Internet protocol n protocole *m* Internet.

Internet radio n radio *f* (par) Internet or en ligne.

Internet Relay Chat n IRC *m* (dialogue en temps réel).

Internet service provider n fournisseur *m* d'accès.

Internet start-up, Internet start-up company n start-up *f*, jeune pousse *f* (d'entreprise) *offic*.

Internet telephony n téléphonie *f* Internet.

Internet television, Internet TV n *(U)* télévision *f* Internet or en ligne.

Internet user n internaute *mf*.

internment [ɪnˈtɜːnmənt] n **1.** [gen] internement *m* (politique) ▸ **internment camp** camp *m* d'internement **2.** [in Ireland] système de détention des personnes suspectées de terrorisme en Irlande du Nord.

🏛 **Internment**

En Irlande du Nord, ce terme désigne l'emprisonnement de terroristes présumés auquel avaient recours les autorités britanniques au début des années 1970 pour contrôler les activités de l'IRA (**Irish Republican Army**). Cette pratique fut abandonnée en 1975.

internship ['ɪntɜːnʃɪp] n US MED internat m ; [with firm] stage m en entreprise.

interpersonal [ˌɪntəˈpɜːsənl] adj interpersonnel / *interpersonal relationships* relations fpl interpersonnelles / *interpersonal skills* qualités fpl relationnelles.

interplay ['ɪntəpleɪ] n [between forces, events, people] interaction f.

Interpol ['ɪntəpɒl] pr n Interpol.

interpret [ɪn'tɜːprɪt] ◆ vt interpréter. ◆ vi servir d'interprète, interpréter.

interpretation [ɪnˌtɜːprɪ'teɪʃn] n interprétation f.

interpretation centre n centre m d'information.

interpreter [ɪn'tɜːprɪtər] n 1. [person] interprète mf 2. COMPUT interpréteur m.

interpreting [ɪn'tɜːprɪtɪŋ] n [occupation] interprétariat m.

interpretive center n US centre m d'information.

interracial [ˌɪntə'reɪʃl] adj [relations] interracial.

interrelate [ˌɪntərɪ'leɪt] ◆ vt mettre en corrélation. ◆ vi être interdépendant, interagir.

interrogate [ɪn'terəgeɪt] vt [gen & COMPUT] interroger.

interrogation [ɪnˌterə'geɪʃn] n [gen & LING & COMPUT] interrogation f ; [by police] interrogatoire m / *she's been under interrogation* elle a subi un interrogatoire.

 interrogation or **interrogatoire?**

The French word **interrogation** has a much broader meaning than in English, meaning simply the act of asking questions or wondering about something (**mon interrogation porte sur les couleurs à utiliser** *I'm wondering which colours we should use*). When you want to talk about an interrogation, a series of probing questions asked in a formal context, for example by the police, the French equivalent is **un interrogatoire**.

interrogation mark n point m d'interrogation.

interrogative [ˌɪntə'rɒgətɪv] ◆ adj 1. [inquiring] interrogateur 2. LING interrogatif. ◆ n [word] interrogatif m ; [grammatical form] interrogative f / *in the interrogative* à la forme interrogative.

interrogator [ɪn'terəgeɪtər] n interrogateur m, -trice f.

interrupt [ˌɪntə'rʌpt] ◆ vt 1. [person, lecture, conversation] interrompre 2. [process, activity] interrompre 3. [uniformity] rompre. ◆ vi interrompre. ◆ n COMPUT interruption f.

interruption [ˌɪntə'rʌpʃn] n interruption f.

intersect [ˌɪntə'sekt] ◆ vi se couper, se croiser / *intersecting lines* MATH lignes intersectées. ◆ vt couper, croiser.

intersection [ˌɪntə'sekʃn] n 1. [road junction] carrefour m, croisement m 2. MATH intersection f.

intersperse [ˌɪntə'spɜːs] vt parsemer, semer.

interstate ['ɪntəsteɪt] ◆ adj [commerce, highway] entre États. ◆ n US autoroute f.

intertwine [ˌɪntə'twaɪn] ◆ vt entrelacer. ◆ vi s'entrelacer.

interval ['ɪntəvl] n 1. [period of time] intervalle m ▸ *at intervals* par intervalles, de temps en temps 2. [interlude] pause f ; UK THEAT entracte m ; SPORT mi-temps f 3. [distance] intervalle m, distance f 4. METEOR ▸ *sunny intervals* éclaircies fpl.

intervene [ˌɪntə'viːn] vi 1. [person, government] intervenir 2. [event] survenir 3. [time] s'écouler 4. [interrupt] intervenir.

intervening [ˌɪntə'viːnɪŋ] adj [period of time] intermédiaire.

intervention [ˌɪntə'venʃn] n intervention f.

interventionist [ˌɪntə'venʃənɪst] ◆ adj interventionniste. ◆ n interventionnisme m.

interview ['ɪntəvjuː] ◆ n 1. [for job, university place, etc.] entrevue f, entretien m 2. PRESS, RADIO & TV interview f. ◆ vt 1. [for university place, job, etc.] avoir une entrevue or un entretien avec ; [for opinion poll] interroger, sonder 2. PRESS, RADIO & TV interviewer 3. [subj: police] interroger, questionner. ◆ vi [interviewer] faire passer un entretien ; [candidate] : *he interviews well / badly* il s'en sort / ne s'en sort pas bien aux entretiens.

interviewee [ˌɪntəvjuː'iː] n interviewé m, -e f.

interviewer ['ɪntəvjuːər] n 1. [for media] interviewer m, intervieweur m, -euse f ; [for opinion poll] enquêteur m, -euse, -trice f 2. [for job] : *the interviewer asked me what my present salary was* la personne qui m'a fait passer l'entretien or l'entrevue m'a demandé quel était mon salaire actuel.

interwar [ˌɪntə'wɔːr] adj ▸ *the interwar period* or *years* l'entre-deux-guerres m.

interweave [ˌɪntə'wiːv] (pt interwove [-'wəʊv] or interweaved, pp interwoven [-'wəʊvn] or interweaved) ◆ vt entrelacer ▸ *interwoven with* entrelacé de. ◆ vi s'entrelacer, s'entremêler.

intestate [ɪn'testeɪt] adj intestat (inv) ▸ *to die intestate* décéder intestat.

intestinal [ɪn'testɪnl] adj intestinal.

intestine [ɪn'testɪn] n (usu pl) intestin m.

intimacy ['ɪntɪməsɪ] (pl intimacies) n 1. [closeness, warmth] intimité f 2. [privacy] intimité f 3. (U) euph & fml [sexual relations] relations fpl sexuelles, rapports mpl.

intimate ◆ adj ['ɪntɪmət] 1. [friend, relationship] intime 2. [small and cosy] intime 3. euph & fml [sexually] : *they were intimate on more than one occasion* ils ont eu des rapports (intimes) à plusieurs reprises 4. [personal, private] intime 5. [thorough] profond, approfondi 6. [close, direct] étroit. ◆ n ['ɪntɪmət] intime mf. ◆ vt ['ɪntɪmeɪt] [hint, imply] laisser entendre, intimer.

intimately ['ɪntɪmətlɪ] adv 1. [talk, behave - in a friendly way] intimement 2. [know - thoroughly] à fond ; [- closely, directly] étroitement.

intimation [ˌɪntɪ'meɪʃn] n fml [suggestion] suggestion f ; [sign] indice m, indication f ; [premonition] pressentiment m.

intimidate [ɪn'tɪmɪdeɪt] vt intimider.

intimidating [ɪn'tɪmɪdeɪtɪŋ] adj intimidant.

intimidation [ɪnˌtɪmɪ'deɪʃn] n (U) intimidation f, menaces fpl.

into ['ɪntʊ] prep 1. [indicating direction, movement, etc.] dans / *come into my office* venez dans mon bureau 2. [indicating collision] dans / *the truck ran* or *crashed into the wall* le camion est rentré dans or s'est écrasé contre le mur 3. [indicating division] en / *cut it into three* coupe-le en trois / *6 into 10 won't go* on ne peut pas diviser 10 par 6 4. [indicating elapsed time] : *we worked well into the night* nous avons travaillé (jusque) tard dans la nuit / *he must be well into his forties* il doit avoir la quarantaine bien passée or sonnée / *a week into her holiday and she's bored already* il y a à peine une semaine qu'elle est en vacances et elle s'ennuie déjà 5. inf [fond of] ▸ *to be into sthg* être passionné par qqch / *is he into drugs?* est-ce qu'il se drogue ? 6. [curious about] : *the baby's into everything* le bébé est curieux de tout.

intolerable [ɪn'tɒlrəbl] adj intolérable, insupportable.

intolerably [ɪn'tɒlrəblɪ] adv intolérablement, insupportablement.

intolerance [ɪn'tɒlərəns] n [gen & MED] intolérance f.

intolerant [ɪn'tɒlərənt] adj intolérant.

intonation [ˌɪntə'neɪʃn] n intonation f.

intone [ɪn'təʊn] vt entonner.

intoxicated [ɪn'tɒksɪkeɪtɪd] adj **1.** [drunk] ivre, en état d'ébriété fml **2.** fig ivre / she was intoxicated by success son succès l'avait grisée or lui avait fait tourner la tête.

intoxicating [ɪn'tɒksɪkeɪtɪŋ] adj lit enivrant ; fig grisant, enivrant, excitant.

intoxication [ɪnˌtɒksɪ'keɪʃn] n lit & fig ivresse f.

intractable [ɪn'træktəbl] adj **1.** [person] intraitable, intransigeant **2.** [problem] insoluble ; [situation] inextricable, sans issue.

intramural [ˌɪntrə'mjʊərəl] adj SCH & UNIV [courses, sports] interne (à l'établissement).

intramuscular [ˌɪntrə'mʌskjʊləʳ] adj intramusculaire.

intranet ['ɪntrənet] n intranet m.

intransigence [ɪn'trænzɪʤəns] n intransigeance f.

intransigent [ɪn'trænzɪʤənt] ◆ adj intransigeant. ◆ n intransigeant m, -e f.

intransitive [ɪn'trænzətɪv] ◆ adj intransitif. ◆ n intransitif m.

intrastate [ˌɪntrə'steɪt] adj à l'intérieur d'un même État.

intrauterine device n stérilet m.

intravenous [ˌɪntrə'viːnəs] adj intraveineux / intravenous drugs user usager m de drogue par voie intraveineuse ▶ **intravenous injection** (injection f) intraveineuse f.

intravenously [ˌɪntrə'viːnəslɪ] adv par voie intraveineuse.

in-tray UK, **in-basket** US, **in-box** US n corbeille f de courrier à traiter or « arrivée ».

intrepid [ɪn'trepɪd] adj intrépide.

intricacy ['ɪntrɪkəsɪ] (pl intricacies) n **1.** [complicated detail] complexité f **2.** [complexity] complexité f.

intricate ['ɪntrɪkət] adj complexe, compliqué.

intricately ['ɪntrɪkətlɪ] adv de façon complexe or compliquée.

intrigue [ɪn'triːg] ◆ n **1.** [plotting] intrigue f **2.** [plot, treason] complot m **3.** [love affair] intrigue f. ◆ vt intriguer. ◆ vi intriguer, comploter.

intriguing [ɪn'triːgɪŋ] adj bizarre, curieux.

intriguingly [ɪn'triːgɪŋlɪ] adv bizarrement, curieusement.

intrinsic [ɪn'trɪnsɪk] adj intrinsèque.

intrinsically [ɪn'trɪnsɪklɪ] adv intrinsèquement.

intro ['ɪntrəʊ] (pl intros) n inf introduction f, intro f.

introduce [ˌɪntrə'djuːs] vt **1.** [present -one person to another] présenter / she introduced me to her sister elle m'a présenté à sa sœur / I don't think we've been introduced, have we? nous n'avons pas été présentés, je crois ? **2.** [radio or TV programme] présenter **3.** [bring in] introduire **4.** [laws, legislation] déposer, présenter ; [reform] introduire **5.** [initiate] initier ▶ **to introduce sb to sthg** initier qqn à qqch, faire découvrir qqch à qqn.

introduction [ˌɪntrə'dʌkʃn] n **1.** [of one person to another] présentation f **2.** [first part -of book, speech, piece of music] introduction f **3.** [basic textbook, course] introduction f, initiation f **4.** [bringing in] introduction f **5.** [of bill, law] introduction f, présentation f.

introductory [ˌɪntrə'dʌktrɪ] adj [remarks] préliminaire ; [chapter, course] d'introduction ▶ **introductory offer** COMM offre f de lancement ▶ **introductory price** COMM prix m de lancement.

introspection [ˌɪntrə'spekʃn] n introspection f.

introspective [ˌɪntrə'spektɪv] adj introspectif.

introvert ['ɪntrəvɜːt] ◆ n PSYCHOL introverti m, -e f. ◆ vt rendre introverti.

introverted ['ɪntrəvɜːtɪd] adj PSYCHOL introverti.

intrude [ɪn'truːd] vi **1.** [disturb] déranger, s'imposer / I hope I'm not intruding j'espère que je ne vous dérange pas **2.** [interfere with] : I don't let my work intrude on my private life je ne laisse pas mon travail empiéter sur ma vie privée.

intruder [ɪn'truːdəʳ] n [criminal] cambrioleur m ; [outsider] intrus m, -e f, importun m, -e f.

intrusion [ɪn'truːʒn] n [gen] intrusion f, ingérence f.

intrusive [ɪn'truːsɪv] adj [person] importun.

intubate ['ɪntjubeɪt] vt MED intuber.

intuition [ˌɪntjuː'ɪʃn] n intuition f.

intuitive [ɪn'tjuːɪtɪv] adj intuitif.

Inuit ['ɪnuɪt] (pl Inuit or Inuits) ◆ n Inuit mf. ◆ adj inuit.

inundate ['ɪnʌndeɪt] vt lit & fig inonder / we've been inundated with phone calls / letters nous avons été submergés de coups de fil / courrier / I'm inundated with work just now pour l'instant je suis débordé (de travail) or je croule sous le travail.

inure [ɪ'njʊəʳ] ◆ vt aguerrir ▶ **to become inured to** s'habituer à. ◆ vi [law] entrer en vigueur.

invade [ɪn'veɪd] vt **1.** MIL envahir **2.** fig envahir ▶ **to invade sb's privacy** s'immiscer dans la vie privée de qqn.

invader [ɪn'veɪdəʳ] n envahisseur m, -euse f.

invading [ɪn'veɪdɪŋ] adj **1.** [army] d'invasion **2.** [plants, insects] envahissant.

invalid¹ ◆ n ['ɪnvəlɪd] [disabled person] infirme mf, invalide mf ; [ill person] malade mf. ◆ adj ['ɪnvəlɪd] [disabled] infirme, invalide ; [ill] malade.

invalid² [ɪn'vælɪd] adj **1.** [passport, ticket] non valide, non valable **2.** [law, marriage, election] nul **3.** [argument] non valable.

invalidate [ɪn'vælɪdeɪt] vt **1.** [contract, agreement, etc.] invalider, annuler **2.** [argument] infirmer.

invalidity [ˌɪnvə'lɪdətɪ] n **1.** MED invalidité f **2.** [of contract, agreement, etc.] manque m de validité, nullité f **3.** [of argument] manque m de fondement.

invalidity benefit n UK prestation f d'invalidité (aujourd'hui remplacée par l'« incapacity benefit »).

invaluable [ɪn'væljʊəbl] adj inestimable, très précieux.

invariable [ɪn'veərɪəbl] ◆ adj invariable. ◆ n MATH constante f.

invariably [ɪn'veərɪəblɪ] adv invariablement.

invasion [ɪn'veɪʒn] n **1.** MIL invasion f, envahissement m **2.** fig invasion f, intrusion f / he considered it an invasion of privacy il l'a ressenti comme une intrusion dans sa vie privée.

invasive [ɪn'veɪsɪv] adj MED [surgery] invasif ; fig envahissant.

invective [ɪn'vektɪv] n (U) invective f, invectives fpl.

inveigle [ɪn'veɪgl] vt manipuler / he had been inveigled into letting them in on l'avait adroitement manipulé pour qu'il les laisse entrer.

invent [ɪn'vent] vt **1.** [new machine, process] inventer **2.** [lie, excuse] inventer.

invention [ɪnˈvenʃn] n **1.** [discovery, creation] invention f **2.** [untruth] invention f, fabrication f.

inventive [ɪnˈventɪv] adj [person, mind] inventif ; [plan, solution] ingénieux.

inventor [ɪnˈventər] n inventeur m, -trice f.

inventory [ˈɪnvəntrɪ] (pl **inventories,** pt & pp **inventoried**) ◆ n **1.** [list] inventaire m **2.** (U) 🇺🇸 [stock] stock m, stocks mpl. ◆ vt inventorier.

inverse [ɪnˈvɜːs] ◆ adj inverse. ◆ n inverse m, contraire m ; MATH inverse m.

inversion [ɪnˈvɜːʃn] n [gen] inversion f ; [of roles, relations] renversement m.

invert vt [ɪnˈvɜːt] [turn upside down or inside out] inverser, retourner ; [switch around] intervertir ; [roles] intervertir, renverser.

invertebrate [ɪnˈvɜːtɪbreɪt] ◆ adj invertébré. ◆ n invertébré m.

inverted commas [ɪnˈvɜːtɪd-] pl n 🇬🇧 guillemets mpl / in inverted commas entre guillemets.

inverted snob n 🇬🇧 personne d'origine modeste qui affiche du mépris pour les valeurs bourgeoises.

invest [ɪnˈvest] ◆ vi investir / to invest in shares / in the oil industry / on the stock market investir en actions / dans l'industrie pétrolière / en Bourse. ◆ vt **1.** [money] investir, placer / they invested five million dollars in new machinery ils ont investi cinq millions de dollars dans de nouveaux équipements **2.** [time, effort] investir / we've invested a lot of time and energy in this project nous avons investi beaucoup de temps et d'énergie dans ce projet **3.** fml [confer on] investir / invested with the highest authority investi de la plus haute autorité **4.** MIL [besiege, surround] investir.

investigate [ɪnˈvestɪgeɪt] ◆ vt [allegation, crime, accident] enquêter sur ; [problem, situation] examiner, étudier. ◆ vi enquêter, mener une enquête.

investigation [ɪnˌvestɪˈgeɪʃn] n [into crime, accident] enquête f ; [of problem, situation] examen m, étude f.

investigative [ɪnˈvestɪgətɪv] adj PRESS, RADIO & TV d'investigation ▶ **investigative reporter** journaliste mf or reporter m d'investigation.

investigator [ɪnˈvestɪgeɪtər] n enquêteur m, -euse, -trice f.

investiture [ɪnˈvestɪtʃər] n investiture f.

investment [ɪnˈvestmənt] n **1.** [of money, capital] investissement m, placement m **2.** [of time, effort] investissement m.

investment analyst n analyste mf en placements.

investment bank n banque f d'affaires.

investment trust n société f de placement.

investor [ɪnˈvestər] n investisseur m ; [shareholder] actionnaire mf.

inveterate [ɪnˈvetərət] adj **1.** [habit, dislike] invétéré ; [hatred] tenace **2.** [drinker, gambler] invétéré ; [bachelor, liar, smoker] impénitent.

invidious [ɪnˈvɪdɪəs] adj [unfair] injuste ; [unpleasant] ingrat, pénible.

invigilate [ɪnˈvɪdʒɪleɪt] vi & vt 🇬🇧 SCH & UNIV surveiller (pendant un examen).

invigilator [ɪnˈvɪdʒɪleɪtər] n 🇬🇧 SCH & UNIV surveillant m, -e f (d'un examen).

invigorate [ɪnˈvɪgəreɪt] vt revigorer, vivifier.

invigorating [ɪnˈvɪgəreɪtɪŋ] adj [air, climate] tonique, tonifiant, vivifiant ; [walk] revigorant ; [bath] tonifiant ; [discussion] enrichissant.

invincible [ɪnˈvɪnsɪbl] adj [army, troops] invincible ; [belief] inébranlable.

invisible [ɪnˈvɪzɪbl] adj **1.** invisible / invisible to the naked eye invisible à l'œil nu **2.** COMM [unrecorded] ▶ **invisible earnings** revenus mpl invisibles.

invisible ink n encre f invisible or sympathique.

invitation [ˌɪnvɪˈteɪʃn] n invitation f ▶ **at the invitation of** à l'invitation de / by invitation only sur invitation seulement / prison conditions are an (open) invitation to violence fig les conditions de détention sont une véritable incitation à la violence.

invite ◆ vt [ɪnˈvaɪt] **1.** [ask to come] inviter / to invite sb for lunch inviter qqn à déjeuner **2.** [ask to do sthg] demander, solliciter **3.** [solicit] : he invited comment on his book il a demandé aux gens leur avis sur son livre / we invite applications from all qualified candidates nous invitons tous les candidats ayant le profil requis à postuler **4.** [trouble, defeat, disaster] aller au devant de ; [doubt, sympathy] appeler, attirer. ◆ n [ˈɪnvaɪt] inf invitation f. ◆ **invite out** vt sep inviter (à sortir).

inviting [ɪnˈvaɪtɪŋ] adj [gesture] d'invitation ; [eyes, smile] engageant ; [display] attirant, attrayant ; [idea] tentant, séduisant ; [place, fire] accueillant.

in vitro fertilization [ˌɪnˈviːtrəʊ-] n fécondation f in vitro.

invoice [ˈɪnvɔɪs] ◆ n COMM facture f. ◆ vt [goods] facturer ▶ **to invoice sb for sthg** facturer qqch à qqn.

invoicing [ˈɪnvɔɪsɪŋ] n COMM [of goods, etc.] facturation f ▶ **invoicing address** adresse f de facturation.

invoke [ɪnˈvəʊk] vt **1.** [cite] invoquer **2.** [call upon] en appeler à, faire appel à **3.** [conjure up] invoquer.

involuntarily [ɪnˈvɒləntrəlɪ] adv involontairement.

involuntary [ɪnˈvɒləntrɪ] adj involontaire.

involve [ɪnˈvɒlv] vt **1.** [entail] impliquer, comporter **2.** [concern, affect] concerner, toucher **3.** [bring in, implicate] impliquer **4.** [absorb, engage] absorber.

involved [ɪnˈvɒlvd] adj **1.** [complicated] compliqué, complexe **2.** [implicated] impliqué **3.** [absorbed] absorbé **4.** [emotionally] ▶ **to be involved with sb** avoir une liaison avec qqn.

involvement [ɪnˈvɒlvmənt] n **1.** [participation] participation f **2.** [commitment] investissement m, engagement m **3.** [relationship] liaison f **4.** [complexity] complexité f, complication f.

invulnerable [ɪnˈvʌlnərəbl] adj invulnérable / invulnerable to attack invulnérable à toute attaque, inattaquable.

inward [ˈɪnwəd] ◆ adj **1.** [thoughts, satisfaction] intime, secret **2.** [movement] vers l'intérieur. ◆ adv 🇺🇸 = **inwards.**

inward investment n investissement m étranger.

inward-looking adj [person] introverti, replié sur soi ; [group] replié sur soi, fermé ; [philosophy] introspectif ; pej nombriliste.

inwardly [ˈɪnwədlɪ] adv [pleased, disgusted] secrètement.

inwards [ˈɪnwədz] adv **1.** [turn, face] vers l'intérieur **2.** [into one's own heart, soul, etc.] : my thoughts turned inwards je me suis replié sur moi-même.

in-your-face adj **1.** [uncompromising - documentary, film] cru **2.** [aggressive - attitude, personality] agressif.

I/O (written abbr of **input/output**) E/S.

IOC (abbr of **International Olympic Committee**) pr n CIO m.

iodine [🇬🇧 ˈaɪədiːn 🇺🇸 ˈaɪədaɪn] n iode m ; PHARM teinture f d'iode.

IOM written abbr of **Isle of Man.**

ion [ˈaɪən] n ion m.

ionizer [ˈaɪənaɪzər] n ioniseur m.

iota [aɪˈəʊtə] n **1.** [Greek letter] iota m **2.** [tiny bit] brin m, grain m, iota m.

IOU (abbr of **I owe you**) n reconnaissance de dette.

IOW 1. MESSAGING written abbr of **in other words 2.** written abbr of **Isle of Wight.**

Iowa [ˈaɪəʊə] pr n Iowa m / in Iowa dans l'Iowa.

IP (abbr of **Internet Protocol**) n ▶ **IP address** adresse *f* IP ▶ **IP number** numéro *m* IP.

IPA (abbr of **International Phonetic Alphabet**) n API *m*.

iPod® [ˈaɪpɒd] n iPod® *m*.

IPP (abbr of **Internet Presence Provider**) n *fournisseur d'accès à Internet proposant l'hébergement de sites Web.*

ipse, **IPSE** (abbr of **integrated project support environment**) n outils *mpl* logiciels.

IQ (abbr of **intelligence quotient**) n QI *m*.

IRA pr n (abbr of **Irish Republican Army**) IRA *f*.

 IRA

L'IRA est une organisation luttant pour la réunification de l'Irlande. En 1969, elle s'est scindée en deux et a donné naissance à la **Provisional IRA** et à l'**Official IRA**. En 1994, le processus de paix progressant, l'IRA s'est engagée à ne plus recourir à la violence. Le cessez-le-feu a été rompu plusieurs fois depuis, mais l'IRA, dans sa majorité, a suivi le Sinn Féin dans cette marche vers la paix (marquée en particulier par la signature de l'accord de paix d'Ulster, en avril 1998, le **Good Friday Agreement**). En 2005, l'IRA a annoncé la cessation de la lutte armée en faveur d'un dialogue démocratique visant la réunification de l'Irlande.

Iran [ɪˈrɑːn] pr n Iran *m* **/** *in Iran* en Iran.

Iranian [ɪˈreɪnjən] ◆ n **1.** [person] Iranien *m*, -enne *f* **2.** LING iranien *m*. ◆ adj iranien.

Iraq [ɪˈrɑːk] pr n Iraq *m*, Irak *m* **/** *in Iraq* en Iraq.

Iraqi [ɪˈrɑːkɪ] ◆ n Irakien *m*, -enne *f*, Iraquien *m*, -enne *f*. ◆ adj irakien.

irascible [ɪˈræsəbl] adj irascible, coléreux.

irate [aɪˈreɪt] adj furieux **/** *she got most irate about it* cela l'a rendue furieuse.

IRC (abbr of **Internet Relay Chat**) n IRC *m* (*dialogue en temps réel*).

IRC channel n canal *m* IRC, canal *m* de dialogue en temps réel.

Ireland [ˈaɪələnd] pr n Irlande *f* **/** *in Ireland* en Irlande ▶ **the Republic of Ireland** la république d'Irlande.

iridescent [ˌɪrɪˈdesənt] adj irisé, iridescent *liter*.

iris [ˈaɪərɪs] n **1.** (*pl* **irises** or **irides** [ɪrɪdiːz]) ANAT iris *m* **2.** (*pl* **irises**) BOT iris *m* **3.** PHOT ▶ **iris (diaphragm)** iris *m*.

Irish [ˈaɪrɪʃ] ◆ pl n ▶ **the Irish** les Irlandais. ◆ n LING irlandais *m*. ◆ adj irlandais ▶ **the Irish Free State** l'État *m* libre d'Irlande.

 The Irish Free State

En 1921, après deux ans de guerre civile, la partition de l'Irlande donna naissance à l'Irlande du Nord et à l'État libre d'Irlande, membre du Commonwealth.

Irish coffee n irish-coffee *m*.

Irishman [ˈaɪrɪʃmən] (*pl* **Irishmen** [-mən]) n Irlandais *m*.

Irish Sea pr n ▶ **the Irish Sea** la mer d'Irlande.

Irish stew n ≃ ragoût *m* de mouton.

Irishwoman [ˈaɪrɪʃˌwumən] (*pl* **Irishwomen** [-ˌwɪmɪn]) n Irlandaise *f*.

irk [ɜːk] vt irriter, agacer.

irksome [ˈɜːksəm] adj irritant, agaçant.

IRL MESSAGING written abbr of **in real life**.

IRN (abbr of **Independent Radio News**) pr n *agence de presse radiophonique en Grande-Bretagne.*

iron [ˈaɪən] ◆ adj **1.** [made of, containing iron] de fer, en fer **2.** *fig* [strong] de fer, d'acier. ◆ vt [laundry] repasser. ◆ vi [laundry] se repasser. ◆ n **1.** [mineral] fer *m* **2.** [for laundry] fer *m* (à repasser) ; [action] : *your shirt needs an iron* ta chemise a besoin d'un coup de fer or d'être repassée **3.** [tool, appliance] fer *m* ▶ **to have many irons in the fire** avoir plusieurs fers au feu, jouer sur plusieurs tableaux **4.** [golf club] fer *m*. ◆ **iron out** vt sep **1.** [crease] repasser **2.** *fig* [problem, difficulty] aplanir ; [differences] faire disparaître.

Iron Age n ▶ **the Iron Age** l'âge *m* du fer.

Iron Curtain ◆ n ▶ **the Iron Curtain** HIST le rideau *m* de fer. ◆ adj ▶ **the Iron Curtain countries** les pays *mpl* du bloc soviétique.

ironic(al) [aɪˈrɒnɪk(l)] adj ironique.

📋 Note that **il est ironique que** is followed by a verb in the subjunctive:
It's ironic that he's now so popular. *Il est ironique qu'il soit si populaire aujourd'hui.*

ironically [aɪˈrɒnɪklɪ] adv **1.** [smile, laugh] ironiquement **2.** [paradoxically] : *ironically enough, he was the only one to remember* paradoxalement, il était le seul à s'en souvenir.

ironing [ˈaɪənɪŋ] n repassage *m* ▶ **to do the ironing** faire le repassage, repasser.

ironing board n planche *f* or table *f* à repasser.

iron lung n MED poumon *m* d'acier.

ironmonger [ˈaɪənˌmʌŋgəʳ] n UK quincaillier *m*.

iron-on transfer n transfert *m* (*appliqué au fer à repasser*).

iron-willed adj à la volonté de fer.

ironworks [ˈaɪənwɜːks] (*pl* **ironworks**) n usine *f* sidérurgique.

irony [ˈaɪrənɪ] (*pl* **ironies**) n [gen & LITER] ironie *f*.

irradiate [ɪˈreɪdɪeɪt] vt **1.** MED & PHYS [expose to radiation] irradier ; [food] irradier **2.** [light up] illuminer, éclairer.

irrational [ɪˈræʃənl] adj **1.** [person, behaviour, feeling] irrationnel ; [fear] irraisonné ; [creature, being] incapable de raisonner **2.** MATH irrationnel.

irrationally [ɪˈræʃnəlɪ] adv irrationnellement.

irreconcilable [ɪˈrekənsaɪləbl] adj **1.** [aims, views, beliefs] inconciliable, incompatible **2.** [conflict, disagreement] insoluble.

irreconcilably [ɪˌrekənˈsaɪləblɪ] adv : *they are irreconcilably divided* il y a entre eux des divisions irréconciliables.

irrefutable [ˌɪrɪˈfjuːtəbl] adj [argument, proof] irréfutable ; [fact] certain, indéniable.

irregular [ɪˈregjuləʳ] ◆ adj **1.** [object, shape, etc.] irrégulier ; [surface] inégal **2.** [intermittent, spasmodic] irrégulier **3.** *fml* [unorthodox] irrégulier **4.** LING irrégulier. ◆ n **1.** MIL irrégulier *m* **2.** US COMM article *m* de second choix.

irregularity [ɪˌregjuˈlærətɪ] (*pl* **irregularities**) n [of surface, work, breathing] irrégularité *f*. ◆ **irregularities** pl n [errors, intringements] irrégularités *fpl*.

irregularly [ɪ'regjʊləlɪ] adv **1.** [spasmodically] irrégulièrement **2.** [unevenly] inégalement.

irrelevance [ɪ'reləvəns] n **1.** [of fact, comment] manque m de rapport, non-pertinence f **2.** [pointless fact or matter] inutilité f.

irrelevancy [ɪ'reləvənsɪ] (pl **irrelevancies**) = irrelevance.

irrelevant [ɪ'reləvənt] adj sans rapport, hors de propos.

irreparable [ɪ'repərəbl] adj irréparable.

irreplaceable [ˌɪrɪ'pleɪsəbl] adj irremplaçable.

irrepressible [ˌɪrɪ'presəbl] adj **1.** [need, desire] irrépressible ; [good humour] à toute épreuve **2.** [person] jovial, plein d'entrain.

irreproachable [ˌɪrɪ'prəʊtʃəbl] adj irréprochable.

irresistible [ˌɪrɪ'zɪstəbl] adj irrésistible.

irresistibly [ˌɪrɪ'zɪstəblɪ] adv irrésistiblement.

irresolute [ɪ'rezəlu:t] adj irrésolu, indécis.

irrespective [ˌɪrɪ'spektɪv] ❖ **irrespective of** prep phr sans tenir compte de.

irresponsible [ˌɪrɪ'spɒnsəbl] adj [person] irresponsable ; [act] irréfléchi.

irresponsibly [ˌɪrɪ'spɒnsəblɪ] adv [act, behave] de manière irresponsable.

irretrievable [ˌɪrɪ'tri:vəbl] adj [object] introuvable ; [loss, harm, damage] irréparable.

irretrievably [ˌɪrɪ'tri:vəblɪ] adv irréparablement, irrémédiablement.

irreverence [ɪ'revərəns] n irrévérence f.

irreverent [ɪ'revərənt] adj irrévérencieux.

irreversible [ˌɪrɪ'vɜ:səbl] adj irréversible.

irrevocable [ɪ'revəkəbl] adj irrévocable.

irrigate ['ɪrɪgeɪt] vt [gen & MED] irriguer.

irrigation [ˌɪrɪ'geɪʃn] n [gen & MED] irrigation f.

irritability [ˌɪrɪtə'bɪlətɪ] n irritabilité f.

irritable ['ɪrɪtəbl] adj [gen & MED] irritable.

irritably ['ɪrɪtəblɪ] adv avec irritation.

irritant ['ɪrɪtənt] ❖ adj irritant. ❖ n irritant m.

irritate ['ɪrɪteɪt] vt **1.** [annoy] irriter, contrarier, énerver **2.** MED irriter.

irritated ['ɪrɪteɪtɪd] adj **1.** [annoyed] irrité, agacé **2.** MED [eyes, skin] irrité.

irritating ['ɪrɪteɪtɪŋ] adj **1.** [annoying] irritant, contrariant, énervant **2.** MED irritant, irritatif.

irritation [ɪrɪ'teɪʃn] n **1.** [annoyance] irritation f, agacement m **2.** MED irritation f.

IRS (abbr of **Internal Revenue Service**) pr n ▶ **the IRS** le fisc américain.

is [ɪz] ⟶ be.

IS n abbr of **information system**.

ISA (abbr of **individual savings account**) n 🇬🇧 plan m d'épargne défiscalisé.

ISBN (abbr of **International Standard Book Number**) n ISBN m.

ISDN (abbr of **integrated services digital network**) n RNIS m.

Islam ['ɪzlɑ:m] n islam m, Islam m.

Islamic [ɪz'læmɪk] adj islamique.

Islamic fundamentalist n fondamentaliste mf islamiste, intégriste mf islamiste.

Islamicize, Islamicise [ɪz'læmɪsaɪz] vt islamiser.

Islamism ['ɪzləmɪzəm] n islamisme m.

Islamist ['ɪzləmɪst] adj & n islamiste mf.

Islamization [ˌɪzləmaɪ'zeɪʃən] n islamisation f.

Islamophobia [ɪz,læmə'fəʊbɪə] n islamophobie f.

Islamophobic [ɪz,læmə'fəʊbɪk] adj islamophobe.

island ['aɪlənd] n GEOG île f.

islander ['aɪləndə] n insulaire mf.

isle [aɪl] n île f.

Isle of Man pr n ▶ **the Isle of Man** l'île f de Man / **in** or **on the Isle of Man** à l'île de Man.

Isle of Wight [-waɪt] pr n ▶ **the Isle of Wight** l'île f de Wight / **in** or **on the Isle of Wight** à l'île de Wight.

isn't ['ɪznt] abbr of **is not**.

ISO (abbr of **International Organization for Standardization**) n ISO f.

isolate ['aɪsəleɪt] vt [gen & MED] isoler.

isolated ['aɪsəleɪtɪd] adj **1.** [alone, remote] isolé **2.** [single] unique, isolé.

isolation [aɪsə'leɪʃn] n isolement m / **in isolation** en soi, isolément.

isolationism [ˌaɪsə'leɪʃənɪzm] n isolationnisme m.

isosceles [aɪ'sɒsɪli:z] adj isocèle ▶ **an isosceles triangle** un triangle isocèle.

isotope ['aɪsətəʊp] n isotope m.

ISP n (abbr of **Internet service provider**) FAI m.

Israel ['ɪzreɪəl] pr n Israël m / **in Israel** en Israël.

Israeli [ɪz'reɪlɪ] (pl **Israeli** or **Israelis**) ❖ n Israélien m, -enne f ❖ adj israélien.

Israelite ['ɪzrəlaɪt] n Israélite mf.

ISS ['aɪ'es'es] (abbr of **In School Suspension**) n 🇺🇸 SCH exclusion f interne.

issue ['ɪʃu:] ❖ n **1.** [matter, topic] question f, problème m ▶ **at issue** en question **2.** [cause of disagreement] différend m ▶ **to make an issue of sthg** monter qqch en épingle ▶ **to take issue with sb / sthg** être en désaccord avec qqn / qqch **3.** [edition - of newspaper, magazine, etc.] numéro m **4.** [distribution - of supplies] distribution f ; [- of tickets, official document] délivrance f ; [- of shares, money, stamps] émission f **5.** fml [result, outcome] issue f, résultat m. ❖ vt **1.** [book, newspaper] publier, sortir ; [official document, passport] délivrer ; LAW [warrant, writ] lancer ; [statement, proclamation] publier / **the government has issued a denial** le gouvernement a publié un démenti ; [shares, money, stamps] émettre **2.** [distribute - supplies, tickets, etc.] distribuer.

Istanbul [ˌɪstæn'bʊl] pr n Istanbul.

isthmus ['ɪsməs] (pl **isthmuses** or **isthmi** [-maɪ]) n isthme m.

it [ɪt] ❖ pron **1.** [referring to specific thing, animal, etc. - as subject] il (elle) ; [- as direct object] le (la), l' (before vowel or silent 'h') ; [- as indirect object] lui / **I'd lend you my watch but it's broken** je te prêterais bien ma montre mais elle est cassée **2.** [after preposition] : **he told me all about it** il m'a tout raconté / **there was nothing inside it** il n'y avait rien dedans or à l'intérieur / **I left the bag under it** j'ai laissé le sac dessous **3.** [impersonal uses] : **it's me!** c'est moi ! / **it's raining / snowing** il pleut / neige / **I like it here** je me plais beaucoup ici / **I couldn't bear it if she left** je ne supporterais pas qu'elle parte / **it might look rude if I don't go** si je n'y vais pas cela pourrait être considéré comme une impolitesse / **it's a goal!** but ! ❖ n inf [most important person] : **he thinks he's it (and a bit)** il s'y croit.

IT n (abbr of **information technology**) informatique f ▶ **IT guy** inf informaticien m ▶ **IT manager** responsable mf du service informatique ▶ **IT support** support m informatique.

Italian [ɪ'tæljən] ❖ n **1.** [person] Italien m, -enne f **2.** LING italien m. ❖ adj italien.

Italian dressing n vinaigrette f aux fines herbes.

italic [ɪ'tælɪk] ◆ adj italique. ◆ n italique m / *in italics* en italique. ❖ **Italic** ◆ adj [of ancient Italy] italique. ◆ n LING italique m.

italicize, italicise [ɪ'tælɪsaɪz] vt mettre en italique.

Italy ['ɪtəlɪ] pr n Italie f / *in Italy* en Italie.

itch [ɪtʃ] ◆ n **1.** *lit* démangeaison f **2.** *inf & fig* [desire] envie f. ◆ vi **1.** [physically] avoir des démangeaisons ; [insect bite, part of body] : *does it itch?* est-ce que cela te démange ? **2.** *inf & fig* [desire] ▸ *to be itching to do sthg* : *I was itching to tell her* ça me démangeait de lui dire.

itching ['ɪtʃɪŋ] n démangeaison f.

itchy ['ɪtʃɪ] (*compar* **itchier**, *superl* **itchiest**) adj qui gratte, qui démange / *I've got an itchy leg* ma jambe me démange.

it'd ['ɪtəd] **1.** abbr of **it would 2.** abbr of **it had**.

item ['aɪtəm] n **1.** [object] article m / *an item of clothing* un vêtement **2.** [point, issue] point m, question f **3.** [in newspaper] article m ; [on TV or radio] point m or sujet m d'actualité **4.** COMPUT article m **5.** [couple] : *are they an item?* est-ce qu'ils sortent ensemble ?

itemize, itemise ['aɪtəmaɪz] vt détailler.

it-girl n *inf* jeune femme fortement médiatisée.

itinerant [ɪ'tɪnərənt] ◆ adj itinérant ; [actors] ambulant, itinérant ▸ **itinerant teacher** 🇺🇸 professeur m remplaçant. ◆ n nomade mf.

itinerary [aɪ'tɪnərərɪ] (*pl* **itineraries**) n itinéraire m.

it'll [ɪtl] abbr of **it will**.

ITN (abbr of **Independent Television News**) pr n *service d'actualités télévisées pour les chaînes relevant de l'IBA.*

its [ɪts] det son m, sa f, ses mf.

it's [ɪts] **1.** abbr of **it is 2.** abbr of **it has**.

IAD8 MESSAGING written abbr of **it's a date**.

itself [ɪt'self] pron **1.** [reflexive use] se, s' *(before vowel or silent 'h')* / *the cat was licking itself clean* le chat faisait sa toilette **2.** [emphatic use] lui-même m, elle-même f / *she's kindness itself* c'est la gentillesse même **3.** [after preposition] : *it switches off by itself* ça s'éteint tout seul / *it's not dangerous in itself* ce n'est pas dangereux en soi.

ITV (abbr of **Independent Television**) n *sigle désignant les programmes diffusés par les chaînes relevant de l'IBA.*

ITYS MESSAGING written abbr of **I think you stink**.

IUCD (abbr of **intrauterine contraceptive device**) n stérilet m.

IUD (abbr of **intrauterine device**) n stérilet m.

IUSS MESSAGING written abbr of **if you say so**.

IV (abbr of **intravenous**) adj MED ▸ **IV drip** perfusion f.

I've [aɪv] abbr of **I have**.

IVF (abbr of **in vitro fertilization**) n FIV f.

ivory ['aɪvərɪ] (*pl* **ivories**) ◆ adj **1.** [made of ivory] d'ivoire, en ivoire **2.** [ivory-coloured] (couleur) ivoire (*inv*). ◆ n **1.** [substance] ivoire m **2.** [object] ivoire m. ❖ **ivories** pl n *inf* [piano keys] touches fpl.

Ivory Coast pr n ▸ **the Ivory Coast** la Côte-d'Ivoire / *in the Ivory Coast* en Côte-d'Ivoire.

ivory tower n tour f d'ivoire.

ivy ['aɪvɪ] (*pl* **ivies**) n lierre m.

Ivy League n groupe des huit universités les plus prestigieuses du nord-est des États-Unis. ❖ **Ivy-League** adj : *he had an Ivy-League education* il a fait ses études dans une grande université.

IWB n abbr of **interactive whiteboard**.

IYD MESSAGING written abbr of **in your dreams**.

J/A written abbr of joint account.

jab [dʒæb] (pt & pp **jabbed**, cont **jabbing**) ◆ vt [pierce] piquer / *he jabbed my arm with a needle* or *he jabbed a needle into my arm* il m'a piqué le bras avec une aiguille, il m'a enfoncé une aiguille dans le bras ; [poke] : *you almost jabbed me in the eye with that knife!* tu as failli m'éborgner avec ce couteau ! ; [brandish] pointer, brandir (*d'une façon menaçante*). ◆ vi **1.** [stick] s'enfoncer / *something jabbed into my ribs* j'ai reçu un coup sec dans les côtes **2.** [gesture] : *he jabbed at me with his umbrella* il essaya de me donner un coup de parapluie **3.** [in boxing] : *he's jabbing with (his) right and left* il lui envoie un direct du droit et du gauche. ◆ n **1.** [poke] coup *m* (*donné avec un objet pointu*) ; [in boxing] (coup *m*) droit *m* or direct *m* **2.** inf MED piqûre *f*.

jabber [ˈdʒæbər] inf ◆ vi [idly] jacasser, caqueter *pej* ; [inarticulately] bredouiller, bafouiller ; [in foreign tongue] baragouiner. ◆ vt ▶ **to jabber (out)** bredouiller, bafouiller.

jack [dʒæk] ◆ vt MECH soulever avec un vérin ; AUTO mettre sur cric. ◆ n **1.** MECH & MIN [tool] vérin *m* ; AUTO cric *m* **2.** [playing card] valet *m* **3.** [in bowls] cochonnet *m* **4.** ELEC [male] = **jack plug** ; [female] = **jack socket** **5.** US v inf [money] blé *m*, fric *m*. ◆ **jack in** vt sep UK inf plaquer. ◆ **jack up** vt sep **1.** [car] lever avec un cric **2.** inf [price, wage] augmenter, monter.

jackal [ˈdʒækəl] n *lit & fig* chacal *m*.

jackass [ˈdʒækæs] n **1.** [donkey] âne *m*, baudet *m* **2.** inf [imbecile] imbécile *mf*.

jackdaw [ˈdʒækdɔː] n choucas *m*.

jacket [ˈdʒækɪt] n **1.** [for men] veste *f* ; [for women] veste *f*, jaquette *f* ▶ **leather jacket** blouson *m* de cuir **2.** [of book] jaquette *f* ; US [of record] pochette *f* **3.** CULIN ▶ **jacket potato, potato (cooked) in its jacket** pomme de terre *f* en robe des champs or en robe de chambre **4.** TECH [of boiler] chemise *f*.

jackhammer [ˈdʒæk,hæmər] n US marteau piqueur *m*.

jack-in-the-box n diable *m* (à ressort).

jackknife [ˈdʒæknaɪf] (pl **jackknives** [-naɪvz]) ◆ n couteau *m* de poche. ◆ vi : *the truck jackknifed* le camion s'est mis en travers de la route.

jackknife dive n SPORT saut *m* de carpe.

jack-of-all-trades n *pej* homme *m* à tout faire.

jack plug n jack *m* (mâle), fiche *f* jack.

jackpot [ˈdʒækpɒt] n gros lot *m* ; [in cards] pot *m*.

jacksie [ˈdʒæksɪ] n UK v inf [buttocks] fesses *fpl*, popotin *m*.

Jacobean [,dʒækəˈbɪən] adj jacobéen *m*, -enne *f* (*de l'époque de Jacques Iᵉ d'Angleterre*).

Jacobite [ˈdʒækəbaɪt] ◆ adj jacobite ▶ **the Jacobite Rising** *nom donné aux deux tentatives conduites par les Stuarts pour s'emparer du trône d'Angleterre, en 1715 et 1745.* ◆ n jacobite *mf*.

🏛 **The Jacobites**

Membres du parti légitimiste anglais qui soutint, après la révolution de 1688, d'abord la cause de Jacques II contre Guillaume d'Orange, puis celle des derniers Stuarts contre la maison de Hanovre.

Jacuzzi® [dʒəˈkuːzɪ] (pl **Jacuzzis**) n Jacuzzi® *m*, bain *m* à remous.

jade [dʒeɪd] ◆ n **1.** [stone] jade *m* **2.** [colour] vert jade *m* inv. ◆ adj **1.** [made of jade] de or en jade **2.** [colour] vert jade (inv).

jaded [ˈdʒeɪdɪd] adj [person] désabusé, blasé, éreinté ; [appetite] écœuré, saturé.

jagged [ˈdʒægɪd] adj [edge, coastline] déchiqueté ; [tear] irrégulier ; [rock] râpeux, rugueux.

jaguar [ˈdʒægjuər] n jaguar *m*.

jail [dʒeɪl] ◆ n prison *f* ▶ **to be in jail** être en prison. ◆ vt emprisonner, mettre en prison, incarcérer.

jailbait [ˈdʒeɪlbeɪt] n (U) US inf mineur *m*, -e *f* / *she's jailbait* c'est un coup à se retrouver en taule (*pour détournement de mineur*).

jailbird [ˈdʒeɪlbɜːd] n inf récidiviste *mf*.

jailbreak [ˈdʒeɪlbreɪk] n évasion *f*.

jailer [ˈdʒeɪlər] n geôlier *m*, -ère *f*.

jailhouse [ˈdʒeɪlhaʊs] (pl [-hauzɪz]) n US prison *f*.

Jakarta [dʒəˈkɑːtə] pr n Djakarta, Jakarta.

jalapeño [dʒælæˈpiːnəʊ] n US petit piment *m*.

jam [dʒæm] (pt & pp **jammed**, cont **jamming**) ◆ n **1.** [preserve] confiture *f* **2.** [congestion] encombrement *m* **3.** inf [predicament] pétrin *m*. ◆ comp [tart, pudding, sandwich] à la confiture. ◆ vt **1.** [crowd, cram] entasser, tasser ; [push roughly, ram] fourrer **2.** [make stick] coincer, bloquer **3.** [congest] encombrer, bloquer, boucher **4.** RADIO brouiller. ◆ vi **1.** [crowd] se tasser, s'entasser **2.** [become stuck - gen] se coincer, se bloquer ; [-gun] s'enrayer ; [-brakes] se bloquer **3.** inf [play in a jam session] faire un bœuf **4.** US inf ▶ **to be jamming** aller très bien / *she's jammin'* elle va super bien. ◆ **jam on** vt sep inf ▶ **to jam on the brakes** piler.

Jamaica [dʒəˈmeɪkə] pr n Jamaïque *f* / *in Jamaica* à la Jamaïque.

Jamaican [dʒəˈmeɪkn] ◆ n Jamaïcain *m*, -e f, Jamaïquain *m*, -e f. ◆ adj jamaïcain, jamaïquain.

jamb [dʒæm] n montant m.

jamboree [ˌdʒæmbə'riː] n 1. [gathering] grande fête f 2. [scout rally] jamboree m.

jam-full adj inf bourré, archiplein.

jamjar ['dʒæmdʒɑːʳ] n pot m à confiture.

jamming ['dʒæmɪŋ] n 1. coincement m ; [of brakes] blocage m 2. RADIO brouillage m.

jammy ['dʒæmɪ] (compar **jammier**, superl **jammiest**) adj UK inf 1. [sticky with jam] poisseux 2. [lucky] chanceux.

jam-packed = jam-full.

jams [dʒæmz] pl n US [shorts] bermuda m.

jam session n inf bœuf m, jam-session f.

Jan. (written abbr of **January**) janv.

jangle ['dʒæŋgl] ◆ vi retentir (avec un bruit métallique or avec fracas) ; [more quietly] cliqueter. ◆ vt faire retentir ; [more quietly] faire cliqueter. ◆ n [of bells] tintamarre m ; [of money] bruit m, cliquetis m.

janitor ['dʒænɪtəʳ] n US & Scot [caretaker] gardien m, concierge m ; dated [doorkeeper] portier m.

January ['dʒænjʊərɪ] n janvier m. **See also February**.

japan [dʒə'pæn] ◆ n ART laque f. ◆ vt laquer.

Japan [dʒə'pæn] pr n Japon m / **in Japan** au Japon.

Japanese [ˌdʒæpə'niːz] (pl **Japanese**) ◆ n 1. [person] Japonais m, -e f 2. LING japonais m. ◆ adj japonais.

jape [dʒeɪp] n inf & dated farce f, blague f.

jar [dʒɑːʳ] (pt & pp **jarred**, cont **jarring**) ◆ n 1. [container - glass] bocal m ; [-for jam] pot m ; [-earthenware] pot m, jarre f 2. UK inf [drink] pot m 3. [jolt] secousse f, choc m. ◆ vi 1. [make harsh noise] grincer, crisser 2. [clash - note] détonner ; [-colour] jurer. ◆ vt [shake - structure] secouer, ébranler.

jargon ['dʒɑːgən] n jargon m.

jarring ['dʒɑːrɪŋ] adj [sound] discordant ; [colour] criard.

Jas. written abbr of **James**.

jasmine ['dʒæzmɪn] n jasmin m.

jaundice ['dʒɔːndɪs] n 1. (U) MED jaunisse f 2. fig [bitterness] amertume f.

jaundiced ['dʒɔːndɪst] adj [bitter] aigri, cynique ; [disapproving] désapprobateur.

jaunt [dʒɔːnt] ◆ n balade f. ◆ vi : she's always jaunting off to Paris elle est toujours en balade entre ici et Paris.

jauntily ['dʒɔːntɪlɪ] adv [cheerfully] joyeusement, jovialement ; [in a sprightly way] lestement.

jaunty ['dʒɔːntɪ] (compar **jauntier**, superl **jauntiest**) adj [cheerful] joyeux, enjoué, jovial ; [sprightly] leste, allègre.

java ['dʒɑːvə] n US inf [coffee] caoua m, café m.

Java ['dʒɑːvə] pr n Java m / **in Java** à Java.

Java script n COMPUT (langage m) Javascript m.

javelin ['dʒævlɪn] n [weapon] javelot m, javeline f ; SPORT javelot m ▸ **javelin thrower** lanceur m, -euse f de javelot.

jaw [dʒɔː] n 1. ANAT mâchoire f 2. [of tool] mâchoire f.

jawbone ['dʒɔːbəʊn] n maxillaire m.

jay [dʒeɪ] n ORNITH geai m.

jaywalk ['dʒeɪwɔːk] vi US marcher en dehors des passages pour piétons.

jaywalker ['dʒeɪwɔːkəʳ] n US piéton qui traverse en dehors des passages pour piétons.

jazz [dʒæz] ◆ n 1. MUS jazz m ▸ **the Jazz Age** l'âge d'or du jazz américain 2. inf [rigmarole] baratin m, blabla m ▸ **and all that jazz** et tout le bataclan. ◆ comp [club, album, singer] de jazz ▸ **jazz band** jazz-band m. ❖ **jazz up** vt sep 1. MUS : to jazz up a song mettre une chanson sur un rythme (de) jazz 2. inf [enliven] égayer.

jazzy ['dʒæzɪ] (compar **jazzier**, superl **jazziest**) adj 1. [music] (de) jazz (inv), sur un rythme de jazz 2. inf [gaudy] tapageur, voyant ; [smart] chic (inv).

JCB® n tractopelle f.

JCR (abbr of **junior common room**) n UK UNIV 1. [place] ≃ foyer m des étudiants 2. [students] ▸ **the JCR** les étudiants.

JCS pl n abbr of **Joint Chiefs of Staff**.

JD ◆ pr n 1. abbr of **Justice Department** 2. abbr of **Doctor of Jurisprudence**. ◆ n US ≃ docteur m en droit.

jealous ['dʒeləs] adj 1. [envious] jaloux ▸ **to be jealous of sb** être jaloux de qqn 2. [possessive] jaloux, possessif.

jealously ['dʒeləslɪ] adv jalousement.

jealousy ['dʒeləsɪ] (pl **jealousies**) n jalousie f.

jeans [dʒiːnz] pl n jean m, blue-jean m ▸ **a pair of jeans** un jean.

Jedda ['dʒedə] pr n Djedda.

Jeep® [dʒiːp] n Jeep® f.

jeer [dʒɪəʳ] ◆ vi [scoff] railler, se moquer ; [boo, hiss] pousser des cris hostiles or de dérision / everybody jeered at me ils se sont tous moqués de moi. ◆ vt huer, conspuer. ◆ n [scoffing] raillerie f ; [boo, hiss] huée f.

jeering ['dʒɪərɪŋ] ◆ adj railleur, moqueur. ◆ n (U) [scoffing] railleries fpl ; [boos, hisses] huées fpl.

jeez [dʒiːz] interj US inf purée !

Jehovah [dʒɪ'həʊvə] pr n Jéhovah ▸ **Jehovah's Witness** témoin de Jéhovah.

Jell-o® ['dʒeləʊ] n US = jelly.

jelly ['dʒelɪ] (pl **jellies**) ◆ n 1. [gen] gelée f 2. UK CULIN [dessert] gelée f 3. US CULIN [jam] confiture f, gelée f. ◆ vt gélifier.

jelly baby (pl **jelly babies**) n UK bonbon m gélifié (en forme de bébé).

jelly bean n dragée f à la gelée de sucre.

jellyfish ['dʒelɪfɪʃ] (pl **jellyfish** or **jellyfishes**) n méduse f.

jelly roll n US [gâteau m] roulé m.

jemmy ['dʒemɪ] (pl **jemmies**, pt & pp **jemmied**) UK inf ◆ n pince-monseigneur f. ◆ vt ▸ **to jemmy a door (open)** forcer une porte avec une pince-monseigneur.

jeopardize, jeopardise ['dʒepədaɪz] vt compromettre, mettre en péril.

jeopardy ['dʒepədɪ] n danger m, péril m / our future is in jeopardy notre avenir est en péril or menacé or compromis.

jerk [dʒɜːk] ◆ vt 1. [pull] tirer d'un coup sec, tirer brusquement 2. [shake] secouer. ◆ vi 1. [jolt] cahoter, tressauter 2. [person - jump] sursauter ; [person, muscle - twitch] se contracter. ◆ n 1. [bump] secousse f, saccade f 2. [wrench] coup m sec 3. [brusque movement] mouvement m brusque 4. US v inf [person] con m 5. = **jerky** (noun). ❖ **jerk off** vi vulg se branler.

jerkily ['dʒɜːkɪlɪ] adv par à-coups.

jerkin ['dʒɜːkɪn] n blouson m ; HIST pourpoint m.

jerky ['dʒɜːkɪ] (compar **jerkier**, superl **jerkiest**) ◆ n US viande f séchée ▸ **beef jerky** bœuf m séché. ◆ adj [bumpy] saccadé.

jerry-built adj pej [house, building] construit en carton-pâte, peu solide.

jersey ['dʒɜːzɪ] n 1. [pullover] pull-over m, tricot m ; SPORT maillot m 2. [fabric] jersey m.

Jersey ['dʒɜːzɪ] ◆ pr n Jersey / **in Jersey** à Jersey. ◆ n = **Jersey cow**.

Jersey cow n vache f jersiaise.

Jerusalem [dʒə'ru:sələm] pr n Jérusalem.

Jerusalem artichoke n topinambour m.

jest [dʒest] ◆ n plaisanterie f ▶ **to say sthg in jest** dire qqch pour rire or pour plaisanter. ◆ vi plaisanter.

jester ['dʒestər] n bouffon m, fou m (du roi).

Jesuit ['dʒezjuɪt] ◆ n jésuite m. ◆ adj jésuite.

Jesus ['dʒi:zəs] pr n Jésus ▶ **Jesus Christ** Jésus-Christ.

jet [dʒet] (pt & pp **jetted**, cont **jetting**) ◆ n **1.** [aircraft] avion m à réaction, jet m **2.** [stream - of liquid] jet m, giclée f ; [- of gas, steam] jet m **3.** [nozzle, outlet] gicleur m ; [on gas cooker] brûleur m **4.** [gem] jais m. ◆ comp **1.** [fighter, bomber] à réaction ; [transport, travel] en avion (à réaction) ▶ **jet fuel** kérosène m **2.** [made of jet - earrings, necklace] en jais. ◆ vi **1.** inf [travel by jet] voyager en avion (à réaction) **2.** [issue forth - liquid] gicler, jaillir.

jet-black adj jais (inv), noir de jais.

jet engine n moteur m à réaction.

jetfoil ['dʒetfɔɪl] n hydroglisseur m.

jetlag ['dʒetlæg] n fatigue f due au décalage horaire.

jet-lagged [-lægd] adj fatigué par le décalage horaire.

jet-propelled adj à réaction.

jetsam ['dʒetsəm] n (U) jet m à la mer.

jet set n inf jet-set m.

jet-setter n inf membre m du jet-set.

jetski ['dʒetski] n scooter m de mer, jetski m.

jettison ['dʒetɪsən] vt **1.** NAUT jeter à la mer, jeter par-dessus bord ; AERON [bombs, cargo] larguer **2.** fig [unwanted possession] se débarrasser de ; [theory, hope] abandonner.

jet trail n traînée f de condensation.

jetty ['dʒetɪ] (pl **jetties**) n [landing stage] embarcadère m, débarcadère m ; [breakwater] jetée f, môle m.

Jew [dʒu:] n Juif m, -ive f.

jewel ['dʒu:əl] n **1.** [precious stone] bijou m, joyau m, pierre f précieuse ; [in clockmaking] rubis m **2.** fig [person, thing] bijou m, perle f.

jewel box, jewel case n boîte f de CD.

jeweled 🇺🇸 = jewelled.

jeweler 🇺🇸 = jeweller.

jewelled 🇬🇧, **jeweled** 🇺🇸 ['dʒu:əld] adj orné de bijoux ; [watch] à rubis.

jeweller 🇬🇧, **jeweler** 🇺🇸 ['dʒu:ələr] n bijoutier m, -ère f, joaillier m, -ère f ▶ **jeweller's (shop)** bijouterie f.

jewellery 🇬🇧, **jewelry** 🇺🇸 ['dʒu:əlrɪ] n (U) bijoux mpl / **a piece of jewellery** un bijou.

Jewess ['dʒu:ɪs] n arch & pej Juive f.

Jewish ['dʒu:ɪʃ] adj juif.

JFK¹ (abbr of **John Fitzgerald Kennedy International Airport**) pr n aéroport de New York.

JFK² MESSAGING written abbr of **just for kicks**.

jib [dʒɪb] (pt & pp **jibbed**, cont **jibbing**) ◆ n **1.** NAUT foc m **2.** [of crane] flèche f, bras m. ◆ vi 🇬🇧 [horse] regimber ; [person] ▶ **to jib (at sthg)** regimber or rechigner (à qqch).

jibe [dʒaɪb] ◆ vi **1.** 🇺🇸 inf [agree] s'accorder, coller **2.** = gibe. ◆ n = gibe.

Jidda ['dʒɪdə] = Jedda.

jiffy ['dʒɪfɪ] (pl **jiffies**), **jiff** [dʒɪf] n inf ▶ **to do sthg in a jiffy** faire qqch en un rien de temps or en moins de deux.

Jiffy bag® n enveloppe f matelassée.

jig [dʒɪg] (pt & pp **jigged**, cont **jigging**) ◆ n **1.** [dance] gigue f **2.** TECH gabarit m **3.** FISHING leurre m. ◆ vi **1.** [dance] danser allègrement **2.** 🇬🇧 ▶ **to jig (around** or **about)** sautiller, se trémousser.

jiggle ['dʒɪgl] ◆ vt secouer (légèrement). ◆ vi ▶ **to jiggle (about** or **around)** se trémousser. ◆ n secousse f.

jiggy ['dʒɪgɪ] adj 🇺🇸 inf [cool] cool.

jigsaw ['dʒɪgsɔ:] n [game] : **the pieces of the jigsaw were beginning to fall into place** fig peu à peu tout devenait clair ▶ **jigsaw (puzzle)** puzzle m.

jihad [dʒɪ'hɑ:d] n djihad m.

jilt [dʒɪlt] vt quitter.

jimmy ['dʒɪmɪ] (pl **jimmies**, pt & pp **jimmied**) 🇺🇸 = jemmy.

jingle ['dʒɪŋgl] ◆ n **1.** [sound] tintement m **2.** RADIO & TV jingle m. ◆ vi tinter. ◆ vt faire tinter.

jingoism ['dʒɪŋgəʊɪzm] n pej chauvinisme m.

jingoistic [,dʒɪŋgəʊ'ɪstɪk] adj pej chauvin, cocardier.

jinx [dʒɪŋks] inf ◆ n malchance f, sort m. ◆ vt porter malheur à, jeter un sort à ▶ **to be jinxed** être poursuivi par le mauvais sort.

JIT (abbr of **just in time**) adj juste à temps, JAT.

jitters ['dʒɪtəz] pl n inf frousse f.

jittery ['dʒɪtərɪ] adj inf [person] nerveux ; [situation] tendu, délicat.

jiu-jitsu [dʒu:'dʒɪtsu:] = ju-jitsu.

jive [dʒaɪv] ◆ n **1.** [dance] swing m **2.** [slang] ▶ **jive (talk)** argot m (employé par les Noirs américains, surtout les musiciens de jazz) **3.** 🇺🇸 inf [lies, nonsense] baratin m, blabla m. ◆ vt 🇺🇸 inf [deceive, mislead] baratiner, charrier. ◆ vi [dance] danser le swing. ◆ adj 🇺🇸 inf [phoney, insincere] bidon (inv).

JK MESSAGING written abbr of **just kidding**.

JNCC (abbr of **Joint Nature Conservation Committee**) n organisme britannique de protection de la nature.

Jnr (written abbr of **Junior**) : Michael Roberts Jnr Michael Roberts fils.

job [dʒɒb] (pt & pp **jobbed**, cont **jobbing**) ◆ n **1.** [occupation, employment] emploi m, travail m / **to find a job** trouver du travail or un emploi / **to look for a job** chercher un emploi or du travail ▶ **to be out of a job** être sans emploi or au chômage / **a Saturday / summer job** un boulot or un job pour le samedi / l'été / **he really knows his job** il connaît bien son métier or son boulot ▶ **jobs for the boys** copinage m **2.** [piece of work, task] travail m, tâche f / **to do a good job** faire du bon travail or du bon boulot / **she made a good job of fixing the car** elle s'en est bien sortie pour réparer la voiture / **it's not perfect but it does the job** fig ce n'est pas parfait mais ça fera l'affaire ▶ **on the job** [working] pendant le travail **3.** [role, responsibility] travail m / **it's not my job** ce n'est pas mon travail / **it's not my job to answer questions** je ne suis pas là pour répondre à des questions / **she had the job of breaking the bad news** c'est elle qui était chargée d'annoncer les mauvaises nouvelles **4.** [difficult time] ▶ **to have a job doing sthg** avoir du mal à faire qqch **5.** [state of affairs] : **it's a good job they were home** heureusement qu'ils étaient à la maison / **thanks for the map, it's just the job** merci pour la carte, c'est exactement ce qu'il me fallait **6.** inf [crime] coup m **7.** inf [item, specimen] : **he drives a flashy Italian job** il conduit un petit bolide italien **8.** COMPUT tâche f. ◆ vi [do piecework] travailler à la pièce ; [work irregularly] faire des petits travaux or boulots. ◆ vt 🇬🇧 ST. EX négocier.

job action n 🇺🇸 = industrial action.

jobbing ['dʒɒbɪŋ] adj 🇬🇧 : *jobbing gardener* jardinier *m* à la journée / *jobbing workman* ouvrier *m* à la tâche.

Jobcentre ['dʒɒb,sentə] n 🇬🇧 *agence locale pour l'emploi* ; ≃ Pôle *m* emploi.

job creation n création *f* d'emplois ▶ **job creation scheme** programme *m* de création d'emplois.

job description n description *f* de poste.

jobholder ['dʒɒb,həʊldə] n salarié *m*, -e *f*.

job-hop (*pt & pp* **job-hopped**, *cont* **job-hopping**) vi 🇺🇸 aller d'un emploi à l'autre.

jobhunter ['dʒɒb,hʌntə] = **jobseeker**.

job hunting n recherche *f* d'un emploi.

jobless ['dʒɒblɪs] ◆ adj au chômage, sans emploi. ◆ pl n ▶ **the jobless** les chômeurs *mpl*, les demandeurs *mpl* d'emploi.

job lot n 🇬🇧 COMM lot *m*.

job satisfaction n satisfaction *f* professionnelle.

job security n sécurité *f* de l'emploi.

jobseeker ['dʒɒbsi:kə] n 🇬🇧 demandeur *m* d'emploi ▶ **jobseeker's allowance** indemnité *f* de chômage.

job-share ◆ n partage *m* du travail. ◆ vi partager le travail.

jobsharing ['dʒɒbʃeərɪŋ] n partage *m* du travail.

jobsworth ['dʒɒbzwəθ] n 🇬🇧 *inf* petit chef *m* (*qui invoque le règlement pour éviter toute initiative*).

Joburg, Jo'burg ['dʒəʊbɜ:g] abbr of **Johannesburg**.

jock [dʒɒk] n *inf* **1.** 🇺🇸 [sporty type] sportif *m* **2.** [disc jockey] disc-jockey *m*, animateur *m*, -trice *f*.

Jock [dʒɒk] n *inf* [Scotsman] *terme injurieux ou humoristique désignant un Écossais.*

jockey ['dʒɒkɪ] ◆ n **1.** SPORT jockey *m* **2.** 🇺🇸 *inf* [driver] conducteur *m*, -trice *f* ; [operator] opérateur *m*, -trice *f*. ◆ vt **1.** [horse] monter **2.** [trick] manipuler, manœuvrer. ◆ vi ▶ **to jockey for position** *lit & fig* essayer de se placer avantageusement.

Jockey shorts® pl n slip *m* kangourou.

jockstrap ['dʒɒkstræp] n slip *m* de sport ; MED suspensoir *m*.

jocular ['dʒɒkjʊlə] adj **1.** [jovial] gai, jovial, enjoué **2.** [facetious] facétieux, badin.

jodhpurs ['dʒɒdpəz] pl n jodhpurs *mpl*.

Joe Bloggs 🇬🇧 [-blɒgz], **Joe Blow** 🇺🇸 & 🇦🇺 n *inf* Monsieur Tout le Monde.

Joe Public n *inf* Monsieur Tout le Monde.

jog [dʒɒg] (*pt & pp* **jogged**, *cont* **jogging**) ◆ n **1.** [slow run] jogging *m* ; EQUIT petit trot *m* / **to go for a jog** aller faire un jogging **2.** [push] légère poussée *f* ; [nudge] coup *m* de coude. ◆ vi **1.** [run] courir à petites foulées ; [for fitness] faire du jogging / *she jogs to work every morning* tous les matins, elle va travailler en joggant **2.** [bump] se balancer. ◆ vt [nudge] donner un léger coup à ▶ **to jog sb's memory** rafraîchir la mémoire de qqn. ❖ **jog along** vi **1.** EQUIT trottiner, aller au petit trot **2.** *fig* suivre son cours.

jogger ['dʒɒgə] n jogger *mf*, joggeur *m*, -euse *f*.

jogging ['dʒɒgɪŋ] n jogging *m* / **to go jogging** faire du jogging ▶ **jogging suit** jogging *m*.

joggle ['dʒɒgl] ◆ vt [shake] secouer (légèrement). ◆ vi cahoter, ballotter. ◆ n [shake, jolt] secousse *f*.

Johannesburg [dʒə'hænɪsbɜ:g] pr n Johannesburg.

john [dʒɒn] n 🇺🇸 **1.** *inf* [lavatory] waters *mpl*, W-C *mpl* **2.** *v inf* [prostitute's client] micheton *m*.

John [dʒɒn] pr n ▶ **Saint John** saint Jean.

John Hancock [-'hænkɒk] n 🇺🇸 *inf* signature *f*.

John Q Public n 🇺🇸 Monsieur Tout le Monde.

join [dʒɔɪn] ◆ vt **1.** [political party, club, etc.] adhérer à ; [armed forces] s'engager dans **2.** [join company with, meet] rejoindre ; [in activity or common purpose] se joindre à **3.** [attach, fasten] joindre, raccorder **4.** [unite] relier, unir / *to be joined in marriage* or *matrimony* être uni par les liens du mariage / *she joined forces with her brother* elle s'est alliée à son frère **5.** [intersect with] rejoindre. ◆ vi **1.** [become a member] devenir membre **2.** [meet, come together] se rejoindre **3.** [form an alliance] s'unir, se joindre. ◆ n [in broken china, wallpaper] (ligne *f* de) raccord *m* ; SEW couture *f*. ❖ **join in** ◆ vi : *she started singing and the others joined in* elle a commencé à chanter et les autres se sont mis à chanter avec elle. ◆ vt insep participer à. ❖ **join on** vi s'attacher. ◆ vt sep attacher, ajouter. ❖ **join up** ◆ vi **1.** MIL s'engager **2.** [meet] ▶ **to join up with sb** rejoindre qqn. ◆ vt sep = **join** (*vt*).

joined-up [dʒɔɪnd-] adj : *can you do joined-up writing yet?* tu sais lier les lettres ?

joiner ['dʒɔɪnə] n **1.** [carpenter] menuisier *m* **2.** *inf* [person who joins clubs] : *he's not really a joiner* il n'est pas très sociable.

joinery ['dʒɔɪnərɪ] n menuiserie *f*.

joint [dʒɔɪnt] ◆ n **1.** [gen & CONSTR] assemblage *m* ; MECH joint *m* **2.** ANAT articulation *f*, jointure *f* **3.** 🇬🇧 CULIN rôti *m* **4.** *inf* [night club] boîte *f* ; [bar] troquet *m*, bouiboui *m* ; [gambling house] tripot *m pej* / *strip joint* club *m* de strip-tease **5.** 🇺🇸 *inf* [house] baraque *f* **6.** 🇺🇸 *inf* taule *f* **7.** *drugs sl* joint *m*. ◆ adj **1.** [united, combined] conjugué, commun **2.** [shared, collective] joint, commun ▶ **joint account** BANK compte *m* joint ▶ **joint custody** LAW garde *f* conjointe ▶ **joint ownership** copropriété *f* ▶ **joint responsibility** or **liability** responsabilité *f* conjointe / *the project is their joint responsibility* le projet relève de leur responsabilité à tous les deux ▶ **joint tenancy** location *f* commune **3.** [associate] ▶ **joint author** coauteur *m* ▶ **joint heir** cohéritier *m* ▶ **joint owner** copropriétaire *mf*. ◆ vt **1.** MECH assembler, emboîter **2.** 🇬🇧 CULIN découper.

Joint Chiefs of Staff pl pr n ▶ **the Joint Chiefs of Staff** *organe consultatif du ministère américain de la Défense, composé des chefs d'état-major des trois armes.*

jointed ['dʒɔɪntɪd] adj articulé.

join-the-dots n (U) 🇬🇧 jeu qui consiste à *relier des points numérotés pour découvrir un dessin.*

jointly ['dʒɔɪntlɪ] adv conjointement.

joint-stock company n 🇬🇧 société *f* par actions.

joint venture n coentreprise *f*, société *f* en participation, joint-venture *m*.

joist [dʒɔɪst] n solive *f*.

jojoba [həʊ'həʊbə] n jojoba *m*.

joke [dʒəʊk] ◆ n **1.** [verbal] plaisanterie *f* ▶ **to make a joke of** or **about sthg** plaisanter sur or à propos de qqch **2.** [prank] plaisanterie *f*, farce *f* ▶ **to play a joke on sb** jouer un tour à qqn, faire une farce à qqn **3.** [laughing stock] risée *f*. ◆ vi plaisanter ▶ **to joke about sthg** se moquer de qqch.

joker ['dʒəʊkə] n **1.** [funny person] farceur *m*, -euse *f* ; *pej* [frivolous person] plaisantin *m* **2.** [in cards] joker *m* **3.** *v inf* [man] type *m*, mec *m*.

jokey ['dʒəʊkɪ] (*compar* **jokier**, *superl* **jokiest**) adj *inf* comique.

jokingly ['dʒəʊkɪŋlɪ] adv en plaisantant, pour plaisanter.

jollies ['dʒɒlɪz] pl n 🇺🇸 ▶ **to get one's jollies (doing sthg)** *inf* prendre son pied (à faire qqch).

jollity ['dʒɒlətɪ] (*pl* **jollities**) n entrain *m*, gaieté *f*.

jolly ['dʒɒlɪ] (compar **jollier**, superl **jolliest**, pt & pp **jollied**) ◆ adj **1.** [person] gai, joyeux, jovial **2.** 🇬🇧 [enjoyable] agréable, plaisant. ◆ adv 🇬🇧 rudement, drôlement. ◆ vt 🇬🇧 [coax] enjôler, entortiller. ❖ **jolly up** vt sep 🇬🇧 égayer.

jolt [dʒəʊlt] ◆ vt **1.** [physically] secouer **2.** [mentally] secouer, choquer. ◆ vi cahoter. ◆ n **1.** [jar] secousse f, coup m **2.** [start] sursaut m, choc m.

jones [dʒəʊnz] vi 🇺🇸 inf ▶ **to jones for sthg** avoir très envie de qqch / I'm jonesing for a night out j'ai super envie de sortir.

Joneses ['dʒəʊnzɪz] pl n ▶ **to keep up with the Joneses** inf vouloir faire aussi bien que le voisin, ne pas vouloir être en reste.

Jordan ['dʒɔ:dn] pr n Jordanie f / **in Jordan** en Jordanie ▶ **the (River) Jordan** le Jourdain.

Jordanian [dʒɔ:'deɪnjən] ◆ n Jordanien m, -enne f. ◆ adj jordanien.

joss stick [dʒɒs-] n bâtonnet m d'encens.

jostle ['dʒɒsl] ◆ vi se bousculer. ◆ vt bousculer, heurter. ◆ n bousculade f.

jot [dʒɒt] (pt & pp **jotted**, cont **jotting**) n : there isn't a jot of truth in what he says il n'y a pas un brin de vérité dans ce qu'il raconte. ❖ **jot down** vt sep noter, prendre note de.

jotter ['dʒɒtə'] n 🇬🇧 [exercise book] cahier m, carnet m ; [pad] bloc-notes m.

jottings ['dʒɒtɪŋz] pl n notes fpl.

joule [dʒu:l] n joule m.

journal ['dʒɜ:nl] n **1.** [publication] revue f **2.** [diary] journal m intime **3.** NAUT [logbook] journal m de bord.

journalese [,dʒɜ:nə'li:z] n pej jargon m journalistique.

journalism ['dʒɜ:nəlɪzm] n journalisme m.

journalist ['dʒɜ:nəlɪst] n journaliste mf.

journalistic [dʒɜ:nə'lɪstɪk] adj journalistique.

journey ['dʒɜ:nɪ] ◆ n **1.** [gen] voyage m ▶ **to set out on a journey** partir en voyage **2.** [shorter distance] trajet m. ◆ vi fml voyager.

joust [dʒaʊst] ◆ n joute f. ◆ vi jouter.

jovial ['dʒəʊvjəl] adj jovial, enjoué.

jowls [dʒaʊlz] pl n bajoues fpl.

joy [dʒɔɪ] n **1.** [pleasure] joie f, plaisir m **2.** inf [luck, satisfaction] : they had no joy at the casino ils n'ont pas eu de chance au casino.

joyful ['dʒɔɪfʊl] adj joyeux, enjoué.

joyfully ['dʒɔɪfʊlɪ] adv joyeusement.

joyless ['dʒɔɪlɪs] adj [unhappy] triste, sans joie ; [dull] morne, maussade.

joyous ['dʒɔɪəs] adj liter joyeux.

joyously ['dʒɔɪəslɪ] adv joyeusement.

joyride ['dʒɔɪraɪd] (pt **joyrode** [-rəʊd], pp **joyridden** [-rɪdn]) ◆ n : they went for a joyride ils ont volé une voiture pour aller faire un tour. ◆ vi ▶ **to go joyriding** faire une virée dans une voiture volée.

joyrider ['dʒɔɪraɪdə'] n personne qui vole une voiture pour faire un tour.

joystick ['dʒɔɪstɪk] n **1.** AERON manche m à balai **2.** COMPUT manette f (de jeux), manche m à balai.

JP (abbr of **Justice of the Peace**) n 🇬🇧 ≃ juge d'instance.

 Justice of the Peace

Les **JPs** sont nommés par le **Lord Chancellor**. Il s'agit en général de notables locaux (médecins, professeurs à la retraite...) jouissant d'une bonne réputation, bien que théoriquement chacun ait le droit de poser sa candidature.

JPEG (abbr of **Joint Photographic Experts Group**) n COMPUT (format m) JPEG m.

Jr. (written abbr of **Junior**) 🇺🇸 junior, fils.

JROTC ['dʒeɪɑ:r'əʊti:'si:] (abbr of **Junior Reserve Officers' Training Corps**) n 🇺🇸 SCH programme fédéral dont le but est d'instiller chez les lycéens le sens du patriotisme, de la citoyenneté et le goût de l'exercice afin d'effectuer plus facilement une carrière militaire.

JSA [,dʒeɪes'eɪ] (abbr of **Jobseekers' Allowance**) n 🇬🇧 allocation f chômage.

JTPA (abbr of **Job Training Partnership Act**) n programme gouvernemental américain de formation.

jubilant ['dʒu:bɪlənt] adj débordant de joie, radieux.

jubilation [,dʒu:bɪ'leɪʃn] n (U) [rejoicing] joie f, jubilation f ; [celebration] réjouissances fpl.

jubilee ['dʒu:bɪli:] n jubilé m.

Judaism ['dʒu:deɪ,ɪzm] n judaïsme m.

Judas ['dʒu:dəs] n [traitor] judas m.

judder ['dʒʌdə'] ◆ vi 🇬🇧 [gen] vibrer ; [brakes, clutch] brouter / the bus juddered to a halt le bus s'est arrêté en cahotant. ◆ n trépidation f ; [of vehicle, machine] broutement m.

judge [dʒʌdʒ] ◆ n **1.** LAW juge m ▶ **presiding judge** président m du tribunal **2.** [in a competition] membre m du jury ; SPORT juge m / the judges were divided le jury était partagé **3.** fig juge m. ◆ vt **1.** [pass judgment on, adjudicate] juger **2.** [consider] juger, considérer ; [estimate] évaluer, estimer. ◆ vi juger. ❖ **Judges** n ▶ **(the) book of Judges** BIBLE (le livre des) Juges.

judgment ['dʒʌdʒmənt] n **1.** LAW & RELIG jugement m ▶ **to pass judgment on sb / sthg** porter un jugement sur qqn / qqch ▶ **to sit in judgment on** juger **2.** [opinion] jugement m, opinion f, avis m ▶ **to reserve judgment on sthg** réserver son jugement or opinion sur qqch.

judgmental [dʒʌdʒ'mentl] adj [person - by nature] enclin à juger or à critiquer / I'm not being judgmental ce n'est pas une critique que je vous fais.

judicial [dʒu:'dɪʃl] adj LAW judiciaire ▶ **to take** or **to bring judicial proceedings against sb** attaquer qqn en justice ▶ **judicial review a)** 🇺🇸 [of ruling] examen m d'une décision de justice (par une juridiction supérieure) **b)** [of law] examen de la constitutionnalité d'une loi ▶ **judicial separation** séparation f de corps.

judiciary [dʒu:'dɪʃərɪ] ◆ adj judiciaire. ◆ n **1.** [judicial authority] pouvoir m judiciaire **2.** [judges collectively] magistrature f.

judicious [dʒu:'dɪʃəs] adj judicieux.

judo ['dʒu:dəʊ] n judo m.

jug [dʒʌg] (pt & pp **jugged**, cont **jugging**) ◆ n **1.** [small - for milk] pot m ; [- for water] carafe f ; [- for wine] pichet m, carafe f ; [large - earthenware] cruche f ; [- metal, plastic] broc m **2.** 🇬🇧 v inf [jail] tôle f, taule f, cabane f **3.** 🇺🇸 [narrow-necked] bonbonne f **4.** v inf [breasts] ▶ **jugs** nichons mpl, roberts mpl. ◆ vt CULIN cuire à l'étouffée or à l'étuvée.

juggernaut [ˈdʒʌgənɔːt] n **1.** 🇬🇧 [large lorry] gros poids lourd m **2.** [force] force f fatale.

juggle [ˈdʒʌgl] ◆ vi [as entertainment] jongler ▶ **to juggle with** [figures, dates] jongler avec. ◆ vt lit & fig jongler avec. ◆ n jonglerie f.

juggler [ˈdʒʌgləʳ] n [entertainer] jongleur m, -euse f.

juggling [ˈdʒʌglɪŋ], **jugglery** [ˈdʒʌglərɪ] n lit & fig jonglerie f.

jugular [ˈdʒʌgjʊləʳ] ◆ adj jugulaire ▶ **jugular vein** jugulaire f. ◆ n jugulaire f ▶ **to go for the jugular** inf attaquer qqn sur ses points faibles.

jug wine n 🇺🇸 vin m ordinaire.

juice [dʒuːs] ◆ n **1.** CULIN jus m / grapefruit juice jus de pamplemousse **2.** BIOL suc m **3.** inf [electricity] jus m; [petrol] essence f **4.** 🇺🇸 inf [spirits] tord-boyaux m; [wine] pinard m. ◆ vt [fruit] presser.

juicer [ˈdʒuːsəʳ] n presse-fruits m inv.

juicy [ˈdʒuːsɪ] (compar **juicier**, superl **juiciest**) adj **1.** [fruit] juteux **2.** inf [profitable] juteux **3.** inf [racy] savoureux.

ju-jitsu [dʒuːˈdʒɪtsuː] n jiu-jitsu m inv.

jukebox [ˈdʒuːkbɒks] n juke-box m.

Jul. (written abbr of July) juill.

July [dʒuːˈlaɪ] n juillet m. See also **February**.

jumbal [ˈdʒʌmbəl] n 🇺🇸 CULIN petit gâteau en forme d'anneau.

jumble [ˈdʒʌmbl] ◆ n **1.** [confusion, disorder] fouillis m, désordre m / my things are all in a jumble mes affaires sont tout en désordre **2.** 🇬🇧 [articles for jumble sale] bric-à-brac m **3.** 🇺🇸 CULIN = **jumbal**. ◆ vt **1.** [objects, belongings] mélanger **2.** [thoughts, ideas] embrouiller.

jumble sale n 🇬🇧 vente de charité où sont vendus des articles d'occasion et des produits faits maison.

jumbo [ˈdʒʌmbəʊ] (pl **jumbos**) inf ◆ n **1.** [elephant] éléphant m, pachyderme m **2.** = **jumbo jet**. ◆ adj énorme, géant.

jumbo jet n (avion m) gros-porteur m, jumbo m, jumbo-jet m.

jumbo-size(d) adj énorme, géant.

jump [dʒʌmp] ◆ vi **1.** [leap] sauter, bondir / they jumped across the crevasse ils ont traversé la crevasse d'un bond / to jump back faire un bond en arrière / she jumped into / out of her car elle a sauté dans / hors de sa voiture / he jumped off the bridge il s'est jeté du haut du pont / he jumped up or he jumped to his feet il se leva d'un bond **2.** [start] sursauter, tressauter **3.** [rise sharply] grimper or monter en flèche **4.** 🇺🇸 inf [be lively] être très animé. ◆ vt **1.** [leap over] sauter **2.** [horse] faire sauter **3.** [omit, skip] sauter **4.** inf [attack] sauter sur, agresser **5.** inf [leave, abscond from] ▶ **to jump ship** lit & fig quitter le navire ▶ **to jump bail** ne pas comparaître au tribunal (après avoir été libéré sous caution) **6.** [not wait one's turn at] : to jump the queue ne pas attendre son tour, resquiller / she jumped the lights elle a grillé or brûlé le feu (rouge) **7.** inf [not pay for, take illegally] ▶ **to jump a train** 🇺🇸 voyager sans billet. ◆ n **1.** [leap, bound] saut m, bond m **2.** [sharp rise] bond m, hausse f **3.** EQUIT [fence, obstacle] obstacle m **4.** COMPUT saut m. ◆ **jump about** 🇬🇧, **jump around** vi sautiller. ◆ **jump at** vt insep sauter sur, saisir. ◆ **jump in** vi **1.** lit [into vehicle] monter; [into water, hole] sauter **2.** inf & fig [intervene] intervenir. ◆ **jump on** vt insep **1.** lit [bicycle, horse] sauter sur; [bus, train] sauter dans; [person] sauter sur **2.** fig [mistake] repérer.

jumped-up [ˈdʒʌmpt-] adj 🇬🇧 inf parvenu.

jumper [ˈdʒʌmpəʳ] n **1.** 🇬🇧 [sweater] pull-over m **2.** 🇺🇸 [dress] robe-chasuble f **3.** [person] sauteur m, -euse f.

jumper cables 🇺🇸 = jump leads.

jumper leads pl n 🇬🇧 & 🇦🇺🇸 = jump leads.

jumping-off point, **jumping-off place** n point m de départ, tremplin m.

jump jet n 🇬🇧 avion m à décollage vertical.

jump leads pl n 🇬🇧 câbles mpl de démarrage.

jump rope n 🇺🇸 corde f à sauter.

jump-start vt ▶ **to jump-start a car** a) [by pushing or rolling] faire démarrer une voiture en la poussant or en la mettant dans une pente b) [with jump leads] faire démarrer une voiture avec des câbles (branchés sur la batterie d'une autre voiture).

jumpsuit [ˈdʒʌmpsuːt] n combinaison-pantalon f.

jumpy [ˈdʒʌmpɪ] (compar **jumpier**, superl **jumpiest**) adj **1.** inf [edgy] nerveux **2.** ST. EX instable, fluctuant.

Jun. 1. written abbr of June **2.** (written abbr of Junior) 🇺🇸 junior, fils.

junction [ˈdʒʌŋkʃn] n **1.** [of roads] carrefour m, croisement m; [of railway lines, traffic lanes] embranchement m; [of rivers, canals] confluent m **2.** ELEC [of wires] jonction f, raccordement m.

junction box n 🇬🇧 boîte f de dérivation.

juncture [ˈdʒʌŋktʃəʳ] n **1.** fml [moment] conjoncture f / at this juncture dans la conjoncture actuelle, dans les circonstances actuelles **2.** LING joncture f, jointure f, frontière f **3.** TECH jointure f.

June [dʒuːn] n juin m. See also **February**.

June beetle, **June bug** n hanneton m.

jungle [ˈdʒʌŋgl] ◆ n **1.** [tropical forest] jungle f **2.** fig jungle f **3.** MUS jungle f. ◆ comp [animal] de la jungle.

jungle gym n ensemble de jeux pour les enfants (balançoires, toboggans, etc.).

junior [ˈdʒuːnjəʳ] ◆ n **1.** [younger person] cadet m, -ette f / he is five years her junior il est de cinq ans son cadet, il a cinq ans de moins qu'elle **2.** [subordinate] subordonné m, -e f, subalterne mf **3.** 🇬🇧 [pupil] écolier m, -ère f (entre 7 et 11 ans) **4.** 🇺🇸 SCH élève de troisième année; 🇺🇸 UNIV étudiant m, -e f de première année **5.** 🇺🇸 inf [term of address] fiston m. ◆ comp 🇬🇧 [teaching, teacher] dans le primaire. ◆ adj **1.** [younger] cadet, plus jeune **2.** [lower in rank] subordonné, subalterne / he's junior to her in the department il est son subalterne dans le service ▶ **junior doctor** interne mf ▶ **junior executive** cadre m débutant, jeune cadre ▶ **the junior faculty** 🇺🇸 UNIV les enseignants non titulaires ▶ **junior minister** sous-secrétaire m d'État ▶ **junior partner** associé m adjoint **3.** [juvenile] jeune. ◆ **Junior** = **Jnr**.

Junior College n [in US] établissement d'enseignement supérieur où l'on obtient un diplôme en deux ans.

junior high school n 🇺🇸 ≃ collège m d'enseignement secondaire.

junior school n 🇬🇧 école f élémentaire (pour les enfants de 7 à 11 ans) ▶ **a junior school teacher** instituteur m, institutrice f.

juniper [ˈdʒuːnɪpəʳ] n genévrier m ▶ **juniper berry** baie f de genièvre.

junk [dʒʌŋk] ◆ n **1.** (U) inf [anything poor-quality or worthless] pacotille f, camelote f **2.** (U) [second-hand, inexpensive goods] bric-à-brac m **3.** (U) inf [stuff] trucs mpl, machins mpl **4.** [boat] jonque f. ◆ vt inf jeter (à la poubelle), balancer.

junk e-mail n messages mpl publicitaires, spams mpl, pourriels mpl.

junker [ˈdʒʌŋkəʳ] n 🇺🇸 inf [old car] vieille bagnole f.

junket ['dʒʌŋkɪt] ◆ n **1.** inf & pej [official journey] voyage m aux frais de la princesse **2.** inf [festive occasion] banquet m, festin m **3.** CULIN ≃ fromage m frais (sucré et parfumé). ◆ vi voyager aux frais de la princesse.

junk food n inf nourriture f de mauvaise qualité.

junkie ['dʒʌŋkɪ] n inf **1.** [drug addict] drogué m, -e f, junkie mf **2.** fig dingue mf, accro mf.

junk mail n **1.** [postal] publicité f (reçue par courrier) **2.** = junk e-mail.

junk shop n magasin m de brocante / at the junk shop chez le brocanteur.

junkyard ['dʒʌŋkjɑːd] n **1.** [for scrap metal] entrepôt m de ferraille / at the junkyard chez le ferrailleur **2.** [for discarded objects] dépotoir m.

Junr. = Jnr.

junta [UK 'dʒʌntə US 'hʊntə] n junte f.

Jupiter ['dʒuːpɪtər] pr n **1.** ASTRON Jupiter f **2.** MYTH Jupiter.

jurisdiction [,dʒʊərɪs'dɪkʃn] n LAW & ADMIN juridiction f ▶ to come or to fall within the jurisdiction of relever de la juridiction de.

jurisprudence [,dʒʊərɪs'pruːdəns] n jurisprudence f.

juror ['dʒʊərər] n juré m.

jury ['dʒʊərɪ] (pl **juries**) ◆ n **1.** LAW jury m ▶ to serve on a jury faire partie d'un jury **2.** [in contest] jury m. ◆ adj NAUT de fortune, improvisé.

jury box n sièges mpl des jurés.

jury duty US = jury service.

jury-rigging n LAW truquage m d'un jury.

jury service n participation f à un jury.

just¹ [dʒʌst] adv **1.** [indicating immediate past] juste / just last week pas plus tard que la semaine dernière / they had (only) just arrived ils venaient (tout) juste d'arriver / he's just been to Mexico il revient or rentre du Mexique **2.** [indicating present or immediate future] juste / I was just going to phone you j'allais juste or justement te téléphoner, j'étais sur le point de te téléphoner / I'm just off inf je m'en vais / just coming! inf j'arrive tout de suite ! / I'm just making tea, do you want some? je suis en train de faire du thé, tu en veux ? **3.** [only, merely] juste, seulement / just a little juste un peu / just a minute or a moment or a second, please une (petite) minute or un (petit) instant, s'il vous plaît ▶ he was just trying to help il voulait juste or simplement rendre service **4.** [exactly, precisely] exactement, juste / just at that moment juste à ce moment-là / that's just what I needed **a)** c'est exactement or juste ce qu'il me fallait **b)** iro il ne me manquait plus que ça / just what are you getting at? où veux-tu en venir exactement ? / he's just like his father c'est son père tout craché **5.** [barely] (tout) juste, à peine / I could just make out what they were saying je parvenais tout juste à entendre ce qu'ils disaient ; [a little] : it's just after / before two o'clock il est un peu plus / moins de deux heures / just afterwards juste après **6.** [possibly] : I may or might just be able to do it il n'est pas impossible que je puisse le faire **7.** [emphatic use] : just think what might have happened! imagine un peu ce qui aurait pu arriver ! / it just isn't good enough c'est loin d'être satisfaisant, c'est tout. ◆ **just about** adv phr **1.** [very nearly] presque, quasiment **2.** [barely] (tout) juste / his handwriting is just about legible son écriture est tout juste or à peine lisible. ◆ **just as** conj phr **1.** [at the same time as] juste au moment où **2.** [exactly as] : just as I thought / predicted comme je le pensais / prévoyais. ◆ **just in case** ◆ conj phr juste au cas où / just in case we don't see each other juste au cas où nous ne nous verrions pas. ◆ adv phr au cas où / take a coat, just in case prends un manteau, on ne sait jamais or au cas où. ◆ **just now** adv phr **1.** [at this moment] : I'm busy just now je suis occupé pour le moment **2.** [a short time ago] : when did this happen? — just now quand cela s'est-il passé ? — à l'instant. ◆ **just on** adv phr UK exactement. ◆ **just so** ◆ adv phr fml [expressing agreement] c'est exact. ◆ adj phr UK [properly arranged] parfait / she likes everything (to be) just so elle aime que tout soit parfait. ◆ **just then** adv phr à ce moment-là. ◆ **just the same** adv phr [nonetheless] quand même.

just² [dʒʌst] ◆ adj **1.** [fair, impartial] juste, équitable ; [reasonable, moral] juste, légitime / a just cause une juste cause / he has just cause for complaint il a de bonnes raisons pour se plaindre **2.** [deserved] juste, mérité ▶ to get one's just deserts he got his just deserts il n'a eu que ce qu'il méritait, ce n'est que justice **3.** [accurate] juste, exact **4.** RELIG [righteous] juste. ◆ pl n ▶ the just les justes mpl ▶ to sleep the sleep of the just dormir du sommeil du juste.

J4F MESSAGING written abbr of just for fun.

justice ['dʒʌstɪs] n **1.** LAW justice f ▶ to bring sb to justice traduire qqn en justice ▶ the Justice Department or the Department of Justice US ≃ le ministère de la Justice **2.** [fairness] justice f, équité f ▶ to do sb / sthg justice [represent fairly] rendre justice à qqn / qqch **3.** [punishment, vengeance] justice f **4.** [judge] juge m ▶ Justice of the Peace = JP.

justifiable ['dʒʌstɪ,faɪəbl] adj justifiable ; LAW légitime.

justifiable homicide n [killing in self-defence] homicide m justifiable.

justifiably ['dʒʌstɪ,faɪəblɪ] adv légitimement, à juste titre.

justification [,dʒʌstɪfɪ'keɪʃn] n **1.** [gen] justification f **2.** COMPUT & TYPO justification f.

justify ['dʒʌstɪfaɪ] (pt & pp **justified**) vt **1.** [gen] justifier / she tried to justify her behaviour to her parents elle a essayé de justifier son comportement aux yeux de ses parents **2.** COMPUT & TYPO justifier **3.** LAW : to justify a lawsuit justifier une action en justice.

just-in-time adj ECON juste à temps.

just-in-time distribution n ECON distribution f juste à temps.

just-in-time production n ECON production f juste à temps.

just-in-time purchasing n ECON achat m juste à temps.

justly ['dʒʌstlɪ] adv **1.** [fairly] justement, avec justice **2.** [accurately, deservedly] à juste titre.

justness ['dʒʌstnɪs] n [of claim, demand] bien-fondé m, légitimité f ; [of idea, reasoning] justesse f.

jut [dʒʌt] (pt & pp **jutted**, cont **jutting**) vi ▶ to jut out dépasser, faire saillie.

jute [dʒuːt] n [textile] jute m.

Jute [dʒuːt] n Jute mf.

juvenile ['dʒuːvənaɪl] ◆ adj **1.** [young, for young people] jeune, juvénile fml ▶ juvenile lead jeune premier m **2.** [immature] puéril, enfantin. ◆ n **1.** fml mineur m, -e f **2.** THEAT jeune acteur m, -trice f.

juvenile court n tribunal m pour enfants (10-16 ans).

juvenile delinquency n délinquance f juvénile.

juvenile delinquent n jeune délinquant m, -e f, mineur m délinquant, mineure f délinquante.

juvie ['dʒuːvɪ] US inf **1.** abbr of juvenile court **2.** abbr of juvenile delinquent.

juxtapose [,dʒʌkstə'pəʊz] vt juxtaposer.

juxtaposition [,dʒʌkstəpə'zɪʃn] n juxtaposition f.

K ◆ **1.** (written abbr of **kilobyte**) K, Ko **2.** written abbr of **Knight**. ◆ n (abbr of **thousand**) K.

kabbala, kabbalism 1. = cabala **2.** = cabalism.

Kabul ['kɑ:bʊl] pr n Kaboul, Kabul.

kaffee klatch ['kæfɪklætʃ] n US réunion de femmes qui se retrouvent autour d'un café chez l'une d'entre elles.

kaftan ['kæftæn] n caftan m, cafetan m.

kahuna [kə'hu:nə] n US inf ▶ **the big kahuna** le patron, le big boss.

Kalahari Desert [ˌkælə'hɑ:rɪ-] pr n ▶ **the Kalahari Desert** le (désert du) Kalahari.

kalashnikov [kə'læʃnɪkɒv] n kalachnikov m.

kale [keɪl] n chou m frisé.

kaleidoscope [kə'laɪdəskəʊp] n lit & fig kaléidoscope m.

kamikaze [ˌkæmɪ'kɑ:zɪ] ◆ n kamikaze m. ◆ adj **1.** lit ▶ **kamikaze pilot** kamikaze m ▶ **kamikaze plane** kamikaze m, avion-suicide m **2.** fig suicidaire.

Kampala [kæm'pɑ:lə] pr n Kampala.

Kampuchea [ˌkæmpu'tʃɪə] pr n Kampuchéa m / in Kampuchea au Kampuchéa.

Kampuchean [ˌkæmpu:'tʃɪən] ◆ n Cambodgien m, -enne f. ◆ adj cambodgien.

kangaroo [ˌkæŋgə'ru:] n kangourou m.

Kansas ['kænzəs] pr n Kansas m / in Kansas dans le Kansas.

kaolin ['keɪəlɪn] n kaolin m.

kaput [kə'pʊt] adj inf fichu, foutu.

karaoke [ˌkærə'əʊkɪ] n karaoké m.

karat US = carat.

karate [kə'rɑ:tɪ] n karaté m ▶ **karate chop** coup m de karaté (donné avec le tranchant de la main).

karma ['kɑ:mə] n karma m, karman m.

kasbah ['kæzbɑ:] n casbah f.

Kashmir [kæʃ'mɪə] n GEOG Cachemire m, Kashmir m.

Katar ['kætɑ:r] pr n Katar m, Qatar m / in Katar au Qatar.

kayak ['kaɪæk] n kayak m.

Kazakhstan [ˌkæzæk'stɑ:n] pr n Kazakhstan m / in Kazakhstan au Kazakhstan.

KB (written abbr of **Kilobyte**) n COMPUT ko m, Ko m.

KC¹ (abbr of **King's Counsel**) n US avocat de la Couronne.

KC² MESSAGING written abbr of **keep cool**.

kcal (written abbr of **kilocalorie**) Kcal.

KD (abbr of **knocked down**) adj livré en kit, à monter soi-même.

kebab [kɪ'bæb] n [gen] brochette f ; [in Turkish or Greek cuisine] chiche-kebab m ▶ **kebab house** restaurant grec ou turc.

kedgeree ['kedʒəri:] n UK plat anglo-indien à base de riz, de poisson et d'œufs.

keel [ki:l] n NAUT quille f. ◆ **keel over** ◆ vi **1.** NAUT chavirer **2.** [fall] s'effondrer ; [faint] s'évanouir. ◆ vt sep NAUT faire chavirer, cabaner.

keen [ki:n] ◆ adj **1.** UK [eager, enthusiastic] passionné, enthousiaste / she's a keen gardener c'est une passionnée de jardinage / he was keen to talk to her il tenait à or voulait absolument lui parler / I'm not so keen on the idea l'idée ne m'enchante or ne m'emballe pas vraiment / Susan is really keen on Tom Susan a vraiment le béguin pour Tom **2.** [senses, mind, wit] fin, vif **3.** [fierce -competition, rivalry] acharné **4.** UK [cold -wind] glacial **5.** [sharp -blade, knife] affilé **6.** [intense] intense, profond **7.** UK [very competitive] ▶ **keen prices** des prix mpl imbattables. ◆ vi & vt regional [mourn] pleurer. ◆ n regional [dirge] mélopée f funèbre.

keenly ['ki:nlɪ] adv UK **1.** [deeply, intensely] vivement, profondément ; [fiercely] âprement **2.** [eagerly] ardemment, avec enthousiasme ; [attentively] attentivement.

keenness ['ki:nnɪs] n **1.** UK [enthusiasm] enthousiasme m, empressement m, ardeur f **2.** [sharpness - of blade, senses] acuité f, finesse f / keenness of mind perspicacité f, finesse f **3.** [intensity, fierceness] intensité f, âpreté f.

keep [ki:p] (pt & pp **kept** [kept])
◆ vt

1. [retain -receipt, change] garder ▶ **to keep sthg to o.s.** garder qqch pour soi / they keep themselves very much to themselves ce sont des gens plutôt discrets **2.** [save] garder / we've kept some cake for you on t'a gardé du gâteau **3.** [store, put] mettre, garder / she keeps her money in the bank elle met son argent à la banque / how long can you keep fish in the freezer? combien de temps peut-on garder or conserver du poisson au congélateur ? / where do you keep the playing cards? où est-ce que vous rangez les cartes à jouer ?

1. (with adj complement) [maintain in the specified state or place] : to keep sb quiet faire tenir qqn tranquille / to keep sthg warm garder qqch au chaud ; (with adv complement) : a well- / badly-kept office un bureau bien / mal tenu ; (with present participle) : to keep sb waiting faire attendre qqn / keep the engine running n'arrêtez pas le moteur / to keep sthg going a) [organization, business] faire marcher qqch b) [music, conversation] ne pas laisser qqch s'arrêter **2.** [delay] retenir /

what kept you? qu'est-ce qui t'a retenu ? **3.** [not allow to leave] garder / *to keep sb in hospital / prison* garder qqn à l'hôpital / en prison.

C. SUPPORT 1. [support] : *he hardly earns enough to keep himself* il gagne à peine de quoi vivre / *she has a husband and six children to keep* elle a un mari et six enfants à nourrir **2.** [run - shop, business] tenir **3.** COMM [have in stock] vendre **4.** [farm animals] élever **5.** [diary, list, etc.] tenir / *my secretary keeps my accounts* ma secrétaire tient or s'occupe de ma comptabilité.

D. FULFIL OR GUARD 1. [fulfil - a promise, one's word] tenir **2.** [observe - silence] observer ; [- the Sabbath] respecter ; [- law] respecter, observer **3.** [uphold, maintain] maintenir / *to keep order / the peace* maintenir l'ordre / la paix **4.** [guard] garder.

E. PREVENT 1. [prevent] ▶ **to keep sb from doing sthg** empêcher qqn de faire qqch **2.** [withhold] ▶ **to keep sthg from sb** cacher qqch à qqn / *to keep information from sb* dissimuler des informations à qqn.

◆ vi **1.** (with present participle) [continue] continuer / *letters keep pouring in* les lettres continuent d'affluer / *to keep going* [not give up] continuer / *keep going till you get to the crossroads* allez jusqu'au croisement **2.** [stay, remain] rester, se tenir / *keep calm!* restez calmes !, du calme ! / *to keep in touch with sb* rester en contact avec qqn ▶ **to keep to o.s.** se tenir à l'écart **3.** [last, stay fresh] se conserver, se garder / *it will keep for a week in the refrigerator* vous pouvez le garder or conserver au réfrigérateur pendant une semaine / *the news will keep (until tomorrow)* fig la nouvelle peut attendre (jusqu'à demain) **4.** [in health] aller / *I'm keeping well* je vais bien, ça va (bien).

◆ n **1.** [board and lodging] : *he gives his mother £50 a week for his keep* il donne 50 livres par semaine à sa mère pour sa pension ▶ **to earn one's keep** payer ou travailler pour être nourri et logé **2.** [in castle] donjon m **3.** PHR **for keeps** *inf* pour de bon. ❖ **keep at** ◆ vt insep **1.** [pester] harceler **2.** PHR **to keep at it** persévérer. ◆ vt sep ▶ **to keep sb at it** : *the sergeant kept us hard at it all morning* le sergent nous a fait travailler toute la matinée. ❖ **keep away** ◆ vt sep tenir éloigné, empêcher d'approcher. ◆ vi ne pas s'approcher / *keep away from those people* évitez ces gens-là. ❖ **keep back** ◆ vt sep **1.** [keep at a distance - crowd, spectators] tenir éloigné, empêcher de s'approcher **2.** [not reveal - names, facts] cacher / *I'm sure he's keeping something back (from us)* je suis sûr qu'il (nous) cache quelque chose **3.** [retain] retenir **4.** [detain] retenir **5.** [restrain] retenir. ◆ vi rester en arrière, ne pas s'approcher. ❖ **keep down** ◆ vt sep **1.** [not raise] ne pas lever / *keep your head down!* ne lève pas la tête !, garde la tête baissée ! / *keep your voices down!* parlez doucement ! **2.** [prevent from increasing] limiter / *our aim is to keep prices down* notre but est d'empêcher les prix d'augmenter **3.** [repress] réprimer ; [control - vermin, weeds] empêcher de proliférer **4.** [food] garder / *she can't keep solid foods down* son estomac ne garde aucun aliment solide. ◆ vi ne pas se lever. ❖ **keep from** vt insep s'empêcher de, se retenir de. ❖ **keep in** vt sep [not allow out] empêcher de sortir ; SCH donner une consigne à, garder en retenue. ❖ **keep in with** vt insep ▶ **to keep in with sb** rester en bons termes avec qqn. ❖ **keep off** ◆ vt sep **1.** [dogs, birds, trespassers] éloigner ; [rain, sun] protéger de / *keep your hands off!* pas touche !, bas les pattes ! **2.** [coat, hat] ne pas remettre. ◆ vt insep **1.** [avoid] éviter / *keep off drink and food* évitez l'alcool et le tabac **2.** [keep at a distance from] ne pas s'approcher de. ◆ vi **1.** [keep at a distance] ne pas s'approcher **2.** [weather] : *the rain / snow kept off* il n'a pas plu / neigé. ❖ **keep on** ◆ vt sep **1.** [coat, hat] garder **2.** [employee] garder. ◆ vi **1.** [continue] continuer / *they kept on talking* ils ont conti-

nué à parler **2.** *inf* [talk continually] parler sans cesse / *he keeps on about his kids* il n'arrête pas de parler de ses gosses. ❖ **keep on at** vt insep [pester] harceler. ❖ **keep out** ◆ vt sep empêcher d'entrer / *a guard dog to keep intruders out* un chien de garde pour décourager les intrus / *a scarf to keep the cold out* une écharpe pour vous protéger du froid. ◆ vi ne pas entrer / **'keep out'** 'défense d'entrer', 'entrée interdite' / *to keep out of an argument* ne pas intervenir dans une discussion. ❖ **keep to** vt insep **1.** [observe, respect] respecter / *you must keep to the deadlines* vous devez respecter les délais **2.** [not deviate from] ne pas s'écarter de **3.** [stay in] garder. ❖ **keep up** ◆ vt sep **1.** [prevent from falling - shelf, roof] maintenir / *it's to keep the troops' morale up* c'est pour maintenir le moral des troupes **2.** [maintain - attack, bombardment] poursuivre ; [- correspondence, contacts, conversation] entretenir / *she kept up a constant flow of questions* elle ne cessait de poser des questions ▶ **to keep it up** : *you're doing well, keep it up!* c'est bien, continuez ! / *once they start talking politics, they can keep it up all night* une fois lancés sur la politique, ils sont capables d'y passer la nuit **3.** [prevent from going to bed] empêcher de dormir **4.** [not allow to deteriorate - house, garden] entretenir / *she goes to evening classes to keep up her French* elle suit des cours du soir pour entretenir son français. ◆ vi **1.** [continue] continuer **2.** [not fall] se maintenir **3.** [not fall behind] suivre / *he's finding it hard to keep up in his new class* il a du mal à suivre dans sa nouvelle classe. ❖ **keep up with** vt insep **1.** [stay abreast of] : *to keep up with the news* se tenir au courant de l'actualité **2.** [keep in touch with] rester en contact avec.

keeper ['kiːpər] n **1.** [gen] gardien m, -enne f ; [in museum] conservateur m, -trice f ▶ **am I my brother's keeper?** BIBLE suis-je le gardien de mon frère ? **2.** [goalkeeper] goal m, gardien m de but **3.** TECH [safety catch] cran m de sûreté.

keep-fit n culture f physique, gymnastique f (d'entretien).

keeping ['kiːpɪŋ] n **1.** [care, charge] garde f / *he left the manuscript in his wife's keeping* il a confié le manuscrit à son épouse ▶ **in safe keeping** en sécurité, sous bonne garde **2.** [observing - of rule, custom, etc.] observation f. ❖ **in keeping** adj phr conforme à / *their dress was not at all in keeping with the seriousness of the occasion* leur tenue ne convenait pas du tout à la gravité de la circonstance. ❖ **in keeping with** prep phr conformément à. ❖ **out of keeping** adj phr ▶ **to be out of keeping with** être en désaccord avec.

keepsake ['kiːpseɪk] n souvenir m (objet).

keg [keg] n **1.** [barrel] tonnelet m, baril m ; [of fish] baril ; [of beer] tonnelet ; [of herring] caque f **2.** [beer] bière f (à la) pression.

kegger ['kegər] n US inf [party with beer] soirée f bière.

kelp [kelp] n varech m.

ken [ken] (*pt & pp* **kenned**, *cont* **kenning**) n *dated & hum* ▶ **it is beyond my ken** cela dépasse mon entendement.

kennel ['kenl] (UK *pt & pp* **kennelled** ; US *pt & pp* **kenneled**) ◆ n **1.** [doghouse] niche f **2.** US [for boarding or breeding] chenil m. ◆ vt mettre dans un chenil. ❖ **kennels** n UK [for boarding or breeding] chenil m.

Kentucky [ken'tʌkɪ] pr n Kentucky m / *in Kentucky* dans le Kentucky ▶ **the Kentucky Derby** course pour chevaux de trois ans qui a lieu chaque année à Louisville.

Kenya ['kenjə] pr n Kenya m / *in Kenya* au Kenya.

Kenyan ['kenjən] ◆ n Kenyan m, -e f. ◆ adj kenyan.

kept [kept] ◆ pt & pp ⟶ **keep.** ◆ adj *hum & pej* ▶ **a kept man** un homme entretenu ▶ **a kept woman** une femme entretenue.

kerb UK, **curb** US [kɜːb] n bord m du trottoir.

kerb crawler n *individu qui longe le trottoir en voiture à la recherche d'une prostituée.*

kerb crawling n *fait de longer le trottoir en voiture à la recherche d'une prostituée.*

kerbstone 🇬🇧, **curbstone** 🇺🇸 ['kɜːbstəʊn] n bordure f de trottoir.

kerfuffle [kə'fʌfl] n 🇬🇧 *inf* [disorder] désordre m, chahut m ; [fight] bagarre f.

kernel ['kɜːnl] n **1.** [of nut, fruit stone] amande f ; [of cereal] graine f **2.** *fig* [heart, core] cœur m, noyau m.

kerosene, kerosine ['kerəsiːn] ◆ n 🇺🇸 [for aircraft] kérosène m ; [for lamps, stoves] pétrole m. ◆ comp [lamp, stove] à pétrole.

kestrel ['kestrəl] n crécerelle f.

ketch [ketʃ] n ketch m.

ketchup ['ketʃəp] n ketchup m.

kettle ['ketl] n **1.** [for water] bouilloire f ▶ **to put the kettle on** mettre de l'eau à chauffer **2.** [for fish] poissonnière f.

kettledrum ['ketldrʌm] n timbale f.

kewl adj 🇺🇸 *inf* cool.

key [kiː] ◆ n **1.** [for lock] clé f, clef f ; [for clock, mechanism, etc.] clé f, remontoir m / *the key to the drawer* la clé du tiroir **2.** *fig* [means] clé f, clef f / *the key to happiness* la clé du bonheur **3.** [on typewriter, computer, piano, organ] touche f ; [on wind instrument] clé f, clef f **4.** MUS ton m / *in the key of B minor* en si mineur ▶ **to play in** / **off key** jouer dans le ton / dans le mauvais ton ▶ **to sing in** / **off key** chanter juste / faux **5.** [on map, diagram] légende f **6.** [answers] corrigé m, réponses fpl **7.** TECH clé f or clef f (de serrage) **8.** [island] îlot m ; [reef] (petit) récif m *(qui s'étend au sud de la Floride).* ◆ adj clé, clef / *key industries* industries clés, industries-clés / *a key factor* un élément décisif / *one of the key issues in the election* un des enjeux fondamentaux de ces élections. ◆ vt **1.** [data, text] saisir, entrer **2.** [adjust, adapt] adapter. ◆✣ **key in** vt sep COMPUT [word, number] entrer ; [data, text] saisir.

key account n grand compte m.

keyboard ['kiːbɔːd] ◆ n [of instrument, typewriter, computer] clavier m / *who's on keyboards?* qui est aux claviers ? ▶ **keyboard instrument** instrument m à clavier ▶ **keyboard operator** claviste mf. ◆ vt saisir.

keyboarder ['kiːbɔːdər] n TYPO claviste mf.

keyboard shortcut n raccourci m clavier.

key card n badge m.

key case n porte-clés m.

keyed up [kiːd-] adj surexcité.

keyguard ['kiːgɑːd] n [on mobile phone] verrouillage m du clavier.

keyhole ['kiːhəʊl] n trou m de serrure.

keyhole surgery n cœliochirurgie f.

keylogger ['kiːlɒgər] n enregistreur m de frappe.

key man n homme m clé.

keynote ['kiːnəʊt] ◆ n **1.** [main point] point m capital **2.** MUS tonique f. ◆ adj [address] introductif ; [speaker] principal ▶ **keynote speech** discours m introductif or liminaire. ◆ vt insister sur, mettre en relief.

keypad ['kiːpæd] n pavé m numérique.

keypal ['kiːpæl] n correspondant m, -e f *(avec qui l'on correspond via Internet).*

keypunch ['kiːpʌntʃ] n perforatrice f à clavier.

key ring n porte-clés m inv.

key skill n SCH compétence f de base.

keystage ['kiːsteɪdʒ] n 🇬🇧 SCH *une des cinq étapes-clés du parcours scolaire en Grande-Bretagne.*

keystone ['kiːstəʊn] n CONSTR & *fig* clé f or clef f de voûte.

keystroke ['kiːstrəʊk] n frappe f *(d'une touche).*

kg (written abbr of **kilogram**) kg.

KGB pr n KGB m.

khaki ['kɑːkɪ] ◆ adj kaki *(inv).* ◆ n [colour] kaki m ; [material] treillis m. ◆ pl n 🇺🇸 treillis mpl.

Khmer [kmeər] ◆ n **1.** [person] Khmer m, -ère f ▶ **Khmer Rouge** Khmer rouge **2.** LING khmer m. ◆ adj khmer.

KHz (abbr of **kilohertz**) n KHz m.

kibbutz [kɪ'bʊts] n (pl **kibbutzes** or **kibbutzim** [kɪbʊt'sɪm]) n kibboutz m.

kibosh ['kaɪbɒʃ] n *inf* ▶ **to put the kibosh on sthg** ficher qqch en l'air v inf.

kick [kɪk] ◆ vt **1.** donner un coup de pied à or dans / *I kicked the door open* j'ai ouvert la porte d'un coup de pied / *he had been kicked to death* il avait été tué à coups de pied / *to kick a penalty* a) [in rugby] marquer or réussir une pénalité b) [in football] tirer un penalty **2.** [PHR] **to kick the bucket** *inf* passer l'arme à gauche, casser sa pipe ▶ **to kick a habit** *inf:* *I used to smoke but I've managed to kick the habit* je fumais, mais j'ai réussi à m'arrêter ▶ **to kick o.s.** : *I could have kicked myself!* je me serais donné des gifles ! / *they must be kicking themselves* ils doivent s'en mordre les doigts. ◆ vi **1.** donner or lancer un coup de pied / *they dragged him away kicking and screaming* il se débattait comme un beau diable quand ils l'ont emmené **2.** [in dance] lancer les jambes en l'air **3.** [gun] reculer. ◆ n **1.** coup m de pied ▶ **to aim a kick at sb** / **sthg** lancer or donner un coup de pied en direction de qqn / qqch ▶ **a kick in the teeth** *inf:* *it was a real kick in the teeth for him* ça lui a fait un sacré coup **2.** *inf* [thrill] plaisir m ▶ **to get a kick from** or **out of doing sthg** prendre son pied à faire qqch ▶ **to do sthg for kicks** faire qqch pour rigoler or pour s'amuser **3.** *inf* [strength of drink] : *his cocktail had quite a kick* son cocktail était costaud. ◆✣ **kick about** vi 🇬🇧 *inf* traîner. ◆ vt sep = **kick around.** ◆✣ **kick around** ◆ vt sep **1.** *lit* : *to kick a ball around* jouer au ballon **2.** *inf & fig* [idea] débattre / *we kicked a few ideas around* on a discuté à bâtons rompus **3.** *inf & fig* [mistreat] malmener, maltraiter. ◆ vi 🇬🇧 *inf* traîner. ◆✣ **kick in** ◆ vt sep défoncer à coups de pied / *I'll kick his teeth in!* *inf* je vais lui casser la figure ! ◆ vi *inf* entrer en action. ◆✣ **kick off** ◆ vt sep **1.** [shoes] enlever d'un coup de pied **2.** SPORT donner le coup d'envoi à. ◆ vi **1.** SPORT donner le coup d'envoi / *they kicked off an hour late* le match a commencé avec une heure de retard **2.** *inf & fig* [start] démarrer, commencer. ◆✣ **kick out** vt sep *inf & fig* [person] chasser à coups de pied ; *fig* foutre dehors. ◆✣ **kick up** vt sep **1.** [dust, sand] faire voler (du pied) **2.** *inf & fig* ▶ **to kick up a fuss** or **a row (about sthg)** faire toute une histoire or tout un plat au sujet de qqch).

kick-ass adj *inf* super.

kickback ['kɪkbæk] n **1.** *inf* [bribe] dessous-de-table m inv, pot-de-vin m **2.** TECH recul m **3.** [backlash] contre-coup m.

kickoff ['kɪkɒf] n **1.** SPORT coup m d'envoi **2.** 🇺🇸 *inf & fig* ▶ **for a kickoff** pour commencer.

kickstand ['kɪkstænd] n béquille f (de moto).

kick-start ◆ n = **kick-starter.** ◆ vt démarrer (au kick) / *measures to kick-start the economy* fig des mesures pour faire repartir l'économie.

kick-starter n kick m.

kid [kɪd] (pt & pp **kidded**, cont **kidding**) ◆ n **1.** *inf* [child, young person] gosse mf, môme mf, gamin m, -e f / *listen to me, kid!* écoute-moi bien, petit ! **2.** [young goat] chevreau *m*, chevrette *f* **3.** [hide] chevreau *m*. ◆ *adj* **1.** *inf* [young] : *kid brother* petit frère *m*, frérot *m* / *kid sister* petite sœur *f*, sœurette *f* **2.** [coat, jacket] en chevreau. ◆ *vi* *inf* [joke] blaguer / *I won it in a raffle — no kidding!* or *you're kidding!* je l'ai gagné dans une tombola — sans blague ! or tu rigoles ! / *don't get upset, I was just kidding* ne te fâche pas, je plaisantais or c'était une blague. ◆ *vt* *inf* **1.** [tease] taquiner, se moquer de / *they kidded him about his accent* ils se moquaient de lui à cause de son accent **2.** [deceive, mislead] charrier, faire marcher / *don't kid yourself!* il ne faut pas te leurrer or te faire d'illusions ! / *who do you think you're kidding?* tu te fous de moi ? / *you're not kidding!* je ne te le fais pas dire ! ❖ **kid around** *vi inf* raconter des blagues, rigoler.

kiddie ['kɪdɪ] *inf* = **kiddy**.

kiddo ['kɪdəʊ] (*pl* **kiddos**) *n inf* [addressing boy or young man] mon grand ; [addressing girl or young woman] ma grande.

kiddy ['kɪdɪ] (*pl* **kiddies**) *n inf* gosse *mf*, gamin *m*, -e *f*.

kid gloves *pl n* gants *mpl* de chevreau ▸ **to handle** or **to treat sb with kid gloves** prendre des gants avec qqn.

kidnap ['kɪdnæp] (🇬🇧 *pt* & *pp* **kidnapped**, *cont* **kidnapping** ; 🇺🇸 *pt* & *pp* **kidnaped**, *cont* **kidnaping**) ◆ *vt* enlever, kidnapper / '**Kidnapped**' Stevenson 'Enlevé'. ◆ *n* enlèvement *m*, rapt *m*, kidnapping *m*.

kidnapper 🇬🇧, **kidnaper** 🇺🇸 ['kɪdnæpər] *n* ravisseur *m*, -euse *f*, kidnappeur *m*, -euse *f*.

kidnapping 🇬🇧, **kidnaping** 🇺🇸 ['kɪdnæpɪŋ] *n* enlèvement *m*, rapt *m*, kidnapping *m*.

kidney ['kɪdnɪ] ◆ *n* **1.** ANAT rein *m* **2.** CULIN rognon *m* **3.** 🇬🇧 *liter* [temperament] nature *f*, caractère *f*. ◆ *comp* ANAT [ailment, trouble] des reins, rénal ▸ **kidney specialist** néphrologue *mf* ▸ **kidney stone** calcul *m* rénal.

kidney bean *n* haricot *m* rouge or de Soissons.

kidney machine *n* rein *m* artificiel / *he's on a kidney machine* il est sous rein artificiel or en dialyse or en hémodialyse.

kidult *n inf* jeune adulte *mf*.

Kilimanjaro [ˌkɪlɪmənˈdʒɑːrəʊ] *pr n* ▸ **(Mount) Kilimanjaro** le Kilimandjaro.

kill [kɪl] ◆ *vt* **1.** [person, animal] tuer ▸ **to kill o.s.** se tuer, se donner la mort *fml* ; *fig* tuer **2.** *inf* & *fig* [cause pain to] faire très mal à **3.** [put an end to] tuer, mettre fin à **4.** [alleviate, deaden] atténuer, soulager **5.** *inf* POL [defeat] rejeter, faire échouer **6.** *inf* [cancel, remove] supprimer, enlever ; [computer file] effacer **7.** *inf* [switch off] arrêter, couper / *to kill the lights* éteindre les lumières. ◆ *vi* tuer. ◆ *n* **1.** mise *f* à mort ▸ **to be in at the kill** assister au coup de grâce **2.** [prey - killed by animal] proie *f* ; [- killed by hunter] chasse *f*. ❖ **kill off** *vt sep* tuer, exterminer.

killer ['kɪlər] ◆ *n* **1.** *lit* tueur *m*, -euse *f* **2.** PHR a real killer *inf*: *the exam was a real killer* l'examen était d'une difficulté incroyable. ◆ *comp* [disease] meurtrier ▸ **a killer shark** un requin tueur. ◆ *adj* 🇺🇸 *v inf* [excellent] d'enfer.

killer instinct *n fig* 🇺🇸 *v inf* [excellent] : *he's got the killer instinct* c'est un battant / *he lacks the killer instinct* il manque d'agressivité or de combativité, il a trop de scrupules.

killer whale *n* épaulard *m*, orque *m*.

killing ['kɪlɪŋ] ◆ *n* **1.** [of person] assassinat *m*, meurtre *m* **2.** *inf* [profit] ▸ **to make a killing** se remplir les poches, s'en mettre plein les poches. ◆ *adj* 🇬🇧 *inf* **1.** [tiring] crevant, tuant **2.** *dated* [hilarious] tordant, bidonnant.

killjoy ['kɪldʒɔɪ] *n* trouble-fête *mf*.

kiln [kɪln] *n* four *m* (*à céramique, à briques, etc.*).

kilo ['kiːləʊ] (*pl* **kilos**) (**abbr of kilogram**) *n* kilo *m*.

kilo- ['kɪlə] *pref* kilo-.

kilobyte ['kɪləbaɪt] *n* kilobyte *m*, kilo-octet *m*.

kilocalorie ['kɪlə,kælərɪ] *n* kilocalorie *f*, grande calorie *f*.

kilogram(me) 🇬🇧, **kilogram** 🇺🇸 ['kɪlə,græm] *n* kilogramme *m*.

kilohertz ['kɪlə,hɜːts] *n* kilohertz *m*.

kilojoule ['kɪlə,dʒuːl] *n* kilojoule *m*.

kilometre 🇬🇧, **kilometer** 🇺🇸 ['kɪlə,miːtər or kɪˈlɒmɪtər] *n* kilomètre *m*.

kilowatt ['kɪlə,wɒt] *n* kilowatt *m*.

kilt [kɪlt] *n* kilt *m*.

kilter ['kɪltər] ❖ **out of kilter** *adj phr* en dérangement, en panne.

kimono [kɪˈməʊnəʊ] (*pl* **kimonos**) *n* kimono *m*.

kin [kɪn] *pl n* parents *mpl*, famille *f*.

kind¹ [kaɪnd] *n* **1.** [sort, type] sorte *f*, type *m*, genre *m* / *hundreds of different kinds of books* des centaines de livres de toutes sortes / *have you got any other kind?* en avez-vous d'autres ? / *all kinds of people* toutes sortes de gens / *it's a different kind of problem* c'est un tout autre problème, c'est un problème d'un autre ordre / *what kind of computer have you got?* qu'est-ce que vous avez comme (marque d')ordinateur ? / *what kind of person do you think I am?* pour qui me prenez-vous ? / *Las Vegas is my kind of town* Las Vegas est le genre de ville que j'aime ▸ **nothing of the kind**: *I said nothing of the kind!* je n'ai rien dit de pareil or de tel ! / *you were drunk last night — I was nothing of the kind!* tu étais ivre hier soir — absolument pas or mais pas du tout ! **2.** [class of person, thing] : *it's one of the finest of its kind* **a)** [animal] c'est l'un des plus beaux spécimens de son espèce **b)** [object] c'est l'un des plus beaux dans son genre **3.** PHR **a kind of** une sorte de, une espèce de / *I had a kind of (a) feeling you'd come* j'avais comme l'impression que tu viendrais ▸ **kind of** *inf* plutôt / *it's kind of big and round* c'est plutôt or dans le genre grand et rond / *I'm kind of sad about it* ça me rend un peu triste / *did you hit him? — well, kind of* tu l'as frappé ? — oui, si on veut ▸ **of a kind**: *they're two of a kind* ils sont de la même espèce / *one of a kind* unique (en son genre). ❖ **in kind** *adv phr* **1.** [with goods, services] en nature ▸ **to pay sb in kind** payer qqn en nature **2.** [in similar fashion] de même.

kind² [kaɪnd] *adj* **1.** [good-natured, considerate] gentil, aimable ▸ **to be kind to sb** être gentil avec qqn / *it's very kind of you to take an interest* c'est très gentil à vous or vous y intéresser / *she was kind enough to say nothing* elle a eu la gentillesse de ne rien dire / *would you be so kind as to post this for me?* auriez-vous l'amabilité de mettre ceci à la poste pour moi ? ; [favourable] favorable **2.** [delicate, not harmful] doux (douce) / *a detergent that is kind to your hands* une lessive qui n'abîme pas les mains.

kinda ['kaɪndə] 🇺🇸 *v inf* **abbr of kind of**.

kindergarten ['kɪndə,gɑːtn] *n* 🇺🇸 jardin *m* d'enfants, (école *f*) maternelle *f*.

kindergartner ['kɪndə,gɑːtnər] *n* [child] enfant *m* de maternelle.

kind-hearted *adj* bon, généreux.

kindle ['kɪndl] ◆ *vt* **1.** [wood] allumer, faire brûler **2.** *fig* [interest] susciter ; [passion] embraser, enflammer ; [hatred, jealousy] attiser, susciter. ◆ *vi* **1.** [wood] s'enflammer, brûler **2.** *fig* [passion, desire] s'embraser, s'enflammer ; [interest] s'éveiller.

kindling ['kɪndlɪŋ] *n* petit bois *m*, bois *m* d'allumage.

kindly ['kaɪndlɪ] (*compar* **kindlier**, *superl* **kindliest**) ◆ *adv* **1.** [affably, warmly] chaleureusement, affablement **2.** [obligingly] gentiment, obligeamment **3.** [favourably]

to look kindly on sthg voir qqch d'un bon œil **4.** [in polite requests] : *kindly refrain from smoking* prière de ne pas fumer ; [in anger or annoyance] : *will you kindly sit down!* asseyez-vous, je vous prie ! ◆ adj [person, attitude] gentil ; [smile] bienveillant.

kindness ['kaɪndnɪs] n **1.** [thoughtfulness] bonté f, gentillesse f **2.** 🇬🇧 [considerate act] service m **to do sb a kindness** rendre service à qqn.

kindred ['kɪndrɪd] ◆ n *arch & liter* [relationship] parenté f ; [family] famille f, parents mpl. ◆ adj [related] apparenté ; [similar] similaire, analogue **kindred spirits** âmes fpl sœurs.

kinetic [kɪ'netɪk] adj cinétique.

kinfolk ['kɪnfəʊk] 🇺🇸 = kinsfolk.

king [kɪŋ] n **1.** roi m **King Henry the Eighth** le roi Henri VIII **the King of Spain / Belgium** le roi d'Espagne / des Belges **2.** [in cards and chess] roi m ; [in draughts] dame f. **Kings** n **(the book of) Kings** BIBLE (le livre des) Rois.

kingdom ['kɪŋdəm] n **1.** [realm] royaume m **2.** [division] règne m.

kingfisher ['kɪŋ,fɪʃəʳ] n martin-pêcheur m.

kingpin ['kɪŋpɪn] n **1.** TECH pivot m **2.** fig pivot m, cheville f ouvrière.

king prawn n (grosse) crevette f.

king-size(d) adj [bed, mattress] (très) grand ; [cigarette] long (longue) ; [packet, container] géant.

kink [kɪŋk] ◆ n **1.** [in rope, wire] nœud m ; [in hair] boucle f, frisette f **2.** inf & fig [sexual deviation] perversion f, aberration f ; [quirk] bizarrerie f, excentricité f **3.** 🇺🇸 inf [flaw] problème m. ◆ vt [rope, cable] entortiller, emmêler. ◆ vi [rope, cable] s'entortiller, s'emmêler.

kinky ['kɪŋkɪ] (compar **kinkier**, superl **kinkiest**) adj **1.** inf [behaviour] farfelu ; [sexually] vicieux, pervers **2.** [rope, cable] entortillé, emmêlé ; [hair] crépu, frisé.

kinsfolk ['kɪnzfəʊk] pl n parents mpl, famille f.

kinship ['kɪnʃɪp] n [relationship] parenté f ; fig [closeness] intimité f.

kinsman ['kɪnzmən] (pl **kinsmen** [-mən]) n parent m.

kinswoman ['kɪnz,wʊmən] (pl **kinswomen** [-,wɪmɪn]) n parente f.

kiosk ['kiːɒsk] n [for newspapers, magazines] kiosque m ; 🇺🇸 [for advertisements] ≃ colonne f Morris.

kip [kɪp] (pt & pp **kipped**, cont **kipping**) 🇬🇧 inf ◆ n [sleep] roupillon m **to have a** or **to get some kip** faire or piquer un roupillon. ◆ vi roupiller. **kip down** vi inf se pieuter.

kipper ['kɪpəʳ] ◆ n hareng m fumé, kipper m. ◆ vt [fish] fumer.

kirby-grip ['kɜːbɪ-] n 🇬🇧 pince f à cheveux.

Kiribati ['kɪrɪbæti] n Kiribati m.

kirk [kɜːk] n 🅂🄲🄾🄽 église f.

kirsch [kɪəʃ] n Kirsch m.

kiss [kɪs] ◆ n baiser m / *they gave her a kiss* ils l'ont embrassée. ◆ vt **1.** [with lips] embrasser / *he kissed her on the lips / forehead* il l'embrassa sur la bouche / sur le front / *he kissed her hand* il lui a baisé la main, il lui a fait le baisemain *liter* **2.** *liter* [touch lightly] caresser. ◆ vi s'embrasser. **kiss away** vt sep : *she kissed away my tears* ses baisers ont séché mes larmes.

kissagram ['kɪsəgræm] n baiser m par porteur spécial (service utilisé à l'occasion d'un anniversaire, etc.).

kiss-and-tell adj PRESS : *another kiss-and-tell story by an ex-girlfriend* encore des révélations intimes faites or des secrets d'alcôve dévoilés par une ancienne petite amie.

kiss curl n 🇬🇧 accroche-cœur m.

kisser ['kɪsəʳ] n **1.** [person] : *is he a good kisser?* est-ce qu'il embrasse bien ? **2.** inf [face, mouth] tronche f.

kit [kɪt] (pt & pp **kitted**, cont **kitting**) n **1.** [set] trousse f **tool / sewing kit** trousse à outils / à couture **2.** [equipment] affaires fpl, matériel m / *have you got your squash kit?* as-tu tes affaires de squash ? **3.** [soldier's gear] fourniment m / *in full battle kit* en tenue de combat **kit inspection** revue f de détail **4.** [parts to be assembled] kit m / *it's sold in kit form* c'est vendu en kit / *model aircraft kit* maquette f d'avion. **kit out, kit up** vt sep 🇬🇧 inf équiper.

KIT MESSAGING written abbr of **keep in touch**.

kit bag n 🇬🇧 musette f, sac m de toile.

kitchen ['kɪtʃɪn] ◆ n cuisine f. ◆ comp [salt, scissors, table, utensil] de cuisine **kitchen floor** sol m de la cuisine **kitchen shop** magasin m d'articles de cuisine.

kitchenette [,kɪtʃɪ'net] n kitchenette f, cuisinette f offic.

kitchen foil n aluminium m ménager, papier m d'aluminium or d'alu.

kitchen garden n 🇬🇧 (jardin m) potager m.

kitchen paper, kitchen roll n 🇬🇧 essuie-tout m, Sopalin® m.

kitchen sink n évier m.

kitchen unit n élément m (de cuisine).

kitchenware ['kɪtʃɪnweəʳ] n vaisselle f et ustensiles mpl de cuisine.

kite [kaɪt] n **1.** [toy] cerf-volant m **2.** ORNITH milan m.

Kite mark n label représentant un petit cerf-volant apposé sur les produits conformes aux normes officielles britanniques.

kitesurfing ['kaɪtsɜːfɪŋ] n kitesurf m.

kith [kɪθ] pl n **kith and kin** amis mpl et parents mpl.

kitsch [kɪtʃ] ◆ adj kitsch. ◆ n kitsch m.

kitten ['kɪtn] n chaton m.

kitten heel n petit talon m.

kitty ['kɪtɪ] (pl **kitties**) n **1.** inf [kitten] chaton m **2.** [funds held in common] cagnotte f, caisse f (commune) ; [in gambling] cagnotte f.

kitty-corner 🇺🇸 = cater-corner.

kiwi ['kiːwiː] n **1.** ORNITH kiwi m, aptéryx m **2.** [fruit] kiwi m. **Kiwi** n inf [New Zealander] Néo-Zélandais m, -e f **the Kiwis** [rugby team] les Kiwis.

KK MESSAGING OK.

KKK pr n abbr of **Ku Klux Klan**.

Klaxon® ['klæksn] n 🇬🇧 AUTO Klaxon® m.

Kleenex® ['kliːneks] n Kleenex® m inv, mouchoir m en papier.

kleptomania [,kleptə'meɪnɪə] n kleptomanie f, cleptomanie f.

kleptomaniac [,kleptə'meɪnɪæk] ◆ adj kleptomane, cleptomane. ◆ n kleptomane mf, cleptomane mf.

klutz [klʌts] n inf balourd m, -e f, godiche f.

km (written abbr of **kilometre**) km.

km/h (written abbr of **kilometres per hour**) km/h.

knack [næk] n tour m de main, truc m.

knacker ['nækəʳ] 🇬🇧 ◆ vt v inf crever. ◆ n [slaughterer] équarrisseur m **knacker's yard** équarrissoir m, abattoir m.

knackered ['nækəd] adj v inf [tired] crevé ; [engine] mort.

knapsack ['næpsæk] n havresac m, sac m à dos.

knave [neɪv] n **1.** arch [rogue] fripon m liter, canaille f **2.** fml CARDS valet m.

knead [niːd] vt [dough, clay] pétrir, malaxer ; [massage -body] pétrir, malaxer.

knee [ni:] ◆ n **1.** ANAT genou *m* ▶ **to go down on one's knees** or **to fall to one's knees** se mettre à genoux ▶ **to be on one's knees** *lit & fig* être à genoux **2.** [of trousers] genou *m* **3.** [lap] genou *mpl.* ◆ vt donner un coup de genou à.

kneecap ['ni:kæp] (*pt & pp* kneecapped, *cont* kneecapping) ◆ n ANAT rotule *f.* ◆ vt : *he was kneecapped* on lui a brisé les rotules.

knee-deep adj : *the snow was knee-deep* on avait de la neige jusqu'aux genoux / *we were knee-deep in water* l'eau nous arrivait or nous étions dans l'eau jusqu'aux genoux.

knee-high adj [grass] à hauteur de genou / *knee-high socks* chaussettes *fpl* montantes / *the grass was knee-high* l'herbe nous arrivait (jusqu')aux genoux.

knee jerk n réflexe *m* rotulien. ❖ **knee-jerk** adj automatique / *knee jerk reaction* *fig & pej* réflexe *m*, automatisme *m.*

kneel [ni:l] (*pt & pp* knelt [nelt] or kneeled) vi s'agenouiller, se mettre à genoux. ❖ **kneel down** vi se mettre à genoux, s'agenouiller.

knee-length adj : *a knee-length skirt* une jupe qui descend jusqu'au genou.

knee pad n genouillère *f.*

knees-up n UK *inf* [dance] danse *f* (agitée) ; [party] fête *f.*

knell [nel] n *liter* glas *m.*

knelt [nelt] pt & pp ⟶ kneel.

knew [nju:] pt ⟶ know.

knickerbocker glory ['nɪkəbɒkə-] n *coupe de glace avec fruits et crème Chantilly.*

knickerbockers ['nɪkəbɒkəz] pl n knickers *mpl* ; [for golf] culotte *f* de golf.

knickers ['nɪkəz] ◆ pl n UK [underwear] ▶ **(pair of) knickers** culotte *f*, slip *m* (de femme). ◆ interj UK *inf & dated* ▶ **knickers!** mon œil !

knick-knack ['nɪknæk] n [trinket] bibelot *m* ; [brooch] colifichet *m.*

knife [naɪf] (*pl* knives [naɪvz]) ◆ n **1.** [for eating] couteau *m* / *a knife and fork* une fourchette et un couteau **2.** [as a weapon] couteau *m.* ◆ comp ▶ **a knife wound / attack** une blessure / une attaque à coups de couteau. ◆ vt donner un coup de couteau à.

knife crime n attaques *fpl* à l'arme blanche.

knife-edge n [blade] fil *m* d'un couteau / *we were on a knife-edge* *fig* on était sur des charbons ardents / *his decision was (balanced) on a knife-edge* sa décision ne tenait qu'à un fil.

knife-point n ▶ **at knife-point** sous la menace du couteau.

knifing ['naɪfɪŋ] n agression *f* à coups de couteau.

knight [naɪt] ◆ n **1.** HIST chevalier *m* **2.** UK [honorary title] chevalier *m* **3.** [chess piece] cavalier *m.* ◆ vt faire chevalier.

knighthood ['naɪthʊd] n **1.** UK [title] titre *m* de chevalier **2.** HIST chevalerie *f.*

knit [nɪt] (*pt & pp* knit or knitted, *cont* knitting) ◆ vt **1.** tricoter **2.** [in instructions] : *knit 2 purl 2* (tricoter) 2 mailles à l'endroit, 2 mailles à l'envers **3.** [unite] unir **4.** PHR **to knit one's brows** froncer les sourcils. ◆ vi tricoter. ❖ **knit together** ◆ vi [heal - bones] se souder. ◆ vt sep [unite] unir ; MED [bones] souder. ❖ **knit up** ◆ vi [yarn] : *this wool knits up easily* cette laine se tricote facilement. ◆ vt sep [garment] tricoter.

knitted ['nɪtɪd] adj tricoté, en tricot.

knitting ['nɪtɪŋ] ◆ n **1.** [garment] tricot *m* **2.** [activity] tricot *m* ; [on industrial scale] tricotage *m.* ◆ comp [wool] à tricoter ; [pattern] de tricot ; [factory] de tricotage.

knitting machine n machine *f* à tricoter.

knitting needle, knitting pin n aiguille *f* à tricoter.

knitwear ['nɪtweə] n [garments] tricots *mpl*, pulls *mpl* ; [in department store] rayon *m* pulls / *knitwear manufacturer* fabricant *m* de tricots.

knives [naɪvz] pl ⟶ knife.

knob [nɒb] n **1.** [handle - of door, drawer] poignée *f*, bouton *m* **2.** [control - on appliance] bouton *m* **3.** [ball-shaped end - of walking stick] pommeau *m* ; [- on furniture] bouton *m* **4.** [of butter] noix *f* **5.** [hillock] monticule *m* **6.** UK *vulg* [penis] queue *f*, bite *f.*

knobbly UK ['nɒblɪ] (*compar* knobblier, *superl* knobbliest), **knobby** US ['nɒbɪ] (*compar* knobbier, *superl* knobbiest) adj noueux ▶ **knobbly knees** genoux couverts de bosses.

knock [nɒk] ◆ vt **1.** [hit] : *to knock a nail in* enfoncer un clou / *the force of the explosion knocked us to the floor* la force de l'explosion nous a projetés à terre ▶ **to knock sb unconscious** or **cold** *inf* assommer qqn ; [bump] heurter, cogner / *I knocked my head on* or *against the low ceiling* je me suis cogné la tête contre le or au plafond **2.** *fig* : *maybe it will knock some sense into him* cela lui mettra peut-être du plomb dans la cervelle, cela le ramènera peut-être à la raison / *he knocked all our hopes on the head* UK il a réduit nos espoirs à néant / *he can knock spots off me at chess / tennis* UK il me bat à plate couture aux échecs / au tennis **3.** *inf* [criticize - author, film] éreinter ; [- driving, cooking] critiquer / *knocking your colleagues isn't going to help* ce n'est pas en débinant vos collègues ou en cassant du sucre sur le dos de vos collègues que vous changerez quoi que ce soit **4.** UK *v inf* [have sex with] se faire, se taper. ◆ vi **1.** [hit] frapper ▶ **to knock on** or **at the door** frapper (à la porte) **2.** [bump] ▶ **to knock against** or **into** heurter, cogner / *she knocked into the desk* elle s'est heurtée ou cognée contre le bureau **3.** [make symptomatic sound] cogner / *my heart was knocking* je sentais mon cœur cogner dans ma poitrine, j'avais le cœur qui cognait / *his knees were knocking* *hum* ses genoux jouaient des castagnettes. ◆ n **1.** [blow] coup *m* / *give it a knock with a hammer* donne un coup de marteau dessus / *there was a knock at the door / window* on a frappé à la porte / fenêtre ; [bump] coup *m* / *I got a nasty knock on the elbow* **a)** [in fight, accident] j'ai reçu un sacré coup au coude **b)** [by one's own clumsiness] je me suis bien cogné le coude **2.** [setback] coup *m* / *his reputation has taken a hard knock* sa réputation en a pris un sérieux coup **3.** *inf* [criticism] critique *f* / *she's taken a few knocks from the press* la presse n'a pas toujours été très tendre avec elle. ❖ **knock about** UK, **knock around** ◆ vi *inf* [loiter] traîner / *I knocked about in Australia for a while* j'ai bourlingué ou roulé ma bosse en Australie pendant quelque temps. ◆ vt sep *inf* traîner dans. ◆ vt sep **1.** [beat] battre ; [ill-treat] malmener **2.** [jolt, shake] ballotter **3.** *inf* [discuss] débattre. ❖ **knock about with** UK, **knock around with** vt insep *inf* fréquenter. ❖ **knock back** vt sep *inf* **1.** [drink] descendre / *she could knock back five cognacs in an hour* elle pouvait s'envoyer cinq cognacs en une heure **2.** [cost] coûter. ❖ **knock down** vt sep **1.** [person] renverser ; [in fight] envoyer par terre, étendre / *she was knocked down by a bus* elle a été renversée par un bus **2.** [hurdle, vase, pile of books] faire tomber, renverser **3.** [demolish - building] démolir ; [- wall] démolir, abattre ; [- argument] démolir **4.** [price] baisser ; [salesman] faire baisser. ❖ **knock off** ◆ vt sep **1.** [from shelf, wall, etc.] faire tomber / *he was knocked off his bicy-*

cle le choc l'a fait tomber de son vélo ▶ **to knock sb's block off** *inf* casser la figure à qqn **2.** [reduce by] faire une réduction de / *the salesman knocked 10% off (for us)* le vendeur nous a fait un rabais or une remise de 10 % **3.** *v inf* [kill] descendre, buter **4.** 🇬🇧 *v inf* [steal] piquer, faucher ; [rob] braquer **5.** [PHR] **knock it off!** *inf* [stop] arrête ton char ! ◆ *vi inf* [stop work] cesser le travail / *we knock off at 5* on finit à 17 h. ❖ **knock out** vt sep **1.** [nail] faire sortir ; [wall] abattre / *one of his teeth was knocked out* il a perdu une dent **2.** [make unconscious] assommer ; [in boxing] mettre K-O ; *inf* [subj: drug, pill] assommer, mettre K-O **3.** [eliminate] éliminer **4.** [put out of action] mettre hors service **5.** *inf* [exhaust] crever. ❖ **knock over** vt sep ◆ renverser, faire tomber. ❖ **knock up** ◆ vt sep **1.** 🇬🇧 *inf* [make quickly] faire à la hâte / *he knocked up a delicious meal in no time* en un rien de temps, il a réussi à nous préparer quelque chose de délicieux **2.** *v inf* [make pregnant] mettre en cloque. ◆ *vi* 🇬🇧 [in ball games] faire des balles.

knockabout ['nɒkəbaʊt] adj turbulent, violent / *a knockabout comedy* or *farce* une grosse farce / *a knockabout comedian* un clown.

knockdown ['nɒk,daʊn] ◆ adj **1.** [forceful] : *a knockdown blow* un coup à assommer un bœuf / *a knockdown argument* un argument massue **2.** 🇬🇧 [reduced] : *for sale at knockdown prices* en vente à des prix imbattables or défiant toute concurrence / *I got it for a knockdown price* je l'ai eu pour trois fois rien **3.** [easy to dismantle] démontable. ◆ n [in boxing] knock-down *m*.

knocker ['nɒkə] n **1.** [on door] heurtoir *m*, marteau *m* (de porte) **2.** *inf* [critic] débineur *m*, -euse *f*. ❖ **knockers** pl n *v inf* [breasts] nichons *mpl*.

knocking ['nɒkɪŋ] n **1.** [noise] bruit *m* de coups, cognement *m* ; AUTO cognement *m*, cliquetis *m* **2.** 🇬🇧 *inf* [injury, defeat] ▶ **to take a knocking a)** [in fight] se faire rouer de coups **b)** [in match] se faire battre à plate couture or plates coutures.

knocking copy n (U) publicité *f* comparative.

knocking-off time n 🇬🇧 *inf* : *it's knocking-off time* c'est l'heure de se tirer.

knock-kneed [-'ni:d] adj cagneux.

knock-on ◆ n RUGBY en-avant *m inv*. ◆ adj ▶ **knock-on effect** répercussion *f* ▶ **to have a knock-on effect** déclencher une réaction en chaîne.

knockout ['nɒkaʊt] ◆ n **1.** [in boxing] knock-out *m*, K-O *m* / *to win by a knockout* gagner par K-O **2.** *inf* [sensation] ▶ **to be a knockout** être sensationnel or génial **3.** SPORT tournoi *m* (par élimination directe). ◆ adj **1.** ▶ **knockout blow** coup *m* qui met K-O ▶ **knockout drops** *inf* soporifique *m*, somnifère *m* **2.** SPORT ▶ **knockout competition** tournoi *m* par élimination **3.** *inf* [great] génial.

knock-up n 🇬🇧 SPORT [in ball games] échauffement *m* ▶ **to have a knock-up** faire des balles.

knot [nɒt] (*pt & pp* **knotted**, *cont* **knotting**) ◆ n **1.** [fastening] nœud *m* ; *fig* [bond] lien *m* ▶ **to tie sthg in a knot, to tie a knot in sthg** nouer qqch, faire un nœud à qqch ▶ **to tie** / **to untie a knot** faire / défaire un nœud **2.** [tangle] nœud *m* **3.** [in wood] nœud *m* **4.** ANAT & MED nœud *m*, nodule *m* **5.** [cluster of people] petit groupe *m* **6.** NAUT nœud *m* / *we are doing 15 knots* nous filons 15 nœuds. ◆ vt [string] nouer, faire un nœud dans ; [tie] nouer. ◆ vi [stomach] se nouer ; [muscles] se contracter, se raidir.

knotted ['nɒtɪd] adj noué ▶ **get knotted!** *v inf* va te faire voir !

knotty ['nɒtɪ] (*compar* **knottier**, *superl* **knottiest**) adj [wood, hands] noueux ; [wool, hair] plein de nœuds ; [problem] épineux.

know [nəʊ] (*pt* **knew** [nju:], *pp* **known** [nəʊn]) ◆ vt **1.** [person] connaître ▶ **to know sb by sight** / **by reputation** connaître qqn de vue / de réputation / *knowing him, he'll still be in bed* tel que je le connais, il sera encore au lit **2.** [place] connaître **3.** [fact, information] : *do you know her phone number?* vous connaissez son numéro de téléphone ? / *I don't know that it's the best solution* je ne suis pas certain or sûr que ce soit la meilleure solution / *I know what I'm talking about* je sais de quoi je parle / *I'll let you know how it turns out* je te dirai comment ça s'est passé / *it's not an easy job — don't I know it!* *inf* ce n'est pas un travail facile — à qui le dis-tu ! ▶ **you know what I mean** tu vois ce que je veux dire ▶ **well, what do you know!** *inf* ça alors !, ça par exemple ! / *there's no knowing how he'll react* on ne peut pas savoir comment il réagira **4.** [language, skill] : *he knows French* il comprend le français ▶ **to know how to do sthg** savoir faire qqch **5.** [recognize] reconnaître / *she knows a bargain when she sees one* elle sait reconnaître une bonne affaire **6.** [distinguish] distinguer, discerner **7.** [experience] connaître **8.** [nickname, call] : *Ian White, known as "Chalky"* Ian White, connu sous le nom de « Chalky » **9.** [regard] considérer / *she's known as one of our finest singers* elle est considérée comme l'une de nos meilleures chanteuses. ◆ vi savoir / *not that I know (of)* pas que je sache / *you never know* on ne sait jamais ▶ **to know about sthg** être au courant de qqch / *do you know of a good bookshop?* vous connaissez une bonne librairie ? ◆ n ▶ **to be in the know** *inf* être au courant. ❖ **as far as I know** adv phr (pour) autant que je sache / *not as far as I know* pas que je sache. ❖ **you know** adv phr **1.** [for emphasis] : *I was right, you know* j'avais raison, tu sais **2.** [indicating hesitancy] : *he was just, you know, a bit boring* il était juste un peu ennuyeux, si tu vois ce que je veux dire **3.** [to add information] : *it was that blonde woman, you know, the one with the dog* c'était la femme blonde, tu sais, celle qui avait un chien **4.** [to introduce a statement] : *you know, sometimes I wonder why I do this* tu sais, parfois je me demande pourquoi je fais ça.

know-all 🇬🇧, **know-it-all** 🇺🇸 n *inf & pej* je-sais-tout *mf*, monsieur *m* or madame *f* or mademoiselle *f* je-sais-tout.

know-how n savoir-faire *m*.

knowing ['nəʊɪŋ] adj [look, laugh] entendu, complice.

knowingly ['nəʊɪŋlɪ] adv **1.** [act] sciemment, consciemment **2.** [smile, laugh] d'un air entendu.

know-it-all 🇺🇸 *inf* = **know-all**.

knowledge ['nɒlɪdʒ] n **1.** [learning] connaissance *f*, savoir *m* ; [total learning] connaissances *fpl* / *she has a good knowledge of English* elle a une bonne connaissance de l'anglais **2.** [awareness] connaissance *f* / *it has come to my knowledge that...* j'ai appris que... ▶ **to (the best of) my knowledge** (pour) autant que je sache, à ma connaissance / *not to my knowledge* pas que je sache / *without my knowledge* à mon insu, sans que je le sache.

knowledgeable ['nɒlɪdʒəbl] adj **1.** [well researched] bien documenté **2.** [expert] bien informé / *he's very knowledgeable about computing* il connaît bien l'informatique, il s'y connaît en informatique.

knowledgeably ['nɒlɪdʒəblɪ] adv en connaisseur.

knowledge engineering n ingénierie *f* des connaissances.

knowledge management n gestion *f* des connaissances.

knowledge retrieval n récupération *f* des connaissances.

known [nəʊn] ➤ pp ⟶ know. ➤ adj [notorious] connu, notoire ; [recognized] reconnu / *it's a known fact* c'est un fait établi ▶ **to let it be known** faire savoir.

knuckle ['nʌkl] n **1.** [of human] articulation f or jointure f (du doigt) ; [of animal] première phalange f **2.** [joint of meat] jarret m. ❖ **knuckles** pl n ⟨US⟩ = knuckle-duster. ❖ **knuckle down** vi ⟨UK⟩ s'y mettre. ❖ **knuckle under** vi céder, se soumettre.

knuckle-duster n coup-de-poing m américain.

KO (*pl* KO's, *pt* & *pp* KO'd, *cont* KO'ing) (abbr of **knockout**) ➤ vt mettre K-O ; [in boxing] battre par K-O. ➤ n K-O m.

koala [kəʊ'ɑːlə] n ▶ **koala (bear)** koala m.

Komodo dragon, Komodo lizard [kə'məʊdəʊ-] n ZOOL dragon m de Komodo.

kook [kuːk] n ⟨US⟩ inf dingo m, cinglé m, -e f.

kookie, kooky ['kuːkɪ] (*compar* kookier, *superl* kookiest) adj ⟨US⟩ inf fêlé, malade.

Koran [kɒ'rɑːn] n ▶ **the Koran** le Coran.

Korea [kə'rɪə] pr n Corée f / *in Korea* en Corée ▶ **the Democratic People's Republic of Korea** la République démocratique populaire de Corée.

Korean [kə'rɪən] ➤ n **1.** [person] Coréen m, -enne f **2.** LING coréen m. ➤ adj coréen ▶ **the Korean War** la guerre de Corée.

The Korean War

Conflit qui opposa, de 1950 à 1953, la Corée du Nord (régime communiste) aux forces des Nations unies (soutenant la Corée du Sud), dirigées au début par le général Mac-Arthur, et largement composées de soldats américains. Un traité mit fin à cette guerre en établissant la frontière entre les deux pays sur la ligne de front.

korma ['kɔːmə] n CULIN : *chicken / prawn korma* poulet m / crevettes fpl korma.

kosher ['kəʊʃər] ➤ adj **1.** RELIG kasher, cacher *(inv)* **2.** inf [honest] honnête, régulier. ➤ n nourriture f kasher.

Kosovan ['kɒsəvən], **Kosovar** ['kɒsəvər] ➤ n Kosovar m, -e f. ➤ adj kosovar.

Kosovo ['kɒsəvəʊ] n Kosovo m.

KOTC (written abbr of **hugs and kisses**) MESSAGING biz.

KOTL MESSAGING written abbr of **kiss on the lips**.

Koweit [kə'weɪt] = Kuwait.

kowtow [ˌkaʊ'taʊ] vi ▶ **to kowtow to sb** faire des courbettes à qqn.

KP (abbr of **kitchen police**) n : *looks like we're on KP tonight* fig on dirait qu'on est de corvée de cuisine ce soir.

kph (written abbr of **kilometres per hour**) km/h.

Krakow ['krækɒv] = Cracow.

Kremlin ['kremlɪn] pr n Kremlin m.

Kriss Kringle [-'krɪŋgl] pr n ⟨US⟩ le père Noël.

krypton ['krɪptɒn] n krypton m.

KS ➤ n abbr of **Kaposi's sarcoma**. ➤ written abbr of **Kansas**.

Kt written abbr of **Knight**.

K-12 [ˌkeɪ'twelv] n ⟨US⟩ SCH terme désignant l'ensemble de l'enseignement public du jardin d'enfant à la fin du secondaire.

Kuala Lumpur [ˌkwɑːləˈlʊmˌpʊər] pr n Kuala Lumpur.

kudos ['kjuːdɒs] n gloire f, prestige m.

Ku Klux Klan [ˌkuːklʌksˈklæn] pr n Ku Klux Klan m.

kumquat ['kʌmkwɒt] n kumquat m.

kung fu [ˌkʌŋ'fuː] n kung-fu m.

Kurd [kɜːd] n Kurde mf.

Kurdish ['kɜːdɪʃ] ➤ n LING kurde m. ➤ adj kurde.

Kurdistan [ˌkɜːdɪ'stɑːn] pr n Kurdistan m / *in Kurdistan* au Kurdistan.

Kuwait [kʊ'weɪt] pr n **1.** [country] Koweït m / *in Kuwait* au Koweït **2.** [town] Koweït City.

Kuwaiti [kʊ'weɪtɪ] ➤ n Koweïtien m, -enne f. ➤ adj koweïtien.

kW (written abbr of **kilowatt**) kW.

KY written abbr of **Kentucky**.

l (written abbr of **litre**) l.

I (pl **I's** or **Is**), **L** (pl **L's** or **Ls**) [el] n [letter] l *m*, L *m*. See also **f**.

L **1.** written abbr of **lake** **2.** written abbr of **large** **3.** (written abbr of **left**) g **4.** (written abbr of **learner**) *lettre apposée sur une voiture et signalant un apprenti conducteur (en Grande-Bretagne).*

la [lɑː] n MUS la *m*.

LA ◆ pr n abbr of **Los Angeles**. ◆ written abbr of **Louisiana**.

lab [læb] *inf* ◆ n (abbr of **laboratory**) labo *m*. ◆ comp [book] de laboratoire ▸ **a lab assistant** un laborantin, une laborantine, un assistant de laboratoire, une assistante de laboratoire ▸ **lab coat** blouse f ▸ **lab technician** technicien *m*, -enne f de laboratoire ▸ **lab results** : *I got my lab results back* J'ai eu les résultats de mes analyses.

Lab [læb] written abbr of **Labour/Labour Party**.

label ['leɪbl] (US pt & pp **labelled**, cont **labelling** ; US pt & pp **labeled**, cont **labeling**) ◆ n *lit & fig* étiquette f ▸ **designer label** marque f, griffe f. ◆ vt **1.** [suitcase, jar] étiqueter **2.** *fig* [person] étiqueter, cataloguer.

labelling US, **labeling** US ['leɪblɪŋ] n étiquetage *m*.

labelmate ['leɪblmeɪt] n personne qui travaille pour le même label.

labor US = **labour**.

laboratory [US lə'bɒrətrɪ US 'læbrə,tɔːrɪ] (pl **laboratories**) ◆ n laboratoire *m*. ◆ comp [assistant, equipment, technician] de laboratoire ▸ **laboratory conditions** : *tested under laboratory conditions* testé en laboratoire.

laboratory-tested adj testé en laboratoire.

Labor Day n fête f du travail *(aux États-Unis, célébrée le premier lundi de septembre)*.

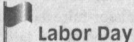 **Labor Day**

La fête du travail aux États-Unis est célébrée le premier lundi de septembre, jour férié dans l'ensemble des États. Ses origines remontent aux années 1880, lorsque le **Central Labor Union**, puissant syndicat new-yorkais, cherche à imposer un jour chômé pour les ouvriers. Aujourd'hui cette fête n'a plus la même dimension politique ; pour la plupart des Américains, elle marque symboliquement la fin de l'été et fournit l'occasion de diverses activités de loisir : pique-niques et barbecues en famille, feux d'artifice, dernières fêtes d'adolescents avant la rentrée. Certaines villes organisent un défilé (**Labor Day Parade**).

laborious [lə'bɔːrɪəs] adj laborieux.

laboriously [lə'bɔːrɪəslɪ] adv laborieusement.

labor union n US syndicat *m*.

labour UK, **labor** US ['leɪbər] ◆ n **1.** [work] travail *m* ; [hard effort] labeur *m* **2.** INDUST [manpower] main-d'œuvre f ; [workers] ouvriers mpl, travailleurs mpl **3.** POL ▸ **Labour** le parti travailliste britannique / **to vote Labour** voter travailliste **4.** MED travail *m* ▸ **to be in labour** être en travail ▸ **to go into labour** commencer le travail ▸ **labour pains** douleurs fpl de l'accouchement ▸ **labour ward** salle f d'accouchement. ◆ comp **1.** [dispute, movement] social ; [market] du travail ; [shortage] de main-d'œuvre **2.** POL [government, victory] travailliste. ◆ vi **1.** [work] travailler dur **2.** [struggle - person] : *he laboured up the stairs* il monta péniblement l'escalier ; [move with difficulty - vehicle] peiner. ◆ vt [stress] insister sur / *there's no need to labour the point* ce n'est pas la peine de t'étendre or d'insister là-dessus.

labour camp n camp *m* de travail.

laboured UK, **labored** US ['leɪbəd] adj **1.** [breathing] pénible, difficile **2.** [clumsy] lourd, laborieux.

labourer UK, **laborer** US ['leɪbərər] n [gen] ouvrier *m*, -ère f ; [on building site] manœuvre *m*.

labour force n [in country] population f active ; [in firm] main-d'œuvre f.

Labour Party n parti *m* travailliste.

 Labour Party

Les origines du parti travailliste britannique remontent à 1900. D'abord résolument socialiste et proche des syndicats, le parti mène une campagne de nationalisations dans les années 1960 et 1970 (gouvernements de Harold Wilson et James Callaghan) avant le retour au pouvoir des conservateurs sous Margaret Thatcher en 1979. Dans les années 1980 et 1990, le parti réoriente sa politique sociale pour devenir davantage un parti de centre gauche. Mené par Tony Blair, le **New Labour**, centriste et social-démocrate, remporte une victoire écrasante aux élections de 1997.

labour relations pl n relations fpl sociales.

laboursaving UK, **laborsaving** US ['leɪbə,seɪvɪŋ] adj ▸ **laboursaving device** a) [in home] appareil *m* ménager b) [at work] appareil permettant un gain de temps.

Labrador ['læbrədɔːʳ] pr n GEOG Labrador *m* / *in Labrador* au Labrador. ❖ **labrador** n [dog] labrador *m*.

labyrinth ['læbərɪnθ] n labyrinthe *m*, dédale *m*.

lace [leɪs] ◆ n **1.** TEXT dentelle *f* **2.** [in shoe, corset] lacet *m*. ◆ comp [handkerchief, tablecloth, etc.] en dentelle. ◆ vt **1.** [tie] lacer ; [put laces in] mettre les lacets à **2.** [add sthg to] : *he laced my orange juice with gin* il a mis du gin dans mon jus d'orange / *laced with irony / humour* teinté d'ironie / d'humour. ❖ **lace together** vt sep entrelacer. ❖ **lace up** vt sep [UK] [shoes] lacer.

lacemaking ['leɪs,meɪkɪŋ] n industrie *f* dentellière.

lacerate ['læsəreɪt] vt lacérer.

laceration [,læsə'reɪʃn] n **1.** [action] lacération *f* **2.** MED [gash] : *he had deep lacerations on his back* il avait le dos profondément lacéré or entaillé.

lace-up adj [shoe, boot] à lacets. ❖ **lace-ups** pl n [UK] chaussures *fpl* à lacets.

lack [læk] ◆ n manque *m* ▶ **through** or **for lack of** par manque de, faute de. ◆ vt manquer de. ❖ **lack for** vt insep manquer de.

lackadaisical [,lækə'deɪzɪkl] adj [person - apathetic] apathique ; [- lazy] indolent ; [work] tranquille.

lackey ['lækɪ] n laquais *m* ; *pej* larbin *m*.

lacklustre [UK], **lackluster** [US] ['læk,lʌstəʳ] adj terne.

laconic [lə'kɒnɪk] adj laconique.

lacquer ['lækəʳ] ◆ n **1.** [varnish, hairspray] laque *f* **2.** [varnished object] laque *m*. ◆ vt [wood] laquer ; [hair] mettre de la laque sur.

lacrosse [lə'krɒs] ◆ n lacrosse *f*, crosse *f* ▶ **lacrosse stick** crosse. ◆ comp [player] de crosse.

lactate vi [læk'teɪt] sécréter du lait.

lactic acid ['læktɪk-] n CHEM acide *m* lactique.

lacto-ovo-vegetarian [læktəʊəʊvəʊ-] n lacto-ovo-végétarien *m*, -enne *f*.

lactose ['læktəʊs] n lactose *m* ▶ **to be lactose intolerant** être intolérant au lactose.

lacto-vegetarian [læktəʊ-] n lacto-végétarien *m*, -enne *f*.

lacy ['leɪsɪ] (*compar* **lacier**, *superl* **laciest**) adj [lace-like] semblable à de la dentelle ; [made of lace] en dentelle.

lad [læd] n **1.** [young boy] garçon *m* ; [son] fils *m* **2.** [UK] inf [friend] copain *m* ; [colleague] collègue *m*, gars *m* **3.** [UK] inf [rake] noceur *m*.

ladder ['lædəʳ] ◆ n **1.** lit & fig échelle *f* **2.** [UK] [in stocking] maille *f* filée. ◆ vi & vt [UK] filer.

ladderproof ['lædəpruːf] adj [UK] indémaillable.

laddish ['lædɪʃ] adj [UK] macho.

laddism ['lædɪzəm] n [UK] machisme *m*.

laden ['leɪdn] adj chargé ▶ **laden with** chargé de.

ladette [læ'det] n [UK] inf nénette *f*.

la-di-da [,lɑːdɪ'dɑː] adj inf & pej [manner] snob, prétentieux ; [voice] maniéré.

ladies ['leɪdɪz] n [UK] [toilet] toilettes *fpl* pour dames.

Ladies' Day pr n [in UK] *troisième jour des courses d'Ascot.*

ladies' man n don Juan *m*, homme *m* à femmes.

ladies room [US] = **ladies**.

lading ['leɪdɪŋ] n [cargo] cargaison *f*, chargement *m*.

ladle ['leɪdl] ◆ n louche *f*. ◆ vt servir (à la louche). ❖ **ladle out** vt sep [UK] **1.** [soup] servir (à la louche) **2.** inf & fig [money, advice] distribuer à droite et à gauche.

ladleful ['leɪdlfʊl] n pleine louche *f*.

lad mag n [UK] inf magazine *m* masculin.

lady ['leɪdɪ] (*pl* **ladies**) ◆ n **1.** [woman] dame *f* / *Ladies and Gentlemen* Mesdames et Messieurs / *young lady* **a)** [girl] jeune fille **b)** [young woman] jeune femme ; [by birth or upbringing] dame *f* ; [term of address] ▶ **my Lady** Madame ; [as title] : *Lady Patricia* Lady Patricia **2.** [US] [term of address] madame *f* **3.** RELIG ▶ **Our Lady** Notre-Dame *f*. ◆ comp femme ▶ **a lady doctor** une femme médecin.

ladybird ['leɪdɪbɜːd] n [UK] coccinelle *f*.

ladybug ['leɪdɪbʌg] n [US] coccinelle *f*.

ladyfinger ['leɪdɪfɪŋgəʳ] n [US] [biscuit] boudoir *m*.

lady-in-waiting n dame *f* d'honneur.

ladykiller ['leɪdɪ,kɪləʳ] n inf bourreau *m* des cœurs.

ladylike ['leɪdɪlaɪk] adj [person] distingué, bien élevé ; [manners] raffiné, élégant.

ladyship ['leɪdɪʃɪp] n ▶ **Your** or **Her Ladyship a)** lit Madame (la baronne / la vicomtesse / la comtesse) **b)** fig & hum la maîtresse de ces lieux.

lag [læg] (*pt & pp* **lagged**, *cont* **lagging**) ◆ n **1.** [gap] décalage *m* **2.** [UK] v inf [convict] ▶ **an old lag** un cheval de retour. ◆ vi rester en arrière, traîner. ◆ vt [pipe] calorifuger. ❖ **lag behind** ◆ vi [dawdle] traîner, lambiner ; [be at the back] rester derrière ; [be outdistanced] se laisser distancer. ◆ vt insep [competitor] traîner derrière, avoir du retard sur.

lager ['lɑːgəʳ] n [UK] bière *f* blonde ▶ **lager lout** *jeune qui, sous l'influence de l'alcool, cherche la bagarre ou commet des actes de vandalisme.* ⟶ **beer**

lagging ['lægɪŋ] n isolant *m*, calorifuge *m*.

lagoon [lə'guːn] n [gen] lagune *f* ; [in coral reef] lagon *m*.

Lagos ['leɪgɒs] pr n Lagos.

lah-di-dah [,lɑːdɪ'dɑː] = **la-di-da**.

laid [leɪd] pt & pp ⟶ **lay**.

laid-back adj inf décontracté, cool.

lain [leɪn] pp ⟶ **lie**.

lair [leəʳ] n [for animals] tanière *f* ; fig repaire *m*, tanière *f*.

lairy ['leərɪ] adj **1.** inf [object] tape à l'œil (*inv*) **2.** [noisy] bruyant.

laisser-faire, **laissez-faire** [,leseɪ'feə] ◆ n non-interventionnisme *m*. ◆ comp ▶ **laisser-faire economy** économie *f* basée sur le non-interventionnisme ▶ **laisser-faire policy** politique *f* du laisser-faire.

laity ['leɪətɪ] n (*U*) **1.** RELIG laïcs *mpl* **2.** [non-specialists] profanes *mpl*.

lake [leɪk] n GEOG lac *m*. ❖ **Lakes** pl pr n ▶ **the Lakes** [UK] la région des lacs.

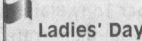

Ladies' Day

Troisième jour de la célèbre rencontre hippique d'Ascot en Angleterre, le fameux **Ladies' Day** est avant tout un événement mondain et une occasion de sortir ses plus beaux atours. Les chapeaux des femmes, sublimes, insolites ou grotesques, attirent toujours l'attention des médias.

Lakes	
Lake Erie	le lac Érié
Lake Geneva	le lac Léman
Lake Huron	le lac Huron
Lake Michigan	le lac Michigan
Lake Ontario	le lac Ontario
Lake Superior	le lac Supérieur

Lake District pr n ▶ **the Lake District** le Lake District, la région des lacs *(dans le nord-ouest de l'Angleterre).*

lakeside ['leɪksaɪd] ◆ n rive f or bord m d'un lac. ◆ comp [hotel] (situé) au bord d'un lac.

lama ['lɑːmə] n RELIG lama m.

lamb [læm] ◆ n **1.** ZOOL agneau m **2.** [meat] agneau m **3.** fig [innocent person] agneau m ; [lovable person] : *be a lamb and fetch my glasses* sois un ange or sois gentil, va me chercher mes lunettes **4.** RELIG ▶ **the Lamb of God** l'Agneau de Dieu. ◆ comp [chop, cutlet] d'agneau. ◆ vi agneler, mettre bas.

lambast [læm'bæst], **lambaste** [læm'beɪst] vt [scold] réprimander ; [thrash] battre, rosser.

lambing ['læmɪŋ] n agnelage m.

lambskin ['læmskɪn] ◆ n (peau f d')agneau m. ◆ comp [coat, gloves] en agneau.

lambswool ['læmzwʊl] comp [scarf, sweater, etc.] en laine d'agneau, en lambswool.

lame [leɪm] ◆ adj **1.** [person, horse] boiteux / *to be lame* boiter / *to go lame* se mettre à boiter **2.** [weak - excuse] piètre, bancal ; [- argument, reasoning] boiteux ; [- plot] boiteux, bancal **3.** US inf [conventional] vieux jeu *(inv).* ◆ vt estropier. ◆ pl n ▶ **the lame** les boiteux *mpl.*

lamé ['lɑːmeɪ] n lamé m.

lame duck n fig **1.** [gen & INDUST] canard m boiteux **2.** US POL candidat sortant non réélu qui attend l'arrivée de son successeur. ◆ **lame-duck** comp ▶ **a lame-duck president** un président sortant non réélu.

lamely ['leɪmlɪ] adv de façon peu convaincante, maladroitement.

lament [lə'ment] ◆ vt [feel sorrow for] regretter, pleurer ; [complain about] se lamenter sur, se plaindre de / *"I'll never finish in time!", she lamented* « je n'aurai jamais fini à temps ! », gémit-elle. ◆ vi se lamenter. ◆ n **1.** [lamentation, complaint] lamentation f **2.** [poem] élégie f ; [song] complainte f.

lamentable ['læməntəbl] adj [regrettable] regrettable ; [poor] lamentable.

laminate ◆ ['læmɪneɪt] vt TECH [bond in layers] laminer ; [veneer] plaquer. ◆ n stratifié m.

laminated ['læmɪneɪtɪd] adj [wood] stratifié ; [glass] feuilleté ; [document] plastifié.

lamp [læmp] n **1.** [gen] lampe f ; [street-lamp] réverbère m ; [on car, train] lumière f, feu m **2.** MED lampe f ▶ **infrared lamp** lampe à infrarouges.

lamplight ['læmplaɪt] n : *her hair shone in the lamplight* la lumière de la lampe faisait briller ses cheveux / *to read by lamplight* lire à la lumière d'une or de la lampe.

lampoon [læm'puːn] ◆ n [satire] satire f ; [written] pamphlet m. ◆ vt ridiculiser, tourner en dérision.

lamppost ['læmppəʊst] n réverbère m.

lampshade ['læmpʃeɪd] n abat-jour m inv.

LAN (abbr of **local area network**) n COMPUT réseau m local.

lance [lɑːns] ◆ n [weapon] lance f. ◆ vt MED percer, inciser.

lance corporal n caporal m *(dans l'armée britannique).*

lancet ['lɑːnsɪt] n MED lancette f, bistouri m.
◆ **the Lancet** UK PRESS importante revue médicale.

Lancs written abbr of Lancashire.

land [lænd] ◆ vi **1.** AERON & ASTRONAUT atterrir / *to land on the moon* atterrir sur la Lune, alunir / *to land in the sea* amerrir / *to land on an aircraft carrier* apponter (sur un porte-avions) **2.** NAUT [boat] arriver à quai ; [passengers] débarquer **3.** [ball, high jumper] tomber, retomber ;

[falling object, bomb, parachutist] tomber ; [bird] se poser / *an apple landed on her head* elle a reçu une pomme sur la tête **4.** inf [finish up] finir, atterrir. ◆ vt **1.** [plane] poser ; [cargo, passengers] débarquer **2.** [fish - onto bank] hisser sur la rive ; [- onto boat] hisser dans le bateau **3.** inf [job, contract] décrocher **4.** inf [put, place] ficher / *this could land us in real trouble* ça pourrait nous attirer de gros ennuis or nous mettre dans le pétrin **5.** [blow] flanquer / *I landed him a blow* or *landed him one on the nose* je lui ai flanqué or collé mon poing dans la figure **6.** inf [encumber] ▶ **to get landed with sthg** : *I got landed with the job of organizing the party* c'est moi qui me suis retrouvé avec la fête à organiser, c'est moi qui me suis tapé l'organisation de la fête. ◆ n **1.** [for farming, building, etc.] terre f / *he works on the land* il travaille la terre / *this is good farming land* c'est de la bonne terre ▶ **building land** terrain constructible / *a piece of land* a) [for farming] un lopin de terre b) [for building] un terrain (à bâtir) **2.** [property] terre f, terres fpl **3.** [area, region] région f **4.** [not sea] terre f / *we travelled by land to Cairo* nous sommes allés au Caire par la route / *over land and sea* sur terre et sur mer **5.** [nation, country] pays m **6.** fig [realm] royaume m, pays m **7.** PHR **Land of Hope and Glory** chanson patriotique anglaise sur un air d'Elgar, traditionnellement chantée lors de la *Last Night of the Proms* ▶ **Land of My Fathers** hymne du pays de Galles. ◆ comp [prices - in town] du terrain ; [- in country] de la terre ; [reform] agraire ; [tax, ownership] foncier ; UK HIST [army] de terre ; [worker] agricole. ◆ **lands** pl n = **land** (noun). ◆ **land up** vi = **land** (vi).

 terre or **terrain**?

When translating **land**, note that **terre** and **terrain** are not interchangeable. **Terre** is used to refer to **land** in general whereas **terrain** is used when talking about the quality of the soil or to refer to a plot of **land**.

landed ['lændɪd] adj UK foncier ▶ **the landed gentry** la noblesse terrienne.

landfall ['lændfɔːl] n NAUT ▶ **to make landfall** apercevoir la terre, arriver en vue d'une côte.

landfill ['lændfɪl] n ensevelissement m de déchets.

landfill gas n gaz m d'enfouissement.

landing ['lændɪŋ] n **1.** [of plane, spacecraft] atterrissage m ; [on moon] alunissage m ; [of passengers, foods] débarquement m ; SPORT [of skier, high jumper] réception f ▶ **the Normandy landings** HIST le Débarquement (en Normandie) **2.** [in staircase] palier m ; [floor] étage m **3.** [jetty] débarcadère m, embarcadère m.

landing card n carte f de débarquement.

landing craft n navire m de débarquement.

landing gear n AERON train m d'atterrissage.

landing lights pl n [on plane] phares mpl d'atterrissage ; [at airport] balises fpl (d'atterrissage).

landing stage n débarcadère m.

landing strip n piste f d'atterrissage.

landlady ['lænd,leɪdɪ] (pl **landladies**) n [owner] propriétaire f ; [in lodgings] logeuse f ; [in pub, guesthouse] patronne f.

land-line n TELEC ligne f terrestre / *call me on my land-line* appelle-moi sur mon fixe.

landlocked ['lændlɒkt] adj [country] enclavé, sans accès à la mer ; [sea] intérieur.

landlord [ˈlændlɔːd] n [owner] propriétaire *m* ; [in lodgings] logeur *m* ; [in pub, guesthouse] patron *m*.

landmark [ˈlændmɑːk] ◆ n **1.** *lit* point *m* de repère **2.** *fig* étape *f* décisive, jalon *m*. ◆ comp [decision, event] qui fait date.

landmass [ˈlændmæs] n zone *f* terrestre / *the American landmass* le continent américain.

landmine [ˈlændmaɪn] n mine *f* (terrestre).

landowner [ˈlænd,əʊnə*] n propriétaire *m* foncier, propriétaire *f* foncière.

land registry n cadastre *m*.

Land Rover® n Land-Rover® *f*.

landscape [ˈlændskeɪp] ◆ n **1.** [gen] paysage *m* **2.** PRINT **▶ to print in landscape** imprimer à l'italienne. ◆ adj **1.** ART **▶ landscape painter** (peintre *m*) paysagiste *m* **▶ landscape painting** le paysage **2.** HORT **▶ landscape architect** architecte *mf* paysagiste **▶ landscape gardener** jardinier *m* paysagiste, jardinière *f* paysagiste **▶ landscape gardening** paysagisme *m* **3.** PRINT à l'italienne. ◆ vt [garden] dessiner ; [waste land] aménager.

landslide [ˈlændslaɪd] ◆ n glissement *m* de terrain. ◆ comp [election victory] écrasant **▶ to win by a landslide** remporter une victoire écrasante.

landslip [ˈlændslɪp] n éboulement *m*.

lane [leɪn] n **1.** [road -in country] chemin *m* ; [-in street names] rue *f*, allée *f* **2.** [for traffic] voie *f* ; [line of vehicles] file *f* ; [for shipping, aircraft] couloir *m* ; [in athletics, swimming] couloir *m*.

langoustine [ˈlæŋɡəstiːn] n langoustine *f*.

language [ˈlæŋɡwɪdʒ] ◆ n **1.** [means of communication] langage *m* **2.** [specific tongue] langue *f* ; SCH & UNIV [area of study] langue *f* **3.** [code] langage *m* / *a computer language* un langage machine **4.** [terminology] langue *f*, langage *m* ; [manner of expression] expression *f*, langue *f* ; [rude words] gros mots *mpl*, grossièretés *fpl*. ◆ comp [acquisition] du langage ; [course] de langues ; [barrier] linguistique ; [student] en langues.

 langue or **langage?**

In everyday French, **une langue** is a natural language, while machine languages and animal languages are usually called **langages**. The language used by specific professional groups can be **langage** or **langue** (**la langue** / **le langage juridique**). In linguistics, Ferdinand de Saussure distinguished between **le langage** (the ability to communicate using language) and **la langue** (a particular language that exists thanks to that ability).

language laboratory, **language lab** n laboratoire *m* de langues.

languid [ˈlæŋɡwɪd] adj langoureux, alangui.

languidly [ˈlæŋɡwɪdlɪ] adv langoureusement.

languish [ˈlæŋɡwɪʃ] vi **1.** [suffer] languir **2.** [become weak] dépérir **3.** *liter* [pine] languir.

languorous [ˈlæŋɡərəs] adj langoureux.

lank [læŋk] adj [hair] terne, mou *(before vowel or silent 'h' mol, f molle)* ; [plant] étiolé, grêle.

lanky [ˈlæŋkɪ] (*compar* **lankier**, *superl* **lankiest**) adj dégingandé.

lanolin(e) [ˈlænəlɪn] n lanoline *f*.

lantern [ˈlæntən] n lanterne *f*.

Lao [laʊ] = **Laotian**.

Laos [ˈlaːɒs] pr n Laos *m* / *in Laos* au Laos.

Laotian [ˈlaːʃn] ◆ n [person] Laotien *m*, -enne *f*. ◆ adj laotien.

lap [læp] (*pt & pp* **lapped**, *cont* **lapping**) ◆ n **1.** [knees] genoux *mpl* **2.** SPORT tour *m* de piste **3.** [of journey] étape *f* **▶ to be on the last lap** : *we're on the last lap* a) *lit* c'est le dernier tour b) *fig* on arrive au bout de nos peines. ◆ vt **1.** SPORT [competitor, car] dépasser, prendre un tour d'avance sur ; [time] chronométrer **2.** [milk] laper **3.** [subj: waves] clapoter contre. ◆ vi **1.** SPORT tourner, faire un tour de circuit **2.** [waves] clapoter. ✦ **lap over** vt insep [tiles] chevaucher sur. ◆ vi se chevaucher. ✦ **lap up** vt sep **1.** [milk] laper **2.** *inf & fig* [praise] boire ; [information] avaler, gober.

laparoscopy [,læpəˈrɒskəpɪ] n laparoscopie *f*, péritonéoscopie *f*.

La Paz [læˈpæz] pr n La Paz.

lap dance ◆ vi danser *(pour les clients d'un bar)*. ◆ n lap dance *f*.

lap dancer n danseuse *f* de bar.

lap dancing n danse érotique exécutée sur les genoux des clients.

lapdog [ˈlæpdɒg] n **1.** *lit* petit chien *m* d'appartement **2.** *pej* toutou *m*, caniche *m*.

lapel [ləˈpel] n revers *m*.

lapis lazuli [,læpɪsˈlæzjʊlaɪ] n lapis *m*, lapis-lazuli *m inv*.

Lapland [ˈlæplænd] pr n Laponie *f* / *in Lapland* en Laponie.

Lapp [læp] ◆ n **1.** [person] Lapon *m*, -one *f* **2.** LING lapon *m*. ◆ adj lapon *m*.

lapse [læps] ◆ n **1.** [failure] : *lapse of memory* trou *m* de mémoire / *lapse in* or *of concentration* moment *m* d'inattention **2.** [in behaviour] écart *m* (de conduite) **3.** [interval] laps *m* de temps, intervalle *m* **4.** [of contract] expiration *f* ; [of custom] disparition *f* ; [of legal right] déchéance *f*. ◆ vi **1.** [decline] baisser, chuter **2.** [drift] tomber / *to lapse into bad habits* prendre de mauvaises habitudes / *to lapse into silence* garder le silence, s'enfermer dans le silence / *she kept lapsing into Russian* elle se remettait sans cesse à parler russe **3.** [pass -time] passer **4.** [law, custom] tomber en désuétude ; [licence, passport] se périmer ; [subscription] prendre fin, expirer **5.** RELIG [lose faith] abandonner or perdre la foi.

lapsed [læpst] adj [law] caduc ; [passport] périmé / *a lapsed Catholic* un catholique qui ne pratique plus.

laptop [ˈlæptɒp] n **▶ laptop (computer)** portable *m*.

larceny [ˈlɑːsənɪ] (*pl* **larcenies**) n LAW vol *m* simple.

larch [lɑːtʃ] n mélèze *m*.

lard [lɑːd] ◆ n saindoux *m*. ◆ vt larder / *an essay larded with quotations* *fig* une rédaction truffée de citations.

larder [ˈlɑːdə*] n [room] cellier *m* ; [cupboard] garde-manger *m inv*.

large [lɑːdʒ] ◆ adj **1.** [in size] grand ; [family] grand, nombreux ; [person] gros (grosse), grand ; [organization] gros (grosse), grand ; [in number, amount] grand, important / *a large number of* beaucoup de **2.** [extensive -changes] considérable, important. ◆ adv **▶ to loom large** menacer, sembler imminent **▶ to be writ large** être évident. ✦ **at large** ◆ adj phr [at liberty] en liberté ; [prisoner] en fuite. ◆ adv phr [as a whole] dans son ensemble / *the country at large* le pays dans son ensemble. ✦ **by and large** adv phr de manière générale, dans l'ensemble.

largely ['lɑːʤlɪ] adv [mainly] en grande partie, pour la plupart ; [in general] en général, en gros.

large-scale adj à grande échelle.

largesse [lɑːˈʤes], **largess** US n (U) largesse f, largesses fpl.

lark [lɑːk] n **1.** ZOOL alouette f **2.** inf [joke] rigolade f ; [prank] blague f, farce f / for a lark pour blaguer, pour rigoler **3.** inf [rigmarole, business] histoire f. ❖ **lark about, lark around** vi US inf faire le fou.

larva ['lɑːvə] (pl **larvae** [-viː]) n larve f.

laryngitis [ˌlærɪnˈʤaɪtɪs] n (U) laryngite f / to have laryngitis avoir une laryngite.

larynx ['lærɪŋks] n larynx m.

lasagne, lasagna [ləˈzænjə] n (U) lasagnes fpl.

lascivious [ləˈsɪvɪəs] adj lascif, lubrique.

lasciviously [ləˈsɪvɪəslɪ] adv lascivement.

laser ['leɪzər] n laser m ▸ **laser surgery** chirurgie f (au) laser.

laser beam n rayon m or faisceau m laser.

laser disc n disque m laser.

laser printer n imprimante f (à) laser.

laser proof n épreuve f laser.

laser show n spectacle m laser.

laser weapon n arme f laser.

lash [læʃ] ❖ n **1.** [whip] lanière f ; [blow from whip] coup m de fouet **2.** fig [of scorn, criticism] : he'd often felt the lash of her tongue il avait souvent été la cible de ses propos virulents **3.** [of rain, sea] : the lash of the rain on the windows le bruit de la pluie qui fouette les vitres / the lash of the waves against the shore le déferlement des vagues sur la grève **4.** [eyelash] cil m. ❖ vt **1.** [with whip] fouetter **2.** [subj: rain, waves] battre, fouetter **3.** [move] : the tiger lashed its tail le tigre fouettait l'air de sa queue **4.** [tie] attacher. ❖ vi : its tail lashed wildly il fouettait l'air furieusement de sa queue / the hail lashed against the window la grêle cinglait la vitre. ❖ **lash down** ❖ vt sep [cargo] arrimer, fixer. ❖ vi [rain, hail] s'abattre, tomber avec violence. ❖ **lash out** vi **1.** [struggle - with fists] donner des coups de poing ; [- with feet] donner des coups de pied **2.** fig [verbally] : he lashed out at his critics il a fustigé ses détracteurs **3.** UK inf [spend] ▸ **to lash out (on sthg)** dépenser un fric monstre (pour qqch).

lass [læs] n Scot [girl] fille f.

lassi n lassi m (yaourt à boire, spécialité indienne).

lassitude ['læsɪtjuːd] n lassitude f.

lasso, lassoo ['læˈsuː] ❖ n lasso m. ❖ vt prendre au lasso.

last¹ [lɑːst] ❖ adj **1.** [with dates, times of day] dernier / last Monday lundi dernier / last week / year la semaine / l'année dernière / last July en juillet dernier, l'année dernière au mois de juillet / last night a) [at night] cette nuit b) [in the evening] hier soir **2.** [final] dernier / that was the last time I saw him c'était la dernière fois que je le voyais / at the last minute or moment à la dernière minute / to the last detail dans les moindres détails / she was on her last legs elle était au bout du rouleau / your car is on its last legs votre voiture ne va pas tarder à vous lâcher / I'll get my money back if it's the last thing I do je récupérerai mon argent coûte que coûte ▸ **last thing** : I always clean my teeth last thing at night je me brosse toujours les dents juste avant de me coucher / we finished the work last thing on Tuesday afternoon on a terminé le travail juste avant de partir mardi après-midi **3.** [most recent] : I've been here for the last five years je suis ici depuis cinq ans, cela fait cinq ans que je suis ici **4.** [least likely] : he's the last person I expected to see c'est bien la dernière personne que je m'attendais à voir / that's the last thing I wanted je n'avais vraiment pas besoin de ça **5.** PHR Last Night of

the Proms concert à l'Albert Hall qui clôt la saison des **Promenade Concerts**. ❖ adv **1.** [finally] : she arrived last elle est arrivée la dernière or en dernier ▸ **..., and last but not least...** ... et en dernier, mais non par ordre d'importance,... **2.** [most recently] : when did you last see him? quand l'avez-vous vu pour la dernière fois ? **3.** = lastly. ❖ n & pron **1.** [final one] dernier m, -ère f / she was the last to arrive elle est arrivée la dernière / the next to last or the last but one l'avant-dernier **2.** [previous one] : each more handsome than the last tous plus beaux les uns que les autres / the day before last avant-hier **3.** [end] : that was the last I saw of her c'était la dernière fois que je la voyais / I'll never see the last of this! je n'en verrai jamais la fin !, je n'en viendrai jamais à bout ! / you haven't heard the last of this! vous aurez de mes nouvelles ! ▸ **till last** : leave the pans till last gardez les casseroles pour la fin, lavez les casseroles en dernier **4.** [remainder] reste m / we drank the last of the wine on a bu ce qui restait de vin. ❖ **at last** adv phr enfin / free at last enfin libre ▸ **at long last** enfin. ❖ **to the last** adv phr jusqu'au bout.

> Note word order, which is reversed with respect to English : les quatre derniers jours the last four days.

🚩 **Last Night of the Proms**

Les **Henry Wood Promenade Concerts**, communément appelés **The Proms**, désignent une saison annuelle de concerts classiques organisés principalement à l'**Albert Hall** à Londres. Les **Promenade Concerts** se distinguent par le fait que beaucoup de spectateurs sont debout (notamment au parterre), ce qui confère une atmosphère décontractée et chaleureuse à la manifestation. Le festival se termine par la célèbre **Last Night of the Proms** à l'Albert Hall, grande manifestation populaire où les spectateurs en liesse agitent des drapeaux en chantant des airs patriotiques (**Land of Hope and Glory, Rule Britannia, Jerusalem, God Save the Queen...**).

last² [lɑːst] ❖ vi **1.** [continue to exist or function] durer / it lasted (for) ten days cela a duré dix jours / how long can we last without water? combien de temps tiendrons-nous sans eau ? / he won't last long a) [in job] il ne tiendra pas longtemps b) [will soon die] il n'en a plus pour longtemps / built / made to last construit / fait pour durer **2.** [be enough] : we've got enough food to last another week nous avons assez à manger pour une semaine encore **3.** [keep fresh - food] se conserver / these flowers don't last (long) ces fleurs ne tiennent or ne durent pas (longtemps). ❖ vt : have we got enough to last us until tomorrow? en avons-nous assez pour tenir or aller jusqu'à demain ? / that fountain pen will last you a lifetime vous pourrez garder ce stylo plume toute votre vie. ❖ n [for shoes] forme f. ❖ **last out** ❖ vi **1.** [survive] tenir **2.** [be enough] suffire / will our supplies last out till the end of the month? les provisions suffiront-elles jusqu'à la fin du mois ? ❖ vt sep : he didn't last the night out il n'a pas passé la nuit, il est mort pendant la nuit / will the play last out the month? est-ce que la pièce tiendra le mois ?

last chance saloon n : *these talks are seen as the last chance saloon by many observers* pour beaucoup d'observateurs, il s'agit des négociations de la dernière chance.

last-ditch adj [ultimate] ultime ; [desperate] désespéré.

lasting ['lɑːstɪŋ] adj durable / *to their lasting regret / shame* à leur plus grand regret / plus grande honte.

lastly ['lɑːstlɪ] adv enfin, en dernier lieu.

last-minute adj de dernière minute.

last name n nom *m* de famille.

last post n 🇬🇧 MIL [at night] extinction *f* des feux ; [at funeral] sonnerie *f* aux morts.

last rites pl n derniers sacrements *mpl*.

last straw n ▸ *it was the last straw* cela a été la goutte (d'eau) qui fait déborder le vase.

Last Supper n ▸ *the Last Supper* la (sainte) Cène.

Las Vegas [ˌlæsˈveɪɡəs] pr n Las Vegas.

latch [lætʃ] ◆ n loquet *m* / *the door was on the latch* la porte n'était pas fermée à clé. ◆ vt fermer au loquet. ◆ vi se fermer. ❖ **latch on** vi *inf* piger. ❖ **latch onto** vt insep *inf* **1.** [attach o.s. to] s'accrocher à **2.** 🇬🇧 [understand] piger **3.** 🇺🇸 [obtain] se procurer, obtenir.

latchkey ['lætʃkiː] n clef *f* (de la porte d'entrée).

latchkey child n enfant dont les parents travaillent et ne sont pas là quand il rentre de l'école.

L8 MESSAGING written abbr of late.

late [leɪt] ◆ adj **1.** [behind schedule] en retard / *to be late* être en retard / *to be 10 minutes late* avoir 10 minutes de retard / *to make sb late* retarder qqn, mettre qqn en retard / *we apologize for the late arrival of flight 906* nous vous prions d'excuser le retard du vol 906 **2.** [in time] tardif / *in the late afternoon* dans l'après-midi, en fin d'après-midi / *she's in her late fifties* elle approche la soixantaine / *in the late seventies* à la fin des années soixante-dix / *at this late stage* à ce stade avancé / *to have a late lunch* déjeuner tard / *he was a late developer* **a)** [physically] il a eu une croissance tardive **b)** [intellectually] son développement intellectuel fut un peu tardif ; [news, edition] dernier ▸ **late booking** réservation *f* de dernière minute **3.** [former] ancien, précédent ; [deceased] : *the late Mr Fox* le défunt M. Fox, feu M. Fox *fml* / *her late husband* son défunt mari, feu son mari *fml* **4.** [recent] récent, dernier. ◆ adv **1.** [in time] tard / *to arrive / to go to bed late* arriver / se coucher tard / *to arrive 10 minutes late* arriver avec 10 minutes de retard / *it's getting late* il se fait tard / *late in the afternoon* tard dans l'après-midi / *she came to poetry late in life* elle est venue à la poésie sur le tard / *it's rather late in the day to be thinking about that* *fig* c'est un peu tard pour penser à ça **2.** [recently] récemment. ❖ **of late** adv phr récemment / *I haven't seen him of late* je ne l'ai pas vu récemment or ces derniers temps.

late adopter n utilisateur tardif *m*, utilisatrice *f* tardive.

late-blooming adj BOT à floraison tardive.

latecomer ['leɪtˌkʌmər] n retardataire *mf* / *'latecomers will not be admitted'* ≃ le placement n'est plus assuré après le début de la représentation.

late-flowering adj BOT à floraison tardive.

lately ['leɪtlɪ] adv récemment, ces derniers temps, dernièrement.

lateness ['leɪtnɪs] n **1.** [of bus, train, person] retard *m* **2.** [late time] heure *f* tardive.

late-night adj [play, show, film] ≃ de minuit ▸ **late-night opening** COMM nocturne *f* ▸ **late-night shopping** courses *fpl* en nocturne.

latent ['leɪtənt] adj latent.

late payment n retard *m* de paiement.

L8r, L8R MESSAGING written abbr of later.

later ['leɪtər] *(compar of late)* ◆ adj ultérieur / *we can always catch a later train* on peut toujours prendre un autre train, plus tard / *at a later date* à une date ultérieure / *at a later stage* à un stade plus avancé / *in later life* plus tard dans la vie. ◆ adv plus tard / *later that day* plus tard dans la journée ▸ **later on** plus tard / *see you later!* à plus tard ! ◆ interj *inf* ciao, à plus, à tout'.

lateral ['lætərəl] adj latéral.

lateral thinking n approche *f* originale.

latest ['leɪtɪst] ◆ adj *(superl of late)* dernier / *the latest date / time* la date / l'heure limite / *the latest news* les dernières nouvelles. ◆ n **1.** [most recent - news] : *have you heard the latest?* vous connaissez la dernière ? **2.** [in time] ▸ **at the latest** au plus tard.

latex ['leɪteks] n latex *m*.

lath [lɑːθ] n [wooden] latte *f* ; [in venetian blind] lame *f*.

lathe [leɪð] ◆ n tour *m* (*à bois ou à métal*) ▸ **lathe operator** tourneur *m*. ◆ vt tourner.

lather ['lɑːðər] ◆ n **1.** [from soap] mousse *f* **2.** [foam - on horse, seawater] écume *f*. ◆ vt [clean] savonner. ◆ vi **1.** [soap] mousser **2.** [horse] écumer.

Latin ['lætɪn] ◆ n **1.** [person] Latin *m*, -e *f* ▸ **the Latins a)** [in Europe] les Latins **b)** [in US] les Latino-américains *mpl* **2.** LING latin *m*. ◆ adj latin ; [alphabet] latin ▸ **the Latin Quarter** le Quartier latin.

Latin America pr n Amérique *f* latine / *in Latin America* en Amérique latine.

Latin American ◆ n Latino-américain *m*, -e *f*. ◆ adj latino-américain.

latitude ['lætɪtjuːd] n **1.** ASTRON & GEOG latitude *f* / *at a latitude of 50° south* à 50° de latitude sud **2.** [freedom] latitude *f*.

latrines [ləˈtriːnz] pl n latrines *fpl*.

latte ['læteɪ] n café *m* au lait.

latter ['lætər] ◆ adj **1.** [in relation to former] dernier, second **2.** [later] dernier, second / *in the latter years of her life* au cours des dernières années de sa vie. ◆ n ▸ **the former... the latter** le premier... le second, celui-là... celui-ci.

latter-day adj d'aujourd'hui / *a latter-day St Francis* un saint François moderne ▸ **Church of the latter-day Saints** Église *f* de Jésus-Christ des saints des derniers jours.

latterly ['lætəlɪ] adv [recently] récemment, dernièrement ; [towards the end] vers la fin.

lattice ['lætɪs] n [fence, frame] treillage *m* ; [design] treillis *m*.

lattice window n fenêtre *f* à croisillons.

Latvia ['lætvɪə] pr n Lettonie *f* / *in Latvia* en Lettonie.

Latvian ['lætvɪən] ◆ n **1.** [person] Letton *m*, -onne *f* **2.** LING letton *m*. ◆ adj letton.

laudable ['lɔːdəbl] adj louable, digne de louanges.

laugh [lɑːf] ◆ vi **1.** [in amusement] rire ▸ **to burst out laughing** éclater de rire / *we laughed about it afterwards* après coup, cela nous a fait bien rire, on en a ri après coup **2.** [in contempt, ridicule] rire / *they laughed in my face* ils m'ont ri au nez **3.** *fig* [be confident] : *once we get the contract, we're laughing* une fois qu'on aura empoché le contrat, on sera tranquilles. ◆ vt **1.** [in amusement] ▸ **to laugh o.s. silly** se tordre de rire, être plié en deux de rire **2.** [in ridicule] : *he was laughed off the stage / out of the room* il a quitté la scène / la pièce sous les rires moqueurs. ◆ n **1.** [of amusement] rire *m* ; [burst of laughter] éclat *m* de rire ▸ **to give a laugh** rire / *we had a good laugh about it* ça nous a bien fait rire ; [of contempt] rire *m* **2.** 🇬🇧 *inf* [fun] rigolade *f* ▸ **to have (a bit of) a laugh** rigoler or se marrer un peu / *he's always good for a laugh* avec lui, on se marre bien **3.** *inf* [joke] : *we did it for a laugh or just for laughs* on l'a fait pour rigoler. ❖ **laugh at** vt insep **1.** [in amusement] : *we all laughed at the joke / the film* la blague / le film nous a tous fait rire **2.** [mock] se moquer de, rire de **3**. [disregard] rire de, rester indifférent à. ❖ **laugh off** vt sep [difficulty] rire de, se moquer de ; [difficult situation] désamorcer.

laughable ['lɑːfəbl] adj ridicule, dérisoire.

laughably ['lɑːfəblɪ] adv : *laughably inadequate* or *low* dérisoire, ridiculement bas / *laughably stupid* d'une stupidité affligeante.

laughing gas n gaz *m* hilarant.

laughingly ['lɑːfɪŋlɪ] adv **1**. [cheerfully] en riant **2**. [inappropriately] : *this noise is laughingly called folk music* c'est ce bruit qu'on appelle le plus sérieusement du monde de la musique folk.

laughing stock n : *they were the laughing stock of the whole neighbourhood* ils étaient la risée de tout le quartier / *they made laughing stocks of themselves* ils se sont couverts de ridicule.

laugh lines n rides *fpl* du sourire.

laughter ['lɑːftər] n (U) rire *m*, rires *mpl* / *a burst of laughter* un éclat de rire.

launch [lɔːntʃ] ❖ n **1**. [boat] vedette *f* ; [long boat] chaloupe *f* **2**. [of ship, spacecraft, new product] lancement *m*. ❖ vt **1**. [boat - from ship] mettre à la mer ; [- from harbour] faire sortir ; [- for first time] lancer **2**. COMM lancer ; FIN [shares] émettre **3**. [start] : *that was the audition that launched me on my career* cette audition a donné le coup d'envoi de ma carrière / *to launch a military offensive* déclencher or lancer une attaque. ❖ **launch into** vt insep [start] se lancer dans. ❖ **launch out** vi se lancer.

launcher ['lɔːntʃər] n ASTRONAUT & MIL lanceur *m*.

launching ['lɔːntʃɪŋ] n **1**. [of ship, spacecraft] lancement *m* ; [of lifeboat - from ship] mise *f* à la mer ; [- from shore] sortie *f* **2**. [of new product] lancement *m*.

launching pad = **launch pad**.

launch pad n rampe *f* de lancement.

launder ['lɔːndər] vt **1**. [clothes] laver ; [at laundry] blanchir **2**. *fig* [money] blanchir.

Launderette® [ˌlɔːndəˈret] = **laundrette**.

laundrette [lɔːnˈdret] n UK laverie *f* automatique.

Laundromat® ['lɔːndrəmæt] n US laverie *f* automatique.

laundry ['lɔːndrɪ] (*pl* **laundries**) n **1**. [shop] blanchisserie *f* ; [in house] buanderie *f* **2**. [washing] linge *m* ▶ **to do the laundry** faire la lessive.

laundry basket n panier *m* à linge.

laureate ['lɔːrɪət] n **1**. [prize winner] lauréat *m* ▶ **a Nobel laureate** un prix Nobel **2**. [poet] poète *m* lauréat.

laurel ['lɔrəl] ❖ n [tree] laurier *m*. ❖ comp [crown, wreath] de lauriers. ❖ **laurels** pl n [honours] lauriers *mpl* ▶ **to look to one's laurels** ne pas s'endormir sur ses lauriers ▶ **to rest on one's laurels** se reposer sur ses lauriers.

Lautro ['lautrəʊ] (abbr of Life Assurance and Unit Trust Regulatory Organization) n *organisme britannique contrôlant les activités de compagnies d'assurance-vie et de SICAV.*

lava ['lɑːvə] n lave *f* ▶ **lava flow** coulée *f* de lave.

lavatory ['lævətrɪ] (*pl* **lavatories**) ❖ n UK toilettes *fpl*, cabinets *mpl* ; [bowl] cuvette *f* ▶ **to go to the lavatory** aller aux toilettes. ❖ adj des W-C ; [humour] scatologique.

lavatory paper n UK papier *m* hygiénique.

lavatory seat n UK abattant *m* de W-C.

lavender ['lævəndər] ❖ n lavande *f*. ❖ adj [colour] lavande.

lavish ['lævɪʃ] ❖ adj **1**. [abundant] copieux, abondant ; [luxurious] somptueux, luxueux **2**. [generous] généreux, magnanime. ❖ vt prodiguer.

lavishly ['lævɪʃlɪ] adv **1**. [generously, extravagantly] généreusement, sans compter **2**. [luxuriously] luxueusement, somptueusement.

law [lɔː] ❖ n **1**. [legal provision] loi *f* / *a law against gambling* une loi qui interdit les jeux d'argent ▶ **the Law Commission** en Grande-Bretagne, commission des lois indépendante ayant pour mission de recommander des réformes juridiques ▶ **Law Lords** UK membres de la chambre des lords siégeant en tant que cour d'appel de dernière instance ▶ **the Law Society** association de soutien et de conseil aux **solicitors** dans les pays de **common law**. **2**. [legislation] loi *f* / *it's against the law to sell alcohol* la vente d'alcool est illégale ▶ **by law** selon la loi / *in* or *under British law* selon la loi britannique **3**. [legal system] droit *m* **4**. [justice] justice *f*, système *m* juridique ▶ **to go to law** UK aller en justice ; [police] ▶ **the law** *inf* les flics *mpl* **5**. [rule - of club, sport] règle *f* **6**. SCI [principle] loi *f*. ❖ comp [faculty, school] de droit.

law-abiding adj respectueux de la loi / *a law-abiding citizen* un honnête citoyen.

law and order n l'ordre public *m*.

law-breaker n personne *f* qui transgresse la loi.

law centre n bureau *m* d'aide judiciaire.

law court n tribunal *m*, cour *f* de justice.

law-enforcement adj US chargé de faire respecter la loi ▶ **law-enforcement officer** représentant d'un service chargé de faire respecter la loi.

lawful ['lɔːful] adj [legal] légal ; [legitimate] légitime ; [valid] valide / *by all lawful means* par tous les moyens légaux / *my lawful wedded wife* mon épouse légitime ▶ **lawful permanent resident** US résident *m* permanent étranger, résidente *f* permanente étrangère.

lawfully ['lɔːfulɪ] adv légalement, de manière légale.

lawless ['lɔːlɪs] adj [person] sans foi ni loi ; [activity] illégal ; [country] livré à l'anarchie.

lawlessness ['lɔːlɪsnɪs] n non-respect *m* de la loi ; [anarchy] anarchie *f* ; [illegality] illégalité *f*.

lawmaker ['lɔːˌmeɪkər] n législateur *m*, -trice *f*.

lawn [lɔːn] n **1**. [grass] pelouse *f*, gazon *m* **2**. TEXT linon *m*.

lawn furniture n mobilier *m* de jardin.

lawnmower ['lɔːnˌməʊər] n tondeuse *f* à gazon.

lawn party n US garden party *f*.

lawn tennis ❖ n tennis *m* sur gazon. ❖ comp [club] de tennis.

lawsuit ['lɔːsuːt] n action *f* en justice ▶ **to bring a lawsuit against sb** intenter une action (en justice) contre qqn.

lawyer ['lɔːjər] n **1**. [barrister] avocat *m*, homme *m* de loi **2**. [solicitor - for wills, conveyancing, etc.] notaire *m* **3**. [legal expert] juriste *mf* ; [adviser] conseil *m* juridique.

 **Lawyer**

Aux États-Unis comme en Angleterre, le terme **lawyer** désigne un avocat (les Américains utilisent plus formellement le synonyme **attorney**). Au Royaume-Uni, il existe deux types d'avocats: le **solicitor** (ou « intermédiaire ») exerce dans un cabinet et représente ses clients devant certaines cours en cas de divorce ou de transfert de biens ; le **barrister** (ou « avocat ») défend son client à la cour devant un juge. Aux États-Unis, un avocat membre du barreau d'un État n'est pas toujours autorisé à exercer en dehors de sa juridiction ; toutefois, tout citoyen peut être représenté par un avocat dans l'État où il réside.

lax [læks] adj **1.** [person] négligent ; [behaviour, discipline] relâché ; [justice] laxiste ▸ **to be lax about sthg** négliger qqch **2.** [not tense - string] lâche, relâché ; LING [phoneme] lâche, relâché ; MED [bowels] relâché **3.** [imprecise - definition] imprécis, vague.

LAX n sigle désignant l'aéroport international de Los Angeles.

laxative ['læksətɪv] ◆ adj laxatif. ◆ n laxatif m.

laxity ['læksətɪ], **laxness** ['læksnɪs] n [slackness] relâchement m ; [negligence] négligence f.

lay [leɪ] (pt & pp **laid** [leɪd]) ◆ pt → **lie**. ◆ vt **1.** [in specified position] poser, mettre / he laid the baby on the bed il a couché l'enfant sur le lit / she laid her head on my shoulder elle a posé sa tête sur mon épaule ; [spread out] étendre / she laid the blanket on the ground elle a étendu la couverture par terre ▸ **to lay it on the line** ne pas y aller par quatre chemins **2.** [tiles, bricks, pipes, cable, carpet] poser ; [foundations] poser ; [wreath] déposer ; [mine] poser, mouiller **3.** [set - table] mettre / lay the table for six mettez la table pour six (personnes), mettez six couverts **4.** [prepare, arrange - fire] préparer / they laid a trap for him ils lui ont tendu un piège **5.** [egg] pondre **6.** [impose - burden, duty] imposer ▸ **to lay emphasis** or **stress on sthg** mettre l'accent sur qqch **7.** LAW [lodge] porter ▸ **to lay an accusation against sb** porter une accusation contre qqn **8.** [present, put forward] : she laid the scheme before him elle lui soumit le projet **9.** [bet] parier **10.** vulg [have sex with] baiser ▸ **to get laid** baiser **11.** [with adjective complements] ▸ **to lay o.s. open to criticism** s'exposer à la critique. ◆ vi **1.** [bird, fish, etc.] pondre **2.** = **lie** (vi). ◆ n vulg [person] : he's / she's a good lay c'est un bon coup. ⁌ **lay aside** vt sep **1.** [put down] mettre de côté / you should lay aside any personal opinions you might have fig vous devez faire abstraction de toute opinion personnelle **2.** [save] mettre de côté. ⁌ **lay down** vt sep **1.** [put down] poser / to lay down one's arms déposer or rendre les armes **2.** [renounce, relinquish] renoncer à / to lay down one's life se sacrifier **3.** [formulate, set out - plan, rule] formuler, établir ; [- condition] imposer / as laid down in the contract, the buyer keeps exclusive rights il est stipulé or il est bien précisé dans le contrat que l'acheteur garde l'exclusivité. ⁌ **lay in** vt sep [stores] faire provision de. ⁌ **lay into** vt insep inf [attack - physically] tomber (à bras raccourcis) sur ; [- verbally] prendre à partie, passer un savon à. ⁌ **lay off** ◆ vt sep [employees] licencier. ◆ vt insep laisser tomber / lay off it, will you! laisse tomber, tu veux ! / I told her to lay off my husband je lui ai dit de laisser mon mari tranquille. ◆ vi inf laisser tomber. ⁌ **lay on** vt sep **1.** [provide] fournir / the meal was laid on by our hosts le repas nous fut offert par nos hôtes / they had transport laid on for us ils s'étaient occupés de nous procurer un moyen de transport **2.** UK [install] installer, mettre **3.** [spread - paint, plaster] étaler ▸ **to lay it on thick** inf & fig en rajouter. ⁌ **lay out** vt sep **1.** [arrange, spread out] étaler / he laid his wares out on the ground il a étalé or déballé sa marchandise sur le sol **2.** [present, put forward] exposer, présenter / her ideas are clearly laid out in her book ses idées sont clairement exposées dans son livre **3.** [design] concevoir / the house is badly laid out la maison est mal conçue **4.** inf [spend] mettre **5.** inf [knock out] assommer, mettre K-O. ⁌ **lay up** vt sep UK **1.** [store, save] mettre de côté **2.** inf [confine to bed] aliter / she's laid up with mumps elle est au lit avec les oreillons.

layabout ['leɪəbaʊt] n UK inf paresseux m, -euse f, fainéant m, -e f.

lay-by (pl **lay-bys**) n UK AUTO aire f de stationnement.

layer ['leɪə] ◆ n **1.** [of skin, paint, wood] couche f ; [of fabric, clothes] épaisseur f **2.** GEOL strate f, couche f **3.** HORT marcotte f **4.** [hen] pondeuse f. ◆ vt [hair] couper en dégradé ; HORT marcotter.

layered ['leɪəd] adj : layered hair cheveux coupés en dégradé / a layered skirt une jupe à volants ▸ **the layered look** a) [hair] la coupe dégradée b) [clothes] le look superposé.

layette [leɪ'et] n layette f.

layman ['leɪmən] (pl **laymen** [-mən]) n **1.** [non-specialist] profane mf, non-initié m, -e f **2.** [non-clerical] laïc m, laïque f.

lay-off n **1.** [sacking] licenciement m **2.** [inactivity] chômage m technique.

layout ['leɪaʊt] n **1.** [gen] disposition f ; [of building, park] disposition f, agencement m ; [of essay] plan m **2.** TYPO maquette f ▸ **layout artist** maquettiste mf **3.** [diagram] schéma m.

layover ['leɪəʊvə] n US escale f, halte f.

lay preacher n prédicateur m laïque.

laze [leɪz] ◆ vi [relax] se reposer ; [idle] paresser. ◆ n farniente m. ⁌ **laze about** UK, **laze around** vi paresser, fainéanter.

lazily ['leɪzɪlɪ] adv paresseusement, avec paresse.

laziness ['leɪzɪnɪs] n paresse f, fainéantise f.

lazy ['leɪzɪ] (compar **lazier**, superl **laziest**) adj **1.** [idle] paresseux, fainéant ; [relaxed] indolent, nonchalant **2.** [movement] paresseux, lent.

lazybones ['leɪzɪbəʊnz] n inf fainéant m, -e f.

lb (written abbr of **pound**) : 3 lb or lbs 3 livres.

LB written abbr of **Labrador**.

lbw (abbr of **leg before wicket**) n au cricket, faute d'un joueur qui met une jambe devant le guichet.

lc (written abbr of **lower case**) bdc.

LC pr n abbr of **Library of Congress**.

L/C written abbr of **letter of credit**.

LCD (abbr of **liquid crystal display**) n LCD m.

Ld written abbr of **lord**.

LDC n abbr of **least developed country**.

LDR MESSAGING written abbr of **long distance relationship**.

L-driver (abbr of **learner-driver**) n UK personne qui apprend à conduire.

L-driver

En Grande-Bretagne, la lettre « L » apposée sur l'arrière d'un véhicule indique que le conducteur n'a pas encore son permis de conduire mais qu'il est en conduite accompagnée.

LDS (abbr of **Licentiate in Dental Surgery**) n (titulaire d'un) diplôme en chirurgie dentaire.

lea [liː] n liter pré m.

LEA n abbr of **local education authority**.

lead[1] [liːd] (pt & pp **led** [led]) ◆ vt **1.** [take, guide] mener, emmener, conduire ▸ **to lead sb somewhere** mener or conduire qqn quelque part / she led him down the stairs elle lui fit descendre l'escalier / the captain led the team onto the field le capitaine a conduit son équipe sur le terrain ▸ **to lead the way** montrer le chemin **2.** [be leader of] être à la tête de, diriger ; SPORT [be in front of] mener / Stardust is *leading Black Beauty by 10 lengths* Stardust a pris 10 longueurs d'avance sur Black Beauty **3.** [induce] amener ▶ **to lead sb to do sthg** amener qqn à faire qqch / *he led me to believe (that) he was innocent* il m'a amené à croire qu'il était innocent / *everything leads us to believe (that) she is still alive* tout porte à croire or nous avons toutes les raisons de croire qu'elle est encore en vie **4.** [life] mener. ◆ vi **1.** [go] mener / *the stairs lead to the cellar* l'escalier mène or conduit à la cave / *that road leads nowhere* cette route ne mène nulle part **2.** SPORT mener, être en tête / *to lead by 2 metres* avoir 2 mètres d'avance / *to lead by 3 points to 1* mener par 3 points à 1 **3.** [go in front] aller devant / *if you lead, I'll follow* allez-y, je vous suis **4.** [in dancing] conduire. ◆ n **1.** SPORT tête f ▶ **to be in the lead** être en tête, mener ▶ **to go into** or **to take the lead a)** [in race] prendre la tête **b)** [in match] mener / *to have a 10-point / 10-length lead* avoir 10 points / 10 longueurs d'avance **2.** [initiative] initiative f / *take your lead from me* prenez exemple sur moi ▶ **to follow sb's lead** suivre l'exemple de qqn **3.** [indication, clue] indice m, piste f / *the police have several leads* la police tient plusieurs pistes **4.** UK PRESS gros titre m / *the news made the lead in all the papers* la nouvelle était à la une de tous les journaux **5.** CIN & THEAT [role] rôle m principal ; [actor] premier rôle m masculin ; [actress] premier rôle m féminin **6.** [for dog] laisse f / **'dogs must be kept on a lead'** 'les chiens doivent être tenus en laisse' **7.** ELEC fil m. ◆ adj [actor, singer] principal, premier ; PRESS [article] de tête. ❖ **lead away** vt sep emmener / *he led her away from the scene of the accident* il l'éloigna du lieu de l'accident. ❖ **lead back** vt sep ramener, reconduire. ❖ **lead off** ◆ vi [in conversation] commencer, débuter ; [at dance] ouvrir le bal. ◆ vt insep **1.** [begin] commencer, entamer **2.** [go from] partir de / *several avenues lead off the square* plusieurs avenues partent de la place. ◆ vt sep conduire / *they were led off to jail* ils ont été conduits or emmenés en prison. ❖ **lead on** ◆ vi aller or marcher devant. ◆ vt sep **1.** [trick] ▶ **to lead sb on** faire marcher qqn **2.** [bring on] faire entrer **3.** [in progression] amener. ❖ **lead to** vt insep [result in, have as consequence] mener or aboutir à / *one thing led to another* une chose en amenait une autre / *several factors led to his decision to leave* plusieurs facteurs le poussèrent or l'amenèrent à décider de partir / *this could lead to some confusion* ça pourrait provoquer une certaine confusion. ❖ **lead up to** vt insep **1.** [path, road] conduire à, mener à / *a narrow path led up to the house* un étroit sentier menait jusqu'à la maison **2.** [in reasoning] : *what are you leading up to?* où voulez-vous en venir ? **3.** [precede, cause] : *the events leading up to the war* les événements qui devaient déclencher la guerre / *in the months leading up to her death* pendant les mois qui précédèrent sa mort.

lead[2] [led] ◆ n **1.** [metal] plomb m / *it's made of lead* c'est en plomb ▶ **lead oxide** oxyde m de plomb **2.** inf [bullets] plomb m / *they pumped him full of lead* ils l'ont flingué **3.** [in pencil] mine f **4.** [piece of lead - for sounding] plomb m (de sonde) ; [- on car wheel, fishing line] plomb m ; TYPO interligne m. ◆ vt **1.** [seal] plomber **2.** TYPO interligner. ◆ adj [made of lead] de or en plomb ; [containing lead] plombifère ▶ **lead pipe / shot** tuyau m / grenaille f de plomb.

leaded ['lɛdɪd] adj **1.** [door, box, billiard cue] plombé / *leaded window* fenêtre f avec verre cathédrale **2.** [petrol] au plomb **3.** TYPO interligné.

leaden ['lɛdn] adj **1.** [made of lead] de or en plomb **2.** [dull - sky] de plomb, plombé ; [heavy - sleep] de plomb ; [- heart] lourd ; [oppressive - atmosphere] lourd, pesant ; [- silence] de mort.

leader ['liːdə] n **1.** [head] chef m ; POL chef m, leader m, dirigeant m, -e f ; [of association] dirigeant m, -e f ; [of strike,

protest] meneur m, -euse f ▶ **the Leader of the House a)** [in the Commons] parlementaire de la majorité chargé de certaines fonctions dans la mise en place du programme gouvernemental **b)** [in the Lords] porte-parole du gouvernement ▶ **the Leader of the Opposition** le chef de l'opposition **2.** SPORT [horse] cheval m de tête ; [athlete] coureur m de tête ; [in championship] leader m **3.** MUS ▶ **leader of the orchestra a)** UK premier violon m **b)** US chef m d'orchestre **4.** [in newspapers - editorial] éditorial m **5.** COMM produit m d'appel **6.** [for film, tape] amorce f **7.** [in climbing] premier m de cordée.

leaderboard ['liːdəbɔːd] n leaderboard (*bannière publicitaire grand format utilisée sur une page Web*).

leadership ['liːdəʃɪp] n **1.** [direction] direction f / *during* or *under her leadership* sous sa direction **2.** [leaders] direction f, dirigeants mpl **3.** PHR ▶ **leadership battle** or **contest** POL lutte f pour la position de leader ▶ **leadership election** POL élections fpl du leader.

lead-free [led-] adj [paint, petrol] sans plomb ; [toy] (garanti) sans plomb.

lead guitar n première guitare f.

lead-in [liːd-] n **1.** US [introductory remarks] introduction f, remarques fpl préliminaires **2.** [wire] descente f d'antenne.

leading[1] ['liːdɪŋ] adj **1.** [prominent] premier, de premier plan ; [major] majeur, principal, dominant / *to play the leading role in a film* être la vedette d'un film **2.** SPORT [in race] de tête ; [in championship] premier ▶ **to be in the leading position** être en tête **3.** MATH [coefficient] premier.

leading[2] ['lɛdɪŋ] n TYPO [process] interlignage m ; [space] interligne m.

leading article ['liːdɪŋ-] n UK éditorial m ; US article m leader or de tête.

leading lady ['liːdɪŋ-] n CIN & THEAT premier rôle m (féminin).

leading light ['liːdɪŋ-] n personnage m (de marque).

leading man ['liːdɪŋ-] n CIN & THEAT premier rôle m (masculin).

leading question ['liːdɪŋ-] n question f orientée.

lead pencil [led-] n crayon m noir or à papier or à mine de plomb.

lead poisoning [led-] n MED intoxication f par le plomb, saturnisme m.

lead time [liːd-] n INDUST délai m de préparation ; COMM délai m de livraison.

lead user n utilisateur m, -trice f pilote.

leaf [liːf] (pl **leaves** [liːvz]) n **1.** [on plant, tree] feuille f ▶ **to come into leaf** se couvrir de feuilles / *the trees are in leaf* les arbres sont en feuilles **2.** [page] feuillet m, page f **3.** [on table - dropleaf] abattant m ; [- inserted board] allonge f, rallonge f **4.** [of metal] feuille f. ❖ **leaf through** vt insep [book, magazine] feuilleter, parcourir.

leaflet ['liːflɪt] ◆ n **1.** [brochure] prospectus m, dépliant m ; [political] tract m ▶ **leaflet drop** largage m de prospectus or de tracts (*par avion*) **2.** [instruction sheet] notice f (explicative), mode m d'emploi **3.** BOT foliole f. ◆ vt distribuer des prospectus or des tracts à.

leafy ['liːfɪ] (*compar* **leafier**, *superl* **leafiest**) adj [tree] feuillu ; [woodland] boisé, vert / *a leafy avenue* une avenue bordée d'arbres / *a leafy suburb* une banlieue verdoyante.

league [liːg] n **1.** [alliance] ligue f ▶ **to be in league (with sb)** être de mèche (avec qqn) ▶ **League Against Cruel Sports** association britannique qui s'oppose aux activités entraînant la souffrance des animaux : chasse, tauromachie, etc. ▶ **the League of Nations** HIST la Société des Nations ▶ **League of Women Voters** association citoyenne américaine qui a vocation d'informer les gens sur les enjeux politiques et de les encourager à voter **2.** SPORT [competition] championnat *m* ; [division] division *f* **3.** *fig* [class] classe *f* / *he's not in the same league as his father* il n'a pas la classe de son père **4.** *arch* [distance] lieue *f*.

league table n (classement *m* du) championnat *m*.

leak [liːk] ◆ n **1.** [in pipe, tank, roof] fuite *f* ; [in boat] voie *f* d'eau **2.** [disclosure - of information, secret] fuite *f* **3.** PHR **to go for** or **to take a leak** *v inf* [urinate] pisser un coup. ◆ vi [pen, pipe] fuir ; [boat, shoe] prendre l'eau / *the roof leaks* il y a une fuite dans le toit ; [gas, liquid] fuir, s'échapper. ◆ vt **1.** [liquid] répandre, faire couler **2.** [information] divulguer. ✧ **leak in** vi s'infiltrer. ✧ **leak out** vi **1.** [liquid, gas] fuir, s'échapper **2.** [news, secret] filtrer, transpirer.

leakage n (U) fuite *f*.

leakproof ['liːkpruːf] adj étanche.

leaky ['liːkɪ] (*compar* **leakier**, *superl* **leakiest**) adj [boat, shoes] qui prend l'eau ; [pen, roof, bucket] qui fuit.

lean [liːn] (UK *pt & pp* **leaned** or **leant** [lent] ; US *pt & pp* **leaned**) ◆ vi [be on incline] pencher, s'incliner / *she / a ladder was leaning (up) against the wall* elle / une échelle était appuyée contre le mur. ◆ vt **1.** [prop - ladder, bicycle] appuyer / *he leant the ladder / bike (up) against the tree* il appuya l'échelle / le vélo contre un arbre **2.** [rest - head, elbows] appuyer / *she leant her head on his shoulder* elle posa sa tête sur son épaule **3.** [incline] pencher / *to lean one's head to one side* pencher ou incliner la tête. ◆ adj **1.** [animal, meat] maigre ; [person - thin] maigre ; [- slim] mince **2.** [poor - harvest] maigre, pauvre ; [- period of time] difficile **3.** [deficient - ore, mixture] pauvre. ◆ n **1.** [slope] inclinaison *f* **2.** [meat] maigre *m*. ✧ **lean back** ◆ vi **1.** [person] se pencher en arrière **2.** [chair] basculer. ◆ vt sep pencher en arrière. ✧ **lean forward** ◆ vi se pencher en avant. ◆ vt sep pencher en avant. ✧ **lean on, lean upon** vt insep **1.** [depend] s'appuyer sur **2.** UK *inf* [pressurize] faire pression sur. ✧ **lean out** ◆ vi se pencher au dehors / *don't lean out of the window!* ne te penche pas par la fenêtre ! ◆ vt sep pencher au dehors / *he leaned his head out of the window* il a passé la tête par la fenêtre. ✧ **lean over** vi [person] se pencher en avant ; [tree, wall] pencher, être penché. ✧ **lean towards** vt insep [tend] pencher pour.

lean body mass n masse *f* corporelle.

leaning ['liːnɪŋ] ◆ n (usu pl) tendance *f*, penchant *m*. ◆ adj [tree, wall] penché ▶ **the Leaning Tower of Pisa** la tour de Pise.

leant [lent] pt & pp UK ⟶ **lean**.

lean-to n UK ▶ **a lean-to (shed)** un appentis.

leap [liːp] (UK *pt & pp* **leaped** or **leapt** [lept] ; US *pt & pp* **leaped**) ◆ vi **1.** [person, animal] bondir, sauter ; [flame] jaillir / *to leap to one's feet* se lever d'un bond **2.** *fig* faire un bond / *the price of petrol leapt by 10%* le prix du pétrole a fait un bond de 10 %. ◆ vt **1.** [fence, stream] sauter (par-dessus), franchir d'un bond **2.** [horse] faire sauter. ◆ n **1.** [jump] saut *m*, bond *m* **2.** [in prices] bond *m*. ✧ **leap about** UK, **leap around** ◆ vt insep gambader dans. ◆ vi gambader. ✧ **leap at** vt insep **1.** [in attack] sauter sur **2.** *fig* : *she leapt at the chance* elle a sauté sur l'occasion. ✧ **leap out** vi bondir ▶ **to leap out at sb** bondir sur qqn. ✧ **leap up** vi **1.** [into the air] sauter (en l'air) ; [to one's feet] se lever d'un bond.

leapfrog ['liːpfrɒg] (*pt & pp* **leapfrogged**, *cont* **leapfrogging**) ◆ n saute-mouton *m* / *to play leapfrog* jouer à saute-mouton. ◆ vi UK ▶ **to leapfrog over sb** sauter par-dessus qqn. ◆ vt UK *fig* dépasser.

leapt [lept] pt & pp UK ⟶ **leap**.

leap year n année *f* bissextile.

learn [lɜːn] (UK *pt & pp* **learned** or **learnt** [lɜːnt] ; US *pt & pp* **learned**) ◆ vt **1.** [by instruction] apprendre ▶ **to learn (how) to do sthg** apprendre à faire qqch ▶ **to learn sthg by heart** apprendre qqch par cœur **2.** [discover, hear] apprendre. ◆ vi **1.** [by instruction, experience] apprendre ▶ **to learn about sthg** apprendre qqch **2.** [be informed] ▶ **to learn of sthg** apprendre qqch. ✧ **learn up** vt sep UK *inf* bûcher, potasser.

learned adj **1.** ['lɜːnɪd] [erudite - person] savant, érudit ; [- subject, book, society] savant **2.** ['lɜːnɪd] LAW [lawyer] ▶ **my learned friend** mon éminent confrère **3.** [lɜːnd] PSYCHOL [behaviour] acquis.

learner ['lɜːnər] n apprenant *m*, -e *f* / *to be a quick learner* apprendre vite ▶ **learner (driver)** UK apprenti *m* conducteur, apprentie *f* conductrice.

learning ['lɜːnɪŋ] n **1.** [erudition] érudition *f*, savoir *m* **2.** [acquisition of knowledge] étude *f* / *language learning* l'étude ou l'apprentissage *m* des langues ▶ **learning difficulties** or **learning disability** US SCH difficultés *fpl* d'apprentissage ▶ **learning resources centre** centre *m* de documentation pédagogique.

learning curve n courbe *f* d'apprentissage.

learning style n style *m* d'apprentissage.

learnt [lɜːnt] UK ◆ pt & pp ⟶ **learn**. ◆ adj PSYCHOL acquis.

lease [liːs] ◆ n **1.** LAW bail *m* ▶ **to take (out) a lease on a house** or **to take a house on lease** prendre une maison à bail **2.** PHR *the trip has given her a new lease of* UK or *on* US *life* le voyage l'a remise en forme ou lui a redonné du tonus. ◆ vt [house] louer à bail ; [car, sailboard] louer.

leaseback ['liːsbæk] n cession-bail *f*.

leasehold ['liːshəʊld] ◆ n [lease] bail *m* ; [property] location *f* à bail. ◆ adj loué à bail.

leaseholder ['liːs,həʊldər] n [tenant] locataire *mf*.

leash [liːʃ] n [for dog] laisse *f*.

leasing ['liːsɪŋ] n crédit-bail *m*, leasing *m*.

least [liːst] ◆ det & pron (*superl* of **little**) **1.** [in quantity, size] : *he's got the least* c'est lui qui en a le moins **2.** [slightest] : *the least thing upsets her* un rien la contrarie / *it was the least we could do* c'était la moindre des choses / *that's the least of our worries* c'est le moindre ou c'est le cadet de nos soucis. ◆ adv (le) moins / *the least interesting film I've ever seen* le film le moins intéressant que j'aie jamais vu / *it's what we least expected* c'est ce à quoi nous nous attendions le moins. ✧ **at least** adv phr **1.** [not less than] au moins / *at least $500* au moins 500 dollars **2.** [as a minimum] au moins / *at the very least he might have phoned us* la moindre des choses aurait été de nous téléphoner **3.** [indicating an advantage] au moins, du moins / *at least we've got an umbrella* au moins ou du moins on a un parapluie **4.** [used to qualify] du moins / *I didn't like him, at least not at first* il ne m'a pas plu, en tout cas ou du moins pas au début. ✧ **in the least** adv phr (with neg) ▶ **not in the least** pas du tout, pas le moins du monde / *she didn't seem to mind in the least* ça ne semblait pas la déranger le moins du monde. ✧ **least of all** adv phr surtout pas / *nobody could understand it, Jim least of all* or *least of all Jim* personne ne comprenait, surtout pas Jim ou Jim encore moins que les autres. ✧ **not least** adv phr : *many politicians, not least the Foreign Secretary, are in favour* de nombreux hommes politiques y sont favorables, notamment le ministre des Affaires étrangères.

least developed country n pays *m* moins développé ▶ **the least developed countries** les pays parmi les moins développés.

leather ['leðər] ◆ n **1.** [material] cuir *m* / *made of leather* de ou en cuir **2.** [for polishing] ▶ (**wash** or **window**)

leather peau *f* de chamois **3.** *inf* [sexual fetish] : *he's into leather* c'est un fétichiste du cuir. ◆ comp **1.** [jacket, shoes, sofa, bag] de or en cuir ▶ **leather goods a)** [ordinary] articles *mpl* en cuir **b)** [finer] maroquinerie *f* **2.** [bar, club] cuir *(inv.)* ◆ *vt* [punish] tanner le cuir à.

leatherbound ['leðəbaʊnd] *adj* relié (en) cuir.

leatherette [ˌleðə'ret] ◆ *n* similicuir *m*. ◆ *adj* en similicuir.

leathery ['leðərɪ] *adj* [meat] coriace ; [skin] parcheminé, tanné.

leave¹ [liːv] *(pt & pp* **left** [left]) ◆ *vi* [depart] partir / *when did you leave?* quand est-ce que vous êtes partis ? / *we're leaving for Mexico tomorrow* nous partons pour le Mexique demain. ◆ *vt* **1.** [depart from - place] quitter / *she left London yesterday* elle est partie de or elle a quitté Londres hier / *he left the room* il est sorti de or il a quitté la pièce / *to leave the table* se lever de table **2.** [quit - job, institution] quitter / *I left home at 18* je suis parti de chez moi or de chez mes parents à 18 ans / *to leave school* quitter l'école **3.** [in specified place or state] laisser / *he left her asleep on the sofa* elle était endormie sur le canapé lorsqu'il la quitta / *I left him to his reading* je l'ai laissé à sa lecture / *just leave me alone!* laissez-moi tranquille ! **4.** [abandon - person] quitter / *she left him for another man* elle l'a quitté pour un autre ; *fml* [take leave of - person] laisser / *it's getting late, I must leave you now* il se fait tard, je dois vous laisser **5.** [deposit, set down] laisser **6.** [for somebody's use, information, etc.] laisser / *he's out, do you want to leave a message?* il n'est pas là, voulez-vous laisser un message ? **7.** [forget] laisser, oublier / *I must have left my gloves at the café* j'ai dû oublier mes gants au café **8.** [allow or cause to remain] laisser / *leave yourself an hour to get to the airport* prévoyez une heure pour aller à l'aéroport / *don't leave things to the last minute* n'attendez pas la dernière minute (pour faire ce que vous avez à faire) / *their behaviour leaves a lot to be desired* leur conduite laisse beaucoup à désirer ; *(passive use)* ▶ **to be left** rester / *I've got £10 / 10 minutes left* il me reste 10 livres / 10 minutes ; [mark, trace] laisser / *the wine left a stain* le vin a fait une tache **9.** [allow] : *can I leave you to deal with it, then?* vous vous en chargez, alors ? / *she leaves me to get on with things* elle me laisse faire / *right then, I'll leave you to it* bon, eh bien, je te laisse **10.** [entrust] laisser / *can I leave my suitcase with you for a few minutes?* puis-je vous confier ma valise quelques instants ? / *leave it to me!* je m'en occupe !, je m'en charge ! / *leave it with me* laissez-moi faire, je m'en charge **11.** 🇺🇸 MATH : *9 from 16 leaves 7* 16 moins 9 égale 7 **12.** [bequeath] léguer **13.** [be survived by] : *he leaves a wife and two children* il laisse une femme et deux enfants. ◆ *n* **1.** [from work] congé *m* ; MIL permission *f* ▶ **to be / to go on leave a)** [gen] être / partir en congé **b)** MIL être / partir en permission ▶ **leave of absence a)** congé (exceptionnel) **b)** [without pay] congé sans solde **2.** *fml* [permission] permission *f*, autorisation *f* / *by or with your leave* avec votre permission **3.** [farewell] congé *m* ▶ **to take one's leave (of sb)** prendre congé (de qqn) ▶ **to take leave of one's senses** *fig* perdre la tête or la raison. ◆ **leave behind** *vt sep* **1.** [not take] laisser / *it's hard to leave all your friends and relations behind* c'est dur de laisser tous ses amis et sa famille derrière soi ; [forget] laisser, oublier **2.** [outstrip] distancer, devancer / *if you don't work harder you'll soon get left behind* si tu ne travailles pas plus, tu vas vite te retrouver loin derrière les autres. ◆ **leave in** *vt sep* [word, paragraph] garder, laisser. ◆ **leave off** ◆ *vi* [stop] s'arrêter / *we'll carry on from where we left off* nous allons reprendre là où nous nous étions arrêtés / *leave off, will you!* 🇺🇸 *inf* arrête, tu veux ! ◆ *vt insep* 🇺🇸 *inf* [stop] ▶ **to leave off doing sthg** arrêter de faire qqch. ◆ *vt sep* **1.** [not put on] ne pas

remettre **2.** [not switch or turn on - tap, gas] laisser fermé ; [-light] laisser éteint ; [not plug in - appliance] laisser débranché. ◆ **leave on** *vt sep* **1.** [not take off - garment] garder ; [-top, cover] laisser **2.** [not switch or turn off - tap, gas] laisser ouvert ; [-light] laisser allumé ; [not unplug - appliance] laisser branché. ◆ **leave out** *vt sep* **1.** [omit] omettre **2.** [exclude] exclure / *I felt completely left out at the party* j'ai eu le sentiment d'être totalement tenu à l'écart or exclu de leur petite fête **3.** [not put away - by accident] ne pas ranger ; [-on purpose] laisser sorti, ne pas ranger ; [leave outdoors] laisser dehors **4.** PHR **leave it out!** 🇬🇧 *v inf* lâche-moi ! ◆ **leave over** *vt sep* [allow or cause to remain] laisser ▶ **to be left over** rester.

leave² [liːv] *(pt & pp* **leaved***, cont* **leaving**) *vi* BOT [produce leaves] feuiller.

leaves [liːz] *pl* ⟶ **leaf**.

leaving ['liːvɪŋ] *n* départ *m*.

Lebanese [ˌlebə'niːz] *(pl* **Lebanese**) ◆ *n* Libanais *m*, -e *f*. ◆ *adj* libanais.

Lebanon ['lebənən] *pr n* Liban *m* / *in (the) Lebanon* au Liban.

lech [letʃ] *inf* ◆ *vi* : *he's always leching after my secretary* il n'arrête pas de reluquer ma secrétaire. ◆ *n* obsédé *m* (sexuel).

lecher ['letʃər] *n* obsédé *m* (sexuel).

lecherous ['letʃərəs] *adj* lubrique.

lecherously ['letʃərəslɪ] *adv* lubriquement, avec lubricité.

lechery ['letʃərɪ] *n* lubricité *f*.

lectern ['lektən] *n* lutrin *m*.

lecture ['lektʃər] ◆ *n* **1.** [talk] conférence *f*, exposé *m* ; UNIV [as part of course] cours *m* (magistral) / *she gave a very good lecture on Yeats* elle a fait un très bon cours sur Yeats **2.** *fig* [sermon] sermon *m*, discours *m* ▶ **to give sb a lecture** sermonner qqn, faire des remontrances à qqn. ◆ comp [notes] de cours ▶ **lecture hall** or **theatre** salle *f* de cours, amphithéâtre *m* ▶ **lecture circuit** : *to be on the lecture circuit* faire des tournées de conférences. ◆ *vi* [talk] faire or donner une conférence ; [teach] faire (un) cours / *she lectures in linguistics* elle enseigne la or donne des cours de linguistique. ◆ *vt* [reprimand] réprimander, sermonner.

lecturer ['lektʃərər] *n* 🇬🇧 [speaker] conférencier *m*, -ère *f* ; UNIV [teacher] assistant *m*, -e *f* / *she's a lecturer in English at the University of Dublin* elle est professeur d'anglais à l'université de Dublin ▶ **assistant lecturer** ≃ maître-assistant *m* ▶ **senior lecturer** ≃ maître *m* de conférences.

lecture room *n* salle *f* de cours or de conférences.

lectureship ['lektʃəʃɪp] *n* UNIV poste *m* d'assistant ▶ **senior lectureship** ≃ poste de maître de conférences.

led [led] *pt & pp* ⟶ **lead¹**.

LED (abbr of **light-emitting diode**) *n* LED *f* ▶ **LED display** affichage *m* (par) LED.

ledge [ledʒ] *n* **1.** [shelf] rebord *m* **2.** GEOG [on mountain] saillie *f* ; [on rock or cliff face] corniche *f* ; [on seabed] haut-fond *m* **3.** GEOL [vein] filon *m*.

ledger ['ledʒər] *n* COMM & FIN grand livre *m*.

lee [liː] *n* **1.** NAUT bord *m* sous le vent **2.** [shelter] abri *m*. ◆ *adj* sous le vent.

leech [liːtʃ] ◆ *n* *lit & fig* sangsue *f*. ◆ *vt* MED saigner (avec des sangsues).

leek [liːk] *n* poireau *m*.

Leek
Le poireau est un emblème du pays de Galles.

leer [lɪəʳ] ◆ n [malevolent] regard m méchant; [lecherous] regard m concupiscent or lubrique. ◆ vi ▸ **to leer at sb** lorgner qqn.

Leeward Islands pl pr n ▸ **the Leeward Islands** les îles fpl Sous-le-Vent / *in the Leeward Islands* aux îles Sous-le-Vent.

leeway ['liːweɪ] n (U) **1.** [margin] marge f (de manœuvre) **2.** [lost time] retard m **3.** AERON & NAUT [drift] dérive f.

left¹ [left] pt & pp ⟶ **leave.**

left² [left] ◆ adj [foot, eye] gauche / *on the left side* sur la gauche, du côté gauche / *to make a left turn* tourner à gauche ▸ **left back** / **half** SPORT arrière m / demi m gauche. ◆ adv **1.** [gen] à gauche / *turn left at the junction* tournez or prenez à gauche au croisement **2.** POL à gauche. ◆ n **1.** [gen] gauche f ▸ **on the left** sur la gauche, à gauche **2.** POL gauche f **3.** [in boxing] gauche m.

left-click vi cliquer gauche.

left field n [US] SPORT ▸ **to play left field** être ailier gauche ▸ **to be out in left field** inf être complètement à l'ouest.

left fielder n [US] SPORT ailier m gauche.

left-footed [-'fʊtɪd] adj gaucher (du pied).

left-hand adj gauche ▸ **on the left-hand side** à gauche, sur la gauche ▸ **left-hand drive** conduite f à gauche.

left-handed [-'hændɪd] ◆ adj **1.** [person] gaucher **2.** [scissors, instrument, golf club] pour gauchers **3.** [US] ▸ **a left-handed compliment** un faux compliment. ◆ adv de la main gauche.

left-hander [-'hændəʳ] n [person] gaucher m, -ère f; [blow] coup m (donné de la main gauche).

leftist ['leftɪst] ◆ n [gen] homme m de gauche, femme f de gauche; [extreme left-winger] gauchiste mf. ◆ adj [gen] de gauche; [extremely left-wing] gauchiste.

left luggage n (U) [UK] [cases] bagages mpl en consigne; [office] consigne f ▸ **the left luggage lockers** la consigne automatique.

left-of-centre adj POL de centre gauche.

leftover ['leftəʊvəʳ] ◆ adj [food, material] qui reste; [stock] en surplus. ◆ n [throwback, vestige] vestige m.

leftovers ['leftəʊvəz] pl n [food] restes mpl.

left wing n **1.** POL gauche f / *the left wing of the party* l'aile f gauche du parti **2.** SPORT [position] aile f gauche; [player] ailier m gauche. ◆ **left-wing** adj POL de gauche / *she's very left-wing* elle est très à gauche.

left-winger n **1.** POL homme m de gauche, femme f de gauche **2.** SPORT ailier m gauche.

lefty ['leftɪ] (pl **lefties**) n inf **1.** pej homme m de gauche, femme f de gauche **2.** [US] [left-handed person] gaucher m, -ère f.

leg [leg] (pt & pp **legged**, cont **legging**) ◆ n **1.** ANAT [of human, horse] jambe f; [of smaller animals and birds] patte f **2.** CULIN [of lamb] gigot m; [of pork, beef] rôti m; [of chicken] cuisse f ▸ **frog's legs** cuisses de grenouille **3.** [of chair, table] pied m **4.** [of trousers, pyjamas] jambe f **5.** [stage - of journey] étape f; [- of competition] manche f. ◆ vt ▸ **to leg it** a) inf [run] courir b) [walk] aller à pied c) [flee] se sauver, se tirer.

legacy ['legəsɪ] (pl **legacies**) n **1.** LAW legs m ▸ **to leave sb a legacy** faire un legs or laisser un héritage à qqn **2.** fig héritage m.

legal ['liːgl] adj **1.** [lawful] légal; [legitimate] légal, légitime ▸ **to make sthg legal** légaliser qqch **2.** [judicial - mind, matter, question] juridique; [- power, investigation, error] judiciaire / *to take legal action* engager des poursuites judiciaires, intenter un procès / *to take legal advice* consulter

un juriste or un avocat / *he's a member of the legal profession* c'est un homme de loi / *legal secretary* secrétaire mf juridique / *legal system* système m juridique.

legal aid n assistance f judiciaire.

legal costs pl n frais mpl de procédure.

legal currency n monnaie f légale.

legal eagle n inf & hum avocat m, -e f.

legal fees pl n frais mpl de procédure.

legality [liː'gælɪtɪ] n légalité f.

legalization, legalisation [ˌliːgəlaɪ'zeɪʃn] n légalisation f.

legalize, legalise ['liːgəlaɪz] vt légaliser, rendre légal.

legalized alien n [US] résident étranger en situation régulière.

legally ['liːgəlɪ] adv légalement / *to be legally binding* avoir force de loi, être juridiquement contraignant.

legal opinion n avis m juridique.

legal proceedings pl n poursuites fpl judiciaires.

legal separation n LAW séparation f de corps.

legal tender n monnaie f légale.

legation [lɪ'geɪʃn] n légation f.

legend ['ledʒənd] n **1.** [myth] légende f **2.** [inscription] légende f.

legendary ['ledʒəndrɪ] adj légendaire.

leggings ['legɪŋz] pl n caleçon m (porté comme pantalon).

leggy ['legɪ] (compar **leggier**, superl **leggiest**) adj [person] tout en jambes; [colt, young animal] haut sur pattes.

legibility [ˌledʒɪ'bɪlɪtɪ] n lisibilité f.

legible ['ledʒəbl] adj lisible.

legibly ['ledʒəblɪ] adv lisiblement.

legion ['liːdʒən] ◆ n MIL & fig légion f. ◆ adj fml légion (inv).

legionnaire's disease n maladie f du légionnaire.

legislate ['ledʒɪsleɪt] vi légiférer.

legislation [ˌledʒɪs'leɪʃn] n législation f / *a piece of legislation* une loi ▸ **to bring in legislation in favour of / against sthg** légiférer en faveur de / contre qqch.

legislative ['ledʒɪslətɪv] adj législatif.

legislator ['ledʒɪsleɪtəʳ] n législateur m, -trice f.

legislature ['ledʒɪsleɪtʃəʳ] n (corps m) législatif m.

legit [lə'dʒɪt] adj inf réglo.

legitimacy [lɪ'dʒɪtɪməsɪ] n légitimité f.

legitimate ◆ adj [lɪ'dʒɪtɪmət] **1.** [legal, lawful] légitime **2.** [valid] légitime, valable / *it would be perfectly legitimate to ask them to pay* on serait tout à fait en droit d'exiger qu'ils paient **3.** [theatre] sérieux. ◆ vt [lɪ'dʒɪtɪmeɪt] légitimer.

legitimately [lɪ'dʒɪtɪmətlɪ] adv **1.** [legally, lawfully] légitimement **2.** [justifiably] légitimement, avec raison.

legitimize, legitimise [lɪ'dʒɪtɪmaɪz] vt légitimer.

legless ['leglɪs] adj **1.** [without legs] cul-de-jatte **2.** [UK] inf [drunk] bourré, soûl.

leg-pull n inf canular m, farce f.

legroom ['legrʊm] n place f pour les jambes.

leg-up n ▸ **to give sb a leg-up** a) lit faire la courte échelle à qqn b) fig donner un coup de main or de pouce à qqn.

legwarmers ['leg,wɔːməz] pl n jambières fpl.

legwork ['legwɜːk] n inf : *who's going to do the legwork?* qui va se taper la marche ?

Leics written abbr of **Leicestershire**.

leisure [[UK] 'leʒəʳ [US] 'liːʒər] ◆ n (U) **1.** [spare time] loisir m, loisirs mpl, temps m libre ▸ **to be at leisure to do**

sthg avoir (tout) le loisir de faire qqch / *I'll read it at (my) leisure* je le lirai à tête reposée **2.** [relaxation] loisir *m* / *to lead a life of leisure* mener une vie oisive / *he's a man of leisure* il mène une vie de rentier. ◆ comp [activity, clothes] de loisir or loisirs ▸ **leisure industry** industrie *f* des loisirs.

leisure centre n centre *m* de loisirs.

leisurely [🇬🇧 'leʒəlɪ 🇺🇸 'liːʒərlɪ] ◆ adj [gesture] mesuré, nonchalant ; [lifestyle] paisible, indolent / *at a leisurely pace* sans se presser. ◆ adv [calmly] paisiblement, tranquillement ; [unhurriedly] sans se presser.

leisure suit n tailleur-pantalon très en vogue, notamment aux États-Unis, dans les années 1970.

leisurewear ['leʒəweər] n vêtements *mpl* de sport.

lemming ['lemɪŋ] n lemming *m*.

lemon ['lemən] ◆ n **1.** [fruit] citron *m* ; [tree] citronnier *m* ▸ **lemon juice a)** jus *m* de citron **b)** [lemon squash] citronnade *f* **c)** [freshly squeezed] citron pressé ▸ **lemon squash** citronnade *f*, sirop *m* de citron ▸ **lemon tea** thé *m* au citron **2.** [colour] jaune citron *m inv* **3.** 🇬🇧 *inf* [awkward person] idiot *m*, -e *f*. ◆ adj [colour] (jaune) citron (*inv*) ; [flavour] citron (*inv*).

lemonade [,lemə'neɪd] n [in UK] limonade *f* ; [in US] citron *m* pressé.

lemon cheese, **lemon curd** n lemon curd *m*, crème *f* au citron.

lemongrass ['lemənɡrɑːs] n (U) citronnelle *f*.

lemon sole n limande-sole *f*.

lemon squeezer n presse-citron *m*.

lemony ['lemənɪ] adj [smell, taste] citronné.

lemur ['liːmər] n lémur *m*, maki *m*.

lend [lend] (*pt & pp* **lent** [lent]) vt **1.** [money, book] prêter ▸ **to lend sthg to sb, to lend sb sthg** prêter qqch à qqn **2.** [contribute] apporter, conférer **3.** [give - support] apporter ; [- name] prêter ▸ **to lend a hand** donner un coup de main à qqn **4.** [adapt - to circumstances, interpretation] : *the novel doesn't lend itself to being filmed* le roman ne se prête pas à une adaptation cinématographique.

lender ['lendər] n prêteur *m*, -euse *f*.

lending library n bibliothèque *f* de prêt.

lending limit n plafond *m* de prêt.

lending rate n taux *m* (d'un prêt).

length [leŋθ] n **1.** [measurement, distance] longueur *f* / *the room is 20 metres in length* la pièce fait 20 mètres de long or de longueur / *a river 200 kilometres in length* un fleuve long de 200 kilomètres **2.** [effort] ▸ **to go to considerable** or **great lengths to do sthg** se donner beaucoup de mal pour faire qqch **3.** [duration] durée *f*, longueur *f* **4.** [of text] longueur *f* **5.** SPORT [in racing, rowing] longueur *f* / *to win by a length* gagner d'une longueur ; [in swimming] longueur *f* (de bassin) **6.** [piece of string, tubing] morceau *m*, bout *m* ; [- of wallpaper] lé *m* ; [- of fabric] pièce *f* **7.** LING [of syllable, vowel] longueur *f*. ◆ **at length** adv phr [finally] finalement, enfin ; [in detail, for a long time] longuement.

-length suffix à hauteur de ▸ **knee-length socks** chaussettes *fpl* (montantes), mi-bas *mpl*.

lengthen ['leŋθən] ◆ vi [shadow] s'allonger ; [day] rallonger ; [holiday, visit] se prolonger. ◆ vt [garment] allonger, rallonger ; [holiday, visit] prolonger ; LING [vowel] allonger.

lengthily ['leŋθɪlɪ] adv longuement.

lengthways ['leŋθweɪz], **lengthwise** ['leŋθwaɪz] ◆ adv dans le sens de la longueur, longitudinalement. ◆ adj en longueur, longitudinal.

lengthy ['leŋθɪ] (*compar* **lengthier**, *superl* **lengthiest**) adj (très) long.

leniency ['liːnjənsɪ] n clémence *f*, indulgence *f*.

lenient ['liːnjənt] adj [jury, sentence] clément ; [attitude, parent] indulgent / *you shouldn't be so lenient with them* vous devriez être plus strict avec eux.

leniently ['liːnjəntlɪ] adv avec clémence or indulgence.

Lenin ['lenɪn] pr n Lénine.

lens [lenz] n **1.** OPT [in microscope, telescope] lentille *f* ; [in spectacles] verre *m* ; [in camera] objectif *m* ; [contact lens] lentille *f* or verre *m* (de contact) **2.** ANAT [in eye] cristallin *m*.

lens cap n bouchon *m* d'objectif.

lent [lent] pt & pp ⟶ **lend**.

Lent [lent] n RELIG le carême.

lentil ['lentɪl] n BOT & CULIN lentille *f* ▸ **lentil soup** soupe *f* aux lentilles.

Leo ['liːəʊ] ◆ pr n ASTROL & ASTRON Lion *m*. ◆ n : *he's a Leo* il est (du signe du) Lion.

leopard ['lepəd] n léopard *m*.

leopardess ['lepədɪs] n léopard *m* femelle.

leopard skin ◆ n peau *f* de léopard. ◆ adj [coat, rug] en (peau de) léopard.

leotard ['liːətɑːd] n body *m* (pour le sport).

leper ['lepər] n lépreux *m*, -euse *f* ; fig pestiféré *m*, -e *f* ▸ **leper colony** léproserie *f*.

leprechaun ['leprəkɔːn] n lutin *m* (dans la tradition irlandaise).

leprosy ['leprəsɪ] n lèpre *f*.

lesbian ['lezbɪən] ◆ adj lesbien. ◆ n lesbienne *f*.

lesbianism ['lezbɪənɪzm] n lesbianisme *m*.

lesion ['liːʒn] n lésion *f*.

Lesotho [lə'suːtuː] pr n Lesotho *m* / *in Lesotho* au Lesotho.

less [les] ◆ det (*compar of little*) moins de / *less money* / *time* / *bread* moins d'argent / de temps / de pain / *of less importance* / *value* de moindre importance / valeur / *I seem to have less and less energy* on dirait que j'ai de moins en moins d'énergie. ◆ pron (*compar of little*) moins / *there was less than I expected* il y en avait moins que je m'y attendais ▸ **less than** : *it took me less than five minutes* ça m'a pris moins de cinq minutes / *nothing less than a four-star hotel is good enough for them* il leur faut au moins un quatre étoiles. ◆ adv moins / *the blue dress costs less* la robe bleue coûte moins cher / *less and less interesting* de moins en moins intéressant / *I don't think any (the) less of her* or *I think no less of her because of what happened* ce qui s'est passé ne l'a pas fait baisser dans mon estime. ◆ prep : *that's £300 less ten per cent for store card holders* ça fait 300 livres moins dix pour cent avec la carte du magasin. ◆ **no less** adv phr rien de moins / *he won the Booker prize, no less!* il a obtenu le Booker prize, rien de moins que ça ! ◆ **no less than** adv phr pas moins de / *taxes rose by no less than 15%* les impôts ont augmenté de 15 %, ni plus ni moins.

less-developed country n pays *m* moins développé.

lessee [le'siː] n preneur *m*, -euse *f* (à bail).

lessen ['lesn] ◆ vt [cost, importance] diminuer, réduire ; [impact, effect] atténuer, amoindrir ; [shock] amortir. ◆ vi s'atténuer, s'amoindrir.

lesser ['lesər] adj **1.** [gen] moindre / *to a lesser extent* dans une moindre mesure **2.** BOT, GEOG & ZOOL petit.

lesser-known adj moins connu.

lesson ['lesn] n **1.** [gen] leçon *f* ; SCH leçon *f*, cours *m* / *an English lesson* une leçon or un cours d'anglais / *a dancing* / *driving lesson* une leçon de danse / de conduite ▸ **to give a lesson** donner un cours or une leçon / *private lessons* cours *mpl* particuliers **2.** [example] leçon *f*

/ *her downfall was a lesson to us all* sa chute nous a servi de leçon à tous ▸ **to teach sb a lesson** donner une (bonne) leçon à qqn **3.** RELIG leçon *f*, lecture *f*.

lessor [le'sɔːr] *n* bailleur *m*, -eresse *f*.

less-than sign *n* signe *m* inférieur à.

lest [lest] *conj liter* de peur que, de crainte que.

let¹ [let] (*pt & pp* **let**, *cont* **letting**) ◆ *vt* **1.** UK [rent] louer / **'to let'** 'à louer' **2.** *arch* MED ▸ **to let (sb's) blood** faire une saignée (à qqn). ◆ *n* **1.** [rental] location *f* / *she took a six-month let on a house* elle a loué une maison pour six mois **2.** SPORT [in tennis, squash] ▸ **let (ball)** let *m* / *the ball was a let* la balle était let **3.** *fml* [hindrance] ▸ **without let or hindrance** librement, sans entrave. ❖ **let out** *vt sep* [rent] louer.

let² [let] (*pt & pp* **let**, *cont* **letting**) *vt* **1.** [permit] laisser, permettre / *she let them watch the programme* elle les a laissés regarder l'émission / *I couldn't come because my parents wouldn't let me* je ne suis pas venu parce que mes parents ne me l'ont pas permis ; [allow] laisser / *let me buy you all a drink* laissez-moi vous offrir un verre / *don't let me stop you going* je ne vous empêche d'y aller ▸ **to let sb have sthg** donner qqch à qqn / *don't be selfish, let him have a cake!* ne sois pas égoïste, donne-lui un gâteau ! / *she let him know what she thought of him* elle lui a fait savoir ce qu'elle pensait de lui ▸ **to let sb have it a)** *inf* [physically] casser la figure à qqn **b)** [verbally] dire ses quatre vérités à qqn ▸ [followed by 'go'] ▸ **to let sb go a)** [allow to leave] laisser partir qqn **b)** [release] relâcher qqn **c)** *euph* [dismiss, fire] licencier qqn / *let me go!* or *let me go of me!* lâchez-moi ! / *give me £5 and we'll let it go at that* donne-moi 5 livres et on n'en parle plus **3.** [in making suggestions] : *let's go!* allons-y ! / *don't let's go out* or *let's not go out tonight* ne sortons pas ce soir / *shall we have a picnic?* — *yes, let's!* si on faisait un pique-nique ? — d'accord ! **4.** [to focus attention] : *let me start by saying how pleased I am to be here* laissez-moi d'abord vous dire combien je suis ravi d'être ici **5.** [in hesitation] : *let me think* attends, voyons voir / *let me see* or *let's see* voyons **6.** [to express criticism or defiance] : *let them talk!* laisse-les dire ! **7.** [in threats] : *don't let me catch you at it again!* que je ne t'y reprenne plus ! **8.** [in commands] : *let them be!* laisse-les tranquilles !, fiche-leur la paix ! **9.** [in making assumptions] : *let us suppose that…* supposons que… ❖ **let down** *vt sep* **1.** [disappoint] décevoir / *I felt really let down* j'étais vraiment déçu / *she let us down badly* elle nous a proprement laissés tomber **2.** [lower, let fall - object] baisser, (faire) descendre ; [- hair] dénouer **3.** SEW rallonger / *to let (the hem of) a dress down* rallonger une robe **4.** [deflate] dégonfler. ❖ **let in** *vt sep* **1.** [person, animal] laisser entrer ▸ **to let sb in** ouvrir (la porte) à qqn, faire entrer qqn / *here's the key to let yourself in* voici la clé pour entrer **2.** [air, water] laisser passer / *the roof lets the rain in* le toit laisse entrer or passer la pluie. ❖ **let in for** *vt sep* : *he didn't realize what he was letting himself in for* il ne savait pas à quoi il s'engageait. ❖ **let in on** *vt sep* ▸ **to let sb in on sthg** mettre qqn au courant de qqch. ❖ **let off** *vt sep* **1.** [excuse] dispenser ▸ **to let sb off doing sthg** dispenser qqn de faire qqch **2.** [allow to leave] laisser partir ; [allow to disembark] laisser descendre **3.** [criminal, pupil, child] ne pas punir / *she was let off with a fine* elle s'en est tirée avec une amende **4.** [bomb, explosive] faire exploser ; [firework] faire partir ; [gun] laisser partir **5.** [release - steam, liquid] laisser échapper. ❖ **let on** *vi inf* : *she never let on* elle ne l'a jamais dit / *somebody let on about the wedding to the press* quelqu'un a parlé du mariage à or a révélé le mariage à la presse. ◆ *vt sep* [allow to embark] laisser monter. ❖ **let out** *vt sep* **1.** [allow to leave] laisser sortir / *the teacher let us out early* le professeur nous a laissés sortir plus tôt / *my*

secretary will let you out ma secrétaire va vous reconduire **2.** [water, air] laisser échapper / *someone's let the air out of the tyres* quelqu'un a dégonflé les pneus **3.** [shout, oath, whistle] laisser échapper **4.** [secret] révéler **5.** SEW [dress, trousers] élargir. ❖ **let up** *vi* **1.** [stop] arrêter ; [diminish] diminuer / *the rain didn't let up all day* il n'a pas cessé or arrêté de pleuvoir de toute la journée **2.** [relax] : *he never lets up* il ne s'accorde aucun répit. ❖ **let up on** *vt insep inf* ▸ **to let up on sb** lâcher la bride à qqn.

letdown ['letdaʊn] *n inf* déception *f*.

lethal ['liːθl] *adj* fatal, mortel ; MED létal.

lethally ['liːθəlɪ] *adv* mortellement.

lethargic [lə'θɑːdʒɪk] *adj* [person, sleep] léthargique ; [atmosphere] soporifique.

lethargy ['leθədʒɪ] *n* léthargie *f*.

let-out *n* UK [excuse] prétexte *m* ; [way out] échappatoire *f*.

let's [lets] (*abbr of* **let us**) ⟶ **let**.

letter ['letər] ◆ *n* **1.** [of alphabet] lettre *f* / *a six-letter word* un mot de six lettres **2.** *fig* [exact meaning] lettre *f* ▸ **the letter of the law** la lettre de la loi / *she obeyed the instructions to the letter* elle a suivi les instructions à la lettre or au pied de la lettre **3.** [communication] lettre *f* ; [mail] courrier *m* / *by letter* par lettre or courrier / *letters to the editor* [in newspapers, magazines] courrier des lecteurs ▸ **letter of credit** COMM lettre de crédit ▸ **the letters page** le courrier des lecteurs. ◆ *vt* [write] inscrire des lettres sur ; [engrave] graver (des lettres sur) ; [manuscript] enluminer. ❖ **letters** *pl n fml* [learning] belles-lettres *fpl* ▸ **a man of letters a)** [scholar] un lettré **b)** [writer] un homme de lettres.

letter bomb *n* lettre *f* piégée.

letterbox ['letəbɒks] *n* UK boîte *f* à or aux lettres ▸ **letterbox format** TV format *m* boîte aux lettres.

letterhead ['letəhed] *n* en-tête *m inv* (de lettre).

lettering ['letərɪŋ] *n* (U) [inscription] inscription *f* ; [characters] caractères *mpl*.

letter opener *n* coupe-papier *m inv*.

letter-perfect *adj* US [person] qui connaît son texte parfaitement ; [text] parfait.

letter quality *n* COMPUT qualité *f* courrier ▸ **near letter quality** qualité quasi-courrier (*pour une imprimante*). ❖ **letter-quality** *adj* qualité courrier (*inv*).

letters patent *pl n* patente *f*.

letting ['letɪŋ] *n* [of house, property] location *f*.

lettuce ['letɪs] *n* [gen & CULIN] salade *f* ; BOT laitue *f*.

letup ['letʌp] *n* [stop] arrêt *m*, pause *f* ; [abatement] répit *m*.

leukaemia UK, **leukemia** US [luː'kiːmɪə] *n* (U) leucémie *f*.

levee ['levɪ] *n* **1.** US [embankment] levée *f* ; [surrounding field] digue *f* **2.** US [landing place] quai *m* **3.** HIST [in royal chamber] lever *m* (du roi) ; UK [at court] réception *f* à la cour.

level ['levl] (UK *pt & pp* **levelled**, *cont* **levelling** ; US *pt & pp* **leveled**, *cont* **leveling**) ◆ *n* **1.** [height - in a horizontal plane] niveau *m* ; [- in a vertical plane] hauteur *f* **2.** [amount] niveau *m* ; [percentage] taux *m* **3.** [rank] niveau *m*, échelon *m* / *at a regional level* au niveau régional **4.** [standard] niveau *m* **5.** [point of view] : *on a personal level, I really like him* sur le plan personnel, je l'aime beaucoup / *on a practical level* du point de vue pratique **6.** [storey] niveau *m*, étage *m* **7.** [flat land] plat *m* **8.** [for woodwork, building, etc.] ▸ **(spirit) level** niveau *m* (à bulle) **9.** *inf* PHR **on the level** [honest] honnête, réglo. ◆ *adj* **1.** [flat] plat / *a level spoonful* une cuillerée rase ▸ **to make sthg level** aplanir qqch **2.** [at the same height] au même niveau, à la même hauteur ; [at the same standard] au même niveau / *the terrace is level with the pool* la terrasse est au même niveau que or de plain-pied avec la piscine **3.** [in horizontal position] : *hold the tray level* tenez le plateau à l'horizontale or bien à plat / *to fly level* AERON voler en palier **4.** [equal] à égalité **5.** [calm, steady] calme, mesuré **6.** *inf* [honest] honnête, réglo **7.** *inf* PHR **to do one's level best** faire de son mieux. ◆ vt **1.** [flatten] aplanir, niveler **2.** [aim] ▸ **to level a gun at sb** braquer une arme sur qqn. ◆ vi ▸ **to level with sb** *inf* être franc avec qqn, jouer franc jeu avec qqn. ◈ **level down** vt sep [surface] aplanir, niveler ; [standard] niveler par le bas. ◈ **level off** ◆ vi **1.** [production, rise, development] s'équilibrer, se stabiliser **2.** AERON amorcer un palier. ◆ vt sep [flatten] aplatir, niveler. ◈ **level out** vi **1.** [road, surface] s'aplanir **2.** [stabilize] se stabiliser. ◆ vt sep niveler. ◈ **level up** vt sep niveler (par le haut).

level crossing n UK passage m à niveau.

level-headed [-'hedɪd] adj équilibré, pondéré, réfléchi.

lever [UK 'liːvəʳ US 'levəʳ] ◆ n *lit & fig* levier m ; [smaller] manette f. ◆ vt manœuvrer à l'aide d'un levier. ◈ **lever out** vt sep extraire or extirper (à l'aide d'un levier) ; *fig* : *they levered the president out of office* ils ont délogé le président de son poste. ◈ **lever up** vt sep soulever (au moyen d'un levier).

leverage [UK 'liːvərɪdʒ US 'levərɪdʒ] ◆ n **1.** MECH force f (de levier) **2.** [influence] : *the committee's findings give us considerable (political) leverage* les conclusions de la commission constituent pour nous des moyens de pression considérables (sur le plan politique) **3.** US ECON effet m de levier. ◆ vt **1.** [exploit, use profitably] tirer profit de **2.** [finance with debt] ▸ **to leverage a company** augmenter le ratio d'endettement d'une entreprise.

leveraged buyout [ˌlevərɪdʒd'baɪaʊt] n leveraged buy out *(rachat des actions d'une entreprise financé par une très large part d'endettement)*.

leveraged management buyout n rachat m d'entreprise par les salariés.

lever-arch file n classeur m à levier.

leviathan [lɪ'vaɪəθn] n [ship] navire m géant ; [institution, organization] institution f or organisation f géante.

levitate ['levɪteɪt] ◆ vi léviter. ◆ vt faire léviter, soulever par lévitation.

levitation [ˌlevɪ'teɪʃn] n lévitation f.

levity ['levətɪ] (*pl* **levities**) n légèreté f, manque m de sérieux.

levy ['levɪ] (*pl* **levies**, *pt & pp* **levied**) ◆ n **1.** [levying] prélèvement m **2.** [tax, duty] impôt m, taxe f **3.** MIL levée f. ◆ vt **1.** [impose - tax] prélever ; [- fine] imposer, infliger **2.** [collect -taxes, fine] lever, percevoir **3.** MIL [troops] lever **4.** [wage] : *to levy war on small states* faire la guerre à de petits États.

lewd [ljuːd] adj [behaviour] lubrique ; [speech, gesture, act] obscène.

lexical ['leksɪkl] adj lexical.

lexicographer [ˌleksɪ'kɒgrəfəʳ] n lexicographe mf.

lexicography [ˌleksɪ'kɒgrəfɪ] n lexicographie f.

lexicon ['leksɪkən] n lexique m.

ley line n *ensemble de repères indiquant le tracé probable d'un chemin préhistorique.*

LI written abbr of Long Island.

liability [ˌlaɪə'bɪlətɪ] (*pl* **liabilities**) n **1.** (*U*) LAW [responsibility] responsabilité f (légale) / *he refused to admit liability for the damage* il refusa d'endosser la responsabilité des dégâts **2.** (*U*) [eligibility] assujettissement m / *liability for tax* assujettissement à l'impôt / *liability for*

military service obligations fpl militaires **3.** [hindrance] gêne f, handicap m. ◈ **liabilities** pl n FIN [debts] passif m, engagements mpl financiers.

liable ['laɪəbl] adj **1.** LAW [responsible] responsable ▸ **to be held liable for sthg** être tenu (pour) responsable de qqch ▸ **to be liable for sb's debts** répondre des dettes de qqn **2.** [likely] ▸ **liable to** : *the programme is liable to change* le programme est susceptible d'être modifié, il se peut que le programme subisse des modifications / *he's liable to arrive at any moment* il peut arriver d'une minute à l'autre **3.** ADMIN : *to be liable for tax* **a)** [person] être assujetti à or redevable de l'impôt **b)** [goods] être assujetti à une taxe / *offenders are liable to a fine* les contrevenants sont passibles d'une amende / *he is liable to be prosecuted* il s'expose à des poursuites judiciaires ; MIL : *to be liable for military service* être astreint au service militaire.

liaise [lɪ'eɪz] vi ▸ **to liaise with sb** assurer la liaison avec qqn.

liaison [lɪ'eɪzɒn] n liaison f.

liar ['laɪəʳ] n menteur m, -euse f.

lib [lɪb] n *inf* abbr of liberation.

Lib [lɪb] abbr of Liberal.

Lib Dem [-dem] n abbr of Liberal Democrat.

libel ['laɪbl] (UK *pt & pp* **libelled**, *cont* **libelling** ; US *pt & pp* **libeled**, *cont* **libeling**) ◆ n LAW [act of publishing] diffamation f ; [publication] écrit m diffamatoire ; *fig* [calumny] calomnie f, mensonge m. ◆ vt LAW diffamer ; *fig* calomnier.

libellous UK, **libelous** US ['laɪbələs] adj diffamatoire.

liberal ['lɪbərəl] ◆ adj **1.** [tolerant - person] libéral, large d'esprit ; [- ideas, mind] libéral, large ; [- education] libéral ▸ **liberal studies** culture f générale *(matière enseignée à l'université)* **2.** [generous] libéral, généreux ; [copious - helping, portion] abondant, copieux. ◆ n [moderate] : *she's a liberal* elle est de centre gauche. ◈ **Liberal** ◆ adj POL [19th century] libéral ; [today] de centre gauche ▸ **the Liberal Party** le parti libéral ▸ **the Liberal Democrats** parti centriste britannique. ◆ n [party member] libéral m, -e f.

 Liberal Democratic Party

Troisième parti politique en Grande-Bretagne, les **Lib Dems** ont vu le jour en 1988 suite à la fusion du **Liberal Party** et du **Social Democratic Party**. Parti pro-européen prônant le libéralisme social, les **Lib Dems** sont notamment en faveur de la représentation proportionnelle et du remplacement de la Chambre des lords par une assemblée d'élus.

liberal arts pl n ▸ **the liberal arts** US les sciences humaines.

liberalism ['lɪbərəlɪzm] n libéralisme m.

liberalize, liberalise ['lɪbərəlaɪz] vt libéraliser.

liberally ['lɪbərəlɪ] adv libéralement.

liberal-minded [-maɪndɪd] adj large d'esprit.

liberate ['lɪbəreɪt] vt [gen] libérer ; CHEM libérer, dégager.

liberated ['lɪbəreɪtɪd] adj libéré.

liberating ['lɪbəreɪtɪŋ] adj libérateur.

liberation [ˌlɪbə'reɪʃn] n libération f.

liberator ['lɪbəreɪtəʳ] n libérateur m, -trice f.

Liberia [laɪ'bɪərɪə] pr n Liberia m / *in Liberia* au Liberia.

Liberian [laɪ'bɪərɪən] ◆ n Libérien m, -enne f. ◆ adj libérien.

libertarian [ˌlɪbəˈteərɪən] ◆ adj libertaire. ◆ n libertaire *mf*.

libertine [ˈlɪbətiːn] ◆ adj libertin. ◆ n libertin *m*, -e *f*.

liberty [ˈlɪbətɪ] (*pl* **liberties**) n [in behaviour] liberté *f* ▸ **to take liberties with sb** prendre or se permettre des libertés avec qqn. ❖ **at liberty** adj phr : *the criminals are still at liberty* les criminels sont toujours en liberté or courent toujours / *I'm not at liberty to say* il ne m'est pas possible or permis de le dire. ❖ **Liberty** pr n [UK organisation] *association britannique de défense des droits du citoyen, anciennement appelée* **The National Council for Civil Liberties**.

libido [lɪˈbiːdəʊ] (*pl* **libidos**) n libido *f*.

Libra [ˈliːbrə] ◆ pr n ASTROL & ASTRON Balance *f*. ◆ n : *he's a Libra* il est (du signe de la) Balance.

librarian [laɪˈbreərɪən] n bibliothécaire *mf*.

librarianship [laɪˈbreərɪənʃɪp] n [science] bibliothéconomie *f*.

library [ˈlaɪbrərɪ] (*pl* **libraries**) ◆ n **1.** [gen] bibliothèque *f* ▸ **the Library of Congress** la bibliothèque du Congrès (*équivalent américain de la Bibliothèque Nationale*) **2.** [published series] bibliothèque *f*, collection *f* **3.** COMPUT bibliothèque *f*. ◆ comp [book, card] de bibliothèque.

library book n livre *m* de bibliothèque.

libretto [lɪˈbretəʊ] (*pl* **librettos** or **libretti** [-tɪ]) n MUS livret *m*, libretto *m*.

Libya [ˈlɪbɪə] pr n Libye *f* / *in Libya* en Libye.

Libyan [ˈlɪbɪən] ◆ n Libyen *m*, -enne *f*. ◆ adj libyen.

lice [laɪs] pl ⟶ **louse**.

licence 🇬🇧, **license** 🇺🇸 [ˈlaɪsəns] n **1.** [permit] permis *m* ; [for marriage] certificat *m* de publication des bans ; [for trade, bar] licence *f* ; [for TV, radio] redevance *f* ; [for pilot] brevet *m* ; [for driver] permis *m* (de conduire) / *a licence to sell alcoholic drinks* une licence de débit de boissons **2.** ADMIN & COMM [permission] licence *f*, autorisation *f* ▸ **to marry by special licence** ≃ se marier sans publication de bans **3.** [liberty] licence *f*, liberté *f* ▸ **artistic licence** licence artistique **4.** [immoral behaviour] licence *f*, débordements *mpl*.

licence number n [on vehicle] numéro *m* d'immatriculation ; [on driving licence] numéro *m* de permis de conduire.

license [ˈlaɪsəns] ◆ n 🇺🇸 = **licence**. ◆ vt **1.** ADMIN & COMM [premises, trader] accorder une licence or une autorisation à / *licensed to practise medicine* habilité à exercer la médecine / *to license a car* immatriculer une voiture **2.** [allow] ▸ **to license sb to do sthg** autoriser qqn à faire qqch, permettre à qqn de faire qqch.

licensed [ˈlaɪsənst] adj **1.** COMM fabriqué sous licence ; [for alcohol] : *these premises are licensed to sell alcoholic drinks* cet établissement est autorisé à vendre des boissons alcoolisées ▸ **licensed premises a)** [bar, pub] débit *m* de boissons **b)** [restaurant, cafeteria] établissement *m* autorisé à vendre des boissons alcoolisées ▸ **licensed product** produit *m* sous licence **2.** [pilot] breveté ; [driver] qui a son permis (de conduire).

licensee [ˌlaɪsənˈsiː] n [gen] titulaire *mf* d'une licence or d'un permis ; [pub-owner, landlord] débitant *m*, -e *f* (de boissons).

license plate n 🇺🇸 plaque *f* minéralogique or d'immatriculation.

licensing [ˈlaɪsənsɪŋ] n [of car] immatriculation *f* ; [of activity] autorisation *f* ▸ **licensing agreement** accord *m* de licence ▸ **licensing authority** *organisme chargé de la délivrance des licences*.

licensing hours pl n [in UK] *heures d'ouverture des pubs*.

licensing laws pl n [in UK] *lois réglementant la vente d'alcools*.

licentious [laɪˈsenʃəs] adj licencieux.

lichee [ˌlaɪˈtʃiː] n = **lychee**.

lichen [ˈlaɪkən] n lichen *m*.

lick [lɪk] ◆ vt **1.** [ice-cream] lécher ; [stamp] humecter **2.** inf [defeat] battre à plate couture ; [in fight] donner une raclée à. ◆ n **1.** [with tongue] coup *m* de langue ▸ **to give sthg a lick** lécher qqch **2.** 🇬🇧 inf [speed] ▸ **at a tremendous lick** à fond la caisse or de train **3.** AGR pierre *f* à lécher.

licking [ˈlɪkɪŋ] n inf [thrashing] raclée *f*, dégelée *f* ; [defeat] déculottée *f*.

licorice 🇺🇸 = **liquorice**.

lid [lɪd] n **1.** [gen] couvercle *m* **2.** ANAT [eyelid] paupière *f* **3.** inf [hat] galure *m*, galurin *m* ; [helmet] casque *m* **4.** inf 🅿🅷🆁 *the scandal put the lid on the Chicago operation* le scandale mit fin à l'opération de Chicago / *the firm is keeping a lid on expenses* l'entreprise met un frein aux dépenses.

lido [ˈliːdəʊ] (*pl* **lidos**) n [pool] piscine *f* découverte ; [resort] station *f* balnéaire.

lie [laɪ] (*pt* **lay** [leɪ], *pp* **lain** [leɪn], *cont* **lying**) ◆ vi **1.** (*pp* **lied**) [tell untruth] mentir **2.** [person, animal - recline] se coucher, s'allonger, s'étendre / *she was lying on the couch* elle était couchée or allongée sur le divan / *lie still!* ne bouge pas ! / *I like lying in bed on Sunday mornings* j'aime rester au lit or faire la grasse matinée le dimanche matin **3.** [corpse] reposer / *he will lie in state at Westminster Abbey* son corps sera exposé solennellement à l'abbaye de Westminster / *'here lies John Smith'* 'ci-gît John Smith' **4.** [thing - be, be placed] : *a folder lay open on the desk before her* un dossier était ouvert devant elle sur le bureau / *snow lay (thick) on the ground* il y avait une (épaisse) couche de neige / *the castle now lies in ruins* le château est aujourd'hui en ruines **5.** [stay - remain, stay] rester / *our machines are lying idle* nos machines sont arrêtées or ne tournent pas **6.** [place - be situated] se trouver, être ; [land - stretch, extend] s'étendre / *a vast desert lay before us* un immense désert s'étendait devant nous **7.** [future event] : *who knows what may lie in store for us* qui sait ce qui nous attend or ce que l'avenir nous réserve **8.** [answer, explanation, duty, etc.] : *the problem lies in getting them motivated* le problème, c'est de réussir à les motiver / *responsibility for the strike lies with the management* la responsabilité de la grève incombe à la direction. ◆ n **1.** [untruth] mensonge *m* ▸ **to tell lies** dire des mensonges, mentir / *it was in June, no, I tell a lie, in July* c'était en juin, non, c'est faux, en juillet **2.** [of land] configuration *f*, disposition *f*. ❖ **lie about** 🇬🇧, **lie around** vi **1.** [person] traîner **2.** [thing] traîner / *don't leave your things lying about* ne laisse pas traîner tes affaires. ❖ **lie back** vi : *he lay back in his armchair* il s'est renversé dans son fauteuil / *just lie back and take it easy!* fig reposetoi un peu ! ❖ **lie behind** vt insep se cacher derrière. ❖ **lie down** vi se coucher, s'allonger, s'étendre ▸ **to take**

sthg lying down accepter qqch sans réagir or sans broncher / *I won't take this lying down!* je ne vais pas me laisser faire comme ça ! ❖ **lie in** vi [sleep in] faire la grasse matinée.

Liechtenstein ['lɪktənstaɪn] pr n Liechtenstein *m* / *in Liechtenstein* au Liechtenstein.

lie detector n détecteur *m* de mensonges.

lie-down n 🇬🇧 *inf* ▶ **to have a lie-down** se coucher, s'allonger.

lie-in n 🇬🇧 *inf* ▶ **to have a lie-in** faire la grasse matinée.

lieu [lju: or lu:] ❖ **in lieu** adv phr : *take Monday off in lieu* prends ton lundi pour compenser. ❖ **in lieu of** prep phr au lieu de, à la place de.

Lieut. (written abbr of **lieutenant**) lieut.

lieutenant [🇬🇧 lef'tenənt 🇺🇸 lu:'tenənt] n **1.** MIL [in army] lieutenant *m* ; [in navy] lieutenant *m* de vaisseau **2.** [in US police] inspecteur *m* (de police) **3.** *fig* lieutenant *m*, second *m* **4.** 🇬🇧 HIST lieutenant *m*.

lieutenant colonel n lieutenant-colonel *m*.

life [laɪf] (*pl* **lives** [laɪvz]) ❖ n **1.** [existence] vie *f* / *it's a matter of life and death* c'est une question de vie ou de mort / *I've worked hard all my life* j'ai travaillé dur toute ma vie / *life is hard* la vie est dure / *how's life?* inf comment ça va ? / *I began life as a labourer* j'ai débuté dans la vie comme ouvrier / *I want to live my own life* je veux vivre ma vie ▶ **to live life to the full** 🇬🇧 or **fullest** 🇺🇸 croquer la vie à belles dents / *hundreds lost their lives* des centaines de personnes ont trouvé la mort ▶ **to save sb's life** sauver la vie à qqn ▶ **to risk one's life (to do sthg)** risquer sa vie (à faire qqch) ▶ **to take sb's life** tuer qqn ▶ **to run for one's life** or **for dear life** s'enfuir à toutes jambes / *for the life of me I can't remember where we met* rien à faire, je n'arrive pas à me rappeler où nous nous sommes rencontrés ▶ **not on your life!** jamais de la vie ! ▶ **that's life!** c'est la vie ! ▶ **this is the life!** (ça, c'est) la belle vie ! ▶ **to have the time of one's life** : *I had the time of my life* je ne me suis jamais autant amusé **2.** [mode of existence] vie *f* / *she's not used to city life* elle n'a pas l'habitude de vivre en ville / *married life* la vie conjugale **3.** [living things collectively] vie *f* / *is there life on Mars?* y a-t-il de la vie sur Mars ? **4.** [liveliness] vie *f* / *there's a lot more life in Sydney than in Wellington* Sydney est nettement plus animé que Wellington ▶ **to come to life** s'animer ▶ **to be the life and soul of the party** : *she was the life and soul of the party* c'est elle qui a mis de l'ambiance dans la soirée **5.** [durability] (durée de) vie *f*. ❖ comp [post, member, president] à vie. ❖ **for life** adv phr : *he was crippled for life* il a été estropié à vie / *a job for life* un emploi à vie.

life-and-death adj : *this is a life-and-death decision* c'est une décision vitale / *a life-and-death struggle* un combat à mort, une lutte désespérée.

life assurance 🇬🇧 = **life insurance**.

life belt n bouée *f* de sauvetage.

lifeblood ['laɪfblʌd] n élément *m* vital.

lifeboat ['laɪfbəʊt] n [shore-based] canot *m* de sauvetage ; [on ship] chaloupe *f* de sauvetage.

lifeboatman ['laɪfbəʊtmən] (*pl* **lifeboatmen** [-mən]) n sauveteur *m* (en mer).

life buoy n bouée *f* de sauvetage.

life coach n coach *m* de vie.

life cycle n cycle *m* de vie.

life drawing n dessin *m* d'après nature.

life expectancy n [of human, animal] espérance *f* de vie ; [of machine] durée *f* de vie probable.

life-form n forme *f* de vie.

life-giving adj qui insuffle la vie, vivifiant.

lifeguard ['laɪfɡɑːd] n maître-nageur *m*.

life history n vie *f*.

life imprisonment n prison *f* à vie.

life insurance n assurance-vie *f*.

life jacket n gilet *m* de sauvetage.

lifeless ['laɪflɪs] adj **1.** [dead body] sans vie **2.** [where no life exists] sans vie **3.** [dull - eyes] éteint ; [- hair] terne ; [- town] mort ; [- style] sans énergie.

lifelike ['laɪflaɪk] adj **1.** [portrait] ressemblant **2.** [seeming alive] : *the new robots are extremely lifelike* ces nouveaux robots ont l'air or paraissent vraiment vivants.

lifeline ['laɪflaɪn] n **1.** NAUT [thrown to boat] remorque *f* ; [stretched across deck] sauvegarde *f*, filière *f* de mauvais temps or de sécurité **2.** [for diver] corde *f* de sécurité **3.** *fig* lien *m* vital.

lifelong ['laɪflɒŋ] adj de toute une vie ▶ **lifelong learning** formation *f* continue.

life-or-death = **life-and-death**.

life peer n 🇬🇧 membre de la Chambre des lords dont le titre n'est pas héréditaire.

life preserver n 🇺🇸 [life belt] bouée *f* de sauvetage ; [life jacket] gilet *m* de sauvetage.

lifer ['laɪfə] n *inf* condamné *m*, -e *f* à perpète.

life raft n canot *m* pneumatique (de sauvetage).

lifesaver ['laɪf,seɪvə] n **1.** [lifeguard] maître-nageur *m* **2.** *inf & fig* : *thank you, you're a lifesaver!* merci, tu m'as sauvé la vie !

life-saving adj : *life-saving apparatus* appareils *mpl* or engins *mpl* de sauvetage / *life-saving vaccine* vaccin *m* qui sauve la vie.

life sentence n condamnation *f* à vie or à perpétuité.

life-size(d) adj grandeur nature *(inv)*.

life span n durée *f* de vie.

life story n biographie *f*.

lifestyle ['laɪfstaɪl] n style *m* or mode *m* de vie ▶ **lifestyle disease** maladie *f* liée au mode de vie ▶ **lifestyle drug** médicament *m* du bien-être ▶ **lifestyle programme a)** [way of living] programme *m* de vie **b)** TV émission traitant de l'art de vivre (habillement, décoration, cuisine, voyages, etc.).

life-support system n MED respirateur *m* artificiel ; AERON & ASTRON équipement *m* de vie.

life-threatening adj [illness] qui peut être mortel.

lifetime ['laɪftaɪm] n vie *f*.

LIFO abbr of **last in first out**.

lift [lɪft] ❖ vt **1.** [object] soulever, lever ; [part of body] lever ; *fml* [voice] élever **2.** [spirits, heart] remonter **3.** [end - blockade, embargo, etc.] lever ; [- control, restriction] supprimer **4.** *inf* [steal] piquer, faucher ; [plagiarize] plagier, piquer **5.** AGR [bulbs, potatoes, turnips] arracher **6.** 🇺🇸 [debt] rembourser **7.** [face] : *she's had her face lifted* elle s'est fait faire un lifting. ❖ vi **1.** [rise] se lever, se soulever **2.** [fog, mist] se lever, se dissiper. ❖ n **1.** [act of lifting] ▶ **to give sthg a lift** soulever qqch **2.** [in morale, energy] ▶ **to give sb a lift** remonter le moral à qqn **3.** 🇬🇧 [elevator] ascenseur *m* ▶ **goods lift** monte-charge *m inv* **4.** [free ride] : *can I give you a lift home?* est-ce que je peux te raccompagner chez toi (en voiture) ? ❖ **lift off** ❖ vi [plane, rocket] décoller. ❖ vt sep [hat, lid] enlever, ôter. ❖ **lift up** vt sep soulever, lever ; [part of body] lever ; *fml* [voice] élever ; *fml* [heart] élever.

lifting ['lɪftɪŋ] n **1.** [of weight] levage *m* / *I can't do any heavy lifting* je ne peux pas porter de charges lourdes ▶ **lifting gear** appareil *m* de levage ▶ **lifting jack** cric *m* (de levage) **2.** [of blockade, embargo, etc.] levée *f* ; [of control, restriction] suppression *f* **3.** AGR arrachage *m*, récolte *f*.

lift-off n décollage *m*.

ligament ['lɪɡəmənt] n ligament *m*.

ligature ['lɪɡətʃə] ❖ n **1.** [gen & MED] & TYPO ligature *f* **2.** MUS liaison *f*. ❖ vt ligaturer.

light [laɪt] ◆ n **1.** [luminosity, brightness] lumière f / *by the light of our flashlamps* à la lumière de nos lampes de poche / *the light was beginning to fail* le jour commençait à baisser ▸ **at first light** au point ou au lever du jour / *you're (standing) in my light* tu me fais de l'ombre ; *fig* ▸ **to bring to light** mettre en lumière ▸ **to be brought** or **to come to light** être découvert or révélé / *can you throw any light on this problem?* peux-tu apporter tes lumières sur ce problème ?, peux-tu éclaircir cette question ? ▸ **to see the light a)** [understand] comprendre **b)** [be converted] trouver le chemin de la vérité **2.** [light source] lumière f ; [lamp] lampe f / *turn the light on* / *off* allume / éteins (la lumière) **3.** *fig* [in sb's eyes] lueur f **4.** AUTO [gen] feu m ; [headlamp] phare m ▸ **parking** / **reversing lights** feux de stationnement / de recul **5.** [traffic light] ▸ **the lights** le feu (de signalisation) / *she jumped the lights* elle a brûlé le feu rouge **6.** [aspect, viewpoint] jour m / *in a good* / *bad* / *new light* sous un jour favorable / défavorable / nouveau **7.** [flame] feu m / *could you give me a light?* pouvez-vous me donner du feu ? ▸ **to set light to sthg** mettre le feu à qqch. ◆ adj **1.** [bright, well-lit] clair / *it's getting light already* il commence déjà à faire jour **2.** [pale] clair / *light yellow* / *brown* jaune / marron clair *(inv)* **3.** [in weight] léger ▸ **to be light on one's feet** être leste **4.** [comedy, music, etc.] léger, facile **5.** [not intense, strong, etc.] léger / *I had a light lunch* j'ai mangé légèrement à midi, j'ai déjeuné léger / *I'm a light sleeper* j'ai le sommeil léger ▸ **to make light of sthg** prendre qqch à la légère. ◆ adv ▸ **to travel light** voyager avec peu de bagages. ◆ vt *(pt & pp* lit [lɪt] *or* lighted) **1.** [illuminate] éclairer / *I'll light the way for you* je vais t'éclairer le chemin **2.** [lamp, candle, cigarette] allumer ; [match] craquer / *to light a fire* allumer un feu, faire du feu. ◆ vi *(pt & pp* lit [lɪt] *or* lighted) **1.** [lamp] s'allumer ; [match] s'enflammer ; [fire, coal] prendre **2.** *liter* [alight] se poser. ❖ **in (the) light of** prep phr : *in the light of these new facts* à la lumière de ces faits nouveaux. ❖ **light on, light upon** vt insep tomber (par hasard) sur, trouver par hasard. ❖ **light up** vt sep éclairer. ◆ vi **1.** [lamp] s'allumer **2.** [face, eyes] s'éclairer, s'illuminer **3.** *inf* [have a cigarette] allumer une cigarette.

light ale n 〔UK〕 bière brune *légère*.

light bulb n ampoule f (électrique).

lighted ['laɪtɪd] adj [room] éclairé ; [candle] allumé.

light-emitting diode [-ɪ'mɪtɪŋ-] n diode f électroluminescente.

lighten ['laɪtn] ◆ vt **1.** [make brighter] éclairer, illuminer **2.** [make paler] éclaircir **3.** [make less heavy] alléger. ◆ vi **1.** [become light] s'éclairer, s'éclaircir **2.** [load, burden] s'alléger. ❖ **lighten up** vi *inf* se remettre.

lighter ['laɪtə'] ◆ n **1.** [for cigarettes] briquet m ; [for gas] allume-gaz m inv **2.** [barge] allège f, chaland m **3.** ⟶ **firelighter**. ◆ comp [flint, fuel] à briquet.

light-fingered [-'fɪŋgəd] adj chapardeur.

light fitting n applique f (électrique).

light-footed [-'fʊtɪd] adj au pied léger, à la démarche légère.

light-headed adj [dizzy] étourdi ; [tipsy] ivre, enivré.

light-headedness [-'hedɪdnɪs] n [dizziness] vertige m ; [tipsiness] ivresse f.

light-hearted adj [person, atmosphere] enjoué, gai ; [poem, irony] léger.

lighthouse ['laɪthaʊs] *(pl* [-haʊzɪz]) n phare m ▸ **lighthouse keeper** gardien m de phare.

lighting ['laɪtɪŋ] n **1.** [gen] éclairage m **2.** (U) THEAT éclairages mpl ▸ **lighting effects** effets mpl d'éclairage or de lumière ▸ **lighting engineer** éclairagiste mf.

lighting-up time n 〔UK〕 heure où les automobilistes doivent obligatoirement allumer leurs phares.

lightly ['laɪtlɪ] adv **1.** [not heavily] légèrement **2.** [casually] légèrement, à la légère **3.** 〔PHR〕 **to get off lightly** s'en tirer à bon compte.

light meter n posemètre m.

lightness ['laɪtnɪs] n **1.** [brightness, light] clarté f **2.** [of object, tone, step, etc.] légèreté f.

lightning ['laɪtnɪŋ] ◆ n (U) éclairs mpl, foudre f ▸ **a flash of lightning** un éclair ▸ **to be struck by lightning** être frappé par la foudre or foudroyé. ◆ adj [raid, visit] éclair *(inv)* / *with* or *at lightning speed* à la vitesse de l'éclair, en un éclair.

lightning conductor, lightning rod n paratonnerre m.

lightning strike n grève f surprise *(inv)*.

light opera n opéra m comique, opérette f.

light pen n crayon m optique, photostyle m.

light pollution n pollution f lumineuse.

light-sensitive adj PHYS photosensible.

lightship ['laɪtʃɪp] n bateau-feu m, bateau-phare m.

light show n spectacle m de lumière.

lights-out n extinction f des feux.

light switch n interrupteur m.

lightweight ['laɪtweɪt] ◆ n **1.** [in boxing] poids m léger **2.** [insignificant person] personne f sans envergure. ◆ adj **1.** [clothes, equipment] léger **2.** [in boxing] poids léger *(inv)*.

light-year n année-lumière f / *it seems light-years away* ça paraît si loin.

likable ['laɪkəbl] = **likeable**.

like¹ [laɪk] vt **1.** [find pleasant] aimer (bien) / *I like her, but I don't love her* je l'aime bien, mais je ne suis pas amoureux d'elle / *I don't like him* je ne l'aime pas beaucoup, il ne me plaît pas / *what do you like about him?* qu'est-ce qui te plaît chez lui ? / *what's not to like? inf* il faudrait être difficile pour ne pas aimer ça **2.** [enjoy - activity] ▸ **to like doing** or **to do sthg** aimer faire qqch / *I don't like being talked at* je n'aime pas qu'on me fasse des discours / *how would* HE *like being kept waiting in the rain?* ça lui plairait, à lui, qu'on le fasse attendre sous la pluie ? **3.** [approve of] aimer / *I like people to be frank with me* j'aime qu'on soit franc avec moi / *I don't like you swearing* or *I don't like it when you swear* je n'aime pas que tu dises des gros mots / *whether you like it or not!* que ça te plaise ou non ! / *well, I like that!* iro ça, c'est le bouquet ! / *I like the way you say "don't worry"* hum « ne t'inquiète pas », c'est facile à dire **4.** [want, wish] aimer, vouloir / *do what you like* fais ce que tu veux or ce qui te plaît / *I didn't like to say anything, but...* je ne voulais rien dire mais... / *I'd like your opinion on this wine* j'aimerais savoir ce que tu penses de ce vin ; [in polite offers, requests] : *would you like to go out tonight?* ça te dirait de or tu as envie de sortir ce soir ? / *would you like tea or coffee?* voulez-vous du thé ou du café ? / *would you like me to do it for you?* veux-tu que je le fasse à ta place ? / *I'd like to speak to Mr Smith, please* je voudrais parler à M. Smith, s'il vous plaît **5.** [asking opinion] : *how do you like my jacket?* comment trouves-tu ma veste ? / *how would you like a trip to Paris?* ça te dirait d'aller à Paris ? **6.** [asking preference] : *how do you like your coffee, black or white?* vous prenez votre café noir ou avec du lait ? **7.** [in generalizations] : *I like to be in bed by 10 p.m.* j'aime être couché pour 10 h / *one doesn't like to interrupt* c'est toujours délicat d'interrompre quelqu'un.

When translating 'would like someone to do something', note that vouloir que, aimer que and souhaiter que are all followed by a verb in the subjunctive :
I'd like you to pay more attention. Je voudrais que / J'aimerais que / Je souhaiterais que tu *sois plus attentif.*

like² [laɪk] ◆ prep **1.** [similar to] comme / *there's a car like ours* voilà une voiture comme la nôtre / *she's nothing like her sister* elle ne ressemble pas du tout à sa sœur / *it's shaped like an egg* ça a la forme d'un œuf / *it looks like rain* on dirait qu'il va pleuvoir **2.** [asking for opinion or description] : *what's your new boss like?* comment est ton nouveau patron ? / *what's the weather like?* quel temps fait-il ? / *what does it taste like?* quel goût ça a ? **3.** [such as] comme / *I'm useless at things like sewing* je ne suis bon à rien quand il s'agit de couture et de choses comme ça **4.** [indicating typical behaviour] : *kids are like that, what do you expect?* les gosses sont comme ça, qu'est-ce que tu veux ! / *it's not like him to be rude* ça ne lui ressemble pas or ce n'est pas son genre d'être impoli / *it's just like him not to show up!* c'est bien son style or c'est bien de lui de ne pas venir ! **5.** [in the same manner as] comme / *do it like this / that* voici / voilà comment il faut faire **6.** [in approximations] : *it cost something like £200* ça a coûté dans les 200 livres / *it was more like midnight when we got home* il était plus près de minuit quand nous sommes arrivés à la maison. ◆ adj : *we were treated in like manner* on nous a traités de la même façon. ◆ conj *inf* **1.** [as] comme / *like I was saying* inf comme je disais / *they don't make them like they used to!* ils / elles ne sont plus ce qu'ils / elles étaient ! **2.** [as if] comme si / *he acted like he was in charge* il se comportait comme si c'était lui le chef. ◆ adv UK v *inf* : *I was hungry, like, so I went into this café* j'avais faim, tu vois, alors je suis entré dans un café. ◆ n : *you can only compare like with like* on ne peut comparer que ce qui est comparable / *she goes in for macramé, yoga and the like* elle fait du macramé, du yoga et d'autres choses comme ça / *I've never seen the like of it!* je n'ai jamais rien vu de pareil ! / *he was a president the like* or *likes of which we will probably never see again* li-ter c'était un président comme on n'en verra probablement plus jamais. ❖ **likes** pl n **1.** [preferences] goûts *mpl* / *try to discover their likes and dislikes* essayez de découvrir ce qu'ils aiment et ce qu'ils n'aiment pas **2.** PHR **the likes of us / them, etc.** inf les gens comme nous / eux, etc.

-like suffix : *dream-like* onirique, de rêve / *ghost-like* fantomatique.

likeable ['laɪkəbl] adj sympathique, agréable.

likelihood ['laɪklɪhʊd] n probabilité f / *there is little likelihood of us still being here* or *that we'll still be here in August* il y a peu de chances (pour) que nous soyons encore là en août. ❖ **in all likelihood** adv phr vraisemblablement, selon toute vraisemblance.

likely ['laɪklɪ] (*compar* likelier, *superl* likeliest) ◆ adj **1.** [probable] probable / *it's not* or *hardly likely to happen* il est peu probable or il y a peu de chances que cela se produise **2.** [promising] prometteur. ◆ adv probablement, sans doute / *would you do it again? — not likely!* inf tu recommencerais ? — ça risque pas or y a pas de risque !

Note that il est probable que and il y a des chances que are followed by a verb in the subjunctive :
It's likely that no one survived. Il est probable que personne n'ait survécu.
He's likely to go to Paris later in the year. Il y a des chances qu'il aille à Paris plus tard dans l'année.

like-minded [-'maɪndɪd] adj : *like-minded people* des gens ayant la même vision des choses.

liken ['laɪkn] vt comparer.

likeness ['laɪknɪs] n **1.** [resemblance] ressemblance f **2.** [portrait] portrait m.

likewise ['laɪkwaɪz] adv **1.** [similarly] de même / *pleased to meet you — likewise* ravi de vous rencontrer — moi de même **2.** [by the same token] de même, de plus, en outre.

liking ['laɪkɪŋ] n **1.** [affection] sympathie f, affection f ▶ **to take a liking to sb** se prendre d'amitié pour qqn **2.** [taste] goût m, penchant m / *is everything to your liking?* est-ce que tout est à votre convenance ?

lilac ['laɪlək] ◆ n [colour, flower] lilas m. ◆ adj [colour] lilas (inv).

Lilo® ['laɪləʊ] (pl **Lilos**) n matelas m pneumatique.

lilt [lɪlt] n **1.** [in voice] modulation f **2.** [in music] rythme m, cadence f.

lilting ['lɪltɪŋ] adj **1.** [voice, accent] mélodieux **2.** [music, tune] chantant, mélodieux.

lily ['lɪlɪ] (pl **lilies**) n lis m, lys m ▶ **lily of the valley** muguet m.

lily-livered [-'lɪvəd] adj inf froussard.

Lima ['liːmə] pr n Lima.

limb [lɪm] n **1.** ANAT membre m **2.** [of tree] (grosse) branche f.

limber ['lɪmbər] ◆ adj souple, agile. ◆ n [of gun carriage] avant-train m. ❖ **limber up** vi SPORT s'échauffer, faire des assouplissements.

limbo ['lɪmbəʊ] n **1.** (U) RELIG limbes mpl **2.** COMPUT ▶ **limbo file** fichier m temporaire **3.** (pl **limbos**) DANCE limbo m **4.** fig ▶ **to be in (a state of) limbo** être dans l'incertitude.

lime [laɪm] ◆ n **1.** AGR & CHEM chaux f **2.** [fruit] citron m vert, lime f, limette f ▶ **lime cordial / juice** sirop m / jus m de citron vert ▶ **lager and lime** bière f blonde au sirop de citron vert **3.** [citrus tree] limettier m **4.** [linden] ▶ **lime (tree)** tilleul m. ◆ vt **1.** AGR [soil] chauler **2.** [with birdlime - branch, bird] engluer.

lime green n vert m citron.

limelight ['laɪmlaɪt] n (U) THEAT feux mpl de la rampe ▶ **to be in the limelight** être sous les feux de la rampe, occuper le devant de la scène.

limerick ['lɪmərɪk] n limerick m (*poème absurde ou indécent en cinq vers, dont les rimes doivent suivre un ordre précis*).

Limerick

Le **limerick** est un petit poème humoristique de cinq vers dont les rimes suivent la séquence « aabba ». La forme fut popularisée par l'écrivain **Edward Lear** (1812-1888). Parmi ses limericks les plus connus, on trouve :

There was an Old Man with a beard,
Who said, "It is just as I feared!
Two Owls and a Hen,
Four Larks and a Wren,
Have all built their nests in my beard!".

Aujourd'hui les limericks ont souvent un caractère grivois.

limestone ['laɪmstəʊn] n calcaire m, roche f calcaire.

limey ['laɪmɪ] ◆ n 🇺🇸 *inf & pej* [English person] ≃ Angliche *mf*. ◆ adj ≃ angliche.

limit ['lɪmɪt] ◆ n **1.** [boundary, greatest extent, maximum] limite *f* / *I know my limits* je connais mes limites, je sais ce dont je suis capable / *our resources are stretched to the limit* nos ressources sont utilisées au maximum / *I'd like to help but there are limits* je veux bien aider mais il y a des limites / *I agree with you, within limits* je suis d'accord avec toi, jusqu'à un certain point ▸ **off limits** interdit d'accès ▸ **that's the (absolute) limit!** c'est le comble ! / *she really is the limit!* elle dépasse vraiment les bornes ! **2.** [restriction] limitation *f* ▸ **to put** or **to set a limit on sthg** limiter qqch ▸ **weight limit** limitation de poids ▸ **to be over the limit** 🇬🇧 [driver] dépasser le taux d'alcoolémie autorisé. ◆ vt limiter.

limitation [,lɪmɪ'teɪʃn] n **1.** [restriction, control] limitation *f*, restriction *f* ▸ **arms limitation talks** négociations *fpl* sur la limitation des armements **2.** [shortcoming] limite *f* **3.** LAW prescription *f*.

limited ['lɪmɪtɪd] adj [restricted] limité, restreint / *to a limited extent* jusqu'à un certain point.

limited company n société *f* à responsabilité limitée, SARL *f*.

limited edition n édition *f* à tirage limité.

limited liability company = **limited company**.

limitless ['lɪmɪtlɪs] adj illimité.

limo ['lɪməʊ] (*pl* limos) *inf* = **limousine**.

limousine ['lɪməziːn] n limousine *f*.

limp [lɪmp] ◆ vi boiter ; [slightly] clopiner. ◆ n ▸ **to walk with a limp** boiter. ◆ adj **1.** [cloth, lettuce, handshake] mou (*before vowel or silent 'h'* **mol**, *f* **molle**) ; [skin] flasque **2.** [book - cover, binding] souple.

limpet ['lɪmpɪt] n ZOOL patelle *f*, bernique *f*, chapeau *m* chinois.

limpid ['lɪmpɪd] adj limpide.

limply ['lɪmplɪ] adv mollement.

limp-wristed [-'rɪstɪd] adj *pej* efféminé.

linchpin ['lɪntʃpɪn] n *fig* [person] pivot *m*.

Lincs written abbr of **Lincolnshire**.

linctus ['lɪŋktəs] n sirop *m* (pour la toux).

line [laɪn] ◆ n **1.** [mark, stroke] ligne *f*, trait *m* ; [wrinkle] ride *f* ; MATH, SPORT & TV ligne / *to draw a line* tracer or tirer une ligne / *straight line* **a)** MATH droite *f* **b)** [gen] ligne *f* droite **2.** [path] ligne *f* / *light travels in a straight line* la lumière se propage en ligne droite ▸ **line of thinking** : *I don't follow your line of thinking* je ne suis pas ton raisonnement ▸ **line of duty** : *it's all in the line of duty* cela fait partie de mes fonctions / *the problems I meet in the line of duty* les problèmes auxquels je suis confronté dans l'exercice de mes fonctions / *there's been a terrible mistake somewhere along the line* il s'est produit une erreur grave quelque part / *I'll support them all along* or *right down the line* je les soutiendrai jusqu'au bout or sur toute la ligne / *the population is split along religious lines* la population est divisée selon des critères religieux / *another idea along the same lines* une autre idée dans le même genre / *we seem to be thinking along the same lines* il semble que nous voyions les choses de la même façon ▸ **to be on the right lines** être sur la bonne voie **3.** [row - side by side] ligne *f*, rang *m*, rangée *f* ; [-one behind another] rang *m*, file *f* ▸ **to step into line** se mettre en rang ; 🇺🇸 [queue] file *f* (d'attente), queue *f* ; *fig* : *he's in line for promotion* il est sur les rangs pour une promotion **4.** *fig* [conformity] : *it's in / out of line with company policy* c'est conforme / ce n'est pas conforme à la politique de la société / *it's more or less in line with what we'd*

expected cela correspond plus ou moins à nos prévisions / *the rebels have been brought into line* les rebelles ont été mis au pas / *to fall into line with government policy* accepter la politique gouvernementale ▸ **to step out of line** s'écarter du droit chemin **5.** [of writing, text] ligne *f* / *she gave me 100 lines* SCH elle m'a donné 100 lignes (à faire) ; [of poem, song] vers *m* ; THEAT réplique *f* **6.** [rope] corde *f* ; NAUT bout *m* ; FISHING ligne *f* / *to hang the washing on the line* mettre le linge à sécher, étendre le linge **7.** 🇬🇧 RAIL [track] voie *f* ; [single rail] rail *m* **8.** [travel route] ligne *f* / *there's a new coach line to London* il y a un nouveau service d'autocars pour Londres / *to keep the lines of communication open* maintenir ouvertes les lignes de communication ; [transport company] compagnie *f* **9.** ELEC ligne *f* / *the power station comes on line in June* la centrale entre en service en juin **10.** TELEC ligne *f* / *the line went dead* la communication a été coupée / *I was on the line to Paris* je téléphonais à Paris / *then a voice came on the other end of the line* alors une voix a répondu à l'autre bout du fil ▸ **hold the line** ne quittez pas ▸ **on line** COMPUT en ligne **11.** [outline] ligne *f* / *can you explain the main* or *broad lines of the project to me?* pouvez-vous m'expliquer les grandes lignes du projet ? **12.** [policy] ligne *f* / *they took a hard* or *tough line on terrorism* ils ont adopté une politique de fermeté envers le terrorisme **13.** MIL ligne *f* **14.** [boundary] frontière *f*, limite *f* / *the (dividing) line between frankness and rudeness* la limite entre la franchise et l'impolitesse ▸ **the poverty line** le seuil de pauvreté **15.** [field of activity] branche *f* ; [job] métier *m* / *she's in the same line (of work) as you* elle travaille dans la même branche que toi / *what line (of business) are you in?* or *what's your line (of business)?* qu'est-ce que vous faites dans la vie ? ; [field of interest] domaine *m* / *that's more in Katy's line* c'est plus du domaine de Katy / *opera isn't really my line* l'opéra n'est pas vraiment mon genre **16.** [range - of products] ligne *f* / *they produce* or *do an interesting line in chairs* ils produisent une gamme intéressante de chaises ▸ **product line** gamme *f* or ligne de produits **17.** [lineage, ancestry] lignée *f* ▸ **line of descent** filiation *f*. ◆ vt **1.** [road, river] border / *the avenue is lined with trees* l'avenue est bordée d'arbres / *crowds lined the streets* la foule était or s'était massée sur les trottoirs **2.** [paper] régler, ligner **3.** [clothes, curtains] doubler ; [container, drawer, cupboard] tapisser, garnir ; [brakes] garnir / *lined with silk* doublé de soie / *walls lined with books* des murs tapissés de livres ▸ **to line one's pockets** *inf* s'en mettre plein les poches. ◆ **line up** ◆ vt sep **1.** [put in line - objects] aligner, mettre en ligne ; [- people] faire aligner **2.** [bring into alignment] aligner **3.** *inf* [prepare, arrange] préparer, prévoir / *I've got a treat lined up for the kids* j'ai préparé une surprise pour les gosses. ◆ vi [stand in line] s'aligner, se mettre en ligne ; 🇺🇸 [queue up] faire la queue.

lineage ['lɪnɪɪdʒ] n [ancestry] ascendance *f*, famille *f* ; [descendants] lignée *f*, descendance *f*.

linear ['lɪnɪə*r*] adj linéaire.

linebacker ['laɪn,bækə*r*] n SPORT secondeur *m*, -euse *f*.

lined [laɪnd] adj **1.** [paper] réglé **2.** [face, skin] ridé **3.** [jacket] doublé ; [box] tapissé.

line dancing n line *m* dancing.

line drawing n dessin *m* au trait.

line feed n saut *m* de ligne.

line judge n SPORT juge *m* de ligne.

linen ['lɪnɪn] ◆ n **1.** [fabric] (toile *f* de) lin *m* **2.** [sheets, tablecloths, towels, etc.] linge *m* (de maison) ; [underclothes] linge *m* (de corps) ▸ **table linen** linge de table. ◆ comp de fil, de lin.

linen basket n corbeille *f* à linge.

line-out n SPORT touche *f*, remise *f* en jeu.

line printer n imprimante f ligne à ligne.

liner ['laɪnəʳ] n **1.** [ship] paquebot m (de grande ligne) **2.** [eyeliner] eye-liner m **3.** [for clothing] doublure f **4.** TECH chemise f.

linesman ['laɪnzmən] (pl **linesmen** [-mən]) n **1.** SPORT [in rugby, football] juge m or arbitre m de touche ; [in tennis] juge m de ligne **2.** UK ELEC & TELEC monteur m or ouvrier m de ligne.

lineup ['laɪnʌp] n **1.** [identity parade] séance f d'identification ; [line of suspects] rangée f de suspects **2.** [composition] : the England lineup for tonight's match la composition de l'équipe anglaise pour le match de ce soir / we have an all-star lineup for tonight's programme nous avons un plateau de vedettes pour l'émission de ce soir.

linger ['lɪŋgəʳ] vi **1.** [persist] persister, subsister **2.** [tarry] s'attarder, traîner **3.** [stay alive] : she might linger on for years yet il se pourrait qu'elle tienne encore des années.

lingerie ['lænʒərɪ] n lingerie f.

lingering ['lɪŋgrɪŋ] adj [long] long (longue) ; [persistent] persistant ; [slow] lent.

lingo ['lɪŋgəʊ] (pl **lingoes**) n inf : I don't speak the lingo je ne parle pas la langue du pays.

lingonberry ['lɪŋgənberɪ] n airelle f rouge.

linguist ['lɪŋgwɪst] n **1.** [in foreign languages - student] étudiant m, -e f en langues étrangères ; [- specialist] spécialiste mf en langues étrangères **2.** [in linguistics] linguiste mf.

linguistic [lɪŋ'gwɪstɪk] adj linguistique.

linguistics [lɪŋ'gwɪstɪks] n (U) linguistique f.

liniment ['lɪnɪmənt] n pommade f.

lining ['laɪnɪŋ] n **1.** [of clothes, curtains] doublure f **2.** [of container, bearing] revêtement m ; [of brake, clutch] garniture f **3.** ANAT paroi f interne.

link [lɪŋk] ◆ n **1.** [of chain] chaînon m, maillon m **2.** [bond, relationship] lien m / she's severed all links with her family elle a coupé les ponts avec sa famille / the link between inflation and unemployment le lien or rapport entre l'inflation et le chômage **3.** [physical connection] liaison f ▶ a road / rail / radio link une liaison routière / ferroviaire / radio. ◆ vt **1.** [relate] lier **2.** [connect physically] relier. ❖ **link up** ◆ vi **1.** [meet - persons] se rejoindre ; [- troops] effectuer une jonction ; [- spacecraft] s'arrimer **2.** [form a partnership] s'associer **3.** [be connected] se relier. ◆ vt sep relier.

linkage ['lɪŋkɪdʒ] n lien m, rapport m.

link road n route f de jonction.

link rot n INTERNET problème de validité d'un lien hypertexte qui pointe vers une ressource qui n'existe plus.

links [lɪŋks] pl n (terrain m or parcours m de) golf m, links mpl.

linkup ['lɪŋkʌp] n **1.** [physical connection] liaison f **2.** [of spacecraft, troops] jonction f.

lino ['laɪnəʊ] n UK lino m.

linoleum [lɪ'nəʊljəm] n linoléum m.

linseed ['lɪnsiːd] n graine f de lin.

lint [lɪnt] n (U) **1.** [fabric] tissu m gratté ▶ **lint bandage** charpie f **2.** US [fluff] peluches fpl.

lintel ['lɪntl] n linteau m.

lion ['laɪən] n **1.** ZOOL lion m **2.** fig [courageous person] lion m, lionne f ; [celebrity] célébrité f.

lion cub n lionceau m.

lioness ['laɪənes] n lionne f.

lionize, lionise ['laɪənaɪz] vt [treat like a celebrity] porter aux nues.

lion-tamer n dompteur m, -euse f (de lions).

lip [lɪp] n **1.** [human] lèvre f ; [animal] lèvre f, babine f **2.** [of jug] bec m ; [of cup, bowl] rebord m ; [of wound] lèvre f, bord m ; [of crater] bord m **3.** inf [impertinence] culot m.

lip balm n baume m pour les lèvres.

lip gloss n brillant m à lèvres.

liposuction ['lɪpəʊ,sʌkʃn] n liposuccion f.

-lipped [lɪpt] suffix : thin-lipped aux lèvres minces or fines.

lippy ['lɪpɪ] (compar **lippier**, superl **lippiest**) adj inf insolent, culotté.

lip-read ['lɪpriːd] (pt & pp **lip-read** ['lɪpred]) ◆ vi lire sur les lèvres. ◆ vt lire sur les lèvres de.

lip-reading n lecture f sur les lèvres.

lip salve n pommade f or baume m pour les lèvres.

lipstick ['lɪpstɪk] n **1.** [substance] rouge m à lèvres ▶ **lipstick lesbian** inf lesbienne f très féminine **2.** [stick] (tube m de) rouge m à lèvres.

lip-synch [-sɪŋk] ◆ vi chanter en play-back. ◆ vt ▶ **to lip-synch a song** chanter une chanson en play-back.

liquefy ['lɪkwɪfaɪ] (pt & pp **liquefied**) ◆ vt liquéfier. ◆ vi se liquéfier.

liqueur [lɪ'kjʊəʳ] n liqueur f.

liquid ['lɪkwɪd] ◆ adj **1.** [fluid] liquide **2.** FIN liquide ▶ **liquid assets** liquidités fpl **3.** [clear - eyes, sound] limpide **4.** LING [consonant] liquide. ◆ n **1.** [fluid] liquide m **2.** LING [consonant] liquide f.

liquidate ['lɪkwɪdeɪt] ◆ vt **1.** euph [kill, eliminate] liquider, éliminer **2.** FIN & LAW [debt, company, estate] liquider ; [capital] mobiliser. ◆ vi FIN & LAW entrer en liquidation, déposer son bilan.

liquidation [,lɪkwɪ'deɪʃn] n **1.** euph [killing, elimination] liquidation f **2.** FIN & LAW [of debt, company, estate] liquidation f ; [of capital] mobilisation f ▶ **to go into liquidation** entrer en liquidation, déposer son bilan.

liquidator ['lɪkwɪdeɪtəʳ] n liquidateur m, -trice f.

liquid crystal display n affichage m à cristaux liquides.

liquidity [lɪ'kwɪdətɪ] n liquidité f.

liquidize, liquidise ['lɪkwɪdaɪz] vt **1.** CULIN passer au mixeur **2.** PHYS liquéfier.

liquidizer, liquidiser ['lɪkwɪdaɪzəʳ] n UK mixer m, mixeur m.

liquefied petroleum gas ['lɪkwɪfaɪd-] n gaz m de pétrole liquéfié.

liquor ['lɪkəʳ] n **1.** US [alcohol] alcool m, boissons fpl alcoolisées **2.** CULIN jus m, bouillon m **3.** PHARM solution f aqueuse.

liquorice UK, **licorice** US ['lɪkərɪs] n [plant, root] réglisse f ; [sweet] réglisse f ▶ **liquorice allsorts** bonbons à la réglisse de différentes couleurs.

liquor store n US magasin m de vins et spiritueux.

lira ['lɪərə] (pl **lire** [-rɪ] or **liras**) n lire f.

Lisbon ['lɪzbən] pr n Lisbonne.

lisp [lɪsp] ◆ vi parler avec un cheveu sur la langue, zézayer. ◆ vt dire en zézayant. ◆ n ▶ **to speak with** or **to have a lisp** avoir un cheveu sur la langue, zézayer.

list [lɪst] ◆ n **1.** [record] liste f ▶ **to make** or **to write a list** faire or dresser une liste **2.** [lean] inclinaison f ; NAUT gîte f, bande f. ◆ vt **1.** [make list of] dresser la liste de ; [enumerate] énumérer ; [enter in a list] inscrire (sur une liste) **2.** [classify] classer / they are listed by family name ils sont classés par nom de famille **3.** [price] : what are the new *laptops listed at?* les nouveaux portables sont vendus combien ? **4.** COMPUT lister **5.** ST. EX [shares] coter. ◆ vi [lean] pencher, être incliné ; NAUT [ship] gîter, donner de la bande.

list administrator n INTERNET administrateur *m*, -trice *f* de liste.

listed building ['lɪstɪd-] Ⓤ monument *m* classé.

listed company ['lɪstɪd-] n Ⓤ société *f* cotée en Bourse.

listen ['lɪsn] ◆ vi **1.** [to sound] écouter ▶ **to listen to sb / sthg** écouter qqn / qqch **2.** [take notice - of advice] écouter / *if only I'd listened to my mother!* si seulement j'avais écouté ma mère or suivi les conseils de ma mère ! ◆ n *inf* : *have a listen to their latest album* écoute un peu leur dernier album. ❖ **listen (out) for** vt insep guetter, être à l'affût de. ❖ **listen in** vi **1.** [to radio] écouter, être à l'écoute **2.** [eavesdrop] écouter / *it's rude to listen in on other people's conversations* c'est impoli d'écouter les conversations. ❖ **listen up** vi *inf* : *hey you guys, listen up!* hé, écoutez un peu !

listener ['lɪsnə*] n **1.** personne *f* qui écoute / *he's a good / bad listener* il sait / il ne sait pas écouter (les autres) **2.** RADIO auditeur *m*, -trice *f*.

listening device n dispositif *m* d'écoute.

listeria [lɪs'tiːrɪə] n listeria *f*.

listing ['lɪstɪŋ] n **1.** [gen - list] liste *f* ; [- entry] entrée *f* / *I found no listing for the company in the directory* je n'ai pas trouvé la société dans l'annuaire **2.** COMPUT listing *m*, listage *m*. ❖ **listings** pl n ▶ **cinema / TV listings** programme *m* des films / émissions de la semaine ▶ **listings magazine / website** magazine *m* / site *m* de programmes télé et cinéma.

listless ['lɪstlɪs] adj [torpid, unenergetic] apathique, endormi, avachi ; [weak] mou *(before vowel or silent 'h' mol, f molle)*, inerte ; [bored] indolent, alangui ; [indifferent] indifférent, insensible.

listlessly ['lɪstlɪslɪ] adv [without energy] sans énergie or vigueur, avec apathie ; [weakly] mollement ; [without interest] d'un air absent.

list price n prix *m* du catalogue.

list server n serveur *m* de liste (de diffusion).

lit [lɪt] ◆ pt & pp ⟶ **light**. ◆ adj **1.** éclairé **2.** Ⓤ *inf* [drunk] soûl, allumé. ◆ n (**abbr of literature**) *inf* : *she teaches English lit* elle enseigne la littérature anglaise.

litany ['lɪtənɪ] *(pl litanies)* n *lit & fig* litanie *f*.

liter Ⓤ = **litre**.

literacy ['lɪtərəsɪ] n [of individual] capacité *f* de lire et d'écrire ; [of population] alphabétisation *f* ▶ **adult literacy** l'alphabétisation des adultes.

literal ['lɪtərəl] adj [meaning] propre, littéral ; [translation] littéral, mot à mot.

literally ['lɪtərəlɪ] adv **1.** [not figuratively] littéralement, au sens propre ; [word for word] littéralement **2.** [in exaggeration] littéralement.

literary ['lɪtərərɪ] adj **1.** [style, work, etc.] littéraire **2.** [formal, written - language] littéraire.

literary agent n agent *m* littéraire.

literate ['lɪtərət] adj **1.** [able to read and write] capable de lire et d'écrire **2.** [educated] instruit, cultivé.

-literate suffix ▶ **to be computer-literate** avoir des connaissances en informatique.

literati [ˌlɪtə'rɑːtɪ] pl n *fml* gens *mpl* de lettres, lettrés *mpl*.

literature ['lɪtrətʃə*] n (U) **1.** [creative writing] littérature *f* **2.** [printed material] documentation *f* ▶ **sales literature** documentation *f*, brochures *fpl* de vente.

lithe [laɪð] adj [movement, person] agile ; [body] souple.

lithium ['lɪθɪəm] n lithium *m*.

lithograph ['lɪθəgrɑːf] ◆ n lithographie *f (estampe)*. ◆ vt lithographier.

lithography [lɪ'θɒgrəfɪ] n lithographie *f (procédé)*.

Lithuania [ˌlɪθjʊ'eɪnjə] pr n Lituanie *f* / *in Lithuania* en Lituanie.

Lithuanian [ˌlɪθjʊ'eɪnjən] ◆ n **1.** [person] Lituanien *m*, -enne *f* **2.** LING lituanien *m*. ◆ adj lituanien.

litigant ['lɪtɪgənt] n LAW plaideur *m*, -euse *f*, partie *f*.

litigate ['lɪtɪgeɪt] ◆ vt LAW contester (en justice). ◆ vi LAW plaider, intenter une action en justice.

litigation [ˌlɪtɪ'geɪʃn] n LAW litige *m*.

litigious [lɪ'tɪdʒəs] adj *fml & pej* [fond of lawsuits] procédurier.

litmus ['lɪtməs] n tournesol *m*.

litre Ⓤ, **liter** Ⓤ ['liːtə*] n litre *m*.

litter ['lɪtə*] ◆ n **1.** (U) [rubbish] détritus *mpl*, ordures *fpl* ; [dropped in street] papiers *mpl* (gras) / **'no litter'** 'respectez la propreté des lieux' **2.** [clutter] fouillis *m* **3.** ZOOL portée *f* **4.** [material - to bed animals] litière *f* ; [- to protect plants] paille *f*, paillis *m* ▶ **litter tray** caisse *f* (pour litière). ◆ vt **1.** [make untidy - public place] laisser des détritus dans ; [- house, room] mettre du désordre dans ; [- desk] encombrer **2.** (usu passive) [cover, strew] joncher, couvrir ; *fig* parsemer. ◆ vi Ⓤ [with rubbish] / **'no littering'** 'respectez la propreté des lieux'.

litter bin n Ⓤ poubelle *f*.

litter lout Ⓤ, **litterbug** Ⓤ ['lɪtəbʌg] n *inf* personne qui jette des papiers ou des détritus par terre.

little¹ ['lɪtl] adj **1.** [in size, quantity] petit / *would you like a little drop of gin?* tu veux un peu de gin ? / *would you like a little something to eat?* voudriez-vous manger un petit quelque chose ? ▶ **the little hand** [of clock] la petite aiguille **2.** [young - child, animal] petit / *when I was little* quand j'étais petit / *my little sister* ma petite sœur **3.** [short - time, distance] : *we spent a little time in France* nous avons passé quelque temps en France / *a little while ago* a) [moments ago] il y a quelques instants b) [days, months ago] il y a quelque temps / *she only stayed (for) a little while* elle n'est pas restée très longtemps / *the shop is a little way along the street* le magasin se trouve un peu plus loin dans la rue **4.** [unimportant] petit / *they had a little argument* ils se sont un peu disputés **5.** [expressing affection, pleasure, irritation] petit / *what a nice little garden!* quel joli petit jardin ! / *a little old lady* une petite vieille / *poor little thing!* pauvre petit !

little² ['lɪtl] (compar **less** [les], superl **least** [liːst]) ◆ det [opposite of 'much'] peu de / *very little time / money* très peu de temps / d'argent / *I watch very little television* je regarde très peu la télévision / *I'm afraid there's little hope left* je crains qu'il n'y ait plus beaucoup d'espoir / *with no little difficulty* *fml* non sans peine. ◆ pron **1.** [small amount] peu grand-chose / *there's little one can say* il n'y a pas grand-chose à dire / *very little is known about his childhood* on ne sait pas grand-chose or on ne sait que très peu de choses sur son enfance / *so little* si peu ▶ **to make little of** a) [fail to understand] ne pas comprendre grand-chose à b) [not emphasize] minimiser c) [scorn] faire peu de cas de **2.** [certain amount] : *a little of everything* un peu de tout / *the little I saw looked excellent* le peu que j'en ai vu paraissait excellent. ◆ adv **1.** [rarely] peu / *we go there as little as possible* nous y allons le moins possible / *we talk very little now* nous ne nous parlons presque plus **2.** *fml* [never] : *I little thought or little did I think we would be friends one day* jamais je n'aurais cru que nous serions amis un jour. ❖ **a little**

◆ det phr un peu de / *I speak a little French* je parle quelques mots de français. ◆ pron phr un peu. ◆ adv phr **1.** [slightly] un peu / *I'm a little tired* je suis un peu fatigué **2.** [for a short time or distance] un peu. ❖ **a little bit** adv phr *inf* = **a little.** ❖ **little by little** adv phr peu à peu, petit à petit.

little finger n auriculaire *m*, petit doigt *m*.

little-known adj peu connu.

little toe n petit orteil *m*.

liturgy ['lɪtədʒɪ] (*pl* **liturgies**) n liturgie *f*.

livable ['lɪvəbl] adj *inf* **1.** [inhabitable] habitable **2.** [bearable] supportable.

live¹ [lɪv] ◆ vi **1.** [be or stay alive] vivre / *as long as I live* tant que je vivrai, de mon vivant / *she didn't live long after her son died* elle n'a pas survécu longtemps à son fils / *you'll live!* *iro* tu n'en mourras pas ! **2.** [have a specified way of life] vivre / *to live dangerously* vivre dangereusement / *they lived happily ever after* ils vécurent heureux jusqu'à la fin de leurs jours / *she lives for her children / for skiing* elle ne vit que pour ses enfants / que pour le ski ▶ **live and let live!** *prov* laisse faire ! ▶ **well, you live and learn!** on en apprend tous les jours ! **3.** [reside] habiter / *they live in Rome* ils habitent (à) Rome, ils vivent à Rome / *to live in a flat / a castle* habiter (dans) un appartement / un château / *I live in or on Bank Street* j'habite Bank Street **4.** [support o.s.] vivre / *he lives by teaching* il gagne sa vie en enseignant **5.** [exist fully, intensely] vivre / *she really knows how to live* elle sait vraiment profiter de la vie / *if you haven't been to New York, you haven't lived!* si tu n'es jamais allé à New York, tu n'as rien vu / ◆ vt vivre / *to live a life of poverty* vivre dans la pauvreté / *to live a solitary life* mener une vie solitaire ▶ **to live a lie** être dans une situation fausse ▶ **to live it up** *inf* faire la fête. ❖ **live down** vt sep [recover from - error, disgrace] : *they'll never let him live that down* ils ne lui passeront or pardonneront jamais cela / *you'll never live this down!* [ridicule] tu n'as pas fini d'en entendre parler ! ❖ **live off** vt insep **1.** [sponge off] vivre aux crochets de **2.** [savings] vivre de ; [nuts, berries] se nourrir de / *to live off the land* vivre de la terre. ❖ **live on** ◆ vi [person] continuer à vivre ; [custom, ideal] persister. ◆ vt insep **1.** [food] vivre de, se nourrir de **2.** [salary] vivre de / *to live on $800 a month* vivre avec 800 dollars par mois. ❖ **live out** vt sep **1.** [spend] passer **2.** [fulfil] vivre / *he lived out his destiny* sa destinée s'est accomplie, il a suivi son destin. ◆ vi : *he studies here but lives out* il est étudiant ici mais il n'habite pas sur le campus. ❖ **live through** vt insep connaître / *they've lived through war and famine* ils ont connu la guerre et la famine. ❖ **live together** vi [as a couple] vivre ensemble, cohabiter. ❖ **live up to** vt insep [name, reputation] se montrer à la hauteur de ; [expectation] être or se montrer à la hauteur de, répondre à / *we have a reputation to live up to!* nous avons une réputation à défendre ! ❖ **live with** vt insep **1.** [cohabit with] vivre avec **2.** [put up with] : *she's not easy to live with* elle n'est pas facile à vivre / *I don't like the situation, but I have to live with it* cette situation ne me plaît pas, mais je n'ai pas le choix.

live² [laɪv] ◆ adj **1.** [alive - animal, person] vivant / *a real live cowboy* *inf* un cow-boy, un vrai de vrai / *a live contender* un concurrent sérieux ▶ **live births** naissances *fpl* viables ▶ **live yoghurt** yaourt *m* actif **2.** MUS, RADIO & TV [programme, interview, concert] en direct / *Sinatra live at the Palladium* Sinatra en concert au Palladium / *recorded before a live audience* enregistré en public ▶ **live music** musique *f* live ▶ **live recording** enregistrement *m* live or public **3.** ELEC [connected] sous tension / *live circuit* circuit *m* alimenté or sous tension **4.** [unexploded] non explosé / *live ammunition* balles *fpl* réelles **5.** [still burning - coals, embers] ardent **6.** [not extinct - volcano] actif **7.** [controver-

sial] controversé / *a live issue* un sujet controversé. ◆ adv en direct / *the match can be seen / is going out live at 3.30 p.m.* on peut suivre le match / le match est diffusé en direct à 15 h 30.

lived-in ['lɪvdɪn] adj [comfortable] confortable ; [occupied] habité.

live-in ['lɪv-] adj [maid] logé et nourri ; [nurse, governess] à demeure.

livelihood ['laɪvlɪhʊd] n *(U)* moyens *mpl* d'existence, gagne-pain *m inv*.

liveliness ['laɪvlɪnɪs] n [of person] vivacité *f* ; [of conversation, party] animation *f* ; [of debate, style] vigueur *f* ; [of music, dance] gaieté *f*, allégresse *f* ; [of colours] éclat *m*, gaieté *f*.

lively ['laɪvlɪ] (*compar* **livelier,** *superl* **liveliest**) adj **1.** [full of life - person] vif, plein d'entrain ; [- kitten, puppy] plein de vie, espiègle ; [- horse] fringant ; [- music] gai, entraînant **2.** [keen - mind, curiosity, imagination] vif ▶ **to take a lively interest in sthg** s'intéresser vivement à qqch **3.** [exciting - place, event, discussion] animé **4.** [eventful - day, time] mouvementé, agité **5.** [brisk - pace] vif **6.** [vivid - colour] vif, éclatant.

liven up ['laɪvn] ◆ vt sep **1.** [make cheerful - person, room] égayer **2.** [stimulate, make interesting] animer. ◆ vi s'animer.

liver ['lɪvər] n **1.** ANAT foie *m* **2.** CULIN foie *m* ▶ **liver pâté** pâté *m* de foie **3.** [colour] rouge brun *m inv*, brun roux *m inv* **4.** [person] ▶ **fast** or **high liver** fêtard *m*, -e *f*, noceur *m*, -euse *f*.

Liverpudlian [,lɪvə'pʌdlɪən] ◆ n habitant de Liverpool. ◆ adj de Liverpool.

liver sausage n 🇬🇧 pâté *m* de foie.

liver spot n tache *f* de vieillesse.

liverwurst ['lɪvəwɜːst] 🇺🇸 = **liver sausage.**

livery ['lɪvərɪ] (*pl* **liveries**) n **1.** [uniform] livrée *f* **2.** [of company] couleurs *fpl*.

lives [laɪvz] pl ⟶ **life.**

livestock ['laɪvstɒk] n *(U)* bétail *m*, cheptel *m*.

live wire ['laɪv-] n **1.** ELEC fil *m* sous tension **2.** *inf & fig* : *she's a real live wire* elle déborde d'énergie.

livid ['lɪvɪd] adj **1.** [blue-grey] livide **2.** *inf* [angry] furax.

living ['lɪvɪŋ] ◆ n **1.** [livelihood] vie *f* / *I have to work for a living* je suis obligé de travailler pour vivre / *what do you do for a living?* qu'est-ce que vous faites dans la vie ? **2.** [life, lifestyle] vie *f* **3.** 🇬🇧 RELIG bénéfice *m*. ◆ adj [alive] vivant. ◆ pl n ▶ **the living** les vivants *mpl*. ◆ comp **1.** [conditions] de vie ▶ **living expenses** frais *mpl* de subsistance ▶ **living standards** niveau *m* de vie **2.** [place] ▶ **living area** : *the living area is separated from the bedrooms* la partie séjour est séparée des chambres ▶ **living environment** cadre *m* de vie ▶ **living quarters** [for servants] logements *mpl* ; [on ship] partie *f* habitée.

living-flame adj : *living-flame gas fire* chauffage au gaz à flammes réelles, imitant un feu de charbon.

living room n (salle *f* de) séjour *m*.

living wage n ▶ **a living wage** le minimum vital.

lizard ['lɪzəd] ◆ n lézard *m*. ◆ comp [belt, shoes] en lézard.

llama ['lɑːmə] n ZOOL lama *m*.

LLB (abbr of **Bachelor of Laws**) n ≈ (titulaire d'une) licence de droit.

LLD (abbr of **Doctor of Laws**) n ≈ docteur en droit.

LLDC (abbr of **least-developed country**) n PMD *m*.

LMAO (written abbr of **laughing my ass off**) MESSAGING MDR.

LMBO (abbr of **leveraged management buyout**) n RES *m*.

LMT (abbr of **Local Mean Time**) n *heure locale*.

lo [ləʊ] interj PHR **lo and behold** : *and lo and behold there he was!* et voilà, il était là !

load [ləʊd] ◆ vt **1.** [person, animal, vehicle] charger ▸ **to load sthg with sthg** charger qqch sur qqch / *load the bags into the car* chargez or mettez les sacs dans la voiture **2.** [camera, gun, machine] charger / *to load a film / tape* mettre une pellicule / une cassette / *load the cassette into the recorder* introduisez la cassette dans le magnétophone **3.** [insurance premium] majorer, augmenter. ◆ vi **1.** [receive freight] charger **2.** [camera, gun] se recharger ; [computer program] se charger. ◆ n **1.** [cargo] charge *f*, chargement *m* ; [carrying capacity] charge *f* **2.** fig [burden] fardeau *m*, charge *f* **3.** [batch of laundry] machine *f* **4.** ELEC, CONSTR & TECH charge *f*. ◆ comp COMPUT [program] de chargement ; [module] chargeable ▸ **load mode** mode *m* chargement. **a load of** det phr : *what a load of rubbish!* inf c'est vraiment n'importe quoi ! **loads** adv inf beaucoup. **loads of** det phr inf des tas or des masses de. **load down** vt sep charger (lourdement) / *he was loaded down with packages* il avait des paquets plein les bras. **load up** ◆ vt sep charger / *load the wheelbarrow up with bricks* remplissez la brouette de briques. ◆ vi charger.

loaded [ˈləʊdɪd] adj **1.** [laden] chargé **2.** fig ▸ **to be loaded with** être chargé de or plein de **3.** [gun, camera] chargé **4.** [dice] pipé **5.** [statement, comment] insidieux ▸ **loaded question** question *f* piège **6.** inf [rich] plein aux as **7.** v inf [drunk] plein, bourré ; [high on drugs] défoncé, cassé.

loading bay n aire *f* de chargement.

loaf [ləʊf] (pl **loaves** [ləʊvz]) ◆ n **1.** [of bread] pain *m* ; [large round loaf] miche *f* **2.** PHR **use your loaf!** UK inf fais travailler tes méninges ! ◆ vi inf fainéanter, traîner.

loafer [ˈləʊfər] n **1.** inf [person] fainéant *m*, -e *f* **2.** [shoe] mocassin *m*.

loam [ləʊm] n **1.** AGR & HORT terreau *m* **2.** CONSTR pisé *m*.

loan [ləʊn] ◆ n **1.** [money lent] prêt *m* ; [money borrowed] emprunt *m* **2.** [act of lending] : *may I have the loan of your typewriter?* UK peux-tu me prêter ta machine à écrire ? / *I have three books on loan from the library* j'ai emprunté trois livres à la bibliothèque / *the book you want is out on loan* le livre que vous voulez est sorti **3.** = **loanword**. ◆ vt prêter ▸ **to loan sb sthg, to loan sthg to sb** prêter qqch à qqn.

loan account n compte *m* de prêt.

loan capital n capital *m* d'emprunt.

loan shark n pej usurier *m*, -ère *f*.

loanword [ˈləʊnwɜːd] n LING (mot *m* d')emprunt *m*.

loath [ləʊθ] adj ▸ **to be loath to do sthg** ne pas être disposé à faire qqch.

loathe [ləʊð] vt détester / *I loathe having to get up in the mornings* j'ai horreur d'être obligé de me lever le matin.

loathing [ˈləʊðɪŋ] n aversion *f*, répugnance *f*.

loathsome [ˈləʊðsəm] adj [behaviour] abominable ; [person] détestable.

loaves [ləʊvz] pl ⟶ **loaf**.

lob [lɒb] (pt & pp **lobbed**, cont **lobbing**) ◆ n SPORT lob *m*. ◆ vt **1.** [throw] lancer **2.** SPORT [ball] envoyer haut ; [opponent] lober. ◆ vi SPORT [player] faire un lob.

lobby [ˈlɒbɪ] (pl **lobbies**, pt & pp **lobbied**) ◆ n **1.** [in hotel] hall *m* ; THEAT foyer *m* ; [in large house, apartment block] entrée *f* **2.** POL [pressure group] groupe *m* de pression, lobby *m* ; [action] pression *f* **3.** UK POL [hall] salle *f* des pas perdus. ◆ vi : *ecologists are lobbying for the closure of the plant* les écologistes font pression pour obtenir la fermeture de la centrale. ◆ vt [person, parliament] exercer une pression sur.

lobbying [ˈlɒbɪɪŋ] n (U) POL pressions *fpl*.

lobbyist [ˈlɒbɪɪst] n lobbyiste *mf*, membre *m* d'un groupe de pression.

lobe [ləʊb] n ANAT, BOT & RADIO lobe *m*.

lobelia [ləˈbiːljə] n BOT lobélie *f*.

lobotomy [ləˈbɒtəmɪ] (pl **lobotomies**) n lobotomie *f*, leucotomie *f*.

lobster [ˈlɒbstər] (pl **lobster** or **lobsters**) n homard *m*.

local [ˈləʊkl] ◆ adj **1.** [of the immediate area - tradition] local ; [- hospital, shop] de quartier ; [- inhabitants] du quartier, du coin **2.** ADMIN & POL [services, council] local, communal, municipal **3.** MED [infection, pain] localisé. ◆ n **1.** [person] habitant *m*, -e *f* (du lieu) ▸ **the locals** les gens *m* du pays or du coin **2.** UK inf [pub] troquet *m* du coin **3.** US [train] omnibus *m* ; [bus] bus *m* local **4.** US [union branch] section *f* syndicale **5.** inf MED anesthésie *f* locale **6.** US PRESS [item] nouvelle *f* locale.

local anaesthetic, local anesthetic US n anesthésie *f* locale.

local area network n COMPUT réseau *m* local.

local authority n administration *f* locale ; [in town] municipalité *f*.

local call n communication *f* urbaine.

local colour n couleur *f* locale.

locale [ləʊˈkɑːl] n [place] endroit *m*, lieu *m* ; [scene, setting] cadre *m*.

local education authority n direction *f* régionale de l'enseignement (en Angleterre et au pays de Galles).

local government n administration *f* municipale ▸ **local government elections** élections *fpl* municipales ▸ **local government official** fonctionnaire *mf* de l'administration municipale.

 Local government

■ *Au Royaume-Uni*

Chaque comté (**county**) en Angleterre est géré par un conseil municipal (**county council**). Les comtés sont divisés en **districts** (chacun ayant son **district council**), divisés à leur tour en **parishes** (paroisses). Les comtés où se trouvent les plus grandes villes (Birmingham, Sheffield, Leeds...) ont le statut de **metropolitan counties** et bénéficient d'une gestion spécifique. Londres a son propre système de gouvernement, avec une assemblée élue (**the London Assembly**) et un maire; onze autres municipalités ont également un maire élu. Les **councils** sont constitués de membres élus, avec un **council leader** (sauf dans les 12 municipalités gérées par des maires) et un cabinet de **councillors** qui se réunissent au **town hall** ou au **county hall**.

Le pays de Galles est divisé en **counties** et en **county boroughs**, l'Irlande du Nord en **districts**, et l'Écosse en **council areas**.

■ *Aux États-Unis*

La plupart des États ont une Constitution qui définit les pouvoirs exécutif, législatif et judiciaire. À la tête de l'exécutif se trouve le gouverneur (**governor**). La branche législative est généralement bicamérale, chaque État ayant son Sénat (**Senate**) et sa Chambre des représentants (**Chamber of Representatives**). Le pouvoir judiciaire dans chaque État est organisé autour d'une Cour suprême d'État (**State Supreme Court**). Les États sont divisés en **counties**, ayant tous leur propre **county government**. À la tête de la plupart des **counties** se trouve une assemblée élue appelée **Board of Commissioners** ou **Board of Supervisors**. Par ailleurs, la plupart des villes américaines ont un maire élu et un conseil municipal.

locality [lə'kælətɪ] (*pl* **localities**) n **1.** [neighbourhood] voisinage *m*, environs *mpl* ; [general area] région *f* **2.** [location - of building, place] lieu *m*, site *m* ; [- of species] localité *f*.
localization, localisation [,ləʊkəlaɪ'zeɪʃn] n COMPUT localisation *f*.
localize, localise ['ləʊkəlaɪz] vt **1.** [pinpoint, locate] localiser, situer **2.** [confine] localiser, limiter **3.** [concentrate - power, money] concentrer.
localized, localised ['ləʊkəlaɪzd] adj localisé.
locally ['ləʊkəlɪ] adv localement.
local time n heure *f* locale.
locate [ləʊ'keɪt] US ['ləʊkeɪt] ◆ vt **1.** [find] repérer, trouver, localiser **2.** *(usu passive)* [situate] situer. ◆ vi **1.** COMM [company, factory] s'établir, s'implanter **2.** US [settle] s'installer, s'établir.
location [ləʊ'keɪʃn] n **1.** [place, site] emplacement *m*, site *m* ; [whereabouts] : *what is your present location?* où te trouves-tu en ce moment ? **2.** CIN extérieurs *mpl* ▶ **shot on location** tourné en extérieur ▶ **location shot** extérieur *m* **3.** [finding, discovery] repérage *m*, localisation *f* **4.** COMPUT position *f* ▶ **memory location** position (en) mémoire.
locavore ['ləʊkəvɔːr] n locavore *mf (personne qui ne mange que des produits locaux)*.
loc. cit. (**written abbr of loco citato**) loc. cit.
loch [lɒk or lɒx] n Scot loch *m*, lac *m*.
lock [lɒk] ◆ vt **1.** [door, drawer, car, etc.] fermer à clef **2.** [valuables, person] enfermer **3.** [hold tightly] serrer **4.** [device, wheels, brakes] bloquer **5.** COMPUT [file] verrouiller. ◆ vi **1.** [door, drawer, car, etc.] (se) fermer à clef **2.** [engage] se joindre **3.** [wheels, brakes, nut] se bloquer. ◆ n **1.** [on door, drawer, etc.] serrure *f* ▶ **under lock and key** [object] sous clef **2.** [on canal] écluse *f* **3.** [grip - gen] prise *f* ; [in wrestling] clef *f*, prise *f* **4.** UK AUTO (rayon *m* de) braquage *m* / *on full lock* braqué à fond **5.** TECH [device - gen] verrou *m* ; [- on gun] percuteur *m* ; [- on keyboard] ▶ **shift** or **caps lock** touche *f* de verrouillage majuscule **6.** COMPUT verrouillage *m* **7.** RUGBY ▶ **lock (forward)** deuxième ligne *m* **8.** [curl] boucle *f* ; [stray strand] mèche *f* **9.** PHR ▶ **lock, stock and barrel** en entier. ❖ **locks** pl n *liter* chevelure *f*. ❖ **lock away** vt sep [valuables] mettre sous clef ; [criminal] incarcérer, mettre sous les verrous. ❖ **lock in** vt sep enfermer / *he locked himself in* il s'est enfermé (à l'intérieur). ❖ **lock onto** vt insep [subj: radar] capter ; [subj: homing device] se caler sur ; [subj: missile] se fixer or se verrouiller sur. ❖ **lock out** vt sep **1.** [accidentally] enfermer dehors ; [deliberately] laisser dehors / *I've locked myself out* j'ai fermé la porte en laissant les clés à l'intérieur, je me suis enfermé dehors **2.** INDUST [workers] lock-outer. ❖ **lock up** ◆ vt sep **1.** [house, shop] fermer à clef **2.** [valuables, criminal] = **lock away 3.** [capital] immobiliser. ◆ vi fermer à clef.
lockable ['lɒkəbl] adj qu'on peut fermer à clef.
lockdown ['lɒkdaʊn] n [in prison, hospital] confinement *m* ▶ **to be in lockdown** faire l'objet de mesures de confinement ▶ **to go into lockdown** [school, airport terminal] empêcher d'en sortir ou d'y entrer.
locked-in syndrome n MED locked-in syndrome *m*, syndrome *m* d'enfermement.
locker ['lɒkər] n **1.** [for clothes, valuables, etc.] casier *m*, petit placard *m* **2.** US [freezer] congélateur *m*.
locker room n US vestiaire *m (avec casiers)*. ❖ **locker-room** adj [humour, joke] corsé, salé.
locket ['lɒkɪt] n pendentif *m*.
lock gate n porte *f* d'écluse.
lockjaw ['lɒkdʒɔː] n tétanos *m*.
lock keeper n éclusier *m*, -ère *f*.
lockout ['lɒkaʊt] n [of workers] lock-out *m inv*.
locksmith ['lɒksmɪθ] n serrurier *m*.
lockup ['lɒkʌp] n **1.** US [jail] prison *f* ; [cell] cellule *f* **2.** UK [garage] garage *m* **3.** [act of locking up] fermeture *f*.
loco ['ləʊkəʊ] (*pl* **locos**) ◆ adj US *v inf* dingue, cinglé. ◆ n UK *inf* RAIL loco *f*.
locomotive [,ləʊkə'məʊtɪv] ◆ n locomotive *f*. ◆ adj automobile ; ANAT locomoteur.
locum ['ləʊkəm] n UK remplaçant *m*, -e *f (de prêtre, de médecin)*.
locust ['ləʊkəst] ◆ n **1.** [insect] locuste *f*, criquet *m* migrateur **2.** = **locust tree**. ◆ comp ▶ **locust bean** caroube *f*.
locust tree n **1.** [false acacia] robinier *m* **2.** [carob tree] caroubier *m*.
lodge [lɒdʒ] ◆ vt **1.** [house] héberger, loger **2.** [stick, embed] loger / *a fish bone had lodged itself in his throat* une arête s'était logée dans sa gorge **3.** [make, file - claim] déposer ▶ **to lodge a complaint** porter plainte ▶ **to lodge an accusation against sb** LAW porter plainte contre qqn **4.** [deposit for safekeeping] déposer, mettre en sûreté **5.** [invest - power, authority, etc.] investir. ◆ vi **1.** [stay] loger, être logé / *he is lodging at Mrs Smith's* or *with Mrs Smith* **a)** il loge chez Mrs Smith **b)** [with board] il est en pension chez Mme Smith **2.** [stick, become embedded] se loger. ◆ n **1.** [cabin - for hunters] pavillon *m* ; [- for skiers] chalet *m* **2.** UK [on country estate] maison *f* du gardien ; [of porter] loge *f* **3.** US [in park, resort] bâtiment *m* central **4.** [Masonic] loge *f* **5.** [hotel] hôtel *m*, relais *m* **6.** [beavers'] hutte *f*.
lodger ['lɒdʒər] n locataire *mf* ; [with board] pensionnaire *mf*.
lodging ['lɒdʒɪŋ] n hébergement *m* ▶ **full board and lodging** pension *f* complète. ❖ **lodgings** pl n UK chambre *f* meublée or chambres *fpl* meublées *(chez un particulier)*.
loft [lɒft] ◆ n **1.** [attic] grenier *m* ▶ **loft conversion** combles *mpl* aménagés **2.** [elevated space - in church] tribune *f*, galerie *f* **3.** [warehouse space] loft *m*. ◆ vt SPORT [hit] lancer très haut.
lofty ['lɒftɪ] (*compar* **loftier**, *superl* **loftiest**) adj **1.** [high - summit, building, etc.] haut, élevé **2.** [supercilious - manner] hautain, dédaigneux, méprisant **3.** [exalted - in spirit] noble, élevé ; [- in rank, position] éminent **4.** [elevated - style, prose] élevé, noble.

log [lɒɡ] (*pt & pp* **logged**, *cont* **logging**) ◆ n **1.** [of wood] rondin *m* ; [for firewood] bûche *f* **2.** [record] journal *m*, registre *m* ; NAUT journal *m* or livre *m* de bord ; AERON carnet *m* de vol ; [lorry driver's] carnet *m* de route **3.** (abbr of **logarithm**) log *m* **4.** [cake] ▶ **Yuletide** or **Christmas log** bûche *f* de Noël. ◆ comp ▶ **log fire** feu *m* de bois. ◆ vt **1.** [information - on paper] consigner, inscrire ; [- in computer memory] entrer **2.** [speed, distance, time] : *he has logged 2,000 hours flying time* il a 2 000 heures de vol à son actif, il totalise 2 000 heures de vol **3.** [tree] tronçonner ; [forest] mettre en coupe. ◆ vi [company] exploiter une forêt ; [person] travailler comme bûcheron. ❖ **log in** ◆ vi COMPUT se connecter. ❖ vt sep [user name, password] entrer, introduire. ❖ **log off** = **log out.** ❖ **log on** = **log in.** ❖ **log out** vi COMPUT se déconnecter. ❖ **log up** vt sep 🇬🇧 [do, achieve] avoir à son actif.

loganberry ['lɒɡənbərı] (*pl* **loganberries**) n [plant] framboisier *m* (hybride) ; [fruit] mûre-framboise *f*.

logarithm ['lɒɡərɪðm] n logarithme *m*.

logbook ['lɒɡbʊk] n **1.** [record] journal *m* ; NAUT journal *m* or livre *m* de bord ; AERON carnet *m* de vol **2.** 🇬🇧 AUTO ≃ carte *f* grise.

log cabin n cabane *f* en rondins.

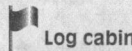

Log cabin

Certains hommes politiques américains prétendent être nés dans une **log cabin** comme Abraham Lincoln, exprimant ainsi leur souci de proximité vis-à-vis des Américains d'origine modeste.

---

loggerheads ['lɒɡəhedz] pl n ▶ **to be at loggerheads (with sb)** : *he's at loggerheads with the management over the issue* il est en complet désaccord avec la direction sur cette question.

logic ['lɒdʒɪk] n [gen & COMPUT] logique *f* ; [reasoning] raisonnement *m*.

logical ['lɒdʒɪkl] adj logique.

📋 Note that **il est logique que** and **il est normal que** are followed by a verb in the subjunctive:

It's logical that he should be upset. *Il est logique / normal qu'il soit contrarié.*

---

logically ['lɒdʒɪklı] adv logiquement.

login n connexion *f* / *since your last login* depuis votre dernière connexion ▶ **login name** (nom *m* de) login *m*.

logistical [lə'dʒɪstɪkl] adj logistique.

logistically [lə'dʒɪstɪklı] adv sur le plan logistique.

logistics [lə'dʒɪstɪks] pl n logistique *f*.

logjam ['lɒdʒæm] n **1.** [in river] bouchon *m* de bois flottés **2.** *fig* [deadlock] impasse *f*.

logo ['ləʊɡəʊ] (*pl* **logos**) n logo *m*.

logrolling ['lɒɡrəʊlɪŋ] n 🇺🇸 *pej* échange *m* de faveurs (*accord entre hommes politiques selon lequel on se rend mutuellement des services*).

logy ['ləʊɡı] (*compar* **logier**, *superl* **logiest**) adj 🇺🇸 *inf* patraque.

loin [lɔɪn] n CULIN [of pork] longe *f*, échine *f*, filet *m* ; [of beef] aloyau *m* ; [of veal] longe *f* ; [of lamb] carré *m*. ❖ **loins** pl n ANAT reins *mpl* ; *euph* [genitals] parties *fpl*.

loincloth ['lɔɪnklɒθ] n pagne *m*.

loiter ['lɔɪtər] vi **1.** [hang about] traîner ; [lurk] rôder **2.** [dawdle] traîner ; [lag behind] traîner (en route).

LOL MESSAGING **1.** (written abbr of **laughing out loud**) LOL, MDR **2.** written abbr of **lots of love.**

loll [lɒl] vi [lounge] se prélasser. ❖ **loll about** 🇬🇧, **loll around** vi [in grass, armchair, etc.] se prélasser. ❖ **loll out** vi [tongue] pendre (mollement).

lollipop ['lɒlɪpɒp] n **1.** [sweet] sucette *f* **2.** 🇬🇧 [ice lolly] esquimau *m*, sucette *f* glacée.

lollipop lady, **lollipop man** n *inf* en *Grande-Bretagne, personne chargée d'aider les enfants à traverser une rue en arrêtant la circulation à l'aide d'un panneau en forme de sucette.*

lollop ['lɒləp] vi [person] marcher lourdement ; [animal] galoper.

lolly ['lɒlı] (*pl* **lollies**) n **1.** 🇬🇧 *inf* = **lollipop 2.** 🇬🇧 *v inf* [money] fric *m*, pognon *m*.

London ['lʌndən] ◆ pr n Londres. ◆ comp [museums, shops, traffic] londonien ; [life] à Londres ▶ **London (Regional) Transport** régie des transports publics londoniens.

Londoner ['lʌndənər] n Londonien *m*, -enne *f*, habitant *m*, -e *f* de Londres.

lone [ləʊn] adj [unaccompanied - rider, stag] solitaire ; [isolated - house] isolé ; [single, unique] unique, seul ▶ **lone parent** parent *m* unique.

loneliness ['ləʊnlɪnɪs] n [of person] solitude *f*, isolement *m* ; [of place] isolement *m*.

lonely ['ləʊnlı] (*compar* **lonelier**, *superl* **loneliest**) adj **1.** [sad - person] seul ; [- life] solitaire **2.** [unfrequented - spot] isolé ; [- street] peu fréquenté, vide.

lonely hearts adj : *lonely hearts club* club *m* de rencontres / *lonely hearts column* rubrique *f* rencontres (*des petites annonces*).

loner ['ləʊnər] n *inf* [person] solitaire *mf*.

lonesome ['ləʊnsəm] ◆ adj 🇺🇸 = **lonely.** ◆ n ▶ **on one's lonesome** *inf* tout seul.

long [lɒŋ] (*compar* **longer** ['lɒŋɡər], *superl* **longest** ['lɒŋɡɪst]) ◆ adj **1.** [in space - road, garment, letter] long (longue) / *how long is the pool?* quelle est la longueur de la piscine ?, la piscine fait combien de long ? / *the pool's 33 metres long* la piscine fait 33 mètres de long / *the article is 80 pages long* l'article fait 80 pages / *is it a long way (away)?* est-ce loin (d'ici) ? / *to get* or *grow longer* a) [shadows] s'allonger b) [hair, beard] pousser **2.** [in time - pause, speech, separation] long (longue) / *how long will the flight be / was the meeting?* combien de temps durera le vol / a duré la réunion ? / *her five-year-long battle with the authorities* sa lutte de cinq années contre les autorités / *I've had a long day* j'ai eu une journée bien remplie / *I've known her (for) a long time* or *while* je la connais depuis longtemps, cela fait longtemps que je la connais ▶ **at long last!** enfin ! ◆ n ▶ PHR **the long and the short of it is that I got fired** enfin bref, j'ai été viré. ◆ adv **1.** [a long time] longtemps / *they live longer than humans* ils vivent plus longtemps que les êtres humains / *I haven't been here long* je viens d'arriver, j'arrive juste / *how long will he be / was he in jail?* (pendant) combien de temps restera-t-il / est-il resté en prison ? / *how long has he been in jail?* ça fait combien de temps qu'il est en prison ?, depuis combien de temps est-il en prison ? / *as long ago as 1937* déjà en 1937 / *long before you were born* bien avant que tu sois né / *the decision had been taken long before* la décision avait été prise depuis longtemps / *colleagues long since promoted* des collègues promus depuis longtemps / *we talked long into the night* nous avons parlé jusque tard dans la nuit ; [with 'be', 'take'] : *will you be long?* tu en as pour longtemps ? / *he took* or *it took him so long to make up his mind...* il a mis si longtemps à se décider..., il lui a fallu tellement de temps pour se décider... / *how long does it take to get there?* combien de temps faut-il pour y aller ? / *this won't take long* ça va être vite fait ; [in wishes, toasts, etc.] : *long live the Queen!* vive la reine ! **2.** [for a long time] depuis longtemps / *it has long been known that...* on sait depuis longtemps que... **3.** [throughout] : *all day / week long* toute la journée / la semaine. ◆ vi ▸ **to long for sb / sthg** : *I long for him* il me manque énormément / *we were longing for a cup of tea* nous avions très envie d'une tasse de thé ▸ **to long** or **to be longing to do sthg** être impatient or avoir hâte de faire qqch / *I was longing to tell her the truth* je mourais d'envie de lui dire la vérité. ◆ **as long as** conj phr **1.** [during the time that] aussi longtemps que, tant que / *as long as he's in power, there will be no hope* tant qu'il sera au pouvoir, il n'y aura aucun espoir **2.** [providing] à condition que, pourvu que / *you can have it as long as you give me it back* vous pouvez le prendre à condition que or pourvu que vous me le rendiez. ◆ **before long** adv phr [soon] dans peu de temps, sous peu ; [soon afterwards] peu (de temps) après. ◆ **for long** adv phr longtemps / *he's still in charge here, but not for long* c'est encore lui qui s'en occupe, mais plus pour longtemps. ◆ **no longer** adv phr ne... plus. ◆ **not any longer** adv phr plus maintenant / *I can't wait any longer* je ne peux pas attendre plus longtemps, je ne peux plus attendre. ◆ **so long as** = **as long as**.

long. (written abbr of longitude) long.

long-awaited [-ə'weɪtɪd] adj très attendu.

longboat ['lɒŋbəʊt] n chaloupe f.

long-distance ◆ adj **1.** [phone call] interurbain **2.** [runner, race] de fond ; [pilot, lorry driver] au long cours ; [journey] vers un pays lointain **3.** [device] (à) longue portée ; [aircraft] long-courrier. ◆ adv ▸ **to call** or **phone long-distance** appeler or téléphoner par l'interurbain.

long division n MATH division f posée.

long-drawn-out adj très long, interminable, qui n'en finit pas.

long drink n long drink m ; [non-alcoholic] grand verre de jus de fruits, de limonade, etc.

longed-for ['lɒŋd-] adj très attendu.

longevity [lɒn'ʤevətɪ] n longévité f.

long-forgotten adj oublié depuis longtemps.

long-grain rice n riz m long.

long-haired adj [person] aux cheveux longs ; [animal] à longs poils.

longhand ['lɒŋhænd] n écriture f courante.

long-haul adj [aircraft] long-courrier.

longing ['lɒŋɪŋ] ◆ n envie f, désir m / *I had a longing to see the sea* j'avais très envie de voir la mer. ◆ adj d'envie, de désir.

longingly ['lɒŋɪŋlɪ] adv [with desire] avec désir or envie ; [with regret] avec regret.

Long Island pr n Long Island / *on Long Island* à Long Island.

longitude ['lɒŋɪtjuːd] n longitude f / *at a longitude of 60° east* par 60° de longitude est.

long johns pl n inf caleçon m long, caleçons mpl longs.

long jump n UK SPORT saut m en longueur.

long-lasting adj durable, qui dure longtemps.

long-life adj [milk] longue conservation (inv) ; [lightbulb, battery] longue durée (inv).

longlist ['lɒŋlɪst] n première liste f.

long-lived [-lɪvd] adj [family, species] d'une grande longévité ; [friendship] durable ; [prejudice] tenace, qui a la vie dure.

long-lost adj [friend, cousin] perdu de vue depuis longtemps ; [object] perdu depuis longtemps.

long-playing record n 33 tours m inv, microsillon m.

long-range adj **1.** [weapon] à longue portée ; [vehicle, aircraft] à long rayon d'action **2.** [forecast, plan] à long terme.

long-running adj [show] qui tient l'affiche ; [battle, conflict, rivalry] qui existe depuis longtemps, de longue date.

longshoreman ['lɒŋʃɔːmən] (pl **longshoremen** [-mən]) n US docker m.

long shot n **1.** [in race -runner, horse] concurrent qui ne figure pas parmi les favoris **2.** [bet] pari m risqué **3.** CIN plan m éloigné **4.** fig entreprise f hasardeuse.

longsighted [,lɒŋ'saɪtɪd] adj **1.** MED hypermétrope, presbyte **2.** fig [well-judged] prévoyant.

longsightedness [,lɒŋ'saɪtɪdnɪs] n **1.** MED hypermétropie f, presbytie f **2.** fig [good judgement] prévoyance f, discernement m.

long-sleeved adj à manches longues.

long-standing adj de longue date.

long-suffering adj (extrêmement) patient, d'une patience à toute épreuve ; [resigned] résigné.

long term ◆ **long-term** adj à long terme ; [situation] prolongé ; [unemployment, illness] longue durée ▸ **long-term car park** UK parking m longue durée ▸ **long-term memory** mémoire f à long terme. ◆ **in the long term** adv phr à long terme.

long-time adj [friend, acquaintance] de longue date ; [interest, affiliation] ancien, qui dure depuis longtemps.

long vacation n UNIV grandes vacances fpl, vacances fpl d'été.

long view n prévisions fpl à long terme ▸ **to take the long view** voir le long terme.

long wave n RADIO grandes ondes fpl ▸ **on (the) long wave** sur les grandes ondes. ◆ **long-wave** adj ▸ **long-wave broadcasts** émissions fpl sur grandes ondes.

longways ['lɒŋweɪz] adv longitudinalement, dans le sens de la longueur.

longwearing [,lɒŋ'weərɪŋ] adj US solide, résistant.

long weekend n week-end m prolongé.

long-winded adj [person] prolixe, bavard ; [article, essay, lecture] interminable ; [style] verbeux, diffus.

loo [luː] n UK inf toilettes fpl ▸ **loo roll** rouleau m de papier hygiénique.

loofa(h) ['luːfə] n luffa m, loofa m.

look [lʊk] ◆ vi **1.** [gen] regarder / *look, there's Brian!* regarde, voilà Brian ! / *what's happening outside? let me look* qu'est-ce qui se passe dehors ? laissez-moi voir / *I'm just looking* [in shop] je jette un coup d'œil / *she looked along the row* elle a parcouru la rangée / la liste du regard ▸ **look before you leap** prov il faut réfléchir deux fois avant d'agir **2.** [search] chercher / *you can't have looked hard enough* tu n'as pas dû beaucoup chercher **3.** [in imperative -listen, pay attention] écouter / *look, I can't pay you back just yet* écoute, je ne peux pas te rembourser tout de suite ▶ **look here!** dites donc ! **4.** [seem, appear] avoir l'air / *you look* or *are looking better today* tu as l'air (d'aller) mieux aujourd'hui / *how do I look?* comment tu me trouves ? / *it makes him look ten years older / younger* ça le vieillit / rajeunit de dix ans / *he's 70, but he doesn't look it* il a 70 ans mais il n'en a pas l'air or mais il ne les fait pas / *it'll look bad if I don't contribute* ça fera mauvaise impression si je ne contribue pas / *things are looking black for the economy* les perspectives économiques sont assez sombres / *I must have looked a fool* j'ai dû passer pour un imbécile / *to make sb look a fool* or *an idiot* tourner qqn en ridicule ▶ **to look like sb / sthg** [resemble] ressembler à qqn / qqch / *what does she look like?* **a)** [describe her] comment est-elle ? **b)** [she looks a mess] non mais, à quoi elle ressemble ! ▶ **it looks like rain** on dirait qu'il va pleuvoir / *it looks (to me) like he was lying* j'ai l'impression qu'il mentait / *is this our room? — it looks like it* c'est notre chambre ? — ça m'en a tout l'air / *it doesn't look as if they're coming* on dirait qu'ils ne vont pas venir ▶ **to look good**: *you're looking good* tu as l'air en forme **5.** [face - house, window] : *to look (out) onto a park* donner sur un parc / *to look north / west* être exposé au nord / à l'ouest **6.** [intend] ▶ **to be looking to do sthg** chercher à faire qqch. ◆ **vt 1.** [in imperative] : *look who's coming!* regarde qui arrive ! / *look who's talking!* tu peux parler, toi ! / *look what you're doing / where you're going!* regarde un peu ce que tu fais / où tu vas ! **2.** (PHR) **to look sb up and down** regarder qqn de haut en bas, toiser qqn du regard. ◆ **n 1.** [gen] coup *m* d'œil ▶ **to have** or **to take a look (at sthg)** jeter un coup d'œil (sur) or à qqch, regarder (qqch) / *it's worth a quick look* ça vaut le coup d'œil / *and now a look ahead to next week's programmes* et maintenant, un aperçu des programmes de la semaine prochaine / *do you mind if I take a look around?* ça vous gêne si je jette un coup d'œil ? **2.** [search] ▶ **to have a look for sthg** chercher qqch / *have another look* cherche encore **3.** [glance] regard *m* / *she gave me a dirty look* elle m'a jeté un regard mauvais / *he didn't say anything, but if looks could kill!* il n'a pas dit un mot, mais il y a des regards qui tuent ! **4.** [appearance, air] air *m* / [expression] : *he had a strange look in his eyes* il avait un drôle de regard / *by the look* or *looks of her, I'd say she failed the exam* à la voir or rien qu'en la voyant, je dirais qu'elle a raté son examen / *I don't like the look of it* ça ne me dit rien de bon or rien qui vaille **5.** [fashion] mode *f*, look *m*. ◆ **looks** pl n [beauty] : *she's got everything, looks, intelligence, youth…* elle a tout pour elle, elle est belle, intelligente, jeune… / *he's lost his looks* il n'est plus aussi beau qu'avant. ◆ **look after** vt insep **1.** [take care of] s'occuper de / *you should look after your clothes more carefully* tu devrais prendre plus grand soin de tes vêtements ; *fig* : *look after yourself!* fais bien attention à toi ! / *don't worry, he can look after himself* ne t'inquiète pas, il est capable de se débrouiller tout seul **2.** [be responsible for] s'occuper de **3.** [keep temporarily - child] garder ; [- object] surveiller / *can you look after my luggage for a few minutes?* pouvez-vous surveiller mes bagages quelques instants ? ◆ **look ahead** vi regarder vers l'avenir / *let's look ahead to the next century / to next month's meeting* pensons au siècle prochain / à la réunion du mois prochain. ◆ **look around** = **look round.** ◆ **look at** vt insep **1.** *lit* regarder / *she looked at herself in the mirror* elle se regarda dans la glace / *it's not much to look at* ça ne paie pas de mine / *you wouldn't think, to look at him, that he's a multimillionaire* à le voir, on ne croirait pas avoir affaire à un multimillionnaire **2.** [consider] considérer / *that's not the way I look at it* ce n'est pas comme ça que je vois les choses **3.** [check] vérifier, regarder / *to have one's teeth*

looked at se faire examiner les dents. ◆ **look away** vi détourner les yeux. ◆ **look back** vi **1.** [in space] regarder derrière soi / *she walked away without looking back* elle est partie sans se retourner **2.** [in time] regarder en arrière / *the author looks back on the war years* l'auteur revient sur les années de guerre / *it seems funny now we look back on it* ça semble drôle quand on y pense aujourd'hui / *after she got her first job she never looked back* fig à partir du moment où elle a trouvé son premier emploi, tout lui a réussi. ◆ **look down** vi regarder en bas ; [in embarrassment] baisser les yeux / *we looked down on* or *at the valley* nous regardions la vallée en dessous. ◆ **look down on** vt insep [despise] mépriser. ◆ **look for** vt insep **1.** [seek] chercher / *are you looking for a fight?* tu cherches la bagarre ? **2.** [expect] attendre / *it's not the result we were looking for* ce n'est pas le résultat que nous attendions. ◆ **look forward to** vt insep attendre avec impatience ▶ **to look forward to doing sthg** être impatient de faire qqch / *I look forward to hearing from you soon* [in letter] dans l'attente de votre réponse / *I'm not looking forward to the operation* la perspective de cette opération ne m'enchante guère. ◆ **look in** vi **1.** [inside] regarder à l'intérieur **2.** [pay a visit] passer ▶ **to look in on sb** rendre visite à or passer voir qqn. ◆ **look into** vt insep examiner, étudier / *it's a problem that needs looking into* c'est un problème qu'il faut examiner or sur lequel il faut se pencher. ◆ **look on** ◆ vi regarder / *the passers-by just looked on* les passants se sont contentés de regarder. ◆ vt insep considérer / *I look on him as my brother* je le considère comme mon frère ▶ **to look on sb / sthg with favour / disfavour** voir qqn / qqch d'un œil favorable / défavorable. ◆ **look out** ◆ vi **1.** [person] regarder dehors **2.** [be careful] faire attention / *look out, it's hot!* attention, c'est chaud ! ◆ vt sep (UK) : *I'll look / I've looked that book out for you* je te chercherai / je t'ai trouvé ce livre. ◆ **look out for** vt insep **1.** [be on watch for] guetter / *she's always looking out for bargains* elle est toujours à la recherche or à l'affût d'une bonne affaire / *you have to look out for snakes* il faut faire attention or se méfier, il y a des serpents **2.** *inf* (PHR) **to look out for o.s.** penser à soi. ◆ **look over** vt insep [glance over] jeter un coup d'œil sur ; [examine] examiner, étudier. ◆ **look round** ◆ vi **1.** [look at surroundings] regarder (autour de soi) / *I'm just looking round* je ne fais que jeter un coup d'œil, je jette simplement un coup d'œil / *I looked round for an exit* j'ai cherché une sortie **2.** [look back] regarder derrière soi, se retourner. ◆ vt insep [museum, cathedral, factory] visiter ; [shop, room] jeter un coup d'œil dans. ◆ **look through** vt insep **1.** [window, screen] regarder à travers **2.** [book, report] jeter un coup d'œil sur or à, regarder **3.** *fig* [person] : *he looked straight through me* il m'a regardé comme si je n'étais pas là. ◆ **look to** vt insep **1.** [turn to] se tourner vers / *it's best to look to an expert* il est préférable de consulter un expert or de demander l'avis d'un expert / *don't look to her for help* ne compte pas sur elle pour t'aider **2.** *fml* [attend to] veiller à. ◆ **look up** ◆ vi **1.** [raise one's eyes] lever les yeux **2.** [improve] s'améliorer / *things are looking up for the economy* les perspectives économiques semblent meilleures. ◆ vt sep **1.** [in reference work, directory, etc.] chercher / *look it up on the Web* cherche-le sur Internet **2.** [visit] passer voir, rendre visite à / *look us up when you're in New York* passe nous voir quand tu seras à New York. ◆ **look upon** = **look on** (vt insep). ◆ **look up to** vt insep respecter, avoir du respect pour.

lookalike ['lukə,laɪk] n [double] sosie *m* / *a John Major lookalike* un sosie de John Major.

looker ['lukər] n *inf* canon *m*.

look-in n <small>UK</small> inf [chance] : *she talked so much that I didn't get a look-in* elle ne m'a pas laissé le temps de placer un mot or d'en placer une.

looking glass n dated miroir m, glace f.

lookout ['lʊkaʊt] n **1.** [watcher -gen] guetteur m ; MIL guetteur m, sentinelle f ; NAUT vigie f **2.** [watch] guet m ▸ **to keep (a) lookout** faire le guet ▸ **to keep a lookout** or **to be on the lookout for sthg** guetter qqch, être à l'affût de qqch **3.** MIL [observation post] poste m de guet ; NAUT poste m de vigie **4.** <small>UK</small> inf [prospect] : *it's a poor lookout when even doctors are on the dole* il y a de quoi s'inquiéter quand même les médecins sont au chômage.

lookup ['lʊkʌp] n COMPUT recherche f, consultation f ▸ **lookup query** requête f ▸ **lookup table** table f de recherche.

loom [luːm] ◆ vi **1.** [appear] surgir **2.** [approach] être imminent **3.** ▸ **to loom large** [threaten] menacer. ◆ n TEXT métier m à tisser. ❖ **loom up** vi apparaître indistinctement, surgir.

LOOM [luːm] (abbr of **Loyal Order of the Moose**) pr n *association caritative américaine*.

looming ['luːmɪŋ] adj **1.** [cliffs, mountains, etc.] imposant **2.** [deadline] qui s'approche dangereusement.

loony ['luːnɪ] (compar **loonier**, superl **looniest**, pl **loonies**) inf ◆ adj dingue, loufoque. ◆ n dingue mf, malade mf.

loony bin n inf & hum asile m.

loop [luːp] ◆ n **1.** [in string, rope] boucle f ; [in river] méandre m ; [in drainpipe] siphon m **2.** COMPUT boucle f **3.** ELEC [closed circuit] circuit m fermé **4.** [contraceptive device] stérilet m. ◆ vt **1.** [in string, rope, etc.] faire une boucle à / *loop the rope around your waist / through the ring* passez la corde autour de votre taille / dans l'anneau **2.** AERON ▸ **to loop the loop** faire un looping. ◆ vi [road] zigzaguer ; [river] faire des méandres or des boucles.

loophole ['luːphəʊl] n [gap, defect] lacune f, faille f / a *loophole in the law* un vide législatif.

loopy ['luːpɪ] (compar **loopier**, superl **loopiest**) adj inf [crazy] dingue, cinglé.

loose [luːs] ◆ adj **1.** [not tightly fixed -nail] mal enfoncé ; [-screw, bolt] desserré ; [-button] qui pend, mal cousu ; [-knot] qui se défait ; [-floor tile] décollé ; [-shelf] mal fixé ; [-handle, brick] branlant ; [-floorboard] disjoint ; [-slate] mal fixé ; [-tooth] qui bouge / *to work loose* a) [nail] sortir b) [screw, bolt] se desserrer c) [knot] se défaire d) [tooth, slate] bouger e) [button] se détacher ▸ **loose connection** ELEC mauvais contact m **2.** [free, unattached] libre ; COMM [not packaged] en vrac **3.** [slack -grip, hold] mou *(before vowel or silent 'h' mol, molle)* ; [-skin, flesh] flasque ; [-bowstring, rope] lâche ; fig [discipline] relâché **4.** [not tight-fitting -dress, jacket] ample, flottant **5.** [weak -connection, link] vague ; [informal -organization] peu structuré ; [-agreement] officieux **6.** [imprecise, broad -thinking, application] peu rigoureux ; [-translation, terminology] approximatif **7.** pej [woman] facile ; [morals] léger **8.** [not dense or compact -earth] meuble ; [-knit, weave] lâche **9.** [relaxed -muscles] détendu, relâché, au repos ▸ **to have loose bowels** avoir la diarrhée **10.** FIN disponible. ◆ n [in rugby] ▸ **in the loose** dans la mêlée ouverte. ◆ vt **1.** [unleash -dogs] lâcher ; [-panic, chaos] semer ; [let fly -bullet] tirer ; [-arrow] décocher **2.** [undo -knot] défaire ; [-hair] détacher ; [unfasten -boat, raft] démarrer, détacher. ❖ **on the loose** adj phr ▸ **to be on the loose** a) [gen] être en liberté b) [on the run] être en fuite. ❖ **loose off** ◆ vt sep [bullet] tirer ; [arrow] décocher ; [gun] décharger ; [curses] lâcher.

◆ vi [with gun] tirer ; <small>US</small> fig [with insults, criticism, etc.] ▸ **to loose off at sb** se déchaîner contre qqn, s'en prendre violemment à qqn.

loose change n petite monnaie f.

loose cover n <small>UK</small> [for armchair, sofa] housse f.

loose end n : *I have a few loose ends to tie up* j'ai encore quelques petits détails à régler ▸ **to be at a loose end** <small>UK</small> or **at loose ends** <small>US</small> être dans un moment creux.

loose-fitting adj ample, large, flottant.

loose-leaf(ed) adj à feuilles mobiles or volantes.

loosely ['luːslɪ] adv **1.** [not firmly -pack, fit, hold, wrap] sans serrer ; [not closely -knit, weave] lâchement **2.** [apply, interpret] mollement / *loosely translated* a) [freely] traduit librement b) [inaccurately] mal traduit **3.** [vaguely -connect, relate] vaguement.

loosen ['luːsn] ◆ vt **1.** [make less tight -knot, screw, lid] desserrer ; [-rope, cable] détendre ; [-grip, reins] relâcher ; [weaken] affaiblir **2.** [liberalize -rules, restrictions] assouplir. ◆ vi [become less tight -knot, screw] se desserrer ; [-grip] se relâcher, se desserrer. ❖ **loosen up** ◆ vi **1.** [get less severe] se montrer moins sévère / *to loosen up on discipline* relâcher la discipline **2.** [relax socially] se détendre **3.** [limber up -athlete, musician] s'échauffer. ◆ vt sep [muscles] échauffer.

loot [luːt] ◆ vt [town, goods, tomb] piller. ◆ vi piller, se livrer au pillage. ◆ n **1.** [stolen goods] butin m **2.** v inf [money] pognon m, fric m.

looter ['luːtər] n [in war, riot] pillard m, -e f ; [of tombs, churches] pilleur m, -euse f.

looting ['luːtɪŋ] n pillage m.

lop [lɒp] (pt & pp **lopped**, cont **lopping**) vt **1.** [tree] élaguer, tailler ; [branch] couper **2.** fig [budget] élaguer, faire des coupes sombres dans ; [sum of money, item of expenditure] retrancher, supprimer. ❖ **lop off** vt sep **1.** [branch] couper, tailler **2.** fig [price, time] réduire.

lope [ləʊp] ◆ vi [runner] courir à grandes foulées ; [animal] courir en bondissant. ◆ n [of runner] pas m de course *(rapide et souple)* ; [of animal] course f *(avec des bonds)*.

lopsided adj **1.** [crooked -nose, grin] de travers ; [out of line -wall, roof, building] de travers ; [asymmetric] asymétrique ; [of uneven proportions] disproportionné **2.** [unevenly weighted] mal équilibré ; [unequal -debate, contest] inégal, déséquilibré.

lord [lɔːd] n [master] seigneur m ; [nobleman] noble m. ❖ **Lord** ◆ n <small>UK</small> [title] lord m / *Lord (Peter) Snow* lord (Peter) Snow ; [term of address] ▸ **my Lord** a) [to judge] monsieur le juge b) [to nobleman] monsieur le comte / marquis / duc c) [to bishop] monseigneur. ◆ pr n RELIG ▸ **the Lord** le Seigneur ; [in interjections and expressions] ▸ **Good Lord!** inf Seigneur ! ▸ **oh Lord!** inf mon Dieu ! ◆ vt ▸ **to lord it over sb** <small>UK</small> prendre des airs supérieurs avec qqn.

 Lord

Le titre de **Lord** est donné aux **peers** («pairs», membres de la Chambre des lords), sauf lorsqu'ils ont par ailleurs le titre de **Duke**. L'expression **my Lord** est employée pour s'adresser aux pairs, aux évêques et aux juges ; dans ce dernier cas, elle est généralement abrégée en **M'Lud**.

Lord Chancellor n lord *m* chancelier.

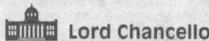

Lord Chancellor

Le **Lord Chancellor** (ou **Lord High Chancellor**) est l'officier d'État traditionnellement responsable de l'indépendance et du bon fonctionnement des tribunaux. La création d'un ministère de la Justice en 2007 a réduit le périmètre du rôle afférent à ce titre ; même s'il se trouve que le ministre de la Justice est également **Lord Chancellor**, il faut se garder de traduire **Lord Chancellor** par « ministre de la Justice ».

Le **Lord Chancellor** était autrefois président (**Speaker**) de la Chambre des lords, mais depuis 2005 il n'a plus cette fonction, désormais assurée par le **Lord Speaker**.

lordly ['lɔːdlɪ] adj **1.** [arrogant] arrogant, hautain / *with lordly indifference* avec une indifférence souveraine **2.** [noble - gesture] noble, auguste ; [splendid - feast, occasion, life style] somptueux.

Lord Mayor n lord-maire *m*, maire *m*.

Lord Mayor

Le **Lord Mayor** est élu par le conseil municipal de certaines villes d'Angleterre et du pays de Galles. Ses fonctions sont purement cérémonielles (présence lors des manifestations civiques, remises de médailles...). Il ne faut pas confondre le **Lord Mayor** avec le **Mayor** (maire élu responsable de la gestion municipale dans 12 villes anglaises et galloises).

Le **Lord Mayor** de Londres, dont la résidence officielle est **Mansion House**, est surtout célèbre pour deux manifestations cérémonielles qui marquent son élection : le **Lord Mayor's Show** voit le nouveau **Lord Mayor** en costume d'apparat défiler dans les rues de Londres en carrosse doré, et le **Lord Mayor's Banquet** est un dîner officiel donné à l'occasion de son élection, où le Premier ministre fait traditionnellement un discours.

lordship ['lɔːdʃɪp] n **1.** [form of address] ▶ **Your / His Lordship a)** [to noble] monsieur le marquis, monsieur le baron **b)** [to judge] monsieur le juge **c)** [to bishop] Excellence / Son Excellence **2.** [lands, rights] seigneurie *f* ; [power] autorité *f*.

Lord's Prayer n ▶ **the Lord's Prayer** le Notre Père.

lore [lɔːʳ] n **1.** [folk legend] tradition *f*, traditions *fpl*, coutume *f*, coutumes *fpl* **2.** [traditional knowledge] science *f*, savoir *m*.

lorry ['lɒrɪ] (*pl* lorries) n ⓤⓀ camion *m*, poids lourd *m*.

lorry driver n ⓤⓀ chauffeur *m* de camion, routier *m*.

lorry-load n ⓤⓀ chargement *m*.

Los Angeles [lɒsˈændʒɪliːz] pr n Los Angeles.

lose [luːz] (*pt & pp* lost [lɒst]) ◆ vt **1.** [gen - limb, job, money, patience, etc.] perdre ▶ **to lose one's way** se perdre,

s'égarer ▶ **to lose one's voice** avoir une extinction de voix **2.** [not win] perdre **3.** [shed, get rid of] perdre ▶ **to lose weight** perdre du poids ; [elude, shake off] semer **4.** [cause to lose] coûter, faire perdre / *it lost him his job* ça lui a fait perdre son emploi **5.** [subj: clock, watch] : *my watch loses five minutes a day* ma montre prend cinq minutes de retard par jour. ◆ vi **1.** perdre / *they lost by one goal* ils ont perdu d'un but / *either way, I can't lose* je suis gagnant à tous les coups / *I lost on the deal* j'ai été perdant dans l'affaire **2.** [clock, watch] retarder. ◆ **lose out** vi perdre, être perdant ▶ **to lose out on a deal** être perdant dans une affaire.

loser ['luːzəʳ] ◆ n **1.** [gen & SPORT] perdant *m*, -e *f* / *he's not a very good loser* il est mauvais perdant or joueur **2.** inf [failure - person] raté *m*, -e *f*, loser *mf*. ◆ adj ⓤⓈ inf : *a real loser guy* un vrai loser.

losing ['luːzɪŋ] adj **1.** [gen & SPORT] perdant ▶ **to fight a losing battle** engager une bataille perdue d'avance **2.** [unprofitable] : *the business was a losing concern* cette entreprise n'était pas viable.

loss [lɒs] n **1.** [gen] perte *f* / *the party suffered heavy losses in the last elections* le parti a subi de lourdes pertes or a perdu de nombreux sièges lors des dernières élections ▶ **to sell at a loss** vendre à perte **2.** [feeling of pain, unhappiness] malheur *m*, chagrin *m* **3.** [in insurance] sinistre *m* **4.** ⓟⒽⓡ **to be at a loss** ne pas savoir quoi faire, être déconcerté or dérouté :

loss adjuster n [for insurance] expert *m* ; NAUT dispatcheur *m*.

loss leader n COMM *article vendu à perte dans le but d'attirer la clientèle.*

lossless ['lɒslɪs] adj COMPUT ▶ **lossless compression** compression *f* sans perte.

lossmaker ['lɒsmeɪkəʳ] n gouffre *m* financier.

loss-making adj ⓤⓀ COMM qui tourne à perte, déficitaire.

lossy adj COMPUT ▶ **lossy compression** compression *f* avec perte.

lost [lɒst] ◆ pt & pp —→ lose. ◆ adj **1.** [keys, money, etc.] perdu **2.** [person - in direction] perdu, égaré / *can you help me, I'm lost* pouvez-vous m'aider, je me suis perdu or égaré ▶ **to get lost** se perdre ▶ **lost in action** MIL mort au combat ▶ **get lost!** inf va te faire voir ! **3.** fig [engrossed] perdu, plongé, absorbé / *lost in a daydream* perdu dans une rêverie **4.** [wasted - time] perdu ; [- opportunity] perdu, manqué ; [- youth] gâché **5.** [confused, bewildered] perdu ; [disconcerted] désorienté **6.** [oblivious] insensible.

lost-and-found n ▶ **lost-and-found (office)** ⓤⓈ bureau *m* des objets trouvés.

lost cause n cause *f* perdue.

lost property n objets *mpl* trouvés.

lost property office n ⓤⓀ bureau *m* des objets trouvés.

lot [lɒt] n **1.** inf [group of people] : *come here, you lot!* venez ici, vous autres ! / *he's a bad lot* c'est un sale type **2.** [group of things] : *take all this lot and dump it in my office* prends tout ça et mets-le dans mon bureau **3.** [item in auction, in lottery] lot *m* **4.** [destiny, fortune] sort *m*, destin *m* / *to be content with one's lot* être content de son sort ▶ **to throw in one's lot with sb** se mettre du côté de qqn **5.** [random choice] : *the winners are chosen by lot* les gagnants sont choisis par tirage au sort ▶ **to draw** or **cast lots** tirer au sort **6.** ⓤⓈ [plot of land] terrain *m* / *a vacant lot* un terrain vague / *a used car lot* un parking de voitures d'occasion. ◆ **lots** inf ◆ pron beaucoup / *do you need any paper / envelopes? I've got lots* est-ce que tu as besoin de papier / d'enveloppes ? j'en ai plein. ◆ adv beaucoup.

❖ **a lot** ◆ pron phr beaucoup / *there's a lot still to be done* il y a encore beaucoup à faire / *there's not a lot you can do about it* tu n'y peux pas grand-chose / *what a lot of people!* quelle foule !, que de monde ! / *we see a lot of them* nous les voyons beaucoup or souvent. ◆ adv phr beaucoup / *a lot better* / *more* beaucoup mieux / plus / *thanks a lot!* merci beaucoup ! / *a (fat) lot she cares!* iro elle s'en fiche pas mal ! ❖ **the lot** pron phr le tout / *there isn't much, take the lot* il n'y en a pas beaucoup, prenez tout.

loth [ləʊθ] = **loath**.

lotion ['ləʊʃn] n lotion f.

lottery ['lɒtəri] n **1.** loterie f ▶ **lottery ticket** billet m de loterie **2.** fig [matter of luck] loterie f.

lotto ['lɒtəʊ] n loto m *(jeu de société).*

lotus ['ləʊtəs] n lotus m.

lotus position n position f du lotus.

loud [laʊd] ◆ adj **1.** [noise, shout] grand, puissant ; [voice, music] fort ; [explosion] fort, violent ; [vigorous - protest, applause] vif ; pej [loudmouthed, brash] bruyant, tapageur **2.** [garish - colour] criard, voyant ; [- pattern] voyant. ◆ adv fort / *can you speak a little louder?* pouvez-vous parler un peu plus fort ? / *the music was turned up loud* on avait mis la musique à fond / *to read out loud* lire à haute voix / *I was thinking out loud* je pensais tout haut.

loudhailer [,laʊd'heɪlər] n 🇬🇧 porte-voix m inv, mégaphone m.

loudly ['laʊdli] adv **1.** [noisily - speak] d'une voix forte ; [- laugh] bruyamment ; [vigorously] avec force or vigueur **2.** [garishly] de façon tapageuse or voyante.

loudmouth ['laʊdmaʊθ] *(pl* [-maʊðz]*)* n inf **1.** [noisy person] braillard m, -e f, gueulard m, -e f **2.** [boaster] crâneur m, -euse f, frimeur m, -euse f.

loudmouthed ['laʊdmaʊðd] adj inf **1.** [noisy] fort en gueule **2.** [boastful] grande gueule, qui l'ouvre.

loudness ['laʊdnɪs] n **1.** [of sound] intensité f, force f ; [of voice] intensité f ; [of cheers] vigueur f **2.** [on hi-fi system] ▶ **loudness control** correcteur m physiologique.

loudspeaker [,laʊd'spiːkər] n haut-parleur m ; [on stereo] enceinte f, baffle m.

Louisiana [luː,iːzi'ænə] pr n Louisiane f / *in Louisiana* en Louisiane.

lounge [laʊndʒ] ◆ n **1.** [room - in private house, on ship, in hotel] salon m ; [- at airport] salle f d'attente ; [bar] (salle f de) bar m ; 🇬🇧 [in pub] = **lounge bar 2.** [rest] : *to have a lounge in the sun* paresser or se prélasser au soleil **3.** MUS ▶ **lounge (music)** (musique f) lounge m. ◆ vi **1.** [recline] s'allonger, se prélasser ; [sprawl] être allongé **2.** [laze] paresser ; [hang about] traîner ; [stroll] flâner. ❖ **lounge about** 🇬🇧, **lounge around** = **lounge** (*vi*).

lounge bar n 🇬🇧 salon dans un pub *(plus confortable et plus cher que le « public bar »).*

lounger ['laʊndʒər] n **1.** [sunbed] chaise f longue, bain m de soleil **2.** [person] paresseux m, -euse f.

lounge suit n 🇬🇧 costume m de ville ; [on invitation] tenue f de ville.

louse [laʊs] n **1.** (*pl* lice [laɪs]) [insect] pou m **2.** (*pl* louses) v inf [person] salaud m, chienne f. ❖ **louse up** vt sep v inf [spoil] foutre en l'air.

lousy ['laʊzi] (*compar* lousier, *superl* lousiest) adj **1.** inf [appalling - film, singer] nul ; [- weather] pourri / *I feel lousy this morning* je suis mal fichu ce matin / *I'm lousy at tennis* or *I'm a lousy tennis player* je suis nul au tennis, je joue au tennis comme un pied / *you're a lousy liar* **a)** [lie badly] tu ne sais pas mentir **b)** [as intensifier] tu n'es

qu'un sale menteur ; [annoying] fichu, sacré **2.** inf [mean] vache **3.** inf & dated [full] : *the town was lousy with police* la ville grouillait de flics **4.** [lice-infested] pouilleux.

lout [laʊt] n [bumpkin] rustre m ; [hooligan] voyou m.

loutish ['laʊtɪʃ] adj [behaviour] grossier ; [manners] de rustre, mal dégrossi.

louvre 🇬🇧, **louver** 🇺🇸 ['luːvər] n [slat] lamelle f ; [window] jalousie f, volet m à claire-voie, persienne f.

louvred 🇬🇧, **louvered** 🇺🇸 ['luːvəd] adj à claire-voie.

lovable ['lʌvəbl] adj charmant, sympathique, attachant.

love [lʌv] ◆ vt **1.** [sweetheart] aimer ; [friends, relatives] aimer beaucoup or bien **2.** [enjoy] aimer, adorer / *I love lying* or *to lie in bed on Sunday mornings* j'adore faire la grasse matinée le dimanche / *I'd love to come* j'aimerais beaucoup venir / *I'd love you to come* j'aimerais beaucoup que or cela me ferait très plaisir que tu viennes / *would you like to come too? — I'd love to* voudriez-vous venir aussi ? — avec grand plaisir **3.** [prize - one's country, freedom, etc.] aimer. ◆ n **1.** [for person] amour m / *it was love at first sight* ce fut le coup de foudre ▶ **to be in love (with sb)** être amoureux (de qqn) ▶ **to fall in love (with sb)** tomber amoureux (de qqn) ▶ **to make love** faire l'amour / *(lots of) love from Jane* or *all my love, Jane* [in letter] affectueusement, Jane **2.** [for jazz, one's country, etc.] amour m **3.** [beloved person] amour m / *she's the love of his life* c'est la femme de sa vie ; [favourite activity] passion f **4.** [term of address] : *thank you, (my) love* inf merci, mon chou ; [to stranger] : *wait a minute, love!* **a)** 🇬🇧 inf [to child] attends une minute, mon petit ! **b)** [to adult] attendez une minute **5.** SPORT zéro m.

love affair n liaison f (amoureuse) ; fig passion f / *his love affair with Paris* sa passion pour Paris.

lovebird ['lʌvbɜːd] n **1.** ORNITH perruche f ▶ **lovebirds** inséparables mpl **2.** hum [lover] amoureux m, -euse f.

lovebite ['lʌvbaɪt] n 🇬🇧 suçon m.

love child n enfant mf de l'amour.

loved up [lʌvd-] adj 🇬🇧 drugs sl tout gentil *(sous l'effet de l'ecstasy).*

love handles pl n inf poignées fpl d'amour.

love-hate adj ▶ **a love-hate relationship** une relation d'amour-haine.

love-in n **1.** dated [hippie gathering] rassemblement m de hipppies **2.** fig situation dans laquelle des gens passent leur temps à se faire des compliments les uns aux autres.

loveless ['lʌvlɪs] adj [marriage] sans amour ; [person - unloved] mal aimé ; [- unloving] sans cœur, incapable d'aimer.

love letter n lettre f d'amour, billet m doux.

love life n vie f sentimentale.

lovelorn ['lʌvlɔːn] adj malheureux en amour.

lovely ['lʌvli] (*compar* lovelier, *superl* loveliest) ◆ adj **1.** [in appearance - person] beau *(before vowel or silent 'h' bel, f belle)*, joli ; [- child] joli, mignon ; [- home, scenery] joli **2.** [view, evening, weather] beau *(before vowel or silent 'h' bel, f belle)* ; [holiday] (très) agréable ; [dress] joli ; [meal] excellent / *it's lovely to see you* je suis enchanté or ravi de vous voir / *it's lovely and warm by the fire* 🇬🇧 il fait bon près de la cheminée / *it sounds lovely* cela a l'air très bien / *would you like to come to dinner next week? — that'd be lovely* tu veux venir dîner la semaine prochaine ? — ça serait vraiment bien or avec plaisir **3.** [in character] charmant, très aimable. ◆ n inf mignonne f.

lovemaking ['lʌv,meɪkɪŋ] n [sexual intercourse] ébats mpl (amoureux).

lover ['lʌvər] n **1.** [sexual partner] amant m, -e f **2.** dated [suitor] amoureux m, soupirant m / *the young lovers* les jeunes amoureux *mpl* **3.** [enthusiast] amateur *m*, -trice *f* / *he's a real music lover* c'est un mélomane / *I'm not a dog lover myself* moi-même je n'aime pas beaucoup les chiens.

lovesick ['lʌvsɪk] *adj* : *to be lovesick* se languir d'amour.

love song *n* chanson *f* d'amour.

love story *n* histoire *f* d'amour.

love triangle *n* triangle *m* amoureux.

lovey-dovey ['lʌvɪdʌvɪ] *adj* *inf & pej* doucereux.

loving ['lʌvɪŋ] *adj* [affectionate] affectueux ; [tender] tendre.

lovingly ['lʌvɪŋlɪ] *adv* [affectionately] affectueusement ; [tenderly] tendrement ; [passionately] avec amour, amoureusement ; [with great care] soigneusement, avec soin.

low [ləʊ] ◆ *adj* **1.** [in height] bas / *this room has a low ceiling* cette pièce est basse de plafond / *low hills* collines peu élevées / *a low neckline* un décolleté **2.** [in scale - temperature] bas ; [-level] faible / *the temperature is in the low twenties* il fait un peu plus de vingt degrés / *I've reached a low point in my career* j'ai atteint un creux dans ma carrière / *low gear* [US] première (vitesse) *f* ; [in degree, intensity - probability, visibility] faible ; [- fire] bas ; [- lighting] faible, tamisé / *cook on a low heat* faire cuire à feu doux ; [in value, amount - figure, price] bas, faible ; [- profit] faible, maigre / *attendance was low* il y avait peu de monde / *we're rather low on whisky* on n'a plus beaucoup de whisky / *low in calories* pauvre en calories **3.** [poor - intelligence, standard] faible ; [- opinion] faible, piètre ; [- in health] mauvais, médiocre ; [- in quality] mauvais / *I'm in rather low spirits* or *I feel rather low* je n'ai pas le moral, je suis assez déprimé **4.** [in rank] bas, inférieur **5.** [vulgar - behaviour] grossier ; [- tastes] vulgaire / *that was a low trick* c'était un sale tour **6.** [soft - voice, music] bas, faible ; [- light] faible / *keep your voice low* ne parlez pas trop fort / *turn the radio down low* mettez la radio moins fort / *turn the lights down low* baissez les lumières **7.** [deep - note, voice] bas. ◆ *adv* **1.** [in height] bas ▶ **lower down** plus bas / *a helicopter flew low over the town* un hélicoptère a survolé la ville à basse altitude / *he bowed low* il s'inclina profondément **2.** [in intensity] bas / *stocks are running low* les réserves baissent / *the batteries are running low* les piles sont usées **3.** [morally] : *I wouldn't stoop* or *sink so low as to tell lies* je ne m'abaisserais pas à mentir. ◆ *n* **1.** [in height] bas *m* ; [in intensity] minimum *m* / *the heating is on low* le chauffage est au minimum **2.** [low point] niveau *m* bas, point *m* bas / *the dollar has reached a record low* le dollar a atteint son niveau le plus bas / *relations between them are at an all-time low* leurs relations n'ont jamais été si mauvaises **3.** METEOR dépression *f*.

low-alcohol *adj* à faible teneur en alcool.

low-angle shot *n* TV & CIN contre-plongée *f*.

lowbrow ['ləʊbraʊ] ◆ *n* *pej* personne *f* sans prétentions intellectuelles or terre à terre. ◆ *adj* [person] peu intellectuel, terre à terre ; [book, film] sans prétentions intellectuelles.

low-budget *adj* économique.

low-calorie, low-cal *adj* (à) basses calories.

Low Church *adj* à tendance évangélique *(dans l'Église anglicane)*.

low-cost *adj* (à) bon marché ; [airline] low cost.

Low Countries *pl pr n* ▶ **the Low Countries** les Pays-Bas *mpl*.

low-cut *adj* décolleté.

low-density housing *n* zones *fpl* d'habitation peu peuplées.

lowdown ['ləʊdaʊn] *n* (U) *inf* renseignements *mpl* / *can you give me the lowdown on what happened?* tu peux me

mettre au courant de ce qui s'est passé ? ↔ **low-down** *adj* **1.** [shameful] honteux, bas ; [mean] mesquin **2.** [US] [depressed] cafardeux.

low-end *adj* bas de gamme.

lower¹ ['ləʊə] ◆ *adj (compar of low)* inférieur, plus bas ▶ **the lower back** le bas du dos ▶ **the lower classes** les classes inférieures ▶ **the lower House** or **Chamber** [UK] POL la Chambre basse or des communes. ◆ *adv (compar of low)* ▶ **the lower paid** la tranche inférieure du salariat. ◆ *vt* **1.** [blind] baisser ; [eyes] baisser ; [sails] abaisser, amener ; [lifeboat] mettre à la mer **2.** [reduce - price, pressure, standard] baisser, diminuer / *lower your voice* parlez moins fort, baissez la voix **3.** [morally] : *she wouldn't lower herself to talk to them* elle ne s'abaisserait pas au point de leur adresser la parole. ◆ *vi* [diminish - pressure] diminuer ; [- price] baisser.

lower² ['laʊə] *vi* **1.** [sky, weather] se couvrir **2.** [person] regarder d'un air menaçant.

lower-case ['ləʊə-] ◆ *adj* TYPO en bas de casse, minuscule. ◆ *n* bas *m* de casse.

lower-class ['ləʊə-] *adj* populaire.

lowest ['ləʊɪst] *adj (superl of low)* le plus bas / *the lowest of the low* le dernier des derniers / *the newspaper panders to the views of the lowest in society* *fig* ce journal flatte les instincts les plus bas de la société ▶ **the lowest common multiple** le plus petit commun multiple ▶ **the lowest common denominator** le plus petit dénominateur commun.

low-fat *adj* [yoghurt, crisps] allégé ; [milk] demi-écrémé.

low-flying *adj* volant à basse altitude.

low-frequency *adj* (à) basse fréquence.

low-grade *adj* [in quality] de qualité inférieure ; [in rank] (de rang) inférieur, subalterne.

low-heeled *adj* à talons plats.

low-income *adj* à faibles revenus.

low-interest *adj* FIN [credit, loan] à taux réduit.

low-key *adj* [style] discret (discrète) ; [person] réservé.

lowland ['ləʊlənd] *n* plaine *f*, basse terre *f* ▶ **the Lowlands** les Basses Terres.

low-level *adj* [talks] à bas niveau ; [operation] de faible envergure ▶ **low-level flying** AERON vol *m* à basse altitude ▶ **low-level language** COMPUT langage *m* non évolué or de bas niveau ▶ **low-level radiation** NUCL irradiation *f* de faible intensité ▶ **low-level radioactive waste** déchets *mpl* radioactifs de faible activité.

low life *n* [underworld] pègre *f*. ↔ **low-life** ◆ *adj* du milieu. ◆ *n* [despicable person] ordure *f* v *inf*.

lowlights ['ləʊlaɪts] *pl n* **1.** [in hair] mèches *fpl* **2.** *inf* [worst points] points *mpl* noirs.

low-loader *n* RAIL wagon *m* à plate-forme surbaissée ; AUTO camion *m* à plate-forme surbaissée.

lowly ['ləʊlɪ] *(compar* **lowlier**, *superl* **lowliest**) *adj* [modest] modeste ; [meek] humble ; [simple] sans prétention or prétentions.

low-lying *adj* [land - gen] bas ; [- below sea level] au-dessous du niveau de la mer ; [cloud] bas.

low-maintenance *adj* [pet] qui ne demande pas beaucoup de soins ; [garden, hairstyle] qui ne demande pas beaucoup d'entretien ; *hum* [friend] peu exigeant.

Low Mass *n* RELIG messe *f* basse.

low-necked *adj* décolleté.

low-octane fuel *n* carburant *m* à faible indice d'octane.

low-paid ◆ *adj* mal payé. ◆ *pl n* ▶ **the low-paid** les petits salaires *mpl*.

low-powered adj de faible puissance.

low profile n ▸ **to keep a low profile** garder un profil bas. ❖ **low-profile** adj **1.** = **low-key 2.** AUTO ▸ **low-profile tyre** pneu *m* à profil bas.

low-res [ləʊrez] *inf* abbr of **low-resolution**.

low-resolution adj à basse résolution.

low-rise adj [buildings] de faible hauteur, bas.

low season n ▸ **the low season** la basse saison.

low-slung adj [furniture] bas ; AUTO [chassis] surbaissé.

low-start mortgage n UK crédit *m* immobilier à faible taux initial.

low-sulphur petrol n essence *f* à basse teneur en soufre.

low-tar adj ▸ **low-tar cigarettes** cigarettes *fpl* à faible teneur en goudron.

low-tech adj rudimentaire.

low tide n marée *f* basse / **at low tide** à marée basse.

low-voltage adj à faible voltage, à faible tension.

low water n *(U)* basses eaux *fpl*.

loyal ['lɔɪəl] adj loyal, fidèle ▸ **to be loyal to sb** être loyal envers qqn, faire preuve de loyauté envers qqn.

loyalist ['lɔɪəlɪst] ❖ n loyaliste *mf*. ❖ adj loyaliste. ❖ **Loyalist** n loyaliste *mf*.

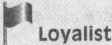 **Loyalist**

Dans le contexte britannique, le mot **Loyalist** désigne un protestant d'Irlande du Nord souhaitant que son pays reste rattaché au Royaume-Uni.

loyally ['lɔɪəlɪ] adv loyalement, fidèlement.

loyalty ['lɔɪəltɪ] *(pl* **loyalties)** n **1.** [faithfulness] loyauté *f*, fidélité *f* **2.** [tie] : *tribal loyalties* liens *mpl* tribaux.

loyalty card n carte *f* de fidélité.

lozenge ['lɒzɪndʒ] n **1.** [sweet] pastille *f* ▸ **throat lozenge** pastille pour la gorge **2.** [rhombus] losange *m*.

LP (abbr of **long-play**) n ▸ **an LP** un 33 tours.

LPG [ˌelpiː'dʒiː] (abbr of **liquified petroleum gas**) n GPL *m*.

LPI written abbr of **lines per inch**.

L-plate n UK plaque apposée sur la voiture d'un conducteur qui n'a pas encore son permis (L signifie «learner», apprenti).

LPN (abbr of **licensed practical nurse**) n aide-soignant(e) diplômé(e).

LRAM (abbr of **Licentiate of the Royal Academy of Music**) n membre de la Royal Academy of Music.

LSAT (abbr of **Law School Admission(s) Test**) n test d'admission aux études de droit.

LSD[1] (abbr of **lysergic acid diethylamide**) n LSD *m*.

LSD[2], lsd, Lsd (abbr of **librae, solidi, denarii**) n symboles représentant les pounds, les shillings et les pence de l'ancienne monnaie britannique avant l'adoption du système décimal en 1971.

LSE (abbr of **London School of Economics and Political Science**) pr n prestigieux établissement universitaire dépendant de l'Université de Londres, spécialisé dans l'économie et les sciences politiques.

LSKOL MESSAGING written abbr of **long slow kiss on the lips**.

LSO (abbr of **London Symphony Orchestra**) pr n orchestre symphonique de Londres.

LT (written abbr of **low tension**) BT.

Lt. (written abbr of **lieutenant**) Lieut.

Ltd, ltd (written abbr of **limited**) ≃ SARL.

LTNC MESSAGING written abbr of **long time no see**.

LTNS MESSAGING written abbr of **long time no see**.

lubricant ['lu:brɪkənt] ❖ adj lubrifiant. ❖ n lubrifiant *m*.

lubricate ['lu:brɪkeɪt] vt [gen] lubrifier ; [mechanism] lubrifier, graisser, huiler.

lubrication [ˌlu:brɪ'keɪʃn] n [gen] lubrification *f* ; [of mechanism] lubrification f, graissage *m*, huilage *m*.

lucid ['lu:sɪd] adj **1.** [clear-headed] lucide / *he has his lucid moments* il a des moments de lucidité **2.** [clear] clair, limpide / *she gave a lucid account of events* elle donna un compte rendu net et précis des événements.

lucidity [lu:'sɪdətɪ] n **1.** [of mind] lucidité *f* **2.** [of style, account] clarté *f*, limpidité *f*.

lucidly ['lu:sɪdlɪ] adv lucidement, avec lucidité.

luck [lʌk] n **1.** [fortune] chance *f* / *to have good luck* avoir de la chance ▸ **good luck!** bonne chance ! ; [good fortune] : *that's a bit of luck!* c'est de la chance ! / *you're in luck* or *your luck's in* vous avez de la chance / *we're out of luck* on n'a pas de chance / *better luck next time* vous aurez plus de chance la prochaine fois / *any luck?* alors, ça a marché ? ; [bad fortune] : *it's bad luck to spill salt* renverser du sel porte malheur ▸ **bad** or **hard** or **tough luck!** pas de chance ! / *we thought the exam was cancelled — no such luck* nous croyions que l'examen était annulé — ç'aurait été trop beau ▸ **with (any) luck** avec un peu de chance ▸ **worse luck** tant pis **2.** [chance, opportunity] hasard *m* ▸ **it's the luck of the draw** c'est une question de chance ▸ **to try one's luck** tenter sa chance ▸ **as luck would have it a)** [by chance] par hasard **b)** [by good luck] par bonheur **c)** [by bad luck] par malheur. ❖ **luck out** vi US inf [succeed] avoir de la veine.

luckily ['lʌkɪlɪ] adv heureusement, par chance / *luckily for him, he escaped* heureusement pour lui, il s'est échappé.

luckless ['lʌklɪs] adj [person] malchanceux ; [escapade, attempt] malheureux.

lucky ['lʌkɪ] *(compar* **luckier**, *superl* **luckiest)** adj **1.** [fortunate - person] chanceux ; [- encounter, winner] heureux ▸ **to be lucky** avoir de la chance ▸ **to get lucky** inf avoir un coup de bol / *what a lucky escape!* on l'a échappé belle ! / *it was lucky for them that we were there* heureusement pour eux que nous étions là / *it's lucky he heard you* heureusement qu'il t'as entendu, c'est une chance qu'il t'ait entendu ▸ **a lucky break** inf un coup de pot ou de bol ▸ **it's my lucky day** c'est mon jour de chance ▸ **you lucky devil** or **thing!** inf sacré veinard ! ▸ **lucky you!** vous en avez de la chance ! **2.** [token, number] porte-bonheur *(inv)* **3.** [guess] heureux.

Note that **c'est une chance que** is followed by a verb in the subjunctive:
It's lucky no one was killed. C'est une chance que personne n'ait été tué.

lucky dip n UK jeu d'enfant consistant à chercher des cadeaux enfouis dans une caisse remplie de sciure.

lucrative ['lu:krətɪv] adj [job] bien rémunéré, lucratif ; [activity, deal] lucratif, rentable.

ludicrous ['lu:dɪkrəs] adj ridicule, absurde.

ludicrously ['luːdɪkrəslɪ] adv ridiculement.

ludo ['luːdəʊ] n ≃ (jeu m des) petits chevaux mpl.

lug [lʌg] (pt & pp **lugged**, cont **lugging**) ◆ vt inf [carry, pull] trimbaler. ◆ ◆ n **1.** [for fixing] ergot m, (petite) patte f ; [handle] anse f, poignée f **2.** 🇬🇧 v inf = **lughole 3.** 🇺🇸 [blockhead] niais m. ❖ **lug about** 🇬🇧, **lug around** vt sep inf trimbaler.

luggage ['lʌgɪdʒ] n (U) bagages mpl ▶ **luggage compartment** compartiment m à bagages.

luggage handler n 🇬🇧 bagagiste mf.

luggage rack n 🇬🇧 RAIL [shelf] porte-bagages m inv ; [net] filet m (à bagages) ; AUTO galerie f (de toit).

luggage van n 🇬🇧 RAIL fourgon m (à bagages).

lughole ['lʌghəʊl] n 🇬🇧 v inf [ear] esgourde f.

lugubrious [luːˈguːbrɪəs] adj lugubre.

lukewarm ['luːkwɔːm] adj [water, soup] tiède / a lukewarm reception **a)** [of person] un accueil peu chaleureux **b)** [of book, film] un accueil mitigé.

lull [lʌl] ◆ ◆ n [in weather] accalmie f ; [in fighting] accalmie f, pause f ; [in conversation] pause f. ◆ vt [calm - anxiety, person] calmer, apaiser / she lulled the child to sleep elle berça l'enfant jusqu'à ce qu'il s'endorme.

lullaby ['lʌləbaɪ] (pl **lullabies**) n berceuse f.

lumbago [lʌmˈbeɪgəʊ] n (U) lumbago m, lombalgie f.

lumber ['lʌmbər] ◆ ◆ n **1.** 🇺🇸 [cut wood] bois m (d'œuvre) ; [ready for use] bois m de construction or de charpente **2.** 🇬🇧 [junk] bric-à-brac m inv. ◆ vt 🇺🇸 [logs] débiter ; [tree] abattre, couper. ◆ vi **1.** [large person, animal] marcher pesamment ; [heavy vehicle] : the tanks lumbered into the centre of the town la lourde colonne de chars avançait vers le centre de la ville **2.** 🇺🇸 [fell trees] abattre des arbres (pour le bois). ❖ **lumber with** vt sep (usu passive) 🇬🇧 inf [encumber] ▶ **to lumber sb with sthg** refiler qqch à qqn.

lumbering ['lʌmbərɪŋ] ◆ ◆ n 🇺🇸 exploitation f forestière. ◆ adj [heavy - step] pesant, lourd ; [- person] lourd, maladroit.

lumberjack ['lʌmbədʒæk] n bûcheron m, -onne f ▶ **lumberjack shirt** chemise f de bûcheron (chemise épaisse à grands carreaux).

lumbermill ['lʌmbəˌmɪl] n 🇺🇸 scierie f.

lumber room n 🇬🇧 débarras m.

lumberyard ['lʌmbəjɑːd] n 🇺🇸 dépôt m de bois.

luminary ['luːmɪnərɪ] (pl **luminaries**) n [celebrity] lumière f, sommité f.

luminescent [ˌluːmɪˈnesənt] adj luminescent.

luminosity [ˌluːmɪˈnɒsətɪ] n luminosité f.

luminous ['luːmɪnəs] adj [paint, colour, sky] lumineux ; fig [explanation, argument] lumineux, limpide.

lump [lʌmp] ◆ ◆ n **1.** [of sugar] morceau m / one lump or two? un ou deux sucres ? **2.** [of solid matter - small] morceau m ; [- large] masse f ; [in food] grumeau m ; [of marble] bloc m **3.** [bump on surface] bosse f **4.** MED [swelling] grosseur f, protubérance f **5.** [of money] : you don't have to pay it all in one lump vous n'êtes pas obligé de tout payer en une seule fois **6.** inf & pej [clumsy person] empoté m, -e f. ◆ vt inf [put up with] : if you don't like it you can lump it! si ça ne te plaît pas, tant pis pour toi ! ❖ **lump together** vt sep **1.** [gather together] réunir, rassembler **2.** [consider the same] mettre dans la même catégorie.

lumpectomy [ˌlʌmˈpektəmɪ] n ablation f d'une tumeur au sein.

lump sum n somme f forfaitaire.

lumpy ['lʌmpɪ] (compar **lumpier**, superl **lumpiest**) adj [sauce] plein de grumeaux ; [mattress] plein de bosses, défoncé.

lunacy ['luːnəsɪ] (pl **lunacies**) n **1.** [madness] démence f, folie f **2.** [folly] folie f / it would be lunacy to accept such a proposal ce serait de la folie d'accepter pareille proposition.

lunar ['luːnər] adj [rock, month, cycle] lunaire ; [eclipse] de la Lune ▶ **lunar landing** alunissage m ▶ **lunar month** lunaison f.

lunatic ['luːnətɪk] ◆ ◆ n **1.** [madman] aliéné m, -e f, dément m, -e f **2.** inf [fool] cinglé m, -e f. ◆ adj **1.** [insane] fou (before vowel or silent 'h' **fol**, f **folle**), dément **2.** inf [crazy - person] cinglé, dingue ; [- idea] insensé.

lunatic asylum n asile m d'aliénés.

lunatic fringe n pej extrémistes mpl fanatiques.

lunch [lʌntʃ] ◆ ◆ n déjeuner m ▶ **to have lunch** déjeuner / she's gone out for lunch elle est partie déjeuner / what did you have for lunch? qu'est-ce que tu as mangé à midi ? ◆ vi déjeuner.

lunchbox ['lʌntʃbɒks] n **1.** [for sandwiches, etc.] boîte dans laquelle on transporte son déjeuner **2.** inf bijoux mpl de famille.

luncheon ['lʌntʃən] n fml déjeuner m.

luncheonette [ˌlʌntʃəˈnet] n 🇺🇸 snack m, snack-bar m.

luncheon meat, **lunchmeat** 🇺🇸 n bloc de viande de porc en conserve.

luncheon voucher n 🇬🇧 Ticket-Restaurant® m.

lunch hour n heure f du déjeuner.

lunchpail ['lʌntʃpeɪl] 🇺🇸 = **lunchbox**.

lunchtime ['lʌntʃtaɪm] n heure f du déjeuner / I saw him at lunchtime je l'ai vu à midi or à l'heure du déjeuner.

lung [lʌŋ] ◆ ◆ n poumon m. ◆ comp [artery, congestion, disease] pulmonaire ; [transplant] du poumon ▶ **lung cancer** cancer m du poumon.

lunge [lʌndʒ] ◆ ◆ n **1.** [sudden movement] ▶ **to make a lunge for sthg** se précipiter vers qqch **2.** FENCING fente f (avant) **3.** EQUIT longe f. ◆ vi [move suddenly] faire un mouvement brusque en avant / she lunged at him with a knife elle se précipita sur lui avec un couteau. ◆ vt [horse] mener à la longe.

lungful ['lʌŋfʊl] n : take a lungful of air inspirez à fond.

lupin ['luːpɪn] n 🇬🇧 lupin m.

lupine ['luːpaɪn] ◆ ◆ n 🇺🇸 = **lupin**. ◆ adj de loup.

lurch [lɜːtʃ] ◆ ◆ vi [person] tituber, chanceler ; [car - swerve] faire une embardée ; [- jerk forwards] avancer par à-coups ; [ship] tanguer. ◆ n : the car gave a sudden lurch and left the road la voiture fit une embardée et quitta la route.

lure [ljʊər] ◆ ◆ n **1.** [attraction] attrait m ; [charm] charme m ; [temptation] tentation f **2.** FISHING & HUNT leurre m. ◆ vt [person] attirer (sous un faux prétexte) / he lured them into a trap il les a attirés dans un piège. ❖ **lure away** vt sep : she invited me over in order to lure me away from the office elle m'a invité chez elle pour m'éloigner du bureau.

lurid ['ljʊərɪd] adj **1.** [sensational - account, story] macabre, atroce, horrible ; [salacious] salace, malsain **2.** [glaring - sky, sunset] sanglant, rougeoyant ; [- wallpaper, shirt] criard, voyant.

lurk [lɜːk] vi [person, animal] se tapir ; [danger] se cacher, menacer ; [doubt, worry] persister ▶ **to lurk in chatrooms** suivre des forums sans y participer.

lurker n [on Internet] personne qui suit les chats dans un forum sans y participer.

lurking ['lɜːkɪŋ] adj [suspicion] vague ; [danger] mena-çant.

Lusaka [luːˈsɑːkə] pr n Lusaka.

luscious ['lʌʃəs] adj **1.** [fruit] succulent ; [colour] riche **2.** [woman] séduisant ; [lips] pulpeux.

lush [lʌʃ] ◆ adj **1.** [vegetation] riche, luxuriant ; [fruit] suc-culent ; *fig* [description] riche **2.** [luxurious] luxueux. ◆ n US *v inf* poivrot *m*, -e *f*.

lust [lʌst] n **1.** [sexual desire] désir *m* sexuel, concupis-cence *f* ; [as sin] luxure *f* **2.** [greed] soif *f*, convoitise *f* / *lust for power* soif de pouvoir. ❖ **lust after** vt insep [person] désirer, avoir envie de, convoiter ; [money, property] convoi-ter. ❖ **lust for** vt insep [money] convoiter ; [revenge, power] avoir soif de.

luster US = **lustre**.

lustful ['lʌstful] adj [lecherous] concupiscent, lascif.

lustily ['lʌstɪlɪ] adv [sing, shout] à pleine gorge, à pleins poumons.

lustre UK, **luster** US ['lʌstər] n **1.** [sheen] lustre *m*, brillant *m* **2.** *fig* [glory] éclat *m*.

lusty ['lʌstɪ] (*compar* lustier, *superl* lustiest) adj [strong - person, baby] vigoureux, robuste ; [- voice, manner] vigoureux.

lute [luːt] n MUS luth *m*.

luv [lʌv] n & vt UK *inf* = **love**.

LUV MESSAGING written abbr of **love**.

luvvie ['lʌvɪ] n *inf & hum* acteur *m* prétentieux, actrice *f* prétentieuse.

Luxembourg ['lʌksəmbɜːg] pr n **1.** [country] Luxem-bourg *m* / *in Luxembourg* au Luxembourg **2.** [town] Luxembourg.

Luxemburger ['lʌksəmbɜːgər] n Luxembourgeois *m*, -e *f*.

luxuriant [lʌgˈʒʊərɪənt] adj **1.** [luxurious - surround-ings] luxueux, somptueux **2.** [vegetation] luxuriant ; [crops, undergrowth] abondant, riche ; [countryside] couvert de végétation, luxuriant ; *fig* [style] luxuriant, riche **3.** [flowing - hair, beard] abondant.

luxuriate [lʌgˈʒʊərɪeɪt] vi **1.** [take pleasure] ▶ **to luxuri-ate in sthg** se délecter de qqch **2.** *liter* [proliferate, flourish] proliférer.

luxurious [lʌgˈʒʊərɪəs] adj **1.** [opulent - house, decor, clothes] luxueux, somptueux ; [- car] luxueux **2.** [voluptuous] voluptueux.

luxury ['lʌkʃərɪ] (*pl* luxuries) ◆ n **1.** [comfort] luxe *m* ▶ **to live in luxury** or **to lead a life of luxury** vivre dans le luxe **2.** [treat] luxe *m*. ◆ comp [car, restaurant, kitchen] de luxe ; [apartment] de luxe, de standing.

luxury goods pl n articles *mpl* de luxe.

LV 1. COMM written abbr of **luncheon voucher 2.** MESSAGING written abbr of **love**.

LW (written abbr of **long wave**) GO.

lychee [ˌlaɪˈtʃiː] n litchi *m*, lychee *m*.

Lycra® ['laɪkrə] n Lycra® *m*.

lying ['laɪɪŋ] ◆ cont ⟶ **lie**. ◆ adj **1.** [reclining] couché, étendu, allongé **2.** [dishonest - person] menteur ; [- story] mensonger, faux (fausse). ◆ n **1.** [corpse] ▶ **ly-ing in state** exposition *f* du corps **2.** *(U)* [dishonesty] men-songes *mpl*.

lying-in n MED couches *fpl*.

lymph gland, lymph node n ganglion *m* lympha-tique.

lynch [lɪntʃ] vt lyncher ▶ **lynch mob** lyncheurs *mpl*.

lynching ['lɪntʃɪŋ] n lynchage *m*.

lynchpin ['lɪntʃpɪn] = **linchpin**.

lynx [lɪŋks] (*pl* lynx or lynxes) n lynx *m inv*.

Lyon [liːɔ̃], **Lyons** ['laɪənz] pr n Lyon.

lyre ['laɪər] n lyre *f*.

lyric ['lɪrɪk] ◆ adj lyrique. ◆ n [poem] poème *m* lyrique. ❖ **lyrics** pl n [of song] paroles *fpl*.

lyrical ['lɪrɪkl] adj **1.** *lit* lyrique **2.** *fig* passionné / *he was positively lyrical about his visit to China* son séjour en Chine l'a véritablement enthousiasmé.

lyricist ['lɪrɪsɪst] n [of poems] poète *m* lyrique ; [of song, opera] parolier *m*, -ère *f*.

m **1.** (written abbr of metre) m **2.** (written abbr of million) M **3.** written abbr of mile.

M ◆ (abbr of motorway) UK ▶ **the M5** l'autoroute M5. ◆ (written abbr of medium) M.

ma [mɑ:] n inf maman f.

MA ◆ n (abbr of Master of Arts) [in England, Wales and US] ≃ (titulaire d'une) maîtrise de lettres ; [in Scotland] premier examen universitaire, équivalent de la licence. ◆ written abbr of Massachusetts.

ma'am [mæm] n madame f.

mac [mæk] inf (abbr of macintosh) UK imper m.

macabre [mə'kɑ:brə] adj macabre.

macadamia nut [,mækə'deɪmɪə-] n noix f de macadamia.

macaroni [,mækə'rəʊnɪ] n (U) macaronis mpl ▶ **macaroni cheese** gratin m de macaronis.

macaroon [,mækə'ru:n] n CULIN macaron m.

macaw [mə'kɔ:] n ara m.

macchiato [mæk'jɑ:təʊ] n café m macchiato ; ≃ café m noisette.

Mace® [meɪs] ◆ n [spray] gaz m lacrymogène. ◆ vt US inf bombarder au gaz lacrymogène.

mace [meɪs] n **1.** [spice] macis m **2.** [club] massue f, masse f d'armes ; [ceremonial] masse f.

Macedonia [,mæsɪ'dəʊnjə] pr n Macédoine f / **in Macedonia** en Macédoine.

machete [mə'ʃetɪ] n machette f.

Machiavellian [,mækɪə'velɪən] adj machiavélique.

machinations [,mækɪ'neɪʃnz] pl n machinations fpl.

machine [mə'ʃi:n] ◆ n **1.** [mechanical device] machine f ▶ **to do sthg by machine** or **on a machine** faire qqch à la machine ; fig & pej [person] machine f, automate m **2.** [organization] machine f, appareil m **3.** [car, motorbike] machine f ; [plane] appareil m. ◆ comp ▶ **the machine age** l'ère f de la machine. ◆ vt SEW coudre à la machine ; INDUST [manufacture] fabriquer à la machine ; [work on machine] usiner.

machine code n code m machine.

machine gun n mitrailleuse f. ❖ **machine-gun** vt mitrailler.

machine language n langage m machine.

machine-readable adj COMPUT exploitable par machine.

machine room n salle f des machines.

machinery [mə'ʃi:nərɪ] n (pl machineries) n **1.** (U) [machines] machines fpl, machinerie f ; [mechanism] mécanisme m **2.** fig rouages mpl.

machine shop n atelier m d'usinage.

machine tool n machine-outil f.

machine washable adj lavable à la or en machine.

machinist [mə'ʃi:nɪst] n INDUST opérateur m, -trice f (sur machine) ; SEW mécanicien m, -enne f.

machismo [mə'tʃɪzməʊ or mə'kɪzməʊ] n machisme m.

macho ['mætʃəʊ] inf ◆ adj macho. ◆ n macho m.

mackerel ['mækrəl] n (pl mackerel or mackerels) n maquereau m.

mackintosh ['mækɪntɒʃ] n UK imperméable m.

macramé ['mækrəmeɪ] n macramé m.

macro ['mækrəʊ] n (pl macros) n COMPUT macro-instruction f, macro f.

macrobiotic [,mækrəʊbaɪ'ɒtɪk] adj macrobiotique. ❖ **macrobiotics** n (U) macrobiotique f.

macroclimate ['mækrəʊ,klaɪmət] n macroclimat m.

macrocosm ['mækrəʊkɒzm] n macrocosme m.

macroeconomics ['mækrəʊ,i:kə'nɒmɪks] n (U) macro-économie f.

macroinstruction ['mækrəʊɪn,strʌkʃn] = macro.

macromarketing ['mækrəʊ,mɑ:kɪtɪŋ] n macromarketing m.

mad [mæd] ◆ adj **1.** UK [crazy] fou (before vowel or silent 'h' fol, f folle) ▶ **to go mad** devenir fou / **to be mad with joy / grief** être fou de joie / douleur ▶ **to drive sb mad** rendre qqn fou **2.** [absurd - ambition, plan] fou (before vowel or silent 'h' fol, f folle), insensé **3.** [angry] en colère, furieux / **he went mad when he saw them** il s'est mis dans une colère noire en les voyant ▶ **to be mad at** or **with sb** être en colère or fâché contre qqn / **she makes me mad** elle m'énerve / **don't get mad** ne vous fâchez pas **4.** [frantic] : **there was a mad rush for the door** tous les gens se sont rués vers la porte comme des fous / **I'm in a mad rush** inf je suis très très pressé, je suis à la bourre / **don't go mad and try to do it all yourself** fig tu ne vas pas te tuer à essayer de tout faire toi-même ? ▶ **like mad** inf : **to run like mad** courir comme un fou or un dératé **5.** UK inf [enthusiastic, keen] fou (before vowel or silent 'h' fol, f folle) ▶ **to be mad about** or **on sthg** être fou de qqch / **he's mad about her** il est fou d'elle **6.** [dog] enragé ; [bull] furieux. ◆ adv UK ▶ **to be mad keen on** or **about sthg** inf être dingue or être un mordu de qqch.

MAD [mæd] (abbr of mutual assured destruction) n destruction f mutuelle assurée.

Madagascan [,mædə'gæskn] ◆ n Malgache mf. ◆ adj malgache.

Madagascar [,mædə'gæskə] pr n Madagascar / **in Madagascar** à Madagascar.

madam ['mædəm] n **1.** *fml* madame *f* / *Dear Madam* (Chère) Madame / *madam Chairman* Madame la présidente **2.** *pej* : *she's a little madam* c'est une petite effrontée **3.** [in brothel] tenancière *f*.

madcap ['mædkæp] ◆ adj fou *(before vowel or silent 'h' fol, f folle)*, insensé. ◆ n fou *m*, folle *f*, hurluberlu *m*, -e *f*.

mad cow disease n maladie *f* de la vache folle.

madden ['mædn] vt [drive insane] rendre fou ; [exasperate] exaspérer, rendre fou.

maddening ['mædnɪŋ] adj exaspérant.

made [meɪd] pt & pp ⟶ **make**.

-made in comp ▶ **factory-made** industriel ▶ **British-made** fabriqué au Royaume-Uni.

Madeira [mə'dɪərə] ◆ pr n [island] Madère / *in Madeira* à Madère. ◆ n [wine] madère *m*.

made-to-measure adj (fait) sur mesure.

made-to-order adj (fait) sur commande.

made-up adj **1.** [wearing make-up] maquillé **2.** [invented -story] fabriqué ; [-evidence] faux (fausse) **3.** 🇬🇧 *inf* [happy] super content.

madhouse ['mædhaʊs] *(pl* [-haʊzɪz]*)* n *inf* asile *m* d'aliénés, maison *f* de fous ; *fig* maison de fous.

madly ['mædlɪ] adv **1.** [passionately] follement / *madly in love* éperdument or follement amoureux / *madly jealous* fou de jalousie **2.** [frantically] comme un fou, frénétiquement ; [wildly] comme un fou, follement ; [desperately] désespérément.

madman ['mædmən] *(pl* **madmen** [-mən]*)* n fou *m*, aliéné *m*.

madness ['mædnɪs] n **1.** [insanity] folie *f*, démence *f* **2.** [folly] folie *f* / *it's madness even to think of going away now* il faut être fou pour songer à partir maintenant.

Madonna [mə'dɒnə] pr n RELIG Madone *f* ; [image] madone *f*.

madrasah, madrassa [mə'dræsə] n madrasa *f*, école *f* coranique.

madras curry n curry très épicé.

Madrid [mə'drɪd] pr n Madrid.

madwoman ['mæd,wʊmən] *(pl* **madwomen** [-,wɪmɪn]*)* n folle *f*, aliénée *f*.

maestro ['maɪstrəʊ] *(pl* **maestros**) n maestro *m*.

mafia ['mæfɪə] n *lit & fig* mafia *f*, maffia *f*.

mag [mæg] n *inf* abbr of **magazine**.

magazine [,mægə'ziːn] n **1.** [publication] magazine *m*, revue *f* ; TV magazine *m* **2.** [in gun] magasin *m* ; [cartridges] chargeur *m* **3.** MIL [store] magasin *m* ; [for weapons] dépôt *m* d'armes ; [munitions] munitions *fpl* **4.** PHOT magasin *m* ; [for slides] panier *m*, magasin *m*.

magazine rack n porte-revues *m*.

maggot ['mægət] n asticot *m*.

Maghreb ['mɑːgrəb] pr n ▶ **the Maghreb** le Maghreb / *in the Maghreb* au Maghreb.

magic ['mædʒɪk] ◆ n **1.** [enchantment] magie *f* ▶ **like** or **as if by magic** *fig* comme par enchantement or magie / *the medicine worked like magic* le remède a fait merveille ; [conjuring] magie *f*, prestidigitation *f* **2.** [special quality] magie *f* / *discover the magic of Greece* découvrez les merveilles de la Grèce. ◆ adj **1.** [supernatural] magique / *a magic spell* un sortilège / *just say the magic words* il suffit de dire la formule magique ▶ **the Magic Kingdom** surnom de Disneyland ▶ **magic number** / **square** nombre *m* / carré *m* magique **2.** [special -formula, moment] magique **3.** *inf* [marvellous] génial. ◆ vt faire apparaître comme par magie / *you can't expect me to just magic it out of*

thin air! tu ne peux pas me demander de le faire apparaître comme par magie ! ◆❖ **magic away** vt sep faire disparaître comme par enchantement. ◆❖ **magic up** vt sep faire comme par magie / *she magicked up a wonderful meal* elle a confectionné un repas somptueux, comme par magie.

magical ['mædʒɪkl] adj magique.

magically ['mædʒɪklɪ] adv magiquement / *don't think it will just happen magically* ne t'imagine pas que cela va se produire comme par enchantement.

magic carpet n tapis *m* volant.

magic eye n œil *m* cathodique or magique.

magician [mə'dʒɪʃn] n magicien *m*, -enne *f*.

magic mushroom n *inf* champignon *m* hallucinogène.

magic wand n baguette *f* magique.

magistrate ['mædʒɪstreɪt] n magistrat *m*.

magistrates' court n tribunal *m* de première instance.

magna cum laude [,mægnəkum'laudeɪ] adv UNIV avec mention très bien.

magnanimity [,mægnə'nɪmətɪ] n magnanimité *f*.

magnanimous [mæg'nænɪməs] adj magnanime.

magnanimously [mæg'nænɪməslɪ] adv avec magnanimité, magnanimement.

magnate ['mægneɪt] n magnat *m* / *a press magnate* un magnat de la presse.

magnesium [mæg'niːzɪəm] n magnésium *m* ▶ **magnesium oxide** magnésie *f*, oxyde *m* de magnésium.

magnet ['mægnɪt] n **1.** *lit* aimant *m* **2.** *fig* : *this place is a magnet for tourists* cet endroit attire beaucoup de touristes / *he's a girl magnet* *inf* il attire les filles / *she's a loser magnet* inf elle n'attire que des losers.

magnetic [mæg'netɪk] adj magnétique / *a magnetic personality* *fig* une personnalité fascinante or charismatique.

magnetic disk n disque *m* magnétique.

magnetic field n champ *m* magnétique.

magnetic storm n orage *m* magnétique.

magnetic tape n bande *f* magnétique.

magnetism ['mægnɪtɪzm] n magnétisme *m*.

magnification [,mægnɪfɪ'keɪʃn] n OPT grossissement *m*.

magnificence [mæg'nɪfɪsəns] n magnificence *f*, splendeur *f*.

magnificent [mæg'nɪfɪsənt] adj magnifique, splendide.

magnify ['mægnɪfaɪ] *(pt & pp* **magnified**) vt **1.** OPT grossir ; ACOUST amplifier **2.** [exaggerate] exagérer, grossir / *the incident was magnified out of all proportion* on a terriblement exagéré l'importance de cet incident.

magnifying glass ['mægnɪfaɪŋ-] n loupe *f*.

magnitude ['mægnɪtjuːd] n [scale] ampleur *f*, étendue *f* ; ASTRON & GEOL magnitude *f* ; [of problem -importance] importance *f* ; [-size] ampleur *f*.

magnolia [mæg'nəʊljə] ◆ n magnolia *m*. ◆ adj couleur magnolia *(inv)*, blanc rosé *(inv)*.

magnum ['mægnəm] n [wine bottle, gun] magnum *m*.

magpie ['mægpaɪ] n **1.** ORNITH pie *f* **2.** *inf & fig* [chatterbox] pie *f*, moulin *m* à paroles ; 🇬🇧 [hoarder] chiffonnier *m*, -ère *f fig*.

maharaja(h) [,mɑːhə'rɑːdʒə] n maharaja *m*, maharadjah *m*.

mahogany [mə'hɒgənɪ] *(pl* **mahoganies**) ◆ n acajou *m* ▶ **mahogany tree** acajou *m*. ◆ adj **1.** ▶ **mahogany (coloured)** acajou *(inv)* **2.** [furniture] en acajou.

maid [meɪd] n [servant] bonne f, domestique f ; [in hotel] femme f de chambre ▶ **maid of honour** demoiselle f d'honneur.

maiden ['meɪdn] ◆ n [young girl] jeune fille f ; [virgin] vierge f. ◆ comp [flight] inaugural.

maiden aunt n tante f célibataire.

maiden name n nom m de jeune fille.

maiden over n au cricket, série de balles où aucun point n'a été marqué.

maiden speech n UK premier discours prononcé par un parlementaire nouvellement élu.

maiden voyage n voyage m inaugural.

mail [meɪl] ◆ n **1.** [postal service] poste f / the parcel got lost in the mail le colis a été égaré par la poste / your cheque is in the mail votre chèque a été posté **2.** [letters] courrier m / the mail is only collected twice a week il n'y a que deux levées par semaine **3.** [e-mail] courrier m électronique **4.** (U) [armour] mailles fpl. ◆ vt **1.** [parcel, goods, cheque] envoyer or expédier par la poste ; [letter] poster **2.** [send by e-mail] envoyer (par courrier électronique). ❖ **Mail** pr n ▶ **the Mail** PRESS nom abrégé du « Daily Mail » ▶ **the Mail on Sunday** PRESS hebdomadaire de centre droit paraissant le dimanche.

mailbag ['meɪlbæg] n sac m postal.

mail bomb n US [letter] lettre f piégée ; [parcel] colis m piégé.

mailbot ['meɪlbɒt] n mailbot m (logiciel de gestion de courrier électronique).

mailbox ['meɪlbɒks] n **1.** US [postbox] boîte f à lettres **2.** US [letterbox] boîte f aux lettres.

mail carrier n US facteur m, -trice f.

mail drop n boîte f à or aux lettres.

mailing ['meɪlɪŋ] n **1.** [posting] expédition f, envoi m par la poste ▶ **mailing address** adresse f postale **2.** COMM & COMPUT mailing m, publipostage m.

mailing list n fichier m d'adresses / are you on our mailing list? est-ce que vous êtes sur notre fichier ?

mailing shot = mailshot.

mailman ['meɪlmən] (pl **mailmen** [-mən]) n US facteur m.

mail merge n COMPUT publipostage m, mailing m.

mail order n vente f par correspondance ▶ **to buy sthg by mail order** acheter qqch par correspondance or sur catalogue. ❖ **mail-order** adj ▶ **mail-order catalogue** catalogue m de vente par correspondance ▶ **mail-order firm** maison f de vente par correspondance ▶ **mail-order goods** marchandises fpl vendues or achetées par correspondance.

mailroom ['meɪlruːm] n service m du courrier.

mail server n serveur m de courrier électronique, serveur m mail.

mailshot ['meɪlʃɒt] n mailing m, publipostage m.

mail train n train m postal.

mail truck n US camionnette f or fourgonnette f des postes.

mail van n UK AUTO camionnette f or fourgonnette f des postes ; RAIL voiture-poste f.

maim [meɪm] vt [disable] mutiler, estropier ; [injure] blesser / people were badly maimed in the attack des gens ont été grièvement blessés au cours de l'attaque ; [psychologically] marquer, perturber.

main [meɪn] ◆ adj [principal] principal ; [largest] principal, plus important ; [essential - idea, theme, reason] principal, essentiel / the main points les points principaux / the main thing we have to consider is his age la première chose à prendre en compte, c'est son âge / you're safe, that's the

main thing tu es sain et sauf, c'est le principal / he always has an eye to the main chance inf il ne perd jamais de vue ses propres intérêts ▶ **main course** a) plat m de résistance b) [on menu] plat m ▶ **main office** a) [gen] bureau m principal b) [headquarters] siège m. ◆ n [for gas, water - public] canalisation f principale ; [for electricity] conducteur m principal. ❖ **in the main** adv phr en gros, dans l'ensemble.

Maine [meɪn] pr n le Maine / in Maine dans le Maine.

mainframe ['meɪnfreɪm] n ▶ **mainframe (computer)** gros ordinateur m, processeur m central.

mainland ['meɪnlənd] ◆ n continent m / the Danish mainland le Danemark continental. ◆ adj continental / in mainland Britain en Grande-Bretagne proprement dite (par opposition aux îles qui l'entourent).

main line n RAIL grande ligne f ; US [road] grande route f. ❖ **main-line** adj [train, station] de grande ligne.

mainline ['meɪnlaɪn] drugs sl ◆ vi se piquer, se shooter. ◆ vt : to mainline heroin se shooter à l'héroïne.

mainly ['meɪnlɪ] adv [chiefly] principalement, surtout ; [in the majority] pour la plupart, dans l'ensemble.

main road n grande route f, route à grande circulation ; ≃ nationale f.

mains [meɪnz] ◆ n (with sg or pl vb) **1.** [main supply] réseau m / where's the mains? où est la conduite principale ? / did you turn the electricity / gas off at the mains? as-tu fermé l'arrivée de gaz / d'électricité ? **2.** ELEC secteur m / my shaver works on battery or mains mon rasoir marche sur piles ou sur (le) secteur. ◆ comp ▶ **mains electricity** : the village doesn't have mains electricity le village n'est pas raccordé au réseau électrique ▶ **mains gas** gaz m de ville ▶ **mains supply** réseau m de distribution de gaz / d'eau / d'électricité ▶ **mains water** eau f courante.

mainsail ['meɪnseɪl or 'meɪnsəl] n NAUT grand-voile f.

mains-operated adj fonctionnant sur secteur.

mainspring ['meɪnsprɪŋ] n **1.** TECH ressort m moteur **2.** fig moteur m / his courage was the mainspring of his success son courage était la raison profonde de son succès.

mainstay ['meɪnsteɪ] n **1.** NAUT étai m (de grand mât) **2.** fig soutien m, point m d'appui / maize is the mainstay of their diet le maïs constitue la base de leur alimentation.

mainstream ['meɪnstriːm] ◆ adj : mainstream French politics le courant dominant de la politique française / mainstream America la majorité des Américains / their music is hardly what you'd call mainstream! leur musique se démarque de ce qu'on entend habituellement ! ◆ n courant m / the mainstream of modern European literature la tendance qui prédomine dans la littérature européenne moderne / to live outside the mainstream of society vivre en marge de la société.

mainstreaming ['meɪnstriːmɪŋ] n ▶ (gender) mainstreaming approche f intégrée de l'égalité.

main street n **1.** lit rue f principale, grande rue f **2.** US fig ▶ Main Street les petits commerçants.

maintain [meɪnˈteɪn] ◆ vt **1.** [retain - institution, tradition] conserver, préserver ; [preserve - peace, standard] maintenir / to maintain law and order maintenir l'ordre / to maintain a position MIL & fig tenir une position ; [look after - roads, machinery] entretenir **2.** [uphold, keep - correspondence, friendship] entretenir ; [- silence, advantage, composure] garder ; [- reputation] défendre **3.** [financially - dependents] entretenir / they have two children at university to maintain ils ont deux enfants à charge à l'université **4.** [assert - opinion] soutenir, défendre ; [- innocence] affirmer / I still maintain she's innocent je soutiens or je maintiens toujours qu'elle est innocente. ◆ vi US ▶ I'm maintaining! [I'm fine] ça va !

maintainable [meɪnˈteɪnəbl] adj [attitude, opinion, position] soutenable, défendable.

maintained school [meɪnˈteɪnd-] adj 🇬🇧 ≃ école f publique.

maintenance [ˈmeɪntənəns] ◆ n **1.** [of roads, building] entretien m ; [of machinery, computer] maintenance f **2.** [financial support] entretien m **3.** LAW [alimony] pension f alimentaire **4.** [of order] maintien m ; [of regulations] application f ; [of situation] maintien m. ◆ comp [costs, crew] d'entretien ▶ **maintenance man** ouvrier m chargé de l'entretien or de la maintenance.

maintenance allowance n [to student] bourse f d'études ; [to businessman] indemnité f pour frais de déplacement.

maintenance grant = maintenance allowance.

maintenance order n obligation f alimentaire.

maisonette [ˌmeɪzəˈnet] n 🇬🇧 [small house] maisonnette f ; [flat] duplex m.

maître d' [ˌmetrəˈdiː], **maître d'hôtel** [ˌmetrədəʊˈtel] n maître m d'hôtel.

maize [meɪz] n maïs m.

Maj. (written abbr of **Major**) ≃ Cdt.

majestic [məˈdʒestɪk] adj majestueux.

majestically [məˈdʒestɪklɪ] adv majestueusement.

majesty [ˈmædʒəstɪ] (pl **majesties**) n majesté f ▶ **His Majesty the King** Sa Majesté le Roi ▶ **Her Majesty the Queen** Sa Majesté la Reine.

major [ˈmeɪdʒər] ◆ adj **1.** [main] : the major part of our research l'essentiel de nos recherches / the major portion of my time is devoted to politics la majeure partie or la plus grande partie de mon temps est consacrée à la politique ▶ **major road** route f principale or à grande circulation ; ≃ nationale f **2.** [significant - decision, change, factor, event] majeur / don't worry, it's not a major problem ne t'inquiète pas, ce n'est pas très grave / of major importance d'une grande importance, d'une importance capitale / a major role **a)** [in play, film] un grand rôle **b)** [in negotiations, reform] un rôle capital or essentiel **3.** [serious - obstacle, difficulty] majeur / she underwent major surgery elle a subi une grosse opération **4.** MUS majeur / a sonata in E major une sonate en mi majeur ▶ **in a major key** en (mode) majeur. ◆ n **1.** MIL [in air force] commandant m ; [in infantry] chef m de bataillon ; [in cavalry] chef m d'escadron **2.** 🇺🇸 UNIV [subject] matière f principale / Tina is a physics major Tina fait des études de physique **3.** 🇺🇸 [big company] : the oil majors les grandes compagnies pétrolières ▶ **the Majors** [film companies] les cinq sociétés de production les plus importantes à Hollywood. ◆ vi 🇺🇸 UNIV [specialize] : [be a student] : she majored in sociology elle a fait des études de sociologie.

Majorca [məˈdʒɔːkə or məˈjɔːkə] pr n Majorque / in Majorca à Majorque.

majority [məˈdʒɒrətɪ] (pl **majorities**) ◆ n [of a group] majorité f, plupart f / the majority of people la plupart des gens / the majority was or were in favour la majorité or la plupart d'entre eux était pour / the vast majority of the tourists were Japanese les touristes, dans leur très grande majorité, étaient des Japonais ; [in voting, opinions] majorité f ▶ **to be in a majority** être majoritaire / the proposition had an overwhelming majority la proposition a recueilli une écrasante majorité / she was elected by a majority of 6 elle a été élue avec une majorité de 6 voix or par 6 voix de majorité. ◆ comp majoritaire ▶ **majority government** gouvernement m majoritaire ▶ **majority rule** gouvernement m à la majorité absolue, système m majoritaire ▶ **majority shareholder** actionnaire mf majoritaire ▶ **majority verdict** verdict m majoritaire.

Major League 🇺🇸 ◆ n [gen] première division f ▶ **Major League team** grande équipe (sportive) ; [in base-ball] une des deux principales divisions de base-ball professionnel aux États-Unis. ◆ adj [significant] de premier rang ; [as intensifier] : he's a major-league jerk c'est un imbécile de première.

make [meɪk] (pt & pp **made** [meɪd])
◆ vt

A. FORM OR CREATE **1.** [construct, create, manufacture] faire, fabriquer / to make a meal préparer un repas / 'made in Japan' 'fabriqué au Japon' / a vase made of or from clay un vase en or de terre cuite / what's it made of? en quoi est-ce que c'est fait ? ▶ **they're made for each other** ils sont faits l'un pour l'autre **2.** [cause to appear or happen - hole, tear, mess, mistake, noise] faire / he's always making trouble il faut toujours qu'il fasse des histoires **3.** [establish - law, rule] établir, faire / I don't make the rules ce n'est pas moi qui fais les règlements **4.** [indicating action performed] : to make one's bed [tidy] faire son lit / to make a note of sthg prendre note de qqch / to make an offer faire une offre / to make a phone call passer un coup de fil.

B. CAUSE **1.** (with adj or pp complement) [cause to be] rendre / to make sb happy / mad rendre qqn heureux / fou / this will make things easier cela facilitera les choses / it makes her tired ça la fatigue **2.** (with noun complement or with 'into') [change into] faire / the film made her (into) a star le film a fait d'elle une vedette / I can't come in the morning, shall we make it 2 pm? je ne peux pas venir le matin, est-ce que 14 h vous conviendrait ? **3.** (with verb complement) [cause] faire / what makes you think they're wrong? qu'est-ce qui te fait penser qu'ils ont tort ? **4.** [force, oblige] ▶ **to make sb do sthg a)** faire faire qqch à qqn **b)** [stronger] forcer or obliger or contraindre qqn à faire qqch / they made me wait or I was made to wait ils m'ont fait attendre.

C. ACHIEVE OR GAIN **1.** [attain, achieve - goal] atteindre / you won't make the team if you don't train tu n'entreras jamais dans l'équipe si tu ne t'entraînes pas **2.** [arrive at, get to - place] atteindre / did you make your train? as-tu réussi à avoir ton train ? **3.** [be available for] : I won't be able to make lunch je ne pourrai pas déjeuner avec toi / elle / vous, etc. / can you make Friday afternoon? vendredi après-midi, ça vous convient ? **4.** [earn, win] faire, gagner / how much do you make a month? combien gagnes-tu par mois ?

D. AMOUNT TO **1.** [amount to, add up to] faire / 17 and 19 make or makes 36 17 plus 19 font or égalent 36 **2.** [reckon to be] : I make the answer 257 d'après moi, ça fait 257 / what time do you make it? quelle heure as-tu ? **3.** (with noun complement) [fulfil specified role, function, etc.] faire / he'll make somebody a good husband ce sera un excellent mari / they make a handsome couple ils forment un beau couple.

E. MAKE OR BE SUCCESSFUL [make successful] faire le succès de / you've got it made! tu n'as plus de souci à te faire ! / what happens today will make or break us notre avenir dépend entièrement de ce qui va se passer aujourd'hui.

F. OTHER SENSES PHR ▶ **to make it a)** [arrive] arriver **b)** [be successful] réussir **c)** [be able to attend] être là / I'll never make it for 10 o'clock je ne pourrai jamais y être pour 10 h / I can't make it for supper tomorrow je ne peux pas dîner avec eux / toi, etc. demain.
◆ vi [act] ▶ **to make (as if)** faire mine de / she made (as if) to stand up elle fit mine de se lever / make like you're asleep! inf fais semblant de dormir ! ▶ **to make believe** imaginer ▶ **to make do (with) a)** [manage] se débrouiller (avec) **b)** [be satisfied] se contenter (de) / it's broken but we'll just have to make do c'est cassé mais il faudra faire avec.

◆ n **1.** [brand] marque f **2.** PHR **to be on the make a)** inf [for power, profit] avoir les dents longues **b)** [looking for sexual partner] draguer. ❖ **make for** vt insep **1.** [head towards] se diriger vers ; [hastily] se précipiter vers **2.** [contribute to] mener à / *the treaty should make for a more lasting peace* le traité devrait mener or aboutir à une paix plus durable / *this typeface makes for easier reading* cette police permet une lecture plus facile. ❖ **make of** ◆ vt sep **1.** [understand] comprendre à / *can you make anything of these instructions?* est-ce que tu comprends quelque chose à ce mode d'emploi ? **2.** [give importance to] : *I think you're making too much of a very minor problem* je pense que tu exagères l'importance de ce petit problème. ◆ vt insep [think of] penser de / *what do you make of the Smiths?* qu'est-ce que tu penses des Smith ? ❖ **make off** vi partir. ❖ **make out** ◆ vt sep **1.** [see] distinguer ; [hear] entendre, comprendre ; [read] déchiffrer **2.** [understand] comprendre / *I can't make her out at all* je ne la comprends pas du tout **3.** [claim] prétendre / *she made out that she was busy* elle a fait semblant d'être occupée **4.** [fill out - form, cheque] remplir / *who shall I make the cheque out to?* je fais le chèque à quel ordre ? ◆ vi **1.** inf [manage] se débrouiller **2.** US vinf [neck, pet] se peloter ▶ **to make out with sb** [have sex] s'envoyer qqn. ❖ **make over** vt sep **1.** [transfer] transférer, céder **2.** US [convert - room, house] réaménager **3.** US [change the appearance of] transformer. ❖ **make up** ◆ vi **1.** [put on make-up] se maquiller **2.** [become reconciled] se réconcilier. ◆ vt sep **1.** [put make-up on] maquiller ▶ **to make o.s. up** se maquiller **2.** [prepare] faire, préparer / *the chemist made up the prescription* le pharmacien a préparé l'ordonnance **3.** [invent] inventer **4.** PHR **to make (it) up with sb** se réconcilier avec qqn. ◆ vt insep **1.** [constitute] composer, constituer / *the different ethnic groups that make up our organization* les différents groupes ethniques qui constituent notre organisation / *the cabinet is made up of 11 ministers* le cabinet est composé de 11 ministres **2.** [compensate for - losses] compenser / *to make up lost ground* regagner le terrain perdu / *he's making up time* il rattrape son retard **3.** [complete] : *we need two more players to make up the team* nous avons besoin de deux joueurs de plus pour que l'équipe soit au complet / *I'll make up the difference* je mettrai la différence. ❖ **make up for** vt insep compenser / *how can I make up for all the trouble I've caused you?* que puis-je faire pour me faire pardonner tous les ennuis que je vous ai causés ? / *she's making up for lost time now!* lit & fig elle est en train de rattraper le temps perdu ! ❖ **make up to** vt sep ▶ **to make it up to sb** : *I promise I'll make it up to you someday* je te promets que je te revaudrai ça (un jour).

make-believe ◆ n : *it's only make-believe* ce n'est qu'illusion / *a world of make-believe* un monde d'illusions. ◆ adj imaginaire / *they turned the bed into a make-believe raft* ils imaginèrent que le lit était un radeau.

makeover ['meɪkəʊvər] n lit & fig [transformation] relookage m / *they've given their garden a complete makeover* ils ont complètement transformé leur jardin ▶ **cosmetic makeover** démonstration f de maquillage.

maker ['meɪkər] n **1.** [craftsman] fabricant m, -e f **2.** RELIG ▶ **Maker** Créateur m ▶ **to go to meet one's Maker** euph & hum passer de vie à trépas.

-maker in comp **1.** [manufacturer] fabricant m ▶ **dressmaker** couturière f **2.** [machine] ▶ **electric coffee-maker** cafetière f électrique ▶ **ice cream-maker** sorbetière f.

makeshift ['meɪkʃɪft] ◆ adj de fortune / *a makeshift shelter* un abri de fortune / *the accommodation was very makeshift* le logement était plutôt improvisé. ◆ n expédient m.

make-up n **1.** [cosmetics] maquillage m, fard m / *she had a lot of make-up on* elle était très maquillée ▶ **eye make-up** fard pour les yeux ▶ **make-up artist** maquilleur m, -euse f ▶ **make-up bag** trousse f de maquillage ▶ **make-up remover** démaquillant m **2.** [constitution] constitution f ▶ **genetic make-up** caractéristiques fpl génétiques **3.** [nature, character] nature f, caractère m **4.** US [test, exam] ▶ **make-up (test)** examen m de rattrapage.

makeweight ['meɪkweɪt] n [on scales] complément m de poids / *I'm only here as a makeweight* fig je ne suis là que pour faire nombre.

making ['meɪkɪŋ] n **1.** [manufacture, creation] fabrication f / *the situation is entirely of his own making* il est entièrement responsable de la situation dans laquelle il se trouve / *the incident was to be the making of his career as a politician* l'incident devait être à l'origine de sa carrière d'homme politique **2.** [preparation - of cake] confection f, préparation f ; [- of film] tournage m. ❖ **in the making** adj phr [idea] en gestation ; [plan] à l'étude ; [building] en construction / *it's history in the making* c'est une page d'histoire qui s'écrit sous nos yeux. ❖ **makings** pl n [essential elements] ingrédients mpl / *his war stories have the makings of a good film* il y a de quoi faire un bon film avec ses récits de guerre ; [potential] : *that child has the makings of a genius* cet enfant présente toutes les caractéristiques du génie.

maladjusted [,mælə'dʒʌstɪd] adj **1.** PSYCHOL [child] inadapté **2.** [engine, TV picture] mal réglé ; [mechanism] mal ajusté.

malaise [mæ'leɪz] n malaise m.

malaria [mə'leərɪə] n malaria f, paludisme m.

malarkey [mə'lɑːkɪ] n (U) inf bêtises fpl, sottises fpl.

Malawi [mə'lɑːwɪ] pr n Malawi m / *in Malawi* au Malawi.

Malawian [mə'lɑːwɪən] ◆ n Malawite mf. ◆ adj malawite.

Malay [mə'leɪ] ◆ n [person] Malais m, -e f. ◆ adj malais.

Malaya [mə'leɪə] pr n Malaisie f, Malaysia f Occidentale / *in Malaya* en Malaisie.

Malayan [mə'leɪən] ◆ n Malais m, -e f. ◆ adj malais.

Malaysia [mə'leɪzɪə] pr n Malaysia f / *in Malaysia* en Malaysia.

Malaysian [mə'leɪzɪən] ◆ n Malais m, -e f. ◆ adj malais.

Maldives ['mɔːldaɪvz] pl pr n ▶ **the Maldives** les (îles fpl) Maldives fpl / *in the Maldives* aux Maldives.

male [meɪl] ◆ adj **1.** ZOOL & BOT mâle / *male attitudes* l'attitude des hommes / *when I phoned her, a male voice answered* quand je l'ai appelée, c'est une voix d'homme qui a répondu / *the male sex* le sexe masculin ▶ **male voice choir** chœur m d'hommes **2.** [virile] mâle, viril **3.** TECH [plug] mâle. ◆ n ZOOL & BOT mâle m ; [gen - man] homme m.

male chauvinism n phallocratie f.

male chauvinist n phallocrate m ▶ **male chauvinist pig!** sale phallocrate !

malevolence [mə'levələns] n malveillance f.

malevolent [mə'levələnt] adj malveillant.

malevolently [mə'levələntlɪ] adv avec malveillance.

malformation [,mælfɔː'meɪʃn] n malformation f.

malfunction [mæl'fʌŋkʃn] ◆ n [fault] fonctionnement m défectueux ; [breakdown] panne f, défaillance f. ◆ vi [go wrong] mal fonctionner ; [break down] tomber en panne.

Mali ['mɑːlɪ] pr n Mali m / *in Mali* au Mali.

malice ['mælɪs] n méchanceté f, malveillance f / I don't bear any malice towards them or I don't bear them any malice je ne leur en veux pas, je ne leur veux aucun mal / out of or through malice par méchanceté, par malveillance ▸ **with malice aforethought** LAW avec préméditation.

⚠ The French word **malice** means mischievousness, **not** malice.

malicious [mə'lɪʃəs] adj **1.** [gen] méchant, malveillant / malicious gossip médisances fpl **2.** LAW criminel ▸ **malicious damage** 🇬🇧, **malicious mischief** 🇺🇸 ≃ dommage m causé avec intention de nuire.

⚠ **Malicieux** means mischievous, **not** malicious.

maliciously [mə'lɪʃəslɪ] adv **1.** [gen] méchamment, avec malveillance **2.** LAW avec préméditation, avec intention de nuire.

malign [mə'laɪn] ◆ vt [slander] calomnier ; [criticize] critiquer, dire du mal de / the much-maligned government le gouvernement, dont on dit beaucoup de mal or que l'on a souvent critiqué. ◆ adj **1.** [evil] pernicieux, nocif **2.** MED malin (maligne).

malignant [mə'lɪɡnənt] adj **1.** [person, behaviour, intentions] malveillant, malfaisant, méchant **2.** MED malin (maligne) ▸ **malignant tumour** tumeur f maligne.

malinger [mə'lɪŋɡər] vi simuler la maladie, faire semblant d'être malade.

malingerer [mə'lɪŋɡərər] n faux malade m, personne f qui fait semblant d'être malade.

mall [mɔːl] n **1.** [avenue] mail m, avenue f **2.** 🇺🇸 = shopping mall. ❖ **Mall** pr n ▸ **the Mall** a) [in London] large avenue reliant Buckingham Palace à Trafalgar Square b) [in Washington] jardin public sur lequel donnent les principaux musées de la ville.

malleable ['mælɪəbl] adj [substance] malléable ; [person] influençable, malléable.

mallet ['mælɪt] n maillet m.

mallrat ['mɔːlræt] n 🇺🇸 adolescent qui traîne dans les centres commerciaux.

malnourished [,mæl'nʌrɪʃt] adj sous-alimenté.

malnutrition [,mæln'trɪʃn] n malnutrition f.

malpractice [,mæl'præktɪs] n (U) [professional] faute f professionnelle ; [financial] malversation f, malversations fpl ; [political] fraude f.

malpractice suit n 🇺🇸 LAW procès pour faute ou négligence professionnelle.

malt [mɔːlt] ◆ n **1.** [substance] malt m **2.** = malt whisky **3.** 🇺🇸 [milk shake] milk-shake m au malt. ◆ comp [extract, sugar, vinegar] de malt. ◆ vt malter.

Malta ['mɔːltə] pr n Malte / in Malta à Malte.

Maltese [,mɔːl'tiːz] ◆ n **1.** [person] Maltais m, -e f **2.** LING maltais m. ◆ adj maltais ▸ **the Maltese Cross** la croix de Malte.

maltreat [,mæl'triːt] vt maltraiter.

malt whisky n whisky m au malt.

malware ['mælweər] n logiciels mpl malveillants / a piece of malware un logiciel malveillant.

mammal ['mæml] n mammifère m.

mammogram ['mæməɡræm] n mammographie f.

mammoth ['mæməθ] ◆ n mammouth m. ◆ adj immense, colossal, gigantesque / a mammoth task un travail de Titan.

mammy ['mæmɪ] (pl mammies) n inf [mother] maman.

man [mæn] (pl men [men], pt & pp manned, cont manning) ◆ n **1.** [adult male] homme m / a young man un jeune homme / an old man un vieillard / he seems a nice man il a l'air gentil / a blind man un aveugle ▸ he's a man's man il aime bien être avec ses copains ▸ he's a man of the world c'est un homme d'expérience **2.** [type] homme m / he's not a betting / drinking man ce n'est pas un homme qui parie / boit **3.** [appropriate person] homme m / I'm your man je suis votre homme / he's not the man for that kind of work il n'est pas fait pour ce genre de travail **4.** [professional] ▸ a medical man un médecin ▸ a man of learning un savant ▸ a man of letters un homme de lettres **5.** [with manly qualities] homme m / he took the news like a man il a pris la nouvelle avec courage / this will separate or sort the men from the boys c'est là qu'on verra les vrais hommes **6.** [person, individual] homme m, individu m / what more can a man do? qu'est-ce qu'on peut faire de plus ? / any man would have reacted in the same way n'importe qui aurait réagi de la même façon / all men are born equal tous les hommes naissent égaux ▸ it's every man for himself c'est chacun pour soi ▸ the man in the street l'homme de la rue **7.** [as husband, father] homme m ▸ man and wife mari et femme ▸ to live as man and wife vivre maritalement or en concubinage ; hum le pater familias ▸ my old man inf a) [husband] mon homme b) [father] mon vieux **8.** [boyfriend, lover] homme m / have you met her young man? a) [boyfriend] avez-vous rencontré son petit ami ? b) [fiancé] avez-vous rencontré son fiancé ? **9.** [inhabitant, native] : I'm a Dublin man je suis de Dublin **10.** [employee - in industry, on farm] ouvrier m ; [- in business, shop] employé m / a TV repair man un réparateur télé **11.** [mankind] homme m / primitive / modern man l'homme primitif / moderne **12.** [as term of address] : hey, man, how are you doing? v inf salut, mon pote, comment tu vas ? / good man! c'est bien ! **13.** [in chess] pièce f ; [in draughts] pion m. ◆ vt **1.** MIL [ship] armer, équiper ; [pumps] armer ; [cannon] servir / the tanker was manned by Greek seamen le pétrolier avait un équipage grec / can you man the fort while I'm at lunch? hum pouvez-vous prendre la relève or me remplacer pendant que je vais déjeuner ? **2.** [staff - machine] faire tourner, s'occuper de ; [- switchboard] assurer le service or la permanence de / who's manning the telephone? qui assure la permanence téléphonique ? ◆ interj 🇺🇸 inf : man, was it big! bon sang, qu'est-ce que c'était grand ! ❖ **to a man** adv phr sans exception. ❖ **man up** vi 🇺🇸 inf : you need to man up and get over that girl il faut que tu trouves la force d'oublier cette fille / I manned up and confessed j'ai pris mon courage à deux mains et j'ai avoué / she should man up il faudrait qu'elle assume ses responsabilités.

man-about-town (pl men-about-town) n 🇬🇧 homme m du monde, mondain m.

manage ['mænɪdʒ] ◆ vt **1.** [business, hotel, shop] gérer, diriger ; [property, estate] gérer ; [team] être le manager de, diriger ; [finances, resources] s'occuper de / I'm very bad at managing money je suis incapable de gérer un budget ; [crisis, illness] gérer **2.** [accomplish] réussir / you'll manage it ça ira / she managed a smile elle trouva la force de sourire ▸ to manage to do sthg réussir or parvenir or arriver à faire qqch / he managed to keep a straight face il est parvenu à garder son sérieux / he always manages to arrive at meal times il se débrouille toujours pour arriver or il trouve toujours le moyen d'arriver à l'heure des repas **3.** [handle - person, animal] savoir s'y prendre avec / she's *a difficult child to manage* c'est une enfant difficile, c'est une enfant dont on ne fait pas ce qu'on veut ; [manipulate - machine, tool] manier, se servir de **4.** [be available for] : *can you manage 9 o'clock / next Saturday?* pouvez-vous venir à 9 h / samedi prochain ? / *can you manage lunch tomorrow?* pouvez-vous déjeuner avec moi demain ? / *can you manage lunch* **5.** [cope with] : *I can't manage all this extra work* je ne peux pas faire face à ce surcroît de travail / *can you manage that rucksack?* pouvez-vous porter ce sac à dos ? / *he can't manage the stairs any more* il n'arrive plus à monter l'escalier ; [eat or drink] : *I think I could manage another slice* j'en reprendrais volontiers une tranche / *I couldn't manage another thing* je ne peux plus rien avaler ; [financially] : *can you manage £10?* pouvez-vous aller jusqu'à 10 livres ? ◆ vi [cope] se débrouiller, y arriver / *can you manage?* ça ira ? / *give me a fork, I can't manage with chopsticks* donne-moi une fourchette, je ne m'en sors pas avec des baguettes / *we had to manage without heating* nous avons dû nous passer de chauffage ; [financially] se débrouiller, s'en sortir.

manageable ['mænɪdʒəbl] adj [size, amount] raisonnable ; [tool, car, boat] maniable ; [hair] facile à coiffer.

management ['mænɪdʒmənt] n **1.** [control - of firm, finances, property] gestion f, direction f / *under Gordon's management sales have increased significantly* depuis que c'est Gordon qui s'en occupe, les ventes ont considérablement augmenté / *who looks after the management of the farm?* qui s'occupe de l'exploitation de la ferme ? ; [handling] : *she was praised for her management of the situation* on a applaudi la façon dont elle s'est comportée dans cette situation ; [of crisis, illness, etc.] gestion f ▶ **man management** 🇬🇧 gestion des ressources humaines **2.** [of shop, hotel, etc.] direction f / *'the management cannot accept responsibility for any loss or damage'* 'la direction décline toute responsabilité en cas de perte ou de dommage' / *'under new management'* 'changement de direction or de propriétaire' ; INDUST patronat m.

management buy-in n management buy-in m *(achat d'une société, le plus souvent par endettement, accompagné de l'arrivée d'une nouvelle équipe)*.

management buyout n 🇬🇧 rachat m d'une entreprise par les salariés.

management consultancy n [activity] conseil m en gestion (d'entreprise) ; [firm] cabinet m (de) conseil.

management consultant n conseiller m, -ère f en or de gestion (d'entreprise).

management information system n COMPUT système m intégré de gestion.

manager ['mænɪdʒər] n **1.** [of firm, bank] directeur m, -trice f ; [of shop] directeur m, -trice f, gérant m ; [of restaurant] gérant m, -e f ; [of pop star, football team] manager m ; FIN directeur m, -trice f / *fund manager* directeur financier / *he's been made manager* il est passé cadre **2.** [organizer] : *she's a good home manager* elle sait tenir une maison.

manageress [,mænɪdʒə'res] n [of shop] directrice f, gérante f ; [of restaurant] gérante f ; [of bank] directrice f.

managerial [,mænɪ'dʒɪərɪəl] adj gestionnaire ▶ **managerial staff** cadres mpl, encadrement m ▶ **managerial skills** qualités fpl de gestionnaire.

managing director ['mænɪdʒɪŋ-] n directeur m général, directrice f générale, P-DG m.

managing editor n rédacteur m, -trice f en chef.

manbag ['mænbæg] n sacoche f.

Mancunian [mæŋ'kjuːnjən] ◆ n [inhabitant] habitant m, -e f de Manchester ; [native] natif m, -ive f de Manchester. ◆ adj de Manchester.

mandarin ['mændərɪn] n **1.** HIST & *fig* mandarin m **2.** BOT [tree] mandarinier m **3.** [fruit] ▶ **mandarin (orange)** mandarine f. ◆ **Mandarin** n LING ▶ **Mandarin (Chinese)** mandarin m.

man date n *inf* sortie f entre hommes.

mandate ◆ n ['mændeɪt] **1.** POL mandat m / *the government has no mandate to introduce the new tax* le gouvernement n'a pas été mandaté pour mettre en place ce nouvel impôt **2.** [country] (territoire m sous) mandat m **3.** [task] tâche f, mission f. ◆ vt [,mæn'deɪt] **1.** [give authority] mandater ▶ **to mandate sb to do sthg** donner mandat à qqn de faire qqch **2.** [country] mettre sous mandat, administrer par mandat.

mandatory ['mændətrɪ] (*pl* **mandatories**) ◆ adj **1.** [obligatory] obligatoire **2.** [of a mandate] découlant d'un mandat ▶ **mandatory powers** pouvoirs mpl donnés par mandat. ◆ n mandataire mf.

man-day n 🇬🇧 jour-homme m / *30 man-days* 30 journées fpl de travail.

mane [meɪn] n [of horse, lion] crinière f / *a mane of golden hair* une crinière blonde.

man-eater n [animal] anthropophage m ; [cannibal] cannibale m, anthropophage m ; *hum* [woman] dévoreuse f d'hommes, mante f religieuse.

man-eating adj [animal] mangeur d'hommes, anthropophage ; [people] cannibale, anthropophage.

maneuver 🇺🇸 = manoeuvre.

manfully ['mænfʊlɪ] adv [courageously] vaillamment, courageusement.

manganese ['mæŋgəniːz] n manganèse m.

mange [meɪndʒ] n gale f.

manger ['meɪndʒər] n [trough] mangeoire f ; RELIG crèche f.

mangle ['mæŋgl] ◆ vt **1.** [body] mutiler, déchiqueter ; [vehicle] rendre méconnaissable ; [quotation, text] estropier, mutiler / *the mangled wreckage of the two cars* les carcasses déchiquetées des deux voitures **2.** [laundry, linen] essorer. ◆ n essoreuse f (à rouleaux).

mango ['mæŋgəʊ] (*pl* **mangos** or **mangoes**) n **1.** [fruit] mangue f **2.** [tree] manguier m.

mangrove ['mæŋgrəʊv] n manglier m, palétuvier m ▶ **mangrove swamp** mangrove f.

mangy ['meɪndʒɪ] (*compar* **mangier**, *superl* **mangiest**) adj **1.** [having mange - animal] galeux **2.** [shabby - coat, carpet] miteux, pelé.

manhandle ['mæn,hændl] vt **1.** [treat roughly] maltraiter, malmener **2.** [move] porter or transporter (à bras d'homme).

manhole ['mænhəʊl] n regard m ; [into sewer] bouche f d'égout ▶ **manhole cover** plaque f d'égout.

manhood ['mænhʊd] n **1.** [age] âge m d'homme **2.** [virility] virilité f **3.** [men collectively] hommes mpl, population f masculine.

man-hour n 🇬🇧 heure-homme f / *300 man-hours* 300 heures fpl de travail.

manhunt ['mænhʌnt] n chasse f à l'homme.

mania ['meɪnjə] n **1.** PSYCHOL manie f ; [obsession] obsession f **2.** [zeal] manie f *pej*, passion f / *he has a mania for collecting old photographs* il a la manie de collectionner les vieilles photos.

maniac ['meɪnɪæk] n **1.** [dangerous person] fou m, folle f ; [sexual] obsédé m, -e f / *to drive like a maniac* conduire comme un fou **2.** [fan] fou m, folle f / *he's a football maniac* c'est un fan ou un mordu de football.

manic ['mænɪk] adj **1.** [crazy] fou *(before vowel or silent 'h' fol, f folle)* **2.** PSYCHOL maniaque.

manic depression n psychose f maniaco-dépressive.

manic-depressive ◆ adj maniaco-dépressif. ◆ n maniaco-dépressif m, -ive f.

manicure ['mænɪˌkjʊəʳ] ◆ n soins mpl des mains ▸ **to give sb a manicure** faire les mains de qqn, manucurer qqn. ◆ comp [case, scissors] de manucure, à ongles ▸ **manicure set** onglier m. ◆ vt faire les mains à, manucurer / she was manicuring her nails elle était en train de se faire les ongles / a manicured lawn une pelouse impeccable.

manicurist ['mænɪˌkjʊərɪst] n manucure mf.

manifest ['mænɪfest] ◆ adj fml manifeste, évident. ◆ vt manifester / how did this mania manifest itself? comment cette obsession s'est-elle manifestée ? ◆ vi [ghost, spirit] se manifester.

manifestation [ˌmænɪfes'teɪʃn] n manifestation f.

manifestly ['mænɪfestlɪ] adv manifestement, à l'évidence.

manifesto [ˌmænɪ'festəʊ] (pl manifestos or manifestoes) n manifeste m.

manifold ['mænɪfəʊld] adj fml [numerous] multiple, nombreux ; [varied] varié, divers.

Manila [mə'nɪlə] pr n Manille.

manil(l)a [mə'nɪlə] ◆ n [hemp] chanvre m de Manille ; [paper] papier m kraft. ◆ comp ▸ **manilla envelope** enveloppe f en papier kraft.

manipulate [mə'nɪpjʊleɪt] vt **1.** [equipment] manœuvrer, manipuler ; [tool] manier ; [vehicle] manœuvrer **2.** pej [person] manipuler, manœuvrer ; [facts, figures] manipuler / he skilfully manipulated situations (to his own end) il avait l'art de tirer profit de toutes les situations **3.** MED : to manipulate bones pratiquer des manipulations.

manipulation [məˌnɪpjʊ'leɪʃn] n [of equipment] manœuvre f, manipulation f ; pej [of people, facts, situation] manipulation f ; MED manipulation f.

manipulative [mə'nɪpjʊlətɪv] adj pej : he can be very manipulative il n'hésite pas à manipuler les gens.

mankind [mæn'kaɪnd] n **1.** [species] humanité f, espèce f humaine **2.** [men in general] hommes mpl.

manky ['mæŋkɪ] (compar mankier, superl mankiest) adj UK v inf [worthless] nul ; [dirty] miteux, pourri.

manlike ['mænlaɪk] adj **1.** [virile] viril, masculin **2.** [woman] masculin.

manliness ['mænlɪnɪs] n virilité f.

manly ['mænlɪ] (compar manlier, superl manliest) adj viril, mâle.

man-made adj [fibre] synthétique ; [construction, lake] artificiel ; [landscape] modelé ou façonné par l'homme.

manna ['mænə] n manne f ▸ **manna from heaven** fig manne céleste.

manned [mænd] adj [ship, machine] ayant un équipage / manned spacecraft vaisseau m spatial habité.

mannequin ['mænɪkɪn] n mannequin m.

manner ['mænəʳ] n **1.** [way] manière f, façon f / in the same manner de la même manière ou façon / it's just a manner of speaking c'est juste une façon de parler / she dealt with them in a very gentle manner elle a été d'une grande douceur avec eux / to keep sb in the manner to which he is accustomed permettre à qqn de maintenir son train de vie **2.** [attitude] attitude f, manière f ; [behaviour] comportement m, manière f, manière f de se conduire / to have a pleasant manner avoir des manières agréables / I don't like his manner je n'aime pas ses façons / he has a good telephone manner il fait bonne impression au téléphone ▸ **in a manner of speaking** pour ainsi dire, dans un certain sens ▸ **by all manner of means** [of course] bien entendu ▸ **not by any manner of means** en aucune manière,

aucunement ▸ **to the manner born** vraiment fait pour ça **3.** [style] manière f / in the manner of Rembrandt dans le style ou à la manière de Rembrandt **4.** [kind] sorte f, genre m / all manner of rare books toutes sortes de livres rares. ❖ **manners** pl n [social etiquette] manières fpl / to have good table manners savoir se tenir à table / it's bad manners to talk with your mouth full c'est mal élevé ou ce n'est pas poli de parler la bouche pleine / she has no manners elle n'a aucune éducation, elle est mal élevée / where are your manners? **a)** [say thank you] qu'est-ce qu'on dit quand on est bien élevé ? **b)** [behave properly] est-ce que c'est une façon de se tenir ?

mannered ['mænəd] adj maniéré, affecté, précieux.

mannerism ['mænərɪzm] n tic m, manie f.

mannish ['mænɪʃ] adj [woman] masculin.

manoeuvrable UK, **maneuvrable** US [mə'nu:vrəbl] adj manœuvrable, maniable.

manoeuvre UK, **maneuver** US [mə'nu:vəʳ] ◆ n manœuvre f ▸ **to be on manoeuvres** MIL être en manœuvres / it was only a manoeuvre to get him to resign ce n'était qu'une manœuvre pour l'amener à démissionner / room for manoeuvre marge f de manœuvre. ◆ vt **1.** [physically] manœuvrer / they manoeuvred the animal into the pen ils ont fait entrer l'animal dans l'enclos **2.** [by influence, strategy] manœuvrer / she manoeuvred her way to the top elle a réussi à se hisser jusqu'au sommet. ◆ vi manœuvrer / to manoeuvre for position manœuvrer pour se placer avantageusement.

manor ['mænəʳ] n [house] ▸ **manor (house)** manoir m, château m.

manpower ['mænˌpaʊəʳ] n (U) [personnel] main-d'œuvre f ; MIL effectifs mpl / we don't have the necessary manpower nous ne disposons pas des effectifs nécessaires.

manservant ['mænsɜ:vənt] n [gen] domestique m ; [valet] valet m (de chambre).

mansion ['mænʃn] n [in town] hôtel m particulier ; [in country] château m, manoir m ▸ **mansion block** résidence f de standing.

man-size(d) adj [job, task] ardu, difficile ; [meal] copieux ▸ **man-sized tissues** grands mouchoirs mpl (en papier).

manslaughter ['mænˌslɔ:təʳ] n homicide m involontaire.

manta ray ['mæntə-] n raie f manta f, mante f.

mantelpiece ['mæntlpi:s] n **1.** [surround] (manteau m de) cheminée f **2.** [shelf] (tablette f de) cheminée f.

mantle ['mæntl] n [cloak] cape f ; fig manteau m ▸ **to take on** ou **to assume the mantle of** fig assumer le rôle de.

man-to-man ◆ adj [discussion] entre hommes, d'homme à homme. ◆ adv entre hommes, d'homme à homme.

mantra ['mæntrə] n mantra m inv.

manual ['mænjʊəl] ◆ adj manuel ▸ **manual worker** travailleur m manuel ▸ **manual labour** travail m manuel. ◆ n [handbook] manuel m.

manually ['mænjʊəlɪ] adv manuellement, à la main.

manufacture [ˌmænjʊ'fæktʃəʳ] ◆ n **1.** [making] fabrication f ; [of clothes] confection f **2.** TECH [product] produit m manufacturé. ◆ vt **1.** [produce] fabriquer, produire ; [clothes] confectionner ▸ **manufactured goods** produits mpl manufacturés **2.** [invent - news, story] inventer ; [- evidence] fabriquer.

manufacturer [ˌmænjʊ'fæktʃərəʳ] n fabricant m, -e f.

manufacturing [ˌmænjʊ'fæktʃərɪŋ] ◆ adj [city, area] industriel ▸ **manufacturing industry** les industries fpl manufacturières ou de transformation. ◆ n fabrication f.

manure [mə'njʊər] n [farmyard] fumier *m* ; [fertilizer] engrais *m* ▶ **liquid manure** purin *m*, lisier *m* ▶ **manure heap** tas *m* de fumier.

manuscript ['mænjʊskrɪpt] ◆ n manuscrit *m* ; [for music] ▶ **manuscript (paper)** papier *m* à musique. ◆ adj manuscrit, (écrit) à la main.

Manx [mæŋks] ◆ pl n ▶ **the Manx** les Manxois *mpl*. ◆ adj manxois.

many ['menɪ] (*compar* **more** [mɔː], *superl* **most** [məʊst]) ◆ det & pron beaucoup de, de nombreux / *many people* beaucoup de or bien des gens / *many of them* beaucoup d'entre eux / *many's the time* bien des fois / *as many again* encore autant / *twice* / *three times as many* deux / trois fois plus / *how many?* combien ? / *so many people* tant de gens / *too many people* trop de gens / *a good many* un bon nombre. ◆ pl n [masses] ▶ **the many** la majorité / *the many who loved her* tous ceux qui l'aimaient.

Maori ['maʊrɪ] (*pl* **Maori** or **Maoris**) ◆ n **1.** [person] Maori *m*, -e f **2.** LING maori *m*. ◆ adj maori.

map [mæp] (*pt & pp* **mapped**, *cont* **mapping**) ◆ n [of country] carte f ; [of town, network] plan *m*. ◆ vt [country, region] faire or dresser la carte de ; [town] faire or dresser le plan de. ❖ **map out** vt sep [itinerary] tracer ; [essay] faire le plan de ; [plan] établir les grandes lignes de ; [career, future] organiser, prévoir.

MAP (*abbr of* **Modified American Plan**) n *dans un hôtel américain, séjour en demi-pension.*

maple ['meɪpl] n érable *m*.

maple leaf n feuille f d'érable.

maple syrup n sirop *m* d'érable.

mar [maːr] (*pt & pp* **marred**, *cont* **marring**) vt gâter, gâcher.

Mar. written abbr of **March**.

marathon ['mærəθn] ◆ n SPORT marathon *m*. ◆ comp ▶ **marathon runner** coureur *m*, -euse f de marathon, marathonien *m*, -enne f. ◆ adj marathon (*inv*).

marauder [mə'rɔːdər] n [person] maraudeur *m*, -euse f ; [animal, bird] maraudeur *m*, prédateur *m*.

marauding [mə'rɔːdɪŋ] adj maraudeur, en maraude.

marble ['maːbl] ◆ n **1.** [stone, sculpture] marbre *m* **2.** [for game] bille f / *to play marbles* jouer aux billes ▶ **to lose one's marbles** *inf* perdre la boule. ◆ comp [fireplace, staircase, statue] de or en marbre ; [industry] marbrier ▶ **marble quarry** marbrière f, carrière f de marbre.

march [maːtʃ] ◆ n **1.** MIL marche f **2.** [demonstration] manifestation f, marche f **3.** [music] marche f **4.** (*usu pl*) [frontier] frontière f. ◆ vi **1.** MIL marcher (au pas) ; [at a ceremony, on parade] défiler ; *fig* [time, seasons] avancer, s'écouler **2.** [walk briskly] avancer d'un pas ferme or résolu **3.** [in demonstration] manifester. ◆ vt **1.** MIL faire marcher au pas **2.** [lead forcibly] : *the prisoner was marched away* / *back to his cell* on conduisit / ramena le prisonnier dans sa cellule.

March [maːtʃ] n (mois *m* de) mars *m*. See also **February**.

marcher ['maːtʃər] n [in demonstration] manifestant *m*, -e f.

marching orders pl n **1.** MIL ordre *m* de route **2.** 🇬🇧 *inf & fig* ▶ **to give sb his** / **her marching orders** flanquer qqn à la porte.

march-past n défilé *m* (militaire).

Mardi Gras [,maːdɪ'graː] n mardi *m* gras, carnaval *m*.

mare [meər] n jument f.

margarine [,maːdʒə'riːn or ,maːdʒəˈriːn] n margarine f.

marge [maːdʒ] 🇬🇧 *inf* = **margarine**.

margin ['maːdʒɪn] n **1.** [on page] marge f **2.** [leeway] marge f / *a margin of safety* une marge d'erreur / de sécurité ; [distance, gap] marge f / *they won by a narrow* / *wide margin* ils ont gagné de justesse / avec une marge confortable.

marginal ['maːdʒɪnl] ◆ adj **1.** [slight -improvement] léger ; [-effect] minime, insignifiant ; [-improvement] mineur, secondaire ; [-case] limite ; [-problem] d'ordre secondaire **2.** COMM [business, profit] marginal. ◆ n POL = **marginal seat**.

marginalize, marginalise ['maːdʒɪnəlaɪz] vt marginaliser.

marginally ['maːdʒɪnəlɪ] adv à peine, légèrement.

marginal seat n POL *en Grande-Bretagne, circonscription dont le député ne dispose que d'une majorité très faible.*

marigold ['mærɪɡəʊld] n [African] rose f d'Inde ; [French] œillet *m* d'Inde.

marihuana, marijuana [,mærɪ'waːnə] n marihuana f, marijuana f.

marina [mə'riːnə] n marina f.

marinade [,mærɪ'neɪd] ◆ n CULIN marinade f. ◆ vt mariner.

marinate ['mærɪneɪt] vt & vi CULIN mariner.

marine [mə'riːn] ◆ adj [underwater] marin ▶ **marine biology** biologie f marine. ◆ n **1.** [ships collectively] marine f **2.** [soldier] fusilier *m* marin ; [British or American] marine *m*.

marital ['mærɪtl] adj [vows, relations, duty] conjugal ; [problem] conjugal, matrimonial ▶ **marital status** situation f de famille.

maritime ['mærɪtaɪm] adj maritime.

Maritime Provinces, Maritimes pl pr n ▶ **the Maritime Provinces** les Provinces *fpl* Maritimes.

marjoram ['maːdʒərəm] n marjolaine f, origan *m*.

mark [maːk] ◆ n **1.** [symbol, sign] marque f, signe *m* ▶ **to make a mark on sthg** faire une marque sur qqch, marquer qqch ; [on scale, in number, level] marque f, niveau *m* / *sales topped the 5 million mark* les ventes ont dépassé la barre des 5 millions / *gas mark 6* 🇬🇧 CULIN thermostat 6 ; [feature] marque f ; [token] marque f, signe *m* / *a mark of affection* une marque d'affection / *as a mark of my esteem* / *friendship* en témoignage de mon estime / de mon amitié / *as a mark of respect* en signe de respect **2.** [trace] trace f, marque f ; [stain, blemish] tache f, marque f ; [wound] trace f de coups / *there wasn't a mark on the body* le corps ne portait aucune trace de coups **3.** SCH [grade] note f / *the mark is out of 100* la note est sur 100 ▶ **to get full marks** obtenir la meilleure note (possible) ; [point] point *m* ; *fig* : *it will be a black mark against his name* ça va jouer contre lui, ça ne va pas jouer en sa faveur **4.** [impact] empreinte f, impression f ▶ **to make one's mark** s'imposer, se faire un nom / *they left their mark on 20th-century history* ils ont profondément marqué l'histoire du XXᵉ siècle ; [distinction] marque f **5.** 🇬🇧 [standard] ▶ **to be up to the mark** a) [be capable] être à la hauteur b) [meet expectations] être satisfaisant ; [in health] : *I still don't feel quite up to the mark* je ne suis pas encore en pleine forme **6.** [target] but *m*, cible f ▶ **to hit** / **to miss the mark** atteindre / manquer la cible **7.** SPORT : *on your marks, (get) set, go!* à vos marques, prêts, partez ! ; 🇬🇧 *fig* ▶ **to be quick** / **slow off the mark** : *she is quick* / *slow off the mark* a) [clever] elle est / n'est pas très maligne, elle a / n'a pas l'esprit très vif b) [in reactions] elle est / n'est pas très rapide **8.** [currency] mark *m*. ◆ vt **1.** [label] marquer / *mark the text with your initials* inscrivez vos initiales sur ce texte / *shall I mark her absent?* est-ce que je la marque absente ? **2.** [stain] tacher, marquer ; [face, hands] marquer / *the scandal marked him for life* [mentally] le scandale l'a marqué pour la vie **3.** [indicate] indiquer, marquer / *X marks the spot* l'endroit est marqué d'un X **4.** [celebrate - anniversary, event] célébrer, marquer / *let's have some champagne to mark the occasion* ouvrons une bouteille de champagne pour fêter l'événement **5.** [distinguish] marquer / *he has all the qualities that mark a good golfer* il possède toutes les qualités d'un bon golfeur **6.** SCH [essay, homework] corriger ; [student] noter ▸ **to mark sthg wrong / right** marquer qqch comme étant faux / juste **7.** [pay attention to] ▸ **(you) mark my words!** souvenez-vous de ce que je vous dis ! **8.** PHR **to mark time a)** MIL marquer le pas **b)** *fig* attendre son heure or le moment propice. ◆ vi [garment] être salissant, se tacher facilement. ◆ **mark down** vt sep **1.** [write] noter, prendre note de, inscrire **2.** [reduce - price] baisser ; [- article] baisser le prix de ; SCH [essay, student] baisser la note de. ◆ **mark off** vt sep **1.** [divide, isolate - area, period of time] délimiter **2.** [measure - distance] mesurer **3.** UK [distinguish] distinguer **4.** [on list] cocher. ◆ **mark out** vt sep **1.** [with chalk, paint - court, pitch] tracer les lignes de ; [with stakes] jalonner ; [with lights, flags] baliser / *his path in life is clearly marked out fig* son avenir est tout tracé **2.** [designate] désigner / *Brian was marked out for promotion* Brian était désigné pour obtenir une promotion **3.** UK [distinguish] distinguer. ◆ **mark up** vt sep **1.** [on notice] marquer **2.** [increase - price] augmenter, majorer ; [- goods] augmenter le prix de, majorer **3.** [annotate] annoter.

markdown ['mɑːkdaʊn] n démarque f.

marked [mɑːkt] adj **1.** [noticeable] accentué, marqué, sensible ; [accent] prononcé **2.** [bearing a mark] marqué.

markedly ['mɑːkɪdlɪ] adv d'une façon marquée, sensiblement, ostensiblement.

marker ['mɑːkə] n **1.** [pen] feutre m, marqueur m **2.** [indicator, landmark] jalon m, balise f **3.** [scorekeeper] marqueur m, -euse f **4.** [page marker] marque-page m, signet m **5.** SPORT marqueur m.

marker pen n marqueur m.

market ['mɑːkɪt] ◆ n **1.** [gen] marché m ▸ **market square** place f du marché ▸ **market day** jour m de marché **2.** ECON marché m / *the job market* le marché de l'emploi / *the property market* le marché immobilier ▸ **to put sthg on the market** mettre qqch en vente or sur le marché / *she's in the market for Persian rugs* elle cherche à acheter des tapis persans, elle est acheteuse de tapis persans ; [demand] demande f, marché m ; [outlet] débouché m, marché m ; [clientele] marché m, clientèle f **3.** ST. EX marché m ; [index] indice m ; [prices] cours mpl ▸ **to play the market** jouer en Bourse, spéculer. ◆ vt [sell] vendre, commercialiser ; [launch] lancer or mettre sur le marché. ◆ vi US [go shopping] faire le marché ▸ **to go marketing** aller faire ses courses.

marketability [,mɑːkɪtə'bɪlətɪ] n possibilité f de commercialisation.

marketable ['mɑːkɪtəbl] adj vendable, commercialisable ; ST. EX négociable.

market analysis n analyse f de marché.

market conditions n conditions fpl du marché.

market-driven adj répondant aux besoins du marché, orienté marché.

market economy n économie f de marché or libérale.

marketeer [,mɑːkə'tɪə] n ▸ **black marketeer** trafiquant m, -e f (au marché noir).

market forces pl n forces fpl du marché.

market garden n UK jardin m maraîcher.

marketing ['mɑːkɪtɪŋ] n [selling] commercialisation f, distribution f ; [promotion, research] marketing m.

marketing campaign n campagne f marketing.

marketing department n service m or département m marketing.

marketing director n directeur m, -trice f marketing.

market leader n [firm, product] leader m du marché.

marketplace ['mɑːkɪtpleɪs] n **1.** [in town] place f du marché **2.** COMM marché m.

market research n étude f or études fpl de marché.

market researcher n personne qui fait des études de marché.

market share n part f de marché.

market survey n enquête f de marché.

market town n bourg m.

market trader n marchand m, -e f.

market value n COMM valeur f marchande ; ST. EX valeur f boursière or en Bourse.

marking ['mɑːkɪŋ] n **1.** ZOOL tache f, marque f **2.** SCH correction f **3.** SPORT marquage m.

marksman ['mɑːksmən] (pl marksmen [-mən]) n tireur m d'élite.

marksmanship ['mɑːksmənʃɪp] n habileté f au tir.

markswoman ['mɑːks,wʊmən] (pl markswomen [-,wɪmɪn]) n tireuse f d'élite.

markup ['mɑːkʌp] n majoration f, augmentation f (de prix).

marmalade ['mɑːməleɪd] n [gen] confiture f d'agrumes ; [orange] marmelade f d'orange.

maroon [mə'ruːn] ◆ vt [abandon] abandonner (sur une île ou une côte déserte) ▸ **to be marooned** [shipwrecked] faire naufrage. ◆ adj [colour] bordeaux (inv).

marquee [mɑː'kiː] n **1.** UK [tent] grande tente f ; [for circus] chapiteau m **2.** US [canopy at hotel, theatre] marquise f.

marquess ['mɑːkwɪs] n marquis m.

marquis ['mɑːkwɪs] = **marquess**.

marriage ['mærɪdʒ] ◆ n **1.** mariage m ; [ceremony] mariage m, noces fpl **2.** fig [union] mariage m, alliance f. ◆ comp conjugal, matrimonial ▸ **marriage ceremony** cérémonie f de mariage ▸ **marriage vows** vœux mpl de mariage.

marriage bureau n agence f matrimoniale.

marriage certificate n extrait m d'acte de mariage.

marriage guidance n conseil m conjugal ▸ **marriage guidance counsellor** conseiller m conjugal, conseillère f conjugale.

marriage of convenience n mariage m de raison.

married ['mærɪd] adj [man, woman] marié, mariée ; [life] conjugal ▸ **married name** nom m d'épouse.

marrow ['mærəʊ] n **1.** BIOL & fig moelle f ▸ **frozen** or **chilled to the marrow** gelé jusqu'à la moelle des os **2.** [vegetable] courge f.

marrowbone ['mærəʊbəʊn] n os f à moelle.

marry ['mærɪ] (pt & pp married) ◆ vt **1.** [subj: fiancé] épouser, se marier avec ▸ **to get married** se marier ▸ **to be married (to sb)** être marié (avec qqn) / *they have been married for five years* ils sont mariés depuis cinq ans **2.** [subj: priest] marier **3.** fig [styles] marier, allier. ◆ vi se marier ▸ **to marry for money** faire un mariage d'argent ▸ **to marry again** se remarier. ◆ **marry off** vt sep marier. ◆ **marry up** vt sep [join together] marier. ◆ vi s'associer.

Mars [mɑːz] pr n ASTRON & MYTH Mars.

marsh [mɑːʃ] n marais m, marécage m.

marshal ['mɑːʃl] (UK pt & pp marshalled, cont marshalling ; US pt & pp marshaled, cont marshaling)

◆ n **1.** MIL maréchal m **2.** [at public event] membre m du service d'ordre ; [in law court] huissier m ; [at race-track] commissaire m **3.** US [police chief] commissaire m de police ; [fire chief] capitaine m des pompiers ; [district police officer] commissaire m. ◆ vt **1.** MIL [troops] masser, rassembler ; [people, group] canaliser, diriger **2.** [organize - arguments, thoughts] rassembler.

marshalling yard ['mɑːʃəlɪŋ-] n UK centre m or gare f de triage.

marshland ['mɑːʃlænd] n marais m, terrain m marécageux.

marshmallow [UK mɑːʃ'mæləʊ US 'mɑrʃ,meləʊ] n BOT guimauve f ; CULIN [sweet] guimauve f.

marshy ['mɑːʃɪ] (compar **marshier**, superl **marshiest**) adj marécageux.

marsupial [mɑː'suːpjəl] ◆ adj marsupial. ◆ n marsupial m.

martial ['mɑːʃl] adj [military] martial ; [warlike] martial, guerrier.

martial art n art m martial.

martial law n loi f martiale.

Martian ['mɑːʃn] ◆ n Martien m, -enne f. ◆ adj martien.

martin ['mɑːtɪn] n martinet m.

Martinique [,mɑːtɪ'niːk] pr n Martinique f / in Martinique à la or en Martinique.

martyr ['mɑːtər] ◆ n martyr m, -e f ; fig : she's always making a martyr of herself elle joue toujours les martyres / he's a martyr to rheumatism ses rhumatismes lui font souffrir le martyre. ◆ vt martyriser.

martyrdom ['mɑːtədəm] n RELIG martyre m ; fig martyre m, calvaire m.

marvel ['mɑːvl] (UK pt & pp **marvelled**, cont **marvelling** ; US pt & pp **marveled**, cont **marveling**) ◆ n **1.** [miracle] merveille f, miracle m, prodige m **2.** [marvellous person] : you're a marvel! tu es une vraie petite merveille ! ◆ vi ▸ **to marvel at sthg** s'émerveiller de qqch. ◆ vt : he marvelled that she had kept so calm il n'en revenait pas qu'elle ait pu rester si calme.

marvellous UK, **marvelous** US ['mɑːvələs] adj [amazing] merveilleux, extraordinaire ; [miraculous] miraculeux.

marvellously UK, **marvelously** US ['mɑːvələslɪ] adv merveilleusement, à merveille.

Marxism ['mɑːksɪzm] n marxisme m.

Marxist ['mɑːksɪst] ◆ adj marxiste. ◆ n marxiste mf.

Maryland ['meərɪlənd] pr n Maryland m / in Maryland dans le Maryland.

marzipan ['mɑːzɪpæn] ◆ n pâte f d'amandes. ◆ comp [cake, sweet, etc.] à la pâte d'amandes.

mascara [mæs'kɑːrə] n mascara m.

mascot ['mæskət] n mascotte f.

masculine ['mæskjʊlɪn] ◆ adj [gen] masculin ; [virile] viril. ◆ n GRAM masculin m.

masculinity [,mæskjʊ'lɪnətɪ] n masculinité f.

mash [mæʃ] ◆ n **1.** UK inf CULIN purée f (de pommes de terre) **2.** inf [pulp] pulpe f, bouillie f. ◆ vt **1.** [crush] écraser, broyer **2.** CULIN faire une purée de ▸ **mashed potato** or **potatoes** purée f (de pommes de terre).

MASH [mæʃ] (abbr of mobile army surgical hospital) n hôpital militaire de campagne.

mask [mɑːsk] ◆ n **1.** lit & fig masque m ; PHOT cache m **2.** COMPUT masque m. ◆ vt **1.** [face] masquer **2.** [truth,

feelings] masquer, cacher, dissimuler **3.** [house] masquer, cacher ; [view] boucher, masquer ; [flavour, smell] masquer, recouvrir.

masked [mɑːskt] adj [face, man] masqué.

masking tape ['mɑːskɪŋ-] n papier m à maroufler.

masochism ['mæsəkɪzm] n masochisme m.

masochist ['mæsəkɪst] ◆ adj masochiste. ◆ n masochiste mf.

masochistic [,mæsə'kɪstɪk] adj masochiste.

mason ['meɪsn] n [stoneworker] maçon m. ❖ **Mason** n [Freemason] maçon m, franc-maçon m.

Masonic [mə'sɒnɪk] adj maçonnique, franc-maçonnique.

masonry ['meɪsnrɪ] n [stonework, skill] maçonnerie f. ❖ **Masonry** n [Freemasonry] Maçonnerie f, franc-maçonnerie f.

masquerade [,mæskə'reɪd] ◆ n lit & fig mascarade f. ◆ vi ▸ **to masquerade as** a) [pretend to be] se faire passer pour b) [disguise o.s. as] se déguiser en.

mass [mæs] ◆ n **1.** PHYS masse f **2.** [large quantity or amount] masse f, quantité f ; [bulk] masse f **3.** [majority] majorité f, plupart f. ◆ adj [for all - communication, education] de masse ; [large-scale - starvation, unemployment] à or sur une grande échelle ; [involving many - resignation] massif, en masse ; [collective - funeral] collectif ▸ **mass grave** charnier m ▸ **mass hypnosis / hysteria** hypnose f / hystérie f collective ▸ **mass murder** tuerie f ▸ **mass murderer** tueur m fou. ◆ vi [people] se masser ; [clouds] s'amonceler. ◆ vt [troops] masser.

Mass [mæs] n RELIG **1.** [music] messe f **2.** [ceremony] messe f ▸ **to go to Mass** aller à la messe.

Massachusetts [,mæsə'tʃuːsɪts] pr n Massachusetts m / in Massachusetts dans le Massachusetts.

massacre ['mæsəkər] ◆ vt **1.** [kill] massacrer **2.** inf SPORT écraser. ◆ n massacre m.

massage [UK 'mæsɑːʒ US mə'sɑːʒ] ◆ n massage m ; [of scalp] friction f. ◆ vt lit masser ; fig [statistics, facts] manipuler.

massage parlour n salon m de massage.

massed [mæst] adj **1.** [crowds, soldiers] massé, regroupé **2.** [collective] de masse.

masses ['mæsɪz] pl n **1.** ▸ **the masses** les masses fpl **2.** inf [large amount] ▸ **masses of** des masses de, plein de.

masseur [UK mæ'sɜːr US mæ'suər] n masseur m.

masseuse [UK mæ'sɜːz US mæ'suːz] n masseuse f.

massive ['mæsɪv] adj [in size] massif, énorme ; [dose, increase] massif ; [majority] écrasant ; [change, explosion] énorme ; [sound] retentissant.

massively ['mæsɪvlɪ] adv massivement.

mass mailing n envoi m en nombre, publipostage m.

mass-market adj grand public (inv).

mass media n & pl n mass media mpl.

mass-produce vt fabriquer en série.

mass-produced adj fabriqué en série.

mass production n fabrication f or production f en série.

mass unemployment n chômage m massif.

mast [mɑːst] n [on ship, for flag] mât m ; [for radio or TV aerial] pylône m.

mastectomy [mæs'tektəmɪ] (pl **mastectomies**) n mastectomie f, mammectomie f.

master ['mɑːstər] ◆ n **1.** [of household, dog, servant, situation] maître m ▸ **master of ceremonies** a) [at reception] maître des cérémonies b) [on TV show] présentateur m **2.** [expert] maître m **3.** SCH [in primary school] instituteur *m*, maître *m* d'école ; [in secondary school] professeur *m* ; [private tutor] maître *m* **4.** UNIV ▶ **Master of Arts / Science a)** [diploma] ≃ maîtrise *f* ès lettres / *ès sciences* **b)** [person] ≃ titulaire *mf* d'une maîtrise de lettres / *de sciences* **5.** dated & fml [boy's title] monsieur *m*. ◆ vt **1.** [person, animal] maîtriser, dompter ; [problem, difficulty] surmonter, venir à bout de ; [emotions] maîtriser, surmonter ; [situation] maîtriser, se rendre maître de **2.** [subject, technique] maîtriser. ◆ adj **1.** [overall] directeur, maître ▶ **master plan** stratégie *f* globale **2.** [in trade] maître ▶ **master chef / craftsman** maître chef *m* / artisan *m* ▶ **a master thief / spy** un voleur / un espion de génie **3.** [controlling] principal ▶ **master switch** interrupteur *m* général **4.** [original] original ▶ **master copy** original *m*.

master bedroom n chambre *f* principale.

master class n cours *m* de maître ; MUS master class *m*.

master (disk) n COMPUT disque *m* d'exploitation.

master file n COMPUT fichier *m* principal or maître.

masterful ['mɑːstəful] adj **1.** [dominating] autoritaire **2.** = **masterly**.

master key n passe-partout *m* inv.

masterly ['mɑːstəli] adj magistral.

mastermind ['mɑːstəmaɪnd] ◆ n [genius] cerveau *m*, génie *m* ; [of crime, operation] cerveau *m*. ◆ vt diriger, organiser.

masterpiece ['mɑːstəpiːs] n lit & fig chef-d'œuvre *m*.

masterstroke ['mɑːstəstrəʊk] n coup *m* de maître.

masterwork ['mɑːstəwɜːk] n chef-d'œuvre *m*.

mastery ['mɑːstəri] (pl **masteries**) n **1.** [domination, control] maîtrise *f*, domination *f* / *mastery of* or *over a situation* maîtrise d'une situation / *mastery of an opponent* supériorité *f* sur un adversaire **2.** [of art, subject, language] maîtrise *f*, connaissance *f*.

masthead ['mɑːsthed] n **1.** NAUT tête *f* de mât **2.** PRESS titre *m*.

masticate ['mæstɪkeɪt] vi & vt mastiquer, mâcher.

mastiff ['mæstɪf] n mastiff *m*.

masturbate ['mæstəbeɪt] ◆ vi se masturber. ◆ vt masturber.

masturbation [,mæstə'beɪʃn] n masturbation *f*.

mat [mæt] (pt & pp **matted**, cont **matting**) ◆ adj = **matt**. ◆ n **1.** [floor covering] (petit) tapis *m*, carpette *f* ; [doormat] paillasson *m* ; [in gym] tapis *m* **2.** [for sleeping on] natte *f* **3.** [on table] set *m* de table ; [for hot dishes] dessous-de-plat *m* inv.

MAT (abbr of machine-assisted translation) n TAO *f*.

match [mætʃ] ◆ n **1.** SPORT match *m*, rencontre *f* **2.** [equal] égal *m*, -e *f* **3.** [couple] couple *m* ; [marriage] mariage *m* / *they are* or *make a good match* ils vont bien ensemble **4.** [combination] : *these colours are a good match* ces couleurs se marient bien or vont bien ensemble **5.** [for lighting] allumette *f*. ◆ vt **1.** [be equal to] être l'égal de, égaler **2.** [go with - subj: clothes, colour] s'assortir à, aller (bien) avec, se marier (harmonieusement) avec **3.** [coordinate] : *I'm trying to match this paint* je cherche une peinture identique à celle-ci / *can you match the names with the photographs?* pouvez-vous attribuer à chaque photo le nom qui lui correspond ? **4.** [oppose] ▶ **to match sb against sb** opposer qqn à qqn **5.** [find equal to] égaler / *to match an offer* égaler une offre / *this restaurant can't be matched for quality* ce restaurant n'a pas son pareil pour ce qui est de la qualité. ◆ vi aller (bien) ensemble, être bien assorti. ❖ **match up** ◆ vt sep = **match** (vt). ◆ vi [dates, figures] correspondre ; [clothes, colours] aller (bien)

ensemble, être bien assorti. ❖ **match up to** vt insep valoir / *the hotel didn't match (up to) our expectations* l'hôtel nous a déçus or ne répondait pas à notre attente.

matchbox ['mætʃbɒks] n boîte *f* d'allumettes.

match-fit adj : *they only have ten match-fit players* ils n'ont que dix joueurs en état de jouer.

match-fixing n : *they were accused of match-fixing* on les a accusés d'avoir truqué le match.

matching ['mætʃɪŋ] adj assorti.

matchmaker ['mætʃ,meɪkə*r*] n [gen] entremetteur *m*, -euse *f* ; [for marriage] marieur *m*, -euse *f*.

match play n GOLF match-play *m*. ❖ **match-play** adj ▶ **match-play tournament** match-play *m*.

match point n TENNIS balle *f* de match.

matchstick ['mætʃstɪk] n allumette *f* ▶ **matchstick men** personnages *mpl* stylisés (*dessinés de simples traits*).

match-winner n atout *m* pour gagner, joker *m*.

M8 MESSAGING written abbr of **mate**.

mate [meɪt] ◆ n **1.** & inf [friend] pote *m*, copain *m* ; [term of address] : *listen, mate!* écoute, mon vieux ! **2.** [colleague] camarade *mf* (de travail) **3.** [workman's helper] aide *mf* ▶ **plumber's mate** aide-plombier *m* **4.** NAUT [in navy] second maître *m* ; [on merchant vessel] ▶ **(first) mate** second *m* ▶ **second mate** lieutenant *m* **5.** ZOOL mâle *m*, femelle *f* ; hum [husband] époux *m* ; [wife] épouse *f* ; [lover] partenaire *mf* **6.** [in chess] mat *m*. ◆ vt **1.** ZOOL accoupler / *to mate a cow with a bull* accoupler une vache à un taureau **2.** [in chess] mettre échec et mat, mater. ◆ vi s'accoupler.

material [mə'tɪərɪəl] ◆ n **1.** [wood, plastic, stone, etc.] matière *f*, substance *f* ; [as constituent] matériau *m* / *building materials* matériaux de construction **2.** [cloth] tissu *m*, étoffe *f* **3.** (U) [ideas, data] matériaux *mpl*, documentation *f* **4.** [finished work] : *a comic who writes his own material* un comique qui écrit ses propres textes or sketches **5.** [necessary equipment] matériel *m* / *teaching materials* SCH supports *mpl* pédagogiques / *writing material* matériel pour écrire **6.** [suitable person or persons] : *is he officer / university material?* a-t-il l'étoffe d'un officier / universitaire ? ◆ adj **1.** [concrete] matériel **2.** fml [relevant] pertinent ▶ **material evidence** LAW preuve *f* matérielle or tangible.

matériel, matériau or **matière?**

The word **matière** is a generic word for materials in the sense of substances (**matières premières** *raw materials* ; **une matière résistante** *a resilient material*). The word **matériau** refers more specifically to a material used to make something (**matériaux de construction** *building materials* ; **des matériaux de revêtement intérieur** *indoor wall and floor covering materials*). The word **matériel** generally refers to material in the sense of equipment (**matériel pédagogique** *teaching material*).

materialism [mə'tɪərɪəlɪzm] n matérialisme *m*.

materialistic [mə,tɪərɪə'lɪstɪk] adj matérialiste.

materialize, materialise [mə'tɪərɪəlaɪz] vi **1.** [become fact] se matérialiser, se réaliser ; [take shape] prendre forme **2.** inf [arrive] : *he eventually materialized around ten* il a fini par se pointer vers dix heures **3.** [ghost, apparition] se matérialiser.

materially [mə'tɪərɪəli] adv matériellement.

maternal [mə'tɜːnl] adj **1.** [motherly] maternel **2.** [related through mother] maternel.

maternity [mə'tɜːnətɪ] ◆ n maternité f. ◆ comp [dress] de grossesse ; [ward] de maternité ▸ **maternity home** or **hospital** maternité f.

maternity allowance n allocation de maternité versée par l'État à une femme n'ayant pas droit à la « maternity pay ».

maternity benefit n ≃ allocations fpl de maternité.

maternity leave n congé m (de) maternité.

maternity pay n allocation de maternité versée par l'employeur.

math [mæθ] US maths fpl.

mathematical [ˌmæθə'mætɪkl] adj mathématique.

mathematically [ˌmæθə'mætɪklɪ] adv mathématiquement.

mathematician [ˌmæθəmə'tɪʃn] n mathématicien m, -enne f.

mathematics [ˌmæθə'mætɪks] ◆ n (U) [science, subject] mathématiques fpl. ◆ pl n [calculations involved] : can you explain the mathematics of it to me? pouvez-vous m'expliquer comment on parvient à ce résultat ?

mathlete ['mæθliːt] n US inf matheux m, -euse f.

maths [mæθs] (**abbr of mathematics**) n (U) UK maths fpl.

matinee, matinée ['mætɪneɪ] n CIN & THEAT matinée f.

mating ['meɪtɪŋ] ◆ n accouplement m. ◆ comp ▸ **mating call** appel m du mâle or de la femelle ▸ **mating instinct** instinct m sexuel ▸ **mating season** saison f des amours.

matriarch ['meɪtrɪɑːk] n [ruler, head of family] chef m de famille (dans un système matriarcal) ; [old woman] matrone f.

matriarchal [ˌmeɪtrɪ'ɑːkl] adj matriarcal.

matriarchy ['meɪtrɪɑːkɪ] (pl **matriarchies**) n matriarcat m.

matrices ['meɪtrɪsiːz] pl ⟶ **matrix**.

matriculate [mə'trɪkjʊleɪt] vi [register] s'inscrire, se faire immatriculer ; [at university] s'inscrire.

matriculation [mə,trɪkjʊ'leɪʃn] n [registration] inscription f, immatriculation f ; [at university] inscription f.

matrimonial [ˌmætrɪ'məʊnjəl] adj matrimonial, conjugal.

matrimony ['mætrɪmənɪ US 'mætrɪməʊnɪ] (pl **matrimonies**) n fml mariage m.

matrix ['meɪtrɪks] (pl **matrixes** or **matrices** ['meɪtrɪsiːz]) n matrice f.

matron ['meɪtrən] n **1.** UK [in hospital] infirmière f en chef ; [in school] infirmière f **2.** liter [married woman] matrone f, mère f de famille **3.** [in retirement home] surveillante f **4.** US [in prison] gardienne f, surveillante f.

matronly ['meɪtrənlɪ] adj : she looks very matronly elle a tout de la matrone.

matt [mæt] adj UK mat / matt paint peinture f mate.

matte [mæt] adj UK = matt.

matted ['mætɪd] adj [material] feutré ; [hair] emmêlé.

matter ['mætər] ◆ n **1.** [affair] affaire f ; [subject] sujet m / business matters affaires fpl / money matters questions fpl d'argent **2.** [question] question f / a matter of life and death une question de vie ou de mort / that's quite another matter or that's a different matter altogether ça c'est une (tout) autre affaire / that's a matter of opinion ça c'est une question d'opinion / as a matter of course tout naturellement / as a matter of principle par

principe / as a matter of urgency d'urgence **3.** [physical substance] matière f **4.** [written material] : printed matter a) texte m imprimé b) [sent by post] imprimés mpl **5.** MED [pus] pus m **6.** PHR what's the matter? qu'est-ce qu'il y a ?, qu'est-ce qui ne va pas ? / what's the matter with Jim? qu'est-ce qu'il a, Jim ? / what's the matter with your eyes? qu'est-ce que vous avez aux yeux ? / what's the matter with the way I dress? qu'est-ce que vous me reprochez à ma façon de m'habiller ? / what's the matter with telling him the truth? quel mal y a-t-il à lui dire la vérité ? / there's something the matter with my leg j'ai quelque chose à la jambe ▸ **is there something** or **is anything the matter?** il y a quelque chose qui ne va pas ?, il y a un problème ? ▸ **nothing's the** or **there's nothing the matter** il n'y a rien, tout va bien / no matter what I do quoi que je fasse / no matter what the boss thinks peu importe ce qu'en pense le patron ▸ **no matter what** quoi qu'il arrive / no matter how hard I try quels que soient les efforts que je fais. ◆ vi importer, avoir de l'importance / what does it matter? quelle importance est-ce que ça a ?, qu'importe ? / it doesn't matter cela n'a pas d'importance, ça ne fait rien / it doesn't matter to me what you do with your money ce que tu fais de ton argent m'est égal / money is all that matters to him il n'y a que l'argent qui l'intéresse / she matters a lot to him il tient beaucoup à elle, elle compte beaucoup pour lui. ❖ **matters** pl n : as matters stand les choses étant ce qu'elles sont / getting angry won't help matters at all se mettre en colère n'arrangera pas les choses. ❖ **as a matter of fact** adv phr en fait, à vrai dire, en réalité. ❖ **for that matter** adv phr d'ailleurs.

Matterhorn ['mætəhɔːn] pr n ▸ **the Matterhorn** le mont Cervin.

matter-of-fact adj [down-to-earth] terre à terre (inv) ; [prosaic] prosaïque ; [unemotional] neutre.

matter-of-factly [-'fæktlɪ] adv [in a down-to-earth manner] de façon pragmatique ; [prosaically] prosaïquement ; [unemotionally] d'un air détaché.

matting ['mætɪŋ] n (U) [used as mat] natte f, tapis m.

mattress ['mætrɪs] n matelas m.

mature [mə'tjʊər] ◆ adj **1.** [person - physically] mûr ; [- mentally] mûr, mature **2.** [cheese] fait ; [wine, spirits] arrivé à maturité **3.** FIN échu **4.** MED [cell] mature. ◆ vi **1.** [person, attitude] mûrir **2.** [wine] arriver à maturité ; [cheese] se faire **3.** FIN arriver à échéance, échoir. ◆ vt [cheese] faire mûrir, affiner ; [wine, spirits] faire vieillir.

⚠ The French adjective **mature** is used to refer to psychological maturity and in some technical terms. In other contexts, use **mûr**.

mature student n UNIV adulte qui fait des études.

maturity [mə'tjʊərətɪ] n **1.** [gen] maturité f ▸ **to reach maturity** [person] devenir majeur **2.** FIN ▸ **maturity (date)** échéance f.

maudlin ['mɔːdlɪn] adj larmoyant, sentimental.

maul [mɔːl] vt **1.** [attack - subj: animal] mutiler ; [- subj: person, crowd] malmener **2.** inf [handle clumsily] tripoter **3.** [criticize] démolir, mettre en pièces.

Maundy Thursday ['mɔːndɪ-] n RELIG jeudi m saint.

Mauritania [ˌmɒrɪ'teɪnjə] pr n Mauritanie f / in Mauritania en Mauritanie.

Mauritanian [ˌmɒrɪ'teɪnjən] ◆ n Mauritanien m, -enne f. ◆ adj mauritanien.

Mauritian [mə'rɪʃn] ◆ n Mauricien m, -enne f. ◆ adj mauricien.

Mauritius [mə'rɪʃəs] pr n l'île f Maurice / in Mauritius à l'île Maurice.

mausoleum [ˌmɔːsəˈlɪəm] n mausolée m.

mauve [məʊv] ◆ adj mauve. ◆ n mauve m.

maverick [ˈmævərɪk] ◆ n [person] franc-tireur m, indépendant m, -e f. ◆ adj non-conformiste, indépendant.

mawkish [ˈmɔːkɪʃ] adj [sentimental] mièvre ; [nauseating] écœurant.

max adv inf maximum / three days max trois jours grand maximum. ❖ **max out** US vt sep : I maxed out my credit card j'ai atteint la limite sur ma carte de crédit / with two kids and a dog, I'm maxed out avec deux gosses et un chien, les fins de mois sont difficiles.

max. (written abbr of **maximum**) max.

maxim [ˈmæksɪm] n maxime f.

maxima [ˈmæksɪmə] pl ⟶ **maximum**.

maximal [ˈmæksɪml] adj maximal.

maximize, maximise [ˈmæksɪmaɪz] vt maximiser, maximaliser.

maximum [ˈmæksɪməm] (pl **maximums** or **maxima** [ˈmæksɪmə]) ◆ n maximum m / to the maximum au maximum. ◆ adj maximum, maximal / maximum load charge f maximale or limite ▶ **maximum security prison** prison f de haute sécurité. ◆ adv au maximum.

may [meɪ] modal vb **1.** [expressing possibility] : this may take some time ça prendra peut-être or il se peut que ça prenne du temps / symptoms may disappear after a few days les symptômes peuvent disparaître après quelques jours / you may well be right il est fort possible or il se peut bien que vous ayez raison / what he says may be true ce qu'il dit est peut-être vrai **2.** [expressing permission] : you may sit down vous pouvez vous asseoir / only close relatives may attend seuls les parents proches sont invités à assister à la cérémonie / if I may say so si je peux or puis me permettre cette remarque **3.** [in polite questions, suggestions] : may I interrupt? puis-je vous interrompre ?, vous permettez que je vous interrompe ? / may I? vous permettez ? **4.** [expressing wishes, hopes] : may she rest in peace qu'elle repose en paix **5.** PHR **may as well** : can I go home now? — you may as well est-ce que je peux rentrer chez moi maintenant ? — tu ferais aussi bien / we may as well have another drink tant qu'à faire, autant prendre un autre verre.

 Note that il se peut / pourrait que is followed by a verb in the subjunctive:
This may just be the house we've always dreamed of. Il se peut / pourrait que ce soit la maison de nos rêves.

May [meɪ] n mai m. See also **February**.

maybe [ˈmeɪbiː] adv peut-être ▶ **maybe so** peut-être bien que oui ▶ **maybe not** peut-être bien que non.

May Day n le Premier Mai.

Mayday [ˈmeɪdeɪ] n [SOS] SOS m.

Mayflower [ˈmeɪflaʊər] pr n ▶ **the Mayflower** US HIST le Mayflower ▶ **the Mayflower Compact** déclaration des principes du nouvel établissement signée par une quarantaine de passagers du Mayflower.

The Mayflower Compact

Accord signé à bord du **Mayflower** par les Pères pèlerins en novembre 1620, avant leur débarquement à Plymouth. Cette convention officialisait la création d'un gouvernement indépendant; elle est considérée comme la première Constitution de l'Amérique du Nord.

mayfly [ˈmeɪflaɪ] (pl **mayflies**) n éphémère m.

mayhem [ˈmeɪhem] n [disorder] désordre m.

mayn't [meɪnt] UK abbr of **may not**.

mayo [ˈmeɪəʊ] n US inf mayonnaise f.

mayonnaise [ˌmeɪəˈneɪz] n mayonnaise f.

mayor [meər] n maire m, mairesse f.

mayoress [ˈmeərɪs] n femme f du maire.

maypole [ˈmeɪpəʊl] n ≃ arbre m de mai (mât autour duquel on danse le Premier mai).

may've [ˈmeɪəv] inf abbr of **may have**.

maze [meɪz] n lit & fig labyrinthe m, dédale m.

MB (written abbr of **megabyte**) Mo.

MBA (abbr of **Master of Business Administration**) n MBA m.

MBBS (abbr of **Bachelor of Medicine and Surgery**) n (titulaire d'une) licence de médecine et de chirurgie.

MBE (abbr of **Member of the Order of the British Empire**) n (membre de) l'ordre de l'Empire britannique (titre honorifique).

MBI (abbr of **management buy-in**) n MBI m.

MC n **1.** abbr of **master of ceremonies 2.** US abbr of **Member of Congress**.

MCAT (abbr of **Medical College Admissions Test**) n test d'admission aux études de médecine.

McCarthyism [məˈkɑːθɪɪzm] n POL maccartisme m, maccarthysme m.

 McCarthyism

Cette campagne anticommuniste vit le jour dans les années 1950 aux États-Unis, et donna lieu à une chasse aux sorcières dans les milieux artistiques, professionnels et politiques. Elle tire son nom du sénateur McCarthy. Celui-ci fut désavoué en 1954 par le Sénat.

McCoy [məˈkɔɪ] n ▶ **it's the real McCoy** inf c'est du vrai de vrai, c'est de l'authentique.

MCP (abbr of **male chauvinist pig**) n inf phallo m.

MD ◆ n **1.** abbr of **Doctor of Medicine 2.** abbr of **managing director**. ◆ written abbr of **Maryland**.

me¹ [miː] pron **1.** [direct or indirect object - unstressed] me, m' (before vowel or silent 'h') ; [- stressed] moi / do you love me? tu m'aimes ? / give me a light donne-moi du feu **2.** [after preposition] moi / they're talking about me ils parlent de moi **3.** [used instead of 'I'] moi / it's me c'est moi / she's bigger than me elle est plus grande que moi.

me² [miː] MUS = **mi**.

ME ◆ n (abbr of **myalgic encephalomyelitis**) (U) myélo-encéphalite f. ◆ written abbr of **Maine**.

mead [miːd] n [drink] hydromel m.

meadow [ˈmedəʊ] n pré m, prairie f.

meagre UK, **meager** US [ˈmiːgər] adj maigre.

meal [miːl] n **1.** repas m / have a nice meal! or enjoy your meal! bon appétit ! ▶ **evening meal** dîner m / we have our evening meal early nous dînons tôt ▶ **to make a meal of sthg** inf faire tout un plat de qqch **2.** [flour] farine f.

meals on wheels n service de repas à domicile à l'intention des invalides et des personnes âgées.

meal ticket n **1.** US ticket m restaurant **2.** inf [source of income] gagne-pain m inv.

mealtime ['miːltaɪm] n [lunch] heure f du déjeuner ; [dinner] heure f du dîner / **at mealtimes** aux heures des repas.

mealy-mouthed [-'mauðd] adj doucereux, patelin.

mean [miːn] (pt & pp **meant** [ment]) ◆ adj **1.** [miserly] avare, radin, pingre / **they're very mean about pay rises** ils accordent les augmentations de salaire au compte-gouttes **2.** [nasty, unkind] méchant, vache / **don't be mean to your sister!** ne sois pas méchant avec ta sœur ! / **to play a mean trick on sb** jouer un sale tour à qqn **3.** [inferior] : **the meanest intelligence** l'esprit le plus borné / **he's no mean architect / guitarist** c'est un architecte / guitariste de talent / **it was no mean feat** ce n'était pas un mince exploit **4.** [average] moyen **5.** v inf [excellent] terrible, super / **she plays a mean guitar** comme guitariste, elle est super. ◆ n **1.** [middle point] milieu m, moyen terme m ▶ **the golden** or **happy mean** le juste milieu **2.** MATH moyenne f. ◆ vt **1.** [signify - subj: word, gesture] vouloir dire, signifier ; [- subj: person] vouloir dire / **what do you mean?** qu'est-ce que tu veux dire ? / **what do you mean by "wrong"?** qu'entendez-vous par «faux» ? / **what do you mean you don't like the cinema?** comment ça, vous n'aimez pas le cinéma ? / **how do you mean?** qu'entendez-vous par là ? / **that doesn't mean a thing!** ça ne veut (strictement) rien dire ! ; [requesting or giving clarification] : **do you mean it?** tu es sérieux ? ▶ **I mean** [that's to say] je veux dire **2.** [imply, entail - subj: event, change] signifier / **she's never known what it means to be loved** elle n'a jamais su ce que c'est que d'être aimée **3.** [matter, be of value] compter / **your friendship means a lot to her** votre amitié compte beaucoup pour elle / **you mean everything to me** tu es tout pour moi / **he means nothing to me** il n'est rien pour moi / **$20 means a lot to me** 20 dollars, c'est une grosse somme or c'est beaucoup d'argent pour moi **4.** [refer to] : **do you mean us?** tu veux dire nous ? **5.** [intend] avoir l'intention de, vouloir, compter / **I only meant to help** je voulais seulement me rendre utile / **I didn't mean it!** a) [action] je ne l'ai pas fait exprès ! b) [words] je n'étais pas sérieux ! / **without meaning to** involontairement / **I meant it as a joke** c'était une plaisanterie / **the present was meant for your brother** le cadeau était destiné à ton frère / **they're meant for each other** ils sont faits l'un pour l'autre / **it's meant to be a horse** c'est censé représenter un cheval / **it was meant to be** c'était écrit / **he means well** il a de bonnes intentions **6.** [consider, believe] : **it's meant to be good for arthritis** il paraît que c'est bon pour l'arthrite **7.** [suppose] : **that box isn't meant to be in here** cette boîte n'est pas censée être ici.

meander [mɪ'ændər] ◆ vi **1.** [river] serpenter, faire des méandres **2.** [person] errer (sans but), se promener au hasard. ◆ n méandre m.

meaning ['miːnɪŋ] ◆ n sens m, signification f. ◆ adj [look, smile] significatif, éloquent.

meaningful ['miːnɪŋful] adj **1.** [expressive - gesture] significatif, éloquent **2.** [comprehensible - explanation] compréhensible ; [significant] significatif **3.** [profound - experience, relationship] profond.

meaningfully ['miːnɪŋfulɪ] adv de façon significative.

meaningless ['miːnɪŋlɪs] adj **1.** [devoid of sense] dénué de sens, sans signification **2.** [futile] futile, vain.

meanness ['miːnnɪs] n **1.** [stinginess] avarice f **2.** US [nastiness, spitefulness] méchanceté f, mesquinerie f.

means [miːnz] (pl **means**) ◆ n [way, method] moyen m ▶ **a means of doing sthg** un moyen de faire qqch / **it's just a means to an end** ce n'est qu'un moyen d'arriver au but / **by means of a screwdriver** à l'aide d'un tournevis / **they communicate by means of signs** ils communiquent par signes ▶ **means of transport** moyen de transport.

◆ pl n [money, resources] moyens mpl, ressources fpl / **to live within one's means** vivre selon ses moyens / **to live beyond one's means** vivre au-dessus de ses moyens. ❖ **by all means** adv mais certainement, bien sûr. ❖ **by no means** adv nullement, en aucune façon / **it's by no means easy** c'est loin d'être facile.

mean-spirited adj mesquin.

means test n enquête f sur les revenus (d'une personne désirant bénéficier d'une allocation d'État). ❖ **means-test** vt : **is unemployment benefit means-tested?** les allocations de chômage sont-elles attribuées en fonction des ressources or des revenus du bénéficiaire ?

meant [ment] pt & pp ⟶ **mean**.

meantime ['miːntaɪm] adv pendant ce temps. ❖ **in the meantime** adv phr entre-temps. ❖ **for the meantime** adv phr pour l'instant.

meanwhile ['miːnwaɪl] adv entre-temps, pendant ce temps.

measles ['miːzlz] n rougeole f.

measly ['miːzlɪ] (compar **measlier**, superl **measliest**) adj inf minable, misérable.

measurable ['meʒərəbl] adj **1.** [rate, change, amount] mesurable **2.** [noticeable, significant] sensible, perceptible.

measurably ['meʒərəblɪ] adv [noticeably, significantly] sensiblement, notablement.

measure ['meʒər] ◆ n **1.** [measurement] mesure f / **linear / square / cubic measure** mesure de longueur / de superficie / de volume **2.** [degree] mesure f / **in some measure** dans une certaine mesure, jusqu'à un certain point / **in large measure** dans une large mesure, en grande partie **3.** [device - ruler] mètre m, règle f ; [- container] mesure f **4.** [portion] portion f, dose f **5.** [step, legislation] mesure f **6.** MUS & LITER mesure f. ◆ vt **1.** [take measurement of] mesurer **2.** [judge] jauger, mesurer, évaluer ▶ **to measure oneself** or **one's strength against sb** se mesurer à qqn. ◆ vi mesurer / **the room measures 18 feet by 12** la pièce mesure 18 pieds sur 12. ❖ **measure off** vt sep mesurer. ❖ **measure out** ◆ vt sep mesurer ▶ **to measure sb up** fig jauger qqn, prendre la mesure de qqn. ◆ vi être or se montrer à la hauteur ▶ **to measure up to sb's expectations** répondre aux espérances de qqn.

measured ['meʒəd] adj **1.** [distance, length, etc.] mesuré **2.** [careful, deliberate] mesuré.

measurement ['meʒəmənt] n **1.** [dimension] mesure f / **to take (down) the measurements of a piece of furniture** prendre les dimensions d'un meuble / **waist / hip measurement** tour m de taille / de hanches / **what are her measurements?** quelles sont ses mensurations ? **2.** [act] mesurage m.

measuring jug n verre m gradué, doseur m.

measuring tape n mètre m à ruban.

meat [miːt] n **1.** viande f ▶ **cooked** or **cold meats** viande froide **2.** liter [food] nourriture f / **that's meat and drink to him!** pour lui, c'est du gâteau ! / **one man's meat is another man's poison** prov ce qui est bon pour les uns ne l'est pas forcément pour les autres.

meatball ['miːtbɔːl] n CULIN boulette f (de viande).

meat-eater n carnivore mf.

meat-eating adj carnivore.

meat loaf (pl **meat loaves**) n pain m de viande.

meat pie n pâté m de viande en croûte.

meaty ['miːtɪ] (compar **meatier**, superl **meatiest**) adj **1.** [taste] de viande / **a good, meaty meal** [full of meat] un bon repas riche en viande **2.** [rich in ideas] substantiel, étoffé.

Mecca ['mekə] pr n la Mecque. ❖ **mecca** n *fig* : *it's a Mecca for book lovers* c'est la Mecque des bibliophiles / *the Mecca of country music* le haut lieu de la country.

mechanic [mɪ'kænɪk] n mécanicien *m*, -enne *f*.

⚠ The feminine noun **mécanique** means mechanics. A mechanic is **un(e) mécanicien(ne)**.

mechanical [mɪ'kænɪkl] adj **1.** [device, process] mécanique / *mechanical shovel* pelle *f* mécanique, pelleteuse *f* **2.** [machine-like] machinal, mécanique.

mechanical engineer n ingénieur *m* mécanicien.

mechanical engineering n [study] mécanique *f* ; [industry] construction *f* mécanique.

mechanically [mɪ'kænɪklɪ] adv mécaniquement ; *fig* machinalement, mécaniquement.

mechanics [mɪ'kænɪks] ❖ n *(U)* [study] mécanique *f*. ❖ pl n [functioning] mécanisme *m*.

mechanism ['mekənɪzm] n mécanisme *m*.

mechanization, mechanisation [,mekənaɪ'zeɪʃn] n mécanisation *f*.

mechanize, mechanise ['mekənaɪz] vt **1.** [equip with machinery] mécaniser **2.** MIL [motorize] motoriser.

MEd [,em'ed] **(abbr of Master of Education)** n ≃ (titulaire d'une) maîtrise en sciences de l'éducation.

Med [med] pr n ᴜᴋ *inf* ▸ **the Med** la Méditerranée.

medal ['medl] n médaille *f*.

medalist ᴜs = medallist.

medallion [mɪ'dæljən] n médaillon *m*.

medallist ᴜᴋ, **medalist** ᴜs ['medəlɪst] n [winner of medal] médaillé *m*, -e *f*.

meddle ['medl] vi **1.** [interfere] ▸ **to meddle in sthg** se mêler de qqch **2.** [tamper] ▸ **to meddle with sthg** toucher à qqch, tripoter qqch.

meddler ['medlər] n **1.** [busybody] : *she's such a meddler* il faut toujours qu'elle fourre son nez partout **2.** [tamperer] touche-à-tout *mf*.

meddlesome ['medlsəm] adj indiscret (indiscrète), qui se mêle de tout.

meddling ['medlɪŋ] ❖ n [action] ingérence *f* *(in/ dans)*. ❖ adj indiscret, qui se mêle de tout.

media ['miːdjə] ❖ pl n **1.** (*often sg*) ▸ **the media** les médias *mpl* ▸ **the news media** la presse **2.** ⟶ **medium**. ❖ comp des médias ; [interest, coverage, event] médiatique ▸ **media centre** COMPUT centre *m* multimédia ▸ **media circus** cirque *m* médiatique ▸ **media coverage** couverture *f* médiatique ▸ **media event** événement *m* médiatique ▸ **media officer** responsable *mf* des relations presse ▸ **media studies** études de communication.

mediaeval [,medɪ'iːvl] = medieval.

media-friendly adj ▸ **to be media-friendly** avoir de bonnes relations avec les médias.

mediagenic ['miːdjə,dʒenɪk] adj [person] médiatique.

median ['miːdjən] ❖ adj médian. ❖ n **1.** MATH médiane *f* **2.** ᴜs AUTO = median strip.

median strip n ᴜs terre-plein *m* central.

media-savvy adj *inf* ▸ **to be media-savvy** bien connaître le fonctionnement des médias.

mediascape ['miːdɪəskeɪp] n paysage *m* médiatique.

media-shy adj : *she's media-shy* elle n'aime pas être interviewée.

mediaspeak ['miːdɪəspiː,k] n jargon *m* des médias.

mediate ['miːdɪeɪt] ❖ vi [act as a peacemaker] servir de médiateur / *to mediate in a dispute* servir de médiateur dans un conflit ▸ **to mediate between** servir d'intermédiaire entre. ❖ vt **1.** [agreement, peace] obtenir par médiation ; [dispute] servir de médiateur dans, se faire le médiateur de **2.** [moderate] modérer.

mediation [,miːdɪ'eɪʃn] n médiation *f*.

mediator ['miːdɪeɪtər] n médiateur *m*, -trice *f*.

media-wise adj ▸ **to be media-wise** bien connaître le fonctionnement des médias.

medic ['medɪk] n *inf* **1.** [doctor] toubib *m* **2.** ᴜᴋ [medical student] étudiant *m* en médecine.

Medicaid ['medɪkeɪd] pr n ᴜs assistance *f* médicale.

medical ['medɪkl] ❖ adj médical ▸ **medical board** a) commission *f* médicale b) MIL conseil *m* de révision ▸ **medical history** [of patient] a) [file] dossier *m* médical b) [previous problems] antécédents *mpl* médicaux ▸ **medical insurance** assurance *f* maladie ▸ **medical officer** a) INDUST médecin *m* du travail b) MIL médecin *m* militaire ▸ **medical practitioner** (médecin *m*) généraliste *mf* ▸ **the medical profession** le corps médical ▸ **medical school** faculté *f* de médecine ▸ **medical student** étudiant *m*, -e *f* en médecine. ❖ n visite *f* médicale ▸ **to have a medical** passer une visite médicale ▸ **to pass / fail a medical** être déclaré apte / inapte à un travail après un bilan de santé.

medical certificate n certificat *m* médical.

medical examination n visite *f* médicale.

medical examiner n ᴜs médecin *m* légiste.

medically ['medɪklɪ] adv médicalement.

Medical Research Council pr n *organisme public de financement des centres de recherche médicale et des hôpitaux en Grande-Bretagne*.

Medicare ['medɪkeər] pr n *aux États-Unis, programme fédéral d'assistance médicale pour personnes âgées qui a largement contribué à réhabiliter socialement le 3ᵉ âge*.

medicated ['medɪkeɪtɪd] adj traitant.

medication [,medɪ'keɪʃn] n médication *f* ▸ **to be on medication** être sous médicaments.

medicinal [me'dɪsɪnl] adj médicinal.

medicine ['medsɪn] n **1.** [art] médecine *f* ▸ **to practise medicine** exercer la médecine **2.** [substance] médicament *m*, remède *m* / *don't forget to take your medicine* n'oublie pas de prendre tes médicaments ▸ **to give sb a dose** or **taste of his / her own medicine** rendre à qqn la monnaie de sa pièce.

medicine cabinet, medicine chest n (armoire *f* à) pharmacie *f*.

medicine man n sorcier *m*, medicine-man *m*.

medieval [,medɪ'iːvl] adj médiéval.

mediocre [,miːdɪ'əʊkər] adj médiocre.

mediocrity [,miːdɪ'ɒkrətɪ] (*pl* mediocrities) n **1.** [gen] médiocrité *f* **2.** [mediocre person] médiocre *mf*, incapable *mf*.

meditate ['medɪteɪt] vi **1.** [practise meditation] méditer **2.** [reflect, ponder] réfléchir, songer ▸ **to meditate on** or **upon sthg** réfléchir or songer à qqch.

meditation [,medɪ'teɪʃn] n méditation *f*, réflexion *f*.

meditative ['medɪtətɪv] adj méditatif.

Mediterranean [,medɪtə'reɪnjən] ❖ pr n ▸ **the Mediterranean (Sea)** la (mer) Méditerranée. ❖ adj méditerranéen.

medium ['miːdjəm] ❖ n **1.** (*pl* media ['miːdjə]) [means of communication] moyen *m* (de communication) **2.** (*pl* mediums) [spiritualist] médium *m* **3.** (*pl* mediums) [middle course] milieu *m* ▸ **the happy medium** le juste milieu **4.** (*pl* **mediums**) [size] taille *f* moyenne. ◆ *adj* **1.** [gen] moyen **2.** CULIN [meat] à point.

medium-dry *adj* [wine] demi-sec.

medium-haul *adj* [flight, route] moyen-courrier.

medium-range *adj* : *medium-range missile* missile *m* à moyenne portée.

medium-rare *adj* CULIN [meat] entre saignant et à point.

medium-sized *adj* moyen, de taille moyenne.

medium-term *adj* à moyen terme.

medium-wave *adj* [broadcast] sur ondes moyennes ; [station, transmitter] émettant sur ondes moyennes.

medley ['medlɪ] *n* **1.** [mixture] mélange *m* **2.** MUS potpourri *m* **3.** [in swimming] quatre nages *m inv*.

medspeak ['medspiːk] *n* jargon *m* médical.

meek [miːk] *adj* doux (douce), docile ▸ **meek and mild** doux comme un agneau.

meekly ['miːklɪ] *adv* doucement, docilement.

meet [miːt] (*pt & pp* **met** [met]) ◆ *vt* **1.** [by chance] rencontrer / *to meet sb on the stairs* croiser qqn dans l'escalier ; [by arrangement] rejoindre, retrouver / *I'll meet you on the platform in 20 minutes* je te retrouve sur le quai dans 20 minutes / *I'm meeting Gregory this afternoon* j'ai rendez-vous avec Gregory cet après-midi **2.** [wait for, collect] attendre, aller or venir chercher / *nobody was at the station to meet me* personne ne m'attendait à la gare / *he'll meet us at the station* il viendra nous chercher à la gare **3.** [greet] : *she came to meet us* elle est venue à notre rencontre **4.** [make acquaintance of] rencontrer, faire la connaissance de / *I'd like you to meet Mr Jones* j'aimerais vous présenter M. Jones / *(I'm very) glad or pleased to meet you* enchanté (de faire votre connaissance) **5.** [satisfy] satisfaire, répondre à ▸ **to meet sb halfway** *fig* trouver un compromis avec qqn ; [settle] régler / *I couldn't meet the payments* je n'ai pas pu régler or payer les échéances **6.** [face] rencontrer, affronter / *how are we going to meet the challenge?* comment allons-nous relever le défi ? / *to meet one's death* trouver la mort **7.** [come in contact with] rencontrer / *my eyes met his* nos regards se croisèrent or se rencontrèrent **8.** [treat] accueillir / *his suggestion was met with howls of laughter* sa proposition a été accueillie par des éclats de rire. ◆ *vi* **1.** [by chance] se rencontrer ; [by arrangement] se retrouver, se rejoindre, se donner rendez-vous / *shall we meet at the station?* on se retrouve or on se donne rendez-vous à la gare ? / *until we meet again!* à la prochaine ! **2.** [become acquainted] se rencontrer, faire connaissance / *have you two met?* est-ce que vous vous connaissez déjà ?, vous vous êtes déjà rencontrés ? **3.** [assemble] se réunir / *the committee meets once a month* le comité se réunit une fois par mois **4.** [join - lines, wires] se rencontrer, se joindre / *their eyes met* leurs regards se rencontrèrent or se croisèrent. ◆ *n* **1.** UK [in hunting] rendezvous *m* (de chasse) **2.** US SPORT rencontre *f*. ❖ **meet up** *vi* [by chance] se rencontrer ; [by arrangement] se retrouver, se donner rendez-vous ▸ **to meet up with sb** retrouver qqn. ❖ **meet with** *vt insep* **1.** [encounter] rencontrer / *they met with considerable difficulties* ils ont rencontré d'énormes difficultés / *to meet with a refusal* se heurter à or essuyer un refus / *I'm afraid your dog has met with an accident* j'ai bien peur que votre chien n'ait eu un (petit) accident **2.** US = meet (*vt*).

meeting ['miːtɪŋ] *n* **1.** [assembly] réunion *f* ; POL assemblée *f*, meeting *m* ; UK SPORT rencontre *f*, meeting *m* ▸ **to hold a meeting** tenir une réunion ▸ **athletics meeting** rencontre *f* or meeting *m* d'athlétisme ▸ **committee meeting**

réunion du comité **2.** [encounter] rencontre *f* **3.** [arranged] rendez-vous *m* / *I have a meeting with the boss this morning* j'ai rendez-vous avec le patron ce matin.

meeting place *n* [for gatherings] lieu *m* de réunion ; [for rendez-vous] (lieu *m* de) rendez-vous *m*.

mega- ['megə-] *in comp inf* super, méga-.

megabit ['megəbɪt] *n* COMPUT méga-bit *m*.

megabucks ['megəbʌks] *n inf* un fric fou, une fortune.

megabyte ['megəbaɪt] *n* mégaoctet *m*.

megahertz ['megəhɜːts] (*pl* **megahertz**) *n* mégahertz *m*.

megalomania [,megələ'meɪnjə] *n* mégalomanie *f*.

megalomaniac [,megələ'meɪnɪæk] ◆ *adj* mégalomane. ◆ *n* mégalomane *mf*.

megaphone ['megəfəʊn] *n* porte-voix *m inv*, mégaphone *m*.

megapixel ['megəpɪksl] *n* mégapixel.

megastar ['megəstɑːʳ] *n inf* superstar *f*.

megastore ['megəstɔːʳ] *n* très grand magasin *m*.

megaton ['megətʌn] *n* mégatonne *f*.

megawatt ['megəwɒt] *n* mégawatt *m*.

melamine ['meləmiːn] *n* mélamine *f*.

melancholy ['melənkəlɪ] ◆ *n liter* mélancolie *f*. ◆ *adj* [person, mood] mélancolique ; [news, sight, thought] sombre, triste.

melanin ['melənɪn] *n* mélanine *f*.

melanoma [,melə'nəʊmə] *n* mélanome *m*.

melatonin [,melə'təʊnɪn] *n* PHYSIOL mélatonine *f*.

melee, mêlée ['meleɪ] *n* mêlée *f*.

mellow ['meləʊ] ◆ *adj* **1.** [fruit] mûr ; [wine] velouté **2.** [bricks] patiné ; [light] doux (douce), tamisé ; [colour] doux (douce) ; [voice, music] doux (douce), mélodieux **3.** [person, mood] serein, tranquille / *to become* or *to grow mellow* s'adoucir **4.** *inf* [relaxed] cool, relax, relaxe **5.** *inf* [tipsy] éméché, gai. ◆ *vt* [subj: age, experience] adoucir ; [subj: food, alcohol] détendre, décontracter. ◆ *vi* **1.** [fruit] mûrir ; [wine] devenir moelleux, se velouter **2.** [light, colour] s'adoucir ; [stone, brick, building] se patiner ; [sound, music] s'adoucir, devenir plus mélodieux **3.** [person] : *he's mellowed (with age)* il s'est adouci avec l'âge ; [with food, alcohol] se décontracter. ❖ **mellow out** *vi* [relax] *inf* se calmer, se détendre.

mellowing ['meləʊɪŋ] *adj* adoucissant.

melodic [mɪ'lɒdɪk] *adj* mélodique.

melodious [mɪ'ləʊdjəs] *adj* mélodieux.

melodrama ['melədrɑːmə] *n* mélodrame *m*.

melodramatic [,melədrə'mætɪk] *adj* mélodramatique / *don't be so melodramatic!* n'en fais pas tout un drame ! ❖ **melodramatics** *pl n* mélo *m inf* / *I'm fed up with his melodramatics* j'en ai asez de son cinéma.

melody ['melədɪ] (*pl* **melodies**) *n* mélodie *f*.

melon ['melən] *n* melon *m*.

melt [melt] ◆ *vi* **1.** [become liquid] fondre **2.** [disappear] ▸ **to melt (away)** disparaître, s'évaporer **3.** [blend] se fondre / *he tried to melt into the crowd* il a essayé de se fondre or de disparaître dans la foule. ◆ *vt* [gen] (faire) fondre ; [metal] fondre ▸ **to melt sb's heart** attendrir (le cœur de) qqn. ❖ **melt down** *vt sep & vi* fondre.

meltdown ['meltdaʊn] *n* NUCL fusion *f* (du cœur) ; *fig* effondrement *m*.

melted cheese ['meltɪd-] *n* fromage *m* fondu / *a melted cheese sandwich* un sandwich au fromage fondu.

melting point *n* point *m* de fusion.

melting pot n creuset m.

member ['membər] ◆ n **1.** [of club, union, political party, etc.] membre m, adhérent m, -e f **2.** [of group, family, class] membre m / *you're practically a member of the family now* tu fais presque partie de la famille maintenant / *a member of the audience* un spectateur / *a member of the public* un membre du public **3.** ANAT, ARCHIT & MATH membre m. ◆ comp ▶ **member country** / **state** pays m / État m membre. ◆ **Member** n [of legislative body] ▶ **Member of Parliament** membre m de la Chambre des communes ; ≃ député m / *the Member (of Parliament) for Leicester* le député de Leicester ▶ **Member of Congress** membre m du Congrès ▶ **Member of the House of Representatives** membre m de la Chambre des représentants ▶ **Member of the European Parliament** député m européen, membre m du Parlement européen.

membership ['membəʃɪp] n **1.** [condition] adhésion f ▶ **membership card** carte f d'adhérent or de membre ▶ **membership fee** cotisation f **2.** [body of members] : *our club has a large membership* notre club compte de nombreux adhérents or membres.

membrane ['membreɪn] n membrane f.

memento [mɪ'mentəʊ] (pl **mementos** or **mementoes**) n souvenir m.

memo ['meməʊ] (pl **memos**) n note f.

memoir ['memwɑː'] n **1.** [biography] biographie f **2.** [essay, monograph] mémoire m. ◆ **memoirs** pl n [autobiography] mémoires mpl.

memo pad n bloc-notes m.

memorabilia [ˌmemərə'bɪliə] pl n souvenirs mpl.

memorable ['memərəbl] adj mémorable, inoubliable.

memorably ['memərəbli] adv : *a memorably hot summer* un été torride dont on se souvient encore.

memorandum [ˌmemə'rændəm] (pl **memoranda** [-də]) n **1.** COMM note f **2.** [diplomatic communication] mémorandum m.

memorial [mɪ'mɔːriəl] ◆ n [monument] monument m (commémoratif), mémorial m. ◆ adj [commemorative] commémoratif ▶ **memorial service** commémoration f.

Memorial Day n US dernier lundi du mois de mai (férié aux États-Unis en l'honneur des soldats américains morts pour la patrie).

memorize, memorise ['meməraɪz] vt mémoriser.

memory ['meməri] (pl **memories**) n **1.** [capacity to remember] mémoire f ▶ **to have a good / bad memory** avoir (une) bonne / mauvaise mémoire ▶ **to have a short memory** avoir la mémoire courte ▶ **to lose one's memory** perdre la mémoire **2.** [recollection] souvenir m ▶ **to have good / bad memories of sthg** garder un bon / mauvais souvenir de qqch ▶ **to the memory of** à la mémoire de **3.** COMPUT mémoire f ▶ **memory dump** vidage m de mémoire. ◆ **in memory of** prep phr en souvenir de.

memory bank n bloc m de mémoire.

memory card n COMPUT carte f d'extension mémoire ▶ **memory card slot** fente f d'extension.

memory leak n COMPUT fuite f mémoire.

memory module n COMPUT module m de mémoire.

memory stick n carte f mémoire.

men [men] pl ⟶ **man**.

menace ['menəs] ◆ n **1.** [source of danger] danger m **2.** [threat] menace f **3.** inf [annoying person or thing] plaie f. ◆ vt menacer.

menacing ['menəsɪŋ] adj menaçant.

menacingly ['menəsɪŋli] adv [speak, act] de manière menaçante ; [look] d'un air menaçant.

menagerie [mɪ'nædʒəri] n ménagerie f.

mend [mend] ◆ vt **1.** [repair - machine, television, broken vase] réparer ; [- clothes] raccommoder ; [- hem] recoudre ; [darn - socks] repriser, ravauder ▶ **to get** or **to have sthg mended** faire réparer qqch **2.** [rectify] rectifier, réparer ▶ **to mend one's ways** s'amender. ◆ vi [improve - patient] se remettre, être en voie de guérison ; [- weather] s'améliorer. ◆ n **1.** [darn] reprise f ; [patch] pièce f **2.** PHR **to be on the mend a)** inf s'améliorer **b)** [patient] se remettre, être en voie de guérison.

mending ['mendɪŋ] n raccommodage m.

menfolk ['menfəʊk] pl n hommes mpl.

menial ['miːnjəl] adj : *menial tasks* tâches fpl ingrates or sans intérêt.

meningitis [ˌmenɪn'dʒaɪtɪs] n méningite f.

menopause ['menəpɔːz] n ménopause f ▶ **the male menopause** l'andropause f.

menservants ['mensɜːvənts] pl ⟶ **manservant**.

men's room n US toilettes fpl (pour hommes).

menstrual ['menstrʊəl] adj menstruel ▶ **menstrual cycle** cycle m menstruel.

menstruate ['menstrʊeɪt] vi avoir ses règles.

menstruation [ˌmenstrʊ'eɪʃn] n menstruation f, règles fpl.

menswear ['menzweə'] n (U) vêtements mpl pour hommes.

mental ['mentl] adj **1.** [intellectual] mental / *he has a mental age of seven* il a un âge mental de sept ans **2.** [in the mind] mental ▶ **to make a mental note of sthg** prendre note de qqch **3.** [psychiatric] mental ▶ **mental block** blocage m (psychologique) ▶ **mental illness** maladie f mentale ▶ **mental nurse** infirmier m, -ère f psychiatrique ▶ **mental patient** malade m mental, malade f mentale **4.** v inf [crazy] malade, timbré.

mental arithmetic n calcul m mental.

mental health n santé f mentale.

mental home, mental hospital n hôpital m psychiatrique.

mentality [men'tæləti] (pl **mentalities**) n mentalité f.

mentally ['mentəli] adv mentalement ▶ **the mentally disabled** or **handicapped** les handicapés mentaux ▶ **mentally ill** malade (mentalement) ▶ **mentally disturbed** déséquilibré (mental).

menthol ['menθɒl] n menthol m ▶ **menthol cigarette** cigarette f au menthol or mentholée.

mentholated ['menθəleɪtɪd] adj au menthol, mentholé.

mention ['menʃn] ◆ vt [talk about] mentionner, faire mention de, parler de / *I'll mention it to him sometime* je lui en toucherai un mot à l'occasion / *thank you very much — don't mention it!* merci beaucoup — il n'y a pas de quoi ! or je vous en prie ! / *it's not worth mentioning* ça ne vaut pas la peine d'en parler ; [remark, point out] signaler ; [name, cite] mentionner, citer, nommer / *just mention my name to her* dites-lui que c'est de ma part / *to mention sb in one's will* coucher qqn sur son testament. ◆ n mention f ▶ **honourable mention** mention f. ◆ **not to mention** prep phr sans parler de.

mentor ['mentɔː'] n mentor m.

menu ['menjuː] n **1.** [in restaurant] menu m, carte f / *on the menu* au menu **2.** COMPUT menu m.

menu bar n COMPUT barre f de menu.

menu-controlled adj COMPUT contrôlé par menu.

meow [miː'aʊ] US = **miaow**.

MEP (abbr of **Member of the European Parliament**) n député m européen, membre m du Parlement européen.

mercantile ['mɜːkəntaɪl] adj **1.** COMM ▸ **mercantile law** droit *m* commercial **2.** ECON [concerning mercantilism] mercantiliste.

mercenary ['mɜːsɪnrɪ] (*pl* **mercenaries**) ◆ n mercenaire *m*. ◆ adj **1.** *pej* intéressé **2.** MIL mercenaire.

merchandise ['mɜːtʃəndaɪz] ◆ n *(U)* marchandises *fpl*. ◆ vt commercialiser.

merchandising ['mɜːtʃəndaɪzɪŋ] n merchandising *m*, marchandisage *m*.

merchant ['mɜːtʃənt] ◆ n **1.** [trader] négociant *m*, -e *f* ; [shopkeeper] marchand *m*, -e *f* / *wool merchant* lainier *m*, négociant en laines / *'The Merchant of Venice' Shakespeare* 'le Marchand de Venise' **2.** *fig* : *merchant of death* marchand de mort / *a doom merchant* un prophète de malheur. ◆ adj marchand.

merchant bank n banque *f* d'affaires.

merchant banker n banquier *m* d'affaires.

merchant marine n US marine *f* marchande.

merchant navy n UK marine *f* marchande.

merchant seaman n marin *m* de la marine marchande.

merciful ['mɜːsɪfʊl] adj clément, miséricordieux ▸ **to be merciful to** or **towards sb** faire preuve de clémence or de miséricorde envers qqn.

mercifully ['mɜːsɪfʊlɪ] adv **1.** [luckily] heureusement, par bonheur **2.** [with clemency] avec clémence.

merciless ['mɜːsɪlɪs] adj impitoyable, implacable.

mercurial [mɜːˈkjʊərɪəl] adj **1.** [changeable] versatile, d'humeur inégale, changeant **2.** [lively] vif, plein de vie, gai.

mercury ['mɜːkjʊrɪ] n CHEM mercure *m*. ❖ **Mercury** pr n ASTRON & MYTH Mercure.

mercy ['mɜːsɪ] (*pl* **mercies**) ◆ n **1.** [clemency] clémence *f*, pitié *f*, indulgence *f* ▸ **to have mercy on sb** avoir pitié de qqn ; RELIG miséricorde *f* **2.** [blessing] chance *f*, bonheur *m* / *it's a mercy that he doesn't know* heureusement qu'il ne sait pas, c'est une chance qu'il ne sache pas **3.** [power] merci *f* ▸ **to be at sb's / sthg's mercy** être à la merci de qqn / qqch. ◆ comp humanitaire, de secours ▸ **mercy mission** : *on a mercy mission* en mission humanitaire.

mercy killing n euthanasie *f*.

mere [mɪə*r*] adj seul, simple, pur / *I'm a mere beginner* je ne suis qu'un débutant.

merely ['mɪəlɪ] adv seulement, (tout) simplement / *I'm merely a beginner* je ne suis qu'un débutant.

merge [mɜːdʒ] ◆ vi **1.** [join - rivers] se rejoindre, confluer ; [-roads] se rejoindre ; [-colours, voices] se confondre ; [-cultures] se mélanger ; POL s'unir **2.** [vanish] se perdre / *the thief merged into the crowd* le voleur s'est fondu dans la foule **3.** COMM fusionner. ◆ vt joindre, fusionner ; COMM & COMPUT fusionner ; POL unifier.

merger ['mɜːdʒə*r*] n COMM fusion *f*.

meridian [məˈrɪdɪən] n **1.** ASTRON, GEOG & MED méridien *m* **2.** *fig* [zenith] zénith *m*, sommet *m*, apogée *m*.

meringue [məˈræŋ] n meringue *f*.

merit ['merɪt] ◆ n mérite *m*. ◆ vt mériter.

meritocracy [ˌmerɪˈtɒkrəsɪ] (*pl* **meritocracies**) n méritocratie *f*.

mermaid ['mɜːmeɪd] n MYTH sirène *f*.

merrily ['merɪlɪ] adv [happily] joyeusement, gaiement ; [blithely] allègrement.

merriment ['merɪmənt] n [joy] joie *f*, gaieté *f* ; [laughter] rire *m*, rires *mpl*, hilarité *f*.

merry ['merɪ] (*compar* **merrier**, *superl* **merriest**) adj **1.** [happy] joyeux, gai ▸ **Merry Christmas!** Joyeux Noël ! ▸ **the more the merrier** *prov* plus on est de fous, plus on rit *prov* **2.** *inf* [tipsy] éméché, pompette.

merry-go-round n UK manège *m* ; *fig* [whirl] tourbillon *m*.

merrymaking ['merɪˌmeɪkɪŋ] n *(U)* réjouissances *fpl*, festivités *fpl*.

mesh [meʃ] ◆ n **1.** [of net] mailles *fpl* ; [of sieve] grille *f* / *a mesh shopping bag* un filet à provisions **2.** [fabric] tissu *m* à mailles. ◆ vi **1.** [be in harmony] s'harmoniser, s'accorder **2.** [tally, coincide] cadrer, concorder **3.** MECH [gears] s'engrener.

mesmerize, mesmerise ['mezməraɪz] vt **1.** [hypnotise] hypnotiser **2.** [entrance] ensorceler, envoûter.

mess [mes] ◆ n **1.** [untidiness] désordre *m*, fouillis *m* ; [dirtiness] saleté *f*, saletés *fpl* **2.** [muddle] gâchis *m* / *to make a mess of a job* gâcher un travail **3.** *inf* [predicament] pétrin *m* **4.** MIL [canteen] mess *m* **5.** MIL [food] ordinaire *m*, gamelle *f*. ◆ vt [dirty] salir, souiller. ◆ vi **1.** *inf* [meddle] ▸ **to mess with sb** embêter qqn **2.** MIL manger or prendre ses repas au mess. ❖ **mess about, mess around** *inf* ◆ vi UK **1.** [waste time] perdre son temps ; [dawdle, hang around] traîner ; [potter] bricoler ; [play the fool] faire l'imbécile **2.** [meddle, fiddle] tripoter, tripatouiller / *don't mess about with my computer* ne tripote pas mon ordinateur ; *fig* ▸ **to mess about with sb a)** [annoy] embêter qqn **b)** [have an affair] coucher avec qqn. ◆ vt sep [person] embêter. ❖ **mess up** vt sep **1.** [make disorderly - room, papers] mettre en désordre **2.** *inf* [spoil] ficher en l'air **3.** [dirty] salir, souiller.

message ['mesɪdʒ] ◆ n **1.** [communication] message *m*, commission *f* ; [written] message *m*, mot *m* **2.** [theme - of book, advert] message *m* ; [teaching - of prophet] message *m*, enseignement *m* **3.** Scot commission *f*, course *f* **4.** LING message *m*. ◆ vt [send SMS to] envoyer un SMS à.

message switching [-ˈswɪtʃɪŋ] n COMPUT commutation *f* de messages.

messaging ['mesɪdʒɪŋ] n COMPUT messagerie *f*.

messenger ['mesɪndʒə*r*] n [gen] messager *m*, -ère *f* ; [errand boy - in office] coursier *m* ; [in hotel] chasseur *m*, coursier *m* / *by special messenger* par porteur spécial ▸ **bike** or **bicycle messenger** coursier *m*, -ère *f* à vélo ▸ **messenger boy** coursier *m*, garçon *m* de courses ▸ **messenger service** messagerie *f*.

messenger bag n sacoche *f*.

messiah [mɪˈsaɪə] n messie *m*. ❖ **Messiah** n Messie *m*.

messily ['mesɪlɪ] adv **1.** [untidily] mal, de façon peu soignée ; [in a disorganized way] n'importe comment **2.** [dirtily] comme un cochon.

Messrs, Messrs. ['mesəz] MM, Messieurs.

messy ['mesɪ] (*compar* **messier**, *superl* **messiest**) adj **1.** [dirty - hands, clothes] sale, malpropre ; [-job] salissant / *don't get all messy* ne te salis pas **2.** [untidy - place] en désordre, désordonné, mal tenu ; [-person] peu soigné, négligé, débraillé ; [-hair] ébouriffé, en désordre, en bataille **3.** [badly done] bâclé **4.** *fig* compliqué, embrouillé, délicat.

met [met] pt & pp —→ **meet**.

Met [met] pr n *inf* **1.** US abbr of Metropolitan Opera **2.** US abbr of Metropolitan Museum **3.** UK abbr of Metropolitan Police.

metabolic [ˌmetəˈbɒlɪk] adj métabolique.

metabolism [mɪˈtæbəlɪzm] n métabolisme *m*.

metabolize, metabolise [mɪˈtæbəlaɪz] vt métaboliser.

metadata ['metədeɪtə] pl n métadonnées *fpl.*

metafile ['metəfaɪl] n métafichier *m.*

metal ['metl] (UK *pt & pp* **metalled,** *cont* **metalling ;** US *pt & pp* **metaled,** *cont* **metaling)** ◆ n [gen & CHEM] métal *m / made of metal* en métal. ◆ adj en métal, métallique.

metal detector n détecteur *m* de métaux.

metallic [mɪ'tælɪk] adj **1.** CHEM métallique **2.** [colour] : *metallic blue / grey* bleu / gris métallisé **3.** [voice] métallique ; [sound] métallique, grinçant.

metallurgy [me'tælədʒɪ] n métallurgie *f.*

metalwork ['metəlwɜ:k] n **1.** [objects] ferronnerie *f* **2.** [activity] travail *m* des métaux **3.** [metal framework] tôle *f,* métal *m* ; [of crashed car, plane] carcasse *f.*

metalworker ['metəl,wɜ:kər] n **1.** [in factory] métallurgiste *m,* métallo *m* **2.** [craftsman] ferronnier *m.*

metamorphose [,metə'mɔ:fəʊz] ◆ vi se métamorphoser ▶ **to metamorphose into sthg** se métamorphoser en qqch. ◆ vt métamorphoser.

metamorphosis [,metə'mɔ:fəsɪs or ,metəmɔ:'fəʊsɪs] *(pl* **metamorphoses** [-si:z]) n métamorphose *f.*

metaphor ['metəfər] n métaphore *f.*

metaphorical [,metə'fɒrɪkl] adj métaphorique.

metaphorically [,metə'fɒrɪklɪ] adv métaphoriquement.

metaphysical [,metə'fɪzɪkl] adj LITER & PHILOS métaphysique ; *fig* [abstract] métaphysique, abstrait.

metaphysics [,metə'fɪzɪks] n (U) métaphysique *f.*

meta-search n COMPUT métarecherche *f* ▶ **metasearch engine** moteur *m* de métarecherche.

mete [mi:t] ❖ **mete out** vt sep [punishment] infliger ; [judgment, justice] rendre.

meteor ['mi:tɪər] n météore *m* ▶ **meteor shower** pluie *f* d'étoiles filantes, averse *f* météorique.

meteoric [mi:tɪ'ɒrɪk] adj **1.** ASTRON météorique **2.** *fig* fulgurant, très rapide.

meteorite ['mi:tɪəraɪt] n météorite *f.*

meteorological [,mi:tjərə'lɒdʒɪkl] adj météorologique.

meteorologist [,mi:tjə'rɒlədʒɪst] n météorologue *mf,* météorologiste *mf.*

meteorology [,mi:tjə'rɒlədʒɪ] n météorologie *f.*

meter ['mi:tər] n **1.** [for water, gas, electricity] compteur *m* **2.** US = metre.

metered ['mi:təd] adj décompté à la minute.

methadone ['meθədəʊn] n méthadone *f.*

methane ['mi:θeɪn] n méthane *m.*

methinks [mɪ'θɪŋks] *(pt* **methought** [-'θɔ:t]) vb *arch & hum* ce me semble.

method ['meθəd] n **1.** [means] méthode *f,* moyen *m* ; [manner] manière *f* ; [instruction] méthode *f,* mode *m* d'emploi ▶ **method of doing sthg** manière de faire qqch, méthode (employée) pour faire qqch **2.** [procedure] méthode *f,* procédé *m* ; [theory] théorie *f,* méthode *f* **3.** [organization] méthode *f,* organisation *f / there's method in her madness* elle n'est pas aussi folle qu'elle en a l'air. ❖ **Method** n ▶ **Method acting** la méthode Stanislavski.

methodical [mɪ'θɒdɪkl] adj méthodique.

methodically [mɪ'θɒdɪklɪ] adv méthodiquement, de façon méthodique, avec méthode.

Methodist ['meθədɪst] ◆ adj méthodiste. ◆ n méthodiste *mf.*

methodological [,meθədə'lɒdʒɪkl] adj méthodologique.

methodology [,meθə'dɒlədʒɪ] *(pl* **methodologies)** n méthodologie *f.*

meths [meθs] **(abbr of methylated spirits)** n UK *inf* alcool *m* à brûler.

methylated spirits ['meθɪleɪtɪd] n alcool *m* à brûler.

meticulous [mɪ'tɪkjʊləs] adj méticuleux.

meticulously [mɪ'tɪkjʊləslɪ] adv méticuleusement.

meticulousness [mɪ'tɪkjʊləsnɪs] n minutie *f,* méticulosité *f liter / with great meticulousness* avec un soin tout particulier.

Met Office [met-] **(abbr of Meteorological Office)** pr n *les services météorologiques britanniques.*

metonymic [,metə'nɪmɪk] adj métonymique.

me-too adj MARKETING [product, brand] me-too.

metre UK, **meter** US ['mi:tər] n **1.** [measurement] mètre *m* **2.** LITER mètre *m* ▶ **in iambic metre** en vers *mpl* iambiques **3.** MUS mesure *f.*

metric ['metrɪk] adj MATH métrique ▶ **to go metric** adopter le système métrique ▶ **metric hundredweight** 50 kilogrammes *mpl* ▶ **metric ton** tonne *f.*

metric system n ▶ **the metric system** le système métrique.

metro ['metrəʊ] *(pl* **metros)** n métro *m.*

metronome ['metrənəʊm] n métronome *m.*

metropolis [mɪ'trɒpəlɪs] *(pl* **metropolises** [-i:z]) n métropole *f,* grande ville *f,* grand centre *m* urbain.

metropolitan [,metrə'pɒlɪtn] ◆ adj **1.** GEOG métropolitain **2.** RELIG métropolitain ▶ **metropolitan bishop** métropolitain *m.* ◆ n RELIG métropolitain *m* ; [in orthodox church] métropolite *m.*

Metropolitan Police n UK police *f* londonienne.

metrosexual [,metrə'sekʃʊəl] ◆ n métrosexuel *m.* ◆ adj métrosexuel.

mettle ['metl] n courage *m.*

mew [mju:] ◆ vi [cat] miauler ; [gull] crier. ◆ n **1.** [of cat] miaulement *m* ; [of gull] cri *m* **2.** [gull] mouette *f.*

mews [mju:z] n UK **1.** [flat] appartement chic aménagé dans une écurie rénovée **2.** [street] ruelle *f.*

Mexican ['meksɪkn] ◆ n Mexicain *m,* -aine *f.* ◆ adj mexicain ▶ **the Mexican War** la guerre du Mexique.

 The Mexican War

Conflit qui opposa les États-Unis au Mexique de 1846 à 1848. Vaincu, celui-ci renonça à ses prétentions sur le Texas et céda un vaste territoire comprenant plusieurs États américains actuels (dont le Nouveau-Mexique et la Californie).

Mexican wave n ola *f.*

Mexico ['meksɪkəʊ] pr n Mexique *m / in Mexico* au Mexique.

Mexico City pr n Mexico.

mezzanine ['metsəni:n] n **1.** mezzanine *f* **2.** US [in theatre] corbeille *f.*

mezzo-soprano *(pl* **mezzo-sopranos)** n **1.** [singer] mezzo-soprano *f* **2.** [voice] mezzo-soprano *m.*

MFA (abbr of Master of Fine Arts) n *(titulaire d'une) maîtrise en beaux-arts.*

MFL n **abbr of modern foreign languages.**

mfr written abbr of **manufacturer.**

mg (written abbr of milligram) mg.

MGB MESSAGING written abbr of may god bless.

Mgr 1. (written abbr of Monseigneur, Monsignor) Mgr **2. written abbr of** manager.

MHOTY MESSAGING written abbr of my hat's off to you.

MHR n abbr of Member of the House of Representatives.

MHz (written abbr of megahertz) MHz.

mi [miː] n MUS mi *m inv.*

MI written abbr of Michigan.

MI5 (abbr of Military Intelligence section 5) pr n *service de contre-espionnage britannique.*

MI6 (abbr of Military Intelligence section 6) pr n *service de renseignements britannique.*

MIA (abbr of missing in action) adj *expression indiquant qu'une personne a disparu lors d'un combat.*

miaow [miːˈaʊ] 🇬🇧 ◆ vi miauler. ◆ n miaulement *m.* ◆ interj miaou.

mice [maɪs] pl ⟶ mouse.

Mich. written abbr of Michigan.

Michigan [ˈmɪʃɪɡən] pr n Michigan *m* / *in Michigan* dans le Michigan.

mickey [ˈmɪkɪ] n **1.** 🇬🇧 ▶ **to take the mickey out of sb** *inf* se payer la tête de qqn **2.** *v inf* = Mickey Finn.

MICR (abbr of magnetic ink character recognition) n *reconnaissance magnétique de caractères.*

micro [ˈmaɪkrəʊ] (pl micros) ◆ adj très petit, microscopique. ◆ n [microcomputer] micro-ordinateur *m,* micro *m.*

micro- [ˈmaɪkrəʊ] pref micro-.

microbe [ˈmaɪkrəʊb] n microbe *m.*

microbiologist [ˌmaɪkrəʊbaɪˈɒlədʒɪst] n microbiologiste *mf.*

microbiology [ˌmaɪkrəʊbaɪˈɒlədʒɪ] n microbiologie *f.*

microblog [ˈmaɪkrəʊˌblɒɡ] n microblog *m.*

microblogger [ˈmaɪkrəʊˌblɒɡə] n microblogeur *m,* -euse *f.*

microblogging [ˈmaɪkrəʊˌblɒɡɪŋ] n microblogging *m.*

microchip [ˈmaɪkrəʊtʃɪp] n microprocesseur *m.*

microcircuit [ˈmaɪkrəʊˌsɜːkɪt] n microcircuit *m.*

microcomputer [ˌmaɪkrəʊkəmˈpjuːtə] n micro-ordinateur *m.*

microcomputing [ˌmaɪkrəʊkəmˈpjuːtɪŋ] n micro-informatique *f.*

microcosm [ˈmaɪkrəʊˌkɒzm] n microcosme *m.*

microcredit [ˈmaɪkrəʊkredɪt] n microcrédit *m.*

microeconomics [ˈmaɪkrəʊˌiːkəˈnɒmɪks] n *(U)* micro-économie *f.*

microelectronics [ˈmaɪkrəʊˌlekˈtrɒnɪks] n microélectronique *f.*

microfibre 🇬🇧, **microfiber** 🇺🇸 [ˈmaɪkrəˌfaɪbə] n microfibre *f.*

microfiche [ˈmaɪkrəʊfiːʃ] n microfiche *f.*

microfilm [ˈmaɪkrəʊfɪlm] ◆ n microfilm *m.* ◆ vt microfilmer, mettre sur microfilm.

microlight [ˈmaɪkrəlaɪt] n AERON ultra-léger motorisé *m,* ULM *m.*

micromesh [ˈmaɪkrəʊmeʃ] adj [tights] surfin.

micron [ˈmaɪkrɒn] (pl microns or micra [-krə]) n micron *m.*

microorganism [ˌmaɪkrəʊˈɔːɡənɪzm] n micro-organisme *m.*

microphone [ˈmaɪkrəfəʊn] n microphone *m.*

microprocessor [ˈmaɪkrəʊˌprəʊsesə] n microprocesseur *m.*

microprogram [ˈmaɪkrəʊˌprəʊɡræm] n microprogramme *m.*

micro scooter n trottinette *f* pliante.

microscope [ˈmaɪkrəskəʊp] n microscope *m.*

microscopic [ˌmaɪkrəˈskɒpɪk] adj **1.** [tiny] microscopique **2.** [using a microscope] au microscope, microscopique.

microscopically [ˌmaɪkrəˈskɒpɪklɪ] adv [examine] au microscope.

microsecond [ˈmaɪkrəʊˌsekənd] n microseconde *f.*

microsurgery [ˌmaɪkrəʊˈsɜːdʒərɪ] n microchirurgie *f.*

microwave [ˈmaɪkrəweɪv] ◆ n **1.** PHYS micro-onde *f* **2.** = microwave oven. ◆ vt faire cuire au micro-ondes.

microwaveable [ˈmaɪkrəʊˌweɪvəbl] adj micro-ondable.

microwave oven n four *m* à micro-ondes.

mid [mɪd] adj **1.** [middle] : *in mid October* à la mi-octobre, au milieu du mois d'octobre / *he's in his mid fifties* il a environ 55 ans **2.** [half] : *mid green* vert ni clair ni foncé **3.** [central] central, du milieu / *mid Wales* le centre or la région centrale du pays de Galles.

mid- [mɪd] pref : *mid-height* mi-hauteur / *mid-morning* milieu de la matinée / *mid-winter* plein hiver.

midair [mɪdˈeə] ◆ adj en plein ciel. ◆ n : *in midair* en plein ciel.

mid-Atlantic ◆ adj [accent] américanisé. ◆ n : *(the) mid-Atlantic* au milieu de l'Atlantique.

midday [ˈmɪddeɪ] n midi *m* / *at midday* à midi / *midday meal* repas *m* de midi.

middle [ˈmɪdl] ◆ n **1.** [in space] milieu *m,* centre *m* ▶ **in the middle (of)** au milieu (de), au centre (de) **2.** [in time] milieu *m* / *in the middle of the week* au milieu de la semaine ; [in activity] ▶ **to be in the middle of (doing) sthg** être en train de faire qqch **3.** [stomach] ventre *m* ; [waist] taille *f.* ◆ adj **1.** [in the centre] du milieu **2.** [average] moyen ; [intermediate] moyen, intermédiaire.

middle age n la cinquantaine / *to reach middle age* avoir un certain âge. ❖ **middle-age** comp ▶ **middle-age spread**: *he's got middle-age spread* il prend de l'embonpoint.

middle-aged adj d'une cinquantaine d'années.

Middle Ages pl n Moyen Âge *m* / *in the Middle Ages* au Moyen Âge.

Middle America pr n **1.** GEOG Amérique *f* centrale **2.** SOCIOL l'Amérique *f* moyenne ; *pej* l'Amérique *f* bien pensante.

middlebrow [ˈmɪdlbraʊ] ◆ n *pej* [reader] lecteur *m* moyen, lectrice *f* moyenne ; [audience] spectateur *m* moyen, spectatrice *f* moyenne. ◆ adj [reader, audience] moyen.

middle class n ▶ **the middle class** or **the middle classes** la classe moyenne, les classes moyennes. ❖ **middle-class** adj des classes moyennes.

middle distance n ▶ **in the middle distance a)** à mi-distance **b)** [in picture] au second plan. ❖ **middle-distance** adj SPORT ▶ **middle-distance runner/race** coureur *m,* -euse *f*/course *f* de demi-fond.

middle ear n ANAT oreille *f* moyenne.

Middle East pr n ▶ **the Middle East** le Moyen-Orient / *in the Middle East* au Moyen-Orient.

Middle Eastern adj moyen-oriental.

Middle England n l'Angleterre *f* moyenne.

middle finger n majeur *m.*

middle ground n **1.** [in picture] second plan *m* **2.** *fig* terrain *m* neutre.

middleman ['mɪdlmæn] (pl **middlemen** [-men]) n intermédiaire mf.

middle management n (U) cadres mpl moyens.

middle name n deuxième prénom m.

middle-of-the-road adj [opinions, policies] modéré ; pej timide, circonspect ▸ **middle-of-the-road music** variétés fpl or musique f passe-partout pej.

middle school n UK cycle d'enseignement à cheval sur le primaire et le secondaire (8 à 13 ans) ; US enseignement secondaire correspondant au premier cycle (10 à 13 ans) ; ≃ collège.

middleweight ['mɪdlweɪt] ◆ n poids m moyen. ◆ adj [championship] de poids moyen.

middling ['mɪdlɪŋ] adj inf [average] moyen ; [mediocre] médiocre ; [in health] : how are you? — fair to middling ça va ? — on fait aller.

Middx written abbr of **Middlesex**.

Mideast [,mɪd'i:st] US = **Middle East**.

midfield [,mɪd'fi:ld] n SPORT milieu m du terrain.

midge [mɪdʒ] n moucheron m.

midget ['mɪdʒɪt] ◆ n [dwarf] nain m, naine f. ◆ adj nain, minuscule.

midi system n mini-chaîne f.

Midlands ['mɪdləndz] pl pr n ▸ **the Midlands** les Midlands (comtés du centre de l'Angleterre).

midlife crisis n : he's having or going through a midlife crisis il a du mal à passer le cap de la cinquantaine.

midnight ['mɪdnaɪt] ◆ n minuit m / at midnight à minuit. ◆ adj [mass, swim] de minuit ▸ **to burn the midnight oil** travailler tard dans la nuit.

midpoint ['mɪdpɔɪnt] n [in space, time] milieu m.

mid-price ['mɪd,praɪs] adj COMM milieu de gamme (inv) ▸ **mid-price computers** des ordinateurs milieu de gamme.

mid-range adj COMM [computer, car] de milieu de gamme.

midriff ['mɪdrɪf] n 1. [stomach] ventre m 2. ANAT diaphragme m.

midst [mɪdst] n 1. [in space] milieu m, cœur m ▸ **in the midst of** au milieu or au cœur de 2. [in time] : in the midst of the crisis en pleine crise.

midstream [mɪd'stri:m] n ▸ **in midstream** lit au milieu du courant / he stopped talking in midstream fig il s'arrêta au beau milieu d'une phrase.

midsummer ['mɪd,sʌmə'] n : in midsummer au milieu de l'été, en été.

Midsummer Day, Midsummer's Day n le solstice d'été.

midterm [mɪd'tɜ:m] n 1. SCH & UNIV milieu m du trimestre 2. MED [of pregnancy] milieu m 3. POL ▸ **midterm elections** aux États-Unis, élections législatives qui ont lieu au milieu de mandat présidentiel.

midway ◆ adv [,mɪd'weɪ] à mi-chemin / she was midway through writing the first chapter elle avait déjà écrit la moitié du premier chapitre ▸ **midway between** à mi-chemin entre. ◆ adj ['mɪdweɪ] ▸ **midway point** [in time, space] milieu m.

midweek ◆ adv [mɪd'wi:k] [travel, arrive, meet] au milieu de la semaine ; RAIL ≃ en période bleue. ◆ adj ['mɪdwi:k] [travel, prices, performance] au milieu de la semaine ; RAIL ≃ (en) période bleue.

midweight ['mɪdweɪt] adj 1. [garment] (assez) léger 2. [in job ads: designer, developer] assez expérimenté.

Midwest [,mɪd'west] pr n ▸ **the Midwest** le Midwest / in the Midwest dans le Midwest.

Midwestern [,mɪd'westən] adj du Midwest.

midwife ['mɪdwaɪf] (pl **midwives** [-waɪvz]) n sage-femme f.

midwifery ['mɪd,wɪfərɪ] n obstétrique f.

midwinter [,mɪd'wɪntə'] n [solstice] solstice m d'hiver / in midwinter au milieu de l'hiver.

miffed [mɪft] adj inf [person] piqué, fâché ; [expression] froissé, fâché.

might¹ [maɪt] modal vb 1. [expressing possibility] : you might well be right il se pourrait bien que vous ayez raison / I might be home late tonight je rentrerai peut-être tard ce soir / she might have decided not to go il se peut qu'elle ait décidé de ne pas y aller 2. [past form of 'may'] : we feared you might be dead nous avons eu peur que vous ne soyez mort 3. [in polite questions or suggestions] : might I interrupt? puis-je me permettre de vous interrompre ? / might I or if I might make a suggestion? puis-je me permettre de suggérer quelque chose ? / you might try using a different approach altogether vous pourriez adopter une approche entièrement différente 4. [commenting on a statement made] : that, I might add, was not my idea cela n'était pas mon idée, soit dit en passant 5. [ought to] : I might have known he'd be the last (to arrive) j'aurais dû savoir qu'il serait le dernier (à arriver) / you might have warned me! tu aurais pu me prévenir ! 6. PHR we might as well go home (as stay here) nous ferions aussi bien de rentrer chez nous (plutôt que de rester ici).

> 📋 Note that il se peut / pourrait que is followed by a verb in the subjunctive:
> **This might just be the perfect solution.** Il se peut / pourrait que ce soit la solution parfaite.

might² [maɪt] n 1. [power - of nation] pouvoir m, puissance f ; [- of army] puissance f 2. [physical strength] force f ▸ **with all one's might** de toutes ses forces / he started yelling with all his might il se mit à crier à tue-tête.

mightn't ['maɪtənt] abbr of might not.

might've ['maɪtəv] abbr of might have.

mighty ['maɪtɪ] (compar mightier, superl mightiest) ◆ adj 1. [powerful] puissant 2. [impressive] imposant ; [enormous] énorme. ◆ adv US inf rudement.

migraine ['mi:greɪn or 'maɪgreɪn] n migraine f.

migrant ['maɪgrənt] ◆ n 1. [bird, animal] migrateur m 2. [worker - in agriculture] (travailleur m) saisonnier m ; [- foreign] travailleur m immigré. ◆ adj 1. [bird, animal] migrateur 2. [person] ▸ **migrant worker a)** [seasonal] (travailleur m) saisonnier m, (travailleuse f) saisonnière f **b)** [foreign] travailleur m immigré, travailleuse f immigrée.

migrate [UK maɪ'greɪt US 'maɪgreɪt] ◆ vi 1. [bird, animal] migrer 2. [person, family] migrer, se déplacer, émigrer. ◆ vt [data] transférer, migrer.

migration [maɪ'greɪʃn] n migration f.

migratory ['maɪgrətrɪ] adj 1. [bird, fish] migrateur 2. [habit, movement] migratoire.

mike [maɪk] (abbr of **microphone**) n inf micro m.

mild [maɪld] ◆ adj 1. [person, manner, voice] doux (douce) 2. [in taste - cheese] doux (douce) ; [- curry] pas très fort or épicé ; [soap, shampoo] doux (douce) ; [in strength - sedative, cigarette] léger 3. [clement - winter] doux (douce) / the weather's mild for the time of year il fait (un temps) doux pour la saison 4. [punishment] léger ; [criticism] clément. ◆ n UK bière moins riche en houblon et plus foncée que la « bitter ».

mildew ['mɪldjuː] n **1.** [on cereals, flowers] rouille f ; [on vines, potatoes, tomatoes] mildiou m **2.** [on paper, leather, food] moisissure f.

mildly ['maɪldlɪ] adv **1.** [in manner, voice] doucement, avec douceur **2.** [slightly] modérément, légèrement / *that's putting it mildly!* c'est le moins qu'on puisse dire !

mild-mannered adj mesuré, calme.

mildness ['maɪldnɪs] n **1.** [of manner] douceur f **2.** [in taste] : *she appreciated the mildness of the curry* elle apprécia le fait que le curry n'était pas trop épicé **3.** [of weather] douceur f **4.** [of rebuke] indulgence f, clémence f.

mile [maɪl] n **1.** [measurement] mille m *(1 609,33 m)* ; [in athletics] mile m / *she lives 30 miles from Birmingham* elle habite à une cinquantaine de kilomètres de Birmingham **2.** [long distance] : *you can see it a mile off* ça se voit de loin / *it's miles from anywhere* c'est un endroit complètement isolé / *you can see for miles and miles* on voit à des kilomètres à la ronde / *we walked (for) miles and miles* on a fait des kilomètres (à pied) **3.** fig : *they're miles ahead of their competitors* ils ont une avance considérable sur leurs concurrents **4.** *(adverbial use)* inf [much] : *she's miles better than me at languages* elle est bien plus forte que moi en langues.

mileage ['maɪlɪdʒ] n **1.** AUTO [distance] ≃ kilométrage m / *the car's got a very high mileage* la voiture a beaucoup roulé *or* a un kilométrage élevé / *the papers got tremendous mileage out of the scandal* fig les journaux ont exploité le scandale au maximum **2.** [consumption] consommation f (d'essence).

mileage allowance n indemnité f kilométrique.

mileometer [maɪ'lɒmɪtər] n ≃ compteur m (kilométrique).

milepost ['maɪlpəʊst] n ≃ borne f (kilométrique).

milestone ['maɪlstəʊn] n **1.** lit ≃ borne f (kilométrique) **2.** fig [important event] jalon m, étape f importante.

MILF (abbr of **mother I'd like to fuck**) n v inf MILF f, cougar f.

milieu [UK 'miːljɜː : US miːl'juː] n environnement m (social).

militancy ['mɪlɪtənsɪ] n militantisme m.

militant ['mɪlɪtənt] ◆ adj militant. ◆ n [gen] militant m, -e f.

militarism ['mɪlɪtərɪzm] n militarisme m.

militaristic [,mɪlɪtə'rɪstɪk] adj militariste.

militarized zone ['mɪlɪtəraɪzd-] n zone f militarisée.

military ['mɪlɪtrɪ] ◆ adj militaire ▶ **military academy** école f militaire ▶ **military service** service m militaire. ◆ n ▶ **the military** l'armée f.

military police n police f militaire.

militate ['mɪlɪteɪt] ❖ **militate against** vt insep [facts, actions] militer contre.

militia [mɪ'lɪʃə] n **1.** [body of citizens] milice f **2.** US [reserve army] réserve f.

militiaman [mɪ'lɪʃəmən] (pl **militiamen** [-mən]) n milicien m.

milk [mɪlk] ◆ n lait m. ◆ comp [bottle, churn, jug, etc. -empty] à lait ; [-full] de lait. ◆ vt **1.** [cow, goat] traire **2.** fig : *to milk a country of its resources* dépouiller un pays de ses ressources / *to milk the applause* faire durer les applaudissements.

milk chocolate n chocolat m au lait.

milk float n UK camionnette f du laitier.

milking ['mɪlkɪŋ] n traite f.

milking machine n machine f à traire, trayeuse f.

milkman ['mɪlkmən] (pl **milkmen** [-mən]) n [who delivers milk] laitier m ; UK [who milks] vacher m, trayeur m.

milk powder n lait m en poudre.

milk round n UK **1.** [for milk delivery] tournée f du laitier **2.** UNIV tournée des universités par les employeurs pour recruter des étudiants en fin d'études.

milk shake n milk-shake m.

milk tooth n dent f de lait.

milk truck US = **milk float**.

milky ['mɪlkɪ] (compar **milkier**, superl **milkiest**) adj **1.** [taste] laiteux, de lait ; [dessert] lacté, à base de lait ; [tea, coffee] avec du lait **2.** [colour] laiteux ; [skin] d'un blanc laiteux **3.** [cloudy - liquid] laiteux, lactescent.

Milky Way pr n ▶ **the Milky Way** la Voie lactée.

mill [mɪl] ◆ n **1.** [for flour] moulin m ; [on industrial scale] meunerie f, minoterie f **2.** [factory] usine f ▶ **steel mill** aciérie f **3.** [domestic - for coffee, pepper] moulin m. ◆ vt [grain] moudre ; [ore] broyer. ❖ **mill about** UK, ❖ **mill around** vi [crowd, people] grouiller.

millenarian [,mɪlɪ'neərɪən] ◆ adj millénariste. ◆ n millénariste mf.

millennial [mɪ'lenɪəl] adj du millenium.

millennium [mɪ'lenɪəm] (pl **millenniums** or **millennia** [-nɪə]) n **1.** [thousand years] millénaire m **2.** RELIG & fig ▶ **the millennium** le millénium.

millepede ['mɪlɪpiːd] = **millipede**.

miller ['mɪlər] n meunier m, -ère f.

millet ['mɪlɪt] n millet m.

milli- ['mɪlɪ] pref milli-.

millibar ['mɪlɪbɑːr] n millibar m.

milligram(me) ['mɪlɪgræm] n milligramme m.

millilitre UK, **milliliter** US ['mɪlɪ,liːtər] n millilitre m.

millimetre UK, **millimeter** US ['mɪlɪ,miːtər] n millimètre m.

million ['mɪljən] n **1.** lit million m / *two million dollars* deux millions de dollars / *millions of pounds* des millions de livres / *his secretary is one in a million* sa secrétaire est une perle rare **2.** [enormous number] : *there were simply millions of people at the concert!* il y avait un monde fou au concert ! / *I've told you a million times not to do that* je t'ai dit cent fois de ne pas faire ça. ❖ **millions** pl n [masses] masses fpl.

millionaire [,mɪljə'neər] n ≃ milliardaire mf.

millionairess [,mɪljə'neərɪs] n ≃ milliardaire f.

million-selling adj : *a million-selling album* un album qui s'est vendu à plus d'un million d'exemplaires.

millionth ['mɪljənθ] ◆ det millionième. ◆ n **1.** [ordinal] millionième mf **2.** [fraction] millionième m.

millipede ['mɪlɪpiːd] n mille-pattes m inv.

millisecond ['mɪlɪ,sekənd] n milliseconde f, millième m de seconde.

millstone ['mɪlstəʊn] n **1.** lit meule f **2.** fig fardeau m.

millwheel ['mɪlwiːl] n roue f (d'un moulin).

milometer [maɪ'lɒmɪtər] = **mileometer**.

mime [maɪm] ◆ n [actor, play] mime m / *to explain something in mime* expliquer quelque chose par gestes. ◆ vi **1.** THEAT faire du mime **2.** [pop singer] chanter en play-back. ◆ vt mimer ; [derisively] singer.

mimic ['mɪmɪk] (pt & pp **mimicked**, cont **mimicking**) ◆ vt [gestures] mimer ; [satirically] parodier, singer. ◆ n imitateur m, -trice f.

mimicry ['mɪmɪkrɪ] n **1.** [imitation] imitation f **2.** BIOL mimétisme m.

min. 1. (written abbr of **minute**) mn, min 2. (written abbr of **minimum**) min.

Min. written abbr of **ministry**.

minaret [mɪnəˈret] n minaret m.

mince [mɪns] ◆ vt 1. CULIN hacher 2. PHR *he doesn't mince his words* il ne mâche pas ses mots. ◆ n 1. UK [meat] viande f hachée, haché m 2. US = **mincemeat**.

mincemeat [ˈmɪnsmiːt] n 1. [meat] viande f hachée 2. [sweet filling] *mélange de fruits secs et d'épices qui sert de garniture à des tartelettes* 3. PHR **to make mincemeat of sb** inf réduire qqn en bouillie or en chair à pâté.

mince pie n tartelette fourrée avec un mélange de fruits secs et d'épices que l'on sert à Noël en Grande-Bretagne.

mincer [ˈmɪnsər] n hachoir m, hache-viande m inv.

mind [maɪnd] ◆ n 1. [reason] esprit m / *the power of mind over matter* le pouvoir de l'esprit sur la matière ▶ **to be of sound mind** être sain d'esprit ▶ **to be / to go out of one's mind** être / devenir fou / *he was out of his mind with worry* il était fou d'inquiétude 2. [thoughts] : *there's something on her mind* il y a quelque chose qui la tracasse / *I have a lot on my mind* j'ai beaucoup de soucis ▶ **at the back of one's mind** : *I've had it* or *it's been at the back of my mind for ages* j'y pense depuis longtemps, ça fait longtemps que ça me travaille / *I just can't get him out of my mind* je n'arrive absolument pas à l'oublier ▶ **to have sb / sthg in mind** penser à qqn / qqch de précis / *what kind of holiday did you have in mind?* qu'est-ce que tu voulais or voudrais faire pour les vacances ? / *you must put the idea out of your mind* tu dois te sortir cette idée de la tête / *a drink will take your mind off the accident* bois un verre, ça te fera oublier l'accident 3. [attention] : *keep your mind on the job* ne vous laissez pas distraire 4. [memory] : *my mind has gone blank* j'ai un trou de mémoire / *it brings to mind the time we were in Spain* cela me rappelle l'époque où nous étions en Espagne / *Churchill's words come to mind* on pense aux paroles de Churchill / *it went clean* or *right out of my mind* cela m'est complètement sorti de l'esprit or de la tête 5. [intellect] esprit m ; [intelligent person, thinker] esprit m, cerveau m ▶ **great minds think alike** hum les grands esprits se rencontrent 6. [opinion] ▶ **to be of the same** or **of like** or **of one mind** être du même avis ▶ **to have sb in mind** à mon avis, selon moi ▶ **to make up one's mind** se décider, prendre une décision ▶ **to make up one's mind to do sthg** se décider à faire qqch 7. [desire] : *I've half a mind to give up* j'ai à moitié envie de renoncer / *I've a good mind to tell him what I think* j'ai bien envie de lui dire ce que je pense ; [intention] : *nothing was further from my mind* je n'en avais nullement l'intention. ◆ vt 1. [look after -children] garder ; [-bags, possessions] garder, surveiller ; [-shop, business] garder, tenir ; [-plants, garden] s'occuper de, prendre soin de 2. [pay attention to] faire attention à / *mind your own business!* occupe-toi de ce qui te regarde !, mêle-toi de tes oignons ! / *mind your language!* surveille ton langage ! / **'mind the step'** *'attention à la marche'* 3. (with verb phrase) [be sure of] faire attention à / *mind you don't break it* fais bien attention de ne pas le casser / *mind what you're doing!* regarde ce que tu fais ! ; [remember] : *mind you post my letter* n'oubliez surtout pas de poster ma lettre 4. [bother about] faire attention à, s'inquiéter de or pour / *I really don't mind what he says / thinks* je me fiche de ce qu'il peut dire / penser 5. [object to] : *I don't mind him* il ne me dérange pas / *do you mind me smoking?* cela ne vous ennuie or dérange pas que je fume ? / *I wouldn't mind a cup of tea* je prendrais bien or volontiers une tasse de thé 6. PHR *mind (you), I'm not surprised* remarque or tu sais, cela ne m'étonne pas / *never mind the consequences* ne vous préoccupez pas des conséquences, peu importent les conséquences / *never mind what people say / think* peu importe ce que disent / pensent les gens. ◆ vi 1. [object -esp in requests] : *do you mind if I open the window?* cela vous dérange si j'ouvre la fenêtre ? / *I don't mind in the least* cela ne me dérange pas le moins du monde / *I don't mind if I do* [in reply to offer] volontiers, je ne dis pas non, ce n'est pas de refus 2. [care, worry] : *if you don't mind, I haven't finished* si cela ne vous fait rien, je n'ai pas terminé ▶ **never mind** a) [it doesn't matter] cela ne fait rien, tant pis b) [don't worry] ne vous en faites pas ▶ **never you mind!** a) [don't worry] ne vous en faites pas ! b) [mind your own business] ce n'est pas votre affaire ! 3. US [be careful] faire attention.

MIND [maɪnd] pr n *organisme d'aide aux handicapés mentaux*.

mind-altering [-ˈɒltərɪŋ] adj [drug] psychotrope.

mind-bending [-bendɪŋ] adj inf 1. [complicated] compliqué 2. [drugs] psychotrope.

mind-blowing adj inf [amazing] époustouflant.

mind-boggling adj extraordinaire, stupéfiant.

-minded [ˌmaɪndɪd] in comp 1. (with adj) : *they're so narrow-minded* ils sont tellement étroits d'esprit 2. (with adv) : *to be politically-minded* s'intéresser beaucoup à la politique 3. (with noun) : *my parents are very money-minded* mes parents ont un faible pour l'argent or sont très portés sur l'argent.

minder [ˈmaɪndər] n 1. UK inf [bodyguard] gorille m 2. [gen] gardien m, -enne f, surveillant m, -e f.

mindful [ˈmaɪndfʊl] adj fml : *mindful of her feelings on the subject, he fell silent* attentif à ce qu'elle ressentait à ce sujet, il se tut.

mindless [ˈmaɪndlɪs] adj 1. [stupid -film, book] idiot, stupide ; [senseless -cruelty, violence] insensé, sans nom 2. [boring] bête, ennuyeux 3. [heedless] : *mindless of the danger, he dived into the river* insouciant du danger, il plongea dans la rivière.

mind-numbing [-nʌmɪŋ] adj abrutissant.

mind reader n : *he must be a mind reader* il lit dans les pensées comme dans un livre.

mindset [ˈmaɪndset] n mentalité f.

mine¹ [maɪn] pron le mien m, la mienne f, les miens mpl, les miennes f / *this bag is mine* ce sac m'appartient or est à moi / *he's an old friend of mine* c'est un vieil ami à moi / *where did that brother of mine get to?* mais où est-ce que mon frère est encore passé ?

mine² [maɪn] ◆ n 1. [for coal, gold, salt, etc.] mine f / *he went down the mine* or *mines at 16* il est descendu à la mine à 16 ans 2. fig [valuable source] mine f / *she's a mine of information* c'est une véritable mine de renseignements 3. [explosive] mine f / *to clear a road of mines* déminer une route. ◆ vt 1. GEOL [coal, gold, etc.] extraire / *they mine coal in the area* il y a des mines de charbon dans la région 2. MIL [road, sea] miner ; [destroy] : *their jeep was mined* leur jeep a sauté sur une mine 3. [undermine -fortification] saper. ◆ vi exploiter une mine / *to mine for uranium* a) [prospect] chercher de l'uranium, prospecter pour trouver de l'uranium b) [extract] exploiter une mine d'uranium.

mine detector n détecteur m de mines.

minefield [ˈmaɪnfiːld] n 1. lit champ m de mines 2. fig : *a political minefield* une situation épineuse du point de vue politique.

minelayer [ˈmaɪnˌleɪər] n mouilleur m de mines.

miner [ˈmaɪnər] n MIN mineur m.

mineral [ˈmɪnərəl] ◆ n 1. GEOL minéral m 2. UK [soft drink] boisson f gazeuse (non alcoolique), soda m. ◆ adj minéral.

mineralogist [ˌmɪnəˈrælədʒɪst] n minéralogiste *mf*.

mineralogy [ˌmɪnəˈrælədʒɪ] n minéralogie *f*.

mineral water n eau *f* minérale.

mineshaft [ˈmaɪnʃɑːft] n puits *m* de mine.

minestrone (soup) [ˌmɪnɪˈstrəʊnɪ-] n minestrone *m*.

minesweeper [ˈmaɪnˌswiːpəʳ] n dragueur *m* de mines.

mineworker [ˈmaɪnˌwɜːkəʳ] n ouvrier *m*, -ère *f* de la mine, mineur *m*.

minging [ˈmɪŋɪŋ] adj 🇬🇧 *v inf* horrible.

mingle [ˈmɪŋgl] ◆ vt mélanger, mêler. ◆ vi se mêler (aux autres) ; [at party] : *excuse me, I must mingle* excusez-moi, il faut que je salue d'autres invités.

mini [ˈmɪnɪ] ◆ n *inf* **1.** [skirt] minijupe *f* **2.** COMPUT mini-ordinateur *m*, mini *m*. ◆ adj mini *(inv)*.

mini- [ˈmɪnɪ] pref mini-.

miniature [ˈmɪnətʃəʳ] ◆ adj [in miniature] en miniature ; [model] miniature ; [tiny] minuscule ▸ **miniature golf** golf *m* miniature ▸ **miniature poodle** caniche *m* nain. ◆ n [gen & ART] miniature *f* / *in miniature* en miniature.

miniaturized [ˈmɪnətʃəraɪzd] adj miniaturisé.

minibar [ˈmɪnɪbɑːʳ] n minibar *m*.

mini-break n [holiday] mini-séjour *m*.

minibus [ˈmɪnɪbʌs] *(pl* **minibuses)** n minibus *m*.

minicab [ˈmɪnɪkæb] n 🇬🇧 *voiture de série convertie en taxi*.

minicam [ˈmɪnɪkæm] n caméra *f* de télévision miniature.

minicomputer [ˌmɪnɪkəmˈpjuːtəʳ] n mini-ordinateur *m*.

mini-cruise n mini-croisière *f*.

MiniDisc® [ˈmɪnɪdɪsk] n Minidisc® *m*.

MiniDisc® player n lecteur de MiniDiscs® *m*.

minidish [ˈmɪnɪdɪʃ] n TV mini antenne *f* parabolique.

minidisk [ˈmɪnɪdɪsk] n mini-disquette *f*.

minidress [ˈmɪnɪdres] n mini-robe *f*.

minigolf [ˈmɪnɪgolf] n minigolf *m*.

minikini [ˈmɪnɪkiːnɪ] n minikini *m*.

minim [ˈmɪnɪm] n 🇬🇧 MUS blanche *f*.

minima [ˈmɪnɪmə] pl ⟶ **minimum**.

minimal [ˈmɪnɪml] adj minimal.

minimalism [ˈmɪnɪməlɪzm] n minimalisme *m*.

minimalist [ˈmɪnɪməlɪst] n minimaliste *mf*.

minimally [ˈmɪnɪməlɪ] adv à peine.

minimarket [ˈmɪnɪˌmɑːkɪt], **minimart** [ˈmɪnɪmɑːt] n supérette *f*, petit supermarché *m*.

minimize, minimise [ˈmɪnɪˌmaɪz] vt **1.** [reduce - size, amount] réduire au minimum, diminuer le plus possible **2.** [diminish - importance, achievement] minimiser **3.** COMPUT [display window] minimiser.

minimum [ˈmɪnɪməm] *(pl* **minimums** *or* **minima** [ˈmɪnɪmə]) ◆ n minimum *m* / *costs were reduced to the* or *a minimum* les coûts furent réduits au minimum / *at the (very) minimum it will cost £2,000* (en mettant les choses) au mieux, cela coûtera 2 000 livres. ◆ adj minimum, minimal.

minimum charge n tarif *m* minimum.

minimum deposit n acompte *m* minimum.

minimum lending rate n 🇬🇧 taux *m* d'escompte or de base.

minimum payment n paiement *m* minimum.

minimum wage n salaire *m* minimum *(légal)* ; ≃ SMIC *m*.

mining [ˈmaɪnɪŋ] ◆ n MIN exploitation *f* minière, extraction *f*. ◆ adj [town, company] minier ; [family] de mineurs.

mining engineer n ingénieur *m* des mines.

minion [ˈmɪnjən] n *pej* laquais *m*.

minipill [ˈmɪnɪpɪl] n minipilule *f*.

mini-roundabout [mɪnɪˈraʊndəbaʊt] n 🇬🇧 petit rond-point *m*.

mini-series n TV mini-feuilleton *m*.

miniskirt [ˈmɪnɪskɜːt] n minijupe *f*.

minister [ˈmɪnɪstəʳ] ◆ n **1.** 🇬🇧 POL ministre *m* ▸ **the Minister of Education / Defence** le ministre de l'Éducation / de la Défense ▸ **minister of state** secrétaire *mf* d'État ▸ **minister without portfolio** ministre *m* sans portefeuille **2.** RELIG pasteur *m*, ministre *m*. ◆ vi [provide care] ▸ **to minister to sb** secourir qqn, donner des soins à qqn ▸ **to minister to sb's needs** pourvoir aux besoins de qqn.

ministerial [ˌmɪnɪˈstɪərɪəl] adj **1.** 🇬🇧 POL [project, crisis] ministériel ; [post] de ministre **2.** RELIG pastoral, sacerdotal.

ministry [ˈmɪnɪstrɪ] *(pl* **ministries)** n **1.** 🇬🇧 POL [department] ministère *m* **2.** [government] gouvernement *m* **3.** RELIG [collective body] sacerdoce *m*, saint ministère *m* ▸ **to join the ministry a)** [Roman Catholic] se faire ordonner prêtre **b)** [Protestant] devenir pasteur ; [period of office] ministère *m*.

minivan [ˈmɪnɪvæn] n fourgonnette *f*.

mink [mɪŋk] ◆ n [animal, fur] vison *m* ; [coat] manteau *m* en or de vison, vison *m*. ◆ comp [coat, stole] en or de vison.

Minnesota [ˌmɪnɪˈsəʊtə] pr n Minnesota *m* / *in Minnesota* dans le Minnesota.

minnow [ˈmɪnəʊ] *(pl* **minnow** *or* **minnows)** n **1.** [specific fish] vairon *m* ; [any small fish] fretin *m (U)* **2.** 🇬🇧 *fig* [insignificant person] (menu) fretin *m*.

minor [ˈmaɪnəʳ] ◆ adj **1.** [secondary - road, role, position] secondaire ; [- writer] mineur ; [- importance, interest] secondaire, mineur ; [- share] petit, mineur **2.** [unimportant - problem, worry] mineur, peu important **3.** [small - alteration, disagreement] mineur, petit ; [- detail, expense] mineur, petit, menu **4.** [not serious - accident] mineur, petit ; [- illness, injury] bénin (bénigne) ▸ **minor offence** LAW délit *m* mineur ▸ **to have a minor operation** MED subir une petite intervention chirurgicale or une intervention chirurgicale bénigne **5.** MUS mineur **6.** 🇺🇸 UNIV [subject] facultatif. ◆ n **1.** [in age] mineur *m*, -e *f* **2.** 🇺🇸 UNIV matière *f* secondaire. ◆ vi 🇺🇸 UNIV : *she minored in French* elle a pris le français comme matière secondaire.

Minorca [mɪˈnɔːkə] pr n Minorque / *in Minorca* à Minorque.

minority [maɪˈnɒrətɪ] *(pl* **minorities)** ◆ n **1.** [small group] minorité *f* ▸ **to be in a** or **the minority** être dans la minorité **2.** LAW [age] minorité *f*. ◆ comp [government, movement, tastes] minoritaire ▸ **minority group** minorité *f* ▸ **minority verdict** LAW verdict *m* de la minorité.

minority shareholder 🇬🇧, **minority stockholder** 🇺🇸 n actionnaire *mf* minoritaire.

minor league ◆ n 🇺🇸 SPORT ≃ division *f* d'honneur. ◆ adj *fig* secondaire, de peu d'importance.

minster [ˈmɪnstəʳ] n [abbey church] (église *f*) abbatiale *f* ; [cathedral] cathédrale *f*.

minstrel [ˈmɪnstrəl] n ménestrel *m*, troubadour *m*.

mint [mɪnt] ◆ n **1.** BOT menthe *f* **2.** [sweet] bonbon *m* à la menthe **3.** [for coins] ▸ **the Mint** l'Hôtel *m* de la Monnaie, la Monnaie **4.** *inf* [fortune] fortune *f* ▸ **to make a mint** faire fortune. ◆ comp [chocolate, sauce, tea] à la menthe. ◆ adj [stamps, coins] (tout) neuf ▸ **in mint condition** *fig* en parfait état, à l'état neuf. ◆ vt [coins] fabriquer, frapper, battre.

minted [ˈmɪntɪd] adj 🇬🇧 *inf* plein aux as, bourré de fric.

minuet [ˌmɪnjʊˈet] n menuet *m*.

minus ['maɪnəs] (pl **minuses** or **minusses**) ◆ prep **1.** MATH moins **2.** [in temperature] : *it's minus 5 ° outside* il fait moins 5 ° dehors **3.** inf [without] : *he came home minus his shopping* il est rentré sans ses achats. ◆ n **1.** [sign] moins *m* **2.** [drawback] inconvénient *m*.

minuscule ['mɪnəskju:l] ◆ adj **1.** [tiny] minuscule **2.** [lower-case] en (lettres) minuscules. ◆ n minuscule *f*.

minus sign n signe *m* moins.

minute¹ ['mɪnɪt] n **1.** [period of 60 seconds] minute *f* ; [in telling the time] : *two minutes past / to ten* dix heures deux / moins deux **2.** [moment] instant *m*, minute *f* / *I'll be back in a minute* je reviens dans une minute or dans un instant or tout de suite / *wait a minute, please* attendez un instant, s'il vous plaît / *I'll talk to him the minute he arrives* je lui parlerai dès qu'il arrivera / *any minute now* d'un instant à l'autre / *right up till the last minute* jusqu'à la toute dernière minute **3.** GEOM [of degree] minute *f*. ❖ **minutes** pl n **1.** [of meeting] procès-verbal *m*, compte rendu *m* **2.** [report] note *f*.

minute² [maɪ'nju:t] adj **1.** [tiny] minuscule, infime ; [very slight - difference, improvement] infime, minime **2.** [precise] minutieux, détaillé / *in minute detail* par le menu.

minute hand ['mɪnɪt-] n grande aiguille *f*, aiguille *f* des minutes.

minutely [maɪ'nju:tlɪ] adv **1.** [carefully] minutieusement, avec un soin minutieux ; [in detail] en détail, par le menu **2.** [fold] tout petit ; [move] imperceptiblement, très légèrement.

minute steak ['mɪnɪt-] n entrecôte *f* minute.

minutiae [maɪ'nju:ʃɪaɪ] pl n menus détails *mpl*, petits détails *mpl* ; pej [trivialities] vétilles *fpl*, riens *mpl*.

miracle ['mɪrəkl] ◆ n RELIG & fig miracle *m* / *it was a miracle (that) she survived* c'est un miracle qu'elle ait survécu. ◆ comp [drug] miracle ; [cure] miraculeux ▶ **miracle worker** faiseur *m*, -euse *f* de miracles.

miraculous [mɪ'rækjʊləs] adj miraculeux / *they had a miraculous escape* c'est un miracle qu'ils s'en soient tirés (vivants).

mirage [mɪ'rɑ:ʒ] n mirage *m*.

mire [maɪə^r] liter n boue *f* ; [deep] bourbier *m*.

mirror ['mɪrə^r] ◆ n **1.** [looking glass] miroir *m*, glace *f* ; AUTO rétroviseur *m* **2.** COMPUT site *m* miroir **3.** PRESS ▶ **the Mirror** nom abrégé du « *Daily Mirror* ». ◆ vt [reflect] réfléchir, refléter.

mirrorball ['mɪrəbɔ:l] n boule *f* à facettes.

mirrored ['mɪrəd] adj [ceiling] couvert de miroirs ▶ **mirrored glasses** lunettes *fpl* métallisées.

mirror image n image *f* en miroir, image *f* spéculaire ; fig copie *f* conforme.

mirror site n COMPUT site *m* miroir.

mirth [mɜ:θ] n (U) rires *mpl*, hilarité *f*.

mirthless ['mɜ:θlɪs] adj liter triste, sombre, morne ; [laugh] faux, forcé.

MIS (abbr of management information system) n COMPUT système intégré *m* de gestion, SIG *m*.

misadventure [,mɪsəd'ventʃə^r] n [accident] mésaventure *f* ; [misfortune] malheur *m*.

misaligned [,mɪsə'laɪnd] adj mal aligné.

misanthropic [,mɪsən'θrɒpɪk] adj [person] misanthrope ; [thoughts] misanthropique.

misanthropist [mɪ'sænθrəpɪst] n misanthrope *mf*.

misanthropy [mɪ'sænθrəpɪ] n misanthropie *f*.

misapprehension ['mɪs,æprɪ'henʃn] n fml malentendu *m* / *I'm afraid you are under a* or *some misapprehension* je crains que vous ne vous mépreniez.

misappropriate [,mɪsə'prəʊprɪeɪt] vt fml [money, funds] détourner ; [property] voler.

misappropriation ['mɪsə,prəʊprɪ'eɪʃn] n fml détournement *m*.

misbehave [,mɪsbɪ'heɪv] vi ▶ **to misbehave (o.s.)** se conduire mal.

misbehaviour 🇬🇧, **misbehavior** 🇺🇸 [,mɪsbɪ'heɪvjə^r] n mauvaise conduite *f*.

misc written abbr of miscellaneous.

miscalculate [,mɪs'kælkjʊleɪt] ◆ vt [amount, distance] mal calculer ; fig mal évaluer. ◆ vi MATH se tromper dans ses calculs ; fig [judge wrongly] se tromper.

miscalculation [,mɪskælkjʊ'leɪʃn] n MATH erreur *f* de calcul ; fig mauvais calcul *m*.

miscarriage [,mɪs'kærɪdʒ] n **1.** MED fausse couche *f* ▶ **to have a miscarriage** faire une fausse couche **2.** [failure] échec *m* ▶ **miscarriage of justice** erreur *f* judiciaire.

miscarry [,mɪs'kærɪ] (pt & pp **miscarried**) vi MED faire une fausse couche.

miscast [,mɪs'kɑ:st] (pt & pp **miscast**) vt CIN & THEAT [play] se tromper dans la distribution de ; [actor] mal choisir le rôle de.

miscellaneous [,mɪsə'leɪnɪəs] adj [assorted] divers, varié ; [jumbled] hétérogène, hétéroclite, disparate ▶ **miscellaneous expenses** frais *mpl* divers.

miscellany [🇬🇧 mɪ'selənɪ 🇺🇸 'mɪsəleɪnɪ] (pl **miscellanies**) n [mixture, assortment] amalgame *m*, mélange *m*.

mischance [,mɪs'tʃɑ:ns] n fml malheur *m*, malchance *f*.

mischief ['mɪstʃɪf] n **1.** (U) [naughtiness] espièglerie *f*, malice *f* ▶ **to get up to mischief** faire des bêtises or sottises ▶ **to keep sb out of mischief** occuper qqn **2.** (U) [trouble] ▶ **to make mischief** semer la zizanie **3.** 🇬🇧 [injury] ▶ **to do o.s. a mischief** se blesser, se faire mal.

mischief-maker n faiseur *m* d'histoires or d'embarras.

mischievous ['mɪstʃɪvəs] adj [child, trick] espiègle, malicieux ; [look] taquin, narquois ; [thought] malicieux.

mischievously ['mɪstʃɪvəslɪ] adv [naughtily, teasingly] malicieusement.

misconceived [,mɪskən'si:vd] adj [plan] mal conçu ; [idea] faux (fausse), erroné.

misconception [,mɪskən'sepʃn] n [poor understanding] mauvaise compréhension *f* ; [complete misunderstanding] idée fausse *f*, méprise *f*.

misconduct n [,mɪs'kɒndʌkt] [bad behaviour] mauvaise conduite *f* ; [immoral behaviour] inconduite *f* ; [adultery] adultère *m*.

misconstruction [,mɪskən'strʌkʃn] n [gen] fausse interprétation *f*.

misconstrue [,mɪskən'stru:] vt mal interpréter.

miscount ◆ vt [,mɪs'kaʊnt] mal compter, faire une erreur en comptant. ◆ vi [,mɪs'kaʊnt] se tromper dans le compte. ◆ n ['mɪskaʊnt] mécompte *m* / *there was a miscount* POL une erreur s'est produite dans le décompte des voix.

misdeed [,mɪs'di:d] n fml méfait *m* ; LAW délit *m*.

misdemeanour 🇬🇧, **misdemeanor** 🇺🇸 [,mɪsdɪ'mi:nə^r] n méfait *m* ; LAW délit *m*, infraction *f*.

misdiagnose [,mɪs'daɪəgnəʊz] vt MED & fig se tromper dans le diagnostic de.

misdirect [,mɪsdɪ'rekt] vt **1.** [to destination - traveller] mal orienter, mal renseigner ; [- letter] mal adresser **2.** [misuse - efforts, talents] mal employer, mal orienter / *misdirected energy* énergie mal utilisée.

miser ['maɪzə^r] n [person] avare *mf*.

miserable ['mɪzrəbl] adj **1.** [unhappy] malheureux, triste **2.** [unpleasant - evening, sight] pénible ; [- weather, summer] épouvantable, pourri ; [- conditions, holiday] déplorable, lamentable **3.** [poor - hotel] miteux ; [- tenement] misérable ; [- meal] maigre **4.** [mean - reward] minable, misérable ; [- salary] de misère ; [- donation, amount] dérisoire **5.** pej méchant.

miserably ['mɪzrəblɪ] adv **1.** [extremely - unhappy, cold] extrêmement ; [very badly - play] de façon lamentable or déplorable ; [- fail] lamentablement ; [- pay] très mal **2.** [unhappily] malheureusement, d'un air malheureux **3.** [in poverty] misérablement, dans la misère.

miserly ['maɪzəlɪ] adj avare.

misery ['mɪzərɪ] (pl miseries) n **1.** [unhappiness] malheur m, tristesse f ▶ **to make sb's life a misery** rendre la vie insupportable à qqn **2.** [suffering] : she begged to be put out of her misery elle suppliait qu'on mît fin à ses souffrances **3.** [misfortune] malheur m, misère f **4.** [poverty] misère f.

misery-guts n inf rabat-joie m.

misfire vi [,mɪs'faɪər] **1.** [gun] faire long feu ; fig [plan, joke] rater, échouer **2.** [engine] avoir des problèmes d'allumage or des ratés.

misfit ['mɪsfɪt] n inadapté m, -e f, marginal m, -e f.

misfortune [mɪs'fɔ:tʃu:n] n **1.** [bad luck] malchance f, infortune f **2.** [unfortunate event] malheur m.

misgiving [mɪs'gɪvɪŋ] n doute m, appréhension f ▶ **to have misgivings about** avoir des doutes quant à, douter de.

misguided [,mɪs'gaɪdɪd] adj [attempt] malencontreux ; [decision] peu judicieux ; [attack] malavisé, maladroit ; [idealist] égaré ; [nationalism] dévoyé.

mishandle [,mɪs'hændl] vt **1.** [equipment] mal utiliser, mal se servir de ; [resources, information] mal exploiter ; [affair] mal gérer / the case was mishandled from the outset l'affaire a été mal menée depuis le début **2.** [treat insensitively - customer] malmener, traiter avec rudesse.

mishap ['mɪshæp] n [misadventure] mésaventure f, accident m.

mishear [,mɪs'hɪər] (pt & pp misheard [-'hɜ:d]) vt mal entendre, mal comprendre.

mishit [,mɪs'hɪt] (pt & pp mishit) ◆ vt SPORT [ball] mal frapper. ◆ n ['mɪshɪt] mauvais coup m, coup m manqué.

mishmash ['mɪʃmæʃ] n inf méli-mélo m, mic-mac m.

misinform [,mɪsɪn'fɔ:m] vt [unintentionally] mal renseigner ; [intentionally] donner de faux renseignements à, tromper.

misinformation [,mɪsɪnfə'meɪʃn] n (U) fausse information f, intox m inf.

misinterpret [,mɪsɪn'tɜ:prɪt] vt mal comprendre, mal interpréter.

misinterpretation ['mɪsɪn,tɜ:prɪ'teɪʃn] n erreur f d'interprétation.

misjudge [,mɪs'dʒʌdʒ] vt [distance, reaction] mal juger, mal évaluer ; [person] mal juger.

miskey ◆ n ['mɪskiː] faute f de frappe. ◆ vt [,mɪs'kiː] ne pas taper correctement.

miskick ◆ vt [,mɪs'kɪk] SPORT : he miskicked the ball il a raté son coup de pied. ◆ vi [,mɪs'kɪk] rater le ballon. ◆ n ['mɪskɪk] coup m de pied raté.

mislay [,mɪs'leɪ] (pt & pp mislaid [-'leɪd]) vt égarer.

mislead [,mɪs'liːd] (pt & pp misled [-'led]) vt tromper, induire en erreur.

misleading [,mɪs'liːdɪŋ] adj [false] trompeur, fallacieux ; [confusing] équivoque.

misled [-'led] pt & pp ⟶ **mislead**.

mismanage [,mɪs'mænɪdʒ] vt mal gérer.

mismanagement [,mɪs'mænɪdʒmənt] n mauvaise gestion f.

mismatch ◆ vt [,mɪs'mætʃ] **1.** [colours, clothes] mal assortir **2.** [in marriage] : they were totally mismatched **a)** [socially] ils étaient vraiment mal assortis **b)** [by temperament] ils n'étaient absolument pas faits pour s'entendre. ◆ n ['mɪsmætʃ] [clash] : the colours are a mismatch ces couleurs ne vont vraiment pas ensemble or sont vraiment mal assorties.

misnomer [,mɪs'nəʊmər] n nom m inapproprié.

misogynist [mɪ'sɒdʒɪnɪst] n misogyne mf.

misogyny [mɪ'sɒdʒɪnɪ] n misogynie f.

misplace [,mɪs'pleɪs] vt **1.** [put in wrong place] mal placer **2.** [mislay] égarer **3.** [trust, confidence] mal placer.

misplaced [,mɪs'pleɪst] adj [trust, confidence] mal placé.

misprint ◆ n ['mɪsprɪnt] faute f d'impression, coquille f ◆ vt [,mɪs'prɪnt] : my name was misprinted in the newspaper il y a eu une coquille dans mon nom sur le journal.

mispronounce [,mɪsprə'naʊns] vt [word] mal prononcer, prononcer incorrectement ; [name] estropier, écorcher.

misquote vt [,mɪs'kwəʊt] [author, text] citer inexactement ; [speaker] déformer les propos de.

misread vt [,mɪs'riːd] (pt & pp misread [-red]) [word, text] mal lire ; fig [actions, motives] mal interpréter, mal comprendre.

misreport [,mɪsrɪ'pɔ:t] ◆ n rapport m inexact. ◆ vt rapporter inexactement.

misrepresent ['mɪs,reprɪ'zent] vt [facts, events] déformer ; [person] donner une image fausse de.

miss [mɪs] ◆ vt **1.** [bus, film, target] manquer, rater ; [opportunity, turn] manquer, laisser passer / we missed the train by five minutes on a manqué le train de cinq minutes / this film is not to be missed c'est un film à ne pas manquer or à ne manquer sous aucun prétexte / you didn't miss much vous n'avez pas manqué grand-chose ▶ **to miss the boat** rater une occasion, manquer le coche / you're going to miss the boat if you delay your application vous allez manquer le coche si vous tardez à poser votre candidature **2.** [fail to do, find, see, etc.] manquer / to miss school manquer l'école / it's at the end of the street, you can't miss it c'est au bout de la rue, vous ne pouvez pas le manquer / I missed the beginning of your question je n'ai pas entendu le début de votre question / you've missed or you're missing the point! vous n'avez rien compris ! / they never or don't miss a trick [UK] rien ne leur échappe **3.** [escape, manage to avoid] : I narrowly or just missed being killed j'ai bien failli me faire tuer **4.** [regret the absence of] : I miss her elle me manque / I miss the warm weather / the sea la chaleur / la mer me manque **5.** [be short of, lack] manquer de / I'm missing two books from my collection il me manque deux livres dans ma collection, deux livres de ma collection ont disparu **6.** [notice disappearance of] : when did you first miss your passport? quand est-ce que vous vous êtes aperçu que la première fois de la perte de or que vous aviez perdu votre passeport ? / he's got so many records he won't miss one il a tellement de disques qu'il ne s'apercevra pas qu'il lui en manque un. ◆ vi **1.** [fail to hit target] manquer or rater son coup **2.** [engine] avoir des ratés **3.** [PHR] **to be missing** manquer / two of the children are still missing il manque encore deux enfants, deux enfants manquent encore. ◆ n **1.** [gen & SPORT] coup m raté or manqué **2.** inf [girl] jeune fille f **3.** TEXT [size] junior **4.** [PHR] **to give sthg a miss a)** [UK] [do without] se passer de qqch **b)** [avoid] éviter qqch / why don't you give the

TV a miss tonight? pourquoi ne pas te passer de (la) télé ce soir ? ❖ **Miss** n [term of address] mademoiselle *f.* ❖ **miss out** ◆ vt sep [omit] omettre, sauter ; [forget] oublier ; [in distribution] oublier, sauter. ◆ vi : *he missed out because he couldn't afford to go to college* il a été désavantagé parce qu'il n'avait pas les moyens de poursuivre ses études. ❖ **miss out on** vt insep [advantage, opportunity] manquer, rater.

misshapen [,mɪs'ʃeɪpn] adj difforme, tordu, déformé.

missile [UK 'mɪsaɪl US 'mɪsəl] n **1.** MIL missile *m* **2.** [object thrown] projectile *m.*

missile launcher n lance-missiles *m inv.*

missing ['mɪsɪŋ] adj **1.** [lacking] manquant / *the table had one leg missing* il manquait un pied à la table **2.** [lost -person] disparu ; [-object] manquant, égaré, perdu ▶ **to go missing** a) disparaître b) [in war] être porté disparu ▶ **missing person** a) personne *f* disparue b) MIL & POL disparu *m.*

missing link n chaînon *m* manquant.

mission ['mɪʃn] n **1.** [delegation] mission *f* **2.** [job, vocation] mission *f* **3.** [organization, charity] mission *f* **4.** RELIG [campaign, building] mission *f* **5.** MIL, COMM & ASTRONAUT mission *f.*

missionary ['mɪʃənrɪ] (*pl* **missionaries**) ◆ n missionnaire *mf.* ◆ adj [work] missionnaire ; [zeal] de missionnaire.

mission control n centre *m* de contrôle.

mission statement n ordre *m* de mission.

missis ['mɪsɪz] = **missus.**

Mississippi [,mɪsɪ'sɪpɪ] pr n **1.** [river] ▶ **the Mississippi (River)** le Mississippi **2.** [state] Mississippi *m* / *in Mississippi* dans le Mississippi.

Missouri [mɪ'zʊərɪ] pr n **1.** [river] ▶ **the Missouri (river)** le Missouri **2.** [state] Missouri *m* / *in Missouri* dans le Missouri.

misspell [,mɪs'spel] (*pt & pp* **misspelt** [,mɪs'spelt] *or* **misspelled**) vt [in writing] mal écrire, mal orthographier ; [in speaking] mal épeler.

misspelling [,mɪs'spelɪŋ] n faute *f* d'orthographe.

misspelt [,mɪs'spelt] pt & pp ⟶ **misspell.**

misspend [,mɪs'spend] (*pt & pp* **misspent** [-'spent]) vt [money, talents] gaspiller, gâcher / *my misspent youth* mes folles années de jeunesse.

missus ['mɪsɪz] n UK inf **1.** [wife] bourgeoise *f* **2.** [woman] : *eh, missus!* dites, m'dame or ma p'tite dame !

mist [mɪst] ◆ n **1.** [fog] brume *f* **2.** [vapour -on window, glasses] buée *f* ; [-from spray] brouillard *m*, nuage *m.* ◆ vt ▶ **to mist (over** or **up)** embuer. ◆ vi ▶ **to mist (over** or **up)** [window, glasses, eyes] s'embuer.

mistake [mɪ'steɪk] (*pt* **mistook** [-'stʊk], *pp* **mistaken** [-'steɪkn]) ◆ n **1.** [error] erreur *f* ; [in grammar, spelling] faute *f* ▶ **to make a mistake** faire une erreur or une faute / *I made the mistake of losing my temper* j'ai commis l'erreur de or j'ai eu le tort de me fâcher / *you're making a big mistake* vous faites une grave erreur / *make no mistake (about it)* ne vous y trompez pas / *there must be some mistake* il doit y avoir erreur or un malentendu **2.** [inadvertence] ▶ **by** or UK **in mistake** par mégarde or erreur **3.** PHR *he's a big man and no mistake!* UK pour être costaud, il est costaud ! ◆ vt **1.** [misunderstand -meaning, intention] mal comprendre, se tromper sur / *there's no mistaking what she said* on ne peut pas se méprendre sur le sens de ses propos **2.** [fail to distinguish] se tromper sur / *you can't mistake our house, it has green shutters* vous ne pouvez pas vous tromper or il n'y a pas de confusion

possible, notre maison a des volets verts **3.** [date, route] se tromper de ; [person] : *I'm often mistaken for my sister* on me prend souvent pour ma sœur.

mistaken [-'steɪkn] ◆ pp ⟶ **mistake.** ◆ adj [wrong -idea, conclusion] erroné, faux (fausse) ▶ **to be mistaken** se tromper, être dans l'erreur / *if I'm not mistaken* si je ne me trompe, si je ne m'abuse / *it was a case of mistaken identity* il y avait erreur sur la personne.

mistakenly [mɪ'steɪknlɪ] adv [in error] par erreur ; [wrongly] à tort.

mister ['mɪstə*] n inf monsieur *m.*

mistime [,mɪs'taɪm] vt mal calculer (le moment de).

mistletoe ['mɪsltəʊ] n gui *m.*

mistook [-'stʊk] pt ⟶ **mistake.**

mistranslate [,mɪstræns'leɪt] ◆ vt mal traduire. ◆ vi faire des contresens.

mistranslation [,mɪstræns'leɪʃn] n **1.** [mistake] contresens *m*, faute *f* or erreur *f* de traduction **2.** [faulty text] traduction *f* inexacte, mauvaise traduction *f.*

mistreat [,mɪs'tri:t] vt maltraiter.

mistreatment [,mɪs'tri:tmənt] n mauvais traitement *m.*

mistress ['mɪstrɪs] n **1.** [woman in control] maîtresse *f* **2.** [lover] maîtresse *f* **3.** UK SCH [in primary school] maîtresse *f* ; [in secondary school] professeure *f* **4.** [of pet] maîtresse *f.*

mistrial ['mɪstraɪəl] n erreur *f* judiciaire ; US [with hung jury] procès annulé par manque d'unanimité parmi les jurés.

mistrust [,mɪs'trʌst] ◆ n méfiance *f*, défiance *f.* ◆ vt [be suspicious, wary of] se méfier de ; [doubt] douter de, ne pas avoir confiance en.

mistrustful [,mɪs'trʌstfʊl] adj méfiant ▶ **to be mistrustful of sb** se méfier de qqn.

misty ['mɪstɪ] (*compar* **mistier**, *superl* **mistiest**) adj **1.** [weather, morning] brumeux **2.** [window, eyes] embué ; [horizon, mountain] embrumé **3.** [vague -idea, memory] flou, nébuleux **4.** [like mist] vaporeux.

misunderstand [,mɪsʌndə'stænd] (*pt & pp* **misunderstood** [-'stʊd]) vt **1.** [misinterpret] mal comprendre, comprendre de travers **2.** *(usu passive)* [misjudge, underrate] méconnaître.

misunderstanding [,mɪsʌndə'stændɪŋ] n **1.** [misapprehension] méprise *f*, quiproquo *m*, malentendu *m* **2.** euph [quarrel] mésentente *f*, brouille *f.*

misunderstood [-'stʊd] pt & pp ⟶ **misunderstand.**

misuse ◆ vt [,mɪs'ju:z] **1.** [privilege, position, etc.] abuser de ; [word, phrase] employer abusivement ; [equipment, gun] mal employer, mal utiliser ; [money, time] mal employer **2.** [funds] détourner **3.** [ill-treat] maltraiter, malmener. ◆ n [,mɪs'ju:s] **1.** [of privilege, one's position] abus *m* ; [of word, phrase] emploi *m* abusif ; [of equipment, gun] mauvais usage *m*, mauvaise utilisation *f* ; [of money, time] mauvais emploi *m* **2.** [of funds] détournement *m.*

MIT (abbr of **Massachusetts Institute of Technology**) pr n MIT *m* (*prestigieux Institut de Technologie du Massachusetts*).

mite [maɪt] n **1.** [insect] mite *f* **2.** [little bit] grain *m*, brin *m*, tantinet *m* **3.** inf [child] mioche *mf.*

miter US = **mitre.**

mitigate ['mɪtɪgeɪt] vt [anger, grief, pain] adoucir, apaiser, alléger ; [conditions, consequences, harm] atténuer.

mitigating ['mɪtɪgeɪtɪŋ] adj ▶ **mitigating circumstances** LAW circonstances *fpl* atténuantes.

mitigation [ˌmɪtɪˈgeɪʃn] n *fml* [of anger, grief, pain] adoucissement *m*, allègement *m* ; [of conditions, consequences, harm] atténuation *f*, mitigation *f*.

mitre UK, **miter** US ['maɪtə'] n RELIG mitre *f*.

mitt [mɪt] n **1.** = **mitten 2.** [glove] gant *m* ; [boxing glove] gant *m* (de boxe) **3.** *inf* [hand] paluche *f*.

mitten ['mɪtn] n [with fingers joined] moufle *f* ; [with cut-off fingers] mitaine *f* ; [boxing glove] gant *m* (de boxe), mitaine *f*.

mix [mɪks] ◆ vt **1.** [combine, blend] mélanger **2.** [prepare - cocktail, medicine] préparer ; [- cement, plaster] malaxer **3.** [stir - salad] tourner **4.** CIN, ELECTRON & MUS mixer. ◆ vi **1.** [combine, blend] se mélanger **2.** [go together] aller ensemble, faire bon ménage **3.** [socialize] : *he mixes with a strange crowd* il fréquente de drôles de gens. ◆ n **1.** [combination, blend] mélange *m* **2.** UK [act of mixing] : *give the paint a (good) mix* mélangez (bien) la peinture **3.** CULIN [in package] préparation *f* ; [batter] pâte *f*. ◆ **mix in** vt sep mélanger. ◆ vi : *she makes no effort to mix in* elle ne fait aucun effort pour se montrer sociable. ◆ **mix up** vt sep **1.** [mistake] confondre ; [baffle, confuse] embrouiller **2.** *(usu passive)* [involve] impliquer **3.** [disorder] mélanger **4.** [combine, blend] mélanger.

mix-and-match adj [clothes] que l'on peut coordonner à volonté.

mixed [mɪkst] adj **1.** [assorted] mélangé ▶ **mixed economy** économie *f* mixte ▶ **mixed farming** polyculture *f* ▶ **mixed metaphor** mélange *m* de métaphores ▶ **mixed vegetables** jardinière *f* de légumes **2.** [not wholly positive] mitigé / *I have mixed feelings about it* je ne sais pas très bien ce que j'en pense, je suis partagé à ce sujet ▶ **it's a bit of a mixed bag** *inf* il y a un peu de tout ▶ **it's a mixed blessing** il y a du pour et du contre **3.** [sexually, racially] mixte ▶ **mixed marriage** mariage *m* mixte ▶ **mixed school / doubles** école *f* / double *m* mixte.

mixed-ability adj [class, teaching] sans niveaux.

mixed-media adj multimédia.

mixed-up adj [confused] désorienté, déboussolé.

mixer ['mɪksə'] n **1.** [device - gen] mélangeur *m* ; CULIN [mechanical] batteur *m* ; [electric] mixeur *m*, mixer *m* ; CIN, ELECTRON & MUS mixeur *m*, mélangeur *m* de signaux **2.** [sociable person] ▶ **to be a good / poor mixer** être sociable / peu sociable **3.** [soft drink] boisson *f* gazeuse *(servant à la préparation des cocktails)*.

mixer tap n [robinet *m*] mélangeur *m*.

mixing ['mɪksɪŋ] n **1.** [gen] mélange *m* **2.** CIN, ELECTRON & MUS mixage *m* ▶ **mixing desk** table *f* de mixage.

mixing bowl n [big] saladier *m* ; [smaller] bol *m*.

mixologist [mɪkˈsɒlədʒɪst] n barman spécialisé dans les cocktails.

mixture ['mɪkstʃə'] n **1.** [gen] mélange *m* **2.** MED mixture *f*.

mix-up n confusion *f*.

MJPEG (abbr of Motion Joint Photographic Expert Group) n COMPUT (format *m*) MJPEG *m*.

mk, MK written abbr of mark.

mkt written abbr of market.

ml (written abbr of millilitre) ml.

MLitt [em'lɪt] (abbr of Master of Literature, Master of Letters) n ≃ (titulaire d'une) maîtrise de lettres.

MLR n abbr of minimum lending rate.

mm (written abbr of millimetre) mm.

MMR [ˌemem'ɑːr] (abbr of measles, mumps & rubella) n MED ROR *m*.

MMX (abbr of multimedia extensions) n COMPUT MMX *m*.

MN ◆ n abbr of Merchant Navy. ◆ written abbr of Minnesota.

mnemonic [nɪˈmɒnɪk] ◆ adj **1.** [aiding memory] mnémonique, mnémotechnique **2.** [relating to memory] mnémonique. ◆ n formule *f* mnémotechnique, aide *f* à la mémoire ; COMPUT mnémonique *m*.

mo, mo' [məʊ] n *inf* moment *m*, instant *m*.

MO ◆ n **1.** abbr of medical officer **2.** abbr of modus operandi **3.** written abbr of money order. ◆ written abbr of Missouri.

moan [məʊn] ◆ vi **1.** [in pain, sadness] gémir **2.** [grumble] ronchonner, grogner / *what are you moaning about now?* de quoi te plains-tu encore ? ◆ vt maugréer. ◆ n [of pain, sadness] gémissement *m* ; [of complaint] plainte *f* ▶ **to have a moan about sthg** se plaindre de qqch.

moaner ['məʊnə'] n *inf* grognon *m*, -onne *f*, râleur *m*, -euse *f*.

moat [məʊt] n douves *fpl*, fossé *m*, fossés *mpl*.

mob [mɒb] (pt & pp mobbed) ◆ n **1.** [crowd] foule *f*, cohue *f* ▶ **mob rule** loi *f* de la rue **2.** *pej* [common people] ▶ **the mob** la populace **3.** [of criminals] gang *m* ▶ **the Mob** la Mafia **4.** *inf* [bunch, clique] bande *f*, clique *f pej*. ◆ vt [person] attaquer, agresser ; [place] assiéger.

Mob MESSAGING written abbr of mobile.

mobile ['məʊbaɪl] ◆ adj **1.** mobile ▶ **mobile library** bibliobus *m* **2.** [features, face] mobile, expressif **3.** [socially] : *the middle classes tend to be particularly mobile* les classes moyennes se déplacent plus facilement que les autres **4.** *inf* [having transport] : *are you mobile?* tu es motorisé ? ◆ n **1.** ART mobile *m* **2.** UK *inf* = **mobile phone**.

mobile home n caravane *f*.

mobile phone n UK (téléphone *m*) portable *m*, (téléphone *m*) mobile *m*.

mobile phone mast n antenne-relais *f* *(de téléphonie mobile)*.

mobile shop n marchand *m* ambulant.

mobility [məˈbɪlətɪ] n mobilité *f* ▶ **mobility allowance** indemnité *f* de déplacement *(versée aux personnes handicapées)*.

mobilize, mobilise ['məʊbɪlaɪz] vi & vt mobiliser.

moccasin ['mɒkəsɪn] n **1.** [shoe] mocassin *m* **2.** ZOOL mocassin *m*.

mocha ['mɒkə] n moka *m*.

mock [mɒk] ◆ vt **1.** [deride] se moquer de, tourner en dérision **2.** [imitate] singer, parodier. ◆ vi se moquer. ◆ adj **1.** [imitation] faux (fausse), factice **2.** [feigned] feint **3.** [as practice] ▶ **mock examination** examen *m* blanc. ◆ n UK *inf* [examination] examen *m* blanc. ◆ **mock up** vt sep UK faire une maquette de.

mockery ['mɒkərɪ] (pl mockeries) n **1.** [derision] moquerie *f*, raillerie *f* **2.** [travesty] parodie *f* ▶ **to make a mockery of sthg** rendre qqch ridicule, enlever toute crédibilité à qqch.

mocking ['mɒkɪŋ] ◆ n moquerie *f*, raillerie *f*. ◆ adj moqueur, railleur.

mockingbird ['mɒkɪŋbɜːd] n ORNITH moqueur *m*.

mock-up n maquette *f*.

MoD, MOD pr n UK abbr of Ministry of Defence.

mod cons [-kɒnz] (abbr of modern conveniences) pl n *inf* ▶ **all mod cons** tout confort, tt. conf.

mode [məʊd] n **1.** [manner] mode *m*, manière *f* ▶ **modes of transport** moyens de transport **2.** GRAM, PHILOS & MATH mode *m* **3.** COMPUT mode *m* **4.** [prevailing fashion] mode *f*.

model ['mɒdl] (UK *pt & pp* **modelled**, *cont* **modelling** ; US *pt & pp* **modeled**, *cont* **modeling**) ◆ n **1.** [copy, representation] modèle *m*, maquette *f* ; [theoretical pattern] modèle *m* **2.** [perfect example] modèle *m* **3.** ART & PHOT [sitter] modèle *m* **4.** [in fashion show] mannequin *m* **5.** COMM modèle *m* **6.** US [showhouse] résidence *f* témoin. ◆ vt **1.** [shape] modeler ▸ **to model o.s. on sb** prendre modèle sur qqn **2.** [in fashion show] : *she models clothes* elle est mannequin. ◆ vi [for artist, photographer] poser ; [in fashion show] être mannequin. ◆ adj **1.** [miniature] (en) miniature ▸ **model aeroplane** maquette *f* d'avion ▸ **model car a)** [toy] petite voiture *f* **b)** [for collectors] modèle *m* réduit **2.** [exemplary] modèle.

modelling UK, **modeling** US ['mɒdəlɪŋ] n **1.** [building models] modelage *m* ; [as a hobby] construction *f* de maquettes **2.** [in fashion shows] : *modelling is extremely well-paid* le travail de mannequin est très bien payé, les mannequins sont très bien payés.

modem ['məʊdem] n modem *m*.

moderate ◆ adj ['mɒdərət] **1.** [restrained, modest] modéré **2.** [average] moyen **3.** METEOR tempéré. ◆ n ['mɒdərət] POL modéré *m*, -e *f*. ◆ vt ['mɒdəreɪt] [make less extreme] modérer.

moderately ['mɒdərətlɪ] adv [with moderation] modérément, avec modération ; [slightly] moyennement.

moderation [,mɒdə'reɪʃn] n modération *f* ▸ *to drink in* or *with moderation* boire avec modération.

moderator ['mɒdəreɪtər] n [president] président *m*, -e *f* ; [mediator] médiateur *m*, -trice *f* ; RELIG modérateur *m*.

modern ['mɒdən] ◆ adj moderne ▸ **modern dance** HIST modern dance *f* ▸ **modern languages** langues *fpl* vivantes. ◆ n [person] moderne *mf*.

modern art n art *m* moderne.

modern-day adj d'aujourd'hui.

modernism ['mɒdənɪzm] n **1.** modernisme *m* **2.** [expression, word] néologisme *m*.

modernist ['mɒdənɪst] ◆ adj moderniste. ◆ n moderniste *mf*.

modernity [mɒ'dɜːnətɪ] n modernité *f*.

modernization, modernisation [,mɒdənaɪ'zeɪʃn] n modernisation *f*.

modernize, modernise ['mɒdənaɪz] ◆ vt moderniser. ◆ vi se moderniser.

modest ['mɒdɪst] adj **1.** [unassuming] modeste **2.** [small, moderate, simple] modeste ; [meagre] modique **3.** [decorous] pudique.

modestly ['mɒdɪstlɪ] adv **1.** [unassumingly] modestement, avec modestie **2.** [simply] modestement, simplement **3.** [with decorum] avec pudeur, pudiquement.

modesty ['mɒdɪstɪ] n **1.** [lack of conceit] modestie *f* ▸ *in all modesty* en toute modestie ▸ *false modesty* fausse modestie **2.** [moderation] modestie *f* ; [meagreness] modicité *f* **3.** [decorum] pudeur *f*.

modicum ['mɒdɪkəm] n minimum *m*.

modification [,mɒdɪfɪ'keɪʃn] n modification *f*.

modify ['mɒdɪfaɪ] (*pt & pp* **modified**) vt **1.** [alter] modifier **2.** [moderate] modérer **3.** GRAM modifier.

modish ['məʊdɪʃ] adj à la mode.

modular ['mɒdjʊlər] adj modulaire ▸ **modular degree** ≃ licence *f* à UV ▸ **modular furniture** mobilier *m* modulaire or à éléments.

modulate ['mɒdjʊleɪt] vt **1.** ELECTRON & MUS moduler ; [voice] moduler **2.** [moderate, tone down] adapter, ajuster.

modulation [,mɒdjʊ'leɪʃn] n modulation *f*.

module ['mɒdjuːl] n **1.** [gen] module *m* **2.** UNIV ≃ unité *f* de valeur ; ≃ UV *f*.

moggie, moggy ['mɒgɪ] (*pl* **moggies**) n UK inf minou *m*.

mogul ['məʊgl] n **1.** [magnate] magnat *m* **2.** [on ski slope] bosse *f*.

MOH (abbr of **Medical Officer of Health**) n UK directeur *m*, -trice *f* de la santé publique.

mohair ['məʊheər] ◆ n mohair *m*. ◆ adj en or de mohair.

Mohican [məʊ'hiːkən or 'məʊɪkən] (*pl* **Mohican** or **Mohicans**) n [person] Mohican *m*, -e *f*. ❖ **mohican** n [hairstyle] coupe *f* à l'iroquoise.

moist [mɔɪst] adj [skin, air, heat] moite ; [climate, soil, surface] humide ; [cake] moelleux.

moisten ['mɔɪsn] ◆ vt humecter, mouiller. ◆ vi [eyes] se mouiller ; [palms] devenir moite.

moisture ['mɔɪstʃər] n humidité *f* ; [on mirror, window, etc.] buée *f*.

moisturize, moisturise ['mɔɪstʃəraɪz] vt [skin] hydrater ; [air] humidifier.

moisturizer, moisturiser ['mɔɪstʃəraɪzər] n crème *f* hydratante.

mojo ['məʊdʒəʊ] n US inf [energy] peps *m*.

molar ['məʊlər] ◆ adj [quantity, solution] molaire. ◆ n [tooth] molaire *f*.

molasses [mə'læsɪz] n (U) mélasse *f*.

mold US = **mould**.

Moldavia [mɒl'deɪvjə] pr n Moldavie *f* ▸ *in Moldavia* en Moldavie.

Moldova [mɒl'dəʊvə] pr n ▸ **the Republic of Moldova** la république de Moldova.

mole [məʊl] n **1.** [on skin] grain *m* de beauté **2.** ZOOL taupe *f* **3.** *fig* [spy] taupe *f*.

molecular [mə'lekjʊlər] adj moléculaire.

molecule ['mɒlɪkjuːl] n molécule *f*.

molehill ['məʊlhɪl] n taupinière *f*.

molest [mə'lest] vt [bother] importuner, tracasser ; [more violently] molester, malmener ; [sexually] agresser (sexuellement).

molester [mə'lestər] n agresseur *m* ▸ **child molester** pédophile *mf*.

mollify ['mɒlɪfaɪ] (*pt & pp* **mollified**) vt apaiser, amadouer.

mollusc UK, **mollusk** US ['mɒləsk] n mollusque *m*.

mollycoddle ['mɒlɪ,kɒdl] vt UK inf & pej dorloter, materner.

Molotov cocktail ['mɒlətɒf-] n cocktail *m* Molotov.

molt US = **moult**.

molten ['məʊltn] adj [metal, lava] en fusion.

mom [mɑːm] n US inf maman *f*.

moment ['məʊmənt] n [period of time] moment *m*, instant *m* ▸ *at the moment* en ce moment ▸ *at that moment* à ce moment-là ▸ *at this (very) moment* en ce moment même ▸ *at this moment in time* à l'heure qu'il est ▸ *from that moment on* désormais ▸ *I'll do it in a moment* je le ferai dans un instant ▸ *I didn't believe them for a* or *one moment* je ne les ai pas crus un seul instant ▸ *one moment, please* a) un instant, s'il vous plaît b) [on telephone] ne quittez pas ▸ *just a moment, you haven't paid yet* un instant, vous n'avez pas encore payé ▸ *she's just this moment gone out* elle vient de sortir ▸ *the moment of truth* l'heure de vérité.

momentarily [UK 'məʊməntərɪlɪ US ,məʊmen'terɪlɪ] adv **1.** [briefly, temporarily] momentanément **2.** US [immediately] immédiatement, tout de suite.

momentary ['məʊməntrɪ] adj [brief, temporary] momentané.

momentous [mə'mentəs] adj capital, d'une importance capitale.

momentum [mə'mentəm] n **1.** [impetus] vitesse f, élan m **2.** MECH & PHYS moment m.

momma ['mɒmə] n US inf maman f.

mommy ['mɒmɪ] US inf = **mummy.**

Mon. (written abbr of Monday) lun.

Monaco ['mɒnəkəʊ] pr n Monaco.

monarch ['mɒnək] n [gen & ENTOM] monarque m.

monarchist ['mɒnəkɪst] ◆ adj monarchiste. ◆ n monarchiste mf.

monarchy ['mɒnəkɪ] (pl **monarchies**) n monarchie f.

monastery ['mɒnəstrɪ] (pl **monasteries**) n monastère m.

monastic [mə'næstɪk] adj monastique.

Monday ['mʌndeɪ] n lundi m. **See also Friday.**

monetarism ['mʌnɪtərɪzm] n monétarisme m.

monetarist ['mʌnɪtərɪst] ◆ adj monétariste. ◆ n monétariste mf.

monetary ['mʌnɪtrɪ] adj monétaire.

money ['mʌnɪ] (pl **moneys** or **monies**) ◆ n **1.** [gen] argent m ▶ **to put money into sthg** investir dans qqch / it's money well spent c'est une bonne affaire ▶ **to make money a)** [person] gagner de l'argent **b)** [business, investment] rapporter / how did she make her money? comment a-t-elle gagné son argent ? / we paid good money for it cela nous a coûté cher / you can earn big money selling carpets on peut gagner beaucoup d'argent en vendant des tapis / I'm not made of money, you know tu as l'air de croire que je roule sur l'or ▶ **to be in the money** inf être plein aux as ▶ **put your money where your mouth is** il est temps de joindre le geste à la parole ▶ **to have money to burn** avoir de l'argent à jeter par les fenêtres ▶ **money is the root of all evil** prov l'argent est la source de tous les maux **2.** FIN [currency] monnaie f. ◆ comp [problems, matters] d'argent, financier. ◆◆ **moneys, monies** pl n LAW [sums] sommes fpl (d'argent) ▶ **public moneys** deniers mpl publics.

money-back guarantee n garantie f de remboursement.

money-back offer n offre f de remboursement.

money belt n ceinture f portefeuille.

moneybox ['mʌnɪbɒks] n tirelire f.

moneyed ['mʌnɪd] adj riche, nanti.

money-grubbing [-,grʌbɪŋ] inf ◆ n radinerie f. ◆ adj radin.

moneylender ['mʌnɪ,lendə'] n FIN prêteur m, -euse f; [usurer] usurier m, -ère f; [pawnbroker] prêteur m, -euse f sur gages.

moneymaker ['mʌnɪ,meɪkə'] n affaire f qui rapporte, mine f d'or fig.

moneymaking ['mʌnɪ,meɪkɪŋ] adj lucratif.

money market n marché m monétaire.

money order n mandat m.

money-spinner ['mʌnɪ,spɪnə'] UK inf = **moneymaker.**

money supply n masse f monétaire.

Mongolia [mɒŋ'gəʊlɪə] pr n Mongolie f / in Mongolia en Mongolie ▶ **Inner / Outer Mongolia** Mongolie-Intérieure /-Extérieure.

mongoose ['mɒŋguːs] n mangouste f.

mongrel ['mʌŋgrəl] ◆ adj [dog] bâtard ; [other animal] hybride. ◆ n [dog] bâtard m ; [other animal] hybride m.

monitor ['mɒnɪtə'] ◆ n **1.** MED & TECH [checking device] moniteur m **2.** COMPUT & TV [screen] moniteur m. ◆ vt **1.** [check] suivre, surveiller / their progress is carefully monitored leurs progrès sont suivis de près / this instrument monitors the pulse rate cet instrument surveille le pouls du patient **2.** [listen in to - broadcasts] écouter ▶ **monitoring station** station f d'écoute.

monk [mʌŋk] n moine m, religieux m.

monkey ['mʌŋkɪ] n **1.** [animal] singe m ▶ **to make a monkey out of sb** inf se payer la tête de qqn ▶ **to have a monkey on one's back** US inf être accro **2.** inf [scamp] polisson m, -onne f, galopin m.

monkey bars n US cage f d'écureuil.

monkey business n (U) inf [suspect activity] combines fpl ; [mischief] bêtises fpl.

monkey nut n UK cacahouète f, cacahuète f.

monkey wrench n clef f anglaise or à molette.

monkfish ['mʌŋkfɪʃ] (pl **monkfish** or **monkfishes**) n [angler fish] baudroie f, lotte f ; [angel shark] ange m de mer.

mono ['mɒnəʊ] (pl **monos**) adj (abbr of **monophonic**) mono (inv), monophonique.

monochrome ['mɒnəkrəʊm] n **1.** [technique] monochromie f ; PHOT & TV noir et blanc m ; ART camaïeu m **2.** [photograph] photographie f en noir et blanc ; [painting] camaïeu m ; [in modern art] monochrome m.

monocle ['mɒnəkl] n monocle m.

monogamous [mɒ'nɒgəməs] adj monogame.

monogamy [mɒ'nɒgəmɪ] n monogamie f.

monogram ['mɒnəgræm] (pt & pp **monogrammed,** cont **monogramming**) ◆ n monogramme m. ◆ vt marquer d'un monogramme.

monograph ['mɒnəgrɑːf] n monographie f.

monolingual [,mɒnə'lɪŋgwəl] adj monolingue.

monolith ['mɒnəlɪθ] n monolithe m.

monolithic [,mɒnə'lɪθɪk] adj monolithique.

monologue UK, **monolog** US ['mɒnəlɒg] ◆ n monologue m. ◆ vi monologuer.

mononucleosis ['mɒnəʊ,njuːklɪ'əʊsɪs] n (U) mononucléose f (infectieuse).

monopolistic [mə,nɒpə'lɪstɪk] adj monopoliste, monopolistique.

monopolize, monopolise [mə'nɒpəlaɪz] vt monopoliser.

monopoly [mə'nɒpəlɪ] (pl **monopolies**) n monopole m ▶ **to have a monopoly of** or **in** or **on sthg** avoir le monopole de qqch.

monorail ['mɒnəreɪl] n monorail m.

monosodium glutamate [,mɒnə'səʊdjəm'gluːtəmeɪt] n CULIN glutamate m (de sodium).

monosyllable ['mɒnə,sɪləbl] n monosyllabe m.

monotheism ['mɒnəθiː,ɪzm] n monothéisme m.

monotone ['mɒnətəʊn] ◆ n ton m monocorde. ◆ adj monocorde.

monotonous [mə'nɒtənəs] adj monotone.

monotonously [mə'nɒtənəslɪ] adv de façon monotone.

monotony [mə'nɒtənɪ] (pl **monotonies**) n monotonie f.

monoxide [mɒ'nɒksaɪd] n monoxyde m.

Monroe Doctrine [mən'rəʊ-] n ▶ **the Monroe Doctrine** la doctrine de Monroe.

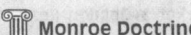 **Monroe Doctrine**

La doctrine de Monroe, énoncée en 1823, inaugura une période isolationniste aux États-Unis, pendant laquelle le continent américain se ferma à l'Europe colonialiste et se détourna délibérément des affaires européennes.

monsoon [mɒnˈsuːn] n mousson f ▸ **the monsoon season** la mousson.

monster ['mɒnstər] ◆ n monstre m. ◆ adj colossal, monstre.

monstrosity [mɒnˈstrɒsətɪ] (pl **monstrosities**) n **1.** [monstrous nature] monstruosité f **2.** [ugly person, thing] horreur f.

monstrous ['mɒnstrəs] adj **1.** [appalling] monstrueux, atroce **2.** [enormous] colossal, énorme **3.** [abnormal] monstrueux.

monstrously ['mɒnstrəslɪ] adv affreusement.

montage ['mɒntɑːʒ] n ART, CIN & PHOT montage m.

Montana [mɒnˈtænə] pr n Montana m / **in Montana** dans le Montana.

Mont Blanc [ˌmɔ̃ˈblɑ̃] pr n mont Blanc m.

Montenegro [ˌmɒntɪˈniːgrəʊ] pr n Monténégro m.

Montevideo [ˌmɒntɪvɪˈdeɪəʊ] pr n Montevideo.

month [mʌnθ] n mois m / **how much does she earn a month?** combien gagne-t-elle par mois ? / **every month** tous les mois / **in a month's time** dans un mois / **by the month** au mois.

monthly ['mʌnθlɪ] (pl **monthlies**) ◆ adj mensuel. ◆ n [periodical] mensuel m. ◆ adv [meet, occur] tous les mois ; [pay] mensuellement.

Montreal [ˌmɒntrɪˈɔːl] pr n Montréal.

monument ['mɒnjʊmənt] n **1.** [memorial] monument m **2.** [historic building] monument m historique.

monumental [ˌmɒnjʊˈmentl] adj monumental.

monumentally [ˌmɒnjʊˈmentəlɪ] adv **1.** [build] de façon monumentale **2.** [extremely] extrêmement.

moo [muː] vi meugler, beugler, mugir.

mooch [muːtʃ] inf vt 🇺🇸 [cadge] taper / **to mooch $10 off** or **from sb** taper qqn de 10 dollars. ❖ **mooch about**, **mooch around** vi 🇬🇧 inf [loaf] traîner.

mood [muːd] n **1.** [humour] humeur f, disposition f ▸ **to be in a good / bad mood** être de bonne / mauvaise humeur / **are you in the mood for a hamburger?** un hamburger, ça te dit ? / **I'm not in the mood** or **I'm in no mood to hear his life story** je ne suis pas d'humeur à l'écouter raconter (l'histoire de) sa vie **2.** [bad temper, sulk] mauvaise humeur f, bouderie f ▸ **to be in a mood** être de mauvaise humeur **3.** [atmosphere] ambiance f, atmosphère f ▸ **mood music** musique f d'ambiance **4.** GRAM mode m.

mood elevator n [drug] stimulant m.

moodily ['muːdɪlɪ] adv [behave] maussadement, d'un air morose ; [talk, reply] d'un ton maussade.

mood swing n saute f d'humeur.

moody ['muːdɪ] (compar **moodier**, superl **moodiest**) adj **1.** [sullen] de mauvaise humeur, maussade, grincheux **2.** [temperamental] versatile, d'humeur changeante.

moon [muːn] ◆ n lune f ▸ **the Moon** la Lune ▸ **to be over the moon** inf être aux anges. ◆ comp [base, flight, rocket] lunaire. ◆ vi inf [show one's buttocks] montrer son derrière or ses fesses. ❖ **moon about** 🇬🇧, **moon**

around vi inf [idly] paresser, traîner, flemmarder ; [dreamily] rêvasser ; [gloomily] se morfondre. ❖ **moon over** vt insep inf soupirer après.

moonbeam ['muːnbiːm] n rayon m de lune.

moon-faced adj joufflu, aux joues rebondies.

moon landing n atterrissage m sur la Lune, alunissage m.

moonlight ['muːnlaɪt] ◆ n clair m de lune / **they took a walk by moonlight** ils se sont promenés au clair de (la) lune. ◆ vi inf [have second job] avoir un deuxième emploi ; [illegally] travailler au noir.

moonlight flit n 🇬🇧 inf ▸ **to do a moonlight flit** déménager à la cloche de bois.

moonlighting ['muːnlaɪtɪŋ] n [illegal work] travail m au noir.

moonlit ['muːnlɪt] adj éclairé par la lune.

moonscape ['muːnskeɪp] n paysage m lunaire.

moonshine ['muːnʃaɪn] n (U) **1.** = moonlight (noun) **2.** inf [foolishness] sornettes fpl, sottises fpl, bêtises fpl **3.** 🇺🇸 [illegally made spirits] alcool m de contrebande.

moon shot n lancement m d'un vaisseau lunaire.

moonstone ['muːnstəʊn] n pierre f de lune, adulaire f.

moonstruck ['muːnstrʌk] adj [dreamy] dans la lune ; [mad] fou (before vowel or silent 'h' **fol**, f **folle**), détraqué.

moony ['muːnɪ] (compar **moonier**, superl **mooniest**) adj inf [dreamy] rêveur, dans la lune.

moor [mʊə] ◆ vt [boat] amarrer ; [buoy] mouiller. ◆ vi mouiller. ◆ n lande f.

moorhen ['mɔːhen] n **1.** [waterfowl] poule f d'eau **2.** [female grouse] grouse f d'Écosse.

mooring ['mɔːrɪŋ] n [place] mouillage m. ❖ **moorings** pl n [cables, ropes, etc.] amarres fpl.

Moorish ['mɔːrɪʃ] adj maure.

moorland ['mɔːlənd] n lande f.

moose [muːs] (pl **moose**) n orignal m.

moot [muːt] vt [question, topic] soulever.

moot point n ▸ **that's a moot point** c'est discutable or ce n'est pas sûr.

mop [mɒp] (pt & pp **mopped**, cont **mopping**) ◆ n **1.** [for floor - string, cloth] lave-pont m, balai m (à franges) ; [-sponge] balai-éponge m ; [for dishes] lavette f (à vaisselle) **2.** [of hair] tignasse f. ◆ vt [floor] laver ; [table, face, spilt liquid] essuyer, éponger. ❖ **mop up** vt sep **1.** [floor, table, spilt liquid] essuyer, éponger **2.** inf [win, make off with] rafler.

mope [məʊp] vi broyer du noir / **he's been moping around** or **about all week** il a passé la semaine à broyer du noir.

moped ['məʊped] n 🇬🇧 Mobylette® f, cyclomoteur m, vélomoteur m.

mophead ['mɒphed] n [scruffy person] épouvantail m fig.

mopping-up operation ['mɒpɪŋ-] n opération f de nettoyage.

moral ['mɒrəl] ◆ adj moral / **he complains about the decline in moral standards** il se plaint du déclin des valeurs morales or du relâchement des mœurs / **we have a moral duty to help them** nous sommes moralement obligés de les aider ▸ **to give sb moral support** soutenir qqn moralement ▸ **moral philosophy** morale f, éthique f. ◆ n [lesson] morale f. ❖ **morals** pl n [standards] sens m moral, moralité f.

morale [məˈrɑːl] n moral m.

morale-booster n : **it was a morale-booster** ça nous / leur, etc. a remonté le moral.

moralist ['mɒrəlɪst] n moraliste *mf*.

morality [mə'rælətɪ] (*pl* **moralities**) n moralité *f*.

moralize, moralise ['mɒrəlaɪz] ◆ vi moraliser ▶ **to moralize about sthg** moraliser sur qqch. ◆ vt moraliser.

moralizing, moralising ['mɒrəlaɪzɪŋ] ◆ adj moralisateur, moralisant. ◆ n (*U*) leçons *fpl* de morale, prêches *mpl pej*.

morally ['mɒrəlɪ] adv moralement.

moral majority n ▶ **the moral majority** les néo-conservateurs *mpl* (*surtout aux États-Unis*).

morass [mə'ræs] n [disordered situation] bourbier *m* ; [of paperwork, information] fouillis *m*, fatras *m*.

moratorium [,mɒrə'tɔːrɪəm] (*pl* **moratoriums** or **moratoria** [-rɪə]) n **1.** [suspension of activity] moratoire *m* **2.** ECON & LAW moratoire *m* ; [of debt] moratoire, suspension *f*.

morbid ['mɔːbɪd] adj [gen] morbide ; [curiosity] malsain.

morbidly ['mɔːbɪdlɪ] adv maladivement.

more [mɔːr] ◆ det **1.** (*compar of many, much*) [greater in number, amount] plus de, davantage de / *there were more boys than girls* il y avait plus de garçons que de filles **2.** [further, additional] : *you should eat more fish* tu devrais manger davantage de or plus de poisson / *three more people arrived* trois autres personnes sont arrivées / *do you have any more stamps?* est-ce qu'il vous reste des timbres ? / *there have been several more incidents in the same area* plusieurs autres incidents se sont produits dans le même quartier / *would you like some more soup?* voulez-vous un peu plus de soupe ? ◆ pron **1.** (*compar of many, much*) [greater amount] plus, davantage ; [greater number] plus / *he earns more than I do* or *than me* il gagne plus que moi **2.** [additional amount] plus, encore / *there's more if you want it* il y en a encore si tu veux / *I couldn't eat any more, thanks* je ne pourrais plus rien avaler, merci / *please can I have some more?* [food] puis-je en reprendre, s'il vous plaît ? / *something / nothing more* quelque chose / rien de plus / *I have something / nothing more to say* j'ai encore quelque chose / je n'ai plus rien à dire ▶ **no more no less** ni plus ni moins. ◆ adv **1.** [forming comparatives] plus / *more intelligent* plus intelligent **2.** [to a greater extent, degree] plus, davantage / *you should read more* tu devrais lire plus or davantage ; [rather] plutôt / *she was more disappointed than angry* elle était plus déçue que fâchée **3.** [again] : *once / twice more* encore une / deux fois. ❖ **more or less** adv phr **1.** [roughly] plus ou moins **2.** [almost] presque. ❖ **more than** ◆ prep phr [with numbers, measurements, etc.] plus de / *for little more than £500* pour à peine plus de 500 livres. ◆ adv phr plus que / *I'd be more than happy to do it* je serais ravi de le faire. ❖ **no more** adv phr **1.** [neither] non plus **2.** [as little] pas plus / *she's no more a spy than I am!* elle n'est pas plus espionne que moi ! **3.** *liter* [no longer] : *the Empire is no more* l'Empire n'est plus. ❖ **not... any more** adv phr : *we don't go there any more* nous n'y allons plus. ❖ **the more** adv phr *fml* d'autant plus ▶ **the more so because...** d'autant plus que... ❖ **the more... the more** conj phr plus... plus / *the more they have, the more they want* plus ils en ont, plus ils en veulent. ❖ **what is more, what's more** adv phr qui plus est.

moreish ['mɔːrɪʃ] adj *UK inf* appétissant.

morello [mə'reləʊ] (*pl* **morellos**) n ▶ **morello (cherry)** griotte *f*.

moreover [mɔː'rəʊvər] adv de plus.

mores ['mɔːreɪz] pl n *fml* mœurs *fpl*.

morgue [mɔːg] n [mortuary] morgue *f*.

MORI ['mɒrɪ] (*abbr of* Market & Opinion Research Institute) pr n *institut de sondage britannique*.

moribund ['mɒrɪbʌnd] adj moribond.

Mormon ['mɔːmən] ◆ n mormon *m*, -e *f*. ◆ adj mormon.

morning ['mɔːnɪŋ] ◆ n matin *m*, matinée *f* / *at three / ten o'clock in the morning* à trois / dix heures du matin / *I worked all morning* j'ai travaillé toute la matinée / *every Saturday / Sunday morning* tous les samedis / dimanches matin / *from morning till night* du matin jusqu'au soir / *there's a flight in the morning* a) [before noon] il y a un vol le matin b) [sometime during] il y a un vol dans la matinée c) [tomorrow] il y a un vol demain matin / *it's open in the morning* or *mornings* c'est ouvert le matin / *see you in the morning!* à demain matin ! / *the previous morning* or *the morning before* la veille au matin / *the next morning* or *the morning after* le lendemain matin. ◆ comp [dew, sun, bath] matinal, du matin ; [newspaper, broadcast] du matin ▶ **morning coffee** : *we have morning coffee around 11* nous faisons une pause-café vers 11 h du matin.

morning-after pill n pilule *f* du lendemain.

morning dress n **1.** (*U*) *UK* [suit] habit porté lors des occasions importantes et comportant queue-de-pie, pantalon gris et haut-de-forme gris **2.** *US* [dress] robe *f* d'intérieur.

mornings ['mɔːnɪŋz] adv *US* le matin.

morning sickness n nausées *fpl* matinales or du matin.

morning star n étoile *f* du matin.

Moroccan [mə'rɒkən] ◆ n Marocain *m*, -e *f*. ◆ adj marocain.

Morocco [mə'rɒkəʊ] pr n Maroc *m* / *in Morocco* au Maroc.

moron ['mɔːrɒn] n *v inf* [stupid person] imbécile *mf*, crétin *m*, -e *f*.

moronic [mə'rɒnɪk] adj imbécile, stupide.

morose [mə'rəʊs] adj morose.

morphine ['mɔːfiːn], **morphia** ['mɔːfjə] n morphine *f*.

morphing ['mɔːfɪŋ] n COMPUT morphing *m*.

morphology [,mɔː'fɒlədʒɪ] n BIOL & LING morphologie *f*.

morris ['mɒrɪs] n ▶ **morris dancing** danses *folkloriques anglaises*.

Morse [mɔːs] n ▶ **Morse (code)** morse *m*.

morsel ['mɔːsl] n [gen] morceau *m* ; [mouthful] bouchée *f*.

mortal ['mɔːtl] ◆ adj **1.** [not immortal] mortel **2.** [fatal - blow, disease, injury] mortel, fatal ; [deadly - enemy, danger] mortel **3.** [very great] : *he lived in mortal fear of being found out* il vivait dans une peur mortelle d'être découvert. ◆ n mortel *m*, -elle *f*.

mortality [mɔː'tælətɪ] (*pl* **mortalities**) n [loss of life] mortalité *f* ▶ **the mortality rate** le taux de mortalité.

mortar ['mɔːtər] n CONSTR, MIL & PHARM mortier *m*.

mortarboard ['mɔːtəbɔːd] n SCH & UNIV ≃ mortier *m* (*couvre-chef de professeur, d'universitaire*).

mortgage ['mɔːgɪdʒ] ◆ n **1.** [to buy house] crédit *m* (immobilier) ▶ **to take out** or **raise a mortgage** souscrire un crédit immobilier **2.** [surety] hypothèque *f*. ◆ vt *lit & fig* hypothéquer, prendre une hypothèque sur.

mortgage broker n courtier *m* en prêts hypothécaires.

mortgage lender n prêteur *m* hypothécaire.

mortgage rate n taux *m* de crédit immobilier.

mortgage relief n exonération fiscale sur un crédit immobilier.

mortician [mɔː'tɪʃn] n US entrepreneur m de pompes funèbres.

mortified ['mɔːtɪfaɪd] adj mortifié, gêné.

mortify ['mɔːtɪfaɪ] (pt & pp **mortified**) vt mortifier.

mortifying ['mɔːtɪfaɪɪŋ] adj humiliant.

mortise lock n serrure f encastrée.

mortuary ['mɔːtʃʊərɪ] (pl **mortuaries**) ◆ n morgue f. ◆ adj mortuaire.

mosaic [məʊ'zeɪɪk] ◆ n mosaïque f. ◆ adj en mosaïque.

Moscow ['mɒskəʊ] pr n Moscou.

Moses basket n couffin m.

mosey ['məʊzɪ] vi US inf [amble] marcher d'un pas tranquille.

Moslem ['mɒzləm] ◆ n musulman m, -e f. ◆ adj musulman.

mosque [mɒsk] n mosquée f.

mosquito [mə'skiːtəʊ] (pl **mosquitos** or **mosquitoes**) n moustique m ▶ **mosquito bite** piqûre f de moustique.

mosquito net n moustiquaire f.

moss [mɒs] n BOT mousse f.

mossy ['mɒsɪ] (compar **mossier**, superl **mossiest**) adj moussu, couvert de mousse.

most [məʊst] ◆ det (superl of **many, much**) **1.** [greatest in number, degree, etc.] : the candidate who gets (the) most votes le candidat qui obtient le plus de voix ou le plus grand nombre de voix **2.** [the majority of] la plupart de, la majorité de / I like most kinds of fruit j'aime presque tous les fruits. ◆ pron (superl of **many, much**) **1.** [the greatest amount] : which of the three applicants has (the) most to offer? lequel des trois candidats a le plus à offrir ? ▶ **to make the most of** a) [advantage, chance, good weather] profiter de b) [bad situation, ill-luck] tirer le meilleur parti de c) [resources, skills] employer ou utiliser au mieux / he knows how to make the most of himself il sait se mettre en valeur **2.** [the greater part] la plus grande ou la majeure partie ; [the greater number] la plupart or majorité / most of the snow has melted presque toute la neige a fondu / most of us / them la plupart d'entre nous / eux. ◆ adv **1.** [forming superlatives] : it's the most beautiful house I've ever seen c'est la plus belle maison que j'aie jamais vue **2.** [as intensifier] bien, fort / a most interesting theory une théorie fort intéressante / most certainly you may! mais bien entendu ! **3.** US inf [almost] presque. ❖ **at (the) most** adv phr au plus, au maximum ▶ **at the very most** tout au plus, au grand maximum.

most-favoured nation n nation f la plus favorisée.

mostly ['məʊstlɪ] adv **1.** [mainly] principalement, surtout **2.** [usually] le plus souvent, la plupart du temps.

MOT (abbr of **Ministry of Transport**) UK ◆ n AUTO ▶ **MOT (certificate)** contrôle technique annuel obligatoire pour les véhicules de plus de trois ans / that old car of yours will never pass its MOT ta vieille voiture n'obtiendra jamais son certificat de contrôle technique. ◆ vt (pt & pp **MOT'd** [ˌeməʊ'tiːd], cont **MOT'ing** [ˌeməʊ'tiːɪŋ]) ▶ **to have one's car MOT'd** soumettre sa voiture au contrôle technique.

motel [məʊ'tel] n motel m.

moth [mɒθ] n **1.** ENTOM papillon m (nocturne) **2.** [in clothes] mite f.

mothball ['mɒθbɔːl] ◆ n boule f de naphtaline. ◆ vt [project] mettre en suspens.

moth-eaten adj **1.** lit [clothing] mité **2.** inf & fig [shabby] miteux.

mother ['mʌðə'] ◆ n **1.** [parent] mère f **2.** RELIG [woman in authority] mère f ▶ **mother superior** Mère f

supérieure ; [Virgin Mary] ▶ **Mother of God** Mère f de Dieu **3.** [original cause, source] mère f **4.** US v inf [character] type m **5.** US v inf = **motherfucker**. ◆ adj [as parent] : the mother bird feeds her young l'oiseau (femelle) nourrit ses petits ▶ **mother hen** mère f poule. ◆ vt [take care of] servir de mère à ; [coddle] dorloter, materner.

motherboard ['mʌðəbɔːd] n COMPUT carte f mère.

mother country n (mère) patrie f.

mother figure n figure f maternelle.

motherfucker ['mʌðəˌfʌkə'] n US vulg [person] enculé m, -e f ; [thing] saloperie f.

motherfucking ['mʌðəˌfʌkɪŋ] adj US vulg foutu / open up or I'll kick the motherfucking door in! ouvre ou j'enfonce cette putain de porte !

motherhood ['mʌðəhʊd] n maternité f.

Mothering Sunday ['mʌðərɪŋ-] n UK la fête des Mères.

mother-in-law (pl **mothers-in-law**) n belle-mère f.

motherland ['mʌðəlænd] n (mère) patrie f, pays m natal.

motherless ['mʌðəlɪs] adj sans mère.

motherly ['mʌðəlɪ] adj maternel.

Mother Nature n la Nature.

mother-of-pearl n nacre f.

Mother's Day n la fête des Mères.

mother-to-be (pl **mothers-to-be**) n future maman f.

mother tongue n langue f maternelle.

motif [məʊ'tiːf] n ART, LITER & MUS motif m.

motion ['məʊʃn] ◆ n **1.** [movement] mouvement m **2.** [gesture] geste m, mouvement m ▶ **to go through the motions (of doing sthg)** faire qqch machinalement **3.** [proposal] motion f, résolution f **4.** LAW [application] requête f. ◆ vi ▶ **to motion to sb (to do sthg)** faire signe à qqn (de faire qqch). ❖ **in motion** n [moving] en mouvement ; [working] en marche. ◆ adv phr : to set the wheels in motion mettre les choses en route.

motionless ['məʊʃənlɪs] adj immobile.

motion picture n US CIN film m.

motion sickness n US mal m des transports.

motivate ['məʊtɪveɪt] vt motiver.

motivated ['məʊtɪveɪtɪd] adj motivé.

motivating ['məʊtɪveɪtɪŋ] adj motivant.

motivation [ˌməʊtɪ'veɪʃn] n motivation f.

motivational [ˌməʊtɪ'veɪʃənl] adj motivationnel.

motive ['məʊtɪv] ◆ n [reason] motif m, raison f ; LAW mobile m. ◆ adj moteur.

motiveless ['məʊtɪvlɪs] adj immotivé, injustifié.

motley ['mɒtlɪ] adj [diverse, assorted] hétéroclite, composite, disparate.

motocross ['məʊtəkrɒs] n motocross m.

motor ['məʊtə'] ◆ n **1.** [engine] moteur m **2.** UK inf [car] auto f, automobile f, voiture f (automobile). ◆ adj **1.** [equipped with motor] à moteur ▶ **motor launch** vedette f ▶ **motor vehicle** véhicule m automobile **2.** UK [concerning cars] automobile **3.** ANAT [nerve, muscle] moteur.

Motorail ['məʊtəreɪl] n train m autocouchette or autoscouchettes.

motorbike ['məʊtəbaɪk] n moto f.

motorboat ['məʊtəbəʊt] n canot m automobile or à moteur.

motorcade ['məʊtəkeɪd] n cortège m (de voitures).

motor car n fml automobile f, voiture f.

motorcycle ['məʊtə,saɪkl] ← n motocyclette f, moto f ▸ **motorcycle racing** motocyclisme m ▸ **motorcycle cop** US inf motard m (de la police). ← vi aller en moto.

motorcyclist ['məʊtə,saɪklɪst] n motocycliste mf.

motor home n US camping-car m.

motoring ['məʊtərɪŋ] n l'automobile f (U).

motorist ['məʊtərɪst] n automobiliste mf.

motorize, motorise ['məʊtəraɪz] vt motoriser.

motor lodge n US motel m.

motor mechanic n mécanicien m.

motormouth ['məʊtə,maʊθ] n v inf : he's a bit of a motormouth c'est un véritable moulin à paroles.

motor neurone disease n maladie f de Charcot.

motor racing n courses fpl automobiles.

motor scooter n scooter m.

motorsport ['məʊtəspɔ:t] n sport m mécanique.

motorway ['məʊtəweɪ] n UK autoroute f.

mottled ['mɒtld] adj tacheté, moucheté ; [skin] marbré.

motto ['mɒtəʊ] (pl mottos or mottoes) n [maxim] devise f.

mould UK, **mold** US [məʊld] ← vt 1. [fashion - statue, vase] façonner, modeler ▸ **to mould sb's character** fig façonner or former le caractère de qqn 2. ART & METALL [make in a mould] mouler. ← n 1. ART & METALL [hollow form] moule m ; [prototype] modèle m, gabarit m ; [moulded article] pièce f moulée 2. fig [pattern] moule m ▸ **to break the mould** sortir des sentiers battus 3. [mildew] moisissure f.

moulding UK, **molding** US ['məʊldɪŋ] n 1. ARCHIT [decorative] moulure f ; [at join of wall and floor] baguette f, plinthe f 2. [moulded article] objet m moulé, pièce f moulée 3. [act of shaping] moulage m.

mouldy UK, **moldy** US ['məʊldɪ] (UK compar mouldier, superl mouldiest ; US compar moldier, superl moldiest) adj moisi / it smells mouldy ça sent le moisi.

moult UK, **molt** US [məʊlt] ← vi ZOOL muer ; [cat, dog] perdre ses poils. ← n mue f.

mound [maʊnd] n 1. [of earth, stones] butte f, monticule m, tertre m 2. [heap] tas m.

mount [maʊnt] ← vt 1. [climb - slope, steps] monter ; [climb onto - horse, bicycle] monter sur, enfourcher ; [-stage, throne, etc.] monter sur 2. [organize, put on - exhibition, campaign, etc.] monter, organiser 3. [fix, support] monter 4. COMPUT [disk] monter. ← vi 1. [onto horse] monter (à cheval), se mettre en selle 2. [rise, increase] monter, augmenter, croître. ← n 1. [mountain] mont m, montagne f 2. GEOG ▸ **the Mount of Olives** le mont des Oliviers ▸ **Mount Rushmore** le mont Rushmore 3. [horse] monture f 4. [support - of photo] carton m, support m ; [- of gem, lens, tool] monture f ; [- of machine] support m ; [- for stamp in collection] charnière f ; [- for object under microscope] lame f. ⬧ **mount up** vi 1. [increase] monter, augmenter, s'accroître 2. [accumulate] s'accumuler, s'amonceler.

mountain ['maʊntɪn] ← n 1. montagne f / we spent a week in the mountains on a passé une semaine à la montagne ▸ **to make a mountain out of a molehill** se faire une montagne d'un rien ▸ **they've got a huge (mountain) to climb** ils ont du pain sur la planche 2. [heap, accumulation] montagne f, tas m / I've got mountains of work to get through j'ai un travail fou or monstre à terminer. ← comp [people] montagnard ; [resort, stream, guide] de montagne ; [air] de la montagne ; [life] en montagne ; [flora, fauna] de montagne, des montagnes ▸ **mountain rescue** : a mountain rescue team une équipe de secours en montagne.

mountain bike n vélo m tout terrain, vélocross m.

mountaineer [,maʊntɪ'nɪə] n alpiniste mf.

mountaineering [,maʊntɪ'nɪərɪŋ] n alpinisme m.

mountainous ['maʊntɪnəs] adj 1. [region] montagneux 2. fig [huge] énorme, colossal.

mountain pass n col m, défilé m.

mountain range n chaîne f de montagnes.

mountainside ['maʊntɪnsaɪd] n flanc m or versant m d'une montagne.

mountain top n sommet m, cime f.

mounted ['maʊntɪd] adj [troops] monté, à cheval.

Mountie, Mounty ['maʊntɪ] (pl Mounties) n inf membre m de la police montée (au Canada) ▸ **the Mounties** la police montée (au Canada).

mourn [mɔ:n] ← vi [feel grief] pleurer ; [be in mourning] être en deuil, porter le deuil. ← vt [person] pleurer, porter le deuil de ; [death, loss] pleurer.

mourner ['mɔ:nə] n [friend, relative] proche mf du défunt.

mournful ['mɔ:nfʊl] adj [person, eyes, mood] triste, mélancolique ; [tone, voice] lugubre ; [place] lugubre, sinistre.

mourning ['mɔ:nɪŋ] ← n (U) [period] deuil m ; [clothes] (vêtements mpl de) deuil m ▸ **to be in mourning** être en deuil, porter le deuil ▸ **to be in mourning for sb** porter le deuil de qqn. ← comp [dress, suit] de deuil.

mouse [maʊs] (pl mice [maɪs]) n 1. souris f 2. [shy person] timide mf, timoré m, -e f 3. COMPUT souris f.

mouse mat, mouse pad n COMPUT tapis m de souris.

mousetrap ['maʊstræp] n souricière f.

moussaka [mu:'sɑ:kə] n moussaka f.

mousse [mu:s] n mousse f.

moustache UK [mə'stɑ:ʃ], **mustache** US ['mʌstæʃ] n moustache f, moustaches fpl.

mousy ['maʊsɪ] (compar mousier, superl mousiest) adj 1. pej [shy] timide, effacé 2. pej [in colour - hair] châtain clair.

mouth ['maʊθ] (pl mouths [maʊðz]) ← n [maʊθ] 1. [of person] bouche f ; [of animal] gueule f / he didn't open his mouth once during the meeting il n'a pas ouvert la bouche or il n'a pas dit un mot pendant toute la réunion / keep your mouth shut n'en parlez à personne, gardez-le pour vous ▸ **me and my big mouth!** j'ai encore perdu une occasion de me taire ! 2. [of river] embouchure f, bouche f, bouches fpl 3. [opening - gen] ouverture f, orifice m, bouche f ; [- of bottle] goulot m ; [- of cave] entrée f. ← vt [maʊð] 1. [silently - insults, obscenities] dire à voix basse, marmonner 2. [pompously] déclamer ; [mechanically] débiter ; [insincerely - excuses] dire qqch du bout des lèvres ; [- regrets] formuler sans conviction. ⬧ **mouth off** vi inf 1. [brag] la ramener 2. [be insolent] se montrer insolent.

-mouthed [maʊðd] in comp ▸ **wide-mouthed** [bottle] à large goulot.

mouthful ['maʊθfʊl] n 1. [of food] bouchée f ; [of liquid] gorgée f / I couldn't eat another mouthful! je ne pourrais rien avaler de plus ! 2. inf [word] mot m difficile à prononcer.

mouth organ n harmonica m.

mouthpiece ['maʊθpi:s] n 1. [of musical instrument] bec m, embouchure f ; [of pipe] tuyau m ; [of telephone] microphone m 2. [spokesperson] porte-parole m inv ; [newspaper, magazine] organe m, porte-parole m inv.

mouth-to-mouth adj ▸ **to give sb mouth-to-mouth resuscitation** faire du bouche-à-bouche à qqn.

mouth ulcer n aphte m.

mouthwash ['maʊθwɒʃ] n [for cleansing] bain *m* de bouche ; [for gargling] gargarisme *m*.

mouth-watering adj appétissant, alléchant.

movable ['muːvəbl] ◆ adj mobile. ◆ n ▸ **movables** LAW effets *mpl* mobiliers, biens *mpl* meubles.

move [muːv] ◆ vt **1.** [put elsewhere - object] déplacer ; [- part of body] bouger, remuer / *we moved all the chairs indoors / outdoors* nous avons rentré / sorti toutes les chaises / *move all those papers off the table!* enlève tous ces papiers de la table !, débarrasse la table de tous ces papiers ! / *move your head to the left* inclinez la tête vers la gauche ; GAMES jouer ▸ **move it!** *inf* grouille-toi ! **2.** [send elsewhere - prisoner, troops, etc.] transférer / *move all these people out of the courtyard* faites sortir tous ces gens de la cour / *she's been moved to the New York office / to accounts* elle a été mutée au bureau de New York / affectée à la comptabilité **3.** [change time or date of] déplacer / *the meeting has been moved to Friday* a) [postponed] la réunion a été remise à vendredi b) [brought forward] la réunion a été avancée à vendredi **4.** [to new premises, location] ▸ **to move house** or **flat** UK déménager **5.** [affect, touch] émouvoir / *I was deeply moved* j'ai été profondément ému or touché **6.** [motivate, prompt] pousser, inciter ▸ **to move sb to do sthg** pousser or inciter qqn à faire qqch **7.** [propose] proposer / *I move that we vote on it* je propose que nous procédions au vote. ◆ vi **1.** [shift, change position] bouger / *the handle won't move* la poignée ne bouge pas / *she wouldn't move out of my way* elle ne voulait pas s'écarter de mon chemin ; [be in motion - vehicle] : *the line of cars was moving slowly down the road* la file de voitures avançait lentement le long de la route / *the truck started moving backwards* le camion a commencé à reculer ; [travel in specified direction] : *the guests moved into / out of the dining room* les invités passèrent dans / sortirent de la salle à manger / *small clouds moved across the sky* de petits nuages traversaient le ciel / *the earth moves round the sun* la Terre tourne autour du Soleil **2.** [leave] partir / *it's getting late, I ought to be* or *get moving* il se fait tard, il faut que j'y aille or que je parte **3.** GAMES [player] jouer ; [piece] se déplacer **4.** [to new premises, location] déménager / *when are you moving to your new apartment?* quand est-ce que vous emménagez dans votre nouvel appartement ? **5.** [develop, progress] avancer, progresser ▸ **to get things moving** faire avancer les choses **6.** [take action] agir / *I'll get moving on it first thing tomorrow* je m'en occuperai demain à la première heure. ◆ n **1.** [movement] mouvement *m* / *one move out of you and you're dead!* un seul geste et tu es mort ! / *she made a move to leave* elle se leva pour partir / *it's late, I ought to be making a move* il se fait tard, il faut que j'y aille ▸ **get a move on!** *inf* grouille-toi !, active ! **2.** [change of home, premises] déménagement *m* **3.** [change of job] changement *m* d'emploi **4.** [step, measure] pas *m*, démarche *f* / *she made the first move* elle a fait le premier pas / *the new management's first move was to increase all salaries* la première mesure de la nouvelle direction a été de relever tous les salaires / *what do you think their next move will be?* selon vous, que vont-ils faire maintenant ? **5.** GAMES [turn to move] tour *m* / *it's my move* c'est à moi (de jouer) ; [act of moving] coup *m* ; [way piece moves] marche *f* ▸ **to be on the move** être en déplacement / *I've been on the move all day* je n'ai pas arrêté de la journée. ❖ **move about** UK ◆ vi se déplacer, bouger / *I can hear somebody moving about upstairs* j'entends des bruits de pas là-haut. ◆ vt sep déplacer. ❖ **move along** ◆ vi avancer / *move along there, please!* circulez, s'il vous plaît ! ◆ vt sep [bystanders, busker] faire circuler. ❖ **move around** = **move about**. ❖ **move away** ◆ vi **1.** [go in opposite direction] s'éloi-

gner, partir **2.** [change address] déménager. ◆ vt sep éloigner. ❖ **move back** ◆ vi **1.** [back away] reculer **2.** [return to original position] retourner / *they've moved back to the States* ils sont retournés habiter or ils sont rentrés aux États-Unis. ◆ vt sep **1.** [push back - person, crowd] repousser ; [- chair] reculer **2.** [return to original position] remettre. ❖ **move down** ◆ vi **1.** [from higher level, floor, etc.] descendre **2.** [make room] se pousser. ◆ vt insep : *move down the bus, please* avancez jusqu'au fond de l'autobus, s'il vous plaît. ◆ vt sep **1.** [from higher level, floor, etc.] descendre / *he was moved down a class* SCH on l'a fait passer dans la classe inférieure. ❖ **move forward** ◆ vi avancer. ◆ vt sep avancer. ❖ **move in** ◆ vi **1.** [into new home, premises] emménager **2.** [close in, approach] avancer, s'approcher **3.** [take control] : *the unions moved in and stopped the strike* les syndicats prirent les choses en main et mirent un terme à la grève. ◆ vt sep [furniture] installer. ❖ **move off** vi s'éloigner, partir / *the train finally moved off* le train partit or s'ébranla enfin. ❖ **move on** ◆ vi **1.** [proceed on one's way] poursuivre son chemin **2.** [progress - to new job, new subject, etc.] : *can we move on to the second point?* pouvons-nous passer au deuxième point ? / *he's finding it hard to move on* [after relationship] il a du mal à tourner la page. ◆ vt sep [bystanders, busker] faire circuler. ❖ **move out** ◆ vi **1.** [of home, premises] déménager **2.** MIL [troops] se retirer. ◆ vt sep MIL [troops] retirer. ❖ **move over** vi **1.** [make room] se pousser **2.** [change over] : *we're moving over to mass production* nous passons à la fabrication en série. ❖ **move up** ◆ vi **1.** [make room] se pousser **2.** [in hierarchy] monter ; [in company] avoir de l'avancement ▸ **to move up a class** SCH passer dans la classe supérieure. ◆ vt sep **1.** [in order to make room] pousser, écarter **2.** [in hierarchy] faire monter.

🗒 **déménager** or **emménager?**

Although **bouger** has the general meaning of to move (**ne bouge pas!** *don't move !*), when moving into a house or flat, or moving out, you should instead choose the verbs **emménager** and **déménager**.

■ *From one place to another*
Je déménage (pour aller) à Bordeaux. *I'm moving to Bordeaux.*

■ *Out of a place*
On déménage la semaine prochaine. *We're moving out next week.*

■ *Into a place*
De l'autre côté de la rue je vois des gens qui emménagent. *Over on the other side of the street I can see people moving into a house.*

---

moveable ['muːvəbl] = movable.

movement ['muːvmənt] n **1.** [change of position] mouvement *m* / *his movements are being watched* ses déplacements sont surveillés / *I'm not sure what my movements are going to be over the next few weeks* je ne sais pas exactement ce que je vais faire or quel sera mon emploi du temps dans les quelques semaines à venir ; [gesture] mouvement *m*, geste *m* **2.** [change, tendency] mouvement *m*, tendance *f* / *there's a growing movement towards privatization* la tendance à la privatisation s'accentue / *the upward / downward movement of interest rates* la hausse / baisse des taux d'intérêts **3.** [group] mouvement *m* **4.** MED [faeces] selles *fpl*.

mover ['muːvər] n **1.** [physical] : *she's a lovely mover* inf elle bouge bien / *he's a fast mover* inf c'est un tombeur ▸ **the movers and the shakers** [key people] les hommes mpl et les femmes fpl d'action **2.** [of a proposal, motion] motionnaire mf **3.** US [removal company] déménageur.

movie ['muːvɪ] US ◆ n film m. ◆ comp [actor] de cinéma ▸ **movie buff** inf cinéphile mf ▸ **movie camera** caméra f ▸ **movie house** or **theatre** (salle f de) cinéma m ▸ **movie director** cinéaste mf, réalisateur m, -trice f ▸ **the movie industry** l'industrie f cinématographique ou du cinéma ▸ **movie rights** droits mpl cinématographiques. ❖ **movies** pl n ▸ **to go to the movies** aller au cinéma / *she's in the movies* elle travaille dans le cinéma.

moviegoer ['muːvɪ,gəʊər] n US cinéphile mf.

moving ['muːvɪŋ] adj **1.** [in motion] en mouvement ; [vehicle] en marche ; [target] mouvant ▸ **slow-** / **fast-moving** qui se déplace lentement / rapidement **2.** [not fixed] mobile ▸ **moving parts** pièces fpl mobiles **3.** [touching] émouvant, touchant **4.** [motivating] : *she's the moving force* or *spirit behind the project* c'est elle l'instigatrice ou le moteur du projet **5.** [for moving house] de déménagement ▸ **moving van** US camion m de déménageurs.

moving staircase n escalier m roulant, escalator m.

moving walkway n trottoir m roulant.

mow [məʊ] (*pt* mowed, *pp* mowed *or* mown [məʊn]) vt [lawn] tondre ; [hay] faucher. ❖ **mow down** vt sep faucher, abattre.

mower ['məʊər] n [person] faucheur m, -euse f ; [machine - for lawn] tondeuse f ; [- for hay] faucheuse f.

mown [məʊn] pp ⟶ **mow**.

moxie ['mɒksɪ] n US inf [guts] cran m.

Mozambican [,məʊzæm'biːkn] ◆ n Mozambicain m, -e f. ◆ adj mozambicain.

Mozambique [,məʊzæm'biːk] pr n Mozambique m / *in Mozambique* au Mozambique.

mozzie ['mɒzɪ] n inf [mosquito] moustique m.

MP n **1.** (abbr of Military Police) PM f **2.** (abbr of Member of Parliament) UK & CAN ≃ député m **3.** CAN abbr of Mounted Police.

MP3 [,empiː'θriː] n COMPUT MP3 m.

MP4 n MP4.

MPEG ['empeg] (abbr of Moving Picture Experts Group) n COMPUT MPEG m.

mpg (abbr of miles per gallon) n consommation f d'essence / *my old car did 20 mpg* mon ancienne voiture faisait or consommait 3,5 litres au cent.

mph (abbr of miles per hour) n miles mpl à l'heure.

MPhil [,em'fɪl] (abbr of Master of Philosophy) n ≃ (titulaire d'une) maîtrise de lettres.

Mr ['mɪstər] (written abbr of Mister) M., Monsieur / *Mr Brown* M. Brown ▸ **Mr President** monsieur le président.

MRC (abbr of Medical Research Council) pr n institut de recherche médicale situé à Londres.

MRCP n abbr of Member of the Royal College of Physicians.

MRCS n abbr of Member of the Royal College of Surgeons.

MRCVS n abbr of Member of the Royal College of Veterinary Surgeons.

MRI (abbr of magnetic resonance imaging) n IRM f.

Mr Right n inf l'homme idéal, le prince charmant.

Mrs ['mɪsɪz] Mme, Madame / *Mrs Brown* Mme Brown.

Ms [mɪz] titre que les femmes peuvent utiliser au lieu de **Mrs** ou **Miss** pour éviter la distinction entre les femmes mariées et les célibataires.

MS ◆ n **1.** (abbr of multiple sclerosis) SEP f **2.** (abbr of Master of Science) US ≃ (titulaire d'une) maîtrise de sciences. ◆ **1.** written abbr of Mississippi **2.** (written abbr of manuscript) ms.

MSA (abbr of Master of Science in Agriculture) n ≃ (titulaire d'une) maîtrise en sciences agricoles.

MSB (abbr of most significant bit/byte) n bit de poids fort.

MSc (abbr of Master of Science) n ≃ (titulaire d'une) maîtrise de sciences.

msg n written abbr of message.

MSG n abbr of monosodium glutamate.

Msgr (written abbr of Monsignor or Monseigneur) Mgr.

MSP n written abbr of Member of the Scottish Parliament.

MST n abbr of Mountain Standard Time.

MSW (abbr of Master of Social Work) n ≃ (titulaire d'une) maîtrise en travail social.

Mt (written abbr of mount) Mt.

MT ◆ n (abbr of machine translation) TA f. ◆ written abbr of Montana.

MTE MESSAGING written abbr of my thoughts exactly.

MTG MESSAGING written abbr of meeting.

MU MESSAGING written abbr of miss you.

much [mʌtʃ] ◆ det beaucoup de / *the tablets didn't do much good* les comprimés n'ont pas servi à grand-chose or n'ont pas fait beaucoup d'effet / *much good may it do you!* iro grand bien vous fasse ! ◆ pron beaucoup / *is there any left? — not much* est-ce qu'il en reste ? — pas beaucoup / *there's still much to be decided* il reste encore beaucoup de choses à décider / *there's not much anyone can do about it* personne n'y peut grand-chose / *I agreed with much of what she said* j'étais d'accord avec presque tout ce qu'elle a dit ; [used to intensify] : *I'm not much of a hiker* je ne suis pas un très bon marcheur ▸ **to make much of sb** / **sthg**: *the defence made much of the witness's criminal record* la défense a beaucoup insisté sur le casier judiciaire du témoin / *I don't think much of him* / *of his technique* je n'ai pas une très haute opinion de lui / de sa technique / *there's much to be said for the old-fashioned method* la vieille méthode a beaucoup d'avantages / *it's not up to much* ça ne vaut pas grand-chose / *he's not up to much* ce n'est pas une lumière / *there's not much in it* il n'y a pas une grande différence. ◆ adv beaucoup / *much happier* / *more slowly* beaucoup plus heureux / plus lentement / *much to my surprise* à mon grand étonnement / *it's much the best* / *the fastest* c'est le meilleur / le plus rapide de beaucoup ▸ **much the same** presque pareil / *I feel much the same as you* je pense plutôt comme vous. ❖ **as much** ◆ pron phr [that, the same] : *I thought* / *suspected as much* c'est bien ce que je pensais / soupçonnais. ◆ adv phr [with multiples, fractions] : *twice* / *three times as much* deux / trois fois plus / *half as much* moitié (de ça). ❖ **as much... as** ◆ det phr [the same amount as] ▸ **as much... as** autant de... que. ◆ conj phr autant que / *he's as much to blame as her* elle n'est pas plus responsable que lui, il est responsable autant qu'elle. ❖ **as much as** ◆ pron phr [the same as] : *it costs as much as the Japanese model* ça coûte le même prix que le modèle japonais. ◆ conj phr autant que / *I hate it as much as you do* ça me déplaît autant qu'à vous / *I don't* *dislike them as much as all that* ils ne me déplaisent pas autant que ça. ❖ **however much** ❖ pron phr : *however much they offer, take it* quelle que soit la somme qu'ils proposent, acceptez-la. ❖ adv phr : *however much you dislike the idea...* quelle que soit votre aversion pour cette idée... ❖ **how much** ❖ det phr combien de. ❖ pron phr combien / *how much do you want? a)* [gen] combien en voulez-vous ? **b)** [money] combien voulez-vous ? ❖ **much as** conj phr : *much as I admire him, I have to admit that...* malgré toute mon admiration pour lui, je dois admettre que... ❖ **so much** ❖ det phr tant de, tellement de / *it's just so much nonsense* c'est tellement bête. ❖ pron phr [such a lot] tant / *I've learnt so much on this course* j'ai vraiment appris beaucoup (de choses) en suivant ces cours / *there's still so much to do* il y a encore tant à faire. ❖ **so much for** prep phr : *so much for that idea!* on peut oublier cette idée ! ❖ **that much** ❖ pron phr : *was there much damage? — not that much* y a-t-il eu beaucoup de dégâts ? — pas tant que ça. ❖ adv phr *(with compar)* **1.** [a lot] beaucoup plus / *not that much better* pas beaucoup mieux **2.** [this amount] : *she's that much taller than me* elle est plus grande que moi de ça. ❖ **this much** ❖ det phr : *there was this much coffee left* il restait ça de café. ❖ pron phr **1.** [this amount] : *I had to cut this much off the hem of my skirt* j'ai dû raccourcir ma jupe de ça **2.** [one thing] une chose / *I'll say this much for her, she's got guts* il faut reconnaître une chose, c'est qu'elle a du cran. ❖ **too much** ❖ det phr trop de. ❖ pron phr trop / *don't expect too much a)* [be too demanding] ne soyez pas trop exigeant, n'en demandez pas trop **b)** [be too hopeful] ne vous faites pas trop d'illusions / *she's too much!* inf elle est trop ! ❖ adv phr [work, speak] trop.

much-loved adj bien-aimé.

muchness ['mʌtʃnɪs] n ▸ **to be much of a muchness** 🇬🇧 inf: *they're all pretty much of a muchness a)* [objects] c'est du pareil au même **b)** [people] ils se valent.

muck [mʌk] *(U)* inf n **1.** [mud] boue f, gadoue f; [dirt] saletés fpl; [manure] fumier m; [dung - of horse] crottin m; [- of dog] crotte f **2.** fig [inferior literature, films, etc.] saletés fpl; [bad food] cochonneries fpl. ❖ **muck about, muck around** 🇬🇧 inf ❖ vi **1.** [waste time] traîner, perdre son temps **2.** [be stupid] faire l'imbécile **3.** [interfere] ▸ **to muck about with sthg a)** [equipment] toucher à qqch, tripoter qqch **b)** [belongings] déranger qqch, mettre la pagaille dans qqch. ❖ vt sep [person - waste time of] faire perdre son temps à; [- be inconsiderate to] malmener; [belongings, papers] déranger, toucher à. ❖ **muck in** vi 🇬🇧 inf [share task] mettre la main à la pâte, donner un coup de main; [share costs] participer aux frais. ❖ **muck out** vt sep 🇬🇧 [horse, stable] nettoyer, curer. ❖ **muck up** vt sep inf **1.** [dirty] cochonner **2.** [ruin] bousiller, foutre en l'air.

muckraking ['mʌkreɪkɪŋ] n pej : *it's the kind of paper that specializes in muckraking* c'est le type de journal spécialisé dans les scandales.

mucky ['mʌkɪ] *(compar* **muckier,** *superl* **muckiest)** adj inf **1.** [dirty, muddy - hands] sale, crasseux; [- shoes] sale, crotté; [- water, road] sale, boueux **2.** [obscene - book, film] obscène.

mucous ['mjuːkəs] adj muqueux ▸ **mucous membrane** muqueuse f.

mucus ['mjuːkəs] n mucus m, mucosité f; [from nose] morve f.

mud [mʌd] *(pt & pp* **mudded,** *cont* **mudding)** n [gen] boue f; [in river, lake] vase f / *my car got stuck in the mud* ma voiture s'est embourbée ▸ **to drag sb** or **sb's name through the mud** traîner qqn dans la boue.

mudbath ['mʌdbɑːθ] n bain m de boue.

muddle ['mʌdl] ❖ n [confusion] confusion f; [mess] désordre m, fouillis m / *Peter was in a real muddle over the holiday plans* Peter ne savait plus où il en était dans ses projets de vacances / *there must have been a muddle over the train times* quelqu'un a dû se tromper dans les horaires de train. ❖ vt **1.** [mix up - dates] confondre, mélanger; [- facts] embrouiller, mélanger / *the dates got muddled* il y a eu une confusion dans les dates **2.** [confuse - person] embrouiller (l'esprit or les idées de) / *now you've got me muddled* maintenant, je ne sais plus où j'en suis. ❖ **muddle along** vi se débrouiller. ❖ **muddle through** vi se tirer d'affaire. ❖ **muddle up** vt sep = **muddle** *(vt).*

muddleheaded [,mʌdl'hedɪd] adj [person] désordonné, brouillon, écervelé; [idea, speech, essay] confus.

muddy ['mʌdɪ] *(compar* **muddier,** *superl* **muddiest)** ❖ adj [hand, car] plein or couvert de boue; [shoes] plein de boue, crotté; [road, stream] boueux. ❖ vt **1.** [hands, shoes] salir, couvrir de boue; [road, stream] rendre boueux **2.** [situation] compliquer, embrouiller.

mudflap ['mʌdflæp] n [on car] bavette f; [on truck] pare-boue m inv.

mudflat ['mʌdflæt] n laisse f or banc m de boue.

mudguard ['mʌdɡɑːd] n 🇬🇧 garde-boue m inv.

mud hut n case f en pisé or en terre.

mudpack ['mʌdpæk] n masque m à l'argile.

mudslide ['mʌdslaɪd] n coulée f de boue.

mudslinging ['mʌd,slɪŋɪŋ] n calomnie f.

mud-spattered adj couvert or maculé de boue.

muesli ['mjuːzlɪ] n muesli m.

muezzin [muː'ezɪn] n muezzin m.

muff [mʌf] ❖ n [for hands] manchon m; [for ears] oreillette f. ❖ vt [bungle] rater, manquer.

muffin ['mʌfɪn] n muffin m.

muffle ['mʌfl] vt [quieten - sound] étouffer, assourdir; [- engine] étouffer le bruit de.

muffled ['mʌfld] adj [sound, voice] sourd, étouffé.

muffler ['mʌflər] n 🇺🇸 AUTO silencieux m.

mug [mʌɡ] *(pt & pp* **mugged,** *cont* **mugging)** ❖ n **1.** [cup, beer glass] chope f **2.** v inf [face] gueule f **3.** 🇬🇧 inf [dupe] poire f; [fool] nigaud m, -e f **4.** 🇺🇸 inf [thug] gangster m, voyou m **5.** = **mugshot.** ❖ vt agresser. ❖ **mug up** 🇬🇧 inf vt sep potasser, bosser.

mugger ['mʌɡər] n agresseur m.

mugging ['mʌɡɪŋ] n agression f.

muggy ['mʌɡɪ] *(compar* **muggier,** *superl* **muggiest)** adj METEOR lourd et humide.

mugshot ['mʌɡʃɒt] n inf photo f d'identité judiciaire; *pej & hum* photo f d'identité.

Muhammad [mə'hæmɪd] pr n Mohammed, Mahomet.

mujaheddin [,muːdʒəhe'diːn] n moudjahid m.

mulatto [mjuː'lætəʊ] *(pl* **mulattos** or **mulattoes)** ❖ adj mulâtre. ❖ n mulâtre m, mulâtresse f.

mulberry ['mʌlbərɪ] n **1.** [fruit] mûre f; [tree] mûrier m **2.** [colour] violet m foncé.

mule [mjuːl] n **1.** [animal - male] mulet m; [- female] mule f **2.** [slipper] mule f **3.** [drug carrier] mule f, fourmi f.

mulish ['mjuːlɪʃ] adj têtu, entêté.

mull over [mʌl] vt sep réfléchir (longuement) à.

mullah ['mʌlə] n mollah m.

mulled ['mʌld] adj ▸ **mulled wine** vin m chaud.

mullet ['mʌlɪt] n *(pl* **mullet** or **mullets)** [fish - grey] muge m, mulet m gris; [- red] rouget m, mulet m rouge.

mulligatawny [,mʌlɪɡə'tɔːnɪ] n 🇬🇧 mulligatawny m, soupe f au curry.

multi- ['mʌltɪ] pref multi-.

multiaccess [,mʌltɪ'ækses] adj COMPUT multiaccès *(inv)*.

multichannel [,mʌltɪ'tʃænl] adj multicanal.

multicoloured UK, **multicolored** US ['mʌltɪ,kʌləd] adj multicolore.

multicultural [,mʌltɪ'kʌltʃərəl] adj multiculturel.

multidisciplinary ['mʌltɪ,dɪsɪ'plɪnərɪ] adj UK pluridisciplinaire, multidisciplinaire.

multiethnic [,mʌltɪ'eθnɪk] adj pluriethnique.

multifaceted [,mʌltɪ'fæsɪtɪd] adj présentant de multiples facettes.

multifaith ['mʌltɪfeɪθ] adj multiconfessionnel.

multifarious [,mʌltɪ'feərɪəs] adj [varied] (très) divers or varié ; [numerous] (très) nombreux.

multifunction [,mʌltɪ'fʌŋkʃən] adj multifonction(s).

multigym ['mʌltɪdʒɪm] n [equipment] appareil *m* de musculation ; [room] salle *f* de musculation.

multilateral [,mʌltɪ'lætərəl] adj multilatéral.

multilayered [,mʌltɪ'leɪəd] adj [cake] à plusieurs couches ; [structure, hierarchy] stratifié ; [film, novel] qui fonctionne sur plusieurs niveaux.

multilevel [mʌltɪ'levl] adj COMPUT multiniveau.

multilingual [,mʌltɪ'lɪŋgwəl] adj multilingue.

multimedia [,mʌltɪ'miːdjə] ◆ n multimédia *m*. ◆ comp multimédia.

multi-million adj : *a multi-million pound / dollar project* un projet de plusieurs millions de livres / dollars.

multimillionaire ['mʌltɪ,mɪljə'neə'] n multimillionnaire *mf*.

multinational [,mʌltɪ'næʃənl] ◆ adj multinational. ◆ n multinationale *f*.

multi-ownership n multipropriété *f*.

multiparty ['mʌltɪ,pɑːtɪ] adj ▶ **the multiparty system** le pluripartisme.

multiplatform [,mʌltɪ'plætfɔːm] adj multiplateforme.

multiple ['mʌltɪpl] ◆ n MATH multiple *m*. ◆ adj [gén] multiple.

multiple-choice adj à choix multiples.

multiple occupancy n [by tenants] colocation *f* ; [by owners] copropriété *f*.

multiple ownership n multipropriété *f* //.

multiple sclerosis n sclérose *f* en plaques.

multiplex ['mʌltɪpleks] ◆ n **1.** TELEC multiplex *m* **2.** CIN complexe *m* multisalles. ◆ comp **1.** TELEC multiplex *m* **2.** CIN ▶ **multiplex cinema** complexe *m* multisalles.

multiplexing ['mʌltɪpleksɪŋ] n multiplexage *m*.

multiplication [,mʌltɪplɪ'keɪʃn] n [gen & MATH] multiplication *f*.

multiplication sign n signe *m* de multiplication.

multiplication table n table *f* de multiplication.

multiplicity [,mʌltɪ'plɪsətɪ] n multiplicité *f*.

multiplier ['mʌltɪplaɪə'] n **1.** ECON, ELECTRON & MATH multiplicateur *m* **2.** COMPUT multiplieur *m*.

multiply ['mʌltɪplaɪ] (*pt & pp* **multiplied**) ◆ vt multiplier. ◆ vi **1.** MATH faire des multiplications **2.** [reproduce, increase] se multiplier.

multiprocessing ['mʌltɪprəʊsesɪŋ] n COMPUT multitraitement *m*.

multiprocessor [,mʌltɪ'prəʊsesə'] n COMPUT multiprocesseur *m*.

multiprogramming [,mʌltɪ'prəʊgræmɪŋ] n COMPUT multiprogrammation *f*.

multipurpose [,mʌltɪ'pɜːpəs] adj à usages multiples, polyvalent.

multiracial [,mʌltɪ'reɪʃl] adj multiracial.

multiresistant bacteria [,mʌltɪrɪ'zɪstənt-] n bactérie *f* multirésistante.

multi-speed adj à plusieurs vitesses ▶ **multi-speed Europe** une Europe à plusieurs vitesses.

multistandard [,mʌltɪ'stændəd] adj TV multistandard.

multistorey UK [,mʌltɪ'stɔːrɪ], **multistoried** US [,mʌltɪ'stɔːrɪd], **multistory** US [,mʌltɪ'stɔːrɪ] adj ▶ **multistorey car park** parking *m* à plusieurs niveaux.

multi-talented adj aux talents multiples.

multitasking [,mʌltɪ'tɑːskɪŋ] ◆ n multitâche *f*. ◆ comp multitâche.

multitude ['mʌltɪtjuːd] n **1.** [large number - of people, animals] multitude *f* ; [- of details, reasons] multitude *f*, foule *f* **2.** [ordinary people] ▶ **the multitude** la multitude, la foule.

multiuser [,mʌltɪ'juːzə'] adj multiutilisateurs *(inv)*.

multivitamin [UK 'mʌltɪvɪtəmɪn US 'mʌltɪvaɪtəmɪn] n multivitamine *f*.

mum [mʌm] ◆ adj ▶ **to keep mum** garder le silence ▶ **mum's the word!** *inf* motus et bouche cousue ! ◆ n UK *inf* [mother] maman *f*.

mumble ['mʌmbl] ◆ vi marmonner. ◆ vt marmonner. ◆ n paroles *fpl* indistinctes, marmonnement *m*, marmonnements *mpl*.

mumbo jumbo [,mʌmbəʊ'dʒʌmbəʊ] n *pej* langage *m* incompréhensible, charabia *m*.

mummify ['mʌmɪfaɪ] (*pt & pp* **mummified**) ◆ vt momifier. ◆ vi se momifier.

mummy ['mʌmɪ] (*pl* **mummies**) n **1.** [body] momie *f* **2.** UK *inf* [mother] maman *f*.

mumps [mʌmps] n (U) oreillons *mpl*.

munch [mʌntʃ] ◆ vt [crunchy food] croquer ; [food in general] mâcher. ◆ vi : *to munch on an apple* croquer une pomme / *she was munching away at some toast* elle mâchonnait un toast.

mundane [mʌn'deɪn] adj [gen] banal, ordinaire ; [task] prosaïque.

mung bean [mʌŋ-] n mungo *m*, ambérique *f*.

municipal [mju:'nɪsɪpl] adj municipal, de la ville.

municipality [mju:,nɪsɪ'pælətɪ] (*pl* **municipalities**) n municipalité *f*.

munitions [mju:'nɪʃnz] pl n munitions *fpl* ▶ **munitions dump** dépôt *m* de munitions ▶ **munitions factory** fabrique *f* de munitions.

mural ['mjʊərəl] ◆ n [painting] mural *m*, peinture *f* murale. ◆ adj mural.

murder ['mɜːdə'] ◆ n **1.** *lit* meurtre *m*, assassinat *m* ▶ **murder trial** procès *m* pour meurtre ▶ **the murder weapon** l'arme *f* du crime ▶ **to get away with murder** faire n'importe quoi impunément **2.** *inf & fig* calvaire *m*, enfer *m* / *the traffic is murder on Fridays* il y a une circulation épouvantable le vendredi. ◆ vt **1.** [kill] tuer, assassiner ; [slaughter] tuer, massacrer **2.** *fig* [language, play] massacrer.

murderer ['mɜːdərə'] n meurtrier *m*, -ère *f*, assassin *m*.

murderess ['mɜːdərɪs] n meurtrière *f*.

murderous ['mɜːdərəs] adj **1.** [deadly - regime, attack, intention] meurtrier **2.** [hateful - look, expression] meurtrier, assassin, de haine **3.** [dangerous - road, bend] meurtrier, redoutable **4.** *inf* [hellish] infernal, épouvantable.

murky ['mɜːkɪ] (*compar* murkier, *superl* murkiest) adj **1.** [dark - sky, night] noir, sombre ; [muddy - water] boueux, trouble ; [dirty - windows, weather] sale **2.** *fig* [shameful] : *a murky episode* une histoire sombre or trouble.

murmur ['mɜːmər] ◆ vi murmurer ▶ **to murmur at** or **against sthg** murmurer contre qqch. ◆ vt murmurer. ◆ n **1.** [sound] murmure *m* ; [of conversation] bruit *m*, bourdonnement *m* / *without a murmur* sans broncher **2.** MED [of heart] souffle *m*.

Murphy's law ['mɜːfɪz-] n loi *f* de l'emmerdement maximum.

MusB ['mʌzbiː], **MusBac** ['mʌzbæk] (*abbr of* Bachelor of Music) n (titulaire d'une) licence de musique.

muscle ['mʌsl] n **1.** ANAT & ZOOL muscle *m* ; [strength] muscle *m*, force *f* **2.** [influence, power] puissance *f*, poids *m*. ❖ **muscle in** vi *inf* intervenir ▶ **to muscle in on sthg** intervenir autoritairement dans qqch.

muscleman ['mʌslmæn] (*pl* musclemen [-men]) n [strongman] hercule *m* ; [bodyguard] garde *m* du corps, homme *m* de main.

muscle strain n MED élongation *f*.

muscular ['mʌskjʊlər] adj **1.** [body] musclé **2.** [pain, tissue] musculaire.

muscular dystrophy n (U) myopathie *f*.

MusD ['mʌzdiː], **MusDoc** ['mʌzdɒk] (*abbr of* Doctor of Music) n (titulaire d'un) doctorat en musique.

muse [mjuːz] ◆ n muse *f* ▶ **the Muses** les Muses. ◆ vi rêvasser, songer ▶ **to muse on** or **upon** or **over sthg** songer à qqch. ◆ vt : *"I wonder what happened to him", she mused* « je me demande bien ce qu'il est devenu », dit-elle d'un air songeur.

museum [mjuːˈziːəm] n musée *m*.

museum piece n *lit* & *fig* pièce *f* de musée.

mush¹ [mʌʃ] n **1.** [food] bouillie *f* ; US [porridge] bouillie *f* de maïs **2.** *inf* & *fig* [sentimentality] mièvrerie *f*.

mush² [muʃ] n UK *v inf* **1.** [face] poire *f*, trombine *f* **2.** [term of address] : *oi, mush!* eh, machin !

mushroom ['mʌʃrʊm] ◆ n BOT & NUCL champignon *m*. ◆ comp **1.** [soup, omelette] aux champignons **2.** *fig* ▶ **mushroom growth** poussée *f* or croissance *f* rapide ▶ **mushroom town** ville *f* champignon. ◆ vi **1.** [spring up] pousser comme des champignons **2.** [grow quickly] s'étendre, prendre de l'ampleur.

mushroom cloud n champignon *m* atomique.

mushy ['mʌʃɪ] (*compar* mushier, *superl* mushiest) adj **1.** [vegetables] ramolli ; [fruit] trop mûr, blet ; [ground] détrempé ▶ **mushy peas** purée *f* de petits pois **2.** *inf* & *fig* [sentimental] à l'eau de rose, mièvre.

music ['mjuːzɪk] ◆ n musique *f* ; [score] partition *f*, musique *f*. ◆ comp [teacher, lesson, festival] de musique.

musical ['mjuːzɪkl] ◆ adj **1.** [evening, taste, composition] musical ; [instrument] de musique **2.** [person] musicien **3.** [pleasant - voice, chimes] musical. ◆ n = musical comedy.

musical box UK = music box.

musical chairs n **1.** [game] jeu *m* des chaises musicales **2.** *fig* va-et-vient *m inv*, remue-ménage *m inv* ; POL remaniements *mpl*.

musical comedy n comédie *f* musicale, musical *m*.

musical instrument n instrument *m* de musique.

musically ['mjuːzɪklɪ] adv [in a musical way] musicalement ; [from a musical viewpoint] musicalement, d'un point de vue musical.

music box n boîte *f* à musique.

music centre n chaîne *f* (midi).

music hall ◆ n **1.** [theatre] théâtre *m* de variétés **2.** [entertainment] music-hall *m*. ◆ comp [song, artist] de music-hall.

musician [mjuːˈzɪʃn] n musicien *m*, -enne *f*.

music-lover n mélomane *mf*.

music piracy n piratage *m* musical.

music stand n pupitre *m* (à musique).

music video n clip *m* (vidéo).

musk [mʌsk] n musc *m*.

musket ['mʌskɪt] n mousquet *m*.

muskrat ['mʌskræt] (*pl* muskrat or muskrats) n **1.** ZOOL rat *m* musqué, ondatra *m* **2.** [fur] rat *m* d'Amérique, loutre *f* d'Hudson.

musky ['mʌskɪ] (*compar* muskier, *superl* muskiest) adj musqué.

Muslim ['muzlɪm] ◆ adj musulman. ◆ n musulman *m*, -e *f*.

muslin ['mʌzlɪn] ◆ n TEXT mousseline *f*. ◆ comp de or en mousseline ▶ **muslin bag** CULIN nouet *m*.

MUSM MESSAGING written abbr of miss you so much.

musquash ['mʌskwɒʃ] = muskrat.

muss [mʌs] vt US *inf* [rumple] friper, froisser ; [dirty] salir.

mussel ['mʌsl] ◆ n moule *f*. ◆ comp ▶ **mussel farm** moulière *f* ▶ **mussel bed** parc *m* à moules.

must (*weak form* [məs], [məst], *strong form* [mʌst]) ◆ modal vb **1.** [expressing necessity, obligation] devoir / *you must lock the door* vous devez fermer or il faut que vous fermiez la porte à clé / *I must go now* il faut que je parte (maintenant) / *I must admit the idea intrigues me* je dois avouer que l'idée m'intrigue / *if I / you, etc. must* s'il le faut / *must you be so rude?* es-tu obligé d'être aussi grossier ? / *you mustn't smoke* il est interdit de fumer **2.** [suggesting, inviting] : *you must meet my wife* il faut que vous rencontriez or fassiez la connaissance de ma femme **3.** [expressing likelihood] devoir / *you must be Alison* vous devez être Alison / *you must be joking!* tu plaisantes ! **4.** (*with 'have'* + *pp*) [making assumptions] : *she must have forgotten* elle a dû oublier, elle a sans doute oublié / *has she forgotten? — she must have* elle a oublié ? — sans doute or certainement / *you must have known!* vous le saviez sûrement ! ◆ n *inf* : *sunglasses are a must* les lunettes de soleil sont absolument indispensables.

> 📋 Note that **falloir que** is followed by a verb in the subjunctive:
> **I must go now.** *Il faut que je m'en aille maintenant.*

mustache US ['mʌstæʃ] = moustache.

mustard ['mʌstəd] ◆ n moutarde *f* ▶ **mustard and cress** mélange de cresson alénois et de pousses de moutarde blanche utilisé en salade. ◆ adj [colour] moutarde (*inv*).

muster ['mʌstər] ◆ vt **1.** [gather - troops] rassembler, réunir ; [- courage, energy] rassembler ; [- finance, cash] réunir **2.** [take roll-call] faire l'appel de. ◆ vi se rassembler. ◆ n **1.** MIL revue *f*, inspection *f* **2.** [assembly] rassemblement *m*. ❖ **muster up** vt insep [courage] rassembler.

must-have ◆ n must *m*. ◆ adj : *the latest must-have accessory* le must en matière d'accessoires.

mustn't ['mʌsnt] abbr of must not.

must-see ◆ n : *that film / TV programme is a must-see* il ne faut surtout pas manquer ce film / cette émission de télévision, ce film / cette émission de télévision est à voir absolument. ◆ adj : *the latest must-see film / TV series* le dernier film / la dernière série télévisée à voir absolument or à ne pas manquer.

must've ['mʌstəv] **abbr of must have.**

musty ['mʌstɪ] (*compar* **mustier,** *superl* **mustiest**) adj **1.** [smell] de moisi ; [room] qui sent le renfermé **2.** *fig* [old-fashioned] suranné, vieux jeu (*inv*).

mutant ['mjuːtənt] ◆ adj mutant. ◆ n mutant *m*, -e *f*.

mutate [mjuː'teɪt] vi & vt muter.

mutation [mjuː'teɪʃn] n mutation *f*.

mute [mjuːt] ◆ adj **1.** MED muet **2.** LING [vowel, letter] muet **3.** [silent - person] muet, silencieux ; [unspoken - feeling] muet. ◆ n MUS sourdine *f*.

muted ['mjuːtɪd] adj **1.** [sound] assourdi, amorti, atténué ; [voice] feutré, sourd ; [colour] doux (douce), pâle ; [criticism, protest] voilé ; [applause] faible **2.** MUS en sourdine.

mutilate ['mjuːtɪleɪt] vt **1.** [maim - body] mutiler ; [- face] défigurer **2.** [damage - property, thing] mutiler, dégrader, détériorer **3.** [adulterate - text] mutiler.

mutilation [ˌmjuːtɪ'leɪʃn] n **1.** [of body] mutilation *f* **2.** [of property] détérioration *f*, dégradation *f* **3.** [of text] mutilation *f*, altération *f*.

mutinous ['mjuːtɪnəs] adj **1.** [rebellious - crew, soldiers] mutiné, rebelle **2.** [unruly - child] indiscipliné, rebelle.

mutiny ['mjuːtɪnɪ] (*pl* **mutinies**) ◆ n [on ship] mutinerie *f* ; [in prison, barracks] rébellion *f*, mutinerie *f* ; [in city] soulèvement *m*, révolte *f*. ◆ vi se mutiner, se rebeller.

mutt [mʌt] n *inf* **1.** [dog] clébard *m* **2.** [fool] crétin *m*, -e *f*.

mutter ['mʌtər] ◆ vt [mumble] marmonner, grommeler. ◆ vi **1.** [mumble] marmonner, parler dans sa barbe or entre ses dents ▸ **to mutter to o.s.** marmonner tout seul **2.** [grumble] grommeler, grogner. ◆ n murmure *m*, murmures *mpl*, marmonnement *m*.

mutton ['mʌtn] ◆ n CULIN mouton *m*. ◆ comp [chop, stew] de mouton.

mutual ['mjuːtʃʊəl] adj [reciprocal - admiration, help] mutuel, réciproque ; [shared - friend, interest] commun.

mutual fund n US [unit trust] fonds *m* commun de placement.

mutually ['mjuːtʃʊəlɪ] adv mutuellement, réciproquement.

Muzak® ['mjuːzæk] n musique *f* de fond, fond *m* sonore.

muzzle ['mʌzl] ◆ n **1.** [for dog, horse] muselière *f* **2.** [of gun] canon *m* **3.** [mouth of animal] gueule *f*. ◆ vt **1.** [dog, horse] museler, mettre une muselière à **2.** *fig* [speaker] museler, empêcher de s'exprimer librement ; [press] bâillonner, museler.

muzzy ['mʌzɪ] (*compar* **muzzier,** *superl* **muzziest**) adj UK [person] aux idées embrouillées ; [mind, head] confus ; [ideas] embrouillé, flou.

MVP (abbr of most valuable player) n US titre décerné au meilleur joueur d'une équipe.

MW (written abbr of medium wave) PO.

my [maɪ] det [belonging to me] mon *m*, ma *f*, mes (*pl*) / *my dog / car / ear* mon chien / ma voiture / mon oreille / *I never use my own car* je n'utilise jamais ma voiture (personnelle) / *I have a car of my own* j'ai une voiture (à moi) / *this is* MY *chair* cette chaise est à moi / *I've broken my arm* je me suis cassé le bras.

Myanmar [ˌmaɪæn'mɑːr] pr n Myanmar *m* / *in Myanmar* au Myanmar.

MYOB MESSAGING written abbr of mind your own business.

myopic [maɪ'ɒpɪk] adj myope.

myriad ['mɪrɪəd] ◆ adj *liter* innombrable. ◆ n myriade *f*.

myrrh [mɜːr] n myrrhe *f*.

myrtle ['mɜːtl] n myrte *m*.

myself [maɪ'self] pron **1.** [reflexive use] : *may I help myself?* puis-je me servir ? **2.** [replacing 'me'] : *it is meant for people like myself* c'est fait pour les gens comme moi / *I'm not (feeling) myself today* je ne me sens pas très bien or je ne suis pas dans mon assiette aujourd'hui **3.** [emphatic use] : *I'm not a great fan of opera myself* personnellement, je ne suis pas un passionné d'opéra / *I was left all by myself* on m'a laissé tout seul **4.** [unaided, alone] moi-même / *I can do it myself* je peux le faire moi-même or tout seul.

mysterious [mɪ'stɪərɪəs] adj mystérieux.

mysteriously [mɪ'stɪərɪəslɪ] adv mystérieusement.

mystery ['mɪstərɪ] (*pl* **mysteries**) ◆ n **1.** [strange or unexplained event] mystère *m* **2.** [strangeness] mystère *m* **3.** THEAT & RELIG mystère *m*. ◆ comp [man, voice] mystérieux.

mystery story n mystère *m*, histoire *f* à suspense, intrigue *f* policière.

mystery tour n excursion dont la destination est inconnue des participants.

mystic ['mɪstɪk] ◆ adj mystique. ◆ n mystique *mf*.

mystical ['mɪstɪkl] adj **1.** PHILOS & RELIG mystique **2.** [occult] occulte.

mysticism ['mɪstɪsɪzm] n mysticisme *m*.

mystified ['mɪstɪfaɪd] adj perplexe.

mystify ['mɪstɪfaɪ] (*pt & pp* **mystified**) vt [puzzle] déconcerter, laisser or rendre perplexe ; [deceive] mystifier.

mystifying ['mɪstɪfaɪɪŋ] adj inexplicable, déconcertant.

myth [mɪθ] n mythe *m*.

mythical ['mɪθɪkl] adj mythique.

mythological [ˌmɪθə'lɒdʒɪkl] adj mythologique.

mythology [mɪ'θɒlədʒɪ] (*pl* **mythologies**) n mythologie *f*.

n n MATH n *m.*

N (written abbr of **North**) N.

n/a, N/A (written abbr of **not applicable**) s.o.

NA¹ (abbr of **Narcotics Anonymous**) pr n *association américaine d'aide aux toxicomanes.*

NA² MESSAGING written abbr of **no access.**

NAACP (abbr of **National Association for the Advancement of Colored People**) pr n *ligue américaine pour la défense des droits de la population noire.*

naan (bread) [nɑːn-] n *pain plat indien.*

nab [næb] (*pt & pp* **nabbed,** *cont* **nabbing**) vt *inf* **1.** [catch in wrongdoing] pincer, choper **2.** [catch - to speak to] coincer, agrafer **3.** [steal, take] chiper, faucher ; [occupy - seat] prendre, accaparer ; [- parking place] piquer.

nadir [ˈneɪˌdɪəʳ] n **1.** ASTRON nadir *m* **2.** *fig* [lowest point] point *m* le plus bas or profond.

naff [næf] adj 🇬🇧 *inf* [very bad] nul, bidon ; [in poor taste] ringard. ⟐ **naff off** vi 🇬🇧 *inf* ▸ **naff off! a)** [go away] tire-toi ! **b)** [as refusal] arrête ton char !

NAFTA [ˈnæftə] (abbr of **North American Free Trade Agreement**) n ALENA *m.*

nag [næg] (*pt & pp* **nagged,** *cont* **nagging**) ⟐ vt **1.** [pester] houspiller, harceler **2.** [subj: pain, sorrow] ronger, travailler ; [subj: doubt] tourmenter, ronger. ⟐ vi trouver à redire, maugréer ▸ **to nag at sb** harceler qqn. ⟐ n. *inf* [person] rouspéteur *m,* -euse *f,* râleur *m,* -euse *f* **2.** [horse] rosse *f.*

nagging [ˈnægɪŋ] ⟐ adj **1.** [wife, husband] grincheux, acariâtre **2.** [doubt, feeling] tenace, harcelant ; [pain] tenace. ⟐ n (U) plaintes *fpl* continuelles.

nail [neɪl] ⟐ n **1.** [pin] clou *m* **2.** ANAT ongle *m.* ⟐ vt **1.** [attach] clouer **2.** *inf* [catch, trap - person] pincer, coincer **3.** *inf* [expose - rumour] démentir ; [- lie] dénoncer, révéler **4.** *inf* [hit] ▸ **to nail sb with sthg** balancer qqch sur qqn. ⟐ **nail down** vt sep **1.** [fasten] clouer, fixer avec des clous **2.** [make definite - details, date] fixer (définitivement) ; [- agreement] parvenir à, arriver à ; [- person] amener à se décider. ⟐ **nail up** vt sep **1.** [shut - door, window] condamner (*en fixant avec des clous*) ; [- box] clouer **2.** [fix to wall, door - picture, photo, etc.] fixer (avec un clou) ; [- notice] clouer, afficher.

nail-biter n **1.** [person] personne *f* qui se ronge les ongles **2.** *fig* [situation] situation *f* au suspense insoutenable.

nail-biting ⟐ n [habit] manie *f* de se ronger les ongles ; *fig* nervosité *f,* inquiétude *f.* ⟐ adj [situation] angoissant, stressant ; [finish] haletant.

nailbrush [ˈneɪlbrʌʃ] n brosse *f* à ongles.

nail clippers pl n coupe-ongles *m inv,* pince *f* à ongles.

nail enamel n 🇺🇸 = **nail polish.**

nail file n lime *f* à ongles.

nail polish n vernis *m* à ongles ▸ **nail polish remover** dissolvant *m.*

nail scissors pl n ciseaux *mpl* à ongles.

nail varnish n 🇬🇧 vernis *m* à ongles ▸ **nail varnish remover** dissolvant *m* (pour vernis à ongles).

Nairobi [naɪˈrəʊbɪ] pr n Nairobi.

naive, naïve [naɪˈiːv] adj naïf.

naively, naïvely [naɪˈiːvlɪ] adv naïvement, avec naïveté.

naivety [naɪˈiːvtɪ] n naïveté *f.*

naked [ˈneɪkɪd] adj **1.** [unclothed - body, leg] nu ; [bare - tree] nu, dénudé, sans feuilles ; [- landscape] nu, dénudé ; [- wall, room] nu ; [unprotected - flame, light, sword] nu ; [- wire] nu, dénudé **2.** [undisguised - reality, truth] tout nu, tout cru ; [- facts] brut ; [- fear] pur et simple ; [- aggression] délibéré **3.** [eye] nu **4.** BOT & ZOOL nu.

nakedness [ˈneɪkɪdnɪs] n nudité *f.*

Nam [næm] pr n 🇺🇸 *inf* Viêt Nam *m.*

namby-pamby [ˌnæmbɪˈpæmbɪ] *inf* ⟐ adj [person] gnangnan (*inv*), cucul (*inv*) ; [style] à l'eau de rose, fadasse. ⟐ n lavette *f,* gnangnan *mf.*

name [neɪm] ⟐ n **1.** nom *m* / *what's your name?* quel est votre nom ?, comment vous appelez-vous ? / *my name's Richard* je m'appelle Richard / *he writes novels under the name of A.B. Alderman* il écrit des romans sous le pseudonyme d'A.B. Alderman / *have you put your name down for evening classes?* est-ce que vous vous êtes inscrit aux cours du soir ? / *she was his wife in all but name* ils n'étaient pas mariés, mais c'était tout comme ▸ **to call sb names** injurier or insulter qqn ▸ **the name of the game** : *money is the name of the game* c'est une affaire d'argent / *ah well, that's the name of the game* c'est comme ça !, c'est la vie ! **2.** [reputation - professional or business] nom *m,* réputation *f* ▸ **to make** or **to win a name for o.s.** se faire un nom or une réputation ▸ **to have a bad name** avoir (une) mauvaise réputation **3.** [famous person] nom *m,* personnage *m* / *he's a big name in the art world* c'est une figure de proue du monde des arts. ⟐ comp COMM [product] de marque. ⟐ vt **1.** [give name to - person, animal] nommer, appeler, donner un nom à ; [- ship, discovery] baptiser / *she wanted to name her son after the President* elle voulait donner à son fils le prénom du président, elle voulait que son fils porte le prénom du président **2.** [give name of] désigner, nommer / *the journalist refused to name his source* le journaliste a refusé de révéler or de donner le nom de son informateur ; [cite] citer, mentionner / *he is named as one of the consultants* son nom est cité or mentionné en tant que consultant **3.** [appoint] nommer, désigner / *she has been named as president* elle a été nommée présidente / *name your price* votre prix sera le mien, dites votre prix **4.** 🇬🇧 POL ▸ **to name an MP** ≃ suspendre un député.

name-calling n *(U)* insultes *fpl*, injures *fpl*.

name-dropper n : *she's an awful name-dropper* à la croire, elle connaît tout le monde.

name-dropping n *allusion fréquente à des personnes connues dans le but d'impressionner.*

nameless ['neɪmlɪs] adj **1.** [anonymous, unmentioned] sans nom, anonyme ; [unknown - grave, writer] anonyme, inconnu **2.** [indefinable - fear, regret] indéfinissable, indicible **3.** [atrocious - crime] innommable, sans nom, inouï.

namely ['neɪmlɪ] adv c'est-à-dire, à savoir.

nameplate ['neɪmpleɪt] n plaque *f*.

namesake ['neɪmseɪk] n homonyme *m*.

Namibia [nə'mɪbɪə] pr n Namibie *f* / *in Namibia* en Namibie.

Namibian [nə'mɪbɪən] ◆ n Namibien *m*, -enne *f*. ◆ adj namibien.

naming ['neɪmɪŋ] n **1.** [gen] attribution *f* d'un nom ; [of ship] baptême *m* **2.** [citing] mention *f*, citation *f* **3.** [appointment] nomination *f*.

nan 🇬🇧 [næn], **nana** ['nænə] n *inf* [grandmother] mémé *f*.

nan (bread) [nɑː-] n = **naan (bread)**.

nanny ['nænɪ] *(pl* **nannies)** n **1.** [nurse] nurse *f*, bonne *f* d'enfants ▸ **the nanny state** l'État *m* paternaliste **2.** 🇬🇧 *inf* [grandma] mémé *f*, mamie *f*.

nanny goat n chèvre *f*.

nanoengineering [ˌnænəʊendʒɪ'nɪərɪŋ] n nano-ingénierie *f*.

nanometre, nanometer 🇺🇸 ['nænəʊˌmiːtər] n nanomètre *m*.

nanoscale ['nænəʊskeɪl] n nano-échelle *f* / *at nanoscale* à nano-échelle, à l'échelle nano.

nanoscopic [ˌnænəʊ'skɒpɪk] adj nanoscopique.

nanosecond ['nænəʊˌsekənd] n nanoseconde *f*.

nanotechnology ['nænəʊˌteknɒlədʒɪ] n nanotechnologie *f*.

nap [næp] *(pt & pp* **napped,** *cont* **napping)** ◆ n [sleep] somme *m* ▸ **to take** or **to have a nap** faire un (petit) somme / *to take an afternoon nap* faire la sieste. ◆ vi [sleep - gen] faire un (petit) somme ; [- in afternoon] faire la sieste.

napalm ['neɪpɑːm] ◆ n napalm *m* ▸ **napalm bomb** bombe *f* au napalm. ◆ vt bombarder au napalm.

nape [neɪp] n ▸ **the nape of the neck** la nuque *f*.

napkin ['næpkɪn] n **1.** [on table] serviette *f* (de table) **2.** 🇬🇧 [for baby] couche *f*.

nappy ['næpɪ] *(pl* **nappies)** ◆ n 🇬🇧 couche *f* (pour bébé). ◆ adj 🇺🇸 [fabric] feutré.

nappy liner n 🇬🇧 change *m* (jetable).

nappy rash n 🇬🇧 érythème *m* fessier.

narcissi [nɑː'sɪsaɪ] pl ⟶ **narcissus**.

narcissism [nɑː'sɪsɪzm] n narcissisme *m*.

narcissistic [ˌnɑːsɪ'sɪstɪk] adj narcissique.

narcissus [nɑː'sɪsəs] *(pl* **narcissus** or **narcissuses** or **narcissi** [nɑː'sɪsaɪ]) n narcisse *m*.

narcodollars ['nɑːkəʊˌdɒləz] pl n narcodollars *mpl*.

narcotic [nɑː'kɒtɪk] ◆ adj narcotique. ◆ n **1.** PHARM narcotique *m* **2.** 🇺🇸 [illegal drug] stupéfiant *m* ▸ **narcotics squad** brigade *f* des stups.

nark [nɑːk] vt *inf* [annoy] mettre en boule or en rogne.

narky ['nɑːkɪ] *(compar* **narkier,** *superl* **narkiest)** adj 🇬🇧 *inf* rouspéteur, grognon.

narrate [🇬🇧 nə'reɪt 🇺🇸 'næreɪt] vt **1.** [relate - story] raconter, narrer *liter* ; [- event] faire le récit de, relater **2.** [read commentary for] : *the film was narrated by an American actor* le commentaire du film a été dit or lu par un acteur américain.

narration [🇬🇧 nə'reɪʃn 🇺🇸 næ'reɪʃn] n **1.** [narrative] narration *f* **2.** [commentary] commentaire *m*.

narrative ['nærətɪv] ◆ adj narratif. ◆ n **1.** LITER narration *f* **2.** [story] histoire *f*, récit *m*.

narrator [🇬🇧 nə'reɪtə 🇺🇸 'næreɪtər] n narrateur *m*, -trice *f*.

narrow ['nærəʊ] ◆ adj **1.** [not wide - street, passage, valley] étroit ; [tight - skirt, shoe] étroit, serré ; [long - nose] mince ; [- face] allongé **2.** [scant, small - advantage, budget, majority] petit, faible ; [close - result] serré / *it was another narrow victory / defeat for the French side* l'équipe française l'a encore emporté de justesse / a encore perdu de peu / *we had a narrow escape* on l'a échappé belle **3.** [restricted - scope, field, research] restreint, limité ; [strict - sense, interpretation] restreint, strict **4.** [bigoted, illiberal - mind, attitude] borné, étroit ; [- person] borné. ◆ vt **1.** [make narrow - road] rétrécir **2.** [reduce - difference, gap] réduire, restreindre ; [limit - search] limiter, restreindre. ◆ vi **1.** [become narrow - road, space] se rétrécir, se resserrer **2.** [be reduced - difference, choice] se réduire, se limiter ; [number, majority] s'amenuiser, se réduire. ❖ **narrow down** ◆ vt sep [limit - choice, search] limiter, restreindre ; [reduce - majority, difference] réduire. ◆ vi [search] se limiter, se restreindre.

narrow-band adj à bande étroite.

narrow boat n péniche *f* (étroite).

narrow gauge n voie *f* étroite. ❖ **narrow-gauge** adj [track, line] à voie étroite.

narrowly ['nærəʊlɪ] adv **1.** [barely] de justesse, de peu **2.** [closely] de près, étroitement **3.** *fml* [strictly] de manière stricte, rigoureusement.

narrow-minded adj [person] étroit d'esprit, borné ; [attitude, opinions] borné.

narrow-mindedness [-'maɪndɪdnɪs] n étroitesse *f* d'esprit.

narrowness ['nærəʊnɪs] n étroitesse *f*.

NAS **(abbr of National Academy of Sciences)** pr n *académie américaine des sciences.*

NASA ['næsə] **(abbr of National Aeronautics and Space Administration)** pr n NASA *f*.

nasal ['neɪzl] ◆ adj **1.** ANAT & LING nasal **2.** [voice, sound] nasillard. ◆ n LING nasale *f*.

nascent ['neɪsənt] adj [in early stages] naissant.

Nasdaq ['næzdæk] **(abbr of National Association of Securities Dealers Automated Quotation)** n ST. EX Nasdaq *(Bourse américaine des valeurs technologiques).*

nastily ['nɑːstɪlɪ] adv [unpleasantly - answer, remark] méchamment, avec méchanceté.

nastiness ['nɑːstɪnɪs] n **1.** [of character] méchanceté *f* **2.** [of injury] gravité *f* **3.** [obscenity] obscénité *f*, indécence *f* **4.** [unpleasantness - of smell, taste] caractère *m* très désagréable.

nasturtium [nəs'tɜːʃəm] n capucine *f*.

nasty ['nɑːstɪ] *(compar* **nastier,** *superl* **nastiest,** *pl* **nasties)** adj **1.** [mean, spiteful - person] mauvais, méchant ; [- remark, rumour] désagréable, désobligeant ▸ **to be nasty to sb** être méchant avec qqn / *he's got a nasty temper* il a un sale caractère **2.** [unpleasant - smell, taste] mauvais, désagréable ; [- impression, surprise] désagréable, déplaisant ;

[- weather, job] sale / *things started to turn nasty* la situation a pris une vilaine tournure ; [in child language - dragon, giant, wolf] vilain, méchant **3.** [ugly, in bad taste] vilain, laid **4.** [serious - sprain, burn, disease] grave **5.** [dangerous - bend, junction] dangereux **6.** [difficult - problem, question] difficile, épineux **7.** [book, film, scene - violent] violent, dur ; [- obscene] obscène, indécent.

natatorium [ˌneɪtəˈtɔːrɪəm] n US piscine f.

nation [ˈneɪʃn] n **1.** [country] pays m, nation f **2.** [people] nation f.

national [ˈnæʃənl] ◆ adj national. ◆ n **1.** [person] ressortissant m, -e f **2.** [newspaper] journal m national.

national anthem n hymne m national.

National Curriculum n ▶ the National Curriculum *programme introduit en 1988 définissant au niveau national (Angleterre et pays de Galles) le contenu de l'enseignement primaire et secondaire.*

national debt n ▶ the national debt UK la dette publique.

national dress n costume m national.

national grid n **1.** UK ELEC réseau m national d'électricité **2.** GEOG réseau m.

National Guard pr n [in the US] Garde f nationale *(armée nationale américaine composée de volontaires).*

National Health Service, National Health pr n *inf système créé en 1946 en Grande-Bretagne et financé par l'État, assurant la gratuité des soins et des services médicaux* ; ≃ Sécurité f sociale.

national insurance n UK *système britannique de sécurité sociale (maladie, retraite) et d'assurance chômage* ▶ **national insurance contributions** cotisations fpl à la sécurité sociale ▶ **national insurance number** numéro m de sécurité sociale.

nationalism [ˈnæʃnəlɪzm] n nationalisme m.

nationalist [ˈnæʃnəlɪst] ◆ adj nationaliste. ◆ n nationaliste mf.

nationalistic [ˌnæʃnəˈlɪstɪk] adj nationaliste.

nationality [ˌnæʃəˈnælətɪ] (pl nationalities) n nationalité f.

nationalization, nationalisation [ˌnæʃnəlaɪˈzeɪʃn] n nationalisation f.

nationalize, nationalise [ˈnæʃnəlaɪz] vt nationaliser.

nationalized, nationalised [ˈnæʃnəlaɪzd] adj nationalisé.

National League pr n *l'une des deux ligues professionnelles de base-ball aux États-Unis.*

National Lottery n Loto m britannique.

nationally [ˈnæʃnəlɪ] adv nationalement.

national park n parc m national.

national press n presse f nationale.

national service n UK service m militaire.

national socialism n national-socialisme m.

national socialist ◆ adj national-socialiste. ◆ n national-socialiste mf.

National Trust pr n ▶ the National Trust *organisme non gouvernemental britannique assurant la conservation de certains paysages et monuments historiques.*

nationhood [ˈneɪʃnhʊd] n statut m de nation.

nation-state n État-nation m.

nationwide [ˈneɪʃənwaɪd] ◆ adj national, à travers tout le pays. ◆ adv à l'échelle nationale, dans tout le pays.

native [ˈneɪtɪv] ◆ n **1.** [of country] natif m, -ive f, autochtone mf ; [of town] natif m, -ive f **2.** BOT [plant] plante f indigène ; ZOOL [animal] animal m indigène ; [species] espèce f indigène. ◆ adj **1.** [by birth] natif ; [of birth - coun-

try] natal ; [- language] maternel **2.** [indigenous - resources] du pays ; [- tribe, customs] indigène **3.** [innate - ability, attraction] inné, naturel **4.** BOT & ZOOL indigène, originaire / *native to India* originaire de l'Inde.

Native American n Indien m, -enne f d'Amérique, Amérindien m, -enne f.

Native Australian n Aborigène mf.

native file n COMPUT fichier m natif.

native speaker n LING locuteur m natif, locutrice f native.

nativity [nəˈtɪvətɪ] (pl nativities) n **1.** RELIG ▶ the Nativity la Nativité **2.** [birth] horoscope m.

Nativity play n *pièce jouée par des enfants et représentant l'histoire de la Nativité.*

NATO [ˈneɪtəʊ] (abbr of North Atlantic Treaty Organization) pr n OTAN f.

natter [ˈnætər] inf ◆ vi UK papoter. ◆ n papotage m.

natty [ˈnætɪ] (compar nattier, superl nattiest) adj inf **1.** [smart, neat - person] bien sapé ; [- dress] chic, qui a de l'allure **2.** [clever - device] astucieux.

natural [ˈnætʃrəl] ◆ adj **1.** [created by nature - scenery, resources] naturel ; [wild - prairie, woodland] à l'état naturel, sauvage **2.** [not artificial - wood, finish] naturel **3.** [normal - explanation, reaction, wish] naturel, normal / *it's only natural for her to be worried* or *that she should be worried* il est tout à fait normal or il est tout naturel qu'elle se fasse du souci **4.** [unaffected - person, manner] naturel, simple **5.** [innate - talent] inné, naturel **6.** [free of additives] naturel **7.** [child] naturel **8.** [real - parents] naturel **9.** INDUST ▶ **natural wastage** départs mpl naturels. ◆ n MUS bécarre m.

> 📝 Note that il est naturel que is followed by a verb in the subjunctive:
> **It's only natural they should be upset.** *Il est tout à fait naturel qu'ils soient vexés.*

natural childbirth n accouchement m naturel.

natural disaster n catastrophe f naturelle.

natural gas n gaz m naturel.

natural history n histoire f naturelle.

naturalism [ˈnætʃrəlɪzm] n naturalisme m.

naturalist [ˈnætʃrəlɪst] n naturaliste mf.

naturalize, naturalise [ˈnætʃrəlaɪz] ◆ vt [person, expression, custom] naturaliser ; [plant, animal] acclimater. ◆ vi BIOL s'acclimater.

naturalized, naturalised [ˈnætʃrəlaɪzd] adj [person] naturalisé.

naturally [ˈnætʃrəlɪ] adv **1.** [of course] naturellement, bien sûr, bien entendu **2.** [by nature - lazy] de nature, par tempérament ; [- difficult] naturellement, par sa nature / *she's got naturally curly hair* elle a les cheveux qui frisent naturellement **3.** [unaffectedly] naturellement, de manière naturelle.

naturalness [ˈnætʃrəlnɪs] n **1.** [unaffectedness] naturel m, simplicité f **2.** [natural appearance] naturel m.

natural science n **1.** (U) sciences fpl naturelles **2.** (C) : *botany is a natural science* la botanique fait partie des sciences naturelles.

natural selection n sélection f naturelle.

nature [ˈneɪtʃər] n **1.** nature f ▶ **to let nature take its course** laisser faire la nature **2.** [character] nature f, caractère m **3.** [type] nature f, type m, genre m. ◈ **in the nature of** prep phr en guise de, à titre de.

-natured ['neɪtʃəd] in comp d'une nature..., d'un caractère... / *she's good / ill-natured* elle a bon / mauvais caractère.

nature lover n amoureux *m*, -euse *f* de la nature.

nature reserve n réserve *f* naturelle.

nature trail n sentier *m* (de découverte de la) nature.

naturism ['neɪtʃərɪzm] n naturisme *m*.

naturist ['neɪtʃərɪst] ◆ adj naturiste. ◆ n naturiste *mf*.

naturopathy [,neɪtʃə'rɒpəθɪ] n naturothérapie *f*, naturopathie *f*.

naughtily ['nɔːtɪlɪ] adv **1.** [mischievously] avec malice, malicieusement **2.** [suggestively] avec grivoiserie.

naughtiness ['nɔːtɪnɪs] n **1.** [disobedience] désobéissance *f* ; [mischievousness] malice *f* **2.** [indecency] grivoiserie *f*, gaillardise *f*.

naughty ['nɔːtɪ] (*compar* **naughtier**, *superl* **naughtiest**) adj **1.** [badly behaved - child] méchant, désobéissant, vilain ; [mischievous] coquin, malicieux **2.** [indecent - joke, story, postcard] paillard, grivois, osé.

nausea ['nɔːsjə] n nausée *f*.

nauseam ['nɔːzɪæm] ⟶ **ad nauseam**.

nauseate ['nɔːsɪeɪt] vt *lit & fig* donner la nausée à, écœurer.

nauseating ['nɔːsɪeɪtɪŋ] adj [food, sight, idea] écœurant, qui donne la nausée ; [smell] écœurant, nauséabond ; [person, behaviour] écœurant, dégoûtant, répugnant.

nauseatingly ['nɔːsɪeɪtɪŋlɪ] adv à vous donner la nausée, à vous écœurer.

nauseous [🇬🇧 'nɔːsjəs 🇺🇸 'nɔːʃəs] adj **1.** [revolting - smell] nauséabond, qui donne la nausée, écœurant **2.** [unwell - person] écœuré **3.** 🇺🇸 *inf* [disgusting] dégueulasse.

nautical ['nɔːtɪkl] adj nautique.

nautical mile n mille *m* marin.

naval ['neɪvl] adj [gen] naval ; [power] maritime ▸ **naval base** base *f* navale ▸ **naval officer** officier *m* de marine.

nave [neɪv] n [of church] nef *f*.

navel ['neɪvl] n nombril *m*.

navigable ['nævɪgəbl] adj [water] navigable ; [craft] dirigeable.

navigate ['nævɪgeɪt] ◆ vt **1.** [chart course of - ship] calculer le parcours de ; [- car, aircraft] être le navigateur de **2.** [sail] : *to navigate the Atlantic* traverser l'Atlantique (en bateau). ◆ vi **1.** [plot course] naviguer **2.** COMPUT naviguer, surfer.

navigation [,nævɪ'geɪʃn] n **1.** [act, skill of navigating] navigation *f* **2.** 🇺🇸 [shipping] navigation *f*, trafic *m* (maritime) **3.** COMPUT navigation *f*, surf *m* sur l'Internet.

navigational [,nævɪ'geɪʃnl] adj de (la) navigation.

navigator ['nævɪgeɪtə'] n navigateur *m*, -trice *f*.

navvy ['nævɪ] (*pl* **navvies**) n 🇬🇧 *inf* terrassier *m*.

navy ['neɪvɪ] (*pl* **navies**) ◆ n **1.** [service] marine *f* (nationale) **2.** [warships collectively] marine *f* de guerre ; [fleet] flotte *f* **3.** = **navy blue**. ◆ adj **1.** de la marine **2.** = **navy-blue**.

navy blue n bleu *m* marine. ◆ **navy-blue** adj bleu marine (*inv*).

naysayer ['neɪ,seɪə'] n *personne qui a l'esprit de contradiction*.

Nazi ['nɑːtsɪ] ◆ adj nazi. ◆ n nazi *m*, -e *f*.

Nazism ['nɑːtsɪzm], **Naziism** ['nɑːtsɪ,ɪzm] n nazisme *m*.

NB 1. (written abbr of **nota bene**) NB **2.** written abbr of **New Brunswick**.

NBA pr n **1.** (abbr of **National Basketball Association**) *fédération américaine de basket-ball* **2.** (abbr of **National Boxing Association**) *fédération américaine de boxe*.

NBC ◆ pr n (abbr of **National Broadcasting Company**) *chaîne de télévision américaine*. ◆ adj (abbr of **nuclear, biological and chemical**) NBC.

NBD MESSAGING written abbr of **no big deal**.

NC 1. written abbr of **no charge 2.** written abbr of **North Carolina 3.** (abbr of **network computer**) NC *m* **4.** MESSAGING written abbr of **no comment**.

NCO (abbr of **non-commissioned officer**) n sous-officier *m*.

ND written abbr of **North Dakota**.

NDP (abbr of **net domestic product**) n ECON PIN *m*.

NE 1. written abbr of **Nebraska 2.** written abbr of **New England 3.** (written abbr of **north-east**) N-E **4.** MESSAGING written abbr of **any**.

Neanderthal, neanderthal [nɪ'ændətɑːl] ◆ adj **1.** ANTHR néandertalien, de Neandertal **2.** [uncivilized] fruste, inculte, primitif. ◆ n néandertalien *m*.

neap tide n (marée *f* de) morte-eau *f*.

near [nɪə'] (*compar* **nearer**, *superl* **nearest**) ◆ prep **1.** [in space] près de / *don't go near the fire* ne t'approche pas du feu / *is there a chemist's near here?* est-ce qu'il y a un pharmacien près d'ici or dans le coin ? / *near the end of the book* vers la fin du livre / *I haven't been near a horse since the accident* je n'ai pas approché un cheval depuis l'accident **2.** [in time] près de, proche de / *it's getting near Christmas* c'est bientôt Noël **3.** [similar to] près de / *that would be nearer the truth* ce serait plus près de la vérité **4.** [on the point of] près de, au bord de / *it's near freezing* il ne fait pas loin de zéro, la température avoisine zéro degré. ◆ adv **1.** [in space] près, à côté, à proximité ▸ **to draw near** s'approcher **2.** [in time] proche, près / *as the time grew* or *drew near* à mesure que le moment approchait **3.** PHR **near enough** ça va comme ça / *it's near enough 50 lbs* ça pèse dans les 50 livres / *it's nowhere near good enough* c'est loin d'être suffisant. ◆ adj **1.** [in space] proche / *the near edge* le bord le plus proche **2.** [in time] proche / *in the near future* dans un proche avenir **3.** [virtual] : *it was a near disaster* on a frôlé la catastrophe / *he found himself in near darkness* il s'est retrouvé dans une obscurité quasi totale ▸ **it was a near thing** on l'a échappé belle, il était moins une / *I caught the train, but it was a near thing* j'ai eu mon train de justesse **4.** [in amount, number] : *to the nearest £10* à 10 livres près. ◆ vt [approach - place, date, event] approcher de ; [- state] être au bord de / *the book is nearing completion* le livre est sur le point d'être terminé.

near- in comp ▸ **near-perfect** pratiquement or quasi parfait ▸ **near-complete** pratiquement or quasi complet.

nearby ◆ adv [,nɪə'baɪ] [near here] près d'ici ; [near there] près de là. ◆ adj ['nɪəbaɪ] : *we stopped at a nearby post office* nous nous sommes arrêtés dans un bureau de poste situé non loin de là.

near-death experience n expérience *f* aux frontières de la mort.

Near East pr n ▸ **the Near East** le Proche-Orient.

nearly ['nɪəlɪ] adv **1.** [almost] presque, à peu près / *he's nearly 80* il a presque 80 ans / *I nearly fell* j'ai failli tomber / *he was nearly crying* or *in tears* il était au bord des larmes **2.** [with negative] : *I didn't buy nearly enough food for everyone* je suis loin d'avoir acheté assez de provisions pour tout le monde / *it's not nearly as difficult as I thought* c'est bien moins difficile que je ne l'imaginais.

near miss n **1.** [gen & SPORT] coup *m* qui a raté de peu / *it was a near miss* **a)** FOOT il s'en est fallu de peu qu'on marque, on a failli marquer un but **b)** [answer] la réponse était presque bonne **c)** [accident] on a frôlé l'accident **2.** [between planes, vehicles, etc.] quasi-collision *f*.

nearness ['nɪənɪs] n proximité *f*.

nearside ['nɪəsaɪd] ᵁᴷ ◆ adj AUTO [when driving on right] (du côté) droit, du côté trottoir ; [when driving on left] (du côté) gauche, du côté trottoir. ◆ n [when driving on right] côté *m* droit ; [when driving on left] côté *m* gauche.

nearsighted [,nɪə'saɪtɪd] adj ᵁˢ myope.

neat [niːt] adj **1.** [tidy - in dress] net, soigné ; [- desk, room] net, bien rangé ; [- garden] bien tenu or entretenu, soigné ; [careful - work, handwriting] soigné **2.** [smart, pretty] joli **3.** [effective - organization] net, efficace ; [- system, plan] bien conçu ; [- solution] élégant **4.** ᵁˢ inf [great] chouette **5.** [undiluted - spirits] sec (sèche), sans eau.

neatly ['niːtlɪ] adv **1.** [tidily] avec soin or ordre ; [carefully - write, work] avec soin, soigneusement **2.** [skilfully] habilement, adroitement.

neatness ['niːtnɪs] n **1.** [tidiness - of dress] soin *m*, netteté *f* ; [- of room] ordre *m* ; [carefulness - of work] soin *m* **2.** [skilfulness - of phrase, solution] élégance *f* ; [- of scheme] habileté *f*.

Nebraska [nɪ'bræskə] pr n Nebraska *m* / *in Nebraska* dans le Nebraska.

nebula ['nebjʊlə] (*pl* **nebulas** or **nebulae** [-liː]) n ASTRON nébuleuse *f*.

nebulous ['nebjʊləs] adj [vague] vague, flou, nébuleux.

NEC (abbr of **National Exhibition Centre**) pr n centre de conférences et d'expositions près de Birmingham en Angleterre.

necessarily [,nesə'serɪlɪ] adv nécessairement, forcément.

necessary ['nesəsrɪ] (*pl* **necessaries**) ◆ adj **1.** [essential] nécessaire, essentiel ; [indispensable] indispensable ; [compulsory] obligatoire / *water is necessary to* or *for life* l'eau est indispensable à la vie / *it is necessary for him to come* il est nécessaire qu'il vienne, il faut qu'il vienne / *if necessary* **a)** [if forced] s'il le faut **b)** [if need arises] le cas échéant, si besoin est / *will you make the necessary arrangements?* pouvez-vous prendre les dispositions nécessaires ? **2.** [inevitable] nécessaire, inéluctable. ◆ n **1.** ᵁᴷ inf **▶ to do the necessary** faire le nécessaire **2.** ᵁᴷ inf [cash] : *have you got the necessary?* tu as de quoi payer ?

> 📋 Note that il est nécessaire que is followed by a verb in the subjunctive:
> **It is necessary for all concerned to be extremely cautious.** *Il est nécessaire que toutes les personnes concernées soient très prudentes.*

necessitate [nɪ'sesɪteɪt] vt nécessiter, rendre nécessaire.

necessity [nɪ'sesətɪ] (*pl* **necessities**) n **1.** [need] nécessité *f*, besoin *m* / *in case of absolute necessity* en cas de force majeure **▶ out of** or **by** or **through necessity** par nécessité, par la force des choses **2.** [essential] chose *f* nécessaire or essentielle / *the basic* or *bare necessities of life* les choses qui sont absolument essentielles or indispensables à la vie. **◆ of necessity** adv phr nécessairement.

neck [nek] ◆ n **1.** ANAT cou *m* ; *fig* : *they were up to their necks in debt* ils étaient endettés jusqu'au cou / **▶ to risk one's neck** risquer sa peau **▶ to stick one's neck out** prendre des risques **2.** CULIN [of lamb] collet *m* ; [of beef] collier *m* **3.** SPORT **▶ to win by a neck** gagner d'une encolure **▶ to be neck and neck** être à égalité **4.** [narrow part or extremity - of bottle, flask] goulot *m*, col *m* ; [- of pipe] tuyau *m* ; [- of womb, femur] col *m* ; [- of violin] manche *m* **5.** [of dress, pullover] col *m*, encolure *f* **6.** ᵁᴷ inf [cheek] toupet *m*, culot *m*. ◆ vi inf se bécoter, se peloter.

neckerchief ['nekətʃɪf] n foulard *m*.

necklace ['neklɪs] n collier *m*.

neckline ['neklaɪn] n col *m*, encolure *f* / *her dress had a low / plunging neckline* elle avait une robe décolletée / très décolletée.

necktie ['nektaɪ] n ᵁˢ cravate *f*.

nectar ['nektə⁻] n BOT & fig nectar *m*.

nectarine ['nektərɪn] n nectarine *f*.

need [niːd] ◆ vt **1.** [as basic requirement] avoir besoin de / *have you got everything you need?* est-ce que tu as tout ce qu'il te faut ? / *you only need to ask* vous n'avez qu'à demander / *the carpet needs cleaning* la moquette a besoin d'être nettoyée **2.** [would benefit from] : *I need a drink / a shower* j'ai besoin de boire quelque chose / de prendre une douche / *it's just what I need* c'est exactement ce qu'il me faut / *that's all we need!* iro il ne nous manquait plus que ça ! / *liquid nitrogen needs careful handling* or *to be handled with care* l'azote liquide demande à être manié avec précaution **3.** [expressing obligation] **▶ to need to do sthg** avoir besoin de or être obligé de faire qqch / *you need to try harder* tu vas devoir faire or il va falloir que tu fasses un effort supplémentaire. ◆ modal vb : *you needn't come if you don't want to* vous n'avez pas besoin de or vous n'êtes pas obligé de venir si vous n'en avez pas envie / *I needn't tell you how important it is* je n'ai pas besoin de vous dire or vous savez à quel point c'est important / *the accident need never have happened* cet accident aurait pu être évité / *need I say more?* ai-je besoin d'en dire davantage or plus ? / *need that be the case?* est-ce nécessairement or forcément le cas ? ◆ n **1.** [necessity] besoin *m* / *phone me if you feel the need for a chat* appelle-moi si tu as besoin de parler / *there's no need to panic* or *for any panic* inutile de paniquer **▶ to be in need of sthg** avoir besoin de qqch **▶ should the need arise** si cela s'avérait nécessaire, si le besoin s'en faisait sentir / *your need is greater than mine* hum vous en avez plus besoin que moi **2.** [requirement] besoin *m* / *he saw to her every need* il subvenait à ses moindres besoins **3.** [poverty] besoin *m*, nécessité *f* ; [adversity] adversité *f*, besoin *m* **▶ to be in need** être dans le besoin. **◆ if need(s) be** adv phr si besoin est, le cas échéant.

> 📋 Note that avoir besoin que is followed by a verb in the subjunctive:
> **We need everybody to make an effort.** *Nous avons besoin que tout le monde fasse un effort.*

needle ['niːdl] ◆ n **1.** MED & SEW aiguille *f* ; [for record player] pointe *f* de lecture, saphir *m* ; [of pine-tree] aiguille *f* ; [spine - of hedgehog] piquant *m* **▶ it's like looking for a needle in a haystack** c'est comme si l'on cherchait une aiguille dans une botte de foin **2.** [as indicator - in compass, on dial] aiguille *f* **3.** GEOL [rocky outcrop] aiguille *f*, pic *m* **4.** [monument] aiguille *f*, flèche *f*. ◆ vt inf [annoy] asticoter ; [tease] chambrer.

needle bank n distributeur-échangeur *m* de seringues.

needlecord ['niːdlkɔːd] n velours *m* côtelé.

needless ['niːdlɪs] adj [unnecessary - expense, effort, fuss] superflu, inutile ; [- remark] inopportun, déplacé / *needless to say I won't go* il va sans dire que je n'irai pas.

needlessly ['niːdlɪslɪ] adv inutilement.

needlework ['niːdlwɜːk] n *(U)* travaux *mpl* d'aiguille, couture *f*.

needn't [niːdnt] *abbr of* **need not**.

needs-based adj fondé sur les besoins.

need-to-know adj : *information is given on a need-to-know basis* les renseignements ne sont donnés qu'aux personnes concernées.

needy ['niːdɪ] *(compar* **needier***, superl* **neediest)** ◆ adj [financially] nécessiteux, dans le besoin ; [emotionally] en manque d'affection. ◆ pl n ▶ **the needy** les nécessiteux *mpl*.

ne'er-do-well n bon à rien, bonne *f* à rien.

negative ['negətɪv] ◆ adj négatif. ◆ n **1.** GRAM négation *f* / *in the negative* à la forme négative **2.** [answer] réponse *f* négative, non *m* / *to reply in the negative* répondre négativement or par la négative **3.** PHOT négatif *m*.

negative equity n *(U)* situation où l'acquéreur d'un bien immobilier reste redevable de l'emprunt contracté alors que son logement enregistre une moins-value.

negative growth n ECON croissance *f* négative.

negatively ['negətɪvlɪ] adv négativement.

negative sign n signe *m* moins or négatif.

negatory [nɪ'geɪtərɪ] adj 🇺🇸 *inf* négatif.

neglect [nɪ'glekt] ◆ n **1.** [lack of attention, care - of building, garden] abandon *m*, manque *m* de soins or d'entretien ; [- of child, invalid] manque *m* de soins or d'attention ; [- of people's demands, needs] manque *m* d'égards / *through neglect* par négligence *f* ; [bad condition - of building, garden] délabrement *m* **2.** [disregard - of duty, promise, rules] manquement *m*. ◆ vt **1.** [fail to attend to, to care for - building, garden] négliger, laisser à l'abandon ; [- work] négliger ; [- child, invalid, friend] délaisser, négliger **2.** [disregard - duty, promise] manquer à ; [- advice] ignorer ; [omit, overlook] omettre, oublier ▶ **to neglect to do sthg** oublier or omettre de faire qqch.

neglected [nɪ'glektɪd] adj **1.** [uncared for - garden] (laissé) à l'abandon, mal entretenu ; [- building] (laissé) à l'abandon, délabré ; [- appearance] négligé, peu soigné **2.** [emotionally - child, wife] délaissé, abandonné.

neglectful [nɪ'glektfʊl] adj [person, attitude] négligent / *to be neglectful of one's duty* négliger ses devoirs.

negligence ['neglɪdʒəns] n [inattention] négligence *f* / *due to or through negligence* par négligence ; [of duties, rules] négligence *f*, manquement *m*.

negligent ['neglɪdʒənt] adj **1.** [neglectful] négligent / *to be negligent of one's duties* manquer à or négliger ses devoirs **2.** [nonchalant - attitude, manner] nonchalant, négligent.

negligently ['neglɪdʒəntlɪ] adv **1.** [carelessly] négligemment **2.** [nonchalantly] négligemment, nonchalamment.

negligible ['neglɪdʒəbl] adj négligeable, insignifiant.

negotiable [nɪ'gəʊʃjəbl] adj FIN [bonds] négociable ; [price, salary] négociable, à débattre.

negotiate [nɪ'gəʊʃɪeɪt] ◆ vt **1.** [gen & FIN] négocier **2.** [manoeuvre round - bend] négocier ; [- rapids, obstacle] franchir ; *fig* [difficulty] franchir, surmonter. ◆ vi négocier.

negotiating table [nɪ'gəʊʃɪeɪtɪŋ-] n table *f* des négociations.

negotiation [nɪ,gəʊʃɪ'eɪʃn] n [discussion] négociation *f*, pourparlers *mpl* ▶ **to enter into negotiation** or **negotiations with sb** entamer des négociations avec qqn.

negotiator [nɪ'gəʊʃɪeɪtər] n négociateur *m*, -trice *f*.

Negro ['niːgrəʊ] *(pl* **Negroes)** ◆ n nègre *m* (attention : le terme «Negro» est considéré comme raciste, sauf dans le domaine de l'anthropologie). ◆ adj nègre.

neigh [neɪ] ◆ vi hennir. ◆ n hennissement *m*.

neighbor 🇺🇸 = **neighbour**.

neighbour 🇬🇧**, neighbor** 🇺🇸 ['neɪbər] ◆ n **1.** voisin *m*, -e *f* **2.** [fellow man] prochain *m*, -e *f*. ◆ comp ▶ **neighbour states** pays *mpl* voisins. ◆ **neighbour on** vt insep [adjoin] avoisiner, être contigu à.

neighbourhood 🇬🇧**, neighborhood** 🇺🇸 ['neɪbəhʊd] ◆ n **1.** [district] voisinage *m*, quartier *m* / *in the neighbourhood of the station* près de la gare **2.** *fig* : *it'll cost you in the neighbourhood of $1,000* cela vous coûtera dans les or environ 1 000 dollars. ◆ comp [police, shop, school] du quartier.

Neighbourhood Watch n système par lequel les habitants d'un quartier s'entraident pour en assurer la surveillance et la sécurité.

neighbouring 🇬🇧**, neighboring** 🇺🇸 ['neɪbərɪŋ] adj avoisinant, voisin.

neighbourly 🇬🇧**, neighborly** 🇺🇸 ['neɪbəlɪ] adj [person] amical ; [relations, visit] de bon voisinage / *to be neighbourly* être bon voisin, entretenir de bonnes relations avec ses voisins.

neither [🇬🇧 'naɪðər 🇺🇸 'niːðər] ◆ pron : *neither of us* aucun de nous (deux) / *which do you prefer? — neither!* lequel des deux préfères-tu ? — ni l'un ni l'autre ! ◆ conj ▶ **neither... nor...** ni... ni... / *I like neither tea nor coffee* je n'aime ni le thé ni le café ▶ *that's neither here nor there* a) [unimportant] c'est sans importance b) [irrelevant] là n'est pas la question ▶ *I neither know nor care* c'est vraiment le cadet de mes soucis. ◆ adv non plus / *neither did / do / were we* (et) nous non plus. ◆ det aucun (des deux), ni l'un ni l'autre / *neither one of them has accepted* ni l'un ni l'autre n'a accepté.

neo- ['niːəʊ] pref néo-.

neoclassical [,niːəʊ'klæsɪkl] adj néoclassique.

neoclassicism [,niːəʊ'klæsɪsɪzm] n néoclassicisme *m*.

neo-con ◆ n néoconservateur *m*, -trice *f*. ◆ adj néoconservateur.

neofascism [,niːəʊ'fæʃɪzm] n néofascisme *m*.

neofascist [,niːəʊ'fæʃɪst] ◆ adj néofasciste. ◆ n néofasciste *mf*.

neo-liberal ◆ n néolibéral *m*, -e *f*. ◆ adj néolibéral.

neolithic, Neolithic [,niːə'lɪθɪk] ◆ adj néolithique. ◆ n néolithique *m*.

neologism [niː'ɒlədʒɪzm] n néologisme *m*.

neon ['niːɒn] ◆ n néon *m*. ◆ comp [lamp] au néon ▶ **neon lights** néons *mpl*.

neonatal [,niːəʊ'neɪtl] adj néonatal.

neo-Nazi [,niːəʊ'nɑːtsɪ] ◆ n néonazi *m*, -e *f*. ◆ adj néonazi.

neorealist [niə'rɪəlɪst] adj néoréaliste.

Nepal [nɪ'pɔːl] pr n Népal *m* / *in Nepal* au Népal.

Nepalese [,nepə'liːz] *(pl* **Nepalese)** ◆ n Népalais *m*, -e *f*. ◆ adj népalais.

Nepali [nɪ'pɔːlɪ] *(pl* **Nepali** or **Nepalis)** ◆ n [person] Népalais *m*, -e *f*. ◆ adj népalais.

nephew ['nefjuː] n neveu *m*.

nepotism ['nepətɪzm] n népotisme *m*.

Neptune ['neptjuːn] pr n ASTRON & MYTH Neptune.

nerd [nɜːd] n *inf* [stupid] crétin *m* ▶ **computer nerd** accro *m* d'informatique ; [studious] binoclard *m*.

nerdy ['nɜːdɪ] adj *inf & pej* [unfashionable] ringard ; [foolish] débile.

nerve [nɜːv] n **1.** ANAT nerf *m* **2.** [courage] courage *m* ; [boldness] audace *f* ; [self-control] assurance *f*, sangfroid *m* / *he didn't have the nerve to say no* il n'a pas osé dire non, il n'a pas eu le courage de dire non **3.** [cheek, audacity] culot *m* / *he had the nerve to refuse* il a eu le culot de refuser / *you've got a nerve coming here!* *inf* tu es gonflé de venir ici ! **4.** [vein - in leaf, marble] veine *f*, nervure *f*. ❖ **nerves** *pl* n **1.** [agitated state] nerfs *mpl* ; [anxiety] nervosité *f* ; [before concert, exam, interview] trac *m* ▶ **to have a fit of nerves** avoir le trac / *I'm a bundle of nerves* je suis un paquet de nerfs **2.** [self-control] nerfs *mpl* ▶ **to have strong nerves / nerves of steel** avoir les nerfs solides / des nerfs d'acier ▶ **to get on sb's nerves** *inf*: *he gets on my nerves* il me tape sur les nerfs or sur le système.

nerve cell n cellule *f* nerveuse.

nerve centre n **1.** ANAT centre *m* nerveux **2.** *fig* [headquarters] quartier *m* général, poste *m* de commandement.

nerve ending n terminaison *f* nerveuse.

nerve gas n gaz *m* neurotoxique.

nerve-racking, nerve-wracking [-,rækɪŋ] adj *inf* angoissant, stressant.

nervous ['nɜːvəs] adj **1.** [anxious, worried] anxieux, appréhensif ; [shy] timide, intimidé ; [uneasy] mal à l'aise ; [agitated] agité, tendu ; [tense] tendu / *he is nervous of Alsatians* les bergers allemands lui font peur / *I'm nervous about speaking in public* j'ai peur or j'appréhende de parler en public / *he's a nervous wreck* *inf* il est à bout de nerfs, il est à cran **2.** ANAT [strain, illness] nerveux ▶ **the nervous system** le système nerveux ▶ **nervous exhaustion a)** fatigue nerveuse **b)** [serious] surmenage *m*.

nervous breakdown n dépression *f* nerveuse ▶ **to have a nervous breakdown** avoir or faire une dépression nerveuse.

nervously ['nɜːvəslɪ] adv [anxiously] anxieusement, avec inquiétude ; [tensely] nerveusement.

nervy ['nɜːvɪ] (*compar* **nervier**, *superl* **nerviest**) adj *inf* **1.** 🇬🇧 [tense] énervé, excité **2.** 🇺🇸 [cheeky] culotté.

nest [nest] ❖ n [for birds, wasps, snakes, etc.] nid *m* ; [occupants - esp birds] nichée *f*. ❖ vi [bird] (se) nicher, faire son nid.

nested ['nestɪd] adj COMPUT & TYPO imbriqué.

nest egg n économies *fpl*, bas *m* de laine, pécule *m*.

nestle ['nesl] vi **1.** [against person] se blottir ; [in comfortable place] se pelotonner **2.** [land, house] être niché or blotti.

net [net] (*pt & pp* **netted**, *cont* **netting**) ❖ n **1.** [gen, for fishing, butterflies, etc.] filet *m* ; [fig] [trap] filet *m*, piège *m* **2.** SPORT filet *m*. ❖ vt **1.** [catch - fish, butterfly] prendre or attraper (au filet) ; [- terrorist, criminal] arrêter **2.** [acquire - prize] ramasser, gagner ; [- fortune] amasser **3.** [income, salary] toucher or gagner net ; [profit] rapporter net. ❖ adj **1.** [income, price, weight] net **2.** [result] final.

Net ❖ n ▶ **the Net** le Net, l'Internet *m*. ❖ comp ▶ **Net surfer** or **user** internaute *mf*.

netball ['netbɔːl] n net-ball *m* (*sport féminin proche du basket-ball*).

net curtain n rideau *m* (de tulle or en filet), voilage *m*.

nethead ['nethed] n *inf* fada *mf* or accro *mf* d'Internet.

Netherlands ['neðələndz] pl pr n ▶ **the Netherlands** les Pays-Bas *m* / *in the Netherlands* aux Pays-Bas.

netiquette ['netɪket] n COMPUT nétiquette *f*.

netizen ['netɪzən] n COMPUT cybercitoyen *m*, -enne *f*.

net receipts n recettes *fpl* nettes.

netspeak ['netspiːk] n COMPUT langage *m* du Net, cyberjargon *m*.

nett [net] = **net** *(noun)*.

netting ['netɪŋ] n (U) [for strawberries, trees] filet *m*, filets *mpl* ; [fencing] treillis *m* (métallique), grillage *m*.

nettle ['netl] ❖ n ortie *f*. ❖ vt 🇬🇧 agacer, énerver.

network ['netwɜːk] ❖ n **1.** [gen & ELEC] & RAIL réseau *m* ; [of shops, hotels] réseau *m*, chaîne *f* ; [of streets] lacis *m* ▶ **road network** réseau routier **2.** TV [national] réseau *m* ; [channel] chaîne *f* **3.** COMPUT réseau *m*. ❖ vt TV diffuser sur l'ensemble du réseau or sur tout le territoire ; COMPUT mettre en réseau. ❖ vi [make contacts] établir un réseau de contacts professionnels, réseauter.

network computer n ordinateur *m* réseau.

networking ['netwɜːkɪŋ] n **1.** [of computers] mise *f* en réseau **2.** [gen & COMM] établissement *m* d'un réseau de liens or de contacts **3.** [via social, networking site] networking *m*, réseautage *m*.

network software n COMPUT logiciel *m* de réseau.

network TV n réseau *m* (de télévision) national.

neural ['njʊərəl] adj neural.

neuralgia [njʊəˈrældʒə] n (U) névralgie *f*.

neurological [,njʊərəˈlɒdʒɪkl] adj neurologique.

neurologist [,njʊəˈrɒlədʒɪst] n neurologue *mf*.

neuron ['njʊərɒn], **neurone** ['njʊərəʊn] n neurone *m*.

neuroscientist [,njʊərəʊˈsaɪəntɪst] n spécialiste *mf* en neurosciences.

neurosis [,njʊəˈrəʊsɪs] (*pl* **neuroses** [-siːz]) n névrose *f*.

neurosurgeon ['njʊərəʊ,sɜːdʒən] n neurochirurgien *m*, -enne *f*.

neurosurgery [,njʊərəʊˈsɜːdʒərɪ] n neurochirurgie *f*.

neurotic [,njʊəˈrɒtɪk] ❖ n névrosé *m*, -e *f*. ❖ adj [person] névrosé ; [disease] névrotique.

neurotoxic [,njʊərəʊˈtɒksɪk] adj neurotoxique.

neuter ['njuːtər] ❖ adj neutre. ❖ n GRAM neutre *m*. ❖ vt châtrer.

neutral ['njuːtrəl] ❖ adj neutre ; [policy] de neutralité. ❖ n **1.** AUTO point *m* mort / *in neutral* au point mort **2.** POL [person] habitant *m*, -e *f* d'un pays neutre ; [state] pays *m* neutre.

neutrality [njuːˈtrælətɪ] n neutralité *f*.

neutralize, neutralise ['njuːtrəlaɪz] vt neutraliser.

neutron ['njuːtrɒn] n neutron *m*.

neutron bomb n bombe *f* à neutrons.

Nevada [nɪˈvɑːdə] pr n Nevada *m* / *in Nevada* dans le Nevada.

never ['nevər] ❖ adv **1.** [not ever] jamais / *I never saw her again* je ne l'ai plus jamais revue / *you never know* on ne sait jamais ▶ **never before a)** [until that moment] jamais auparavant or avant or jusque-là **b)** [until now] jamais jusqu'ici or jusqu'à présent / *I'll never ever speak to him again* plus jamais de ma vie je ne lui adresserai la parole / *never again!* plus jamais ça ! **2.** [used instead of 'did not'] : *she never turned up* elle n'est pas venue ▶ **that will never do! a)** [it is unacceptable] c'est inadmissible ! **b)** [it is insufficient] ça ne va pas ! **3.** ▶ **well I never (did)!** çà alors !, par exemple ! ❖ interj ▶ **never!** (ce n'est) pas possible !

never-ending adj interminable, qui n'en finit pas.

nevermind ['nevəmaɪnd] n 🇺🇸 ▶ **it makes no nevermind a)** [to me] ça m'est égal **b)** [in general] ça n'a pas d'importance.

never-never *inf* ❖ n 🇬🇧 ▶ **to buy sthg on the never-never** acheter qqch à crédit or à tempérament. ❖ adj imaginaire, chimérique ▶ **never-never land** pays *m* de cocagne.

nevertheless [,nevəðəˈles] adv néanmoins ; [at start of clause or sentence] cependant.

new [njuː] (*compar* **newer**, *superl* **newest**) ❖ adj **1.** [gen] nouveau (*before vowel or silent 'h'* **nouvel**, *f* **nouvelle**) ; [different] nouveau (nouvelle), autre ; [unused] neuf, nouveau (*before vowel or silent 'h'* **nouvel**, *f* **nouvelle**) (nouvelle) / *he's wearing his new suit for the first time* il porte son nouveau costume or son costume neuf pour la première fois / *there are new people in the flat next door* il y a de nouveaux occupants dans l'appartement d'à côté ▸ **as good as new (again) a)** [clothing, carpet] (à nouveau) comme neuf **b)** [watch, electrical appliance] (à nouveau) en parfait état de marche ▸ **to feel like a new woman / man** se sentir revivre **2.** [latest, recent - issue, recording, baby] nouveau *(before vowel or silent 'h'* **nouvel**, *f* **nouvelle**) / *is there anything new on the catastrophe?* est-ce qu'il y a du nouveau sur la catastrophe ? ; [modern] nouveau *(before vowel or silent 'h'* **nouvel**, *f* **nouvelle**), moderne ▸ **what's new?** quoi de neuf ? **3.** [unfamiliar - experience, environment] nouveau *(before vowel or silent 'h'* **nouvel**, *f* **nouvelle**) ▸ **to be new to sb** : *everything's still very new to me here* tout est encore tout nouveau pour moi ici ▸ **that's a new one on me!** **a)** *inf* [joke] celle-là, on ne me l'avait jamais faite ! **b)** [news] première nouvelle ! **c)** [experience] on en apprend tous les jours ! **4.** [recently arrived] nouveau *(before vowel or silent 'h'* **nouvel**, *f* **nouvelle**) ; [novice] novice / *you're new here, aren't you?* vous êtes nouveau ici, n'est-ce pas ? / *she's new to the job* elle débute dans le métier / *we're new to this area* nous venons d'arriver dans la région **5.** CULIN [wine] nouveau *(before vowel or silent 'h'* **nouvel**, *f* **nouvelle**) ; [potatoes, carrots] nouveau *(before vowel or silent 'h'* **nouvel**, *f* **nouvelle**). ◆ *n* nouveau *m*.

New Age ◆ *n* New Age *m*. ◆ adj New Age *(inv)* ▸ **New Age traveller** nomade *mf* New Age.

NEway MESSAGING **written abbr of** anyway.

newbie ['njuːbɪ] *n* inf **1.** néophyte *mf* **2.** COMPUT internaute *mf* novice, cybernovice *mf*.

new blood *n* inf sang *m* neuf.

newborn ['njuːbɔːn] ◆ adj nouveau-né. ◆ *pl n* ▸ **the newborn** les nouveau-nés *mpl*.

New Brunswick pr n Nouveau-Brunswick *m* / *in New Brunswick* dans le Nouveau-Brunswick.

new-build adj neuf ▸ **new-build flats** des programmes de logements neufs.

New Caledonia pr n Nouvelle-Calédonie *f* / *in New Caledonia* en Nouvelle-Calédonie.

New Caledonian ◆ *n* Néo-Calédonien *m*, -enne *f*. ◆ adj néo-calédonien.

newcomer ['njuːˌkʌmər] *n* **1.** [new arrival] nouveau venu *m*, nouvelle venue *f* **2.** [beginner] novice *mf*.

New Deal pr n ▸ **the New Deal** le New Deal *(programme de réformes sociales mises en place aux États-Unis par le président Roosevelt au lendemain de la grande dépression des années 1930).*

New Delhi pr n New Delhi.

New England pr n Nouvelle-Angleterre *f* / *in New England* en Nouvelle-Angleterre.

newfangled [ˌnjuːˈfæŋgld] adj *pej* [idea, device] nouveau *(before vowel or silent 'h'* **nouvel**, *f* **nouvelle**), dernier cri *(inv)*.

new-found adj nouveau *(before vowel or silent 'h'* **nouvel**, *f* **nouvelle**), récent.

Newfoundland ['njuːfəndlənd] pr n **1.** GEOG Terre-Neuve / *in Newfoundland* à Terre-Neuve **2.** [dog] terre-neuve *m inv*.

New Guinea pr n Nouvelle-Guinée *f* / *in New Guinea* en Nouvelle-Guinée.

New Hampshire [-ˈhæmpʃər] pr n New Hampshire *m* / *in New Hampshire* dans le New Hampshire.

New Hebrides *pl pr n* Nouvelles-Hébrides *fpl* / *in the New Hebrides* aux Nouvelles-Hébrides.

New Jersey pr n New Jersey *m* / *in New Jersey* dans le New Jersey.

New Labour pr n [in UK] New Labour *m*.

new-look adj new-look *(inv)*.

newly ['njuːlɪ] adv nouvellement, récemment.

newlyweds ['njuːlɪwedz] *pl n* jeunes mariés *mpl*.

new media *pl n* ▸ **the new media** les nouveaux médias.

New Mexico pr n Nouveau-Mexique *m* / *in New Mexico* au Nouveau-Mexique.

new moon *n* nouvelle lune *f*.

New Orleans [-ˈɔːlɪənz] pr n La Nouvelle-Orléans.

New Quebec pr n Nouveau-Québec *m* / *in New Quebec* au Nouveau-Québec.

news [njuːz] ◆ *n (U)* **1.** [information] nouvelles *fpl*, informations *fpl* / *a piece of news* une nouvelle, une information / *is there any more news about* or *on the explosion?* est-ce qu'on a plus d'informations sur l'explosion ? / *that's good / bad news* c'est une bonne / mauvaise nouvelle / *have you had any news of her?* avez-vous eu de ses nouvelles ? / *what's your news?* quoi de neuf (chez vous) ? ▸ **have I got news for you!** j'ai du nouveau (à vous annoncer) ! ▸ **it's news to me!** première nouvelle !, je l'ignorais ! ▸ **to break the news (of sthg) to sb** annoncer la nouvelle (de qqch) à qqn / *he's bad news* inf on a toujours des ennuis avec lui **2.** RADIO & TV actualités *fpl*, informations *fpl* ; [bulletin] chronique *f*, journal *m*, page *f* / *I heard it on the news* je l'ai entendu aux informations / *the sports / financial news* la page sportive / financière. ◆ comp ▸ **news desk** (salle *f* de) rédaction *f* ▸ **news editor** rédacteur *m*, -trice *f* ▸ **news item** information *f*.

news agency *n* agence *f* de presse.

newsagent 🇬🇧 ['njuːzˌeɪdʒənt], **newsdealer** 🇺🇸 ['njuːzdiːlər] *n* marchand *m*, -e *f* de journaux.

news bulletin *n* bulletin *m* d'informations.

newscast ['njuːzkɑːst] *n* bulletin *m* d'informations ; TV journal *m* télévisé, informations *fpl*.

newscaster ['njuːzkɑːstər] *n* présentateur *m*, -trice *f* du journal.

news conference *n* conférence *f* de presse.

newsdealer ['njuːzdiːlər] 🇺🇸 = newsagent.

newsfeed ['njuːzfiːd] *n* INTERNET newsfeed *m*.

newsflash ['njuːzflæʃ] *n* flash *m* d'informations.

newsgroup ['njuːzgruːp] *n* COMPUT forum *m* de discussion.

news headlines *pl n* titres *mpl* de l'actualité.

newshound ['njuːzhaʊnd] *n* inf reporter *m*, journaliste *mf*.

newsletter ['njuːzˌletər] *n* lettre *f*, bulletin *m*.

newsman ['njuːzmən] *(pl* **newsmen** [-mən]) *n* journaliste *m*.

New South Wales pr n Nouvelle-Galles du Sud *f* / *in New South Wales* en Nouvelle-Galles du Sud.

newspaper ['njuːzˌpeɪpər] ◆ *n* **1.** [publication] journal *m* / *in the newspaper* dans le journal **2.** [paper] : *wrapped in newspaper* enveloppé dans du papier journal. ◆ comp [article, report] de journal ▸ **newspaper reporter** reporter *m* (de la presse écrite).

newspaperman ['njuːzˌpeɪpəmæn] *(pl* **newspapermen** [-men]) *n* journaliste *m* (de la presse écrite).

newspaperwoman ['njuːzˌpeɪpəˌwʊmən] *(pl* **newspaperwomen** [-ˌwɪmɪn]) *n* journaliste *f* (de la presse écrite).

newsprint ['njuːzprɪnt] *n* papier *m* journal.

newsreader ['njuːzˌriːdər] = newscaster.

newsreel ['njuːzriːl] *n* film *m* d'actualités.

news report *n* bulletin *m* d'informations.

newsroom ['nju:zru:m] n **1.** PRESS salle f de rédaction **2.** RADIO & TV studio m.

news service n US agence de presse qui publie ses informations par le biais d'un syndicat de distribution.

newssheet ['nju:zʃi:t] = newsletter.

newsstand ['nju:zstænd] n kiosque m (à journaux).

newswoman ['nju:z,wumən] (pl **newswomen** [-,wɪmɪn]) n journaliste f.

newsworthy ['nju:z,wɜ:ðɪ] adj : *it's not newsworthy* cela n'a aucun intérêt médiatique.

newt [nju:t] n ZOOL triton m.

new technology n nouvelle technologie f, technologie f de pointe.

New Testament pr n Nouveau Testament m.

new town n UK ville f nouvelle.

new wave n [in cinema] nouvelle vague f; [in pop music] new wave f. ◈ **new-wave** adj [cinema] nouvelle vague (inv); [pop music] new-wave (inv).

New World pr n ▶ **the New World** le Nouveau Monde.

New Year n Nouvel An m ▶ **happy New Year!** bonne année !

New Year's Day n jour m de l'an.

New Year's Eve n Saint-Sylvestre f.

New York pr n **1.** [city] ▶ **New York (City)** New York ▶ **the New York subway** le métro new-yorkais ▶ **the New York Times** quotidien américain de qualité **2.** [state] ▶ **New York (State)** l'État m de New York / *in (the State of) New York* or *in New York (State)* dans l'État de New York.

New Yorker [-'jɔ:kə*r*] n New-Yorkais m, -e f ▶ **the New Yorker** US PRESS hebdomadaire culturel et littéraire new-yorkais.

New Zealand [-'zi:lənd] pr n Nouvelle-Zélande f / *in New Zealand* en Nouvelle-Zélande / *New Zealand butter* beurre néo-zélandais.

New Zealander [-'zi:ləndə*r*] n Néo-Zélandais m, -e f.

next [nekst] ◈ adj **1.** [in time - coming] prochain ; [- already past] suivant / *keep quiet about it for the next few days* n'en parlez pas pendant les quelques jours qui viennent / *I had to stay in bed for the next ten days* j'ai dû garder le lit pendant les dix jours qui ont suivi / *(the) next day* le lendemain / *(the) next morning / evening* le lendemain matin / soir / *next Sunday* or *Sunday next* dimanche prochain / *the next Sunday* le dimanche suivant ▶ **next time** : *(the) next time I see him* la prochaine fois que je le vois or verrai / *(the) next time I saw him* quand je l'ai revu **2.** [in series - in future] prochain ; [- in past] suivant / *translate the next sentence* traduisez la phrase suivante / *the next 10 pages* les 10 pages suivantes / *the next before last* l'avant-dernier ; [in space - house, street] prochain, suivant / *take the next street on the left* prenez la prochaine à gauche / *after the kitchen, it's the next room on your right* après la cuisine, c'est la première pièce à votre droite ; [in queue, line] : *I'm next* c'est (à) mon tour, c'est à moi / *who's next?* à qui le tour ? / *I'm next after you* je suis (juste) après vous ▶ **(the) next thing** ensuite / *and (the) next thing I knew, I woke up in hospital* et l'instant d'après je me suis réveillé à l'hôpital. ◈ adv **1.** [afterwards] ensuite, après / *what did you do with it next?* et ensuite, qu'en avez-vous fait ? / *next on the agenda* is the question of finance la question suivante à l'ordre du jour est celle des finances / *what* or *whatever next?* [indignantly or in mock indignation] et puis quoi encore ? **2.** [next time - in future] la prochaine fois ; [- in past] la fois suivante or d'après / *when we next met* quand nous nous sommes revus **3.** [with superlative adj] : *the next youngest / oldest child* l'enfant le plus jeune / le plus âgé ensuite / *the next* **largest size** la taille juste au-dessus. ◈ n [next train, person, child] prochain m, -e f / *next please!* au suivant, s'il vous plaît ! ▶ **next of kin** plus proche parent m. ◈ prep US = next to. ◈ **next to** prep **1.** [near] à côté de / *come and sit next to me* venez vous asseoir à côté de or près de moi / *I love the feel of silk next to my skin* j'adore le contact de la soie sur ma peau ; [in series] : *next to last* avant-dernier **2.** [in comparisons] après **3.** [almost] presque / *next to impossible* presque or quasiment impossible / *I bought it for next to nothing* je l'ai acheté pour trois fois rien or presque rien.

next door ◈ adv : *they live next door to us* ils habitent à côté de chez nous, ce sont nos voisins / *the girl / boy next door* la fille / le garçon d'à côté. ◈ n la maison d'à côté. ◈ **next-door** adj ▶ **next-door neighbour** a) [in private house] voisin m, -e f (de la maison d'à côté) b) [in apartment building] voisin m, -e f de palier.

next-of-kin n [relative] parent m le plus proche ; [family] famille f / *to inform the next-of-kin* prévenir la famille.

NF ◈ pr n abbr of National Front. ◈ written abbr of Newfoundland.

NFL (abbr of National Football League) pr n fédération nationale de football américain.

NFU (abbr of National Farmers' Union) pr n syndicat britannique d'exploitants agricoles.

NG pr n US abbr of National Guard.

NGO (abbr of non-governmental organization) n ONG f.

NH written abbr of New Hampshire.

NHL (abbr of National Hockey League) pr n fédération nationale américaine de hockey sur glace.

NHS (abbr of National Health Service) pr n UK Sécurité sociale.

NI ◈ n UK abbr of national insurance. ◈ written abbr of Northern Ireland.

Niagara [naɪ'ægərə] pr n ▶ **Niagara Falls** les chutes fpl du Niagara.

nib [nɪb] n [of fountain pen] plume f; [of ballpoint, tool] pointe f.

nibble ['nɪbl] ◈ vt **1.** [subj: person, caterpillar] grignoter ; [subj: rodent] grignoter, ronger ; [subj: goat, sheep] brouter **2.** [playfully - ear] mordiller. ◈ vi **1.** [eat] ▶ **to nibble at** or **on sthg** grignoter qqch **2.** [bite] ▶ **to nibble at sthg** mordiller qqch **3.** fig [show interest] ▶ **to nibble at an offer** être tenté par une offre. ◈ n **1.** FISHING touche f **2.** [snack] ▶ **to have a nibble** grignoter quelque chose ▶ **nibbles** amuse-gueule(s) mpl.

Nicaragua [,nɪkə'rægjuə] pr n Nicaragua m / *in Nicaragua* au Nicaragua.

Nicaraguan [,nɪkə'rægjuən] ◈ n Nicaraguayen m, -enne f. ◈ adj nicaraguayen.

nice [naɪs] ◈ adj **1.** [expressing approval - good] bien, chouette ; [- attractive] beau (before vowel or silent 'h' bel, f belle) ; [- pretty] joli ; [- car, picture] beau (before vowel or silent 'h' bel, f belle) ; [- food] bon ; [- idea] bon ; [- weather] beau (before vowel or silent 'h' bel, f belle) / *they have a nice house* ils ont une belle maison / *very nice* a) [visually] très joli b) [food] très bon / *to smell nice* sentir bon / *she was wearing a very nice hat* elle portait un très joli chapeau / *she always looks nice* elle est toujours bien habillée or mise / *we had a nice meal* on a bien mangé ; [pleasant - gen] agréable, bien ; [- person] bien, sympathique / *she's very nice* elle est très sympa / *have a nice time* amusez-vous bien / *it's nice to be back again* cela fait plaisir d'être de retour / *(it was) nice meeting you* (j'ai été) ravi de faire votre connaissance **2.** [kind] gentil, aimable ▶ **to be nice to sb**

être gentil avec qqn / *that's nice of her* c'est gentil or aimable de sa part / *it's nice of you to say so* vous êtes bien aimable de le dire / *he was nice enough to carry my case* il a eu la gentillesse or l'obligeance de porter ma valise **3.** [respectable] bien (élevé), convenable **4.** [ironic use] : *he made a nice mess of the job* il a fait un travail de cochon / *we're in a nice mess* nous sommes dans de beaux draps or un beau pétrin **5.** [subtle -distinction, point] subtil, délicat. ◆ adv [as intensifier] : *a nice cold drink* une boisson bien fraîche / *to have a nice long nap* faire une bonne sieste ; [with 'and'] : *take it nice and easy* allez-y doucement / *it's nice and warm in here* il fait bon ici.

nice-looking adj joli, beau (*before vowel or silent 'h'* **bel**, *f* **belle**).

nicely ['naɪslɪ] adv **1.** [well] bien ; [pleasantly] gentiment, agréablement **2.** [politely -behave, eat] bien, comme il faut **3.** [exactly] exactement, avec précision ; [subtly] avec précision.

nicety ['naɪsətɪ] (*pl* **niceties**) n **1.** [precision] justesse *f*, précision *f* **2.** (*usu pl*) [subtlety] subtilité *f*, finesse *f*.

niche [niːʃ] n **1.** [recess -in church, cliff] niche *f* **2.** COMM créneau *m*.

nick [nɪk] ◆ n **1.** [notch] encoche *f* ; [chip -in crockery] ébréchure *f* ; [cut -on skin] (petite) coupure *f* **2.** UK v inf [police station] poste *m* (de police) ; [prison] taule *f* **3.** UK inf [condition] état *m* **4.** PHR **in the nick of time** à point nommé. ◆ vt **1.** [cut -deliberately] faire une entaille or une encoche sur ; [accidentally -crockery] ébrécher ; [-metal, paint] faire des entailles dans ; [-skin, face] entailler, couper (légèrement) **2.** UK v inf [arrest] épingler **3.** UK inf [steal] faucher, chiper.

nickel ['nɪkl] (UK *pt & pp* **nickelled**, *cont* **nickelling** ; US *pt & pp* **nickeled**, *cont* **nickeling**) ◆ n **1.** [metal] nickel *m* **2.** US [coin] pièce *f* de 5 cents. ◆ vt nickeler.

nickname ['nɪkneɪm] ◆ n [gen] surnom *m*, sobriquet *m* ; [short form] diminutif *m*. ◆ vt surnommer.

nicotine ['nɪkətiːn] n nicotine *f* ▶ **nicotine addiction** tabagisme *m*.

nicotine patch n patch *m* or timbre *m* antitabac.

niece [niːs] n nièce *f*.

nifty ['nɪftɪ] (*compar* **niftier**, *superl* **niftiest**) adj inf **1.** [stylish] chouette, classe (*inv*) **2.** [clever -solution] génial **3.** [quick] rapide ; [agile] agile.

Niger pr n **1.** [niː'ʒeə'] [country] Niger *m* / *in Niger* au Niger **2.** ['naɪdʒə'] [river] ▶ **the (River) Niger** le Niger.

Nigeria [naɪ'dʒɪərɪə] pr n Nigeria *m* / *in Nigeria* au Nigeria.

Nigerian [naɪ'dʒɪərɪən] ◆ n Nigérian *m*, -e *f*. ◆ adj nigérian.

Nigerien [niː'ʒeərɪən] ◆ n Nigérien *m*, -enne *f*. ◆ adj nigérien.

niggardly ['nɪgədlɪ] adj [person] avare, pingre, ladre ; [quantity] parcimonieux, chiche.

niggle ['nɪgl] ◆ vi **1.** [fuss over details] ergoter ▶ **to niggle over** or **about sthg** ergoter sur qqch **2.** [nag] trouver à redire. ◆ vt **1.** [worry -subj: conscience] harceler, travailler **2.** [nag] harceler. ◆ n **1.** [small criticism] objection *f* mineure **2.** [small worry, doubt] léger doute *m*. ◆ **niggle at** vt insep : *it's been niggling at me all day* ça me travaille depuis ce matin.

niggling ['nɪglɪŋ] ◆ adj **1.** [petty -person] tatillon ; [-details] insignifiant **2.** [fastidious -job] fastidieux **3.** [nagging -pain, doubt] tenace. ◆ n chicanerie *f*, pinaillage *m*.

nigh [naɪ] liter ◆ adv : *well nigh 80 years* près de 80 ans / *well nigh impossible* presque impossible. ◆ adj proche. ◆ **nigh on** adv phr presque.

night [naɪt] ◆ n [late] nuit *f* ; [evening] soir *m*, soirée *f* ▶ *at night* a) [evening] le soir b) [late] la nuit / *ten o'clock at night* dix heures du soir / *all night (long)* toute la nuit ▶ *by night* de nuit / *during* or *in the night* pendant l[a] nuit / *(on) Tuesday night* a) [evening] mardi soir b) [during night] dans la nuit de mardi à mercredi / *last night* a) [evening] hier soir b) [during night] cette nuit / *the night before* a) [evening] la veille au soir b) [late] la nuit précédente. ◆ comp [duty, flight, sky] de nuit. ◆ **nights** ad[v] de nuit.

nightcap ['naɪtkæp] n **1.** [drink -gen] boisson *f* (que l'o[n] prend avant d'aller se coucher) ; [-alcoholic] dernier verre *m* (avant d'aller se coucher) **2.** [headgear] bonnet *m* de nuit.

nightclothes ['naɪtkləʊðz] pl n [pyjamas] pyjama *m* ; [nightdress] chemise *f* de nuit.

nightclub ['naɪtklʌb] n night-club *m*, boîte *f* de nuit.

nightclubbing ['naɪtklʌbɪŋ] n ▶ **to go nightclubbing** sortir en boîte.

nightdress ['naɪtdres] n chemise *f* de nuit.

nightfall ['naɪtfɔːl] n tombée *f* de la nuit or du jour.

nightgown ['naɪtgaʊn] = nightdress.

nightie ['naɪtɪ] n inf chemise *f* de nuit.

nightingale ['naɪtɪŋgeɪl] n rossignol *m*.

nightlife ['naɪtlaɪf] n vie *f* nocturne.

nightlight ['naɪtlaɪt] n veilleuse *f*.

nightly ['naɪtlɪ] ◆ adj [happening every night] de tou[s] les soirs, de chaque nuit. ◆ adv tous les soirs, chaque soir.

nightmare ['naɪtmeə'] ◆ n lit & fig cauchemar *m*[.] ◆ comp [vision, experience] cauchemardesque, de cauche[mar].

nightmarish ['naɪtmeərɪʃ] adj cauchemardesque, d[e] cauchemar.

night owl n inf couche-tard *mf inv*.

night porter n portier *m* de nuit.

night safe n coffre *m* de nuit.

night school n cours *mpl* du soir / *in* US or *at* U[K] *night school* aux cours du soir.

night shift n [work force] équipe *f* de nuit ; [period o[f] duty] poste *m* de nuit ▶ **to be on the night shift** être d[e] nuit.

nightshirt ['naɪtʃɜːt] n chemise *f* de nuit.

nightspot ['naɪtspɒt] n inf boîte *f* (de nuit).

nightstand ['naɪtstænd] n US table *f* de nuit.

nightstick ['naɪtstɪk] n US matraque *f* (de policier).

night-time n nuit *f* / *at night-time* la nuit.

night vision n vision *f* nocturne.

night watchman n veilleur *m* de nuit.

nightwear ['naɪtweə'] n (U) = nightclothes.

nil [nɪl] ◆ n [gen & SPORT] zéro *m* ; [on written form] néant *m*. ◆ adj nul, zéro (*inv*).

Nile [naɪl] pr n ▶ **the (River) Nile** UK, **the Nile River** US le Nil.

nimble ['nɪmbl] adj **1.** [agile -body, movements] agile ; [-fingers] adroit, habile ; [skilful] habile **2.** [quick -thought, mind] vif, prompt.

nimbly ['nɪmblɪ] adv agilement, lestement, prestement.

nimby ['nɪmbɪ] (*abbr of* not in my backyard) n in[f] riverain s'opposant à tout projet de construction à proximité d[e] chez lui.

nincompoop ['nɪŋkəmpuːp] n inf cruche *f*.

nine [naɪn] ◆ det neuf (*inv*). ◆ n **1.** neuf *m inv* **2.** US SPORT équipe *f* (de base-ball). ◆ pron neuf. **See also** five.

911 1. *numéro de téléphone des urgences dans certains États* *les États-Unis* **2.** MESSAGING *signifie qu'il y a urgence ou que* *on souhaite être contacté rapidement.*

nineteen [,naın'tiːn] ◆ det dix-neuf. ◆ n dix-neuf *m*. ◆ pron dix-neuf. **See also** **five.**

nineteenth [,naın'tiːnθ] ◆ det dix-neuvième. ◆ n **1.** [ordinal] dix-neuvième *mf* **2.** [fraction] dix-neuvième *m*. **See also** **fifth.**

ninetieth ['naıntıəθ] ◆ det quatre-vingt-dixième. ◆ n **1.** [ordinal] quatre-vingt-dixième *mf* **2.** [fraction] quatre-vingt-dixième *m*. **See also** **fifth.**

nine-to-five ◆ adv de neuf heures du matin à cinq heures du soir ▶ **to work nine-to-five** avoir des horaires de bureau. ◆ adj **1.** [job] routinier **2.** [mentality, attitude] de gratte-papier.

ninety ['naıntı] *(pl* **nineties)** ◆ det quatre-vingt-dix. ◆ n quatre-vingt-dix *m*. ◆ pron quatre-vingt-dix. **See also** **fifty.**

ninny ['nını] *(pl* **ninnies)** n *inf* empoté *m*, -e *f*, nigaud *m*, -e *f*, bêta *m*, -asse *f*.

ninth [naınθ] ◆ adj neuvième. ◆ n **1.** [ordinal] neuvième *mf* **2.** [fraction] neuvième *m*. ◆ adv [in contest] en neuvième position, à la neuvième place. **See also** **fifth.**

ninth grade n US SCH *classe de l'enseignement secondaire correspondant à la troisième (13-14 ans).*

nip [nıp] *(pt & pp* **nipped,** *cont* **nipping)** ◆ n **1.** [pinch] pincement *m* ; [bite] morsure *f* **2.** [cold] froid *m* piquant. ◆ vt **1.** [pinch] pincer ; [bite] mordre (légèrement), mordiller **2.** US *inf* [steal] piquer, faucher. ◆ vi **1.** [try to bite] : *the dog nipped at my ankles* le chien m'a mordillé les chevilles **2.** UK *inf* [go] faire un saut ▶ *to nip (across or along or over) to the butcher's* faire un saut chez le boucher / *she nipped in to say hello* elle est passée en vitesse dire bonjour. ◆ **nip off** ◆ vt sep [cut off] couper ; HORT pincer. ◆ vi US *inf* filer.

nipple ['nıpl] n **1.** [on breast] mamelon *m* ; [on animal] tétine *f*, mamelle *f* **2.** [teat - on feeding bottle] tétine *f* **3.** US [baby's dummy] tétine *f*.

nippy ['nıpı] *(compar* **nippier,** *superl* **nippiest)** adj **1.** [weather] frisquet ; [cold] piquant **2.** US *inf* [quick] vif, rapide.

nit [nıt] n **1.** ENTOM lente *f* ; [in hair] pou *m* **2.** UK *inf* [idiot] andouille *f*.

NITING MESSAGING written abbr of **anything.**

nitpick ['nıtpık] vi *inf* couper les cheveux en quatre, chercher la petite bête, pinailler.

nitpicker ['nıt,pıkər] n *inf* chipoteur *m*, -euse *f*.

nitpicking ['nıtpıkıŋ] *inf* ◆ n chicane *f*, pinaillage *m*. ◆ adj chicanier.

nitrate ['naıtreıt] n nitrate *m*, azotate *m*.

nitrogen ['naıtrədʒən] n azote *m*.

nitty-gritty [,nıtı'grıtı] n *inf* essentiel *m*.

nitwit ['nıtwıt] n *inf* andouille *f*.

nix [nıks] US *inf* ◆ interj [no] non. ◆ n rien *m*. ◆ vt [refuse] rejeter, refuser ; [veto] opposer un veto à.

NJ written abbr of **New Jersey.**

NJoy MESSAGING written abbr of **enjoy.**

NLF (abbr of **National Liberation Front**) pr n FLN *m*.

NLQ (abbr of **near letter quality**) n qualité quasi-courrier.

NLRB (abbr of **National Labor Relations Board**) pr n *commission américaine d'arbitrage en matière d'emploi.*

NM written abbr of **New Mexico.**

no [nəʊ] *(pl* **noes** or **nos)** ◆ adv **1.** [expressing refusal, disagreement] non / *do you like spinach? — no, I*

don't aimez-vous les épinards ? — non **2.** [with comparative adj or adv] : *I can go no further* je ne peux pas aller plus loin / *you're no better than he is* vous ne valez pas mieux que lui / *call me, if you're (feeling) no better in the morning* appelez-moi si vous ne vous sentez pas mieux demain matin / *this car is no more expensive than the other one* cette voiture ne coûte pas plus cher que l'autre. ◆ det **1.** [not any, not one] : *I have no family* je n'ai pas de famille / *she has no intention of leaving* elle n'a aucune intention de partir / *there are no letters for you today* il n'y a pas de courrier or aucune lettre pour toi aujourd'hui / *no sensible person would dispute this* quelqu'un de raisonnable ne discuterait pas / *it's of no importance / interest* ça n'a aucune importance / aucun intérêt / *there's no telling* nul ne peut le dire **2.** [not a] : *I'm no expert, I'm afraid* malheureusement, je ne suis pas un expert / *she's no friend of mine* ce n'est pas une amie à moi / *it will be no easy task* persuading them ce ne sera pas une tâche facile que de les persuader **3.** [introducing a prohibition] / **'no smoking'** 'défense de fumer' / **'no swimming'** 'baignade interdite'. ◆ n non *m* inv / *the noes have it* les non l'emportent. ◆ interj non.

No., no. (written abbr of **number**) No, no.

Noah ['nəʊə] pr n Noé ▶ **Noah's Ark** l'arche de Noé.

no-ball n SPORT balle *f* nulle.

nobble ['nɒbl] vt UK *inf* **1.** [jury, witness - bribe] graisser la patte à ; [- threaten] manipuler (avec des menaces) **2.** [racehorse] mettre hors d'état de courir ; [with drugs] droguer **3.** [grab, catch - person] accrocher (au passage), agrafer **4.** [steal] faucher, barboter, chiper.

Nobel [nəʊ'bel] comp ▶ **Nobel prize** prix *m* Nobel ▶ **Nobel prizewinner** lauréat *m*, -e *f* du prix Nobel.

nobility [nə'bılətı] *(pl* **nobilities)** n **1.** [aristocracy] noblesse *f*, aristocratie *f* **2.** [loftiness] noblesse *f*, majesté *f*, grandeur *f*.

noble ['nəʊbl] ◆ adj **1.** [aristocratic] noble **2.** [fine, distinguished - aspiration, purpose] noble, élevé ; [- bearing, manner] noble, gracieux, majestueux ; [- person] noble, supérieur ; [- animal] noble ; [- wine] grand **3.** [generous - gesture] généreux, magnanime **4.** [brave - deed, feat] noble, héroïque **5.** [impressive - monument] noble, majestueux. ◆ n noble *mf*, aristocrate *mf*.

nobleman ['nəʊblmən] *(pl* **noblemen** [-mən]) n noble *m*, aristocrate *m*.

noblewoman ['nəʊbl,wʊmən] *(pl* **noblewomen** [-,wımın]) n noble *f*, aristocrate *f*.

nobly ['nəʊblı] adv **1.** [by birth] noblement **2.** [majestically, superbly] majestueusement, superbement **3.** [generously] généreusement, magnanimement **4.** [bravely] noblement, courageusement.

nobody ['nəʊbədı] *(pl* **nobodies)** ◆ pron personne / *nobody came* personne n'est venu / *nobody else* personne d'autre / *nobody famous* personne de célèbre / *she's nobody's fool* elle n'est pas née d'hier ou tombée de la dernière pluie. ◆ n [insignificant person] moins que rien *mf*.

no-brainer [nəʊ'breınər] n US *inf* décision facile à prendre.

no-claim(s) bonus n UK [in insurance] bonus *m*.

nocturnal [nɒk'tɜːnl] adj nocturne.

nod [nɒd] *(pt & pp* **nodded,** *cont* **nodding)** ◆ vt ▶ **to nod one's head a)** [as signal] faire un signe de (la) tête **b)** [in assent] faire oui de la tête, faire un signe de tête affirmatif **c)** [in greeting] saluer d'un signe de tête **d)** [with fatigue] dodeliner de la tête / *she nodded her head in approval* or *nodded her approval* elle manifesta son approbation d'un signe de tête / *the boss nodded him into the office* le chef lui fit signe (de la tête) d'entrer dans le bureau.

◆ vi **1.** [as signal] faire un signe de (la) tête ; [in assent, approval] faire un signe de tête affirmatif, faire oui de la tête ; [in greeting] saluer d'un signe de tête / *she nodded at* or *to him through the window* elle lui fit un signe de tête de derrière la fenêtre **2.** [doze] somnoler / *he was nodding in his chair* il somnolait dans son fauteuil. ◆ n [sign] signe *m* de (la) tête ▶ **to give sb a nod a)** [as signal] faire un signe de tête à qqn **b)** [in assent] faire un signe de tête affirmatif à qqn **c)** [in greeting] saluer qqn d'un signe de tête. ❖ **nod off** vi *inf* s'endormir, s'assoupir.

nodding ['nɒdɪŋ] adj UK ▶ **to have a nodding acquaintance with sb** connaître qqn de vue or vaguement.

node [nəʊd] n ASTRON, BOT, LING & MATH nœud *m*.

no-fault adj US LAW ▶ **no-fault divorce** divorce *m* par consentement mutuel.

no-fly zone n zone *f* d'exclusion aérienne.

no-frills adj sans fioritures, (tout) simple, sommaire.

no-go area n zone *f* interdite.

no-good *inf* ◆ adj propre à rien. ◆ n bon *m* à rien, bonne *f* à rien.

no-holds-barred adj [report, documentary] sans fard.

no-hoper [-'həʊpəʳ] n *inf* raté *m*, -e *f*, minable *mf*.

noise [nɔɪz] n **1.** [sound] bruit *m*, son *m* **2.** [din] bruit *m*, tapage *m*, tintamarre *m* ; [very loud] vacarme *m* **3.** ELEC & TELEC parasites *mpl* ; [on line] friture *f*, sifflement *m* **4.** PHR ▶ **to make a noise about sthg** faire du tapage or beaucoup de bruit autour de qqch. ❖ **noises** pl n *inf* [indications of intentions] : *she made vague noises about emigrating* elle a vaguement parlé d'émigrer.

noiseless ['nɔɪzlɪs] adj silencieux.

noisily ['nɔɪzɪlɪ] adv bruyamment.

noisy ['nɔɪzɪ] (*compar* **noisier**, *superl* **noisiest**) adj **1.** [machine, engine, person] bruyant **2.** [colour] criard.

nomad ['nəʊmæd] n nomade *mf*.

nomadic [nəʊ'mædɪk] adj nomade.

no-man's-land n *lit & fig* no man's land *m inv*.

nominal ['nɒmɪnl] ◆ adj **1.** [in name only - owner, leader] de nom (seulement), nominal ; [- ownership, leadership] nominal **2.** [negligible] insignifiant ; [token] symbolique **3.** GRAM nominal. ◆ n GRAM élément *m* nominal ; [noun phrase] groupe *m* nominal ; [pronoun] nominal *m*.

nominate ['nɒmɪneɪt] vt **1.** [propose] proposer (la candidature de) ▶ **to nominate sb for a post** proposer la candidature de qqn à un poste ; [for award] sélectionner, nominer **2.** [appoint] nommer, désigner.

nomination [,nɒmɪ'neɪʃn] n **1.** [proposal] proposition *f* ; [for award] nomination *f* **2.** [appointment] nomination *f*.

nominee [,nɒmɪ'niː] n **1.** [proposed] candidat *m*, -e *f* **2.** [appointed] personne *f* désignée or nommée.

non- [nɒn] in comp **1.** [not] non- / *all non-French nationals* tous les ressortissants de nationalité autre que française **2.** [against] anti-.

nonacceptance [,nɒnək'septəns] n non-acceptation *f*.

nonaccidental [,nɒnæksɪ'dentl] adj ▶ **nonaccidental injury** [of child, woman] blessures *fpl* dues à de mauvais traitements.

nonaddictive [,nɒnə'dɪktɪv] adj qui ne crée pas de phénomène d'accoutumance.

non-adopter n MARKETING consommateur qui n'essaie jamais de nouveaux produits.

nonaffiliated [,nɒnə'fɪlɪeɪtɪd] adj non affilié, indépendant.

nonaggression [,nɒnə'greʃn] n non-agression *f*.

nonalcoholic [,nɒnælkə'hɒlɪk] adj non alcoolisé, sans alcool.

nonaligned [,nɒnə'laɪnd] adj non-aligné.

nonattendance [,nɒnə'tendəns] n absence *f*.

nonavailable [,nɒnə'veɪləbl] adj non disponible.

nonbeliever [,nɒnbɪ'liːvəʳ] n non-croyant *m*, -e *f*, in croyant *m*, -e *f*.

nonbinding [,nɒn'baɪndɪŋ] adj sans obligation, non contraignant.

nonbiodegradable ['nɒn,baɪəʊdɪ'greɪdəbl] adj non biodégradable.

nonchalant [UK 'nɒnʃələnt US ,nɒnʃə'lɑːnt] adj non chalant.

nonchalantly [UK 'nɒnʃələntlɪ US ,nɒnʃə'lɑːntlɪ] adv nonchalamment, avec nonchalance.

noncommittal [,nɒnkə'mɪtl] adj [statement] évasif, qu n'engage à rien ; [attitude, person] réservé ; [gesture] pe révélateur.

noncompetitive [,nɒnkəm'petɪtɪv] adj qui n'est pa basé sur la compétition.

noncompliance [,nɒnkəm'plaɪəns] n non-respect *m* non-observation *f* / *noncompliance with the treaty le* non-respect du traité.

nonconformist [,nɒnkən'fɔːmɪst] ◆ n [gen non-conformiste *mf*. ◆ adj [gen] non-conformiste ❖ **Nonconformist** ◆ n RELIG non-conformiste *mf* ◆ adj RELIG non-conformiste.

noncooperation ['nɒnkəʊ,ɒpə'reɪʃn] n refus *m* de coopérer.

non-dairy adj qui ne contient aucun produit laitier.

nondeductible [,nɒndɪ'dʌktəbl] adj non déductible.

nondescript [UK 'nɒndɪskrɪpt ,nɒndɪ'skrɪpt] ad quelconque.

nondrinker [,nɒn'drɪŋkəʳ] n abstinent *m*, -e *f*.

nondrip [,nɒn'drɪp] adj antigoutte *(inv)*.

nondriver [,nɒn'draɪvəʳ] n : *I'm a nondriver* a) [neve learnt] je n'ai pas mon permis b) [out of choice] je ne conduis pas.

none [nʌn] pron **1.** [with countable nouns] aucun *m*, -e *f* / *none of the photos is* or *are for sale* aucune des photos n'est à vendre / *he looked for clues but found none* il cher cha des indices mais n'en trouva aucun / *there are none left* il n'en reste plus ; [with uncountable nouns] : *none of the mail is for you* il n'y a rien pour vous au courrier / *I've done a lot of work but you've done none* j'ai beaucoup travaillé, mais toi tu n'as rien fait ▶ **none of that!** [stop it] pas de ça ! / *she would have none of it* elle ne voulait rien savoir **2.** [not one person] aucun *m*, -e *f* / *none of us understood his explanation* aucun de nous n'a compris son explication. ❖ **none other than** prep phr personne d'autre que / *he received a letter from none other than the Prime Minister himself* il reçut une lettre dont l'auteur n'était autre que le Premier ministre en personne. ❖ **none the** adv phr (with compar adj) : *I feel none the better* / *worse for it* je ne me sens pas mieux / plus mal pour autant / *she's none the worse for her adventure* son aventure ne lui a pas fait de mal. ❖ **none too** adv phr : *he's none too bright* il est loin d'être brillant / *I was none too pleased with them* j'étais loin d'être content d'eux / *and none too soon!* ce n'est pas trop tôt !

nonentity [nɒn'entətɪ] (*pl* **nonentities**) n **1.** [insignificant person] personne *f* insignifiante, nullité *f* **2.** [insignificance] inexistence *f*.

nonessential [,nɒnɪ'senʃl] ◆ adj accessoire, non essentiel. ◆ n ▶ **the nonessentials** l'accessoire *m*, le superflu.

nonetheless [,nʌnðə'les] = **nevertheless.**

non-event n non-événement *m*.

non-executive adj [director] externe.

nonexistent [ˌnɒnɪɡ'zɪstənt] adj non-existant, inexistant.

nonfat ['nɒnfæt] adj sans matière grasse or matières grasses.

nonfattening [ˌnɒn'fætnɪŋ] adj qui ne fait pas grossir.

nonfiction [ˌnɒn'fɪkʃn] ◆ n (U) ouvrages mpl non romanesques. ◆ comp ▶ **nonfiction section** [of bookshop] rayon m des ouvrages généraux.

nonflammable [ˌnɒn'flæməbl] adj ininflammable.

non-habit-forming [-ˌfɔːmɪŋ] adj qui ne crée pas de phénomène d'accoutumance.

noninfectious [ˌnɒnɪn'fekʃəs] adj qui n'est pas infectieux.

noninflammable [ˌnɒnɪn'flæməbl] = nonflammable.

noninterference [ˌnɒnɪntə'fɪərəns], **nonintervention** [ˌnɒnɪntə'venʃn] n non-intervention f, non-ingérence f.

noninterventionist [ˌnɒnɪntə'venʃənɪst] adj [policy] non interventionniste, de non-intervention.

non-iron adj qui ne nécessite aucun repassage.

nonmalignant [ˌnɒnmə'lɪɡnənt] adj bénin.

nonmember ['nɒnˌmembə] n non-membre m; [of a club] personne f étrangère (au club) / **open to nonmembers** ouvert au public.

non-native adj non-indigène ▶ **non-native speaker** locuteur m étranger or non natif, locutrice étrangère or non native.

non-negotiable adj non négociable.

no-no n inf interdit m / **that subject is a no-no** ce sujet est tabou.

no-nonsense adj [efficient] pratique.

nonoperational [ˌnɒnɒpə'reɪʃənl] adj non-opérationnel.

nonparticipation [ˌnɒnpɑːtɪsɪ'peɪʃn] n non-participation f.

nonpayment [ˌnɒn'peɪmənt] n non-paiement m, défaut m de paiement.

nonplussed, nonplused [ˌnɒn'plʌst] US adj dérouté, perplexe.

nonpolluting [ˌnɒnpə'luːtɪŋ] adj non polluant, propre.

nonprofit [ˌnɒn'prɒfɪt] US = non-profitmaking.

non-profitmaking adj UK à but non lucratif.

nonproliferation [ˌnɒnprəˌlɪfə'reɪʃn] n non-prolifération f.

non-reflecting adj antireflet (inv).

nonrefundable [ˌnɒnrɪ'fʌndəbl] adj non remboursable.

nonrenewable [ˌnɒnrɪ'njuːəbl] adj [resources] non renouvelable.

nonresident [ˌnɒn'rezɪdənt] ◆ n 1. [of country] non-résident m, -e f 2. [of hotel] : **the dining room is open / closed to nonresidents** le restaurant est ouvert au public // réservé aux clients. ◆ adj non résident.

nonreturnable [ˌnɒnrɪ'tɜːnəbl] adj [bottle, container] non consigné.

nonsectarian [ˌnɒnsek'teəriən] adj tolérant, ouvert.

nonsense ['nɒnsəns] ◆ n (U) 1. [rubbish, absurdity] absurdités fpl, non-sens m inv, sottises fpl 2. [foolishness] sottises fpl, bêtises fpl, enfantillages mpl. ◆ interj tarata! ◆ adj dénué de sens.

nonsensical [nɒn'sensɪkl] adj [talk, idea, action] absurde, qui n'a pas de sens, inepte.

non sequitur [ˌnɒn'sekwɪtə] n illogisme m.

nonsexist [ˌnɒn'seksɪst] ◆ adj non sexiste. ◆ n non-sexiste mf.

nonshrink [ˌnɒn'ʃrɪŋk] adj irrétrécissable.

nonskid [ˌnɒn'skɪd] adj antidérapant.

nonslip [ˌnɒn'slɪp] adj antidérapant.

nonsmoker [ˌnɒn'sməʊkə] n 1. [person] non-fumeur m, -euse f 2. RAIL compartiment m non-fumeurs.

nonsmoking [ˌnɒn'sməʊkɪŋ] adj [area] (pour les) non-fumeurs.

nonspecialist [ˌnɒn'speʃəlɪst] ◆ n non-spécialiste mf. ◆ adj non spécialiste.

nonstandard [ˌnɒn'stændəd] adj 1. LING [use of word] critiqué / **in nonstandard English** a) [colloquial] en anglais familier or populaire b) [dialectal] en anglais dialectal 2. [product, size, shape, etc.] non-standard.

nonstarter [ˌnɒn'stɑːtə] n 1. [horse] non-partant m 2. inf & fig : **this project is a nonstarter** ce projet est condamné d'avance.

nonstick [ˌnɒn'stɪk] adj [coating] antiadhérent, antiadhésif; [pan] qui n'attache pas.

nonstop [ˌnɒn'stɒp] ◆ adj [journey] sans arrêt; [flight] direct, sans escale, non-stop; [train] direct; [radio programme] non-stop, sans interruption. ◆ adv sans arrêt.

nontaxable [ˌnɒn'tæksəbl] adj non imposable.

nontoxic [ˌnɒn'tɒksɪk] adj non-toxique.

nontransferable [ˌnɒntræns'fɜːrəbl] adj nominatif.

nonverbal [ˌnɒn'vɜːbl] adj non verbal.

nonviolence [ˌnɒn'vaɪələns] n non-violence f.

nonviolent [ˌnɒn'vaɪələnt] adj non-violent.

nonvoter [ˌnɒn'vəʊtə] n 1. [person not eligible to vote] personne f qui n'a pas le droit de vote 2. [person not exercising the right to vote] abstentionniste mf.

nonvoting [ˌnɒn'vəʊtɪŋ] adj 1. [person - not eligible to vote] qui n'a pas le droit de vote; [- not exercising the right to vote] abstentionniste 2. FIN [shares] sans droit de vote.

nonwhite [ˌnɒn'waɪt] ◆ n personne f de couleur. ◆ adj de couleur.

noodle ['nuːdl] n 1. CULIN : **chicken noodle soup** soupe f de poulet aux vermicelles 2. inf [fool] andouille f, nouille f 3. US inf [head] tronche f. ❖ **noodles** pl n nouilles fpl.

nook [nʊk] n 1. [corner] coin m, recoin m ▶ **in every nook and cranny** dans le moindre recoin 2. liter [secluded spot] retraite f.

noon [nuːn] ◆ n [midday] midi m / **come at noon** venez à midi. ◆ comp [break, heat, sun] de midi.

No1 MESSAGING **written abbr of** no one.

no one, no-one = nobody.

noose [nuːs] n [gen] nœud m coulant; [snare] collet m; [lasso] lasso m.

nope [nəʊp] adv inf non.

no-place US = nowhere.

nor [nɔː] ◆ conj [following 'neither', 'not'] ni / **neither he nor his wife has ever spoken to me** mi lui mi sa femme ne m'ont jamais adressé la parole / **she neither drinks nor smokes** elle ne boit ni ne fume. ◆ adv : I **don't believe him, nor do I trust him** je ne le crois pas, et je n'ai pas confiance en lui non plus / **I don't like fish — nor do I** je n'aime pas le poisson — moi non plus.

Nordic ['nɔːdɪk] ◆ n Nordique mf. ◆ adj nordique.

Norf written abbr of Norfolk.

norm [nɔːm] n norme f.

normal ['nɔːml] ◆ adj 1. [common, typical, standard] normal; [habitual] habituel, normal 2. MATH [in statistics, geometry] normal. ◆ n 1. [gen] normale f, état m normal 2. GEOM normale f.

normality [nɔː'mælətɪ], **normalcy** US ['nɔːməlsɪ] n normalité f.

normalization, normalisation [ˌnɔːməlaɪ'zeɪʃn] n normalisation f.

normalize, normalise [ˈnɔːməlaɪz] vt normaliser.

normally [ˈnɔːməli] adv 1. [in a normal manner] normalement 2. [ordinarily] en temps normal, d'ordinaire.

Norman [ˈnɔːmən] ◆ n 1. [person] Normand m, -e f 2. LING normand m. ◆ adj GEOG & HIST normand ▶ **the Norman Conquest** la conquête normande (de l'Angleterre).; ARCHIT roman, anglo-normand.

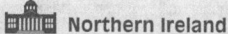

The Norman Conquest

Conquête de l'Angleterre par Guillaume le Conquérant, inaugurée par sa victoire sur le roi Harold II à la bataille de Hastings, en 1066. Désormais gouverné et régi par les Normands, le pays subit de grands changements dans les domaines politique et social, se voyant notamment imposer le français comme langue officielle.

Normandy [ˈnɔːməndi] pr n Normandie f / in Normandy en Normandie.

north [nɔːθ] ◆ n GEOG nord m / the region to the north of Sydney la région au nord de Sydney / in the north of India dans le nord de l'Inde / the wind is in the north le vent est au nord. ◆ adj 1. GEOG nord (inv), du nord / in North London dans le nord de Londres 2. [wind] du nord. ◆ adv au nord, vers le nord / the ranch lies north of the town le ranch est situé au nord de la ville.

North Africa pr n Afrique f du Nord / in North Africa en Afrique du Nord.

North African ◆ n Nord-Africain m, -e f. ◆ adj nord-africain, d'Afrique du Nord.

North America pr n Amérique f du Nord.

North American ◆ n Nord-Américain m, -e f. ◆ adj nord-américain, d'Amérique du Nord.

Northants written abbr of Northamptonshire.

northbound [ˈnɔːθbaʊnd] adj en direction du nord.

North Carolina pr n Caroline f du Nord / in North Carolina en Caroline du Nord.

North Country pr n 1. [in England] Angleterre f du Nord 2. [in America] l'Alaska, le Yukon et les Territoires du Nord-Ouest.

Northd written abbr of Northumberland.

North Dakota pr n Dakota m du Nord / in North Dakota dans le Dakota du Nord.

northeast [ˌnɔːθˈiːst] ◆ n GEOG nord-est m. ◆ adj 1. GEOG nord-est (inv), du nord-est 2. [wind] de nord-est. ◆ adv au nord-est, vers le nord-est.

northeasterly [ˌnɔːθˈiːstəli] (pl **northeasterlies**) ◆ adj 1. GEOG nord-est (inv), du nord-est 2. [wind] de nord-est. ◆ adv au nord-est, vers le nord-est.

northeastern [ˌnɔːθˈiːstən] adj nord-est (inv), du nord-est.

northerly [ˈnɔːðəli] (pl **northerlies**) ◆ adj 1. GEOG nord (inv), du nord 2. [wind] du nord. ◆ adv vers le nord. ◆ n vent m du nord.

northern [ˈnɔːðən] adj 1. GEOG nord (inv), du nord 2. [wind] du nord.

Northerner [ˈnɔːðənə] n 1. [gen] homme m /femme f du nord 2. US HIST nordiste mf.

northern hemisphere n hémisphère m nord or boréal.

Northern Ireland pr n Irlande f du Nord / in Northern Ireland en Irlande du Nord.

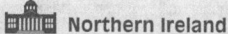

Northern Ireland

Partie de l'Irlande à majorité protestante, restée rattachée à la Grande-Bretagne lors de la partition du pays, en 1921. Depuis les émeutes sanglantes de Belfast et de Londonderry, en 1969, le pays a connu trente années de confrontations violentes entre les nationalistes de l'IRA, les extrémistes protestants et les autorités britanniques. En 1985, l'accord anglo-irlandais a donné à la République d'Irlande un droit de regard sur les affaires de l'Irlande du Nord, sans qu'une véritable solution pour la paix ne soit proposée. En 1993, la déclaration faite par le Premier ministre à Downing Street (**Downing Street Declaration**) préparait la voie pour l'arrêt des confrontations et, le 31 août 1994, l'IRA promettait de ne plus recourir à la violence. Cette déclaration fut suivie d'un cessez-le-feu loyaliste, rompu par la suite en plusieurs occasions, mais le processus de paix a finalement conduit à la signature de l'accord de paix d'Ulster, en avril 1998 (**Good Friday Agreement**), activement suivi par le Sinn Féin et la majorité des partis unionistes.

northern lights pl n aurore f boréale.

northernmost [ˈnɔːðənməʊst] adj le plus au nord.

Northern Territory pr n Territoire m du Nord / in Northern Territory dans le Territoire du Nord.

North Korea pr n Corée f du Nord.

North Korean ◆ n Nord-Coréen m, -enne f. ◆ adj nord-coréen.

North Pole pr n ▶ **the North Pole** le pôle Nord.

North Sea ◆ pr n ▶ **the North Sea** la mer du Nord. ◆ comp [oil, gas] de la mer du Nord.

North Star pr n ▶ **the North Star** l'étoile f Polaire.

North Vietnam pr n Nord Viêt Nam m / in North Vietnam au Nord Viêt Nam.

North Vietnamese ◆ n Nord-Vietnamien m, -enne f. ◆ adj nord-vietnamien.

northward [ˈnɔːθwəd] ◆ adj au nord. ◆ adv = **northwards**.

northwards [ˈnɔːθwədz] adv vers le nord, en direction du nord.

northwest [ˌnɔːθˈwest] ◆ n nord-ouest m. ◆ adj 1. GEOG nord-ouest (inv), du nord-ouest 2. [wind] de nord-ouest. ◆ adv au nord-ouest, vers le nord-ouest.

northwesterly [ˌnɔːθˈwestəli] (pl **northwesterlies**) ◆ adj 1. GEOG nord-ouest (inv), du nord-ouest 2. [wind] du nord-ouest. ◆ adv au nord-ouest, vers le nord-ouest.

northwestern [ˌnɔːθˈwestən] adj nord-ouest (inv), du nord-ouest.

Northwest Territories pl pr n Territoires mpl du Nord-Ouest.

North Yemen pr n Yémen m du Nord / in North Yemen au Yémen du Nord.

Norway [ˈnɔːweɪ] pr n Norvège f / in Norway en Norvège.

Norwegian [nɔːˈwiːdʒən] ◆ n 1. [person] Norvégien m, -enne f 2. LING norvégien m. ◆ adj norvégien.

Nos., nos. (written abbr of numbers) no.

nose [nəʊz] ◆ n **1.** ANAT nez m **2.** [sense of smell] odorat m, nez m **3.** [aroma - of wine] arôme m, bouquet m,
nez m **4.** [forward part - of aircraft, ship] nez m ; [-of car]
avant m ; [-of bullet, missile, tool] pointe f ; [-of gun] canon m. ◆ vt **1.** [smell] flairer, renifler **2.** [push with nose]
pousser du nez. ◆ vi **1.** [advance with care] avancer précautionneusement **2.** inf [snoop] fouiner. ◆ **nose about**
UK, **nose around** vi inf [snoop] fureter, fouiner. ◆ **nose**
out vt sep **1.** [discover - by smell] flairer ; [-by cunning, in-
tuition] dénicher, débusquer **2.** inf [beat narrowly] battre
d'une courte tête.

nosebag ['nəʊzbæg] n UK musette f, mangeoire f portative.

nosebleed ['nəʊzbliːd] n saignement m de nez, épis-
taxis f spec.

-nosed [nəʊzd] in comp au nez… ◆ **red-nosed** au nez
rouge.

nosedive ['nəʊzdaɪv] ◆ n **1.** [of plane, bird] piqué m
2. inf & fig [sharp drop] chute f, dégringolade f. ◆ vi
1. [plane] piquer, descendre en piqué **2.** fig [popularity,
prices] être en chute libre, chuter.

nose job n inf intervention f de chirurgie esthétique sur
le nez.

nose stud n piercing m or boucle f de nez.

nosey ['nəʊzɪ] inf = nosy.

nosh [nɒʃ] inf & dated ◆ n bouffe f. ◆ vi bouffer.

no-show n [for flight, voyage] passager qui ne se présente
pas à l'embarquement ; [for show] spectateur qui a réservé sa
place et qui n'assiste pas au spectacle / there were so many
no-shows that they cancelled the flight il y a eu tellement
de défections que le vol a été annulé.

nosh-up n UK infgueuleton m.

nostalgia [nɒ'stældʒə] n nostalgie f.

nostalgic [nɒ'stældʒɪk] adj nostalgique ▶ **to be** or **feel**
nostalgic for sthg regretter qqch.

nostril ['nɒstrɪl] n [gen] narine f ; [of horse, cow, etc.]
naseau m.

no-strings adj **1.** inf [contract, agreement] sans pièges
2. [relationship] sans lendemain.

nosy ['nəʊzɪ] (compar nosier, superl nosiest) adj inf
curieux.

not [nɒt] adv **1.** [after verb or auxiliary] ne… pas / we are
not or **aren't** sure nous ne sommes pas sûrs / do not or
don't believe her ne la croyez pas / you've been there already, haven't you or fml have you not? vous y êtes déjà
allé, non or n'est-ce pas ? ; [with infinitive] ne pas / I'll
try not to cry j'essaierai de ne pas pleurer **2.** [as phrase or
clause substitute] non, pas / we hope not nous espérons que
non / will it rain? — I think not fml est-ce qu'il va pleuvoir ? — je crois que non or je ne crois pas **3.** [with adj, adv,
noun, etc.] pas / it's Thomas, not Jake c'est Thomas, pas
Jake / not all her books are good ses livres ne sont pas tous
bons, tous ses livres ne sont pas bons / not I fml pas moi
4. [in double negatives] : not without some difficulty non
sans quelque difficulté, non sans mal / it's not unusual for
him to be late il n'est pas rare qu'il soit en retard.

> 📋 **Note that** non (pas) que **is followed by a
> verb in the subjunctive:**
> … not that we're angry, of course! … non
> (pas) que nous soyons fâchés, bien entendu !

notable ['nəʊtəbl] ◆ adj [thing] notable, remarquable ;
[person] notable, éminent. ◆ n notable m.

notably ['nəʊtəblɪ] adv **1.** [particularly] notamment, en
particulier **2.** [markedly] manifestement, de toute évidence.

notary ['nəʊtərɪ] (pl notaries) n ▶ **notary (public)**
notaire m.

notation [nəʊ'teɪʃn] n **1.** [sign system] notation f
▶ **mathematical notation** symboles mpl mathématiques
2. US [jotting] notation f, note f.

notch [nɒtʃ] n **1.** [cut - in stick] entaille f, encoche f ; [hole
- in belt] cran m **2.** [degree] cran m **3.** US [gorge] défilé m.
◆ **notch up** vt sep [achieve] accomplir.

note [nəʊt] ◆ n **1.** [record, reminder] note f **2.** [short
letter] mot m **3.** [formal communication] note f **4.** [anno-
tation, commentary] note f, annotation f **5.** UK [banknote]
billet m (de banque) **6.** [sound, tone] ton m, note f ; fig [feel-
ing, quality] note f **7.** MUS note f ; UK [piano key] touche f
8. [notice, attention] ▶ **to take note of sthg** prendre (bonne)
note de qqch. ◆ vt **1.** [observe, notice] remarquer, noter
2. [write down] noter, écrire **3.** [mention] (faire) remarquer
or observer. ◆ **of note** adj phr : a musician of note un
musicien éminent or renommé / nothing of note has happened il ne s'est rien passé d'important, aucun événement
majeur ne s'est produit. ◆ **note down** vt sep = note
(vt).

notebook ['nəʊtbʊk] n carnet m, calepin m ; SCH cahier m, carnet m ▶ **notebook computer** ordinateur m bloc-
notes.

noted ['nəʊtɪd] adj [person] éminent, célèbre ; [place, ob-
ject] réputé, célèbre ; [fact, idea] reconnu / to be noted for
one's integrity être connu pour son intégrité.

notepad ['nəʊtpæd] n [for notes] bloc-notes m ; [for let-
ters] bloc m de papier à lettres.

notepaper ['nəʊtpeɪpə] n papier m à lettres.

noteworthy ['nəʊt,wɜːðɪ] adj notable, remarquable.

not-for-profit adj US à but non lucratif.

nothing ['nʌθɪŋ] ◆ pron ne… rien / she forgets nothing elle n'oublie rien / nothing has been decided rien n'a
été décidé / I have nothing else to say je n'ai rien d'autre
à dire / nothing serious rien de grave / they're always
fighting over nothing ils passent leur temps à se disputer
pour des broutilles or des riens / reduced to nothing réduit
à néant / there's nothing for it but to start again il n'y a
plus qu'à recommencer / there's nothing in or to these
rumours ces rumeurs sont dénuées de tout fondement /
there's nothing to it! [it's easy] c'est simple (comme bonjour) ! / she says he's nothing or he means nothing to her
elle dit qu'il n'est rien pour elle / I'll take what's due to
me, nothing more, nothing less je prendrai mon dû, rien
ni moins. ◆ n **1.** [trifle] rien m, vétille f / $500 may be
a mere nothing to you 500 dollars ne représentent peut-
être pas grand-chose pour vous **2.** inf [person] nullité f,
zéro m **3.** US inf [worthless] nul. ◆ adj inf **for**
nothing adv phr **1.** [gratis] pour rien / I got it for nothing
at the flea market je l'ai eu pour (trois fois) rien aux puces
2. [for no purpose] pour rien **3.** [for no good reason] pour
rien. ◆ **nothing but** adv phr : that car's been nothing but trouble cette voiture ne m'a attiré que des ennuis /
nothing but a miracle can save us seul un miracle pourrait
nous sauver. ◆ **nothing like** prep phr **1.** [completely
unlike] : she's nothing like her mother elle ne ressemble en
rien à sa mère **2.** [nothing as good as] : there's nothing like
a nice cup of tea! rien de tel qu'une bonne tasse de thé !

notice ['nəʊtɪs] ◆ n **1.** [written announcement] annonce f ; [sign] écriteau m, pancarte f ; [poster] affiche f ; [in
newspaper - article] entrefilet m ; [-advertisement] annonce f
2. [attention] attention f ▶ **to take notice of** faire or prêter
attention à ▶ **to bring sthg to sb's notice** faire remarquer
qqch à qqn, attirer l'attention de qqn sur qqch ▶ **to escape**
or **to avoid notice** passer inaperçu **3.** [notification, warning]

avis *m*, notification *f* ; [advance notification] préavis *m* ▸ **without previous** or **prior notice** sans prévenir ▸ **at a moment's notice** sur-le-champ, immédiatement ▸ **at short notice** très rapidement ▸ **until further notice** jusqu'à nouvel ordre or avis **4.** [notifying document] avis *m*, notification *f* ; [warning document] avertissement *m* ▸ **notice of receipt** COMM accusé *m* de réception **5.** [intent to terminate contract - by employer, landlord, tenant] congé *m* ; [- by employee] démission *f* **6.** [review] critique *f*. ◆ *vt* **1.** [spot, observe] remarquer, s'apercevoir de **2.** [take notice of] faire attention à.

> ⚠ The French word **notice** means a note in a printed text, not a notice.

noticeable ['nəʊtɪsəbl] *adj* [mark, defect] visible ; [effect, change, improvement] sensible.

noticeably ['nəʊtɪsəblɪ] *adv* sensiblement.

noticeboard ['nəʊtɪsbɔːd] *n* panneau *m* d'affichage.

notifiable ['nəʊtɪfaɪəbl] *adj* [disease] à déclaration obligatoire.

notification [ˌnəʊtɪfɪˈkeɪʃn] *n* notification *f*, avis *m* / *you will receive notification by mail* vous serez averti par courrier.

notify ['nəʊtɪfaɪ] (*pt* & *pp* **notified**) *vt* notifier, avertir ▸ **to notify sb of sthg** avertir qqn de qqch, notifier qqch à qqn.

notion ['nəʊʃn] *n* **1.** [concept] notion *f*, concept *m* **2.** [opinion] idée *f*, opinion *f* **3.** [vague idea] notion *f*, idée *f* **4.** [thought, whim] idée *f* ; [urge] envie *f*, désir *m*. ❖ **notions** *pl n* 🇺🇸 [haberdashery] (articles *mpl* de) mercerie *f* ▸ **notions store** mercerie *f* (*boutique*).

notional ['nəʊʃənl] *adj* **1.** 🇬🇧 [hypothetical] théorique, notionnel **2.** [imaginary] imaginaire **3.** 🇺🇸 [fanciful] capricieux.

notoriety [ˌnəʊtəˈraɪətɪ] (*pl* **notorieties**) *n* [ill fame] triste notoriété *f* ; [fame] notoriété *f*.

notorious [nəʊˈtɔːrɪəs] *adj pej* [ill-famed - person] tristement célèbre ; [- crime] célèbre ; [- place] mal famé ; [well-known] connu / *she's notorious for being late* elle est connue pour ne jamais être à l'heure / *the area is notorious for muggings* il est bien connu que c'est un quartier où il y a beaucoup d'agressions.

notoriously [nəʊˈtɔːrɪəslɪ] *adv* notoirement.

Notts written abbr of **Nottinghamshire**.

notwithstanding [ˌnɒtwɪθˈstændɪŋ] *fml* ◆ *prep* en dépit de. ◆ *adv* malgré tout, néanmoins.

nougat ['nuːgɑː] *n* nougat *m*.

nought [nɔːt] *n* 🇬🇧 [zero] zéro *m*.

noun [naʊn] *n* nom *m*, substantif *m* ▸ **common / proper noun** nom commun / propre.

nourish ['nʌrɪʃ] *vt* **1.** [feed] nourrir **2.** [entertain, foster] nourrir, entretenir.

nourishing ['nʌrɪʃɪŋ] *adj* nourrissant, nutritif.

nourishment ['nʌrɪʃmənt] *n* (U) **1.** [food] nourriture *f*, aliments *mpl* **2.** [act of nourishing] alimentation *f*.

Nov. (written abbr of **November**) nov.

Nova Scotia [ˌnəʊvəˈskəʊʃə] *pr n* Nouvelle-Écosse *f* / *in Nova Scotia* en Nouvelle-Écosse.

Nova Scotian [ˌnəʊvəˈskəʊʃn] ◆ *n* Néo-Écossais *m*, -e *f*. ◆ *adj* néo-écossais.

novel ['nɒvl] ◆ *n* roman *m*. ◆ *adj* nouveau (*before vowel or silent 'h' nouvel, f nouvelle*), original.

novelist ['nɒvəlɪst] *n* romancier *m*, -ère *f*.

novelty ['nɒvltɪ] (*pl* **novelties**) *n* **1.** [newness] nouveauté *f*, originalité *f* ▸ **novelty value** attrait *m* de la nou-

veauté **2.** [thing, idea] innovation *f*, nouveauté *f* / *it was a real novelty* c'était une nouveauté, c'était tout nouveau **3.** [trinket] nouveauté *f*, article *m* fantaisie ; [gadget] gadget *m*.

November [nəˈvembər] *n* novembre *m*. See also **February**.

novice ['nɒvɪs] *n* **1.** [beginner] débutant *m*, -e *f*, novice *mf* **2.** RELIG novice *mf*.

now [naʊ] ◆ *adv* **1.** [at this time] maintenant / *she'll be here any moment* or *any time now* elle va arriver d'un moment or instant à l'autre / *we are now entering enemy territory* nous sommes désormais en territoire ennemi ▸ **it's now or never** c'est le moment ou jamais / *I'd never met them before now* je ne les avais jamais rencontrés auparavant / *between now and next August* / *next year* d'ici le mois d'août prochain / l'année prochaine / *they must have got the letter by now* ils ont dû recevoir la lettre à l'heure qu'il est / *that's all for now* c'est tout pour le moment / *in a few years from now* d'ici quelques années ▸ **from now on** désormais, dorénavant, à partir de maintenant / *we've had no problems till now* or *until now* or *up to now* nous n'avons eu aucun problème jusqu'ici **2.** [nowadays] maintenant, aujourd'hui, actuellement **3.** [marking a specific point in the past] maintenant, alors, à ce moment-là / *by now we were all exhausted* nous étions alors tous épuisés **4.** [introducing information] or / *now a Jaguar is a very fast car* or, la Jaguar est une voiture très rapide **5.** [to show enthusiasm] : *now that's what I call a car!* voilà ce que j'appelle une voiture ! ; [to show surprise] : *well now!* ça alors ! ; [to mark a pause] : *now, what was I saying?* voyons, où en étais-je ? / *now let me see* voyons voir. ◆ *conj* maintenant que, à présent que / *now you come to mention it* maintenant que tu le dis. ❖ **now and again, now and then** *adv phr* de temps en temps, de temps à autre.

NOW [naʊ] (**abbr of National Organization for Women**) *pr n* organisation féministe américaine.

nowadays ['naʊədeɪz] *adv* aujourd'hui, de nos jours.

nowhere ['nəʊweər] *adv* **1.** [no place] nulle part / *he goes nowhere without her* il ne va nulle part sans elle / *there's nowhere to hide* il n'y a nulle part où se cacher ▸ **nowhere else** nulle part ailleurs / *my watch is nowhere to be found* impossible de retrouver ma montre / *she / the book was nowhere to be seen* elle / le livre avait disparu ; *fig* : *we're getting nowhere fast* *inf* on pédale dans la choucroute or la semoule / *he's going nowhere fast* il n'ira pas loin **2.** PHR **nowhere near** : *the hotel was nowhere near the beach* l'hôtel était bien loin de la plage / *I've nowhere near enough time* je suis loin d'avoir assez de temps.

no-win situation *n* situation *f* sans issue.

noxious ['nɒkʃəs] *adj* [gas, substance] nocif ; [influence] néfaste.

nozzle ['nɒzl] *n* [gen] bec *m*, embout *m* ; [for hose, paint gun] jet *m*, buse *f* ; [in carburettor] gicleur *m* ; [in turbine] tuyère *f*.

NP 1. written abbr of **notary public 2.** MESSAGING written abbr of **no problem**.

NPD (abbr of **new product development**) *n* développement *m* de nouveaux produits.

NQT *n* 🇬🇧 abbr of **newly qualified teacher**.

nr written abbr of **near**.

NRN MESSAGING written abbr of **no reply necessary**.

NS written abbr of **Nova Scotia**.

NSC (abbr of **National Security Council**) *pr n* organisme chargé de superviser la politique militaire de défense du gouvernement des États-Unis.

NSF ◆ pr n **abbr of** National Science Foundation. ◆ **written abbr of** non-sufficient funds.

NSPCC (**abbr of** National Society for the Prevention of Cruelty to Children) pr n *association britannique de protection de l'enfance.*

NSW written abbr of New South Wales.

NT ◆ n (**abbr of** New Testament) NT. ◆ pr n **1. abbr** of National Trust **2.** (**abbr of** Royal National Theatre) *grand théâtre londonien subventionné par l'État.*

nth [enθ] adj **1.** MATH ▸ **to the nth power** à la puissance n **2.** *inf* [umpteenth] énième.

nuance [nju:'ɑ:ns] n nuance f.

nuclear ['nju:klɪə] adj **1.** PHYS nucléaire ▸ **nuclear power station** centrale f nucléaire or atomique **2.** MIL nucléaire ▸ **nuclear bomb** bombe f nucléaire ▸ **nuclear capability** puissance f or potentiel m nucléaire ▸ **France's nuclear deterrent** la force de dissuasion nucléaire française ▸ **nuclear disarmament** désarmement m nucléaire ▸ **nuclear energy** énergie f nucléaire ▸ **nuclear fission** fission f nucléaire ▸ **nuclear fusion** fusion f nucléaire ▸ **nuclear physics** (U) physique f nucléaire ▸ **nuclear power** nucléaire m, énergie f nucléaire ▸ **nuclear reactor** réacteur m nucléaire ▸ **nuclear testing** essais mpl nucléaires ▸ **nuclear war** guerre f atomique ▸ **nuclear weapons** armes fpl nucléaires ▸ **nuclear winter** hiver m nucléaire **3.** BIOL nucléaire.

nuclear family n SOCIOL famille f nucléaire.

nuclear-free zone n périmètre dans lequel une collectivité locale interdit l'utilisation, le stockage ou le transport des matières radioactives.

nuclear-powered adj à propulsion nucléaire ▸ **nuclear-powered submarine** sous-marin m nucléaire.

nucleus ['nju:klɪəs] (*pl* nucleuses or nuclei ['nju:klɪaɪ]) n **1.** BIOL & PHYS noyau m **2.** *fig* [kernel] noyau m, cœur m.

nude [nju:d] ◆ adj [naked] nu. ◆ n **1.** ART nu m **2.** [being nude] : *I was in the nude* j'étais (tout) nu ▸ **to pose in the nude** poser nu.

nudge [nʌdʒ] ◆ vt **1.** [with elbow] pousser du coude **2.** [push] pousser **3.** [encourage] encourager, pousser **4.** [approach] approcher (de). ◆ n **1.** [with elbow] coup m de coude ; [with foot, stick, etc.] petit coup m (de pied), de bâton, etc. ▸ **to give sb a nudge** pousser qqn du coude **2.** [encouragement] : *he needs a nudge in the right direction* il a besoin qu'on le pousse dans la bonne direction.

nudist ['nju:dɪst] ◆ adj nudiste, naturiste ▸ **nudist colony / beach** camp m / plage f de nudistes. ◆ n nudiste mf, naturiste mf.

nudity ['nju:dətɪ] n nudité f.

nufn (**written abbr of** nothing) MESSAGING r1.

nugget ['nʌgɪt] n **1.** [piece] pépite f **2.** *fig* : *nuggets of wisdom* des trésors de sagesse / *an interesting nugget of information* un (petit) renseignement intéressant.

nuisance ['nju:sns] n **1.** [annoying thing, situation] : *that noise is a nuisance* ce bruit est énervant / *it's (such) a nuisance having to attend all these meetings* c'est (vraiment) pénible de devoir assister à toutes ces réunions / *what a nuisance!* c'est énervant ! ▸ **nuisance call** appel m anonyme **2.** [annoying person] empoisonneur m, -euse f ▸ **to make a nuisance of o.s.** embêter or empoisonner le monde / *stop being a nuisance* arrête de nous embêter **3.** [hazard] nuisance f ▸ **public nuisance** : *that rubbish dump is a public nuisance* cette décharge est une calamité.

NUJ (**abbr of** National Union of Journalists) pr n *syndicat britannique des journalistes.*

nuke [nju:k] *inf* ◆ vt **1.** [bomb] lâcher une bombe atomique sur **2.** [microwave] cuire au micro-ondes. ◆ n **1.** [weapon] arme f nucléaire **2.** US [power plant] centrale f nucléaire.

null [nʌl] adj **1.** LAW [invalid] nul ; [lapsed] caduc ▸ **null and void** nul et non avenu **2.** [insignificant] insignifiant, sans valeur ; [amounting to nothing] nul **3.** MATH ▸ **null set** ensemble m vide.

nullify ['nʌlɪfaɪ] (*pt & pp* nullified) vt **1.** LAW [claim, contract, election] annuler, invalider **2.** [advantage] neutraliser.

NUM (**abbr of** National Union of Mineworkers) pr n *syndicat britannique des mineurs.*

numb [nʌm] ◆ adj engourdi / *we were numb with cold* nous étions transis de froid / *numb with terror* *fig* paralysé par la peur / *he was numb with shock* *fig* il était sous le choc. ◆ vt [person, limbs, senses] engourdir ; [pain] atténuer, apaiser.

number ['nʌmbə] ◆ n **1.** [gen & MATH] nombre m ; [figure, numeral] chiffre m **2.** [as identifier] numéro m / *have you got my work number?* avez-vous mon numéro (de téléphone) au travail ? / *the winning number* le numéro gagnant / *we live at number 80* nous habitons au (numéro) 80 **3.** [quantity] nombre m ▸ **to be equal in number** être à nombre égal / *a large number of people* un grand nombre de gens, de nombreuses personnes **4.** [group] ▸ **one of their / our number** un des leurs / des nôtres **5.** [issue -of magazine, paper] numéro m **6.** *inf* [job] boulot m **7.** [song, dance, act] numéro m **8.** *inf* [thing, person] : *this number is a hot seller* ce modèle se vend comme des petits pains / *she was wearing a little black number* elle portait une petite robe noire **9.** GRAM nombre m. ◆ vt **1.** [assign number to] numéroter **2.** [include] compter **3.** [total] compter **4.** [count] compter. ◆ vi : *she numbers among the great writers of the century* elle compte parmi les grands écrivains de ce siècle. ◆ **any number of** adj phr un grand nombre de. ◆ **numbers** n US = **numbers game**. ◆ **number off** vi se numéroter.

number-crunching [-krʌntʃɪŋ] n *inf* COMPUT traitement m en masse des chiffres.

numbering ['nʌmbərɪŋ] n numérotation f, numérotage m.

number one ◆ adj premier / *it's our number one priority* c'est la première de nos priorités / *the number one hit in the charts* le numéro un au hit-parade. ◆ n **1.** *inf* [boss] boss m, patron m, -onne f **2.** *inf* [oneself] ▸ **to look out for** or **to take care of number one** penser à soi **3.** [in hit parade] : *her album got to number one* son album a été classé numéro un au hit-parade.

numberplate ['nʌmbəpleɪt] n UK AUTO plaque f minéralogique or d'immatriculation.

number portability n TELEC portage m or conservation f du numéro.

numbers game n US loterie f clandestine.

Number Ten pr n ▸ **Number Ten (Downing Street)** *résidence officielle du Premier ministre britannique.*

numbhead ['nʌmhed], **numbskull** ['nʌmskʌl] *inf* = numskull.

numbness ['nʌmnɪs] n [physical] engourdissement m ; [mental] torpeur f, engourdissement m.

numeracy ['nju:mərəsɪ] n (U) UK notions fpl d'arithmétique.

numeral ['nju:mərəl] n chiffre m, nombre m.

numerate ['nju:mərət] adj UK [skilled] bon en mathématiques ; [having basics] sachant compter.

numerical [nju:'merɪkl] adj numérique / *in numerical order* par ordre numérique.

numerically [nju:'merɪklɪ] adv numériquement.

numeric keypad n COMPUT pavé m numérique.

numero uno [,nu:mərəʊ'u:nəʊ] US inf ◆ n : *it's the numero uno* c'est le top du top / *he's the numero uno* c'est le meilleur. ◆ adj : *she's the numero uno actress in Bollywood* c'est l'actrice la plus en vogue à Bollywood.

numerous ['nju:mərəs] adj nombreux / *for numerous reasons* pour de nombreuses raisons.

numskull ['nʌmskʌl] n inf andouille f.

nun [nʌn] n religieuse f ▶ **to become a nun** prendre le voile.

nunnery ['nʌnərɪ] (pl nunneries) n couvent m or monastère m (de femmes).

nuptial ['nʌpʃl] adj nuptial. ◇ **nuptials** pl n liter noce f, noces fpl.

nurse [nɜ:s] ◆ n 1. MED [in hospital] infirmier m, -ère f ; [at home] infirmier m, -ère f, garde-malade mf 2. UK [nanny] gouvernante f, nurse f 3. [wet nurse] nourrice f. ◆ vt 1. MED soigner 2. [harbour, foster -grudge, hope, desire] entretenir ; [-scheme] mijoter, couver 3. [breast-feed] allaiter 4. [hold] bercer (dans ses bras). ◆ vi 1. MED être infirmier / infirmière 2. [infant] téter.

nursemaid ['nɜ:smeɪd] n gouvernante f, nurse f ▶ **to play nursemaid to sb** fig tenir qqn par la main.

nursery ['nɜ:sərɪ] (pl nurseries) n 1. [room] nursery f, chambre f d'enfants 2. [day-care centre] crèche f, garderie f 3. [school] école f maternelle ▶ **nursery teacher** instituteur m, -trice f de maternelle 4. [for plants, trees] pépinière f.

nursery nurse n puéricultrice f.

nursery rhyme n comptine f.

nursery school n UK école f maternelle ▶ **nursery school teacher** instituteur m, -trice f de maternelle.

nursery slopes pl n UK pistes fpl pour débutants.

nursing ['nɜ:sɪŋ] ◆ n 1. [profession] profession f d'infirmier 2. [care] soins mpl 3. [breast-feeding] allaitement m. ◆ adj 1. MED d'infirmier ▶ **the nursing staff** le personnel soignant 2. [suckling] allaitant.

nursing home n 1. [for aged] maison f de retraite ; [for convalescents] maison f de repos ; [for mentally ill] maison f de santé 2. UK [private clinic] hôpital m privé, clinique f privée.

nurture ['nɜ:tʃə] ◆ vt 1. [bring up] élever, éduquer ; [nourish] nourrir 2. [foster -hope, desire] entretenir ; [-plan, scheme] mijoter, couver. ◆ n [upbringing] éducation f.

nurturing ['nɜ:tʃərɪŋ] adj attentionné, maternel.

NUS (abbr of National Union of Students) n union nationale des étudiants de Grande-Bretagne.

nut [nʌt] (pt & pp nutted, cont nutting) ◆ n 1. BOT & CULIN fruit m à coque 2. TECH écrou m 3. inf [crazy person] dingue mf, timbré m, -e f, taré m, -e f ; [enthusiast] fana 4. inf [head] tronche f, poire f 5. [small lump of coal] noix f, tête-de-moineau f. ◆ vt inf donner un coup de boule à v inf.

NUT (abbr of National Union of Teachers) pr n synd cat britannique d'enseignants.

nutcase ['nʌtkeɪs] n inf dingue mf, timbré m, -e f, taré m, -e f

nutcracker ['nʌt,krækə] n casse-noix m inv, casse noisettes m inv.

nutcrackers ['nʌt,krækəz] pl n = nutcracker.

nutmeg ['nʌtmeg] ◆ n 1. BOT [nut] (noix f de) mus cade f ; [tree] muscadier m 2. [football] petit pont m. ◆ v [football] ▶ **to nutmeg a player** faire un petit pont à u joueur.

nutrient ['nju:trɪənt] ◆ n substance f nutritive. ◆ ac nutritif.

nutrition [nju:'trɪʃn] n nutrition f.

nutritional [nju:'trɪʃənl] adj [disorder, process, value nutritif ; [science, research] nutritionnel.

nutritionist [nju:'trɪʃənɪst] n nutritionniste m f.

nutritious [nju:'trɪʃəs] adj nutritif, nourrissant.

nuts [nʌts] ◆ adj inf dingue, timbré, fêlé ▶ **to go nut** [crazy, angry] piquer une crise ▶ **to be nuts about** or **on** être fou or dingue de. ◆ pl n v inf [testicles] couilles fpl, rou pettes fpl. ◆ interj v inf ▶ **nuts!** des clous !

nutshell ['nʌtʃel] n coquille f de noix (de noisette, etc ▶ **in a nutshell** en un mot ▶ **to put it in a nutshell** pou résumer l'histoire (en un mot).

nutter ['nʌtə] n UK inf malade mf, timbré m, -e f, taré m -e f.

nutty ['nʌtɪ] (compar nuttier, superl nuttiest) ad 1. [tasting of or containing nuts] aux noix (aux amandes, au noisettes, etc.) 2. inf [crazy] dingue, timbré.

nuzzle ['nʌzl] ◆ vt [push with nose] pousser du nez [sniff at] renifler ; [subj: animal] pousser du museau. ◆ v 1. ▶ **to nuzzle up against, to nuzzle at** = nuzzle (v 2. [nestle] se blottir.

NV written abbr of Nevada.

NVQ (abbr of National Vocational Qualification) r UK examen sanctionnant une formation professionnelle.

NW (written abbr of north-west) N-O.

NWO MESSAGING written abbr of no way out.

n-word n ▶ **the n-word** le mot « nigger ».

NWT written abbr of Northwest Territories.

NY written abbr of New York.

NYC written abbr of New York City.

nylon ['naɪlɒn] ◆ n Nylon® m. ◆ comp [thread, shirt stockings] de or en Nylon®. ◇ **nylons** pl n [stockings] bas mpl (de) Nylon®.

nymph [nɪmf] n MYTH & ZOOL nymphe f.

nymphomaniac [,nɪmfə'meɪnɪæk] ◆ adj nympho mane. ◆ n nymphomane f.

NYPD [,enwaɪpi:'di:] (abbr of New York Police Department) n police f new-yorkaise.

NYSE pr n abbr of New York Stock Exchange.

NZ written abbr of New Zealand.

O [əʊ] (pl O's or Os), **O** (pl O's or Os) n [letter] o m, O m ▸ **O positive / negative** MED O positif /négatif. **See also** f.

O n [zero] zéro m ▸ **agent double O seven** agent 007.

O & M (abbr of **organization and methods**) n O et M f.

oaf [əʊf] n [dull, clumsy man] lourdaud m ; [uncouth man] rustre m, goujat m.

oak [əʊk] ◆ n chêne m. ◆ comp [furniture, door, panelling] de or en chêne ▸ **oak tree** chêne m.

oaky ['əʊkɪ] adj [wine] boisé, aux arômes boisés.

OAP (abbr of **old age pensioner**) n UK retraité m, -e f.

oar [ɔːr] n 1. [instrument] rame f, aviron m 2. [person] rameur m, -euse f.

oarsman ['ɔːzmən] (pl oarsmen [-mən]) n rameur m.

oarswoman ['ɔːz,wʊmən] (pl oarswomen [-,wɪmɪn]) n rameuse f.

OAS (abbr of **Organization of American States**) pr n OEA f.

oasis [əʊ'eɪsɪs] (pl oases [-siːz]) n lit & fig oasis f ▸ **an oasis of calm** une oasis or un havre de paix.

oat [əʊt] n [plant] avoine f. ✣ **oats** pl n avoine f.

oatcake ['əʊtkeɪk] n gâteau m sec (d'avoine).

oath [əʊθ] (pl [əʊðz]) n 1. [vow] serment m ▸ **to be on** or **under oath** LAW être sous serment, être assermenté ▸ **to put sb on** or **under oath** LAW faire prêter serment à qqn 2. [swearword] juron m.

oatmeal ['əʊtmiːl] ◆ n (U) [flakes] flocons mpl d'avoine ; [flour] farine f d'avoine ▸ **oatmeal porridge** bouillie f d'avoine, porridge m. ◆ adj [colour] grège.

OB n abbr of **outside broadcast**.

obdurate ['ɒbdjʊrət] adj fml 1. [hardhearted] insensible, dur 2. [obstinate] obstiné, entêté ; [unyielding] inflexible.

OBE (abbr of **Officer of the Order of the British Empire**) n distinction honorifique britannique.

obedience [ə'biːdjəns] n 1. obéissance f ▸ **to show obedience to sb** obéir à qqn ▸ **to owe obedience to sb** liter devoir obédience à qqn / **in obedience to her wishes** conformément à ses vœux ▸ **to command obedience** savoir se faire obéir 2. RELIG obédience f.

obedient [ə'biːdjənt] adj obéissant, docile ▸ **to be obedient to sb** obéir à qqn.

obediently [ə'biːdjəntlɪ] adv docilement.

obelisk ['ɒbəlɪsk] n 1. [column] obélisque m 2. TYPO croix f (d'évêque), obel m.

obese [əʊ'biːs] adj obèse.

obesity [əʊ'biːsətɪ], **obeseness** [əʊ'biːsnɪs] n obésité f.

obey [ə'beɪ] ◆ vt obéir à / **he always obeyed his mother / his intuition / the law** il a toujours obéi à sa mère / à son intuition / aux lois / **the plane is no longer obeying the controls** l'avion ne répond plus. ◆ vi obéir, obtempérer.

⚠ **Note the use of the preposition when translating the transitive verb obey: obéis à ta mère; il lui a obéi.**

obituary [ə'bɪtjʊərɪ] (pl obituaries) ◆ n nécrologie f, notice f nécrologique ▸ **the obituary column, the obituaries** la rubrique nécrologique. ◆ adj nécrologique.

object¹ ['ɒbdʒɪkt] n 1. [thing] objet m, chose f 2. [aim] objet m, but m, fin f / **with this object in mind** dans ce but, à cette fin 3. [focus] objet m 4. GRAM [of verb] complément m d'objet ; [of preposition] objet m.

object² [əb'dʒekt] ◆ vi élever une objection ; [stronger] protester ▸ **to object to sthg** protester contre qqch / **they object to working overtime** ils ne sont pas d'accord pour faire des heures supplémentaires / **if you don't object** si vous n'y voyez pas d'inconvénient / **you know how your father objects to it!** tu sais combien ton père y est opposé ! / **I object!** je proteste ! / **I object strongly to your attitude** je trouve votre attitude proprement inadmissible / **I wouldn't object to a cup of tea** je ne dirais pas non à or je prendrais volontiers une tasse de thé / **he objects to her smoking** il désapprouve qu'elle fume / **she objects to his coming** elle n'est pas d'accord pour qu'il vienne / **why do you object to all my friends?** pourquoi cette hostilité à l'égard de tous mes amis ? / **it's not her I object to but her husband** ce n'est pas elle qui me déplaît, c'est son mari. ◆ vt objecter.

objection [əb'dʒekʃn] n 1. [argument against] objection f ▸ **to make** or **to raise an objection** faire or soulever une objection / **I have no objection to his coming** je ne vois pas d'objection à ce qu'il vienne / **I have no objection to his friends** je n'ai rien contre ses amis / **if you have no objection** si vous n'y voyez pas d'inconvénient ▸ **objection!** LAW objection ! ▸ **objection overruled!** LAW objection rejetée ! 2. [opposition] opposition f.

objectionable [əb'dʒekʃnəbl] adj [unpleasant] désagréable ; [blameworthy] répréhensible / **to use objectionable language** parler vulgairement / **I find his views objectionable** je n'aime pas sa façon de penser / **what is so objectionable about her behaviour?** qu'est-ce qu'on peut lui reprocher ?

objective [əb'dʒektɪv] ◆ adj 1. [unbiased] objectif, impartial 2. [real, observable] objectif. ◆ n 1. [aim] objectif m, but m 2. PHOT objectif m.

objectively [əb'dʒektɪvlɪ] adv 1. [unbiasedly] objectivement, impartialement 2. [really, externally] objectivement.

objectivity [ˌɒbdʒek'tɪvəti] n objectivité f.

objector [əb'dʒektə'] n opposant m, -e f.

object-oriented adj COMPUT orienté objet ▸ **object-oriented programming** programmation f orientée objet.

obligate ['ɒbligeit] vt **1.** US & UK fml [compel] obliger, contraindre ▸ **to be / to feel obligated to do sthg** être / se sentir obligé de faire qqch **2.** US FIN [funds, credits] affecter.

obligation [ˌɒblɪ'geɪʃn] n obligation f ▸ **to be under an obligation to do sthg** être dans l'obligation de faire qqch / *you are under no obligation to reply* vous n'êtes pas tenu de répondre / *I am under an obligation to her* j'ai une dette envers elle ▸ **to put** or **to place sb under an obligation to do sthg** mettre qqn dans l'obligation de faire qqch.

obligatory [ə'blɪgətrɪ] adj obligatoire.

oblige [ə'blaɪdʒ] ◆ vt **1.** [constrain] obliger ▸ **to oblige sb to do sthg** obliger qqn à faire qqch **2.** [do a favour to] rendre service à, obliger ▸ **much obliged!** merci beaucoup ! ▸ **to be obliged to sb for sthg** savoir gré à qqn de qqch. ◆ vi : *always ready to oblige!* toujours prêt à rendre service !

obliging [ə'blaɪdʒɪŋ] adj serviable, obligeant / *it was very obliging of him* c'était très aimable à lui or de sa part.

obligingly [ə'blaɪdʒɪŋlɪ] adv aimablement, obligeamment.

oblique [ə'bliːk] ◆ adj **1.** GEOM [slanted] oblique **2.** [indirect] indirect **3.** GRAM oblique. ◆ n **1.** GEOM oblique f ; ANAT oblique m **2.** TYPO barre f oblique.

obliquely [ə'bliːklɪ] adv **1.** obliquement, en biais **2.** [indirectly] indirectement.

obliterate [ə'blɪtəreɪt] vt [destroy, erase] effacer ; [cancel - stamp] oblitérer.

oblivion [ə'blɪvɪən] n **1.** [being forgotten] oubli m **2.** [unconsciousness] inconscience f, oubli m.

oblivious [ə'blɪvɪəs] adj inconscient / *she was oblivious of* or *to what was happening* elle n'avait pas conscience de or n'était pas consciente de ce qui se passait.

oblong ['ɒblɒŋ] ◆ adj [rectangular] rectangulaire ; [elongated] allongé, oblong (oblongue). ◆ n [rectangle] rectangle m.

obnoxious [əb'nɒkʃəs] adj [person] odieux, ignoble ; [behaviour] odieux ; [smell] ignoble, infect.

o.b.o. (written abbr of or best offer) à déb.

oboe ['əʊbəʊ] n hautbois m.

oboist ['əʊbəʊɪst] n hautbois m (musicien), hautboïste mf.

obscene [əb'siːn] adj obscène.

obscenely [əb'siːnlɪ] adv d'une manière obscène / *he's obscenely rich* il est tellement riche que c'en est dégoûtant.

obscenity [əb'senətɪ] (pl obscenities) n **1.** (U) [obscene language] obscénité f, obscénités fpl **2.** [obscene word] obscénité f, grossièreté f **3.** fig : *war is an obscenity* la guerre est une chose obscène.

obscure [əb'skjʊə'] ◆ adj **1.** [not clear] obscur ; [little-known] perdu **2.** [dark] obscur, sombre. ◆ vt **1.** [hide] cacher ; [confuse] obscurcir, embrouiller **2.** [darken] obscurcir, assombrir.

obscurely [əb'skjʊəlɪ] adv obscurément.

obscurity [əb'skjʊərɪtɪ] (pl obscurities) n **1.** [insignificance] obscurité f **2.** [difficulty] obscurité f **3.** [darkness] obscurité f, ténèbres fpl.

obsequious [əb'siːkwɪəs] adj fml obséquieux.

obsequiousness [əb'siːkwɪəsnɪs] n fml obséquiosité f.

observable [əb'zɜːvəbl] adj [visible] observable, visible ; [discernible] perceptible, appréciable / *behaviour observable in humans* un comportement observable or que l'on peut observer chez les humains.

observably [əb'zɜːvəblɪ] adv perceptiblement, visiblement.

observance [əb'zɜːvəns] n **1.** [recognition - of custom, law, etc.] observation f, observance f ; [- of anniversary] célébration f **2.** RELIG [rite, ceremony] observance f.

observant [əb'zɜːvnt] adj [alert] observateur / *how observant of him!* comme il est observateur !, rien ne lui échappe !

observation [ˌɒbzə'veɪʃn] n **1.** [study] observation f, surveillance f ▸ **to be under observation** a) [patient] être en observation b) [by police] être surveillé par la police or sous surveillance policière **2.** [comment] observation f, remarque f **3.** [perception] observation f.

observational [ˌɒbzə'veɪʃənl] adj [faculties, powers] d'observation ; [technique, research] observationnel.

observation post n MIL poste m d'observation.

observatory [əb'zɜːvətrɪ] (pl observatories) n observatoire m.

observe [əb'zɜːv] vt **1.** [see, notice] observer, remarquer **2.** [study, pay attention to] observer **3.** [comment, remark] (faire) remarquer, (faire) observer **4.** [abide by, keep] observer, respecter / *to observe a minute's silence* observer une minute de silence.

observer [əb'zɜːvə'] n **1.** [watcher] observateur m, -trice f **2.** [at official ceremony, election] observateur m, -trice f **3.** [commentator] spécialiste mf, expert m ▸ **The Observer** PRESS journal de qualité politiquement indépendant, paraissant le dimanche et comprenant un supplément magazine.

obsess [əb'ses] ◆ vt obséder. ◆ vi ▸ **to obsess about** or **over sthg** être obsédé par qqch.

obsession [əb'seʃn] n [fixed idea] obsession f, idée f fixe / *it's becoming an obsession with him* ça devient une idée fixe or une obsession chez lui / *she has an obsession about punctuality* c'est une maniaque de la ponctualité ; [obsessive fear] hantise f / *his obsession with death* sa hantise de la mort.

obsessional [əb'seʃənl] adj obsessionnel.

obsessive [əb'sesɪv] ◆ adj **1.** [person] obsédé ; MED & PSYCHOL obsessionnel ; [behaviour] obsessionnel **2.** [thought, image] obsédant. ◆ n obsessionnel m, -elle f.

obsessive-compulsive adj PSYCHOL obsessionnel-compulsif / *he's a bit obsessive-compulsive* il est un peu maniaque ▸ **obsessive-compulsive disorder** troubles mpl obsessionnels compulsifs.

obsessively [əb'sesɪvlɪ] adv d'une manière obsessionnelle.

obsolescence [ˌɒbsə'lesns] n [of equipment, consumer goods] obsolescence f ▸ **planned** or **built-in obsolescence** COMM obsolescence planifiée, désuétude f calculée.

obsolescent [ˌɒbsə'lesnt] adj qui tombe en désuétude ; [equipment, consumer goods] obsolescent.

obsolete ['ɒbsəliːt] adj [outmoded] démodé, désuet (désuète) ; [antiquated] archaïque ; [machinery] dépassé.

obstacle ['ɒbstəkl] n obstacle m / *what are the obstacles to free trade?* qu'est-ce qui fait obstacle au libre-échange ? ▸ **to put obstacles in sb's way** mettre des bâtons dans les roues à qqn.

obstacle course, obstacle race n course f d'obstacles.

obstetric [ɒb'stetrɪk] adj obstétrical ; [nurses] en obstétrique.

obstetrician [ˌɒbstə'trɪʃn] n obstétricien m, -enne f.

obstetrics [ɒb'stetrɪks] n (U) obstétrique f.

obstinacy ['ɒbstɪnəsɪ] n 1. [stubbornness] obstination f, entêtement m ; [tenacity] opiniâtreté f, ténacité f 2. [persistence] persistance f.

obstinate ['ɒbstənət] adj 1. [stubborn] obstiné, entêté, têtu ; [tenacious] obstiné, tenace, acharné 2. [persistent] persistant, tenace.

obstinately ['ɒbstənətlɪ] adv [stubbornly] obstinément, avec acharnement.

obstreperous [əb'strepərəs] adj fml & hum [noisy] bruyant ; [disorderly] turbulent ; [recalcitrant] récalcitrant.

obstruct [əb'strʌkt] vt 1. [block - passage, road, traffic] bloquer, obstruer ; [- pipe] boucher ; [- vein, artery] obstruer, boucher 2. [impede - progress, measures] faire obstruction or obstacle à, entraver 3. SPORT [opponent] faire obstruction à.

obstruction [əb'strʌkʃn] n 1. [impeding - of progress, measures] obstruction f 2. [blockage, obstacle - gen] obstacle m ; [- in vein, artery] obstruction f ; [- in pipe] bouchon m 3. SPORT obstruction f 4. LAW obstruction f de la voie publique.

obstructive [əb'strʌktɪv] adj : they are being very obstructive ils nous mettent constamment des bâtons dans les roues.

obtain [əb'teɪn] vt obtenir ; [for oneself] se procurer ▸ to **obtain sthg for sb** obtenir qqch pour qqn, procurer qqch à qqn ▸ to **obtain sthg from sb** obtenir qqch de qqn / the book may be obtained from the publisher on peut se procurer le livre chez l'éditeur.

obtainable [əb'teɪnəbl] adj : where is this drug obtainable? où peut-on se procurer ce médicament ? / the catalogue is obtainable in our branches le catalogue est disponible dans nos agences / obtainable from your local supermarket en vente dans votre supermarché / this result is easily obtainable ce résultat est facile à obtenir.

obtrusive [əb'truːsɪv] adj [intrusive - decor, advertising, hoarding, architecture] trop voyant ; [- smell] tenace, envahissant, pénétrant ; [- person, behaviour] envahissant, importun, indiscret (indiscrète).

obtrusively [əb'truːsɪvlɪ] adv importunément.

obtuse [əb'tjuːs] adj 1. fml [slow-witted] obtus 2. GEOM [angle] obtus ; [triangle] obtusangle.

obverse ['ɒbvɜːs] n [of coin] avers m, face f.

obviate ['ɒbvɪeɪt] vt fml [difficulty, need] obvier à / this obviates the need for further action cela rend toute autre démarche inutile.

obvious ['ɒbvɪəs] ◆ adj 1. [evident] évident / it's obvious that he's wrong il est évident or clair qu'il a tort 2. pej [predictable] prévisible. ◆ n ▸ to **state the obvious** enfoncer une porte ouverte.

obviously ['ɒbvɪəslɪ] adv 1. [of course] évidemment, de toute évidence / she's obviously not lying il est clair or évident qu'elle ne ment pas / obviously not! il semble que non ! / he obviously got the wrong number de toute évidence, il s'est trompé de numéro 2. [plainly, visibly] manifestement / she's not obviously lying il n'est pas sûr qu'elle mente 3. [beginning a sentence] il va de soi / obviously, we won't break even until next year il va de soi que nous ne rentrerons pas dans nos frais avant un an.

occasion [ə'keɪʒn] ◆ n 1. [circumstance, time] occasion f / he was perfectly charming on that occasion cette fois-là, il fut tout à fait charmant / on the occasion of her wedding à l'occasion de son mariage / I have been there on quite a few occasions j'y suis allé à plusieurs occasions or à plusieurs reprises / if the occasion arises or should the occasion arise si l'occasion se présente, le cas échéant / it wasn't a suitable occasion les circonstances n'étaient pas favorables ▸ to **rise to the occasion** se montrer à la hauteur (de la situation) 2. [special event] événement m / his birth-

day is always a big occasion son anniversaire est toujours un événement important 3. [reason, cause] motif m, raison f, occasion f / I had no occasion to suspect her je n'avais aucune raison de la soupçonner / there is no occasion for worry il n'y a pas lieu de s'inquiéter. ◆ vt occasionner, provoquer. ❖ **on occasion(s)** adv phr de temps en temps, de temps à autre.

occasional [ə'keɪʒənl] adj 1. occasionnel, épisodique / he's an occasional visitor / golfer il vient / joue au golf de temps en temps / during his occasional visits to her lorsqu'il allait la voir or lui rendait visite / I have the occasional headache j'ai de temps en temps des maux de tête / I like an or the occasional cigar j'aime (fumer) un cigare à l'occasion or de temps en temps / there will be occasional showers il y aura quelques averses or pluies intermittentes 2. [music, play, etc.] de circonstance.

occasionally [ə'keɪʒnəlɪ] adv de temps en temps, quelquefois, occasionnellement.

occasional table n ⓤⓀ table f d'appoint.

occidental [ˌɒksɪ'dentl] adj liter occidental. ❖ **Occidental** ◆ adj occidental. ◆ n Occidental m, -e f.

occult [ɒ'kʌlt] ◆ adj occulte. ◆ n ▸ **the occult** a) [supernatural] le surnaturel b) [mystical skills] les sciences fpl occultes.

occupancy ['ɒkjʊpənsɪ] (pl occupancies) n occupation f (d'un appartement, etc.).

occupant ['ɒkjʊpənt] n [gen] occupant m, -e f ; [tenant] locataire mf ; [of vehicle] passager m, -ère f ; [of job] titulaire mf.

occupation [ˌɒkjʊ'peɪʃn] n 1. [employment] emploi m, travail m 2. [activity, hobby] occupation f 3. [of building, offices, etc.] occupation f 4. MIL & POL occupation f.

occupational [ˌɒkjuː'peɪʃənl] adj professionnel ▸ **occupational disease** maladie f professionnelle ▸ **occupational hazard** risque m professionnel or du métier.

occupational pension n ⓤⓀ retraite f complémentaire.

occupational therapist n ergothérapeute mf.

occupational therapy n ergothérapie f.

occupied ['ɒkjʊpaɪd] adj [country, town] occupé.

occupier ['ɒkjʊpaɪər] n [gen] occupant m, -e f ; [tenant] locataire mf.

occupy ['ɒkjʊpaɪ] (pt & pp occupied) vt 1. [house, room, etc.] occuper / is this seat occupied? est-ce que cette place est prise ? 2. [keep busy - person, mind] occuper ▸ to **be occupied in** or **with (doing) sthg** être occupé à (faire) qqch 3. [fill, take up - time, space] occuper 4. MIL & POL occuper 5. [hold - office, role, rank] occuper.

occur [ə'kɜːr] (pt & pp occurred, cont occurring) vi 1. [happen] arriver, avoir lieu, se produire 2. [exist, be found] se trouver, se rencontrer 3. [come to mind] ▸ to **occur to sb** venir à l'esprit de qqn.

occurrence [ə'kʌrəns] n 1. [incident] événement m 2. [fact or instance of occurring] : the increasing occurrence of racial attacks le nombre croissant d'agressions racistes.

OCD (abbr of **obsessive-compulsive disorder**) n TOC m.

ocean ['əʊʃn] n GEOG océan m ▸ **the ocean** ⓤⓢ la mer.

oceangoing ['əʊʃnˌɡəʊɪŋ] adj de haute mer.

Oceania [ˌəʊʃɪ'ɑːnɪə] pr n Océanie f / in Oceania en Océanie.

Oceanian [ˌəʊʃɪ'ɑːnɪən] ◆ n Océanien m, -enne f. ◆ adj océanien.

ocean liner n paquebot m.

oceanography [ˌəʊʃə'nɒɡrəfɪ] n océanographie f.

ochre UK, **ocher** US ['əʊkər] ◆ n [ore] ocre f ; [colour] ocre m. ◆ adj ocre (inv).

o'clock [ə'klɒk] adv **1.** [time] : *it's one / two o'clock* il est une heure / deux heures / *at precisely 9 o'clock* à 9 h précises / *a flight at 4 o'clock in the afternoon* un vol à 16 h / *the 8 o'clock bus* le bus de 8 h / *at 12 o'clock* a) [midday] à midi b) [midnight] à minuit **2.** [position] : *enemy fighter at 7 o'clock* chasseur ennemi à 7 h.

OCR n **1.** abbr of **optical character reader 2.** (abbr of **optical character recognition**) ROC f.

Oct. (written abbr of **October**) oct.

octagon ['ɒktəgən] n octogone m.

octagonal [ɒk'tægənl] adj octogonal.

octane ['ɒkteɪn] n octane m ▶ **high-octane petrol** UK or **gas** US super m, supercarburant m ▶ **low-octane petrol** UK or **gas** US ordinaire m, essence f ordinaire.

octave ['ɒktɪv] n FENCING, MUS & RELIG octave f ; LITER huitain m.

October [ɒk'təʊbər] n octobre m. See also **February**.

octogenarian [,ɒktəʊdʒɪ'neərɪən] ◆ adj octogénaire. ◆ n octogénaire mf.

octopus ['ɒktəpəs] (*pl* **octopuses** or **octopi** [-paɪ]) n ZOOL pieuvre f, poulpe m ; CULIN poulpe m.

oculist ['ɒkjʊlɪst] n oculiste mf.

OD (*pt & pp* **OD'd**) ◆ n (abbr of **overdose**) inf overdose f. ◆ vi inf être victime d'une overdose. ◆ **1.** written abbr of **overdrawn 2.** written abbr of **overdraft**.

odd [ɒd] adj **1.** [weird] bizarre, étrange / *the odd thing is that the room was empty* ce qui est bizarre, c'est que la pièce était vide / *it felt odd seeing her again* ça m'a fait (tout) drôle de la revoir **2.** [occasional, incidental] : *at odd moments* de temps en temps / *I smoke the odd cigarette* il m'arrive de fumer une cigarette de temps en temps / *we took the odd photo* nous avons pris deux ou trois photos / *we did get the odd enquiry* on a bien eu une ou deux demandes de renseignements ▶ **odd jobs** petits boulots mpl / *she gives him a few odd jobs from time to time* de temps en temps, elle lui donne une ou deux choses à faire **3.** [not matching] dépareillé / *he was wearing odd socks* ses chaussettes étaient dépareillées, il portait des chaussettes dépareillées **4.** [not divisible by two] impair **5.** (*in combinations*) inf [or so] : *twenty odd* vingt et quelques / *he must be forty-odd* il doit avoir la quarantaine or dans les quarante ans **6.** PHR **the odd one** or **man** or **woman out** l'exception f / *everyone else was in evening dress, I was the odd one out* ils étaient tous en tenue de soirée sauf moi / *they all knew each other so well and I felt the odd one out* ils se connaissaient tous si bien que j'avais l'impression d'être la cinquième roue du carrosse or de la charrette.

ODD n abbr of **optical disc drive**.

oddball ['ɒdbɔːl] inf ◆ n excentrique mf, original m, -e f. ◆ adj excentrique, original.

oddity ['ɒdɪtɪ] (*pl* **oddities**) n **1.** [strange person] excentrique mf, original m, -e f ; [strange thing] curiosité f **2.** [strangeness] étrangeté f, bizarrerie f.

odd-job man UK, **odd jobber** US n homme m à tout faire, factotum m.

odd-looking adj à l'air bizarre.

oddly ['ɒdlɪ] adv bizarrement, curieusement / *oddly shaped* d'une forme bizarre / *oddly enough, he didn't recognize me* chose curieuse, il ne m'a pas reconnu / *the oddly named "Bellevue Hotel"* l'hôtel Bellevue, au nom incongru.

oddment ['ɒdmənt] n COMM [of matched set] article m dépareillé ; [of lot, line] fin f de série ; [of fabric] coupon m.

odds [ɒdz] pl n **1.** [in betting] cote f / *the odds are ten to one against* la cote est de dix contre un / *the odds are ten to one on* la cote est d'un contre dix ▶ **to pay over the odds** UK : *I ended up paying over the odds* en fin de compte, je l'ai payé plus cher qu'il ne valait or que sa valeur **2.** [chances] chances fpl / *what are the odds on him getting the job?* quelles chances a-t-il d'avoir le poste ? / *the odds are she's been lying to us all along* il y a de fortes chances qu'elle nous ait menti depuis le début / *the odds are on / against her accepting* il y a de fortes chances / il y a peu de chances (pour) qu'elle accepte **3.** [great difficulties] ▶ **against all the odds** contre toute attente **4.** UK inf [difference] ▶ **it makes no odds** ça ne change rien / *it makes no odds to me* ça m'est égal **5.** PHR **odds and sods** UK inf, **odds and ends** a) [miscellaneous objects] objets mpl divers, bric-à-brac m inv b) [leftovers] restes mpl / *I've still got a few odds and ends to do* j'ai encore quelques bricoles or petites choses à faire. ◆ **at odds** adj phr en conflit ▶ **at odds with** en conflit avec.

odds-on adj UK : *it's odds-on that he'll win* il y a tout à parier qu'il gagnera ▶ **odds-on favourite** grand favori m.

ode [əʊd] n ode f.

odious ['əʊdɪəs] adj fml odieux.

odometer [əʊ'dɒmɪtər] n US AUTO compteur m kilométrique.

odor US = **odour**.

odour UK, **odor** US ['əʊdər] n **1.** [smell] odeur f **2.** [pervasive quality] odeur f, parfum m, arôme m.

odourless UK, **odorless** US ['əʊdəlɪs] adj inodore.

OECD (abbr of **Organisation for Economic Co-operation and Development**) pr n OCDE f.

oedema UK, **edema** US [iː'diːmə] (UK pl **oedemata** [-mətə] ; US pl **edemata** [-mətə]) n œdème m.

oesophagus UK, **esophagus** US [ɪ'sɒfəgəs] (UK pl **oesophaguses** or **oesophagi** [-gaɪ] ; US pl **esophaguses** or **esophagi** [-gaɪ]) n œsophage m.

oestrogen UK, **estrogen** US ['iːstrədʒən] n œstrogène m.

of (weak form [əv], strong form [ɒv]) prep **1.** [after nouns expressing quantity, number, amount] de / *a loaf of bread* un pain / *a piece of cake* un morceau de gâteau / *a pair of trousers* un pantalon / *there are six of us* nous sommes six / *some / many / few of us were present* quelques-uns / beaucoup / peu d'entre nous étaient présents **2.** [indicating age] de / *a boy / a girl of three* un garçon / une fille de trois ans **3.** [indicating composition, content] de / *a map of Spain* une carte d'Espagne **4.** [with words expressing attitude or emotion] de / *I'm proud of it* j'en suis fier / *I'm afraid of the dark* j'ai peur du noir **5.** [indicating possession, relationship] de / *he's a friend of mine* c'est un ami à moi / *a friend of mine saw me* un de mes amis m'a vu **6.** [indicating subject of action] : *it was kind / mean of him* c'était gentil / méchant de sa part **7.** [with names of places] de / *the city of New York* la ville de New York **8.** [made from] : *a ring of solid gold* une bague en or massif / *a heart of stone* un cœur de pierre **9.** [indicating likeness, similarity] de / *the colour of blood* / *of grass* la couleur du sang / de l'herbe / *it smells of coffee* ça sent le café / *a giant of a man* un homme très grand **10.** [indicating specific point in time or space] de / *the 3rd of May* le 3 mai / *in the middle of August* à la mi-août / *the crash of 1929* le krach de 1929 / *a quarter of nine* US neuf heures moins le quart **11.** [indicating deprivation or absence] : *a lack of food* un manque de nourriture ▶ **to rob sb of sthg** voler qqch à qqn **12.** [indicating information received or passed on] : *I've never heard of him* je n'ai jamais entendu parler de lui / *her knowledge of French* sa connaissance du français.

Ofcom ['ɒfkɒm] pr n *organisme britannique de régulation des télécoms.*

off [ɒf] ◆ adv **1.** [indicating removal] ▸ **to take sthg off** enlever or ôter qqch / *she cut off her hair* elle s'est coupé les cheveux **2.** [indicating departure] ▸ **to run off** partir en courant / *when are you off to Dublin?* quand partez-vous pour Dublin ? / *I'm off!* inf j'y vais ! / *off we go!* c'est parti ! **3.** [indicating movement away from a surface] : *I knocked the glass off with my elbow* j'ai fait tomber le verre d'un coup de coude **4.** [indicating absence, inactivity] : *to take a week off* prendre une semaine de congé / *Monday's my day off* le lundi est mon jour de congé **5.** [indicating distance in time or space] : *Paris / Christmas is still a long way off* Paris / Noël est encore loin / *it's a few miles off* c'est à quelques kilomètres d'ici **6.** [indicating disconnection] ▸ **to put** or **switch** or **turn the light off** éteindre la lumière ▸ **to turn the tap off** fermer le robinet **7.** [indicating price reduction] / **'special offer: £5 off** 'offre spéciale : 5 livres de réduction' / *the salesman gave me $20 / 20% off* le vendeur m'a fait une remise de 20 dollars / 20 %. ◆ prep ◆ **1.** [indicating movement away from] de / *she knocked the vase off the table* elle a fait tomber le vase de la table **2.** [indicating removal] de / *take the top off the bottle* enlève le bouchon de la bouteille **3.** [from the direction of] de / *a cool breeze off the sea* une brise fraîche venant du large **4.** [indicating location] : *a few miles off the coast* à quelques kilomètres de la côte / *we ate in a small restaurant off the main road* nous avons mangé dans un petit restaurant à l'écart de la grand-route / *an alley off Oxford Street* une ruelle qui part d'Oxford Street / *just off Oxford Street there's a pretty little square* à deux pas d'Oxford Street il y a une petite place ravissante **5.** [absent from] : *Mr Dale is off work today* M. Dale est absent aujourd'hui **6.** inf [no longer wanting or needing] ▸ **to be off one's food** ne pas avoir faim / *I'm off whisky* je n'aime plus le whisky. ◆ adj **1.** [not working - electricity, light, radio, TV] éteint ; [-tap] fermé ; [-engine, machine] arrêté, à l'arrêt ; [-handbrake] desserré / *the gas is off* a) [at mains] le gaz est fermé b) [under saucepan] le gaz est éteint c) [for safety reasons] le gaz est coupé / **'off** 'arrêt' / *make sure the switches are in the off position* vérifiez que les interrupteurs sont sur (la position) arrêt / *the "off" button* le bouton d'arrêt **2.** [bad, tainted] mauvais, avarié / *the milk is off* le lait a tourné / *it smells / tastes off* on dirait que ce n'est plus bon **3.** [cancelled] annulé / *if that's your attitude, the deal's off!* si c'est comme ça que vous le prenez, ma proposition ne tient plus ! **4.** inf [unacceptable] : *I say, that's a bit off!* dites donc, vous y allez un peu fort ! / *I thought it was a bit off the way she just ignored me* je n'ai pas apprécié qu'elle m'ignore comme ça. ◆ n inf [start] départ m / *they're ready for the off* ils sont prêts à partir. ❖ **off and on** adv phr par intervalles / *we lived together off and on for three years* on a plus ou moins vécu ensemble pendant trois ans.

off-air ◆ adj hors antenne. ◆ adv hors antenne.

offal ['ɒfl] n (U) **1.** UK CULIN abats mpl **2.** [refuse] ordures fpl, déchets mpl **3.** [carrion] charogne f.

off-balance ◆ adj déséquilibré. ◆ adv ▸ **to throw** or **to knock sb off-balance** a) lit faire perdre l'équilibre à qqn b) fig couper le souffle à or désarçonner qqn.

offbeat ['ɒfbi:t] adj [unconventional] décalé.

off-centre UK, **off-center** US ◆ adj **1.** [painting on wall] décentré ; [rotation] excentrique ; [gun sights] désaligné **2.** fig [unconventional] original. ◆ adv de côté.

off chance ❖ **on the off chance** adv phr au cas où / *I phoned on the off chance of catching him at home*

j'ai appelé en espérant qu'il serait chez lui / *she kept it on the off chance (that) it might prove useful* elle l'a gardé pour le cas où cela pourrait servir.

off-colour adj **1.** UK [ill] mal fichu / *she's looking a little off-colour* elle n'est pas très bien, elle est mal fichue **2.** [indelicate - film, story] de mauvais goût, d'un goût douteux.

offcut ['ɒfkʌt] n [of cloth, wood, paper] chute f ; [of meat] reste m.

off-day n : *he was having an off-day* il n'était pas en forme / *everyone has their off-days* il y a des jours sans.

off-duty adj [policeman, soldier, nurse] qui n'est pas de service / *I'm off duty at 6* je finis mon service à 6 h.

offence UK, **offense** US [ə'fens] n **1.** LAW délit m **2.** [displeasure, hurt] ▸ **to give** or **to cause offence to sb** blesser or offenser qqn ▸ **to take offence at sthg** s'offenser or s'offusquer de qqch ▸ **no offence!** sans vouloir te / vous vexer ! **3.** MIL [attack] attaque f, offensive f **4.** SPORT [attackers] attaque f.

offend [ə'fend] ◆ vt [person] offenser, blesser / *she's easily offended* elle se susceptible, elle se vexe pour un rien ; [eyes, senses, reason] choquer. ◆ vi LAW violer la loi, commettre un délit. ❖ **offend against** vt insep [law, regulation] enfreindre, violer ; [custom] aller à l'encontre de ; [good manners, good taste] être un outrage à.

offended [ə'fendɪd] adj offensé, blessé / *don't be offended if I leave early* ne le prends pas mal si je pars de bonne heure.

offender [ə'fendər] n **1.** LAW délinquant m, -e f ▸ **traffic offenders** contrevenants mpl au Code de la route **2.** [gen - culprit] coupable mf.

offending [ə'fendɪŋ] adj blessant / *the offending word was omitted* le mot choquant a été enlevé / *the offending object / article* l'objet / l'article incriminé.

offense US = offence.

offensive [ə'fensɪv] ◆ adj **1.** [causing indignation, anger] offensant, choquant ▸ **to be offensive to sb** [person] injurier or insulter qqn **2.** [disgusting - smell] repoussant **3.** [aggressive] offensif ▸ **offensive weapon** arme f offensive. ◆ n offensive f.

offensively [ə'fensɪvlɪ] adv **1.** [behave, speak] d'une manière offensante or blessante **2.** MIL & SPORT offensivement.

offer ['ɒfər] ◆ vt **1.** [present] offrir ▸ **to offer sthg to sb, to offer sb sthg** offrir qqch à qqn / *she offered me £800 for my car* elle m'a proposé 800 livres pour ma voiture ▸ **to have a lot to offer** [town, person] avoir beaucoup à offrir **2.** [propose] proposer ▸ **to offer to do sthg** s'offrir pour faire qqch, proposer de faire qqch ▸ **to offer an opinion** émettre une opinion ▸ **to offer sb advice** donner des conseils à qqn. ◆ n offre f / *£500 or near* or *nearest offer* 500 livres, à débattre / *she wants £500, but she's open to offers* elle veut 500 livres, mais elle est prête à négocier / *make me an offer!* faites-moi une offre ! ▸ **to be under offer** faire l'objet d'une proposition d'achat. ❖ **on offer** adv phr : *these goods are on offer this week* ces articles sont en promotion cette semaine.

offering ['ɒfərɪŋ] n **1.** [action] offre f **2.** [thing offered] offre f, don m **3.** RELIG offrande f.

off-guard adj [moment] : *in an off-guard moment* dans un moment d'inattention. ❖ **off guard** adv phr ▸ **to catch** or **to take sb off guard** prendre qqn au dépourvu.

offhand [,ɒf'hænd] ◆ adj **1.** [nonchalant] désinvolte, cavalier **2.** [abrupt] brusque. ◆ adv spontanément, au pied levé.

offhanded [,ɒf'hændɪd] adj = offhand (adj).

offhandedly [ˌɒfˈhændɪdlɪ] adv [nonchalantly] de façon désinvolte or cavalière, avec désinvolture ; [with abruptness] brusquement, sans ménagement.

office [ˈɒfɪs] ◆ n **1.** [of firm] bureau m ▸ **doctor's office** US cabinet m médical ▸ **lawyer's office** cabinet m d'avocat ▸ **office party** réception organisée dans un bureau à l'occasion des fêtes de fin d'année **2.** [government department] bureau m, département m ▸ **the Office of Fair Trading** organisme britannique régulant la concurrence et les prix **3.** [distribution point] bureau m, guichet m **4.** [position, power] fonction f ▸ **to be in** or **to hold office** a) [political party] être au pouvoir b) [mayor, minister, official] être en fonctions ▸ **to be out of office** avoir quitté ses fonctions ▸ **to take office** a) [political party] arriver au pouvoir b) [mayor, minister, official] entrer en fonctions ▸ **to resign / to leave office** se démettre de / quitter ses fonctions ▸ **to run for** or **to seek office** se présenter aux élections **5.** RELIG office m. ◆ comp [furniture, job, staff] de bureau. ❖ **offices** pl n [help, actions] : *I got the job through the (good) offices of Mrs Katz* j'ai obtenu ce travail grâce aux bons offices de Mᵐᵉ Katz.

office administrator n chef m de bureau.

office assistant n assistant m, -e f.

office automation n bureautique f.

office bearer n UK [in club, association] membre m du bureau.

officeholder [ˈɒfɪsˌhəʊldəʳ] n **1.** POL titulaire mf d'une fonction **2.** US = office bearer.

office junior n stagiaire mf (en secrétariat).

officer [ˈɒfɪsəʳ] n **1.** MIL officier m **2.** [policeman] agent m de police ; [as form of address - to policeman] Monsieur l'agent ; [- to policewoman] Madame l'agent **3.** [official - in local government] fonctionnaire mf ; [- of trade union] représentant m permanent ; [- of company] membre m de la direction ; [- in job titles] responsable mf ; [- of association, institution] membre m du bureau.

official [əˈfɪʃl] ◆ adj **1.** [formal] officiel ▸ **official strike** grève soutenue par la direction du syndicat ▸ **the Official Secrets Act** loi britannique sur le secret défense **2.** [alleged] officiel. ◆ n [representative] officiel m ; [civil servant] fonctionnaire mf ; [subordinate employee] employé m, -e f ; SPORT [referee] arbitre m ▸ **a bank / club / union official** un représentant de la banque / du club / du syndicat.

officially [əˈfɪʃəlɪ] adv **1.** [formally] officiellement **2.** [allegedly] théoriquement, en principe.

officiate [əˈfɪʃɪeɪt] vi **1.** [gen] : *she officiated at the ceremony* elle a présidé la cérémonie **2.** RELIG officier.

officious [əˈfɪʃəs] adj [overbearing] impérieux, autoritaire ; [interfering] importun ; [zealous] zélé, empressé.

offie [ˈɒfɪ] n UK inf = off-licence.

offing [ˈɒfɪŋ] n **1.** NAUT large m **2.** PHR **to be in the offing** être imminent, être dans l'air.

off-key ◆ adj **1.** MUS faux (fausse) **2.** fig [remark] hors de propos, sans rapport. ◆ adv faux.

off-licence n UK [shop] magasin autorisé à vendre des boissons alcoolisées à emporter.

off-line ◆ adj **1.** COMPUT [website] hors ligne ; [storage, processing] autonome **2.** INDUST [production] hors ligne. ◆ adv ▸ **to go off-line** [website, contact] se mettre hors ligne ▸ **to work off-line** travailler hors ligne.

offload [ɒfˈləʊd] vt **1.** [unload - passengers] débarquer ; [- cargo] décharger **2.** [dump - work, blame] : *she tends to offload responsibility onto other people* elle a tendance à se décharger de ses responsabilités sur les autres.

off-message adj ▸ **to be off-message** ne pas être dans la ligne officielle.

off-peak adj [consumption, rate, train] aux heures creuses, en dehors des périodes d'affluence or de pointe ▸ **off-peak hours** or **times** heures fpl creuses.

off-piste adj & adv SPORT hors-piste.

off-putting [-pʊtɪŋ] adj UK [smell] repoussant ; [manner] rébarbatif ; [person, description] peu engageant.

off-ramp n US sortie f d'autoroute.

off-road ◆ adj [driving] hors route (inv). ◆ adv [drive, cycle] hors route ▸ **off-road vehicle** véhicule m tout-terrain.

off sales pl n UK vente à emporter de boissons alcoolisées.

offscreen ◆ adj [ˈɒfskriːn] CIN & TV [out of sight] hors champ, off. ◆ adv [ɒfˈskriːn] **1.** CIN & TV hors champ, off **2.** [in private life] dans le privé.

off-season ◆ n morte-saison f. ◆ adj hors saison (inv).

offset [ˈɒfset] (pt & pp offset, cont offsetting) vt [make up for] contrebalancer, compenser / *the advantages tend to offset the difficulties* les avantages compensent presque les inconvénients.

offshoot [ˈɒfʃuːt] n [of organization, movement] ramification f ; [spin-off] application f secondaire ; fig [consequence] retombée f ; [subsidiary] : *the company has offshoots in Asia* la société a des succursales en Asie.

offshore [ˈɒfʃɔːʳ] ◆ adj **1.** [in or on sea] marin ; [near shore - shipping, fishing, waters] côtier ; [- island] près de la côte ; PETR offshore (inv), marin ▸ **offshore rig** plate-forme f offshore **2.** FIN ▸ **offshore fund** fonds m off-shore ▸ **offshore investment** investissement m off-shore. ◆ adv PETR [live, drill] en mer, au large / *20 miles offshore* à 20 milles de la côte.

offside ◆ adj & adv [ˌɒfˈsaɪd] SPORT hors jeu (inv). ◆ n [ˈɒfsaɪd] AUTO [when driving on right] côté m gauche, côté m rue ; [when driving on left] côté m droit, côté m rue.

offspring [ˈɒfsprɪŋ] (pl offspring) pl n [descendants] progéniture f.

offstage ◆ adv [ˌɒfˈsteɪdʒ] **1.** THEAT dans les coulisses / *she ran offstage* elle quitta la scène en courant **2.** [in private life] en privé. ◆ adj [ˈɒfˌsteɪdʒ] dans les coulisses.

off-the-cuff ◆ adj impromptu, improvisé. ◆ adv au pied levé, à l'improviste.

off-the-peg, off-the-rack US adj prêt à porter ▸ **off-the-peg clothes** prêt-à-porter m. ❖ **off the peg, off the rack** US adv ▸ **to buy one's clothes off the peg** acheter du prêt-à-porter.

off-the-record adj [not to be made public] confidentiel ; [not to be put in minutes] à ne pas faire figurer dans le compte rendu.

off-the-shelf adj [goods] disponible dans le commerce.

off-the-shoulder adj qui dégage les épaules.

off-the-wall adj inf [crazy] loufoque, dingue ; [unexpected] original, excentrique.

off-white ◆ adj blanc cassé (inv). ◆ n blanc m cassé.

Ofgem [ˈɒfdʒem] (abbr of Office of Gas and Electricity Markets) n organisme britannique chargé de réguler les marchés du gaz et de l'électricité.

Ofsted [ˈɒfsted] (abbr of Office for Standards in Education, Children's Services and Skills) pr n organisme britannique chargé de contrôler le système d'éducation nationale.

oft [ɒft] adv liter maintes fois, souvent.

oft- in comp ▸ **oft-quoted** souvent cité.

OFT abbr of Office of Fair Trading.

often [ˈɒfn or ˈɒftn] adv souvent / *how often do I have to tell you?* combien de fois faudra-t-il que je te le répète ? / *how often does he write to you?* est-ce qu'il t'écrit souvent ? / *she's said that once too often* elle l'a dit une fois de trop. ❖ **as often as not** adv phr la plupart du temps. ❖ **every so often** adv phr de temps en temps, de temps à autre.

Ofwat ['ɒfwɒt] pr n *organisme britannique chargé de contrôler les activités des compagnies régionales de distribution des eaux.*

ogle ['əʊgl] vt lorgner.

ogre ['əʊgə'] n ogre *m*.

oh [əʊ] interj oh, ah / *oh really?* vraiment ?, ah bon ? / *oh no!* oh non !

OH written abbr of Ohio.

Ohio [əʊ'haɪəʊ] pr n Ohio *m* / *in Ohio* dans l'Ohio.

ohm [əʊm] n ohm *m*.

OHMS (written abbr of On His/Her Majesty's Service) *tampon apposé sur le courrier administratif britannique.*

OHP n abbr of overhead projector.

OIC MESSAGING written abbr of oh, I see.

oil [ɔɪl] ❖ n 1. [petroleum] pétrole *m* 2. [in food, as lubricant] huile *f* ; [as fuel] mazout *m*, fuel *m* or fioul *m* domestique / *sardines in oil* sardines *fpl* à l'huile ▶ **to change the oil** AUTO faire la vidange ▶ **to pour oil on troubled waters** ramener le calme 3. ART [paint] (peinture *f* à l')huile *f* ; [picture] huile *f*. ❖ comp 1. [industry, production, corporation] pétrolier ; [drum, deposit, reserves] de pétrole ; [magnate, sheikh] du pétrole 2. [level, pressure] d'huile ; [filter] à huile ; [heating, burner] à mazout. ❖ vt [machine, engine] lubrifier, graisser ; [hinge, wood] huiler ; [skin] graisser, huiler.

oilcan ['ɔɪlkæn] n [drum] bidon *m* d'huile ; [oiler] burette *f* (à huile).

oil change n vidange *f*.

oilcloth ['ɔɪlklɒθ] n toile *f* cirée.

oil-dependent adj pétrodépendant.

oiled [ɔɪld] adj 1. [machine] lubrifié, graissé ; [hinge, silk] huilé 2. *inf* [drunk] ▶ **to be well oiled** être complètement bourré.

oilfield ['ɔɪlfiːld] n gisement *m* de pétrole or pétrolier.

oil-fired [-ˌfaɪəd] adj à mazout.

oil gauge n [for measuring level] jauge *f* or indicateur *m* de niveau d'huile ; [for measuring pressure] indicateur *m* de pression d'huile.

oil lamp n [burning oil] lampe *f* à huile ; [burning paraffin] lampe *f* à pétrole.

oilman ['ɔɪlmən] (*pl* oilmen [-mən]) n pétrolier *m* (*personne*).

oil paint n peinture *f* à l'huile (*substance*).

oil painting n peinture *f* à l'huile.

oil-producing adj producteur de pétrole ▶ **the oil-producing countries** les pays producteurs de pétrole.

oil refinery n raffinerie *f* de pétrole.

oilrich ['ɔɪl,rɪtʃ] adj 1. [made rich by oil trade] enrichi par le pétrole 2. [rich in oil resources] riche en gisements pétrolifères.

oil rig n [onshore] derrick *m* ; [offshore] plate-forme *f* pétrolière.

oilskin ['ɔɪlskɪn] ❖ n 1. [cloth] toile *f* cirée 2. [garment] ciré *m*. ❖ comp en toile cirée.

oil slick n [on sea] nappe *f* de pétrole ; [on beach] marée *f* noire.

oil tanker n [ship] pétrolier *m*, tanker *m* ; [lorry] camion-citerne *m* (*pour le pétrole*).

oil well n puits *m* de pétrole.

oily ['ɔɪlɪ] (*compar* oilier, *superl* oiliest) adj 1. [substance] huileux ; [rag, fingers] graisseux ; [cooking, hair, skin] gras (grasse) ▶ **oily fish** poisson *m* gras 2. *pej* [smile, person] mielleux, doucereux.

ointment ['ɔɪntmənt] n pommade *f*, onguent *m*.

oiro (written abbr of offers in the region of) : *oiro £100* 100 livres à débattre.

OJ n abbr of orange juice.

OK [,əʊ'keɪ] (*pt & pp* OKed [,əʊ'keɪd], *cont* OKing [,əʊ'keɪɪŋ]) ❖ interj *inf* OK, d'accord, d'ac. ❖ adj *inf* : *you look very pale, are you OK?* tu es très pâle, tu te sens bien ? / *that idea sounds OK to me* ça me semble être une bonne idée / *it's OK but it could be better* ce n'est pas mal, mais ça pourrait être mieux / *I'll bring my husband if that's OK with* or *by you* je viendrai avec mon mari, si ça ne vous gêne pas / *thanks for your help — that's OK!* merci de votre aide — de rien ! or il n'y a pas de quoi ! / *he's OK* or *he's an OK guy* c'est un type sympa. ❖ adv *inf* bien. ❖ vt *inf* [approve] approuver ; [initial] parafer, parapher. ❖ n *inf* [agreement] accord *m* ; [approval] approbation *f* / *I gave him the OK* je lui ai donné le feu vert. ❖ written abbr of Oklahoma.

okay [,əʊ'keɪ] = OK.

Oklahoma [,əʊklə'həʊmə] pr n Oklahoma *m* / *in Oklahoma* dans l'Oklahoma.

okra ['əʊkrə] n gombo *m*.

old [əʊld] (*compar* older, *superl* oldest) ❖ adj 1. [not new or recent] vieux (*before vowel or silent 'h' vieil, f vieille*) 2. [not young] vieux (*before vowel or silent 'h' vieil, f vieille*) / *old people* personnes *fpl* âgées ▶ **to get** or **grow old** vieillir / *who will look after me in my old age?* qui s'occupera de moi quand je serai vieux ? / *I've got a little money put aside for my old age* j'ai quelques économies de côté pour mes vieux jours ▶ **old people's home** maison *f* de retraite 3. [referring to a particular age] : *how old is she?* quel âge a-t-elle ? ▶ **to be old enough to do sthg** être en âge de faire qqch / *she's two years older than him* elle a deux ans de plus que lui / *the older generation* la vieille génération / *my older sister* ma sœur aînée / *she's 6 months / 25 years old* elle a 6 mois / 25 ans, elle est âgée de 6 mois / 25 ans / *they have a 14-year-old boy* ils ont un garçon de 14 ans 4. [former] ancien 5. *inf* [expressing familiarity or affection] vieux (*before vowel or silent 'h' vieil, f vieille*) 6. *inf* [as intensifier] : *it's a funny old life!* la vie est drôle, quand même ! / *silly old bat* espèce de vieille folle ! / *any old bit of wood will do* n'importe quel vieux bout de bois fera l'affaire. ❖ pl n ▶ **the old** les vieux *mpl*. ❖ **of old** adv phr 1. *liter* [of former times] : *in days of old* autrefois, jadis 2. [for a long time] : *I know them of old* je les connais depuis longtemps.

old age pension n 🇬🇧 (pension *f* de) retraite *f*.

old age pensioner n 🇬🇧 retraité *m*, -e *f*.

Old Bailey pr n ▶ **the Old Bailey** *la cour d'assises de Londres.*

Old Bill pl n 🇬🇧 v *inf* ▶ **the Old Bill** les flics *mpl*.

old boy n 🇬🇧 [ex-pupil of school] ancien élève *m*.

olden ['əʊldn] adj *arch & liter* d'autrefois, d'antan ▶ **in olden times** or **days** autrefois, jadis.

old-fashioned [-'fæʃnd] ❖ adj 1. [out-of-date] suranné, désuet (désuète), démodé ; [idea] périmé, démodé 2. [of the past] d'autrefois, ancien. ❖ n 🇺🇸 old-fashioned *m* (*cocktail au whisky*).

old flame n ancien béguin *m*.

old girl n 🇬🇧 [ex-pupil] ancienne élève *f*.

Old Glory pr n 🇺🇸 *surnom du drapeau américain.*

old hand n expert m, vieux routier m ▶ **to be an old hand at sthg** avoir une grande expérience de qqch.

old hat adj inf dépassé, vieux *(before vowel or silent 'h' vieil, f vieille)*.

old maid n pej vieille fille f.

old master n [painter] grand maître m (de la peinture); [painting] tableau m de maître.

old media n anciens médias mpl.

old school n ▶ **of the old school** de la vieille école.

old school tie n 🇬🇧 **1.** lit cravate f aux couleurs de son ancienne école **2.** fig & pej attitudes et système de valeurs typiques des anciens élèves des écoles privées britanniques.

old-style adj à l'ancienne (mode).

Old Testament n Ancien Testament m.

old-time adj d'autrefois, ancien.

old-timer n **1.** 🇺🇸 inf [old person] vieillard m, ancien m, -enne f **2.** [veteran] vétéran m, vieux m de la vieille.

old wives' tale n conte m de bonne femme.

old-world adj [of the past] d'antan, d'autrefois; [quaint] pittoresque / *a village full of old-world charm* un village au charme suranné.

Old World pr n ▶ **the Old World** l'Ancien Monde.

O-level n 🇬🇧 SCH examen qui sanctionnait autrefois la fin des études au niveau de la seconde; ≃ BEPC m.

olive ['ɒlɪv] ◆ n [fruit] olive f; [tree] olivier m ▶ **olive (wood)** (bois m d')olivier m ▶ **olive grove** olivaie f, oliveraie f. ◆ adj [colour] (vert) olive *(inv)* / *he has an olive complexion* il a le teint olive.

olive branch n rameau m d'olivier ▶ **to hold out an olive branch to sb** proposer à qqn de faire la paix.

olive green n vert m olive. ◆ **olive-green** adj vert olive *(inv)*.

olive oil n huile f d'olive.

ollie ['ɒlɪ] n [in skateboarding] ollie m.

Olympic [ə'lɪmpɪk] adj olympique ▶ **the Olympic Games** les jeux Olympiques. ◆ **Olympics** pl n ▶ **the Olympics** les jeux Olympiques.

OM abbr of **Order of Merit**.

Oman [əʊ'mɑːn] pr n Oman / *in Oman* à Oman.

OMB (abbr of **Office of Management and Budget**) pr n organisme fédéral américain chargé de préparer le budget.

ombudsman ['ɒmbʊdzmən] (pl **ombudsmen** [-mən]) n ombudsman m, médiateur m; [in Quebec] protecteur m du citoyen.

omega ['əʊmɪɡə] n oméga m.

omelette 🇬🇧, **omelet** 🇺🇸 ['ɒmlɪt] n omelette f.

omen ['əʊmen] n augure m, présage m.

OMG MESSAGING written abbr of oh, my god.

ominous ['ɒmɪnəs] adj [threatening] menaçant, inquiétant; [boding ill] de mauvais augure, de sinistre présage.

ominously ['ɒmɪnəslɪ] adv de façon inquiétante or menaçante.

omission [ə'mɪʃn] n [exclusion - accidental] omission f, oubli m; [-deliberate] exclusion f.

omit [ə'mɪt] (pt & pp **omitted**, cont **omitting**) vt omettre / *a name was omitted from the list* un nom a été omis sur la liste ▶ **to omit to do sthg** omettre de faire qqch.

omnibus ['ɒmnɪbəs] ◆ n **1.** dated [bus] omnibus m **2.** RADIO & TV rediffusion en continu des épisodes d'un feuilleton. ◆ adj 🇬🇧 [edition] complet (complète).

omnipotence [ɒm'nɪpətəns] n omnipotence f.

omnipotent [ɒm'nɪpətənt] ◆ adj omnipotent, toutpuissant. ◆ n ▶ **the Omnipotent** le Tout-Puissant.

omnipresent [ˌɒmnɪ'prezənt] adj omniprésent.

omniscient [ɒm'nɪsɪənt] adj omniscient.

omnivorous [ɒm'nɪvərəs] adj ZOOL omnivore; fig insatiable, avide.

on [ɒn]
◆ prep

A. IN SPACE 1. [specifying position] sur / *on the floor* par terre / *on the ceiling* au plafond / *there are posters on the walls* il y a des affiches aux or sur les murs / *on the left / right* à gauche / droite **2.** [indicating general location, area] : *he works on a building site* il travaille sur un chantier / *they live on a farm* ils habitent une ferme **3.** [indicating movement, direction] : *the mirror fell on the floor* la glace est tombée par terre.

B. WORN OR CARRIED [indicating thing carried] sur / *I only had £10 on me* je n'avais que 10 livres sur moi.

C. INDICATING INTEREST OR ACTIVITY 1. [indicating purpose of money, time, effort spent] sur / *she spent £1,000 on her new stereo* elle a dépensé 1 000 livres pour acheter sa nouvelle chaîne hi-fi **2.** [indicating activity undertaken] : *he's off on a trip to Brazil* il part pour un voyage au Brésil / *she was sent on a course* on l'a envoyé suivre des cours.

D. SUBJECT, CAUSE OR METHOD 1. [about, on the subject of] sur / *we all agree on that point* nous sommes tous d'accord sur ce point **2.** [indicating means of transport] : *on the bus / train* dans le bus / train / *she arrived on the midday bus / train* elle est arrivée par le bus / train de midi **3.** [indicating instrument played] : *who's on guitar / on drums?* qui est à la guitare / à la batterie ? **4.** RADIO, TV & THEAT : *I heard it on the radio / on television* je l'ai entendu à la radio / à la télévision / *what's on the other channel* or *side?* qu'est-ce qu'il y a sur l'autre chaîne ?

E. IN TIME : *on the 6th of July* le 6 juillet / *on Christmas Day* le jour de Noël / *I'll see her on Monday* je la vois lundi / *I don't work on Mondays* je ne travaille pas le lundi / *it's just on five o'clock* il est cinq heures pile.

F. INDICATING SOURCE 1. [indicating source of payment] : *have a drink on me* prenez un verre, c'est moi qui offre **2.** [indicating drugs, medicine prescribed] : *I'm still on antibiotics* je suis toujours sous antibiotiques / *the doctor put her on tranquillizers* le médecin lui a prescrit des tranquillisants.

◆ adv **1.** [in place] : *the lid wasn't on* le couvercle n'était pas mis / *put the top back on afterwards* remets le capuchon ensuite **2.** [referring to clothes] : *why have you got your gloves on?* pourquoi as-tu mis tes gants ? **3.** [indicating continued action] : *to read on* continuer à lire / *the car drove on* la voiture ne s'est pas arrêtée **4.** inf PHR **to be** or **go on about sthg** parler de qqch sans arrêt / *he's on about his new car again* le voilà reparti sur sa nouvelle voiture / *what's she on about?* qu'est-ce qu'elle raconte ? ▶ **to be** or **go on at sb (about sthg)** : *my parents are always on at me about my hair* mes parents n'arrêtent pas de m'embêter avec mes cheveux.

◆ adj **1.** [working - electricity, light, radio, TV] allumé; [-gas, tap] ouvert; [-engine, machine] en marche; [-handbrake] serré / *the radio was on very loud* la radio hurlait / *make sure the switches are in the "on" position* vérifiez que les interrupteurs sont sur (la position) « marche » / *the "on" button* le bouton de mise en marche **2.** [happening, under way] : *there's a conference on next week* il y a une conférence la semaine prochaine / *the match is still on* a) [on TV] le match n'est pas terminé b) [going ahead] le match n'a pas été annulé / *it's on at the local cinema* ça passe au cinéma du quartier / *your favourite TV programme is on tonight* il y a ton émission préférée à la télé ce soir **3.** inf [in agreement] : *are you still on for dinner tonight?* ça marche toujours pour le dîner de ce soir ? / *shall we say*

£10? — *you're on!* disons 10 livres ? — d'accord or tope là ! ❖ **on and off** adv phr : *we went out together on and off for a year* on a eu une relation irrégulière pendant un an. ❖ **on and on** adv phr sans arrêt / *the play dragged on and on* la pièce n'en finissait plus.

ON written abbr of **Ontario**.

on-air ◆ adj TV & RADIO à l'antenne. ◆ adv TV & RADIO à l'antenne.

on-board adj COMPUT [built-in] intégré.

ONC (abbr of **Ordinary National Certificate**) n *brevet de technicien en Grande-Bretagne.*

on-camera ◆ adj TV & CIN à l'image. ◆ adv TV & CIN à l'image.

1NC MESSAGING written abbr of **once**.

once [wʌns] ◆ adv **1.** [on a single occasion] une fois / *I've been there once before* j'y suis déjà allé une fois / *once or twice* une ou deux fois / *I see her once every three months* je la vois tous les trois mois ▶ **once in a while** occasionnellement, une fois de temps en temps ▶ **once more** or **again** encore une fois, une fois de plus ▶ **for once** : *for once he isn't late* pour une fois, il n'est pas en retard ▶ **once a liar always a liar** qui a menti mentira **2.** [formerly] jadis, autrefois ▶ **once upon a time there was...** il était une fois... ◆ predet : *once a month / year* une fois par mois / an. ◆ conj une fois que, dès que / *it'll be easy once we've started* une fois qu'on aura commencé, ce sera facile / *give me a call once you get there* passe-moi un coup de fil quand tu arrives. ◆ n ▶ **(just) this once** (juste) pour cette fois-ci, (juste) pour une fois. ❖ **at once** adv phr **1.** [at the same time] à la fois, en même temps **2.** [immediately] tout de suite. ❖ **once and for all** adv phr une fois pour toutes.

once-only adj : *a once-only offer* une offre unique.

once-over n inf **1.** [glance] coup *m* d'œil / *I gave the morning paper the once-over* j'ai jeté un coup d'œil sur le journal du matin / *I could see her giving me the once-over* je la voyais qui me regardait des pieds à la tête **2.** [clean] : *give the stairs / the bookcase a quick once-over* passe un coup dans l'escalier / sur la bibliothèque.

oncologist [ɒŋ'kɒlədʒɪst] n oncologue *mf*, oncologiste *mf*.

oncoming ['ɒn,kʌmɪŋ] ◆ adj **1.** [traffic, vehicle] venant en sens inverse **2.** [year, season] qui arrive, qui approche. ◆ n approche *f.*

OND (abbr of **Ordinary National Diploma**) n *brevet de technicien supérieur en Grande-Bretagne.*

one [wʌn] ◆ det **1.** (as numeral) [in expressions of age, date, measurement, etc.] un *m*, une *f* / *one and a half kilos* un kilo et demi / *one thousand* mille / *at one o'clock* à une heure / *I'll be one (year old) in June* il aura un an en juin / *on page one* a) [of book] (à la) page un b) [of newspaper] à la une ▶ **one or two** [a few] un / une ou deux **2.** [referring to a single object or person] un *m*, une *f* / *only one answer is correct* il n'y a qu'une seule bonne réponse / *one car looks much like another to me* pour moi, toutes les voitures se ressemblent **3.** [only, single] seul, unique / *the one woman who knows* la seule femme qui soit au courant **4.** [same] même / *the two wanted men are in fact one and the same person* les deux hommes recherchés sont en fait une seule et même personne **5.** [instead of 'a'] : *if there's one thing I hate it's rudeness* s'il y a une chose que je n'aime pas, c'est bien la grossièreté / *for one thing it's too late* d'abord, c'est trop tard **6.** [indicating indefinite time] : *early one morning* un matin de bonne heure. ◆ pron **1.** [person, thing] : *which one* lequel *m*, laquelle *f* / *this one* celui-ci *m*, celle-ci *f* / *the other one* l'autre *mf* / *the right one* le bon (la bonne) / *he's the*

one who did it c'est lui qui l'a fait / *one of my colleagues is sick* (l')un / (l')une de mes collègues est malade / *she's one of us* elle est des nôtres / *I've only got one* je n'en ai qu'un / qu'une / *the mother and her little ones* la mère et ses petits / *I'm not much of a one* or *I'm not a great one for cheese* inf je ne raffole pas du fromage / *she's a great one for computers* c'est une mordue d'informatique / *I'm not one to gossip but...* je ne suis pas du genre commère mais... ▶ **to get one over on sb** inf avoir l'avantage sur qqn **2.** [joke, story, question, etc.] : *that's a good one!* elle est bien bonne celle-là ! / *that's an easy one* c'est facile **3.** fml [as subject] on ; [as object or after preposition] vous / *one can only do one's* or US *his best* on fait ce qu'on peut / *it certainly makes one think* ça fait réfléchir, c'est sûr. ❖ **for one** adv phr : *I for one am disappointed* pour ma part, je suis déçu. ❖ **in one** adv phr **1.** [combined] ▶ **all in one** à la fois **2.** [at one attempt] du premier coup. ❖ **in ones and twos** adv phr : *people stood around in ones and twos* les gens se tenaient là par petits groupes. ❖ **one another** pron phr l'un l'autre (l'une l'autre), les uns les autres (les unes les autres) / *they didn't dare talk to one another* ils n'ont pas osé se parler / *we love one another* nous nous aimons. ❖ **one by one** adv phr un par un (une par une).

one-armed bandit n machine *f* à sous.

1DAY MESSAGING written abbr of **one day**.

one-dimensional adj unidimensionnel.

one-hit wonder n *groupe ou chanteur qui n'a eu qu'un seul tube.*

one-liner n [quip] bon mot *m.*

one-man adj [vehicle, canoe] monoplace ; [task] pour un seul homme ; [expedition] en solitaire ▶ **one-man show** a) [by artist] exposition *f* individuelle b) [by performer] spectacle *m* solo, one-man-show *m* inv.

one-man band n homme-orchestre *m.*

oneness ['wʌnnɪs] n **1.** [singleness] unité *f* ; [uniqueness] unicité *f* **2.** [agreement] accord *m* **3.** [wholeness] intégrité *f* **4.** [sameness] identité *f.*

one-night stand n **1.** MUS & THEAT représentation *f* unique **2.** inf [brief affair] aventure *f* (sans lendemain).

one-off ◆ adj unique. ◆ n [original] : *it's a one-off* a) [object] c'est unique b) [situation] c'est exceptionnel.

one-on-one US = **one-to-one**.

one-parent family n famille *f* monoparentale.

one-party adj POL à parti unique.

one-piece ◆ adj une pièce *(inv).* ◆ n vêtement *m* une pièce.

onerous ['ɒnərəs] adj fml lourd, pénible.

⚠ **Onéreux** means **expensive, not onerous.**

oneself [wʌn'self] pron **1.** [reflexive] se, s' (before vowel or silent 'h') ; [after preposition] soi, soi-même ; [emphatic] soi-même / *to wash oneself* se laver / *to be pleased with oneself* être content de soi or soi-même **2.** [one's normal self] soi-même **3.** PHR **to be (all) by oneself** être tout seul.

one-shot US inf = **one-off** *(adj).*

one-sided adj **1.** [unequal] inégal **2.** [biased] partial **3.** [unilateral] unilatéral.

one-size adj taille unique *(inv).*

one-stop adj [shop, service] où l'on trouve tout ce dont on a besoin ▶ **one-stop buying** or **shopping** achats réalisés au même endroit.

one-time adj ancien.

one-to-one ◆ adj [discussion, meeting] seul à seul, en tête à tête / *I'd prefer to talk to you on a one-to-one basis* je préférerais vous parler seul à seul / *one-to-one tuition* cours *mpl* particuliers. ◆ n [meeting] entretien *m* (individuel).

one-touch dialling 🇬🇧, **one-touch dialing** 🇺🇸 n numérotation *f* rapide.

one-track adj 🅿🅷🆁 **to have a one-track mind** : *he's got a one-track mind* a) *inf* [thinks only of one thing] c'est une obsession chez lui b) [thinks only of sex] il ne pense qu'à ça.

one-up (*pt & pp* one-upped, *cont* one-upping) ◆ adj : *we're one-up on our competitors* nous avons pris l'avantage sur nos concurrents. ◆ vt 🇺🇸 *inf* marquer un point sur.

one-upmanship [-'ʌpmənʃɪp] n comportement d'une personne qui ne supporte pas de voir d'autres faire mieux qu'elle.

one-way adj **1.** [street] à sens unique ; [traffic] en sens unique **2.** [ticket] simple **3.** [mirror] sans tain **4.** [reaction, current] irréversible ; [decision] unilatéral **5.** [relationship, feeling] à sens unique.

ongoing ['ɒn,gəʊɪŋ] adj [continuing] continu ; [current, in progress] en cours.

onion ['ʌnjən] n oignon *m*.

on-line adj & adv COMPUT en ligne.

online banking n banque *f* en ligne.

online community n communauté *f* en ligne.

online retailer n détaillant *m* en ligne.

online shopping n téléachats *mpl*, achats *mpl* sur Internet.

onlooker ['ɒn,lʊkər] n [during event] spectateur *m*, -trice *f* ; [after accident] badaud *m*, -e *f*, curieux *m*, -euse *f*.

only ['əʊnlɪ] ◆ adj seul, unique / *he's | she's an only child* il est fils / elle est fille unique / *she was the only woman there* c'était la seule femme / *her only answer was to shrug her shoulders* pour toute réponse, elle a haussé les épaules / *the only thing is, I won't be there* le seul problème, c'est que je ne serai pas là. ◆ adv **1.** [exclusively] seulement / *there are only two people I trust* il n'y a que deux personnes en qui j'aie confiance / **'staff only'** 'réservé au personnel' **2.** [just, merely] : *he's only a child!* ce n'est qu'un enfant ! / *it's only me!* c'est moi ! / *it's only natural she should want to see him* c'est tout naturel qu'elle veuille le voir / *I only hope we're not too late* j'espère seulement que nous n'arrivons pas trop tard **3.** [to emphasize smallness of amount, number, etc.] ne… que / *it only cost me £5* ça ne m'a coûté que 5 livres **4.** [to emphasize recentness of event] : *I only found out this morning* je n'ai appris ça que ce matin. ◆ conj *inf* **1.** [but, except] mais **2.** [were it not for the fact that] mais, seulement. ◆ **not only** conj phr ▶ **not only… but also** non seulement… mais aussi. ◆ **only if, only… if** conj phr seulement si / *he'll only agree if the money's good enough* il n'acceptera que si on lui propose assez d'argent. ◆ **only just** adv phr **1.** [not long before] : *I've only just woken up* je viens (tout) juste de me réveiller **2.** [barely] tout juste / *I only just finished in time* je n'ai fini qu'au dernier moment. ◆ **only too** adv phr : *I was only too aware of my own shortcomings* je n'étais que trop conscient de mes propres imperfections.

O4U MESSAGING written abbr of **only for you.**

on-message adj ▶ **to be on-message** être dans la ligne officielle.

o.n.o. (abbr of **or near/nearest offer**) adv 🇬🇧 : *£100 o.n.o.* 100 livres à débattre.

on-off adj **1.** ELEC ▶ **on-off button** bouton *m* de marchearrêt **2.** [intermittent] : *they have a very on-off relationship* ils ont une relation très peu suivie.

on-screen adj & adv COMPUT à l'écran ▶ **on-screen help** aide *f* en ligne.

onset ['ɒn,set] n **1.** [assault] attaque *f*, assaut *m* **2.** [beginning] début *m*, commencement *m*.

onshore ['ɒn'ʃɔːr] adj **1.** [on land] sur terre, terrestre ▶ **onshore oil production** production *f* pétrolière à terre **2.** [moving towards land] ▶ **onshore wind** vent *m* de mer.

onside [,ɒn'saɪd] adj & adv SPORT qui n'est pas hors jeu ou en position de hors-jeu.

on-site adj sur place.

onslaught ['ɒn,slɔːt] n attaque *f*, assaut *m*.

onstage ['ɒnsteɪdʒ] adj & adv sur scène.

Ont. written abbr of **Ontario.**

on-target earnings pl n [of salesperson] salaire *m* plus commission.

Ontario [ɒn'teərɪəʊ] pr n Ontario *m* / *in Ontario* dans l'Ontario.

on-the-job adj [training] en entreprise ; [experience] sur le tas.

onto ['ɒntuː] prep **1.** [gen] sur / *the bedroom looks out onto a garden* la chambre donne sur un jardin / *let's move onto the next point* passons au point suivant / *get onto the bus* montez dans le bus **2.** [indicating discovery] : *let's just hope the authorities don't get onto us* espérons qu'on ne sera pas découverts par les autorités / *we're onto something big* nous sommes sur le point de faire une importante découverte / *he'd better watch out, I'm onto him!* qu'il fasse attention, je l'ai dans mon or le collimateur ! **3.** [in contact with] : *you should get onto head office about this* vous devriez contacter le siège à ce sujet.

on-trend adj dans le vent, branché.

onus ['əʊnəs] n [responsibility] responsabilité *f* ; [burden] charge *f*.

onward ['ɒnwəd] ◆ adj : *the onward journey* la suite du voyage / *there is an onward flight to Chicago* il y a une correspondance pour Chicago. ◆ adv 🇺🇸 = **onwards.** ◆ interj en avant.

onwards ['ɒnwədz] adv [forwards] en avant ; [further on] plus loin ▶ **to go onwards** avancer. ◆ **from… onwards** adv phr à partir de / *from her childhood onwards* dès ou depuis son enfance / *from now onwards* désormais, dorénavant, à partir de maintenant / *from then onwards* à partir de ce moment-là.

onyx ['ɒnɪks] ◆ n onyx *m*. ◆ comp en onyx, d'onyx.

oodles ['uːdlz] pl n *inf* des masses *fpl*, des tas *mpl*.

ooh [uː] ◆ interj oh ! ◆ vi : *they were all oohing and aahing over her baby* ils poussaient tous des cris d'admiration devant son bébé.

oomph [ʊmf] n *inf* **1.** [energy] punch *m* **2.** [sex appeal] sexappeal *m*.

oops [ups ou uːps], **oops-a-daisy** [,ʊpsə'deɪzɪ] interj *inf* oh la la la !

ooze [uːz] ◆ vi suinter. ◆ vt : *the walls ooze moisture* l'humidité suinte des murs. ◆ n boue *f*, vase *f*.

op [ɒp] (abbr of **operation**) n *inf* MED & MIL opération *f*.

opal ['əʊpl] ◆ n opale *f*. ◆ comp [brooch, ring] en opale.

opaque [əʊ'peɪk] adj **1.** *lit* opaque **2.** *fig* [text] inintelligible, obscur ; [person] stupide.

OPEC ['əʊpek] (abbr of **Organization of the Petroleum Exporting Countries**) pr n OPEP *f*.

op-ed ['ɒped] n [in newspaper] page contenant les tribunes libres située en face de l'éditorial.

open ['əʊpn] ◆ adj **1.** [not shut -window, cupboard, suitcase, jar, box, sore, valve] ouvert / her eyes were slightly open / wide open ses yeux étaient entrouverts / grands ouverts / he kicked the door open il a ouvert la porte d'un coup de pied **2.** [not fastened -coat, fly, packet] ouvert / his shirt was open to the waist sa chemise était ouverte or déboutonnée jusqu'à la ceinture **3.** [spread apart, unfolded -arms, book, magazine, umbrella] ouvert ; [-newspaper] ouvert, déplié ; [-legs, knees] écarté / the book lay open at page six le livre était ouvert à la page six **4.** [for business] ouvert / are you open on Saturdays? ouvrez-vous le samedi ? **5.** [not covered -carriage, wagon, bus] découvert ; [-car] décapoté ; [-grave] ouvert ; [-boat] ouvert, non ponté ; [-courtyard, sewer] à ciel ouvert **6.** [not enclosed -hillside, plain] : our neighbourhood lacks open space notre quartier manque d'espaces verts / the wide open spaces of Texas les grands espaces du Texas / they were attacked in open country ils ont été attaqués en rase campagne / ahead lay a vast stretch of open water au loin s'étendait une vaste étendue d'eau ▸ **the open air** : in the open air en plein air / nothing beats life in the open air il n'y a rien de mieux que la vie au grand air **7.** [unobstructed -road, passage] dégagé ; [-mountain pass] ouvert, praticable ; [-waterway] ouvert à la navigation ; [-view] dégagé / only one lane on the bridge is open il n'y a qu'une voie ouverte à la circulation sur le pont **8.** [unoccupied, available -job] vacant ; [-period of time] libre / we have two positions open nous avons deux postes à pourvoir / I'll keep this Friday open for you je vous réserverai ce vendredi **9.** [unrestricted -competition] ouvert (à tous) ; [-meeting, trial] public ; [-society] ouvert, démocratique / club membership is open to anyone aucune condition particulière n'est requise pour devenir membre du club ▸ **open seating** AERON & THEAT places fpl non réservées ▸ **open ticket** billet m open **10.** [unprotected, unguarded -flank, fire] ouvert ; [-wiring] non protégé ▸ **to lay o.s. open to criticism** prêter le flanc à la critique **11.** [undecided -question] non résolu, non tranché / he wanted to leave the date open il n'a pas voulu fixer de date **12.** [liable] : his speech is open to misunderstanding son discours peut prêter à confusion / the prices are not open to negotiation les prix ne sont pas négociables **13.** [receptive] : to be open to suggestions être ouvert aux suggestions / I try to keep an open mind about such things j'essaie de ne pas avoir de préjugés sur ces questions **14.** [candid -person, smile, countenance] ouvert, franc (franche) ; [-discussion] franc (franche) **15.** [blatant -contempt, criticism] ouvert ; [-attempt] non dissimulé ; [-scandal] public ; [-rivalry] déclaré. ◆ vt **1.** [window, lock, shop, eyes, border] ouvrir ; [wound] rouvrir ; [bottle, can] ouvrir, déboucher ; [wine] déboucher / she opened her eyes very wide elle ouvrit grand les yeux, elle écarquilla les yeux **2.** [unfasten -coat, envelope, gift, collar] ouvrir **3.** [unfold, spread apart -book, umbrella, penknife, arms, hand] ouvrir ; [-newspaper] ouvrir, déplier ; [-legs, knees] écarter **4.** [pierce -hole] percer ; [-breach] ouvrir ; [-way, passage] ouvrir, frayer **5.** [start -campaign, discussion, account, trial] ouvrir, commencer ; [-negotiations] ouvrir, engager ; [-conversation] engager, entamer **6.** [set up -shop, business] ouvrir ; [inaugurate -hospital, airport, library] ouvrir, inaugurer **7.** [clear, unblock -road, lane, passage] dégager ; [-mountain pass] ouvrir. ◆ vi **1.** [door, window] (s')ouvrir ; [suitcase, valve, padlock, eyes] s'ouvrir / the window opens outwards la fenêtre (s')ouvre vers l'extérieur ▸ **open wide!** ouvrez grand ! / both rooms open onto the corridor les deux chambres donnent or ouvrent sur le couloir **2.** [unfold, spread apart -book, umbrella, parachute] s'ouvrir ; [-bud, leaf] s'ouvrir, s'épanouir **3.** [gape -chasm] s'ouvrir **4.** [for business] ouvrir / what time do you open on Sundays? à quelle heure ouvrez-vous le dimanche ?

5. [start -campaign, meeting, discussion, concert, play, story] commencer / the film opens next week le film sort la semaine prochaine. ◆ n **1.** [outdoors, open air] ▸ **(out) in the open** a) [gen] en plein air, dehors b) [in countryside] au grand air / to sleep in the open dormir à la belle étoile **2.** [public eye] ▸ **to bring sthg (out) into the open** exposer or étaler qqch au grand jour **3.** SPORT ▸ **the British Open** l'open m or le tournoi open de Grande-Bretagne. ❖ **open out** ◆ vi **1.** [unfold -bud, petals] s'ouvrir, s'épanouir ; [-parachute] s'ouvrir ; [-sail] se gonfler **2.** [lie -vista, valley] s'étendre, s'ouvrir **3.** [widen -path, stream] s'élargir. ◆ vt sep [unfold -newspaper, deck chair, fan] ouvrir. ❖ **open up** ◆ vi **1.** [unlock the door] ouvrir / open up in there! ouvrez, là-dedans ! **2.** [become available -possibility] s'ouvrir / we may have a position opening up in May il se peut que nous ayons un poste disponible en mai **3.** [for business -shop, branch, etc.] (s')ouvrir **4.** [become less reserved -person] s'ouvrir ; [-discussion] s'animer / he needs to open up about his feelings il a besoin de dire ce qu'il a sur le cœur or de s'épancher. ◆ vt sep **1.** [crate, gift, bag, tomb] ouvrir **2.** [for business] ouvrir **3.** [for development -isolated region] désenclaver ; [-quarry, oilfield] ouvrir, commencer l'exploitation de ; [-new markets] ouvrir / a discovery which opens up new fields of research une découverte qui crée de nouveaux domaines de recherche.

open-air adj [market, concert] en plein air ; [sports] de plein air / open-air swimming pool piscine f découverte / open-air museum écomusée m.

open-and-shut adj [choice] simple, évident / it's an open-and-shut case la solution est évidente or ne fait pas l'ombre d'un doute.

opencast ['əʊpnkɑːst] adj 🇬🇧 MIN à ciel ouvert.

open day n 🇬🇧 journée f portes ouvertes.

open-door adj [policy] de la porte ouverte.

open-ended [-'endɪd] adj [flexible -offer] flexible ; [-plan] modifiable ; [-question] ouvert / an open-ended discussion une discussion libre / open-ended contract contrat m à durée indéterminée.

opener ['əʊpnər] n **1.** [tool] outil m or dispositif m servant à ouvrir ; [for cans] ouvre-boîtes m inv **2.** [person -in cards, games] ouvreur m, -euse f **3.** [first song, act, etc.] lever m de rideau **4.** 🅟🅗🅡 **for openers** 🇬🇧 inf pour commencer.

open-handed adj généreux.

open-hearted [-'hɑːtɪd] adj **1.** [candid] franc (franche), sincère **2.** [kind] bon, qui a bon cœur.

open-heart surgery n chirurgie f à cœur ouvert.

open house n **1.** 🇺🇸 = open day **2.** 🇺🇸 [party] grande fête f **3.** 🅟🅗🅡 **to keep open house** 🇬🇧 tenir table ouverte.

opening ['əʊpnɪŋ] ◆ adj [part, chapter] premier ; [day, hours] d'ouverture ; [ceremony] d'ouverture, d'inauguration ; [remark] préliminaire, préalable ▸ **opening balance** solde m d'ouverture ▸ **opening prices** ST. EX prix mpl à l'ouverture. ◆ n **1.** [act of opening] ouverture f **2.** [gap, hole, entrance] ouverture f **3.** 🇺🇸 = clearing **4.** [start, first part] ouverture f, début m **5.** [opportunity -gen] occasion f ; [-for employment] débouché m.

opening night n THEAT première f.

opening time n COMM heure f d'ouverture.

open letter n lettre f ouverte.

openly ['əʊpənlɪ] adv visiblement.

open market n marché m libre.

open-minded adj [receptive] ouvert (d'esprit) ; [unprejudiced] sans préjugés.

open-mindedness [-'maɪndɪdnɪs] n ouverture f d'esprit.

open-mouthed [-'maʊðd] ◆ adj [person] stupéfait, interdit. ◆ adv ▶ **to watch open-mouthed** regarder bouche bée.

open-neck(ed) adj à col ouvert.

openness ['əʊpənnɪs] n 1. [candidness] franchise f; [receptivity] ouverture f 2. [spaciousness] largeur f.

open-plan adj ARCHIT [design, house] à plan ouvert, sans cloisons ▶ **open-plan kitchen** cuisine f américaine ▶ **open-plan office** bureau m paysager.

open primary n US POL élection primaire ouverte à tous les électeurs y compris à ceux non membres d'un parti.

open prison n prison f ouverte.

open sandwich n [gen] tartine f; [cocktail food] canapé m.

open season n saison f.

open secret n UK secret m de Polichinelle.

open sesame ◆ interj ▶ **open sesame!** sésame, ouvre-toi ! ◆ n UK [means to success] sésame m.

open shop n INDUST UK [open to non-union members] entreprise ne pratiquant pas le monopole d'embauche.

open source adj COMPUT à code source libre, open-source.

open-toe, open-toed [-təʊd] adj [shoe] ouvert.

open-top adj décapotable.

open-topped bus n autobus m à impériale.

Open University n UK ≃ Université f ouverte à tous (pratiquant le télé-enseignement).

open verdict n LAW verdict m de décès sans cause déterminée.

opera ['ɒpərə] n 1. [musical play] opéra m 2. [art of opera] opéra m ▶ **opera singer** chanteur m, -euse f d'opéra 3. [opera house] opéra m.

operable ['ɒprəbl] adj MED opérable.

opera glasses pl n jumelles fpl de théâtre.

operagoer ['ɒprə.gəʊə] n amateur m d'opéra.

opera house n (théâtre m de l')opéra m.

operate ['ɒpəreɪt] ◆ vt 1. [machine, device] faire fonctionner, faire marcher 2. [business] gérer, diriger ; [mine] exploiter ; [drug ring] contrôler. ◆ vi 1. [machine, device] marcher, fonctionner ; [system, process, network] fonctionner 2. MED opérer ▶ **to operate on sb (for sthg)** opérer qqn (de qqch) 3. [be active] opérer 4. [produce an effect] opérer, agir ; [be operative] s'appliquer.

> ⚠ **Note that no preposition must be used when translating** to operate on somebody: **Ils vont opérer sa mère demain** They're going to operate on his mother tomorrow.

operatic [.ɒpə'rætɪk] adj d'opéra ▶ **operatic repertoire / role** répertoire / rôle lyrique.

operating ['ɒpəreɪtɪŋ] adj [costs, methods, etc.] d'exploitation / *the factory has reached full operating capacity* l'usine a atteint sa pleine capacité de production ▶ **operating instructions** mode m d'emploi ▶ **operating profit** bénéfice m d'exploitation.

operating room n US salle f d'opération.

operating system n COMPUT système m d'exploitation.

operating table n table f d'opération.

operating theatre n UK salle f d'opération.

operation [.ɒpə'reɪʃn] n 1. [functioning - of machine, device] fonctionnement m, marche f; [- of process, system] fonctionnement m; [- of drug, market force] action f ▶ **to be in operation** a) [machine, train service] être en service b) [firm, group, criminal] être en activité c) [law] être en vigueur ▶ **to put into operation** a) [machine, train service] mettre en service b) [plan] mettre en application or en œuvre c) [law] faire entrer en vigueur ▶ **to come into operation** a) [machine, train service] entrer en service b) [law] entrer en vigueur 2. [running, management - of firm] gestion f; [- of mine] exploitation f; [- of process, system] application f; [- of machine] fonctionnement m 3. [act, activity, deal, etc.] opération f; MIL opération f 4. [company] entreprise f, société f 5. MED opération f, intervention f / *he had a heart operation* il a subi une opération or il a été opéré du cœur 6. COMPUT & MATH opération f.

operational [.ɒpə'reɪʃənl] adj 1. MIL [gen] opérationnel ▶ **operational costs** a) frais mpl opérationnels b) COMM frais mpl d'exploitation 2. [equipment, engine, system] opérationnel.

operations manager n directeur m, -trice f des opérations.

operative ['ɒprətɪv] ◆ adj 1. [operational - system, scheme, skill] opérationnel 2. PHR **the operative word** le mot qui convient. ◆ n 1. opérateur m, -trice f ▶ **machine operative** conducteur m, -trice f de machine ▶ **textile operative** ouvrier m, -ère f du textile 2. US [secret agent] agent m secret ; [detective] (détective m) privé m.

operator ['ɒpəreɪtə] n 1. [technician] opérateur m, -trice f ▶ **radio operator** radio mf 2. TELEC opérateur m, -trice f 3. COMM [director] directeur m, -trice f, dirigeant m, -e f; [organizer] organisateur m, -trice f 4. MATH opérateur m.

operetta [.ɒpə'retə] n opérette f.

ophthalmic optician n opticien m, -enne f (optométriste).

ophthalmologist [.ɒfθæl'mɒlədʒɪst] n oculiste mf, ophtalmologiste mf, ophtalmologue mf.

ophthalmology [.ɒfθæl'mɒlədʒɪ] n ophtalmologie f.

opinion [ə'pɪnjən] n 1. [estimation] opinion f, avis m ; [viewpoint] point m de vue / *in my opinion* à mon avis / *what is your opinion on* or *about the elections?* que pensez-vous des élections ? ▶ **to have a good / bad opinion of sthg** avoir une bonne / mauvaise opinion de qqch 2. [conviction, belief] opinion f ▶ **a matter of opinion** une affaire d'opinion ; LAW avis m 3. [advice] opinion f, avis m.

opinionated [ə'pɪnjəneɪtɪd] adj pej borné, têtu.

opinion poll n sondage m d'opinion.

opium ['əʊpjəm] n opium m.

opium den n fumerie f d'opium.

opponent [ə'pəʊnənt] n [gen & POL] [SPORT] adversaire mf; [rival] rival m, -e f; [competitor] concurrent m, -e f; [in debate] adversaire mf / **political opponent** a) [democratic] adversaire politique b) [of regime] opposant m, -e f politique.

opportune ['ɒpətjuːn] adj fml 1. [coming at the right time] opportun 2. [suitable for a particular purpose] propice.

opportunism [.ɒpə'tjuːnɪzm] n opportunisme m.

opportunist [.ɒpə'tjuːnɪst] ◆ adj opportuniste. ◆ n opportuniste mf.

opportunistic [.ɒpətjuː'nɪstɪk] adj opportuniste.

opportunity [.ɒpə'tjuːnətɪ] (pl **opportunities**) n 1. [chance] occasion f ▶ **to have an opportunity to do** or **of doing sthg** avoir l'occasion de faire qqch / *we don't have much opportunity of practising hang-gliding* nous avons rarement l'occasion de faire du deltaplane / *if ever you get the opportunity* si jamais vous en avez l'occasion

▸ **to give sb an opportunity of doing sthg** or **the opportunity to do sthg** donner à qqn l'occasion de faire qqch / *I took every opportunity of travelling* je n'ai manqué aucune occasion de or j'ai saisi toutes les occasions de voyager / *I'd like to take this opportunity to thank everyone* j'aimerais profiter de cette occasion pour remercier tout le monde **2.** [prospect] perspective f / *the opportunities for advancement are excellent* les perspectives d'avancement sont excellentes.

oppose [ə'pəʊz] vt **1.** [decision, plan, bill, etc.] s'opposer à, être hostile à ; [verbally] parler contre **2.** [in contest, fight] s'opposer à ; [combat] combattre **3.** [contrast] opposer.

opposed [ə'pəʊzd] adj opposé, hostile ▸ **to be opposed to sthg** être opposé or hostile à qqch. ⬦ **as opposed to** prep phr par opposition à, plutôt que.

opposing [ə'pəʊzɪŋ] adj **1.** [army, team] adverse ; [factions] qui s'opposent ; [party, minority] d'opposition / *they're on opposing sides* ils sont adversaires, ils ne sont pas du même côté **2.** [contrasting -views] opposé, qui s'oppose.

opposite ['ɒpəzɪt] ◆ adj **1.** [facing] d'en face, opposé / *the opposite side of the road* l'autre côté de la rue **2.** [opposing -direction, position] inverse, opposé ; [rival -team] adverse / *it's in the opposite direction* c'est dans la direction opposée **3.** [conflicting -attitude, character, opinion] contraire, opposé / *his words had just the opposite effect* ses paroles eurent exactement l'effet contraire **4.** BOT opposé **5.** MATH opposé. ◆ adv en face / *the houses opposite* les maisons d'en face / *they live just opposite* ils habitent juste en face. ◆ prep **1.** en face de / *our houses are opposite each other* nos maisons se font face or sont en face l'une de l'autre / *they sat opposite each other* ils étaient assis l'un en face de l'autre / *we have a park opposite our house* nous avons un parc en face de chez nous **2.** CIN & THEAT ▸ **to play opposite sb** donner la réplique à qqn. ◆ n opposé m, contraire m / *I understood quite the opposite* j'ai compris exactement le contraire / *what's the opposite of "optimistic"?* quel est le contraire d'«optimiste» ?

opposite number n homologue mf.

opposite sex n sexe m opposé.

opposition [ˌɒpə'zɪʃn] ◆ n **1.** [physical] opposition f, résistance f ; [moral] opposition f ▸ **in opposition to** en opposition avec **2.** POL ▸ **the opposition** l'opposition f / *Labour spent the 1980s in opposition* les travaillistes furent dans l'opposition pendant toutes les années 1980 **3.** [rivals] adversaires mpl ; SPORT adversaires mpl ; COMM concurrents mpl, concurrence f **4.** [contrast] (mise f en) opposition f. ◆ comp [committee, spokesperson, etc.] de l'opposition.

oppress [ə'pres] vt **1.** [tyrannize] opprimer **2.** liter [torment -subj: anxiety, atmosphere] accabler, oppresser.

oppressed [ə'prest] pl n ▸ **the oppressed** les opprimés mpl.

oppression [ə'preʃn] n **1.** [persecution] oppression f **2.** [sadness] angoisse f, malaise m.

oppressive [ə'presɪv] adj **1.** POL [regime, government] oppressif, tyrannique ; [law, tax] oppressif **2.** [hard to bear -debt, situation] accablant **3.** [weather] lourd, étouffant.

oppressively [ə'presɪvlɪ] adv d'une manière oppressante or accablante.

oppressor [ə'presə'] n oppresseur m.

opt [ɒpt] vi ▸ **to opt for sthg** opter pour qqch, choisir qqch / *she opted to study maths* elle a choisi d'étudier les maths. ⬦ **opt in** vi [gen] s'engager ; [accept emails] accepter les mails. ⬦ **opt out** vi **1.** [gen] se désengager, retirer sa participation **2.** POL [school, hospital] *choisir l'autonomie vis-à-vis des pouvoirs publics* **3.** [refuse emails] refuser les mails.

optic ['ɒptɪk] adj optique ▸ **optic nerve** nerf m optique.

optical ['ɒptɪkl] adj [lens] optique ; [instrument] optique.

optical character reader n lecteur m optique de caractères.

optical character recognition n reconnaissance f optique de caractères.

optical disc (drive) n disque m optique.

optical fibre n fibre f optique.

optical illusion n illusion f or effet m d'optique.

optical media pl n supports mpl optiques.

optical resolution n résolution f optique.

optical zoom n zoom m optique.

optician [ɒp'tɪʃn] n opticien m, -enne f / *at the optician's* chez l'opticien.

optics ['ɒptɪks] n (U) optique f.

optimal ['ɒptɪml] adj optimal.

optimism ['ɒptɪmɪzm] n optimisme m.

optimist ['ɒptɪmɪst] n optimiste mf.

optimistic [ˌɒptɪ'mɪstɪk] adj [person, outlook] optimiste ; [period] d'optimisme.

optimistically [ˌɒptɪ'mɪstɪklɪ] adv avec optimisme, d'une manière optimiste.

optimize, optimise ['ɒptɪmaɪz] vt optimiser, optimaliser.

optimum ['ɒptɪməm] (pl **optimums**, pl formal **optima** [-mə]) ◆ adj optimum, optimal. ◆ n optimum m.

option ['ɒpʃn] n **1.** [alternative] choix m / *he has no option* il n'a pas le choix / *I have no option but to refuse* je ne peux faire autrement que de refuser / *they were given the option of adopting a child* on leur a proposé d'adopter un enfant **2.** [possible choice] option f, possibilité f ▸ **to keep** or **leave one's options open** ne pas prendre de décision, ne pas s'engager ; SCH (matière f à) option f ; [accessory] option f **3.** COMM & FIN option f ▸ **to take an option on sthg** prendre une option sur qqch ▸ **to take up an option** lever une option **4.** COMPUT option f.

optional ['ɒpʃənl] adj **1.** facultatif ▸ **optional extra** option f **2.** SCH facultatif, optionnel.

opt-out n POL [of school, hospital] décision de choisir l'autonomie vis-à-vis des pouvoirs publics / *Britain's opt-out from the Social Chapter* la décision de la Grande-Bretagne de ne pas souscrire au chapitre social européen.

opt-out clause n clause f d'exemption.

opulence ['ɒpjʊləns] n opulence f.

opulent ['ɒpjʊlənt] adj [lifestyle, figure] opulent ; [abundant] abondant, luxuriant ; [house, clothes] somptueux.

opus ['əʊpəs] (pl **opuses**) n opus m.

or [ɔː'] conj [in positive statements] ou ; [in negative statements] ni / *I can go today or tomorrow* je peux y aller aujourd'hui ou demain / *have you got any brothers or sisters?* avez-vous des frères et sœurs / *he never laughs or smiles* il ne rit ni ne sourit jamais. ⬦ **or else** ◆ conj phr **1.** [otherwise] sinon **2.** [offering an alternative] ou bien. ◆ adv phr inf : *give us the money, or else...* donne-nous l'argent, sinon... ⬦ **or so** adv phr environ / *ten minutes or so* environ dix minutes.

OR written abbr of **Oregon**.

oracle ['ɒrəkl] n oracle m.

oral ['ɔːrəl] ◆ adj **1.** [spoken] oral **2.** ANAT [of mouth] buccal, oral ▸ **oral sex** rapports mpl bucco-génitaux ; PHARM [medicine] à prendre par voie orale ▸ **oral contraceptive** contraceptif m oral. ◆ n (examen m) oral m.

orally ['ɔːrəlɪ] adj **1.** [verbally] oralement, verbalement, de vive voix **2.** SCH oralement ; MED par voie orale.

orange ['ɒrɪndʒ] ◆ n **1.** [fruit] orange f **2.** [drink] boisson f à l'orange **3.** [colour] orange m. ◆ adj **1.** [colour] orange (inv), orangé **2.** [taste] d'orange ; [liqueur, sauce] à l'orange ▸ **orange blossom** fleur f or fleurs fpl d'oranger ▸ **orange juice** jus m d'orange ▸ **orange marmalade** marmelade f d'orange, confiture f d'orange or d'oranges ▸ **orange peel** a) écorce f or peau f d'orange b) fig [cellulite] peau f d'orange ▸ **orange tree** oranger m.

orangeade [,ɒrɪndʒ'eɪd] n [still] orangeade f ; [fizzy] soda m à l'orange.

Orangeman ['ɒrɪndʒmən] (pl **Orangemen** [-mən]) n **1.** UK HIST orangiste m (partisan de la maison d'Orange) **2.** [in Ireland] orangiste m (protestant).

Orange march n UK défilé m des orangistes.

orang-(o)utan [ɔ:'ræŋatan], **orang-(o)utang** [ɔ:'ræŋ atəŋ] n orang-outan m, orang-outang m.

oration [ɔ:'reɪʃn] n (long) discours m, allocution f.

orator ['ɒrətə] n orateur m, -trice f.

oratorio [,ɒrə'tɔ:rɪəʊ] (pl **oratorios**) n oratorio m.

oratory ['ɒrətrɪ] n **1.** [eloquence] art m oratoire, éloquence f **2.** RELIG oratoire m.

orb [ɔ:b] n **1.** [sphere] globe m **2.** ASTRON & liter orbe m.

orbit ['ɔ:bɪt] ◆ n **1.** ASTRON orbite f ▸ **to put a satellite into orbit** mettre un satellite sur or en orbite ▸ **in orbit** en orbite **2.** [influence] orbite f **3.** ANAT & PHYS [of eye, electron] orbite f. ◆ vt [subj: planet, comet] graviter or tourner autour de ; [subj: astronaut] : the first man to orbit the Earth le premier homme à être placé or mis en orbite autour de la Terre. ◆ vi décrire une orbite.

orbital ['ɔ:bɪtl] adj orbital ▸ **orbital motorway** UK (autoroute f) périphérique m.

orchard ['ɔ:tʃəd] n verger m.

orchestra ['ɔ:kɪstrə] n **1.** [band] orchestre m **2.** [in theatre, cinema] fauteuils mpl d'orchestre, parterre m.

orchestral [ɔ:'kestrəl] adj d'orchestre, orchestral.

orchestra pit n fosse f d'orchestre.

orchestrate ['ɔ:kɪstreɪt] vt MUS & fig orchestrer.

orchid ['ɔ:kɪd] n orchidée f.

ordain [ɔ:'deɪn] vt **1.** RELIG ordonner **2.** [order] ordonner, décréter ; [declare] décréter, déclarer ; [decide] dicter, décider.

ordeal [ɔ:'di:l] n épreuve f, calvaire m.

order ['ɔ:də] ◆ n **1.** [sequence, arrangement] ordre m / in alphabetical / chronological order par ordre alphabétique / chronologique / let's do things in order faisons les choses en ordre / in order of appearance a) THEAT par ordre d'entrée en scène b) CIN & TV par ordre d'apparition à l'écran **2.** [organization, tidiness] ordre m / to put one's affairs / books in order mettre de l'ordre dans ses affaires / livres, ranger ses affaires / livres **3.** [command] ordre m ; [instruction] instruction f ▸ **to give sb orders to do sthg** ordonner à qqn de faire qqch / I don't have to take orders from you je n'ai pas d'ordres à recevoir de vous / orders are orders les ordres sont les ordres / on doctor's orders sur ordre du médecin ; MIL ordre m, consigne f **4.** COMM [request for goods] commande f ▸ **to place an order for sthg** passer (une) commande de qqch ; [goods ordered] marchandises fpl commandées / your order has now arrived votre commande est arrivée ; [in restaurant] : can I take your order? avez-vous choisi ? ; US [portion] part f / an order of French fries une portion de frites **5.** FIN ▸ **(money) order** mandat m / pay to the order of A. Jones payez à l'ordre de A. Jones **6.** LAW ordonnance f, arrêté m **7.** [discipline, rule] ordre m, discipline f ▸ **to keep order** a) [police] maintenir l'ordre b) SCH maintenir la discipline / children need to be kept in order les enfants ont besoin de discipline ▸ **to restore order** rétablir l'ordre ; [in meeting] ordre m ▸ **to call**

sb to order rappeler qqn à l'ordre ▸ **order!** de l'ordre ! / he's out of order ce qu'il a dit / fait était déplacé **8.** [system] ordre m établi ▸ **order of the day** POL ordre m du jour **9.** [functioning state] : in working order en état de marche or de fonctionnement **10.** [class] classe f, ordre m ; [rank] ordre m / research work of the highest order un travail de recherche de tout premier ordre ; [kind] espèce f, genre m **11.** [decoration] ordre m ▸ **the Order of the Garter** / **of Merit** l'ordre de la Jarretière / du Mérite **12.** RELIG ordre m. ◆ vt **1.** [command] ordonner ▸ **to order sb to do sthg** ordonner à qqn de faire qqch / the government ordered an inquiry into the disaster le gouvernement a ordonné l'ouverture d'une enquête sur la catastrophe ; MIL ▸ **to order sb to do sthg** donner l'ordre à qqn de faire qqch / the troops were ordered to the Mediterranean les troupes ont reçu l'ordre de gagner la Méditerranée **2.** COMM [meal, goods] commander **3.** [organize - society] organiser ; [- ideas, thoughts] mettre de l'ordre dans ; [- affairs] régler, mettre en ordre. ◆ vi commander, passer une commande / would you like to order now? [in restaurant] voulez-vous commander maintenant ? **◈ in order** adj phr **1.** [valid] en règle **2.** [acceptable] approprié, admissible / an apology is in order des excuses s'imposent. **◈ in order that** conj phr afin que. **◈ in order to** conj phr afin de / in order not to upset you pour éviter de vous faire de la peine. **◈ out of order** adj phr [machine, TV] en panne ; [phone] en dérangement / 'out of order' 'hors service', 'en panne'. **◈ to order** adv phr sur commande / he had a suit made to order il s'est fait faire un costume sur mesures. **◈ order about** UK, **order around** vt sep commander / he likes ordering people about il adore régenter son monde.

📝 Note that ordonner que is followed by a verb in the subjunctive:
He ordered all the prisoners to be executed. Il a ordonné que tous les prisonniers soient exécutés.

---

order book n carnet m de commandes.

order form n bon m de commande.

orderly ['ɔ:dəlɪ] (pl **orderlies**) ◆ adj **1.** [tidy - room] ordonné, rangé **2.** [organized - person, mind, lifestyle] ordonné, méthodique **3.** [well-behaved] ordonné, discipliné. ◆ n **1.** MIL officier m d'ordonnance **2.** MED aide-infirmier m.

order number n numéro m de commande.

ordinal ['ɔ:dɪnl] ◆ adj ordinal. ◆ n ordinal m.

ordinance ['ɔ:dɪnəns] n ordonnance f, décret m.

ordinarily ['ɔ:dənrɪlɪ] US [,ɔ:rdn'erəlɪ] adv **1.** [in an ordinary way] ordinairement, d'ordinaire **2.** [normally] normalement, en temps normal.

ordinary ['ɔ:dənrɪ] adj **1.** [usual] ordinaire, habituel ; [normal] normal **2.** [average] ordinaire, moyen / Miss Brodie was no ordinary teacher Miss Brodie était un professeur peu banal or qui sortait de l'ordinaire **3.** [commonplace] ordinaire, quelconque pej / it's a very ordinary-looking car c'est une voiture qui n'a rien de spécial. **◈ out of the ordinary** adj phr : as a pianist, she's really out of the ordinary c'est vraiment une pianiste exceptionnelle or hors du commun / nothing out of the ordinary ever happens here il ne se passe jamais rien de bien extraordinaire ici.

ordinary degree n UK ≃ licence f sans mention or avec la mention passable.

Ordinary level = O-level.

ordinary share n action f ordinaire.

ordination [,ɔːdɪ'neɪʃn] n ordination f.

ordnance ['ɔːdnəns] n **1.** [supplies] (service m de l')équipement m militaire **2.** [artillery] artillerie f.

Ordnance Survey pr n UK service m national de cartographie ; ≃ IGN m ▶ **Ordnance Survey map** carte f d'état-major.

ore [ɔːʳ] n minerai m.

oregano [UK ,ɒrɪ'gɑːnəʊ US ə'regənəʊ] n BOT & CULIN origan m.

Oregon ['ɒrɪgən] pr n Oregon m / *in Oregon* dans l'Oregon.

organ ['ɔːgən] n **1.** MUS orgue m ; [large] (grandes) orgues fpl **2.** ANAT organe m ▶ **organ donor** donneur m, -euse f d'organes ▶ **organ transplant** greffe f d'organe **3.** fig [means] organe m, instrument m ; [mouthpiece] organe m, porte-parole m inv.

organ grinder n joueur m, -euse f d'orgue de Barbarie.

organic [ɔː'gænɪk] adj **1.** BIOL & CHEM organique **2.** [natural - produce] bio, biologique.

organically [ɔː'gænɪklɪ] adv **1.** BIOL & CHEM organiquement ▶ **organically grown** cultivé sans engrais chimiques, biologique **2.** fig organiquement.

organic chemistry n chimie f organique.

organic farming n agriculture f bio, culture f biologique.

organism ['ɔːgənɪzm] n BIOL organisme m.

organist ['ɔːgənɪst] n organiste mf.

organization, organisation [,ɔːgənaɪ'zeɪʃn] n **1.** [organizing] organisation f ▶ **organization and method** INDUST organisation f scientifique du travail, OST f **2.** [association] organisation f, association f ; [official body] organisme m, organisation f **3.** ADMIN [personnel] cadres mpl.

organizational, organisational [,ɔːgənaɪ'zeɪʃnl] adj [skills, methods] organisationnel, d'organisation ; [expenses] d'organisation ; [change] dans l'organisation, structurel.

organize, organise ['ɔːgənaɪz] vt [sort out] organiser ▶ **to get organized** s'organiser.

organized, organised ['ɔːgənaɪzd] adj **1.** [trip] organisé **2.** [unionized] syndiqué ▶ **organized labour** main-d'œuvre f syndiquée **3.** [orderly] organisé ; [methodical] méthodique.

organized crime n le crime organisé.

organizer, organiser ['ɔːgənaɪzəʳ] n **1.** [person] organisateur m, -trice f **2.** [diary] agenda m modulaire, Filofax® m **3.** COMPUT organiseur m, agenda m électronique.

organza [ɔː'gænzə] n organdi m.

orgasm ['ɔːgæzm] n orgasme m.

orgy ['ɔːdʒɪ] (pl orgies) n orgie f.

orient ['ɔːrɪənt] vt orienter ▶ **to orient o.s.** s'orienter / *our firm is very much oriented towards the American market* notre société est très orientée vers le marché américain.

Orient ['ɔːrɪənt] pr n ▶ **the Orient** [gen] l'Orient m ; [the Far East] l'Extrême-Orient.

oriental [,ɔːrɪ'entl] adj oriental ▶ **oriental rug** tapis m d'Orient.

orientate ['ɔːrɪenteɪt] vt UK orienter ▶ **to orientate o.s.** s'orienter / *the course is very much orientated towards the sciences* le cours est très orienté vers or axé sur les sciences.

-orientated ['ɔːrɪenteɪtɪd] UK = -oriented.

orientation [,ɔːrɪen'teɪʃn] n orientation f ▶ **sexual orientation** orientation f sexuelle.

-oriented in comp orienté vers..., axé sur... / *ours is a money-oriented society* c'est l'argent qui mène notre société / *pupil-oriented teaching* enseignement adapté aux besoins des élèves.

orienteering [,ɔːrɪen'tɪərɪŋ] n course f d'orientation.

orifice ['ɒrɪfɪs] n orifice m.

origami [,ɒrɪ'gɑːmɪ] n origami m.

origin ['ɒrɪdʒɪn] n **1.** [source] origine f / *country of origin* pays m d'origine / *of unknown origin* d'origine inconnue **2.** [ancestry] origine f / *he is of Canadian origin* il est d'origine canadienne.

original [ɒ'rɪdʒɪnl] ◆ adj **1.** [initial] premier, d'origine, initial **2.** [unusual] original ; [strange] singulier **3.** [new - play, writing] original, inédit. ◆ n **1.** [painting, book] original m / *the film was shown in the original* le film a été projeté en version originale / *I prefer to read Proust in the original* je préfère lire Proust dans le texte **2.** [model - of hero, character] : *Betty was the original of the novel's heroine* Betty inspira le personnage de l'héroïne du roman **3.** [unusual person] original m, -e f, excentrique mf.

 original or **originel?**

The French adjective **original** is close in meaning to its English counterpart, although when applied to a person it also means eccentric. **Originel** is a much rarer word meaning early, primeval or primitive.

originality [ə,rɪdʒə'nælətɪ] (pl originalities) n originalité f.

originally [ə'rɪdʒənəlɪ] adv **1.** [initially] à l'origine, au début, initialement **2.** [unusually, inventively] d'une façon or d'une manière originale, originalement.

original sin n péché m originel.

originate [ə'rɪdʒəneɪt] vi [idea, rumour] ▶ **to originate in** avoir or trouver son origine dans ▶ **to originate from** tirer son origine de / *the conflict originated in the towns* le conflit est né dans les villes ; [goods] provenir.

originator [ə'rɪdʒəneɪtəʳ] n [of crime] auteur m ; [of idea] initiateur m, -trice f, auteur m.

Orinoco [,ɒrɪ'nəʊkəʊ] pr n ▶ **the (River) Orinoco** l'Orénoque m.

Orkney Islands ['ɔːknɪ-], **Orkneys** ['ɔːknɪz] pl pr n ▶ **the Orkney Islands** les Orcades fpl / *in the Orkney Islands* dans les Orcades.

ornament n ['ɔːnəmənt] [decorative object] objet m décoratif, bibelot m ; [jewellery] colifichet m.

ornamental [,ɔːnə'mentl] adj [decorative] ornemental, décoratif ; [plant] ornemental ; [garden] d'agrément.

ornate [ɔː'neɪt] adj [decoration] (très) orné ; [style] orné, fleuri ; [lettering] orné.

ornery ['ɔːnərɪ] adj US inf **1.** [nasty] méchant **2.** [stubborn] obstiné, entêté.

ornithologist [,ɔːnɪ'θɒlədʒɪst] n ornithologiste mf, ornithologue mf.

ornithology [,ɔːnɪ'θɒlədʒɪ] n ornithologie f.

orphan ['ɔːfn] ◆ n **1.** [person] orphelin m, -e f **2.** TYPO ligne f orpheline. ◆ adj orphelin. ◆ vt ▶ **to be orphaned** se retrouver or devenir orphelin.

orphanage ['ɔːfənɪdʒ] n orphelinat m.

orthodontics [,ɔːθə'dɒntɪks] n (U) orthodontie f.

orthodontist [,ɔːθə'dɒntɪst] n orthodontiste mf.

orthodox ['ɔːθədɒks] adj orthodoxe.

Orthodox Church n ▶ the Orthodox Church l'Église f orthodoxe.

orthodoxy ['ɔ:θədɒksɪ] (pl **orthodoxies**) n orthodoxie f.

orthopaedic UK, **orthopedic** [,ɔ:θə'pi:dɪk] adj orthopédique ▶ **orthopaedic surgeon** chirurgien m, -enne f orthopédiste mf.

orthopaedics UK, **orthopedics** [,ɔ:θə'pi:dɪks] n (U) orthopédie f.

orthopaedist UK, **orthopedist** [,ɔ:θə'pi:dɪst] n orthopédiste mf.

OS ◆ n **1.** abbr of **ordinary seaman 2.** abbr of **operating system.** ◆ pr n (abbr of **Ordnance Survey**) ≃ IGN m. ◆ written abbr of **outsize**.

O/S written abbr of **out of stock**.

Oscar ['ɒskər] n CIN Oscar m.

Oscar-winning adj : an Oscar-winning picture un film primé aux oscars / in her Oscar-winning role dans le rôle qui lui a valu l'oscar.

oscillate ['ɒsɪleɪt] vi **1.** ELEC & PHYS osciller **2.** [person] osciller.

OSD (abbr of **optical scanning device**) n lecteur m optique.

OSHA (abbr of **Occupational Safety and Health Administration**) pr n aux États-Unis, direction de la sécurité et de l'hygiène au travail.

Oslo ['ɒzləʊ] pr n Oslo.

osmosis [ɒz'məʊsɪs] n osmose f.

ossified ['ɒsɪfaɪd] adj [cartilage] ossifié ; fig [mind, ideas, social system] sclérosé ; [person] à l'esprit sclérosé.

Ostend [ɒs'tend] pr n Ostende.

ostensible [ɒ'stensəbl] adj [apparent] apparent ; [pretended] prétendu ; [so-called] soi-disant (inv).

ostensibly [ɒ'stensəblɪ] adv [apparently] apparemment ; [supposedly] prétendument, soi-disant ; [on the pretext] : he left early, ostensibly because he was sick il est parti tôt, prétextant une indisposition.

ostentation [,ɒstən'teɪʃn] n ostentation f.

ostentatious [,ɒstən'teɪʃəs] adj **1.** [showy - display, appearance, decor] ostentatoire, plein d'ostentation ; [manner, behaviour] prétentieux, ostentatoire **2.** [exaggerated] exagéré, surfait.

ostentatiously [,ɒstən'teɪʃəslɪ] adv avec ostentation.

osteopath ['ɒstɪəpæθ] n ostéopathe mf.

osteopathy [,ɒstɪ'ɒpəθɪ] n ostéopathie f.

osteoporosis [,ɒstɪəʊpɔ:'rəʊsɪs] n ostéoporose f.

ostracism ['ɒstrəsɪzm] n ostracisme m.

ostracize, ostracise ['ɒstrəsaɪz] vt frapper d'ostracisme, ostraciser.

ostrich ['ɒstrɪtʃ] n autruche f.

OT n **1.** (abbr of **Old Testament**) AT **2.** abbr of **occupational therapy**.

OTC ◆ pr n (abbr of **Officer Training Corps**) section de formation des officiers en Grande-Bretagne. ◆ adj abbr of **over-the-counter**.

other ['ʌðər] ◆ adj **1.** [different] autre, différent / it's the same in other countries c'est la même chose dans les autres pays / I had no other choice je n'avais pas le choix or pas d'autre solution / he doesn't respect other people's property il ne respecte pas le bien d'autrui **2.** [second of two] autre / give me the other one donnez-moi l'autre **3.** [additional] autre / some other people came d'autres personnes sont arrivées **4.** [remaining] autre / the other three men les trois autres hommes **5.** [in expressions of

time] autre **6.** [opposite] : on the other side of the room / of the river de l'autre côté de la pièce / de la rivière. ◆ pron **1.** [additional person, thing] autre / some succeed, others fail certains réussissent, d'autres échouent **2.** [opposite, far end] autre **3.** [related person] autre. ◆ **other than** ◆ conj phr **1.** [apart from, except] autrement que / we had no alternative other than to accept their offer nous n'avions pas d'autre possibilité que celle d'accepter leur offre **2.** [differently from] différemment de / she can't be other than she is elle est comme ça, c'est tout. ◆ prep phr sauf, à part / other than that à part cela.

otherwise ['ʌðəwaɪz] ◆ adv **1.** [differently] autrement **2.** [in other respects] autrement, à part cela ; [in other circumstances] sinon, autrement **3.** [in other words] autrement / Louis XIV, otherwise known as the Sun King Louis XIV, surnommé le Roi-Soleil **4.** [in contrast, opposition] : through diplomatic channels or otherwise par voie diplomatique ou autre. ◆ conj [or else] sinon, autrement. ◆ adj autre. ◆ **or otherwise** adv phr : it is of no interest, financial or otherwise ça ne présente aucun intérêt, que ce soit financier ou autre.

otherworldly [,ʌðə'wɜ:ldlɪ] adj **1.** [unrealistic] peu réaliste **2.** [mystical] mystique **3.** [ethereal] éthéré.

OTOH MESSAGING written abbr of **on the other hand**.

OTT (abbr of **over-the-top**) adj UK inf ▶ that's a bit OTT! c'est pousser le bouchon un peu loin !, c'est un peu fort !

Ottawa ['ɒtəwə] pr n Ottawa.

otter ['ɒtər] n loutre f.

OU pr n abbr of **Open University**.

ouch [aʊtʃ] interj ▶ ouch! aïe !, ouille !, ouïe !

ought [ɔ:t] modal vb **1.** [indicating morally right action] : you ought to tell her vous devriez le lui dire / she thought she ought to tell you elle a pensé qu'il valait mieux te le dire ; [indicating sensible or advisable action] : I really ought to be going il faut vraiment que je m'en aille **2.** [expressing expectation, likelihood] : they ought to be home now à l'heure qu'il est, ils devraient être rentrés **3.** [followed by 'to have'] : you ought to have told me! vous auriez dû me le dire ! / they ought not to have been allowed in on n'aurait pas dû les laisser entrer.

oughtn't [ɔ:tnt] abbr of **ought not**.

ounce [aʊns] n **1.** [weight] once f **2.** fig : there isn't an ounce of truth in what she says il n'y a pas une once de vérité dans ce qu'elle raconte / you haven't got an ounce of common sense tu n'as pas (pour) deux sous de bon sens / it took every ounce of strength she had cela lui a demandé toutes ses forces.

our ['aʊər] det notre (sg), nos (pl) / this is OUR house cette maison est à nous / we have a car of our own nous avons une voiture à nous.

ours ['aʊəz] pron le nôtre m, la nôtre f, les nôtres mf / that house is ours a) [we live there] cette maison est la nôtre b) [we own it] cette maison est à nous or nous appartient / those books are ours ces livres à nous / it must be one of ours ce doit être un des nôtres / she's a friend of ours c'est une de nos amies.

ourselves [aʊə'selvz] pron **1.** [reflexive use] nous / we enjoyed ourselves nous nous sommes bien amusés / we built ourselves a log cabin nous avons construit une cabane en rondins / we said to ourselves, why not wait here? nous nous sommes dit or on s'est dit : pourquoi ne pas attendre ici ? **2.** [emphatic use] nous-mêmes / we ourselves have much to learn nous-mêmes avons beaucoup à apprendre / we want to see for ourselves nous avons envie de nous en rendre compte (par) nous-mêmes ▶ (all) by ourselves tout seuls / *we had the flat to ourselves* nous avions l'appartement pour nous tout seuls **3.** [replacing 'us'] nous-mêmes / *people like ourselves* des gens comme nous.

oust [aust] vt **1.** [opponent, rival] évincer, chasser **2.** [tenant, squatter] déloger, expulser ; [landowner] déposséder.

out [aut]
◆ adv

A. IN SPACE **1.** [indicating movement from inside to outside] dehors / *to go out* sortir **2.** [away from home, office, etc.] : *Mr Powell's out, do you want to leave a message?* M. Powell est sorti, voulez-vous laisser un message ? / *he stayed out all night* il n'est pas rentré de la nuit **3.** [indicating view from inside] : *I stared out of the window* je regardais par la fenêtre **4.** [in the open air] dehors **5.** [indicating distance from land, centre, town, etc.] : *on the trip out* à l'aller / *they live a long way out* ils habitent loin du centre **6.** [indicating extended position] : *he lay stretched out on the bed* il était allongé (de tout son long) sur le lit / *hold your arms / your hand out* tendez les bras / la main **7.** [of tide] : *the tide's on its way out* la mer se retire, la marée descend.

B. DISTRIBUTION OR TRANSMISSION **1.** [indicating distribution] : *she handed out some photocopies* elle a distribué des photocopies **2.** [indicating source of light, smell, sound, etc.] : *it gives out a lot of heat* ça dégage beaucoup de chaleur **3.** [loudly, audibly] : *read out the first paragraph* lisez le premier paragraphe à haute voix.

C. EXCLUSION OR EXTINCTION **1.** [indicating exclusion or rejection] : *throw him out!* jetez-le dehors ! **2.** [extinguished] : *put* or *turn the lights out* éteignez les lumières.

D. PUBLISHED OR MADE PUBLIC **1.** [revealed, made public] : *the secret is out* le secret a été éventé ▸ *out with it!* inf alors, t'accouches ? **2.** [published, on sale] : *the new model will be* or *come out next month* le nouveau modèle sort le mois prochain.

◆ adj **1.** [flowering] en fleurs **2.** [shining] : *the sun is out* il y a du soleil **3.** [finished] : *before the year is out* avant la fin de l'année **4.** [on strike] en grève **5.** GAMES & SPORT : *the ball was out* la balle était dehors or sortie, la balle était faute / *she went out in the first round* elle a été éliminée au premier tour **6.** [tide] bas **7.** [wrong] : *your calculations are (way) out* or *you're (way) out in your calculations* vous vous êtes (complètement) trompé dans vos calculs **8.** inf [impossible] : *that plan's out because of the weather* ce projet est à l'eau à cause du temps **9.** inf [unfashionable] : *long hair's (right) out* les cheveux longs c'est (carrément) dépassé **10.** inf [unconscious] ▸ *to be out* être K-O **11.** [extinguished] éteint **12.** inf [openly gay] qui ne cache pas son homosexualité.

◆ interj **1.** [leave] ▸ *out!* dehors ! **2.** TELEC ▸ *(over and) out!* terminé !

◆ prep inf hors de / *she went out that door* elle est sortie par cette porte / *look out the window* regarde par la fenêtre.

◆ vt ▸ **to out sb** révéler l'homosexualité de qqn.

◆ **out and about** adv phr : *where have you been?* — *oh, out and about* où étais-tu ? — oh, je suis allé faire un tour. ◆ **out of** prep phr **1.** [indicating movement from inside to outside] hors de / *she came out of the office* elle est sortie du bureau / *to look / to fall out of a window* regarder / tomber par une fenêtre **2.** [indicating location] : *we drank out of china cups* nous avons bu dans des tasses de porcelaine / *he's out of town* il n'est pas en ville / *it's a long way out of town* c'est loin de la ville **3.** [indicating raw material] : *it's made out of mahogany* c'est en acajou / *plastic is made out of petroleum* on obtient le plastique à partir du pétrole **4.** [indicating motive] par **5.** [lacking] : *I'm out of cigarettes* je n'ai plus de cigarettes **6.** [in proportions, marks, etc.] sur / *ninety-nine times out of a hundred* quatre-vingt-dix-neuf fois sur cent / *out of all the people there, only*

one spoke German parmi toutes les personnes présentes, une seule parlait allemand **7.** [indicating similarity to book, film, etc.] : *it was like something out of a Fellini film* on se serait cru dans un film de Fellini **8.** [indicating exclusion or rejection] : *he's out of the race* il n'est plus dans la course / *you keep out of this!* mêlez-vous de ce qui vous regarde ! **9.** [indicating avoidance] : *come in out of the rain* ne reste pas dehors sous la pluie / *stay out of the sun* ne restez pas au soleil **10.** PHR **to be out of it a)** [unaware of situation] être à côté de la plaque **b)** [drunk] être bourré / *I felt really out of it* [excluded] je me sentais complètement exclu.

outage ['autɪdʒ] n US [breakdown] panne f ; ELEC coupure f or panne f de courant.

out-and-out adj complet (complète), total / *it was an out-and-out disaster* ce fut un désastre complet.

outback ['autbæk] n AUSTR arrière-pays m inv, intérieur m du pays.

outbid [aut'bɪd] (pt outbid, pp outbid or outbidden [-'bɪdn], cont outbidding) vt enchérir sur.

outboard ['autbɔːd] ◆ adj [position, direction] horsbord ▸ **outboard motor** moteur m hors-bord. ◆ n [motor, boat] hors-bord m inv.

outbound ['autbaund] adj qui quitte le centre-ville.

out box n [for e-mail] boîte f de départ, éléments mpl envoyés.

outbreak ['autbreɪk] n **1.** [of fire, storm, war] début m ; [of violence, disease, epidemic] éruption f **2.** METEOR [sudden shower] : *there will be outbreaks of rain / snow in many places* il y aura des chutes de pluie / de neige un peu partout.

outbuildings ['autbɪldɪŋz] pl n dépendances fpl.

outburst ['autbɜːst] n accès m, explosion f.

outcast ['autkɑːst] ◆ n paria m. ◆ adj proscrit, banni.

outclass [ˌaut'klɑːs] vt surclasser, surpasser.

outcome ['autkʌm] n [of election, competition] résultat m ; [of sequence of events] conséquence f.

outcrop (pt & pp outcropped, cont outcropping) n ['autkrɒp] GEOL affleurement m.

outcry ['autkraɪ] (pl outcries) n tollé m.

outdated [ˌaut'deɪtɪd] adj [idea, attitude] démodé, dépassé ; [clothes] démodé ; [expression] désuet (désuète).

outdid [ˌaut'dɪd] pt —→ outdo.

outdistance [ˌaut'dɪstəns] vt laisser derrière soi.

outdo [ˌaut'duː] (pt outdid [ˌaut'dɪd], pp outdone [-'dʌn]) vt surpasser, faire mieux que, l'emporter sur / *Mark, not to be outdone, decided to be ill as well* Mark, pour ne pas être en reste, décida d'être malade lui aussi.

outdoor ['autdɔːr] adj **1.** [open-air - games, sports] de plein air ; [- work] d'extérieur ; [- swimming pool] en plein air, découvert **2.** [clothes] d'extérieur ▸ **outdoor shoes a)** [warm] grosses chaussures **b)** [waterproof] chaussures imperméables **c)** [for walking] chaussures de marche **3.** [person] ▸ **to lead an outdoor life** vivre au grand air.

outdoors [aut'dɔːz] ◆ n ▸ **the great outdoors** les grands espaces naturels. ◆ adv dehors, au dehors / *the scene takes place outdoors* la scène se déroule à l'extérieur / *to sleep outdoors* coucher à la belle étoile. ◆ adj [activity] en or de plein air.

outdoorsman [aut'dɔːsmən] (pl outdoorsmen [aut-'dɔːsmn]) n ▸ **to be an outdoorsman** aimer la nature.

outer ['autər] adj **1.** [external] extérieur, externe ▸ **outer garments** vêtements mpl de dessus **2.** [peripheral] périphérique ▸ **outer London** la banlieue londonienne **3.** [furthest - limits] externe ; [- planets] extérieur.

Outer Mongolia pr n Mongolie-Extérieure f / *in Outer Mongolia* en Mongolie-Extérieure.

outermost ['aʊtəməʊst] adj [most distant] le plus (à l')extérieur ; [most isolated] le plus reculé or isolé.

outer space n espace m intersidéral, cosmos m.

outfit ['aʊtfɪt] (pt & pp **outfitted**, cont **outfitting**) ◆ n **1.** [clothes] ensemble m, tenue f ; [child's disguise] panoplie f **2.** [equipment, kit - for camping, fishing] matériel m, équipement m ; [tools] outils mpl, outillage m ; [case] trousse f **3.** inf [group] équipe f, bande f **4.** MIL équipe f. ◆ vt [with equipment] équiper.

outfitter ['aʊtfɪtər] n UK [shop] ▶ **school outfitter** or **outfitter's** magasin qui vend des uniformes et autres vêtements scolaires ▶ **(gentlemen's) outfitter** or **outfitter's** magasin de vêtements d'homme.

outgoing ['aʊt,gəʊɪŋ] adj **1.** [departing - government, minister, tenant] sortant ; [- following resignation] démissionnaire **2.** [train, ship] en partance ; [letters] à expédier **3.** [tide] descendant **4.** [extrovert] extraverti, plein d'entrain.

outgoings ['aʊt,gəʊɪŋz] pl n dépenses fpl, frais mpl.

outgrow [,aʊt'grəʊ] (pt **outgrew** [-'gruː], pp **outgrown** [-'grəʊn]) vt **1.** [grow faster than] grandir plus (vite) que / the world is outgrowing its resources la population mondiale croît plus vite que les ressources dont elle dispose **2.** [clothes] devenir trop grand pour **3.** [game, habit, hobby] ne plus s'intéresser à (en grandissant) ; [attitude, behaviour, phase] abandonner (en grandissant or en prenant de l'âge).

outhouse ['aʊthaʊs] (pl [-haʊzɪz]) n **1.** UK [outbuilding] remise f **2.** US [toilet] toilettes fpl extérieures.

outing ['aʊtɪŋ] n **1.** [trip] sortie f ; [organized] excursion f ▶ **to go on an outing** faire une excursion **2.** [of homosexuals] révélation f de l'homosexualité.

outlandish [aʊt'lændɪʃ] adj [eccentric - appearance, behaviour, idea] bizarre, excentrique ; pej [language, style] barbare.

outlast [,aʊt'lɑːst] vt [subj: person] survivre à ; [subj: machine] durer plus longtemps que.

outlaw ['aʊtlɔː] ◆ n hors-la-loi m inv. ◆ vt [person] mettre hors la loi ; [behaviour] proscrire, interdire ; [organization] interdire.

outlay ◆ n ['aʊtleɪ] [expense] dépense f ; [investment] investissement m, mise f de fonds. ◆ vt [aʊt'leɪ] (pt & pp **outlaid** [-'leɪd]) [spend] dépenser ; [invest] investir / to outlay $10,000 capital faire une mise de fonds de 10 000 dollars.

outlet ['aʊtlet] ◆ n **1.** [for liquid, air, smoke] bouche f ; [tap] vanne f d'écoulement **2.** [for feelings, energy] exutoire m **3.** [for talent] débouché m **4.** COMM [market] débouché m ; [sales point] point m de vente **5.** US ELEC prise f (de courant). ◆ comp [for liquid] d'écoulement ; [for gas, smoke] d'échappement.

outline ['aʊtlaɪn] ◆ n **1.** [contour, shape] silhouette f, contour m ; [of building, of mountains] silhouette f ; [of face, figure] profil m ; ART [sketch] esquisse f, ébauche f **2.** [plan - of project, essay] plan m d'ensemble, esquisse f ; [- of book] canevas m ; [general idea] idée f générale, grandes lignes fpl ; [overall view] vue f d'ensemble ▶ **to give sb an outline of sthg** expliquer les grandes lignes de qqch à qqn / she gave us an outline of or she explained to us in outline what she intended to do elle nous a expliqué dans les grandes lignes ce qu'elle avait l'intention de faire. ◆ vt **1.** [plan, theory] expliquer dans les grandes lignes ; [facts] résumer, passer en revue / he outlined the situation briefly il dressa un bref bilan de la situation **2.** [person, building, mountain] : the trees were outlined against the blue sky les arbres se détachaient sur le fond bleu du ciel **3.** ART esquisser (les traits de), tracer.

outlive [,aʊt'lɪv] vt survivre à / she outlived her husband by only six months elle n'a survécu à son mari que six mois / the measures have outlived their usefulness les mesures n'ont plus de raison d'être.

outlook ['aʊtlʊk] n **1.** [prospect] perspective f ; ECON & POL horizon m, perspectives fpl (d'avenir) / the outlook for the New Year is promising cette nouvelle année s'annonce prometteuse / it's a bleak outlook for the unemployed pour les sans-emploi, les perspectives d'avenir ne sont guère réjouissantes ; METEOR prévision f, prévisions fpl / the outlook for March is cold and windy pour mars, on prévoit un temps froid avec beaucoup de vent **2.** [viewpoint] point de vue m, conception f **3.** [view - from window] perspective f, vue f.

outlying ['aʊt,laɪɪŋ] adj [remote - area, village] isolé, à l'écart ; [far from centre - urban areas] périphérique.

outmanoeuvre UK, **outmaneuver** US [,aʊtmə-'nuːvər] vt MIL se montrer meilleur tacticien que ; fig déjouer les manœuvres de.

outmoded [,aʊt'məʊdəd] adj démodé, désuet (désuète).

outnumber [,aʊt'nʌmbər] vt être plus nombreux que.

out-of-body experience n expérience f hors du corps, EHC f, autoscopie f.

out-of-bounds adj **1.** [barred] interdit **2.** US SPORT hors (du) terrain.

out-of-court adj ▶ **out-of-court settlement** arrangement m à l'amiable.

out-of-date adj **1.** = **outdated 2.** [expired] périmé.

out-of-doors UK ◆ adv = **outdoors**. ◆ adj = **outdoor**.

out-of-hand adj US inf [extraordinary] génial, géant.

out-of-pocket adj : I'm £5 out of pocket j'en suis pour 5 livres de ma poche.

out-of-the-ordinary adj insolite.

out-of-the-way adj **1.** [isolated] écarté, isolé ; [unknown to most people] peu connu ; [not popular] peu fréquenté **2.** [uncommon] insolite.

out-of-town adj [shopping centre, retail park] situé à la périphérie d'une ville.

out-of-towner [-'taʊnər] n US inf étranger m, -ère f à la ville.

out-of-work adj au chômage.

outpace [,aʊt'peɪs] vt [run faster than] courir plus vite que ; [overtake] dépasser, devancer.

outpatient ['aʊt,peɪʃnt] n malade mf en consultation externe ▶ **outpatients' clinic** or **department** service m de consultation externe.

outperform [,aʊtpə'fɔːm] vt avoir de meilleures performances que, être plus performant que.

outplay [,aʊt'pleɪ] vt jouer mieux que, dominer (au jeu).

outpost ['aʊtpəʊst] n avant-poste m.

outpouring ['aʊt,pɔːrɪŋ] n épanchement m ▶ **outpourings** effusions fpl.

output ['aʊtpʊt] (pt & pp **output**, cont **outputting**) ◆ n **1.** [production] production f ; [productivity] rendement m ; [power - of machine] rendement m, débit m **2.** ELEC puissance f ; [of amplifier] puissance f (de sortie) ; COMPUT [device] sortie f ; [printout] sortie f papier, tirage m. ◆ vt COMPUT [data] sortir. ◆ vi COMPUT sortir des données.

outrage ['aʊtreɪdʒ] ◆ n **1.** [affront] outrage m, affront m / it's an outrage against humanity / society c'est un affront à l'humanité / à la société ; [scandal] scandale m

2. [indignation] indignation *f* **3.** [brutal act] atrocité *f*, acte *m* de brutalité or de violence. ◆ vt [person] outrager ; [moral sensibility] outrager, faire outrage à.

outraged ['aʊtreɪdʒd] adj outré, scandalisé ▸ **to be outraged** at or by sthg être outré or scandalisé par qqch.

outrageous [aʊt'reɪdʒəs] adj **1.** [scandalous - behaviour, manners] scandaleux ; [atrocious - crime, attack, etc.] monstrueux, atroce **2.** [slightly offensive - humour, style] choquant ; [- joke, remark] outrageant **3.** [extravagant - person, colour] extravagant **4.** [price] exorbitant.

outrageously [aʊt'reɪdʒəslɪ] adv **1.** [scandalously] de façon scandaleuse, scandaleusement ; [atrociously] atrocement, monstrueusement **2.** [extravagantly] de façon extravagante.

outran [ˌaʊt'ræn] pt ⟶ **outrun**.

outreach n ['aʊtriːtʃ] ADMIN *recherche des personnes qui ne demandent pas l'aide sociale dont elles pourraient bénéficier* ▸ **outreach worker** *employé ou bénévole dans un bureau d'aide sociale.*

outrider ['aʊtˌraɪdə*] n UK [motorcyclist] motard *m* (d'escorte).

outright ◆ adj ['aʊtraɪt] **1.** [absolute, utter - dishonesty, hypocrisy] pur (et simple), absolu ; [- liar] fieffé ; [frank - denial, refusal] net, catégorique **2.** [clear - win, winner] incontesté. ◆ adv [aʊt'raɪt] **1.** [frankly - refuse] net, carrément ; [- ask] carrément, franchement **2.** [totally - oppose] absolument **3.** [clearly - win] nettement, haut la main **4.** [instantly] : *they were killed outright* ils ont été tués sur le coup.

outrun [ˌaʊt'rʌn] (*pt* outran [ˌaʊt'ræn], *pp* outrun, *cont* outrunning) vt **1.** [run faster than] courir plus vite que ; [pursuer] distancer **2.** [ability, energy, resources] excéder, dépasser.

outsell [ˌaʊt'sel] (*pt* & *pp* outsold [-'səʊld]) vt [subj: article] se vendre mieux que ; [subj: company] vendre davantage que.

outset ['aʊtset] n ▸ **at the outset** au début, au départ ▸ **from the outset** dès le début, d'emblée.

outshine [ˌaʊt'ʃaɪn] (*pt* & *pp* outshone [-'ʃɒn]) vt [subj: star] briller plus que ; *fig* [rival] éclipser, surpasser.

outside ◆ adv [aʊt'saɪd] **1.** [outdoors] dehors, à l'extérieur ▸ *it's cold outside* il fait froid dehors ▸ *to go outside* sortir **2.** [on other side of door] dehors. ◆ prep [aʊt'saɪd or 'aʊtsaɪd] **1.** [on or to the exterior] à l'extérieur de, hors de / *nobody is allowed outside the house* personne n'a le droit de quitter la maison / *put the eggs outside the window* / *door* mettez les œufs sur le rebord de la fenêtre / devant la porte **2.** [away from] : *we live some way outside the town* nous habitons assez loin de la ville / *I don't think anybody outside France has heard of him* je ne pense pas qu'il soit connu ailleurs qu'en France **3.** [beyond] en dehors de, au-delà de / *it's outside his field* ce n'est pas son domaine / *outside office hours* en dehors des heures de bureau. ◆ adj ['aʊtsaɪd] **1.** [exterior] extérieur / *she has few outside interests* elle s'intéresse à peu de choses à part son travail / *an outside toilet* des toilettes (situées) à l'extérieur / *the outside edge* le bord extérieur ▸ **outside lane** a) [driving on left] file *f* or voie *f* de droite b) [driving on right] file *f* or voie *f* de gauche ▸ **an outside line** [on telephone] une ligne extérieure **2.** [from elsewhere - help, influence] extérieur ▸ **to get an outside opinion** demander l'avis d'un tiers **3.** [poor - possibility] faible / *she has only an outside chance of winning* elle n'a que très peu de chances de gagner. ◆ n [aʊt'saɪd or 'aʊtsaɪd] **1.** [exterior - of building, container] extérieur *m*, dehors *m* / *the arms were flown in from outside* les armes ont été introduites dans le pays par avion ; *fig* : *looking at the problem from (the) outside* quand on considère le problème de l'extérieur **2.** AUTO

▸ **to overtake on the outside** a) [driving on left] doubler à droite b) [driving on right] doubler à gauche **3.** [outer edge] extérieur *m*. ◆ **outside of** prep phr US **1.** = outside **2.** [except for] en dehors de / *nobody, outside of a few close friends, was invited* personne, en dehors de or à part quelques amis intimes, n'était invité.

outside broadcast n reportage *m*.

outsider [ˌaʊt'saɪdə*] n **1.** [person] étranger *m*, -ère *f* **2.** SPORT outsider *m*.

outsize ['aʊtsaɪz] adj **1.** [large] énorme, colossal **2.** [in clothes sizes] grande taille (*inv*).

outsized ['aʊtsaɪzd] adj énorme, colossal.

outskirts ['aʊtskɜːts] pl n [of town] banlieue *f*, périphérie *f* ; [of forest] orée *f*, lisière *f* / *we live on the outskirts of Copenhagen* nous habitons la banlieue de Copenhague.

outsmart [ˌaʊt'smɑːt] vt se montrer plus malin que.

outsource ['aʊtsɔːs] vt COMM sous-traiter, externaliser.

outspoken [ˌaʊt'spəʊkn] adj franc (franche) ▸ **to be outspoken** parler franchement, avoir son franc-parler / *he has always been an outspoken critic of the reforms* il a toujours ouvertement critiqué les réformes.

outspread [ˌaʊt'spred] adj écarté.

outstanding [ˌaʊt'stændɪŋ] adj **1.** [remarkable - ability, performance] exceptionnel, remarquable ; [notable - event, feature] marquant, mémorable **2.** [unresolved - problem] non résolu, en suspens ; [unfinished - business, work] inachevé, en cours ; ADMIN en souffrance, en attente ; [unpaid - bill] impayé ▸ **outstanding payment** impayé *m* ▸ **outstanding interest** / **rent** arriérés *mpl* d'intérêt / de loyer.

outstandingly [ˌaʊt'stændɪŋlɪ] adv exceptionnellement, remarquablement.

outstay [ˌaʊt'steɪ] vt [subj: guests] rester plus longtemps que ▸ **to outstay one's welcome** abuser de l'hospitalité de ses hôtes.

outstretched [ˌaʊt'stretʃt] adj [limbs, body] étendu, allongé ; [wings] déployé.

outstrip [ˌaʊt'strɪp] (*pt* & *pp* outstripped, *cont* outstripping) vt UK dépasser, surpasser.

outtake ['aʊtteɪk] n CIN & TV coupure *f*.

out tray n corbeille *f* sortie.

outvote [ˌaʊt'vəʊt] vt [bill, reform] rejeter (à la majorité des voix) ; [person] mettre en minorité.

outward ['aʊtwəd] ◆ adj **1.** [external] extérieur, externe ; [apparent] apparent **2.** [in direction] vers l'extérieur ▸ **the outward journey** le voyage aller, l'aller *m*. ◆ adv vers l'extérieur ▸ **outward bound** [ship, train] en partance.

outward bound course n école *f* d'endurcissement (en plein air).

outwardly ['aʊtwədlɪ] adv en apparence.

outwards ['aʊtwədz] adv UK vers l'extérieur.

outweigh [aʊt'weɪ] vt l'emporter sur.

outwit [ˌaʊt'wɪt] (*pt* & *pp* outwitted, *cont* outwitting) vt se montrer plus malin que.

outworker ['aʊtˌwɜːkə*] n UK travailleur *m* à domicile.

oval ['əʊvl] ◆ adj (en) ovale. ◆ n ovale *m*. ◆ **Oval** pr n ▸ **the Oval** célèbre terrain de cricket dans le centre de Londres.

Oval Office pr n [office] Bureau *m* ovale ; [authority] présidence *f* des États-Unis.

ovarian [əʊ'veərɪən] adj ovarien.

ovary ['əʊvərɪ] (*pl* ovaries) n ovaire *m*.

ovation [əʊ'veɪʃn] n ovation *f* ▸ **to give sb an ovation** faire une ovation à qqn.

oven ['ʌvn] n four *m*.

oven chips, oven fries pl n frites *fpl* au four.

oven glove, oven mitt n gant *m* isolant.

ovenproof ['ʌvnpruːf] adj allant or qui va au four.

oven-ready adj prêt à cuire or à mettre au four.

over ['əʊvəʳ]

◆ prep

A. IN SPACE 1. [above] au-dessus de 2. [on top of, covering] sur, par-dessus / *she wore a cardigan over her dress* elle portait un gilet par-dessus sa robe 3. [across the entire surface of] : *to cross over the road* traverser la rue / *they live over the road from me* ils habitent en face de chez moi 4. [on the far side of] : *the village over the hill* le village de l'autre côté de la colline.

B. QUANTITY OR VOLUME [with specific figure or amount - more than] plus de / *it took me well / just over an hour* j'ai mis bien plus / un peu plus d'une heure / *children over (the age of) 7* les enfants (âgés) de plus de 7 ans / *think of a number over 100* pensez à un chiffre supérieur à 100.

C. IN TIME [during] : *I've got a job over the long vacation* je vais travailler pendant les grandes vacances / *what are you doing over Easter?* qu'est-ce que tu fais pour Pâques ? / *over the next few decades* au cours des prochaines décennies / *we discussed it over a drink / over a game of golf* nous en avons discuté autour d'un verre /en faisant une partie de golf.

D. ABOUT OR VIA 1. [concerning] au sujet de / *they're always quarrelling over money* ils se disputent sans cesse pour des questions d'argent 2. [by means of, via] : *I heard it over the radio* je l'ai entendu à la radio.

E. RECOVERED FROM : *are you over your bout of flu?* est-ce que tu es guéri or tu t'es remis de ta grippe ? / *he's over the shock now* il s'en est remis maintenant / *we'll soon be over the worst* le plus dur sera bientôt passé.

◆ adv 1. [indicating movement or location, across distance or space] : *an eagle flew over* un aigle passa au-dessus de nous / *she walked over to him and said hello* elle s'approcha de lui pour dire bonjour / *over there* là-bas / *come over here!* viens (par) ici ! / *has Bill been over?* est-ce que Bill est passé ? / *she drove over to meet us* elle est venue nous rejoindre en voiture / *let's have* or *invite them over for dinner* si on les invitait à dîner ? / *we have guests over from Morocco* nous avons des invités qui viennent du Maroc 2. [indicating movement from a higher to a lower level] : *I fell over* je suis tombé (par terre) / *she knocked her glass over* elle a renversé son verre 3. TELEC ▶ **over (to you)!** à vous ! ▶ **over and out!** terminé ! 4. [left, remaining] : *there were / I had a few pounds (left) over* il restait /il me restait quelques livres 5. [with specific figure or amount - more] plus / *men of 30 and over* les hommes âgés de 30 ans et plus 6. [again, more than once] encore / *I had to do the whole thing over* [US] j'ai dû tout refaire / *she won the tournament five times over* elle a gagné le tournoi à cinq reprises.

◆ adj fini. ❖ **over and above** prep phr en plus de. ❖ **over and over** adv phr : *I've told you over and over (again)* je te l'ai répété je ne sais combien de fois.

over- in comp 1. [excessive] ▶ **over-activity** suractivité *f* ▶ **over-cautious** trop prudent, d'une prudence excessive 2. [more than] ▶ **the over-fifties**: *a club for the over-fifties* un club pour les plus de cinquante ans.

overachiever [,əʊvərə'tʃiːvəʳ] n surdoué *m*, -e *f*.

overact [,əʊvər'ækt] vi forcer la note, avoir un jeu outré.

overactive [,əʊvər'æktɪv] adj ▶ **to have an overactive thyroid** faire de l'hyperthyroïdie.

overall ◆ adv [,əʊvər'ɔːl] 1. [in general - consider, examine] en général, globalement 2. [measure] de bout en bout, d'un bout à l'autre ; [cost, amount] en tout 3. [in competition, sport] au classement général. ◆ adj 1. [general] global, d'ensemble / *my overall impression* mon impression d'ensemble 2. [total - cost, amount] total ; [-measurement] total, hors tout. ◆ n ['əʊvərɔːl] [protective coat] blouse *f* ; [US] [boiler suit] bleu *m* de travail. ❖ **overalls** pl n [UK] [boiler suit] bleu *m* de travail ; [US] [dungarees] salopette *f*.

overambitious [,əʊvəræm'bɪʃəs] adj trop ambitieux.

overanxious [,əʊvər'æŋkʃəs] adj 1. [worried] trop inquiet 2. [keen] trop soucieux.

overarm ['əʊvərɑːm] adv [serve, bowl] par-dessus l'épaule.

overate [,əʊvər'et] pt ⟶ **overeat.**

overawe [,əʊvər'ɔː] vt intimider, impressionner.

overbalance [,əʊvə'bæləns] ◆ vi [person] perdre l'équilibre ; [load, pile] basculer, se renverser ; [car] capoter ; [boat] chavirer. ◆ vt [person] faire perdre l'équilibre à ; [pile, vehicle] renverser, faire basculer.

overbearing [,əʊvə'beərɪŋ] adj autoritaire, impérieux.

overblown [,əʊvə'bləʊn] adj 1. [flower, beauty] qui commence à se faner 2. *pej* [prose, style] boursouflé, ampoulé, pompier.

overboard ['əʊvəbɔːd] adv NAUT par-dessus bord ▶ **to jump overboard** sauter à la mer ▶ **man overboard!** un homme à la mer !

overbook [,əʊvə'bʊk] ◆ vt [flight, hotel] surréserver. ◆ vi [airline, hotel] surréserver.

overbooking [,əʊvə'bʊkɪŋ] n surréservation *f*, surbooking *m*.

overborrow [,əʊvə'bɒrəʊ] vi FIN [company] emprunter de façon excessive.

overborrowing [,əʊvə'bɒrəʊɪŋ] n [of company] surendettement *m*.

overburden [,əʊvə'bɜːdn] vt surcharger, accabler / *overburdened with debts* criblé de dettes.

overcame [,əʊvə'keɪm] pt ⟶ **overcome.**

overcapitalize, overcapitalise [,əʊvə'kæpɪtəlaɪz] vt surcapitaliser.

overcast (*pt & pp* **overcast**) ◆ vt [,əʊvə'kɑːst] SEW surfiler. ◆ adj ['əʊvəkɑːst] [sky] sombre, couvert ; [weather] couvert.

overcautious [,əʊvə'kɔːʃəs] adj trop prudent, prudent à l'excès.

overcharge [,əʊvə'tʃɑːdʒ] ◆ vt 1. [customer] faire payer trop cher 2. ELEC [circuit] surcharger. ◆ vi faire payer trop cher.

overcoat ['əʊvəkəʊt] n manteau *m*, pardessus *m*.

overcome [,əʊvə'kʌm] (*pt* **overcame** [,əʊvə'keɪm], *pp* **overcome**) ◆ vt 1. [vanquish - enemy, opposition] vaincre, triompher de ; [-difficulty, shyness] surmonter ; [-fear, repulsion, prejudice] vaincre, surmonter, maîtriser ; [master - nerves] maîtriser, contrôler 2. [debilitate, weaken] accabler 3. (*usu passive*) [overwhelm] : *to be overcome by fear* être paralysé par la peur / *to be overcome with joy* être comblé de joie. ◆ vi vaincre.

overcompensate [,əʊvə'kɒmpənseɪt] vt surcompenser.

overcomplicated [,əʊvə'kɒmplɪkeɪtɪd] adj trop or excessivement compliqué.

overconfident [,əʊvə'kɒnfɪdənt] adj 1. [arrogant] suffisant, présomptueux 2. [trusting] trop confiant / *I'm not overconfident of his chances of recovery* je ne crois pas trop en ses chances de guérison.

overconsume [,əʊvəkən'sjuːm] vt consommer trop de.

overcook [,əʊvə'kʊk] ◆ vt faire trop cuire. ◆ vi trop cuire.

overcritical [ˌəʊvə'krɪtɪkəl] adj trop critique.

overcrowded [ˌəʊvə'kraʊdɪd] adj [bus, train, room] bondé, comble ; [city, country, prison] surpeuplé ; [streets] plein de monde ; [class] surchargé.

overcrowding [ˌəʊvə'kraʊdɪŋ] n surpeuplement *m*, surpopulation *f* ; [in housing] entassement *m* ; [in bus, train, etc.] entassement *m* des voyageurs, affluence *f* ; [in schools] effectifs *mpl* surchargés ; [in prisons] surpeuplement *m*.

overdevelop [ˌəʊvədɪ'veləp] vt [gen & PHOT] surdévelopper / *parts of the coastline have been overdeveloped* par endroits, le littoral est trop construit.

overdeveloped [ˌəʊvədɪ'veləpt] adj [gen & PHOT] surdéveloppé.

overdevelopment [ˌəʊvədɪ'veləpmənt] n surdéveloppement *m*.

overdo [ˌəʊvə'duː] (*pt* **overdid** [-'dɪd], *pp* **overdone** [-'dʌn]) vt **1.** [exaggerate] exagérer, pousser trop loin **2.** [eat, drink too much of] : *don't overdo the whisky* n'abuse pas du whisky **3.** CULIN trop cuire **4.** PHR **to overdo it** or **to overdo things** se surmener.

overdone [-'dʌn] ◆ pp ⟶ **overdo.** ◆ adj **1.** [exaggerated] exagéré, excessif **2.** CULIN trop cuit.

overdose ◆ n ['əʊvədəʊs] *lit* dose *f* massive or excessive ; *fig* dose *f.* ◆ vi [ˌəʊvə'dəʊs] prendre une overdose / *he overdosed on heroin / LSD* il a pris une overdose d'héroïne / de LSD. ◆ vt [ˌəʊvə'dəʊs] [patient] administrer une dose excessive à ; [drug] prescrire une dose excessive de.

overdraft ['əʊvədrɑːft] n découvert *m* (bancaire).

overdrawn [-'drɔːn] adj à découvert ⟩ **to be** or **to go overdrawn** être or se mettre à découvert.

overdressed [ˌəʊvə'drest] adj habillé avec trop de recherche.

overdrive ['əʊvədraɪv] n AUTO (vitesse *f*) surmultipliée *f*, overdrive *m* ⟩ **to go into overdrive** *fig* mettre les bouchées doubles.

overdue [ˌəʊvə'djuː] adj **1.** [bus, flight, person] en retard ; [payment, rent] en retard, impayé ; [library book] non retourné **2.** [apology] tardif ; [change, reform] qui tarde, qui se fait attendre **3.** [in pregnancy] ⟩ **to be overdue** être en retard.

overeager [ˌəʊvər'iːgər] adj trop empressé / *he is overeager to please* il est trop soucieux or désireux de plaire.

over easy adj US ⟩ **eggs over easy** œufs sur le plat saisis des deux côtés.

overeat [ˌəʊvər'iːt] (*pt* **overate** [ˌəʊvər'et], *pp* **overeaten** [-'iːtn]) vi [once] trop manger, faire un repas trop copieux ; [habitually] se suralimenter.

overeating [ˌəʊvər'iːtɪŋ] n [habitual] suralimentation *f.*

overegg [ˌəʊvər'eg] vt UK ⟩ **to overegg the pudding** en faire trop.

overemphasize, overemphasise [ˌəʊvər'emfəsaɪz] vt trop mettre l'accent sur, trop insister sur.

overenthusiastic ['əʊvərɪnˌθjuːzɪ'æstɪk] adj trop enthousiaste.

overestimate [ˌəʊvər'estɪmeɪt] vt surestimer.

overexcited [ˌəʊvərɪk'saɪtɪd] adj surexcité ⟩ **to become** or **to get overexcited** (trop) s'énerver.

overexert [ˌəʊvərɪg'zɜːt] vt surmener ⟩ **to overexert o.s.** se surmener, s'éreinter.

overexpose [ˌəʊvərɪk'spəʊz] vt *lit & fig* surexposer.

overexposure [ˌəʊvərɪk'spəʊʒər] n *lit & fig* surexposition *f.*

overfamiliar [ˌəʊvəfə'mɪljər] adj **1.** [too intimate, disrespectful] trop familier **2.** [conversant] : *I'm not overfamiliar with the system* je ne connais pas très bien le système.

overfeed [ˌəʊvə'fiːd] (*pt & pp* **overfed** [-'fed]) ◆ vt suralimenter. ◆ vi se suralimenter, trop manger.

overfeeding [ˌəʊvə'fiːdɪŋ] n suralimentation *f.*

overfill [ˌəʊvə'fɪl] vt trop remplir.

overfish [ˌəʊvə'fɪʃ] vt [fishing ground] surexploiter.

overfishing [ˌəʊvə'fɪʃɪŋ] n surpêche *f.*

overflow ◆ vi [ˌəʊvə'fləʊ] **1.** [with liquid - container, bath] déborder ; [river] déborder, sortir de son lit / *the glass is full to overflowing* le verre est plein à ras bord ; [with people - room, vehicle] déborder, être plein à craquer / *the streets were overflowing with people* les rues regorgeaient de monde / *the shop was full to overflowing* le magasin était plein à craquer ; [with objects - box, wastebin] déborder **2.** *fig* [with emotion] déborder / *his heart was overflowing with joy* son cœur débordait de joie. ◆ n ['əʊvəfləʊ] **1.** [drain - from sink, cistern] trop-plein *m* ; [- large-scale] déversoir *m* **2.** [excess - of population, production] excédent *m*, surplus *m* ; [- of energy, emotion] trop-plein *m*, débordement *m* **3.** [flooding] inondation *f* ; [excess] trop-plein *m.*

overflow pipe n trop-plein *m*, tuyau *m* d'écoulement.

overgenerous [ˌəʊvə'dʒenərəs] adj [person, act] (trop) généreux, prodigue ; [portion] trop copieux, excessif.

overgrown [ˌəʊvə'grəʊn] adj [garden, path, etc.] ⟩ **overgrown with** envahi par.

overhang (*pt & pp* **overhung** [-'hʌŋ]) ◆ vt [ˌəʊvə'hæŋ] **1.** [subj: cliff, ledge, balcony] surplomber, faire saillie au-dessus de ; [subj: cloud, mist, smoke] planer sur, flotter au-dessus de **2.** *fig* [subj: threat, danger] planer sur, menacer. ◆ n ['əʊvəhæŋ] surplomb *m.*

overhanging [ˌəʊvə'hæŋɪŋ] adj **1.** [cliff, ledge, balcony] en surplomb, en saillie **2.** *fig* [threat] imminent.

overhaul ◆ n ['əʊvəhɔːl] [of car, machine] révision *f* ; [of institution, system] révision *f*, remaniement *m.* ◆ vt [ˌəʊvə'hɔːl] **1.** [car, machine] réviser ; [system] revoir, remanier **2.** [catch up] rattraper ; [overtake] dépasser ; NAUT gagner.

overhead ◆ adv [ˌəʊvə'hed] au-dessus. ◆ adj ['əʊvəhed] **1.** [cable, railway] aérien ; [lighting] au plafond ; SPORT [racket stroke] smashé ; FOOT [kick] retourné **2.** COMM ⟩ **overhead costs** frais *mpl* généraux. ◆ n US = **overheads.** ⟿ **overheads** pl n UK frais *mpl* généraux.

overhead light n plafonnier *m.*

overhead projector n rétroprojecteur *m.*

overhear [ˌəʊvə'hɪər] (*pt & pp* **overheard** [-'hɜːd]) vt [gen] entendre par hasard ; [conversation] surprendre / *I couldn't help overhearing what you were saying* malgré moi, j'ai entendu votre conversation / *she overheard them talking about her* elle les a surpris à parler d'elle.

overheat [ˌəʊvə'hiːt] ◆ vt surchauffer. ◆ vi chauffer.

overheated [ˌəʊvə'hiːtɪd] adj **1.** [too hot - room] surchauffé, trop chauffé ; [- engine] qui chauffe **2.** *fig* [angry] passionné, violent, exalté.

overhung [-'hʌŋ] pt & pp ⟶ **overhang.**

overimpress [ˌəʊvərɪm'pres] vt : *she wasn't overimpressed by the film* le film ne l'a pas particulièrement impressionnée.

overindulge [ˌəʊvərɪn'dʌldʒ] ◆ vt **1.** [appetite, desire] céder à, succomber à, se laisser aller à **2.** [person] (trop) gâter. ◆ vi [overeat] trop manger ; [drink] trop boire.

overjoyed [ˌəʊvəˈdʒɔɪd] adj comblé, transporté, ravi / *she was overjoyed at being home again* elle était ravie d'être rentrée / *I was overjoyed at the news* cette nouvelle m'a ravi ou transporté.

overkill [ˈəʊvəkɪl] n **1.** MIL surarmement *m* **2.** *fig* exagération *f*, excès *m* ▸ **media overkill** médiatisation *f* excessive.

overladen [ˌəʊvəˈleɪdn] ◆ pp ⟶ **overload.** ◆ adj surchargé.

overlaid [ˌəʊvəˈleɪd] pt & pp ⟶ **overlay.**

overland [ˈəʊvəlænd] adj & adv par voie de terre / *the overland route to India* le voyage en Inde par la route.

overlap (*pt* & *pp* **overlapped,** *cont* **overlapping**) ◆ vi [ˌəʊvəˈlæp] [gen] (se) chevaucher, se recouvrir en partie. ◆ vt [ˌəʊvəˈlæp] [in space] faire se chevaucher ; [in time] empiéter sur. ◆ n [ˈəʊvəlæp] [gen] chevauchement *m*.

overlay vt [ˌəʊvəˈleɪ] (*pt* & *pp* **overlaid** [ˌəʊvəˈleɪd]) recouvrir.

overleaf [ˌəʊvəˈliːf] adv au dos, au verso / **'see overleaf'** 'voir au verso' / **'continued overleaf'** [in book, magazine] 'suite page suivante'.

overload ◆ vt [ˌəʊvəˈləʊd] (*pp* **overloaded**) **1.** (*pp* **overloaded** *or* **overladen** [ˌəʊvəˈleɪdn]) [animal, vehicle] surcharger **2.** (*pp* **overloaded**) [electric circuit] surcharger ; [engine, machine] surmener ; *fig* [with work] surcharger, écraser. ◆ n [ˈəʊvələʊd] surcharge *f*.

overlong [ˌəʊvəˈlɒŋ] ◆ adj trop ou excessivement long. ◆ adv trop longtemps.

overlook [ˌəʊvəˈlʊk] vt **1.** [have view of] avoir vue sur, donner sur **2.** [fail to notice - detail, small thing] laisser échapper, oublier / *it's easy to overlook the small print* on oublie souvent de lire ce qui est en petits caractères ; [neglect] négliger, ne pas prendre en compte / *they overlooked the language problem* ils n'ont pas pris en compte le problème de la langue ; [ignore] laisser passer, passer sur / *I'll overlook it this time* je veux bien fermer les yeux cette fois-ci.

overly [ˈəʊvəlɪ] adj trop.

overmanning [ˌəʊvəˈmænɪŋ] n (*U*) sureffectifs *mpl.*

overmuch [ˌəʊvəˈmʌtʃ] adv outre mesure, trop / *I don't like it overmuch* ça ne me plaît pas trop.

overnight ◆ adv [ˌəʊvəˈnaɪt] **1.** [during the night] pendant la nuit / *to drive / to fly overnight* rouler / voler de nuit ; [until next day] jusqu'au lendemain / *they stopped or stayed overnight in Birmingham* ils ont passé la nuit à Birmingham **2.** *fig* [suddenly] du jour au lendemain. ◆ adj [ˈəʊvənaɪt] **1.** [stay, guest] d'une nuit ; [clothes, journey] de nuit / *we had an overnight stay in Paris* nous avons passé une nuit à Paris **2.** *fig* [sudden] soudain, subit / *there has been an overnight improvement in the situation* la situation s'est subitement améliorée.

overnight bag n sac *m* ou nécessaire *m* de voyage.

overoptimistic [ˌəʊvəˌɒptɪˈmɪstɪk] adj excessivement ou par trop optimiste / *I am not overoptimistic about their chances* je ne crois pas qu'ils aient de grandes chances.

overpaid [ˌəʊvəˈpeɪd] pt & pp ⟶ **overpay.**

overparticular [ˌəʊvəpəˈtɪkjʊlər] adj (par) trop exigeant / *he's not overparticular about these things* il se moque un peu de ces choses-là.

overpass [ˈəʊvəpɑːs] n AUTO saut-de-mouton *m* (route).

overpay [ˌəʊvəˈpeɪ] (*pt* & *pp* **overpaid** [ˌəʊvəˈpeɪd]) vt [bill, employee] surpayer, trop payer.

overplay [ˌəʊvəˈpleɪ] ◆ vt [importance] exagérer ▸ **to overplay one's hand** présumer de ses forces ou de ses capacités. ◆ vi exagérer son rôle.

overpopulated [ˌəʊvəˈpɒpjʊleɪtɪd] adj surpeuplé.

overpopulation [ˈəʊvəˌpɒpjʊˈleɪʃn] n surpeuplement *m*, surpopulation *f*.

overpower [ˌəʊvəˈpaʊər] vt **1.** [physically - enemy, opponent] maîtriser, vaincre **2.** [subj: smell] suffoquer ; [subj: heat, emotion] accabler.

overpowering [ˌəʊvəˈpaʊərɪŋ] adj **1.** [heat, sensation] accablant, écrasant ; [smell] suffocant ; [perfume] entêtant **2.** [desire, passion] irrésistible ; [grief] accablant **3.** [force] irrésistible **4.** [personality, charisma] dominateur, irrésistible.

overpriced [ˌəʊvəˈpraɪst] adj excessivement cher / *those books are really overpriced* le prix de ces livres est vraiment excessif ou trop élevé.

overproduction [ˌəʊvəprəˈdʌkʃn] n surproduction *f*.

overprotective [ˌəʊvəprəˈtektɪv] adj trop protecteur, protecteur à l'excès / *she is overprotective of* or *towards her son* elle couve trop son fils.

overqualified [ˌəʊvəˈkwɒlɪfaɪd] adj surqualifié.

overran [ˌəʊvəˈræn] pt ⟶ **overrun.**

overrated [ˌəʊvəˈreɪtɪd] adj [person] : *he is rather overrated as a novelist* sa réputation de romancier est assez surfaite ; [book, film] : *I think champagne is really overrated* je pense que le champagne ne mérite pas sa réputation ou que la réputation du champagne est surfaite.

overreach [ˌəʊvəˈriːtʃ] vt ▸ **to overreach o.s.** présumer de ses forces, viser trop haut.

overreact [ˌəʊvərɪˈækt] vi [gen] réagir de façon excessive, dramatiser ; [panic] s'affoler.

override [ˌəʊvəˈraɪd] (*pt* **overrode** [-ˈrəʊd], *pp* **overridden** [-ˈrɪdn]) vt **1.** [instruction, desire, authority] passer outre à, outrepasser ; [decision] annuler ; [rights] fouler aux pieds, bafouer / *my objection was overridden* il n'a été tenu aucun compte de mon objection **2.** [fact, factor] l'emporter sur.

overriding [ˌəʊvəˈraɪdɪŋ] adj [importance] primordial, capital ; [belief, consideration, factor] prépondérant, premier, dominant.

overripe [ˌəʊvəˈraɪp] adj [fruit] trop mûr ; [cheese] trop fait.

overrode [-ˈrəʊd] pt ⟶ **override.**

overrule [ˌəʊvəˈruːl] vt [decision] annuler ; [claim, objection] rejeter / *I was overruled* mon avis a été rejeté.

overrun ◆ vt [ˌəʊvəˈrʌn] (*pt* **overran** [ˌəʊvəˈræn], *pp* **overrun,** *cont* **overrunning**) **1.** [invade] envahir **2.** [exceed - time limit] dépasser / *the programme overran the allotted time by ten minutes* l'émission a dépassé de dix minutes le temps qui lui était imparti ; [overshoot] dépasser, aller au-delà de. ◆ vi [ˌəʊvəˈrʌn] (*pt* **overran** [ˌəʊvəˈræn], *pp* **overrun,** *cont* **overrunning**) [programme, speech] dépasser le temps alloué ou imparti ; [meeting] dépasser l'heure prévue / *the speech overran by ten minutes* le discours a duré dix minutes de plus que prévu. ◆ n [ˈəʊvərʌn] [in time, space] dépassement *m*.

oversaw [ˌəʊvəˈsɔː] pt ⟶ **oversee.**

overseas ◆ adv [ˌəʊvəˈsiːz] à l'étranger. ◆ adj [ˈəʊvəsiːz] [student, tourist, market] étranger ; [travel, posting] à l'étranger ; [mail - from overseas] (en provenance) de l'étranger ; [- to an overseas country] pour l'étranger ; [trade] extérieur ; [colony, possession] d'outre-mer.

oversee [ˌəʊvəˈsiː] (*pt* **oversaw** [ˌəʊvəˈsɔː], *pp* **overseen** [-ˈsiːn]) vt [watch] surveiller, contrôler ; [supervise] superviser.

overseer [ˈəʊvəˌsiːər] n [foreman] contremaître *m*, chef *m* d'équipe.

oversensitive [ˌəʊvəˈsensɪtɪv] adj trop sensible ou susceptible, hypersensible.

oversexed [,əʊvə'sekst] adj : *he's oversexed* il ne pense qu'au sexe.

overshadow [,əʊvə'ʃædəʊ] vt **1.** [eclipse - person, event] éclipser **2.** [darken] ombrager / *their lives had been overshadowed by the death of their father* fig leur vie avait été endeuillée par la mort de leur père.

overshare ['əʊvəʃeəʳ] US ◆ vi donner trop de détails personnels / *never overshare on your first date* ne donnez pas trop de détails sur votre vie privée lors d'un premier rendez-vous. ◆ n détail *m* en trop / *that qualifies as an overshare* tu aurais pu nous faire grâce de ce détail / *avoid overshare at work* évitez de trop parler de votre vie privée avec vos collègues.

overshoot vt [,əʊvə'ʃu:t] (*pt & pp* **overshot** [-'ʃɒt]) dépasser, aller au-delà de.

oversight ['əʊvəsaɪt] n **1.** [error] omission *f*, oubli *m* **ı by** or **through an oversight** par mégarde, par négligence **2.** [supervision] surveillance *f*, supervision *f*.

oversimplification ['əʊvə,sɪmplɪfɪ'keɪʃn] n simplification *f* excessive.

oversimplify [,əʊvə'sɪmplɪfaɪ] (*pt & pp* **oversimplified**) vt simplifier à l'excès.

oversize(d) [,əʊvə'saɪz(d)] adj **1.** [very big] énorme, démesuré **2.** [too big] trop grand. .

oversleep [,əʊvə'sli:p] (*pt & pp* **overslept** [-'slept]) vi se réveiller en retard, ne pas se réveiller à temps.

overspend (*pt & pp* **overspent** [-'spent]) ◆ n ['əʊvəspend] **1.** [gen] dépenses *fpl* excessives, prodigalités *fpl* **2.** FIN dépassement *m* budgétaire or du budget. ◆ vi [,əʊvə'spend] [gen] trop dépenser ; FIN être en dépassement budgétaire.

overspill ◆ vi [,əʊvə'spɪl] déborder, se répandre. ◆ n ['əʊvəspɪl] excédent *m* de population (urbaine). ◆ comp **ı overspill population** excédent *m* de population.

overstaffed [,əʊvə'stɑ:ft] adj en sureffectif / *the firm is overstaffed* le personnel de la firme est trop nombreux, la firme connaît un problème de sureffectifs.

overstate [,əʊvə'steɪt] vt exagérer.

overstatement [,əʊvə'steɪtmənt] n exagération *f*.

overstay [,əʊvə'steɪ] vt **ı to overstay one's welcome** abuser de l'hospitalité de ses hôtes.

overstep [,əʊvə'step] (*pt & pp* **overstepped**, cont **overstepping**) vt dépasser, outrepasser **ı to overstep one's authority** outrepasser ses pouvoirs **ı to overstep the mark** or **the limit** fig dépasser les bornes, aller trop loin.

overstretched [əʊvə'stretʃt] adj [person] débordé ; [budget] extrêmement serré.

oversubscribe [,əʊvəsəb'skraɪb] vt **ı to be oversubscribed** [concert, play] être en surlocation / *the school trip is oversubscribed* il y a trop d'élèves inscrits à l'excursion organisée par l'école.

overt ['əʊvɜ:t or əʊ'vɜ:t] adj manifeste, évident.

overtake [,əʊvə'teɪk] (*pt* **overtook** [-'tʊk], *pp* **overtaken** [-'teɪkn]) vt **1.** [pass beyond] dépasser, devancer ; UK AUTO dépasser, doubler **2.** [surprise] surprendre ; [strike] frapper.

overtaking [,əʊvə'teɪkɪŋ] n UK dépassement *m* **ı 'no overtaking'** 'défense de doubler'.

overtax [,əʊvə'tæks] vt **1.** FIN [person] surimposer ; [goods] surtaxer **2.** [strain - patience, hospitality] abuser de ; [- person, heart] surmener / *don't overtax your strength* or *yourself* ne te fatigue pas inutilement, ne te surmène pas.

overtaxation [,əʊvətæk'seɪʃən] n FIN surcharge *m* d'impôts, surimposition *f*.

over-the-counter adj [medicines] vendu sans ordonnance, en vente libre.

overthrow vt [,əʊvə'θrəʊ] (*pt* **overthrew** [-'θru:], *pp* **overthrown** [-'θrəʊn]) [regime, government] renverser ; [rival, enemy army] vaincre ; [values, standards] bouleverser ; [plans] réduire à néant.

overtime ['əʊvətaɪm] n *(U)* **1.** [work] heures *fpl* supplémentaires **ı to do** or **to work overtime** faire des heures supplémentaires / *your imagination seems to have been working overtime* on dirait que tu as laissé ton imagination s'emballer **2.** [overtime pay] rémunération *f* des heures supplémentaires **ı to be paid overtime** être payé en heures supplémentaires **3.** US SPORT prolongations *fpl* / *the match went into overtime* ils ont joué les prolongations.

overtime pay = **overtime**.

overtly [əʊ'vɜ:tlɪ] adv franchement, ouvertement.

overtone ['əʊvətəʊn] n [nuance] nuance *f*, accent *m* / *his speech was full of racist overtones* son discours était truffé de sous-entendus racistes.

overtook [-'tʊk] pt → **overtake**.

overture ['əʊvə,tjʊəʳ] n **1.** MUS ouverture *f* **2.** fig [proposal] ouverture *f*, avance *f* **ı to make overtures to sb** faire des avances à qqn **3.** fig [prelude] prélude *m*, début *m*.

overturn [,əʊvə'tɜ:n] ◆ vt **1.** [lamp, car, furniture] renverser ; [ship] faire chavirer **2.** [overthrow - regime, government, plans] renverser ; LAW [judgment, sentence] casser. ◆ vi [lamp, furniture] se renverser ; [car] se retourner, capoter ; [ship] chavirer.

overuse ◆ vt [,əʊvə'ju:z] abuser de. ◆ n [,əʊvə'ju:s] abus *m*, usage *m* excessif.

overview ['əʊvəvju:] n vue *f* d'ensemble.

overwater [,əʊvə'wɔ:təʳ] vt [plant] trop arroser.

overweight adj [,əʊvə'weɪt] [person] (trop) gros (grosse) / *I'm a few pounds overweight* j'ai quelques kilos de trop ; [luggage, parcel] trop lourd.

overwhelm [,əʊvə'welm] vt **1.** [devastate] accabler, terrasser ; [astound] bouleverser / *overwhelmed with grief* accablé de chagrin **2.** [submerge] submerger / *our switchboard has been overwhelmed by the number of calls* notre standard a été submergé par les appels / *I'm completely overwhelmed with work* je suis débordé de travail **3.** [defeat] écraser.

overwhelming [,əʊvə'welmɪŋ] adj **1.** [crushing - victory, defeat] écrasant / *the overwhelming majority (of people) oppose these measures* la grande majorité des gens est opposée à ces mesures **2.** [extreme, overpowering - grief, heat] accablant ; [-joy] extrême ; [-love] passionnel ; [-desire, urge, passion] irrésistible / *an overwhelming sense of frustration* un sentiment d'extrême frustration.

overwhelmingly [,əʊvə'welmɪŋlɪ] adv **1.** [crushingly] de manière écrasante **2.** [as intensifier] extrêmement ; [predominantly] surtout.

overwinter [,əʊvə'wɪntəʳ] vi [birds, animals] hiverner ; [people] passer l'hiver.

overwork ◆ vt [,əʊvə'wɜ:k] **1.** [person] surmener **2.** [word] abuser de, utiliser trop souvent. ◆ vi [,əʊvə'wɜ:k] se surmener. ◆ n ['əʊvə,wɜ:k] surmenage *m*.

overwrite [,əʊvə'raɪt] (*pt* **overwrote** [-'rəʊt], *pp* **overwritten** [-'rɪtn]) vt COMPUT [file] écraser.

overwrought [,əʊvə'rɔ:t] adj sur les nerfs, à bout.

overzealous [,əʊvə'zeləs] adj trop zélé.

ovulate ['ɒvjʊleɪt] vi ovuler.

ovulation [,ɒvjʊ'leɪʃn] n ovulation *f*.

ovum ['əʊvəm] (*pl* **ova** ['əʊvə]) n BIOL ovule *m*.

ow [aʊ] interj aïe.

owe [əʊ] ◆ vt devoir **ı to owe sthg to sb, to owe sb sthg** devoir qqch à qqn / *how much do we still owe him for* or *on the car?* combien nous reste-t-il à lui payer pour la voiture ? / *I owe you a beer* je te dois une bière / *we owe them an apology* nous leur devons des excuses / *you owe it to yourself to try again* tu te dois d'essayer encore une fois / *to what do we owe the honour of your visit?* qu'est-ce qui nous vaut l'honneur de votre visite ? / *I owe it all to my parents* je suis redevable de tout cela à mes parents. ◆ vi être endetté.

owing ['əʊɪŋ] adj *(after noun)* dû / *the sum owing on the car* la somme qui reste due sur le prix de la voiture. ❖ **owing to** prep phr à cause de, en raison de.

owl [aʊl] n hibou *m*, chouette *f*.

own [əʊn] ◆ adj propre / *I have my very own bedroom* j'ai une chambre pour moi tout seul / *a flat with its own entrance* un appartement avec une porte d'entrée indépendante / *these are my own skis* ces skis sont à moi or m'appartiennent / *it's all my own work* c'est moi qui ai tout fait / *it's your own fault!* tu n'as à t'en prendre qu'à toi-même ! / *you'll have to make up your own mind* c'est à toi et à toi seul de décider, personne ne pourra prendre cette décision à ta place. ◆ pron : *is that car your own?* est-ce que cette voiture est à vous ? / *I don't need a pen, I've brought my own* je n'ai pas besoin de stylo, j'ai apporté le mien / *a house / a room / a garden of one's (very) own* une maison / une pièce / un jardin (bien) à soi / *their son has a car of his own* leur fils a sa propre voiture / *the town has a character of its own* or *all (of) its own* la ville possède un charme qui lui est propre or un charme bien à elle / *my time is not my own* je ne suis pas maître de mon temps / *I haven't a single thing I can call my own* je n'ai rien à moi / *you're on your own now!* à toi de jouer maintenant ! ▸ **to come into one's own** a) [show one's capabilities] montrer de quoi on est capable b) [inherit] toucher son héritage ▸ **to get one's own back (on sb)** se venger (de qqn) / *I'll get my own back on him for that* je lui revaudrai ça ▸ **to look after one's own** s'occuper des siens ▸ **to make sthg one's own** s'approprier qqch. ◆ vt [possess] posséder / *does she own the house?* est-elle propriétaire de la maison ? / *who owns this car?* à qui appartient cette voiture ? / *they walked in as if they owned the place* inf ils sont entrés comme (s'ils étaient) chez eux. ❖ **on one's own** adj phr (tout) seul / *I'm trying to get him on his own* j'essaie de le voir seul à seul / *I did it (all) on my own* je l'ai fait tout seul. ❖ **own up** vi avouer, faire des aveux ▸ **to own up to sthg** avouer qqch / *he owned up to his mistake* il a reconnu son erreur.

own-brand adj ▸ **own-brand products** *produits vendus sous la marque du distributeur.*

owner ['əʊnə*ʳ*] n propriétaire *mf* / *at the owner's risk* aux risques du propriétaire / *who is the owner of this jacket?* à qui appartient cette veste ? / *they are all car owners* ils possèdent or ils ont tous une voiture.

owner-occupancy n *fait d'être propriétaire du logement qu'on occupe* / *owner-occupancy has increased* de plus en plus de gens sont propriétaires de leurs logements.

owner-occupier n occupant *m*, -e *f* propriétaire.

ownership ['əʊnəʃɪp] n possession *f* / *we require proof of ownership* nous demandons un titre de propriété / *the government encourages home ownership* le gouvernement encourage l'accession à la propriété / '**under new ownership**' 'changement de propriétaire'.

own-label = **own-brand**.

ox [ɒks] n (pl **oxen** ['ɒksn]) n bœuf *m* ▸ **(as) strong as an ox** fort comme un bœuf.

Oxbridge ['ɒksbrɪdʒ] pr n *désignation collective des universités d'Oxford et de Cambridge* / *Oxbridge graduates* diplômés des universités d'Oxford ou de Cambridge.

oxen ['ɒksn] pl ⟶ **ox**.

Oxfam ['ɒksfæm] (abbr of **Oxford Committee for Famine Relief**) pr n *association caritative britannique.*

oxfords ['ɒksfədz] pl n chaussures *fpl* à lacets.

oxide ['ɒksaɪd] n oxyde *m*.

oxidize, oxidise ['ɒksɪdaɪz] ◆ vt oxyder. ◆ vi s'oxyder.

Oxo ® ['ɒksəʊ] pr n *marque anglaise de bouillon cube.*

Oxon written abbr of **Oxfordshire**.

oxtail ['ɒksteɪl] n queue *f* de bœuf ▸ **oxtail soup** potage *m* oxtail.

ox tongue n langue *f* de bœuf.

oxyacetylene [ˌɒksɪə'setɪliːn] adj oxyacétylénique ▸ **oxyacetylene burner** or **lamp** or **torch** chalumeau *m* oxyacétylénique.

oxygen ['ɒksɪdʒən] n oxygène *m*.

oxygenate ['ɒksɪdʒəneɪt] vt oxygéner.

oxygenation [ˌɒksɪdʒə'neɪʃn] n oxygénation *f*.

oxygen mask n masque *m* à oxygène.

oxygen tent n tente *f* à oxygène.

oxymoron [ˌɒksɪ'mɔːrɒn] (pl **oxymora** [-rə]) n oxymoron *m*.

oyster ['ɔɪstə*ʳ*] n huître *f* ▸ **oyster farming** ostréiculture *f* / *the world is her oyster* le monde lui appartient.

oyster bed n parc *m* à huîtres.

oz. written abbr of **ounce**.

ozone ['əʊzəʊn] n **1.** [gas] ozone *m* ▸ **ozone layer** or **shield** couche *f* d'ozone **2.** inf [sea air] bon air *m* marin.

ozone-friendly adj qui préserve la couche d'ozone.

ozone-safe adj qui préserve la couche d'ozone.

p [piː] (*pl* p's *or* ps), **P** (*pl* P's *or* Ps) n [letter] p *m*, P *m*
▶ **to mind one's p's and q's** UK *inf* se tenir à carreau. See
also f.

p ◆ (written abbr of page) p. ◆ n abbr of penny,
abbr of pence.

P 1. written abbr of president 2. (written abbr of
prince) Pce.

p & h US written abbr of postage and handling.

p & p written abbr of postage and packing.

pa [pɑː] n US *inf* papa *m*.

p.a. (written abbr of per annum) p.a.

PA ◆ n 1. (abbr of personal assistant) UK secrétaire *mf* de direction 2. (abbr of public address system) système *m* de sonorisation, sono *f*. ◆ pr n abbr of
Press Association. ◆ written abbr of Pennsylvania.

PAC (abbr of political action committee) n *aux États-
Unis, comité qui réunit des fonds pour soutenir une cause politique.*

pace [peɪs] ◆ n 1. [speed] allure *f*, vitesse *f*, train *m* /
she quickened her pace elle pressa le pas / *the slower pace
of country life* le rythme plus paisible de la vie à la campagne / *to keep pace with new developments* se tenir au
courant des derniers développements / *he couldn't stand
or take the pace* il n'arrivait pas à suivre le rythme / *do it
at your own pace* faites-le à votre propre rythme ▶ **to make**
or **to set the pace** a) SPORT donner l'allure, mener le train
b) *fig* donner le ton 2. [step] pas *m* / *take two paces to
the left* faites deux pas à gauche ▶ **to put sb through his /
her paces** UK mettre qqn à l'épreuve. ◆ vi marcher (à pas
mesurés) / *he paced up and down the corridor* il arpentait
le couloir. ◆ vt 1. [corridor, cage, room] arpenter 2. [regu-
late] régler l'allure de.

pacemaker ['peɪsˌmeɪkə'] n 1. SPORT meneur *m*, -euse *f*
de train ; *fig* [leader] leader *m* 2. MED pacemaker *m*, stimulateur *m* cardiaque.

pacesetter ['peɪsˌsetə'] US = pacemaker.

Pacific [pə'sɪfɪk] ◆ pr n ▶ **the Pacific (Ocean)** le Pacifique, l'océan *m* Pacifique. ◆ adj du Pacifique.

Pacific Rim pr n ▶ **the Pacific Rim** *groupe de pays situés
au bord du Pacifique, particulièrement les pays industrialisés
d'Asie.*

pacifier ['pæsɪfaɪə'] n US [for baby] tétine *f*, sucette *f*.

pacifism ['pæsɪfɪzm] n pacifisme *m*.

pacifist ['pæsɪfɪst] ◆ adj pacifiste. ◆ n pacifiste *mf*.

pacify ['pæsɪfaɪ] (*pt & pp* pacified) vt 1. [soothe] apaiser, calmer 2. MIL [subdue] pacifier.

pack [pæk] ◆ vt 1. [bags] faire ▶ **to pack one's case**
or **suitcase** faire sa valise / *she packed her bags and left*

elle a fait ses bagages et elle est partie, elle a plié bagage
2. [container, crate] remplir 3. [put in bags - clothes, be-
longings] : *I've already packed the towels* j'ai déjà mis les
serviettes dans la valise / *shall I pack the camera?* est-ce
que j'emporte or je prends l'appareil photo ? 4. [wrap up
- goods for transport] emballer 5. [cram tightly - cupboard,
container] bourrer ; [- belongings, people] entasser 6. [crowd
into - subj: spectators, passengers] s'entasser dans 7. [com-
press - soil] tasser 8. *inf* [have, carry] : *he packs a lot of
influence in cabinet / ministerial circles* il a beaucoup d'influence au conseil des ministres / dans les milieux ministériels
▶ **to pack a gun** US être armé. ◆ vi 1. [for journey] faire
sa valise or ses bagages / *have you finished packing?* as-tu
fini tes bagages ? 2. [fit - into container] rentrer / *the keyboard will pack easily into a briefcase* on peut facilement
faire tenir le clavier dans un attaché-case 3. [crowd together
- spectators, passengers] s'entasser / *we all packed into her
car* nous nous sommes tous entassés dans sa voiture. ◆ n
1. [for carrying - rucksack] sac *m* à dos ; [- bundle] ballot *m* ;
[- bale] balle *f* ; [- on animal] charge *f* 2. [packet] paquet *m*
3. UK [deck of cards] jeu *m* 4. [group - of children, wolves]
bande *f* ; [- of cub scouts] meute *f* ; [- of hunting hounds]
meute *f* 5. SPORT [in rugby] pack *m*, paquet *m* (d'avant)
6. PHR **that's a pack of lies!** UK c'est un tissu de mensonges ! ◆ **pack away** ◆ vt sep 1. [tidy up] ranger 2. *inf* [eat] bouffer 3. = pack off. ◆ vi se ranger
facilement, être escamotable. ◆ **pack in** ◆ vt sep UK
1. [crowd in] entasser 2. *inf* [task] arrêter ; [job, boyfriend,
girlfriend] plaquer ▶ **pack it in!** laisse tomber !, arrête !
◆ vi 1. [crowd in] s'entasser (à l'intérieur) 2. UK *inf* [break
down - machine, engine] tomber en rade. ◆ **pack off**
vt sep *inf* expédier. ◆ **pack up** ◆ vi 1. [pack one's suit-
case] faire sa valise or ses bagages 2. UK *inf* [break down]
tomber en rade 3. UK *inf* [give up] laisser tomber. ◆ vt sep
1. [suitcase, bags] faire 2. [clothes, belongings, tools] ranger
3. UK *inf* [stop] arrêter.

package ['pækɪdʒ] ◆ n 1. [small parcel] paquet *m*,
colis *m* ; US [packet] paquet *m* 2. [set of proposals] ensemble *m* / *the offer is part of a larger package* l'offre fait
partie d'un ensemble plus important / *a new package of
measures to halt inflation* un nouvel ensemble or un nouveau train de mesures visant à stopper l'inflation 3. COMPUT
▶ **(software) package** progiciel *m*. ◆ vt 1. [wrap] emballer, conditionner 2. [in advertising] fabriquer l'image (de
marque) de.

package deal n transaction *f* globale, accord *m* global.

package holiday n voyage *m* organisé or à prix forfaitaire.

packager ['pækɪdʒə'] n [in advertising, publishing] packager *m*, packageur *m*.

package tour = package holiday.

packaging ['pækɪʤɪŋ] n **1.** [wrapping materials] emballage m, conditionnement m **2.** [in advertising, publishing] packaging m.

packed [pækt] adj **1.** [crowded - train, room] bondé ; [- theatre] comble **2.** [with luggage ready] : *I'm packed and ready to leave* j'ai fait mes bagages, je suis prête.

packed lunch n panier-repas m, casse-croûte m inv.

packer ['pækər] n [worker] emballeur m, -euse f, conditionneur m, -euse f ; [machine] embulleuse f, conditionneuse f.

packet ['pækɪt] n **1.** [box] paquet m ; [bag, envelope] sachet m ▶ **packet soup** soupe f en sachet **2.** [parcel] paquet m, colis m **3.** ⓤⓈ inf [lot of money] paquet m / *that must have cost you a packet* ça a dû te coûter les yeux de la tête or un paquet d'argent ▶ **to make a packet** gagner un fric fou or monstre **4.** NAUT ▶ **packet (boat** or **steamer)** paquebot m.

packet switching [-,swɪtʃɪŋ] n COMPUT commutation f par paquets.

packhorse ['pækhɔːs] n cheval m de bât.

pack ice n pack m, banquise f.

packing ['pækɪŋ] n (U) **1.** [of personal belongings] : *have you done your packing?* as-tu fait tes bagages ? / *the removal men will do the packing* les déménageurs se chargeront de l'emballage **2.** [of parcel] emballage m ; [of commercial goods] emballage m, conditionnement m **3.** [wrapping material] emballage m.

packing case n caisse f d'emballage.

pact [pækt] n pacte m / *we made a pact to stop smoking* nous avons convenu de nous arrêter de fumer.

pad [pæd] (*pt & pp* **padded,** *cont* **padding**) ▶ n **1.** [to cushion shock] coussinet m **2.** [for absorbing liquid, polishing, etc.] tampon m **3.** ZOOL [underside of foot] coussinet m **4.** [of paper] bloc m **5.** AERON & ASTRONAUT aire f **6.** inf [flat] appart m ; [room] piaule f **7.** ⓤⓈ inf [sanitary towel] serviette f hygiénique. ◆ vt **1.** [clothing] matelasser ; [shoulder] rembourrer ; [door, wall] capitonner **2.** = **pad out.** ◆ vi [walk] avancer à pas feutrés. ◆ **pad out** vt sep **1.** = **pad** (*vt*) **2.** fig [essay, article, speech] délayer.

padded ['pædɪd] adj **1.** [door, bench, steering wheel] capitonné ; [garment, envelope, oven glove] matelassé ; [sofa] bien rembourré ▶ **padded bra** soutien-gorge m à bonnets renforcés ▶ **padded cell** cellule f capitonnée ▶ **padded shoulders** épaules fpl rembourrées **2.** [fat] : *he's well padded* il est bien en chair.

padding ['pædɪŋ] n **1.** [fabric] ouate f, ouatine f, garnissage m **2.** fig [in essay, speech] délayage m, remplissage m.

paddle ['pædl] ◆ n **1.** [for boat, canoe] pagaie f **2.** [of waterwheel] palette f, aube f **3.** ⓤⓈ [table tennis bat] raquette f (de ping-pong) **4.** [wade] ▶ **to go for** or **to have a paddle** aller barboter. ◆ vi **1.** [in canoe] pagayer / *he paddled across the lake* il a traversé le lac en pagayant **2.** [wade] barboter. ◆ **paddle along** vi [in canoe] pagayer.

paddle boat n **1.** = **paddle steamer 2.** [pedalo] Pédalo® m.

paddle steamer n bateau m à roues.

paddling pool n pataugeoire f.

paddock ['pædək] n [gen] enclos m ; [at racetrack] paddock m.

paddy field n rizière f.

paddy wagon n ⓤⓈ inf panier m à salade.

padlock ['pædlɒk] ◆ n [for door, gate] cadenas m ; [for bicycle] antivol m. ◆ vt [door, gate] cadenasser ; [bicycle] mettre un antivol à.

paederast ⓤⓀ ['pedəræst] = **pederast.**

paediatric ⓤⓀ [,piːdɪ'ætrɪk] = **pediatric.**

paedophile ⓤⓀ ['piːdəʊ,faɪl] = **pedophile.**

paella [paɪ'elə] n paella f.

paeony ['piːənɪ] ⓤⓀ = **peony.**

pagan ['peɪgən] ◆ n païen m, -enne f. ◆ adj païen.

page [peɪʤ] ◆ n **1.** [of book, newspaper, etc.] page f / *on page two* **a)** [of book] (à la) page deux **b)** [of newspaper] (en) page deux **2.** [at court] page m ; [at wedding] page m. ◆ vt [call] appeler (par haut-parleur) / *paging Mrs Clark!* on demande Mme Clark !

pageant ['pæʤənt] n [historical parade, show] reconstitution f historique ; [grand display] spectacle m fastueux ; [beauty contest] concours m de beauté.

pageantry ['pæʤəntrɪ] n apparat m, pompe f.

page boy n **1.** [at wedding] page m **2.** [hairstyle] ▶ **page boy (cut)** coupe f à la Jeanne d'Arc.

pager ['peɪʤər] n TELEC bip m.

page-turner n inf [book] livre m passionnant, livre m captivant.

pagoda [pə'gəʊdə] n pagode f.

paid [peɪd] ◆ pt & pp ⟶ **pay.** ◆ adj **1.** payé, rémunéré **2.** ⓟⒽⓇ **to put paid to sthg** gâcher or ruiner qqch.

paid-up adj [member] à jour de ses cotisations ; fig [committed] : *he's a (fully) paid-up member of the Communist Party* il a sa carte au Parti communiste.

pail [peɪl] n [bucket] seau m.

pain [peɪn] ◆ vt [cause distress to] peiner, faire de la peine à ; [hurt] faire souffrir. ◆ n **1.** [physical] douleur f / *are you in pain?* avez-vous mal ?, est-ce que vous souffrez ? ▶ **to cry out in pain** crier or hurler de douleur **2.** [emotional] peine f, douleur f, souffrance f **3.** inf [annoying person or thing] : *what a pain he is!* qu'est-ce qu'il est enquiquinant ! / *it's a (real)* or *such a pain trying to cross London during the rush hour* traverser Londres aux heures de pointe, c'est la galère **4.** LAW ▶ **on pain of death** sous peine de mort. ◆ **pains** pl n [efforts] peine f, mal m / *he went to great pains to help us* il s'est donné beaucoup de mal pour nous aider / *is that all we get for our pains?* c'est comme cela que nous sommes récompensés de nos efforts ?

pained [peɪnd] adj peiné, affligé.

painful ['peɪnfʊl] adj **1.** [sore] douloureux / *is your back still painful?* avez-vous toujours mal au dos ? **2.** [upsetting] pénible **3.** [laborious] pénible, difficile, laborieux.

painfully ['peɪnfʊlɪ] adv **1.** [hit, strike, rub] durement ; [move, walk] péniblement **2.** [distressingly] douloureusement ; [laboriously] laborieusement, avec difficulté **3.** [as intensifier] horriblement / *it was painfully obvious that he didn't understand* il n'était que trop évident qu'il ne comprenait pas / *she's painfully shy* elle est d'une timidité maladive.

painkiller ['peɪn,kɪlər] n analgésique m, calmant m.

painless ['peɪnlɪs] adj **1.** [injection, operation] sans douleur, indolore ; [death] sans souffrance **2.** [unproblematic] facile.

pain relief n soulagement m.

painstaking ['peɪnz,teɪkɪŋ] adj [research, care] rigoureux, méticuleux ; [worker] assidu, soigneux.

paint [peɪnt] ◆ n **1.** [for a room, furniture, picture] peinture f **2.** pej [make-up] peinture f. ◆ vt **1.** [room, furniture, picture] peindre / *the door was painted yellow* la porte était peinte en jaune ▶ **to paint one's nails** se vernir les ongles ▶ **to paint the town red** inf faire la noce or la foire **2.** [apply - varnish] appliquer (au pinceau) **3.** fig [describe] dépeindre, décrire / *the author paints a bleak pic-*

ture of suburban life l'auteur dresse un sombre portrait or brosse un sombre tableau de la vie des banlieusards. ◆ vi peindre, faire de la peinture ▶ **to paint in oils** faire de la peinture à l'huile ▶ **to paint in watercolours** faire de l'aquarelle. ◆ **paint out, paint over** vt sep recouvrir (d'une couche) de peinture.

paintball ['peɪntbɔːl] n paintball *m*.

paintbox ['peɪntbɒks] n boîte *f* de couleurs.

paintbrush ['peɪntbrʌʃ] n pinceau *m*.

painter ['peɪntər] n **1.** [artist, decorator] peintre *m* ▶ **painter and decorator** peintre-décorateur **2.** NAUT amarre *f*.

painting ['peɪntɪŋ] n **1.** [activity] peinture *f* **2.** [picture] peinture *f*, tableau *m*.

paint stripper n décapant *m*.

paintwork ['peɪntwɜːk] n *(U)* peinture *f*.

pair [peər] ◆ n **1.** [two related objects or people] paire *f* ▶ **to work in pairs** travailler par deux / **line up in pairs!** mettez-vous en rang (deux) par deux ! / **I've only got one pair of hands!** je n'ai que deux mains ! **2.** [single object in two parts] : *a pair of trousers / shorts / tights* un pantalon / short / collant / *a pair of scissors* une paire de ciseaux **3.** [husband and wife] couple *m* **4.** [of animals] paire *f* ; [of birds] couple *m* **5.** MATH paire *f* **6.** [in cards, dice] paire *f*. ◆ vt [socks] assortir ; [animal, birds] apparier, accoupler. ◆ **pair off** ◆ vt [arrange in couples - dancers] répartir en couples ; [- team members, children in class] mettre deux par deux. ◆ vi [dancers] former des couples ; [team members, children in class] se mettre deux par deux. ◆ **pair up** ◆ vt sep [socks] assortir. ◆ vi [people] se mettre par deux.

paisley ['peɪzlɪ] n [pattern] (impression *f*) cachemire *m* ; [material] tissu *m* cachemire / *a paisley tie* une cravate impression cachemire.

pajama US = pyjama.

Paki ['pækɪ] n US *offens terme raciste désignant un Pakistanais.*

Paki-basher n US *offens auteur d'agressions racistes contre les personnes d'origine pakistanaise.*

Pakistan [US ˌpɑːkɪˈstɑːn US ˈpækɪstæn] pr n Pakistan *m* / *in Pakistan* au Pakistan.

Pakistani [US ˌpɑːkɪˈstɑːnɪ US ˌpækɪˈstænɪ] ◆ n Pakistanais *m*, -e *f*. ◆ adj pakistanais.

pal [pæl] (*pt & pp* **palled,** *cont* **palling**) n *inf* **1.** [friend] copain *m*, copine *f*, pote *m* **2.** [term of address] : *thanks, pal* merci mon pote. ◆ **pal up** vi US *inf* : *he / she palled up with George* il est devenu le copain / elle est devenue la copine de George.

palace ['pælɪs] n palais *m* ▶ **the Palace** US [Buckingham Palace] le palais de Buckingham (*et par extension ses habitants*) ▶ **the Palace of Westminster** le palais de Westminster (*siège du Parlement britannique*).

⚠ The French word **palace** means a luxury hotel, **not** a palace.

palatable ['pælətəbl] adj **1.** [food, drink - tasty] savoureux ; [- edible] mangeable **2.** *fig* [idea] acceptable.

palate ['pælət] n **1.** ANAT palais *m* **2.** [sense of taste] palais *m*.

palatial [pəˈleɪʃl] adj grandiose, magnifique.

palaver [pəˈlɑːvər] US *inf* n *(U)* [rigmarole, fuss] chichis *mpl*, histoire *f*, histoires *fpl* / *all the palaver of passports, customs and immigration* toutes ces histoires de passeports, de formalités de douane et d'immigration / *what a palaver!* quelle affaire !, que de chichis !

pale [peɪl] ◆ adj **1.** [face, complexion] pâle ; [from fright, shock, sickness] blême, blafard / *he turned pale* il a pâli or blêmi **2.** [colour] pâle, clair ; [light] pâle, blafard **3.** [feeble] pâle. ◆ vi [person, face] pâlir, blêmir ; [sky, colour] pâlir / *our problems pale into insignificance beside hers* nos problèmes sont insignifiants comparés aux siens or à côté des siens.

pale ale n pale-ale *f*, bière *f* blonde légère.

paleness ['peɪlnɪs] n pâleur *f*.

pale-skinned adj à la peau claire.

Palestine ['pæləˌstaɪn] pr n Palestine *f* / *in Palestine* en Palestine.

Palestinian [ˌpæləˈstɪnɪən] ◆ n Palestinien *m*, -enne *f*. ◆ adj palestinien.

palette ['pælət] n ART palette *f*.

palette knife n ART couteau *m* (à palette) ; CULIN palette *f*.

palimony ['pælɪmənɪ] n pension *f* alimentaire (*accordée à un ex-concubin ou une ex-concubine*).

pall [pɔːl] ◆ n [cloud - of smoke] voile *m* ▶ **to cast a pall over** [event, celebration] assombrir. ◆ vi US perdre son charme.

pallet ['pælɪt] n **1.** [bed] grabat *m* ; [mattress] paillasse *f* **2.** [for loading, transportation] palette *f* **3.** [potter's instrument] palette *f*.

palliative ['pælɪətɪv] ◆ adj palliatif. ◆ n palliatif *m*.

palliative care n *(U)* MED soins *mpl* palliatifs.

pallid ['pælɪd] adj **1.** [wan] pâle, blême, blafard **2.** [lacking vigour] insipide.

pally ['pælɪ] (*compar* **pallier,** *superl* **palliest**) adj *inf* ▶ **to be pally with sb** être copain / copine avec qqn.

palm [pɑːm] ◆ n **1.** [of hand] paume *f* ▶ **to read sb's palm** lire les lignes de la main à qqn ▶ **to have sb in the palm of one's hand**: *he had them in the palm of his hand* il les tenait à sa merci or sous sa coupe **2.** [tree] palmier *m* **3.** [branch] palme *f* ; RELIG rameau *m*. ◆ vt [coin] cacher dans le creux de la main. ◆ **palm off** vt sep *inf* [unwanted objects] refiler ; [inferior goods] fourguer ▶ **to palm sb off with sth, to palm sth off on sb** refiler qqch à qqn.

palm oil n huile *f* de palme.

Palm Sunday n (le dimanche des) Rameaux *mpl*.

palmtop ['pɑːmtɒp] n COMPUT ordinateur *m* de poche.

palm tree n palmier *m*.

palpable ['pælpəbl] adj **1.** [tangible] palpable, tangible **2.** [obvious] évident, manifeste, flagrant.

palpitation [ˌpælpɪˈteɪʃn] n palpitation *f* ▶ **to have** or **to get palpitations** MED avoir des palpitations / *I get palpitations whenever I see her* *hum* mon cœur bat la chamade or s'emballe chaque fois que je la vois.

paltry ['pɔːltrɪ] adj **1.** [meagre - wage, sum] misérable, dérisoire **2.** [worthless - person, attitude] insignifiant, minable.

pamper ['pæmpər] vt choyer, dorloter ▶ **to pamper o.s.** se dorloter / *pamper yourself with a bubble bath* faites-vous plaisir, prenez un bain moussant.

pamphlet ['pæmflɪt] n [gen] brochure *f* ; POL pamphlet *m*.

pan [pæn] (*pt & pp* **panned,** *cont* **panning**) ◆ n **1.** CULIN casserole *f* ▶ **cake pan** US moule *m* à gâteau **2.** US [toilet bowl] ▶ **(lavatory) pan** cuvette *f* de W-C **3.** CIN & TV panoramique *m*. ◆ vi [camera] faire un panoramique. ◆ vt *inf* [criticize] descendre. ◆ **pan out** vi US *inf* [work out] se dérouler, marcher ; [succeed] réussir.

panacea [ˌpænəˈsɪə] n panacée *f*.

panache [pəˈnæʃ] n panache *m*.

Panama ['pænəmɑː] ◆ pr n Panamá *m* / *in Panama* au Panamá. ◆ n = Panama hat.

Panama Canal pr n ▶ **the Panama Canal** le canal de Panamá.

Panama City pr n Panamá.

Panama hat n panama *m*.

Panamanian [ˌpænəˈmeɪnjən] ◆ n Panaméen *m*, -enne *f*. ◆ adj panaméen.

Pan-American adj panaméricain ▶ **the Pan-American Highway** la route panaméricaine.

pancake ['pænkeɪk] ◆ n **1.** CULIN [in UK] crêpe *f* ; [in US] *sorte de petite galette épaisse servie au petit déjeuner* **2.** *inf* [make-up] fond *m* de teint épais **3.** AERON = pancake landing. ◆ vi AERON atterrir sur le ventre.

Pancake Day n 🇬🇧 Mardi gras *m*.

pancake landing n atterrissage *m* à plat or brutal.

pancake roll n rouleau *m* de printemps.

Pancake Tuesday n mardi gras *m*.

pancreas ['pæŋkrɪəs] n pancréas *m*.

panda ['pændə] n panda *m* ▶ **panda (car)** 🇬🇧 voiture *f* de police.

pandemic [pæn'demɪk] ◆ adj MED pandémique. ◆ n MED pandémie *f*.

pandemonium [ˌpændɪˈməʊnjəm] n *(U)* [chaos] chaos *m* ; [uproar] tumulte *m*, tohu-bohu *m*.

pander ['pændər] vi ▶ **to pander to** [person, weaknesses] flatter (bassement).

Pandora [pæn'dɔːrə] pr n Pandore ▶ **Pandora's box** la boîte de Pandore.

pane [peɪn] n **1.** [of glass] vitre *f*, carreau *m* **2.** COMPUT fenêtre.

panel ['pænl] (🇬🇧 *pt & pp* panelled, *cont* panelling ; 🇺🇸 *pt & pp* paneled, *cont* paneling) ◆ n **1.** [flat section - of wood, glass, etc.] panneau *m* **2.** [group, committee - gen] comité *m* ; [-to judge exam, contest] jury *m* ; [-in radio or TV quiz] invités *mpl* ; [-in public debate] panel *m* ; [-in public inquiry] commission *f* (d'enquête) **3.** [set of controls] ▶ **(control) panel** tableau *m* de bord ▶ **(instrument) panel** AERON & AUTO tableau *m* de bord. ◆ vt [wall, hall] lambrisser, revêtir de panneaux / *a panelled door* une porte à panneaux / *the room is in panelled oak* la pièce est lambrissée de chêne.

panel discussion n débat *m*, tribune *f*.

panel game n 🇬🇧 RADIO jeu *m* radiophonique ; TV jeu *m* télévisé.

panelling 🇬🇧, **paneling** 🇺🇸 ['pænəlɪŋ] n *(U)* panneaux *mpl*, lambris *m*.

panellist 🇬🇧, **panelist** 🇺🇸 ['pænəlɪst] n [jury member] juré *m* ; [in radio or TV quiz] invité *m*, -e *f* ; [in public debate] panéliste *mf*.

panel truck n 🇺🇸 camionnette *f*.

pan-fry vt (faire) sauter, poêler.

pang [pæŋ] n **1.** [of emotion] coup *m* au cœur, pincement de cœur / *I felt a pang of sadness* j'ai eu un serrement de cœur / *to feel pangs of conscience* or *guilt* éprouver des remords **2.** [of pain] élancement *m* ▶ **hunger pangs** tiraillements *mpl* d'estomac.

panhandle ['pæn,hændl] 🇺🇸 ◆ n GEOG *nom donné à la partie longue et étroite de certains États ou parcs américains* ▶ **the Alaska panhandle** la région sud de l'Alaska. ◆ vi *inf* faire la manche. ◆ vt *inf* ▶ **to panhandle money from sb, to panhandle sb** taper qqn.

panhandler ['pæn,hændlər] n 🇺🇸 *inf* mendiant *m*, -e *f*.

panic ['pænɪk] (*pt & pp* panicked, *cont* panicking) ◆ n **1.** [alarm, fear] panique *f*, affolement *m* / *she was close to panic* elle était au bord de l'affolement ▶ **to get into a panic** paniquer **2.** *inf* [rush] hâte *f* / *I was in a mad panic to get to the airport* c'était la panique pour aller à l'aéroport **3.** 🇺🇸 *inf* [sthg funny] : *it was a panic!* c'était à hurler de rire ! ◆ vi s'affoler / *don't panic!* ne vous affolez pas ! / *he's starting to panic about the wedding* il commence à s'affoler à la perspective de ce mariage. ◆ vt affoler / *they were panicked by the prospect of...* ils étaient pris de panique à la perspective de...

panic attack n crise *f* de panique.

panic button n signal *m* d'alarme.

panic buying n *(U)* achats *mpl* en catastrophe or de dernière minute.

panicky ['pænɪkɪ] adj *inf* [person, crowd] paniqué ; [voice, message] affolé ; [feeling, reaction] de panique / *I get panicky every time I have to speak to him* je panique chaque fois que je dois lui parler.

panic stations pl n *inf* : *it was panic stations!* ça a été la panique générale !

panic-stricken adj affolé, pris de panique.

pannier ['pænɪər] n [bag - on bicycle, motorbike] sacoche *f*.

panorama [ˌpænəˈrɑːmə] n *lit & fig* panorama *m*.

panoramic [ˌpænəˈræmɪk] adj panoramique.

panpipes ['pænpaɪps] pl n flûte *f* de Pan.

pan scrubber n tampon *m* à récurer.

pansy ['pænzɪ] (*pl* pansies) n BOT pensée *f*.

pant [pænt] ◆ vi [puff] haleter, souffler. ◆ vt [say] dire en haletant or d'une voix haletante. ◆ **pant for** vt insep mourir d'envie de.

pantechnicon [pæn'teknɪkən] n 🇬🇧 [van] camion *m* de déménagement.

pantheon ['pænθɪən] n panthéon *m*.

panther ['pænθər] (*pl* panther or panthers) n **1.** [leopard] panthère *f* **2.** 🇺🇸 [puma] puma *m*.

pantie hose = panty hose.

panties ['pæntɪz] pl n (petite) culotte *f*.

pantihose 🇺🇸 = panty hose.

panto ['pæntəʊ] (*pl* pantos) n 🇬🇧 *inf* = pantomime.

pantomime ['pæntəmaɪm] n **1.** 🇬🇧 [Christmas show] *spectacle de Noël pour enfants* ▶ **pantomime dame** *rôle de la vieille dame tenu par un homme, dans la pantomime anglaise* ▶ **pantomime horse** *personnage de cheval joué par deux comédiens* **2.** [mime] pantomime *f* **3.** *inf & fig* comédie *f*, cirque *m* / *there was a bit of a pantomime over who should pay* ça a été tout un cirque pour savoir qui devait payer.

 Pantomime

La **pantomime** est un spectacle britannique traditionnel, avec des personnages-types et des interventions du public très codifiées. Le héros (**principal boy**) doit, selon la tradition, être joué par une jeune actrice, alors que le rôle comique, celui de la vieille dame (**pantomime dame**), est tenu par un acteur. Tout au long de la pièce, les spectateurs interviennent au moyen de répliques connues de tous : **Behind you!** - **Oh, yes he is!** - **Oh, no he isn't!** Jouée au moment des fêtes de fin d'année, elle s'inspire des contes de fées.

pantry ['pæntrɪ] (*pl* **pantries**) n [cupboard] garde-manger *m inv* ; [walk-in cupboard] cellier *m*, office *m*.

pants [pænts] pl n **1.** UK [underpants] ▸ **(pair of) pants** slip *m*, culotte *f* **2.** US [trousers] ▸ **(pair of) pants** pantalon *m* ▸ **to catch sb with his pants down** *inf* surprendre qqn dans une situation embarrassante ▸ **to wear the pants** : *it's his wife who wears the pants* c'est sa femme qui porte la culotte ▸ **to bore the pants off sb** *inf* : *he bores the pants off me* il me rase.

pantsuit ['pæntsuːt] US tailleur-pantalon *m*.

panty hose US, **pantihose** US ['pæntɪˌhəʊz] pl n collant *m*, collants *mpl*.

panty liner n protège-slip *m*.

papa [pə'pɑː or 'pæpə] n papa *m*.

papacy ['peɪpəsɪ] (*pl* **papacies**) n [system, institution] papauté *f* ; [term of office] pontificat *m*.

papadum ['pæpədəm] = popadum.

papal ['peɪpl] adj papal.

paparazzi [ˌpæpə'rætsɪ] pl n paparazzi *mpl*.

papaya [pə'paɪə] n **1.** [fruit] papaye *f* **2.** [tree] papayer *m*.

paper ['peɪpər] ◆ n **1.** (*U*) [material] papier *m* ▸ **a piece / sheet of paper** un bout / une feuille de papier / *he wants it on paper* il veut que ce soit écrit / *don't put anything down on paper!* ne mettez rien par écrit ! / *on paper, they're by far the better side* sur le papier or a priori, c'est de loin la meilleure équipe **2.** [newspaper] journal *m* **3.** (*usu pl*) [document] papier *m*, document *m* ▸ **(identity) papers** papiers (d'identité) **4.** SCH & UNIV [exam paper] devoir *m*, épreuve *f* ; [student's answers] copie *f* **5.** [academic treatise - published] article *m* ; [-oral] communication *f* ▸ **to give** or **to read a paper on sthg** faire un exposé sur qqch **6.** [wallpaper] papier peint *m*. ◆ adj **1.** [napkin, towel] en or de papier ; [plate] en carton ▸ **paper currency** billets *mpl* (de banque) **2.** [theoretical] sur le papier, théorique ▸ **paper qualifications** diplômes *mpl*. ◆ vt [room, walls] tapisser. ❖ **paper over** vt sep **1.** *lit* recouvrir de papier peint **2.** *fig* [dispute, facts] dissimuler ▸ *they tried to paper over the cracks* ils ont essayé de masquer les désaccords.

paperback ['peɪpəbæk] ◆ n livre *m* de poche / *it's in paperback* c'est en (édition de) poche. ◆ adj [book, edition] de poche.

paper bag n sac *m* en papier.

paperboy ['peɪpəbɔɪ] n [delivering papers] livreur *m* de journaux ; [selling papers] vendeur *m* or crieur *m* de journaux.

paper clip n trombone *m*.

paper cup n gobelet *m* en carton.

paper feed n COMPUT & TYPO alimentation *f* en papier.

papergirl ['peɪpəgɜːl] n [delivering papers] livreuse *f* de journaux ; [selling papers] vendeuse *f* de journaux.

paper handkerchief n mouchoir *m* en papier.

paper knife n coupe-papier *m inv*.

paper lantern n lampion *m*.

paperless ['peɪpəlɪs] adj [electronic -communication, record-keeping] informatique ▸ **the paperless office** le bureau entièrement informatisé.

papermill ['peɪpəmɪl] n papeterie *f*, usine *f* à papier.

paper money n papier-monnaie *m*.

paper round UK, **paper route** US n ▸ **to do a paper round** livrer les journaux à domicile.

paper shop n marchand *m* de journaux.

paper-thin adj extrêmement mince or fin.

paper towel n serviette *f* en papier.

paper trail n traces *fpl* écrites.

paper tray n [in printer] bac *m* à papier.

paperweight ['peɪpəweɪt] n presse-papiers *m inv*.

paperwork ['peɪpəwɜːk] n travail *m* de bureau ; *pej* paperasserie *f*.

papier-mâché [ˌpæpjeɪ'mæʃeɪ] n papier *m* mâché.

paprika ['pæprɪkə] n paprika *m*.

Papuan ['pæpjʊən] ◆ n [person] Papou *m*, -e *f*. ◆ adj papou.

Papua New Guinea pr n Papouasie-Nouvelle-Guinée *f* / *in Papua New Guinea* en Papouasie-Nouvelle-Guinée.

par [pɑːr] (*pt* & *pp* **parred**, *cont* **parring**) ◆ n **1.** [equality] égalité *f* ▸ **to be on a par (with sb / sthg)** être au même niveau (que qqn / qqch) **2.** [normal, average] normale *f*, moyenne *f* / *I'm feeling a bit below* or *under par these days* je ne me sens pas en forme ces jours-ci / *your work is below* or *not up to par* votre travail laisse à désirer **3.** SPORT [in golf] par *m* / *that's about par for the course inf* [typical] ça n'a rien de surprenant / *his behaviour was about par for the course* ça ne m'étonne pas de lui. ◆ vt [in golf -hole] faire le par à.

para ['pærə] (**abbr of** paratrooper) n UK *inf* para *m*.

paraben ['pærəben] n paraben *m*.

parable ['pærəbl] n RELIG parabole *f*.

parabola [pə'ræbələ] n MATH parabole *f*.

paracetamol [ˌpærə'siːtəmɒl] n paracétamol *m*.

parachute ['pærəʃuːt] ◆ n parachute *m*. ◆ comp [harness] de parachute ; [troops, regiment] de parachutistes ▸ **parachute drop** or **landing** parachutage *m* ▸ **parachute jump** saut *m* en parachute. ◆ vt parachuter. ◆ vi sauter en parachute ▸ **to go parachuting** SPORT faire du parachutisme.

parachutist ['pærəʃuːtɪst] n parachutiste *mf*.

parade [pə'reɪd] ◆ n **1.** [procession -gen] défilé *m* ; MIL défilé *m*, parade *f* ▸ **to be on parade** MIL défiler **2.** [street -of shops] rangée *f* de magasins ; [-public promenade] promenade *f* **3.** [show, ostentation] étalage *m* **4.** = parade ground. ◆ vi **1.** [march -gen & MIL] défiler **2.** [strut] se pavaner, parader. ◆ vt **1.** [troops, prisoners, etc.] faire défiler **2.** [streets] défiler dans **3.** [show off] faire étalage de.

parade ground n terrain *m* de manœuvres.

paradigm ['pærədaɪm] n paradigme *m* ▸ **paradigm shift** changement *m* radical.

paradigmatic [ˌpærədɪg'mætɪk] adj paradigmatique.

paradise ['pærədaɪs] n **1.** [heaven] paradis *m* ; [Eden] le paradis terrestre **2.** *fig* paradis *m*.

paradox ['pærədɒks] n paradoxe *m*.

paradoxical [ˌpærə'dɒksɪkl] adj paradoxal.

paradoxically [ˌpærə'dɒksɪklɪ] adv paradoxalement.

paraffin ['pærəfɪn] ◆ n **1.** UK [fuel -for lamp] pétrole *m* ; [-for stove] mazout *m* ; [-for aircraft] kérosène *m* **2.** = paraffin wax. ◆ comp [lamp] à pétrole ; [heater] à mazout.

paraffin wax n paraffine *f*.

paraglider ['pærəglaɪdər] n **1.** [person] parapentiste *mf* **2.** [parachute] parapente *m*.

paragliding ['pærəˌglaɪdɪŋ] n parapente *m* ▸ **to go paragliding** faire du parapente.

paragon ['pærəgən] n modèle *m* ▸ **paragon of virtue** modèle or parangon *m liter* de vertu.

paragraph ['pærəgrɑːf] ◆ n **1.** [in writing] paragraphe *m*, alinéa *m* / *begin* or *start a new paragraph* (allez) à la ligne **2.** [short article] entrefilet *m*. ◆ vt diviser en paragraphes or en alinéas.

Paraguay ['pærəgwaɪ] pr n Paraguay *m* / *in Paraguay* au Paraguay.

Paraguayan [,pærə'gwaɪən] ◆ n Paraguayen *m*, -enne *f*. ◆ adj paraguayen.

parakeet ['pærəkiːt] n perruche *f* (ondulée).

parallel ['pærəlel] ◆ adj **1.** [gen & MATH] parallèle ▸ **to run parallel to sthg** longer qqch **2.** [concomitant - change, event] parallèle **3.** COMPUT [interface, operation] parallèle ▸ **parallel port** port *m* parallèle. ◆ n **1.** [equivalent] équivalent *m* ; [similarity] ressemblance *f*, similitude *f* ▸ **in parallel / to** or **with sthg** parallèlement à qqch **2.** [comparison] parallèle *m* ▸ **to draw a parallel between** faire or établir un parallèle entre.

parallel bars pl n barres *fpl* parallèles.

parallel cable n câble *m* parallèle.

parallelogram [,pærə'leləgræm] n parallélogramme *m*.

parallel processing n traitement *m* en parallèle or en simultanéité.

parallel turn n [in skiing] virage *m* parallèle.

Paralympics [,pærə'lɪmpɪks] pl n : **the Paralympics** les jeux *mpl* Paralympiques.

paralyse UK, **paralyze** US ['pærəlaɪz] vt **1.** MED paralyser **2.** *fig* [city, industry, etc.] paralyser, immobiliser ; [person] paralyser, pétrifier.

paralysed UK, **paralyzed** US ['pærəlaɪzd] adj **1.** MED paralysé / *both his legs are paralysed* or *he's paralysed in both legs* il est paralysé des deux jambes, il a les deux jambes paralysées **2.** *fig* [city, industry, etc.] paralysé, immobilisé ; [person] paralysé, pétrifié / *paralysed with* or *by shyness* paralysé par la timidité.

paralysis [pə'rælɪsɪs] n **1.** MED paralysie *f* **2.** *fig* [of industry, business] immobilisation *f* ; [of government] paralysie *f*.

paralytic [,pærə'lɪtɪk] ◆ adj **1.** MED paralytique **2.** UK *inf* [drunk] ivre mort. ◆ n paralytique *mf*.

paralyze US = paralyse.

paramedic [,pærə'medɪk] ◆ n aide-soignant *m*, -e *f* *(membre du personnel paramédical).* ◆ adj = paramedical.

paramedical [,pærə'medɪkl] adj paramédical.

parameter [pə'ræmɪtər] n [gen & LING] & MATH paramètre *m* / *within the parameters of...* dans les limites de...

paramilitary [,pærə'mɪlɪtrɪ] *(pl* **paramilitaries)** ◆ adj paramilitaire. ◆ n [group] formation *f* paramilitaire ; [person] membre *m* d'une formation paramilitaire.

paramount ['pærəmaʊnt] adj [asset, concern] primordial ▸ **to be of paramount importance** être de la plus haute importance.

paranoia [,pærə'nɔɪə] n *(U)* paranoïa *f*.

paranoiac [,pærə'nɔɪæk], **paranoic** [,pærə'nɔʊɪk] ◆ adj paranoïaque. ◆ n paranoïaque *mf*.

paranoid ['pærənɔɪd] ◆ adj [disorder] paranoïde ; [person] paranoïaque. ◆ n paranoïaque *mf*.

paranormal [,pærə'nɔːml] ◆ adj paranormal. ◆ n ▸ **the paranormal** le paranormal.

parapet ['pærəpɪt] n ARCHIT parapet *m*, garde-fou *m* ; MIL parapet *m*.

paraphernalia [,pærəfə'neɪljə] n *(U)* **1.** [equipment] attirail *m* ; [belongings] fourbi *m* **2.** *inf* [trappings] tralala *m*.

paraphrase ['pærəfreɪz] ◆ n paraphrase *f*. ◆ vt paraphraser.

paraplegic [,pærə'pliːdʒɪk] ◆ adj paraplégique. ◆ n paraplégique *mf*.

parapsychology [,pærəsaɪ'kɒlədʒɪ] n parapsychologie *f*.

Paraquat® ['pærəkwɒt] n Paraquat® *m*.

parasailing ['pærə,seɪlɪŋ] n parachute *m* ascensionnel *(tracté par bateau).*

parascending ['pærə,sendɪŋ] n parachute *m* ascensionnel *(tracté par véhicule).*

parasite ['pærəsaɪt] n BOT & ZOOL parasite *m* ; *fig* parasite *m*.

parasitic [,pærə'sɪtɪk] adj **1.** [plant, animal] parasite ; *fig* [person] parasite ; [existence] de parasite **2.** [illness - caused by parasites] parasitaire.

parasol ['pærəsɒl] n [for woman] ombrelle *f* ; [for beach, table] parasol *m*.

paratrooper ['pærətruːpər] n MIL parachutiste *m*.

parcel ['pɑːsl] (UK pt & pp **parcelled**, cont **parcelling** ;US pt & pp **parceled**, cont **parceling**) ◆ n **1.** [package] colis *m*, paquet *m* **2.** [portion of land] parcelle *f* **3.** [group, quantity - gen] groupe *m*, lot *m* ; [- of shares] paquet *m*. ◆ vt **1.** UK [wrap up] emballer, faire un colis de **2.** [divide up] diviser en parcelles. ◆ **parcel out** vt sep **1.** [share out] distribuer, partager **2.** [divide up] diviser en parcelles, lotir. ◆ **parcel up** vt sep emballer, mettre en colis.

parcel bomb n colis *m* piégé.

parcel post n ▸ **to send sthg by parcel post** envoyer qqch par colis postal or en paquet-poste.

parched [pɑːtʃt] adj **1.** [very dry - grass] desséché ; [- throat, lips] sec (sèche) **2.** *inf* [person] : *I'm parched* je crève de soif.

parchment ['pɑːtʃmənt] n [material, document] parchemin *m*.

pardon ['pɑːdn] ◆ vt **1.** [forgive] pardonner ▸ **to pardon sb for sthg** pardonner qqch à qqn / *pardon me for asking, but...* excusez-moi de vous poser cette question, mais... **2.** LAW gracier. ◆ n **1.** [forgiveness] pardon *m*. ◆ interj ▸ **pardon (me)?** [what?] pardon ?, comment ? ▸ **pardon (me)!** [sorry] pardon !, excusez-moi !

pardonable ['pɑːdnəbl] adj pardonnable, excusable.

pare [peər] vt **1.** [fruit, vegetable] peler, éplucher ; [nails] ronger, couper **2.** [reduce - budget] réduire. ◆ **pare down** vt sep [expenses, activity] réduire ; [text, speech] raccourcir.

pared-down ['peəd-] adj [style, design] dépouillé, épuré.

parent ['peərənt] ◆ n [mother] mère *f* ; [father] père *m* ▸ **parents** parents *mpl* ▸ **parents' evening** réunion *f* de parents d'élèves. ◆ comp **1.** [cooperation, participation] des parents, parental **2.** [organization] mère.

parentage ['peərəntɪdʒ] n origine *f* / *a child of unknown parentage* un enfant de père et mère inconnus.

parental [pə'rentl] adj parental, des parents.

parent company n COMM société *f* or maison *f* mère.

parent directory n COMPUT répertoire *m* parent.

parenthesis [pə'renθɪsɪs] *(pl* **parentheses** [-siːz]) n parenthèse *f* / *in parenthesis* entre parenthèses.

parenthood ['peərənthʊd] n [fatherhood] paternité *f* ; [motherhood] maternité *f* / *the responsibilities of parenthood* les responsabilités parentales.

parenting ['peərəntɪŋ] n fait *m* or art *m* d'élever un enfant ▸ **parenting skills** capacités *fpl* à élever des enfants.

parent-teacher association n *association regroupant les parents d'élèves et les enseignants.*

pariah [pə'raɪə] n paria *m*.

Paris ['pærɪs] pr n GEOG Paris.

parish ['pærɪʃ] ◆ n **1.** RELIG paroisse *f* **2.** POL ≃ commune *f* *(en Angleterre).* ◆ comp RELIG [hall, funds] paroissial.

parish council n ≃ conseil *m* municipal *(d'une petite commune en Angleterre)*.

parishioner [pə'rɪʃənəʳ] n paroissien *m*, -enne *f*.

parish priest n [Catholic] curé *m* ; [Protestant] pasteur *m*.

Parisian [pə'rɪzjən] ◆ n Parisien *m*, -enne *f*. ◆ adj parisien.

parity ['pærətɪ] *(pl* **parities)** n **1.** [equality] égalité *f*, parité *f* **2.** ECON & FIN parité *f* **3.** COMPUT, MATH & PHYS parité *f*.

park [pɑːk] ◆ n [public] parc *m* ; [smaller] jardin *m* public ; [private estate] parc *m*, domaine *m*. ◆ vt **1.** AUTO garer **/** *behind the parked coaches* derrière les cars en stationnement **2.** *inf* [dump - person, box] laisser **/** *she parked her bags in the hall* elle a laissé ses sacs dans l'entrée **/** *he parked himself on the sofa* il s'installa sur le canapé. ◆ vi AUTO se garer, stationner **/** *I couldn't find anywhere to park* je n'ai pas trouvé à me garer.

parka ['pɑːkə] n parka *m*.

park-and-ride n *système de contrôle de la circulation qui consiste à garer les voitures à l'extérieur des grandes villes, puis à utiliser les transports en commun.*

parking ['pɑːkɪŋ] ◆ n stationnement *m* **/** **'no parking'** 'stationnement interdit', 'défense de stationner' **/** *parking is a problem in town* il est difficile de se garer or de stationner en ville. ◆ comp [area] de stationnement **▸ parking space** or **place** place *f* de stationnement **/** *to look for* **/** *to find a parking place* chercher **/** trouver à se garer.

parking attendant n [in car park] gardien *m*, -enne *f* ; [at hotel] voiturier *m*.

parking brake n US frein *m* à main.

parking deck n US parking *m (à plusieurs étages)*.

parking garage n US parking *m* couvert.

parking light n US feu *m* de position.

parking lot n US parking *m*, parc *m* de stationnement.

parking meter n parcmètre *m*, parcomètre *m*.

parking offence n infraction *f* aux règles de stationnement.

parking ticket n contravention *f (pour stationnement irrégulier)*, P-V *m*.

Parkinson's disease [pɑːkɪnsnz-] n maladie *f* de Parkinson.

park keeper n gardien *m*, -enne *f* de jardin public.

parkland ['pɑːklænd] n *(U)* espace *m* vert, espaces *mpl* verts.

parkway ['pɑːkweɪ] n US route *f* paysagère (à plusieurs voies).

parky ['pɑːkɪ] *(compar* **parkier,** *superl* **parkiest)** adj UK *inf* [cold] frisquet.

parlance ['pɑːləns] n *fml* langage *m*, parler *m*.

parliament ['pɑːləmənt] n parlement *m* **/** *she was elected to Parliament in 2012* elle a été élue député en 2012 **/** *the French Parliament* l'Assemblée nationale (française).

parliamentarian [pɑːləmen'teərɪən] ◆ adj parlementaire. ◆ n parlementaire *mf*.

parliamentary [pɑːlə'mentərɪ] adj [system, debate, democracy] parlementaire **▸ parliamentary elections** élections *fpl* législatives **▸ parliamentary candidate** candidat *m* aux (élections) législatives.

parlor US = **parlour**.

parlour UK, **parlor** US ['pɑːləʳ] n **1.** *dated* [in house] salon *m* **2.** *dated* [in hotel, club] salon *m* **3.** US COMM **▸ beer parlour** bar *m*.

parlour game n UK jeu *m* de société.

parlous ['pɑːləs] adj lamentable **/** *in a parlous state* dans un état lamentable.

Parma ['pɑːmə] pr n Parme **▸ Parma ham** jambon *m* de Parme.

Parmesan (cheese) [pɑːmɪ'zæn-] n parmesan *m*.

parochial [pə'rəʊkjəl] adj **1.** RELIG paroissial **2.** *pej* borné.

parochialism [pə'rəʊkjəlɪzm] n *pej* esprit *m* de clocher, étroitesse *f* d'esprit.

parochial school n US école *f* catholique.

parody ['pærədɪ] *(pl* **parodies,** *pt & pp* **parodied)** ◆ n parodie *f*. ◆ vt parodier.

parole [pə'rəʊl] ◆ n LAW liberté *f* conditionnelle or sur parole **/** *she was released on parole* elle a été mise en liberté conditionnelle or libérée sur parole. ◆ vt mettre en liberté conditionnelle, libérer sur parole.

parole board n UK ≃ comité *m* de probation et d'assistance aux libérés.

paroxysm ['pærəksɪzm] n **1.** [outburst - of rage, despair] accès *m* ; [- of tears] crise *f* **2.** MED paroxysme *m*.

parquet ['pɑːkeɪ] n **1.** CONSTR **▸ parquet (floor** or **flooring)** parquet *m* **2.** US THEAT parterre *m*.

parrot ['pærət] n perroquet *m*.

parrot fashion adv comme un perroquet.

parry ['pærɪ] *(pt & pp* **parried,** *pl* **parries)** vt **1.** [in boxing, fencing, etc.] parer **2.** [problem] tourner, éviter ; [question] éluder ; [manoeuvre] parer à, contrer.

parse [pɑːz] vt faire l'analyse grammaticale de.

parser ['pɑːzəʳ] n COMPUT analyseur *m* syntaxique.

parsimonious [pɑːsɪ'məʊnjəs] adj *fml* parcimonieux.

parsley ['pɑːslɪ] n persil *m* **▸ parsley sauce** sauce *f* au persil or persillée.

parsnip ['pɑːsnɪp] n panais *m (légume courant dans l'alimentation britannique)*.

parson ['pɑːsn] n [gen] ecclésiastique *m* ; [Protestant] pasteur *m*.

parson's nose [pɑːsnz-] n CULIN croupion *m*.

part [pɑːt] ◆ n **1.** [gen - portion, subdivision] partie *f* **/** *(a) part of the garden is flooded* une partie du jardin est inondée **/** *that's only part of the problem* ce n'est qu'un des aspects du problème **/** *we've finished the hardest part* nous avons fait le plus dur **▸ to be (a) part of sthg** [be involved with] faire partie de qqch **▸ to be part and parcel of sthg** faire partie (intégrante) de qqch **2.** [role] rôle *m* **/** *he's just playing a part fig* il joue la comédie **/** *work plays a large part in our lives* le travail joue un rôle important dans notre vie **▸ to take part (in sthg)** prendre part or participer (à qqch) **/** *I had no part in that affair* je n'ai joué aucun rôle dans cette affaire **/** *Joe had no part in it* Joe n'y était pour rien **▸ for my** / **his part** pour ma / sa part **3.** [component - of machine] pièce *f* **4.** [area - of country, town, etc.] : *which part of England are you from?* vous êtes d'où en Angleterre ?, de quelle région de l'Angleterre venez-vous ? **5.** [instalment - of encyclopedia] fascicule *m* ; [- of serial] épisode *m* **6.** [measure] mesure *f* **7.** [side] parti *m*, part *f* **8.** US [in hair] raie *f*. ◆ comp [payment] partiel **▸ part owner** copropriétaire *mf*. ◆ adv en partie, partiellement **/** *the jacket is part cotton, part polyester* la veste est un mélange de coton et de polyester or un mélange coton-polyester **/** *he's part English, part Chinese* il est moitié anglais, moitié chinois. ◆ vi **1.** [move apart - lips, curtains] s'ouvrir ; [- branches, legs, crowd] s'écarter ; [disengage - fighters] se séparer **2.** [leave one another] se quitter **3.** [break - rope] se casser ; [tear - fabric] se déchirer. ◆ vt **1.** [move apart, open - lips, curtains] ouvrir ; [- branches, legs, crowd] écarter **/** *her lips were slightly parted* ses lèvres étaient entrouvertes

2. [separate] séparer / *the children were parted from their parents* les enfants ont été séparés de leurs parents **3.** [hair] faire une raie à. ❖ **for the most part** adv phr dans l'ensemble. ❖ **in part** adv phr en partie. ❖ **in parts** adv phr par endroits. ❖ **part with** vt insep se séparer de.

partake [pɑːˈteɪk] (*pt* partook [-ˈtʊk], *pp* partaken [-ˈteɪkn]) vi *arch & fml* **1.** [eat, drink] ▶ **to partake of** prendre **2.** [participate] ▶ **to partake in** a) [event] participer à b) [joy, grief] partager **3.** [share quality] ▶ **to partake of** relever de, tenir à.

part exchange n COMM reprise f.

Parthenon [ˈpɑːθɪnən] pr n ▶ **the Parthenon** le Parthénon.

partial [ˈpɑːʃl] adj **1.** [incomplete] partiel **2.** [biased] partial **3.** [fond] ▶ **to be partial to sthg** avoir un penchant or un faible pour qqch.

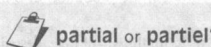

partial or **partiel**?

French **partial** means partial in the sense of biased, while **partiel** means partial in the sense of only in part.

partial eclipse n éclipse f partielle.

partially [ˈpɑːʃəlɪ] adv **1.** [partly] en partie, partiellement **2.** [in biased way] partialement, avec partialité.

partially sighted ❖ adj malvoyant. ❖ pl n ▶ **the partially sighted** les malvoyants mpl.

participant [pɑːˈtɪsɪpənt] n participant m, -e f.

participate [pɑːˈtɪsɪpeɪt] vi participer, prendre part ▶ **to participate in** [race, discussion] prendre part à, participer à.

participation [pɑːˌtɪsɪˈpeɪʃn] n participation f.

participle [ˈpɑːtɪsɪpl] n participe m.

particle [ˈpɑːtɪkl] n [tiny piece] particule f, parcelle f ; [of dust] grain m ; *fig* [jot] brin m, grain m.

particle accelerator n accélérateur m de particules.

particle physics n (U) physique f des particules.

parti-coloured [ˈpɑːtɪ-] adj bariolé, bigarré.

particular [pəˈtɪkjʊləʳ] ❖ adj **1.** [specific, distinct] particulier / *in this particular case* dans ce cas particulier / *for no particular reason* sans raison particulière / *only that particular colour will do* il n'y a que cette couleur-là qui fasse l'affaire **2.** [exceptional, special] particulier, spécial / *it's an issue of particular importance to us* c'est une question qui revêt une importance toute particulière à nos yeux **3.** [fussy] : *to be particular about hygiene / manners* attacher beaucoup d'importance à l'hygiène / aux bonnes manières / *to be particular about one's food* être difficile pour la nourriture. ❖ n **1.** [specific] : *from the general to the particular* du général au particulier **2.** [facts, details] détails mpl, points mpl / *correct in all particulars* correct en tout point / *for further particulars phone this number* pour de plus amples renseignements, appelez ce numéro. ❖ **in particular** adv phr en particulier.

particularity [pəˌtɪkjʊˈlærətɪ] (*pl* **particularities**) n particularité f.

particularly [pəˈtɪkjʊləlɪ] adv particulièrement / *not particularly* pas particulièrement or spécialement.

partied out [ˈpɑːtɪd-] adj *inf* : *I'm partied out!* a) [exhausted] j'ai trop fait la fête, je suis crevé ! b) [had enough of parties] ras-le-bol de faire la fête !

parting [ˈpɑːtɪŋ] ❖ n **1.** [leave-taking] séparation f ▶ **a parting of the ways** : *we came to a parting of the ways*

nous sommes arrivées à la croisée des chemins **2.** [opening - in clouds] trouée f **3.** 🇬🇧 [in hair] raie f. ❖ adj *liter* [words, kiss] d'adieu.

parting shot n *fig* flèche f du Parthe / *that was his parting shot* et sur ces mots, il s'en alla.

partisan [ˌpɑːtɪˈzæn] ❖ adj partisan. ❖ n partisan m.

partition [pɑːˈtɪʃn] ❖ n **1.** [wall] cloison f ; [screen] paravent m **2.** [of country] partition f ; [of property] division f ; [of power] répartition f, morcellement m **3.** COMPUT partition f. ❖ vt **1.** [room] diviser, cloisonner **2.** [country] diviser, démembrer. ❖ **partition off** vt sep [part of room] cloisonner.

partly [ˈpɑːtlɪ] adv en partie, partiellement.

partner [ˈpɑːtnəʳ] ❖ n **1.** [spouse] conjoint m, -e f ; [lover] compagnon m, compagne f ▶ **sexual partner** partenaire mf (sexuel) **2.** [in game, dance] partenaire mf **3.** [in common undertaking] partenaire mf ; [in firm, medical practice, etc.] associé m, -e f. ❖ vt **1.** [be the partner of] être partenaire de **2.** [dance with] danser avec ; [play with] faire équipe avec, être le partenaire de.

partnership [ˈpɑːtnəʃɪp] n [gen] association f ; [between companies] partenariat m ▶ **to work in partnership with** sb / sthg travailler en association or en partenariat avec qqn / qqch ▶ **to go into partnership with** sb s'associer avec qqn.

part of speech n partie f du discours.

partook [-ˈtʊk] pt —→ partake.

part payment n acompte m.

partridge [ˈpɑːtrɪdʒ] (*pl* partridge or partridges) n perdrix f ; [immature] perdreau m.

part-time adj & adv à temps partiel / *she's got a part-time job* elle travaille à temps partiel.

part-timer n travailleur m, -euse f à temps partiel.

partway [ˌpɑːtˈweɪ] adv en partie, partiellement / *partway along* or *there* à mi-chemin / *partway through the year, she resigned* elle a démissionné en cours d'année / *I'm only partway through the book* je n'ai pas fini le livre.

party [ˈpɑːtɪ] (*pl* parties, *pt & pp* partied) ❖ n **1.** [social event] fête f ; [more formal] soirée f, réception f ▶ **to give a party** a) [formal] donner une réception or une soirée b) [informal] faire une fête ▶ **to have** or **to throw a party for** sb organiser une fête en l'honneur de qqn **2.** POL parti m **3.** [group of people] groupe m **4.** *fml* LAW [individual, participant] partie f ▶ **to be a party to** a) [discussion] prendre part à b) [crime] être complice de c) [conspiracy, enterprise] être mêlé à, tremper dans **5.** [person] individu m. ❖ comp **1.** [atmosphere, clothes] de fête ▶ **party dress** robe f habillée ▶ **party invitations** invitations fpl ▶ **party snacks** amuse-gueule mpl **2.** POL [leader, leadership, funds] du parti ; [system] des partis. ❖ vi faire la fête.

party animal n *inf* fêtard m.

partygoer [ˈpɑːtɪgəʊə] n fêtard m, -e f.

partying [ˈpɑːtɪŋ] n : *she's a great one for partying* *inf* elle adore faire la fête.

party line n **1.** POL ligne f du parti ▶ **to toe** or **follow the party line** suivre la ligne du parti **2.** TELEC ligne f commune (à plusieurs abonnés).

party piece n *inf* chanson f or poème m de circonstance (à l'occasion d'une fête).

party political adj [broadcast] réservé à un parti politique ; [issue] de parti politique.

party politics pl n politique f de parti ; *pej* politique f politicienne.

party pooper n *inf* rabat-joie m inv.

party wall n mur m mitoyen.

pascal [ˈpæskl] n PHYS pascal m.

PASCAL [pæ'skæl] n PASCAL m.

pashmina [pæʃ'mi:nə] n pashmina f.

pass [pɑ:s] ◆ vi **1.** [move in specified direction] passer / his life passed before his eyes il a vu sa vie défiler devant ses yeux **2.** [move past, go by] passer / I happened to be passing, so I thought I'd call in il s'est trouvé que je passais, alors j'ai eu l'idée de venir vous voir **3.** [overtake] dépasser, doubler. **4.** [elapse - months, years] (se) passer, s'écouler ; [- holiday] se passer / time passed rapidly le temps a passé très rapidement **5.** [be transformed] passer, se transformer **6.** [take place] se passer, avoir lieu / the party, if it ever comes to pass, should be quite something la fête, si elle a jamais lieu, sera vraiment un grand moment **7.** [end, disappear - pain, crisis, fever] passer ; [- anger, desire] disparaître, tomber ; [- dream, hope] disparaître **8.** [be transferred - power, responsibility] passer ; [- inheritance] passer, être transmis **9.** [get through, be approved - proposal] être approuvé ; [- bill, law] être voté ; [- motion] être adopté ; SCH [& UNIV - student] être reçu or admis **10.** [go unchallenged] passer / the insult passed unnoticed personne ne releva l'insulte / I don't like it, but I'll let it pass je n'aime pas ça, mais je préfère ne rien dire or me taire **11.** [be adequate, acceptable - behaviour] convenir, être acceptable ; [- repair job] passer / in a grey suit you might just pass avec ton costume gris, ça peut aller **12.** [substitute] : you could easily pass for your sister on pourrait très bien te prendre pour ta sœur / he could pass for 35 on lui donnerait 35 ans **13.** SPORT faire une passe **14.** GAMES passer. ◆ vt **1.** [move past, go by - building] passer devant ; [- person] croiser / I passed her on the stairs je l'ai croisée dans l'escalier **2.** [go beyond - finishing line, frontier] passer ; [overtake] dépasser, doubler / we've passed the right exit nous avons dépassé la sortie que nous aurions dû prendre **3.** [move, run] passer / she passed her hand over her hair elle s'est passé la main dans les cheveux **4.** [hand] passer / pass me the sugar, please passez-moi le sucre, s'il vous plaît ; [transmit - message] transmettre / can you pass her the message? pourriez-vous lui transmettre or faire passer le message ? **5.** [spend - life, time, visit] passer **6.** [succeed in - exam, driving test] être reçu à, réussir / he didn't pass his history exam il a échoué or il a été recalé à son examen d'histoire **7.** [approve - bill, law] voter ; [- motion, resolution] adopter ; SCH [& UNIV - student] recevoir, admettre **8.** [pronounce - judgment, verdict, sentence] prononcer, rendre ; [- remark, compliment] faire / he declined to pass comment il s'est refusé à tout commentaire **9.** [counterfeit money, stolen goods] écouler **10.** SPORT [ball, puck] passer **11.** PHYSIOL ▶ **to pass water** uriner. ◆ n **1.** [in mountains] col m, défilé m **2.** [authorization - for worker, visitor] laissez-passer m inv ; THEAT invitation f, billet m de faveur ; [MIL - for leave of absence] permission f ; [- for safe conduct] sauf-conduit m ▶ **press pass** carte f de presse ▶ **rail / bus pass** carte f d'abonnement (de train) / de bus **3.** SCH & UNIV [in exam] moyenne f, mention f passable **4.** [state of affairs] situation f ▶ **things have come to a pretty** or **fine** or **sorry pass** on est dans une bien mauvaise passe, la situation s'est bien dégradée **5.** SPORT [with ball, puck] passe f ; [in fencing] botte f ; [in bullfighting] passe f **6.** PHR ▶ **to make a pass at sb** inf faire des avances à qqn. ❖ **pass around** vt sep [cake, cigarettes] (faire) passer ; [petition] (faire) circuler ; [supplies] distribuer. ❖ **pass away** vi euph [die] s'éteindre euph, décéder. ❖ **pass by** ◆ vi **1.** [move past, go by] : he passed by without a word! il est passé à côté de moi sans dire un mot ! **2.** [visit] passer. ◆ vt sep [disregard] ignorer, négliger / she felt life had passed her by elle avait le sentiment d'avoir raté sa vie. ❖ **pass down** vt sep **1.** [reach down] descendre / he passed me down my suitcase il m'a tendu or passé ma valise **2.** [transmit - inheritance, disease, tradition] transmettre, passer. ❖ **pass off** ◆ vi **1.** [take place - conference, attack]

se passer, se dérouler **2.** [end - fever, fit] passer. ◆ vt sep [represent falsely] faire passer / he passes himself off as an actor il se fait passer pour un acteur. ❖ **pass on** ◆ vi **1.** euph [die] trépasser, s'éteindre euph **2.** [proceed] passer. ◆ vt sep **1.** [hand on - box, letter] passer **2.** [transmit - disease, tradition] transmettre / they pass the costs on to their customers ils répercutent les coûts sur leurs clients. ❖ **pass out** ◆ vi **1.** [faint] s'évanouir, perdre connaissance ; [from drunkenness] tomber ivre mort ; [go to sleep] s'endormir **2.** MIL [cadet] ≃ finir ses classes. ◆ vt sep [hand out] distribuer. ❖ **pass over** ◆ vt sep [not take - opportunity] négliger, ignorer ; [overlook - person] : he was passed over for promotion on ne lui a pas accordé la promotion qu'il attendait. ◆ vt insep **1.** [overlook - fault, mistake] passer sur, ne pas relever **2.** [skip - paragraph] sauter. ❖ **pass round** = pass around. ❖ **pass through** ◆ vi passer / are you in Boston for some time or are you just passing through? êtes-vous à Boston pour quelque temps ou êtes-vous juste de passage ? ◆ vt insep [difficult period] traverser ; [barrier] franchir. ❖ **pass up** vt sep **1.** [hand up] passer **2.** [forego - job, opportunity] manquer, laisser passer.

passable ['pɑ:səbl] adj **1.** [acceptable] passable, acceptable **2.** [road] praticable ; [river, canyon] franchissable.

passage ['pæsɪdʒ] n **1.** [way through] passage m **2.** [corridor] passage m, couloir m ; [alley] ruelle f **3.** [in book, music] passage m **4.** [passing - gen] passage m ; [- of bill] adoption f / their friendship has survived the passage of time leur amitié a survécu au temps **5.** [voyage] voyage m ; [crossing] traversée f / she worked her passage to Rio elle a payé son voyage à Rio en travaillant à bord du navire.

passageway ['pæsɪdʒweɪ] n [corridor] passage m, couloir m ; [alleyway] ruelle f.

passbook ['pɑ:sbʊk] n [bankbook] livret m (d'épargne).

pass degree n en Grande-Bretagne, licence obtenue avec mention passable (par opposition au «honours degree»).

passenger ['pæsɪndʒər] n **1.** [in car, bus, aircraft, ship] passager m, -ère f ; [in train] voyageur m, -euse f **2.** UK pej [worker, team member] poids m mort.

passenger door n [of car] portière f avant côté passager.

passenger list n liste f des passagers.

passenger pigeon n pigeon m voyageur.

passenger seat n AUTO [in front] siège m du passager ; [in back] siège m arrière.

passenger train n train m de voyageurs.

passer-by [,pɑ:sə'baɪ] (pl **passers-by**) n passant m, -e f.

passing ['pɑ:sɪŋ] ◆ adj **1.** [going by] qui passe / with each passing day he grew more worried son inquiétude croissait de jour en jour / she flagged down a passing car elle a fait signe à une voiture qui passait de s'arrêter **2.** [fleeting] éphémère, passager / a passing whim un caprice passager **3.** [cursory, casual] [rel] en passant / he made only a passing reference to her absence il a fait mention de son absence en passant **4.** [slight] : to have a passing acquaintance with sb connaître qqn de vue / to bear a passing resemblance to sb ressembler vaguement à qqn. ◆ n **1.** [of time] passage m, fuite f / with the passing of time the pain will ease la douleur s'atténuera avec le temps **2.** [of train, crowd] passage m ; [overtaking - of another car] dépassement m **3.** euph [death] trépas m, mort f. ❖ **in passing** adv phr en passant.

passing lane n US AUTO voie f de dépassement.

passing place n voie f de dépassement, aire f de croisement.

passion ['pæʃn] n **1.** [love] passion f / I have a passion for Chinese food j'adore la cuisine chinoise **2.** [emotion, feeling] passion f.

passionate ['pæʃənət] adj passionné.

passionately ['pæʃənətlɪ] adv passionnément.

passion fruit n fruit m de la Passion.

passion killer n tue-l'amour m inv.

passive ['pæsɪv] ◆ adj **1.** [gen & CHEM & ELECTRON] passif **2.** GRAM passif. ◆ n GRAM passif m / in the passive au passif.

passive-aggressive adj PSYCHOL passif-agressif.

passive graphics n COMPUT infographie f passive.

passively ['pæsɪvlɪ] adv **1.** [gen] passivement **2.** GRAM au passif.

passiveness ['pæsɪvnɪs], **passivity** [pæ'sɪvətɪ] n passivité f.

passive resistance n résistance f passive.

passive smoking n tabagisme m passif.

passkey ['pɑːskiː] n passe-partout m inv.

pass mark n SCH moyenne f.

Passover ['pɑːsˌəʊvər] n Pâque f (juive), Pessah f.

passport ['pɑːspɔːt] n **1.** passeport m / British passport holders les détenteurs de passeports britanniques ▸ **passport control** contrôle m des passeports ▸ **passport photo** photo f d'identité **2.** fig clé f / the passport to happiness la clé du bonheur.

pass-the-parcel n 🇬🇧 jeu où l'on se passe un colis contenant soit un gage, soit un cadeau.

password ['pɑːswɜːd] n mot m de passe.

password-protected adj COMPUT protégé par mot de passe.

past [pɑːst] ◆ n **1.** [former time] ▸ **in the past** a) dans le passé b) [longer ago] autrefois ▸ **to live in the past** vivre dans le passé ▸ **to be** / **to become a thing of the past** : politeness seems to have become a thing of the past la politesse semble avoir été une chose démodée **2.** GRAM passé m / in the past au passé. ◆ adj **1.** [gone by - life] antérieur ; [-quarrels, differences] vieux (before vowel or silent 'h' vieil, f vieille), d'autrefois ; [-generation, centuries, mistakes, event] passé ▸ **in past time** or **times past** autrefois, (au temps) jadis ; [ended, over] ▸ **to be past** être passé or terminé **2.** [last] dernier / this past month has been very busy le mois qui vient de s'achever a été très chargé / I've not been feeling well for the past few days ça fait quelques jours que je ne me sens pas très bien / he has spent the past five years in China il a passé ces cinq dernières années en Chine **3.** [former] ancien **4.** GRAM passé. ◆ prep **1.** [in time] après / it's ten / quarter / half past six 🇬🇧 il est six heures dix / et quart / et demie / it's already past midnight il est déjà plus de minuit or minuit passé / he's past 50 il a plus de 50 ans, il a dépassé la cinquantaine ▸ **to be past it** inf avoir passé l'âge **2.** [further than] plus loin que, au-delà de / turn right just past the school prenez à droite juste après l'école **3.** [by, in front of] devant **4.** [beyond scope of] au-delà de **5.** [no longer capable of] : I'm past caring ça ne me fait plus ni chaud ni froid / I wouldn't put it past him il en est bien capable. ◆ adv [by] : to go past passer / they ran past ils passèrent en courant / the years flew past les années passaient à une vitesse prodigieuse. ◆ **in the past** adv phr autrefois, dans le temps.

pasta ['pæstə] n (U) pâtes fpl (alimentaires).

paste [peɪst] ◆ n **1.** [substance - gen] pâte f **2.** CULIN [dough] pâte f ; [mashed meat, fish] pâté m ▸ **tomato paste** concentré m de tomate **3.** [glue] colle f **4.** [for jewellery] strass m, stras m ▸ **paste necklace** / **diamonds** collier / diamants en stras or strass. ◆ vt **1.** [stick - stamp] coller ;

[spread glue on] encoller, enduire de colle **2.** [cover - wall] recouvrir **3.** COMPUT coller / to paste text into a document insérer un texte dans un document. ❖ **paste up** vt sep [poster] coller ; [list] afficher ; [wallpaper] poser.

pastel ['pæstl] ◆ n pastel m. ◆ adj pastel (inv).

paste-up n TYPO maquette f.

pasteurize, pasteurise ['pɑːstʃəraɪz] vt pasteuriser.

pasteurized, pasteurised ['pɑːstʃəraɪzd] adj **1.** [milk, beer] pasteurisé **2.** pej [version, description] édulcoré, aseptisé.

past historic n passé m simple.

pastille, pastil ['pæstɪl] n pastille f ▸ **cough pastilles** pastilles pour or contre la toux.

pastime ['pɑːstaɪm] n passe-temps m.

pasting ['peɪstɪŋ] n inf [beating, defeat] raclée f.

past master n expert m / he's a past master at doing as little as possible hum il est passé maître dans l'art d'en faire le moins possible.

pastor ['pɑːstər] n RELIG pasteur m.

pastoral ['pɑːstərəl] adj **1.** [gen & ART & LITER] pastoral **2.** RELIG pastoral **3.** SCH ▸ **pastoral care** ≃ tutorat m / teachers also have a pastoral role les enseignants ont également un rôle de conseillers.

past participle n participe m passé.

past perfect n plus-que-parfait m.

pastrami [pə'strɑːmɪ] n pastrami m.

pastry ['peɪstrɪ] (pl **pastries**) n **1.** [dough] pâte f **2.** [cake] pâtisserie f, gâteau m.

pastry case n croûte f.

pastry cook n pâtissier m, -ère f.

past tense n passé m.

pasture ['pɑːstʃər] ◆ n pâture f, pré m, pâturage m ▸ **to leave for greener pastures** or **pastures new** partir vers des horizons plus favorables. ◆ vt [animal] faire paître.

pastureland ['pɑːstʃəlænd] n herbages mpl, pâturages mpl.

pasty[1] ['peɪstɪ] (compar **pastier**, superl **pastiest**) adj [texture] pâteux ; [sallow] terreux ; [whitish] blanchâtre.

pasty[2] ['pæstɪ] (pl **pasties**) n 🇬🇧 CULIN ≃ petit pâté m.

pasty-faced ['peɪstɪ-] adj au teint terreux.

pat [pæt] (pt & pp **patted**, cont **patting**) ◆ vt tapoter ▸ **to pat sb on the back** a) lit tapoter qqn or donner une petite tape à qqn dans le dos b) fig féliciter or complimenter qqn. ◆ n **1.** [tap] (légère) tape f / you deserve a pat on the back fig tu mérites un coup de chapeau **2.** [lump] ▸ **a pat of butter** une noix de beurre. ◆ adj [glib - remark] tout fait ; [-answer] tout prêt. ◆ adv **1.** [exactly] parfaitement, avec facilité ▸ **to have sthg off pat** apprendre qqch à la perfection or par cœur **2.** 🇺🇸 [unbending] ▸ **to stand pat** [on decision] rester intraitable.

Patagonia [ˌpætə'gəʊnjə] pr n Patagonie f / in Patagonia en Patagonie.

patch [pætʃ] ◆ n **1.** [of fabric] pièce f ; [on inner tube] Rustine® f ▸ **to be not a patch on sb** / **sthg** : it isn't a patch on his first film ça ne vaut pas du tout son premier film **2.** [over eye] bandeau m **3.** [sticking plaster] pansement m (adhésif) **4.** [plot of land] parcelle f, lopin m **5.** [small expanse - of light, colour] tache f ; [-of fog] nappe f, poche f ; [of ice] plaque f ; [of water] flaque f / there were damp patches on the ceiling il y avait des taches d'humidité au plafond **6.** 🇬🇧 [period] période f, moment m ▸ **to go through a bad** or **sticky** or **rough patch** traverser une période difficile or une mauvaise passe **7.** 🇬🇧 [district, beat] secteur m **8.** COMPUT rustine f **9.** MED patch m, timbre m. ◆ vt **1.** [mend - clothes] rapiécer ; [-tyre, canoe] réparer

2. COMPUT [program] modifier. ❖ **patch together**
vt sep : *they managed to patch together a government / story* ils sont parvenus à former un gouvernement
de fortune / à construire une histoire de toutes pièces.
❖ **patch up** vt sep **1.** [repair - clothes] rapiécer ; [-car,
boat] réparer ; [-in makeshift way] rafistoler **2.** [relation-
ship] : *he's trying to patch things up with his wife* il essaie
de se rabibocher avec sa femme.

patch program n COMPUT rustine *f*.

patchwork ['pætʃwɜːk] ◆ n **1.** SEW patchwork *m* ; *fig*
[of colours, fields] mosaïque *f* **2.** [collection] collection *f*.
◆ adj [quilt] en patchwork.

patchy ['pætʃɪ] (*compar* **patchier**, *superl* **patchiest**)
adj **1.** [not uniform] inégal, irrégulier **2.** [incomplete - evi-
dence] incomplet (incomplète) ; [-knowledge] imparfait.

pâté ['pæteɪ] n pâté *m*.

patent [UK 'peɪtənt, US 'pætənt] ◆ n **1.** [on invention]
brevet *m* ▸ **to take out a patent on sthg** prendre un brevet
sur qqch, faire breveter qqch / **'patent pending'** demande
de brevet déposée **2.** = **patent leather 3.** US [on land]
concession *f*. ◆ adj **1.** [product, procedure] breveté **2.** [bla-
tant] patent, manifeste. ◆ vt faire breveter.

patent leather n cuir *m* verni, vernis *m*.

patently [UK 'peɪtəntlɪ, US 'pætəntlɪ] adv manifestement, de toute évidence ▸ **patently obvious** absolument
évident.

Patent Office n ≃ Institut *m* national de la propriété
industrielle.

paternal [pə'tɜːnl] adj paternel.

paternalistic [pə,tɜːnə'lɪstɪk] adj paternaliste.

paternally [pə'tɜːnəlɪ] adv paternellement.

paternity [pə'tɜːnətɪ] n paternité *f*.

paternity leave n congé *m* de paternité.

paternity suit n action *f* en recherche de paternité.

paternity test n test *m* de recherche de paternité.

path [pɑːθ] (*pl* **paths** [pɑːðz]) n **1.** [in garden, park]
allée *f* ; [in country] chemin *m*, sentier *m* ; [along road] trottoir *m* **2.** [way ahead or through] chemin *m*, passage *m* /
the hurricane destroyed everything in its path l'ouragan a
tout détruit sur son passage / *the path to fame* *fig* la route
or le chemin qui mène à la gloire **3.** [trajectory - of projectile, planet] trajectoire *f* **4.** COMPUT chemin *m* (d'accès).

path-breaking adj révolutionnaire.

pathetic [pə'θetɪk] adj **1.** [pitiable - lament, waif, smile,
story] pitoyable / *it was pathetic to see how they lived* cela
serrait le cœur or c'était un crève-cœur de voir dans quelles
conditions ils vivaient **2.** *pej* [worthless] minable, lamentable.

pathetically [pə'θetɪklɪ] adv pitoyablement.

pathname ['pɑːθneɪm] n nom *m* (d'accès).

pathological [,pæθə'lɒdʒɪkl] adj pathologique.

pathologist [pə'θɒlədʒɪst] n pathologiste *mf*.

pathology [pə'θɒlədʒɪ] (*pl* **pathologies**) n pathologie *f*.

pathos ['peɪθɒs] n pathétique *m*.

pathway ['pɑːθweɪ] n [in garden] allée *f* ; [in country]
chemin *m*, sentier *m* ; [beside road] trottoir *m*.

patience ['peɪʃns] n **1.** patience *f* ▸ **to lose patience
(with sb)** perdre patience (avec qqn) / *he has no patience
with children* les enfants l'exaspèrent / *my patience is
wearing thin* ma patience a des limites, je suis à bout de
patience **2.** UK [card game] réussite *f* / *she was playing
patience* elle faisait des réussites.

patient ['peɪʃnt] ◆ adj patient / *be patient!* (un peu de)
patience !, soyez patient ! ◆ n MED malade *mf*, patient *m*,
-e *f*.

patiently ['peɪʃntlɪ] adv patiemment.

patio ['pætɪəʊ] (*pl* **patios**) n patio *m*.

patio doors pl n portes *fpl* vitrées (*donnant sur un patio*).

Patna rice ['pætnə-] n *variété de riz à grains longs.*

patois ['pætwɑː] (*pl* **patois** ['pætwɑː]) n patois *m*.

patriarch ['peɪtrɪɑːk] n patriarche *m*.

patriarchal [,peɪtrɪ'ɑːkl] adj patriarcal.

patrimony [UK 'pætrɪmənɪ, US 'pætrɪməʊnɪ] (*pl* patri-
monies) n patrimoine *m*.

patriot [UK 'pætrɪət, US 'peɪtrɪət] n patriote *mf*.

Patriot Act n *loi qui donne aux agences gouvernementales américaines des pouvoirs exceptionnels dans la lutte
contre le terrorisme.*

patriotic [UK ,pætrɪ'ɒtɪk, US ,peɪtrɪ'ɒtɪk] adj [person]
patriote ; [song, action, etc.] patriotique.

patriotism [UK 'pætrɪətɪzm, US 'peɪtrɪətɪzm] n patriotisme *m*.

patrol [pə'trəʊl] (*pt & pp* **patrolled**, *cont* **patrolling**)
◆ n **1.** [group] patrouille *f* **2.** [task] patrouille *f* ▸ **to be
on patrol** être de patrouille. ◆ vi patrouiller. ◆ vt [area,
streets] patrouiller dans.

patrol car n voiture *f* de police.

patrolman [pə'trəʊlmən] (*pl* **patrolmen** [-mən]) n **1.**
US agent *m* de police (*qui fait sa ronde*) **2.** UK dépanneur
employé par une association d'automobilistes.

patrol wagon n US, Austr & NZ fourgon *m* cellulaire.

patrolwoman [pə'trəʊl,wʊmən] (*pl* **patrolwomen**
[-,wɪmɪn]) n US femme *f* agent de police (*qui fait sa ronde*).

patron ['peɪtrən] n **1.** [sponsor - of the arts] mécène *m* ;
[-of a festival] parrain *m*, sponsor *m* **2.** [customer - of restaurant, hotel, shop] client *m*, -e *f* ; [-of library] usager *m* ; [-of
museum] visiteur *m*, -euse *f* ; [-of theatre, cinema] spectateur *m*, -trice *f* / **'patrons only'** 'réservé aux clients'.

patronage ['peɪtrənɪdʒ] n [support, sponsorship] patronage *m*, parrainage *m*.

patronize, patronise ['pætrənaɪz] vt **1.** [business]
donner sa clientèle à ; [cinema] fréquenter **2.** [condescend
to] traiter avec condescendance **3.** [sponsor] patronner, parrainer.

patronizing, patronising ['pætrənaɪzɪŋ] adj
condescendant.

patronizingly, patronisingly ['pætrənaɪzɪŋlɪ] adv
[smile] avec condescendance ; [say] d'un ton condescendant.

patron saint n (saint *m*) patron *m*, (sainte *f*) patronne *f*.

patter ['pætə'] ◆ n **1.** [sound] crépitement *m*, (petit)
bruit *m* **2.** *inf* [of salesman] baratin *m*, boniment *m* ; [of
entertainer] bavardage *m*, baratin *m*. ◆ vi [raindrops] tambouriner.

pattern ['pætən] n **1.** [design - decorative] motif *m* ;
[-natural] dessin *m* ; [-on animal] marques *fpl* / *a geometric / herringbone pattern* un motif géométrique / à chevrons
2. [physical arrangement] disposition *f*, configuration *f* ▸ **to
form a pattern** former un motif or un dessin **3.** [abstract
arrangement] système *m*, configuration *f* / *sometimes
there seems to be no pattern to our lives* notre existence
semble parfois être régie par le hasard / *there is a definite
pattern to the burglaries* on observe une constante bien
précise dans les cambriolages / *the evening followed the
usual pattern* la soirée s'est déroulée selon le schéma habituel **4.** SEW patron *m* **5.** *fig* [example] exemple *m*, modèle *m*
▸ **to set a pattern for** a) [subj: company, method, work]
servir de modèle (à) b) [subj: person] instaurer un modèle
(pour).

patterned ['pætənd] adj à motifs.

pattie, patty ['pætɪ] (*pl* **patties**) n **1.** US ▸ **(hamburger) pattie** *portion de steak haché* **2.** [pasty] (petit) pâté *m*.

patty pan, patty tin n CULIN petit moule *m*.

paucity ['pɔːsətɪ] n *fml* pénurie *f*.

paunch [pɔːntʃ] n *pej & hum* [stomach] (gros) ventre *m*, bedaine *f*.

pauper ['pɔːpər] n pauvre *mf*, pauvresse *f*, indigent *m*, -e *f* ▸ **to end up in a pauper's grave** finir à la fosse commune.

pause [pɔːz] ◆ n [break] pause *f*, temps *m* d'arrêt ; [on tape recorder] 'pause' / *there will be a ten minute pause after the second lecture* il y aura or nous ferons une pause de dix minutes après le deuxième cours / *without a pause* sans s'arrêter, sans interruption. ◆ vi faire or marquer une pause / *we paused for lunch* nous avons fait une pause-déjeuner / *without pausing for breath* sans même reprendre son souffle.

pave [peɪv] vt [street, floor - with flagstones, tiles] paver ; [- with concrete, asphalt] revêtir.

paved [peɪvd] adj ▸ **paved in** or **with a)** [flagstones, tiles] pavé de **b)** [concrete, asphalt] revêtu de.

pavement ['peɪvmənt] n **1.** UK [footpath] trottoir *m* ▸ **pavement café** café *m*, terrasse *f* d'un café **2.** US [roadway] chaussée *f* **3.** [surfaced area - of cobbles, stones] pavé *m* ; [- of marble, granite] dallage *m* ; [- of concrete] (dalle *f* de) béton *m* ; [- of mosaic] pavement *m*.

pavement artist n UK artiste *mf* de trottoir.

pavilion [pə'vɪljən] n **1.** [building] pavillon *m* ; [at sports ground] vestiaires *mpl* ▸ **(cricket) pavilion** *bâtiment abritant les vestiaires et le bar sur un terrain de cricket* **2.** [tent] pavillon *m*, tente *f*.

paving ['peɪvɪŋ] ◆ n [cobbles, flagstones] pavé *m* ; [tiles] carrelage *m* ; [concrete] dallage *m*, béton *m*. ◆ adj [measure, legislation] préparatoire.

paving stone n pavé *m*.

paw [pɔː] ◆ n **1.** [of animal] patte *f* **2.** *inf* [hand] pince *f*, patte *f*. ◆ vt **1.** [animal] donner un coup de patte à **2.** *inf* [touch, maul] tripoter ; [sexually] peloter. ◆ vi : *the dog pawed at the door* le chien grattait à la porte.

pawn [pɔːn] ◆ n **1.** [in chess] pion *m* **2.** [at pawnbroker's] : *my watch is in pawn* ma montre est en gage. ◆ vt mettre or laisser en gage.

pawnbroker ['pɔːnˌbrəʊkər] n prêteur *m* sur gages / *at the pawnbroker's* au mont-de-piété.

pawnshop ['pɔːnʃɒp] n boutique *f* de prêteur sur gages, mont-de-piété *m*.

pawpaw ['pɔːpɔː] n papaye *f*.

pay [peɪ] (*pt & pp* **paid** [peɪd]) ◆ vt **1.** [person] payer / *she's paid £2,000 a month* elle est payée or elle touche 2 000 livres par mois **2.** [sum of money] payer / *I paid her £20* je lui ai payé 20 livres / *he paid £20 for the watch* il a payé la montre 20 livres **3.** [bill, debt] payer, régler ; [fine, taxes, fare] payer ▸ **to pay one's way** payer sa part **4.** *fig* [benefit] rapporter à / *it'll pay you to start now* vous avez intérêt à commencer tout de suite / *it'll pay you to keep quiet!* tu as intérêt à tenir ta langue ! **5.** [with various noun objects] : *pay attention!* faites attention ! ▸ **to pay a call on sb, to pay sb a visit** rendre visite à qqn. ◆ vi payer ▸ **to pay by cheque** payer par chèque ▸ **to pay (by) cash** payer en espèces / *the job pays very well* le travail est très bien payé / *after two years the business was beginning to pay* après deux ans, l'affaire était devenue rentable / *it pays to be honest* ça rapporte d'être honnête. ◆ n paie *f*, paye *f*. ◆ comp **1.** [demand, negotiations] salarial ; [increase, cut] de salaire **2.** [not free] payant. ❖ **pay back** vt sep **1.** [loan, lender] rembourser **2.** [retaliate against] rendre la monnaie de sa pièce à. ❖ **pay for** vt insep **1.** [item,

task] payer **2.** [crime, mistake] payer ▸ **to make sb pay for sthg** faire payer qqch à qqn. ❖ **pay in** vt sep UK [cheque] déposer sur un compte. ❖ **pay into** ◆ vt sep [money] : *I'd like to pay this cheque into my account* j'aimerais déposer ce chèque sur mon compte. ◆ vt insep ▸ **to pay into a pension scheme** cotiser à un plan de retraite. ❖ **pay off** ◆ vt sep **1.** [debt] payer, régler, s'acquitter de ; [loan] rembourser **2.** [dismiss, lay off] licencier, congédier **3.** *inf* [bribe] acheter. ◆ vi payer, rapporter. ❖ **pay out** vt sep **1.** [money] payer, débourser **2.** [rope] laisser filer. ◆ vi payer.

payable ['peɪəbl] adj payable / *cheques should be made payable to Mr Brown* les chèques devraient être libellés or établis à l'ordre de M. Brown.

pay-and-display adj ▸ **pay-and-display car park** parking *m* à horodateur ▸ **pay-and-display machine** horodateur *m*.

pay-as-you-earn = PAYE.

pay-as-you-go n paiement *m* à l'usage.

payback ['peɪbæk] n **1.** FIN rapport *m* (*d'un investissement*) **2.** [revenge] revanche *f*.

paybed ['peɪbed] n UK lit *m* (d'hôpital) privé.

pay channel n chaîne *f* payante.

pay check US = **pay packet**.

pay cheque n UK paie *f*.

pay claim n revendication *f* salariale.

payday ['peɪdeɪ] n jour *m* de paie.

PAYE (abbr of **pay-as-you-earn**) n prélèvement *m* à la source (*des impôts*).

payee [peɪ'iː] n bénéficiaire *mf*.

pay envelope US = **pay packet**.

payer ['peɪər] n **1.** [gen] payeur *m*, -euse *f* **2.** [of cheque] tireur *m*, -euse *f*.

PAYG n abbr of **pay-as-you-go**.

pay increase n augmentation *f* de salaire.

paying ['peɪɪŋ] ◆ n paiement *m*. ◆ adj **1.** [who pays] payant **2.** [profitable] payant, rentable.

paying guest n hôte *m* payant.

paying-in book n carnet *m* de versement.

paying-in slip n UK bordereau *m* de versement.

payload ['peɪləʊd] n [gen] chargement *m*.

payment ['peɪmənt] n **1.** [sum paid, act of paying] paiement *m*, versement *m* / *to make a payment* effectuer un paiement / *48 monthly payments* 48 versements mensuels, 48 mensualités / *on payment of a deposit* moyennant des arrhes / *in payment of your invoice* en règlement de votre facture / *they offered their services without payment* ils ont offert leurs services à titre gracieux **2.** [reward, compensation] récompense *f*.

payoff ['peɪɒf] n **1.** [profit] bénéfice *m*, profit *m* **2.** [consequence] conséquence *f*, résultat *m* ; [reward] récompense *f* **3.** *inf* [bribe] pot-de-vin *m*.

payola [peɪ'əʊlə] n (U) US *inf* pots-de-vin *mpl*, dessous-de-table *mpl*.

pay packet n UK [envelope] enveloppe *f* contenant le salaire ; [money] paie *f*, salaire *m*.

pay-per-view ◆ adj TV à péage ▸ **pay-per-view channel** chaîne *f* à la carte or à la séance or en pay per view. ◆ n TV système *m* de télévison à la carte or à la séance.

payphone ['peɪfəʊn] n téléphone *m* public.

pay rise UK, **pay raise** US n augmentation *f* de salaire.

payroll ['peɪrəʊl] n **1.** [personnel] personnel m **2.** [list] registre m du personnel.

payslip ['peɪslɪp] n fiche f or feuille f or bulletin m de paie.

pay station 🇺🇸 = payphone.

paystub ['peɪstʌb] n bulletin m de salaire.

pay television n chaîne f à péage.

pay TV n abbr of pay television.

PBS (abbr of Public Broadcasting Service) pr n société américaine de production télévisuelle.

pc (written abbr of per cent) p. cent.

pc, PC n **1.** (abbr of personal computer) PC m, micro m **2.** abbr of postcard.

PC ◆ n **1.** abbr of police constable **2.** abbr of privy councillor. ◆ adj abbr of politically correct.

PCB n **1.** abbr of printed circuit board **2.** (abbr of polychlorinated biphenyl) PCB m.

PCC (abbr of Press Complaints Commission) n organisme britannique de contrôle de la presse.

PC card n carte f PC.

PC-compatible adj COMPUT compatible PC.

pcm (written abbr of per calendar month) par mois.

PCM MESSAGING written abbr of please call me.

PCME MESSAGING written abbr of please call me.

PCV (abbr of passenger carrying vehicle) n 🇺🇰 véhicule m de transport en commun.

pd written abbr of paid.

PD n 🇺🇸 abbr of police department.

PDF (abbr of portable document format) n COMPUT PDF m.

pdq (abbr of pretty damn quick) adv inf illico presto.

PDSA (abbr of People's Dispensary for Sick Animals) pr n association de soins aux animaux malades.

PDT [,pi:di:'ti:] (abbr of Pacific Daylight Time) n heure f du Pacifique.

PE (abbr of physical education) n EPS f.

pea [pi:] n BOT pois m ; CULIN (petit) pois m ▶ **pea soup** soupe f aux pois ▶ **to be as alike as two peas in a pod** : they are as alike as two peas in a pod ils se ressemblent comme deux gouttes d'eau.

peace [pi:s] ◆ n **1.** [not war] paix f / the country is at peace now la paix est maintenant rétablie dans le pays ▶ **to make peace** faire la paix / he made (his) peace with his father fig il a fait la paix or il s'est réconcilié avec son père ; [treaty] (traité m de) paix f **2.** [tranquillity] paix f, tranquillité f ▶ **to be at peace with oneself / the world** être en paix avec soi-même / le reste du monde / all I want is a bit of peace and quiet tout ce que je veux, c'est un peu de tranquillité ▶ **to have peace of mind** avoir l'esprit tranquille / he'll give you no peace until you pay him tant que tu ne l'auras pas payé, il ne te laissera pas tranquille / leave us in peace! laisse-nous tranquilles !, laisse-nous en paix ! ◆ comp [treaty] de paix ; [rally, movement] pour la paix ▶ **peace talks** pourparlers mpl de paix.

peaceable ['pi:səbl] adj **1.** [peace-loving - nation, person] pacifique **2.** [calm - atmosphere] paisible, tranquille ; [- demonstration, methods] pacifique ; [- discussion] calme.

peaceably ['pi:səblɪ] adv [live] paisiblement, tranquillement ; [discuss, listen] calmement, paisiblement ; [assemble, disperse] pacifiquement, sans incident.

peace campaigner n militant m, -e pour la paix ; [for nuclear disarmament] militant m, -e pour le désarmement nucléaire.

Peace Corps pr n organisation américaine de coopération avec les pays en voie de développement.

peaceful ['pi:sfʊl] adj **1.** [calm, serene] paisible, tranquille **2.** [non-violent] pacifique / for peaceful purposes à des fins pacifiques / to do sthg by peaceful means faire qqch en utilisant des moyens pacifiques.

peacefully ['pi:sfʊlɪ] adv [live, rest] paisiblement, tranquillement ; [protest] pacifiquement.

peacekeeper ['pi:s,ki:pə*] n [soldier] soldat m de la paix ; [of United Nations] Casque m bleu.

peacekeeping ['pi:s,ki:pɪŋ] ◆ n maintien m de la paix. ◆ adj de maintien de la paix.

peacemaker ['pi:s,meɪkə*] n pacificateur m, -trice f, conciliateur m, -trice f.

peace offering n offrande f de paix.

peacetime ['pi:staɪm] n temps m de paix / in peacetime en temps de paix.

peach [pi:tʃ] ◆ n **1.** [fruit] pêche f ; [tree] pêcher m **2.** [colour] couleur f pêche. ◆ adj [colour] pêche (inv).

peachy ['pi:tʃɪ] (compar peachier, superl peachiest) adj **1.** [taste, flavour] de pêche **2.** inf [nice] chouette.

peacock ['pi:kɒk] (pl peacock or peacocks) n [bird] paon m.

pea green n vert m pomme. ◆ **pea-green** adj vert pomme (inv).

peahen ['pi:hen] n paonne f.

pea jacket n caban m.

peak [pi:k] ◆ n **1.** [mountain top] pic m, sommet m ; [mountain] pic m **2.** [high point - of fame, career] sommet m, apogée m ; [- on graph] sommet m / emigration was at its peak in the 1890s l'émigration a atteint son point culminant or son sommet dans les années 1890 / the party was at its peak la fête battait son plein / sales have reached a new peak les ventes ont atteint un nouveau record **3.** [of cap] visière f. ◆ vi [production, demand] atteindre un maximum. ◆ adj maximum ▶ **peak condition** : the team is in peak condition l'équipe est à son top niveau ▶ **peak hours** or **period** or **time** a) [of electricity use] période f de pointe b) [of traffic] heures fpl de pointe or d'affluence c) [in restaurant] coup m de feu ▶ **peak rate** plein tarif m ▶ **peak season** pleine saison f ▶ **peak time** TV heures fpl de grande écoute.

peaked [pi:kt] adj [roof] pointu ; [cap] à visière.

peaky ['pi:kɪ] (compar peakier, superl peakiest) adj 🇺🇰 inf [unwell] (un peu) malade ; [tired] fatigué.

peal [pi:l] ◆ n **1.** [sound] ▶ **the peal of bells** la sonnerie de cloches, le carillon ▶ **a peal of thunder** un coup de tonnerre / peals of laughter came from the living room des éclats de rire se faisaient entendre du salon **2.** [set of bells] carillon m. ◆ vi ▶ **to peal (out)** a) [bells] carillonner b) [thunder] gronder.

peanut ['pi:nʌt] n [nut] cacahuète f, cacahuète f ; [plant] arachide f ▶ **peanuts** inf [small sum] clopinettes fpl / to work for peanuts travailler pour des clopinettes / it's worth peanuts ça ne vaut pas un clou / £100 is peanuts for a return ticket 100 livres, ce n'est rien pour un billet aller-retour.

peanut butter n beurre m de cacahuètes.

peanut oil n huile f d'arachide.

pear [peə*] n [fruit] poire f ; [tree, wood] poirier m.

pearl [pɜ:l] ◆ n **1.** [gem] perle f **2.** [mother-of-pearl] nacre f **3.** fig perle f ▶ **pearls of wisdom** trésors mpl de sagesse. ◆ adj **1.** [made of pearls] de perles **2.** [made of mother-of-pearl] de or en nacre.

pearl barley n orge m perlé.

pearl grey n gris m perle. ◆ **pearl-grey** adj gris perle (inv).

pearly ['pɜːlɪ] (*compar* pearlier, *superl* pearliest) adj **1.** [pearl-like] nacré / *pearly white teeth* dents de perle ou éclatantes **2.** [decorated with pearls] perlé ; [made of mother-of-pearl] en or de nacre.

pear-shaped adj en forme de poire, piriforme *liter* / *she's pear-shaped* elle a de fortes hanches ▸ **to go pear-shaped** *inf* tourner mal.

peasant ['peznt] ◆ n paysan *m*, -anne *f*. ◆ adj paysan ▸ **peasant farmer** paysan.

peashooter ['piːˌʃuːtəʳ] n sarbacane *f*.

peat [piːt] n tourbe *f*.

peat bog n tourbière *f*.

pebble ['pebl] n [stone] caillou *m* ; [waterworn] galet *m* ▸ **a pebble beach** une plage de galets / *he's not the only pebble on the beach* un de perdu, dix de retrouvés.

pebbledash ['pebldæʃ] UK ◆ n crépi *m* (*incrusté de cailloux*). ◆ vt crépir.

pecan [UK 'piːkən, US pɪ'kæn] ◆ n [nut] (noix *f* de) pecan *m*, (noix *f* de) pacane *f* ; [tree] pacanier *m*. ◆ adj [pie, ice cream] à la noix de pecan.

peck [pek] ◆ vt **1.** [pick up] picorer, picoter ; [strike with beak] donner un coup de bec à **2.** [kiss] faire une bise à. ◆ n **1.** [with beak] coup *m* de bec **2.** [kiss] bise *f*, (petit) baiser *m* / *she gave me a peck on the forehead* elle m'a fait une bise sur le front. ❖ **peck at** vt insep **1.** = peck (*vt*) **2.** ▸ **to peck at one's food** manger du bout des dents.

pecking order ['pekɪŋ-] n [among birds] ordre *m* hiérarchique ; [among people] hiérarchie *f*.

peckish ['pekɪʃ] adj UK *inf* ▸ **to be** ou **to feel peckish** avoir un petit creux.

pecs [peks] pl n *inf* [pectorals] pectoraux *mpl*.

peculiar [pɪ'kjuːljəʳ] adj **1.** [strange] étrange, bizarre **2.** [specific, exclusive] particulier ▸ **to be peculiar to** être spécifique à ; [particular] spécial, particulier.

peculiarity [pɪˌkjuːlɪ'ærətɪ] (*pl* peculiarities) n **1.** [oddness] étrangeté *f*, bizarrerie *f* **2.** [specific characteristic] particularité *f*.

peculiarly [pɪ'kjuːljəlɪ] adv **1.** [oddly] étrangement, bizarrement **2.** [especially] particulièrement, singulièrement.

pecuniary [pɪ'kjuːnjərɪ] adj pécuniaire.

pedal ['pedl] (UK *pt & pp* pedalled, *cont* pedalling ; US *pt & pp* pedaled, *cont* pedaling) ◆ n **1.** [on bicycle, piano, etc.] pédale *f* ▸ **clutch / brake pedal** pédale d'embrayage / de frein ▸ **loud / soft pedal** [of piano] pédale droite ou forte / gauche ou douce **2.** MUS = pedal point. ◆ vi pédaler. ◆ vt faire avancer en pédalant.

pedal bin n UK poubelle *f* à pédale.

pedal boat n pédalo *m*.

pedal car n voiture *f* à pédales.

pedalo ['pedələʊ] (*pl* pedalos or pedaloes) n pédalo *m*.

pedal point n MUS pédale *f*.

pedal pushers pl n (pantalon *m*) corsaire *m*.

pedant ['pedənt] n [pettifogger] pinailleur *m*, -euse *f*.

⚠ A **pédant** is someone who likes showing off knowledge, not someone who splits hairs; the adjective **pédant** means pretentious, not pettifogging; and **pédantisme** is showing off knowledge, not hair-splitting.

pedantic [pɪ'dæntɪk] adj [pettifogging] pinailleur.

peddle ['pedl] vt **1.** dated [wares] colporter **2.** [drugs] revendre, faire le trafic de **3.** *pej* [promote - idea, opinion] propager ; [- gossip, scandal] colporter.

peddler ['pedləʳ] n **1.** [seller] colporteur *m*, -euse *f* **2.** [drug pusher] trafiquant *m*, -e *f* (de drogue), revendeur *m*, -euse *f*.

pederast ['pedəræst] n pédéraste *m*.

pedestal ['pedɪstl] n *lit & fig* piédestal *m* ▸ **to place** or **to put sb on a pedestal** mettre qqn sur un piédestal / *that knocked him off his pedestal* cela l'a fait tomber de son piédestal.

pedestrian [pɪ'destrɪən] ◆ n piéton *m* / **'pedestrians only'** 'réservé aux piétons'. ◆ comp [street, area] piéton, piétonnier ▸ **pedestrian overpass** passerelle *f*. ◆ adj **1.** [prosaic] prosaïque ; [commonplace] banal **2.** [done on foot - exercise, outing] pédestre, à pied.

pedestrian-controlled crossing n passage *m* pour piétons à bouton d'appel.

pedestrian crossing n UK passage *m* clouté or (pour) piétons.

pedestrianize, pedestrianise [pə'destrɪənaɪz] vt transformer en zone piétonne or piétonnière.

pedestrian precinct UK, **pedestrian zone** US n zone *f* piétonnière.

pediatric [ˌpiːdɪ'ætrɪk] adj pédiatrique.

pediatrician [ˌpiːdɪə'trɪʃn] n pédiatre *m*.

pediatrics [ˌpiːdɪ'ætrɪks] n pédiatrie *f*.

pedicure ['pedɪˌkjʊəʳ] n [treatment] pédicurie *f*.

pedigree ['pedɪgriː] ◆ n **1.** [descent - of animal] pedigree *m* ; [- of person] ascendance *f*, lignée *f* **2.** [document for animal] pedigree *m*. ◆ adj [horse, cat, dog] de race.

pedlar ['pedləʳ] UK = peddler.

pedophile ['piːdəʊˌfaɪl] n pédophile *m*.

pedophile ring n réseau *m* de pédophiles.

pedophilia [ˌpiːdəʊ'fɪlɪə] n pédophilie *f*.

pee [piː] *inf* ◆ n pipi *m* ▸ **to have** or **to take a pee** faire pipi. ◆ vi faire pipi.

peek [piːk] ◆ vi [glance] jeter un coup d'œil ; [look furtively] regarder furtivement ▸ **to peek at sthg** jeter un coup d'œil à ou sur qqch / *turn around and no peeking!* retourne-toi et n'essaie pas de voir ce que je fais ! ◆ n coup *m* d'œil ▸ **to have** or **to take a peek at sthg** jeter un coup d'œil à ou sur qqch.

peel [piːl] ◆ n [of banana] peau *f* ; [of orange, lemon] écorce *f* ; [of apple, onion, potato] pelure *f*. ◆ vt [fruit, vegetable] peler, éplucher ; [boiled egg] écaler, éplucher ; [shrimp] décortiquer. ◆ vi **1.** [fruit, vegetable] se peler **2.** [plaster on wall, ceiling, etc.] s'écailler, se craqueler ; [paint, varnish] s'écailler ; [wallpaper] se décoller **3.** [skin on back, face, etc.] peler. ❖ **peel away** ◆ vi = peel (*vi*). ◆ vt sep [label, wallpaper] détacher, décoller ; [bandage] enlever, ôter. ❖ **peel back** vt sep [label, wallpaper] détacher, décoller. ❖ **peel off** ◆ vi **1.** = peel (*vi*) **2.** [turn away] se détacher. ◆ vt sep **1.** = peel away **2.** [item of clothing] enlever.

peeler ['piːləʳ] n [device] éplucheur *m* ; [electric] éplucheuse *f*.

peelings ['piːlɪŋz] pl n épluchures *fpl*, pelures *fpl*.

peep [piːp] ◆ vi **1.** [glance] jeter un coup d'œil ▸ **to peep at / over / under sthg** jeter un coup d'œil (furtif) à / par-dessus / sous qqch **2.** [emerge] se montrer **3.** [bird] pépier. ◆ n **1.** [glance] coup d'œil ▸ **to have a peep at sthg** jeter un coup d'œil à qqch **2.** [of bird] pépiement *m* ; *fig* : *any news from him? — not a peep!* *inf* tu as eu de ses nouvelles ? — pas un mot ou que dalle !

pee-pee n US *baby talk* ▸ **to go pee-pee** faire pipi.

peephole ['piːphəʊl] n trou *m* ; [in house door, cell] judas *m*.

peeping Tom [ˌpiːpɪŋˈtɒm] n voyeur m.

peep-toe(d) shoes pl n escarpins mpl à bout découpé.

peer [pɪər] ◆ n **1.** [nobleman] pair m, noble mf **2.** [equal] pair m / as a negotiator she has no peer c'est une négociatrice hors pair. ◆ vi [look - intently] regarder attentivement ; [- with difficulty] s'efforcer de voir.

peerage [ˈpɪərɪdʒ] n **1.** [title] pairie f **2.** [body of peers] pairs mpl, noblesse f.

peeress [ˈpɪərɪs] n pairesse f.

peer group n SOCIOL pairs mpl.

peerless [ˈpɪəlɪs] adj sans pareil.

peer pressure n influence f des pairs or du groupe.

peer-to-peer adj peer-to-peer.

peeved [piːvd] adj inf énervé.

peevish [ˈpiːvɪʃ] adj [person] irritable, grincheux ; [report, expression] irrité.

peevishly [ˈpiːvɪʃlɪ] adv [say, refuse] d'un ton irrité ; [behave] de façon désagréable.

peg [peg] (pt & pp pegged, cont pegging) ◆ n **1.** [for hat, coat] patère f **2.** 🔲 [clothespeg] pince f à linge **3.** [dowel - wooden] cheville f ; [- metal] fiche f **4.** [for tent] piquet m **5.** fig [degree, notch] degré m, cran m ▶ to bring or to take sb down a peg or two rabattre le caquet à qqn. ◆ vt **1.** [fasten - gen] attacher ; [- with dowels] cheviller ; [insert - stake] enfoncer, planter **2.** [set - price, increase] fixer **3.** 🇺🇸 inf [classify] classer.

PEI written abbr of Prince Edward Island.

pejorative [pɪˈdʒɒrətɪv] ◆ adj péjoratif. ◆ n péjoratif m.

Pekinese [ˌpiːkəˈniːz], **Pekingese** [ˌpiːkɪŋˈiːz] ◆ n [dog] pékinois m. ◆ adj pékinois.

Peking [ˌpiːˈkɪŋ] pr n Pékin.

pelican [ˈpelɪkən] n pélican m.

pelican crossing n 🔲 passage piétons à commande manuelle.

pellet [ˈpelɪt] n **1.** [for gun] (grain m de) plomb m **2.** [of animal food] granulé m.

pell-mell [ˌpelˈmel] adv 🔲 [pile, throw] pêle-mêle / the crowd ran pell-mell into the square la foule s'est ruée sur la place dans une cohue indescriptible.

pelmet [ˈpelmɪt] n [for curtains] cantonnière f ; [wood, board] lambrequin m.

pelt [pelt] ◆ vt [person, target] bombarder / they were pelting each other with snowballs ils se lançaient des boules de neige. ◆ vi inf **1.** [rain] : it was pelting or pelting down with rain il pleuvait à verse, il tombait des cordes **2.** [run] courir à fond de train or à toute allure / she came pelting up the stairs elle grimpa l'escalier quatre à quatre / she came pelting down the stairs elle dévala l'escalier. ◆ n **1.** [skin] peau f ; [fur] fourrure f **2.** 🅿🅷🆁 at full pelt 🔲 à fond de train.

pelvic [ˈpelvɪk] adj pelvien ▶ pelvic bone ilion m.

pelvis [ˈpelvɪs] (pl pelvises or pelves [-viːz]) n bassin m, pelvis m.

pen [pen] (pt & pp penned, cont penning) ◆ n **1.** [for writing] stylo m ▶ to put pen to paper écrire, prendre sa plume **2.** [for animals] enclos m, parc m ▶ sheep pen parc à moutons **3.** (abbr of penitentiary) 🇺🇸 inf taule f, tôle f. ◆ vt **1.** [write] écrire **2.** [enclose] ▶ to pen in or up a) [livestock] parquer, enfermer dans un enclos b) [dog] enfermer c) [person] enfermer, cloîtrer, claquemurer.

penal [ˈpiːnl] adj **1.** [law] pénal ; [establishment] pénitentiaire **2.** [severe - taxation, fine] écrasant.

penal code n Code m pénal.

penalize, penalise [ˈpiːnəlaɪz] vt **1.** [punish] pénaliser, sanctionner **2.** [disadvantage] pénaliser, défavoriser, désavantager.

penalty [ˈpenltɪ] (pl penalties) n **1.** LAW peine f **2.** ADMIN & COMM [for breaking contract] pénalité f, sanction f **3.** fig [unpleasant consequence] ▶ to pay the penalty (for sthg) subir les conséquences (de qqch) **4.** SPORT [gen] pénalisation f ; [kick - in football] penalty m ; [- in rugby] pénalité f.

penalty area n FOOT surface f de réparation.

penalty box n **1.** [in football] = penalty area **2.** [in ice hockey] banc m de pénalité.

penalty goal n [in rugby] but m sur pénalité.

penalty kick n [in football] penalty m ; [in rugby] (coup m de pied de) pénalité f.

penalty points pl n [in quiz, game] gage m ; [for drivers] points mpl de pénalité (dans le système du permis à points).

penance [ˈpenəns] n pénitence f ▶ to do penance for one's sins faire pénitence.

pence [pens] n (pl of penny) pence mpl.

penchant [🔲 pɑ̃ʃɑ̃ 🇺🇸 ˈpentʃənt] n penchant m, goût m ▶ to have a penchant for sthg avoir un faible pour qqch.

pencil [ˈpensl] (🔲 pt & pp pencilled, cont pencilling ; 🇺🇸 pt & pp penciled, cont penciling) ◆ n [for writing, makeup] crayon m ▶ pencil case trousse f ▶ pencil sharpener taille-crayon m. ◆ comp au crayon. ◆ vt écrire au crayon ; [hastily] crayonner. ❖ **pencil in** vt sep [date, name, address] noter or inscrire au crayon ; fig fixer provisoirement.

pendant [ˈpendənt] ◆ n **1.** [necklace] pendentif m **2.** [piece of jewellery - on necklace] pendentif m ; [- on earring] pendeloque f ▶ pendant earrings pendants mpl d'oreille **3.** [chandelier] lustre m. ◆ adj = pendent.

pendent [ˈpendənt] adj fml **1.** [hanging] pendant, qui pend **2.** [overhanging] en surplomb, en saillie.

pending [ˈpendɪŋ] ◆ adj **1.** [waiting to be settled - gen] en attente ; LAW en instance, pendant **2.** [imminent] imminent. ◆ prep en attendant.

pending tray n 🔲 corbeille f des dossiers en attente.

pendulum [ˈpendjʊləm] n pendule m ; [in clock] balancier m.

penetrate [ˈpenɪtreɪt] ◆ vt **1.** [find way into or through - jungle] pénétrer dans ; [- blockade, enemy defences] pénétrer **2.** [infiltrate - party, movement] s'infiltrer dans, noyauter **3.** [pierce - subj: missile] percer, transpercer / the bullet penetrated his right lung la balle lui a perforé le poumon droit **4.** [pass through - subj: sound, light, etc.] traverser, transpercer / the cold wind penetrated her clothing le vent glacial passait à travers ses vêtements **5.** COMM s'introduire sur / to penetrate the market faire une percée sur or s'introduire sur le marché **6.** [see through - darkness, disguise, mystery] percer. ◆ vi **1.** [break through] pénétrer / the troops penetrated deep into enemy territory les troupes ont pénétré très avant en territoire ennemi **2.** [sink in] : I had to explain it to him several times before it finally penetrated j'ai dû le lui expliquer plusieurs fois avant qu'il (ne) finisse par comprendre.

penetrating [ˈpenɪtreɪtɪŋ] adj **1.** [sound - pleasant] pénétrant ; [- unpleasant] perçant **2.** [cold] pénétrant, perçant ; [rain] pénétrant **3.** [look, mind, question] pénétrant.

penetration [ˌpenɪˈtreɪʃn] n **1.** [gen & COMM] pénétration f **2.** MIL percée f.

penetrative ['penɪtrətɪv] adj [force] de pénétration ▶ **penetrative sex** pénétration f.

pen friend n 🇬🇧 correspondant m, -e f (épistolaire).

penguin ['peŋgwɪn] n manchot m.

penicillin [,penɪ'sɪlɪn] n pénicilline f.

peninsula [pə'nɪnsjulə] n [large] péninsule f; [small] presqu'île f.

penis ['piːnɪs] (pl **penises** or **penes** [-ɪz]) n pénis m.

penitence ['penɪtəns] n pénitence f.

penitent ['penɪtənt] adj [gen] contrit.

penitentiary [,penɪ'tenʃərɪ] (pl **penitentiaries**) n 🇺🇸 [prison] prison f.

penknife ['pennaɪf] (pl **penknives** [-naɪvz]) n canif m.

pen name n nom m de plume, pseudonyme m.

pennant ['penənt] n 1. [flag - gen] fanion m 2. NAUT [for identification] flamme f; [for signalling] pavillon m 3. 🇺🇸 SPORT drapeau servant de trophée dans certains championnats.

penniless ['penɪlɪs] adj sans le sou.

Pennines ['penaɪnz] pl pr n ▶ **the Pennines** les Pennines fpl.

Pennsylvania [,pensɪl'veɪnjə] pr n Pennsylvanie f / **in Pennsylvania** en Pennsylvanie.

penny ['penɪ] n 1. (pl **pence**) [unit of currency - in Britain, Ireland] penny m / it cost me 44 pence ça m'a coûté 44 pence 2. (pl **pennies**) [coin - in Britain, Ireland] penny m, pièce f d'un penny; [- in US] cent m, pièce f d'un cent / it was expensive, but it was worth every penny c'était cher, mais j'en ai vraiment eu pour mon argent / they haven't got a penny to their name or two pennies to rub together ils n'ont pas un sou vaillant ▶ **to be two** or **ten a penny** 🇬🇧 inf: people like him are two or ten a penny des gens comme lui, ce n'est pas ça qui manque or il y en a à la pelle ▶ **a penny for your thoughts** à quoi penses-tu ? ▶ **suddenly the penny dropped** 🇬🇧 inf d'un seul coup ça a fait tilt ▶ **in for a penny in for a pound** prov quand le vin est tiré, il faut le boire prov.

penny arcade n 🇺🇸 galerie f de jeux.

penny loafers pl n 🇺🇸 mocassins mpl.

penny-pinching [-,pɪntʃɪŋ] inf ◆ n économies fpl de bouts de chandelle. ◆ adj qui fait des économies de bouts de chandelle, pingre, radin.

penny whistle n pipeau m.

pen pal n inf correspondant m, -e f (épistolaire).

pension ['penʃn] n [for retired people] retraite f; [for disabled people] pension f ▶ **disability pension** pension d'invalidité. ◆ **pension off** vt sep 🇬🇧 1. [person] mettre à la retraite 2. hum [old car, machine] mettre au rancart.

pensionable ['penʃənəbl] adj [person - gen] qui a droit à une pension; [- for retirement] qui a atteint l'âge de la retraite.

pensioner ['penʃənər] n 🇬🇧 ▶ **(old age) pensioner** retraité m, -e f.

⚠ **Pensionnaire** means boarder, not pensioner.

pension fund n caisse f de retraite.

pension plan, **pension scheme** n régime m de retraite.

pensive ['pensɪv] adj pensif, méditatif, songeur.

pentagon ['pentəgən] n GEOM pentagone m. ◆ **Pentagon** pr n POL ▶ **the Pentagon** le Pentagone.

 The Pentagon

Le Pentagone, immense bâtiment à cinq façades situé à Washington, abrite le secrétariat à la Défense et l'état-major des forces armées des États-Unis. Il fut attaqué lors des attentats du 11 septembre 2001. Le terme désigne plus généralement les autorités militaires américaines.

pentathlon [pen'tæθlɒn] n pentathlon m.

Pentecost ['pentɪkɒst] n Pentecôte f.

Pentecostal [,pentɪ'kɒstl] = **Pentecostalist**.

Pentecostalist [,pentɪ'kɒstəlɪst] ◆ adj pentecôtiste. ◆ n pentecôtiste mf.

penthouse ['penthaʊs] (pl [-haʊzɪz]) n [flat] appartement de luxe avec terrasse généralement au dernier étage d'un immeuble ▶ **penthouse suite** [in hotel] suite f avec terrasse.

pent-up adj [emotion] refoulé, réprimé; [force] contenu, réprimé.

penultimate [pe'nʌltɪmət] adj [gen] avant-dernier.

penury ['penjʊrɪ] n fml 1. [poverty] indigence f, dénuement m 2. [scarcity] pénurie f.

peony ['piːənɪ] (pl **peonies**) n pivoine f.

people ['piːpl] ◆ pl n 1. [gen] personnes fpl, gens mpl / 500 people 500 personnes / there were people everywhere il y avait des gens or du monde partout / there were a lot of people there il y avait beaucoup de monde / some people think it's true certaines personnes or certains pensent que c'est vrai / many / most people disagree beaucoup de gens / la plupart des gens ne sont pas d'accord ▶ **you people**: are you people coming or not? alors, vous venez ou pas ? 2. [in indefinite uses] on / people say it's impossible on dit que c'est impossible 3. [with qualifier] gens mpl / clever / sensitive people les gens intelligents / sensibles / rich / poor / blind people les riches / pauvres / aveugles / young people les jeunes / old people les personnes âgées / city / country people les citadins / campagnards / people who know her ceux qui la connaissent / they are theatre / circus people ce sont des gens de théâtre / du cirque; [inhabitants, nationals]: Danish people les Danois / the people of Brazil les Brésiliens / the people of Glasgow les habitants de Glasgow / the people of Yorkshire les gens du Yorkshire; [employed in a specified job]: I'll call the electricity / gas people tomorrow je téléphonerai à la compagnie d'électricité / de gaz demain 4. POL ▶ **the people** le peuple 5. dated [family] famille f, parents mpl. ◆ n 1. [nation] peuple m, nation f 2. [ethnic group] population f. ◆ comp ▶ **to have people skills** avoir le sens du contact ▶ **to be a people person**: she's a real people person elle a vraiment le sens du contact. ◆ vt 1. (usu passive) [inhabit] peupler 2. fig: the monsters that people his dreams les monstres qui hantent ses rêves.

people carrier n [car] monospace m.

people trafficking n trafic m d'êtres humains.

pep [pep] (pt & pp **pepped**, cont **pepping**) n inf punch m. ◆ **pep up** vt sep inf 1. [person - depressed] remonter le moral à; [- ill, tired] requinquer, retaper 2. [business] faire repartir, dynamiser; [party] dynamiser, remettre de l'entrain dans; [conversation] égayer, ranimer, relancer.

pepper ['pepər] ◆ n 1. [condiment] poivre m 2. [vegetable - sweet] poivron m; [- hot] piment m. ◆ vt 1. CULIN poivrer 2. [scatter, sprinkle] émailler, parsemer / her text was peppered with quotations son texte était émaillé de citations.

pepperbox ['pepəbɒks] n 🇺🇸 poivrier m.

peppercorn ['pepəkɔːn] n grain m de poivre.

pepper mill n moulin m à poivre.

peppermint ['pepəmɪnt] ◆ n **1.** BOT menthe f poivrée **2.** [sweet] bonbon m à la menthe. ◆ adj à la menthe.

pepperoni [pepə'rəʊnɪ] n pepperoni m.

pepper pot UK, **peppershaker** US n CULIN poivrier m, poivrière f.

peppery ['pepərɪ] adj **1.** CULIN poivré **2.** [quick-tempered] coléreux, irascible.

pep pill n inf stimulant m, excitant m.

pep talk n inf discours m d'encouragement.

peptic ulcer ['peptɪk-] n spec ulcère m gastro-duodénal or de l'estomac.

per [pɜːʳ] prep [for each] par / per person par personne / per head par tête / per day / week / month / year par jour / semaine / mois / an / they are paid £6 per hour ils sont payés 6 livres de l'heure / 100 miles per hour ≃ 160 kilomètres à l'heure / it costs £8 per kilo ça coûte 8 livres le kilo. ◆ **as per** prep prep phr suivant, selon ▶ **as per normal** or **usual** inf comme d'habitude.

per annum [pərˈænəm] adv par an, annuellement.

P-E ratio, P/E ratio (abbr of price-earnings ratio) n PER m.

per capita [pə'kæpɪtə] fml ◆ adj par personne / per capita income is higher in the south le revenu par habitant est plus élevé dans le Sud. ◆ adv par personne.

perceive [pə'siːv] vt **1.** [see] distinguer ; [hear, smell, etc.] percevoir **2.** [notice] s'apercevoir de, remarquer **3.** [conceive, understand] percevoir, comprendre / their presence is perceived as a threat leur présence est perçue comme une menace.

per cent [pə'sent] (pl per cent) adv pour cent / prices went up (by) 10 per cent les prix ont augmenté de 10 pour cent / it's 50 per cent cotton il y a a 50 pour cent de coton, c'est du coton à 50 pour cent / I'm 99 per cent certain j'en suis sûr à 99 pour cent ▶ **to give 100 per cent** se donner à fond or à cent pour cent.

percentage [pə'sentɪdʒ] ◆ n **1.** [proportion] pourcentage m / a high percentage of the staff une grande partie du personnel **2.** [share of profits, investment] pourcentage m ▶ **to get a percentage on sthg** toucher un pourcentage sur qqch. ◆ adj US [profitable] payant.

perceptible [pə'septəbl] adj perceptible.

perception [pə'sepʃn] n **1.** [faculty] perception f ▶ **visual / aural perception** perception visuelle / auditive **2.** [notion, conception] perception f, conception f / her perception of the problem is different from mine sa façon de voir le problème diffère de la mienne / the general public's perception of the police l'image que le grand public a de la police **3.** [insight] perspicacité f, intuition f / a man of great perception un homme très perspicace.

perceptive [pə'septɪv] adj [observant - person] perspicace ; [- remark] judicieux.

perch [pɜːtʃ] ◆ n **1.** [for bird - in cage] perchoir m ; [- on tree] branche f **2.** (pl perch or perches) [fish] perche f. ◆ vi [bird, person] se percher.

percolate ['pɜːkəleɪt] vi **1.** [liquid] filtrer, s'infiltrer ; [coffee] passer **2.** [ideas, news] se répandre **3.** US inf [be excited] être (tout) excité.

percolator ['pɜːkəleɪtə] n cafetière f à pression.

percussion [pə'kʌʃn] n **1.** MUS percussion f ▶ **the percussion section** les percussions fpl **2.** [collision, shock] percussion f, choc m **3.** MED & MIL percussion f.

percussion instrument n MUS instrument m à percussion.

percussionist [pə'kʌʃənɪst] n MUS percussionniste mf.

peremptory [pə'remptərɪ] adj [tone, manner] péremptoire.

perennial [pə'renjəl] ◆ adj **1.** BOT vivace **2.** fig [everlasting] éternel ; [recurrent, continual] perpétuel, sempiternel. ◆ n BOT plante f vivace.

perfect ◆ adj ['pɜːfɪkt] **1.** [flawless - person, performance, etc.] parfait / in perfect health en excellente or parfaite santé / her hearing is still perfect elle entend encore parfaitement / nobody's perfect personne n'est parfait **2.** [complete - agreement, mastery, etc.] parfait, complet (complète) / there was perfect silence il y avait un silence total / you have a perfect right to be here vous avez parfaitement or tout à fait le droit d'être ici ; [as intensifier] véritable, parfait **3.** [fine, lovely - conditions] parfait, idéal ; [- weather] idéal, superbe **4.** [fitting, right - gift, example] parfait, approprié / Monday is perfect for me lundi me convient parfaitement **5.** [exemplary - gentleman, host] parfait, exemplaire **6.** GRAM [participle] passé ▶ **perfect participle** participe m passé ▶ **the perfect tense** le parfait. ◆ n ['pɜːfɪkt] GRAM parfait m / in the perfect au parfait. ◆ vt [pə'fekt] **1.** [improve - knowledge, skill] perfectionner, parfaire **2.** [bring to final form - plans, method] mettre au point.

perfection [pə'fekʃn] n [quality] perfection f ▶ **to do sthg to perfection** faire qqch à la perfection.

perfectionism [pə'fekʃənɪzm] n perfectionnisme m.

perfectionist [pə'fekʃənɪst] ◆ adj perfectionniste. ◆ n perfectionniste mf.

perfectly ['pɜːfɪktlɪ] adv **1.** [speak, understand] parfaitement **2.** [as intensifier] : you are perfectly right vous avez parfaitement or tout à fait raison / it's a perfectly good raincoat cet imperméable est tout à fait mettable.

perfect pitch n MUS ▶ **to have perfect pitch** avoir l'oreille absolue.

perfidious [pə'fɪdɪəs] adj liter perfide.

perforate ['pɜːfəreɪt] vt [pierce] perforer, percer.

perforated ['pɜːfəreɪtɪd] adj perforé, percé / to have a perforated eardrum avoir un tympan perforé or crevé / tear along the perforated line détacher suivant les pointillés.

perforation [ˌpɜːfə'reɪʃn] n perforation f.

perform [pə'fɔːm] ◆ vt **1.** [carry out - manoeuvre, task] exécuter, accomplir ; [- calculation] effectuer, faire ; [- miracle] accomplir ; [- wedding, ritual] célébrer **2.** [fulfil - function, duty] remplir **3.** [stage - play] jouer, donner ; [- ballet, opera] interpréter, jouer ; [- concert] donner ; [- solo] exécuter. ◆ vi **1.** [actor, comedian, musician] jouer ; [dancer] danser ; [singer] chanter **2.** [in job, situation] se débrouiller / to perform well / badly **a)** [person] bien / ne pas bien s'en tirer **b)** [company] avoir de bons / mauvais résultats **3.** [function - vehicle, machine] marcher, fonctionner.

performance [pə'fɔːməns] n **1.** [show] spectacle m, représentation f ; CIN séance f / afternoon performance matinée f **2.** [rendition - by actor, musician, dancer] interprétation f **3.** [showing - by sportsman, politician, etc.] performance f, prestation f / the country's poor economic performance les mauvais résultats économiques du pays ; [by pupil, economy, company] résultats mpl, performances fpl ; [by employee] rendement m, performance f **4.** [of machine, computer, car] performance f **5.** [carrying out - of task, manoeuvre] exécution f ; [- of miracle, duties] accomplissement m ; [- of ritual] célébration f / to perform well **6.** inf [rigmarole] histoire f, cirque m.

performance appraisal n [system] système m d'évaluation ; [individual] évaluation f.

performance art n spectacle m total.

performance-enhancing drug n produit m dopant.

performance pay n prime f de mérite or de résultat.

performance-related adj en fonction du mérite or résultat ▶ **performance-related pay** salaire m au mérite.

performer [pəˈfɔːməʳ] n [singer, dancer, actor] interprète mf / nightclub performer artiste mf de cabaret.

performing [pəˈfɔːmɪŋ] adj [bear, dog, etc.] savant.

performing arts pl n arts mpl du spectacle.

perfume ◆ n [ˈpɜːfjuːm] 1. [bottled] parfum m ▶ **perfume spray** atomiseur m de parfum 2. [smell] parfum m. ◆ vt [pəˈfjuːm] parfumer.

perfunctory [pəˈfʌŋktərɪ] adj [gesture] négligent; [greeting, kiss] détaché; [explanation, apology, letter] sommaire; [effort] de pure forme; [interrogation, search] fait pour la forme.

perhaps [pəˈhæps] adv peut-être / perhaps they've forgotten ils ont peut-être oublié, peut-être ont-ils oublié / perhaps not peut-être que non; [used in polite requests, offers] : perhaps you'd be kind enough... peut-être aurais-tu la gentillesse...

peril [ˈperɪl] n péril m, danger m ▶ **to be in peril** être en danger / you do it at your peril UK c'est à vos risques et périls.

perilous [ˈperələs] adj périlleux, dangereux.

perilously [ˈperələslɪ] adv périlleusement, dangereusement / he came perilously close to defeat / drowning il s'en est fallu d'un cheveu qu'il ne perde / qu'il ne se noie.

perimeter [pəˈrɪmɪtəʳ] n périmètre m.

perimeter fence n grillage m.

period [ˈpɪərɪəd] ◆ n 1. [length of time] période f; [historical epoch] période f, époque f / within a period of a few months en l'espace de quelques mois / the Elizabethan period l'époque élisabéthaine / after a short period in hospital après un court séjour à l'hôpital / the holiday period la période des vacances / at that period in her life à cette époque de sa vie 2. GEOL période f 3. SCH [lesson] cours m ▶ **a free period** a) [for pupil] une heure de permanence b) [for teacher] une heure de battement 4. [menstruation] règles fpl 5. US [full stop] point m / I said no, period j'ai dit non, point final 6. CHEM [in periodic table] période f 7. MUS période f. ◆ comp [furniture, costume] d'époque; [novel] historique.

periodic [ˌpɪərɪˈɒdɪk] adj 1. [gen] périodique 2. CHEM & MATH périodique.

periodical [ˌpɪərɪˈɒdɪkl] ◆ n [publication] périodique m. ◆ adj périodique.

periodically [ˌpɪərɪˈɒdɪklɪ] adv périodiquement, de temps en temps.

periodic table n classification f périodique (des éléments), tableau m de Mendeleïev.

period pains pl n règles fpl douloureuses.

peripatetic [ˌperɪpəˈtetɪk] adj 1. [itinerant] itinérant 2. UK SCH ▶ **peripatetic teacher** professeur qui enseigne dans plusieurs établissements scolaires.

peripheral [pəˈrɪfərəl] ◆ adj périphérique. ◆ n COMPUT ▶ **peripheral (device** or **unit)** (unité f) périphérique m.

periphery [pəˈrɪfərɪ] (pl peripheries) n 1. [of circle, vision, city, etc.] périphérie f / on the periphery à la périphérie 2. [of group, movement] frange f / on the periphery of society en marge de la société.

periscope [ˈperɪskəup] n périscope m.

perish [ˈperɪʃ] vi 1. UK [rot - rubber, leather, etc.] s'abîmer, se détériorer; [- food] se gâter, pourrir 2. liter [die] périr ▶ **perish the thought** hum : you're not pregnant, are you? — perish the thought! tu n'es pas enceinte au moins? — tu veux rire or j'espère que bien que non ! / and that, perish the thought, would mean giving up your weekends et pour ça, comble de l'horreur, tu devrais renoncer à tes weekends.

perishable [ˈperɪʃəbl] adj périssable. ❖ **perishables** pl n denrées fpl périssables.

perished [ˈperɪʃt] UK inf [cold] frigorifié.

perishing [ˈperɪʃɪŋ] adj UK inf [cold - person, hands] frigorifié / it's perishing (cold) il fait un froid de canard or de loup.

peritonitis [ˌperɪtəˈnaɪtɪs] n (U) péritonite f / to have peritonitis avoir une péritonite.

perjure [ˈpɜːdʒəʳ] vt ▶ **to perjure o.s.** faire un faux témoignage.

perjurer [ˈpɜːdʒərəʳ] n faux témoin m.

perjury [ˈpɜːdʒərɪ] (pl perjuries) n ▶ **to commit perjury** faire un faux témoignage.

perk [pɜːk] inf ◆ n [from job] avantage m en nature; [advantage - gen] avantage m. ◆ vi & vt [coffee] passer. ❖ **perk up** vt sep [cheer up] remonter, ragaillardir, revigorer; [liven up] revigorer. ◆ vi 1. [cheer up] se ragaillardir, retrouver le moral 2. [become interested] dresser l'oreille or la tête.

perky [ˈpɜːkɪ] (compar perkier, superl perkiest) adj gai, vif.

perm [pɜːm] ◆ vt [hair] permanenter / I've had my hair permed je me suis fait faire une permanente. ◆ n permanente f ▶ **to have a perm** se faire faire une permanente.

permanence [ˈpɜːmənəns] n permanence f, caractère m permanent.

permanent [ˈpɜːmənənt] ◆ adj permanent ▶ **permanent address** domicile m / are you here on a permanent basis? êtes-vous ici à titre définitif ? ▶ **a permanent post** a) [gen] un emploi permanent b) [in public service] un poste de titulaire. ◆ n US [in hair] permanente f.

permanently [ˈpɜːmənəntlɪ] adv 1. [constantly] en permanence, constamment 2. [definitively] définitivement, à titre définitif.

permeable [ˈpɜːmjəbl] adj perméable.

permeate [ˈpɜːmɪeɪt] ◆ vt 1. [subj: gas, smell] se répandre dans 2. [subj: liquid] s'infiltrer dans 3. fig [subj: ideas] se répandre dans, se propager à travers; [subj: feelings] envahir, emplir. ◆ vi 1. [gas] se répandre, se diffuser; [smell] se répandre 2. [liquid] filtrer 3. fig [ideas, feelings] se répandre, se propager.

permissible [pəˈmɪsəbl] adj fml 1. [allowed] permis, autorisé 2. [tolerable - behaviour] admissible, acceptable.

permission [pəˈmɪʃn] n permission f, autorisation f ▶ **to ask for permission to do sthg** demander la permission or l'autorisation de faire qqch ▶ **to have permission to do sthg** avoir la permission or l'autorisation de faire qqch ▶ **to give sb permission to do sthg** donner à qqn la permission de faire qqch / with your permission avec votre permission, si vous le permettez.

permissive [pəˈmɪsɪv] adj [tolerant - behaviour, parent, etc.] permissif ▶ **the permissive society** la société permissive.

permissiveness [pəˈmɪsɪvnɪs] n [morally] permissivité f.

permit [pəˈmɪt] (pt & pp permitted, cont permitting) ◆ vt 1. [allow] permettre, autoriser ▶ **to permit sb to do sthg** permettre à qqn de faire qqch, autoriser qqn à faire qqch / she was permitted to take two weeks off on l'a autorisée à prendre deux semaines de congé / you are not permitted to enter the building vous n'avez pas le droit de pénétrer dans l'immeuble / smoking is not permitted upstairs il est interdit de fumer à l'étage; [tolerate] tolérer

2. [enable] permettre. ◆ vi permettre ▶ **weather permitting** si le temps le permet / *if time permits* si j'ai / nous avons, etc. le temps. ◆ n ['pɜːmɪt] [authorization] autorisation f ; ADMIN permis m ; [pass] laissez-passer m inv ▶ **'permit holders only'** 'réservé aux personnes autorisées'.

permutation [ˌpɜːmjuːˈteɪʃn] n MATH permutation f.

pernicious [pəˈnɪʃəs] adj **1.** [harmful] pernicieux **2.** [malicious - gossip, lie] malveillant.

pernickety UK [pəˈnɪkətɪ], **persnickety** US [pəˈsnɪkɪtɪ] adj inf **1.** pej [person - fussy] tatillon, chipoteur ; [- hard to please] difficile **2.** [job - fiddly] délicat, minutieux.

peroxide [pəˈrɒksaɪd] n **1.** CHEM peroxyde m **2.** [for hair] eau f oxygénée.

peroxide blonde n [woman] blonde f décolorée.

perp [pɜːp] (**abbr of perpetrator**) n US inf & crime sl auteur m.

perpendicular [ˌpɜːpənˈdɪkjʊləʳ] ◆ adj **1.** GEOM perpendiculaire **2.** [vertical - cliff] escarpé, abrupt, à pic ; [- slope] raide, à pic. ◆ n perpendiculaire f.

perpetrate ['pɜːpɪtreɪt] vt fml [commit - crime] commettre, perpétrer liter.

perpetrator ['pɜːpɪtreɪtəʳ] n fml auteur m.

perpetual [pəˈpetʃʊəl] adj **1.** [state, worry] perpétuel ; [noise, questions] continuel, incessant **2.** HORT perpétuel.

perpetually [pəˈpetʃʊəlɪ] adv perpétuellement, sans cesse.

perpetuate [pəˈpetʃʊeɪt] vt perpétuer.

perpetuation [pəˌpetʃʊˈeɪʃn] n perpétuation f.

perpetuity [ˌpɜːpɪˈtjuːətɪ] (pl **perpetuities**) n [eternity] perpétuité f liter ▶ **in** or **for perpetuity** à perpétuité.

perplex [pəˈpleks] vt [puzzle] rendre or laisser perplexe.

perplexed [pəˈplekst] adj perplexe / *I'm perplexed about what to do* je ne sais pas trop quoi faire.

perplexing [pəˈpleksɪŋ] adj inexplicable, incompréhensible.

per se [pɜːˈseɪ] adv [as such] en tant que tel ; [in itself] en soi.

persecute ['pɜːsɪkjuːt] vt **1.** [oppress] persécuter **2.** [pester] persécuter, harceler.

persecution [ˌpɜːsɪˈkjuːʃn] n persécution f.

perseverance [ˌpɜːsɪˈvɪərəns] n persévérance f.

persevere [ˌpɜːsɪˈvɪəʳ] vi persévérer / *persevere in your efforts* persévérez dans vos efforts / *you must persevere with your studies* il faut persévérer dans vos études.

Persia ['pɜːʃə] pr n Perse f / *in Persia* en Perse.

Persian ['pɜːʃn] ◆ n **1.** [person] Persan m, -e f ; ANTIQ Perse mf **2.** LING [modern] persan m ; [ancient] perse m. ◆ adj persan ; ANTIQ perse.

Persian carpet n tapis m persan.

Persian cat n chat m persan.

Persian Gulf pr n ▶ **the Persian Gulf** le golfe Persique.

persist [pəˈsɪst] vi **1.** [person] persister ▶ **to persist in doing sthg** persister or s'obstiner à faire qqch / *he persists in the belief that...* il persiste à croire que... **2.** [weather, problem, etc.] persister.

persistence [pəˈsɪstəns], **persistency** [pəˈsɪstənsɪ] n **1.** [perseverance] persistance f, persévérance f ; [insistence] persistance f, insistance f ; [obstinacy] obstination f / *his persistence in asking awkward questions* son obstination à poser des questions embarrassantes **2.** [continuation - of rain, problem, etc.] persistance f.

persistent [pəˈsɪstənt] adj **1.** [continual - demands, rain etc.] continuel, incessant ▶ **persistent offender** récidiviste mf **2.** [lingering - smell, fever, etc.] persistant, tenace **3.** [persevering] persévérant **4.** BOT persistant.

persistently [pəˈsɪstəntlɪ] adv **1.** [continually] continuellement, sans cesse / *they persistently insult him* ils ne cessent de l'insulter **2.** [perseveringly] avec persévérance or persistance, obstinément.

persnickety US inf = **pernickety**.

person ['pɜːsn] (pl **people** ['piːpl]) (pl formal **persons**) n **1.** personne f / *a young person* a) [female] une jeune personne b) [male] un jeune homme / *he's a good worker, but I don't really like him as a person* sur le plan du travail il est bien, mais je n'aime pas trop sa personnalité or mais sur le plan personnel je ne l'aime pas trop / *he's not that sort of person* ce n'est pas du tout son genre / *I'm not a great eating-out person* inf je n'aime pas beaucoup manger au restaurant **2.** fml [body] personne f ▶ **to have sthg on** or **about one's person** avoir qqch sur soi **3.** GRAM personne f / *in the first person plural* à la première personne du pluriel. ◆ **in person** adv phr en personne.

persona [pəˈsəʊnə] (pl **personas** or **personae** [-niː]) n LITER & PSYCHOL personnage m.

personable ['pɜːsnəbl] adj plaisant, charmant.

personage ['pɜːsənɪdʒ] n fml personnage m (individu).

personal ['pɜːsənl] ◆ adj **1.** [individual - experience, belief, etc.] personnel / *she tries to give her work a personal touch* elle essaie de donner une touche personnelle à son travail / *my personal opinion is that he drowned* personnellement, je crois qu'il s'est noyé **2.** [in person] personnel / *we were expecting a personal appearance by the Prime Minister* nous pensions que le Premier ministre ferait une apparition en personne **3.** [private - message, letter] personnel **4.** [for one's own use] personnel / *this is for my personal use* ceci est destiné à mon usage personnel ▶ **personal belongings** or **possessions** objets mpl personnels, affaires fpl ▶ **personal effects** effets mpl personnels ▶ **personal loan** prêt m personnel ▶ **personal pension plan** retraite f personnelle **5.** [intimate - feelings, reasons, life] personnel / *I'd like to see her on a personal matter* je voudrais la voir pour des raisons personnelles / *just a few personal friends* rien que quelques amis intimes **6.** [offensive] désobligeant / *nothing personal!* ne le prenez pas pour vous !, n'y voyez rien de personnel ! / *the discussion was getting rather personal* la discussion prenait un tour un peu trop personnel **7.** [bodily - hygiene] corporel **8.** GRAM personnel ▶ **personal pronoun** pronom m personnel. ◆ n US [advert] petite annonce f (pour rencontres).

personal account n compte m personnel.

personal ad n inf petite annonce f (pour rencontres).

personal assistant n secrétaire m particulier, secrétaire f particulière.

personal best n SPORT record m personnel.

personal call n TELEC appel m personnel or privé.

personal column n petites annonces fpl (pour rencontres) ▶ **to put an ad in the personal column** passer une petite annonce.

personal computer n ordinateur m individuel or personnel, PC m.

personal details pl n [name, address] coordonnées fpl personnelles.

personal identification number n code m confidentiel (d'une carte bancaire).

personality [ˌpɜːsəˈnælətɪ] (pl **personalities**) n **1.** [character] personnalité f, caractère m ; [of thing, animal, etc.] caractère m / *a woman with a lot of personality* une femme dotée d'une forte personnalité **2.** [famous person] personnalité f ; CIN & TV vedette f **3.** PSYCHOL personnalité f.

personality cult n culte m de la personnalité.

personality disorder n trouble m de la personnalité.

personality profile n profil *m* de personnalité.

personalize, personalise ['pɜːsənəlaɪz] vt **1.** [make personal - gen] personnaliser ; [-luggage, clothes] marquer (à son nom) **2.** [argument, campaign] donner un tour personnel à **3.** [personify] personnifier.

personally ['pɜːsnəlɪ] adv **1.** [speaking for oneself] personnellement, pour ma / sa etc. part **2.** [in person, directly] en personne, personnellement **3.** [not officially] sur le plan personnel **4.** [individually] personnellement ▸ **to take things personally** prendre les choses trop à cœur.

personal organizer n organiseur *m*.

personal stereo n baladeur *m offic*, Walkman® *m*.

personal trainer n coach *m* personnel.

person-hour n = man-hour.

personification [pə,sɒnɪfɪ'keɪʃn] n personnification *f*.

personify [pə'sɒnɪfaɪ] (*pt & pp* personified) vt personnifier / *he is evil personified* c'est le mal personnifié or en personne.

personnel [,pɜːsə'nel] n **1.** [staff] personnel *m* ▸ **personnel officer** responsable *m* du personnel **2.** [department] service *m* du personnel.

person-to-person ◆ adv US : *I'd like to speak to her person-to-person* je voudrais lui parler en particulier or seule à seul. ◆ adj **1.** [conversation] personnel **2.** TELEC ▸ **person-to-person call** communication *f* avec préavis (*se dit d'un appel téléphonique où la communication n'est établie et facturée que lorsque la personne à qui l'on veut parler répond*).

perspective [pə'spektɪv] ◆ n **1.** ARCHIT & ART perspective *f* ▸ **to draw sthg in perspective** dessiner qqch en perspective **2.** [opinion, viewpoint] perspective *f*, optique *f* **3.** [proportion] : *we must try to keep our (sense of) perspective* or *to keep things in perspective* nous devons nous efforcer de garder notre sens des proportions ▸ **to get things out of perspective** perdre le sens des proportions **4.** [view, vista] perspective *f*, panorama *m*, vue *f* **5.** [prospect] perspective *f*. ◆ adj [drawing] perspectif.

Perspex® ['pɜːspeks] ◆ n US Plexiglas *m*. ◆ comp [window, windscreen, etc.] en Plexiglas.

perspicacious [,pɜːspɪ'keɪʃəs] adj *fml* [person] perspicace ; [remark, judgment] pénétrant, lucide.

perspicacity [,pɜːspɪ'kæsətɪ] n *fml* perspicacité *f*.

perspire [pə'spaɪə] vi transpirer / *his hands were perspiring* il avait les mains moites.

persuade [pə'sweɪd] vt persuader, convaincre ▸ **to persuade sb to do sthg** persuader or convaincre qqn de faire qqch ▸ **to persuade sb not to do sthg** persuader qqn de ne pas faire qqch, dissuader qqn de faire qqch / *I managed to persuade him (that) I was right* j'ai réussi à le persuader or convaincre que j'avais raison.

persuasion [pə'sweɪʒn] n **1.** [act of convincing] persuasion *f* / *I wouldn't need much persuasion to give it up* il ne faudrait pas insister beaucoup pour que j'abandonne / *I'm open to persuasion* je suis prêt à me laisser convaincre **2.** RELIG [belief] confession *f*, religion *f* ; POL tendance *f* / *people, regardless of their political persuasion* les gens, quelles que soient leurs convictions politiques.

persuasive [pə'sweɪsɪv] adj [manner, speaker] persuasif, convaincant ; [argument] convaincant.

persuasively [pə'sweɪsɪvlɪ] adv de façon convaincante or persuasive.

persuasiveness [pə'sweɪsɪvnəs] n force *f* de persuasion.

pert [pɜːt] adj [person, reply] effronté.

pertain [pə'teɪn] vi **1.** [apply] s'appliquer **2.** ▸ **to pertain to** avoir rapport à, se rapporter à.

pertinence ['pɜːtɪnəns] n pertinence *f*.

pertinent ['pɜːtɪnənt] adj pertinent, à propos.

perturb [pə'tɜːb] vt [worry] inquiéter, troubler.

perturbed [pə'tɜːbd] adj troublé, inquiet (ète) / *I was perturbed to hear that...* ça m'a troublé or inquiété d'apprendre que...

perturbing [pə'tɜːbɪŋ] adj inquiétant, troublant.

Peru [pə'ruː] pr n Pérou *m* / *in Peru* au Pérou.

perusal [pə'ruːzl] n [thorough reading] lecture *f* approfondie, examen *m* ; [quick reading] lecture *f* sommaire, survol *m*.

peruse [pə'ruːz] vt [read thoroughly] lire attentivement, examiner ; [read quickly] parcourir, survoler.

Peruvian [pə'ruːvjən] ◆ n Péruvien *m*, -enne *f*. ◆ adj péruvien.

pervade [pə'veɪd] vt **1.** [subj: gas, smell] se répandre dans **2.** [subj: ideas] se répandre dans, se propager à travers ; [subj: feelings] envahir.

pervading [pə'veɪdɪŋ] adj [smell] pénétrant ; [influence, feeling, idea] dominant.

pervasive [pə'veɪsɪv] adj [feeling] envahissant ; [influence] omniprésent ; [effect] général ; [smell] envahissant, omniprésent.

perverse [pə'vɜːs] adj [stubborn - person] têtu, entêté ; [-desire] tenace ; [contrary, wayward] contrariant / *she takes a perverse delight in doing this* elle y prend un malin plaisir.

perversely [pə'vɜːslɪ] adv [stubbornly] obstinément ; [unreasonably, contrarily] par esprit de contradiction.

perverseness [pə'vɜːsnɪs] n [stubbornness] entêtement *m*, obstination *f* ; [unreasonableness, contrariness] esprit *m* de contradiction.

perversion [UK pə'vɜːʃn US pə'vɜːrʒn] n **1.** [sexual abnormality] perversion *f* ▸ **sexual perversions** perversions *fpl* sexuelles **2.** [distortion - of truth] déformation *f* ▸ **a perversion of justice** un simulacre de justice.

perversity [pə'vɜːsətɪ] (*pl* perversities) n = perverseness.

pervert ◆ vt [pə'vɜːt] **1.** [corrupt morally - person] pervertir, corrompre ; PSYCHOL pervertir **2.** [distort - truth] déformer ; [-words] dénaturer ▸ **to pervert the course of justice** LAW entraver le cours de la justice. ◆ n ['pɜːvɜːt] pervers *m*, -e *f*.

perverted [pə'vɜːtɪd] adj PSYCHOL pervers.

peseta [pə'seɪtə] n peseta *f*.

pesky ['peskɪ] (*compar* peskier, *superl* peskiest) adj US *inf* fichu.

peso ['peɪsəʊ] (*pl* pesos) n peso *m*.

pessary ['pesərɪ] (*pl* pessaries) n MED pessaire *m*.

pessimism ['pesɪmɪzm] n pessimisme *m*.

pessimist ['pesɪmɪst] n pessimiste *mf*.

pessimistic [,pesɪ'mɪstɪk] adj pessimiste.

pest [pest] n **1.** [insect] insecte *m* nuisible ; [animal] animal *m* nuisible ▸ **pest control a)** lutte *f* contre les animaux nuisibles **b)** [of insects] désinsectisation *f* **2.** *inf* [nuisance] plaie *f*, peste *f*.

pester ['pestə] vt importuner, harceler / *stop pestering your mother!* laisse ta mère tranquille ! / *to pester sb with questions* harceler qqn de questions / *they're always pestering me for money* ils sont toujours à me réclamer de l'argent / *the children pestered me to tell them a story* les enfants n'ont eu de cesse que je leur raconte une histoire / *he pestered me into buying him a computer* il m'a harcelé jusqu'à ce que je lui achète un ordinateur.

pesticide [ˈpestɪsaɪd] n pesticide m.

pestilence [ˈpestɪləns] n liter peste f, pestilence f liter.

pestle [ˈpesl] n CULIN pilon m.

pesto [ˈpestəʊ], **pesto sauce** n pesto m.

pet [pet] (pt & pp petted, cont petting) ⬥ n 1. [animal] animal m domestique ▸ pet food aliments mpl pour animaux de compagnie 2. [favourite] favori m, -ite f, chouchou m, -oute f pej ▸ the teacher's pet le chouchou du prof 3. inf [term of endearment] : how are you, pet? comment ça va, mon chou ? ⬥ adj 1. [hawk, snake, etc.] apprivoisé 2. inf [favourite - project, theory] favori / his pet subject or topic son dada ▸ pet hate or peeve US bête f noire. ⬥ vt 1. [stroke - animal] câliner, caresser 2. inf [caress sexually] caresser.

petal [ˈpetl] n pétale m.

peter [ˈpiːtə] n US v inf [penis] quéquette f. ⬦ **peter out** vi [run out - supplies, money] s'épuiser ; [come to end - path] se perdre ; [- stream] tarir ; [- line] s'estomper, s'évanouir ; [- conversation] tarir.

petfood [ˈpetfuːd] n aliments mpl pour animaux de compagnie.

petite [pəˈtiːt] adj menue.

petition [pɪˈtɪʃn] n [with signatures] pétition f.

petitioner [pɪˈtɪʃənə] n 1. LAW pétitionnaire mf ; [in divorce] demandeur m, -eresse f de divorce 2. [on petition] signataire mf.

pet name n surnom m.

petrified [ˈpetrɪfaɪd] adj [terrified] paralysé or pétrifié de peur ; [weaker use] terrifié.

petrify [ˈpetrɪfaɪ] (pt & pp petrified) vt 1. [fossilize] pétrifier 2. [terrify] paralyser or pétrifier de peur ; [weaker use] terrifier.

petrochemical [ˌpetrəʊˈkemɪkl] adj pétrochimique.

petrodollar [ˈpetrəʊˌdɒlə] n pétrodollar m.

petrol [ˈpetrəl] UK ⬥ n essence f. ⬥ comp [fumes, rationing, shortage] d'essence.

⚠ **Pétrole** means oil or petroleum, not petrol.

---

petrolatum [ˌpetrəˈleɪtəm] n US vaseline f.

petrol bomb n cocktail m Molotov. ⬦ **petrol-bomb** vt attaquer au cocktail Molotov, lancer un cocktail Molotov contre or sur.

petrol can n UK bidon m d'essence.

petrol cap n UK bouchon m d'essence.

petrol-driven adj UK [engine] à essence.

petrol engine n UK moteur m à essence.

petroleum [pɪˈtrəʊljəm] ⬥ n pétrole m. ⬥ comp [industry] du pétrole ; [imports] de pétrole.

petroleum jelly n UK vaseline f.

petrol gauge n UK jauge f à essence.

petrol pump n UK [at service station] pompe f à essence.

petrol station n UK station-service f.

petrol tank n UK AUTO réservoir m (d'essence).

petrol tanker n UK 1. [lorry] camion-citerne m 2. [ship] pétrolier m, tanker m.

pet shop n magasin m d'animaux domestiques, animalerie f.

petticoat [ˈpetɪkəʊt] n [waist slip] jupon m ; [full-length slip] combinaison f.

pettiness [ˈpetɪnɪs] n [small-mindedness] mesquinerie f, étroitesse f d'esprit.

petting [ˈpetɪŋ] n (U) inf [sexual] caresses fpl / there was a lot of heavy petting going on ça se pelotait dans tous les coins.

petty [ˈpetɪ] (compar pettier, superl pettiest) adj 1. pej [trivial - detail] insignifiant, mineur ; [- difficulty] mineur ; [- question] tatillon ; [- regulation] tracassier ; [- ambitions] médiocre 2. pej [mean - behaviour, mind, spite] mesquin 3. [minor, small-scale] petit.

petty cash n petite monnaie f.

petty crime n 1. [illegal activities] petite délinquance f 2. [illegal act] délit m mineur.

petty criminal adj n petit malfaiteur m.

petty-minded adj borné, mesquin.

petty officer n UK ≃ second maître m.

petulant [ˈpetjʊlənt] adj [bad-tempered - person] irritable, acariâtre ; [- remark] acerbe, désagréable ; [- behaviour] désagréable, agressif ; [sulky] maussade / in a petulant mood de mauvaise humeur.

pew [pjuː] n banc m d'église.

pewter [ˈpjuːtə] ⬥ n [metal] étain m. ⬥ comp [tableware, tankard] en étain.

PG ⬥ n (abbr of parental guidance) CIN désigne un film dont certaines scènes peuvent choquer. ⬥ adj (abbr of pregnant) US inf enceinte.

pH n pH m.

PH n abbr of Purple Heart.

phalanx [ˈfælæŋks] (pl phalanxes or phalanges [-lændʒiːz]) n 1. ANTIQ & MIL phalange f 2. ANAT phalange f 3. POL phalange f.

phallic [ˈfælɪk] adj phallique.

phantom [ˈfæntəm] ⬥ n 1. [ghost] fantôme m, spectre m 2. [threat, source of dread] spectre m. ⬥ adj 1. [gen] imaginaire, fantôme 2. MED ▸ phantom pregnancy UK grossesse f nerveuse.

pharaoh [ˈfeərəʊ] n pharaon m.

pharmaceutical [ˌfɑːməˈsjuːtɪkl] ⬥ adj pharmaceutique. ⬥ n médicament m.

pharmacist [ˈfɑːməsɪst] n pharmacien m, -enne f.

pharmacology [ˌfɑːməˈkɒlədʒɪ] n pharmacologie f.

pharmacy [ˈfɑːməsɪ] (pl pharmacies) n 1. [science] pharmacie f 2. [dispensary, shop] pharmacie f.

pharming [ˈfɑːmɪŋ] n 1. COMPUT pharming m 2. PHARM culture ou élevage de plantes ou animaux génétiquement modifiés pour la fabrication de produits pharmaceutiques.

pharyngitis [ˌfærɪnˈdʒaɪtɪs] n (U) pharyngite f.

pharynx [ˈfærɪŋks] (pl pharynxes or pharynges [fæˈrɪndʒiːz]) n pharynx m.

phase [feɪz] ⬥ n 1. [period - gen] phase f, période f ; [- of illness] phase f, stade m ; [- of career, project] étape f ; [- of civilization] période f / the project is going through a critical phase le projet traverse une phase critique / their daughter's going through a difficult phase leur fille traverse une période difficile / don't worry, it's just a phase she's going through ne vous inquiétez pas, ça lui passera 2. CHEM, ELEC & PHYS phase f ▸ to be out of phase lit & fig être déphasé. ⬥ vt 1. [changes, new methods] introduire progressivement ; [project] développer en phases successives ; [schedule, introduction of technology] échelonner / the closure of the plant will be phased over three years la fermeture de l'usine se fera progressivement sur trois ans 2. [synchronize] synchroniser, faire coïncider. ⬦ **phase in** vt sep introduire progressivement or par étapes. ⬦ **phase out** vt sep [stop using - machinery, weapon] cesser progressivement d'utiliser ; [stop producing - car, model] abandonner progressivement la production de ; [do away with - jobs, tax] supprimer progressivement or par étapes ; [- grant] retirer progressivement.

phased [feɪzd] adj [withdrawal, development] progressif, par étapes.

phase-out n suppression f progressive.

phat [fæt] adj US inf [very good] génial, top.

PhD (abbr of Doctor of Philosophy) n ≃ (titulaire d'un) doctorat de 3ᵉ cycle.

pheasant ['feznt] (pl pheasant or pheasants) n faisan m ; [hen] (poule f) faisane f.

phenomena [fɪ'nɒmɪnə] pl ⟶ phenomenon.

phenomenal [fɪ'nɒmɪnl] adj phénoménal.

phenomenally [fɪ'nɒmɪnəlɪ] adv phénoménalement.

phenomenon [fɪ'nɒmɪnən] (pl phenomena [fɪ'nɒm-ɪnə]) n phénomène m.

pheromone ['ferəməʊn] n phéromone f, phérormone f.

phew [fju:] interj [in relief] ouf ; [from heat] pff ; [in disgust] berk, beurk.

phial ['faɪəl] n fiole f.

Philadelphia [,fɪlə'delfjə] pr n Philadelphie / in Philadelphia à Philadelphie.

philanderer [fɪ'lændərər] n pej coureur m (de jupons).

philanthropic [,fɪlən'θrɒpɪk] adj philanthropique.

philanthropist [fɪ'lænθrəpɪst] n philanthrope mf.

philanthropy [fɪ'lænθrəpɪ] n philanthropie f.

philatelist [fɪ'lætəlɪst] n philatéliste mf.

philately [fɪ'lætəlɪ] n philatélie f.

Philippines ['fɪlɪpi:nz] pl pr n ‣ **the Philippines** les Philippines fpl / in the Philippines aux Philippines.

Philistine [US 'fɪlɪstaɪn US 'fɪlɪsti:n] n fig philistin m liter, béotien m, -enne f.

Phillips® ['fɪlɪps] comp ‣ **Phillips screw / screw-driver** vis f / tournevis m cruciforme.

Philly ['fɪlɪ] pr n US inf Philadelphie.

philologist [fɪ'lɒlədʒɪst] n philologue mf.

philology [fɪ'lɒlədʒɪ] n philologie f.

philosopher [fɪ'lɒsəfər] n philosophe mf ‣ **the philosopher's stone** la pierre philosophale.

philosophic(al) [,fɪlə'sɒfɪk(l)] adj 1. PHILOS philosophique 2. [calm, resigned] philosophe.

philosophically [,fɪlə'sɒfɪklɪ] adv 1. PHILOS philosophiquement 2. [calmly] philosophiquement, avec philosophie.

philosophize, philosophise [fɪ'lɒsəfaɪz] vi philosopher ‣ **to philosophize about sthg** philosopher sur qqch.

philosophy [fɪ'lɒsəfɪ] (pl philosophies) n philosophie f.

phishing ['fɪʃɪŋ] n COMPUT phishing m.

phlegm [flem] n MED [in respiratory passages] glaire f.

phlegmatic [fleg'mætɪk] adj flegmatique.

phobia ['fəʊbjə] n phobie f.

phobic ['fəʊbɪk] ◆ adj phobique. ◆ n phobique mf.

phoenix ['fi:nɪks] n phénix m.

phone [fəʊn] ◆ n [telephone] téléphone m / just a minute, I'm on the phone un instant, je suis au téléphone / you're wanted on the phone on vous demande au téléphone. ◆ comp [bill] de téléphone ; [line, message] téléphonique. ◆ vi US téléphoner. ◆ vt US téléphoner à. ✢ **phone back** vt sep & vi rappeler. ✢ **phone in** ◆ vi téléphoner, appeler / he phoned in sick il a appelé pour dire qu'il était malade et qu'il ne viendrait pas travailler.

◆ vt : phone in your answers donnez vos réponses par téléphone. ✢ **phone up** ◆ vi téléphoner. ◆ vt sep téléphoner à.

phone book n annuaire m (téléphonique).

phone booth n cabine f téléphonique.

phone box n UK cabine f téléphonique.

phone call n coup m de téléphone, appel m (téléphonique).

phonecard ['fəʊnkɑ:d] n Télécarte® f.

phonecasting ['fəʊnkɑ:stɪŋ] n phonecasting m.

phone-in n RADIO & TV ‣ **phone-in (programme)** émission au cours de laquelle les auditeurs ou les téléspectateurs peuvent intervenir par téléphone.

phone number n numéro m de téléphone.

phone-tapping [-,tæpɪŋ] n (U) écoute f téléphonique, écoutes fpl téléphoniques.

phonetic [fə'netɪk] adj phonétique.

phonetically [fə'netɪklɪ] adv phonétiquement.

phonetic alphabet n alphabet m phonétique.

phonetics [fə'netɪks] n (U) phonétique f.

phoney ['fəʊnɪ] (compar phonier, superl phoniest, pl phonies) inf ◆ adj 1. [false - banknote, jewel, name] faux (fausse) ; [- title, company, accent] bidon ; [- tears] de crocodile ; [- laughter] qui sonne faux ‣ **the phoney war** la drôle de guerre 2. [spurious - person] bidon. ◆ n [charlatan] charlatan m.

phony ['fəʊnɪ] = phoney.

phosphate ['fɒsfeɪt] n AGR & CHEM phosphate m.

phosphorescent [,fɒsfə'resnt] adj phosphorescent.

phosphorus ['fɒsfərəs] n phosphore m.

photo ['fəʊtəʊ] (pl photos) (abbr of photograph) n photo f.

photo album n album m de photos.

photobooth ['fəʊtəʊbu:ð] n Photomaton®.

photocall ['fəʊtəʊkɔ:l] n séance f photo (avec des photographes de presse).

photocard ['fəʊtəʊkɑ:d] n carte portant une photo d'identité du titulaire.

photocopier ['fəʊtəʊ,kɒpɪər] n photocopieur m, photocopieuse f.

photocopy ['fəʊtəʊ,kɒpɪ] (pl photocopies, pt & pp photocopied) ◆ n photocopie f. ◆ vt photocopier.

photoelectric [,fəʊtəʊɪ'lektrɪk] adj photoélectrique ‣ **photoelectric cell** cellule f photoélectrique.

photo finish n 1. SPORT arrivée f groupée 2. fig partie f serrée.

Photofit® ['fəʊtəʊfɪt] n ‣ **Photofit (picture)** photo-robot f, portrait-robot m.

photo frame n cadre m photo.

photogenic [,fəʊtəʊ'dʒenɪk] adj photogénique.

photograph ['fəʊtəgrɑ:f] ◆ n photographie f (image), photo f (image) ‣ **to take a photograph** prendre or faire une photo ‣ **to take a photograph of sb** prendre qqn en photo, photographier qqn / they took our photograph ils nous ont pris en photo ‣ **to have one's photograph taken** se faire photographier / I'm in this photograph je suis sur cette photo / we took a lot of good photographs on holiday nous avons pris or fait beaucoup de bonnes photos pendant les vacances / she takes a good photograph [is photogenic] elle est photogénique. ◆ vt photographier, prendre en photo / she doesn't like being photographed elle n'aime pas qu'on la prenne en photo.

⚠ **Photographe** means photographer, not photograph.

photograph album n album *m* de photos.
photographer [fə'tɒgrəfər] n photographe *mf*.
photographic [,fəʊtə'græfɪk] adj photographique ▸ **to have a photographic memory** avoir une bonne mémoire visuelle.
photography [fə'tɒgrəfɪ] n photographie *f (art)*, photo *f (art)*.
photojournalism [,fəʊtəʊ'dʒɜːnəlɪzm] n photojournalisme *m*.
photomontage [,fəʊtəʊmɒn'tɑːʒ] n photomontage *m*.
photon ['fəʊtɒn] n photon *m*.
photo opportunity n séance *f* photoprotocolaire.
photosensitive [,fəʊtəʊ'sensɪtɪv] adj photosensible.
photoshoot ['fəʊtəʊʃuːt] n prise *f* de vue.
photosynthesis [,fəʊtəʊ'sɪnθəsɪs] n photosynthèse *f*.
photosynthesize, photosynthesise [,fəʊtəʊ-'sɪnθəsaɪz] vt fabriquer par photosynthèse.
phrasal verb n verbe *m* à particule.
phrase [freɪz] ◆ n **1.** [expression] expression *f*, locution *f* **2.** LING syntagme *m*, groupe *m* **3.** MUS phrase *f*. ◆ vt **1.** [letter] rédiger, tourner ; [idea] exprimer, tourner / *couldn't you phrase it differently?* ne pourriez-vous pas trouver une autre formule ? / *he phrased it very elegantly* il a trouvé une tournure très élégante (pour le dire) **2.** MUS phraser.
phrasebook ['freɪzbʊk] n guide *m* de conversation.
phrasing ['freɪzɪŋ] n **1.** [expressing] choix *m* des mots **2.** MUS phrasé *m*.
phreaker ['friːkər] n *inf* TELEC pirate *m* du téléphone.
phreaking ['friːkɪŋ] n *inf* TELEC piratage *m* du téléphone.
Phys Ed ['fɪzed] (abbr of physical education) n 🇺🇸 ≃ EPS *f*.
physiatrics [,fɪzɪ'ætrɪks] n *(U)* 🇺🇸 kinésithérapie *f*.
physiatrist [,fɪzɪ'ætrɪst] n 🇺🇸 kinésithérapeute *mf*.
physical ['fɪzɪkl] ◆ adj **1.** [bodily - fitness, strength, sport] physique ▸ **a physical examination** un examen médical, une visite médicale / *I don't get enough physical exercise* je ne fais pas assez d'exercice (physique) ▸ **physical abuse** sévices *mpl* ▸ **physical attraction** attirance *f* physique ▸ **physical handicap** infirmité *f* **2.** [natural, material - forces, property, presence] physique ; [- manifestation, universe] physique, matériel / *it's a physical impossibility* c'est physiquement or matériellement impossible **3.** CHEM & PHYS physique **4.** GEOG physique. ◆ n visite *f* médicale.
physical education n éducation *f* physique.
physical jerks pl n 🇬🇧 *inf* ▸ **to do physical jerks** faire des mouvements de gym.
physically ['fɪzɪklɪ] adv physiquement ▸ **to be physically fit** être en bonne forme physique / *she is physically handicapped* elle a un handicap physique.
physical sciences pl n sciences *fpl* physiques.
physical therapist n kinésithérapeute *mf*.
physical therapy n kinésithérapie *f* ; [after accident or illness] rééducation *f*.
physical training = physical education.
physician [fɪ'zɪʃn] n médecin *m*.

⚠ **Physicien(ne)** means physicist, not physician.

physicist ['fɪzɪsɪst] n physicien *m*, -enne *f*.
physics ['fɪzɪks] n *(U)* physique *f*.
physio ['fɪzɪəʊ] n *inf* **1.** (abbr of physiotherapy) kiné *f* **2.** (abbr of physiotherapist) kiné *mf*.
physiological [,fɪzɪə'lɒdʒɪkl] adj physiologique.
physiology [,fɪzɪ'ɒlədʒɪ] n physiologie *f*.
physiotherapist [,fɪzɪəʊ'θerəpɪst] n kinésithérapeute *mf*.
physiotherapy [,fɪzɪəʊ'θerəpɪ] n kinésithérapie *f* ; [after accident or illness] rééducation *f*.
physique [fɪ'ziːk] n constitution *f* physique, physique *m*.
pi [paɪ] n MATH pi *m*.
PI n 🇺🇸 abbr of private investigator.
pianist ['pɪənɪst] n pianiste *mf*.
piano¹ [pɪ'ænəʊ] (*pl* pianos) ◆ n piano *m*. ◆ comp [duet, lesson, stool, teacher, tuner] de piano ; [music] pour piano ; [lid, leg] du piano.
piano² ['pjɑːnəʊ] adj & adv [softly] piano *(inv)*.
piano accordion [pɪ'ænəʊ-] n accordéon *m* (à touches).
pic [pɪk] (*pl* pics or pix [pɪks]) n *inf* [photograph] photo *f* ; [picture] illustration *f* ; [film] film *m*.
Picardy ['pɪkədɪ] pr n Picardie *f* / *in Picardy* en Picardie.
piccalilli [,pɪkə'lɪlɪ] n piccalilli *m (sauce piquante à base de pickles et de moutarde)*.
piccolo ['pɪkələʊ] (*pl* piccolos) n piccolo *m*, picolo *m*.
pick [pɪk] ◆ vt **1.** [select] choisir / *she's been picked for the England team* elle a été sélectionnée dans l'équipe d'Angleterre ▸ **to pick a winner** [in racing] choisir un cheval gagnant / *you really (know how to) pick them!* *iro* tu les choisis bien ! ▸ **to pick one's way**: *they picked their way along the narrow ridge* ils avancèrent prudemment le long de la crête étroite **2.** [gather - fruit, flowers] cueillir ; [- mushrooms] ramasser **3.** [remove] enlever ; [remove bits of food, debris, etc. from] ▸ **to pick one's nose** se mettre les doigts dans le nez ▸ **to pick one's teeth** se curer les dents **4.** [provoke] ▸ **to pick a fight** chercher la bagarre ▸ **to pick a quarrel with sb** chercher noise or querelle à qqn **5.** [lock] crocheter. ◆ vi ▸ **to pick and choose**: *I like to be able to pick and choose* j'aime bien avoir le choix / *he always has to pick and choose* *pej* il faut toujours qu'il fasse le difficile. ◆ n **1.** [choice] choix *m* / *take your pick* faites votre choix / *you can have your pick of them* vous pouvez choisir celui qui vous plaît ▸ **the pick of the bunch** *inf* le dessus du panier, le gratin **2.** [tool] pic *m*, pioche *f*.
❖ **pick at** vt insep **1.** [pull at - loose end] tirer sur ; [- flake of paint, scab] gratter **2.** [food] manger du bout des dents / *he only picked at the fish* il a à peine touché au poisson **3.** [criticize pettily] être sur le dos de. ❖ **pick off** vt sep **1.** [shoot one by one] abattre (un par un) **2.** [remove - scab, paint] gratter. ❖ **pick on** vt insep **1.** [victimize] harceler, s'en prendre à **2.** [single out] choisir. ❖ **pick out** vt sep **1.** [choose] choisir **2.** [spot, identify] repérer, reconnaître **3.** [highlight, accentuate] rehausser / *the stitching is picked out in bright green* un vert vif fait ressortir les coutures. ❖ **pick over, pick through** vt insep [fruit, vegetables, etc.] trier. ❖ **pick up** vt sep **1.** [lift] ramasser ▸ **to pick up the telephone** décrocher le téléphone ▸ **to pick o.s. up** se relever ▸ **to pick up the bill** 🇬🇧 or **the tab** 🇺🇸: *they left me to pick up the bill* ils m'ont laissé l'addition ▸ **to pick up the pieces** recoller les morceaux **2.** [give lift to] prendre **3.** [collect, fetch] : *my father picked me up at the station* mon père est venu me chercher à la gare / *I have to pick up a parcel at the post office* je dois passer prendre un colis à la poste **4.** [acquire - skill] apprendre / *to pick up bad habits* prendre de mauvaises habitudes ; [win - reputation] gagner, acquérir ; [- prize] gagner, remporter **5.** [glean

- idea, information] glaner 6. *inf* [buy cheaply] ▶ **to pick up a bargain** dénicher une bonne affaire 7. [catch - illness, infection] attraper 8. *inf* [arrest] pincer 9. *inf* [start relationship with] draguer 10. [detect] détecter / *the dogs picked up the scent again* les chiens ont retrouvé la piste 11. RADIO & TV [receive] capter 12. [notice] relever 13. [criticize] : *nobody picked him up on his sexist comments* personne n'a relevé ses remarques sexistes 14. [resume] reprendre 15. [return to] revenir sur, reprendre 16. [gather - speed, momentum] prendre 17. *inf* [revive] remonter, requinquer. ◆ vi 1. [get better - sick person] se rétablir, se sentir mieux 2. [improve - business, weather] s'arranger, s'améliorer ; [- trade] reprendre / *the market is picking up after a slow start* COMM après avoir démarré doucement le marché commence à prendre 3. [resume] continuer, reprendre.

pickaxe 🇬🇧, **pickax** 🇺🇸 ['pɪkæks] n pic *m*, pioche *f*.

picker ['pɪkər] n [of fruit, cotton, etc.] cueilleur *m*, -euse *f*, ramasseur *m*, -euse *f* ▶ **grape-picker** vendangeur *m*, -euse *f*.

picket ['pɪkɪt] ◆ n 1. INDUST [group] piquet *m* de grève ; [individual] gréviste *mf*, piquet *m* de grève 2. [outside embassy, ministry - group] groupe *m* de manifestants ; [- individual] manifestant *m*, -e *f* 3. [stake] piquet *m*. ◆ vt INDUST [workplace, embassy] : *the strikers picketed the factory* les grévistes ont mis en place un piquet de grève devant l'usine / *demonstrators picketed the consulate at the week-end* des manifestants ont bloqué le consulat ce week-end. ◆ vi INDUST mettre en place un piquet de grève.

picket fence n clôture *f* de piquets, palissade *f*.

picketing ['pɪkətɪŋ] n *(U)* 1. [of workplace] piquets *mpl* de grève 2. [of ministry, embassy] : *there was picketing outside the embassy today* aujourd'hui, il y a eu des manifestations devant l'ambassade.

picket line n piquet *m* de grève.

pickings ['pɪkɪŋz] pl n *inf* [spoils] grapillage *m*, gratte *f* / *there are rich* or *easy pickings to be had* on pourrait se faire pas mal d'argent, ça pourrait rapporter gros.

pickle ['pɪkl] ◆ n 1. 🇺🇸 [gherkin] cornichon *m* 2. *inf* [mess, dilemma] pétrin *m* ▶ **to be in a (pretty) pickle** être dans le pétrin or dans de beaux draps 3. *(U)* 🇬🇧 [food] pickles *mpl* (*petits oignons, cornichons, morceaux de choux-fleurs, etc., macérés dans du vinaigre*). ◆ vt CULIN [in vinegar] conserver dans le vinaigre ; [in brine] conserver dans la saumure.

pickled ['pɪkld] adj 1. CULIN [in vinegar] au vinaigre ; [in brine] conservé dans la saumure ▶ **pickled cabbage** chou *m* rouge au vinaigre ▶ **pickled herring** rollmops *m inv* ▶ **pickled onion** oignon *m* au vinaigre 2. *inf* [drunk] bourré, rond.

pick-me-up n *inf* remontant *m*.

pickpocket ['pɪk,pɒkɪt] n pickpocket *m*, voleur *m*, -euse *f* à la tire.

pick-up n 1. AUTO [vehicle] ▶ **pick-up (truck)** pick-up *m inv*, camionnette *f* (découverte) 2. [act of collecting] ▶ **pick-up point** a) [for cargo] aire *f* de chargement b) [for passengers] point *m* de ramassage, lieu *m* de rendez-vous.

picky ['pɪkɪ] (*compar* **pickier**, *superl* **pickiest**) adj *inf* difficile.

pick-your-own adj [farm] où l'on peut cueillir soi-même ses fruits et ses légumes ; [strawberries, raspberries] cueilli à la ferme.

picnic ['pɪknɪk] (*pt & pp* **picnicked**, *cont* **picnicking**) ◆ n 1. *lit* pique-nique *m* ▶ **to go on** or **for a picnic** faire un pique-nique 2. *inf & fig* [easy task] : *it's no picnic showing tourists around London* ce n'est pas une partie de plaisir que de faire visiter Londres aux touristes. ◆ vi pique-niquer.

picnic basket, **picnic hamper** n panier *m* à pique-nique.

picnicker ['pɪknɪkər] n pique-niqueur *m*, -euse *f*.

pictorial [pɪk'tɔːrɪəl] adj [in pictures] en images ; [magazine, newspaper] illustré.

picture ['pɪktʃər] ◆ n 1. [gen] image *f* ; [drawing] dessin *m* ; [painting] peinture *f*, tableau *m* ; [in book] illustration *f* ▶ **to draw / to paint a picture (of sthg)** dessiner / peindre (qqch) ; [photograph] photo *f*, photographie *f* ▶ **to take a picture of sb, to take sb's picture** prendre une photo de qqn, prendre qqn en photo ▶ **to have one's picture taken** se faire prendre en photo ; [on television] image *f* 2. [film] film *m* ▶ **to go to the pictures** *inf* aller au ciné 3. [description] tableau *m*, portrait *m* / *the picture he painted was a depressing one* il a brossé or fait un tableau déprimant de la situation 4. [idea, image] image *f* / *he's the picture of health* il respire la santé, il est resplendissant de santé 5. [situation] situation *f* 6. PHR **to be in the picture** être au courant ▶ **to put sb in the picture** *inf* mettre qqn au courant / *I get the picture!* je comprends !, j'y suis ! / *doesn't she look a picture!* n'est-elle pas adorable or ravissante ! / *her face was a real picture when she heard the news!* il fallait voir sa tête quand elle a appris la nouvelle ! ◆ vt [imagine] s'imaginer, se représenter / *I can't quite picture him as a teacher* j'ai du mal à me l'imaginer comme enseignant / *just picture the scene* imaginez un peu la scène.

picture book n livre *m* d'images.

picture frame n cadre *m* (pour tableaux).

picture messaging n messagerie *f* photo.

picture rail n cimaise *f*.

picturesque [,pɪktʃə'resk] adj pittoresque.

picture window n fenêtre *f* or baie *f* panoramique.

piddling ['pɪdlɪŋ], **piddly** ['pɪdlɪ] adj *inf* [details] insignifiant ; [job, pay] minable.

pidgin ['pɪdʒɪn] n LING pidgin *m*.

pie [paɪ] n [with fruit] tarte *f* ; [with meat, fish, etc.] tourte *f* ▶ **chicken pie** tourte au poulet ▶ **it's just pie in the sky** *inf* ce sont des paroles or promesses en l'air.

piebald ['paɪbɔːld] ◆ adj pie (*inv*). ◆ n cheval *m* pie.

piece [piːs] n 1. [bit - of chocolate, paper, wood] morceau *m*, bout *m* ; [- of land] parcelle *f*, lopin *m* ; [with uncountable nouns] : *a piece of bread* un morceau de pain / *a piece of advice* un conseil / *pieces of advice / information / news* des conseils / renseignements / nouvelles / *that was a real piece of luck* cela a vraiment été un coup de chance ▶ **to be in pieces** a) [in parts] être en pièces détachées b) [broken] être en pièces or en morceaux ▶ **to be in one piece** a) [undamaged] être intact b) [uninjured] être indemne c) [safe] être sain et sauf ▶ **to be all of a piece** a) [in one piece] être tout d'une pièce or d'un seul tenant b) [consistent] être cohérent c) [alike] se ressembler / *his actions are of a piece with his opinions* ses actes sont conformes à ses opinions ▶ **to pull sthg to pieces** a) *lit* [doll, garment, book] mettre qqch en morceaux b) [flower] effeuiller qqch c) *fig* [argument, suggestion, idea] démolir qqch ▶ **to come to pieces** a) [into separate parts] se démonter b) [break] se briser ▶ **to fall to pieces** partir en morceaux ▶ **to go (all) to pieces** a) *inf* [person] s'effondrer, craquer b) [team] se désintégrer c) [market] s'effondrer ▶ **to give sb a piece of one's mind** : *I gave him a piece of my mind* a) *inf* [spoke frankly] je lui ai dit son fait or ce que j'avais sur le cœur b) [spoke harshly] je lui ai passé un savon 2. [item] pièce *f* / *a piece of furniture* un meuble 3. [part - of mechanism, set] pièce *f* ; [- of jigsaw] pièce *f*, morceau *m* / *an 18-piece band* un orchestre de 18 musiciens 4. GAMES [in chess] pièce *f* ; [in draughts, checkers] pion *m* 5. [performance] morceau *m* ; [musical composition] morceau *m*, pièce *f*; [sculpture] pièce *f* (de sculpture) / *a piano piece* un morceau pour piano **6.** [newspaper article] article *m* **7.** [coin] pièce *f* / *a 50p piece* une pièce de 50 pence. ✦ **piece together** vt sep **1.** [from parts - broken object] recoller; [-jigsaw] assembler **2.** [story, facts] reconstituer.

⚠ The French word **pièce** cannot always be used to translate piece. See the entry for details.

piecemeal ['piːsmiːl] ✦ adv [little by little] peu à peu, petit à petit / *the town was rebuilt piecemeal after the war* la ville a été reconstruite par étapes après la guerre / *the collection was sold piecemeal* les pièces de la collection ont été vendues séparément. ✦ adj [fragmentary] fragmentaire, parcellaire ▸ **in piecemeal fashion** en plusieurs étapes.

piecework ['piːswɜːk] n travail *m* à la pièce ▸ **to be on piecework** travailler à la pièce.

pie chart n graphique *m* circulaire, camembert *m*.

pie dish n plat *m* à tarte; [for meat] terrine *f*; [ovenproof] plat *m* allant au four.

pie-eyed adj inf bourré.

pie plate n US plat *m* allant au four.

pier [pɪər] n **1.** US [at seaside] jetée *f* **2.** [jetty] jetée *f*; [landing stage] embarcadère *m*; [breakwater] digue *f* **3.** [pillar] pilier *m*, colonne *f*; [of bridge] pile *f*.

pierce [pɪəs] vt **1.** [make hole in] percer, transpercer **2.** [subj: sound, scream] percer; [subj: light] percer **3.** [penetrate - defence, barrier] percer.

pierced [pɪəst] adj percé.

piercing ['pɪəsɪŋ] adj **1.** [scream, eyes, look] perçant; [question] lancinant; [wind] glacial **2.** [body art] ▸ **(body) piercing** piercing *m*.

piety ['paɪətɪ] (*pl* **pieties**) n piété *f*.

piffling ['pɪflɪŋ] adj UK inf [excuse, amount] insignifiant.

pig [pɪg] (*pt & pp* **pigged**, *cont* **pigging**) ✦ n **1.** ZOOL cochon *m*, porc *m* ▸ **pigs might fly!** quand les poules auront des dents! ▸ **to make a pig's ear of sthg** : quand le travail de sagouin! **2.** inf [greedy person] goinfre *m*; [dirty eater] cochon *m*, -onne *f* ▸ **to make a pig of o.s.** se goinfrer, s'empiffrer **3.** [dirty person] cochon *m*, -onne *f* **4.** inf [unpleasant person] ordure *f*. ✦ vt inf [stuff] ▸ **to pig o.s.** : *we really pigged ourselves at Christmas* on s'en est mis plein la lampe à Noël. ✦ **pig out** vi inf se goinfrer, s'empiffrer.

pigeon ['pɪdʒɪn] n **1.** ORNITH pigeon *m* ▸ **pigeon fancier** colombophile *mf* ▸ **pigeon loft** pigeonnier *m* **2.** UK inf [business] : *it's not my pigeon* ce n'est pas mon problème **3.** inf & fig [dupe] pigeon *m*.

pigeonhole ['pɪdʒɪnhəʊl] ✦ n casier *m* (à courrier). ✦ vt **1.** [file] classer **2.** [postpone] différer, remettre (à plus tard) **3.** [classify] étiqueter, cataloguer.

pigeon-toed adj : *to be pigeon-toed* avoir les pieds tournés en dedans.

pig farmer n éleveur *m*, -euse *f* de porcs.

piggy ['pɪgɪ] (*pl* **piggies**) inf n : *I'm tired of being piggy in the middle* j'en ai assez d'être pris entre deux feux.

piggyback ['pɪgɪbæk] ✦ adv ▸ **to ride** or **to be carried piggyback** se faire porter sur le dos de qqn. ✦ n ▸ **to give sb a piggyback** porter qqn sur le dos. ✦ adj [ride] sur le dos.

piggybacking ['pɪgɪbækɪŋ] n FIN portage *m*.

piggybank ['pɪgɪbæŋk] n tirelire *f* (en forme de petit cochon).

pig-headed [-'hedɪd] adj têtu, obstiné.

piglet ['pɪglɪt] n cochonnet *m*, porcelet *m*.

pigment ✦ n ['pɪgmənt] pigment *m*. ✦ vt [pɪg'ment] pigmenter.

Pigmy ['pɪgmɪ] = **Pygmy**.

pigpen ['pɪgpen] n US lit & fig porcherie *f*.

pigskin ['pɪgskɪn] ✦ n **1.** [leather] peau *f* de porc **2.** US [football] ballon *m* (de football américain). ✦ comp [bag, watchstrap] en (peau de) porc.

pigsty ['pɪgstaɪ] (*pl* **pigsties**) n lit & fig porcherie *f*.

pigtail ['pɪgteɪl] n natte *f*.

pike [paɪk] (*pl* **pike** or **pikes**) n [fish] brochet *m*.

Pilates [pɪ'lɑːtiːz] n [gymnastics] Pilates *f*.

pilchard ['pɪltʃəd] n pilchard *m*.

pile [paɪl] ✦ n **1.** [stack] pile *f*; [heap] tas *m* / *she left her clothes / records in a pile on the floor* elle a laissé ses vêtements / disques en tas par terre **2.** (usu pl) inf [large quantity] tas *m* ou *mpl*, masses *fpl* **3.** inf [fortune] ▸ **to make one's pile** faire fortune **4.** [large building] édifice *m* **5.** CONSTR pieu *m*; [for bridge] pile *f* **6.** (U) TEXT fibres *fpl*, poil *m*. ✦ vt [stack] empiler / *she piled her clothes neatly on the chair* elle empila soigneusement ses habits sur la chaise / *the table was piled high with papers* il y avait une grosse pile de papiers sur la table / *he piled spaghetti onto his plate* il a rempli son assiette de spaghettis. ✦ vi : *they all piled off / onto the bus* ils sont tous descendus du bus / montés dans le bus en se bousculant. ✦ **pile in** vi inf [enter] entrer en se bousculant; [join fight] : *once the first punch was thrown we all piled in* après le premier coup de poing, on s'est tous lancés dans la bagarre. ✦ **pile into** vt insep inf **1.** [crash] rentrer dans **2.** [attack - physically] rentrer dans, foncer dans; [-verbally] rentrer dans, tomber sur. ✦ **pile off** vi inf [from bus, train] descendre en se bousculant. ✦ **pile on** inf ✦ vi [onto bus, train] s'entasser, monter en s'entassant. ✦ vt sep **1.** [increase - suspense] faire durer; [-pressure] augmenter **2.** PHR **to pile it on** [exaggerate] exagérer, en rajouter ▸ **to pile on the pounds** or **pile it on** inf: *she's been piling on the pounds* or *she's been piling it on* elle a vachement grossi. ✦ **pile out** vi inf [off bus, train] descendre en se bousculant; [from cinema, lecture hall] sortir en se bousculant. ✦ **pile up** ✦ vi **1.** [crash - car] s'écraser **2.** [accumulate - work, debts] s'accumuler, s'entasser; [-washing, clouds] s'amonceler. ✦ vt sep **1.** [stack] empiler **2.** [accumulate - evidence, examples] accumuler.

piles [paɪlz] pl n MED hémorroïdes *fpl*.

pileup ['paɪlʌp] n carambolage inf *m*.

pilfer ['pɪlfər] vi & vt voler (des objets sans valeur).

pilfering ['pɪlfərɪŋ] n vol *m* (d'objets sans valeur).

pilgrim ['pɪlgrɪm] n pèlerin *m*.

pilgrimage ['pɪlgrɪmɪdʒ] n pèlerinage *m* ▸ **to make** or **to go on a pilgrimage** faire un pèlerinage.

Pilgrim Fathers pl pr n ▸ **the Pilgrim Fathers** les Pères pèlerins *mpl*.

 The Pilgrim Fathers

Puritains persécutés en Angleterre, les Pères pèlerins parvinrent en Amérique en 1620 à bord du **Mayflower** et fondèrent la première colonie du Nouveau Monde, à Plymouth, dans ce qui devait devenir l'État du Massachusetts.

pill [pɪl] n **1.** MED pilule f, comprimé m **2.** [contraceptive pill] ▶ **the pill** la pilule ▶ **to go on the pill** commencer à prendre la pilule ▶ **to be on the pill** prendre la pilule.

pillage ['pɪlɪdʒ] ◆ vt mettre à sac, piller. ◆ vi se livrer au pillage. ◆ n pillage m.

pillar ['pɪlər] n **1.** [structural support] pilier m ; [ornamental] colonne f / he was sent from pillar to post on l'a envoyé à droite et à gauche **2.** [of smoke] colonne f ; [of water] trombe f ; [mainstay] pilier m ▶ **a pillar of society** un pilier de la société.

pillar box n UK boîte f à lettres.

pillar-box red adj UK rouge vif.

pillbox ['pɪlbɒks] n **1.** MED boîte f à pilules **2.** MIL blockhaus m inv, casemate f **3.** [hat] toque f.

pillion ['pɪljən] ◆ n [on motorbike] ▶ **pillion (seat)** siège m arrière. ◆ adv ▶ **to ride pillion** voyager sur le siège arrière.

pillory ['pɪlərɪ] (pl pillories, pt & pp pilloried) ◆ n pilori m. ◆ vt HIST & fig mettre or clouer au pilori.

pillow ['pɪləʊ] ◆ n **1.** [on bed] oreiller m **2.** TEXT [for lace] carreau m (de dentellière) **3.** US [on chair, sofa] coussin m. ◆ vt [rest] reposer.

pillowcase ['pɪləʊkeɪs] n taie f d'oreiller.

pillowslip UK ['pɪləʊslɪp], **pillow sham** US = pillowcase.

pillow talk n (U) confidences fpl sur l'oreiller.

pilot ['paɪlət] ◆ n **1.** AERON & NAUT pilote m ; fig [guide] guide m **2.** = **pilot light**. ◆ comp [error] de pilotage. ◆ vt **1.** AERON & NAUT piloter **2.** [guide] piloter, guider. ◆ adj [trial - study, programme, scheme] d'essai, pilote, expérimental.

pilot burner = pilot light.

pilot light n veilleuse f.

pilot study n avant-projet m.

pimento [pɪ'mentəʊ] (pl pimentos) n piment m.

pimp [pɪmp] inf n maquereau m, souteneur m.

pimple ['pɪmpl] n bouton m.

pimply ['pɪmplɪ] (compar pimplier, superl pimpliest) adj boutonneux.

pin [pɪn] (pt & pp pinned, cont pinning) ◆ n **1.** [for sewing] épingle f ; [safety pin] épingle f ; [drawing pin] punaise f ; [hairpin] épingle f / for two pins I'd let the whole thing drop il ne faudrait pas beaucoup me pousser pour que je laisse tout tomber / you could have heard a pin drop on aurait entendu voler une mouche **2.** US [brooch] broche f ; [badge] insigne m **3.** [peg - in hand grenade] goupille f **4.** ELEC [on plug] broche f ▶ **two-pin plug** prise f à deux broches **5.** MED [for broken bone] broche f. ◆ vt **1.** [attach - with pin or pins] épingler ; [- with drawing pin or pins] punaiser ; fig ▶ **to pin one's hopes on sb / sthg** mettre ses espoirs dans qqn / qqch / they pinned the blame on the shop assistant ils ont rejeté la responsabilité sur la vendeuse, ils ont mis ça sur le dos de la vendeuse / they can't pin anything on me ils ne peuvent rien prouver contre moi **2.** [immobilize] immobiliser, coincer / they pinned his arms behind his back ils lui ont coincé les bras derrière le dos ▶ **to pin sb to the ground / against a wall** clouer qqn au sol / contre un mur. ◆ **pin down** vt sep **1.** [define clearly - difference, meaning] mettre le doigt sur, cerner avec précision **2.** [commit] amener à se décider / try to pin her down to a definite schedule essayez d'obtenir d'elle un planning définitif. ◆ **pin together** vt sep épingler, attacher avec une épingle or des épingles. ◆ **pin up** vt sep **1.** [poster] punaiser ; [results, names] afficher **2.** [hem] épingler ; [hair] relever (avec des épingles).

PIN [pɪn] (abbr of **personal identification number**) n ▶ **pin (number)** code m PIN.

pinafore ['pɪnəfɔːr] n UK **1.** [apron] tablier m **2.** = pinafore dress.

pinafore dress n robe f chasuble.

pinball ['pɪnbɔːl] n [game] flipper m ▶ **pinball machine** or **table** flipper.

pincer ['pɪnsər] n [of crab] pince f. ◆ **pincers** pl n [tool] tenaille f, tenailles fpl ▶ **a pair of pincers** une tenaille, des tenailles.

pinch [pɪntʃ] ◆ vt **1.** [squeeze] pincer **2.** US inf [steal] piquer, faucher ▶ **to pinch sthg from sb** piquer qqch à qqn **3.** inf [arrest] pincer. ◆ vi **1.** [shoes] serrer, faire mal (aux pieds) **2.** [economize] ▶ **to pinch and scrape** économiser sur tout, regarder (de près) à la dépense. ◆ n **1.** [squeeze] pincement m ▶ **to feel the pinch** : we're beginning to feel the pinch nous commençons à devoir nous priver **2.** [of salt, snuff] pincée f ▶ **to take sthg with a pinch of salt** : you must take what he says with a pinch of salt il ne faut pas prendre ce qu'il dit pour argent comptant. ◆ **at a pinch** UK, **in a pinch** US adv phr à la rigueur.

pinched [pɪntʃt] adj [features] tiré.

pinch-hitter n US SPORT remplaçant m, -e f.

pincushion ['pɪn,kʊʃn] n pelote f à épingles.

pine [paɪn] ◆ n BOT [tree, wood] pin m. ◆ comp [furniture] en pin. ◆ vi **1.** [long] ▶ **to pine for sthg** désirer qqch ardemment, soupirer après qqch **2.** [grieve] languir. ◆ **pine away** vi dépérir.

pineapple ['paɪn,æpl] ◆ n ananas m. ◆ comp [juice, chunks] d'ananas ; [ice cream] à l'ananas.

pine cone n pomme de pin f.

pine kernel = pine nut.

pine needle n aiguille f de pin.

pine nut = pine kernel.

ping [pɪŋ] ◆ n & onomat **1.** [gen] ding m **2.** COMPUT ping m. ◆ vi **1.** faire ding ; [timer] sonner **2.** US [car engine] cliqueter.

ping-pong, ping pong ['pɪŋpɒŋ] n ping-pong m.

pinhole ['pɪnhəʊl] n trou m d'épingle.

pinion ['pɪnjən] vt [hold fast] retenir de force / we were pinioned against the wall by the crowd la foule nous coinçait contre le mur.

pink [pɪŋk] ◆ n **1.** [colour] rose m **2.** fig ▶ **to be in the pink (of health)** se porter à merveille **3.** [flower] œillet m. ◆ adj **1.** [in colour] rose / to go or to turn pink with anger / embarrassment rougir de colère / confusion **2.** inf POL [left-wing] de gauche, gauchisant. ◆ vi UK [car engine] cliqueter.

pink economy n marché que représentent les homosexuels.

pink gin n cocktail m de gin et d'angustura.

pinkie ['pɪŋkɪ] US & Scot = pinky.

pinking scissors, pinking shears pl n SEW ciseaux mpl à cranter.

pink pound n UK ▶ **the pink pound** le pouvoir d'achat des homosexuels.

pink slip n US inf lettre f or avis m de licenciement ▶ **to get a pink slip** se faire renvoyer.

pinky ['pɪŋkɪ] (pl pinkies) n US & Scot inf petit doigt m.

pin money n argent m de poche.

pinnacle ['pɪnəkl] n fig [of fame, career] apogée m, sommet m ; [of technology] fin m du fin.

pin number n code m confidentiel.

pinny ['pɪnɪ] (pl pinnies) n inf tablier m.

pinpoint ['pɪnpɔɪnt] vt **1.** [locate -smell, leak] localiser ; [-on map] localiser, repérer **2.** [identify -difficulty] mettre le doigt sur.

pinprick ['pɪnprɪk] n **1.** [puncture] piqûre f d'épingle **2.** [irritation] agacement m, tracasserie f.

pins and needles n (U) inf fourmillements mpl / I've got pins and needles in my arm j'ai des fourmis dans le bras, je ne sens plus mon bras ▶ **to be on pins and needles** US trépigner d'impatience, ronger son frein.

pinstripe ['pɪnstraɪp] ◆ n TEXT rayure f (très fine). ◆ adj = pinstriped.

pinstriped ['pɪnstraɪpt] adj rayé.

pint [paɪnt] n **1.** [measure] pinte f (UK = 0,568 litres, US = 0,473 litres) ; ≃ demi-litre m **2.** UK inf [beer] bière f / I had a few pints last night j'ai bu quelques bières hier soir.

pint-sized adj inf & pej tout petit, minuscule.

pinup ['pɪnʌp] ◆ n pin-up f inv. ◆ adj [photo] de pin-up.

pioneer [ˌpaɪə'nɪər] ◆ n **1.** [explorer, settler] pionnier m, -ère f **2.** [of technique, activity] pionnier m, -ère f / she was a pioneer in the field of psychoanalysis elle a été une pionnière de la psychanalyse / they were pioneers in the development of heart surgery ils ont ouvert la voie en matière de chirurgie cardiaque **3.** MIL pionnier m, sapeur m. ◆ comp [work, research] novateur, original. ◆ vt : to pioneer research in nuclear physics être à l'avant-garde de la recherche en physique nucléaire.

pioneering [ˌpaɪə'nɪərɪŋ] adj [work, spirit] novateur, original.

pious ['paɪəs] adj **1.** [person, act, text] pieux **2.** [falsely devout] cagot liter, hypocrite **3.** [unrealistic] irréel.

piously ['paɪəslɪ] adv pieusement.

pip [pɪp] (pt & pp pipped, cont pipping) ◆ n **1.** [in fruit] pépin m **2.** UK [sound] bip m ; [during telephone call] tonalité f (indiquant une unité supplémentaire) ; TELEC [time signal] ▶ **the pips** le signal sonore, le signal horaire. ◆ vt UK [defeat] battre, vaincre ▶ **to pip sb at the post** coiffer qqn au poteau.

pipe [paɪp] ◆ n **1.** [for smoking] pipe f / he smokes a pipe il fume la pipe **2.** [for gas, liquid, etc.] tuyau m, conduite f ; [for stove] tuyau m / the pipes have frozen les canalisations ont gelé **3.** MUS [gen] pipeau m ; [on organ] tuyau m ▶ **the pipes** [bagpipes] la cornemuse. ◆ comp [bowl, stem] de pipe ; [tobacco] à pipe. ◆ vt **1.** [convey -liquid] acheminer par tuyau **2.** MUS [tune] jouer **3.** CULIN : to pipe cream onto a cake décorer un gâteau de crème fouettée (à l'aide d'une poche à douille). ◆ vi MUS [on bagpipes] jouer de la cornemuse ; [on simple pipe] jouer du pipeau. ❖ **pipe down** vi inf la mettre en sourdine. ❖ **pipe up** vi **1.** [person] se faire entendre **2.** [band] se mettre à jouer.

pipe bomb n bombe artisanale fabriquée à partir d'un morceau de tuyau contenant des explosifs.

pipe cleaner n cure-pipe m.

piped music [paɪpt-] n musique f d'ambiance.

pipe dream n chimère f.

pipeline ['paɪplaɪn] n **1.** [gen] pipeline m ; [for oil] oléoduc m ; [for gas] gazoduc m **2.** fig : he's got another film / project in the pipeline il travaille actuellement sur un autre film / projet / changes are in the pipeline for next year des changements sont prévus pour l'année prochaine.

piper ['paɪpər] n [gen] joueur m, -euse f de pipeau ; [of bagpipes] joueur m, -euse f de cornemuse, cornemuseur m.

piping ['paɪpɪŋ] ◆ n **1.** [system of pipes] tuyauterie f, canalisations fpl / a piece of copper piping un tuyau de cuivre **2.** MUS [gen] son m du pipeau or de la flûte ; [of bagpipes] son de la cornemuse. ◆ adv [as intensifier] ▶ **piping hot** très chaud, brûlant.

pipsqueak ['pɪpskwi:k] n inf & pej demi-portion f.

piquant ['pi:kənt] adj piquant.

pique [pi:k] ◆ n dépit m, ressentiment m / he resigned in a fit of pique il a démissionné par pur dépit, il était tellement dépité qu'il a démissionné. ◆ vt **1.** [vex] dépiter, irriter, froisser **2.** [arouse] piquer, exciter.

piracy ['paɪrəsɪ] (pl piracies) n **1.** [of vessel] piraterie f **2.** [of software, book, tape, etc.] piratage m ; [of idea] copie f, vol m.

piranha [pɪ'rɑ:nə] (pl piranha or piranhas) n piranha m, piraya m.

pirate ['paɪrət] ◆ n **1.** [person] pirate m ; [ship] navire m de pirates **2.** [of software, book, tape, etc.] pirate m ; [of idea] voleur m, -euse f. ◆ comp [raid, flag] de pirates ; [video, tape, copy] pirate. ◆ vt [software, book, tape, etc.] pirater ; [idea] s'approprier, voler.

pirate radio n radio f pirate.

pirouette [ˌpɪrʊ'et] ◆ n pirouette f. ◆ vi pirouetter.

Pisa ['pi:zə] pr n Pise.

Pisces ['paɪsi:z] ◆ pr n ASTROL & ASTRON Poissons mpl. ◆ n : she's (a) Pisces elle est Poissons.

piss [pɪs] v inf ◆ vi **1.** [urinate] pisser **2.** [rain] : it's pissing with rain il pleut comme vache qui pisse. ◆ vt pisser. ◆ n pisse f ▶ **to have** or **to take a piss** pisser (un coup) ▶ **to go on the piss** se soûler la gueule ▶ **to take the piss out of sb** a) UK [mock] se foutre de la gueule de qqn b) US [calm down] calmer qqn. ❖ **piss about** UK v inf, **piss around** v inf ◆ vi déconner, faire le con. ◆ vt sep emmerder. ❖ **piss away** vt [waste] gaspiller. ❖ **piss down** v inf [rain] : it's pissing (it) down il pleut comme vache qui pisse. ❖ **piss off** v inf ◆ vi foutre le camp ▶ **piss off!** fous or fous-moi le camp ! ◆ vt sep faire chier ▶ **to be pissed off** a) [bored] s'emmerder b) [angry] être en rogne ▶ **to be pissed off with sb** en avoir plein le cul de qqn.

pissed [pɪst] adj v inf **1.** UK [drunk] beurré, schlass ▶ **to get pissed** se soûler la gueule **2.** US [angry] en rogne.

pisshead ['pɪshed] n v inf UK [drunkard] poivrot m, -e f, soûlard m, -e f.

piss-take n UK v inf [mockery] mise f en boîte ; [of book, film] parodie f.

piss-up n UK v inf ▶ **to go on** or **to have a piss-up** se biturer, se soûler la gueule.

pissy ['pɪsɪ] adj v inf ▶ **to be pissy** être de mauvais poil.

pistachio [pɪ'stɑ:ʃɪəʊ] (pl pistachios) ◆ n **1.** [nut] pistache f ; [tree] pistachier m **2.** [colour] (vert m) pistache m. ◆ adj [vert] pistache (inv).

piste [pi:st] n piste f (de ski) ▶ **off piste** hors piste.

pistol ['pɪstl] n pistolet m.

pistol-whip vt frapper (au visage) avec un pistolet.

piston ['pɪstən] n MECH piston m.

pit [pɪt] (pt & pp pitted, cont pitting) ◆ n **1.** [hole in ground] fosse f, trou m ; [pothole in road] nid m de poule **2.** [shallow mark - in metal] marque f, piqûre f ; [-on skin] cicatrice f, marque f **3.** [mine] mine f, puits m ; [mineshaft] puits m de mine ▶ **to work down the pit** travailler à la mine **4.** UK THEAT [for orchestra] fosse f (d'orchestre) ; [seating section] parterre m **5.** US ST. EX parquet m (de la Bourse) **6.** (usu pl) AUTO [at race track] stand m (de ravitaillement) ▶ **to make a pit stop** s'arrêter au stand **7.** ANAT creux m ▶ **the pit of the stomach** le creux de l'estomac **8.** US [in fruit] noyau m **9.** liter [hell] ▶ **the pit** l'enfer m. ◆ comp [closure] de mine ; [worker] de fond ; [accident] minier.

◆ vt **1.** [mark] marquer / *a road pitted with potholes* une route criblée de nids-de-poule / *pitted with rust* piqué par la rouille **2.** [oppose] opposer, dresser / *she was pitted against the champion* on l'a opposée à la championne ▸ **to pit o.s. against sb** se mesurer à qqn ▸ **to pit one's wits against sb** se mesurer à *or* avec qqn **3.** US [fruit] dénoyauter. ❖ **pits** pl n *inf* [awful thing, place] : *it's the pits!* c'est l'horreur !

pita = pitta.

PITA MESSAGING written abbr of pain in the ass.

pit bull, pit bull terrier n pitbull *m*.

pitch [pɪtʃ] ◆ vt **1.** [throw] lancer, jeter **2.** MUS [note] donner ; [tune] donner le ton de ; [one's voice] poser **3.** [set level of] : *we must pitch the price at the right level* il faut fixer le prix au bon niveau **4.** [set up - camp] établir / *to pitch a tent* dresser une tente **5.** [in cricket] lancer ; [in golf] pitcher **6.** *inf* [tell] raconter. ◆ vi **1.** [fall over] tomber / *the passengers pitched forwards / backwards* les passagers ont été projetés en avant / en arrière **2.** [bounce - ball] rebondir **3.** AERON & NAUT tanguer **4.** [in baseball] lancer, être lanceur **5.** [slope - roof] être incliné. ◆ n **1.** [tone] ton *m* **2.** [particular level or degree] niveau *m*, degré *m* ; [highest point] comble *m* **3.** UK [sports field] terrain *m* **4.** UK *inf* [street vendor's place] place *f*, emplacement *m* **5.** *inf* [spiel] boniment *m* **6.** [slope - of roof, etc.] pente *f*, inclinaison *f* **7.** [movement - of boat, aircraft] tangage *m* **8.** [natural tar] poix *f* **9.** US *inf* PHR **to make a pitch for sthg** jeter son dévolu sur qqch. ❖ **pitch in** vi [start work] s'attaquer au travail ; [lend a hand] donner un coup de main. ❖ **pitch into** vt insep [attack] : *they pitched into me* ils me sont tombés dessus / *they pitched into the meal* ils ont attaqué le repas. ❖ **pitch out** vt sep [rubbish] jeter ; [person] expulser, mettre à la porte.

pitch-and-putt n pitch-and-putt *m* (*forme simplifiée du golf*).

pitch-black adj [water] noir comme de l'encre ; [hair] noir ébène *(inv)* ; [night] noir / *it's pitch-black in here* il fait noir comme dans un four ici.

pitch-dark adj [night] noir / *it was pitch-dark inside* à l'intérieur, il faisait noir comme dans un four.

pitched [pɪtʃt] adj [roof] en pente.

pitched battle n MIL & *fig* bataille *f* rangée.

pitcher ['pɪtʃə^r] n **1.** [jug - earthenware] cruche *f* ; [- metal, plastic] broc *m* ; US [smaller - for milk] pot *m* **2.** US [in baseball] lanceur *m* ▸ **pitcher's mound** monticule *m*.

pitchfork ['pɪtʃfɔːk] ◆ n fourche *f* (à foin). ◆ vt **1.** [hay] fourcher **2.** *fig* [person] propulser.

pitch invasion n SPORT invasion *f* de terrain.

piteous ['pɪtɪəs] adj pitoyable.

pitfall ['pɪtfɔːl] n **1.** [hazard] embûche *f*, piège *m* **2.** HUNT piège *m*, trappe *f*.

pith [pɪθ] n [in citrus fruit] peau *f* blanche (*sous l'écorce des agrumes*).

pithead ['pɪthed] n carreau *m* de mine.

pithy ['pɪθɪ] (*compar* pithier, *superl* pithiest) adj [comment, writing] concis, lapidaire.

pitiable ['pɪtɪəbl] adj **1.** [arousing pity] pitoyable **2.** [arousing contempt] piteux, lamentable.

pitiful ['pɪtɪfʊl] adj **1.** [arousing pity] pitoyable **2.** [arousing contempt] piteux, lamentable.

pitifully ['pɪtɪfʊlɪ] adv **1.** [touchingly] pitoyablement **2.** [contemptibly] lamentablement.

pitiless ['pɪtɪlɪs] adj [person] impitoyable, sans pitié ; [weather] rude, rigoureux.

pitta (bread) ['pɪtə-] n pita *m*.

pittance ['pɪtəns] n somme *f* misérable *or* dérisoire.

pitted ['pɪtɪd] adj [olives, cherries] dénoyauté.

pitter-patter ['pɪtə,pætə^r] ◆ n [of rain, hail] crépitement *m* ; [of feet] trottinement *m* ; [of heart] battement *m*. ◆ adv ▸ **to go pitter-patter** a) [feet] trottiner b) [heart] palpiter.

pituitary [pɪ'tjuːɪtrɪ] ◆ n ▸ **pituitary (gland)** glande *f* pituitaire, hypophyse *f*. ◆ adj pituitaire.

pity ['pɪtɪ] (*pl* pities, *pt & pp* pitied) ◆ n **1.** [compassion] pitié *f*, compassion *f* ▸ **to take** *or* **to have pity on sb** avoir pitié de qqn **2.** [mercy] pitié *f*, miséricorde *f* ▸ **for pity's sake!** a) [entreaty] pitié ! b) [annoyance] par pitié ! **3.** [misfortune, shame] dommage *m* / *what a pity!* c'est dommage ! / *it's a pity (that) she isn't here* quel dommage qu'elle ne soit pas là / *it seems a pity not to finish the bottle* ce serait dommage de ne pas finir la bouteille / *we're leaving tomorrow, more's the pity* nous partons demain, malheureusement. ◆ vt avoir pitié de, s'apitoyer sur.

> 📋 **Note that** il est / c'est dommage que **is** followed by a verb in the subjunctive:
> **It's a pity they can't come.** C'est dommage qu'ils ne *puissent* pas venir.

pitying ['pɪtɪɪŋ] adj [look, smile] de pitié.

pityingly ['pɪtɪɪŋlɪ] adv avec pitié.

pivot ['pɪvət] ◆ n *lit & fig* pivot *m*. ◆ vi **1.** *lit* pivoter **2.** *fig* : *his life pivots around his family* toute son existence tourne autour de sa famille. ◆ vt faire pivoter. ❖ **pivot on** vt insep *fig* dépendre de.

pivotal ['pɪvətl] adj [crucial] crucial, central.

pixel ['pɪksl] n pixel *m*.

pixelate ['pɪksəleɪt], **pixelize** ['pɪksəlaɪz] vt pixéliser.

pixelisation, pixelization [,pɪksəlaɪ'zeɪʃn] n [image defect] pixélisation *f* ; TV [to hide identity] mosaïquage *m*.

pixel(l)ated ['pɪksəleɪtɪd] adj COMPUT [image] pixélisé, bitmap, en mode point.

pixie ['pɪksɪ] n fée *f*, lutin *m*.

pixilated ['pɪksɪleɪtɪd] adj US *inf* [drunk] bourré, pété.

pixy ['pɪksɪ] (*pl* pixies) = pixie.

pizza ['piːtsə] n pizza *f*.

pizzazz [pɪ'zæz] n *inf* [dynamism] tonus *m*, punch *m* ; [panache] panache *m*.

pl written abbr of plural.

Pl. written abbr of place.

placard ['plækɑːd] n [on wall] affiche *f*, placard *m* ; [hand-held] pancarte *f*. ◆ vt [wall, town] placarder.

placate [plə'keɪt] vt apaiser, calmer.

placatory [plə'keɪtərɪ] adj apaisant, conciliant.

place [pleɪs] ◆ n **1.** [gen - spot, location] endroit *m*, lieu *m* / *keep the documents in a safe place* gardez les documents en lieu sûr / *this is neither the time nor the place to discuss it* ce n'est ni le moment ni le lieu pour en discuter / *I had no particular place to go* je n'avais nulle part où aller ▸ **to go places** [travel] aller quelque part / *that girl will go places!* *inf* cette fille ira loin ! ▸ **place of birth** lieu de naissance **2.** US [in adverbial phrases] : *no place* nulle part / *some place* quelque part / *I've looked every place* j'ai cherché partout **3.** [locality] : *do you know the place well?* est-ce que tu connais bien le coin ? / *how long have you been working in this place?* depuis combien de temps travaillez-vous ici ? ▸ **place of work** lieu *m* de travail / *we had lunch at a little place in the country* nous avons déjeuné dans un petit restaurant de campagne **4.** [house] maison *f* ; [flat] appartement *m* / *nice place you've got* *here* c'est joli chez vous / *your place or mine?* on va chez toi ou chez moi ? 5. [proper or assigned position] place *f* / *take your places!* prenez vos places ! / *suddenly everything fell* or *clicked into place* a) *fig* [I saw the light] tout à coup, ça a fait tilt b) [everything went well] tout d'un coup, tout s'est arrangé / *I'll soon put him in his place* j'aurai vite fait de le remettre à sa place 6. [role, function] place *f* / *what would you do (if you were) in my place?* que feriez-vous (si vous étiez) à ma place ? / *if she leaves there's nobody to take* or *to fill her place* si elle part, il n'y a personne pour la remplacer 7. [seat -on train, in theatre, etc.] place *f* ; [-on committee] siège *m* 8. [table setting] couvert *m* 9. [post, vacancy] place *f*, poste *m* / *to get a place at university* être admis à l'université 10. [ranking -in competition, hierarchy, etc.] place *f* / *Brenda took third place in the race / exam* Brenda a terminé troisième de la course / a été reçue troisième à l'examen / *the team is in fifth place* l'équipe est en cinquième position / *for me, work takes second place to my family* pour moi, la famille passe avant le travail 11. [in book, speech, etc.] : *I've lost my place* je ne sais plus où j'en étais 12. [PHR] **to take place** avoir lieu. ❖ *vt* 1. [put, set] placer, mettre / *he placed an ad in the local paper* il a fait passer or mis une annonce dans le journal local 2. [find work or a home for] placer 3. *(usu passive)* [situate] placer, situer / *you are better placed to judge than I am* vous êtes mieux placé que moi pour en juger 4. *(usu passive)* [rank -in competition, race, etc.] placer, classer / *the runners placed in the first five go through to the final* les coureurs classés dans les cinq premiers participent à la finale / *the horse we bet on wasn't even placed* le cheval sur lequel nous avions parié n'est même pas arrivé placé 5. [identify] (se) remettre / *I can't place him* je n'arrive pas à (me) le remettre 6. [order] placer, passer ; [bet] placer. ❖ **all over the place** adv phr 1. [everywhere] partout, dans tous les coins 2. [in disorder] en désordre 3. [very erratic, inaccurate] pas au point *hum*. ❖ **in place** adv phr 1. [steady] en place 2. [on the spot -run, jump] sur place. ❖ **in place of** prep phr à la place de. ❖ **in places** adv phr par endroits. ❖ **in the first place** adv phr : *what drew your attention to it in the first place?* qu'est-ce qui a attiré votre attention à l'origine or en premier lieu ? / *I didn't want to come in the first place* d'abord, je ne voulais même pas venir / *in the first place, it's too big, and in the second place...* premièrement, c'est trop grand, et deuxièmement..., primo, c'est trop grand, et secundo... ❖ **out of place** adj phr : *he felt out of place amongst so many young people* il ne se sentait pas à sa place parmi tous les jeunes / *such remarks are out of place at a funeral* de telles paroles sont déplacées lors d'un enterrement.

⚠ **The French word place can rarely be used to translate place. See the entry for details.**

placebo [pləˈsiːbəʊ] *(pl* placebos *or* placeboes) n *lit & fig* placebo *m*.

place card n *carte marquant la place des convives à table*.

place mat n set *m* (de table).

placement [ˈpleɪsmənt] n 1. [job-seeking] placement *m* ❯ **placement office** [US] UNIV centre *m* d'orientation (professionnelle) 2. [work experience] stage *m* en entreprise.

placename [ˈpleɪsneɪm] n toponyme *m* ❯ **the study of placenames** la toponymie.

placenta [pləˈsentə] *(pl* placentas *or* placentae [-tiː]) n placenta *m*.

place setting n couvert *m*.

placid [ˈplæsɪd] adj [person, attitude] placide ; [lake, town] tranquille, calme.

placidly [ˈplæsɪdlɪ] adv placidement.

plagiarism [ˈpleɪdʒjərɪzm] n plagiat *m*.

plagiarize, plagiarise [ˈpleɪdʒəraɪz] vt plagier.

plague [pleɪg] ❖ n 1. [bubonic] ❯ **the plague** la peste ❯ **to avoid sb like the plague** fuir qqn comme la peste 2. [epidemic] épidémie *f* 3. [scourge] fléau *m* ; BIBLE plaie *f* / *a plague of rats* une invasion de rats 4. *inf* [annoying person] enquiquineur *m*, -euse *f*. ❖ vt 1. [afflict] tourmenter / *the region is plagued by floods* la région est en proie aux inondations / *we are plagued with tourists in the summer* l'été, nous sommes envahis par les touristes / *we are plagued with mosquitoes in the summer* l'été, nous sommes infestés de moustiques 2. [pester] harceler / *to plague sb with telephone calls* harceler qqn de coups de téléphone.

plaice [pleɪs] *(pl* plaice *or* plaices) n carrelet *m*, plie *f*.

plaid [plæd] ❖ n 1. [fabric, design] tartan *m*, tissu *m* écossais 2. [worn over shoulder] plaid *m*. ❖ adj (en tissu) écossais.

plain [pleɪn] ❖ n 1. plaine *f* 2. [in knitting] maille *f* à l'endroit. ❖ adj 1. [not patterned, unmarked] uni / *plain blue wallpaper* papier peint bleu uni / *under plain cover* or *in a plain envelope* sous pli discret / *plain paper* a) [unheaded] papier sans en-tête b) [unruled] papier non réglé 2. [simple, not fancy] simple / *I like good plain cooking* j'aime la bonne cuisine bourgeoise or simple ; [with nothing added -omelette, rice, yoghurt] nature *(inv)* 3. [clear, obvious] clair, évident, manifeste / *the facts are plain* c'est clair, les choses sont claires / *she made her intentions plain* elle n'a pas caché ses intentions / *he made it plain to us that he wasn't interested* il nous a bien fait comprendre que cela ne l'intéressait pas / *I thought I'd made myself plain* je croyais avoir été assez clair / *in plain language* de manière claire 4. [blunt, unambiguous] franc (franche) / *let me be plain with you* je vais être franc avec vous / *I want a plain yes or no answer* je veux une réponse claire et nette / *the time has come for plain words* or *speaking* le moment est venu de parler franchement / *I told him in plain English what I thought* je lui ai dit ce que je pensais sans mâcher mes mots 5. [unattractive] pas très beau, quelconque 6. [in knitting] : *plain one, purl two* une maille à l'endroit, deux à l'envers. ❖ adv 1. [clearly] franchement, carrément / *you couldn't have put it any plainer* tu n'aurais pas pu être plus clair 2. [US] *inf* [utterly] complètement, carrément / *he's just plain crazy* il est complètement cinglé / *I just plain forgot!* j'ai tout bonnement oublié !

plain chocolate n chocolat *m* noir or à croquer.

plain clothes pl n ❯ **to be in** or **to wear plain clothes** être en civil. ❖ **plain-clothes** adj en civil.

plain flour n farine *f* (sans levure).

plainly [ˈpleɪnlɪ] adv 1. [manifestly] clairement, manifestement 2. [distinctly -remember, hear] clairement, distinctement 3. [simply -dress, lunch] simplement 4. [bluntly, unambiguously] franchement, carrément, sans ambages.

plainness [ˈpleɪnnɪs] n 1. [of clothes, cooking] simplicité *f* 2. [clarity, obviousness] clarté *f* 3. [unattractiveness] physique *m* quelconque or ingrat.

plain-paper adj [fax, printer] à papier ordinaire.

plain sailing n : *it's plain sailing from now on* maintenant ça va marcher tout seul or comme sur des roulettes.

plain-spoken [-ˈspəʊkn] adj qui a son franc-parler.

plain text n COMPUT texte seul.

plaintiff [ˈpleɪntɪf] n LAW demandeur *m*, -eresse *f*, plaignant *m*, -e *f*.

plaintive [ˈpleɪntɪv] adj [voice, sound] plaintif.

plait [plæt] ❖ n [of hair] natte *f*, tresse *f* ; [of straw] tresse *f*. ❖ vt [hair, rope, grass] natter, tresser ; [garland] tresser.

plan [plæn] (*pt & pp* planned, *cont* planning) ◆ n **1.** [strategy] plan *m*, projet *m* ‣ **to draw up** or **to make a plan** dresser or établir un plan ‣ **to go according to plan** se dérouler comme prévu or selon les prévisions **2.** [intention, idea] projet *m* / *I had to change my holiday plans* j'ai dû changer mes projets de vacances / *we had made plans to stay at a hotel* nous avions prévu de descendre à l'hôtel / *what are your plans for Monday?* qu'est-ce que tu as prévu pour lundi ? **3.** [diagram, map] plan *m* **4.** [outline - of book, essay, lesson] plan *m* ‣ **rough plan** canevas *m*, esquisse *f* **5.** ARCHIT plan *m*. ◆ vt **1.** [organize in advance - project] élaborer ; [-concert, conference] organiser, monter ; [-crime, holiday, trip, surprise] préparer ; ECON planifier / *plan your time carefully* organisez votre emploi du temps avec soin / *they're planning a surprise for you* ils te préparent une surprise / *everything went as planned* tout s'est déroulé comme prévu **2.** [intend] projeter / *we're planning to go to the States* nous projetons d'aller aux États-Unis **3.** [design - house, garden, town] concevoir, dresser les plans de **4.** [make outline of - book, essay] faire le plan de, esquisser ; [-lesson] préparer. ◆ vi faire des projets / *it is important to plan ahead* il est important de faire des projets pour l'avenir. ❖ **plan for** vt insep prévoir / *we didn't plan for this many people* nous n'avions pas prévu or nous n'attendions pas autant de monde / *you must plan for everything* vous devez tout prévoir or parer à toute éventualité. ❖ **plan on** vt insep **1.** [intend] projeter / *what are you planning on doing?* qu'est-ce que vous projetez de faire or vous avez l'intention de faire ? **2.** [expect] compter sur / *we hadn't planned on it raining* nous n'avions pas prévu qu'il pleuvrait. ❖ **plan out** vt sep préparer dans le détail.

plane [pleɪn] ◆ n **1.** [aeroplane] avion *m* ‣ **plane crash** accident d'avion **2.** ARCHIT, ART & MATH plan *m* **3.** [level, degree] plan *m* **4.** [tool] rabot *m* **5.** BOT ‣ **plane (tree)** platane *m*. ◆ adj [flat] plan, plat ; MATH plan. ◆ vi **1.** [glide] planer **2.** *inf* [travel by plane] voyager par or en avion. ◆ vt [in carpentry] ‣ **to plane (down)** raboter.

planet ['plænɪt] n planète *f*.

planetarium [ˌplænɪ'teərɪəm] (*pl* planetariums or planetaria [-rɪə]) n planétarium *m*.

planetary ['plænɪtrɪ] adj planétaire.

plank [plæŋk] ◆ n **1.** [board] planche *f* **2.** POL article *m* **3.** [UK] *inf* [stupid person] andouille *f*. ◆ vt [floor, room] planchéier.

plankton ['plæŋktən] n plancton *m*.

pl& MESSAGING written abbr of planned.

planned [plænd] adj [trip] projeté ; [murder] prémédité ; [baby] désiré, voulu ‣ **planned economy** ECON économie *f* planifiée or dirigée ‣ **planned obsolescence** INDUST obsolescence *f* planifiée, désuétude *f* calculée ‣ **planned parenthood** planning *m* familial.

planner ['plænər] n **1.** [gen & ECON] planificateur *m*, -trice *f* ‣ **(town) planner** urbaniste *mf* **2.** [in diary, on wall] planning *m*.

planning ['plænɪŋ] n **1.** [of concert, conference] organisation *f* ; [of lesson, menu] préparation *f* ; [of campaign] organisation *f*, préparation *f* **2.** [of economy, production] planification *f* **3.** [of town, city] urbanisme *m*.

planning permission n (U) permis *m* de construire.

plant [plɑːnt] ◆ n **1.** BOT plante *f* **2.** [factory] usine *f* **3.** (U) [industrial equipment] équipement *m*, matériel *m* ; [buildings and equipment] bâtiments et matériel **4.** *inf* [frame-up] coup *m* monté **5.** *inf* [infiltrator] agent *m* infiltré, taupe *f*. ◆ comp BOT ‣ **plant food** engrais *m* (*pour plantes d'appartement*) ‣ **plant life** flore *f*. ◆ vt **1.** [flowers, crops, seed] planter **2.** *inf* [firmly place] planter / *she planted herself in the doorway* elle se planta or se campa dans l'entrée **3.** *inf* [give -kick, blow] envoyer, donner ; [-kiss] planter

4. [in someone's mind] mettre, introduire / *her talk planted doubts in their minds* son discours a semé le doute dans leur esprit / *who planted that idea in your head?* qui t'a mis cette idée dans la tête ? **5.** [hide -bomb] mettre, placer ; [-microphone] cacher ; [infiltrate -spy] infiltrer / *he says the weapons were planted in his flat* il prétend que les armes ont été placées dans son appartement pour le compromettre ‣ **to plant evidence on sb** cacher un objet compromettant sur qqn pour l'incriminer. ❖ **plant out** vt sep [young plants] repiquer.

plantation [plæn'teɪʃn] n plantation *f* ‣ **sugar plantation** plantation de canne à sucre.

planter ['plɑːntər] n **1.** [person] planteur *m*, -euse *f* **2.** [machine] planteuse *f* **3.** [flowerpot holder] cache-pot *m inv* ; [for several plants] bac *m* à fleurs.

plant pot n pot *m* (de fleurs).

plaque [plɑːk] n **1.** [on wall, monument] plaque *f* **2.** DENT ‣ **(dental) plaque** plaque *f* dentaire.

plasma ['plæzmə] n MED & PHYS plasma *m*.

plasma screen n TV écran *m* (à) plasma.

plasma TV n télévision *f* à plasma.

plaster ['plɑːstər] ◆ n **1.** [for walls, modelling] plâtre *m* ‣ **plaster of Paris** plâtre de Paris or à mouler **2.** [for broken limbs] plâtre *m* / *her arm was in plaster* [UK] elle avait le bras dans le plâtre **3.** [UK] [for cut] ‣ **(sticking) plaster** pansement *m* (adhésif). ◆ comp [model, statue] de or en plâtre. ◆ vt **1.** CONSTR & MED plâtrer **2.** [smear -ointment, cream] enduire / *she had plastered make-up on her face* or *her face was plastered with make-up* elle avait une belle couche de maquillage sur la figure **3.** [make stick] coller **4.** [cover] ‣ **to plaster sthg with** couvrir qqch de / *her name was plastered over the front pages* son nom s'étalait en première page. ❖ **plaster over, plaster up** vt sep [hole, crack] boucher (avec du plâtre).

plasterboard ['plɑːstəbɔːd] n Placoplâtre® *m*.

plaster cast n **1.** MED plâtre *m* **2.** ART moule *m* (en plâtre).

plastered ['plɑːstəd] adj *inf* [drunk] bourré ‣ **to get plastered** se soûler.

plasterer ['plɑːstərər] n plâtrier *m*.

plastering ['plɑːstərɪŋ] n CONSTR plâtrage *m*.

plastic ['plæstɪk] ◆ n **1.** [material] plastique *m*, matière *f* plastique **2.** (U) *inf* [credit cards] cartes *fpl* de crédit. ◆ adj [made of plastic] en or de plastique / *plastic cups* gobelets *mpl* en plastique.

plastic bullet n balle *f* en plastique.

plastic explosive n plastic *m*.

Plasticine® ['plæstɪsiːn] n pâte *f* à modeler.

plasticize, plasticise ['plæstɪsaɪz] vt plastifier.

plastic money n (U) *inf* cartes *fpl* de crédit.

plastic surgeon n [cosmetic] chirurgien *m*, -enne *f* esthétique ; [therapeutic] plasticien *m*, -enne *f*.

plastic surgery n [cosmetic] chirurgie *f* esthétique ; [therapeutic] chirurgie *f* plastique or réparatrice / *she had plastic surgery on her nose* elle s'est fait refaire le nez.

plastic wrap n [US] film *m* alimentaire.

plate [pleɪt] ◆ n **1.** [for eating] assiette *f* ; [for serving] plat *m* / *he ate a huge plate of spaghetti* il a mangé une énorme assiette de spaghetti ‣ **to hand sthg to sb on a plate** donner or apporter qqch à qqn sur un plateau (d'argent) / *she was handed the job on a plate* on lui a offert cet emploi sans qu'elle ait à lever le petit doigt ‣ **to have a lot on one's plate** avoir du pain sur la planche **2.** [piece of metal, glass, etc.] plaque *f* ; [rolled metal] tôle *f* **3.** [with inscription] plaque *f* **4.** [on cooker] plaque *f* (de cuisson) **5.** [dishes, cutlery -silver] vaisselle *f* en argent ; [-gold] vaisselle *f* en or **6.** [coated metal] plaqué *m* ; [metal coating] placage *m*. ◆ vt **1.** [coat with metal] plaquer **2.** [cover with metal plates] garnir de plaques ; [armour plate] blinder.

plateau ['plætəʊ] (*pl* **plateaus** *or* **plateaux** [-təʊz]) n GEOG & *fig* plateau *m* ▶ **to reach a plateau** [activity, process] atteindre un palier.

plateful ['pleɪtfʊl] n assiettée *f*, assiette *f*.

plate glass n verre *m* (à vitres). ◆ **plate-glass** adj en verre ▶ **plate glass window** vitrine *f*.

plate rack n égouttoir *m*.

plate tectonics n (*U*) tectonique *f* des plaques.

platform ['plætfɔːm] n **1.** [stage] estrade *f* ; [for speakers] tribune *f* ; *fig* tribune *f* **2.** [raised structure] plateforme *f* ▶ **loading platform** quai *m* de chargement **3.** [at station] quai *m* **4.** POL [programme] plate-forme *f* ▶ **electoral platform** plate-forme électorale **5.** UK [on bus] plate-forme *f* **6.** COMPUT plate-forme *f*.

platform-agnostic adj multiplateformes.

platform shoes pl n chaussures *fpl* à semelle compensée.

platform soles pl n semelles *fpl* compensées.

platform ticket n ticket *m* de quai.

plating ['pleɪtɪŋ] n [gen] placage *m* ; [in gold] dorage *m*, dorure *f* ; [in silver] argentage *m*, argenture *f* ; [in nickel] nickelage *m*.

platinum ['plætɪnəm] ◆ n platine *m*. ◆ comp [jewellery, pen] en platine. ◆ adj [colour] platine (*inv*).

platinum blonde n blonde *f* platine. ◆ **platinum-blonde** adj [blond] platine (*inv*).

platinum disc, platinum record n MUS disque *m* de platine.

platitude ['plætɪtjuːd] n [trite remark] platitude *f*, lieu *m* commun.

platonic [plə'tɒnɪk] adj [love, relationship] platonique.

platoon [plə'tuːn] n MIL section *f* ; [of bodyguards, firemen, etc.] armée *f*.

platter ['plætər] n **1.** [for serving] plat *m* ▶ **seafood platter** plateau *m* de fruits de mer **2.** US *inf* [record] disque *m*.

platypus ['plætɪpəs] n ornithorynque *m*.

plaudits ['plɔːdɪts] pl n *fml* **1.** [applause] applaudissements *mpl* **2.** [praise] éloges *mpl*.

plausibility [,plɔːzə'bɪlətɪ] n plausibilité *f*.

plausible ['plɔːzəbl] adj [excuse, alibi, theory] plausible ; [person] crédible.

plausibly ['plɔːzəblɪ] adv de façon convaincante.

play [pleɪ] ◆ vt **1.** [games, cards] jouer à / **to play tennis / poker / dominoes** jouer au tennis / au poker / aux dominos / **how about playing some golf after work?** si on faisait une partie de golf après le travail ? / **do you play any sports?** pratiquez-vous un sport ? ▶ **to play the game** a) SPORT jouer selon les règles b) *fig* jouer le jeu ▶ **to play it cool** *inf* ne pas s'énerver, garder son calme ▶ **to play (it) safe** ne pas prendre de risque, jouer la sécurité **2.** [opposing player or team] jouer contre, rencontrer / **I played him at chess** j'ai joué aux échecs avec lui **3.** [match] jouer, disputer ▶ **to play a match against sb** disputer un match avec or contre qqn / **the next game will be played on Sunday** la prochaine partie aura lieu dimanche **4.** [card, chess piece] jouer **5.** [shot, stroke] jouer / **he played the ball to me** il m'a envoyé la balle **6.** [gamble on - stock market, slot machine] jouer à / **he played the red / the black** il a misé sur le rouge / le noir **7.** [joke, trick] jouer ▶ **to play a trick / joke on sb** jouer un tour / faire une farce à qqn **8.** CIN & THEAT [act - role, part] jouer, interpréter / **who played the godfather in Coppola's film?** qui jouait le rôle du parrain dans le film de Coppola ? ; *fig* ▶ **to play a part** or **role in sthg** prendre part or contribuer à qqch **9.** CIN & THEAT [perform at - theatre, club] : **they played Broadway last year** ils ont joué à Broadway l'année dernière **10.** [act as] : **to play the fool** faire l'idiot or l'imbécile / **to play the hero** jouer les héros **11.** [instrument] jouer de ; [note, melody, waltz] jouer / **to play the blues** jouer du blues / **they're playing our song / Strauss** ils jouent notre chanson / du Strauss **12.** [put on - record, tape] passer, mettre ; [- radio] mettre, allumer ; [- tapedeck, jukebox] faire marcher **13.** [direct - beam, nozzle] diriger. ◆ vi **1.** jouer, s'amuser ; [frolic - children, animals] folâtrer, s'ébattre **2.** GAMES & SPORT jouer / **it's her (turn) to play** c'est à elle de jouer, c'est (à) son tour ▶ **to play in a tournament** participer à un tournoi ▶ **to play into sb's hands** faire le jeu de qqn ▶ **to play for time** essayer de gagner du temps **3.** [gamble] jouer ▶ **to play for drinks / for money** jouer les consommations / de l'argent **4.** MUS [person, band, instrument] jouer ; [record] passer / **I heard a guitar playing** j'entendais le son d'une guitare ; [radio, stereo] : **a radio was playing upstairs** on entendait une radio en haut **5.** CIN & THEAT [act] jouer **6.** CIN & THEAT [show, play, film] se jouer **7.** [feign] faire semblant ▶ **to play dead** faire le mort **8.** [breeze, sprinkler, light] ▶ **to play (on)** jouer (sur) / **a smile played on** or **about** or **over his lips** un sourire jouait sur ses lèvres. ◆ n **1.** [fun, recreation] jeu *m* ▶ **play on words** jeu *m* de mots, calembour *m* **2.** SPORT [course, conduct of game] jeu *m* / **play was interrupted by a shower** le match a été interrompu par une averse / **there was some nice play from Brooks** Brooks a réussi de belles actions or a bien joué **3.** [turn] tour *m* **4.** [manoeuvre] stratagème *m* ▶ **to make a play for sthg** : **he is making a play for the presidency** il se lance dans la course à la présidence ▶ **to make a play for sb** : **she made a play for my boyfriend** elle a fait des avances à mon copain **5.** [gambling] jeu *m* **6.** [activity, interaction] jeu *m* ▶ **to come into play** entrer en jeu ▶ **to bring sthg into play** mettre qqch en jeu **7.** THEAT pièce *f* (de théâtre) ▶ **to be in a play** jouer dans une pièce / **it's been ages since I've seen** or **gone to see a play** ça fait des années que je ne suis pas allé au théâtre ▶ **television play** dramatique *f* **8.** TECH [slack, give] jeu *m* ▶ **to give** or **to allow full play to sthg** *fig* donner libre cours à qqch. ◆ **play about** vi UK [have fun - children] jouer, s'amuser ; [frolic] s'ébattre, folâtrer. ◆ **play about with** vt insep **1.** [fiddle with, tamper with] ▶ **to play about with sthg** jouer avec or tripoter qqch **2.** [juggle - statistics, figures] jouer avec ; [consider - possibilities, alternatives] envisager, considérer. ◆ **play along** vi [cooperate] coopérer ▶ **to play along with sb** or **with sb's plans** entrer dans le jeu de qqn. ◆ **play around** vi **1.** = **play about 2.** *inf* [have several lovers] coucher à droite et à gauche. ◆ **play around with** = **play about with**. ◆ **play at** vt insep **1.** [subj: child] jouer à / **just what do you think you're playing at?** *fig* à quoi tu joues exactement ? **2.** [dally in - politics, journalism] faire en dilettante. ◆ **play back** vt sep [cassette, film] repasser. ◆ **play down** vt sep [role, difficulty, victory] minimiser / **we've been asked to play down the political aspects of the affair** on nous a demandé de ne pas insister sur le côté politique de l'affaire. ◆ **play off** vi [teams, contestants] jouer les barrages. ◆ **play off against** vt sep : **he played Bill off against his father** il a monté Bill contre son père. ◆ **play on** ◆ vt insep [weakness, naivety, trust] jouer sur. ◆ vi continuer à jouer. ◆ **play up** ◆ vt sep **1.** [exaggerate - role, importance] exagérer ; [stress] souligner, insister sur **2.** UK *inf* [bother] tracasser / **my back is playing me up** mon dos me joue encore des tours. ◆ vi UK *inf* [cause problems] : **he plays up when his mother leaves** il pique une crise chaque fois que sa mère s'en va / **the car is playing up at the moment** la voiture fait des siennes en ce moment. ◆ **play with** vt insep **1.** [toy with - pencil, hair] jouer avec / **he only played with his meat** il a à peine touché à sa viande ▶ **to play with fire** jouer avec le feu **2.** [manipulate - words] jouer sur ; [- rhyme, language] manier

3. [consider - idea] caresser / *we're playing with the idea of buying a house* nous pensons à acheter une maison **4.** [treat casually - someone's affections] traiter à la légère **5.** [have available - money, time] disposer de / *how much time have we got to play with?* de combien de temps disposons-nous ?

playable ['pleɪəbl] adj jouable.

play-act vi **1.** *fig* [pretend] jouer la comédie / *stop play-acting!* arrête ton cinéma or de jouer la comédie ! **2.** [act in plays] faire du théâtre.

play-acting n **1.** [pretence] (pure) comédie f *fig*, cinéma m *fig* **2.** [acting in play] théâtre m.

playback ['pleɪbæk] n **1.** [replay] enregistrement m **2.** [function] lecture f / *put it on playback* mettez-le en position lecture ▸ **playback head** tête f de lecture.

playbill ['pleɪbɪl] n **1.** [poster] affiche f (de théâtre) **2.** [programme] programme m.

playboy ['pleɪbɔɪ] n play-boy m.

Play-Doh® ['pleɪ,dəʊ] n *sorte de pâte à modeler.*

player ['pleɪə'] n **1.** [of game, sport] joueur m, -euse f / *are you a poker player?* est-ce que vous jouez au poker ? **2.** [of musical instrument] joueur m, -euse f **3.** [participant] participant m, -e f / *France has been a major player in this debate* la France a eu un rôle clé dans ce débat **4.** [actor] acteur m, -trice f.

playful ['pleɪfʊl] adj [lively - person] gai, espiègle ; [- animal] espiègle ; [good-natured - nudge, answer] taquin / *to be in a playful mood* être d'humeur enjouée.

playfully ['pleɪfʊlɪ] adv [answer, remark] d'un ton taquin ; [act] avec espièglerie.

playgoer ['pleɪ,gəʊə'] n amateur m de théâtre.

playground ['pleɪgraʊnd] n [at school] cour f de récréation ; [in park] aire f de jeu.

playgroup ['pleɪgruːp] n *réunion régulière d'enfants d'âge préscolaire généralement surveillés par une mère.*

playhouse ['pleɪhaʊs] (pl [-haʊzɪz]) n **1.** [theatre] théâtre m **2.** US [children's] maison f de poupée.

playing ['pleɪɪŋ] n MUS : *the pianist's playing was excellent* le pianiste jouait merveilleusement bien / *guitar playing is becoming more popular* de plus en plus de gens jouent de la guitare.

playing card ['pleɪɪŋ-] n carte f à jouer.

playing field ['pleɪɪŋ] n UK terrain m de sport ▸ **to have a level playing field** *fig* être sur un pied d'égalité.

playlist ['pleɪlɪst] n RADIO playlist f (*programme des disques à passer*).

playmate ['pleɪmeɪt] n camarade mf (de jeu).

play-off n SPORT (match m de) barrage m.

playpen ['pleɪpen] n parc m (pour bébés).

playroom ['pleɪrum] n [in house] salle f de jeu.

playschool ['pleɪskuːl] = playgroup.

plaything ['pleɪθɪŋ] n *lit & fig* jouet m.

playtime ['pleɪtaɪm] n récréation f / *at playtime* pendant la récréation.

playwright ['pleɪraɪt] n dramaturge m, auteur m dramatique.

plaza ['plɑːzə] n **1.** [open square] place f **2.** US [shopping centre] centre m commercial ▸ **toll plaza** péage m (d'autoroute).

plc, PLC (abbr of **public limited company**) n UK ≃ SARL f.

plea [pliː] n **1.** [appeal] appel m, supplication f **2.** LAW [argument] argument m ; [defence] défense f ▸ **to enter a plea of guilty / not guilty / insanity** plaider coupable / non coupable / la démence **3.** [excuse, pretext] excuse f, prétexte f.

plead [pliːd] (UK pt & pp **pleaded** ; US pt & pp **pleaded** or **pled** [pled]) ◆ vi **1.** [beg] supplier ▸ **to plead for forgiveness** implorer le pardon / *she pleaded to be given more time* elle supplia qu'on lui accorde plus de temps ▸ **to plead with sb** supplier or implorer qqn **2.** LAW plaider ▸ **to plead guilty / not guilty** plaider coupable / non coupable. ◆ vt **1.** [beg] implorer, supplier **2.** [gen & LAW] plaider ▸ **to plead sb's case** a) défendre qqn b) *fig* plaider la cause de qqn ▸ **to plead self-defence** plaider la légitime défense **3.** [put forward as excuse] invoquer, alléguer ; [pretend] prétexter / *we could always plead ignorance* nous pourrions toujours prétendre que nous ne savions pas.

pleasant ['pleznt] adj **1.** [enjoyable, attractive] agréable, plaisant / *thank you for a most pleasant evening* merci pour une très agréable soirée / *it was pleasant to be out in the countryside again* c'était agréable de se retrouver de nouveau à la campagne **2.** [friendly - person, attitude, smile] aimable, agréable / *she was very pleasant to us as a rule* elle était en général très aimable à notre égard.

pleasantly ['plezntlɪ] adv **1.** [attractively] agréablement / *the room was pleasantly arranged* la pièce était aménagée de façon agréable **2.** [enjoyably] agréablement / *pleasantly surprised* agréablement surpris, surpris en bien **3.** [kindly - speak, smile] aimablement.

pleasantry ['plezntrɪ] (pl **pleasantries**) n [agreeable remark] propos m aimable ▸ **to exchange pleasantries** échanger des civilités.

please [pliːz] ◆ adv **1.** [requesting or accepting] s'il vous / te plaît / *another cup of tea? — (yes) please!* une autre tasse de thé ? — oui, s'il vous plaît ! or volontiers ! / *may I sit beside you? — please do* puis-je m'asseoir près de vous ? — mais bien sûr / *please, make yourselves at home* faites comme chez vous, je vous en prie / *please carry on* continuez, s'il vous plaît or je vous en prie **2.** [pleading] : *please don't hurt him* je vous en prie, ne lui faites pas de mal **3.** [remonstrating] : *Henry, please, we've got guests!* Henry, voyons, nous avons des invités ! **4.** [hoping] : *please let them arrive safely!* faites qu'ils arrivent sains et saufs ! ◆ vt **1.** [give enjoyment to] plaire à, faire plaisir à ; [satisfy] contenter / *he only did it to please his mother* il ne l'a fait que pour faire plaisir à sa mère / *you can't please everybody* on ne peut pas faire plaisir à tout le monde **2.** PHR ▸ **to please oneself** faire comme on veut / *please yourself!* comme tu veux ! ◆ vi **1.** [give pleasure] plaire, faire plaisir ▸ **to be eager to please** chercher à faire plaisir **2.** [choose] : *she does as* or *what she pleases* elle fait ce qu'elle veut or ce qui lui plaît / *I'll talk to whoever I please!* je parlerai avec qui je veux !

pleased [pliːzd] adj content, heureux ▸ **to be pleased with sthg / sb** être content de qqch / qqn / *you're looking very pleased with yourself!* tu as l'air très content de toi ! / *I am not at all pleased with the results* je ne suis pas du tout satisfait des résultats / *I'm very pleased to be here this evening* je suis très heureux d'être ici ce soir / *I'm very pleased (that) you could come* je suis ravi que tu aies pu venir ▸ **pleased to meet you!** enchanté (de faire votre connaissance) !

pleasing ['pliːzɪŋ] adj agréable, plaisant.

pleasurable ['pleʒərəbl] adj agréable, plaisant.

pleasure ['pleʒə'] n [enjoyment, delight] plaisir m ▸ **to write / to paint for pleasure** écrire / peindre pour le plaisir ▸ **to take** or **to find pleasure in doing sthg** prendre plaisir or éprouver du plaisir à faire qqch / *I'd accept your invitation with pleasure, but...* j'accepterais votre invitation avec plaisir, seulement... / *another beer? — with pleasure!* une autre bière ? — avec plaisir or volontiers ! / *thank you very much — my pleasure!* or *it's a pleasure!* merci beaucoup — je vous en prie ! / *it's a great pleasure (to meet you)* ravi de faire votre connaissance / *Mr and Mrs Evans request the pleasure of your company at their son's wed-*

ding fml : M. et Mme Evans vous prient de leur faire l'honneur d'assister au mariage de leur fils. ◆ comp [yacht] de plaisance ; [park] de loisirs ; [cruise, tour] d'agrément ▶ **pleasure boat** bateau m de plaisance ▶ **pleasure trip** excursion f.

pleat [pliːt] ◆ n pli m. ◆ vt plisser.

pleated [ˈpliːtɪd] adj plissé / a pleated skirt une jupe plissée.

pleb [pleb] n pej [plebeian] plébéien m, -enne f / it's not for the plebs ce n'est pas pour n'importe qui !!

plebiscite [ˈplebɪsaɪt] n plébiscite m.

plectrum [ˈplektrəm] (pl plectrums or plectra [-trə]) n médiator m, plectre m.

pled [pled] pt & pp US → plead.

pledge [pledʒ] ◆ vt 1. [promise] promettre 2. [offer as security] donner en garantie ; [pawn] mettre en gage, engager. ◆ n 1. [promise] promesse f / I am under a pledge of secrecy j'ai juré de garder le secret ▶ **to sign** or **to take the pledge** [stop drinking] cesser de boire 2. [security, collateral] gage m, garantie f / in pledge en gage 3. [token, symbol] gage m.

plenary [ˈpliːnəri] ◆ adj 1. POL ▶ **plenary powers** pleins pouvoirs mpl 2. [meeting] plénier / in plenary session en séance plénière. ◆ n [plenary meeting] réunion f plénière ; [plenary session] séance f plénière.

plentiful [ˈplentɪfʊl] adj [gen] abondant ; [meal] copieux / we have a plentiful supply of food nous avons de la nourriture en abondance.

plenty [ˈplenti] ◆ pron 1. [enough] (largement) assez, plus qu'assez / no thanks, I've got plenty non merci, j'en ai (largement) assez / £20 should be plenty 20 livres devraient suffire (amplement) / we've got plenty of time nous avons largement le temps 2. [a great deal] beaucoup. ◆ n liter [abundance] abondance f. ◆ adv inf 1. [a lot] beaucoup / there's plenty more food in the fridge il y a encore plein de choses à manger dans le frigo 2. [easily] : the room is plenty big enough for two la pièce est largement assez grande pour deux. ◆ det US regional [a lot of] plein de. ❖ **in plenty** adv phr en abondance.

plethora [ˈpleθərə] n pléthore f.

pleurisy [ˈplʊərəsi] n (U) pleurésie f.

Plexiglas® [ˈpleksɪglɑːs] n Plexiglas® m.

pliable [ˈplaɪəbl] adj 1. [material] flexible, pliable 2. [person] malléable, accommodant, docile.

pliant [ˈplaɪənt] = pliable.

pliers [ˈplaɪəz] pl n pince f ▶ **a pair of pliers** une pince.

plight [plaɪt] n [bad situation] situation f désespérée.

plimsoll [ˈplɪmsəl] n UK tennis m.

plinth [plɪnθ] n [of statue] socle m ; [of column, pedestal] plinthe f.

PLO (abbr of Palestine Liberation Organization) pr n OLP f.

plod [plɒd] (pt & pp plodded, cont plodding) ◆ vi 1. [walk] marcher lourdement 2. inf [carry on] : he'd been plodding along in the same job for years ça faisait des années qu'il faisait le même boulot / she kept plodding on until it was finished elle s'est acharnée jusqu'à ce que ce soit fini. ◆ n : we maintained a steady plod nous avons gardé un pas régulier.

plodder [ˈplɒdə] n pej : he's a bit of a plodder il est plutôt lent à la tâche.

plodding [ˈplɒdɪŋ] adj pej [walk, rhythm, style] lourd, pesant ; [worker] lent.

plonk [plɒŋk] ◆ n 1. [heavy sound] bruit m sourd 2. UK inf [cheap wine] piquette f. ◆ vt inf [put down] poser

bruyamment / she plonked herself down on the sofa elle s'est affalée sur le canapé. ◆ vi ▶ **to plonk away on the piano** jouer du piano (mal et assez fort).

plop [plɒp] (pt & pp plopped, cont plopping) ◆ n plouf m, floc m. ◆ vi [splash] faire plouf or floc. ◆ vt [put] poser, mettre.

plot [plɒt] (pt & pp plotted, cont plotting) ◆ n 1. [conspiracy] complot m, conspiration f 2. [story line - of novel, play] intrigue f 3. [piece of land] terrain m 4. US [graph] graphique m 5. US ARCHIT plan m. ◆ vt 1. [conspire] comploter 2. [course, position] déterminer 3. [graph] tracer, faire le tracé de 4. [map, plan] lever. ◆ vi [conspire] comploter, conspirer ▶ **to plot against** conspirer contre.

plotter [ˈplɒtə] n 1. [conspirator] conspirateur m, -trice f 2. [device - gen] traceur m ; COMPUT table f traçante, traceur m de courbes.

plough UK, **plow** US [plaʊ] ◆ n 1. charrue f 2. ASTRON ▶ **the Plough** la Grande Ourse. ◆ vt 1. [land] labourer ; [furrow] creuser 2. fig [invest] investir ▶ **to plough money into sthg** investir de l'argent dans qqch. ◆ vi 1. AGR labourer 2. [crash] emboutir, percuter / the truck ploughed into the wall le camion percuta le mur. ❖ **plough back** vt sep [profits] réinvestir. ❖ **plough in** vt sep [earth, crops, stubble] enfouir (en labourant). ❖ **plough on** vi continuer péniblement or laborieusement. ❖ **plough through** vt insep [documents, papers] éplucher. ❖ **plough under** = plough in. ❖ **plough up** vt sep 1. AGR [field, footpath] labourer 2. [rip up] labourer.

ploughback UK, **plowback** US [ˈplaʊbæk] n FIN bénéfices mpl réinvestis.

ploughman UK, **plowman** US [ˈplaʊmən] (pl ploughmen [-mən] ; US pl plowmen [-mən]) n laboureur m.

ploughman's (lunch) n assiette de fromage, de pain et de pickles (généralement servie dans un pub).

ploughshare UK, **plowshare** US [ˈplaʊʃeə] n soc m.

plow US = plough.

ploy [plɔɪ] n [stratagem, trick] ruse f, stratagème m.

PLR (abbr of Public Lending Right) pr n droit d'auteur versé pour les ouvrages prêtés par les bibliothèques.

PLS (written abbr of please), **PLZ** MESSAGING stp, svp.

pluck [plʌk] ◆ vt 1. [pick - flower, fruit] cueillir 2. [pull] tirer, retirer 3. [chicken] plumer ; [feathers] arracher 4. [instrument] pincer les cordes de ; [string] pincer 5. [eyebrow] épiler. ◆ vi : he plucked at my sleeve il m'a tiré par la manche / she was plucking at (the strings of) her guitar elle pinçait les cordes de sa guitare. ◆ n 1. [courage] courage m 2. [tug] petite secousse f. ❖ **pluck up** vt sep 1. [uproot] arracher, extirper 2. fig ▶ **to pluck up (one's) courage** prendre son courage à deux mains ▶ **to pluck up the courage to do sthg** trouver le courage de faire qqch.

plucky [ˈplʌki] (compar pluckier, superl pluckiest) adj courageux.

plug [plʌg] (pt & pp plugged, cont plugging) ◆ n 1. ELEC [on appliance, cable] fiche f, prise f (mâle) ; [socket - in wall] prise f (de courant) 2. [stopper - gen] bouchon m ; [- in barrel] bonde f ; [- for nose] tampon m 3. [for sink, bath] bonde f 4. AUTO ▶ **(spark) plug** bougie f 5. inf [advertising] coup m de pub 6. US ▶ **(fire) plug** bouche f d'incendie. ◆ vt 1. [block - hole, gap] boucher ; [- leak] colmater 2. [insert] enficher / plug the cable into the socket branchez le câble sur la prise 3. inf [advertise] faire de la pub à 4. US v inf [shoot] flinguer. ❖ **plug away** vi travailler dur. ❖ **plug in** vt sep brancher. ◆ vi 1. se brancher / the TV plugs in over there la télé se branche là-bas 2. US fig : we try to plug in to people's needs nous essayons d'être à l'écoute des besoins de la population. ❖ **plug into** ◆ vt sep [connect] : *to plug sthg into sthg* brancher qqch sur qqch. ◆ vt insep [connect] : *the TV plugs into that socket* la télé se branche sur cette prise.

plug-and-play ◆ n COMPUT plug-and-play m. ◆ adj COMPUT plug-and-play.

plughole ['plʌghəʊl] n trou m d'écoulement ▶ *to go down the plughole* UK inf : *that's all our work gone down the plughole!* tout notre travail est fichu !!

plug-in ◆ adj [radio] qui se branche sur le secteur ;; [accessory for computer, stereo, etc.] qui se branche sur l'appareil. ◆ n COMPUT périphérique m prêt à brancher.

plum [plʌm] ◆ n 1. [fruit] prune f 2. ▶ **plum (tree)** prunier m 3. [colour] couleur f lie-de-vin. ◆ comp [tart] aux prunes. ◆ adj 1. [colour] lie-de-vin (*inv*), prune (*inv*) 2. inf [desirable] : *it's a plum job* c'est un boulot en or.

plumage ['plu:mɪdʒ] n plumage m.

plumb [plʌm] ◆ n 1. [weight] plomb m 2. [verticality] aplomb m / *the wall is out of plumb* le mur n'est pas d'aplomb or à l'aplomb. ◆ adj [vertical] vertical, à l'aplomb. ◆ adv 1. [in a vertical position] à l'aplomb, d'aplomb ▶ **plumb with** d'aplomb avec 2. UK inf [exactly, right] exactement, en plein 3. US inf [utterly, completely] complètement, tout à fait. ◆ vt [measure depth of] sonder / *his films plumb the depths of bad taste* ses films sont de très mauvais goût. ❖ **plumb in** vt sep UK effectuer le raccordement de ;; [washing machine] raccorder.

plumber ['plʌmə^r] n [workman] plombier m.

plumbing ['plʌmɪŋ] n 1. [job] plomberie f 2. [pipes] plomberie f, tuyauterie f.

plumb line n CONSTR fil m à plomb ;; NAUT sonde f.

plume [plu:m] n 1. [feather] plume f 2. [on helmet] plumet m, panache m ;; [on hat] plumet m ;; [on woman's hat] plume f 3. [of smoke] volute f ;; [of water] jet m.

plummet ['plʌmɪt] vi 1. [plunge, dive] tomber, plonger, piquer 2. [drop, go down - price, rate, amount] chuter, dégringoler.

plummy ['plʌmɪ] (*compar* plummier, *superl* plummiest) adj 1. UK pej [voice, accent] snob 2. [colour] prune (*inv*).

plump [plʌmp] ◆ adj [person] rondelet, dodu ;; [arms, legs] dodu, potelé ;; [fowl] dodu, bien gras ;; [fruit] charnu. ◆ vt [pillow, cushion] retaper. ❖ **plump down** vt sep : *she plumped herself // her bag down next to me* elle s'est affalée // a laissé tomber son sac à côté de moi. ❖ **plump for** vt insep inf arrêter son choix sur, opter en faveur de. ❖ **plump up** vt sep = plump (vt).

plum pudding n plum-pudding m.

plum tomato n olivette f.

plunder ['plʌndə^r] ◆ vt piller. ◆ n 1. [booty] butin m 2. [act of pillaging] pillage m.

plunderer ['plʌndərə^r] n pillard m, -e f.

plundering ['plʌndərɪŋ] ◆ n pillage m. ◆ adj pillard.

plunge [plʌndʒ] ◆ vi 1. [dive] plonger 2. [throw o.s.] se jeter, se précipiter ;; [fall, drop] tomber, chuter / *the bus plunged into the river* le bus est tombé dans la rivière / *to plunge to one's death* faire une chute mortelle 3. fig : *sales have plunged by 30%* les ventes ont chuté de 30 %. ◆ vt 1. [immerse] plonger 2. fig plonger / *he was plunged into despair by the news* la nouvelle l'a plongé dans le désespoir / *the office was plunged into darkness* le bureau fut plongé dans l'obscurité. ◆ n 1. [dive] plongeon m ▶ *to take the plunge* se jeter à l'eau 2. [fall, drop] chute f.

plunge pool n mini-piscine f.

plunger ['plʌndʒə^r] n 1. [for sinks, drains] ventouse f, déboucheur m 2. [piston] piston m.

plunging ['plʌndʒɪŋ] adj plongeant.

pluperfect [,plu:'pɜ:fɪkt] ◆ adj ▶ **the pluperfect tense** le plus-que-parfait. ◆ n plus-que-parfait m / *in the pluperfect* au plus-que-parfait.

plural ['plʊərəl] ◆ adj 1. GRAM [form, ending] pluriel, du pluriel ;; [noun] au pluriel 2. [multiple] multiple ;; [heterogeneous] hétérogène, pluriel. ◆ n GRAM pluriel m / *in the plural* au pluriel.

pluralism ['plʊərəlɪzm] n 1. [gen & PHILOS] pluralisme m 2. [holding of several offices] cumul m.

pluralist ['plʊərəlɪst] n [gen & PHILOS] pluraliste mf.

pluralistic [,plʊərə'lɪstɪk] adj pluraliste.

plurality [plʊə'rælətɪ] (*pl* pluralities) n 1. [multiplicity] pluralité f 2. US POL majorité f relative 3. = pluralism.

plus [plʌs] (*pl* pluses *or* plusses) ◆ prep 1. MATH plus 2. [as well as] plus. ◆ adj 1. ELEC & MATH positif 2. [good, positive] positif / *on the plus side, it's near the shops* un des avantages, c'est que c'est près des magasins / *it certainly is a big plus point* c'est incontestablement un gros avantage 3. [after noun] [over, more than] : *children of twelve plus* les enfants de douze ans et plus / *B plus* [in school marks] B plus. ◆ n 1. MATH plus m 2. [bonus, advantage] plus m, avantage m. ◆ conj inf (et) en plus.

plus fours pl n pantalon m de golf.

plush [plʌʃ] ◆ adj 1. inf [luxurious] luxueux 2. [made of plush] en peluche. ◆ n peluche f.

plus sign n signe m plus.

Pluto ['plu:təʊ] pr n Pluton.

plutocrat ['plu:təkræt] n ploutocrate mf.

plutonium [plu:'təʊnɪəm] n plutonium m.

ply [plaɪ] (*pl* plies, *pt* & *pp* plied) ◆ n 1. [thickness - gen] épaisseur f ;; [layer - of plywood] pli m ;; [strand - of rope, wool] brin m 2. inf = plywood. ◆ vt 1. [supply insistently] ▶ *to ply sb with sthg* : *she plied us with food all evening* elle nous a gavés toute la soirée 2. liter [perform, practise] exercer. ◆ vi 1. [seek work] ▶ *to ply for hire* [taxi] prendre des clients 2. [travel - ship, boat] ▶ *to ply between* faire la navette entre.

plywood ['plaɪwʊd] n contreplaqué m.

p.m. (*abbr of* post meridiem) adv : *3 p.m.* 3 h de l'après-midi, 15 h / *11 p.m.* 11 h du soir, 23 h.

PM n abbr of Prime Minister.

PMS (abbr of premenstrual syndrome) = PMT.

PMT (abbr of premenstrual tension) n syndrome m prémenstruel.

pneumatic [nju:'mætɪk] adj pneumatique ▶ **pneumatic brakes** freins mpl à air comprimé.

pneumatic drill n UK marteau piqueur m.

pneumonia [nju:'məʊnjə] n (U) pneumonie f / *you'll catch* or *get pneumonia!* tu vas attraper une pneumonie !!

po [pəʊ] (*pl* pos) n UK inf pot m (de chambre).

PO 1. written abbr of post office **2.** written abbr of postal order.

POA ◆ pr n (abbr of Prison Officers' Association) syndicat des agents pénitentiaires en Grande-Bretagne. ◆ n US abbr of power of attorney.

poach [pəʊtʃ] ◆ vt 1. [hunt illegally] prendre en braconnant 2. fig [steal - idea] voler ;; [- employee] débaucher 3. CULIN pocher ▶ **poached egg** œuf m poché. ◆ vi braconner.

poacher ['pəʊtʃə^r] n 1. [person] braconnier m 2. CULIN pocheuse f ▶ **egg poacher** pocheuse.

poaching ['pəʊtʃɪŋ] n braconnage m.

POB, PO Box (abbr of **post office box**) n boîte f postale, BP f.

pocket ['pɒkɪt] ◆ n **1.** [on clothing] poche f; [on car door] compartiment m / I went through his pockets j'ai fouillé or regardé dans ses poches ▸ **to line one's pockets** se remplir les poches, s'en mettre plein les poches ▸ **to be out of pocket** en être de sa poche **2.** fig [financial resources] portefeuille m, porte-monnaie m **3.** [small area] poche f / pocket of air trou m d'air **4.** [on billiard or pool table] blouse f. ◆ comp [diary, camera, revolver, etc.] de poche. ◆ vt **1.** [put in one's pocket] mettre dans sa poche, empocher **2.** [steal] : somebody must have pocketed the money quelqu'un a dû mettre l'argent dans sa poche **3.** [in billiards, pool] mettre dans le trou or la blouse spec **4.** US POL ▸ **to pocket a bill** garder un projet de loi sous le coude pour l'empêcher d'être adopté.

pocket billiards n billard m américain.

pocketbook ['pɒkɪtbʊk] n **1.** [notebook] calepin m, carnet m **2.** US [handbag] pochette f.

pocket calculator n calculatrice f de poche.

pocketful ['pɒkɪtfʊl] n poche f pleine.

pocket-handkerchief n mouchoir m de poche.

pocketknife ['pɒkɪtnaɪf] (pl **pocketknives** [-naɪvz]) n canif m.

pocket money n UK argent m de poche.

pocket-size(d) adj **1.** [book, revolver, etc.] de poche **2.** [tiny] tout petit, minuscule.

pockmark ['pɒkmɑːk] n [on surface] marque f, petit trou m; [from smallpox] cicatrice f de variole / his face is covered with pockmarks il a le visage grêlé or variolé.

pockmarked ['pɒkmɑːkt] adj [face] grêlé ; [surface] criblé de petits trous / pockmarked with rust piqué par la rouille.

pod [pɒd] (pt & pp **podded**, cont **podding**) n BOT cosse f.

podcast ['pɒdkɑːst] n COMPUT podcast m.

podgy ['pɒdʒɪ] (compar **podgier**, superl **podgiest**) adj UK dodu, replet (replète).

podiatrist [pə'daɪətrɪst] n US pédicure mf.

podiatry [pə'daɪətrɪ] n US pédicurie f.

podium ['pəʊdɪəm] (pl **podiums** or **podia** [-dɪə]) n [stand] podium m.

POE n **1.** abbr of **port of embarkation 2.** abbr of **port of entry.**

poem ['pəʊɪm] n poème m.

poet ['pəʊɪt] n poète m.

poetic(al) [pəʊ'etɪkl] adj poétique.

poetic justice n justice f immanente / it's poetic justice that they ended up losing ce n'est que justice qu'ils aient fini par perdre.

poetry ['pəʊɪtrɪ] n poésie f.

po-faced ['pəʊfeɪst] adj UK inf à l'air pincé.

pogo stick ['pəʊgəʊ-] n bâton m sauteur (jeu).

pogrom ['pɒgrəm] n pogrom m.

poignancy ['pɔɪnjənsɪ] n caractère m poignant.

poignant ['pɔɪnjənt] adj poignant.

poignantly ['pɔɪnjəntlɪ] adv de façon poignante.

poinsettia [pɔɪn'setɪə] n poinsettia m.

point [pɔɪnt] ◆ n **1.** [tip - of sword, nail, pencil, etc.] pointe f / trim one end of the stick into a point taillez un des bouts de la branche en pointe **2.** [small dot] point m **3.** [specific place] point m, endroit m / point of intersection or intersection point point d'intersection ▸ **to pass / to reach the point of no return** passer / atteindre le point de non-retour / at that point you'll see a church on the left à ce moment-là, vous verrez une église sur votre gauche **4.** [particular moment] moment m; [particular period] période f / we are at a critical point nous voici à un point critique / there comes a point when a decision has to be made il arrive un moment où il faut prendre une décision / at that point, I was still undecided à ce moment-là, je n'avais pas encore pris de décision **5.** [stage in development or process] point m / I was on the point of admitting everything j'étais sur le point de tout avouer / she had worked to the point of exhaustion elle avait travaillé jusqu'à l'épuisement **6.** [for discussion or debate] point m / are there any points I haven't covered? y a-t-il des questions que je n'ai pas abordées ? ▸ **to make** or **to raise a point** faire une remarque / all right, you've made your point! d'accord, on a compris ! / I see or take your point je vois ce que vous voulez dire or où vous voulez en venir ▸ **point taken!** c'est juste ! / he may not be home — you've got a point there! il n'est peut-être pas chez lui — ça c'est vrai ! ; [precise detail] ▸ **to make a point of doing sthg** tenir à faire qqch **7.** [essential part, heart -of argument, explanation] essentiel m; [conclusion -of joke] chute f ▸ **to get the point:** I get the point je comprends, je vois / the point is (that) we're overloaded with work le fait est que nous sommes débordés de travail / we're getting off or away from the point nous nous éloignons or écartons du sujet ▸ **that's the (whole) point!** a) [that's the problem] c'est là (tout) le problème ! b) [that's the aim] c'est ça, le but ! ▸ **to be beside the point:** the money is / your feelings are beside the point l'argent n'a / vos sentiments n'ont rien à voir là-dedans ▸ **to come to** or **get to the point:** get to the point! dites ce que vous avez à dire !, ne tournez pas autour du pot ! / I'll come straight to the point je serai bref ▸ **to keep to the point** ne pas s'écarter du sujet **8.** [purpose] but m; [meaning, use] sens m, intérêt m / there's no point in asking him now ça ne sert à rien or ce n'est pas la peine de le lui demander maintenant / what's the point of all this? à quoi ça sert tout ça ? / oh, what's the point anyway? oh, et puis à quoi bon, après tout ! **9.** [feature, characteristic] point m / the boss has his good points le patron a ses bons côtés / it's my weak / strong point c'est mon point faible / fort **10.** [unit -in scoring, measuring] point m **11.** [in decimals] virgule f **12.** [punctuation mark] point m ▸ **three** or **ellipsis points** points mpl de suspension **13.** AUTO vis f platinée **14.** UK ELEC [socket] ▸ **(power) point** prise f (de courant). ◆ vi **1.** [person] tendre le doigt ▸ **to point at** or **to** or **towards sthg** montrer qqch du doigt / it's rude to point ce n'est pas poli de montrer du doigt **2.** [roadsign, needle on dial] : a compass needle always points north l'aiguille d'une boussole indique toujours le nord / the weather vane is pointing north la girouette est orientée au nord **3.** [be directed, face -gun, camera] être braqué ; [-vehicle] être dirigé, être tourné. ◆ vt **1.** [direct, aim -vehicle] diriger ; [-flashlight, hose] tourner, braquer ; [-finger] pointer, tendre ▸ **to point one's finger at sb / sthg** montrer qqn / qqch du doigt / he pointed the rifle / the camera at me il braqua le fusil / l'appareil photo sur moi ; [send -person] : if anybody shows up, just point them in my direction si quelqu'un arrive, tu n'as qu'à me l'envoyer / just point him to the nearest bar tu n'as qu'à lui indiquer le chemin du bar le plus proche **2.** DANCE ▸ **to point one's toes** faire des pointes **3.** CONSTR [wall, building] jointoyer **4.** PHR ▸ **to point the way a)** [subj: arrow, signpost] indiquer la direction or le chemin **b)** fig [subj: person] montrer le chemin / they point the way (in) which reform must go ils indiquent la direction dans laquelle les réformes doivent aller. ◆ **points** pl n **1.** UK RAIL aiguilles fpl ▸ **points failure** panne f d'aiguillage **2.** DANCE [chaussons mpl à] pointes fpl / she's already (dancing) on points elle fait déjà des pointes. ◆ **at this point in time** adv phr pour l'instant. ◆ **in point of fact** adv phr en fait, à vrai dire. ◆ **to the point** adj phr pertinent. ◆ **up to a point** adv phr jusqu'à un certain point. ◆ **point out** vt sep

1. [indicate] indiquer, montrer **2.** [mention, call attention to] signaler, faire remarquer **/** *I'd like to point out that it was my idea in the first place* je vous ferai remarquer que l'idée est de moi. ❖ **point to** vt insep **1.** [signify, denote] signifier, indiquer ; [foreshadow] indiquer, annoncer **/** *the facts point to only one conclusion* les faits ne permettent qu'une seule conclusion **/** *all the evidence points to him* toutes les preuves indiquent que c'est lui **2.** [call attention to] attirer l'attention sur. ❖ **point up** vt sep [subj: person, report] souligner, mettre l'accent sur ; [subj: event] faire ressortir.

point-and-click n pointer-cliquer *m*.

point-blank ❖ adj **1.** [shot] (tiré) à bout portant **/** *he was shot at point-blank range* on lui a tiré dessus à bout portant **2.** [refusal, denial] catégorique ; [question] (posé) de but en blanc, (posé) à brûle-pourpoint. ❖ adv **1.** [shoot] à bout portant **2.** [refuse, deny] catégoriquement ; [ask] de but en blanc, à brûle-pourpoint.

point-by-point adj méthodique.

point duty n 🇬🇧 ▶ **to be on point duty** diriger la circulation.

pointed ['pɔɪntɪd] adj **1.** [sharp] pointu ▶ **pointed arch** ARCHIT arche *f* en ogive ▶ **pointed style** ARCHIT style *m* gothique **2.** [meaningful - look, comment] insistant ; [- reference] peu équivoque **3.** [marked] ostentatoire.

pointedly ['pɔɪntɪdlɪ] adv **1.** [meaningfully - look, comment] de façon insistante **2.** [markedly] de façon marquée or prononcée.

pointer ['pɔɪntər] n **1.** [for pointing - stick] baguette *f* ; [- arrow] flèche *f* **2.** [on dial] aiguille *f* **3.** [indication, sign] indice *m*, signe *m* **/** *all the pointers indicate an impending economic recovery* tout indique que la reprise économique est imminente **/** *he gave me a few pointers on how to use the computer* il m'a donné quelques tuyaux sur la façon d'utiliser l'ordinateur **4.** COMPUT pointeur *m* **5.** [dog] pointer *m*.

pointing ['pɔɪntɪŋ] n (U) CONSTR [act, job] jointoiement *m* ; [cement work] joints *mpl*.

pointing device n COMPUT dispositif *m* de pointage.

pointless ['pɔɪntlɪs] adj [gen] inutile, vain ; [crime, violence, vandalism] gratuit **/** *it's pointless trying to convince him* ça ne sert à rien or il est inutile d'essayer de le convaincre.

pointlessness ['pɔɪntlɪsnɪs] n [gen] inutilité *f* ; [of remark] manque *m* d'à-propos ; [of crime, violence, vandalism] gratuité *f*.

point-of-purchase adj sur le lieu de vente.

point-of-sale adj sur le point or sur le lieu de vente ▶ **point-of-sale advertising** publicité *f* sur le lieu de vente, PLV *f* ▶ **point-of-sale promotion** promotion *f* sur le lieu de vente.

point of view n point *m* de vue **/** *from my point of view, it doesn't make much difference* en ce qui me concerne, ça ne change pas grand-chose.

point-to-point n 🇬🇧 *rallye hippique pour cavaliers amateurs*.

poise [pɔɪz] n **1.** [composure, coolness] calme *m*, aisance *f*, assurance *f* **/** *to recover one's poise* retrouver son calme **2.** [physical bearing] port *m*, maintien *m* ; [gracefulness] grâce *f*.

poised [pɔɪzd] adj **1.** [balanced] en équilibre ; [suspended] suspendu **2.** [ready, prepared] prêt **/** *poised for action* prêt à agir **3.** [composed, self-assured] calme, assuré.

poison ['pɔɪzn] ❖ n **1.** poison *m* ; [of reptile] venin *m* **2.** *fig* poison *m*, venin *m*. ❖ comp [mushroom, plant] vénéneux ; [gas] toxique. ❖ vt **1.** *lit* empoisonner ▶ **to poison sb with sthg** empoisonner qqn à qqch **2.** *fig* envenimer, gâcher.

poisoning ['pɔɪznɪŋ] n empoisonnement *m* ▶ **mercury poisoning** empoisonnement au mercure.

poison ivy n sumac *m* vénéneux.

poisonous ['pɔɪznəs] adj **1.** [mushroom, plant] vénéneux ; [snake, lizard] venimeux ; [gas, chemical] toxique **2.** *fig* [person] malveillant, venimeux ; [remark, allegation] venimeux.

 vénéneux or **venimeux?**

Be careful not to confuse these two very similar adjectives: **vénéneux** means poisonous, and refers to toxic plants or substances. **Venimeux** means venomous, and refers to animals that produce venom.

poison-pen letter n lettre *f* anonyme.

poke [pəʊk] ❖ vt **1.** [push, prod - gen] donner un coup à ; [- with elbow] donner un coup de coude à **2.** [stick, thrust] enfoncer ▶ **to poke a hole in sthg** faire un trou dans qqch **3.** [fire] tisonner **4.** *inf* [punch] flanquer un coup de poing à **5.** [person on networking site] envoyer un poke à. ❖ n **1.** [push, prod] poussée *f*, (petit) coup *m* **2.** 🇺🇸 *inf* [punch] gnon *m*, marron *m* **3.** [on networking site] poke *m*. ❖ **poke about, poke around** vi fouiller, fourrager. ❖ **poke along** vi 🇺🇸 avancer lentement. ❖ **poke at** vt insep [with finger] pousser (du doigt) ; [with stick] pousser (avec un bâton). ❖ **poke out** ❖ vi [stick out] dépasser. ❖ vt sep [remove] déloger ▶ **to poke sb's eye out** crever un œil à qqn.

poker ['pəʊkər] n **1.** [card game] poker *m* **2.** [for fire] tisonnier *m*.

poker-faced adj (au visage) impassible.

poky ['pəʊkɪ] (*compar* **pokier**, *superl* **pokiest**) adj *inf* **1.** 🇬🇧 [house, room - cramped] exigu (exiguë) **2.** 🇺🇸 [slow] lambin.

Poland ['pəʊlənd] pr n Pologne *f* **/** *in Poland* en Pologne.

polar ['pəʊlər] adj **1.** CHEM, ELEC, GEOG & MATH polaire **2.** *fig* [totally opposite - opinions, attitudes] diamétralement opposé.

polar bear n ours *m* polaire or blanc.

polarity [pəʊˈlærətɪ] (*pl* **polarities**) n polarité *f*.

polarization, polarisation [ˌpəʊləraɪˈzeɪʃn] n polarisation *f*.

polarize, polarise ['pəʊləraɪz] ❖ vt polariser. ❖ vi se polariser.

pole [pəʊl] ❖ n **1.** ELEC & GEOG pôle *m* ▶ **to be poles apart** : *they are poles apart* ils n'ont absolument rien en commun **/** *their positions on disarmament are poles apart* leurs positions sur le désarmement sont diamétralement opposées **2.** [rod] bâton *m*, perche *f* ; [for tent] montant *m* ; [in fence, construction] poteau *m*, pieu *m* ; [for gardening] tuteur *m* ; [for climbing plants] rame *f* ; [for pole-vaulting, punting] perche *f* ; [for skier] bâton *m* **3.** [mast - for phonelines] poteau *m* ; [- for flags] mât *m* **4.** [for climbing] mât *m* ; [in fire-station] perche *f* **/** *he's driving me up the pole!* 🇬🇧 il me rend dingue ! **5.** [unit of measure] ≃ perche *f*. ❖ vt [punt] faire avancer (avec une perche).

Pole [pəʊl] n Polonais *m*, -e *f*.

poleaxed ['pəʊlækst] adj *inf* [surprised] baba, épaté.

polecat ['pəʊlkæt] (*pl* **polecat** or **polecats**) n **1.** [European, African] putois *m* **2.** 🇺🇸 [skunk] moufette *f*, mouffette *f*.

pole dancing n danse *f* de poteau.

pole jump = pole vault.

polemical [pə'lemɪkl] adj polémique.

polemicist [pə'lemɪsɪst] n polémiste *mf*.

polenta [pə'lentə] n polenta *f*.

pole position n [in motor racing] pole position *f* ▸ **to be in pole position** être en pole position.

Pole Star n (étoile *f*) Polaire *f*.

pole vault n saut *m* à la perche. ❖ **pole-vault** vi [as activity] faire du saut à la perche ; [on specific jump] faire un saut à la perche.

pole-vaulter [-,vɔ:ltə'] n perchiste *mf*.

police [pə'li:s] ❖ pl n police *f* / *the police are on their way* la police arrive, les gendarmes arrivent / *18 police were injured* 18 policiers ont été blessés. ❖ comp [vehicle, patrol, spy] de police ; [protection, work] de la police, policier ; [harassment] policier / *he was taken into police custody* il a été emmené en garde à vue. ❖ vt **1.** [subj: policemen] surveiller, maintenir l'ordre dans / *the match was heavily policed* d'importantes forces de police étaient présentes lors du match ; [subj: guards, vigilantes] surveiller, maintenir l'ordre dans ; [subj: army, international organization] surveiller, contrôler / *the area is policed by army patrols* des patrouilles militaires veillent au maintien de l'ordre dans la région **2.** [regulate - prices] contrôler ; [-agreement] veiller à l'application or au respect de **3.** 🇺🇸 [clean - military camp] nettoyer.

police academy n 🇺🇸 école *f* de police.

police car n voiture *f* de police.

police chief n ≃ préfet *m* de police.

police commissioner n 🇺🇸 commissaire *m* de police.

police constable n 🇬🇧 ≃ gardien *m* de la paix ; ≃ agent *m* (de police).

police department n 🇺🇸 service *m* de police.

police dog n chien *m* policier.

police force n police *f* ▸ **to join the police force** entrer dans la police.

police inspector n inspecteur *m*, -trice *f* de police.

policeman [pə'li:smən] (*pl* policemen [-mən]) n agent *m* (de police), policier *m*.

police officer n policier *m*, agent *m* de police.

police record n casier *m* judiciaire.

police state n État *m* or régime *m* policier.

police station n [urban] poste *m* de police, commissariat *m* (de police) ; [rural] gendarmerie *f*.

policewoman [pə'li:s,wʊmən] (*pl* policewomen [-,wɪmɪn]) n femme *f* policier.

policing [pə'li:sɪŋ] n [by police] maintien *m* de l'ordre.

policy [pɒləsɪ] (*pl* policies) ❖ n **1.** POL politique *f* / *the government's economic policies* la politique économique du gouvernement **2.** COMM [of company, organization] politique *f*, orientation *f* **3.** [personal principle, rule of action] principe *m*, règle *f* **4.** [for insurance] police *f* ▸ **to take out a policy** souscrire une assurance. ❖ comp [decision, statement] de principe ; [debate] de politique générale.

⚠ The French word **police** only means a policy in the insurance sense.

policy-holder [pɒləsɪ,həʊldə'] n assuré *m*, -e *f*.

policymaker [pɒləsɪ,meɪkə'] n POL responsable *mf* politique ; COMM décideur *m*.

policy statement n déclaration *f* de principe.

polio [pəʊlɪəʊ] n (*U*) polio *f*.

polish [pɒlɪʃ] ❖ vt **1.** [furniture] cirer, encaustiquer ; [brass, car] astiquer ; [mirror] astiquer ; [shoes] cirer, brosser ;

[gemstone] polir **2.** *fig* [perfect] polir, perfectionner **3.** [person] parfaire l'éducation de. ❖ n **1.** [for wood, furniture] encaustique *f*, cire *f* ; [for shoes] cirage *m* ; [for brass, car, silverware] produit d'entretien pour le cuivre, la voiture, l'argenterie, etc ; [for fingernails] vernis *m* **2.** [act of polishing] ▸ **to give sthg a polish** astiquer qqch **3.** [shine, lustre] brillant *m*, éclat *m* ▸ **to put a polish on sthg** faire briller qqch **4.** *fig* raffinement *m*, élégance *f*. ❖ **polish off** vt sep *inf* **1.** [finish - meal] finir, avaler **2.** [complete - job] expédier ; [-book, essay] en finir avec **3.** [defeat] se débarrasser de, écraser ; [kill] liquider, descendre. ❖ **polish up** vi : *brass polishes up well* le cuivre est facile à faire briller. ❖ vt sep **1.** [furniture, shoes] faire briller ; [diamond] polir **2.** *fig* [perfect - maths, language] perfectionner, travailler ; [-technique] parfaire, améliorer.

Polish [pəʊlɪʃ] ❖ n LING polonais *m*. ❖ pl n [people] ▸ **the Polish** les Polonais. ❖ adj polonais.

polished [pɒlɪʃt] adj **1.** [surface] brillant, poli **2.** [person] qui a du savoir-vivre, raffiné ; [manners] raffiné **3.** [performer] accompli ; [performance] parfait, impeccable ; [style] raffiné, élégant.

polite [pə'laɪt] adj **1.** [person] poli, courtois ; [remark, conversation] poli, aimable ▸ **to be polite to sb** être poli envers or avec qqn / *it is polite to ask first* quand on est poli, on demande d'abord ▸ **to make polite conversation** faire la conversation / *she was very polite about my poems* elle s'est montrée très diplomate dans ses commentaires sur mes poèmes **2.** [refined - manners] raffiné, élégant ▸ **polite society** la bonne société, le beau monde.

politely [pə'laɪtlɪ] adv poliment, de manière courtoise.

politeness [pə'laɪtnɪs] n politesse *f*, courtoisie *f* / *out of politeness* par politesse.

politic [pɒlətɪk] adj *fml* [shrewd] habile, avisé ; [wise] judicieux, sage.

political [pə'lɪtɪkl] adj **1.** politique **2.** [interested in politics] : *he's always been very political* il s'est toujours intéressé à la politique.

political asylum n droit *m* d'asile (politique) ▸ **to ask for political asylum** demander le droit d'asile (politique).

political correctness n le politiquement correct.

political establishment n classe *f* politique dirigeante.

political geography n géographie *f* politique.

politically [pə'lɪtɪklɪ] adv politiquement.

politically correct adj politiquement correct.

political prisoner n prisonnier *m* politique.

political science n (*U*) sciences *fpl* politiques.

politician [,pɒlɪ'tɪʃn] n **1.** [gen] homme *m* politique, femme *f* politique **2.** 🇺🇸 *pej* politicien *m*, -enne *f*.

politicization, politicisation [pə,lɪtɪsaɪ'zeɪʃn] n politisation *f*.

politicize, politicise [pə'lɪtɪsaɪz] ❖ vt politiser / *the whole issue has become highly politicized* on a beaucoup politisé toute cette question. ❖ vi faire de la politique.

politicking [pɒlətɪkɪŋ] n *pej* politique *f* politicienne.

politics [pɒlətɪks] ❖ n (*U*) **1.** [as a profession] ▸ **to go into politics** faire de la politique ▸ **to be in politics** faire de la politique **2.** [art or science] politique *f* / *she studied politics at university* elle a étudié les sciences politiques à l'université ▸ **to talk politics** parler politique **3.** [activity] politique *f* ▸ **sexual politics** ensemble des idées et des problèmes touchant aux droits des femmes, des homosexuels, etc. ❖ pl n [opinions] idées *fpl* or opinions *fpl* politiques / *what exactly are her politics?* quelles sont ses opinions politiques au juste ?

polka [pɒlkə] ❖ n polka *f*. ❖ vi danser la polka.

polka dot n TEXT pois *m*. ❖ **polka-dot** adj à pois.

poll [pəʊl] ❖ n **1.** POL [elections] élection *f*, élections *fpl*, scrutin *m* ▶ **to go to the polls** voter, se rendre aux urnes ; [vote] vote *m* ; [votes cast] suffrages *mpl* (exprimés), nombre *m* de voix **2.** [survey - of opinion, intentions] sondage *m* ▶ **to conduct a poll on** or **about sthg** faire un sondage d'opinion sur qqch, effectuer un sondage auprès de la population concernant qqch **3.** [count, census] recensement *m* **4.** [list - of taxpayers] rôle *m* nominatif ; [-of electors] liste *f* électorale. ❖ vt **1.** POL [votes] recueillir, obtenir **2.** [person] sonder, recueillir l'opinion de **3.** US [assembly] inscrire le vote de. ❖ vi [receive votes] : *the party polled well* le parti a obtenu un bon score.

pollen ['pɒlən] n pollen *m*.

pollen count n indice *m* pollinique (de l'air).

pollinate ['pɒləneɪt] vt polliniser.

pollination [,pɒlɪ'neɪʃn] n pollinisation *f*.

polling ['pəʊlɪŋ] n (U) **1.** POL [voting] vote *m*, suffrage *m* ; [elections] élections *fpl*, scrutin *m* / *the first round of polling* le premier tour de scrutin or des élections / *polling is up on last year* la participation au vote est plus élevée que l'année dernière **2.** [for opinion poll] sondage *m*.

polling booth n isoloir *m*.

polling day n jour *m* des élections or du scrutin.

polling station n bureau *m* de vote.

pollster ['pəʊlstər] n inf enquêteur *m*, -euse, -trice *f*, sondeur *m*, -euse *f*.

poll tax n **1.** [in UK] impôt local aboli en 1993, basé sur le nombre d'occupants adultes d'un logement **2.** [in US] impôt, aboli en 1964, donnant droit à être inscrit sur les listes électorales.

pollutant [pə'luːtnt] n polluant *m*.

pollute [pə'luːt] vt polluer / *the rivers are polluted with toxic waste* les cours d'eau sont pollués par les déchets toxiques.

polluter [pə'luːtər] n pollueur *m*, -euse *f*.

pollution [pə'luːʃn] n **1.** [of environment] pollution *f* ▶ **air pollution** pollution de l'air **2.** (U) [pollutants] polluants *mpl*.

polo ['pəʊləʊ] (pl polos) ❖ n **1.** SPORT polo *m* **2.** US [shirt] = polo shirt. ❖ comp [match, stick] de polo.

polo neck n UK [collar] col *m* roulé ; [sweater] (pull *m* à) col *m* roulé. ❖ **polo-neck(ed)** adj UK à col roulé.

polo shirt n polo *m* (chemise).

poltergeist ['pɒltəgaɪst] n esprit *m* frappeur, poltergeist *m*.

poly ['pɒlɪ] (pl polys) UK inf = polytechnic.

poly bag n UK inf sac *m* en plastique.

polyester [,pɒlɪ'estər] ❖ n polyester *m*. ❖ adj (de or en) polyester.

polyethylene [,pɒlɪ'eθiliːn] = polythene.

polygamist [pə'lɪgəmɪst] n polygame *m*.

polygamous [pə'lɪgəməs] adj polygame.

polygamy [pə'lɪgəmɪ] n polygamie *f*.

polymer ['pɒlɪmər] n polymère *m*.

Polynesia [,pɒlɪ'niːzjə] pr n Polynésie *f* / *in Polynesia* en Polynésie ▶ **French Polynesia** la Polynésie française.

Polynesian [,pɒlɪ'niːzjən] ❖ n **1.** [person] Polynésien *m*, -enne *f* **2.** LING polynésien *m*. ❖ adj polynésien.

polyp ['pɒlɪp] n polype *m*.

polystyrene [,pɒlɪ'staɪriːn] n polystyrène *m* ▶ **polystyrene tiles** carreaux *mpl* de polystyrène.

polytechnic [,pɒlɪ'teknɪk] n en Grande-Bretagne, avant 1993, établissement d'enseignement supérieur qui appartenait à un système différent de celui des universités. Depuis 1993, les «polytechnics» ont acquis le statut d'universités.

polythene ['pɒlɪθiːn] ❖ n UK polyéthylène *m*, Polythène *m*. ❖ comp en plastique, en polyéthylène spec, en Polythène spec ▶ **polythene bag** sac *m* (en) plastique.

polytunnel ['pɒlɪtʌnəl] n AGR polytunnel *m*.

polyunsaturated [,pɒlɪʌn'sætʃəreɪtɪd] adj polyinsaturé.

polyurethane [,pɒlɪ'jʊərəθeɪn] n polyuréthane *m*, polyuréthanne *m*.

pom [pɒm] Austr & NZ inf = pommie.

pomander [pə'mændər] n [bag] sachet *m* aromatique ; [orange stuck with cloves] pomme *f* d'amour.

pomegranate ['pɒmɪ,grænɪt] n grenade *f* (fruit) ▶ **pomegranate tree** grenadier *m*.

pommel ['pɒml] (UK pt & pp pommelled, cont pommelling ; US pt & pp pommeled, cont pommeling) ❖ n pommeau *m*. ❖ vt = pummel.

pommie, pommy ['pɒmɪ] (pl pommies) ❖ n Austr & NZ inf & hum angliche *mf* pej. ❖ adj angliche pej.

pomp [pɒmp] n pompe *f*, faste *m* ▶ **with great pomp (and circumstance)** en grande pompe.

pompom ['pɒmpɒm] n [flower, bobble] pompon *m*.

pomposity [pɒm'pɒsətɪ] (pl pomposities) n **1.** (U) [of manner] comportement *m* pompeux, manières *fpl* pompeuses **2.** [of ceremony] apparat *m*, pompe *f* ; [of style] caractère *m* pompeux.

pompous ['pɒmpəs] adj [pretentious] pompeux, prétentieux.

pompously ['pɒmpəslɪ] adv pompeusement.

ponce [pɒns] UK inf ❖ n **1.** [pimp] maquereau *m* **2.** pej [effeminate man] homme *m* efféminé. ❖ vi **1.** [pimp] faire le maquereau **2.** pej [behave effeminately] faire des simagrées, minauder. ❖ **ponce about, ponce around** vi inf [mess around] traîner.

poncey, poncy ['pɒnsɪ] adj UK inf & pej efféminé.

poncho ['pɒntʃəʊ] (pl ponchos) n poncho *m*.

pond [pɒnd] n [small] mare *f* ; [large] étang *m* ; [in garden] bassin *m* ▶ **pond life** la faune des étangs ▶ **the pond** inf [the Atlantic] l'Atlantique *m*.

ponder ['pɒndər] ❖ vi [think] réfléchir ; [meditate] méditer. ❖ vt réfléchir à or sur / *I sat down and pondered what to do* je m'assis et considérai ce que j'allais faire.

ponderous ['pɒndərəs] adj [heavy] pesant, lourd ; [slow] lent, laborieux ; [dull] lourd.

pong [pɒŋ] UK inf ❖ n puanteur *f*. ❖ vi cocoter.

pontiff ['pɒntɪf] n souverain pontife *m*, pape *m*.

pontificate vi [pɒn'tɪfɪkeɪt] [gen & RELIG] pontifier / *he's always pontificating about* or *on something or other* pej il faut toujours qu'il pontifie.

pontoon [pɒn'tuːn] n **1.** [float] ponton *m* ; [on seaplane] flotteur *m* **2.** [card game] vingt-et-un *m*.

pontoon bridge n pont *m* flottant.

pony ['pəʊnɪ] (pl ponies) n **1.** ZOOL poney *m* **2.** [glass] verre *m* à liqueur **3.** US inf SCH [crib] antisèche *f*.

ponytail ['pəʊnɪteɪl] n queue de cheval *f*.

pony-trekking [-,trekɪŋ] n randonnée *f* à dos de poney ▶ **to go pony-trekking** faire une randonnée à dos de poney.

Ponzi scheme ['pɒnzɪ] n chaîne *f* de Ponzi (escroquerie sous forme de vente pyramidale).

poo [puː] n & vi inf = pooh.

pooch [puːtʃ] n US inf toutou *m*.

poodle ['pu:dl] n caniche m.

poof [puf] ◆ n **UK** v inf & pej pédé m. ◆ interj : and then it was gone, poof, just like that et puis hop ! il a disparu d'un coup.

pooh [pu:] **UK** inf ◆ interj [with disgust] pouah ; [with disdain] peuh. ◆ n baby talk caca m. ◆ vi baby talk faire caca.

pooh-pooh vt **UK** inf rire de, ricaner de.

pool [pu:l] ◆ n **1.** [pond -small] mare f ; [-large] étang m ; [-ornamental] bassin m **2.** [puddle] flaque f / a pool of light un rond de lumière **3.** [swimming pool] piscine f ▶ **pool party** fête organisée autour d'une piscine **4.** [in harbour] bassin m ; [in canal, river] plan m d'eau **5.** [of money] cagnotte f ; [in card games] cagnotte f, poule f **6.** [of workmen, babysitters] groupe m, groupement m ; [of experts] équipe f ; [of typists] pool m ; [of cars -in firm] parc m ; [of ideas] réserve f ; [of talent] pépinière f, réserve f **7.** [consortium] cartel m, pool m ; [group of producers] groupement m de producteurs **8.** **US** FIN [group] groupement m ; [agreement] entente f, accord m **9.** [American billiards] billard m américain ▶ **to shoot pool** **US** jouer au billard américain. ◆ vt [resources, cars] mettre en commun ; [efforts, ideas] unir.

poolroom ['pu:l,ru:m] n salle f de billard.

pools [pu:lz] pl n **UK** ▶ **the (football) pools** les concours de pronostics (au football) ▶ **to win the (football) pools** gagner aux pronostics (au football) ▶ **pools coupon** fiche f de pari, grille f de pronostics (au football).

pool table n (table f de) billard m.

pooped [pu:pt] adj **US** inf ▶ **pooped (out)** vanné, HS.

poor [pʊə˟] ◆ adj **1.** [financially - person, area, country] pauvre **2.** [mediocre in quantity - gen] maigre ; [- output, sale figures] faible, médiocre ; [mediocre in quality - land, soil] maigre, pauvre ; [- effort, excuse] piètre ; [- piece of work] médiocre ; [- results] médiocre, piètre ; [- weather, summer] médiocre ; [- quality, condition] mauvais / the joke was in extremely poor taste la plaisanterie était du plus mauvais goût / the team put in a poor performance l'équipe n'a pas très bien joué / our chances of success are very poor nos chances de réussite sont bien maigres **3.** [weak - memory, sight] mauvais ; [to be in poor health être en mauvaise santé / I have rather poor sight j'ai une mauvaise vue **4.** [in ability] peu doué / I'm a poor cook je ne suis pas doué pour la cuisine / my spelling / French is poor je ne suis pas fort en orthographe / en français **5.** [inadequate] faible **6.** [pitiful] pauvre / you poor thing! mon pauvre ! ◆ pl n ▶ **the poor** les pauvres mpl.

poorly ['pʊəlɪ] (compar **poorlier**, superl **poorliest**) ◆ adj **UK** malade, souffrant. ◆ adv [badly] mal ▶ **to think poorly of sb** avoir une mauvaise opinion de qqn.

poor relation n **UK** fig parent m pauvre.

pop [pɒp] (pt & pp **popped**, cont **popping**) ◆ onomat pan ▶ **to go pop a)** [cork] sauter **b)** [balloon] éclater. ◆ n **1.** MUS musique f pop **2.** [sound] bruit m de bouchon qui saute, bruit m sec **3.** [drink] boisson f gazeuse or pétillante **4.** **US** inf [father] papa m. ◆ comp [singer, video] pop (inv) ▶ **pop concert** concert m rock ▶ **pop group** groupe m pop ▶ **pop music** musique f pop, pop music f. ◆ vi **1.** [cork, buttons] sauter ; [bulb, balloon] éclater ▶ **to pop open a)** [box, bag] s'ouvrir tout d'un coup **b)** [buttons] sauter **2.** [ears] se déboucher d'un seul coup ; [eyes] s'ouvrir tout grand **3.** **UK** inf [go] faire un saut / to pop into town faire un saut en ville **4.** **US** inf [pay] payer / who's going to pop for the ice cream? qui va payer les glaces ? ◆ written abbr of **population**. ◆ vt **1.** [balloon, bag] crever ; [button, cork] faire sauter ; [corn] faire éclater **2.** inf [put] mettre, fourrer / just pop the paper through the letterbox glissez juste le journal dans la boîte aux lettres / she

kept popping tablets into her mouth elle n'arrêtait pas de se fourrer des comprimés dans la bouche / he popped his head over the wall sa tête surgit en haut du mur **3.** drugs sl ▶ **to pop pills** prendre des comprimés (pour se droguer). ❖ **pop in** vi **UK** inf faire une petite visite ▶ **to pop in to see sb** passer voir qqn. ❖ **pop off** vi inf **1.** [leave] s'en aller, filer **2.** [die] casser sa pipe. ❖ **pop out** vi inf sortir un instant. ❖ **pop over** vi inf passer, faire une petite visite. ❖ **pop round** vi inf passer / pop round anytime passe n'importe quand / they popped round to see us ils sont passés nous voir. ❖ **pop up** vi inf **1.** [go upstairs] faire un saut en haut or à l'étage, monter / pop up to see me sometime monte donc me voir un de ces jours **2.** [crop up] surgir / his name seems to pop up everywhere on ne parle que de lui.

POP (abbr of **point of purchase**) n lieu m d'achat or de vente.

popadum ['pɒpədəm] n galette indienne.

popcorn ['pɒpkɔ:n] n pop-corn m inv.

pope [pəup] n **1.** [in Catholic Church] pape m **2.** [in Eastern Orthodox Church] pope m.

pop-eyed adj inf ébahi, aux yeux écarquillés.

popgun ['pɒpgʌn] n pistolet m (d'enfant) à bouchon.

poplar (tree) ['pɒplə˟-] n peuplier m.

poplin ['pɒplɪn] ◆ n popeline f. ◆ adj en popeline.

popper ['pɒpə˟] n **UK** [press-stud] bouton-pression m, pression f. ❖ **poppers** pl n [drugs] poppers mpl.

poppet ['pɒpɪt] n **UK** inf chéri m, -e f, mignon m, -onne f.

poppy ['pɒpɪ] (pl **poppies**) n **1.** [flower] coquelicot m ; [opium poppy] pavot m ; [paper flower] coquelicot m en papier (vendu le jour de l'Armistice) ▶ **poppy seed** graine f de pavot **2.** [colour] rouge m coquelicot (inv).

Poppy Day pr n journée de commémoration pendant laquelle on porte un coquelicot en papier en souvenir des soldats britanniques morts lors des guerres mondiales.

Popsicle® ['pɒpsɪkl] n **US** glace f en bâtonnet.

populace ['pɒpjʊləs] n **1.** [population] population f **2.** [masses] masses fpl, peuple m.

popular ['pɒpjʊlə˟] adj **1.** [well-liked - person] populaire / she's very popular with her pupils elle est très populaire auprès de ses élèves, ses élèves l'aiment beaucoup / I'm not going to be very popular when they find out it's my fault! je ne vais pas être bien vu quand ils découvriront que c'est de ma faute ! **2.** [appreciated by many - product, colour] populaire ; [- restaurant, resort] très couru, très fréquenté / the film was very popular in Europe le film a été un très grand succès en Europe / the most popular book of the year le livre le plus vendu or le best-seller de l'année **3.** [common] courant, répandu ; [general] populaire ▶ **on** or **by popular demand** à la demande générale **4.** [aimed at ordinary people] populaire.

popularity [,pɒpjʊ'lærətɪ] n popularité f.

popularization, popularisation [,pɒpjʊləraɪ'zeɪʃn] n **1.** [of trend, activity] popularisation f ; [of science, philosophy] vulgarisation f **2.** [book] œuvre f de vulgarisation.

popularize, popularise ['pɒpjʊləraɪz] vt **1.** [make popular] populariser **2.** [science, philosophy] vulgariser.

popularly ['pɒpjʊləlɪ] adv généralement ; [commonly] couramment, communément.

populate ['pɒpjʊleɪt] vt [inhabit] peupler, habiter ; [colonize] peupler, coloniser / a town populated by miners and their families une ville habitée par des mineurs et leurs familles / a densely populated country un pays fortement peuplé or à forte densité de population.

population [ˌpɒpjʊˈleɪʃn] ◆ n population f / *the prison population* la population carcérale. ◆ comp [control, fall, increase] démographique, de la population ▶ **population explosion** explosion f démographique.

populism [ˈpɒpjʊlɪzm] n populisme m.

populist [ˈpɒpjʊlɪst] n populiste mf.

populous [ˈpɒpjʊləs] adj populeux.

pop-up ◆ adj [book, card] en relief ; [toaster] automatique ▶ **pop-up book** livre m animé ▶ **pop-up menu** COMPUT menu m local. ◆ n COMPUT pop-up m.

porcelain [ˈpɔːsəlɪn] ◆ n porcelaine f. ◆ comp [dish, vase, lamp] en porcelaine.

porch [pɔːtʃ] n **1.** [entrance] porche m **2.** 🇺🇸 [veranda] véranda f.

porcupine [ˈpɔːkjʊpaɪn] n porc-épic m.

pore [pɔːr] ◆ n [in skin, plant, fungus, rock] pore m. ◆ vi ▶ **to pore over a)** [book] être plongé dans or absorbé par **b)** [picture, details] étudier de près.

pork [pɔːk] ◆ n CULIN porc m. ◆ comp [chop, sausage] de porc.

pork pie n ≃ pâté m en croûte (*à la viande de porc*).

porky [ˈpɔːkɪ] (*compar* **porkier**, *superl* **porkiest**) ◆ adj *inf & pej* [fat] gros (grosse), gras (grasse), adipeux *pej*. ◆ n 🇬🇧 *inf* [lie] bobard m.

porn [pɔːn] *inf* ◆ n porno m ▶ **hard / soft porn** porno m hard / soft ▶ **porn shop** sex-shop m. ◆ adj *inf* porno ▶ **porn actor / actress** acteur m, -trice f de porno, hardeur m, -euse f ▶ **porn star** star f du porno.

porno [ˈpɔːnəʊ] adj *inf* porno.

pornographic [ˌpɔːnəˈɡræfɪk] adj pornographique.

pornography [pɔːˈnɒɡrəfɪ] n pornographie f.

porous [ˈpɔːrəs] adj poreux.

porpoise [ˈpɔːpəs] (*pl* **porpoise** *or* **porpoises**) n marsouin m.

porridge [ˈpɒrɪdʒ] n **1.** CULIN porridge m **2.** 🇬🇧 *prison sl* peine f de prison ▶ **to do porridge** faire de la tôle v *inf*.

port [pɔːt] ◆ n **1.** [harbour] port m ▶ **to come into port** entrer dans le port ▶ **any port in a storm** nécessité fait loi *prov* **2.** [wine] porto m **3.** [window - on ship, plane] hublot m **4.** COMPUT port m **5.** NAUT [left side] bâbord m. ◆ comp [authorities, activity, facilities] portuaire ; [bow, quarter] de bâbord.

portability [ˌpɔːtəˈbɪlɪtɪ] n portabilité f.

portable [ˈpɔːtəbl] ◆ adj **1.** portatif, portable ▶ **portable TV (set)** télévision f portative **2.** COMPUT [software, program] compatible. ◆ n [typewriter] machine f portative ; [TV] télévision f portative ; [computer] ordinateur m portatif.

Portacrib® [ˈpɔːtəˌkrɪb] n 🇺🇸 moïse m, porte-bébé m.

Portakabin® [ˈpɔːtəˌkæbɪn] n [gen] baraquement m préfabriqué.

portal [ˈpɔːtl] n *liter or* COMPUT portail m.

portcullis [ˌpɔːtˈkʌlɪs] n herse f (*de château fort*).

portentous [pɔːˈtentəs] adj *liter* **1.** [ominous - sign] de mauvais présage or augure **2.** [momentous - event] capital, extraordinaire **3.** [serious] grave, solennel **4.** [pompous] pompeux.

porter [ˈpɔːtər] n **1.** [of luggage] porteur m **2.** 🇬🇧 [door attendant - in hotel] portier m ; [- in block of flats] concierge mf, gardien m, -enne f ; [- on private estate] gardien m, -enne f ; [- in university, college] appariteur m **3.** 🇺🇸 RAIL [on train] employé m, -e f des wagons-lits **4.** [beer] porter m, bière f brune.

portfolio [ˌpɔːtˈfəʊljəʊ] (*pl* **portfolios**) n **1.** [briefcase] porte-documents m *inv* **2.** [dossier - of artist] dossier m **3.** POL portefeuille m **4.** ST. EX portefeuille m (financier) or d'investissements.

porthole [ˈpɔːthəʊl] n hublot m.

portico [ˈpɔːtɪkəʊ] (*pl* **porticos** *or* **porticoes**) n ARCHIT portique m.

portion [ˈpɔːʃn] n **1.** [part, section] partie f **2.** [share] part f ; [measure] mesure f, dose f / *he cut the cake into five portions* il a coupé le gâteau en cinq (parts) **3.** [helping - of food] portion f. ◆ **portion out** vt sep distribuer, répartir.

portly [ˈpɔːtlɪ] (*compar* **portlier**, *superl* **portliest**) adj corpulent, fort.

port of call n NAUT escale f.

portrait [ˈpɔːtreɪt] ◆ n **1.** [gen & ART] portrait m **2.** PRINT ▶ **to print in portrait** imprimer à la française. ◆ comp ▶ **portrait gallery** galerie f de portraits ▶ **portrait painter** portraitiste mf ▶ **portrait painting** le portrait ▶ **portrait photograph** portrait m photographique, photo-portrait f ▶ **portrait photographer** photographe m d'art. ◆ adj PRINT à la française.

portraitist [ˈpɔːtreɪtɪst] n portraitiste mf.

portray [pɔːˈtreɪ] vt **1.** [represent] représenter **2.** [act role of] jouer le rôle de **3.** [depict in words] dépeindre **4.** [artist] peindre, faire le portrait de.

portrayal [pɔːˈtreɪəl] n **1.** [description] portrait m, description f **2.** ART portrait m **3.** THEAT interprétation f.

Portugal [ˈpɔːtʃʊɡl] pr n Portugal m / *in Portugal* au Portugal.

Portuguese [ˌpɔːtʃʊˈɡiːz] (*pl* **Portuguese**) ◆ n **1.** [person] Portugais m, -e f **2.** LING portugais m. ◆ adj portugais.

POS (abbr of **point of sale**) n PDV m.

pose [pəʊz] ◆ n **1.** [position - gen & ART] & PHOT pose f ▶ **to take up** or **to strike a pose** prendre une pose **2.** [pretence] façade f. ◆ vi **1.** ART & PHOT poser ▶ **to pose for a photograph / for an artist** poser pour une photographie / pour un artiste **2.** [masquerade] : *he posed as a hero* il s'est posé en héros, il s'est fait passer pour un héros / *a man posing as a policeman* un homme se faisant passer pour un policier. ◆ vt [constitute - problem] poser, créer ; [- threat] constituer ; [set - question] poser ; [put forward - claim, idea] formuler.

poser [ˈpəʊzər] n *inf* **1.** [question - thorny] question f épineuse ; [- difficult] colle f / *that's a bit of a poser!* alors ça, c'est une colle ! **2.** *pej* [show-off] poseur m, -euse f.

poseur [pəʊˈzɜːr] n *pej* poseur m, -euse f.

posh [pɒʃ] 🇬🇧 *inf* ◆ adj [clothes] chic ; [person] BCBG ; [car] chic ; [house] de riches ; [restaurant] huppé ; [area] chic ; [accent] snob / *posh people don't usually come here* généralement les gens de la haute ne viennent pas ici. ◆ adv ▶ **to talk posh** parler avec un accent snob.

posit [ˈpɒzɪt] vt *fml* [idea] avancer ; [theory] avancer, postuler.

position [pəˈzɪʃn] ◆ n **1.** [place] position f, place f, emplacement m ▶ **to change** or **to shift position** changer de place **2.** [pose, angle, setting] position f / *hold the spray can in an upright position* tenez le vaporisateur en position verticale / *the lever should be in the off position* le levier devrait être en position arrêt **3.** [circumstances] situation f, position f ▶ **to be in a bad / good position** être en mauvaise / bonne posture / *you're in a bad position* or *in no position to judge* vous êtes mal placé pour (en) juger ▶ **to be in a position to do sthg** être en mesure de faire qqch / *put yourself in my position* mettez-vous à ma place **4.** [rank - in table, scale] place f, position f / *they're* *in tenth position in the championship* ils sont à la dixième place or ils occupent la dixième place du championnat ; [in hierarchy] position *f*, situation *f* ; [social standing] position *f*, place *f* **5.** [standpoint] position *f*, point *m* de vue ‣ **to take up a position on sthg** adopter une position or prendre position sur qqch **6.** [job] poste *m*, situation *f* / *there were four candidates for the position of manager* il y avait quatre candidats au poste de directeur / *it is a position of great responsibility* c'est un poste à haute responsabilité **7.** ADMIN [in bank, post office] guichet *m* **8.** SPORT [in team, on field] position *f* / *he can play in any position* il peut jouer à n'importe quelle position or place **9.** MIL position *f* / *the men took up position on the hill* les hommes prirent position sur la colline. ◆ vt **1.** [put in place - cameras, equipment] mettre en place, placer, disposer ; [- precisely] mettre en position ; [- guests, officials] placer / *he positioned himself on the roof* il a pris position sur le toit **2.** *(usu passive)* [situate - house, building] situer, placer ; SPORT placer **3.** [post - guards] placer, poster **4.** COMM [product] positionner.

positioning n [of product] positionnement *m*.

positive ['pɒzətɪv] ◆ adj **1.** [sure] sûr, certain / *are you positive about that?* en êtes-vous sûr ? / *are you absolutely sure? — yes, positive* en êtes-vous absolument sûr ? — sûr et certain **2.** [constructive] positif, constructif ‣ **positive thinking** idées *fpl* constructives **3.** [affirmative - reply, response] positif, affirmatif ; [- test, result] positif **4.** [definite - fact, progress] réel, certain ; [clear - change, advantage] réel, effectif ; [precise - instructions] formel, clair / *we have positive evidence of his involvement* nous avons des preuves irréfutables de son implication **5.** [as intensifier - absolute] absolu, véritable, pur **6.** [assured] assuré, ferme. ◆ n **1.** GRAM positif *m* / *in the positive* à la forme positive **2.** [answer] réponse *f* positive or affirmative, oui *m* ‣ **to reply in the positive** répondre par l'affirmative or affirmativement.

positive discrimination n *(U)* discrimination *f* positive *(mesures favorisant les membres de groupes minoritaires)*.

positively ['pɒzətɪvlɪ] adv **1.** [absolutely] absolument, positivement ; [definitely] incontestablement, positivement **2.** [constructively] positivement **3.** [affirmatively] affirmativement ; [with certainty] avec certitude, positivement.

positive vetting [-'vetɪŋ] n contrôle *m* or enquête *f* de sécurité *(sur un candidat à un poste touchant à la sécurité nationale)*.

positivism ['pɒzɪtɪvɪzm] n positivisme *m*.

posse ['pɒsɪ] n **1.** [US] HIST petit groupe d'hommes rassemblés par le shérif en cas d'urgence ‣ **to get up a posse** réunir un groupe d'hommes **2.** *v inf* [group of friends] bande *f*.

possess [pə'zes] vt **1.** [have possession of - permanently] posséder, avoir ; [- temporarily] être en possession de, détenir, avoir **2.** [obsess] obséder / *what on earth possessed him to do such a thing?* qu'est-ce qui lui a pris de faire une chose pareille ?

possessed [pə'zest] adj [controlled - by an evil spirit] possédé / *she / her soul is possessed by the devil* elle / son âme est possédée du démon.

possession [pə'zeʃn] n **1.** [gen] possession *f* ‣ **to be in possession of sthg** être en possession de qqch ‣ **to take possession of sthg a)** [acquire] prendre possession de qqch **b)** [by force] s'emparer de or s'approprier qqch **c)** [confiscate] confisquer qqch **2.** LAW [of property] possession *f*, jouissance *f* **3.** [by evil] possession *f*. ❖ **possessions** pl n **1.** [belongings] affaires *fpl*, biens *mpl* **2.** [colonies] possessions *fpl* ; [land] terres *fpl*.

possessive [pə'zesɪv] ◆ adj **1.** [gen] possessif / *he's possessive about his belongings* il a horreur de prêter ses affaires / *she's possessive about her children* c'est une

mère possessive **2.** GRAM possessif ‣ **possessive adjective / pronoun** adjectif *m* / pronom *m* possessif. ◆ n GRAM [case] (cas *m*) possessif *m* ; [word] possessif *m*.

possessively [pə'zesɪvlɪ] adv de manière possessive.

possessiveness [pə'zesɪvnɪs] n caractère *m* possessif, possessivité *f*.

possessor [pə'zesəʳ] n possesseur *m*, propriétaire *mf*.

possibility [,pɒsə'bɪlətɪ] *(pl* **possibilities)** n **1.** [chance] possibilité *f*, éventualité *f* / *there's no possibility of that happening* il n'y a aucune chance or aucun risque que cela se produise / *there's a strong possibility we'll know the results tomorrow* il est fort possible que nous connaissions les résultats demain **2.** [person - for job] candidat *m*, -e *f* possible ; [- as choice] choix *m* possible. ❖ **possibilities** pl n [potential] possibilités *fpl*.

po$bl MESSAGING written abbr of **possible**.

possible ['pɒsɪbl] ◆ adj **1.** [which can be done] possible / *if possible* si possible / *it isn't possible for her to come* il ne lui est pas possible or il lui est impossible de venir ; *(in comparisons) : as far as possible* **a)** [within one's competence] dans la mesure du possible **b)** [at maximum distance] aussi loin que possible / *as long as possible* aussi longtemps que possible / *as much* or *as many as possible* autant que possible / *as soon as possible* dès que possible, le plus tôt or le plus vite possible **2.** [conceivable, imaginable] possible, imaginable / *it's possible (that) he won't come* il se peut qu'il ne vienne pas ; [feasible] possible, faisable **3.** [potential] éventuel / *possible risks* des risques éventuels. ◆ n **1.** [activity] possible *m* **2.** [choice] choix *m* possible ; [candidate] candidature *f* susceptible d'être retenue ; SPORT [player] joueur *m* susceptible d'être choisi.

> Note that **il est possible que** is followed by a verb in the subjunctive:
> **It's possible I may be late.** *Il est possible que je sois en retard.*

possibly ['pɒsɪblɪ] adv **1.** [perhaps] peut-être / *possibly (so)* / *possibly not, but he had no other choice* peut-être (bien) / peut-être pas, mais il n'avait pas le choix / *will you be there tomorrow? — possibly* vous serez là demain ? — c'est possible / *could you possibly lend me £5?* vous serait-il possible de me prêter 5 livres ? **2.** *(with modal verbs)* : *she can't possibly get here on time* elle ne pourra jamais arriver à l'heure / *where can they possibly have got to?* où peuvent-ils bien être passés ? / *I couldn't possibly accept your offer* je ne puis accepter votre proposition / *she might possibly still be here* il se pourrait qu'elle soit encore ici.

possum ['pɒsəm] n [American] opossum *m* ; [Australian] phalanger *m* ‣ **to play possum** *inf* faire le mort.

post [pəʊst] ◆ n **1.** [UK] [letters] courrier *m* ; [postal service] poste *f*, courrier *m* / *has the post come?* est-ce que le facteur est passé ? / *did it come through the post* or *by post?* est-ce que c'est arrivé par la poste ? / *I sent it by post* je l'ai envoyé par la poste / *can you put the cheque in the post?* pouvez-vous poster le chèque ? ; [delivery] (distribution *f* du) courrier *m* / *a parcel came in this morning's post* un paquet est arrivé au courrier de ce matin ; [collection] levée *f* (du courrier) / *I don't want to miss the post* je ne veux pas manquer la levée / *will we still catch the post?* pourrons-nous poster le courrier à temps or avant la levée ? ; [post office] poste *f* ; [letterbox] boîte *f* à lettres / *can you take the letters to the post?* **a)** [post office] pouvez-vous porter les lettres à la poste ? **b)** [post them] pouvez-vous poster les lettres or mettre les lettres à la boîte ? **2.** [station] relais *m* de poste ; [rider] courrier *m* **3.** [of sign, street lamp, fence] poteau *m* ; [of four-poster bed] colonne *f* ; [upright - of door] montant *m* **4.** [in racing] poteau *m* **5.** FOOT poteau *m*, montant *m* ▶ **the near / far post** le premier / deuxième poteau **6.** [job] poste *m*, emploi *m* / *a university / diplomatic post* un poste universitaire / de diplomate / *a government post* un poste au gouvernement **7.** [duty station] poste *m* / *a sentry post* un poste de sentinelle **8.** US [trading post] comptoir *m*. ◆ vt **1.** [letter - put in box] poster, mettre à la poste ; [- send by post] envoyer par la poste ▶ **to post sthg to sb** envoyer qqch à qqn par la poste, poster qqch à qqn **2.** [station] poster **3.** UK [transfer - employee] muter, affecter **4.** [publish - banns, names] publier ; [- on bulletin board] afficher **5.** BANK & ADMIN inscrire, enregistrer ▶ **to post an entry** passer une écriture **6.** US [issue] ▶ **to post bail** déposer une caution **7.** COMPUT poster ▶ **to post sthg on a blog** poster or publier qqch sur un blog. ❖ **post on** vt sep [letters] faire suivre. ❖ **post up** vt sep **1.** [notice] afficher **2.** [ledger] mettre à jour *(les écritures)*.

post- [pəʊst] pref post-.

postage ['pəʊstɪdʒ] ◆ n (U) [postal charges] tarifs *mpl* postaux or d'affranchissement ; [cost of posting] frais *mpl* d'expédition or d'envoi or de port / *what's the postage on this parcel?* c'est combien pour envoyer ce paquet ? ▶ **postage and packing** UK or **handling** US frais de port et d'emballage ▶ **postage paid** franco. ◆ comp [rates] postal.

postage stamp n timbre *m*, timbre-poste *m*.

postal ['pəʊstl] adj **1.** [charge, code, district] postal ; [administration, service, strike] des postes ; [delivery] par la poste ▶ **postal charges** frais *mpl* d'envoi or de port ▶ **postal vote** UK vote *m* par correspondance ▶ **postal worker** employé *m*, -e *f* des postes **2.** ▶ **to go postal** inf péter les plombs.

postal order n UK mandat *m* postal.

postbag ['pəʊstbæg] n UK **1.** [sack] sac *m* postal **2.** [correspondence] courrier *m*.

postbox ['pəʊstbɒks] n UK boîte *f* à or aux lettres.

postcard ['pəʊstkɑ:d] n carte *f* postale.

postcode ['pəʊstkəʊd] n UK code *m* postal.

postdate [,pəʊst'deɪt] vt **1.** [letter, cheque] postdater **2.** [event] assigner une date postérieure à.

post-edit vt réviser.

poster ['pəʊstər] n [informative] affiche *f* ; [decorative] poster *m*.

poster boy, poster child, poster girl n **1.** *lit* enfant malade dont l'image est reproduite sur les affiches d'une association caritative **2.** *fig* : *he's the poster boy of the revolutionary movement* il symbolise à lui seul le mouvement révolutionnaire.

poster campaign n campagne *f* d'affichage.

poste restante [,pəʊst'restɑ:nt] n poste *f* restante.

posterior [pɒ'stɪərɪər] ◆ adj **1.** *fml* [in time] postérieur **2.** TECH [rear] arrière. ◆ n *inf & hum* [of a person] postérieur *m*, arrière-train *m*.

posterity [pɒ'sterətɪ] n postérité *f* / *for posterity* pour la postérité ▶ **to go down to posterity** entrer dans la postérité or l'histoire.

poster paint n gouache *f*.

post-feminism n postféminisme *m*.

post-feminist adj & n postféministe *mf*.

post-free ◆ adj **1.** UK [prepaid] port payé **2.** [free of postal charge] dispensé d'affranchissement. ◆ adv **1.** UK [prepaid] en port payé **2.** [free of postal charge] en franchise postale.

postgraduate [,pəʊst'grædʒuət] ◆ n étudiant *m*, -e *f* de troisième cycle. ◆ adj [diploma, studies] de troisième cycle.

posthaste [,pəʊst'heɪst] adv *liter* à toute vitesse, en toute hâte.

posthumous ['pɒstjuməs] adj posthume.

posthumously ['pɒstjuməslɪ] adj après la mort / *the prize was awarded posthumously* le prix a été décerné à titre posthume.

postimpressionism [,pəʊstɪm'preʃnɪzm] n postimpressionnisme *m*.

postimpressionist [,pəʊstɪm'preʃnɪst] ◆ n postimpressionniste *mf*. ◆ adj postimpressionniste.

postindustrial [,pəʊstɪn'dʌstrɪəl] adj postindustriel.

posting ['pəʊstɪŋ] n **1.** UK [of diplomat] nomination *f*, affectation *f* ; [of soldier] affectation *f* **2.** COMM [in ledger] inscription *f*, enregistrement *m* **3.** UK [of letter] expédition *f* par la poste.

Post-it® (note) n Post-it® *m*.

postman ['pəʊstmən] (*pl* postmen [-mən]) n facteur *m* ; ADMIN préposé *m*.

postmark ['pəʊstmɑ:k] ◆ n [on letter] cachet *m* de la poste ▶ **date as postmark** le cachet de la poste faisant foi. ◆ vt oblitérer / *the letter is postmarked Phoenix* la lettre vient de or a été postée à Phoenix.

postmaster ['pəʊst,mɑ:stər] n receveur *m* des Postes.

Postmaster General (*pl* Postmasters General) n ≃ ministre *m* des Postes et Télécommunications.

postmistress ['pəʊst,mɪstrɪs] n receveuse *f* des Postes.

post-modern adj postmoderne.

post-modernism n postmodernisme *m*.

post-modernist ◆ n postmoderniste *mf*. ◆ adj postmoderniste.

postmortem [,pəʊst'mɔ:təm] ◆ n **1.** MED autopsie *f* ▶ **to carry out a postmortem** pratiquer une autopsie **2.** *fig* autopsie *f*. ◆ adj après le décès ▶ **postmortem examination** autopsie *f*.

postnatal [,pəʊst'neɪtl] adj postnatal ▶ **postnatal depression** dépression *f* postnatale.

post office n [place] (bureau *m* de) poste *f* ; [service] (service *m* des) postes *fpl*, poste *f* ▶ **the Post Office** la Poste ▶ **post office and general stores** petite épicerie de village faisant office de bureau de poste.

post office box n boîte *f* postale.

postoperative [,pəʊst'ɒpərətɪv] adj postopératoire.

postpaid [,pəʊst'peɪd] adj & adv franco, franc de port.

postpone [,pəʊst'pəʊn] vt [meeting, holiday] remettre (à plus tard) ; [match, game] reporter ; [decision] différer / *the meeting was postponed for three weeks / until a later date* la réunion a été reportée de trois semaines / remise à une date ultérieure.

postponement [,pəʊst'pəʊnmənt] n [of meeting, match] renvoi *m* (à une date ultérieure), report *m* ; [of holiday] report *m*.

postproduction [,pəʊstprə'dʌkʃn] n postproduction *f*.

postscript ['pəʊsskrɪpt] n post-scriptum *m* inv.

post-traumatic stress disorder n (U) névrose *f* post-traumatique.

postulate *fml* ◆ vt ['pɒstjuleɪt] **1.** [hypothesize] poser comme hypothèse **2.** [take as granted] postuler, poser comme principe. ◆ n ['pɒstjʊlət] postulat *m*.

posture ['pɒstʃər] ◆ n **1.** [body position] posture *f*, position *f* **2.** *fig* [attitude] attitude *f*. ◆ vi se donner des airs, poser.

posturing ['pɒstʃərɪŋ] n pose *f*, affectation *f*.

postviral syndrome [ˌpəʊst'vaɪərl-] n syndrome m postviral.

postwar [ˌpəʊst'wɔːr] adj d'après-guerre, après la guerre ▸ **the postwar period** l'après-guerre m ou f / **in the immediate postwar period** au cours des années qui ont immédiatement suivi la guerre, tout de suite après la guerre.

postwoman ['pəʊst,wʊmən] (pl **women**) n factrice f.

posy ['pəʊsɪ] (pl **posies**) n petit bouquet m (de fleurs).

pot [pɒt] (pt & pp **potted**, cont **potting**) ◆ vt **1.** [jam] mettre en pot or pots ; [fruit] mettre en conserve **2.** [plant] mettre en pot **3.** UK [in snooker] ▸ **to pot the ball** mettre la bille dans la poche or la blouse **4.** UK [shoot] tuer. ◆ vi **1.** [do pottery] faire de la poterie **2.** UK [shoot] ▸ **to pot at sthg** tirer sur qqch. ◆ n **1.** [container - for paint, plant, jam, etc.] pot m ; [teapot] théière f ; [coffeepot] cafetière f / **I'll make another pot of tea / coffee** je vais refaire du thé / café / **a pot of tea for two** du thé pour deux personnes **2.** [saucepan] casserole f ▸ **pots and pans** batterie f de cuisine ▸ **(cooking) pot** marmite f, fait-tout m inv **3.** [pottery object] poterie f, pot m ▸ **to throw a pot** tourner une poterie **4.** inf SPORT [trophy] trophée m, coupe f **5.** US [kitty] cagnotte f **6.** inf [belly] bedaine f, brioche f **7.** UK inf [shot] ▸ **to take a pot at sthg** tirer sur qqch **8.** inf [marijuana] herbe f **9.** ELEC potentiomètre m **10.** PHR **to go to pot a)** inf [country] aller à la dérive **b)** [morals] dégénérer **c)** [plans] tomber à l'eau **d)** [person] se laisser aller / **everything has gone to pot** tout est fichu. ◆ **pots** pl n UK inf [large amount] tas mpl, tonnes fpl ▸ **to have pots of money** avoir plein de fric, être plein aux as.

potash ['pɒtæʃ] n (U) potasse f.

potassium [pə'tæsɪəm] n (U) potassium m.

potato [pə'teɪtəʊ] (pl **potatoes**) ◆ n pomme f de terre ▸ **the potato famine** UK HIST la disette de la pomme de terre. ◆ comp [farming, salad] de pommes de terre.

🏛 **The potato famine**

Famine qui sévit en Irlande en 1845, à la suite d'une épidémie qui détruisit les stocks de pommes de terre, aliment de base de la population. Plongeant le pays dans la misère, cette catastrophe poussa plus d'un million de personnes à émigrer aux États-Unis.

---

potato chip n **1.** UK [French fry] (pomme f) frite f **2.** US [crisp] (pomme f) chips f.

potato crisp n UK (pomme f) chips f.

potato masher n presse-purée m inv.

potato peeler n [tool] éplucheur m, épluche-légumes m, (couteau m) Économe m ; [machine] éplucheuse f.

potbellied ['pɒt,belɪd] adj **1.** [person] bedonnant / **to be potbellied** avoir du ventre **2.** ▸ **potbellied stove** poêle m.

potbelly ['pɒt,belɪ] (pl **potbellies**) n **1.** [stomach] ventre m, bedon m / **to have a potbelly** avoir du ventre **2.** US [stove] poêle m.

potboiler ['pɒt,bɔɪlər] n inf gagne-pain m.

pot-bound adj [plant] qui a besoin d'être rempoté.

potency ['pəʊtənsɪ] (pl **potencies**) n **1.** [strength - of spell, influence, argument] force f, puissance f ; [- of medicine] efficacité f ; [- of drink] (forte) teneur f en alcool **2.** [virility] puissance f, virilité f.

potent ['pəʊtənt] adj **1.** [spell, influence] fort, puissant ; [argument] convaincant ; [medicine, poison, antidote] actif ; [drink] fort (en alcool) **2.** [virile] viril.

potentate ['pəʊtənteɪt] n POL potentat m ; fig magnat m.

potential [pə'tenʃl] ◆ adj **1.** [possible] possible, potentiel **2.** LING potentiel **3.** ELEC & PHYS potentiel. ◆ n **1.** (U) [of person] promesse f, possibilités fpl (d'avenir) / **your son has potential** votre fils a de l'avenir or un avenir prometteur / **she has the potential to succeed** elle a la capacité de réussir / **she has great potential as an actress** or **great acting potential** elle a toutes les qualités d'une grande actrice ▸ **to fulfil one's potential** donner toute sa mesure ; [of concept, discovery, situation] possibilités fpl ; [of place] possibilités fpl **2.** ELEC & MATH potentiel m.

potentially [pə'tenʃəlɪ] adv potentiellement.

pothole ['pɒthəʊl] n **1.** [in road] fondrière f, nid-de-poule m **2.** [underground] caverne f, grotte f.

potholer ['pɒt,həʊlər] n UK spéléologue mf.

potholing ['pɒt,həʊlɪŋ] n (U) UK spéléologie f ▸ **to go potholing** faire de la spéléologie.

potion ['pəʊʃn] n **1.** MED potion f **2.** fig potion f, breuvage m.

potluck [ˌpɒt'lʌk] n inf ▸ **to take potluck a)** [for meal] manger à la fortune du pot **b)** [take what one finds] s'en remettre au hasard.

pot plant n UK plante f d'intérieur.

potpourri [ˌpəʊ'pʊərɪ] n pot-pourri m.

pot roast n rôti m à la cocotte.

pot shot n ▸ **to take a pot shot at sthg a)** [fire at] tirer à l'aveuglette sur qqch **b)** [attempt] faire qqch à l'aveuglette.

potted ['pɒtɪd] adj **1.** HORT en pot ▸ **potted plant** plante f verte **2.** CULIN [cooked] (cuit) en terrine ; [conserved] (conservé) en terrine or en pot ▸ **potted meat** ≃ terrine f ▸ **potted shrimps** crevettes fpl en conserve **3.** inf [condensed - version] condensé, abrégé.

potter ['pɒtər] ◆ n potier m, -ère f ▸ **potter's clay** argile f de potier, terre f glaise ▸ **potter's wheel** tour m de potier ▸ **potter's field** US cimetière m des pauvres. ◆ vi UK inf s'occuper de choses et d'autres, bricoler. ◆ **potter about** UK inf ◆ vi s'occuper, bricoler. ◆ vt insep ▸ **to potter about the house / garden** faire de petits travaux or bricoler dans la maison / le jardin. ◆ **potter along** vi UK inf aller son petit bonhomme de chemin. ◆ **potter around** UK inf = potter about.

Potteries ['pɒtərɪz] pl n ▸ **the Potteries** la région des poteries dans le Staffordshire (en Angleterre).

pottery ['pɒtərɪ] (pl **potteries**) n **1.** (U) [craft] poterie f **2.** (U) [earthenware] poterie f, poteries fpl ; [ceramics] céramiques fpl / **a beautiful piece of pottery** une très belle poterie **3.** [workshop] atelier m de poterie.

potting ['pɒtɪŋ] n (U) **1.** HORT rempotage m ▸ **potting compost** terreau m **2.** [pottery] poterie f.

potty ['pɒtɪ] (pl **potties**, compar **pottier**, superl **pottiest**) ◆ n [for children] pot m (de chambre). ◆ adj UK inf fou (before vowel or silent 'h' **fol**, f **folle**), cinglé, dingue ▸ **to be potty about sthg** être toqué de qqch / **he's absolutely potty about her** il est absolument fou d'elle.

potty-train vt ▸ **to potty-train a child** apprendre à un enfant à aller sur son pot.

potty-trained adj propre.

pouch [paʊtʃ] n **1.** [bag] (petit) sac m ; [for tobacco] blague f ; [for money] sac m, bourse f ; [for ammunition] cartouchière f, giberne f ; [for gunpowder] sacoche f, sac m ; [for mail] sac m (postal) **2.** ZOOL [of marsupial, in cheeks] poche f, abajoue f ; [pocket of skin] poche f **3.** US [for diplomats] valise f diplomatique.

pouf(fe) [puːf] n UK **1.** [cushion] pouf m **2.** UK v inf = **poof** (noun).

poultice ['pəʊltɪs] ◆ n MED cataplasme *m*. ◆ vt mettre un cataplasme à.

poultry ['pəʊltrɪ] ◆ n *(U)* [meat] volaille *f*. ◆ pl n [birds] volaille *f*, volailles *fpl*.

poultry farm n élevage *m* de volaille or de volailles.

poultry farmer n éleveur *m*, -euse *f* de volaille or de volailles, aviculteur *m*, -trice *f*.

pounce [paʊns] ◆ vi sauter, bondir. ◆ n bond *m*. ❖ **pounce on, pounce upon** vt insep 1. [subj: animal] se jeter sur, bondir sur ; [subj: bird] se jeter sur, fondre sur ; [subj: police] saisir, arrêter 2. [in criticism] bondir sur, sauter sur 3. [seize - opportunity] sauter sur, saisir.

pound [paʊnd] ◆ n 1. [weight] livre *f* ▶ **to sell goods by the pound** vendre des marchandises à la livre / *two dollars a pound* deux dollars la livre 2. [money] livre *f* / *two for a pound* deux livres pour une livre ▶ **pound coin** pièce *f* d'une livre ▶ **the pound sterling** la livre sterling 3. [for dogs, cars] fourrière *f*. ◆ vt 1. [crush, pulverize - grain] broyer, concasser ; [- rocks] concasser, écraser 2. [hammer, hit] cogner sur, marteler / *the waves pounded the rocks / boat* les vagues battaient les rochers / venaient s'écraser violemment contre le bateau / *he began pounding the typewriter keys* il commença à taper sur or à marteler le clavier de la machine à écrire 3. [bombard, shell] bombarder, pilonner / *they pounded the enemy positions with mortar fire* ils ont bombardé les positions ennemies au mortier 4. [walk - corridor] faire les cent pas dans, aller et venir dans ▶ **to pound the streets** battre le pavé ▶ **to pound the beat** faire sa ronde. ◆ vi 1. [hammer - on table, ceiling] cogner, taper ; [- on piano, typewriter] taper / *we had to pound on the door before anyone answered* il a fallu frapper à la porte à coups redoublés avant d'obtenir une réponse / *the waves pounded against the rocks* les vagues venaient s'écraser sur or fouettaient les rochers / *the rain was pounding on the roof* la pluie tambourinait sur le toit 2. [rhythmically - drums] battre ; [- heart] battre fort ; [- with fear, excitement] battre la chamade / *my head was pounding from the noise* le bruit me martelait la tête 3. [more heavily] : *he pounded down the stairs* il descendit l'escalier bruyamment. ❖ **pound away** vi 1. [at task] travailler avec acharnement 2. [on typewriter, piano, drums] taper 3. [with artillery] : *to pound away at the enemy lines* pilonner sans arrêt les lignes ennemies. ❖ **pound down** vt sep 1. [crush] piler, concasser 2. [flatten - earth] pilonner, tasser. ❖ **pound out** vt sep ⓤⓀ 1. [rhythm] marteler 2. [letter, document] taper (avec fougue).

-pounder ['paʊndər] in comp ▶ **a fifteen-pounder** [fish] un poisson de 15 livres ▶ **a six-pounder** [gun] un canon or une pièce de six.

pounding ['paʊndɪŋ] ◆ adj : *with pounding heart* le cœur battant à tout rompre / *a pounding headache* un violent mal de tête. ◆ n 1. [noise] martèlement *m* 2. *(U)* [beating - of heart] battements *mpl* 3. *inf* [battering] rossée *f* 4. *inf* [severe defeat] déculottée *f*, piquette *f*.

pound sign n 1. ⓤⓀ *symbole de la livre sterling* 2. ⓤⓈ [on telephone] dièse *m*.

pour [pɔːr] ◆ vt 1. [liquid] verser / *she poured milk into their mugs* elle a versé du lait dans leurs tasses ; [serve] servir, verser ▶ **to pour a drink for sb** servir à boire à qqn 2. [invest] investir / *he poured all his energy into the project* il a mis toute son énergie dans le projet. ◆ vi 1. [light, liquid] se déverser, couler à flots / *water poured from the gutters* l'eau débordait des gouttières / *tears poured down her face* elle pleurait à chaudes larmes / *blood poured from the wound* la blessure saignait abondamment / *light poured into the church* l'église était inondée de lumière / *smoke poured out of the blazing building* des nuages de fumée s'échappaient de l'immeuble en flammes 2. [rain]

pleuvoir très fort / *it's pouring (down)* or *it's pouring with rain* il pleut des cordes or à torrents / *the rain poured down* il pleuvait à torrents 3. [crowd] affluer / *spectators poured into* or *out of the cinema* une foule de spectateurs entrait dans le cinéma / sortait du cinéma 4. [pan, jug] ▶ **to pour well / badly** verser bien / mal. ❖ **pour away** vt sep [empty] vider ; [throw out] jeter. ❖ **pour down** vi = **pour** *(vi)*. ❖ **pour in** vi 1. [rain, light] entrer à flots 2. [cars, refugees, spectators] arriver en masse ; [information, reports] affluer, arriver en masse / *offers of help poured in from all sides* des offres d'aide ont afflué de toutes parts / *money poured in for the disaster victims* des milliers de dons ont été envoyés pour les victimes de la catastrophe. ❖ **pour off** vt sep [liquid, excess] vider. ❖ **pour out** ◆ vt sep 1. [liquid] verser 2. [information, propaganda] répandre, diffuser ; [substances] : *the industry pours out tons of dangerous chemicals* l'industrie déverse des tonnes de produits chimiques dangereux 3. [emotions] donner libre cours à / *she poured out all her troubles to me* elle m'a raconté tout ce qu'elle avait sur le cœur ▶ **to pour out one's heart to sb** parler à qqn à cœur ouvert. ◆ vi [water] jaillir, couler à flots ; [tears] couler abondamment ; [light] jaillir.

pouring ['pɔːrɪŋ] adj 1. [rain] battant, diluvien / *we were stranded in the pouring rain* nous étions coincés sous une pluie battante 2. [cream] liquide.

pout [paʊt] ◆ vi faire la moue. ◆ vt dire en faisant la moue. ◆ n [facial expression] moue *f*.

POV written abbr of **point of view**.

poverty ['pɒvətɪ] n 1. [financial] pauvreté *f*, misère *f* ▶ **to live in poverty** vivre dans le besoin 2. [shortage - of resources] manque *m* ; [- of ideas, imagination] pauvreté *f*, manque *m* ; [weakness - of style, arguments] pauvreté *f*, faiblesse *f* 3. [of soil] pauvreté *f*, aridité *f*.

poverty line n seuil *m* de pauvreté ▶ **to live on / below the poverty line** vivre à la limite / en dessous du seuil de pauvreté.

poverty-stricken adj [person] dans la misère, dans le plus grand dénuement ; [areas] misérable, où sévit la misère.

poverty trap n *situation inextricable de ceux qui dépendent de prestations sociales qu'ils perdent s'ils trouvent une activité, même peu rémunérée.*

pow [paʊ] onomat [from collision] vlan, v'lan ; [from gun] pan.

POW n abbr of **prisoner of war**.

powder ['paʊdər] ◆ n [gen & MIL] poudre *f*. ◆ vt 1. [crush, pulverize] pulvériser, réduire en poudre 2. [make up] poudrer ▶ **to powder one's face** se poudrer le visage ▶ **to powder one's nose** *euph* [go to the toilet] aller se repoudrer le nez 3. [sprinkle] saupoudrer.

powder blue n bleu *m* pastel. ❖ **powder-blue** adj bleu pastel *(inv)*.

powder compact n poudrier *m*.

powdered ['paʊdəd] adj 1. [milk] en poudre ; [coffee] instantané ▶ **powdered sugar** ⓤⓈ sucre *m* glace 2. [hair, face] poudré.

powder keg n [of gunpowder] baril *m* de poudre ; *fig* poudrière *f*.

powder puff n houppette *f*.

powder room n *euph* toilettes *fpl* (pour dames).

powdery ['paʊdərɪ] adj 1. [covered in powder] couvert de poudre 2. [like powder] poudreux ▶ **powdery snow** (neige *f*) poudreuse *f* 3. [crumbling] friable.

power ['paʊər] ◆ n 1. [strength, force - gen] puissance *f*, force *f* ; PHYS [of engine, lens, microscope] puissance *f* ▶ **at full power** à plein régime 2. [influence] pouvoir *m*, puissance *f* / *I'll do everything in my power to help you* je ferai tout mon possible or tout ce qui est en mon pouvoir pour vous aider ; [control] pouvoir *m* ▸ **to have sb in one's power** avoir qqn en son pouvoir ; POL pouvoir *m* ▸ **to be in power** être au pouvoir ▸ **to come to / to take power** arriver au / prendre le pouvoir **3.** [authority] autorité *f*, pouvoir *m* ; [of assembly] pouvoir *m* ▸ **to have the power to decide / judge** avoir le pouvoir de décider / juger, avoir autorité pour décider / juger ; [influential group or person] puissance *f* **4.** POL [state] puissance *f* **5.** [ability, capacity] capacité *f*, pouvoir *m* / *he has great powers as an orator* or *great oratorical powers* il a de grands talents oratoires ; [faculty] faculté *f*, pouvoir *m* ▸ **the power of speech** : *he lost the power of speech* il a perdu l'usage de la parole **6.** ELEC [current] courant *m* **7.** ELEC & PHYS [energy] énergie *f* ▸ **nuclear / solar power** énergie nucléaire / solaire **8.** LAW [proxy] pouvoir *m* **9.** MATH puissance *f* / *5 to the power (of)* 6 5 puissance 6 **10.** PHR a power of good *inf* : *the holiday did me a power of good* les vacances m'ont fait énormément de bien. ◆ comp [source, consumption] d'énergie ; [cable] électrique ; [brakes, steering] assisté ▸ **power breakfast** petit déjeuner *m* d'affaires ▸ **power dressing** façon de s'habiller qu'adoptent certaines femmes cadres dans le but de projeter une image d'autorité. ◆ vt [give power to] faire fonctionner or marcher ; [propel] propulser. ◆ vi avancer à toute vitesse, foncer.

power-assisted adj assisté.

power base n assise *f* politique.

powerboat ['paʊəbəʊt] n [outboard] hors-bord *m inv* ; [inboard] vedette *f* (rapide) ▸ **powerboat racing** courses *fpl* offshore.

powerbrand ['paʊəbrænd] n marque *f* forte.

power broker n décideur *m* politique.

power cut n coupure *f* de courant.

-powered ['paʊəd] in comp ▸ **high / low-powered** de haute / faible puissance ▸ **a high-powered executive** un cadre très haut placé ▸ **steam / wind-powered** mû par la vapeur / le vent.

power failure n panne *f* de courant.

powerful ['paʊəfʊl] adj **1.** [strong - gen] puissant ; [-smell] fort ; [-kick] violent ; [-imagination] débordant **2.** [influential - person] fort, influent ; [-country, firm] puissant.

powerfully ['paʊəfʊlɪ] adv puissamment.

power game n lutte *f* d'influence, course *f* au pouvoir.

powerhouse ['paʊəhaʊs] *(pl* [-hauzɪz)] n **1.** ELEC centrale *f* électrique **2.** *fig* [person] personne *f* énergique, locomotive *f* ; [place] pépinière *f*.

powerless ['paʊəlɪs] adj impuissant, désarmé / *they were powerless to prevent the scandal* ils n'ont rien pu faire pour éviter le scandale.

power line n ligne *f* à haute tension.

power of attorney n LAW procuration *f*.

power plant n **1.** [factory] centrale *f* électrique **2.** [generator] groupe *m* électrogène **3.** [engine] groupe *m* moteur.

power point n prise *f* de courant.

power sharing [-,ʃeərɪŋ] n POL partage *m* du pouvoir.

power station n centrale *f* (électrique).

power steering n direction *f* assistée.

power struggle n lutte *f* pour le pouvoir.

power supply n ELEC alimentation *f* électrique.

power tool n outil *m* électrique.

power worker n employé *m*, -e *f* de l'électricité.

powwow ['paʊwaʊ] n [of American Indians] assemblée *f* ; *fig & hum* [meeting] réunion *f* ; [discussion] discussion *f*, pourparlers *mpl*.

pp (written abbr of *per procurationem*) pp.

PPE (abbr of philosophy, politics, and economics) n UK *philosophie, science politique et science économique (matière à l'université).*

PPI abbr of pixels per inch.

PPL MESSAGING written abbr of people.

ppm 1. (abbr of parts per million) ppm **2.** (abbr of pages per minute) ppm.

PPS ◆ n UK abbr of parliamentary private secretary. ◆ (written abbr of post postscriptum) PPS.

PPV, ppv (abbr of pay-per-view) n système *m* de télévison à la carte or à la séance or pay per view.

PQ written abbr of Province of Quebec.

PR ◆ n **1.** abbr of proportional representation **2.** abbr of public relations **3.** US *pej* abbr of Puerto Rican. ◆ written abbr of Puerto Rico.

Pr. (written abbr of prince) Pce.

practicability [,præktɪkə'bɪlətɪ] n **1.** [of plan, action] faisabilité *f*, viabilité *f* **2.** [of road] praticabilité *f*.

practicable ['præktɪkəbl] adj **1.** [feasible] réalisable, praticable ; [possible] possible **2.** [road] praticable.

practical ['præktɪkl] ◆ adj **1.** [convenient, easy to use] pratique, commode **2.** [sensible, commonsense - person] pragmatique, doué de sens pratique ; [-mind, suggestion] pratique **3.** [training, experience, question] pratique, concret (concrète) ▸ **practical nurse** aide-soignant *m*, -e *f* **4.** [virtual] : *it's a practical impossibility* c'est pratiquement impossible. ◆ n UK SCH & UNIV [class] travaux *mpl* pratiques, TP *mpl* ; [exam] épreuve *f* pratique.

practicality [,præktɪ'kælətɪ] *(pl* practicalities) n [of person] sens *m* pratique ; [of ideas] nature *f* pratique. ❖ **practicalities** pl n [details] détails *mpl* pratiques.

practical joke n farce *f* ▸ **to play a practical joke on sb** faire une farce or jouer un tour à qqn.

practical joker n farceur *m*, -euse *f*.

practically ['præktɪklɪ] adv **1.** [sensibly] de manière pratique **2.** [based on practice] pratiquement **3.** [almost] presque, pratiquement **4.** [in practice] dans la pratique.

practice ['præktɪs] ◆ n **1.** [habit] pratique *f*, habitude *f* ; [custom] pratique *f*, coutume *f*, usage *m* **2.** [exercise - of profession, witchcraft, archery] pratique *f* **3.** [training] entraînement *m* ; [rehearsal] répétition *f* ; [study - of instrument] étude *f*, travail *m* ▸ **to be in practice** être bien entraîné ▸ **to be out of practice** manquer d'entraînement **4.** [training session] (séance *f* d')entraînement *m* ; [rehearsal - of choir] répétition *f* **5.** [practical application] pratique *f* ▸ **to put sthg in** or **into practice** mettre qqch en pratique ▸ **in practice** dans la pratique **6.** [professional activity] exercice *m* **7.** [office, surgery] cabinet *m* ; [clientele] clientèle *f*. ◆ comp [game, run, session] d'entraînement. ◆ vt & vi US = practise.

practiced US = practised.

practicing US = practising.

practise UK, **practice** US ['præktɪs] ◆ vt **1.** [for improvement - musical instrument] s'exercer à, travailler ; [-song] travailler, répéter ; [-foreign language] travailler, pratiquer ; [-stroke, shot] travailler / *to practise speaking French* s'entraîner à parler français **2.** [put into practice - principle, virtue] pratiquer, mettre en pratique **3.** [profession] exercer, pratiquer **4.** [inflict] infliger **5.** [customs, beliefs] observer, pratiquer **6.** RELIG pratiquer **7.** [magic] pratiquer. ◆ vi **1.** [gen & MUS] s'entraîner, s'exercer ; SPORT s'entraîner / *to practise on the guitar* faire des exercices à la guitare **2.** [professionally] exercer **3.** RELIG être pratiquant.

practised 🇬🇧, **practiced** 🇺🇸 ['præktɪst] adj **1.** [experienced] expérimenté, chevronné ; [skilled] habile **2.** [expert -aim, movement] expert ; [-ear, eye] exercé **3.** [artificial -smile, charm] factice, étudié.

practising 🇬🇧, **practicing** 🇺🇸 ['præktɪsɪŋ] adj **1.** RELIG pratiquant **2.** [professionally -doctor] exerçant ; [-lawyer, solicitor] en exercice **3.** [homosexual] actif.

practitioner [præk'tɪʃnə] n **1.** MED ▶ **(medical) practitioner** médecin m **2.** [gen] praticien m, -enne f.

PR agency n agence f de communication.

pragmatic [præg'mætɪk] adj pragmatique.

pragmatism ['prægmətɪzm] n pragmatisme m.

Prague [prɑːg] pr n Prague.

prairie ['preərɪ] n plaine f (herbeuse). ⬦ **Prairie** pr n ▶ **the Prairie** or **Prairies** a) [in US] la Grande Prairie b) [in Canada] les Prairies fpl.

praise [preɪz] ⬦ n **1.** [compliments] éloge m, louanges fpl / she was full of praise for their kindness elle ne tarissait pas d'éloges sur leur gentillesse / we have nothing but praise for the way in which he handled the matter nous ne pouvons que le féliciter de la façon or nous n'avons que des éloges à lui faire pour la façon dont il s'est occupé de l'affaire **2.** RELIG louange f, louanges fpl, gloire f. ⬦ vt **1.** louer, faire l'éloge de **2.** RELIG louer, glorifier, rendre gloire à. ⬦ **in praise of** prep phr : the director spoke in praise of his staff le directeur fit l'éloge de son personnel.

praiseworthy ['preɪz,wɜːðɪ] adj [person] digne d'éloges ; [action, intention, sentiment] louable, méritoire.

praline ['prɑːliːn] n praline f.

pram [præm] n **1.** 🇬🇧 [for baby] voiture f d'enfant, landau m **2.** NAUT prame f.

PRAM ['piːræm] (abbr of phase-change random access memory) n RAM f programmable.

prance [prɑːns] ⬦ vi **1.** [cavort -horse] caracoler, cabrioler ; [-person] caracoler, gambader **2.** [strut] se pavaner, se dandiner. ⬦ n sautillement m.

prang [præŋ] inf ⬦ vt 🇬🇧 [car] esquinter ; [plane] bousiller. ⬦ n : he had a prang a) [in car] il a eu un accident (de voiture) or un accrochage b) [in plane] son avion s'est planté.

prank [præŋk] n farce f, tour m ▶ **to play a prank on sb** jouer un tour or faire une farce à qqn.

prat [præt] n 🇬🇧 v inf couillon m.

prattish ['prætɪʃ] adj 🇬🇧 inf crétin, idiot.

prattle ['prætl] 🇬🇧 inf & pej ⬦ vi [babble] babiller, jacasser ; [converse] papoter. ⬦ n [babble] babillage m ; [conversation] papotage m, bavardage m.

prawn [prɔːn] n crevette f (rose), bouquet m.

prawn cocktail n cocktail m de crevettes.

prawn cracker n beignet m de crevette.

pray [preɪ] ⬦ vi prier ▶ **to pray for sb / for sb's soul** prier pour qqn / pour l'âme de qqn. ⬦ vt RELIG : we pray the rain will stop nous prions pour que la pluie cesse.

prayer [preə] n **1.** RELIG prière f ▶ **to be at prayer** être en prière, prier ▶ **to kneel in prayer** prier à genoux, s'agenouiller pour prier ▶ **to say a prayer for sb** dire une prière pour qqn ▶ **to say one's prayers** faire sa prière **2.** [wish] souhait m. ⬦ **prayers** pl n [at church] office m (divin), prière f ; 🇬🇧 SCH prière f du matin.

prayer book n bréviaire m.

prayer mat n tapis m de prière.

prayer meeting n réunion f de prière.

praying mantis ['preɪŋ-] n mante f religieuse.

pre- [priː] pref pré-.

preach [priːtʃ] ⬦ vi **1.** RELIG prêcher ▶ **to preach to sb** prêcher qqn **2.** [lecture] prêcher, sermonner. ⬦ vt **1.** RELIG prêcher ▶ **to preach a sermon** prêcher, faire un sermon **2.** fig [recommend] prêcher, prôner.

preacher ['priːtʃə] n [gen] prédicateur m ; 🇺🇸 [minister] pasteur m.

preamble [priː'æmbl] n préambule m.

prearrange [,priːə'reɪndʒ] vt fixer or régler à l'avance.

precancerous [,priː'kænsərəs] adj précancéreux.

precarious [prɪ'keərɪəs] adj précaire.

precariously [prɪ'keərɪəslɪ] adv précairement / precariously balanced en équilibre précaire.

precariousness [prɪ'keərɪəsnɪs] n précarité f.

precast [,priː'kɑːst] adj [concrete element] préfabriqué.

precaution [prɪ'kɔːʃn] n précaution f / as a precaution par précaution ▶ **to take precautions** prendre des précautions.

precautionary [prɪ'kɔːʃənərɪ] adj de précaution / as a precautionary measure par mesure de précaution ▶ **to take precautionary measures** or **steps against sthg** prendre des mesures préventives contre qqch.

precede [prɪ'siːd] vt **1.** [in order, time] précéder **2.** [in importance, rank] avoir la préséance sur, prendre le pas sur **3.** [preface] (faire) précéder.

precedence ['presɪdəns], **precedency** ['presɪdənsɪ] n (U) **1.** [priority] priorité f ▶ **to take** or **to have precedence over sthg** avoir la priorité sur qqch / her health must take precedence over all other considerations sa santé doit passer avant toute autre considération **2.** [in rank, status] préséance f ▶ **to have** or **to take precedence over sb** avoir la préséance or prendre le pas sur qqn.

precedent ['presɪdənt] n **1.** LAW précédent m, jurisprudence f ▶ **to set a precedent** faire jurisprudence ▶ **to follow a precedent** s'appuyer sur un précédent, suivre la jurisprudence **2.** [example case] précédent m ▶ **to create** or **to set** or **to establish a precedent** créer un précédent / without precedent sans précédent **3.** [tradition] tradition f ▶ **to break with precedent** rompre avec la tradition.

preceding [prɪ'siːdɪŋ] adj précédent / the preceding day le jour précédent, la veille.

precept ['priːsept] n précepte m.

precinct ['priːsɪŋkt] n **1.** [area -round castle, cathedral] enceinte f **2.** 🇬🇧 [shopping area] zone f commerciale **3.** [boundary] pourtour m **4.** 🇺🇸 ADMIN arrondissement m, circonscription f administrative ▶ **precinct (station)** commissariat m de quartier or d'arrondissement **5.** 🇺🇸 POL circonscription f électorale. ⬦ **precincts** pl n environs mpl, alentours mpl.

precious ['preʃəs] ⬦ adj **1.** [jewel, material, object] précieux, de grande valeur **2.** [friend, friendship, moment] précieux **3.** [affected -style, person] précieux **4.** inf [expressing irritation] : I don't want your precious advice je ne veux pas de vos fichus conseils. ⬦ adv inf très / there's precious little chance of that happening il y a bien peu or très peu de chances (pour) que cela se produise. ⬦ n ▶ **my precious** mon trésor.

precious metal n métal m précieux.

precious stone n pierre f précieuse.

precipice ['presɪpɪs] n lit précipice m ; fig catastrophe f.

precipitate ⬦ vt [prɪ'sɪpɪteɪt] **1.** [downfall, ruin, crisis] précipiter, hâter **2.** [person, vehicle, object] précipiter **3.** CHEM précipiter. ⬦ n [prɪ'sɪpɪteɪt] précipité m. ⬦ adj [prɪ'sɪpɪtət] **1.** [hasty -action] précipité ; [-decision, judgment] hâtif ; [-remark] irréfléchi **2.** [steep] abrupt, à pic.

precipitation [prɪ,sɪpɪ'teɪʃn] n (U) **1.** [haste] précipitation f **2.** CHEM précipitation f **3.** METEOR précipitations fpl.

precipitous [prɪ'sɪpɪtəs] adj **1.** [steep -cliff] à pic, escarpé ; [-road, stairs] raide ; [-fall] à pic **2.** [hasty] précipité.

precipitously [prɪˈsɪpɪtəslɪ] adv **1.** [steeply] à pic, abruptement **2.** [hastily] précipitamment.
précis [⬛ ˈpreɪsiː: ⬛ ˈpresiː] (*pl* **précis** [⬛ ˈpreɪsiː: ⬛ ˈpresiː:]) ◆ n précis *m*, résumé *m*. ◆ vt faire un résumé de.
precise [prɪˈsaɪs] adj **1.** [exact - amount, detail] précis ; [- location] exact ; [- pronunciation] exact, juste / *he was very precise in his description* il a donné une description très précise or détaillée / *at that precise moment* à ce moment précis **2.** [meticulous - person, manner, mind, movement] précis, méticuleux **3.** *pej* [fussy] pointilleux, maniaque.
precisely [prɪˈsaɪslɪ] ◆ adv [exactly - explain] précisément, exactement ; [measure] précisément, avec précision / *that's precisely the reason (why) I'm not going* c'est précisément pourquoi je n'y vais pas / *she speaks very precisely* elle s'exprime avec beaucoup de précision / *at 4 o'clock precisely* à 4 h précises. ◆ interj précisément, exactement / *do you think it's too risky? — precisely!* pensez-vous que ce soit trop risqué ? — tout à fait ! or exactement !
precision [prɪˈsɪʒn] ◆ n précision *f*. ◆ comp [instrument, engineering, tool, bombing] de précision.
precision-engineered, precision-made adj de (haute) précision.
preclude [prɪˈkluːd] vt *fml* exclure, prévenir / *the crisis precludes her (from) going to Moscow* la crise rend impossible son départ pour Moscou or la met dans l'impossibilité de partir pour Moscou.
precocious [prɪˈkəʊʃəs] adj précoce.
precociousness [prɪˈkəʊʃəsnɪs], **precocity** [prɪˈkɒsətɪ] n précocité *f*.
precognition [ˌpriːkɒgˈnɪʃn] n [gift] prescience *f*, don *m* de seconde vue ; [knowledge] connaissance *f* préalable.
preconceived [ˌpriːkənˈsiːvd] adj préconçu ▶ **preconceived idea** idée *f* préconçue.
preconception [ˌpriːkənˈsepʃn] n préconception *f*, idée *f* préconçue.
precondition [ˌpriːkənˈdɪʃn] ◆ n condition *f* préalable, condition *f* sine qua non. ◆ vt conditionner.
precooked [priːˈkʊkt] adj précuit.
precursor [ˌpriːˈkɜːsər] n [person] précurseur *m* ; [invention, machine] ancêtre *m* ; [event] signe *m* avant-coureur or précurseur.
precut [priːˈkʌt] adj [ham, cheese, bread] prédécoupé, pré-tranché.
predate [priːˈdeɪt] vt **1.** [give earlier date to - cheque] antidater ; [- historical event] attribuer une date antérieure à **2.** [precede] être antérieur à.
predator [ˈpredətər] n **1.** [animal, bird] prédateur *m* **2.** *fig* [person] rapace *m*.
predatory [ˈpredətrɪ] adj **1.** [animal, bird] prédateur **2.** *fig* [gen - person, instinct] rapace ; [- attacker] pillard.
predatory pricing n pratique de prix prédateurs.
predecease [ˌpriːdɪˈsiːs] vt mourir avant.
predecessor [ˈpriːdɪsesər] n [person, model] prédécesseur *m* ; [event] précédent *m*.
predestination [priːˌdestɪˈneɪʃn] n prédestination *f*.
predestine [ˌpriːˈdestɪn] vt prédestiner.
predetermination [ˈpriːdɪˌtɜːmɪˈneɪʃn] n prédétermination *f*.
predetermine [ˌpriːdɪˈtɜːmɪn] vt prédéterminer.
predetermined [ˌpriːdɪˈtɜːmɪnd] adj déterminé / *at a predetermined date* à une date déterminée or arrêtée d'avance.
predicament [prɪˈdɪkəmənt] n situation *f* difficile or malencontreuse ▶ **to be in a predicament** être dans une situation difficile.
predict [prɪˈdɪkt] vt prédire.
predictability [prɪˌdɪktəˈbɪlətɪ] n prévisibilité *f*.

predictable [prɪˈdɪktəbl] adj prévisible.
predictably [prɪˈdɪktəblɪ] adv de manière prévisible / *predictably, she forgot to tell him* comme on pouvait le prévoir or comme on pouvait s'y attendre, elle a oublié de le lui dire.
prediction [prɪˈdɪkʃn] n [gen] prévision *f* ; [supernatural] prédiction *f*.
predictive texting [prɪˈdɪktɪv-] n TELEC [on mobile phone] écriture *f* prédictive, T9 *m*.
predilection [ˌpriːdɪˈlekʃn] n prédilection *f* ▶ **to have a predilection for sthg** avoir une prédilection or un faible pour qqch.
predispose [ˌpriːdɪsˈpəʊz] vt prédisposer ▶ **to be predisposed to do sthg** être prédisposé à faire qqch / *I was not predisposed in his favour* je n'étais pas prédisposé en sa faveur.
predisposition [ˈpriːˌdɪspəˈzɪʃn] n prédisposition *f* ▶ **to have a predisposition to** or **towards sthg** avoir une prédisposition à qqch.
predominance [prɪˈdɒmɪnəns], **predominancy** [prɪˈdɒmɪnənsɪ] n prédominance *f*.
predominant [prɪˈdɒmɪnənt] adj prédominant.
predominantly [prɪˈdɒmɪnəntlɪ] adv principalement.
predominate [prɪˈdɒmɪneɪt] vi **1.** [be greater in number] prédominer **2.** [prevail] prédominer, prévaloir, l'emporter.
pre-eminence [ˌpriːˈemɪnəns] n prééminence *f*.
pre-eminent [ˌpriːˈemɪnənt] adj prééminent.
pre-eminently [ˌpriːˈemɪnəntlɪ] adv de façon prépondérante, avant tout.
pre-empt [ˌpriːˈempt] vt **1.** [plan, decision] anticiper, devancer **2.** [land, property] acquérir par (droit de) préemption.
pre-emptive [ˌpriːˈemptɪv] adj [right] de préemption ; [strike] préventif.
preen [priːn] vt **1.** [plumage] lisser / *the bird was preening its feathers* or *was preening itself* l'oiseau se lissait les plumes ▶ **to preen o.s.** *fig* se faire beau, se pomponner **2.** [pride] ▶ **to preen o.s. on sthg** s'enorgueillir de qqch.
preexist [ˌpriːɪgˈzɪst] vt préexister à.
pre-existent adj préexistant.
prefab [ˈpriːfæb] n *inf* (bâtiment *m*) préfabriqué *m*.
prefabricate [ˌpriːˈfæbrɪkeɪt] vt préfabriquer.
prefabricated [ˌpriːˈfæbrɪkeɪtɪd] adj ▶ **prefabricated houses** maisons *fpl* en préfabriqué.
preface [ˈprefɪs] ◆ n [to text] préface *f*, avant-propos *m inv* ; [to speech] introduction *f*, préambule *m*. ◆ vt [book] préfacer ; [speech] faire précéder.
prefect [ˈpriːfekt] n **1.** ⬛ SCH élève *chargé de la discipline* **2.** [in France, Italy, etc.] préfet *m*.
prefer [prɪˈfɜːr] vt **1.** préférer, aimer mieux / *I prefer Paris to London* je préfère Paris à Londres, j'aime mieux Paris que Londres / *she prefers living* or *to live alone* elle préfère vivre seule / *he prefers to walk rather than take the bus* il préfère marcher plutôt que prendre le bus / *do you mind if I smoke? — I'd prefer (that) you didn't* cela vous dérange si je fume ? — j'aimerais mieux que vous ne le fassiez pas / *I'd prefer you not to go* je préférerais que vous n'y alliez pas **2.** LAW ▶ **to prefer charges against sb a)** [civil action] porter plainte contre qqn **b)** [police action] ≃ déférer qqn au parquet.

▱ Note that **préférer que** and **aimer mieux que** are followed by a verb in the subjunctive: **I'd prefer you to come alone** / **I'd prefer it if you came alone.** *Je préférerais que tu viennes seule. J'aimerais mieux que tu viennes seule.*

preferable ['prefrəbl] adj préférable / *it is preferable to book seats* il est préférable de or il vaut mieux retenir des places.

preferably ['prefrəblı] adv de préférence, préférablement.

preference ['prefərəns] n **1.** [liking] préférence *f* ▸ **to have** or **to show a preference for sthg** avoir une préférence pour qqch / *in order of preference* par ordre de préférence **2.** [priority] préférence *f*, priorité *f* ▸ **to have** or **to be given preference over** avoir la priorité sur.

preferential [,prefə'renʃl] adj préférentiel, privilégié ▸ **to get preferential treatment** bénéficier d'un traitement de faveur.

preferential rate n tarif *m* préférentiel.

preferred [prɪ'fɜːd] adj [best liked] préféré ▸ **preferred customer** client *m*, -e *f* privilégié(e).

prefigure [priː'fɪgəʳ] vt **1.** [foreshadow] préfigurer **2.** [foresee] se figurer or s'imaginer (d'avance).

prefix ['priːfɪks] ◆ n préfixe *m*. ◆ vt préfixer.

pregnancy ['pregnənsɪ] (*pl* **pregnancies**) n [of woman] grossesse *f* ; [of animal] gestation *f*.

pregnancy test n test *m* de grossesse.

pregnant ['pregnənt] adj **1.** [woman] enceinte ; [animal] pleine, grosse ▸ **to get** or **to become pregnant** tomber enceinte ▸ **to get a woman pregnant** faire un enfant à une femme / *to be six months pregnant* être enceinte de six mois / *she was pregnant with Brian then* à cette époque, elle attendait Brian **2.** *fig* [silence - with meaning] lourd or chargé de sens ; [- with tension] tendu.

preheat [,priː'hiːt] vt préchauffer.

preheated [,priː'hiːtɪd] adj préchauffé.

prehistoric [,priːhɪ'stɒrɪk] adj *lit & fig* préhistorique.

prehistory [,priː'hɪstərɪ] n préhistoire *f*.

pre-industrial adj préindustriel.

preinstalled [,priːɪn'stɔːld] adj [software] préinstallé.

prejudge [,priː'dʒʌdʒ] vt [issue, topic] préjuger (de) ; [person] porter un jugement prématuré sur.

prejudice ['predʒudɪs] ◆ n **1.** [bias] préjugé *m* ▸ **to have a prejudice in favour of** / **against** avoir un préjugé en faveur de / contre **2.** [detriment] préjudice *m*, tort *m*. ◆ vt **1.** [influence] influencer, prévenir ▸ **to prejudice sb against** / **in favour of sthg** prévenir qqn contre / en faveur de qqch **2.** [jeopardize] compromettre, porter préjudice à, nuire à.

⚠ **Préjudice** can only be used to translate prejudice when it means detriment.

prejudiced ['predʒudɪst] adj [person] qui a des préjugés or des idées préconçues ▸ **to be prejudiced against sthg** avoir des préjugés contre qqch ; [opinion] partial, préconçu.

prejudicial [,predʒu'dɪʃl] adj préjudiciable, nuisible.

prelate ['prelɪt] n prélat *m*.

preliminary [prɪ'lɪmɪnərɪ] (*pl* **preliminaries**) ◆ adj préliminaire, préalable ▸ **preliminary hearing** LAW première audience *f* ▸ **preliminary investigation** LAW instruction *f* (d'une affaire). ◆ n **1.** [gen] préliminaire *m* ▸ **as a preliminary** en guise de préliminaire, au préalable **2.** [eliminating contest] épreuve *f* éliminatoire.

prelude ['prelju:d] n [gen & MUS] prélude *m*.

premarital [,priː'mærɪtl] adj prénuptial, avant le mariage ▸ **premarital sex** rapports *mpl* sexuels avant le mariage.

premature ['premə,tjuəʳ] adj **1.** [birth, child] prématuré, avant terme / *three months premature* né trois mois

avant terme **2.** [death, decision, judgment] prématuré / *don't you think you're being a bit premature?* vous ne trouvez pas que c'est un peu prématuré ?

premature ejaculation n éjaculation *f* précoce.

prematurely ['premə,tjuːəlɪ] adv prématurément / *he was born prematurely* il est né avant terme / *to be prematurely bald* / *grey* être chauve / avoir les cheveux gris avant l'âge.

premeditate [,priː'medɪteɪt] vt préméditer.

premeditated [,priː'medɪteɪtɪd] adj prémédité.

premeditation [priː,medɪ'teɪʃn] n préméditation *f* / *without premeditation* sans préméditation.

premenstrual [priː'menstruəl] adj prémenstruel.

premenstrual tension 🇬🇧, **premenstrual syndrome** 🇺🇸 n syndrome *m* prémenstruel.

premier ['premjəʳ] ◆ adj premier, primordial. ◆ n Premier ministre *m*.

premiere ['premɪeəʳ] ◆ n CIN & THEAT première *f* / *the film's London* / *television premiere* la première londonienne / télévisée du film. ◆ vt donner la première de / *the opera was premiered in Paris* la première de l'opéra a eu lieu à Paris.

Premier League pr n *championnat anglais de football disputé par les plus grands clubs professionnels.*

premiership ['premjəʃɪp] n poste *m* de Premier ministre / *during her premiership* alors qu'elle était Premier ministre.

premise ['premɪs] ◆ n [hypothesis] prémisse *f* ▸ **on the premise that...** en partant du principe que... ◆ vt *fml* ▸ **to premise that** poser comme hypothèse que ▸ **to be premised on** être fondé sur.

premises ['premɪsɪz] pl n [place] locaux *mpl*, lieux *mpl* ▸ **business premises** locaux commerciaux ▸ **on the premises** sur les lieux, sur place.

premium ['priːmjəm] ◆ n **1.** [insurance payment] prime *f* (d'assurance) **2.** [bonus, extra cost] prime *f* / *fresh fruit is (selling) at a premium* les fruits frais sont très recherchés ▸ **to put** or **to place a (high) premium on sthg** attacher beaucoup de valeur à or faire grand cas de qqch **3.** 🇺🇸 [fuel] supercarburant *m*. ◆ comp ▸ **premium bond** obligation *f* à prime ▸ **premium quality** qualité *f* extra.

premonition [,premə'nɪʃn] n prémonition *f*, pressentiment *m* ▸ **to have a premonition of sthg** pressentir qqch, avoir le pressentiment de qqch / *I had a premonition he wouldn't come* j'avais le pressentiment qu'il ne viendrait pas.

prenatal [,priː'neɪtl] adj prénatal.

prenup ['priːnʌp] (abbr of pre-nuptial agreement or contract) n *inf* contrat *m* de mariage.

prenuptial [,priː'nʌpʃl] adj prénuptial ▸ **prenuptial agreement** or **contract** contrat *m* de mariage.

preoccupation [priː,ɒkju'peɪʃn] n préoccupation *f* / *I don't understand his preoccupation with physical fitness* je ne comprends pas qu'il soit si préoccupé par sa forme physique.

preoccupied [priː'ɒkjupaɪd] adj préoccupé ▸ **to be preoccupied by** or **with sthg** être préoccupé par or de *liter* qqch.

preoccupy [priː'ɒkjupaɪ] (*pt & pp* **preoccupied**) vt préoccuper.

preordain [,priːɔː'deɪn] vt : *our defeat was preordained* il était dit que nous perdrions.

pre-owned adj d'occasion.

prep [prep] *inf* ◆ n *(U)* 🇬🇧 SCH **1.** [homework] devoirs *mpl* **2.** [study period] étude *f (après les cours).* ◆ vi 🇺🇸 SCH faire ses études dans un établissement privé.

pre-packaged adj préconditionné, préemballé.

pre-packed adj préconditionné, préemballé.

prepaid *(pt, pp* [ˌpriːˈpeɪd]) ◆ pt & pp ⟶ **prepay.** ◆ adj [ˈpriːpeɪd] payé (d'avance).

preparation [ˌprepəˈreɪʃn] n **1.** *(U)* préparation *f* ▶ **to be in preparation** être en préparation / *in preparation for Christmas* pour préparer Noël **2.** *(C)* CHEM & PHARM préparation *f.* ❖ **preparations** pl n [arrangements] préparatifs *mpl,* dispositions *fpl / preparations for war* préparatifs de guerre.

preparatory [prɪˈpærətrɪ] adj [work] préparatoire ; [measure] préalable, préliminaire / *the report is still at the preparatory stage* le rapport en est encore au stade préliminaire or préparatoire.

preparatory school n **1.** [in UK] école *f* primaire privée *(pour enfants de sept à treize ans, préparant généralement à entrer dans une «public school»)* **2.** [in US] école privée qui prépare à l'enseignement supérieur.

prepare [prɪˈpeər] ◆ vt [plan, food, lesson] préparer / *to prepare a meal for sb* préparer un repas à or pour qqn / *to prepare the way / the ground for negotiations* ouvrir la voie à / préparer le terrain pour des négociations / *we are preparing to leave tomorrow* nous nous préparons à partir demain ; [person] préparer ▶ **to prepare o.s. for sthg** se préparer à qqch. ◆ vi ▶ **to prepare for sthg** faire des préparatifs en vue de or se préparer à qqch ▶ **to prepare to do sthg** se préparer or s'apprêter à faire qqch.

prepared [prɪˈpeəd] adj [ready - gen] préparé, prêt ; [- answer, excuse] tout prêt / *I was prepared to leave* j'étais préparé or prêt à partir / *he wasn't prepared for what he saw* a) [hadn't expected] il ne s'attendait pas à ce spectacle b) [was shocked] il n'était pas préparé à voir cela / *you must be prepared for anything* il faut s'attendre à tout ; [willing] prêt, disposé.

preparedness [prɪˈpeədnɪs] n : *preparedness for war* préparation *f* à la guerre / *lack of preparedness* manque *m* de préparation.

preponderance [prɪˈpɒndərəns] n [in importance] prépondérance *f* ; [in number] supériorité *f* numérique.

preponderantly [prɪˈpɒndərəntlɪ] adv [in importance] de façon prépondérante ; [especially] surtout.

preposition [ˌprepəˈzɪʃn] n préposition *f.*

prepossessing [ˌpriːpəˈzesɪŋ] adj [person] avenant ; [smile, behaviour] avenant, engageant.

preposterous [prɪˈpɒstərəs] adj absurde, grotesque.

preposterously [prɪˈpɒstərəslɪ] adv absurdement, ridiculement.

preppie, preppy 🇺🇸 [ˈprepɪ] *inf* ◆ n *(pl* **preppies)** : *he's a preppie* il est BCBG. ◆ adj *(compar* **preppier,** *superl* **preppiest)** BCBG.

preprogrammed [ˌpriːˈprəʊɡræmd] adj préprogrammé.

prep school n abbr of **preparatory school.**

prepubescent [ˌpriːpjuːˈbesənt] adj prépubère.

prequel [ˈpriːkwəl] n *inf* film dont l'action est antérieure à celle d'une œuvre existante.

prerecord [ˌpriːrɪˈkɔːd] vt préenregistrer.

prerecorded [ˌpriːrɪˈkɔːdɪd] adj préenregistré.

preregistration [ˌpriːredʒɪˈstreɪʃn] n UNIV préinscription *f.*

prerequisite [ˌpriːˈrekwɪzɪt] ◆ n (condition *f)* préalable *m,* condition *f* sine qua non ▶ **to be a prerequisite for** or **of sthg** être une condition préalable à qqch. ◆ adj ▶ **prerequisite condition** condition *f* préalable.

prerogative [prɪˈrɒɡətɪv] n prérogative *f,* apanage *m* ▶ **to exercise one's prerogative** exercer ses prérogatives.

Pres. written abbr of **president.**

presage [ˈpresɪdʒ] ◆ n présage *m.* ◆ vt présager, annoncer.

Presbyterian [ˌprezbɪˈtɪərɪən] ◆ adj presbytérien. ◆ n presbytérien *m,* -enne *f.*

presbytery [ˈprezbɪtrɪ] n **1.** [house] presbytère *m* **2.** [court] presbyterium *m* **3.** [part of church] presbyterium *m.*

preschool [ˌpriːˈskuːl] ◆ adj [playgroup, age] préscolaire ; [child] d'âge préscolaire. ◆ n 🇺🇸 école *f* maternelle.

preschooler [ˌpriːˈskuːləʳ] n 🇺🇸 enfant *mf* d'âge préscolaire.

prescribe [prɪˈskraɪb] vt **1.** MED prescrire ▶ **to prescribe sthg for sb** prescrire qqch à qqn **2.** [advocate] préconiser, recommander **3.** [set - punishment] infliger ; 🇬🇧 [SCH - books] inscrire au programme **4.** LAW prescrire.

prescription [prɪˈskrɪpʃn] ◆ n **1.** MED ordonnance *f* ▶ **to get sthg on prescription** obtenir qqch sur ordonnance **2.** [recommendation] prescription *f.* ◆ comp ▶ **a prescription drug** un médicament délivré seulement sur ordonnance.

prescription charge n 🇬🇧 ≃ ticket *m* modérateur.

prescriptive [prɪˈskrɪptɪv] adj **1.** LING [grammar, rule] normatif **2.** [dogmatic] dogmatique, strict.

preselect [ˌpriːsəˈlekt] vt [tracks, channels] prérégler.

presence [ˈprezns] n **1.** présence *f* ▶ **in the presence of sb** en présence de qqn ▶ **presence of mind** présence *f* d'esprit **2.** [number of people present] présence *f* **3.** [personality, magnetism] présence *f* **4.** [entity] présence *f.*

present ◆ n [ˈpreznt] **1.** [gift] cadeau *m* ▶ **to give sb a present** faire un cadeau à qqn ▶ **to make sb a present of sthg** faire cadeau de qqch à qqn / *it's for a present* [in shop] c'est pour offrir **2.** [in time] présent *m / at present* actuellement, à présent / *up to the present* jusqu'à présent, jusqu'à maintenant / *as things are* or *stand at present* au point où en sont les choses / *that's enough for the present* ça suffit pour le moment or pour l'instant / *to live only in* or *for the present* vivre pour l'instant présent or au présent **3.** GRAM présent *m / in the present* au présent. ◆ vt [prɪˈzent] **1.** [gift] donner, offrir ; [prize] remettre, décerner ▶ **to present sthg to sb** or **sb with sthg** donner or offrir qqch à qqn / *the singer was presented with a bunch of flowers* la chanteuse s'est vu offrir or remettre un bouquet de fleurs **2.** *fml* [introduce] présenter ▶ **to present sb to sb** présenter qqn à qqn / *to be presented at Court* être présenté à la Cour **3.** [put on - play, film] donner ; [- exhibition] présenter, monter **4.** RADIO & TV présenter **5.** [offer - entertainment] présenter **6.** [put forward - apology, view, report] présenter ; [plan] soumettre ; [orally] exposer / *I wish to present my complaint in person* je tiens à déposer plainte moi-même / *to present a bill in Parliament* présenter or introduire un projet de loi au parlement **7.** [pose, offer - problem, difficulty] présenter, poser ; [- chance, view] offrir / *if the opportunity presents itself* si l'occasion se présente **8.** [show - passport, ticket] présenter ▶ **present arms!** MIL présentez armes ! **9.** [arrive, go] ▶ **to present o.s.** se présenter **10.** MED / *the foetus presented itself normally* la présentation (fœtale) était normale. ◆ vi [prɪˈzent] présenter. ◆ adj [ˈpreznt] **1.** [in attendance] présent / *to be present at a meeting* être présent à or assister à une réunion / *present company excepted* à l'exception des personnes présentes **2.** [current - job, government, price] actuel / *in the present case* dans le cas présent / *at the present time* actuellement, à l'époque actuelle / *up to the present day* jusqu'à présent, jusqu'à aujourd'hui / *given the present circumstances* étant donné les circonstances actuelles, dans l'état actuel des choses / *in the present writer's opinion* de l'avis de l'auteur de ces lignes **3.** GRAM au présent ▸ **indicative present** or **present indicative** présent *m* de l'indicatif.

presentable [prɪ'zentəbl] adj [person, room] présentable ; [clothes] présentable, mettable / *make yourself presentable* arrange-toi un peu.

presentation [,prezn'teɪʃn] n **1.** [showing] présentation *f* / *on presentation of this voucher* sur présentation de ce bon ; [putting forward - of ideas, facts] présentation *f*, exposition *f* ; [- of petition] présentation *f*, soumission *f* **2.** COMM [of product, policy] présentation *f* **3.** [introduction] présentation *f* **4.** [performance - of play, film] représentation *f* **5.** [of piece of work] présentation *f* **6.** [award - of prize, diploma] remise *f* ▸ **to make sb a presentation of sthg** remettre qqch à qqn **7.** [award ceremony] = **presentation ceremony 8.** MED [of foetus] présentation *f*.

presentation ceremony n cérémonie *f* de remise (*d'un prix*).

presentation copy n [specimen] spécimen *m* (gratuit) ; [from writer] exemplaire *m* gratuit.

presentation pack n coffret *m* de présentation.

present-day adj actuel, contemporain.

presenter [prɪ'zentə'] n présentateur *m*, -trice *f*.

presentiment [prɪ'zentɪmənt] n pressentiment *m*.

presently ['prezntlɪ] adv **1.** 🇬🇧 [soon] bientôt, tout à l'heure **2.** [now] à présent, actuellement.

present perfect n passé *m* composé / *in the present perfect* au passé composé.

present tense n présent *m* / *in the present tense* au présent.

preservation [,prezə'veɪʃn] n **1.** [upkeep, maintenance - of tradition] conservation *f* ; [- of leather, building, wood] entretien *m* ; [- of peace, life] maintien *m* **2.** [of food] conservation *f* **3.** [protection] préservation *f*.

preservation order n ▸ **to put a preservation order on a building** classer un édifice (*monument historique*).

preservative [prɪ'zɜ:vətɪv] ◆ n agent *m* conservateur or de conservation, conservateur *m*. ◆ adj conservateur.

⚠ Un **préservatif** is a **condom**, not a preservative.

preserve [prɪ'zɜ:v] ◆ vt **1.** [maintain - tradition, building] conserver ; [- leather] conserver, entretenir ; [- silence] garder, observer ; [- peace, life] maintenir ; [- dignity] garder, conserver ▸ **to be well preserved a)** [building, specimen] être en bon état de conservation **b)** [person] être bien conservé **2.** [protect] préserver, protéger **3.** CULIN mettre en conserve ▸ **preserved fruit** fruits *mpl* en conserve. ◆ n **1.** HUNT réserve *f* (de chasse) **2.** [privilege] privilège *m*, apanage *m* **3.** CULIN [fruit] confiture *f* ; [vegetable] conserve *f*. ⬪ **preserves** pl n CULIN [jam] confitures *fpl* ; [vegetables, fruit] conserves *fpl* ; [pickles] pickles *mpl*.

preset [,pri:'set] [*pt & pp* **preset**] ◆ vt prérégler, régler à l'avance. ◆ adj préréglé, réglé d'avance.

preshrunk [,pri:'ʃrʌŋk] adj irrétrécissable.

preside [prɪ'zaɪd] vi présider ▸ **to preside at a meeting** / **at table** présider une réunion / la table. ⬪ **preside over** vt insep **1.** [meeting] présider ; [changes] présider à **2.** [subj: statue, building] dominer.

presidency ['prezɪdənsɪ] (*pl* **presidencies**) n présidence *f*.

president ['prezɪdənt] n **1.** [of state] président *m*, -e *f* / *President Simpson* le président Simpson **2.** [of organization, club] président *m*, -e *f* **3.** 🇺🇸 [of company, bank] président-directeur général *m*, P-D G *m*.

president-elect n titre du président des États-Unis nouvellement élu (en novembre) jusqu'à la cérémonie d'investiture présidentielle (le 20 janvier).

presidential [,prezɪ'denʃl] adj [elections, candidate] présidentiel ; [aeroplane, suite] présidentiel, du président / *it's a presidential year* c'est l'année des élections présidentielles.

President's Day n jour férié aux États-Unis, le troisième lundi de février, en l'honneur des anniversaires des présidents Washington et Lincoln.

press [pres] ◆ vt **1.** [push - button, bell, trigger, accelerator] appuyer sur / *he pressed the lid shut* il a fermé le couvercle (en appuyant dessus) / *to press sthg flat* aplatir qqch / *he was pressed (up) against the railings* il s'est trouvé coincé contre le grillage / *I pressed myself against the wall* je me suis collé contre le mur / *she pressed a note into my hand* elle m'a glissé un billet dans la main / *he pressed his nose (up) against the windowpane* il a collé son nez à la vitre **2.** [squeeze - hand, arm] presser, serrer ; [- grapes, olives] presser / *she pressed her son to her* elle serra son fils contre elle **3.** [urge] presser, pousser ▸ **to press sb for an answer** presser qqn de répondre ; [harass] harceler, talonner **4.** [force] forcer, obliger / *I was pressed into signing the contract* j'ai été obligé de signer le contrat **5.** [impose, push forward - claim, advantage] appuyer, pousser ; [- opinions] insister sur ▸ **to press (home) an advantage** profiter d'un avantage ▸ **to press charges against sb** LAW engager des poursuites contre qqn **6.** [iron - shirt, tablecloth] repasser **7.** [manufacture in mould - component] mouler ; [- record] presser **8.** [preserve by pressing - flower] presser, faire sécher (dans un livre ou un pressoir) **9.** [in weightlifting] soulever **10.** [enlist by force] recruter or enrôler de force ▸ **to press into service** fig réquisitionner. ◆ vi **1.** [push] appuyer **2.** lit [be a burden] faire pression ; fig [troubles] peser **3.** [insist, campaign] : *he pressed hard to get the grant* il a fait des pieds et des mains pour obtenir la bourse **4.** [surge] : *the crowd pressed against the barriers* / *round the President* la foule se pressait contre les barrières / autour du président / *they pressed forward to get a better view* ils poussaient pour essayer de mieux voir **5.** [iron] se repasser **6.** ☐PHR *time presses!* le temps presse ! ◆ n **1.** [newspapers] presse *f* / *the national* / *local press* la presse nationale / locale / *they advertised in the press* ils ont fait passer une annonce dans les journaux ▸ **the Press Association** la principale agence de presse britannique ▸ **the Press Complaints Commission** organisme britannique de contrôle de la presse ▸ **the Press Council** organisme indépendant veillant au respect de la déontologie dans la presse britannique **2.** [journalists] presse *f* / *the press were there* la presse était là / *she's a member of the press* elle a une carte de presse **3.** [report, opinion] presse *f* ▸ **to get (a) good** / **bad press** avoir bonne / mauvaise presse ▸ **to give sb (a) good** / **bad press** faire l'éloge / la critique de qqn **4.** [printing] presse *f* ▸ **to go to press a)** [book] être mis sous presse **b)** [newspaper] partir à l'impression **5.** [machine] ▸ **(printing) press** presse *f* **6.** [publisher] presses *fpl* **7.** [for tennis racket, handicrafts, woodwork, trousers] presse *f* ; [for cider, wine] pressoir *m* **8.** [push] : *the machine dispenses hot coffee at the press of a button* il suffit d'appuyer sur un bouton pour que la machine distribue du café chaud **9.** [squeeze] serrement *m* / *he gave my hand a quick press* il m'a serré la main rapidement **10.** [crowd] foule *f* ; [rush] bousculade *f* **11.** [ironing] coup *m* de fer ▸ **to give sthg a press** donner un coup de fer à qqch **12.** [cupboard] placard *m*

13. [in weightlifting] développé *m* **14.** INDUST [forming machine] presse *f*. ◆ comp [campaign, card, reporter, photographer] de presse ; [advertising, coverage] dans la presse.
◆◆ **press ahead** = press on. ◆◆ **press for** vt insep [demand] exiger, réclamer. ◆◆ **press in** vt sep enfoncer. ◆◆ **press on** vi [on journey] poursuivre or continuer son chemin ; [in enterprise, job] poursuivre, persévérer / *we pressed on regardless* nous avons continué malgré tout. ◆◆ **press on with** vt insep [job, negotiations] continuer, poursuivre.

press agency n agence *f* de presse.

press agent n attaché *m*, -e *f* de presse.

press baron n magnat *m* de la presse.

press box n tribune *f* de (la) presse.

press clipping = press cutting.

press conference n conférence *f* de presse.

press corps n US journalistes *mpl*.

press cutting n coupure *f* de presse or de journal.

pressed [prest] adj **1.** [flower] pressé, séché **2.** [hurried] pressé ; [overworked] débordé. ◆◆ **pressed for** adj phr [short of] à court de / *we're pressed for space* nous manquons de place / *we're rather pressed for time* le temps nous est compté.

press gallery n tribune *f* de (la) presse (*par exemple au Parlement*).

press-gang ['pres-] ◆ n MIL & HIST racoleurs *mpl*, recruteurs *mpl*. ◆ vt **1.** UK [force] ▶ **to press-gang sb into doing sthg** obliger qqn à faire qqch (contre son gré) **2.** MIL & HIST racoler, recruter de force.

pressing ['presɪŋ] ◆ adj **1.** [urgent - appointment, business, debt] urgent **2.** [insistent - demand, danger, need] pressant **3.** [imminent - danger] imminent. ◆ n **1.** [of fruit, record] pressage *m* **2.** [ironing] repassage *m*.

press kit n dossier *m* de presse (*distribué aux journalistes*).

pressman ['presmæn] (*pl* **pressmen** [-men]) n **1.** [journalist] journaliste *m* **2.** [printer] typographe *m*.

press officer n responsable *mf* des relations avec la presse.

press release n communiqué *m* de presse.

pressroom ['presrʊm] n salle *f* de presse.

press secretary n POL ≃ porte-parole *m inv* du gouvernement.

press stud n UK bouton-pression *m*, pression *f*.

press-up n UK SPORT pompe *f* ▶ **to do press-ups** faire des pompes.

pressure ['preʃər] ◆ n **1.** METEOR & PHYS pression *f* ; [of blood] tension *f* **2.** [squeezing] pression *f* **3.** *fig* [force, influence] ▶ **to bring pressure to bear** *fml* or *to put pressure on sb* faire pression or exercer une pression sur qqn **4.** *fig* [strain, stress - of circumstances, events] pression *f* ; [- of doubts, worries] poids *m* / *we're under pressure to finish on time* on nous presse de respecter les délais / *she's under a lot of pressure just now* elle est vraiment sous pression en ce moment. ◆ vt faire pression sur / *they pressured him into resigning* ils l'ont contraint à démissionner.

pressure cooker n cocotte-minute *f*, autocuiseur *m*.

pressure gauge n jauge *f* de pression, manomètre *m*.

pressure group n groupe *m* de pression.

pressurization, pressurisation [,preʃəraɪ'zeɪʃn] n pressurisation *f*.

pressurize, pressurise ['preʃəraɪz] vt **1.** [person, government] faire pression sur ▶ **to pressurize sb to do sthg** or **into doing sthg** faire pression sur qqn pour qu'il fasse qqch **2.** AERON & ASTRONAUT pressuriser.

pressurized, pressurised ['preʃəraɪzd] adj [container] pressurisé ; [liquid, gas] sous pression.

prestige [pre'stiːʒ] ◆ n prestige *m*. ◆ adj de prestige.

prestigious [pre'stɪdʒəs] adj prestigieux.

presto ['prestəʊ] adv presto ▶ **hey presto!** et voilà, le tour est joué !

prestressed concrete [,priː'strest-] n béton *m* précontraint.

presumably [prɪ'zjuːməblɪ] adv vraisemblablement / *presumably, he isn't coming* apparemment, il ne viendra pas.

presume [prɪ'zjuːm] ◆ vt **1.** [suppose] présumer, supposer / *I presume he isn't coming* je présume or suppose qu'il ne viendra pas **2.** [take liberty] oser, se permettre **3.** [presuppose] présupposer. ◆ vi : *I don't want to presume* je ne voudrais pas m'imposer ▶ **to presume on** or **upon sb** abuser de la gentillesse de qqn.

presumption [prɪ'zʌmpʃn] n **1.** [supposition] présomption *f*, supposition *f* **2.** (U) [arrogance] audace *f*, présomption *f*, prétention *f*.

presumptuous [prɪ'zʌmptʃʊəs] adj présomptueux, arrogant.

presuppose [,priːsə'pəʊz] vt présupposer.

pre-tax [,priː'tæks] adj brut, avant (le prélèvement des) impôts ▶ **pre-tax profits** bénéfices *mpl* bruts or avant impôts.

pre-teen ◆ adj [sizes, fashions] pour préadolescents ; [problems] des préadolescents ▶ **pre-teen child** préadolescent *m*, -e *f*. ◆ n préadolescent *m*, -e *f*.

pretence UK, **pretense** US [prɪ'tens] n **1.** [false display] simulacre *m* ▶ **to make a pretence of doing sthg** faire semblant or mine de faire qqch **2.** [pretext] prétexte *m* ▶ **under** or **on the pretence of doing sthg** sous prétexte de faire qqch **3.** [claim] prétention *f*.

pretend [prɪ'tend] ◆ vt **1.** [make believe] ▶ **to pretend to do sthg** faire semblant de faire qqch, feindre de faire qqch / *she pretends that everything is all right* elle fait comme si tout allait bien **2.** [claim] prétendre / *I don't pretend to be an expert* je ne prétends pas être un expert, je n'ai pas la prétention d'être un expert **3.** [feign - indifference, ignorance] feindre, simuler. ◆ vi **1.** [feign] faire semblant **2.** [lay claim] prétendre ▶ **to pretend to sthg** prétendre à qqch. ◆ adj *inf* [child language - money, fight] pour faire semblant, pour jouer / *it was only pretend!* c'était pour rire or pour faire semblant !

⚠ **Prétendre** can only be used to translate **to pretend** when it means **to claim**.

pretense US = pretence.

pretension [prɪ'tenʃn] n **1.** [claim] prétention *f* ▶ **to have pretensions to sthg** avoir des prétentions or prétendre à qqch **2.** (U) [pretentiousness] prétention *f*.

pretentious [prɪ'tenʃəs] adj prétentieux.

pretentiously [prɪ'tenʃəslɪ] adv prétentieusement.

pretentiousness [prɪ'tenʃəsnɪs] n (U) prétention *f*.

preterite ['pretərət] ◆ adj [form] du prétérit ▶ **the preterite tense** le prétérit. ◆ n prétérit *m* / *in the preterite* au prétérit.

pretext ['priːtekst] n prétexte *m* ▶ **on** or **under the pretext of doing sthg** sous prétexte de faire qqch.

Pretoria [prɪ'tɔːrɪə] pr n Pretoria.

prettify ['prɪtɪfaɪ] (*pt & pp* **prettified**) vt *pej* [room, garden] enjoliver ▶ **to prettify o.s.** se pomponner.

prettily ['prɪtɪlɪ] adv joliment.

prettiness ['prɪtɪnɪs] n **1.** [of appearance] beauté f **2.** pej [of style] mièvrerie f.

pretty ['prɪtɪ] (compar **prettier**, superl **prettiest**, pt & pp **prettied**) ◆ adj **1.** [attractive - clothes, girl, place] joli **2.** iro : this is a pretty state of affairs! c'est du joli or du propre ! **3.** pej [dainty - style, expression] précieux ; [effeminate - boy] mignon **4.** PHR a pretty penny : it cost a pretty penny ça a coûté une jolie petite somme. ◆ adv inf **1.** [quite] assez **2.** [almost] presque, à peu près, pratiquement **3.** PHR to be sitting pretty avoir la partie belle.

pretzel ['pretsl] n bretzel m.

prevail [prɪ'veɪl] vi **1.** [triumph] l'emporter, prévaloir liter ▸ to prevail against sb l'emporter or prévaloir contre qqn ▸ to prevail over sb l'emporter or prévaloir sur qqn **2.** [exist, be widespread - situation, opinion, belief] régner, avoir cours. ◆ prevail on, prevail upon vt insep fml persuader.

prevailing [prɪ'veɪlɪŋ] adj **1.** [wind] dominant **2.** [belief, opinion] courant, répandu ; [fashion] en vogue.

prevalence ['prevələns] n [widespread existence] prédominance f ; [of disease] prévalence f ; [frequency] fréquence f.

prevalent ['prevələnt] adj **1.** [widespread] répandu, courant ; [frequent] fréquent ▸ to become prevalent se généraliser **2.** [current - today] actuel, d'aujourd'hui ; [- in past] de or à l'époque.

prevaricate [prɪ'værɪkeɪt] vi fml tergiverser, user de faux-fuyants.

prevarication [prɪ,værɪ'keɪʃn] n fml tergiversation f, faux-fuyant m, faux-fuyants mpl.

prevent [prɪ'vent] vt [accident, catastrophe, scandal, illness] éviter, prévenir ▸ to prevent sb (from) doing sthg empêcher qqn de faire qqch / we were unable to prevent the bomb from exploding nous n'avons rien pu faire pour empêcher la bombe d'exploser / I couldn't prevent her je n'ai pas pu l'en empêcher.

⚠ **Prévenir** is used (as well as **empêcher**) to talk about preventing things from happening (illnesses, crises, etc.). When talking about preventing someone from doing something, use **empêcher**.

📋 Note that **empêcher que** is followed by a verb in the subjunctive (preceded by ne in affirmative clauses):
... to **prevent it from going rotten** ... pour empêcher que cela ne pourrisse.

preventable [prɪ'ventəbl] adj évitable.

preventative [prɪ'ventətɪv] adj préventif.

prevention [prɪ'venʃn] n prévention f / the prevention of cruelty to animals la protection des animaux.

preventive [prɪ'ventɪv] ◆ adj **1.** [medicine] préventif, prophylactique ; [measure] préventif **2.** UK LAW ▸ preventive detention peine de prison allant de 5 à 14 ans. ◆ n **1.** [measure] mesure f préventive / as a preventive à titre préventif **2.** MED médicament m préventif or prophylactique.

preview ['pri:vju:] ◆ n **1.** [preliminary showing - of film, show, exhibition] avant-première f ; [- of art exhibition] vernissage m **2.** US CIN [trailer] bande-annonce f. ◆ vt : to preview a film a) [put on] donner un film en avant-première b) [see] voir un film en avant-première.

previous ['pri:vjəs] ◆ adj **1.** [prior] précédent / on a previous occasion auparavant / I have a previous en-

gagement j'ai déjà un rendez-vous, je suis déjà pris / she has had several previous accidents elle a déjà eu plusieurs accidents / do you have any previous experience of this kind of work? avez-vous déjà une expérience de ce genre de travail ? / the two months previous to your arrival les deux mois précédant votre arrivée ; LAW : he has no previous convictions il n'a pas de casier judiciaire, il a un casier judiciaire vierge / he has had several previous convictions il a déjà fait l'objet de plusieurs condamnations **2.** [former] antérieur / in a previous life dans une vie antérieure / his previous marriages ended in divorce ses autres mariages se sont soldés par des divorces **3.** [with days and dates] précédent / the previous Monday le lundi précédent / the previous June au mois de juin précédent / the previous day le jour précédent, la veille **4.** US inf [premature, hasty - decision, judgement] prématuré, hâtif ; [- person] expéditif. ◆ adv antérieurement / previous to his death fml avant sa mort, avant qu'il ne meure.

previously ['pri:vjəslɪ] adv **1.** [in the past] auparavant, précédemment / six weeks previously six semaines auparavant or plus tôt **2.** [already] déjà.

prewar [,pri:'wɔːr] adj d'avant-guerre ▸ the prewar years l'avant-guerre m ou f.

prey [preɪ] n (U) lit & fig proie f / hens are often (a) prey to foxes les poules sont souvent la proie des renards / to be (a) prey to doubts / nightmares être en proie au doute / à des cauchemars. ◆ prey on, prey upon vt insep **1.** [subj: predator] faire sa proie de **2.** [subj: fear, doubts] ronger.

price [praɪs] ◆ n **1.** [cost] prix m / petrol has gone down in price le prix de l'essence a baissé / I got the chair at a reduced / at half price j'ai eu la chaise à prix réduit / à moitié prix **2.** [value] prix m, valeur f ▸ to argue over the price of sthg débattre le prix de qqch ▸ to put a price on sthg a) [definite] fixer le prix or la valeur de qqch b) [estimate] évaluer le prix or estimer la valeur de qqch **3.** ST. EX cours m, cote f **4.** fig [penalty] prix m **5.** [chance, odds] cote f **6.** [quotation] devis m. ◆ comp [bracket, range] de prix ; [rise, level] des prix. ◆ vt **1.** [set cost of] fixer or établir or déterminer le prix de / the book is priced at £17 le livre coûte 17 livres **2.** [indicate cost of] marquer le prix de ; [with label] étiqueter **3.** [ascertain price of] demander le prix de, s'informer du prix de. ◆ at any price adv phr : she wants a husband at any price elle veut un mari à tout prix or coûte que coûte / he wouldn't do it at any price! il ne voulait le faire à aucun prix or pour rien au monde ! ◆ at a price adv phr en y mettant le prix. ◆ price down vt sep ▸ baisser le prix de, démarquer. ◆ price out vt sep ▸ to price o.s. or one's goods out of the market perdre son marché or sa clientèle à cause de ses prix trop élevés / he priced himself out of the job il n'a pas été embauché parce qu'il a demandé un salaire trop élevé. ◆ price up vt sep US [raise cost of] augmenter or majorer le prix de, majorer ; [on label] indiquer un prix plus élevé sur.

price bid n offre f de prix.

price bracket n gamme f de prix ▸ within my price bracket dans mes prix.

price bubble n bulle f des prix.

price ceiling n plafond m de prix.

price cut n rabais m, réduction f (de prix).

price-cutting n (U) réductions fpl de prix.

-priced [praɪst] in comp ▸ high-priced à prix élevé, (plutôt) cher ▸ low-priced à bas prix, peu cher ▸ over-priced trop cher.

price differential n écart m de prix.

price discrimination n tarif m discriminatoire.

price-earnings ratio n ST. EX ratio m cours-bénéfices, rapport m cours-bénéfices.

price-fixing [-fɪksɪŋ] n [control] contrôle *m* des prix ; [rigging] entente *f* sur les prix.

price freeze n gel *m* des prix.

price increase n hausse *f* or augmentation *f* des prix.

price index n indice *m* des prix.

priceless ['praɪslɪs] adj **1.** [precious - jewels, friendship] d'une valeur inestimable **2.** *inf* [funny - joke] tordant, bidonnant ; [-person] impayable.

price list n tarif *m*, liste *f* des prix.

price range n gamme *f* de prix ❱ **within my price range** dans mes prix.

price tag n **1.** [label] étiquette *f* de prix **2.** [value] prix *m*, valeur *f*.

price war n guerre *f* des prix.

pricey ['praɪsɪ] (*compar* **pricier**, *superl* **priciest**) adj *inf* chérot.

pricing ['praɪsɪŋ] n détermination *f* du prix, fixation *f* du prix ❱ **pricing policy** politique *f* de(s) prix.

prick [prɪk] ❖ vt **1.** [jab, pierce] piquer, percer / *she pricked her finger / herself with the needle* elle s'est piqué le doigt / elle s'est piquée avec l'aiguille ❱ **to prick holes in sthg** faire des trous dans qqch **2.** [irritate] piquer, picoter. ❖ vi **1.** [pin, cactus, thorn] piquer **2.** [be irritated] picoter. ❖ n **1.** [from insect, pin, thorn] piqûre *f* **2.** *vulg* [penis] bite *f* **3.** *v inf* [person] con *m*, connard *m*. ❖ **prick up** ❖ vi [ears] se dresser. ❖ vt sep dresser.

prickle ['prɪkl] ❖ n **1.** [on rose, cactus] épine *f*, piquant *m* ; [on hedgehog, porcupine] piquant *m* **2.** [sensation] picotement *m*. ❖ vt piquer. ❖ vi [skin] picoter, fourmiller.

prickly ['prɪklɪ] (*compar* **pricklier**, *superl* **prickliest**) adj **1.** [cactus, plant] épineux ; [hedgehog] couvert de piquants ; [beard] piquant ; [clothes] qui pique **2.** *inf* [irritable - person] ombrageux, irritable ; [-character] ombrageux **3.** [delicate - subject, topic] épineux, délicat.

prickly heat n (*U*) fièvre *f* miliaire.

pricktease ['prɪkti:z], **prickteaser** ['prɪkti:zə¹] n *vulg* allumeuse *f*.

pride [praɪd] ❖ n **1.** [satisfaction] fierté *f* ❱ **to take (a) pride in one's appearance** prendre soin de sa personne ❱ **to take (a) pride in doing sthg** mettre de la fierté à faire qqch, s'enorgueillir de faire qqch **2.** [self-respect] fierté *f*, amour-propre *m* **3.** *pej* [arrogance] orgueil *m* **4.** [most valuable thing] orgueil *m*, fierté *f* / *she is her parents' pride and joy* elle fait la fierté de ses parents ❱ **to have or to take pride of place** occuper la place d'honneur **5.** [of lions] groupe *m*. ❖ vt ❱ **to pride o.s. on** or **upon sthg** être fier or s'enorgueillir de qqch / *she prided herself on being the youngest member of the team* elle s'enorgueillissait or était fière d'être la plus jeune de l'équipe.

priest [pri:st] n prêtre *m*.

priestess ['pri:stɪs] n prêtresse *f*.

priesthood ['pri:sthʊd] n [as vocation] prêtrise *f* ; [clergy] clergé *m* ❱ **to enter the priesthood** être ordonné prêtre.

prig [prɪg] n 🇬🇧 : *he's such a prig!* il fait toujours son petit saint !

prim [prɪm] (*compar* **primmer**, *superl* **primmest**) adj *pej* **1.** [affectedly proper - person] collet monté *(inv)* **1.** [-attitude, behaviour] guindé, compassé ; [-voice] affecté / *she's very prim and proper* elle est très collet monté **2.** [neat - clothes] (très) comme il faut, (très) classique ; [-house, hedge, lawn] impeccable.

primacy ['praɪməsɪ] (*pl* **primacies**) n **1.** [preeminence] primauté *f*, prééminence *f* **2.** RELIG primatie *f*.

prima donna [,pri:mə'dɒnə] n **1.** [opera singer] prima donna *f* **2.** *pej* diva *f* **3.** [star] star *f*.

primaeval [praɪ'mi:vəl] = **primeval**.

prima facie [,praɪmə'feɪʃi:] ❖ adv à première vue, de prime abord. ❖ adj LAW ❱ **a prima facie case** une affaire simple a priori ❱ **prima facie evidence** commencement *m* de preuve.

primal ['praɪml] adj **1.** [original] primitif, premier ❱ **primal scream** PSYCHOL cri *m* primal **2.** [main] primordial, principal.

primarily [🇬🇧 'praɪmərɪlɪ 🇺🇸 praɪ'merəlɪ] adv [mainly] principalement, avant tout.

primary ['praɪmərɪ] (*pl* **primaries**) ❖ adj **1.** [main] principal, premier ; [basic] principal, fondamental **2.** SCI primaire **3.** SCH primaire ❱ **primary education** enseignement *m* primaire **4.** ECON primaire. ❖ n **1.** POL [in US] ❱ **primary (election)** (élection *f*) primaire *f* **2.** [school] école *f* primaire **3.** [colour] couleur *f* primaire.

 Primaries

Les primaires américaines sont des élections, directes ou indirectes selon les États, pour sélectionner les candidats représentant les deux grands partis nationaux (démocrate et républicain) à l'élection présidentielle.

primary carer, **primary caregiver** n *personne qui s'occupe d'un proche dépendant.*

primary care trust n 🇬🇧 *administration qui gère les services de santé au niveau local.*

primary colour n couleur *f* primaire.

primary market n marché *m* primaire.

primary school n école *f* primaire ❱ **primary school teacher** instituteur *m*, -trice *f*.

primate ['praɪmeɪt] n **1.** ZOOL primate *m* **2.** RELIG primat *m* ❱ **the Primate of All England** titre officiel de l'archevêque de Cantorbéry.

prime [praɪm] ❖ adj **1.** [foremost] premier, primordial ; [principal] premier, principal ; [fundamental] fondamental **2.** [perfect] parfait ; [excellent] excellent ❱ **prime quality** de première qualité ❱ **prime beef** bœuf *m* de première catégorie **3.** MATH [number] premier. ❖ n **1.** [best moment] ❱ **to be in one's prime** or **in the prime of life** être dans la fleur de l'âge **2.** MATH nombre *m* premier. ❖ vt **1.** [gun, machine, pump] amorcer ❱ **to prime sb with drink** faire boire qqn **2.** [brief - person] mettre au courant, briefer ❱ **to prime sb for a meeting** préparer qqn à une réunion **3.** [with paint, varnish] apprêter.

Prime Minister n Premier ministre *m*.

prime ministership, **prime ministry** n fonctions *fpl* de Premier ministre / *during her prime ministership* pendant qu'elle était Premier ministre.

prime mover n **1.** PHYS force *f* motrice **2.** PHILOS cause *f* première **3.** *fig* [person] instigateur *m*, -trice *f*.

prime number n nombre *m* premier.

primer ['praɪmə¹] n **1.** [paint] apprêt *m* **2.** [for explosives] amorce *f* **3.** [book - elementary] manuel *m* (élémentaire) ; [-for reading] abécédaire *m*.

prime rate n taux *m* d'escompte bancaire préférentiel, prime rate *m*.

prime time n heure *f* de grande écoute, prime time *m*. ❖ **prime-time** adj [TV programme, advertising] diffusé à une heure de grande écoute, de prime time.

primeval [praɪ'mi:vl] adj **1.** [prehistoric] primitif, des premiers âges or temps **2.** [primordial - fears, emotions] atavique, instinctif.

primitive ['prɪmɪtɪv] ❖ adj primitif. ❖ n **1.** [primitive person] primitif *m*, -ive *f* **2.** [artist] primitif *m* **3.** COMPUT & MATH primitive *f*.

primly ['prɪmlɪ] adv *pej* d'une manière guindée or collet monté.

primordial [praɪ'mɔːdjəl] adj primordial ▸ **primordial ooze** or **soup** soupe f primitive.

primrose ['prɪmrəʊz] ◆ n **1.** BOT primevère f **2.** [colour] jaune m pâle. ◆ adj jaune pâle *(inv)*.

Primus® ['praɪməs] n [UK] ▸ **Primus (stove)** réchaud m (de camping).

prince [prɪns] n *lit & fig* prince m ▸ **Prince Rupert** le prince Rupert ▸ **the Prince of Wales** le prince de Galles.

Prince Charming n le Prince Charmant.

Prince Edward Island pr n l'île f du Prince-Édouard.

princely ['prɪnslɪ] adj princier / *a princely sum* une somme princière.

prince regent n prince m régent.

princess [prɪn'ses] n princesse f ▸ **Princess Anne** la princesse Anne ▸ **the Princess of Wales** la princesse de Galles.

principal ['prɪnsəpl] ◆ adj [gen] principal ; MUS [violin, oboe] premier. ◆ n **1.** [head - of school] directeur m, -trice f ; [-of university] doyen m, -enne f **2.** [main character - in play] acteur m principal, actrice f principale ; [-in orchestra] chef m de pupitre ; [-in crime] auteur m **3.** FIN [capital - gen] capital m ; [-of debt] principal m.

principal boy n *jeune héros d'une pantomime dont le rôle est traditionnellement joué par une femme.*

principality [,prɪnsɪ'pælətɪ] n principauté f ▸ **the Principality** [Wales] le pays de Galles.

principally ['prɪnsəplɪ] adv principalement.

principle ['prɪnsəpl] n **1.** [for behaviour] principe m / *on principle* or *as a matter of principle* par principe / *it's against my principles to eat meat* j'ai pour principe de ne pas manger de viande ▸ **to stick to one's principles** rester fidèle à ses principes **2.** [fundamental law] principe m **3.** [theory] principe m ▸ **in principle** en principe.

principled ['prɪnsəpld] adj : *a principled man* un homme de principes or qui a des principes ▸ **to take a principled stand** adopter une position de principe.

print [prɪnt] ◆ n **1.** [of publications] ▸ **to appear in print** être publié or imprimé ▸ **to see o.s.** / **one's name in print** voir ses écrits imprimés / son nom imprimé ; [of book] ▸ **to be in** / **out of print** être disponible / épuisé / *the newspapers had already gone to print before the news broke* les journaux étaient déjà sous presse lorsque la nouvelle est tombée **2.** (U) [characters] caractères mpl / *in large print* en gros caractères / *in bold print* en caractères gras **3.** (U) [text] texte m (imprimé) ▸ **the small** or **fine print on a contract** les lignes en petits caractères en bas d'un contrat **4.** PHOT épreuve f, tirage m **5.** ART [engraving] gravure f, estampe f ; [reproduction] poster m **6.** TEXT [fabric] imprimé m ; [dress] robe f imprimée **7.** [mark - from tyre, foot] empreinte f ; [fingerprint] empreinte f digitale. ◆ comp **1.** TYPO ▸ **the print unions** les syndicats mpl des typographes **2.** COMPUT ▸ **print cartridge** cartouche f ▸ **print menu** menu m d'impression. ◆ adj [dress] en tissu imprimé. ◆ vt **1.** [book, newspaper, money] imprimer ; [publish - story, article] publier / *the novel is being printed* le roman est sous presse or en cours d'impression / *1,000 copies of the book have already been printed* on a déjà tiré le livre à 1 000 exemplaires / *printed in France* imprimé en France **2.** [write] écrire en caractères d'imprimerie / *print your name clearly* écrivez votre nom lisiblement **3.** PHOT tirer **4.** TEXT imprimer **5.** [mark] imprimer ; *fig* [in memory] graver, imprimer. ◆ vi **1.** imprimer / *tomorrow's newspapers haven't started printing yet* les journaux de demain ne sont pas encore sous presse or à l'impression **2.** [in handwriting] écrire en caractères d'imprimerie **3.** PHOT [negative] ▸ **to print well** sortir bien au tirage. ❖ **print off** vt sep **1.** TYPO imprimer, tirer **2.** PHOT tirer. ❖ **print out** vt sep COMPUT imprimer.

printable ['prɪntəbl] adj imprimable, publiable / *my opinion on the matter is not printable* mon avis sur la question n'est pas très agréable à entendre.

printed ['prɪntɪd] adj **1.** [gen] imprimé ▸ **printed matter** imprimés mpl ▸ **the printed word** l'écrit m **2.** [notepaper] à en-tête.

printed circuit (board) n circuit m imprimé.

printer ['prɪntər] n **1.** [person - gen] imprimeur m ; [- typographer] typographe mf ; [- compositor] compositeur m, -trice f / *it's at the printer's* c'est chez l'imprimeur or à l'impression ▸ **printer's error** coquille f ▸ **printer's ink** encre f d'imprimerie ▸ **printer's mark** marque f d'imprimeur **2.** COMPUT imprimante f ▸ **printer cable** câble m d'imprimante ▸ **printer driver** programme m de commande d'impression ▸ **printer port** port m d'imprimante **3.** PHOT tireuse f.

printing ['prɪntɪŋ] n **1.** [activity] imprimerie f **2.** [copies printed] impression f, tirage m **3.** PHOT tirage m **4.** (U) [handwriting] (écriture f en) caractères mpl d'imprimerie.

printing press n presse f (d'imprimerie).

printout ['prɪntaʊt] n [act of printing out] tirage m, sortie f sur imprimante ▸ **to do a printout** sortir un document sur imprimante, imprimer (un document) ; [printed version] sortie f papier, tirage m ; [results of calculation] listing m.

print preview n COMPUT aperçu m avant impression.

print queue n COMPUT liste f d'attente or queue f d'impression.

prior ['praɪər] adj **1.** [earlier] antérieur, précédent / *she had a prior engagement* elle était déjà prise ; [preliminary] préalable / *without prior notice* sans préavis **2.** [more important] ▸ **to have a prior claim to** or **on sthg** avoir un droit de priorité or d'antériorité sur qqch. ❖ **prior to** prep phr avant, antérieurement à, préalablement à.

prioritize, prioritise [praɪ'ɒrɪtaɪz] vt donner or accorder la priorité à.

priority [praɪ'ɒrətɪ] (pl **priorities**) n priorité f ▸ **to give priority to** donner or accorder la priorité à ▸ **to have** or **to take priority over** avoir la priorité sur ▸ **to do sthg as a (matter of) priority** faire qqch en priorité / *the matter has top priority* l'affaire a la priorité absolue or est absolument prioritaire / *you should get your priorities right* il faudrait que tu apprennes à distinguer ce qui est important de ce qui ne l'est pas.

priory ['praɪərɪ] (pl **priories**) n prieuré m.

prise [praɪz] vt [UK] ▸ **to prise sthg open** ouvrir qqch à l'aide d'un levier / *we managed to prise the information out of her* fig on a réussi à lui arracher le renseignement.

prism ['prɪzm] n prisme m.

prison ['prɪzn] ◆ n prison f ▸ **to be in prison** être en prison / *he's been in prison* il a fait de la prison ▸ **to go to prison** aller en prison, être emprisonné ▸ **to send sb to prison, to put sb in prison** envoyer or mettre qqn en prison / *to sentence sb to three years in prison* condamner qqn à trois ans de prison. ◆ comp [director, warder, cell] de prison ; [food, conditions] en prison, dans les prisons ; [system, regulations, administration] pénitentiaire, carcéral ▸ **prison sentence** peine f de prison.

prison camp n camp m de prisonniers.

prisoner ['prɪznər] n prisonnier m, -ère f, détenu m, -e f ▸ **to take sb prisoner** faire qqn prisonnier ▸ **to hold sb prisoner** retenir qqn prisonnier, détenir qqn ▸ **to be taken prisoner** être fait prisonnier ▸ **to be held prisoner** être détenu ▸ **political prisoner** prisonnier or détenu politique ▸ **prisoner of conscience** prisonnier m d'opinion ▸ **prisoner of war** prisonnier de guerre.

prison officer n gardien m, -enne f de prison.

prissy ['prɪsɪ] adj *inf* prude, bégueule.

pristine ['prɪstiːn] adj **1.** [immaculate] parfait, immaculé / *in pristine condition* en parfait état **2.** [original] primitif, premier.

privacy [UK 'prɪvəsɪ US 'praɪvəsɪ] n **1.** [seclusion] solitude f / *lack of privacy* manque m d'intimité / *I have no privacy here* je ne peux jamais être seul ici / *can I have some privacy for a few hours?* pouvez-vous me laisser seul quelques heures ? ; [private life] vie f privée / *I value my privacy* je tiens à ma vie privée / *an intrusion on sb's privacy* une ingérence dans la vie privée de qqn / *the papers have no respect for people's privacy* les journaux ne respectent pas la vie privée des gens / *in the privacy of one's own home* dans l'intimité de son foyer / *there's no privacy in this world* tout se sait dans ce bas monde **2.** [secrecy] intimité f, secret m / *to get married in the strictest privacy* se marier dans la plus stricte intimité **3.** [confidentiality] confidentialité f ▶ **on-line privacy** confidentialité f en ligne ▶ **privacy policy** politique f de confidentialité or de protection des données personnelles ▶ **privacy statement** déclaration f de confidentialité.

private ['praɪvɪt] ◆ adj **1.** [not for the public] privé ▶ **private land** terrain m privé ▶ **private road** voie f privée / **'private'** 'privé', 'interdit au public' **2.** [independent, not run or controlled by the state] privé **3.** [personal] privé, personnel / *for private reasons* pour des raisons personnelles / *it's my private opinion* c'est mon opinion personnelle / *it's a private joke* c'est une blague que vous ne pouvez pas comprendre **4.** [confidential] privé, confidentiel, personnel **5.** [individual - bank account] personnel ; [- bathroom, lessons, tuition] particulier / *private pupil* élève mf (à qui l'on donne des cours particuliers) / *private teacher* précepteur m, -trice f / *this is a private house* c'est une maison particulière or qui appartient à des particuliers ▶ **private car** voiture f personnelle **6.** [quiet, intimate] intime, privé ▶ **private bar** *salon dans un pub* **7.** [ordinary] ▶ **a private citizen** un (simple) citoyen, un particulier ▶ **private soldier** (simple) soldat m. ◆ n MIL (simple) soldat m, soldat m de deuxième classe. ◆ **privates** pl n *inf & euph* parties fpl (génitales). ❖ **in private** adv phr [confidentially] en privé, en confidence ; [in private life] en privé, dans la vie privée ; [personally] en privé, personnellement.

private company n entreprise f or société f privée.

private detective n détective m privé.

private enterprise n libre entreprise f.

private eye n *inf* privé m ▶ **Private Eye** PRESS *magazine satirique britannique.*

private income n rentes fpl ▶ **to live on** or **off a private income** vivre de ses rentes.

private investigator = private detective.

private life n vie f privée / *in (his) private life* dans sa vie privée, en privé.

privately ['praɪvɪtlɪ] adv **1.** [not publicly] : *a privately owned company* une entreprise privée / *they were married privately* leur mariage a eu lieu dans l'intimité / *to be privately educated* a) [at school] faire ses études dans une école privée b) [with tutor] avoir un précepteur **2.** [personally] dans mon / son, etc. for intérieur, en moi-même / soi-même, etc. ; [secretly] secrètement **3.** [confidentially] en privé **4.** [as a private individual] à titre personnel.

private member's bill n UK proposition f de loi.

private parts *inf* = privates.

private pension n retraite f complémentaire.

private practice n médecine f privée or non conventionnée / *she's in private practice* elle a un cabinet (médical) privé.

private property n propriété f privée.

private school n ≃ école f libre.

private sector n ▶ **the private sector** le secteur privé. ❖ **private-sector** comp [business, pay, bosses] privé.

privation [praɪ'veɪʃn] n privation f.

privatization, **privatisation** [ˌpraɪvɪtaɪ'zeɪʃn] n privatisation f.

privatize, **privatise** ['praɪvɪtaɪz] vt privatiser.

privet ['prɪvɪt] n troène m ▶ **privet hedge** haie f de troènes.

privilege ['prɪvɪlɪdʒ] ◆ n **1.** [right, advantage] privilège m ▶ **to grant sb the privilege of doing sthg** accorder à qqn le privilège de faire qqch ; *(U)* [unfair advantage] : *a struggle against privilege* une lutte contre les privilèges **2.** [honour] honneur m / *it was a privilege to do business with you* ce fut un honneur de travailler avec vous / *I had the privilege of attending his wedding* j'ai eu le bonheur or la chance d'assister à son mariage **3.** POL ▶ **parliamentary privilege** immunité f parlementaire. ◆ vt privilégier.

privileged ['prɪvɪlɪdʒd] ◆ adj [person] privilégié. ◆ pl n ▶ **the privileged** les privilégiés mpl.

privy ['prɪvɪ] *(pl* privies*)* ◆ adj *fml* [informed] ▶ **to be privy to sthg** *fml* être instruit de qqch, être au courant de qqch. ◆ n *arch & hum* [toilet] lieux mpl d'aisances.

Privy Council n ▶ **the Privy Council** le Conseil privé du souverain en Grande-Bretagne.

 Privy Council

Présidé par le souverain, le **Privy Council** compte environ 400 membres. En font partie tous les ministres du gouvernement ainsi que d'autres hautes personnalités de la politique. Théoriquement, il peut assumer les pouvoirs du gouvernement en cas de crise nationale, mais en pratique ses fonctions sont purement honorifiques. Les membres du Privy Council ont droit à l'appellation **Right Honourable (Rt Hon)** devant leur nom.

Privy Purse n cassette f royale.

prize [praɪz] ◆ n **1.** [for merit] prix m ▶ **to award a prize to sb** décerner un prix à qqn ▶ **to win (the) first prize in a contest** remporter le premier prix d'un concours **2.** [in game] lot m **3.** NAUT prise f. ◆ vt **1.** [for value] chérir, attacher une grande valeur à ; [for quality] priser **2.** = **prise**. ◆ adj **1.** [prizewinning] primé, médaillé **2.** [excellent] parfait, typique ; [complete] : *a prize fool* *inf* un parfait imbécile **3.** [valuable] de valeur ; [cherished] prisé.

prize day n UK SCH (jour m de la) distribution f des prix.

prize draw n tombola f, loterie f.

prizefight ['praɪzfaɪt] n combat m professionnel.

prizefighter ['praɪzfaɪtə'] n boxeur m professionnel.

prizefighting ['praɪzfaɪtɪŋ] n boxe f professionnelle.

prize-giving n distribution f or remise f des prix.

prize money n prix m en argent.

prizewinner ['praɪzwɪnə'] n [of exam, essay contest] lauréat m, -e f ; [of game, lottery] gagnant m, -e f.

prizewinning ['praɪzwɪnɪŋ] adj [novel, entry] primé ; [ticket, number, contestant] gagnant.

pro [prəʊ] *(pl* pros*)* ◆ n *inf* **1.** (abbr of professional) [gen & SPORT] pro mf ▶ **to turn pro** passer pro **2.** (abbr of prostitute) UK professionnelle f. ◆ prep [in favour of] pour. ❖ **pros** pl n ▶ **the pros and cons** le pour et le contre ▶ **the pros and the antis** ceux qui sont pour et ceux qui sont contre.

pro- in comp [in favour of] pro- ▶ **pro-American** proaméricain.

PRO n **1. abbr of** public relations officer **2. abbr of** Public Records Office.

proactive [prəʊ'æktɪv] adj [firm, industry, person] dynamique ; PSYCHOL proactif.

proactively [ˌprəʊ'æktɪvlɪ] adv de manière dynamique.

pro-am ['prəʊ'æm] adj SPORT professionnel et amateur ▶ **a pro-am golf tournament** un open de golf.

probability [ˌprɒbə'bɪlətɪ] (pl **probabilities**) n [likelihood] probabilité f / the probability is that he won't come il est probable qu'il ne viendra pas, il y a de fortes chances (pour) qu'il ne vienne pas / there is a strong probability of that happening il y a de fortes chances que cela se produise ▶ **in all probability** selon toute probabilité.

probability sample n échantillon m probabiliste.

probable ['prɒbəbl] ◆ adj **1.** [likely] probable, vraisemblable / it's highly probable that we won't arrive before 2 o'clock il est fort probable or plus que probable que nous n'arriverons pas avant 14 h **2.** [plausible] vraisemblable. ◆ n : he's a probable for the team next Saturday il y a de fortes chances pour qu'il joue dans l'équipe samedi prochain.

probably ['prɒbəblɪ] adv probablement, vraisemblablement, selon toute probabilité / probably not probablement pas / will you be able to come? — probably pourrez-vous venir ? — probablement / will he write to you? — very probably il t'écrira ? — c'est très probable / she's probably left already elle est probablement déjà partie, il est probable qu'elle soit déjà partie.

probate ['prəʊbeɪt] ◆ n [authentification] homologation f, authentification f, validation f. ◆ vt 🇺🇸 [will] homologuer, faire authentifier.

probation [prə'beɪʃn] n **1.** LAW probation f ; ≃ condamnation f avec sursis et mise à l'épreuve ▶ **to be on probation** ≃ être en sursis avec mise à l'épreuve ▶ **to put sb on probation** ≃ condamner qqn avec mise à l'épreuve **2.** [trial employment] essai m ▶ **to be on probation** être en période d'essai.

probationary [prə'beɪʃnrɪ] adj [trial] d'essai ▶ **probationary period** période f d'essai ▶ **probationary teacher** professeur m stagiaire.

probationer [prə'beɪʃnər] n [employee] employé m, -e f à l'essai or en période d'essai ; 🇬🇧 [teacher] (professeur m) stagiaire mf ; [trainee nurse] élève m infirmier, élève f infirmière.

probation officer n ≃ agent m de probation.

probe [prəʊb] ◆ n **1.** [investigation] enquête f, investigation f **2.** [question] question f, interrogation f **3.** ASTRONAUT, ELECTRON & MED sonde f ; ZOOL trompe f. ◆ vt **1.** [investigate] enquêter sur **2.** [examine, sound out - person, motive, reasons] sonder ▶ **to probe sb about sthg** sonder qqn sur qqch **3.** [explore, poke around in] explorer, fouiller, sonder ; MED sonder. ◆ vi **1.** [investigate] enquêter, faire une enquête ▶ **to probe into sthg** enquêter sur qqch **2.** MED faire un sondage.

probing ['prəʊbɪŋ] ◆ adj [look] inquisiteur, perçant ; [mind] pénétrant, clairvoyant ; [remark, question] perspicace. ◆ n (U) **1.** [investigation] enquête f, investigations fpl ; [questioning] questions fpl, interrogatoire m **2.** MED sondage m.

probity ['prəʊbətɪ] n probité f.

problem ['prɒbləm] ◆ n problème m ▶ **to cause problems for sb** causer des ennuis or poser des problèmes à qqn / thanks for doing that for me — no problem! inf merci d'avoir fait ça pour moi — pas de problème ! ◆ comp [child, family, hair] à problèmes ; [play] à thèse / it's a real problem case c'est un cas qui pose de réels problèmes.

problematic(al) [ˌprɒblə'mætɪk(l)] adj problématique, incertain.

problem-free adj sans problème.

problem page n 🇬🇧 courrier m du cœur.

problem-solving [-ˌsɒlvɪŋ] n résolution f de problèmes.

pro bono [-bəʊnəʊ] adj 🇺🇸 LAW [legal work] à titre gratuit ; [lawyer] exerçant à titre gratuit.

procedural [prə'siːdʒərəl] adj de procédure, procédural.

procedure [prə'siːdʒər] n **1.** procédure f / what's the correct procedure? comment doit-on procéder ?, quelle est la marche à suivre ? ▶ **criminal / civil (law) procedure** LAW procédure f pénale / civile **2.** COMPUT procédure f, sous-programme m.

proceed [prə'siːd] vi **1.** [continue] continuer, poursuivre **2.** [happen] se passer, se dérouler **3.** [move on] passer / let's proceed to item 32 passons à la question 32 ▶ **to proceed to do sthg a)** [start] se mettre à faire qqch **b)** [do next] passer à qqch **4.** [act] procéder, agir **5.** [go, travel] avancer, aller ; [car] avancer, rouler **6.** LAW ▶ **to proceed with charges against sb** poursuivre qqn en justice, intenter un procès contre qqn **7.** [originate] ▶ **to proceed from** provenir de, découler de. ❖ **proceed against** vt insep LAW engager des poursuites contre.

proceedings [prə'siːdɪŋz] pl n **1.** [happening, event] événement m **2.** [meeting] réunion f, séance f **3.** [records - of meeting] compte rendu m, procès-verbal m ; [- of learned society] actes mpl **4.** LAW [legal action] procès m, poursuites fpl ▶ **to take** or **to institute (legal) proceedings against sb** intenter une action (en justice) contre qqn, engager des poursuites contre qqn ; [legal process] procédure f / legal proceedings are very slow in this country la procédure judiciaire est très lente dans ce pays.

proceeds ['prəʊsiːdz] pl n recette f, somme f recueillie.

process ◆ n ['prəʊses] **1.** [series of events, operation] processus m **2.** [method] procédé m, méthode f / by a process of elimination par élimination / by a process of trial and error en procédant par tâtonnements ▶ **to be in process** être en cours **3.** LAW [legal action] procès m, action f en justice ; [writ, summons] citation f (en justice), assignation f (en justice) **4.** BIOL [outgrowth] processus m. ◆ vt ['prəʊses] **1.** [transform - raw materials] traiter, transformer ; [- cheese, meat, milk] traiter ; [- nuclear waste] retraiter ; [COMPUT - data] traiter ; PHOT développer **2.** ADMIN & COMM [deal with - order, information, cheque] traiter **3.** fig [come to terms with] faire face à. ◆ vi ['prɑːses] [march] défiler ; RELIG défiler en procession. ❖ **in the process** adv phr : I managed to rescue the cat but I twisted my ankle in the process j'ai réussi à sauver le chat, mais je me suis tordu la cheville (en le faisant). ❖ **in the process of** prep phr en train de ▶ **to be in the process of doing sthg** être en train de faire qqch.

processed ['prəʊsest] adj [food] traité, industriel pej ▶ **processed cheese a)** [for spreading] fromage m à tartiner **b)** [in slices] fromage m en tranches.

processing ['prəʊsesɪŋ] n [gen & COMPUT] traitement m ▶ **processing plant** [for sewage, nuclear waste, etc.] usine f de traitement.

procession [prə'seʃn] n **1.** [ceremony] procession f, cortège m ; RELIG procession f **2.** [demonstration] défilé m, cortège m **3.** [continous line] procession f, défilé m.

processor ['prəʊsesər] n **1.** COMPUT processeur m **2.** CULIN robot m ménager.

pro-choice ['prəʊ'tʃɔɪs] adj favorable au droit de pratiquer l'avortement et/ou l'euthanasie.

pro-choicer n personne favorable au droit de pratiquer l'avortement et / ou l'euthanasie.

proclaim [prə'kleɪm] vt **1.** [declare] proclamer, déclarer / *to proclaim independence* proclamer l'indépendance / *many proclaimed that he was mad* or *proclaimed him to be mad* beaucoup de gens ont déclaré qu'il était fou / *he proclaimed himself emperor* il s'est proclamé empereur / *she proclaimed her innocence* elle a clamé son innocence **2.** [reveal] révéler, manifester, trahir.

proclamation [ˌprɒklə'meɪʃn] n proclamation *f*, déclaration *f* ▶ **to issue** or **to make a proclamation** faire une proclamation.

proclivity [prə'klɪvətɪ] (*pl* **proclivities**) n *fml* propension *f*, inclination *f*, tendance *f* ▶ **to have a proclivity to** or **towards sthg** avoir une propension à qqch.

procrastinate [prə'kræstɪneɪt] vi tergiverser, atermoyer, temporiser.

procrastination [prəˌkræstɪ'neɪʃn] n procrastination *f* *liter*, tendance *f* à tout remettre au lendemain.

procreate ['prəʊkrɪeɪt] *fml* ◆ vi procréer. ◆ vt engendrer.

procreation [ˌprəʊkrɪ'eɪʃn] n *fml* procréation *f*.

proctor ['prɒktə'] ◆ n **1.** LAW [agent] ≃ fondé *m* de pouvoir **2.** UNIV [in UK] représentant *m*, -e *f* du conseil de discipline ; [in US -invigilator] surveillant *m*, -e *f* (à un examen) **3.** RELIG procureur *m*. ◆ vi & vt [US] surveiller.

procurator fiscal n [Scot] LAW *en Écosse, magistrat qui fait office de procureur et qui remplit les fonctions du «coroner» en Angleterre* ; ≃ procureur *m* de la République.

procure [prə'kjʊə'] ◆ vt **1.** *fml* [obtain] procurer, obtenir ; [buy] (se) procurer, acheter ▶ **to procure sthg (for o.s.)** se procurer qqch ▶ **to procure sthg for sb** procurer qqch à qqn **2.** LAW [prostitutes] procurer, prostituer. ◆ vi LAW se livrer au proxénétisme.

procurement [prə'kjʊəmənt] n **1.** [acquisition] obtention *f*, acquisition *f* **2.** COMM [buying] achat *m*, acquisition *f* ; MIL acquisition *f* de matériel.

prod [prɒd] (*pt & pp* **prodded**, *cont* **prodding**) ◆ n **1.** [with finger] petit coup *m* avec le doigt ; [with stick] petit coup *m* de bâton **2.** *fig* [urging] : *he needs a prod to make him work* il faut le pousser pour qu'il travaille **3.** [stick] bâton *m*, pique *f*. ◆ vt **1.** [with finger] donner un coup avec le doigt à, pousser du doigt ; [with stick] pousser avec la pointe d'un bâton **2.** *fig* [urge] pousser, inciter ▶ **to prod sb into doing sthg** pousser or inciter qqn à faire qqch.

Prod [prɒd] n [Ir] *v inf* & *pej* Protestant *m*, -e *f*.

prodigal ['prɒdɪgl] ◆ adj prodigue ▶ **the prodigal son** BIBLE le fils prodigue. ◆ n prodigue *mf*.

prodigious [prə'dɪdʒəs] adj prodigieux.

prodigy ['prɒdɪdʒɪ] (*pl* **prodigies**) n **1.** [person] prodige *m* ▶ **child** or **infant prodigy** enfant *mf* prodige **2.** [marvel] prodige *m*.

produce ◆ vt [prə'dju:s] **1.** [manufacture, make] produire, fabriquer **2.** [yield - minerals, crops] produire ; [-interest, profit] rapporter **3.** [bring out -book, recording] produire, sortir ; [publish] publier, éditer **4.** BIOL [give birth to -subj: woman] donner naissance à ; [-subj: animal] produire, donner naissance à ; [secrete -saliva, sweat, etc.] sécréter **5.** [bring about -situation, problem] causer, provoquer, créer ; [-illness, death] causer, provoquer ; [-anger, pleasure, reaction] susciter, provoquer ; [-effect] provoquer, produire **6.** [present, show -evidence, documents] présenter, produire **7.** [film] produire ; [play -organize, finance] produire ; [-direct] réaliser, mettre en scène ; [radio or TV programme -organize, finance] produire ; [-direct] réaliser, mettre en scène **8.** GEOM [line] prolonger, continuer **9.** CHEM, ELEC & PHYS [reaction, spark] produire ; [discharge] produire, provoquer ; [vacuum] faire, créer. ◆ vi [prə'dju:s] **1.** [yield -factory, mine] produire, rendre **2.** THEAT assurer la mise en scène ;

CIN [financer] assurer la production ; [director] assurer la réalisation. ◆ n ['prɒdju:s] *(U)* produits *mpl* (alimentaires) ▶ **agricultural** / **dairy produce** produits agricoles / laitiers ▶ **farm produce** produits agricoles or de la ferme ▶ **produce of Spain** produit en Espagne.

producer [prə'dju:sə'] n **1.** AGR & INDUST producteur *m*, -trice *f* **2.** [of film] producteur *m*, -trice *f* ; [of play, of TV or radio programme -organizer, financer] producteur *m*, -trice *f* ; [-director] réalisateur *m*, -trice *f*.

-producing [prəˌdju:sɪŋ] in comp producteur de.

product ['prɒdʌkt] n **1.** AGR, CHEM & INDUST produit *m* ▶ **finished product a)** INDUST produit fini **b)** [piece of work] résultat *m* final / *food products* produits alimentaires, denrées *fpl* alimentaires / *product of India* produit d'Inde **2.** [result] produit *m*, résultat *m* **3.** MATH produit *m*.

product awareness n notoriété *f* or mémorisation *f* du produit.

product bundling n groupage *m* de produits.

production [prə'dʌkʃn] n **1.** [process of producing -of goods] production *f*, fabrication *f* ; [-of crops, electricity, heat] production *f* **2.** [amount produced] production *f* **3.** [of film] production *f* ; [of play, of radio or TV programme -organization, financing] production *f* ; [-artistic direction] réalisation *f*, mise *f* en scène **4.** CIN & THEAT [show, work of art] spectacle *m* ; RADIO & TV production *f* ; ART & LITER œuvre *f* **5.** [presentation -of document, passport, ticket] présentation *f*.

production line n chaîne *f* de fabrication.

production manager n directeur *m*, -trice *f* de la production.

productive [prə'dʌktɪv] adj **1.** [gen & ECON] productif **2.** [fertile -land] fertile ; [-imagination] fertile, fécond ; [prolific -writer, artist] prolifique **3.** [useful] fructueux, utile **4.** [of situation, feeling, etc.] ▶ **to be productive of** engendrer, créer.

productively [prə'dʌktɪvlɪ] adv **1.** ECON d'une manière productive **2.** [usefully] utilement ; [fruitfully] fructueusement, profitablement, avec profit.

productivity [ˌprɒdʌk'tɪvətɪ] ◆ n productivité *f*, rendement *m*. ◆ comp [deal, fall, level] de productivité ▶ **productivity bonus** prime *f* de rendement or de productivité.

product life cycle n cycle *m* de vie du produit.

product management n gestion *f* de produits.

product manager n chef *m* de produit, directeur *m*, -trice *f* de produit.

product mix n assortiment *m* or mix *m* de produits.

product placement n CIN & TV placement *m* de produits.

product range n gamme *f* de produits.

product testing n essais *mpl* de produits.

Prof. (written abbr of **professor**) Pr.

profane [prə'feɪn] ◆ adj **1.** [irreligious] sacrilège, impie *liter dated* **2.** [secular] profane, laïque **3.** [uninitiated] profane **4.** [vulgar -language] vulgaire, grossier. ◆ vt profaner.

profanity [prə'fænətɪ] (*pl* **profanities**) n **1.** [profane nature of text] nature *f* or caractère *m* profane ; [-of action] impiété *f* **2.** [oath] grossièreté *f*, juron *m* ▶ **to utter profanities** proférer des grossièretés.

profess [prə'fes] vt **1.** [declare] professer *liter*, déclarer, proclamer ▶ **to profess ignorance** avouer son ignorance **2.** [claim] prétendre, déclarer / *she professes to speak French* elle prétend parler le français.

professed [prə'fest] adj **1.** [avowed] déclaré **2.** [alleged] supposé, prétendu.

profession [prə'feʃn] n **1.** [occupation] profession *f* / *she's a lawyer by profession* elle exerce la profession d'avocat, elle est avocate (de profession) ▸ **the (liberal) professions** les professions libérales **2.** [body] (membres *mpl* d'une) profession *f*, corps *m* / *the teaching profession* le corps enseignant, les enseignants *mpl* **3.** [declaration] profession *f*, déclaration *f* / *profession of faith* profession de foi.

professional [prə'feʃənl] ◆ adj **1.** [relating to a profession] professionnel ▸ **to take** *or* **to get professional advice a)** [gen] consulter un professionnel **b)** [from doctor / lawyer] consulter un médecin / un avocat **2.** [as career, full-time] professionnel, de profession / *he's a professional painter* il vit de sa peinture / *a professional soldier / diplomat* un militaire / diplomate de carrière / *a professional army* une armée de métier ; SPORT professionnel ▸ **to go** *or* **to turn professional** passer professionnel **3.** [in quality, attitude] professionnel. ◆ n professionnel *m*, -elle *f*.

professional foul n FOOT faute *f* délibérée.

professionalism [prə'feʃnəlɪzm] n professionnalisme *m*.

professionalization [prə,feʃnəlaɪ'zeɪʃən] n professionnalisation *f*.

professionalize [prə'feʃnəlaɪz] vt professionnaliser.

professionally [prə'feʃnəlɪ] adv **1.** [as profession] professionnellement / *he plays professionally* SPORT c'est un joueur professionnel **2.** [skilfully, conscientiously] professionnellement, de manière professionnelle.

professor [prə'fesər] n UNIV [in UK - head of department] titulaire *mf* d'une chaire, professeur *m* ; [in US - lecturer] enseignant *m*, -e *f* (de faculté) *or* d'université.

professorship [prə'fesəʃɪp] n chaire *f*.

proffer ['prɒfər] vt *fml* **1.** [offer, present - drink, present] offrir, tendre ; [- resignation] présenter, offrir, remettre ; [- advice] donner ; [- excuses] présenter, offrir ▸ **to proffer one's hand to sb** tendre la main à qqn **2.** [put forward - idea, opinion] émettre ; [- remark, suggestion] émettre, faire.

proficiency [prə'fɪʃənsɪ] n compétence *f*, maîtrise *f*.

proficient [prə'fɪʃənt] adj [worker] compétent, expérimenté ; [driver] expérimenté, chevronné / *I used to be quite proficient in French* j'avais un assez bon niveau en français.

profile ['prəʊfaɪl] ◆ n **1.** ART & ARCHIT profil *m* ▸ **to look at / to draw sb in profile** regarder / dessiner qqn de profil **2.** [description - of person] profil *m*, portrait *m* **3.** [of candidate, employee] profil *m* ; [level of prominence] profil *m* ▸ **to keep a high profile** occuper le devant de la scène, faire parler de soi ▸ **to keep a low profile** adopter un profil bas, se faire tout petit **4.** [graph] profil *m* **5.** GEOG & GEOL profil *m*. ◆ vt **1.** [show in profile] profiler / *his shadow was profiled against the wall* son ombre se profilait *or* se découpait sur le mur **2.** [write profile of - person] établir le profil de, brosser le portrait de.

profit ['prɒfɪt] ◆ n **1.** [financial gain] profit *m*, bénéfice *m* ▸ **to make a profit out of sthg** faire un bénéfice sur qqch ▸ **to be in profit** être bénéficiaire ▸ **to move into profit** devenir bénéficiaire ▸ **to make** *or* **to turn out a profit** réaliser un bénéfice ▸ **to show a profit** rapporter (un bénéfice *or* des bénéfices) ▸ **to sell sthg at a profit** vendre qqch à profit, faire un profit sur la vente de qqch ▸ **profit and loss account** compte *m* de pertes et profits **2.** *fml* [advantage] profit *m*, avantage *m* ▸ **to turn sthg to one's profit, to gain profit from sthg** tirer profit *or* avantage de qqch ▸ **to do sthg for profit** faire qqch dans un but intéressé. ◆ vt *fml & arch* profiter à, bénéficier à. ◆ vi profiter, tirer un profit *or* avantage ▸ **to profit from** *or* **by sthg** tirer profit *or* avantage de qqch, profiter de qqch.

profitability [,prɒfɪtə'bɪlətɪ] n FIN rentabilité *f* ; [of ideas, action] caractère *m* profitable *or* fructueux.

profitable ['prɒfɪtəbl] adj **1.** [lucrative] rentable, lucratif / *it wouldn't be very profitable for me to sell* pour moi il ne serait pas très rentable de vendre, cela ne me rapporterait pas grand-chose de vendre **2.** [beneficial] profitable, fructueux.

profitably ['prɒfɪtəblɪ] adv **1.** FIN avec profit, d'une manière rentable **2.** [usefully] utilement, avec profit, profitablement.

profit centre n centre *m* de profit.

profit-driven adj COMM poussé par les profits.

profiteer [,prɒfɪ'tɪər] ◆ n profiteur *m*, -euse *f*. ◆ vi faire des bénéfices exorbitants.

profiteering [,prɒfɪ'tɪərɪŋ] n : *they were accused of profiteering* on les a accusés de faire des bénéfices excessifs.

profit-making adj **1.** [aiming to make profit] à but lucratif ▸ **non profit-making organization** association *f* à but non lucratif **2.** [profitable] rentable.

profit margin n marge *f* bénéficiaire.

profit motive n recherche *f* du profit.

profit-related pay n rémunération *f* liée aux résultats.

profit-sharing n participation *f* *or* intéressement *m* aux bénéfices.

profligate ['prɒflɪgɪt] *fml* ◆ adj **1.** [dissolute] débauché, dévergondé **2.** [extravagant] (très) prodigue, dépensier ; [wasteful] (très) gaspilleur. ◆ n **1.** [dissolute person] débauché *m*, -e *f*, libertin *m*, -e *f* **2.** [spendthrift] dépensier *m*, -ère *f*.

pro forma [,prəʊ'fɔːmə] ◆ adj pro forma *(inv)*. ◆ adv pour la forme. ◆ n = **pro forma invoice**.

profound [prə'faʊnd] adj profond.

profoundly [prə'faʊndlɪ] adv profondément ▸ **the profoundly deaf** les sourds profonds.

profundity [prə'fʌndətɪ] (*pl* **profundities**) n profondeur *f*.

profuse [prə'fjuːs] adj **1.** [abundant, copious] abondant, profus *liter* **2.** [generous - praise, apologies] prodigue, profus / *to be profuse in one's compliments* se répandre en compliments / *to be profuse in one's apologies* se confondre en excuses.

profusely [prə'fjuːslɪ] adv **1.** [abundantly, copiously] abondamment, en abondance, à profusion **2.** [generously, extravagantly] : *they thanked her profusely* ils la remercièrent avec effusion / *she was profusely apologetic* elle s'est confondue en excuses.

profusion [prə'fjuːʒn] n profusion *f*, abondance *f* / *in profusion* à profusion, en abondance.

progeny ['prɒdʒənɪ] n *fml* [offspring] progéniture *f* ; [descendants] descendants *mpl*, lignée *f*.

progesterone [prə'dʒestərəʊn] n progestérone *f*.

prognosis [prɒg'nəʊsɪs] (*pl* **prognoses** [-siːz]) n *fml* MED pronostic *m*.

prognostication [prɒg,nɒstɪ'keɪʃn] n pronostic *m*.

program ['prəʊgræm] (*pt & pp* **programmed** *or* **programed**, *cont* **programming** *or* **programing**) ◆ n **1.** US = **programme 2.** COMPUT programme *m* ▸ **program manager** gestionnaire *m* de programmes. ◆ vt **1.** US = **programme 2.** COMPUT programmer. ◆ vi COMPUT programmer.

programmable UK, **programable** US [prəʊ'græməbl] adj programmable ▸ **programmable function key** touche *f* de fonction programmable.

programme UK, **program** US ['prəʊgræm] ◆ n **1.** MUS, POL & THEAT programme *m* **2.** [booklet] programme *m* ; [syllabus] programme *m* ; [timetable] emploi *m* du temps **3**. RADIO & TV [broadcast] émission *f* ; [TV station] chaîne *f* ; [radio station] station *f*. ◆ vt programmer / *the heating is programmed to switch itself off at night* le chauffage est programmé pour s'arrêter la nuit.

programmer 🇺🇸, **programer** 🇺🇸 ['prəʊgræməʳ] n COMPUT **1**. [person] programmeur *m*, -euse *f* **2**. [device] programmateur *m*.

programming ['prəʊgræmɪŋ] n programmation *f* ▸ **programming language** langage *m* de programmation.

progress ◆ n ['prəʊgres] *(U)* **1**. [headway] progrès *mpl* / *he is making progress in English* il fait des progrès en anglais **2**. [evolution] progrès *m* **3**. [forward movement] progression *f*. ◆ vi [prə'gres] **1**. [make headway - negotiations, research] progresser, avancer ; [- situation] progresser, s'améliorer ; [- patient] aller mieux ; [- student] progresser, faire des progrès **2**. [move forward] avancer ▸ **to progress towards a place / an objective** se rapprocher d'un lieu / d'un objectif. ◆ **in progress** adj phr ▸ **to be in progress** être en cours.

progression [prə'greʃn] n **1**. [advance - of disease, army] progression *f* **2**. MATH & MUS progression *f* **3**. [series, sequence] série *f*, suite *f*.

progressive [prə'gresɪv] ◆ adj **1**. [forward-looking - idea, teacher, jazz] progressiste ; [- education, method] nouveau *(before vowel or silent 'h' nouvel, f nouvelle)*, moderne **2**. [gradual - change] progressif ▸ **progressive income tax** impôt *m* progressif ; MED [disease] progressif **3**. GRAM [aspect] progressif. ◆ n **1**. POL progressiste *mf* **2**. GRAM forme *f* progressive, progressif *m* / *in the progressive* à la forme progressive.

progressively [prə'gresɪvlɪ] adv **1**. POL & SCH d'une manière progressiste **2**. [gradually] progressivement, graduellement, petit à petit.

progress report n [gen] compte-rendu *m* ; [on work] rapport *m* sur l'avancement des travaux ; [on patient] bulletin *m* de santé ; [on pupil] bulletin *m* scolaire.

prohibit [prə'hɪbɪt] vt **1**. [forbid] interdire, défendre, prohiber ▸ **to prohibit sb from doing sthg** interdire or défendre à qqn de faire qqch **2**. [prevent] interdire, empêcher / *his pacifism prohibits him from joining the army* son pacifisme lui interdit or l'empêche de s'engager dans l'armée.

prohibition [,prəʊɪ'bɪʃn] n interdiction *f*, prohibition *f*. ◆ **Prohibition** n 🇺🇸 HIST la prohibition.

🏛 **Prohibition**

Le 18ᵉ amendement à la Constitution américaine instituant la prohibition (interdiction de consommer et de vendre de l'alcool) fut voté en 1919 sous la pression de groupes religieux et conservateurs. La prolifération de bars clandestins (**speakeasies**) et l'apparition d'une guerre des gangs (les **bootleggers**) pour le monopole de la vente d'alcool incitèrent le Congrès à voter l'annulation de cette mesure en 1933, et les États l'abandonnèrent progressivement.

---

prohibitive [prə'hɪbətɪv] adj prohibitif.

prohibitively [prə'hɪbətɪvlɪ] adv : *prohibitively expensive* d'un coût prohibitif.

project ◆ n ['prɒdʒekt] **1**. [plan] projet *m* ; [enterprise, undertaking] opération *f*, entreprise *f* **2**. SCH [class work] travaux *mpl* pratiques ; [individual work] dossier *m* **3**. [study,

research] étude *f* **4**. 🇺🇸 ▸ **(housing) project** cité *f* HLM. ◆ vt [prə'dʒekt] **1**. [plan] prévoir **2**. [foresee, forecast] prévoir **3**. [send forth - gen] projeter, envoyer ; [- film, slide, etc.] projeter ▸ **to project one's voice** projeter sa voix **4**. [present] présenter, projeter **5**. PSYCHOL [transfer] projeter ▸ **to project one's feelings onto sb** projeter ses sentiments sur qqn **6**. [cause to jut out] faire dépasser **7**. GEOM projeter. ◆ vi [prə'dʒekt] **1**. [protrude, jut out] faire saillie, dépasser **2**. PSYCHOL se projeter **3**. [as personality] : *she doesn't project well* elle présente mal **4**. [with voice] ▸ **to learn to project** apprendre à projeter sa voix.

⚠ **Un projet** is not always the correct translation for a project, as the entry shows.

project administrator n administrateur *m*, -trice *f* de projet.

project coordinator n coordinateur *m*, -trice *f* de projet, chef *mf* de projet.

projected [prə'dʒektɪd] adj **1**. [planned - undertaking, visit] prévu **2**. [forecast - figures, production] prévu.

projectile [prə'dʒektaɪl] n projectile *m*.

projection [prə'dʒekʃn] n **1**. CIN, GEOM & PSYCHOL projection *f* **2**. FIN [estimate] projection *f*, prévision *f* **3**. [protrusion] saillie *f*, avancée *f* ; [overhang] surplomb *m*.

projectionist [prə'dʒekʃənɪst] n projectionniste *mf*.

projection room n cabine *f* de projection.

project manager n [gen] chef *m* de projet ; CONSTR maître *m* d'œuvre.

projector [prə'dʒektəʳ] n projecteur *m*.

proletarian [,prəʊlɪ'teərɪən] ◆ n prolétaire *mf*. ◆ adj **1**. ECON, POL & SOCIOL prolétarien **2**. *pej* de prolétaire.

proletariat [,prəʊlɪ'teərɪət] n prolétariat *m*.

pro-life ['prəʊ'laɪf] adj contre l'avortement et l'euthanasie.

pro-lifer [prəʊ'laɪfəʳ] n *personne qui s'oppose au droit de pratiquer l'avortement et / ou l'euthanasie.*

proliferate [prə'lɪfəreɪt] vi proliférer.

proliferation [prə,lɪfə'reɪʃn] n **1**. [rapid increase] prolifération *f* **2**. [large amount or number] grande quantité *f*.

prolific [prə'lɪfɪk] adj prolifique.

prolog ['prəʊlɒg] 🇺🇸 = **prologue**.

prologue ['prəʊlɒg] *lit & fig* prologue *m*, prélude *m*.

prolong [prə'lɒŋ] vt prolonger.

prolongation [,prəʊlɒŋ'geɪʃn] n [in time] prolongation *f* ; [in space] prolongement *m*, extension *f*.

prolonged [prə'lɒŋd] adj long (longue).

prom [prɒm] n *inf* **1**. = **promenade 2**. 🇬🇧 abbr of **promenade concert**. ◆ **proms** pl n *inf festival de concerts-promenades* ▸ **the Last Night of the Proms** 🇬🇧 *le dernier des concerts-promenades de la saison londonienne, au cours duquel le public se joint aux musiciens pour chanter des airs très connus.*

PROM [prɒm] (abbr of **programmable read only memory**) n COMPUT PROM *f inv*.

promenade [,prɒmə'nɑːd] ◆ n **1**. 🇬🇧 [at seaside] front *m* de mer, promenade *f* **2**. 🇺🇸 MUS = **promenade concert 3**. [walk] promenade *f*. ◆ vi *fml & hum* se promener. ◆ vt *fml & hum* promener.

promenade concert n concert-promenade *m* *(où certains auditeurs se tiennent debout dans un promenoir).*

prominence ['prɒmɪnəns] n **1**. [importance] importance *f* ; [fame] célébrité *f* ▸ **to rise to prominence** se hisser au premier rang ▸ **to come into** or **to prominence**

a) [become important] prendre de l'importance **b)** [become famous] devenir célèbre **2.** [protuberance] proéminence f **3.** ASTRON protubérance f solaire.

prominent ['prɒmɪnənt] adj **1.** [well-known] célèbre ; [eminent] éminent ; [important] important **2.** [striking, salient - detail, difference] frappant, remarquable ; [- fact, feature] saillant, marquant **3.** [clearly visible - bones, muscles] saillant ; [- land, structure, nose] proéminent ; [- teeth] qui avance, proéminent.

prominently ['prɒmɪnəntlɪ] adv bien en vue / *he figures prominently in French politics* il occupe une position importante or de premier plan dans la vie politique française / *the medal was prominently displayed* la médaille était mise en évidence.

promiscuity [,prɒmɪ'skjuːətɪ] n promiscuité f sexuelle.

promiscuous [prɒ'mɪskjuəs] adj **1.** [sexually - person] **▶ to be promiscuous** avoir des mœurs sexuelles libres / *promiscuous behaviour* promiscuité f sexuelle **2.** fig [disorderly] confus.

promise ['prɒmɪs] **◆** n **1.** [pledge] promesse f **▶ to make** or **to give sb a promise** faire une promesse à qqn, donner sa parole à qqn / *she always keeps her promises* elle tient toujours ses promesses, elle tient toujours (sa) parole **▶ to break one's promise** manquer à sa parole, ne pas tenir ses promesses **2.** [hope, potential] promesse f **▶ to hold out the promise of sthg to sb** promettre qqch à qqn, faire espérer or miroiter qqch à qqn. **◆** vt **1.** [pledge] promettre **▶ to promise sthg to sb, to promise sb sthg** promettre qqch à qqn **▶ to promise sb to do sthg** promettre à qqn de faire qqch **2.** [indicate] promettre, annoncer **3.** [in marriage] : *she was promised to the King's son at birth* dès sa naissance, elle fut promise au fils du roi. **◆** vi **1.** promettre **2.** fig **▶ to promise well a)** [enterprise] promettre, s'annoncer bien **b)** [person] être prometteur or plein de promesses **c)** [results, harvest, negotiations] s'annoncer bien.

Promised Land ['prɒmɪst-] n BIBLE & fig Terre f promise.

promising ['prɒmɪsɪŋ] adj **1.** [full of potential - person] prometteur, qui promet, plein de promesses **2.** [encouraging] prometteur, qui promet.

promisingly ['prɒmɪsɪŋlɪ] adv d'une façon prometteuse.

promissory note ['prɒmɪsərɪ-] n billet m à ordre.

promo ['prəʊməʊ] (pl promos) (abbr of promotion) n inf clip m (promotionnel).

promontory ['prɒməntrɪ] (pl promontories) n promontoire m.

promote [prə'məʊt] vt **1.** [in profession, army] promouvoir **▶ to be** or **to get promoted** être promu, monter en grade, obtenir de l'avancement / *she's been promoted (to) regional manager* elle a été promue (au poste de) directrice régionale **2.** SPORT : *the Rovers were promoted to the second division* les Rovers sont montés en deuxième division **3.** [foster] promouvoir, favoriser, encourager **4.** COMM [advertise, publicize] promouvoir, faire la promotion de.

promoter [prə'məʊtər] n **1.** COMM promoteur m, -trice f (des ventes) **2.** [organizer - of match, concert] organisateur m, -trice f ; [- of scheme] promoteur m, -trice f, instigateur m, -trice f **3.** [of peace] promoteur m, -trice f.

promotion [prə'məʊʃn] n **1.** [advancement] promotion f, avancement m **▶ to get promotion** être promu, obtenir de l'avancement / *there are good prospects of promotion in this company* il y a de réelles possibilités de promotion or d'avancement dans cette société **2.** SPORT promotion f / *the team won promotion to the first division* l'équipe a gagné sa place en première division **3.** [en-

couragement, development] promotion f, développement m **4.** COMM promotion f **▶ sales promotion** promotion f des ventes **5.** [in chess] promotion f.

promotional [prə'məʊʃənl] adj [material] promotionnel, publicitaire.

prompt [prɒmpt] **◆** adj **1.** [quick] rapide, prompt **▶ prompt payment** COMM paiement m dans les délais **2.** [punctual] exact, à l'heure. **◆** adv inf [exactly] : *we begin at 9 o'clock prompt* nous commençons à 9 h précises. **◆** vt **1.** [provoke, persuade] pousser, inciter / *what prompted you to suggest such a thing?* qu'est-ce qui vous a incité à proposer une chose pareille ? **2.** THEAT souffler. **◆** n **1.** THEAT **▶ to give an actor a prompt** souffler une réplique à un acteur **2.** COMPUT message-guide m (au début de la ligne de commande).

prompter ['prɒmptər] n souffleur m, -euse f ; TV téléprompteur m.

prompting ['prɒmptɪŋ] n **1.** [persuasion] incitation f **2.** THEAT : *some actors need frequent prompting* certains acteurs ont souvent recours au souffleur.

promptly ['prɒmptlɪ] adv **1.** [quickly] promptement, rapidement **2.** [punctually] ponctuellement **3.** [immediately] aussitôt, tout de suite.

promptness ['prɒmptnɪs] n **1.** [quickness] promptitude f, rapidité f **2.** [punctuality] ponctualité f.

promulgate ['prɒmlgeɪt] vt fml **1.** [decree, law] promulguer **2.** [belief, idea, opinion] répandre, diffuser.

prone [prəʊn] adj **1.** [inclined] sujet, enclin **▶ to be prone to do sthg** être sujet or enclin à faire qqch / *to be prone to accidents / illness* être sujet aux accidents / à la maladie **2.** [prostrate] à plat ventre / *in a prone position* couché sur le ventre.

prong [prɒŋ] n [of fork] dent f ; [of tuning fork] branche f ; [of antler] pointe f ; [of attack, argument] pointe f.

pronoun ['prəʊnaʊn] n pronom m.

pronounce [prə'naʊns] **◆** vt **1.** [say] prononcer **2.** [declare] déclarer, prononcer / *the doctor pronounced him dead* le médecin l'a déclaré mort. **◆** vi **1.** [articulate] prononcer **2.** [declare] se prononcer **▶ to pronounce for / against sthg a)** [gen] se prononcer pour / contre qqch **b)** LAW prononcer pour / contre qqch **▶ to pronounce on** or **upon sthg** se prononcer sur qqch.

pronounced [prə'naʊnst] adj prononcé, marqué.

pronouncement [prə'naʊnsmənt] n déclaration f.

pronto ['prɒntəʊ] adv inf illico.

pronunciation [prə,nʌnsɪ'eɪʃn] n prononciation f.

proof [pruːf] **◆** n **1.** (U) [evidence] preuve f **▶ to show** or **to give proof of sthg** faire or donner la preuve de qqch / *do you have any proof?* vous en avez la preuve or des preuves ? / *you need proof of identity* vous devez fournir une pièce d'identité **▶ proof of purchase** reçu m **2.** PHOT & TYPO épreuve f **3.** [of alcohol] teneur f (en alcool) / *45% proof brandy* ≃ cognac à 45 degrés. **◆** adj 🇬🇧 **▶ to be proof against a)** [fire, acid, rust] être à l'épreuve de **b)** [danger, temptation] être à l'abri de or insensible à. **◆** vt **1.** [cloth] imperméabiliser **2.** TYPO [proofread] corriger les épreuves de ; [produce proof of] préparer les épreuves de.

-proof [pruːf] in comp à l'épreuve de.

proofread ['pruːfriːd] (pt & pp proofread [-red]) vt corriger (les épreuves de).

proofreader ['pruːf,riːdər] n correcteur m, -trice f (d'épreuves or d'imprimerie).

proofreading ['pruːf,riːdɪŋ] n correction f (d'épreuves) **▶ proofreading mark** or **symbol** signe m de correction.

prop [prɒp] (pt & pp propped, cont propping) **◆** n **1.** [gen] support m ; CONSTR [for tunnel, wall] étai m, étançon *m*; [in pit] étai *m* **2.** [pole, stick - for plant, flowers] tuteur *m*; [-for beans, peas] rame *f*; [-for vines] échalas *m*; [-for washing line] perche *f* **3.** RUGBY pilier *m* **4.** *fig* soutien *m* **5.** (abbr of property) THEAT accessoire *m* **6.** *inf* abbr of **propeller**. ◆ vt **1.** [lean] appuyer / *she propped her bike (up) against the wall* elle a a appuyé son vélo contre le mur **2.** [support] ▶ **to prop (up)** a) [wall, tunnel] étayer, étançonner, consolider b) [plants] mettre un tuteur à c) [peas, beans] ramer ▶ **to prop sthg open**: *I propped the door open with a chair* j'ai maintenu la porte ouverte avec une chaise. ◆◈ **prop up** vt sep [regime, family, business] soutenir.

prop. written abbr of **proprietor**.

propaganda [ˌprɒpə'gændə] ◆ n propagande *f*. ◆ comp [film, machine, material, exercise] de propagande.

propagandist [ˌprɒpə'gændɪst] ◆ adj propagandiste. ◆ n propagandiste *mf*.

propagate ['prɒpəgeɪt] ◆ vt propager. ◆ vi se propager.

propagation [ˌprɒpə'geɪʃn] n propagation *f*.

propane ['prəʊpeɪn] n propane *m*.

propel [prə'pel] (*pt & pp* **propelled**, *cont* **propelling**) vt **1.** [machine, vehicle, etc.] propulser, faire avancer **2.** [person] propulser, pousser.

propellant, propellent [prə'pelənt] ◆ n [for rocket] propergol *m*; [for gun] poudre *f* propulsive; [in aerosol] (agent *m*) propulseur *m*. ◆ adj propulsif, propulseur.

propeller [prə'pelər] n hélice *f*.

propellerhead [prə'peləhed] n US *inf scientifique ou informaticien considéré comme socialement inapte*; geek *m*.

propelling pencil [prə'pelɪŋ-] n UK portemine *m*.

propensity [prə'pensətɪ] (*pl* **propensities**) n *fml* propension *f*, tendance *f*, penchant *m* / *he has a propensity for* or *towards drink* il a tendance à boire (plus que de raison).

proper ['prɒpər] ◆ adj **1.** [correct] bon, juste, correct / *she didn't come at the proper time* elle s'est trompée d'heure / *you're not doing it in the proper way* vous ne vous y prenez pas comme il faut ▶ **to think it proper to do sthg** juger bon de faire qqch / *do as you think proper* faites comme bon vous semble **2.** [appropriate] convenable, approprié / *that wasn't the proper thing to say* / *to do* ce n'était pas ce qu'il fallait dire / faire / *you must go through the proper channels* il faut suivre la filière officielle **3.** [real] vrai, véritable **4.** UK *inf* [as intensifier] vrai, véritable, complet (complète) / *I gave him a proper telling-off* je lui ai passé un bon savon **5.** [respectable] correct, convenable, comme il faut **6.** [predicative use - specifically] proprement dit / *he lives outside the city proper* il habite en dehors de la ville même or proprement dite **7.** [characteristic] ▶ **proper to** propre à, typique de. ◆ adv *v inf* **1.** UK [correctly] comme il faut **2.** UK *regional* [very] très, vraiment, complètement.

properly ['prɒpəlɪ] adv **1.** [well, correctly] bien, juste, correctement / *the lid isn't on properly* le couvercle n'est pas bien mis / *the engine isn't working properly* le moteur ne marche pas bien **2.** [decently] correctement, convenablement, comme il faut / *patrons must be properly dressed* une tenue vestimentaire correcte est exigée de nos clients / *I haven't thanked you properly* je ne vous ai pas remercié comme il faut or comme il convient **3.** [strictly] proprement / *he isn't properly speaking an expert* il n'est pas à proprement parler un expert **4.** UK *inf* [as intensifier] vraiment, complètement, tout à fait.

proper name, proper noun n nom *m* propre.

property ['prɒpətɪ] (*pl* **properties**) ◆ n **1.** *(U)* [belongings] propriété *f*, biens *mpl*; LAW biens *mpl*; [objects] objets *mpl* **2.** *(U)* [buildings] propriété *f*; [real es-

tate] biens *mpl* immobiliers, immobilier *m*; [land] terres *fpl* **3.** [plot of land] terrain *m*; [house, building] propriété *f* **4.** [quality] propriété *f* **5.** THEAT accessoire *m*. ◆ comp [speculator] immobilier; [owner, tax] foncier ▶ **property developer** promoteur *m* (immobilier).

property ladder n ▶ **to get a foot on the property ladder** accéder à la propriété, devenir propriétaire.

property market n marché *m* immobilier.

prophecy ['prɒfɪsɪ] (*pl* **prophecies**) n prophétie *f*.

prophesy ['prɒfɪsaɪ] (*pt & pp* **prophesied**) ◆ vt prophétiser, prédire ▶ **to prophesy that sthg will happen** prédire que qqch va arriver. ◆ vi faire des prophéties.

prophet ['prɒfɪt] n prophète *m*. ◆◈ **Prophets** n BIBLE ▶ **(the Book of) Prophets** le livre des Prophètes.

prophetic [prə'fetɪk] adj prophétique.

prophylactic [ˌprɒfɪ'læktɪk] adj prophylactique.

propitious [prə'pɪʃəs] adj *fml* propice, favorable ▶ **propitious for sthg** propice à or favorable à qqch.

proponent [prə'pəʊnənt] n avocat *m*, -e *f* *fig*, partisan *m*, -e *f*.

proportion [prə'pɔːʃn] ◆ n **1.** [gen] [MATH - ratio] proportion *f*, rapport *m* / *the sentence is out of all proportion to the crime* la peine est disproportionnée par rapport au or est sans commune mesure avec le délit **2.** [perspective] proportion *f* ▶ **to have a sense of proportion** avoir le sens des proportions **3.** [dimension] proportion *f*, dimension *f* **4.** [share, part] partie *f*, part *f*, pourcentage *m*. ◆ vt proportionner. ◆◈ **in proportion to, in proportion with** prep phr par rapport à.

proportional [prə'pɔːʃənl] adj proportionnel, en proportion ▶ **proportional to** proportionnel à.

proportionally [prə'pɔːʃnəlɪ] adv proportionnellement.

proportional representation n représentation *f* proportionnelle.

proportionate adj [prə'pɔːʃnət] proportionné.

proportionately [prə'pɔːʃnətlɪ] adv proportionnellement, en proportion.

proposal [prə'pəʊzl] n **1.** [offer] proposition *f*, offre *f* ▶ **to make a proposal** faire or formuler une proposition; [of marriage] demande *f* en mariage **2.** [suggestion] proposition *f*, suggestion *f* **3.** [plan, scheme] proposition *f*, projet *m*, plan *m* / *the proposal for a car park* / *to build a car park* le projet de parking / de construction d'un parking.

propose [prə'pəʊz] ◆ vt **1.** [suggest] proposer, suggérer ▶ **to propose sthg to sb** proposer qqch à qqn ▶ **to propose doing sthg** proposer de faire qqch / *I propose (that) we all go for a drink* je propose or suggère que nous allions tous prendre un verre **2.** [present - policy, resolution, scheme] proposer, présenter, soumettre ▶ **to propose sb's health, to propose a toast to sb** porter un toast à (la santé de) qqn / *I propose Jones as* or *for treasurer* je propose Jones comme trésorier; [in marriage] ▶ **to propose marriage to sb** demander qqn en mariage, faire une demande en mariage à qqn **3.** [intend] se proposer, avoir l'intention, compter / *I propose taking* or *to take a few days off work* je me propose de prendre quelques jours de congé. ◆ vi [offer marriage] faire une demande en mariage ▶ **to propose to sb** demander qqn en mariage.

📝 Note that **proposer que** is followed by a verb in the subjunctive:
I propose we stop the meeting now. *Je propose que nous mettions fin à cette réunion tout de suite.*

proposed [prə'pəʊzd] adj projeté.

proposition [ˌprɒpə'zɪʃn] ◆ n **1.** [proposal, statement] proposition f **2.** [task] affaire f **3.** [available choice] solution f **4.** [offer of sex] proposition f **5.** MATH proposition f. ◆ vt faire des propositions (malhonnêtes) or des avances à.

propound [prə'paʊnd] vt fml [argument, theory] avancer, mettre en avant ; [opinion] avancer, émettre ; [problem] poser.

proprietary [prə'praɪətrɪ] adj **1.** COMM de marque déposée ▸ **proprietary brand** marque f déposée **2.** [attitude, behaviour, function] de propriétaire.

proprietor [prə'praɪətəʳ] n propriétaire mf.

propriety [prə'praɪətɪ] (pl **proprieties**) n fml **1.** [decorum] bienséance f, convenance f **2.** [suitability - of action, measure] opportunité f ; [- of word, remark] justesse f, propriété f **3.** [rectitude] rectitude f.

propulsion [prə'pʌlʃn] n propulsion f.

pro rata [ˌprəʊ'rɑːtə] adj & adv au prorata.

prosaic [prəʊ'zeɪɪk] adj prosaïque.

prosaically [prəʊ'zeɪɪklɪ] adv prosaïquement.

Pros. Atty written abbr of prosecuting attorney.

proscribe [prəʊ'skraɪb] vt proscrire.

prose [prəʊz] n **1.** LITER prose f ▸ **to write in prose** écrire en prose, faire de la prose **2.** UK SCH thème m.

prosecute ['prɒsɪkjuːt] ◆ vt **1.** LAW poursuivre (en justice), engager des poursuites contre ▸ **to prosecute sb for sthg** poursuivre qqn (en justice) pour qqch **2.** fml [pursue - war, investigation] poursuivre. ◆ vi LAW [lawyer - in civil case] représenter la partie civile ; [- in criminal case] représenter le ministère public or le parquet.

prosecuting attorney ['prɒsɪkjuːtɪŋ-] n US ≃ procureur m (de la République).

prosecution [ˌprɒsɪ'kjuːʃn] n **1.** LAW [proceedings] poursuites fpl (judiciaires) ; [indictment] accusation f ▸ **to be liable to prosecution** s'exposer à des poursuites (judiciaires) ▸ **to bring a prosecution against sb** poursuivre qqn en justice **2.** LAW [lawyer - in civil case] avocat m or avocats mpl représentant les plaignants or la partie plaignante ; [- in criminal case] ministère m public, accusation f ▸ **witness for the prosecution** témoin m à charge **3.** fml [pursuit] poursuite f.

prosecutor ['prɒsɪkjuːtəʳ] n [person bringing case] plaignant m, -e f ; [lawyer] ▸ **(public) prosecutor** UK procureur m.

prospect ◆ n ['prɒspekt] **1.** [possibility] chance f, perspective f / **there's little prospect of their winning the match** ils ont peu de chances de remporter or il y a peu d'espoir (pour) qu'ils remportent le match **2.** [impending event, situation] perspective f / **I don't relish the prospect of working for him** la perspective de travailler pour lui ne m'enchante guère ▸ **to have sthg in prospect** avoir qqch en vue or en perspective **3.** (usu pl) [chance of success] perspectives fpl d'avenir **4.** [person - customer] client m potentiel or éventuel, prospect m ; [- marriage partner] parti m dated ; [- candidate] espoir m **5.** [view] perspective f, vue f. ◆ vi [prə'spekt] prospecter / **to prospect for oil** chercher du pétrole. ◆ vt [prə'spekt] [area, land] prospecter.

prospecting [prə'spektɪŋ] n MIN & PETR prospection f.

prospective [prə'spektɪv] adj **1.** [future] futur **2.** [possible] potentiel, éventuel **3.** [intended, expected] en perspective.

prospector [prə'spektəʳ] n prospecteur m, -trice f, chercheur m, -euse f.

prospectus [prə'spektəs] n prospectus m.

prosper ['prɒspəʳ] vt prospérer.

prosperity [prɒ'sperətɪ] n prospérité f.

prosperous ['prɒspərəs] adj [business, area, family] prospère ; [period] prospère, de prospérité.

prostate (gland) ['prɒsteɪt-] n prostate f.

prosthesis [prɒs'θiːsɪs] (pl **prostheses** [-siːz]) n MED prothèse f.

prosthetic [prɒs'θetɪk] adj MED prothétique.

prostitute ['prɒstɪtjuːt] ◆ n prostituée f ▸ **male prostitute** prostitué m. ◆ vt fig & lit prostituer ▸ **to prostitute o.s.** se prostituer.

prostitution [ˌprɒstɪ'tjuːʃn] n prostitution f.

prostrate ◆ adj ['prɒstreɪt] **1.** [lying flat] (couché) à plat ventre ; [in submission] prosterné ▸ **to lie prostrate before sb** être prosterné devant qqn **2.** [exhausted] épuisé, abattu ; [overwhelmed] prostré, accablé, atterré. ◆ vt [prɒ'streɪt] **1.** [in obedience, respect] ▸ **to prostrate o.s. before sb** se prosterner devant qqn **2.** [overwhelm] accabler, abattre.

protagonist [prə'tægənɪst] n protagoniste mf.

protect [prə'tekt] vt protéger ▸ **to protect sb / sthg from** or **against sthg** protéger qqn / qqch de or contre qqch.

protected [prə'tektɪd] adj protégé / **protected species** espèce f protégée.

protection [prə'tekʃn] n **1.** [safeguard] protection f / **this drug offers protection against** or **from the virus** ce médicament vous protège or vous immunise contre le virus / **cyclists often wear face masks for protection against car fumes** les cyclistes portent souvent des masques pour se protéger des gaz d'échappement des voitures / **she travelled under police protection** elle a voyagé sous la protection de la police / **environmental protection** protection f de l'environnement **2.** [insurance] protection f / **protection against fire and theft** protection contre l'incendie et le vol **3.** [run by gangsters] ▸ **protection (money)** argent m versé aux racketteurs ▸ **protection racket** racket m.

protection factor n [of sun cream] indice m de protection.

protectionism [prə'tekʃənɪzm] n protectionnisme m.

protectionist [prə'tekʃənɪst] ◆ adj protectionniste. ◆ n protectionniste mf.

protective [prə'tektɪv] adj **1.** [person] protecteur ; [behaviour, attitude] protecteur, de protection / **she's too protective towards her children** elle a trop tendance à couver ses enfants **2.** [material, clothes] de protection ; [cover] protecteur, de protection **3.** ECON [duty, measure] protecteur.

protective custody n détention f dans l'intérêt de la personne.

protectively [prə'tektɪvlɪ] adv [behave, act] de façon protectrice ; [speak] d'un ton protecteur, d'une voix protectrice ; [look] d'un œil protecteur.

protectiveness [prə'tektɪvnɪs] n attitude f protectrice.

protector [prə'tektəʳ] n **1.** [person] protecteur m, -trice f **2.** [on machine] dispositif m de protection, protecteur m.

protégé ['prɒtəʒeɪ] n protégé m, -e f.

protein ['prəʊtiːn] n protéine f ▸ **protein content** teneur f en protéines ▸ **protein deficiency** carence f en protéines.

pro tem [ˌprəʊ'tem] inf, **pro tempore** ['prəʊ'tempərɪ] ◆ adv temporairement. ◆ adj intérimaire, temporaire.

protest ◆ n ['prəʊtest] **1.** [gen] protestation f ▸ **to make a protest against** or **about sthg** élever une protestation contre qqch, protester contre qqch ▸ **to register** or **to lodge a protest with sb** protester auprès de qqn ▸ **in protest against** or **at sthg** en signe de protestation contre qqch ▸ **to stage a protest a)** [complaint] organiser une protestation **b)** [demonstration] organiser une manifestation ▸ **to do sthg under protest** faire qqch en protestant **2.** COMM & LAW protêt m. ◆ comp [letter, meeting] de protestation

▶ **protest demonstration** or **march** manifestation *f* ▶ **protest vote** vote *m* de protestation. ◆ vt [prə'test] **1.** [innocence, love, etc.] protester de / *"no one told me", she protested* «personne ne me l'a dit», protesta-t-elle / *she protested that it was unfair* elle déclara que ce n'était pas juste **2.** 🇺🇸 [measures, law, etc.] protester contre. ◆ vi protester ▶ **to protest at** or **against** / **about sthg** protester contre qqch.

Protestant ['prɒtɪstənt] ◆ adj protestant ▶ **the Protestant Church** l'Église *f* protestante. ◆ n protestant *m*, -e *f*.

Protestantism ['prɒtɪstəntɪzm] n protestantisme *m*.

protestation [,prɒte'steɪʃn] n protestation *f*.

protester, protestor [prə'testər] n [demonstrator] manifestant *m*, -e *f*; [complainer] protestataire *mf*.

protocol ['prəʊtəkɒl] n protocole *m*.

proton ['prəʊtɒn] n proton *m*.

prototype ['prəʊtətaɪp] n prototype *m*.

protracted [prə'træktɪd] adj [stay] prolongé; [argument, negotiations] qui dure, (très) long.

protractor [prə'træktər] n GEOM rapporteur *m*.

protrude [prə'truːd] ◆ vi [rock, ledge] faire saillie; [eyes, chin] saillir; [teeth] avancer. ◆ vt avancer, pousser en avant.

protruding [prə'truːdɪŋ] adj [ledge] en saillie; [chin, ribs] saillant; [eyes] globuleux; [teeth] proéminent, protubérant; [belly] protubérant.

protrusion [prə'truːʒn] n [ledge] saillie *f*; [bump] bosse *f*.

protuberance [prə'tjuːbərəns] n *fml* protubérance *f*.

protuberant [prə'tjuːbərənt] adj *fml* protubérant.

proud [praʊd] ◆ adj **1.** [pleased] fier ▶ **to be proud of sb** / **sthg** être fier de qqn / qqch / *he was proud to have won* or *of having won* il était fier d'avoir gagné / *I'm proud (that) you didn't give up* je suis fier que tu n'aies pas abandonné **2.** [arrogant] fier, orgueilleux **3.** *liter* [stately - tree, mountain] majestueux, altier; [-bearing, stallion, eagle] fier, majestueux **4.** 🇬🇧 [protruding] qui dépasse / *it's a few millimetres proud* ça dépasse de quelques millimètres. ◆ adv *inf* ▶ **to do sb proud a)** [entertain lavishly] recevoir qqn comme un roi / une reine **b)** [honour] faire honneur à qqn.

> 📋 Note that **être fier que** is followed by a verb in the subjunctive:
> **I'm so proud he won.** *Je suis si fier qu'il ait gagné.*

proudly ['praʊdlɪ] adv **1.** [with pride] fièrement, avec fierté **2.** [arrogantly] orgueilleusement **3.** [majestically] majestueusement.

provable ['pruːvəbl] adj prouvable, démontrable.

prove [pruːv] (🇬🇧 *pt & pp* proved; 🇺🇸 *pt* proved, *pp* proved *or* proven ['pruːvn]) ◆ vt **1.** [verify, show] prouver / *the facts prove her (to be) guilty* les faits prouvent qu'elle est coupable ▶ **to prove sb right** / **wrong** donner raison / tort à qqn **2.** LOGIC & MATH [proposition, theorem] démontrer **3.** [put to the test] mettre à l'épreuve ▶ **to prove o.s.** faire ses preuves **4.** 🇬🇧 [will] homologuer. ◆ vi **1.** [turn out] s'avérer, se révéler / *your suspicions proved (to be) well-founded* vos soupçons se sont avérés fondés / *it has proved impossible to find him* il a été impossible de le retrouver **2.** CULIN [dough] lever.

proven ['pruːvn] ◆ pp ➤ **prove.** ◆ adj **1.** [tested] éprouvé / *a candidate with proven experience* un candidat qui a déjà fait ses preuves / *a proven method* une méthode qui a fait ses preuves **2.** LAW ▶ **a verdict of not proven** ≃ un non-lieu.

provenance ['prɒvənəns] n provenance *f*.

Provençal [,prɒvɒn'sɑːl] ◆ n **1.** [person] Provençal *m*, -e *f* **2.** LING provençal *m*. ◆ adj provençal.

Provence [prɒ'vɒs] pr n Provence *f* / *in Provence* en Provence.

proverb ['prɒvɜːb] n proverbe *m*.

proverbial [prə'vɜːbjəl] adj proverbial, légendaire.

provide [prə'vaɪd] ◆ vt **1.** [supply] pourvoir, fournir ▶ **to provide sthg for sb, to provide sb with sthg** fournir qqch à qqn **2.** [offer, afford] offrir, fournir **3.** [stipulate - subj: contract, law] stipuler. ◆ vi ▶ **to provide against sthg** se prémunir contre qqch. ✧ **provide for** vt insep **1.** [support] ▶ **to provide for sb** pourvoir or subvenir aux besoins de qqn / *I have a family to provide for* j'ai une famille à nourrir / *an insurance policy that will provide for your children's future* une assurance qui subviendra aux besoins de vos enfants / *his widow was left well provided for* sa veuve était à l'abri du besoin **2.** [prepare] ▶ **to provide for sthg** se préparer à qqch **3.** [contract, law] ▶ **to provide for sthg** stipuler or prévoir qqch.

provided [prə'vaɪdɪd] conj ▶ **provided (that)** pourvu que, à condition que.

> 📋 Note that **pourvu que** is followed by a verb in the subjunctive:
> ... **provided that no one objects, of course.**
> ... *pourvu que personne n'y voie d'inconvénient, bien entendu.*

providence ['prɒvɪdəns] n **1.** [fate] providence *f* **2.** [foresight] prévoyance *f*; [thrift] économie *f*.

provident ['prɒvɪdənt] adj [foresighted] prévoyant; [thrifty] économe.

providential [,prɒvɪ'denʃl] adj providentiel.

providentially [,prɒvɪ'denʃəlɪ] adv providentiellement.

providently ['prɒvɪdəntlɪ] adv avec prévoyance, prudemment.

provider [prə'vaɪdər] n [gen] fournisseur *m*, -euse *f*; COMPUT fournisseur *m* (d'accès), provider *m*.

providing [prə'vaɪdɪŋ] = **provided.**

province ['prɒvɪns] n **1.** [region, district] province *f* ▶ **the Maritime** / **Prairie Provinces** [of Canada] les Provinces maritimes / des Prairies **2.** [field, sphere - of activity] domaine *m*; [- of responsability] compétence *f* **3.** RELIG province *f* ecclésiastique. ✧ **provinces** pl n 🇬🇧 [not the metropolis] ▶ **the provinces** la province / *in the provinces* en province.

provincial [prə'vɪnʃl] ◆ adj provincial. ◆ n **1.** [from provinces] provincial *m*, -e *f* **2.** RELIG provincial *m*.

proving ground ['pruːvɪŋ-] n terrain *m* d'essai.

provision [prə'vɪʒn] ◆ vt approvisionner, ravitailler. ◆ n **1.** [act of supplying] approvisionnement *m*, fourniture *f*, ravitaillement *m* **2.** [stock, supply] provision *f*, réserve *f* **3.** [arrangement] disposition *f* **4.** [condition, clause] disposition *f*, clause *f*. ✧ **provisions** pl n [food] vivres *mpl*, provisions *fpl*.

provisional [prə'vɪʒənl] adj provisoire ▶ **provisional (driving) licence** 🇬🇧 permis *m* de conduire provisoire (*autorisation que l'on doit obtenir avant de prendre des leçons*). ✧ **Provisional** ◆ adj POL ▶ **the Provisional IRA** l'IRA *f* provisoire. ◆ n membre *m* de l'IRA provisoire.

provisionally [prə'vɪʒnəlɪ] adv provisoirement.

proviso [prə'vaɪzəʊ] (*pl* provisos *or* provisoes) n stipulation *f*, condition *f*.

provisory [prə'vaizəri] adj **1.** [conditional] conditionnel **2.** = **provisional.**

Provo ['prəʊvəʊ] (pl **Provos**) n 🇬🇧 inf POL membre m de l'IRA provisoire.

provocation [ˌprɒvə'keiʃn] n provocation f.

provocative [prə'vɒkətiv] adj **1.** [challenging] provocateur, provocant **2.** [seductive] provocant **3.** [obscene] : a provocative gesture un geste obscène.

provocatively [prə'vɒkətivli] adv [write, dress] d'une manière provocante ; [say] sur un ton provocateur or provocant.

provoke [prə'vəʊk] vt **1.** [goad] provoquer ▶ to provoke sb into doing sthg pousser qqn à faire qqch ; [infuriate] enrager ; [vex] exaspérer **2.** [cause - accident, quarrel, anger] provoquer.

provoking [prə'vəʊkiŋ] adj [situation] contrariant ; [person, behaviour] exaspérant.

provost n ['prɒvəst] **1.** 🇬🇧 UNIV ≃ recteur m ; 🇺🇸 ≃ doyen m **2.** Scot maire m.

prow [praʊ] n proue f.

prowess ['praʊis] n (U) **1.** [skill] (grande) habileté f / sexual prowess prouesses fpl sexuelles **2.** [bravery] vaillance f.

prowl [praʊl] ◆ vi rôder. ◆ vt [street, jungle] rôder dans. ◆ n ▶ to be on the prowl rôder. ✧ prowl about 🇬🇧, prowl around ◆ vi rôder. ◆ vt insep = prowl (vt).

prowl car n 🇺🇸 voiture f de police en patrouille.

prowler ['praʊlə'] n rôdeur m, -euse f.

proximity [prɒk'siməti] n proximité f / in proximity to or in the proximity of à proximité de.

proxy ['prɒksi] (pl **proxies**) n **1.** [person] mandataire mf, fondé m, -e f de pouvoir ; [authorization] procuration f, mandat m ▶ to vote by proxy voter par procuration **2.** COMPUT proxy m, dispositif m de passerelle sécurisée.

proxy server n COMPUT serveur m proxy, serveur m mandataire.

proxy vote n vote m par procuration.

Prozac® ['prəʊzæk] n Prozac® m.

PRP n abbr of performance-related pay.

PRT MESSAGING written abbr of party.

prude [pru:d] n prude f.

prudence ['pru:dns] n prudence f, circonspection f.

prudent ['pru:dnt] adj prudent, circonspect.

prudently ['pru:dntli] adv prudemment.

prudish ['pru:diʃ] adj prude, pudibond.

prudishness ['pru:diʃnis] n pruderie f, pudibonderie f.

prune [pru:n] ◆ n **1.** [fruit] pruneau m **2.** 🇬🇧 inf [fool] patate f, ballot m. ◆ vt **1.** [hedge, tree] tailler ; [branch] élaguer **2.** fig [text, budget] élaguer, faire des coupes sombres dans.

⚠ The French word **prune** means plum, not prune.

pruning ['pru:niŋ] n [of hedge, tree] taille f ; [of branches] élagage m ; fig [of budget, staff] élagage m.

prurient ['prʊəriənt] adj lubrique, lascif.

Prussia ['prʌʃə] pr n Prusse f / in Prussia en Prusse.

Prussian ['prʌʃn] ◆ n Prussien m, -enne f. ◆ adj prussien.

PRW MESSAGING written abbr of parents are watching.

pry [prai] (pt & pp **pried**) ◆ vt 🇺🇸 = **prise.** ◆ vi fouiller, fureter / I didn't mean to pry je ne voulais pas être indiscret.

prying ['praiiŋ] adj indiscret (indiscrète) ▶ away from prying eyes à l'abri des regards indiscrets.

PS (abbr of postscript) n PS m.

psalm [sa:m] n psaume m ▶ (the Book of) Psalms (le livre des) Psaumes.

pseud [sju:d] inf ◆ n poseur m, -euse f, prétentieux m, -euse f. ◆ adj = **pseudo.**

pseudo ['sju:dəʊ] adj inf [kindness, interest] prétendu ; [person] faux (fausse).

pseudo- in comp pseudo-.

pseudonym ['sju:dənim] n pseudonyme m.

PSHE (abbr of personal, social and health education) n 🇬🇧 SCH éducation f civique et sexuelle.

psi (abbr of pounds per square inch) n livres au pouce carré (mesure de pression).

PSNI (abbr of Police Service of Northern Ireland) n corps de police d'Irlande du Nord.

psoriasis [sɒ'raiəsis] n (U) psoriasis m.

psst [pst] interj psitt, pst.

PST n 🇺🇸 abbr of Pacific Standard Time.

psych [saik] vt inf **1.** [psychoanalyse] psychanalyser **2.** 🇺🇸 [excite] : I'm really psyched about my vacation je suis surexcité à l'idée de partir en vacances. ✧ psych out vt sep inf **1.** [sense - sb's motives] deviner ; [- situation] comprendre, piger **2.** [intimidate] : he soon psyched out his opponent and the game was his très vite, il a décontenancé son adversaire et il a gagné. ✧ psych up vt sep inf [motivate] ▶ to psych o.s. up for sthg / to do sthg se préparer psychologiquement à qqch / à faire qqch.

psyche¹ ['saiki] n [mind] psyché f, psychisme m.

psyche² [saik] = **psych.**

psychedelic [ˌsaiki'delik] adj psychédélique.

psychiatric [ˌsaiki'ætrik] adj psychiatrique ▶ psychiatric nurse infirmier m, -ère f psychiatrique ▶ psychiatric patient patient m, -e f en psychiatrie.

psychiatrist [sai'kaiətrist] n psychiatre mf.

psychiatry [sai'kaiətri] n psychiatrie f.

psychic ['saikik] ◆ adj **1.** [supernatural] parapsychique ▶ to be psychic, to have psychic powers avoir le don de double vue or un sixième sens **2.** [mental] psychique. ◆ n médium m.

psycho ['saikəʊ] (pl **psychos**) inf ◆ n psychopathe mf. ◆ adj psychopathe.

psychoactive [ˌsaikəʊ'æktiv] adj psychotrope.

psychoanalyse 🇬🇧, **psychoanalyze** 🇺🇸 [ˌsaikəʊ'ænəlaiz] vt psychanalyser.

psychoanalysis [ˌsaikəʊə'næləsis] n psychanalyse f.

psychoanalyst [ˌsaikəʊ'ænəlist] n psychanalyste mf.

psychoanalytic(al) ['saikəʊˌænə'litik(l)] adj psychanalytique.

psychodrama ['saikəʊˌdra:mə] n psychodrame m.

psychological [ˌsaikə'lɒdʒikl] adj psychologique.

psychological block n blocage m psychologique.

psychologically [ˌsaikə'lɒdʒikli] adv psychologiquement.

psychological profile n profil m psychologique.

psychological warfare n guerre f psychologique.

psychologist [sai'kɒlədʒist] n psychologue mf.

psychology [sai'kɒlədʒi] n psychologie f.

psychopath ['saikəpæθ] n psychopathe mf.

psychopathic [ˌsaɪkəˈpæθɪk] adj [person] psychopathe ; [disorder, personality] psychopathique.

psychosis [saɪˈkəʊsɪs] (pl **psychoses** [-siːz]) n psychose f.

psychosomatic [ˌsaɪkəʊsəˈmætɪk] adj psychosomatique.

psychotherapist [ˌsaɪkəʊˈθerəpɪst] n psychothérapeute mf.

psychotherapy [ˌsaɪkəʊˈθerəpɪ] n psychothérapie f.

psychotic [saˈkɒtɪk] ◆ adj psychotique. ◆ n psychotique mf.

pt 1. written abbr of **pint 2.** written abbr of **point.**

PT n **1.** (abbr of **physical training**) dated EPS f ▸ **PT instructor** professeur m d'éducation physique **2.** US abbr of **physical therapy 3.** US abbr of **physical therapist.**

Pt. (written abbr of **point**) [on map] Pte.

PTA (abbr of **parent-teacher association**) n association de parents d'élèves et de professeurs.

PTB MESSAGING written abbr of **please text back.**

Pte. US MIL written abbr of **private.**

PTO (written abbr of **please turn over**) US TSVP.

PTV n **1.** (abbr of **pay television**) télévision à péage **2.** (abbr of **public television**) programmes télévisés éducatifs.

pub [pʌb] (abbr of **public house**) n pub m ▸ **pub lunch**: we had a pub lunch nous avons déjeuné dans un pub ▸ **pub grub** inf nourriture (relativement simple) servie dans un pub. ⟶ **beer**

 Pub

Dans l'ensemble des îles Britanniques, le **pub** est un des grands foyers de la vie sociale, surtout le vendredi soir et le samedi soir. Ces établissements – généralement interdits aux personnes de moins de 18 ans non accompagnées – étaient soumis à des horaires stricts, mais ceux-ci se sont beaucoup assouplis récemment (voir **licensing hours**). De simple débit de boissons, qu'il était souvent, le **pub** évolue de plus en plus vers une sorte de brasserie servant des repas légers. Certains sont devenus de véritables restaurants. Voir aussi **beer.**

---

pub. written abbr of **published.**

pub crawl n US inf ▸ **to go on a pub crawl** ≃ faire la tournée des bars.

puberty [ˈpjuːbətɪ] n puberté f ▸ **to reach puberty** atteindre l'âge de la puberté.

pubes[1] [ˈpjuːbiːz] (pl **pubes**) n [region] pubis m, région f pubienne ; [hair] poils mpl pubiens ; [bones] (os m du) pubis m.

pubes[2] [pjuːbz] pl n inf poils mpl (pubiens).

pubescent [pjuːˈbesnt] adj **1.** [at puberty] pubère **2.** [plant, animal] pubescent.

pubic [ˈpjuːbɪk] adj pubien ▸ **pubic bone** symphyse f pubienne ▸ **pubic louse** pou m du pubis ▸ **pubic hair** poils mpl pubiens or du pubis.

public [ˈpʌblɪk] ◆ adj **1.** [of, by the state - education, debt] public ▸ **public bill** US POL ≃ projet m de loi d'intérêt général ▸ **public housing** US logements mpl sociaux ; ≃ HLM f inv ▸ **public housing project** US ≃ cité f HLM ▸ **public money** deniers mpl or fonds mpl publics ▸ **to hold public office** avoir des fonctions officielles ▸ **public official**

fonctionnaire mf ▸ **public ownership** nationalisation f, étatisation f ▸ **the public purse** US le Trésor (public) ▸ **public television** US (télévision f du) service m public **2.** [open or accessible to all - place, meeting] public ▸ **public baths** bains mpl publics ▸ **public library** bibliothèque f municipale ▸ **public phone** cabine f téléphonique **3.** [of, by the people] public / in the public interest dans l'intérêt général / to restore public confidence regagner la confiance de la population / public awareness of the problem has increased le public est plus sensible au problème maintenant / the bill has public support l'opinion publique est favorable au projet de loi ▸ **to be in the public eye** occuper le devant de la scène (publique) **4.** [publicly known, open] public ▸ **to make sthg public** rendre qqch public ▸ **a public figure** une personnalité très connue ▸ **public spirit** sens m civique, civisme m **5.** ST. EX ▸ **to go public** être coté en Bourse. ◆ n public m / the public is or are tired of political scandals la population est lasse des scandales politiques / the film-going public les amateurs de or les gens qui vont au cinéma. ◆ **in public** adv phr en public.

public-address system n (système m de) sonorisation f.

publican [ˈpʌblɪkən] n US [pub owner] patron m, -onne f de pub ; [manager] tenancier m, -ère f de pub.

public assistance n US aide f sociale.

publication [ˌpʌblɪˈkeɪʃn] n **1.** [of book, statistics, banns] publication f ; [of edict] promulgation f **2.** [work] publication f, ouvrage m publié.

public bar n US salle f de bar (moins confortable et moins chère que le « lounge bar » ou le « saloon bar »).

public company n ≃ société f anonyme par actions.

public convenience n US toilettes fpl publiques.

public debt n dette f publique or de l'État.

public defender n US avocat m commis d'office.

public domain n ▸ **to be in the public domain** [publication] être dans le domaine public.

public gallery n tribune f réservée au public.

public health n santé f publique.

public holiday n jour m férié, fête f légale.

public house n US [pub] pub m, bar m ; US [inn] auberge f.

public inquiry n enquête f officielle.

publicist [ˈpʌblɪsɪst] n [press agent] (agent m) publicitaire mf.

publicity [pʌbˈlɪsɪtɪ] ◆ n publicité f. ◆ comp [agent, campaign] publicitaire, de publicité ; [manager] de publicité ▸ **publicity stunt** coup m de pub.

publicity-seeking [-siːkɪŋ] adj [person] qui cherche à se faire de la publicité ; [operation, manœuvre] publicitaire.

publicize, publicise [ˈpʌblɪsaɪz] vt **1.** [make known] he doesn't like to publicize the fact that he's been in prison il n'aime pas qu'on dise qu'il a fait de la prison / his much publicized blunders don't help his image ses célèbres gaffes ne font rien pour arranger son image de marque / the government's environmental reforms have been well publicized in the press la presse a beaucoup parlé des réformes du gouvernement en matière d'environnement **2.** [advertise - product, event] faire de la publicité pour.

public lavatory n US toilettes fpl publiques.

public limited company n société f à responsabilité limitée.

publicly [ˈpʌblɪklɪ] adv publiquement, en public ▸ **publicly owned** ECON nationalisé.

public nuisance n **1.** [act] : the pub's late opening hours were creating a public nuisance les heures d'ouverture tardives du pub portaient atteinte à la tranquillité générale **2.** [person] fléau m public, empoisonneur m, -euse f.

public opinion n opinion *f* publique ▸ **public opinion poll** sondage *m* (d'opinion).

public property n [land, etc.] bien *m* public.

public prosecutor n ≈ procureur *m* général ; ≈ ministère *m* public.

Public Records Office [ˌpʌblɪkˈrekɔːdzˌɒfɪs] n ▸ **the Public Records Office** les Archives nationales du Royaume-Uni.

public relations ◆ n *(U)* communication *f*, relations *fpl* publiques. ◆ adj ▸ **public relations consultant** conseil *m* en communication or en relations publiques ▸ **public relations exercise** opération *f* de communication or de relations publiques ▸ **public relations officer** responsable *mf* de la communication or des relations publiques.

public school n **1.** [in UK] public school *f*, école *f* privée (prestigieuse) **2.** [in US] école *f* publique.

Public school

En Angleterre et au pays de Galles, le terme **public school** désigne une école privée de type traditionnel ; certaines de ces écoles (comme Eton et Harrow, par exemple) sont très réputées. Les **public schools** ont pour vocation de former l'élite de la nation. Aux États-Unis, le terme désigne une école publique.

public sector n secteur *m* public ▸ **public sector borrowing requirement** emprunts *mpl* d'État.

public servant n fonctionnaire *mf*.

public service n **1.** 🇬🇧 [civil service] fonction *f* publique **2.** [amenity] service *m* public or d'intérêt général ; ADMIN : *our organization performs a public service* notre association assure un service d'intérêt général. ❖ **public-service** adj ▸ **a public-service message** or **announcement** RADIO & TV un communiqué (d'un ministère) ▸ **Public-Service Commission** 🇺🇸 commission chargée de la réglementation des sociétés privées assurant des services publics ▸ **public-service corporation** 🇺🇸 société privée assurant un service public et réglementée par une commission d'État ▸ **public-service vehicle** 🇬🇧 autobus *m*.

public speaking n prise *f* de parole en public.

public spending n *(U)* dépenses *fpl* publiques or de l'État.

public-spirited adj [gesture] d'esprit civique ; [person] ▸ **to be public-spirited** faire preuve de civisme.

public transport 🇬🇧, **public transportation** 🇺🇸 n *(U)* transports *mpl* en commun ▸ *he went by public transport* [bus] il est allé en bus ; [train] il est allé en train.

public utility n 🇺🇸 **1.** [company] société privée assurant un service public et réglementée par une commission d'État **2.** [amenity] service *m* public.

public works pl n travaux *mpl* publics.

publish [ˈpʌblɪʃ] ◆ vt **1.** [book, journal] publier, éditer ; [author] éditer **2.** [subj: author] : *he's published poems in several magazines* ses poèmes ont été publiés dans plusieurs revues **3.** [make known - statistics, statement, banns] publier. ◆ vi **1.** [newspaper] paraître **2.** [author] être publié.

publishable [ˈpʌblɪʃəbl] adj publiable.

publisher [ˈpʌblɪʃər] n [person] éditeur *m*, -trice *f* ; [company] maison *f* d'édition.

publishing [ˈpʌblɪʃɪŋ] ◆ n **1.** [industry] édition *f* ▸ *she's* or *she works in publishing* elle travaille dans l'édition **2.** [of book, journal] publication *f*. ◆ comp ▸ **publishing company** or **house** maison *f* d'édition.

puce [pjuːs] ◆ n couleur *f* puce. ◆ adj puce *(inv)*.

puck [pʌk] n **1.** [in ice hockey] palet *m* **2.** [sprite] lutin *m*, farfadet *m*.

pucker [ˈpʌkər] ◆ vi [face, forehead] se plisser ; [fabric, collar] goder, godailler. ◆ vt [face, forehead] plisser ; [fabric, collar] faire goder, faire godailler. ◆ n [crease] pli *m*. ❖ **pucker up** ◆ vi **1.** = **pucker** *(vi)* **2.** *inf* [for kiss] avancer les lèvres. ◆ vt sep = **pucker** *(vt)*.

pudding [ˈpʊdɪŋ] n **1.** [sweet dish] ▸ **rice / tapioca pudding** riz *m* / tapioca *m* au lait **2.** 🇬🇧 [part of meal] dessert *m* **3.** [savoury dish] *tourte cuite à la vapeur* **4.** [sausage] boudin *m* ▸ **white pudding** boudin *m* blanc **5.** 🇬🇧 *inf* [podgy person] boudin *m*.

pudding basin, pudding bowl n 🇬🇧 *jatte dans laquelle on fait cuire le pudding* ▸ **pudding basin haircut** coupe *f* au bol.

puddle [ˈpʌdl] ◆ n flaque *f*. ◆ vt [clay] malaxer.

pudgy [ˈpʌdʒɪ] *(compar* **pudgier**, *superl* **pudgiest)** = **podgy**.

puerile [ˈpjʊəraɪl] adj puéril.

Puerto Rican [ˌpwɜːtəʊˈriːkən] ◆ pr n Portoricain *m*, -e *f*. ◆ adj portoricain.

Puerto Rico [ˌpwɜːtəʊˈriːkəʊ] pr n Porto Rico, Puerto Rico *f* ▸ *in Puerto Rico* à Porto Rico, à Puerto Rico.

puff¹ [pʌf] ◆ vt **1.** [smoke - cigar, pipe] tirer des bouffées de **2.** [emit, expel] ▸ **to puff (out) smoke / steam** envoyer des nuages de fumée / des jets de vapeur **3.** [pant] : *"I can't go on", he puffed* «je n'en peux plus», haleta-t-il **4.** [swell - sail, parachute] gonfler. ◆ vi **1.** [blow - person] souffler ; [- wind] souffler en bourrasques **2.** [pant] haleter ; [breathe heavily] souffler / *he was puffing and panting* il soufflait comme un phoque **3.** [smoke] ▸ **to puff on one's cigar** tirer sur son cigare **4.** [issue - smoke, steam] sortir **5.** [train] : *the train puffed into the station* le train entra en gare dans un nuage de fumée. ◆ n **1.** [gust, whiff] bouffée *f* ; [gasp] souffle *m* **2.** [on cigarette, pipe] bouffée *f* ▸ **to have** or **take a puff** tirer une bouffée **3.** [sound - of train] teuf-teuf *m* **4.** 🇬🇧 *inf* [breath] souffle *m* ▸ **to be out of puff** être à bout de souffle or essoufflé **5.** [fluffy mass] : *puffs of cloud in the sky* des moutons or des petits nuages dans le ciel **6.** [for make-up] ▸ **(powder) puff** houppe *f* (à poudrer), houpette *f* **7.** [pastry] chou *m* **8.** 🇺🇸 [eiderdown] édredon *m*. ❖ **puff out** ◆ vt sep **1.** [extinguish] souffler, éteindre (en soufflant) **2.** [inflate, make rounded - cheeks, sail] gonfler ; [- chest] bomber ; [- cushion, hair] faire bouffer **3.** [emit] ▸ **to puff out smoke / steam** envoyer des nuages de fumée / de vapeur. ◆ vi **1.** [parachute, sail] se gonfler **2.** [be emitted - smoke] s'échapper. ❖ **puff up** ◆ vt sep **1.** = **puff out 2.** *(usu passive)* [swell - lip, ankle, etc.] enfler / *her eyes were puffed up* elle avait les yeux bouffis ▸ **to be puffed up with pride** *fig* être bouffi d'orgueil. ◆ vi [lip, ankle, etc.] enfler, bouffir.

puff² [pʊf] = **poof**.

Puffa jacket® [ˈpʌfə-] n blouson *m* de rappeur.

puffed [pʌft] adj **1.** [rice, oats] soufflé ▸ **puffed wheat cereal** céréale *f* de blé soufflé **2.** 🇬🇧 *inf* [out of breath] essoufflé, à bout de souffle.

puffed sleeves = **puff sleeves**.

puffin [ˈpʌfɪn] n macareux *m*.

puffiness [ˈpʌfɪnɪs] n boursouflure *f*.

puff pastry 🇬🇧 [pʌf-], **puff paste** 🇺🇸 [pʌf-] n [for pies] pâte *f* feuilletée ; [for puffs] pâte *f* à choux.

puff sleeves [pʌf-] pl n manches *fpl* ballon.

puffy [ˈpʌfɪ] *(compar* **puffier**, *superl* **puffiest)** adj [lip, cheek] enflé ; [eye] bouffi.

pug [pʌg] n [dog] carlin *m*.

pugnacious [pʌgˈneɪʃəs] adj *fml* pugnace, agressif.

puke [pjuːk] v inf ◆ vt dégueuler, gerber / *you make me puke!* tu me dégoûtes ! ◆ vi dégueuler. ◆ n dégueulis m.
◆ **puke up** ◆ vt sep dégueuler. ◆ vi dégueuler.

pukka ['pʌkə] adj **UK** dated & hum **1.** [genuine] vrai, authentique, véritable **2.** [done well] bien fait, très correct ; [excellent] de premier ordre **3.** [socially acceptable] (très) comme il faut.

Pulitzer Prize ['pjuːlɪtsər-] n ▶ **the Pulitzer Prize** le prix Pulitzer.

pull [pʊl] ◆ vt **1.** [object - yank, tug] tirer ; [-drag] traîner / *she pulled my hair* elle m'a tiré les cheveux / *he pulled his chair closer to the fire* il approcha sa chaise de la cheminée / *she came in and pulled the door shut behind her* elle entra et ferma la porte derrière elle ; [person] tirer, entraîner ; [remove forcibly] arracher / *she pulled her hand from mine* elle retira (brusquement) sa main de la mienne ▶ **pull the other one (it's got bells on)!** **UK** inf mon œil !, à d'autres ! ▶ **to pull sthg to bits** or **pieces a)** lit démonter qqch **b)** fig démolir qqch **2.** [operate - lever, handle] tirer **3.** [tow, draw - load, trailer, carriage, boat] tirer, remorquer **4.** [take out - tooth] arracher, extraire ; [-weapon] tirer, sortir / *he pulled a gun on me* il a braqué un revolver sur moi **5.** [strain - muscle, tendon] : *she pulled a muscle* elle s'est déchiré un muscle, elle s'est fait un claquage **6.** inf [bring off] réussir ▶ **to pull a trick on sb** jouer un tour à qqn **7.** [hold back] ▶ **to pull one's punches** lit & fig retenir ses coups, ménager son adversaire / *she didn't pull any punches* elle n'y est pas allée de main morte **8.** [gut - fowl] vider **9.** inf [withdraw] retirer **10.** inf [attract - customers, spectators] attirer / *the festival pulled a big crowd* le festival a attiré beaucoup de monde **11.** **UK** [serve - draught beer] tirer **12.** **UK** v inf [seduce] lever. ◆ vi **1.** [exert force, tug] tirer / *pull harder!* tirez plus fort ! / *the steering pulls to the right* la direction tire à droite **2.** [go, move - vehicle, driver] : *pull into the space next to the Mercedes* mettez-vous or garez-vous à côté de la Mercedes / *when the train pulls out of the station* quand le train quitte la gare **3.** [strain, labour - vehicle] peiner ; [-horse] tirer sur le mors **4.** [row] ramer **5.** v inf [have sex] : *did you pull last night?* tu as tiré la nuit dernière ? ◆ n **1.** [tug, act of pulling] coup m ▶ **to give sthg a pull, to give a pull on sthg** tirer (sur) qqch **2.** [physical force - of machine] traction f ; [-of sun, moon, magnet] attraction f / *we fought against the pull of the current* nous luttions contre le courant qui nous entraînait **3.** [psychological, emotional attraction] attrait m **4.** inf [influence, power] influence f **5.** [climb] montée f / *it'll be a long pull to the summit* la montée sera longue (et difficile) pour atteindre le sommet **6.** [at cigar] bouffée f ; [at drink, bottle] gorgée f ; [on cigarette, pipe] ▶ **to take a pull at** or **on** tirer sur **7.** [knob, handle] poignée f ; [cord] cordon m ; [strap] sangle f. ◆ **pull apart** vt sep **1.** [take to pieces - machine, furniture] démonter **2.** [destroy, break] mettre en morceaux or en pièces / *tell him where it's hidden or he'll pull the place apart* inf dites-lui où c'est (caché) sinon il va tout saccager **3.** fig [demolish - essay, theory] démolir **4.** [separate - fighters, dogs] séparer ; [-papers] détacher, séparer **5.** [make suffer] déchirer. ◆ **pull around** vt sep **1.** [cart, toy, suitcase] tirer derrière soi **2.** [make turn] tourner, faire pivoter. ◆ **pull at** vt insep [strain at, tug at] tirer sur / *I pulled at his sleeve* je lui ai tiré par la manche. ◆ **pull away** ◆ vi **1.** [withdraw - person] s'écarter, se détourner / *he had me by the arm but I managed to pull away* il me tenait par le bras mais j'ai réussi à me dégager **2.** [move off - vehicle, ship] démarrer ; [-train, convoy] s'ébranler **3.** [get ahead - runner, competitor] prendre de l'avance. ◆ vt sep [withdraw - covering, hand] retirer ; [grab] arracher. ◆ **pull back** ◆ vi **1.** [withdraw - troops, participant] se retirer **2.** [step backwards] reculer **3.** [jib - horse, person] regimber. ◆ vt sep **1.** [draw backwards or towards one] retirer / *she pulled back the curtains* elle ouvrit les rideaux **2.** [withdraw - troops] retirer. ◆ **pull down** vt sep

1. [lower - lever, handle] tirer (vers le bas) ; [-trousers, veil] baisser ; [-suitcase, book] descendre ; [-blind, window] baisser / *pull the blind / the window down* baissez le store / la vitre / *with his hat pulled down over his eyes* son chapeau rabattu sur les yeux **2.** [demolish - house, wall] démolir, abattre **3.** inf [weaken - subj: illness] affaiblir, abattre ; [depress] déprimer, abattre. ◆ **pull in** ◆ vi [vehicle, driver - stop] s'arrêter ; [-park] se garer ; [-move to side of road] se rabattre ; [train] entrer en gare. ◆ vt sep **1.** [line, fishing net] ramener ▶ **to pull sb in a)** [into building, car] tirer qqn à l'intérieur, faire entrer qqn **b)** [into water] faire tomber qqn à l'eau ; [stomach] rentrer **2.** [attract - customers, investors, investment] attirer / *her show is really pulling them in* son spectacle attire les foules **3.** inf [arrest] arrêter, embarquer. ◆ **pull off** ◆ vi **1.** [move off] démarrer ; [after halt] redémarrer **2.** [leave main road] quitter la route ; [stop] s'arrêter. ◆ vt sep **1.** [clothes, boots, ring] enlever, retirer ; [cover, bandage, knob] enlever ; [page from calendar, sticky backing] détacher ; [wrapping, wallpaper] enlever **2.** inf [accomplish - deal, stratagem, mission, shot] réussir ; [-press conference, negotiations] mener à bien ; [-plan] réaliser / *will she (manage to) pull it off?* est-ce qu'elle va y arriver ? ◆ **pull on** ◆ vt sep [clothes, boots, pillow slip] mettre, enfiler. ◆ vt insep **1.** [tug at - rope, handle, etc.] tirer sur **2.** [draw on - cigarette, pipe] tirer sur. ◆ **pull out** ◆ vi **1.** [withdraw - troops, ally, participant] se retirer / *they've pulled out of the deal* ils se sont retirés de l'affaire **2.** [move off - car, ship] démarrer ; [-train, convoy] s'ébranler ; [move towards centre of road] : *he pulled out to overtake* il a déboîté pour doubler. ◆ vt sep **1.** [remove - tooth, hair, weeds] arracher ; [-splinter, nail] enlever ; [-plug, cork] ôter, enlever ; [produce - wallet, weapon] sortir, tirer / *to pull the country out of recession* sortir le pays de la récession **2.** [draw towards one - drawer] tirer ; [unfold] déplier / *he pulled a chair out from under the table* il a écarté une chaise de la table **3.** [withdraw - troops, contestant] retirer. ◆ **pull over** ◆ vt sep **1.** [draw into specified position] tirer, traîner / *pull the chair over to the window* amenez la chaise près de la fenêtre **2.** [make fall - pile, person, table] faire tomber, renverser **3.** (usu passive) [stop - vehicle, driver] arrêter / *I got pulled over for speeding* je me suis fait arrêter pour excès de vitesse. ◆ vi [vehicle, driver - stop] s'arrêter ; [-move to side of road] se ranger, se rabattre. ◆ **pull round** **UK** ◆ vt sep **1.** = **pull around** ◆ vi [revive] ranimer. ◆ vi [regain consciousness] revenir à soi, reprendre connaissance ; [recover] se remettre. ◆ **pull through** ◆ vi [recover] s'en sortir, s'en tirer. ◆ vt sep **1.** [draw through - rope, thread] faire passer **2.** [help survive or surmount] tirer d'affaire. ◆ **pull together** ◆ vi [on rope] tirer ensemble ; [on oars] ramer à l'unisson ; fig [combine efforts] concerter ses efforts, agir de concert. ◆ vt sep **1.** [place together, join] joindre **2.** [organize - demonstration, rescue team] organiser ; [prepare] préparer **3.** **PHR** ▶ **to pull o.s. together** se reprendre, se ressaisir / *pull yourself together!* ressaisissez-vous !, ne vous laissez pas aller ! ◆ **pull up** ◆ vi **1.** [stop] s'arrêter ▶ **to pull up short** s'arrêter net or brusquement **2.** [draw even] rattraper. ◆ vt sep **1.** [draw upwards - trousers, sleeve, blanket, lever] remonter ; [hoist] hisser **2.** [move closer - chair] approcher **3.** [uproot - weeds] arracher ; [-bush, stump, tree] arracher, déraciner ; [rip up - floorboards] arracher **4.** [stop - person, vehicle, horse] arrêter ; [check - person] retenir / *he was about to tell them everything but I pulled him up (short)* il était sur le point de tout leur dire mais je lui ai coupé la parole **5.** inf [improve - score, mark] améliorer ; [-average] remonter **6.** **UK** inf [rebuke] réprimander, enguirlander.

pulldown ['pʊldaʊn] adj [bench, counter] à abattant ▶ **pulldown menu** COMPUT menu m déroulant ▶ **pulldown seat** strapontin m.

pulley ['pʊlɪ] n [wheel, device] poulie f ; TECH [set of parallel wheels] molette f.

pulling power ['pʊlɪŋ-] n ▣ inf pouvoir m de séduction.

pullout ['pʊlaʊt] ◆ n 1. [magazine supplement] supplément m détachable 2. [fold-out] hors-texte m inv (qui se déplie) 3. [withdrawal - gen & MIL] retrait m ; [- of candidate] désistement m ; [evacuation] évacuation f 4. AERON rétablissement m. ◆ adj [magazine section] détachable ; [map, advertising page] hors texte (inv) ; [legs, shelf] rétractable ▶ **pullout bed** canapé-lit m.

pullover ['pʊl‚əʊvə‛] n pull-over m, pull m.

pulmonary ['pʌlmənərɪ] adj pulmonaire.

pulp [pʌlp] ◆ n 1. [in fruit] pulpe f ; [for paper] pâte f à papier, pulpe f ; [in tooth] pulpe f 2. [mush] bouillie f ▶ **to beat** or **to smash to a pulp** réduire en bouillie ou en marmelade 3. MIN pulpe f. ◆ comp pej [novel, fiction] de hall de gare. ◆ vt 1. [crush - wood] réduire en pâte ; [- fruit, vegetables] réduire en pulpe ; [- book] mettre au pilon 2. [remove pulp from] ôter la pulpe de.

pulpit ['pʊlpɪt] n RELIG chaire f ; fig [clergy] ▶ **the pulpit** le clergé, les ecclésiastiques mpl.

pulsar ['pʌlsɑː‛] n pulsar m.

pulsate [pʌl'seɪt] vi 1. [throb - heart] battre fort ; [- music, room] vibrer 2. MED pulser.

pulse [pʌls] ◆ n 1. MED pouls m ; [single throb] pulsation f / he took my pulse il a pris mon pouls 2. ELECTRON & PHYS [series] série f d'impulsions ; [single] impulsion f 3. [vibration] rythme m régulier 4. [bustle, life] animation f 5. BOT [plant] légumineuse f. ◆ vi [blood] battre ; [music, room] vibrer.

pulverize, pulverise ['pʌlvəraɪz] vt lit & fig pulvériser.

puma ['pjuːmə] (pl puma or pumas) n puma m.

pumice ['pʌmɪs] ◆ n ▶ **pumice (stone)** (pierre f) ponce f. ◆ vt poncer, passer à la pierre ponce.

pummel ['pʌml] (▣ pt & pp pummelled, cont pummelling ; ▣ pt & pp pummeled, cont pummeling) vt 1. [punch] donner des coups de poing à, marteler à coups de poing 2. [massage] masser, palper 3. [knead - dough] pétrir.

pump [pʌmp] ◆ n 1. MECH pompe f ▶ **pump attendant** pompiste mf 2. [shoe - for dancing] ballerine f ; [- for gym] tennis m 3. ▣ inf [heart] cœur m, palpitant v inf m. ◆ vt 1. [displace - liquid, gas] pomper ▶ **to pump sthg out of sthg** pomper ou aspirer qqch de qqch 2. [empty - stomach] vider 3. [inflate - tyre, ball, etc.] gonfler 4. [move back and forth - pedal, handle] appuyer sur or actionner (plusieurs fois) 5. inf [shoot] ▶ **to pump sb full of lead** cribler qqn de plomb 6. inf [money] investir 7. inf [interrogate] interroger, tirer les vers du nez à 8. ⌊PHR⌋ **to pump iron** inf faire de la gonflette. ◆ vi 1. [machine, person] pomper ; [heart] battre fort 2. [liquid] couler à flots, jaillir. ◈ **pumps** pl n [shoes] escarpins mpl. ◈ **pump in** vt sep 1. [liquid, gas] refouler 2. inf [funds, capital] investir, injecter. ◈ **pump out** ◆ vt sep 1. [liquid, gas] pomper ; [stomach] vider 2. inf & pej [mass-produce - music, graduates, products] produire ; [- books, essays] produire à la chaîne, pondre en série. ◆ vi [liquid, blood] couler à flots. ◈ **pump up** vt sep 1. [liquid, mixture] pomper 2. [inflate] gonfler 3. ▣ inf [excite] ▶ **to be all pumped up** être tout excité.

pump-action shotgun n fusil m à pompe.

pumped [pʌmpt] adj ▣ inf [excited] excité.

pumpernickel ['pʌmpənɪkl] n pumpernickel m ; ≃ pain m noir.

pumpkin ['pʌmpkɪn] n potiron m ; [smaller] citrouille f.

pump prices pl n [of petrol] prix mpl à la pompe.

pun [pʌn] (pt & pp punned, cont punning) ◆ n calembour m, jeu m de mots. ◆ vi faire des calembours.

punch [pʌntʃ] ◆ n 1. [blow] coup m de poing 2. fig [effectiveness - of person] punch m ; [of speech, cartoon, play] mordant m 3. [for holes - in paper] perforateur m ; [- in metal] poinçonneuse f ; [for tickets - by hand] poinçonneuse f ; [- machine] composteur m ; [steel rod, die] poinçon m 4. [for stamping design] machine f à estamper 5. [for nails, bolts] chasse-clou m 6. [drink] punch m. ◆ vt 1. [hit - once] donner un coup de poing à ; [- repeatedly] marteler à coups de poing 2. [key, button] appuyer sur 3. [pierce - ticket] poinçonner ; [- in machine] composter ; [- paper, computer card] perforer ; [- sheet metal] poinçonner 4. [stamp] estamper. ◆ vi [strike] frapper. ◈ **punch in** ◆ vt sep 1. [enter - code, number] taper, composer ; [- figures, data] introduire 2. [knock in - door] défoncer (à coups de poing) ; [- nails] enfoncer. ◆ vi ▣ [on time clock] pointer (en arrivant). ◈ **punch out** ◆ vt sep 1. [enter - code, number] taper, composer 2. [cut out - form, pattern] découper 3. [stamp] estamper, emboutir 4. ▣ inf [beat up] tabasser 5. inf AERON [subj: pilot] s'éjecter. ◆ vi ▣ [on time clock] pointer (en partant).

Punch [pʌntʃ] pr n ≃ Polichinelle ▶ **Punch and Judy show** ≃ (spectacle m de) guignol m.

Punch and Judy

Le **Punch and Judy show** est un spectacle de marionnettes très apprécié des enfants en Grande-Bretagne. Les représentations ont le plus souvent lieu dans un jardin public ou sur une plage. On y retrouve les personnages de Punch le Bossu, de sa femme Judy, avec qui il se querelle constamment, de leur bébé et de leur chien, Toby.

punch bag ['pʌntʃ‚bæg] n ▣ 1. SPORT sac m de sable, punching-bag m 2. fig [victim] souffre-douleur m inv.

punch ball n ▣ punching-ball m.

punch bowl n bol m à punch.

punch-drunk adj [boxer] groggy ; fig abruti, sonné.

punched card ['pʌntʃt-] n ▣ COMPUT carte f perforée.

punching bag ['pʌntʃɪŋ-] ▣ = punch bag.

punch line n fin f (d'une plaisanterie), chute f.

punch-up n inf bagarre f.

punchy ['pʌntʃɪ] (compar punchier, superl punchiest) adj inf 1. [stimulating, lively] plein de punch 2. = punch-drunk.

punctilious [pʌŋk'tɪlɪəs] adj pointilleux.

punctual ['pʌŋktʃʊəl] adj [bus] à l'heure ; [person] ponctuel.

punctuality [‚pʌŋktʃʊ'ælətɪ] n ponctualité f, exactitude f.

punctually ['pʌŋktʃʊəlɪ] adv [begin, arrive] à l'heure ; [pay] ponctuellement.

punctuate ['pʌŋktʃʊeɪt] vt ponctuer.

punctuation [‚pʌŋktʃʊ'eɪʃn] n ponctuation f.

punctuation mark n signe m de ponctuation.

puncture ['pʌŋktʃə‛] ◆ n 1. ▣ [in tyre, ball, balloon] crevaison f / I had a puncture on the way to work j'ai crevé en allant travailler ▶ **puncture repair kit** trousse f de réparation pour crevaisons 2. [gen - hole] perforation f 3. MED ponction f. ◆ vt 1. [gen] perforer 2. [tyre, ball, balloon] crever 3. fig [pride, self-esteem] blesser, porter atteinte à. ◆ vi crever.

pundit ['pʌndɪt] n 1. [expert] expert m (qui pontifie) 2. [Brahmin] pandit m.

pungency ['pʌndʒənsɪ] n 1. [of smell, taste] âcreté f ; [of food] piquant m 2. [of wit, remark] causticité f, mordant m.

pungent ['pʌndʒənt] adj **1.** [smell, taste - sour] âcre ; [- spicy] piquant **2.** [wit, remark] caustique, mordant.

punish ['pʌnɪʃ] vt **1.** [person, crime] punir **2.** inf [attack relentlessly - opponent, enemy, etc.] malmener.

punishable ['pʌnɪʃəbl] adj punissable.

punishing ['pʌnɪʃɪŋ] ◆ n **1.** [punishment] punition f **2.** inf [relentless attack] ▶ **to take a punishing a)** [opponent, team] se faire malmener **b)** hum [bottle] en prendre un coup. ◆ adj [heat, climb, effort] exténuant ; [defeat] écrasant.

punishment ['pʌnɪʃmənt] n **1.** [act of punishing] punition f, châtiment m **2.** [means of punishment] punition f, châtiment m, sanction f ; LAW peine f **3.** inf [heavy use] : the landing gear can take a lot of punishment même soumis à rude épreuve, le train d'atterrissage tiendra le coup.

punitive ['pju:nətɪv] adj **1.** [expedition] punitif **2.** [measures, tax] écrasant ▶ **to take punitive action** avoir recours à des sanctions ▶ **punitive damages** dommages mpl et intérêts mpl dissuasifs.

Punjab [,pʌn'dʒɑːb] pr n ▶ **the Punjab** le Pendjab / in the Punjab au Pendjab.

Punjabi [,pʌn'dʒɑːbɪ] ◆ n **1.** [person] Pendjabi mf **2.** LING pendjabi m. ◆ adj pendjabi, du Pendjab.

punk [pʌŋk] ◆ n **1.** [music, fashion] punk m **2.** [punk rocker] punk mf **3.** US v inf [worthless person] vaurien m, -enne f ; [hoodlum] voyou m. ◆ adj **1.** [music, fashion] punk (inv) ▶ **punk rock** punk m ▶ **punk rocker** punk mf **2.** US inf [worthless] nul.

punnet ['pʌnɪt] n UK barquette f.

punt¹ [pʌnt] ◆ n [boat] longue barque à fond plat manœuvrée à la perche. ◆ vt [boat] faire avancer à la perche. ◆ vi **1.** [in boat] ▶ **to go punting** faire un tour en barque **2.** UK [gamble] jouer.

punt² [pʊnt] n [former currency] livre f irlandaise.

punter ['pʌntər] n UK **1.** [gambler] parieur m, -euse f **2.** inf [customer] client m, -e f **3.** v inf [prostitute's client] micheton m.

puny ['pju:nɪ] (compar **punier**, superl **puniest**) adj **1.** [frail - person, animal, plant] malingre, chétif ; [- arms, legs] maigre, grêle **2.** [feeble - effort] pitoyable.

pup [pʌp] (pt & pp **pupped**, cont **pupping**) ◆ n **1.** [young dog] chiot m ; [young animal] jeune animal m ▶ **seal pup** jeune or bébé phoque m ▶ **to be in pup** [bitch] être pleine **2.** inf [youth] blanc-bec m. ◆ vi mettre bas.

pupil ['pju:pl] ◆ n **1.** [gen] élève mf ; [of primary school] écolier m, -ère f ; [of lower secondary school] collégien m, -enne f ; [of upper secondary school] lycéen m, -enne f ; [of painter, musician] élève mf **2.** LAW [minor ward] pupille mf **3.** ANAT pupille f. ◆ comp SCH [participation, power] des élèves.

puppet ['pʌpɪt] ◆ n **1.** [gen] marionnette f ; [string puppet] fantoche m, pantin m ▶ **puppet theatre** théâtre m de marionnettes **2.** fig pantin m, fantoche m. ◆ comp **1.** [theatre] de marionnettes ▶ **puppet show** (spectacle m de) marionnettes fpl **2.** POL [government, president] fantoche.

puppetry ['pʌpɪtrɪ] n [art - of making] fabrication f de marionnettes ; [- of manipulating] art m du marionnettiste.

puppy ['pʌpɪ] (pl **puppies**) n chiot m.

puppy fat n (U) UK rondeurs fpl de l'adolescence.

purchase ['pɜːtʃəs] ◆ vt acheter ▶ **to purchase sthg from sb** acheter qqch à qqn ▶ **to purchase sthg for sb, to purchase sb sthg** acheter qqch à or pour qqn. ◆ n **1.** [buy, buying] achat m **2.** [grip] prise f.

purchase order n bon m de commande.

purchase price n prix m d'achat.

purchaser ['pɜːtʃəsər] n acheteur m, -euse f.

purchase tax n taxe f à l'achat.

purchasing behaviour n comportement m d'achat.

purchasing decision n décision f d'achat.

purchasing department n service m des achats.

purchasing power ['pɜːtʃəsɪŋ-] n pouvoir m d'achat.

purdah ['pɜːdə] n purdah m (chez certains peuples hindous et musulmans, système qui astreint les femmes à une vie retirée) ▶ **to be in purdah a)** lit être reclus **b)** fig vivre en reclus.

pure [pjʊər] adj **1.** [unadulterated, untainted] pur ▶ **as pure as the driven snow** blanc comme neige **2.** [science, maths, research] pur **3.** [as intensifier] pur.

purebred ['pjʊəbred] adj de race (pure).

puree, purée ['pjʊəreɪ] ◆ n purée f. ◆ vt (pt & pp **pureed** or **puréed**, cont **pureeing** or **puréeing**) réduire en purée.

purely ['pjʊəlɪ] adj purement.

pureness ['pjʊənɪs] n pureté f.

purgative ['pɜːgətɪv] ◆ n purgatif m. ◆ adj purgatif.

purgatory ['pɜːgətrɪ] n RELIG purgatoire m ; fig enfer m.

purge [pɜːdʒ] ◆ vt **1.** POL [party, organization] purger, épurer ; [undesirable elements] éliminer **2.** [free, rid] débarrasser, délivrer **3.** LAW [clear] disculper, innocenter **4.** dated MED [bowels] purger. ◆ n **1.** [gen & POL] purge f, épuration f **2.** MED purge f.

purification [,pjʊərɪfɪ'keɪʃn] n **1.** [of water, oil] épuration f **2.** RELIG purification f.

purifier ['pjʊərɪfaɪər] n [device - for water, oil] épurateur m ; [- for air, atmosphere] purificateur m.

purify ['pjʊərɪfaɪ] (pt & pp **purified**) vt [water, oil] épurer ; [air, soul] purifier.

purist ['pjʊərɪst] ◆ adj puriste. ◆ n puriste mf.

puritan ['pjʊərɪtən] ◆ n puritain m, -e f. ◆ adj puritain. ◆ **Puritan** ◆ n RELIG puritain m, -e f. ◆ adj RELIG puritain.

The Puritans

Ces protestants anglais radicaux sont apparus au XVIᵉ siècle. Ils souhaitaient débarrasser l'Église anglicane des éléments de faste du culte catholique. Soutenus par la Chambre des communes mais rejetés par Élisabeth Iʳᵉ, ils réussirent à s'imposer pendant la période du Protectorat (1653 à 1659).

puritanical [,pjʊərɪ'tænɪkl] adj puritain.

purity ['pjʊərətɪ] n pureté f.

purl [pɜːl] ◆ n [in knitting] ▶ **purl (stitch)** maille f à l'envers. ◆ vt tricoter à l'envers / knit one, purl one une maille à l'endroit, une maille à l'envers.

purloin [pɜː'lɔɪn] vt fml & hum dérober, voler.

purple ['pɜːpl] ◆ n **1.** [colour] violet m **2.** [dye, cloth] pourpre f **3.** [high rank] ▶ **the purple** la pourpre. ◆ adj **1.** [in colour] violet ▶ **purple state** US POL État où aucun des deux partis ne domine le vote populaire **2.** [prose] emphatique, ampoulé.

Purple Heart n US médaille décernée aux blessés de guerre.

purport fml ◆ vt [pə'pɔːt] [claim] prétendre ; [subj: film, book] se vouloir / he purports to be an expert il prétend être un expert, il se fait passer pour un expert. ◆ n ['pɜːpɔːt] signification f, teneur f.

purportedly [pə'pɔːtɪdlɪ] adv fml prétendument.

purpose ['pɜːpəs] ◆ n **1.** [objective, reason] but m, objet m / for this purpose dans ce but, à cet effet **2.** [use, function] usage *m* ; [end, result] fin *f* **3.** [determination] résolution *f*, détermination *f*. ◆ vt *liter* avoir l'intention de. ❖ **on purpose** adv phr exprès.

purpose-built adj 🇬🇧 construit or conçu pour un usage spécifique.

purposeful ['pɜːpəsfʊl] adj [person] résolu ; [look, walk] résolu, décidé ; [act] réfléchi.

purposefully ['pɜːpəsfʊlɪ] adv [for a reason] dans un but précis, délibérément ; [determinedly] d'un air résolu.

purposeless ['pɜːpəslɪs] adj [life] sans but, vide de sens ; [act, violence] gratuit.

purposely ['pɜːpəslɪ] adv exprès, délibérément.

purr [pɜːr] ◆ vi [cat, engine] ronronner. ◆ vt susurrer. ◆ n [of cat] ronronnement *m*, ronron *m* ; [of engine] ronronnement *m*.

purse [pɜːs] ◆ n **1.** 🇬🇧 [for coins] porte-monnaie *m inv* **2.** 🇺🇸 [handbag] sac *m* à main **3.** FIN [wealth, resources] bourse *f* ▸ **to hold** or **to control the purse strings** *fig* tenir les cordons de la bourse **4.** SPORT [prize money] bourse *f*. ◆ vt [lips] pincer.

purser ['pɜːsər] n NAUT commissaire *m* de bord.

purse snatching n 🇺🇸 vol *m* à l'arraché.

pursue [pəˈsjuː] vt **1.** [chase, follow] poursuivre ; *fig* suivre, poursuivre **2.** [strive for] poursuivre, rechercher **3.** [carry out] exécuter, mettre en œuvre ; [practise] exercer **4.** [take further] poursuivre.

pursuer [pəˈsjuːər] n poursuivant *m*, -e *f*.

pursuit [pəˈsjuːt] n **1.** [chasing] poursuite *f* / *they went out in pursuit of the vandals* ils se sont lancés à la poursuite des vandales / *with a pack of dogs in hot pursuit* avec une meute de chiens à leurs trousses **2.** [striving after] poursuite *f*, quête *f*, recherche *f* **3.** [pastime] occupation *f* **4.** SPORT [cycle race] poursuite *f*.

purvey [pəˈveɪ] vt **1.** [sell] vendre, fournir ▸ **to purvey sthg to sb** fournir qqch à qqn, approvisionner qqn en qqch **2.** [communicate - information, news] communiquer ; [- lies, rumours] colporter.

purveyor [pəˈveɪər] n *fml* **1.** [supplier] fournisseur *m*, -euse *f* **2.** [spreader - of gossip, lies] colporteur *m*, -euse *f*.

pus [pʌs] n pus *m*.

push [pʊʃ] ◆ vt **1.** [shove, propel] pousser / *she pushed the door open / shut* elle ouvrit / ferma la porte (en la poussant) / *he pushed the branches apart* il a écarté les branches / *she pushed her way to the bar* elle se fraya un chemin jusqu'au bar **2.** [insert] enfoncer, introduire ; [thrust] enfoncer / *push all that mess under the bed* pousse tout ce bazar sous le lit **3.** [press - doorbell, pedal, button] appuyer sur ▸ **to push sb's buttons** *inf*: *he pushed all my buttons* a) [turned me on] il a fait tout ce qu'il fallait pour m'exciter b) [annoyed me] il a fait tout ce qu'il fallait pour m'énerver **4.** [cause to move in specified direction] : *the crisis is pushing the country towards chaos* la crise entraîne le pays vers le chaos / *he is pushing the party to the right* il fait glisser le parti vers la droite **5.** [pressurize] pousser ; [force] forcer, obliger, contraindre ▸ **to push sb to do sthg** pousser qqn à faire qqch ▸ **to push sb into doing sthg** forcer or obliger qqn à faire qqch / *I like to push myself hard* j'aime me donner à fond / *he won't do it if he's pushed too hard* il ne le fera pas si l'on insiste trop **6.** [advocate, argue for - idea, method] prôner, préconiser ; [promote - product] promouvoir / *he's trying to push his own point of view* il essaie d'imposer son point de vue personnel **7.** [stretch, exaggerate - argument, case] présenter avec insistance, insister sur ▸ **that's pushing it a bit!** *inf* c'est un peu fort ! **8.** *inf* [approach] friser / *to be pushing thirty* friser la trentaine. ◆ vi **1.** [shove] pousser / *no pushing please!* ne poussez pas, s'il vous plaît ! /

people were pushing to get in les gens se bousculaient pour entrer / *he pushed through the crowd to the bar* il s'est frayé un chemin jusqu'au bar à travers la foule **2.** [press - on button, bell, knob] appuyer **3.** [advance] avancer ; [progress] évoluer **4.** [extend - path, fence] s'étendre. ◆ n **1.** [shove] poussée *f* ▸ **to give sb / sthg a push** pousser qqn / qqch / *would you give me a push?* pourriez-vous me pousser ? ▸ **to give sb the push** a) 🇬🇧 *inf* [from job] virer qqn b) [in relationship] plaquer qqn ▸ **when it comes to the push** *inf*, **when push comes to shove** *inf* au moment critique or crucial ▸ **at a push** *inf*: *I can do it at a push* je peux le faire si c'est vraiment nécessaire **2.** [act of pressing] : *the door opens at the push of a button* il suffit d'appuyer sur un bouton pour que la porte s'ouvre / *he expects these things to happen at the push of a button* *fig* il s'attend à ce que ça se fasse sur commande **3.** *fig* [trend] : *the push towards protectionism is gathering strength* la tendance au protectionnisme se renforce **4.** [encouragement] mot *m* d'encouragement / *he just needs a push in the right direction* il a juste besoin qu'on le mette sur la bonne voie **5.** [campaign] campagne *f*. ❖ **push about** vt sep 🇬🇧 **1.** [physically] malmener **2.** [bully] donner des ordres à. ❖ **push ahead** vi [make progress] : *they decided to push ahead with the plans to extend the school* ils ont décidé d'activer les projets d'extension de l'école. ❖ **push around** = **push about**. ❖ **push aside** vt sep **1.** [objects] pousser **2.** [reject - proposal] écarter, rejeter ; [neglect - problem] : *I pushed my doubts aside* je n'ai pas tenu compte de mes doutes. ❖ **push away** vt sep repousser. ❖ **push back** vt sep **1.** [person] repousser (en arrière) ; [bedclothes] rejeter, repousser **2.** [repulse - troops] repousser **3.** [postpone] repousser. ❖ **push down** vt sep **1.** [lever, handle] abaisser ; [pedal] appuyer sur **2.** [knock over] renverser, faire tomber. ❖ **push for** vt insep [argue for] demander ; [campaign for] faire campagne pour ; [agitate for] militer pour. ❖ **push forward** ◆ vt sep *lit* pousser (en avant) ▸ **to push o.s. forward** *fig* se mettre en avant, se faire valoir. ◆ vi **1.** [advance - person, car] se frayer un chemin ; [- crowd, herd] se presser en avant **2.** = **push ahead**. ❖ **push in** ◆ vt sep **1.** [drawer] pousser ; [electric plug, key] enfoncer, introduire ; [disk] insérer ; [knife, stake, spade] enfoncer ; [button, switch] appuyer sur **2.** [person] : *they pushed me in the water* ils m'ont poussé dans l'eau **3.** [break down - panel, cardboard] enfoncer. ◆ vi [in queue] se faufiler. ❖ **push off** ◆ vi *inf* [go away] filer / *push off!* de l'air !, dégage ! ◆ vt sep **1.** [knock off] faire tomber **2.** [boat] déborder. ❖ **push on** vi [on journey - set off again] reprendre la route, se remettre en route ; [- continue] poursuivre or continuer son chemin ; [keep working] continuer, persévérer. ❖ **push out** vt sep **1.** [person, object] : *they pushed the car out of the mud* ils ont désembourbé la voiture en la poussant ▸ **to push the boat out** a) *lit* déborder l'embarcation b) *fig* faire la fête **2.** [stick out - hand, leg] tendre **3.** [oust] évincer ; [dismiss from job] mettre à la porte. ❖ **push over** vt sep **1.** [pass - across table, floor] pousser **2.** [knock over] faire tomber, renverser ; [from ledge, bridge] pousser, faire tomber. ❖ **push through** vt sep **1.** [project, decision] faire accepter ; [deal] conclure ; [bill, budget] réussir à faire voter or passer **2.** [thrust - needle] passer / *she eventually managed to push her way through (the crowd)* elle réussit finalement à se frayer un chemin (à travers la foule). ❖ **push up** vt sep **1.** [push upwards - handle, lever] remonter, relever ; [- sleeves] remonter, retrousser **2.** [increase - taxes, sales, demand] augmenter ; [- prices, costs, statistics] faire monter.

pushbike ['pʊʃbaɪk] n 🇬🇧 *inf* vélo *m*, bécane *f*.

push button n bouton *m*. ❖ **push-button** adj [telephone] à touches ; [car window] à commande automatique ▶ **push-button controls** commandes *fpl* automatiques.

pushcart ['puʃkɑːt] n US charrette *f* à bras.

pushchair ['puʃtʃeər] n UK poussette *f*.

pushed [puʃt] adj **1.** *inf* [lacking - money, time] ▶ **to be pushed for sthg** manquer de or être à court de qqch **2.** [in difficulty] ▶ **to be hard pushed to do sthg** avoir du mal à faire qqch.

pusher ['puʃər] n *inf* [drug dealer] trafiquant *m*, -e *f* (de drogue), dealer *m*.

pushing ['puʃɪŋ] n bousculade *f*.

pushover ['puʃ,əʊvər] n **1.** *inf* [easy thing] jeu *m* d'enfant **2.** *inf* [sucker] pigeon *m* / *he's a pushover* il se laisse facilement faire.

push-start ❖ n AUTO ▶ **to give sb a push-start** pousser la voiture de qqn pour la faire démarrer. ❖ vt faire démarrer en poussant.

push technology n COMPUT technologie *f* du push de données.

push-up n pompe *f* (exercice physique) ▶ **to do push-ups** faire des pompes.

pushy ['puʃɪ] (compar **pushier**, superl **pushiest**) adj *inf & pej* **1.** [ambitious] arriviste ; [attention-seeking] qui cherche à se faire valoir or mousser **2.** [self-assertive] : *you have to be pretty pushy in this work* il faut savoir s'imposer dans ce travail **3.** [insistent - salesman] : *he was very pushy* il a fait du rentre-dedans *inf*.

puss [pus] n **1.** *inf* [cat] minou *m* **2.** *inf* [girl, woman] meuf *f*.

pussycat ['pusɪkæt] n *inf* minou *m*.

pussyfoot ['pusɪfʊt] vi *inf* atermoyer, tergiverser.

pussy-whip vt US *v inf* : *he's pussy-whipped* sa femme le mène par le bout du nez.

pussy willow n saule *m* blanc.

put [put] (pt & pp **put**, cont **putting**)
❖ vt

A. PLACE OR IMPOSE 1. [into specified place or position] mettre / *put the chairs nearer the table* approche les chaises de la table / *he put his arm around my shoulders* il passa son bras autour de mes épaules ; [send] : *to put a child to bed* mettre un enfant au lit, coucher un enfant ; *fig* : *I didn't know where to put myself!* je ne savais plus où me mettre ! **2.** [push or send forcefully] : *he put a bullet through his head* il s'est mis une balle dans la tête **3.** [impose - responsibility, tax] mettre / *the new tax will put 5p on a packet of cigarettes* la nouvelle taxe augmentera de 5 pence le prix d'un paquet de cigarettes **4.** [into specified state] mettre / *music always puts him in a good mood* la musique le met toujours de bonne humeur / *to put sb out of a job* mettre qqn au chômage **5.** [write down] mettre, écrire **6.** [bring about] ▶ **to put an end** or **a stop to sthg** mettre fin or un terme à qqch.

B. EXPRESS 1. [say, express] dire, exprimer / *let me put it this way* laissez-moi l'exprimer ainsi / *it was, how shall I put it, rather long* c'était, comment dirais-je, un peu long / *he put it better than that* il l'a dit or formulé mieux que ça **2.** [present, submit - suggestion, question] soumettre ; [- motion] proposer, présenter / *he put his case very well* il a très bien présenté son cas.

C. CLASSIFY IN HIERARCHY placer, mettre / *I put my family above my job* je fais passer ma famille avant mon travail.

D. APPLY OR INVEST 1. [set to work] : *they put her on the Jones case* ils l'ont mise sur l'affaire Jones **2.** [apply, invest - effort] investir, consacrer ▶ **to put a lot of time / energy into sthg** consacrer beaucoup de temps / d'énergie à qqch, investir beaucoup de temps / d'énergie dans qqch **3.** [invest - money] placer, investir **4.** [bet] parier, miser.

E. OTHER USES SPORT ▶ **to put the shot** or **the weight** lancer le poids.

❖ vi NAUT ▶ **to put to sea** lever l'ancre, appareiller / *we put into port at Bombay* nous avons fait escale à Bombay. ❖ **put about** ❖ vt sep **1.** [spread - gossip, story] faire courir **2.** UK *inf* [sexually] ▶ **to put o.s. about** coucher à droite à gauche. ❖ vi NAUT virer de bord. ❖ **put across** vt sep [communicate] faire comprendre ▶ **to put sthg across to sb** faire comprendre qqch à qqn / *she's good at putting herself across* elle sait se mettre en valeur. ❖ **put aside** vt sep **1.** [stop - activity, work] mettre de côté, poser **2.** [disregard, ignore] écarter, laisser de côté **3.** [save] mettre de côté / *we have a little money put aside* nous avons un peu d'argent de côté. ❖ **put away** vt sep **1.** [tidy] ranger **2.** [lock up - in prison] mettre sous les verrous ; [- in mental home] enfermer **3.** *inf* [eat] enfourner, s'envoyer ; [drink] descendre, écluser **4.** [save] mettre de côté. ❖ **put back** vt sep **1.** [replace, return] remettre **2.** [postpone] remettre **3.** [slow down, delay] retarder / *the strike has put our schedule back at least a month* la grève nous a fait perdre au moins un mois sur notre planning **4.** [turn back - clock] retarder. ❖ vi NAUT ▶ **to put back (to port)** rentrer au port. ❖ **put by** vt sep [save] mettre de côté. ❖ **put down** ❖ vt sep **1.** [on table, floor, etc.] poser / *put that down!* laisse (ça) ! / *it's one of those books you just can't put down* c'est un de ces livres que tu ne peux pas poser avant de l'avoir fini **2.** [drop off - passenger] déposer, laisser **3.** [write down] écrire, inscrire / *it's never been put down in writing* ça n'a jamais été mis par écrit **4.** [quell] réprimer, étouffer **5.** [belittle] rabaisser, critiquer **6.** UK *euph* [kill] ▶ **to put a cat / dog down** faire piquer un chat / chien. ❖ vi [land - plane, pilot] atterrir, se poser. ❖ **put down as** vt sep classer parmi. ❖ **put down for** vt sep inscrire pour. ❖ **put down to** vt sep mettre sur le compte de. ❖ **put forth** vt insep **1.** *liter* [sprout - shoots, leaves] produire **2.** *fml* [state] avancer. ❖ **put forward** vt sep **1.** [suggest - proposal, idea, hypothesis] avancer ; [- candidate] proposer / *she put her name forward for the post of treasurer* elle a posé sa candidature au poste de trésorière **2.** [turn forward - clock, hands of clock] avancer **3.** [bring forward] avancer. ❖ **put in** ❖ vt sep **1.** [place inside bag, container, cupboard] mettre dans **2.** [insert, include] insérer, inclure **3.** [interject] placer **4.** [install] installer **5.** [devote - time] passer / *I've put in a lot of work on that car* j'ai beaucoup travaillé sur cette voiture **6.** [appoint] nommer **7.** [submit - request, demand] déposer, soumettre / *to put in an application for a job* déposer sa candidature pour or se présenter pour un emploi. ❖ vi NAUT faire escale. ❖ **put in for** vt insep ▶ **to put in for sthg a)** [post] poser sa candidature pour qqch **b)** [leave, promotion] faire une demande de qqch, demander qqch. ❖ **put off** vt sep **1.** [postpone] repousser, remettre / *the meeting has been put off until tomorrow* la réunion a été renvoyée or remise à demain / *I kept putting off telling him the truth* je continuais à repousser le moment de lui dire la vérité **2.** [dissuade] : *once he's made up his mind nothing in the world can put him off* une fois qu'il a pris une décision, rien au monde ne peut le faire changer d'avis **3.** [distract] déranger, empêcher de se concentrer / *the noise put her off her service* le bruit l'a gênée or dérangée pendant son service **4.** [repel] dégoûter, rebuter / *it put me off skiing for good* ça m'a définitivement dégoûté du ski / *it put me off my dinner* ça m'a coupé l'appétit. ❖ **put on** vt sep **1.** [clothes, make-up, ointment] mettre **2.** [present, stage - play, opera] monter ; [- poetry reading, whist drive, slide show] organiser **3.** [lay on, provide] : *they have put on 20 extra trains* ils ont ajouté 20 trains **4.** [gain - speed, weight] prendre **5.** [turn on, cause to function - light, radio, gas] allumer ; [-CD, song] mettre ; [-handbrake] mettre, serrer / *to put on the brakes* freiner **6**. [start cooking] mettre (à cuire) / *I've put the kettle on for tea* j'ai mis de l'eau à chauffer pour le thé **7**. [bet] parier **8**. [assume] prendre / *to put on airs* prendre des airs / *don't worry, he's just putting it on* ne t'inquiète pas, il fait semblant **9**. US *inf* [tease] faire marcher **10**. [add] ajouter / *the tax increase will put another 10p on a gallon of petrol* l'augmentation de la taxe va faire monter le prix du gallon d'essence de 10 pence. ✧ **put onto** vt sep [help find] indiquer à ▸ **to put the police / taxman onto sb** dénoncer qqn à la police / au fisc / *what put you onto the butler, detective inspector?* qu'est-ce qui vous a amené à soupçonner le maître d'hôtel, commissaire ? ✧ **put out** ✦ vt sep **1**. [place outside] mettre dehors, sortir **2**. [issue - apology, announcement] publier ; [- story, rumour] faire circuler ; [broadcast] émettre **3**. [extinguish - fire, light, candle] éteindre ; [- cigarette] éteindre, écraser **4**. [lay out, arrange] sortir **5**. [stick out, stretch out - arm, leg] étendre, allonger ; [- hand] tendre ; [- tongue] tirer **6**. [dislocate] ▸ **to put one's shoulder out** se démettre l'épaule **7**. [annoy, upset] ▸ **to be put out about sthg** être fâché à cause de qqch **8**. [inconvenience] déranger **9**. [sprout - shoots, leaves] produire **10**. [make unconscious - with drug, injection] endormir **11**. [subcontract] sous-traiter. ✦ vi **1**. NAUT prendre le large ▸ **to put out to sea** appareiller, prendre la mer **2**. US *inf* [sexually] : *everyone knows she puts out* tout le monde sait qu'elle est prête à coucher. ✧ **put over** = **put across**. ✧ **put round** vt sep [spread - gossip, story] faire courir. ✧ **put through** vt sep **1**. TELEC [connect] passer la communication à / *I'll put you through to Mrs Powell* je vous passe Mme Powell **2**. [carry through, conclude] conclure **3**. [subject to] soumettre à / *I'm sorry to put you through this* je suis désolé de vous imposer ça ▸ **to put sb through it** *inf* en faire voir de toutes les couleurs **4**. [pay for] : *he put himself through college* il a payé ses études. ✧ **put together** vt sep **1**. *(usu passive)* [combine] mettre ensemble, réunir / *he's more trouble than the rest of them put together* il nous crée plus de problèmes à lui seul que tous les autres réunis **2**. [assemble - kit, furniture, engine] monter, assembler ▸ **to put sthg (back) together again** remonter qqch **3**. [compile - dossier] réunir ; [- proposal, report] préparer ; [- story, facts] reconstituer **4**. [organize - show, campaign] organiser, monter. ✧ **put up** vt sep **1**. [raise, hoist - hand] lever ; [- flag] hisser ; [- hood] relever ; [- umbrella] ouvrir **2**. [erect, build - tent] dresser, monter ; [- house, factory] construire ; [- monument, statue] ériger **3**. [install, put in place] mettre **4**. [display - sign] mettre ; [- poster] afficher **5**. [show - resistance] offrir, opposer ▸ **to put up a good show** bien se défendre ▸ **to put up a struggle** se défendre, se débattre **6**. [present - argument, proposal] présenter **7**. [offer for sale] ▸ **to put sthg up for sale / auction** mettre qqch en vente / aux enchères **8**. [put forward - candidate] présenter ; [- person, name] proposer (comme candidat) **9**. [provide - capital] : *who's putting the money up for the new business?* qui finance la nouvelle entreprise ? **10**. [increase] faire monter, augmenter **11**. [give hospitality to] loger **12**. [urge, incite] ▸ **to put sb up to (doing) sthg** pousser qqn à (faire) qqch. ✧ **put up with** vt insep supporter, tolérer.

putative ['pjuːtətɪv] adj *fml* présumé, putatif.

put-down n *inf* [snub] rebuffade *f*.

put-on ✦ adj affecté, simulé. ✦ n *inf* **1**. [pretence] simulacre *m* **2**. [hoax] canular *m* **3**. US [charlatan] charlatan *m*.

putrefaction [ˌpjuːtrɪ'fækʃn] n putréfaction *f*.

putrefy ['pjuːtrɪfaɪ] (*pt & pp* **putrefied**) ✦ vi se putréfier. ✦ vt putréfier.

putrid ['pjuːtrɪd] adj **1**. [decaying] putride **2**. *inf* [awful] dégueulasse.

putsch [pʊtʃ] n putsch *m*, coup *m* d'État.

putt [pʌt] ✦ n putt *m*. ✦ vi & vt putter.

putter ['pʌtər] ✦ n SPORT **1**. [club] putter *m* **2**. [person] : *he's a good putter* il putte bien. ✦ vi **1**. [vehicle] avancer en faisant teuf-teuf **2**. US = **potter**. ✧ **putter about, putter around** vi US bricoler.

putting ['pʌtɪŋ] n SPORT putting *m*.

putting green n green *m*.

putty ['pʌtɪ] ✦ n [for cracks, holes] mastic *m* ; [for walls] enduit *m*. ✦ vt mastiquer.

put-up adj UK *inf* ▸ **put-up job** coup *m* monté.

put-upon adj UK exploité.

puzzle ['pʌzl] ✦ n **1**. [game - gen] jeu *m* de patience ; [jigsaw] puzzle *m* ; [brainteaser] casse-tête *m* inv ; [riddle] devinette *f* **2**. [problem] question *f* (difficile) ; [enigma, mystery] énigme *f*, mystère *m* **3**. [perplexity] perplexité *f*. ✦ vt laisser perplexe. ✦ vi [wonder] se poser des questions ; [ponder] réfléchir. ✧ **puzzle out** vt sep UK [meaning, solution, route, way] trouver, découvrir ; [code, enigma, handwriting] déchiffrer ; [problem] résoudre ; [behaviour, intentions] comprendre. ✧ **puzzle over** vt insep [answer, explanation] essayer de trouver ; [absence, letter, theory] essayer de comprendre ; [enigma, crossword] essayer de résoudre ; [code, handwriting] essayer de déchiffrer.

puzzled ['pʌzld] adj perplexe.

puzzling ['pʌzlɪŋ] adj [behaviour, remark] curieux, qui laisse perplexe ; [symbol, machine] incompréhensible.

PVC (abbr of **polyvinyl chloride**) n PVC *m*.

Pvt. written abbr of **private**.

pw (written abbr of **per week**) p.sem.

PWR (abbr of **pressurized water reactor**) n REP *m*.

PX (abbr of **post exchange**) n US MIL économat pour les militaires et leurs familles.

pygmy ['pɪgmɪ] (*pl* **pygmies**) ✦ n **1**. ZOOL [small animal] nain *m*, -e *f* **2**. *fig & pej* [person] nain *m*. ✦ adj pygmée. ✧ **Pygmy** ✦ n Pygmée *mf*. ✦ adj pygmée.

pyjama UK, **pajama** US [pə'dʒɑːmə] comp [jacket, trousers] de pyjama. ✧ **pyjamas** UK, **pajamas** US pl n pyjama *m* ▸ **a pair of pyjamas** un pyjama / *he was in his pyjamas* il était en pyjama.

pylon ['paɪlən] n [gen & ARCHEOL] pylône *m*.

pyramid ['pɪrəmɪd] ✦ n pyramide *f*. ✦ vt **1**. [build in pyramid form] ériger en forme de pyramide **2**. FIN [companies] structurer en holdings.

pyramid scheme n opération *f* de vente pyramidale.

pyramid selling n vente *f* pyramidale.

pyre ['paɪər] n ▸ **(funeral) pyre** bûcher *m* funéraire.

Pyrenean [ˌpɪrə'niːən] adj pyrénéen.

Pyrenees [ˌpɪrə'niːz] pl pr n ▸ **the Pyrenees** les Pyrénées *fpl*.

Pyrex® ['paɪreks] ✦ n Pyrex® *m*. ✦ comp [dish] en Pyrex.

pyromaniac [ˌpaɪrə'meɪnɪæk] n pyromane *mf*.

pyrotechnics [ˌpaɪrəʊ'teknɪks] ✦ n *(U)* [process] pyrotechnie *f*. ✦ pl n **1**. [display] feu *m* d'artifice **2**. *fig* [display of skill] performance *f* éblouissante.

Pyrrhic victory ['pɪrɪk-] n victoire *f* à la Pyrrhus.

python ['paɪθn] n python *m*.

pzazz [pə'zæz] n *inf* = **pizzazz**.

Q (written abbr of **Queen**) [in chess] D.

Qatar ['kætɑːr] pr n Qatar m.

QC n **1.** (abbr of **Queen's Counsel**)  ≃ avocat (e) de la Couronne **2.** abbr of **quality control**.

QED (abbr of **quod erat demonstrandum**) adv CQFD.

QM n abbr of **quartermaster**.

qt¹ written abbr of **quart**.

qt², **QT** (abbr of **quiet**) ◈ **on the qt** adv phr inf en douce.

QT³ MESSAGING written abbr of **cutie**.

Q-tip® n US Coton-Tige® m.

qty (written abbr of **quantity**) qté.

quack [kwæk] ◆ vi [duck] cancaner, faire coin-coin. ◆ n **1.** [of duck] coin-coin m inv **2.** [charlatan] charlatan m **3.** UK & Austr inf & hum [doctor] toubib m. ◆ adj [medicine, method] de charlatan, charlatanesque ▶ **quack doctor** charlatan m. ◆ onomat ▶ **quack (quack)!** coin-coin !

quad [kwɒd] n **1.** abbr of **quadruplet 2.** abbr of **quadrangle 3.** abbr of **quadraphonic 4.** TYPO cadrat m.

quad bike n (moto f) quad.

quadrangle ['kwɒdræŋgl] n **1.** GEOM quadrilatère m **2.** [courtyard] cour f.

quadrant ['kwɒdrənt] n **1.** GEOM quadrant m **2.** ASTRON & NAUT quart-de-cercle m, quadrant m.

quadraphonic [,kwɒdrə'fɒnɪk] adj quadriphonique.

quadrilateral [,kwɒdrɪ'lætərəl] ◆ adj quadrilatère, quadrilatéral. ◆ n quadrilatère m.

quadriplegic [,kwɒdrɪ'pliːdʒɪk] ◆ adj tétraplégique. ◆ n tétraplégique mf.

quadrophonic [,kwɒdrə'fɒnɪk] = **quadraphonic**.

quadruped ['kwɒdruped] ◆ adj quadrupède. ◆ n quadrupède m.

quadruple [kwɒ'druːpl] ◆ adj quadruple. ◆ n quadruple m. ◆ vi & vt quadrupler.

quadruplet ['kwɒdruplɪt] n quadruplé m, -e f.

quagmire ['kwægmaɪər] n lit & fig bourbier m.

quail [kweɪl] ◆ (pl **quail** or **quails**) ◆ n [bird] caille f. ◆ vi [feel afraid] trembler ; [give way, lose heart] perdre courage ▶ **to quail before sb / sthg** trembler devant qqn / qqch.

quaint [kweɪnt] adj **1.** [picturesque] pittoresque ; [old-fashioned] au charme désuet **2.** [odd] bizarre, étrange.

quaintly ['kweɪntlɪ] adv **1.** [picturesquely] de façon pittoresque **2.** [oddly] bizarrement, étrangement.

quaintness ['kweɪntnɪs] n **1.** [picturesqueness] pittoresque m ; [old-fashioned charm] charme m vieillot or désuet **2.** [oddness] bizarrerie f, étrangeté f.

quake [kweɪk] ◆ vi **1.** [person] trembler, frémir ▶ **to quake with fear** trembler de peur **2.** [earth] trembler. ◆ n inf tremblement m de terre.

Quaker ['kweɪkər] ◆ n quaker m, -eresse f. ◆ adj des quakers.

qualification [,kwɒlɪfɪ'keɪʃn] n **1.** [diploma] diplôme m **2.** [ability, quality] aptitude f, compétence f ; [for job] qualification f **3.** [restriction] réserve f **4.** [act of qualifying] qualification f.

qualified ['kwɒlɪfaɪd] adj **1.** [trained] qualifié, diplômé **2.** [able, competent] compétent, qualifié / I don't feel qualified to discuss such matters ces questions sont hors de ma compétence **3.** [limited, conditional] mitigé, nuancé.

qualifier ['kwɒlɪfaɪər] n **1.** SPORT [person] qualifié m, -e f ; [contest] (épreuve f) éliminatoire f **2.** GRAM qualificatif m.

qualify ['kwɒlɪfaɪ] (pt & pp **qualified**) ◆ vi **1.** [pass exams, complete training] obtenir son diplôme **2.** [be eligible] : to qualify for a pension avoir droit à la retraite **3.** [in competition] se qualifier. ◆ vt **1.** [make able or competent] qualifier, habiliter **2.** [modify - statement, criticism] mitiger, atténuer ; [put conditions on] poser des conditions **3.** GRAM qualifier.

qualifying ['kwɒlɪfaɪɪŋ] adj **1.** [gen] ▶ **qualifying examination** a) [at end of course] examen m de fin d'études b) [to get onto course] examen m d'entrée ▶ **qualifying heat** or **round** SPORT (épreuve f) éliminatoire f **2.** GRAM qualificatif.

qualitative ['kwɒlɪtətɪv] adj qualitatif.

qualitatively ['kwɒlɪtətɪvlɪ] adv qualitativement.

qualitative research n études fpl qualitatives.

quality ['kwɒlətɪ] (pl **qualities**) ◆ n **1.** [standard, nature] qualité f **2.** [high standard, excellence] qualité f **3.** [feature, attribute] qualité f. ◆ comp [goods, work, shop] de qualité ▶ **quality paper** UK quotidien ou journal du dimanche de qualité (par opposition à la presse populaire).

quality control n contrôle m de qualité.

quality time n : I only spend an hour in the evening with my kids, but it's quality time je ne passe qu'une heure avec mes gosses le soir, mais je profite bien d'eux.

qualm [kwɑːm] n **1.** [scruple] scrupule m ; [misgiving] appréhension f, inquiétude f / I occasionally have qualms about the job I do il m'arrive d'avoir des scrupules à faire le travail que je fais **2.** [pang of nausea] haut-le-cœur m inv, nausée f.

quandary ['kwɒndərɪ] (pl **quandaries**) n dilemme m.

quango ['kwæŋgəʊ] (abbr of quasi-autonomous non-governmental organization) n organisme semi-public.

> **Quango**
>
> Un **quango** est un organisme semi-public financé majoritairement par l'État mais disposant d'une certaine autonomie, tel le British Council.

quantifiable [kwɒntɪ'faɪəbl] adj quantifiable.

quantify ['kwɒntɪfaɪ] (pt & pp **quantified**) vt **1.** [estimate] quantifier, évaluer quantitativement **2.** LOGIC quantifier.

quantitative ['kwɒntɪtətɪv], **quantitive** ['kwɒntətɪv] adj quantitatif.

quantitative research n études fpl quantitatives.

quantity ['kwɒntətɪ] (pl **quantities**) n [gen & LING] & MATH quantité f ▶ **in quantity** en (grande) quantité.

quantity surveyor n métreur m.

quantum computer n ordinateur m quantique.

quantum jump, quantum leap n progrès m énorme, bond m en avant.

quantum theory n théorie f des quanta or quantique.

quarantine ['kwɒrənti:n] ◆ n MED quarantaine f / our dog is in quarantine notre chien est en quarantaine. ◆ vt mettre en quarantaine.

quark [kwɑ:k] n **1.** PHYS quark m **2.** [cheese] fromage m blanc.

quarrel ['kwɒrəl] (UK pt & pp **quarrelled**, cont **quarrelling** ; US pt & pp **quarreled**, cont **quarreling**) ◆ n **1.** [dispute] querelle f, dispute f / they had a quarrel over money ils se sont disputés pour des histoires d'argent ▶ **to pick a quarrel with sb** chercher querelle à qqn **2.** [cause for complaint] : my only quarrel with the plan is its cost la seule chose que je reproche à ce projet, c'est son coût / I have no quarrel with her proposal je n'ai rien contre sa proposition. ◆ vi **1.** [argue] se disputer, se quereller / I don't want to quarrel with you over or about this je ne veux pas me disputer avec toi à ce sujet or à propos de cela **2.** [take issue] : I can't quarrel with your figures je ne peux pas contester vos chiffres.

quarrelling UK, **quarreling** US ['kwɒrəlɪŋ] n (U) disputes fpl, querelles fpl.

quarrelsome ['kwɒrəlsəm] adj querelleur.

quarry ['kwɒrɪ] (pl **quarries**, pt & pp **quarried**) ◆ n **1.** [excavation] carrière f **2.** [prey] proie f. ◆ vt **1.** [sand, slate, marble, etc.] extraire **2.** [land, mountain] exploiter. ◆ vi exploiter / they are quarrying for marble ils exploitent une carrière de marbre.

quarry tile n carreau m.

quart [kwɔ:t] n ≈ litre m.

quarter ['kwɔ:tə'] ◆ adj ▶ **a quarter hour / century / pound** un quart d'heure / de siècle / de livre. ◆ vt **1.** [divide into four] diviser en quatre **2.** [divide by four] diviser par quatre **3.** [lodge] loger ; MIL cantonner **4.** [dismember] écarteler **5.** [subj: hunting dog] ▶ **to quarter the ground** quêter. ◆ n **1.** [one fourth] quart m / a quarter of a century / of an hour un quart de siècle / d'heure **2.** [in telling time] quart m / (a) quarter to six, (a) quarter of six US six heures moins le quart / (a) quarter past six UK, (a) quarter after six US six heures et quart **3.** [3 months] trimestre m **4.** [US and Canadian money] (pièce f de) vingt-cinq cents mpl **5.** [weight - quarter of hundredweight] ≈

12 kg ; [- quarter pound] quart m de livre, 113 g **6.** [direction] direction f, côté m **7.** [part of town] quartier m **8.** [phase of moon] quartier m **9.** SPORT [period of play] quart-temps m inv **10.** [part of butchered animal] quartier m **11.** (usu neg) liter [mercy] quartier m. ◆ **quarters** pl n [accommodation] domicile m, résidence f.

quarterback ['kwɔ:təbæk] ◆ n US SPORT quarterback m. ◆ vt US **1.** SPORT [team] jouer quarterback dans **2.** fig être le stratège de, diriger la stratégie de.

quarterdeck ['kwɔ:tədek] n **1.** NAUT [part of ship] plage f arrière **2.** [personnel] ▶ **the quarterdeck** les officiers.

quarterfinal [,kwɔ:tə'faɪnl] n quart m de finale.

quarterfinalist ['kwɔ:təfaɪnəlɪst] n quart-de-finaliste mf.

quarterlight ['kwɔ:təlaɪt] n AUTO [in UK] déflecteur m.

quarterly ['kwɔ:təlɪ] ◆ adj trimestriel. ◆ n publication f trimestrielle. ◆ adv trimestriellement, tous les trois mois.

quartermaster ['kwɔ:tə,mɑ:stə'] n **1.** [in army] commissaire m ; HIST intendant m **2.** [in navy] officier m de manœuvre.

quarter note n US MUS noire f.

quarter-pounder n CULIN gros hamburger.

quarter sessions pl n **1.** [in England and Wales] ≈ cour f d'assises (remplacée en 1972 par la Crown Court) **2.** [in US] dans certains États, tribunal local à compétence criminelle, pouvant avoir des fonctions administratives.

quartet [kwɔ:'tet] n **1.** [players - classical] quatuor m ; [- jazz] quartette m **2.** [piece of music] quatuor m **3.** [group of four people] quatuor m.

quarto ['kwɔ:təʊ] (pl **quartos**) ◆ n in-quarto m inv. ◆ adj in quarto (inv).

quartz [kwɔ:ts] ◆ n quartz m. ◆ comp [clock, watch] à quartz.

quasar ['kweɪzɑ:'] n quasar m.

quash [kwɒʃ] vt UK **1.** [annul - verdict] casser ; [- decision] annuler **2.** [suppress - revolt] étouffer, écraser ; [- emotion] réprimer, refouler ; [- suggestion] rejeter, repousser.

quasi- ['kweɪzaɪ] in comp quasi.

quaver ['kweɪvə'] ◆ vi [voice] trembloter, chevroter ; [person] parler d'une voix tremblotante or chevrotante. ◆ n **1.** [of sound, in voice] chevrotement m, tremblement m **2.** UK MUS croche f.

quavering ['kweɪvərɪŋ] ◆ adj tremblotant, chevrotant. ◆ n tremblement m, chevrotement m.

quay [ki:] n quai m.

quayside ['ki:saɪd] n quai m.

queasiness ['kwi:zɪnɪs] n (U) **1.** [nausea] nausée f **2.** [uneasiness] scrupules mpl.

queasy ['kwi:zɪ] (compar **queasier**, superl **queasiest**) adj **1.** [nauseous] nauséeux **2.** [uneasy] mal à l'aise, gêné.

Quebec [kwɪ'bek] pr n **1.** [province] Québec m / in Quebec au Québec **2.** [city] Québec.

Quebecker, Quebecer [kwɪ'bekə'] n Québécois m, -e f.

Quebecois, Québécois [kebe'kwɑ:] (pl **Quebecois**) n Québécois m, -e f.

queen [kwi:n] ◆ n **1.** [sovereign, king's wife] reine f ▶ **the Queen of England / Spain / Belgium** la reine d'Angleterre / d'Espagne / de Belgique ▶ **Queen Elizabeth II** la reine Élisabeth II **2.** [woman considered best] reine f **3.** [in cards, chess] dame f, reine f **4.** [of bees, ants] reine f **5.** v inf & pej [homosexual] tante f, pédale f. ◆ vt **1.** [in chess] ▶ **to queen a pawn** aller à dame f. **2.** PHR **to queen it** UK inf prendre des airs de (grande) marquise.

queen bee n reine f des abeilles.

queencake ['kwiːnkeɪk] n US petit gâteau aux raisins secs.

queen mother n reine f mère.

Queen's Counsel n avocat m, -e f de la Couronne.

Queen's English n l'anglais britannique correct.

Queen's evidence n UK ▸ **to turn Queen's evidence** témoigner contre ses complices.

queen-size bed n grand lit m double (de 2 mètres sur 1,50 mètre).

Queen's Speech n [in UK] ▸ **the Queen's Speech** allocution prononcée par la reine (mais préparée par le gouvernement) lors de la rentrée parlementaire et dans laquelle elle définit les grands axes de la politique gouvernementale.

queer [kwɪər] ◆ adj **1.** [strange] étrange, bizarre ▸ **he's a queer fish!** c'est un drôle d'individu ! **2.** [suspicious] suspect, louche **3.** inf & dated [queasy] mal fichu, patraque **4.** inf [crazy] timbré, cinglé **5.** v inf & pej [homosexual] pédé m ; [as used by homosexuals - culture, activism, politics] gay (inv), gai **6.** US inf [counterfeit] ▸ **queer money** fausse monnaie f. ◆ n v inf homo m ; pej pédé m. ◆ vt inf gâter, gâcher ▸ **to queer sb's pitch** UK couper l'herbe sous le pied de qqn.

queer-bashing [-ˌbæʃɪŋ] n UK v inf & pej chasse f aux pédés.

quell [kwel] vt **1.** [quash - revolt, opposition] réprimer, étouffer **2.** [overcome - emotion] dompter, maîtriser **3.** [allay - pain] apaiser, soulager ; [- doubts, fears] dissiper.

quench [kwentʃ] vt **1.** lit ▸ **to quench one's thirst** étancher sa soif, se désaltérer **2.** [fire] éteindre **3.** METALL tremper.

querulous ['kwerʊləs] adj [person] pleurnicheur ; [voice, tone] plaintif, gémissant.

query ['kwɪəri] ◆ n (pl queries) **1.** [question] question f ; [doubt] doute m **2.** UK [question mark] point m d'interrogation. ◆ vt (pt & pp queried) **1.** [express doubt about] mettre en doute **2.** [ask] demander **3.** US [interrogate] interroger.

query language n COMPUT langage m d'interrogation.

quest [kwest] ◆ n quête f. ◆ vi liter ▸ **to quest for** or **after sthg** se mettre en quête de qqch.

question ['kwestʃn] ◆ n **1.** [query] question f ▸ **to ask sb a question** poser une question à qqn **2.** [matter, issue] question f ; [problem] problème m / it raises the question of how much teachers should be paid cela soulève or pose le problème du salaire des enseignants / the place / time in question le lieu / l'heure en question / the person in question is away at the moment la personne en question est absente en ce moment / but that's not the question mais là n'est pas la question / it's a question of how much you want to spend tout dépend de la somme que vous voulez mettre **3.** (U) [doubt] doute m ▸ **to bring** or **to call sthg into question** remettre qqch en question **4.** [possibility] : there's no question of his coming with us or it's out of the question that he should come with us il est hors de question qu'il vienne avec nous. ◆ vt **1.** [interrogate] interroger, poser des questions à ; [subj: police] interroger ; SCH interroger **2.** [doubt - motives, honesty, wisdom] mettre en doute, remettre en question ; [- statement, claim] mettre en doute, contester.

questionable ['kwestʃənəbl] adj **1.** [doubtful] contestable, douteux **2.** [suspicious - motives] douteux, louche ; [- behaviour] louche **3.** [strange - taste, style] douteux.

questioner ['kwestʃənər] n [gen, in quiz show] animateur m, -trice f ; LAW interrogateur m, -trice f.

questioning ['kwestʃənɪŋ] ◆ adj interrogateur. ◆ n interrogation f.

questioningly ['kwestʃənɪŋli] adv de manière interrogative.

question mark n point m d'interrogation ; fig : a question mark hangs over the future of this country il est impossible de prédire quel sort attend ce pays or sera réservé à ce pays.

question master n meneur m de jeu ; RADIO & TV animateur m, -trice f (d'un jeu).

questionnaire [ˌkwestʃə'neər] n questionnaire m.

queue [kjuː] ◆ n UK queue f, file f d'attente / they were standing in a queue ils faisaient la queue. ◆ vi UK faire la queue. ◆▸ **queue up** vi UK faire la queue.

queue-jump vi UK essayer de passer avant son tour, resquiller.

queue-jumper n UK resquilleur m, -euse f (qui n'attend pas son tour).

quibble ['kwɪbl] ◆ vi chicaner ▸ **to quibble over details** chicaner sur des détails. ◆ n chicane f.

quiche [kiːʃ] n quiche f.

quick [kwɪk] ◆ adj **1.** [rapid] rapide ; [easy - profits] rapide, facile **2.** [sharp] alerte, éveillé, vif / he is quick to learn il apprend vite **3.** [hasty - judgment] hâtif, rapide / he is quick to take offence il est prompt à s'offenser, il se vexe pour un rien. ◆ adv rapidement. ◆ n [of fingernail] vif m.

quick-acting, **quick-action** adj [mechanism] à action rapide or immédiate ; [drug, medication] à action rapide.

quick-drying adj [paint, concrete] qui sèche rapidement.

quicken ['kwɪkn] ◆ vt **1.** [hasten] accélérer, hâter ; MUS [tempo] presser **2.** [stir - imagination] stimuler ; [- hatred, desire] exciter ; [- appetite, interest] stimuler ; [- resolve] hâter. ◆ vi [step, pulse] s'accélérer.

quickfire ['kwɪkfaɪər] adj : a series of quickfire questions un feu roulant de questions.

quick fix n solution f miracle.

quickie ['kwɪkɪ] ◆ n inf **1.** [gen] truc m vite fait ; [question] question f rapide **2.** [sex] coup m en vitesse or entre deux portes **3.** [drink] pot m rapide.

quickie divorce n divorce m rapide.

quickly ['kwɪklɪ] adv rapidement, vite.

quickness ['kwɪknɪs] n **1.** [rapidity - of movement, pulse] rapidité f ; [- of thought, reaction] rapidité, vivacité f **2.** [acuteness - of sight, wit] vivacité f ; [- of hearing] finesse f **3.** [hastiness] : his quickness of temper sa promptitude à s'emporter.

quicksand ['kwɪksænd] n sables mpl mouvants.

quick-setting adj [cement] à prise rapide ; [jelly] qui prend rapidement.

quicksilver ['kwɪkˌsɪlvər] ◆ n vif-argent m, mercure m. ◆ adj [mind] très vif, comme du vif-argent.

quickstep ['kwɪkstep] n quickstep m.

quick-tempered adj : he is quick-tempered il s'emporte facilement.

quick-witted adj à l'esprit vif.

quid [kwɪd] n **1.** (pl quid) UK inf [pound] livre f **2.** [tobacco] chique f.

quid pro quo [ˌkwɪdprəʊ'kwəʊ] (pl quid pro quos) n contrepartie f, récompense f.

quiet ['kwaɪət] ◆ adj **1.** [silent - person] tranquille, silencieux / be or keep quiet! taisez-vous ! ; [subdued, soft] tranquille **2.** [calm, tranquil] calme, tranquille, paisible ; FIN [market, business] calme **3.** [docile - animal] docile ; [easy - baby] calme ; [uncommunicative] silencieux, peu communicatif **4.** [private - wedding] dans l'intimité ; [- party] avec quelques intimes, avec peu d'invités ; [secret] secret (secrète), dissimulé **5.** [subtle, discreet - irony] discret (discrète) ; [- optimism] tranquille ; [- anger] sourd ; [- despair, resentment] secret (se-crète) **6.** [muted - colour, style] sobre. ◆ n silence *m*. ◆ vt [calm] calmer ; [silence] faire taire. ◆ **on the quiet** adv phr 🇬🇧 [in secrecy] en douce, en cachette ; [discreetly] discrètement, en douceur ; [in confidence] en confiance. ◆ **quiet down** vi 🇺🇸 se calmer.

quieten ['kwaɪətn] ◆ vt 🇬🇧 [child, audience] calmer, apaiser ; [conscience] tranquilliser, apaiser ; [doubts] dis-siper. ◆ vi [child] se calmer ; [music] devenir plus doux. ◆ **quieten down** ◆ vi **1.** [become quiet - person] se calmer ; [- storm, wind] se calmer, s'apaiser **2.** [become rea-sonable] s'assagir. ◆ vt sep [calm] calmer, apaiser ; [shut up] faire taire.

quietly ['kwaɪətlɪ] adv [silently] silencieusement, sans bruit ; [gently, softly] doucement, calmement ; [peacefully] tranquillement, paisiblement.

quietness ['kwaɪətnɪs] n [stillness] tranquillité *f*, calme *m* ; [silence] silence *m*.

quiff [kwɪf] n [hairstyle] banane *f*.

quill pen n plume *f* d'oie.

quilt [kwɪlt] n [eiderdown] édredon *m* ; [bedspread] dessus-de-lit *m inv* ; [duvet] couette *f*.

quilted ['kwɪltɪd] adj matelassé.

quince [kwɪns] ◆ n [fruit] coing *m* ; [tree] cognassier *m*. ◆ comp [jam, jelly] de coing.

quinine [kwɪ'niːn] n quinine *f*.

quinoa [kiː'nəʊə] n BOT & CULIN quinoa *m*.

quint [kwɪnt] **(abbr of quintuplet)** n 🇺🇸 quintuplé *m*, -e *f*.

quintessence [kwɪn'tesns] n quintessence *f*.

quintessential [kwɪntə'senʃl] adj typique, type.

quintet [kwɪn'tet] n quintette *m*.

quintuplet [kwɪn'tjuːplɪt] n quintuplé *m*, -e *f*.

quip [kwɪp] **(pt & pp quipped, cont quipping)** ◆ n [remark - witty] bon mot *m*, mot *m* d'esprit ; [- sarcastic] sar-casme *m* ; [gibe] quolibet *m*. ◆ vt : *"only if I'm asked", he quipped* «seulement si on me le demande», lança-t-il d'un air malicieux.

quire ['kwaɪəʳ] n [in bookbinding] cahier *m* ; [of paper] main *f* (de papier).

quirk [kwɜːk] n **1.** [idiosyncrasy] manie *f*, excentricité *f* **2.** [accident] bizarrerie *f*, caprice *m*.

quirky ['kwɜːkɪ] adj bizarre, original.

quit [kwɪt] **(pt & pp quit or quitted, cont quitting)** ◆ vt **1.** [leave] quitter **2.** 🇺🇸 [give up, stop] quitter, cesser / *I've quit smoking* j'ai arrêté or cessé de fumer / *quit it!* arrête !, ça suffit ! ◆ vi **1.** [give up] renoncer, abandonner ; [resign] démissionner **2.** 🇺🇸 [leave] partir **3.** COMPUT quitter. ◆ adj ▸ **to be quit of sb / sthg** être débarrassé de qqn / qqch.

quite [kwaɪt] adv & predet **1.** [moderately] assez / *the film is quite good* le film est assez bon / *I'd quite like to go* ça me plairait assez d'y aller / *quite a difficult job* un tra-vail assez difficile / *quite a lot of people seem to believe it* un bon nombre de gens semblent le croire / *I've been here for quite some time* je suis ici depuis un bon moment or depuis assez longtemps **2.** [completely, absolutely] parfaite-ment, tout à fait / *the story isn't quite true* l'histoire n'est pas tout à fait or entièrement vraie / *I quite understand* je comprends tout à fait or parfaitement / *that's quite an-other matter!* ça, c'est autre chose ! / *you've had quite enough* vous en avez eu largement assez / *that's quite enough!* ça suffit comme ça !

quits [kwɪts] adj quitte / *I'm quits with her now* mainte-nant, je suis quitte envers elle / *now we're quits* maintenant nous sommes quittes / *let's call it quits* a) [financially] disons que nous sommes quittes b) [in fight, argument] restons-en là.

quitter ['kwɪtəʳ] n inf dégonflé *m*, -e *f*.

quiver ['kwɪvəʳ] ◆ vi **1.** [tremble - person] frémir, trem-bler ; [- lips, hands, voice] trembler / *to quiver with fear / rage* trembler de peur / rage / *to quiver with emotion* frissonner d'émotion **2.** [flutter - heart] trembler, frémir ; [- leaves] frémir, frissonner ; [- flame] trembler, vaciller. ◆ n **1.** [tremble] tremblement *m* ; [of violin] trémolo *m*, frémisse-ment *m* **2.** [for arrows] carquois *m*.

quivering ['kwɪvərɪŋ] adj frissonnant.

Quixote ['kwɪksət] pr n ▸ **Don Quixote** Don Quichotte.

quixotic [kwɪk'sɒtɪk] adj [idealistic] idéaliste, chimé-rique ; [chivalrous] généreux, chevaleresque.

quiz [kwɪz] **(pl quizzes, pt & pp quizzed, cont quiz-zing)** ◆ n **1.** [game - on TV] jeu *m* télévisé ; [- on radio] jeu *m* radiophonique ; [- in newspaper] questionnaire *m* ▸ **quiz shows** or **programmes** les jeux télévisés ▸ **general knowledge quiz** test *m* de culture générale **2.** 🇺🇸 SCH [test] interrogation *f* écrite. ◆ vt **1.** [question] interroger, ques-tionner ▸ **to quiz sb about sthg** interroger qqn au sujet de qqch **2.** 🇺🇸 SCH [test] interroger.

quizmaster ['kwɪz,mɑːstəʳ] n RADIO & TV animateur *m*, -trice *f* (d'un jeu).

quizzical ['kwɪzɪkl] adj [questioning] interrogateur ; [ironic] ironique, narquois.

quizzically ['kwɪzɪklɪ] adv [questioningly] d'un air inter-rogateur ; [ironically] d'un air ironique or narquois.

quoit [kɔɪt] n [in game] anneau *m* ▸ **to play quoits** jouer aux anneaux.

Quonset hut® ['kwɑːnsɪt-] n 🇺🇸 abri *m* préfabriqué (en tôle ondulée).

Quorn® [kwɔːn] n aliment aux protéines végétales servant de substitut à la viande.

quorum ['kwɔːrəm] n quorum *m*.

quota ['kwəʊtə] n **1.** [limited quantity] quota *m*, contin-gent *m* **2.** [share] part *f*, quota *m*.

quotable ['kwəʊtəbl] adj **1.** [worth quoting] digne d'être cité **2.** [on the record] que l'on peut citer **3.** ST. EX cotable.

quotation [kwəʊ'teɪʃn] n **1.** [remark, sentence] cita-tion *f* **2.** ST. EX cours *m*, cotation *f* **3.** COMM [estimate] de-vis *m* ; [for insurance] cotation *f*.

quotation marks pl n guillemets *mpl*.

quote [kwəʊt] ◆ vt **1.** [cite - words, example, statistics] ci-ter **2.** ADMIN & COMM : *please quote this reference (num-ber)* prière de mentionner cette référence **3.** [specify - price] indiquer ; ST. EX coter. ◆ vi **1.** [cite] faire des citations **2.** COMM ▸ **to quote for a job** faire un devis pour un tra-vail. ◆ n **1.** [quotation] citation *f* ; [statement] déclaration *f* **2.** [estimate] devis *m* **3.** [quotation mark] guillemet *m* / *in quotes* entre guillemets.

quoted company ['kwəʊtɪd-] n 🇬🇧 société *f* cotée en Bourse.

quotient ['kwəʊʃnt] n quotient *m*.

qv (written abbr of quod vide) cf. (expression renvoyant le lecteur à une autre entrée dans une encyclopédie).

qwerty, Qwerty ['kwɜːtɪ] n ▸ **qwerty keyboard** cla-vier *m* qwerty.

r (*pl* r's *or* rs), **R** (*pl* R's *or* Rs) [ɑːʳ] n [letter] r *m*, R *m* ▶ **the three Rs** la lecture, l'écriture et l'arithmétique *(qui constituent les fondements de l'enseignement primaire)*. See also f.

R ◆ **1.** (written abbr of **right**) dr. **2.** written abbr of **river 3.** US written abbr of **Republican 4.** (written abbr of **Rex**) UK *suit le nom d'un roi* **5.** (written abbr of **Regina**) UK *suit le nom d'une reine* **6.** written abbr of **radius 7.** written abbr of **road 8.** written abbr of **registered (trademark) 9.** MESSAGING written abbr of **are**. ◆ adj (abbr of **restricted**) US *indique qu'un film est interdit aux moins de 17 ans.*

R & B (abbr of **rhythm and blues**) n R & B *m*.

R & D (abbr of **research and development**) n R & D *f*.

RA ◆ n **1.** abbr of **rear admiral 2.** (abbr of **Royal Academician**) *membre de la Royal Academy*. ◆ pr n **abbr of Royal Academy**.

RAAF [ræf] (abbr of **Royal Australian Air Force**) pr n *armée de l'air australienne.*

Rabat [rəˈbɑːt] pr n Rabat.

rabbi [ˈræbaɪ] n rabbin *m* ▶ **chief rabbi** grand rabbin.

rabbit [ˈræbɪt] ◆ n [animal] lapin *m*, -e *f* ▶ **doe rabbit** lapine *f* ▶ **young rabbit** lapereau *m* ▶ **wild rabbit** lapin de garenne. ◆ comp [coat] en (peau de) lapin ▶ **rabbit food** aliments *mpl* pour lapins ▶ **rabbit stew** ragoût *m* or gibelotte *f* de lapin. ◆ vi ▶ **to go rabbiting** chasser le lapin. ❖ **rabbit on** vi *inf* [talk] jacasser / *he's been rabbiting on about his money problems* il me rebat les oreilles de ses problèmes d'argent / *what's she rabbiting on about?* de quoi elle cause ?

rabbit burrow, rabbit hole n terrier *m* (de lapin).

rabbit hutch n clapier *m*, cage *f* or cabane *f* à lapins ; *fig* [housing] cage *f* à lapins.

rabbit warren n **1.** *lit* garenne *f* **2.** *fig* labyrinthe *m*, dédale *m*.

rabble [ˈræbl] n **1.** [mob] ▶ **the rabble** *pej* la populace, la racaille **2.** TECH [in foundry] râble *m*.

rabble-rousing ◆ n démagogie *f*. ◆ adj démagogique.

rabid [ˈræbɪd or ˈreɪbɪd] adj **1.** MED [animal] enragé ; [person] atteint de la rage **2.** *fig* [extremist, revolutionary] enragé ; [hatred] farouche ; [anger] féroce.

rabies [ˈreɪbiːz] n (U) MED rage *f*.

RAC (abbr of **Royal Automobile Club**) pr n ▶ **the RAC** *un des deux grands clubs automobiles de Grande-Bretagne.*

raccoon [rəˈkuːn] ◆ n raton *m* laveur. ◆ comp [coat, stole] en (fourrure de) raton laveur.

race [reɪs] ◆ n **1.** [competition] course *f* / *an 800 metre race* une course de or sur 800 mètres ▶ **to have** or **to run a race** courir, participer à une course / *a race against time* une course contre la montre / *it'll be a race to finish on time* il faudra se dépêcher pour finir à temps / *the race for the Presidency* la course à la présidence / *it's a race to the bottom* *hum* c'est une course vers la médiocrité **2.** [ethnic group] race *f* ; [in anthropology] ethnie *f* **3.** *liter* [passing - of sun, moon] course *f* ; [- of life] cours *m* **4.** [current] fort courant *m* ; [in sea channel] raz *m* (de courant). ◆ comp [discrimination, hatred, prejudice] racial ▶ **race issue** question *f* raciale. ◆ vi **1.** [compete] faire la course / *the cars / drivers were racing against each other* les voitures / conducteurs faisaient la course **2.** [go fast, rush] aller à toute allure or vitesse ▶ **to race in / out / past** entrer / sortir / passer à toute allure ▶ **to race for a bus** courir pour attraper un bus / *she raced downstairs* elle a dévalé l'escalier / *my pulse was racing* mon cœur battait à tout rompre / *a thousand ideas raced through her mind* mille idées lui sont passées par la tête **3.** [of engine] s'emballer. ◆ vt **1.** [compete against] faire la course avec / *(I'll) race you there!* à qui y arrivera le premier ! **2.** [rush] : *the casualties were raced to hospital* les blessés ont été transportés d'urgence à l'hôpital **3.** [put into a race] ▶ **to race a horse** faire courir un cheval ▶ **to race pigeons** faire des courses de pigeons **4.** AUTO ▶ **to race the engine a)** accélérer **b)** [excessively] faire s'emballer le moteur.

race car n US voiture *f* de course.

racecourse [ˈreɪskɔːs] n **1.** champ *m* de courses, hippodrome *m* **2.** US [for cars, motorbikes] circuit *m* ; [for runners, cycles] piste *f*.

race driver n US pilote *m* de course.

racehorse [ˈreɪshɔːs] n cheval *m* de course.

race meeting n courses *fpl*.

racer [ˈreɪsər] n [runner] coureur *m*, -euse *f* ; [horse] cheval *m* de course ; [car] voiture *f* de course ; [cycle] vélo *m* de course.

race relations pl n relations *fpl* interraciales ▶ **the Race Relations Act** [in the UK] *loi de 1976 sur le respect des minorités ethniques* ▶ **race relations body** or **board** organisme *m* luttant contre la discrimination raciale.

race riot n émeute *f* raciale.

racetrack [ˈreɪstræk] n [gen] piste *f* ; [for horses] champ *m* de courses, hippodrome *m*.

racewalking [ˈreɪswɔːkɪŋ] n marche *f* athlétique.

racial [ˈreɪʃl] adj **1.** [concerning a race] racial, ethnique **2.** [between races] racial.

racial discrimination n discrimination *f* raciale.

racialism [ˈreɪʃəlɪzm] n racisme *m*.

racialist [ˈreɪʃəlɪst] ◆ adj raciste. ◆ n raciste *mf*.

racially ['reɪʃəlɪ] adv du point de vue racial / *a racially motivated attack* une agression raciste / *racially prejudiced* raciste.

racing ['reɪsɪŋ] ◆ n [of horses] courses *fpl* de chevaux. ◆ comp [bicycle, yacht] de course.

racing car n 🇬🇧 voiture *f* de course.

racing driver n 🇬🇧 coureur *m*, -euse *f* automobile, pilote *mf* (de course).

racism ['reɪsɪzm] n racisme *m*.

racist ['reɪsɪst] ◆ adj raciste. ◆ n raciste *mf*.

rack [ræk] ◆ n **1.** [shelf] étagère *f* ; [for cooling, drying] grille *f*, claie *f* ; [for fodder, bicycles, test tubes, pipes] râtelier *m* ; [for bottles] casier *m* ▶ **(luggage) rack a)** [in train, bus] filet *m* (à bagages) **b)** [on cycle] porte-bagages *m inv* ▶ **(stereo) rack** meuble *m* pour chaîne hi-fi ▶ **(tool) rack** porte-outils *m inv* ; [in shop] présentoir *m* ▶ **(clothes) rack** triangle *m* (à vêtements) ▶ **to buy a suit off the rack** acheter un costume en prêt-à-porter **2.** HIST chevalet *m* ▶ **to put sb on the rack a)** *lit* faire subir à qqn le supplice du chevalet **b)** *fig* mettre qqn au supplice **3.** MECH crémaillère *f* **4.** CULIN ▶ **rack of lamb** carré *m* d'agneau **5.** PHR **to go to rack and ruin a)** [house] tomber en ruine **b)** [garden] être à l'abandon **c)** [person] dépérir **d)** [company] péricliter **e)** [country, institution] aller à vau-l'eau. ◆ vt **1.** [torture] faire subir le supplice du chevalet à ; *fig* tenailler, ronger / *racked by guilt* tenaillé par un sentiment de culpabilité ▶ **to rack one's brains** se creuser la tête **2.** [wine] soutirer. ◆ **rack up** vt sep 🇺🇸 [points] marquer.

racket ['rækɪt] ◆ n **1.** SPORT [bat] raquette *f* **2.** [snowshoe] raquette *f* **3.** *inf* [din] boucan *m* **4.** [extortion] racket *m* ; [fraud] escroquerie *f* ; [traffic] trafic *m* / *this lottery is such a racket* cette loterie, c'est de l'arnaque **5.** *inf* [job] boulot *m* / *is she still in the teaching / publishing racket?* est-ce qu'elle est encore dans l'enseignement / l'édition ? ◆ vi [be noisy] faire du boucan. ◆ **rackets** n *(U)* [game] racket-ball *m*.

racketeering [,rækə'tɪərɪŋ] n racket *m*.

raconteur [,rækɒn'tɜːʳ] n raconteur *m*, -euse *f*.

racquet ['rækɪt] = **racket** *(noun)*.

racy ['reɪsɪ] *(compar* **racier**, *superl* **raciest)** adj **1.** [lively] plein de verve or de brio **2.** [suggestive] osé **3.** [wine] racé.

RADA ['rɑːdə] *(abbr of* Royal Academy of Dramatic Art) pr n conservatoire britannique d'art dramatique.

radar ['reɪdɑːʳ] ◆ n radar *m* ▶ **to navigate by radar** naviguer au radar ▶ **to slip under the radar** passer inaperçu. ◆ comp [image, screen, station] radar ▶ **radar blip** top *m* d'écho (radar) ▶ **radar operator** radariste *mf*.

radar trap n contrôle *m* radar.

radial ['reɪdjəl] ◆ adj radial ▶ **radial roads** routes *fpl* en étoile. ◆ n **1.** [tyre] pneu *m* radial or à carcasse radiale **2.** [line] rayon *m*.

radian ['reɪdjən] n radian *m*.

radiance ['reɪdjəns] n **1.** [of light, sun] éclat *m*, rayonnement *m* ; *fig* [beauty, happiness] éclat *m* **2.** PHYS exitance *f*.

radiant ['reɪdjənt] ◆ adj **1.** *liter* [bright] radieux **2.** [happy] radieux, rayonnant / *he was radiant with joy* il rayonnait de joie **3.** PHYS radiant, rayonnant **4.** BOT rayonnant. ◆ n **1.** PHYS point *m* radiant **2.** ASTRON radiant *m*.

radiantly ['reɪdjəntlɪ] adv [shine, glow] avec éclat ; [smile] d'un air radieux / *radiantly beautiful* d'une beauté éclatante.

radiate ['reɪdɪeɪt] ◆ vi **1.** [emit energy] émettre de l'énergie ; [be emitted] rayonner, irradier **2.** [spread] rayonner. ◆ vt **1.** [heat] émettre, dégager ; [light] émettre **2.** *fig* :

the children radiate good health / happiness les enfants respirent la santé / rayonnent de bonheur / *his manner radiated confidence* il semblait très sûr de lui.

radiation [,reɪdɪ'eɪʃn] n **1.** [energy radiated] rayonnement *m*, rayonnements *mpl* ; NUCL rayons *mpl* ▶ **atomic radiation** radiation *f* or rayonnement atomique ▶ **low-level radiation** radiation de faible intensité ▶ **radiation therapy** radiothérapie *f* **2.** [act of radiating] rayonnement *m*, radiation *f*.

radiation sickness n mal *m* des rayons.

radiator ['reɪdɪeɪtəʳ] n [gen & AUTO] radiateur *m* ▶ **radiator grille** calandre *f*.

radical ['rædɪkl] ◆ adj **1.** [gen] radical **2.** 🇺🇸 *inf* [excellent] génial. ◆ n **1.** POL radical *m*, -e *f* **2.** LING, MATH & CHEM radical *m*.

radical chic n ≃ gauche *f* caviar.

radicalism ['rædɪkəlɪzm] n radicalisme *m*.

radicalize ['rædɪkəlaɪz] vt radicaliser.

radically ['rædɪklɪ] adv radicalement.

radicchio [rə'diːkɪəʊ] n trévise *f*.

radii ['reɪdɪaɪ] pl ⟶ **radius**.

radio ['reɪdɪəʊ] *(pl* **radios)** ◆ n **1.** [apparatus] radio *f* ▶ **to turn the radio on / off** allumer / éteindre la radio **2.** [system] radio *f* / *by radio* par radio ; [industry, activity] radio / *I heard it on the radio* je l'ai entendu à la radio ▶ **to be on the radio** passer à la radio ▶ **the Radio Times** 🇬🇧 PRESS *magazine de radio et de télévision*. ◆ comp [broadcast, play, programme] radiophonique ; [contact, link, silence] radio *(inv)* ; [announcer, technician] à la radio ; [station] de radio. ◆ vt **1.** [person] appeler or contacter par radio **2.** [message] envoyer par radio ; [position, movement] signaler par radio. ◆ vi envoyer un message radio / *she radioed for help / instructions* elle demanda de l'aide / des instructions par radio.

Radio

Les principales stations de radio de la **BBC** sont : **Radio 1** (bulletins d'information, musique pop et rock) ; **Radio 2** (variétés) ; **Radio 3** (musique classique, jazz, musiques du monde) ; **Radio 4** (actualités, reportages, théâtre, programmes éducatifs) ; **Radio 5 Live** (sports, programmes éducatifs, musique pop et rock). La BBC comprend également 41 stations locales. Il existe d'autre part plus de 100 stations indépendantes.

radioactive [,reɪdɪəʊ'æktɪv] adj **1.** *lit* radioactif ▶ **radioactive dating** datation *f* au carbone 14 ▶ **radioactive waste** déchets *mpl* radioactifs or nucléaires **2.** 🇺🇸 *inf & fig* [curry, chilli] super épicé.

radioactivity [,reɪdɪəʊæk'tɪvɪtɪ] n radioactivité *f*.

radio alarm (clock) n radioréveil *m*.

radio cassette n radiocassette *f*.

radio-controlled adj radioguidé.

radio frequency n fréquence *f* radioélectrique, radiofréquence *f*.

radiogram ['reɪdɪəʊˌgræm] n **1.** *dated* [radio and record player] radio *f* avec pick-up **2.** [message] radiogramme *m* **3.** = **radiograph**.

radiograph ['reɪdɪəʊɡrɑːf] n radiographie *f*.

radiographer [,reɪdɪ'ɒɡrəfəʳ] n radiologue *mf*, radiologiste *mf*.

radiography [ˌreɪdɪˈɒɡrəfɪ] n radiographie f.

radiologist [ˌreɪdɪˈɒlədʒɪst] n radiologue mf, radiologiste mf.

radiology [ˌreɪdɪˈɒlədʒɪ] n radiologie f.

radiopaging [ˈreɪdɪəʊˌpeɪdʒɪŋ] n radiomessagerie f.

radiotelephone [ˌreɪdɪəʊˈtelɪfəʊn] n radiotéléphone m.

radiotherapist [ˌreɪdɪəʊˈθerəpɪst] n radiothérapeute mf.

radiotherapy [ˌreɪdɪəʊˈθerəpɪ] n radiothérapie f.

radio wave n onde f hertzienne or radioélectrique.

radish [ˈrædɪʃ] n radis m.

radium [ˈreɪdɪəm] n radium m ▸ **radium therapy** or **treatment** curiethérapie f.

radius [ˈreɪdɪəs] (pl **radiuses** or **radii** [ˈreɪdɪaɪ]) n **1.** [gen & MATH] rayon m / within or in a radius of 20 km dans un rayon de 20 km **2.** ANAT radius m.

radon (gas) [ˈreɪdɒn-] n radon m.

RAF (abbr of **Royal Air Force**) pr n armée de l'air britannique.

raffia [ˈræfɪə] n raphia m.

raffish [ˈræfɪʃ] adj dissolu.

raffle [ˈræfl] ◆ n tombola f ▸ **raffle ticket** billet m de tombola. ◆ vt ▸ **to raffle (off)** mettre en tombola.

raft [rɑːft] ◆ n **1.** [craft - gen] radeau m ; [- inflatable] matelas m pneumatique ; SPORT raft m **2.** [logs] train m de flottage **3.** inf [large amount] tas m, flopée f **4.** CONSTR radier m. ◆ vt : they raft wood down the river ils envoient le bois en aval dans des trains de flottage. ◆ vi voyager en radeau ▸ **to go rafting** SPORT faire du rafting.

rafter [ˈrɑːftər] n CONSTR chevron m.

rag [ræg] (pt & pp **ragged**, cont **ragging**) ◆ n **1.** [cloth] chiffon m / a piece of rag un bout de chiffon ▸ **to chew the rag** inf discuter le bout de gras ▸ **to lose one's rag** inf se mettre en boule ▸ **to be like a red rag to a bull** : when he said that to her it was like a red rag to a bull elle a vu rouge après ce qu'il lui a dit **2.** [worn-out garment] loque f **3.** [shred, scrap] lambeau m / torn to rags mis en lambeaux **4.** inf & pej [newspaper] feuille f de chou **5.** US v inf [sanitary towel] serviette f hygiénique **6.** UK UNIV ▸ **rag (week)** semaine pendant laquelle les étudiants préparent des divertissements, surtout au profit des œuvres charitables **7.** UK [joke] farce f, canular m **8.** MUS ragtime m. ◆ vt [tease] taquiner / they ragged her about her accent ils la taquinaient au sujet de son accent. ❖ **rags** pl n [worn-out clothes] guenilles fpl, haillons mpl, loques fpl ▸ **to go from rags to riches** passer de la misère à la richesse ▸ **a rags-to-riches story** un véritable conte de fées.

ragamuffin [ˈræɡəˌmʌfɪn] n dated [vagrant] va-nu-pieds m inv, gueux m, gueuse f ; [urchin] galopin m, polisson m, -onne f.

rag-and-bone man n UK chiffonnier m.

ragbag [ˈræɡbæɡ] n UK fig ramassis m, bric-à-brac m inv, fouillis m.

rag doll n poupée f de chiffon.

rage [reɪdʒ] ◆ n **1.** [anger] rage f, fureur f / the boss was in a rage le patron était furieux ▸ **to fly into a rage** entrer dans une rage folle ▸ **a fit of rage** un accès or une crise de rage **2.** inf [fashion] mode f ▸ **to be all the rage** faire fureur **3.** [of sea, elements] furie f. ◆ vi **1.** [person] être furieux, s'emporter / he was raging against the Government il pestait contre le gouvernement **2.** [sea] se déchaîner ; [storm, war] faire rage / the plague was raging throughout Europe la peste ravageait l'Europe / the argument still rages la question est toujours très controversée.

ragged [ˈræɡɪd] adj **1.** [tattered - clothes] en lambeaux, en loques, en haillons ; [- person] loqueteux, vêtu de loques or de haillons **2.** [uneven] irrégulier / the ragged coastline la côte échancrée **3.** [erratic - performance] inégal, décousu **4.** PHR **to run sb ragged** inf éreinter or crever qqn.

raging [ˈreɪdʒɪŋ] adj **1.** [intense - pain] insupportable, atroce ; [- fever] violent / I had a raging headache j'avais affreusement mal à la tête / I've got a raging thirst je meurs de soif / raging anticlericalism un anticléricalisme virulent **2.** [storm] déchaîné, violent ; [sea] démonté ; [torrent] furieux **3.** [person] furieux.

ragout [ˈræɡuː] n ragoût m.

rag-roll vt peindre au chiffon.

ragtime [ˈræɡtaɪm] n ragtime m.

ragtop [ˈræɡtɒp] n US inf AUTO décapotable f.

rag trade n inf confection f / he's in the rag trade il est or travaille dans les fringues.

rag week = rag (noun).

raid [reɪd] ◆ n **1.** MIL raid m, incursion f / bombing raid raid aérien / they fear a terrorist raid on the palace ils craignent une attaque terroriste contre le palais **2.** [by police] descente f / a drugs raid une descente de police (pour saisir de la drogue) **3.** [robbery] hold-up m, braquage m / a raid on a bank un hold-up dans une banque **4.** ST. EX raid m. ◆ vt **1.** MIL [subj: army] faire un raid or une incursion dans ; [subj: airforce] bombarder **2.** [subj: police] faire une descente or une rafle dans **3.** [subj: thieves] : to raid a bank dévaliser une banque / to raid the fridge hum dévaliser le frigo.

raider [ˈreɪdər] n **1.** MIL membre m d'un commando / the raiders were repelled le commando a été repoussé **2.** [thief] voleur m, -euse f **3.** ST. EX ▸ **(corporate) raider** raider m.

rail [reɪl] ◆ n **1.** [bar - gen] barre f ; [- in window, on bridge] garde-fou m ; [- on ship] bastingage m ; [- on balcony] balustrade f ; [- on stairway] rampe f ; [- for carpet] tringle f ▸ **towel rail** porte-serviettes m inv **2.** [for train, tram] rail m ; [mode of transport] ▸ **to travel by rail** voyager en train ▸ **to go off the rails** a) [train] dérailler b) fig [person] perdre la tête or le nord **3.** ORNITH râle m. ◆ comp [traffic, transport, link, tunnel] ferroviaire ; [ticket, fare] de train ; [journey, travel] en train ; [employee, union] des chemins de fer ; [strike] des chemins de fer, des cheminots / the rail strike has affected the whole of France la grève SNCF a touché la France entière. ◆ vt [enclose] clôturer. ◆ vi [complain bitterly] ▸ **to rail against** or **at** pester contre. ❖ **rails** pl n [fencing] grille f ; [in horseracing] corde f ▸ **to be on the rails** fig [in difficult situation] être sur la corde raide. ❖ **rail in** vt sep clôturer. ❖ **rail off** vt sep fermer (au moyen d'une barrière).

railcard [ˈreɪlkɑːd] n UK carte permettant de bénéficier de tarifs avantageux sur les chemins de fer britanniques.

railing [ˈreɪlɪŋ] n **1.** [barrier - gen] barrière f ; [- on bridge] garde-fou m ; [- on balcony] balustrade f **2.** [upright bar] barreau m **3.** = railings. ❖ **railings** pl n [fence] grille f / she squeezed through the railings elle se glissa entre les barreaux de la grille.

railroad [ˈreɪlrəʊd] ◆ n US = railway. ◆ vt ▸ **to railroad sb into doing sthg** forcer qqn à faire qqch.

railway [ˈreɪlweɪ] UK ◆ n **1.** [system, organization] chemin m de fer / he works on the railways il est cheminot **2.** [track] voie f ferrée. ◆ comp [bridge, traffic, travel, tunnel] ferroviaire ; [company] ferroviaire, de chemin de fer ; [journey] en train ; [employee, union] des chemins de fer ▸ **railway worker** cheminot m.

railway carriage n UK wagon m, voiture f.

railway crossing n UK passage m à niveau.

railway engine n UK locomotive f.

railway line n ⬚ **1.** [route] ligne *f* de chemin de fer **2.** [track] voie *f* ferrée ; [rail] rail *m*.

railwayman ['reɪlweɪmən] (*pl* **railwaymen** [-mən]) n ⬚ cheminot *m*.

railway station n ⬚ [gen] gare *f* (de chemin de fer) ; [in France] gare *f* SNCF.

railway track n ⬚ voie *f* ferrée.

rain [reɪn] ◆ n **1.** *lit* pluie *f* / *it was pouring with rain* il pleuvait à verse / *the rain was heavy* il pleuvait beaucoup / *a light rain was falling* il tombait une pluie fine / *come in out of the rain* rentre, ne reste pas sous la pluie / *it looks like rain* on dirait qu'il va pleuvoir / *Venice in the rain* Venise sous la pluie ▸ **the rains** la saison des pluies ▸ **come rain or shine** quoi qu'il arrive ▸ **(as) right as rain** *inf*: *don't worry, you'll be as right as rain in a minute* ne t'inquiète pas, ça va passer **2.** *fig* [of projectiles, blows] pluie *f*. ◆ vi pleuvoir / *it's raining* il pleut ▸ **it's raining cats and dogs** *inf & dated* il pleut des cordes, il tombe des hallebardes ▸ **it never rains but it pours** ⬚ *prov*, **when it rains, it pours** ⬚ *prov* tout arrive en même temps *prov* ▸ **to rain on sb's parade** ⬚ *inf*: *he rained on my parade* a) [ruined things] il a tout gâché pour moi b) [dampened my enthusiasm] il m'a cassé mes envies. ◆ vt faire pleuvoir. ❖ **rain down** ◆ vi [projectiles, blows, etc.] pleuvoir. ◆ vt sep [projectiles, blows, etc.] faire pleuvoir. ❖ **rain off** vt sep ⬚ : *the game was rained off* a) [cancelled] la partie a été annulée à cause de la pluie b) [abandoned] la partie a été abandonnée à cause de la pluie. ❖ **rain out** vt sep ⬚ = **rain off**.

rainbow ['reɪnbəʊ] ◆ n arc-en-ciel *m* ▸ **to chase rainbows** se bercer d'illusions. ◆ comp ▸ **rainbow coalition** POL coalition représentant un large éventail de tendances.

rainbow-coloured, **rainbow-hued** adj arc-en-ciel *(inv)*, multicolore.

rainbow trout n truite *f* arc-en-ciel.

rain check n ⬚ bon pour un autre match (ou spectacle) donné par suite d'une annulation à cause de la pluie / *I'll take a rain check on that inf* ça sera pour une autre fois.

rain cloud n nuage *m* de pluie.

raincoat ['reɪnkəʊt] n imperméable *m*.

raindrop ['reɪndrɒp] n goutte *f* de pluie.

rainfall ['reɪnfɔːl] n [amount of rain] pluviosité *f*.

rainforest ['reɪnˌfɒrɪst] n forêt *f* pluviale.

rain gauge n pluviomètre *m*.

rainhat ['reɪnhæt] n chapeau *m* pour la pluie.

rainhood ['reɪnhʊd] n capuche *f* ; [attached to anorak, jacket, etc.] capuchon *m*, capuche *f*.

rainproof ['reɪnpruːf] ◆ adj imperméable. ◆ vt imperméabiliser.

rainstorm ['reɪnstɔːm] n pluie *f* torrentielle.

rainwater ['reɪnˌwɔːtər] n eau *f* de pluie or pluviale.

rainy ['reɪnɪ] (*compar* **rainier**, *superl* **rainiest**) adj pluvieux ▸ **the rainy season** la saison des pluies ▸ **to save sthg for a rainy day** garder qqch pour les mauvais jours.

raise [reɪz] ◆ vt **1.** [lift, move upwards - gen] lever ; [- burden, lid] soulever ▸ **to raise one's head** lever la tête / *she didn't raise her eyes from her book* elle n'a pas levé les yeux de son livre ▸ **to raise the bar** *fig* placer la barre plus haut **2.** [increase - offer, price, tax] augmenter ; [- interest rates] relever ; [- temperature, tension] faire monter / *the speed limit has been raised to 150 km/h* la limitation de vitesse est passée à 150 km/h / *the age limit has been raised to 18* la limite d'âge a été repoussée à 18 ans **3.** [boost, improve] remonter, élever ▸ **to raise sb's spirits** remonter le moral à qqn ▸ **to raise sb's hopes** donner des espoirs à qqn **4.** [promote] élever, promouvoir **5.** [collect - together - support] réunir ; [- army] lever / *we have raised over a million signatures* nous avons recueilli plus d'un million de signatures **6.** [obtain - money] trouver, obtenir ; [- taxes] lever ▸ **to raise funds** collecter des fonds **7.** [make, produce] : *they raised a cheer when she came in* ils ont poussé des bravos quand elle est entrée / *he managed to raise a smile when he saw us* il a réussi à sourire en nous voyant **8.** [cause as reaction - laugh, welt, blister] provoquer / *his jokes didn't even raise a smile* ses plaisanteries n'ont même pas fait sourire **9.** ⬚ [rear - children, family] élever **10.** ⬚ [breed - livestock] élever ; [grow - crops] cultiver **11.** [introduce, bring up - point, subject, question] soulever ; [- doubts] soulever, susciter **12.** [erect] élever, ériger **13.** [resuscitate] ressusciter ; [evoke - spirit] évoquer / *they were making enough noise to raise the dead* ils faisaient un bruit à réveiller les morts **14.** [end - ban, siege] lever **15.** [contact] contacter **16.** [in bridge] monter sur ; [in poker] relancer / *I'll raise you 5 pounds* je relance de 5 livres **17.** CULIN [dough, bread] faire lever **18.** MATH élever **19.** NAUT ▸ **to raise land** arriver en vue de terre. ◆ vi [in bridge] monter, enchérir ; [in poker] relancer. ◆ n **1.** ⬚ [pay increase] augmentation *f* de salaire **2.** [in bridge] enchère *f* ; [in poker] relance *f*. ❖ **raise up** vt sep ▸ **to raise o.s. up** se soulever / *she raised herself up onto the chair* elle se hissa sur la chaise.

raised [reɪzd] adj **1.** [ground, platform, jetty, etc.] surélevé ; [pattern] en relief **2.** CULIN levé, à la levure **3.** LING [vowel] haut **4.** TEXT lainé, gratté.

raisin ['reɪzn] n raisin *m* sec.

Raj [rɑːdʒ] n ▸ **the Raj** l'Empire *m* britannique (en Inde).

rajah ['rɑːdʒə] n raja *m*, rajah *m*, radjah *m*.

rake [reɪk] ◆ n **1.** [in garden, casino] râteau *m* **2.** [libertine] roué *m*, libertin *m* **3.** THEAT pente *f* ; NAUT [of mast, funnel] quête *f*. ◆ vt **1.** [soil, lawn, path] ratisser, râteler / *she raked the leaves into a pile* elle ratissa les feuilles en tas **2.** [search] fouiller (dans) **3.** [scan] balayer / *a searchlight raked the darkness* un projecteur fouilla l'obscurité **4.** [strafe] balayer. ◆ vi **1.** [search] ▸ **to rake among** or **through** fouiller dans **2.** [slope] être en pente, être incliné. ❖ **rake in** vt sep *inf* [money] ramasser ▸ **to be raking it in** toucher un joli paquet. ❖ **rake off** vt sep *inf* [share of profits] empocher, ramasser. ❖ **rake out** vt sep **1.** [fire] enlever les cendres de ; [ashes] enlever **2.** [search out] dénicher. ❖ **rake over** vt sep **1.** [soil, lawn, path] ratisser **2.** *fig* remuer. ❖ **rake up** vt sep **1.** [collect together - leaves, weeds] ratisser ; [- people] réunir, rassembler **2.** [dredge up] déterrer ▸ **to rake up sb's past** fouiller dans le passé de qqn.

rake-off n *inf* petit profit *m*.

rakish ['reɪkɪʃ] adj **1.** [jaunty] désinvolte, insouciant **2.** [boat] à la forme élancée, allongé.

rally ['rælɪ] (*pl* **rallies**, *pt & pp* **rallied**) ◆ n **1.** [gathering - gen] rassemblement *m* ; MIL [during battle] ralliement *m* ; POL rassemblement *m*, (grand) meeting *m* **2.** [recovery - gen] amélioration *f* ; ST. EX reprise *f* **3.** AUTO rallye *m* ▸ **rally driver** pilote *m* de rallye **4.** SPORT (long) échange *m*. ◆ vi **1.** [assemble, gather - gen] se rassembler ; [- troops, supporters] se rallier / *they rallied to the party* / *to the defence of their leader* ils se sont ralliés au parti / pour défendre leur chef **2.** [recover - gen] s'améliorer ; [- sick person] aller mieux, reprendre des forces ; [- currency, share prices] remonter ; [- stock market] se reprendre **3.** AUTO faire des rallyes. ◆ vt **1.** [gather] rallier, rassembler / *she's trying to rally support for her project* elle essaie de rallier des gens pour soutenir son projet **2.** [summon up] rassembler / *to rally one's spirits* reprendre ses esprits ; [boost] ranimer / *the news rallied their morale* la nouvelle leur a remonté le moral **3.** *arch* [tease] taquiner. ❖ **rally around**,

rally round 🇺🇸 ◆ vi : *all her family rallied round* toute sa famille est venue lui apporter son soutien. ◆ vt insep : *they rallied round her* ils lui ont apporté leur soutien.

rallying ['rælɪŋ] adj ▶ **rallying cry** cri *m* de ralliement.

ram [ræm] (*pt* & *pp* **rammed**, *cont* **ramming**) ◆ n **1.** ZOOL bélier *m* **2.** HIST [for breaking doors, walls] bélier *m* **3.** TECH [piston] piston *m* ; [flattening tool] hie *f*, dame *f* ; [pile driver] mouton *m* ; [lifting pump] bélier *m* hydraulique. ◆ vt **1.** [bang into] percuter ; NAUT aborder ; [in battle] éperonner / *the police car rammed them twice* la voiture de police les a percutés deux fois **2.** [push] pousser (violemment) / *she rammed the papers into her bag* elle fourra les papiers dans son sac / *in order to ram home the point* pour enfoncer le clou. ◆ vi ▶ **to ram into sthg** entrer dans or percuter qqch.

RAM [ræm] ◆ n (abbr of random access memory) RAM *f*. ◆ pr n abbr of Royal Academy of Music.

Ramadan [ˌræməˈdæn] n ramadan *m*.

ramble ['ræmbl] ◆ n [hike] randonnée *f* (pédestre) ; [casual walk] promenade *f* ▶ **to go for a ramble** aller faire un tour. ◆ vi **1.** [hike] faire une randonnée **2.** [wander] se balader **3.** [talk] divaguer, radoter / *he rambled on and on about nothing* il n'arrêtait pas de parler pour ne rien dire **4.** [plant] pousser à tort et à travers **5.** [path, stream] serpenter. ❖ **ramble on** vi *pej* radoter.

rambler ['ræmbləʳ] n **1.** [hiker] randonneur *m*, -euse *f* **2.** [in speech] : *he's a bit of a rambler* il est du genre radoteur **3.** BOT plante *f* sarmenteuse.

rambling ['ræmblɪŋ] ◆ adj **1.** [building] plein de coins et de recoins **2.** [conversation, style] décousu ; [ideas, book, thoughts] incohérent, sans suite ; [person] qui divague, qui radote **3.** [plant] sarmenteux ▶ **rambling rose** rosier *m* sarmenteux. ◆ n [hiking] randonnée *f* ▶ **to go rambling** aller en randonnée.

RAMC (abbr of Royal Army Medical Corps) pr n *service de santé des armées britanniques.*

ramekin, ramequin ['ræmɪkɪn] n ramequin *m*.

ramen ['rɑːmən] n CULIN soupe *f* aux nouilles *(spécialité japonaise)*.

ramification [ˌræmɪfɪˈkeɪʃn] n **1.** [implication] implication *f* **2.** [branching] ramification *f*.

ramp [ræmp] n **1.** pente *f*, rampe *f* ; [in road works] dénivellation *f* **2.** 🇺🇸 [access road] rampe *f* d'accès. ❖ **ramp up** vt sep [increase] augmenter.

rampage [ræmˈpeɪdʒ] ◆ n fureur *f* ▶ **to be on the rampage** être déchaîné ▶ **to go on the rampage** se livrer à des actes de violence / *the headmaster's on the rampage!* le directeur est déchaîné ! ◆ vi se déchaîner / *a herd of elephants rampaged through the bush* un troupeau d'éléphants avançait dans la brousse en balayant tout sur son passage / *they rampaged through the town* ils ont saccagé la ville.

rampant ['ræmpənt] adj **1.** [unrestrained] déchaîné, effréné / *corruption is rampant* la corruption sévit / *the disease is rampant* la maladie fait des ravages / *rampant inflation* inflation *f* galopante **2.** [exuberant - vegetation] exubérant, foisonnant **3.** *(after noun)* HERALD rampant.

> ⚠ The French adjective **rampant** only corresponds to the English word rampant in the field of heraldry.

rampart ['ræmpɑːt] ◆ n *lit* & *fig* rempart *m*. ◆ vt fortifier (d'un rempart).

ramraid ['ræmreɪd] n pillage *m*.

ramraider ['ræmˌreɪdəʳ] n *personne qui pille les magasins en fracassant les vitrines avec sa voiture.*

ramshackle ['ræmˌʃækl] adj délabré.

ran [ræn] pt ⟶ **run**.

RAN (abbr of Royal Australian Navy) pr n *marine de guerre australienne.*

ranch [rɑːntʃ] ◆ n ranch *m* ▶ **chicken ranch** élevage *m* de poulets. ◆ comp ▶ **ranch hand** ouvrier *m* agricole ▶ **ranch house** *grande maison basse dite de style ranch.* ◆ vi exploiter un ranch. ◆ vt ▶ **to ranch cattle** élever du bétail (sur un ranch).

rancher ['rɑːntʃəʳ] n [owner] propriétaire *mf* de ranch ; [manager] exploitant *m*, -e *f* de ranch ; [worker] garçon *m* de ranch, cow-boy *m*.

rancid ['rænsɪd] adj rance ▶ **to go** or **to turn rancid** rancir.

rancour 🇬🇧, **rancor** 🇺🇸 ['ræŋkəʳ] n rancœur *f*, rancune *f*.

R and B n (abbr of rhythm and blues) R & B *m*.

R and D n (abbr of research and development) R & D *f*.

random ['rændəm] adj **1.** [aleatory] aléatoire, fait or choisi au hasard / *a random number* un nombre aléatoire / *a random sample* un échantillon pris au hasard / *a random shot* une balle perdue / *random violence* violence *f* aveugle **2.** inf [odd] bizarre / *she did something totally random* elle a fait un truc de ouf. ❖ **at random** adv phr au hasard / *to lash out at random* distribuer des coups à l'aveuglette.

random access n COMPUT accès *m* aléatoire or direct. ❖ **random-access** adj COMPUT à accès aléatoire or direct ▶ **random-access memory** mémoire *f* vive.

randomly ['rændəmlɪ] adv au hasard.

random sampling n échantillonnage *m* aléatoire.

R and R (abbr of rest and recreation) n MIL permission *f* / *I need some R and R* j'ai besoin de me reposer.

randy ['rændɪ] (*compar* **randier**, *superl* **randiest**) adj 🇬🇧 inf excité / *he's a randy devil* c'est un chaud lapin / *a randy old man* un vieux satyre.

rang [ræŋ] pt ⟶ **ring**.

range [reɪndʒ] ◆ n **1.** [of missile, sound, transmitter, etc.] portée *f* ; [of vehicle, aircraft] autonomie *f* ▶ **at long** / **short range** à longue / courte portée ▶ **out of range** hors de portée ▶ **within** or **in range** a) [of guns] à portée de tir b) [of voice] à portée de voix / *it can kill a man at a range of 800 metres* ça peut tuer un homme à une distance de 800 mètres / *it gives you some idea of the range of their powers* ça vous donne une petite idée de l'étendue de leurs pouvoirs **2.** [bracket] gamme *f*, éventail *m*, fourchette *f* ▶ **age range** : *children in the same age range* les enfants dans la même tranche d'âge ▶ **price range** gamme or fourchette de prix / *it's within my price range* c'est dans mes prix **3.** [selection] gamme *f* / *we stock a wide range of office materials* nous avons en stock une large gamme de matériels de bureaux / *it provoked a wide range of reactions* ça a provoqué des réactions très diverses ; COMM : *the new autumn range* [of clothes] la nouvelle collection d'automne / *this car is the top* / *bottom of the range* cette voiture est le modèle haut / bas de gamme **4.** *fig* [scope] champ *m*, domaine *m* / *that is beyond the range of the present inquiry* cela ne relève pas de cette enquête / *that lies outside the range of my responsibility* ça dépasse les limites de ma responsabilité **5.** [of mountains] chaîne *f* **6.** [prairie] prairie *f* **7.** [practice area] champ *m* de tir **8.** MUS [of instrument] étendue *f*, portée *f* ; [of voice] tessiture *f* **9.** [cooker] fourneau *m* (de cuisine) **10.** [row,

line] rang *m*, rangée *f* **11.** BIOL [habitat] habitat *m*. ◆ vi
1. [vary] aller, s'étendre / *their ages range from 5 to 12* or
between 5 and 12 ils ont de 5 à 12 or entre 5 et 12 ans
/ *the quality ranges from mediocre to excellent* la qualité
varie de médiocre à excellent **2.** [roam] ▶ **to range over**
parcourir / *thugs range through the city streets* des voyous
rôdent dans les rues de la ville **3.** [extend] : *the survey
ranged over the whole country* l'enquête couvrait la totalité
du pays / *our conversation ranged over a large number
of topics* nous avons discuté d'un grand nombre de sujets.
◆ vt **1.** [roam] parcourir **2.** [arrange] ranger ; [put in a
row or in rows] mettre or disposer en rang or rangs / *the
desks are ranged in threes* les pupitres sont en rangées de
trois **3.** [join, ally] ranger, rallier **4.** [classify] classer, ranger
5. [aim - cannon, telescope] braquer **6.** TYPO aligner, justifier.
ranger ['reɪndʒə'] n **1.** [in park, forest] garde *m* forestier
2. US [lawman] ≃ gendarme *m* **3.** US [in national park]
gardien *m*, -enne de parc national **4.** US MIL ranger *m*.
◆ **Ranger (Guide)** n guide *m*.
Rangoon [ˌræŋˈguːn] pr n Rangoon.
rangy ['reɪndʒɪ] (*compar* rangier, *superl* rangiest) adj
1. [tall and thin] grand et élancé **2.** [roomy] spacieux.
rank [ræŋk] ◆ n **1.** [grade] rang *m*, grade *m* / *promoted to the rank of colonel* promu (au rang de or au
grade de) colonel / *the rank of manager* le titre de directeur ▶ **to pull rank** faire valoir sa supériorité hiérarchique
2. [quality] rang *m* **3.** [social class] rang *m*, condition *f*
(sociale) / *the lower ranks of society* les couches inférieures
de la société **4.** [row, line] rang *m*, rangée *f* ; [on chessboard]
rangée *f* ▶ **to break ranks a)** MIL rompre les rangs **b)** *fig*
se désolidariser ▶ **to close ranks** MIL & *fig* serrer les rangs
5. US ▶ **(taxi) rank** station *f* (de taxis) **6.** MATH [in matrix]
rang *m*. ◆ vt **1.** [rate] classer / *she is ranked among the
best contemporary writers* elle est classée parmi les meilleurs écrivains contemporains / *I rank this as one of our
finest performances* je considère que c'est une de nos
meilleures représentations / *he is ranked number 3* il est
classé numéro 3 **2.** [arrange] ranger **3.** US [outrank] avoir
un grade supérieur à. ◆ vi **1.** [rate] figurer / *it ranks high /
low on our list of priorities* c'est / ce n'est pas une de nos
priorités / *he hardly ranks as an expert* on ne peut guère
le qualifier d'expert **2.** US MIL être officier supérieur. ◆ adj
1. [as intensifier] complet, véritable / *he is a rank outsider
in this competition* il fait figure d'outsider dans cette compétition **2.** [foul-smelling] infect, fétide ; [rancid] rance / *his
shirt was rank with sweat* sa chemise empestait la sueur
3. [coarse - person, language] grossier **4.** *liter* [profuse -
vegetation] luxuriant ; [-weeds] prolifique. ◆ **ranks** pl n
1. [members] rangs *mpl* / *to join the ranks of the opposition / unemployed* rejoindre les rangs de l'opposition / des
chômeurs **2.** MIL [rank and file] ▶ **the ranks, other ranks**
les hommes du rang / *to come up through* or *to rise from
the ranks* sortir du rang / *to reduce an officer to the ranks*
dégrader un officier.
-rank in comp ▶ **second-rank** petit, mineur ▶ **top-rank**
grand, majeur.
ranking ['ræŋkɪŋ] ◆ n classement *m*. ◆ adj US **1.** MIL
▶ **ranking officer** officier *m* responsable **2.** [prominent] de
premier ordre.
-ranking in comp ▶ **low-ranking** de bas rang or grade.
rankle ['ræŋkl] vi : *their decision still rankles with me*
leur décision m'est restée en travers de la gorge.
ransack ['rænsæk] vt **1.** [plunder] saccager, mettre à sac
2. [search] mettre sens dessus dessous.
ransom ['rænsəm] ◆ n rançon *f* / *they held her to
ransom* ils l'ont kidnappée pour avoir une rançon / *they're
holding the country to ransom* ils tiennent le pays en otage
▶ **a king's ransom** une fortune. ◆ vt rançonner.

rant [rænt] vi fulminer ▶ **to rant at sb** fulminer contre qqn
▶ **to rant and rave** tempêter, tonitruer.
ranting ['ræntɪŋ] ◆ n (U) vociférations *fpl*. ◆ adj déclamatoire.
rap [ræp] (*pt* & *pp* rapped, *cont* rapping) ◆ vt
1. [strike] frapper sur, cogner sur ▶ **to rap sb's knuckles, to
rap sb over the knuckles** *fig* sermonner qqn **2.** [in newspaper headlines] réprimander. ◆ vi **1.** [knock] frapper, cogner
2. US *inf* [chat] bavarder, discuter le bout de gras **3.** MUS
jouer du rap. ◆ n **1.** [blow, sound] coup *m* (sec) ; [rebuke]
réprimande *f* ▶ **to be given a rap over** or **on the knuckles**
fig se faire taper sur les doigts ▶ **to take the rap for sthg** *inf*
écoper pour qqch **2.** US *v inf* [legal charge] accusation *f* /
he's up on a murder / drugs rap il est accusé de meurtre /
dans une affaire de drogue / *it's a bum rap* c'est un coup
monté **3.** US *inf* [chat] ▶ **rap session** bavardage *m* **4.** MUS
rap *m*. ◆ **rap out** vt sep **1.** [say sharply] lancer, lâcher
2. [tap out - message] taper.
rapacious [rəˈpeɪʃəs] adj rapace.
rapaciousness [rəˈpeɪʃəsnɪs], **rapacity** [rəˈpæsətɪ]
n rapacité *f*.
rape [reɪp] ◆ n **1.** [sex crime] viol *m* ▶ **to commit rape**
perpétrer un viol ▶ **rape victim** victime *f* d'un viol / *the
rape of the countryside* la dévastation de la campagne
▶ **rape crisis centre** centre d'accueil pour femmes violées
2. BOT colza *m* **3.** [remains of grapes] marc *m* (de raisin).
◆ vt violer.
rapeseed ['reɪpsiːd] n graine *f* de colza.
rapid ['ræpɪd] adj rapide / *in rapid succession* en une
succession rapide. ◆ **rapids** pl n rapide *m*, rapides *mpl*
▶ **to shoot the rapids** franchir le rapide or les rapides.
rapid eye movement n mouvements oculaires rapides
pendant le sommeil paradoxal.
rapid-fire adj MIL à tir rapide ; *fig* [questions, jokes] qui
se succèdent à toute allure.
rapidity [rəˈpɪdətɪ] n rapidité *f*.
rapidly ['ræpɪdlɪ] adv rapidement.
rapidness ['ræpɪdnɪs] = **rapidity**.
rapist ['reɪpɪst] n violeur *m*.
rapper ['ræpə'] n **1.** [on door] heurtoir *m* **2.** MUS rappeur *m*, -euse *f*.
rapport [ræˈpɔː'] n rapport *m* / *I have a good rapport
with him* j'ai de bons rapports avec lui.
rapprochement [ræˈprɒʃmɒnt] n rapprochement *m*.
rap sheet n US casier *m* judiciaire.
rapt [ræpt] adj **1.** [engrossed] absorbé, captivé / *the
clown held the children rapt* le clown fascinait les enfants
2. [delighted] ravi / *rapt with joy* transporté de joie.
rapture ['ræptʃə'] n ravissement *m*, extase *f* ▶ **to go into
raptures over** or **about sthg** s'extasier sur qqch / *they
were in raptures about their presents* leurs cadeaux les ont
ravis.
rapturous ['ræptʃərəs] adj [feeling] intense, profond ;
[gaze] ravi, extasié ; [praise, applause] enthousiaste.
rapturously ['ræptʃərəslɪ] adv [watch] d'un air ravi, avec
ravissement ; [praise, applaud] avec enthousiasme.
rare [reə'] adj **1.** [uncommon] rare / *it's rare to see such
marital bliss nowadays* un tel bonheur conjugal est rare
de nos jours / *on the rare occasions when I've seen him
angry* les rares fois où je l'ai vu en colère / *a rare opportunity* une occasion exceptionnelle / *he's a rare bird* c'est
un oiseau rare **2.** [exceptional] rare, exceptionnel **3.** *inf* [ex-
treme] énorme ; [excellent] fameux, génial **4.** [meat] saignant
5. [rarefied - air, atmosphere] raréfié.
rarefied ['reərɪfaɪd] adj **1.** [air, atmosphere] raréfié
2. [refined] raffiné.

rarely ['reəlɪ] adv rarement / *it rarely snows here* il neige rarement ici, il est rare qu'il neige ici.

📋 Note that il est rare que is followed by a verb in the subjunctive:
People rarely make the connection. *Il est rare que les gens fassent le lien.*

rareness ['reənɪs] n rareté f.

raring ['reərɪŋ] adj *inf* impatient ▸ **to be raring to go** ronger son frein.

rarity ['reərətɪ] (*pl* **rarities**) n **1.** [uncommon person, thing] rareté f **2.** [scarcity] rareté f.

rascal ['rɑːskl] n **1.** [naughty child] polisson m, -onne f **2.** *liter* [rogue] vaurien m, gredin m.

rash [ræʃ] ◆ n **1.** MED rougeur f, éruption f **2.** [wave, outbreak] vague f. ◆ adj imprudent.

rasher ['ræʃər] n 🇬🇧 tranche f (*de bacon*).

rashly ['ræʃlɪ] adv imprudemment.

rashness ['ræʃnɪs] n imprudence f.

rasp [rɑːsp] ◆ n **1.** [file] râpe f **2.** [sound] bruit m de râpe. ◆ vt **1.** [scrape, file] râper **2.** [say] dire d'une voix rauque. ◆ vi [make rasping noise] grincer, crisser.

raspberry ['rɑːzbərɪ] (*pl* **raspberries**) ◆ n **1.** [fruit] framboise f **2.** *inf* [noise] ▸ **to blow a raspberry** faire pfft (*en signe de dérision*). ◆ comp [jam] de framboises ; [tart] aux framboises ▸ **raspberry bush** or **cane** BOT framboisier m. ◆ adj [colour] framboise (*inv*).

rasping ['rɑːspɪŋ] ◆ adj [noise] grinçant, crissant ; [voice] grinçant. ◆ n [noise] grincement m, crissement m.

Rasta ['ræstə] ◆ n (*abbr of* **Rastafarian**) rasta mf. ◆ adj rasta (*inv*).

Rastafarian [ˌræstə'feərɪən] ◆ n rastafari mf. ◆ adj rastafari (*inv*).

rat [ræt] (*pt & pp* **ratted**, *cont* **ratting**) ◆ n **1.** ZOOL rat m **2.** *inf* [as insult - gen] ordure f. ◆ vi **1.** *lit* ▸ **to go ratting** faire la chasse aux rats **2.** *inf & fig* retourner sa veste. ◆ **rat on** vt insep *inf* **1.** [betray] vendre ; [inform on] moucharder **2.** [go back on] revenir sur.

rat-arsed ['ræ.tɑːst] adj 🇬🇧 *v inf* bourré.

ratbag ['rætbæg] n 🇬🇧 *inf* peau f de vache.

ratchet ['rætʃɪt] n rochet m.

rate [reɪt] ◆ n **1.** [ratio, level] taux m ▸ **rate of exchange** taux de change ▸ **rate of return** taux de rendement ▸ **rate of taxation** taux d'imposition **2.** [cost, charge] tarif m / *his rates have gone up* ses prix ont augmenté / *standard / reduced rate* tarif normal / réduit **3.** [speed] vitesse f, train m. ◆ vt **1.** [reckon, consider] considérer ▸ **to rate sb / sthg highly** avoir une haute opinion de qqn / qqch, faire grand cas de qqn / qqch **2.** [deserve] mériter **3.** *inf* [have high opinion of] : *I don't rate him as an actor* à mon avis, ce n'est pas un bon acteur / *I don't rate their chances much* je ne pense pas qu'ils aient beaucoup de chance **4.** 🇬🇧 [fix rateable value of] fixer la valeur locative imposable de. ◆ vi [rank high] se classer / *he rates highly in my estimation* je le tiens en très haute estime. ◆ **rates** pl n 🇬🇧 dated impôts mpl locaux. ◆ **at any rate** adv phr de toute façon, de toute manière, en tout cas.

rateable ['reɪtəbl] adj ▸ **rateable value** 🇬🇧 ≈ valeur f locative imposable.

ratepayer ['reɪtˌpeɪər] n [in UK] contribuable mf.

rather ['rɑːðər] ◆ adv **1.** [slightly, a bit] assez, un peu / *it's rather too small for me* c'est un peu trop petit pour moi / *she cut me a rather large slice* elle m'a coupé une tranche plutôt grande / *it tastes rather like honey* ça a un peu le goût du miel **2.** [expressing preference] plutôt / *I'd rather not do it today* je préférerais or j'aimerais mieux ne pas le faire aujourd'hui / *shall we go out tonight? — I'd rather not* si on sortait ce soir ? — je n'ai pas très envie ▸ **rather you than me!** je n'aimerais pas être à votre place ! **3.** [more exactly] plutôt, plus exactement. ◆ predet plutôt / *it was rather a long film* le film était plutôt long.

📋 Note that préférer que and aimer mieux que are followed by a verb in the subjunctive:
I'd rather you came alone. *Je préférerais que tu viennes seule. J'aimerais mieux que tu viennes seule.*

ratification [ˌrætɪfɪ'keɪʃn] n ratification f.

ratify ['rætɪfaɪ] (*pt & pp* **ratified**) vt ratifier.

rating ['reɪtɪŋ] n **1.** [ranking] classement m ; FIN [of bank, company] notation f **2.** [appraisal] évaluation f, estimation f **3.** NAUT matelot m. ◆ **ratings** pl n RADIO & TV indice m d'écoute.

ratio ['reɪʃɪəʊ] (*pl* **ratios**) n **1.** [gen] proportion f, rapport m **2.** MATH raison f, proportion f **3.** ECON ratio m.

ration ['ræʃn] ◆ n *lit & fig* ration f. ◆ comp ▸ **ration book** carnet m de tickets de rationnement ▸ **ration card** carte f de rationnement. ◆ vt **1.** [food] rationner **2.** [funds] limiter. ◆ **rations** pl n [food] vivres mpl ▸ **to be on double / short rations** toucher une ration double / réduite ▸ **half rations** demi-rations fpl. ◆ **ration out** vt sep rationner.

rational ['ræʃənl] ◆ adj **1.** [capable of reason] doué de raison, raisonnable **2.** [reasonable, logical - person] raisonnable ; [- behaviour, explanation] rationnel **3.** [of sound mind, sane] lucide **4.** MATH rationnel. ◆ n rationnel m.

rationale [ˌræʃə'nɑːl] n **1.** [underlying reason] logique f **2.** [exposition] exposé m.

rationalist ['ræʃənəlɪst] ◆ adj rationaliste. ◆ n rationaliste mf.

rationalistic [ˌræʃənə'lɪstɪk] adj rationaliste.

rationality [ˌræʃə'nælətɪ] n **1.** [of belief, system, etc.] rationalité f **2.** [faculty] raison f.

rationalization, rationalisation [ˌræʃənəlaɪ'zeɪʃn] n rationalisation f.

rationalize, rationalise ['ræʃənəlaɪz] vt **1.** [gen & COMM] rationaliser **2.** MATH rendre rationnel.

rationally ['ræʃənlɪ] adv rationnellement.

rationing ['ræʃnɪŋ] n [of food] rationnement m.

rat poison n mort-aux-rats f inv.

rat race n jungle f fig.

rattle ['rætl] ◆ vi [gen] faire du bruit ; [car, engine] faire un bruit de ferraille ; [chain, machine, dice] cliqueter ; [gunfire, hailstones] crépiter ; [door, window] vibrer. ◆ vt **1.** [box] agiter (*en faisant du bruit*) ; [key] faire cliqueter ; [chain, dice] agiter, secouer ; [door, window] faire vibrer **2.** [disconcert] ébranler, secouer. ◆ n **1.** [noise - of chains] bruit m ; [- of car, engine] bruit m de ferraille ; [- of keys] cliquetis m ; [- of gunfire, hailstones] crépitement m ; [- of window, door] vibration f, vibrations fpl **2.** [for baby] hochet m ; [for sports fan] crécelle f **3.** ZOOL [of rattlesnake] grelot m. ◆ **rattle around** vi : *you'll be rattling around in that big old house!* tu seras perdu tout seul dans cette grande maison ! ◆ **rattle off** vt sep [speech, list] débiter, réciter à toute allure ; [piece of work] expédier ; [letter, essay] écrire en vitesse. ◆ **rattle on** vi jacasser. ◆ **rattle through** vt insep [speech, meeting, etc.] expédier.

rattler ['rætlər] US *inf* = **rattlesnake**.

rattlesnake ['rætlsneɪk] n serpent *m* à sonnettes, crotale *m*.

rattling ['rætlɪŋ] ◆ n = **rattle** *(noun)*. ◆ adj **1.** [sound] : *there was a rattling noise* on entendait un cliquetis **2.** [fast] rapide. ◆ adv *inf* & *dated* : *this book is a rattling good read* ce livre est vraiment formidable.

rat trap n **1.** *lit* piège *m* à rats, ratière *f* **2.** US [building] taudis *m*.

ratty ['rætɪ] *(compar* **rattier,** *superl* **rattiest)** adj *inf* **1.** UK [irritable] de mauvais poil **2.** US [shabby] miteux.

raucous ['rɔːkəs] adj **1.** [noisy] bruyant **2.** [hoarse] rauque.

raucously ['rɔːkəslɪ] adv **1.** [noisily] bruyamment **2.** [hoarsely] d'une voix rauque.

raunchy ['rɔːntʃɪ] *(compar* **raunchier,** *superl* **raunchiest)** adj *inf* **1.** [woman] d'une sensualité débordante ; [song, film, etc.] torride **2.** US [slovenly] négligé.

ravage ['rævɪdʒ] vt ravager, dévaster. ◇ **ravages** pl n : *the ravages of time* les ravages du temps.

ravaged ['rævɪdʒd] adj ravagé.

rave [reɪv] ◆ vi **1.** [be delirious] délirer **2.** [talk irrationally] divaguer **3.** [shout] se déchaîner **4.** *inf* [praise] s'extasier ▶ **to rave about sthg / sb** s'extasier sur qqch / qqn **5.** UK *inf* [at party] faire la bringue or la fête. ◆ n *inf* **1.** [praise] critique *f* élogieuse **2.** [fashion, craze] mode *f* **3.** UK [party] rave *f*. ◆ adj *inf* [enthusiastic] élogieux / *the play got rave reviews* or *notices* les critiques de la pièce furent très élogieuses. ◇ **rave up** vt sep UK *dated* ▶ **to rave it up** *inf* faire la bringue or la fête.

raven ['reɪvn] ◆ n (grand) corbeau *m*. ◆ adj *liter* noir comme un corbeau or comme du jais.

ravenous ['rævənəs] adj **1.** [hungry] affamé **2.** *liter* [rapacious] vorace.

raver ['reɪvər] n UK *inf* [partygoer] fêtard *m*, -e *f*, noceur *m*, -euse *f*.

rave-up n UK *inf* & *dated* fête *f*.

ravine [rə'viːn] n ravin *m*.

raving ['reɪvɪŋ] ◆ adj **1.** [mad] délirant **2.** [as intensifier] : *he's a raving lunatic inf* c'est un fou furieux, il est fou à lier. ◆ adv *inf* ▶ **raving mad** fou à lier. ◇ **ravings** pl n divagations *fpl*.

ravioli [,rævɪ'əʊlɪ] n (U) ravioli *mpl*, raviolis *mpl*.

ravish ['rævɪʃ] vt *liter* **1.** [delight] ravir, transporter de joie **2.** *arch* & *liter* [rape] violer ; [abduct] ravir.

ravishing ['rævɪʃɪŋ] adj ravissant, éblouissant.

ravishingly ['rævɪʃɪŋlɪ] adv de façon ravissante ; [as intensifier] : *ravishingly beautiful* d'une beauté éblouissante.

raw [rɔː] ◆ adj **1.** [uncooked] cru ; [as hors d'œuvre] crudités *fpl* **2.** [untreated - sugar, latex, leather] brut ; [- milk] cru ; [- spirits] pur ; [- cotton, linen] écru ; [- silk] grège, écru ; [- sewage] non traité **3.** [data, statistics] brut **4.** [sore - gen] sensible, irrité ; [- wound, blister] à vif ; [- nerves] à fleur de peau **5.** [emotion, power, energy] brut **6.** [contact] joindre **7.** [inexperienced] inexpérimenté / *a raw recruit* un bleu **7.** [weather] rigoureux, rude **8.** [forthright] franc (franche), direct **9.** US [rude, coarse] grossier, cru **10.** PHR **to give sb a raw deal** traiter qqn de manière injuste. ◆ n ▶ **in the raw** *inf* à poil.

raw material n (usu pl) matière *f* première.

ray [reɪ] n **1.** [of light] rayon *m* **2.** *fig* lueur *f* **3.** [fish] raie *f* **4.** MUS ré *m*.

rayon ['reɪɒn] ◆ n rayonne *f*. ◆ adj en rayonne.

raze [reɪz] vt raser / *the village was razed to the ground* le village fut entièrement rasé.

razor ['reɪzər] ◆ n rasoir *m*. ◆ vt raser.

razor blade n lame *f* de rasoir.

razor-sharp adj **1.** [blade] tranchant comme un rasoir or comme une lame de rasoir ; [nails] acéré **2.** [person, mind] vif.

razz [ræz] vt US *inf* [tease] se moquer de.

razzle ['ræzl] n UK *inf* ▶ **to be** or **to go on the razzle** faire la bringue or la nouba.

razzmatazz ['ræzmə'tæz] n *inf* clinquant *m*.

RC n abbr of **Roman Catholic**.

RCA pr n abbr of **Royal College of Art**.

RCAF (abbr of **Royal Canadian Air Force**) pr n *armée de l'air canadienne*.

RCMP (abbr of **Royal Canadian Mounted Police**) pr n *police montée canadienne*.

Rd written abbr of **road**.

RDA n abbr of **recommended daily allowance**.

RDC n abbr of **rural district council**.

re¹ [reɪ] n MUS ré *m*.

re² [riː] prep **1.** ADMIN & COMM : *re your letter of the 6th June* en réponse à or suite à votre lettre du 6 juin ; [in letter heading] : *Re: job application* Objet : demande d'emploi **2.** LAW ▶ **(in) re** en l'affaire de.

RE n abbr of **religious education**.

reacclimate [rɪ'æklɪmeɪt] vt US : *I was getting reacclimated* j'étais en train de retrouver mes repères.

reach [riːtʃ] ◆ vt **1.** [arrive at - destination] arriver à **2.** [extend as far as - stage, point, level] arriver à, atteindre **3.** [come to - agreement, decision, conclusion] arriver à, parvenir à ; [- compromise] arriver à, aboutir à **4.** [be able to touch] atteindre **5.** [pass, hand] passer **6.** [contact] joindre. ◆ vi **1.** [with hand] tendre la main / *she reached for her glass* elle tendit la main pour prendre son verre **2.** [extend] s'étendre ; [carry - voice] porter **3.** [be long enough] : *it won't reach* ce n'est pas assez long **4.** NAUT faire une bordée. ◆ n **1.** [range] portée *f*, atteinte *f* ▶ **within reach** à portée de la main / *the house is within easy reach of the shops* la maison est à proximité des magasins / *within everyone's reach* [affordable by all] à la portée de toutes les bourses ▶ **out of reach** hors de portée ▶ **out of reach of** hors de (la) portée de **2.** [in boxing] allonge *f* **3.** NAUT bordée *f*, bord *m*. ◇ **reaches** pl n étendue *f* / *the upper / the lower reaches of a river* l'amont / l'aval d'une rivière / *the upper reaches of society* les échelons supérieurs de la société. ◇ **reach back** vi [in time] remonter. ◇ **reach down** ◆ vt sep descendre. ◆ vi **1.** [person] se baisser **2.** [coat, hair] descendre. ◇ **reach out** ◆ vt sep [arm, hand] tendre, étendre. ◆ vi tendre or étendre le bras. ◇ **reach up** vi **1.** [raise arm] lever le bras **2.** [rise] ▶ **to reach up to** arriver à.

reachable ['riːtʃəbl] adj **1.** [town, destination] accessible **2.** [contactable] joignable.

react [rɪ'ækt] vi réagir ▶ **to react to sthg** réagir à qqch ▶ **to react against sb / sthg** réagir contre qqn / qqch.

reaction [rɪ'ækʃn] n **1.** [gen & CHEM] réaction *f* **2.** [reflex] réflexe *m* **3.** POL réaction *f*.

reactionary [rɪ'ækʃənrɪ] ◆ adj réactionnaire. ◆ n réactionnaire *mf*.

reactivate [rɪ'æktɪveɪt] vt réactiver.

reactive [rɪ'æktɪv] adj [gen & CHEM] & PHYS réactif ; PSYCHOL réactionnel.

reactor [rɪ'æktər] n réacteur *m*.

read¹ [riːd] *(pt* & *pp* **read** [red]) ◆ vt **1.** [book, magazine, etc.] lire / *I read it in the paper* je l'ai lu dans le journal ▶ **to read sb's lips** *lit* lire sur les lèvres de qqn ▶ **read my lips** *fig* écoutez-moi bien ▶ **to take sthg as read** considérer qqch comme allant de soi **2.** [interpret] interpréter, lire **3.** [understand - person, mood] comprendre ▸ **to read sb's thoughts** lire dans les pensées de qqn / *I can read him like a book!* je sais comment il fonctionne ! **4.** [via radio] recevoir / *reading you loud and clear* je vous reçois cinq sur cinq **5.** [at university] étudier / *he read history* il a étudié l'histoire, il a fait des études d'histoire **6.** [gauge, dial, barometer] lire ▸ **to read the meter** relever le compteur **7.** [register - subj: gauge, dial, barometer] indiquer. ◆ vi **1.** [person] lire ▸ **to read to sb** faire la lecture à qqn ▸ **to read to o.s.** lire / *I'd read about it in the papers* je l'avais lu dans les journaux ▸ **to read between the lines** lire entre les lignes **2.** [text] : *her article reads well / badly* son article se lit facilement / ne se lit pas facilement / *the book reads like a translation* à la lecture, on sent que ce roman est une traduction / *article 22 reads as follows* voici ce que dit l'article 22. ◆ n **1.** [act of reading] ▸ **to have a read** lire / *can I have a read of your paper?* est-ce que je peux jeter un coup d'œil sur ton journal ? **2.** [reading matter] : *her books are a good read* ses livres se lisent bien. ◆▸ **read into** vt sep : *you shouldn't read too much into their silence* vous ne devriez pas accorder trop d'importance à leur silence. ◆▸ **read out** vt sep [aloud] lire (à haute voix). ◆▸ **read over** vt sep relire. ◆▸ **read through** vt sep lire *(du début à la fin)*. ◆▸ **read up** vt sep étudier. ◆▸ **read up on** vt insep = **read up.**

read² [red] ◆ pt & pp ⟶ **read.** ◆ adj : *he's widely read* c'est un homme cultivé.

readable ['riːdəbl] adj **1.** [handwriting] lisible **2.** [book] qui se laisse lire.

readdress [ˌriːə'dres] vt [mail] faire suivre.

reader ['riːdər] n **1.** [of book] lecteur *m*, -trice *f* **2.** COMPUT lecteur *m* **3.** [reading book] livre *m* de lecture ; [anthology] recueil *m* de textes **4.** UK UNIV ≃ maître-assistant *m*, -e *f* **5.** US UNIV ≃ assistant *m*, -e *f*.

readership ['riːdəʃɪp] n **1.** [of newspaper, magazine] nombre *m* de lecteurs, lectorat *m* **2.** UK UNIV ≃ poste *m* de maître-assistant **3.** US UNIV ≃ fonction *f* d'assistant.

readies ['rediz] pl n UK inf [cash] fric *m*, liquide *m*.

readily ['redɪlɪ] adv **1.** [willingly] volontiers **2.** [with ease] facilement, aisément.

readiness ['redɪnɪs] n **1.** [preparedness] ▸ **to be in readiness for sthg** être préparé à qqch ▸ **to be in a state of readiness** être fin prêt **2.** [willingness] empressement *m* / *their readiness to assist us* leur empressement à nous aider.

reading ['riːdɪŋ] ◆ n **1.** [activity] lecture *f* **2.** [reading material] lecture *f* **3.** [recital] lecture *f* **4.** [from instrument, gauge] indication *f* **5.** POL lecture *f* **6.** [interpretation] interprétation *f* **7.** [variant] variante *f*. ◆ comp ▸ **reading matter** : *take some reading matter* emmenez de quoi lire.

reading age n UK niveau *m* de lecture.

reading glasses [-glɑːsɪz] pl n [spectacles] lunettes *fpl* pour lire.

reading lamp n lampe *f* de bureau.

reading list n [syllabus] liste *f* des ouvrages au programme ; [for further reading] liste *f* des ouvrages recommandés.

reading room n salle *f* de lecture.

readjust [ˌriːə'dʒʌst] ◆ vt **1.** [readapt] ▸ **to readjust o.s.** se réadapter **2.** [alter - controls, prices, clothing] rajuster, réajuster. ◆ vi se réadapter ▸ **to readjust to sthg** se réadapter à qqch.

readjustment [ˌriːə'dʒʌstmənt] n **1.** [readaptation] réadaptation *f* **2.** [alteration] rajustement *m*, réajustement *m*.

read-me file n COMPUT fichier *m* ouvrez-moi or lisez-moi.

readmit [ˌriːəd'mɪt] vt : *she has been readmitted to hospital* elle a été réadmise à l'hôpital / *he was readmitted to the concert* on l'a relaissé passer à l'entrée du concert.

read-only [riːd-] adj [disk, file] en lecture seule.

read-only memory [riːd-] n mémoire *f* morte.

readout ['riːdaʊt] n COMPUT [gen] lecture *f* ; [on screen] affichage *m* ; [on paper] sortie *f* papier or sur imprimante, listing *m*.

read-through [riːd-] n ▸ **to have a read-through of sthg** lire qqch *(du début à la fin)*.

readvertise [ˌriː'ædvətaɪz] ◆ vt repasser une annonce de. ◆ vi repasser une annonce.

ready ['redɪ] *(compar* **readier,** *superl* **readiest,** *pl* **readies,** *pt* & *pp* **readied)** ◆ adj **1.** [prepared] prêt ▸ **to be ready to do sthg** être prêt à faire qqch / *to be ready for anything* être prêt à tout ▸ **to get sthg ready** préparer qqch ▸ **to get ready to do sthg** se préparer or s'apprêter à faire qqch **2.** [willing] prêt, disposé ▸ **ready to do sthg** prêt à faire qqch **3.** [quick] prompt **4.** [likely] ▸ **ready to do sthg** sur le point de faire qqch **5.** [easily accessible] ▸ **ready to hand a)** [within reach] à portée de main **b)** [available] à disposition ▸ **ready cash** or **money** (argent *m*) liquide *m*. ◆ n UK inf [money] ▸ **the ready, the readies** le fric, le pognon. ◆ adv ▸ **ready cut ham** jambon *m* prétranché ▸ **ready salted peanuts** cacahuètes *fpl* salées. ◆ vt préparer ▸ **to ready o.s. for sthg** se préparer pour qqch. ◆▸ **at the ready** adj phr (tout) prêt.

ready-made ◆ adj **1.** [clothes] de prêt-à-porter ; [food] précuit **2.** [excuse, solution, argument] tout prêt. ◆ n [garment] vêtement *m* de prêt-à-porter.

ready meal n plat *m* cuisiné.

ready-to-wear adj ▸ **ready-to-wear clothing** prêt-à-porter *m*.

reaffirm [ˌriːə'fɜːm] vt réaffirmer.

reafforest [ˌriːə'fɒrɪst] vt reboiser.

reafforestation ['riːəˌfɒrɪ'steɪʃn] n reboisement *m*, reforestation *f*.

real [rɪəl] ◆ adj **1.** [authentic] vrai, véritable **2.** [actually existing] réel / *in real life* dans la réalité **3.** [net, overall] réel / *salaries have fallen in real terms* les salaires ont baissé en termes réels / *real wage* salaire *m* réel **4.** [as intensifier] vrai, véritable / *it was a real surprise* ce fut une vraie surprise / *she's a real pain* elle est vraiment rasante **5.** COMPUT, MATH, PHILOS & PHYS réel **6.** PHR **get real!** *v inf* arrête de délirer ! ◆ adv US inf vachement. ◆ n PHILOS ▸ **the real** le réel. ◆▸ **for real** adv & adj phr *inf* pour de vrai or de bon.

real ale n UK bière *f* artisanale.

real estate n (U) **1.** US [property] biens *mpl* immobiliers **2.** UK LAW biens *mpl* fonciers. ◆▸ **real-estate** comp US immobilier.

realign [ˌriːə'laɪn] ◆ vt aligner (de nouveau) ; POL regrouper. ◆ vi s'aligner (de nouveau) ; POL se regrouper.

realignment [ˌriːə'laɪnmənt] n (nouvel) alignement *m* ; POL regroupement *m*.

realism ['rɪəlɪzm] n réalisme *m*.

realist ['rɪəlɪst] ◆ adj réaliste. ◆ n réaliste *mf*.

realistic [ˌrɪə'lɪstɪk] adj **1.** [reasonable] réaliste **2.** [lifelike] ressemblant.

realistically [ˌrɪə'lɪstɪklɪ] adv de façon réaliste.

reality [rɪ'ælətɪ] *(pl* **realities)** n réalité *f*. ◆▸ **in reality** adv phr en réalité.

reality check n : *take a reality check!* sois réaliste ! / *let's have a reality check here* soyons un peu réalistes !

reality TV n (U) téléréalité *f*.

realization, realisation [ˌrɪəlaɪˈzeɪʃn] n **1.** [awareness] : *there has been a growing realization on the part of the government that...* le gouvernement s'est peu à peu rendu compte que... / *his realization that he was gay* la prise de conscience de son homosexualité **2.** [of aim, dream, project] réalisation *f* **3.** FIN [of assets] réalisation *f*.

realize, realise [ˈrɪəlaɪz] vt **1.** [be or become aware of] se rendre compte de **2.** [achieve] réaliser **3.** FIN [yield financially] rapporter ; [convert into cash] réaliser.

real-life adj vrai.

reallocate [ˌriːˈæləkeɪt] vt [funds, resources] réaffecter, réattribuer ; [task, duties] redistribuer.

really [ˈrɪəlɪ] adv **1.** [actually] vraiment, réellement / *did you really say that?* as-tu vraiment dis ça ? **2.** [as intensifier] vraiment / *these cakes are really delicious* ces gâteaux sont vraiment délicieux **3.** [in surprise, interest] ▶ **(oh) really?** oh, vraiment ?, c'est pas vrai ?

realm [relm] n **1.** [field, domain] domaine *m* **2.** *liter* [kingdom] royaume *m*.

real time n COMPUT temps *m* réel. ❖ **real-time** adj [system, control, processing] en temps réel.

realtor [ˈrɪəltər] n 🇺🇸 agent *m* immobilier.

realty [ˈrɪəltɪ] n (U) 🇺🇸 biens *mpl* immobiliers.

ream [riːm] n [of paper] rame *f* ▶ **to write reams** *inf & fig* écrire des tartines. ❖ vt **1.** TECH fraiser **2.** 🇺🇸 *inf* [person] rouler.

reap [riːp] ❖ vt **1.** [crop] moissonner, faucher **2.** *fig* récolter, tirer. ❖ vi moissonner, faire la moisson.

reaper [ˈriːpər] n **1.** [machine] moissonneuse *f* ▶ **reaper and binder** moissonneuse-lieuse *f* **2.** [person] moissonneur *m*, -euse *f* ▶ **the (Grim) Reaper** *liter* la Faucheuse.

reappear [ˌriːəˈpɪər] vi [person, figure, sun] réapparaître ; [lost object] refaire surface.

reappearance [ˌriːəˈpɪərəns] n réapparition *f*.

reapply [ˌriːəˈplaɪ] (*pt & pp* **reapplied**) vi : *to reapply for a job* poser sa candidature pour un poste.

reappoint [ˌriːəˈpɔɪnt] vt réengager, rengager.

reappraisal [ˌriːəˈpreɪzl] n réexamen *m*.

reappraise [ˌriːəˈpreɪz] vt réexaminer.

rear [rɪər] ❖ n **1.** [of place] arrière *m* / *at the rear of the bus* à l'arrière du bus / *the garden at the rear* 🇬🇧 or *in the rear* 🇺🇸 *of the house* le jardin qui est derrière la maison **2.** MIL arrière *m*, arrières *mpl* **3.** *inf* [buttocks] arrière-train *m*. ❖ adj [door, wheel] arrière *(inv)*, de derrière ; [engine] arrière ; [carriages] de queue ▶ **rear lamp** or **light** 🇬🇧 AUTO feu *m* arrière ▶ **rear window** lunette *f* arrière. ❖ vt **1.** [children, animals] élever ; [plants] cultiver **2.** [head, legs] lever, relever. ❖ vi **1.** [horse] ▶ **to rear (up)** se cabrer **2.** [mountain, skyscraper] ▶ **to rear (up)** se dresser.

rear admiral n contre-amiral *m*.

rear-end vt 🇺🇸 [drive into back of] emboutir.

rearguard action n combat *m* d'arrière-garde.

rearm [riːˈɑːm] ❖ vt [nation, ship] réarmer. ❖ vi réarmer.

rearmament [riːˈɑːməmənt] n réarmement *m*.

rearmost [ˈrɪəməʊst] adj dernier.

rearrange [ˌriːəˈreɪndʒ] vt **1.** [arrange differently - furniture, objects] réarranger, changer la disposition de ; [- flat, room] réaménager **2.** [put back in place] réarranger **3.** [reschedule] changer la date / l'heure de.

rearrangement [ˌriːəˈreɪndʒmənt] n **1.** [different arrangement] réarrangement *m*, réaménagement *m* **2.** [rescheduling] changement *m* de date / d'heure.

rearview mirror [ˈrɪəvjuː-] n rétroviseur *m*.

rear-wheel drive n AUTO traction *f* arrière.

reason [ˈriːzn] ❖ n **1.** [cause, motive] raison *f* / *what is the reason for his absence?* quelle est la raison de son absence ? / *did he give a reason for being so late?* a-t-il donné la raison d'un tel retard ? / *the reason (why) they refused* la raison de leur refus, la raison pour laquelle ils ont refusé / *we have | there is reason to believe he is lying* nous avons de bonnes raisons de croire / il y a lieu de croire qu'il ment / *but that's the only reason I came!* mais c'est pour ça que je suis venue ! / *that's no reason to get annoyed* ce n'est pas une raison pour s'énerver ▶ **for some reason (or other)** pour une raison ou pour une autre **2.** [common sense] raison *f* / *he won't listen to reason* il refuse d'entendre raison **3.** [rationality] raison *f*. ❖ vi raisonner ▶ **to reason with sb** raisonner qqn. ❖ vt **1.** [maintain] maintenir, soutenir ; [work out] calculer, déduire ; [conclude] conclure **2.** [persuade] : *she reasoned me into / out of going* elle m'a persuadé / dissuadé d'y aller. ❖ **by reason of** prep phr en raison de. ❖ **for reasons of** prep phr : *for reasons of space / national security* pour des raisons de place / sécurité nationale. ❖ **within reason** adv phr dans la limite du raisonnable. ❖ **reason out** vt sep résoudre *(par la raison)*.

reasonable [ˈriːznəbl] adj **1.** [sensible - person, behaviour, attitude] raisonnable ; [- explanation, decision] raisonnable, sensé **2.** [moderate - price] raisonnable, correct ; [- restaurant] qui pratique des prix raisonnables **3.** [fair, acceptable - offer, suggestion] raisonnable, acceptable.

reasonably [ˈriːznəblɪ] adv **1.** [behave, argue] raisonnablement **2.** [quite, rather] : *reasonably good* assez bien, pas mal.

reasoned [ˈriːznd] adj [argument, decision] raisonné.

reasoning [ˈriːznɪŋ] n raisonnement *m*.

reassemble [ˌriːəˈsembl] ❖ vt **1.** [people, arguments] rassembler **2.** [machinery] remonter. ❖ vi se rassembler.

reassert [ˌriːəˈsɜːt] vt [authority] réaffirmer.

reassess [ˌriːəˈses] vt **1.** [position, opinion] réexaminer **2.** FIN [damages] réévaluer ; [taxation] réviser.

reassessment [ˌriːəˈsesmənt] n **1.** [of position, opinion] réexamen *m* **2.** FIN [of damages] réévaluation *f* ; [of taxes] révision *f*.

reassign [ˌriːəˈsaɪn] vt réaffecter.

reassurance [ˌriːəˈʃɔːrəns] n **1.** [comforting] réconfort *m* **2.** [guarantee] assurance *f*, confirmation *f*.

reassure [ˌriːəˈʃɔːr] vt **1.** [gen] rassurer **2.** FIN réassurer.

reassuring [ˌriːəˈʃɔːrɪŋ] adj rassurant.

reassuringly [ˌriːəˈʃɔːrɪŋlɪ] adv d'une manière rassurante ; [as intensifier] : *reassuringly simple* d'une grande simplicité.

reawaken [ˌriːəˈweɪkn] ❖ vt [person] réveiller ; [concern, interest] réveiller ; [feelings] faire renaître, raviver. ❖ vi [person] se réveiller de nouveau.

reawakening [ˌriːəˈweɪknɪŋ] n [of sleeper] réveil *m* ; [of interest, concern] réveil *m*.

rebate [ˈriːbeɪt] n [reduction - on goods] remise *f*, ristourne *f* ; [- on tax] dégrèvement *m* ; [refund] remboursement *m*.

rebel (*pt & pp* **rebelled**, *cont* **rebelling**) ❖ n [ˈrebl] [in revolution] rebelle *mf*, insurgé *m*, -e *f* ; *fig* rebelle *mf*. ❖ adj [ˈrebl] [soldier] rebelle ; [camp, territory] des rebelles ; [attack] de rebelles. ❖ vi [rɪˈbel] se rebeller ▶ **to rebel against sthg / sb** se révolter contre qqch / qqn ; *hum* [stomach] : *my stomach rebelled* mon estomac a protesté.

rebellion [rɪˈbeljən] n rébellion *f*, révolte *f* ▶ **to rise (up) in rebellion against sthg / sb** se révolter contre qqch / qqn.

rebellious [rɪˈbeljəs] adj [child, hair] rebelle ; [troops] insoumis.

rebirth [,ri:'bɜ:θ] n renaissance f.

reboot [ri:'bu:t] vt [computer] réinitialiser, réamorcer offic; [programme] relancer.

reborn [,ri:'bɔ:n] adj réincarné ▶ **to be reborn** renaître.

rebound ◆ vi [rɪ'baʊnd] **1.** [ball] rebondir **2.** fig ▶ **to rebound on sb** se retourner contre qqn **3.** [recover - business] reprendre, repartir ; [-prices] remonter. ◆ n ['ri:baʊnd] **1.** [of ball] rebond m **2.** PHR **to be on the rebound a)** [after relationship] être sous le coup d'une déception sentimentale **b)** [after setback] être sous le coup d'un échec.

re-brand vt ▶ **to re-brand something** effectuer le re-branding de qqch.

rebranding [ri:'brændɪŋ] n changement m de marque, rebranding m.

rebuff [rɪ'bʌf] ◆ vt [snub] rabrouer ; [reject] repousser. ◆ n rebuffade f.

rebuild [,ri:'bɪld] (pt & pp **rebuilt** [-'bɪlt]) vt [town, economy] rebâtir, reconstruire ; [relationship, life] reconstruire ; [confidence] faire renaître.

rebuke [rɪ'bju:k] ◆ vt [reprimand] réprimander ▶ **to rebuke sb for sthg** reprocher qqch à qqn ▶ **to rebuke sb for doing** or **having done sthg** reprocher à qqn d'avoir fait qqch. ◆ n reproche m, réprimande f.

rebut [ri:'bʌt] (pt & pp **rebutted**, cont **rebutting**) vt réfuter.

rebuttal [ri:'bʌtl] n réfutation f.

rec. written abbr of **received**.

recalcitrant [rɪ'kælsɪtrənt] adj fml récalcitrant.

recall ◆ vt [rɪ'kɔ:l] **1.** [remember] se rappeler, se souvenir de / **I don't recall seeing** or **having seen her** je ne me rappelle pas l'avoir vue **2.** [evoke - past] rappeler **3.** [send for - actor, ambassador] rappeler ; [-Parliament] rappeler (en session extraordinaire) ; [-library book, hire car] demander le retour de ; [-faulty goods] rappeler **4.** MIL rappeler. ◆ n ['ri:kɔ:l] **1.** [memory] rappel m, mémoire f **2.** MIL rappel m. ◆ comp ▶ **recall button** [on phone] rappel m automatique ▶ **recall rate** taux m de mémorisation ▶ **recall slip** [for library book] fiche f de rappel.

recant [rɪ'kænt] ◆ vt [religion] abjurer ; [opinion] rétracter. ◆ vi [from religion] abjurer ; [from opinion] se rétracter.

recap ['ri:kæp] (pt & pp **recapped**, cont **recapping**) ◆ n [summary] récapitulation f. ◆ vt [summarize] récapituler.

recapitulate [,ri:kə'pɪtjʊleɪt] vt récapituler.

recapture [,ri:'kæptʃər] ◆ vt **1.** [prisoner, town] reprendre ; [animal] capturer **2.** [regain - confidence] reprendre ; [-feeling, spirit] retrouver ; [evoke - subj: film, book, play] recréer, faire revivre **3.** US FIN saisir. ◆ n **1.** [of escapee, animal] capture f ; [of town] reprise f **2.** US FIN saisie f.

recd, **rec'd** written abbr of **received**.

recede [ri:'si:d] ◆ vi **1.** [move away - object] s'éloigner ; [-waters] refluer ; [-tide] descendre **2.** [fade - hopes] s'évanouir ; [-fears] s'estomper ; [-danger] s'éloigner **3.** [hairline] : **his hair has started to recede** son front commence à se dégarnir **4.** FIN baisser. ◆ vt LAW [right] rétrocéder ; [land] recéder.

receding [rɪ'si:dɪŋ] adj **1.** [hair] ▶ **to have a receding hairline** avoir le front qui se dégarnit **2.** FIN en baisse.

receipt [rɪ'si:t] ◆ n **1.** [for purchase] reçu m, ticket m de caisse ; [for bill] acquit m ; [for rent, insurance] quittance f ; [for meal, taxi fare] reçu m ; [from customs] récépissé m **2.** [reception] réception f. ◆ vt US acquitter. ❖ **receipts** pl n [money] recettes fpl.

receivable [rɪ'si:vəbl] adj recevable ; COMM [outstanding] à recevoir ▶ **accounts receivable** comptes mpl clients, créances fpl.

receive [rɪ'si:v] ◆ vt **1.** [gift, letter] recevoir ▶ **to receive sthg from sb** recevoir qqch de qqn **2.** [blow] recevoir ; [insult, refusal] essuyer ; [criticism] être l'objet de **3.** [greet, welcome] accueillir, recevoir ; [into club, organization] admettre **4.** [signal, broadcast] recevoir, capter **5.** SPORT ▶ **to receive service** recevoir le service **6.** LAW [stolen goods] receler **7.** fml [accommodate] recevoir, prendre. ◆ vi **1.** fml [have guests] recevoir **2.** SPORT recevoir, être le receveur **3.** RELIG recevoir la communion **4.** LAW [thief] receler.

Received Pronunciation n UK prononciation f standard (de l'anglais).

Received Standard n US prononciation f standard (de l'américain).

receiver [rɪ'si:vər] n **1.** [gen & SPORT] receveur m, -euse f ; [of consignment] destinataire mf, consignataire mf ; [of stolen goods] receleur m, -euse f **2.** [on telephone] combiné m, récepteur m **3.** TV récepteur m, poste m de télévision ; RADIO récepteur m, poste m de radio **4.** FIN administrateur m judiciaire **5.** CHEM récipient m.

receivership [rɪ'si:vəʃɪp] n FIN ▶ **to go into receivership** être placé sous administration judiciaire.

receiving end n PHR ▶ **to be on the receiving end** inf : **if anything goes wrong, you'll be on the receiving end** si ça tourne mal, c'est toi qui vas payer les pots cassés.

recent ['ri:snt] adj [new] récent, nouveau (before vowel or silent 'h' **nouvel**, f **nouvelle**) ; [modern] récent, moderne.

recently ['ri:sntlɪ] adv récemment, dernièrement, ces derniers temps.

receptacle [rɪ'septəkl] n **1.** fml [container] récipient m **2.** US ELEC prise f de courant (femelle).

reception [rɪ'sepʃn] n **1.** [welcome] réception f, accueil m **2.** [formal party] réception f **3.** [in hotel] réception f ; [in office] accueil m / **at reception** à la réception **4.** RADIO & TV réception f **5.** US SPORT [of ball] réception f **6.** UK SCH ≃ cours m préparatoire ▶ **reception class** première année f de maternelle.

reception centre n UK centre m d'accueil.

reception desk n [in hotel] réception f ; [in office] accueil m.

receptionist [rɪ'sepʃənɪst] n [in hotel] réceptionniste mf ; [in office] hôtesse f d'accueil.

reception room n [in hotel] salle f de réception ; UK [in house] salon m.

receptive [rɪ'septɪv] adj [open] réceptif.

receptiveness [rɪ'septɪvnɪs], **receptivity** [,resep-'tɪvətɪ] n réceptivité f.

recess [UK rɪ'ses US 'ri:ses] ◆ n **1.** [alcove - gen] renfoncement m ; [-in bedroom] alcôve f ; [for statue] niche f ; [in doorway] embrasure f **2.** [of mind, memory] recoin m, tréfonds m **3.** US LAW suspension f d'audience **4.** US SCH récréation f **5.** [closure - of parliament] vacances fpl parlementaires, intersession f parlementaire ; [-of courts] vacances fpl judiciaires, vacations fpl. ◆ vi US LAW suspendre l'audience ; POL suspendre la séance. ◆ vt encastrer.

recessed [UK rɪ'sest US 'ri:sest] adj encastré.

recession [rɪ'seʃn] n **1.** ECON récession f **2.** fml [retreat] recul m, retraite f **3.** RELIG sortie f en procession du clergé **4.** LAW rétrocession f.

recessionary [rɪ'seʃənrɪ] adj ECON de crise, de récession.

recessive [rɪ'sesɪv] adj **1.** [gene] récessif **2.** [backward - measure] rétrograde.

recharge ◆ vt [ˌriːˈtʃɑːdʒ] [battery, rifle] recharger. ◆ n [ˈriːˈtʃɑːdʒ] recharge f.

rechargeable [ˌriːˈtʃɑːdʒəbl] adj rechargeable.

rechip [ˌriːˈtʃɪp] vt [mobile phone] reprogrammer la puce de.

recipe [ˈresɪpɪ] n CULIN recette f; fig recette f ▶ **recipe book** livre m de recettes.

recipient [rɪˈsɪpɪənt] n **1.** [of letter] destinataire mf; [of cheque] bénéficiaire mf; [of award, honour] récipiendaire m **2.** MED [of transplant] receveur m, -euse f.

reciprocal [rɪˈsɪprəkl] adj [mutual] réciproque, mutuel; [bilateral] réciproque, bilatéral; GRAM & MATH réciproque.

reciprocate [rɪˈsɪprəkeɪt] ◆ vt [favour, invitation, smile] rendre; [love, sentiment] répondre à, rendre. ◆ vi [in praise, compliments] retourner le compliment; [in fight] rendre coup pour coup; [in dispute] rendre la pareille; [in argument] répondre du tac au tac.

reciprocity [ˌresɪˈprɒsətɪ] n réciprocité f.

recital [rɪˈsaɪtl] n **1.** MUS & LITER récital m **2.** [narrative] narration f, relation f; [of details] énumération f.

recitation [ˌresɪˈteɪʃn] n récitation f.

recite [rɪˈsaɪt] ◆ vt [play, poem] réciter, déclamer; [details, facts] réciter, énumérer. ◆ vi réciter; US SCH réciter sa leçon.

reckless [ˈreklɪs] adj **1.** [rash] imprudent; [thoughtless] irréfléchi; [fearless] téméraire **2.** ADMIN & LAW ▶ **reckless driving** conduite f imprudente ▶ **reckless driver** conducteur m imprudent, conductrice f imprudente.

recklessly [ˈreklɪslɪ] adv [rashly] imprudemment; [thoughtlessly] sans réfléchir; [fearlessly] avec témérité.

recklessness [ˈreklɪsnɪs] n [rashness] imprudence f; [thoughtlessness] insouciance f, étourderie f; [fearlessness] témérité f.

reckon [ˈrekn] ◆ vt **1.** [estimate] : there were reckoned to be about fifteen hundred demonstrators on a estimé à mille cinq cents le nombre des manifestants **2.** [consider] considérer / I reckon this restaurant to be the best in town je considère ce restaurant comme le meilleur de la ville **3.** inf [suppose, think] croire, supposer **4.** [expect] compter, penser **5.** fml [calculate] calculer. ◆ vi [calculate] calculer, compter. ❖ **reckon on** vt insep **1.** [rely on] compter sur **2.** [expect] s'attendre à, espérer. ❖ **reckon up** ◆ vt sep [bill, total, cost] calculer. ◆ vi faire ses comptes ▶ **to reckon up with sb** régler ses comptes avec qqn. ❖ **reckon with** vt insep **1.** [take into account] tenir compte de, songer à; [as opponent] avoir affaire à **2.** [cope with] compter avec. ❖ **reckon without** vt insep US **1.** [do without] se passer de, se débrouiller sans **2.** inf [ignore, overlook] : he reckoned without the gold price il n'a pas pris en compte le cours de l'or.

reckoning [ˈrekənɪŋ] n **1.** (U) [calculation] calcul m, compte m **2.** [estimation] estimation f; [opinion] avis m.

reclaim [rɪˈkleɪm] ◆ vt **1.** [land - gen] mettre en valeur **2.** [salvage] récupérer; [recycle] recycler **3.** [deposit, baggage] récupérer, réclamer **4.** liter [sinner, drunkard] ramener dans le droit chemin. ◆ n ▶ **to be past** or **beyond reclaim** être irrécupérable.

reclamation [ˌrekləˈmeɪʃn] n **1.** [of land - gen] remise f en valeur; [- from forest] défrichement m; [- from sea, marsh] assèchement m, drainage m; [- from desert] reconquête f **2.** [salvage] récupération f; [recycling] recyclage m.

reclassify [ˌriːˈklæsɪfaɪ] (pt & pp reclassified) vt reclasser.

recline [rɪˈklaɪn] ◆ vt **1.** [head] appuyer **2.** [seat] baisser, incliner. ◆ vi **1.** [be stretched out] être allongé, être étendu; [lie back] s'allonger **2.** [seat] être inclinable, avoir un dossier inclinable.

recliner [rɪˈklaɪnər] n [for sunbathing] chaise f longue; [armchair] fauteuil m à dossier inclinable, fauteuil m relax.

reclining [rɪˈklaɪnɪŋ] adj [seat] inclinable, à dossier inclinable.

recluse [rɪˈkluːs] n reclus m, -e f.

reclusive [rɪˈkluːsɪv] adj reclus.

recognition [ˌrekəɡˈnɪʃn] n **1.** [identification] reconnaissance f / the town has changed beyond or out of all recognition la ville est méconnaissable ▶ **optical / speech / character recognition** COMPUT reconnaissance optique / de la parole / de caractères **2.** [acknowledgment, thanks] reconnaissance f ▶ **in recognition of** en reconnaissance de **3.** [appreciation] ▶ **to win** or **to achieve recognition** être (enfin) reconnu ▶ **public recognition** la reconnaissance du public **4.** [realization - of problem] reconnaissance f **5.** [of state, organization, trade union] reconnaissance f.

recognizable, recognisable [ˈrekəɡnaɪzəbl] adj reconnaissable.

recognizably, recognisably [ˈrekəɡnaɪzəblɪ] adv d'une manière or façon reconnaissable.

recognize, recognise [ˈrekəɡnaɪz] vt **1.** [identify - person, place, etc.] reconnaître; COMPUT reconnaître **2.** [acknowledge - person] reconnaître les talents de; [- achievement] reconnaître **3.** [be aware of, admit] reconnaître **4.** ADMIN & POL [state, diploma] reconnaître **5.** US [in debate] donner la parole à.

recognized, recognised [ˈrekəɡnaɪzd] adj [acknowledged] reconnu, admis; [identified] reconnu; [official] officiel, attitré.

recoil ◆ vi [rɪˈkɔɪl] **1.** [person] reculer ▶ **to recoil from doing sthg** reculer devant l'idée de faire qqch **2.** [firearm] reculer; [spring] se détendre. ◆ n [ˈriːkɔɪl] **1.** [of gun] recul m; [of spring] détente f **2.** [of person] mouvement m de recul; fig répugnance f.

recollect [ˌrekəˈlekt] vt se souvenir de, se rappeler / as far as I (can) recollect autant que je m'en souvienne, autant qu'il m'en souvienne.

recollection [ˌrekəˈlekʃn] n [memory] souvenir m / I have no recollection of it je n'en ai aucun souvenir / to the best of my recollection (pour) autant que je m'en souvienne.

recommence [ˌriːkəˈmens] vi & vt recommencer.

recommend [ˌrekəˈmend] vt **1.** [speak in favour of] recommander / she recommended him for the job elle l'a recommandé pour cet emploi; [think or speak well of] recommander / the book has been highly recommended to me le livre m'a été fortement recommandé / it's a restaurant I can thoroughly recommend c'est un restaurant que je recommande vivement **2.** [advise] recommander, conseiller / not (to be) recommended à déconseiller / to recommend that... recommander que... (+ subjunctive) ▶ **recommended** [in film, book review] à voir / lire ▶ **recommended reading** ouvrages mpl recommandés.

> 🗒 Note that recommander que is followed by a verb in the subjunctive:
> **We recommend that the session should be open to all.** Nous recommandons que la séance soit ouverte à tous.

recommendable [ˌrekəˈmendəbl] adj recommandable.

recommendation [ˌrekəmenˈdeɪʃn] n [personal] recommandation f / on your / his recommendation sur votre / sa recommandation; [of committee, advisory body] recommandation f.

recommended daily allowance or **intake** n apport *m* quotidien recommandé.

recommended retail price [ˌrekə'mendɪd-] n prix *m* de vente conseillé.

recompense ['rekəmpens] ◆ n **1.** [reward] récompense *f* **2.** LAW [compensation] dédommagement *m*, compensation *f*. ◆ vt récompenser ▸ **to recompense sb for sthg a)** [gen] récompenser qqn de qqch **b)** LAW dédommager qqn de or pour qqch.

reconcilable ['rekənsaɪləbl] adj [opinions] conciliable, compatible ; [people] compatible.

reconcile ['rekənsaɪl] vt **1.** [people] réconcilier ; [ideas, opposing principles] concilier **2.** [resign] ▸ **to reconcile o.s.** or **to become reconciled to sthg** se résigner à qqch **3.** [win over] ▸ **to reconcile sb to sthg** faire accepter qqch à qqn **4.** [settle - dispute] régler, arranger.

reconciliation [ˌrekənsɪlɪ'eɪʃn] n [between people] réconciliation *f* ; [between ideas] conciliation *f*, compatibilité *f*.

recondite ['rekəndaɪt] adj *fml* [taste] ésotérique ; [text, style] abscons, obscur ; [writer] obscur.

reconditioned [ˌriːkən'dɪʃnd] adj remis à neuf ; <u>UK</u> [tyre] rechapé ▸ **reconditioned engine** AUTO (moteur *m*) échange *m* standard.

reconfigure [ˌriːkən'fɪɡər] vt COMPUT reconfigurer.

reconnaissance [rɪ'kɒnɪsəns] n MIL reconnaissance *f* ▸ **reconnaissance flight** vol *m* de reconnaissance.

reconnect [ˌriːkə'nekt] vt rebrancher ; TELEC reconnecter.

reconnoitre <u>UK</u>, **reconnoiter** <u>US</u> [ˌrekə'nɔɪtər] ◆ vt MIL reconnaître. ◆ vi effectuer une reconnaissance.

reconquest [ˌriː'kɒŋkwest] n reconquête *f*.

reconsider [ˌriːkən'sɪdər] ◆ vt [decision, problem] réexaminer ; [topic] se repencher sur ; [judgment] réviser, revoir. ◆ vi reconsidérer la question.

reconsideration ['riːkənˌsɪdə'reɪʃn] n [reexamination] nouvel examen *m*, nouveau regard *m* ; [of judgment] révision *f*.

reconstitute [ˌriː'kɒnstɪtjuːt] vt reconstituer.

reconstituted [ˌriː'kɒnstɪtjuːtɪd] adj reconstitué.

reconstruct [ˌriːkən'strʌkt] vt [house, bridge] reconstruire, rebâtir ; [crime, event] reconstituer ; [government, system] reconstituer.

reconstruction [ˌriːkən'strʌkʃn] n [of demolished building] reconstruction *f* ; [of old building] reconstitution *f* ; [of façade, shop] réfection *f* ; [of crime, event] reconstitution *f* ; [of government] reconstitution *f* ▸ **the Reconstruction** <u>US</u> HIST la Reconstruction.

🏛 **The Reconstruction**

Période allant de 1865 à 1877, succédant à la guerre de Sécession et pendant laquelle les États de l'ex-Confédération (États sudistes) étaient réintégrés dans l'Union s'ils avaient adopté les amendements à la Constitution fédérale qui reconnaissaient les droits des Noirs et interdisaient aux confédérés toute activité politique et administrative.

reconstructive surgery [riːkən'strʌktɪv-] n chirurgie *f* réparatrice.

reconvene [ˌriːkən'viːn] ◆ vt reconvoquer. ◆ vi : *the meeting reconvenes at three* la réunion reprend à trois heures.

record ◆ vt [rɪ'kɔːd] **1.** [take note of - fact, complaint, detail] noter, enregistrer ; [- in archives, on computer] enre-

gistrer ; [attest, give account of] attester, rapporter ; [explain, tell] raconter, rapporter **2.** [indicate - measurement] indiquer ; [- permanently] enregistrer **3.** [music, tape, TV programme] enregistrer **4.** SPORT [score] marquer. ◆ vi [rɪ'kɔːd] [on tape, video] enregistrer. ◆ n ['rekɔːd] **1.** [account, report] rapport *m* ; [note] note *f* ; [narrative] récit *m* ▸ **to make a record of sthg** noter qqch ; [testimony] témoignage *m* ; [evidence] preuve *f* ; [from instrument] trace *f* ; [graph] courbe *f* **2.** [past history] passé *m* ; [file] dossier *m* ; [criminal or police file] casier *m* (judiciaire) ; [reputation] réputation *f* ▸ **service** or **army record** MIL états *mpl* de service ▸ **school record** dossier *m* scolaire **3.** [disc] disque *m* ; [recording] enregistrement *m* **4.** [gen & SPORT] record *m* **5.** COMPUT enregistrement *m*. ◆ comp ['rekɔːd] **1.** [company, label, producer, shop] de disques **2.** [summer, temperature] record *(inv)* / *in record time* en un temps record / *a record score* un score record / *to reach record levels* atteindre un niveau record / *a record number of spectators* une affluence record. ◆ **records** pl n [of government, police, hospital] archives *fpl* ; [of history] annales *fpl* ; [of conference, learned society] actes *mpl* ; [register] registre *m* ; [of proceedings, debate] procès-verbal *m*, compte rendu *m* ▸ **public records office** archives *fpl* nationales. ◆ **for the record** adv phr pour mémoire, pour la petite histoire. ◆ **off the record** ◆ adj phr confidentiel. ◆ adv phr : *he admitted off the record that he had known* il a admis en privé qu'il était au courant. ◆ **on record** adv phr enregistré / *I wish to go on record as saying that...* je voudrais dire officiellement or publiquement que... / *it's the wettest June on record* c'est le mois de juin le plus humide que l'on ait connu.

record-breaker n SPORT nouveau recordman *m*, nouvelle recordwoman *f*.

record-breaking adj **1.** SPORT : *a record-breaking jump* un saut qui a établi un nouveau record **2.** [year, temperatures] record *(inv)*.

recorded [rɪ'kɔːdɪd] adj **1.** [music, message, tape] enregistré ; [programme] préenregistré ; [broadcast] transmis en différé **2.** [fact] attesté, noté ; [history] écrit ; [votes] exprimé.

recorded delivery n <u>UK</u> recommandé *m* ▸ **to send (by) recorded delivery** envoyer en recommandé avec accusé de réception.

recorder [rɪ'kɔːdər] n **1.** [apparatus] enregistreur *m* **2.** [musical instrument] flûte *f* à bec **3.** [keeper of records] archiviste *mf* ▸ **court recorder** LAW greffier *m*.

record holder n recordman *m*, recordwoman *f*, détenteur *m*, -trice *f* d'un record.

recording [rɪ'kɔːdɪŋ] ◆ n [of music, data] enregistrement *m*. ◆ comp **1.** MUS & TV [equipment, session, studio] d'enregistrement ; [company] de disques ; [star] du disque **2.** [indicating - apparatus] enregistreur **3.** ADMIN & LAW [official, clerk - in census] chargé du recensement ; [- in court of law] qui enregistre les débats.

recording studio n studio *m* d'enregistrement.

record library n discothèque *f* (de prêt).

record player n tourne-disque *m*, platine *f* (disques).

recount [rɪ'kaunt] vt [story, experience] raconter.

recoup [rɪ'kuːp] vt **1.** [get back - losses, cost] récupérer / *to recoup one's costs* rentrer dans or couvrir ses frais **2.** [pay back] rembourser, dédommager **3.** [from taxes] défalquer, déduire.

recourse [rɪ'kɔːs] n **1.** [gen] recours *m* ▸ **to have recourse to sthg** recourir à qqch, avoir recours à qqch **2.** FIN recours *m*.

recover [rɪ'kʌvər] ◆ vt **1.** [get back - property] récupérer, retrouver ; [- debt, loan, deposit] récupérer, recouvrer ; [take back] reprendre ▸ **to recover sthg from sb** reprendre qqch à qqn ; [regain - territory, ball] regagner ;

[-composure, control, hearing] retrouver ; [-advantage] re-prendre **2.** [salvage -wreck, waste] récupérer ; [-from water] récupérer, repêcher **3.** LAW : *to recover damages* obtenir des dommages-intérêts **4.** [extract -from ore] extraire. ◆ vi **1.** [after accident] se remettre ; [after illness] se rétablir, guérir ▶ **to recover from sthg** se remettre de qqch ; [after surprise, setback] se remettre **2.** [currency, economy] se redresser ; [market] reprendre, se redresser ; [prices, shares] se redresser, remonter **3.** LAW gagner son procès, obtenir gain de cause.

recoverable [rɪ'kʌvrəbl] adj [debt] recouvrable ; [losses, mistake] réparable ; [by-product] récupérable.

recovery [rɪ'kʌvərɪ] *(pl* **recoveries)** n **1.** [of lost property, wreck] récupération *f* ; [of debt] recouvrement *m*, récupération *f* **2.** [from illness] rétablissement *m*, guéri-son *f* **3.** [of economy] relance *f*, redressement *m* ; [of prices, shares] redressement *m*, remontée *f* ; [of currency] redresse-ment *m* ; [of market, business] reprise *f* **4.** [of wreck, waste] récupération *f* ; [from water] récupération *f*, repêchage *m* **5.** COMPUT [of files] récupération *f* **6.** LAW [of damages] obtention *f*.

recovery position n MED position *f* latérale de sécu-rité.

recovery vehicle n 𝖴𝖪 dépanneuse *f*.

re-create [ˌriː'krɪeɪt] vt [past event] reconstituer ; [place, scene] recréer.

recreation [ˌrekrɪ'eɪʃn] n [relaxation] récréation *f*, dé-tente *f* / *she only reads for* or *as recreation* elle ne lit que pour se délasser or se détendre.

recreational [ˌrekrɪ'eɪʃənl] adj de loisir ▶ **recreational drug** drogue *f* douce ▶ **recreational facilities** équipe-ments *mpl* de loisirs.

recreational vehicle 𝖴𝖲 = RV.

recreation ground n terrain *m* de jeu.

recreation room n [in school, hospital] salle *f* de ré-création ; [in hotel] salle *f* de jeu ; [at home] salle *f* de jeu.

recrimination [rɪˌkrɪmɪ'neɪʃn] n *(usu pl)* ▶ **recrimin-ations** récriminations *fpl*.

recrudescence [ˌriːkruː'desns] n *fml* recrudescence *f*.

recruit [rɪ'kruːt] ◆ n [gen & MIL] recrue *f*. ◆ vt [mem-ber, army] recruter ; [worker] recruter, embaucher.

recruiting [rɪ'kruːtɪŋ] n recrutement *m*.

recruitment [rɪ'kruːtmənt] n recrutement *m* ▶ **recruit-ment agency** cabinet *m* de recrutement ▶ **recruitment consultant** consultant *m*, -e *f* en recrutement.

rectangle ['rekˌtæŋgl] n rectangle *m*.

rectangular [rek'tæŋgjʊlər] adj rectangulaire.

rectification [ˌrektɪfɪ'keɪʃn] n **1.** [correction] rectifi-cation *f*, correction *f* **2.** CHEM & MATH rectification *f* ; ELEC redressement *m*.

rectify ['rektɪfaɪ] *(pt & pp* **rectified)** vt [mistake] recti-fier, corriger ; [oversight] réparer ; [situation] redresser.

rectitude ['rektɪtjuːd] n rectitude *f*.

rector ['rektər] n **1.** RELIG [Anglican, Presbyterian] pas-teur *m* ; [Catholic] recteur *m* **2.** 𝖴𝖪 SCH proviseur *m*, direc-teur *m*, -trice *f* **3.** 𝖲𝖼𝗈𝗍 UNIV président *m*, -e *f* d'honneur.

rectory ['rektərɪ] *(pl* **rectories)** n presbytère *m*.

rectum ['rektəm] *(pl* **rectums** or **recta** [-tə])** n rec-tum *m*.

recuperate [rɪ'kuːpəreɪt] ◆ vi se remettre, récupé-rer ; [after illness] se rétablir ▶ **to recuperate from sthg** se remettre de qqch. ◆ vt [materials, money] récupérer ; [loss] compenser ; [strength] reprendre.

recuperation [rɪˌkuːpə'reɪʃn] n **1.** MED rétablisse-ment *m* **2.** [of materials] récupération *f* **3.** FIN [of market] reprise *f*.

recur [rɪ'kɜːr] *(pt & pp* **recurred,** *cont* **recurring)** vi **1.** [occur again] se reproduire ; [reappear] réapparaître, reve-nir **2.** [to memory] revenir à la mémoire **3.** MATH se repro-duire, se répéter.

recurrence [rɪ'kʌrəns] n [of mistake, notion, event] répé-tition *f* ; [of disease, symptoms] réapparition *f* ; [of subject, problem] retour *m*.

recurrent [rɪ'kʌrənt] adj **1.** [repeated] récurrent ▶ **recurrent expenses a)** [gen] dépenses *fpl* courantes **b)** COMM frais *mpl* généraux **2.** ANAT & MED récurrent.

recurring [rɪ'kɜːrɪŋ] adj **1.** [persistent -problem] qui revient or qui se reproduit souvent ; [-dream, nightmare] qui revient sans cesse **2.** MATH périodique.

recyclable [ˌriː'saɪkləbl] adj recyclable.

recycle [ˌriː'saɪkl] vt [materials] recycler ; [money] réinves-tir.

recycle bin n COMPUT poubelle *f*, corbeille *f*.

recycled [ˌriː'saɪkld] adj [materials] recyclé ▶ **recycled paper** papier *m* recyclé.

recycling [ˌriː'saɪklɪŋ] n recyclage *m*.

recycling plant n usine *f* de recyclage.

red [red] *(compar* **redder,** *superl* **reddest)** ◆ adj **1.** [gen] rouge ; [hair] roux (rousse) ▶ **to go red** rougir ▶ **red with anger / shame** rouge de colère / honte ▶ **to be red in the face a)** [after effort] avoir la figure toute rouge **b)** [with embarrassment] être rouge de confusion ▶ **to go into red ink a)** 𝖴𝖲 [person] être à découvert **b)** [company] être en déficit ▶ **to be as red as a beetroot** être rouge comme une pivoine or une écrevisse **2.** *inf* POL rouge. ◆ n **1.** [colour] rouge *m* ▶ **to see red** voir rouge **2.** [in roulette] rouge *m* ; [in snooker] (bille *f*) rouge *f* **3.** [wine] rouge *m* **4.** *inf & pej* [communist] rouge *mf*, coco *mf pej* **5.** [deficit] ▶ **to be in the red** être dans le rouge / *to be £5,000 in the red* **a)** [company] avoir un déficit de 5 000 livres **b)** [person] avoir un découvert de 5 000 livres.

redact [rɪ'dækt] vt **1.** [write] rédiger **2.** [edit] modifier.

redaction [rɪ'dækʃən] n **1.** [writing] rédaction *f* **2.** [edit-ing] modification *f*.

red alert n alerte *f* rouge ▶ **to be on red alert** être en état d'alerte maximale.

Red Army pr n Armée *f* rouge.

red blood cell n globule *m* rouge, hématie *f*.

red-blooded [-'blʌdɪd] adj *inf* vigoureux, viril.

red-brick adj 𝖴𝖪 [building] en brique rouge.

redbrick university ['redbrɪk-] n *en Angleterre, uni-versité de création relativement récente par opposition à Oxford et Cambridge.*

red card n SPORT carton *m* rouge.

red carpet n tapis *m* rouge ▶ **to roll out the red carpet for sb a)** [for VIP] dérouler le tapis rouge en l'honneur de qqn **b)** [for guest] mettre les petits plats dans les grands en l'honneur de qqn ▶ **to give sb the red-carpet treatment** réserver un accueil fastueux or princier à qqn.

red corpuscle n globule *m* rouge, hématie *f*.

Red Crescent pr n Croissant-Rouge *m*.

Red Cross (Society) pr n Croix-Rouge *f*.

redcurrant ['redkʌrənt] n groseille *f* (rouge) ▶ **redcur-rant bush** groseillier *m* rouge ▶ **redcurrant jelly** gelée *f* de groseille.

red deer n cerf *m* commun.

redden ['redn] ◆ vt rougir, rendre rouge ; [hair] teindre en roux. ◆ vi [person, face] rougir, devenir (tout) rouge ; [leaves] devenir roux, roussir.

reddish ['redɪʃ] adj rougeâtre ; [fur] roussâtre ; [hair] rous-sâtre, qui tire sur le roux.

redecorate [ˌriː'dekəreɪt] ◆ vt [gen - room, house] refaire ; [repaint] refaire les peintures de ; [re-wallpaper] retapisser. ◆ vi [repaint] refaire les peintures ; [re-wallpaper] refaire les papiers peints.

redecoration [riːˌdekə'reɪʃn] n [painting] remise f à neuf des peintures ; [wallpapering] remise f à neuf des papiers peints.

redeem [rɪ'diːm] vt **1.** [from pawn] dégager, retirer **2.** [cash - voucher] encaisser ; [- bond, share] réaliser ; [exchange - coupon, savings stamps] échanger ; [- banknote] compenser **3.** [pay - debt] rembourser, s'acquitter de ; [- bill] honorer ; [- loan, mortgage] rembourser **4.** [make up for - mistake, failure] racheter, réparer ; [- crime, sin] expier ▶ **to redeem o.s.** se racheter **5.** [save - situation, position] sauver ; [- loss] récupérer, réparer ; [- honour] sauver ; RELIG [sinner] racheter **6.** [fulfil - promise] s'acquitter de, tenir ; [- obligation] satisfaire à, s'acquitter de **7.** [free - slave] affranchir.

redeemable [rɪ'diːməbl] adj **1.** [voucher] remboursable ; [debt] remboursable, amortissable **2.** [error] réparable ; [sin, crime] expiable, rachetable ; [sinner] rachetable.

redeeming [rɪ'diːmɪŋ] adj [characteristic, feature] qui rachète or compense les défauts.

redefine [ˌriːdɪ'faɪn] vt [restate - objectives, terms] redéfinir ; [modify] modifier.

redemption [rɪ'dempʃn] n **1.** [from pawn] dégagement m **2.** [of debt, loan, mortgage, voucher] remboursement m ; ST. EX [of shares] liquidation f **3.** [gen & RELIG] rédemption f, rachat m ▶ **past** or **beyond redemption a)** [person] perdu à tout jamais, qui ne peut être racheté **b)** [situation, position] irrémédiable, irrécupérable **c)** [book, furniture] irréparable, irrécupérable.

redeploy [ˌriːdɪ'plɔɪ] vt [troops, forces, resources] redéployer ; [workers] reconvertir.

redeployment [ˌriːdɪ'plɔɪmənt] n [of troops, resources] redéploiement m ; [of workers] reconversion f.

redesign [ˌriːdɪ'zaɪn] vt [plan of room, garden, etc.] redessiner ; [layout of furniture, rooms, etc.] réagencer ; [system] repenser ; [book cover, poster, etc.] refaire le design de.

redevelop [ˌriːdɪ'veləp] vt **1.** [region] réexploiter, revitaliser ; [urban area] rénover, reconstruire ; [tourism, industry] relancer **2.** [argument] réexposer **3.** PHOT redévelopper.

redevelopment [ˌriːdɪ'veləpmənt] n **1.** [of region] revitalisation f, développement m ; [of urban area] rénovation f ; [of tourism, industry] relance f **2.** PHOT redéveloppement m.

red eye n (U) PHOT effet m yeux rouges.

redeye ['redaɪ] n [US] inf [night flight] vol m de nuit.

red-eyed adj aux yeux rouges.

red-faced [-'feɪst] adj lit rougeaud ; fig rouge de confusion or de honte.

red-haired [-ˌheəd] adj roux (rousse), aux cheveux roux / a red-haired girl une rousse.

red-handed [-'hændɪd] adv ▶ **to be caught red-handed** être pris en flagrant délit or la main dans le sac.

redhead ['redhed] n roux m, rousse f.

red-headed = **red-haired**.

red herring n **1.** fig diversion f **2.** CULIN hareng m saur.

red-hot adj **1.** [metal] chauffé au rouge **2.** [very hot] brûlant **3.** inf & fig [keen] passionné, enthousiaste **4.** inf [recent - news, information] de dernière minute **5.** inf [sure - tip, favourite] certain, sûr **6.** inf [expert] calé **7.** inf [sensational - scandal, story] croustillant, sensationnel.

redial [ˌriː'daɪəl] ◆ vt ▶ **to redial a number** refaire un numéro. ◆ n ▶ **automatic redial** système m de rappel du dernier numéro ▶ **redial button** touche f bis ▶ **redial facility** rappel m du dernier numéro.

redid [ˌriː'dɪd] pt ⟶ **redo.**

Red Indian n Peau-Rouge mf.

redirect [ˌriːdɪ'rekt] vt **1.** [mail] faire suivre, réexpédier ; [aeroplane, traffic] dérouter **2.** fig [efforts, attentions] réorienter.

rediscover [ˌriːdɪ'skʌvə°] vt redécouvrir.

rediscovery [ˌriːdɪ'skʌvrɪ] (pl **rediscoveries**) n redécouverte f.

redistribute [ˌriːdɪ'strɪbjuːt] vt [money, wealth, objects] redistribuer ; [tasks] réassigner.

redistribution ['riːˌdɪstrɪ'bjuːʃn] n redistribution f.

red-letter day n jour m à marquer d'une pierre blanche.

red light n AUTO feu m rouge ▶ **to go through a red light** passer au rouge, brûler le feu rouge. ◆◇ **red-light** adj ▶ **red-light district** quartier m chaud.

red meat n viande f rouge.

redneck ['rednek] [US] inf & pej ◆ n Américain d'origine modeste qui a des idées réactionnaires et des préjugés racistes. ◆ comp [attitude] de plouc, borné.

redness ['rednɪs] n (U) rougeur f ; [of hair] rousseur f ; [inflammation] rougeurs fpl.

redo [ˌriː'duː] (pt **redid** [ˌriː'dɪd], pp **redone** [-'dʌn]) vt refaire ; [hair] recoiffer ; [repaint] refaire, repeindre.

redolent ['redələnt] adj liter **1.** [perfumed] : redolent of or with lemon qui sent le citron, qui a une odeur de citron **2.** [evocative, reminiscent] : the style is redolent of James Joyce le style rappelle celui de James Joyce.

redone [-'dʌn] pp ⟶ **redo.**

redouble [ˌriː'dʌbl] vt [in intensity] redoubler ▶ **to redouble one's efforts** redoubler ses efforts or d'efforts.

redoubtable [rɪ'daʊtəbl] adj [formidable] redoutable, terrifiant ; [awe-inspiring] impressionnant.

redraft vt [ˌriː'drɑːft] [bill, contract] rédiger de nouveau ; [demand] reformuler ; [text] remanier.

redraw [ˌriː'drɔː] (pt **redrew** [-'druː], pp **redrawn** [-'drɔːn]) vt redessiner.

redress [rɪ'dres] ◆ vt [grievance, errors] réparer ; [wrong] réparer, redresser ; [situation] rattraper ▶ **to redress the balance** rétablir l'équilibre. ◆ n [gen & LAW] réparation f ▶ **to seek redress for sthg** demander réparation de qqch.

redrew [-'druː] pt ⟶ **redraw.**

Red Sea pr n ▶ **the Red Sea** la mer Rouge.

Red Square pr n la place Rouge.

red squirrel n écureuil m (commun d'Europe).

red state ['redwɪŋ] n [US] État qui vote traditionnellement républicain.

red tape n [bureaucracy] paperasserie f.

reduce [rɪ'djuːs] ◆ vt **1.** [risk, scale, time, workload] réduire, diminuer ; [temperature] abaisser ; [speed] réduire, ralentir ; [in length] réduire, raccourcir ; [in size] réduire, rapetisser, diminuer ; [in weight] réduire, alléger ; [in height] réduire, abaisser ; [in thickness] réduire, amenuiser ; [in strength] réduire, affaiblir **2.** COMM & FIN [price] baisser ; [rate, expenses, cost] réduire ; [tax] alléger, réduire ; [goods] solder, réduire le prix de **3.** [render] ▶ **to reduce sthg to ashes / to a pulp** réduire qqch en cendres / en bouillie ▶ **to reduce sb to silence / to tears / to poverty / to submission** réduire qqn au silence / aux larmes / à la pauvreté / à l'obéissance **4.** CULIN [sauce] faire réduire **5.** CHEM & MATH réduire **6.** MED [fracture] réduire ; [swelling] résorber, résoudre **7.** MIL dégrader. ◆ vi **1.** CULIN réduire **2.** [slim] maigrir.

reduced [rɪ'djuːst] adj [price, rate, scale] réduit ; [goods] soldé, en solde / **'reduced to clear'** 'articles en solde' ▶ **to be in reduced circumstances** euph être dans la gêne.

reduction [rɪ'dʌkʃn] n **1.** [lessening - gen] réduction f, diminution f ; [- in temperature] baisse f, diminution f ; [- in length] réduction f, raccourcissement m ; [- in weight] réduction f, diminution f ; [- in strength] réduction f, affaiblissement m ; [- in speed] réduction f, ralentissement m **2.** COMM & FIN [in cost] baisse f, diminution f ; [in rate] baisse f ; [in expenses] réduction f, diminution f ; [in tax] dégrèvement m ; [on goods] rabais m, remise f **3.** CHEM, MATH & PHOT réduction f **4.** MED [of fracture] réduction f ; [of swelling] résorption f **5.** CULIN réduction f.

reductive [rɪ'dʌktɪv] adj réducteur.

redundancy [rɪ'dʌndənsɪ] (pl **redundancies**) ◆ n **1.** 🇬🇧 [layoff] licenciement m ; [unemployment] chômage m **2.** [superfluousness] caractère m superflu ; [tautology] pléonasme m **3.** COMPUT, LING & TELEC redondance f. ◆ comp ▶ **redundancy notice** 🇬🇧 lettre f de licenciement ▶ **redundancy payment** 🇬🇧 indemnité f de licenciement.

redundant [rɪ'dʌndənt] adj **1.** INDUST licencié, au chômage ▶ **to become** or **to be made redundant** être licencié or mis au chômage **2.** [superfluous] redondant, superflu ; [tautologous] pléonastique **3.** COMPUT, LING & TELEC redondant.

redwood ['redwʊd] n séquoia m.

re-echo [,riː'ekəʊ] ◆ vt renvoyer en écho. ◆ vi retentir.

reed [riːd] ◆ n **1.** BOT roseau m **2.** MUS anche f. ◆ comp [chair, mat] en roseau or roseaux, fait de roseaux.

reed instrument n instrument m à anche.

re-educate [riː'edʒʊkeɪt] vt rééduquer.

reedy ['riːdɪ] (compar **reedier**, superl **reediest**) adj **1.** [place] envahi par les roseaux **2.** [sound, voice] flûté, aigu (aiguë).

reef [riːf] n [in sea] récif m, écueil m ; fig écueil m.

reek [riːk] ◆ vi [smell] puer, empester / it reeks of tobacco in here ça empeste or pue le tabac ici. ◆ n puanteur f.

reel [riːl] ◆ n **1.** [for thread, film, tape] bobine f ; [for hose] dévidoir m, enrouleur m ; [for cable] enrouleur m ; [for rope-making] caret m ▶ **(fishing) reel** moulinet m (de pêche) **2.** [film, tape] bande f, bobine f **3.** [dance] quadrille m (écossais ou irlandais) ; MUS branle m (écossais ou irlandais). ◆ vi **1.** [stagger] tituber, chanceler **2.** fig [whirl - head, mind] tournoyer. ◆ vt bobiner. ◆ **reel in** vt sep [cable, hose] enrouler ; [fish] remonter, ramener ; [line] enrouler, remonter. ◆ **reel off** vt sep [poem, speech, story] débiter.

re-elect [,riː'ɪ'lekt] vt réélire.

re-election [,riː'ɪ'lekʃn] n réélection f.

re-emerge [,riː'ɪ'mɜːdʒ] vi [new facts] ressortir ; [idea, clue] réapparaître ; [problem, question] se reposer ; [from hiding, tunnel] ressortir, ressurgir.

re-emergence [,riː'ɪ'mɜːdʒəns] n réapparition f.

re-emphasize, reemphasise [,riː'emfəsaɪz] vt insister une fois de plus sur, souligner une nouvelle fois.

re-enact [,riː'ɪ'nækt] vt **1.** [scene, crime] reconstituer **2.** ADMIN & POL [legislation] remettre en vigueur.

re-enter [,riː'entər] ◆ vi **1.** [gen] rentrer, entrer à nouveau **2.** [candidate] ▶ **to re-enter for an exam** se réinscrire à un examen. ◆ vt [room, country] rentrer dans, entrer à nouveau dans ; [atmosphere] rentrer dans.

re-entry [,riː'entrɪ] (pl **re-entries**) n **1.** [gen & ASTRONAUT] rentrée f **2.** MUS [of theme] reprise f.

re-establish [,riː'ɪ'stæblɪʃ] vt **1.** [order] rétablir ; [practice] restaurer ; [law] remettre en vigueur **2.** [person] réhabi-

liter, réintégrer / the team have re-established themselves as the best in the country l'équipe s'est imposée de nouveau comme la meilleure du pays.

re-examination [,riːɪg'zæmɪneɪʃn] n [of question] réexamen m ; LAW nouvel interrogatoire m.

re-examine [,riːɪg'zæmɪn] vt [question, case] réexaminer, examiner de nouveau ; [witness] réinterroger, interroger de nouveau ; [candidate] faire repasser un examen à.

re-export ◆ vt [,riː'ek'spɔːt] réexporter. ◆ n [,riː'ekspɔːt] **1.** [of goods] réexportation f **2.** [product] marchandise f de réexportation.

ref [ref] n 🇬🇧 inf abbr of referee.

ref, ref. (written abbr of **reference**) réf. / your ref v/réf.

refectory [rɪ'fektərɪ] (pl **refectories**) n réfectoire m.

refer [rɪ'fɜːr] (pt & pp **referred**, cont **referring**) vt **1.** [submit, pass on] soumettre, renvoyer ; [send, direct] renvoyer ; [in writing, reading] renvoyer **2.** MED : the pain may be referred to another part of the body il peut y avoir irradiation de la douleur dans d'autres parties du corps **3.** UNIV [student] refuser, recaler ; [thesis] renvoyer pour révision. ◆ **refer to** vt insep **1.** [allude to] ▶ **to refer to sthg** faire allusion or référence à qqch, parler de qqch / he keeps referring to me as Dr Rayburn il ne cesse de m'appeler Dr Rayburn **2.** [relate to] correspondre à, faire référence à ; [apply, be connected to] s'appliquer à, s'adresser à **3.** [consult - notes] consulter ; [- book, page, instructions] se reporter à ; [- person] / I shall have to refer to my boss je dois en référer à or consulter mon patron.

referee [,refə'riː] ◆ n **1.** SPORT arbitre m ; TENNIS juge m arbitre **2.** 🇬🇧 [for job] répondant m, -e f **3.** LAW conciliateur m, médiateur m. ◆ vt SPORT arbitrer. ◆ vi SPORT être arbitre.

reference ['refrəns] ◆ n **1.** [allusion] allusion f ▶ **to make a reference to sthg** faire allusion à qqch **2.** [consultation] consultation f / without reference to me sans me consulter **3.** [recommendation - for job] recommandation f, référence f **4.** [in code, catalogue] référence f ; [on map] coordonnées fpl ; [footnote] renvoi m ; COMM référence f **5.** [remit - of commission] compétence f, pouvoirs mpl **6.** LING référence f **7.** LAW [of case] renvoi m. ◆ comp [material, section] de référence ; [value, quantity] de référence, étalon. ◆ vt **1.** [refer to] faire référence à **2.** [thesis] établir la liste des citations dans ; [quotation] donner la référence de. ◆ **with reference to, in reference to** prep phr en ce qui concerne.

reference book n ouvrage m de référence.

reference library n bibliothèque f d'ouvrages de référence.

reference number n numéro m de référence.

referendum [,refə'rendəm] (pl **referendums** or **referenda** [-də]) n référendum m ▶ **to hold a referendum** organiser un référendum.

referral [rɪ'fɜːrəl] n **1.** [forwarding] renvoi m **2.** [consultation] consultation f **3.** UNIV [of thesis] renvoi m pour révision **4.** [person] patient m (envoyé par son médecin chez un spécialiste).

refill ◆ vt [,riː'fɪl] [glass] remplir (à nouveau) ; [lighter, canister] recharger. ◆ n ['riːfɪl] [for pen, lighter] (nouvelle) cartouche f ; [for propelling pencil] mine f de rechange ; [for notebook] recharge f ; [drink] : do you need a refill? inf je vous en ressers un ? ◆ comp ['riːfɪl] de rechange.

refillable [,riː'fɪləbl] adj rechargeable.

refinance [,riː'faɪnæns] ◆ vt refinancer. ◆ vi [of company] se refinancer.

refinancing [riː'faɪnænsɪŋ] n refinancement m.

refine [rɪ'faɪn] vt **1.** [oil, sugar] raffiner ; [ore, metal] affiner ; [by distillation] épurer **2.** [model, manners] améliorer ; [judgment, taste] affiner ; [lecture, speech] parfaire, peaufiner.

refined [rɪ'faɪnd] adj **1.** [oil, sugar] raffiné ; [ore] affiné ; [by distillation] épuré **2.** [style, person, taste] raffiné.

refinement [rɪ'faɪnmənt] n **1.** [of oil, sugar] raffinage m ; [of metals, ore] affinage m ; [by distillation] épuration f **2.** [of person] délicatesse f, raffinement m ; [of taste, culture] raffinement m ; [of morals] pureté f **3.** [of style, discourse, language] subtilité f, raffinement m **4.** [improvement] perfectionnement m, amélioration f.

refinery [rɪ'faɪnərɪ] (pl **refineries**) n [for oil, sugar] raffinerie f ; [for metals] affinerie f.

refit (pt & pp **refitted**, cont **refitting**) ◆ vt [,ri:'fɪt] **1.** [repair] remettre en état **2.** [refurbish] rééquiper, renouveler l'équipement de. ◆ vi [,ri:'fɪt] [ship] être remis en état. ◆ n ['ri:fɪt] [of plant, factory] rééquipement m, nouvel équipement m ; [of ship] remise f en état, réparation f.

reflate [,ri:'fleɪt] vt **1.** [ball, tyre] regonfler **2.** ECON relancer.

reflation [,ri:'fleɪʃn] n ECON relance f.

reflationary [,ri:'fleɪʃənrɪ] adj ECON [policy] de relance.

reflect [rɪ'flekt] ◆ vt **1.** [image] refléter ; [sound, heat] renvoyer ; [light] réfléchir **2.** fig [credit] faire jaillir, faire retomber **3.** fig [personality, reality] traduire, refléter **4.** [think] penser, se dire ; [say] dire, réfléchir. ◆ vi [think] réfléchir. ❖ **reflect on, reflect upon** vt insep [negatively] porter atteinte à, nuire à ; [positively] rejaillir sur ; [cast doubt on] mettre en doute, jeter le doute sur.

reflection [rɪ'flekʃn] n **1.** [of light, sound, heat] réflexion f **2.** [image] reflet m **3.** [comment] réflexion f, remarque f, observation f ; [criticism] critique f **4.** [deliberation] réflexion f ; [thought] pensée f ▶ **on reflection** après ou à la réflexion, en y réfléchissant.

reflective [rɪ'flektɪv] adj **1.** OPT [surface] réfléchissant, réflecteur ; [power, angle] réflecteur ; [light] réfléchi **2.** [mind, person] pensif, réfléchi ; [faculty] de réflexion.

reflector [rɪ'flektər] n réflecteur m ; AUTO catadioptre m.

reflex ['ri:fleks] ◆ n **1.** [gen & PHYSIOL] réflexe m **2.** PHOT (appareil m) reflex m. ◆ adj **1.** PHYSIOL réflexe **2.** PHOT reflex (inv).

reflexive [rɪ'fleksɪv] ◆ adj **1.** GRAM réfléchi **2.** PHYSIOL réflexe **3.** LOGIC & MATH réflexif. ◆ n GRAM réfléchi m.

reflexively [rɪ'fleksɪvlɪ] adv GRAM [in meaning] au sens réfléchi ; [in form] à la forme réfléchie.

reflexive verb n verbe m réfléchi.

reflexologist [,ri:flek'splədʒɪst] n réflexologiste mf.

reflexology [,ri:flek'splədʒɪ] n réflexothérapie f.

reflux ['ri:flʌks] n reflux m.

reforest [,ri:'fɒrɪst] = **reafforest**.

reforestation [ri:,fɒrɪ'steɪʃn] = **reafforestation**.

reform [rɪ'fɔ:m] ◆ vt **1.** [modify - law, system, institution] réformer **2.** [person] faire perdre ses mauvaises habitudes à ; [drunkard] faire renoncer à la boisson ; [habits, behaviour] corriger. ◆ vi se corriger, s'amender. ◆ n réforme f.

re-form [ri:'fɔ:m] ◆ vt **1.** MIL [ranks] remettre en rang, reformer ; [men] rallier **2.** [return to original form] rendre sa forme primitive ou originale à ; [in new form] donner une nouvelle forme à ; [form again] reformer. ◆ vi **1.** MIL [men] se remettre en rangs ; [ranks] se reformer **2.** [group, band] se reformer.

reformat [,ri:'fɔ:mæt] (cont **reformatting**, pt & pp **reformatted**) vt COMPUT reformater.

reformation [,refə'meɪʃn] n **1.** [of law, institution] réforme f **2.** [of behaviour] réforme f ; [of criminal, addict, etc.] réinsertion f. ❖ **Reformation** ◆ n ▶ **the Reformation** la Réforme. ◆ comp [music, writer] de la Réforme.

reformatory [rɪ'fɔ:mətrɪ] ◆ adj réformateur. ◆ n **UK** ≃ maison f de redressement ; **US** ≃ centre m d'éducation surveillée.

reformed [rɪ'fɔ:md] adj **1.** [person] qui a perdu ses mauvaises habitudes ; [prostitute, drug addict] ancien **2.** [institution, system] réformé **3.** RELIG [Christian] réformé ; [Jewish] non orthodoxe.

reformer [rɪ'fɔ:mər] n réformateur m, -trice f.

reformist [rɪ'fɔ:mɪst] ◆ adj réformiste. ◆ n réformiste mf.

refract [rɪ'frækt] ◆ vt réfracter. ◆ vi se réfracter.

refraction [rɪ'frækʃn] n [phenomenon] réfraction f ; [property] réfringence f.

refractive [rɪ'fræktɪv] adj réfringent.

refrain [rɪ'freɪn] ◆ vi [hold back] ▶ **to refrain from (doing)** sthg s'abstenir de (faire) qqch. ◆ n refrain m.

reframe [,ri:'freɪm] vt **1.** [approach, point of view] recentrer ; [argument] remanier ; [question] reformuler **2.** [picture] réencadrer.

refreeze [,ri:'fri:z] (pt **refroze** [-'frəuz], pp **refrozen** [-'frəuzn]) vt [ice, ice-cream] remettre au congélateur ; [food] recongeler.

refresh [rɪ'freʃ] vt **1.** [revive - subj: drink, shower, ice] rafraîchir ; [- subj: exercise, swim] revigorer ; [- subj: sleep] reposer, détendre **2.** [memory, experience] rafraîchir **3.** [computer screen] rafraîchir.

refresher course n stage m or cours m de recyclage.

refreshing [rɪ'freʃɪŋ] adj **1.** [physically - drink, breeze] rafraîchissant ; [- exercise] tonique, revigorant ; [- sleep] réparateur, reposant ; [- holiday] reposant **2.** [mentally - idea] original, stimulant ; [- sight] réconfortant ; [- performance] plein de vie.

refreshingly [rɪ'freʃɪŋlɪ] adv : it's refreshingly different c'est un changement agréable / he was refreshingly honest il a été d'une honnêteté qui fait plaisir à voir / the wine is refreshingly dry c'est un vin agréablement sec / a refreshingly cool breeze un petit vent agréablement frais.

refreshment [rɪ'freʃmənt] n [of body, mind] repos m, délassement m / would you like some refreshment? **a)** [food] voulez-vous manger un morceau ? **b)** [drink] voulez-vous boire quelque chose ? ❖ **refreshments** pl n rafraîchissements mpl / **'refreshments available'** 'buvette'.

refresh rate n COMPUT fréquence f de rafraîchissement.

refrigerate [rɪ'frɪdʒəreɪt] vt [in cold store] frigorifier, réfrigérer ; [freeze] congeler ; [put in fridge] mettre au réfrigérateur.

refrigeration [rɪ,frɪdʒə'reɪʃn] n réfrigération f.

refrigerator [rɪ'frɪdʒəreɪtər] ◆ n [in kitchen] réfrigérateur m ; [storeroom] chambre f froide or frigorifique. ◆ comp [ship, lorry, unit] frigorifique.

refrigerator-freezer n **US** réfrigérateur-congélateur m.

refuel [,ri:'fjuəl] (**UK** pt & pp **refuelled**, cont **refuelling** ; **US** pt & pp **refueled**, cont **refueling**) ◆ vt ravitailler (en carburant). ◆ vi se ravitailler en carburant ; fig [eat, drink] se restaurer.

refuelling **UK**, **refueling** **US** [,ri:'fjuəlɪŋ] ◆ n ravitaillement m (en carburant). ◆ comp [boom, tanker] de ravitaillement ▶ **to make a refuelling stop a)** AUTO s'arrêter pour prendre de l'essence **b)** AERON faire une escale technique.

refuge ['refju:ʤ] n **1.** [shelter - gen] refuge *m*, abri *m* ; [- in mountains] refuge *m* ; [-for crossing road] refuge *m* **2.** [protection - from weather] : *to take refuge from the rain* s'abriter de la pluie ; [from attack, reality] ▸ **to seek refuge** chercher refuge.

refugee [,refjʊ'ʤi:] n réfugié *m*, -e *f*.

refugee camp n camp *m* de réfugiés.

refund ◆ vt [rɪ'fʌnd] **1.** [expenses, excess, person] rembourser ▸ **to refund sthg to sb** rembourser qqch à qqn **2.** FIN & LAW [monies] restituer. ◆ n ['ri:fʌnd] **1.** COMM remboursement *m* ▸ **to get** or **to obtain a refund** se faire rembourser **2.** FIN & LAW [of monies] restitution *f* **3.** US [of tax] bonification *f* de trop-perçu.

refundable [ri:'fʌndəbl] adj remboursable.

refurbish [,ri:'fɜ:bɪʃ] vt réaménager.

refurbishment [,ri:'fɜ:bɪʃmənt] n remise *f* à neuf.

refurnish [,ri:'fɜ:nɪʃ] vt [house] remeubler.

refusal [rɪ'fju:zl] n [of request, suggestion] refus *m*, rejet *m* ▸ **to meet with a refusal** essuyer or se heurter à un refus ▸ **to receive a refusal** recevoir une réponse négative.

refuse[1] [rɪ'fju:z] ◆ vt **1.** [turn down - invitation, gift] refuser ; [- offer] refuser, décliner ; [- request, proposition] refuser, rejeter ▸ **to refuse to do sthg** refuser de or se refuser à faire qqch **2.** [deny - permission] refuser (d'accorder) ; [- help, visa] refuser. ◆ vi [person] refuser ; [horse] refuser l'obstacle.

refuse[2] ['refju:s] n UK [household] ordures *fpl* (ménagères) ; [garden] détritus *mpl* ; [industrial] déchets *mpl*.

refuse bin ['refju:s-] n UK poubelle *f*.

refuse chute ['refju:s-] n UK vide-ordures *m inv*.

refuse collection ['refju:s-] n UK ramassage *m* d'ordures.

refuse collector ['refju:s-] n UK éboueur *m*.

refuse dump ['refju:s-] n UK [public] décharge *f* (publique), dépotoir *m*.

refutation [,refju:'teɪʃn] n réfutation *f*.

refute [rɪ'fju:t] vt [disprove] réfuter ; [deny] nier.

reg (written abbr of **registered**) ▸ **reg trademark** marque *f* déposée.

regain [rɪ'geɪn] vt **1.** [territory] reconquérir ; [health] recouvrer ; [strength] retrouver ; [sight, composure] retrouver, recouvrer ; [glory] retrouver / *to regain consciousness* reprendre connaissance / *to regain one's balance* retrouver l'équilibre **2.** *fml* [get back to - road, place, shelter] regagner.

regal ['ri:gl] adj *lit* royal ; *fig* [person, bearing] majestueux ; [banquet, decor] somptueux.

regale [rɪ'geɪl] vt ▸ **to regale sb with sthg** régaler qqn de qqch.

regalia [rɪ'geɪljə] pl n **1.** [insignia] insignes *mpl* **2.** [finery, robes] accoutrement *m*, atours *mpl*.

regard [rɪ'gɑ:d] ◆ vt **1.** [consider] considérer, regarder ; [treat] traiter / *I regard him as* or *like a brother* je le considère comme un frère / *I regard their conclusions as correct* or *to be correct* je tiens leurs conclusions pour correctes ; [esteem] estimer, tenir en estime ▸ **to regard sb highly** tenir qqn en grande estime / *highly regarded* très estimé **2.** *fml* [observe] regarder, observer **3.** [heed - advice, wishes] tenir compte de. ◆ n **1.** [notice, attention] considération *f*, attention *f* ▸ **to pay regard to sthg** tenir compte de qqch, faire attention à qqch **2.** [care, respect] souci *m*, considération *f*, respect *m* ▸ **to have regard for sb** avoir de la considération pour qqn ▸ **out of regard for** par égard pour **3.** [connection] ▸ **in this regard** à cet égard **4.** [esteem] estime *f*, considération *f* **5.** *fml* [eyes, look] regard *m*. ❖ **regards** pl n [in letters] : *regards, Peter* bien cordialement, Peter ▸ **kind regards** UK, **best regards** bien à vous ;

[in greetings] : *give them my regards* transmettez-leur mon bon souvenir / *he sends his regards* vous avez le bonjour de sa part. ❖ **as regards** prep phr en ce qui concerne, pour ce qui est de. ❖ **in regard to, with regard to** prep phr en ce qui concerne.

regarding [rɪ'gɑ:dɪŋ] prep quant à, en ce qui concerne, pour ce qui est de.

regardless [rɪ'gɑ:dlɪs] adv [in any case] quand même, en tout cas ; [without worrying] sans s'occuper or se soucier du reste. ❖ **regardless of** prep phr : *regardless of what you think* a) [without bothering] sans se soucier de ce que vous pensez b) [whatever your opinion] indépendamment de ce que vous pouvez penser / *regardless of the expense* sans regarder à la dépense.

regatta [rɪ'gætə] n régate *f*.

regd = **reg**.

regency ['ri:ʤənsɪ] (*pl* **regencies**) n régence *f*. ❖ **Regency** comp [style, furniture, period] Regency (*inv*), de la Régence anglaise *(1811-1830)*.

regenerate ◆ vt [rɪ'ʤenəreɪt] **1.** [gen] régénérer **2.** [district, urban area] réhabiliter. ◆ vi [rɪ'ʤenəreɪt] se régénérer. ◆ adj [rɪ'ʤenərət] régénéré.

regeneration [rɪ,ʤenə'reɪʃn] n [gen] régénération *f* ; [of interest] regain *m* ; [of urban area] réhabilitation *f*.

regenerative [rɪ'ʤenərətɪv] adj régénérateur.

regent ['ri:ʤənt] n **1.** HIST régent *m*, -e *f* **2.** US membre du conseil d'administration d'une université.

reggae ['regeɪ] ◆ n reggae *m*. ◆ comp [song, group, singer] reggae (*inv*).

Reggaeton [r'egeɪtɒn] n *style musical latino-américain mélangeant reggae, hip-hop et rap.*

regift [ri:'gɪft] vt offrir à quelqu'un d'autre.

regime, régime [reɪ'ʒi:m] n POL & SOCIOL régime *m* / *under the present regime* sous le régime actuel.

regiment ◆ n ['reʤɪmənt] MIL & *fig* régiment *m*. ◆ vt ['reʤɪment] [organize] enrégimenter ; [discipline] soumettre à une discipline trop stricte.

regimental [,reʤɪ'mentl] adj MIL [mess, dress] régimentaire, du régiment ; [band, mascot] du régiment ; *fig* [organization] trop discipliné, enrégimenté.

regimented ['reʤɪmentɪd] adj strict.

region ['ri:ʤən] n **1.** GEOG & ADMIN région *f* **2.** [in body] région *f* **3.** [of knowledge, sentiments] domaine *m*. ❖ **in the region of** prep phr environ.

regional ['ri:ʤənl] adj régional.

regionalism ['ri:ʤənəlɪzm] n régionalisme *m*.

regionally ['ri:ʤnəlɪ] adv à l'échelle régionale.

register ['reʤɪstər] ◆ vt **1.** [record - name] (faire) enregistrer, (faire) inscrire ; [- birth, death] déclarer ; [- vehicle] (faire) immatriculer ; [- trademark] déposer ; [- on list] inscrire ; [- request] enregistrer ; [- readings] relever, enregistrer ; MIL [recruit] recenser ▸ **to register a complaint** déposer une plainte ▸ **to register a protest** protester **2.** [indicate] indiquer ; [subj: person, face] exprimer **3.** [obtain - success] remporter ; [- defeat] essuyer **4.** *inf* [understand] saisir, piger **5.** [parcel, letter] envoyer en recommandé. ◆ vi **1.** [enrol] s'inscrire, se faire inscrire ; [in hotel] s'inscrire sur or signer le registre (de l'hôtel) **2.** [be understood] : *the truth slowly began to register (with me)* petit à petit, la vérité m'est apparue ; [have effect] : *his name doesn't register (with me)* son nom ne me dit rien **3.** [instrument] donner une indication. ◆ n **1.** [book] registre *m* ; [list] liste *f* ; SCH registre *m* de présences, cahier *m* d'appel ; [on ship] livre *m* de bord ▸ **to keep a register** tenir un registre ▸ **electoral register** liste *f* électorale ▸ **register of shipping** registre *m* maritime ▸ **register of births, deaths and marriages**

registre *m* de l'état civil **2.** [gauge] enregistreur *m* ; [counter] compteur *m* ; [cash till] caisse *f* (enregistreuse) **3.** [pitch -of voice] registre *m*, tessiture *f* ; [-of instrument] registre **4.** LING registre *m*, niveau *m* de langue **5.** TYPO registre *m* **6.** ART & COMPUT registre *m*.

registered ['redʒɪstəd] adj **1.** [student, elector] inscrit ; UK [charity] agréé ; FIN [bond, securities] nominatif ▸ **registered childminder** nourrice *f* agréée ▸ **registered company** société *f* inscrite au registre du commerce **2.** [letter, parcel] recommandé.

registered disabled adj UK ▸ **to be registered disabled** avoir une carte d'invalidité.

registered general nurse n [in UK] infirmier *m* diplômé, infirmière *f* diplômée.

Registered Nurse n infirmier *m* diplômé or infirmière *f* diplômée d'État.

registered post UK, **registered mail** US n ▸ **to send sthg by registered post** envoyer qqch en recommandé.

Registered Trademark n marque *f* déposée.

registered user n COMPUT utilisateur *m*, -trice *f* disposant d'une licence.

register office ADMIN = **registry office**.

registrar [,redʒɪ'strɑːʳ] n **1.** UK ADMIN officier *m* de l'état civil / *to inform the registrar's office of a death* déclarer un décès au bureau de l'état civil **2.** UK & NZ MED chef *m* de clinique **3.** LAW greffier *m* **4.** US UNIV chef *m* du service or du bureau des inscriptions ; UK UNIV président *m* (*d'une université*) **5.** COMM & FIN ▸ **companies' registrar** responsable *mf* du registre des sociétés.

registration [,redʒɪ'streɪʃn] n **1.** [of name] enregistrement *m* ; [of student] inscription *f* ; [of trademark] dépôt *m* ; [of vehicle] immatriculation *f* ; [of luggage] enregistrement *m* ; [of birth, death] déclaration *f* **2.** UK SCH appel *m* **3.** [of mail] recommandation *f* **4.** US = **registration document**.

registration document n UK AUTO ≃ carte *f* grise.

registration fee n frais *mpl* or droits *mpl* d'inscription.

registration number n UK AUTO numéro *m* d'immatriculation.

registry ['redʒɪstrɪ] (*pl* **registries**) n **1.** [registration] enregistrement *m* ; UNIV inscription *f* **2.** [office] bureau *m* d'enregistrement **3.** NAUT immatriculation *f*.

registry office n UK bureau *m* de l'état civil.

regress ◆ vi [rɪ'gres] BIOL & PSYCHOL régresser. ◆ n ['riːgres] = **regression**.

regression [rɪ'greʃn] n BIOL & PSYCHOL régression *f*.

regressive [rɪ'gresɪv] adj BIOL, FIN & PSYCHOL régressif ; [movement] de recul.

regret [rɪ'gret] (*pt & pp* **regretted**, *cont* **regretting**) ◆ vt [be sorry about -action, behaviour] regretter / *we regret to inform you* nous avons le regret de vous informer / *I regret ever mentioning it* je regrette d'en avoir parlé / *she regrets that she never met Donovan* elle regrette de n'avoir jamais rencontré Donovan. ◆ n [sorrow, sadness] regret *m* ▸ **to express one's regrets at** or **about sthg** exprimer ses regrets devant qqch.

> 📋 Note that **regretter que** is followed by a verb in the subjunctive:
> **We regret that this should be the case.** *Nous regrettons qu'il en soit ainsi.*

regretful [rɪ'gretfʊl] adj [person] plein de regrets ; [expression, attitude] de regret.

regretfully [rɪ'gretfʊlɪ] adv [sadly] avec regret ; [unfortunately] malheureusement.

regrettable [rɪ'gretəbl] adj [unfortunate] regrettable, malencontreux ; [annoying] fâcheux, ennuyeux / *it is most regrettable that you were not informed* il est fort regrettable que vous n'ayez pas été informé.

> 📋 Note that **il est regrettable que** is followed by a verb in the subjunctive:
> **It is most regrettable that the accused did not mention this.** *Il est tout à fait regrettable que l'accusé n'ait pas mentionné cela.*

regrettably [rɪ'gretəblɪ] adv [unfortunately] malheureusement, malencontreusement ; [irritatingly] fâcheusement.

regroup [,riː'gruːp] ◆ vt regrouper. ◆ vi se regrouper.

regt written abbr of **regiment**.

regular ['regjʊləʳ] ◆ adj **1.** [rhythmical -footsteps, movement, sound] régulier ; [even -breathing, pulse] régulier, égal **2.** [frequent -meetings, service, salary] régulier **3.** [usual -brand, dentist, supplier] habituel ; [-customer] régulier ; [listener, reader] fidèle ; [normal, ordinary -price, model] courant ; [-size] courant, standard ; [-procedure] habituel ; [permanent -agent] attitré, permanent ; [-police force] permanent, régulier ; [-army] de métier ; [-soldier] de carrière ▸ **regular (grade) gas** US AUTO (essence *f*) ordinaire **4.** [even -features, teeth] régulier ; [smooth, level] uni, égal **5.** [ordered -hours] régulier ; [-life] bien réglé **6.** GRAM & MATH régulier **7.** inf [as intensifier] vrai, véritable **8.** US inf [pleasant] sympathique, chouette **9.** RELIG [clergy] régulier **10.** US POL [loyal to party] fidèle au parti. ◆ n **1.** [customer -in bar] habitué *m*, -e *f* ; [-in shop] client *m*, -e *f* fidèle **2.** [contributor, player] : *she's a regular on our column* elle contribue régulièrement à notre rubrique **3.** [soldier] militaire *m* de carrière **4.** RELIG religieux *m* régulier, régulier *m* **5.** US [fuel] ordinaire *m* **6.** US POL [loyal party member] membre *m* fidèle (du parti).

regularity [,regjʊ'lærətɪ] (*pl* **regularities**) n régularité *f*.

regularly ['regjʊləlɪ] adv régulièrement.

regulate ['regjʊleɪt] vt **1.** [control, adjust -machine, expenditure] régler ; [-flow] réguler **2.** [organize -habit, life] régler ; [-with rules] réglementer.

regulation [,regjʊ'leɪʃn] ◆ n **1.** [ruling] règlement *m* / *it's contrary to* or *against (the) regulations* c'est contraire au règlement / *it complies with EU regulations* c'est conforme aux dispositions communautaires **2.** [adjustment, control -of machine] réglage *m* ; [-of flow] régulation *f*. ◆ comp [size, haircut, issue, dress] réglementaire ; [pistol, helmet] d'ordonnance.

regulator ['regjʊleɪtəʳ] n **1.** [person] régulateur *m*, -trice *f* **2.** [apparatus] régulateur *m*.

regulatory ['regjʊlətrɪ] adj réglementaire.

regurgitate [rɪ'gɜːdʒɪteɪt] ◆ vt [food] régurgiter ; fig [facts] régurgiter, reproduire. ◆ vi [bird] dégorger.

rehab ['riːhæb] n US ▸ **to be in rehab** faire une cure de désintoxication ▸ **rehab center** centre *m* de désintoxication.

rehabilitate [,riːə'bɪlɪteɪt] vt **1.** [convict, drug addict, alcoholic] réhabiliter, réinsérer ; [restore to health] rééduquer ; [find employment for] réinsérer **2.** [reinstate -idea, style] réhabiliter **3.** [renovate -area, building] réhabiliter.

rehabilitation ['riːə,bɪlɪ'teɪʃn] n **1.** [of disgraced person, memory, reputation] réhabilitation *f* ; [of convict, alcoholic, drug addict] réhabilitation *f*, réinsertion *f* ; [of disabled person] rééducation *f* ; [of unemployed] réinsertion **2**. [of idea, style] réhabilitation *f* **3**. [of area, building] réhabilitation *f*.

rehabilitation centre n [for work training] centre *m* de réadaptation ; [for drug addicts] centre de réinsertion.

rehash *inf & pej* ◆ vt [,riː'hæʃ] **1**. 🇬🇧 [rearrange] remanier **2**. [repeat - argument] ressasser ; [- programme] reprendre ; [- artistic material] remanier. ◆ n ['riːhæʃ] réchauffé *m*.

rehearsal [rɪ'hɜːsl] n *lit & fig* répétition *f*.

rehearse [rɪ'hɜːs] ◆ vt **1**. [play, music, speech, coup d'état] répéter ; [actors, singers, orchestra] faire répéter **2**. [recite - list, facts, complaints] réciter, énumérer ; [- old arguments] répéter, ressasser. ◆ vi MUS & THEAT répéter.

reheat [,riː'hiːt] vt réchauffer.

re-heel vt [shoes] remettre des talons à.

rehome [,riː'həʊm] vt [child, pet] trouver un nouveau foyer pour.

rehouse [,riː'haʊz] vt reloger.

rehousing [,riː'haʊzɪŋ] n relogement *m*.

reign [reɪn] ◆ n règne *m* ▶ **in** or **under the reign of** sous le règne de. ◆ vi **1**. *lit* régner **2**. *fig* [predominate] régner.

reigning ['reɪnɪŋ] adj **1**. *lit* [monarch, emperor] régnant **2**. [present - champion] en titre.

reimburse [,riːɪm'bɜːs] vt rembourser ▶ **to reimburse sb (for) sthg** rembourser qqch à qqn or qqn de qqch.

reimbursement [,riːɪm'bɜːsmənt] n remboursement *m*.

rein [reɪn] n **1**. [for horse] rêne *f* **2**. *fig* [control] bride *f* ▶ **to give (a) free rein to sb** laisser à qqn la bride sur le cou ▶ **to keep a rein on sthg** tenir qqch en bride, maîtriser qqch. ❖ **reins** pl n [for horse, child] rêne *f* ; *fig* ▶ **to hand over the reins** passer les rênes. ❖ **rein back** ◆ vi tirer sur les rênes, serrer la bride. ◆ vt sep faire ralentir, freiner. ❖ **rein in** ◆ vi ralentir. ◆ vt sep **1**. [horse] serrer la bride à, ramener au pas **2**. *fig* [person] ramener au pas ; [emotions] maîtriser, réfréner.

reincarnate ◆ vt [riː'ɪnkɑːneɪt] réincarner. ◆ adj [,riːɪn'kɑːnɪt] réincarné.

reincarnation [,riːɪnkɑː'neɪʃn] n réincarnation *f*.

reindeer ['reɪn,dɪər] (*pl* **reindeer**) n renne *m*.

reinforce [,riːɪn'fɔːs] vt **1**. MIL renforcer **2**. [gen & CONSTR - wall, heel] renforcer **3**. *fig* [demand] appuyer ; [argument] renforcer.

reinforced concrete [,riːɪn'fɔːst-] n béton *m* armé.

reinforcement [,riːɪn'fɔːsmənt] ◆ n **1**. [gen & MIL] renfort *m* **2**. [gen & CONSTR] armature *f* **3**. *fig* [strengthening] renforcement *m*. ◆ comp [troops, ships, supplies] de renfort.

reinsert [,riːɪn'sɜːt] vt réinsérer.

re-install vt réinstaller.

reinstate [,riːɪn'steɪt] vt [employee] réintégrer, rétablir (dans ses fonctions) ; [idea, system] rétablir, restaurer.

reinstatement [,riːɪn'steɪtmənt] n réintégration *f*.

reintegrate [,riː'ɪntɪgreɪt] vt réintégrer.

reintegration ['riː,ɪntɪ'greɪʃn] n réintégration *f*.

reinterpret [,riːɪn'tɜːprɪt] vt réinterpréter.

reintroduce ['riː,ɪntrə'djuːs] vt réintroduire.

reintroduction ['riː,ɪntrə'dʌkʃn] n réintroduction *f*.

reinvent [,riːɪn'vent] vt réinventer ▶ **to reinvent the wheel** réinventer la roue.

reissue [riː'ɪʃuː] ◆ vt **1**. [book] rééditer ; [film] rediffuser, ressortir **2**. ADMIN & FIN [banknote, shares, stamps] réémettre. ◆ n **1**. [of book] réédition *f* ; [of film] rediffusion *f* **2**. ADMIN & FIN nouvelle émission *f*.

reiterate [riː'ɪtəreɪt] vt répéter, réaffirmer.

reiteration [riː,ɪtə'reɪʃn] n réitération *f*.

reject ◆ vt [rɪ'dʒekt] **1**. [offer, suggestion, unwanted article] rejeter ; [advances, demands] rejeter, repousser ; [application, manuscript] rejeter, refuser ; [suitor] éconduire, repousser ; [belief, system, values] rejeter **2**. MED [foreign body, transplant] rejeter **3**. COMPUT rejeter. ◆ n ['riːdʒekt] **1**. COMM [in factory] article *m* or pièce *f* de rebut ; [in shop] (article *m* de) second choix *m* ; *fig* [person] personne *f* marginalisée **2**. COMPUT rejet *m*. ◆ comp ['riːdʒekt] [merchandise] de rebut ; [for sale] (de) second choix ; [shop] d'articles de second choix.

rejection [rɪ'dʒekʃn] n **1**. [of offer, manuscript] refus *m* ; [of advances, demands] rejet *m* ▶ **to be afraid of rejection** [emotional] avoir peur d'être rejeté **2**. MED rejet *m*.

rejection slip n lettre *f* de refus.

rejig [,riː'dʒɪg] (*pt & pp* **rejigged**, *cont* **rejigging**) vt 🇬🇧 **1**. [reequip] rééquiper, réaménager **2**. [reorganize] réarranger, revoir.

rejoice [rɪ'dʒɔɪs] vi se réjouir ▶ **to rejoice at** or **over sthg** se réjouir de qqch / **he rejoices in the name of French-Edwardes** *hum* il a le privilège de porter le nom de French-Edwardes.

rejoicing [rɪ'dʒɔɪsɪŋ] n réjouissance *f*.

rejoin[1] [,riː'dʒɔɪn] vt **1**. [go back to] rejoindre ▶ **to rejoin ship** NAUT rallier le bord **2**. [join again] rejoindre ; [club] se réinscrire à ▶ **to rejoin the majority** POL rallier la majorité.

rejoin[2] [rɪ'dʒɔɪn] vt & vi [reply] répliquer.

rejoinder [rɪ'dʒɔɪndər] n réplique *f*.

rejuvenate [rɪ'dʒuːvəneɪt] vt rajeunir.

rejuvenation [rɪ,dʒuːvə'neɪʃn] n rajeunissement *m*.

rekindle [,riː'kɪndl] ◆ vt [fire] rallumer, attiser ; *fig* [enthusiasm, desire, hatred] raviver, ranimer. ◆ vi [fire] se rallumer ; *fig* [feelings] se ranimer.

relapse [rɪ'læps] ◆ n MED & *fig* rechute *f* ▶ **to have a relapse** faire une rechute, rechuter. ◆ vi **1**. MED rechuter, faire une rechute **2**. [go back] retomber / **to relapse into silence** redevenir silencieux.

relate [rɪ'leɪt] ◆ vt **1**. [tell - events, story] relater, faire le récit de ; [- details, facts] rapporter **2**. [connect - ideas, events] rapprocher, établir un rapport or un lien entre. ◆ vi **1**. [connect - idea, event] se rapporter, se rattacher / *this relates to what I was just saying* ceci est lié à or en rapport avec ce que je viens de dire **2**. [have relationship, interact] : *at school, they learn to relate to other children* à l'école, ils apprennent à vivre avec d'autres enfants **3**. *inf* [appreciate] : *I can't relate to his music* je n'accroche pas à sa musique.

related [rɪ'leɪtɪd] adj **1**. [in family] parent ▶ **to be related by marriage to sb** être parent de qqn par alliance ; [animal, species] apparenté ; [language] de même famille, proche **2**. [connected] connexe, lié ; [neighbouring] voisin ; ADMIN & LAW afférent ▶ **related to** afférent à.

-related in comp lié à / *business-related activities* des activités liées or ayant rapport aux affaires / *drug-related crime* délits *mpl* liés aux stupéfiants.

relation [rɪ'leɪʃn] n **1**. [member of family] parent *m*, -e *f* / *they have relations in Paris* ils ont de la famille à Paris / *he's a relation of mine* il est de ma famille / *what relation of mine* il n'y a aucun lien de parenté entre nous **2**. [kinship] parenté *f* / *what relation is he to you?* quelle est sa parenté avec vous ? **3**. [connection] rapport *m*, relation *f* ▶ **to have** or **to bear a relation to sthg** avoir (un) rapport à qqch, être en rapport avec qqch **4.** [relationship, contact] rapport *m*, relation *f*; [between people, countries] rapport *m*, rapports *mpl* ▶ **to have (sexual) relations with sb** *fml* avoir des rapports (sexuels) avec qqn ▶ **diplomatic relations** relations diplomatiques **5.** *fml* [narration - of events, story] récit *m*, relation *f*; [- of details] rapport *m*. ❖ **in relation to, with relation to** prep phr par rapport à, relativement à.

relational [rɪ'leɪʃənl] adj relationnel.

relational database n COMPUT base *f* de données relationnelle.

relationship [rɪ'leɪʃnʃɪp] n **1.** [between people, countries] rapport *m*, rapports *mpl*, relation *f*, relations *fpl* ▶ **to have a good / bad relationship with sb** [gen] avoir de bonnes / mauvaises relations avec qqn **2.** [kinship] lien *m* or liens *mpl* de parenté **3.** [connection - between ideas, events, things] rapport *m*, relation *f*, lien *m*.

relationship marketing n marketing *m* relationnel.

relative ['relətɪv] ❖ adj **1.** [comparative] relatif / *to live in relative comfort* vivre dans un confort relatif; [proportional] relatif / *taxation is relative to income* l'imposition est proportionnelle au revenu; [respective] respectif / *the relative qualities of the two candidates* les qualités respectives des deux candidats **3.** [not absolute] relatif **3.** MUS relatif **4.** GRAM relatif ▶ **relative clause** (proposition *f*) relative *f* ▶ **relative pronoun** pronom *m* relatif. ❖ n **1.** [person] parent *m*, -e *f* / *she has relatives in Canada* elle a de la famille au Canada / *he's a relative of mine* il fait partie de ma famille **2.** GRAM relatif *m*. ❖ **relative to** prep phr par rapport à.

relatively ['relətɪvlɪ] adv relativement.

relativism ['relətɪvɪzm] n relativisme *m*.

relativist ['relətɪvɪst] ❖ adj relativiste. ❖ n relativiste *mf*.

relativity [,relə'tɪvətɪ] n relativité *f* ▶ **theory of relativity** théorie *f* de la relativité.

relax [rɪ'læks] ❖ vi **1.** [person] se détendre, se délasser; [in comfort, on holiday] se relaxer, se détendre; [calm down] se calmer, se détendre / *relax!* a) [calm down] du calme ! b) [don't worry] ne t'inquiète pas **2.** [grip] se relâcher, se desserrer; [muscle] se relâcher, se décontracter; TECH [spring] se détendre. ❖ vt **1.** [mind] détendre, délasser; [muscles] relâcher, décontracter **2.** [grip] relâcher, desserrer; MED [bowels] relâcher; [concentration, effort] relâcher **4.** [hair] défriser.

relaxation [,riːlæk'seɪʃn] n **1.** [rest] détente *f*, relaxation *f* **2.** [loosening - of grip] relâchement *m*, desserrement *m*; fig [of authority, law] relâchement *m*, assouplissement *m*.

relaxed [rɪ'lækst] adj **1.** [person, atmosphere] détendu, décontracté; [smile] détendu; [attitude] décontracté **2.** [muscle] relâché; [discipline] assoupli.

relaxing [rɪ'læksɪŋ] adj [restful - atmosphere, afternoon, holiday] reposant.

relay ['riːleɪ] ❖ n **1.** [team - of athletes, workers, horses] relais *m* **2.** RADIO & TV [transmitter] réémetteur *m*, relais *m*; [broadcast] émission *f* relayée **3.** ELEC & TECH relais *m* **4.** SPORT ▶ **relay (race)** (course *f* de) relais *m*. ❖ vt (*pt & pp* **relayed**) **1.** [pass on - message, news] transmettre **2.** RADIO & TV [broadcast] relayer, retransmettre **3.** (*pt & pp* **relaid** [-leɪd]) [cable, carpet] reposer.

relay station n relais *m*.

release [rɪ'liːs] ❖ n **1.** [from captivity] libération *f*; [from prison] libération *f*, mise *f* en liberté; ADMIN élargissement *m*; [from custody] mise *f* en liberté, relaxe *f*; [from work] congé *m* (spécial) ▶ **release on bail** mise en liberté provisoire (sous caution) ▶ **release on parole** libération *f* conditionnelle; fig [from obligation, promise] libération *f*, dis-

pense *f*; [from pain, suffering] délivrance *f* **2.** COMM [from bond, customs] congé *m* **3.** [letting go - of handle, switch] déclenchement *m*; [- of brake] desserrage *m*; [- of bomb] largage *m* **4.** [distribution - of film] sortie *f*; [- of book, album] sortie *f*, parution *f* / *the film is on general release* le film est sorti dans les salles; [new film, book, album] nouveauté *f* / *it's a new release* ça vient de sortir **5.** MECH [lever] levier *m*; [safety catch] cran *m* de sûreté **6.** COMPUT version *f*. ❖ comp [button, switch] de déclenchement. ❖ vt **1.** [prisoner] libérer, relâcher; ADMIN élargir; [from custody] remettre en liberté, relâcher, relaxer; [captive person, animal] libérer; [employee, schoolchild] libérer, laisser partir ▶ **to release sb from captivity** libérer qqn ▶ **to be released on bail** LAW être libéré sous caution; [from obligation] libérer, dégager; [from promise] dégager, relever; [from vows] relever, dispenser **2.** [let go - from control, grasp] lâcher; [- feelings] donner or laisser libre cours à; [bomb] larguer, lâcher; [gas, heat] libérer, dégager **3.** [issue - film] sortir; [- book, recording] sortir **4.** [goods, new model] mettre en vente or sur le marché; [stamps, coins] émettre **5.** [make public - statement] publier; [- information, story] dévoiler, annoncer **6.** [lever, mechanism] déclencher; [brake] desserrer ▶ **to release the clutch** AUTO débrayer **7.** FIN [credits, funds] dégager, débloquer **8.** [property, rights] céder.

relegate ['relɪgeɪt] vt **1.** [person, thought] reléguer ▶ **to relegate sb / sthg to sthg** reléguer qqn / qqch à qqch **2.** SPORT [team] reléguer, déclasser ▶ **to be relegated** FOOT descendre en or être relégué à la division inférieure **3.** [refer - issue, question] renvoyer.

relegation [,relɪ'geɪʃn] n **1.** [demotion - of person, team, thing] relégation *f* **2.** [referral - of issue, matter] renvoi *m*.

relent [rɪ'lent] vi **1.** [person] se laisser fléchir or toucher **2.** [storm] s'apaiser.

relentless [rɪ'lentlɪs] adj **1.** [merciless] implacable, impitoyable **2.** [sustained - activity, effort] acharné, soutenu; [- noise] ininterrompu; [- rain] incessant; [- increase] constant.

relentlessly [rɪ'lentlɪslɪ] adv **1.** [mercilessly] impitoyablement, implacablement **2.** [persistently] avec acharnement or opiniâtreté.

relevance ['reləvəns], **relevancy** ['reləvənsɪ] n **1.** [of facts, remarks] pertinence *f*, intérêt *m* / *I don't see the relevance of your remark* la pertinence de votre remarque m'échappe / *what is the relevance of this to the matter under discussion?* quel est le rapport avec ce dont on parle ? / *this question has little relevance for us* cette question ne nous concerne pas vraiment **2.** [usefulness, significance] intérêt *m* / *many students fail to see the practical relevance of such courses* de nombreux étudiants considèrent que ces formations n'ont pas d'intérêt or d'utilité pratique.

relevant ['reləvənt] adj **1.** [pertinent - comment, beliefs, ideas] pertinent / *facts relevant to the case* des faits en rapport avec l'affaire **2.** [appropriate] approprié / *fill in your name in the relevant space* inscrivez votre nom dans la case correspondante / *she did not have the relevant experience for the job* elle n'avait pas l'expérience requise pour le poste / *you should report the matter to the relevant department* vous devriez en référer au service compétent **3.** [useful, significant] to be / to remain relevant; [book, idea] être / rester d'actualité.

reliability [rɪ,laɪə'bɪlətɪ] n **1.** [of person] sérieux *m*; [of information] sérieux *m*, fiabilité *f*; [of memory, judgment] sûreté *f*, fiabilité *f* **2.** [of clock, engine] fiabilité *f*.

reliable [rɪ'laɪəbl] adj **1.** [trustworthy - friend] sur qui on peut compter, sûr; [- worker] à qui on peut faire confiance, sérieux ; [-witness] digne de confiance or de foi ; [-information] sérieux, sûr ; [-memory, judgment] fiable, auquel on peut se fier **2.** [clock, machine, car] fiable.

reliably [rɪ'laɪəblɪ] adv sérieusement / *we are reliably informed that...* nous avons appris de bonne source or de source sûre que...

reliance [rɪ'laɪəns] n **1.** [trust] confiance f ▸ **to place reliance on sb / sthg** faire confiance à qqn / qqch **2.** [dependence] dépendance f / *her reliance on alcohol* sa dépendance vis-à-vis de l'alcool.

reliant [rɪ'laɪənt] adj **1.** [dependent] dépendant **2.** [trusting] confiant ▸ **to be reliant on sb** faire confiance à or avoir confiance en qqn.

relic ['relɪk] n **1.** RELIG relique f ; [vestige] relique f, vestige m **2.** *fig & pej* [old person] croulant m, vieux débris m.

relief [rɪ'liːf] ◆ n **1.** [from anxiety, pain] soulagement m ▸ **to bring relief to sb** soulager qqn, apporter un soulagement à qqn **2.** [aid] secours m, aide f **3.** US [state benefit] aide f sociale ▸ **to be on relief** recevoir des aides sociales or des allocations **4.** [diversion] divertissement m, distraction f **5.** [of besieged city] libération f, délivrance f **6.** [of guard, team] relève f **7.** ART relief m / *the inscription stood out in relief* l'inscription était en relief ; [contrast] relief m **8.** GEOG relief m **9.** LAW [redress] réparation f ; [exemption] dérogation f, exemption f. ◆ comp **1.** [extra - transport, service] supplémentaire ; [replacement - worker, troops, team] de relève ; [-bus, machine] de remplacement **2.** [for aid -fund] de secours ▸ **relief agency** or **organization** organisation f humanitaire ▸ **relief work** coopération f ▸ **relief worker** membre d'une organisation humanitaire qui travaille sur le terrain.

relief map n carte f en relief.

relief road n itinéraire m bis, route f de délestage.

relieve [rɪ'liːv] vt **1.** [anxiety, distress, pain] soulager, alléger ; [poverty] soulager **2.** [boredom, gloom] dissiper ; [monotony] briser **3.** [unburden] ▸ **to relieve sb of sthg** soulager or débarrasser qqn de qqch **4.** [aid - population, refugees, country] secourir, venir en aide à **5.** [replace - worker, team] relayer, prendre la relève de ; [-guard, sentry] relever **6.** [liberate - fort, city] délivrer, libérer ; [from siege] lever le siège de **7.** *euph* [urinate] ▸ **to relieve o.s.** se soulager.

relieved [rɪ'liːvd] adj soulagé / *we were greatly relieved at the news* nous avons été très soulagés d'apprendre la nouvelle.

religion [rɪ'lɪdʒn] n **1.** RELIG religion f **2.** *fig* [obsession] religion f, culte m ▸ **to make a religion of sthg** se faire une religion de qqch.

religious [rɪ'lɪdʒəs] ◆ adj **1.** [authority, order, ceremony, art] religieux ; [war] de religion ▸ **religious education** or **instruction** instruction f religieuse **2.** [devout] religieux, croyant **3.** *fig* [scrupulous] religieux. ◆ n [monk, nun] religieux m, -euse f.

religiously [rɪ'lɪdʒəslɪ] adv *lit & fig* religieusement.

reline [ˌriː'laɪn] vt [garment] mettre une nouvelle doublure à, redoubler ; [picture] rentoiler ▸ **to reline the brakes** AUTO changer les garnitures de freins.

relinquish [rɪ'lɪŋkwɪʃ] vt **1.** [give up - claim, hope, power] abandonner, renoncer à ; [-property, possessions] se dessaisir de ; [-right] renoncer à **2.** [release - grip, hold] ▸ **to relinquish one's hold of** or **on sthg a)** *lit* lâcher qqch **b)** *fig* relâcher l'étreinte que l'on a sur qqch.

relish ['relɪʃ] ◆ n **1.** [pleasure, enthusiasm] goût m, plaisir m, délectation f ▸ **to do sthg with relish** faire qqch avec délectation or grand plaisir, adorer faire qqch **2.** [condiment, sauce] condiment m, sauce f **3.** [flavour] goût m, saveur f. ◆ vt **1.** [enjoy] savourer ; [look forward to] : *I don't relish the idea* or *prospect* or *thought of seeing them again*

l'idée or la perspective de les revoir ne m'enchante or ne me réjouit guère **2.** [savour - food, drink] savourer, se délecter de.

relive [ˌriː'lɪv] vt revivre.

reload [ˌriː'ləʊd] vt recharger.

relocate [ˌriː'ləʊ'keɪt] ◆ vt installer ailleurs, délocaliser. ◆ vi s'installer ailleurs, déménager.

relocation [ˌriː'ləʊ'keɪʃn] n [of premises, industry] délocalisation f, déménagement m ; [of population] relogement m ▸ **relocation expenses** indemnité f de déménagement.

reluctance [rɪ'lʌktəns] n **1.** [unwillingness] répugnance f ▸ **to do sthg with reluctance** faire qqch à contrecœur or de mauvais gré **2.** PHYS réluctance f.

reluctant [rɪ'lʌktənt] adj **1.** [unwilling] peu enclin or disposé ▸ **to be reluctant to do sthg** être peu enclin à faire qqch, n'avoir pas envie de faire qqch **2.** [against one's will - commitment, promise, approval] accordé à contrecœur.

reluctantly [rɪ'lʌktəntlɪ] adv à contrecœur.

rely [rɪ'laɪ] (pt & pp relied) ◆❖ **rely on**, **rely upon** vt insep **1.** [depend on] compter sur, faire confiance à / *I'm relying on you to find a solution* je compte sur vous pour trouver une solution **2.** LAW [call on] invoquer.

REM (abbr of rapid eye movement) n & comp mouvements oculaires rapides pendant le sommeil paradoxal ▸ **REM sleep** sommeil m paradoxal.

remain [rɪ'meɪn] vi **1.** [be left] rester / *that remains to be seen* cela reste à voir / *it only remains for me to thank you* il ne me reste plus qu'à vous remercier **2.** [stay] rester, demeurer / *to remain silent* garder le silence, rester silencieux.

remainder [rɪ'meɪndər] ◆ n **1.** [leftover - supplies, time] reste m ; [-money] solde m ; [-debt] reliquat m ; [-people] / *the remainder went on a picnic* les autres sont allés pique-niquer **2.** MATH reste m **3.** [unsold book] invendu m ; [unsold product] fin f de série **4.** LAW usufruit m avec réversibilité. ◆ vt COMM solder.

remaining [rɪ'meɪnɪŋ] adj qui reste, restant / *the only remaining member of her family* la seule personne de sa famille (qui soit) encore en vie / *the remaining guests* le reste des invités / *it's our only remaining hope* c'est le seul espoir qui nous reste, c'est notre dernier espoir.

remains [rɪ'meɪnz] pl n **1.** [of meal, fortune] restes mpl ; [of building] restes mpl, vestiges mpl **2.** *euph & fml* [corpse] restes mpl, dépouille f mortelle.

remake (pt & pp remade [-'meɪd]) ◆ vt [ˌriː'meɪk] refaire. ◆ n ['riːmeɪk] [film] remake m.

remand [rɪ'mɑːnd] UK ◆ vt LAW [case] renvoyer ; [defendant] déférer ▸ **to remand sb in custody** placer qqn en détention préventive ▸ **to remand sb on bail** mettre qqn en liberté or libérer qqn sous caution. ◆ n renvoi m ▸ **to be on remand a)** [in custody] être en détention préventive **b)** [on bail] être libéré sous caution.

remand centre n UK centre de détention préventive.

remark [rɪ'mɑːk] ◆ n **1.** [comment] remarque f, réflexion f ▸ **to make** or **to pass a remark** faire une remarque ▸ **to make** or **to pass remarks about sthg / sb** faire des réflexions sur qqch / qqn **2.** *fml* [attention] attention f, intérêt m. ◆ vt **1.** [comment] (faire) remarquer, (faire) observer **2.** *fml* [notice] remarquer. ❖ **remark on**, **remark upon** vt insep ▸ **to remark on** or **upon sthg a)** [comment] faire un commentaire or une observation sur qqch **b)** [criticize] faire des remarques sur qqch.

remarkable [rɪ'mɑːkəbl] adj [quality, aspect] remarquable ; [event, figure] remarquable, marquant / *they are remarkable for their modesty* ils sont d'une rare modestie or remarquablement modestes.

remarkably [rɪˈmɑːkəblɪ] adv remarquablement.
remarket [riːˈmɑːkɪt] vt recommercialiser.
remarketing [riːˈmɑːkɪtɪŋ] n marketing *m* de relance.
remarriage [ˌriːˈmærɪdʒ] n remariage *m*.
remarry [ˌriːˈmærɪ] *(pt & pp* **remarried)** vi se remarier.
remedial [rɪˈmiːdjəl] adj **1.** [action] réparateur ; [measures] de redressement **2.** UK SCH [classes, education] de rattrapage, de soutien ; [pupil, student] qui n'a pas le niveau ▸ **remedial teaching** rattrapage *m* scolaire **3.** MED [treatment] correctif, curatif ▸ **remedial exercises** gymnastique *f* corrective.
remediation [rɪmiːdɪˈeɪʃn] n US SCH rattrapage *m* scolaire.
remedy [ˈremədɪ] *(pl* **remedies,** *pt & pp* **remedied)** ◆ n **1.** *lit & fig* remède *m* ▸ **to find a remedy for sthg** trouver un remède à qqch **2.** LAW recours *m* ▸ **to have no remedy at law against sb** n'avoir aucun recours légal contre qqn. ◆ vt MED remédier à ; *fig* rattraper, remédier à.
remember [rɪˈmembər] ◆ vt **1.** [recollect - face, person, past event] se souvenir de, se rappeler / *I don't remember ever going* or *having gone there* je ne me rappelle pas y être jamais allé / *do you remember me knocking on your door?* vous souvenez-vous que j'ai frappé à votre porte ? **2.** [not forget] penser à, songer à / *remember to close the door* n'oubliez pas de or pensez à fermer la porte **3.** [give regards to] : *remember me to your parents* rappelez-moi au bon souvenir de vos parents **4.** [give tip or present to] : *please remember the driver* n'oubliez pas le chauffeur / *she always remembers me on my birthday* elle n'oublie jamais le jour de mon anniversaire / *he remembered me in his will* il a pensé à moi dans son testament **5.** [commemorate - war] commémorer ; [- victims] se souvenir de. ◆ vi se souvenir / *as far as I can remember* autant qu'il m'en souvienne / *not that I remember* pas que je m'en souvienne / *if I remember rightly* si je me or si je m'en souviens bien, si j'ai bonne mémoire.
remembrance [rɪˈmembrəns] n **1.** [recollection] souvenir *m*, mémoire *f* **2.** [memory] souvenir *m* **3.** [keepsake] souvenir *m* **4.** [commemoration] souvenir *m*, commémoration *f* ▸ **remembrance service, service of remembrance** cérémonie *f* du souvenir, commémoration *f*. ◆ **in remembrance of** prep phr ▸ **in remembrance of sthg / sb** en souvenir or en mémoire de qqch / qqn.
Remembrance Day, Remembrance Sunday n UK (commémoration *f* de l')Armistice *m* *(le dimanche avant ou après le 11 novembre).*

> ## Remembrance Sunday
>
> Commémorant l'armistice de la Première Guerre mondiale, **Remembrance Sunday** est célébré chaque année au Royaume-Uni le dimanche qui précède ou suit le 11 novembre. Dans les premiers jours de novembre, on porte un coquelicot **(poppy)** en papier en souvenir des soldats britanniques morts lors des guerres mondiales.

remind [rɪˈmaɪnd] vt **1.** [tell] rappeler à ▸ **to remind sb to do sthg** rappeler à qqn de faire qqch, faire penser à qqn qu'il faut faire qqch ▸ **to remind sb about sthg** rappeler qqch à qqn / *that reminds me!* à propos !, pendant que j'y pense ! **2.** [be reminiscent of] : *she reminds me of my sister* elle me rappelle ma sœur.

reminder [rɪˈmaɪndər] n [spoken] rappel *m* ; [written] pense-bête *m* ; ADMIN & COMM rappel *m* ▸ **to give sb a reminder to do sthg** rappeler à qqn qu'il doit faire qqch.
reminisce [ˌremɪˈnɪs] vi raconter ses souvenirs / *to reminisce about the past* évoquer le passé or parler du passé.
reminiscent [ˌremɪˈnɪsnt] adj [suggestive] ▸ **reminiscent of** qui rappelle, qui fait penser à.
remiss [rɪˈmɪs] adj *fml* négligent / *it was rather remiss of you to forget her birthday* c'était un peu négligent or léger de votre part d'oublier son anniversaire.
remission [rɪˈmɪʃn] n **1.** UK LAW [release - from prison sentence] remise *f* (de peine) ; [- from debt, claim] remise *f* ; ADMIN [dispensation] dispense *f* **2.** MED & RELIG rémission *f*.
remit *(pt & pp* **remitted,** *cont* **remitting)** ◆ vt [rɪˈmɪt] **1.** [release - from penalty, sins] remettre ▸ **to remit sb's sentence** accorder une remise de peine à qqn ; [dispense, exonerate - fees, tax] remettre **2.** [send - money] envoyer **3.** LAW [case] renvoyer. ◆ n [ˈriːmɪt] attributions *fpl*, pouvoirs *mpl* / *that's outside their remit* cela n'entre pas dans (le cadre de) leurs attributions / *our remit is to...* il nous incombe de...
remittance [rɪˈmɪtns] n **1.** [payment] versement *m* ; [settlement] paiement *m*, règlement *m* **2.** [delivery - of papers, documents] remise *f*.
remix ◆ vt [ˌriːˈmɪks] [song, recording] remixer, refaire le mixage de. ◆ n [ˈriːmɪks] remix *m*.
remnant [ˈremnənt] n [remains - of meal, material] reste *m* ; [vestige - of beauty, culture] vestige *m*. ◆ **remnants** pl n COMM [unsold goods] invendus *mpl* ; [fabric] coupons *mpl* (de tissus) ; [oddments] fins *fpl* de série.
remodel [ˌriːˈmɒdl] (UK *pt & pp* **remodelled,** *cont* **remodelling** ; US *pt & pp* **remodeled,** *cont* **remodeling)** vt remodeler.
remonstrate [ˈremənstreɪt] vi *fml* protester ▸ **to remonstrate with sb** faire des remontrances à qqn ▸ **to remonstrate against sthg** protester contre qqch.
remorse [rɪˈmɔːs] n remords *m* / *he was filled with remorse at what he had done* il était pris de remords en songeant à ce qu'il avait fait / *she felt no remorse* elle n'éprouvait aucun remords / *without remorse* **a)** [with no regret] sans remords **b)** [pitilessly] sans pitié.
remorseful [rɪˈmɔːsful] adj plein de remords.
remorsefully [rɪˈmɔːsfulɪ] adv avec remords.
remorseless [rɪˈmɔːslɪs] adj **1.** [with no regret] sans remords **2.** [relentless] implacable, impitoyable.
remorselessly [rɪˈmɔːslɪslɪ] adv **1.** [with no regret] sans remords **2.** [relentlessly] impitoyablement, implacablement.
remortgage [ˌriːˈmɔːgɪdʒ] vt [house, property] hypothéquer de nouveau, prendre une nouvelle hypothèque sur.
remote [rɪˈməut] adj **1.** [distant - place] éloigné, lointain ; [- time, period] lointain, reculé ; [- ancestor] éloigné **2.** [aloof - person, manner] distant, froid ; [faraway - look] lointain, vague ; [- voice] lointain **3.** [unconnected - idea, comment] éloigné **4.** [slight - chance] petit, faible ; [- resemblance] vague, lointain / *I haven't the remotest idea* je n'en ai pas la moindre idée **5.** COMPUT [terminal] commandé à distance ▸ **remote access** accès *m* à distance ▸ **remote user** utilisateur *m* distant.
remote control n télécommande *f*, commande *f* à distance.
remote-controlled [-kənˈtrəuld] adj télécommandé.
remotely [rɪˈməutlɪ] adv **1.** [slightly] faiblement, vaguement **2.** [distantly] : *they are remotely related* ils sont parents éloignés **3.** [aloofly] de façon distante or hautaine ; [dreamily] vaguement, de façon songeuse.

remoteness [rɪ'məʊtnɪs] n **1.** [distance - in space] éloignement *m*, isolement *m*; [- in time] éloignement *m* **2.** [aloofness - of person] distance *f*, froideur *f*.

remould 🇬🇧, **remold** 🇺🇸 ◆ vt [,riː'məʊld] **1.** ART & TECH remouler, refaçonner **2.** AUTO [tyre] rechaper **3.** *fig* [person, character] changer, remodeler. ◆ n ['riːməʊld] [tyre] pneu *m* rechapé.

removable [rɪ'muːvəbl] adj **1.** [detachable - lining, cover] amovible, détachable **2.** [transportable - furniture, fittings] mobile, transportable.

removal [rɪ'muːvl] ◆ n **1.** [of garment, stain, object] enlèvement *m*; [of abuse, evil, threat] suppression *f*; MED [of organ, tumour] ablation *f* **2.** [change of residence] déménagement *m*; [transfer] transfert *m* **3.** [dismissal] ▶ **removal from office** révocation *f*, renvoi *m*. ◆ comp [expenses, firm] de déménagement ▶ **removal man** 🇬🇧 déménageur *m* ▶ **removal van** camion *m* de déménagement.

remove [rɪ'muːv] ◆ vt **1.** [take off, out - clothes, object] enlever, retirer, ôter; [- stain] enlever, faire partir; [MED - organ, tumour] enlever, retirer / *to remove one's make-up* se démaquiller; [take or send away - object] enlever; [- person] faire sortir; [dismiss - employee] renvoyer; [- official] révoquer, destituer **2.** [suppress - clause, paragraph] supprimer; [- suspicion, doubt, fear] dissiper; *euph* [kill] faire disparaître, tuer. ◆ vi *fml* [firm, premises, family] déménager. ◆ n [distance] distance *f* / *this is but one remove from blackmail* ça frôle le chantage.

removed [rɪ'muːvd] adj ▶ **to be far removed from** être très éloigné or loin de ▶ **first cousin once / twice removed** cousin *m*, cousine *f* au premier / deuxième degré.

remover [rɪ'muːvə] n **1.** [of furniture] déménageur *m* **2.** [solvent] ▶ **paint remover** décapant *m* (*pour peinture*).

remunerate [rɪ'mjuːnəreɪt] vt rémunérer.

remuneration [rɪ,mjuːnə'reɪʃn] n rémunération *f* ▶ **to receive remuneration for sthg** être rémunéré or payé pour qqch ▶ **remuneration package** package *m* de rémunération.

remunerative [rɪ'mjuːnərətɪv] adj rémunérateur.

renaissance [rə'neɪsns] ◆ n renaissance *f* ▶ **the Renaissance** ART & HIST la Renaissance. ◆ comp [art, painter] de la Renaissance; [palace, architecture, style] Renaissance (*inv*).

renal ['riːnl] adj rénal.

rename [,riː'neɪm] vt **1.** [person, street] rebaptiser **2.** COMPUT [file, directory] renommer.

rend [rend] (*pt & pp* rent [rent]) vt *liter* [tear - fabric] déchirer; [- wood, armour] fendre; *fig* [silence, air] déchirer.

render ['rendə'] vt **1.** [deliver - homage, judgment, verdict] rendre; [- assistance] prêter; [- help] fournir; [submit - bill, account] présenter, remettre ▶ **account rendered** COMM facture *f* de rappel **2.** [cause to become] rendre **3.** [perform - song, piece of music] interpréter; [convey - atmosphere, spirit] rendre, évoquer **4.** [translate] rendre, traduire / *rendered into English* rendu or traduit en anglais **5.** CULIN faire fondre **6.** CONSTR crépir, enduire de crépi. ❖ **render up** vt sep *liter* [fortress] rendre; [hostage] libérer, rendre; [secret] livrer.

rendering ['rendərɪŋ] n **1.** [performance - of song, play, piece of music] interprétation *f* **2.** [evocation - of atmosphere, spirit] évocation *f* **3.** [translation] traduction *f* **4.** CONSTR crépi *m*.

rendezvous ['rɒndɪvuː] (*pl* rendezvous ['rɒndɪvuːz]) ◆ n **1.** [meeting] rendez-vous *m* **2.** [meeting place] lieu *m* de rendez-vous. ◆ vi [friends] se retrouver; [group, party] se réunir ▶ **to rendezvous with sb** rejoindre qqn.

rendition [ren'dɪʃn] n **1.** [of poem, piece of music] interprétation *f* **2.** [translation] traduction *f* **3.** ▶ **(extraordinary) rendition** [of suspect] remise (*d'un suspect*) *par une autorité à une autre*.

renegade ['renɪgeɪd] ◆ n renégat *m*, -e *f*. ◆ adj renégat.

renege [rɪ'niːg] vi [in cards] faire une renonce. ❖ **renege on** vt insep [responsibilities] manquer à; [agreement] revenir sur.

renegotiate [,riːnɪ'gəʊʃɪeɪt] vi & vt renégocier.

renew [rɪ'njuː] vt **1.** [extend validity - passport, library book] renouveler; [- contract, lease] renouveler, reconduire **2.** [repeat - attack, promise, threat] renouveler; [restart - correspondence, negotiations] reprendre; [increase - strength] reconstituer, reprendre **3.** [replace - supplies] renouveler, remplacer; [- batteries, mechanism] remplacer, changer.

renewable [rɪ'njuːəbl] adj renouvelable ▶ **renewable energy** énergie *f* renouvelable ▶ **renewable resource** ressource *f* renouvelable.

renewal [rɪ'njuːəl] n **1.** [extension - of validity] renouvellement *m*; [restart - of negotiations, hostilities] reprise *f*; [- of acquaintance] fait *m* de renouer; [increase - of energy, hope] regain *m*; [repetition - of promise, threat] renouvellement *m* **2.** [renovation] rénovation *f* **3.** RELIG renouveau *m*.

rennet ['renɪt] n [for cheese, junket] présure *f*.

renounce [rɪ'naʊns] ◆ vt [claim, title] abandonner, renoncer à; [faith, principle, habit] renoncer à, renier; [treaty] dénoncer. ◆ vi [in cards] renoncer.

renovate ['renəveɪt] vt remettre à neuf, rénover.

renovation [,renə'veɪʃn] n remise *f* à neuf, rénovation *f*.

renown [rɪ'naʊn] n renommée *f*, renom *m*.

renowned [rɪ'naʊnd] adj renommé, célèbre, réputé ▶ **to be renowned for sthg** être connu or célèbre pour qqch.

rent [rent] ◆ pt & pp ⟶ **rend.** ◆ vt **1.** [subj: tenant, hirer] louer, prendre en location ▶ **to rent sthg from sb** louer qqch à qqn / **'to rent'** 🇺🇸 'à louer' **2.** [subj: owner] louer, donner en location ▶ **to rent sthg (out) to sb** louer qqch à qqn. ◆ vi 🇺🇸 se louer. ◆ n **1.** [for flat, house] loyer *m*; [for farm] loyer *m*, fermage *m*; [for car, TV] (prix *m* de) location *f* ▶ **(up) for rent** à louer **2.** ECON loyer *m* **3.** [tear] déchirure *f* **4.** [split - in movement, party] rupture *f*, scission *f*.

> ⚠ The French word **rente** never means rent.

rental ['rentl] ◆ n **1.** [hire agreement - for car, house, TV, telephone] location *f* **2.** [payment - for property, land] loyer *m*; [- for TV, car, holiday accommodation] (prix *m* de) location *f*; [- for telephone] abonnement *m*, redevance *f* **3.** [income] (revenu *m* des) loyers *mpl* **4.** 🇺🇸 [apartment] appartement *m* en location; [house] maison *f* en location; [land] terrain *m* en location. ◆ adj [agency] de location ▶ **rental agreement** contrat *m* de location ▶ **rental charge a)** [for telephone] abonnement *m* **b)** [for TV, car] prix *m* de location ▶ **rental library** 🇺🇸 bibliothèque *f* de prêt.

rent book n carnet *m* de quittances de loyer.

rent boy n jeune prostitué *m* (*pour hommes*).

rent collector n receveur *m*, -euse *f* des loyers.

rented ['rentɪd] adj loué, de location / *the high cost of rented accommodation in London* le prix élevé des loyers londoniens.

rent-free ◆ adj exempt de loyer. ◆ adv sans payer de loyer, sans avoir de loyer à payer.

rent rebate n réduction *f* de loyer.

renumber [,riː'nʌmbə'] vt renuméroter.

renunciation [rɪ,nʌnsɪ'eɪʃn] n [of authority, claim, title] renonciation f, abandon m ; [of faith, religion] renonciation f, abjuration f ; [of principle] abandon m, répudiation f ; [of treaty] dénonciation f.

reoccupy [,ri:'ɒkjʊpaɪ] (pt & pp **reoccupied**) vt réoccuper.

reoccurrence [,ri:ə'kʌrəns] = **recurrence**.

reopen [,ri:'əʊpn] ◆ vt **1.** [door, border, book, bank account] rouvrir **2.** [restart - hostilities] reprendre ; [- debate, negotiations] reprendre, rouvrir. ◆ vi **1.** [door, wound] se rouvrir ; [shop, theatre] rouvrir ; [school - after holiday] reprendre **2.** [negotiations] reprendre.

reopening [,ri:'əʊpnɪŋ] n [of shop] réouverture f ; [of negotiations] reprise f.

reorder ◆ vt [,ri:'ɔ:dəʳ] **1.** COMM [goods, supplies] commander de nouveau, faire une nouvelle commande de **2.** [rearrange - numbers, statistics, objects] reclasser, réorganiser. ◆ n ['ri:ɔ:dəʳ] COMM nouvelle commande f.

reorganization, reorganisation ['ri:,ɔ:gənaɪ'zeɪʃn] n réorganisation f.

reorganize, reorganise [,ri:'ɔ:gənaɪz] ◆ vt réorganiser. ◆ vi se réorganiser.

rep [rep] n **1.** (abbr of **representative**) inf COMM VRP m **2.** abbr of **repertory 3.** abbr of **repetition**.

Rep 🇺🇸 **1.** written abbr of **Representative 2.** written abbr of **Republican**.

repackage [,ri:'pækɪʤ] vt **1.** [goods] remballer **2.** 🇺🇸 [public image] redorer fig.

repaginate [,ri:'pæʤɪneɪt] vt remettre en pages ; [renumber] repaginer.

repaid [ri:'peɪd] pt & pp ⟶ **repay**.

repaint [,ri:'peɪnt] vt repeindre.

repair [rɪ'peəʳ] ◆ vt **1.** [mend - car, tyre, machine] réparer ; [- road, roof] réparer, refaire ; [- clothes] raccommoder ; [- hull] radouber, caréner ; [- tights] repriser / to have one's shoes repaired faire réparer ses chaussures **2.** [make amends for - error, injustice] réparer, remédier à. ◆ vi fml & hum aller, se rendre. ◆ n **1.** [mending - of car, machine, roof] réparation f, remise f en état ; [- of clothes] raccommodage m ; [- of shoes] réparation f ; [- of road] réfection f, remise f en état ; NAUT radoub m ▸ to carry out repairs to or on sthg effectuer des réparations sur qqch ▸ to be under repair être en réparation ▸ repair kit trousse f à outils **2.** [condition] état m ▸ to be in good / bad repair être en bon / mauvais état.

repairman [rɪ'peəmən] (pl **repairmen** [-mən]) n réparateur m.

repaper [,ri:'peɪpəʳ] vt retapisser.

reparation [,repə'reɪʃn] n **1.** fml [amends] réparation f ▸ to make reparations for sthg réparer qqch fig **2.** (usu pl) [damages - after war, invasion, etc.] réparations fpl.

reparcelling [ri:'pɑ:slɪŋ] n [of land] remembrement m.

repartee [,repɑ:'ti:] n **1.** [witty conversation] esprit m, repartie f **2.** [witty comment] repartie f, réplique f.

repatriate ◆ vt [,ri:'pætrɪeɪt] rapatrier. ◆ n [ri:'pætrɪət] rapatrié m, -e f.

repatriation [,ri:pætrɪ'eɪʃn] n rapatriement m.

repay [ri:'peɪ] (pt & pp **repaid** [ri:'peɪd]) vt **1.** [refund - creditor, loan] rembourser ▸ to repay a debt a) lit rembourser une dette b) fig s'acquitter d'une dette **2.** [return - visit] rendre ; [- hospitality, kindness] rendre, payer de retour ; [reward - efforts, help] récompenser.

repayable [ri:'peɪəbl] adj remboursable / repayable in five years remboursable sur cinq ans or en cinq annuités.

repayment [ri:'peɪmənt] n **1.** [of money, loan] remboursement m ▸ repayment options formules fpl de remboursement **2.** [reward - for kindness, effort] récompense f.

repayment mortgage n prêt-logement m.

repeal [rɪ'pi:l] ◆ vt [law] abroger, annuler ; [prison sentence] annuler ; [decree] rapporter, révoquer. ◆ n [law] abrogation f ; [prison sentence] annulation f ; [decree] révocation f.

repeat [rɪ'pi:t] ◆ vt **1.** [say again - word, secret, instructions] répéter ; [- demand, promise] répéter, réitérer **2.** [redo, reexecute - action, attack, mistake] répéter, renouveler ; MUS reprendre **3.** RADIO & TV [broadcast] rediffuser **4.** COMM [order, offer] renouveler **5.** SCH & UNIV [class, year] redoubler. ◆ vi **1.** [say again] répéter **2.** [recur] se répéter, se reproduire ; MATH se reproduire périodiquement **3.** [food] donner des renvois **4.** 🇺🇸 POL voter plus d'une fois (à une même élection) **5.** [watch, clock] être à répétition. ◆ n **1.** [gen] répétition f **2.** MUS [passage] reprise f ; [sign] signe m de reprise **3.** RADIO & TV [broadcast] rediffusion f, reprise f. ◆ comp [order, visit] renouvelé ▸ repeat offender récidiviste mf ▸ repeat prescription ordonnance f (de renouvellement d'un médicament) / she gave me a repeat prescription elle a renouvelé mon ordonnance.

repeated [rɪ'pi:tɪd] adj répété.

repeatedly [rɪ'pi:tɪdlɪ] adv à plusieurs or maintes reprises.

repeat performance n THEAT deuxième représentation f / we don't want a repeat performance of last year's chaos fig nous ne voulons pas que le désordre de l'année dernière se reproduise.

repel [rɪ'pel] (pt & pp **repelled**, cont **repelling**) ◆ vt **1.** [drive back - attacker, advance, suggestion] repousser **2.** [disgust - subj: unpleasant sight, smell, etc.] rebuter, dégoûter **3.** ELEC & PHYS repousser. ◆ vi ELEC & PHYS se repousser.

repellent, repellant [rɪ'pelənt] ◆ adj repoussant, répugnant ▸ to find sb / sthg repellent éprouver de la répugnance pour qqn / qqch. ◆ n **1.** [for insects] insecticide m ; [for mosquitoes] antimoustiques m inv ; [for waterproofing] imperméabilisant m.

repent [rɪ'pent] ◆ vi se repentir ▸ to repent of sthg se repentir de qqch. ◆ vt se repentir de.

repentance [rɪ'pentəns] n repentir m.

repentant [rɪ'pentənt] adj repentant.

repercussion [,ri:pə'kʌʃn] n [consequence] répercussion f, retentissement m, contrecoup m ▸ to have repercussions on avoir des répercussions sur.

repertoire ['repətwɑ:ʳ] n lit & fig répertoire m.

repertory ['repətrɪ] (pl **repertories**) n **1.** THEAT ▸ to be or to act in repertory faire partie d'une troupe de répertoire, jouer dans un théâtre de répertoire ▸ repertory (theatre) théâtre m de répertoire **2.** = **repertoire**.

repertory company n compagnie f or troupe f de répertoire.

repetition [,repɪ'tɪʃn] n **1.** [of words, orders] répétition f **2.** [of action] répétition f, renouvellement m **3.** MUS reprise f.

repetitious [,repɪ'tɪʃəs] adj plein de répétitions or de redites.

repetitive [rɪ'petɪtɪv] adj [activity, work, rhythm] répétitif, monotone ; [song, speech] plein de répétitions ; [person] qui se répète.

repetitive strain injury,   repetitive stress injury = RSI.

rephrase [,ri:'freɪz] vt reformuler.

replace [rɪˈpleɪs] vt **1.** [put back] replacer, remettre (à sa place or en place) ▶ **to replace the receiver** [on telephone] reposer le combiné, raccrocher (le téléphone) **2.** [person] remplacer ; [mechanism, tyres] remplacer.

 replacer or **remplacer?**

Replacer qqch means to put sthg back in its place, while **remplacer qqch** means to replace sthg (i.e., to change it for sthg else).

replacement [rɪˈpleɪsmənt] ◆ n **1.** [putting back] remise f en place **2.** [substitution] remplacement m **3.** [person] remplaçant m, -e f **4.** [engine or machine part] pièce f de rechange ; [product] produit m de remplacement. ◆ comp [part] de rechange.

replaster [ˌriːˈplɑːstər] vt replâtrer, recrépir.

replay ◆ n [ˈriːpleɪ] **1.** TV ralenti m **2.** SPORT match m rejoué. ◆ vt [ˌriːˈpleɪ] [match] rejouer ; [recording, piece of film, video] repasser.

replenish [rɪˈplenɪʃ] vt fml **1.** [restock - cellar, stock] réapprovisionner **2.** [refill - glass] remplir de nouveau.

replete [rɪˈpliːt] adj fml **1.** [full] rempli, plein ; [person - full up] rassasié.

replica [ˈreplɪkə] n [of painting, model, sculpture] réplique f, copie f ; [of document] copie f (exacte).

replicate [ˈreplɪkeɪt] vt [reproduce] reproduire.

replication [ˌreplɪˈkeɪʃn] n [gen] reproduction f.

reply [rɪˈplaɪ] (pl **replies**, pt & pp **replied**) ◆ n **1.** [answer] réponse f ; [retort] réplique f **2.** LAW réplique f. ◆ vt [answer] répondre ; [retort] répliquer, rétorquer. ◆ vi répondre ▶ **to reply to sb** répondre à qqn. ◆ **in reply to** prep phr en réponse à.

reply card, reply coupon n coupon-réponse m.

reply-paid adj 🇬🇧 avec réponse payée.

repo [ˈriːpəʊ] (**abbr of repossession**) n 🇺🇸 inf recouvrement m ▶ **repo man** agent m de recouvrement ▶ **repo woman** agente f de recouvrement.

repopulate [ˌriːˈpɒpjʊleɪt] vt repeupler.

repopulation [ˌriːpɒpjʊˈleɪʃən] n repeuplement m.

report [rɪˈpɔːt] ◆ vt **1.** [announce] annoncer, déclarer, signaler **2.** [subj: press, media - event, match] faire un reportage sur ; [- winner] annoncer ; [- debate, speech] faire le compte rendu de / the newspapers report heavy casualties les journaux font état de nombreuses victimes / our correspondent reports that troops have left the city notre correspondant nous signale que des troupes ont quitté la ville ; [unconfirmed news] : it is reported that a woman drowned une femme se serait noyée / he is reported to have left or as having left the country il aurait quitté le pays **3.** [give account of] faire état de, rendre compte de / the police have reported some progress in the fight against crime la police a annoncé des progrès dans la lutte contre la criminalité ▶ to report one's findings a) [in research] rendre compte des résultats de ses recherches b) [in inquiry, commission] présenter ses conclusions **4.** [burglary, disappearance, murder] signaler ; [wrongdoer] dénoncer, porter plainte contre / to report sb missing (to the police) signaler la disparition de qqn (à la police) / to be reported missing / dead être porté disparu / au nombre des morts / they were reported to the police for vandalism on les a dénoncés à la police pour vandalisme. ◆ vi **1.** [make a report - committee] faire son rapport, présenter ses conclusions ; [- police] faire un rapport ; [- journalist] faire un reportage ▶ **to report on sthg a)** ADMIN faire un rapport sur qqch **b)** PRESS faire un reportage sur qqch **2.** [in hierarchy]

▶ **to report to sb** être sous les ordres de qqn / I report directly to the sales manager je dépends directement du chef des ventes **3.** [present o.s.] se présenter ▶ **to report for duty** prendre son service, se présenter au travail ▶ **to report to barracks** or **to one's unit** MIL rallier son unité ▶ **to report sick** se faire porter malade. ◆ n **1.** [account, review] rapport m ▶ **to draw up** or **to make a report on sthg** faire un rapport sur qqch / he gave an accurate report of the situation il a fait un rapport précis sur la situation ; [summary - of speech, meeting] compte rendu m ; [official record] procès-verbal m ; COMM & FIN [review] rapport m ; [balance sheet] bilan m **2.** [in media] reportage m ; [investigation] enquête f ; [bulletin] bulletin m ▶ **to do a report on sthg** faire un reportage or une enquête sur qqch / according to newspaper / intelligence reports selon les journaux / les services de renseignements ; [allegation] allégation f, rumeur f ; [news] nouvelle f / there are reports of civil disturbances in the North il y aurait des troubles dans le Nord / reports are coming in of an earthquake on parle d'un tremblement de terre **3.** 🇬🇧 SCH ▶ **(school) report** bulletin m (scolaire) ▶ **end of term report** bulletin m trimestriel **4.** LAW [of court proceedings] procès-verbal m ▶ **law reports** recueil m de jurisprudence **5.** fml [repute] renom m, réputation f **6.** [sound - of explosion, shot] détonation f. ◆ **report back** ◆ vi **1.** [return - soldier] regagner ses quartiers, rallier son régiment ; [- journalist, salesman] rentrer / to report back to headquarters a) MIL rentrer au quartier général b) [salesman, clerk] rentrer au siège **2.** [present report] présenter son rapport / the commission must first report back to the minister la commission doit d'abord présenter son rapport au ministre. ◆ vt sep [results, decision] rapporter, rendre compte de. ◆ **report out** vt sep 🇺🇸 POL [bill, legislation] renvoyer après examen.

⚠ The French noun **report** never means a report. The expression **reporter à qqn** (to report to sb) is sometimes used in business contexts, but it is an anglicism that many find unacceptable.

reportage [ˌrepɔːˈtɑːʒ] n reportage m.

report card n SCH bulletin m or carnet m scolaire.

reported [rɪˈpɔːtɪd] adj : there have been reported sightings of dolphins off the coast on aurait vu des dauphins près des côtes / what was their last reported position? où ont-ils été signalés pour la dernière fois ?

reportedly [rɪˈpɔːtɪdlɪ] adv : 300 people have reportedly been killed 300 personnes auraient été tuées.

reported speech n GRAM style m or discours m indirect / in reported speech en style indirect.

reporter [rɪˈpɔːtər] n **1.** [for newspaper] journaliste mf, reporter m ; RADIO & TV reporter m **2.** [scribe - in court] greffier m, -ère f ; [- in parliament] sténographe mf.

reporting [rɪˈpɔːtɪŋ] n [of news] reportage m / she is noted for her objective reporting elle est connue pour l'objectivité de ses reportages ▶ **reporting restrictions** LAW restrictions fpl imposées aux médias (lors de la couverture d'un procès).

repose [rɪˈpəʊz] ◆ vt fml [place - confidence, trust] mettre, placer. ◆ vi **1.** [rest - person] se reposer ; [- the dead] reposer **2.** [be founded - belief, theory] reposer. ◆ n fml repos m / in repose au or en repos.

reposition [ˌriːpəˈzɪʃn] vt repositionner.

repositioning n [of brand, product] repositionnement m.

repository [rɪ'pɒzɪtrɪ] (*pl* **repositories**) n **1.** [storehouse - large] entrepôt *m* ; [- smaller] dépôt *m* **2.** [of knowledge, secret] dépositaire *mf*.

repossess [,ri:pə'zes] vt reprendre possession de ; LAW saisir / *they have* or *their house has been repossessed* leur maison a été mise en saisie immobilière.

repossession [,ri:pə'zeʃn] n reprise *f* de possession ; LAW saisie *f*.

repossession order n ordre *m* de saisie.

reprehensible [,reprɪ'hensəbl] adj répréhensible.

reprehensibly [,reprɪ'hensəblɪ] adv de façon répréhensible.

represent [,reprɪ'zent] vt **1.** [symbolize - subj: diagram, picture, symbol] représenter **2.** [depict] représenter, dépeindre ; [describe] décrire **3.** [constitute - achievement, change] représenter, constituer **4.** POL [voters, members] représenter ; [be delegate for - subj: person] représenter ; [opinion] représenter ; [in numbers] représenter **5.** [express, explain - advantages, prospect, theory] présenter **6.** THEAT [subj: actor] jouer, interpréter.

representation [,reprɪzen'teɪʃn] n **1.** POL représentation *f* ▸ **proportional representation** représentation proportionnelle **2.** [description, presentation] représentation *f*. ❖ **representations** pl n [complaints] plaintes *fpl*, protestations *fpl* ; [intervention] démarche *f*, intervention *f* ▸ **to make representations to sb a)** [complain] se plaindre auprès de qqn **b)** [intervene] faire des démarches auprès de qqn.

representational [,reprɪzen'teɪʃənl] adj [gen] représentatif ; ART figuratif.

representative [,reprɪ'zentətɪv] ❖ adj **1.** [typical] typique, représentatif ▸ **to be representative of sthg** être représentatif de qqch / *is this a representative sample of your results?* est-ce un échantillon représentatif de vos résultats ? **2.** POL représentatif. ❖ n **1.** [gen] représentant *m*, -e *f* **2.** COMM ▸ **(sales) representative** représentant *m*, -e *f* (de commerce) **3.** US POL ≃ député *m*, -e *f* ; ⟶ **House of Representatives**.

repress [rɪ'pres] vt [rebellion] réprimer ; PSYCHOL refouler.

repressed [rɪ'prest] adj [gen] réprimé ; PSYCHOL refoulé.

repression [rɪ'preʃn] n [gen] répression *f* ; PSYCHOL refoulement *m*.

repressive [rɪ'presɪv] adj [authority, system] répressif ; [measures] de répression, répressif.

reprieve [rɪ'pri:v] ❖ vt **1.** LAW [prisoner - remit] gracier ; [- postpone] accorder un sursis à **2.** *fig* [give respite to - patient] accorder un répit or un sursis à ; [- company] accorder un sursis à. ❖ n **1.** LAW remise *f* de peine, grâce *f* **2.** *fig* [respite - from danger, illness] sursis *m*, répit *m* ; [extra time] délai *m*.

reprimand ['reprɪmɑ:nd] ❖ vt réprimander / *he was reprimanded for being late* **a)** [worker] il a reçu un blâme pour son retard **b)** [schoolchild] on lui a donné un avertissement pour son retard. ❖ n [rebuke] réprimande *f* ; [professional] blâme *m*.

reprint ❖ vt [,ri:'prɪnt] réimprimer. ❖ n ['ri:prɪnt] réimpression *f*.

reprisal [rɪ'praɪzl] n représailles *fpl* ▸ **to take reprisals (against sb)** user de représailles or exercer des représailles (contre qqn) ▸ **by way of** or **in reprisal, as a reprisal** par représailles.

reproach [rɪ'prəʊtʃ] ❖ n **1.** [criticism] reproche *m* ▸ **above** or **beyond reproach** au-dessus de tout reproche, irréprochable **2.** [source of shame] honte *f* ▸ **to be a reproach to** être la honte de. ❖ vt faire des reproches à ▸ **to reproach sb with sthg** reprocher qqch à qqn.

reproachful [rɪ'prəʊtʃfʊl] adj [voice, look, attitude] réprobateur ; [tone, words] de reproche, réprobateur.

reproachfully [rɪ'prəʊtʃfʊlɪ] adv avec reproche / *to look at sb reproachfully* lancer des regards réprobateurs à qqn.

reprobate ['reprəbeɪt] ❖ adj dépravé. ❖ n dépravé *m*, -e *f*.

reprocess [,ri:'prəʊses] vt retraiter.

reprocessing [,ri:'prəʊsesɪŋ] n retraitement *m* ▸ **nuclear reprocessing** retraitement des déchets nucléaires.

reproduce [,ri:prə'dju:s] ❖ vt reproduire. ❖ vi se reproduire.

reproduction [,ri:prə'dʌkʃn] ❖ n **1.** BIOL reproduction *f* **2.** [of painting, document] reproduction *f*, copie *f*. ❖ comp ▸ **reproduction furniture** reproduction *f* or copie *f* de meubles d'époque.

reproductive [,ri:prə'dʌktɪv] adj [organs, cells, process] reproducteur, de reproduction.

reprogram [,ri:'prəʊgræm] vt reprogrammer, programmer de nouveau.

reprogrammable [,ri:,prəʊ'græməbəl] adj COMPUT [key] reprogrammable.

reproof [rɪ'pru:f] n réprimande *f*, reproche *m*.

reprove [rɪ'pru:v] vt [person] réprimander ; [action, behaviour] réprouver / *he was reproved for his conduct* on lui a reproché sa conduite.

reproving [rɪ'pru:vɪŋ] adj réprobateur.

reprovingly [rɪ'pru:vɪŋlɪ] adv [look] d'un air réprobateur or de reproche ; [say] d'un ton réprobateur or de reproche.

reptile ['reptaɪl] ❖ adj reptile. ❖ n reptile *m*.

Repub. US abbr of **Republican**.

republic [rɪ'pʌblɪk] n république *f*.

republican [rɪ'pʌblɪkən] ❖ adj républicain. ❖ n républicain *m*, -e *f*.

republicanism [rɪ'pʌblɪkənɪzm] n républicanisme *m*.

repudiate [rɪ'pju:dɪeɪt] vt [reject - opinion, belief] renier, désavouer ; [- evidence] réfuter ; [- authority, accusation, charge] rejeter ; [- spouse] répudier ; [- friend] désavouer ; [- gift, offer] refuser, repousser ; [go back on - obligation, debt, treaty] refuser d'honorer.

repudiation [rɪ,pju:dɪ'eɪʃn] n **1.** [of belief, opinion] reniement *m*, désaveu *m* ; [of spouse] répudiation *f* ; [of friend, accusation] rejet *m* ; [of gift, offer] refus *m*, rejet *m* **2.** [of obligation, debt] refus *m* d'honorer.

repugnance [rɪ'pʌgnəns] n répugnance *f*.

repugnant [rɪ'pʌgnənt] adj répugnant / *I find the idea repugnant* cette idée me répugne.

repulse [rɪ'pʌls] ❖ vt [attack, offer] repousser. ❖ n MIL [defeat] défaite *f*, échec *m* ; *fig* [refusal] refus *m*, rebuffade *f*.

repulsion [rɪ'pʌlʃn] n répulsion *f*.

repulsive [rɪ'pʌlsɪv] adj [idea, sight, appearance] répugnant, repoussant ; PHYS répulsif.

repulsively [rɪ'pʌlsɪvlɪ] adv de façon repoussante or répugnante / *repulsively ugly* d'une laideur repoussante.

repurpose [,ri:'pɜ:pəs] n récupérer / *his flat is furnished with repurposed furniture* son appartement est meublé avec des meuble srécupérés or avec de la récup *inf*.

repurposing [,ri:'pɜ:pəsɪŋ] n récupération *f*, récup *f inf*.

reputable ['repjʊtəbl] adj [person, family] qui a bonne réputation, honorable, estimable ; [firm, tradesman] qui a bonne réputation ; [profession] honorable ; [source] sûr.

reputation [,repjʊ'teɪʃn] n réputation *f* / *she has a reputation as a cook* sa réputation de cuisinière n'est plus à faire / *they have a reputation for good service* ils sont réputés pour la qualité de leur service / *she has a reputation for being difficult* elle a la réputation d'être difficile.

repute [rɪ'pjuːt] ◆ n réputation f, renom m. ◆ vt [rumoured] : *she is reputed to be wealthy* elle passe pour riche.

reputed [rɪ'pjuːtɪd] adj réputé ▶ **reputed father** LAW père m putatif.

reputedly [rɪ'pjuːtɪdlɪ] adv d'après ce qu'on dit / *he is reputedly a millionaire* on le dit milliardaire.

reqd written abbr of **required**.

request [rɪ'kwest] ◆ n **1.** [demand] demande f, requête f ▶ **at sb's request** à la demande or requête de qqn / *tickets are available on request* des billets peuvent être obtenus sur simple demande **2.** [song - on radio] chanson demandée par un auditeur ; [- at dance] chanson demandée par un membre du public ▶ **to play a request for sb** passer un morceau à l'intention de qqn. ◆ vt demander ▶ **to request sb to do sthg** demander à qqn or prier qqn de faire qqch / *I enclose a cheque for £5, as requested* selon votre demande, je joins un chèque de 5 livres ▶ **to request sthg of sb** fml demander qqch à qqn.

request stop n UK arrêt m facultatif.

requiem mass n messe f de requiem.

require [rɪ'kwaɪər] vt **1.** [need - attention, care, etc.] exiger, nécessiter, demander **2.** [demand - qualifications, standard, commitment] exiger, requérir, réclamer ▶ **to require sthg of sb** exiger qqch de qqn ▶ **to require sb to do sthg** exiger que qqn fasse qqch.

required [rɪ'kwaɪəd] adj [conditions, qualifications, standard] requis, exigé / *in* or *by the required time* dans les délais (prescrits) / *required reading* SCH & UNIV lectures fpl à faire.

requirement [rɪ'kwaɪəmənt] n **1.** [demand] exigence f, besoin m / *this doesn't meet our requirements* ceci ne répond pas à nos exigences ; [necessity] besoin m, nécessité f / *energy requirements* besoins énergétiques **2.** [condition, prerequisite] condition f requise / *she doesn't fulfil the requirements for the job* elle ne remplit pas les conditions requises pour le poste / *what are the course requirements?* **a)** [for enrolment] quelles conditions faut-il remplir pour s'inscrire à ce cours ? **b)** [as student] quel niveau doit-on avoir pour suivre ce cours ?

requisite ['rekwɪzɪt] adj requis, nécessaire.

requisition [,rekwɪ'zɪʃn] ◆ n **1.** MIL réquisition f **2.** COMM demande f. ◆ vt MIL & fig réquisitionner.

reran [,riː'ræn] pt ⟶ **rerun**.

reread [,riː'riːd] (pt & pp **reread** [-'red]) vt relire.

rerecord [,riːrɪ'kɔːd] vt réenregistrer.

rerelease [,riːrɪ'liːs] ◆ vt [film, recording] ressortir. ◆ n [film, recording] reprise f.

reroute [,riː'ruːt] vt dérouter, changer l'itinéraire de.

rerun ◆ n ['riːrʌn] [of film] reprise f ; [of TV serial] rediffusion f. ◆ vt [,riː'rʌn] (pt **reran** [,riː'ræn], pp **rerun**, cont **rerunning**) **1.** [film] passer de nouveau ; [TV series] rediffuser **2.** [race] courir de nouveau.

resale ['riːseɪl] n revente f.

resale price maintenance n vente f au détail à prix imposé.

resale value n valeur f à la revente.

resat [,riː'sæt] pt & pp ⟶ **resit**.

reschedule [UK ,riː'ʃedjuːl US ,riː'skedʒul] vt **1.** [appointment, meeting] modifier l'heure or la date de ; [bus, train, flight] modifier l'horaire de ; [plan, order] modifier le

programme de / *the meeting has been rescheduled for next week* la réunion a été déplacée à la semaine prochaine **2.** FIN [debt] rééchelonner.

rescind [rɪ'sɪnd] vt fml [judgment] casser, annuler ; [agreement] annuler ; [law] abroger ; [contract] résilier.

rescue ['reskjuː] ◆ vt [from danger] sauver ; [from captivity] délivrer ; [in need, difficulty] secourir, venir au secours de / *to rescue sb from drowning* sauver qqn de la noyade. ◆ n [from danger, drowning] sauvetage m ; [from captivity] délivrance f ; [in need, difficulty] secours m ▶ **to go** / **to come to sb's rescue** aller / venir au secours or à la rescousse de qqn. ◆ comp [attempt, mission, operation, party, team] de sauvetage, de secours ▶ **rescue worker** sauveteur m.

rescuer ['reskjuər] n sauveteur m.

reseal [,riː'siːl] vt [envelope] recacheter ; [jar] refermer hermétiquement.

resealable [,riː'siːləbl] adj qui peut être recacheté.

research [rɪ'sɜːtʃ] ◆ n (U) recherche f, recherches fpl ▶ **to do research into sthg** faire des recherches sur qqch ▶ **research and development** recherche f et développement m, recherche-développement f. ◆ comp [establishment, work] de recherche ▶ **research worker** chercheur m, -euse f. ◆ vt [article, book, problem, subject] faire des recherches sur. ◆ vi faire des recherches or de la recherche.

researcher [rɪ'sɜːtʃər] n chercheur m, -euse f.

research student n étudiant m, -e f qui fait de la recherche (après la licence).

resell [,riː'sel] (pt & pp **resold** [-'sould]) vt revendre.

resemblance [rɪ'zembləns] n ressemblance f ▶ **to bear a resemblance to sb** ressembler vaguement à qqn.

resemble [rɪ'zembl] vt ressembler à.

resent [rɪ'zent] vt [person] en vouloir à, éprouver de la rancune à l'égard de ; [remark, criticism] ne pas apprécier ▶ **to resent sthg strongly** un vif ressentiment à l'égard de qqch / *I resent that!* je proteste !

resentful [rɪ'zentfʊl] adj plein de ressentiment ▶ **to feel resentful about** or **at sthg** éprouver du ressentiment à l'égard de qqch, mal accepter qqch ▶ **to be resentful about** or **of sb's achievements** envier sa réussite à qqn.

resentfully [rɪ'zentfʊlɪ] adv avec ressentiment.

resentment [rɪ'zentmənt] n ressentiment m.

reservation [,rezə'veɪʃn] ◆ n **1.** [doubt] réserve f, restriction f ▶ **to have reservations about** or **about sthg** avoir or émettre des réserves sur qqch / *without reservation* or *reservations* sans réserve **2.** [booking] réservation f ▶ **to make a reservation a)** [on train] réserver une or sa place **b)** [in hotel] réserver or retenir une chambre **c)** [in restaurant] réserver une table **3.** [enclosed area] réserve f ▶ **Indian reservation** réserve indienne. ◆ comp [desk] des réservations.

reserve [rɪ'zɜːv] ◆ vt **1.** [keep back] réserver, mettre de côté **2.** [book] réserver, retenir. ◆ n **1.** [store - of energy, money, provisions] réserve f **2.** [storage] réserve f ▶ **to have** or **to keep in reserve** avoir or garder en réserve **3.** UK [doubt, qualification] réserve f **4.** [reticence] réserve f, retenue f **5.** MIL réserve f **6.** [area of land] réserve f **7.** SPORT remplaçant m, -e f **8.** [at auction] prix m minimum. ◆ comp **1.** FIN [funds, currency, resources, bank] de réserve **2.** SPORT remplaçant ▶ **the reserve team** l'équipe f de réserve.

reserve bank n banque f de réserve.

reserve currency n fonds m de réserve.

reserved [rɪ'zɜːvd] adj **1.** [shy - person] timide, réservé **2.** [doubtful] : *he has always been rather reserved about the scheme* il a toujours exprimé des doutes sur ce projet **3.** [room, seat] réservé ▶ **all rights reserved** tous droits réservés.

reserve price n prix m minimum.

reservist [rɪ'zɜːvɪst] n réserviste m.

reservoir ['rezəvwɑːr] n lit & fig réservoir m.

reset ◆ vt [ˌriː'set] (pt & pp reset, cont resetting) 1. [jewel] remonter 2. [watch, clock] remettre à l'heure ; [alarm] réenclencher ; [counter] remettre à zéro 3. COMPUT réinitialiser 4. [limb] remettre en place ; [fracture] réduire 5. [lay] ▶ to reset the table a) [in restaurant] remettre le couvert b) [in home] remettre la table. ◆ n ['riːset] COMPUT réinitialisation f ▶ reset button bouton m de réinitialisation.

resettle [ˌriː'setl] ◆ vt [refugees, population] établir or implanter (dans une nouvelle région) ; [territory] repeupler. ◆ vi se réinstaller.

resettlement [ˌriː'setlmənt] n [of people] établissement m or implantation f (dans une nouvelle région) ; [of territory] repeuplement m.

reshape [ˌriː'ʃeɪp] vt [clay, material] refaçonner ; [novel, policy] réorganiser, remanier.

reshuffle [ˌriː'ʃʌfl] ◆ vt 1. POL [cabinet] remanier 2. [cards] rebattre, battre de nouveau. ◆ n 1. POL remaniement m ▶ a Cabinet reshuffle un remaniement ministériel 2. [in cards] ▶ to have a reshuffle battre les cartes à nouveau.

reside [rɪ'zaɪd] vi fml 1. [live] résider / they reside in New York ils résident or ils sont domiciliés à New York 2. fig [be located] : authority resides in or with the Prime Minister c'est le Premier ministre qui est investi de l'autorité.

residence ['rezɪdəns] n 1. [home] résidence f, demeure f ▶ to be in residence [monarch] être en résidence ▶ writer / artist in residence écrivain m / artiste mf en résidence ▶ place of residence [on form] domicile m 2. UNIV ▶ (university) residence résidence f (universitaire) 3. [period of stay] résidence f, séjour m.

residence hall n US résidence f (universitaire).

residence permit n ≃ permis m or carte f de séjour.

resident ['rezɪdənt] ◆ n 1. [of town] habitant m, -e f ; [of street] riverain m, -e f ; [in hotel, hostel] pensionnaire mf ; [foreigner] résident m, -e f / 'residents only' a) [in street] 'interdit sauf aux riverains' b) [in hotel] 'réservé à la clientèle de l'hôtel' 2. US MED interne mf 3. ZOOL résident m. ◆ adj 1. [as inhabitant] résidant ▶ to be resident in a country résider dans un pays 2. [staff] qui habite sur place, à demeure 3. COMPUT résident.

residential [ˌrezɪ'denʃl] adj [district, accommodation] résidentiel ; [status] de résident ; [course, job] sur place ▶ residential care mode d'hébergement supervisé pour handicapés, délinquants, etc. ▶ residential treatment facility US fml hôpital m psychiatrique.

residents' association n association f de locataires.

residual [rɪ'zɪdjʊəl] adj [gen] restant.

residue ['rezɪdjuː] n [leftovers] reste m, restes mpl ; [of money] reliquat m ; CHEM & PHYS résidu m ; MATH reste m, reliquat m.

resign [rɪ'zaɪn] ◆ vi 1. [from post] démissionner, donner sa démission / she resigned from her job / from the committee elle a démissionné de son emploi / du comité 2. CHESS abandonner. ◆ vt 1. [give up - advantage] renoncer à ; [-job] démissionner de ; [-function] se démettre de, démissionner de 2. [give away] céder ▶ to resign sthg to sb céder qqch à qqn 3. [reconcile] : I had resigned myself to going alone je m'étais résigné à y aller seul.

resignation [ˌrezɪg'neɪʃn] n 1. [from job] démission f ▶ to hand in or to tender fml one's resignation donner sa démission 2. [acceptance - of fact, situation] résignation f.

resigned [rɪ'zaɪnd] adj résigné ▶ to become resigned to (doing) sthg se résigner à (faire) qqch / she gave me a resigned look / smile elle m'a regardé / souri avec résignation.

resilience [rɪ'zɪlɪəns] n 1. [of rubber, metal - springiness] élasticité f ; [-toughness] résistance f 2. [of character, person] énergie f, ressort m ; [of institution] résistance f.

resilient [rɪ'zɪlɪənt] adj 1. [rubber, metal - springy] élastique ; [-tough] résistant 2. [person - in character] qui a du ressort, qui ne se laisse pas abattre or décourager ; [-in health, condition] très résistant.

resin ['rezɪn] n résine f.

resist [rɪ'zɪst] ◆ vt [temptation, attack, change, pressure] résister à ; [reform] s'opposer à / he couldn't resist having just one more drink il n'a pas pu résister à l'envie de prendre un dernier verre / I can't resist it! c'est plus fort que moi ! / he was charged with resisting arrest fml il a été inculpé de résistance aux forces de l'ordre. ◆ vi résister, offrir de la résistance.

resistance [rɪ'zɪstəns] ◆ n [gen & ELEC], MED, PHYS & PSYCHOL résistance f / their resistance to all reform leur opposition (systématique) à toute réforme / her resistance to infection is low elle offre peu de résistance à l'infection ▶ air / wind resistance résistance de l'air / du vent. ◆ comp [movement] de résistance ; [group] des résistants ▶ resistance fighter résistant m, -e f.

resistant [rɪ'zɪstənt] ◆ adj [gen & ELEC], MED & PHYS résistant / she is very resistant to change elle est très hostile au changement. ◆ n résistant m, -e f.

-resistant in comp ▶ flame-resistant ignifugé.

resistor [rɪ'zɪstər] n ELEC résistance f (objet).

resit ◆ vt [ˌriː'sɪt] (pt & pp resat [ˌriː'sæt], cont resitting) [exam] repasser. ◆ n ['riːsɪt] examen m de rattrapage.

resize [ˌriː'saɪz] vt COMPUT [window] redimensionner ▶ resize box case f de redimensionnement.

resold [-'səʊld] pt & pp ⟶ resell.

resolute ['rezəluːt] adj [determined - person, expression, jaw] résolu ; [steadfast - faith, courage, refusal] inébranlable.

resolutely ['rezəluːtlɪ] adv [oppose, struggle, believe] résolument ; [refuse] fermement.

resolution [ˌrezə'luːʃn] n 1. [decision] résolution f, décision f 2. [formal motion] résolution f 3. [determination] résolution f 4. [settling, solving] résolution f 5. COMPUT, OPT & TV résolution f 6. MED & MUS résolution f.

resolve [rɪ'zɒlv] ◆ vt 1. [work out - quarrel, difficulty, dilemma] résoudre ; [-doubt] dissiper ; [MATH - equation] résoudre 2. [decide] (se) résoudre ▶ to resolve to do sthg décider de or se résoudre à faire qqch / it was resolved that... il a été résolu or on a décidé que... 3. [break down, separate] résoudre, réduire 4. MED résoudre, faire disparaître. ◆ vi [separate, break down] se résoudre. ◆ n 1. [determination] résolution f 2. [decision] résolution f, décision f.

resonance ['rezənəns] n résonance f.

resonant ['rezənənt] adj 1. [loud, echoing] retentissant, sonore 2. ACOUST, MUS & PHYS résonant, résonnant.

resonate ['rezəneɪt] vi [noise, voice, laughter, place] résonner, retentir / the valley resonated with their cries la vallée retentissait de leurs cris.

resort [rɪ'zɔːt] ◆ n 1. [recourse] recours m / without resort to threats sans avoir recours aux menaces / as a last resort en dernier ressort 2. [for holidays] station f ▶ ski resort station de sports d'hiver ▶ luxury resort hotel hôtel m de tourisme de luxe 3. [haunt, hang-out] repaire m. ◆ resort to vt insep [violence, sarcasm, etc.] avoir recours à, recourir à.

resound [rɪ'zaʊnd] vi **1.** [noise, words, explosion] retentir, résonner **2.** [hall, cave, hills, room] retentir **3.** *fml & liter* [spread - rumour] se propager.

resounding [rɪ'zaʊndɪŋ] adj **1.** [loud - noise, blow, wail] retentissant ; [-voice] sonore, claironnant ; [explosion] violent **2.** [unequivocal] retentissant, éclatant.

resoundingly [rɪ'zaʊndɪŋlɪ] adv **1.** [loudly] bruyamment **2.** [unequivocally - win] d'une manière retentissante or décisive ; [-criticize, condemn] sévèrement / *the team was resoundingly beaten* l'équipe a été battue à plate couture.

resource [rɪ'sɔːs] ◆ n **1.** [asset] ressource f ▶ **natural / energy resources** ressources naturelles / énergétiques **2.** [human capacity] ressource f **3.** [ingenuity] ressource f. ◆ comp SCH & UNIV ▶ **resource** or **resources centre / room** centre m / salle f de documentation ▶ **resource materials a)** [written] documentation f **b)** [audio-visual] aides fpl pédagogiques.

resourceful [rɪ'sɔːsfʊl] adj ingénieux, plein de ressource or ressources.

resourcefully [rɪ'sɔːsfʊlɪ] adv ingénieusement.

resourcefulness [rɪ'sɔːsfʊlnɪs] n ressource f, ingéniosité f.

respect [rɪ'spekt] ◆ vt **1.** [esteem - person, judgment, right, authority] respecter **2.** [comply with - rules, customs, wishes] respecter. ◆ n **1.** [esteem] respect m, estime f **2.** [care, politeness] respect m, égard m ▶ **to do sthg out of respect for sthg / sb** faire qqch par respect pour qqch / qqn **3.** [regard, aspect] égard m / *in every respect* à tous les égards **4.** [compliance, observance] respect m, observation f. ◆ **respects** pl n [salutations] respects mpl, hommages mpl ▶ **to pay one's respects to sb** présenter ses respects or ses hommages à qqn. ◆ **with respect to** prep phr quant à, en ce qui concerne.

respectability [rɪ,spektə'bɪlətɪ] n respectabilité f.

respectable [rɪ'spektəbl] adj **1.** [socially proper, worthy] respectable, convenable, comme il faut ▶ **to be outwardly respectable** avoir l'apparence de la respectabilité ▶ **to make o.s. (look) respectable** se préparer **2.** [fair - speech, athlete] assez bon ; [-amount, wage, etc.] respectable, correct.

respectably [rɪ'spektəblɪ] adv [properly] convenablement, comme il faut.

respected [rɪ'spektɪd] adj respecté.

respecter [rɪ'spektə] n : *she is no respecter of tradition* elle ne fait pas partie de ceux qui respectent la tradition / *disease is no respecter of class* nous sommes tous égaux devant la maladie.

respectful [rɪ'spektfʊl] adj respectueux.

respectfully [rɪ'spektfʊlɪ] adv respectueusement.

respective [rɪ'spektɪv] adj respectif.

respectively [rɪ'spektɪvlɪ] adv respectivement.

respiration [,respə'reɪʃn] n respiration f.

respirator ['respəreɪtə] n [mask, machine] respirateur m.

respiratory [ⓤⱪ rɪ'spɪrətrɪ ⓤⱼ 'respərətɔːrɪ] adj respiratoire ▶ **respiratory problem** or **problems** troubles mpl respiratoires.

respite ['respaɪt] n **1.** [pause, rest] répit m / *without respite* sans répit or relâche ▶ **respite care** (U) accueil temporaire, dans un établissement médicalisé, de personnes malades, handicapées, etc., destiné à prendre le relais des familles **2.** [delay] répit m, délai m ; [stay of execution] sursis m.

resplendent [rɪ'splendənt] adj [splendid] magnifique, splendide ; [shining] resplendissant.

respond [rɪ'spɒnd] ◆ vi **1.** [answer - person, guns] répondre ▶ **to respond to a request** répondre à une demande

2. [react] répondre, réagir ; [person] : *he doesn't respond well to criticism* il réagit mal à la critique. ◆ vt répondre. ◆ n **1.** ARCHIT [for arch] pilier m butant ; [ending colonnade] colonne f engagée **2.** RELIG répons m.

respondent [rɪ'spɒndənt] n **1.** LAW défendeur m, -eresse f **2.** [in opinion poll] sondé m, -e f / *10% of the respondents* 10 % de ces personnes interrogées.

response [rɪ'spɒns] n **1.** [answer] réponse f / *have you had any response to your request yet?* avez-vous obtenu une réponse à votre demande ? / *he smiled in response* il a répondu par un sourire **2.** [reaction] réponse f, réaction f **3.** [in bridge] réponse f **4.** RELIG répons m **5.** MED réaction f. ◆ **in response to** prep phr en réponse à.

response time n COMPUT temps m de réponse ; MED & PSYCHOL temps m de réaction.

responsibility [rɪ,spɒnsə'bɪlətɪ] (pl **responsibilities**) n **1.** [control, authority] responsabilité f ▶ **to have responsibility for sthg** avoir la charge or la responsabilité de qqch **2.** [accountability] responsabilité f / *I take full responsibility for the defeat* je prends (sur moi) l'entière responsabilité de la défaite **3.** [task, duty] responsabilité f ▶ **to have a responsibility to sb** avoir une responsabilité envers qqn ▶ **to shirk one's responsibilities** fuir ses responsabilités.

responsible [rɪ'spɒnsəbl] adj **1.** [in charge, in authority] responsable / *who's responsible for research?* qui est chargé de la recherche ? / *he was responsible for putting the children to bed* c'était lui qui couchait les enfants / a *responsible position* un poste à responsabilité **2.** [accountable] responsable ▶ **responsible for sthg** responsable de qqch **3.** [serious, trustworthy] sérieux, responsable / *it wasn't very responsible of him* ce n'était pas très sérieux de sa part.

responsibly [rɪ'spɒnsəblɪ] adv de manière responsable.

responsive [rɪ'spɒnsɪv] adj **1.** [person - sensitive] sensible ; [-receptive] ouvert ; [-enthusiastic] enthousiaste ; [-affectionate] affectueux **2.** [brakes, controls, keyboard] sensible / *the patient isn't proving responsive to treatment* le malade ne réagit pas au traitement **3.** [answering - smile, nod] en réponse.

respray ◆ vt [,riː'spreɪ] [car] repeindre. ◆ n ['riːspreɪ] : *I took the car in for a respray* j'ai donné la voiture à repeindre.

rest [rest] ◆ n **1.** [remainder] : *take the rest of the cake* prenez le reste or ce qui reste du gâteau / *take the rest of the cakes* prenez les autres gâteaux or les gâteaux qui restent **2.** [relaxation] repos m ; [pause] repos m, pause f ▶ **rest and recuperation a)** ⓤ⒮ MIL permission f **b)** hum vacances fpl ▶ **to put** or **to set sb's mind at rest** tranquilliser or rassurer qqn **3.** [motionlessness] repos m ▶ **to come to rest a)** [vehicle, pendulum, ball] s'immobiliser, s'arrêter **b)** [bird, falling object] se poser **4.** euph [death] paix f / *he's finally at rest* il a finalement trouvé la paix ▶ **to lay sb to rest** porter qqn en terre **5.** [support] support m, appui m ; [in snooker] repose-queue m **6.** MUS silence m / *minim* ⓤⓚ or *half* ⓤ⒮ *rest* demi-pause f **7.** [in poetry] césure f. ◆ vi **1.** [relax, stop working] se reposer **2.** [be held up or supported] reposer ; [lean - person] s'appuyer ; [-bicycle, ladder] être appuyé **3.** [depend, be based - argument, hope] reposer **4.** [be, remain] être / *rest assured we're doing our best* soyez certain que nous faisons de notre mieux / *can't you let the matter rest?* ne pouvez-vous pas abandonner cette idée ? **5.** [reside, belong] résider **6.** [alight - eyes, gaze] se poser **7.** euph [lie dead] reposer / **'rest in peace'** 'repose en paix' **8.** LAW : *the defence rests* la défense conclut sa plaidoirie **9.** AGR [lie fallow] être en repos or en jachère. ◆ vt **1.** [allow to relax] laisser reposer **2.** [support, lean] appuyer **3.** ⓅⱧⱤ **I rest my case a)** LAW j'ai conclu mon plaidoyer **b)** fig je n'ai rien d'autre à ajouter. ❖ **for the rest** adv phr pour le reste, quant au reste. ❖ **rest up** vi inf se reposer (un peu), prendre un peu de repos.

rest area n AUTO aire f de repos.

restart ◆ vt [ˌriːˈstɑːt] **1.** [activity] reprendre, recommencer ; [engine, mechanism] remettre en marche **2.** COMPUT [system] relancer, redémarrer ; [program] relancer. ◆ vi [ˌriːˈstɑːt] **1.** [job, project] reprendre, recommencer ; [engine, mechanism] redémarrer **2.** COMPUT [system] redémarrer ; [program] reprendre. ◆ n [ˈriːstɑːt] **1.** [of engine, mechanism] remise f en marche **2.** COMPUT [of system] redémarrage m ; [of program] reprise f ▸ **restart point** point m de reprise.

restate [ˌriːˈsteɪt] vt **1.** [reiterate - argument, case, objection] répéter, réitérer ; [- one's intentions, innocence, faith] réaffirmer **2.** [formulate differently] reformuler.

restaurant [ˈrestərɒnt] n restaurant m.

restaurant car n wagon-restaurant m, voiture-restaurant f.

restaurateur [ˌrestɒrəˈtɜːr] n restaurateur m, -trice f (tenant un restaurant).

rest cure n cure f de repos.

rested [ˈrestɪd] adj reposé.

restful [ˈrestfʊl] adj reposant, délassant, paisible.

rest home n maison f de retraite.

resting place [ˈrestɪŋ-] n **1.** lit lieu m de repos **2.** fig & liter [grave] dernière demeure f.

restitution [ˌrestɪˈtjuːʃn] n restitution f.

restive [ˈrestɪv] adj **1.** [nervous, fidgety] nerveux, agité **2.** [unmanageable] rétif, difficile.

restless [ˈrestlɪs] adj **1.** [fidgety] nerveux, agité ; [impatient] impatient **2.** [constantly moving] agité **3.** [giving no rest] : a restless night une nuit agitée.

restlessly [ˈrestlɪslɪ] adv **1.** [nervously] nerveusement ; [impatiently] impatiemment, avec impatience **2.** [sleeplessly] : she tossed restlessly all night elle a eu une nuit très agitée.

restlessness [ˈrestlɪsnɪs] n [fidgeting, nervousness] nervosité f, agitation f ; [impatience] impatience f.

restock [ˌriːˈstɒk] vt **1.** [with food, supplies] réapprovisionner **2.** [with fish] empoissonner ; [with game] réapprovisionner en gibier.

restoration [ˌrestəˈreɪʃn] n **1.** [giving back] restitution f **2.** [re-establishment] restauration f, rétablissement m **3.** [repairing, cleaning - of work of art, building] restauration f. ❖ **Restoration** ◆ n HIST ▸ **the Restoration** la Restauration anglaise. ◆ comp HIST [literature, drama] de (l'époque de) la Restauration (anglaise).

> 🏛 **The Restoration**
>
> La restauration, en 1660, de la monarchie britannique avec l'avènement de Charles II mit fin à la période d'austérité qui avait débuté sous le Protectorat de Cromwell.

restorative [rɪˈstɒrətɪv] ◆ adj fortifiant, remontant. ◆ n fortifiant m, remontant m.

restore [rɪˈstɔːr] vt **1.** [give back] rendre, restituer / the jewels have been restored to their rightful owners les bijoux ont été rendus or restitués à leurs propriétaires légitimes **2.** [re-establish - peace, confidence, etc.] restaurer, rétablir ; [- monarchy] restaurer ; [- monarch] remettre sur le trône / restored to his former post rétabli or réintégré dans ses anciennes fonctions **3.** [repair, clean - work of art, building] restaurer.

restorer [rɪˈstɔːrər] n ART restaurateur m, -trice f (de tableaux).

restrain [rɪˈstreɪn] vt **1.** [hold back, prevent] retenir, empêcher / I couldn't restrain myself from making a remark je n'ai pas pu m'empêcher de faire une remarque **2.** [overpower, bring under control - person] maîtriser **3.** [repress - emotion, anger, laughter] contenir, réprimer **4.** [imprison] interner, emprisonner.

restrained [rɪˈstreɪnd] adj **1.** [person] retenu, réservé ; [emotion] contenu, maîtrisé **2.** [colour, style] sobre, discret (discrète).

restraint [rɪˈstreɪnt] n **1.** [self-control] retenue f / with remarkable restraint avec une retenue remarquable **2.** [restriction] restriction f, contrainte f **3.** [control] contrôle m / a policy of price restraint une politique de contrôle des prix.

restrict [rɪˈstrɪkt] vt restreindre, limiter.

restricted [rɪˈstrɪktɪd] adj **1.** [limited] limité, restreint ▸ **restricted area a)** [out of bounds] zone f interdite **b)** 🇬🇧 AUTO [with parking restrictions] zone f à stationnement réglementé **c)** [with speed limit] zone f à vitesse limitée **2.** ADMIN [secret - document, information] secret (secrète), confidentiel **3.** [narrow - ideas, outlook] étroit, borné.

restriction [rɪˈstrɪkʃn] n **1.** [limitation] restriction f, limitation f ▸ **to put** or **to place** or **to impose restrictions on sthg** imposer des restrictions sur qqch ▸ **speed restriction** limitation de vitesse **2.** LOGIC & MATH condition f.

restrictive [rɪˈstrɪktɪv] adj **1.** [clause, list] restrictif, limitatif ; [interpretation] strict **2.** LING [clause] déterminatif.

restrictive practice n [by union] pratique f syndicale restrictive ; [by traders] atteinte f à la libre concurrence.

rest room n 🇺🇸 toilettes fpl.

restructure [ˌriːˈstrʌktʃər] vt restructurer.

restructuring [ˌriːˈstrʌktʃərɪŋ] n restructuration f.

restyle [ˌriːˈstaɪl] vt [car] changer le design de ; [hair, clothes] changer de style de ; [magazine] changer la présentation de.

result [rɪˈzʌlt] ◆ n **1.** [consequence] résultat m, conséquence f **2.** [success] résultat m **3.** [of match, exam, election] résultat m **4.** MATH [of sum, equation] résultat m. ◆ vi résulter / the fire resulted from a short circuit c'est un court-circuit qui a provoqué l'incendie ▸ **to result in** avoir pour résultat. ❖ **as a result** adv phr : as a result, I missed my flight à cause de cela, j'ai manqué mon avion. ❖ **as a result of** prep phr à cause de.

resume [rɪˈzjuːm] ◆ vt [seat, activity, duties, etc.] reprendre ; [story, journey] poursuivre. ◆ vi reprendre, continuer.

> ⚠ **Résumer means** to sum up, **not** to resume.

résumé [ˈrezjuːmeɪ] n **1.** [summary] résumé m **2.** 🇺🇸 [curriculum vitae] curriculum vitae m inv.

resumption [rɪˈzʌmpʃn] n reprise f.

resurface [ˌriːˈsɜːfɪs] ◆ vi lit & fig refaire surface. ◆ vt [road] refaire.

resurgence [rɪˈsɜːdʒəns] n réapparition f, renaissance f.

resurgent [rɪˈsɜːdʒənt] adj renaissant.

resurrect [ˌrezəˈrekt] vt lit & fig ressusciter.

resurrection [ˌrezəˈrekʃn] n résurrection f.

resuscitate [rɪˈsʌsɪteɪt] vt ranimer, réanimer.

> ⚠ **Ressusciter means** to bring back from the dead, **not** to resuscitate.

resuscitation [rɪˌsʌsɪˈteɪʃn] n réanimation f.

retail ['ri:teɪl] ◆ n (vente f au) détail m. ◆ adj de détail ▶ **retail goods** marchandises fpl vendues au détail ▶ **retail outlet** point m de vente (au détail) ▶ **the retail price** le prix de or au détail ▶ **retail price index** [UK] indice m des prix de détail ▶ **retail therapy**: to do some retail therapy inf faire du shopping pour se remonter le moral ▶ **retail trade** commerce m (de détail). ◆ adv au détail. ◆ vt **1.** COMM vendre au détail **2.** fml [story, event, experience] raconter; [gossip, scandal] répandre, colporter pej. ◆ vi [goods] se vendre (au détail) / they retail at £10 each ils se vendent à 10 livres la pièce.

retailer ['ri:teɪlə] n détaillant m, -e f.

retail park n [UK] centre m commercial.

retain [rɪ'teɪn] vt **1.** [keep] garder **2.** [hold, keep in place] retenir **3.** [remember] retenir, garder en mémoire **4.** [reserve - place, hotel room] retenir, réserver **5.** [engage - solicitor] engager ▶ **retaining fee** provision f or avance f sur honoraires.

retainer [rɪ'teɪnə] n **1.** [retaining fee] provision f **2.** [nominal rent] loyer m nominal.

retaining wall [rɪ'teɪnɪŋ-] n mur m de soutènement.

retake (pt retook [-'tʊk], pp retaken [-'teɪkn]) ◆ vt [ˌri:'teɪk] **1.** [town, fortress] reprendre **2.** [exam] repasser **3.** CIN [shot] reprendre, refaire ; [scene] refaire une prise (de vues). ◆ n ['ri:teɪk] **1.** [of exam] nouvelle session f **2.** CIN nouvelle prise f (de vues).

retaliate [rɪ'tælɪeɪt] vi se venger, riposter.

retaliation [rɪˌtælɪ'eɪʃn] n (U) représailles fpl, vengeance f ▶ **in retaliation (for sthg)** en or par représailles (contre qqch).

retaliatory [rɪ'tælɪətrɪ] adj de représailles, de rétorsion.

retardant [rɪ'tɑ:dnt] ◆ n SCI retardateur m. ◆ adj fml or SCI retardateur.

retarded [rɪ'tɑ:dɪd] adj **1.** [mentally] arriéré **2.** [delayed] retardé.

retch [retʃ] ◆ vi avoir un or des haut-le-cœur. ◆ n haut-le-cœur m inv.

retention [rɪ'tenʃn] n **1.** [keeping] conservation f **2.** MED [holding] rétention f ▶ **fluid retention** rétention d'eau **3.** [memory] rétention f.

retentive [rɪ'tentɪv] adj [memory] qui retient bien.

rethink (pt & pp rethought [-'θɔ:t]) ◆ vt [ˌri:'θɪŋk] repenser. ◆ n ['ri:θɪŋk] ▶ **to have a rethink about sthg** réfléchir de nouveau à qqch.

reticence ['retɪsəns] n réticence f.

reticent ['retɪsənt] adj réticent.

retina ['retɪnə] (pl retinas or retinae [-ni:]) n rétine f.

retinue ['retɪnju:] n suite f, cortège m.

retire [rɪ'taɪə] ◆ vi **1.** [from job] prendre sa retraite ; [from business, politics] se retirer / to retire from the political scene se retirer de la scène politique **2.** fml & hum [go to bed] aller se coucher **3.** [leave] se retirer / shall we retire to the lounge? si nous passions au salon ? / to retire hurt SPORT abandonner à la suite d'une blessure **4.** MIL [pull back] se replier. ◆ vt **1.** [employee] mettre à la retraite **2.** MIL [troops] retirer **3.** FIN [coins, bonds, shares] retirer de la circulation.

retired [rɪ'taɪəd] adj **1.** [from job] retraité, à la retraite **2.** [secluded] retiré.

retirement [rɪ'taɪəmənt] n **1.** [from job] retraite f ▶ **to take early retirement** partir en préretraite **2.** [seclusion] isolement m, solitude f.

retirement age n âge m de la retraite.

retirement benefit n indemnité f de départ en retraite, prime f de mise à la retraite.

retirement home n maison f de retraite.

retirement pension n (pension f de) retraite f.

retirement plan n [US] régime m de retraite.

retiring [rɪ'taɪərɪŋ] adj **1.** [reserved] réservé **2.** [leaving - official, MP] sortant **3.** [employee] qui part à la retraite.

retort [rɪ'tɔ:t] ◆ vi & vt rétorquer, riposter. ◆ n **1.** [reply] riposte f, réplique f **2.** CHEM cornue f.

retouch [ˌri:'tʌtʃ] vt [gen & PHOT] retoucher.

retrace [rɪ'treɪs] vt **1.** [go back over - route] refaire ▶ **to retrace one's steps** rebrousser chemin, revenir sur ses pas **2.** [reconstitute - past events, sb's movements] reconstituer.

retract [rɪ'trækt] ◆ vt **1.** [withdraw - statement, confession] retirer, rétracter liter ; [go back on - promise, agreement] revenir sur **2.** [draw in - claws, horns] rétracter, rentrer ; [AERON - wheels] rentrer, escamoter. ◆ vi **1.** [recant] se rétracter, se désavouer **2.** [be drawn in - claws, horns] se rétracter ; [AERON - wheels] rentrer.

retractable [rɪ'træktəbl] adj **1.** [aerial, undercarriage] escamotable **2.** [statement] que l'on peut rétracter or désavouer.

retraction [rɪ'trækʃn] n [of false information] démenti m.

retrain [ˌri:'treɪn] ◆ vt recycler. ◆ vi se recycler.

retraining [ˌri:'treɪnɪŋ] n recyclage m.

retread ◆ vt [ˌri:'tred] (pt retrod [-'trɒd], pp retrodden [-'trɒdn] or retrod [-'trɒd]) AUTO rechaper. ◆ n ['ri:tred] pneu m rechapé.

retreat [rɪ'tri:t] ◆ vi **1.** MIL battre en retraite, se replier **2.** [gen] se retirer / to retreat to the country se retirer à la campagne. ◆ n **1.** [gen & MIL] retraite f, repli m ▶ **to beat / to sound the retreat** battre / sonner la retraite **2.** [refuge] refuge m, asile m **3.** RELIG retraite f ▶ **to go on a retreat** faire une retraite.

retrenchment [ri:'trentʃmənt] n [of costs, expenses] réduction f, compression f.

retrial [ˌri:'traɪəl] n nouveau procès m.

retribution [ˌretrɪ'bju:ʃn] n punition f, châtiment m.

⚠ **Rétribution** means payment, not retribution.

retrieval [rɪ'tri:vl] n **1.** [getting back - of object] récupération f ; [- of fortune, health] recouvrement m **2.** COMPUT récupération f, extraction f ▶ **data retrieval** recherche f de données **3.** [making good - of mistake] réparation f / the situation is beyond retrieval il n'y a plus rien à faire (pour sauver la situation).

retrieve [rɪ'tri:v] ◆ vt **1.** [get back - lost object] récupérer ; [- health, fortune] recouvrer, retrouver **2.** [save] sauver **3.** COMPUT [data] récupérer, extraire **4.** [make good - mistake] réparer ; [- situation] rattraper, sauver **5.** HUNT rapporter. ◆ vi HUNT rapporter le gibier.

retriever [rɪ'tri:və] n [gen] retriever m ; [golden retriever] Golden retriever m ; [Labrador retriever] Labrador retriever.

retro ['retrəʊ] adj rétro (inv).

retroactive [ˌretrəʊ'æktɪv] adj rétroactif.

retrofit ['retrəʊfɪt] (pt & pp retrofitted) ◆ vt [machine] équiper après fabrication ; [building, factory] mettre aux normes. ◆ vi [building, factory] se mettre aux normes. ◆ n **1.** [adding components] ajout m d'équipements **2.** [added component] équipement m ajouté **3.** [of building, factory] mise f aux normes.

retrograde ['retrəgreɪd] ◆ adj rétrograde. ◆ vi **1.** [gen] rétrograder **2.** [US] MIL [retreat] battre en retraite.

retrogressive [ˌretrə'gresɪv] adj rétrogressif, régressif.

retrospect ['retrəspekt] ❖ **in retrospect** adv phr rétrospectivement, avec le recul.

retrospective [,retrə'spektɪv] ❖ adj rétrospectif. ❖ n ART rétrospective f.

retrospectively [,retrə'spektɪvlɪ] adv rétrospectivement.

retry [,ri:'traɪ] (pt & pp **retried**) vt LAW refaire le procès de, juger à nouveau.

return [rɪ'tɜ:n] ❖ vi **1.** [go back] retourner ; [come back] revenir **2.** [to subject, activity, former state] revenir / let's return to your question revenons à votre question / to return to work reprendre le travail / she returned to her reading elle reprit sa lecture / the situation should return to normal next week la situation devrait redevenir normale la semaine prochaine **3.** [reappear - fever, pain, good weather, fears] réapparaître. ❖ vt **1.** [give back] rendre ; [take back] rapporter ; [send back] renvoyer, retourner **2.** [replace, put back] remettre **3.** [repay - greeting, kindness, compliment] rendre (en retour) ; [reciprocate - affection] rendre **4.** SPORT [hit or throw back] renvoyer **5.** 🇬🇧 [elect] élire / she was returned as member for Tottenham elle a été élue député de Tottenham **6.** [reply] répondre **7.** LAW [pronounce - verdict] rendre, prononcer **8.** FIN [yield - profit, interest] rapporter **9.** [in bridge] rejouer. ❖ adj [fare] aller (et) retour ; [trip, flight] de retour / the return journey le (voyage du) retour. ❖ n **1.** [going or coming back] retour m / on her return à son retour ❱ **the point of no return** le point de non-retour **2.** [giving or taking back] retour m ; [sending back] renvoi m, retour m ❱ **by return (of post)** 🇬🇧 par retour du courrier **3.** 🇬🇧 [round trip] aller et retour m **4.** [to subject, activity, earlier state] retour m / a return to normal un retour à la normale / the strikers' return to work la reprise du travail par les grévistes **5.** [reappearance - of fever, pain, good weather] réapparition f, retour m **6.** FIN [yield] rapport m / a 10% return on investment un rendement de 10 % sur la somme investie **7.** [for income tax] (formulaire m de) déclaration f d'impôts **8.** SPORT [esp in tennis] retour m **9.** ARCHIT retour m. ❖ **returns** pl n **1.** [results] résultats mpl ; [statistics] statistiques fpl, chiffres mpl **2.** [birthday greetings] ❱ **many happy returns (of the day)!** bon or joyeux anniversaire ! ❖ **in return** adv phr en retour, en échange. ❖ **in return for** prep phr en échange de.

returnable [rɪ'tɜ:nəbl] adj **1.** [container, bottle] consigné **2.** [document] à retourner.

returning officer [rɪ'tɜ:nɪŋ-] n président m, -e f du bureau de vote.

return key n COMPUT touche f entrée.

return match n match m retour.

return ticket n 🇬🇧 (billet m d')aller (et) retour m.

reunification [,ri:ju:nɪfɪ'keɪʃn] n réunification f.

reunify [,ri:'ju:nɪfaɪ] (pt & pp **reunified**) vt réunifier.

reunion [,ri:'ju:njən] n réunion f.

Reunion [,ri:'ju:njən] pr n ❱ **Reunion (Island)** (l'île f de) La Réunion / in Reunion à La Réunion.

reunite [,ri:ju:'naɪt] ❖ vt réunir. ❖ vi se réunir.

reupholster [,ri:ʌp'həʊlstər] vt rembourrer (de nouveau).

reusable [ri:'ju:zəbl] adj réutilisable, recyclable.

re-use ❖ vt [,ri:'ju:z] réutiliser, remployer, recycler. ❖ n [,ri:'ju:s] réutilisation f, remploi m, recyclage m.

rev [rev] (pt & pp **revved**, cont **revving**) inf ❖ n (abbr of **revolution**) AUTO tour m. ❖ vt & vi = **rev up**. ❖ **rev up** inf ❖ vt sep [engine] emballer. ❖ vi [driver] appuyer sur l'accélérateur ; [engine] s'accélérer.

Rev. written abbr of **Reverend**.

revalue [,ri:'vælju:] vt **1.** [currency] réévaluer **2.** [property] réévaluer, estimer à nouveau la valeur de.

revamp [,ri:'væmp] vt inf rafistoler, retaper.

rev counter n inf compte-tours m inv.

Revd written abbr of **reverend**.

reveal [rɪ'vi:l] vt **1.** [disclose, divulge] révéler **2.** [show] révéler, découvrir, laisser voir.

revealing [rɪ'vi:lɪŋ] adj **1.** [experience, action] révélateur **2.** [dress] décolleté, qui ne cache rien ; [neckline] décolleté.

revealingly [rɪ'vi:lɪŋlɪ] adv **1.** [significantly] : revealingly, not one of them speaks a foreign language il est révélateur qu'aucun d'entre eux ne parle une langue étrangère **2.** [exposing the body] : a revealingly short dress une robe courte qui laisse tout voir.

reveille [🇬🇧 rɪ'vælɪ 🇺🇸 'revəlɪ] n MIL réveil m.

revel ['revl] (🇬🇧 pt & pp **revelled**, cont **revelling** ; 🇺🇸 pt & pp **reveled**, cont **reveling**) vi **1.** [bask, wallow] se délecter ❱ **to revel in sthg** se délecter de or à qqch **2.** [make merry] s'amuser. ❖ **revels** pl n festivités fpl.

revelation [,revə'leɪʃn] n révélation f.

reveller, **reveler** 🇺🇸 ['revələr] n fêtard m, -e f, noceur m, -euse f.

revelry ['revlrɪ] n festivités fpl.

revenge [rɪ'vendʒ] ❖ n **1.** [vengeance] vengeance f, revanche f / I'll get or I'll take my revenge on him for this! il va me le payer ! / she did it out of revenge elle l'a fait pour se venger or par vengeance **2.** SPORT revanche f. ❖ vt venger / how can I revenge myself on them for this insult? comment leur faire payer cette insulte ?

revenue ['revənju:] ❖ n **1.** [gen] revenu m ❱ **state revenue** or **revenues** les recettes publiques or de l'État **2.** inf ❱ **the Revenue** (the Internal Revenue) le fisc. ❖ comp [department, official] du fisc ❱ **revenue expenditure** dépenses fpl de fonctionnement.

revenue stream n source f de revenus.

reverberate [rɪ'vɜ:bəreɪt] vi **1.** [sound] résonner, retentir / the building reverberated with their cries l'immeuble retentissait de leurs cris **2.** [light] se réverbérer **3.** fig [spread] retentir.

reverberation [rɪ,vɜ:bə'reɪʃn] n **1.** [of sound, light] réverbération f **2.** fig [repercussion] retentissement m, répercussion f.

revere [rɪ'vɪər] vt révérer, vénérer.

reverence ['revərəns] ❖ n **1.** [respect] révérence f, vénération f **2.** [term of address] : Your Reverence mon révérend (Père) / His Reverence the Archbishop Son Excellence l'archevêque.

reverend ['revərənd] ❖ adj **1.** RELIG ❱ **a reverend gentleman** un révérend père / the Reverend Paul James le révérend Paul James **2.** [gen - respected] vénérable, révéré. ❖ n [Protestant] pasteur m ; [Catholic] curé m.

Reverend Mother n Révérende Mère f.

reverent ['revərənt] adj respectueux, révérencieux liter.

reverential [,revə'renʃl] adj révérenciel.

reverently ['revərəntlɪ] adv avec révérence, révérencieusement liter.

reverie ['revərɪ] n liter [gen & MUS] rêverie f.

revers [rɪ'vɪər] (pl **revers** [rɪ'vɪəz]) n revers m.

reversal [rɪ'vɜ:sl] n **1.** [change - of situation] retournement m ; [- of opinion] revirement m ; [- of order, roles] interversion f, inversion f ; [- of policy] changement m **2.** [setback] revers m.

reverse [rɪ'vɜ:s] ❖ vt **1.** [change - process, trend] renverser ; [- situation] retourner ; [- order, roles, decline] inverser **2.** [turn round - garment] retourner ; [- photo] inverser

3. [annul -decision] annuler ; LAW casser, annuler **4.** [cause to go backwards -car] mettre en marche arrière ; [-machine] renverser la marche de **5.** UK TELEC ▸ **to reverse the charges** appeler en PCV. ◆ vi AUTO [car, driver] faire marche arrière. ◆ n **1.** AUTO marche *f* arrière / *in reverse* en marche arrière **2.** [contrary] contraire *m*, inverse *m*, opposé *m* **3.** [other side -of cloth, leaf] envers *m* ; [-of sheet of paper] verso *m* ; [-of coin, medal] revers *m* **4.** [setback] revers *m*, échec *m* ; [defeat] défaite *f*. ◆ adj **1.** [opposite, contrary] inverse, contraire, opposé **2.** [back] ▸ **the reverse side a)** [of cloth, leaf] l'envers **b)** [of sheet of paper] le verso **c)** [of coin, medal] le revers **3.** [turned around] inversé ▸ **a reverse image** une image inversée **4.** AUTO ▸ **reverse gear** marche *f* arrière.

reverse-charge call n UK appel *m* en PCV.

reverse discrimination n discrimination à l'encontre d'un groupe normalement privilégié.

reversible [rɪ'vɜːsəbl] adj [coat, process] réversible ; [decision] révocable.

reversing light [rɪ'vɜːsɪŋ-] n feu *m* de recul.

revert [rɪ'vɜːt] vi retourner, revenir / *he soon reverted to his old ways* il est vite retombé dans or il a vite repris ses anciennes habitudes / *to revert to childhood* retomber en enfance / *the property reverts to the spouse* LAW les biens reviennent à l'époux ▸ **to revert to type** retrouver sa vraie nature.

review [rɪ'vjuː] ◆ n **1.** [critical article] critique *f* **2.** [magazine] revue *f* ; [radio or TV programme] magazine *m* **3.** [assessment -of situation, conditions] étude *f*, examen *m*, bilan *m* / *pollution controls are under review* on est en train de réexaminer la réglementation en matière de pollution ▸ **review board** commission *f* d'étude **4.** [reassessment -of salary, prices, case] révision *f* / *all our prices are subject to review* tous nos prix sont susceptibles d'être révisés / *my salary comes* or *is up for review next month* mon salaire doit être révisé le mois prochain **5.** MIL [inspection] revue *f* **6.** US SCH & UNIV [revision] révision *f* **7.** = revue. ◆ vt **1.** [write critical article on] faire la critique de **2.** [assess] examiner, étudier, faire le bilan de ; [reassess] réviser ; LAW [case] réviser **3.** [go back over, look back on] passer en revue **4.** MIL [troops] passer en revue **5.** [revise] réviser.

review copy n exemplaire *m* de service de presse.

reviewer [rɪ'vjuːə'] n PRESS critique *m*.

revile [rɪ'vaɪl] vt *liter* vilipender, injurier.

revise [rɪ'vaɪz] ◆ vt **1.** [alter -policy, belief, offer, price] réviser **2.** [read through -text, manuscript] revoir, corriger **3.** [update] mettre à jour, corriger UK SCH & UNIV réviser. ◆ vi UK SCH & UNIV réviser.

revised [rɪ'vaɪzd] adj **1.** [figures, estimate] révisé **2.** [edition] revu et corrigé.

revision [rɪ'vɪʒn] n **1.** [alteration, etc.] révision *f* **2.** UK SCH & UNIV révision *f*.

revisionism [rɪ'vɪʒnɪzm] n révisionnisme *m*.

revisionist [rɪ'vɪʒnɪst] ◆ adj révisionniste. ◆ n révisionniste *mf*.

revisit [ˌriː'vɪzɪt] vt [place] revisiter ; [person] retourner voir.

revitalize, revitalise [ˌriː'vaɪtəlaɪz] vt revitaliser.

revival [rɪ'vaɪvl] n **1.** [resurgence] renouveau *m*, renaissance *f* / *a religious revival* un renouveau de la religion ▸ **revival tent** US chapiteau sous lequel se tiennent des réunions religieuses **2.** [bringing back -of custom, language] rétablissement *m* **3.** [of play, TV series] reprise *f* **4.** [from a faint] reprise *f* de connaissance ; [from illness] récupération *f*.

revive [rɪ'vaɪv] ◆ vi **1.** [regain consciousness] reprendre connaissance, revenir à soi ; [regain strength or form] récu-

pérer **2.** [flourish again -business, the economy] reprendre ; [-movement, group] renaître, ressusciter ; [-custom, expression] réapparaître. ◆ vt **1.** [restore to consciousness] ranimer ; MED réanimer ; [restore strength to] remonter **2.** [make flourish again -discussion, faith, etc.] ranimer, raviver ; [-business, the economy] relancer, faire redémarrer ; [-interest, hope, etc.] raviver, faire renaître **3.** [bring back -law] remettre en vigueur ; [-fashion] relancer ; [-style, look] remettre en vogue ; [-custom, language, movement] raviver, ressusciter **4.** [play, TV series] reprendre.

revocation [ˌrevə'keɪʃn] n [of decision] annulation *f* ; [of measure, law] abrogation *f*, annulation *f*, révocation *f* ; [of will] révocation *f*, annulation *f* ; [of title, diploma, permit] retrait *m*.

revoke [rɪ'vəuk] vt [decision] annuler ; [measure, law] abroger, annuler, révoquer ; [will] révoquer, annuler ; [title, diploma, permit] retirer.

revolt [rɪ'vəult] ◆ vi [rise up] se révolter, se rebeller, se soulever. ◆ vt dégoûter / *she is revolted by the idea* l'idée la dégoûte or la révolte / *the sight of food revolts me at the moment* la vue de la nourriture m'écœure or me dégoûte en ce moment. ◆ n [uprising] révolte *f*, rébellion *f*.

revolting [rɪ'vəultɪŋ] adj **1.** [disgusting -story, scene] dégoûtant ; [-person, act] ignoble ; [-food, mess] écœurant, immonde **2.** *inf* [nasty] affreux.

revoltingly [rɪ'vəultɪŋlɪ] adv de façon dégoûtante ; [as intensifier] : *she's so revoltingly clever!* ça m'écœure qu'on puisse être aussi intelligent !

revolution [ˌrevə'luːʃn] n **1.** POL & *fig* révolution *f* **2.** [turn] révolution *f*, tour *m* ; [turning] révolution *f*.

revolutionary [ˌrevə'luːʃnərɪ] (*pl* **revolutionaries**) ◆ adj révolutionnaire. ◆ n révolutionnaire *mf*.

revolutionize, revolutionise [ˌrevə'luːʃənaɪz] vt **1.** [change radically] révolutionner **2.** POL [country] faire une révolution dans ; [people] insuffler des idées révolutionnaires à.

revolve [rɪ'vɒlv] ◆ vi **1.** [rotate] tourner / *the moon revolves around* or *round the earth* la Lune tourne autour de la Terre **2.** [centre, focus] tourner / *their conversation revolved around* or *round two main points* leur conversation tournait autour de deux points principaux **3.** [recur] revenir / *the seasons revolve* les saisons se succèdent. ◆ vt **1.** [rotate] faire tourner **2.** *fml* [ponder] considérer, ruminer.

revolver [rɪ'vɒlvə'] n revolver *m*.

revolving [rɪ'vɒlvɪŋ] adj [gen] tournant ; [chair] pivotant ; TECH rotatif ; ASTRON en rotation.

revolving door n tambour *m* (porte).

revue [rɪ'vjuː] n THEAT revue *f*.

revulsion [rɪ'vʌlʃn] n **1.** [disgust] répulsion *f*, dégoût *m* **2.** [recoiling] (mouvement *m* de) recul *m* **3.** MED révulsion *f*.

reward [rɪ'wɔːd] ◆ n récompense *f*. ◆ vt récompenser.

rewarding [rɪ'wɔːdɪŋ] adj gratifiant / *a very rewarding experience* / *career* une expérience / carrière très gratifiante / *the conference was most rewarding* le colloque était très enrichissant / *financially rewarding* rémunérateur, lucratif.

rewind (*pt* & *pp* **rewound** [ˌriː'waund]) ◆ vt [ˌriː'waɪnd] rembobiner. ◆ vi [ˌriː'waɪnd] se rembobiner. ◆ n ['riːwaɪnd] rembobinage *m* / *it has automatic rewind* ça se rembobine automatiquement ▸ **rewind button** bouton *m* de rembobinage.

rewire [ˌriː'waɪə'] vt [house] refaire l'électricité dans ; [machine] refaire les circuits électriques de.

reword [ˌriː'wɜːd] vt reformuler.

rework [ˌriː'wɜːk] vt **1.** [speech, text] retravailler **2.** INDUST retraiter.

reworking [ˌriːˈwɜːkɪŋ] n reprise f.

rewound [ˌriːˈwaʊnd] pt & pp ⟶ **rewind**.

rewritable [ˌriːˈraɪtəbl] adj COMPUT réinscriptible.

rewrite ◆ vt [ˌriːˈraɪt] (pt **rewrote** [-ˈrəʊt], pp **rewritten** [-ˈrɪtn]) récrire, réécrire ; [for publication] récrire, rewriter. ◆ n [ˈriːraɪt] **1.** inf [act] réécriture f, rewriting m **2.** [text] nouvelle version f.

rewriting [ˌriːˈraɪtɪŋ] n PRESS récriture f, rewriting m.

REX (abbr of **real-time executive**) n superviseur en temps réel.

Rex [reks] n 🇬🇧 : Edward / George Rex le roi Édouard / Georges, Édouard / Georges Roi / Rex v Gibson LAW la Couronne contre Gibson.

Reykjavik [ˈrekjəvɪk] pr n Reykjavik.

RFC (abbr of **Rugby Football Club**) n club de rugby.

RGDS MESSAGING written abbr of **regards**.

RGN (abbr of **registered general nurse**) n en Grande-Bretagne, infirmier ou infirmière diplômé(e) d'État.

Rh (written abbr of **rhesus**) Rh.

rhapsody [ˈræpsədɪ] (pl **rhapsodies**) n **1.** [ecstasy] extase f **2.** MUS & LITER rhapsodie f, rapsodie f.

rhesus baby [ˈriːsəs-] n bébé souffrant de la maladie hémolytique du nouveau-né.

rhesus factor n facteur m Rhésus.

rhesus negative adj Rhésus négatif.

rhesus positive adj Rhésus positif.

rhetoric [ˈretərɪk] n rhétorique f.

rhetorically [rɪˈtɒrɪklɪ] adv en rhétoricien / "who knows?", she asked rhetorically « qui sait ? », demanda-t-elle sans vraiment attendre de réponse / I was only asking rhetorically je demandais ça simplement pour la forme.

rhetorical question n question f posée pour la forme.

rheumatic [ruːˈmætɪk] ◆ adj [symptom] rhumatismal ; [person] rhumatisant ; [limbs] atteint de rhumatismes. ◆ n rhumatisant m, -e f.

rheumatism [ˈruːmətɪzm] n rhumatisme m.

rheumatoid arthritis n polyarthrite f rhumatoïde.

Rhine [raɪn] pr n ▶ **the (River) Rhine** le Rhin.

Rhineland [ˈraɪnlænd] pr n Rhénanie f.

rhinestone [ˈraɪnstəʊn] n fausse pierre f ; [smaller] strass m.

rhino [ˈraɪnəʊ] (pl **rhino** or **rhinos**) n rhinocéros m.

rhinoceros [raɪˈnɒsərəs] (pl **rhinoceros** or **rhinoceroses** or **rhinoceri** [-raɪ]) n rhinocéros m.

Rhode Island [rəʊd-] pr n Rhode Island m / in Rhode Island dans le Rhode Island.

Rhodes [rəʊdz] pr n Rhodes / in Rhodes à Rhodes.

rhododendron [ˌrəʊdəˈdendrən] n rhododendron m.

rhombus [ˈrɒmbəs] (pl **rhombuses** or **rhombi** [-baɪ]) n losange m.

Rhône [rəʊn] pr n ▶ **the (River) Rhône** le Rhône.

rhubarb [ˈruːbɑːb] n BOT rhubarbe f.

rhyme [raɪm] ◆ n **1.** [sound] rime f ▶ **without rhyme or reason** sans rime ni raison **2.** (U) [poetry] vers mpl / in rhyme en vers **3.** [poem] poème m. ◆ vi **1.** [word, lines] rimer **2.** [write verse] écrire or composer des poèmes. ◆ vt faire rimer.

rhyming slang [ˈraɪmɪŋ-] n sorte d'argot qui consiste à remplacer un mot par un groupe de mots choisis pour la rime.

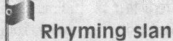
Rhyming slang

Cet argot londonien, qui consiste à remplacer un mot par une expression avec laquelle il rime, est traditionnellement employé par les **Cockneys**, mais certaines expressions sont passées dans la langue courante, comme **pork pie** (pour dire **lie**), **brown bread (dead)**, etc. On ne retient parfois que le premier élément de l'expression : **my old china** (qui vient de **china plate** pour dire **mate**); **to have a butcher's (butcher's hook** pour **look**).

---

rhythm [ˈrɪðm] n rythme m.

rhythm and blues n rhythm and blues m inv.

rhythm guitar n guitare f rythmique.

rhythmic(al) [ˈrɪðmɪk(l)] adj [pattern, exercice] rythmique ; [music, noise] rythmé.

rhythmically [ˈrɪðmɪklɪ] adv rythmiquement.

RI written abbr of **Rhode Island**.

rib [rɪb] (pt & pp **ribbed**, cont **ribbing**) ◆ n **1.** ANAT côte f **2.** CULIN côte f **3.** [of vault, leaf, aircraft or insect wing] nervure f ; [of ship's hull] couple m, membre m ; [of umbrella] baleine f **4.** [in knitting] côte f **5.** [on mountain - spur] éperon m ; [- crest] arête f **6.** [vein of ore] veine f, filon m. ◆ vt inf [tease] taquiner, mettre en boîte.

ribald [ˈrɪbəld] adj liter [joke, language] grivois, paillard ; [laughter] égrillard.

ribbed [rɪbd] adj **1.** [leaf, vault] à nervures **2.** [sweater, fabric] à côtes.

ribbing [ˈrɪbɪŋ] n **1.** (U) TEXT côtes fpl **2.** inf [teasing] taquinerie f, mise f en boîte.

ribbon [ˈrɪbən] n **1.** [for hair, typewriter, parcel, etc.] ruban m **2.** fig [of road] ruban m ; [of land] bande f ; [of cloud] traînée f.

ribcage [ˈrɪbkeɪdʒ] n cage f thoracique.

rib-eye n : rib-eye (steak) faux-filet m.

rib-tickler n inf & hum plaisanterie f.

rice [raɪs] n riz m ▶ **rice paddy** rizière f.

ricefield [ˈraɪsfiːld] n rizière f.

rice-growing adj [country, region] rizicole.

rice paper n papier m de riz.

rice pudding n riz m au lait.

rice wine n alcool m de riz, saké m.

rich [rɪtʃ] ◆ adj **1.** [wealthy, affluent] riche **2.** [elegant, luxurious] riche, luxueux, somptueux **3.** [abundant, prolific] riche, abondant / rich in vitamins / proteins riche en vitamines / protéines **4.** [fertile] riche, fertile **5.** [full, eventful] riche **6.** [strong, intense - colour] riche, chaud, vif ; [- voice, sound] chaud, riche ; [- smell] fort **7.** [food] riche ; [meal] lourd **8.** [funny] drôle / I say, that's a bit rich! inf c'est un peu fort (de café) !, ça, c'est le comble ! ◆ pl n ▶ **the rich** les riches mpl. ⟷ **riches** pl n richesses fpl.

-rich in comp riche en... / vitamin-rich foods aliments mpl riches en vitamines.

richly [ˈrɪtʃlɪ] adv **1.** [handsomely, generously] largement, richement **2.** [thoroughly] largement, pleinement **3.** [abundantly] abondamment, richement **4.** [elegantly, luxuriously] somptueusement, luxueusement **5.** [vividly] : richly coloured aux couleurs riches or vives.

richness [ˈrɪtʃnɪs] n **1.** [wealth, affluence] richesse f **2.** [elegance, luxury] luxe m, richesse f **3.** [abundance] abondance f, richesse f **4.** [fertility] richesse f, fertilité f **5.** [fullness, eventfulness] richesse f **6.** [strength, intensity -of colour, sound] richesse f ; [-of smell] intensité f.

Richter scale ['rɪktə-] n échelle f de Richter.

rickets ['rɪkɪts] n *(U)* rachitisme m.

rickety ['rɪkətɪ] adj **1.** [shaky -structure] branlant ; [-chair] bancal ; [-vehicle] (tout) bringuebalant **2.** [feeble -person] frêle, chancelant **3.** MED rachitique.

rickshaw ['rɪkʃɔː] n [pulled] pousse m inv, poussepousse m inv ; [pedalled] cyclo-pousse m inv.

ricochet ['rɪkəʃeɪ] (*pt & pp* **ricocheted** [-ʃeɪd] or **ricochetted** [-ʃetɪd], *cont* **ricocheting** [-ʃeɪɪŋ] or **ricochetting** [-ʃetɪŋ]) ◆ n ricochet m. ◆ vi ricocher ▶ **to ricochet off sthg** ricocher sur qqch.

rid [rɪd] (*pt & pp* **rid** or **ridded**, *cont* **ridding**) ◆ vt débarrasser / *we must rid the country of corruption* il faut débarrasser le pays de la corruption. ◆ adj ▶ **to get rid of** se débarrasser de ▶ **to be rid of** être débarrassé de.

riddance ['rɪdəns] n débarras m ▶ **good riddance (to bad rubbish)!** inf bon débarras !

ridden ['rɪdn] ◆ pp ⟶ **ride.** ◆ adj affligé, atteint.

-ridden in comp ▶ **debt-ridden** criblé de dettes ▶ **disease-ridden** infesté de maladies ▶ **flea-ridden** infesté de puces.

riddle ['rɪdl] ◆ n **1.** [poser] devinette f ▶ **to ask sb a riddle** poser une devinette à qqn **2.** [mystery] énigme f ▶ **to talk** or **to speak in riddles** parler par énigmes **3.** [sieve] crible m, tamis m. ◆ vt **1.** [pierce] cribler / *they riddled the car with bullets* ils criblèrent la voiture de balles **2.** [sift] passer au crible, cribler.

riddled ['rɪdld] adj plein ▶ **riddled with** plein de.

ride [raɪd] (*pt* **rode** [rəʊd], *pp* **ridden** ['rɪdn]) ◆ vt **1.** [horse] monter à ; [camel, donkey, elephant] monter à dos de / *they were riding horses / donkeys / camels* ils étaient à cheval / à dos d'âne / à dos de chameau **2.** [bicycle, motorcycle] monter sur / *I don't know how to ride a bike / a motorbike* je ne sais pas faire du vélo / conduire une moto / *she was riding a motorbike* elle était en moto / *she rides her bike everywhere* elle se déplace toujours à vélo **3.** [go about -fields, valleys] parcourir **4.** [participate in -race] faire **5.** US [have a go on -roundabout, fairground attraction] faire un tour de ; [lift, ski lift] prendre **6.** US [travel on -bus, subway, train, ferry] prendre **7.** US [give a lift to] amener / *hop in and I'll ride you home* monte, je te ramène chez toi. ◆ vi **1.** [ride a horse] monter (à cheval), faire du cheval / *I was stiff after riding all day* j'avais des courbatures après avoir chevauché toute la journée or après une journée entière à cheval **2.** [go -on horseback] aller (à cheval) ; [-by bicycle] aller (à vélo) ; [-by car] aller (en voiture) / *we rode along the canal and over the bridge* nous avons longé le canal et traversé le pont / *he rode by on a bicycle / on a white horse / on a donkey* il passa à vélo / sur un cheval blanc / monté sur un âne ▶ **to ride off a)** [leave] partir **b)** [move away] s'éloigner **3.** [float, sail] voguer ▶ **we'll have to ride with it** inf il faudra faire avec **4.** [be sustained -person] être porté / *she was riding on a wave of popularity* elle était portée par une vague de popularité **5.** [depend] dépendre / *my reputation is riding on the outcome* ma réputation est en jeu **6.** [money in bet] miser **7.** [continue undisturbed] : *he decided to let the matter ride* il a décidé de laisser courir. ◆ n **1.** [trip -for pleasure] promenade f, tour m ▶ **to go for a car / motorcycle ride** (aller) faire un tour or une promenade en voiture / en moto / *we went on long bicycle / horse rides* nous avons fait de longues promenades à vélo / à cheval / *how about a ride in my new car?* et si on faisait un tour dans ma nouvelle voiture ? ; [when talking about distance] parcours m, trajet m / *she has a long car / bus ride to work* elle doit faire un long trajet

en voiture / en bus pour aller travailler / *it's a 30-minute ride by bus / train / car* il faut 30 minutes en bus / train / voiture **2.** ▶ **to give sb a rough ride**: *the journalists gave her a rough ride* les journalistes ne l'ont pas ménagée **3.** US [lift -in car] : *can you give me a ride to the station?* peux-tu me conduire à la gare ? / *don't accept rides from strangers* ne montez pas dans la voiture de quelqu'un que vous ne connaissez pas **4.** [in fairground -attraction] manège m ; [-turn] tour m / *to have a ride on the big wheel* faire un tour sur la grande roue **5.** PHR ▶ **to take sb for a ride** inf **a)** [deceive] faire marcher qqn **b)** [cheat] arnaquer or rouler qqn **c)** US [kill] descendre or liquider qqn. ◆ **ride out** vt insep [difficulty, crisis] surmonter ; [recession] survivre à ▶ **to ride out the storm a)** NAUT étaler la tempête **b)** *fig* surmonter la crise, tenir.

rider ['raɪdə] n **1.** [of horse, donkey] cavalier m, -ère f ; [of bicycle] cycliste mf ; [of motorcycle] motocycliste mf **2.** [proviso] condition f, stipulation f **3.** [annexe -to contract] annexe f ; UK LAW [jury recommendation] recommandation f **4.** [on scales] curseur m.

ridge [rɪdʒ] ◆ n **1.** [of mountains] crête f, ligne f de faîte ; [leading to summit] crête f, arête f **2.** [raised strip or part] arête f, crête f ; AGR [in ploughed field] crête f / *a ridge of high pressure* METEOR une crête de haute pression, une dorsale barométrique *spec* **3.** [of roof] faîte m. ◆ vt [crease] sillonner, rider.

ridicule ['rɪdɪkjuːl] ◆ n ridicule m. ◆ vt ridiculiser, tourner en ridicule.

ridiculous [rɪ'dɪkjʊləs] ◆ adj ridicule. ◆ n ▶ **the ridiculous** le ridicule.

ridiculously [rɪ'dɪkjʊləslɪ] adv ridiculement.

ridiculousness [rɪ'dɪkjʊləsnɪs] n ridicule m.

riding ['raɪdɪŋ] ◆ n **1.** EQUIT ▶ **(horse) riding** équitation f ▶ **to go riding** faire de l'équitation or du cheval **2.** [in Yorkshire] division f administrative **3.** [in Canada, New Zealand] circonscription f électorale. ◆ comp [boots, jacket] de cheval ; [techniques] d'équitation.

riding crop n cravache f.

riding habit n tenue f d'amazone.

riding school n centre m équestre.

rife [raɪf] adj **1.** [widespread] répandu **2.** [full] ▶ **rife with** abondant en.

riffraff ['rɪfræf] n racaille f.

rifle ['raɪfl] ◆ vt **1.** [search] fouiller (dans) **2.** [rob] dévaliser **3.** [steal] voler **4.** [gun barrel] rayer. ◆ vi ▶ **to rifle through sthg** fouiller dans qqch. ◆ n [gun] fusil m. ◆ comp [bullet, butt, shot] de fusil.

rifle range n **1.** [for practice] champ m de tir **2.** [distance] ▶ **within rifle range** à portée de tir or de fusil.

rift [rɪft] ◆ n **1.** [gap, cleavage] fissure f, crevasse f ; GEOL [fault] faille f / *a rift in the clouds* une trouée dans les nuages **2.** *fig* [split] cassure f, faille f ; POL scission f ; [quarrel] désaccord m, querelle f. ◆ vt scinder. ◆ vi se scinder.

rift vault n fossé m d'effondrement.

Rift Valley pr n ▶ **the Rift Valley** la Rift Valley.

rig [rɪg] (*pt & pp* **rigged**, *cont* **rigging**) ◆ vt **1.** [fiddle] truquer / *to rig a jury* manipuler un jury **2.** NAUT gréer **3.** [install] monter, bricoler. ◆ n **1.** [gen -equipment] matériel m **2.** NAUT gréement m **3.** PETR [on land] derrick m ; [offshore] plate-forme f **4.** inf [clothes] tenue f, fringues fpl **5.** US [truck] semi-remorque m. ◆ **rig out** vt sep **1.** inf [clothe] habiller **2.** [equip] équiper. ◆ **rig up** vt sep [install] monter, installer.

rigamarole ['rɪgəmərəʊl] n = **rigmarole**.

rigging ['rɪgɪŋ] n **1.** NAUT gréement m **2.** THEAT machinerie f **3.** [fiddling] trucage m.

right [raɪt] ◆ adj **1.** [indicating location, direction] droit **/** *raise your right hand* levez la main droite **/** *take the next right (turn)* prenez la prochaine à droite **2.** [accurate, correct - prediction] juste, exact ; [- answer, address] bon **/** *he didn't give me the right change* il ne m'a pas rendu la monnaie exacte **/** *the clock is right* l'horloge est juste or à l'heure **/** *the sentence doesn't sound* **/** *look quite right* la phrase sonne / a l'air un peu bizarre **/** *there's something not quite right in what he says* il y a quelque chose qui cloche dans ce qu'il dit ; [person] ▶ **to be right** avoir raison **/** *you were right about him* vous aviez raison à son sujet **/** *that's right* c'est juste, oui **/** *he got the pronunciation* **/** *spelling right* il l'a bien prononcé / épelé **/** *she got the answer right* elle a donné la bonne réponse ▶ **to put sb right (about sthg / sb)** détromper qqn (au sujet de qqch / qqn) ▶ **to put things** or **matters right a)** [politically, financially, etc.] redresser or rétablir la situation **b)** [in relationships] arranger les choses **/** *he made a mess of it and I had to put things right* il a raté son coup et j'ai dû réparer les dégâts **3.** [appropriate - diploma, tool, sequence, moment] bon ; [best - choice, decision] meilleur **/** *are we going in the right direction?* est-ce que nous allons dans le bon sens ? **/** *when the time is right* au bon moment, au moment voulu **/** *I can't find the right word* je ne trouve pas le mot juste **/** *she's the right woman for the job* c'est la femme qu'il faut pour ce travail **/** *it wasn't the right thing to say* ce n'était pas la chose à dire **/** *you've done the right thing to tell us about it* vous avez bien fait de nous en parler **/** *he did the right thing, but for the wrong reasons* il a fait le bon choix, mais pour de mauvaises raisons **/** *you're not doing it the right way!* ce n'est pas comme ça qu'il faut faire or s'y prendre ! **4.** [fair, just] juste, équitable ; [morally good] bien *(inv)* ; [socially correct] correct **/** *it's not right to separate the children* ce n'est pas bien de séparer les enfants **/** *I don't think capital punishment is right* je ne crois pas que la peine de mort soit juste **/** *I thought it right to ask you first* j'ai cru bon de vous demander d'abord **/** *it's only right that you should know* il est juste que vous le sachiez **/** *I only want to do what is right* je ne cherche qu'à bien faire ▶ **to do the right thing (by sb)** bien agir (avec qqn) **5.** [functioning properly] : *there's something not quite right with the motor* le moteur ne marche pas très bien **6.** [healthy] bien *(inv)* **/** *my knee doesn't feel right* j'ai quelque chose au genou ▶ **to be right in the head** *inf : he's not quite right in the head* ça ne va pas très bien dans sa tête **/** *nobody in their right mind would refuse such an offer!* aucune personne sensée ne refuserait une telle offre ! **7.** [satisfactory] bien *(inv)* **/** *things aren't right between them* ça ne va pas très bien entre eux **8.** **UK** *inf* [as intensifier] vrai, complet **/** *I felt like a right idiot* je me sentais vraiment bête. ◆ adv **1.** [in directions] à droite **/** *turn right at the traffic lights* tournez à droite au feu (rouge) **/** *the party is moving further right* le parti est en train de virer plus à droite **2.** [accurately, correctly - hear] bien ; [- guess] juste ; [- answer, spell] bien, correctement **/** *if I remember right* si je me rappelle bien **3.** [properly] bien, comme il faut **/** *the top isn't on right* le couvercle n'est pas bien mis **/** *nothing is going right today* tout va de travers aujourd'hui **/** *he can't do anything right* il ne peut rien faire correctement or comme il faut **4.** [emphasizing precise location] : *the lamp's shining right in my eyes* j'ai la lumière de la lampe en plein dans les yeux or en pleine figure **/** *it's right opposite the post office* c'est juste en face de la poste **/** *it's right in front of* / *behind you* c'est droit devant vous / juste derrière vous **/** *I'm right behind you there* *fig* je suis entièrement d'accord avec vous là-dessus **5.** [emphasizing precise time] juste, exactement **/** *I arrived right at that moment* je suis arrivé juste à ce moment-là **/** *right in the middle of the fight* au beau milieu de la bagarre **6.** [all the way] : *it's right at the back of the drawer* / *at the front of the book*

c'est tout au fond du tiroir / juste au début du livre **/** *right from the start* dès le début **/** *we worked right up until the last minute* nous avons travaillé jusqu'à la toute dernière minute **7.** [immediately] tout de suite **/** *I'll be right over* je viens tout de suite **8.** [justly, fairly] bien ; [properly, fittingly] correctement **/** *you did right* tu as bien fait ▶ **to do right by sb** agir correctement envers qqn. ◆ n **1.** [in directions] droite f **/** *look to the* or *your right* regardez à droite or sur votre droite **/** *keep to the* or *your right* restez à droite **/** *from right to left* de droite à gauche **2.** POL droite f **3.** [entitlement] droit m **/** *the right to vote* / *of asylum* le droit de vote / d'asile ▶ **to have a right to sthg** avoir droit à qqch ▶ **to have a** or **the right to do sthg** avoir le droit de faire qqch **/** *you have every right to be angry* tu as toutes les raisons d'être en colère ▶ **in one's own right** : *she's rich in her own right* elle a une grande fortune personnelle **/** *he became a leader in his own right* il est devenu leader par son seul talent **4.** [what is good, moral] bien m ▶ **to know right from wrong** distinguer ce qui est bien de ce qui est mal ▶ **to be in the right** être dans le vrai, avoir raison. ◆ interj : *come tomorrow — right (you are)!* venez demain — d'accord ! **/** *right, let's get to work!* bon or bien, au travail ! ◆ vt **1.** [set upright again - chair, ship] redresser **2.** [redress - situation] redresser, rétablir ; [- damage] réparer ; [- injustice] réparer ▶ **to right a wrong** redresser un tort. ◆ **rights** pl n **1.** [political, social] droits *mpl* **/** *read him his rights* **US** [on arresting a suspect] prévenez-le de ses droits **2.** COMM droits *mpl* **/** *who has the mineral* / *film* / *distribution rights?* qui détient les droits miniers / d'adaptation cinématographique / de distribution ? **3.** **PHR** **to put** or **to set to rights a)** [room] mettre en ordre **b)** [firm, country] redresser **c)** [situation] arranger ▶ **to set the world to rights** *hum* refaire le monde. ◆ **by right(s)** adv phr en principe. ◆ **right away** adv phr [at once] tout de suite, aussitôt ; [from the start] dès le début ; [first go] du premier coup. ◆ **right now** adv phr **1.** [at once] tout de suite **2.** [at the moment] pour le moment. ◆ **right off** **US** = **right away.**

right angle n angle m droit **/** *a line at right angles to the base* une ligne perpendiculaire à la base.

right-angled triangle n **UK** triangle m rectangle.

right-click ◆ vt COMPUT cliquer avec le bouton droit de la souris sur. ◆ vi COMPUT cliquer avec le bouton droit de la souris.

righteous ['raɪtʃəs] adj **1.** [just] juste ; [virtuous] vertueux **2.** *pej* [self-righteous] suffisant **/** *righteous indignation* colère indignée.

righteousness ['raɪtʃəsnɪs] n vertu f, rectitude f.

rightful ['raɪtfʊl] adj légitime.

rightfully ['raɪtfʊlɪ] adv légitimement.

right-hand adj droit **/** *on the right-hand side* à droite **/** *the right-hand side of the road* le côté droit de la route **/** *it's in the right-hand drawer* c'est dans le tiroir de droite **/** *a right-hand bend* un virage à droite.

right-hand drive n AUTO conduite f à droite **/** *a right-hand drive vehicle* un véhicule avec la conduite à droite.

right-handed [-'hændɪd] adj **1.** [person] droitier **2.** [punch] du droit **3.** [scissors, golf club] pour droitiers ; [screw] fileté à droite.

right-hand man n bras m droit.

Right Honourable adj **UK** titre utilisé pour s'adresser à certains hauts fonctionnaires ou à quelqu'un ayant un titre de noblesse.

rightly ['raɪtlɪ] adv **1.** [correctly] correctement, bien **/** *I don't rightly know* *inf* je ne sais pas bien **2.** [with justification] à juste titre, avec raison **/** *he was rightly angry* or *he was angry and rightly so* il était en colère à juste titre.

right-minded adj raisonnable, sensé.

rightness ['raɪtnɪs] n **1.** [accuracy - of answer] exactitude f, justesse f ; [-of guess] justesse f **2.** [justness - of decision, judgment] équité f ; [-of claim] légitimité f **3.** [appropriateness - of tone, dress] justesse f, caractère m approprié.

righto ['raɪtəʊ] interj 🇬🇧 inf OK, d'ac.

right-of-centre adj centre droit.

right of way (pl **rights of way**) n **1.** AUTO priorité f ▸ **to have (the) right of way** avoir (la) priorité **2.** [right to cross land] droit m de passage **3.** [path, road] chemin m ; 🇺🇸 [for power line, railroad, etc.] voie f.

right-on adj inf idéologiquement correct.

rightsize ['raɪtsaɪz] vt dégraisser.

rightsizing ['raɪt,saɪzɪŋ] n dégraissage m.

right-thinking adj raisonnable, sensé.

right-to-life adj [movement, candidate] antiavortement.

right wing n **1.** POL droite f / the right wing of the party l'aile droite du parti **2.** SPORT [position] aile f droite ; [player] ailier m droit. ❖ **right-wing** adj POL de droite.

right-winger n **1.** POL homme m, femme f de droite **2.** SPORT ailier m droit.

rigid ['rɪdʒɪd] adj **1.** [structure, material] rigide ; [body, muscle] raide / he was rigid with fear il était paralysé par la peur / it shook me rigid! inf ça m'a fait un de ces coups ! **2.** [person, ideas, policy] rigide, inflexible ; [discipline] strict, sévère.

rigidity [rɪ'dʒɪdətɪ] n **1.** [of structure, material] rigidité f ; [of body, muscle] raideur f **2.** [of person, ideas, policy] rigidité f, inflexibilité f ; [of discipline] sévérité f.

rigidly ['rɪdʒɪdlɪ] adv rigidement, avec raideur.

rigmarole ['rɪgmərəʊl] n inf **1.** [procedure] cirque m **2.** [talk] charabia m, galimatias m.

rigor ['rɪgə] n 🇺🇸 = **rigour**.

rigorous ['rɪgərəs] adj rigoureux.

rigorously ['rɪgərəslɪ] adv rigoureusement, avec rigueur.

rigour 🇬🇧, **rigor** 🇺🇸 ['rɪgə] n rigueur f.

rile [raɪl] vt [person] agacer, énerver.

Riley ['raɪlɪ] pr n ▸ **to live the life of Riley** inf mener une vie de pacha.

rim [rɪm] (pt & pp **rimmed**, cont **rimming**) ❖ n **1.** [of bowl, cup] bord m ; [of eye, lake] bord m, pourtour m ; [of well] margelle f **2.** [of spectacles] monture f **3.** [of wheel] jante f **4.** [of dirt] marque f. ❖ vt border.

rimless ['rɪmlɪs] adj [spectacles] sans monture.

-rimmed [rɪmd] in comp : gold / steel-rimmed spectacles lunettes fpl à monture en or / d'acier.

rind [raɪnd] n [on bacon] couenne f ; [on cheese] croûte f ; [on fruit] écorce f ; [of bark] couche f extérieure.

ring [rɪŋ] ❖ n **1.** [sound of bell] sonnerie f / there was a ring at the door on a sonné (à la porte) **2.** [sound] son m ; [resounding] retentissement m ; fig [note] note f, accent m **3.** [telephone call] coup m de téléphone / give me a ring tomorrow passez-moi un coup de téléphone or appelez-moi demain **4.** [set of bells] jeu m de cloches **5.** [on finger] anneau m, bague f ; [in nose, ear] anneau m **6.** [round object] anneau m ; [for serviette] rond m ; [for swimmer] bouée f ; [for identifying bird] bague f ; [of piston] segment m ▸ **the rings** [in gym] les anneaux mpl **7.** [circle] cercle m, rond m ; [of smoke] rond m ; [in or around tree trunk] anneau m **8.** [for boxing, wrestling] ring m ; [in circus] piste f **9.** 🇬🇧 [for cooking - electric] plaque f ; [-gas] feu m, brûleur m **10.** [group of people] cercle m, clique f pej : spy / drug ring réseau m d'espions / de trafiquants de drogue **11.** CHEM [of atoms] chaîne f fermée. ❖ vt **1.** (pt rang [ræŋ], pp rung [rʌŋ]) [bell, alarm] sonner / I rang the doorbell j'ai sonné à la porte **2.** (pt rang [ræŋ], pp rung [rʌŋ]) 🇬🇧 [phone] téléphoner à, appeler **3.** [surround] entourer, encercler **4.** [draw circle round] entourer d'un cercle **5.** [bird] baguer ; [bull, pig] anneler **6.** [in quoits, hoopla - throw ring round] lancer un anneau sur. ❖ vi (pt rang [ræŋ], pp rung [rʌŋ]) **1.** [chime, peal - bell, telephone, alarm] sonner ; [with high pitch] tinter ; [long and loud] carillonner / the doorbell rang on a sonné (à la porte) **2.** [resound] résonner, retentir / my ears are ringing j'ai les oreilles qui bourdonnent ▸ **to ring true / false / hollow** sonner vrai / faux / creux **3.** [summon] sonner / to ring for the maid sonner la bonne **4.** 🇬🇧 [phone] téléphoner. ❖ **ring around** = **ring round**. ❖ **ring back** vi & vt sep 🇬🇧 [phone back] rappeler. ❖ **ring in** ❖ vi 🇬🇧 [phone] téléphoner. ❖ vt sep PHR **to ring the New Year in** sonner les cloches pour annoncer la nouvelle année. ❖ **ring off** vi 🇬🇧 raccrocher. ❖ **ring out** ❖ vi retentir. ❖ vt sep ▸ **to ring out the old year** sonner les cloches pour annoncer la fin de l'année. ❖ vt insep ▸ **to ring out the old and ring in the new** se débarrasser du vieux pour faire place au neuf. ❖ **ring round** vt insep 🇬🇧 téléphoner à, appeler. ❖ **ring up** vt sep 🇬🇧 **1.** [phone] téléphoner à, appeler **2.** [on cash register - sale, sum] enregistrer.

ring binder n classeur m (à anneaux).

ring-bound adj [notebook, file] à anneaux.

ringer ['rɪŋə] n **1.** [of bells] sonneur m, carillonneur m, -euse f **2.** inf [double] sosie m / he's a (dead) ringer for you vous vous ressemblez comme deux gouttes d'eau.

ring-fence vt [money to be spent, fund] allouer ; [bad debt, assets] isoler ; [project] délimiter, définir le périmètre de.

ring finger n annulaire m.

ringing ['rɪŋɪŋ] ❖ adj sonore, retentissant. ❖ n **1.** [of doorbell, phone, alarm] sonnerie f ; [of cowbell] tintement m ; [of church bells] carillonnement m **2.** [of cries, laughter] retentissement m ; [in ears] bourdonnement m.

ringing tone n sonnerie f, signal m d'appel.

ringleader ['rɪŋ,li:də] n meneur m, -euse f.

ringlet ['rɪŋlɪt] n boucle f (de cheveux).

ringmaster ['rɪŋ,mɑːstə] n ≃ Monsieur Loyal m.

ring-pull n 🇬🇧 anneau m, bague f (sur une boîte de boisson).

ring road n 🇬🇧 rocade f.

ringside ['rɪŋsaɪd] n (U) SPORT premiers rangs mpl.

ringtone ['rɪŋtəʊn] n sonnerie f.

ringway ['rɪŋweɪ] 🇬🇧 = **ring road**.

ringworm ['rɪŋwɜːm] n teigne f.

rink [rɪŋk] n [for ice-skating] patinoire f ; [for roller-skating] piste f (pour patins à roulettes).

rinse [rɪns] ❖ vt rincer. ❖ n **1.** [gen] rinçage m / I gave the shirt a good rinse j'ai bien rincé la chemise **2.** [for hair] rinçage m. ❖ **rinse out** vt sep rincer.

Rio ['riːəʊ], **Rio de Janeiro** [,riːəʊdʒə'nɪərəʊ] pr n Rio de Janeiro.

Rio Grande [,riːəʊ'grændɪ] pr n ▸ **the Rio Grande** le Rio Grande.

Rio Negro [,riːəʊ'neɪgrəʊ] pr n ▸ **the Rio Negro** le Rio Negro.

riot ['raɪət] ❖ n **1.** [civil disturbance] émeute f **2.** inf [funny occasion] : the party was a riot on s'est éclatés à la fête ; [funny person] : Jim's a riot Jim est désopilant or impayable **3.** [profusion] profusion f / the garden is a riot of colour le jardin offre une véritable débauche de couleurs. ❖ vi participer à or faire une émeute. ❖ adv ▸ **to run riot** : a group of youths ran riot un groupe de jeunes a provoqué une émeute / her imagination ran riot son imagination s'est déchaînée.

rioter ['raɪətəʳ] n émeutier m, -ère f.

rioting ['raɪətɪŋ] n (U) émeutes fpl.

riotous ['raɪətəs] adj **1.** [mob] déchaîné ; [behaviour] séditieux **2.** [debauched] débauché ; [exuberant, noisy] tapageur, bruyant **3.** [funny] désopilant, tordant.

riotously ['raɪətəslɪ] adv **1.** [seditiously] de façon séditieuse **2.** [noisily] bruyamment **3.** [as intensifier] : *it's riotously funny* inf c'est à mourir ou à hurler de rire.

riot police pl n police f or forces fpl antiémeutes.

riot shield n bouclier m antiémeutes.

riot squad n brigade f antiémeutes.

rip [rɪp] (pt & pp ripped, cont ripping) ◆ vt **1.** [tear] déchirer (violemment) / *he ripped the envelope open* il déchira l'enveloppe ▶ **to rip sthg to shreds** or **pieces** mettre qqch en morceaux ou en lambeaux **2.** [snatch] arracher **3.** US inf [rob] voler **4.** COMPUT ▶ **to rip a CD** graver un CD. ◆ vi **1.** [tear] se déchirer **2.** inf [go fast] aller à fond de train ou à fond la caisse. ◆ n déchirure f. ❖ **rip off** vt sep **1.** [tear off] arracher **2.** inf [cheat, overcharge] arnaquer **3.** inf [rob] dévaliser ; [steal] faucher, piquer. ❖ **rip out** vt sep arracher. ❖ **rip through** vt insep [subj: explosion, noise] déchirer. ❖ **rip up** vt sep [paper, cloth] déchirer (violemment), mettre en pièces ; [road surface, street] éventrer.

RIP ◆ (written abbr of **rest in peace**) RIP. ◆ n abbr of **Raster Image Processor**.

ripcording ['rɪpkɔːdɪŋ] n enregistrement de musique en ligne sous forme de fichiers MP3.

ripe [raɪp] adj **1.** [fruit, vegetable] mûr ; [cheese] fait, à point **2.** [age] ▶ **to live to a ripe old age** vivre jusqu'à un âge avancé **3.** [ready] prêt, mûr **4.** [full - lips] sensuel, charnu ; [breasts] plantureux **5.** [pungent - smell] âcre **6.** inf [vulgar] égrillard.

ripen ['raɪpn] ◆ vi [gen] mûrir ; [cheese] se faire. ◆ vt [subj: sun] mûrir ; [subj: farmer] (faire) mûrir.

ripeness ['raɪpnɪs] n maturité f.

rip-off n inf **1.** [swindle] escroquerie f, arnaque f **2.** [theft] vol m, fauche f.

ripped [rɪpt] adj US inf ▶ **to be ripped, to have a ripped body** être super musclé.

ripple ['rɪpl] ◆ n **1.** [on water] ride f, ondulation f ; [on wheatfield, hair, sand] ondulation f **2.** [sound - of waves] clapotis m ; [- of brook] gazouillis m ; [- of conversation] murmure m **3.** [repercussion] répercussion f, vague f ▶ **ripple effect** effet m de vague **4.** CULIN ▶ **strawberry / chocolate ripple (ice cream)** glace f marbrée à la fraise / au chocolat. ◆ vi **1.** [undulate - water] se rider ; [- wheatfield, hair] onduler ▶ **rippling muscles** muscles saillants ou puissants **2.** [murmur - water, waves] clapoter **3.** [resound, have repercussions] se répercuter. ◆ vt [water, lake] rider.

rip-roaring adj inf [noisy] bruyant, tapageur ; [great, fantastic] génial, super / *a rip-roaring success* un succès monstre.

rise [raɪz] (pt rose [rəʊz], pp risen ['rɪzn]) ◆ vi **1.** [get up - from chair, bed] se lever ; [- from knees, after fall] se relever / *he rose (from his chair) to greet me* il s'est levé (de sa chaise) pour me saluer ▶ **to rise to one's feet** se lever, se mettre debout ▶ **rise and shine!** debout ! **2.** [sun, moon, fog] se lever ; [smoke, balloon] s'élever, monter ; [tide, river level] monter ; [river] prendre sa source ; [land] s'élever ; [fish] mordre ; THEAT [curtain] se lever ; CULIN [dough] lever ; [soufflé] monter ▶ **to rise to the surface** [swimmer, whale] remonter à la surface / *the colour rose in* or *to her cheeks* le rouge lui est monté aux joues ▶ **to rise from the dead** RELIG ressusciter d'entre les morts ▶ **to rise to the occasion** se montrer à la hauteur de la situation **3.** [increase - value] augmenter ; [- number, amount] augmenter, monter ; [- prices,

costs] monter, augmenter, être en hausse ; [- temperature, pressure] monter ; [- barometer] monter, remonter ; [- wind] se lever ; [- tension, tone, voice] monter ; [- feeling, anger, panic] monter, grandir / *his spirits rose when he heard the news* il a été soulagé or heureux d'apprendre la nouvelle **4.** [mountains, buildings] se dresser, s'élever **5.** [socially, professionally] monter, réussir ▶ **to rise to fame** devenir célèbre ▶ **to rise in sb's esteem** monter dans l'estime de qqn ▶ **to rise from the ranks** sortir du rang **6.** [revolt] se soulever, se révolter ▶ **to rise in revolt (against sb / sthg)** se révolter (contre qqn / qqch). ◆ n **1.** [high ground] hauteur f, éminence f ; [slope] pente f ; [hill] côte f **2.** [of moon, sun, curtain] lever m ; [to power, influence] montée f, ascension f ; INDUST [development] essor m / *the rise and fall of the Roman Empire* la croissance et la chute or la grandeur et la décadence de l'Empire romain **3.** [increase - of price, crime, accidents] hausse f, augmentation f ; [- in bank rate, interest] relèvement m, hausse f ; [- of temperature, pressure] hausse f ; [- of affluence, wealth] augmentation f ▶ **to be on the rise** être en hausse / *there has been a steep rise in house prices* les prix de l'immobilier ont beaucoup augmenté / *rise in value* appréciation f ; UK [in salary] augmentation f (de salaire) ▶ **to be given a rise** être augmenté **4.** PHR ▶ **to give rise to sthg** donner lieu à qqch, entraîner qqch ▶ **to get** or **to take a rise out of sb** UK inf faire réagir qqn, faire marcher qqn. ❖ **rise above** vt insep [obstacle, fear] surmonter ; [figure] dépasser. ❖ **rise up** vi **1.** [get up] se lever ; [go up] monter, s'élever **2.** [revolt] se soulever, se révolter / *to rise up against an oppressor* se soulever contre un oppresseur **3.** [appear] apparaître.

riser ['raɪzəʳ] n [person] ▶ **to be an early / late riser** être un lève-tôt (inv) / lève-tard (inv).

rising ['raɪzɪŋ] ◆ n **1.** [revolt] insurrection f, soulèvement m **2.** [of sun, moon, of theatre curtain] lever m **3.** [of prices] augmentation f, hausse f **4.** [of river] crue f ; [of ground] élévation f **5.** [from dead] résurrection f **6.** [of Parliament, an assembly] ajournement m, clôture f de séance. ◆ adj **1.** [sun] levant **2.** [tide] montant ; [water level] ascendant **3.** [ground, road] qui monte **4.** [temperature, prices] en hausse ; FIN [market] orienté à la hausse **5.** [up-and-coming] : *he's a rising celebrity* c'est une étoile montante **6.** [emotion] croissant.

risk [rɪsk] ◆ n **1.** [gen] risque m ▶ **to take a risk** prendre un risque ▶ **to run the risk** courir le risque / *the government runs the risk of losing support* le gouvernement (court le) risque de ne plus être soutenu **2.** [in insurance] risque m ▶ **fire risk** risque d'incendie. ◆ vt [endanger, hazard] fml. ❖ **at risk** adj phr : *there's too much at risk* les risques or les enjeux sont trop importants / *all our jobs are at risk* tous nos emplois sont menacés ▶ **to be at risk** MED & SOCIOL être vulnérable ; une personne à risque.

risk assessment n évaluation f des risques.

risk-taking n (U) prise f de risques.

risky ['rɪskɪ] (compar riskier, superl riskiest) adj [hazardous] risqué, hasardeux.

risotto [rɪ'zɒtəʊ] (pl risottos) n risotto m.

risqué ['riːskeɪ] adj [story, joke] risqué, osé, scabreux.

rissole ['rɪsəʊl] n CULIN rissole f.

rite [raɪt] n rite m ▶ **rite of passage** cérémonie f d'initiation.

ritual ['rɪtʃʊəl] ◆ n rituel m. ◆ adj rituel.

ritualistic [ˌrɪtʃʊə'lɪstɪk] adj ritualiste.

rival ['raɪvl] (UK pt & pp rivalled, cont rivalling ; US pt & pp rivaled, cont rivaling) ◆ n [gen] rival m, -e f ; COMM rival m, -e f, concurrent m, -e f. ◆ adj [gen] rival ; COMM concurrent, rival. ◆ vt [gen] rivaliser avec ; COMM être en concurrence avec.

rivalry ['raɪvlrɪ] (*pl* **rivalries**) n rivalité *f*.

river ['rɪvər] ◆ n **1.** [as tributary] rivière *f* ; [flowing to sea] fleuve *m* **2.** *fig* [of mud, lava] coulée *f*. ◆ comp [port, system, traffic] fluvial ; [fish] d'eau douce.

riverbank ['rɪvəbæŋk] n rive *f*, berge *f*.

riverbed ['rɪvəbed] n lit *m* de rivière or de fleuve.

riverside ['rɪvəsaɪd] ◆ n bord *m* d'une rivière or d'un fleuve, rive *f*. ◆ adj au bord d'une rivière or d'un fleuve.

rivet ['rɪvɪt] ◆ n rivet *m*. ◆ vt **1.** TECH riveter, river **2.** *fig* ▶ **to be riveted to the spot** rester cloué or rivé sur place **3.** [fascinate] fasciner.

riveting ['rɪvɪtɪŋ] adj fascinant, passionnant, captivant.

Riviera [ˌrɪvɪ'eərə] pr n ▶ **the French Riviera** la Côte d'Azur / *on the French Riviera* sur la Côte d'Azur ▶ **the Italian Riviera** la Riviera italienne / *on the Italian Riviera* sur la Riviera italienne.

Riyadh ['riːæd] pr n Riyad, Riad.

RLR MESSAGING **written abbr of** earlier.

rly MESSAGING **written abbr of** really.

RMB (**written abbr of** ring my bell) MESSAGING ça veut dire quoi ?

RMT (**abbr of** National Union of Rail, Maritime and Transport Workers) pr n *syndicat britannique des cheminots et des gens de mer*.

RN ◆ pr n **abbr of** Royal Navy. ◆ n UK **1.** (**abbr of** registered nurse) [nurse] infirmier *m* diplômé (d'État) ; infirmière *f* diplômée (d'État) **2.** [qualification] diplôme *m* (d'État) d'infirmier.

RNA (**abbr of** ribonucleic acid) n ARN *m*.

RNLI (**abbr of** Royal National Lifeboat Institution) pr n *société britannique de sauvetage en mer*.

RNZAF (**abbr of** Royal New Zealand Air Force) pr n *armée de l'air néo-zélandaise*.

RNZN (**abbr of** Royal New Zealand Navy) pr n *marine de guerre néo-zélandaise*.

roach [rəʊtʃ] n **1.** (*pl* **roach** or **roaches**) [fish] gardon *m* **2.** US *inf* [cockroach] cafard *m*, cancrelat *m* **3.** *drugs sl* [of marijuana cigarette] filtre *m* ▶ **roach clip** fume-joint *m*.

road [rəʊd] ◆ n **1.** *lit* route *f* ; [small] chemin *m* / *by road* par la route ; [street] rue *f* / *he lives just down the road* il habite un peu plus loin dans la même rue ; [roadway] route *f*, chaussée *f* **2.** *fig* [path] chemin *m*, voie *f* ▶ **to be on the road to success / recovery** être sur le chemin de la réussite / en voie de guérison / *you're in my road!* a) UK *inf* [I can't pass] vous me bouchez le passage ! b) [I can't see] vous me bouchez la vue ! **3.** US [railway] chemin de fer *m*, voie *f* ferrée **4.** (*usu pl*) NAUT rade *f* **5.** [in mine] galerie *f*. ◆ comp [traffic, transport, bridge] routier ; [accident] de la route ; [conditions, construction, repairs] des routes ▶ **road atlas** atlas *m* routier ▶ **road maintenance** voirie *f*.

roadblock ['rəʊdblɒk] n barrage *m* routier.

road-fund licence n UK vignette *f* (automobile).

road hog n *inf* chauffard *m*.

roadholding ['rəʊd,həʊldɪŋ] n tenue *f* de route.

roadie ['rəʊdɪ] n *inf* technicien qui accompagne les groupes de rock en tournée.

road kill n animal écrasé par une voiture.

road manager n responsable *m* de tournée (d'un chanteur ou d'un groupe pop).

road map n carte *f* routière.

road rage n agressivité *f* au volant (se traduisant parfois par un acte de violence).

road roller n rouleau *m* compresseur.

road safety n sécurité *f* routière.

road sense n [for driver] sens *m* de la conduite ; [for pedestrian] : *children have to be taught road sense* on doit apprendre aux enfants à faire attention à la circulation.

roadshow ['rəʊdʃəʊ] n [gen] tournée *f* ; [radio show] *animation en direct proposée par une station de radio en tournée*.

roadside ['rəʊdsaɪd] ◆ n bord *m* de la route, bas-côté *m*. ◆ adj au bord de la route.

road sign n panneau *m* de signalisation.

roadsweeper ['rəʊd,swiːpər] n [person] balayeur *m*, -euse *f* ; [vehicle] balayeuse *f*.

road tax n UK taxe *f* sur les automobiles ▶ **road tax disc** vignette *f* (automobile).

road test n essai *m* sur route. ◆ **road-test** vt essayer sur route.

roadtrip ['rəʊdtrɪp] n US [short] promenade *f* en voiture ; [-longer] voyage *m* en voiture.

road-user n usager *m*, -ère *f* de la route.

roadway ['rəʊdweɪ] n chaussée *f*.

road works pl n travaux *mpl* (d'entretien des routes).

roadworthy ['rəʊd,wɜːðɪ] adj [vehicle] en état de rouler.

roam [rəʊm] ◆ vt **1.** [travel - world] parcourir ; [- streets] errer dans **2.** [hang about - streets] traîner dans. ◆ vi [wander] errer, voyager sans but. ◆ **roam about** UK **, roam around** vi **1.** [travel] vagabonder, bourlinguer **2.** [aimlessly] errer, traîner.

roaming ['rəʊmɪŋ] ◆ adj [vagrant] vagabond, errant ; [-dog, wild animal] errant ; [- reporter, photographer] itinérant. ◆ n **1.** [vagrancy] vagabondage *m* **2.** TELEC itinérance *f*.

roar [rɔːr] ◆ vi [lion] rugir ; [bull] beugler, mugir ; [elephant] barrir ; [person] hurler, crier ; [crowd] hurler ; [radio, music] beugler, hurler ; [sea, wind] mugir ; [storm, thunder] gronder ; [fire] ronfler ; [cannon] tonner ; [car, motorcycle, engine] vrombir. ◆ vt [feelings, order] hurler. ◆ n [of lion] rugissement *m* ; [of bull] mugissement *m*, beuglement *m* ; [of elephant] barrissement *m* ; [of sea, wind] mugissement *m* ; [of thunder, storm] grondement *m* ; [of fire] ronflement *m* ; [of cannons] grondement *m* ; [of crowd] hurlements *mpl* ; [of engine] vrombissement *m*.

roaring ['rɔːrɪŋ] ◆ adj **1.** [lion] rugissant ; [bull] mugissant, beuglant ; [elephant] qui barrit ; [person, crowd] hurlant ; [sea, wind] mugissant ; [thunder, storm] qui gronde ; [engine] vrombissant ▶ **a roaring fire** une bonne flambée **2.** *fig* [excellent] ▶ **a roaring success** un succès fou ▶ **to do a roaring trade** UK faire des affaires en or. ◆ adv *inf* ▶ **roaring drunk** ivre mort, complètement bourré.

roast [rəʊst] ◆ vt **1.** [meat] rôtir ; [peanuts, almonds, chestnuts] griller, faire griller ; [coffee] griller, torréfier **2.** [minerals] calciner **3.** *fig* [by sun, fire] griller, rôtir **4.** US *inf* [make fun of] se moquer (gentiment) de. ◆ vi **1.** [meat] rôtir **2.** *fig* [person] avoir très chaud. ◆ adj rôti ▶ **roast beef** rôti *m* de bœuf, rosbif *m* ▶ **roast chestnuts** marrons *mpl* chauds ▶ **roast chicken** poulet *m* rôti ▶ **roast potatoes** pommes de terre *fpl* rôties au four ▶ **medium roast coffee** café *m* torréfié. ◆ n **1.** [joint of meat] rôti *m* **2.** US [barbecue] barbecue *m*.

roasting ['rəʊstɪŋ] ◆ n **1.** [of meat] rôtissage *m* ; [of coffee] torréfaction *f* ▶ **roasting spit** tournebroche *m* ▶ **roasting tin** plat *m* à rôtir **2.** UK *inf & fig* [harsh criticism] ▶ **to give sb a roasting** passer un savon à qqn. ◆ adj *inf* [weather] torride.

rob [rɒb] (*pt & pp* **robbed**, *cont* **robbing**) vt **1.** [person] voler ; [bank] dévaliser ; [house] cambrioler ▶ **to rob sb of sthg** voler or dérober qqch à qqn **2.** *fig* [deprive] priver ▶ **to rob sb of sthg** priver qqn de qqch.

robber ['rɒbəʳ] n [of property] voleur m, -euse f.

robbery ['rɒbərı] (pl robberies) n **1.** [of property] vol m ; [of bank] hold-up m ; [of house] cambriolage m ▸ **robbery with violence** vol m avec coups et blessures, vol m qualifié spec **2.** inf [overcharging] vol m.

robe [rəʊb] ◆ n **1.** US [dressing gown] peignoir m, robe f de chambre **2.** [long garment - gen] robe f ; [- for judge, academic] robe f, toge f. ◆ vt [dress - gen] habiller, vêtir ; [- in robe] vêtir d'une robe. ◆ vi [judge] revêtir sa robe.

robin ['rɒbın] n **1.** [European] ▸ **robin (redbreast)** rouge-gorge m **2.** [American] merle m américain.

robot ['rəʊbɒt] ◆ n lit & fig [automaton] robot m, automate m. ◆ comp [pilot, vehicle, system] automatique.

robotic [rəʊ'bɒtık] adj robotique.

robotics [rəʊ'bɒtıks] n (U) robotique f.

robust [rəʊ'bʌst] adj [person] robuste, vigoureux, solide ; [health] solide ; [appetite] robuste, solide ; [wine] robuste, corsé ; [structure] solide ; [economy, style, car] robuste ; [response, defence] vigoureux, énergique.

robustly [rəʊ'bʌstlı] adv solidement, avec robustesse.

rock [rɒk] ◆ n **1.** [substance] roche f, roc m **2.** [boulder] rocher m ▸ **to be on the rocks** a) inf [person] être dans la dèche b) [firm] être en faillite c) [enterprise, marriage] mal tourner, tourner à la catastrophe ▸ **on the rocks** [drink] avec des glaçons **3.** [music, dance] rock m **4.** [in place names] rocher m, roche f ▸ **the Rock** le rocher de Gibraltar **5.** US [stone] pierre f **6.** UK [sweet] ≃ sucre m d'orge **7.** v inf [diamond] diam m. ◆ comp [film] rock ; [band, album] (de) rock ; [radio station] de rock ▸ **a rock guitarist** un guitariste rock. ◆ vt **1.** [swing to and fro - baby] bercer ; [- chair] balancer ; [- lever] basculer ; [- boat] ballotter, tanguer / to rock a baby to sleep bercer un bébé pour l'endormir ▸ **to rock the boat** jouer les trouble-fête, semer le trouble **2.** [shake] secouer, ébranler **3.** US inf : you really rock that outfit! cette tenue te va super bien ! ◆ vi **1.** [sway] se balancer **2.** [quake] trembler ▸ **to rock with laughter** se tordre de rire **3.** [jive] danser le rock **4.** inf [be very good] : this really rocks! ça décoiffe !

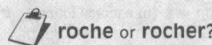 **roche** or **rocher**?

Un rocher is the everyday term for a rock. **Une roche** can have the same meaning, but used uncountably (**de la roche**) it means rock in the geological sense.

---

rockabilly ['rɒkə,bılı] n rockabilly m.

rock and roll n rock m (and roll).

rock bottom n fig ▸ **to hit rock bottom** a) [person] avoir le moral à zéro, toucher le fond b) [firm, funds] atteindre le niveau le plus bas. ◆ **rock-bottom** adj [price] défiant toute concurrence, le plus bas.

rock bun, rock cake n rocher m (gâteau).

rock climber n varappeur m, -euse f.

rock climbing n escalade f (de rochers), varappe f.

rock dash n US [pebbledash] crépi m.

rocker ['rɒkəʳ] n **1.** [of cradle, chair] bascule f **2.** [rocking chair] fauteuil m à bascule **3.** UK [youth] rocker m.

rockery ['rɒkərı] (pl rockeries) n (jardin m de) rocaille f.

rocket ['rɒkıt] ◆ n **1.** AERON & ASTRONAUT fusée f **2.** MIL [missile] roquette f **3.** [signal, flare] fusée f **4.** [firework] fusée f **5.** BOT & CULIN roquette f. ◆ comp [propulsion] par fusée ; [engine] de fusée. ◆ vt **1.** [missile, astronaut] lancer (dans l'espace) **2.** [record, singer] faire monter en flèche. ◆ vi [price, sales] monter en flèche.

rocket attack n attaque f à la roquette.

rocket launcher n AERON & ASTRONAUT lance-fusées m inv ; MIL lance-roquettes m inv.

rocket science n **1.** lit science f des fusées **2.** fig ▸ **it's hardly rocket science** inf c'est pas sorcier.

rocket scientist n **1.** lit spécialiste mf de la science des fusées **2.** fig ▸ **he's no rocket scientist** inf il n'a pas inventé la poudre.

rock face n paroi f rocheuse.

rockfall ['rɒkfɔ:l] n chute f de pierres or de rochers.

rock-hard adj dur comme le roc.

Rockies ['rɒkız] pl pr n ▸ **the Rockies** les Rocheuses fpl.

rocking ['rɒkıŋ] n [of chair, boat] balancement m ; [of baby] bercement m ; [of head - to rhythm] balancement m.

rocking chair n fauteuil m à bascule, rocking-chair m.

rocking horse n cheval m à bascule.

rock music n rock m.

rock'n'roll [,rɒkn'rəʊl] = **rock and roll**.

rock pool n petite flaque f d'eau de mer dans les rochers.

rock salt n sel m gemme.

rock slide n éboulis m.

rock-solid adj inébranlable.

rock star n rock star f.

rocksteady [,rɒk'stedı] n MUS rocksteady m.

rocky ['rɒkı] (compar rockier, superl rockiest) adj **1.** [seabed, mountain] rocheux ; [path, track] rocailleux **2.** [unstable - situation] précaire, instable ▸ **to be going through a rocky patch** traverser une période difficile ; [government] peu stable.

Rocky Mountains pl pr n ▸ **the Rocky Mountains** les montagnes fpl Rocheuses.

rococo [rə'kəʊkəʊ] ◆ adj rococo. ◆ n rococo m.

rod [rɒd] n [of iron] barre f ; [of wood] baguette f ; [for curtains, carpet] tringle f ; [for fishing] canne f ; [for punishment] baguette f ; [flexible] verge f ; SCH [pointer] baguette f.

rode [rəʊd] pt ⟶ **ride**.

rodent ['rəʊdənt] ◆ adj rongeur. ◆ n rongeur m.

rodent control n dératisation f.

rodeo ['rəʊdıəʊ] (pl rodeos) n rodéo m.

roe [rəʊ] (pl roe or roes) n (U) [eggs] œufs mpl de poisson ; [sperm] laitance f ▸ **cod roe** œufs de cabillaud.

roe deer n chevreuil m.

Roe vs Wade ['rəʊvɜ:səs'weıd] pr n arrêt de 1973 de la Cour suprême reconnaissant l'avortement comme un droit constitutionnel dans tous les États américains.

ROFL (written abbr of **rolling on the floor laughing**) MESSAGING MDR.

ROFLOL (written abbr of **rolling on the floor laughing out loud**) MESSAGING MDR.

rogan josh [,rəʊgən'dʒɒʃ] n variété de curry d'agneau, spécialité indienne.

rogue [rəʊg] ◆ n **1.** [scoundrel] escroc m, filou m ; [mischievous child] polisson m, -onne f, coquin m, -e f **2.** [animal] solitaire m. ◆ adj **1.** [animal] solitaire **2.** US [delinquent] dévoyé **3.** PHR ▸ **rogue state** état m voyou ▸ **rogue trader** trader m voyou.

roguish ['rəʊgıʃ] adj [mischievous] espiègle, malicieux, coquin.

roguishness ['rəʊgıʃnıs] n [dishonesty] malhonnêteté f ; [mischievousness] côté m farceur ; [of child] espièglerie f.

role, rôle [rəʊl] n rôle m ▸ **role model** modèle m ▸ **role play** SCH & PSYCHOL jeu m de rôles ▸ **role playing** (U) jeux mpl de rôles.

roll [rəʊl] ◆ vt **1.** [ball] (faire) rouler ; [dice] jeter, lancer ; [cigarette, umbrella] rouler ; [coil] enrouler / the hedgehog *rolled itself into a tight ball* le hérisson s'est mis en boule / *he rolled his sleeves above his elbows* il a roulé or retroussé ses manches au-dessus du coude ▸ **to roll one's r's** rouler les r ▸ **to roll one's eyes in fright** rouler les yeux de frayeur / *she's a company executive, wife and house-keeper all rolled into one* fig elle cumule les rôles de cadre dans sa société, d'épouse et de ménagère ▸ **to roll one's own** UK [cigarettes] rouler ses cigarettes **2.** [flatten - grass] rouler ; [- pastry, dough] étendre ; [- gold, metal] laminer ; [- road] cylindrer. ◆ vi **1.** [ball] rouler / *to roll in the mud* **a)** [gen] se rouler dans la boue **b)** [wallow] se vautrer dans la boue / *the car rolled down the hill / the slope* la voiture dévalait la colline / la pente / *the car rolled to a halt* la voiture s'est arrêtée lentement ; [sweat] dégouliner ; [tears] rouler / *tears rolled down her face* des larmes roulaient sur ses joues ▸ **to be rolling in money** or **rolling in it** inf rouler sur l'or, être plein aux as **2.** [ship] avoir du roulis ; [plane - with turbulence] avoir du roulis **3.** [machine, camera] tourner ▸ **to get** or **to start things rolling** mettre les choses en marche **4.** US inf : *that's how I roll* je suis comme ça. ◆ n **1.** [of carpet, paper] rouleau m ; [of banknotes] liasse f ; [of tobacco] carotte f ; [of butter] coquille f ; [of fat, flesh] bourrelet m ; [of film] rouleau m, bobine f ; [of tools] trousse f **2.** ▸ **(bread) roll** petit pain m **3.** [of ball] roulement m ; [of dice] lancement m ; [of car, ship] roulis m ; [of plane - in turbulence] roulis m ; [- in aerobatics] tonneau m ; [of hips, shoulders] balancement m ; [of sea] houle f ; [somersault] galipette f **4.** [list - of members] liste f, tableau m ; ADMIN & NAUT rôle m ; SCH liste f des élèves ▸ **to call the roll** faire l'appel ▸ **roll of honour a)** MIL liste des combattants morts pour la patrie **b)** SCH tableau m d'honneur **5.** [of drum] roulement m ; [of thunder] grondement m **6.** inf PHR **to be on a roll** avoir le vent en poupe. ❖ **roll about** vi UK rouler ça et là / *to roll about on the floor / grass* se rouler par terre / dans l'herbe. ❖ **roll in** ◆ vi **1.** [arrive] arriver ; [come back] rentrer **2.** [car] entrer ; [waves] déferler **3.** inf [money] rentrer ; [crowds] affluer. ◆ vt sep [bring in] faire entrer ; [barrel, car] faire entrer en roulant. ❖ **roll off** ◆ vi [fall] tomber en roulant ; [on floor] rouler par terre. ◆ vt sep [print] imprimer. ◆ vt insep TYPO ▸ **to roll off the presses** sortir des presses. ❖ **roll on** vi **1.** [ball] continuer à rouler **2.** [time] s'écouler **3.** UK PHR *roll on Christmas!* vivement (qu'on soit à) Noël ! ❖ **roll out** ◆ vi sortir / *to roll out of bed* [person] sortir du lit. ◆ vt sep [ball] rouler (dehors) ; [car] rouler or pousser dehors ; [map] dérouler ; [pastry] étendre (au rouleau). ❖ **roll over** ◆ vi [person, animal] se retourner ; [car] faire un tonneau ▸ **to roll over and over a)** [in bed] se retourner plusieurs fois **b)** [car] faire une série de tonneaux. ◆ vt sep retourner. ◆ vt insep rouler sur ; [subj: car] écraser. ❖ **roll up** ◆ vt sep [map, carpet] rouler ; [sleeves] retrousser ; [trousers] remonter, retrousser ; [window] remonter. ◆ vi [carpet] se rouler.

roll bar n arceau m de sécurité.

roll call n appel m ▸ **to take (the) roll call** faire l'appel.

rolled [rəʊld] adj **1.** [paper] en rouleau ; [carpet] roulé **2.** [iron, steel] laminé **3.** [tobacco] en carotte ▸ **rolled oats** flocons mpl d'avoine.

rolled gold n plaqué m or.

rolled-up adj roulé, enroulé.

roller ['rəʊlə'] n **1.** [cylinder - for paint, pastry, garden, hair] rouleau m ; [- for blind] enrouleur m ; [- of typewriter] rouleau m, cylindre m ; TEXT calandre f ; METALL laminoir m **2.** [wheel - for marking, furniture] roulette f ; [- in machine] galet m **3.** [of sea] rouleau m.

rollerblade ['rəʊləbleɪd] vi SPORT faire du roller.

rollerblader ['rəʊlə,bleɪdə'] n patineur m, -euse f en rollers.

Rollerblades® pl n rollers mpl.

rollerblading ['rəʊləbleɪdɪŋ] n (U) SPORT roller m.

roller blind n store m à enrouleur.

roller coaster n montagnes fpl russes, grand huit m.

roller skate n patin m à roulettes. ❖ **roller-skate** vi faire du patin à roulettes.

roller-skating n patinage m à roulettes.

roller towel n essuie-mains m (monté sur un rouleau).

rollicking ['rɒlɪkɪŋ] inf ◆ adj [joyful] joyeux ; [noisy] bruyant / *we had a rollicking (good) time* on s'est amusés comme des fous. ◆ n UK ▸ **to get a rollicking** se faire enguirlander.

rolling ['rəʊlɪŋ] ◆ adj **1.** [object] roulant, qui roule **2.** [countryside, hills] ondulant **3.** [sea] houleux ; [boat] qui a du roulis **4.** [fog] enveloppant ; [thunder] grondant **5.** [mobile - target] mobile, mouvant **6.** [boil] ▸ **a rolling boil** : *bring to a rolling boil* maintenir à ébullition **7.** [strikes] tournant. ◆ n **1.** [of ball, marble] roulement m ; [of dice] lancement m **2.** [of boat] roulis m **3.** [of drum] roulement m ; [of thunder] grondement m. ◆ adv UK inf ▸ **to be rolling drunk** être complètement soûl.

rolling credits, rolling titles pl n CIN & TV générique m déroulant.

rolling mill n [factory] usine f de laminage ; [equipment] laminoir m.

rolling pin n rouleau m à pâtisserie.

rolling stock n matériel m roulant.

rolling titles pl n = **rolling credits.**

roll neck n col m roulé. ❖ **roll-neck** = **roll-necked.**

roll-necked adj à col roulé.

roll-on ◆ n **1.** [deodorant] déodorant m à bille **2.** [corset] gaine f, corset m. ◆ adj ▸ **roll-on deodorant** déodorant m à bille.

roll-on/roll-off ◆ n [ship] (navire m) transbordeur m, ferry-boat m ; [system] roll on-roll off m inv, manutention f par roulage. ◆ adj [ferry] transbordeur, ro-ro (inv).

rollover ['rəʊləʊvə'] ◆ n UK [in national lottery] remise f en jeu des prix. ◆ adj UK [in national lottery] : *it's a rollover week* cette semaine il y a remise en jeu des prix.

roly-poly [,rəʊlɪ'pəʊlɪ] (pl **roly-polies**) ◆ adj inf grassouillet, rondelet. ◆ n **1.** inf [plump person] : *she's a real roly-poly* elle est vraiment grassouillette **2.** CULIN ▸ **roly-poly (pudding)** gâteau m roulé à la confiture.

ROM [rɒm] (abbr of read only memory) n ROM f.

romaine [rəʊ'meɪn] n US ▸ **romaine (lettuce)** (laitue f) romaine f.

roman ['rəʊmən] ◆ n TYPO romain m. ◆ adj TYPO romain.

Roman ['rəʊmən] ◆ n Romain m, -e f. ◆ adj **1.** [gen & RELIG] romain **2.** [nose] aquilin.

Roman alphabet n alphabet m romain.

Roman candle n chandelle f romaine.

Roman Catholic ◆ adj catholique. ◆ n catholique mf.

Roman Catholicism n catholicisme m.

romance [rəʊ'mæns] ◆ n **1.** [love affair] liaison f (amoureuse) ▸ **to have a romance with sb a)** [affair] avoir une liaison avec qqn **b)** [idyll] vivre un roman d'amour avec qqn **2.** [love] amour m (romantique) **3.** [romantic novel] roman m d'amour, roman m à l'eau de rose pej ; [film] film m romantique, film m à l'eau de rose pej ▸ **historical romance** roman d'amour situé à une époque ancienne **4.** [attraction, charm] charme m, poésie f ; [excitement] attrait m **5.** [fantasy] fantaisie f ; [invention] invention f **6.** LITER roman m **7.** MUS romance f. ◆ comp ▸ **romance writer** romancier m, -ère f, auteur m d'histoires romanesques. ◆ vi laisser vagabonder son imagination, fabuler. ◆ vt courtiser.

Roman Empire n ▸ **the Roman Empire** l'Empire *m* romain.

Romanesque [ˌrəʊmə'nesk] adj ARCHIT roman.

Romani ['rəʊmənɪ] = **Romany** *(noun)*.

Romania [ruː'meɪnjə] pr n Roumanie *f* / *in Romania* en Roumanie.

Romanian [ruː'meɪnjən] ◆ n **1.** [person] Roumain *m* Roumain, e **2.** LING roumain *m*. ◆ adj roumain.

Roman numeral n chiffre *m* romain.

romantic [rəʊ'mæntɪk] ◆ adj **1.** romantique **2.** [unrealistic] romanesque. ◆ n romantique *mf*.

romantically [rəʊ'mæntɪklɪ] adv de manière romantique, romantiquement *liter*.

romanticism [rəʊ'mæntɪsɪzm] n romantisme *m*.

romanticize, romanticise [rəʊ'mæntɪsaɪz] vt [idea, event] idéaliser.

Romany ['rəʊmənɪ] *(pl* **Romanies)** ◆ n **1.** [person] Bohémien *m*, -enne *f*, Rom *mf* **2.** LING rom *m*. ◆ adj bohémien, rom.

Rome [rəʊm] pr n Rome.

romp [rɒmp] ◆ vi s'ébattre (bruyamment) ▸ **to romp home** [candidate, horse, runner] gagner haut la main. ◆ n **1.** [frolic] ébats *mpl*, gambades *fpl* **2.** [film, play] farce *f*, comédie *f* **3.** [UK] *inf* [easy win] : *it was a romp* c'était du gâteau. ◆ **romp through** vt insep : *she romped through the test* elle a réussi le test haut la main.

rompers ['rɒmpəz], **romper suit** n barboteuse *f*.

roof [ruːf] *(pl* **roofs** or **rooves** [ruːvz]) ◆ n **1.** [of building] toit *m* ; [of cave, tunnel] plafond *m* ; [of branches, trees] voûte *f* ; [of car] toit *m*, pavillon *m* ▸ **to live under the same roof** vivre sous le même toit ▸ **to be without a roof over one's head** être à la rue ▸ **to go through** or **to hit the roof a)** *inf* [person] piquer une crise, sortir de ses gonds **b)** [prices] flamber **2.** [roof covering] toiture *f* **3.** ANAT ▸ **roof of the mouth** voûte *f* du palais. ◆ vt couvrir d'un toit.

roof garden n jardin *m* sur le toit.

roofing ['ruːfɪŋ] n toiture *f*, couverture *f*.

roof rack n AUTO galerie *f*.

rooftop ['ruːftɒp] n toit *m* ▸ **to shout** or **to proclaim sthg from the rooftops** *fig* crier qqch sur les toits.

rook [rʊk] ◆ n **1.** [bird] freux *m*, corbeau *m* **2.** [in chess] tour *f*. ◆ vt *inf* rouler, escroquer.

rookie ['rʊkɪ] n [US] *inf* [recruit] bleu *m* ; [inexperienced person] novice *mf*.

room [ruːm or rʊm] ◆ n **1.** [in building, public place] salle *f* ; [in house] pièce *f* ; [in hotel] chambre *f* ▸ **room and board** chambre avec pension **2.** [space, place] place *f* ▸ **to make room for sb a)** faire une place or de la place pour qqn **b)** *fig* laisser la place à qqn **3.** [people in room] salle *f*. ◆ vi [US] loger ▸ **to room with sb a)** [share flat] partager un appartement avec qqn **b)** [in hotel] partager une chambre avec qqn.

---

 pièce, salle or **chambre?**

A room can be referred to as a **pièce**, a **salle** or a **chambre**, depending on what kind of space it is.

■ *Pièce*

Use **pièce** when the room in question is not seen from the point of view of someone's attachment to it. For example, **pièce** is used in technical descriptions of properties by estate

agents. Avoid **pièce** when talking about someone's room. Use **bureau** if you are referring to their office or **chambre** if you are referring to their bedroom.

■ *Salle*

Except in compound words like **salle d'attente, salle de bains, salle d'eau, salle de séjour, salle de jeu** and **salle à manger**, the word **salle** is reserved for large rooms in public places, such as station waiting rooms, hospitals wards or museum galleries.

■ *Chambre*

This is strictly speaking a room where somebody sleeps, either a hotel room, or a bedroom which is part of a flat or house which has rooms for other uses. If someone's room is more than just a bedroom but does not really fit the definition of a flat | apartment or of a house (for example a student's digs, or a bachelor pad), use a word that describes more specifically the type of lodging it is : **studio, garçonnière**, etc.

-roomed [ruːmd] in comp : *a five-roomed flat* un appartement de cinq pièces, un cinq-pièces.

roomer ['ruːmər] n [US] pensionnaire *mf*.

roomful ['ruːmfʊl] n pleine salle *f* or pièce *f* / *a roomful of furniture* une pièce pleine de meubles.

roomie ['ruːmɪ] n [US] *inf* colocataire *mf*.

rooming house ['ruːmɪŋ-] n [US] immeuble *m* *(avec chambres à louer)*.

roommate ['ruːmmeɪt] n [in boarding school, college] camarade *mf* de chambre ; [US] [in flat] personne avec qui l'on partage un logement.

room service n service *m* dans les chambres *(dans un hôtel)*.

room temperature n température *f* ambiante / '**to be served at room temperature**' [wine] 'servir chambré'.

roomy ['ruːmɪ] *(compar* **roomier,** *superl* **roomiest)** adj [house, office] spacieux ; [suitcase, bag] grand ; [coat] ample.

roost [ruːst] ◆ n perchoir *m*, juchoir *m*. ◆ vi [bird] se percher, (se) jucher.

rooster ['ruːstər] n [US] coq *m*.

root [ruːt] ◆ n **1.** BOT & *fig* racine *f* ▸ **to pull up a plant by its roots** déraciner une plante ▸ **to take root** BOT & *fig* prendre racine ▸ **to put down roots** BOT & *fig* prendre racine, s'enraciner **2.** ANAT [of tooth, hair, etc.] racine *f* **3.** [source] source *f* ; [cause] cause *f* ; [bottom] fond *m* ▸ **to get at** or **to the root of the problem** aller au fond du problème / *poor housing is at the root of much delinquency* la mauvaise qualité des logements est souvent à l'origine de la délinquance **4.** LING [in etymology] racine *f* ; [baseform] radical *m*, base *f* **5.** MATH racine *f*. ◆ comp [problem] fondamental, de base ▸ **root cause** cause *f* première. ◆ vt enraciner / *he stood rooted to the spot* *fig* il est resté cloué sur place. ◆ vi **1.** [plant] s'enraciner, prendre racine **2.** [pigs] fouiller *(avec le groin)*. ◆ **roots** pl n [of person - origin] racines *fpl*, origines *fpl* / *their actual roots are in Virginia* en fait, ils sont originaires de Virginie. ◆ **root about, root around** vi [animal] fouiller *(avec le museau)* ; [person] fouiller ▸ **to root about for sthg** fouiller pour trouver qqch. ◆ **root for** vt insep [team] encourager, soutenir.

❖ **root out** vt sep **1.** [from earth] déterrer ; [from hiding place] dénicher **2.** [suppress] supprimer, extirper. ❖ **root up** vt sep [plant] déraciner ; [subj: pigs] déterrer.

root beer n US boisson gazeuse à base d'extraits végétaux.

root cellar n US cellier m pour conserver les légumes.

root crop n racine f comestible.

root directory n COMPUT répertoire m racine.

rooted ['ru:tɪd] adj [prejudice, belief, habits] enraciné.

rootless ['ru:tlɪs] adj sans racine or racines.

root vegetable n racine f comestible.

rope [rəʊp] ❖ n **1.** [gen] corde f ; [collectively] cordage m ; [of steel, wire] filin m ; [cable] câble m ; [for bell, curtains] cordon m ▸ **a piece** or **length of rope** un bout de corde, une corde **2.** [in mountaineering] cordée f **3.** [of pearls] collier m ; [of onions] chapelet m. ❖ vt **1.** [package] attacher avec une corde, corder / *the climbers were roped together* les alpinistes étaient encordés **2.** US [cattle, horses] prendre au lasso. ❖ **ropes** pl n **1.** BOX cordes fpl ▸ **to be on the ropes** a) [boxer] être dans les cordes b) fig être aux abois **2.** [know-how] ▸ **to know the ropes** connaître les ficelles or son affaire ▸ **to show** or **to teach sb the ropes** montrer les ficelles du métier à qqn ▸ **to learn the ropes** se mettre au courant, apprendre à se débrouiller. ❖ **rope in** vt sep fig ▸ **to rope sb in to do sthg** enrôler qqn pour faire qqch. ❖ **rope off** vt sep [part of hall, of church] délimiter par une corde ; [street, building] interdire l'accès de. ❖ **rope up** ❖ vi s'encorder. ❖ vt sep [climbers] encorder.

rope ladder n échelle f de corde.

rop(e)y ['rəʊpɪ] (*compar* **ropier**, *superl* **ropiest**) adj UK inf [mediocre] médiocre, pas fameux ; [ill] mal fichu.

rosary ['rəʊzərɪ] (*pl* **rosaries**) n RELIG [beads] chapelet m, rosaire m ; [prayers] rosaire m ▸ **to tell** or **to say the rosary** dire son rosaire.

rose [rəʊz] ❖ pt ⟶ **rise.** ❖ n **1.** BOT [flower] rose f ; [bush] rosier m **2.** [rose shape - on hat, dress] rosette f ; [-on ceiling] rosace f **3.** [colour] rose m **4.** [on hosepipe, watering can] pomme f. ❖ adj rose, de couleur rose.

rosé ['rəʊzeɪ] n (vin m) rosé m.

rosebed ['rəʊzbed] n parterre m or massif m de roses.

rosebud ['rəʊzbʌd] n bouton m de rose.

rosebush ['rəʊzbʊʃ] n rosier m.

rose-coloured adj rose, rosé ▸ **to see life through rose-coloured spectacles** voir la vie en rose.

rose garden n roseraie f.

rose hip n gratte-cul m, cynorhodon m spec ▸ **rose hip syrup** sirop m d'églantine.

rosemary ['rəʊzmərɪ] (*pl* **rosemaries**) n romarin m.

rose-tinted adj teinté en rose.

rosette [rəʊ'zet] n **1.** [made of ribbons] rosette f ; SPORT cocarde f **2.** ARCHIT rosace f **3.** BOT rosette f.

rosewater ['rəʊz,wɔ:tə] n eau f de rose.

rose window n rosace f.

rosewood ['rəʊzwʊd] ❖ n bois m de rose. ❖ comp en bois de rose.

RoSPA ['rɒspə] (abbr of Royal Society for the Prevention of Accidents) pr n association britannique pour la prévention des accidents.

roster ['rɒstə] ❖ n [list] liste f ; [for duty] tableau m de service. ❖ vt inscrire au tableau de service or au planning.

rostrum ['rɒstrəm] (*pl* **rostrums** or **rostra** [-trə]) n [platform - for speaker] estrade f, tribune f ; [-for conductor] estrade f ; SPORT podium m.

rosy ['rəʊzɪ] (*compar* **rosier**, *superl* **rosiest**) adj [in colour] rose, rosé ; fig [future, situation] brillant, qui se présente bien.

rot [rɒt] (*pt* & *pp* **rotted**, *cont* **rotting**) ❖ vi **1.** [fruit, vegetable] pourrir, se gâter ; [teeth] se carier **2.** fig [person] pourrir. ❖ vt [vegetable, fibres] (faire) pourrir ; [tooth] carier, gâter. ❖ n **1.** [of fruit, vegetable] pourriture f ; [of tooth] carie f **2.** fig [in society] pourriture f ▸ **to stop the rot** redresser la situation **3.** (*U*) [nonsense - spoken] bêtises fpl, sottises fpl ; [-written] bêtises fpl ; [-on TV] émission f idiote, émissions fpl idiotes. ❖ **rot away** vi tomber en pourriture.

rota ['rəʊtə] n roulement m ; [for duty] tableau m de service, planning m / **on a rota basis** à tour de rôle, par roulement.

rotary ['rəʊtərɪ] ❖ (*pl* **rotaries**) ❖ adj rotatif. ❖ n US rond-point m.

rotate ❖ vt [rəʊ'teɪt] **1.** [turn] faire tourner ; [on pivot] faire pivoter **2.** AGR [crops] alterner **3.** [staff] faire un roulement de ; [jobs] faire à tour de rôle or par roulement. ❖ vi [rəʊ'teɪt] **1.** [turn] tourner ; [on pivot] pivoter **2.** [staff] changer de poste par roulement.

rotating [rəʊ'teɪtɪŋ] adj **1.** lit tournant, rotatif **2.** AGR ▸ **rotating crops** cultures fpl alternantes or en rotation.

rotation [rəʊ'teɪʃn] n **1.** [of machinery, planets] rotation f **2.** [of staff, jobs] roulement m / **in** or **by rotation** par roulement, à tour de rôle **3.** [of crops] rotation f.

rote [rəʊt] ❖ n routine f ▸ **to learn sthg by rote** apprendre qqch par cœur. ❖ adj ▸ **rote learning** apprentissage m par cœur.

ROTG (written abbr of rolling on the ground) MESSAGING MDR.

rotisserie [rəʊ'ti:sərɪ] n [spit] rôtissoire f.

rotor ['rəʊtə] n rotor m.

rotor blade n pale f de rotor.

rotten ['rɒtn] adj **1.** [fruit, egg, wood] pourri ; [tooth] carié, gâté **2.** [corrupt] pourri, corrompu **3.** inf [person - unfriendly] rosse, peu aimable ▸ **to be rotten to sb** être dur avec qqn / *I feel rotten about what happened* je ne suis pas très fier de ce qui s'est arrivé **4.** inf [ill] mal en point / *I feel rotten* je ne me sens pas du tout dans mon assiette **5.** inf [bad] lamentable, nul ; [weather] pourri ; [performer] mauvais, nul ; [in indignation] fichu.

rotting ['rɒtɪŋ] adj qui pourrit, pourri.

rotund [rəʊ'tʌnd] adj **1.** [shape] rond, arrondi ; [person] rondelet **2.** [style, speech] grandiloquent.

rouble ['ru:bl] n rouble m.

rouge [ru:ʒ] ❖ n rouge m (à joues). ❖ vt : *she had rouged cheeks* elle s'était mis du rouge aux joues.

rough [rʌf] ❖ adj **1.** [uneven - surface, skin] rugueux, rêche ; [-road] accidenté, rocailleux ; [-coast] accidenté ; [-cloth] rêche ; [-edge] rugueux ▸ **rough ground** a) [bumpy] terrain m rocailleux or raboteux b) [waste] terrain m vague **2.** [violent, coarse - behaviour] brutal ; [-manners] rude, fruste ; [-neighbourhood] dur, mal fréquenté **3.** [unpleasant, harsh] rude, dur / *she's had a rough time of it* elle en a vu des dures or de toutes les couleurs / *we got a rough deal* on n'a pas eu de veine / *rough justice* justice f sommaire **4.** [not finalized] ▸ **rough draft** or **work** brouillon m ▸ **rough sketch** croquis m, ébauche f ▸ **rough paper** papier m brouillon ; [approximate] approximatif / *at a rough guess* grosso modo, approximativement ; [crude - equipment] grossier, rudimentaire **5.** [sea] agité, houleux ; [climate] rude ▸ **rough weather** gros temps m **6.** [sound, voice] rauque ; [tone] brusque ; [speech, accent] rude, grossier **7.** [taste] âcre **8.** [ill] mal en point. ❖ n **1.** [ground] terrain m rocailleux ; GOLF rough m **2.** [draft] brouillon m ▸ **in rough** à l'état de brouillon or d'ébauche **3.** inf [hoodlum] dur m, voyou m. ❖ adv [play] brutalement ; [speak] avec rudesse ▸ **to live rough** vivre à la dure ▸ **to sleep rough** UK coucher à la dure. ❖ vt ▸ **to rough it** UK inf vivre à la dure. ❖ **rough out** vt sep 🇬🇧 [drawing, plan] ébaucher, esquisser. ❖ **rough up** vt sep inf [person] tabasser, passer à tabac.

roughage ['rʌfɪdʒ] n (U) fibres fpl (alimentaires).

rough-and-ready adj **1.** [makeshift - equipment, apparatus] rudimentaire, de fortune ; [careless - work] grossier, fait à la hâte ; [- methods] grossier, expéditif **2.** [unrefined - person] sans façons, rustre ; [- living conditions] dur.

rough-and-tumble ◆ adj [life - hectic] mouvementé ; [- disorderly] désordonné. ◆ n [fight] bagarre f ; [hurly-burly] tohu-bohu m inv.

roughcast ['rʌfkɑːst] ◆ adj crépi. ◆ n crépi m. ◆ vt crépir.

rough diamond n lit diamant m brut / he's a rough diamond 🇬🇧 fig il est bourru mais il a un cœur d'or.

roughen ['rʌfn] ◆ vt [surface] rendre rugueux ; [hands] rendre rugueux or rêche. ◆ vi devenir rugueux.

roughly ['rʌflɪ] adv **1.** [brutally] avec brutalité, brutalement **2.** [sketchily - draw] grossièrement ; [crudely - make] grossièrement, sans soin **3.** [approximately] approximativement, à peu près.

roughneck ['rʌfnek] n **1.** 🇺🇸 inf [brute] brute f **2.** [worker] ouvrier (non qualifié).

roughness ['rʌfnɪs] n **1.** [of surface, hands] rugosité f ; [of road, ground] inégalités fpl **2.** [of manner] rudesse f ; [of reply, speech] brusquerie f ; [of person] rudesse f, brutalité f ; [of living conditions] rudesse f, dureté f **3.** [of sea] agitation f.

roughshod ['rʌfʃɒd] adv ▸ **to ride** or **run roughshod over** faire peu de cas de.

roulette [ruːˈlet] n roulette f.

round [raʊnd] ◆ adj **1.** [circular] rond, circulaire ; [spherical] rond, sphérique **2.** [figures] rond / 500, in round numbers 500 tout rond / a round dozen une douzaine tout rond. ◆ prep **1.** [on all sides of] autour de / to sit round the fire / table s'asseoir autour du feu / de la table **2.** [measuring the circumference of] : the pillar is three feet round the base la base du pillier fait trois pieds de circonférence **3.** [in the vicinity of, near] autour de / they live somewhere round here ils habitent quelque part par ici **4.** [to the other side of] : the nearest garage is just round the corner le garage le plus proche est juste au coin de la rue / to go round the corner passer le coin, tourner au coin / there must be a way round the problem fig il doit y avoir un moyen de contourner ce problème **5.** [so as to cover] : he put a blanket round her legs il lui enveloppa les jambes d'une couverture **6.** [so as to encircle] autour de / he put his arm round her shoulders / waist il a passé son bras autour de ses épaules / de sa taille **7.** [all over, everywhere in] : to walk round the town faire le tour de la ville (à pied) **8.** [approximately] environ, aux environs de / round 6 o'clock aux environs de or vers les 6 h / round Christmas aux environs de Noël. ◆ adv **1.** [on all sides] autour / there are trees all the way round il y a des arbres tout autour **2.** [to other side] : you'll have to go round, the door's locked il faudra faire le tour, la porte est fermée à clé **3.** [in a circle or cycle] : turn the wheel right round or all the way round faites faire un tour complet à la roue / all year round tout au long de or toute l'année **4.** [in the opposite direction] : turn round and look at me retournez-vous et regardez-moi **5.** [to a particular place] : she came round to see me elle est passée me voir / let's invite some friends round et si on invitait des amis ? / come round for supper some time viens dîner un soir. ◆ n **1.** [circle] rond m, cercle m **2.** [one in a series - of discussions, negotiations] série f ; [- of elections] tour m ; [- of increases] série f, train m / the next round of talks will be held in Moscow les prochains pourparlers auront lieu à Moscou **3.** [delivery] ronde f ▸ a paper / milk round une distribution de journaux / de lait ▸ to do or make the rounds circuler /

she's doing or making the rounds of literary agents elle fait le tour des agents littéraires ▸ to go on one's rounds a) [paperboy, milkman] faire sa tournée b) [doctor] faire ses visites ▸ to go the rounds circuler **4.** [in golf] partie f **5.** [in boxing, wrestling] round m, reprise f **6.** [in cards] partie f **7.** [stage of competition] tour m, manche f **8.** [of drinks] tournée f / it's my round c'est ma tournée **9.** [of cheering] salve f ▸ a round of applause des applaudissements mpl. ◆ vt **1.** [lips, vowel] arrondir **2.** [corner] tourner. ❖ **round about** ◆ prep near environ / round about midnight vers minuit. ◆ adv phr alentour, des alentours. ❖ **round and round** ◆ adv phr : to go round and round tourner / my head was spinning round and round j'avais la tête qui tournait. ◆ prep phr : we drove round and round the field on a fait plusieurs tours dans le champ. ❖ **round down** vt sep arrondir au chiffre inférieur. ❖ **round off** vt sep [finish, complete] terminer, clore / he rounded off his meal with a glass of brandy il a terminé son repas par un verre de cognac. ❖ **round up** vt sep **1.** [cattle, people] rassembler ; [criminals] ramasser **2.** [figures] arrondir au chiffre supérieur.

roundabout ['raʊndəbaʊt] ◆ n 🇬🇧 **1.** [at fair] manège m **2.** AUTO rond-point m. ◆ adj détourné, indirect.

rounded ['raʊndɪd] adj **1.** [shape] arrondi ; [cheeks] rebondi ; [vowel] arrondi **2.** [number] arrondi **3.** [style] harmonieux.

rounders ['raʊndəz] n (U) 🇬🇧 sport proche du base-ball.

round-eyed adj lit aux yeux ronds ; fig [surprised] avec des yeux ronds.

Roundhead ['raʊndhed] n HIST ▸ **the Roundheads** les têtes rondes (partisans du Parlement pendant la guerre civile anglaise, de 1642 à 1646).

roundly ['raʊndlɪ] adv [severely] vivement, sévèrement ; 🇬🇧 [plainly] carrément.

round robin n **1.** [letter] pétition f (où les signatures sont disposées en rond) **2.** 🇺🇸 [contest] poule f.

round-shouldered [-'ʃəʊldəd] adj : to be round-shouldered avoir le dos rond, être voûté.

round table n table f ronde. ❖ **round-table** adj ▸ round-table discussions or negotiations table f ronde. ❖ **Round Table** pr n ▸ the Round Table la Table ronde.

round-the-clock adj 24 heures sur 24 / a round-the-clock vigil une permanence nuit et jour. ❖ **round the clock** adv 24 heures sur 24 / we worked round the clock nous avons travaillé 24 heures d'affilée.

round trip n (voyage m) aller et retour m.

round-trip ticket n 🇺🇸 (billet m) aller-retour m.

roundup ['raʊndʌp] n **1.** [of cattle, people] rassemblement m ; [of criminals] rafle f **2.** [of news] résumé m de l'actualité.

rouse [raʊz] vt **1.** [wake - person] réveiller **2.** [provoke - interest, passion] éveiller, exciter ; [- hope] éveiller ; [- suspicion] éveiller, susciter ; [- admiration, anger, indignation] susciter, provoquer ▸ **to rouse sb to action** pousser or inciter qqn à agir **3.** HUNT [game] lever.

rousing ['raʊzɪŋ] adj [speech] vibrant, passionné ; [march, music] entraînant ; [applause] enthousiaste.

rout [raʊt] ◆ n MIL déroute f, débâcle f. ◆ vt MIL mettre en déroute or en fuite ; fig [team, opponent] battre à plate couture, écraser. ◆ vi fouiller. ❖ **rout about** vi fouiller. ❖ **rout out** vt sep **1.** [find] dénicher **2.** [remove, force out] déloger, expulser.

route [🇬🇧 ruːt 🇺🇸 raʊt] ◆ n **1.** [way - gen] route f, itinéraire m ▸ **sea** / **air route** voie maritime / aérienne **2.** [for buses] trajet m, parcours m ▸ **bus route** : we need a map of the bus routes il nous faut un plan des lignes d'autobus **3.** MED voie f **4.** 🇺🇸 [for deliveries] tournée f **5.** 🇺🇸 [highway] ≃ route f (nationale) ; ≃ nationale f.

♦ vt 1. [procession, motorist] fixer l'itinéraire de, diriger ; [train, bus] fixer l'itinéraire de **2.** [luggage, parcel] expédier, acheminer. **♦ en route** adv phr en route.

route map n [for roads] carte *f* routière ; [for buses] plan *m* du réseau ; [for trains] carte *f* du réseau.

route march n marche *f* d'entraînement.

router ['ruːtə US 'rautər] n COMPUT routeur *m*.

routine [ruːˈtiːn] **♦** n **1.** [habit] routine *f*, habitude *f* **2.** *pej* routine *f* **3.** [formality] formalité *f* **4.** [dance, play] numéro *m*, séquence *f* **5.** [insincere act] : *don't give me that old routine!* arrête, je la connais celle-là ! **6.** COMPUT sous-programme *m*, routine *f*. **♦** adj **1.** [ordinary, regular -flight, visit] de routine ; [-investigation] de routine, d'usage **2.** [everyday] de routine **3.** [monotonous] routinier, monotone.

routinely [ruːˈtiːnlɪ] adv systématiquement.

roux [ruː] (*pl* roux [ruː]) n CULIN roux *m*.

rove [rəuv] **♦** vi **1.** [person] errer, vagabonder **2.** [eyes] errer. **♦** vt [country] parcourir, errer dans ; [streets] errer dans.

roving ['rəuvɪŋ] **♦** adj vagabond, nomade **▶ roving reporter** reporter *m* **▶ to have a roving eye (for the girls)** : *he has a roving eye* il aime bien reluquer les filles. **♦** n vagabondage *m*.

row¹ [rəu] **♦** n **1.** [of chairs, trees] rangée *f* ; [of vegetables, seeds] rang *m* ; [of people - next to one another] rangée *f* ; [-behind one another] file *f*, queue *f* ; [of cars] file *f* ; [in knitting] rang *m* / *for the third time in a row* pour la troisième fois de suite / *they sat / stood in a row* ils étaient assis / debout en rang **2.** [in cinema, hall] rang *m* / *in the third row* au troisième rang **3.** UK [in street names] rue *f* **4.** COMPUT ligne *f* **5.** [in boat] promenade *f* (en bateau à rames). **♦** vi [in boat] ramer ; SPORT faire de l'aviron. **♦** vt [boat] faire avancer à la rame or à l'aviron ; [passengers] transporter en canot **▶ to row a race** faire une course d'aviron. **♦ row back** vi : *they've been forced to row back on the plan* ils ont été obligés de faire marche arrière.

row² [rau] **♦** n UK **1.** [quarrel] dispute *f*, querelle *f* **▶ to have a row with sb** se disputer avec qqn **▶ to get into a row** se faire gronder **2.** [din] tapage *m*, vacarme *m* **▶ to make a row** faire du tapage or du vacarme. **♦** vi se disputer **▶ to row with sb** se disputer avec qqn.

rowboat ['rəubəut] n US bateau *m* à rames.

rowdiness ['raudɪnɪs] n tapage *m*, chahut *m*.

rowdy ['raudɪ] (*compar* rowdier, *superl* rowdiest, *pl* rowdies) **♦** adj [person] chahuteur, bagarreur ; [behaviour] chahuteur. **♦** n bagarreur *m*, voyou *m* ; [at football matches] hooligan *m*.

rower ['rəuər] n rameur *m*, -euse *f*.

row house [rəu-] n US maison attenante aux maisons voisines.

rowing ['rəuɪŋ] n [gen] canotage *m* ; SPORT aviron *m*.

rowing boat n UK bateau *m* à rames.

rowing machine n rameur *m*.

royal ['rɔɪəl] **♦** adj **1.** *lit* [seal, residence] royal ; [horse, household, vehicle] royal, du roi, de la reine **▶ the Royal Family** la famille royale **2.** *fig & fml* [splendid] royal, princier. **♦** n *inf* membre de la famille royale **▶ the Royals** la famille royale.

Royal Academy (of Arts) pr n Académie *f* royale britannique.

Royal Air Force pr n armée *f* de l'air britannique.

royal blue n bleu roi *m*. **♦ royal-blue** adj bleu roi (*inv*).

Royal Highness n : *His Royal Highness, the Prince of Wales* Son Altesse Royale, le prince de Galles.

royalist ['rɔɪəlɪst] **♦** adj royaliste. **♦** n royaliste *mf*.

royal jelly n gelée *f* royale.

royally ['rɔɪəlɪ] adv *lit & fig* royalement ; [like a king] en roi ; [like a queen] en reine.

Royal Mail pr n **▶ the Royal Mail** la Poste britannique.

Royal Marines pl pr n Marines *mpl* (britanniques).

Royal Navy pr n marine *f* nationale britannique.

royalty ['rɔɪəltɪ] **♦** n **1.** [royal family] famille *f* royale **2.** [rank] royauté *f*. **♦** comp **▶ royalty payments a)** [for writer] (paiement *m* des) droits *mpl* d'auteur **b)** [for patent] (paiement *m* des) royalties *fpl*. **♦ royalties** pl n [for writer, musician] droits *mpl* d'auteur ; [for patent] royalties *fpl*, redevance *f*.

Royal Ulster Constabulary pr n **▶ the Royal Ulster Constabulary** corps de police d'Irlande du Nord.

RP (abbr of received pronunciation) n *prononciation standard de l'anglais britannique*.

RPI (abbr of retail price index) n UK indice *m* des prix à la consommation.

rpm (written abbr of revolutions per minute) tr/min.

RR US written abbr of railroad.

RRP written abbr of recommended retail price.

RSA (abbr of Royal Society of Arts) pr n société *f* royale des arts.

RSC (abbr of Royal Shakespeare Company) pr n *célèbre troupe de théâtre basée à Stratford-upon-Avon et à Londres*.

RSI (abbr of repetitive strain/stress injury) n *(U)* TMS *mpl*.

RSN US MESSAGING abbr of real soon now.

RSPB (abbr of Royal Society for the Protection of Birds) pr n *ligue britannique pour la protection des oiseaux*.

RSPCA (abbr of Royal Society for the Prevention of Cruelty to Animals) pr n *société britannique protectrice des animaux* ; ≃ SPA *f*.

RST (abbr of Royal Shakespeare Theatre) pr n *célèbre théâtre à Stratford-upon-Avon*.

RSVP (written abbr of répondez s'il vous plaît) RSVP.

Rt Hon written abbr of Right Honourable.

Rt Rev written abbr of Right Reverend.

RU¹ (abbr of Rugby Union) **♦** n SPORT rugby *m* (à quinze). **♦** pr n [authority] fédération *f* de rugby.

RU² MESSAGING written abbr of are you?

rub [rʌb] (*pt & pp* rubbed, *cont* rubbing) **♦** vt **1.** [gen] frotter **▶ to rub one's eyes** se frotter les yeux **▶ to rub one's hands (in delight)** se frotter les mains (de joie) **▶ to rub sb the wrong way** US prendre qqn à rebrousse-poil **2.** [ointment, lotion] : *rub the ointment into the skin* faire pénétrer la pommade / *rub your chest with the ointment* frottez-vous la poitrine avec la pommade **3.** [polish] astiquer, frotter. **♦** vi frotter. **♦** n **1.** [rubbing] frottement *m* ; [massage] friction *f*, massage *m* / *can you give my back a rub?* pouvez-vous me frotter le dos ? **2.** [with rag, duster] coup *m* de chiffon ; [with brush] coup *m* de brosse ; [with teatowel] coup *m* de torchon / *give the table / glasses a rub* passez un coup de chiffon sur la table / les verres **3.** UK PHR **▶ there's the rub!** voilà le nœud du problème !, c'est là que le bât blesse ! **♦ rub along** vi UK *inf* **1.** [manage] se débrouiller **2.** [get on -people] s'entendre. **♦ rub away** **♦** vt sep **1.** [stain, writing] faire disparaître en frottant **2.** [wipe - tears, sweat] essuyer. **♦** vi disparaître en frottant. **♦ rub down** vt sep **1.** [horse] bouchonner ; [dog] frotter (*pour sécher*) **▶ to rub o.s. down** se sécher **2.** [clean - wall] frotter, nettoyer en frottant ; [with sandpaper] frotter, poncer. **♦ rub in** vt sep [lotion, oil] faire pénétrer (en frottant). **♦ rub off** **♦** vt sep [erase - writing] effacer ; [- mark, dirt] enlever en frottant. **♦** vi **1.** [mark] s'en aller, partir / *the red dye has rubbed off on my shirt / hands* la teinture rouge a déteint sur ma chemise / m'a déteint sur les mains **2.** *fig* [quality] déteindre / *with a bit of luck, her common* *sense will rub off on him* avec un peu de chance, son bon sens déteindra sur lui. ❖ **rub on** vt sep [spread] étaler (en frottant) ; [apply] appliquer (en frottant). ❖ **rub out** ◆ vt sep **1.** [erase - stain, writing] effacer **2.** 🇺🇸 v inf [kill] liquider, descendre. ◆ vi [mark, stain] partir, s'en aller (en frottant). ❖ **rub together** vt sep frotter l'un contre l'autre. ❖ **rub up** ◆ vi [animal] se frotter ▶ **to rub up against sb** fig côtoyer qqn, coudoyer qqn. ◆ vt sep [polish] frotter, astiquer.

rubber ['rʌbər] ◆ adj [ball, gloves, hose] en or de caoutchouc ; [bullet] en caoutchouc ▶ **rubber boots** 🇺🇸 bottes fpl en caoutchouc ▶ **rubber dinghy** canot m pneumatique ▶ **rubber ring** bouée f (de natation). ◆ n **1.** [material] caoutchouc m ▶ **this is where the rubber meets the road** 🇺🇸 c'est le moment décisif **2.** 🇺🇰 [eraser - for pencil] gomme f ▶ **(board) rubber** tampon m (pour essuyer le tableau) **3.** 🇺🇸 inf [condom] préservatif m, capote f. ❖ **rubbers** pl n 🇺🇸 [boots] caoutchoucs mpl, bottes fpl en caoutchouc.

rubber band n élastique m.

rubber cheque n inf & fig chèque m sans provision, chèque m en bois.

rubberize, rubberise ['rʌbəraɪz] vt caoutchouter.

rubberneck ['rʌbənek] inf ◆ n **1.** [onlooker] badaud m, -e f **2.** [tourist] touriste mf. ◆ vi faire le badaud.

rubber plant n caoutchouc m, ficus m.

rubber stamp n tampon m or timbre m en caoutchouc. ❖ **rubber-stamp** vt **1.** lit tamponner **2.** fig [decision] approuver sans discussion.

rubber tree n hévéa m.

rubbery ['rʌbərɪ] adj caoutchouteux.

rubbing ['rʌbɪŋ] n **1.** [gen] frottement m **2.** ART décalque m / **to take a rubbing of an inscription** décalquer une inscription (en frottant).

rubbish ['rʌbɪʃ] 🇺🇰 ◆ n (U) **1.** [from household] ordures fpl (ménagères) ; [from garden] détritus mpl ; [from factory] déchets mpl ; [from building site] gravats mpl ▶ **rubbish van** 🇺🇰 camion m d'éboueurs **2.** inf [worthless goods] camelote f, pacotille f **3.** inf [nonsense] bêtises fpl, sottises fpl / *rubbish!* mon œil !, et puis quoi encore ! / *this film is absolute rubbish!* ce film est complètement nul ! ◆ vt inf débiner.

rubbish bin n 🇺🇰 poubelle f.

rubbish dump n 🇺🇰 décharge f (publique), dépotoir m.

rubbish tip = rubbish dump.

rubbishy ['rʌbɪʃɪ] adj 🇺🇰 inf [poor quality - goods] de pacotille ; [stupid - idea, book] débile, quelle émission débile !

rubble ['rʌbl] n (U) **1.** [ruins] décombres mpl ; [debris] débris mpl ; [stones] gravats mpl / *the building was reduced to (a heap of) rubble* l'immeuble n'était plus qu'un amas de décombres **2.** [for roadmaking, building] blocage m, blocaille f.

rubdown ['rʌbdaʊn] n friction f ▶ **to give sb a rubdown** frictionner qqn.

rubella [ru:'belə] n (U) MED rubéole f.

rubric ['ru:brɪk] n rubrique f.

ruby ['ru:bɪ] (pl rubies) ◆ n **1.** [jewel] rubis m **2.** [colour] couleur f (de) rubis, couleur f vermeille. ◆ adj **1.** [in colour] vermeil, rubis (inv) ▶ **ruby (red) lips** des lèvres vermeilles ▶ **ruby port** porto m rouge **2.** [made of rubies] de rubis **3.** [anniversary] ▶ **ruby wedding (anniversary)** noces fpl de vermeil.

ruched [ru:ʃt] adj à ruchés.

rucksack ['rʌksæk] n sac m à dos.

ructions ['rʌkʃnz] pl n inf grabuge m.

rudder ['rʌdər] n [of boat, plane] gouvernail m.

ruddy ['rʌdɪ] (compar **ruddier**, superl **ruddiest**) adj [red - gen] rougeâtre, rougeoyant ; [- face] rougeaud, rubicond ▶ **to have a ruddy complexion** avoir le teint rouge, être rougeaud.

rude [ru:d] adj **1.** [ill-mannered] impoli, mal élevé ; [stronger] grossier ; [insolent] insolent ▶ **to be rude to sb** être impoli envers qqn / *he was very rude about my new hairstyle* il a fait des commentaires très désagréables sur ma nouvelle coiffure **2.** [indecent, obscene] indécent, obscène, grossier / *a rude joke* une histoire grivoise or scabreuse / *rude words* gros mots mpl **3.** [sudden] rude, violent, brutal / *it was a rude awakening for us* nous avons été rappelés brutalement à la réalité.

⚠ The French word **rude** means rough, harsh or tough, not rude.

rudely ['ru:dlɪ] adv **1.** [impolitely] impoliment, de façon mal élevée ; [stronger] grossièrement ; [insolently] insolemment **2.** [indecently, obscenely] indécemment, d'une manière obscène **3.** [suddenly] violemment, brutalement **4.** [in a rudimentary way] grossièrement.

rudeness ['ru:dnɪs] n **1.** [impoliteness] impolitesse f ; [stronger] grossièreté f ; [insolence] insolence f **2.** [indecency, obscenity] indécence f, obscénité f **3.** [suddenness] violence f, brutalité f **4.** [rudimentary nature] caractère m rudimentaire ; [primitive nature] caractère m primitif.

rudimentary [,ru:dɪ'mentərɪ] adj [gen & ANAT] rudimentaire.

rudiments ['ru:dɪmənts] pl n [of a language, a skill] rudiments mpl, notions fpl élémentaires.

rue [ru:] vt liter & hum regretter / *I rue the day I met him* je maudis le jour où je l'ai rencontré.

rueful ['ru:fʊl] adj [sad] triste, chagrin liter.

ruefully ['ru:fʊlɪ] adv [sadly] tristement ; [regretfully] avec regret.

ruffian ['rʌfjən] n voyou m ; hum [naughty child] petit vaurien m.

ruffle ['rʌfl] ◆ vt **1.** [hair, fur, feathers] ébouriffer ; [clothes] friper, froisser, chiffonner ▶ **to ruffle sb's feathers** froisser qqn **2.** [lake, sea, grass] agiter **3.** [upset - person] troubler, décontenancer. ◆ n **1.** [frill - on dress] ruche f **2.** [ripple - on lake, sea] ride f.

ruffled ['rʌfld] adj **1.** [flustered] décontenancé **2.** [rumpled - sheets] froissé ; [- hair] ébouriffé **3.** [decorated with frill] ruché, plissé.

rug [rʌg] n **1.** [for floor] carpette f, (petit) tapis m ▶ **to pull the rug from under sb's feet** couper l'herbe sous le pied à qqn ▶ **to sweep sthg under the rug** 🇺🇸 fig enterrer qqch **2.** [blanket] couverture f ▶ **tartan rug** plaid m.

rugby ['rʌgbɪ] ◆ n ▶ **rugby (football)** rugby m. ◆ comp [ball, match, team] de rugby ▶ **rugby player** joueur m, -euse f de rugby, rugbyman m ▶ **rugby shirt** maillot m de rugby.

rugby league n rugby m or jeu m à treize.

rugby tackle n plaquage m. ❖ **rugby-tackle** vt plaquer.

rugby union n rugby m à quinze.

rugged ['rʌgɪd] adj **1.** [countryside, region] accidenté ; [road, path - bumpy] cahoteux, défoncé ; [- rocky] rocailleux ; [coastline] échancré, découpé **2.** [face, features] rude / *he had rugged good looks* il était d'une beauté sauvage **3.** [unrefined - person, character, manners] rude, mal dégrossi ; [- lifestyle] rude, fruste ; [determined - resistance] acharné **4.** [healthy] vigoureux, robuste ; [tough - clothing, equipment, vehicle] solide, robuste.

ruggedness ['rʌgɪdnɪs] n (U) **1.** [of countryside, region] caractère m accidenté ; [of road, path] inégalités fpl ; [of coastline] échancrures *fpl* / *the ruggedness of the terrain* les inégalités du terrain **2.** [of face, features] irrégularité *f* **3.** [of person, manners, lifestyle] rudesse *f*.

rugger ['rʌgəʳ] n 🇬🇧 *inf* rugby *m*.

rugrat ['rʌgræt] n 🇺🇸 *inf* [child] mioche *mf*.

ruin ['ruːɪn] ◆ n **1.** *(usu pl)* [remains] ruine *f* / *the ruins of an old castle* les ruines d'un vieux château ▸ **in ruins** en ruine **2.** [destruction] ruine *f* / *this spelt the ruin of our hopes* c'était la fin de nos espoirs ▸ **to fall into ruin** tomber en ruine / *you will be my ruin* or *the ruin of me* tu me perdras **3.** [bankruptcy] ruine *f* / *the business was on the brink of (financial) ruin* l'affaire était au bord de la ruine. ◆ vt **1.** [destroy] ruiner, détruire, abîmer ; [spoil] gâter, gâcher / *that's ruined our chances* ça nous a fait perdre toutes nos chances / *you're ruining your eyesight* tu es en train de t'abîmer la vue or les yeux **2.** [bankrupt] ruiner.

ruination [ruːɪ'neɪʃn] n ruine *f*, perte *f* / *the ruination of the countryside* la destruction de la campagne.

ruined [ruːɪnd] adj **1.** [house, reputation, health] en ruine, ruiné ; [clothes] abîmé **2.** [person - financially] ruiné.

ruinous ['ruːɪnəs] adj **1.** [expensive] ruineux **2.** [disastrous] désastreux.

ruinously ['ruːɪnəslɪ] adv de façon ruineuse / *ruinously expensive* ruineux.

rule [ruːl] ◆ n **1.** [law, tenet] règle *f* ; [regulation] règlement *m* / *the rules of chess / grammar* les règles du jeu d'échecs / de la grammaire ▸ **to break the rules** ne pas respecter les règles ▸ **to play according to the rules** or **by the rules (of the game)** jouer suivant les règles (du jeu) ▸ **the rules and regulations** le règlement / *smoking is against the rules* or *it's against the rules to smoke* le règlement interdit de fumer ▸ **to stretch** or **to bend the rules (for sb)** faire une entorse au règlement (pour qqn) ▸ **rule of three** règle *f* de trois ▸ **rule of thumb** point *m* de repère **2.** [convention, guideline] règle *f* / *rules of conduct* règles de conduite / *the rules for a happy marriage* comment réussir son mariage / *he makes it a rule not to trust anyone* il a comme or pour règle de ne faire confiance à personne **3.** [normal state of affairs] règle *f* / *tipping is the rule here* les pourboires sont de règle ici / *long hair was the rule in those days* tout le monde avait les cheveux longs à cette époque **4.** [government] gouvernement *m*, autorité *f* ; [reign] règne *m* / *a return to majority* / *mob rule* un retour à la démocratie / à l'anarchie / *the territories under French rule* les territoires sous autorité française ▸ **the rule of law** (l'autorité de) la loi **5.** [for measuring] règle *f* ▸ **folding rule** mètre *m* pliant ▸ **metre rule** mètre *m*. ◆ vt **1.** [govern - country] gouverner / *if I ruled the world* si j'étais maître du monde **2.** [dominate - person] dominer ; [- emotion] maîtriser / *their lives are ruled by fear* leur vie est dominée par la peur / *don't be ruled by what he says* ce n'est pas à lui de vous dire ce que vous avez à faire ▸ **to rule the roost** faire la loi **3.** [judge, decide] juger, décider **4.** [draw - line, margin] tirer à la règle ; [draw lines on - paper] régler. ◆ vi **1.** [govern - monarch, dictator] régner ; [- elected government] gouverner / *he ruled over a vast kingdom* il régna sur un vaste royaume / *Chelsea rule OK!* *inf* vive l'équipe de Chelsea ! / *'Rule Britannia'* chant patriotique britannique **2.** [prevail] régner **3.** LAW [decide] statuer ▸ **to rule on a dispute** statuer sur un litige ▸ **to rule against** / **in favour of sb** décider or prononcer contre / en faveur de qqn. ❖ **as a (general) rule** adv phr en règle générale. ❖ **rule off** vt sep tirer une ligne sous. ❖ **rule out** vt sep [possibility, suggestion, suspect] exclure, écarter / *she cannot be ruled out of the inquiry* elle n'a pas encore été mise hors de cause / *the injury rules him out of Saturday's game* sa blessure ne lui permettra pas de jouer samedi.

rulebook ['ruːlbʊk] n règlement *m* ▸ **to do sthg by the rulebook** faire qqch strictement selon les règles ▸ **to go by the rulebook** suivre scrupuleusement le règlement.

ruled [ruːld] adj [paper, block] réglé.

rule-governed [-gʌvənd] adj qui suit des règles.

ruler ['ruːləʳ] n **1.** [sovereign] souverain *m*, -e *f* ; [president, prime minister, etc.] homme *m* d'État, dirigeant *m* **2.** [for measuring] règle *f*.

ruling ['ruːlɪŋ] ◆ adj **1.** [governing - monarch] régnant ; [- party] au pouvoir ; [- class] dirigeant / *football's ruling body* les instances dirigeantes du football **2.** [dominant - passion, factor] dominant. ◆ n LAW [finding] décision *f*, jugement *m*.

rum [rʌm] (compar **rummer**, superl **rummest**) ◆ n [drink] rhum *m*. ◆ comp [ice cream, toddy] au rhum.

Rumania [ruː'meɪnjə] = **Romania**.

rumba ['rʌmbə] ◆ n rumba *f*. ◆ vi danser la rumba.

rumble ['rʌmbl] ◆ n **1.** [of thunder, traffic, cannons] grondement *m* ; [of conversation] murmure *m*, bourdonnement *m* ; [in stomach] borborygme *m*, gargouillis *m*, gargouillement *m* **2.** 🇺🇸 *inf* [street fight] bagarre *f*, castagne *f* (entre gangs). ◆ vi [thunder, traffic, cannons] gronder ; [stomach] gargouiller / *trucks were rumbling past all night* toute la nuit, on entendait le grondement des camions. ◆ vt **1.** 🇬🇧 *inf* [discover - plan] découvrir ; [understand - person, trick] piger **2.** [mutter - comment, remark] grommeler, bougonner. ❖ **rumble on** vi [person] palabrer ; [conversation, debate] ne pas en finir / *the dispute's been rumbling on for weeks now* le conflit dure depuis des semaines.

rumbling ['rʌmblɪŋ] n [of thunder, traffic, cannons] grondement *m* ; [of stomach] borborygmes *mpl*, gargouillis *mpl*, gargouillements *mpl*. ❖ **rumblings** pl n [of discontent] grondement *m*, grondements *mpl* ; [omens] présages *mpl*.

rumbustious [rʌm'bʌstʃəs] adj 🇬🇧 *inf* [boisterous] exubérant, tapageur, bruyant ; [unruly] turbulent, indiscipliné.

ruminate ['ruːmɪneɪt] ◆ vi **1.** ZOOL ruminer **2.** *fml* [person] ruminer ▸ **to ruminate over** or **about** or **on** réfléchir longuement. ◆ vt **1.** ZOOL ruminer **2.** *fml* [person] ruminer.

ruminative ['ruːmɪnətɪv] adj [person] pensif, méditatif ; [look, mood] pensif.

rummage ['rʌmɪdʒ] ◆ n **1.** [search] ▸ **to have a rummage through** or **around in sthg** fouiller (dans) qqch **2.** 🇺🇸 [jumble] bric-à-brac *m*. ◆ vi fouiller / *he rummaged in* or *through his pockets* il fouilla dans ses poches. ❖ **rummage about** 🇬🇧, **rummage around** = **rummage** (vi).

rummage sale n 🇺🇸 vente *f* de charité.

rumour 🇬🇧, **rumor** 🇺🇸 ['ruːməʳ] ◆ n rumeur *f*, bruit *m* (qui court) / *there's a rumour going round* or *rumour has it that he's going to resign* le bruit court qu'il va démissionner. ◆ vt : *it is rumoured that...* le bruit court que... / *she is rumoured to be extremely rich* on la dit extrêmement riche.

rump [rʌmp] n **1.** [of mammal] croupe *f* ; CULIN culotte *f* ; [of bird] croupion *m* ; *hum* [of person] postérieur *m*, derrière *m* **2.** [remnant] : *the organization was reduced to a rump* il ne restait pas grand-chose de l'organisation.

rumple ['rʌmpl] vt [clothes] friper, froisser, chiffonner ; [banknote, letter] froisser ; [hair, fur] ébouriffer.

rump steak n romsteck *m*, rumsteck *m*.

rumpus ['rʌmpəs] n *inf* raffut *m*, boucan *m* / *the announcement caused a rumpus* la nouvelle fit l'effet d'une bombe ▸ **to kick up a rumpus** faire du chahut or des histoires.

rumpus room n 🇺🇸 salle *f* de jeu (souvent située au sous-sol et également utilisée pour des fêtes).

run [rʌn] (pt ran [ræn], pp run, cont running) ◆ vi

A. PHYSICAL ACTION 1. [gen] courir / *they ran out of the house* ils sont sortis de la maison en courant ▸ **to run upstairs / downstairs** monter / descendre l'escalier en courant / *I had to run for the train* j'ai dû courir pour attraper le train

▶ **to run to meet sb** courir or se précipiter à la rencontre de qqn ; *fig* : *don't come running to me with your problems* ne viens pas m'embêter avec tes problèmes **2.** [compete in race] courir ▶ **to run in a race** [horse, person] participer à une course ; [be positioned in race] arriver ; [in cricket, baseball] marquer **3.** [flee] se sauver, fuir / *if the night watchman sees you, run (for it)* inf! si le veilleur de nuit te voit, tire-toi or file ! / *run for your lives!* sauve qui peut !

B. EXTEND, TRAVEL OR SPREAD **1.** [road, railway, boundary] passer / *the railway line runs through a valley / over a viaduct* le chemin de fer passe dans une vallée / sur un viaduc / *the road runs alongside the river / parallel to the coast* la route longe la rivière / la côte / *a high fence runs around the building* une grande barrière fait le tour du bâtiment **2.** [hand, fingers] : *her eyes ran down the list* elle parcourut la liste des yeux **3.** [travel - thoughts, sensation] : *a shiver ran down my spine* un frisson me parcourut le dos **4.** [occur - inherited trait, illness] : *twins run in our family* les jumeaux sont courants dans la famille **5.** [spread - rumour, news] se répandre **6.** [move or travel freely - ball, vehicle] rouler.

C. WITH LIQUID **1.** [flow - water, tap, nose] couler ; [paint] goutter / *your bath is running* ton bain est en train de couler / *your nose is running* tu as le nez qui coule / *their faces were running with sweat* 🇬🇧 leurs visages ruisselaient de transpiration / *tears ran down her face* elle avait le visage couvert de larmes **2.** [river, stream] couler / *the Jari runs into the Amazon* le Jari se jette dans l'Amazone **3.** [butter, ice cream, wax] fondre ; [cheese] couler **4.** [in wash - colour, fabric] déteindre **5.** [tide] monter.

D. WITH MACHINE OR OPERATION **1.** [operate - engine, machine, business] marcher, fonctionner ▶ **to run on** or **off electricity / gas / diesel** fonctionner à l'électricité / au gaz / au diesel / *leave the engine running* laissez tourner le moteur / *everything is running smoothly* fig tout marche très bien **2.** [public transport] circuler / *some bus lines run all night* certaines lignes d'autobus sont en service toute la nuit.

E. DURATION OR RANGE **1.** [last] durer **2.** [be performed - play, film] tenir l'affiche / *this soap opera has been running for 20 years* ça fait 20 ans que ce feuilleton est diffusé **3.** [be valid, remain in force - contract] être or rester valide ; [- agreement] être or rester en vigueur / *the lease has another year to run* le bail n'expire pas avant un an **4.** FIN [be paid, accumulate - interest] courir **5.** [range] aller.

F. STATE OR SITUATION **1.** [indicating current state or condition] : *feelings were running high* les passions étaient exacerbées ▶ **to run late** être en retard, avoir du retard **2.** [reach] : *inflation was running at 18%* le taux d'inflation était de 18 %.

G. IN ELECTIONS [be candidate, stand] se présenter ▶ **to run for president** or **the presidency** être candidat aux élections présidentielles or à la présidence.

◆ vt

A. MANAGE OR OPERATE **1.** [manage - company, office] diriger, gérer ; [- shop, restaurant, club] tenir, diriger ; [- theatre] diriger ; [- house] tenir ; [- country] gouverner, diriger / *the library is run by volunteer workers* la bibliothèque est tenue par des bénévoles / *I wish she'd stop trying to run my life!* j'aimerais bien qu'elle arrête de me dire comment vivre ma vie ! **2.** [organize, lay on - service, course, contest] organiser ; [train, bus] mettre en service / *several private companies run buses to the airport* plusieurs sociétés privées assurent un service d'autobus pour l'aéroport **3.** [operate, work - piece of equipment] faire marcher, faire fonctionner ; [vehicle] : *I can't afford to run a car any more* 🇬🇧 je n'ai plus les moyens d'avoir une voiture **4.** [conduct - experiment, test] effectuer **5.** COMPUT [program] exécuter.

B. PHYSICAL ACTION **1.** [do or cover at a run - race, distance] courir / *I can still run 2 km in under 7 minutes* j'arrive encore à courir or à couvrir 2 km en moins de 7 minutes / *the children were running races* les enfants faisaient la course / *he'd run a mile if he saw it* il prendrait ses jambes à son

cou s'il voyait ça **2.** [cause to run] ▶ **to be run off one's feet** être débordé **3.** [enter for race - horse, greyhound] faire courir **4.** [chase] chasser **5.** [hunt] chasser.

C. TRANSPORT OR DRIVE **1.** [transport - goods] transporter ; [give lift to - person] accompagner / *I'll run you to the bus stop* je vais te conduire à l'arrêt de bus **2.** [drive - vehicle] conduire / *I ran my car into a lamppost* je suis rentré dans un réverbère (avec ma voiture).

D. PASS OVER SURFACE OR VIA ROUTE **1.** [pass, quickly or lightly] passer / *he ran his hand / a comb through his hair* il passa sa main / un peigne dans ses cheveux / *she ran her finger down the list / her eye over the text* elle parcourut la liste du doigt / le texte des yeux **2.** [send via specified route] : *it would be better to run the wires under the floorboards* ce serait mieux de faire passer les fils sous le plancher.

E. OTHER SENSES **1.** [go through or past - blockade] forcer ; [- rapids] franchir ; 🇺🇸 [red light] brûler **2.** [cause to flow] faire couler ▶ **to run a bath** faire couler un bain **3.** [publish] publier **4.** [enter for election] présenter **5.** [expose o.s. to] ▶ **to run the danger** or **risk of doing sthg** courir le risque de faire qqch.

◆ n **1.** [action] course f ▶ **to go for a run** aller faire du jogging / *to go for a five-mile run* courir huit kilomètres / *two policemen arrived at a run* deux policiers sont arrivés au pas de course ▶ **to make a run for it** prendre la fuite, se sauver ▶ **to have the run of sthg** : *we have the run of the house while the owners are away* nous disposons de toute la maison pendant l'absence des propriétaires ▶ **to be on the run** : *the murderer is on the run* le meurtrier est en cavale / *she was on the run from her creditors / the police* elle essayait d'échapper à ses créanciers / à la police / *we've got them on the run!* MIL & SPORT nous les avons mis en déroute ! **2.** [race] course f **3.** [drive] excursion f, promenade f / *she took me for a run in her new car* elle m'a emmené faire un tour dans sa nouvelle voiture **4.** [route, itinerary] trajet m, parcours m / *the buses on the London to Glasgow run* les cars qui font le trajet or qui assurent le service Londres-Glasgow **5.** AERON [flight] vol m, mission f ▶ **bombing run** mission de bombardement **6.** SPORT [in cricket, baseball] point m **7.** [track - for skiing, bobsleighing] piste f **8.** [series, continuous period] série f, succession f, suite f / *they've had a run of ten defeats* ils ont connu dix défaites consécutives / *you seem to be having a run of good / bad luck* on dirait que la chance est / n'est pas de ton côté en ce moment ; [series of performances] : *the play had a triumphant run on Broadway* la pièce a connu un succès triomphal à Broadway ▶ **in the long / short run** à long / court terme **9.** [general tendency, trend] tendance f / *I was lucky and got the run of the cards* j'avais de la chance, les cartes m'étaient favorables / *the usual run of colds and upset stomachs* les rhumes et les maux de ventre habituels **10.** [ladder - in stocking, tights] échelle f, maille f filée **11.** [enclosure - for animals] enclos m. ❖ **run about** 🇬🇧 vi courir (çà et là). ❖ **run across** ◆ vi traverser en courant. ◆ vt insep [meet - acquaintance] rencontrer par hasard, tomber sur ; [find - book, reference] trouver par hasard, tomber sur. ❖ **run after** vt insep *lit & fig* courir après. ❖ **run along** vi [go away] s'en aller, partir. ❖ **run around** vi **1.** = run about **2.** [husband] courir après les femmes ; [wife] courir après les hommes. ❖ **run away** vi **1.** [flee] se sauver, s'enfuir / *their son has run away from home* leur fils a fait une fugue / *to run away from one's responsibilities* fig fuir ses responsabilités **2.** [elope] partir. ❖ **run away with** vt insep **1.** [secretly or illegally] partir avec **2.** [overwhelm] : *she tends to let her imagination run away with her* elle a tendance à se laisser emporter par son imagination **3.** [get - idea] : *don't go running away with the idea* or the notion that it will be easy n'allez pas vous imaginer que ce sera facile **4.** [win - race, match] emporter haut la main ; [- prize] remporter. ❖ **run by** vt sep ▶ **to run sthg by**

sb [submit] soumettre qqch à qqn. ❖ **run down** ❖ vi
1. *lit* descendre en courant **2.** [clock, machine] s'arrêter ;
[battery - through use] s'user ; [-through a fault] se décharger. ❖ vt sep **1.** [reduce, diminish] réduire **2.** *inf* [criticize, denigrate] rabaisser **3.** AUTO [pedestrian, animal] renverser, écraser. ❖ **run into** vt insep **1.** [encounter - problem, difficulty] rencontrer **2.** [meet - acquaintance] rencontrer (par hasard), tomber sur **3.** [collide with - subj: car, driver] percuter, rentrer dans **4.** [amount to] s'élever à **5.** [merge into] se fondre dans, se confondre avec. ❖ **run out** vi **1.** *lit* [person, animal] sortir en courant ; [liquid] s'écouler **2.** [be used up - supplies, money, etc.] s'épuiser, (venir à) manquer ; [-time] filer / *hurry up, time is running out!* dépêchez-vous, il ne reste plus beaucoup de temps ! / *their luck finally ran out* la chance a fini par tourner, leur chance n'a pas duré **3.** [expire - contract, passport, agreement] expirer, venir à expiration. ❖ **run out of** vt insep manquer de / *to run out of patience* être à bout de patience / *he's run out of money* il n'a plus d'argent / *to run out of petrol* tomber en panne d'essence. ❖ **run out on** vt insep [spouse, colleague] laisser tomber, abandonner. ❖ **run over** ❖ vt sep [pedestrian, animal] écraser, renverser. ❖ vt insep [review] revoir ; [rehearse] répéter ; [recap] récapituler / *let's run over the arguments one more time before the meeting* reprenons les arguments une dernière fois avant la réunion. ❖ vi **1.** [overflow] déborder **2.** [run late] dépasser l'heure. ❖ **run past** ❖ vi passer en courant. ❖ vt sep = **run by.** ❖ **run through** vt insep **1.** *lit* traverser en courant **2.** [pervade - thought, feeling] : *a strange idea ran through my mind* une idée étrange m'a traversé l'esprit / *a thrill of excitement ran through her* un frisson d'émotion la parcourut **3.** [review] revoir ; [rehearse] répéter ; [recap] / *she ran through the arguments in her mind* elle repassa les arguments dans sa tête **4.** [read quickly] parcourir (des yeux), jeter un coup d'œil sur. ❖ **run to** vt insep **1.** [amount to] se chiffrer à / *her essay ran to 20 pages* sa dissertation faisait 20 pages **2.** [afford, be enough for] : *your salary should run to a new computer* ton salaire devrait te permettre d'acheter un nouvel ordinateur. ❖ **run up** ❖ vi [climb rapidly] monter en courant ; [approach] approcher en courant. ❖ vt sep **1.** [debt, bill] laisser s'accumuler / *I've run up a huge overdraft* j'ai un découvert énorme **2.** [flag] hisser **3.** [sew quickly] coudre (rapidement) or à la hâte. ❖ **run up against** vt insep [encounter] se heurter à.

runaround ['rʌnəraʊnd] *inf* ▶ **to give sb the runaround** a) raconter des salades à qqn b) [husband, wife] tromper qqn.

runaway ['rʌnəweɪ] ❖ n [gen] fugitif *m*, -ive *f* ; [child - from home, school, etc.] fugueur *m*, -euse *f*. ❖ adj **1.** [convict] fugitif ; [child] fugueur ; [horse] emballé ; [train, car] fou *(before vowel or silent 'h' fol, f folle)* ▶ **a runaway marriage** un mariage clandestin **2.** [rampant, extreme - inflation] galopant ; [-success] fou *(before vowel or silent 'h' fol, f folle)* / *a runaway victory* une victoire remportée haut la main.

rundown ['rʌndaʊn] n **1.** [reduction] réduction *f*, déclin *m* **2.** *inf* [report] compte rendu *m* ▶ **to give sb a rundown** of or on sthg mettre qqn au courant de qqch.

run-down adj *inf* **1.** [tired] vanné, crevé / *I think you're just a bit run-down* je pense que c'est juste un peu de surmenage **2.** [dilapidated] délabré.

rung [rʌŋ] ❖ pp ⟶ **ring.** ❖ n [of ladder] barreau *m*, échelon *m* ; [of chair] barreau *m* ; *fig* [in hierarchy] échelon *m*.

run-in n *inf* [quarrel] engueulade *f*, prise *f* de bec / *I had a bit of a run-in with the police last week* j'ai eu un petit accrochage avec la police la semaine dernière.

runner ['rʌnər] n **1.** [in race - person] coureur *m*, -euse *f* ; [-horse] partant *m* / *he's a good / fast runner* il court bien / vite **2.** [messenger] coursier *m*, -ère *f* **3.** *(usu in compounds)* [smuggler] contrebandier *m*, -ère *f*, trafiquant *m*, -e *f* ▶ **drug runner** trafiquant *m* de drogue **4.** [slide - for door, drawer,

etc.] glissière *f* ; [-on sledge] patin *m* ; [-on skate] lame *f* **5.** BOT coulant *m*, stolon *m* **6.** [stair carpet] tapis *m* d'escalier **7.** ⟨PHR⟩ **to do a runner** ⟨UK⟩ *inf* partir sans payer.

runner bean n ⟨UK⟩ haricot *m* d'Espagne.

runner-up *(pl* **runners-up)** n second *m*, -e *f* / *her novel was runner-up for the Prix Goncourt* son roman était le second favori pour le prix Goncourt / *there will be 50 consolation prizes for the runners-up* il y aura 50 lots de consolation pour les autres gagnants.

running ['rʌnɪŋ] ❖ n **1.** SPORT course *f* (à pied) / *running is forbidden in the corridors* il est interdit de courir dans les couloirs ▶ **to make the running** a) SPORT mener le train b) *fig* prendre l'initiative ▶ **to be in the running for sthg** être sur les rangs pour obtenir qqch ▶ **to be out of the running** ne plus être dans la course **2.** [management] gestion *f*, direction *f* ; [organization] organisation *f* **3.** [working, functioning] marche *f*, fonctionnement *m* **4.** [operating] conduite *f*, maniement *m* **5.** [smuggling] contrebande *f* ▶ **drug running** trafic *m* de drogue ▶ comp [shoe, shorts, track] de course (à pied). ❖ adj **1.** [at a run - person, animal] courant, qui court ▶ **running jump** *lit* saut *m* avec élan ▶ **(go) take a running jump!** *inf* va te faire voir (ailleurs) ! **2.** *(after noun)* [consecutive] de suite / *three times / weeks / years running* trois fois / semaines / années de suite **3.** [continuous] continu, ininterrompu ▶ **running account** FIN compte *m* courant ▶ **running battle** lutte *f* continuelle ▶ **running total** montant *m* à reporter **4.** [flowing] : *the sound of running water* le bruit de l'eau qui coule / *all the rooms have running water* toutes les chambres ont l'eau courante ▶ **a running sore** une plaie suppurante **5.** [working, operating] ▶ **in running order** en état de marche ▶ **to be up and running** être opérationnel ▶ **running costs** a) frais *mpl* d'exploitation b) [of car] frais *mpl* d'entretien ▶ **running repairs** réparations *fpl* courantes **6.** [cursive - handwriting] cursif.

running commentary n RADIO & TV commentaire *m* en direct / *she gave us a running commentary on what the neighbours were doing* *fig* elle nous a expliqué en détail ce que les voisins étaient en train de faire.

running mate n ⟨US⟩ POL candidat *m* à la vice-présidence.

running order n ordre *m* de passage.

running time n durée *f*.

runny ['rʌnɪ] *(compar* **runnier,** *superl* **runniest)** adj **1.** [sauce, honey] liquide ; [liquid] (très) fluide ; [omelette] baveux / *a runny egg* un œuf dont le jaune coule **2.** [nose] qui coule ; [eye] qui pleure / *I've got a runny nose* j'ai le nez qui coule.

run-off n **1.** SPORT [final] finale *f* ; [after tie] belle *f* **2.** [water] trop-plein *m*.

run-of-the-mill adj ordinaire, banal.

run-on n **1.** [in printed matter] texte *m* composé à la suite *(sans alinéa)* **2.** [in dictionary] sous-entrée *f*.

runt [rʌnt] n **1.** [animal] avorton *m* **2.** *inf* [person] avorton *m*.

run-through n [review] révision *f* ; [rehearsal] répétition *f* ; [recap] récapitulation *f*.

runtime ['rʌntaɪm] n COMPUT durée *f* d'utilisation ▶ **runtime system** système *m* en phase d'exécution ▶ **runtime version** version *f* exécutable.

run-up n **1.** SPORT élan *m* **2.** [period before] période *f* préparatoire / *the run-up to the elections* la période qui précède les élections ou pré-électorale **3.** ⟨US⟩ [increase] augmentation *f*, hausse *f*.

runway ['rʌnweɪ] n AERON piste *f* (d'atterrissage or d'envol) ▶ **runway lights** feux *mpl* de piste.

RUOK? MESSAGING written abbr of **are you OK?**

rupee [ruː'piː] n roupie *f*.

rupture ['rʌptʃər] ❖ n **1.** [split] rupture *f* **2.** [hernia] hernie *f*. ❖ vt **1.** [split] rompre **2.** MED ▶ **to rupture o.s.** se faire une hernie.

rural ['ruərəl] adj [life, country, scenery] rural.

ruse [ruːz] n ruse f.

rush [rʌʃ] ◆ vi **1.** [hurry, dash - individual] se précipiter ; [-crowd] se ruer, se précipiter ; [-vehicle] foncer / *people rushed out of the blazing house* les gens se ruèrent hors de la maison en flammes / *there's no need to rush* pas besoin de se presser / *passers-by rushed to help the injured man* des passants se sont précipités au secours du blessé / *he rushed in / out / past* il est entré précipitamment / sorti précipitamment / passé à toute allure **2.** [act overhastily] : *to rush into a decision* prendre une décision à la hâte / *now don't rush into anything* ne va pas foncer tête baissée **3.** [surge - air] s'engouffrer ; [-liquid] jaillir / *the cold water rushed over her bare feet* l'eau froide déferla sur ses pieds nus / *the blood rushed to her head* le sang lui est monté à la tête. ◆ vt **1.** [do quickly] expédier ; [do overhastily] faire à la hâte or à la va-vite / *don't rush your food* ne mange pas trop vite **2.** [cause to hurry] bousculer, presser ; [pressurize] faire pression sur, forcer la main à / *don't rush me!* ne me bouscule pas ! ▸ **to rush sb into sthg** or **doing sthg** forcer qqn à faire qqch à la hâte / *don't be rushed into signing* ne signez pas sous la pression **3.** [attack - person] attaquer, agresser ; [-place] attaquer, prendre d'assaut **4.** [transport quickly] transporter d'urgence ; [send quickly] envoyer or expédier d'urgence **5.** US *inf* [court] courtiser. ◆ n **1.** [hurry] précipitation f, hâte f ▸ **to do sthg in a rush** faire qqch à la hâte ▸ **to be in a rush** être (très) pressé / *what's the rush?* pourquoi tant de précipitation ? / *there's no (great) rush* rien ne presse / *it'll be a bit of a rush, but we should make it* il faudra se dépêcher mais on devrait y arriver / *your essay was written in too much of a rush* vous avez fait votre dissertation à la va-vite **2.** [stampede] ruée f, bousculade f / *there was a rush for the door* tout le monde s'est rué vers la porte ; [great demand] ruée / *there's been a rush on or for tickets* les gens se sont rués sur les billets / *there's a rush on that particular model* ce modèle est très demandé **3.** [busy period] heure f de pointe or d'affluence / *the six o'clock rush* la foule de six heures ; [in shops, post office, etc.] : *I try to avoid the lunchtime rush* j'essaie d'éviter la foule de l'heure du déjeuner / *the holiday rush* **a)** [leaving] les grands départs en vacances **b)** [returning] les embouteillages des retours de vacances **4.** [attack] attaque f, assaut m ▸ **to make a rush at** or **for sb** se jeter sur qqn **5.** [surge - of water] jaillissement m ; [-of air] bouffée f ; [-of emotion, nausea] accès m, montée f / *I could hear nothing above the rush of water* le bruit de l'eau (qui bouillonnait) m'empêchait d'entendre quoi que ce soit / *she had a rush of blood to the head* le sang lui est monté à la tête **6.** BOT jonc m ; [for seats] paille f ▸ **rush mat** natte f (de jonc) / *the floor is covered with rush matting* des nattes (de jonc) recouvrent le sol **7.** *drugs sl* [from drugs] flash m. ◆ adj **1.** [urgent] urgent / *it's a rush job for Japan* c'est un travail urgent pour le Japon / *rush order* commande f urgente **2.** [hurried] fait à la hâte or à la va-vite / *I'm afraid it's a bit of a rush job* je suis désolé, le travail a été fait un peu vite or a été un peu bâclé **3.** [busy - period] de pointe, d'affluence. ❖ **rushes** pl n CIN rushes mpl, épreuves fpl de tournage. ❖ **rush about** UK, ❖ **rush around** vi courir çà et là. ❖ **rush in** vi **1.** *lit* entrer précipitamment or à toute allure **2.** [decide overhastily] : *you always rush in without thinking first* tu fonces toujours tête baissée sans réfléchir. ❖ **rush out** ◆ vi sortir précipitamment or à toute allure. ◆ vt sep [book, new product] sortir rapidement. ❖ **rush through** vt sep [job] expédier ; [goods ordered] envoyer d'urgence ; [order, application] traiter d'urgence ; [bill, legislation] faire voter à la hâte. ❖ **rush up** ◆ vi accourir. ◆ vt sep envoyer d'urgence / *troops were rushed up as reinforcements* on envoya d'urgence des troupes en renfort.

rushed [rʌʃt] adj [person] bousculé ; [work] fait à la hâte or à la va-vite, bâclé / *he doesn't like to be rushed* il n'aime pas qu'on le bouscule / *the meal was a bit rushed* on a dû se dépêcher pour manger.

rush hour n heure f de pointe or d'affluence. ❖ **rush-hour** comp [crowds, traffic] des heures de pointe or d'affluence.

rush job n [urgent] travail m urgent ; [hurried] travail m bâclé / *I'm afraid it's a bit of a rush job* je suis désolé, le travail a été fait un peu vite or a été un peu bâclé.

rush week n US UNIV *semaine pendant laquelle les associations d'étudiants américains essaient de recruter de nouveaux membres.*

rusk [rʌsk] n biscotte f.

russet ['rʌsɪt] ◆ n **1.** [colour] brun roux m inv **2.** [apple] reinette f. ◆ adj [colour] brun-roux *(inv).*

Russia ['rʌʃə] pr n Russie f / *in Russia* en Russie.

Russian ['rʌʃn] ◆ n **1.** [person] Russe mf **2.** LING russe m. ◆ adj russe.

Russian Federation n ▸ **the Russian Federation** la Fédération de Russie.

Russian roulette n roulette f russe.

rust [rʌst] ◆ n **1.** BOT [on metal] rouille f **2.** [colour] couleur f rouille. ◆ adj rouille *(inv).* ◆ vi rouiller, se rouiller. ◆ vt rouiller. ❖ **rust up** vi rouiller, se rouiller.

Rust Belt pr n ▸ **the Rust Belt** *États du nord-est des États-Unis (principalement le Michigan et l'Illinois) dont l'industrie (automobile et sidérurgie) a périclité.*

rusted ['rʌstɪd] adj US rouillé.

rustic ['rʌstɪk] ◆ adj rustique. ◆ n paysan m, -anne f, campagnard m, -e f.

rustle ['rʌsl] ◆ vi **1.** [make sound - gen] produire un froissement or bruissement ; [-leaves] bruire ; [-dress, silk] froufrouter **2.** US [steal cattle] voler du bétail. ◆ vt **1.** [leaves] faire bruire ; [papers] froisser ; [dress, silk] faire froufrouter **2.** [cattle] voler. ◆ n [sound - gen] froissement m, bruissement m ; [-of dress, silk] froufrou m, froufroutement m. ❖ **rustle up** vt sep *inf* [meal] faire en vitesse.

rustproof ['rʌstpruːf] ◆ adj [metal, blade] inoxydable ; [paint] antirouille *(inv).* ◆ vt traiter contre la rouille.

rusty ['rʌstɪ] *(compar* **rustier,** *superl* **rustiest)** adj lit & fig rouillé.

rut [rʌt] *(pt & pp* **rutted,** *cont* **rutting)** ◆ n **1.** [in ground] ornière f **2.** fig routine f ▸ **to be (stuck) in a rut** s'encroûter **3.** ZOOL rut m / *in rut* en rut. ◆ vt [ground] sillonner. ◆ vi ZOOL être en rut.

rutabaga [ˌruːtəˈbeɪgə] n US rutabaga m, chou-navet m.

ruthless ['ruːθlɪs] adj [person, behaviour - unpitying] impitoyable, cruel ; [-determined] résolu, acharné ; [criticism] impitoyable, implacable.

ruthlessly ['ruːθlɪslɪ] adv [pitilessly] impitoyablement, sans pitié ; [relentlessly] implacablement.

ruthlessness ['ruːθlɪsnɪs] n [of person, behaviour - pitilessness] caractère m impitoyable, dureté f ; [-determination] acharnement m ; [of criticism] dureté f.

rutted ['rʌtɪd] adj sillonné.

RV n **1.** abbr of Revised Version **2.** (abbr of recreational vehicle) US camping-car m.

Rwanda [ruˈændə] pr n GEOG Rwanda m, Ruanda m / *in Rwanda* au Rwanda.

Rwandan [ruˈændən] ◆ n Rwandais m, -e f. ◆ adj rwandais.

rye [raɪ] n **1.** [cereal] seigle m **2.** [drink] = rye whiskey.

rye bread n pain m de seigle.

ryegrass ['raɪgrɑːs] n ray-grass m inv.

rye whiskey n whisky m (de seigle).

S (*pl* **s's** *or* **ss**), **S** (*pl* **S's** *or* **Ss**) [es] n [letter] s *m*, S *m* ; See also **f**.

S (written abbr of **south**) S.

SA ◆ **1.** written abbr of **South Africa 2.** written abbr of **South America.** ◆ pr n abbr of **Salvation Army.**

SAA MESSAGING written abbr of **silly and awkard.**

Saar [sɑːr] pr n ▶ **the Saar** la Sarre.

Sabbath ['sæbəθ] n RELIG [Christian] dimanche *m*, jour *m* du Seigneur ; [Jewish] sabbat *m*.

sabbatical [sə'bætɪkl] ◆ adj [gen & RELIG] sabbatique. ◆ n congé *m* sabbatique.

saber 🇺🇸 = **sabre.**

sabotage ['sæbətɑːʒ] ◆ n sabotage *m*. ◆ vt saboter.

saboteur [,sæbə'tɜːr] n saboteur *m*, -euse *f*.

sabre 🇬🇧, **saber** 🇺🇸 ['seɪbər] n sabre *m*.

sabre-toothed tiger n machairodonte *m*.

saccharine ['sækərɪn] ◆ adj **1.** CHEM saccharin **2.** *fig & pej* [exaggeratedly sweet - smile] mielleux ; [-politeness] onctueux ; [-sentimentality] écœurant, sirupeux. ◆ n = **saccharin.**

sachet ['sæʃeɪ] n sachet *m*.

sack [sæk] ◆ n **1.** [bag] (grand) sac *m* **2.** 🇬🇧 *inf* [dismissal] licenciement *m* ▶ **to give sb the sack** virer qqn **3.** [pillage] sac *m*, pillage *m* **4.** *inf* [bed] pieu *m*, plumard *m* **5.** *arch* [wine] vin *m* blanc sec. ◆ vt **1.** *inf* [dismiss] mettre à la porte, virer **2.** [pillage] mettre à sac, piller. ❖ **sack out** vi 🇺🇸 *inf* s'endormir.

sackful ['sækful] n sac *m*.

sacking ['sækɪŋ] n **1.** TEXT toile *f* à sac or d'emballage **2.** *inf* [dismissal] licenciement *m* **3.** [pillaging] sac *m*, pillage *m*.

sacrament ['sækrəmənt] n sacrement *m*. ❖ **Sacrament** n ▶ **the Blessed** or **holy Sacrament** le saint sacrement.

sacred ['seɪkrɪd] adj **1.** [holy] sacré, saint ▶ **sacred music** musique *f* sacrée or religieuse **2.** [solemn, important - task, duty] sacré, solennel ; [- promise, right] inviolable, sacré ; [- revered, respected] sacré.

sacred cow n *fig* vache *f* sacrée.

sacrifice ['sækrɪfaɪs] ◆ n RELIG & *fig* sacrifice *m*. ◆ vt RELIG & *fig* sacrifier.

sacrificial [,sækrɪ'fɪʃl] adj [rite, dagger] sacrificiel ; [victim] du sacrifice.

sacrilege ['sækrɪlɪʤ] n *lit & fig* sacrilège *m*.

sacrilegious [,sækrɪ'lɪʤəs] adj *lit & fig* sacrilège.

sacrosanct ['sækrəusæŋkt] adj *lit & fig* sacro-saint.

sad [sæd] (*compar* **sadder**, *superl* **saddest**) adj **1.** [unhappy, melancholy] triste ; [stronger] affligé / **it makes me sad to see what's become of them** ça me rend triste or m'attriste de voir ce qu'ils sont devenus / **I shall be sad to see you leave** je serai désolé de vous voir partir **2.** [depressing - news, day, story] triste ; [- sight, occasion] triste, attristant ; [- painting, music, etc.] lugubre, triste ; [- loss] cruel, douloureux / **but sad to say it didn't last long** mais, malheureusement, cela n'a pas duré **3.** [regrettable] triste, regrettable / **it's a sad reflection on modern society** ça n'est pas flatteur pour la société moderne **4.** *inf* [pathetic] minable ▶ **to be a sad case** être minable.

📋 Note that **être triste que** is followed by a verb in the subjunctive:
I'm sad you've got to leave straight away. *Je suis triste que tu doives nous quitter tout de suite.*

SAD n (abbr of **seasonal affective disorder**) TAS *m*.

sadden ['sædn] vt rendre triste, attrister ; [stronger] affliger.

saddle ['sædl] ◆ n **1.** [on horse, bicycle] selle *f* ▶ **to be in the saddle** *lit & fig* être en selle / **you'll soon be back in the saddle again** vous allez bientôt pouvoir vous remettre en selle **2.** CULIN [of lamb, mutton] selle *f* ; [of hare] râble *m*. ◆ vt **1.** [horse] seller **2.** *inf* [lumber] ▶ **to saddle sb with sthg** refiler qqch à qqn / **I always get saddled with doing the nasty jobs** c'est toujours moi qui fais le sale boulot. ❖ **saddle up** vi seller sa monture.

saddlebag ['sædlbæg] n [for bicycle, motorcycle] sacoche *f* ; [for horse] sacoche *f* de selle.

saddler ['sædlər] n sellier *m*.

sadism ['seɪdɪzm] n sadisme *m*.

sadist ['seɪdɪst] n sadique *mf*.

sadistic [sə'dɪstɪk] adj sadique.

sadly ['sædlɪ] adv **1.** [unhappily] tristement **2.** [unfortunately] malheureusement **3.** [regrettably] déplorablement / **you are sadly mistaken** vous vous trompez du tout au tout / **compassion is sadly lacking in our society** la compassion fait tristement défaut dans notre société.

sadness ['sædnɪs] n tristesse *f*.

sadomasochism [,seɪdəu'mæsəkɪzm] n sadomasochisme *m*.

sadomasochist [,seɪdəu'mæsəkɪst] n sadomasochiste *mf*.

sadomasochistic ['seɪdəu,mæsə'kɪstɪk] adj sadomasochiste.

s.a.e., sae n 🇬🇧 abbr of **stamped addressed envelope.**

safari [sə'fɑːrɪ] n safari *m* / **they've gone on** or **they're on safari** ils font un safari.

safari park n safari park m.

safe [seɪf] ◆ adj **1.** [harmless, not dangerous - car, machine, area] sûr ; [-structure, building, fastening] solide ; [-beach] pas dangereux / *is it safe to swim here?* est-ce qu'on peut or est-ce dangereux de nager ici ? / *the bomb has been made safe* la bombe a été désamorcée / *to make a building safe* assurer la sécurité d'un bâtiment / *the police kept the crowd at a safe distance* les policiers ont empêché la foule d'approcher de trop près ▶ **safe sex** le sexe sans risque **2.** [not risky, certain - course of action] sans risque or risques, sans danger ; [-investment] sûr ; [-guess] certain ; [-estimate] raisonnable / *I played it safe and arrived an hour early* pour ne pas prendre de risques, je suis arrivé une heure en avance / *it's a safe bet that he'll be late* on peut être sûr qu'il arrivera en retard / *I think it's safe to say that everybody enjoyed themselves* je pense que l'on peut dire avec certitude que ça a plu à tout le monde / *take an umbrella (just) to be on the safe side* prends un parapluie, c'est plus sûr or au cas où ▶ **safe seat** UK POL siège de député qui traditionnellement va toujours au même parti **3.** [secure - place] sûr / *in safe hands* en mains sûres ▶ **safe house** [for spies, wanted man] lieu m sûr **4.** [reliable] : *is he safe with the money / the children?* est-ce qu'on peut lui confier l'argent / les enfants (sans crainte) ? / *she's a very safe driver* c'est une conductrice très sûre, elle ne prend pas de risques au volant **5.** [protected, out of danger] en sécurité, hors de danger ▶ **keep safe!** US prends bien soin de toi ! ▶ **(have a) safe journey!** bon voyage ! **6.** [unharmed, undamaged] sain et sauf / *he arrived safe (and sound)* il est arrivé sain et sauf. ◆ n **1.** [for money, valuables, etc.] coffre-fort m **2.** [for food] garde-manger m inv.

safe area n zone f de sécurité.

safebreaker ['seɪf,breɪkər] n perceur m, -euse f de coffres-forts.

safe-conduct [-'kɒndʌkt] n sauf-conduit m.

safe-deposit box n coffre m (dans une banque).

safeguard ['seɪfɡɑːd] ◆ vt sauvegarder ▶ **to safeguard sb / sthg against sthg** protéger qqn / qqch contre qqch. ◆ n sauvegarde f / *as a safeguard against theft* comme précaution contre le vol.

safe haven n **1.** [area of country] zone f de sécurité **2.** [asylum] asile m **3.** [refuge] refuge m **4.** FIN valeur f refuge.

safekeeping [,seɪf'kiːpɪŋ] n (bonne) garde f.

safely ['seɪflɪ] adv **1.** [without danger] sûrement **2.** [confidently, certainly] avec confiance or certitude **3.** [securely] en sécurité, à l'abri **4.** [without incident] sans incident.

safety ['seɪftɪ] ◆ n [absence of danger] sécurité f. ◆ comp [device, feature, measures, etc.] de sécurité / *as a safety measure* par mesure de sécurité.

safety belt n ceinture f de sécurité.

safety catch n [on gun] cran m de sécurité.

safety chain n [on door] chaîne f de sûreté ; [on bracelet] chaînette f de sûreté.

safety-conscious adj : *she's very safety-conscious* elle se préoccupe beaucoup de tout ce qui a trait à la sécurité.

safety curtain n THEAT rideau m de fer.

safety-deposit box = safe-deposit box.

safety glass n verre m de sécurité.

safety helmet n casque m (de protection).

safety island n US refuge m (sur une route).

safety lock n serrure f de sécurité.

safety match n allumette f de sûreté.

safety net n lit & fig filet m.

safety pin n **1.** [fastener] épingle f de nourrice or de sûreté **2.** [of grenade, bomb] goupille f de sûreté.

safety valve n lit & fig soupape f de sûreté.

saffron ['sæfrən] ◆ n **1.** BOT & CULIN safran m **2.** [colour] jaune m safran. ◆ adj (jaune) safran (inv).

sag [sæg] (pt & pp **sagged**, cont **sagging**) ◆ vi **1.** [rope] être détendu ; [roof, beam, shelf, bridge] s'affaisser ; [branch] ployer ; [jowls, cheeks, hemline] pendre ; [breasts] tomber **2.** [prices, stocks, demand] fléchir, baisser ; [conversation] traîner. ◆ n [in prices, stocks, demand] fléchissement m, baisse f.

saga ['sɑːɡə] n **1.** [legend, novel, film] saga f **2.** [complicated story] : *it's a saga of bad management and wrong decisions* c'est une longue histoire de mauvaise gestion et de mauvaises décisions.

sage [seɪdʒ] ◆ n **1.** liter [wise person] sage m **2.** BOT & CULIN sauge f. ◆ adj liter [wise] sage, judicieux.

sagging ['sæɡɪŋ], **saggy** ['sæɡɪ] adj **1.** [rope] détendu ; [bed, roof, bridge] affaissé ; [shelf, beam] qui ploie ; [hemline] qui pend ; [jowls, cheeks] pendant ; [breasts] tombant **2.** [prices, demand] en baisse ; [spirits] abattu, découragé.

Sagittarius [,sædʒɪ'teərɪəs] ◆ pr n ASTROL & ASTRON Sagittaire m. ◆ n : *he's a Sagittarius* il est (du signe de) Sagittaire.

Sahara [sə'hɑːrə] pr n ▶ **the Sahara (Desert)** le (désert du) Sahara.

Saharan [sə'hɑːrən] adj saharien.

said [sed] ◆ pt & pp ⟶ say. ◆ adj : *the said Howard Riley* le dit or dénommé Howard Riley / *the said articles* les dits articles.

sail [seɪl] ◆ n **1.** [on boat] voile f ▶ **to set sail a)** [boat] prendre la mer, appareiller **b)** [person] partir (en bateau) **2.** [journey] voyage m en bateau ; [pleasure trip] promenade f en bateau **3.** [of windmill] aile f. ◆ vi **1.** [move over water - boat, ship] naviguer **2.** [set off - boat, passenger] partir, prendre la mer, appareiller **3.** [travel by boat] voyager (en bateau) **4.** [as sport or hobby] ▶ **to sail** or **to go sailing** faire de la voile **5.** fig : *a sports car sailed past me* une voiture de sport m'a doublé à toute vitesse / *she sailed across the room to greet me* elle traversa la pièce d'un pas majestueux pour venir à ma rencontre. ◆ vt **1.** [boat - subj: captain] commander ; [- subj: helmsman, yachtsman] barrer **2.** [cross - sea, lake] traverser. ⬥ **sail into** vt insep inf [attack] tomber à bras raccourcis sur. ⬥ **sail through** vt insep & vi [succeed] réussir haut la main.

sailboard ['seɪlbɔːd] n planche f à voile.

sailboarder ['seɪl,bɔːdər] n véliplanchiste mf.

sailboarding ['seɪl,bɔːdɪŋ] n planche f à voile (activité).

sailboat ['seɪlbəʊt] n US voilier m, bateau m à voile.

sailcloth ['seɪlklɒθ] n toile f à voile or à voiles.

sailing ['seɪlɪŋ] n **1.** [activity] navigation f ; [hobby] voile f, navigation f de plaisance ; [sport] voile f **2.** [departure] départ m **3.** PHR it's plain sailing from now on, it's clear sailing from here on out US tout va marcher comme sur des roulettes à partir de maintenant.

sailing boat n UK voilier m, bateau m (à voiles).

sailing ship n (grand) voilier m, bateau m à voile or à voiles.

sailor ['seɪlər] n **1.** [gen] marin m, navigateur m, -trice f / *I'm a good / bad sailor* j'ai / je n'ai pas le pied marin **2.** [as rank] matelot m.

sailor suit n costume m marin.

saint [seɪnt] n saint m, -e f ▶ **Saint David** saint David ▶ **Saint David's day** la Saint-David.

Saint Helena [-ɪ'liːnə] pr n Sainte-Hélène / *on Saint Helena* à Sainte-Hélène.

sainthood ['seɪnthʊd] n sainteté f.

Saint Lawrence [-'lɒrəns] pr n ▶ **the Saint Lawrence (River)** le Saint-Laurent.

Saint Lucia [-'luːʃə] pr n Sainte-Lucie.

saintly ['seɪntlɪ] (compar **saintlier**, superl **saintliest**) adj [life, behaviour, humility, virtue] de saint.

Saint Patrick's Day [-'pætrɪks-] n la Saint-Patrick.

saint's day n fête f (d'un saint).

sake¹ [seɪk] n ▶ **for sb's sake a)** [for their good] pour (le bien de) qqn **b)** [out of respect for] par égard pour qqn **c)** [out of love for] pour l'amour de qqn / **for old times' sake** en souvenir du passé / **for the sake of argument, let's assume it costs £100** (pour les besoins de la discussion,) admettons que ça coûte 100 livres ▶ **for goodness** or **God's** or **Christ's** or **pity's** or **heaven's sake!** pour l'amour du ciel or de Dieu !

sake² ['sɑːkɪ] n [drink] saké m.

salacious [sə'leɪʃəs] adj fml [joke, book, look] salace, grivois, obscène.

salad ['sæləd] n salade f.

salad bar n [restaurant] restaurant où l'on mange des salades ; [area] salad bar m.

salad bowl n saladier m.

salad cream n UK sorte de mayonnaise (vendue en bouteille).

salad dressing n [gen] sauce f (pour salade) ; [French dressing] vinaigrette f.

salad oil n huile f pour assaisonnement.

salad spinner n essoreuse f à salade.

salamander ['sælə,mændə'] n salamandre f.

salami [sə'lɑːmɪ] n salami m, saucisson m sec.

salaried ['sælərɪd] adj salarié.

salary ['sælərɪ] (pl **salaries**) ◆ n salaire m. ◆ comp [bracket, level, scale] des salaires ▶ **salary earner** salarié m, -e f.

sale [seɪl] ◆ n **1.** [gen] vente f / **'for sale'** 'à vendre' ▶ **to put sthg up for sale** mettre qqch en vente ▶ **on sale** en vente ▶ **sale of work** vente f de charité **2.** [event] soldes mpl / **the January sales attract huge crowds** les soldes de janvier attirent les foules / **the sales are on in London** les soldes ont commencé à Londres / **I got it in a sale** je l'ai acheté en solde ▶ **sale price** prix m soldé **3.** [auction] vente f (aux enchères). ◆ comp [goods] soldé. ◆ **sales** comp [department, executive] des ventes, commercial ; [drive, force, team] de vente ; [promotion] des ventes ▶ **sales assistant, sales associate** assistant m commercial, assistante f commerciale ▶ **sales conference** réunion f commerciale ▶ **sales figures** chiffres mpl de ventes ▶ **sales forecast** prévision f des ventes.

saleability [,seɪlə'bɪlɪtɪ] n facilité f de vente or d'écoulement.

saleroom ['seɪlrʊm] n UK salle f des ventes.

salesclerk ['seɪlzklɑːrk] n US vendeur m, -euse f.

salesman ['seɪlzmən] (pl **salesmen** [-mən]) n [in shop] vendeur m ; [rep] représentant m (de commerce) / **an insurance salesman** un représentant en assurances.

sales manager n directeur m commercial, directrice f commerciale.

salesmanship ['seɪlzmənʃɪp] n art m de la vente, technique f de vente.

salesperson ['seɪlz,pɜːsn] (pl **salespeople** [-,piːpl]) n [in shop] vendeur m, -euse f ; [rep] représentant m, -e f (de commerce).

sales pitch = sales talk.

sales rep, sales representative n représentant m, -e f (de commerce).

salesroom ['seɪlzrʊm] US = saleroom.

sales slip n US ticket m de caisse.

sales talk n boniment m.

sales tax n US ≃ TVA f.

saleswoman ['seɪlz,wʊmən] (pl **saleswomen** [-,wɪmɪn]) n [in shop] vendeuse f ; [rep] représentante f (de commerce).

salient ['seɪljənt] ◆ adj saillant. ◆ n ARCHIT & MIL saillant m.

saline ['seɪlaɪn] adj salin ▶ **saline drip** MED perfusion f saline.

Salisbury steak ['sɔːlzbərɪ-] n US CULIN steak haché assaisonné servi en sauce.

saliva [sə'laɪvə] n salive f.

salivate ['sælɪveɪt] vi saliver.

sallow ['sæləʊ] ◆ adj [gen] jaunâtre ; [face, complexion] jaunâtre, cireux. ◆ n BOT saule m.

sally ['sælɪ] (pl **sallies**, pt & pp **sallied**) n **1.** [gen & MIL] sortie f **2.** fml [quip] saillie f liter. ◆ **sally forth, sally out** vi liter sortir.

salmon ['sæmən] (pl **salmon** or **salmons**) n saumon m.

salmonella [,sælmə'nelə] (pl **salmonellae** [-liː]) n salmonella f inv, salmonelle f ▶ **salmonella poisoning** salmonellose f.

salmon pink n (rose m) saumon m. ◆ **salmon-pink** adj (rose) saumon (inv).

salon ['sælɒn] n salon m.

saloon [sə'luːn] n **1.** UK = saloon car **2.** [public room] salle f, salon m ; [on ship] salon m **3.** US [bar] bar m ; [in Wild West] saloon m **4.** UK = saloon bar.

saloon bar n UK salon m (dans un pub).

saloon car n UK conduite f intérieure, berline f.

salopettes [,sælə'pets] pl n combinaison f de ski.

salt [sɔːlt or sɒlt] ◆ n **1.** CHEM & CULIN sel m **2.** inf [sailor] ▶ **old salt** (vieux) loup m de mer. ◆ vt **1.** [food] saler **2.** [roads] saler, répandre du sel sur. ◆ adj salé. ◆ **salts** pl n PHARM sels mpl. ◆ **salt away** vt sep inf & fig [money] mettre de côté. ◆ **salt down** vt sep saler, conserver dans du sel.

SALT [sɔːlt or sɒlt] (abbr of Strategic Arms Limitation Talks/Treaty) n SALT m ▶ **SALT talks** négociations fpl SALT.

salt cellar n UK salière f.

salted ['sɔːltɪd] adj salé.

saltpetre UK, **saltpeter** US [,sɔːlt'piːtə'] n salpêtre m.

salt shaker n US salière f.

salt water n eau f salée. ◆ **saltwater** adj [fish, plant] de mer.

salty ['sɔːltɪ] (compar **saltier**, superl **saltiest**) adj [food, taste] salé ; [deposit] saumâtre.

salubrious [sə'luːbrɪəs] adj **1.** [respectable] respectable, bien **2.** [healthy] salubre, sain.

salutary ['sæljʊtrɪ] adj salutaire.

salute [sə'luːt] ◆ n **1.** MIL [with hand] salut m ; [with guns] salve f **2.** [greeting] salut m, salutation f **3.** [tribute] hommage m. ◆ vt **1.** MIL [with hand] saluer ; [with guns] tirer une salve en l'honneur de **2.** [greet] saluer **3.** [acknowledge, praise] saluer, acclamer. ◆ vi MIL faire un salut.

Salvadorean, Salvadorian [,sælvə'dɔːrɪən] ◆ n Salvadorien m, -enne f. ◆ adj salvadorien.

salvage ['sælvɪdʒ] ◆ vt **1.** [vessel, cargo, belongings] sauver ; [old newspapers, scrap metal] récupérer **2.** fig [mistake, meal] rattraper ; [situation] rattraper, sauver. ◆ n **1.** [recovery - of vessel, cargo, belongings, furniture] sauvetage m ; [- of old newspapers, scrap metal] récupération f **2.** (U) [things recovered - from shipwreck, disaster] objets mpl sauvés ; [- for re-use, recycling] objets mpl récupérés **3.** [payment] indemnité f or prime f de sauvetage. ◆ comp [company, operation, vessel] de sauvetage.

salvation [sæl'veɪʃn] n **1.** RELIG salut m **2.** fig salut m.

Salvation Army pr n ▶ **the Salvation Army** l'Armée f du salut.

salve [sælv] ◆ n **1.** [ointment] baume m, pommade f **2.** fig [relief] baume m liter, apaisement m. ◆ vt [relieve] calmer, soulager.

salver ['sælvə'] n plateau m (de service).

salvo ['sælvəʊ] (pl **salvos** or **salvoes**) n **1.** MIL salve f **2.** fig [of applause] salve f ; [of laughter] éclat m ; [of insults] torrent m.

Samaritan [sə'mærɪtn] ◆ n RELIG Samaritain m, -e f. ◆ adj samaritain. ❖ **Samaritans** pl pr n ▶ **the Samaritans** association proposant un soutien moral par téléphone aux personnes déprimées ; ≃ SOS Amitié.

samba ['sæmbə] ◆ n samba f. ◆ vi danser la samba.

same [seɪm] ◆ adj même / the two suitcases are exactly the same colour / shape les deux valises sont exactement de la même couleur / ont exactement la même forme / they are one and the same thing c'est une seule et même chose / it all boils down to the same thing cela revient au même / they come out with the same old rubbish every time inf ils ressortent les mêmes conneries à chaque fois ▶ it's the same old story! inf, it's the same old, same old! US inf c'est toujours la même histoire ! ▶ same difference! inf c'est du pareil au même ! ◆ pron **1.** ▶ the same [unchanged] le même m, la même f, les mêmes mf / it's the same as before c'est comme avant / life's just not the same now they're gone les choses ont changé depuis qu'ils sont partis ; [identical] identique / the two vases are exactly the same les deux vases sont identiques **2.** [used in comparisons] ▶ the same la même chose / it's always the same c'est toujours la même chose or toujours pareil ▶ the very same: aren't you Freddie Fortescue? — the very same vous n'êtes pas Freddie Fortescue ? — lui-même ▶ (the) same again, please la même chose (, s'il vous plaît) / if it's all the same to you, I'll go now si cela ne vous fait rien, je vais partir maintenant / it's all or just the same to me what you do tu peux faire ce que tu veux, ça m'est bien égal ▶ the same is true of or the same holds for il en va de même pour ▶ same here! inf: I was really cross — same here! j'étais vraiment fâché — et moi donc ! ▶ (and the) same to you!: Happy Christmas — and the same to you! Joyeux Noël — à vous aussi or de même ! ❖ **all the same**, **just the same** adv phr quand même / all the same, I still like her je l'aime bien quand même / thanks all the same merci quand même.

same-day adj COMM [processing, delivery] dans la journée.

sameness ['seɪmnɪs] n **1.** [similarity] similitude f, ressemblance f **2.** [tedium] monotonie f, uniformité f.

same-sex adj homosexuel.

samey ['seɪmɪ] adj US inf & pej monotone, ennuyeux.

Samoa [sə'məʊə] pr n Samoa m / in Samoa à Samoa.

Samoan [sə'məʊən] ◆ n **1.** [person] Samoan m, -e f **2.** LING samoan m. ◆ adj samoan.

samosa [sə'məʊsə] (pl **samosa** or **samosas**) n samosa m (petit pâté indien à la viande ou aux légumes).

sample ['sɑːmpl] ◆ n **1.** [gen & COMM & SOCIOL] échantillon m **2.** GEOL, MED & SCI échantillon m, prélèvement m ; [of blood] prélèvement m ; [of urine] échantillon m ▶ **to take a sample** prélever un échantillon, faire un prélèvement ▶ **to take a blood sample** faire une prise de sang. ◆ comp ▶ **a sample bottle / pack, etc.** un échantillon / we'll send you a sample bottle of our shampoo nous vous enverrons un échantillon de notre shampooing ▶ **sample question**: a sample question from last year's exam paper un exemple de question tiré de l'examen de l'année dernière ▶ **sample section**: a sample section of the population un échantillon représentatif de la population. ◆ vt **1.** [food, drink] goûter (à), déguster ; [experience] goûter à **2.** MUS échantillonner, sampler.

sampler ['sɑːmplə'] n **1.** SEW modèle m de broderie **2.** [collection of samples] échantillonnage m, sélection f **3.** MUS échantillonneur m, sampler m.

sampling ['sɑːmplɪŋ] n [gen & COMPUT] échantillonnage m ; MUS échantillonnage m, sampling m.

sanatorium [ˌsænə'tɔːrɪəm] (pl **sanatoriums** or **sanatoria** [-rɪə]) n [nursing home] sanatorium m ; [sick bay] infirmerie f.

sanctify ['sæŋktɪfaɪ] (pt & pp **sanctified**) vt sanctifier.

sanctimonious [ˌsæŋktɪ'məʊnjəs] adj moralisateur.

sanction ['sæŋkʃn] ◆ n **1.** [approval] sanction f, accord m, consentement m **2.** [punitive measure] sanction f. ◆ vt sanctionner, entériner ; [behaviour] approuver.

sanctity ['sæŋktətɪ] n [of person, life] sainteté f ; [of marriage, property, place - holiness] caractère m sacré ; [- inviolability] inviolabilité f.

sanctuary ['sæŋktʃʊərɪ] (pl **sanctuaries**) n **1.** [holy place] sanctuaire m **2.** [refuge] refuge m, asile m ▶ **wildlife sanctuary** réserve f animale.

sanctum ['sæŋktəm] (pl **sanctums** or **sancta** ['sæŋktə]) n **1.** [holy place] sanctuaire m **2.** hum [private place] retraite f, tanière f.

sand [sænd] ◆ n **1.** [substance] sable m ▶ **to build on sand** fig bâtir sur le sable **2.** US v inf [courage] cran m. ◆ comp [dune] de sable. ◆ vt **1.** [polish, smooth] poncer **2.** [spread sand on] sabler. ❖ **sand down** vt sep [wood, metal] poncer au papier de verre, décaper.

sandal ['sændl] n **1.** [footwear] sandale f **2.** = **sandalwood**.

sandalwood ['sændlwʊd] n bois m de santal.

sandbag ['sændbæg] (pt & pp **sandbagged**) ◆ n sac m de sable or de terre. ◆ vt **1.** [shore up] renforcer avec des sacs de sable ; [protect] protéger avec des sacs de sable **2.** inf [hit] assommer **3.** US inf [coerce] ▶ **to sandbag sb into doing sthg** forcer qqn à faire qqch.

sandbank ['sændbæŋk] n banc m de sable.

sandblast ['sændblɑːst] ◆ vt décaper à la sableuse, sabler. ◆ n jet m de sable.

sandbox ['sændbɒks] n **1.** RAIL sablière f **2.** [for children] bac m à sable.

sandcastle ['sænd,kɑːsl] n château m de sable.

sander ['sændə'] n [tool] ponceuse f.

S and M n inf sadomasochisme m, SM m.

sandpaper ['sænd,peɪpə'] ◆ n papier m de verre. ◆ vt poncer (au papier de verre).

sandpit ['sændpɪt] n US **1.** [for children] bac m à sable **2.** [quarry] sablonnière f.

sandstone ['sændstəʊn] n grès m.

sandstorm ['sændstɔːm] n tempête f de sable.

sand trap n US bunker m (de sable).

sandwich ['sænwɪdʒ] ◆ n [bread] sandwich m / a ham sandwich un sandwich au jambon ▶ **the sandwich generation** la génération-sandwich (personnes s'occupant de leurs parents âgés tout en ayant des enfants à charge). ◆ vt **1.** inf [place] intercaler **2.** inf [trap] prendre en sandwich, coincer.

sandwich bar n ⬛ sandwicherie f.

sandwich board n panneau m publicitaire (porté par un homme-sandwich).

sandwich cake n ⬛ gâteau m fourré.

sandwich course n ⬛ formation en alternance.

sandwich loaf n ≃ pain m de mie.

sandwich man n homme-sandwich m.

sandy ['sændɪ] (compar sandier, superl sandiest) adj **1.** [beach, desert] de sable ; [soil, road] sablonneux ; [water, alluvium] sableux ; [floor, clothes] couvert de sable **2.** [in colour] (couleur) sable (inv) / he has sandy or sandy-coloured hair il a les cheveux blond roux.

sand yacht n char m à voile.

sand-yachting n char m à voile / to go sand-yachting faire du char à voile.

sane [seɪn] adj **1.** [person] sain d'esprit **2.** [action] sensé ; [attitude, approach, policy] raisonnable, sensé.

sanely ['seɪnlɪ] adv raisonnablement.

sang [sæŋ] pt ⟶ **sing**.

sangfroid [,sɒŋ'frwɑː] n sang-froid m.

sanguine ['sæŋgwɪn] ◆ adj **1.** [optimistic - person, temperament] optimiste, confiant **2.** liter [ruddy - complexion] sanguin, rubicond. ◆ n ART sanguine f.

sanitary ['sænɪtrɪ] adj **1.** [hygienic] hygiénique **2.** [arrangements, conditions, measures, equipment] sanitaire.

sanitary inspector n inspecteur m de la santé publique.

sanitary towel ⬛, **sanitary napkin** ⬛ n serviette f hygiénique.

sanitation [,sænɪ'teɪʃn] n [public health] hygiène f publique ; [sewers] système m sanitaire ; [plumbing] sanitaires mpl.

sanitation worker n ⬛ éboueur m.

sanitize, sanitise ['sænɪtaɪz] vt **1.** [disinfect] désinfecter **2.** fig [expurgate] expurger.

sanitorium [,sænɪ'tɔːrɪəm], **sanitarium** [,sænɪ'teərɪəm] ⬛ = **sanatorium**.

sanity ['sænətɪ] n **1.** [mental health] santé f mentale **2.** [reasonableness] bon sens m, rationalité f.

sank [sæŋk] pt ⟶ **sink**.

San Marino [,sænmə'riːnəʊ] pr n Saint-Marin.

San Salvador [,sæn'sælvədɔːr] pr n San Salvador.

Sanskrit ['sænskrɪt] ◆ adj sanskrit. ◆ n sanskrit m.

Santa ['sæntə] inf, **Santa Claus** ['sæntə,klɔːz] pr n le père Noël.

sap [sæp] (pt & pp sapped, cont sapping) ◆ n **1.** BOT sève f **2.** ⬛ inf [fool] bêta m, -asse f, andouille f ; [gullible person] nigaud m, -e f **3.** ⬛ inf [cosh] matraque f, gourdin m **4.** MIL sape f. ◆ vt **1.** fig [strength, courage] saper, miner **2.** ⬛ inf [cosh] assommer (d'un coup de gourdin) **3.** MIL saper.

sapling ['sæplɪŋ] n **1.** BOT jeune arbre m **2.** liter [youth] jouvenceau m.

sapphire ['sæfaɪər] ◆ n [gem, colour] saphir m. ◆ comp [ring, pendant] de saphir. ◆ adj [in colour] saphir (inv).

Sarajevo [,særə'jeɪvəʊ] pr n Sarajevo.

sarcasm ['sɑːkæzm] n (U) sarcasme m.

sarcastic [sɑː'kæstɪk] adj sarcastique.

sarcastically [sɑː'kæstɪklɪ] adv d'un ton sarcastique.

sarcophagus [sɑː'kɒfəgəs] (pl sarcophaguses or sarcophagi [-gaɪ]) n sarcophage m.

sardine [sɑː'diːn] n sardine f / we were packed in like sardines nous étions serrés comme des sardines.

Sardinia [sɑː'dɪnjə] pr n Sardaigne f / in Sardinia en Sardaigne.

sardonic [sɑː'dɒnɪk] adj sardonique.

sardonically [sɑː'dɒnɪklɪ] adv sardoniquement.

Sargasso Sea pr n ▶ **the Sargasso Sea** la mer des Sargasses.

sari ['sɑːrɪ] n sari m.

sarky ['sɑːkɪ] (compar sarkier, superl sarkiest) adj ⬛ inf sarcastique.

sarnie ['sɑːnɪ] (abbr of sandwich) n ⬛ v inf sandwich m.

sarong [sə'rɒŋ] n sarong m.

SARS ['særz] (abbr of severe acute respiratory syndrome) n SRAS m.

sarsaparilla [,sɑːspə'rɪlə] n [plant] salsepareille f ; [drink] boisson f à la salsepareille.

sartorial [sɑː'tɔːrɪəl] adj vestimentaire / his sartorial elegance son élégance vestimentaire, l'élégance de sa mise.

SAS (abbr of Special Air Service) pr n commando d'intervention spéciale de l'armée britannique.

SASE n ⬛ abbr of self-addressed stamped envelope.

sash [sæʃ] n **1.** [belt] ceinture f (en étoffe) ; [sign of office] écharpe f **2.** [frame of window, door] châssis m, cadre m.

sashay ['sæʃeɪ] vi ⬛ inf [saunter] flâner ; [strut] parader, se pavaner / he sashayed in and said hello **a)** [casually] il entra d'un pas nonchalant et dit bonjour **b)** [ostentatiously] il entra en se pavanant et dit bonjour.

sash window n fenêtre f à guillotine.

Saskatchewan [sæs'kætʃɪwən] pr n Saskatchewan m / in Saskatchewan dans le Saskatchewan.

sassy ['sæsɪ] (compar sassier, superl sassiest) adj ⬛ inf culotté, gonflé.

sat [sæt] pt & pp ⟶ **sit**.

SAT [sæt] (abbr of Scholastic Aptitude Test) n examen d'entrée à l'université aux États-Unis.

Sat. (written abbr of Saturday) sam.

Satan ['seɪtn] pr n Satan.

satanic [sə'tænɪk] adj satanique / 'The Satanic Verses' Rushdie 'les Versets sataniques'.

satanism ['seɪtənɪzm] n satanisme m.

satanist ['seɪtənɪst] ◆ adj sataniste. ◆ n sataniste mf.

satchel ['sætʃəl] n cartable m.

sated ['seɪtɪd] adj [person] rassasié ; [hunger] assouvi ; [thirst] étanché.

satellite ['sætəlaɪt] ◆ n **1.** ASTRON & TELEC satellite m / broadcast live by satellite transmis en direct par satellite **2.** [country] pays m satellite **3.** [in airport] satellite m. ◆ comp **1.** [broadcasting, network, relay, navigation] par satellite ▶ **satellite broadcast** émission f retransmise par satellite ▶ **satellite channel** chaîne f (de télévision) par satellite ▶ **satellite dish** antenne f de télévision par satellite ▶ **satellite link** liaison f par satellite ▶ **satellite television** télévision f par satellite **2.** [country] satellite ▶ **satellite state** état m satellite.

satiate ['seɪʃɪeɪt] vt *liter* **1.** [satisfy - hunger, desire] assouvir ; [-thirst] étancher **2.** [gorge] rassasier / *satiated with pleasure* repu de plaisir.

satin ['sætɪn] ◆ n satin *m*. ◆ comp **1.** [dress, shirt] en or de satin **2.** [finish] satiné.

satire ['sætaɪəʳ] n satire *f* / *it's a satire on the English* c'est une satire contre les Anglais / *her novels are full of satire* ses romans sont pleins d'observations satiriques.

satirical [sə'tɪrɪkl] adj satirique.

satirically [sə'tɪrɪklɪ] adv satiriquement.

satirist ['sætərɪst] n satiriste *mf*.

satirize, satirise ['sætəraɪz] vt faire la satire de.

satisfaction [,sætɪs'fækʃn] n **1.** [fulfilment - of curiosity, hunger, demand, conditions] satisfaction *f*; [-of contract] exécution *f*, réalisation *f*; [-of debt] acquittement *m*, remboursement *m* **2.** [pleasure] satisfaction *f*, contentement *m* / *is everything to your satisfaction?* est-ce que tout est à votre convenance ? / *the plan was agreed to everyone's satisfaction* le projet fut accepté à la satisfaction générale / *to the satisfaction of the court* d'une manière qui a convaincu le tribunal / *I don't get much job satisfaction* je ne tire pas beaucoup de satisfaction de mon travail **3.** [pleasing thing] satisfaction *f* **4.** [redress - of a wrong] réparation *f*; [-of damage] dédommagement *m* ; [-of an insult] réparation *f*.

satisfactorily [,sætɪs'fæktərəlɪ] adv de façon satisfaisante.

satisfactory [,sætɪs'fæktərɪ] adj satisfaisant / *their progress is only satisfactory* leurs progrès sont satisfaisants, sans plus / *I hope she has a satisfactory excuse* j'espère qu'elle a une excuse valable / *the patient's condition is satisfactory* l'état du malade n'est pas inquiétant.

satisfied ['sætɪsfaɪd] adj **1.** [happy] satisfait, content / *a satisfied customer* un client satisfait / *a satisfied sigh* un soupir de satisfaction / *the teacher isn't satisfied with their work* le professeur n'est pas satisfait de leur travail / *are you satisfied now you've made her cry?* tu es content de l'avoir fait pleurer ? / *they'll have to be satisfied with what they've got* ils devront se contenter de ce qu'ils ont **2.** [convinced] convaincu, persuadé / *I'm not entirely satisfied with the truth of his story* je ne suis pas tout à fait convaincu que son histoire soit vraie.

satisfy ['sætɪsfaɪ] (*pt & pp* **satisfied**) ◆ vt **1.** [please] satisfaire, contenter / *Richard Fox has satisfied the examiners in the following subjects* SCH Richard Fox a été reçu dans les matières suivantes **2.** [fulfil - curiosity, desire, hunger] satisfaire ; [-thirst] étancher ; [-demand, need, requirements] satisfaire à, répondre à ; [-conditions, terms of contract] remplir ; [-debt] s'acquitter de **3.** [prove to - gen] persuader, convaincre ; [-authorities] prouver à / *I satisfied myself that all the windows were closed* je me suis assuré que toutes les fenêtres étaient fermées. ◆ vi donner satisfaction.

satisfying ['sætɪsfaɪɪŋ] adj [job, outcome, evening] satisfaisant ; [meal] substantiel.

satnav ['sætnæv] n GPS *m*.

satsuma [,sæt'su:mə] n 🇬🇧 mandarine *f*.

saturate ['sætʃəreɪt] vt **1.** *fig* [swamp] saturer ▶ **to saturate sb with sthg** saturer qqn de qqch **2.** [drench] tremper **3.** CHEM saturer.

saturated ['sætʃəreɪtɪd] adj **1.** CHEM saturé ▶ **saturated fats** graisses *fpl* saturées **2.** [very wet] trempé **3.** PHOT ▶ **saturated colours** couleurs *fpl* saturées.

saturation [,sætʃə'reɪʃn] n saturation *f*.

saturation bombing n bombardement *m* intensif.

saturation coverage n TV couverture *f* maximale.

saturation point n point *m* de saturation / *we've reached saturation point* nous sommes arrivés à saturation / *the market is at* or *has reached saturation point* le marché est saturé.

Saturday ['sætədeɪ] n samedi *m* / **'Saturday Night Fever'** *Badham* 'la Fièvre du samedi soir'. See also **Friday**.

Saturday girl n vendeuse *f* (*travaillant le samedi*).

Saturn ['sætən] pr n ASTRON & MYTH Saturne.

sauce [sɔ:s] n **1.** CULIN [with savoury dishes] sauce *f*; [with desserts] coulis *m* ▶ **raspberry sauce** coulis de framboises ▶ **chocolate sauce** sauce au chocolat ▶ **what's sauce for the goose is sauce for the gander** *prov* ce qui est bon pour l'un est bon pour l'autre **2.** *inf* [insolence] culot *m*, toupet *m*.

sauce boat n saucière *f*.

saucepan ['sɔ:spən] n casserole *f*.

saucer ['sɔ:səʳ] n soucoupe *f*.

saucy ['sɔ:sɪ] (*compar* **saucier**, *superl* **sauciest**) adj *inf* **1.** [cheeky] effronté **2.** [provocative - action] provocant ; [-postcard, joke] grivois.

Saudi Arabia pr n Arabie Saoudite *f* / *in Saudi Arabia* en Arabie Saoudite.

Saudi (Arabian) ['saʊdɪ-] ◆ n Saoudien *m*, -enne *f*. ◆ adj saoudien.

sauerkraut ['saʊəkraʊt] n choucroute *f*.

sauna ['sɔ:nə] n sauna *m*.

saunter ['sɔ:ntəʳ] ◆ vi se promener d'un pas nonchalant, flâner / *I think I'll saunter down to the library* je pense que je vais aller faire un petit tour jusqu'à la bibliothèque. ◆ n petite promenade *f*.

sausage ['sɒsɪdʒ] n saucisse *f*; [of pre-cooked meats] saucisson *m* ▶ **pork sausages** saucisses *fpl* de porc ▶ **not a sausage!** 🇬🇧 *inf* que dalle !, des clous !

sausage meat n chair *f* à saucisse.

sausage roll n sorte de friand à la saucisse.

sauté [🇬🇧 'saʊteɪ 🇺🇸 saʊ'teɪ] (*pt & pp* **sautéed**, *cont* **sautéing**) ◆ vt faire sauter. ◆ adj ▶ **sauté potatoes** pommes de terre sautées. ◆ n sauté *m*.

savage ['sævɪdʒ] ◆ adj **1.** [ferocious - person] féroce, brutal ; [-dog] méchant ; [-fighting, tiger] féroce ; [reply, attack] violent, féroce / *he came in for some savage criticism from the press* il a été violemment critiqué dans la presse / *the new policy deals a savage blow to the country's farmers* la nouvelle politique porte un coup très dur or fatal aux agriculteurs **2.** [primitive - tribe] primitif ; [-customs] barbare, primitif. ◆ n sauvage *mf*. ◆ vt **1.** [subj: animal] attaquer / *she was savaged by a tiger* elle a été attaquée par un tigre **2.** [subj: critics, press] attaquer violemment.

savagely ['sævɪdʒlɪ] adv sauvagement, brutalement.

savageness ['sævɪdʒnɪs] = **savagery**.

savagery ['sævɪdʒrɪ] n **1.** [brutality] sauvagerie *f*, férocité *f*, brutalité *f* **2.** [primitive state] : *the tribe still lives in savagery* la tribu vit toujours à l'état sauvage.

savanna(h) [sə'vænə] n savane *f*.

save [seɪv] ◆ vt **1.** [rescue] sauver / *she saved my life* elle m'a sauvé la vie ▶ **to save sb from a fire / from drowning** sauver qqn d'un incendie / de la noyade / *the doctors managed to save her eyesight* les médecins ont pu lui sauver la vue / *he saved me from making a terrible mistake* il m'a empêché de faire une erreur monstrueuse / *to save a species from extinction* sauver une espèce en voie de disparition ▶ **saved by the bell!** sauvé par le gong ! ▶ **to save one's neck** or **skin** or **hide** or **bacon** *inf* sauver sa peau ▶ **to save face** sauver la face ▶ **to save the day** sauver la mise **2.** [put by - money] économiser, épargner, mettre de côté / *how much money have you got saved?* à combien se montent vos économies ?, combien d'argent avez-vous mis de côté ? ; [collect] collectionner / *do you still save stamps?* est-ce que tu collectionnes toujours les timbres ? **3.** [economize on - fuel, electricity] économiser, faire des économies de ; [-money] économiser ; [-effort] économiser ; [-time, space] gagner ; [-strength] ménager, économiser / *their advice saved me a fortune* leurs conseils m'ont fait économiser une fortune / *a computer would save you a lot of time* un ordinateur vous ferait gagner beaucoup de temps **4.** [spare - trouble, effort] éviter, épargner ; [-expense] éviter / *thanks, you've saved me a trip / having to go myself* merci, vous m'avez évité un trajet / d'y aller moi-même **5.** [protect - eyes, shoes] ménager **6.** [reserve] garder, mettre de côté / *I'll save you a place* je te garderai une place / *I always save the best part till last* je garde toujours le meilleur pour la fin **7.** FOOT [shot, penalty] arrêter ▶ **to save a goal** arrêter *or* bloquer un tir **8.** RELIG [sinner, mankind] sauver, délivrer ; [soul] sauver **9.** COMPUT sauvegarder, enregistrer / **'save as'** 'enregistrer sous'. ◆ vi **1.** [spend less] faire des économies, économiser / *to save on fuel* économiser sur le carburant **2.** [put money aside] faire des économies, épargner / *I'm saving for a new car* je fais des économies pour acheter une nouvelle voiture. ◆ n **1.** FOOT arrêt *m* **2.** COMPUT sauvegarde *f.* ◆ prep *fml* sauf, hormis. ❖ **save for** prep phr à part / *save for the fact we lost, it was a great match* à part le fait qu'on a perdu, c'était un très bon match. ❖ **save up** ◆ vt sep = **save** (vt). ◆ vi = **save** (vi).

save as you earn n UK plan *m* d'épargne *(avec prélèvements automatiques sur le salaire).*

saveloy ['sævələɪ] n cervelas *m.*

saver ['seɪvər] n **1.** [person] épargnant *m*, -e *f* **2.** [product] bonne affaire *f* ▶ **super saver (ticket)** billet *m* à tarif réduit.

-saver in comp : *it's a real money-saver* ça permet d'économiser de l'argent *or* de faire des économies.

saving ['seɪvɪŋ] ◆ n **1.** [thrift] épargne *f* **2.** [money saved] économie *f* ▶ **to make a saving** faire une économie / *he drew all his savings out of the bank* il a retiré toutes ses économies de la banque. ◆ prep *fml* sauf, hormis.

saving grace n : *her sense of humour is her saving grace* on lui pardonne tout parce qu'elle a de l'humour.

savings account n compte *m* sur livret.

savings and loan association n US caisse *f* d'épargne logement.

savings bank n caisse *f* d'épargne.

saviour UK, **savior** US ['seɪvjər] n sauveur *m* ▶ **the Saviour** le Sauveur.

savoir-faire [ˌsævwɑːˈfeər] n [know-how] savoir-faire *m* ; [social skills] savoir-vivre *m.*

savor US = **savour.**

savory ['seɪvərɪ] n BOT sarriette *f.*

savour UK, **savor** US ['seɪvər] ◆ n **1.** [taste] goût *m*, saveur *f* **2.** [interest, charm] saveur *f.* ◆ vt [taste] goûter (à), déguster ; [enjoy - food, experience, one's freedom] savourer. ◆ vi ▶ **to savour of sthg** sentir qqch.

savoury UK, **savory** US ['seɪvərɪ] ◆ adj **1.** [salty] salé ; [spicy] épicé ▶ **savoury biscuits** biscuits salés **2.** US [appetizing] savoureux **3.** *fml* [wholesome] : *it's not a very savoury subject* c'est un sujet peu ragoûtant / *he's not a very savoury individual* c'est un individu peu recommandable. ◆ n petit plat salé servi soit comme hors-d'œuvre, soit en fin de repas après le dessert.

Savoy [səˈvɔɪ] ◆ pr n Savoie *f* / *in Savoy* en Savoie. ◆ adj savoyard.

savoy cabbage n chou *m* frisé.

savvy ['sævɪ] *inf* ◆ n [know-how] savoir-faire *m* ; [shrewdness] jugeote *f*, perspicacité *f.* ◆ adj US [well-informed] bien informé, calé ; [shrewd] perspicace, astucieux.

saw [sɔː] (UK pt **sawed,** pp **sawed** *or* **sawn** [sɔːn] ; US pt & pp **sawed**) ◆ pt ⟶ **see.** ◆ n **1.** [tool] scie *f* ▶ **to cut sthg up with a saw** couper *or* débiter qqch à la scie ▶ **metal saw** scie à métaux **2.** [saying] dicton *m.* ◆ vt : *to saw a tree into logs* débiter un arbre en rondins / *he sawed the table in half* il a scié la table en deux / *his arms sawed the air* *fig* il battait l'air de ses bras. ◆ vi scier / *he was sawing away at the cello* *fig* il raclait le violoncelle. ❖ **saw down** vt sep [tree] abattre. ❖ **saw off** vt sep scier, enlever à la scie. ❖ **saw up** vt sep scier en morceaux, débiter à la scie.

sawdust ['sɔːdʌst] n sciure *f* (de bois).

sawed-off ['sɔːd-] US = **sawn-off.**

sawmill ['sɔːmɪl] n scierie *f.*

sawn [sɔːn] pp ⟶ **saw.**

sawn-off adj [truncated] scié, coupé (à la scie) ▶ **sawn-off shotgun** carabine *f* à canon scié.

sax [sæks] **(abbr of saxophone)** n *inf* saxo *m.*

Saxon ['sæksn] ◆ n **1.** [person] Saxon *m*, -onne *f* **2.** LING saxon *m.* ◆ adj saxon.

saxophone ['sæksəfəʊn] n saxophone *m.*

saxophonist [US sækˈsɒfənɪst US ˈsæksəfəʊnɪst] n saxophoniste *mf.*

say [seɪ] *(pt & pp* **said** [sed]*, pres (3rd pers sing)* **says** [sez])
◆ vt

A. SPEAK 1. [put into words] dire ▶ **to say sthg (to sb)** dire qqch (à qqn) / *I wouldn't say no!* je ne dis pas non !, ce n'est pas de refus ! ; [expressing fact, idea, comment] : *what did you say in reply?* qu'avez-vous répondu ? / *I can't think of anything to say* je ne trouve rien à dire / *I have nothing to say* a) [gen] je n'ai rien à dire b) [no comment] je n'ai aucune déclaration à faire / *let's say no more about it* n'en parlons plus / *can you say that again?* pouvez-vous répéter ce que vous venez de dire ? / *say what you mean* dites ce que vous avez à dire / *he didn't have a good word to say about the plan* il n'a dit que du mal du projet / *he certainly has a lot to say for himself* il n'a pas la langue dans la poche ▶ **to say nothing of...** : *to say nothing of the overheads* sans parler des frais ▶ **just say the word, you only have to say (the word)** UK vous n'avez qu'un mot à dire ▶ **having said that** ceci (étant) dit ▶ **it goes without saying that...** : *it goes without saying that we shall travel together* il va sans dire *or* il va de soi que nous voyagerons ensemble ▶ **you can say that again!** c'est le cas de le dire !, je ne vous le fais pas dire ! ▶ **enough said** [I understand] je vois **2.** [with direct or indirect speech] dire / *they said it was going to rain* ils ont annoncé de la pluie **3.** [claim, allege] dire / *you know what they say, no smoke without fire* tu sais ce qu'on dit, il n'y a pas de fumée sans feu / *don't say you've forgotten!* ne (me) dites pas que vous avez oublié ! / *who can say?* qui sait ? **4.** [expressing personal opinion] dire / *so he says* c'est ce qu'il dit / *I must say she's been very helpful* je dois dire qu'elle nous a beaucoup aidés / *I'll say this for him, he certainly tries hard* je dois reconnaître qu'il fait tout son possible / *if you say so* si *or* puisque tu le dis ▶ **to say the least** c'est le moins qu'on puisse dire / *there's something to be said for the idea* l'idée a du bon / *there's not much to be said for the idea* l'idée ne vaut pas grand-chose ▶ **that's not saying much** ça ne veut pas dire grand-chose / *it doesn't say much for his powers of observation* cela en dit long sur son sens de l'observation.

B. THINK, SUPPOSE OR INDICATE 1. [think] dire, penser / *what do you say we drive over* or *to driving over to see them?* que diriez-vous de prendre la voiture et d'aller les voir ? / *what do you say?* [do you agree?] qu'en dites-vous ? / *when would you say would be the best time for us to leave?* quel serait le meilleur moment pour partir, à votre avis ? / *to look at them, you wouldn't say they were a day over forty* à les voir, on ne leur donnerait pas plus de quarante ans 2. [suppose, assume] : *(let's) say your plan doesn't work, what then?* admettons que votre plan ne marche pas, qu'est-ce qui se passe ? / *say he doesn't arrive, who will take his place?* si jamais il n'arrive pas, qui prendra sa place ? 3. [indicate, register] indiquer, marquer / *the clock says 10.40* la pendule indique 10 h 40 4. [express - subj: intonation, eyes] exprimer, marquer 5. [mean] : *that's not to say I don't like it* cela ne veut pas dire que je ne l'aime pas. ◆ vi [tell] dire / *he won't say* il ne veut pas le dire / *I'd rather not say* je préfère ne rien dire / *it's not for me to say* a) [speak] ce n'est pas à moi de le dire b) [decide] ce n'est pas à moi de décider ▶ **I say!** a) [expressing surprise] eh bien ! b) [to attract attention] dites ! ▶ **you don't say!** *inf* sans blague !, ça alors !
◆ n ▶ **to have a say in sthg** avoir son mot à dire dans qqch / *I had no say in choosing the wallpaper* on ne m'a pas demandé mon avis pour le choix du papier peint ▶ **to have one's say** dire ce qu'on a à dire.
◆ interj **US** dites donc ! ❖ **when all's said and done** *adv phr* tout compte fait, au bout du compte.

SAYE n *abbr of* save as you earn.

saying ['seɪɪŋ] n dicton m, proverbe m ▶ **as the saying goes** a) [proverb] comme dit le proverbe b) [as we say] comme on dit.

say-so n **UK** 1. [authorization] : *I'm not going without her say-so* je n'irai pas sans qu'elle m'y autorise or sans son accord / *he refused to do it without the boss's say-so* il a refusé de le faire sans avoir l'aval du patron 2. [assertion] : *I won't believe it just on his say-so* ce n'est pas parce qu'il l'a dit que j'y crois.

SBNA (abbr of **Small Business Administration**) n *organisme fédéral américain d'aide aux petites entreprises.*

SC 1. written abbr of **South Carolina** 2. MESSAGING written abbr of **stay cool.**

S/C written abbr of **self-contained.**

scab [skæb] (*pt & pp* **scabbed**, *cont* **scabbing**) ◆ n 1. MED [from cut, blister] croûte f 2. BOT & ZOOL gale f 3. *inf & pej* [strikebreaker] jaune mf 4. *inf* [cad] crapule f, sale type m. ◆ vi 1. MED former une croûte 2. **UK** *inf & pej* briser une grève, refuser de faire grève.

scabby ['skæbɪ] (*compar* **scabbier**, *superl* **scabbiest**) adj 1. MED [skin] croûteux, recouvert d'une croûte 2. *inf & pej* [mean - person] mesquin ; [- attitude] moche.

scabies ['skeɪbiːz] n (U) gale f.

scaffold ['skæfəʊld] n 1. CONSTR échafaudage m 2. [for execution] échafaud m ▶ **to go to the scaffold** monter à l'échafaud.

scaffolding ['skæfəldɪŋ] n [framework] échafaudage m.

scalawag ['skæləwæg] n **US** = scallywag.

scald [skɔːld] ◆ vt 1. [hands, skin] ébouillanter / *the hot tea scalded my tongue* le thé bouillant m'a brûlé la langue 2. CULIN [tomatoes] ébouillanter ; [milk] porter presque à ébullition 3. [sterilize] stériliser. ◆ vi brûler. ◆ n brûlure f *(causée par un liquide, de la vapeur)* / *I got a nasty scald* je me suis bien ébouillanté.

scalding ['skɔːldɪŋ] ◆ adj 1. [water] bouillant ; [metal, tea, soup, tears] brûlant 2. [sun] brûlant ; [heat] suffocant, torride ; [weather] très chaud, torride 3. [criticism] cinglant, acerbe. ◆ adv ▶ **scalding hot** a) [coffee] brûlant b) [weather] torride.

scale [skeɪl] ◆ n 1. [of model, drawing] échelle f / *the sketch was drawn to scale* l'esquisse était à l'échelle / *the scale of the map is 1 to 50,000* la carte est au 50 millième / *the drawing is out of scale* or *is not to scale* le croquis n'est pas à l'échelle 2. [for measurement, evaluation] échelle f ; [of salaries, taxes] échelle f, barème m ; [of values] échelle m / *the social scale* l'échelle sociale / *at the top of the scale* en haut de l'échelle ; [graduation] échelle f (graduée), graduation f ▶ **to be off the scale** or **to go off the scale** atteindre des niveaux extrêmes 3. [extent] échelle f, étendue f ; [size] importance f / *the scale of the devastation* l'étendue des dégâts / *the sheer scale of the problem* l'ampleur même du problème ▶ **to do sthg on a large scale** faire qqch sur une grande échelle / *on an industrial scale* à l'échelle industrielle ▶ **economies of scale** économies d'échelle 4. MUS gamme f ▶ **to practise** or **to do one's scales** faire ses gammes 5. [of fish, reptile] écaille f ; [of epidermis] squame f / *the scales fell from her eyes* fig les écailles lui sont tombées des yeux 6. [in kettle, pipes] tartre m, [dépôt m] calcaire m ; [on teeth] tartre m 7. [of paint, plaster, rust] écaille f, écaillure f 8. [scale pan] plateau m (de balance) 9. **US** [for weighing] pèse-personne m, balance f. ◆ vt 1. [climb over - wall, fence] escalader 2. [drawing] dessiner à l'échelle 3. [test] graduer, pondérer 4. [fish, paint] écailler ; [teeth, pipes] détartrer. ◆ vi [paint, rust] s'écailler ; [skin] peler. ❖ **scales** pl n [for food] balance f ; [for letters] pèse-lettre m ; [for babies] pèse-bébé m ; [public] bascule f ▶ **(a pair of) kitchen scales** une balance de cuisine ▶ **(a pair of) bathroom scales** un pèse-personne. ❖ **scale down** vt sep 1. [drawing] réduire l'échelle de 2. [figures, demands] réduire, baisser, diminuer. ❖ **scale off** ◆ vi [paint, rust] s'écailler. ◆ vt sep écailler. ❖ **scale up** vt sep 1. [drawing] augmenter l'échelle de 2. [figures, demands] réviser à la hausse, augmenter.

scale diagram n plan m à l'échelle.

scale drawing n dessin m à l'échelle.

scale model n [of car, plane] modèle m réduit ; [of buildings, town centre] maquette f.

scallion ['skæljən] n **US** CULIN [spring onion] oignon m blanc ; [leek] poireau m ; [shallot] échalote f.

scallop ['skɒləp] ◆ vt 1. CULIN [fish, vegetable] gratiner 2. SEW [edge, hem] festonner. ◆ n CULIN & ZOOL coquille Saint-Jacques f. ❖ **scallops** pl n SEW festons mpl.

scallywag ['skælɪwæg] n *inf* [rascal] voyou m, coquin m.

scalp [skælp] ◆ n 1. [top of head] cuir m chevelu 2. [Indian trophy] scalp m 3. *fig* [trophy] trophée m ; HUNT trophée m de chasse. ◆ vt 1. [person, animal] scalper 2. **US** [tickets] vendre en réalisant un bénéfice substantiel ▶ **to scalp shares** or **securities US** boursicoter 3. *inf* [cheat] arnaquer 4. **US** *inf* [defeat] battre à plate couture.

scalpel ['skælpəl] n scalpel m.

scalper ['skælpər] n **US** revendeur m, -euse f de tickets à la sauvette *(pour un concert, un match, etc.).*

scam [skæm] ◆ n v *inf* escroquerie f, arnaque f ▶ **mail scam** arnaque f par mail. ◆ vi ▶ **to scam on sb US** *inf* [hit on] draguer qqn.

scamp [skæmp] n *inf* [child] garnement m, coquin m, -e f ; [rogue] voyou m.

scamper ['skæmpər] ◆ vi 1. [small animal] trottiner ; [children] gambader, galoper / *the kids scampered into the house* / *up the stairs* les gosses sont entrés dans la maison / ont monté l'escalier en courant 2. *inf* [work quickly] : *I positively scampered through the book* j'ai lu le livre à toute vitesse. ◆ n trottinement m. ❖ **scamper about** vi [animal] courir or trottiner çà et là ; [children] gambader. ❖ **scamper away, scamper off** vi détaler, se sauver.

scampi ['skæmpɪ] n (U) scampi mpl.

scan [skæn] (*pt & pp* **scanned**, *cont* **scanning**) ◆ vt 1. [look carefully at] scruter, fouiller du regard ; [read carefully] lire attentivement 2. [consult quickly - report, notes] lire en diagonale, parcourir rapidement ; [-magazine] feuilleter ; [-screen, image] balayer ; [-tape, memory] lire **3.** PHYS [spectrum] balayer, parcourir ; [subj: radar, searchlight] balayer **4.** MED examiner au scanner, faire une scanographie de **5.** ELECTRON & TV balayer **6.** LITER scander **7.** COMPUT scanner. ◆ vi LITER se scander. ◆ n **1.** MED scanographie f, examen m au scanner **2.** LITER scansion f **3.** ELECTRON & TV balayage m. ❖ **scan in** vt sep COMPUT insérer par scanneur.

scandal ['skændl] n **1.** [disgrace] scandale m ▶ **to cause a scandal** provoquer un scandale / *it's a scandal that people like them should be let free* c'est scandaleux de laisser des gens pareils en liberté / *it's a national scandal* c'est une honte nationale or un scandale public **2.** (U) [gossip] ragots mpl ; [evil] médisance f, médisances fpl, calomnie f / *this newspaper specializes in scandal* c'est un journal à scandale / *the latest society scandal* les derniers potins mondains.

scandalize, scandalise ['skændəlaɪz] vt scandaliser, choquer / *he was scandalized by what she said* il a été scandalisé par ses propos / *she's easily scandalized* elle se scandalise or s'indigne vite.

scandalous ['skændələs] adj **1.** [conduct] scandaleux, choquant ; [news, price] scandaleux / *it's absolutely scandalous!* c'est un véritable scandale ! **2.** [gossip] calomnieux.

scandalously ['skændələslɪ] adv **1.** [act] scandaleusement **2.** [speak, write] de manière diffamatoire.

Scandinavia [,skændɪ'neɪvjə] pr n Scandinavie f / *in Scandinavia* en Scandinavie.

Scandinavian [,skændɪ'neɪvjən] ◆ n **1.** [person] Scandinave mf **2.** LING scandinave m. ◆ adj scandinave.

scanner ['skænər] n **1.** MED & ELECTRON scanner m **2.** [for radar] antenne f **3.** COMPUT ▶ **(optical) scanner** scanner m.

scant [skænt] ◆ adj maigre ▶ **to pay scant attention to sb / sthg** ne prêter que peu d'attention à qqn / qqch / *they showed scant regard for our feelings* ils ne se sont pas beaucoup souciés or ils se sont peu souciés de ce que nous pouvions ressentir / *a scant teaspoonful* une cuillerée à café rase. ◆ vt **1.** [skimp on] lésiner sur ; [restrict] restreindre **2.** [treat superficially] traiter de manière superficielle.

scantily ['skæntɪlɪ] adv [furnished] pauvrement, chichement ; [dressed] légèrement.

scanty ['skæntɪ] (compar **scantier**, superl **scantiest**) adj **1.** [small in number, quantity -meal, crops] maigre, peu abondant ; [-income, payment] maigre, modeste ; [-information, knowledge] maigre, limité ; [-applause] maigre, peu fourni ; [-audience] clairsemé ; [-praise, aid] limité **2.** [brief -clothing] léger / *she was wearing only a scanty negligee* elle ne portait qu'un négligé qui ne cachait pas grand-chose *hum.*

scapegoat ['skeɪpgəʊt] n bouc m émissaire.

scar [skɑːr] (pt & pp **scarred**, cont **scarring**) ◆ n **1.** [from wound, surgery] cicatrice f ; [from deep cut on face] balafre f **2.** fig [on land, painted surface, tree] cicatrice f, marque f ; [emotional] cicatrice f / *the scars of battle* les traces de la bataille / *the mine was like an ugly scar on the landscape* la mine déparait terriblement le paysage **3.** [rock] rocher m escarpé ; [in river] écueil m. ◆ vt **1.** [skin, face] laisser une cicatrice sur / *his hands were badly scarred* il avait sur les mains de profondes cicatrices / *smallpox had scarred his face* il avait le visage grêlé par la variole **2.** fig [surface] marquer ; [emotionally] marquer / *she was permanently scarred by the experience* cette expérience l'avait marquée pour la vie. ◆ vi [form scar] se cicatriser ; [leave scar] laisser une cicatrice. ❖ **scar over** vi [form scar] former une cicatrice ; [close up] se cicatriser.

scarce ['skeəs] ◆ adj [rare] rare ; [infrequent] peu fréquent ; [in short supply] peu abondant / *sugar is scarce at the moment* il y a une pénurie de sucre en ce moment ▶ **to become scarce** se faire rare / *water is becoming scarce* l'eau commence à manquer / *rain is scarce in this region* il ne pleut pas souvent dans cette région ▶ **to make o.s. scarce** a) inf [run away] se sauver, décamper b) [get out] débarrasser le plancher / *can you make yourself scarce for half an hour?* peux-tu disparaître pendant une demi-heure ? ◆ adv *liter* à peine.

scarcely ['skeəslɪ] adv **1.** [no sooner] à peine / *we had scarcely begun or scarcely had we begun when the bell rang* nous avions tout juste commencé quand or à peine avions-nous commencé que la cloche a sonné **2.** [barely] : *he scarcely spoke to me* c'est tout juste s'il m'a adressé la parole / *she's scarcely more than a child* elle n'est encore qu'une enfant / *scarcely any* presque pas de / *scarcely anybody* presque personne / *scarcely anything* presque rien / *I know scarcely any of those people* je ne connais pratiquement personne parmi ces gens or pratiquement aucune de ces personnes / *he has scarcely any hair left* il n'a presque plus de cheveux **3.** [indicating difficulty] à peine, tout juste / *I could scarcely tell his mother, now could I!* je ne pouvais quand même pas le dire à sa mère, non ? / *I scarcely know where to begin* je ne sais pas trop par où commencer / *I can scarcely wait to meet her* j'ai hâte de la rencontrer / *I can scarcely believe what you're saying* j'ai du mal à croire ce que vous dites.

scarcity ['skeəsətɪ] (pl **scarcities**) n [rarity] rareté f ; [lack] manque m ; [shortage] manque m, pénurie f / *there is a scarcity of new talent today* les nouveaux talents se font rares.

scare [skeər] ◆ vt effrayer, faire peur à / *thunder really scares me* le tonnerre me fait vraiment très peur ▶ **to scare sb stiff** inf: *the film scared me stiff!* le film m'a flanqué une de ces frousses ! ▶ **to scare the wits** or **the living daylights** or **the life out of sb** inf flanquer une peur bleue or une trouille pas possible à qqn ▶ **to scare the hell** inf or **the shit** vulg **out of sb** : *he scared the hell out of me* il m'a foutu les jetons. ◆ vi s'effrayer, prendre peur / *I don't scare easily* je ne suis pas peureux. ◆ n **1.** [fright] peur f, frayeur f ▶ **to give sb a scare** effrayer qqn, faire peur à qqn **2.** [alert] alerte f ; [rumour] bruit m alarmiste, rumeur f ▶ **a takeover scare** des rumeurs concernant une possible OPA ▶ **a bomb / fire scare** une alerte à la bombe / au feu ▶ **beef / poultry scare** alerte f alimentaire à propos du bœuf / du poulet. ◆ comp [sensational -headlines] alarmiste. ❖ **scare away, scare off** vt sep [bird, customer] faire fuir. ❖ **scare up** vt sep US inf dénicher.

scarecrow ['skeəkrəʊ] n [for birds] épouvantail m ; fig [person -thin] squelette m ; [-badly dressed] épouvantail m.

scared ['skeəd] adj [frightened] effrayé ; [nervous] craintif, peureux ▶ **to be scared (of sthg)** avoir peur (de qqch) / *he was scared to ask* il avait peur de demander / *he's scared of being told off / that she might tell him off* il craint de se faire gronder / qu'elle ne le gronde ▶ **to be scared stiff** inf or **to death** inf avoir une peur bleue / *I was scared out of my wits!* inf j'étais mort de peur !

> 📋 Note that avoir peur que and craindre que are followed by a verb in the subjunctive, usually preceded by ne:
> **I'm scared he might get angry if I tell him.** *J'ai peur qu'il ne se mette en colère si je le lui dis.*
> **I'm scared they might have got lost.** *Je crains qu'ils ne se soient perdus.*

scaremongering ['skeə,mʌŋgrɪŋ] n alarmisme m.

scare story n histoire f pour faire peur.

scare tactics n manœuvres fpl d'intimidation.

scarey ['skeərɪ] = scary.

scarf [skɑːf] n **1.** (pl scarfs or scarves [skɑːvz]) [long] écharpe f ; [headscarf, cravat] foulard m **2.** CONSTR [cut] entaille f. ❖ **scarf down** vt sep 🇺🇸 inf [eat] avaler.

scarlet ['skɑːlət] ❖ adj [gen] écarlate ; [face - from illness, effort] cramoisi ; [- from shame] écarlate, cramoisi. ❖ n écarlate f.

scarlet fever n (U) scarlatine f.

scarper ['skɑːpə‍ʳ] vi 🇬🇧 inf déguerpir, se barrer.

scarves [skɑːvz] pl ⟶ scarf.

scary ['skeərɪ] (compar scarier, superl scariest) adj inf **1.** [frightening - place, person] effrayant ; [- story] qui donne le frisson **2.** [fearful] peureux.

scathing ['skeɪðɪŋ] adj [criticism, remark] caustique, cinglant ▶ **to give sb a scathing look** foudroyer qqn du regard / **he can be very scathing** il sait se montrer acerbe or cinglant.

scathingly ['skeɪðɪŋlɪ] adv [retort, criticize] de manière cinglante.

scatter ['skætə‍ʳ] ❖ vt **1.** [strew] éparpiller, disperser / papers had been scattered all over the desk le bureau était jonché or couvert de papiers **2.** [spread] répandre ; [sprinkle] saupoudrer / she scattered crumbs for the birds elle a jeté des miettes de pain aux oiseaux / to scatter seeds semer des graines à la volée **3.** [disperse - crowd, mob] disperser ; [- enemy] mettre en fuite ; [- clouds] dissiper, disperser **4.** PHYS [light] disperser. ❖ vi **1.** [people, clouds] se disperser / they told us to scatter ils nous ont dit de partir **2.** [beads, papers] s'éparpiller. ❖ n **1.** [of rice, bullets] pluie f / a scatter of farms on the hillside quelques fermes éparpillées à flanc de coteau **2.** [in statistics] dispersion f. ❖ **scatter about** 🇬🇧, **scatter around** vt sep éparpiller.

scatterbrain ['skætəbreɪn] n tête f de linotte, étourdi m, -e f.

scatterbrained ['skætəbreɪnd] adj écervelé, étourdi.

scatter cushion n petit coussin m.

scattered ['skætəd] adj **1.** [strewn] éparpillé / papers / toys lying scattered all over the floor des papiers / des jouets éparpillés par terre **2.** [sprinkled] parsemé / the tablecloth was scattered with crumbs la nappe était parsemée de miettes **3.** [dispersed - population] dispersé, disséminé ; [- clouds] épars ; [- villages, houses] épars ; [- light] diffus ; [- fortune] dissipé / she tried to collect her scattered thoughts elle essaya de mettre de l'ordre dans ses idées ▶ **scattered showers** averses fpl intermittentes **4.** 🇺🇸 = scatterbrained.

scatter-gun n fusil m de chasse.

scattering ['skætərɪŋ] n **1.** [small number] : a scattering of followers une poignée d'adeptes / there was a scattering of farms il y avait quelques fermes çà et là **2.** [dispersion] dispersion f.

scatty ['skætɪ] (compar scattier, superl scattiest) adj inf [forgetful] étourdi, écervelé ; [silly] bêta (bêtasse).

scavenge ['skævɪndʒ] ❖ vi **1.** [bird, animal] ▶ **to scavenge (for food)** chercher sa nourriture **2.** [person] : he was scavenging among the dustbins il fouillait dans or faisait les poubelles. ❖ vt **1.** [material, metals] récupérer / he managed to scavenge a meal il a finalement trouvé quelque chose à se mettre sous la dent **2.** [streets] nettoyer.

scavenger ['skævɪndʒə‍ʳ] n **1.** ZOOL charognard m **2.** [salvager] ramasseur m d'épaves ; [in rubbish] pilleur m de poubelles **3.** 🇬🇧 [street cleaner] éboueur m.

SCE (abbr of Scottish Certificate of Education) n certificat de fin d'études secondaires en Écosse.

scenario [sɪˈnɑːrɪəʊ] (pl scenarios) n scénario m.

scene [siːn] n **1.** [sphere of activity, milieu] scène f, situation f / the world political scene la scène politique internationale / she's a newcomer on or to the sports scene c'est une nouvelle venue sur la scène sportive or dans le monde du sport / the drug scene le monde de la drogue / she came on the scene just when we needed her elle est arrivée juste au moment où nous avions besoin d'elle / he disappeared from the scene for a few years il a disparu de la circulation or de la scène pendant quelques années **2.** CIN & THEAT [in film] scène f, séquence f ; [in play] scène f ▶ **to set the scene** planter le décor / the scene is set or takes place in Bombay la scène se passe or l'action se déroule à Bombay ▶ **behind the scenes** en coulisses / the scene was set for the arms negotiations fig tout était prêt pour les négociations sur les armements **3.** [place, spot] lieu m, lieux mpl, endroit m / the scene of the disaster l'endroit où s'est produite la catastrophe / the scene of the crime le lieu du crime / the police were soon on the scene la police est rapidement arrivée sur les lieux or sur place ▶ **scene of operations** MIL théâtre m des opérations **4.** [image] scène f, spectacle m ; [incident] scène f, incident m / scenes of horror / violence scènes d'horreur / de violence / scenes from or of village life scènes de la vie villageoise / just picture the scene essayez de vous représenter la scène ; [view] spectacle m, perspective f, vue f / a change of scene will do you good un changement d'air or de décor vous fera du bien ; ART tableau m, scène f / city / country scenes scènes de ville / champêtres **5.** [fuss, row] scène f ▶ **to make a scene** faire une scène ▶ **to have a scene with sb** se disputer avec qqn / he made an awful scene about it il en a fait toute une histoire **6.** inf [favourite activity] : jazz isn't really my scene le jazz, ça n'est pas vraiment mon truc.

scenery ['siːnərɪ] n **1.** [natural setting] paysage m / mountain scenery paysage de montagne / the scenery round here is lovely les paysages sont très beaux par ici / she needs a change of scenery fig elle a besoin de changer de décor or d'air **2.** THEAT décor m, décors mpl.

scenic ['siːnɪk] adj **1.** [surroundings] pittoresque / let's take the scenic route prenons la route touristique **2.** ART & THEAT scénique.

scent [sent] ❖ n **1.** [smell] parfum m, odeur f **2.** HUNT [of animal] fumet m ; [of person] odeur f ; [track] trace f, piste f / the hounds are on the scent or have picked up the scent of a fox les chiens sont sur la trace d'un renard or ont dépisté un renard / they've lost the scent ils ont perdu la piste ▶ **to put** or **to throw sb off the scent** semer qqn / we're on the scent of a major scandal nous flairons un gros scandale **3.** 🇬🇧 [perfume] parfum m. ❖ vt **1.** [smell - prey] flairer ; [detect - danger, treachery] flairer, subodorer **2.** [perfume] parfumer / scented notepaper papier m à lettres parfumé.

scepter 🇺🇸 = sceptre.

sceptic 🇬🇧, **skeptic** 🇺🇸 ['skeptɪk] ❖ adj sceptique. ❖ n sceptique mf.

sceptical 🇬🇧, **skeptical** 🇺🇸 ['skeptɪkl] adj sceptique.

scepticism 🇬🇧, **skepticism** 🇺🇸 ['skeptɪsɪzm] n scepticisme m.

sceptre 🇬🇧, **scepter** 🇺🇸 ['septə‍ʳ] n sceptre m.

SCF pr n abbr of Save the Children Fund.

schadenfreude ['ʃɑːdən,frɔɪdə] n joie maligne qu'on éprouve face au malheur d'autrui.

schedule [🇬🇧 'ʃedjuːl 🇺🇸 'skedʒʊl] ❖ n **1.** [programme] programme m ; [calendar] programme m, calendrier m ; [timetable] programme m, emploi m du temps ;

[plan] prévisions *fpl*, plan *m* / *I have a busy schedule* **a)** [for visit] j'ai un programme chargé **b)** [in general] j'ai un emploi du temps chargé **c)** [over period] j'ai un calendrier chargé / *everything went according to schedule* tout s'est déroulé comme prévu / *the work was carried out according to schedule* le travail a été effectué selon les prévisions / *we are on schedule* or *up to schedule* nous sommes dans les temps / *our work is ahead of / behind schedule* nous sommes en avance / en retard dans notre travail / *the bridge was opened on / ahead of schedule* le pont a été ouvert à la date prévue / en avance sur la date prévue ▸ **to fall behind schedule** prendre du retard sur les prévisions de travail **2.** [timetable - for transport] horaire *m* / *the train is on / is running behind schedule* le train est à l'heure / a du retard **3.** [list - of prices] barème *m* ; [- of contents] inventaire *m* ; [- of payments] échéancier *m* ; [for taxes] rôle *m* ▸ **schedule of charges** tarifs *mpl* **4.** LAW [annexe] annexe *f*, avenant *m*. ◆ *vt* **1.** [plan - event] fixer la date or l'heure de ; [- appointment] fixer / *the meeting was scheduled for 3 o'clock / Wednesday* la réunion était prévue pour 15 heures / mercredi / *the plane was scheduled to touch down at 18.45* il était prévu que l'avion arrive or l'arrivée de l'avion était prévue à 18 h 45 / *which day is the film scheduled for?* quel jour a été retenu pour le film ? / *it's scheduled for Saturday* il est programmé pour samedi / *you aren't scheduled to sing until later* d'après le programme, vous devez chanter plus tard (dans la soirée) **2.** [period, work, series] organiser / *to schedule one's time* aménager or organiser son temps / *to schedule a morning* établir l'emploi du temps d'une matinée / *that lunch hour is already scheduled* ce déjeuner est déjà réservé **3.** [topic, item] inscrire / *it's scheduled as a topic for the next meeting* c'est inscrit à l'ordre du jour de la prochaine réunion **4.** UK ADMIN [monument] classer.

scheduled [UK 'ʃedju:ld US 'skedʒuld] adj **1.** [planned] prévu / *at the scheduled time* à l'heure prévue / *we announce a change to our scheduled programmes* TV nous annonçons une modification de nos programmes **2.** [regular - flight] régulier ; [- stop, change] habituel **3.** [official - prices] tarifé **4.** UK ADMIN ▸ **scheduled building** bâtiment *m* classé (monument historique) ▸ **the scheduled territories** la zone sterling.

scheduling [UK 'ʃedju:lɪŋ US 'skedʒu:lɪŋ] n TV & RADIO programmation *f* ▸ **scheduling director** TV & RADIO directeur *m*, -trice *f* des programmes.

schematic [skɪ'mætɪk] ◆ adj schématique. ◆ n schéma *m*.

scheme [ski:m] ◆ n **1.** [plan] plan *m*, projet *m* / *a scheme to get rich quick* un procédé pour s'enrichir rapidement / *he's always dreaming up mad schemes for entertaining the children* il a toujours des idées lumineuses pour distraire les enfants ▸ **the scheme of things** l'ordre des choses / *where does he fit into the scheme of things?* quel rôle joue-t-il dans cette affaire ? / *it just doesn't fit into her scheme of things* cela n'entre pas dans sa conception des choses **2.** [plot] intrigue *f*, complot *m* ; [unscrupulous] procédé *m* malhonnête **3.** UK ADMIN plan *m*, système *m* / *the firm has a profit-sharing / a pension scheme* l'entreprise a un système de participation aux bénéfices / un régime de retraites complémentaires / *government unemployment schemes* plans antichômage du gouvernement ▸ **National Savings Scheme** ≃ Caisse *f* nationale d'épargne **4.** [arrangement] disposition *f*, schéma *m*. ◆ vi intriguer ▸ **to scheme to do sthg** projeter de faire qqch. ◆ vt combiner, manigancer.

scheming ['ski:mɪŋ] ◆ n (U) intrigues *fpl*, machinations *fpl*. ◆ adj intrigant, conspirateur.

schism ['sɪzm or 'skɪzm] n schisme *m*.

schizo ['skɪtsəʊ] (*pl* **schizos**) *v inf* ◆ adj schizophrène, schizo. ◆ n schizophrène *mf*, schizo *mf*.

schizophrenia [ˌskɪtsə'fri:njə] n schizophrénie *f* / *to suffer from schizophrenia* être atteint de schizophrénie, être schizophrène.

schizophrenic [ˌskɪtsə'frenɪk] ◆ adj schizophrène. ◆ n schizophrène *mf*.

schlep(p) [ʃlep] (*pt & pp* **schlepped**, *cont* **schlepping**) US *v inf* vt trimbaler / *I've got to schlepp all this stuff over to the office* il faut que je trimballe or transbahute tous ces trucs au bureau.

schmal(t)z [ʃmɔ:lts] n *inf* sentimentalité *f*.

schmal(t)zy ['ʃmɔ:ltsɪ] adj *inf* à l'eau de rose.

schmuck [ʃmʌk] n US *v inf* connard *m*.

schnitzel ['ʃnɪtsəl] n côtelette *f* de veau.

scholar ['skɒlə] n **1.** [academic] érudit *m*, -e *f*, savant *m* ; [specialist] spécialiste *mf* ; [intellectual] intellectuel *m*, -elle *f* **2.** [holder of grant] boursier *m*, -ère *f*.

scholarly ['skɒləlɪ] adj **1.** [person] érudit, cultivé **2.** [article, work] savant **3.** [approach] rigoureux, scientifique **4.** [circle] universitaire.

scholarship ['skɒləʃɪp] n **1.** SCH & UNIV [grant] bourse *f* / *to win a scholarship to Stanford* obtenir une bourse pour Stanford (sur concours) ▸ **scholarship student** or **holder** boursier *m*, -ère *f* **2.** [knowledge] savoir *m*, érudition *f*.

scholastic [skə'læstɪk] ◆ adj **1.** [ability, record, supplier] scolaire ; [profession] d'enseignant ; [competition] interécoles **2.** [philosophy, approach, argument] scolastique. ◆ n scolastique *m*.

school [sku:l] ◆ n **1.** [educational establishment] école *f*, établissement *m* scolaire ; [secondary school - to age 15] collège *m* ; [- 15 to 18] lycée *m* ▸ **to go to school** aller à l'école or au collège or au lycée ▸ **to be at** or **in school** être à l'école or en classe ▸ **to go back to school a)** [after illness] reprendre l'école **b)** [after holidays] rentrer ▸ **to send one's children to school** envoyer ses enfants à l'école / *I was at school with him* j'étais en classe avec lui, c'était un de mes camarades de classe ; [classes] école *f*, classe *f*, classes *fpl*, cours *mpl* / *there's no school today* il n'y a pas (d')école or il n'y a pas classe aujourd'hui / *school starts back next week* c'est la rentrée (scolaire or des classes) la semaine prochaine ; [pupils] école *f* / *the whole school is* or *are invited* toute l'école est invitée ; *fig* école *f* ▸ **schools broadcasting** émissions *fpl* scolaires **2.** [institute] école *f*, académie *f* ▸ **school of dance, dancing school** académie or école de danse ▸ **school of music a)** [gen] école de musique **b)** [superior level] conservatoire *m* ▸ **school of motoring** auto-école *f*, école *f* de conduite **3.** UNIV [department] département *m*, institut *m* ; [faculty] faculté *f* ; [college] collège *m* ; US [university] université *f* ▸ **school of medicine** faculté de médecine ▸ **London School of Economics** prestigieux établissement universitaire dépendant de l'Université de Londres, spécialisé dans l'économie et les sciences politiques / *she's at law school* elle fait des études de droit, elle fait son droit ; [at Oxbridge] salle *f* d'examens **4.** [of art, literature] école *f* ▸ **school of thought a)** *lit* école *f* de pensée **b)** *fig* théorie *f* **5.** [of fish, porpoise] banc *m*. ◆ comp [doctor, report] scolaire ▸ **school board** US conseil *m* d'établissement ▸ **school day** journée *f* scolaire or d'école ▸ **school dinners** repas *mpl* servis à la cantine (de l'école) ▸ **school fees** frais *mpl* de scolarité ▸ **school governor** UK membre *m* du conseil de gestion de l'école ▸ **school record** dossier *m* scolaire ▸ **school trip** sortie *f* scolaire. ◆ vt **1.** [send to school] envoyer à l'école, scolariser **2.** [train - person] entraîner ; [- animal] dresser / *to be schooled in monetary / military matters* être rompu aux questions monétaires / militaires / *she schooled herself to listen to what others said* elle a appris à écouter (ce que disent) les autres.

 Comprehensive schools

Les **comprehensive schools** furent établies en Grande-Bretagne au cours des années 1960 et 1970 par les gouvernements travailliste et conservateur. Elles devaient remplacer le système bipolaire des **grammar schools** (l'équivalent des lycées) et **secondary moderns** (l'équivalent des CES) qui ne profitait qu'à une minorité d'élèves. En accueillant dans un même établissement des élèves de tous les niveaux de compétence, les **comprehensives** ont réalisé d'assez bons résultats sur le plan social et éducatif. Cependant, leur caractère souvent impersonnel (beaucoup d'entre elles comptant plus de 1 000 élèves) et leur tendance à refléter les problèmes sociaux du milieu environnant ont suscité de vives critiques de la part des parents et des enseignants. On évolue aujourd'hui vers un système qui se caractérisera par un plus grand éventail d'écoles diverses, mais où le recrutement sélectif aura fait sa réapparition.

school age n âge *m* scolaire ▶ **school-age children** des enfants d'âge scolaire.

schoolbag ['sku:lbæg] n cartable *m*.

schoolbook ['sku:lbʊk] n livre *m* or manuel *m* scolaire.

schoolboy ['sku:lbɔɪ] n écolier *m* ▶ **schoolboy slang** argot *m* scolaire.

school bus n car *m* de ramassage scolaire.

schoolchild ['sku:ltʃaɪld] (*pl* **schoolchildren** [-tʃɪldrən]) n écolier *m*, -ère *f*.

schooldays ['sku:ldeɪz] pl n années *fpl* d'école.

school district n *aux États-Unis, autorité locale décisionnaire dans le domaine de l'enseignement primaire et secondaire.*

school friend n camarade *mf* d'école.

schoolgirl ['sku:lgɜ:l] ◆ n écolière *f*. ◆ comp ▶ **schoolgirl crush**: *she had the usual schoolgirl crush on the gym teacher* comme toutes les filles de son âge, elle était tombée amoureuse de son prof de gym.

school holiday n jour *m* de congé scolaire / *during the school holidays* pendant les vacances or congés scolaires.

school hours pl n heures *fpl* de classe or d'école / *in school hours* pendant les heures de classe / *out of school hours* en dehors des heures de classe.

schoolhouse ['sku:lhaʊs] (*pl* [-haʊzɪz]) n école *f* (du village).

schooling ['sku:lɪŋ] n **1.** [education] instruction *f*, éducation *f* ; [enrolment at school] scolarité *f* **2.** [of horse] dressage *m*.

schoolkid ['sku:lkɪd] n *inf* écolier *m*, -ère *f*.

school-leaver [-ˌli:vəʳ] n ⬛⬛ *jeune qui entre dans la vie active à la fin de sa scolarité.*

school-leaving age [-'li:vɪŋ-] n fin *f* de la scolarité obligatoire / *the school-leaving age was raised to 16* l'âge légal de fin de scolarité a été porté à 16 ans.

schoolma'am, **schoolmarm** ['sku:lmɑ:m] n *inf* **1.** *hum* [teacher] maîtresse *f* d'école **2.** ⬛⬛ *pej* [prim woman] bégueule *f*.

schoolmaster ['sku:lˌmɑ:stəʳ] n ⬛⬛ [at primary school] maître *m*, instituteur *m* ; [at secondary school] professeur *m*.

schoolmate ['sku:lmeɪt] n camarade *mf* d'école.

schoolmistress ['sku:lˌmɪstrɪs] n ⬛⬛ [primary school] maîtresse *f*, institutrice *f* ; [secondary school] professeur *m*.

schoolroom ['sku:lrʊm] n (salle *f* de) classe *f*.

school run n ⬛⬛ ▶ **to do the school run** emmener les enfants à l'école.

school spirit ['sku:lˌspɪrɪt] n ⬛⬛ SCH esprit *m* d'école.

schoolteacher ['sku:lˌti:tʃəʳ] n [at any level] enseignant *m*, -e *f* ; [at primary school] instituteur *m*, -trice *f* ; [at secondary school] professeur *m*.

schoolteaching ['sku:lˌti:tʃɪŋ] n enseignement *m*.

schooltime ['sku:ltaɪm] n [school hours] heures *fpl* d'école ; [outside holidays] année *f* scolaire.

school uniform n uniforme *m* scolaire.

schoolwork ['sku:lwɜ:k] n (*U*) travail *m* scolaire ; [at home] devoirs *mpl*, travail *m* à la maison.

schoolyard n ⬛⬛ cour *f* de récréation.

school year n année *f* scolaire / *my school years* ma scolarité, mes années d'école.

schooner ['sku:nəʳ] n **1.** NAUT schooner *m* **2.** [for sherry, beer] grand verre *m*.

schtum [ʃtʊm] adj : ⬛⬛ *inf* **to keep schtum** ne pas piper mot.

sciatica [saɪˈætɪkə] n (*U*) sciatique *f*.

science ['saɪəns] ◆ n (*U*) [gen] science *f*, sciences *fpl* ; [branch] science *f*. ◆ comp [exam] de science ; [teacher] de science, de sciences ; [student] en sciences ; [lab, subject] scientifique.

science fiction n science-fiction *f*.

science park n parc *m* scientifique.

scientific [ˌsaɪənˈtɪfɪk] adj **1.** [research, expedition] scientifique **2.** [precise, strict] scientifique, rigoureux.

scientifically [ˌsaɪənˈtɪfɪklɪ] adv scientifiquement, de manière scientifique.

scientist ['saɪəntɪst] n [worker] scientifique *m* ; [academic] scientifique *mf*, savant *m*.

Scientologist [ˌsaɪənˈtɒlədʒɪst] n scientologiste *mf*.

sci-fi [ˌsaɪˈfaɪ] n *inf* abbr of **science fiction**.

Scilly Isles ['sɪlɪ-], **Scillies** ['sɪlɪz] pl pr n ▶ **the Scilly Isles** les îles *fpl* Sorlingues / *in the Scilly Isles* aux îles Sorlingues.

scintillating ['sɪntɪleɪtɪŋ] adj [conversation, wit] brillant, pétillant, étincelant ; [person, personality] brillant.

scissors ['sɪzəʳz] pl n ▶ **(a pair of) scissors** (une paire de) ciseaux *mpl*.

scissors-and-paste adj ▶ **it's just a scissors-and-paste job** c'est du montage.

sclerosis [skləˈrəʊsɪs] n (*U*) BOT & MED & *fig* sclérose *f*.

SCNR MESSAGING written abbr of **sorry, could not resist**.

scoff [skɒf] ◆ vi **1.** [mock] se moquer, être méprisant / *they scoffed at my efforts / ideas* ils se sont moqués de mes efforts / idées **2.** *inf* [eat] s'empiffrer. ◆ vt ⬛⬛ *inf* [eat] bouffer, s'empiffrer de.

scold [skəʊld] ◆ vt gronder, réprimander. ◆ vi rouspéter.

scone [skɒn] n scone m (petit pain rond).

scoop [sku:p] ◆ n **1.** PRESS scoop m, exclusivité f ▶ **to get** or **to make a scoop** faire un scoop **2.** [utensil, ladle - for ice-cream, potatoes] cuillère f à boule ; [- for flour, grain] pelle f ; [- for water] écope f ; [on crane, dredger] pelle f ; [on bulldozer] lame f **3.** [amount scooped - of ice-cream, potatoes] boule f ; [- of flour, grain] pelletée f ; [- of earth, rocks] pelletée f. ◆ vt **1.** [take, measure, put] prendre (avec une mesure) ; [serve] servir (avec une cuillère) **2.** PRESS [story] publier en exclusivité ; [competitor] publier avant, devancer. ❖ **scoop out** vt sep **1.** [take - with scoop] prendre (avec une cuillère) ; [- with hands] prendre (avec les mains) **2.** [hollow - wood, earth] creuser ; [empty, remove] vider. ❖ **scoop up** vt sep **1.** [take, pick up - in scoop] prendre or ramasser à l'aide d'une pelle or d'un récipient ; [- in hands] prendre or ramasser dans les mains **2.** [gather together] entasser.

scoop neck n décolleté m.

scoot [sku:t] inf vi filer ▶ **to scoot over** [move over] se pousser, se décaler ▶ **scoot!** fichez le camp !, allez, ouste !

scooter ['sku:tər] n **1.** [child's] trottinette f **2.** [moped] ▶ **(motor) scooter** scooter m **3.** ☒ [ice yacht] yacht m à glace.

scope [skəʊp] n **1.** [range] étendue f, portée f ; [limits] limites fpl ; [size, extent - of change] étendue f ; [- of undertaking] étendue f, envergure f **2.** [opportunity, room] occasion f, possibilité f **3.** inf [telescope] télescope m ; [microscope] microscope m ; [periscope] périscope m. ❖ **scope out** vt sep ☒ [look at] observer.

scorch [skɔ:tʃ] ◆ vt **1.** [with iron - clothing, linen] roussir, brûler légèrement ; [with heat - skin] brûler ; [- meat] brûler, carboniser ; [- woodwork] brûler, marquer **2.** [grass, vegetation - with sun] roussir, dessécher ; [- with fire] brûler. ◆ vi **1.** [linen] roussir **2.** ☒ inf [in car] filer à toute allure ; [on bike] pédaler comme un fou or à fond de train. ◆ n [on linen] marque f de roussi ; [on hand, furniture] brûlure f ▶ *there's a scorch (mark) on my shirt* ma chemise a été roussie.

scorched-earth policy n politique f de la terre brûlée.

scorcher ['skɔ:tʃər] n inf [hot day] journée f torride.

scorching ['skɔ:tʃɪŋ] ◆ adj **1.** [weather, tea, surface] brûlant **2.** [criticism] cinglant. ◆ adv : *a scorching hot day* une journée torride.

score [skɔ:r] ◆ n **1.** SPORT score m ; CARDS points mpl ; [in exam, test - mark] note f ; [- result] résultat m **2.** fig [advantage - in debate] avantage m, points mpl **3.** [debt] compte m **4.** [subject, cause] sujet m, titre m ▶ *don't worry on that score* ne vous inquiétez pas à ce sujet **5.** [twenty] vingtaine f ; [many] : *scores of people* beaucoup de gens **6.** MUS partition f ; CIN & THEAT musique f **7.** [mark - on furniture] rayure f ; [notch, deep cut] entaille f ; [in leather] entaille f, incision f ; GEOL strie f. ◆ vt **1.** SPORT [goal, point] marquer ▶ **to score a hit a)** [with bullet, arrow, bomb] atteindre la cible **b)** [in fencing] toucher **c)** fig réussir ; [in test, exam - marks] obtenir **2.** [scratch] érafler ; [make shallow cut in - paper] marquer ; [- rock] strier ; [- pastry, meat] inciser, faire des incisions dans **3.** MUS [symphony, opera] orchestrer ; CIN & THEAT composer la musique de **4.** ☒ [grade, mark - test] noter. ◆ vi **1.** SPORT [team, player] marquer un point or des points ; FOOT marquer un but or des buts ; [scorekeeper] marquer les points ; [in test] ▶ **to score high** / **low** obtenir un bon / mauvais score **2.** [succeed] avoir du succès, réussir **3.** v inf [sexually] avoir une touche. ❖ **score off** ◆ vt insep prendre l'avantage sur, marquer des points sur. ◆ vt sep rayer, barrer. ❖ **score over**

vt insep **1.** = **score off** *(vt insep)* **2.** [be more successful than] avoir l'avantage sur. ❖ **score out, score through** vt sep biffer, barrer.

scoreboard ['skɔ:bɔ:d] n tableau m d'affichage (du score).

scorecard ['skɔ:kɑ:d] n [for score - in game] fiche f de marque or de score ; [- in golf] carte f de parcours.

score draw n FOOT match m nul (où chaque équipe a marqué).

scoreless ['skɔ:lɪs] adj : *the game was scoreless* aucun point or but n'a été marqué.

scoreline ['skɔ:laɪn] n score m.

scorer ['skɔ:rər] n **1.** FOOT [regularly] buteur m ; [of goal] marqueur m **2.** [scorekeeper] marqueur m, -euse f **3.** [in test, exam] : *the highest scorer* le candidat qui obtient le meilleur score.

scoring ['skɔ:rɪŋ] n (U) **1.** [of goals] marquage m d'un but ; [number scored] buts mpl (marqués) **2.** CARDS & GAMES [scorekeeping] marquage m des points, marque f ; [points scored] points mpl marqués **3.** [scratching] rayures fpl, éraflures fpl ; [notching] entaille f, entailles fpl ; GEOL striage m **4.** MUS [orchestration] orchestration f ; [arrangement] arrangement m ; [composition] écriture f.

scorn [skɔ:n] ◆ n [contempt] mépris m, dédain m. ◆ vt **1.** [be contemptuous of] mépriser **2.** [reject - advice, warning] rejeter, refuser d'écouter ; [- idea] rejeter ; [- help] refuser, dédaigner.

scornful ['skɔ:nfʊl] adj dédaigneux, méprisant.

scornfully ['skɔ:nfʊlɪ] adv avec mépris, dédaigneusement.

Scorpio ['skɔ:pɪəʊ] ◆ pr n ASTROL & ASTRON Scorpion m. ◆ n : *he's a Scorpio* il est Scorpion.

scorpion ['skɔ:pjən] n ZOOL scorpion m.

Scot [skɒt] n Écossais m, -e f.

scotch [skɒtʃ] vt [suppress - revolt, strike] mettre fin à, réprimer, étouffer ; [- rumour] étouffer.

Scotch [skɒtʃ] ◆ n [whisky] scotch m. ◆ pl n [people] ▶ **the Scotch** les Écossais mpl. ◆ adj écossais.

Scotch broth n soupe écossaise à base de légumes et d'orge perlée.

Scotch egg n œuf dur entouré de chair à saucisse et enrobé de chapelure.

Scotch mist n bruine f.

Scotch tape® n ☒ Scotch® m. ❖ **scotch-tape** vt scotcher.

scot-free adj impuni ▶ **to get off** or **be let off scot-free** : *they were let off scot-free* on les a relâchés sans les punir.

Scotland ['skɒtlənd] pr n Écosse f ▶ *in Scotland* en Écosse.

Scotland Yard pr n ancien nom du siège de la police à Londres (aujourd'hui New Scotland Yard).

Scots [skɒts] ◆ n [language - Gaelic] écossais m, erse m ; [- Lallans] anglais m d'Écosse. ◆ adj [accent, law, etc.] écossais.

Scotsman ['skɒtsmən] (pl Scotsmen [-mən]) n Écossais m ▶ **the Scotsman** PRESS un des grands quotidiens écossais.

Scotswoman ['skɒtswʊmən] (pl Scotswomen [-ˌwɪmɪn]) n Écossaise f.

Scottish ['skɒtɪʃ] ◆ n LING écossais m. ◆ pl n ▶ **the Scottish** les Écossais mpl. ◆ adj écossais.

Scottish National Party pr n parti indépendantiste écossais fondé en 1934.

Scottish Office pr n ministère des affaires écossaises, basé à Édimbourg.

Scottish Parliament n Parlement *m* écossais.

scoundrel ['skaʊndrəl] n bandit *m*, vaurien *m* ; [child] vilain *m*, -e *f*, coquin *m*, -e *f*.

scour ['skaʊəʳ] ◆ vt **1.** [clean - pan] récurer ; [- metal surface] décaper ; [- floor] lessiver, frotter ; [- tank] vidanger, purger **2.** [scratch] rayer **3.** [subj: water, erosion] creuser **4.** [search - area] ratisser, fouiller. ◆ n : *give the pans a good scour* récurez bien les casseroles.

scourer ['skaʊərəʳ] n tampon *m* à récurer.

scourge [skɜːdʒ] ◆ n **1.** [bane] fléau *m* **2.** [person] peste *f* **3.** [whip] fouet *m*. ◆ vt **1.** [afflict] ravager **2.** [whip] fouetter.

scouring pad ['skaʊərɪŋ-] n tampon *m* à récurer.

scouring powder n poudre *f* à récurer.

Scouse [skaʊs] 🇬🇧 inf ◆ n **1.** [person] surnom donné aux habitants de Liverpool **2.** [dialect] dialecte de la région de Liverpool. ◆ adj de Liverpool.

scout [skaʊt] ◆ n **1.** [boy] scout *m*, éclaireur *m* ; [girl] scoute *f*, éclaireuse *f* **2.** MIL [searcher] éclaireur *m* ; [watchman] sentinelle *f*, guetteur *m* ; [ship] vedette *f* ; [aircraft] avion *m* de reconnaissance **3.** [for players, models, dancers] dénicheur *m* de vedettes **4.** [exploration] tour *m* ◗ **to have** or **to take a scout around** (aller) reconnaître le terrain. ◆ comp [knife, uniform] (de) scout, d'éclaireur ◗ **scout camp** camp *m* scout ◗ **the scout movement** le mouvement scout, le scoutisme. ◆ vt [area] explorer ; MIL reconnaître. ◆ vi partir en reconnaissance. ◇ **scout about** 🇬🇧, **scout around** vi explorer les lieux ; MIL partir en reconnaissance. ◇ **Scout** = scout.

scoutmaster ['skaʊt,mɑːstəʳ] n chef *m* scout.

scowl [skaʊl] ◆ n [angry] mine *f* renfrognée or hargneuse, air *m* renfrogné ; [threatening] air *m* menaçant. ◆ vi [angrily] se renfrogner, faire la grimace ; [threateningly] prendre un air menaçant ◗ **to scowl at sb** jeter un regard mauvais à qqn.

scowling ['skaʊlɪŋ] adj [face] renfrogné, hargneux.

SCR (abbr of **senior common room**) n 🇬🇧 **1.** [room] salle des étudiants de 3ᵉ cycle **2.** [students] expression désignant l'ensemble des étudiants de 3ᵉ cycle.

Scrabble® ['skræbl] n Scrabble® *m*.

scrabble ['skræbl] vi **1.** [search] : *she was scrabbling in the grass for the keys* elle cherchait les clés à tâtons dans l'herbe / *the man was scrabbling for a handhold on the cliff face* l'homme cherchait désespérément une prise sur la paroi de la falaise **2.** [scrape] gratter. ◆ n [scramble] : *there was a wild scrabble for the food* les gens se ruèrent sur la nourriture. ◇ **scrabble about** 🇬🇧, **scrabble around** vi [grope] fouiller, tâtonner.

scraggy ['skrægɪ] (compar **scraggier**, superl **scraggiest**) adj **1.** [thin - neck, person] efflanqué, maigre, décharné ; [- horse, cat] efflanqué, étique *liter* **2.** [jagged] déchiqueté.

scram [skræm] (pt & pp **scrammed**, cont **scramming**) vi [get out] déguerpir, ficher le camp.

scramble ['skræmbl] ◆ vi **1.** [verb of movement - hurriedly or with difficulty] : *he scrambled to his feet* il s'est levé précipitamment ◗ **to scramble down** dégringoler ◗ **to scramble up** grimper avec difficulté **2.** [scrabble, fight] : *to scramble for seats* se bousculer pour trouver une place assise, se ruer sur les places assises **3.** AERON & MIL décoller sur-le-champ **4.** SPORT ◗ **to go scrambling** faire du trial. ◆ vt **1.** RADIO & TELEC brouiller **2.** [jumble] mélanger **3.** AERON & MIL ordonner le décollage immédiat de **4.** CULIN [eggs] brouiller. ◆ n **1.** [rush] bousculade *f*, ruée *f* **2.** SPORT [on motorbikes] course *f* de trial **3.** AERON & MIL décollage *m* immédiat **4.** [in rock climbing] grimpée *f* à quatre pattes.

scrambled eggs *(pl n)*, **scrambled egg** ['skræmbld-] n œufs *mpl* brouillés.

scrambler ['skræmbləʳ] n RADIO & TELEC brouilleur *m*.

scrambling ['skræmblɪŋ] n **1.** 🇬🇧 SPORT trial *m* **2.** [in rock climbing] grimpée *f* à quatre pattes.

scrap [skræp] *(pt & pp* **scrapped**, cont **scrapping)** ◆ n **1.** [small piece - of paper, cloth] bout *m* ; [- of bread, cheese] petit bout *m* ; [- of conversation] bribe *f* / *scraps of news* / *of information* des bribes de nouvelles / d'informations / *there isn't a scrap of truth in the story* il n'y a pas une parcelle de vérité or il n'y a absolument rien de vrai dans cette histoire / *it didn't do me a scrap of good* a) [action] cela ne m'a servi absolument à rien b) [medicine] cela ne m'a fait aucun bien / *what I say won't make a scrap of difference* ce que je dirai ne changera rien du tout **2.** [waste] : *we sold the car for scrap* on a vendu la voiture à la ferraille or à la casse **3.** inf [fight] bagarre *f* ◗ **to get into** or **to have a scrap with sb** se bagarrer avec qqn. ◆ comp ◗ **scrap lead** plomb *m* de récupération ◗ **scrap iron** or **metal** ferraille *f* ◗ **scrap merchant** 🇬🇧 ferrailleur *m* ◗ **scrap (metal) dealer** ferrailleur *m* ◗ **scrap value** valeur *f* à la casse. ◆ vt **1.** [discard - shoes, furniture] jeter ; [- idea, plans] renoncer à, abandonner ; [- system] abandonner, mettre au rancart ; [- machinery] mettre au rebut or au rancart **2.** [send for scrap - car, ship] envoyer or mettre à la ferraille or à la casse. ◆ vi inf [fight] se bagarrer. ◇ **scraps** pl n [food] restes *mpl* ; [fragments] débris *mpl*.

scrapbook ['skræpbʊk] n album *m* (de coupures de journaux, de photos, etc.).

scrape [skreɪp] ◆ vt **1.** [rasp, rub - boots, saucepan, earth] gratter, racler ; [- tools] gratter, décaper ; [- vegetables, windows] gratter ; [drag] traîner **2.** [touch lightly] effleurer, frôler ; [scratch - paint, table, wood] rayer **3.** [skin, knee] érafler **4.** [with difficulty] ◗ **to scrape a living** arriver tout juste à survivre, vivoter. ◆ vi **1.** [rub] frotter ; [rasp] gratter **2.** fig [avoid with difficulty] : *the ambulance just scraped past* l'ambulance est passée de justesse **3.** [economize] faire des petites économies **4.** [be humble] faire des courbettes or des ronds de jambes. ◆ n **1.** [rub, scratch] : *he had a nasty scrape on his knee* il avait une méchante éraflure au genou, il s'était bien éraflé le genou / *just give the saucepan a quick scrape* frotte or gratte un peu la casserole **2.** inf [dilemma, trouble] pétrin *m* ◗ **to get into a scrape** se mettre dans le pétrin **3.** [scraping] grattement *m*, grincement *m* **4.** = **scraping** (noun). ◇ **scrape along** vi [financially] se débrouiller, vivre tant bien que mal. ◇ **scrape away** vt sep enlever en grattant. ◇ **scrape by** vi [financially] se débrouiller. ◇ **scrape in** vi [in election] être élu de justesse. ◇ **scrape into** vt insep : *he just scraped into university* / *parliament* il est entré à l'université / au parlement d'extrême justesse. ◇ **scrape off** vt sep [mud, paint] enlever au grattoir or en grattant ; [skin] érafler. ◆ vi s'enlever au grattoir. ◇ **scrape out** vt sep **1.** [saucepan] récurer, racler ; [residue] enlever en grattant or raclant **2.** [hollow] creuser. ◇ **scrape through** ◆ vt insep [exam] réussir de justesse ; [doorway, gap] passer (de justesse). ◆ vi [in exam] réussir de justesse ; [in election] être élu or l'emporter de justesse ; [financially] se débrouiller tout juste ; [through gap] passer de justesse. ◇ **scrape together** vt sep **1.** [two objects] frotter l'un contre l'autre **2.** [into pile] mettre en tas **3.** [collect - supporters, signatures] réunir or rassembler à grand-peine ; [- money for o.s.] réunir en raclant les fonds de tiroirs ; [- money for event] réunir avec beaucoup de mal. ◇ **scrape up** = scrape together.

scraper ['skreɪpəʳ] n grattoir *m* ; [for muddy shoes] décrottoir *m*.

scrapheap ['skræphi:p] n **1.** *lit* décharge *f* **2.** *fig* rebut *m* ▸ **to be thrown on** or **consigned to the scrapheap** être mis au rebut / *he ended up on the scrapheap* on l'a mis au rebut.

scrap paper n ⓊⓀ (papier *m*) brouillon *m*.

scrapple ['skræpl] n ⓊⓈ CULIN *plat régional (Pennsylvanie, New Jersey, Maryland) à base de porc et de farine de maïs frits.*

scrappy ['skræpɪ] (*compar* **scrappier**, *superl* **scrappiest**) adj **1.** [disconnected] décousu **2.** ⓊⓈ *inf* [quarrelsome] bagarreur, chamailleur.

scrapyard ['skræpjɑːd] n chantier *m* de ferraille, casse *f*.

scratch [skrætʃ] ◆ vt **1.** [itch, rash] gratter ; [earth, surface] gratter **2.** [subj: cat] griffer ; [subj: thorn, nail] égratigner, écorcher ; [mark - woodwork, marble] rayer, érafler ; [- glass, CD] rayer **3.** [irritate] gratter **4.** SPORT [cancel - match] annuler **5.** ⓊⓈ POL rayer de la liste. ◆ vi **1.** [person, monkey] se gratter **2.** [hen] gratter (le sol) ; [pen] gratter **3.** [cat] griffer ; [brambles, nail] griffer, écorcher. ◆ n **1.** [for itch] grattement *m* **2.** [from cat] coup *m* de griffe ; [from fingernails] coup *m* d'ongle ; [from thorns, nail] égratignure *f*, écorchure *f* **3.** [mark - on furniture] rayure *f*, éraflure *f* ; [- on glass, CD] rayure *f* **4.** ⓅⒽⓇ **to be up to scratch a)** [in quality] avoir la qualité voulue **b)** [in level] avoir le niveau voulu. ◆ adj [team, meal] improvisé ; [player] scratch *(inv)*, sans handicap ; [shot] au hasard. ❖ **scratch up** vt sep ⓊⓈ rayer. ❖ **from scratch** adv phr à partir de rien or de zéro. ❖ **scratch off** vt sep enlever en grattant. ❖ **scratch out** vt sep [name] raturer ▸ **to scratch sb's eyes out** arracher les yeux à qqn. ❖ **scratch together** vt sep ⓊⓀ [team] réunir (difficilement) ; [sum of money] réunir or rassembler (en raclant les fonds de tiroir). ❖ **scratch up** vt sep **1.** [dig up - bone, plant] déterrer **2.** ⓊⓀ [money] réunir (en raclant les fonds de tiroir).

scratch card ['skrætʃkɑːd] n carte *f* à gratter.

scratchpad ['skrætʃpæd] n ⓊⓈ bloc-notes *m* ▸ **scratchpad memory** COMPUT mémoire *f* bloc-notes.

scratch paper ⓊⓈ = **scrap paper**.

scratchproof ['skrætʃpruːf] adj inrayable.

scratchy ['skrætʃɪ] (*compar* **scratchier**, *superl* **scratchiest**) adj **1.** [prickly - jumper, blanket] rêche, qui gratte ; [- bush] piquant **2.** [pen] qui gratte **3.** [drawing, writing] griffonné **4.** [record] rayé.

scrawl [skrɔːl] ◆ n griffonnage *m*, gribouillage *m*. ◆ vt griffonner, gribouiller. ◆ vi gribouiller.

scrawny ['skrɔːnɪ] (*compar* **scrawnier**, *superl* **scrawniest**) adj **1.** [person, neck] efflanqué, décharné ; [cat, chicken] efflanqué, étique *liter* **2.** [vegetation] maigre.

scream [skriːm] ◆ vi **1.** [shout] pousser des cris, hurler ; [baby] crier, hurler ; [birds, animals] crier ▸ **to scream at sb** crier après qqn ▸ **to scream in anger / with pain** hurler de colère / de douleur / *she screamed for help* elle cria à l'aide or au secours / *they were screaming with laughter* ils se tordaient de rire, ils riaient aux éclats **2.** [tyres] crisser ; [engine, siren] hurler. ◆ vt **1.** [shout] hurler **2.** [order, answer] hurler **3.** [newspaper] étaler. ◆ n **1.** [cry] cri *m* perçant, hurlement *m* / *screams of laughter* des éclats de rire **2.** [of tyres] crissement *m* ; [of sirens, engines] hurlement *m* **3.** [person] : *he's an absolute scream* il est vraiment désopilant or impayable ; [situation, event] : *the party was a scream* on s'est amusés comme des fous à la soirée. ❖ **scream out** ◆ vi pousser de grands cris ▸ **to be screaming out for sthg** *fig* avoir sacrément besoin de qqch. ◆ vt sep hurler.

screaming ['skriːmɪŋ] adj [fans] qui crie, qui hurle ; [tyres] qui crisse ; [sirens, jets] qui hurle ; [need] criant / *screaming headlines* grandes manchettes *fpl*.

scree [skriː] n *(U)* éboulis *m*, pierraille *f*.

screech [skriːtʃ] ◆ vi **1.** [owl] ululer, hululer, huer ; [gull] crier, piailler ; [parrot] crier ; [monkey] hurler **2.** [person - in high voice] pousser des cris stridents or perçants ; [- loudly] hurler ; [singer] crier, chanter d'une voie stridente **3.** [tyres] crisser ; [brakes, machinery] grincer (bruyamment) ; [siren, jets] hurler. ◆ vt [order] hurler, crier à tue-tête. ◆ n **1.** [of owl] ululement *m*, hululement *m* ; [of gull] cri *m*, piaillement *m* ; [of parrot] cri *m* ; [of monkey] hurlement *m* **2.** [of person] cri *m* strident or perçant ; [with pain, rage] hurlement *m* **3.** [of tyres] crissement *m* ; [of brakes] grincement *m* ; [of sirens, jets] hurlement *m*.

screen [skriːn] ◆ n **1.** CIN, PHOT & TV écran *m* **2.** [for protection - in front of fire] pare-étincelles *m inv* ; [- over window] moustiquaire *f* **3.** [for privacy] paravent *m* **4.** *fig* [mask] écran *m*, masque *m* **5.** [sieve] tamis *m*, crible *m* ; [filter - for employees, candidates] filtre *m*, crible *m* **6.** SPORT écran *m*. ◆ comp [actor, star] de cinéma. ◆ vt **1.** CIN & TV [film] projeter, passer **2.** [shelter, protect] protéger ; [hide] cacher, masquer ▸ **to screen sthg from sight** cacher or masquer qqch aux regards **3.** [filter, check - employees, applications, suspects] passer au crible **4.** [sieve - coal, dirt] cribler, passer au crible. ❖ **screen off** vt sep **1.** [put screens round - patient] abriter derrière un paravent ; [- bed] entourer de paravents **2.** [divide, separate - with partition] séparer par une cloison ; [- with curtain] séparer par un rideau ; [- with folding screen] séparer par un paravent **3.** [hide - with folding screen] cacher derrière un paravent ; [- with curtain] cacher derrière un rideau ; [- behind trees, wall] cacher. ❖ **screen out** vt sep filtrer, éliminer.

screen break n COMPUT pause *f*.

screen door n ⓊⓈ porte *f* avec moustiquaire.

screen dump n COMPUT vidage *m* d'écran.

screening ['skriːnɪŋ] n **1.** CIN projection *f* (en salle) ; TV passage *m* (à l'écran), diffusion *f* **2.** [of applications, candidates] tri *m*, sélection *f* ; [for security] contrôle *m* ; MED [for cancer, tuberculosis] test *m* or tests *mpl* de dépistage **3.** [mesh] grillage *m* **4.** [of coal] criblage *m*.

screen memory n souvenir écran *m*.

screenplay ['skriːnpleɪ] n scénario *m*.

screen print n sérigraphie *f*.

screen printing n sérigraphie *f*.

screen process n sérigraphie *f*.

screen saver n COMPUT économiseur *m* (d'écran).

screenshot ['skriːnʃɒt] n copie *f* or capture *f* d'écran.

screen test n CIN bout *m* d'essai. ❖ **screen-test** vt faire faire un bout d'essai à.

screenwriter ['skriːnˌraɪtər] n scénariste *mf*.

screw [skruː] ◆ n **1.** [for wood] vis *f* ; [bolt] boulon *m* ; [in vice] vis *f* **2.** [turn] tour *m* de vis **3.** [thread] pas *m* de vis **4.** [propeller] hélice *f* **5.** ⓊⓀ [of salt, tobacco] cornet *m* **6.** *v inf & prison sl* [guard] maton *m* **7.** ⓊⓀ *v inf* [salary] salaire *m*, paye *f* **8.** *vulg* [sexual] ▸ **to have a screw** ⓊⓀ baiser, s'envoyer en l'air. ◆ vt **1.** [bolt, screw] visser ; [handle, parts] fixer avec des vis ; [lid on bottle] visser **2.** [crumple] froisser, chiffonner **3.** [wrinkle - face] : *he screwed his face into a grimace* une grimace lui tordit le visage **4.** *inf* [obtain] arracher ▸ **to screw a promise / an agreement out of sb** arracher une promesse / un accord à qqn **5.** *v inf* [con] arnaquer, baiser **6.** *vulg* [sexually] baiser **7.** *v inf* [as invective] : *screw the expense!* et merde, je peux bien m'offrir ça ! / *screw you!* va te faire foutre ! ◆ vi **1.** [bolt, lid] se visser **2.** *vulg* [sexually] baiser. ❖ **screw around** vi **1.** ⓊⓈ *v inf* [waste time] glander ; [fool about] déconner **2.** *vulg* [sleep around] baiser avec n'importe qui, coucher à droite à gauche. ❖ **screw down** ◆ vt sep visser. ◆ vi se visser. ❖ **screw off** ◆ vt sep dévisser. ◆ vi se dévisser. ❖ **screw on** vt sep visser.

◆ vi se visser. ◆ **screw together** vt sep [parts] visser ensemble **/ to screw sthg together** assembler qqch avec des vis. ◆ **screw up** vt sep **1.** [tighten, fasten] visser **2.** [crumple - handkerchief, paper] chiffonner, faire une boule de **3.** 🇬🇧 [eyes] plisser ▶ **to screw up one's courage** prendre son courage à deux mains **4.** inf [mess up - plans, chances] bousiller, foutre en l'air ; [- person] faire perdre ses moyens à, angoisser, mettre dans tous ses états.

screwball ['skru:bɔ:l] 🇺🇸 inf ◆ n **1.** [crazy] cinglé m, -e f, dingue mf **2.** [in baseball] balle qui dévie de sa trajectoire. ◆ adj cinglé, dingue.

screwdriver ['skru:,draɪvər] n **1.** [tool] tournevis m **2.** [drink] vodka-orange f.

screwed-up adj **1.** [crumpled] froissé, chiffonné **2.** inf [confused] paumé ; [neurotic] perturbé, angoissé.

screwtop jar ['skru:tɒp-] n pot m à couvercle à pas de vis.

screwy ['skru:ɪ] (compar **screwier**, superl **screwiest**) adj inf [person] timbré, cinglé ; [situation] bizarre.

scribble ['skrɪbl] ◆ vt [note, drawing] gribouiller, griffonner. ◆ vi gribouiller. ◆ n gribouillis m, gribouillage m, griffonnage m. ◆ **scribble down** vt sep [address, number] griffonner, noter (rapidement). ◆ **scribble out** vt sep **1.** [cross out] biffer, raturer **2.** [write] griffonner.

scribbling ['skrɪblɪŋ] n gribouillis m, gribouillage m.

scribe [skraɪb] ◆ n scribe m. ◆ vt graver.

scrimp [skrɪmp] vi lésiner **/ she scrimps on food** elle lésine sur la nourriture ▶ **to scrimp and save** économiser sur tout, se serrer la ceinture.

scrip [skrɪp] n ST. EX titre m provisoire.

script [skrɪpt] ◆ n **1.** [text] script m, texte m ; CIN script m **2.** (U) [handwriting] script m, écriture f script ; [lettering, characters] écriture f, caractères mpl, lettres fpl **/ Arabic script** caractères arabes, écriture arabe **/ in italic script** en italique **3.** LAW [copy] original m ; UNIV copie f (d'examen). ◆ vt CIN écrire le script de.

scripted ['skrɪptɪd] adj [speech, interview, etc.] (dont le texte a été) écrit d'avance.

Scripture ['skrɪptʃər] n **1.** [Christian] Écriture f (sainte) **2.** [non-Christian] ▶ **the Scriptures** les textes mpl sacrés.

scriptwriter ['skrɪpt,raɪtər] n scénariste m.

scroll [skrəʊl] ◆ n **1.** [of parchment] rouleau m **2.** [manuscript] manuscrit m (ancien) **3.** [on column, violin, woodwork] volute f. ◆ vt COMPUT faire défiler. ◆ vi COMPUT défiler. ◆ **scroll down** vt COMPUT faire défiler l'écran vers le bas. ◆ **scroll through** vt insep COMPUT faire défiler d'un bout à l'autre. ◆ **scroll up** vi COMPUT faire défiler l'écran vers le haut.

scroll bar n COMPUT barre f de défilement.

scrolling ['skrəʊlɪŋ] n COMPUT défilement m.

scrooge [skru:dʒ] n grippe-sou m, harpagon m.

scrotum ['skrəʊtəm] (pl **scrotums** or **scrota** [-tə]) n scrotum m.

scrounge [skraʊndʒ] inf ◆ vt [sugar, pencil] emprunter, piquer ; [meal] se faire offrir ; [money] se faire prêter **/ he tried to scrounge $10 off me** il a essayé de me taper de 10 dollars. ◆ vi ▶ **to scrounge on** or **off sb** [habitually] vivre aux crochets de qqn. ◆ n ▶ **to be on the scrounge a)** [for food] venir quémander de quoi manger **b)** [for cigarette] venir quémander une cigarette.

scrounger ['skraʊndʒər] n inf pique-assiette mf, parasite m.

scrub [skrʌb] (pt & pp **scrubbed**, cont **scrubbing**) ◆ vt **1.** [clean, wash] brosser (avec de l'eau et du savon) ; [floor, carpet] nettoyer à la brosse, frotter avec une brosse ; [saucepan, sink] frotter, récurer ; [clothes, face, back]

frotter ; [fingernails] brosser **2.** [cancel - order] annuler ; [- plans, holiday] annuler, laisser tomber ; [recording, tape] effacer **3.** TECH [gas] laver. ◆ vi : **I spent the morning scrubbing** j'ai passé la matinée à frotter les planchers ou les sols. ◆ n **1.** [with brush] coup m de brosse **2.** [vegetation] broussailles fpl **3.** 🇺🇸 SPORT [team] équipe f de seconde zone ; [player] joueur m, -euse f de second ordre. ◆ **scrub away** ◆ vt sep [mark, mud] faire partir en brossant. ◆ vi partir à la brosse. ◆ **scrub down** vt sep [wall, paintwork] lessiver ; [horse] bouchonner. ◆ **scrub out** ◆ vt sep **1.** [dirt, stain] faire partir à la brosse ; [bucket, tub] nettoyer à la brosse ; [pan] récurer ; [ears] nettoyer, bien laver **2.** [erase - graffiti, comment] effacer ; [- name] barrer, biffer. ◆ vi partir à la brosse. ◆ **scrub up** vi MED [before operation] se laver les mains.

scrubbing brush 🇬🇧 ['skrʌbɪŋ-], **scrub brush** 🇺🇸 n brosse f à récurer.

scrubland ['skrʌblænd] n maquis m, garrigue f.

scruff [skrʌf] n **1.** 🇬🇧 inf [untidy person] individu m débraillé or dépenaillé or peu soigné ; [ruffian] voyou m **2.** 🅿🅷🆁 ▶ **by the scruff of the neck** par la peau du cou.

scruffily ['skrʌfɪlɪ] adv : **scruffily dressed** dépenaillé, mal habillé.

scruffy ['skrʌfɪ] (compar **scruffier**, superl **scruffiest**) adj [appearance, clothes] dépenaillé, crasseux ; [hair] ébouriffé ; [building, area] délabré, miteux.

scrum [skrʌm] (pt & pp **scrummed**, cont **scrumming**) ◆ n **1.** RUGBY mêlée f **2.** [brawl] mêlée f, bousculade f. ◆ vi former une mêlée. ◆ **scrum down** vi former une mêlée ▶ **scrum down!** [as instruction] mêlée !

scrumhalf [,skrʌm'hɑ:f] n demi m de mêlée.

scrumptious ['skrʌmpʃəs] adj inf délicieux, succulent.

scrunch [skrʌntʃ] ◆ vt [biscuit, apple] croquer ; [snow, gravel] faire craquer or crisser ; [paper - noisily] froisser (bruyamment). ◆ vi [footsteps - on gravel, snow] craquer, faire un bruit de craquement ; [gravel, snow - underfoot] craquer, crisser. ◆ n [of gravel, snow, paper] craquement m, bruit m de craquement. ◆ onomat crac ! crac ! ◆ **scrunch up** vt sep **1.** [crumple - paper] froisser **/ he scrunched up his face in disgust** il a fait une grimace de dégoût **2.** 🇺🇸 [hunch] : **she was sitting with her shoulders scrunched up** elle était assise, les épaules rentrées.

scrunchie, scrunchy ['skrʌntʃɪ] n chouchou m.

scruple ['skru:pl] n scrupule m ▶ **to act without scruple** agir sans scrupule.

scrupulous ['skru:pjʊləs] adj **1.** [meticulous] scrupuleux, méticuleux **2.** [conscientious] scrupuleux.

scrupulously ['skru:pjʊləslɪ] adv [meticulously] scrupuleusement, parfaitement ; [honestly] scrupuleusement, avec scrupule.

scrutinize, scrutinise ['skru:tɪnaɪz] vt scruter, examiner attentivement.

scrutiny ['skru:tɪnɪ] (pl **scrutinies**) n [examination] examen m approfondi ; [watch] surveillance f ; [gaze] regard m insistant ▶ **to be under scrutiny a)** [prisoners] être sous surveillance **b)** [accounts, staff] faire l'objet d'un contrôle.

scuba ['sku:bə] n scaphandre m autonome.

scuba dive vi faire de la plongée sous-marine.

scuba diver n plongeur m sous-marin, plongeuse f sous-marine.

scuba diving n plongée f sous-marine.

scud [skʌd] (pt & pp **scudded**, cont **scudding**) vi glisser, filer.

scuff [skʌf] ◆ vt **1.** [shoe, leather] érafler, râper **2.** [drag] ▶ **to scuff one's feet** marcher en traînant les pieds, traîner les pieds. ◆ vi marcher en traînant les pieds. ◆ n ▶ **scuff (mark)** éraflure f.

scuffle ['skʌfl] ◆ n **1.** [fight] bagarre f, échauffourée f **2.** [of feet] piétinement. ◆ vi **1.** [fight] se bagarrer, se battre **2.** [with feet] marcher en traînant les pieds. ◆ vt : *they stood at the door, scuffling their feet* ils piétinaient devant la porte.

scull [skʌl] ◆ n **1.** [double paddle] godille f ; [single oar] aviron m **2.** [boat] yole f. ◆ vt [with double paddle] godiller ; [with oars] ramer. ◆ vi ramer en couple ▶ **to go sculling** faire de l'aviron.

scullery ['skʌlərɪ] (pl **sculleries**) n 🇬🇧 arrière-cuisine f.

sculpt [skʌlpt] ◆ vt sculpter. ◆ vi faire de la sculpture.

sculptor ['skʌlptər] n sculpteur m.

sculptural ['skʌlptʃərəl] adj sculptural.

sculpture ['skʌlptʃər] ◆ n **1.** [art] sculpture f **2.** [object] sculpture f. ◆ vt sculpter. ◆ vi sculpter / *to sculpture in bronze* sculpter dans le bronze.

scum [skʌm] ◆ n [on liquid, sea] écume f ; [in bath] (traînées fpl de) crasse f ; METALL écume f, scories fpl ▶ **to take the scum off a)** [liquid] écumer **b)** [bath] nettoyer. ◆ pl n inf [people] rebut m, lie f ▶ **the scum of the earth** le rebut de l'humanité.

scumbag ['skʌmbæg] n v inf salaud m, ordure f.

scummy ['skʌmɪ] (compar **scummier**, superl **scummiest**) adj **1.** [liquid] écumeux **2.** v inf [person] salaud ; [object] crade.

scupper ['skʌpər] ◆ vt 🇬🇧 **1.** [ship] saborder **2.** [plans, attempt] saborder, faire capoter. ◆ n NAUT dalot m.

scurf [skɜːf] n (U) [dandruff] pellicules fpl ; [on skin] squames fpl ; [on plant] lamelles fpl.

scurrilous ['skʌrələs] adj [lying] calomnieux, mensonger ; [insulting] outrageant, ignoble ; [bitter] fielleux ; [vulgar] grossier, vulgaire.

scurry ['skʌrɪ] (pt & pp **scurried**, pl **scurries**) ◆ vi se précipiter, courir. ◆ n **1.** [rush] course f (précipitée), débandade f **2.** [sound - of feet] bruit m de pas précipités. ◆ **scurry away**, **scurry off** vi [animal] détaler ; [person] décamper, prendre ses jambes à son cou. ◆ **scurry out** vi [animal] détaler ; [person] sortir à toute vitesse.

scurvy ['skɜːvɪ] (compar **scurvier**, superl **scurviest**) n (U) scorbut m.

scuttle ['skʌtl] ◆ vi [run] courir à pas précipités, se précipiter. ◆ vt **1.** NAUT saborder **2.** [hopes] ruiner ; [plans] saborder, faire échouer. ◆ n **1.** [run] course f précipitée, débandade f **2.** ▶ **(coal) scuttle** seau m à charbon **3.** NAUT écoutille f. ◆ **scuttle away**, **scuttle off** vi [animal] détaler ; [person] déguerpir, se sauver. ◆ **scuttle out** vi sortir précipitamment.

scythe [saɪð] ◆ n faux f. ◆ vt faucher.

SD written abbr of **South Dakota**.

SDI (abbr of **Strategic Defense Initiative**) pr n IDS f.

SE (written abbr of **south-east**) S-E.

sea [siː] ◆ n **1.** GEOG mer f ▶ **to travel by sea** voyager par mer or par bateau ▶ **at sea a)** [boat, storm] en mer **b)** [as sailor] de or comme marin ▶ **to swim in the sea** nager or se baigner dans la mer ▶ **to put (out) to sea** appareiller, prendre la mer ▶ **to go to sea a)** [boat] prendre la mer **b)** [sailor] se faire marin ▶ **to look out to sea** regarder vers le large / *the little boat was swept* or *washed out to sea* le petit bateau a été emporté vers le large ▶ **across** or **over the sea** or **seas** outre-mer ▶ **to be (all) at sea a)** 🇬🇧 inf [be lost] nager **b)** [be mixed-up] être déboussolé or déso-

rienté / *when it comes to computers, I'm all at sea* je ne connais strictement rien aux ordinateurs / *he's been all at sea since his wife left him* il est complètement déboussolé or il a complètement perdu le nord depuis que sa femme l'a quitté **2.** [seaside] bord m de la mer / *they live by* or *beside the sea* ils habitent au bord de la mer **3.** [large quantity - of blood, mud] mer f ; [- of problems, faces] multitude f. ◆ comp [fish] de mer ▶ **sea battle** bataille f navale ▶ **sea breeze** brise f marine ▶ **sea traffic** navigation f or trafic m maritime ▶ **sea view** vue f sur la mer.

SEA (abbr of **Single European Act**) pr n AUE m.

sea air n air m marin or de la mer.

sea anemone n anémone f de mer.

sea bass n bar m, loup m.

seabed ['siːbed] n fond m de la mer or marin.

seabird ['siːbɜːd] n oiseau m de mer.

seaboard ['siːbɔːd] n littoral m, côte f.

sea bream n daurade f, dorade f.

sea change n changement m radical, profond changement m.

seafaring ['siːˌfeərɪŋ] ◆ adj [nation] maritime, de marins ; [life] de marin. ◆ n vie f de marin.

seafloor ['siːflɔːr] n fond m de (la) mer or marin.

seafood ['siːfuːd] n (U) (poissons mpl et) fruits mpl de mer.

seafront ['siːfrʌnt] n bord m de mer, front m de mer.

seagoing ['siːˌgəʊɪŋ] adj [trade, nation] maritime ; [life] de marin ▶ **a seagoing ship** un navire de haute mer, un (navire) long-courrier.

seagull ['siːgʌl] n mouette f ; [large] goéland m.

seahorse ['siːhɔːs] n hippocampe m.

seal [siːl] ◆ n **1.** ZOOL phoque m **2.** [tool] sceau m, cachet m ; [on document, letter] sceau m ; [on crate] plombage m ; [on battery, gas cylinder] bande f de garantie ; [on meter] plomb m **3.** (U) LAW [on door] scellé m, scellés mpl **4.** COMM label m ▶ **seal of quality** label de qualité **5.** [joint - for engine, jar, sink] joint m d'étanchéité ; [putty] mastic m. ◆ vt **1.** [document] apposer son sceau à, sceller **2.** [close - envelope, package] cacheter, fermer ; [-with sticky tape] coller, fermer ; [-jar] sceller, fermer hermétiquement ; [-can] souder ; [-tube, mineshaft] sceller ; [window, door - for insulation] isoler ▶ **sealed orders** des ordres scellés sous pli **3.** LAW [door] apposer des scellés sur ; [evidence] mettre sous scellés ; [at customs - goods] (faire) sceller **4.** CULIN [meat] saisir. ◆ vi ZOOL ▶ **to go sealing** aller à la chasse au phoque. ◆ **seal in** vt sep enfermer hermétiquement. ◆ **seal off** vt sep [passage, road] interdire l'accès de ; [entrance] condamner. ◆ **seal up** vt sep [close - envelope] cacheter, fermer ; [-with sticky tape] coller, fermer ; [-jar] sceller, fermer hermétiquement ; [-can] souder ; [-tube, mineshaft] sceller ; [window, door - for insulation] isoler.

sealable ['siːlɪbl] adj qui peut être fermé hermétiquement.

sea lane n couloir m de navigation.

sealant ['siːlənt] n [paste, putty] produit m d'étanchéité ; [paint] enduit m étanche ; [for radiator] antifuite m.

sealed [siːld] adj [document] scellé ; [envelope] cacheté ; [orders] scellé sous pli ; [jar] fermé hermétiquement ; [mineshaft] obturé, bouché ; [joint] étanche.

sea level n niveau m de la mer / *above* / *below sea level* au-dessus / au-dessous du niveau de la mer.

sealing ['siːlɪŋ] n **1.** [hunting] chasse f aux phoques **2.** [of document] cachetage m ; [of crate] plombage m ; [of door] scellage m ; [of shaft, mine] fermeture f, obturation f.

sealing wax n cire f à cacheter.

sea lion n otarie f.

sealskin ['si:lskɪn] ◆ n peau f de phoque. ◆ adj en peau de phoque.

seam [si:m] ◆ n **1.** [on garment, stocking] couture f; [in airbed, bag] couture f, joint m; [weld] soudure f; [between planks] joint m **2.** [of coal, ore] filon m, veine f; [in rocks] couche f. ◆ comp [in cricket] ▶ **a seam bowler** un lanceur qui utilise les coutures de la balle pour la faire dévier. ◆ vt [garment] faire une couture dans, coudre; [plastic, metal, wood] faire un joint à.

seaman ['si:mən] (pl **seamen** [-mən]) n **1.** [sailor] marin m **2.** [in US Navy] quartier-maître m de 2e classe.

seamanship ['si:mənʃɪp] n (U) qualités fpl de marin.

sea mist n brume f de mer.

seamless ['si:mlɪs] adj sans couture; fig homogène, cohérent.

seamstress ['semstrɪs] n couturière f.

seamy ['si:mɪ] (compar **seamier**, superl **seamiest**) adj sordide, louche.

séance ['seɪɑ:ns] n [for raising spirits] séance f de spiritisme.

seaplane ['si:pleɪn] n hydravion m.

seaport ['si:pɔ:t] n port m maritime.

sear [sɪə^r] vt **1.** [burn] brûler; [brand] marquer au fer rouge; MED cautériser / the scene seared itself on my memory la scène est restée gravée or marquée dans ma mémoire **2.** CULIN [meat, etc.] saisir.

search [sɜ:tʃ] ◆ vt **1.** [look in - room] chercher (partout) dans; [- pockets, drawers] fouiller (dans), chercher dans **2.** [subj: police, customs] fouiller; [with warrant] perquisitionner, faire une perquisition dans **3.** [examine, consult - records] chercher dans; [- memory] chercher dans, fouiller; [- conscience] sonder; COMPUT [file] consulter. ◆ vi chercher ▶ **to search for** or **after sthg** chercher qqch, rechercher qqch; COMPUT : to search for a file rechercher un fichier / **'searching'** 'recherche'. ◆ n **1.** [gen] recherche f, recherches fpl ▶ **search and rescue operation** opération f de recherche et secours **2.** [by police, customs - of house, person, bags] fouille f; [- with warrant] perquisition f **3.** COMPUT recherche f. ◆ **in search of** prep phr à la recherche de. ◆ **search out** vt sep [look for] rechercher; [find] trouver, dénicher. ◆ **search through** vt insep [drawer, pockets] fouiller (dans); [case, documents] fouiller; [records] consulter, faire des recherches dans; [memory] fouiller, chercher dans.

searchable ['sɜ:tʃəbl] adj interrogeable.

search engine n COMPUT moteur m de recherche.

searcher ['sɜ:tʃə^r] n chercheur m, -euse f.

searching ['sɜ:tʃɪŋ] adj **1.** [look, eyes] pénétrant **2.** [examination] rigoureux, minutieux.

searchingly ['sɜ:tʃɪŋlɪ] adv [look] de façon pénétrante; [examine] rigoureusement; [question] minutieusement.

searchlight ['sɜ:tʃlaɪt] n projecteur m.

search party n équipe f de secours.

search warrant n mandat m de perquisition.

searing ['sɪərɪŋ] adj **1.** [pain] fulgurant; [light] éclatant, fulgurant **2.** [attack, criticism] sévère, impitoyable.

sea salt n sel m marin or de mer.

sea scout n scout m marin.

sea shanty n chanson f de marins.

seashell ['si:ʃel] n coquillage m.

seashore ['si:ʃɔ:^r] n [edge of sea] rivage m, bord m de (la) mer; [beach] plage f.

seasick ['si:sɪk] adj : to be seasick avoir le mal de mer.

seasickness ['si:sɪknɪs] n mal m de mer.

seaside ['si:saɪd] ◆ n bord m de (la) mer / we live by or at the seaside nous habitons au bord de la mer. ◆ comp [holiday, vacation] au bord de la mer, à la mer; [town, hotel] au bord de la mer, de bord de mer.

seaside resort n station f balnéaire.

season ['si:zn] ◆ n **1.** [summer, winter, etc.] saison f **2.** [for trade] saison f ▶ **the low / high season** la basse / haute saison ▶ **in season** en saison ▶ **off season** hors saison **3.** [for fruit, vegetables] saison f / strawberries are in / out of season les fraises sont / ne sont pas de saison, c'est / ce n'est pas la saison des fraises **4.** [for breeding] époque f, période f ▶ **to be in season** [animal] être en chaleur **5.** [for sport, entertainment] saison f; [for show, actor] saison f; [for hunting] saison f, période f / the start of the season **a)** HUNT l'ouverture de la chasse **b)** FISHING l'ouverture de la pêche; [for socializing] saison f / the social season la saison mondaine **6.** [Christmas] / 'Season's Greetings' 'Joyeux Noël et Bonne Année'. ◆ vt **1.** [food - with seasoning] assaisonner; [- with spice] épicer **2.** [timber] (faire) sécher, laisser sécher; [cask] abreuver.

seasonable ['si:znəbl] adj **1.** [weather] de saison **2.** [opportune] à propos, opportun.

seasonal ['si:zənl] adj saisonnier ▶ **seasonal worker** saisonnier m ▶ **seasonal affective disorder** troubles mpl de l'humeur saisonniers.

seasonal adjustment n correction f des variations saisonnières.

seasonally ['si:znəlɪ] adv de façon saisonnière ▶ **seasonally adjusted statistics** statistiques corrigées des variations saisonnières, statistiques désaisonnalisées.

seasoned ['si:znd] adj **1.** [food] assaisonné, épicé **2.** [wood] desséché, séché **3.** [experienced] expérimenté, chevronné, éprouvé.

seasoning ['si:znɪŋ] n **1.** [for food] assaisonnement m **2.** [of wood] séchage m; [of cask] abreuvage m.

season ticket n (carte f d')abonnement m ▶ **season ticket holder** abonné m, -e f.

seat [si:t] ◆ n **1.** [chair, stool] siège m; [on bicycle] selle f; [in car - single] siège m; [- bench] banquette f; [on train, at table] place f **2.** [accommodation, place - in theatre, cinema, train] place f; [space to sit] place f assise **3.** [of trousers] fond m; [of chair] siège m; [buttocks] derrière m **4.** POL siège m **5.** [centre - of commerce] centre m; ADMIN siège m; MED [- of infection] foyer m **6.** [manor] ▶ **(country) seat** manoir m **7.** EQUIT ▶ **to have a good seat** se tenir bien en selle, avoir une bonne assiette ▶ **to lose one's seat** être désarçonné. ◆ vt **1.** [passengers, children] faire asseoir; [guests - at table] placer / please be seated veuillez vous asseoir **2.** [accommodate] avoir des places assises pour.

seat belt n ceinture f de sécurité.

-seater ['si:tə^r] in comp ▶ **two / four-seater (car)** voiture f à deux / quatre places.

seating ['si:tɪŋ] ◆ n (U) **1.** [seats] sièges mpl; [benches, pews] bancs mpl **2.** [sitting accommodation] places fpl (assises) / there's seating for 300 in the hall il y a 300 places dans la salle **3.** [plan] affectation f des places **4.** [material - cloth, canvas] (tissu m du) siège m; [- wicker] cannage m. ◆ comp ▶ **seating accommodation** or **capacity** nombre m de places assises ▶ **the seating arrangements** le placement m or la disposition f des gens ▶ **seating plan a)** [in theatre] plan m de la disposition des places **b)** [at table] plan m de table.

seat-of-the-pants adj inf : the project has been a bit of a seat-of-the-pants operation le projet a été mené au pif.

sea trout n truite f de mer.

sea urchin n oursin m.

sea wall n digue *f*.

seawater ['siː,wɔːtər] n eau *f* de mer.

seaweed ['siːwiːd] n *(U)* algues *fpl*.

seaworthy ['siː,wɜːðɪ] adj [boat] en état de naviguer.

sebaceous [sɪ'beɪʃəs] adj sébacé.

sec [sek] **(abbr of second)** n *inf* seconde *f*, instant *m* / **in a sec!** une seconde !

SEC **(abbr of Securities and Exchange Commission)** pr n commission *f* américaine des opérations de Bourse ; ≃ COB *f*.

Sec. written abbr of **second**.

secateurs [,sekə'tɜːz] pl n 🇬🇧 ▶ **(pair of) secateurs** sécateur *m*.

secede [sɪ'siːd] vi faire sécession, se séparer.

secession [sɪ'seʃn] n sécession *f*, scission *f*.

secluded [sɪ'kluːdɪd] adj [village] retiré, à l'écart ; [garden] tranquille.

seclusion [sɪ'kluːʒn] n **1.** [isolation - chosen] solitude *f*, isolement *m* **2.** [isolation - imposed] isolement *m*.

second¹ ['sekənd] ◆ n **1.** [unit of time] seconde *f* **2.** [instant] seconde *f*, instant *m* / *I'll be with you in a second* je serai à vous dans un instant / *I'll only be a second* j'en ai seulement pour deux secondes **3.** MATH seconde *f* **4.** [in order] second *m*, -e *f*, deuxième *mf* / *I was the second to arrive* je suis arrivé deuxième or le deuxième ▶ *to come a close second* [in race] être battu de justesse **5.** [in duel] témoin *m*, second *m* ; [in boxing] soigneur *m* **6.** AUTO seconde *f* / *in second* en seconde **7.** 🇬🇧 UNIV ▶ **an upper / lower second** une licence avec mention bien / assez bien **8.** MUS seconde *f*. ◆ det **1.** [in series] deuxième ; [of two] second / *every second person* une personne sur deux / *to be second in command* a) [in hierarchy] être deuxième dans la hiérarchie b) MIL commander en second / *second floor* a) 🇬🇧 deuxième étage *m* b) 🇺🇸 premier étage / *in the second person singular / plural* GRAM à la deuxième personne du singulier / pluriel ▶ **second violin** MUS deuxième violon *m* **2.** [additional, extra] deuxième, second, autre / *to take a second helping* se resservir / *they have a second home in France* ils ont une résidence secondaire en France / *I'd like a second opinion* a) [doctor] je voudrais prendre l'avis d'un confrère b) [patient] je voudrais consulter un autre médecin. ◆ adv **1.** [in order] en seconde place / *to come second* [in race] arriver en seconde position **2.** [with superl adj] : *the second-oldest* le cadet / *the second-largest / second-richest* le second par la taille / second par le revenu **3.** [secondly] en second lieu, deuxièmement. ◆ vt [motion] appuyer ; [speaker] appuyer la motion de. ◆ **seconds** pl n **1.** [goods] marchandises *fpl* de second choix ; [crockery] vaisselle *f* de second choix **2.** *inf* [of food] rab *m*.

second² [sɪ'kɒnd] vt 🇬🇧 [employee] affecter (provisoirement), envoyer en détachement ; MIL détacher.

secondary ['sekəndrɪ] *(pl* **secondaries***)* adj **1.** [gen & MED] secondaire ; [minor] secondaire, de peu d'importance ▶ **secondary colour** couleur *f* secondaire or binaire **2.** SCH secondaire *m* ▶ **secondary education** enseignement *m* secondaire or du second degré.

secondary modern (school) n 🇬🇧 HIST établissement secondaire d'enseignement général et technique, aujourd'hui remplacé par la « comprehensive school ».

secondary picketing n *(U)* 🇬🇧 INDUST piquets *mpl* de grève de solidarité.

secondary school n établissement secondaire ▶ **secondary school teacher** professeur *m* du secondaire.

second best ◆ n pis-aller *m inv*. ◆ adv ▶ **to come off second best** être battu, se faire battre. ◆ **second-best** adj [clothes, objects] de tous les jours.

second chamber n [gen] deuxième chambre *f* ; [in UK] Chambre *f* des lords ; [in US] Sénat *m*.

second class n RAIL seconde *f* (classe *f*). ◆ **second-class** ◆ adj **1.** RAIL de seconde (classe) / *two second-class returns to Glasgow* deux allers (et) retours pour Glasgow en seconde (classe) **2.** [hotel] de seconde catégorie **3.** [mail] à tarif réduit or lent **4.** 🇬🇧 UNIV ▶ **a second-class honours degree** ≃ une licence avec mention (assez) bien **5.** [inferior] de qualité inférieure. ◆ adv **1.** RAIL en seconde (classe) **2.** [for mail] ▶ **to send a parcel second-class** expédier un paquet en tarif réduit.

second-class citizen n citoyen *m*, -enne *f* de seconde zone.

second cousin n cousin *m*, -e *f* au second degré, cousin *m* issu or cousine *f* issue de germains.

second-degree burn n brûlure *f* au deuxième degré.

seconder ['sekəndər] n **1.** [in debate - of motion] personne *f* qui appuie une motion **2.** [of candidate] deuxième parrain *m*.

second-generation adj [immigrant, computer] de la seconde génération.

second grade n 🇺🇸 SCH classe de l'enseignement primaire correspondant au CE1 (6-7 ans).

second-guess vt *inf* **1.** [after event] comprendre après coup **2.** [before event] essayer de prévoir or d'anticiper.

second hand n [of watch, clock] aiguille *f* des secondes, trotteuse *f*. ◆ **second-hand** ◆ adj **1.** [car, clothes, books] d'occasion ▶ **second-hand shop** magasin *m* d'occasions ▶ **second-hand clothes shop** friperie *f* **2.** [information] de seconde main. ◆ adv **1.** [buy] d'occasion **2.** [indirectly] : *I heard the news second-hand* j'ai appris la nouvelle indirectement.

second-in-command n MIL commandant *m* en second ; NAUT second *m*, officier *m* en second ; [in hierarchy] second *m*, adjoint *m*.

second language n langue *f* seconde.

secondly ['sekəndlɪ] adv deuxièmement, en deuxième lieu.

secondment [sɪ'kɒndmənt] n 🇬🇧 *fml* détachement *m*, affectation *f* provisoire ▶ **to be on secondment** a) [teacher] être en détachement b) [diplomat] être en mission.

second name n nom *m* de famille.

second-rate adj [goods, equipment] de qualité inférieure ; [film, book] médiocre ; [politician, player] médiocre, de second ordre.

second sight n seconde or double vue *f* / *to have second sight* avoir un don de double vue.

second-string adj 🇺🇸 SPORT remplaçant.

second thought n ▶ **to have second thoughts** avoir des doutes / *he left his family without a second thought* il a quitté sa famille sans réfléchir or sans se poser de questions ▶ **on second thoughts** 🇬🇧 or **on second thought** 🇺🇸 : *on second thoughts I'd better go myself* toute réflexion faite, il vaut mieux que j'y aille moi-même.

secrecy ['siːkrəsɪ] n *(U)* secret *m* ; [mystery] mystère *m*.

secret ['siːkrɪt] ◆ n **1.** [information kept hidden] secret *m* / *I have no secrets from her* je ne lui cache rien / *can you keep a secret?* pouvez-vous garder un secret ? / *I'll tell you* or *I'll let you into a secret* je vais vous dire or révéler un secret **2.** [explanation] secret *m* **3.** [mystery] secret *m*, mystère *m*. ◆ adj **1.** [meeting, plan] secret (secrète) ▶ **to keep sthg secret** tenir qqch secret ; [personal] secret (secrète) ▶ **secret ballot** vote *m* à bulletin secret

secret weapon arme f secrète **2.** [hidden - door] caché, dérobé ; [- compartment, safe] caché **3.** [identity] inconnu **4.** [secluded - beach, garden] retiré, secret (ète). **in secret** adv phr en secret, secrètement.

secret agent n agent m secret.

secretarial [ˌsekrə'teərɪəl] adj [tasks] de secrétaire, de secrétariat ; [course, college] de secrétariat **secretarial skills** notions fpl de secrétariat **the secretarial staff** le secrétariat.

secretariat [ˌsekrə'teərɪət] n secrétariat m.

secretary [UK 'sekrətrɪ US 'sekrə,terɪ] (pl secretaries) n **1.** [gen & COMM] secrétaire mf **2.** POL [in UK - minister] ministre m ; [- non-elected official] secrétaire m d'État ; [in US] secrétaire m d'État **secretary of state a)** [in UK] ministre **b)** [in US] secrétaire m d'État, ministre des Affaires étrangères **3.** [diplomat] secrétaire m d'ambassade.

secretary-general n secrétaire m général, secrétaire f générale.

secrete [sɪ'kriːt] vt **1.** ANAT & MED sécréter **2.** fml [hide] cacher.

secretion [sɪ'kriːʃn] n ANAT & MED sécrétion f.

secretive ['siːkrətɪv] adj [nature] secret (ète) ; [behaviour] cachottier.

secretively ['siːkrətɪvlɪ] adv en cachette, secrètement.

secretly ['siːkrɪtlɪ] adv [do, act] en secret, secrètement ; [believe, think] en son for intérieur, secrètement.

secret police n police f secrète.

secret service n services mpl secrets. **Secret Service** n [in US] **the secret service** service de protection du président, du vice-président des États-Unis et de leurs familles.

sect [sekt] n secte f.

sectarian [sek'teərɪən] adj sectaire **sectarian violence** violence f d'origine religieuse.

sectarianism [sek'teərɪənɪzm] n sectarisme m.

section ['sekʃn] n **1.** [sector] section f, partie f ; [division - of staff, services] section f ; [- in army] groupe m de combat ; [- in orchestra] section f **2.** [component part - of furniture] élément m ; [- of tube] section f ; [- of track, road] section f, tronçon m ; RAIL section f **3.** [subdivision - of law] article m ; [- of book, exam, text] section f, partie f ; [- of library] section f ; [of newspaper - page] page f ; [- pages] pages fpl ; [in department store] rayon m **4.** US RAIL [train] train m supplémentaire ; [sleeper] compartiment-lits m **5.** [cut, cross-section - drawing] coupe f, section f ; GEOM section f ; [for microscope] coupe f, lamelle f ; [in metal] profilé m **6.** MED sectionnement m **7.** US [land] division (administrative) d'un mille carré. vt **1.** [divide into sections] sectionner **2.** UK [confine to mental hospital] interner. **section off** vt sep séparer.

sector ['sektər] n **1.** [area, realm] secteur m, domaine m ; ECON secteur m ; [part, subdivision] secteur m, partie f ; COMPUT [of screen] secteur m **2.** MIL secteur m, zone f **3.** GEOM secteur m **4.** [for measuring] compas m de proportion. vt diviser en secteurs ; ADMIN & GEOG sectoriser.

secular ['sekjʊlər] adj **1.** [life, clergy] séculier **2.** [education, school] laïque **3.** [music, art] profane **4.** [ancient] séculaire **5.** ASTRON séculaire.

secularism ['sekjʊlərɪzm] n [policy] laïcité f ; [doctrine] laïcisme m.

secularize, secularise ['sekjʊləraɪz] vt séculariser ; [education] laïciser.

secure [sɪ'kjʊər] adj **1.** [protected] sûr, en sécurité, en sûreté **2.** [guaranteed - job] sûr ; [- victory, future] assuré **3.** [calm, confident] tranquille, sécurisé **4.** [solid - investment, base] sûr ; [- foothold, grasp] sûr, ferme ; [solidly fastened - bolt, window] bien fermé ; [- scaffolding, aerial] solide, qui tient bien ; [- knot] solide **5.** COMPUT **secure electronic transaction** paiement m sécurisé **secure server** serveur m sécurisé. vt **1.** fml [obtain] se procurer, obtenir ; [agreement] obtenir ; [loan] obtenir, se voir accorder **2.** [fasten, fix - rope] attacher ; [- parcel] ficeler ; [- ladder, aerial] bien fixer ; [- window, lock] bien fermer **3.** [guarantee - future] assurer ; [- debt] garantir **4.** [from danger] préserver, protéger.

secured [sɪ'kjʊəd] adj FIN [debt, loan] garanti.

securely [sɪ'kjʊəlɪ] adv **1.** [firmly] fermement, solidement **2.** [safely] en sécurité, en sûreté.

secure unit n [in psychiatric hospital] quartier m de haute sécurité ; [for young offenders] centre m d'éducation surveillée.

security [sɪ'kjʊərətɪ] (pl securities) n **1.** [safety] sécurité f ; [police measures, protection, etc.] sécurité f / there was maximum security for the President's visit des mesures de sécurité exceptionnelles ont été prises pour la visite du président **2.** (U) [assurance] sécurité f **to have security of tenure a)** [in job] être titulaire, avoir la sécurité de l'emploi **b)** [as tenant] avoir un bail qui ne peut être résilié **3.** [guarantee] garantie f, caution f / have you anything to put up as security? qu'est-ce que vous pouvez fournir comme garantie ? ; [guarantor] garant m, -e f **to stand security for sb** UK se porter garant de qqn **to stand security for a loan** avaliser un prêt **4.** [department] sécurité f **5.** COMPUT sécurité f. comp [measures, forces] de sécurité **security camera** caméra f de surveillance **security device** dispositif m de sécurité. **securities** pl n FIN titres mpl, actions fpl, valeurs fpl **government securities** titres mpl d'État **the securities market** le marché des valeurs.

security blanket n doudou m.

security-coded adj **1.** [radio] codé, à code de sécurité **2.** AUTO **security-coded immobilizer** antidémarrage m codé.

Security Council n Conseil m de Sécurité.

security gate n [at airport] portique m.

security guard n garde m (chargé de la sécurité) ; [for armoured van] convoyeur m de fonds.

security risk n : she's considered to be a security risk on considère qu'elle représente un risque pour la sécurité.

secy (written abbr of secretary) secr.

sedan [sɪ'dæn] n **1.** US [car] berline f **2.** [chair] **sedan (chair)** chaise f à porteurs.

sedate [sɪ'deɪt] adj [person, manner] calme, posé ; [behaviour] calme, pondéré. vt donner des sédatifs à.

sedation [sɪ'deɪʃn] n sédation f **under sedation** sous calmants.

sedative ['sedətɪv] adj calmant. n calmant m.

sedentary ['sedntrɪ] adj sédentaire.

sediment ['sedɪmənt] n **1.** GEOL sédiment m **2.** [in liquid] sédiment m, dépôt m ; [in wine] dépôt m, lie f. vt déposer. vi se déposer.

sedition [sɪ'dɪʃn] n sédition f.

seditious [sɪ'dɪʃəs] adj séditieux.

seduce [sɪ'djuːs] vt **1.** [sexually] séduire **2.** [attract] séduire, attirer ; [draw] entraîner.

seduction [sɪ'dʌkʃn] n séduction f.

seductive [sɪ'dʌktɪv] adj [person] séduisant ; [personality] séduisant, attrayant ; [voice, smile] aguichant, séducteur ; [offer] séduisant, alléchant.

seductively [sɪ'dʌktɪvlɪ] adv [dress] d'une manière séduisante ; [smile] d'une manière enjôleuse.

see [siː] (pt saw [sɔː], pp seen [siːn])

◆ vt

A. PERCEIVE WITH EYES 1. [perceive with eyes] voir / *can you see me?* est-ce que tu me vois ? / *she could see a light in the distance* elle voyait une lumière au loin / *I see her around a lot* je la croise assez souvent / *there wasn't a car to be seen* il n'y avait pas une seule voiture en vue ; [imagine] : *there's nothing there, you're seeing things!* il n'y a rien, tu as des hallucinations ! ▶ **to see one's way (clear) to doing sthg**: *could you see your way clear to lending me £20?* est-ce que vous pourriez me prêter 20 livres ? ▶ **to see the back** or **last of sthg** en avoir fini avec qqch **2.** [watch - film, play, programme] voir **3.** [refer to - page, chapter] voir / *see page 317* voir page 317.

B. MEET OR VISIT 1. [meet by arrangement, consult] voir / *you should see a doctor* tu devrais voir or consulter un médecin **2.** [meet by chance] voir, rencontrer **3.** [visit - person, place] voir / *to see the world* voir le monde **4.** [receive a visit from] recevoir, voir **5.** [spend time with socially] voir / *is he seeing anyone at the moment?* [going out with] est-ce qu'il a quelqu'un en ce moment ? **6.** *inf* PHR **see you!**, **(I'll) be seeing you!** salut ! ▶ **see you later!** à tout à l'heure ! ▶ **see you around!** à un de ces jours ! ▶ **see you tomorrow!** à demain !

C. IMAGINE OR UNDERSTAND 1. [understand] voir, comprendre / *I see what you mean* je vois or comprends ce que vous voulez dire / *can I borrow the car?* — *I don't see why not* est-ce que je peux prendre la voiture ? — je n'y vois pas d'inconvénients / *I could see his point* je voyais ce qu'il voulait dire **2.** [consider, view] voir / *we see things differently* nous ne voyons pas les choses de la même façon / *as I see it, it's the parents who are to blame* à mon avis, ce sont les parents qui sont responsables **3.** [imagine, picture] voir, s'imaginer / *I can't see him getting married* je ne le vois pas or je ne me l'imagine pas se mariant.

D. TRY, DISCOVER OR CHECK 1. [try to find] voir / *I'll see if I can fix it* je vais voir si je peux le réparer **2.** [become aware of] voir / *what can she possibly see in him?* qu'est-ce qu'elle peut bien lui trouver ? **3.** [discover, learn] voir / *as we shall see in a later chapter* comme nous le verrons dans un chapitre ultérieur **4.** [make sure] s'assurer, veiller à / *see that all the lights are out before you leave* assurez-vous or veillez à ce que toutes les lumières soient éteintes avant de partir.

E. WITNESS OR EXPERIENCE 1. [experience] voir, connaître / *he thinks he's seen it all* il croit tout savoir **2.** [witness] voir / *I never thought I'd see the day when he'd admit he was wrong* je n'aurais jamais cru qu'un jour il admettrait avoir tort.

F. ACCOMPANY 1. [accompany] accompagner / *he saw her into a taxi / onto the train* il l'a mise dans un taxi / le train **2.** [in poker] voir.

◆ vi **1.** [perceive with eyes] voir / *I can't see without (my) glasses* je ne vois rien sans mes lunettes **2.** [find out] voir **3.** [understand] voir, comprendre / *it makes no difference as far as I can see* autant que je puisse en juger, ça ne change rien / *I was tired, you see, and...* j'étais fatigué, voyez-vous, et... / *I haven't quite finished — so I see* je n'ai pas tout à fait terminé — c'est ce que je vois **4.** [indicating a pause or delay] : *let me* or *let's see* voyons voir. ❖ **see about** vt insep s'occuper de / *I'll see about making the reservations* je m'occuperai des réservations / *they're sending someone to see about the gas* ils envoient quelqu'un pour vérifier le gaz / *they won't let us in — we'll (soon) see about that!* inf ils ne veulent pas nous laisser entrer — c'est ce qu'on va voir ! ❖ **see in** vt sep **1.** [escort] faire entrer **2.** [celebrate] ▶ **to see in the New Year** fêter le Nouvel An. ◆ vi voir à l'intérieur. ❖ **see off** vt sep **1.** [say goodbye to] dire au revoir à **2.** [chase away] chasser **3.** [repel - attack] repousser. ❖ **see out** vt sep [accompany to the door] reconduire or raccompagner à la porte / *can you see yourself*

out? pouvez-vous trouver la sortie tout seul ? / *goodbye, I'll see myself out* au revoir, ce n'est pas la peine de me raccompagner. ❖ **see through** ◆ vt insep **1.** [window, fabric] voir à travers **2.** [be wise to - person] ne pas être dupe de, voir dans le jeu de ; [- trick, scheme, behaviour] ne pas se laisser tromper par. ◆ vt sep **1.** [bring to a successful end] mener à bonne fin **2.** [support, sustain] : *I've got enough money to see me through the week* j'ai assez d'argent pour tenir jusqu'à la fin de la semaine. ❖ **see to** vt insep **1.** [look after] s'occuper de / *see to it that everything's ready by 5 p.m.* veillez à ce que tout soit prêt pour 17 h **2.** [repair] réparer.

seed [si:d] ◆ n **1.** (C) BOT & HORT graine f ; (U) graines fpl, semence f ▶ **grass seed** semence pour gazon ▶ **to go** or **to run to seed a)** HORT monter en graine **b)** fig [physically] se laisser aller, se décatir **c)** [mentally] perdre ses facultés **2.** [in fruit, tomatoes] pépin m **3.** [source] germe m **4.** liter BIBLE [offspring] progéniture f ; [sperm] semence f **5.** SPORT tête f de série / *the top seeds* les meilleurs joueurs classés. ◆ vt **1.** BOT & HORT [garden, field] ensemencer ; [plants] planter **2.** [take seeds from - raspberries, grapes] épépiner **3.** SPORT ▶ **seeded player** tête f de série. ◆ vi [lettuce] monter en graine ; [corn] grener.

seedless ['si:dlɪs] adj sans pépins.

seedling ['si:dlɪŋ] n [plant] semis m, jeune plant m ; [tree] jeune plant m.

seedy ['si:dɪ] (compar **seedier**, superl **seediest**) adj **1.** [person, hotel, clothes] miteux, minable ; [area] délabré **2.** [fruit] plein de pépins.

seeing ['si:ɪŋ] ◆ n [vision] vue f, vision f. ◆ conj vu que / *seeing (that* or *as how) no-one came, we left* vu que or étant donné que personne n'est venu, nous sommes partis.

seeing eye (dog) n US chien m d'aveugle.

seeing-to n UK inf : *to give sb a good seeing-to* **a)** [beat up] tabasser qqn **b)** [have sex with] faire passer qqn à la casserole.

seek [si:k] (pt & pp **sought** [sɔːt]) ◆ vt **1.** [search for - job, person, solution] chercher, rechercher **2.** [ask for - advice, help] demander, chercher **3.** [attempt] ▶ **to seek to do sthg** chercher à faire qqch, tenter de faire qqch **4.** [move towards] chercher / *water seeks its own level* c'est le principe des vases communicants. ◆ vi chercher. ❖ **seek after** vt insep rechercher. ❖ **seek out** vt sep **1.** [go to see] aller voir **2.** [search for] chercher, rechercher ; [dig out] dénicher.

seeker ['si:kər] n chercheur m, -euse f.

seem [si:m] vi

A. GIVE IMPRESSION 1. [with adjective] sembler, paraître, avoir l'air / *he seems very nice* il a l'air très gentil / *things aren't always what they seem (to be)* les apparences sont parfois trompeuses / *how does the situation seem to you?* — *it seems hopeless* que pensez-vous de la situation ? — elle me semble désespérée **2.** [with infinitive] sembler, avoir l'air / *the door seemed to open by itself* la porte sembla s'ouvrir toute seule / *he didn't seem to know* or *he seemed not to know* il n'avait pas l'air de savoir ; [used to soften a statement, question, etc.] : *I seem to remember (that)...* je crois bien me souvenir que... ; [with 'can't', 'couldn't'] : *I can't seem to do it* je n'y arrive pas **3.** [with noun, often with 'like'] sembler, paraître / *he seems (like) a nice boy* il a l'air très sympathique or d'un garçon charmant / *it seems like only yesterday* il me semble que c'était hier.

B. IMPERSONAL USE 1. [impersonal use] : *it seemed that* or *as if nothing could make her change her mind* il semblait que rien ne pourrait la faire changer d'avis / *it seemed as though we'd known each other for years* nous avions l'impression de nous connaître depuis des années / *it seems* *to me that...* j'ai l'impression or il me semble que... / *there seems to be some mistake* on dirait qu'il y a une erreur / *we've been having a spot of bother — so it seems* or *would seem!* nous avons eu un petit problème — on dirait bien ! **2.** [indicating that information is hearsay or second-hand] paraître / *it seems* or *it would seem (that) he already knew* il semble or il semblerait qu'il était déjà au courant ‣ *it would seem so* il paraît que oui ‣ *it would seem not* il paraît que non, apparemment pas.

📋 Note that il semble(rait) que is followed by a verb in the subjunctive:
It seems no one thought to warn them. // *semblerait que personne n'ait pensé à les avertir.*

seeming ['siːmɪŋ] adj apparent.

seemingly ['siːmɪŋlɪ] adv **1.** [judging by appearances] apparemment, en apparence **2.** [from reports] à ce qu'il paraît ‣ **seemingly so / not** il paraît que oui / non.

seemly ['siːmlɪ] (*compar* **seemlier**, *superl* **seemliest**) adj *liter* **1.** [of behaviour] convenable, bienséant **2.** [of dress] décent.

seen [siːn] pp —→ **see**.

seep [siːp] vi filtrer, s'infiltrer. ❖ **seep away** vi s'écouler goutte à goutte. ❖ **seep in** vi **1.** [liquid] s'infiltrer **2.** *fig* faire son effet. ❖ **seep out** vi **1.** [blood, liquid] suinter ; [gas, smoke] se répandre **2.** [information, secret] filtrer.

seer ['sɪə˞] n *liter* prophète *m*, prophétesse *f*.

seersucker ['sɪə˞ˌsʌkə˞] n crépon *m* de coton, seersucker *m*.

seesaw ['siːsɔː] ❖ n balançoire *f* (à bascule). ❖ comp [motion] de bascule. ❖ vi osciller.

seethe [siːð] vi **1.** [liquid, lava] bouillir, bouillonner ; [sea] bouillonner **2.** [with anger, indignation] bouillir / *he was seething with anger* il bouillait de rage **3.** [teem] grouiller / *the streets seethed with shoppers* les rues grouillaient de gens qui faisaient leurs courses.

seething ['siːðɪŋ] adj **1.** [liquid, sea] bouillonnant **2.** [furious] furieux **3.** [teeming] grouillant.

see-through adj transparent.

CUL8R MESSAGING (written abbr of **see you later**) @+.

segment ❖ n ['segmənt] **1.** [piece - gen & ANAT & GEOM] segment *m* ; [- of fruit] quartier *m* / *in segments* par segments **2.** [part - of book, film, programme] partie *f*. ❖ vt [seg'ment] segmenter, diviser or partager en segments. ❖ vi [seg'ment] se segmenter.

segmentation [ˌsegmen'teɪʃn] n segmentation *f*.

segmented [seg'mentɪd] adj segmentaire.

segregate ['segrɪgeɪt] ❖ vt [separate] séparer ; [isolate] isoler. ❖ vi [in genetics] se diviser.

segregated ['segrɪgeɪtɪd] adj POL où la ségrégation raciale est pratiquée.

segregation [ˌsegrɪ'geɪʃn] n **1.** POL ségrégation *f* **2.** [separation - of sexes, patients] séparation *f* **3.** [in genetics] division *f*.

segregationist [ˌsegrɪ'geɪʃnɪst] ❖ adj ségrégationniste. ❖ n ségrégationniste *mf*.

segue ['segweɪ] ❖ n [transition] transition *f* ; [between pieces of music] enchaînement *m* / *a segue between the old and the new* une transition entre l'ancien et le moderne. ❖ vi : *to segue between two songs* enchaîner deux morceaux / *he segued into a joke / into a solo career* il a enchaîné sur une histoire drôle / sur une carrière en solo /

the film then segues into farce le film bascule alors dans la farce. ❖ vt : *to segue a playlist* enchaîner les morceaux d'une playlist.

seine [seɪn] n ‣ **seine (net)** senne *f*.

Seine [seɪn] pr n ‣ **the (River) Seine** la Seine.

seismic ['saɪzmɪk] adj sismique, séismique.

seismograph ['saɪzməɡrɑːf] n sismographe *m*, séismographe *m*.

seize [siːz] ❖ vt **1.** [grasp] attraper, saisir ; [in fist] saisir, empoigner ‣ **to seize hold of sthg** saisir or attraper qqch **2.** [by force] s'emparer de, saisir / *to seize power* s'emparer du pouvoir **3.** [arrest - terrorist, smuggler] se saisir de, appréhender, capturer ; [capture, confiscate - contraband, arms] se saisir de, saisir ; LAW [property] saisir **4.** [opportunity] saisir, sauter sur **5.** [understand - meaning] saisir **6.** [overcome] saisir. ❖ vi [mechanism] se gripper. ❖ **seize on**, ❖ **seize upon** vt insep [opportunity] saisir, sauter sur ; [excuse] saisir ; [idea] saisir, adopter. ❖ **seize up** vi **1.** [machinery] se gripper **2.** [system] se bloquer **3.** [leg] s'ankyloser ; [back] se bloquer ; [heart] s'arrêter. ❖ **seize upon** = **seize on**.

seizure ['siːʒə˞] n **1.** (U) [of goods, property] saisie *f* ; [of city, fortress] prise *f* ; [of ship] capture *f* ; [arrest] arrestation *f* **2.** MED crise *f*, attaque *f* / *to have a seizure* *lit* & *fig* avoir une attaque.

seldom ['seldəm] adv rarement.

select [sɪ'lekt] ❖ vt **1.** [gen] choisir ; [team] sélectionner **2.** COMPUT sélectionner. ❖ adj **1.** [elite - restaurant, neighbourhood] chic, sélect ; [- club] fermé, sélect **2.** [in quality - goods] de (premier) choix.

select committee n POL commission *f* d'enquête parlementaire.

selected [sɪ'lektɪd] adj [friends, poems] choisi ; [customers] privilégié ; [fruit, cuts of meat] de (premier) choix.

selection [sɪ'lekʃn] ❖ n **1.** [choice] choix *m*, sélection *f* ; [of team] sélection *f* **2.** [of stories, music] choix *m*, sélection *f* / *selections from Balzac* morceaux *mpl* choisis de Balzac **3.** COMPUT sélection *f*. ❖ comp [committee, criteria] de sélection.

selective [sɪ'lektɪv] adj **1.** [gen] sélectif ‣ **selective entry** SCH sélection *f* ‣ **selective service** 🇺🇸 service *m* militaire obligatoire, conscription *f* **2.** ELECTRON sélectif.

selectively [sɪ'lektɪvlɪ] adv sélectivement, de manière sélective.

selector [sɪ'lektə˞] n **1.** [gen & SPORT] sélectionneur *m* **2.** TELEC & TV sélecteur *m*.

self [self] (*pl* **selves** [selvz]) ❖ n **1.** [individual] : *she's back to her old* or *usual self* elle est redevenue elle-même or comme avant / *she's only a shadow of her former self* elle n'est plus que l'ombre d'elle-même / *he was his usual tactless self* il a fait preuve de son manque de tact habituel / *they began to reveal their true selves* ils ont commencé à se montrer sous leur véritable jour **2.** PSYCHOL moi *m* **3.** [on cheque] ‣ **pay self** payez à l'ordre de soi-même. ❖ adj [matching] assorti.

self- in comp **1.** [of o.s.] de soi-même, auto- ‣ **self-accusation** autoaccusation *f* ‣ **self-actualization** épanouissement *m* de la personnalité **2.** [by o.s.] auto-, par soi-même ‣ **self-financing** autofinancé, qui s'autofinance **3.** [automatic] auto-, automatique ‣ **self-checking** à contrôle automatique ‣ **self-opening** à ouverture automatique.

self-absorbed [-əb'sɔːbd] adj égocentrique.

self-addressed [-ə'drest] adj : *send three self-addressed (stamped) envelopes* envoyez trois enveloppes (timbrées) à votre adresse.

self-adhesive adj autocollant, autoadhésif.

self-adjusting adj à autoréglage, à réglage automatique.

self-aggrandizement n autoglorification f.

self-appointed [-ə'pɔɪntɪd] adj qui s'est nommé or proclamé lui-même.

self-appraisal n auto-évaluation f.

self-assembly adj [furniture] en kit.

self-assertion n affirmation f de soi.

self-assertive adj sûr de soi, impérieux.

self-assertiveness n affirmation f de soi.

self-assessment n 1. [gen] auto-évaluation f 2. 🆄🅺 [for taxes] *système de déclaration des revenus pour le paiement des impôts, par opposition au prélèvement à la source.*

self-assurance n confiance f en soi, aplomb m.

self-assured adj : *he's very self-assured* il est très sûr de lui.

self-aware adj conscient de soi-même.

self-awareness n conscience f de soi.

self-belief n confiance f en soi.

self-betterment n [material] amélioration f de sa condition ; [spiritual] progrès mpl spirituels.

self-catering adj 🆄🅺 [flat, accommodation] indépendant (avec cuisine) ; [holiday] dans un appartement or un logement indépendant.

self-censorship n autocensure f.

self-centred 🆄🅺, **self-centered** 🆄🅂 [-'sentəd] adj égocentrique.

self-centredness 🆄🅺, **self-centeredness** 🆄🅂 [-'sentədnɪs] n égocentrisme m.

self-check routine n COMPUT routine f d'autotest.

self-cleaning adj autonettoyant.

self-coloured 🆄🅺, **self-colored** 🆄🅂 adj uni.

self-composed adj posé, calme.

self-confessed [-kən'fest] adj [murderer, rapist] qui reconnaît sa culpabilité.

self-confidence n confiance f en soi, assurance f.

self-confident adj sûr de soi, plein d'assurance.

self-confidently adv avec assurance or aplomb.

self-congratulation n autosatisfaction f.

self-congratulatory adj satisfait de soi.

self-conscious adj 1. [embarrassed] timide, gêné ▸ **to make sb feel self-conscious** intimider qqn / *he's very self-conscious about his red hair* il fait un complexe de ses cheveux roux / *I feel very self-conscious in front of all these people* je me sens très mal à l'aise devant tous ces gens **2.** [style] appuyé.

self-consciously adv timidement.

self-consciousness n timidité f, gêne f.

self-contained adj 1. [device] autonome 2. [flat] indépendant 3. [person] réservé.

self-contempt n mépris m de soi-même.

self-content n contentement m de soi.

self-contented adj content de soi.

self-contentment n contentement m de soi.

self-contradictory adj qui se contredit.

self-control n sang-froid m, maîtrise f de soi.

self-controlled adj maître de soi.

self-correcting [-kə'rektɪŋ] adj à correction automatique, autocorrecteur.

self-deceit, self-deception n aveuglement m.

self-declared adj autoproclamé.

self-defeating [-dɪ'fiːtɪŋ] adj contraire au but recherché.

self-defence n 1. [physical] autodéfense f 2. LAW légitime défense f / *it was self-defence* j'étais / il était, etc. en état de légitime défense ▸ **to act in self-defence** agir en état de légitime défense / *I shot him in self-defence* j'ai tiré sur lui en état de légitime défense.

self-delusion n illusion f.

self-denial n abnégation f, sacrifice m de soi.

self-denying [-dɪ'naɪɪŋ] adj qui fait preuve d'abnégation.

self-deprecating [-'deprɪkeɪtɪŋ] adj : *to be self-deprecating* se déprécier.

self-deprecation n [ironic] autodérision f ; [from sense of inferiority] dénigrement m de soi-même.

self-deprecatory = self-deprecating.

self-destruct ◆ vi s'autodétruire. ◆ adj [mechanism] autodestructeur.

self-destructive adj autodestructeur.

self-determination n POL autodétermination f.

self-discipline n [self-control] maîtrise f de soi ; [good behaviour] autodiscipline f.

self-disciplined adj [self-controlled] maître de soi ; [well-behaved] qui fait preuve d'autodiscipline.

self-doubt n doute m de soi-même.

self-drive adj ▸ **self-drive car** voiture f sans chauffeur.

self-educated adj autodidacte.

self-effacing [-ɪ'feɪsɪŋ] adj modeste, effacé.

self-elected adj élu or nommé par soi-même.

self-employed ◆ adj indépendant, qui travaille à son compte. ◆ pl n ▸ **the self-employed** les travailleurs mpl indépendants.

self-employment n travail m en indépendant, travail m à son propre compte.

self-esteem n respect m de soi, amour-propre m ▸ **to have low / high self-esteem** avoir une mauvaise / bonne opinion de soi-même.

self-evident adj évident, qui va de soi, qui saute aux yeux.

self-examination n examen m de conscience ; [of breasts, testicles] autopalpation f.

self-explanatory adj qui se passe d'explications, évident.

self-expression n expression f libre.

self-focusing [-'fəʊkəsɪŋ] adj autofocus (inv), à mise au point automatique.

self-fulfilling adj ▸ **self-fulfilling prophecy** prophétie défaitiste qui se réalise.

self-governing adj POL autonome.

self-government n POL autonomie f.

self-harm ◆ n automutilation f. ◆ vi s'automutiler.

self-hatred n haine f de soi.

self-help ◆ n autonomie f ; [in welfare] entraide f. ◆ comp ▸ **self-help group** groupe m d'entraide ▸ **self-help guide** guide m pratique.

self-ignition n AUTO autoallumage m.

self-image n image f de soi-même.

self-importance n suffisance f.

self-important adj vaniteux, suffisant.

self-imposed [-ɪm'pəʊzd] adj que l'on s'impose à soi-même / *self-imposed exile* exil m volontaire.

self-improvement n perfectionnement m des connaissances personnelles.

self-induced adj que l'on provoque soi-même.

self-indulgence n complaisance f envers soi-même, habitude f de ne rien se refuser.

self-indulgent adj [person] qui ne se refuse rien ; [book, film] complaisant.

self-inflicted [-ın'flıktıd] adj : *his wounds were self-inflicted* il s'était auto-infligé ses blessures.

self-interest n intérêt m personnel.

self-interested adj intéressé, qui agit par intérêt personnel.

selfish ['selfıʃ] adj égoïste.

selfishness ['selfıʃnıs] n égoïsme m.

self-justification n autojustification f.

self-knowledge n connaissance f de soi.

selfless ['selflıs] adj altruiste, désintéressé.

selflessly ['selflıslı] adv de façon désintéressée, avec désintéressement.

self-loading adj [gun] automatique.

self-loathing n dégoût m de soi-même.

self-locking adj à verrouillage automatique.

self-made adj qui a réussi tout seul or par ses propres moyens ▶ **a self-made man** un self-made man.

self-medication n automédication f.

self-motivated adj capable de prendre des initiatives.

self-motivation n motivation f.

self-obsessed adj obsédé par soi-même.

self-opinionated adj sûr de soi.

self-perpetuating [-pə'petʃueıtıŋ] adj qui se perpétue.

self-pity n apitoiement m sur son sort.

self-pitying adj qui s'apitoie sur son (propre) sort.

self-portrait n [in painting] autoportrait m ; [in book] portrait m de l'auteur par lui-même.

self-possessed adj maître de soi, qui garde son sang-froid.

self-possession n sang-froid m.

self-praise n éloge m de soi-même.

self-preservation n instinct m de conservation.

self-proclaimed [-prə'kleımd] adj : *she's a self-proclaimed art critic* elle se proclame critique d'art.

self-promotion n autopromotion f.

self-propelled [-prə'peld], **self-propelling** [-prə'pelıŋ] adj autopropulsé.

self-protection n autoprotection f ▶ **out of self-protection** pour se défendre.

self-publicist n : *he is an accomplished self-publicist* il sait soigner sa publicité.

self-raising UK [-,reızıŋ], **self-rising** US [-,raızıŋ] adj ▶ **self-raising flour** farine f avec levure incorporée.

self-realization n prise f de conscience de soi-même.

self-regard n égoïsme m.

self-regarding adj qui ne considère que soi-même / *from self-regarding motives* par intérêt.

self-regulating [-'regjuleıtıŋ] adj autorégulateur.

self-regulation n autorégulation f.

self-reliance n indépendance f.

self-reliant adj indépendant.

self-replicating [-'replıkeıtıŋ] adj autoreproducteur.

self-respect n respect m de soi, amour-propre m.

self-respecting [-rı'spektıŋ] adj qui se respecte.

self-restrained adj retenu, qui sait se contenir.

self-restraint n retenue f.

self-righteous adj suffisant.

self-righteousness n suffisance f, pharisaïsme m *fml*.

self-rising US = **self-raising**.

self-rule n POL autonomie f.

self-sacrifice n abnégation f.

selfsame ['selfseım] adj même, identique.

self-satisfaction n suffisance f, contentement m de soi, fatuité f.

self-satisfied adj [person] suffisant, content de soi ; [look, smile, attitude] suffisant, satisfait.

self-sealing adj [envelope] autocollant, autoadhésif ; [tank] à obturation automatique.

self-seeking [-'si:kıŋ] adj égoïste.

self-serve adj US = **self-service**.

self-service ◆ adj en self-service, en libre service ▶ **self-service restaurant** self-service m ▶ **self-service shop** libre-service m. ◆ n [restaurant] self-service m ; [garage, shop] libre-service m.

self-serving adj intéressé.

self-starter n **1.** AUTO starter m automatique **2.** [person] personne f pleine d'initiative.

self study ◆ n apprentissage m autonome / *this book is ideal for self study* ce livre est idéal pour apprendre seul. ◆ adj d'autoformation.

self-styled [-'staıld] adj prétendu, soi-disant.

self-sufficiency n **1.** [of person - independence] indépendance f ; [- self-assurance] suffisance f **2.** ECON [of nation, resources] autosuffisance f ; POL ▶ **(economic) self-sufficiency** autarcie f.

self-sufficient adj **1.** [person - independent] indépendant ; [- self-assured] plein de confiance en soi, suffisant **2.** ECON [nation] autosuffisant ; POL autarcique.

self-supporting adj **1.** [financially] indépendant **2.** [framework] autoporteur, autoportant.

self-taught adj autodidacte.

self-test n COMPUT test m imprimante.

self-timer n PHOT retardateur m.

self-worth n : *to have a sense of self-worth* avoir confiance en soi / *he has no sense of self-worth* il n'a aucune confiance en lui.

sell [sel] (*pt & pp* **sold** [səuld]) ◆ vt **1.** [goods] vendre ▶ **to sell sb sthg** or **sthg to sb** vendre qqch à qqn **2.** [promote - idea] faire accepter **3.** [make enthusiastic about] convaincre **4.** PHR ▶ **to sell sb short a)** *inf* [cheat] rouler qqn **b)** [disparage] débiner qqn. ◆ vi se vendre / *the cakes sell for* or *at 70 pence each* les gâteaux se vendent (à) or valent 70 pence pièce / *sorry, I'm not interested in selling* désolé, je ne cherche pas à vendre. ◆ n **1.** COMM vente f **2.** *inf* [disappointment] déception f ; [hoax] attrape-nigaud m. ❖ **sell back** vt sep revendre. ❖ **sell off** vt sep [at reduced price] solder ; [clear] liquider ; [get cash] vendre ; [privatize] privatiser. ❖ **sell on** vt sep revendre (en faisant du bénéfice). ❖ **sell out** ◆ vt sep **1.** (*usu passive*) [concert, match] : *the match was sold out* le match s'est joué à guichets fermés **2.** [betray] trahir **3.** ST. EX vendre, réaliser. ◆ vi **1.** COMM [sell business] vendre son commerce ; [sell stock] liquider (son stock) ; [run out] vendre tout le stock / *my father sold out and retired* mon père a vendu son affaire et a pris sa retraite / *he sold out to some Japanese investors* il a vendu à des investisseurs japonais / *we've sold out of sugar* nous n'avons plus de sucre, nous avons écoulé tout notre stock de sucre **2.** [be traitor] trahir / *to sell out to the enemy* passer à l'ennemi. ❖ **sell up** ◆ vt sep **1.** FIN & LAW [goods] opérer la vente forcée de, procéder à la liquidation de **2.** COMM [business] vendre, liquider. ◆ vi [shopkeeper] vendre son fonds de commerce or son affaire ; [businessman] vendre son affaire.

sellable ['seləbl] adj vendable.

sell-by date n date f limite de vente.

seller ['selər] n **1.** [person -gen] vendeur m, -euse f ; [-merchant] vendeur m, -euse f, marchand m, -e f ▶ **it's a seller's market** c'est un marché vendeur or favorable aux vendeurs **2.** [goods] : *it's one of our biggest sellers* c'est un des articles qui se vend le mieux.

selling ['selɪŋ] n (U) vente f.

selling point n avantage m, atout m, point m fort.

selling power n puissance f de vente.

selling price n prix m de vente.

selloff ['selɒf] n [gen] vente f ; [of shares] dégagement m.

Sellotape® ['seləteɪp] UK Scotch® m, ruban m adhésif. ◆ **sellotape** vt UK scotcher, coller avec du ruban adhésif.

sell-out n **1.** COMM liquidation f **2.** [betrayal] trahison f ; [capitulation] capitulation f **3.** [of play, concert, etc.] : *it was a sell-out* on a vendu tous les billets / *the match was a sell-out* le match s'est joué à guichets fermés.

seltzer ['seltsər] n ▶ **seltzer (water)** eau f de Seltz.

selves [selvz] pl ⟶ self.

semantic [sɪ'mæntɪk] adj sémantique.

semantics [sɪ'mæntɪks] n (U) sémantique f.

semaphore ['seməfɔ:r] ◆ n **1.** (U) [signals] signaux mpl à bras **2.** RAIL & NAUT sémaphore m. ◆ vt transmettre par signaux à bras.

semblance ['sembləns] n semblant m, apparence f.

semen ['si:men] n (U) sperme m, semence f.

semester [sɪ'mestər] n US semestre m.

semi ['semɪ] n **1.** UK inf abbr of **semidetached house 2.** inf abbr of **semifinal**.

semi- in comp [partly] semi-, demi- / *in semi-darkness* dans la pénombre or la semi-obscurité / *he's in semi-retirement* il est en semi-retraite.

semi-annual adj semestriel ; BOT semi-annuel.

semi-automatic ◆ adj semi-automatique. ◆ n arme f semi-automatique.

semicircle ['semɪ,sɜ:kl] n demi-cercle m.

semicircular [,semɪ'sɜ:kjələr] adj demi-circulaire, semi-circulaire.

semicolon [,semɪ'kəʊlən] n point-virgule m.

semiconductor [,semɪkən'dʌktər] n semi-conducteur m.

semiconscious [,semɪ'kɒnʃəs] adj à demi or moitié conscient.

semidetached [,semɪdɪ'tætʃt] adj ▶ **semidetached house** maison f jumelée.

semifinal [,semɪ'faɪnl] n demi-finale f.

semifinalist [,semɪ'faɪnəlɪst] n demi-finaliste mf.

seminal ['semɪnl] adj **1.** ANAT & BOT séminal **2.** [important] majeur, qui fait école.

seminar ['semɪnɑ:r] n **1.** [conference] séminaire m, colloque m **2.** UNIV [class] séminaire m, travaux mpl dirigés.

seminary ['semɪnərɪ] (pl seminaries) n RELIG & SCH [for boys, priests] séminaire m ; [for girls] pensionnat m de jeunes filles.

semiofficial [,semɪə'fɪʃəl] adj semi-officiel.

semiotics [,semɪ'ɒtɪks] n (U) sémiotique f.

semiprecious ['semɪ,preʃəs] adj semi-précieux.

semi-retirement n préretraite f progressive.

semiskilled [,semɪ'skɪld] adj [worker] spécialisé.

semi-skimmed [-'skɪmd] adj [milk] demi-écrémé.

semitrailer [,semɪ'treɪlər] n US semi-remorque f.

semolina [,semə'li:nə] n semoule f ▶ **semolina pudding** gâteau m de semoule.

sen. written abbr of **senior**.

SEN (abbr of **State Enrolled Nurse**) n infirmier ou infirmière diplômé(e) d'État.

Sen. written abbr of **Senator**.

senate ['senɪt] n **1.** POL sénat m ▶ **the United States Senate** le Sénat américain **2.** UNIV Conseil m d'Université.

 Senate

Le Sénat constitue, avec la Chambre des représentants, l'organe législatif américain ; il est composé de 100 membres (deux par État). Le mandat d'un sénateur est de six ans.

senator ['senətər] n sénateur m.

send [send] (pt & pp sent [sent]) vt **1.** [letter, parcel, money] envoyer, expédier ▶ **to send sb a letter, to send a letter to sb** envoyer une lettre à qqn / *he sent (us) word that he would be delayed* il (nous) a fait savoir qu'il aurait du retard / *she sends her love* or *regards* elle vous envoie ses amitiés / *we sent help to the refugees* nous avons envoyé des secours aux réfugiés ; [to carry out task] envoyer / *she sent her daughter for the meat* or *to get the meat* elle a envoyé sa fille chercher la viande ▶ **to send sb packing** inf or **about his business** envoyer promener qqn, envoyer qqn sur les roses **2.** [to a specific place] envoyer / *send the children indoors* faites rentrer les enfants / *the collision sent showers of sparks / clouds of smoke into the sky* la collision fit jaillir une gerbe d'étincelles / provoqua des nuages de fumée / *the sound sent shivers down my spine* le bruit m'a fait froid dans le dos ; [order] : *I was sent to bed / to my room* on m'a envoyé me coucher / dans ma chambre ▶ **to send sb home** renvoyer qqn chez lui ▶ **to send sb to prison** envoyer qqn en prison **3.** (with present participle) [propel] envoyer, expédier / *I sent the cup flying* j'ai envoyé voler la tasse / *the blow sent me flying* le coup m'a envoyé rouler par terre **4.** [into a specific state] rendre / *the news sent them into a panic* les nouvelles les ont fait paniquer ▶ **to send sb to sleep** lit & fig endormir qqn. ◆ **send away** ◆ vt sep **1.** [letter, parcel] expédier, mettre à la poste **2.** [person] renvoyer, faire partir / *the children were sent away to school* les enfants furent mis en pension. ◆ vi ▶ **to send away for sthg** a) [by post] se faire envoyer qqch b) [by catalogue] commander qqch par correspondance or sur catalogue. ◆ **send back** vt sep **1.** [return -books, goods] renvoyer **2.** [order -person] : *we sent her back to fetch a coat* or *for a coat* nous l'avons envoyée prendre un manteau. ◆ **send down** vt sep **1.** [person, lift] faire descendre, envoyer en bas **2.** [prices, temperature] faire baisser, provoquer la baisse de **3.** inf [to prison] envoyer en prison. ◆ **send for** vt insep **1.** [doctor, taxi] faire venir, appeler ; [mother, luggage] faire venir ; [police] appeler ; [help] envoyer chercher ; [food, drink] commander **2.** [by post, from catalogue] se faire envoyer, commander ; [catalogue, price list] demander. ◆ **send in** vt sep **1.** [visitor] faire entrer ; [troops, police] envoyer **2.** [submit -report, form] envoyer ; [-suggestions, resignation] envoyer, soumettre. ◆ **send off** ◆ vt sep **1.** [by post] expédier, mettre à la poste **2.** [person] envoyer / *they sent us off to bed / to get washed* ils nous ont envoyés nous coucher / nous laver **3.** SPORT expulser. ◆ vi ▶ **to send off for sthg** a) [by catalogue] commander qqch par correspondance or sur catalogue b) [by post] se faire envoyer qqch. ◆ **send on**

vt sep [mail] faire suivre ; [luggage] expédier. ❖ **send out** ◆ vt sep **1.** [by post - invitations] expédier, poster **2.** [messengers, search party] envoyer, dépêcher ; [patrol] envoyer ; [transmit - message, signal] envoyer **3.** [outside] envoyer dehors ; [on errand, mission] envoyer / *we sent her out for coffee* nous l'avons envoyée chercher du café **4.** [produce, give out - leaves] produire ; [- light, heat] émettre, répandre, diffuser ; [- fumes, smoke] répandre. ◆ vi : *to send out for coffee / sandwiches* [to shop] envoyer quelqu'un chercher du café / des sandwiches. ❖ **send round** vt sep **1.** [circulate - petition] faire circuler **2.** [dispatch - messenger, repairman] envoyer ; [- message] faire parvenir. ❖ **send up** vt sep **1.** [messenger, luggage, drinks] faire monter ; [rocket, flare] lancer ; [plane] faire décoller ; [smoke] répandre **2.** [raise - price, pressure, temperature] faire monter **3.** *inf* [ridicule] mettre en boîte, se moquer de **4.** 🇬🇧 *inf* [imitate] imiter.

sender ['sendər] n expéditeur *m*, -trice *f* ▶ **return to sender** retour à l'expéditeur.

send-off n ▶ **to give sb a send-off** dire au revoir à qqn, souhaiter bon voyage à qqn.

send-up n *inf* parodie *f*.

Senegal [ˌsenɪ'gɔːl] pr n Sénégal *m* / *in Senegal* au Sénégal.

Senegalese [ˌsenɪgə'liːz] (*pl* Senegalese) ◆ n Sénégalais *m*, -e *f*. ◆ adj sénégalais.

senile ['siːnaɪl] adj sénile ▶ **senile dementia** démence *f* sénile.

senility [sɪ'nɪlətɪ] n sénilité *f*.

senior ['siːnjər] ◆ adj **1.** [in age] plus âgé, aîné ; [in rank] (de grade) supérieur / *I am senior to them* **a)** [higher position] je suis leur supérieur **b)** [longer service] j'ai plus d'ancienneté qu'eux ▶ **senior clerk** commis *m* principal, chef *m* de bureau ▶ **senior executive** cadre *m* supérieur ▶ **senior government official** haut fonctionnaire *m* **2.** SCH ▶ **senior master** 🇬🇧 professeur *m* principal ; 🇺🇸 ▶ **senior high school** lycée *m* ▶ **senior year** terminale *f*, dernière année *f* d'études secondaires. ◆ n **1.** [older person] aîné *m*, -e *f* / *he is my senior by six months* or *he is six months my senior* il a six mois de plus que moi, il est de six mois mon aîné **2.** 🇺🇸 SCH élève *mf* de terminale ; UNIV étudiant *m*, -e *f* de licence **3.** 🇬🇧 SCH ▶ **the seniors** ≃ les grands *mpl* ; ≃ les grandes *fpl* **4.** [in hierarchy] supérieur *m*, -e *f*. ❖ **Senior** adj [in age] : *John Brown senior* John Brown père.

senior citizen n personne *f* âgée or du troisième âge.

Senior Common Room n 🇬🇧 UNIV salle *f* des professeurs.

seniority [ˌsiːnɪ'ɒrətɪ] n **1.** [in age] priorité *f* d'âge **2.** [in rank] supériorité *f* ▶ **to have seniority over sb** être le supérieur de qqn ; [length of service] ancienneté *f* / *according to* or *by seniority* en fonction de or à l'ancienneté.

sensation [sen'seɪʃn] n **1.** (*U*) [sensitivity] sensation *f* **2.** [impression] impression *f*, sensation *f* **3.** [excitement, success] sensation *f* ▶ **to cause** or **to be a sensation** faire sensation.

sensational [sen'seɪʃənl] adj **1.** [causing a sensation] sensationnel, qui fait sensation **2.** [press] à sensation **3.** [wonderful] formidable, sensationnel.

sensationalism [sen'seɪʃnəlɪzm] n **1.** [in press, novels, etc.] sensationnalisme *m* **2.** PHILOS sensationnisme *m*.

sensationalist [sen'seɪʃnəlɪst] ◆ n [writer] auteur *m* à sensation ; [journalist] journaliste *mf* à sensation. ◆ adj à sensation.

sensationally [sen'seɪʃnəlɪ] adv d'une manière sensationnelle ; [as intensifier] : *we found this sensationally good restaurant* inf on a découvert un restaurant vraiment génial.

sense [sens] ◆ n **1.** [faculty] sens *m* ▶ **sense of hearing** ouïe *f* ▶ **sense of sight** vue *f* ▶ **sense of smell** odorat *m* ▶ **sense of taste** goût *m* ▶ **sense of touch** toucher *m* **2.** [sensation] sensation *f* ; [feeling] sentiment *m* ; [notion] sens *m*, notion *f* / *I lost all sense of time* j'ai perdu toute notion de l'heure / *to have a (good) sense of direction* avoir le sens de l'orientation / *he has a good sense of humour* il a le sens de l'humour **3.** [practicality, reasonableness] bon sens *m* ▶ **to show good sense** faire preuve de bon sens ▶ **to see sense** entendre raison / *there's no sense in all of us going* cela ne sert à rien or c'est inutile d'y aller tous **4.** [meaning - of word, expression] sens *m*, signification *f* ; [- of text] sens *m* **5.** [coherent message] sens *m* ▶ **to make sense a)** [words] avoir un sens **b)** [be logical] tenir debout, être sensé / *it makes / doesn't make sense to wait* c'est une bonne idée / idiot d'attendre ▶ **to talk sense** dire des choses sensées **6.** [way] ▶ **in a sense** dans un sens ▶ **in no sense** en aucune manière ▶ **in the sense that...** en ce sens que..., dans le sens où... ◆ vt **1.** [feel - presence] sentir ; [- danger, catastrophe] pressentir **2.** ELECTRON détecter ; COMPUT lire. ❖ **senses** pl n [sanity, reason] raison *f* ▶ **to come to one's senses a)** [become conscious] reprendre connaissance **b)** [be reasonable] revenir à la raison ▶ **to take leave of one's senses** perdre la raison or la tête ▶ **to bring sb to his / her senses** ramener qqn à la raison.

senseless ['senslɪs] adj **1.** [futile] insensé, absurde / *it's senseless trying to persuade her* inutile d'essayer or on perd son temps à essayer de la persuader **2.** [unconscious] sans connaissance ▶ **to knock sb senseless** assommer qqn.

senselessly ['senslɪslɪ] adv stupidement, de façon absurde.

sensibility [ˌsensɪ'bɪlətɪ] (*pl* sensibilities) n [physical or emotional] sensibilité *f*. ❖ **sensibilities** pl n susceptibilité *f*, susceptibilités *fpl*.

sensible ['sensəbl] adj **1.** [reasonable - choice] judicieux, sensé ; [- reaction] sensé, qui fait preuve de bon sens ; [- person] sensé, doué de bon sens **2.** [practical - clothes, shoes] pratique **3.** *fml* [notable - change] sensible, appréciable **4.** *fml & liter* [aware] : *I am sensible of the fact that things have changed between us* j'ai conscience du fait que les choses ont changé entre nous.

⚠️ When **sensible** means *wise*, it is not translated by **sensible** in French, which usually means *sensitive*.

sensibly ['sensəblɪ] adv **1.** [reasonably] raisonnablement ▶ **to be sensibly dressed** porter des vêtements pratiques **2.** *fml* [perceptibly] sensiblement, perceptiblement.

sensitive ['sensɪtɪv] adj **1.** [eyes, skin] sensible / *my eyes are very sensitive to bright light* j'ai les yeux très sensibles à la lumière vive **2.** [emotionally] sensible ▶ **to be sensitive to sthg** sensible à qqch **3.** [aware] sensibilisé / *the seminar made us more sensitive to the problem* le séminaire nous a sensibilisés au problème **4.** [touchy - person] susceptible ; [- age] où l'on est susceptible ; [- public opinion] sensible / *she's very sensitive about her height* elle n'aime pas beaucoup qu'on lui parle de sa taille ; [difficult - issue, topic] délicat, épineux ; [information] confidentiel **5.** [instrument] sensible ; PHOT [film] sensible ; [paper] sensibilisé **6.** ST. EX [market] instable.

-sensitive in comp sensible ▶ **heat-sensitive** sensible à la chaleur, thermosensible ▶ **price-sensitive** sensible aux fluctuations des prix ▶ **voice-sensitive** sensible à la voix.

sensitively ['sensɪtɪvlɪ] adv avec sensibilité.

sensitivity [ˌsensɪ'tɪvətɪ] n **1.** [physical] sensibilité *f* **2.** [emotional] sensibilité *f* ; [touchiness] susceptibilité *f* **3.** [of equipment] sensibilité *f* **4.** ST. EX instabilité *f*.

sensitize, sensitise ['sensɪtaɪz] vt sensibiliser, rendre sensible.

sensor ['sensər] n détecteur m, capteur m.

sensory ['sensərɪ] adj [nerve, system] sensoriel ▸ **sensory deprivation** isolation f sensorielle.

sensual ['sensjʊəl] adj sensuel.

sensuality [,sensjʊ'ælətɪ] n sensualité f.

sensuous ['sensjʊəs] adj [music, arts] qui affecte les sens ; [lips, person] sensuel.

sent [sent] pt & pp ⟶ **send**.

sentence ['sentəns] ◆ n **1.** GRAM phrase f ▸ **sentence structure** structure f de phrase **2.** LAW condamnation f, peine f, sentence f ▸ **to pass sentence on sb** prononcer une condamnation contre qqn. ◆ vt LAW condamner ▸ **to sentence sb to life imprisonment** condamner qqn à la prison à perpétuité.

sententious [sen'tenʃəs] adj sentencieux, pompeux.

sentiment ['sentɪmənt] n **1.** [feeling] sentiment m ; [opinion] sentiment m, avis m, opinion f / **my sentiments exactly** c'est exactement ce que je pense, voilà mon sentiment **2.** [sentimentality] sentimentalité f.

sentimental [,sentɪ'mentl] adj sentimental.

sentimentalism [,sentɪ'mentəlɪzm] n sentimentalisme m.

sentimentality [,sentɪmen'tælətɪ] (pl **sentimentalities**) n sentimentalité f, sensiblerie f pej.

sentimentalize, sentimentalise [,sentɪ'mentəlaɪz] ◆ vt [to others] présenter de façon sentimentale ; [to o.s.] percevoir de façon sentimentale. ◆ vi faire du sentiment.

sentimentally [,sentɪ'mentəlɪ] adv sentimentalement, de manière sentimentale.

sentinel ['sentɪnl] n sentinelle f, factionnaire m.

sentry ['sentrɪ] (pl **sentries**) n sentinelle f, factionnaire m.

Seoul [səʊl] pr n Séoul.

SEP MESSAGING written abbr of **somebody else's problem**.

Sep. (written abbr of September) sept.

separable ['seprəbl] adj séparable.

separate ◆ adj ['seprət] [different, distinct - category, meaning, issue] distinct, à part ; [- incident] différent / **that's quite a separate matter** ça, c'est une toute autre affaire / **they sleep in separate rooms a)** [children] ils ont chacun leur chambre **b)** [couple] ils font chambre à part / **administration and finance are in separate departments** l'administration et les finances relèvent de services différents / **the canteen is separate from the main building** la cantine se trouve à l'extérieur du bâtiment principal / **begin each chapter on a separate page** commencez chaque chapitre sur une nouvelle page / **it happened on four separate occasions** cela s'est produit à quatre reprises / **she likes to keep her home life separate from the office** elle tient à ce que son travail n'empiète pas sur sa vie privée / **the peaches must be kept separate from the lemons** les pêches et les citrons ne doivent pas être mélangés / **he was kept separate from the other children** on le tenait à l'écart or on l'isolait des autres enfants ; [independent - entrance, living quarters] indépendant, particulier ; [- existence, organization] indépendant / **they lead very separate lives** ils mènent chacun leur vie / **they went their separate ways a)** lit [after meeting] ils sont partis chacun de leur côté **b)** fig [in life] chacun a suivi sa route. ◆ n ['seprət] **1.** [in stereo] élément m séparé **2.** US [offprint] tiré m à part. ◆ vt ['sepəreɪt] **1.** [divide, set apart] séparer / **the Bosphorus separates Europe from Asia** le Bosphore sépare l'Europe

de l'Asie / **the seriously ill were separated from the other patients** les malades gravement atteints étaient isolés des autres patients / **the records can be separated into four categories** les disques peuvent être divisés or classés en quatre catégories ; [detach - parts, pieces] séparer, détacher / **the last three coaches will be separated from the rest of the train** les trois derniers wagons seront détachés du reste du train **2.** [keep distinct] séparer, distinguer / **to separate reality from myth** distinguer le mythe de la réalité, faire la distinction entre le mythe et la réalité **3.** CULIN [milk] écrémer ; [egg] séparer. ◆ vi ['sepəreɪt] **1.** [go different ways] se quitter, se séparer **2.** [split up - couple] se séparer, rompre ; [- in boxing, duel] rompre ; POL [party] se scinder **3.** [come apart, divide - liquid] se séparer ; [- parts] se séparer, se détacher, se diviser / **the boosters separate from the shuttle** les propulseurs auxiliaires se détachent de la navette / **the model separates into four parts** la maquette se divise en quatre parties. ◇◇ **separates** pl n [clothes] coordonnés mpl. ◇◇ **separate out** ◆ vt sep séparer, trier. ◆ vi se séparer.

separated ['sepəreɪtɪd] adj [not living together] séparé.

separately ['seprətlɪ] adv **1.** [apart] séparément, à part **2.** [individually] séparément.

separation [,sepə'reɪʃn] n **1.** [division] séparation f **2.** [of couple] séparation f.

separatism ['seprətɪzm] n séparatisme m.

separatist ['seprətɪst] ◆ adj séparatiste. ◆ n séparatiste mf.

sepia ['si:pjə] ◆ n [pigment, print] sépia f. ◆ adj sépia (inv).

Sept. (written abbr of September) sept.

September [sep'tembər] n septembre m. See also **February**.

septet [sep'tet] n septuor m.

septic ['septɪk] adj septique ; [wound] infecté ▸ **to go** or **to become septic** s'infecter ▸ **septic poisoning** septicémie f.

septicaemia UK, **septicemia** US [,septɪ'si:mɪə] n (U) septicémie f.

septic tank n fosse f septique.

sepulcher US = **sepulchre**.

sepulchre UK, **sepulcher** US ['sepəlkər] n sépulcre m.

sequel ['si:kwəl] n **1.** [result, aftermath] conséquence f, suites fpl, conséquences fpl ; [to illness, war] séquelles fpl / **as a sequel to this event** à la suite de cet événement **2.** [to novel, film, etc.] suite f.

sequence ['si:kwəns] ◆ n **1.** [order] suite f, ordre m ▸ **in sequence a)** [in order] par ordre, en série **b)** [one after another] l'un après l'autre ▸ **sequence of tenses** GRAM concordance f des temps **2.** [series] série f ; [in cards] séquence f ▸ **the sequence of events** le déroulement or l'enchaînement des événements **3.** CIN & MUS séquence f ▸ **dance sequence** numéro m de danse **4.** LING & MATH séquence f **5.** BIOL & CHEM séquençage m. ◆ vt **1.** [order] classer, ordonner **2.** BIOL & CHEM faire le séquençage de.

sequencer ['si:kwənsər] n séquenceur m.

sequential [sɪ'kwenʃl] adj **1.** COMPUT séquentiel **2.** fml [following] subséquent.

sequester [sɪ'kwestər] vt **1.** fml [set apart] isoler, mettre à part **2.** fml [shut away] séquestrer **3.** LAW [goods, property] séquestrer, placer sous séquestre.

sequestrate [sɪ'kwestreɪt] vt **1.** LAW séquestrer, placer sous séquestre **2.** fml [confiscate] saisir.

sequin ['si:kwɪn] n paillette f.

Serb [sɜ:b] ◆ n Serbe mf. ◆ adj serbe.

Serbia ['sɜ:bjə] pr n Serbie f / *in Serbia* en Serbie.

Serbian ['sɜ:bjən] ◆ n **1.** [person] Serbe *mf* **2.** LING serbe *m*. ◆ adj serbe.

Serbo-Croat [,sɜ:bəʊ'krəʊæt], **Serbo-Croatian** [,sɜ:bəʊkrəʊ'eɪʃn] ◆ n LING serbo-croate *m*. ◆ adj serbo-croate.

serenade [,serə'neɪd] ◆ n sérénade f. ◆ vt [sing] chanter une sérénade à ; [play] jouer une sérénade à.

serendipity [,serən'dɪpətɪ] n *liter* don de faire des découvertes *(accidentelles)*.

serene [sɪ'ri:n] adj [person, existence, sky] serein ; [sea, lake] calme ▶ **His / Her Serene Highness** *fml* Son Altesse Sérénissime.

serenely [sɪ'ri:nlɪ] adv sereinement, avec sérénité.

serenity [sɪ'renətɪ] n sérénité f.

serf [sɜ:f] n serf *m*, serve f.

serge [sɜ:dʒ] ◆ n serge f. ◆ comp [cloth, trousers] de or en serge.

sergeant ['sɑ:dʒənt] n **1.** [in army] sergent *m* ; US [in air force] sergent-chef *m* ; US caporal-chef *m* **2.** [in police] brigadier *m*.

sergeant major n sergent-chef *m*.

serial ['sɪərɪəl] ◆ n **1.** RADIO & TV feuilleton *m* ▶ **TV serial** feuilleton télévisé ; [in magazine] feuilleton *m* / *published in serial form* publié sous forme de feuilleton **2.** [periodical] périodique *m*. ◆ adj **1.** [in series] en série ; [from series] d'une série ; [forming series] formant une série **2.** [music] sériel **3.** COMPUT [processing, transmission] série *(inv)* ▶ **serial cable** câble f série ▶ **serial port** port *m* série.

serialization, serialisation [,sɪərɪəlaɪ'zeɪʃn] n [of book] publication f en feuilleton ; [of play, film] adaptation f en feuilleton.

serialize, serialise ['sɪərɪəlaɪz] vt [book] publier en feuilleton ; [play, film] adapter en feuilleton ; [in newspaper] publier or faire paraître en feuilleton.

serial killer n tueur *m* en série.

serial killing n ▶ **serial killings** meurtres *mpl* en série.

serially ['sɪərɪəlɪ] adv **1.** MATH en série **2.** PRESS [as series] en feuilleton, sous forme de feuilleton ; [periodically] périodiquement, sous forme de périodique.

serial monogamy n succession f de relations monogamiques.

serial number n [of car, publication] numéro *m* de série ; [of cheque, voucher] numéro *m* ; [of soldier] (numéro *m*) matricule *m*.

series ['sɪərɪ:z] *(pl* series) n **1.** [set, group - gen & CHEM & GEOL] série f ; [sequence - gen & MATH] séquence f, suite f **2.** LING & MUS série f, séquence f **3.** [of cars, clothes] série f **4.** RADIO & TV série f ▶ **TV series** série télévisée ; [in magazine, newspaper] série f d'articles **5.** [collection - of stamps, coins, books] collection f, série f **6.** ELEC série f / *wired in series* branché en série **7.** SPORT série f de matches.

serious ['sɪərɪəs] adj **1.** [not frivolous - suggestion, subject, worker, publication, writer, theatre] sérieux ; [- occasion] solennel / *can I have a serious conversation with you?* est-ce qu'on peut parler sérieusement ? / *she's a serious actress* a) [cinema] elle fait des films sérieux b) [theatre] elle joue dans des pièces sérieuses **2.** [in speech, behaviour] sérieux / *I'm quite serious* je suis tout à fait sérieux, je ne plaisante absolument pas / *is she serious about Peter?* est-ce que c'est sérieux avec Peter ? **3.** [thoughtful - person, expression] sérieux, plein de sérieux ; [- voice, tone] sérieux, grave / *don't look so serious* ne prends pas cet air sérieux ; [careful - examination] sérieux, approfondi ; [- consideration] sérieux, sincère / *to give serious thought* or *consideration to sthg* songer sérieusement à qqch **4.** [grave - mistake, problem,

illness] sérieux, grave / *the situation is serious* la situation est préoccupante / *serious crime* crime *m* / *his condition is described as serious* MED son état est jugé préoccupant ; [considerable - damage] important, sérieux ; [- loss] lourd ; [- doubt] sérieux **5.** *inf* [as intensifier] : *we're talking serious money here* il s'agit de grosses sommes d'argent / *they go in for some really serious drinking at the weekends* le week-end, qu'est-ce qu'ils descendent ! *inf.*

seriously ['sɪərɪəslɪ] adv **1.** [earnestly] sérieusement, avec sérieux ▶ **to take sb / sthg seriously** prendre qqn / qqch au sérieux **2.** [severely - damage] sérieusement, gravement ; [- ill] gravement ; [- injured, wounded] grièvement **3.** *v inf* [very] : *he's seriously rich* il est bourré de fric.

seriousness ['sɪərɪəsnɪs] n **1.** [of person, expression] sérieux *m* ; [of voice, manner] (air *m*) sérieux *m* ; [of intentions, occasion, writing] sérieux *m* ▶ **in all seriousness** sérieusement, en toute sincérité **2.** [of illness, situation, loss] gravité f ; [of allegation] sérieux *m* ; [of damage] importance f, étendue f.

sermon ['sɜ:mən] n **1.** RELIG sermon *m* ▶ **to give** or **to preach a sermon** faire un sermon ▶ **the Sermon on the Mount** BIBLE le Sermon sur la Montagne **2.** *fig & pej* sermon *m*, laïus *m*.

seronegative [,sɪərəʊ'negətɪv] adj séronégatif.

seropositive [,sɪərəʊ'pɒzɪtɪv] adj séropositif.

serotonin [,serə'təʊnɪn] n BIOL & CHEM sérotonine f.

serpent ['sɜ:pənt] n serpent *m*.

SERPS ['sɜ:ps] (abbr of **State Earnings-Related Pension Scheme**) n UK ≃ régime *m* de retraite minimal en Grande-Bretagne.

serrated [sɪ'reɪtɪd] adj [edge] en dents de scie, dentelé ; [scissors, instrument] cranté, en dents de scie ▶ **serrated knike** couteau-scie *m*.

serum ['sɪərəm] *(pl* **serums** or **sera** [-rə]) n sérum *m*.

servant ['sɜ:vənt] n **1.** [in household] domestique *mf* ; [maid] bonne f, servante f ▶ **servants' quarters** appartements *mpl* des domestiques **2.** [of God, of people] serviteur *m*.

serve [sɜ:v] ◆ vt **1.** [employer, monarch, country, God] servir **2.** [in shop, restaurant - customer] servir ▶ **to serve sb with sthg** servir qqch à qqn / *are you being served?* est-ce qu'on s'occupe de vous ? **3.** [provide - with electricity, gas, water] alimenter ; [- with transport service] desservir **4.** [food, drink] servir ▶ **to serve mass** RELIG servir la messe **5.** [be suitable for] servir / *the plank served him as a rudimentary desk* la planche lui servait de bureau rudimentaire / *it serves no useful purpose* cela ne sert à rien de spécial **6.** [term, apprenticeship] faire / *he has served two terms (of office) as president* il a rempli deux mandats présidentiels ▶ **to serve one's time** MIL faire son service ; [prison sentence] faire ▶ **to serve time** faire de la prison **7.** LAW [summons, warrant, writ] notifier, remettre ▶ **to serve sb with a summons, to serve a summons on sb** remettre une assignation à qqn ▶ **to serve sb with a writ, to serve a writ on sb** assigner qqn en justice **8.** SPORT servir **9.** AGR servir **10.** PHR **it serves you right** c'est bien fait pour toi. ◆ vi **1.** [in shop or restaurant, at table] servir ; [be in service - maid, servant] servir **2.** [as soldier] servir ; [in profession] : *he served as treasurer for several years* il a exercé les fonctions de trésorier pendant plusieurs années ; [on committee] : *she serves on the housing committee* elle est membre de la commission au logement **3.** [function, act - as example, warning] servir / *let that serve as a lesson to you!* que cela vous serve de leçon ! ; [be used as] : *their bedroom had to serve as a cloakroom for their guests* leur chambre a dû servir or faire office de vestiaire pour leurs invités **4.** SPORT servir, être au service **5.** RELIG servir la messe. ◆ n SPORT service *m*. ❖ **serve out** ◆ vt sep **1.** [food] servir ;

[provisions] distribuer **2.** [period of time] faire. ◆ vi SPORT sortir son service. ❖ **serve up** vt sep [meal, food] servir ; *fig* [facts, information] servir, débiter.

server ['sɜːvər] n **1.** [at table] serveur *m*, -euse *f* **2.** SPORT serveur *m*, -euse *f* **3.** RELIG servant *m* **4.** [utensil] couvert *m* de service **5.** COMPUT serveur *m*.

service ['sɜːvɪs] ◆ n **1.** [to friend, community, country, God] service *m* ▶ **to offer one's services** proposer ses services ▶ **at your service** à votre service, à votre disposition ▶ **to be of service to sb** rendre service à qqn, être utile à qqn ▶ **to do sb a service** rendre (un) service à qqn **2.** [employment - in firm] service *m* ; [as domestic servant] service ▶ **to be in service** être domestique **3.** [in shop, hotel, restaurant] service *m* / **'10% service included / not included'** 'service 10 % compris / non compris' **4.** MIL service *m* / *he saw active service in Korea* il a servi en Corée, il a fait la campagne de Corée ▶ **the services** les (différentes branches des) forces armées **5.** ADMIN [department, scheme] service *m* **6.** RELIG [Catholic] service *m*, office *m* ; [Protestant] service *m*, culte *m* **7.** [of car, machine - upkeep] entretien *m* ; [- overhaul] révision *f* **8.** [working order - esp of machine] service *m* ▶ **to come into service** [system, bridge] entrer en service **9.** [set of tableware] service *m* **10.** SPORT service *m* **11.** LAW [of summons, writ] signification *f*, notification *f*. ◆ comp **1.** [entrance, hatch, stairs] de service **2.** AUTO & MECH [manual, record] d'entretien **3.** MIL [family, pay] de militaire ; [conditions] dans les forces armées. ◆ vt **1.** [overhaul - central heating, car] réviser **2.** FIN [debt] assurer le service de **3.** AGR [subj: bull, stallion] servir. ❖ **services** npl **1.** UK [on motorway] aire *f* de service **2.** COMM & ECON services *mpl* / *more and more people will be working in services* de plus en plus de gens travailleront dans le tertiaire.

serviceable ['sɜːvɪsəbl] adj **1.** [durable - clothes, material] qui fait de l'usage, qui résiste à l'usure ; [- machine, construction] durable, solide **2.** [useful - clothing, tool] commode, pratique **3.** [usable] utilisable, qui peut servir **4.** [ready for use] prêt à servir.

service area n **1.** AUTO [on motorway] aire *f* de service **2.** RADIO zone *f* desservie or de réception.

service charge n service *m*.

service industry n industrie *f* de services.

serviceman ['sɜːvɪsmən] (*pl* **servicemen** [-mən]) n **1.** MIL militaire *m* **2.** US [mechanic] dépanneur *m*.

service provider n **1.** [gen] fournisseur *m* de services **2.** [for Internet] fournisseur *m* d'accès.

service station n station-service *f*.

servicewoman ['sɜːvɪs,wʊmən] (*pl* **servicewomen** [-,wɪmɪn]) n femme *f* soldat.

servicing ['sɜːvɪsɪŋ] n **1.** [of heating, car] entretien *m* **2.** [by transport] desserte *f*.

serviette [,sɜːvɪ'et] n UK serviette *f* (de table) ▶ **serviette ring** rond *m* de serviette.

servile ['sɜːvaɪl] adj [person, behaviour] servile, obséquieux ; [admiration, praise] servile ; [condition, task] servile, d'esclave.

servility [sɜː'vɪlətɪ] n servilité *f*.

serving ['sɜːvɪŋ] ◆ n **1.** [of drinks, meal] service *m* ▶ **serving dish** plat *m* de service **2.** [helping] portion *f*, part *f* ▶ **serving spoon** grande cuillère *f* (pour servir). ◆ adj ADMIN [member, chairman] actuel, en exercice.

sesame ['sesəmɪ] n sésame *m* ▶ **open sesame!** Sésame, ouvre-toi !

sesame seed n graine *f* de sésame.

session ['seʃn] n **1.** ADMIN, LAW & POL séance *f*, session *f* / *this court is now in session* l'audience est ouverte / *the House is not in session during the summer months* la Chambre ne siège pas pendant les mois d'été

▶ **to go into secret session** siéger à huis clos **2.** [interview, meeting, sitting] séance *f* ; [for painter, photographer] séance *f* de pose / *a drinking session* une beuverie **3.** SCH [classes] cours *mpl* **4.** US & Scot UNIV [term] trimestre *m* ; [year] année *f* universitaire **5.** RELIG conseil *m* presbytéral.

session musician n musicien *m*, -enne *f* de studio.

SET® (abbr of secure electronic transaction) n COMPUT SET® *f*.

set [set] (*pt & pp* set, *cont* setting) ◆ vt

A. PLACE, LOCATE OR RANK **1.** [put in specified place or position] mettre, poser / *she set the steaming bowl before him* elle plaça le bol fumant devant lui **2.** (*usu passive*) [locate, situate - building, story] situer / *the house is set in large grounds* la maison est située dans un grand parc / *the story is set in Tokyo* l'histoire se passe or se déroule à Tokyo **3.** [adjust - gen] régler ; [- mechanism] mettre / *I've set the alarm for six* j'ai mis le réveil à (sonner pour) six heures / *I set my watch to New York time* j'ai réglé ma montre à l'heure de New York **4.** [fix into position] mettre, fixer ; [jewel, diamond] sertir, monter ▶ **to set a bone** réduire une fracture **5.** [lay, prepare in advance - table] mettre ; [- trap] poser, tendre **6.** [place - in hierarchy] placer / *they set a high value on creativity* ils accordent une grande valeur à la créativité **7.** [establish - date, schedule, price, terms] fixer, déterminer ; [- rule, guideline, objective, target] établir ; [- mood, precedent] créer / *you've set yourself a tough deadline* or *a tough deadline for yourself* vous vous êtes fixé un délai très court ▶ **to set a new world record** établir un nouveau record mondial.

B. CHANGE OF STATE OR ACTIVITY **1.** ▶ **to set sthg alight** or **on fire** mettre le feu à qqch ▶ **to set sb against sb** monter qqn contre qqn ▶ **to set the dogs on sb** lâcher les chiens sur qqn / *it will set the country on the road to economic recovery* cela va mettre le pays sur la voie de la reprise économique / *his failure set him thinking* son échec lui a donné à réfléchir **2.** [make firm, rigid] : *his face was set in a frown* son visage était figé dans une grimace renfrognée **3.** [hair] ▶ **to set sb's hair** faire une mise en plis à qqn.

C. POSE OR ASSIGN **1.** [pose - problem] poser ; [assign - task] fixer / *I've set myself the task of writing to them regularly* je me suis fixé la tâche de leur écrire régulièrement **2.** UK SCH [exam] composer, choisir les questions de ; [books, texts] mettre au programme / *she set the class a maths exercise* or *she set a maths exercise for the class* elle a donné un exercice de maths à la classe.

◆ vi **1.** [sun, stars] se coucher **2.** [become firm - glue, cement, plaster, jelly, yoghurt] prendre **3.** [bone] se ressouder **4.** (*with infinitive*) [start] se mettre / *he set to work* il s'est mis au travail.

◆ n **1.** [of facts, conditions, characteristics] ensemble *m* ; [of people] groupe *m* ; [of events, decisions, questions] série *f*, suite *f* ; [of numbers, names, instructions, stamps, weights] série *f* ; [of tools, keys, golf clubs, sails] jeu *m* ; [of books] collection *f* ; [of furniture] ensemble *m* ; [of dishes] service *m* ; [of tyres] train *m* ; PRINT [of proofs, characters] jeu *m* / *they make a set* ils vont ensemble / *given another set of circumstances, things might have turned out differently* dans d'autres circonstances, les choses auraient pu se passer différemment / *a full set of the encyclopedia* une encyclopédie complète / *the cups / the chairs are sold in sets of six* les tasses / les chaises sont vendues par six / *a set of matching luggage* un ensemble de valises assorties / *a set of table / bed linen* une parure de table / de lit ▶ **badminton / chess set** jeu de badminton / d'échecs **2.** [social group] cercle *m*, milieu *m* **3.** MATH ensemble *m* **4.** [electrical device] appareil *m* ; RADIO & TV poste *m* ▶ **a colour TV set** un poste de télévision or un téléviseur couleur **5.** SPORT set *m*, manche *f* **6.** CIN, THEAT &

TV [scenery] décor *m* ; [place & CIN & TV] plateau *m* ; THEAT scène *f* ▸ **on (the) set a)** CIN & TV sur le plateau **b)** THEAT sur scène. ✧ adj **1.** [specified, prescribed - rule, quantity, sum, wage] fixe / *meals are at set times* les repas sont servis à heures fixes ▸ **set menu** or **meal** 🇬🇧 menu *m* **2.** [fixed, rigid - ideas, views] arrêté ; [-smile, frown] figé / *her day followed a set routine* sa journée se déroulait selon un rituel immuable ▸ **set expression** or **phrase** GRAM expression *f* figée **3.** [intent, resolute] résolu, déterminé ▸ **to be set on** or **upon sthg** vouloir qqch à tout prix / *I'm (dead) set on finishing it tonight* je suis (absolument) déterminé à le finir ce soir / *he's dead set against it* il s'y oppose formellement **4.** [ready, in position] prêt **5.** [likely] probablement. ✧ **set about** vt insep **1.** [start - task] se mettre à / *I didn't know how to set about it* je ne savais pas comment m'y prendre **2.** [attack] attaquer, s'en prendre à. ✧ **set against** vt sep [friends, family] monter contre. ✧ **set apart** vt sep **1.** *(usu passive)* [place separately] mettre à part or de côté **2.** [distinguish] distinguer. ✧ **set aside** vt sep **1.** [put down - knitting, book] poser **2.** [reserve, keep - time, place] réserver ; [-money] mettre de côté **3.** [arable land] mettre en friche **3.** [overlook, disregard] mettre de côté, oublier, passer sur **4.** [reject - dogma, proposal, offer] rejeter ; [annul - contract, will] annuler ; LAW [verdict, judgment] casser. ✧ **set back** vt sep **1.** [delay - plans, progress] retarder / *his illness set him back a month in his work* sa maladie l'a retardé d'un mois dans son travail **2.** *inf* [cost] coûter. ✧ **set down** vt sep **1.** [tray, bag, etc.] poser **2.** 🇬🇧 [passenger] déposer **3.** [note, record] noter, inscrire **4.** [establish - rule, condition] établir, fixer. ✧ **set forth** ✦ vi *liter* = **set off.** ✧ vt insep *fml* [expound - plan, objections] exposer, présenter. ✧ **set in** vi [problems] survenir, surgir ; [disease] se déclarer ; [winter] commencer ; [night] tomber / *the bad weather has set in for the winter* le mauvais temps s'est installé pour tout l'hiver / *panic set in* **a)** [began] la panique éclata **b)** [lasted] la panique s'installa. ✧ **set off** ✦ vi partir, se mettre en route / *after lunch, we set off again* après le déjeuner, nous avons repris la route. ✦ vt sep **1.** [alarm] déclencher ; [bomb] faire exploser ; [fireworks] faire partir **2.** [reaction, process, war] déclencher, provoquer / *to set sb off laughing* faire rire qqn **3.** [enhance] mettre en valeur. ✧ **set on** = **set upon.** ✧ **set out** ✦ vi **1.** = **set off 2.** [undertake course of action] entreprendre / *he has trouble finishing what he sets out to do* il a du mal à terminer ce qu'il entreprend / *I can't remember now what I set out to do* je ne me souviens plus de ce que je voulais faire à l'origine. ✦ vt sep **1.** [arrange - chairs, game pieces] disposer ; [spread out - merchandise] étaler **2.** [design] concevoir **3.** [present] exposer, présenter. ✧ **set to** vi [begin work] commencer, s'y mettre. ✧ **set up** ✦ vt sep **1.** [install - equipment, computer] installer ; [put in place - roadblock] installer, disposer ; [-experiment] préparer / *everything's set up for the show* tout est préparé or prêt pour le spectacle ; *fig* : *to set up a meeting* organiser une réunion **2.** [erect, build - tent, furniture kit, crane, flagpole] monter ; [-shed, shelter] construire ; [-monument, statue] ériger ▸ **to set up camp** installer or dresser le camp **3.** [start up, institute - business, scholarship] créer ; [-hospital, school] fonder ; [-committee, task force] constituer ; [-system of government, republic] instaurer ; [-programme, review process, system] mettre en place ; [-inquiry] ouvrir ▸ **to set up house** or **home** s'installer **4.** [financially, in business] installer, établir / *she could finally set herself up as an accountant* elle pourrait enfin s'installer comme comptable **5.** [provide] : *she can set you up with a guide / the necessary papers* elle peut vous procurer un guide / les papiers qu'il vous faut **6.** [restore energy to] remonter, remettre sur pied **7.** *inf* [frame] monter un coup contre / *she claims she was set up* elle prétend

qu'elle est victime d'un coup monté. ✦ vi s'installer, s'établir. ✧ **set upon** vt insep [physically or verbally] attaquer, s'en prendre à.

setaside n mise *f* en jachère.

setback ['setbæk] n revers *m*, échec *m* ; [minor] contretemps *m*.

SETE MESSAGING written abbr of **smiling ear to ear.**

set piece n **1.** ART, LITER & MUS morceau *m* de bravoure **2.** [fireworks] pièce *f* (de feu) d'artifice **3.** [of scenery] élément *m* de décor.

set point n TENNIS balle *f* de set.

setsquare ['setskweər] n équerre *f* (à dessiner).

settee [se'tiː] n canapé *m*.

setter ['setər] n **1.** [dog] setter *m* **2.** [of jewels] sertisseur *m*.

setting ['setɪŋ] n **1.** [of sun, moon] coucher *m* **2.** [situation, surroundings] cadre *m*, décor *m* ; THEAT décor *m* / *they photographed the foxes in their natural setting* ils ont photographié les renards dans leur milieu naturel / *the film has Connemara as its setting* le film a pour cadre le Connemara **3.** [position, level - of machine, instrument] réglage *m* **4.** [for jewels] monture *f* ; [of jewels] sertissage *m* **5.** [at table] set *m* de table **6.** MUS [of poem, play] mise *f* en musique ; [for instruments] arrangement *m*, adaptation *f* **7.** [of fracture] réduction *f* ; [in plaster] plâtrage *m* **8.** [of jam] prise *f* ; [of cement] prise *f*, durcissement *m* **9.** TYPO composition *f*.

settle ['setl] ✦ vt **1.** [solve - question, issue] régler ; [-dispute, quarrel, differences] régler, trancher **2.** [determine, agree on - date, price] fixer / *that's settled then, I'll meet you at 8 o'clock* alors c'est entendu or convenu, on se retrouve à 8 h / *that settles it, he's fired* trop c'est trop, il est renvoyé ! **3.** [pay - debt, account, bill] régler **4.** [install] installer ▸ **to get settled** s'installer (confortablement) ; [arrange, place - on table, surface] installer, poser (soigneusement) **5.** [colonize] coloniser **6.** [calm - nerves, stomach] calmer, apaiser **7.** LAW [money, allowance, estate] constituer ▸ **to settle an annuity on sb** constituer une rente à qqn. ✦ vi **1.** [go to live - gen] s'installer, s'établir ; [-colonist] s'établir **2.** [become calm - nerves, stomach, storm] s'apaiser, se calmer ; [-situation] s'arranger **3.** [install o.s. - in new flat, bed] s'installer ; [adapt - to circumstances] s'habituer **4.** [come to rest - snow] tenir ; [-dust, sediment] se déposer ; [-bird, insect, eyes] se poser **5.** [spread] : *an eerie calm settled over the village* un calme inquiétant retomba sur le village **6.** CONSTR [road, wall, foundations] se tasser **7.** [financially] ▸ **to settle with sb for sthg** régler le prix de qqch à qqn ▸ **to settle out of court** régler une affaire à l'amiable **8.** [decide] se décider / *they've settled on a Volkswagen* ils se sont décidés pour une Volkswagen / *they've settled on Rome for their honeymoon* ils ont décidé d'aller passer leur lune de miel à Rome. ✦ n [seat] banquette *f* à haut dossier. ✧ **settle down** ✦ vi **1.** [in armchair, at desk] s'installer ; [in new home] s'installer, se fixer ; [at school, in job] s'habituer, s'adapter **2.** *fig* [become stable - people] se ranger, s'assagir **3.** [concentrate, apply o.s.] ▸ **to settle down to do sthg** se mettre à faire qqch **4.** [become calm - excitement] s'apaiser ; [-situation] s'arranger. ✦ vt sep [person] installer. ✧ **settle for** vt insep accepter, se contenter de. ✧ **settle in** vi [at new house] s'installer ; [at new school, job] s'habituer, s'adapter. ✧ **settle into** ✦ vt insep [job, routine] s'habituer à, s'adapter à. ✦ vt sep installer dans. ✧ **settle up** ✦ vi régler (la note). ✦ vt sep régler.

settled ['setld] adj **1.** [stable, unchanging - person] rangé, établi ; [-life] stable, régulier ; [-habits] régulier / *he's very settled in his ways* il est très routinier, il a ses petites habitudes **2.** METEOR [calm] beau *(before vowel or silent 'h'*

bel, f belle) / *the weather will remain settled* le temps demeurera au beau fixe **3.** [inhabited] peuplé ; [colonized] colonisé **4.** [fixed - population] fixe, établi **5.** [account, bill] réglé.

settlement ['setlmənt] n **1.** [resolution - of question, dispute] règlement *m*, solution *f* ; [of problem] solution *f* **2.** [payment] règlement *m* ▸ **out-of-court settlement** règlement à l'amiable **3.** [agreement] accord *m* ▸ **to reach a settlement** parvenir à or conclure un accord ▸ **wage settlement** accord salarial **4.** [decision - on details, date] décision *f* **5.** LAW [financial] donation *f* ; [dowry] dot *f* ; [of annuity] constitution *f* ▸ **to make a settlement on sb** faire une donation à or en faveur de qqn **6.** [colony] colonie *f* ; [village] village *m* ; [dwellings] habitations *fpl* **7.** [colonization] colonisation *f*, peuplement *m* **8.** [of contents, road] tassement *m* ; [of sediment] dépôt *m*.

settler ['setlər] n colonisateur *m*, -trice *f*, colon *m*.

set-to *(pl* set-tos*)* n *inf* [fight] bagarre *f* ; [argument] prise *f* de bec.

set-top box n décodeur *m*.

set-up n **1.** [arrangement, system] organisation *f*, système *m* / *the project manager explained the set-up to me* le chef de projet m'a expliqué comment les choses fonctionnaient or étaient organisées / *this is the set-up* voici comment ça se passe / *it's an odd set-up* c'est une drôle de situation **2.** *inf* [frame-up] coup *m* monté.

set-up costs n frais *mpl* de lancement.

set-up fee n FIN frais *mpl* d'inscription.

setup file n fichier *m* de configuration.

setup program n COMPUT programme *m* d'installation.

seven ['sevn] ◆ det sept. ◆ n sept *m inv*. ◆ pron sept. See also **five**.

seventeen [,sevn'ti:n] ◆ det dix-sept. ◆ n dix-sept *m inv*. ◆ pron dix-sept. See also **five**.

seventeenth [,sevn'ti:nθ] ◆ det dix-septième. ◆ n [ordinal] dix-septième *mf* ; [fraction] dix-septième *m*. See also **fifth**.

seventh ['sevnθ] ◆ det septième. ◆ n [ordinal] septième *mf* ; [fraction] septième *m* ; MUS septième *f*. ◆ adv [in contest] en septième position, à la septième place. See also **fifth**.

seventh grade n ⓤⓈ SCH *classe de l'enseignement secondaire correspondant à la cinquième (11-12 ans).*

seventh heaven n le septième ciel ▸ **to be in (one's) seventh heaven** être au septième ciel.

seventieth ['sevntjəθ] ◆ det soixante-dixième. ◆ n [ordinal] soixante-dixième *mf* ; [fraction] soixante-dixième *m*. See also **fifth**.

seventy ['sevntɪ] *(pl* seventies*)* ◆ det soixante-dix. ◆ n soixante-dix *m inv*. ◆ pron soixante-dix. See also **fifty**.

sever ['sevər] ◆ vt **1.** [cut off - rope, limb] couper, trancher **2.** [cease - relationship, contact] cesser, rompre. ◆ vi se rompre, casser, céder.

several ['sevrəl] ◆ det plusieurs. ◆ pron plusieurs / *several of us* plusieurs d'entre nous / *there are several of them* ils sont plusieurs. ◆ adj LAW [separate] distinct.

severance ['sevrəns] n [of relations] rupture *f*, cessation *f* ; [of communications, contact] interruption *f*, rupture *f*.

severance pay n *(U)* indemnité *f* or indemnités *fpl* de licenciement.

severe [sɪ'vɪər] adj **1.** [harsh - criticism, punishment, regulations] sévère, dur ; [- conditions] difficile, rigoureux ; [- storm] violent ; [- winter, climate] rude, rigoureux ; [- frost] intense ; [- competition] rude, serré ; [strict - tone, person]

sévère **2.** [serious - illness, handicap] grave, sérieux ; [- defeat] grave ; [- pain] vif, aigu (aiguë) **3.** [austere - style, dress, haircut] sévère, strict.

severely [sɪ'vɪəlɪ] adv **1.** [harshly - punish, treat, criticize] sévèrement, durement ; [strictly] strictement, sévèrement **2.** [seriously - ill, injured, disabled] gravement, sérieusement **3.** [austerely] d'une manière austère, sévèrement.

severity [sɪ'verətɪ] n **1.** [harshness - of judgment, treatment, punishment, criticism] sévérité *f*, dureté *f* ; [- of climate, weather] rigueur *f*, dureté *f* ; [- of frost, cold] intensité *f* **2.** [seriousness - of illness, injury, handicap] gravité *f*, sévérité *f* **3.** [austerity] austérité *f*, sévérité *f*.

sew [səʊ] *(pt* sewed, *pp* sewn [səʊn] *or* sewed*)* ◆ vt coudre / *to sew a button on (to) a shirt* coudre or recoudre un bouton sur une chemise. ◆ vi coudre, faire de la couture. ❖ **sew up** vt sep **1.** [tear, slit] coudre, recoudre ; [seam] faire ; MED [wound] coudre, recoudre, suturer ; [hole] raccommoder **2.** *inf & fig* [arrange, settle - contract] régler ; [- details] régler, mettre au point ; [control] contrôler, monopoliser.

sewage ['su:ɪdʒ] n *(U)* vidanges *fpl*, eaux *fpl* d'égout, eaux-vannes *fpl* ▸ **the sewage system** les égouts *mpl* ▸ **sewage disposal** évacuation *f* des eaux usées.

sewage farm ⓤⓀ, **sewage works** ⓤⓀ, **sewage plant** ⓤⓈ n champs *mpl* d'épandage.

sewer ['suər] n [drain] égout *m*.

sewerage ['suərɪdʒ] n *(U)* **1.** [disposal] évacuation *f* des eaux usées **2.** [system] égouts *mpl*, réseau *m* d'égouts **3.** [sewage] eaux *fpl* d'égout.

sewing ['səʊɪŋ] ◆ n **1.** [activity] couture *f* **2.** [piece of work] couture *f*, ouvrage *m*. ◆ comp [basket, kit] à couture ; [cotton] à coudre ; [class] de couture.

sewing machine n machine *f* à coudre.

sewn [səʊn] pp ⟶ sew.

sex [seks] ◆ n **1.** [gender] sexe *m* / *the club is open to both sexes* le club est ouvert aux personnes des deux sexes ▸ **single sex school** établissement *m* scolaire non mixte **2.** *(U)* [sexual intercourse] relations *fpl* sexuelles, rapports *mpl* (sexuels) ▸ **to have sex with sb** avoir des rapports (sexuels) or faire l'amour avec qqn **3.** [sexual activity] sexe *m*. ◆ comp sexuel ▸ **sex discrimination** discrimination *f* sexuelle ▸ **sex life** vie *f* sexuelle ▸ **sex scandal** affaire *f* de mœurs ▸ **sex worker** prostitué *m*, -e *f*. ◆ vt [animal] déterminer le sexe de. ❖ **sex up** vt sep **1.** [image, style] rendre plus sexy **2.** *fig* [text, document, story] enjoliver.

sex abuse n *(U)* sévices or abus *mpl* sexuels.

sex appeal n sex-appeal *m*.

sex change n changement *m* de sexe / *to have a sex change* changer de sexe.

sexed [sekst] adj BIOL & ZOOL sexué ▸ **to be highly sexed** [person] avoir une forte libido.

sex education n éducation *f* sexuelle.

sexism ['seksɪzm] n sexisme *m*.

sexist ['seksɪst] ◆ adj sexiste. ◆ n sexiste *mf*.

sex maniac n obsédé *m* sexuel, obsédée *f* sexuelle.

sex object n objet *m* sexuel.

sex offender n auteur *m* d'un délit sexuel.

sex pest n *inf* dragueur *m* infernal.

sexploits ['seksplɔɪts] pl n *inf & hum* aventures *fpl* sexuelles.

sex shop n sex-shop *m*.

sex symbol n sex-symbol *m*.

sextet [seks'tet] n sextuor *m*.

sexting ['sekstɪŋ] n ⓤⓈ envoi de SMS à caractère sexuel.

sex tourism n tourisme *m* sexuel.

sex toy n gadget *m* érotique, sex-toy *m*.

sextuplet ['sekstjʊplɪt] n sextuplé *m*, -e *f*.

sexual ['seksʊəl] adj sexuel.

sexual abuse n *(U)* sévices or abus *mpl* sexuels.

sexual assault n agression *f* sexuelle.

sexual equality n égalité *f* des sexes.

sexual harassment n harcèlement *m* sexuel.

sexual intercourse n *(U)* rapports *mpl* sexuels.

sexuality [,seksʊ'ælətɪ] n sexualité *f*.

sexually ['seksʊəlɪ] adv sexuellement ▸ **to be sexually assaulted** être victime d'une agression sexuelle ▸ **sexually transmitted disease** maladie *f* sexuellement transmissible.

sexual orientation n orientation *f* sexuelle.

sex-worker n travailleur *m* sexuel, travailleuse *f* sexuelle.

sexy ['seksɪ] (*compar* sexier, *superl* sexiest) adj *inf & lit* [person] sexy (*inv*) ; *inf & fig* [product] sympa.

Seychelles [seɪ'ʃelz] pl pr n ▸ **the Seychelles** les Seychelles *fpl* / **in the Seychelles** aux Seychelles.

SF [es'ef] (*abbr of* science-fiction) n *(U)* SF *f*.

SFO (*abbr of* Serious Fraud Office) n *service britannique de la répression des fraudes.*

SG n *abbr of* Surgeon General.

Sgt (*written abbr of* sergeant) Sgt.

sh [ʃ] interj ▸ **sh!** chut !

shabby ['ʃæbɪ] (*compar* shabbier, *superl* shabbiest) adj **1.** [clothes] râpé, élimé ; [carpet, curtains] usé, élimé ; [person] pauvrement vêtu ; [hotel, house] miteux, minable ; [furniture] pauvre, minable ; [street, area] misérable, miteux **2.** [mean - behaviour, treatment] mesquin, vil, bas **3.** [medio-cre - excuse] piètre ; [- reasoning] médiocre.

shack [ʃæk] n cabane *f*, case *f*, hutte *f*. ❖ **shack up** vi *inf* ▸ **to shack up with sb** s'installer avec qqn.

shackle ['ʃækl] vt *lit* enchaîner, mettre aux fers ; *fig* entraver. ❖ **shackles** pl n *lit* chaînes *fpl*, fers *mpl* ; *fig* chaînes *fpl*, entraves *fpl*.

shade [ʃeɪd] ❖ n **1.** [shadow] ombre *f* / *45 degrees in the shade* 45 degrés à l'ombre / *in the shade of a tree* à l'ombre d'un arbre / *these trees give plenty of shade* ces arbres font beaucoup d'ombre ; ART ombre *f*, ombres *fpl* / *the use of light and shade in the painting* l'utilisation des ombres et des lumières or du clair-obscur dans le tableau ▸ **to put sb in the shade** éclipser qqn **2.** [variety - of colour] nuance *f*, ton *m* ; [nuance - of meaning, opinion] nuance *f* / *all shades of political opinion were represented* toutes les nuances politiques étaient représentées, tous les courants politiques étaient représentés **3.** [for lamp] abat-jour *m inv* ; [for eyes] visière *f* ; US [blind - on window] store *m* **4.** *liter* [spirit] ombre *f*. ❖ vt **1.** [screen - eyes, face] abriter ; [- place] ombrager, donner de l'ombre à / *he shaded his eyes (from the sun) with his hand* il a mis sa main devant ses yeux pour se protéger du soleil **2.** [cover - light, light-bulb] masquer, voiler **3.** ART [painting] ombrer ; [by hatching] hachurer / *I've shaded the background green* j'ai coloré l'arrière-plan en vert. ❖ vi [merge] se dégrader, se fondre / *the blue shades into purple* le bleu se fond en violet. ❖ **shades** pl n **1.** *liter* [growing darkness] : *the shades of evening* les ombres du soir **2.** *inf* [sunglasses] lunettes *fpl* de soleil **3.** [reminder, echo] échos *mpl*. ❖ **a shade** adv phr : *she's a shade better today* elle va un tout petit peu mieux aujourd'hui. ❖ **shade in** vt sep [background] hachurer, tramer ; [with colour] colorer.

shading ['ʃeɪdɪŋ] n *(U)* ART [in painting] ombres *fpl* ; [hatching] hachure *f*, tramage *m*, hachures *fpl* ; *fig* [differ-ence] nuance *f*.

shadow ['ʃædəʊ] ❖ n **1.** [of figure, building] ombre *f* / *the shadow of suspicion fell on them* on a commencé à les soupçonner / *she's a shadow of her former self* elle n'est plus que l'ombre d'elle-même ▸ **to live in sb's shadow** vivre dans l'ombre de qqn ▸ **to cast a shadow on** or **over sthg** *lit & fig* projeter or jeter une ombre sur qqch **2.** [under eyes] cerne *m* **3.** [shade] ombre *f*, ombrage *m* / *she was standing in (the) shadow* elle se tenait dans l'ombre **4.** [slightest bit] ombre *f* ▸ **without** or **beyond a** or **the shadow of a doubt** sans l'ombre d'un doute **5.** [detective] : *I want a shadow put on him* je veux qu'on le fasse suivre **6.** [companion] ombre *f* / *he follows me everywhere like a shadow* il me suit comme mon ombre, il ne me lâche pas d'une semelle **7.** MED [on lung] voile *m*. ❖ vt **1.** [follow secretly] filer, prendre en filature **2.** *liter* [screen from light] ombrager. ❖ adj UK POL ▸ **shadow cabinet** cabinet *m* fan-tôme ▸ **the Shadow Education Secretary** / **Defence Secretary** le porte-parole de l'opposition pour l'éducation / pour la défense nationale. ❖ **shadows** pl n *liter* [darkness] ombre *f*, ombres *fpl*, obscurité *f*.

 Shadow cabinet

Le cabinet fantôme est composé des parle-mentaires du principal parti de l'opposition, qui deviendraient ministres si leur parti arrivait au pouvoir.

shadowy ['ʃædəʊɪ] adj **1.** [shady - woods, path] ombragé **2.** [vague - figure, outline] vague, indistinct ; [- plan] vague, imprécis.

shady ['ʃeɪdɪ] (*compar* shadier, *superl* shadiest) adj **1.** [place] ombragé **2.** *inf* [person, behaviour] louche, sus-pect ; [dealings] louche.

shaft [ʃɑːft] ❖ n **1.** [of spear] hampe *f* ; [of feather] tuyau *m* ; ARCHIT [of column] fût *m* ; ANAT [of bone] diaphyse *f* **2.** [of axe, tool, golf club] manche *m* **3.** [of cart, carriage] brancard *m*, limon *m* **4.** MECH [for propeller, in ma-chine] arbre *m* **5.** [in mine] puits *m* ; [of ventilator, chimney] puits *m*, cheminée *f* ; [of lift] cage *f* **6.** [of light] rai *m* **7.** *liter* [arrow] flèche *f* **8.** PHR ▸ **to get the shaft** US *v inf*: *he got the shaft* **a)** [got shouted at] qu'est-ce qu'il s'est pris ! **b)** [got fired] il s'est fait virer. ❖ vt **1.** *v inf* [cheat] ▸ **to get shafted** se faire rouler **2.** *vulg* [have sex with] baiser.

shag [ʃæg] (*pt & pp* shagged) ❖ n **1.** [of hair, wool] toison *f* ▸ **shag (pile) carpet** moquette *f* à poils longs **2.** ▸ **shag (tobacco)** tabac *m* (très fort) **3.** ORNITH cormo-ran *m* huppé **4.** *vulg* [sex] ▸ **to have a shag** baiser **5.** US [ballboy] ramasseur *m* de balles. ❖ vt **1.** *v inf* [tire] cre-ver ▸ **to be shagged (out)** être complètement crevé or HS **2.** *vulg* [have sex with] baiser **3.** US [fetch] aller chercher. ❖ vi *vulg* [have sex with] baiser.

shagged [ʃægd], **shagged out** adj UK *inf* [ex-hausted] crevé.

shaggy ['ʃægɪ] (*compar* shaggier, *superl* shaggiest) adj [hair, beard] hirsute, touffu ; [eyebrows] hérissé, broussail-leux ; [dog, pony] à longs poils (rudes) ; [carpet, rug] à longs poils.

shaggy-dog story n histoire *f* sans queue ni tête.

shake [ʃeɪk] (*pt* shook [ʃʊk], *pp* shaken ['ʃeɪkn]) ❖ vt **1.** [rug, tablecloth, person] secouer ; [bottle, cocktail, dice] agiter ; [subj: earthquake, explosion] ébranler, faire trembler / *he shook his head* **a)** [in refusal] il a dit or fait non de la tête **b)** [in resignation, sympathy] il a hoché la tête **2.** [brandish] brandir / *he shook his fist at him* il l'a menacé du poing **3.** [hand] serrer ▸ **to shake hands with sb, to shake sb's hand** serrer la main à qqn / *they shook* *hands* ils se sont serré la main **4.** [upset - faith, confidence, health, reputation] ébranler **5.** [amaze] bouleverser, ébranler. ◆ *vi* **1.** [ground, floor, house] trembler, être ébranlé ; [leaves, branches] trembler, être agité **2.** [with emotion - voice] trembler, frémir ; [- body, knees] trembler */ to shake with laughter* se tordre de rire */ to shake with fear* trembler de peur **3.** [in agreement] : *let's shake on it!* tope-là ! */ they shook on the deal* ils ont scellé leur accord par une poignée de main. ◆ *n* **1.** secousse *f*, ébranlement *m* ▶ **to give sb / sthg a shake** secouer qqn / qqch */ with a shake of his head* [in refusal, in resignation, sympathy] avec un hochement de tête **2.** *inf* [moment] instant *m* ▶ **in two shakes (of a lamb's tail)** en un clin d'œil **3.** ⓤⓢ *inf* [earthquake] tremblement *m* de terre **4.** ⓤⓢ *inf* [milk shake] milkshake *m* **5.** ⓤⓢ *inf* [deal] : *he'll give you a fair shake* il ne te roulera pas **6.** MUS trille *m*. ❖ **shake down** ◆ *vi* **1.** *inf* [go to bed] coucher **2.** *inf* [adapt - to new situation, job] s'habituer. ◆ *vt sep* **1.** [from tree] faire tomber en secouant **2.** ⓤⓢ *inf* ▶ **to shake sb down a)** [rob] racketter qqn **b)** [search] fouiller qqn **3.** ⓤⓢ *inf* [test] essayer, tester. ❖ **shake off** *vt sep* **1.** [physically] secouer ▶ **to shake the sand / water off sthg** secouer le sable / l'eau de qqch **2.** [get rid of - cold, pursuer, depression] se débarrasser de ; [- habit] se défaire de, se débarrasser de. ❖ **shake out** *vt sep* **1.** [tablecloth, rug] (bien) secouer ; [sail, flag] déferler, déployer ; [bag] vider en secouant **2.** [rouse - person] : *I can't seem to shake him out of his apathy* je n'arrive pas à le tirer de son apathie. ❖ **shake up** *vt sep* **1.** [physically - pillow] secouer, taper ; [- bottle] agiter **2.** *fig* [upset - person] secouer, bouleverser **3.** [rouse - person] secouer **4.** *inf* [overhaul - organization, company] remanier, réorganiser de fond en comble. ❖ **shakes** *pl n inf* ▶ **to have the shakes** avoir la tremblote */ it's no great shakes* [film, book, restaurant, etc.] ça ne casse pas des briques */ he's no great shakes* il est insignifiant.

shakedown ['ʃeɪkdaʊn] ◆ *n* **1.** [bed] lit *m* improvisé or de fortune **2.** *inf* [of ship, plane - test] essai *m* ; [flight, voyage] voyage *m* or vol *m* d'essai **3.** ⓤⓢ *v inf* [search] fouille *f* **4.** ⓤⓢ *v inf* [extortion] racket *m*. ◆ *adj* [test, flight, voyage] d'essai.

shaken ['ʃeɪkn] ◆ *pp* ⟶ **shake.** ◆ *adj* [upset] secoué ; [stronger] bouleversé, ébranlé.

shakeout ['ʃeɪkaʊt] *n* ECON dégraissage *m*.

Shakespearean [ʃeɪk'spɪərɪən] *adj* shakespearien.

shake-up *n inf* **1.** [of company, organization] remaniement *m*, restructuration *f* **2.** [emotional] bouleversement *m*.

shakily ['ʃeɪkɪlɪ] *adv* **1.** [unsteadily - walk] d'un pas chancelant or mal assuré ; [- write] d'une main tremblante ; [- speak] d'une voix tremblante or chevrotante **2.** [uncertainly] d'une manière hésitante or peu assurée.

shaky ['ʃeɪkɪ] (*compar* **shakier,** *superl* **shakiest**) *adj* **1.** [unsteady - chair, table] branlant, peu solide ; [- ladder] branlant, peu stable ; [- hand] tremblant, tremblotant ; [- writing] tremblé ; [- voice] tremblotant, chevrotant ; [- steps] chancelant **2.** [uncertain, weak - health, faith] précaire, vacillant ; [- authority, regime] incertain, chancelant ; [- future, finances] incertain, précaire ; [- business] incertain.

shale [ʃeɪl] *n* argile *f* schisteuse, schiste *m* argileux.

shall (*weak form* [ʃəl], *strong form* [ʃæl]) *modal vb* **1.** [as future auxiliary] : *I shall* or *I'll come tomorrow* je viendrai demain */ I shall not* or *I shan't be able to come* je ne pourrai pas venir **2.** [in suggestions, questions] : *shall I open the window?* voulez-vous que j'ouvre la fenêtre ? */ I'll shut that window, shall I?* je peux fermer cette fenêtre, si vous voulez */ we'll all go then, shall we?* dans ce cas, pourquoi n'y allons-nous pas tous ? **3.** *fml* [emphatic use] : *it shall be done* ce sera fait.

shallot [ʃə'lɒt] *n* échalote *f*.

shallow ['ʃæləʊ] *adj* **1.** [water, soil, dish] peu profond ▶ **the shallow end** [of swimming pool] le petit bain **2.** [superficial - person, mind, character] superficiel, qui manque de profondeur ; [- conversation] superficiel, futile ; [- argument] superficiel **3.** [breathing] superficiel. ❖ **shallows** *pl n* bas-fond *m*, bas-fonds *mpl*, haut-fond *m*, hauts-fonds *mpl*.

shallowness ['ʃæləʊnɪs] *n* **1.** [of water, soil, dish] faible profondeur *f* **2.** [of mind, character, sentiments] manque *m* de profondeur ; [of person] esprit *m* superficiel, manque *m* de profondeur ; [of talk, ideas] futilité *f*.

sham [ʃæm] (*pt & pp* **shammed,** *cont* **shamming**) ◆ *n* **1.** [pretence - of sentiment, behaviour] comédie *f*, farce *f*, faux-semblant *m* **2.** [impostor - person] imposteur *m* ; [- organization] imposture *f*. ◆ *adj* **1.** [pretended - sentiment, illness] faux (fausse), feint, simulé ; [- battle] simulé **2.** [mock - jewellery] imitation *(adj)*, faux (fausse). ◆ *vt* feindre, simuler. ◆ *vi* faire semblant, jouer la comédie.

shambles ['ʃæmblz] *n* **1.** [place] désordre *m* **2.** [situation, event] désastre *m*.

shambolic [ʃæm'bɒlɪk] *adj* ⓤⓚ désordonné.

shame [ʃeɪm] ◆ *n* **1.** [feeling] honte *f* / *to my great shame* à ma grande honte **2.** [disgrace, dishonour] honte *f* ▶ **to bring shame on one's family / country** déshonorer sa famille / sa patrie, couvrir sa famille / sa patrie de honte ▶ **to put sb to shame** faire honte à qqn **3.** [pity] dommage *m* ▶ **it's a shame!** c'est dommage ! ▶ **what a shame!** quel dommage ! */ it's a shame he can't come* c'est dommage qu'il ne puisse pas venir. ◆ *vt* [disgrace - family, country] être la honte de, faire honte à, déshonorer ; [put to shame] faire honte à, humilier ▶ **to shame sb into doing sthg** obliger qqn à faire qqch en lui faisant honte.

 Note that **il est / c'est dommage que** is followed by a verb in the subjunctive:
It's a shame they can't come. *C'est dommage qu'ils ne puissent pas venir.*

shamefaced [ˌʃeɪm'feɪst] *adj* honteux, penaud.

shameful ['ʃeɪmfʊl] *adj* honteux, indigne.

shamefully ['ʃeɪmfʊlɪ] *adv* honteusement, indignement.

shameless ['ʃeɪmlɪs] *adj* effronté, sans vergogne.

shamelessly ['ʃeɪmlɪslɪ] *adv* sans honte, sans vergogne, sans pudeur.

shammy ['ʃæmɪ] *n* ▶ **shammy (leather)** peau *f* de chamois.

shampoo [ʃæm'pu:] ◆ *n* shampooing *m* ▶ **shampoo and set** shampooing *m* (et) mise en plis *f*. ◆ *vt* [person, animal] faire un shampooing à ; [carpet] shampouiner ▶ **to shampoo one's hair** se faire un shampooing, se laver les cheveux.

shamrock ['ʃæmrɒk] *n* trèfle *m*.

🚩 **Shamrock**

Le trèfle est l'emblème de l'Irlande.

shandy ['ʃændɪ] (*pl* **shandies**) *n* ⓤⓚ panaché *m*.

shan't [ʃɑːnt] *abbr of* shall not.

shanty ['ʃæntɪ] (*pl* **shanties**) *n* **1.** [shack] baraque *f*, cabane *f* **2.** [song] chanson *f* de marins.

shantytown ['ʃæntɪtaʊn] *n* bidonville *m*.

shape [ʃeɪp] ◆ *n* **1.** [outer form] forme *f* / *a sweet in the shape of a heart* un bonbon en forme de cœur **2.** [figure, silhouette] forme *f*, silhouette *f* **3.** [abstract form or structure] forme *f* ▶ **to take shape** prendre forme or tournure ▶ **to give shape to sthg** donner forme à qqch **4.** [guise] forme *f* **5.** [proper condition, fitness, effectiveness, etc.] forme *f* ▶ **to be in good / bad shape a)** [person] être en bonne / mauvaise forme, être / ne pas être en forme **b)** [business, economy] marcher bien / mal ▶ **to keep o.s.** or **to stay in shape** garder la or rester en forme / *what sort of shape was he in?* dans quel état était-il ?, comment allait-il ? **6.** [apparition, ghost] apparition *f*, fantôme *m* **7.** [mould - gen] moule *m* ; [- for hats] forme *f*. ◆ vt **1.** [mould - clay] façonner, modeler ; [- wood, stone] façonner, tailler **2.** [influence - events, life, future] influencer, déterminer ▶ **to shape sb's character** former le caractère de qqn **3.** [plan - essay] faire le plan de ; [- excuse, explanation, statement] formuler. ◆ vi [develop - plan] prendre forme or tournure ; [person] se débrouiller. ❖ **shape up** vi **1.** [improve] se secouer **2.** US [get fit again] retrouver la forme **3.** [progress, develop] prendre (une bonne) tournure / *the business is beginning to shape up* les affaires commencent à bien marcher / *the new team is shaping up well* la nouvelle équipe commence à bien fonctionner / *she isn't shaping up too badly* elle ne se débrouille or ne s'en sort pas trop mal.

SHAPE [ʃeɪp] (abbr of **Supreme Headquarters Allied Powers Europe**) pr n SHAPE *m.*

shaped [ʃeɪpt] adj **1.** [garment] ajusté ; [wooden or metal object] travaillé **2.** [in descriptions] : *shaped like a triangle* en forme de triangle.

-shaped in comp en forme de.

shapeless [ˈʃeɪplɪs] adj [mass, garment, heap] informe / *to become shapeless* se déformer.

shapelessness [ˈʃeɪplɪsnɪs] n absence *f* de forme, aspect *m* informe.

shapely [ˈʃeɪplɪ] (compar **shapelier**, superl **shapeliest**) adj [legs] bien galbé, bien tourné ; [figure, woman] bien fait.

shard [ʃɑːd] n [of glass] éclat *m* ; [of pottery] tesson *m.*

share [ʃeəʳ] ◆ vt **1.** [divide - money, property, food, chores] partager **2.** [use jointly - tools, flat, bed] partager ▶ **shared line** TELEC ligne *f* partagée, raccordement *m* collectif **3.** [have in common - interest, opinion] partager ; [- characteristic] avoir en commun ; [- worry, sorrow] partager, prendre part à, compatir à ▶ **shared experience** expérience *f* partagée. ◆ vi partager ▶ **to share in a)** [cost, work] participer à, partager **b)** [profits] avoir part à **c)** [credit, responsibility] partager **d)** [joy, sorrow] prendre part à, partager **e)** [grief] compatir à. ◆ n **1.** [portion - of property, cost, food, credit, blame] part *f* ▶ **to have a share in a business** être l'un des associés dans une affaire **2.** [part, role - in activity, work] part *f* ▶ **to do one's share (of the work)** faire sa part du travail ▶ **to have a share in doing sthg** contribuer à faire qqch **3.** ST. EX action *f* **4.** AGR soc *m* (de charrue). ❖ **share out** vt sep partager, répartir.

share capital n capital-actions *m.*

share certificate n certificat *m* or titre *m* d'actions.

share dealing n opérations *fpl* de Bourse.

share economy n économie *f* de partage.

shareholder [ˈʃeə,həʊldəʳ] n actionnaire *mf.*

shareholding [ˈʃeə,həʊldɪŋ] n actionnariat *m.*

share index n indice *m* boursier.

share-out n partage *m*, répartition *f.*

share prices n cours *mpl* des actions.

shareware [ˈʃeəweəʳ] n (U) COMPUT sharewares *mpl*, logiciels *mpl* contributifs or libres / *a piece of shareware* un logiciel contributif.

sharia law [ˈʃɑːrɪə] n charia *f.*

sharing [ˈʃeərɪŋ] ◆ adj [person] partageur. ◆ n [of money, power] partage *m.*

shark [ʃɑːk] n **1.** ZOOL requin *m* **2.** *inf & fig* [swindler] escroc *m*, filou *m* ; [predator - in business] requin *m* **3.** US *inf* [genius] génie *m* ▶ **to be a shark at sthg** être calé en qqch **4.** US [at match] revendeur *m* de billets à la sauvette.

sharp [ʃɑːp] ◆ adj **1.** [blade, scissors, razor] affûté, bien aiguisé ; [edge] tranchant, coupant ; [point] aigu (aiguë), acéré ; [teeth, thorn] pointu ; [claw] acéré ; [needle, pin - for sewing] pointu ; [- for pricking] qui pique ; [pencil] pointu, bien taillé ; [nose] pointu / *she has sharp features* elle a des traits anguleux ▶ **the sharp end** la première ligne **2.** [clear - photo, line, TV picture] net ; [- contrast, distinction] net, marqué **3.** [abrupt, sudden - blow, bend, turn] brusque ; [- rise, fall, change] brusque, soudain **4.** [piercing - wind, cold] vif, fort **5.** [intense - pain, disappointment] vif **6.** [sour, bitter - taste, food] âpre, piquant **7.** [harsh - words, criticism] mordant, cinglant ; [- reprimand] sévère ; [- voice, tone] âpre, acerbe ; [- temper] vif / *he can be very sharp with customers* il lui arrive d'être très brusque avec les clients / *she has a sharp tongue* elle a la langue bien affilée **8.** [keen - eyesight] perçant ; [- hearing, senses] fin / *he has a sharp eye* il a le coup d'œil ; [in intellect, wit - person] vif ; [- child] vif, éveillé ; [- judgment] vif / *she was too sharp for them* elle était trop maligne pour eux **9.** [quick, brisk - reflex, pace] ▶ **be sharp (about it)!** dépêche-toi ! **10.** [shrill - sound, cry] aigu (aiguë), perçant **11.** MUS : *C sharp minor* ut dièse mineur ▶ **to be sharp a)** [singer] chanter trop haut **b)** [violinist] jouer trop haut **12.** *pej* [unscrupulous - trading, lawyer] peu scrupuleux, malhonnête ▶ **sharp practice** : *accused of sharp practice* accusé de procédés indélicats or malhonnêtes **13.** *inf* [smart] classe / *he's always been a sharp dresser* il s'est toujours habillé très classe. ◆ adv **1.** [precisely] : *at 6 o'clock sharp* à 6 h pile or précises **2.** [in direction] : *turn sharp left* tournez tout de suite à gauche / *the road turns sharp left* la route tourne brusquement à gauche **3.** MUS [sing, play] trop haut, faux **4.** PHR ▶ **look sharp (about it)!** *inf* dépêche-toi !, grouille-toi ! *inf*. ◆ n MUS dièse *m.* ◆ vt US MUS [sharpen] diéser.

sharpen [ˈʃɑːpn] ◆ vt **1.** [blade, knife, razor] affiler, aiguiser, affûter ; [pencil] tailler ; [stick] tailler en pointe **2.** [appetite, pain] aviver, aiguiser ; [intelligence] affiner **3.** [outline, image] mettre au point, rendre plus net ; [contrast] accentuer, rendre plus marqué **4.** UK MUS diéser. ◆ vi [tone, voice] devenir plus vif or âpre ; [pain] s'aviver, devenir plus vif ; [appetite] s'aiguiser ; [wind, cold] devenir plus vif.

sharpener [ˈʃɑːpnəʳ] n [for knife - machine] aiguisoir *m* (à couteaux) ; [- manual] fusil *m* (à aiguiser) ; [for pencil] taille-crayon *m inv.*

sharp-eyed adj [with good eyes] qui a l'œil vif ; [with insight] à qui rien n'échappe.

sharpish [ˈʃɑːpɪʃ] adv UK *inf* [quickly] en vitesse, sans tarder ▶ **look sharpish!** grouille-toi !

sharply [ˈʃɑːplɪ] adv **1.** : *sharply pointed* **a)** [knife] pointu **b)** [pencil] à pointe fine, taillé fin **c)** [nose, chin, shoes] pointu **2.** [contrast, stand out] nettement ; [differ] nettement, clairement **3.** [abruptly, suddenly - curve, turn] brusquement ; [- rise, fall, change] brusquement, soudainement **4.** [harshly - speak] vivement, sèchement, de façon brusque ; [- criticize] vivement, sévèrement ; [- reply, retort] vertement, vivement.

sharpness [ˈʃɑːpnɪs] n **1.** [of blade, scissors, razor] tranchant *m* ; [of needle, pencil, thorn] pointe *f* aiguë ; [of features] aspect *m* anguleux **2.** [of outline, image, contrast] netteté *f* **3.** [of bend, turn] angle *m* brusque ; [of rise, fall, change] soudaineté *f* **4.** [of word, criticism, reprimand] sévérité *f* ; [of tone, voice] brusquerie *f*, aigreur *f* **5.** [of eyesight, hearing, senses] finesse *f*, acuité *f*; [of appetite, pain] acuité *f*; [of mind, intelligence] finesse *f*, vivacité *f*; [of irony, wit] mordant *m*.

sharpshooter [ˈʃɑːpˌʃuːtər] n tireur *m* d'élite.

sharp-tongued [-ˈtʌŋd] adj caustique.

sharp-witted [-ˈwɪtɪd] adj à l'esprit vif or fin.

shat [ʃæt] pt & pp *vulg* ⟶ shit.

shatter [ˈʃætər] ◆ vt 1. [break - glass, window] briser, fracasser; [-door] fracasser / *the noise shattered my eardrums* le bruit m'a assourdi 2. *fig* [destroy - career, health] briser, ruiner; [-nerves] démolir, détraquer; [-confidence, faith, hope] démolir, détruire / *they were shattered by the news* or *the news shattered them* ils ont été complètement bouleversés par la nouvelle, la nouvelle les a complètement bouleversés. ◆ vi [glass, vase, windscreen] voler en éclats.

shattered [ˈʃætəd] adj 1. [upset] bouleversé / *shattered dreams* des rêves brisés 2. 🆄🅺 *inf* [exhausted] crevé.

shattering [ˈʃætərɪŋ] adj 1. [emotionally - news, experience] bouleversant; [disappointment] fort, cruel 2. [extreme - defeat] écrasant / *a shattering blow* a) *lit* un coup violent b) *fig* un grand coup 3. 🆄🅺 *inf* [tiring] crevant.

shatterproof [ˈʃætəpruːf] adj ▸ **shatterproof glass** verre *m* sans éclats or Securit®.

shave [ʃeɪv] ◆ vt 1. raser ▸ **to shave one's legs** / **one's head** se raser les jambes / la tête 2. [wood] raboter ▸ **shaved parmesan** / **chocolate** CULIN copeaux *mpl* de parmesan / de chocolat 3. [graze] raser, frôler 4. [reduce] réduire. ◆ vi se raser. ◆ n ▸ **to have a shave** se raser ▸ **to give sb a shave** raser qqn. ❖ **shave off** vt sep 1. ▸ **to shave off one's beard** / **moustache** / **hair** se raser la barbe / la moustache / la tête 2. = shave (vt).

shaven [ˈʃeɪvn] adj [face, head] rasé.

shaver [ˈʃeɪvər] n [razor] rasoir *m* (électrique).

shaver outlet 🆄🆂, **shaver point** n prise *f* pour rasoir électrique.

shaving [ˈʃeɪvɪŋ] ◆ n [act] rasage *m*. ◆ comp [cream, foam, gel] à raser ▸ **shaving brush** blaireau *m* ▸ **shaving soap** savon *m* à barbe. ❖ **shavings** pl n [of wood] copeaux *mpl*; [of metal] copeaux *mpl*, rognures *fpl*; [of paper] rognures *fpl*.

shawl [ʃɔːl] n châle *m*.

she [ʃiː] ◆ pron [referring to woman, girl] elle / *she's a teacher* / *an engineer* elle est enseignante / ingénieure / *she's a very interesting woman* c'est une femme très intéressante / *she can't do it* elle ? elle ne peut pas le faire. ◆ n [referring to animal, baby] : *it's a she* a) [animal] c'est une femelle b) [baby] c'est une fille.

s/he (written abbr of she/he) il ou elle.

sheaf [ʃiːf] (*pl* sheaves [ʃiːvz]) ◆ n 1. [of papers, letters] liasse *f* 2. [of barley, corn] gerbe *f*; [of arrows] faisceau *m*. ◆ vt gerber, engerber.

shear [ʃɪər] (*pt* sheared, *pp* sheared *or* shorn [ʃɔːn]) ◆ vt 1. [sheep, wool] tondre 2. [metal] couper (net), cisailler. ◆ vi céder. ❖ **shears** pl n [for gardening] cisaille *f*; [for sewing] grands ciseaux *mpl*; [for sheep] tondeuse *f* ▸ **a pair of shears** a) HORT une paire de cisailles b) SEW une paire de grands ciseaux. ❖ **shear off** ◆ vt sep [wool, hair] tondre; [branch] couper, élaguer; [something projecting] couper, enlever. ◆ vi [part, branch] se détacher.

sheath [ʃiːθ] (*pl* sheaths [ʃiːðz]) n 1. [scabbard, case - for sword] fourreau *m*; [-for dagger] gaine *f*; [-for scissors, tool] étui *m* 2. [covering - for cable] gaine *f*; [-for water pipe] gaine *f*, manchon *m*; BOT, ANAT & ZOOL gaine *f* 3. 🆄🅺 [condom] préservatif *m* 4. = sheath dress.

sheath dress n (robe *f*) fourreau *m*.

sheathe [ʃiːð] vt 1. [sword, dagger] rengainer 2. [cable] gainer; [water pipe] gainer, mettre dans un manchon protecteur / *she was sheathed from head to foot in black satin* *fig* elle était moulée dans du satin noir de la tête aux pieds.

sheath knife n couteau *m* à gaine.

sheaves [ʃiːvz] pl ⟶ sheaf.

shed [ʃed] (*pt & pp* shed, *cont* shedding) ◆ n 1. [in garden] abri *m*, remise *f*, resserre *f*; [lean-to] appentis *m* 2. [barn] grange *f*, hangar *m*; [for trains, aircraft, vehicles] hangar *m* 3. [in factory] atelier *m*. ◆ vt 1. [cast off - leaves, petals] perdre; [-skin, shell] se dépouiller de; [-water] ne pas absorber; [take off - garments] enlever 2. [get rid of - inhibitions, beliefs] se débarrasser de, se défaire de; [-staff] congédier 3. [tears, blood] verser, répandre; [weight] perdre 4. [eject, lose] déverser; ASTRONAUT larguer 5. 🅟🅗🅡 **to shed light on** a) *lit* éclairer b) *fig* éclairer, éclaircir.

she'd (weak form [ʃɪd], strong form [ʃiːd]) 1. abbr of she had 2. abbr of she would.

sheen [ʃiːn] n [on satin, wood, hair, silk] lustre *m*; [on apple] poli *m*.

sheep [ʃiːp] (*pl* sheep) ◆ n mouton *m*; [ewe] brebis *f*. ◆ comp [farm, farming] de moutons.

sheepdog [ˈʃiːpdɒg] n chien *m* de berger.

sheepfold [ˈʃiːpfəʊld] n parc *m* à moutons, bergerie *f*.

sheepish [ˈʃiːpɪʃ] adj penaud.

sheepishly [ˈʃiːpɪʃlɪ] adv d'un air penaud.

sheepskin [ˈʃiːpskɪn] ◆ n 1. TEXT peau *f* de mouton 2. 🆄🆂 *inf* UNIV [diploma] parchemin *m*. ◆ comp [coat, rug] en peau de mouton.

sheer [ʃɪər] ◆ adj 1. [as intensifier] pur / *by sheer accident* or *chance* tout à fait par hasard, par pur hasard 2. [steep - cliff] à pic, abrupt 3. TEXT [stockings] extra fin. ◆ adv à pic, abruptement. ◆ vi NAUT [ship] faire une embardée. ❖ **sheers** pl n 🆄🆂 [curtains] voilages *mpl*. ❖ **sheer away** vi 1. [ship] larguer les amarres, prendre le large 2. [animal, shy person] filer, détaler ▸ **to sheer away from** éviter. ❖ **sheer off** vi 1. [ship] faire une embardée 2. *fig* [person] changer de chemin or de direction.

sheet [ʃiːt] ◆ n 1. [for bed] drap *m*; [for furniture] housse *f*; [shroud] linceul *m*; [tarpaulin] bâche *f* 2. [of paper] feuille *f*; [of glass, metal] feuille *f*, plaque *f*; [of cardboard, plastic] feuille *f*; [of iron, steel] tôle *f*, plaque *f* 3. [of water, snow] nappe *f*, étendue *f*; [of rain] rideau *m*, torrent *m*; [of flames] rideau *m* / *a sheet of ice* a) une plaque de glace b) [on road] une plaque de verglas 4. CULIN ▸ **baking sheet** plaque *f* de four or à gâteaux 5. NAUT écoute *f*. ◆ vt [figure, face] draper, couvrir d'un drap; [furniture] couvrir de housses. ❖ **sheet down** vi [rain, snow] tomber à torrents.

sheet feed n COMPUT alimentation *f* feuille à feuille.

sheet feeder n COMPUT dispositif *m* d'alimentation en papier.

sheet ice n plaque *f* de glace; [on road] (plaque *f* de) verglas *m*.

sheeting [ˈʃiːtɪŋ] n 1. [cloth] toile *f* pour draps 2. [plastic, polythene] feuillet *m*; [metal] feuille *f*, plaque *f*.

sheet lightning n éclair *m* en nappe or en nappes.

sheet metal n tôle *f*.

sheet music n (U) partitions *fpl*.

sheik(h) [ʃeɪk] n cheikh *m*.

shelf [ʃelf] (*pl* shelves [ʃelvz]) n 1. [individual] planche *f*, étagère *f*; [as part of set, in fridge] étagère *f*; [short] tablette *f*; [in oven] plaque *f*; [in shop] étagère *f*, rayon *m* ▸ **to buy sthg off the shelf** acheter qqch tout fait

‣ **to be left on the shelf a)** [woman] rester vieille fille **b)** [man] rester vieux garçon **2.** GEOL banc *m*, rebord *m*, saillie *f* ; [under sea] écueil *m*, plate-forme *f*.

shelf life n COMM durée *f* de conservation avant vente / *bread has a short shelf life* le pain ne se conserve pas très longtemps / *to have a short shelf life* [idea, pop group] avoir une durée de vie assez courte, ne pas durer longtemps.

shell [ʃel] ◆ n **1.** BIOL [gen - of egg, mollusc, nut] coquille *f* ; [- of peas] cosse *f* ; [- of crab, lobster, tortoise] carapace *f* ; [empty - on seashore] coquillage *m* **2.** [of building] carcasse *f* ; [of car, ship, machine] coque *f* **3.** CULIN fond *m* (de tarte) **4.** MIL obus *m* ; US [cartridge] cartouche *f* **5.** [boat] outrigger *m*. ◆ comp [ornament, jewellery] de or en coquillages. ◆ vt **1.** [peas] écosser, égrener ; [nut] décortiquer, écaler ; [oyster] ouvrir ; [prawn, crab] décortiquer **2.** MIL bombarder (d'obus). ❖ **shell out** *inf* ◆ vi casquer ‣ **to shell out for sthg** casquer pour qqch, payer qqch. ◆ vt insep payer, sortir.

---

 coquille or **coquillage?**

Une **coquille** is an empty shell, while **un coquillage** is a shellfish or a shell on the seashore. An exception is **coquille Saint-Jacques**, which means a scallop or a scallop shell.

---

she'll [ʃiːl] abbr of **she will.**

shellfire [ˈʃelfaɪə] n (U) tirs *mpl* d'obus.

shellfish [ˈʃelfɪʃ] (*pl* **shellfish**) n **1.** ZOOL [crab, lobster, shrimp] crustacé *m* ; [mollusc] coquillage *m* **2.** (U) CULIN fruits *mpl* de mer.

shelling [ˈʃelɪŋ] n MIL pilonnage *m*.

shellproof [ˈʃelpruːf] adj MIL blindé, à l'épreuve des obus.

shell shock n (U) psychose *f* traumatique (*due à une explosion*).

shell-shocked [-,ʃɒkt] adj commotionné (*après une explosion*) / *I'm still feeling pretty shell-shocked by it all* je suis encore sous le choc après toute cette histoire.

shell suit n survêtement *m* (*en polyamide froissé et doublé*).

shelter [ˈʃeltə] ◆ n **1.** [cover, protection] abri *m* ‣ **to take** or **to get under shelter** se mettre à l'abri or à couvert ; [accommodation] asile *m*, abri *m* ‣ **to give shelter to sb a)** [hide] donner asile à or cacher qqn **b)** [accommodate] héberger qqn **2.** [enclosure - gen] abri *m* ; [- for sentry] guérite *f* ‣ **(bus) shelter** Abribus *m*. ◆ vt [protect - from rain, sun, bombs] abriter ; [- from blame, suspicion] protéger ‣ **to shelter sb from sthg** protéger qqn de qqch ; [give asylum to - fugitive, refugee] donner asile à, abriter. ◆ vi s'abriter, se mettre à l'abri ; [from bullets] se mettre à couvert. ❖ **Shelter** pr n *association britannique d'aide aux sans-abri.*

sheltered [ˈʃeltəd] adj **1.** [place] abrité **2.** [protected - industry] protégé (*de la concurrence*) ; [- work] dans un centre pour handicapés ‣ **to lead a sheltered life** vivre à l'abri des soucis.

sheltered accommodation, sheltered housing n *logement dans une résidence pour personnes âgées ou handicapées.*

shelve [ʃelv] ◆ vt **1.** [put aside, suspend] laisser en suspens **2.** [books - in shop] mettre sur les rayons ; [- at home] mettre sur les étagères **3.** [wall, room - in shop] garnir de rayons ; [- at home] garnir d'étagères. ◆ vi [ground] être en pente douce.

shelves [ʃelvz] pl ⟶ **shelf.**

shelving [ˈʃelvɪŋ] n (U) [in shop] rayonnage *m*, rayonnages *mpl*, étagères *fpl* ; [at home] étagères *fpl*.

shenanigans [ʃɪˈnænɪɡənz] pl n *inf* **1.** [mischief] malice *f*, espièglerie *f* **2.** [scheming, tricks] manigances *fpl*, combines *fpl*.

shepherd [ˈʃepəd] ◆ n **1.** berger *m*, pâtre *m* *liter* ‣ **shepherd's crook** bâton *m* de berger, houlette *f* **2.** *liter* RELIG pasteur *m*, berger *m* ‣ **the Good Shepherd** le Bon Pasteur. ◆ vt **1.** [tourists, children] guider, conduire ‣ **to shepherd sb out of a room** escorter qqn jusqu'à la porte **2.** [sheep] garder, surveiller.

shepherd's pie n hachis *m* Parmentier.

sherbet [ˈʃɜːbət] n **1.** UK [powder] poudre *f* acidulée **2.** US [ice] sorbet *m*.

sheriff [ˈʃerɪf] n **1.** US [in Wild West and today] shérif *m* **2.** UK [crown officer] shérif *m*, officier *m* de la Couronne **3.** Scot LAW ≃ juge *m* au tribunal de grande instance.

sherry [ˈʃerɪ] (*pl* **sherries**) n sherry *m*, xérès *m*, vin *m* de Xérès.

she's [ʃiːz] **1.** abbr of she has **2.** abbr of she is.

Shetland [ˈʃetlənd] ◆ pr n GEOG ‣ **the Shetlands** or **the Shetland Isles** or **the Shetland Islands** les (îles *fpl*) Shetland *fpl* / *in the Shetlands* or *the Shetland Isles* or *the Shetland Islands* dans les Shetland. ◆ adj **1.** GEOG shetlandais **2.** TEXT [pullover] en shetland ‣ **Shetland wool** laine *f* d'Écosse or de Shetland.

shh [ʃ] interj chut.

shield [ʃiːld] ◆ n **1.** [carried on arm] écu *m* ; HERALD bouclier *m* **2.** *fig* bouclier *m*, paravent *m* ‣ **to provide a shield against sthg** protéger contre qqch **3.** TECH [on machine] écran *m* de protection or de sécurité ; [on nuclear reactor, spacecraft] bouclier *m* ‣ **nuclear shield** bouclier atomique ‣ **sun shield** pare-soleil *m inv* **4.** [trophy] trophée *m*. ◆ vt protéger ‣ **to shield sb from sthg** protéger qqn de or contre qqch.

shift [ʃɪft] ◆ vt **1.** [move, put elsewhere] déplacer, bouger ; [part of body] bouger, remuer / *shift yourself!* **a)** *inf* [move] pousse-toi !, bouge-toi ! **b)** [hurry] remue-toi !, grouille-toi ! ; [employee - to new job or place of work] muter ; [- to new department] affecter ; [scenery] changer **2.** [change] changer de ‣ **to shift gears** US changer de vitesse **3.** [remove - stain] enlever, faire partir **4.** *inf* COMM [sell] écouler. ◆ vi **1.** [move] se déplacer, bouger **2.** [change, switch - gen] changer ; [- wind] tourner / *to shift into fourth (gear)* US AUTO passer en quatrième (vitesse) **3.** *inf* [travel fast] filer **4.** [manage] ‣ **to shift for o.s.** se débrouiller tout seul **5.** [stain] partir, s'enlever **6.** UK *inf* COMM [sell] se vendre. ◆ n **1.** [change] changement *m* ‣ **(gear) shift** US AUTO changement *m* de vitesse **2.** [move] déplacement *m* **3.** [turn, relay] relais *m* ‣ **to do sthg in shifts** se relayer **4.** INDUST [period of time] poste *m*, équipe *f* / *I'm on the night / morning shift* je suis dans l'équipe de nuit / du matin ‣ **to work shifts, to be on shifts** travailler en équipe, faire les trois-huit ; [group of workers] équipe *f*, brigade *f* **5.** US & UK *dated* [woman's slip] combinaison *f* ; [dress] (robe *f*) fourreau *m* **6.** COMPUT [in arithmetical operation] décalage *m* ; [in word processing, telegraphy, etc.] touche *f* de majuscule **7.** US AUTO = shift stick. ❖ **shift over, shift up** vi *inf* se pousser, se déplacer.

shift key n touche *f* de majuscule.

shiftless [ˈʃɪftlɪs] adj [lazy] paresseux, fainéant ; [apathetic] apathique, mou (*before vowel or silent 'h' mol, f molle*) ; [helpless] sans ressource, perdu.

shift stick n US AUTO levier *m* de (changement de) vitesse.

shift work n travail m en équipe / *she does shift work* elle fait les trois-huit.

shift worker n *personne qui fait les trois-huit.*

shifty ['ʃɪftɪ] (*compar* **shiftier,** *superl* **shiftiest**) adj *inf* [look] sournois, furtif, fuyant / *he looks a shifty customer* il a l'air louche.

Shiite ['ʃiːaɪt] ◆ n ▶ **Shiite (Muslim)** chiite mf. ◆ adj chiite.

shilling ['ʃɪlɪŋ] n **1.** shilling m (*ancienne pièce britannique valant 12 pence, soit un vingtième de livre*) **2.** [in Kenya, Tanzania, etc.] shilling m.

shilly-shally ['ʃɪlɪˌʃælɪ] (*pt & pp* **shilly-shallied**) vi *inf & pej* hésiter.

shimmer ['ʃɪmər] ◆ vi [sequins, jewellery, silk] chatoyer, scintiller ; [water] miroiter. ◆ n [of sequins, jewellery, silk] chatoiement m, scintillement m ; [of water] miroitement m.

shimmering ['ʃɪmərɪŋ] adj [light] scintillant ; [jewellery, silk] chatoyant ; [water] miroitant.

shin [ʃɪn] ◆ n **1.** ANAT tibia m **2.** CULIN [of beef] gîte m or gîte-gîte m (de bœuf) ; [of veal] jarret m (de veau). ◆ vi (*pt & pp* **shinned**) grimper ▶ **to shin (up) a lamp post** grimper à un réverbère / *I shinned down the drainpipe* je suis descendu le long de la gouttière.

shinbone ['ʃɪnbəʊn] n tibia m.

shindig ['ʃɪndɪg] n *inf* **1.** [party] (grande) fête f **2.** [fuss] tapage m.

shine [ʃaɪn] ◆ vi (*pt & pp* **shone** [ʃɒn]) **1.** [sun, moon, lamp, candle] briller ; [surface, glass, hair] briller, luire **2.** [excel] briller. ◆ vt **1.** (*pt & pp* **shone** [ʃɒn]) [focus] braquer, diriger **2.** (*pt & pp* **shined**) [polish] faire briller, faire reluire, astiquer. ◆ n **1.** [polished appearance] éclat m, brillant m, lustre m ▶ **to put a shine on sthg, to give sthg a shine** faire reluire or briller qqch ▶ **to take a shine to sb** a) *inf* [take a liking to] se prendre d'amitié pour qqn b) [get a crush on] s'enticher de qqn **2.** [polish] polissage m. ❖ **shine down** vi briller. ❖ **shine out,** **shine through** vi [light] jaillir ; *fig* [courage, skill, generosity] rayonner, briller. ❖ **shine up to** vt insep [US] *inf* faire de la lèche à.

shingle ['ʃɪŋgl] ◆ n **1.** (U) [pebbles] galets mpl ▶ **shingle beach** plage f de galets **2.** CONSTR [for roofing] bardeau m, aisseau m ▶ **shingle roof** toit m en bardeaux **3.** [US] [nameplate] plaque f. ◆ vt [roof] couvrir de bardeaux or d'aisseaux.

shingles ['ʃɪŋglz] n (U) MED zona m.

shinguard ['ʃɪngɑːd] = shinpad.

shining ['ʃaɪnɪŋ] adj **1.** [gleaming - glass, metal, shoes] luisant, reluisant ; [- eyes] brillant ; [- face] rayonnant **2.** [outstanding] éclatant, remarquable.

shinny ['ʃɪnɪ] (*pt & pp* **shinnied**) [US] = shin (vi).

shinpad ['ʃɪnpæd] n jambière f.

shiny ['ʃaɪnɪ] (*compar* **shinier,** *superl* **shiniest**) adj **1.** [gleaming - glass, metal, shoes] luisant, reluisant **2.** [clothing - with wear] lustré.

ship [ʃɪp] (*pt & pp* **shipped**) ◆ n **1.** NAUT navire m, vaisseau m, bateau m ▶ **on board** or **aboard ship** à bord ▶ **the ship's papers** les papiers mpl de bord **2.** [airship] dirigeable m ; [spaceship] vaisseau m (spatial). ◆ vt **1.** [send by ship] expédier (par bateau or par mer) ; [carry by ship] transporter (par bateau or par mer) **2.** [send by any means] expédier ; [carry by any means] transporter **3.** [embark - passengers, cargo] embarquer **4.** [take into boat - gangplank, oars] rentrer ; [- water] embarquer. ◆ vi **1.** [passengers, crew] embarquer, s'embarquer **2.** COMM [product] sortir de l'usine. ❖ **ship off** vt sep *inf* expédier.

shipbuilder ['ʃɪpˌbɪldər] n constructeur m, -trice f de navires.

shipbuilding ['ʃɪpˌbɪldɪŋ] n construction f navale.

ship canal n canal m maritime.

shipment ['ʃɪpmənt] n **1.** [goods sent] cargaison f **2.** [sending of goods] expédition f.

shipper ['ʃɪpər] n [charterer] affréteur m, chargeur m ; [transporter] transporteur m ; [sender] expéditeur m, -trice f.

shipping ['ʃɪpɪŋ] ◆ n (U) **1.** [ships] navires mpl ; [traffic] navigation f **2.** [transport - gen] transport m ; [- by sea] transport m maritime **3.** [loading] chargement m, embarquement m. ◆ comp [company, line] maritime, de navigation ; [sport, trade, intelligence] maritime ▶ **shipping forecast** météo f or météorologie f marine.

shipping agent n agent m maritime.

shipping lane n voie f de navigation.

shipshape ['ʃɪpʃeɪp] adj en ordre, rangé.

shipwreck ['ʃɪprek] ◆ n **1.** [disaster at sea] naufrage m **2.** [wrecked ship] épave f. ◆ vt **1.** *lit* : *they were shipwrecked on a desert island* ils ont échoué sur une île déserte **2.** *fig* [ruin, spoil] ruiner.

shipwrecked ['ʃɪprekt] adj : *to be shipwrecked* a) [boat] faire naufrage b) [crew, passenger] être naufragé.

shipyard ['ʃɪpjɑːd] n chantier m naval.

shire ['ʃaɪər] n [UK] **1.** [county] comté m **2.** = shire horse. ❖ **Shires** pl pr n ▶ **the Shires** les comtés (ruraux) du centre de l'Angleterre.

shire horse n shire m.

shirk [ʃɜːk] ◆ vt [work, job, task] éviter de faire, échapper à ; [duty] se dérober à ; [problem, difficulty, question] esquiver, éviter. ◆ vi tirer au flanc.

shirker ['ʃɜːkər] n tire-au-flanc mf.

shirt [ʃɜːt] n [gen] chemise f ; [footballer's, cyclist's, etc.] maillot m.

shirtsleeves ['ʃɜːtsliːvz] pl n ▶ **to be in (one's) shirtsleeves** être en manches or bras de chemise.

shirttail ['ʃɜːteɪl] n pan m de chemise.

shirty ['ʃɜːtɪ] (*compar* **shirtier,** *superl* **shirtiest**) adj [UK] *inf* désagréable.

shit [ʃɪt] (*pt & pp* **shat** [ʃæt], *cont* **shitting**) *vulg* ◆ n **1.** [excrement] merde f ▶ **to have a shit** (aller) chier ▶ **to have the shits** avoir la chiasse ▶ **to kick** or **to beat** or **to knock the shit out of sb** casser la gueule à qqn ▶ **to scare the shit out of sb** foutre la trouille à qqn ▶ **I don't give a shit** je m'en fous, j'en ai rien à foutre ▶ **to be in the shit** être dans la merde ▶ **shit happens** ce sont des choses qui arrivent ▶ **no shit?** [US] sans blague ? ▶ **when the shit hits the fan** quand ça va éclater **2.** (U) [nonsense, rubbish] conneries fpl ▶ **that's a load of shit!** c'est des conneries, tout ça ! ▶ **to be full of shit** raconter des conneries **3.** [disliked person] salaud m, salope f, connard m, connasse f **4.** *drugs sl* [hashish] shit m, hasch m **5.** [US] [anything] : *I can't see shit* j'y vois que dalle. ◆ vi chier. ◆ vt ▶ **to shit oneself** chier dans son froc. ◆ interj merde *inf*.

shitfaced ['ʃɪtfeɪst] adj *vulg* [drunk] bourré.

shithole ['ʃɪthəʊl] n v *inf* [dirty place] porcherie f, taudis m / *this town's a complete shithole* [boring, ugly] cette ville est un vrai trou.

shitless ['ʃɪtlɪs] adj *vulg* ▶ **to be scared shitless** avoir une trouille bleue ▶ **to be bored shitless** se faire chier à mort.

shitload ['ʃɪtləʊd] n *vulg* ▶ **shitloads of sthg** des tonnes de qqch.

shit-scared adj *vulg* : *to be shit-scared* avoir une trouille bleue.

shit-stirrer n [UK] v *inf* fouteur m, -euse f de merde.

shitter ['ʃɪtər] n ⬛ *vulg* chiottes *fpl.*

shitty ['ʃɪtɪ] (*compar* shittier, *superl* shittiest) adj *vulg* **1.** [worthless] merdique **2.** [mean] dégueulasse.

shiver ['ʃɪvər] ◆ vi **1.** [with cold, fever, fear] grelotter, trembler ; [with excitement] frissonner, trembler **2.** [splinter] se fracasser, voler en éclats. ◆ n **1.** [from cold, fever, fear] frisson m, tremblement m ; [from excitement] frisson m ▶ **to give sb the shivers** *inf*: *it gives me the shivers* ça me donne le frisson or des frissons **2.** [fragment] éclat m.

shivery ['ʃɪvərɪ] adj [cold] frissonnant ; [frightened] frissonnant, tremblant ; [feverish] fiévreux, grelottant de fièvre.

shoal [ʃəʊl] ◆ n **1.** [of fish] banc m **2.** *fig* [large numbers] foule f **3.** [shallows] haut-fond m **4.** [sandbar] barre f ; [sandbank] banc m de sable. ◆ vi [fish] se mettre or se rassembler en bancs.

shock [ʃɒk] ◆ n **1.** [surprise] choc m, surprise f **2.** [upset] choc m **3.** ELEC décharge f (électrique) ▶ **to get a shock** recevoir or prendre une décharge (électrique) **4.** [impact - of armies, vehicles] choc m, heurt m ; [vibration - from explosion, earthquake] secousse f **5.** MED choc m ▶ **to be in a state of shock, to be suffering from shock** être en état de choc **6.** ⬛ *inf* AUTO = shock absorber **7.** [bushy mass] ▶ **a shock of hair** une tignasse. ◆ comp [measures, argument, headline] choc *(inv)* ; [attack] surprise *(inv)* ; [result, defeat] inattendu. ◆ vt **1.** [stun] stupéfier, bouleverser, secouer **2.** [offend, scandalize] choquer, scandaliser **3.** [incite, force] ▶ **to shock sb out of sthg** secouer qqn pour le sortir de qqch ▶ **to shock sb into action** pousser qqn à agir ▶ **to shock sb into doing sthg** secouer qqn jusqu'à ce qu'il fasse qqch **4.** ELEC donner une secousse or un choc électrique à.

shock absorber [-əb,zɔːbər] n amortisseur m.

shocked [ʃɒkt] adj **1.** [stunned] bouleversé, stupéfait **2.** [offended, scandalized] choqué, scandalisé.

> 📋 Note that être choqué que is followed by
> a verb in the subjunctive:
> **I'm shocked that you didn't inform me of this.**
> *Je suis choqué que vous ne m'en ayez pas informé.*

shocker ['ʃɒkər] n *inf* **1.** [book] livre m à sensation ; [film] film m à sensation ; [news] nouvelle f sensationnelle ; [play] pièce f à sensation ; [story] histoire f sensationnelle **2.** *hum* [atrocious person] : *you little shocker!* petit monstre !

shock-horror adj *inf* [story, headline] à sensation.

shocking ['ʃɒkɪŋ] ◆ adj **1.** [scandalous] scandaleux, choquant **2.** [horrifying] atroce, épouvantable **3.** *inf* [very bad] affreux, épouvantable. ◆ adv *inf* : *it was raining something shocking!* il fallait voir ce qu'il or comme ça tombait !

shockingly ['ʃɒkɪŋlɪ] adv **1.** [as intensifier] affreusement, atrocement **2.** [extremely badly] très mal, lamentablement.

shocking pink ◆ n rose m bonbon. ◆ adj rose bonbon *(inv).*

shock jock n *inf* présentateur de radio qui cherche à choquer son auditoire.

shockproof ['ʃɒkpruːf] adj résistant aux chocs.

shock resistant adj résistant aux chocs.

shock tactics pl n ▶ **to use shock tactics** employer la manière forte.

shock therapy, shock treatment n MED (traitement m par) électrochoc m, sismothérapie f.

shock troops pl n troupes *fpl* de choc.

shock wave n onde f de choc ; *fig* répercussion f.

shod [ʃɒd] pt & pp ⟶ **shoe.**

shoddy ['ʃɒdɪ] (*compar* shoddier, *superl* shoddiest) ◆ adj **1.** [of inferior quality] de mauvaise qualité / *shoddy workmanship* du travail mal fait / *a shoddy imitation* une piètre or médiocre imitation **2.** [mean, petty] sale. ◆ n tissu m shoddy or de Renaissance.

shoe [ʃuː] (*pt & pp* shod [ʃɒd]) ◆ n **1.** [gen] chaussure f ▶ **a pair of shoes** une paire de chaussures ▶ **to put on one's shoes** mettre ses chaussures, se chausser **2.** ▶ **(horse) shoe** fer m (à cheval) **3.** [in casino - for baccarat, etc.] sabot m **4.** [on electric train] frotteur m. ◆ comp [cream, leather] pour chaussures ▶ **shoe repairer** cordonnier m ▶ **shoe size** pointure f. ◆ vt **1.** [horse] ferrer **2.** *(usu passive) liter* [person] chausser.

shoebrush ['ʃuːbrʌʃ] n brosse f à chaussures.

shoehorn ['ʃuːhɔːn] n chausse-pied m.

shoelace ['ʃuːleɪs] n lacet m (de chaussures).

shoemaker ['ʃuːˌmeɪkər] n [craftsman] bottier m ; [manufacturer] fabricant m, -e f de chaussures, chausseur m.

shoemender ['ʃuːˌmendər] n cordonnier m, -ère f.

shoe polish n cirage m.

shoe shop n magasin m de chaussures.

shoestring ['ʃuːstrɪŋ] ◆ n **1.** [shoelace] lacet m (de chaussure) **2.** *inf* ⬚ᴾᴴᴿ **on a shoestring** avec trois fois rien. ◆ comp ▶ **shoestring budget** petit budget m.

shoetree ['ʃuːtriː] n embauchoir m.

shone [ʃɒn] pt & pp ⟶ **shine.**

shoo [ʃuː] (pt & pp shooed) ◆ interj oust, ouste. ◆ vt chasser ▶ **to shoo sb / sthg away** chasser qqn / qqch.

shook [ʃʊk] pt ⟶ **shake.**

shoot [ʃuːt] (*pt & pp* shot [ʃɒt]) ◆ vi **1.** [with gun] tirer ▶ **to shoot at sb / sthg** tirer sur qqn / qqch **2.** ⬛ [hunt] chasser ▶ **to go shooting** aller à la chasse **3.** [go fast] : *the rabbit shot into its burrow* le lapin s'est précipité dans son terrier / *the car shot out in front of us* a) [changed lanes] la voiture a déboîté tout d'un coup devant nous b) [from another street] la voiture a débouché devant nous / *the water shot out of the hose* l'eau a jailli du tuyau d'arrosage / *a violent pain shot up my leg* j'ai senti une violente douleur dans la jambe **4.** CIN tourner / *shoot!* moteur !, on tourne ! **5.** SPORT tirer, shooter **6.** *inf* [go ahead, speak] : *can I ask you something? — shoot!* je peux te poser une question ? — vas-y ! **7.** BOT [sprout] pousser ; [bud] bourgeonner **8.** ⬛ ▶ **to shoot for** or **at** [aim for] viser. ◆ vt **1.** [hit] atteindre ; [injure] blesser / *she was shot in the arm / leg* elle a reçu une balle dans le bras / la jambe ; [kill] abattre, descendre, tuer (d'un coup de pistolet or de fusil) ▶ **to shoot o.s.** se tuer, se tirer une balle ; [execute by firing squad] fusiller **2.** [fire - gun] tirer un coup de ; [- bullet] tirer ; [- arrow] tirer, lancer, décocher ; [- rocket, dart, missile] lancer ▶ **to shoot questions at sb** *fig* bombarder or mitrailler qqn de questions / *she shot a shy smile at him* *fig* elle lui jeta un petit sourire timide **3.** ⬛ [hunt] chasser, tirer **4.** CIN tourner ; PHOT prendre (en photo) **5.** ⬛ GAMES & SPORT [play] jouer ▶ **to shoot pool** jouer au billard américain ▶ **to shoot dice** jouer aux dés ; [score] marquer ▶ **to shoot a goal / basket** marquer un but / panier **6.** [send] envoyer / *the explosion shot debris high into the air* l'explosion a projeté des débris dans les airs / *she shot out a hand* elle a étendu le bras d'un geste vif **7.** [go through - rapids] franchir ; [- traffic lights] / *the car shot the lights* la voiture a brûlé le feu rouge **8.** [bolt - close] fermer ; [- open] ouvrir, tirer **9.** *drugs sl* [drugs] se shooter à. ◆ n **1.** BOT pousse f **2.** ⬛ HUNT [party] partie f de chasse ; [land] (terrain m de) chasse f **3.** ⬛ [chute - for coal, rubbish, etc.] glissière f **4.** MIL tir m **5.** CIN tournage m **6.** PHOT séance f photo, prise f de vues. ◆ interj ⬛ *inf* zut, mince.

⬧ **shoot down** vt sep [person, plane, helicopter] abattre.

❖ shoot off ◆ vi s'enfuir à toutes jambes. **◆** vt sep **1.** [weapon] tirer, décharger **2.** [limb] emporter, arracher **3.** v inf **PHR** **to shoot one's mouth off** ouvrir sa gueule. **❖ shoot up ◆** vi **1.** [move skywards - flame, geyser, lava] jaillir ; [- rocket] monter en flèche **2.** [increase - inflation, price] monter en flèche **3.** [grow - plant] pousser rapidement or vite ; [- person] grandir **4.** drugs sl [with drug] se shooter. **◆** vt sep **1.** **US** inf [with weapon - saloon, town] terroriser en tirant des coups de feu **2.** drugs sl [drug] se shooter à.

shoot-em-up n jeu m vidéo violent.

shooting ['ʃuːtɪŋ] **◆** n **1.** (U) [firing] coups mpl de feu, fusillade f **2.** [incident] fusillade f ; [killing] meurtre m **3.** [ability to shoot] tir m **4.** **US** HUNT chasse f **5.** CIN tournage m. **◆** comp **1.** [with weapon] **▶ shooting incident** fusillade f **▶ shooting practice** entraînement m au tir **2.** HUNT de chasse **▶ the shooting season** la saison de la chasse. **◆** adj [pain] lancinant.

shooting gallery n stand m de tir.

shooting match n concours m de tir **▶ the whole shooting match** **US** inf tout le tintouin.

shooting range n champ m de tir.

shooting star n étoile f filante.

shooting stick n canne-siège f.

shoot-out n inf fusillade f.

shop [ʃɒp] (pt & pp **shopped,** cont **shopping**) **◆** n **1.** **UK** [store] magasin m ; [smaller] boutique f **2.** [shopping trip] **▶ to do one's weekly shop** faire les courses or les achats de la semaine **3.** **UK** [workshop] atelier m. **◆** vi [for food, necessities] faire les or ses courses ; [for clothes, gifts, etc.] faire les magasins, faire du shopping **▶ to go shopping** faire des courses, courir les magasins. **◆** vt **UK** inf [to the police] donner, balancer. **❖ shop around** vi comparer les prix **▶ to shop around for sthg** comparer les prix avant d'acheter qqch.

shopaholic [ˌʃɒpəˈhɒlɪk] n : he's a real shopaholic il adore faire les boutiques.

shop assistant n **UK** vendeur m, -euse f.

shop floor n [place] atelier m ; [workers] **▶ the shop floor** les ouvriers mpl. **❖ shop-floor** comp **▶ shop floor worker** ouvrier m, -ère f / the decision was taken at shop floor level la décision a été prise par la base.

shopfront ['ʃɒpfrʌnt] n **UK** devanture f (de magasin).

shopkeeper ['ʃɒpˌkiːpə'] n **UK** commerçant m, -e f **▶ small shopkeeper** petit commerçant.

shoplift ['ʃɒplɪft] vt voler à l'étalage.

shoplifter ['ʃɒpˌlɪftə'] n voleur m, -euse f à l'étalage.

shoplifting ['ʃɒpˌlɪftɪŋ] n vol m à l'étalage.

shopper ['ʃɒpə'] n **1.** [person] personne f qui fait ses courses **2.** [shopping bag] cabas m.

shopping ['ʃɒpɪŋ] **◆** n (U) **1.** [for food, necessities] courses fpl ; [for clothes, gifts, etc.] courses fpl, shopping m / we're going into town to do some shopping nous allons en ville pour faire des courses or pour faire le tour des magasins / to do a bit of shopping faire quelques (petites) courses or emplettes **2.** [goods bought] achats mpl, courses fpl, emplettes fpl. **◆** comp [street, area] commerçant.

shopping bag n sac m or filet m à provisions, cabas m.

shopping basket n **1.** panier m (à provisions) **2.** [on commercial website] panier m.

shopping cart n **US** = shopping trolley.

shopping centre **UK**, **shopping mall** **US**, **shopping plaza** **US** [-ˌplɑːzə] n centre m commercial.

shopping channel n TV chaîne f de télé-achat.

shopping list n liste f des courses.

shopping mall, shopping plaza **US** = shopping centre.

shopping precinct n **UK** centre m commercial.

shopping spree n : to go on a shopping spree aller faire du shopping.

shopping trolley n chariot m, Caddie® m.

shopsoiled ['ʃɒpsɔɪld] adj **UK** lit & fig défraîchi.

shop steward n délégué syndical m, déléguée syndicale f.

shopwalker ['ʃɒpˌwɔːkə'] n **UK** chef m de rayon.

shop window n vitrine f (de magasin) / a shop window for British exports fig une vitrine pour les exportations britanniques.

shopworn ['ʃɒpwɔːn] **US** = shopsoiled.

shore [ʃɔːr] **◆** n **1.** [edge, side - of sea] rivage m, bord m ; [- of lake, river] rive f, rivage m, bord m ; [coast] côte f, littoral m ; [dry land] terre f **▶ to go on shore** débarquer **2.** [prop] étai m, étançon m. **◆** vt étayer, étançonner. **❖ shores** pl n liter [country] rives fpl. **❖ shore up** vt sep **UK** **1.** lit étayer, étançonner **2.** fig étayer, appuyer, consolider.

shore leave n permission f à terre.

shoreline ['ʃɔːlaɪn] n littoral m.

shorn [ʃɔːn] **◆** pp ⟶ shear. **◆** adj **1.** [head, hair] tondu **2.** fig **▶ shorn of** dépouillé de.

short [ʃɔːt] **◆** adj **1.** [in length] court **▶ to have short hair** avoir les cheveux courts / the editor made the article shorter by a few hundred words le rédacteur a raccourci l'article de quelques centaines de mots / she made a short speech elle a fait un court or petit discours / I'd just like to say a few short words j'aimerais dire quelques mots très brefs **▶ short and to the point** bref et précis **▶ short and sweet** inf court mais bien **2.** [in distance] court, petit / to go for a short walk faire une petite promenade / at short range à courte portée / it's only a short distance from here ce n'est pas très loin (d'ici) **3.** [in height] petit, de petite taille **4.** [period, interval] court, bref / a short stay un court séjour / after a short time après un court intervalle or un petit moment / I met him a short time or while later je l'ai rencontré peu (de temps) après / it's rather short notice to invite them for tonight c'est un peu juste pour les inviter ce soir / the days are getting shorter les jours raccourcissent / to demand shorter hours / a shorter working week exiger une réduction des heures de travail / une réduction du temps de travail hebdomadaire **▶ in the short run** à court terme **5.** [abbreviated] : HF is short for high frequency HF est l'abréviation de haute fréquence / Bill is short for William Bill est un diminutif de William **6.** [gruff] brusque, sec (sèche) / she tends to be a bit short with people elle a tendance à être un peu brusque avec les gens **▶ to have a short temper** être irascible **7.** [sudden - sound, action] brusque **8.** [lacking, insufficient] **▶ to give sb short weight** ne pas donner le bon poids à qqn / whisky is in short supply on manque or on est à court de whisky / I'm a bit short (of money) at the moment je suis un peu à court (d'argent) en ce moment. **◆** adv **1.** [suddenly] **▶ to stop short** s'arrêter net **2.** **PHR** **to fall short of a)** [objective, target] ne pas atteindre **b)** [expectations] ne pas répondre à **▶ to go short (of sthg)** manquer (de qqch) **▶ to run short (of sthg)** être à court (de qqch). **◆** vt ELEC court-circuiter. **◆** vi ELEC se mettre en court-circuit. **◆** n **1.** inf ELEC court-circuit m **2.** **UK** [drink] alcool servi dans de petits verres **3.** CIN court-métrage m. **❖ shorts** pl n [short trousers] short m / a pair of khaki shorts un short kaki ; **US** [underpants] caleçon m. **❖ for short** adv phr : they call him Ben for short on l'appelle Ben pour faire plus court / trinitrotoluene, or TNT for short le trinitrotoluène ou TNT en abrégé. ❖ **in short** adv phr (en) bref.

❖ **short of** prep phr sauf / *he would do anything short of stealing* il ferait tout sauf voler / *nothing short of a miracle can save him now* seul un miracle pourrait le sauver maintenant.

shortage ['ʃɔːtɪdʒ] n [of labour, resources, materials] manque *m*, pénurie *f* ; [of food] disette *f*, pénurie *f* ; [of money] manque *m* / *the housing / energy shortage* la crise du logement / de l'énergie / *there's no shortage of good restaurants in this part of town* les bons restaurants ne manquent pas dans ce quartier.

short back and sides n coupe *f* courte or dégagée sur la nuque et derrière les oreilles.

shortbread ['ʃɔːtbred] n sablé *m* ▸ **shortbread biscuit** 🇬🇧 sablé *m*.

short-change vt **1.** *lit* ▸ **to short-change sb** ne pas rendre assez (de monnaie) à qqn **2.** *inf* [swindle] rouler, escroquer.

short circuit n court-circuit *m*. ❖ **short-circuit** ◆ vt ELEC & *fig* court-circuiter. ◆ vi se mettre en court-circuit.

shortcoming ['ʃɔːtˌkʌmɪŋ] n défaut *m*.

shortcrust pastry ['ʃɔːtkrʌst-] n pâte *f* brisée.

short cut n *lit & fig* raccourci *m* ▸ **to take a short cut** prendre un raccourci ▸ **keyboard short cut** COMPUT raccourci *m* clavier.

shorten ['ʃɔːtn] ◆ vt **1.** [in length - garment, string] raccourcir ; [- text, article, speech] raccourcir, abréger / *the name James is often shortened to Jim* Jim est un diminutif courant de James **2.** [in time] écourter. ◆ vi **1.** [gen] (se) raccourcir **2.** [in betting - odds] devenir moins favorable.

shortening ['ʃɔːtnɪŋ] n **1.** CULIN matière *f* grasse **2.** [of garment, string] raccourcissement *m* ; [of text, speech] raccourcissement *m*, abrègement *m* ; [of time, distance] réduction *f*.

shortfall ['ʃɔːtfɔːl] n insuffisance *f*, manque *m*.

short-haired adj [person] à cheveux courts ; [animal] à poil ras.

shorthand ['ʃɔːthænd] n sténographie *f*, sténo *f* ▸ **to take notes in shorthand** prendre des notes en sténo.

shorthanded [ˌʃɔːt'hændɪd] adj à court de personnel.

shorthand typist n sténodactylo *mf*.

short-haul adj [transport] à courte distance ▸ **short-haul aircraft** court-courrier *m*.

short list n 🇬🇧 liste *f* de candidats présélectionnés. ❖ **short-list** 🇬🇧 vt : *five candidates have been short-listed* cinq candidats ont été présélectionnés.

short-lived [-'lɪvd] adj [gen] de courte durée, éphémère, bref ; [animal, species] éphémère.

shortly ['ʃɔːtlɪ] adv **1.** [soon] bientôt, sous peu, avant peu / *shortly afterwards* peu (de temps) après **2.** [gruffly] sèchement, brusquement **3.** [briefly] brièvement, en peu de mots.

shortness ['ʃɔːtnɪs] n **1.** [in length] manque *m* de longueur ; [in height] petite taille *f* ; [in time] brièveté *f* ; [of speech, essay] brièveté.

short-range adj **1.** [weapon] de courte portée ; [vehicle, aircraft] à rayon d'action limité **2.** [prediction, outlook] à court terme.

shortsighted [ˌʃɔːt'saɪtɪd] adj **1.** *lit* myope **2.** *fig* [person] qui manque de perspicacité or de prévoyance ; [plan, policy] à courte vue.

shortsightedness [ˌʃɔːt'saɪtɪdnɪs] n **1.** *lit* myopie *f* **2.** *fig* myopie *f*, manque *m* de perspicacité or de prévoyance.

short-sleeved adj à manches courtes.

short-staffed [-'stɑːft] adj à court de personnel.

short-stay adj ▸ **short-stay car park** parking *m* courte durée ▸ **short-stay patient** patient *m* hospitalisé pour une courte durée.

short story n nouvelle *f*.

short-tempered adj irascible, irritable.

short-term adj à court terme ; [contract, parking] de courte durée.

short wave n onde *f* courte / *on short wave* sur ondes courtes. ❖ **short-wave** comp [radio] à ondes courtes ; [programme, broadcasting] sur ondes courtes.

shot [ʃɒt] ◆ pt & pp ⟶ **shoot.** ◆ n **1.** [instance of firing] coup *m* (de feu) ▸ **to have** or **to fire** or **to take a shot at sthg** tirer sur qqch ▸ **it was a shot in the dark** j'ai / il a, etc. dit ça au hasard / *the dog was off like a shot* le chien est parti comme une flèche / *I'd accept the offer like a shot* inf j'accepterais l'offre sans la moindre hésitation **2.** [sound of gun] coup *m* de feu **3.** (U) [shotgun pellets] plomb *m*, plombs *mpl* **4.** [marksman] tireur *m*, -euse *f*, fusil *m* **5.** SPORT [at goal - in football, hockey, etc.] tir *m* ; [stroke - in tennis, cricket, billiards, etc.] coup *m* ; [throw - in darts] lancer *m* ▸ **good shot!** bien joué ! ▸ **to call the shots** mener le jeu **6.** SPORT ▸ **to put the shot** lancer le poids **7.** ASTRONAUT [launch] tir *m* **8.** PHOT photo *f* ; CIN plan *m*, prise *f* de vue **9.** inf [try] tentative *f*, essai *m* / *I'd like to have a shot at it* j'aimerais tenter le coup / *give it your best shot* fais pour le mieux / *I gave it my best shot* j'ai fait ce que j'ai pu / *it's worth a shot* ça vaut le coup d'essayer **10.** [injection] piqûre *f* **11.** [drink] (petit) verre *m*, shot *m*. ◆ adj **1.** 🇬🇧 [rid] ▸ **to get shot of sthg / sb** inf se débarrasser de qqch / qqn **2.** [streaked] strié ▸ **shot silk** soie *f* changeante **3.** inf [exhausted] épuisé, crevé ; [broken, spoilt] fichu, bousillé / *my nerves are shot* je suis à bout de nerfs.

🚩 **The shot heard around the world**

Titre d'un poème de Ralph Waldo Emerson, en hommage au premier coup de feu échangé entre les **Minutemen** américains et les forces anglaises, en avril 1775, à Lexington. L'écrivain y loue la détermination des colons et salue l'avènement d'une nouvelle nation.

---

shot glass n verre *m* à shots.

shotgun ['ʃɒtgʌn] ◆ n fusil *m* de chasse. ◆ adj forcé ▸ **a shotgun merger** une fusion imposée. ◆ adv 🇺🇸 ▸ **to ride shotgun** voyager comme passager.

shot put n lancer *m* du poids.

should [ʃʊd] modal vb **1.** [indicating duty, necessity] : *I should be working, not talking to you* je devrais être en train de travailler au lieu de parler avec vous ; [indicating likelihood] : *they should have arrived by now* ils devraient être arrivés maintenant ; [indicating what is acceptable, desirable, etc.] : *you shouldn't have done that!* tu n'aurais pas dû faire ça ! / *should he tell her?* — yes he should est-ce qu'il devrait le lui dire ? — oui, sans aucun doute / *I'm very sorry — and so you should be!* je suis vraiment désolé — il y a de quoi ! **2.** (forming conditional tense) [would] : *I should like to meet your parents* j'aimerais rencontrer vos parents / *I should have thought the answer was obvious* j'aurais pensé que la réponse était évidente / *how should I know?* comment voulez-vous que je le sache ? / *I should think so / not!* j'espère bien / bien que non ! **3.** [after 'that' and in expressions of feeling, opinion, etc.] : *it's strange* *(that) she should do that* c'est bizarre qu'elle fasse cela **4.** *(after 'who' or 'what')* [expressing surprise] : *and who should I meet but Betty!* et sur qui je tombe ? Betty !

shoulder ['ʃəʊldər] ◆ n **1.** [part of body, of garment] épaule f **2.** CULIN épaule f **3.** [along road] accotement m, bas-côté m **4.** [on hill, mountain] replat m ; [of bottle] renflement m. ◆ vt **1.** [pick up] charger sur son épaule ▶ **to shoulder arms** MIL se mettre au port d'armes ▶ **shoulder arms!** MIL portez armes ! **2.** *fig* [take on - responsibility, blame] assumer ; [cost] faire face à **3.** [push] pousser (de l'épaule).

shoulder bag n sac m à bandoulière.

shoulder blade n omoplate f.

shoulder-high adj qui arrive (jusqu') à l'épaule.

shoulder-length adj [hair] mi-long, qui arrive (jusqu')aux épaules.

shoulder pad n [in garment] épaulette f *(coussinet de rembourrage)* ; SPORT protège-épaule m.

shoulder strap n [on dress, bra, accordion] bretelle f ; [on bag] bandoulière f.

shouldn't ['ʃʊdnt] abbr of **should not**.

should've ['ʃʊdəv] abbr of **should have**.

shout [ʃaʊt] ◆ n **1.** [cry] cri m, hurlement m / *give me a shout if you need a hand* appelle-moi si tu as besoin d'un coup de main **2.** UK & Austr inf [round of drinks] tournée f. ◆ vi **1.** [cry out] crier, hurler ▶ **to shout at the top of one's voice** crier à tue-tête ▶ **to shout (out) for help** appeler au secours / *he shouted (out) to her to be careful* il lui a crié de faire attention **2.** UK & Austr inf [pay for drinks] : *I'll shout* c'est ma tournée. ◆ vt **1.** [cry out] crier / *the sergeant shouted (out) an order* le sergent hurla un ordre **2.** UK & Austr inf [treat] ▶ **to shout sb a meal** inviter qqn. ◆ **shout down** vt sep [speaker] empêcher de parler en criant ; [speech] couvrir par des cris.

shouting ['ʃaʊtɪŋ] n (U) cris mpl, vociférations fpl ▶ **it's all over bar the shouting** l'affaire est dans le sac.

shove [ʃʌv] ◆ vt **1.** [push] pousser ; [push roughly] pousser sans ménagement ; [insert, stick] enfoncer **2.** inf [put hurriedly or carelessly] mettre, flanquer, ficher. ◆ vi **1.** [push] pousser ; [jostle] se bousculer **2.** UK inf [move up] se pousser / *shove up* or *over* or *along a bit* pousse-toi un peu. ◆ n **1.** [push] poussée f ▶ **to give sb / sthg a shove** pousser qqn / qqch **2.** inf PHR **to give sb the shove** sacquer qqn ▶ **to get the shove** se faire sacquer. ◆ **shove about** UK, **shove around** vt sep [jostle] bousculer ; [mistreat] malmener. ◆ **shove off** ◆ vi **1.** inf [go away] se casser, se tirer **2.** [boat] pousser au large. ◆ vt sep [boat] pousser au large, déborder.

shovel ['ʃʌvl] (UK pt & pp **shovelled**, cont **shovelling**, US pt & pp **shoveled**, cont **shoveling**) ◆ n pelle f ; [on excavating machine] pelle f, godet m. ◆ vt [coal, earth, sand] pelleter ; [snow] déblayer (à la pelle) ▶ **shovel food into one's mouth** inf enfourner de la nourriture.

show [ʃəʊ] (pt **showed**, pp **shown** [ʃəʊn]) ◆ vt **1.** [display, present] montrer, faire voir ▶ **to show sthg to sb, to show sb sthg** montrer qqch à qqn / *you have to show your pass / your ticket on the way in* il faut présenter son laissez-passer / son billet à l'entrée / *I had very little to show for my efforts* mes efforts n'avaient donné que peu de résultats / *if he ever shows himself round here again, I'll kill him!* si jamais il se montre encore par ici, je le tue ! ▶ **to show one's age** faire son âge ; [reveal - talent, affection, readiness, reluctance] montrer, faire preuve de / **to show a preference for sthg** manifester une préférence pour qqch / *they will be shown no mercy* ils seront traités sans merci **2.** [prove] montrer, démontrer, prouver / *it just goes to*

show that nothing's impossible c'est la preuve que rien n'est impossible **3.** [register - subj: instrument, dial, clock] marquer, indiquer **4.** [represent, depict] montrer, représenter **5.** [point out, demonstrate] montrer, indiquer / *show me how to do it* montrez-moi comment faire ▶ **to show (sb) the way** montrer le chemin (à qqn) ▶ **I'll show you!** inf tu vas voir ! **6.** [escort, accompany] : *let me show you to your room* je vais vous montrer votre chambre / *will you show this gentleman to the door?* veuillez reconduire Monsieur à la porte **7.** [profit, loss] faire **8.** [put on - film, TV programme] passer / *the film has never been shown on television* le film n'est jamais passé à la télévision **9.** [exhibit - work of art, prize, produce] exposer. ◆ vi **1.** [be visible - gen] se voir ; [-petticoat] dépasser / *she doesn't like him, and it shows* elle ne l'aime pas, et ça se voit **2.** [be on - film, TV programme] passer **3.** US inf [turn up] arriver, se pointer. ◆ n **1.** [demonstration, display] démonstration f, manifestation f ; [pretence] semblant m, simulacre m / *she put on a show of indifference* elle a fait semblant d'être indifférente ; [ostentation] ostentation f, parade f ▶ *the metal strips are just for show* les bandes métalliques ont une fonction purement décorative ▶ **a show of strength** une démonstration de force ▶ **a show of hands** un vote à main levée **2.** THEAT spectacle m ; TV émission f ▶ **the show must go on** THEAT & fig le spectacle continue **3.** [exhibition] exposition f ; [trade fair] foire f, salon m / *I dislike most of the paintings on show* je n'aime pas la plupart des tableaux exposés ▶ **the agricultural / motor show** le salon de l'agriculture / de l'auto **4.** inf [business, affair] affaire f ▶ **let's get this show on the road!** il faut y aller maintenant ! **5.** [achievement, performance] performance f, prestation f / *the team put up a pretty good show* l'équipe s'est bien défendue. ◆ **show around** vt sep faire visiter. ◆ **show in** vt sep faire entrer. ◆ **show off** ◆ vi crâner, frimer, se faire remarquer. ◆ vt sep **1.** [parade] faire étalage de / *to show off one's skill* faire étalage de son savoir-faire **2.** [set off] mettre en valeur. ◆ **show out** vt sep reconduire or raccompagner (à la porte). ◆ **show round** = **show around**. ◆ **show up** ◆ vi **1.** inf [turn up, arrive] arriver **2.** [be visible] se voir, être visible / *the difference is so slight it hardly shows up at all* la différence est tellement minime qu'elle se remarque à peine. ◆ vt sep UK **1.** [unmask] démasquer **2.** [draw attention to - deficiency, defect] faire apparaître, faire ressortir **3.** [embarrass] faire honte à.

showbiz ['ʃəʊbɪz] n inf show-biz m, monde m du spectacle.

show business n show-business m, monde m du spectacle.

showcase ['ʃəʊkeɪs] ◆ n vitrine f. ◆ adj [role] prestigieux ; [operation] de prestige. ◆ vt servir de vitrine à *fig*.

showdown ['ʃəʊdaʊn] n **1.** [confrontation] confrontation f, épreuve f de force **2.** [in poker] étalement m du jeu.

shower ['ʃaʊər] ◆ n **1.** [for washing] douche f ▶ **to have** or **to take a shower** prendre une douche **2.** METEOR averse f ▶ **a snow shower** une chute de neige **3.** [stream - of confetti, sparks, gravel] pluie f ; [-of praise, abuse] avalanche f ; [-of blows] pluie f, volée f, grêle f **4.** US [party] fête au cours de laquelle les invités offrent des cadeaux **5.** UK inf & pej [group] bande f. ◆ vi **1.** [have a shower] prendre une douche, se doucher **2.** [rain] pleuvoir par averses **3.** fig [rain down] pleuvoir. ◆ vt : *passers-by were showered with broken glass* des passants ont été atteints par des éclats de verre / *they showered him with gifts* or *they showered gifts on him* ils l'ont comblé de cadeaux ▶ **to shower sb with praise** encenser qqn.

shower cap n bonnet m de douche.

shower curtain n rideau m de douche.

shower gel n gel m douche.

shower head n pomme f de douche.
showerproof ['ʃaʊəpruːf] adj imperméable.
shower room n salle f d'eau.
shower unit n bloc-douche m.
showery ['ʃaʊərɪ] adj : *it will be rather a showery day tomorrow* il y aura des averses demain.
show flat n [UK] appartement m témoin.
showground ['ʃaʊgraʊnd] n parc m d'expositions.
show house n maison f témoin.
showily ['ʃaʊɪlɪ] adv de façon voyante or ostentatoire.
showing ['ʃaʊɪŋ] n **1.** [of paintings, sculpture] exposition f ; [of film] projection f, séance f **2.** [performance] performance f, prestation f.
showing off n : *I've had enough of his showing off* j'en ai assez de sa vantardise.
show jumper n [rider] cavalier m, -ère f *(participant à des concours de saut d'obstacles)* ; [horse] sauteur m.
show jumping n jumping m, concours m de saut d'obstacles.
showman ['ʃaʊmən] *(pl* showmen [-mən]) n THEAT metteur m en scène ; [in fairground] forain m ; [circus manager] propriétaire m de cirque.
showmanship ['ʃaʊmənʃɪp] n sens m de la mise en scène.
shown [ʃaʊn] pp ⟶ show.
show-off n inf frimeur m, -euse f.
showpiece ['ʃaʊpiːs] n : *the showpiece of his collection* le joyau de sa collection / *the school had become a showpiece of educational excellence* l'école est devenue un modèle quant à la qualité de l'enseignement.
showroom ['ʃaʊrʊm] n salle f or salon m d'exposition.
show-stopping adj sensationnel.
show trial n procès m à grand spectacle.
showy ['ʃaʊɪ] *(compar* showier, *superl* showiest) adj voyant, ostentatoire.
shrank [ʃræŋk] pt ⟶ shrink.
shrapnel ['ʃræpnl] n **1.** *(U)* [fragments] éclats mpl d'obus / *a piece of shrapnel* un éclat d'obus **2.** [shell] shrapnel m.
shred [ʃred] ◆ n **1.** [of paper, fabric, etc.] lambeau m ▶ **in shreds** en lambeaux ▶ **to tear sthg to shreds a)** *lit* déchirer qqch en petits morceaux **b)** *fig* démolir qqch **2.** [of truth, evidence] parcelle f. ◆ vt **1.** [tear up - paper, fabric] déchiqueter **2.** CULIN râper.
shredder ['ʃredər] n **1.** CULIN [manual] râpe f ; [in food processor] disque-râpeur m **2.** [for documents] destructeur m de documents.
shrew [ʃruː] n **1.** ZOOL musaraigne f **2.** pej [woman] mégère f, harpie f.
shrewd [ʃruːd] adj [person - astute] perspicace ; [-crafty] astucieux, rusé, habile ; [judgment] perspicace / *to make a shrewd guess* deviner juste / *a shrewd investment* un placement judicieux.
shrewdly ['ʃruːdlɪ] adv [act] avec perspicacité or sagacité ; [answer, guess] astucieusement.
shrewdness ['ʃruːdnɪs] n [astuteness] perspicacité f ; [craftiness] habileté f, ruse f.
shriek [ʃriːk] ◆ vi hurler, crier / *to shriek with pain* pousser un cri de douleur / *to shriek with laughter* hurler de rire. ◆ vt hurler, crier.
shrift [ʃrɪft] n [PHR] **to give sb short shrift** envoyer promener qqn.
shrill [ʃrɪl] ◆ adj perçant, aigu (aiguë), strident. ◆ vi [siren, whistle] retentir. ◆ vt crier d'une voix perçante.

shrimp [ʃrɪmp] ◆ n **1.** ([US] *pl* shrimp) ZOOL crevette f ▶ **shrimp cocktail** cocktail m de crevettes **2.** inf & pej [small person] minus m, avorton m. ◆ vi ▶ **to go shrimping** aller aux crevettes.
shrine [ʃraɪn] n **1.** [place of worship] lieu m saint **2.** [container for relics] reliquaire m **3.** [tomb] tombe f, mausolée m **4.** fig haut lieu m.
shrink [ʃrɪŋk] *(pt* shrank [ʃræŋk], *pp* shrunk [ʃrʌŋk]) ◆ vi **1.** [garment, cloth] rétrécir **2.** [grow smaller - gen] rétrécir, rapetisser ; [-economy] se contracter ; [-meat] réduire ; [-person] rapetisser ; [-numbers, profits, savings] diminuer, baisser ; [-business, trade] se réduire **3.** [move backwards] reculer ▶ **to shrink into o.s.** se refermer or se replier sur soi-même **4.** [shy away] se dérober ; [hesitate] répugner. ◆ vt (faire) rétrécir. ◆ n inf & pej [psychiatrist, psychoanalyst] psy mf.
shrinkage ['ʃrɪŋkɪdʒ] n *(U)* **1.** [gen] rétrécissement m, contraction f **2.** COMM [of goods in transit] pertes fpl ; [of goods stolen] vol m (des stocks).
shrink-wrap *(pt & pp* shrink-wrapped, *cont* shrink-wrapping) vt emballer sous film plastique.
shrink-wrapped adj emballé sous film plastique.
shrink-wrapping n **1.** [process] emballage m sous film plastique **2.** [material] film m plastique.
shrivel ['ʃrɪvl] ([UK] *pt & pp* shrivelled, *cont* shrivelling ; [US] *pt & pp* shriveled, *cont* shriveling) ◆ vi [fruit, vegetable] se dessécher, se ratatiner ; [leaf] se recroqueviller ; [flower, crops] se flétrir ; [face, skin] se flétrir ; [meat, leather] se racornir. ◆ vt [fruit, vegetable] dessécher, ratatiner ; [leaf] dessécher ; [flower, crops] flétrir ; [face, skin] flétrir, rider, parcheminer ; [meat, leather] racornir. ❖ **shrivel up** vi & vt sep = shrivel.
shrivelled ['ʃrɪvld] pp = shrivel.
shrivelled ['ʃrɪvld] adj ratatiné.
shroud [ʃraʊd] ◆ n **1.** [burial sheet] linceul m, suaire m **2.** fig [covering] voile m, linceul m **3.** [shield - for spacecraft] coiffe f **4.** [rope, cord - for aerial, mast, etc.] hauban m ; [-on parachute] suspente f. ◆ vt **1.** [body] envelopper dans un linceul or suaire **2.** [obscure] voiler, envelopper.
Shrove Tuesday [ʃrəʊv-] pr n Mardi gras.
shrub [ʃrʌb] n arbrisseau m, arbuste m.
shrubbery ['ʃrʌbərɪ] *(pl* shrubberies) n [shrub garden] jardin m d'arbustes ; [scrubland] maquis m.
shrug [ʃrʌg] *(pt & pp* shrugged, *cont* shrugging) ◆ vt ▶ **to shrug one's shoulders** hausser les épaules. ◆ vi hausser les épaules. ◆ n haussement m d'épaules. ❖ **shrug off** vt sep [disregard] dédaigner / *to shrug off an illness* se débarrasser d'une maladie / *to shrug off one's problems* faire abstraction de ses problèmes.
shrunk [ʃrʌŋk] pp ⟶ shrink.
shrunken ['ʃrʌŋkn] adj [garment, fabric] rétréci ; [person, body] ratatiné, rapetissé ; [head] réduit.
shtick [ʃtɪk] n [US] inf numéro m.
shtum = schtum.
shucks [ʃʌks] interj [US] inf (ah) zut.
shudder ['ʃʌdər] vi **1.** [person] frissonner, frémir, trembler / *I shudder to think how much it must have cost!* je frémis rien que de penser au prix que ça a dû coûter ! **2.** [vehicle, machine] vibrer ; [stronger] trépider / *the train shuddered to a halt* le train s'arrêta dans une secousse.
shuffle ['ʃʌfl] ◆ vi **1.** [walk] traîner les pieds **2.** [fidget] remuer, s'agiter **3.** [in card games] battre les cartes. ◆ vt **1.** [walk] ▶ **to shuffle one's feet** traîner les pieds **2.** [move round - belongings, papers] remuer **3.** [cards] battre, brasser ; [dominoes] mélanger, brasser. ◆ n **1.** [walk] pas m traînant **2.** [of cards] battage m. ❖ **shuffle off** ◆ vi partir en traînant les pieds. ◆ vt sep [responsibility] se dérober à.

shun [ʃʌn] (*pt & pp* **shunned**, *cont* **shunning**) vt fuir, éviter.

shunt [ʃʌnt] ◆ vt **1.** [move] déplacer **2.** ⬛ RAIL [move about] manœuvrer ; [direct] aiguiller ; [marshal] trier **3.** ELEC [circuit] shunter, monter en dérivation ; [current] dériver. ◆ vi **1.** RAIL manœuvrer **2.** [travel back and forth] faire la navette. ◆ n **1.** RAIL manœuvre f (de triage) **2.** ELEC shunt m, dérivation f **3.** MED shunt m **4.** ⬛ inf [car crash] collision f.

shunter [ˈʃʌntə'] n locomotive f de manœuvre.

shush [ʃʊʃ] ◆ interj chut. ◆ vt : *he kept shushing us* il n'arrêtait pas de nous dire de nous taire.

shut [ʃʌt] (*pt & pp* **shut**, *cont* **shutting**) ◆ vt **1.** [close] fermer ▸ **shut your mouth** or **your face!** *inf* boucle-la !, la ferme ! **2.** [trap] : *her skirt got shut in the door* sa robe est restée coincée dans la porte / *I shut my finger in the door* je me suis pris le doigt dans la porte. ◆ vi **1.** [door, window, container, etc.] (se) fermer **2.** [shop, gallery, etc.] fermer. ◆ adj fermé ▸ **keep your mouth** or **trap shut!** *inf* ferme-la !, boucle-la ! ◆ **shut away** vt sep [criminal, animal] enfermer ; [precious objects] mettre sous clé. ◆ **shut down** vt sep [store, factory, cinema] fermer ; [machine, engine] arrêter. ◆ vi [store, factory, cinema] fermer. ◆ **shut in** vt sep enfermer. ◆ **shut off** ◆ vt sep **1.** [cut off - supplies, water, electricity] couper ; [- radio, machine] éteindre, arrêter ; [- light] éteindre **2.** [isolate] couper, isoler **3.** [block] boucher. ◆ vi se couper, s'arrêter. ◆ **shut out** vt sep **1.** [of building, room] : *she shut us out* elle nous a enfermés dehors / *we got shut out* nous ne pouvions plus rentrer **2.** [exclude] exclure **3.** [block out - thought, feeling] chasser (de son esprit) **4.** SPORT [opponent] empêcher de marquer. ◆ **shut up** ◆ vi **1.** *inf* [be quiet] se taire **2.** [close] fermer. ◆ vt sep **1.** [close - shop, factory] fermer **2.** [lock up] enfermer **3.** *inf* [silence] faire taire.

shutdown [ˈʃʌtdaʊn] n fermeture f définitive.

shut-eye n *inf* ▸ **to get a bit of shut-eye** faire un somme, piquer un roupillon.

shutoff [ˈʃʌtɒf] n **1.** [device] : *the automatic shutoff didn't work* le dispositif d'arrêt automatique n'a pas fonctionné **2.** [action] arrêt m.

shutter [ˈʃʌtə'] n **1.** [on window] volet m **2.** PHOT obturateur m.

shuttered [ˈʃʌtəd] adj [with shutters fitted] à volets ; [with shutters closed] aux volets fermés.

shutter release n déclencheur m d'obturateur.

shutter speed n vitesse f d'obturation.

shuttle [ˈʃʌtl] ◆ n **1.** [vehicle, service] navette f / *there is a shuttle bus service from the station to the stadium* il y a une navette d'autobus entre la gare et le stade **2.** [on weaving loom, sewing machine] navette f **3.** = **shuttlecock**. ◆ vi faire la navette. ◆ vt : *passengers are shuttled to the airport by bus* les passagers sont transportés en bus à l'aéroport.

shuttlecock [ˈʃʌtlkɒk] n volant m (*au badminton*).

shuttle diplomacy n navette f diplomatique.

shuttle service n (service m de) navettes fpl.

shy [ʃaɪ] (*compar* **shyer**, *superl* **shyest**, *pt & pp* **shied**) ◆ adj **1.** [person - timid] timide ; [- ill at ease] gêné, mal à l'aise ; [- unsociable] sauvage ▸ **to make sb shy** intimider qqn **2.** [animal, bird] peureux **3.** ⬛ [short, lacking] ▸ **to be shy of** manquer de, être à court de. ◆ n ⬛ [throw] lancer m, jet m. ◆ vi [horse] broncher. ◆ vt lancer, jeter. ◆ **shy away from** vt insep éviter de.

shyly [ˈʃaɪlɪ] adv timidement.

shyness [ˈʃaɪnɪs] n timidité f.

shyster [ˈʃaɪstə'] ⬛ *inf* ◆ n [crook] escroc m, filou m ; [corrupt lawyer] avocat m marron ; [politician] politicien véreux m, politicienne f véreuse. ◆ adj malhonnête, véreux.

Siam [ˌsaɪˈæm] pr n Siam m / *in Siam* au Siam.

Siamese [ˌsaɪəˈmiːz] (*pl* **Siamese**) ◆ n **1.** [person] Siamois m, -e f **2.** LING siamois m **3.** = **Siamese cat**. ◆ adj siamois.

Siamese cat n chat m siamois.

Siamese twins pl n [male] frères mpl siamois ; [female] sœurs fpl siamoises.

Siberia [saɪˈbɪərɪə] pr n Sibérie f / *in Siberia* en Sibérie.

Siberian [saɪˈbɪərɪən] ◆ n Sibérien m, -enne f. ◆ adj sibérien.

sibling [ˈsɪblɪŋ] ◆ n [brother] frère m ; [sister] sœur f / *all his siblings* sa fratrie *spec*, tous ses frères et sœurs. ◆ adj ▸ **sibling rivalry** rivalité f entre frères et sœurs.

sic [sɪk] ◆ adv sic. ◆ interj ⬛ [to dog] ▸ **sic!** attaque ! ◆ vt ⬛ ▸ **to sic a dog onto sb** dire à un chien d'attaquer qqn.

Sicilian [sɪˈsɪljən] ◆ n **1.** [person] Sicilien m, -enne f **2.** LING sicilien m. ◆ adj sicilien.

Sicily [ˈsɪsɪlɪ] pr n Sicile f / *in Sicily* en Sicile.

7K MESSAGING written abbr of **sick**.

sick [sɪk] ◆ adj **1.** [unwell - person, plant, animal] malade ; [- state] maladif ▸ **to fall sick, to get** or **to take sick** ⬛ tomber malade / *my secretary is off sick* ma secrétaire est en congé de maladie ▸ **to go** *inf* or **to report sick** MIL se faire porter malade or pâle ▸ **to be sick with fear / worry** être malade de peur / d'inquiétude **2.** [nauseous] ▸ **to be sick** vomir ▸ **to feel sick** avoir envie de vomir or mal au cœur **3.** [fed up, disgusted] écœuré, dégoûté / *I'm sick (and tired) of telling you!* j'en ai assez de te le répéter ! / *you make me sick!* tu m'écœures or me dégoûtes ! ▸ **to be sick to death of sb / sthg** *inf* en avoir vraiment assez or ras le bol de qqn / qqch **4.** *inf* [unwholesome] malsain, pervers ; [morbid - humour] malsain ; [- joke] macabre. ◆ pl n ▸ **the sick** les malades mpl. ◆ n ⬛ *inf* [vomit] vomi m. ◆ **sick up** vt sep ⬛ *inf* vomir, rendre.

sickbag [ˈsɪkbæg] n sac m à vomi.

sickbay [ˈsɪkbeɪ] n infirmerie f.

sickbed [ˈsɪkbed] n lit m de malade.

sick building syndrome n syndrome m du bâtiment malsain.

sicken [ˈsɪkn] ◆ vt **1.** [disgust, distress] écœurer, dégoûter **2.** [make nauseous] donner mal au cœur à, écœurer ; [make vomit] faire vomir. ◆ vi **1.** [fall ill - person, animal] tomber malade ; [- plant] dépérir / *he's sickening for something* ⬛ il couve quelque chose **2.** *liter* [become weary] se lasser.

sickening [ˈsɪknɪŋ] adj **1.** [nauseating - smell, mess] nauséabond, écœurant ; [- sight] écœurant **2.** *fig* écœurant, répugnant.

sickeningly [ˈsɪknɪŋlɪ] adv : *he's sickeningly pious* il est d'une piété écœurante / *she's sickeningly successful* hum elle réussit si bien que c'en est écœurant.

sickie [ˈsɪkɪ] n ⬛, Austr & NZ *inf* : *to take a sickie* se faire porter pâle (*lorsqu'on est bien portant*) / *he threw a sickie* il n'est pas allé travailler, faisant croire qu'il était malade.

sickle [ˈsɪkl] n faucille f ▸ **a sickle moon** un mince croissant de lune.

sick leave n congé m (de) maladie ▸ **to be (away) on sick leave** être en congé de (de) maladie.

sickly ['sɪklɪ] (*compar* **sicklier,** *superl* **sickliest**) adj **1.** [person] chétif, maladif ; [complexion, pallor] maladif ; [plant] chétif ; [dawn, light, glare] blafard ; [smile] pâle **2.** [nauseating] écœurant ; [sentimentality] mièvre.

sick-making adj ▥ *inf* dégueulasse / *it's absolutely sick-making* c'est à vous donner la nausée.

sickness ['sɪknɪs] n **1.** [nausea] nausée *f* **2.** [illness] maladie *f*.

sickness benefit n (U) ▥ prestations *fpl* de l'assurance maladie ; ≃ indemnités *fpl* journalières.

sick note n mot d'absence (*pour cause de maladie*).

sicko ['sɪkəʊ] adj ▣ dérangé, malade.

sick-out n ▣ grève où *tous les employés prétendent être malades le même jour.*

sick pay n indemnité *f* de maladie (*versée par l'employeur*).

sickroom ['sɪkrʊm] n [sickbay] infirmerie *f* ; [in home] chambre *f* de malade.

side [saɪd] ◆ n **1.** [part of body - human] côté *m* ; [- animal] flanc *m* ▶ *lie on your side* couchez-vous sur le côté / *I've got a pain in my right side* j'ai mal au côté droit / *I sat down at* or *by his side* je me suis assis à ses côtés or à côté de lui ▶ *to get on sb's good / bad side* s'attirer la sympathie / l'antipathie de qqn **2.** [as opposed to top, bottom, front, back] côté *m* / *the bottle was on its side* la bouteille était couchée / *her hair is cut short at the sides* ses cheveux sont coupés court sur les côtés **3.** [outer surface - of cube, pyramid] côté *m*, face *f* ; [flat surface - of biscuit, sheet of paper, cloth] côté *m* ; [- of coin, record, tape] côté *m*, face *f* / *write on both sides of the paper* écrivez recto verso / **'this side up'** 'haut' / *the right / wrong side of the cloth* l'endroit *m* / l'envers *m* du tissu ; [inner surface - of bathtub, cave, stomach] paroi *f* **4.** [edge - of triangle, lawn] côté *m* ; [- of road, pond, river, bed] bord *m* **5.** [slope - of mountain, hill, valley] flanc *m*, versant *m* **6.** [opposing part] côté *m* / *on the other side of the room / wall* de l'autre côté de la pièce / du mur / *you're driving on the wrong side!* vous conduisez du mauvais côté ! ▶ *to take sb to one side* prendre qqn à part / *leaving that on one side for the moment...* en laissant cela de côté pour l'instant... / *Manhattan's Lower East Side* le quartier sud-est de Manhattan / *on every side* or *on all sides* de tous côtés, de toutes parts / *he's on the right / wrong side of forty* il n'a pas encore / il a dépassé la quarantaine / *I can't see myself finishing the work this side of Easter* je ne me vois pas finir ce travail d'ici à Pâques **7.** [facet, aspect - of problem] aspect *m*, côté *m* ; [- of person] côté *m* / *to examine all sides of an issue* examiner un problème sous tous ses aspects / *she's very good at the practical side of things* elle est excellente sur le plan pratique / *she has her good side* elle a ses bons côtés / *she showed an unexpected side of herself* elle a révélé une facette inattendue de sa personnalité **8.** [group, faction] côté *m*, camp *m* ; [team] équipe *f* ; POL [party] parti *m* / *the winning side* le camp des vainqueurs ▶ *to pick* or *to choose sides* former des équipes / *whose side is he on?* de quel côté est-il ? ▶ *to go over to the other side, to change sides* changer de camp / *time is on their side* le temps joue en leur faveur ▶ *to take sides* prendre parti **9.** [position, point of view] point *m* de vue / *there are two sides to every argument* dans toute discussion il y a deux points de vue / *he's told me his side of the story* il m'a donné sa version de l'affaire **10.** ▥ [page of text] page *f* **11.** ▥ *inf* [TV channel] chaîne *f*. ◆ vi ▶ *to side with sb* se ranger or se mettre du côté de qqn, prendre parti pour qqn / *they all sided against her* ils ont fait cause commune contre elle. ◆ adj **1.** [situated on one side - panel, window] latéral, de côté ▶ **side door** porte *f* latérale ▶ **side pocket** poche *f* extérieure **2.** [directional - view] de côté,

de profil ; [- elevation, kick] latéral **3.** [additional] en plus / *a side order of toast* une portion de toast en plus or en supplément. ❖ **on the side** adv phr : *to make a bit of money on the side* a) [gen] se faire un peu d'argent en plus or supplémentaire b) [dishonestly] se remplir les poches / *a hamburger with salad on the side* un hamburger avec une salade. ❖ **side by side** adv phr côte à côte.

sidebar ['saɪdbɑ:ʳ] n COMPUT menu *m* latéral.

sideboard ['saɪdbɔːd] n [for dishes] buffet *m* bas. ❖ **sideboards** ▥ = sideburns.

sideburns ['saɪdbɜːnz] pl n pattes *fpl*.

sidecar ['saɪdkɑːʳ] n **1.** [on motorbike] side-car *m* **2.** [drink] side-car *m* (*cocktail composé de cognac, de Cointreau et de jus de citron*).

-sided ['saɪdɪd] in comp : *three / five-sided* à trois / cinq côtés / *a many-sided figure* une figure polygonale / *a glass-sided box* une boîte à parois de verre / *elastic-sided boots* bottes avec de l'élastique sur les côtés / *a steep-sided valley* une vallée encaissée.

side dish n plat *m* d'accompagnement.

side effect n effet *m* secondaire.

side issue n question *f* secondaire.

sidekick ['saɪdkɪk] n *inf* acolyte *m*.

sidelight ['saɪdlaɪt] n **1.** ▥ AUTO feu *m* de position **2.** NAUT feu *m* de position **3.** [information] ▶ *to give (sb) a sidelight on sthg* donner à qqn un aperçu de qqch.

sideline ['saɪdlaɪn] ◆ n **1.** SPORT [gen] ligne *f* de côté ; [touchline] (ligne *f* de) touche *f*, ligne *f* de jeu **2.** [job] activité *f* or occupation *f* secondaire **3.** COMM [product line] ligne *f* de produits secondaires. ◆ vt SPORT & *fig* mettre sur la touche.

sidelong ['saɪdlɒŋ] ◆ adj oblique, de côté. ◆ adv en oblique, de côté.

side-on ◆ adv de profil / *the car was hit side-on* la voiture a subi un choc latéral. ◆ adj [photo] de profil ; [collision] latéral.

side order n ▣ portion *f* / *I'd like a side order of fries* je voudrais aussi des frites.

side plate n petite assiette *f* (*que l'on met à gauche de chaque convive*).

side road n [minor road - in country] route *f* secondaire ; [- in town] petite rue *f* ; [road at right angles] rue *f* transversale.

sidesaddle ['saɪd,sædl] ◆ n selle *f* de femme. ◆ adv ▶ *to ride sidesaddle* monter en amazone.

side salad n salade *f* (*pour accompagner un plat*).

sideshow ['saɪdʃəʊ] n **1.** [in fair - booth] stand *m*, baraque *f* foraine ; [- show] attraction *f* **2.** [minor event] détail *m*.

sidesplitting ['saɪd,splɪtɪŋ] adj *inf* [story, joke] tordant, bidonnant.

sidesplittingly ['saɪd,splɪtɪŋlɪ] adv *inf* : *sidesplittingly funny* à se tordre de rire.

sidestep ['saɪdstep] (*pt & pp* **sidestepped,** *cont* **sidestepping**) ◆ n crochet *m* ; SPORT esquive *f*. ◆ vt **1.** [opponent, tackle - in football, rugby] crocheter ; [- in boxing] esquiver **2.** [issue, question] éluder, éviter ; [difficulty] esquiver. ◆ vi **1.** [dodge] esquiver **2.** [in skiing] : *to sidestep up a slope* monter une pente en escalier **3.** [be evasive] rester évasif.

side street n [minor street] petite rue *f* ; [at right angles] rue *f* transversale.

sidetrack ['saɪdtræk] ◆ vt [person - in talk] faire dévier de son sujet ; [- in activity] distraire ; [enquiry, investigation] détourner. ◆ n **1.** [digression] digression *f* **2.** ▣ RAIL [in yard] voie *f* de garage ; [off main line] voie *f* d'évitement.

sidewalk ['saɪdwɔːk] n US trottoir *m*.

sidewalk artist n US artiste *mf* de rue *(qui dessine à la craie sur le trottoir)*.

sidewalk café n US café *m* avec terrasse.

sideways ['saɪdweɪz] ◆ adv [lean] d'un côté ; [glance] obliquement, de côté ; [walk] en crabe / *to step sideways* faire un pas de côté / *I was thrown sideways* j'ai été projeté sur le côté / *I now turn sideways* maintenant mettez-vous de profil / *the pieces can move only sideways* les pièces ne peuvent que se déplacer latéralement ▸ *to knock sb sideways*: *the news really knocked him sideways* a) *inf* [astounded him] la nouvelle l'a vraiment époustouflé b) [upset him] la nouvelle l'a vraiment mis dans tous ses états. ◆ adj [step] de côté ; [look] oblique, de côté / *the job is a sideways move* c'est une mutation et non pas une promotion.

sideyard ['saɪdɑːd] n US jardin *m* *(à côté d'une maison)*.

siding ['saɪdɪŋ] n **1.** RAIL [in yard] voie *f* de garage ; [off main track] voie *f* d'évitement **2.** US CONSTR pavement *m*.

sidle ['saɪdl] vi se faufiler ▸ *to sidle in / out* entrer / sortir furtivement ▸ *to sidle up* or *over to sb* se glisser vers or jusqu'à qqn.

SIDS (abbr of **sudden infant death syndrome**) n MSN *f*.

siege [siːdʒ] ◆ n MIL & *fig* siège *m* ▸ *to lay siege to sthg* assiéger qqch ▸ *to be under siege* être assiégé. ◆ comp [machine, warfare] de siège ▸ *to have a siege mentality* être toujours sur la défensive.

Sierra Leone [sɪ'erəlɪ'əun] pr n Sierra Leone *f* / *in Sierra Leone* en Sierra Leone.

Sierra Leonean [sɪ'erəlɪ'əunjən] ◆ n habitant de la Sierra Leone. ◆ adj de la Sierra Leone.

siesta [sɪ'estə] n sieste *f* ▸ *to have* or *to take a siesta* faire la sieste.

sieve [sɪv] ◆ n [gen] tamis *m* ; [kitchen utensil] passoire *f* ; [for gravel, ore] crible *m* ▸ *to have a memory* or *mind like a sieve*: *I've got a memory like a sieve!* ma mémoire est une vraie passoire ! ◆ vt [flour, sand, powder] tamiser, passer au tamis ; [purée, soup] passer ; [gravel, ore] cribler, passer au crible.

sift [sɪft] ◆ vt **1.** [ingredients, soil] tamiser, passer au tamis ; [gravel, seed, ore] cribler, passer au crible **2.** [scrutinize - evidence, proposal] passer au crible *fig* **3.** = **sift out**. ◆ vi **1.** [search] fouiller **2.** [pass, filter] filtrer. ◆ **sift out** vt sep **1.** [remove - lumps, debris] enlever (à l'aide) d'un tamis or d'un crible **2.** [distinguish] dégager, distinguer.

sigh [saɪ] ◆ vi **1.** [gen] soupirer, pousser un soupir **2.** *liter* [lament] se lamenter ▸ *to sigh over sthg* se lamenter sur qqch ; [grieve] soupirer ▸ *to sigh for* or *over sb* / *sthg* soupirer pour qqn / qqch **3.** [wind] murmurer ; [tree, reed] bruire. ◆ vt : *"it's so lovely here", she sighed* « c'est tellement joli ici », soupira-t-elle. ◆ n soupir *m* ▸ *to give* or *to heave a sigh of relief* pousser un soupir de soulagement.

sighing ['saɪɪŋ] n *(U)* [of person] soupirs *mpl* ; [of wind] murmure *m* ; [of trees] bruissement *m*.

sight [saɪt] ◆ n **1.** [faculty, sense] vue *f* ▸ *to lose / to recover one's sight* perdre / recouvrer la vue **2.** [act, instance of seeing] vue *f* ▸ *to catch sight of sb / sthg* apercevoir or entrevoir qqn / qqch ▸ *to lose sight of sb / sthg* perdre qqn / qqch de vue / *at first sight the place seemed abandoned* à première vue, l'endroit avait l'air abandonné ▸ *to know sb by sight* connaître qqn de vue **3.** [range of vision] (portée *f* de) vue *f* / *the plane was still in sight* l'avion était encore en vue ▸ *out of sight* hors de vue **4.** [spectacle] spectacle *m* ; [you look awful] tu fais vraiment peine à voir **5.** [tourist attraction] curiosité *f* **6.** *liter* [opinion, judgment] avis *m*, opinion *f* / *in my father's sight she could do no wrong* aux

yeux de mon père, elle était incapable de faire du mal **7.** *inf* [mess] pagaille *f* ; [ridiculously dressed person] tableau *m* *fig* **8.** [aiming device] viseur *m* ; [on mortar] appareil *m* de pointage ▸ *to have sthg in one's sights* a) *lit* avoir qqch dans sa ligne de tir b) *fig* avoir qqch en vue. ◆ vt **1.** [see] voir, apercevoir ; [spot] repérer **2.** [aim - gun] pointer. ◆ **a sight** adv phr UK *inf* beaucoup / *you'd earn a sight more money working in industry* votre salaire serait beaucoup plus important si vous travailliez dans l'industrie.

sighted ['saɪtɪd] adj voyant ▸ **partially sighted** malvoyant.

sighting ['saɪtɪŋ] n : *UFO sightings have increased* un nombre croissant de personnes déclarent avoir vu des ovnis.

sight-read [-riːd] (*pt & pp* **sight-read** [-red]) vi & vt MUS déchiffrer.

sightseeing ['saɪt,siːɪŋ] ◆ n tourisme *m* ▸ *to do some sightseeing* a) faire du tourisme b) [in town] visiter la ville. ◆ comp ▸ **sightseeing tour**: *I went on a sightseeing tour of Rome* j'ai fait une visite guidée de Rome.

sightseer ['saɪt,siːər] n touriste *mf*.

sign [saɪn] ◆ n **1.** [gen & LING], MATH & MUS signe *m* **2.** [gesture, motion] signe *m*, geste *m* ▸ *to make a sign to sb* faire signe à qqn **3.** [arranged signal] signal *m* **4.** [written notice - gen & AUTO] panneau *m* ; [- hand-written] écriteau *m* ; [- on shop, bar, cinema, etc.] enseigne *f* ▸ **traffic signs** panneau *m* de signalisation **5.** [evidence, indication] signe *m*, indice *m* ; MED signe *m* / *as a sign of respect* en témoignage or en signe de respect **6.** ASTROL signe *m* / *what sign are you?* de quel signe êtes-vous ? **7.** RELIG [manifestation] signe *m* / *a sign from God* un signe de Dieu. ◆ vt **1.** [document, book] signer **2.** SPORT [contract] signer ; [player] engager **3.** [provide with signs] signaliser. ◆ vi **1.** [write name] signer **2.** [signal] ▸ *to sign to sb to do sthg* faire signe à qqn de faire qqch **3.** [use sign language] communiquer par signes. ◆ **sign away** vt sep [right, land, inheritance] se désister de ; [independence] renoncer à ; [power, control] abandonner. ◆ **sign in** ◆ vi **1.** [at hotel] remplir sa fiche (d'hôtel) ; [in club] signer le registre **2.** [worker] pointer (en arrivant). ◆ vt sep **1.** [guest] faire signer en arrivant **2.** [file, book] rendre, retourner. ◆ **sign for** vt insep **1.** [accept] signer / *to sign for a delivery / a registered letter* signer un bon de livraison / le récépissé d'une lettre recommandée **2.** [undertake work] signer (un contrat d'engagement). ◆ **sign off** vi **1.** RADIO & TV terminer l'émission **2.** [in letter] : *I'll sign off now* je vais conclure ici. ◆ **sign on** UK ◆ vi **1.** = **sign up** *(vi)*. **2.** [register as unemployed] s'inscrire au chômage. ◆ vt sep = **sign up** *(vt sep)*. ◆ **sign out** ◆ vi [gen] signer le registre (en partant) ; [worker] pointer (en partant). ◆ vt sep **1.** [file, car] retirer (contre décharge) ; [library book] emprunter **2.** [hospital patient] autoriser le départ de. ◆ **sign over** vt sep transférer. ◆ **sign up** ◆ vt sep **1.** [for job] se faire embaucher **2.** MIL [enlist] s'engager **3.** [enrol] s'inscrire. ◆ vt sep **1.** [employee] embaucher ; MIL [recruit] engager **2.** [student, participant] inscrire.

signal ['sɪgnl] (UK *pt & pp* **signalled**, cont **signalling** ; US *pt & pp* **signaled**, cont **signaling**) ◆ n **1.** [indication] signal *m* ▸ *to give sb the signal to do sthg* donner à qqn le signal de faire qqch **2.** RAIL sémaphore *m* **3.** RADIO, TELEC & TV signal *m*. ◆ comp **1.** NAUT ▸ **signal book** code *m* international des signaux ▸ **signal beacon** or **light** AERON & NAUT balise *f* **2.** RADIO & TELEC [strength, frequency] de signal. ◆ adj *fml* insigne. ◆ vt **1.** [send signal to] envoyer un signal à **2.** [indicate - refusal] indiquer, signaler ; [- malfunction] signaler, avertir de **3.** [announce, mark - beginning, end, change] marquer. ◆ vi **1.** [gesture] faire des signes ▸ *to signal to sb to do sthg* faire signe à qqn de faire qqch **2.** [send signal] envoyer un signal **3.** AUTO [with indicator] mettre son clignotant ; [with arm] indiquer de la main un changement de direction.

signal box n 🇬🇧 RAIL poste *m* de signalisation.

signaling 🇺🇸 = signalling.

signalling 🇬🇧, **signaling** 🇺🇸 ['sɪgnəlɪŋ] ◆ n **1.** AERON, AUTO, NAUT & RAIL signalisation *f* **2.** [warning] avertissement *m* **3.** [of electronic message] transmission *f*. ◆ comp [error, equipment] de signalisation ▸ **signalling flag a)** NAUT pavillon *m* de signalisation **b)** MIL drapeau *m* de signalisation.

signally ['sɪgnəlɪ] adv *fml* : *they have signally failed to achieve their goal* ils n'ont manifestement pas pu atteindre leur but.

signalman ['sɪgnlmən] (*pl* **signalmen** [-mən]) n RAIL aiguilleur *m* ; MIL & NAUT signaleur *m*.

signal tower n 🇺🇸 poste *m* d'aiguillage or de signalisation.

signatory ['sɪgnətrɪ] (*pl* **signatories**) ◆ n signataire *mf* / *Namibia is a signatory to* or *of the treaty* la Namibie a ratifié le traité. ◆ adj signataire.

signature ['sɪgnətʃər] n **1.** [name] signature *f* ▸ **to put one's signature to sthg** apposer sa signature sur qqch **2.** [signing] signature *f* ▸ **to witness a signature** signer comme témoin **3.** 🇺🇸 PHARM [instructions] posologie *f* **4.** TYPO [section of book] cahier *m* ; [mark] signature *f*.

signature tune n 🇬🇧 RADIO & TV indicatif *m* (musical).

signet ring n chevalière *f*.

significance [sɪg'nɪfɪkəns] n **1.** [importance, impact] importance *f*, portée *f* / *what happened?* — *nothing of any significance* qu'est-ce qui s'est passé ? — rien d'important or de spécial / *his decision is of no significance to our plans* sa décision n'aura aucune incidence sur nos projets **2.** [meaning] signification *f*, sens *m*.

significant [sɪg'nɪfɪkənt] adj **1.** [notable - change, amount, damage] important, considérable ; [- discovery, idea, event] de grande portée ▸ **significant other** partenaire *mf* (*dans une relation affective*) **2.** [meaningful, indicative - look, pause] significatif **3.** [in statistics] significatif.

significantly [sɪg'nɪfɪkəntlɪ] adv **1.** [differ, change, increase] considérablement, sensiblement **2.** [nod, frown, wink] de façon significative **3.** [in statistics] de manière significative.

signification [,sɪgnɪfɪ'keɪʃn] n signification *f*.

signify ['sɪgnɪfaɪ] (*pt* & *pp* **signified**) ◆ vt **1.** [indicate, show] signifier, indiquer **2.** [mean] signifier, vouloir dire. ◆ vi *inf* être important.

signing ['saɪnɪŋ] n **1.** [sign language] traduction simultanée en langage par signes / *her signing is excellent* elle connaît très bien le langage des signes **2.** SPORT [transfer] transfert *m* ; [player] recrue *f*.

sign language n (*U*) langage *m* des signes ▸ **to speak in sign language** parler par signes / *using sign language, he managed to ask for food* (en s'exprimant) par signes, il s'est débrouillé pour demander à manger.

signpost ['saɪnpəʊst] ◆ n **1.** *lit* poteau *m* indicateur **2.** *fig* [guide] repère *m* ; [omen] présage *m*. ◆ vt *lit & fig* [indicate] indiquer ; [provide with signs] signaliser, baliser.

signwriter ['saɪn,raɪtər] n peintre *m* en lettres.

Sikh [siːk] ◆ n Sikh *mf*. ◆ adj sikh.

Sikhism ['siːkɪzm] n sikhisme *m*.

silage ['saɪlɪdʒ] n ensilage *m*.

silence ['saɪləns] ◆ n silence *m*. ◆ vt **1.** [person] réduire au silence, faire taire ; [sound] étouffer ; [guns] faire taire **2.** [stifle - opposition] réduire au silence ; [- conscience, rumours, complaints] faire taire.

silencer ['saɪlənsər] n **1.** [on gun] silencieux *m* **2.** 🇬🇧 AUTO pot *m* d'échappement, silencieux *m*.

silent ['saɪlənt] ◆ adj **1.** [saying nothing] silencieux ▸ **to fall silent** se taire ▸ **to keep** or **to be silent** garder le silence, rester silencieux **2.** [taciturn] silencieux, taciturne **3.** [unspoken - prayer, emotion, reproach] muet **4.** [soundless - room, forest] silencieux, tranquille ; [- tread] silencieux ; [- film] muet **5.** LING muet. ◆ n CIN film *m* muet ▸ **the silents** le (cinéma) muet.

silently ['saɪləntlɪ] adv silencieusement.

silent majority n majorité *f* silencieuse.

silent partner n 🇺🇸 COMM (associé *m*) commanditaire *m*, bailleur *m* de fonds.

silhouette [,sɪluː'et] ◆ n silhouette *f*. ◆ vt (*usu passive*) ▸ **to be silhouetted against sthg** se découper contre qqch / *she stood at the window, silhouetted against the light* elle se tenait à la fenêtre, sa silhouette se détachant à contre-jour.

silicon ['sɪlɪkən] n silicium *m*.

silicon chip n puce *f*.

silicone ['sɪlɪkəʊn] n silicone *f* ▸ **silicone implant** : *she's had a silicone implant* elle s'est fait poser des implants en silicone.

Silicon Valley pr n Silicon Valley *f*.

silk [sɪlk] ◆ n **1.** [fabric] soie *f* ; [thread] fil *m* de soie **2.** [filament - from insect, on maize] soie *f* **3.** 🇬🇧 LAW ▸ **to take silk** être nommé avocat de la couronne. ◆ comp [scarf, blouse, etc.] de or en soie. ✧ **silks** pl n [jockey's jacket] casaque *f*.

silk screen n ▸ **silk screen (printing** or **process)** sérigraphie *f*. ✧ **silk-screen** vt sérigraphier, imprimer en sérigraphie.

silkworm ['sɪlkwɜːm] n ver *m* à soie ▸ **silkworm breeding** sériciculture *f*.

silky ['sɪlkɪ] (*compar* **silkier**, *superl* **silkiest**) adj **1.** [like silk - hair, cheek] soyeux **2.** [suave - tone, manner] doux (douce) **3.** [made of silk] de or en soie.

sill [sɪl] n **1.** [ledge - gen] rebord *m* ; [- of window] rebord *m*, appui *m* ; [- of door] seuil *m* **2.** AUTO marchepied *m* **3.** MIN [deposit] filon *m*, gisement *m*.

silliness ['sɪlɪnɪs] n bêtise *f*, stupidité *f*.

silly ['sɪlɪ] (*compar* **sillier**, *superl* **silliest**) ◆ adj **1.** [foolish - person] bête, stupide ; [- quarrel, book, grin, question] bête, stupide, idiot ; [infantile] bébête / *I'm sorry, it was a silly thing to say* excusez-moi, c'était bête de dire ça / *don't do anything silly* ne fais pas de bêtises / *how silly of me!* que je suis bête ! / *it's silly to worry* c'est idiot de s'inquiéter / *you silly idiot!* espèce d'idiot or d'imbécile ! / *you look silly in that tie* tu as l'air ridicule avec cette cravate **2.** [comical - mask, costume, voice] comique, drôle. ◆ adv *inf* [senseless] : *the blow knocked me silly* le coup m'a étourdi / *I was bored silly* je m'ennuyais à mourir / *I was scared silly* j'avais une peur bleue / *he drank himself silly* il s'est complètement soûlé.

silo ['saɪləʊ] (*pl* **silos**) n AGR & MIL silo *m*.

silt [sɪlt] n GEOL limon *m* ; [mud] vase *f*. ✧ **silt up** ◆ vi [with mud] s'envaser ; [with sand] s'ensabler. ◆ vt sep [subj: mud] envaser ; [subj: sand] ensabler.

silver ['sɪlvər] ◆ n **1.** [metal] argent *m* **2.** (*U*) [coins] pièces *fpl* (d'argent) ▸ **silver collection** quête *f* **3.** (*U*) [dishes] argenterie *f* ; [cutlery - gen] couverts *mpl* ; [- made of silver] argenterie *f*, couverts *mpl* en argent **4.** [colour] (couleur *f*) argent *m* **5.** SPORT [medal] médaille *f* d'argent. ◆ comp ▸ **silver mine** mine *f* d'argent ▸ **silver ore** minerai *m* argentifère. ◆ adj **1.** [of silver] d'argent, en argent **2.** [in colour] argenté, argent (*inv*) **3.** [sound] argentin ▸ **to have a silver tongue** : *she has a silver tongue* elle sait parler. ◆ vt *lit & fig* argenter.

silver birch n bouleau *m* blanc.

silver bullet n *fig* solution f miracle / *it's no silver bullet, but it'll help* ce n'est pas une solution miracle, mais ça aidera.

silver foil n papier m d'aluminium.

silver jubilee n (fête f du) vingt-cinquième anniversaire m / *the Queen's silver jubilee* le vingt-cinquième anniversaire de l'accession au trône de la reine.

silver lining n : *to have a silver lining* avoir de bons côtés.

silver medal n SPORT médaille f d'argent.

silver medallist n médaillé m, -e d'argent.

silver paper n papier m d'aluminium.

silver-plated [-'pleɪtɪd] adj argenté, plaqué argent / *silver-plated tableware* argenterie f.

silver screen n *dated* ▶ **the silver screen** le grand écran, le cinéma.

silversmith ['sɪlvəsmɪθ] n orfèvre m.

silver surfer n *inf* internaute mf senior.

silverware ['sɪlvəweəʳ] n **1.** [gen] argenterie f **2.** US [cutlery] couverts mpl.

silver wedding n ▶ **silver wedding (anniversary)** noces fpl d'argent.

sim n GAMES abbr of simulation.

SIM (abbr of subscriber identity module) n TELEC ▶ **SIM card** carte f SIM.

similar ['sɪmɪləʳ] adj **1.** [showing resemblance] similaire, semblable / *they're very similar* ils se ressemblent beaucoup / *other customers have had similar problems* d'autres clients ont eu des problèmes similaires or analogues or du même ordre / *they are very similar in content* leurs contenus sont pratiquement identiques / *the print is similar in quality to that of a typewriter* la qualité de l'impression est proche de celle d'une machine à écrire / *it's an assembly similar to the US Senate* c'est une assemblée comparable au Sénat américain / *a fruit similar to the orange* un fruit voisin de l'orange **2.** GEOM [triangles] semblable.

similarity [,sɪmɪ'lærətɪ] n [resemblance] ressemblance f, similarité f / *there is a certain similarity to her last novel* ça ressemble un peu à son dernier roman / *there are points of similarity in their strategies* leurs stratégies ont des points communs or présentent des similitudes. ❖ **similarities** pl n [features in common] ressemblances fpl, points mpl communs.

similarly ['sɪmɪləlɪ] adv **1.** [in a similar way] d'une façon similaire / *the houses are similarly constructed* les maisons sont construites sur le même modèle **2.** [likewise] de même.

simile ['sɪmɪlɪ] n LITER comparaison f.

simmer ['sɪməʳ] ❖ vi **1.** [water, milk, sauce] frémir ; [soup, stew] mijoter, mitonner ; [vegetables] cuire à petit feu **2.** [smoulder - violence, quarrel, discontent] couver, fermenter ; [seethe - with anger, excitement] être en ébullition **3.** [be hot] rôtir ; [when humid] mijoter. ❖ vt [milk, sauce] laisser frémir ; [soup, stew] mijoter, mitonner ; [vegetables] faire cuire à petit feu. ❖ n faible ébullition f. ❖ **simmer down** vi *inf* [person] se calmer.

simper ['sɪmpəʳ] ❖ vi minauder. ❖ vt : *"of course, madam", he simpered* « bien sûr, chère Madame », dit-il en minaudant. ❖ n sourire m affecté.

simpering ['sɪmpərɪŋ] n (U) minauderies fpl.

simple ['sɪmpl] adj **1.** [easy] simple, facile ; [uncomplicated] simple **2.** [plain - tastes, ceremony, life, style] simple **3.** [unassuming] simple, sans façons **4.** [naive] simple, naïf ; [feeble-minded] simple, niais **5.** [basic, not compound - substance, fracture, sentence] simple ; BIOL [eye] simple ▶ **simple equation** MATH équation f du premier degré.

simple interest n (U) intérêts mpl simples.

simple-minded adj [naive] naïf, simplet ; [feeble-minded] simple d'esprit / *it's a very simple-minded view of society* c'est une vision très simpliste de la société.

simple tense n temps m simple.

simpleton ['sɪmpltən] n *dated* nigaud m, -e f.

simplicity [sɪm'plɪsətɪ] (pl **simplicities**) n simplicité f / *the instructions are simplicity itself* les instructions sont simples comme bonjour or tout ce qu'il y a de plus simple.

simplification [,sɪmplɪfɪ'keɪʃn] n simplification f.

simplify ['sɪmplɪfaɪ] (pt & pp **simplified**) vt simplifier.

simplistic [sɪm'plɪstɪk] adj simpliste.

simplistically [sɪm'plɪstɪklɪ] adv de manière simpliste.

simply ['sɪmplɪ] adv **1.** [in a simple way] simplement, avec simplicité / *put quite simply, it's a disaster* c'est tout simplement une catastrophe **2.** [just, only] simplement, seulement / *it's not simply a matter of money* ce n'est pas une simple question d'argent **3.** [as intensifier] absolument / *simply don't understand you* je ne vous comprends vraiment pas / *we simply must go now* il faut absolument que nous partions maintenant.

simulate ['sɪmjʊleɪt] vt **1.** [imitate - blood, battle, sound] simuler, imiter **2.** [feign - pain, pleasure] simuler, feindre **3.** COMPUT & TECH simuler.

simulated ['sɪmjʊleɪtɪd] adj simulé.

simulation [,sɪmjʊ'leɪʃn] n simulation f ▶ **simulation model** COMPUT modèle m de simulation.

simulator ['sɪmjʊleɪtəʳ] n simulateur m.

simulcast [UK 'sɪməlkɑːst US 'saɪməlkæst] ❖ vt diffuser simultanément à la télévision et à la radio. ❖ adj radiotélévisé. ❖ n émission f radiotélévisée.

simultaneous [UK ,sɪməl'teɪnjəs US ,saɪməl'teɪnjəs] adj simultané ▶ **simultaneous translation** traduction f simultanée.

simultaneously [UK ,sɪməl'teɪnjəslɪ US ,saɪməl'teɪnjəslɪ] adv simultanément, en même temps.

sin [sɪn] (pt & pp **sinned**, cont **sinning**) ❖ n péché m ▶ **to commit a sin** pécher, commettre un péché / *it's a sin to tell a lie* mentir or le mensonge est un péché / *it would be a sin to sell it* ce serait un crime de le vendre ▶ **to live in sin** RELIG & *hum* vivre dans le péché. ❖ vi pécher ▶ **to sin against sthg** pécher contre qqch.

sin bin n *inf* SPORT banc m des pénalités, prison f.

since [sɪns] ❖ prep depuis / *he has been talking about it since yesterday / since before Christmas* il en parle depuis hier / depuis avant Noël / *the fair has been held annually ever since 1950* la foire a lieu chaque année depuis 1950 / *how long is it since their divorce?* ça fait combien de temps qu'ils ont divorcé ? / *since when have you been married?* depuis quand êtes-vous marié ? ❖ conj **1.** [in time] depuis que / *I've worn glasses since I was six* je porte des lunettes depuis que j'ai six ans or depuis l'âge de six ans / *how long has it been since you last saw Hal?* ça fait combien de temps que tu n'as pas vu Hal ? **2.** [expressing cause] puisque, comme / *she used to be his assistant, but she's since been promoted* elle était son assistante, mais depuis elle a été promue. ❖ **ever since** ❖ conj phr depuis que / *ever since she resigned, things have been getting worse* depuis qu'elle a démissionné or depuis sa démission, les choses ont empiré. ❖ prep phr depuis / *ever since that day he's been afraid of dogs* depuis ce jour-là, il a peur des chiens. ❖ adv phr depuis / *he arrived at 9 o'clock and he's been sitting there ever since* il est arrivé à 9 h et il est assis là depuis.

sincere [sɪn'sɪəʳ] adj sincère / *please accept my sincere apologies* veuillez accepter mes sincères excuses.

sincerely [sɪn'sɪəlɪ] adv sincèrement / *sincerely held views* des opinions auxquelles on croit sincèrement / *I sincerely hope we can be friends* j'espère sincèrement que nous serons amis ▶ **Yours sincerely a)** [formally] je vous prie d'agréer, Monsieur (or Madame), mes sentiments les meilleurs **b)** [less formally] bien à vous.

sincerity [sɪn'serətɪ] n sincérité f / *in all sincerity, I must admit that...* en toute sincérité, je dois admettre que...

sinecure ['saɪnɪˌkjʊəʳ] n sinécure f.

sinew ['sɪnjuː] n [tendon] tendon m ; [muscle] muscle m ; *liter* [strength] force f, forces fpl. ❖ **sinews** pl n *liter* [source of strength] nerf m, vigueur f.

sinewy ['sɪnjuːɪ] adj **1.** [muscular - person, body, arm] musclé ; [- neck, hands] nerveux **2.** [with tendons - tissue] tendineux **3.** *liter* [forceful - style] vigoureux, nerveux.

sinful ['sɪnfʊl] adj [deed, urge, thought] coupable, honteux ; [world] plein de péchés, souillé par le péché / *his sinful ways* sa vie de pécheur / *sinful man* pécheur m.

sing [sɪŋ] (*pt* sang [sæŋ], *pp* sung [sʌŋ]) ❖ vi **1.** [person] chanter **2.** [bird, kettle] chanter ; [wind, arrow] siffler ; [ears] bourdonner, siffler **3.** 🇺🇸 *inf* [act as informer] parler. ❖ vt **1.** [song, note, mass] chanter ▶ **to sing sb to sleep** chanter pour endormir qqn. [laud] célébrer, chanter ▶ **to sing sb's praises** chanter les louanges de qqn. ❖ **sing along** vi chanter (tous) ensemble / *to sing along to* or *with the radio* chanter en même temps que la radio. ❖ **sing out** vi **1.** [sing loudly] chanter fort **2.** *inf* [shout] crier / *when you're ready, sing out* quand tu seras prêt, fais-moi signe. ❖ **sing up** vi chanter plus fort.

Singapore [ˌsɪŋə'pɔːʳ] pr n Singapour.

Singaporean [ˌsɪŋə'pɔːrɪən] ❖ n Singapourien m, -enne f. ❖ adj singapourien.

singe [sɪndʒ] (*cont* singeing) ❖ vt **1.** [gen] brûler légèrement ; [shirt, fabric, paper] roussir **2.** CULIN [carcass, chicken] flamber, passer à la flamme. ❖ vi [fabric] roussir. ❖ n [burn] brûlure f (légère) ▶ **singe (mark)** marque f de brûlure.

singer ['sɪŋəʳ] n chanteur m, -euse f / *I'm a terrible singer* je chante affreusement mal.

Singhalese [ˌsɪŋhə'liːz] = **Sinhalese**.

singing ['sɪŋɪŋ] ❖ n **1.** [of person, bird] chant m ; [of kettle, wind] sifflement m ; [in ears] bourdonnement m, sifflement m **2.** [art] chant m. ❖ adj [lesson, teacher, contest] de chant.

singing telegram n vœux présentés sous forme chantée, généralement à l'occasion d'un anniversaire.

single ['sɪŋgl] ❖ adj **1.** [sole] seul, unique ▶ **single currency** monnaie f unique ▶ **the Single European Act** l'Acte unique européen ▶ **the Single Market** le Marché unique (européen) **2.** [individual, considered discretely] individuel, particulier / *every single apple* or *every single one of the apples was rotten* toutes les pommes sans exception étaient pourries **3.** [not double - flower, thickness] simple ; [- combat] singulier **4.** [for one person] ▶ **single room** chambre f pour une personne or individuelle ▶ **a single sheet** un drap pour un lit d'une personne ▶ **single supplement** [in hotel] supplément m chambre individuelle **5.** [unmarried] célibataire **6.** 🇺🇰 [one way] ▶ **single ticket**: *a single ticket to Oxford* un aller (simple) pour Oxford. ❖ n **1.** [hotel room] chambre f pour une personne or individuelle **2.** [record] 45 tours m inv, single m **3.** 🇺🇰 [ticket] billet m, aller m simple **4.** (*usu pl*) 🇺🇰 [money] pièce f d'une livre ; 🇺🇸 billet m d'un dollar **5.** [in cricket] point m. ❖ **single out** vt sep [for attention, honour] sélectionner, distinguer.

single bed n lit à une place.

single-breasted [-'brestɪd] adj [jacket, coat] droit.

single-click ❖ n clic m. ❖ vi cliquer une fois. ❖ vt cliquer une seule fois sur.

single cream n 🇺🇰 crème f (fraîche) liquide.

single-decker [-'dekəʳ] n ▶ **single-decker (bus)** autobus m sans impériale.

single file n file f indienne ▶ **to walk in single file** marcher en file indienne or à la queue leu leu.

single-handed [-'hændɪd] ❖ adv [on one's own] tout seul, sans aucune aide. ❖ adj **1.** [unaided - voyage] en solitaire **2.** [using one hand] à une main.

single-handedly [-'hændɪdlɪ] adv **1.** [on one's own] tout seul **2.** [with one hand] d'une seule main.

single-lane adj [traffic] à voie unique.

single-minded adj résolu, déterminé ▶ **to be single-minded about sthg** aborder qqch avec beaucoup de ténacité or de détermination / *he is single-minded in his efforts to block the project* il fait tout ce qu'il peut pour bloquer le projet.

single-mindedly [-'maɪndɪdlɪ] adv avec détermination.

single mother, single mum n mère f célibataire.

single parent n parent m isolé / *he's a single parent* c'est un père célibataire.

single-parent family n famille f monoparentale.

single-phase adj [current] monophasé.

single quotes pl n guillemets mpl.

singles ['sɪŋglz] (*pl* singles) ❖ n SPORT simple m / *the men's singles champion* le champion du simple messieurs. ❖ comp [bar, club, magazine] pour célibataires.

single-sex adj SCH non mixte.

singlet ['sɪŋglɪt] n 🇺🇰 [undergarment] maillot m de corps ; SPORT maillot m.

single-user licence n COMPUT licence f individuelle d'utilisation.

singly ['sɪŋglɪ] adv **1.** [one at a time] séparément **2.** [alone] seul **3.** [individually - packaged] individuellement.

singsong ['sɪŋsɒŋ] ❖ n **1.** [melodious voice, tone] ▶ **to speak in a singsong** parler d'une voix chantante **2.** 🇺🇰 [singing] chants mpl (en chœur) / *let's have a singsong* chantons tous ensemble or en chœur. ❖ adj [voice, accent] chantant.

singular ['sɪŋgjʊləʳ] ❖ adj **1.** [remarkable] singulier ; [odd] singulier, bizarre **2.** GRAM singulier. ❖ n GRAM singulier m / *in the third person singular* à la troisième personne du singulier.

singularly ['sɪŋgjʊləlɪ] adv singulièrement.

Sinhalese [ˌsɪnhə'liːz] ❖ n **1.** [person] Cinghalais m, -e f **2.** LING cinghalais m. ❖ adj cinghalais.

sinister ['sɪnɪstəʳ] adj **1.** [ominous, evil] sinistre **2.** HERALD senestre, sénestre.

sink [sɪŋk] (*pt* sank [sæŋk], *pp* sunk [sʌŋk]) ❖ n **1.** [for dishes] évier m ; [for hands] lavabo m ▶ **double sink** évier à deux bacs ▶ **sink board** 🇺🇸 égouttoir m **2.** [cesspool] puisard m **3.** GEOL doline f. ❖ vi **1.** [below surface - boat] couler, sombrer ; [- person, stone, log] couler **2.** [in mud, snow, etc.] s'enfoncer **3.** [subside - level, water, flames] baisser ; [- building, ground] s'affaisser **4.** [sag, slump - person] s'affaler, s'écrouler ; [- hopes] s'écrouler ▶ **to sink to the ground** s'effondrer **5.** [decrease, diminish - wages, rates, temperature] baisser ; [more dramatically] plonger, chuter ; [voice] se faire plus bas **6.** [slip, decline] sombrer, s'enfoncer / *to sink into apathy / depression* sombrer dans l'apathie / dans la dépression / *how could you sink to this?* comment as-tu pu tomber si bas ? **7.** [penetrate - blade, arrow] s'enfoncer. ◆ vt **1.** [boat, submarine] couler, envoyer par le fond **2.** [ruin -plans] faire échouer **3.** [forget] oublier **4.** [plunge, drive -knife, spear] enfoncer **5.** [dig, bore -well, mine shaft] creuser, forer **6.** [invest -money] mettre, investir ; [-extravagantly] engloutir **7.** SPORT [score -basket] marquer ; [-putt] réussir ▶ **to sink a shot a)** [in snooker] couler une bille **b)** [in basketball] réussir un tir or un panier **8.** [debt] s'acquitter de, payer ; FIN amortir **9.** 🔲 *inf* [drink down] s'envoyer, siffler. ❖ **sink in** vi **1.** [nail, blade] s'enfoncer **2.** [soak -varnish, cream] pénétrer **3.** [register -news] être compris or assimilé ; [-allusion] faire son effet.

sinking ['sɪŋkɪŋ] ◆ n **1.** [of ship -accidental] naufrage *m* ; [-deliberate] torpillage *m* **2.** [of building, ground] affaissement *m* **3.** [of money] engloutissement *m*. ◆ adj ▶ **sinking feeling** : *I experienced that sinking feeling you get when you've forgotten something* j'ai eu cette angoisse que l'on ressent quand on sait que l'on a oublié quelque chose.

sinking fund n FIN caisse *f* or fonds *mpl* d'amortissement.

sink school n *inf & pej* école *f* poubelle.

sink unit n bloc-évier *m*.

sinner ['sɪnər] n pécheur *m*, -eresse *f*.

Sinn Féin [ˌʃɪn'feɪn] pr n le Sinn Féin *(branche politique de l'IRA)*.

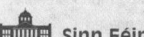 Sinn Féin

Mouvement nationaliste et républicain irlandais fondé en 1905, luttant pour l'indépendance et la renaissance de la culture gaélique. Force politique vitale en Irlande à partir de 1916, il devient, après la Seconde Guerre mondiale, la branche politique de l'IRA (**Irish Republican Army**).

sinuous ['sɪnjʊəs] adj [road, neck, movement, reasoning] sinueux.

sinus ['saɪnəs] n sinus *m*.

sinusitis [ˌsaɪnə'saɪtɪs] n *(U)* sinusite *f*.

sip [sɪp] *(pt & pp* sipped, *cont* sipping) ◆ vt [drink slowly] boire à petites gorgées or à petits coups ; [savour] siroter. ◆ vi : *he was at the bar, sipping at a cognac* il était au comptoir, sirotant un cognac. ◆ n petite gorgée *f*.

siphon ['saɪfn] ◆ n siphon *m*. ◆ vt **1.** [liquid, petrol] siphonner **2.** [money, resources] transférer ; [illicitly] détourner. ❖ **siphon off** vt sep **1.** [liquid, petrol] siphonner **2.** [remove -money] absorber, éponger ; [divert illegally] détourner.

sir [sɜːr] n **1.** [term of address] monsieur *m* / *no, sir* **a)** [gen & SCH] non, monsieur **b)** MIL [to officer] non, mon général / mon colonel, etc. ▶ **(Dear) Sir** [in letter] (Cher) Monsieur **2.** [title of knight, baronet] : *Sir Ian Hall* sir Ian Hall ▶ **to be made a sir** être anobli **3.** 🔲 *inf* [male teacher] : *Sir's coming!* le maître arrive !

siren ['saɪərən] n **1.** [device] sirène *f* ▶ **ambulance / police siren** sirène d'ambulance / de voiture de police **2.** MYTH sirène *f*; *fig* [temptress] sirène *f*, femme *f* fatale.

sirloin ['sɜːlɔɪn] n aloyau *m* ▶ **a sirloin steak** un bifteck dans l'aloyau.

sisal ['saɪsl] ◆ n sisal *m*. ◆ adj en or de sisal.

sissy ['sɪsɪ] *(pl* sissies) ◆ n [coward] peureux *m*, -euse *f* ; [effeminate person] : *he's a real sissy* c'est une vraie mauviette. ◆ adj [cowardly] peureux ; [effeminate] : *don't be so sissy* t'es une mauviette, ou quoi ?

sister ['sɪstər] ◆ n **1.** sœur *f* / *my big / little sister* ma grande / petite sœur **2.** [nun] religieuse *f*, (bonne) sœur *f* / *Sister Pauline* sœur Pauline **3.** 🔲 [nurse] infirmière *f* en chef **4.** POL [comrade] sœur *f* **5.** [to address woman] ma fille. ◆ adj *(especially with f nouns)* sœur ; *(especially with m nouns)* frère ▶ **sister company** société *f* sœur ▶ **sister countries** pays *mpl* frères, nations *fpl* sœurs ▶ **sister ship a)** [belonging to same company] navire *m* de la même ligne **b)** [identical] navire-jumeau *m*, sister-ship *m*.

sisterhood ['sɪstəhʊd] n **1.** [group of women -gen & RELIG] communauté *f* de femmes **2.** [solidarity] solidarité *f* entre femmes.

sister-in-law *(pl* sisters-in-law) n belle-sœur *f*.

sisterly ['sɪstəlɪ] adj [kiss, hug] sororal *liter*, fraternel ; [advice] de sœur.

sit [sɪt] *(pt & pp* sat [sæt], *cont* sitting) ◆ vi **1.** [take a seat] s'asseoir ; [be seated] être assis / *she came and sat next to me* elle est venue s'asseoir à côté de moi / *sit still!* tiens-toi or reste tranquille ! ▶ **sit!** [to dog] assis ! / *he sits in front of the television all day* il passe toute la journée devant la télévision **2.** ART & PHOT [pose] poser **3.** [be a member] ▶ **to sit on a board** faire partie or être membre d'un conseil d'administration **4.** [be in session] être en séance, siéger / *the council was still sitting at midnight* à minuit, le conseil siégeait toujours or était toujours en séance **5.** 🔲 SCH & UNIV [be a candidate] ▶ **to sit for an exam** se présenter à or passer un examen **6.** [be situated -building] être, se trouver ; [-vase] être posé **7.** [remain inactive or unused] rester **8.** [fit -coat, dress] tomber / *the jacket sits well on you* la veste vous va parfaitement ; *fig* : *the thought sat uneasily on my conscience* cette pensée me pesait sur la conscience **9.** [bird -perch] se percher, se poser ; [-brood] couver. ◆ vt **1.** [place] asseoir, installer / *he sat the child in the pram* il a assis l'enfant dans le landau **2.** [invite to be seated] faire asseoir **3.** 🔲 [examination] se présenter à, passer. ❖ **sit about** 🔲, **sit around** vi rester à ne rien faire, traîner. ❖ **sit back** vi **1.** [relax] s'installer confortablement / *just sit back and close your eyes* installe-toi bien et ferme les yeux **2.** [refrain from intervening] : *I can't just sit back and watch!* je ne peux pas rester là à regarder sans rien faire ! ❖ **sit by** vi rester sans rien faire. ❖ **sit down** ◆ vi s'asseoir / *please sit down* asseyez-vous, je vous en prie ▶ **to sit down to table** se mettre à table, s'attabler. ◆ vt sep [place -person] asseoir, installer. ❖ **sit in** vi **1.** [attend] ▶ **to sit in on a meeting / a class** assister à une réunion / un cours **2.** [replace] ▶ **to sit in for sb** remplacer qqn **3.** [hold a sit-in] faire un sit-in. ❖ **sit on** vt insep *inf* **1.** [suppress, quash -file, report] garder le silence sur ; [-suggestion, proposal] repousser, rejeter **2.** [take no action on] ne pas s'occuper de **3.** [silence -person] faire taire ; [rebuff] rabrouer. ❖ **sit out** ◆ vi [sit outside] s'asseoir or se mettre dehors. ◆ vt sep **1.** [endure] attendre la fin de **2.** [not take part in] : *I think I'll sit the next one out* **a)** [dance] je crois que je ne vais pas danser la prochaine danse **b)** [in cards] je crois que je ne jouerai pas la prochaine main. ❖ **sit through** vt insep attendre la fin de. ❖ **sit up** ◆ vi **1.** [raise o.s. to sitting position] s'asseoir ; [sit straight] se redresser / *she was sitting up in bed reading* elle lisait, assise dans son lit / *sit up straight!* redresse-toi !, tiens-toi droit ! **2.** [not go to bed] rester debout, ne pas se coucher / *I'll sit up with her until the fever passes* je vais rester avec elle jusqu'à ce que sa fièvre tombe **3.** *inf* [look lively] : *the public began to sit up and take notice* le public a commencé à montrer un certain intérêt. ◆ vt sep [child, patient] asseoir, redresser.

sitcom ['sɪtkɒm] n comédie *f* de situation, sitcom *m*.

SITD MESSAGING **written abbr of still in the dark.**

sit-down ◆ n inf [rest] pause f. ◆ adj ▶ **sit-down din-ner** dîner pris à table ▶ **sit-down strike** 🇬🇧 grève f sur le tas.

site [saɪt] ◆ n **1.** [piece of land] terrain m **2.** [place, location] emplacement m, site m **3.** CONSTR ▶ **(building) site** chantier m ▶ **demolition site** chantier de démolition **4.** ARCHEOL site m **5.** INTERNET site m. ◆ comp CONSTR [office, inspection, visit] de chantier. ◆ vt placer, situer. ❖ **on site** adv phr sur place.

sit-in n **1.** [demonstration] sit-in m inv ▶ **to stage** or **to hold a sit-in** faire un sit-in **2.** [strike] grève f sur le tas.

sitter ['sɪtər] n **1.** [babysitter] baby-sitter mf **2.** ART [model] modèle m **3.** [hen] couveuse f **4.** 🇬🇧 inf SPORT [easy chance] coup m facile.

sitting ['sɪtɪŋ] ◆ n [for meal] service m; ART [for portrait] séance f de pose; [of assembly, committee] séance f / I read the book at or in one sitting j'ai lu le livre d'une traite. ◆ adj **1.** [seated] assis **2.** [in office] en exercice / the sitting member for Leeds le député actuel de Leeds.

sitting duck n inf [target] cible f facile; [victim] proie f facile, pigeon m.

sitting room n 🇬🇧 salon m, salle f de séjour.

sitting tenant n 🇬🇧 locataire mf en place.

situate ['sɪtjʊeɪt] vt fml [in place] situer, implanter; [in context] resituer.

situated ['sɪtjʊeɪtɪd] adj **1.** [physically] situé / the house is conveniently situated for shops and public transport la maison est située à proximité des commerces et des transports en commun / the town is well / badly situated for tourist development la situation de la ville est / n'est pas favorable à son développement touristique **2.** [circumstantially] : how are we situated as regards the competition? comment est-ce qu'on est situés par rapport à la concurrence?

situation [ˌsɪtjʊ'eɪʃn] n **1.** [state of affairs] situation f / I've got myself into a ridiculous situation je me suis mis dans une situation ridicule / what would you do in my situation? qu'est-ce que tu ferais à ma place ou dans ma situation? / the firm's financial situation isn't good la situation financière de la société n'est pas bonne / a crisis situation une situation de crise / it won't work in a classroom situation ça ne marchera pas dans une salle de classe **2.** [job] situation f, emploi m / situations vacant / wanted offres fpl / demandes fpl d'emploi **3.** [location] situation f, emplacement m.

situation comedy n comédie f de situation.

sit-up n SPORT redressement m assis.

six [sɪks] ◆ n **1.** [number] six m ▶ **to be at sixes and sevens** 🇬🇧 être sens dessus dessous ▶ **it's six of one and half a dozen of the other** inf c'est blanc bonnet et bonnet blanc, c'est kif-kif ▶ **to get six of the best** 🇬🇧 inf & dated SCH recevoir six coups de canne **2.** [ice hockey team] équipe f; [cub or brownie patrol] patrouille f **3.** [in cricket] six points mpl. ◆ det six ▶ **to be six feet under** inf être six pieds sous terre, manger les pissenlits par la racine. ◆ pron six. See also **five**.

six-pack n pack m de six.

six-shooter n 🇺🇸 inf pistolet m à six coups, six-coups m inv.

sixteen [sɪks'tiːn] ◆ det seize ▶ **sweet sixteen**: she was sweet sixteen c'était une jolie jeune fille de seize ans. ◆ n seize m. ◆ pron seize. See also **fifteen**.

sixteenth [sɪks'tiːnθ] ◆ det seizième. ◆ n **1.** [ordinal] seizième mf **2.** [fraction] seizième m. See also **fifteenth**.

sixth [sɪksθ] ◆ det sixième. ◆ n **1.** [ordinal] sixième mf **2.** [fraction] sixième m **3.** MUS sixte f **4.** 🇬🇧 SCH ▶ **to be in**

the lower / upper sixth ≃ être en première / en terminale. ◆ adv **1.** [in contest] en sixième position, à la sixième place **2.** = **sixthly**. See also **fifth**.

sixth form n 🇬🇧 SCH dernière classe de l'enseignement secondaire en Grande-Bretagne, préparant aux A-levels et correspondant aux classes de première et de terminale. ❖ **sixth-form** adj [student, teacher, subject] de première or terminale ▶ **sixth-form college** établissement préparant aux A-levels.

sixth former n 🇬🇧 SCH élève mf de première or de terminale.

sixth grade n 🇺🇸 SCH classe du primaire pour les 10-11 ans.

sixth sense n sixième sens m / some sixth sense told me she wouldn't come j'avais l'intuition qu'elle ne viendrait pas.

sixtieth ['sɪkstɪəθ] ◆ det soixantième. ◆ n **1.** [ordinal] soixantième mf **2.** [fraction] soixantième m. See also **fifth**.

sixty ['sɪkstɪ] (pl **sixties**) ◆ det soixante. ◆ n soixante m / she's in her sixties elle a entre soixante et soixante-dix ans / sixties pop music la musique pop des années soixante. ◆ pron soixante. See also **fifty**.

size [saɪz] ◆ n **1.** [gen] taille f; [of ball, tumour] taille f, grosseur f; [of region, desert, forest] étendue f, superficie f; [of difficulty, operation, protest movement] importance f, ampleur f; [of debt, bill, sum] montant m, importance f / the two rooms are the same size les deux pièces sont de la même taille or les mêmes dimensions / it's about the size of a dinner plate c'est à peu près de la taille d'une assiette / my garden is half the size of hers mon jardin fait la moitié du sien / the tumour is increasing in size la tumeur grossit **2.** [of clothes -gen] taille f; [of shoes, gloves, hat] pointure f, taille f / what size are you? or what size do you take? quelle taille faites-vous ? / I take (a) size 40 je fais du 40 **3.** [for paper, textiles, leather] apprêt m; [for plaster] enduit m. ◆ vt **1.** [sort] trier selon la taille **2.** [make] fabriquer aux dimensions voulues **3.** [paper, textiles, leather] apprêter; [plaster] enduire. ❖ **size up** vt sep [stranger, rival] jauger; [problem, chances] mesurer.

-size = **-sized**.

sizeable ['saɪzəbl] adj [piece, box, car] assez grand; [apple, egg, tumour] assez gros (assez grosse); [sum, income, quantity, crowd] important; [town] assez important; [error] de taille / they were elected by a sizeable majority ils ont été élus à une assez large majorité.

-sized [-saɪzd] in comp : small and medium-sized businesses petites et moyennes entreprises fpl, PME fpl / a fair-sized crowd une foule assez nombreuse.

sizzle ['sɪzl] ◆ vt **1.** [sputter] grésiller **2.** inf [be hot] : the city sizzled in the heat la ville étouffait sous la chaleur. ◆ n grésillement m.

sizzling ['sɪzlɪŋ] ◆ adj **1.** [sputtering] grésillant **2.** inf [hot] brûlant. ◆ adv inf ▶ **sizzling hot** brûlant.

SK written abbr of **Saskatchewan**.

skanky ['skæŋkɪ] adj **1.** 🇺🇸 v inf [filthy] dégueulasse **2.** [ugly] moche **3.** [slutty] : she's real skanky c'est une vraie salope.

skate [skeɪt] ◆ n **1.** [ice] patin m à glace; [roller] patin m à roulettes **2.** (pl **skate** or **skates**) [fish] raie f. ◆ vi **1.** [gen] patiner ▶ **to go skating** a) [ice] faire du patin or du patinage b) [roller] faire du patin à roulettes **2.** [slide -pen, plate] glisser **3.** [person] glisser. ❖ **skate around**, **skate over** vt insep [problem, issue] esquiver, éviter.

skateboard ['skeɪtbɔːd] ◆ n skateboard m, planche f à roulettes. ◆ vi faire du skateboard or de la planche à roulettes.

skateboarder ['skeɪtbɔːdər] n personne qui fait du skateboard or de la planche à roulettes.

skateboarding ['skeɪtbɔːdɪŋ] n ▶ **to go skateboarding** faire de la planche à roulettes or du skateboard.

skater ['skeɪtər] n [on ice] patineur *m*, -euse *f* ; [on roller skates] patineur *m*, -euse *f* à roulettes.

skating ['skeɪtɪŋ] ◆ n [on ice] patin *m* (à glace) ; [on roller skates] patin *m* (à roulettes). ◆ adj de patinage.

skating rink n [for ice skating] patinoire *f* ; [for roller skating] piste *f* pour patin à roulettes.

skein [skeɪn] n **1.** [of wool, silk] écheveau *m* **2.** [flight - of geese] vol *m*.

skeletal ['skelɪtl] adj squelettique.

skeleton ['skelɪtn] ◆ n **1.** ANAT squelette *m* **2.** CONSTR & CHEM [structure] squelette *m* **3.** [outline - of book, report] ébauche *f*, esquisse *f* ; [- of project, strategy, speech] schéma *m*, grandes lignes *fpl*. ◆ comp [team] (réduit au) minimum, squelettique *pej* / *a skeleton staff* UK or *crew* US des effectifs réduits au minimum.

skeleton contract n contrat-type *m*.

skeleton key n passe-partout *m inv*, passe *m*.

skeptic US = **sceptic**.

sketch [sketʃ] ◆ n **1.** [drawing] croquis *m*, esquisse *f* **2.** [brief description] résumé *m* ; [preliminary outline - of book] ébauche *f* ; [- of proposal, speech, campaign] grandes lignes *fpl* **3.** THEAT sketch *m*. ◆ vt **1.** [person, scene] faire un croquis or une esquisse de, croquer, esquisser ; [line, composition, form] esquisser, croquer ; [portrait, illustration] faire (rapidement) **2.** [book] ébaucher, esquisser ; [proposal, speech] ébaucher, préparer dans les grandes lignes. ❖ **sketch in** vt sep **1.** [provide - background, main points] indiquer **2.** [draw] ajouter, dessiner. ❖ **sketch out** vt sep **1.** [book] ébaucher, esquisser ; [plan, speech] ébaucher, préparer dans les grandes lignes ; [details, main points] indiquer **2.** [draw] ébaucher.

sketchbook ['sketʃbʊk] n carnet *m* à dessins.

sketchpad ['sketʃpæd] n carnet *m* à dessins.

sketchy ['sketʃɪ] (*compar* **sketchier**, *superl* **sketchiest**) adj [description, account] sommaire ; [research, work, knowledge] superficiel ; [idea, notion] vague ; [plan] peu détaillé.

skew [skjuː] ◆ vt [distort - facts, results] fausser ; [- idea, truth] dénaturer ; [- statistics] / *it will skew the sample* ça va fausser l'échantillonnage. ◆ vi [oblique, dévier de sa trajectoire. ◆ adj UK **1.** [crooked - picture] de travers ; [- pole] penché **2.** [distorted - notion, view] partial ▶ **skew distribution** [in statistics] distribution *f* asymétrique **3.** [angled, slanting] oblique, en biais. ◆ n UK ▶ **to be on the skew** être de travers.

skewed [skjuːd] = **skew** (*adj*).

skewer ['skjuːər] ◆ n CULIN brochette *f* ; [larger] broche *f*. ◆ vt CULIN [roast, duck] embrocher ; [meat, mushrooms, tomatoes] mettre en brochette ; *fig* [person] transpercer.

skew-whiff [,skjuː'wɪf] adj & adv UK *inf* de traviole, de travers.

ski [skiː] ◆ n **1.** SPORT ski *m* (*equipment*) ▶ **(a pair of) skis** (une paire de) skis **2.** AERON patin *m*, ski *m*. ◆ vi faire du ski, skier ▶ **to go skiing a)** [activity] faire du ski **b)** [on holiday] partir aux sports d'hiver or faire du ski. ◆ comp [clothes, boots, lessons] de ski ▶ **ski instructor** moniteur *m*, -trice *f* de ski ▶ **ski pass** forfait *m* de remonte-pente ▶ **ski pole** or **stick** bâton *m* de ski ▶ **ski slope** piste *f* de ski ▶ **ski suit** combinaison *f* (de ski) ▶ **ski wax** fart *m* (pour skis). ◆ vt : *I've never skied the red run* je n'ai jamais descendu la piste rouge.

skibob ['skiːbɒb] n ski-bob *m*, véloski *m*.

skid [skɪd] (*pt & pp* **skidded**, *cont* **skidding**) ◆ vi **1.** [on road - driver, car, tyre] déraper ▶ **to skid to a halt** s'arrêter en dérapant **2.** [slide - person, object] déraper, glisser. ◆ n **1.** AUTO dérapage *m* ▶ **to go into a skid** partir en dérapage, déraper ▶ **to get out of** or **to correct a skid** redresser or contrôler un dérapage **2.** [wedge] cale *f* **3.** US [log] rondin *m* ; [dragging platform] traîneau *m* ; ≃ schlitte *f*.

skid mark n trace *f* de pneus (*après un dérapage*).

skidproof ['skɪdpruːf] adj antidérapant.

skid row n US *inf* quartier *m* des clochards / *you'll end up on skid row!* tu es sur une mauvaise pente ! ▶ **a skid-row bum** un zonard.

skier ['skiːər] n skieur *m*, -euse *f*.

skiing ['skiːɪŋ] ◆ n ski *m* (activité). ◆ comp [lessons, accident, clothes] de ski ▶ **to go on a skiing holiday** partir aux sports d'hiver ▶ **skiing instructor** moniteur *m*, -trice *f* de ski ▶ **skiing resort** station *f* de sports d'hiver.

ski jump ◆ n [ramp] tremplin *m* de ski ; [event, activity] saut *m* à skis. ◆ vi faire du saut à skis.

skilful UK, **skillful** US ['skɪlfʊl] adj habile, adroit.

skilfully UK, **skillfully** US ['skɪlfʊlɪ] adv habilement, avec habileté, adroitement.

ski lift n [gen] remontée *f* mécanique ; [chair lift] télésiège *m*.

skill [skɪl] n **1.** [ability] compétence *f*, aptitude *f* ; [dexterity] habileté *f*, adresse *f* ; [expertise] savoir-faire *m inv* **2.** [learned technique] aptitude *f*, technique *f* ; [knowledge] connaissances *fpl*. ❖ **skill up** vi [in game] améliorer sa technique.

skilled [skɪld] adj **1.** INDUST [engineer, labour, worker] qualifié ; [task] de spécialiste **2.** [experienced - driver, negotiator] habile, expérimenté ; [expert] habile, expert ; [manually] adroit ; [clever - gesture] habile, adroit ▶ **to be skilled at doing sthg** être doué pour faire qqch.

skillet ['skɪlɪt] n US poêle *f* (à frire).

skillful US = **skilful**.

skim [skɪm] ◆ vt **1.** [milk] écrémer ; [jam] écumer ; [floating matter - with skimmer] écumer, enlever avec une écumoire ; [- with spatula] enlever avec une spatule **2.** [glide over - surface] effleurer, frôler **3.** [stone] faire ricocher **4.** [read quickly - letter, book] parcourir, lire en diagonale ; [- magazine] parcourir, feuilleter. ◆ vi : *to skim over the ground / across the waves* [bird] raser le sol / les vagues / *to skim over* or *across the lake* [stone] faire des ricochets sur le lac. ❖ **skim off** vt sep **1.** [cream, froth] enlever (avec une écumoire) / *the book dealers skimmed off the best bargains* fig les marchands de livres ont fait les meilleures affaires **2.** [steal - money] : *he skimmed a little off the top for himself* il s'est un peu servi au passage. ❖ **skim over** vt insep [letter, report] parcourir, lire en diagonale ; [difficult passage] lire superficiellement, parcourir rapidement. ❖ **skim through** vt insep [letter, page] parcourir, lire en diagonale ; [magazine] feuilleter.

skimmed milk [skɪmd-] n lait *m* écrémé.

skimp [skɪmp] vi lésiner ▶ **to skimp on sthg** lésiner sur qqch.

skimpily ['skɪmpɪlɪ] adv [scantily] ▶ **skimpily dressed** légèrement vêtu.

skimpy ['skɪmpɪ] (*compar* **skimpier**, *superl* **skimpiest**) adj **1.** [mean - meal, offering] maigre, chiche ; [- praise, thanks] maigre, chiche **2.** [clothes, dress - too small] trop juste ; [- light] léger / *a skimpy skirt* une jupe étriquée.

skin [skɪn] (*pt & pp* **skinned**, *cont* **skinning**) ◆ n **1.** [of person] peau *f* / *to have dark / fair skin* avoir la peau brune / claire / *you're nothing but skin and bone* tu n'as que la peau et les os ▶ **to escape by the skin of one's teeth** : *she escaped by the skin of her teeth* elle l'a échappé belle, elle s'en est tirée de justesse ▶ **it's no skin off my nose** *inf* ça ne me coûte rien *fig*, ça ne me gêne pas **2.** [from animal] peau *f* **3.** [on fruit, vegetable, sausage] peau *f*; [on onion] pelure *f* **4.** [on milk, pudding] peau *f* **5.** [of plane] revêtement *m*; [of building] revêtement *m* extérieur; [of drum] peau *f* **6.** [for wine] outre *f* **7.** *inf* [skinhead] skin *mf* **8.** COMPUT [interface] interface *f*. ◆ *comp* [cancer, tone] de la peau ▶ **skin disease** maladie *f* de peau. ◆ *vt* **1.** [animal] dépouiller, écorcher; [vegetable] éplucher **2.** [graze - limb] écorcher **3.** ⓤ *inf* [rob] plumer. ❖ **skin up** *vi inf* rouler un joint.

skincare ['skɪnkeə']' n *(U)* soins *mpl* de la peau.

skincare product n produit *m* (de soin) pour la peau.

skin cream n crème *f* pour la peau.

skin-deep ◆ adj superficiel. ◆ adv superficiellement.

skin diver n plongeur *m*, -euse *f*.

skin diving n plongée *f* sous-marine.

skinflint ['skɪnflɪnt] n avare *mf*.

skin graft n greffe *f* de la peau / *to have a skin graft* subir une greffe de la peau.

skinhead ['skɪnhed] n skinhead *mf*.

-skinned [skɪnd] in *comp* à la peau... / *she's dark-skinned* elle a la peau foncée.

skinny ['skɪnɪ] *(compar* **skinnier**, *superl* **skinniest)** adj **1.** [person] très mince **2.** [belt, tie] très fin; [jeans] très serré.

skinny-dipping [-'dɪpɪŋ] n *inf* baignade *f* à poil.

skint [skɪnt] adj ⓤ *inf* fauché, raide.

skin test n MED cuti-réaction *f*.

skin-tight adj moulant.

skip [skɪp] *(pt & pp* **skipped**, *cont* **skipping)** ◆ vi **1.** [with skipping rope] sauter à la corde **2.** [jump] sautiller **3.** *inf* [go] faire un saut, aller. ◆ vt **1.** [omit] sauter, passer; [miss - meeting, meal] sauter; [SCH - class] sécher ▶ **skip it!** *inf* laisse tomber ! ▶ **to skip bail** ⓤ ne pas comparaître au tribunal **2.** *inf* [leave] fuir, quitter. ◆ n **1.** *inf* = **skipper 2.** [jump] (petit) saut *m* **3.** [on lorry, for rubbish] benne *f*. ❖ **skip off** *vi inf* **1.** [disappear] décamper **2.** [go] faire un saut. ❖ **skip over** vt insep [omit] sauter, passer.

ski pants pl n fuseau *m*, pantalon *m* de ski.

skipper ['skɪpə'] ◆ n **1.** NAUT [gen] capitaine *m*; [of yacht] skipper *m* **2.** SPORT capitaine *m*, chef *m* d'équipe **3.** *inf* [boss] patron *m*. ◆ vt **1.** [ship, plane] commander, être le capitaine de; [yacht] skipper **2.** SPORT [team] être le capitaine de.

skipping ['skɪpɪŋ] n saut *m* à la corde.

skipping rope n ⓤ corde *f* à sauter.

skirmish ['skɜ:mɪʃ] ◆ n MIL & *fig* escarmouche *f*, accrochage *m*. ◆ vi MIL s'engager dans une escarmouche ▶ **to skirmish with sb over sthg** *fig* avoir un accrochage or s'accrocher avec qqn au sujet de qqch.

skirt [skɜ:t] ◆ n **1.** [garment] jupe *f*; [part of coat] pan *m*, basque *f* **2.** MECH jupe *f* **3.** ⓤ [cut of meat] ≃ flanchet *m* **4.** *(U)* ⓤ *v inf* [woman] ▶ **a bit of skirt** une belle nana. ◆ vt **1.** [go around] contourner **2.** [avoid - issue, problem] éluder, esquiver. ❖ **skirt round** vt insep = **skirt** *(vt)*.

skirting (board) ['skɜ:tɪŋ-] n ⓤ plinthe *f*.

ski run n piste *f* de ski.

skit [skɪt] n parodie *f*, satire *f* ▶ **to do a skit on sthg** parodier qqch.

ski tow n téléski *m*.

skittish ['skɪtɪʃ] adj **1.** [person - playful] espiègle; [- frivolous] frivole **2.** [horse] ombrageux, difficile.

skittle ['skɪtl] n quille *f*. ❖ **skittles** n (jeu *m* de) quilles *fpl* / *to play skittles* jouer aux quilles, faire une partie de quilles.

skive [skaɪv] vi ⓤ *inf* [avoid work] tirer au flanc; SCH sécher les cours. ❖ **skive off** ⓤ *inf* ◆ vi se défiler. ◆ vt insep [work, class, school] sécher.

skivvy ['skɪvɪ] *(pl* **skivvies)** ⓤ *inf* ◆ vi faire la boniche. ◆ n *pej* bonne *f* à tout faire. ❖ **skivvies** pl n ⓤ *inf* [for women] dessous *mpl*; [for men] sous-vêtements *mpl* (masculins).

skulduggery [skʌl'dʌgərɪ] n *(U)* combines *fpl* or manœuvres *fpl* douteuses.

skulk [skʌlk] vi rôder ▶ **to skulk away** or **off** s'éclipser.

skull [skʌl] n crâne *m*.

skull and crossbones n [motif] tête *f* de mort; [flag] pavillon *m* à tête de mort.

skullcap ['skʌlkæp] n **1.** [headgear] calotte *f* **2.** BOT scutellaire *f*.

skunk [skʌŋk] ◆ n **1.** *(pl* **skunk** or **skunks)** [animal] moufette *f*, mouffette *f*, sconse *m*; [fur] sconse *m* **2.** *(pl* **skunks)** *inf* [person] canaille *f*, ordure *f*. ◆ vt ⓤ *inf* [opponent] battre à plate couture, flanquer une déculottée à.

sky [skaɪ] *(pl* **skies**, *pt & pp* **skied** or **skyed)** ◆ n [gen] ciel *m*. ◆ vt **1.** FOOT [ball] envoyer au ciel **2.** [in rowing] ▶ **to sky the oars** lever les avirons trop haut. ❖ **skies** pl n [climate] cieux *mpl*; [descriptive] ciels *mpl*.

sky blue n bleu ciel *m*. ❖ **sky-blue** adj bleu ciel *(inv)*.

skycap ['skaɪkæp] n ⓤ porteur *m* *(dans un aéroport)*.

skydiver ['skaɪ,daɪvə'] n parachutiste *mf*.

skydiving ['skaɪ,daɪvɪŋ] n parachutisme *m*.

sky-high ◆ adj *lit* très haut dans le ciel; *fig* [prices] inabordable, exorbitant. ◆ adv **1.** *lit* très haut dans le ciel **2.** *fig* [very high] : *prices soared* or *went sky-high* les prix ont grimpé en flèche / *the explosion blew the building sky-high* l'explosion a complètement soufflé le bâtiment.

skyjack ['skaɪdʒæk] vt [plane] détourner.

skylark ['skaɪlɑ:k] ◆ n alouette *f* des champs. ◆ vi *inf & dated* faire le fou, chahuter.

skylight ['skaɪlaɪt] n lucarne *f*.

skyline ['skaɪlaɪn] n [horizon] ligne *f* d'horizon; [urban] : *the New York skyline* la silhouette (des immeubles) de New York.

sky marshal n ⓤ agent de sécurité à bord d'un avion.

skyscraper ['skaɪ,skreɪpə'] n gratte-ciel *m inv*.

slab [slæb] *(pt & pp* **slabbed**, *cont* **slabbing)** ◆ n **1.** [block - of stone, wood] bloc *m*; [flat] plaque *f*, dalle *f*; [for path] pavé *m* / *a concrete slab* une dalle de béton **2.** [piece - of cake] grosse tranche *f*; [- of chocolate] tablette *f*; [- of meat] pavé *m* **3.** [table, bench - of butcher] étal *m* ▶ **on the slab a)** [in mortuary] sur la table d'autopsie **b)** *inf* [for operation] sur la table d'opération. ◆ vt [cut - stone] tailler en blocs; [- log] débiter.

slack [slæk] ◆ adj **1.** [loose - rope, wire] lâche, insuffisamment tendu; [- knot] mal serré, desserré; [- chain] lâche; [- grip] faible **2.** [careless - work] négligé; [- worker, student] peu sérieux, peu consciencieux **3.** [slow, weak - demand] faible; [- business] calme **4.** [lax - discipline, laws, control] mou *(before vowel or silent 'h' mol, f molle)*, relâché; [- parents] négligent **5.** NAUT ▶ **slack water, slack tide** mer *f* étale. ◆ n **1.** [in rope] mou *m*; [in cable joint] jeu *m*; NAUT [in cable] battant *m* ▶ **to take up the slack in a rope** tendre une corde **2.** *fig* [in economy] secteurs *mpl* affaiblis ▶ **to take up the slack in the economy** relancer les secteurs faibles de l'économie **3.** [still water] eau *f* morte; [tide] mer *f* étale **4.** [coal] poussier *m*. ◆ vi se laisser aller.

slacken ['slækn] ◆ vt **1.** [loosen - cable, rope] détendre, relâcher ; [-reins] relâcher ; [-grip, hold] desserrer **2.** [reduce - pressure, speed] réduire, diminuer ; [-pace] ralentir. ◆ vi **1.** [rope, cable] se relâcher ; [grip, hold] se desserrer **2.** [lessen - speed, demand, interest] diminuer ; [-business] ralentir ; [-wind] diminuer de force ; [-standards] baisser. ❖ **slacken off** vt sep **1.** [rope] relâcher, donner du mou à **2.** [speed, pressure] diminuer ; [efforts] relâcher. ◆ vi **1.** [rope] se relâcher **2.** [speed, demand] diminuer. ❖ **slacken up** vi [speed] diminuer ; [person] se relâcher.

slacker ['slækər] n inf fainéant m, -e f.

slacks [slæks] pl n ▶ **(a pair of) slacks** un pantalon.

slag [slæg] (pt & pp **slagged**, cont **slagging**) n **1.** (U) [waste - from mine] stériles mpl ; [-from foundry] scories fpl, crasses fpl ; [-from volcano] scories fpl volcaniques **2.** UK v inf & pej [woman] garce f, salope f. ❖ **slag off** vt sep UK inf dénigrer, débiner.

slagheap ['slæghi:p] n terril m, crassier m.

slain [sleɪn] ◆ pp ⟶ **slay.** ◆ pl n liter ▶ **the slain** les soldats tombés au champ d'honneur.

slalom ['slɑːləm] ◆ n [gen & SPORT] slalom m. ◆ vi slalomer, faire du slalom.

slam [slæm] (pt & pp **slammed**, cont **slamming**) ◆ vt **1.** [close - window, door] claquer ; [-drawer] fermer violemment **2.** inf [defeat] écraser **3.** inf [criticize] descendre. ◆ vi [door, window] claquer. ◆ n **1.** [of door, window] claquement m **2.** CARDS chelem m. ❖ **slam down** vt sep [lid] refermer en claquant ; [books, keys] poser bruyamment / **to slam the phone down** raccrocher brutalement / **he slammed the phone down on me** il m'a raccroché au nez. ❖ **slam on** vt sep ▶ **to slam on the brakes** freiner brutalement. ❖ **slam to** vt sep refermer en claquant.

slam dunk US ◆ n SPORT smash m au panier, slam-dunk m. ◆ vt & vi SPORT smasher.

slander ['slɑːndər] ◆ vt [gen] calomnier, dire du mal de ; LAW diffamer. ◆ n [gen] calomnie f ; LAW diffamation f.

slanderous ['slɑːndrəs] adj [gen] calomniateur ; LAW diffamatoire.

slang [slæŋ] ◆ n [gen & LING] argot m. ◆ adj argotique, d'argot. ◆ vt UK inf traiter de tous les noms.

slant [slɑːnt] ◆ n **1.** [line] ligne f oblique ; [slope] inclinaison f **2.** [point of view] perspective f, point m de vue. ◆ vt **1.** [news, evidence] présenter avec parti pris or de manière peu objective **2.** [line, perspective] incliner, faire pencher. ◆ vi [line, handwriting] pencher ; [ray of light] passer obliquement.

slanting ['slɑːntɪŋ] adj [floor, table] en pente, incliné ; [writing] penché ; [line] oblique, penché.

slap [slæp] (pt & pp **slapped**, cont **slapping**) ◆ vt **1.** [hit] donner une claque à **2.** [put] : just slap some paint over it passe un coup de pinceau dessus. ◆ vi : the waves slapped against the harbour wall les vagues battaient contre la digue. ◆ n **1.** [smack] claque f ; [on face] gifle f ; [on back] tape f dans le dos **2.** [noise] : the slap of the waves against the side of the boat le clapotis des vagues contre la coque **3.** THEAT [makeup] fard m. ◆ adv inf en plein. ❖ **slap down** vt sep **1.** [book, money] poser avec violence **2.** inf [suggestion] rejeter ; [person] rembarrer, envoyer promener or paître. ❖ **slap on** vt sep **1.** [paint] appliquer n'importe comment or à la va-vite ; [jam, butter] étaler généreusement **2.** [tax, increase] : they slapped on a 3% surcharge ils ont mis une surtaxe de 3 %.

slapdash ['slæpdæʃ] ◆ adv à la va-vite, sans soin, n'importe comment. ◆ adj [work] fait n'importe comment or à la va-vite ; [person] négligent.

slaphead ['slæphed] n v inf chauve m, crâne m d'œuf.

slapper ['slæpər] n UK v inf salope f.

slapstick ['slæpstɪk] ◆ n grosse farce f, bouffonnerie f. ◆ adj [humour] bouffon ▶ **slapstick comedy** comédie f bouffonne.

slap-up adj UK inf ▶ **a slap-up meal** un repas de derrière les fagots.

slash [slæʃ] ◆ vt **1.** [cut - gen] taillader ; [-face] balafrer **2.** [hit - with whip] frapper, cingler ; [-with stick] battre **3.** UK [verbally] critiquer violemment **4.** [prices] casser ; [cost, taxes] réduire considérablement **5.** SEW : a green jacket slashed with blue une veste verte avec des crevés laissant apercevoir du bleu. ◆ vi ▶ **to slash at sb with a knife** donner des coups de couteau en direction de qqn / he slashed at the bushes with a stick il donna des coups de bâton dans les buissons. ◆ n **1.** [with knife] coup m de couteau ; [with sword] coup m d'épée ; [with whip] coup m de fouet ; [with stick] coup m de bâton **2.** [cut] entaille f ; [on face] balafre f **3.** SEW crevé m **4.** TYPO (barre f) oblique f **5.** (U) US [wood chips] copeaux mpl **6.** PHR **to have a slash** UK v inf pisser un coup.

slasher movie n inf film m gore.

slat [slæt] n [in blinds, louvre] lamelle f ; [wooden] latte f ; AERON aileron m.

slate [sleɪt] ◆ n **1.** CONSTR & SCH ardoise f ▶ **to put sthg on the slate** UK inf & fig : put it on the slate mettez-le sur mon compte **2.** US POL liste f provisoire de candidats. ◆ comp [roof] en ardoise or ardoises, d'ardoise ; [industry] ardoisier ▶ **slate quarry** carrière f d'ardoise, ardoisière f. ◆ vt **1.** [cover - roof] couvrir d'ardoises **2.** US POL proposer (un candidat) **3.** US [destine] : she was slated for a gold medal / for victory elle devait remporter une médaille d'or / la victoire ; [expect] prévoir **4.** UK inf [criticize - film, actor] descendre.

slatted ['slætɪd] adj à lattes.

slatternly ['slætənlɪ] adj [woman] mal soigné ; [habit, dress] négligé.

slaughter ['slɔːtər] ◆ vt **1.** [kill - animal] abattre, tuer ; [-people] massacrer, tuer (sauvagement) **2.** inf & fig [defeat - team, opponent] massacrer. ◆ n [of animal] abattage m ; [of people] massacre m, tuerie f.

slaughterhouse ['slɔːtəhaʊs] (pl [-haʊzɪz]) n abattoir m.

Slav [slɑːv] ◆ adj slave. ◆ n Slave mf.

slave [sleɪv] ◆ n lit & fig esclave mf / to be a slave to fashion / habit être esclave de la mode / de ses habitudes. ◆ vi travailler comme un esclave or un forçat, trimer / he slaved over his books all day long il était plongé dans ses livres à longueur de journée.

slaver[1] ['sleɪvər] ◆ n **1.** [trader] marchand m d'esclaves **2.** [ship] (vaisseau m) négrier m.

slaver[2] ['slævər] ◆ vi [dribble] baver. ◆ n [saliva] bave f.

slavery ['sleɪvərɪ] n esclavage m ▶ **to be sold into slavery** être vendu comme esclave.

slave trade n commerce m des esclaves ; [of Africans] traite f des Noirs.

Slavic ['slɑːvɪk] = **Slavonic.**

slavish ['sleɪvɪʃ] adj [mentality, habits] d'esclave ; [devotion] servile ; [imitation] sans aucune originalité, servile.

slavishly ['sleɪvɪʃlɪ] adv [work] comme un forçat ; [copy, worship] servilement.

Slavonic [slə'vɒnɪk] ◆ n LING slave m ; HIST slavon m. ◆ adj slave.

slay [sleɪ] (pt slew [sluː], pp slain [sleɪn]) vt **1.** [kill] tuer **2.** US inf [impress] impressionner **3.** UK inf [amuse] faire crever de rire.

sleaze [sli:z] ◆ n inf [squalidness] aspect m miteux, caractère m sordide ; [pornography] porno m ; POL [corruption] corruption f. ◆ vi [live immoral life] mener une vie dissolue.

sleazebag ['sli:zbæg], **sleazeball** ['sli:zbɔ:l] n inf **1.** [despicable person] ordure f, raclure f **2.** [repulsive man] gros dégueulasse m.

sleaziness ['sli:zɪnɪs] n inf sordide m.

sleazy ['sli:zɪ] (compar **sleazier**, superl **sleaziest**) adj inf [squalid] miteux, sordide ; [disreputable] mal famé.

sled [sled] ◆ n US = **sledge** (noun) ; US = **sledge** (noun). ◆ vi US = **sledge** (vi) ; US = **sledge** (vi). ◆ vt US transporter en luge.

sledge [sledʒ] ◆ n **1.** [for fun or sport] luge f **2.** [pulled by animals] traîneau m. ◆ vi **1.** US [for fun or sport] faire de la luge ▸ **to go sledging** faire de la luge **2.** [pulled by animals] faire du traîneau. ◆ vt US transporter en traîneau.

sledgehammer ['sledʒ,hæmər] n masse f (outil) ▸ **a sledgehammer blow** fig un coup très violent.

sleek [sli:k] adj **1.** [fur, hair] luisant, lustré, lisse ; [feathers] brillant, luisant ; [bird] aux plumes luisantes ; [cat] au poil soyeux or brillant **2.** [person - in appearance] soigné, tiré à quatre épingles ; [- in manner] onctueux, doucereux **3.** [vehicle, plane] aux lignes pures.

sleep [sli:p] (pt & pp **slept** [slept]) ◆ vi **1.** [rest] dormir ▸ **to sleep soundly** dormir profondément or à poings fermés ▸ **to sleep rough** coucher à la dure ; [spend night] coucher, passer la nuit **2.** [daydream] rêvasser, rêver **3.** euph & liter [be dead] dormir du dernier sommeil. ◆ vt **1.** [accommodate] : the sofa bed sleeps two deux personnes peuvent coucher dans le canapé-lit / the house sleeps four on peut loger quatre personnes dans cette maison **2.** PHR I didn't sleep a wink all night je n'ai pas fermé l'œil de la nuit. ◆ n **1.** [rest] sommeil m ▸ **to talk in one's sleep** parler en dormant or dans son sommeil ▸ **to be in a deep sleep** dormir profondément ▸ **to go to sleep** s'endormir **2.** UK [nap] : the children usually have a sleep in the afternoon en général les enfants font la sieste l'après-midi / I could do with a sleep je ferais bien un petit somme **3.** [substance in eyes] chassie f. ◆ **sleep around** vi inf coucher à droite et à gauche. ◆ **sleep in** vi **1.** [lie in - voluntarily] faire la grasse matinée ; [- involuntarily] se lever en retard **2.** [sleep at home] coucher à la maison ; [staff] être logé sur place. ◆ **sleep off** vt sep [hangover, fatigue] dormir pour faire passer. ◆ **sleep on** ◆ vi continuer à dormir. ◆ vt insep ▸ **sleep on it** la nuit porte conseil prov. ◆ **sleep out** vi [away from home] découcher ; [in the open air] coucher à la belle étoile ; [in tent] coucher sous la tente. ◆ **sleep over** vi : can I sleep over? est-ce que je peux rester dormir ? ◆ **sleep through** ◆ vi : he slept through till five o'clock il a dormi jusqu'à cinq heures. ◆ vt insep : I slept through the last act j'ai dormi pendant tout le dernier acte / she slept through her alarm elle n'a pas entendu son réveil. ◆ **sleep together** vi coucher ensemble. ◆ **sleep with** vt insep euph coucher avec.

sleeper ['sli:pər] n **1.** [sleeping person] dormeur m, -euse f ▸ **to be a light / heavy sleeper** avoir le sommeil léger / lourd **2.** [train] train-couchettes m ; [sleeping car] wagon-lit m, voiture-lit f ; [berth] couchette f **3.** US [sofa bed] canapé-lit m **4.** UK RAIL [track support] traverse f **5.** [spy] agent m dormant **6.** UK [earring] clou m **7.** inf [unexpected success] révélation f.

sleepily ['sli:pɪlɪ] adv [look] d'un air endormi ; [speak] d'un ton endormi.

sleepiness ['sli:pɪnɪs] n [of person] envie f de dormir ; [of town] torpeur f.

sleeping ['sli:pɪŋ] adj qui dort, endormi.

sleeping bag n sac m de couchage.

sleeping car n wagon-lit m.

sleeping economy n économie f dormante.

sleeping partner n UK COMM (associé m) commanditaire m, bailleur m de fonds.

sleeping pill n somnifère m.

sleeping policeman n UK casse-vitesse m inv, ralentisseur m.

sleeping suit n US grenouillère f.

sleeping tablet = sleeping pill.

sleepless ['sli:plɪs] adj [without sleep] sans sommeil / I had or spent a sleepless night j'ai passé une nuit blanche, je n'ai pas fermé l'œil de la nuit.

sleeplessness ['sli:plɪsnɪs] n (U) insomnie f, insomnies fpl.

sleep mode n COMPUT mode m de veille.

sleepover ['sli:pəʊvər] n [of child] nuit f chez un ami.

sleepsuit = sleeping suit.

sleepwalk ['sli:pwɔ:k] vi : he was sleepwalking last night il a eu une crise de somnambulisme hier soir.

sleepwalker ['sli:p,wɔ:kər] n somnambule mf.

sleepwalking ['sli:p,wɔ:kɪŋ] n somnambulisme m.

sleepy ['sli:pɪ] (compar **sleepier**, superl **sleepiest**) adj **1.** [person] qui a envie de dormir, somnolent / I'm or I feel sleepy j'ai sommeil, j'ai envie de dormir **2.** [town] plongé dans la torpeur.

sleet [sli:t] ◆ n neige f fondue (tombant du ciel). ◆ vi : it's sleeting il tombe de la neige fondue.

sleeve [sli:v] n **1.** [on garment] manche f **2.** TECH [tube] manchon m ; [lining] chemise f **3.** UK [for record] pochette f.

sleeveless ['sli:vlɪs] adj sans manches.

sleeve notes pl n UK texte figurant au dos des pochettes de disques.

sleigh [sleɪ] n traîneau m ▸ **sleigh ride** promenade f en traîneau.

sleight of hand [,slaɪt-] n [skill] dextérité f ; [trick] tour m de passe-passe / by sleight of hand par un tour de passe-passe.

slender ['slendər] adj **1.** [slim, narrow - figure] mince, svelte ; [- fingers, neck, stem] fin ; [- margin] étroit **2.** [limited - resources] faible, maigre, limité ; [- majority] étroit, faible ; [- hope, chance] maigre, faible.

slept [slept] pt & pp —→ sleep.

sleuth [slu:θ] inf & hum ◆ n (fin) limier m, détective m. ◆ vi enquêter.

slew [slu:] ◆ pt —→ slay. ◆ vi **1.** [pivot - person] pivoter, se retourner **2.** [vehicle - skid] déraper ; [- swerve] faire une embardée ; [- turn] virer. ◆ vt **1.** [turn, twist] faire tourner or pivoter ; NAUT [mast] virer, dévirer **2.** [vehicle] faire déraper. ◆ n inf ▸ **a slew of, slews of** un tas de.

slice [slaɪs] ◆ n **1.** [of bread, meat, cheese] tranche f ; [of pizza] part f ; [round] rondelle f, tranche f **2.** fig [share, percentage] part f, partie f **3.** [utensil] pelle f, spatule f ▸ **cake slice** pelle f à gâteau **4.** SPORT slice m. ◆ vt **1.** [cut into pieces - cake, bread] couper (en tranches) ; [- sausage, banana] couper (en rondelles) **2.** [cut] couper, trancher **3.** SPORT couper, slicer. ◆ vi [knife] couper ; [bread] se couper. ◆ **slice off** vt sep [branch] couper. ◆ **slice through** vt insep **1.** [cut - rope, cable] couper (net), trancher **2.** [go, move] traverser (rapidement), fendre. ◆ **slice up** vt sep [loaf, cake] couper (en tranches) ; [banana] couper (en rondelles).

sliced bread [slaɪst-] n pain m (coupé) en tranches.

slick [slɪk] ◆ adj **1.** *pej* [glib] qui a du bagout ; [in speech] enjôleur ; [in manner] doucereux ; [in content] superficiel **2.** [smoothly efficient] habile **3.** [style, magazine] beau *(before vowel or silent 'h' bel, f belle)* **4.** [smart, chic] chic, tiré à quatre épingles **5.** [hair] lisse, lissé, luisant ; [road surface] glissant, gras ; [tyre] lisse **6.** US [slippery] glissant ; [greasy] gras (grasse) **7.** US [cunning] malin (maligne), rusé. ◆ n **1.** [oil spill - on sea] nappe f de pétrole ; [- on beach] marée f noire **2.** [tyre] pneu m lisse **3.** US [glossy magazine] magazine en papier glacé contenant surtout des articles et des photos sur la vie privée des stars. ❖ **slick back, slick down** vt sep ▶ **to slick one's hair back** or **down** se lisser les cheveux.

slicker [ˈslɪkər] n US [raincoat] imperméable m, ciré m.

slickly [ˈslɪklɪ] adv [answer] habilement ; [perform] brillamment.

slide [slaɪd] *(pt & pp* slid [slɪd]) ◆ vi **1.** [on ice, slippery surface] glisser **2.** [move quietly] : *she slid into / out of the room* elle s'est glissée dans la pièce / hors de la pièce / *the door slid open / shut* la porte s'est ouverte / fermée en glissant **3.** [go gradually] glisser **4.** [prices, value] baisser. ◆ vt faire glisser, glisser. ◆ n **1.** [in playground] toboggan m ; [on ice, snow] glissoire f ; [for logs] glissoire f **2.** [act of sliding] glissade f **3.** [fall - in prices] baisse f **4.** PHOT diapositive f, diapo f ; [for microscope] porte-objet m **5.** US [in hair] barrette f **6.** [runner - in machine, trombone] coulisse f **7.** MUS coulé m. ❖ **slide off** vi **1.** [lid] s'enlever en glissant **2.** [fall] glisser **3.** [go away - visitor] s'en aller discrètement, s'éclipser.

slide projector n projecteur m de diapositives.

slide rule n règle f à calcul.

slide show n diaporama m.

sliding [ˈslaɪdɪŋ] ◆ adj [part] qui glisse ; [movement] glissant ; [door] coulissant ; [panel] mobile. ◆ n glissement m.

sliding scale n [for salaries] échelle f mobile ; [for prices] barème m des prix ; [for tax] barème m des impôts.

slight [slaɪt] ◆ adj **1.** [person - slender] menu, mince ; [- frail] frêle ; [structure] fragile, frêle **2.** [minor, insignificant - error, increase, movement] faible, léger, petit ; [- difference] petit ; [- cut, graze] léger / *there's a slight drizzle / wind* il y a un peu de crachin / de vent / *she has a slight cold* elle est un peu enrhumée ; [in superl form] : *I haven't the slightest idea* je n'en ai pas la moindre idée ▶ **not in the slightest** pas le moins du monde, pas du tout. ◆ vt [snub] manquer d'égards envers ; [insult] insulter ; [offend] froisser, blesser. ◆ n [snub, insult] manque m d'égards, vexation f, affront m.

slightly [ˈslaɪtlɪ] adv **1.** [a little] un peu, légèrement **2.** [slenderly] : *slightly built* fluet, frêle.

slim [slɪm] *(compar* slimmer, *superl* slimmest, *pt & pp* slimmed) ◆ adj **1.** [person, waist, figure] mince, svelte ; [wrist] mince, fin, délicat **2.** [volume, wallet, diary] mince **3.** [faint, feeble - hope, chance] faible, minime ; [- pretext] mince, piètre, dérisoire. ◆ vi [get thin] maigrir, mincir ; [diet] faire or suivre un régime. ◆ vt [subj: diet, exercise] faire maigrir. ❖ **slim down** ◆ vt sep **1.** [subj: diet] faire maigrir ; [subj: clothes] amincir **2.** *fig* [industry] dégraisser ; [workforce] réduire ; [ambitions, plans] limiter, réduire ; [design, car] épurer, alléger. ◆ vi **1.** [person] maigrir, suivre un régime **2.** [industry] être dégraissé.

slime [slaɪm] n [sticky substance] substance f gluante or poisseuse ; [from snail] bave f ; [mud] vase f.

slimeball [ˈslaɪmbɔːl] US *v inf* = **sleazeball**.

slimline [ˈslɪmlaɪn] adj **1.** [butter] allégé ; [milk, cheese] sans matière grasse, minceur *(inv)* ; [soft drink] light *(inv)*

2. *fig* : *clothes for the new slimline you* des vêtements pour votre nouvelle silhouette allégée / *the slimline version of the 2009 model* la version épurée du modèle 2009.

slimmer [ˈslɪmər] n personne f qui suit un régime (amaigrissant).

slimming [ˈslɪmɪŋ] ◆ n amaigrissement m. ◆ adj [diet] amaigrissant ; [cream, product] amincissant ; [exercises] pour maigrir ; [meal] à faible teneur en calories.

slimness [ˈslɪmnɪs] n [of person, waist, figure] minceur f, sveltesse f ; [of wrist, ankle] minceur f, finesse f, délicatesse f.

slimy [ˈslaɪmɪ] *(compar* slimier, *superl* slimiest) adj **1.** [with mud] vaseux, boueux ; [with oil, secretion] gluant, visqueux ; [wall] suintant **2.** US [obsequious - person] mielleux ; [- manners] doucereux, obséquieux.

sling [slɪŋ] *(pt & pp* slung [slʌŋ]) ◆ vt **1.** [fling] jeter, lancer **2.** [lift, hang - load] hisser ; NAUT élinguer. ◆ n **1.** [for broken arm] écharpe f **2.** [for baby] porte-bébé m **3.** NAUT & CONSTR élingue f ; [belt] courroie f ; [rope] corde f, cordage m ; [for removal men] corde f, courroie f ; [for rifle] bretelle f ; [for mast] cravate f **4.** [weapon] fronde f ; [toy] lance-pierres m inv **5.** [for climber] baudrier m **6.** [cocktail] sling m (cocktail à base de spiritueux et de jus de citron, allongé d'eau plate ou gazeuse). ❖ **sling out** vt sep US inf [person] flanquer or ficher à la porte ; [rubbish, magazines, etc.] bazarder, ficher en l'air. ❖ **sling over** vt sep US inf lancer, envoyer.

slingback [ˈslɪŋbæk] n US chaussure f à talon découvert.

slingshot [ˈslɪŋʃɒt] n US lance-pierres m inv.

slink [slɪŋk] *(pt & pp* slunk [slʌŋk]) vi ▶ **to slink in / out** entrer / sortir furtivement ▶ **to slink away** s'éclipser.

slinky [ˈslɪŋkɪ] *(compar* slinkier, *superl* slinkiest) adj *inf* [manner] aguichant ; [dress] sexy *(inv)* ; [walk] ondoyant, chaloupé.

slip [slɪp] *(pt & pp* slipped, cont slipping) ◆ vi **1.** [lose balance, slide] glisser / *I slipped on the ice* j'ai glissé sur une plaque de verglas / *he slipped and fell* il glissa et tomba ; [move unexpectedly] glisser / *my hand slipped* ma main a glissé / *the prize slipped from her grasp* or *from her fingers* fig le prix lui a échappé / *somehow, the kidnappers slipped through our fingers* fig je ne sais comment les ravisseurs nous ont filé entre les doigts **2.** [go gradually] glisser / *the patient slipped into a coma* le patient a glissé or s'est enfoncé peu à peu dans le coma **3.** [go down] baisser **4.** [go discreetly or unnoticed] se glisser, se faufiler / *she slipped quietly into the room* elle s'est glissée discrètement dans la pièce / *some misprints have slipped into the text* des coquilles se sont glissées dans le texte ; [go quickly] se faufiler ; [into clothes] : *I'll slip into something cooler* je vais enfiler or mettre quelque chose de plus léger **5.** [slide - runners, drawer] glisser **6.** inf [be less efficient] : *you're slipping!* tu n'es plus ce que tu étais ! **7.** PHR ▶ **to let slip a)** [opportunity] laisser passer or échapper **b)** [word] lâcher, laisser échapper / *she let (it) slip that she was selling her house* elle a laissé échapper qu'elle vendait sa maison. ◆ vt **1.** [give or put discreetly] glisser / *to slip sb a note* glisser un mot à qqn **2.** [escape] : *it slipped my mind* ça m'est sorti de la tête **3.** [release] : *he slipped the dog's lead* US il a lâché la laisse du chien / *the dog slipped its lead* US le chien s'est dégagé de sa laisse ▶ **to slip a disc, to have a slipped disc** MED avoir une hernie discale **4.** AUTO [clutch] faire patiner. ◆ n **1.** [piece of paper] ▶ **slip (of paper)** feuille f or bout m de papier **2.** [on ice, banana skin] glissade f **3.** [mistake] erreur f ; [blunder] bévue f ; [careless oversight] étourderie f ; [moral] écart m, faute f légère ▶ **slip of the tongue** or **pen** lapsus m **4.** [petticoat - full length] combinaison f, fond m de robe ; [- skirt] jupon m **5.** PHR ▶ **a slip of a girl** US une petite jeune ▶ **a slip of a boy** US un petit jeune ▶ **to give sb the slip** semer qqn. ❖ **slip away**

vi [person] s'éclipser, partir discrètement ; [moment] passer ; [boat] s'éloigner doucement / *I felt my life slipping away* j'avais l'impression que ma vie me glissait entre les doigts. ❖ **slip in** ❖ vi [person] entrer discrètement or sans se faire remarquer ; [boat] entrer lentement / *some misprints have slipped in somehow* des fautes de frappe se sont glissées dans le texte. ❖ vt sep [moving part] faire glisser à sa place ; [quotation, word] glisser, placer. ❖ **slip out** ❖ vi **1.** [leave - person] sortir discrètement, s'esquiver **2.** [escape - animal, child] s'échapper / *the word slipped out before he could stop himself* le mot lui a échappé **3.** [go out] sortir (un instant). ❖ vt sep sortir. ❖ **slip through** vi [person] passer sans se faire remarquer ; [mistake] passer inaperçu. ❖ **slip up** vi faire une erreur.

slip-on ❖ adj [shoe] sans lacets. ❖ n chaussure *f* sans lacets.

slippage ['slɪpɪdʒ] n **1.** MECH patinage *m* **2.** [in targeting] retard *m (par rapport aux prévisions)* ; [in standards] baisse *f*.

slipped disc [,slɪpt-] n hernie *f* discale.

slipper ['slɪpər] ❖ n [soft footwear] chausson *m*, pantoufle *f* ; [mule] mule *f* ; [for dancing] escarpin *m*. ❖ vt 🇬🇧 [hit] ▶ **to slipper sb** donner une fessée à qqn *(avec une pantoufle)*.

slippery ['slɪpərɪ] adj **1.** [surface, soap] glissant **2.** *inf* [person - evasive] fuyant ; [unreliable] sur qui on ne peut pas compter.

slippy ['slɪpɪ] (*compar* **slippier**, *superl* **slippiest**) adj [slippery] glissant.

slip road n 🇬🇧 bretelle *f* d'accès.

slipshod ['slɪpʃɒd] adj [appearance] négligé, débraillé ; [habits, behaviour] négligent ; [style] peu soigné, négligé ; [work] négligé, mal fait.

slipstream ['slɪpstriːm] ❖ n AUTO sillage *m*. ❖ vt [driver] rester dans le sillage de.

slip-up n *inf* erreur *f*.

slipway ['slɪpweɪ] n NAUT [for repairs] cale *f* de halage ; [for launching] cale *f* de lancement.

slit [slɪt] (*pt & pp* **slit**, *cont* **slitting**) ❖ n [narrow opening] fente *f* ; [cut] incision *f*. ❖ vt **1.** [split] fendre ; [cut] inciser, couper ▶ **to slit sb's throat** égorger qqn / *she slit her wrists* elle s'est ouvert les veines **2.** [open - parcel, envelope] ouvrir (avec un couteau or un coupe-papier). ❖ adj [skirt] fendu ; [eyes] bridé.

slither ['slɪðər] vi **1.** [snake] ramper, onduler **2.** [car, person - slide] glisser, patiner ; [- skid] déraper.

sliver ['slɪvər] n **1.** [of glass] éclat *m* **2.** [small slice - of cheese, cake] tranche *f* fine.

slob [slɒb] n *inf* [dirty] souillon *mf* ; [uncouth] plouc *m* ; [lazy] flemmard *m*, -e *f*. ❖ **slob about** 🇬🇧, **slob around** *inf* ❖ vi traînasser. ❖ vt insep traînasser.

slobber ['slɒbər] ❖ vi **1.** [dribble - baby, dog] baver ▶ **to slobber over** baver sur **2.** *fig* ▶ **to slobber over** a) [possession, pet] s'extasier sur or devant b) [person] faire des ronds de jambe à. ❖ n [dribble] bave *f*.

slog [slɒg] (*pt & pp* **slogged**, *cont* **slogging**) *inf* ❖ n **1.** [hard task] travail *m* d'Hercule ; [chore] corvée *f*, travail *m* pénible ; [effort] (gros) effort *m* **2.** 🇬🇧 [hit] grand coup *m*. ❖ vi **1.** [work hard] trimer, bosser **2.** [walk, go] avancer péniblement. ❖ vt **1.** [move] : *we slogged our way through the snow* nous nous sommes péniblement frayé un chemin dans la neige **2.** 🇬🇧 [hit - ball] donner un grand coup dans ; [- person] cogner sur ▶ **to slog it out** a) [fight] se tabasser b) [argue] s'enguirlander.

slogan ['sləugən] n slogan *m*.

slo-mo ['sləuməu] n *inf* ralenti *m* ▶ **in slo-mo** au ralenti.

sloop [sluːp] n sloop *m*.

slop [slɒp] (*pt & pp* **slopped**, *cont* **slopping**) ❖ vi [spill] renverser ; [overflow - liquid] déborder. ❖ vt renverser. ❖ n (*U*) [liquid waste - for pigs] pâtée *f* ; [- from tea, coffee] fond *m* de tasse ; [tasteless food] mixture *f* *pej*. ❖ **slop about** 🇬🇧, **slop around** ❖ vi **1.** [liquid] clapoter **2.** [paddle] patauger **3.** *inf* [be lazy] traînasser. ❖ vt sep [paint] éclabousser ; [tea] renverser. ❖ vt insep *inf* : *he slops about the house doing nothing* il traîne à la maison à ne rien faire. ❖ **slop out** vi [prisoner] vider les seaux hygiéniques.

slope [sləup] ❖ n **1.** [incline - of roof] inclinaison *f*, pente *f* ; [- of ground] pente *f* ▶ **rifle at the slope** MIL fusil sur l'épaule **2.** [hill - up] côte *f*, montée *f* ; [- down] pente *f*, descente *f* ; [mountainside] versant *m*, flanc *m* **3.** [for skiing] piste *f*. ❖ vi [roof] être en pente or incliné ; [writing] pencher. ❖ vt MIL ▶ **slope arms!** portez arme ! ❖ **slope off** vi *inf* filer.

sloping ['sləupɪŋ] adj [table, roof] en pente, incliné ; [writing] penché ; [shoulders] tombant.

sloppily ['slɒpɪlɪ] adv **1.** [work] sans soin ; [dress] de façon négligée **2.** 🇬🇧 *inf* [sentimentally] avec sensiblerie.

sloppy ['slɒpɪ] (*compar* **sloppier**, *superl* **sloppiest**) adj **1.** [untidy - appearance] négligé, débraillé ; [careless - work] bâclé, négligé ; [- writing] peu soigné ; [- thinking] flou, vague, imprécis **2.** *inf* [loose - garment] large, lâche **3.** *inf* [sentimental - person, letter] sentimental ; [- book, film] à l'eau de rose.

slosh [slɒʃ] *inf* ❖ vt **1.** [spill] renverser, répandre ; [pour - onto floor] répandre ; [- into glass, bucket] verser ; [apply - paint, glue] flanquer **2.** 🇬🇧 [hit] flanquer un coup de poing à *v inf*. ❖ vi **1.** [liquid] se répandre **2.** [move - in liquid, mud] patauger. ❖ onomat plouf. ❖ **slosh about** 🇬🇧, **slosh around** vi [liquid] clapoter ; [person] patauger.

sloshed [slɒʃt] adj *inf* rond, soûl ▶ **to get sloshed** prendre une cuite.

slot [slɒt] (*pt & pp* **slotted**, *cont* **slotting**) ❖ n **1.** [opening - for coins, papers] fente *f* ; [groove] rainure *f* **2.** [in schedule, timetable] tranche *f* or plage *f* horaire, créneau *m* ; RADIO & TV créneau *m* ; [opening] créneau *m* **3.** AERON fente *f*. ❖ vt **1.** [insert] emboîter **2.** [find time for, fit] insérer, faire rentrer. ❖ vi **1.** [fit - part] rentrer, s'encastrer, s'emboîter **2.** [in timetable, schedule] rentrer, s'insérer. ❖ **slot in** ❖ vt sep [into schedule] faire rentrer. ❖ vi [part] s'emboîter, s'encastrer ; [programme] s'insérer. ❖ **slot together** ❖ vt sep emboîter, encastrer. ❖ vi s'emboîter, s'encastrer.

sloth [sləuθ] n **1.** [laziness] paresse *f* **2.** ZOOL paresseux *m*.

slot-in card n COMPUT carte *f* enfichable.

slot machine n [for vending] distributeur *m* (automatique) ; [for gambling] machine *f* à sous.

slot meter n 🇬🇧 compteur *m* à pièces.

slotted spoon n écumoire *f*.

slouch [slautʃ] ❖ vi : *she was slouching against the wall* elle était nonchalamment adossée au mur / *stop slouching!* redresse-toi ! ▶ **to slouch in / out** entrer / sortir en traînant les pieds. ❖ vt ▶ **to slouch one's shoulders** rentrer les épaules. ❖ n **1.** [in posture] ▶ **to have a slouch** avoir le dos voûté **2.** *inf* [person] : *he's no slouch* ce n'est pas un empoté. ❖ **slouch about** 🇬🇧, **slouch around** vi se traîner.

slough[1] [slau] n [mud pool] bourbier *m* ; [swamp] marécage *m*.

slough[2] [slʌf] ❖ n **1.** [skin - of snake] dépouille *f*, mue *f* ; MED escarre *f* **2.** CARDS carte *f* défaussée. ❖ vt : *the snake sloughs its skin* le serpent mue. ❖ **slough off** vt sep

[skin] se dépouiller de / *the snake sloughs off its skin* le serpent mue ; *fig* [worries] se débarrasser de ; [habit] perdre, se débarrasser de.

Slovak ['sləʊvæk] ◆ n [person] Slovaque *mf.* ◆ adj slovaque.

Slovakia [slə'vækɪə] pr n Slovaquie *f* / *in Slovakia* en Slovaquie.

Slovakian [slə'vækɪən] ◆ n Slovaque *mf.* ◆ adj slovaque.

Slovenia [slə'viːnjə] pr n Slovénie *f* / *in Slovenia* en Slovénie.

Slovenian [slə'viːnjən] ◆ n Slovène *mf.* ◆ adj slovène.

slovenly ['slʌvnlɪ] adj [appearance] négligé, débraillé ; [habits] relâché ; [work] peu soigné ; [style, expression] relâché, négligé.

slow [sləʊ] ◆ adj **1.** [not fast - movements, speed, service, traffic] lent / *a slow dance* un slow ; [in reactions] lent ; [in progress] lent ; [intellectually] lent ▶ **the slow lane** a) AUTO [when driving on left] la file de gauche b) [when driving on right] la file de droite ▶ **slow train** omnibus *m* **2.** [slack - business, market] calme **3.** [dull - evening, film, party] ennuyeux **4.** [clock] qui retarde / *your watch is (half an hour) slow* ta montre retarde (d'une demi-heure) **5.** CULIN ▶ **slow burner** feu *m* doux. ◆ adv lentement / *the clock is going* or *running slow* l'horloge prend du retard. ◆ vt ralentir. ◆ **slow down** ◆ vt sep **1.** [in speed - bus, machine, progress] ralentir ; [- person] (faire) ralentir ; [in achievement, activity] ralentir **2.** [delay] retarder. ◆ vi [driver, train, speed] ralentir ; *fig* [person] ralentir (le rythme) / *slow down!* moins vite ! ◆ **slow up** = **slow down.**

slow-acting adj à action lente.

slow-burning adj [fuse, fuel] à combustion lente / *fig slow-burning anger* colère *f* froide / *he's got a slow-burning temper* il refoule sa colère jusqu'au moment où il explose.

slowcoach ['sləʊkəʊtʃ] n 🇬🇧 *inf* [in moving] lambin *m*, -e *f*, traînard *m*, -e *f* ; [in thought] balourd *m*, -e *f*, lourdaud *m*, -e *f*.

slow-cook vt mitonner, mijoter.

slowdown ['sləʊdaʊn] n **1.** 🇺🇸 [go-slow] grève *f* perlée **2.** [slackening] ralentissement *m*.

slow handclap n 🇬🇧 applaudissements *mpl* rythmés *(pour montrer sa désapprobation)* / *they gave him the slow handclap* ≃ ils l'ont sifflé.

slowly ['sləʊlɪ] adv **1.** [not fast] lentement ▶ **slowly but surely** lentement mais sûrement **2.** [gradually] peu à peu.

slow motion n CIN & TV ralenti *m* ▶ **in slow motion** au ralenti. ◆ **slow-motion** adj (tourné) au ralenti ▶ **slow-motion replay** TV ralenti *m*.

slow-moving adj [person, car] lent ; [film, plot] dont l'action est lente ; [market] stagnant / *slow-moving target* cible *f* qui bouge lentement.

slowpoke ['sləʊpəʊk] 🇺🇸 *inf* = **slowcoach.**

slow-release adj MED à libération prolongée ; AGR [fertilizer] à action lente.

slow-roast vt confire / *slow-roasted lamb shank* souris d'agneau confite.

slowworm ['sləʊwɜːm] n orvet *m*.

SLR (abbr of **single-lens reflex**) n reflex *m* (monoobjectif).

sludge [slʌdʒ] n *(U)* **1.** [mud] boue *f*, vase *f* ; [snow] neige *f* fondue **2.** [sediment] dépôt *m*, boue *f* **3.** [sewage] vidanges *fpl*.

slug [slʌg] (*pt & pp* **slugged,** *cont* **slugging**) ◆ n **1.** ZOOL limace *f* **2.** *inf & fig* [lazy person] mollusque *m*

3. PRINT [of metal] lingot *m* **4.** 🇺🇸 [token] jeton *m* **5.** *inf* [hit] beigne *f* **6.** *inf* [drink] coup *m* ; [mouthful] lampée *f* / *to take a slug of whisky* boire une gorgée de whisky **7.** *inf* [bullet] balle *f*. ◆ vt *inf* **1.** [hit] frapper (fort), cogner **2.** 🇵🇭🇷 **to slug it out a)** [fight] se taper dessus **b)** [argue] s'enguirlander.

sluggish ['slʌgɪʃ] adj **1.** [lethargic] mou *(before vowel or silent 'h' **mol**, f **molle**)*, apathique **2.** [slow - traffic, growth, reaction] lent ; [- digestion] lent, paresseux ; [- market, business] calme, stagnant **3.** [engine] qui manque de reprise or de nervosité.

sluggishly ['slʌgɪʃlɪ] adv [slowly] lentement ; [lethargically] mollement.

sluice [sluːs] ◆ n **1.** [lock] écluse *f* ; [gate] porte *f* or vanne *f* d'écluse ; [channel] canal *m* à vannes ; *(U)* [lock water] eaux *fpl* retenues par la vanne **2.** [wash] ▶ **to give sth a sluice (down)** laver qqch à grande eau ▶ **to give sb a sluice (down)** asperger qqn d'eau. ◆ vt **1.** [drain] drainer ; [irrigate] irriguer **2.** [wash] laver à grande eau ; MIN [ore] laver ▶ **to sluice sth (down)** laver qqch à grande eau.

slum [slʌm] (*pt & pp* **slummed,** *cont* **slumming**) ◆ n *lit & fig* taudis *m* ; [district] quartier *m* pauvre, bas quartiers *mpl* ▶ **slum dwelling** taudis *m*. ◆ vt 🇬🇧 ▶ **to slum it** *inf* s'encanailler. ◆ vi *inf & hum* : *we're slumming tonight* on va s'encanailler ce soir *hum*.

slumber ['slʌmbər] ◆ n *liter* sommeil *m* (profond). ◆ vi dormir.

slumber party n 🇺🇸 soirée *f* entre copines *(au cours de laquelle on regarde des films, on discute et on reste dormir chez la personne qui a organisé la soirée).*

slumlord ['slʌmlɔːd] n marchand *m* de sommeil.

slump [slʌmp] ◆ n **1.** [in attendance, figures, popularity] chute *f*, forte baisse *f*, baisse *f* soudaine **2.** ECON [depression] crise *f* économique ; [recession] récession *f* ; ST. EX effondrement *m* (des cours), krach *m* (boursier) **3.** 🇺🇸 SPORT passage *m* à vide. ◆ vi **1.** [flop - with fatigue, illness] s'écrouler, s'effondrer **2.** [collapse - business, prices, market] s'effondrer ; [morale, attendance] baisser soudainement. ◆ vt *(usu passive)* : *to be slumped in an armchair* être affalé or affaissé dans un fauteuil / *he was slumped over the wheel* il était affaissé sur le volant.

slumpflation [slʌmp'fleɪʃn] n ECON forte récession accompagnée d'une inflation des prix et des salaires.

slung [slʌŋ] pt & pp ⟶ **sling.**

slunk [slʌŋk] pt & pp ⟶ **slink.**

slur [slɜːr] (*pt & pp* **slurred,** *cont* **slurring**) ◆ n **1.** [insult] insulte *f*, affront *m* ; [blot, stain] tache *f* ▶ **to cast a slur on sb** porter atteinte à la réputation de qqn **2.** MUS liaison *f*. ◆ vt **1.** [speech] mal articuler **2.** [denigrate] dénigrer **3.** MUS lier. ◆ vi [speech, words] devenir indistinct.

slurp [slɜːp] *inf* ◆ vt & vi boire bruyamment. ◆ n : *a loud slurp* un lapement bruyant / *can I have a quick slurp of your tea?* je peux boire une gorgée de ton thé ?

slurred [slɜːd] adj mal articulé / *his speech was slurred* il articulait.

slurry ['slʌrɪ] n [cement, clay] barbotine *f* ; [manure] purin *m*.

slush [slʌʃ] n **1.** [snow] neige *f* fondue ; [mud] gadoue *f* **2.** *inf* [sentimentality] sensiblerie *f*.

slush fund, slush money n 🇺🇸 caisse *f* noire *(servant généralement au paiement des pots-de-vin).*

slushy ['slʌʃɪ] *(compar* **slushier,** *superl* **slushiest)** adj **1.** [snow] fondu ; [ground] détrempé ; [path] couvert de neige fondue **2.** [film, book] à l'eau de rose.

slut [slʌt] n *pej* [slovenly woman] souillon *f* ; [immoral woman] fille *f* facile.

sly [slaɪ] (*compar* **slyer** *or* **slier**, *superl* **slyest** *or* **sliest**)
◆ adj **1.** [cunning, knowing] rusé **2.** [deceitful - person]
sournois ; [- behaviour] déloyal ; [- trick] malhonnête **3.** [mis-
chievous] malin (maligne), espiègle **4.** [secretive] dissimulé /
he's a sly one! c'est un petit cachottier ! ◆ n ▸ **on the sly**
inf en douce.

slyly ['slaɪlɪ] adv **1.** [cunningly] de façon rusée, avec ruse
2. [deceitfully] sournoisement **3.** [mischievously] avec espièglerie, de façon espiègle **4.** [secretly] discrètement.

slyness ['slaɪnɪs] n **1.** [cunning] ruse f **2.** [deceitfulness]
fausseté f **3.** [mischief] espièglerie f **4.** [secrecy] dissimulation f.

s/m n abbr of sadomasochism.

smack [smæk] ◆ n **1.** [slap] grande tape f, claque f ; [on
face] gifle f ; [on bottom] fessée f **2.** [sound] bruit m sec ; [of
whip] claquement m **3.** [taste] léger or petit goût m ; CULIN
soupçon m **4.** [boat] smack m, sémaque m **5.** [kiss] gros
baiser m **6.** *drugs sl* [heroin] poudre f, blanche f. ◆ vt donner une grande tape à, donner une claque à ; [in face] donner une gifle à, gifler ; [on bottom] donner une fessée à ▸ **to
smack sb's bottom a)** [in punishment] donner la fessée à
qqn **b)** [in play] donner une tape sur les fesses à qqn ▸ **to
smack one's lips** se lécher les babines. ◆ vi ▸ **to smack
of sthg** *lit & fig* sentir qqch. ◆ adv **1.** [forcefully] en plein /
she kissed him smack on the lips elle l'a embrassé en plein
sur la bouche **2.** [exactly] en plein / *we arrived smack in
the middle of the meeting* nous sommes arrivés au beau
milieu de la réunion.

smacking ['smækɪŋ] ◆ n fessée f. ◆ adj ⬚ *inf* ▸ **at a
smacking pace** à vive allure, à toute vitesse.

small [smɔːl] ◆ adj **1.** [in size - person, town, garden]
petit / *small children* les jeunes enfants / *in small letters*
en (lettres) minuscules ▸ **to make smaller a)** [garment] diminuer **b)** [hole] réduire ▸ **to make o.s. small** se faire tout
petit ▸ **to feel small** se trouver or se sentir bête ▸ **to make
sb look** or **feel small** humilier qqn **2.** [in number - crowd]
peu nombreux ; [- family] petit ; [- population] faible ; [in
quantity - amount, percentage, resources] petit, faible ; [- sup-
ply] petit ; [- salary, sum] petit, modeste ; [- helping] petit,
peu copieux ; [- meal] léger ▸ **to get or grow smaller**
diminuer, décroître ▸ **to make smaller a)** [income] diminuer
b) [staff] réduire **3.** [in scale, range] petit ; [minor] petit,
mineur / *down to the smallest details* jusqu'aux moindres
détails / *it's no small achievement* c'est une réussite non
négligeable ; COMM ▸ **small businesses a)** [firms] les petites et moyennes entreprises fpl, les PME fpl **b)** [shops] les
petits commerçants mpl **4.** [mean, narrow] petit, mesquin /
they've got small minds ce sont des esprits mesquins.
◆ adv ▸ **to cut sthg up small** couper qqch en tout petits
morceaux ▸ **to roll sthg up small a)** [long] rouler qqch bien
serré **b)** [ball] rouler qqch en petite boule. ◆ n : *I have a
pain in the small of my back* j'ai mal aux reins or au creux
des reins. ◆▸ **smalls** pl n *inf & hum* sous-vêtements mpl.

small ad n petite annonce f.

small arms pl n armes fpl portatives.

small change n petite monnaie f.

small fry n menu fretin m / *he's small fry* ⬚ or *a
small fry* ⬚ il ne compte pas.

smallholder ['smɔːl,həʊldər] n ⬚ petit propriétaire m.

smallholding ['smɔːl,həʊldɪŋ] n ⬚ petite propriété f.

small-minded adj [attitude, person] mesquin.

smallness ['smɔːlnɪs] n **1.** [of child] petite taille f ; [of
hand, room] petitesse f ; [of salary, fee] modicité f ; [of extent]
caractère m limité **2.** [of mind] mesquinerie f.

smallpox ['smɔːlpɒks] n variole f.

small print n : *in small print* en petits caractères, écrit
petit / *make sure you read the small print before you sign*
lisez bien ce qui est écrit en petits caractères avant de signer.

small screen n ▸ **the small screen** le petit écran.

small talk n (U) papotage m, menus propos mpl ▸ **to
make small talk** échanger des banalités.

small-time adj peu important, de petite envergure / *a
small-time thief* / crook un petit voleur / escroc.

small-town adj provincial / *small-town America*
l'Amérique profonde.

smarmy ['smɑːmɪ] (*compar* **smarmier**, *superl*
smarmiest) adj ⬚ *inf & pej* [toadying] lèche-bottes (*inv*) ;
[obsequious] obséquieux.

smart [smɑːt] ◆ adj **1.** ⬚ [elegant - person, clothes]
chic, élégant ; [fashionable - hotel, district] élégant, chic ▸ **the
smart set** les gens chics, le beau monde **2.** [clever - person]
malin (maligne), habile ; [- reply] habile, adroit ; [- shrewd
person] habile, astucieux ; [witty - person, remark] spirituel
3. [impertinent] impertinent, audacieux **4.** [quick - pace,
rhythm] vif, prompt **5.** [sharp - reprimand] bon, bien envoyé
6. COMPUT intelligent **7.** ARM [bomb, weapon] intelligent.
◆ vi **1.** [eyes, wound] picoter, brûler **2.** [person] être piqué
au vif. ◆ n **1.** [pain] douleur f cuisante ; *fig* effet m cinglant
2. ⬚ *inf* [useful hint] tuyau m, combine f.

smart aleck n *inf* je-sais-tout mf. ◆▸ **smart-aleck**
adj *inf* gonflé.

smartarse ⬚, **smartass** ⬚ ['smɑːtɑːs]
v *inf* = **smart aleck.**

smart card n carte f à puce.

smart drug n smart drug f, nootrope m.

smarten ['smɑːtn] vt **1.** [improve appearance] ▸ **to
smarten o.s.** se faire beau **2.** ⬚ [speed up] ▸ **to smarten
one's pace** accélérer l'allure. ◆▸ **smarten up** ◆ vi [per-
son] se faire beau ; [restaurant] devenir plus chic, être retapé ;
[town, street] devenir plus pimpant. ◆ vt sep [person] pomponner ; [room, house, town] arranger, rendre plus élégant
▸ **to smarten o.s. up** se faire beau, soigner son apparence.

smartly ['smɑːtlɪ] adv **1.** [elegantly] avec beaucoup
d'allure or de chic, élégamment **2.** [cleverly] habilement,
adroitement **3.** [briskly - move] vivement ; [- act, work] rapidement, promptement **4.** [sharply - reprimand] vertement ;
[- reply] du tac au tac, sèchement.

smart money n *inf* : *all the smart money is on him
to win the presidency* il est donné pour favori aux élections
présidentielles.

smart set n ▸ **the smart set** les branchés.

smarty-pants (*pl* **smarty-pants**) n *inf* : *you're
a real smarty-pants, aren't you?* tu crois vraiment tout
savoir !

smash [smæʃ] ◆ n **1.** [noise - of breaking] fracas m
2. [blow] coup m or choc m violent **3.** *inf* [collision]
collision f ; [accident] accident m ; [pile-up] carambolage m **4.** SPORT smash m **5.** *inf* [success] succès m bœuf.
◆ onomat patatras. ◆ adv : *to go or to run smash into a
wall* heurter un mur avec violence, rentrer en plein dans un
mur. ◆ vt **1.** [break - cup, window] fracasser, briser ; PHYS
[atom] désintégrer **2.** [crash, hit] écraser / *he smashed his
fist (down) on the table* il lui écrasa son poing sur la table /
they smashed their way in ils sont entrés par effraction (en
enfonçant la porte ou la fenêtre) / *the raft was smashed
against the rocks* le radeau s'est fracassé contre or sur
les rochers **3.** SPORT ▸ **to smash the ball** faire un smash,
smasher **4.** [destroy - conspiracy, organization] briser, démolir ; [- resistance, opposition] briser, écraser ; [- chances, hopes,
career] ruiner, briser ; [- opponent, record] pulvériser. ◆ vi
[break, crash] se briser, se fracasser. ◆▸ **smash down**
vt sep [door] fracasser, écraser. ◆▸ **smash in** vt sep [door,

window] enfoncer. ❖ **smash up** vt sep [furniture] casser, démolir ; [room, shop] tout casser or démolir dans ; [car] démolir.

smash-and-grab (raid) n cambriolage commis en brisant une devanture.

smashed [smæʃt] adj inf [on alcohol] bourré ; [on drugs] défoncé.

smash hit n [song, album] gros succès m.

smashing ['smæʃɪŋ] adj UK inf super, terrible.

smash-up n [accident] accident m ; [pile-up] carambolage m, télescopage m.

smattering ['smætərɪŋ] n (U) [of knowledge] notions fpl vagues ; [of people, things] poignée f, petit nombre m.

SME (abbr of small and medium-sized enterprise) n PME f.

smear [smɪə⁰] ❖ n **1.** [mark - on glass, mirror, wall] trace f, tache f ; [longer] traînée f ; [of ink] pâté m, bavure f **2.** [slander] diffamation f ▶ **to use smear tactics** avoir recours à la calomnie **3.** MED frottis m, prélèvement m. ❖ vt **1.** [spread - butter, oil] étaler ; [coat] barbouiller **2.** [smudge] : the ink on the page was smeared l'encre a coulé sur la page / the mirror was smeared with fingermarks il y avait des traces de doigts sur la glace **3.** [slander] ▶ **to smear sb** salir la réputation de qqn, calomnier qqn **4.** US inf [thrash] battre à plates coutures. ❖ vi [wet paint, ink] se salir, se maculer.

smear campaign n campagne f de diffamation or dénigrement.

smear test n MED frottis m.

smell [smel] (UK pt & pp **smelled** or **smelt** [smelt] ; US pt & pp **smelled**) ❖ vt **1.** [notice an odour of] sentir **2.** fig [sense - trouble, danger] flairer, pressentir **3.** [sniff at - food] sentir, renifler ; [- flower] sentir, humer. ❖ vi **1.** [have odour] sentir ▶ **to smell good** or **sweet** sentir bon / **to smell bad** sentir mauvais / **it smells awful!** ça pue ! / **it smells musty** ça sent le renfermé / **it smells of lavender** ça sent la lavande / **it smells like lavender** on dirait de la lavande **2.** [have bad odour] sentir (mauvais) / **his breath smells** il a mauvaise haleine **3.** [perceive odour] : **he can't smell** il n'a pas d'odorat. ❖ n **1.** [sense - of person] odorat m ; [- of animal] odorat m, flair m ▶ **to have a keen sense of smell** avoir le nez fin **2.** [odour] odeur f ; [bad odour] mauvaise odeur f, relent m ; [stench] puanteur f / **there was a smell of burning in the kitchen** il y avait une odeur de brûlé dans la cuisine / **there was a lovely smell of lavender** ça sentait bon la lavande / **what an awful smell!** qu'est-ce que ça sent mauvais ! **3.** [sniff] : **have a smell of this** sentez-moi ça. ❖ **smell out** vt sep [subj: dog] dénicher en flairant ; fig [subj: person] découvrir, dépister ; [secret, conspiracy] découvrir.

smelly ['smelɪ] (compar **smellier**, superl **smelliest**) adj [person, socks, etc.] qui sent mauvais, qui pue.

smelt [smelt] (pl **smelt** or **smelts**) ❖ pt & pp ⟶ **smell.** ❖ n [fish] éperlan m. ❖ vt METALL [ore] fondre ; [metal] extraire par fusion.

smidgen, smidgin ['smɪdʒɪn] n inf ▶ **a smidgen of** un tout petit peu de.

smile [smaɪl] ❖ n sourire m. ❖ vi sourire ▶ **to smile at sb** sourire à qqn ▶ **to smile to o.s.** sourire pour soi. ❖ vt ▶ **to smile one's approval** exprimer son approbation par un sourire.

smiley ['smaɪlɪ] n smiley m, émoticon m, souriant m.

smiling ['smaɪlɪŋ] adj souriant.

smirk [smɜːk] ❖ vi [smugly] sourire d'un air suffisant or avec suffisance ; [foolishly] sourire bêtement. ❖ n [smug] petit sourire m satisfait or suffisant ; [foolish] sourire m bête.

smith [smɪθ] n [blacksmith - gen] forgeron m ; EQUIT maréchal-ferrant m.

smithereens [,smɪðə'riːnz] pl n morceaux mpl ▶ **to smash sthg to smithereens** briser qqch en mille morceaux.

smithy ['smɪðɪ] (pl **smithies**) n forge f.

smitten ['smɪtn] ❖ pp ⟶ **smite.** ❖ adj : he was with or by her beauty il a été ébloui par sa beauté / he's really smitten (with that girl) il est vraiment très épris (de cette fille).

smock [smɒk] ❖ n [loose garment] blouse f ; [maternity wear - blouse] tunique f de grossesse ; [- dress] robe f de grossesse. ❖ vt faire des smocks à.

smog [smɒg] n smog m.

smoggy ['smɒgɪ] (compar **smoggier**, superl **smoggiest**) adj : it's smoggy il y a du smog.

smoke [sməʊk] ❖ n **1.** [from fire, cigarette] fumée f ▶ **to go up in smoke** a) [building] brûler b) [plans] partir or s'en aller en fumée ▶ **there's no smoke without fire** prov il n'y a pas de fumée sans feu prov **2.** [act of smoking] ▶ **to have a smoke** fumer **3.** inf & dated [cigarette] clope m ou f **4.** drugs sl [hashish] shit m **5.** UK inf [city] ▶ **the Smoke** a) [any city] la grande métropole b) [London] Londres. ❖ vi **1.** [fireplace, chimney, lamp] fumer **2.** [person] fumer ▶ **to smoke like a chimney** inf fumer comme un pompier or un sapeur. ❖ vt **1.** [cigarette, pipe, opium, etc.] fumer / **to smoke a pipe** fumer la pipe **2.** CULIN & INDUST [fish, meat, glass] fumer. ❖ **smoke out** vt sep **1.** [from den, hiding place - fugitive, animal] enfumer ; fig [discover - traitor] débusquer, dénicher ; [- conspiracy, plot] découvrir **2.** [room] enfumer.

smoke alarm n détecteur m de fumée.

smoke bomb n bombe f fumigène.

smoked [sməʊkt] adj fumé ▶ **smoked salmon** saumon m fumé ▶ **smoked glass** verre m fumé.

smoke detector n détecteur m de fumée.

smoke-filled [-fɪld] adj enfumé.

smokeless fuel ['sməʊklɪs-] n combustible m non polluant.

smokeless zone n zone dans laquelle seul l'usage de combustibles non polluants est autorisé.

smoker ['sməʊkə⁰] n **1.** [person] fumeur m, -euse f **2.** [on train] compartiment m fumeurs.

smokescreen ['sməʊkskriːn] n MIL écran m or rideau m de fumée ; fig paravent m, couverture f.

smoke shop n US tabac m.

smokestack ['sməʊkstæk] n cheminée f.

smokestack industry n industrie f lourde.

smoking ['sməʊkɪŋ] n : I've given up smoking j'ai arrêté de fumer / **'no smoking'** 'défense de fumer'.

smoking area n zone f fumeurs.

smoking compartment UK, **smoking car** US n compartiment m fumeurs.

smoking gun n fig [clue] indice m tangible, preuve f flagrante.

smoky ['sməʊkɪ] (compar **smokier**, superl **smokiest**) adj **1.** [atmosphere, room] enfumé **2.** [chimney, lamp, fire] qui fume **3.** [in flavour - food] qui sent le fumé, qui a un goût de fumé **4.** [in colour] gris cendré (inv).

smolder US = **smoulder**.

smooch [smuːtʃ] inf ❖ n ▶ **to have a smooch** a) [kiss] se bécoter b) [pet] se peloter. ❖ vi **1.** [kiss] se bécoter ; [pet] se peloter **2.** UK [dance] danser joue contre joue.

smooth [smuːð] ❖ adj **1.** [surface] lisse ; [pebble, stone] lisse, poli ; [skin] lisse, doux (douce) ; [chin - close-shaven] rasé de près ; [- beardless] glabre, lisse ; [hair, fabric, road]

snap

lisse ; [sea, water] calme **2.** [ride, flight] confortable ; [take-off, landing] en douceur **3.** [steady, regular - flow, breathing, working, supply] régulier ; [- organization] qui marche bien ; [- rhythm, style] coulant **4.** [trouble-free - life, course of events] paisible, calme **5.** CULIN [in texture] onctueux, homogène ; [in taste] moelleux **6.** *pej* [slick, suave] doucereux, onctueux, suave. ◆ vt **1.** [tablecloth, skirt] défroisser ; [hair, feathers] lisser ; [wood] rendre lisse, planer **2.** [rub - oil, cream] masser **3.** [polish] lisser, polir. ❖ **smooth back** vt sep [hair] lisser en arrière ; [sheet] rabattre en lissant. ❖ **smooth down** vt sep [hair] lisser ; [sheets, dress] lisser, défroisser ; [wood] planer, aplanir ; *fig* [person] apaiser, calmer. ❖ **smooth out** vt sep [skirt, sheet, curtains] lisser, défroisser ; [crease, pleat, wrinkle] faire disparaître (en lissant) ; *fig* [difficulties, obstacles] aplanir, faire disparaître. ❖ **smooth over** vt sep **1.** [gravel, sand] rendre lisse (en ratissant) ; [soil] aplanir, égaliser **2.** *fig* [difficulties, obstacles] aplanir ; [embarrassing situation] ▸ **to smooth things over** arranger les choses.

smoothie ['smu:ðɪ] n **1.** *inf & pej* : *he's a real smoothie* **a)** [in manner] il roule les mécaniques **b)** [in speech] c'est vraiment un beau parleur **2.** [drink] smoothie *m*.

smoothly ['smu:ðlɪ] adv **1.** [easily, steadily - operate, drive, move] sans à-coups, en douceur ▸ **to run smoothly a)** [engine] tourner bien **b)** [operation] marcher comme sur des roulettes **2.** [gently - rise, fall] doucement, en douceur **3.** *pej* [talk] doucereusement ; [behave] (trop) suavement.

smoothness ['smu:ðnɪs] n **1.** [of surface] égalité *f*, aspect *m* uni or lisse ; [of fabric, of skin, of hair] douceur *f* ; [of road] surface *f* lisse ; [of sea] calme *m* ; [of stone] aspect *m* lisse or poli ; [of tyre] aspect *m* lisse **2.** [of flow, breathing, pace, supply] régularité *f* ; [of engine, machine] bon fonctionnement *m* ; [of life, course of events] caractère *m* paisible or serein ; *fig* [of temperament] calme *m*, sérénité *f* **3.** CULIN [of texture] onctuosité *f* ; [of taste] moelleux *m*.

smooth sailing n : *it's smooth sailing from now on* maintenant, ça va marcher tout seul or comme sur des roulettes.

smooth-talking [-ˌtɔːkɪŋ] adj doucereux, mielleux.

smoothy ['smu:ðɪ] *inf* = **smoothie**.

smother ['smʌðər] ◆ vt **1.** [suppress - fire, flames] étouffer ; [- sound] étouffer, amortir ; [- emotions, laughter, yawn] réprimer ; [suppress - scandal, opposition] étouffer **2.** [suffocate - person] étouffer **3.** [cover] couvrir, recouvrir / *strawberries smothered in* or *with cream* des fraises couvertes de crème **4.** [overwhelm - with kindness, love] combler / *to smother sb with kisses* couvrir or dévorer qqn de baisers. ◆ vi [person] étouffer.

smoulder UK, **smolder** US ['sməʊldər] vi **1.** [fire - before flames] couver ; [- after burning] fumer **2.** [feeling, rebellion] couver / *her eyes smouldered with passion* son regard était plein de désir.

smouldering UK, **smoldering** US ['sməʊldərɪŋ] adj [fire, anger, passion] qui couve ; [embers, ruins] fumant ; [eyes] de braise.

SMS [ˌesemˈes] **(abbr of short message service)** n TELEC service *m* SMS ▸ **SMS (message)** (message *m*) SMS *m*, texto *m*.

smudge [smʌdʒ] ◆ n **1.** [on face, clothes, surface] (petite) tache *f* ; [of make-up] traînée *f* ; [on page of print] bavure *f* **2.** US [fire] feu *m* (de jardin). ◆ vt [face, hands] salir ; [clothes, surface] tacher, salir ; [ink] répandre ; [writing] étaler. ◆ vi [ink, make-up] faire des taches ; [print] être maculé ; [wet paint] s'étaler.

smug [smʌg] (*compar* **smugger**, *superl* **smuggest**) adj *pej* [person] content de soi, suffisant ; [attitude, manner, voice] suffisant.

smuggle ['smʌgl] ◆ vt [contraband] passer en contrebande ; [into prison - mail, arms] introduire clandestinement ▸ **to smuggle sthg through customs** passer qqch en fraude à la douane ; *fig* [into classroom, meeting, etc.] introduire subrepticement. ◆ vi faire de la contrebande. ❖ **smuggle in** vt sep [on a large scale - drugs, arms] faire entrer or passer en contrebande ; [as tourist - cigarettes, alcohol] introduire en fraude ; [move secretly - books, mail, etc.] introduire clandestinement. ❖ **smuggle out** vt sep [goods] faire sortir en fraude or en contrebande.

smuggler ['smʌglər] n contrebandier *m*, -ère *f* ▸ **drug smuggler** trafiquant *m*, -e *f* de drogue.

smuggling ['smʌglɪŋ] n contrebande *f*.

smugly ['smʌglɪ] adv [say] d'un ton suffisant, avec suffisance ; [look, smile] d'un air suffisant, avec suffisance.

smugness ['smʌgnɪs] n suffisance *f*.

smut [smʌt] (*pt & pp* **smutted**, *cont* **smutting**) n **1.** (U) *inf* [obscenity] cochonneries *fpl* ; [pornography] porno *m* **2.** UK [speck of dirt] poussière *f* ; [smudge of soot] tache *f* de suie **3.** AGR charbon *m* or nielle *f* du blé.

smutty ['smʌtɪ] (*compar* **smuttier**, *superl* **smuttiest**) adj **1.** *inf* [obscene] cochon *m* ; [pornographic] porno **2.** [dirty - hands, face, surface] sali, noirci.

snack [snæk] ◆ n **1.** [light meal] casse-croûte *m inv*, en-cas *m inv* ▸ **to have a snack** casser la croûte, manger un morceau **2.** (*usu pl*) [appetizer - esp at party] amuse-gueule *m*. ◆ vi US grignoter.

snack bar n snack *m*, snack-bar *m*.

snacking ['snækɪŋ] n *fait de manger entre les repas* / *is snacking healthy?* est-ce qu'il est sain de grignoter entre les repas ?

snaffle ['snæfl] ◆ vt **1.** UK *inf* [get] se procurer ; [steal] piquer, faucher **2.** EQUIT mettre un bridon à. ◆ n EQUIT ▸ **snaffle (bit)** mors *m* brisé, bridon *m*.

snag [snæg] (*pt & pp* **snagged**, *cont* **snagging**) ◆ n **1.** [problem] problème *m*, difficulté *f*, hic *m* ▸ **to come across** or **to run into a snag** tomber sur un hic or sur un os **2.** [tear - in garment] accroc *m* ; [- in stocking] fil *m* tiré **3.** [sharp protuberance] aspérité *f* ; [tree stump] chicot *m*. ◆ vt **1.** [tear - cloth, garment] faire un accroc à, déchirer **2.** US *inf* [obtain] s'emparer de. ◆ vi s'accrocher.

snaggle-toothed ['snægl-] adj US *aux dents mal placées*.

snail [sneɪl] n escargot *m* ▸ **at a snail's pace a)** [move] comme un escargot **b)** [change, progress] très lentement.

snail mail n *inf* ▸ **to send sthg by snail mail** envoyer qqch par courrier.

snake [sneɪk] ◆ n **1.** ZOOL serpent *m* **2.** [person] vipère *f* **3.** ECON serpent *m* (monétaire). ◆ vi serpenter, sinuer *liter*. ◆ vt : *the river* / *road snakes its way down to the sea* le fleuve serpente / la route descend en lacets jusqu'à la mer.

snakebite ['sneɪkbaɪt] n **1.** [bite] morsure *f* de serpent **2.** [drink] *mélange de cidre et de bière blonde.*

snake pit n US *fig* fosse *f* aux serpents, nid *m* de vipères.

snakeskin ['sneɪkskɪn] ◆ n peau *f* de serpent. ◆ comp [shoes, handbag] en (peau de) serpent.

snap [snæp] (*pt & pp* **snapped**, *cont* **snapping**) ◆ vt **1.** [break - sharply] casser net ; [- with a crack] casser avec un bruit sec **2.** [make cracking sound] faire claquer **3.** [say brusquely] dire d'un ton sec or brusque **4.** *inf* PHOT prendre une photo de. ◆ vi **1.** [break - branch] se casser net or avec un bruit sec, craquer ; [- elastic band] claquer ; [- rope] se casser, rompre **2.** [make cracking sound - whip, fingers] claquer **3.** *fig* [person, nerves] craquer **4.** [speak brusquely] ▸ **to snap at sb** parler à qqn d'un ton sec **5.** [try to bite] ▸ **to snap at** chercher à or essayer de mordre. ◆ n **1.** [of whip] claquement *m* ; [of sthg breaking, opening, closing] bruit *m* sec

2. [of jaws] ❱ **to make a snap at sb / sthg** essayer de mordre qqn / qqch **3.** *inf* PHOT photo *f*, instantané *m* **4.** 🇬🇧 CARDS ≃ bataille *f* **5.** METEOR : *a cold snap* or *a snap of cold weather* une vague de froid **6.** *inf* [effort] effort *m* ; [energy] énergie *f* **7.** 🇺🇸 *inf* [easy task] : *it's a snap!* c'est simple comme bonjour ! **8.** CULIN biscuit *m*, petit gâteau *m* sec **9.** 🇺🇸 [clasp, fastener] fermoir *m* ; [press stud] bouton-pression *m*. ❖ adj **1.** [vote] éclair ; [reaction] immédiat ; [judgment] irréfléchi, hâtif / *to call a snap election* procéder à une élection surprise **2.** 🇺🇸 *inf* [easy] facile. ❖ adv ❱ **to go snap** casser net. ❖ interj 🇬🇧 **1.** CARDS ❱ **snap!** ≃ bataille ! **2.** *inf* [in identical situation] ❱ **snap!** tiens !, quelle coïncidence ! ❖ **snap off** ❖ vt sep casser. ❖ vi casser net. ❖ **snap on** vt sep 🇺🇸 ❱ **to snap a light on** allumer une lampe. ❖ **snap out** ❖ vi ❱ **to snap out of** a) [depression, mood, trance] se sortir de, se tirer de b) [temper] dominer, maîtriser. ❖ vt sep [question] poser d'un ton sec ; [order, warning] lancer brutalement. ❖ **snap up** vt sep **1.** [subj: dog, fish] happer, attraper **2.** *fig* [bargain, offer, opportunity] sauter sur, se jeter sur **3.** 🇵🇭🇷 **snap it up!** 🇺🇸 *inf* dépêchons !

snap fastener n [press stud] bouton-pression *m*, pression *f* ; [clasp - on handbag, necklace] fermoir *m* (à pression).

snappish ['snæpɪʃ] adj [dog] hargneux, toujours prêt à mordre ; [person] hargneux ; [voice] mordant, cassant ; [reply] brusque, cassant, sec (sèche).

snappy ['snæpɪ] (*compar* **snappier**, *superl* **snappiest**) adj *inf* **1.** [fashionable] : *she's a snappy dresser* elle sait s'habiller **2.** [lively - pace, rhythm] vif, entraînant ; [-dialogue, debate] plein d'entrain, vivant ; [-style, slogan] qui a du punch ; [-reply] bien envoyé ❱ **make it snappy!** et que ça saute ! **3.** [unfriendly - person] hargneux ; [-answer] brusque ; [-voice] cassant / *a snappy little dog* un petit roquet.

snapshot ['snæpʃɒt] n instantané *m*.

snare [sneəʳ] ❖ n **1.** [trap - gen] piège *m* ; [-made of rope, wire] lacet *m*, collet *m*, lacs *m* ; *fig* piège *m*, traquenard *m* **2.** MUS ❱ **snare (drum)** caisse *f* claire. ❖ vt [animal - gen] piéger ; [-in wire or rope trap] prendre au lacet ou au collet ; *fig* [person] prendre au piège, piéger.

snarl [snɑːl] ❖ vi **1.** [dog] gronder, grogner ; [person] gronder **2.** [thread, rope, hair] s'emmêler ; [traffic] se bloquer ; [plan, programme] cafouiller. ❖ vt **1.** [person] lancer d'une voix rageuse, rugir **2.** [thread, rope, hair] enchevêtrer, emmêler ❖ n **1.** [sound] grognement *m*, grondement *m* **2.** [tangle - in thread, wool, hair] nœud *m*, nœuds *mpl*. ❖ **snarl up** ❖ vi = **snarl** (*vi*). ❖ vt sep (*usu passive*) **1.** [thread, rope, hair] emmêler, enchevêtrer **2.** [traffic] bloquer, coincer ; [plans] faire cafouiller.

snarl-up n [of traffic] bouchon *m*, embouteillage *m* ; [of plans] cafouillage *m*.

snatch [snætʃ] ❖ vt **1.** [seize - bag, money] saisir ; [-opportunity] saisir, sauter sur ❱ **to snatch sthg from sb** or **from sb's hands** arracher qqch des mains de qqn **2.** [manage to get - meal, drink] avaler à la hâte ; [-holiday, rest] réussir à avoir ❱ **to snatch some sleep** réussir à dormir un peu ❱ **to snatch a glance at sb** lancer un coup d'œil furtif à qqn **3.** [steal] voler ; [kiss] voler, dérober ; [victory] décrocher **4.** [kidnap] kidnapper. ❖ vi [to child] ❱ **to snatch at sthg** essayer de saisir ou d'attraper qqch. ❖ n **1.** [grab] geste *m* vif de la main (*pour attraper qqch*) ❱ **to make a snatch at sthg** essayer de saisir or d'attraper qqch **2.** 🇬🇧 *inf* [robbery] vol *m* à l'arraché ❱ **bag snatch** vol (de sac) à l'arraché **3.** *inf* [kidnapping] kidnapping *m* **4.** [fragment - of conversation] fragment *m*, bribes *fpl* ; [-of song, music] fragment *m*, mesure *f* ; [-of poetry] fragment *m*, vers *m* **5.** [short spell] courte période *f* / *to sleep in snatches* dormir par intervalles or de façon intermittente **6.** [in weightlifting] arra-

ché *m*. ❖ **snatch away** vt sep [letter, plate, etc.] arracher, enlever d'un geste vif ; [hope] ôter, enlever ❱ **to snatch away from sb** arracher qqch à qqn. ❖ **snatch up** vt sep ramasser vite or vivement or d'un seul coup.

snazzy ['snæzɪ] (*compar* **snazzier**, *superl* **snazziest**) adj *inf* [garment] chic, qui a de l'allure ; [car, house] chouette.

sneak [sniːk] (🇬🇧 *pt* & *pp* **sneaked** ; 🇺🇸 *pt* & *pp* **sneaked** or **snuck** [snʌk]) ❖ vi **1.** [verb of movement] se glisser, se faufiler ; [furtively] se glisser furtivement ; [quietly] se glisser à pas feutrés or sans faire de bruit ; [secretly] se glisser sans se faire remarquer / *to sneak up* / *down the stairs* monter / descendre l'escalier furtivement **2.** 🇬🇧 *inf* SCH moucharder, cafter ❱ **to sneak on sb** moucharder qqn. ❖ vt **1.** [give - letter, message] glisser en douce or sans se faire remarquer **2.** [take] enlever, prendre ❱ **to sneak a look at sthg** lancer or jeter un coup d'œil furtif à qqch **3.** *inf* [steal] chiper, piquer, faucher. ❖ n *inf* **1.** [devious person] faux jeton *m* **2.** 🇬🇧 SCH cafardeur *m*, -euse *f*, mouchard *m*, -e *f*. ❖ adj [attack] furtif. ❖ **sneak away**, **sneak off** vi se défiler, s'esquiver. ❖ **sneak up** vi s'approcher à pas feutrés or furtivement ❱ **to sneak up on** or **behind sb** s'approcher de qqn à pas feutrés.

sneaker ['sniːkəʳ] n 🇺🇸 (chaussure *f* de) tennis *m* ou *f*, basket *m* ou *f*.

sneakily ['sniːkɪlɪ] adv [slyly] sournoisement ; [furtively] en cachette.

sneaking ['sniːkɪŋ] adj [feeling, respect] inavoué, secret (secrète).

sneak preview n avant-première *f* privée.

sneaky ['sniːkɪ] (*compar* **sneakier**, *superl* **sneakiest**) adj [person] sournois ; [action] faite en cachette, faite à la dérobée.

sneer [snɪəʳ] ❖ vi ricaner, sourire avec mépris or d'un air méprisant ❱ **to sneer at sb / sthg** se moquer de qqn / qqch. ❖ n [facial expression] ricanement *m*, rictus *m* ; [remark] raillerie *f*, sarcasme *m*.

sneering ['snɪərɪŋ] ❖ adj ricaneur, méprisant. ❖ n (*U*) ricanement *m*, ricanements *mpl*.

sneeze [sniːz] ❖ n éternuement *m*. ❖ vi éternuer.

sneezing ['sniːzɪŋ] n éternuement *m*.

snicker ['snɪkəʳ] ❖ n **1.** [snigger] ricanement *m* **2.** [of horse] (petit) hennissement *m*. ❖ vi **1.** [snigger] ricaner ❱ **to snicker at sb** se moquer de qqn **2.** [horse] hennir doucement.

snide [snaɪd] adj [sarcastic] narquois, railleur ; [unfriendly] inamical, insidieux.

sniff [snɪf] ❖ vi **1.** [from cold, crying, etc.] renifler **2.** [scornfully] faire la grimace or la moue. ❖ vt **1.** [smell - food, soap] renifler, sentir l'odeur de ; [-rose, perfume] humer, sentir l'odeur de ; [subj: dog] renifler, flairer **2.** [inhale - air] humer, respirer ; [-smelling salts] respirer ; [-cocaine] sniffer, priser ; [-snuff] priser ; [-glue] respirer, sniffer **3.** [say scornfully] dire d'un air méprisant or dédaigneux. ❖ n [gen] reniflement *m* ❱ **to give a sniff** a) *lit* renifler b) [scornfully] faire la grimace or la moue ❱ **to have** or **to take a sniff of sthg** renifler or flairer qqch. ❖ **sniff at** vt insep **1.** *lit* ❱ **to sniff at sthg** a) [subj: person] renifler qqch b) [subj: dog] renifler or flairer qqch **2.** *fig* faire la grimace or la moue devant. ❖ **sniff out** vt sep [subj: dog] découvrir en reniflant or en flairant ; [criminal] découvrir, dépister ; [secret] découvrir.

sniffer dog ['snɪfəʳ-] n chien *m* policier (*dressé pour le dépistage de la drogue, des explosifs*).

sniffle ['snɪfl] ❖ vi [sniff] renifler ; [have runny nose] avoir le nez qui coule. ❖ n [sniff] (léger) reniflement *m* ; [cold] petit rhume *m* de cerveau ❱ **to have the sniffles** *inf* avoir le nez qui coule.

snigger ['snɪgər] ◆ vi ricaner, rire dans sa barbe ▶ **to snigger at a)** [suggestion, remark] ricaner en entendant **b)** [appearance] se moquer de, ricaner à la vue de. ◆ n rire *m* en dessous ; [sarcastic] ricanement *m*.

sniggering ['snɪgərɪŋ] ◆ n *(U)* rires *mpl* en dessous ; [sarcastic] ricanements *mpl*. ◆ adj ricaneur.

snip [snɪp] *(pt & pp* snipped, *cont* snipping) ◆ n **1.** [cut] petit coup *m* de ciseaux, petite entaille *f* or incision *f* **2.** [sound] clic *m* **3.** [small piece -of cloth, paper] petit bout *m* ; [-of hair] mèche *f* (coupée) **4.** UK *inf* [bargain] (bonne) affaire *f* ; [horse] tuyau *m* sûr **5.** UK *inf* [cinch] ▶ **it's a snip!** c'est du gâteau !, c'est simple comme bonjour ! ◆ vt couper *(en donnant de petits coups de ciseaux)*. ◆ vi : *he was snipping at the hedge* il coupait la haie. ❖ **snip off** vt sep couper or enlever (à petits coups de ciseaux).

snipe [snaɪp] *(pl* snipe) ◆ n bécassine *f.* ◆ vi [shoot] tirer (d'une position cachée) ▶ **to snipe at sb a)** *lit* tirer sur qqn **b)** *fig* [criticize] critiquer qqn par derrière.

sniper ['snaɪpər] n tireur *m* embusqué or isolé.

snippet ['snɪpɪt] n [of material, paper] petit bout *m* ; [of conversation, information] bribe *f.*

snivel ['snɪvl] (UK *pt & pp* snivelled, *cont* snivelling ; US *pt & pp* sniveled, *cont* sniveling) ◆ vi [whine] pleurnicher ; [because of cold] renifler (continuellement) ; [with runny nose] avoir le nez qui coule. ◆ vt : *"it wasn't my fault"*, *he snivelled* «ce n'était pas de ma faute», fit-il en pleurnichant. ◆ n [sniffing] reniflement *m*, reniflements *mpl* ; [tears] pleurnichements *mpl*.

snivelling UK, **sniveling** US ['snɪvlɪŋ] ◆ adj pleurnicheur, larmoyant. ◆ n *(U)* [crying] pleurnichements *mpl* ; [because of cold] reniflement *m*, reniflements *mpl*.

snob [snɒb] n snob *mf*.

snobbery ['snɒbərɪ] n snobisme *m*.

snobbish ['snɒbɪʃ] adj snob.

snobby ['snɒbɪ] *(compar* snobbier, *superl* snobbiest) *inf* = snobbish.

snog [snɒg] *(pt & pp* snogged, *cont* snogging) UK *inf* ◆ vi se rouler une pelle. ◆ vt rouler une pelle à. ◆ n ▶ **to have a snog** se rouler une pelle.

snogging ['snɒgɪŋ] n UK *inf* : *there was a lot of snogging going on* ça s'embrassait dans tous les coins.

snooker ['snuːkər] ◆ n snooker *m (sorte de billard joué avec 22 boules)*. ◆ vt **1.** UK *inf* [thwart] mettre dans l'embarras, mettre dans une situation impossible ; [trick] arnaquer, avoir **2.** GAMES laisser dans une position difficile.

snoop [snuːp] *inf* ◆ vi fourrer son nez dans les affaires des autres ▶ **to snoop on sb** espionner qqn. ◆ n **1.** [search] ▶ **to have a snoop around** fouiller, fouiner **2.** = snooper.

snooper ['snuːpər] n fouineur *m*, -euse *f.*

snooty ['snuːtɪ] *(compar* snootier, *superl* snootiest) adj *inf* [person] snobinard ; [restaurant] snob.

snooze [snuːz] *inf* ◆ n petit somme *m*, roupillon *m* ▶ **to have a snooze** faire un petit somme, piquer un roupillon ; [in afternoon] faire la sieste. ◆ vi sommeiller, piquer un roupillon ; [in afternoon] faire la sieste.

snooze button n bouton *m* de veille.

snore [snɔːr] ◆ vi ronfler. ◆ n ronflement *m*.

snoring ['snɔːrɪŋ] n *(U)* ronflement *m*, ronflements *mpl*.

snorkel ['snɔːkl] (UK *pt & pp* snorkelled, *cont* snorkelling ; US *pt & pp* snorkeled, *cont* snorkeling) ◆ n [of swimmer] tuba *m* ; [on submarine] schnorchel *m*, schnorkel *m*. ◆ vi nager sous l'eau *(avec un tuba)*.

snorkelling UK, **snorkeling** US ['snɔːklɪŋ] n ▶ **to go snorkelling** faire de la plongée avec un tuba.

snort [snɔːt] ◆ vi **1.** [horse] s'ébrouer ; [pig] grogner ; [bull] renâcler **2.** [person -in anger] grogner, ronchonner ▶ **to snort with laughter** s'étouffer or pouffer de rire. ◆ vt **1.** [angrily] grogner ; [laughingly] dire en pouffant de rire **2.** *drugs sl* [cocaine] sniffer. ◆ n **1.** [of bull, horse] ébrouement *m* ; [of person] grognement *m* **2.** *inf* [drink] petit verre *m* (d'alcool).

snot [snɒt] n *inf* **1.** [in nose] morve *f* **2.** [person] morveux *m*, -euse *f.*

snotty ['snɒtɪ] *(compar* snottier, *superl* snottiest, *pl* snotties) *inf* adj **1.** [nose] qui coule ; [face, child] morveux **2.** [uppity] crâneur, snobinard.

snotty-nosed adj *inf, lit & fig* morveux.

snout [snaʊt] n **1.** [of pig] groin *m*, museau *m* ; [of other animal] museau *m* **2.** [projection] saillie *f* ; [of gun] canon *m* **3.** *inf & hum* [nose] pif *m*.

snow [snəʊ] ◆ n **1.** *lit* neige *f* **2.** *fig* [on screen] neige *f* **3.** *drugs sl* [cocaine] neige *f drugs sl*. ◆ vi neiger / *it's snowing* il neige. ◆ vt US *inf* [sweet-talk] baratiner. ❖ **snow in** vt sep ▶ **to be snowed in** être bloqué par la neige. ❖ **snow under** vt sep *fig* : *to be snowed under with work* être débordé or complètement submergé de travail / *they're snowed under with applications / offers* ils ont reçu une avalanche de demandes / d'offres. ❖ **snow up** vt sep ▶ **to be snowed up a)** [house, village, family] être bloqué par la neige **b)** [road] être complètement enneigé.

snowball ['snəʊbɔːl] ◆ n **1.** boule *f* de neige / *they had a snowball fight* ils ont fait une bataille de boules de neige **2.** [cocktail] snowball *m (advokaat allongé de limonade)*. ◆ comp ▶ **snowball effect** effet *m* boule de neige. ◆ vt bombarder de boules de neige, lancer des boules de neige à. ◆ vi *fig* faire boule de neige.

snowbank ['snəʊbæŋk] n congère *f.*

snowbike ['snəʊbaɪk] n motoneige *f.*

snow blindness n cécité *f* des neiges.

snowboard ['snəʊˌbɔːd] ◆ n surf *m* des neiges. ◆ vi faire du surf des neiges.

snowboarder ['snəʊˌbɔːdər] n surfeur *m*, -euse *f* (des neiges).

snowboarding ['snəʊˌbɔːdɪŋ] n surf *m* (des neiges).

snow-boot n après-ski *m.*

snowbound ['snəʊbaʊnd] adj [person, house, village] bloqué par la neige ; [road] enneigé.

snow-capped [-kæpt] adj couronné de neige.

snowcat ['snəʊkæt] n autoneige *f*, motoneige *f.*

snowdrift ['snəʊdrɪft] n congère *f.*

snowdrop ['snəʊdrɒp] n perce-neige *m ou f inv.*

snowfall ['snəʊfɔːl] n **1.** [snow shower] chute *f* de neige **2.** [amount] enneigement *m.*

snowflake ['snəʊfleɪk] n flocon *m* de neige.

snowline ['snəʊlaɪn] n limite *f* des neiges éternelles.

snowman ['snəʊmæn] *(pl* snowmen [-men]) n bonhomme *m* de neige.

snowmobile ['snəʊməbiːl] = snowcat.

snow pea n US mange-tout *m inv.*

snowplough UK, **snowplow** US ['snəʊplaʊ] ◆ n **1.** [vehicle] chasse-neige *m inv* **2.** [in skiing] chasse-neige *m inv.* ◆ vi [in skiing] faire du chasse-neige.

snowshoe ['snəʊʃuː] n raquette *f (pour marcher sur la neige).*

snowstorm ['snəʊstɔːm] n tempête *f* de neige.

snow-white adj blanc comme neige.

snowy ['snəʊɪ] *(compar* snowier, *superl* snowiest) adj **1.** [weather, region, etc.] neigeux ; [countryside, roads, etc.] enneigé, couvert or recouvert de neige ; [day] de neige **2.** *fig* [hair, beard] de neige ; [sheets, tablecloth] blanc comme neige.

SNP *pr n abbr of* **Scottish National Party.**

Snr (*written abbr of* **Senior**) *utilisé après le nom de quelqu'un pour le distinguer d'un autre membre de la famille, plus jeune et portant le même nom.*

snub [snʌb] (*pt & pp* **snubbed**, *cont* **snubbing**) ◆ n rebuffade *f.* ◆ vt [person] remettre à sa place, rabrouer ; [offer, suggestion] repousser (dédaigneusement) ▶ **to be snubbed** essuyer une rebuffade. ◆ adj [nose] retroussé.
snub-nosed adj au nez retroussé.

snuck [snʌk] *pt & pp* → **sneak.**

snuff [snʌf] ◆ n tabac *m* à priser ▶ **to take snuff** priser ▶ **a pinch of snuff** une prise (de tabac). ◆ vt **1.** [candle] moucher **2.** [sniff] renifler, flairer **3.** PHR **to snuff it** *inf & hum* casser sa pipe. ◆ **snuff out** vt sep [candle] éteindre, moucher ; *fig* [hope] ôter, supprimer ; [rebellion] étouffer ; [enthusiasm] briser.

snuffle ['snʌfl] ◆ vi **1.** [sniffle] renifler **2.** [in speech] parler du nez, nasiller. ◆ vt dire or prononcer d'une voix nasillarde. ◆ n **1.** [sniffle] reniflement *m* ▶ **to have the snuffles** être un peu enrhumé **2.** [in speech] voix *f* nasillarde.

snuff movie n *inf* film pornographique sadique supposé comporter une scène de meurtre filmée en direct.

snug [snʌg] ◆ adj **1.** [warm and cosy - bed, room] douillet, (bien) confortable ; [-sleeping bag, jacket] douillet, bien chaud **2.** [fit] bien ajusté. ◆ n UK [in pub] petite arrière-salle *f.*

snuggle ['snʌgl] ◆ vi se blottir, se pelotonner. ◆ vt [child, kitten] serrer contre soi, câliner. ◆ n câlin *m.* ◆ **snuggle down** vi se blottir, se pelotonner. ◆ **snuggle up** vi ▶ **to snuggle up to sb** se blottir or se serrer contre qqn.

snugly ['snʌglɪ] adv **1.** [cosily] douillettement, confortablement **2.** [in fit] : *the skirt fits snugly* la jupe est très ajustée / *the two parts fit together snugly* les deux pièces s'emboîtent parfaitement.

so¹ [səʊ] ◆ adv **1.** (*before adj, adv*) [to such an extent] si, tellement / *I'm so glad to see you* ça me fait tellement plaisir or je suis si content de te voir / *his handwriting's so bad (that) it's illegible* il écrit si mal que c'est impossible à lire ; (*with 'that' clause*) : *he was upset, so much so that he cried* il était bouleversé, à tel point qu'il en a pleuré ; (*in negative comparisons*) si, aussi / *I'm not so sure* je n'en suis pas si sûr / *it's not so bad, there's only a small stain* ça n'est pas si grave que ça, il n'y a qu'une petite tache **2.** [indicating a particular size, length, etc.] : *the table is about so high / wide* la table est haute / large comme ça à peu près **3.** [referring to previous statement, question, word, etc.] : *I believe / think / suppose so* je crois / pense / suppose / *I hope so* a) [answering question] j'espère que oui b) [agreeing] j'espère bien, je l'espère / *I told you so!* je vous l'avais bien dit ! / *if so* si oui / *so I believe / see* c'est ce que je crois / vois / *so I've been told / he said* c'est ce qu'on m'a dit / qu'il a dit / *isn't that Jane over there? — why, so it is!* ce ne serait pas Jane là-bas ? — mais si (c'est elle) ! / *he was told to leave the room and did so immediately* on lui a ordonné de quitter la pièce et il l'a fait immédiatement ; [used mainly by children] : *I didn't say that! — you did so!* *inf* je n'ai pas dit ça ! — si, tu l'as dit ! ▶ **so be it!** *arch & hum* soit !, qu'il en soit ainsi ! **4.** [likewise] aussi / *we arrived early and so did he* nous sommes arrivés tôt et lui aussi **5.** [like this, in this way] ainsi / *hold the pen (like) so* tenez le stylo ainsi or comme ceci / *the laptop computer is so called because...* l'ordinateur lap-top tient son nom de... ▶ **it (just) so happens that...** il se trouve

(justement) que... / *she likes everything (to be) just so* elle aime que tout soit parfait **6.** [introducing the next event in a sequence] : *so then she left* alors elle est partie ; [requesting more information] : *so what's the problem?* alors, qu'est-ce qui ne va pas ? ; [in exclamations] alors ; [introducing a concession] et alors / *so?* et alors ?, et après ? / *he'll be angry — so what?* il va se fâcher ! — qu'est-ce que ça peut (me) faire or et alors ? ◆ conj **1.** [indicating result] donc, alors **2.** [indicating purpose] pour que, afin que / *give me some money so I can buy some sweets* donne-moi de l'argent pour que je puisse acheter des bonbons. ◆ adj ainsi, vrai / *is that so?* a) c'est vrai ? b) *iro* vraiment ? / *if that is so* si c'est le cas, s'il en est ainsi. ◆ **or so** adv phr environ, à peu près. ◆ **so as** conj phr *inf* pour que, afin que. ◆ **so as to** conj phr pour, afin de. ◆ **so that** conj phr [in order that] pour que, afin que / *they tied him up so that he couldn't escape* ils l'ont attaché afin qu'il or pour qu'il ne s'échappe pas. ◆ **so to speak, so to say** adv phr pour ainsi dire.

> 📋 Note that **afin que, pour que,** and **de façon (à ce) que** are all followed by a verb in the subjunctive:
> Use a microphone so that everyone can hear you. *Utilisez un micro afin que tout le monde puisse vous entendre.*
> Make a guest list so that no one feels left out. *Préparez une liste d'invités pour que personne ne se sente exclu.*
> They have been asked to step in so that the incident does not turn into a crisis. *On leur a demandé d'intervenir de façon (à ce) que l'incident ne devienne pas une crise.*

so² [səʊ] n MUS sol *m.*
SO n abbr of **standing order.**

soak [səʊk] ◆ vt **1.** [washing, food] faire or laisser tremper **2.** [drench - person, dog, etc.] tremper **3.** *fig* [immerse] imprégner **4.** *inf* [exploit - by swindling] rouler, arnaquer ; [-through taxation] faire casquer. ◆ vi [washing] tremper ▶ **to soak in the bath** faire trempette dans la baignoire. ◆ n **1.** [in water] trempage *m* **2.** *inf* [heavy drinker] soûlard *m*, -e *f*, pochard *m*, -e *f.* ◆ **soak in** vi **1.** [water] pénétrer, s'infiltrer **2.** *inf & fig* [comment, news] faire son effet. ◆ **soak off** vi [dirt, stains] partir (au trempage). ◆ vt sep [dirt, stains] faire disparaître or partir (en faisant tremper). ◆ **soak through** vi [liquid] filtrer au travers, s'infiltrer. ◆ **soak up** vt sep **1.** [absorb] absorber **2.** *inf & hum* [drink] : *he can really soak it up* il peut vraiment boire comme un trou.

soaked [səʊkt] adj *fig* [immersed] imprégné / *the place is soaked in history* l'endroit est imprégné d'histoire.

soaking ['səʊkɪŋ] ◆ adj trempé. ◆ n **1.** [gen] trempage *m* ; *inf* [in rain] ▶ **to get a soaking** se faire tremper or saucer **2.** *inf* [financial loss] perte *f* financière.

so-and-so n *inf* **1.** [referring to stranger] untel *m*, unetelle *f* / *Mr so-and-so* Monsieur Untel / *Mrs so-and-so* Madame Unetelle **2.** [annoying person] : *you little so-and-so!* espèce de petit minable !

soap [səʊp] ◆ n (U) **1.** savon *m* ▶ **a bar of soap** un savon, une savonnette ▶ **soap bubble** bulle *f* de savon **2.** *inf* RADIO & TV = **soap opera 3.** PHR **no soap!** US *inf* des clous !, des nèfles ! ◆ vt savonner. ◆ **soap down** vt sep savonner.

soapbox ['səʊpbɒks] ◆ n **1.** *lit* caisse *f* à savon ; *fig* [for speaker] tribune *f* improvisée or de fortune ▶ **get off your**

soapbox! ne monte pas sur tes grands chevaux ! **2.** [gokart] chariot *m* ; ≃ kart *m (sans moteur)*. ◆ comp [orator] de carrefour ; [oratory] de démagogue.

soapflakes ['səʊpfleɪks] pl n paillettes *fpl* de savon, savon *m* en paillettes.

soap opera n RADIO & TV soap opera *m*.

soap powder n lessive *f* (en poudre), poudre *f* à laver.

soapsuds ['səʊpsʌdz] pl n [foam] mousse *f* de savon ; [soapy water] eau *f* savonneuse.

soapy ['səʊpɪ] (*compar* **soapier**, *superl* **soapiest**) adj **1.** [water, hands, surface] savonneux ; [taste] de savon **2.** *inf* & *fig* [person, manner, voice] doucereux, mielleux.

soar [sɔːr] vi **1.** [bird, plane] monter en flèche ; [flames] jaillir **2.** [spire] se dresser vers le ciel ; [mountain] s'élever vers le ciel **3.** [temperature, profits, prices] monter or grimper en flèche ; [suddenly] faire un bond **4.** [spirits] remonter en flèche ; [hopes, imagination] grandir démesurément ; [reputation] monter en flèche **5.** [sound, music] s'élever.

soaring ['sɔːrɪŋ] ◆ adj **1.** [bird, glider] qui s'élève dans le ciel ; [spire, tower] qui s'élance vers le ciel ; [mountain] qui s'élève vers le ciel **2.** [prices, inflation] qui monte or qui grimpe en flèche ; [imagination] débordant ; [hopes, reputation] grandissant. ◆ n [of bird] essor *m*, élan *m* ; [of plane] envol *m* ; [of prices] envolée *f*, explosion *f*.

sob¹ [sɒb] (*pt* & *pp* **sobbed**, *cont* **sobbing**) ◆ n sanglot *m*. ◆ vi sangloter. ◆ vt ▶ **to sob o.s. to sleep** s'endormir à force de sangloter or en sanglotant / *"I can't remember!", he sobbed* «je ne me rappelle pas», dit-il en sanglotant. ◆ **sob out** vt sep raconter en sanglotant ▶ **to sob one's heart out** sangloter de tout son corps, pleurer à gros sanglots.

sob², **SOB** ['esəʊbiː] **US** *inf* abbr of **son-of-a-bitch**.

sobbing ['sɒbɪŋ] ◆ n *(U)* sanglots *mpl*. ◆ adj sanglotant.

sober ['səʊbər] adj **1.** [not drunk] : *are you sure he was sober?* tu es sûr qu'il n'avait pas bu ? ; [sobered up] dessoûlé **2.** [moderate - person] sérieux, posé, sensé ; [- attitude, account, opinion] modéré, mesuré ; [- manner] sérieux, posé **3.** [serious, solemn - atmosphere, occasion] solennel, plein de solennité ; [- expression] grave, plein de gravité ; [- voice] grave, empreint de gravité ; [- reminder] solennel **4.** [subdued - colour, clothing] discret (discrète), sobre **5.** [plain - fact, reality] (tout) simple ; [- truth] simple, tout nu ; [- tastes] simple, sobre. ◆ **sober up** vi & vt sep dessoûler.

sobering ['səʊbərɪŋ] adj : *it's a sobering thought* cela donne à réfléchir.

soberly ['səʊbəlɪ] adv [act, speak] avec sobriété or modération or mesure ; [dress] sobrement, discrètement.

sobriety [səʊ'braɪətɪ] n **1.** [non-drunkenness] sobriété *f* **2.** [moderation - of person] sobriété *f*, sérieux *m* ; [- of opinion, judgement] mesure *f*, modération *f* ; [- of manner, style, tastes] sobriété *f* **3.** [solemnity - of occasion] solennité *f* ; [- of voice] ton *m* solennel or grave ; [- of mood] sobriété *f* **4.** [of colour, dress] sobriété *f*.

sob story n *inf* & *pej* histoire *f* larmoyante, histoire *f* à vous fendre le cœur.

Soc [sɒk] (abbr of **Society**) n ≃ club *m* (abréviation utilisée dans la langue parlée notamment par les étudiants pour désigner les différents clubs universitaires).

so-called [-kɔːld] adj soi-disant (*inv*), prétendu.

soccer ['sɒkər] ◆ n football *m*, foot *m*. ◆ comp [pitch, match, team] de football, de foot ; [supporter] d'une équipe de foot ▶ **soccer mom** **US** mère de famille blanche de classe moyenne ayant des enfants d'âge scolaire ▶ **soccer player** footballeur *m*, -euse *f*.

sociable ['səʊʃəbl] ◆ adj **1.** [enjoying company] sociable, qui aime la compagnie (des gens) ; [friendly] sociable, amical ; [evening] amical, convivial **2.** SOCIOL & ZOOL sociable. ◆ n **US** fête *f*.

social ['səʊʃl] ◆ adj **1.** [background, behaviour, conditions, reform, tradition] social ; [phenomenon] social, de société / *they move in high or the best social circles* ils évoluent dans les hautes sphères de la société ▶ **social conscience** conscience *f* sociale ▶ **social order** ordre *m* social ▶ **social outcast** paria *m* **2.** [in society - activities] mondain ; [leisure] de loisir or loisirs / *his life is one mad social whirl* il mène une vie mondaine insensée **3.** [evening, function] amical ▶ **social event** rencontre *f* **4.** ZOOL social. ◆ n soirée *f* (dansante).

social climber n arriviste *mf*.

social club n club *m*.

social democracy n **1.** [system] social-démocratie *f* **2.** [country] démocratie *f* socialiste.

social democrat n social-démocrate *mf*.

social fund n caisse d'aide sociale.

social housing n **UK** logements *mpl* sociaux.

social insurance n *(U)* prestations *fpl* sociales.

socialism ['səʊʃəlɪzm] n socialisme *m*.

socialist ['səʊʃəlɪst] ◆ adj socialiste. ◆ n socialiste *mf*.

socialite ['səʊʃəlaɪt] n mondain *m*, -e *f*, personne *f* qui fréquente la haute société.

socialize, socialise ['səʊʃəlaɪz] ◆ vi [go out] sortir, fréquenter des gens ; [make friends] se faire des amis ▶ **to socialize with sb** frayer avec qqn. ◆ vt POL & PSYCHOL socialiser.

socialized medicine ['səʊʃəlaɪzd-] n **US** système de sécurité sociale.

socializing, socialising ['səʊʃəlaɪzɪŋ] n fait *m* de fréquenter des gens.

social life n vie *f* mondaine ▶ **to have a busy social life** **a)** [be fashionable] mener une vie très mondaine **b)** [go out often] sortir beaucoup / *he doesn't have much of a social life* il ne sort pas beaucoup / *there isn't much of a social life in this town* les gens ne sortent pas beaucoup dans cette ville, il ne se passe rien dans cette ville.

socially ['səʊʃəlɪ] adv socialement.

social media pl n médias *mpl* sociaux.

social network n réseau *m* social.

social networking n réseautage *m* social ▶ **social networking site** site *m* de réseautage social.

social science n sciences *fpl* humaines.

social scientist n spécialiste *mf* des sciences humaines.

social security n **1.** [gen] prestations *fpl* sociales ▶ **to be on social security** toucher une aide sociale **2.** **UK** [money paid to unemployed] ≃ allocations *fpl* de chômage.

social security number n **US** numéro *m* de sécurité sociale.

social services pl n services *mpl* sociaux.

social software n logiciels *mpl* sociaux / *a piece of social software* un logiciel social.

social studies pl n sciences *fpl* sociales.

social welfare n protection *f* sociale.

social work n assistance *f* sociale, travail *m* social.

social worker n assistant social *m*, assistante sociale *f*, travailleur social *m*, travailleuse sociale *f*.

society [sə'saɪətɪ] (*pl* **societies**) ◆ n **1.** [social community] société *f* / *it is a danger to society* cela constitue un danger pour la société **2.** [nation, group] société *f* / *Western society* la société occidentale **3.** [fashionable circles] ▶ **(high)**

society la haute société, le (beau or grand) monde **4.** *liter* [company] société *f*, compagnie *f* ▪ **in polite society** dans la bonne société or le (beau) monde **5.** [association, club] société *f*, association *f* ; [for sports] club *m*, association *f* ; SCH & UNIV [for debating, study, etc.] société *f* ▪ **the Society of Friends** la Société des Amis *(les quakers)*. ◆ comp [gossip, news, wedding] mondain ▪ **the society column** PRESS la chronique mondaine ▪ **a society man / woman** un homme / une femme du monde.

socioeconomic ['səʊsɪəʊ,iːkəˈnɒmɪk] adj socio-économique.

sociolinguistics [,səʊsɪəʊlɪŋˈgwɪstɪks] n *(U)* sociolinguistique *f*.

sociological [,səʊsjəˈlɒdʒɪkl] adj sociologique.

sociologist [,səʊsɪˈɒlədʒɪst] n sociologue *mf*.

sociology [,səʊsɪˈɒlədʒɪ] n sociologie *f*.

sock [sɒk] ◆ n **1.** [garment] chaussette *f* ▪ **it'll knock your socks off!** *inf* tu vas tomber à la renverse ! ▪ **to pull one's socks up** *inf* se secouer *inf* (les puces) ▪ **put a sock in it!** US *inf* la ferme ! **2.** AERON & METEOR ▪ **(wind) sock** manche *f* à air **3.** *inf* [blow] gnon *m*, beigne *f*. ◆ vt *inf* [hit] flanquer une beigne à.

socket ['sɒkɪt] n **1.** ELEC [for bulb] douille *f* ; US [in wall] prise *f* (de courant) **2.** TECH cavité *f* ; [in carpentry] mortaise *f* **3.** ANAT [of arm, hipbone] cavité *f* articulaire ; [of tooth] alvéole *f* ; [of eye] orbite *f*.

sod [sɒd] *(pt & pp* **sodded,** *cont* **sodding)** ◆ n **1.** US *v inf* [obnoxious person] enfoiré *m*, con *m* **2.** US *v inf* [fellow] bougre *m*, con *m* **3.** US *v inf* [difficult or unpleasant thing] corvée *f* ▪ **that's sod's law** c'est la poisse **4.** [of turf] motte *f* (de gazon) ; [earth and grass] terre *f* ; [lawn] gazon *m*. ◆ vt US *v inf* ▪ **sod it!** merde ! ▪ **sod him!** qu'il aille se faire foutre ! ◆ **sod off** vi US *v inf* foutre le camp.

soda ['səʊdə] n **1.** CHEM soude *f* **2.** [fizzy water] eau *f* de Seltz ▪ **a whisky and soda** un whisky soda **3.** US [soft drink] soda *m*.

soda siphon n siphon *m* (d'eau de Seltz).

soda water n eau *f* de Seltz.

sodden ['sɒdn] adj [ground] détrempé ; [clothes] trempé.

sodium ['səʊdɪəm] n sodium *m*.

sodomy ['sɒdəmɪ] n sodomie *f*.

sofa ['səʊfə] n sofa *m*, canapé *m*.

sofa bed n canapé-lit *m*.

Sofia ['səʊfjə] pr n Sofia.

soft [sɒft] ◆ adj **1.** [to touch - skin, hands] doux (douce) ; [- wool, fur, pillow] doux (douce), moelleux ; [- leather] souple ; [- material, hair] doux (douce), soyeux **2.** [yielding to pressure - bed, mattress] moelleux ; [- collar, ground, snow] mou *(before vowel or silent 'h' mol, f molle)* ; [- butter] mou *(before vowel or silent 'h' mol, f molle)*, ramolli ; [- muscles, body] ramolli, avachi, flasque ; [too yielding - bed, mattress] mou *(before vowel or silent 'h' mol, f molle)* ▪ **soft cheese** fromage *m* à pâte molle **3.** [malleable - metal, wood, stone] tendre ; [- pencil] gras (grasse), tendre ▪ **soft contact lenses** lentilles *fpl* souples **4.** [gentle - breeze, rain, words] doux (douce) ; [- expression, eyes] doux (douce), tendre ; [- curve, shadow] doux (douce) ; [- climate, weather] doux (douce), clément **5.** [quiet, not harsh - voice, music] doux (douce) ; [- sound, accent] doux (douce), léger ; [- tap, cough] petit, léger ; [- step] feutré **6.** [muted - colour, glow] doux (douce) ; [- shade] doux (douce), pastel *(inv)* ; [- light] doux (douce), tamisé **7.** [blurred - outline] estompé, flou **8.** [kind, gentle - person] doux (douce), tendre ; [- reply] gentil, aimable ; [- glance] doux (douce), gentil ; [lenient] indulgent ▪ **to be soft on sb** se montrer indulgent envers qqn, faire preuve d'indulgence envers qqn **9.** [weak - physically] mou *(before vowel or silent 'h' mol, f molle)*

10. *inf* [mentally] : *you must be soft in the head!* ça va pas, non ? **11.** [fond] ▪ **to be soft on sb** *inf* avoir le béguin pour qqn ▪ **to have a soft spot for sb** avoir un faible pour qqn **12.** [easy - life] doux (douce), tranquille, facile ; [- job] facile **13.** [moderate] modéré **14.** ECON & FIN [currency] faible ; [market] faible, lourd **15.** [water] doux (douce) **16.** LING [consonant] doux (douce) **17.** [drug] doux (douce). ◆ adv **1.** *liter* [softly] doucement **2.** *inf* ▪ **don't talk soft!** ne sois pas idiot !

softball ['sɒftbɔːl] n US [game] sorte de base-ball joué sur un terrain plus petit et avec une balle moins dure.

soft-boiled [-bɔɪld] adj ▪ **soft-boiled egg** œuf *m* (à la) coque.

soft-centre n [chocolate] chocolat *m* fourré.

soft copy n COMPUT copie *f* électronique.

soft-core adj [pornography] soft *(inv)*.

soft drink n boisson *f* non alcoolisée.

soften ['sɒfn] ◆ vt **1.** [butter, ground] ramollir ; [skin, water] adoucir ; [fabric, wool, leather] assouplir **2.** [voice, tone] adoucir, radoucir ; [colour, light, sound] adoucir, atténuer **3.** [make less strict] assouplir **4.** [lessen - pain, emotion] soulager, adoucir, atténuer ; [- shock, effect, impact] adoucir, amoindrir ; [- opposition, resistance] réduire, amoindrir. ◆ vi **1.** [butter, ground, etc.] se ramollir ; [skin] s'adoucir ; [cloth, wool, leather] s'assouplir **2.** [become gentler - eyes, expression, voice] s'adoucir ; [- breeze, rain] s'atténuer ; [- lighting, colour] s'atténuer, s'adoucir ; [- angle, outline] s'adoucir, s'estomper **3.** [become friendlier, more receptive] ▪ **to soften towards sb** se montrer plus indulgent envers qqn. ◆ **soften up** ◆ vt sep **1.** *inf* [make amenable - gen] attendrir, rendre plus souple ; [- by persuasion] amadouer ; [- aggressively] intimider **2.** MIL affaiblir **3.** [make softer - butter, ground] ramollir ; [- skin] adoucir ; [- leather] assouplir. ◆ vi **1.** [ground] devenir mou, se ramollir ; [butter] se ramollir ; [leather] s'assouplir ; [skin] s'adoucir **2.** [become gentler - person, voice] s'adoucir ▪ **to soften up on sb** faire preuve de plus d'indulgence envers qqn.

softener ['sɒfnər] n **1.** [for water] adoucisseur *m* (d'eau) ; [for fabric] assouplissant *m* (textile) **2.** *inf* [bribe] pot-de-vin *m*.

softening ['sɒfnɪŋ] n [of substance, ground] ramollissement *m* ; [of fabric, material] assouplissement *m*, adoucissement *m* ; [of attitude, expression, voice] adoucissement *m* ; [of colours, contrasts] atténuation *f*.

soft focus n PHOT flou *m* artistique.

soft furnishings pl n US tissus *mpl* d'ameublement.

softhearted [,sɒftˈhɑːtɪd] adj (au cœur) tendre.

softie ['sɒftɪ] *(pl* **softies)** n *inf* **1.** [weak] mauviette *f*, mollasson *m*, -onne *f* ; [coward] poule *f* mouillée, dégonflé *m*, -e *f* **2.** [softhearted] sentimental *m*, -e *f*.

softly ['sɒftlɪ] adv **1.** [quietly - breathe, say] doucement ; [- move, walk] à pas feutrés, (tout) doucement **2.** [gently - blow, touch] doucement, légèrement **3.** [fondly - smile, look] tendrement, avec tendresse.

softness ['sɒftnɪs] n **1.** [to touch - of skin, hands, hair] douceur *f* ; [- of fabric, wool, fur, pillow] douceur *f*, moelleux *m* ; [- of leather] souplesse *f* **2.** [to pressure - of bed, ground, snow, butter] mollesse *f* ; [- of collar] souplesse *f* ; [- of wood] tendreté *f* **3.** [gentleness - of breeze, weather, voice, music] douceur *f* ; [- of expression, manner] douceur *f*, gentillesse *f* ; [- of eyes, light, colour] douceur *f* ; [- of outline, curve] flou *m*, douceur *f* **4.** [kindness - of person] douceur *f* ; [- of heart] tendresse *f* ; [indulgence] indulgence *f*.

soft sell n COMM méthodes de vente non agressives.

soft-spoken adj à la voix douce.

soft top n *inf* AUTO (voiture *f*) décapotable *f*.

soft toy n (jouet *m* en) peluche *f*.

software ['sɒftweə'] ◆ n COMPUT logiciels m, software m ▶ **a piece of software** un logiciel. ◆ comp ▶ **software company** fabricant m de logiciels ▶ **software house** société f de services et d'ingénierie informatique ▶ **software piracy** piratage m de logiciels.

software package n logiciel m.

softwood ['sɒftwʊd] n bois m tendre.

softy ['sɒftɪ] inf = **softie**.

soggy ['sɒgɪ] (compar **soggier,** superl **soggiest**) adj [ground] détrempé, imbibé d'eau ; [clothes] trempé ; [bread, cake] mou (before vowel or silent 'h' **mol,** f **molle**) ; [rice] trop cuit, collant.

soil [sɔɪl] ◆ n **1.** [earth] terre f **2.** [type of earth] terre f, sol m **3.** fig [land] terre f, sol m **/** his native soil sa terre natale **/** on Irish soil sur le sol irlandais **4.** (U) [excrement] excréments mpl, ordures fpl ; [sewage] vidange f. ◆ vt **1.** [dirty - clothes, linen, paper] salir ; fig & liter souiller **2.** fig [reputation] salir, souiller, entacher. ◆ vi [clothes, material] se salir.

soiled [sɔɪld] adj [dressings] usagé ; [bedlinen] souillé ; [goods] défraîchi.

solace ['sɒləs] liter ◆ n consolation f, réconfort m. ◆ vt [person] consoler, réconforter ; [pain, suffering] soulager.

solar ['səʊlə'] adj **1.** [of, concerning the sun - heat, radiation] solaire, du soleil ; [- cycle, year] solaire **2.** [using the sun's power - energy, heating] solaire.

solarium [sə'leərɪəm] (pl **solariums** or **solaria** [-rɪə]) n solarium m.

solar panel n panneau m solaire.

solar plexus n plexus m solaire.

solar power n énergie f solaire.

solar-powered [-'paʊəd] adj à énergie solaire.

solar system n système m solaire.

sold [səʊld] ◆ pt & pp ⟶ **sell.** ◆ adj **1.** COMM vendu **2.** inf & fig ▶ **to be sold on sb / sthg** être emballé par qqn / qqch. ◆ **sold out** adj phr **1.** [goods] épuisé **/ 'sold out'** [for play, concert] 'complet' **2.** [stockist] : we're sold out of bread nous avons vendu tout le pain, il ne reste plus de pain.

solder ['səʊldə'] ◆ vt souder. ◆ n soudure f, métal m d'apport.

soldering iron ['səʊldərɪŋ-] n fer m à souder.

soldier ['səʊldʒə'] ◆ n **1.** soldat m, militaire m ▶ **to become a soldier** se faire soldat, entrer dans l'armée ▶ **soldier of fortune** soldat de fortune ▶ **old soldier** MIL vétéran m **2.** ENTOM soldat m **3.** [strip of bread] mouillette f. ◆ vi être soldat, servir dans l'armée. ◆ **soldier on** vi 🇬🇧 continuer or persévérer (malgré tout).

sole [səʊl] ◆ adj **1.** [only] seul, unique **2.** [exclusive] exclusif ▶ **sole agent** COMM concessionnaire mf ▶ **sole legatee** LAW légataire m universel, légataire f universelle ▶ **sole trader** 🇬🇧 COMM entreprise f individuelle or unipersonnelle. ◆ n **1.** [of foot] plante f **2.** [of shoe, sock] semelle f **3.** (pl **sole** or **soles**) [fish] sole f. ◆ vt ressemeler.

solely ['səʊllɪ] adv **1.** [only] seulement, uniquement **2.** [entirely] entièrement.

solemn ['sɒləm] adj **1.** [grave, serious] sérieux, grave, solennel ; [sombre] sobre **2.** [formal - agreement, promise] solennel **3.** [grand - occasion, music] solennel ▶ **solemn mass** grand-messe f, messe f solennelle.

solemnity [sə'lemnətɪ] (pl **solemnities**) n **1.** [serious nature] sérieux m, gravité f **2.** [formality] solennité f **3.** (usu pl) liter [solemn event] solennité f.

solemnly ['sɒləmlɪ] adv **1.** [seriously, gravely] gravement, solennellement **2.** [formally] solennellement **3.** [grandly] solennellement, avec solennité.

solicit [sə'lɪsɪt] ◆ vt **1.** [business, support, information] solliciter ; [opinion] demander **2.** [subj: prostitute] racoler. ◆ vi [prostitute] racoler.

soliciting [sə'lɪsɪtɪŋ] n [by prostitute] racolage m.

solicitor [sə'lɪsɪtə'] n **1.** 🇬🇧 LAW [for sales, wills] ≃ notaire m ; [in divorce, court cases] ≃ avocat m, -e f **2.** [person who solicits] solliciteur m, -euse f.

solicitous [sə'lɪsɪtəs] adj [showing consideration, concern] plein de sollicitude ; [eager, attentive] empressé ; [anxious] soucieux.

solid ['sɒlɪd] ◆ adj **1.** [not liquid or gas] solide **/** frozen solid complètement gelé **2.** [of one substance] massif **/** her necklace is solid gold son collier est en or massif **3.** [not hollow] plein **/** solid tyres pneus pleins **4.** [unbroken, continuous] continu **5.** 🇺🇸 [of one colour] uni **6.** [dense, compact] dense, compact **7.** [powerful - blow] puissant **8.** [sturdy, sound - structure, understanding, relationship] solide ; [- evidence, argument] solide, irréfutable ; [- advice] valable, sûr **9.** [respectable, worthy] respectable, honorable **10.** POL [firm] massif ; [unanimous] unanime **11.** MATH ▶ **solid figure** solide m. ◆ n GEOM & PHYS solide m. ◆ **solids** pl n **1.** [solid food] aliments mpl solides **2.** CHEM particules fpl solides.

solidarity [,sɒlɪ'dærətɪ] ◆ n solidarité f. ◆ comp [strike] de solidarité.

solid fuel n combustible m solide. ◆ **solid-fuel** adj à combustible solide.

solidify [sə'lɪdɪfaɪ] (pt & pp **solidified**) ◆ vi **1.** [liquid, gas] se solidifier **2.** [system, opinion] se consolider. ◆ vt **1.** [liquid, gas] solidifier **2.** [system, opinion] consolider.

solidly ['sɒlɪdlɪ] adv **1.** [sturdily] solidement ; [person] ▶ **to be solidly built** avoir une forte carrure **2.** [thoroughly] très, tout à fait **3.** [massively] massivement, en masse **4.** [continuously] sans arrêt.

soliloquy [sə'lɪləkwɪ] (pl **soliloquies**) n soliloque m, monologue m.

solitaire [,sɒlɪ'teə'] n **1.** [pegboard] solitaire m **2.** 🇺🇸 [card game] réussite f, patience f **3.** [gem] solitaire m.

solitary ['sɒlɪtrɪ] (pl **solitaries**) ◆ adj **1.** [alone - person, life, activity] solitaire **2.** [single] seul, unique **3.** [remote - place] retiré, isolé **4.** [empty of people] vide, désert. ◆ n **1.** inf = **solitary confinement 2.** [person] solitaire mf.

solitary confinement n isolement m (d'un prisonnier).

solitude ['sɒlɪtjuːd] n solitude f.

solo ['səʊləʊ] (pl **solos**) ◆ n **1.** MUS solo m **2.** [flight] vol m solo **3.** = **solo whist.** ◆ adj **1.** MUS solo **/** she plays solo violin elle est soliste de violon, elle est violon solo **2.** [gen] en solitaire **/** a solo act un one-man-show. ◆ adv **1.** MUS en solo **2.** [gen] seul, en solitaire, en solo.

soloist ['səʊləʊɪst] n soliste mf.

Solomon Islands pl pr n ▶ **the Solomon Islands** les îles fpl Salomon **/** in the Solomon Islands dans les îles Salomon.

solo whist n solo m (variante du whist).

solstice ['sɒlstɪs] n solstice m.

solubility [,sɒljʊ'bɪlətɪ] n solubilité f.

soluble ['sɒljʊbl] adj **1.** [substance] soluble **2.** [problem] soluble.

solution [sə'luːʃn] n **1.** [answer - to problem, equation, mystery] solution f **2.** [act of solving - of problem, equation, mystery] résolution f **3.** CHEM & PHARM solution f.

solve [sɒlv] vt [equation] résoudre ; [problem] résoudre, trouver la solution de ; [crime, mystery] élucider.

solvency ['sɒlvənsɪ] n solvabilité f.

solvent ['sɒlvənt] ◆ adj **1.** [financially] solvable **2.** [substance, liquid] dissolvant. ◆ n solvant m, dissolvant m.

solvent abuse n fml usage m de solvants hallucinogènes.

Som. written abbr of Somerset.

Somali [sə'mɑːlɪ] ◆ n **1.** [person] Somalien m, -enne f **2.** LING somali m. ◆ adj somalien.

Somalia [sə'mɑːlɪə] pr n Somalie f / in Somalia en Somalie.

somber US = sombre.

sombre UK, **somber** US ['sɒmbər] adj **1.** [dark - colour, place] sombre **2.** [grave, grim - outlook, person, day] sombre, morne.

some [sʌm] ◆ det **1.** (before uncountable nouns) [a quantity of] : don't forget to buy some cheese / beer / garlic n'oublie pas d'acheter du fromage / de la bière / de l'ail / let me give you some advice laissez-moi vous donner un conseil ; (before plural nouns) [a number of] : we've invited some friends round nous avons invité des amis à la maison **2.** (before uncountable nouns) [not all] : some wine / software is very expensive certains vins / logiciels coûtent très cher ; (before plural nouns) certains mpl, certaines **3.** (before uncountable nouns) [a fairly large amount of] un certain m, une certaine f / I haven't been abroad for some time ça fait un certain temps que je ne suis pas allé à l'étranger / it's some distance from here c'est assez loin d'ici ; (before plural nouns) [a fairly large number of] certains mpl, certaines, quelques mf pl / it happened some years ago ça s'est passé il y a quelques années **4.** (before uncountable nouns) [a fairly small amount of] un peu de / you must have some idea of how much it will cost vous devez avoir une petite idée de combien ça va coûter / I hope I've been of some help to you j'espère que je vous ai un peu aidé ; (before plural nouns) [a fairly small number of] : I'm glad some people understand me! je suis content qu'il y ait quand même des gens qui me comprennent ! **5.** [not known or specified] : we must find some alternative il faut que nous trouvions une autre solution / she works for some publishing company elle travaille pour je ne sais quelle maison d'édition / I'll get even with them some day! je me vengerai d'eux un de ces jours or un jour ou l'autre ! / come back some other time revenez un autre jour **6.** [expressing irritation, impatience] : some people! il y a des gens, je vous assure ! **7.** inf [expressing admiration, approval] : that was some party! ça c'était une fête ! / he's some tennis player! c'est un sacré tennisman ! ◆ pron **1.** [an unspecified number or amount -as subject] quelques-uns mpl, quelques-unes, certains mpl / some say it wasn't an accident certains disent or il y a des gens qui disent que ce n'était pas un accident ; [as object] en / I've got too much cake, do you want some? j'ai trop de gâteau, en voulez-vous un peu ? / can I have some more? est-ce que je peux en reprendre ? / he wants the lot and then some il veut tout et puis le reste **2.** [not all] : some of the snow had melted une partie de la neige avait fondu / some of us / them certains d'entre nous / eux / if you need pencils, take some of these / mine si vous avez besoin de crayons à papier, prenez quelques-uns de ceux-ci / des miens. ◆ adv **1.** [approximately] quelque, environ / it's some fifty kilometres from London c'est à environ cinquante kilomètres or c'est à une cinquantaine de kilomètres de Londres **2.** US inf [a little] un peu ; [a lot] beaucoup, pas mal.

somebody ['sʌmbədɪ] pron **1.** [an unspecified person] quelqu'un ▶ **somebody else** quelqu'un d'autre / somebody big / small quelqu'un de grand / de petit / there's somebody on the phone for you on vous demande au télé-phone / somebody's at the door or there's somebody at the door on a frappé / somebody has left their / his / her umbrella behind quelqu'un a oublié son parapluie ▶ **somebody or other** quelqu'un, je ne sais qui **2.** [an important person] : you really think you're somebody, don't you? tu te crois vraiment quelqu'un, n'est-ce pas ?

someday ['sʌmdeɪ] adv un jour (ou l'autre), un de ces jours.

somehow ['sʌmhaʊ] adv **1.** [in some way or another] d'une manière ou d'une autre, d'une façon ou d'une autre / she'd somehow (or other) managed to lock herself in elle avait trouvé moyen de s'enfermer **2.** [for some reason] pour une raison ou pour une autre, je ne sais pas trop pourquoi.

SUM1 (written abbr of someone) MESSAGING kelk1.

someone ['sʌmwʌn] = somebody.

someplace ['sʌmpleɪs] US = somewhere.

somersault ['sʌməsɔːlt] ◆ n [roll] culbute f ; [by car] tonneau m ; [acrobatic feat -in air] saut m périlleux. ◆ vi faire la culbute or un saut périlleux or des sauts périlleux ; [car] faire un tonneau or des tonneaux.

something ['sʌmθɪŋ] ◆ pron **1.** [an unspecified object, event, action, etc.] quelque chose / I've got something in my eye j'ai quelque chose dans l'œil / I've thought of something j'ai eu une idée ▶ **something else** quelque chose d'autre, autre chose ▶ **something or other** quelque chose / something big / small quelque chose de grand / de petit / he gave them something to eat / drink il leur a donné à manger / boire / they all want something for nothing ils veulent tous avoir tout pour rien / there's something about him / in the way he talks that reminds me of Gary il y a quelque chose chez lui / dans sa façon de parler qui me rappelle Gary / there must be something in or to all these rumours il doit y avoir quelque chose de vrai dans toutes ces rumeurs / he's got a certain something il a un petit quelque chose / I think you've got something there! je crois que vous avez un début d'idée, là ! / at least they've replied to my letter, that's something au moins, ils ont répondu à ma lettre, c'est mieux que rien or c'est toujours ça ▶ **wow, that's something else!** inf ça, c'est génial ! ▶ **well, isn't that something?** inf et bien, ça alors ! / it was really something to see those kids dancing! c'était quelque chose de voir ces gosses danser ! **2.** inf [in approximations] : he's forty something il a dans les quarante ans / it cost £7 something ça a coûté 7 livres et quelques **3.** PHR **something of** : he's something of an expert in the field c'est en quelque sorte un expert dans ce domaine ▶ **to be** or **have something to do with** avoir un rapport avec / I'm sure the weather has something to do with it je suis sûre que le temps y est pour quelque chose or que ça a un rapport avec le temps. ◆ adv **1.** [a little] un peu ; [somewhere] : something in the region of $10,000 quelque chose comme 10 000 dollars **2.** inf [as intensifier] vraiment, vachement / it hurts something awful ça fait vachement mal. ◆◆ **or something** adv phr inf : she must be ill or something elle doit être malade ou quelque chose dans ce genre-là. ◆◆ **something like** prep phr [roughly] environ / it costs something like £500 ça coûte quelque chose comme or dans les 500 livres.

sometime ['sʌmtaɪm] ◆ adv **1.** [in future] un jour (ou l'autre), un de ces jours / I hope we'll meet again sometime soon j'espère que nous nous reverrons bientôt / you'll have to face up to it sometime or other un jour ou l'autre il faudra bien voir les choses en face / sometime after / before next April après le mois / d'ici au mois d'avril / sometime next year dans le courant de l'année prochaine **2.** [in past] : she phoned sometime last week elle a téléphoné (dans le courant de) la semaine dernière / *sometime around 1920* vers 1920. ◆ adj **1.** [former] ancien **2.** US [occasional] intermittent.

sometimes ['sʌmtaɪmz] adv quelquefois, parfois / *sometimes (they're) friendly, sometimes they're not* tantôt ils sont aimables, tantôt (ils ne le sont) pas / *the museum is sometimes closed on Sundays* le musée est parfois fermé le dimanche, il arrive que le musée soit fermé le dimanche.

> 📋 Note that il arrive que is followed by a verb in the subjunctive:
> **These practices are sometimes forbidden.** *Il arrive que ces pratiques soient interdites.*

someway ['sʌmweɪ] US *inf* = **somehow.**

somewhat ['sʌmwɒt] adv quelque peu, un peu / *everybody came, somewhat to my surprise* tout le monde est venu, ce qui n'a pas été sans me surprendre / *I was in somewhat of a hurry to get home* j'étais quelque peu pressé de rentrer chez moi / *it was somewhat of a failure* c'était plutôt un échec.

somewhere ['sʌmweəʳ] adv **1.** [indicating an unspecified place] quelque part / *she's somewhere around* elle est quelque part par là, elle n'est pas loin / *let's go somewhere else* allons ailleurs or autre part / *but it's got to be somewhere or other!* mais il doit bien être quelque part ! / *I'm looking for somewhere to stay* je cherche un endroit où loger ▸ **now we're getting somewhere!** nous arrivons enfin à quelque chose ! **2.** [approximately] environ / *she earns somewhere around $2,000 a month* elle gagne quelque chose comme 2 000 dollars par mois.

son [sʌn] n **1.** fils *m* ▸ **son and heir** héritier *m* **2.** *inf* [term of address] fiston *m*. ◆ **Son** n RELIG Fils *m* ▸ **the Son of God** le Fils de Dieu.

sonar ['səʊnɑːʳ] n sonar *m*.

sonata [sə'nɑːtə] n sonate *f* ▸ **piano / violin sonata** sonate pour piano / violon.

song [sɒŋ] n **1.** chanson *f* ▸ **a song and dance act** un numéro de comédie musicale ▸ **the Song of Songs** or **the Song of Solomon** BIBLE le Cantique des cantiques **2.** [songs collectively, act of singing] chanson *f* / *they all burst into song* ils se sont tous mis à chanter **3.** [of birds, insects] chant *m*.

songbird ['sɒŋbɜːd] n oiseau *m* chanteur.

songbook ['sɒŋbʊk] n recueil *m* de chansons.

songwriter ['sɒŋ,raɪtəʳ] n [of lyrics] parolier *m*, -ère *f*; [of music] compositeur *m*, -trice *f*; [of lyrics and music] auteur-compositeur *m*.

sonic ['sɒnɪk] adj **1.** [involving, producing sound] acoustique **2.** [concerning speed of sound] sonique.

sonic boom n bang *m*.

son-in-law (*pl* **sons-in-law**) n gendre *m*, beau-fils *m*.

sonnet ['sɒnɪt] n sonnet *m*.

sonny ['sʌnɪ] n *inf* fiston *m*.

son-of-a-bitch (*pl* **sons-of-bitches**) n US *v inf* salaud *m*, fils *m* de pute.

sonorous ['sɒnərəs] adj **1.** [resonant] sonore **2.** [grandiloquent] grandiloquent.

soon [suːn] adv **1.** [in a short time] bientôt, sous peu / *(I'll) see you* or *speak to you soon!* à bientôt ! / *I'll be back soon* je serai vite de retour / *she phoned soon after you'd left* elle a téléphoné peu après ton départ **2.** [early] tôt / *it's too soon to make any predictions* il est trop tôt pour se prononcer / *how soon can you finish it?* pour quand pouvez-vous le terminer ? ◆ **as soon as**

conj phr dès que, aussitôt que ▸ **as soon as possible** dès que possible, le plus tôt or le plus vite possible / *he came as soon as he could* il est venu dès or aussitôt qu'il a pu. ◆ **(just) as soon** adv phr : *I'd (just) as soon go by boat as by plane* j'aimerais autant or mieux y aller en bateau qu'en avion.

sooner ['suːnəʳ] adv *(compar of soon)* **1.** [earlier] plus tôt ▸ **the sooner the better** le plus tôt sera le mieux ▸ **no sooner said than done!** aussitôt dit, aussitôt fait ! ▸ **sooner or later**: *it was bound to happen sooner or later* cela devait arriver tôt ou tard **2.** [indicating preference] : *would you sooner I called back tomorrow?* préférez-vous que je rappelle demain ? / *shall we go out tonight? — I'd sooner not* si on sortait ce soir ? — j'aimerais mieux pas / *I'd sooner die than go through that again!* plutôt mourir que de revivre ça !

Sooner ['suːnəʳ] n *habitant ou natif de l'Oklahoma* ▸ **the Sooner State** l'Oklahoma.

soot [sʊt] n suie *f*. ◆ **soot up** vt sep [dirty] couvrir or recouvrir de suie ; [clog] encrasser.

soothe [suːð] vt **1.** [calm, placate] calmer, apaiser **2.** [relieve - pain] calmer, soulager.

soothing ['suːðɪŋ] adj **1.** [music, words, voice] apaisant ; [atmosphere, presence] rassurant **2.** [lotion, ointment] apaisant, calmant.

sooty ['sʊtɪ] (*compar* **sootier**, *superl* **sootiest**) adj **1.** [dirty] couvert de suie, noir de suie **2.** [dark] noir comme de la suie.

sop [sɒp] n [concession] : *they threw in the measure as a sop to the ecologists* ils ont ajouté cette mesure pour amadouer les écologistes.

SOP (abbr of **standard operating procedure**) n procédure *f* à suivre.

sophisticated [sə'fɪstɪkeɪtɪd] adj **1.** [person, manner, tastes - refined] raffiné ; [-chic] chic, élégant ; [-well-informed] bien informé ; [-mature] mûr **2.** [argument, novel, film - subtle] subtil ; [-complicated] complexe **3.** [machine, system, technology - advanced] sophistiqué, perfectionné.

sophistication [sə,fɪstɪ'keɪʃn] n **1.** [of person, manners, tastes - refinement] raffinement *m* ; [-chic] chic *m*, élégance *f* ; [-maturity] maturité *f* **2.** [of argument, novel, film - subtlety] subtilité *f* ; [-complexity] complexité *f* **3.** [of system, technology] sophistication *f*, perfectionnement *m*.

sophomore ['sɒfəmɔːʳ] n US étudiant *m*, -e *f* de seconde année / *in my sophomore year* lorsque j'étais en seconde année.

soporific [,sɒpə'rɪfɪk] ◆ adj soporifique. ◆ n soporifique *m*, somnifère *m*.

sopping ['sɒpɪŋ] adj & adv *inf* ▸ **sopping (wet)** a) [person] trempé (jusqu'aux os) b) [shirt, cloth] détrempé.

soppy ['sɒpɪ] (*compar* **soppier**, *superl* **soppiest**) adj UK *inf* **1.** [sentimental - person] sentimental, fleur bleue *(inv)* ; [-story, picture] sentimental, à l'eau de rose **2.** [silly] nigaud, bébête **3.** [in love] ▸ **to be soppy about sb** avoir le béguin pour qqn.

soprano [sə'prɑːnəʊ] (*pl* **sopranos** or **soprani** [-niː]) ◆ n [singer] soprano *mf* ; [voice, part, instrument] soprano *m* ▸ **to sing soprano** avoir une voix de soprano. ◆ adj [voice, part] de soprano ; [music] pour soprano ▸ **soprano saxophone** saxophone *m* soprano.

SOR written abbr of **sale or return**.

sorbet ['sɔːbeɪ] n **1.** UK sorbet *m* **2.** US *pulpe de fruit glacée*.

sorcerer ['sɔːsərəʳ] n sorcier *m*.

sorcery ['sɔːsərɪ] n sorcellerie *f*.

sordid ['sɔːdɪd] adj **1.** [dirty, wretched] sordide, misérable **2.** [base, loathsome] sordide, infâme, vil.

sore [sɔːʳ] ◆ adj **1.** [aching] douloureux / *I'm sore all over* j'ai mal partout / *I've a sore throat* j'ai mal à la gorge / *my arms / legs are sore* j'ai mal aux bras / jambes, mes bras / jambes me font mal **2.** 🇺🇸 *inf* [angry] en boule / *are you still sore at me?* est-ce que tu es toujours en boule contre moi ? ; [resentful] vexé, amer **3.** *liter* [great] grand ▶ **to be in sore need of sthg** avoir grand besoin de qqch. ◆ n plaie *f.*

sorely ['sɔːlɪ] adv **1.** [as intensifier] grandement **2.** *liter* [painfully] : *sorely wounded* grièvement blessé.

soreness ['sɔːnɪs] n douleur *f.*

sorority [sə'rɒrətɪ] (*pl* **sororities**) n 🇺🇸 UNIV association d'étudiantes très sélective.

sorrel ['sɒrəl] ◆ n **1.** BOT & CULIN oseille *f* **2.** [colour] roux *m*, brun rouge *m* **3.** [horse] alezan *m* clair. ◆ adj [gen] roux ; [horse] alezan clair (*inv*).

sorrow ['sɒrəʊ] ◆ n chagrin *m*, peine *f*, tristesse *f* ; [stronger] affliction *f*, douleur *f.* ◆ vi *liter* éprouver du chagrin or de la peine.

sorrowful ['sɒrəʊfʊl] adj [person] triste ; [look, smile] affligé.

sorrowfully ['sɒrəʊflɪ] adv tristement.

sorry ['sɒrɪ] (*compar* **sorrier,** *superl* **sorriest**) adj **1.** [in apologies] désolé / *I'm sorry we won't be able to fetch you* je regrette que or je suis désolé que nous ne puissions venir vous chercher / *(I'm) sorry to have bothered you* (je suis) désolé de vous avoir dérangé / *ouch, that's my foot!* — *(I'm) sorry!* aïe ! mon pied ! — je suis désolé or excusez-moi ! / *I'm sorry about the mix-up* excusez-moi pour la confusion / *sorry about forgetting your birthday* désolé d'avoir oublié ton anniversaire ▶ **to say sorry** s'excuser / *what's the time?* — *sorry?* quelle heure est-il ? — pardon ? or comment ? / *they're coming on Tuesday, sorry,* Thursday ils viennent mardi, pardon, jeudi **2.** [regretful] : *I'm sorry I ever came here!* je regrette d'être venu ici ! / *you'll be sorry for this* tu le regretteras **3.** [expressing sympathy] désolé, navré, peiné / *I was sorry to hear about your father's death* j'ai été désolé or peiné or navré d'apprendre la mort de votre père **4.** [pity] ▶ **to be** or **to feel sorry for sb** plaindre qqn ▶ **to be** or **to feel sorry for o.s.** s'apitoyer sur soi-même or sur son propre sort **5.** [pitiable, wretched] triste, piteux.

sorry-ass, sorry-assed adj 🇺🇸 v *inf* [inferior, contemptible] à la con.

sort [sɔːt] ◆ n **1.** [kind, type] sorte *f*, espèce *f*, genre *m* ; [brand] marque *f* / *it's a strange sort of film* c'est un drôle de film / *it's a different sort of problem* c'est un autre type de problème / *I've got a sort of feeling about what the result will be* j'ai comme un pressentiment sur ce que sera le résultat / *she's not the sort (of woman) to let you down* elle n'est pas du genre à vous laisser tomber / *they're not our sort (of people)* nous ne sommes pas du même monde / *I know your sort!* les gens de ton espèce, je les connais ! / *what sort of way is that to speak to your grandmother?* en voilà une façon de parler à ta grand-mère ! / *I've heard all sorts of good things about you* j'ai entendu dire beaucoup de bien de vous / *I said nothing of the sort!* je n'ai rien dit de pareil or de tel ! ▶ **to feel out of sorts** : *I feel out of sorts* je ne suis pas dans mon assiette **2.** [gen] [COMPUT - act of sorting] tri *m.* ◆ vt **1.** [classify] classer, trier ; [divide up] répartir ; [separate] séparer ; COMPUT trier / *to sort mail* trier le courrier / *sort the cards into two piles* répartissez les cartes en deux piles **2.** [select and set aside] = **sort out.** ◆ **sort of** adv phr *inf* : *I'm sort of glad that I missed them* je suis plutôt content de les avoir ratés / *it's sort of big and round* c'est du genre grand

et rond / *did you hit him?* — *well, sort of* tu l'as frappé ? — en quelque sorte, oui. ◆ **sort out** vt sep **1.** [classify] = **sort** (*vt*) **2.** [select and set aside] trier **3.** [tidy up - papers, clothes, room, cupboard] ranger ; [put in order - finances, ideas] mettre en ordre / *she needs to get her personal life sorted out* il faut qu'elle règle ses problèmes personnels **4.** [settle, resolve - problem, dispute] régler, résoudre / *everything's sorted out now* tout est arrangé maintenant / *things will sort themselves out in the end* les choses finiront par s'arranger **5.** [work out] : *have you sorted out how to do it?* est-ce que tu as trouvé le moyen de le faire ? ; [arrange] arranger, fixer **6.** 🇬🇧 *inf* [solve the problems of - person] : *she needs time to sort herself out* il lui faut du temps pour régler ses problèmes **7.** 🇬🇧 *inf* [punish] régler son compte à. ◆ **sort through** vt insep trier.

sorta ['sɔːtə] *inf* abbr of **sort of.**

sort code n BANK code *m* guichet.

sorted ['sɔːtɪd] 🇬🇧 *inf* ◆ adj : *to be sorted* a) [psychologically] être équilibré, être bien dans ses baskets or dans sa peau b) [have everything one needs] être paré / *to be sorted for sthg* disposer de qqch. ◆ excl super !, génial !

sortie ['sɔːtiː] n MIL sortie *f.*

sorting ['sɔːtɪŋ] n tri *m.*

sorting office n centre *m* de tri.

sort-out n 🇬🇧 *inf* [tidying] rangement *m.*

SOS (abbr of **save our souls**) n SOS *m* ▶ **to send out an SOS** lancer un SOS.

so-so adj *inf* pas fameux ; [in health] comme ci comme ça, couci-couça.

soufflé ['suːfleɪ] n soufflé *m* ▶ **cheese / chocolate soufflé** soufflé au fromage / au chocolat ▶ **soufflé dish** moule *m* à soufflé.

sought [sɔːt] pt & pp ⟶ **seek.**

sought-after adj recherché.

soul [səʊl] n **1.** RELIG âme *f* ; [emotional depth] profondeur *f* **2.** [leading figure] âme *f* **3.** [perfect example] modèle *m* **4.** [person] personne *f*, âme *f* **5.** [music] (musique *f*) soul *f*, soul music *f.*

soul-destroying [-dɪˌstrɔɪɪŋ] adj [job] abrutissant ; [situation, place] déprimant.

soulful ['səʊlfʊl] adj [song, performance, sigh] émouvant, attendrissant ; [look, eyes] expressif.

soulless ['səʊllɪs] adj **1.** [inhuman - place] inhumain, sans âme ; [- work] abrutissant **2.** [heartless] sans cœur, insensible.

soul mate n âme *f* sœur.

soul music n musique *f* soul, soul music *f.*

soul-searching n introspection *f.*

sound [saʊnd] ◆ n **1.** [noise - of footsteps, thunder, conversation] bruit *m* ; [- of voice, musical instrument] son *m* / *I was woken by the sound of voices / laughter* j'ai été réveillé par un bruit de voix / par des éclats de rires / *don't make a sound!* surtout ne faites pas de bruit ! **2.** PHYS son *m* / *the speed of sound* la vitesse du son **3.** LING son *m* **4.** RADIO & TV son *m* ▶ **to turn the sound up / down** monter / baisser le son or volume **5.** [impression, idea] : *I don't like the sound of these new measures* ces nouvelles mesures ne me disent rien qui vaille. ◆ comp [level, recording] sonore ; [broadcasting] radiophonique ; LING [change] phonologique. ◆ adj **1.** [structure, building, wall - sturdy] solide ; [- in good condition] en bon état, sain **2.** [healthy - person] en bonne santé ; [- body, mind, limbs] sain ▶ **to be of sound mind** être sain d'esprit ▶ **to be as sound as a bell** être en parfaite santé **3.** [sensible, well-founded - advice, idea, strategy] sensé, judicieux ; [- argument, claim] valable, fondé, solide / *to show sound judgment* faire preuve de jugement **4.** [reliable, solid] solide, compétent **5.** [safe - investment] sûr ;

[-company, business] solide **6.** [severe - defeat] total ; [- hiding] bon **7.** [deep - sleep] profond / *I'm a very sound sleeper* j'ai le sommeil profond. ◆ adv ▶ **to be sound asleep** dormir profondément or à poings fermés. ◆ vi **1.** [make a sound] sonner, résonner, retentir / *it sounds hollow if you tap it* ça sonne creux lorsqu'on tape dessus / *their voices sounded very loud in the empty house* leurs voix résonnaient bruyamment dans la maison vide **2.** 🇬🇧 [be pronounced] se prononcer **3.** [seem] sembler, paraître / *it doesn't sound very interesting to me* ça ne m'a pas l'air très intéressant / *(that) sounds like a good idea* ça semble être une bonne idée / *the name sounded French* le nom avait l'air d'être or sonnait français / *you sound as though* or *as if* or *like you've got a cold* on dirait que tu es enrhumé / *it doesn't sound to me as though they want to do it* je n'ai pas l'impression qu'ils veuillent le faire. ◆ vt **1.** [bell, alarm] sonner ; [wind instrument] sonner de ▶ **to sound one's horn** klaxonner ▶ **to sound a warning** lancer un avertissement **2.** [pronounce] prononcer. ❖ **sound off** vi *inf* **1.** [declare one's opinions] crier son opinion sur tous les toits ; [complain] râler ▶ **to sound off at sb** [angrily] passer un savon à *v inf* qqn **2.** [boast] se vanter. ❖ **sound out** vt sep *fig* [person] sonder.

sound barrier n mur *m* du son ▶ **to break the sound barrier** franchir le mur du son.

soundbite ['saʊndbaɪt] n petite phrase *f* (*prononcée par un homme politique à la radio ou à la télévision pour frapper les esprits*).

sound card n COMPUT carte *f* son.

sound effects pl n bruitage *m*.

sound engineer n ingénieur *m* du son.

sounding ['saʊndɪŋ] n **1.** AERON, METEOR & NAUT [measuring] sondage *m* **2.** [of bell, horn] son *m*. ❖ **soundings** pl n [investigations] sondages *mpl* ▶ **to take soundings** faire des sondages.

-sounding in comp : *a foreign-sounding name* un nom à consonance étrangère.

sounding board n **1.** *fig* [person] : *she uses her assistants as a sounding board for any new ideas* elle essaie toutes ses nouvelles idées sur ses assistants **2.** [over pulpit, rostrum] abat-voix *m inv*.

soundly ['saʊndlɪ] adv **1.** [deeply - sleep] profondément **2.** [sensibly - advise, argue] judicieusement, avec bon sens **3.** [safely - invest] de façon sûre, sans risque or risques **4.** [competently - work, run] avec compétence **5.** [thoroughly - defeat] à plate couture or plates coutures.

soundness ['saʊndnɪs] n **1.** [of body, mind] santé *f*, équilibre *m* ; [of health] robustesse *f* **2.** [of building, structure] solidité *f* ; [of business, financial situation] solvabilité *f* ; [of decision, advice] bon sens *m* ; [of argument, reasoning] justesse *f* **3.** [of sleep] profondeur *f*.

soundproof ['saʊndpruːf] ◆ adj insonorisé. ◆ vt insonoriser.

soundproofing ['saʊndpruːfɪŋ] n insonorisation *f*.

sound system n [hi-fi] chaîne *f* hi-fi ; [PA system] sonorisation *f*.

soundtrack ['saʊndtræk] n bande *f* sonore.

sound wave n onde *f* sonore.

soup [suːp] n **1.** CULIN soupe *f* ; [thin or blended] soupe *f*, potage *m* ; [smooth and creamy] velouté *m* / *onion* / *fish* / *leek soup* soupe à l'oignon / de poisson / aux poireaux ▶ **cream of mushroom soup** velouté de champignons ▶ **to be in the soup** *inf* être dans le pétrin ▶ **from soup to nuts** 🇺🇸 *inf* du début à la fin ▶ **everything from soup to nuts** absolument tout **2.** *v inf* [nitroglycerine] nitroglycérine *f*, nitro *f*. ❖ **soup up** vt sep *inf* [engine] gonfler ; [car] gonfler le moteur de ; [machine, computer program] perfectionner.

souped-up [suːpt-] adj *inf* [engine] gonflé, poussé ; [car] au moteur gonflé or poussé ; [machine, computer program] perfectionné.

soup kitchen n soupe *f* populaire.

soup plate n assiette *f* creuse or à soupe.

soup spoon n cuillère *f* or cuiller *f* à soupe.

sour ['saʊər] ◆ adj **1.** [flavour, taste] aigre, sur **2.** [rancid - milk] tourné, aigre ; [- breath] fétide / *the milk has gone* or *turned sour* le lait a tourné **3.** [disagreeable - person, character, mood] aigre, revêche, hargneux ; [- look] hargneux ; [- comment, tone] aigre, acerbe **4.** [wrong, awry] ▶ **to go** or **to turn sour** mal tourner **5.** [too acidic - soil] trop acide. ◆ vi **1.** [wine] surir, s'aigrir ; [milk] tourner, aigrir **2.** [person, character] aigrir ; [relationship] se dégrader, tourner au vinaigre ; [situation] mal tourner. ◆ vt **1.** [milk, wine] aigrir **2.** [person, character] aigrir ; [relationship] gâter, empoisonner ; [situation] gâter. ◆ n whisky *m* sour.

source [sɔːs] ◆ n **1.** [gen] source *f* / *at source* à la source **2.** [of information] source *f* **3.** [of river] source *f*. ◆ comp ▶ **source material** or **materials** [documents] documentation *f*. ◆ vt : *our paper is sourced from sustainable forests* notre papier provient de forêts gérées de façon durable.

source language n **1.** LING langue *f* source **2.** COMPUT langage *m* source.

source program n COMPUT programme *m* source.

sour cream n crème *f* aigre.

sour grapes n jalousie *f*, envie *f*.

sourly ['saʊəlɪ] adj aigrement, avec aigreur.

sourness ['saʊənɪs] n **1.** [of flavour, taste] aigreur *f*, acidité *f* ; [of milk] aigreur *f* **2.** [of person, character, mood] aigreur *f* ; [of speech, comment] ton *m* aigre.

south [saʊθ] ◆ n **1.** GEOG sud *m* / *the region to the south of Birmingham* la région qui est au sud de Birmingham / *I was born in the south* je suis né dans le Sud / *in the South of France* dans le Midi (de la France) / *the wind is in the south* le vent vient du sud ; [in US] ▶ **the South** le Sud, les États du Sud **2.** CARDS sud *m*. ◆ adj **1.** GEOG sud (*inv*), du sud, méridional / *the south coast* la côte sud / *in south India* dans le sud de l'Inde ▶ **the South Atlantic** l'Atlantique *m* **2.** [wind] du sud. ◆ adv au sud, vers le sud / *the village lies south of York* le village est situé au sud de York / *the living room faces south* la salle de séjour est exposée au sud / *the path heads (due) south* le chemin va or mène (droit) vers le sud / *they live down south* ils habitent dans le Sud.

South Africa pr n Afrique *f* du Sud / *in South Africa* en Afrique du Sud ▶ **the Republic of South Africa** la République d'Afrique du Sud.

South African ◆ n Sud-Africain *m*, -e *f*. ◆ adj sud-africain, d'Afrique du Sud.

South America pr n Amérique *f* du Sud / *in South America* en Amérique du Sud.

South American ◆ n Sud-Américain *m*, -e *f*. ◆ adj sud-américain, d'Amérique du Sud.

southbound ['saʊθbaʊnd] adj en direction du sud / *the southbound carriageway of the motorway is closed* l'axe sud de l'autoroute est fermé (à la circulation).

South Carolina pr n Caroline *f* du Sud / *in South Carolina* en Caroline du Sud.

South Dakota pr n Dakota *m* du Sud / *in South Dakota* dans le Dakota du Sud.

southeast [ˌsaʊθˈiːst] ◆ n sud-est *m*. ◆ adj **1.** GEOG sud-est *(inv)*, du sud-est / *in southeast England* dans le sud-est de l'Angleterre **2.** [wind] de sud-est. ◆ adv au sud-est, vers le sud-est / *it's 50 miles southeast of Liverpool* c'est à 80 kilomètres au sud-est de Liverpool.

Southeast Asia pr n Asie f du Sud-Est / *in Southeast Asia* en Asie du Sud-Est.

southeasterly [,saʊθ'iːstəlɪ] (*pl* **southeasterlies**) ◆ adj **1.** GEOG sud-est *(inv)*, du sud-est **2.** [wind] de sud-est. ◆ adv au sud-est, vers le sud-est. ◆ n vent *m* de sud-est.

southeastern [,saʊθ'iːstən] adj sud-est *(inv)*, du sud-est.

southerly ['sʌðəlɪ] (*pl* **southerlies**) ◆ adj **1.** GEOG sud *(inv)*, du sud / *in a southerly direction* vers le sud **2.** [wind] du sud. ◆ adv vers le sud. ◆ n vent *m* du sud.

southern ['sʌðən] adj GEOG sud *(inv)*, du sud, méridional / *he has a southern accent* il a un accent du sud / *southern Africa* l'Afrique f australe / *southern Europe* l'Europe f méridionale / *in southern India* dans le sud de l'Inde ▸ **the southern hemisphere** l'hémisphère *m* Sud or austral ▸ **the Southern States** aux États-Unis, les États entre la Pennsylvanie et la Virginie occidentale.

southerner ['sʌðənə'] n [gen] homme *m*, femme f du sud ; [in continental Europe] méridional *m*, -e f.

southernmost ['sʌðənməʊst] adj le plus au sud.

south-facing adj [house, wall] (exposé) au sud or au midi.

South Korea pr n Corée f du Sud / *in South Korea* en Corée du Sud.

South Korean ◆ n Sud-Coréen *m*, -enne f, Coréen *m*, -enne f du Sud. ◆ adj sud-coréen.

South Pole pr n pôle *m* Sud / *at the South Pole* au pôle Sud.

South Vietnam pr n Sud Viêt Nam *m* / *in South Vietnam* au Sud Viêt Nam.

South Vietnamese ◆ n Sud-Vietnamien *m*, -enne f ▸ **the South Vietnamese** les Sud-Vietnamiens. ◆ adj sud-vietnamien.

southward ['saʊθwəd] ◆ adj au sud. ◆ adv vers le sud, en direction du sud.

southwards ['saʊθwədz] = **southward** *(adv)*.

southwest [,saʊθ'west] ◆ n sud-ouest *m*. ◆ adj **1.** GEOG sud-ouest *(inv)*, du sud-ouest **2.** [wind] de sud-ouest. ◆ adv au sud-ouest, vers le sud-ouest / *it's southwest of London* c'est au sud-ouest de Londres.

southwesterly [,saʊθ'westəlɪ] (*pl* **southwesterlies**) ◆ adj **1.** GEOG sud-ouest *(inv)*, du sud-ouest **2.** [wind] de sud-ouest. ◆ adv au sud-ouest, vers le sud-ouest. ◆ n vent *m* de sud-ouest, suroît *m*.

southwestern [,saʊθ'westən] adj sud-ouest *(inv)*, du sud-ouest / *the southwestern States* les États du sud-ouest.

South Yemen pr n Yémen *m* du Sud / *in South Yemen* au Yémen du Sud.

souvenir [,suː'vɜ'nɪə'] n souvenir *m* (objet).

sou'wester [saʊ'westə'] n **1.** [headgear] suroît *m* **2.** [wind] = **southwesterly**.

sovereign ['sɒvrɪn] ◆ n **1.** [monarch] souverain *m*, -e f **2.** [coin] souverain *m*. ◆ adj POL [state, territory] souverain ; [powers] souverain, suprême ; [rights] de souveraineté.

sovereignty ['sɒvrɪntɪ] (*pl* **sovereignties**) n souveraineté f.

soviet ['saʊvɪət] n [council] soviet *m*. ❖ **Soviet** ◆ n [inhabitant] Soviétique *mf*. ◆ adj soviétique ▸ **the Union of Soviet Socialist Republics** l'Union f des républiques socialistes soviétiques.

Soviet Union pr n ▸ **the Soviet Union** l'Union f soviétique / *in the Soviet Union* en Union soviétique.

sow¹ [saʊ] (*pt* **sowed**, *pp* **sowed** or **sown** [saʊn], *cont* **sowing**) ◆ vt **1.** [seed, crop] semer ; [field] ensemencer **2.** *fig* semer. ◆ vi semer.

sow² [saʊ] n [pig] truie f.

sown [saʊn] pp ⟶ **sow**.

sox [sɒks] pl n US *inf* chaussettes *fpl*.

soya ['sɔɪə] n soja *m* ▸ **soya flour** / **milk** farine f / lait *m* de soja.

soya bean UK, **soybean** US ['sɔɪbiːn] n graine f de soja.

soy sauce n sauce f de soja.

sozzled ['sɒzld] adj UK *inf* soûl, paf.

spa [spɑː] n **1.** [resort] ville f d'eau **2.** [spring] source f minérale **3.** [whirlpool bath] bain *m* à remous **4.** [health club] centre *m* de fitness.

space [speɪs] ◆ n **1.** ASTRON & PHYS espace *m* **2.** [room] espace *m*, place f **3.** [volume, area, distance] espace *m* ▸ **advertising space** espace *m* publicitaire **4.** [gap] espace *m*, place f ; [on page, official form] espace *m*, case f **5.** TYPO [gap between words] espace f, blanc *m* ; [blank type] espace f **6.** [period of time, interval] intervalle *m*, espace *m* (de temps), période f / *in* or *within the space of six months* en (l'espace de) six mois **7.** [seat, place] place f. ◆ comp [programme, research, travel, flight] spatial. ◆ vt = **space out.** ❖ **space out** vt sep **1.** [in space] espacer **2.** [in time] échelonner, espacer.

space age n ▸ **the space age** l'ère f spatiale. ❖ **space-age** adj **1.** SCI de l'ère spatiale **2.** [futuristic] futuriste.

space bar n [on typewriter] barre f d'espacement.

space cadet n *inf* taré *m*, -e f.

space capsule n capsule f spatiale.

spacecraft ['speɪskrɑːft] n vaisseau *m* spatial.

spaced-out adj *v inf* shooté.

spaceman ['speɪsmæn] (*pl* **spacemen** [-men]) n [gen] spationaute *m* ; [American] astronaute *m* ; [Russian] cosmonaute *m*.

space probe n sonde f spatiale.

space-saving adj qui fait gagner de la place.

spaceship ['speɪsʃɪp] n vaisseau *m* spatial habité.

space shuttle n navette f spatiale.

space station n station f spatiale or orbitale.

spacesuit ['speɪssuːt] n combinaison f spatiale.

space travel n voyages *mpl* dans l'espace, astronautique f *spec*.

spacewoman ['speɪs,wʊmən] (*pl* **spacewomen** [-,wɪmɪn]) n [gen] spationaute f, astronaute f ; [Russian] cosmonaute f.

spacing ['speɪsɪŋ] n **1.** [of text on page - horizontal] espacement *m* ; [- vertical] interligne *m* / *typed in single* / *double spacing* tapé avec interligne simple / double **2.** [between trees, columns, buildings, etc.] espacement *m*, écart *m*.

spacious ['speɪʃəs] adj [house, room, office] spacieux, grand ; [park, property] étendu, grand.

spade [speɪd] n **1.** [tool] bêche f **2.** [in cards] pique *m*.

spadework ['speɪdwɜːk] n travail *m* de préparation or de déblayage.

spaghetti [spə'getɪ] n (U) spaghetti *mpl*, spaghettis *mpl*.

Spain [speɪn] pr n Espagne f / *in Spain* en Espagne.

Spam® [spæm] n pâté de jambon en conserve.

spam [spæm] ◆ n inf COMPUT spam m, pourriel m. ◆ vt (pt & pp **spammed**, cont **spamming**) envoyer un spam à.

spammer ['spæmər] n spammeur m.

spamming ['spæmɪŋ] n (U) spam m.

span [spæn] (pt & pp **spanned**, cont **spanning**) ◆ n **1.** [duration] durée f, laps m de temps ; [interval] intervalle m **2.** [range] gamme f **3.** [of hands, arms, wings] envergure f **4.** [of bridge] travée f ; [of arch, dome, girder] portée f **5.** [unit of measurement] empan m **6.** [matched pair - of horses, oxen] paire f. ◆ vt **1.** [encompass, stretch over - in time, extent] couvrir, embrasser **2.** [cross - river, ditch, etc.] enjamber, traverser **3.** [build bridge over] jeter un pont sur. ◆ pt arch ⟶ **spin**.

spandex ['spændeks] n Lycra® m.

spangle ['spæŋgl] ◆ n paillette f. ◆ vt pailleter, décorer de paillettes / stars spangled the night sky le ciel était parsemé d'étoiles.

Spaniard ['spænjəd] n Espagnol m, -e f.

spaniel ['spænjəl] n épagneul m.

Spanish ['spænɪʃ] ◆ adj espagnol ▸ **Spanish guitar** guitare f classique. ◆ n LING espagnol m. ◆ pl n ▸ **the Spanish** les Espagnols mpl.

Spanish America pr n Amérique f hispanophone.

Spanish-American ◆ n **1.** [in the US] Hispanique mf **2.** [in Latin America] Hispano-Américain m, -e f. ◆ adj **1.** [in the US] hispanique **2.** [in Latin America] hispanoaméricain.

Spanish-speaking adj hispanophone.

spank [spæŋk] ◆ vt donner une fessée à, fesser. ◆ vi [go at a lively pace] ▸ **to be** or **to go spanking along** aller bon train or à bonne allure. ◆ n tape f sur les fesses.

spanner ['spænər] n clé f, clef f (outil).

spar [spɑːr] (pt & pp **sparred**, cont **sparring**) ◆ vi **1.** SPORT [in boxing - train] s'entraîner (avec un sparringpartner) ; [- test out opponent] faire des feintes (pour tester son adversaire) **2.** [argue] se disputer. ◆ n **1.** [pole - gen] poteau m, mât m ; NAUT espar m **2.** AERON longeron m **3.** MINER spath m.

spare [speər] ◆ adj **1.** [not in use] dont on ne se sert pas, disponible ; [kept in reserve] de réserve, de rechange ; [extra, surplus] de trop, en trop **2.** [free] libre, disponible **3.** [lean] maigre, sec (sèche) **4.** [uncluttered - style, decor] dépouillé ; [frugal - meal] frugal **5.** UK inf [mad] ▸ **to go spare** devenir dingue. ◆ n [spare part] pièce f de rechange ; [wheel] roue f de secours ; [tyre] pneu m de rechange. ◆ vt **1.** [make available, give] accorder, consacrer ; [do without] se passer de **2.** [refrain from harming, punishing, destroying] épargner ▸ **to spare sb's life** épargner la vie de qqn ▸ **to spare sb's feelings** ménager les sentiments de qqn ▸ **to spare sb's blushes** épargner qqn **3.** [save - trouble, suffering] épargner, éviter **4.** [economize] ménager. ◆ **to spare** adj phr : do you have a few minutes to spare? avez-vous quelques minutes de libres or devant vous ? / we got to the airport with over an hour to spare nous sommes arrivés à l'aéroport avec plus d'une heure d'avance.

spare part n pièce f de rechange, pièce f détachée.

sparerib [speə'rɪb] n travers m de porc.

spare room n chambre f d'amis.

spare time n temps m libre. ◆ **spare-time** adj ▸ **spare-time activities** loisirs mpl.

spare tyre n **1.** AUTO pneu m de secours or de rechange **2.** inf [roll of fat] bourrelet m (à la taille).

spare wheel n roue f de secours.

sparing ['speərɪŋ] adj **1.** [economical - person] économe / she's very sparing with her compliments elle est très avare de compliments **2.** [meagre - quantity] limité, modéré ; [- use] modéré, économe.

sparingly ['speərɪŋlɪ] adv [eat] frugalement ; [drink, use] avec modération ; [praise] chichement, avec parcimonie.

spark [spɑːk] ◆ vt [trigger - interest, argument] susciter, provoquer. ◆ vi **1.** [produce sparks - gen] jeter des étincelles **2.** AUTO [spark plug, ignition system] allumer (par étincelle). ◆ n **1.** [from flame, electricity] étincelle f **2.** [flash, trace - of excitement, wit] étincelle f, lueur f ; [- of interest, enthusiasm] / she hasn't a spark of common sense elle n'a pas le moindre bon sens. ◆ **spark off** vt sep = **spark**.

sparking plug ['spɑːkɪŋ-] UK = **spark plug**.

sparkle ['spɑːkl] ◆ vi **1.** [jewel, frost, glass, star] étinceler, briller, scintiller ; [sea, lake] étinceler, miroiter ; [eyes] étinceler, pétiller **2.** [person] briller ; [conversation] être brillant **3.** [wine, cider, mineral water] pétiller. ◆ n **1.** [of jewel, frost, glass, star] étincellement m, scintillement m ; [of sea, lake] étincellement m, miroitement m ; [of eyes] éclat m **2.** [of person, conversation, wit, performance] éclat m.

sparkler ['spɑːklər] n **1.** [firework] cierge m magique **2.** UK v inf [diamond] diam m.

sparkling ['spɑːklɪŋ] ◆ adj **1.** [jewel, frost, glass, star] étincelant, scintillant ; [sea, lake] étincelant, miroitant ; [eyes] étincelant, pétillant **2.** [person, conversation, wit, performance] brillant **3.** [soft drink, mineral water] gazeux, pétillant. ◆ adv : sparkling clean / white d'une propreté / blancheur éclatante.

sparkling wine n vin m mousseux.

spark plug n AUTO bougie f.

sparring match ['spɑːrɪŋ-] n **1.** [in boxing] combat m d'entraînement **2.** [argument] discussion f animée.

sparring partner n **1.** [in boxing] sparring-partner m **2.** fig adversaire m.

sparrow ['spærəʊ] n moineau m.

sparse [spɑːs] adj clairsemé, rare.

sparsely ['spɑːslɪ] adv [wooded, populated] peu.

spartan ['spɑːtn] adj fig spartiate / a spartan room une chambre austère or sans aucun confort. ◆ **Spartan** ◆ n HIST Spartiate mf. ◆ adj HIST spartiate.

spasm ['spæzm] n **1.** [muscular contraction] spasme m **2.** [fit] accès m.

spasmodic [spæz'mɒdɪk] adj **1.** [intermittent] intermittent, irrégulier **2.** MED [pain, contraction] spasmodique.

spasmodically [spæz'mɒdɪklɪ] adv de façon intermittente, par à-coups.

spastic ['spæstɪk] ◆ n MED [gen] handicapé m, -e f (moteur) ; [person affected by spasms] spasmophile mf. ◆ adj **1.** MED [gen] handicapé (moteur) ; [affected by spasms] spasmophile ▸ **spastic paralysis** tétanie f **2.** v inf & offens [clumsy] empoté, gourde.

spat [spæt] ◆ pt & pp ⟶ **spit**. ◆ n **1.** [gaiter] guêtre f **2.** inf [quarrel] prise f de bec **3.** [shellfish] naissain m.

spate [speɪt] n **1.** [of letters, visitors] avalanche f ; [of abuse, insults] torrent m **2.** UK [flood] crue f / the river was in spate le fleuve était en crue.

spatial ['speɪʃl] adj spatial.

spatter ['spætər] ◆ vt [splash] éclabousser. ◆ vi [liquid] gicler ; [oil] crépiter. ◆ n [on garment] éclaboussure f, éclaboussures fpl ; [sound - of rain, oil, applause] crépitement m.

spatula ['spætjʊlə] n **1.** CULIN spatule f **2.** MED abaisselangue m inv, spatule f.

spawn [spɔːn] ◆ n (U) **1.** ZOOL [of frogs, fish] œufs mpl, frai m **2.** BOT [of mushrooms] mycélium m **3.** fig & pej [offspring] progéniture f. ◆ vt **1.** ZOOL pondre **2.** fig [produce] engendrer. ◆ vi ZOOL frayer.

spay [speɪ] vt stériliser.

SPCA (abbr of Society for the Prevention of Cruelty to Animals) pr n société américaine protectrice des animaux ; ≃ SPA.

SPCC (abbr of Society for the Prevention of Cruelty to Children) pr n société américaine pour la protection de l'enfance.

speak [spiːk] (pt spoke [spəʊk], pp spoken ['spəʊkn]) ◆ vi **1.** [talk] parler ▸ to speak to or 🇺🇸 with sb parler à or avec qqn ▸ to speak about or of sthg parler de qqch ▸ to speak to sb about sthg parler à qqn de qqch ; [on telephone] parler / who's speaking? a) [gen] qui est à l'appareil ? b) [switchboard] c'est de la part de qui ? / Kate Smith speaking Kate Smith à l'appareil, c'est Kate Smith **2.** [in debate, meeting, etc. -make a speech] faire un discours, parler ; [-intervene] prendre la parole, parler **3.** [be on friendly terms] : she isn't speaking to me elle ne me parle plus / I don't know them to speak to je ne les connais que de vue ▸ to be on speaking terms with sb connaître qqn (assez pour lui parler) **4.** [as spokesperson] ▸ to speak for sb a) [on their behalf] parler au nom de qqn b) [in their favour] parler en faveur de qqn **5.** [in giving an opinion] : generally speaking en général / personally speaking en ce qui me concerne, quant à moi ▸ speaking of which justement, à ce propos / financially speaking financièrement parlant, du point de vue financier / speaking as a politician en tant qu'homme politique / he always speaks well / highly of you il dit toujours du bien / beaucoup de bien de vous **6.** fig [give an impression] : his paintings speak of terrible loneliness ses peintures expriment une immense solitude. ◆ vt **1.** [say, pronounce] dire, prononcer ▸ to speak one's mind dire sa pensée or façon de penser ▸ to speak the truth dire la vérité **2.** [language] parler. ❖ not to speak of prep phr sans parler de. ❖ so to speak adv phr pour ainsi dire. ❖ to speak of adv phr : there's no wind / mail to speak of il n'y a presque pas de vent / de courrier. ❖ speak for vt insep (usu passive) : these goods are already spoken for ces articles sont déjà réservés or retenus / she's already spoken for elle est déjà prise. ❖ speak out vi parler franchement, ne pas mâcher ses mots ▸ to speak out for sthg parler en faveur de qqch ▸ to speak out against sthg s'élever contre qqch. ❖ speak up vi **1.** [louder] parler plus fort ; [more clearly] parler plus clairement **2.** [be frank] parler franchement ▸ to speak up for sb parler en faveur de qqn, défendre les intérêts de qqn.

-speak in comp pej ▸ computer-speak langage m or jargon m de l'informatique.

speaker ['spiːkər] n **1.** [gen] celui m / celle f qui parle ; [in discussion] interlocuteur m, -trice f ; [in public] orateur m, -trice f ; [in lecture] conférencier m, -ère f **2.** LING locuteur m, -trice f / native speakers of English ceux dont la langue maternelle est l'anglais / Spanish speaker hispanophone mf **3.** POL speaker m, président m, -e f de l'assemblée ▸ the Speaker (of the House of Commons) le président de la Chambre des communes ▸ the Speaker of the House le président de la Chambre des représentants américaine **4.** [loudspeaker] haut-parleur m ; [in stereo system] enceinte f, baffle m.

 Speaker of the House

Le président de la Chambre des représentants est l'une des personnalités politiques les plus influentes de la Maison-Blanche : il est en deuxième position, après le vice-président, pour remplacer le président des États-Unis en cas de force majeure.

speaker phone n téléphone m avec haut-parleur.

speaking ['spiːkɪŋ] ◆ adj **1.** [involving speech] : do you have a speaking part in the play? est-ce que vous avez du texte ? / she has a good speaking voice elle a une belle voix **2.** [which speaks - robot, machine, doll] parlant. ◆ n art m de parler.

-speaking in comp **1.** [person] : they're both German / Spanish-speaking ils sont tous deux germanophones / hispanophones / a child of Polish-speaking parents un enfant dont les parents sont de langue or d'origine polonaise **2.** [country] : French / English-speaking countries les pays francophones / anglophones / the Arab-speaking world le monde arabophone.

speaking clock n 🇬🇧 horloge f parlante.

spear [spɪər] ◆ n **1.** [weapon] lance f ; [harpoon] harpon m **2.** [of asparagus, broccoli, etc.] pointe f. ◆ vt **1.** [enemy] transpercer d'un coup de lance ; [fish] harponner **2.** [food] piquer.

spearhead ['spɪəhed] ◆ n lit & fig fer m de lance. ◆ vt [attack] être le fer de lance de ; [campaign, movement] mener, être à la tête de.

spearmint ['spɪəmɪnt] ◆ n **1.** [plant] menthe f verte ; [flavour] menthe f **2.** [sweet] bonbon m à la menthe. ◆ adj [flavour] de menthe ; [toothpaste, chewing gum] à la menthe.

spec [spek] n **1.** abbr of specification **2.** PHR on spec 🇬🇧 inf au hasard.

special ['speʃl] ◆ adj **1.** [exceptional, particular - offer, friend, occasion, ability] spécial ; [-reason, effort, pleasure] particulier ; [-powers] extraordinaire ▸ special agent agent m secret ▸ special interest holidays vacances fpl à thème ▸ the special relationship POL relations d'amitié entre les USA et la Grande-Bretagne **2.** [specific - need, problem] spécial, particulier ; [-equipment] spécial ; [-adviser] particulier **3.** [peculiar] particulier **4.** [valued] cher / you're very special to me je tiens beaucoup à toi. ◆ n **1.** [train] train m supplémentaire ; [bus] car m supplémentaire **2.** [in restaurant] spécialité f / today's special le plat du jour **3.** TV émission f spéciale ; PRESS [issue] numéro m spécial ; [feature] article m spécial **4.** 🇺🇸 COMM offre f spéciale / sugar is on special today le sucre est en promotion aujourd'hui.

Special Branch pr n renseignements généraux britanniques.

special constable n 🇬🇧 auxiliaire mf de police.

special correspondent n PRESS envoyé m spécial, envoyée f spéciale.

special delivery n service postal britannique garantissant la distribution du courrier sous 24 heures.

special effects pl n CIN & TV effets mpl spéciaux.

specialism ['speʃəlɪzm] n spécialisation f.

specialist ['speʃəlɪst] ◆ n **1.** [gen & MED] spécialiste mf / she's a heart specialist elle est cardiologue / he's a specialist in rare books c'est un spécialiste en livres rares **2.** 🇺🇸 MIL officier m technicien. ◆ adj [skills, vocabulary] spécialisé, de spécialiste ; [writing, publication] pour spécialistes.

speciality [ˌspeʃɪ'ælətɪ] (pl **specialities**), **specialty** ['speʃltɪ] (pl **specialties**) n 1. [service, product] spécialité f 2. [area of study] spécialité f.

specialization, specialisation [ˌspeʃəlaɪ'zeɪʃn] n spécialisation f.

specialize, specialise ['speʃəlaɪz] vi [company, restaurant, student] se spécialiser ▶ **to specialize in sthg** se spécialiser en or dans qqch.

specialized, specialised ['speʃəlaɪzd] adj spécialisé.

specially ['speʃəlɪ] adv 1. [above all] spécialement, particulièrement, surtout 2. [on purpose, specifically] exprès, spécialement 3. [particularly] spécialement.

special needs pl n ▶ **children with special needs** enfants ayant des difficultés scolaires ▶ **special needs teacher** enseignant m, -e f spécialisé s'occupant d'enfants ayant des difficultés scolaires.

special offer n offre f spéciale, promotion f ▶ **to be on special offer** être en promotion.

Special Olympics pr n ▶ **the Special Olympics** championnats sportifs pour handicapés mentaux.

special school n [for the physically disabled] établissement m d'enseignement spécialisé (pour enfants handicapés) ; [for the mentally disabled] établissement m d'enseignement spécialisé (pour enfants inadaptés).

specialty ['speʃltɪ] (pl **specialties**) n 1. = speciality 2. LAW contrat m sous seing privé.

species ['spi:ʃi:z] (pl **species**) n 1. BIOL espèce f 2. fig espèce f.

specific [spə'sɪfɪk] adj 1. [explicit] explicite ; [precise] précis ; [clear] clair ; [particular] particulier 2. BIOL & BOT ▶ **specific name** nom m spécifique or d'espèce. ◆ **specifics** pl n détails mpl.

specifically [spə'sɪfɪklɪ] adv 1. [explicitly] explicitement ; [precisely] précisément, de façon précise ; [clearly] clairement, expressément 2. [particularly] particulièrement ; [specially] spécialement ; [purposely] exprès, expressément.

specification [ˌspesɪfɪ'keɪʃn] n 1. (often pl) [in contract, of machine, building materials, etc.] spécifications fpl 2. [stipulation] spécification f, précision f.

specify ['spesɪfaɪ] (pt & pp **specified**) vt spécifier, préciser / unless otherwise specified sauf indication contraire / the person previously specified la personne précitée or déjà nommée / on a specified date à une date précise.

specimen ['spesɪmən] ◆ n 1. [sample - of work, handwriting] spécimen m ; [- of blood] prélèvement m ; [- of urine] échantillon m 2. [single example] spécimen m 3. inf & pej [person] spécimen m. ◆ comp [page, letter, reply] spécimen ▶ **specimen copy** spécimen m (livre, magazine).

speck [spek] ◆ n 1. [of dust, dirt] grain m ; [in eye] poussière f 2. [stain, mark - gen] petite tache f ; [- on skin, fruit] tache f, tavelure f ; [- of blood] petite tache f 3. [dot - on horizon, from height] point m noir 4. [tiny amount] tout petit peu m. ◆ vt (usu passive) tacheter.

speckled ['spekld] adj tacheté, moucheté.

specs [speks] (abbr of **spectacles**) pl n inf lunettes fpl, binocles mpl.

spectacle ['spektəkl] n 1. [sight] spectacle m ▶ **to make a spectacle of o.s.** se donner en spectacle 2. CIN, THEAT & TV superproduction f.

spectacles ['spektəklz] pl n lunettes fpl ▶ **a pair of spectacles** une paire de lunettes.

spectacular [spek'tækjʊlər] ◆ adj [event, defeat, result, view] spectaculaire. ◆ n CIN, THEAT & TV superproduction f.

spectacularly [spek'tækjʊləlɪ] adv [big, beautiful] spectaculairement.

spectate [spek'teɪt] vi assister à.

spectator [spek'teɪtər] n spectateur m, -trice f.

spectator sport n sport m grand public.

specter = spectre.

spectre , **specter** ['spektər] n spectre m ▶ **to raise the spectre of unemployment / war** agiter le spectre du chômage / de la guerre.

spectrum ['spektrəm] (pl **spectrums** or **spectra** ['spektrə]) n 1. PHYS spectre m 2. fig [range] gamme f / right across the spectrum sur toute la gamme ▶ **the political spectrum** l'éventail m politique.

speculate ['spekjʊleɪt] vi 1. [wonder] s'interroger, se poser des questions ; [make suppositions] faire des suppositions ; PHILOS spéculer 2. COMM & FIN spéculer ▶ **to speculate on the stock market** spéculer or jouer en Bourse.

speculation [ˌspekjʊ'leɪʃn] n 1. (U) [supposition, conjecture] conjecture f, conjectures fpl, supposition f, suppositions fpl ; PHILOS spéculation f 2. [guess] supposition f, conjecture f 3. COMM & FIN spéculation f.

speculative ['spekjʊlətɪv] adj spéculatif.

speculator ['spekjʊleɪtər] n spéculateur m, -trice f.

sped [sped] pt & pp ⟶ speed.

speech [spi:tʃ] n 1. [ability to speak] parole f ; [spoken language] parole f, langage m parlé 2. [manner of speaking] façon f de parler, langage m ; [elocution] élocution f, articulation f 3. [dialect, language] parler m, langage m 4. [talk] discours m, allocution f fml ; [shorter, more informal] speech m ▶ **to make a speech on** or **about sthg** faire un discours sur qqch 5. THEAT monologue m.

speech bubble n bulle f (de BD).

speech day n SCH distribution f des prix / on speech day le jour de la distribution des prix.

📖 **Speech day**

À la fin de l'année scolaire en Grande-Bretagne, il est de coutume, dans certaines écoles, d'inviter une personnalité qui préside la cérémonie de remise des prix et prononce un discours.

speech-impaired adj muet.

speech impediment n défaut m d'élocution or de prononciation.

speechless ['spi:tʃlɪs] adj 1. [with amazement, disbelief] muet, interloqué ; [with rage, joy] muet ▶ **to leave sb speechless** laisser qqn sans voix 2. [inexpressible - rage, fear] muet.

speechmaking ['spi:tʃˌmeɪkɪŋ] n (U) discours mpl ; pej beaux discours mpl.

speech processing n compréhension f du langage parlé.

speech recognition n COMPUT reconnaissance f de la parole.

speech therapist n orthophoniste mf.

speech therapy n orthophonie f.

speed [spi:d] ◆ n 1. [rate, pace - of car, progress, reaction, work] vitesse f / at (a) great or high speed à toute vitesse, à grande vitesse / at top or full speed a) [drive] à toute vitesse or allure b) [work] très vite, en quatrième vitesse 2. [rapid rate] vitesse f, rapidité f ▶ **to pick up / to lose speed** prendre / perdre de la vitesse 3. [gear - of car, bicycle] vitesse f 4. PHOT [of film] rapidité f, sensibilité f ; [of shutter] vitesse f ; [of lens] luminosité f 5. drugs sl speed m, amphétamines fpl.

◆ vi **1.** (pt & pp **sped** [sped]) [go fast] aller à toute allure **2.** (pt & pp **speeded**) AUTO [exceed speed limit] faire des excès de vitesse, rouler trop vite. ◆ vt (pt & pp **sped** [sped] or **speeded**) [person] ▶ **to speed sb on his way** souhaiter bon voyage à qqn. ◆ **speed up** ◆ vi [gen] aller plus vite ; [driver] rouler plus vite ; [worker] travailler plus vite ; [machine, film] accélérer. ◆ vt sep [worker] faire travailler plus vite ; [person] faire aller plus vite ; [work] activer, accélérer ; [pace] presser ; [production] accélérer, augmenter ; [reaction, film] accélérer.

speedboat ['spiːdbəʊt] n vedette f (rapide) ; [with outboard engine] hors-bord m inv.

speed bump n ralentisseur m, casse-vitesse m.

speed camera n cinémomètre m.

speed dating n speed-dating m.

speed-dialling [UK], **speed-dialing** [US] n (U) TELEC numérotation f rapide.

speedily ['spiːdɪlɪ] adv [quickly] vite, rapidement ; [promptly] promptement, sans tarder ; [soon] bientôt.

speeding ['spiːdɪŋ] ◆ n AUTO excès m de vitesse. ◆ comp ▶ **a speeding ticket** un P-V pour excès de vitesse.

speed limit n limitation f de vitesse / the speed limit is 60 la vitesse est limitée à 60.

speedo ['spiːdəʊ] (pl **speedos**) [UK] inf = **speedometer**.

speedometer [spɪ'dɒmɪtər] n compteur m de vitesse.

speed trap n contrôle m de vitesse ▶ **radar speed trap** contrôle radar.

speedway ['spiːdweɪ] n **1.** [racing] speedway m **2.** [US] [track] piste f de vitesse pour motos **3.** [US] [expressway] voie f express ou rapide.

speedy ['spiːdɪ] (compar **speedier**, superl **speediest**) adj **1.** [rapid] rapide ; [prompt] prompt **2.** [car] rapide, nerveux.

speleology [ˌspiːlɪ'ɒlədʒɪ] n spéléologie f.

spell [spel] ([UK] pt & pp **spelt** [spelt] or **spelled** ; [US] pt & pp **spelled**) ◆ vt **1.** [write] écrire, orthographier ; [aloud] épeler **2.** [subj: letters] former, donner **3.** fig [mean] signifier **4.** ([UK] pt & pp **spelled**) [worker, colleague] relayer. ◆ vi ▶ **to learn to spell** apprendre l'orthographe / he spells badly il est mauvais en orthographe. ◆ n **1.** [period] (courte) période f / scattered showers and sunny spells des averses locales et des éclaircies / he had a dizzy spell il a été pris de vertige **2.** [of duty] tour m **3.** [magic words] formule f magique, incantation f **4.** [enchantment] charme m, sort m, sortilège m ▶ **to cast** or **to put a spell on sb** jeter un sort or un charme à qqn, ensorceler or envoûter qqn ▶ **to break the spell** rompre le charme ▶ **to be under sb's spell** lit & fig être sous le charme de qqn. ◆ **spell out** vt sep **1.** [read out letter by letter] épeler ; [decipher] déchiffrer **2.** [make explicit] expliquer bien clairement.

spellbinding ['spel,baɪndɪŋ] adj ensorcelant, envoûtant.

spellbound ['spelbaʊnd] adj [spectator, audience] captivé, envoûté / the film held me spellbound from start to finish le film m'a tenu en haleine or m'a captivé du début jusqu'à la fin.

spell-check ◆ n vérification f orthographique ▶ **to do** or **run a spell-check on a document** effectuer la vérification orthographique d'un document. ◆ vt faire la vérification orthographique de.

spell-checker n correcteur m or vérificateur m orthographique.

spelling ['spelɪŋ] ◆ n **1.** [word formation] orthographe f / what is the spelling of this word? quelle est l'orthographe de or comment s'écrit ce mot ? **2.** [ability

to spell] : he is good at spelling il est fort en orthographe. ◆ comp [error, test, book] d'orthographe ; [pronunciation] orthographique ▶ **spelling mistake** faute f d'orthographe.

spelling bee n [US] concours m d'orthographe.

spelt [spelt] ◆ pt & pp ⟶ **spell** (vi & vt). ◆ n BOT épeautre m.

spelunking [spɪ'lʌŋkɪŋ] n [US] spéléologie f.

spend [spend] (pt & pp **spent** [spent]) ◆ vt **1.** [money, fortune] dépenser ▶ **to spend money on a)** [food, clothes] dépenser de l'argent en **b)** [house, car] dépenser de l'argent pour, consacrer de l'argent à **2.** [time - pass] passer ; [- devote] consacrer ▶ **to spend time on sthg** / **on doing sthg** passer du temps sur qqch / à faire qqch **3.** [exhaust, use up] épuiser. ◆ vi dépenser, faire des dépenses. ◆ n [US] [allocated money] allocation f.

spender ['spendər] n dépensier m, -ère f / she's a big spender elle est très dépensière.

spending ['spendɪŋ] n (U) dépenses fpl / public or government spending dépenses publiques / a cut in defence spending une réduction du budget de la défense.

spending money n argent m de poche.

spending power n pouvoir m d'achat.

spendthrift ['spendθrɪft] ◆ n dépensier m, -ère f. ◆ adj dépensier.

spent [spent] ◆ pt & pp ⟶ **spend**. ◆ adj **1.** [used up - fuel, bullet, match] utilisé ; [cartridge] brûlé **2.** [tired out] épuisé.

sperm [spɜːm] (pl **sperm** or **sperms**) n **1.** [cell] spermatozoïde m ▶ **sperm count** spermogramme m **2.** [liquid] sperme m.

sperm bank n banque f de sperme.

spermicidal [ˌspɜːmɪ'saɪdl] adj spermicide ▶ **spermicidal cream** / **jelly** crème f / gelée f spermicide.

spermicide ['spɜːmɪsaɪd] n spermicide m.

sperm whale n cachalot m.

spew [spjuː] ◆ vt **1.** v inf & lit dégueuler **2.** fig vomir. ◆ vi **1.** v inf & lit dégueuler **2.** fig [pour out] gicler. ◆ **spew up** vi & vt sep v inf vomir.

SPF (abbr of **sun protection factor**) indice m de protection solaire.

sphere [sfɪər] n **1.** [globe] sphère f ; liter [sky] cieux mpl **2.** fig [of interest, activity] sphère f, domaine m / her sphere of activity a) [professional] son domaine d'activité **b)** [personal] sa sphère d'activité.

spherical ['sferɪkl] adj sphérique.

sphincter ['sfɪŋktər] n sphincter m.

Sphinx [sfɪŋks] pr n ▶ **the Sphinx** le sphinx.

spice [spaɪs] ◆ n **1.** CULIN épice f ▶ **mixed spice** (U) épices fpl mélangées ▶ **spice rack** étagère f or présentoir m à épices **2.** fig piquant m, sel m. ◆ vt **1.** CULIN épicer, parfumer **2.** fig pimenter, corser. ◆ **spice up** vt sep = **spice** (vt).

spick-and-span ['spɪkən,spæn] adj [room] impeccable, reluisant de propreté ; [appearance] tiré à quatre épingles.

spicy ['spaɪsɪ] (compar **spicier**, superl **spiciest**) adj **1.** [food] épicé **2.** fig [book, story] piquant, corsé.

spider ['spaɪdər] n **1.** ZOOL araignée f ▶ **spider's web** toile f d'araignée **2.** [UK] [for luggage] araignée f (à bagages) **3.** [US] CULIN poêle f (à trépied) **4.** COMPUT araignée f.

spider crab n araignée f (de mer).

spider monkey n singe m araignée, atèle m.

spiderweb ['spaɪdəweb] n [US] toile f d'araignée.

spidery ['spaɪdərɪ] adj [in shape] en forme d'araignée ; [finger] long et mince ▶ **spidery writing** pattes fpl de mouches.

spiel [ʃpiːl] inf ◆ n **1.** [speech] laïus m, baratin m **2.** [sales talk] baratin m. ◆ vi baratiner.

spike [spaɪk] ◆ vt **1.** [shoes, railings] garnir de pointes **2.** [impale] transpercer **3.** inf [drink] corser **4.** PRESS [story] rejeter. ◆ vi [in volleyball] smasher. ◆ n **1.** [on railings, shoe] pointe f ; [on cactus] épine f ; [on tyre] clou m ; [for paper] pique-notes m inv **2.** [peak - on graph] pointe f **3.** [nail] gros clou m **4.** [antler] dague f **5.** [in volleyball] smash m. ❖ **spikes** pl n inf [shoes] chaussures fpl à pointes.

spiked [spaɪkt] adj [railings] à pointes de fer ; [shoes] à pointes ; [tyre] clouté, à clous.

spike heels pl n (chaussures fpl à) talons mpl aiguilles.

spiky ['spaɪkɪ] (compar **spikier**, superl **spikiest**) adj **1.** [branch, railings] garni or hérissé de pointes ; [hair] en épis ; [writing] pointu **2.** 🇬🇧 inf [bad-tempered] chatouilleux, ombrageux.

spill [spɪl] (🇬🇧 pt & pp **spilt** [spɪlt] or **spilled** ;🇺🇸 pt & pp **spilled**) ◆ vt **1.** [liquid, salt, etc.] renverser, répandre **2.** fig [secret] dévoiler ▶ **to spill the beans** inf vendre la mèche **3.** [blood] verser, faire couler. ◆ vi **1.** [liquid, salt, etc.] se renverser, se répandre **2.** [crowd] se déverser. ◆ n **1.** [spillage - of liquid] renversement m ; [solid] déversement m **2.** [for fire] longue allumette f. ❖ **spill out** ◆ vt sep **1.** [contents, liquid] renverser, répandre **2.** fig [secret] dévoiler, révéler. ◆ vi **1.** [contents, liquid] se renverser, se répandre **2.** fig [crowd] se déverser, s'échapper. ❖ **spill over** vi **1.** [liquid] déborder, se répandre **2.** fig [overflow] se déverser, déborder.

spillage ['spɪlɪdʒ] n [act of spilling] renversement m, fait m de renverser ; [liquid spilt] liquide m renversé.

spillover ['spɪl,əʊvər] n **1.** [act of spilling] renversement m ; [quantity spilt] quantité f renversée **2.** [excess] excédent m **3.** ECON retombées fpl (économiques).

spilt [spɪlt] pt & pp 🇬🇧 ⟶ **spill**.

spin [spɪn] (pt & pp **spun** [spʌn], cont **spinning**) ◆ vt **1.** [cause to rotate - wheel, chair] faire tourner ; [- top] lancer, faire tournoyer ; [SPORT - ball] donner de l'effet à **2.** [yarn, glass] filer ; [thread] fabriquer **3.** [subj: spider, silkworm] tisser **4.** [invent - tale] inventer, débiter **5.** [in spin-dryer] essorer. ◆ vi **1.** [rotate] tourner, tournoyer ; SPORT [ball] tournoyer **2.** fig [grow dizzy] tourner / my head is spinning j'ai la tête qui (me) tourne **3.** [spinner] filer ; [spider] tisser sa toile **4.** [in spin-dryer] essorer. ◆ n **1.** [rotation] tournoiement m / the plane went into a spin **a)** [accidentally] l'avion a fait une chute en vrille **b)** [in aerobatics] l'avion a effectué une descente en vrille / the car went into a spin la voiture a fait un tête-à-queue / my head is in a spin fig j'ai la tête qui tourne **2.** inf [panic] ▶ **to be in a flat spin** être dans tous ses états **3.** SPORT [on ball] effet m **4.** [in spin-dryer] essorage m **5.** inf [ride - in car] tour m, balade f ▶ **to go for a spin** faire une (petite) balade en voiture **6.** inf [try] ▶ **to give sthg a spin** essayer or tenter qqch **7.** [manipulation of facts] : it was just spin c'était de l'intox inf. ❖ **spin off** vt sep [hive off] : they spun off their own company ils ont monté leur propre affaire. ❖ **spin out** vt sep [story, idea] faire durer, délayer ; [supplies, money] faire durer, économiser / the plane spun out of control l'avion est parti en vrille / the car spun out of control la voiture a dérapé / things are spinning out of control les choses dérapent complètement or partent en vrille. ❖ **spin round** 🇬🇧, **spin around** ◆ vi **1.** [planet, wheel] tourner (sur soi-même) ; [skater, top] tournoyer, tourner **2.** [face opposite direction] se retourner. ◆ vt sep faire tourner.

spina bifida [,spaɪnə'bɪfɪdə] n spina-bifida m inv.

spinach ['spɪnɪdʒ] n (U) épinards mpl.

spinal ['spaɪnl] adj [nerve, muscle] spinal ; [ligament, disc] vertébral ▶ **a spinal injury** une blessure à la colonne vertébrale.

spinal column n colonne f vertébrale.

spinal cord n moelle f épinière.

spindle ['spɪndl] n **1.** [for spinning - by hand] fuseau m ; [- by machine] broche f **2.** TECH broche f, axe m ; [in motor, lathe] arbre m ; [of valve] tige f.

spindly ['spɪndlɪ] (compar **spindlier**, superl **spindliest**) adj [legs] grêle, comme des allumettes ; [body] chétif, maigrichon ; [tree] grêle ; [plant] étiolé.

spin doctor n responsable de la communication d'un parti politique.

spin-dry vi & vt essorer.

spin-dryer n 🇬🇧 essoreuse f.

spine [spaɪn] n **1.** ANAT colonne f vertébrale ; ZOOL épine f dorsale **2.** [prickle - of hedgehog] piquant m ; [- of plant, rose] épine f **3.** [of book] dos m **4.** [of hill] crête f **5.** 🇺🇸 [courage] résolution f, volonté f.

spine-chilling adj à vous glacer le sang, terrifiant.

spineless ['spaɪnlɪs] adj **1.** [weak] mou (before vowel or silent 'h' mol, f molle) ; [cowardly] lâche **2.** ZOOL invertébré **3.** BOT sans épines.

spinelessness ['spaɪnlɪsnɪs] n lâcheté f.

spinner ['spɪnər] n **1.** TEXT [person] fileur m, -euse f **2.** [in fishing] cuiller f **3.** [spin-dryer] essoreuse f (à linge) **4.** 🇬🇧 SPORT [bowler in cricket] lanceur m ; [ball] balle f qui a de l'effet.

spinning ['spɪnɪŋ] ◆ n **1.** TEXT [by hand] filage m ; [by machine] filature f **2.** [in fishing] pêche f à la cuiller. ◆ adj tournant, qui tourne.

spinning top n toupie f.

spin-off n **1.** [by-product] retombée f, produit m dérivé **2.** [work derived from another] : the book is a spin-off from the TV series le roman est tiré de la série télévisée / the TV series gave rise to a number of spin-offs la série télévisée a donné lieu à plusieurs produits dérivés.

spinster ['spɪnstər] n ADMIN & LAW célibataire f ; pej vieille fille f.

spiral ['spaɪərəl] (🇬🇧 pt & pp **spiralled**, cont **spiralling** ;🇺🇸 pt & pp **spiraled**, cont **spiraling**) ◆ n **1.** [gen] spirale f / in a spiral en spirale ▶ **inflationary spiral** spirale f inflationniste **2.** AERON vrille f. ◆ adj [motif, shell, curve] en (forme de) spirale ; [descent, spring] en spirale ▶ **spiral binding** reliure f spirale. ◆ vi **1.** [in flight - plane] vriller ; [- bird] voler en spirale ; [in shape - smoke, stairs] former une spirale **2.** [prices, inflation] s'envoler, monter en flèche ▶ **to spiral downwards** chuter. ❖ **spiral up** vi [plane, smoke] monter en spirale ; [prices] monter en flèche.

spiral staircase n escalier m en colimaçon.

spire ['spaɪər] n ARCHIT flèche f.

spirit ['spɪrɪt] ◆ n **1.** [non-physical part of being, soul] esprit m **2.** [supernatural being] esprit m ▶ **evil spirits** esprits malins ▶ **the spirit world** le monde des esprits **3.** [person] esprit m, âme f **4.** [attitude, mood] esprit m, attitude f ▶ **to enter into the spirit of things a)** [at party] se mettre au diapason **b)** [in work] participer de bon cœur ▶ **that's the spirit!** voilà comment il faut réagir !, à la bonne heure ! **5.** [deep meaning] esprit m, génie m / the spirit of the law l'esprit de la loi **6.** [energy] énergie f, entrain m ; [courage] courage m ; [character] caractère m / he replied with spirit il a répondu énergiquement / a man of spirit un homme de caractère / his spirit was broken il avait perdu courage **7.** (usu pl) 🇬🇧 [alcoholic drink] alcool m, spiritueux m **8.** CHEM essence f, sel m. ◆ vt [move secretly] :

they spirited her in / out by a side door ils l'ont fait entrer / sortir discrètement par une porte dérobée. ❖ **spirits** pl n [mood, mental state] humeur *f*, état *m* d'esprit ; [morale] moral *m* ▸ **to be in good spirits** être de bonne humeur, avoir le moral ▸ **to feel out of spirits** avoir le cafard ▸ **to be in low spirits** être déprimé / *you must keep your spirits up* il faut garder le moral, il ne faut pas vous laisser abattre ▸ **to raise sb's spirits** remonter le moral à qqn. ❖ **spirit away**, **spirit off** vt sep [carry off secretly] faire disparaître (comme par enchantement) ; [steal] escamoter, subtiliser.

spirited ['spɪrɪtɪd] adj **1.** [lively - person] vif, plein d'entrain ; [- horse] fougueux ; [- manner] vif ; [- reply, argument] vif ; [- music, rhythm, dance] entraînant **2.** [courageous - person, action, decision, defence] courageux.

spirit level n niveau *m* à bulle.

spiritual ['spɪrɪtʃʊəl] ◆ adj **1.** [relating to the spirit] spirituel **2.** [religious, sacred] religieux, sacré ▸ **spiritual adviser** conseiller *m* spirituel. ◆ n [song] (negro) spiritual *m*.

spiritualism ['spɪrɪtʃʊəlɪzm] n RELIG spiritisme *m* ; PHILOS spiritualisme *m*.

spiritualist ['spɪrɪtʃʊəlɪst] ◆ adj RELIG spirite ; PHILOS spiritualiste. ◆ n RELIG spirite *mf* ; PHILOS spiritualiste *mf*.

spirituality [,spɪrɪtʃʊ'ælətɪ] n spiritualité *f*.

spiritually ['spɪrɪtʃʊəlɪ] adv spirituellement, en esprit.

spit [spɪt] (*pt & pp* **spit** *or* **spat** [spæt], *cont* **spitting**) ◆ vi **1.** [in anger, contempt] cracher ▸ **to spit at sb** cracher sur qqn ▸ **to spit in sb's face** cracher à la figure de qqn **2.** [while talking] postillonner, envoyer des postillons **3.** [hot fat] sauter, grésiller **4.** [PHR] *it's spitting* (with rain) il bruine, il pleut légèrement. ◆ vt *lit & fig* cracher. ◆ n **1.** (U) [spittle - in mouth] salive *f* ; [- spat out] crachat *m* ; [- ejected while speaking] postillon *m* ; [act of spitting] crachement *m* **2.** [US] *inf* [likeness] ▸ **to be the spit of sb** : *he's the spit of his dad* c'est son père tout craché **3.** [of insects] écume *f* printanière, crachat *m* de coucou **4.** CULIN broche *f* **5.** GEOG pointe *f*, langue *f* de terre. ❖ **spit out** vt sep [food, medicine, words, invective] cracher ▸ **come on, spit it out!** *inf* allez, accouche !

spite [spaɪt] ◆ n [malice] dépit *m*, malveillance *f* ▸ **to do sthg out of spite** faire qqch par dépit. ◆ vt contrarier, vexer. ❖ **in spite of** prep phr en dépit de, malgré.

spiteful ['spaɪtfʊl] adj [person, remark, character] malveillant.

spitefully ['spaɪtfʊlɪ] adv par dépit, par méchanceté, méchamment.

spit roast n rôti *m* à la broche. ❖ **spit-roast** vt faire rôtir à la broche.

spitting ['spɪtɪŋ] n / **'no spitting'** 'défense de cracher'.

spitting image n *inf* ▸ **to be the spitting image of sb** : *he's the spitting image of his father* c'est son père tout craché.

spittle ['spɪtl] n [saliva - of person] salive *f* ; [- of dog] bave *f* ; [- on floor] crachat *m*.

splash [splæʃ] ◆ vt **1.** [with water, mud] éclabousser **2.** [pour carelessly] répandre **3.** [daub] barbouiller **4.** PRESS étaler. ◆ vi **1.** [rain, liquid] faire des éclaboussures **2.** [walk, run, etc.] patauger, barboter. ◆ n **1.** [noise] floc *m*, plouf *m* **2.** [of mud, paint] éclaboussure *f* ; [of colour, light] tache *f* **3.** [small quantity - of whisky] goutte *f* **4.** *inf & fig* [sensation] sensation *f* ▸ **to make a splash** faire sensation. ◆ adv ▸ **to go / to fall splash into the water** entrer / tomber dans l'eau en faisant plouf. ❖ **splash about** [UK], **splash around** ◆ vi [duck, swimmer] barboter. ◆ vt sep [liquid] faire des éclaboussures de ; [money] dépenser sans compter. ❖ **splash down** vi [spaceship] amerrir. ❖ **splash out** *inf* ◆ vi [spend] faire des folies ▸ **to splash out on sthg** se payer qqch. ◆ vt insep [money] claquer.

splashdown ['splæʃdaʊn] n [of spaceship] amerrissage *m*.

splashguard ['splæʃgɑːd] n [US] garde-boue *m inv*.

splashy ['splæʃɪ] adj [US] *inf* tape-à-l'œil.

splat [splæt] ◆ n floc *m*. ◆ adv ▸ **to go splat** faire floc.

splatter ['splætər] ◆ vt éclabousser / *splattered with mud / blood* éclaboussé de boue / sang. ◆ vi [rain] crépiter ; [mud] éclabousser. ◆ n **1.** [mark - of mud, ink] éclaboussure *f* **2.** [sound - of rain] crépitement *m*.

splay [spleɪ] ◆ vt [fingers, legs] écarter ; [feet] tourner en dehors. ◆ vi [fingers, legs] s'écarter ; [feet] se tourner en dehors.

spleen [spliːn] n **1.** ANAT rate *f* **2.** [bad temper] humeur *f* noire, mauvaise humeur *f* ▸ **to vent one's spleen on sthg / sb** décharger sa bile sur qqch / qqn.

splendid ['splendɪd] ◆ adj **1.** [beautiful, imposing - dress, setting, decor] splendide, superbe, magnifique **2.** [very good - idea, meal] excellent, magnifique ; [- work] excellent, superbe. ◆ interj excellent !, parfait !

splendidly ['splendɪdlɪ] adv **1.** [dress, decorate, furnish] magnifiquement, superbement ; [entertain] somptueusement **2.** [perform] superbement.

splendour [UK], **splendor** [US] ['splendər] n splendeur *f*.

splice [splaɪs] ◆ vt **1.** [join] ▸ **to splice (together)** a) [film, tape] coller b) [rope] épisser c) [pieces of wood] enter **2.** [UK] *inf & hum* [marry] ▸ **to get spliced** convoler (en justes noces). ◆ n [in tape, film] collure *f* ; [in rope] épissure *f* ; [in wood] enture *f*.

spliff [splɪf] n *drugs sl* joint *m*.

splint [splɪnt] ◆ n MED éclisse *f*, attelle *f* / *her arm was in a splint* or *in splints* elle avait le bras dans une attelle. ◆ vt éclisser, mettre dans une attelle.

splinter ['splɪntər] ◆ n [of glass, wood] éclat *m* ; [of bone] esquille *f* ; [in foot, finger] écharde *f*. ◆ vt [glass, bone] briser en éclats ; [wood] fendre en éclats. ◆ vi [glass, bone] se briser en éclats ; [marble, wood] se fendre en éclats ; [political party] se scinder, se fractionner.

splinter group n groupe *m* dissident or scissionniste.

split [splɪt] (*pt & pp* **split**, *cont* **splitting**) ◆ vt **1.** [cleave - stone] fendre, casser ; [- slate] cliver ; [- wood] fendre ▸ **to split sthg in two** or **in half** casser or fendre qqch en deux ▸ **to split sthg open** ouvrir qqch (*en le coupant en deux ou en le fendant*) ▸ **to split the atom** PHYS fissionner l'atome **2.** [tear] déchirer **3.** [divide - family] diviser ; [POL - party] diviser, créer or provoquer une scission dans / *we were split into two groups* on nous a divisés en deux groupes **4.** [share - profits] (se) partager, (se) répartir ; [- bill] (se) partager ; [FIN - stocks] faire une redistribution de / *to split the profits four ways* diviser les bénéfices en quatre **5.** GRAM ▸ **to split an infinitive** intercaler un adverbe ou une expression adverbiale entre « to » et le verbe **6.** [US] *v inf* [leave] quitter. ◆ vi **1.** [break - wood, slate] se fendre, éclater / *the ship split in two* le navire s'est brisé (en deux) **2.** [tear - fabric] se déchirer ; [- seam] craquer / *the bag split open* le sac s'est déchiré **3.** [divide - gen] se diviser, se fractionner ; [- political party] se scinder ; [- cell] se diviser ; [- road, railway] se diviser, bifurquer / *the hikers split into three groups* les randonneurs se sont divisés en trois groupes **4.** [separate - couple] se séparer ; [- family, group] s'éparpiller, se disperser **5.** *v inf* [leave] se casser, mettre les bouts. ◆ n **1.** [crack - in wood, rock] fissure *f* **2.** [tear] déchirure *f* **3.** [division] division *f* ; [separation] séparation *f* ; [quarrel] rupture *f* ; POL scission *f*, schisme *m* ; RELIG schisme *m* ; [gap] fossé *m*, écart *m* **4.** [share] part *f* **5.** [US] [bottle] ▸ **soda split** petite bouteille de soda. ◆ adj [lip, skirt] fendu. ❖ **splits** pl n ▸ **to do the splits** [UK], **to do splits** [US] faire le grand écart. ⬦ **split off** ◆ vi **1.** [branch, splinter] se détacher **2.** [separate - person, group] se séparer. ◆ vt sep **1.** [break, cut - branch, piece] enlever (en fendant) **2.** [person, group] séparer. ⬦ **split on** vt insep ⚲ *inf* [inform on] vendre, moucharder. ⬦ **split up** ◆ vi **1.** [wood, marble] se fendre ; [ship] se briser **2.** [couple] se séparer, rompre ; [friends] rompre, se brouiller ; [meeting, members] se disperser ; POL se diviser, se scinder ▶ **to split up with sb** rompre avec qqn. ◆ vt sep **1.** [wood] fendre ; [cake] couper en morceaux **2.** [divide - profits] partager ; [- work] répartir **3.** [disperse] disperser / *the teacher split the boys up* le professeur a séparé les garçons.

split end n fourche *f*.

split-level adj [house, flat] à deux niveaux ▶ **split-level cooker** cuisinière *f* à éléments de cuisson séparés.

split pea n pois *m* cassé.

split personality n double personnalité *f*, dédoublement *m* de la personnalité.

split screen n CIN écran *m* divisé.

split second n : *in a split second* en une fraction de seconde. ⬦ **split-second** adj [timing, reaction] au quart de seconde.

splitting ['splɪtɪŋ] ◆ n **1.** [of wood, marble] fendage *m* ▶ **the splitting of the atom** PHYS la fission de l'atome **2.** [of fabric, seams] déchirure *f* **3.** [division] division *f* **4.** [sharing] partage *m*. ◆ adj : *I have a splitting headache* j'ai un mal de tête atroce.

splodge ['splɒdʒ] *inf* ◆ n **1.** [splash - of paint, ink] éclaboussure *f*, tache *f* ; [- of colour] tache *f* **2.** [dollop - of cream, of jam] bonne cuillerée *f*. ◆ vt éclabousser, barbouiller. ◆ vi s'étaler, faire des pâtés.

splurge [splɜ:dʒ] *inf* ◆ n **1.** [spending spree] folie *f*, folles dépenses *fpl* **2.** [display] fla-fla *m*, tralala *m*. ◆ vt [spend] dépenser ; [waste] dissiper. ⬦ **splurge out** vi faire une folie or des folies ▶ **to splurge out on sthg** se payer qqch.

splutter ['splʌtər] ◆ vi **1.** [spit - speaker] postillonner ; [- flames, fat] crépiter, grésiller ; [- pen, ink] cracher **2.** [stutter - speaker] bredouiller ; [- engine] tousser, avoir des ratés. ◆ vt [protest, apology, thanks] bredouiller, balbutier. ◆ n **1.** [spitting - in speech] crachotement *m* ; [- of fat, flames] crépitement *m*, grésillement *m* **2.** [stutter - in speech] bredouillement *m*, balbutiement *m* ; [- of engine] toussotement *m*.

spoil [spɔɪl] (*pt & pp* spoilt [spɔɪlt] *or* spoiled) ◆ vt **1.** [make less attractive or enjoyable] gâter, gâcher **2.** [damage] abîmer, endommager **3.** [pamper] gâter / *she's spoilt rotten* *inf* elle est super gâtée, c'est une enfant pourrie ▶ **to spoil o.s.** s'offrir une petite folie **4.** POL [ballot paper] rendre nul. ◆ vi [fruit, food] se gâter, s'abîmer ; [in store, hold of ship] s'avarier, devenir avarié. ◆ n (U) **1.** = spoils **2.** [earth, diggings] déblai *m*, déblais *mpl*. ⬦ **spoils** pl n **1.** [loot] butin *m*, dépouilles *fpl* ; [profit] bénéfices *mpl*, profits *mpl* ; [prize] prix *m* / *the spoils of war* les dépouilles de la guerre **2.** ⚲ POL assiette *f* au beurre. ⬦ **spoil for** vt insep ▶ **to be spoiling for a fight / an argument** chercher la bagarre / la dispute.

spoiled [spɔɪld] = spoilt.

spoiler ['spɔɪlər] n **1.** AUTO becquet *m* **2.** AERON aérofrein *m* **3.** PRESS *tactique utilisée pour s'approprier le scoop d'un journal rival.*

spoiler campaign n *campagne lancée par une entreprise pour minimiser l'impact d'une campagne publicitaire menée par une société concurrente.*

spoilsport ['spɔɪlspɔ:t] n trouble-fête *mf*, rabat-joie *m inv*, empêcheur *m*, -euse *f* de tourner en rond.

spoilt [spɔɪlt] ◆ *pt & pp* ⟶ spoil. ◆ adj **1.** [child] gâté ; [behaviour] d'enfant gâté ▶ **to be spoilt for choice** :

we were spoilt for choice nous n'avions que l'embarras du choix **2.** [harvest] abîmé ; [food, dinner] gâché, gâté **3.** POL [ballot paper] nul.

spoke [spəʊk] ◆ *pt* ⟶ speak. ◆ n [in wheel] rayon *m* ; [in ladder] barreau *m*, échelon *m* ; [on ship's wheel] manette *f*.

spoken ['spəʊkn] ◆ *pp* ⟶ speak. ◆ adj [dialogue] parlé, oral ▶ **the spoken word** la langue parlée, la parole ▶ **spoken language** oral *m*.

spokesman ['spəʊksmən] (*pl* spokesmen [-mən]) n porte-parole *m inv*.

spokesperson ['spəʊks,pɜ:sn] n porte-parole *m inv*.

spokeswoman ['spəʊks,wʊmən] (*pl* spokeswomen [-,wɪmɪn]) n porte-parole *m inv* (femme).

spondulicks, spondulix [spɒn'dju:lɪks] pl n *inf* fric *m*, pognon *m*, flouze *m*.

sponge [spʌndʒ] ◆ n **1.** ZOOL [in sea] éponge *f* **2.** [for cleaning, washing] éponge *f* / *I gave the table a sponge* j'ai passé un coup d'éponge sur la table ▶ **to throw in the sponge** jeter l'éponge **3.** *inf & pej* [scrounger] parasite *m* **4.** ⚲ [cake] gâteau *m* de Savoie ▶ **jam / cream sponge** gâteau de Savoie fourré à la confiture / à la crème. ◆ vt **1.** [wipe - table, window] donner un coup d'éponge sur ; [- body] éponger **2.** [soak up] éponger **3.** *inf* [cadge - food, money] taper / *I sponged £20 off or from him* je l'ai tapé de 20 livres. ◆ vi *inf* [cadge] ▶ **to sponge on or from sb** vivre aux crochets de qqn / *she's always sponging* c'est un vrai parasite. ⬦ **sponge down** vt sep éponger, laver à l'éponge.

sponge bag n ⚲ trousse *f* or sac *m* de toilette.

sponge bath n toilette *f* à l'éponge.

sponge cake n gâteau *m* de Savoie.

sponge pudding n *dessert chaud fait avec une pâte de gâteau de Savoie.*

sponger ['spʌndʒər] n *inf & pej* parasite *m*.

spongy ['spʌndʒɪ] (*compar* spongier, *superl* spongiest) adj spongieux.

sponsor ['spɒnsər] ◆ n **1.** COMM & SPORT [of sportsman, team, tournament] sponsor *m* ; [of film, TV programme] sponsor *m*, commanditaire *m* ; [of artist, musician] commanditaire *m*, mécène *m* ; [of student, studies] parrain *m* ; [for charity] donateur *m*, -trice *f* ▶ **to act as sponsor for sb** sponsoriser qqn **2.** [of would-be club member] parrain *m*, marraine *f* ; [guarantor - for loan] répondant *m*, -e *f*, garant *m*, -e *f* ; [backer - for business] parrain *m*, bailleur *m* de fonds **3.** ⚲ [of godchild] parrain *m*, marraine *f*. ◆ vt **1.** COMM & SPORT sponsoriser ; RADIO & TV [programme] sponsoriser, parrainer ; [concert, exhibition] parrainer, commanditer ; [studies, student] parrainer **2.** [for charity] : *I sponsored him to swim 10 miles* je me suis engagé à lui donner de l'argent (pour des œuvres charitables) s'il parcourait 10 milles à la nage **3.** [appeal, proposal] présenter ; [would-be club member] parrainer ; [loan, borrower] se porter garant de ; [firm] patronner ▶ **to sponsor a bill** POL présenter un projet de loi **4.** [godchild] être le parrain / la marraine de.

sponsored walk ['spɒnsəd-] n *marche parrainée.*

⚑ Sponsored walk

Les **sponsored walks** sont destinés à rassembler des fonds, chaque marcheur établissant une liste des personnes ayant accepté de donner une certaine somme d'argent par kilomètre parcouru. On utilise ce principe pour d'autres activités sportives : **sponsored swim, sponsored parachute jump,** etc.

sponsorship ['spɒnsəʃɪp] n **1.** COMM & SPORT sponsoring *m* **2.** [of appeal, proposal] présentation *f*; POL [of bill] proposition *f*, présentation *f*; [of would-be club member, godchild] parrainage *m*; [of loan, borrower] cautionnement *m*.

sponsorship deal n contrat *m* de sponsoring.

spontaneity [,spɒntə'neɪətɪ] n spontanéité *f*.

spontaneous [spɒn'teɪnjəs] adj spontané.

spontaneously [spɒn'teɪnjəslɪ] adv spontanément.

spoof [spu:f] inf ◆ n **1.** [mockery] satire *f*, parodie *f* **2.** [trick] blague *f*, canular *m*. ◆ adj prétendu, fait par plaisanterie. ◆ vt [book, style] parodier; [person] faire marcher.

spook [spu:k] inf ◆ n **1.** [ghost] fantôme *m* **2.** US [spy] barbouze *mf* **3.** US offens terme raciste désignant un Noir; ≈ négro. ◆ vt US **1.** [frighten] faire peur à, effrayer **2.** [haunt] hanter.

spooky ['spu:kɪ] (compar **spookier,** superl **spookiest**) adj inf **1.** [atmosphere] qui donne la chair de poule, qui fait froid dans le dos **2.** US [skittish] peureux **3.** [odd] bizarre.

spool [spu:l] ◆ n [of film, tape, thread] bobine *f*; [for fishing] tambour *m*; [of wire] rouleau *m*; SEW & TEXT cannette *f*. ◆ vt [gen] bobiner; COMPUT spouler.

spoon [spu:n] ◆ n **1.** [utensil] cuiller *f*, cuillère *f* **2.** [quantity] cuillerée *f* **3.** FISHING cuiller *f*, cuillère *f* **4.** [in golf] spoon *m*. ◆ vt [food - serve] servir; [- transfer] verser. ◆> **spoon up** vt sep [eat] manger avec une cuiller; [clear up] ramasser avec une cuiller.

spoon-feed vt **1.** lit [child, sick person] nourrir à la cuiller **2.** fig ▶ **to spoon-feed sb** mâcher le travail à qqn.

spoonful ['spu:nfʊl] n cuillerée *f*.

sporadic [spə'rædɪk] adj sporadique.

sporadically [spə'rædɪklɪ] adv sporadiquement.

sport [spɔ:t] ◆ n **1.** [physical exercise] sport *m* / *she does a lot of sport* elle fait beaucoup de sport, elle est très sportive / *I hated sport* or *sports at school* je détestais le sport or les sports à l'école ▶ **the sport of kings** [horse racing] un sport de rois **2.** liter [hunting] chasse *f*; [fishing] pêche *f* **3.** liter [fun] amusement *m*, divertissement *m* ▶ **to say sthg in sport** dire qqch pour rire or en plaisantant ▶ **to make sport of sb / sthg** se moquer de qqn / qqch, tourner qqn / qqch en ridicule **4.** inf [friendly person] chic type *m*, chic fille *f* / *go on, be a sport!* allez, sois sympa ! **5.** [good loser] ▶ **to be a (good) sport** être beau joueur **6.** BIOL variété *f* anormale. ◆ vt [wear] porter, arborer. ◆ vi liter batifoler, s'ébattre. ◆> **sports** ◆ pl n [athletics meeting] meeting *m* d'athlétisme. ◆ comp [equipment, programme, reporter] sportif; [fan] de sport.

sporting ['spɔ:tɪŋ] adj **1.** SPORT [fixtures, interests] sportif **2.** [friendly, generous - behaviour] chic (inv) **3.** [fairly good - chance] assez bon.

sports car n voiture *f* de sport.

sportscast ['spɔ:tskɑ:st] n US émission *f* sportive.

sports day n UK SCH réunion sportive annuelle où les parents sont invités.

sports jacket n veste *f* sport.

sportsman ['spɔ:tsmən] (pl **sportsmen** [-mən]) n **1.** [player of sport] sportif *m* **2.** [person who plays fair] : *he's a real sportsman* il est très sport or beau joueur.

sportsmanlike ['spɔ:tsmənlaɪk] adj sportif.

sportsmanship ['spɔ:tsmənʃɪp] n sportivité *f*, sens *m* sportif.

sports pages ['spɔ:ts-] pl n pages *fpl* des sports.

sportsperson ['spɔ:ts,pɜ:sn] (pl **sportspeople** [-,pi:pl]) n sportif *m*, sportive *f*.

sportswear ['spɔ:tsweə*r*] n (U) vêtements *mpl* de sport.

sportswoman ['spɔ:ts,wʊmən] (pl **sportswomen** [-,wɪmɪn]) n sportive *f*.

sport-utility vehicle n US 4 x 4 *m*.

sporty ['spɔ:tɪ] (compar **sportier,** superl **sportiest**) adj [person] sportif; [garment] de sport.

spot [spɒt] (pt & pp **spotted,** cont **spotting**) ◆ n **1.** [dot - on material, clothes] pois *m*; [- on leopard, giraffe] tache *f*, moucheture *f*; [- on dice, playing card] point *m* **2.** [stain, unwanted mark] tache *f*; [on fruit] tache *f*, tavelure *f*; [splash] éclaboussure *f* **3.** UK [pimple] bouton *m*; [freckle] tache *f* de son or de rousseur ▶ **to come out in spots** avoir une éruption de boutons ▶ **to suffer from spots** souffrir d'acné **4.** [blemish - on character] tache *f*, souillure *f* **5.** [small amount - of liquid] goutte *f*; [- of salt] pincée *f*; [- of irony, humour] pointe *f*, soupçon *m* **6.** [place] endroit *m*, coin *m*; [site] site *m*; [on body] endroit *m*, point *m* / *a tender* or *sore spot* un point sensible **7.** [aspect, feature, moment] : *the only bright spot of the week* le seul bon moment de la semaine **8.** [position, job] poste *m*, position *f* **9.** inf [difficult situation] embarras *m* ▶ **to be in a spot** être dans l'embarras ▶ **to put sb on the spot** prendre qqn au dépourvu, coincer qqn **10.** RADIO & TV [for artist, interviewee] numéro *m*; [news item] brève *f* ▶ **advertising spot** message *m* or spot *m* publicitaire **11.** [spotlight] spot *m*, projecteur *m* **12.** [in billiards] mouche *f*. ◆ comp **1.** COMM [price] comptant; [transaction, goods] payé comptant **2.** [random - count, test] fait à l'improviste **3.** TV ▶ **spot advertisement** spot *m* publicitaire ▶ **spot announcement** flash *m*. ◆ vt **1.** [notice - friend, object] repérer, apercevoir; [- talent, mistake] trouver, déceler **2.** [stain] tacher; [mark with spots] tacheter **3.** US [opponent] accorder un avantage à **4.** US [remove - stain] enlever / *a chemical for spotting clothes* un produit pour détacher les vêtements. ◆ vi **1.** [garment, carpet] se tacher, se salir **2.** MIL servir d'observateur. ◆> **on the spot** adv phr [at once] sur-le-champ; [at the scene] sur les lieux, sur place / *the man on the spot* a) [employee, diplomat] l'homme qui est sur place or sur le terrain b) [journalist] l'envoyé spécial ▶ **to run on the spot** courir sur place. ◆> **on-the-spot** adj phr [fine] immédiat; [report] sur place or sur le terrain.

spot buying n achats *mpl* au comptant.

spot check n [investigation] contrôle *m* surprise; [for quality] sondage *m*; [by customs] fouille *f* au hasard. ◆> **spot-check** vt contrôler au hasard; [for quality] sonder.

spotless ['spɒtlɪs] adj [room, appearance] impeccable; [character] sans tache.

spotlessly ['spɒtlɪslɪ] adv ▶ **spotlessly clean** reluisant de propreté, d'une propreté impeccable.

spotlight ['spɒtlaɪt] (pt & pp **spotlit** [-lɪt]) ◆ n **1.** [in theatre] spot *m*, projecteur *m* ▶ **in the spotlight** lit & fig sous le feu or la lumière des projecteurs ▶ **to turn the spotlight on sb** a) lit braquer les projecteurs sur qqn b) fig mettre qqn en vedette **2.** [lamp - in home, on car] spot *m*. ◆ vt **1.** THEAT diriger les projecteurs sur **2.** fig [personality, talent] mettre en vedette; [pinpoint - flaws, changes] mettre en lumière, mettre le doigt sur.

spotlit [-lɪt] adj éclairé par des projecteurs.

spot-on inf ◆ adj UK **1.** [correct - remark, guess] en plein dans le mille; [- measurement] pile, très précis **2.** [perfect] parfait. ◆ adv [guess] en plein dans le mille.

spotted ['spɒtɪd] ◆ pt & pp → **spot.** ◆ adj **1.** [leopard, bird] tacheté, moucheté; [apple, pear] tavelé **2.** [tie, dress] à pois **3.** [stained - carpet, wall] taché.

spotting ['spɒtɪŋ] n **1.** : *train / plane spotting* repérage *m* de trains / d'avions **2.** MED petites pertes de sang en dehors des règles.

spotty ['spɒtɪ] (*compar* **spottier**, *superl* **spottiest**) adj **1.** [covered with spots -wallpaper] piqué or tacheté d'humidité ; [-mirror] piqueté, piqué ; [stained] taché ; 🇬🇧 [skin, person] boutonneux **2.** [patterned -fabric, tie] à pois **3.** 🇺🇸 [patchy] irrégulier.

spouse [spaʊs] n *fml* époux *m*, épouse *f* ; ADMIN & LAW conjoint *m*, -e *f*.

spout [spaʊt] ◆ n **1.** [of teapot, kettle, tap, watering can] bec *m* ; [of carton] bec *m* verseur ; [of pump, gutter] dégorgeoir *m* ; [of pipe] embout *m* **2.** [of water -from fountain, geyser] jet *m* ; [-from whale] jet *m*, souffle *m* d'eau ; [of flame] colonne *f* ; [of lava] jet *m* **3.** 🇬🇧 PHR **to be up the spout a)** *inf* [ruined] être fichu or foutu **b)** [pregnant] être enceinte. ◆ vi **1.** [water, oil] jaillir, sortir en jet ; [whale] souffler **2.** *inf & pej* [talk] dégoiser. ◆ vt **1.** [water, oil] faire jaillir un jet de ; [fire, smoke] vomir, émettre un jet de **2.** *inf & pej* [words, poetry] débiter, sortir.

sprain [spreɪn] ◆ vt [joint] fouler, faire une entorse à ; [muscle] étirer / *she has sprained her ankle* or *has a sprained ankle* elle s'est fait une entorse à la cheville or s'est foulé la cheville. ◆ n entorse *f*, foulure *f*.

sprang [spræŋ] pt ⟶ **spring**.

sprat [spræt] n sprat *m*.

sprawl [sprɔːl] ◆ vi **1.** [be sitting, lying] être affalé or vautré ; [sit down, lie down] s'affaler, se laisser tomber **2.** [spread] s'étaler, s'étendre. ◆ vt *(usu passive)* : *she was sprawled in the armchair / on the pavement* elle était vautrée dans le fauteuil / étendue de tout son long sur le trottoir. ◆ n **1.** [position] position *f* affalée **2.** [of city] étendue *f* / *the problem of urban sprawl* le problème de l'expansion urbaine.

sprawling ['sprɔːlɪŋ] adj [body] affalé ; [suburbs, metropolis] tentaculaire ; [handwriting] informe.

spray [spreɪ] ◆ vt **1.** [treat -crops, garden] faire des pulvérisations sur, traiter ; [-field] pulvériser ; [-hair, house plant] vaporiser ; [sprinkle -road] asperger **2.** [apply -water, perfume] vaporiser ; [-paint, insecticide] pulvériser ; [-coat of paint, fixer] mettre, appliquer ; [-graffiti, slogan] écrire, tracer (à la bombe). ◆ vi **1.** [liquid] jaillir **2.** [against crop disease] pulvériser, faire des pulvérisations. ◆ n **1.** [droplets] gouttelettes *fpl* fines ; [from sea] embruns *mpl* **2.** [container -for aerosol] bombe *f*, aérosol *m* ; [-for perfume] atomiseur *m* ; [-for cleaning fluids, water, lotion] vaporisateur *m* **3.** [act of spraying -of crops] pulvérisation *f* ; [-against infestation] traitement *m* (par pulvérisation) ; [-of aerosol product] coup *m* de bombe **4.** *fig* [of bullets] grêle *f* **5.** [cut branch] branche *f* **6.** [bouquet] (petit) bouquet *m* **7.** [brooch] aigrette *f*. ◆ comp [insecticide, deodorant] en aérosol. ❖ **spray on** ◆ vt sep appliquer (à la bombe). ◆ vi [paint, polish, cleaner] s'appliquer (par pulvérisation).

spray can n [for aerosol] bombe *f*, aérosol *m* ; [refillable] vaporisateur *m*.

spray-on adj en bombe, en aérosol.

spray paint n peinture *f* en bombe / *a can of spray paint* une bombe de peinture. ❖ **spray-paint** vt [with can] peindre à la bombe ; [with spray gun] peindre au pistolet.

spread [spred] (*pt & pp* **spread**) ◆ vt **1.** [apply -jam, icing, plaster, glue] étaler ; [-asphalt] répandre ; [-manure] épandre / *he spread butter on a slice of toast* or *a slice of toast with butter* il a tartiné de beurre une tranche de pain grillé **2.** [open out, unfold -wings, sails] étendre, déployer ; [-arms, legs, fingers] écarter ; [-map, napkin, blanket] étaler ; [-rug] étendre ; [-fan] ouvrir **3.** [lay out, arrange -photos, cards, possessions] étaler **3.** [disseminate -disease, fire] propager, répandre ; [-news, idea, faith] propager ; [-rumour] répandre, faire courir ; [-terror, panic] répandre / *to spread the gospel* prêcher or répandre l'Évangile **5.** [scatter -over

an area] répandre ; [-over a period of time] échelonner, étaler / *the floor was spread with straw* le sol était recouvert de paille / *the explosion had spread debris over a large area* l'explosion avait dispersé des débris sur une grande superficie **6.** [divide up -tax burden, work load] répartir **7.** MUS [chord] arpéger. ◆ vi **1.** [stain] s'élargir ; [disease, suburb] s'étendre ; [fire, desert, flood] gagner du terrain, s'étendre ; [rumour, ideas, faith, terror, crime, suspicion] se répandre / *panic spread through the crowd* la panique a envahi or gagné la foule / *the epidemic is spreading to other regions* l'épidémie gagne de nouvelles régions / *the cancer had spread through her whole body* le cancer s'était généralisé **2.** [extend -over a period of time, a range of subjects] s'étendre **3.** [butter, glue] s'étaler. ◆ n **1.** [diffusion, growth -of epidemic, fire] propagation *f*, progression *f* ; [-of technology, idea] diffusion *f*, dissémination *f* ; [-of religion] propagation *f* **2.** [range -of ages, interests] gamme *f*, éventail *m* **3.** [wingspan] envergure *f* **4.** [period] période *f* **5.** [expanse] étendue *f* **6.** CULIN [paste] pâte *f* à tartiner ; [jam] confiture *f* ▶ **salmon spread** beurre *m* de saumon ▶ **chocolate spread** chocolat *m* à tartiner **7.** PRESS & TYPO [two pages] double page *f* ; [advertisement] double page *f* publicitaire **8.** *inf* [meal] festin *m* **9.** 🇺🇸 *inf* [farm] ferme *f* ; [ranch] ranch *m* **10.** ST. EX spread *m* **11.** 🇺🇸 [bedspread] couvre-lit *m*. ◆ adj **1.** [arms, fingers, legs] écarté **2.** LING [vowel] non arrondi. ❖ **spread out** ◆ vi **1.** [town, forest] s'étendre **2.** [disperse] se disperser ; [in formation] se déployer **3.** [open out -sail] se déployer, se gonfler **4.** [make o.s. at ease] s'installer confortablement. ◆ vt sep **1.** *(usu passive)* [disperse] disperser, éparpiller **2.** = **spread** *(vt)*.

spread-eagled [-,iːgld] adj bras et jambes écartés.

spreadsheet ['spredʃiːt] n tableur *m*.

spree [spriː] n fête *f* ▶ **to go** or **to be on a spree** faire la fête ▶ **to go on a shopping spree** faire des folies dans les magasins.

sprig [sprɪg] n brin *m*.

sprightly ['spraɪtlɪ] (*compar* **sprightlier**, *superl* **sprightliest**) adj [person] alerte, guilleret ; [step] vif ; [tune, whistle] gai.

spring [sprɪŋ] (*pt* **sprang** [spræŋ] *or* **sprung** [sprʌŋ], *pp* **sprung**) ◆ n **1.** [season] printemps *m* / *in (the) spring* au printemps **2.** [device, coil] ressort *m* ▶ **the springs** AUTO la suspension **3.** [natural source] source *f* **4.** [leap] bond *m*, saut *m* **5.** [resilience] élasticité *f*. ◆ comp **1.** [flowers, weather, colours] printanier, de printemps ▶ **spring term** SCH & UNIV ≃ dernier trimestre *m* **2.** [mattress] à ressorts ▶ **spring binding** reliure *f* à ressort **3.** [water] de source. ◆ vi **1.** [leap] bondir, sauter ▶ **to spring at** bondir or se jeter sur / *springing out of the armchair* bondissant du fauteuil / *I sprang to my feet* je me suis lèvé d'un bond **2.** [be released] : *to spring shut / open* se fermer / s'ouvrir brusquement / *the branch sprang back* la branche s'est redressée d'un coup **3.** *fig* : *the police sprang into action* les forces de l'ordre passèrent rapidement à l'action / *the engine sprang to* or *into life* le moteur s'est mis soudain en marche or a brusquement démarré / *she sprang to my defence* elle a vivement pris ma défense / *to spring to the rescue* se précipiter pour porter secours / *tears sprang to his eyes* les larmes lui sont montées or venues aux yeux / *just say the first thing which springs to mind* dites simplement la première chose qui vous vient à l'esprit / *where did you spring from?* *inf* d'où est-ce que tu sors ? **4.** [originate] venir, provenir **5.** [plank -warp] gauchir, se gondoler ; [-crack] se fendre **6.** 🇺🇸 *inf* ▶ **to spring for sthg** casquer pour qqch. ◆ vt **1.** [trap] déclencher ; [mine] faire sauter ; [bolt] fermer **2.** [make known -decision, news] annoncer de but en blanc or à brûle-pourpoint ▶ **to spring a question on sb** poser une question à qqn de but en blanc **3.** [develop]

▸ **to spring a leak a)** [boat] commencer à prendre l'eau
b) [tank, pipe] commencer à fuir **4.** [jump over - hedge,
brook] sauter **5.** [plank - warp] gauchir, gondoler ; [- crack]
fendre **6.** HUNT [game] lever **7.** *inf* [prisoner] faire sortir.
❖ **spring up** vi **1.** [get up] se lever d'un bond **2.** [move
upwards] bondir, rebondir **3.** [grow in size, height] pousser
4. [appear - towns, factories] surgir, pousser comme des
champignons ; [- doubt, suspicion, rumour, friendship] naître ;
[- difficulty, threat] surgir ; [- breeze] se lever brusquement.

springboard ['sprɪŋbɔːd] n SPORT & *fig* tremplin *m*.

spring chicken n **1.** 🇺🇸 poulet *m* (à rôtir) **2.** [young
person] : *he's no spring chicken* il n'est plus tout jeune.

spring-clean ❖ vi faire un nettoyage de printemps.
❖ vt nettoyer de fond en comble. ❖ n 🇬🇧 nettoyage *m*
de printemps ▸ **to give the house a spring-clean** nettoyer
la maison de fond en comble.

spring-cleaning n nettoyage *m* de printemps.

spring onion n petit oignon *m* blanc.

spring roll n rouleau *m* de printemps.

spring tide n grande marée *f*; [at equinox] marée *f*
d'équinoxe (de printemps).

springtime ['sprɪŋtaɪm] n printemps *m*.

springy ['sprɪŋɪ] (*compar* springier, *superl* springi-
est) adj [mattress, diving board] élastique ; [step] souple,
élastique ; [floor] souple ; [moss, carpet] moelleux ; [hair] dru.

sprinkle ['sprɪŋkl] ❖ vt **1.** [salt, sugar, spices, breadcrumbs, talc] saupoudrer ; [parsley, raisins] parsemer / *I
sprinkled sugar on* or *over my cereal, I sprinkled my
cereal with sugar* j'ai saupoudré mes céréales de sucre ;
[liquid] : *to sprinkle water on sthg* or *sthg with water*
asperger qqch d'eau **2.** *(usu passive)* [strew, dot] parsemer,
semer. ❖ vi [rain] tomber des gouttes. ❖ n **1.** [rain] petite
pluie *f* **2.** = sprinkling.

sprinkler ['sprɪŋklər] n **1.** AGR & HORT arroseur *m*
(automatique) ▸ **sprinkler truck** arroseuse *f* **2.** [fire-
extinguishing device] sprinkler *m* ▸ **sprinkler system** installation *f* d'extinction automatique d'incendie **3.** [for holy
water] goupillon *m*, aspersoir *m*.

sprinkling ['sprɪŋklɪŋ] n [small quantity] petite quantité *f*; [pinch] pincée *f*.

sprint [sprɪnt] ❖ n SPORT [dash] sprint *m*; [race] course *f*
de vitesse, sprint *m* / *the 60 metre sprint* le 60 mètres ▸ **to
break into** or **to put on a sprint** [gen] piquer un sprint.
❖ vi sprinter.

sprinter ['sprɪntər] n sprinter *m*. ❖ **Sprinter** n 🇬🇧
TRANSP train de banlieue express.

sprite [spraɪt] n MYTH [male] lutin *m*; [female] nymphe *f*
▸ **water sprite** MYTH naïade *f*.

spritzer ['sprɪtsər] n mélange de vin blanc et de soda.

sprocket ['sprɒkɪt] n [wheel] pignon *m*.

sprout [spraʊt] ❖ n **1.** [on plant, from ground]
pousse *f*; [from bean, potato] germe *m* **2.** ▸ **(Brussels)
sprouts** choux *mpl* de Bruxelles. ❖ vi **1.** [germinate - bean,
seed, onion] germer **2.** [grow - leaves, hair] pousser **3.** [ap-
pear] apparaître, surgir. ❖ vt **1.** [grow - leaves] pousser,
produire ; [- beard] faire pousser **2.** [germinate - seeds, beans,
lentils] faire germer. ❖ **sprout up** vi **1.** [grow - grass,
wheat, plant] pousser, pointer ; [- person] pousser **2.** [appear
- towns, factories] pousser comme des champignons, surgir.

spruce [spruːs] ❖ n (*pl* spruce) **1.** BOT épicéa *m*; [tim-
ber] épinette *f*. ❖ adj [person, car, building, town] pimpant ;
[haircut] net ; [garment] impeccable. ❖ **spruce up** vt sep
[car, building, town] donner un coup de neuf à ; [paint-
work] refaire ; [child] faire beau ▸ **to spruce o.s. up, to get
spruced up** se faire beau.

sprung [sprʌŋ] ❖ pt & pp ⟶ **spring.** ❖ adj [mat-
tress] à ressorts.

spry [spraɪ] (*compar* sprier or spryer, *superl* spriest
or spryest) adj [person] alerte, leste.

SPUC [spʌk] (abbr of **Society for the Protection of
Unborn Children**) pr n ligue contre l'avortement.

spud [spʌd] n **1.** *inf* [potato] patate *f* **2.** [gardening tool]
sarcloir *m*.

spun [spʌn] ❖ pt & pp ⟶ **spin.** ❖ adj filé.

spunk [spʌŋk] n **1.** *inf* [pluck] cran *m*, nerf *m* **2.** 🇬🇧 *vulg*
[semen] foutre *m*.

spur [spɜːr] ❖ (*pt & pp* spurred, *cont* spurring) ❖ n
1. EQUIT éperon *m* **2.** *fig* [stimulation] aiguillon *m* ▸ **on the
spur of the moment** sur le coup, sans réfléchir **3.** GEOG
[ridge] éperon *m*, saillie *f* **4.** RAIL [siding] voie *f* latérale or
de garage ; [branch line] embranchement *m* **5.** [on motor-
way] bretelle *f* **6.** [breakwater] brise-lames *m inv*, digue *f*
7. BOT & ZOOL éperon *m*; [on gamecock] ergot *m*. ❖ vt
1. [horse] éperonner **2.** *fig* inciter / *her words spurred me
into action* ses paroles m'ont incité à agir. ❖ **spur on**
vt sep **1.** [horse] éperonner **2.** *fig* éperonner, aiguillonner
▸ **to spur sb on to do sthg** inciter or pousser qqn à faire
qqch.

spurious ['spʊərɪəs] adj **1.** [false - gen] faux (fausse) ;
[- comparison, argument, reason, objection] spécieux **2.** [pre-
tended - enthusiasm, sympathy] simulé ; [- flattery, compli-
ment] hypocrite **3.** [of doubtful origin - text] apocryphe,
inauthentique.

spurn [spɜːn] vt [gen] dédaigner, mépriser ; [suitor] éconduire, rejeter.

spurt [spɜːt] ❖ vi **1.** [water, blood] jaillir, gicler ; [flames,
steam] jaillir **2.** [dash - runner, cyclist] sprinter, piquer un
sprint. ❖ vt [gush - subj: pierced container] laisser jaillir ;
[spit - subj: gun, chimney] cracher. ❖ n **1.** [of steam, water,
flame] jaillissement *m*; [of blood, juice] giclée *f* **2.** [dash] accélération *f*; [at work] coup *m* de collier ; [revival] regain *m*.
❖ **spurt out** vi = spurt *(vi)*.

sputter ['spʌtər] ❖ vi **1.** [motor] toussoter, crachoter ; [fire, candle] crépiter **2.** [stutter] bredouiller, bafouiller
3. [spit - gen] crachoter ; [- when talking] postillonner. ❖ vt
[apology, curses] bredouiller, bafouiller. ❖ n **1.** [of motor]
toussotement *m*, hoquet *m*; [of fire, candle] crépitement *m*
2. [stuttering] bredouillement *m*. ❖ **sputter out** vi [can-
dle, enthusiasm, anger] s'éteindre.

spy [spaɪ] (*pl* spies, *pt & pp* spied) ❖ n espion *m*,
-onne *f*. ❖ comp [novel, film, scandal] d'espionnage ; [net-
work] d'espions ▸ **spy ring** réseau *m* d'espions ▸ **spy satellite** satellite *m* espion. ❖ vi [engage in espionage] faire
de l'espionnage. ❖ vt *liter* [notice] apercevoir ; [make out]
discerner. ❖ **spy on** vt insep espionner. ❖ **spy out**
vt sep [sb's methods, designs] chercher à découvrir (subrepticement) ; [landing sites] repérer.

spying ['spaɪɪŋ] n [gen & INDUST] espionnage *m*.

spyware [spaɪweər] n logiciels *mpl* espions / *a piece of
spyware* un logiciel espion.

sq., Sq. written abbr of **square.**

sq. ft. (written abbr of **square foot/feet**) pied(s)
carré(s).

squabble ['skwɒbl] ❖ vi se disputer, se quereller. ❖ n
dispute *f*, querelle *f*.

squad [skwɒd] n **1.** [group - gen] équipe *f*, escouade *f*
2. MIL escouade *f*, section *f* **3.** [of police detachment] brigade *f*.

squad car n 🇺🇸 voiture *f* de patrouille de police.

squadron ['skwɒdrən] n [in air force] escadron *m* ; [in navy -small] escadrille *f* ; [-large] escadre *f* ; [in armoured regiment, cavalry] escadron *m*.

squadron leader n [in air force] commandant *m*.

squalid ['skwɒlɪd] adj sordide.

squall [skwɔːl] ◆ n **1.** [METEOR -storm] bourrasque *f*, rafale *f* ; NAUT grain *m* ; [rain shower] grain *m* **2.** [argument] dispute *f* **3.** [bawling] braillement *m*. ◆ vi **1.** [bawl] brailler **2.** NAUT : *it was squalling* on a pris un grain. ◆ vt : *"no!",* *he squalled* « non ! », brailla-t-il.

squalor ['skwɒlər] n *(U)* [degrading conditions] conditions *fpl* sordides ; [filth] saleté *f* repoussante ▶ **to live in squalor** vivre dans des conditions sordides or dans une misère noire.

squander ['skwɒndər] vt [resources, time, money] gaspiller ; [inheritance] dissiper ; [opportunity] gâcher, passer à côté de.

square [skweər] ◆ n **1.** [shape -gen & GEOM] carré *m* **2.** [square object -gen] carré *m* ; [-tile] carreau *m* **3.** [square space -in matrix, crossword, board game] case *f* **4.** [open area -with streets] place *f* ; [-with gardens] square *m* ; MIL [parade ground] place *f* d'armes ▶ **the town square** la place, la grand-place **5.** MATH [multiple] carré *m*, -e *f*. ◆ [instrument] équerre *f* **7.** *inf & pej* [person] ringard *m*, -e *f*. ◆ adj **1.** [in shape -field, box, building, face] carré **2.** [mile, inch, etc.] carré / *10 square kilometres* 10 kilomètres carrés / *the room is 15 feet square* la pièce fait 5 mètres sur 5 **3.** [at right angles] à angle droit **4.** [fair, honest] honnête ▶ **to give sb a square deal** agir correctement avec qqn **5.** [frank, blunt -person] franc (franche) ; [-denial] clair, net, catégorique **6.** [even, equal] : *we're all square* [in money] nous sommes quittes / *they were* (all) *square at two games each* SPORT ils étaient à égalité deux parties chacun **7.** *inf* [old-fashioned] vieux jeu. ◆ adv **1.** = **squarely 2.** [at right angles] : *she set the box square with* or *to the edge of the paper* elle a aligné la boîte sur les bords de la feuille de papier **3.** [directly] : *he hit the ball square in the middle of the racket* il frappa la balle avec le milieu de sa raquette / *she looked him square in the face* elle le regarda bien en face. ◆ vt **1.** [make square -pile of paper] mettre droit, aligner ; [-stone] carrer ; [-log] équarrir ; [-shoulders] redresser **2.** MATH carrer, élever au carré **3.** [reconcile] concilier **4.** [settle -account, bill] régler ; [-debt] acquitter ; [-books] balancer, mettre en ordre **5.** SPORT : *his goal squared the match* son but a mis les équipes à égalité **6.** *inf* [arrange] arranger / *can you square it with the committee?* pourriez-vous arranger cela avec le comité ? **7.** *inf* [bribe] soudoyer. ◆ vi cadrer, coïncider / *his story doesn't square with the facts* son histoire ne cadre or ne coïncide pas avec les faits. ◆ **square away** vt sep *(usu passive)* 🇺🇸 *inf* régler, mettre en ordre. ◆ **square off** ◆ vi [opponents, boxers] se mettre en garde. ◆ vt sep **1.** [piece of paper, terrain] quadriller **2.** [stick, log] carrer, équarrir. ◆ **square up** vi **1.** [settle debt] faire les comptes ▶ **to square up with sb** faire ses comptes avec qqn *lit* **2.** = **square off**. ◆ **square up to** vt insep [confront -situation, criticism] faire face or front à ; [-in physical fight] se mettre en position de combat contre.

square bracket n PRINT crochet *m* / *in square brackets* entre crochets.

squared [skweəd] adj [paper] quadrillé.

square dance n quadrille *m* américain.

squarely ['skweəlɪ] adv **1.** [firmly] fermement, carrément ; [directly] en plein / *squarely opposed to* fermement opposé à ▶ **to look sb squarely in the eye** regarder qqn droit dans les yeux **2.** [honestly] honnêtement ▶ **to deal squarely with sb** agir avec qqn de façon honnête.

square meal n : *I haven't had a square meal in days* ça fait plusieurs jours que je n'ai pas fait de vrai repas.

Square Mile pr n ▶ **the Square Mile** la City de Londres, dont la superficie fait environ un mile carré.

square root n racine *f* carrée.

squash [skwɒʃ] ◆ vt **1.** [crush] écraser / *I was squashed between two large ladies* j'étais serré or coincé entre deux grosses dames **2.** [cram, stuff] fourrer **3.** [silence, repress -person] remettre à sa place ; [-objection] écarter ; [-suggestion] repousser ; [-argument] réfuter ; [-hopes] réduire à néant ; [-rumour] mettre fin à ; [-rebellion] réprimer. ◆ vi **1.** [push -people] s'entasser **2.** [fruit, package] s'écraser. ◆ n **1.** [crush of people] cohue *f* / *with five of us it'll be a bit of a squash* à cinq, nous serons un peu serrés **2.** SPORT squash *m* **3.** 🇬🇧 [drink] ▶ **lemon / orange squash** sirop *m* de citron / d'orange **4.** 🇺🇸 [vegetable] courge *f*. ◆ comp [ball, court, champion, racket] de squash ▶ **squash rackets** 🇬🇧 [game] squash *m*. ◆ **squash in** vi [people] s'entasser / *I squashed in between two very fat men* je me suis fait une petite place entre deux hommes énormes. ◆ **squash together** ◆ vi [people] se serrer (les uns contre les autres), s'entasser. ◆ vt sep serrer, tasser.

squat [skwɒt] *(pt & pp* squatted, *cont* squatting, *compar* squatter, *superl* squattest) ◆ vi **1.** [crouch -person] s'accroupir ; [-animal] se tapir **2.** [live] vivre dans un squat. ◆ vt [building] squatter, squattériser. ◆ n **1.** [building] squat *m* ; [action] squat *m*, occupation *f* de logements vides **2.** [crouch] accroupissement *m* **3.** 🇺🇸 *v inf* [nothing] que dalle. ◆ adj [person, figure, building] trapu.

squatter ['skwɒtər] n squatter *m* ; 🇦🇺 [rancher] squatter *m*, éleveur *m*.

squawk [skwɔːk] ◆ vi **1.** [bird] criailler ; [person] brailler **2.** *inf* [complain] criailler, râler **3.** *inf* [inform] moucharder, vendre la mèche. ◆ vt : *"let go of me!",* she squawked « lâchez-moi ! », brailla-t-elle. ◆ n **1.** [of bird] criaillement *m*, cri *m* ; [of person] cri *m* rauque ▶ **to let out** or **to give a squawk** pousser un cri rauque.

squeak [skwiːk] ◆ vi **1.** [floorboard, chalk, wheel] grincer ; [animal] piauler, piailler ; [person] glapir **2.** *inf* [succeed narrowly] : *the team squeaked into the finals* l'équipe s'est qualifiée de justesse pour la finale. ◆ vt : *"who, me?",* he squeaked « qui ? moi ? », glapit-il. ◆ n [of floorboard, hinge, chalk, etc.] grincement *m* ; [of animal] piaillement *m* ; [of person] petit cri *m* aigu, glapissement *m* ; [of soft toy] couinement *m*. ◆ **squeak by, squeak through** vi *inf* **1.** [pass through] se faufiler **2.** [succeed narrowly] réussir de justesse ; [in exam] être reçu de justesse ; [in election] l'emporter de justesse. ◆ **squeak in** vi passer de justesse.

squeaky ['skwiːkɪ] *(compar* squeakier, *superl* squeakiest) adj [floorboard, bed, hinge] grinçant ; [voice] aigu (aiguë).

squeaky clean adj *inf* **1.** [hands, hair] extrêmement propre **2.** [reputation] sans tache.

squeal [skwiːl] ◆ vi **1.** [person] pousser un cri perçant ; [tyres, brakes] crisser ; [pig] couiner ▶ **to squeal with pain** pousser un cri de douleur ▶ **to squeal with laughter** hurler de rire **2.** *v inf* [inform] moucharder ▶ **to squeal on sb** balancer qqn. ◆ vt : *"ouch!",* she squealed « aïe ! », cria-t-elle. ◆ n [of person] cri *m* perçant ; [of tyres, brakes] crissement *m*.

squeamish ['skwiːmɪʃ] adj hypersensible.

squeeze [skwiːz] ◆ vt **1.** [press -tube, sponge, pimple] presser ; [-trigger] presser sur, appuyer sur ; [-package] palper ; [-hand, shoulder] serrer **2.** [extract, press out -liquid] exprimer ; [-paste, glue] faire sortir / *a glass of freshly squeezed orange juice* une orange pressée **3.** *fig* [money, information] soutirer **4.** [cram, force] faire entrer (avec difficulté) / *20 men were squeezed into one small cell*

20 hommes étaient entassés dans une petite cellule / *the airport is squeezed between the sea and the mountains* l'aéroport est coincé entre la mer et les montagnes **5.** [constrain - profits, budget] réduire ; [- taxpayer, workers] pressurer **6.** [in bridge] squeezer. ◆ vi : *the lorry managed to squeeze between the posts* le camion a réussi à passer de justesse entre les poteaux / *they all squeezed onto the bus* ils se sont tous entassés dans le bus / *can you squeeze into that parking space?* y a-t-il assez de place pour te garer là ? ◆ n **1.** [amount - of liquid, paste] quelques gouttes *fpl* / *a squeeze of toothpaste* un peu de dentifrice **2.** [crush of people] cohue *f* / *it was a tight squeeze* a) [in vehicle, room] on était très serré b) [through opening] on est passé de justesse **3.** [pressure, grip] pression *f* ; [handshake] poignée *f* de main ; [hug] étreinte *f* **4.** *inf* [difficult situation] situation *f* difficile **5.** ECON ▸ **(credit) squeeze** resserrement *m* du crédit **6.** [in bridge] squeeze *m* **7.** US *inf* [friend] copain *m*, copine *f*. ❖ **squeeze in** ◆ vi [get in] se faire une petite place. ◆ vt sep [in schedule] réussir à faire entrer / *she's hoping to squeeze in a trip to Rome too* elle espère avoir aussi le temps de faire un saut à Rome / *the dentist says he can squeeze you in* le dentiste dit qu'il peut vous prendre entre deux rendez-vous. ❖ **squeeze out** vt sep **1.** [sponge, wet clothes] essorer **2.** [liquid] exprimer ; TECH [plastic] extruder **3.** [replace - candidate, competitor] l'emporter sur / *the Japanese are squeezing them out of the market* ils sont en train de se faire évincer du marché par les Japonais. ❖ **squeeze past** vi se faufiler. ❖ **squeeze through** vi se faufiler. ❖ **squeeze up** vi se serrer, se pousser.

squeezebox ['skwi:zbɒks] n *inf* [accordion] accordéon *m*, piano *m* à bretelles ; [concertina] concertina *m*.

squeezer ['skwi:zə˟] n CULIN presse-agrumes *m inv*.

squelch [skweltʃ] ◆ vi **1.** [walk - in wet terrain] patauger ; [- with wet shoes] marcher les pieds trempés **2.** [make noise - mud] clapoter. ◆ vt [crush] écraser. ◆ n [noise] clapotement.

squib [skwɪb] n **1.** [firecracker] pétard *m* **2.** [piece of satire] pamphlet *m*.

squid [skwɪd] (*pl* squid *or* squids) n cal(a)mar *m*, encornet *m*.

squidgy ['skwɪdʒɪ] (*compar* squidgier, *superl* squidgiest) adj UK *inf* mou (*before vowel or silent 'h'* mol, *f* molle), spongieux.

squiffy ['skwɪfɪ] (*compar* squiffier, *superl* squiffiest) adj UK *inf & dated* éméché, pompette.

squiggle ['skwɪgl] n **1.** [scrawl, doodle] gribouillis *m* **2.** [wavy line, mark] ligne *f* ondulée.

squiggly ['skwɪglɪ] adj *inf* pas droit, ondulé.

squint [skwɪnt] ◆ n **1.** MED strabisme *m* ▸ **to have a squint** loucher **2.** *inf* [glimpse] coup *m* d'œil. ◆ vi **1.** MED loucher **2.** [half-close one's eyes] plisser les yeux.

squire ['skwaɪə˟] n **1.** [landowner] propriétaire *m* terrien / *Squire Greaves* le squire Greaves **2.** [for knight] écuyer *m* **3.** *dated* [escort] cavalier *m* **4.** UK *inf* [term of address] : *evening, squire!* bonsoir, chef !

squirm [skwɜ:m] ◆ vi **1.** [wriggle] se tortiller **2.** [be ill-at-ease] être gêné, être très mal à l'aise ; [be ashamed] avoir honte / *to squirm with embarrassment* être mort de honte. ◆ n : *she gave a squirm of embarrassment* elle ne put cacher sa gêne.

squirrel [UK 'skwɪrəl US 'skwɜ:rəl] (UK *pt & pp* squirrelled, *cont* squirrelling ; US *pt & pp* squirreled, *cont* squirreling) n **1.** ZOOL écureuil *m* **2.** *fig* [hoarder] : *she's a real squirrel* c'est une vraie fourmi **3.** US *inf* [bizarre person] énergumène *m*. ❖ **squirrel away** vt sep [hoard, store] engranger *fig* ; [hide] cacher.

squirt [skwɜ:t] ◆ vt [liquid] faire gicler ; [mustard, ketchup, washing-up liquid] faire jaillir. ◆ vi [juice, blood, ink] gicler ; [water] jaillir. ◆ n **1.** [of juice, ink] giclée *f* ; [of water] jet *m* ; [of mustard, ketchup, washing-up liquid] dose *f* ; [of oil, perfume] quelques gouttes *fpl* **2.** *inf & pej* [person] minus *m* ; [short person] avorton *m* ; [child] mioche *mf*.

squishy ['skwɪʃɪ] (*compar* squishier, *superl* squishiest) adj *inf* [fruit, wax] mou (*before vowel or silent 'h'* mol, *f* molle) ; [chocolate] ramolli ; [ground] boueux.

Sr 1. (written abbr of **senior**) : *Ralph Todd Sr* Ralph Todd père **2.** written abbr of **sister**.

SRC n (abbr of **students' representative council**) UK comité étudiant.

Sri Lanka [ˌsri:'læŋkə] pr n Sri Lanka *m* / *in Sri Lanka* au Sri Lanka.

Sri Lankan [ˌsri:'læŋkn] ◆ n Sri Lankais *m*, -e *f*. ◆ adj sri lankais.

SRN n abbr of **State Registered Nurse**.

Sry (written abbr of **sorry**) MESSAGING dsl.

SS ◆ (abbr of **steamship**) *initiales précédant le nom des navires de la marine marchande* ▸ **the SS "Norfolk"** le « Norfolk ». ◆ pr n (abbr of **Schutzstaffel**) ▸ **the SS** les SS.

SSA pr n US abbr of **Social Security Administration**.

ssh [ʃ] interj ▸ **ssh!** chut !

SSN n abbr of **social security number**.

SSSI (abbr of **Site of Special Scientific Interest**) n en Grande-Bretagne, site déclaré d'intérêt scientifique.

St 1. (written abbr of **saint**) St, Ste **2.** written abbr of **street**.

ST n abbr of **Standard Time**.

stab [stæb] (*pt & pp* stabbed, *cont* stabbing) ◆ vt **1.** [injure - with knife] donner un coup de couteau à, poignarder ; [- with bayonet] blesser d'un coup de baïonnette ; [- with spear] blesser avec une lance / *he stabbed me in the arm* il me donna un coup de couteau dans le bras / *they were stabbed to death* ils ont été tués à coups de couteau **2.** [thrust, jab] planter / *I stabbed myself in the thumb with a pin* je me suis enfoncé une épingle dans le pouce / *I stabbed my finger in his eye* je lui ai enfoncé mon doigt dans l'œil / *I stabbed a turnip with my fork* j'ai piqué un navet avec ma fourchette. ◆ vi : *he stabbed at the map with his finger* il frappa la carte du doigt / *he stabbed at the leaves with his walking stick* il piquait les feuilles de la pointe de sa canne. ◆ n **1.** [thrust] coup *m* (de couteau or de poignard) ▸ **stab wound** blessure *f* par arme blanche **2.** [of pain] élancement *m* **3.** *inf* [try] ▸ **to have** or **to make** or **to take a stab at (doing) sthg** s'essayer à (faire) qqch.

stabbing ['stæbɪŋ] ◆ n [knife attack] agression *f* (à l'arme blanche). ◆ adj [pain] lancinant.

stability [stə'bɪlətɪ] n stabilité *f*.

stabilize, stabilise ['steɪbəlaɪz] ◆ vt stabiliser. ◆ vi se stabiliser.

stabilizer, stabiliser ['steɪbəlaɪzə˟] n **1.** AERON, AUTO & ELEC [device] stabilisateur *m* ; NAUT stabilisateur *m* ; [on bicycle] stabilisateur *m* **2.** CHEM [in food] stabilisateur *m*, stabilisant *m*.

stable ['steɪbl] ◆ adj **1.** [steady, permanent - gen] stable ; [- marriage] solide **2.** [person, personality] stable, équilibré **3.** CHEM & PHYS stable. ◆ n **1.** [building] écurie *f* ▸ **riding stable** or **stables** centre *m* d'équitation **2.** [group - of racehorses, racing drivers, etc.] écurie *f*. ◆ vt [take to stable] mettre à l'écurie / *her horse is stabled at Dixon's* son cheval est en pension chez Dixon.

stable boy n valet *m* d'écurie, lad *m*.

stable lad n 1. = **stable boy** 2. [in racing stable] lad m.

staccato [stə'kɑːtəʊ] ◆ adj 1. MUS [note] piqué ; [passage] joué en staccato 2. [noise, rhythm] saccadé. ◆ adv MUS staccato.

stack [stæk] ◆ n 1. [pile] tas m, pile f 2. inf [large quantity] tas m 3. AGR [of hay, straw] meule f 4. [chimney] cheminée f 5. AERON avions mpl en attente, empilage m 6. COMPUT [file] pile f 7. MIL [of rifles] faisceau m 8. [in library] ▶ the stack or stacks les rayons mpl 9. PHR to blow one's stack US inf exploser, piquer une crise. ◆ vt 1. [pile - chairs, boxes, etc.] empiler 2. AGR [hay] mettre en meule or meules 3. [fill - room, shelf] remplir 4. COMPUT empiler 5. AERON [planes] mettre en attente (à altitudes échelonnées) 6. [fix, rig - committee] remplir de ses partisans ; [- cards, odds, etc.] ▶ to stack the cards or the deck truquer les cartes. ◆ vi s'empiler. ◆ stacks adv US inf vachement. ◆ stack up ◆ vt sep [pile up] empiler. ◆ vi 1. US inf [add up, work out] : I don't like the way things are stacking up je n'aime pas la tournure que prennent les événements 2. [compare] se comparer / how does he stack up against or with the other candidates? que vaut-il comparé aux autres candidats ?

stackable ['stækəbl] adj empilable.

stadium ['steɪdjəm] (pl stadiums or stadia [-djə]) n stade m.

staff [stɑːf] (pl staffs [stɑːvz]) ◆ n 1. [work force] personnel m ; [teachers] professeurs mpl, personnel m enseignant / is he staff or a member of staff? est-ce qu'il fait partie du personnel ? / staff / student ratio taux m d'encadrement des étudiants 2. MIL & POL état-major m 3. (pl staffs or staves) [rod] bâton m ; [flagpole] mât m ; [for shepherd] houlette f ; [for bishop] crosse f, bâton m pastoral ; UK [in surveying & TECH] jalon m ; fig [support] soutien m 4. (pl staffs or staves) MUS portée f. ◆ comp [canteen, outing, etc.] du personnel. ◆ vt (usu passive) pourvoir en personnel.

staffer ['stɑːfər] n 1. PRESS rédacteur m, -trice f, membre m de la rédaction 2. US [staff member] membre m du personnel.

staffing ['stɑːfɪŋ] n [recruiting] recrutement m ▶ staffing levels effectifs mpl.

staff nurse n infirmier m, -ère f.

staffroom ['stɑːfrʊm] n SCH salle f des enseignants or des professeurs.

Staffs written abbr of Staffordshire.

stag [stæg] (pl stag or stags) n ZOOL cerf m.

stage [steɪdʒ] ◆ n 1. [period, phase - of development, project, etc.] stade m ; [- of illness] stade m, phase f / we'll deal with that at a later stage nous nous en occuperons plus tard / the conflict is still in its early stages le conflit n'en est encore qu'à ses débuts ▶ by or in stages par paliers 2. [stopping place, part of journey] étape f 3. THEAT [place] scène f ▶ the stage [profession, activity] le théâtre ▶ on stage sur scène ▶ stage right / left côté jardin / cour ▶ to go on stage monter sur (la) scène ▶ to go on the stage [as career] monter sur les planches, faire du théâtre ▶ to write for the stage écrire pour la scène ; fig ▶ to set the stage for sthg préparer le terrain pour qqch 4. ASTRONAUT étage m 5. [platform - gen] plate-forme f ; [- on microscope] platine f ; [scaffolding] échafaudage m 6. [stagecoach] diligence f 7. ELECTRON [circuit part] étage m. ◆ comp [design] scénique ; [version] pour le théâtre / she has great stage presence elle a énormément de présence sur scène. ◆ vt 1. THEAT [put on - play] monter ; [set] situer 2. [organize - ceremony, festival] organiser ; [carry out - robbery] organi-

niser / to stage a hijacking détourner un avion / to stage a diversion créer une or faire diversion 3. [fake - accident] monter, manigancer.

⚠ The French word **stage** means a training course, not a stage.

stagecoach ['steɪdʒkəʊtʃ] n diligence f.

stage designer n décorateur m de théâtre.

stage direction n indication f scénique.

stage door n entrée f des artistes.

stage fright n trac m.

stagehand ['steɪdʒhænd] n THEAT machiniste mf.

stage-manage vt 1. THEAT [play, production] s'occuper de la régie de 2. [press conference, appearance] orchestrer, mettre en scène.

stage manager n THEAT régisseur m.

stage name n nom m de scène.

stage set n THEAT décor m.

stagflation [stæg'fleɪʃn] n stagflation f.

stagger ['stægər] ◆ vi [totter - person, horse] chanceler, tituber. ◆ vt 1. (usu passive) [payments] échelonner ; [holidays] étaler ▶ staggered start SPORT [on oval track] départ m décalé ▶ staggered wings AERON ailes fpl décalées 2. (usu passive) [astound] ▶ to be staggered être atterré, être stupéfait / I was staggered to learn of his decision j'ai été stupéfait d'apprendre sa décision. ◆ n [totter] pas m chancelant.

staggering ['stægərɪŋ] ◆ adj [news, amount] stupéfiant, ahurissant ; [problems] énorme / it was a staggering blow lit & fig ce fut un sacré coup. ◆ n 1. [of vacations] étalement m ; [of payments] échelonnement m 2. [unsteady gait] démarche f chancelante.

staging ['steɪdʒɪŋ] ◆ n 1. THEAT [of play] mise f en scène 2. [scaffolding] échafaudage m ; [shelving] rayonnage f 3. ASTRONAUT largage m (d'un étage de fusée). ◆ comp MIL ▶ staging area or point lieu m de rassemblement.

stagnant ['stægnənt] adj 1. [water, pond - still] stagnant ; [- stale] croupissant ; [air - still] confiné ; [- stale] qui sent le renfermé 2. [trade, career] stagnant ; [society] statique, en stagnation.

stagnate [stæg'neɪt] vi 1. [water - be still] stagner ; [- be stale] croupir 2. [economy, career] stagner ; [person] croupir.

stagnation [stæg'neɪʃn] n stagnation f.

stag night, stag party n [gen] soirée f entre hommes ; [before wedding day] : we're having or holding a stag night for Bob nous enterrons la vie de garçon de Bob.

staid [steɪd] adj [person] rangé, collet monté (inv) pej ; [colours] sobre, discret (discrète) ; [job] très ordinaire.

stain [steɪn] ◆ n 1. [mark, spot] tache f ▶ to leave a stain laisser une tache / I couldn't get the stain out je n'ai pas réussi à enlever or faire disparaître la tache 2. fig [on character] tache f / it was a stain on his reputation cela a entaché sa réputation 3. [colour, dye] teinte f, teinture f ▶ a wood stain une teinture pour bois ▶ oak / mahogany stain teinte chêne / acajou. ◆ vt 1. [soil, mark] tacher / the sink was stained with rust l'évier était taché de rouille 2. [honour, reputation] tacher, entacher, ternir 3. [colour, dye - wood] teindre ; [- glass, cell specimen] colorer. ◆ vi 1. [mark - wine, oil, etc.] tacher 2. [become marked - cloth] se tacher.

stained [steɪnd] adj 1. [soiled - collar, sheet] taché ; [- teeth] jauni 2. [coloured - gen] coloré ; [- wood] teint.

-stained in comp taché / his sweat-stained shirt sa chemise tachée de transpiration.

stained glass n vitrail *m*. ❖ **stained-glass** adj ❱ **stained-glass window** vitrail *m*.

stainless steel ❖ n acier *m* inoxydable, Inox® *m*. ❖ comp en acier inoxydable, en Inox®.

stain remover n détachant *m*.

stair [steər] n **1.** [step] marche *f* **/** *the bottom stair* la première marche **2.** *liter* [staircase] escalier *m*. ❖ **stairs** pl n [stairway] escalier *m*, escaliers *mpl* **/** *I slipped on the stairs* j'ai glissé dans l'escalier ❱ **at the top of the stairs** en haut de l'escalier ❱ **at the bottom** or **the foot of the stairs** en bas or au pied de l'escalier ❱ **above / below stairs** 🔒 chez les patrons / les domestiques.

staircase ['steəkeɪs] n escalier *m*.

stairway ['steəweɪ] = **staircase.**

stairwell ['steəwel] n cage *f* d'escalier.

stake [steɪk] ❖ n **1.** [post, pole] pieu *m* ; [for plant] tuteur *m* ; [in surveying] piquet *m*, jalon *m* ; [for tent] piquet *m* ; [for execution] poteau *m* ❱ **to die** or **to be burned at the stake** mourir sur le bûcher **2.** [in gambling] enjeu *m*, mise *f* ❱ **to play for high stakes** jouer gros jeu **3.** [interest, share] intérêt *m*, part *f* ; [investment] investissement *m*, investissements *mpl* ; [shareholding] participation *f* **4.** 🇺🇸 [savings] (petit) pécule *m*, bas *m* de laine. ❖ vt **1.** [bet - sum of money, valuables] jouer, miser ; *fig* [reputation] jouer, risquer **/** *I'd stake my all* or *my life on it* j'en mettrais ma main au feu **2.** 🇺🇸 [aid financially] financer **3.** [fasten - boat, animal] attacher (à) un pieu or un piquet ; [- tent] attacher avec des piquets ; [- plant] tuteurer **4.** [put forward] ❱ **to stake a** or **one's claim to sthg** revendiquer qqch **5.** 🔤 **to be at stake** être en jeu. ❖ **stakes** pl n [horse race] course *f* de chevaux ; [money prize] prix *m*. ❖ **stake off** vt sep = **stake out.** ❖ **stake out** vt sep **1.** [delimit - area, piece of land] délimiter (avec des piquets) ; [- boundary, line] marquer, jalonner ; [- sphere of influence] définir ; [- market] se tailler ; [- job, research field] s'approprier **2.** 🇺🇸 [keep watch on] mettre sous surveillance, surveiller.

stakeholder ['steɪk,həʊldər] n partie *f* prenante ❱ **a stakeholder society** une société citoyenne.

stakeholder pension n épargne-retraite par capitalisation.

stakeout ['steɪkaʊt] n 🇺🇸 [activity] surveillance *f* ; [place] locaux *mpl* sous surveillance.

stalactite ['stæləktaɪt] n stalactite *f*.

stalagmite ['stæləgmaɪt] n stalagmite *f*.

stale [steɪl] adj **1.** [bread, cake] rassis, sec (sèche) ; [chocolate, cigarette] vieux *(before vowel or silent 'h' vieil, f vieille)* ; [cheese - hard] desséché ; [- mouldy] moisi ; [fizzy drink] éventé, plat ; [air - foul] vicié ; [- confined] confiné **/** *stale breath* haleine *f* fétide ❱ **to go stale a)** [bread] (se) rassir **b)** [chocolate, cigarette] perdre son goût **c)** [cheese] se dessécher **d)** [beer] s'éventer **2.** [idea, plot, joke] éculé, rebattu ; [discovery, news] éventé, dépassé ; [pleasure] émoussé, qui n'a plus de goût ; [beauty] fané, défraîchi.

stalemate ['steɪlmeɪt] ❖ n **1.** [in chess] pat *m* **/** *the game ended in stalemate* la partie s'est terminée par un pat **2.** [deadlock] impasse *f* **/** *the argument ended in (a) stalemate* la discussion s'est terminée dans une impasse. ❖ vt *(usu passive)* [in chess - opponent] faire pat à **/** *the negotiations were stalemated* *fig* les négociations étaient dans l'impasse.

staleness ['steɪlnɪs] n [of food, air] manque *m* de fraîcheur ; [of information, joke, etc.] manque *m* de nouveauté.

stalk [stɔːk] ❖ n **1.** BOT [of flower, plant] tige *f* ; [of cabbage, cauliflower] trognon *m* **2.** ZOOL pédoncule *m* **3.** [gen - long object] tige *f*. ❖ vt **1.** [game, fugitive, etc.] traquer **2.** [subj: wolf, ghost] rôder dans **3.** *liter* [subj: disease, terror] régner dans, rôder dans. ❖ vi **1.** [person] : *she stalked out angrily / in disgust* elle sortit d'un air furieux / dégoûté **/** *he was stalking up and down the deck* il arpentait le pont **2.** [prowl - tiger, animal] rôder ; [hunt] chasser.

stalker ['stɔːkər] n [criminal] criminel suivant sa victime à la trace.

stall [stɔːl] ❖ n **1.** [at market] étal *m*, éventaire *m* ; [at fair, exhibition] stand *m* **/** *I bought some peaches at a fruit stall* j'ai acheté des pêches chez un marchand de fruits **/** *flower stall* 🔒 [on street] kiosque *m* de fleuriste **2.** [for animal] stalle *f* ❱ **(starting) stalls** ÉQUIT stalles de départ **3.** [cubicle] cabine *f* **4.** [in church] stalle *f* **5.** 🔒 CIN & THEAT orchestre *m*, fauteuil *m* d'orchestre ❱ **the stalls** l'orchestre **6.** 🇺🇸 [in parking lot] emplacement *m* *(de parking)*. ❖ vi **1.** [motor, vehicle, driver] caler ; [plane] décrocher ; [pilot] faire décrocher son avion **2.** [delay] ❱ **to stall for time** essayer de gagner du temps. ❖ vt **1.** [motor, vehicle] caler ; [plane] faire décrocher **2.** [delay - sale, decision] retarder ; [- person] faire attendre **3.** [animal] mettre à l'étable.

stallholder ['stɔːl,həʊldər] n [in market] marchand *m*, -e *f* de or des quatre-saisons ; [in fair] forain *m*, -e *f* ; [in exhibition] exposant *m*, -e *f*.

stalling ['stɔːlɪŋ] ❖ n *(U)* atermoiements *mpl*, manœuvres *fpl* dilatoires. ❖ adj ❱ **stalling tactic** manœuvre *f* dilatoire.

stallion ['stæljən] n étalon *m* *(cheval)*.

stalwart ['stɔːlwət] ❖ adj [person] robuste ; [citizen, fighter] vaillant, brave ; [work, worker] exemplaire. ❖ n fidèle *mf*.

stamen ['steɪmən] *(pl stamens or stamina* ['stæmɪnə]*)* n BOT étamine *f*.

stamina ['stæmɪnə] n [physical] résistance *f*, endurance *f* ; [mental] force *f* intérieure, résistance *f*.

stammer ['stæmər] ❖ vi [through fear, excitement] balbutier, bégayer ; [through speech defect] bégayer, être bègue. ❖ vt bredouiller, bégayer. ❖ n [through fear, excitement] balbutiement *m*, bégaiement *m* ; [through speech defect] bégaiement *m* ❱ **to have a stammer** bégayer, être bègue.

stammering ['stæmərɪŋ] n [through fear, excitement] bégaiement *m*, balbutiement *m* ; [speech defect] bégaiement *m*.

stamp [stæmp] ❖ n **1.** [sticker, token] timbre *m* ; *television (licence) stamp* timbre pour la redevance ❱ **(national insurance) stamp** 🔒 cotisation *f* de sécurité sociale ❱ **(postage) stamp** timbre, timbre-poste *m* **2.** [instrument - rubber stamp] tampon *m*, timbre *m* ; [- for metal] poinçon *m* ; [- for leather] fer *m* **3.** [mark, impression - in passport, library book, etc.] cachet *m*, tampon *m* ; [- on metal] poinçon *m* ; [- on leather] motif *m* ; [- on antique] estampille *f* ; [postmark] cachet *m* (d'oblitération de la poste) **/** *he has an Israeli stamp in his passport* il y a un tampon de la douane israélienne sur son passeport ❱ **stamp of approval** *fig* approbation *f*, aval *m* **4.** [distinctive trait] marque *f*, empreinte *f* **/** *his story had the stamp of authenticity* son histoire semblait authentique **/** *poverty has left its stamp on him* la pauvreté a laissé son empreinte sur lui or l'a marqué de son sceau **5.** [type, ilk, class] genre *m*, acabit *m* *pej* ; [calibre] trempe *f* **6.** [noise - of boots] bruit *m* (de bottes) ; [- of audience] trépignement *m*. ❖ comp [album, collection, machine] de timbres, de timbres-poste. ❖ vt **1.** [envelope, letter] timbrer, affranchir **2.** [mark - document] tamponner ; [- leather, metal] estamper **/** *incoming mail is stamped with the date received* le courrier qui arrive est tamponné à la date de réception **/** *the machine stamps the time on your ticket* la machine marque or poinçonne l'heure sur votre ticket **3.** [affect, mark - society, person] marquer **/** *as editor she stamped her personality on the magazine* comme rédactrice en chef, elle a marqué la revue du sceau de sa personnalité **4.** [characterise, brand] étiqueter **5.** [foot] : *she stamped her foot in anger* furieuse, elle tapa du pied **/** *the audience were stamping their feet and booing* la salle trépignait et sifflait **/** *he stamped the snow off his boots* il a tapé du pied pour enlever la neige de ses bottes. ◆ vi **1.** [in one place - person] taper du pied ; [-audience] trépigner ; [-horse] piaffer **/** *I stamped on his fingers* je lui ai marché sur les doigts **2.** [walk] ▶ **to stamp in** / **out a)** [noisily] entrer / sortir bruyamment **b)** [angrily] entrer / sortir en colère **/** *he stamped up the stairs* il monta l'escalier d'un pas lourd. ◆ **stamp down** vt sep [loose earth, snow] tasser avec les pieds ; [peg] enfoncer du pied. ◆ **stamp on** vt insep [rebellion] écraser ; [dissent, protest] étouffer ; [proposal] repousser. ◆ **stamp out** vt sep **1.** [fire] éteindre avec les pieds or en piétinant **2.** [end - disease, crime] éradiquer ; [-strike, movement] supprimer ; [-dissent, protest] étouffer ; [-corruption, ideas] extirper **3.** [hole] découper (à l'emporte-pièce) ; [medal] frapper ; [pattern] estamper.

stamp collecting n philatélie f.

stamp collector n collectionneur m, -euse f de timbres or de timbres-poste, philatéliste mf.

stamp duty n 🇬🇧 droit m de timbre.

stamped [stæmpt] adj [letter, envelope] timbré **/** *send a stamped addressed envelope* envoyez une enveloppe timbrée à votre adresse.

stampede [stæm'piːd] ◆ n **1.** [of animals] fuite f, débandade f **2.** [of people - flight] sauve-qui-peut m inv, débandade f ; [-rush] ruée f. ◆ vi [flee] s'enfuir (pris d'affolement) ; [rush] se ruer, se précipiter. ◆ vt **1.** [animals] faire fuir ; [crowd] semer la panique dans **2.** [pressurize] forcer la main à.

stamping ground ['stæmpɪŋ-] n inf lieu m favori.

stance [stæns] n **1.** [physical posture] posture f **2.** [attitude] position f ▶ **to adopt** or **to take a tough stance on sthg** adopter or prendre une position ferme sur qqch.

stand [stænd] (pt & pp stood [stʊd])
◆ vi

A. IN SPACE **1.** [rise to one's feet] se lever, se mettre debout **2.** [be on one's feet] être or se tenir debout **/** *I've been standing all day* je suis resté debout toute la journée **/** *I had to stand all the way* j'ai dû voyager debout pendant tout le trajet ; [in a specified location] être (debout), rester (debout) **/** *don't stand near the edge* ne restez pas près du bord **/** *don't just stand there, do something!* ne restez pas là à ne rien faire ! **/** *stand clear!* écartez-vous ! **/** *they were standing a little way off* ils se tenaient un peu à l'écart **/** *excuse me, you're standing on my foot* excusez-moi, vous me marchez sur le pied ; [in a specified posture] se tenir **/** *I stood perfectly still, hoping they wouldn't see me* je me suis figé sur place en espérant qu'ils ne me verraient pas **/** *stand still!* ne bougez pas !, ne bougez plus ! **3.** [be upright - post, target, etc.] être debout **/** *not a stone was left standing* il ne restait plus une seule pierre debout **4.** [be supported, be mounted] reposer **/** *the house stands on solid foundations* la maison repose or est bâtie sur des fondations solides **5.** [be located - building, tree, statue] se trouver ; [-clock, vase, lamp] être, être posé **/** *the piano stood in the centre of the room* le piano était au centre or occupait le centre de la pièce.

B. SITUATION OR STATE **1.** [indicating current state of affairs, situation] être **/** *how do things stand?* où en est la situation ? **/** *as things stand* telles que les choses se présentent **/** *just print the text as it stands* faites imprimer le texte tel quel **/** *he stands accused of rape* il est accusé de viol **/** *I stand corrected* c'est vous qui avez raison **/** *the party stands united behind him* le parti est uni derrière lui ▶ **to stand at a)** [gauge, barometer] indiquer **b)** [score] être or de **c)** [unemployment] avoir atteint **/** *their turnover now stands at three million pounds* leur chiffre d'affaires atteint désormais

les trois millions de livres **/** *it's the only thing standing between us and financial disaster* c'est la seule chose qui nous empêche de sombrer dans un désastre financier ▶ **to stand in sb's way a)** lit être sur le chemin de qqn **b)** fig gêner qqn **/** *nothing stands in our way now* maintenant, la voie est libre **2.** [on issue] : *how* or *where does he stand on the nuclear issue?* quelle est sa position or son point de vue sur la question nucléaire ? **3.** [be likely] ▶ **to stand to lose** risquer de perdre ▶ **to stand to win** avoir des chances de gagner **/** *they stand to make a huge profit on the deal* ils ont des chances de faire un bénéfice énorme dans cette affaire **4.** [remain] rester ; [be left undisturbed - marinade, dough] reposer ; [-tea] infuser **/** *time stood still* le temps semblait s'être arrêté **/** *the car has been standing in the garage for a year* ça fait un an que la voiture n'a pas bougé du garage **5.** [be valid, effective - offer, law] rester valable ; [-decision] rester inchangé **/** *my invitation still stands* vous êtes toujours le bienvenu **6.** [succeed] : *the government will stand or fall on the outcome of this vote* le maintien ou la chute du gouvernement dépend du résultat de ce vote.

C. MEASURE OR RANK **1.** [measure - person, tree] mesurer **/** *she stands 5 feet in her stocking feet* elle mesure moins de 1,50 m pieds nus **2.** [rank] se classer, compter.

D. IN ELECTION 🇬🇧 [run in election] se présenter, être candidat **/** *she's standing as an independent* elle se présente en tant que candidate indépendante.

◆ vt **1.** [set, place] mettre, poser **/** *she stood her umbrella in the corner* elle a mis son parapluie dans le coin ▶ **to stand sthg on (its) end** faire tenir qqch debout **2.** [endure, withstand] supporter **/** *it will stand high temperatures without cracking* cela peut résister à or supporter des températures élevées sans se fissurer ; fig : *their figures don't stand close inspection* leurs chiffres ne résistent pas à un examen sérieux **3.** [put up with, bear - toothache, cold] supporter ; [-behaviour] supporter, tolérer **/** *I can't stand it any longer!* je n'en peux plus ! **/** *how can you stand working with him?* comment est-ce que vous faites pour or comment arrivez-vous à travailler avec lui ? **/** *if there's one thing I can't stand, it's hypocrisy* s'il y a quelque chose que je ne supporte pas, c'est bien l'hypocrisie **4.** inf [do with, need] supporter, avoir besoin de **5.** [perform duty of] remplir la fonction de **6.** inf [treat to] : *I'll stand you a drink* 🇬🇧, *I'll stand you to a drink* 🇺🇸 je t'offre un verre **7.** PHR *you don't stand a chance!* vous n'avez pas la moindre chance !

◆ n **1.** [stall, booth - gen] stand m ; [-in exhibition] stand m ; [-in market] étal m, éventaire m ; [-for newspapers] kiosque m **2.** [frame, support - gen] support m ; [-for lamp, sink] pied m ; [-on bicycle, motorbike] béquille f ; [-for pipes, guns] râtelier m ; [COMM - for magazines, sunglasses] présentoir m ; [lectern] lutrin m **3.** [platform - gen] plate-forme f ; [-for speaker] tribune f ; [pulpit] chaire f **4.** [in sports ground] tribune f **5.** [for taxis] ▶ **(taxi) stand** station f de taxis **6.** 🇺🇸 [in courtroom] barre f **7.** lit & fig [position] position f ▶ **to take a stand on sthg** prendre position à propos de qqch **/** *he refuses to take a stand* il refuse de prendre position **8.** MIL & fig [defensive effort] résistance f, opposition f ▶ **to make a stand** résister. ◆ **stand about** 🇬🇧, **stand around** vi rester là, traîner pej **/** *we stood about* or *around waiting for the flight announcement* nous restions là à attendre que le vol soit annoncé **/** *I'm not just going to stand about waiting for you to make up your mind!* je n'ai pas l'intention de poireauter là en attendant que tu te décides ! ◆ **stand aside** vi [move aside] s'écarter ▶ **to stand aside in favour of sb a)** [gen] laisser la voie libre à qqn **b)** POL se désister en faveur de qqn. ◆ **stand back** vi **1.** [move back] reculer, s'écarter **/** *stand back from the doors!* écartez-vous des portes ! **2.** [be set back] être en retrait or à l'écart **3.** [take mental distance] prendre du recul.

⟡ stand by ◆ vi **1.** [not intervene] rester là (sans rien faire) **2.** [be ready - person] être or se tenir prêt ; [-vehicle] être prêt ; [-army, embassy] être en état d'alerte / *the police were standing by to disperse the crowd* la police se tenait prête à disperser la foule. ◆ vt insep **1.** [support - person] soutenir / *I'll stand by you through thick and thin* je te soutiendrai or je resterai à tes côtés quoi qu'il arrive **2.** [adhere to - promise, word] tenir ; [-decision, offer] s'en tenir à.

⟡ stand down ◆ vi **1.** 🇬🇧 POL [withdraw] se désister ; [resign] démissionner **2.** [leave witness box] quitter la barre **3.** MIL [troops] être déconsigné *(en fin d'alerte).* ◆ vt sep [workers] licencier. **⟡ stand for** vt insep **1.** [represent] représenter / *what does DNA stand for?* que veut dire l'abréviation ADN ? / *the R stands for Ryan* le R signifie Ryan / *we want our name to stand for quality and efficiency* nous voulons que notre nom soit synonyme de qualité et d'efficacité **2.** [tolerate] tolérer, supporter ; [allow] permettre / *I'm not going to stand for it!* je ne le tolérerai or permettrai pas !

⟡ stand in vi assurer le remplacement ▸ **to stand in for sb** remplacer qqn. **⟡ stand out** vi **1.** [protrude - vein] saillir ; [-ledge] faire saillie, avancer **2.** [be clearly visible - colour, typeface] ressortir, se détacher / *the pink stands out against the green background* le rose ressort or se détache sur le fond vert **3.** [be distinctive] ressortir, se détacher / *she stands out above all the rest* elle surpasse or surclasse tous les autres / *I don't like to stand out in a crowd* je n'aime pas me singulariser **4.** [resist, hold out] tenir bon, tenir ▸ **to stand out against** a) [attack, enemy] résister à b) [change, tax increase] s'opposer avec détermination à. **⟡ stand over** vt insep [watch over] surveiller / *I can't work with someone standing over me* je ne peux pas travailler quand quelqu'un me regarde par-dessus mon épaule. **⟡ stand to** vi MIL se mettre en état d'alerte ▸ **stand to!** à vos postes ! **⟡ stand up** ◆ vi **1.** [rise to one's feet] se lever, se mettre debout ▸ **to stand up and be counted** avoir le courage de ses opinions **2.** [be upright] être debout / *I can't get the candle to stand up straight* je n'arrive pas à faire tenir la bougie droite **3.** [last] tenir, résister **4.** [be valid - argument, claim] être valable, tenir debout / *his evidence won't stand up in court* son témoignage ne sera pas valable en justice. ◆ vt sep **1.** [set upright - chair, bottle] mettre debout **2.** *inf* [fail to meet] poser un lapin à, faire faux bond à. **⟡ stand up for** vt insep défendre ▸ **to stand up for o.s.** se défendre. **⟡ stand up to** vt insep ▸ **to stand up to sthg** résister à qqch ▸ **to stand up to sb** tenir tête à or faire face à qqn.

standalone ['stændələʊn] ◆ adj COMPUT [system] autonome. ◆ n application *f* autonome.

standard ['stændəd] ◆ n **1.** [norm] norme *f* ; [level] niveau *m* ; [criterion] critère *m* / *most of the goods are or come up to standard* la plupart des marchandises sont de qualité satisfaisante / *your work isn't up to standard* or *is below standard* votre travail laisse à désirer / *he sets high standards for himself* il est très exigeant avec lui-même / *it's a difficult task by any standard* or *by anybody's standards* c'est indiscutablement une tâche difficile / *we apply the same standards to all candidates* nous jugeons tous les candidats selon les mêmes critères ▸ **standard of living** niveau de vie **2.** [moral principle] principe *m* / *to have high moral standards* avoir de grands principes moraux **3.** [for measures, currency - model] étalon *m* ; [in coins - proportion] titre *m* **4.** [established item] standard *m* ; [tune] standard *m* / *a jazz standard* un classique du jazz **5.** 🇺🇸 [car] / *I can't drive a standard* je ne sais conduire que les voitures à boîte de vitesse automatique **6.** [flag] étendard *m* ; [of sovereign, noble] bannière *f* **7.** [support - pole] poteau *m* ; [-for flag] mât *m* ; [-for lamp] pied *m* ; [-for power-line] pylône *m* **8.** 🇬🇧 [lamp] lampadaire *m* (de salon) **9.** AGR & HORT [fruit tree] haute-tige *f* **10.** BOT [petal] éten-

dard *m.* ◆ adj **1.** [ordinary, regular - gen] normal ; [- model, size] standard ▸ **standard gear shift** 🇺🇸 AUTO changement *m* de vitesse manuel **2.** [measure - metre, kilogramme, etc.] étalon *(inv)* **3.** [text, work] classique, de base **4.** LING [pronunciation, spelling, etc.] standard / *standard English* l'anglais correct **5.** AGR & HORT [fruit tree, shrub] à haute tige ▸ **standard rose** rose *f* tige.

standard bearer n **1.** [of cause] porte-drapeau *m* ; [of political party] chef *m* de file **2.** [of flag] porte-étendard *m.*

standardization, standardisation [,stændədaɪˈzeɪʃn] n **1.** [gen] standardisation *f* ; [of dimensions, terms, etc.] normalisation *f* **2.** TECH [verification] étalonnage *m.*

standardize, standardise ['stændədaɪz] vt **1.** [gen] standardiser ; [dimensions, products, terms] normaliser **2.** TECH [verify] étalonner.

standard lamp n 🇬🇧 lampadaire *m* (de salon).

standard time n heure *f* légale.

standby ['stændbaɪ] *(pl* **standbys)** ◆ adj **1.** [equipment, provisions, etc.] de réserve ; [generator] de secours / *in standby position* RADIO en écoute **2.** AERON [ticket, fare] stand-by *(inv)* ; [passenger] stand-by *(inv)*, en attente ▸ **standby list** liste *f* d'attente **3.** FIN ▸ **standby agreement** accord *m* stand-by ▸ **standby credit** crédit *m* stand-by or de soutien ▸ **standby loan** prêt *m* conditionnel. ◆ n **1.** [substitute - person] remplaçant *m,* -e *f* ; THEAT [understudy] doublure *f* ▸ **to be on standby** a) [doctor] être de garde or d'astreinte b) [flight personnel, emergency repairman] être d'astreinte c) [troops, police, firemen] être prêt à intervenir **2.** AERON [system] stand-by *m inv* ; [passenger] passager *m,* -ère *f* stand-by *m inv* ▸ **to be on standby** [passenger] être en stand-by or sur la liste d'attente. ◆ adv [travel] en stand-by.

stand-in ◆ n [gen] remplaçant *m,* -e *f* ; CIN [for lighting check] doublure *f* ; [stunt person] cascadeur *m,* -euse *f* ; THEAT [understudy] doublure *f.* ◆ adj [gen] remplaçant ; [office worker] intérimaire ; [teacher] suppléant, qui fait des remplacements.

standing ['stændɪŋ] ◆ adj **1.** [upright - position, person, object] debout *(inv)* ▸ **standing room** or **places** places *fpl* debout ▸ **standing lamp** 🇺🇸 lampadaire *m* (de salon) ▸ **standing ovation** ovation *f* **2.** [stationary] ▸ **standing jump** SPORT saut *m* à pieds joints ▸ **standing start** a) SPORT départ *m* debout b) AUTO départ *m* arrêté ▸ **standing wave** PHYS onde *f* stationnaire **3.** [grain, timber] sur pied **4.** [stagnant - water] stagnant **5.** [permanent - army, offer, etc.] permanent ; [-claim] de longue date / *it's a standing joke with us* c'est une vieille plaisanterie entre nous ▸ **standing committee** comité *m* permanent ▸ **to pay by standing order** 🇬🇧 payer par prélèvement (bancaire) automatique / *I get paid by standing order* je reçois mon salaire par virement bancaire ▸ **standing orders** 🇬🇧 POL règlement *m* intérieur *(d'une assemblée délibérative).* ◆ n **1.** [reputation] réputation *f* ; [status] standing *m* **2.** [ranking] rang *m,* place *f* ; SCH & SPORT [ordered list] classement *m* **3.** [duration] durée *f* / *of long standing* de longue date **4.** 🇺🇸 AUTO / **'no standing'** 'arrêt interdit' **5.** 🇺🇸 LAW position *f* en droit.

standing charges n [on bill] frais *mpl* d'abonnement.

standoff ['stændɒf] n **1.** POL [inconclusive clash] affrontement *m* indécis ; [deadlock] impasse *f* **2.** 🇺🇸 SPORT [tie] match *m* nul.

standoffish [,stænd'ɒfɪʃ] adj distant, froid.

standout ['stændaʊt] ◆ n [person] as *m* / *his article was a real standout* son article sortait vraiment du lot. ◆ adj exceptionnel.

standpipe ['stændpaɪp] n **1.** [in street - for fire brigade] bouche *f* d'incendie ; [-for public] point *m* d'alimentation en eau de secours **2.** [in pumping system] tuyau *m* ascendant, colonne *f* d'alimentation.

standpoint ['stændpɔɪnt] n point *m* de vue.

standstill ['stændstɪl] n arrêt m ▸ **to come to a stand-still a)** [vehicle, person] s'immobiliser **b)** [talks, work, etc.] piétiner ▸ **to bring to a standstill a)** [vehicle, person] arrêter **b)** [talks, traffic] paralyser ▸ **to be at a standstill a)** [talks, career] être au point mort **b)** [traffic] être paralysé **c)** [economy] piétiner, stagner.

stand-up adj [collar] droit ; [meal] (pris) debout ▸ **a stand-up fight a)** [physical] une bagarre en règle **b)** [verbal] une discussion violente ▸ **stand-up comic** or **comedian** comique mf *(qui se produit seul en scène)* ▸ **stand-up counter** or **diner** US buvette f ▸ **a stand-up guy** US [decent, honest] un type réglo.

stank [stæŋk] pt ⟶ **stink**.

stanza ['stænzə] n **1.** [in poetry] strophe f **2.** US SPORT période f.

staple ['steɪpl] ◆ n **1.** [for paper] agrafe f **2.** [for wire] cavalier m, crampillon m **3.** [foodstuff] aliment m or denrée f de base **4.** COMM & ECON [item] article m de base ; [raw material] matière f première **5.** [constituent] partie f intégrante **6.** TEXT fibre f artificielle à filer. ◆ vt **1.** [paper, upholstery, etc.] agrafer **2.** MED ▸ **to have one's stomach stapled** se faire poser un anneau gastrique. ◆ adj **1.** [food, products] de base ; [export, crop] principal / *a staple diet of rice and beans* un régime à base de riz et de haricots **2.** TEXT ▸ **staple fibre** fibre f artificielle à filer.

staple gun n agrafeuse f (professionnelle).

stapler ['steɪplə^r] n agrafeuse f (de bureau).

staple remover n ôte-agrafes m inv.

star [stɑ:^r] *(pt & pp* **starred**, *cont* **starring)** ◆ n **1.** [in sky] étoile f / *to sleep (out) under the stars* dormir or coucher à la belle étoile ▸ **the morning / evening star** l'étoile du matin / du soir ▸ **falling** or **shooting star** étoile filante ▸ **The Star** PRESS *nom abrégé du Daily Star* **2.** [symbol of fate, luck] étoile f ; ASTROL astre m, étoile f ▸ **to be born under a lucky star** être né sous une bonne étoile / *what do my stars say today?* inf que dit mon horoscope aujourd'hui ? **3.** [figure, emblem] étoile f ; SCH bon point m ▸ **the Star of David** l'étoile de David ▸ **the Stars and Bars** le drapeau des États confédérés ▸ **the Stars and Stripes** le drapeau américain **4.** [asterisk] astérisque m **5.** [celebrity] vedette f, star f **6.** [blaze - on animal] étoile f. ◆ comp **1.** CIN & THEAT ▸ **the star attraction**: *the star attraction of tonight's show* la principale attraction du spectacle de ce soir ▸ **the star turn** la vedette ▸ **to give sb star billing** mettre qqn en tête d'affiche ▸ **to give sb star treatment**: *the hotel gives all its clients star treatment* cet hôtel offre à sa clientèle un service de première classe **2.** [salesman, pupil, etc.] meilleur / *he's our star witness* c'est notre témoin-vedette or notre témoin principal **3.** ELEC ▸ **star connection** couplage m en étoile ▸ **star point** point m neutre. ◆ vt **1.** CIN & THEAT avoir comme or pour vedette **2.** [mark with asterisk] marquer d'un astérisque **3.** *liter* [adorn with stars] étoiler. ◆ vi CIN & THEAT être la vedette.

starboard ['stɑ:bəd] ◆ n NAUT tribord m ; AERON tribord m, droite f. ◆ adj NAUT [rail, lights] de tribord ; AERON [door, wing] droit, de tribord. ◆ vt NAUT ▸ **to starboard the helm** or **rudder** mettre la barre à tribord.

starch [stɑ:tʃ] ◆ n **1.** [for laundry] amidon m, empois m **2.** [in cereals] amidon m ; [in root vegetables] fécule f **3.** *(U)* inf [formality] manières fpl guindées **4.** PHR ▸ **to take the starch out of sb** US [critic, bully] rabattre le caquet à qqn. ◆ vt empeser, amidonner.

starched [stɑ:tʃt] adj amidonné.

starchy ['stɑ:tʃɪ] *(compar* **starchier**, *superl* **starchiest)** adj **1.** [diet] riche en féculents ; [taste] farineux ▸ **starchy foods** féculents mpl **2.** pej [person] guindé, compassé.

stardom ['stɑ:dəm] n célébrité f, vedettariat m ▸ **to rise to stardom** devenir célèbre, devenir une vedette.

stare [steə^r] ◆ vi regarder (fixement) ▸ **to stare at sb / sthg** regarder qqn / qqch fixement / *I stared into his eyes* je l'ai regardé dans le blanc des yeux. ◆ vt **1.** [intimidate] ▸ **to stare sb into silence** faire taire qqn en le fixant du regard **2.** PHR *the answer is staring you in the face!* mais la réponse saute aux yeux ! ◆ n regard m (fixe). ◆ **stare out** UK, **stare down** US vt sep faire baisser les yeux à.

starfish ['stɑ:fɪʃ] *(pl* **starfish** or **starfishes)** n étoile f de mer.

starfruit ['stɑ:fru:t] n carambole f.

stargazing ['stɑ:,ɡeɪzɪŋ] n **1.** [astronomy] observation f des étoiles ; [astrology] astrologie f **2.** *(U)* [daydreaming] rêveries fpl, rêvasseries fpl.

staring ['steərɪŋ] ◆ adj [bystanders] curieux / *with staring eyes* **a)** [fixedly] aux yeux fixes **b)** [wide-open] aux yeux écarquillés **c)** [blank] aux yeux vides. ◆ adv = **stark**.

stark [stɑ:k] ◆ adj **1.** [bare, grim - landscape] désolé ; [-branches, hills] nu ; [-crag, rock] âpre, abrupt ; [-room, façade] austère ; [-silhouette] net **2.** [blunt - description, statement] cru, sans ambages ; [-refusal, denial] catégorique ; [harsh - words] dur **3.** [utter - brutality, terror] absolu ; [-madness] pur. ◆ adv complètement ▸ **stark raving** or **staring mad** inf complètement fou or dingue ▸ **stark naked** à poil.

starkly ['stɑ:klɪ] adv [describe] crûment ; [tell] carrément, sans ambages ; [stand out] nettement.

starlight ['stɑ:laɪt] n lumière f des étoiles / *by starlight* à or sous la lumière des étoiles.

starling ['stɑ:lɪŋ] n étourneau m, sansonnet m.

starlit ['stɑ:lɪt] adj [night] étoilé ; [landscape] illuminé par les étoiles ; [beach, sea] baigné par la lumière des étoiles.

starry ['stɑ:rɪ] *(compar* **starrier**, *superl* **starriest)** adj **1.** [adorned with stars] étoilé **2.** [sparkling] étincelant, brillant **3.** *liter & fig* [lofty] élevé.

starry-eyed adj [idealistic] idéaliste ; [naive] naïf, ingénu ; [dreamy] rêveur, dans la lune.

star sign n signe m (du zodiaque).

Star-Spangled Banner n ▸ **the Star-Spangled Banner** la bannière étoilée.

starstruck ['stɑ:strʌk] adj ébloui *(devant une célébrité)*.

star-studded adj [show, film] à vedettes / *a star-studded cast* une distribution où figurent de nombreuses vedettes or a brochette de stars.

start [stɑ:t] ◆ vt **1.** [begin - gen] commencer ; [-climb, descent] amorcer ▸ **to start doing** or **to do sthg** commencer à or se mettre à faire qqch / *it's starting to rain* il commence à pleuvoir / *she started driving* or *to drive again a month after her accident* elle a recommencé à conduire or elle s'est remise à conduire un mois après son accident / *he started life as a delivery boy* il débuta dans la vie comme garçon livreur / *I like to finish anything I start* j'aime aller au bout de tout ce que j'entreprends ▸ **to get started**: *I got started on the dishes* je me suis mis à la vaisselle / *once he gets started there's no stopping him* une fois lancé, il n'y a pas moyen de l'arrêter / *shall we get started on the washing-up?* si on attaquait la vaisselle ? **2.** [initiate, instigate - reaction, revolution, process] déclencher ; [- fashion] lancer ; [- violence] déclencher, provoquer ; [- conversation, discussion] engager, amorcer ; [- rumour] faire naître / *which side started the war?* quel camp a déclenché la guerre ? / *to start a fire* **a)** [in fireplace] allumer le feu **b)** [campfire] faire du feu **c)** [by accident, bomb] mettre le feu **3.** [cause to behave in specified way] faire / *it started her (off) crying / laughing* cela l'a fait pleurer / rire **4.** [set in motion - motor, car] (faire) démarrer, mettre en marche ; [- machine, device] mettre en marche ; [- meal] mettre en route / *how do I get the tape (going)?* comment est-ce que je dois faire pour mettre le magnétophone en marche ? / *I couldn't get the car started* je n'ai pas réussi à faire démarrer la voiture **5.** [begin using - bottle, pack] entamer **6.** [establish, found - business, school, political party] créer, fonder ; [- restaurant, shop] ouvrir ; [- social programme] créer, instaurer **7.** [person - in business, work] installer, établir / *his election success started him on his political career* son succès aux élections l'a lancé dans la carrière d'homme politique **8.** SPORT ▸ **to start the race** donner le signal du départ. ◆ vi **1.** [in time] commencer / *before the New Year / the rainy season starts* avant le début de l'année prochaine / de la saison des pluies / *before the cold weather starts* avant qu'il ne commence à faire froid / *starting (from) next week* à partir de la semaine prochaine ▸ **to start again** or **afresh** recommencer ▸ **to start all over again, to start again from scratch** recommencer à zéro ; [story, speech] : *calm down and start at the beginning* calmez-vous et commencez par le commencement / *I didn't know where to start* je ne savais pas par quel bout commencer ; [in career, job] débuter / *she started in personnel / as an assistant* elle a débuté au service du personnel / comme assistante / *isn't it time you got a job? — don't YOU start!* il serait peut-être temps que tu trouves du travail — tu ne vas pas t'y mettre, toi aussi ! **2.** [in space - desert, fields, slope, street] commencer ; [- river] prendre sa source **3.** [car, motor] démarrer, se mettre en marche / *why won't the car start?* pourquoi la voiture ne veut-elle pas démarrer ? **4.** [set off - person, convoy] partir, se mettre en route ; [- train] s'ébranler / *the tour starts at or from the town hall* la visite part de la mairie **5.** [range - prices] commencer / *houses here start at $100,000* ici, le prix des maisons démarre à 100 000 dollars **6.** [jump involuntarily - person] sursauter ; [- horse] tressaillir, faire un soubresaut ; [jump up] bondir / *he started in surprise* il a tressailli de surprise **7.** [gush] jaillir, gicler / *tears started to his eyes* les larmes lui sont montées aux yeux. ◆ n **1.** [beginning - gen] commencement m, début m ; [- of inquiry] ouverture f / *the start of the school year* la rentrée scolaire / *it was an inauspicious start to his presidency* c'était un début peu prometteur pour sa présidence / *things are off to a bad / good start* ça commence mal / bien, on est mal / bien partis / *to get a good start in life* prendre un bon départ dans la vie or l'existence ▸ **to make a start (on sthg)** commencer (qqch) ▸ **to make** or **to get an early start a)** [gen] commencer de bonne heure **b)** [on journey] partir de bonne heure / *I was lonely at the start* au début je me sentais seule ▸ **from the start** dès le début or commencement ▸ **from start to finish**: *the trip was a disaster from start to finish* le voyage a été un désastre d'un bout à l'autre / *I laughed from start to finish* j'ai ri du début à la fin / *the project was ill-conceived from start to finish* le projet

était mal conçu de bout en bout **2.** SPORT [place] (ligne f de) départ m ; [signal] signal m de départ **3.** [lead, advance] avance f / *he gave him 20 metres' start* or *a 20-metre start* il lui a accordé une avance de 20 mètres **4.** [jump] sursaut m / *she woke up with a start* elle s'est réveillée en sursaut ▸ **to give a start** sursauter, tressaillir ▸ **to give sb a start** faire sursauter or tressaillir qqn. ⬧ **for a start** adv phr d'abord, pour commencer. ⬧ **to start with** adv phr pour commencer, d'abord / *to start (off) with, my name isn't Jo* pour commencer or d'abord, je ne m'appelle pas Jo. ⬧ **start back** vi **1.** [turn back] rebrousser chemin **2.** [start again] recommencer. ⬧ **start off** ◆ vi **1.** [leave] partir, se mettre en route **2.** [begin - speech, film] commencer / *I started off agreeing with him* au début, j'étais d'accord avec lui **3.** [in life, career] débuter / *he started off as a cashier* il a débuté comme caissier. ◆ vt sep **1.** [book, campaign, show] commencer **2.** [person - on new task] : *here's some wool to start you off* voici de la laine pour commencer **3.** [set off] déclencher ▸ **to start sb off laughing / crying** faire rire / pleurer qqn. ⬧ **start on** vt insep **1.** [begin - essay, meal] commencer ; [- task, dishes] se mettre à ; [- new bottle, pack] entamer **2.** [attack, berate] s'en prendre à. ⬧ **start out** vi **1.** = **start off 2.** [begin career] se lancer, s'installer, s'établir / *he started out in business with his wife's money* il s'est lancé dans les affaires avec l'argent de sa femme. ⬧ **start over** vi & vt sep recommencer (depuis le début). ⬧ **start up** ◆ vt sep **1.** [establish, found - business, school, political party] créer, fonder ; [- restaurant, shop] ouvrir **2.** [set in motion - car, motor] faire démarrer ; [- machine] mettre en marche. ◆ vi **1.** [guns, music, noise, band] commencer ; [wind] se lever / *the applause started up again* les applaudissements ont repris **2.** [car, motor] démarrer, se mettre en marche ; [machine] se mettre en marche **3.** [set up business] se lancer, s'installer, s'établir.

starter ['stɑːtə*r*] n **1.** AUTO [motor, button] démarreur m ; [on motorbike] kick m, démarreur m au pied ▸ **starter switch** bouton m de démarrage ▸ **starter handle** US AUTO manivelle f **2.** [runner, horse] partant m ; [in relay race] premier coureur m, première coureuse f **3.** SPORT [official] starter m, juge m de départ ▸ **starter's pistol** or **gun** pistolet m du starter ▸ **to be under starter's orders** [in horseracing] être sous les ordres du starter **4.** [fermenting agent] ferment m **5.** UK [hors d'œuvre] hors-d'œuvre m inv ▸ **for starters a)** [in meal] comme hors-d'œuvre **b)** fig pour commencer.

starter motor n démarreur m.

starter pack n kit m de base.

starting ['stɑːtɪŋ] ◆ n commencement m. ◆ adj initial / *the starting line-up* la composition initiale de l'équipe ▸ **starting salary** salaire m d'embauche.

starting block n starting-block m.

starting point n point m de départ.

starting price n [gen] prix m initial ; [in horseracing] cote f au départ ; [at auction] mise f à prix, prix m d'appel.

startle ['stɑːtl] ◆ vt [person - surprise] surprendre, étonner ; [- frighten, alarm] faire peur à, alarmer ; [- cause to jump] faire sursauter ; [animal, bird, fish] effaroucher. ◆ vi s'effaroucher.

startled ['stɑːtld] adj [person] étonné ; [expression, shout, glance] de surprise ; [animal] effarouché.

startling ['stɑːtlɪŋ] adj étonnant, surprenant ; [contrast, resemblance] saisissant.

start-up ◆ adj [costs] de démarrage ▸ **start-up loan** prêt m initial. ◆ n start-up f, jeune pousse f d'entreprise offic.

starvation [stɑːˈveɪʃn] n faim f ▸ **to die of** or **from starvation** mourir de faim.

starve [stɑːv] ✦ vi [suffer] souffrir de la faim, être affamé
▸ **to starve (to death)** [die] mourir de faim. ✦ vt **1.** [cause
to suffer] affamer **2.** [cause to die] laisser mourir de faim
3. [deprive] priver. ✧ **starve out** vt sep [rebels, inmates]
affamer, réduire par la faim ; [animal] obliger à sortir en
l'affamant.

starving ['stɑːvɪŋ] adj affamé.

Star Wars pr n HIST la guerre des étoiles *(nom donné à
l'Initiative de Défense Stratégique, programme militaire spatial
mis en place dans les années 1980 par le président Reagan).*

stash [stæʃ] inf ✦ vt **1.** [hide] planquer, cacher **2.** [put
away] ranger. ✦ n **1.** [reserve] réserve f **2.** [hiding place]
planque f, cachette f **3.** *drugs sl* cache f. ✧ **stash away**
vt sep inf = **stash** *(vt).*

state [steɪt] ✦ n **1.** [condition] état *m* ▸ **to be in a
good / bad state** a) [road, carpet, car] être en bon / mauvais
état b) [person, economy, friendship] aller bien / mal ▸ **to get
into a state** inf se mettre dans tous ses états **2.** POL [nation,
body politic] État *m* ▸ **the member states** les États membres
▸ **the head of state** le chef de l'État ▸ **state lottery** US loterie d'État dont les gros lots sont soumis à l'impôt et sont ver-
sés au gagnant sur une période de 10 ou 20 ans ▸ **the State
Opening of Parliament** ouverture officielle du Parlement britannique en présence de la reine **3.** [in US, Australia, India,
etc. - political division] État *m* ▸ **the States** inf les États-Unis,
les US / *the State of Ohio* l'État de l'Ohio **4.** US [depart-
ment] ▸ **State** le Département d'État **5.** [pomp] apparat *m*,
pompe f. ✦ comp **1.** [secret] [secret; [subsidy, intervention]
de l'État ; ECON [sector] public / *a state funeral* des funérailles nationales **2.** UK SCH [education system] public **3.** US
[not federal - legislature, policy, law] de l'État / *the state
capital* la capitale de l'État / *state police* police f de l'État
4. [official, ceremonious] officiel. ✦ vt [utter, say] déclarer ;
[express, formulate - intentions] déclarer ; [- demand] formuler ; [- proposition, problem, conclusions, views] énoncer, formuler ; [- conditions] poser. ✧ **in state** adv phr en grand
apparat, en grande pompe ▸ **to lie in state** être exposé
solennellement.

state-controlled adj [industry] nationalisé ; [economy]
étatisé ; [activities] soumis au contrôle de l'État.

stated ['steɪtɪd] adj [amount, date] fixé ; [limit] prescrit ;
[aim] déclaré.

State Department n US ministère *m* des Affaires
étrangères.

Statehouse ['steɪthaʊs] *(pl* [-haʊzɪz]*)* n siège de l'assemblée législative d'un État aux États-Unis.

stateless ['steɪtlɪs] adj apatride ▸ **stateless person** apatride mf.

stately ['steɪtlɪ] *(compar* statelier, *superl* stateliest)
adj [ceremony, building] majestueux, imposant ; [person,
bearing] noble, plein de dignité.

stately home n château ou manoir à la campagne, généralement ouvert au public.

statement ['steɪtmənt] n **1.** [declaration - gen] déclaration f, affirmation f ; [- to the press] communiqué *m* ▸ **to
put out** or **to issue** or **to make a statement about sthg**
émettre un communiqué concernant qqch **2.** [act of stating
- of theory, opinions, policy, aims] exposition f ; [- of prob-
lem] exposé *m*, formulation f ; [- of facts, details] exposé *m*,
compte-rendu *m* **3.** LAW déposition f / *to make a statement to the police* faire une déposition dans un commissariat de police **4.** COMM & FIN relevé *m* **5.** LING affirmation f
6. COMPUT instruction f.

state of affairs n circonstances fpl actuelles / *this is
an appalling state of affairs* c'est une situation épouvantable.

state of emergency *(pl* states of emergency*)* n
état *m* d'urgence.

state of mind *(pl* states of mind*)* n état *m* d'esprit.

State of the Union address n : *the State of the
Union address* le discours sur l'état de l'Union.

▥▥▥▥ **State of the Union address**

Une fois par an, le président des États-Unis
prononce un discours devant le Congrès, dans
lequel il dresse le bilan de son programme
et en définit les orientations. Ce discours
est retransmis à la radio et à la télévision.

state-owned [-'əʊnd] adj nationalisé.

state pension n pension f de l'État.

state-run adj d'état.

state school n UK école f publique.

state's evidence n US ▸ **to turn state's evidence**
témoigner contre ses complices en échange d'une remise de
peine.

stateside ['steɪtsaɪd] adj & adv US inf aux États-Unis ;
≈ au pays.

statesman ['steɪtsmən] *(pl* statesmen [-mən]*)* n homme
m d'État.

statesmanlike ['steɪtsmənlaɪk] adj [protest, reply]
diplomatique ; [solution] de grande envergure ; [caution]
pondéré.

statesmanship ['steɪtsmənʃɪp] n qualités fpl d'homme
d'État.

state trooper n US ≈ gendarme *m*.

state visit n POL visite f officielle.

static ['stætɪk] adj **1.** [stationary, unchanging] stationnaire, stable **2.** ELEC statique ▸ **static electricity** électricité f
statique. ✦ n *(U)* **1.** RADIO & TELEC parasites mpl **2.** ELEC
électricité f statique **3.** US inf [aggravation, criticism] ▸ **to
give sb static about** or **over sthg** passer un savon à qqn
à propos de qqch ▸ **to get a lot of static (about)** or **(over)
sthg** se faire enguirlander (pour qqch).

station ['steɪʃn] ✦ n **1.** TRANSP gare f ; [underground]
station f (de métro) **2.** [establishment, building] station f,
poste *m* **3.** MIL [gen - position] poste *m* ▸ **action** or **battle stations!** à vos postes ! **4.** MIL [base] poste *m*, base f
5. RADIO & TV [broadcaster] station f ; [smaller] poste
m émetteur ▸ **commercial radio station** station de radio
commerciale, radio f commerciale ; [on radio or TV set]
chaîne f ▸ **to change stations** changer de chaîne
6. [social rank] rang *m*, condition f, situation f ▸ **to
marry below one's station** faire une mésalliance
▸ **to marry above one's station** se marier au-dessus de sa
condition sociale **7.** COMPUT station f **8.** RELIG ▸ **the Stations of the Cross** le chemin de la Croix. ✦ comp [buf-
fet, platform, etc.] de gare. ✦ vt **1.** [position] placer, poster
2. MIL [garrison] : *British troops stationed in Germany* les
troupes britanniques stationnées en Allemagne.

stationary ['steɪʃnərɪ] adj **1.** [not moving] stationnaire / *he hit a stationary vehicle* il a heurté un véhicule à
l'arrêt or en stationnement **2.** [fixed] fixe ▸ **stationary engine / shaft** MECH moteur *m* / arbre *m* fixe.

stationer ['steɪʃnə'] n UK papetier *m*, -ère f ▸ **stationer's (shop)** papeterie f / *at the stationer's* à la papeterie.

stationery ['steɪʃnərɪ] n [in general] papeterie f ; [writ-
ing paper] papier *m* à lettres ▸ **school / office stationery**
fournitures fpl scolaires / de bureau.

station house n 🇺🇸 [police station] poste *m* de police, commissariat *m* ; [fire station] caserne *f* de pompiers.

stationmaster ['steɪʃn,mɑːstər] n chef *m* de gare.

station wagon n 🇺🇸 break *m*.

statistic [stə'tɪstɪk] n chiffre *m*, statistique *f*.

statistical [stə'tɪstɪkl] adj [analysis, technique] statistique ; [error] de statistique.

statistically [stə'tɪstɪklɪ] adv statistiquement.

statistician [,stætɪ'stɪʃn] n statisticien *m*, -enne *f*.

statistics [stə'tɪstɪks] ◆ n (U) [science] statistique *f*. ◆ pl n **1.** [figures] statistiques *fpl*, chiffres *mpl* **2.** inf [of woman] mensurations *fpl*.

stats [stæts] inf = **statistics**.

statue ['stætʃuː] n statue *f* ▸ **the Statue of Liberty** la statue de la Liberté.

statuesque [,stætju'esk] adj : *a statuesque woman* une femme d'une beauté sculpturale.

statuette [,stætju'et] n statuette *f*.

stature ['stætʃər] n **1.** [height] stature *f*, taille *f* **2.** [greatness] envergure *f*, calibre *m*.

status [🇬🇧 'steɪtəs 🇺🇸 'stætəs] ◆ n **1.** [position - in society, hierarchy, etc.] rang *m*, position *f*, situation *f* **2.** [prestige] prestige *m*, standing *m* **3.** [legal or official standing] statut *m* ▸ **legal status** statut légal **4.** [general state or situation] état *m*, situation *f*, condition *f* ▸ **to make a status report on sthg** faire le point sur qqch **5.** MED : *HIV-positive status* séropositivité *f*. ◆ comp [car, club] de prestige, prestigieux.

status bar n COMPUT barre *f* d'état.

status quo [,steɪtəs'kwəʊ] n statu quo *m* ▸ **to maintain** or **to preserve the status quo** maintenir le statu quo.

status symbol n marque *f* de prestige.

statute ['stætjuːt] n **1.** LAW loi *f* ▸ **statute of limitations** loi *f* de prescription, prescription *f* légale **2.** [of club, company, university] règle *f* ▸ **the statutes** le règlement, les statuts *mpl*.

statute book n 🇬🇧 code *m* (des lois), recueil *m* de lois / *the new law is not yet on the statute book* la nouvelle loi n'est pas encore entrée en vigueur.

statutory ['stætjʊtrɪ] adj **1.** [regulations] statutaire ; [rights, duties, penalty] statutaire, juridique ; [holiday] légal ; [offence] prévu par la loi ; [price controls, income policy] obligatoire ▸ **statutory rape** 🇺🇸 détournement *m* de mineur ▸ **statutory sick pay** 🇬🇧 indemnité de maladie versée par l'employeur ▸ **statutory tenant** locataire *mf* en place **2.** 🇬🇧 [token] ▸ **the statutory woman** la femme-alibi *(présente pour que soit respectée la réglementation sur l'égalité des sexes)*.

staunch [stɔːntʃ] ◆ adj [loyal] loyal, dévoué ; [unswerving] constant, inébranlable. ◆ vt [liquid, blood] étancher ; [flow] arrêter, endiguer.

staunchly ['stɔːntʃlɪ] adv [loyally] loyalement, avec dévouement ; [unswervingly] avec constance, fermement.

stave [steɪv] (*pt* & *pp* **staved** or **stove** [stəʊv]) n **1.** MUS portée *f* **2.** [stanza] stance *f*, strophe *f* **3.** [part of barrel] douve *f*, douelle *f*. ◆ **stave in** vt sep enfoncer, défoncer. ◆ **stave off** vt sep [defeat] retarder ; [worry, danger] écarter ; [disaster, threat] conjurer ; [misery, hunger, thirst] tromper ; [questions] éluder.

stay [steɪ] ◆ vi **1.** [remain] rester / *stay here* or *stay put until I come back* restez ici or ne bougez pas jusqu'à ce que je revienne / *would you like to stay for* or *to dinner?* voulez-vous rester dîner ? / *let's try and stay calm* essayons de rester calmes / *she managed to stay ahead of the others* elle a réussi à conserver son avance sur les autres / *personal computers have come to stay* or *are here to stay* l'ordinateur personnel est devenu indispensable **2.** [reside temporarily] : *how long are you staying in New York?* combien de temps restez-vous à New York ? / *we decided to stay an extra week* nous avons décidé de rester une semaine de plus or de prolonger notre séjour d'une semaine / *to look for a place to stay* chercher un endroit où loger. ◆ vt **1.** [last out] aller jusqu'au bout de, tenir jusqu'à la fin de ▸ **to stay the course** a) *lit* finir la course b) *fig* tenir jusqu'au bout **2.** [stop] arrêter, enrayer ; [delay] retarder. ◆ n [sojourn] séjour *m* / *enjoy your stay!* bon séjour ! ◆ **stay away** vi ne pas aller, s'abstenir d'aller. ◆ **stay behind** vi rester / *a few pupils stayed behind to talk to the teacher* quelques élèves sont restés (après le cours) pour parler au professeur. ◆ **stay down** vi **1.** [gen] rester en bas **2.** 🇬🇧 SCH redoubler **3.** [food] : *I do eat, but nothing will stay down* je mange, mais je ne peux rien garder. ◆ **stay in** vi **1.** [stay at home] rester à la maison, ne pas sortir ; [stay indoors] rester à l'intérieur, ne pas sortir **2.** [be kept in after school] être consigné, être en retenue **3.** [not fall out] rester en place, tenir. ◆ **stay out** vi **1.** [not come home] ne pas rentrer / *she stayed out all night* elle n'est pas rentrée de la nuit **2.** [remain outside] rester dehors / *get out and stay out!* sors d'ici et ne t'avise pas de revenir ! **3.** [not get involved] ne pas se mêler / *stay out of this!* ne te mêle pas de ça ! ◆ **stay over** vi **1.** [not leave] s'arrêter un certain temps / *we decided to stay over until the weekend* nous avons décidé de prolonger notre séjour jusqu'au week-end **2.** [stay the night] passer la nuit. ◆ **stay up** vi **1.** [not go to bed] veiller, ne pas se coucher **2.** [not fall - building, mast] rester debout ; [- socks, trousers] tenir ; [remain in place - pictures, decorations] rester en place. ◆ **stay with** vt insep inf : *just stay with it, you can do it* accroche-toi, tu peux y arriver.

staycation [steɪ'keɪʃən] n vacances *fpl* passées à la maison.

stayer ['steɪər] n inf : *he's a real stayer* il est drôlement résistant.

staying power ['steɪŋ-] n résistance *f*, endurance *f*.

stay-ups pl n [tights] bas *mpl* autofixants.

St Bernard [🇬🇧 -'bɜːnəd 🇺🇸 -bər'nɑːrd] n [dog] saint-bernard *m inv*.

STD n **1.** (abbr of **subscriber trunk dialling**) 🇬🇧 TELEC automatique *m* (interurbain) ▸ **STD code** indicatif *m* de zone **2.** (abbr of **sexually transmitted disease**) MST *f*.

stead [sted] n 🇬🇧 ▸ **in sb's stead** *fml* à la place de qqn ▸ **to stand sb in good stead** rendre grand service or être très utile à qqn.

steadfast ['stedfɑːst] adj **1.** [unswerving] constant, inébranlable ; [loyal] loyal, dévoué **2.** [steady - stare, gaze] fixe.

Steadicam® ['stedɪkæm] n Steadicam® *m*.

steadily ['stedɪlɪ] adv **1.** [regularly - increase, decline] régulièrement, progressivement ; [- breathe] régulièrement ; [non-stop - rain] sans interruption, sans cesse **2.** [firmly - stand] planté or campé sur ses jambes ; [- walk] d'un pas ferme ; [- gaze] fixement, sans détourner les yeux.

steady ['stedɪ] (*compar* **steadier**, *superl* **steadiest**, *pl* **steadies**, *pt* & *pp* **steadied**) ◆ adj **1.** [regular, constant - growth, increase, decline] régulier, progressif ; [- speed, pace] régulier, constant ; [- pulse] régulier, égal ; [- work] stable ; [- income] régulier / *steady boyfriend* petit ami *m* régulier or attitré **2.** [firm, stable - ladder, boat, relationship] stable ; [- structure, desk, chair] solide, stable / *hold the ladder steady for me* tiens-moi l'échelle ▸ **to have a steady hand** avoir la main sûre ; [calm - voice] ferme ; [- gaze] fixe ; [- nerves] solide **3.** [reliable - person] sérieux. ◆ adv ▸ **to go steady with sb** sortir avec qqn. ◆ interj ▸ **steady (on)!** a) [be careful] attention ! b) [calm down] du calme !

◆ vt **1.** [stabilize] stabiliser ; [hold in place] maintenir, retenir **2.** [calm] calmer. ◆ vi [boat, prices, stock market] se stabiliser ; [pulse, breathing] devenir régulier ; [person - regain balance] retrouver son équilibre ; [- calm down] se calmer.

steak [steɪk] n **1.** [beefsteak - for frying, grilling] steak *m*, bifteck *m* ▶ **steak and chips** steak frites *m* **2.** [beef - for stews, casseroles] bœuf *m* à braiser ▶ **steak and kidney pie** tourte à la viande et aux rognons cuite au four ▶ **steak and kidney pudding** tourte à la viande et aux rognons cuite à la vapeur **3.** [cut - of veal, turkey] escalope *f* ; [- of horse meat] steak *m*, bifteck *m* ; [- of other meat] tranche *f* ; [- of fish] tranche *f*, darne *f*.

steakhouse ['steɪkhaʊs] (*pl* [-haʊzɪz]) n grill *m*, grill-room *m*.

steal [stiːl] (*pt* stole [stəʊl], *pp* stolen ['stəʊln]) ◆ vt **1.** [money, property] voler ▶ **to steal sthg from sb** voler qqch à qqn **2.** fig [time] voler, prendre ; [attention, affection] détourner ▶ **to steal a glance at sb** jeter un regard furtif à qqn. ◆ vi **1.** [commit theft] voler **2.** [move secretively] ▶ **to steal in / out** entrer / sortir à pas furtifs or feutrés ▶ **to steal into a room** se glisser or se faufiler dans une pièce. ◆ n US inf [bargain] affaire *f*. ❖ **steal away** vi partir furtivement, s'esquiver.

stealing ['stiːlɪŋ] n vol *m*.

stealth [stelθ] n **1.** [of animal] ruse *f* **2.** (U) [underhandedness] moyens *mpl* détournés ▶ **stealth tax** impôt indirect et donc invisible.

Stealth bomber, Stealth plane n avion *m* furtif.

stealthily ['stelθɪlɪ] adv furtivement, subrepticement, en catimini.

stealthy ['stelθɪ] (*compar* stealthier, *superl* stealthiest) adj furtif.

steam [stiːm] ◆ n **1.** [vapour] vapeur *f* ; [condensation] buée *f* **2.** MECH & RAIL [as power] vapeur *f* ▶ **to run on** or **to work by steam** marcher à la vapeur ▶ **at full steam** à toute vapeur, à pleine vitesse. ◆ comp [boiler, locomotive, etc.] à vapeur. ◆ vt **1.** [unstick with steam] : *steam the stamps off the envelope* passez l'enveloppe à la vapeur pour décoller les timbres / *to steam open an envelope* décacheter une enveloppe à la vapeur **2.** CULIN (faire) cuire à la vapeur. ◆ vi **1.** [soup, kettle, wet clothes] fumer **2.** [go - train, ship] : *the train steamed into / out of the station* le train entra en gare / quitta la gare / *my brother steamed on ahead* fig mon frère filait devant. ❖ **steam up** ◆ vi [window, glasses] s'embuer, se couvrir de buée. ◆ vt sep [window, glasses] embuer.

steamboat ['stiːmbəʊt] n bateau *m* à vapeur, vapeur *m*.

steamed-up [stiːmd-] adj inf [angry] énervé, dans tous ses états.

steam engine n MECH moteur *m* à vapeur ; RAIL locomotive *f* à vapeur.

steamer ['stiːmər] n **1.** NAUT bateau *m* à vapeur, vapeur *m* **2.** CULIN [pan] marmite *f* à vapeur ; [basket inside pan] panier *m* de cuisson à la vapeur ; ELEC cuit-vapeur *m*.

steam iron n fer *m* (à repasser) à vapeur.

steamroll ['stiːmrəʊl] vt [road] cylindrer.

steamroller ['stiːm,rəʊlər] ◆ n lit & fig rouleau *m* compresseur ▶ **to use steamroller tactics** employer la technique du rouleau compresseur. ◆ vt **1.** [crush - opposition, obstacle] écraser **2.** [force] ▶ **to steamroller a bill through Parliament** faire passer une loi à la Chambre sans tenir compte de l'opposition ▶ **to steamroller sb into doing sthg** forcer qqn à faire qqch **3.** = **steamroll**.

steamroom ['stiːmruːm] n hammam *m*.

steam shovel n US bulldozer *m*.

steamy ['stiːmɪ] (*compar* steamier, *superl* steamiest) adj **1.** [room] plein de vapeur ; [window, mirror] embué **2.** inf [erotic] érotique, d'un érotisme torride.

steel [stiːl] ◆ n **1.** [iron alloy] acier *m* **2.** [steel industry] industrie *f* sidérurgique, sidérurgie *f* **3.** [for sharpening knives] aiguisoir *m* **4.** liter [sword] fer *m*. ◆ comp [industry, plant] sidérurgique ; [strike] des sidérurgistes ▶ **steel manufacturer** sidérurgiste *mf*. ◆ adj [helmet, cutlery, etc.] en acier. ◆ vt **1.** UK [harden] ▶ **to steel o.s. against sthg** se cuirasser contre qqch / *I had steeled myself for the worst* je m'étais préparé au pire **2.** METALL aciérer.

steel wool n paille *f* de fer.

steelworker ['stiːl,wɜːkər] n sidérurgiste *mf*.

steelworks ['stiːlwɜːks] (*pl* steelworks) n aciérie *f*, usine *f* sidérurgique.

steely ['stiːlɪ] adj **1.** [in colour] d'acier, gris acier (inv) **2.** [strong - determination, will] de fer ; [- look] d'acier.

steep [stiːp] ◆ adj **1.** [hill] raide, abrupt, escarpé ; [slope] fort, raide ; [cliff] abrupt ; [road, path] raide, escarpé ; [staircase] raide **2.** [increase, fall] fort **3.** inf [fee, price] excessif, élevé **4.** inf [unreasonable] : *it's a bit steep asking us to do all that work by Friday* c'est un peu fort or un peu raide de nous demander de faire tout ce travail pour vendredi. ◆ vt [soak] (faire) tremper ; CULIN (faire) macérer, (faire) mariner. ◆ vi [gen] tremper ; CULIN macérer, mariner.

steeped [stiːpt] adj : *steeped in tradition / mystery* imprégné de tradition / mystère.

steeple ['stiːpl] n clocher *m*, flèche *f*.

steeplechase ['stiːpltʃeɪs] n [in horse racing, athletics] steeple *m*, steeple-chase *m*.

steeplejack ['stiːpldʒæk] n UK réparateur de clochers et de cheminées.

steeply ['stiːplɪ] adv en pente raide, à pic / *costs are rising steeply* les coûts montent en flèche.

steer ['stɪər] ◆ vt **1.** [car] conduire ; NAUT [boat] gouverner, barrer **2.** [person] guider, diriger **3.** [conversation, project, etc.] diriger. ◆ vi **1.** [driver] conduire ; NAUT [helmsman] gouverner, barrer ▶ **to steer clear of sthg / sb** éviter qqch / qqn **2.** [car] : *this car steers very well / badly* cette voiture a une excellente / très mauvaise direction ; NAUT [boat] se diriger. ◆ n AGR bœuf *m*.

steering ['stɪərɪŋ] ◆ n **1.** AUTO [apparatus, mechanism] direction *f* ; [manner of driving] conduite *f* **2.** NAUT conduite *f*, pilotage *m*. ◆ comp AUTO [arm, lever] de direction.

steering column n colonne *f* de direction.

steering committee n UK comité *m* directeur, comité *m* de pilotage.

steering lock n AUTO **1.** [turning circle] rayon *m* de braquage **2.** [antitheft device] antivol *m* de direction.

steering wheel n **1.** AUTO volant *m* **2.** NAUT roue *f* du gouvernail, barre *f*.

stellar ['stelər] adj **1.** ASTRON stellaire **2.** inf CIN & THEAT : *the play boasts a stellar cast* cette pièce a une distribution éblouissante.

stem [stem] (*pt & pp* stemmed, *cont* stemming) ◆ n **1.** BOT [of plant, tree] tige *f* ; [of fruit, leaf] queue *f* **2.** [of glass] pied *m* **3.** [of tobacco pipe] tuyau *m* **4.** LING [of word] radical *m* **5.** TECH [in lock, watch] tige *f* **6.** [vertical stroke - of letter] hampe *f* ; [- of musical note] queue *f* **7.** NAUT [timber, structure] étrave *f* ; [forward section] proue *f*. ◆ vt **1.** [check, stop - flow, spread, bleeding] arrêter, endiguer ; [- blood] étancher ; [- river, flood] endiguer, contenir **2.** SPORT ▶ **to stem one's skis** faire un stem or stemm. ◆ vi **1.** [derive] ▶ **to stem from** avoir pour cause, être le résultat de **2.** SPORT faire du stem or stemm.

stem cell n MED cellule f souche ▶ **stem cell research** recherche f sur les cellules souches.

stench [stentʃ] n puanteur f, odeur f nauséabonde.

stencil ['stensl] (🇬🇧 pt & pp stencilled, cont stencilling ; 🇺🇸 pt & pp stenciled, cont stenciling) ◆ n 1. [for typing] stencil m 2. [template] pochoir m 3. [pattern] dessin m au pochoir. ◆ vt dessiner au pochoir.

stenographer [stə'nɒgrəfər] n 🇺🇸 sténographe mf.

stenography [stə'nɒgrəfɪ] n 🇺🇸 sténographie f.

step [step] (pt & pp stepped, cont stepping) ◆ n 1. [pace] pas m / take two steps forwards / backwards faites deux pas en avant / en arrière / that's certainly put a spring in her step ça a dû lui donner un peu de ressort / he was following a few steps behind me il me suivait à quelques pas 2. [move, action] pas m ; [measure] mesure f, disposition f / it's a great step forward for mankind c'est un grand pas en avant pour l'humanité ▶ **to take steps to do sthg** prendre des mesures pour faire qqch / it's a step in the right direction c'est un pas dans la bonne direction 3. [stage] étape f / this promotion is a big step up for me cette promotion est un grand pas en avant pour moi / we are still one step ahead of our competitors nous conservons une petite avance sur nos concurrents / we'll support you every step of the way nous vous soutiendrons à fond or sur toute la ligne / one step at a time petit à petit 4. [stair - gen] marche f ; [- into bus, train, etc.] marchepied m ▶ **a flight of steps** un escalier / 'mind the step' 'attention à la marche' 5. DANCE pas m / do try and keep step! essaie donc de danser en mesure ! 6. [in marching] pas m ▶ **in step** au pas ▶ **to march in step** marcher au pas ▶ **out of step** désynchronisé ▶ **to be out of step** ne pas être en cadence ▶ **to fall into step with sb** a) lit s'aligner sur le pas de qqn b) fig se ranger à l'avis de qqn ▶ **to keep step** marcher au pas. ◆ vi 1. [take a single step] faire un pas ; [walk, go] marcher, aller / step this way, please par ici, je vous prie / step inside! entrez ! / I stepped onto / off the train je suis monté dans le / descendu du train / she stepped lightly over the ditch elle enjamba le fossé lestement 2. [put one's foot down, tread] marcher / I stepped on a banana skin / in a puddle j'ai marché sur une peau de banane / dans une flaque d'eau ▶ **step on it!** inf appuie sur le champignon ! ▶ **to step out of line** s'écarter du droit chemin. ▶ **to step out of line** s'écarter du droit chemin. ◆ vt 1. [measure out] mesurer 2. [space out] échelonner. ❖ **steps** pl n 🇬🇧 [stepladder] ▶ **(pair of) steps** escabeau m. ❖ **step aside** vi 1. [move to one side] s'écarter, s'effacer 2. = step down (vi). ❖ **step back** vi 1. lit reculer, faire un pas en arrière 2. fig prendre du recul. ❖ **step down** vi 1. [descend] descendre 2. [quit position, job] se retirer, se désister. ❖ **step forward** vi 1. lit faire un pas en avant 2. fig [volunteer] se présenter, être volontaire. ❖ **step in** vi 1. [enter] entrer 2. [intervene] intervenir. ❖ **step out** vi 1. [go out of doors] sortir 2. [walk faster] presser le pas. ❖ **step up** ◆ vi s'approcher ▶ **to step up to sb** s'approcher de qqn. ◆ vt sep [increase - output, pace] augmenter, accroître ; [- activity, efforts] intensifier.

step aerobics n step m.

stepbrother ['step,brʌðər] n demi-frère m.

step-by-step ◆ adv [gradually] pas à pas, petit à petit. ◆ adj [point by point] : a step-by-step guide to buying your own house un guide détaillé pour l'achat de votre maison.

stepchild ['step,tʃaɪld] (pl stepchildren [-,tʃɪldrən]) n beau-fils m, belle-fille f (fils ou fille du conjoint).

stepdaughter ['step,dɔ:tər] n belle-fille f (fille du conjoint).

stepfather ['step,fɑ:ðər] n beau-père m (conjoint de la mère).

stepladder ['step,lædər] n escabeau m.

stepmother ['step,mʌðər] n belle-mère f (conjointe du père).

stepping-stone ['stepɪŋ-] n 1. lit pierre f de gué 2. fig tremplin m / a stepping-stone to a new career un tremplin pour (se lancer dans) une nouvelle carrière.

stepsister ['step,sɪstər] n demi-sœur f.

stepson ['stepsʌn] n beau-fils m (fils du conjoint d'un précédent mariage).

stereo ['sterɪəʊ] (pl stereos) ◆ n 1. [stereo sound] stéréo f / broadcast in stereo retransmis en stéréo 2. [hifi system] chaîne f (stéréo). ◆ adj [cassette, record, record player] stéréo (inv) ; [recording, broadcast] en stéréo.

stereophonic [,sterɪə'fɒnɪk] adj stéréophonique.

stereo system n chaîne f stéréo.

stereotype ['sterɪətaɪp] ◆ n 1. [idea, trait, convention] stéréotype m 2. TYPO cliché m. ◆ vt 1. [person, role] stéréotyper 2. TYPO clicher.

stereotyped ['sterɪəutaɪpt] adj stéréotypé.

stereotypical [,sterɪəʊ'tɪpɪkl] adj stéréotypé.

stereotyping ['sterɪəʊ,taɪpɪŋ] n : we want to avoid sexual stereotyping nous voulons éviter les stéréotypes sexuels.

sterile ['steraɪl] adj stérile.

sterility [ste'rɪlətɪ] n stérilité f.

sterilization, sterilisation [,sterəlaɪ'zeɪʃn] n stérilisation f.

sterilize ['sterəlaɪz] vt stériliser.

sterilized, sterilised ['sterəlaɪzd] adj [milk] stérilisé.

sterling ['stɜ:lɪŋ] ◆ n 1. [currency] sterling m inv ▶ **sterling area** zone f sterling 2. [standard] titre m 3. [silverware] argenterie f. ◆ comp [reserves, balances] en sterling ; [traveller's cheques] en livres sterling. ◆ adj 1. [gold, silver] fin 2. fml [first-class] excellent, de premier ordre.

stern [stɜ:n] ◆ adj 1. [strict, harsh - person, measure] sévère, strict ; [- appearance] sévère, austère ; [- discipline, punishment] sévère, rigoureux ; [- look, rebuke] sévère, dur ; [- warning] solennel, grave 2. [robust] solide, robuste. ◆ n NAUT arrière m, poupe f.

sternly ['stɜ:nlɪ] adv sévèrement.

steroid ['stɪərɔɪd] n stéroïde m ▶ **steroid abuse** abus m de stéroïdes anabolisants.

stethoscope ['steθəskəʊp] n stéthoscope m.

Stetson® ['stetsn] n Stetson® m, chapeau m de cow-boy.

stevedore ['sti:vədɔ:r] ◆ n 🇺🇸 docker m, débardeur m. ◆ vi travailler comme docker or débardeur.

stew [stju:] ◆ n CULIN ragoût m ▶ **lamb / vegetable stew** ragoût d'agneau / de légumes (mijotés). ◆ vt [meat] préparer en ragoût, cuire (en ragoût) ; [fruit] (faire) cuire en compote. ◆ vi 1. CULIN [meat] cuire en ragoût, mijoter ; [fruit] cuire ; [tea] infuser trop longtemps 2. [worry] ▶ **to stew over sthg** ruminer qqch.

steward ['stjʊəd] n 1. [on aeroplane, ship] steward m 2. [at race, sports event] commissaire m ▶ **steward's enquiry** 🇬🇧 enquête f des commissaires 3. [at dance, social event] organisateur m, -trice f ; [at meeting, demonstration] membre m du service d'ordre 4. [of property] intendant m, -e f ; [estate, finances] régisseur m, -euse f ; [in college] économe mf.

stewardess ['stjʊədɪs] n hôtesse f.

stewed [stju:d] adj 1. CULIN ▶ **stewed meat** ragoût m ▶ **stewed fruit** compote f de fruits 2. [tea] trop infusé 3. inf [drunk] bourré, cuité.

stewing steak [stju:ɪŋ-] n 🇬🇧 bœuf m à braiser.

St. Ex. written abbr of stock exchange.

stg written abbr of sterling.

STI (abbr of sexually transmitted infection) n MED IST *f*.

stick [stɪk] (*pt & pp* stuck [stʌk]) ◆ n **1.** [piece of wood] bout *m* de bois ; [branch] branche *f* ; [twig] petite branche *f*, brindille *f* / *gather some sticks, we'll make a fire* ramassez du bois, on fera du feu **2.** [wooden rod - as weapon] bâton *m* ; [walking stick] canne *f*, bâton *m* ; [drumstick] baguette *f* ; [for plants] rame *f*, tuteur *m* ; [for lollipop] bâton *m* / *his behaviour became a stick to beat him with* son comportement s'est retourné contre lui / *we don't have one stick of decent furniture* nous n'avons pas un seul meuble convenable ▸ **to get (hold of) the wrong end of the stick** mal comprendre, comprendre de travers **3.** [piece - of chalk] bâton *m*, morceau *m* ; [- of cinnamon, incense, liquorice, dynamite] bâton *m* ; [- of charcoal] morceau *m* ; [- of chewing gum] tablette *f* ; [- of glue, deodorant] bâton *m*, stick *m* ; [- of celery] branche *f* ; [- of rhubarb] tige *f* **4.** GAMES & SPORT [in lacrosse] crosse *f* ; [in hockey] crosse *f*, stick *m* ; [ski pole] bâton *m* (de ski) ; [baseball bat] batte *f* ; [billiard cue] queue *f* de billard ; [in pick-up sticks] bâton *m*, bâtonnet *m*, jonchet *m* **5.** (*U*) ⟦UK⟧ *inf* [criticism] critiques *fpl* (désobligeantes) ▸ **to get** or **to come in for a lot of stick** : *the police got a lot of stick from the press* la police s'est fait éreinter or démolir par la presse / *he got a lot of stick from his friends about his new hairstyle* ses amis l'ont bien charrié avec sa nouvelle coupe. ◆ vt **1.** [jab, stab - spear, nail, knife] planter, enfoncer ; [- needle] piquer, planter ; [- pole, shovel] planter ; [- elbow, gun] enfoncer / *don't stick drawing pins in the wall* ne plantez pas de punaises dans le mur / *a ham stuck with cloves* un jambon piqué de clous de girofle **2.** [insert] insérer, mettre, ficher ; [put] mettre / *he stuck a rose in his lapel* il s'est mis une rose à la boutonnière / *here, stick this under the chair leg* tenez, calez la chaise avec ça / *she stuck her head into the office / out of the window* elle a passé la tête dans le bureau / par la fenêtre ; *inf* [put casually] mettre, ficher / *mix it all together and stick it in the oven* mélangez bien (le tout) et mettez au four / *he can stick the job!* ⟦UK⟧ *v inf* il sait où il peut se le mettre, son boulot ! ▸ **stick it!** *v inf* tu peux te le mettre où je pense or quelque part ! **3.** [fasten] fixer ; [pin up] punaiser **4.** [with adhesive] coller / *to stick a stamp on an envelope* coller un timbre sur une enveloppe / *he had posters stuck to the walls with Sellotape* il avait scotché des posters aux murs **5.** ⟦UK⟧ *inf* [bear - person, situation] supporter / *I can't stick him* je ne peux pas le sentir **6.** *inf* [with chore, burden] / *I always get stuck with the dishes* je me retrouve toujours avec la vaisselle sur les bras, c'est toujours moi qui dois me taper la vaisselle. ◆ vi **1.** [arrow, dart, spear] se planter **2.** [attach, adhere - wet clothes, bandage, chewing gum] coller ; [- gummed label, stamp] tenir, coller ; [- burr] s'accrocher / *the dough stuck to my fingers* la pâte collait à mes doigts / *the damp has made the stamps stick together* l'humidité a collé les timbres les uns aux autres / *food won't stick to these pans* ces casseroles n'attachent pas **3.** [become jammed, wedged - mechanism, drawer, key] se coincer, se bloquer / *the lorry stuck fast in the mud* le camion s'est complètement enlisé dans la boue **4.** [remain, keep] rester / *his bodyguards stick close to him at all times* ses gardes du corps l'accompagnent partout or ne le quittent jamais d'une semelle / *stick to the main road* suivez la route principale **5.** *inf* [be upheld] ▸ **to make the charge** or **charges stick** prouver la culpabilité de qqn **6.** [extend, project] : *his ticket was sticking out of his pocket* son billet sortait or dépassait de sa poche. ❖ **sticks** pl n *inf* [backwoods] cambrousse *f* / *they live way out in the sticks* ils habitent en pleine cambrousse. ❖ **stick around** vi *inf* [stay] rester (dans les parages) ;

[wait] attendre. ❖ **stick at** vt insep ▸ **to stick at it** ⟦UK⟧ [persevere] persévérer. ❖ **stick by** vt insep **1.** [person] soutenir / *don't worry, I'll always stick by you* sois tranquille, je serai toujours là pour te soutenir **2.** [one's decision] s'en tenir à. ❖ **stick down** ◆ vt sep **1.** [flap, envelope] coller **2.** ⟦UK⟧ [note down] noter ; [scribble] griffonner **3.** *inf* [place] poser. ◆ vi [flap, envelope] (se) coller. ❖ **stick in** ◆ vt sep **1.** [nail, knife, spear] planter, enfoncer ; [needle] piquer, enfoncer ; [pole, shovel] enfoncer, planter **2.** [insert - coin, bank card] insérer ; [- electric plug] brancher ; [- cork, sink plug] enfoncer ; [- word, sentence] ajouter **3.** [glue in] coller. ◆ vi [dart, arrow, spear] se planter. ❖ **stick on** ◆ vt sep **1.** [fasten on - gummed badge, label, stamp] coller ; [- china handle] recoller ; [- broom head] fixer **2.** *inf* [jacket, boots] enfiler. ◆ vi coller, se coller. ❖ **stick out** ◆ vt sep **1.** [extend - hand, leg] tendre, allonger ; [- feelers, head] sortir ▸ **to stick one's tongue out (at sb)** tirer la langue (à qqn) / *I opened the window and stuck my head out* j'ai ouvert la fenêtre et j'ai passé la tête au dehors **2.** ⟦PHR⟧ **to stick it out** *inf* tenir le coup jusqu'au bout. ◆ vi **1.** [protrude - nail, splinter] sortir ; [- teeth] avancer ; [- plant, shoot] pointer ; [- ledge, balcony] être en saillie / *her ears stick out* elle a les oreilles décollées **2.** [be noticeable - colour] ressortir / *I don't like to stick out in a crowd* je n'aime pas me singulariser or me faire remarquer. ❖ **stick to** vt insep : *it won't be easy to stick to this schedule* ce ne sera pas facile de tenir or respecter ce planning / *once I make a decision I stick to it* une fois que j'ai pris une décision, je m'y tiens or je n'en démords pas / *to stick to one's word* or *promises* tenir (sa) parole / *to stick to one's principles* rester fidèle à ses principes / *stick to the point!* ne vous éloignez pas du sujet ! ❖ **stick together** vi *inf* [people] rester ensemble ; *fig* se serrer les coudes. ❖ **stick up** ◆ vt sep **1.** [sign, notice, poster] afficher ; [postcard] coller ; [with drawing pins] punaiser **2.** [raise - pole] dresser ▸ **to stick one's hand up** lever la main ▸ **stick 'em up!** *inf* haut les mains ! **3.** ⟦US⟧ *inf* [rob - person, bank, supermarket] braquer. ◆ vi [point upwards - tower, antenna] s'élever ; [- plant shoots] pointer. ❖ **stick up for** vt insep ▸ **to stick up for sb** prendre la défense or le parti de qqn / *stick up for yourself!* ne te laisse pas faire ! / *he has trouble sticking up for himself / his rights* il a du mal à défendre ses intérêts / à faire valoir ses droits. ❖ **stick with** vt insep **1.** [activity, subject] s'en tenir à, persister dans **2.** [person] : *stick with me, kid, and you'll be all right* *inf* reste avec moi, petit, et tout ira bien.

sticker ['stɪkə'] n **1.** [adhesive label] autocollant *m* **2.** *inf* [determined person] : *she's a sticker* elle est persévérante, elle va au bout de ce qu'elle entreprend.

stickiness ['stɪkɪnɪs] n [of hands, substance, surface, jamjar] caractère *m* gluant or poisseux.

sticking plaster ['stɪkɪŋ-] n ⟦UK⟧ pansement *m*, sparadrap *m*.

sticking point n *fig* point *m* de friction.

stick insect n phasme *m*.

stick-in-the-mud n *inf* [fogey] vieux croûton *m* ; [killjoy] rabat-joie *m inv*.

stickleback ['stɪklbæk] n épinoche *f* (*de rivière*).

stickler ['stɪklə'] n ▸ **to be a stickler for** a) [regulations, discipline, good manners] être à cheval sur b) [tradition, routine] insister sur.

stick-on adj autocollant.

stickpin ['stɪkpɪn] n ⟦US⟧ épingle *f* de cravate.

stick shift n ⟦US⟧ AUTO levier *m* de vitesse.

stick-shift transmission n ⟦US⟧ AUTO transmission *f* manuelle.

stick-up n ⟦US⟧ *inf* braquage *m*, hold-up *m*.

sticky ['stɪkɪ] (compar **stickier,** super/ **stickiest**) adj **1.** [adhesive] adhésif, gommé **2.** [tacky, gluey - hands, fingers] collant, poisseux ; [- substance, surface, jamjar] gluant, poisseux **3.** [sweaty] moite **4.** [humid - weather] moite, humide **5.** inf [awkward - situation] difficile, délicat ▶ **to be (batting) on a sticky wicket** 🇬🇧 être dans une situation difficile.

sticky tape n ruban m adhésif.

stiff [stɪf] ◆ adj **1.** [rigid] raide, rigide / stiff paper / cardboard papier / carton rigide / a stiff brush une brosse à poils durs **2.** [thick, difficult to stir] ferme, consistant / beat the mixture until it is stiff battez jusqu'à obtention d'une pâte consistante / beat the eggwhites until stiff battre les blancs en neige jusqu'à ce qu'ils soient (bien) fermes **3.** [difficult to move] dur / the drawers have got a bit stiff les tiroirs sont devenus un peu durs à ouvrir **4.** [aching] courbaturé, raide / I'm still stiff after playing squash the other day j'ai encore des courbatures d'avoir joué au squash l'autre jour ▶ **to have a stiff back** avoir mal au dos ▶ **to have a stiff neck** avoir un or le torticolis **5.** [over-formal - smile, welcome] froid ; [- person, manners, behaviour] froid, guindé ; [- style] guindé **6.** [difficult] dur, ardu ▶ **to face stiff competition** avoir affaire à forte concurrence **7.** [severe] sévère / I sent them a stiff letter je leur ai envoyé une lettre bien sentie **8.** [strong - breeze, drink] fort **9.** [high - price, bill] élevé **10.** [determined - resistance, opposition] tenace, acharné ; [- resolve] ferme, inébranlable **11.** 🇬🇧 inf [full] plein (à craquer). ◆ adv inf ▶ **to be bored stiff** mourir d'ennui ▶ **to be worried / scared stiff** être mort d'inquiétude / de peur. ◆ n v inf [corpse] macchabée m.

stiffen ['stɪfn] ◆ vt **1.** [paper, fabric] raidir, renforcer **2.** [thicken - batter, concrete] donner de la consistance à ; [- sauce] lier **3.** [make painful - arm, leg, muscle] courbaturer **4.** [strengthen - resistance, resolve] renforcer. ◆ vi **1.** [harden - paper, fabric] devenir raide or rigide **2.** [tense, stop moving] se raidir **3.** [thicken - batter, concrete] épaissir, devenir ferme ; [- sauce] se lier **4.** [become hard to move - hinge, handle, door] se coincer **5.** [start to ache] s'ankyloser **6.** [strengthen - resistance, resolve] se renforcer ; [- breeze] forcir.

stiffener ['stɪfnər] n **1.** [in collar] baleine f **2.** 🇬🇧 inf [drink] remontant m.

stiffly ['stɪflɪ] adv **1.** [rigidly] : stiffly starched très empesé or amidonné / he stood stiffly to attention il se tenait raide au garde-à-vous **2.** [painfully - walk, bend] avec raideur **3.** [coldly - smile, greet] froidement, d'un air distant.

stiffness ['stɪfnɪs] n **1.** [of paper, fabric] raideur f, rigidité f **2.** [of batter, dough, concrete] consistance f, fermeté f **3.** [of hinge, handle, door] dureté f **4.** [of joints, limbs] raideur f, courbatures fpl **5.** [of manners, smile, welcome] froideur f, distance f ; [of style] caractère m guindé **6.** [difficulty - of exam, competition] difficulté f, dureté f.

stifle ['staɪfl] ◆ vt **1.** [suppress - resistance, creativity, progress] réprimer, étouffer ; [- tears, anger, emotion] réprimer **2.** [suffocate] étouffer, suffoquer. ◆ vi étouffer, suffoquer.

stifling ['staɪflɪŋ] adj suffocant, étouffant.

stigma ['stɪgmə] n **1.** [social disgrace] honte f **2.** BOT, MED & ZOOL stigmate m.

stigmata [stɪg'mɑːtə] pl n RELIG stigmates mpl.

stigmatize, stigmatise ['stɪgmətaɪz] vt stigmatiser.

stile [staɪl] n **1.** [over fence] échalier m **2.** [turnstile] tourniquet m **3.** CONSTR [upright] montant m.

stiletto [stɪ'letəʊ] (pl **stilettos**) n **1.** [heel] talon m aiguille **2.** [knife] stylet m. ◆ **stilettos** pl n (chaussures fpl à) talons mpl aiguilles.

still¹ [stɪl] adv **1.** [as of this moment] encore, toujours / we're still waiting for the repairman to come nous attendons toujours que le réparateur vienne / there's still a bit of cake left il reste encore un morceau de gâteau / the worst was still to come le pire n'était pas encore arrivé **2.** [all the same] quand même / it's a shame we lost — still, it was a good game (c'est) dommage que nous ayons perdu — quand même, c'était un bon match **3.** (with compar) [even] encore / still more / less encore plus / moins / still further or further still encore plus loin / the sea was getting still rougher la mer était de plus en plus agitée.

still² [stɪl] ◆ adj **1.** [motionless - person, air, surface] immobile / be still! arrête de remuer ! ▶ **still waters run deep** prov méfie-toi de l'eau qui dort prov **2.** [calm] calme, tranquille ; [quiet] silencieux **3.** [not fizzy] plat. ◆ adv sans bouger / stand still! ne bougez pas ! / my heart stood still mon cœur a cessé de battre / they're so excited they can't sit still ils sont tellement excités qu'ils ne peuvent pas rester en place / try to hold the camera still essaie de ne pas bouger l'appareil photo. ◆ vt liter **1.** [silence] faire taire **2.** [allay - doubts, fears] apaiser, calmer. ◆ n **1.** liter [silence] silence m **2.** CIN photo f (de plateau) ▶ **still photographer** photographe mf de plateau **3.** [apparatus] alambic m.

stillbirth ['stɪlbɜːθ] n [birth] mort f à la naissance ; [fœtus] enfant m mort-né, enfant f mort-née.

stillborn ['stɪlbɔːn] adj **1.** MED mort-né **2.** fig [idea, plan] avorté.

still life (pl **still lifes**) n nature f morte.

stillness ['stɪlnɪs] n **1.** [motionlessness] immobilité f **2.** [calm] tranquillité f, paix f.

stilt [stɪlt] n **1.** [for walking] échasse f **2.** ARCHIT pilotis m.

stilted ['stɪltɪd] adj [speech, writing, person] guindé, emprunté ; [discussion] qui manque de naturel.

Stilton® ['stɪltn] n stilton m, fromage m de Stilton.

stimulant ['stɪmjʊlənt] ◆ n stimulant m. ◆ adj stimulant.

stimulate ['stɪmjʊleɪt] vt stimuler ▶ **to stimulate sb to do sthg** inciter or encourager qqn à faire qqch.

stimulating ['stɪmjʊleɪtɪŋ] adj **1.** [medicine, drug] stimulant **2.** [work, conversation, experience] stimulant, enrichissant.

stimulation [,stɪmjʊ'leɪʃn] n **1.** [of person] stimulation f **2.** [stimulus] stimulant m.

stimulus ['stɪmjʊləs] (pl **stimuli** [-laɪ or -liː]) n **1.** [incentive] stimulant m, incitation f **2.** PHYSIOL stimulus m.

sting [stɪŋ] (pt & pp **stung** [stʌŋ]) ◆ vt **1.** [subj: insect, nettle, scorpion] piquer ; [subj: smoke] piquer, brûler ; [subj: vinegar, acid, disinfectant] brûler ; [subj: whip, rain] cingler **2.** [subj: remark, joke, criticism] piquer (au vif), blesser ▶ **to sting sb into action** inciter or pousser qqn à agir **3.** inf [cheat] arnaquer / they stung me for £20 ils m'ont arnaqué de 20 livres. ◆ vi **1.** [insect, nettle, scorpion] piquer ; [vinegar, acid, disinfectant] brûler, piquer ; [whip, rain] cingler **2.** [eyes, skin] piquer, brûler. ◆ n **1.** [organ - of bee, wasp, scorpion] aiguillon m, dard m ; [- of nettle] poil m (urticant) **2.** [wound, pain, mark - from insect, nettle, scorpion] piqûre f ; [- from vinegar, acid, disinfectant] brûlure f ; [- from whip] douleur f cinglante **3.** inf [trick] arnaque f ▶ **sting (operation)** coup m monté (où les policiers se font passer pour des complices).

stinging ['stɪŋɪŋ] adj **1.** [wound, pain] cuisant ; [bite, eyes] qui pique ; [lash, rain] cinglant **2.** [remark, joke, criticism] cinglant, mordant.

stinging nettle n ortie f.

stingray ['stɪŋreɪ] n pastenague f.

stingy ['stɪndʒɪ] adj inf [person] radin ; [amount, helping] misérable.

stink [stɪŋk] (pt **stank** [stæŋk], pp **stunk** [stʌŋk]) ◆ vi **1.** [smell] puer, empester **2.** inf [be bad] : I think your *idea stinks!* je trouve ton idée nulle ! / *this town stinks!* cette ville est pourrie ! ◆ n **1.** [stench] puanteur f, odeur f nauséabonde **2.** *inf* [fuss] esclandre m ▶ **to kick up** or **to make** or **to raise a stink about sthg** faire un esclandre or un scandale à propos de qqch. ❖ **stink out** vt sep *inf* **1.** [drive away] chasser par la mauvaise odeur **2.** [fill with a bad smell] empester.

stink-bomb n boule f puante.

stinking ['stɪŋkɪŋ] ◆ adj **1.** [smelly] puant, nauséabond **2.** *inf* [as intensifier] : *I've got a stinking cold* j'ai un rhume carabiné. ◆ adv *inf* vachement ▶ **to be stinking rich** être plein de fric or plein aux as.

stint [stɪnt] ◆ n **1.** [period of work] période f de travail ; [share of work] part f de travail **2.** *fml* [limitation] ▶ **without stint a)** [spend] sans compter **b)** [give] généreusement **c)** [work] inlassablement. ◆ vt 🇬🇧 **1.** [skimp on] lésiner sur **2.** [deprive] priver. ◆ vi 🇬🇧 ▶ **to stint on sthg** lésiner sur qqch.

stipend ['staɪpend] n traitement m, appointements mpl.

stipulate ['stɪpjʊleɪt] ◆ vt stipuler. ◆ vi *fml* ▶ **to stipulate for sthg** stipuler qqch.

stipulation [ˌstɪpjʊ'leɪʃn] n stipulation f.

stir [stɜːr] ◆ (*pt & pp* **stirred**, *cont* **stirring**) ◆ vt **1.** [mix] remuer, tourner **2.** [move] agiter, remuer **3.** [touch] émouvoir **4.** [rouse, excite] éveiller, exciter ▶ **to stir sb to do sthg** inciter or pousser qqn à faire qqch ▶ **to stir sb into action** pousser qqn à agir. ◆ vi **1.** [move - person] bouger, remuer ; [- leaves] remuer **2.** [awaken, be roused - feeling, anger] s'éveiller **3.** *inf* [cause trouble] faire de la provocation or des histoires. ◆ n **1.** [act of mixing] ▶ **to give sthg a stir** remuer qqch **2.** [commotion] émoi m, agitation f ▶ **to cause** or **to create** or **to make quite a stir** soulever un vif émoi, faire grand bruit **3.** [movement] mouvement m. ❖ **stir in** vt sep CULIN ajouter or incorporer en remuant. ❖ **stir up** vt sep **1.** [disturb - dust, mud] soulever **2.** [incite, provoke - trouble] provoquer ; [- emotions] exciter, attiser ; [- dissent] fomenter ; [- memories] réveiller ; [- crowd, followers] ameuter / *he likes stirring it* or *things up* il aime provoquer.

stir-fry ◆ vt CULIN faire sauter à feu vif *(tout en remuant)*. ◆ adj sauté.

stirring ['stɜːrɪŋ] ◆ adj [music, song] entraînant ; [story] excitant, passionnant ; [speech] vibrant. ◆ n : *he felt vague stirrings of guilt* il éprouva un vague sentiment de culpabilité / *the first stirrings of what was to become the Romantic movement* les premières manifestations de ce qui allait devenir le mouvement romantique.

stirrup ['stɪrəp] n EQUIT étrier m ▶ **to put one's feet in the stirrups** chausser les étriers. ❖ **stirrups** pl n MED étriers mpl.

stitch [stɪtʃ] ◆ n **1.** SEW point m ; [in knitting] maille f **2.** MED point m de suture / *I'm having my stitches taken out tomorrow* on m'ôte les fils demain **3.** [pain] point m de côté ▶ **to get a stitch** attraper un point de côté **4.** [PHR] **to be in stitches** *inf* se tordre or être écroulé de rire. ◆ vt **1.** [material, shirt, hem] coudre **2.** MED suturer **3.** [in bookbinding] brocher. ❖ **stitch down** vt sep rabattre. ❖ **stitch up** vt sep **1.** [material, shirt, hem] coudre **2.** MED suturer **3.** *inf* [deal] conclure, sceller **4.** *inf* [frame - person] : *he reckons the police stitched him up* il pense que la police a monté un coup contre lui.

stitching ['stɪtʃɪŋ] n **1.** [gen] couture f **2.** [in bookbinding] brochage m.

stoat [stəʊt] n hermine f.

stock [stɒk] ◆ n **1.** [supply] réserve f, provision f, stock m ; COMM & INDUST stock m / *we got in a stock of food* nous avons fait tout un stock de nourriture ▶ **in stock**

en stock, en magasin ▶ **to keep sthg in stock** stocker qqch ▶ **out of stock** épuisé ▶ **to take stock a)** *lit* faire l'inventaire **b)** *fig* faire le point **2.** [total amount] parc m ▶ **the housing stock** le parc de logements **3.** *(usu pl)* ST. EX [gen] valeur f mobilière ; [share] action f ; [bond] obligation f ▶ **to invest in stocks and shares** investir dans des actions et obligations or en portefeuille ▶ **government stocks** obligations fpl or titres mpl d'État **4.** FIN [equity] capital m **5.** *fig* [value, credit] cote f ▶ **to put stock in sthg** faire (grand) cas de qqch **6.** [descent, ancestry] souche f, lignée f / *of peasant / noble stock* de souche paysanne / noble **7.** AGR [animals] cheptel m **8.** CULIN bouillon m ▶ **vegetable stock** bouillon de légumes **9.** [handle, butt - of gun, plough] fût m ; [- of whip] manche m ; [- of fishing rod] gaule f **10.** BOT giroflée f **11.** [tree trunk] tronc m ; [tree stump] souche f **12.** HORT [stem receiving graft] porte-greffe m, sujet m ; [plant from which graft is taken] plante f mère *(sur laquelle on prélève un greffon)* **13.** [in card games, dominoes] talon m, pioche f **14.** THEAT répertoire m **15.** [neckcloth] lavallière f, foulard m **16.** NAUT [of anchor] jas m. ◆ vt **1.** COMM [have in stock] avoir (en stock), vendre **2.** [supply] approvisionner ; [fill] remplir **3.** [stream, lake] empoissonner ; [farm] monter en bétail. ◆ adj **1.** [common, typical - phrase, expression] tout fait ; [- question, answer, excuse] classique **2.** COMM [kept in stock] en stock ; [widely available] courant ▶ **stock control** contrôle m des stocks **3.** AGR [for breeding] destiné à la reproduction **4.** THEAT [play] du répertoire. ❖ **stocks** pl n **1.** [instrument of punishment] pilori m **2.** NAUT [frame] cale f ▶ **on the stocks** en chantier. ❖ **stock up** ◆ vi s'approvisionner ▶ **to stock up on** or **with sthg** s'approvisionner en. ◆ vt sep approvisionner, garnir.

stockade [stɒ'keɪd] ◆ n **1.** [enclosure] palissade f **2.** 🇺🇸 MIL [prison] prison f (militaire). ◆ vt palissader.

stockboy ['stɒkbɔɪ] n magasinier m.

stockbroker ['stɒkˌbrəʊkər] n agent m de change.

stockbroking ['stɒkˌbrəʊkɪŋ] n commerce m des valeurs en Bourse.

stock car n **1.** AUTO stock-car m ▶ **stock car racing** (courses fpl de) stock-car m **2.** 🇺🇸 RAIL wagon m à bestiaux.

stock company n 🇺🇸 **1.** FIN société f anonyme par actions **2.** THEAT troupe f de répertoire.

stock cube n tablette f de bouillon.

stock exchange n Bourse f. ❖ **stock-exchange** comp boursier, de la Bourse ▶ **stock exchange prices** cours m des actions.

stockgirl ['stɒkgɜːl] n magasinière f.

stockholder ['stɒkˌhəʊldər] n actionnaire mf.

Stockholm ['stɒkhəʊm] pr n Stockholm ▶ **Stockholm syndrome** PSYCHOL syndrome m de Stockholm.

stocking ['stɒkɪŋ] n **1.** [for women] bas m ▶ **stocking mask** bas m *(utilisé par un bandit masqué)* **2.** *dated* [sock] bas m de laine.

stock-in-trade n COMM & *fig* fonds m de commerce.

stockist ['stɒkɪst] n stockiste mf.

stocklist ['stɒklɪst] n inventaire m.

stock market ◆ n Bourse f (des valeurs), marché m financier. ◆ comp boursier, de la Bourse ▶ **stock market boom** boom m du marché boursier ▶ **the stock market crash** le krach boursier ▶ **stock market prices** cours m des actions.

stockpile ['stɒkpaɪl] ◆ n stock m, réserve f. ◆ vt [goods] stocker, constituer un stock de ; [weapons] amasser, accumuler. ◆ vi faire des stocks.

stockpiling ['stɒkpaɪlɪŋ] n ▶ **to accuse sb of stockpiling a)** [food] accuser qqn de faire des réserves de nourriture **b)** [weapon] accuser qqn de faire des réserves d'armes.

stockroom ['stɒkrʊm] n magasin m, réserve f.

stock-still adv (complètement) immobile.

stocktaking ['stɒk,teɪkɪŋ] n **1.** COMM inventaire *m* **2.** *fig* ▸ **to do some stocktaking** faire le point.

stocky ['stɒkɪ] (*compar* stockier, *superl* stockiest) adj trapu, râblé.

stodge [stɒdʒ] n *(U)* UK *inf* **1.** [food] aliments *mpl* bourratifs, étouffe-chrétien *m inv* **2.** [writing] littérature *f* indigeste.

stodgy ['stɒdʒɪ] (*compar* stodgier, *superl* stodgiest) adj *inf* **1.** [food, meal] bourratif, lourd **2.** [style] lourd, indigeste **3.** [person, manners, ideas] guindé.

stoic ['stəʊɪk] ◆ adj stoïque. ◆ n stoïque *mf*. ❖ **Stoic** n PHILOS stoïcien *m*, -enne *f*.

stoical ['stəʊɪkl] adj stoïque.

stoically ['stəʊɪklɪ] adv stoïquement, avec stoïcisme.

stoicism ['stəʊɪsɪzm] n stoïcisme *m*. ❖ **Stoicism** n PHILOS stoïcisme *m*.

stoke [stəʊk] vt **1.** [fire, furnace] alimenter, entretenir ; [locomotive, boiler] chauffer **2.** *fig* [emotions, feelings, anger] entretenir, alimenter. ❖ **stoke up** ◆ vi **1.** [put fuel on -fire] alimenter le feu ; [-furnace] alimenter la chaudière **2.** UK *inf* [fill one's stomach] s'empiffrer. ◆ vt sep = stoke.

stoked [stəkd] adj US *inf* ▸ **to be stoked about sthg** [excited] être tout excité à cause de qqch.

stole [stəʊl] ◆ pt → steal. ◆ n **1.** étole *f*, écharpe *f* **2.** RELIG étole *f*.

stolen ['stəʊln] ◆ pp → steal. ◆ adj [goods, car] volé.

stolid ['stɒlɪd] adj flegmatique, impassible.

stomach ['stʌmək] ◆ n **1.** [organ] estomac *m* ▸ **to have an upset stomach** avoir l'estomac barbouillé / *I can't work on an empty stomach* je ne peux pas travailler l'estomac vide ▸ **to have a pain in one's stomach** a) avoir mal à l'estomac b) [lower] avoir mal au ventre **2.** [region of body] ventre *m* **3.** *(usu neg)* [desire, appetite] envie *f*, goût *m*. ◆ comp [infection] de l'estomac, gastrique ; [ulcer, operation] à l'estomac ; [pain] à l'estomac, au ventre. ◆ vt **1.** [tolerate] supporter, tolérer **2.** [digest] digérer.

stomachache ['stʌməkeɪk] n mal *m* de ventre ▸ **to have (a) stomachache** avoir mal au ventre.

stomach pump n pompe *f* stomacale.

stomp [stɒmp] *inf* ◆ vi marcher d'un pas lourd. ◆ n **1.** [tread] pas *m* lourd **2.** [dance] jazz que l'on danse en frappant du pied pour marquer le rythme.

stomping ground ['stɒmpɪŋ-] = stamping ground.

stone [stəʊn] (*pl* stones) ◆ n **1.** [material] pierre *f* / *the houses are built of stone* les maisons sont en pierre **2.** [piece of rock] pierre *f*, caillou *m* ; [on beach] galet *m* **3.** [memorial] stèle *f*, pierre *f* **4.** [gem] pierre *f* **5.** MED calcul *m* **6.** UK [in fruit] noyau *m* **7.** (*pl* stone *or* stones) [unit of weight] ≃ 6 kg / *she weighs about 8 stone or stones* elle pèse dans les 50 kilos. ◆ adj de or en pierre. ◆ vt **1.** [fruit, olive] dénoyauter **2.** [person, car] jeter des pierres sur, bombarder de pierres ; [as punishment] lapider.

Stone Age n ▸ **the Stone Age** l'âge *m* de (la) pierre. ❖ **Stone-Age** comp [man, dwelling, weapon] de l'âge de (la) pierre.

stone-cold ◆ adj complètement froid. ◆ adv *inf* ▸ **stone-cold sober** pas du tout soûl.

stoned [stəʊnd] adj *v inf* [drunk] bourré, schlass ; [drugged] défoncé.

stonemason ['stəʊn,meɪsn] n tailleur *m* de pierre.

stonewall ['stəʊn,wɔːl] ◆ vi **1.** [filibuster] monopoliser la parole (*pour empêcher les autres de parler*) ; [avoid questions] donner des réponses évasives **2.** SPORT jouer très prudemment, bétonner. ◆ vt bloquer, faire barrage à.

Stonewall ['stəʊn,wɔːl] pr n US HIST Stonewall.

Stonewall

Bar new-yorkais fréquenté par des homosexuels où, en 1969, les incessantes descentes de police provoquèrent des émeutes qui furent à l'origine du mouvement du même nom luttant pour la reconnaissance des droits des homosexuels.

stonewalling ['stəʊnwɔːlɪŋ] n POL obstructionnisme *m*.

stoneware ['stəʊnweər] n (poterie *f* en) grès *m*.

stonewashed ['stəʊnwɒʃt] adj [jeans, denim] délavé (*avant l'achat*).

stonework ['stəʊnwɜːk] n maçonnerie *f*, ouvrage *m* en pierre.

stonking ['stɒŋkɪŋ] adj UK *inf* super, génial, d'enfer.

stony ['stəʊnɪ] (*compar* stonier, *superl* stoniest) adj **1.** [covered with stones -ground, soil, road, land] pierreux, caillouteux, rocailleux ; [-beach] de galets **2.** [stone-like -texture, feel] pierreux **3.** [unfeeling] insensible ; [look, silence] glacial / *a stony heart* un cœur de pierre.

stony-broke adj UK *inf* fauché (comme les blés), à sec.

stony-faced adj au visage impassible.

stood [stʊd] pt & pp → stand.

stooge [stuːdʒ] n **1.** *inf & pej* larbin *m*, laquais *m* **2.** THEAT [straight man] faire-valoir *m inv*.

stool [stuːl] n **1.** [seat] tabouret *m* **2.** MED selle *f* **3.** HORT [tree stump] souche *f* ; [shoot] rejet *m* de souche ; [base of plant] pied *m* de plante **4.** US [windowsill] rebord *m* de fenêtre.

stoop [stuːp] ◆ vi **1.** [bend down] se baisser, se pencher **2.** [stand, walk with a stoop] avoir le dos voûté **3.** [abase o.s.] s'abaisser / *she would stoop to anything* elle est prête à toutes les bassesses **4.** [condescend] daigner **5.** [bird of prey] fondre, plonger. ◆ vt baisser, pencher, incliner. ◆ n **1.** [of person] ▸ **to walk with** or **to have a stoop** avoir le dos voûté **2.** [by bird of prey] attaque *f* en piqué **3.** US [veranda] véranda *f*, porche *m*.

stop [stɒp] (*pt & pp* stopped, *cont* stopping) ◆ vt **1.** [cease, finish] arrêter, cesser / *it hasn't stopped raining all day* il n'a pas arrêté de pleuvoir toute la journée / *stop it, that hurts!* arrête, ça fait mal ! **2.** [prevent] empêcher ▸ **to stop sb (from) doing sthg** empêcher qqn de faire qqch / *it's too late to stop the meeting from taking place* il est trop tard pour empêcher la réunion d'avoir lieu / *she's made up her mind and there's nothing we can do to stop her* elle a pris sa décision et nous ne pouvons rien faire pour l'arrêter **3.** [cause to halt] arrêter / *I managed to stop the car* j'ai réussi à arrêter la voiture / *the sound of voices stopped him short* or *stopped him in his tracks* un bruit de voix le fit s'arrêter net ▸ **stop thief!** au voleur ! **4.** [arrest] arrêter **5.** UK [withhold -sum of money, salary] retenir / *the money will be stopped out of your wages* la somme sera retenue sur votre salaire **6.** [interrupt] interrompre, arrêter ; [suspend] suspendre, arrêter ; [cut off] couper / *once he starts talking about the war there's no stopping him* une fois qu'il commence à parler de la guerre, on ne peut plus l'arrêter ▸ **to stop a cheque** faire opposition à un chèque **7.** [block -hole, gap] boucher. ◆ vi **1.** [halt, pause -person, vehicle, machine] arrêter, s'arrêter / *go on, don't stop* continue, ne t'arrête pas ▶ **to stop dead in one's tracks** s'arrêter net ; *fig* : *she doesn't know* or *when to stop* elle ne sait pas s'arrêter / *they'll stop at nothing to get what they want* ils ne reculeront devant rien pour obtenir ce qu'ils veulent / *she began talking then stopped short* elle commença à parler puis s'arrêta net or brusquement **2.** [come to an end] cesser, s'arrêter, se terminer / *the rain has stopped* la pluie s'est arrêtée **3.** [stay] rester ; [reside] loger / *we've got friends stopping with us* nous avons des amis qui séjournent chez nous en ce moment. ◆ n **1.** [stopping place - for buses] arrêt *m* ; [-for trains] station *f* **2.** [break - in journey, process] arrêt *m*, halte *f* ; [-in work] pause *f* / *we made several stops to pick up passengers* nous nous sommes arrêtés à plusieurs reprises pour prendre des passagers **3.** [standstill] arrêt *m* ▶ **to come to a stop** s'arrêter **4.** [end] ▶ **to put a stop to sthg** mettre fin or un terme à qqch **5.** ⓤⓚ [full stop] point *m* ; [in telegrams] stop *m* **6.** [on organ] jeu *m* (d'orgue) ▶ **to pull out all the stops (to do sthg)** remuer ciel et terre (pour faire qqch). ◆ comp [button, mechanism, signal] d'arrêt. ❖ **stop by** vi *inf* passer / *I'll stop by at the chemist's on my way home* je passerai à la pharmacie en rentrant. ❖ **stop in** vi ⓤⓚ *inf* **1.** [stay at home] ne pas sortir, rester à la maison **2.** = **stop by.** ❖ **stop off** vi s'arrêter, faire une halte. ❖ **stop out** vi ⓤⓚ *inf* ne pas rentrer. ❖ **stop over** vi [gen] s'arrêter, faire une halte ; TRANSP [on flight, cruise] faire escale. ❖ **stop up** vi ⓤⓚ *inf* ne pas se coucher, veiller.

> 📋 Note that empêcher que is followed by ne and a verb in the subjunctive:
> **They have taken steps to stop this happening.** Ils ont pris des dispositions pour empêcher que cela ne se produise.

stop-and-search n fouilles *fpl* dans la rue.
stopcock ['stɒpkɒk] n ⓤⓚ robinet *m* d'arrêt.
stopgap ['stɒpgæp] ◆ n bouche-trou *m*. ◆ adj de remplacement ▶ **a stopgap measure** un palliatif.
stop-go adj ECON ▶ **stop-go policy** politique *f* économique en dents de scie *(alternant arrêt de la croissance et mesures de relance)*, politique *f* du stop-and-go.
stoplight ['stɒplaɪt] n **1.** [traffic light] feu *m* rouge **2.** ⓤⓚ [brake-light] stop *m*.
stopover ['stɒpˌəʊvəʳ] n [gen] halte *f* ; [on flight] escale *f*.
stoppage ['stɒpɪdʒ] n **1.** [strike] grève *f*, arrêt *m* de travail **2.** ⓤⓚ [sum deducted] retenue *f* **3.** [halting, stopping] arrêt *m*, interruption *f* ; FOOT arrêt *m* de jeu **4.** [blockage] obstruction *f* ; MED occlusion *f*.
stopper ['stɒpəʳ] ◆ n **1.** [for bottle, jar] bouchon *m* ; [for sink] bouchon *m*, bonde *f* ; [for pipe] obturateur *m* ; [on syringe] embout *m* de piston **2.** FOOT stoppeur *m* **3.** [in bridge] arrêt *m*. ◆ vt boucher, fermer.
stopping ['stɒpɪŋ] ◆ n **1.** [coming or bringing to a halt] arrêt *m* ▶ **stopping distance** AUTO distance *f* d'arrêt **2.** [blocking] obturation *f* **3.** [cancellation - of payment, leave, etc.] suspension *f* ; [-of service] suppression *f* ; [-of cheque] opposition *f*. ◆ adj [place] où l'on s'arrête.
stop press n nouvelles *fpl* de dernière minute / **'stop press!'** 'dernière minute'.
stop sign n [signal *m* de] stop *m*.
stopwatch ['stɒpwɒtʃ] n chronomètre *m*.
storage ['stɔ:rɪdʒ] ◆ n **1.** [putting into store] entreposage *m*, emmagasinage *m*, stockage *m* ; [keeping, conservation] stockage *m* **2.** COMPUT (mise *f* en) mémoire *f*. ◆ comp **1.** [charges] de stockage, d'emmagasinage **2.** COMPUT de mémoire.

storage heater, storage radiator n radiateur *m* à accumulation.
storage room n [small] cagibi *m* ; [larger] débarras *m*.
storage unit n meuble *m* de rangement.
store [stɔ:ʳ] ◆ n **1.** [large shop] grand magasin *m* ; ⓤⓢ [shop] magasin *m* **2.** [stock - of goods] stock *m*, réserve *f*, provision *f* ; [-of food] provision *f* ; [-of facts, jokes, patience, knowledge] réserve *f* ; [-of wisdom] fonds *m* **3.** [place - warehouse] entrepôt *m*, dépôt *m* ; [-in office, home, shop] réserve *f* ; [-in factory] magasin *m*, réserve *f* **4.** COMPUT [memory] mémoire *f* **5.** [value] ▶ **to lay** or **to put** or **to set great store by sthg** faire grand cas de qqch. ◆ comp **1.** ⓤⓢ [store-bought -gen] de commerce ; [-clothes] de confection **2.** [for storage] ▶ **store cupboard** placard *m* de rangement. ◆ vt **1.** [put away, put in store -goods, food] emmagasiner, entreposer ; [-grain, crop] engranger ; [-heat] accumuler, emmagasiner ; [-electricity] accumuler ; [-files, documents] classer ; [-facts, ideas] engranger, enregistrer dans sa mémoire **2.** [keep] conserver, stocker **3.** [fill with provisions] approvisionner **4.** COMPUT stocker. ❖ **stores** pl n [provisions] provisions *fpl*. ❖ **in store** adv phr : *who knows what the future has in store?* qui sait ce que l'avenir nous réserve ? ❖ **store away, store up** vt sep garder en réserve.

> ⚠ The French word **store** means a blind, not a store.

store card n carte *f* de crédit *(d'un grand magasin)*.
store detective n vigile *m* *(dans un magasin)*.
storefront ['stɔ:frʌnt] n ⓤⓢ devanture *f* de magasin.
storehouse ['stɔ:haʊs] *(pl* [-haʊzɪz]*)* n **1.** *lit* magasin *m*, entrepôt *m*, dépôt *m* **2.** *fig* [of information, memories] mine *f*.
storekeeper ['stɔ:ˌki:pəʳ] n **1.** [in warehouse] magasinier *m*, -ère *f* **2.** ⓤⓢ [shopkeeper] commerçant *m*, -e *f*.
storeroom ['stɔ:rʊm] n **1.** [in office, shop] réserve *f* ; [in factory] magasin *m*, réserve *f* ; [in home] débarras *m* **2.** NAUT soute *f*, magasin *m*.
storey ⓤⓚ, **story** ⓤⓢ ['stɔ:rɪ] (ⓤⓚ *pl* **storeys** ⓤⓢ *pl* **stories**) n étage *m*.
stork [stɔ:k] n cigogne *f*.
storm [stɔ:m] ◆ n **1.** METEOR tempête *f* ; [thunderstorm] orage *m* ; [on Beaufort scale] tempête *f* **2.** *fig* [furore] tempête *f*, ouragan *m* **3.** MIL ▶ **to take by storm** prendre d'assaut. ◆ vi **1.** [go angrily] ▶ **to storm in** / **out** entrer / sortir comme un ouragan **2.** [be angry] tempêter, fulminer **3.** [rain] tomber à verse ; [wind] souffler violemment ; [snow] faire rage. ◆ vt emporter, enlever d'assaut.
storm cloud n **1.** METEOR nuage *m* d'orage **2.** *fig* nuage *m* menaçant.
storm damage n dégâts *mpl* causés par la tempête.
storm door n ⓤⓢ porte *f* extérieure *(qui double la porte de la maison pour éviter les courants d'air)*.
storming ['stɔ:mɪŋ] n [attack] assaut *m* ; [capture] prise *f* (d'assaut) ▶ **the storming of the Bastille** HIST la prise de la Bastille.
stormproof ['stɔ:mpru:f] adj à l'épreuve de la tempête.
stormy ['stɔ:mɪ] *(compar* **stormier**, *superl* **stormiest**)* adj **1.** [weather] orageux, d'orage ; [sea] houleux, démonté **2.** *fig* [relationship] orageux ; [debate] houleux ; [look] furieux ; [career, life] tumultueux, mouvementé.
story ['stɔ:rɪ] *(pl* **stories**) n **1.** [tale, work of fiction - spoken] histoire *f* ; [-written] histoire *f*, conte *m* ▶ **to tell sb a story** raconter une histoire à qqn **2.** [plot - story line] intrigue *f*, scénario *m* **3.** [account] histoire *f* / *the witness*

changed his story le témoin est revenu sur sa version des faits ▸ **to cut** UK or **make** US **a long story short** enfin bref **4.** [history] histoire *f* / *his life story* l'histoire de sa vie **5.** *euph* [lie] histoire *f* **6.** [rumour] rumeur *f*, bruit *m* ▸ **or so the story goes** c'est du moins ce que l'on raconte **7.** PRESS [article] article *m* ; [event, affair] affaire *f* **8.** US = **storey**.

storybook ['stɔːrɪbʊk] ◆ n livre *m* de contes. ◆ adj ▸ **a storybook ending** une fin romanesque ▸ **a storybook romance** une idylle de conte de fées.

story line n intrigue *f*, scénario *m*.

storyteller ['stɔːrɪˌtelər] n **1.** conteur *m*, -euse *f* **2.** *euph* [liar] menteur *m*, -euse *f*.

storytelling ['stɔːrɪˌtelɪŋ] n **1.** [art] art *m* de conter **2.** *euph* [telling lies] mensonges *mpl*.

stout [staʊt] ◆ adj **1.** [corpulent] gros (grosse), corpulent, fort **2.** [strong - stick] solide ; [- structure, material] solide, robuste **3.** [brave] vaillant, courageux ; [firm, resolute - resistance, opposition, enemy] acharné ; [- support, supporter] fidèle, loyal. ◆ n stout *m*, bière *f* brune forte.

stoutness ['staʊtnɪs] n **1.** [corpulence] corpulence *f*, embonpoint *m* **2.** [solidity, strength - of structure, materials] solidité *f*, robustesse *f* **3.** [bravery] vaillance *f*, courage *m* ; [firmness, resolution - of resistance, defence, opposition] acharnement *m* ; [- of support, supporter] fidélité *f*, loyauté *f* ▸ **stoutness of heart** vaillance, courage.

stove [stəʊv] ◆ pt & pp ⟶ **stave.** ◆ n **1.** [for heating] poêle *m* **2.** [cooker - gen] cuisinière *f* ; [- portable] réchaud *m* ; [kitchen range] fourneau *m* **3.** INDUST [kiln] four *m*, étuve *f*.

stow [stəʊ] vt **1.** [store] ranger, stocker ; [in warehouse] emmagasiner ; NAUT [cargo] arrimer ; [equipment, sails] ranger **2.** [pack, fill] remplir. ◆ **stow away** ◆ vi [on ship, plane] s'embarquer clandestinement, être un passager clandestin. ◆ vt sep **1.** = **stow 2.** UK *inf* [food] enfourner.

stowaway ['stəʊəweɪ] n passager *m* clandestin, passagère *f* clandestine.

straddle ['strædl] ◆ vt **1.** [sit astride of - horse, bicycle, chair, wall] chevaucher ; [mount - horse, bicycle] enfourcher ; [step over - ditch, obstacle] enjamber **2.** [span, spread over] enjamber **3.** MIL [target] encadrer **4.** US *inf* ▸ **to straddle the fence** [be noncommittal] ne pas prendre position. ◆ vi US *inf & fig* [sit on the fence] ne pas prendre position.

strafe [strɑːf] vt [with machine guns] mitrailler (au sol) ; [with bombs] bombarder.

straggle ['strægl] ◆ vi **1.** [spread in long line - roots, creeper, branches] pousser de façon désordonnée ; [be scattered - trees, houses] être disséminé ; [hang untidily - hair] pendre (lamentablement) **2.** [linger] traîner, traînasser. ◆ n : *all I saw was a straggle of houses / trees on the hillside* je n'ai aperçu que quelques maisons disséminées / quelques arbres disséminés sur la colline / *a straggle of islands* un long chapelet d'îles.

straggler ['stræglər] n **1.** [lingerer] traînard *m*, -e *f* ; [in race] retardataire *mf* **2.** BOT gourmand *m*.

straggly ['strægli] adj [hair] maigre ; [beard] épars, hirsute ; [roots] long et mince.

straight [streɪt] ◆ adj **1.** [not curved - line, road, nose] droit ; [- hair] raide / *keep your back straight* tiens-toi droit, redresse-toi **2.** [level, upright] droit / *the picture isn't straight* le tableau n'est pas droit or est de travers ▸ **to put** or **to set straight a)** [picture] remettre d'aplomb, redresser **b)** [hat, tie] ajuster **3.** [honest, frank] franc (franche), droit ▸ **to be straight with sb** être franc avec qqn ▸ **to give sb a straight answer** répondre franchement à qqn / *he's always been straight in his dealings with me* il a toujours été honnête avec moi ▸ **to do some straight talking** parler franchement / *are you being straight with me?* est-ce

que tu joues franc jeu avec moi ? **4.** [correct, clear] clair ▸ **to put** or **to set the record straight** mettre les choses au clair / *let's get this straight* entendons-nous bien sur ce point / *have you put her straight?* as-tu mis les choses au point avec elle ? / *now just you get this straight!* mets-toi bien ceci dans la tête !, qu'on se mette bien d'accord sur ce point ! **5.** [tidy, in order - room, desk, accounts] en ordre ▸ **to put** or **to set straight a)** [room, house] mettre en ordre, mettre de l'ordre dans **b)** [affairs] mettre de l'ordre dans **6.** [quits] quitte **7.** [direct] droit, direct ; POL ▸ **straight fight** une élection où ne se présentent que deux candidats ▸ **to vote a straight ticket** US voter pour une liste sans panachage **8.** [pure, utter] pur **9.** [consecutive] consécutif, de suite / *to have three straight wins* gagner trois fois de suite or d'affilée / *a straight flush* CARDS une quinte flush **10.** [neat - whisky, vodka] sec (sèche) **11.** [serious] sérieux ▸ **to keep a straight face** garder son sérieux / *it's the first straight role she's played in years* c'est son premier rôle sérieux depuis des années **12.** *inf* [conventional] vieux jeu *(inv)* ; [heterosexual] hétéro ; [not a drug user] qui ne se drogue pas **13.** AUTO [cylinders] en ligne / *a straight eight engine* un moteur huit cylindres en ligne **14.** GEOM [angle] plat **15.** US SCH ▸ **to get straight As**: *he got straight As all term* il n'a eu que de très bonnes notes tout le semestre ▸ **a straight A student** un étudiant brillant **16.** US *inf* ▸ **I'm straight** [I'm OK] ça va aller. ◆ adv **1.** [in a straight line] droit, en ligne droite / *the rocket shot straight up* la fusée est montée à la verticale or en ligne droite / *to shoot straight* viser juste ; *fig* : *I can't see straight* je ne vois pas bien / *I can't think straight* je n'ai pas les idées claires ▸ **to go straight** *inf* [criminal] revenir dans le droit chemin **2.** [upright - walk, sit, stand] (bien) droit / *sit up straight!* tiens-toi droit or redresse-toi (sur ta chaise) ! **3.** [directly] (tout) droit, directement / *he looked me straight in the eye* il me regarda droit dans les yeux / *it's straight across the road* c'est juste en face / *the car came straight at me* la voiture a foncé droit sur moi / *go straight to bed!* va tout de suite te coucher ! / *the ball went straight through the window* la balle est passée par la fenêtre / *they mostly go straight from school to university* pour la plupart, ils passent directement du lycée à l'université ▸ **to come straight to the point** aller droit au fait ▸ **straight ahead** tout droit / *he looked straight ahead* il regarda droit devant lui ▸ **straight off** *inf* sur-le-champ, tout de suite ▸ **straight on** tout droit **4.** [frankly] franchement, carrément, tout droit / *I told him straight (out) what I thought of him* je lui ai dit franchement ce que je pensais de lui ▸ **straight up** UK *inf* [honestly] sans blague **5.** [neat, unmixed] ▸ **to drink whisky straight** boire son whisky sec. ◆ n **1.** [on racecourse, railway track] ligne *f* droite ▸ **the final** or **home straight** la dernière ligne droite ▸ **to keep to the straight and narrow** rester dans le droit chemin **2.** *inf* [person] : *he's a straight* **a)** [conventional person] il est conventionnel, c'est quelqu'un de conventionnel **b)** [heterosexual] il est hétéro, c'est un hétéro.

straight arrow n US : *he's a straight arrow* **a)** [person of integrity] on peut compter sur lui **b)** [too conventional] il est un peu coincé.

straightaway [ˌstreɪtə'weɪ] ◆ adv tout de suite, sur-le-champ. ◆ adj US droit. ◆ n US ligne *f* droite.

straight-edged adj [blade] à tranchant droit.

straighten ['streɪtn] ◆ vt **1.** [remove bend or twist from - line, wire] redresser ; [- nail] redresser, défausser ; [- wheel] redresser, dévoiler ; [- hair] décrêper **2.** [adjust - picture] redresser, remettre d'aplomb ; [- tie, hat] redresser, ajuster ; [- hem] arrondir, rectifier **3.** [tidy - room, papers] ranger, mettre de l'ordre dans ; [organize - affairs, accounts] mettre en ordre, mettre de l'ordre dans. ◆ vi [person] se dresser, se redresser ; [plant] pousser droit ; [hair] devenir raide ; [road] devenir droit. ◆ **straighten out**

◆ vt sep **1.** [nail, wire] redresser **2.** [situation] débrouiller, arranger ; [problem] résoudre ; [mess, confusion] mettre de l'ordre dans, débrouiller **3.** ▶ **to straighten sb out a)** *inf* [help] remettre qqn dans la bonne voie **b)** [punish] remettre qqn à sa place. ◆ vi [road] devenir droit ; [plant] pousser droit ; [hair] devenir raide. ❖ **straighten up** ◆ vi [person] se dresser, se redresser ; [plant] pousser droit. ◆ vt sep [room, papers] ranger, mettre de l'ordre dans ; [affairs] mettre de l'ordre dans, mettre en ordre.

straight-faced adj qui garde son sérieux, impassible.

straightforward [,streɪt'fɔːwəd] adj **1.** [direct - person] direct ; [-explanation] franc (franche) ; [-account] très clair **2.** [easy, simple - task, problem] simple, facile ; [-instructions] clair **3.** [pure, utter] pur.

straightforwardly [,streɪt'fɔːwədlɪ] adv **1.** [honestly - act, behave] avec franchise ; [-answer] franchement, sans détour **2.** [without complications] simplement, sans anicroche.

straight-to-video adj [movie] sorti directement sur cassette vidéo.

strain [streɪn] ◆ n **1.** [on rope, girder - pressure] pression *f* ; [-tension] tension *f* ; [-pull] traction *f* ; [-weight] poids *m* ▶ **to collapse under the strain** [bridge, animal] s'effondrer sous le poids **2.** [mental or physical effort] (grand) effort *m* ; [overwork] surmenage *m* ; [tiredness] (grande) fatigue *f* / *he's beginning to feel / show the strain* il commence à sentir la fatigue / à donner des signes de fatigue ; [stress] stress *m*, tension *f* or fatigue *f* nerveuse **3.** MED [of muscle] froissement *m* ; [sprain - of ankle, wrist] entorse *f* ▶ **to give one's back a strain** se faire un tour de reins **4.** [breed, variety - of animals] lignée *f*, race *f* ; [of plant, virus, etc.] souche *f* **5.** [style] genre *m*, style *m* **6.** [streak, touch] fond *m*, tendance *f*. ◆ vt **1.** [rope, cable, girder] tendre (fortement) ; [resources, economy, budget] grever **2.** [force - voice] forcer **3.** [hurt, damage - muscle] froisser ; [-eyes] fatiguer ▶ **to strain o.s. a)** [by gymnastics, lifting] se froisser un muscle **b)** [by overwork] se surmener **4.** [force - meaning] forcer ; [-word] forcer le sens de **5.** [test - patience] mettre à l'épreuve, abuser de ; [-friendship, relationship] mettre à l'épreuve, mettre à rude épreuve **6.** CULIN [soup, milk] passer ; [vegetables] (faire) égoutter. ◆ vi **1.** [pull] tirer fort ; [push] pousser fort / *she was straining at the door* **a)** [pull] elle tirait sur la porte de toutes ses forces **b)** [push] elle poussait (sur) la porte de toutes ses forces **2.** [strive] s'efforcer, faire beaucoup d'efforts ▶ **to strain to do sthg** s'efforcer de faire qqch **3.** [rope, cable] se tendre. ❖ **strains** pl n [in music] accents *mpl*, accords *mpl* ; [in verse] accents *mpl*. ❖ **strain off** vt sep [liquid] vider, égoutter.

strained [streɪnd] adj **1.** [forced - manner, laugh] forcé, contraint ; [-voice] forcé ; [-language, style, etc.] forcé, exagéré **2.** [tense - atmosphere, relations, person] tendu **3.** [sprained - ankle, limb] foulé ; [-muscle] froissé / *to have a strained shoulder* s'être froissé un muscle à l'épaule / *to have a strained neck* avoir un torticolis ; [tired - eyes] fatigué **4.** CULIN [liquid] filtré ; [soup] passé ; [vegetables] égoutté ; [baby food] en purée.

strainer ['streɪnər] n passoire *f*.

strait [streɪt] n GEOG ▶ **strait, straits** détroit *m*. ❖ **straits** pl n [difficulties] gêne *f*, situation *f* fâcheuse ▶ **to be in financial straits** avoir des ennuis financiers or des problèmes d'argent.

 **STRAITS**

the Straits of Dover	le pas de Calais
the Strait of Gibraltar	le détroit de Gibraltar
the Strait of Hormuz or Ormuz	le détroit d'Hormuz or d'Ormuz

straitened ['streɪtnd] adj ▶ **in straitened circumstances** dans le besoin or la gêne.

straitjacket ['streɪt,dʒækɪt] n camisole *f* de force.

straitlaced [,streɪt'leɪst] adj collet monté *(inv).*

strand [strænd] ◆ n **1.** [of thread, string, wire] brin *m*, toron *m* ▶ **a strand of hair** une mèche de cheveux **2.** [in argument, plot, sequence] fil *m* **3.** *liter* [beach] plage *f* ; [shore] grève *f*, rivage *m*. ◆ vt **1.** [ship, whale] échouer **2.** *(usu passive)* ▶ **to be stranded** [person, vehicle] rester en plan or coincé.

stranded ['strændɪd] adj **1.** [person, car] bloqué / *the stranded holidaymakers camped out in the airport* les vacanciers, ne pouvant pas partir, campèrent à l'aéroport **2.** BIOL & CHEM [molecule, sequence] torsadé.

strange [streɪndʒ] adj **1.** [odd] étrange, bizarre ; [peculiar] singulier, insolite / *it's strange that he should be so late* c'est bizarre or étrange qu'il ait tant de retard **2.** [unfamiliar] inconnu **3.** [unwell] bizarre ▶ **to look / to feel strange** avoir l'air / se sentir bizarre **4.** PHYS [matter, particle] étrange.

strangely ['streɪndʒlɪ] adv étrangement, bizarrement.

strangeness ['streɪndʒnɪs] n **1.** [of person, situation] étrangeté *f*, bizarrerie *f*, singularité *f* **2.** PHYS étrangeté *f*.

stranger ['streɪndʒər] n **1.** [unknown person] inconnu *m*, -e *f* **2.** [person from elsewhere] étranger *m*, -ère *f* / *I'm a stranger here myself* je ne suis pas d'ici non plus **3.** [novice] novice *m* / *he is no stranger to loneliness / misfortune* il sait ce qu'est la solitude / le malheur.

strangle ['stræŋgl] vt **1.** *lit* étrangler **2.** *fig* [opposition, growth, originality] étrangler, étouffer.

stranglehold ['stræŋglhəʊld] n [grip around throat] étranglement *m*, étouffement *m*, strangulation *f* ; [in wrestling] étranglement *m* ▶ **to have a stranglehold on sb** *lit & fig* tenir qqn à la gorge ▶ **to have a stranglehold on sthg** *fig* tenir qqch à la gorge.

strangling ['stræŋglɪŋ] n **1.** [killing] étranglement *m*, strangulation *f* ; *fig* [of opposition, protest, originality] étranglement *m*, étouffement *m* **2.** [case] : *that brings to five the number of stranglings* cela porte à cinq le nombre de personnes étranglées.

strangulation [,stræŋgjʊ'leɪʃn] n strangulation *f*.

strap [stræp] (*pt & pp* **strapped,** *cont* **strapping**) ◆ n **1.** [belt - of leather] courroie *f*, sangle *f*, lanière *f* ; [-of cloth, metal] sangle *f*, bande *f* **2.** [support - for bag, camera, on harness] sangle *f* ; [fastening - for dress, bra] bretelle *f* ; [-for hat, bonnet] bride *f* ; [-for helmet] attache *f* ; [-for sandal] lanière *f* ; [-under trouser leg] sous-pied *m* ; [-for watch] bracelet *m* **3.** [as punishment] ▶ **to give sb / to get the strap** administrer / recevoir une correction (à coups de ceinture) **4.** [on bus, underground] poignée *f* **5.** = **strop 6.** TECH lien *m*. ◆ vt sangler, attacher. ❖ **strap down** vt sep sangler, attacher avec une sangle or une courroie. ❖ **strap in** vt sep [in car] attacher la ceinture (de sécurité) de ; [child - in high chair, pram] attacher avec un harnais or avec une ceinture. ❖ **strap on** vt sep [bag, watch] attacher. ❖ **strap up** vt sep [suitcase, parcel] sangler ; [limbs, ribs] mettre un bandage à, bander.

strapless ['stræplɪs] adj [dress, bra, etc.] sans bretelles.

strapline ['stræplaɪn] n **1.** [UK] [slogan] slogan *m* **2.** PRESS sous-titre *m*.

strapped [stræpt] adj *inf* ▶ **to be strapped for cash** être fauché.

strapping ['stræpɪŋ] adj *inf* costaud / *a fine strapping girl* un beau brin de fille.

Strasbourg ['stræzbɜːg] pr n Strasbourg.

strata ['strɑːtə] pl ⟶ **stratum**.

stratagem ['strætədʒəm] n stratagème *m*.

strategic [strə'tiːdʒɪk] adj stratégique.

strategically [strə'tiːdʒɪklɪ] adv stratégiquement, du point de vue de la stratégie.

strategist ['strætɪdʒɪst] n stratège *m*.

strategy ['strætɪdʒɪ] (*pl* **strategies**) n [gen & MIL] stratégie *f*.

stratified ['strætɪfaɪd] adj stratifié, en couches.

stratosphere ['strætə,sfɪə] n stratosphère *f*.

stratum ['strɑːtəm] (*pl* **strata** ['strɑːtə]) n 1. GEOL strate *f*, couche *f* 2. *fig* couche *f*.

straw [strɔː] ◆ n 1. AGR paille *f* 2. [for drinking] paille *f* ▶ **to drink sthg through a straw** boire qqch avec une paille 3. PHR **to catch** or **to clutch at a straw** or **at straws** se raccrocher désespérément à la moindre lueur d'espoir ▶ **to draw** or **to get the short straw** être tiré au sort, être de corvée ▶ **that's the last straw** or **the straw that breaks the camel's back** c'est la goutte d'eau qui fait déborder le vase. ◆ comp [gen] de or en paille ; [roof] en chaume.

strawberry ['strɔːbərɪ] (*pl* **strawberries**) ◆ n [fruit] fraise *f* ; [plant] fraisier *m*. ◆ comp [jam] de fraises ; [tart] aux fraises ; [ice cream] à la fraise.

 Strawberries and cream

En Grande-Bretagne, on déguste traditionnellement des fraises à la crème lors de manifestations en plein air, notamment pendant les tournois de tennis à Wimbledon.

---

straw hat n chapeau *m* de paille.

straw poll n [vote] vote *m* blanc ; [opinion poll] sondage *m* d'opinion.

stray [streɪ] ◆ vi 1. [child, animal] errer 2. [speaker, writer] s'éloigner du sujet 3. [thoughts] errer, vagabonder. ◆ n [dog] chien *m* errant or perdu ; [cat] chat *m* errant or perdu ; [cow, sheep] animal *m* égaré ; [child] enfant *m* perdu or abandonné. ◆ adj 1. [lost - dog, cat] perdu, errant ; [- cow, sheep] égaré ; [- child] perdu, abandonné 2. [random - bullet] perdu ; [- thought] vagabond ; [- memory] fugitif 3. [occasional - car, boat] isolé, rare. ❖ **strays** pl n RADIO & TELEC parasites *mpl*, friture *f*.

streak [striːk] ◆ n 1. [smear - of blood, dirt] filet *m* ; [- of ink, paint] traînée *f* ; [line, stripe - of light] trait *m*, rai *m* ; [- of ore] filon *m*, veine *f* ; [- in marble] veine *f* / **streaks of lightning lit up the sky** des éclairs zébraient le ciel 2. [of luck] période *f* 3. [tendency] : **he has a mean streak** or **a streak of meanness in him** il est un peu mesquin ; [trace] trace *f* 4. *inf* [naked dash] ▶ **to do a streak** traverser un lieu public nu en courant. ◆ vt [smear] tacher ; [stripe] strier, zébrer. ◆ vi 1. [go quickly] ▶ **to streak in / out** entrer / sortir comme un éclair ▶ **to streak past** passer en courant d'air 2. [run naked] faire du streaking (traverser un lieu public nu en courant).

streaker ['striːkə] n streaker *mf* (personne nue qui traverse un lieu public en courant).

streaky ['striːkɪ] (*compar* **streakier**, *superl* **streakiest**) adj 1. [colour, surface] marbré, jaspé, zébré ; [rock, marble] veiné 2. CULIN [meat] entrelardé, persillé ▶ **streaky bacon** bacon *m* entrelardé.

stream [striːm] ◆ n 1. [brook] ruisseau *m* 2. [current] courant *m* 3. [flow - of liquid] flot *m*, jet *m* ; [- of air] courant *m* ; [- of blood, lava] ruisseau *m*, flot *m*, cascade *f*, torrent *m* ; [- of people, traffic] flot *m*, défilé *m* (continu) ; [- of tears] ruisseau *m*, torrent *m* ▶ **stream of consciousness** monologue *m* intérieur 4. INDUST & TECH ▶ **to be on / off**

stream être en service / hors service ▶ **to come on stream** être mis en service 5. UK SCH classe *f* de niveau. ◆ vi 1. [flow - water, tears] ruisseler, couler à flots ; [- blood] ruisseler 2. [flutter] flotter, voleter 3. [people, traffic] ▶ **to stream in / out** entrer / sortir à flots. ◆ vt 1. [flow with] ▶ **to stream blood / tears** ruisseler de sang / de larmes 2. UK SCH répartir en classes de niveau 3. COMPUT [music, news] télécharger en streaming.

streamer ['striːmə] n 1. [decoration] serpentin *m* 2. [banner] banderole *f* ; [pennant] flamme *f* 3. ASTRON flèche *f* lumineuse 4. PRESS manchette *f*.

streaming ['striːmɪŋ] ◆ n 1. UK SCH répartition *f* en classes de niveau 2. COMPUT streaming *m*. ◆ adj [surface, window, windscreen] ruisselant / **I've got a streaming cold** UK j'ai attrapé un gros rhume.

streaming video n vidéo *f* streaming.

streamline ['striːmlaɪn] ◆ vt 1. AUTO & AERON donner un profil aérodynamique à, profiler, caréner 2. ECON & INDUST [company, production] rationaliser ; [industry] dégraisser, restructurer. ◆ n 1. AUTO & AERON ligne *f* aérodynamique, forme *f* profilée or carénée 2. PHYS écoulement *m* non perturbé.

streamlined ['striːmlaɪnd] adj 1. AUTO & AERON aérodynamique, profilé, caréné 2. *fig* [building] aux contours harmonieux ; [figure] svelte 3. ECON & INDUST [company, production] rationalisé ; [industry] dégraissé, restructuré.

streamlining ['striːmlaɪnɪŋ] n 1. AUTO & AERON carénage *m* 2. ECON & INDUST [of business, organization] rationalisation *f* ; [of industry] dégraissage *m*, restructuration *f*.

street [striːt] ◆ n rue *f* ▶ **in** UK or **on** US **a street** dans une rue ▶ **to be on the street** or **streets a)** *inf* [as prostitute] faire le trottoir **b)** [homeless person] être à la rue or sur le pavé ▶ **to take to the streets** [protestors] descendre dans la rue ▶ **to walk the streets a)** *inf* [as prostitute] faire le trottoir **b)** [from idleness] battre le pavé, flâner dans les rues **c)** [in search] faire les rues. ◆ comp [noises] de la rue ; [musician] des rues. ◆ adj US *inf* [streetsmart] dégourdi. ❖ **streets** adv *inf* ▶ **to be streets ahead of sb** dépasser qqn de loin.

streetcar ['striːtkɑːr] n US tramway *m*.

street cred [-kred] *inf*, **street credibility** ≃ image *f* cool or branchée.

streetlamp ['striːtlæmp], **streetlight** ['striːtlaɪt] n réverbère *m*.

street lighting n éclairage *m* public.

street map n plan *m* de la ville.

street market n marché *m* en plein air or à ciel ouvert.

street plan = street map.

streetsmart ['striːtsmɑːt] adj *inf* dégourdi.

street value n [of drugs] valeur *f* marchande.

streetwise ['striːtwaɪz] adj *inf* qui connaît la vie de la rue, ses dangers et ses codes.

strength [streŋθ] n 1. (U) [physical power - of person, animal, muscle] force *f*, puissance *f* / **with all my strength** de toutes mes forces ; [health] forces *fpl* ▶ **to get one's strength back** reprendre des or recouvrer ses forces 2. [of faith, opinion, resolution] force *f*, fermeté *f* ; [of emotion, feeling] force *f* ; [of music, art] force *f* ▶ **strength of character** force de caractère ▶ **strength of purpose** résolution *f* 3. [intensity - of earthquake, wind] force *f*, intensité *f* ; [- of current, light] intensité *f* ; [- of sound, voice, lens, magnet] force *f*, puissance *f* 4. [strong point, asset] force *f*, point *m* fort 5. [solidity] solidité *f* ; *fig* [of claim, position, relationship] solidité *f* ; [vigour - of argument, protest] force *f*, vigueur *f* ; FIN [of currency, economy] solidité *f* 6. [of alcohol] teneur *f* en alcool ; [of solution] titre *m* ; [of coffee, tobacco] force *f* 7. (U) [numbers] effectif *m*, effectifs *mpl* **∕** *we're at full strength* nos effectifs sont au complet. **❖ on the strength of** *prep phr* en vertu de, sur la foi de.

strengthen ['streŋθn] **◆** *vt* **1.** [physically - body, muscle] fortifier, raffermir ; [- person] fortifier, tonifier ; [- voice] renforcer ; [improve - eyesight, hearing] améliorer **2.** [reinforce - firm, nation] renforcer ; [- fear, emotion, effect] renforcer, intensifier ; [- belief, argument] renforcer ; [- link, friendship] renforcer, fortifier ; [morally - person] fortifier **3.** [foundation, structure] renforcer, consolider ; [material] renforcer **4.** FIN [currency, economy] consolider. **◆** *vi* **1.** [physically - body] se fortifier, se raffermir ; [- voice] devenir plus fort ; [- grip] se resserrer **2.** [increase - influence, effect, desire] augmenter, s'intensifier ; [- wind] forcir ; [- current] augmenter, se renforcer ; [- friendship, character, resolve] se renforcer, se fortifier **3.** FIN [prices, market] se consolider, se raffermir.

strengthening ['streŋθənɪŋ] **◆** *n* **1.** [physical - of body, muscle] raffermissement *m* ; [- of voice] renforcement *m* ; [- of hold, grip] resserrement *m* **2.** [increase - of emotion, effect, desire] renforcement *m*, augmentation *f*, intensification *f* ; [reinforcement - of character, friendship, position] renforcement *m* ; [- of wind, current] renforcement *m* **3.** [of structure, building] renforcement *m*, consolidation *f* **4.** FIN consolidation *f*. **◆** *adj* fortifiant, remontant ; MED tonifiant.

strenuous ['strenjʊəs] *adj* **1.** [physically - activity, exercise, sport] ardu **2.** [vigorous - opposition, support] acharné, énergique ; [- protest] vigoureux, énergique ; [- opponent, supporter] zélé, très actif **▸ to make strenuous efforts to do sthg** faire des efforts considérables pour faire qqch.

strep [strep] *inf adj* [infection] streptococcique **▸ strep throat** angine *f*.

stress [stres] **◆** *n* **1.** [nervous tension] stress *m*, tension *f* nerveuse **▸ to suffer from stress** être stressé **▸ to be under stress a)** [person] être stressé **b)** [relationship] être tendu **∕** *the stresses and strains of being a parent* les angoisses qu'on éprouve lorsqu'on a des enfants ; [pressure] pression *f* **2.** CONSTR & TECH contrainte *f*, tension *f* **▸ to be in stress** [beam, girder] être sous contrainte **3.** [emphasis] insistance *f* **▸ to lay stress on sthg a)** [fact, point, detail] insister sur, souligner **b)** [qualities, values, manners] insister sur, mettre l'accent sur **4.** LING [gen] accentuation *f* ; [on syllable] accent *m* ; [accented syllable] syllabe *f* accentuée **5.** MUS accent *m*. **◆** *vt* **1.** [emphasize - fact, point, detail] insister sur, faire ressortir, souligner ; [- value, qualities] insister sur, mettre l'accent sur **2.** [in phonetics, poetry, music] accentuer **3.** CONSTR & TECH [structure, foundation] mettre sous tension or en charge ; [concrete, metal] solliciter. **◆** *vi inf* stresser. **❖ stress out** *vt inf* stresser.

stress-buster *n inf* éliminateur *m* de stress.

stressed [strest] *adj* **1.** [person] stressé, tendu ; [relationship] tendu **2.** [syllable, word] accentué.

stressed-out *adj inf* stressé.

stressful ['stresful] *adj* [lifestyle, job, conditions] stressant ; [moments] de stress.

stress management *n* gestion *f* du stress.

stressor ['stresər] *n* ⒰ facteur *m* de stress.

stress-related *adj* dû au stress.

stretch [stretʃ] **◆** *vt* **1.** [pull tight] tendre **∕** *stretch the rope tight* tendez bien la corde **2.** [pull longer or wider - elastic] étirer ; [- garment, shoes] élargir **▸ to stretch sthg out of shape** déformer qqch **3.** [extend, reach to full length] étendre **∕** *stretch your arms upwards* tendez les bras vers le haut **▸ to stretch o.s.** s'étirer **▸ to stretch one's legs** se dégourdir les jambes **4.** [force, strain, bend - meaning, truth] forcer, exagérer ; [- rules] tourner, contourner ; [- principle] faire une entorse à ; [- imagination] faire

un gros effort de **∕** *you're really stretching my patience* ma patience a des limites **∕** *that's stretching it a bit (far)!* là vous exagérez !, là vous allez un peu loin ! **∕** *it would be stretching a point to call him a diplomat* dire qu'il est diplomate serait exagérer or aller un peu loin **∕** *I suppose we could stretch a point and let him stay* je suppose qu'on pourrait faire une entorse au règlement et lui permettre de rester **5.** [budget, income, resources, supplies - get the most from] tirer le maximum de ; [- overload] surcharger, mettre à rude épreuve **∕** *our resources are stretched to the limit* nos ressources sont exploitées or utilisées au maximum **∕** *our staff are really stretched today* le personnel travaille à la limite de ses possibilités aujourd'hui **▸ to be fully stretched a)** [machine, engine] tourner à plein régime **b)** [factory, economy] fonctionner à plein régime **c)** [person, staff] faire son maximum ; [person - use one's talents] : *the job won't stretch you enough* le travail ne sera pas assez stimulant pour vous **6.** MED [ligament, muscle] étirer. **◆** *vi* **1.** [be elastic] s'étirer ; [become longer] s'allonger ; [become wider] s'élargir **∕** *the shoes will stretch with wear* vos chaussures vont se faire or s'élargir à l'usage **∕** *my pullover has stretched out of shape* mon pull s'est déformé **2.** [person, animal - from tiredness] s'étirer ; [- on ground, bed] s'étendre, s'allonger ; [- to reach something] tendre la main **∕** *he had to stretch to reach it* **a)** [reach out] il a dû tendre le bras pour l'atteindre **b)** [stand on tiptoe] il a dû se mettre sur la pointe des pieds pour l'atteindre **3.** [spread, extend - in space, time] s'étendre **∕** *the forest stretches as far as the eye can see* la forêt s'étend à perte de vue **∕** *the road stretched across 500 miles of desert* la route parcourait 800 km de désert **∕** *my salary won't stretch to a new car* mon salaire ne me permet pas d'acheter une nouvelle voiture. **◆** *n* **1.** [expanse - of land, water] étendue *f* **∕** *this stretch of the road is particularly dangerous in the winter* cette partie de la route est très dangereuse en hiver **∕** *a new stretch of road* **∕** *motorway* un nouveau tronçon de route / d'autoroute **∕** *it's a lovely stretch of river* / *scenery* cette partie de la rivière / du paysage est magnifique ; [on racetrack] ligne *f* droite **▸ to go into the final** or **finishing stretch** entamer la dernière ligne droite **2.** [period of time] laps *m* de temps **∕** *for long stretches at a time there was nothing to do* il n'y avait rien à faire pendant de longues périodes **∕** *he did a stretch in Dartmoor* *inf* il a fait de la taule à Dartmoor **3.** [act of stretching] étirement *m* **∕** *he stood up, yawned and had a stretch* il se leva, bâilla et s'étira **▸ to give one's legs a stretch** se dégourdir les jambes **∕** *by no stretch of the imagination* même en faisant un gros effort d'imagination **4.** [elasticity] élasticité *f* **∕** *there's a lot of stretch in these stockings* ces bas sont très élastiques or s'étirent facilement **5.** SPORT [exercise] étirement *m* **∕** *do a couple of stretches before breakfast* faites quelques exercices d'assouplissement avant le petit déjeuner. **◆** *adj* TEXT [material] élastique, stretch *(inv)* ; [cover] extensible. **❖ at a stretch** *adv phr* d'affilée. **❖ at full stretch** *adv phr* **▸ to be at full stretch a)** [factory, machine] fonctionner à plein régime or à plein rendement **b)** [person] se donner à fond, faire son maximum **∕** *we were working at full stretch* nous travaillions d'arrache-pied. **❖ stretch out ◆** *vt sep* **1.** [pull tight] tendre **∕** *the sheets had been stretched out on the line to dry* on avait étendu les draps sur le fil à linge pour qu'ils sèchent **∕** *the plastic sheet was stretched out on the lawn* la bâche en plastique était étalée sur la pelouse **2.** [extend, spread - arms, legs] allonger, étendre ; [- hand] tendre ; [- wings] déployer **∕** *she stretched out her hand towards him* / *for the cup* elle tendit la main vers lui / pour prendre la tasse **∕** *she lay stretched out in front of the television* elle était allongée par terre devant la télévision **3.** [prolong - interview, meeting] prolonger, faire durer ; [- account] allonger **4.** [make last - supplies, income] faire durer. **◆** *vi* **1.** [person, animal] s'étendre, s'allonger **∕**

they stretched out on the lawn in the sun ils se sont allongés au soleil sur la pelouse **2.** [forest, countryside] s'étendre ; [prospects, season] s'étendre, s'étaler / *a nice long holiday stretched out before them* ils avaient de longues vacances devant eux.

stretcher ['stretʃə'] n MED brancard *m*, civière *f* / *he was carried off on a stretcher* on l'a emmené sur une civière or un brancard.

stretcher party n détachement *m* de brancardiers.

stretchmarks ['stretʃmɑːks] pl n vergetures *fpl*.

stretchy ['stretʃɪ] (*compar* **stretchier**, *superl* **stretchiest**) adj élastique, extensible.

strew [struː] (*pt* **strewed**, *pp* **strewn** [struːn] or **strewed**) vt *liter* **1.** [scatter - seeds, flowers, leaves] répandre, éparpiller ; [throw - toys, papers] éparpiller, jeter ; [-debris] éparpiller, disséminer **2.** [cover - ground, floor, path] joncher, parsemer ; [-table] joncher.

stricken ['strɪkn] adj *fml* **1.** [ill] malade ; [wounded] blessé ; [damaged, troubled] ravagé, dévasté **2.** [afflicted] frappé, atteint / *stricken by* or *with blindness* frappé de cécité.

strict [strɪkt] adj **1.** [severe, stern - person, discipline] strict, sévère ; [inflexible - principles] strict, rigoureux ; [- belief, code, rules] strict, rigide **2.** [exact, precise - meaning, interpretation] strict **3.** [absolute - accuracy, hygiene] strict, absolu / *he told me in the strictest confidence* il me l'a dit à titre strictement confidentiel.

strictly ['strɪktlɪ] adv **1.** [severely - act, treat] strictement, avec sévérité **2.** [exactly - interpret, translate] fidèlement, exactement ▸ **strictly speaking** à strictement or à proprement parler **3.** [absolutely, rigorously] strictement, absolument / *strictly forbidden* or *prohibited* formellement interdit.

strictness ['strɪktnɪs] n **1.** [severity - of person, rules, diet] sévérité *f* **2.** [exactness - of interpretation] exactitude *f*, rigueur *f*.

stride [straɪd] (*pt* **strode** [strəʊd], *pp* **stridden** ['strɪdn]) ◆ n **1.** [step] grand pas *m*, enjambée *f*, foulée *f* **2.** *fig* [progress] ▸ **to make great strides** faire de grands progrès, avancer à pas de géant. ◆ vi marcher à grands pas or à grandes enjambées ▸ **to stride away** / **in** / **out** s'éloigner / entrer / sortir à grands pas. ◆ vt [streets, fields, deck] arpenter. ❖ **strides** pl n 🇬🇧 & Austr *inf* [trousers] pantalon *m*.

strident ['straɪdnt] adj strident.

strife [straɪf] n (U) *fml* [conflict] dissensions *fpl* ; [struggles] luttes *fpl* ; [quarrels] querelles *fpl* / *industrial strife* conflits sociaux.

strike [straɪk] (*pt & pp* **struck** [strʌk], *cont* **striking**) ◆ n **1.** [by workers] grève *f* ▸ **to go on strike** se mettre en or faire grève ▸ **to be (out) on strike** être en grève / *coal* or *miners' strike* grève des mineurs / *postal* or *post office strike* grève des postes **2.** MIL raid *m*, attaque *f* ; [nuclear] deuxième frappe *f* ; [by bird of prey, snake] attaque *f* **3.** [of clock - chime, mechanism] sonnerie *f* **4.** [act or instance of hitting] coup *m* ; [sound] bruit *m* **5.** [in baseball] strike *m* ; 🇺🇸 *fig* [black mark] mauvais point *m* / *he has two strikes against him* *fig* il est mal parti **6.** [in bowling] honneur *m* double. ◆ comp [committee, movement] de grève. ◆ vt **1.** [hit] frapper / *he struck me with his fist* il m'a donné un coup de poing / *she took the vase and struck him on* or *over the head* elle saisit le vase et lui donna un coup sur la tête / *she struck him across the face* elle lui a donné une gifle ; [inflict, deliver - blow] donner / *who struck the first blow?* qui a porté le premier coup ?, qui a frappé le premier ? ▸ **to strike a blow for democracy** / **women's rights** **a)** *fig* [law, event] faire progresser la démocratie / les droits de la femme **b)** [person, group] marquer des points en faveur de la démocratie / des droits des femmes **2.** [bump into, collide with] heurter, cogner / *his foot struck the bar on his first jump* son pied a heurté la barre lors de son premier saut / *she fell and struck her head on* or *against the kerb* elle s'est cogné la tête contre le bord du trottoir en tombant **3.** [assail, attain - subj: bullet, torpedo, bomb] toucher, atteindre ; [- subj: lightning] frapper ; [afflict - subj: drought, disease, worry, regret] frapper ; [- subj: storm, hurricane, disaster, wave of violence] s'abattre sur, frapper / *I was struck by* or *with doubts* j'ai été pris de doute, le doute s'est emparé de moi **4.** [occur to] frapper / *only later did it strike me as unusual* ce n'est que plus tard que j'ai trouvé ça or que cela m'a paru bizarre / *a terrible thought struck her* une idée affreuse lui vint à l'esprit **5.** [impress] frapper, impressionner / *what strikes you is the silence* ce qui (vous) frappe, c'est le silence / *how did she strike you?* quelle impression vous a-t-elle faite ?, quel effet vous a-t-elle fait ? **6.** [chime] sonner / *it was striking midnight as we left* minuit sonnait quand nous partîmes **7.** [play - note, chord] jouer ▸ **to strike a false note a)** MUS faire une fausse note **b)** [speech] sonner faux ▸ **to strike a chord**: *does it strike a chord?* est-ce que cela te rappelle or dit quelque chose ? **8.** [arrive at, reach - deal, treaty, agreement] conclure / *I'll strike a bargain with you* je te propose un marché / *it's not easy to strike a balance between too much and too little freedom* il n'est pas facile de trouver un équilibre or de trouver le juste milieu entre trop et pas assez de liberté **9.** [cause a feeling of] ▸ **to strike fear** or **terror into sb** remplir qqn d'effroi **10.** [cause to become] rendre / *I was struck dumb by the sheer cheek of the man!* je suis resté muet devant le culot de cet homme ! **11.** [ignite - match] frotter, allumer ; [- sparks] faire jaillir **12.** [discover - gold] découvrir ; [- oil, water] trouver ▸ **to strike it lucky a)** 🇬🇧 *inf* [material gain] trouver le filon **b)** [be lucky] avoir de la veine ▸ **to strike it rich** *inf* trouver le filon, faire fortune **13.** [mint - coin, medal] frapper. ◆ vi **1.** [hit] frapper ▸ **to strike lucky** *inf* avoir de la veine **2.** [stop working] faire grève / *they're striking for more pay* ils font grève pour obtenir une augmentation de salaire **3.** [attack - gen] attaquer ; [- snake] mordre ; [- wild animal] sauter or bondir sur sa proie ; [- bird of prey] fondre or s'abattre sur sa proie / *these are measures which strike at the root* / *heart of the problem* voici des mesures qui attaquent le problème à la racine / qui s'attaquent au cœur du problème **4.** [chime] sonner **5.** [happen suddenly - illness, disaster, earthquake] survenir, se produire, arriver. ❖ **strike back** vi se venger ; MIL contre-attaquer. ❖ **strike down** vt sep foudroyer, terrasser. ❖ **strike off** ◆ vt sep **1.** [delete, remove - from list] rayer, barrer ; [- from professional register] radier **2.** [sever] couper. ◆ vi [go] : *we struck off into the forest* nous sommes entrés or avons pénétré dans la forêt. ❖ **strike out** ◆ vi **1.** [set up on one's own] s'établir à son compte ; [launch out] se lancer / *they decided to strike out into a new field* ils ont décidé de se lancer dans un nouveau domaine **2.** [go] : *she struck out across the fields* elle prit à travers champs **3.** [swim] : *we struck out for the shore* nous avons commencé à nager en direction de la côte **4.** [aim a blow] : *he struck out at me* il essaya de me frapper. ◆ vt sep [cross out] rayer, barrer. ❖ **strike up** ◆ vt sep [start] ▸ **to strike up a conversation with sb** engager la conversation avec qqn ▸ **to strike up an acquaintance** / **a friendship with sb** lier connaissance / se lier d'amitié avec qqn. ◆ vi [musician, orchestra] commencer à jouer ; [music] commencer.

strikebound ['straɪkbaʊnd] adj [factory, department] bloqué par une or la grève ; [industry, country] bloqué par des grèves.

strikebreaker ['straɪk,breɪkə'] n briseur *m*, -euse *f* de grève, jaune *m*.

strike pay n salaire *m* de gréviste *(versé par le syndicat ou par un fonds de solidarité).*

striker ['straɪkəʳ] n **1.** INDUST gréviste *mf* **2.** FOOT buteur *m* **3.** [device - on clock] marteau *m* ; [- in gun] percuteur *m*.

striking ['straɪkɪŋ] ◆ adj **1.** [remarkable - contrast, resemblance, beauty] frappant, saisissant **2.** [clock] qui sonne les heures ▶ **striking mechanism** sonnerie *f* (des heures) **3.** MIL [force] d'intervention **4.** INDUST en grève **5.** PHR within striking distance à proximité / *she lives within striking distance of London* elle habite tout près de Londres. ◆ n **1.** [of clock] sonnerie *f* (des heures) **2.** [of coins] frappe *f*.

strikingly ['straɪkɪŋlɪ] adv remarquablement.

Strimmer® ['strɪməʳ] n débroussailleuse *f* (à fil).

string [strɪŋ] (*pt & pp* **strung** [strʌŋ]) ◆ n **1.** [gen - for parcel] ficelle *f* ; [-on apron, pyjamas] cordon *m* / *a piece of string* un bout ou un morceau de ficelle ; [for puppet] ficelle *f*, fil *m* **2.** [for bow, tennis racket, musical instrument] corde *f* ▶ **the strings** MUS les cordes **3.** [row, chain - of beads, pearls] rang *m*, collier *m* ; [- of onions, sausages] chapelet *m* ; [- of visitors, cars] file *f* / *a string of islands* un chapelet d'îles / *a string of fairy lights* une guirlande (électrique) / *she owns a string of shops* elle est propriétaire d'une chaîne de magasins / *a string of race horses* une écurie de course **4.** [series - of successes, defeats] série *f* ; [-of lies, insults] kyrielle *f*, chapelet *m* **5.** COMPUT & LING chaîne *f* ; MATH séquence *f*. ◆ comp **1.** MUS [band, instrument, orchestra] à cordes ▶ **string player** musicien *m*, -enne *f* qui joue d'un instrument à cordes ▶ **the string section** les cordes *fpl* ▶ **string quartet** quatuor *m* à cordes **2.** [made of string] de ou en ficelle ▶ **string bag** filet *m* à provisions ▶ **string vest** tricot *m* de corps à grosses mailles. ◆ vt **1.** [guitar, violin] monter, mettre des cordes à ; [racket] corder ; [bow] mettre une corde à **2.** [beads, pearls] enfiler **3.** [hang] suspendre ; [stretch] tendre **4.** CULIN [beans] enlever les fils de. ❖ **string along** *inf* ◆ vi **1.** [tag along] suivre (les autres) **2.** [agree] ▶ **to string along with sb** se ranger à l'avis de qqn. ◆ vt sep [person] faire marcher. ❖ **string out** vt sep [washing, lamps] suspendre (sur une corde). ❖ **string together** vt sep **1.** [beads] enfiler ; [words, sentences] enchaîner **2.** [improvise - story] monter, improviser. ❖ **string up** vt sep **1.** [lights] suspendre ; [washing] étendre **2.** *inf* [hang - person] pendre.

string bean n **1.** [vegetable] haricot *m* vert **2.** *inf* [person] grande perche *f*.

stringed [strɪŋd] adj [instrument] à cordes.

stringent ['strɪndʒənt] n **1.** [rules] rigoureux, strict, sévère ; [measures, conditions] rigoureux, draconien **2.** ECON & FIN [market] tendu.

strip [strɪp] (*pt & pp* **stripped**) ◆ n **1.** [of paper, carpet] bande *f* ; [of metal] bande *f*, ruban *m* ; [of land] bande *f*, langue *f* / *there was a thin strip of light under the door* il y avait un mince rai de lumière sous la porte / *a narrow strip of water* **a)** [sea] un étroit bras de mer **b)** [river] un étroit ruban de rivière / *can you cut off a strip of material?* pouvez-vous couper une bande de tissu ? / *she cut the dough / material into strips* elle coupa la pâte en lamelles / le tissu en bandes ▶ **to tear sthg into strips** déchirer qqch en bandes **2.** US [street with businesses] avenue *f* commerçante **3.** AERON piste *f* **4.** [light] ▶ **neon strip** tube *m* néon **5.** SPORT tenue *f* **6.** [striptease] strip-tease *m*. ◆ vt **1.** [undress] déshabiller, dévêtir / *they were stripped to the waist* ils étaient torse nu, ils étaient nus jusqu'à la ceinture ▶ **to strip sb naked** déshabiller qqn (complètement) **2.** [make bare - tree] dépouiller, dénuder ; [-door, furniture] décaper ; [-wire] dénuder / *the walls need to be stripped*

first **a)** [of wallpaper] il faut d'abord enlever or arracher le papier peint **b)** [of paint] il faut d'abord décaper les murs **3.** [remove cover from] découvrir ; [take contents from] vider ▶ **to strip a bed** défaire un lit **4.** [remove -gen] enlever ; [-paint] décaper / *we stripped the wallpaper from the walls* nous avons arraché le papier peint des murs **5.** [deprive] dépouiller, démunir ▶ **to strip sb of his / her privileges / possessions** dépouiller qqn de ses privilèges / biens / *he was stripped of his rank* il a été dégradé **6.** [dismantle - engine, gun] démonter **7.** TECH [screw, bolt] arracher le filet de ; [gear] arracher les dents de. ◆ vi **1.** [undress] se déshabiller, se dévêtir ▶ **to strip to the waist** se dévêtir jusqu'à la ceinture, se mettre torse nu **2.** [do a striptease] faire un strip-tease. ❖ **strip down** ◆ vt sep **1.** [bed] défaire (complètement) ; [wallpaper] arracher, enlever ; [door, furniture] décaper **2.** [dismantle - engine, mechanism] démonter. ◆ vi se déshabiller / *he stripped down to his underpants* il s'est déshabillé, ne gardant que son slip. ❖ **strip off** ◆ vt sep [gen] enlever, arracher ; [clothes, shirt] enlever ; [paint] décaper / *to strip the leaves off a tree* dépouiller un arbre de ses feuilles. ◆ vi se déshabiller, se mettre nu. ❖ **strip out** vt sep [engine, mechanism] démonter, démanteler.

strip cartoon n UK bande *f* dessinée.

strip club n boîte *f* de strip-tease.

stripe [straɪp] ◆ n **1.** [on animal] zébrure *f* ; [on material, shirt] raie *f*, rayure *f* ; [on car] filet *m* **2.** MIL galon *m*, chevron *m* **3.** [kind] genre *m* **4.** [lash] coup *m* de fouet ; [mark] marque *f* d'un coup de fouet. ◆ vt rayer, marquer de rayures.

striped [straɪpt] adj [animal] tigré, zébré ; [material, shirt, pattern] rayé, à rayures / *striped with blue* avec des rayures bleues.

strip lighting n éclairage *m* fluorescent or au néon.

strip mall n US centre commercial dont les différents magasins sont situés côte à côte le long d'un trottoir.

stripper ['strɪpəʳ] n **1.** [in strip club] strip-teaseuse *f* **2.** [for paint] décapant *m*.

strip show n (spectacle *m* de) strip-tease *m*.

striptease ['striptiːz] n strip-tease *m* ▶ **striptease artist** strip-teaseur *m*, -euse *f*.

stripy ['straɪpɪ] (*compar* **stripier**, *superl* **stripiest**) adj [material, shirt, pattern] rayé, à rayures ; ZOOL tigré, zébré.

strive [straɪv] (*pt* **strove** [strəʊv], *pp* **striven** ['strɪvn]) vt *fml & liter* **1.** [attempt] ▶ **to strive to do sthg** s'évertuer à ou s'acharner à faire qqch ▶ **to strive after** or **for sthg** faire tout son possible pour obtenir qqch, s'efforcer d'obtenir qqch **2.** [struggle] lutter, se battre.

strobe [strəʊb] n **1.** ▶ **strobe (lighting)** lumière *f* stroboscopique **2.** = **stroboscope.**

stroboscope ['strəʊbəskəʊp] n stroboscope *m*.

strode [strəʊd] pt ⟶ **stride.**

stroke [strəʊk] ◆ n **1.** [blow, flick] coup *m* **2.** SPORT [in golf, tennis, cricket, billiards] coup *m* ; [in swimming - movement] mouvement *m* des bras ; [-style] nage *f* ; [in rowing - movement] coup *m* d'aviron ; [-technique] nage *f* **3.** [mark - from pen, pencil] trait *m* ; [from brush] trait *m*, touche *f* ; [on letters, figures] barre *f* ; TYPO [oblique dash] barre *f* oblique / *225 stroke 62* UK 225 barre oblique 62 **4.** [piece, example - of luck] coup *m* ; [- of genius] trait *m* / *she didn't do a stroke (of work) all day* UK elle n'a rien fait de la journée **5.** [of clock, bell] coup *m* / *on the stroke of midnight* sur le coup de minuit / *on the stroke of 6* à 6 h sonnantes or tapantes **6.** MED attaque *f* (d'apoplexie) ▶ **to have a stroke** avoir une attaque **7.** NAUT [oarsman] chef *m* de nage **8.** TECH [of piston] course *f* ▶ **two- / four-stroke engine** un moteur à deux / quatre temps **9.** [caress]

caresse f. ◆ vt **1.** [caress] caresser **2.** [in rowing] ▶ **to stroke a boat** être chef de nage, donner la nage **3.** SPORT [ball] frapper. ◆ vi [in rowing] être chef de nage, donner la nage. ❖ **at a stroke, at one stroke** adv phr d'un seul coup.

stroll [strəʊl] ◆ vi se balader, flâner ▶ **to stroll in / out / past** entrer / sortir / passer sans se presser. ◆ vt ▶ **to stroll the streets** se promener dans les rues. ◆ n petit tour m, petite promenade f ▶ **to go for a stroll** aller faire un tour or une petite promenade.

stroller ['strəʊlə'] n **1.** [walker] promeneur m, -euse f **2.** 🇺🇸 [pushchair] poussette f.

strong [strɒŋ] (compar **stronger** ['strɒŋgə'], superl **strongest** ['strɒŋgɪst]) ◆ adj **1.** [sturdy - person, animal, constitution, arms] fort, robuste ; [- building] solide ; [- cloth, material] solide, résistant ; [- shoes, table] solide, robuste ; [in health - person] en bonne santé ; [- heart] solide, robuste ; [- eyesight] bon **2.** [in degree, force - sea current, wind, light, lens, voice] fort, puissant ; [- magnet] puissant ; [ELEC - current] intense ; [MUS - beat] fort ; [firm - conviction, belief] ferme, fort, profond ; [- protest, support] énergique, vigoureux ; [- measures] énergique, draconien ; [intense, vivid - desire, imagination, interest] vif ; [- colour] vif, fort ; [emotionally, morally - character] fort, bien trempé ; [- feelings] intense, fort ; [- nerves] solide **3.** [striking - contrast, impression] fort, frappant, marquant ; [- accent] fort **4.** [solid - argument, evidence] solide, sérieux **5.** [in taste, smell] fort **6.** [in ability - student, team] fort ; [- candidate, contender] sérieux **7.** [tough, harsh - words] grossier **8.** [in number] : **an army 5,000 strong** une armée forte de 5 000 hommes / **the marchers were 400 strong** les manifestants étaient au nombre de 400 **9.** COMM & ECON [currency, price] solide ; [market] ferme **10.** GRAM [verb, form] fort. ◆ adv inf ▶ **to be going strong a)** [person] être toujours solide or toujours d'attaque **b)** [party] battre son plein **c)** [machine, car] fonctionner toujours bien **d)** [business, economy] être florissant, prospérer ▶ **to come on strong a)** [insist] insister lourdement **b)** [make a pass] faire des avances.

strongarm ['strɒŋɑːm] adj inf [methods] brutal, violent ▶ **to use strongarm tactics** employer la manière forte. ❖ **strong-arm** vt inf faire violence à ▶ **to strong-arm sb into doing sthg** forcer la main à qqn pour qu'il fasse qqch.

strongbox ['strɒŋbɒks] n coffre-fort m.

stronghold ['strɒŋhəʊld] n **1.** MIL forteresse f, fort m **2.** fig bastion m.

strongly ['strɒŋlɪ] adv **1.** [greatly - regret] vivement, profondément ; [- impress, attract] fortement, vivement **2.** [firmly - believe, support] fermement ; [forcefully - attack, defend, protest] énergiquement, vigoureusement, avec force ; [- emphasize] fortement **3.** [sturdily - constructed] solidement / **strongly built a)** [person] costaud, bien bâti **b)** [wall, structure] solide, bien construit.

strongman ['strɒŋmæn] (pl **strongmen** [-men]) n hercule m (de foire).

strong-minded adj résolu, déterminé.

strongroom ['strɒŋrʊm] n 🇬🇧 [in castle, house] chambre f forte ; [in bank] chambre f forte, salle f des coffres.

strong-willed [-'wɪld] adj volontaire, résolu, tenace.

strop [strɒp] (pt & pp **stropped**, cont **stropping**) ◆ n cuir m (à rasoir) ▶ **to be in a strop** fig être de mauvais poil. ◆ vt [razor] repasser sur le cuir.

stroppy ['strɒpɪ] (compar **stroppier**, superl **stroppiest**) adj 🇬🇧 inf : **there's no need to get stroppy!** tu n'as pas besoin de monter sur tes grands chevaux !

strove [strəʊv] pt ⟶ **strive**.

struck [strʌk] ◆ pt & pp ⟶ **strike**. ◆ adj 🇺🇸 [industry] bloqué pour cause de grève ; [factory] fermé pour cause de grève.

structural ['strʌktʃərəl] adj **1.** [gen] structural ; [change, problem] structurel, de structure ; [unemployment] structurel ; LING [analysis] structural, structurel ▶ **structural linguistics / psychology** linguistique f / psychologie f structurale **2.** CONSTR [fault, steel] de construction ; [damage, alterations] structural ▶ **structural engineering** génie m civil.

structuralism ['strʌktʃərəlɪzm] n structuralisme m.

structuralist ['strʌktʃərəlɪst] ◆ n structuraliste mf. ◆ adj structuraliste.

structurally ['strʌktʃərəlɪ] adv **1.** [gen] du point de vue de la structure **2.** CONSTR du point de vue de la construction.

structure ['strʌktʃə'] ◆ n **1.** [composition, framework] structure f ; [of building] structure f, ossature f, armature f **2.** [building] construction f, bâtisse f. ◆ vt structurer.

structured ['strʌktʃəd] adj structuré.

structured query language n COMPUT langage m d'interrogation structuré.

struggle ['strʌgl] ◆ n [gen] lutte f ; [physical fight] bagarre f, lutte f ▶ **power struggle** lutte pour le pouvoir / **they surrendered without a struggle** ils se sont rendus sans opposer de résistance / **I finally succeeded but not without a struggle** j'y suis finalement parvenu, non sans peine / **it was a struggle to convince him** on a eu du mal à le convaincre. ◆ vi **1.** [fight] lutter, se battre **2.** [try hard, strive] lutter, s'efforcer, se démener / **I struggled to open the door** je me suis démené pour ouvrir la porte / **he struggled with the lock** il s'est battu avec la serrure / **she struggled to control her temper** elle avait du mal à garder son calme / **she had to struggle to make ends meet** elle a eu bien du mal à joindre les deux bouts **3.** [expressing movement] : **to struggle to one's feet a)** [old person] se lever avec difficulté or avec peine **b)** [in fight] se relever péniblement / **to struggle up a hill a)** [person] gravir péniblement une colline **b)** [car] peiner dans une côte. ❖ **struggle along** vi lit peiner, avancer avec peine / fig subsister avec difficulté. ❖ **struggle on** vi **1.** = **struggle along 2.** [keep trying] continuer à se battre. ❖ **struggle through** vi [in difficult situation] s'en sortir tant bien que mal.

struggling ['strʌglɪŋ] adj [hard up - painter, writer, etc.] qui tire le diable par la queue, qui a du mal à joindre les deux bouts.

strum [strʌm] (pt & pp **strummed**, cont **strumming**) ◆ vt [guitar] gratter sur ▶ **to strum a tune on the guitar** jouer un petit air à la guitare. ◆ vi [guitarist] gratter. ◆ n [on guitar] raclement m.

strung [strʌŋ] ◆ pt & pp ⟶ **string**. ◆ adj **1.** [guitar, piano] muni de cordes, monté ; [tennis racket] cordé **2.** 🇺🇸 inf à cran.

strung-out adj v inf **1.** drugs sl ▶ **to be strung-out a)** [addicted] être accroché or accro **b)** [high] être shooté, planer **c)** [suffering withdrawal symptoms] être en manque **2.** [uptight] crispé, tendu.

strut [strʌt] (pt & pp **strutted**, cont **strutting**) ◆ n **1.** [support - for roof, wall] étrésillon m, étançon m, contre-fiche f ; [- for building] étai m, support m ; [- between uprights] entretoise f, traverse f ; [- for beam] jambe f de force ; [- in plane wing, model] support m **2.** [crossbar - of chair, ladder] barreau m **3.** [gait] démarche f fière. ◆ vi ▶ **to strut (about)** or **around** plastronner, se pavaner. ◆ vt 🇺🇸 ▶ **to strut one's stuff** inf se montrer en spectacle.

strychnine ['strɪkniːn] n strychnine f.

stub [stʌb] (*pt & pp* **stubbed**, *cont* **stubbing**) ◆ n
1. [stump - of tree] chicot *m*, souche *f* ; [- of pencil] bout *m* ;
[- of tail] moignon *m* ; [- of cigarette] mégot *m* **2.** [counterfoil - of cheque] souche *f*, talon *m* ; [- of ticket] talon *m*. ◆ vt
▶ **to stub one's toe / foot** se cogner le doigt de pied / le
pied. ◆ **stub out** vt sep [cigarette] écraser.
stubble ['stʌbl] n **1.** AGR chaume *m* **2.** [on chin] barbe *f*
de plusieurs jours.
stubbly ['stʌblɪ] (*compar* **stubblier**, *superl* **stubbliest**) adj **1.** [chin, face] mal rasé ; [beard] de plusieurs jours ;
[hair] en brosse **2.** [field] couvert de chaume.
stubborn ['stʌbən] adj **1.** [determined - person] têtu,
obstiné ; [- animal] rétif, récalcitrant ; [- opposition] obstiné,
acharné ; [- refusal, insistence] obstiné **2.** [resistant - cold,
cough, symptoms] persistant, opiniâtre ; [- stain] récalcitrant,
rebelle.
stubbornly ['stʌbənlɪ] adv obstinément, opiniâtrement.
stubby ['stʌbɪ] (*compar* **stubbier**, *superl* **stubbiest**)
◆ adj [finger] boudiné, court et épais ; [tail] très court, tronqué ; [person] trapu. ◆ n (AUSTR) *inf* petite canette *f* de bière.
stucco ['stʌkəʊ] (*pl* **stuccos** *or* **stuccoes**) ◆ n
stuc *m*. ◆ comp [ceiling, wall, façade] de *or* en stuc, stuqué.
◆ vt stuquer.
stuck [stʌk] ◆ pt & pp ⟶ **stick**. ◆ adj **1.** [jammed
- window, mechanism] coincé, bloqué ; [- vehicle, lift] bloqué / *he got his hand stuck inside the jar* il s'est pris or
coincé la main dans le pot / *to get stuck in the mud* s'embourber / *to get stuck in the sand* s'enliser / *to be* or *to
get stuck in traffic* être coincé or bloqué dans les embouteillages ; [stranded] coincé, bloqué / *they were* or *they got
stuck at the airport overnight* ils sont restés bloqués or ils
ont dû passer toute la nuit à l'aéroport **2.** [in difficulty] : *if
you get stuck go on to the next question* si tu sèches, passe
à la question suivante / *he's never stuck for an answer* il a
toujours réponse à tout / *to be stuck for money* être à court
d'argent **3.** [in an unpleasant situation, trapped] coincé /
to be stuck in a boring / dead-end job avoir un boulot
ennuyeux / sans avenir **4.** *inf* [lumbered] ▶ **to get** or **to be
stuck with sthg** se retrouver avec qqch sur les bras **5.** *inf*
[fond, keen] ▶ **to be stuck on sb** être en pincer pour qqn **6.** (UK)
inf (PHR) *he got stuck into his work* il s'est mis au travail /
get stuck in! allez-y !
stuck-up adj *inf* bêcheur, snob.
stud [stʌd] (*pt & pp* **studded**, *cont* **studding**) ◆ n
1. [nail, spike] clou *m* (*à grosse tête*) ; [decorative] clou *m*
(*décoratif*) ; [on shoe] clou *m* (*à souliers*), caboche *f* ; [on belt]
clou *m* ; [on football boots, track shoes] crampon *m* ; [on tyre]
clou *m* **2.** [earring] = **stud earring 3.** [on roadway]
catadioptre *m* **4.** [on shirt] agrafe *f* (*servant à fermer un col,
un plastron, etc.*) **5.** TECH [screw] goujon *m* ; [pin, pivot] tourillon *m* ; [lug] ergot *m* **6.** CONSTR montant *m* **7.** [on chain]
étai *m* **8.** [reproduction] monte *f* ▶ **to put a stallion (out)
to stud** mener un étalon à la monte ▶ **to be at stud** saillir
9. [stud farm] haras *m* **10.** [stallion] étalon *m* **11.** *v inf*
[man - gen] mec *m* ; [promiscuous man] tombeur *m* ; [lover]
jules *m*. ◆ vt [shoes, belt] clouter ; [door, chest] clouter, garnir de clous.
studded ['stʌdɪd] adj **1.** [tyre, belt, jacket] clouté
2. [spangled] ▶ **studded with** émaillé or parsemé de.
stud earring n clou *m* d'oreille.
student ['stjuːdnt] ◆ n UNIV étudiant *m*, -e *f* ; SCH
élève *mf*, lycéen *m*, -enne *f* / *she's a biology student* or *a
student of biology* elle étudie la biologie or est étudiante en
biologie. ◆ comp [life] d'étudiant, estudiantin ; [hall of residence, canteen] universitaire ; UNIV [participation] étudiant ;
SCH des élèves ; [power, union] étudiant ; UNIV [protest]
d'étudiants, étudiant ; SCH d'élèves, de lycéens ; UNIV [attitudes] des étudiants ; SCH des élèves.

student card n carte *f* d'étudiant.
student loan n *prêt bancaire pour étudiants.*
student teacher n [in primary school] instituteur *m*,
-trice *f* stagiaire ; [in secondary school] professeur *m* stagiaire.
student union n **1.** [trade union] syndicat *m* or
union *f* des étudiants **2.** [premises] ≃ foyer *m* des étudiants.

Student union

Dans les universités britanniques et américaines, on appelle **student union** à la fois le
syndicat des étudiants et le local lui-même.
Les syndicats défendent les intérêts des
étudiants et leur offrent différents services.

stud farm n haras *m*.
studied ['stʌdɪd] adj [ease, politeness, indifference] étudié ; [insult, rudeness, negligence] délibéré ; [elegance] recherché ; [manner, pose] étudié, affecté.
studio ['stjuːdɪəʊ] (*pl* **studios**) n [gen & CIN & RADIO]
studio *m*.
studio apartment n (US) studio *m*.
studio audience n public *m* (*présent lors de la diffusion
ou de l'enregistrement d'une émission*).
studio flat n (UK) studio *m*.
studious ['stjuːdjəs] adj **1.** [diligent - person] studieux,
appliqué ; [painstaking - attention, effort] soutenu ; [- piece of
work] soigné, sérieux **2.** [deliberate - indifference] délibéré,
voulu.
studiously ['stjuːdjəslɪ] adv **1.** [diligently - prepare,
work, examine] minutieusement, soigneusement **2.** [deliberately] d'une manière calculée or délibérée.
study ['stʌdɪ] (*pt & pp* **studied**, *pl* **studies**) ◆ vt
1. [gen & SCH & UNIV] étudier **2.** [examine - plan, evidence,
situation] étudier, examiner ; [observe - expression, reactions]
étudier, observer attentivement ; [- stars] observer. ◆ vi
[gen] étudier ; SCH & UNIV étudier, faire ses études ▶ **to
study for an exam** préparer un examen. ◆ n **1.** [gen]
étude *f* **2.** [room] bureau *m*, cabinet *m* de travail **3.** ART,
MUS & PHOT étude *f*. ◆ comp [hour, period, room] d'étude.
◆ **studies** pl n SCH & UNIV études *fpl*.
stuff [stʌf] ◆ n (U) **1.** *inf* [indefinite sense - things]
choses *fpl*, trucs *mpl* ; [- substance] substance *f*, matière *f*
2. *inf & pej* [rubbish, nonsense] bêtises *fpl*, sottises *fpl* **3.** *inf*
[possessions] affaires *fpl* ; [equipment] affaires *fpl*, matériel *m* / *where's my shaving / fishing stuff?* où est mon
matériel de rasage / de pêche ? **4.** *liter* [essence] étoffe *f*
5. *drugs sl* came *f* **6.** *inf* (PHR) ▶ **to do one's stuff** faire ce
qu'on a à faire ▶ **that's the stuff!** c'est ça !, allez-y ! ▶ **to
know one's stuff** connaître son affaire. ◆ vt **1.** *inf* [shove]
fourrer ; [expressing anger, rejection, etc.] : *he told me
I could stuff my report v inf* il m'a dit qu'il se foutait pas
mal de mon rapport ▶ **get stuffed!** *v inf* va te faire voir ! /
stuff him! v inf il peut aller se faire voir ! **2.** *inf* [cram, pack
full] bourrer **3.** [plug - gap] boucher **4.** [cushion, armchair] rembourrer **5.** CULIN farcir **6.** [in taxidermy - animal,
bird] empailler **7.** *inf* [with food] ▶ **to stuff o.s.** or **one's
face** *v inf* bâfrer / *I'm stuffed* je n'ai plus faim
8. (US) POL [ballot box] remplir de bulletins de votes truqués.
◆ **stuff up** vt sep [block] boucher.
stuffed [stʌft] adj **1.** CULIN farci **2.** [chair, cushion] rembourré.
stuffed shirt n prétentieux *m*, -euse *f*.
stuffily ['stʌfɪlɪ] adv **1.** [say, reply] d'un ton désapprobateur.

stuffing ['stʌfɪŋ] n **1.** [for furniture, toys] rembourrage m, bourre f; [for clothes] rembourrage m; [in taxidermy] paille f **2.** CULIN farce f.

stuffy ['stʌfɪ] (compar **stuffier**, superl **stuffiest**) adj **1.** [room] mal aéré, mal ventilé, qui sent le renfermé **2.** pej [person - prim] collet monté (inv); [- old-fashioned] vieux jeu (inv); [atmosphere, reception] guindé **3.** [dull - book, subject, lecture] ennuyeux **4.** [nose] bouché.

stultifying ['stʌltɪfaɪɪŋ] adj [work] abrutissant, assommant; [atmosphere] abrutissant, débilitant.

stumble ['stʌmbl] ◆ vi **1.** [person] trébucher, faire un faux pas; [horse] broncher, faire un faux pas ▶ **to stumble along / in / out** avancer / entrer / sortir en trébuchant **2.** [in speech] trébucher. ◆ n **1.** [in walking] faux pas m **2.** [in speech] : she read the poem without a stumble elle a lu le poème sans se tromper or sans se reprendre une seule fois. ❖ **stumble across, stumble on, stumble upon** vt insep **1.** [meet] rencontrer par hasard, tomber sur **2.** [discover] trouver par hasard, tomber sur.

stumbling block ['stʌmblɪŋ-] n pierre f d'achoppement.

stump [stʌmp] ◆ n **1.** [of tree] chicot m, souche f **2.** [of limb, tail] moignon m; [of tooth] chicot m; [of pencil, blade] (petit) bout m **3.** US POL estrade f (d'un orateur politique) ▶ **to be** or **to go on the stump** faire une tournée électorale **4.** ART estompe f ▶ **stump drawing** estompe f. ◆ vt **1.** inf [bewilder] laisser perplexe; [with question] coller **2.** US POL [constituency, state] faire une tournée électorale dans. ◆ vi **1.** [walk heavily] marcher d'un pas lourd ▶ **to stump in / out** [heavily] entrer / sortir d'un pas lourd **2.** US POL faire une tournée électorale. ❖ **stumps** pl n inf [legs] quilles fpl. ❖ **stump up** UK inf ◆ vi casquer. ◆ vt sep [money] cracher, aligner; [deposit] payer.

stumpy ['stʌmpɪ] (compar **stumpier**, superl **stumpiest**) adj [person] boulot, courtaud; [arms, legs] court et épais; [tail] tronqué.

stun [stʌn] (pt & pp **stunned**, cont **stunning**) vt **1.** [knock out] assommer **2.** fig [astonish] abasourdir, stupéfier.

stung [stʌŋ] pt & pp ⟶ **sting**.

stun grenade n grenade f cataplexiante.

stunk [stʌŋk] pp ⟶ **stink**.

stunned [stʌnd] adj **1.** [knocked out] assommé **2.** fig abasourdi, stupéfait.

stunner ['stʌnə'] n inf [woman] fille f superbe; [car] voiture f fantastique.

stunning ['stʌnɪŋ] adj **1.** [blow] étourdissant **2.** [astounding - news, event] stupéfiant, renversant; [beautiful - dress, car] fantastique; [- woman, figure] superbe.

stunningly ['stʌnɪŋlɪ] adv remarquablement, incroyablement.

stunt [stʌnt] ◆ n **1.** [feat] tour m de force, exploit m spectaculaire; [in plane] acrobatie f (aérienne) **2.** [by stunt man] cascade f ▶ **to do a stunt a)** [in plane] faire des acrobaties **b)** [stunt man] faire une cascade **3.** [trick] truc m; [hoax] farce f, canular m ▶ **to pull a stunt** faire un canular or une farce. ◆ comp ▶ **stunt driver** conducteur m cascadeur, conductrice f cascadeuse ▶ **stunt pilot** aviateur m, -trice f qui fait des cascades, spécialiste mf de l'acrobatie aérienne. ◆ vi **1.** AERON faire des acrobaties **2.** CIN & TV faire des cascades. ◆ vt [impede - growth, development] retarder; [- person] freiner or retarder la croissance de; [- intelligence] freiner le développement de.

stunted ['stʌntɪd] adj [person] chétif; [plant] chétif, rabougri; [growth, intelligence] retardé.

stunt man n cascadeur m.

stunt woman n cascadeuse f.

stupefaction [,stju:pɪ'fækʃn] n stupéfaction f, stupeur f.

stupefied ['stju:pɪfaɪd] adj stupéfait.

stupefy ['stju:pɪfaɪ] (pt & pp **stupefied**) vt **1.** [subj: alcohol, drugs, tiredness] abrutir; [subj: blow] assommer, étourdir **2.** [astound] stupéfier, abasourdir.

stupefying ['stju:pɪfaɪɪŋ] adj stupéfiant.

stupendous [stju:'pendəs] adj [amount, achievement, talent] extraordinaire, prodigieux; [event] prodigieux, extraordinaire; [book, film] extraordinaire.

stupid ['stju:pɪd] ◆ adj **1.** [foolish] stupide, bête / he's always saying / doing stupid things il dit / fait sans arrêt des bêtises **2.** liter [from alcohol, sleep] abruti, hébété; [from blow] étourdi ▶ **to drink o.s. stupid** s'abrutir d'alcool **3.** inf [wretched, confounded] maudit, fichu. ◆ n inf bêta m, -asse f, idiot m, -e f.

stupidity [stju:'pɪdətɪ] (pl **stupidities**) n stupidité f, bêtise f, sottise f.

stupidly ['stju:pɪdlɪ] adv stupidement, bêtement.

stupor ['stju:pə'] n stupeur f, abrutissement m ▶ **to be in a drunken stupor** être abruti par l'alcool.

sturdy ['stɜ:dɪ] (compar **sturdier**, superl **sturdiest**) adj **1.** [robust - person] robuste, vigoureux; [- limbs] robuste; [- table, tree, shoes] robuste, solide **2.** [firm - denial, defence, opposition, support] énergique, vigoureux; [- voice] ferme.

sturgeon ['stɜ:dʒən] (pl **sturgeon**) n esturgeon m.

stutter ['stʌtə'] ◆ n bégaiement m ▶ **to speak with a** or **to have a stutter** bégayer, être bègue. ◆ vi bégayer. ◆ vt ▶ **to stutter (out)** bégayer, bredouiller.

sty [staɪ] (pl **sties**) n **1.** [for pigs] porcherie f **2.** = **stye**.

stye [staɪ] n orgelet m, compère-loriot m.

style [staɪl] ◆ n **1.** [manner] style m, manière f; ART, LITER & MUS style m **2.** [fashion - in clothes] mode f; [model, design] modèle m **3.** [elegance - of person] allure f, chic m; [- of dress, picture, building, film] style m ▶ **to live in style** mener grand train, vivre dans le luxe **4.** [type] genre m **5.** TYPO [in editing] style m **6.** UK fml [title] titre m **7.** BOT style m. ◆ vt **1.** [call] appeler, désigner **2.** [design - dress, jewel, house] créer, dessiner ▶ **to style sb's hair** coiffer qqn **3.** PRESS & TYPO [manuscript] mettre au point (selon les précisions stylistiques de l'éditeur).

-style in comp dans le style de / baroque-style architecture architecture f de style baroque, baroque m.

style bar n COMPUT barre f de style.

styling ['staɪlɪŋ] n [of dress] forme f, ligne f; [of hair] coupe f; [of car] ligne f ▶ **styling gel** gel m coiffant ▶ **styling mousse** mousse f coiffante.

stylish ['staɪlɪʃ] adj [person] élégant, chic (inv); [clothes, hotel, neighbourhood] élégant, chic (inv); [book, film] qui a du style.

stylishly ['staɪlɪʃlɪ] adv [dress] avec chic, avec allure, élégamment; [live] élégamment; [travel] dans le luxe; [write] avec style or élégance.

stylishness ['staɪlɪʃnɪs] n chic m, élégance f.

stylist ['staɪlɪst] n **1.** [designer - for clothes] styliste mf (de mode), modéliste mf; [- for cars, furniture] styliste mf ▶ **(hair) stylist** coiffeur m, -euse f **2.** ART & LITER styliste mf.

stylistic [staɪ'lɪstɪk] adj ART, LITER & LING stylistique.

stylistically [staɪ'lɪstɪklɪ] adv d'un point de vue stylistique.

stylized, stylised ['staɪlaɪzd] adj stylisé.

stylus ['staɪləs] (pl **styluses** or **styli** ['staɪlaɪ]) n [on record player] saphir m; [tool] style m, stylet m.

stymie ['staɪmɪ] ◆ vt **1.** [in golf] barrer le trou à **2.** inf & fig [person] coincer ; [plan] ficher en l'air. ◆ n [in golf] trou m barré ; fig obstacle m, entrave f.

Styrofoam® ['staɪrəfəʊm] n polystyrène m expansé.

suave [swɑ:v] adj **1.** [polite, charming] poli ; pej [smooth] doucereux, mielleux, onctueux **2.** [elegant] élégant, chic.

sub [sʌb] (pt & pp **subbed**, cont **subbing**) ◆ n **1.** abbr of **submarine 2.** abbr of **subeditor 3.** abbr of **subscription 4.** abbr of **substitute 5.** [US] abbr of **submarine sandwich.** ◆ vi & vt **1.** abbr of **subcontract 2.** abbr of **subedit.**

sub- in comp sub-, sous / to run a sub-four minute mile courir le mille en moins de quatre minutes.

subcommittee ['sʌbkə,mɪtɪ] n sous-comité m, sous-commission f.

subconscious [,sʌb'kɒnʃəs] ◆ adj subconscient ▶ the **subconscious mind** le subconscient. ◆ n subconscient m.

subconsciously [,sʌb'kɒnʃəslɪ] adv d'une manière subconsciente, inconsciemment.

subcontinent [,sʌb'kɒntɪnənt] n sous-continent m ▶ the (Indian) Subcontinent le sous-continent indien.

subcontract ◆ vt [,sʌbkən'trækt] [pass on] (faire) sous-traiter. ◆ vi [,sʌbkən'trækt] travailler en sous-traitance. ◆ n [sʌb'kɒntrækt] (contrat m de) sous-traitance f.

subcontracting [,sʌbkən'træktɪŋ] adj sous-traitant.

subcontractor [,sʌbkən'træktə⁻] n sous-traitant m.

subculture ['sʌb,kʌltʃə⁻] n **1.** [gen & SOCIOL] subculture f **2.** BIOL culture f repiquée or secondaire.

subcutaneous [,sʌbkju:'teɪnjəs] adj sous-cutané.

subdivide [,sʌbdɪ'vaɪd] ◆ vt subdiviser. ◆ vi se subdiviser.

subdivision [,sʌbdɪ'vɪʒn] n subdivision f.

subdue [səb'dju:] vt **1.** [country, tribe] assujettir, soumettre ; [rebels] soumettre ; [rebellion] réprimer **2.** [feelings, passions] refréner, maîtriser ; [fears, anxiety] apaiser.

subdued [səb'dju:d] adj **1.** [person] silencieux ; [mood] sombre ; [emotion, feeling] contenu ; [audience] peu enthousiaste **2.** [voice, sound] bas ; [conversation] à voix basse **3.** [light, lighting] tamisé, atténué ; [colours] sobre.

subedit [,sʌb'edɪt] ◆ vt corriger, préparer pour l'impression. ◆ vi travailler comme secrétaire de rédaction.

subeditor [,sʌb'edɪtə⁻] n secrétaire mf de rédaction.

subentry [,sʌb'entrɪ] (pl subentries) n sous-entrée f.

subfolder ['sʌb,fəʊldə⁻] n COMPUT sous-dossier m.

subgroup ['sʌbgru:p] n sous-groupe m.

subhead ['sʌbhed], **subheading** ['sʌb,hedɪŋ] n [title] sous-titre m ; [division] paragraphe m.

subhuman [,sʌb'hju:mən] ◆ adj [intelligence] limité ; [crime] brutal, bestial. ◆ n sous-homme m.

subject ◆ n ['sʌbdʒekt] **1.** [topic] sujet m ▶ on the subject of au sujet de, à propos de / let's come or get back to the subject revenons à nos moutons / don't try and change the subject n'essaie pas de changer de conversation or de sujet / let's drop the subject parlons d'autre chose / while we're on the subject à (ce) propos **2.** [in letters and memos] : subject: recruitment of new staff objet : recrutement de personnel **3.** ART, LITER & PHOT sujet m **4.** GRAM & PHILOS sujet m **5.** SCH & UNIV matière f, discipline f ; [field] domaine m **6.** POL sujet m, -ette f / she is a British subject c'est une ressortissante britannique **7.** MED & PSYCHOL [of test] sujet m **8.** [cause] sujet m, motif m, raison f. ◆ adj ['sʌbdʒekt] **1.** [subordinate] dépendant / we are all subject to the rule of law nous sommes tous soumis à la loi **2.** [liable, prone] ▶ subject to sujet à / subject to tax imposable. ◆ vt [səb'dʒekt] **1.** [country, people] soumettre, assujettir

2. [expose] ▶ to subject to soumettre à. ◆ **subject to** prep phr ['sʌbdʒekt] [save for] sous réserve de, sauf ; [conditional upon] à condition de.

subjection [səb'dʒekʃn] n **1.** [act of subjecting] assujettissement m **2.** [state of being subjected] sujétion f, assujettissement m, soumission f.

subjective [səb'dʒektɪv] ◆ adj **1.** [viewpoint, argument, criticism] subjectif **2.** GRAM [pronoun, case] sujet ; [genitive] subjectif **3.** MED [symptom] subjectif. ◆ n GRAM (cas m) sujet m, nominatif m.

subjectively [səb'dʒektɪvlɪ] adv subjectivement.

subjectivity [,sʌbdʒek'tɪvətɪ] n subjectivité f.

subject matter n [topic] sujet m, thème m ; [substance] substance f, contenu m.

sub judice [-'dʒu:dɪsɪ] adj en instance, pendant.

subjugate ['sʌbdʒʊgeɪt] vt **1.** [people, tribe, country] assujettir, soumettre ; [rebels] soumettre **2.** [feelings] dompter ; [reaction] réprimer.

subjunctive [səb'dʒʌŋktɪv] ◆ adj subjonctif ▶ subjunctive mood mode m subjonctif. ◆ n subjonctif m / in the subjunctive au subjonctif.

sublet [,sʌb'let] (pt & pp **sublet**, cont **subletting**) ◆ vt sous-louer. ◆ n sous-location f.

sublimation [,sʌblɪ'meɪʃn] n sublimation f.

sublime [sə'blaɪm] ◆ adj **1.** [noble, inspiring] sublime **2.** inf [very good] génial, sensationnel **3.** [utter - disregard, contempt, ignorance] suprême, souverain. ◆ n ▶ the sublime le sublime / from the sublime to the ridiculous du sublime au grotesque. ◆ vt sublimer.

sublimely [sə'blaɪmlɪ] adv complètement, totalement.

subliminal [,sʌb'lɪmɪnl] adj infraliminaire, subliminaire, subliminal / subliminal advertising publicité f subliminale or invisible.

submachine gun [,sʌbmə'ʃi:n-] n mitraillette f.

submarine [,sʌbmə'ri:n] ◆ n **1.** sous-marin m **2.** [US] abbr of **submarine sandwich.** ◆ adj sous-marin.

submarine sandwich n [US] grand sandwich m mixte.

submenu ['sʌb,menju:] n COMPUT sous-menu m.

submerge [səb'mɜ:dʒ] ◆ vt **1.** [plunge] submerger, immerger / to submerge o.s. in work fig se plonger dans le travail **2.** [flood] submerger, inonder. ◆ vi [submarine] plonger.

submerged [səb'mɜ:dʒd] adj submergé ▶ a submerged **volcano** un volcan sous-marin.

submersible [səb'mɜ:səbl] ◆ adj submersible. ◆ n submersible m.

submersion [səb'mɜ:ʃn] n **1.** [in liquid] immersion f ; [of submarine] plongée f **2.** [flooding] inondation f.

submission [səb'mɪʃn] n **1.** [yielding] soumission f **2.** [submissiveness] soumission f, docilité f **3.** [referral - gen] soumission f ; LAW [of case] renvoi m **4.** [proposition, argument - gen] thèse f ; LAW plaidoirie f / her submission is that... elle soutient que... **5.** [in wrestling] soumission f.

submissive [səb'mɪsɪv] adj soumis.

submissively [səb'mɪsɪvlɪ] adv [behave, confess, accept] docilement ; [yield, react] avec résignation.

submissiveness [səb'mɪsɪvnɪs] n soumission f, docilité f.

submit [səb'mɪt] (pt & pp **submitted**, cont **submitting**) ◆ vi **1.** lit se rendre, se soumettre **2.** fig se soumettre, se plier. ◆ vt **1.** [propose] soumettre / I submit that... LAW je soutiens or je maintiens que... **2.** [yield] ▶ to **submit o.s. to sb / sthg** se soumettre à qqn / qqch.

subnormal [ˌsʌb'nɔːml] adj **1.** [person] arriéré ▶ **educationally subnormal children** des enfants arriérés *(du point de vue scolaire)* **2.** [temperatures] au-dessous de la normale.

subordinate ◆ n [sə'bɔːdɪnət] subordonné *m*, -e *f*, subalterne *mf*. ◆ adj **1.** [in rank, hierarchy] subordonné, subalterne **2.** [secondary] subordonné, accessoire **3.** GRAM subordonné. ◆ vt [sə'bɔːdɪneɪt] subordonner.

subordinate clause [sə'bɔːdɪnət-] n GRAM (proposition *f*) subordonnée *f*.

subordination [sə,bɔːdɪ'neɪʃn] n subordination *f*.

subplot ['sʌb,plɒt] n intrigue *f* secondaire.

subpoena [sə'piːnə] ◆ n citation *f* *(à comparaître en qualité de témoin)*, assignation *f*. ◆ vt citer *(à comparaître en qualité de témoin)*.

sub-post office n UK petit bureau *m* de poste local.

subprime ['sʌbpraɪm] n US FIN ▶ **subprime (loan** or **mortgage)** subprime *m* *(type de crédit immobilier à risque)*.

subprogram ['sʌb,prəʊgræm] n COMPUT sous-programme *m*.

subroutine ['sʌbruː,tiːn] n COMPUT sous-programme *m*.

sub-Saharan [sʌbsə'hɑːrən] adj GEOG subsaharien ▶ **sub-Saharan Africa** Afrique *f* subsaharienne.

subscribe [səb'skraɪb] ◆ vi **1.** [to magazine, service] s'abonner, être abonné **2.** [to loan, fund, campaign, share issue] souscrire / **to subscribe to a charity** faire des dons à une œuvre de charité. ◆ vt **1.** [donate] donner, faire don de **2.** *fml* [write - one's name, signature] apposer ; [sign - document] signer.

subscriber [səb'skraɪbə'] n **1.** [to newspaper, service, telephone system] abonné *m*, -e *f* **2.** [to fund, campaign, share issue] souscripteur *m*, -trice *f* **3.** [to opinion, belief] partisan *m*, adepte *mf*.

subscript ['sʌbskrɪpt] ◆ n COMPUT, MATH & TYPO indice *m*. ◆ adj en indice.

subscription [səb'skrɪpʃn] n **1.** [to newspaper, magazine] abonnement *m* ▶ **to take out a subscription to a magazine** s'abonner à un magazine **2.** [to fund, campaign, share issue] souscription *f* ; [to club, organization] cotisation *f* **3.** [to opinion, belief] adhésion *f*.

subsection ['sʌb,sekʃn] n [of text, contract, etc.] article *m*, paragraphe *m*.

subsequent ['sʌbsɪkwənt] adj **1.** [next] suivant, subséquent *fml* / **subsequent to 1880** après 1880 / **subsequent to this** par la suite **2.** [consequent] conséquent, consécutif.

subsequently ['sʌbsɪkwəntlɪ] adv par la suite, subséquemment *fml*.

subservient [səb'sɜːvjənt] adj **1.** [servile] servile, obséquieux *pej* **2.** [subjugated] asservi **3.** [secondary] secondaire, accessoire.

subset ['sʌbset] n sous-ensemble *m*.

subside [səb'saɪd] vi **1.** [abate - shooting, laughter] cesser ; [- storm, rage, pain] se calmer ; [recede - water] se retirer, baisser ; [- danger] s'éloigner **2.** [sink - house, land] s'abaisser ; [- wall, foundations] se tasser ; [settle - sediment] se déposer.

subsidence [səb'saɪdns or 'sʌbsɪdns] n [of house, land] affaissement *m* ; [of wall, foundations] tassement *m*.

subsidiarity [sʌb,sɪdɪ'ærɪtɪ] n subsidiarité *f*.

subsidiary [səb'sɪdjərɪ] *(pl* **subsidiaries)** ◆ adj [supplementary] supplémentaire, complémentaire ; [secondary - question, reason] subsidiaire ; [- idea, action] accessoire ▶ **subsidiary company** filiale *f*. ◆ n COMM filiale *f*.

subsidize, subsidise ['sʌbsɪdaɪz] vt subventionner.

subsidized ['sʌbsɪdaɪzd] adj subventionné ▶ **subsidized industry** industrie *f* subventionnée.

subsidy ['sʌbsɪdɪ] *(pl* **subsidies)** n subvention *f* ▶ **government subsidy** subvention de l'État ▶ **export subsidies** primes *fpl* à l'exportation.

subsist [səb'sɪst] vi subsister / **they subsist on fish and rice** ils vivent de poisson et de riz.

subsistence [səb'sɪstəns] ◆ n subsistance *f*, existence *f*. ◆ comp [wage] à peine suffisant pour vivre ; [farming] d'autoconsommation ▶ **subsistence economy** économie *f* de subsistance ▶ **to live at subsistence level** avoir tout juste de quoi vivre.

subsistence allowance n UK [advance] acompte *m* *(perçu avant l'engagement définitif)* ; [expenses] frais *mpl* (de subsistance).

subsoil ['sʌbsɔɪl] n GEOL sous-sol *m*.

substance ['sʌbstəns] n **1.** [matter] substance *f* ▶ **illegal substances** stupéfiants *mpl* **2.** [solidity] solidité *f* **3.** [essential part, gist] essentiel *m*, substance *f* ; [basis] fond *m* **4.** [significance, weight] importance *f*, poids *m* **5.** [wealth] richesses *fpl* ; [power] pouvoir *m* ; [influence] influence *f*. ◆ **in substance** adv phr [generally] en gros, en substance ; [basically] à la base, au fond ; [in brief] en substance, en somme.

substance abuse n *fml* abus *m* de stupéfiants.

substandard [ˌsʌb'stændəd] adj **1.** [work, output] médiocre, en dessous des niveaux requis ; [meal, merchandise] de qualité inférieure ▶ **substandard housing** logements *ne* respectant pas les normes requises **2.** LING non conforme à la norme.

substantial [səb'stænʃl] adj **1.** [large] considérable, important ; LAW [damages] élevé **2.** [nourishing - food] nourrissant ; [-meal] solide, copieux, substantiel **3.** [convincing - argument, evidence] solide, convaincant **4.** [real, tangible] réel, substantiel ; PHILOS substantiel **5.** [solidly built] solide **6.** [rich] riche, aisé ; [powerful] puissant ; [influential] influent ; [well-established] solide, bien établi.

substantially [səb'stænʃəlɪ] adv **1.** [considerably] considérablement **2.** [generally] en gros, en grande partie ; [fundamentally] fondamentalement, au fond **3.** [solidly] solidement **4.** PHILOS [as for the substance] substantiellement.

substantiate [səb'stænʃɪeɪt] vt confirmer, apporter or fournir des preuves à l'appui de.

substantive ◆ adj [sʌb'stæntɪv] **1.** [real, important] substantiel ; [permanent - rank] permanent ; [independent - means, resources] indépendant **2.** GRAM nominal. ◆ n ['sʌbstəntɪv] GRAM substantif *m*.

substitute ['sʌbstɪtjuːt] ◆ n **1.** [person] remplaçant *m*, -e *f* **2.** [thing] produit *m* de remplacement or de substitution **3.** GRAM terme *m* suppléant. ◆ adj remplaçant ▶ **substitute teacher** US suppléant *m*, -e *f*. ◆ vt [gen] substituer, remplacer ; SPORT remplacer ▶ **to substitute sthg for sthg** substituer qqch à qqch. ◆ vi ▶ **to substitute for sb/sthg** remplacer qqn/qqch.

substitution [ˌsʌbstɪ'tjuːʃn] n [gen] remplacement *m*, substitution *f* ; SPORT remplacement *m*.

subterfuge ['sʌbtəfjuːdʒ] n subterfuge *m*.

subterranean [ˌsʌbtə'reɪnjən] adj souterrain.

subtext ['sʌb,tekst] n [of book, film, situation] message *m* sous-jacent.

subtitle ['sʌb,taɪtl] ◆ n CIN, LITER & PRESS sous-titre *m*. ◆ vt sous-titrer.

subtitled ['sʌb,taɪtld] adj sous-titré, avec sous-titrage.

subtitling ['sʌb,taɪtlɪŋ] n sous-titrage *m*.

subtle ['sʌtl] adj subtil.

subtlety ['sʌtltɪ] *(pl* **subtleties)** n **1.** [subtle nature] subtilité *f* **2.** [detail, distinction] subtilité *f*.

subtly ['sʌtlɪ] adv subtilement.

subtotal ['sʌb,təʊtl] n total *m* partiel.

subtract [səb'trækt] vt soustraire, déduire / *subtract 52 from 110* ôtez or retranchez 52 de 110.

subtraction [səb'trækʃn] n soustraction *f*.

subtropical [,sʌb'trɒpɪkl] adj subtropical.

suburb ['sʌbɜːb] n banlieue *f*, faubourg *m* / *in the suburbs* en banlieue / *the outer suburbs* la grande banlieue.

📕 **Suburb**

À la différence du mot « banlieue » qui en est souvent la traduction, le mot « suburb » ne désigne que rarement les quartiers en difficulté. Il évoque plutôt des cités tranquilles, bourgeoises, confortables. Sur le plan social, en faisant la part des différences urbanistiques, les équivalents les plus proches des « banlieues en difficulté » françaises sont, en Grande-Bretagne, les **inner cities** (les centres urbains) et, aux États-Unis, les **housing projects** (proches des cités HLM).

suburban [sə'bɜːbn] adj **1.** [street, railway, dweller] de banlieue ; [population, growth] de banlieue, suburbain **2.** pej [mentality, outlook] de petit-bourgeois.

suburbanite [sə'bɜːbənaɪt] n banlieusard *m*, -e *f*.

suburbia [sə'bɜːbɪə] n la banlieue / *in suburbia* en banlieue.

subversion [səb'vɜːʃn] n subversion *f*.

subversive [səb'vɜːsɪv] ◆ adj subversif. ◆ n élément *m* subversif.

subvert [səb'vɜːt] vt **1.** [undermine - society, state, institution] subvertir *liter*, renverser **2.** [corrupt - individual] corrompre.

subway ['sʌbweɪ] n **1.** 🇬🇧 [pedestrian underpass] passage *m* souterrain **2.** 🇺🇸 [railway] métro *m*.

sub-zero adj au-dessous de zéro.

succeed [sək'siːd] ◆ vi **1.** [manage successfully] réussir ▶ **to succeed in doing sthg** réussir or parvenir or arriver à faire qqch **2.** [work out] réussir **3.** [do well] réussir, avoir du succès **4.** [follow on] succéder ▶ **to succeed to the throne** monter sur le trône. ◆ vt [subj: person] succéder à, prendre la suite de ; [subj: event, thing] succéder à, suivre.

succeeding [sək'siːdɪŋ] adj **1.** [subsequent] suivant, qui suit **2.** [future] futur, à venir.

success [sək'ses] ◆ n réussite *f*, succès *m* / *her success in the elections* sa victoire aux élections / *his success in the exam* son succès à l'examen ▶ **to meet with** or **to achieve success** réussir / *I had no success in trying to persuade them* je n'ai pas réussi à les convaincre / *I tried to convince them, but without success* j'ai essayé de les convaincre, mais sans succès ▶ **to make a success of sthg** mener qqch à bien. ◆ comp [rate] de réussite, de succès.

successful [sək'sesfʊl] adj **1.** [resulting in success - attempt, effort, plan] qui réussit ; [- negotiations] fructueux ; [- outcome] heureux ; [- performance, mission, partnership] réussi / *she was not successful in her application for the post* sa candidature à ce poste n'a pas été retenue / *I was successful in convincing them* j'ai réussi or je suis arrivé or je suis parvenu à les convaincre **2.** [thriving - singer, album, author, book, play] à succès ; [- businessman] qui a réussi, [- life, career] réussi.

successfully [sək'sesfʊlɪ] adv avec succès ▶ **to do sthg successfully** réussir à faire qqch.

succession [sək'seʃn] n **1.** [series] succession *f*, suite *f* / *she made three phone calls in succession* elle a passé trois coups de fil de suite **2.** [ascension to power] succession *f* / *his succession to the post* sa succession au poste **3.** LAW [descendants] descendance *f* ; [heirs] héritiers *mpl*.

successive [sək'sesɪv] adj [attempts, generations] successif ; [days, years] consécutif.

successively [sək'sesɪvlɪ] adv [in turn] successivement, tour à tour, l'un /l'une après l'autre.

successor [sək'sesər] n **1.** [replacement] successeur *m* **2.** [heir] héritier *m*, -ère *f*.

success story n réussite *f*.

succinct [sək'sɪŋkt] adj succinct, concis.

succinctly [sək'sɪŋktlɪ] adv succinctement, avec concision.

succor 🇺🇸 = succour.

succour 🇬🇧, **succor** 🇺🇸 ['sʌkər] ◆ n secours *m*, aide *f*. ◆ vt secourir, aider.

succulent ['sʌkjʊlənt] ◆ adj **1.** [tasty] succulent **2.** BOT succulent. ◆ n plante *f* grasse.

succumb [sə'kʌm] vi **1.** [yield] succomber, céder **2.** [die] succomber, mourir.

such [sʌtʃ] ◆ det & predet **1.** [of the same specified kind] tel, pareil / *such a song* une telle chanson, une chanson pareille or de ce genre / *no such place exists* un tel endroit n'existe pas / *have you ever heard such a thing?* avez-vous jamais entendu une chose pareille ? / *I said no such thing!* je n'ai rien dit de tel or de la sorte ! ; [followed by 'as'] : *there is no such thing as magic* la magie n'existe pas ; [followed by 'that'] : *their timetable is such that we never see them* leur emploi du temps est tel que nous ne les voyons jamais **2.** [as intensifier] tel / *my accounts are in such a mess!* mes comptes sont dans un de ces états ! / *it's such a pity you can't come!* c'est tellement dommage que vous ne puissiez pas venir ! / *such tall buildings* des immeubles aussi hauts / *such a handsome man* un si bel homme / *I didn't realize it was such a long way* je ne me rendais pas compte que c'était si loin ; [followed by 'that'] : *he was in such pain that he fainted* il souffrait tellement qu'il s'est évanoui. ◆ pron : *such were my thoughts last night* voilà où j'en étais hier soir / *such is life!* c'est la vie ! ◆ **and such** adv phr et d'autres choses de ce genre or de la sorte. ◆ **as such** adv phr [strictly speaking] en soi ; [in that capacity] en tant que tel, à ce titre / *she doesn't get a salary as such* elle n'a pas de véritable salaire or pas de salaire à proprement parler / *she's an adult and as such she has rights* elle est majeure et en tant que telle elle a des droits. ◆ **such and such** predet phr tel. ◆ **such as** prep phr tel que, comme / *I can think of lots of reasons — such as?* je vois beaucoup de raisons — comme quoi par exemple ? ◆ **such as it is**, **such as they are** adv phr : *and this is my study, such as it is* et voici ce que j'appelle mon bureau / *I'll give you my opinion, such as it is* je vais vous donner mon avis, prenez-le pour ce qu'il vaut.

suchlike ['sʌtʃlaɪk] ◆ adj semblable, pareil. ◆ pron : *frogs, toads and suchlike* les grenouilles, les crapauds et autres animaux (du même genre).

suck [sʌk] ◆ vt **1.** [with mouth] sucer **2.** [pull] aspirer / *we found ourselves sucked into an argument* fig nous nous sommes trouvés entraînés dans une dispute. ◆ vi **1.** [with mouth] ▶ **to suck at** or **on sthg** sucer or suçoter qqch / *the child was sucking at her breast* l'enfant tétait son sein **2.** 🇺🇸 v inf [be very bad] : *this town sucks!* cette ville est nulle ! ◆ n **1.** [act of sucking - gen] ▶ **to have a suck at sthg** sucer or suçoter qqch ; [at breast] tétée *f* ▶ **to give suck** donner le sein, allaiter **2.** [force] aspiration *f*. ◆ **suck down** vt sep [subj: sea, quicksand, whirlpool] engloutir. ◆ **suck off** vt sep *vulg* sucer, tailler une pipe à.

❖ **suck up** ◆ vt sep [subj: person] aspirer, sucer ; [subj: vacuum cleaner, pump] aspirer ; [subj: porous surface] absorber. ◆ vi inf ▶ **to suck up to sb** lécher les bottes à qqn.

sucker ['sʌkər] ◆ n **1.** inf [dupe] pigeon m, gogo m **2.** UK [suction cup or pad] ventouse f **3.** ZOOL [of insect] suçoir m ; [of octopus, leech] ventouse f **4.** BOT drageon m **5.** US [lollipop] sucette f. ◆ vt **1.** HORT enlever les drageons de **2.** US v inf [dupe] refaire, pigeonner. ◆ vi BOT [plant] drageonner.

suckle ['sʌkl] ◆ vt [child] allaiter, donner le sein à ; [animal] allaiter. ◆ vi téter.

sucrose ['suːkrəuz] n saccharose f.

suction ['sʌkʃn] n succion f, aspiration f.

suction pump n pompe f aspirante.

Sudan [suːˈdɑːn] pr n Soudan m **/ in Sudan** or **in the Sudan** au Soudan.

Sudanese [ˌsuːdəˈniːz] (pl **Sudanese**) ◆ n Soudanais m, -e f. ◆ adj soudanais.

sudden ['sʌdn] adj soudain, subit ▶ **sudden death a)** lit mort f subite **b)** GAMES & SPORT jeu pour départager les ex aequo (où le premier point perdu, le premier but concédé, etc., entraîne l'élimination immédiate). ❖ **all of a sudden** adv phr soudain, subitement, tout d'un coup.

suddenly ['sʌdnlɪ] adv soudainement, subitement, tout à coup.

suddenness ['sʌdnnɪs] n soudaineté f, caractère m subit or imprévu.

sudoku ['suːdəuku:] n sudoku m.

suds [sʌdz] pl n [foam] mousse f ; [soapy water] eau f savonneuse.

sue [suː] ◆ vt poursuivre en justice, intenter un procès à ▶ **to sue sb for** or **over sthg** poursuivre qqn en justice pour qqch ▶ **to be sued for damages / libel** être poursuivi en dommages-intérêts / en diffamation. ◆ vi **1.** LAW intenter un procès, engager des poursuites **/** she threatened to sue for libel elle a menacé d'intenter un procès en diffamation / he's suing for divorce il a entamé une procédure de divorce **2.** fml [solicit] ▶ **to sue for** solliciter.

suede [sweɪd] ◆ n daim m, suède m spec. ◆ comp [jacket, purse, shoes] en or de daim ; [leather] suédé.

suet ['suɪt] n graisse f de rognon.

Suez ['suːɪz] pr n Suez ▶ **the Suez Canal** le canal de Suez ▶ **the Suez crisis** l'affaire du canal de Suez.

suffer ['sʌfər] ◆ vi **1.** [feel pain] souffrir **2.** [be ill, afflicted] souffrir ▶ **to suffer from a)** [serious disease] souffrir de **b)** [cold, headache] avoir **3.** [be affected] : it's the children who suffer in a marriage break-up ce sont les enfants qui souffrent lors d'une séparation / the low-paid will be the first to suffer les petits salaires seront les premiers touchés **4.** [deteriorate] souffrir, se détériorer. ◆ vt **1.** [experience - pain, thirst] souffrir de ; [- hardship] souffrir, subir **2.** [stand, put up with] tolérer, supporter / he doesn't suffer fools gladly il ne tolère pas les imbéciles.

sufferance ['sʌfrəns] n **1.** [tolerance] tolérance f ▶ **on sufferance** par tolérance **2.** [endurance] endurance f, résistance f **3.** [suffering] souffrance f.

sufferer ['sʌfrər] n malade mf, victime f / sufferers from heart disease les personnes cardiaques.

suffering ['sʌfrɪŋ] ◆ n souffrance f, souffrances fpl. ◆ adj souffrant, qui souffre.

suffice [səˈfaɪs] ◆ vi fml suffire, être suffisant / suffice it to say (that) she's overjoyed inutile de dire qu'elle est ravie. ◆ vt suffire à, satisfaire / empty promises will not suffice him il ne se contentera pas de vaines promesses.

sufficiency [səˈfɪʃnsɪ] (pl **sufficiencies**) n quantité f suffisante.

sufficient [səˈfɪʃnt] adj **1.** [gen] suffisant **2.** PHILOS suffisant.

sufficiently [səˈfɪʃntlɪ] adv suffisamment, assez.

suffix ['sʌfɪks] ◆ n suffixe m. ◆ vt suffixer.

suffocate ['sʌfəkeɪt] ◆ vi **1.** [die] suffoquer, étouffer, s'asphyxier **2.** [be hot, lack fresh air] suffoquer, étouffer **3.** fig [with anger, emotion, etc.] s'étouffer, suffoquer. ◆ vt **1.** [kill] suffoquer, étouffer, asphyxier **2.** fig [repress, inhibit] étouffer, suffoquer.

suffocating ['sʌfəkeɪtɪŋ] adj **1.** [heat, room] suffocant, étouffant ; [smoke, fumes] asphyxiant, suffocant **2.** fig étouffant.

suffocation [ˌsʌfəˈkeɪʃn] n suffocation f, étouffement m, asphyxie f ▶ **to die from suffocation** mourir asphyxié.

suffrage ['sʌfrɪdʒ] n **1.** [right to vote] droit m de suffrage or de vote ▶ **universal suffrage** suffrage m universel ▶ **women's suffrage** le droit de vote pour les femmes **2.** fml [vote] suffrage m, vote m.

suffragette [ˌsʌfrəˈdʒet] n suffragette f.

The suffragettes

Militantes britanniques luttant pour le droit de vote des femmes au début du XXᵉ siècle. Menées par Emmeline Pankhurst, elles mirent en œuvre différents moyens d'action (manifestations, interruptions de meetings, attentats, incendies criminels, grèves de la faim) qui eurent finalement raison du Premier ministre Asquith, lequel fit adopter par le Parlement, en 1918, un projet de loi accordant le droit de vote à certaines catégories de femmes (femmes mariées, femmes au foyer et femmes diplômées âgées d'au moins 30 ans). En 1928, une nouvelle loi étendit ce droit à toutes les femmes.

suffuse [səˈfjuːz] vt (usu passive) se répandre sur, baigner / suffused with light inondé de lumière.

sugar ['ʃugər] ◆ n **1.** [gen, & CHEM] sucre m / how many sugars? combien de sucres ? **2.** US inf [to a man] mon chéri ; [to a woman] ma chérie. ◆ vt sucrer. ◆ interj inf ▶ **oh sugar!** mince alors !

sugar beet n betterave f sucrière or à sucre.

sugarcane ['ʃugəkeɪn] n canne f à sucre.

sugar-coated [-ˈkəutɪd] adj dragéifié ▶ **sugar-coated almonds** dragées fpl.

sugared ['ʃugəd] adj **1.** lit sucré **2.** fig mielleux, doucereux.

sugar-free adj sans sucre.

sugar lump n morceau m de sucre.

sugar refinery n raffinerie f de sucre.

sugarsnap peas ['ʃugəsnæp-] pl n pois mpl gourmands.

sugary ['ʃugərɪ] adj **1.** [drink, food] (très) sucré ; [taste] sucré **2.** [manner, tone] mielleux, doucereux.

suggest [səˈdʒest] vt **1.** [propose, put forward] suggérer, proposer / I suggest (that) we do nothing for the moment je suggère or je propose que nous ne fassions rien pour l'instant **2.** [recommend] proposer, conseiller, recommander **3.** [imply, insinuate] suggérer **4.** [indicate, point to] suggérer, laisser supposer **5.** [evoke] évoquer.

suggestion [sə'dʒestʃn] n **1.** [proposal] suggestion *f*, proposition *f* / **'serving suggestion'** 'suggestion de présentation' **2.** [recommendation] conseil *m*, recommandation *f* **3.** [indication] indication *f* **4.** [trace, hint] soupçon *m*, trace *f* **5.** [implication] suggestion *f*, implication *f* **6.** PSYCHOL suggestion *f*.

suggestion box n boîte *f* à suggestions.

suggestive [sə'dʒestɪv] adj **1.** [indicative, evocative] suggestif **2.** [erotic] suggestif.

suggestively [sə'dʒestɪvlɪ] adv de façon suggestive.

suicidal [su:ɪ'saɪdl] adj suicidaire.

suicide ['su:ɪsaɪd] ◆ n [act] suicide *m* ▶ **to commit suicide** se suicider. ◆ comp [mission, plane, squad] suicide ; [attempt, bid, pact] de suicide.

suit [su:t] ◆ n **1.** [outfit - for men] costume *m*, complet *m* ; [- for women] tailleur *m* ; [- for particular activity] combinaison *f* / *he came in a suit and tie* il est venu en costume-cravate ▶ **suit of armour** armure *f* complète ▶ **suit of clothes** tenue *f* **2.** [complete set] jeu *m* **3.** [in card games] couleur *f* ▶ **long** or **strong suit** couleur forte **4.** LAW [lawsuit] action *f*, procès *m* ▶ **to bring** or **to file a suit against sb** intenter un procès à qqn, poursuivre qqn en justice ▶ **criminal suit** action au pénal **5.** *fml* [appeal] requête *f*, pétition *f* ; *liter* [courtship] cour *f* **6.** *inf* [corporate executive] cadre *m*. ◆ vt **1.** [be becoming to - subj: clothes, colour] aller à / *black really suits her* le noir lui va à merveille **2.** [be satisfactory or convenient to] convenir à, arranger / *Tuesday suits me best* c'est mardi qui me convient or qui m'arrange le mieux ▶ **suit yourself!** *inf* faites ce qui vous chante ! **3.** [agree with] convenir à, aller à, réussir à **4.** [be appropriate] convenir à, aller à, être fait pour / *clothes to suit all tastes* des vêtements pour tous les goûts / *the role suits her perfectly* le rôle lui va comme un gant **5.** [adapt] adapter, approprier. ◆ vi [be satisfactory] convenir, aller / *will that date suit?* cette date vous convient-elle or est-elle à votre convenance ? ❖ **suit up** vi [dress - diver, pilot, astronaut, etc.] mettre sa combinaison.

suitability [ˌsu:tə'bɪlətɪ] n [of clothing] caractère *m* approprié ; [of behaviour, arrangements] caractère *m* convenable ; [of act, remark] à-propos *m*, pertinence *f* ; [of time, place] opportunité *f*.

suitable ['su:təbl] adj **1.** [convenient] approprié, adéquat / *will that day be suitable for you?* cette date-là vous convient-elle ? **2.** [appropriate - gen] qui convient ; [- clothing] approprié, adéquat ; [- behaviour] convenable ; [- act, remark] approprié, pertinent ; [- time, place] propice / *suitable for all occasions* qui convient dans toutes les occasions / **'not suitable for children'** 'réservé aux adultes' / *the house is not suitable for a large family* la maison ne conviendrait pas à une famille nombreuse.

suitably ['su:təblɪ] adv [dress] de façon appropriée ; [behave] convenablement, comme il faut.

suitcase ['su:tkeɪs] n valise *f*.

suite [swi:t] n **1.** [rooms] suite *f*, appartement *m* **2.** [furniture] mobilier *m* ▶ **bedroom suite** chambre *f* à coucher **3.** MUS suite *f* ▶ **a cello suite** une suite pour violoncelle **4.** [staff, followers] suite *f* **5.** COMPUT ensemble *m* (de programmes), progiciel *m*.

suited ['su:tɪd] adj **1.** [appropriate] approprié / *he's not suited to teaching* il n'est pas fait pour l'enseignement **2.** [matched] assorti / *they are well suited (to each other)* ils sont faits l'un pour l'autre, ils sont bien assortis.

suitor ['su:tə*r*] n **1.** *dated* [wooer] amoureux *m*, soupirant *m* **2.** LAW plaignant *m*, -e *f*.

sulfate US = sulphate.

sulfur US = sulphur.

sulk [sʌlk] ◆ vi bouder, faire la tête. ◆ n bouderie *f* ▶ **to have a sulk** or **(a fit of) the sulks** faire la tête.

sulkily ['sʌlkɪlɪ] adv [act] en boudant, d'un air maussade ; [answer] d'un ton maussade.

sulky ['sʌlkɪ] (*compar* **sulkier**, *superl* **sulkiest**, *pl* **sulkies**) ◆ adj [person, mood] boudeur, maussade. ◆ n sulky *m*.

sullen ['sʌlən] adj **1.** [person, behaviour, appearance, remark] maussade, renfrogné **2.** [clouds] menaçant.

sullenly ['sʌlənlɪ] adv [behave] d'un air maussade or renfrogné ; [answer, say, refuse] d'un ton maussade ; [agree, obey] de mauvaise grâce, à contrecœur.

sully ['sʌlɪ] (*pt* & *pp* **sullied**) vt **1.** [dirty] souiller **2.** *fig* [reputation] ternir.

sulphate UK, **sulfate** US ['sʌlfeɪt] n sulfate *m* ▶ **copper / zinc sulphate** sulfate *m* de cuivre / de zinc.

sulphur UK, **sulfur** US ['sʌlfə*r*] n soufre *m*.

sulphuric UK, **sulfuric** US [sʌl'fjʊərɪk] adj sulfurique ▶ **sulphuric acid** acide *m* sulfurique.

sultan ['sʌltən] n sultan *m*.

sultana [səl'tɑ:nə] n **1.** UK [raisin] raisin *m* de Smyrne **2.** [woman] sultane *f*.

sultry ['sʌltrɪ] (*compar* **sultrier**, *superl* **sultriest**) adj **1.** [weather] lourd ; [heat] étouffant, suffocant **2.** [person, look, smile] sensuel ; [voice] chaud, sensuel.

sum [sʌm] (*pt* & *pp* **summed**, *cont* **summing**) ◆ n **1.** [amount of money] somme *f* **2.** [total] total *m*, somme *f* **3.** [arithmetical operation] calcul *m* ▶ **to do sums** UK faire du calcul **4.** [gist] somme *f* ▶ **in sum** en somme, somme toute. ◆ vt [add] additionner, faire le total de ; [calculate] calculer. ❖ **sum up** ◆ vt sep **1.** [summarize] résumer, récapituler **2.** [size up] jauger. ◆ vi [gen] récapituler, faire un résumé ; LAW [judge] résumer.

Sumatra [su'mɑ:trə] pr n Sumatra / *in Sumatra* à Sumatra.

Sumatran [su'mɑ:trən] ◆ n Sumatranais *m*, -e *f*. ◆ adj sumatranais.

summarily ['sʌmərəlɪ] adv sommairement.

summarize, summarise ['sʌməraɪz] vt résumer.

summary ['sʌmərɪ] (*pl* **summaries**) ◆ n **1.** [synopsis - of argument, situation] résumé *m*, récapitulation *f* ; [- of book, film] résumé *m* / *there is a news summary every hour* il y a un court bulletin d'information toutes les heures **2.** [written list] sommaire *m*, résumé *m* ; FIN [of accounts] relevé *m*. ◆ adj [gen, & LAW] sommaire.

summation [sʌ'meɪʃn] n **1.** [addition] addition *f* ; [sum] somme *f*, total *m* **2.** [summary] récapitulation *f*, résumé *m*.

summer ['sʌmə*r*] ◆ n [season] été *m* ▶ **in (the) summer** en été. ◆ comp [clothes, residence, day, holidays] d'été ; [heat, sports] estival ▶ **summer house** US maison *f* de campagne. ◆ vi passer l'été. ◆ vt [cattle, sheep] estiver.

summer camp n US colonie *f* de vacances.

summerhouse ['sʌməhaus] (*pl* [-hauzɪz]) n UK pavillon *m* (de jardin).

summer school n stage *m* d'été.

summertime ['sʌmətaɪm] n [season] été *m* / *in the summertime* en été. ❖ **summer time** n heure *f* d'été.

summery ['sʌmərɪ] adj d'été / *it feels quite summery today* il fait un temps d'été aujourd'hui.

summing-up [ˌsʌmɪŋ-] (*pl* **summings-up**) n [gen] résumé *m*, récapitulation *f* ; LAW résumé *m*.

summit ['sʌmɪt] ◆ n **1.** [peak - of mountain] sommet *m*, cime *f* ; [- of glory, happiness, power] apogée *m*, summum *m* **2.** POL [meeting] sommet *m*. ◆ comp [talks, agreement] au sommet.

summon ['sʌmən] vt **1.** [send for - person] appeler, faire venir ; [- help] appeler à, requérir **2.** [convene] convoquer **3.** LAW citer, assigner ▶ **to summon sb to appear in court**

citer qqn en justice / *the court summoned her as a witness* la cour l'a citée comme témoin **4.** [muster -courage, strength] rassembler, faire appel à **5.** *fml* [order] sommer, ordonner à / *she summoned us in / up* elle nous a sommés or ordonné d'entrer / de monter. ❖ **summon up** vt sep **1.** [courage, strength] rassembler, faire appel à **2.** [help, support] réunir, faire appel à **3.** [memories, thoughts] évoquer **4.** [spirits] invoquer.

summons ['sʌmənz] (*pl* **summonses**) ◆ n **1.** LAW citation f, assignation f / *he received* or *got a summons for speeding* il a reçu une citation à comparaître en justice pour excès de vitesse ▸ **to take out a summons against sb** faire assigner qqn en justice **2.** [gen] convocation f **3.** MIL sommation f. ◆ vt LAW citer or assigner (à comparaître) / *she was summonsed to testify* elle a été citée à comparaître en tant que témoin.

sumo ['su:məʊ] ◆ n sumo m. ◆ comp ▸ **sumo wrestler** lutteur m de sumo ▸ **sumo wrestling** sumo m.

sump [sʌmp] n **1.** TECH puisard m ; 🇬🇧 AUTO carter m **2.** [cesspool] fosse f d'aisances.

sumptuous ['sʌmptʃʊəs] adj somptueux.

sumptuously ['sʌmptʃʊəslɪ] adv somptueusement.

sum total n totalité f, somme f totale.

sun [sʌn] (*pt & pp* sunned, *cont* sunning) ◆ n soleil m ▸ **The Sun** PRESS *quotidien britannique à sensation* ⟶ tabloid. ◆ vt ▸ **to sun o.s.** a) [person] prendre le soleil, se faire bronzer b) [animal] se chauffer au soleil.

Sun. (written abbr of Sunday) dim.

sunbathe ['sʌnbeɪð] ◆ vi prendre un bain de soleil, se faire bronzer. ◆ n 🇬🇧 bain m de soleil.

sunbather ['sʌnbeɪðər] n *personne qui prend un bain de soleil.*

sunbathing ['sʌnbeɪðɪŋ] n *(U)* bains mpl de soleil.

sunbeam ['sʌnbi:m] n rayon m de soleil.

sunbed ['sʌnbed] n [in garden, on beach] lit m pliant ; [with tanning lamps] lit m à ultraviolets.

sun block n écran m total.

sunburn ['sʌnbɜ:n] n coup m de soleil.

sunburnt ['sʌnbɜ:nt], **sunburned** ['sʌnbɜ:nd] adj brûlé par le soleil.

sun cream n crème f solaire.

sundae ['sʌndeɪ] n *coupe de glace aux fruits et à la crème Chantilly.*

Sunday ['sʌndeɪ] ◆ n **1.** [day] dimanche m **2.** 🇬🇧 [newspaper] ▸ **the Sundays** les journaux mpl du dimanche. ◆ comp [clothes, newspaper, driver, painter] du dimanche ; [peace, rest, mass] dominical ▸ **the Sunday roast** or **joint** le rôti du dimanche. See also **Friday.**

Sunday papers

Les principaux hebdomadaires britanniques paraissant le dimanche sont :
The Independent on Sunday ;
The Mail on Sunday (tendance conservatrice) ;
The News of the World (journal à sensation) ;
The Observer (tendance centre gauche) ;
The People (journal à sensation) ;
The Sunday Express ;
The Sunday Mirror (tendance centre gauche) ;
The Sunday Telegraph (tendance conservatrice) ;
The Sunday Times (tendance conservatrice).

Sunday school n ≃ catéchisme m.

sundial ['sʌndaɪəl] n cadran m solaire.

sundown ['sʌndaʊn] n coucher m du soleil.

sundrenched ['sʌndrentʃt] adj inondé de soleil.

sundried ['sʌndraɪd] adj séché au soleil ▸ **sundried tomatoes** tomates fpl séchées.

sundry ['sʌndrɪ] ◆ adj divers, différent. ◆ pron : *she told all and sundry about it* elle l'a raconté à qui voulait l'entendre. ❖ **sundries** pl n articles mpl divers.

sunflower ['sʌn,flaʊər] ◆ n tournesol m, soleil m. ◆ comp [oil, seed] de tournesol.

sung [sʌŋ] ◆ pp ⟶ sing. ◆ adj ▸ **sung mass** messe f chantée.

sunglasses ['sʌn,glɑ:sɪz] pl n lunettes fpl de soleil.

sunhat ['sʌnhæt] n chapeau m de soleil.

sunk [sʌŋk] ◆ pp ⟶ sink. ◆ adj inf fichu.

sunken ['sʌŋkən] adj **1.** [boat, rock] submergé ; [garden] en contrebas ; [bathtub] encastré (au ras du sol) **2.** [hollow -cheeks] creux, affaissé ; [-eyes] creux.

sunlamp ['sʌnlæmp] n lampe f à rayons ultraviolets or à bronzer.

sunlight ['sʌnlaɪt] n (lumière f du) soleil m / *in the sunlight* au soleil.

sunlit ['sʌnlɪt] adj ensoleillé.

sun lotion n lait m solaire.

sunlounger ['sʌn,laʊndʒər] n 🇬🇧 chaise f longue (*où l'on s'allonge pour bronzer*).

Sunni ['sʌnɪ] n **1.** [religion] sunnisme m **2.** [person] sunnite mf.

sunny ['sʌnɪ] (*compar* sunnier, *superl* sunniest) adj **1.** [day, place, etc.] ensoleillé / *it's a sunny day* or *it's sunny* il fait (du) soleil or beau ▸ **sunny intervals** or **periods** METEOR éclaircies fpl **2.** fig [cheerful -disposition] heureux ; [-smile] radieux, rayonnant.

sunrise ['sʌnraɪz] n lever m du soleil / *at sunrise* au lever du soleil.

sunrise industry n industrie f de pointe.

sunroof ['sʌnru:f] n toit m ouvrant.

sunscreen ['sʌnskri:n] n [suntan lotion] écran m or filtre m solaire.

sunseeker n *touriste qui part dans un pays chaud à la recherche du soleil, notamment en hiver.*

sunset ['sʌnset] n coucher m du soleil / *at sunset* au coucher du soleil.

sunshade ['sʌnʃeɪd] n [lady's parasol] ombrelle f ; [for table] parasol m ; [on cap] visière f.

sunshine ['sʌnʃaɪn] n **1.** [sunlight] (lumière f du) soleil m / *in the sunshine* au soleil **2.** inf [term of address] : *hello sunshine!* salut ma jolie !, salut mon mignon !

sunspot ['sʌnspɒt] n tache f solaire.

sunstroke ['sʌnstrəʊk] n (U) insolation f ▸ **to have / to get sunstroke** avoir / attraper une insolation.

suntan ['sʌntæn] ◆ n bronzage m ▸ **to have a suntan** être bronzé ▸ **to get a suntan** se faire bronzer, bronzer. ◆ comp [cream, lotion, oil] solaire, de bronzage.

suntanned ['sʌntænd] adj bronzé.

suntrap ['sʌntræp] n coin m abrité et très ensoleillé.

sun-up ['sʌnʌp] n 🇺🇸 inf lever m du soleil / *at sun-up* au lever du soleil.

super ['su:pər] ◆ adj **1.** inf [wonderful] super (*inv*), terrible, génial **2.** [superior] supérieur, super-. ◆ interj inf super, formidable.

superabundance [,su:pərə'bʌndəns] n surabondance f.

superannuated [,su:pə'rænjʊeɪtɪd] adj **1.** [person] à la retraite, retraité **2.** [object] suranné, désuet (désuète).

superannuation [ˌsuːpəˌrænjʊ'eɪʃn] n **1.** [act of retiring] mise f à la retraite **2.** [pension] pension f de retraite **3.** [contribution] versement m or cotisation f pour la retraite ▶ **superannuation fund** caisse f de retraite.

superb [suː'pɜːb] adj superbe, magnifique.

superbly [suː'pɜːblɪ] adv superbement, magnifiquement.

Super Bowl pr n US Superbowl m (finale du championnat des États-Unis de football américain).

superbug ['suːpəbʌg] n bactérie f multirésistante.

supercilious [ˌsuːpə'sɪlɪəs] adj hautain, arrogant, dédaigneux.

supercomputer [ˌsuːpəkəm'pjuːtəʳ] n supercalculateur m, superordinateur m.

supercool ['suːpəkuːl] ◆ vt [liquid] surfondre. ◆ adj inf [very trendy] super branché ; [very relaxed] super génial.

superficial [ˌsuːpə'fɪʃl] adj [knowledge] superficiel ; [differences] superficiel, insignifiant ; [person] superficiel, frivole, léger ; [wound] superficiel, léger.

superficiality ['suːpəˌfɪʃɪ'ælətɪ] n caractère m superficiel, manque m de profondeur.

superficially [ˌsuːpə'fɪʃəlɪ] adv superficiellement.

superfluous [suː'pɜːflʊəs] adj superflu / it is superfluous to say... (il est) inutile de or il va sans dire... / I felt superfluous je me sentais de trop.

superglue ['suːpəgluː] n superglu f.

superhero ['suːpəˌhɪərəʊ] (pl **superheroes**) n superhéros m.

superhighway ['suːpəˌhaɪweɪ] n **1.** US AUTO autoroute f **2.** COMPUT autoroute f.

superhuman [ˌsuːpə'hjuːmən] adj surhumain.

superimpose [ˌsuːpərɪm'pəʊz] vt superposer ▶ **to superimpose sthg on sthg** superposer qqch à qqch.

superintend [ˌsuːpərɪn'tend] vt **1.** [oversee - activity] surveiller ; [- person] surveiller, avoir l'œil sur **2.** [run - office, institution] diriger.

superintendent [ˌsuːpərɪn'tendənt] n **1.** [of institution] directeur m, -trice f ; [of department, office] chef m **2.** UK [of police] ≃ commissaire mf (de police) **3.** US [of apartment building] gardien m, -enne f, concierge mf.

superior [suː'pɪərɪəʳ] ◆ adj **1.** [better, greater] supérieur ▶ **superior to** supérieur à ▶ **superior in number to** supérieur en nombre à, numériquement supérieur à **2.** [senior - officer, position] supérieur ▶ **superior to** supérieur à, au-dessus de **3.** pej [supercilious] suffisant, hautain **4.** [upper] supérieur ▶ **the superior limbs** les membres mpl supérieurs **5.** TYPO ▶ **superior letter** lettre f supérieure or suscrite **6.** BIOL supérieur. ◆ n supérieur m, -e f. ◆ **Superior** pr n ▶ **Lake Superior** le lac Supérieur.

superiority [suːˌpɪərɪ'ɒrətɪ] n **1.** [higher amount, worth] supériorité f **2.** pej [arrogance] supériorité f, arrogance f.

superlative [suː'pɜːlətɪv] ◆ adj **1.** [outstanding - quality, skill, performance] sans pareil ; [- performer, athlete] sans pareil, inégalé **2.** [overwhelming - indifference, ignorance, joy] suprême **3.** GRAM superlatif. ◆ n superlatif m / in the superlative au superlatif.

superlatively [suː'pɜːlətɪvlɪ] adv au plus haut degré, exceptionnellement.

superman ['suːpəmæn] (pl **supermen** [-men]) n PHILOS [gen] surhomme m ; [gen] superman m. ◆ **Superman** pr n ▶ [comic book hero] Superman m.

supermarket ['suːpəˌmɑːkɪt] n supermarché m ▶ **supermarket trolley** Caddie® m.

supermodel ['suːpəmɒdl] n top model m.

supernatural [ˌsuːpə'nætʃrəl] ◆ adj surnaturel. ◆ n surnaturel m.

superpower ['suːpəˌpaʊəʳ] n superpuissance f, super-grand m.

superscript ['suːpəskrɪpt] ◆ n exposant m. ◆ adj en exposant.

supersede [ˌsuːpə'siːd] vt [person - get rid of] supplanter, détrôner ; [- replace] succéder à, remplacer ; [object] remplacer.

supersize ['suːpəsaɪz] adj géant.

supersonic [ˌsuːpə'sɒnɪk] adj supersonique ▶ **supersonic bang** or **boom** bang m (supersonique).

superstar ['suːpəstɑːʳ] n superstar f.

superstition [ˌsuːpə'stɪʃn] n superstition f.

superstitious [ˌsuːpə'stɪʃəs] adj superstitieux ▶ **to be superstitious about sthg** être superstitieux au sujet de qqch.

superstitiously [ˌsuːpə'stɪʃəslɪ] adv superstitieusement.

superstore ['suːpəstɔːʳ] n hypermarché m.

superstructure ['suːpəˌstrʌktʃəʳ] n superstructure f.

supertanker ['suːpəˌtæŋkəʳ] n supertanker m, superpétrolier m.

supertax ['suːpətæks] n ≃ impôt m sur les grandes fortunes.

superuser ['suːpəˌjuːzəʳ] n COMPUT gros utilisateur m.

supervise ['suːpəvaɪz] ◆ vt **1.** [oversee - activity, exam] surveiller ; [- child, staff] surveiller, avoir l'œil sur **2.** [run - office, workshop] diriger. ◆ vi surveiller.

supervision [ˌsuːpə'vɪʒn] n **1.** [of person, activity] surveillance f, contrôle m **2.** [of office] direction f.

supervisor ['suːpəvaɪzəʳ] n [gen] surveillant m, -e f ; COMM [of department] chef m de rayon ; SCH & UNIV [at exam] surveillant m, -e f ; UNIV [of thesis] directeur m, -trice f de thèse ; [of research] directeur m, -trice f de recherches.

supervisory ['suːpəvaɪzərɪ] adj de surveillance / in a supervisory role or capacity à titre de surveillant.

superwoman ['suːpəˌwʊmən] (pl **superwomen** [-ˌwɪmɪn]) n superwoman f. ◆ **Superwoman** pr n [comic book heroine] Superwoman.

supine ['suːpaɪn] adj **1.** liter [on one's back] couché or étendu sur le dos **2.** fig [passive] indolent, mou (before vowel or silent 'h' mol, f molle), passif.

supper ['sʌpəʳ] n [evening meal] dîner m ; [late-night meal] souper m ▶ **to have** or **to eat supper** dîner, souper / we had steak for supper nous avons mangé du steak au dîner ou au souper.

supplant [sə'plɑːnt] vt [person] supplanter, évincer ; [thing] supplanter, remplacer.

supple ['sʌpl] adj souple ▶ **to become supple** s'assouplir.

supplement ◆ n ['sʌplɪmənt] **1.** [additional amount - paid] supplément m ; [- received] complément m ▶ **food supplement** complément m alimentaire **2.** PRESS supplément m **3.** UK ADMIN [allowance] allocation f. ◆ vt ['sʌplɪment] [increase] augmenter ; [complete] compléter.

supplementary [ˌsʌplɪ'mentərɪ] adj **1.** [gen] complémentaire, additionnel ▶ **supplementary to** en plus de ▶ **supplementary income** revenus mpl annexes **2.** GEOM [angle] supplémentaire.

supplementary benefit n UK ancien nom de l'«income support», ; ≃ allocation f supplémentaire.

supplier [sə'plaɪəʳ] n COMM fournisseur m, -euse f ▶ **supplier credit** crédit-fournisseur m.

supply[1] [sə'plaɪ] (pt & pp **supplied**, pl **supplies**) ◆ vt **1.** [provide - goods, services] fournir ▶ **to supply sthg**

to sb fournir qqch à qqn / *to supply electricity | water to a town* alimenter une ville en électricité / eau **2.** [provide sthg to -person, institution, city] fournir, approvisionner ; MIL ravitailler, approvisionner ▶ **to supply sb with sthg** fournir qqch à qqn, approvisionner qqn en qqch **3.** [equip] munir / *all toys are supplied with batteries* des piles sont fournies avec tous les jouets **4.** [make good - deficiency] suppléer à ; [- omission] réparer, compenser ; [satisfy - need] répondre à. ◆ n **1.** [stock] provision *f*, réserve *f* / *water is in short supply in the southeast* on manque d'eau dans le sud-est **2.** [provision - of goods, equipment] fourniture *f* ; [- of fuel] alimentation *f* ; MIL ravitaillement *m*, approvisionnement *m* / *the domestic hot water supply* l'alimentation domestique en eau chaude **3.** ECON offre *f* **4.** 🇬🇧 [clergyman, secretary, teacher] remplaçant *m*, -e *f*, suppléant *m*, -e *f* ▶ **to be on supply** faire des remplacements or des suppléances **5.** *(usu pl)* POL [money] crédits *mpl*. ◆ comp **1.** [convoy, train, truck, route] de ravitaillement ▶ **supply ship** ravitailleur *m* **2.** [secretary] intérimaire ; [clergyman] suppléant. ◆ **supplies** pl n [gen] provisions *fpl* ; [of food] vivres *mpl* ; MIL subsistances *fpl*, approvisionnements *mpl* / *office supplies* fournitures *fpl* de bureau.

supply² ['sʌplɪ] adv souplement, avec souplesse.

supply teacher [sə'plaɪ-] n 🇬🇧 remplaçant *m*, -e *f*.

support [sə'pɔːt] ◆ vt **1.** [back - action, campaign, person] soutenir, appuyer ; [- cause, idea] défendre, soutenir ; SPORT être supporter de, supporter / *he supports Tottenham* c'est un supporter de Tottenham **2.** [assist] soutenir, aider ; CIN & THEAT : *supported by a superb cast* avec une distribution superbe **3.** [hold up] supporter, soutenir / *her legs were too weak to support her* ses jambes étaient trop faibles pour la porter / *she held on to the table to support herself* elle s'agrippa à la table pour ne pas tomber **4.** [provide for financially - person] subvenir aux besoins de ; [- campaign, project] aider financièrement / *she has three children to support* elle a trois enfants à charge / *she earns enough to support herself* elle gagne assez pour subvenir à ses propres besoins **5.** [sustain] faire vivre / *the land has supported four generations of tribespeople* cette terre a fait vivre la tribu pendant quatre générations **6.** [substantiate, give weight to] appuyer, confirmer, donner du poids à / *there is no evidence to support his claim* il n'y a aucune preuve pour appuyer ses dires **7.** [endure] supporter, tolérer **8.** FIN [price, currency] maintenir. ◆ n **1.** [backing] soutien *m*, appui *m* ▶ **to give** or **to lend one's support to sthg** accorder or prêter son appui à qqch / *she gave us her full support* elle nous a pleinement appuyés / *you have my full support on this* je vous soutiens à cent pour cent, vous pouvez compter sur mon soutien inconditionnel / *to speak in support of a motion* appuyer une motion / *they are striking in support of the miners* ils font grève par solidarité avec les mineurs **2.** [assistance, encouragement] appui *m*, aide *f* / *she gave me the emotional support I needed* elle m'a apporté le soutien affectif dont j'avais besoin **3.** [person who offers assistance, encouragement] soutien *m* / *she's been a great support to me* elle m'a été d'un grand soutien **4.** [holding up] soutien *m* / *I was holding his arm for support* je m'appuyais sur son bras / *this bra gives good support* ce soutien-gorge maintient bien la poitrine **5.** [supporting structure, prop] appui *m* ; CONSTR & TECH soutien *m*, support *m* **6.** [funding] soutien *m* / *they depend on the government for financial support* ils sont subventionnés par le gouvernement / *what are your means of support?* quelles sont vos sources de revenus ? / *she is their only means of support* ils n'ont qu'elle pour les faire vivre **7.** [substantiation, corroboration] corroboration *f* / *in support of her theory* à l'appui de or pour corroborer sa théorie **8.** 🇬🇧 ECON [subsidy] subvention *f* **9.** COMPUT assistance *f* **10.** MUS = **support band**. ◆ comp **1.** [troops,

unit] de soutien **2.** [hose, stockings] de maintien ; [bandage] de soutien **3.** CONSTR & TECH [structure, device, frame] de soutien **4.** ADMIN ▶ **support services** services *mpl* d'assistance technique.

support band n groupe *m* en première partie.

supporter [sə'pɔːtər] n **1.** CONSTR & TECH [device] soutien *m*, support *m* **2.** [advocate, follower - of cause, opinion] adepte *mf*, partisan *m* ; [- of political party] partisan *m* ; SPORT supporter *m*, supporteur *m*, -trice *f* **3.** HERALD tenant *m*.

support group n **1.** ADMIN groupe *m* de soutien **2.** MUS = **support band**.

supporting [sə'pɔːtɪŋ] adj **1.** CONSTR & TECH [pillar, structure] d'appui, de soutènement ; [wall] porteur ▶ **supporting beam** CONSTR sommier *m* **2.** CIN & THEAT [role] secondaire, de second plan ; [actor] qui a un rôle secondaire or de second plan **3.** [substantiating] qui confirme, qui soutient.

supportive [sə'pɔːtɪv] adj [person] qui est d'un grand soutien ; [attitude] de soutien ▶ **supportive therapy** MED thérapie *f* de soutien.

suppose [sə'pəʊz] ◆ vt **1.** [assume] supposer / *suppose x equals y* MATH soit x égal à y / *I suppose you think that's funny!* je suppose que vous trouvez ça drôle ! / *let's suppose (that)…* supposons que… **2.** [think, believe] penser, croire / *do you suppose he'll do it?* pensez-vous or croyez-vous qu'il le fera ? / *I suppose so* a) [affirmative response] je suppose que oui b) [expressing reluctance] oui, peut-être / *I suppose not* or *I don't suppose so* je ne (le) pense pas **3.** [imply] supposer. ◆ vi supposer, imaginer / *he's gone, I suppose?* il est parti, je suppose or j'imagine ? / *there were, I suppose, about 50 people there* il y avait, je dirais, une cinquantaine de personnes. ◆ conj si / *suppose they see you?* et s'ils vous voyaient ? / *suppose I'm right and she does come?* mettons or supposons que j'aie raison et qu'elle vienne ?

supposed [sə'pəʊzd] adj **1.** [presumed] présumé, supposé ; [alleged] prétendu **2.** PHR **to be supposed to** : *to be supposed to do sthg* être censé faire qqch.

supposedly [sə'pəʊzɪdlɪ] adv soi-disant *(adv)*.

supposing [sə'pəʊzɪŋ] conj si, à supposer que.

supposition [,sʌpə'zɪʃn] n supposition *f*, hypothèse *f*.

suppository [sə'pɒzɪtrɪ] *(pl* **suppositories**) n suppositoire *m*.

suppress [sə'pres] vt **1.** [put an end to] supprimer, mettre fin à **2.** [withhold] supprimer, faire disparaître ; [conceal] supprimer, cacher / *to suppress the truth | a scandal* étouffer la vérité / un scandale **3.** [withdraw from publication] supprimer, interdire **4.** [delete] supprimer, retrancher **5.** [inhibit - growth, weeds] supprimer, empêcher **6.** [hold back, repress - anger, yawn, smile] réprimer ; [- tears] retenir, refouler ; [- feelings, desires] étouffer, refouler **7.** PSYCHOL refouler **8.** ELECTRON & RADIO antiparasiter.

suppressant [sə'presənt] n MED ▶ **(appetite) suppressant** coupe-faim *m* ▶ **cough suppressant** antitussif *m*.

suppression [sə'preʃn] n **1.** [ending - of rebellion, demonstration] suppression *f*, répression *f* ; [- of rights] suppression *f*, abolition *f* ; [- of a law, decree] abrogation *f* **2.** [concealment - of evidence, information] suppression *f*, dissimulation *f* ; [- of scandal] étouffement *m* **3.** [nonpublication - of document, report] suppression *f*, interdiction *f* ; [- of part of text] suppression *f* **4.** [holding back - of feelings, thoughts] refoulement *m* **5.** PSYCHOL refoulement *m* **6.** ELECTRON & RADIO antiparasitage *m*.

suppressor [sə'presər] n ELEC dispositif *m* antiparasite.

supranational [,suːprə'næʃənl] adj supranational.

supremacist [sʊ'preməsɪst] n *personne qui croit en la suprématie d'un groupe* / *they are white supremacists* ils croient en la suprématie de la race blanche.

supremacy [soˈpreməsɪ] n **1.** [dominance] suprématie f, domination f **2.** [superiority] suprématie f.

supreme [soˈpriːm] adj **1.** [highest in rank, authority] suprême **2.** [great, outstanding] extrême.

Supreme Court pr n ▶ **the Supreme Court** la Cour suprême *(des États-Unis)*.

 Supreme Court

La Cour suprême est l'organe supérieur du pouvoir judiciaire américain. Composée de 9 membres nommés sans limitation de durée par le président des États-Unis, elle détient l'ultime pouvoir de décision et a le droit d'interpréter la Constitution.

supremely [soˈpriːmlɪ] adv suprêmement, extrêmement.

supremo [soˈpriːməʊ] *(pl* **supremos**) n US *inf* (grand) chef m.

Supt. written abbr of superintendent.

surcharge [ˈsɜːʃɑːdʒ] ◆ n **1.** [extra duty, tax] surtaxe f **2.** [extra cost] supplément m **3.** [overprinting - on postage stamp] surcharge f. ◆ vt **1.** [charge extra duty or tax on] surtaxer **2.** [charge a supplement to] faire payer un supplément à **3.** [overprint - postage stamp] surcharger.

sure [ʃʊər] ◆ adj **1.** [convinced, positive] sûr, certain / *are you sure of the facts?* êtes-vous sûr or certain des faits ? / *I'm not sure you're right* je ne suis pas sûr or certain que vous ayez raison / *he's not sure whether he's going to come or not* il n'est pas sûr de venir / *she isn't sure of* or *about her feelings for him* elle n'est pas sûre de ses sentiments pour lui / *he'll win, I'm sure* il gagnera, j'en suis sûr **2.** [confident, assured] sûr / *you can be sure of good service in this restaurant* dans ce restaurant, vous êtes sûr d'être bien servi ▶ **to be sure of o.s.** être sûr de soi, avoir confiance en soi **3.** [certain - to happen] sûr, certain / *one thing is sure, he won't be back in a hurry!* une chose est sûre or certaine, il ne va pas revenir de sitôt ! / *we're sure to meet again* nous nous reverrons sûrement ▶ **sure thing!** US *inf* bien sûr (que oui) !, pour sûr ! / *it's a sure thing* [it's a certainty] c'est dans la poche ▶ **be sure to:** *be sure to be on time tomorrow* il faut que vous soyez à l'heure demain ▶ **to make sure (that):** *we made sure that no one was listening* nous nous sommes assurés or nous avons vérifié que personne n'écoutait / *it is his job to make sure that everyone is satisfied* c'est lui qui veille à ce que tout le monde soit satisfait / *make sure you don't lose your ticket* prends garde à ne pas perdre ton billet **4.** [firm, steady] sûr / *a sure grasp of the subject fig* des connaissances solides en la matière **5.** [reliable, irrefutable] sûr / *insomnia is a sure sign of depression* l'insomnie est un signe incontestable de dépression. ◆ adv **1.** *inf* [of course] bien sûr, pour sûr / *can I borrow your car? — sure (you can)!* (est-ce que) je peux emprunter ta voiture ? — bien sûr (que oui) ! **2.** US *inf* [really] drôlement, rudement / *are you hungry? — I sure am!* as-tu faim ? — plutôt ! or et comment ! **3.** [as intensifier] ▶ **(as) sure as** aussi sûr que. ◆ **for sure** adv phr : *I'll give it to you tomorrow for sure* je te le donnerai demain sans faute / *one thing is for sure, I'm not staying here!* une chose est sûre, je ne reste pas ici ! / *I think he's single but I can't say for sure* je crois qu'il est célibataire, mais je ne peux pas l'affirmer. ◆ **sure enough** adv phr effectivement, en effet / *she said she'd ring and sure enough she did* elle a dit qu'elle appellerait, et c'est ce qu'elle a fait. ◆ **to be sure** adv phr : *to be sure, his offer is well-intentioned* ce qui est certain, c'est que son offre est bien intentionnée.

Note that pas sûr que and pas certain que are followed by a verb in the subjunctive: **I'm not sure this is really fair.** *Je ne suis pas sûr / certain que cela soit tout à fait juste.*

Note that veiller à ce que is followed by a verb in the subjunctive: **Make sure the chicken is cooked right through.** *Veillez à ce que le poulet soit cuit à cœur.*

surefire [ˈʃʊəfaɪər] adj *inf* infaillible, sûr.

surefooted [ˈʃʊəˌfʊtɪd] adj au pied sûr.

surely [ˈʃʊəlɪ] adv **1.** [used to express surprise, incredulity, to contradict] quand même, tout de même **2.** [undoubtedly, assuredly] sûrement, sans (aucun) doute **3.** [steadily] sûrement / *things are improving slowly but surely* les choses s'améliorent lentement mais sûrement **4.** US [of course] bien sûr, certainement.

sureness [ˈʃʊənɪs] n **1.** [certainty] certitude f **2.** [assurance] assurance f **3.** [steadiness] sûreté f ; [accuracy] justesse f, précision f.

surety [ˈʃʊərətɪ] *(pl* **sureties**) n **1.** [guarantor] garant m, -e f, caution f ▶ **to act as** or **to stand surety (for sb)** se porter garant (de qqn) **2.** [collateral] caution f, sûreté f.

surf [sɜːf] ◆ n *(U)* **1.** [waves] vagues *fpl* (déferlantes), ressac m **2.** [foam] écume f. ◆ vt ▶ **to surf the Net** surfer sur le Net. ◆ vi surfer, faire du surf ; COMPUT surfer (sur le Net).

surface [ˈsɜːfɪs] ◆ n **1.** [exterior, top] surface f / *the submarine / diver came to the surface* le sous-marin / plongeur fit surface **2.** [flat area] surface f **3.** [covering layer] revêtement m ▶ **road surface** revêtement m **4.** [outward appearance] surface f, extérieur m, dehors m / *on the surface she seems nice enough* au premier abord elle paraît assez sympathique **5.** GEOM [area] surface f, superficie f. ◆ vi **1.** [submarine, diver, whale] faire surface, monter à la surface ▶ **to surface again** refaire surface, remonter à la surface **2.** [become manifest] apparaître, se manifester / *he surfaced again after many years of obscurity* il a réapparu après être resté dans l'ombre pendant de nombreuses années / *rumours like this tend to surface every so often* ce type de rumeur a tendance à refaire surface de temps à autre **3.** *inf* [get up] se lever, émerger. ◆ vt [put a surface on - road] revêtir ; [- paper] calandrer. ◆ adj **1.** [superficial] superficiel **2.** [exterior] de surface ▶ **surface measurements** superficie f **3.** MIN [workers] de surface, au jour ; [work] à la surface, au jour ; MIL [forces] au sol ; [fleet] de surface.

surface area n surface f, superficie f.

surface mail n [by land] courrier m par voie de terre ; [by sea] courrier m par voie maritime.

surface-to-air adj sol-air *(inv)*.

surfboard [ˈsɜːfbɔːd] n (planche f de) surf m.

surfboarding [ˈsɜːfbɔːdɪŋ] n surf m.

surfeit [ˈsɜːfɪt] ◆ n *fml* [excess] excès m, surabondance f. ◆ vt rassasier.

surfer [ˈsɜːfər] n SPORT surfeur m, -euse f ; COMPUT internaute mf.

surfing [ˈsɜːfɪŋ] n surf m.

surge [sɜːdʒ] ◆ n **1.** [increase - of activity] augmentation f, poussée f ; [- of emotion] vague f, accès m ; [ELEC - of voltage, current] pointe f / *a big surge in demand* une forte augmentation de la demande / *a surge of pain / pity* un accès de douleur / de pitié **2.** [rush, stampede] ruée f **3.** NAUT houle f. ◆ vi **1.** [well up - emotion] monter **2.** [rush - crowd] se ruer, déferler ; [- water] couler à flots or à torrents ; [- waves] déferler **3.** ELEC subir une surtension. ◆ **surge up** vi = **surge** *(vi)*.

surgeon [ˈsɜːdʒən] n chirurgien m, -enne f.

surge protector n ELEC protecteur *m* de surtension.
surgery ['sɜːdʒərɪ] (*pl* **surgeries**) n **1.** [field of medicine] chirurgie *f* **2.** (*U*) [surgical treatment] intervention *f* chirurgicale, interventions *fpl* chirurgicales ▸ **to perform surgery on sb** opérer qqn ▸ **to have brain / heart surgery** se faire opérer du cerveau / du cœur **3.** 🇬🇧 [consulting room] cabinet *m* médical or de consultation ; [building] centre *m* médical ; [consultation] consultation *f* ▸ **surgery hours** heures *fpl* de consultation **4.** 🇬🇧 POL permanence *f*.
surgical ['sɜːdʒɪkl] adj **1.** [operation, treatment] chirurgical ; [manual, treatise] de chirurgie ; [instrument, mask] chirurgical, de chirurgien ; [methods, shock] opératoire **2.** [appliance, boot, stocking] orthopédique **3.** MIL ▸ **surgical strike** frappe *f* « chirurgicale ».
surgically ['sɜːdʒɪklɪ] adv par intervention chirurgicale.
surgical spirit n 🇬🇧 alcool *m* à 90 (degrés).
Surinam [ˌsʊərɪ'næm] pr n Surinam *m*, Suriname *m* / **in Surinam** au Surinam.
surly ['sɜːlɪ] (*compar* **surlier**, *superl* **surliest**) adj [ill-tempered] hargneux, grincheux ; [gloomy] maussade, renfrogné.
surmise [sɜː'maɪz] ◆ vt conjecturer, présumer. ◆ n *fml* conjecture *f*, supposition *f*.
surmount [sɜː'maʊnt] vt **1.** [triumph over] surmonter, vaincre **2.** *fml* [cap, top] surmonter.
surname ['sɜːneɪm] n 🇬🇧 nom *m* (de famille).
surpass [sə'pɑːs] vt **1.** [outdo, outshine] surpasser **2.** [go beyond] surpasser, dépasser.
surplus ['sɜːpləs] ◆ n **1.** [overabundance] surplus *m*, excédent *m* **2.** (*U*) [old military clothes] surplus *mpl* / *an army surplus store* un magasin de surplus de l'armée **3.** FIN [in accounting] boni *m*. ◆ adj **1.** [gen] en surplus, en trop ▸ **to be surplus to requirements** excéder les besoins **2.** COMM & ECON en surplus, excédentaire.
surprise [sə'praɪz] ◆ n **1.** [unexpected event, experience, etc.] surprise *f* / *it was a surprise to me* cela a été une surprise pour moi, cela m'a surpris ▸ **to give sb a surprise** faire une surprise à qqn **2.** [astonishment] surprise *f*, étonnement *m* / *much to my surprise, she agreed* à ma grande surprise et à mon grand étonnement, elle accepta / *he looked at me in surprise* il me regarda d'un air surpris or étonné **3.** [catching unawares] surprise *f* / *their arrival took me by surprise* leur arrivée m'a pris au dépourvu. ◆ comp [attack, present, victory] surprise ; [announcement] inattendu ▸ **surprise party** fête *f* surprise. ◆ vt **1.** [amaze] surprendre, étonner / *it surprised me that they didn't give her the job* j'ai été surpris or étonné qu'ils ne l'aient pas embauchée / *it wouldn't surprise me if they lost* ça ne m'étonnerait pas or je ne serais pas surpris qu'ils perdent **2.** [catch unawares] surprendre.
surprised [sə'praɪzd] adj surpris, étonné / *she was surprised to learn that she had got the job* elle a été surprise d'apprendre qu'on allait l'embaucher / *don't be surprised if she doesn't come* ne vous étonnez pas si elle ne vient pas / *I'm surprised by* or *at his reaction* sa réaction me surprend or m'étonne.

> 📝 Note that être surpris / étonné que and s'étonner que are followed by a verb in the subjunctive:
> **I'm surprised he's so fond of that old car.** *Je suis surpris* / étonné qu'il *tienne autant à cette vieille voiture.*
> **I'm surprised that no one has yet replied.** *Je m'étonne que personne n'ait encore répondu.*

surprising [sə'praɪzɪŋ] adj surprenant, étonnant.

surprisingly [sə'praɪzɪŋlɪ] adv étonnamment.
surreal [sə'rɪəl] ◆ adj **1.** [strange, dreamlike] étrange, onirique **2.** [surrealist] surréaliste. ◆ n ▸ **the surreal** le surréel.
surrealism [sə'rɪəlɪzm] n ART & LITER surréalisme *m*.
surrealist [sə'rɪəlɪst] ◆ adj ART & LITER surréaliste. ◆ n ART & LITER surréaliste *mf*.
surrealistic [səˌrɪəl'ɪstɪk] adj **1.** ART & LITER surréaliste **2.** *fig* surréel, surréaliste.
surrender [sə'rendər] ◆ vi **1.** MIL [capitulate] se rendre, capituler / *they surrendered to the enemy* ils se rendirent à or ils capitulèrent devant l'ennemi **2.** [give o.s. up] se livrer **3.** *fig* [abandon o.s.] se livrer, s'abandonner / *to surrender to temptation* se livrer or s'abandonner à la tentation. ◆ vt **1.** [city, position] livrer ; [relinquish - possessions, territory] céder, rendre ; [- one's seat] céder, laisser ; [- arms] rendre, livrer ; [- claim, authority, freedom, rights] renoncer à ; [- hopes] abandonner ▸ **to surrender o.s. to sthg** se livrer or s'abandonner à qqch **2.** [hand in - ticket, coupon] remettre. ◆ n **1.** [capitulation] reddition *f*, capitulation *f* **2.** [relinquishing - of possessions, territory] cession *f* ; [- of arms] remise *f* ; [- of claim, authority, freedom, rights] renonciation *f*, abdication *f* ; [- of hopes] abandon *m*.
surreptitious [ˌsʌrəp'tɪʃəs] adj subreptice *liter*, furtif, clandestin.
surreptitiously [ˌsʌrəp'tɪʃəslɪ] adv subrepticement *liter*, furtivement, à la dérobée.
surrogacy ['sʌrəgəsɪ] n maternité *f* de remplacement or de substitution.
surrogate ['sʌrəgeɪt] ◆ n **1.** *fml* [substitute - person] remplaçant *m*, -e *f*, substitut *m* ; [- thing] succédané *m* **2.** PSYCHOL substitut *m* **3.** 🇺🇸 LAW magistrat *m* de droit civil *(juridiction locale)* **4.** 🇬🇧 RELIG évêque *m* auxiliaire. ◆ adj de substitution, de remplacement.
surrogate mother n PSYCHOL substitut *m* maternel ; MED mère *f* porteuse.
surround [sə'raʊnd] ◆ vt **1.** [gen] entourer **2.** [subj: troops, police, enemy] encercler, cerner. ◆ n 🇬🇧 [border, edging] bordure *f*.
surrounding [sə'raʊndɪŋ] adj environnant.
◆◇ **surroundings** pl n **1.** [of town, city] alentours *mpl*, environs *mpl* **2.** [setting] cadre *m*, décor *m* **3.** [environment] environnement *m*, milieu *m*.
surtax ['sɜːtæks] n *impôt supplémentaire qui s'applique au-delà d'une certaine tranche de revenus*.
surtitle ['sɜːtaɪtl] n surtitre *m*.
surveillance [sɜː'veɪləns] n surveillance *f* ▸ **to keep sb under constant surveillance** garder qqn sous surveillance continue.
survey ◆ vt [sə'veɪ] **1.** [contemplate] contempler ; [inspect] inspecter, examiner ; [review] passer en revue **2.** [make a study of] dresser le bilan de, étudier **3.** [poll] sonder **4.** [land] arpenter, relever, faire un relèvement de ; 🇬🇧 [house] expertiser, faire une expertise de. ◆ n ['sɜːveɪ] **1.** [study, investigation] étude *f*, enquête *f* **2.** [overview] vue *f* d'ensemble **3.** [poll] sondage *m* **4.** [of land] relèvement *m*, levé *m* ▸ **aerial survey** levé aérien ; 🇬🇧 [of house] expertise *f* ▸ **to have a survey done** faire faire une expertise.
surveying [sə'veɪɪŋ] n [measuring - of land] arpentage *m*, levé *m* ; 🇬🇧 [examination - of buildings] examen *m*.
surveyor [sə'veɪər] n **1.** [of land] arpenteur *m*, géomètre *m* **2.** 🇬🇧 [of buildings] géomètre-expert *m*.
survival [sə'vaɪvl] ◆ n **1.** [remaining alive] survie *f* ▸ **the survival of the fittest** la survie du plus apte **2.** [relic, remnant] survivance *f*, vestige *m*. ◆ comp [course, kit] de survie.

survive [sə'vaɪv] ◆ vi **1.** [remain alive] survivre **2.** [remain, be left] subsister. ◆ vt **1.** [live through] survivre à, réchapper à or de **2.** [cope with, get through] supporter **3.** [outlive, outlast] survivre à **4.** [withstand] survivre à, résister à.

surviving [sə'vaɪvɪŋ] adj survivant / *his only surviving son* son seul fils encore en vie.

survivor [sə'vaɪvər] n **1.** [of an accident, attack] survivant *m*, -e *f*, rescapé *m*, -e *f* **2.** LAW survivant *m*, -e *f*.

susceptibility [sə,septə'bɪlɪtɪ] (*pl* **susceptibilities**) n **1.** [predisposition - to an illness] prédisposition *f* **2.** [vulnerability] sensibilité *f* / *his susceptibility to flattery* sa sensibilité à la flatterie **3.** [sensitivity] sensibilité *f*, émotivité *f* **4.** PHYS susceptibilité *f*.

susceptible [sə'septəbl] adj **1.** [prone - to illness] prédisposé / *I'm very susceptible to colds* je m'enrhume très facilement **2.** [responsive] sensible / *susceptible to flattery* sensible à la flatterie **3.** [sensitive, emotional] sensible, émotif **4.** fml [capable] susceptible.

sushi ['suːʃɪ] n sushi *m* ▶ **sushi bar** sushi-bar *m*.

suspect ◆ vt [sə'spekt] **1.** [presume, imagine] soupçonner, se douter de / *I suspected there would be trouble* je me doutais qu'il y aurait des problèmes / *I suspected as much!* je m'en doutais ! / *what happened, I suspect, is that they had an argument* ce qui s'est passé, j'imagine, c'est qu'ils se sont disputés **2.** [mistrust] douter de, se méfier de ▶ **to suspect sb's motives** avoir des doutes sur les intentions de qqn **3.** [person - of wrongdoing] soupçonner, suspecter ▶ **to be suspected of sthg** être soupçonné de qqch ▶ **to suspect sb of sthg** or **of doing sthg** soupçonner qqn de qqch or d'avoir fait qqch. ◆ n ['sʌspekt] suspect *m*, -e *f*. ◆ adj ['sʌspekt] suspect.

suspected [sə'spektɪd] adj présumé.

suspend [sə'spend] vt **1.** [hang] suspendre / *suspended from the ceiling* suspendu au plafond **2.** [discontinue] suspendre ; [withdraw - permit, licence] retirer (provisoirement), suspendre **3.** [defer] suspendre, reporter ▶ **to suspend judgment** suspendre son jugement ▶ **to suspend one's disbelief** faire taire son incrédulité **4.** [exclude temporarily - official, member, sportsman] suspendre ; [- worker] suspendre, mettre à pied ; [- pupil, student] exclure provisoirement.

suspended animation [sə'spendɪd-] n [natural state] hibernation *f* ; [induced state] hibernation *f* artificielle.

suspended sentence n LAW condamnation *f* avec sursis.

suspender belt n UK porte-jarretelles *m* inv.

suspense [sə'spens] n **1.** [anticipation] incertitude *f* ▶ **to keep** or **to leave sb in suspense** laisser qqn dans l'incertitude ; [in films, literature] suspense *m* **2.** ADMIN & LAW ▶ **in suspense** en suspens.

suspension [sə'spenʃn] n **1.** [interruption] suspension *f* ; [withdrawal] suspension *f*, retrait *m* (provisoire) **2.** [temporary dismissal - from office, political party, club, team] suspension *f* ; [- from job] suspension *f*, mise *f* à pied ; [- from school, university] exclusion *f* provisoire **3.** AUTO & TECH suspension *f* **4.** CHEM suspension *f* / *in suspension* en suspension.

suspension bridge n pont *m* suspendu.

suspicion [sə'spɪʃn] n **1.** [presumption of guilt, mistrust] soupçon *m*, suspicion *f* ▶ **to be above** or **beyond suspicion** être au-dessus de tout soupçon ▶ **to be under suspicion** être soupçonné **2.** [notion, feeling] soupçon *m* / *I had a growing suspicion that he wasn't telling the truth* je soupçonnais de plus en plus qu'il ne disait pas la vérité **3.** [trace, hint] soupçon *m*, pointe *f*.

suspicious [sə'spɪʃəs] adj **1.** [distrustful] méfiant, soupçonneux **2.** [suspect] suspect.

suspiciously [sə'spɪʃəslɪ] adv **1.** [distrustfully] avec méfiance, soupçonneusement **2.** [strangely] de façon suspecte.

suss [sʌs] vt UK inf flairer. ◆ **suss out** vt sep UK inf **1.** [device, situation] piger **2.** [person] saisir le caractère de.

sustain [sə'steɪn] vt **1.** [maintain, keep up - conversation] entretenir ; [- effort, attack, pressure] soutenir, maintenir ; [- sb's interest] maintenir **2.** [support physically] soutenir, supporter **3.** [support morally] soutenir **4.** MUS [note] tenir, soutenir **5.** [nourish] nourrir / *a planet capable of sustaining life* une planète capable de maintenir la vie **6.** [suffer - damage] subir ; [- defeat, loss] subir, essuyer ; [- injury] recevoir ; [withstand] supporter **7.** LAW [accept as valid] admettre / *objection sustained* objection admise / *the court sustained her claim* le tribunal lui accorda gain de cause **8.** [corroborate - assertion, theory, charge] corroborer **9.** THEAT [role] tenir.

sustainability [sə,steɪnə'bɪlɪtɪ] n durabilité *f*.

sustainable [səs'teɪnəbl] adj [development, agriculture, politics, housing] durable ▶ **sustainable resources** ressources *fpl* renouvelables.

sustained [sə'steɪnd] adj [effort, attack] soutenu ; [discussion] prolongé.

sustenance ['sʌstɪnəns] n **1.** [nourishment] valeur *f* nutritive **2.** [means of subsistence] subsistance *f*.

suture ['suːtʃər] ◆ n **1.** MED point *m* de suture **2.** ANAT & BOT suture *f*. ◆ vt MED suturer.

SUV (abbr of sport utility vehicle) n AUTO 4 x 4 *m*.

svelte [svelt] adj svelte.

SW 1. (written abbr of **short wave**) OC **2.** (written abbr of **south-west**) S-O.

swab [swɒb] (*pt* & *pp* **swabbed**, *cont* **swabbing**) ◆ n **1.** MED [cotton] tampon *m* ; [specimen] prélèvement *m* **2.** [mop] serpillière *f*. ◆ vt **1.** MED [clean] nettoyer (avec un tampon) **2.** [mop] laver.

swag [swæg] inf n UK [booty] butin *m*.

swagger ['swægər] ◆ vi **1.** [strut] se pavaner **2.** [boast] se vanter, fanfaronner, plastronner. ◆ n [manner] air *m* arrogant ; [walk] démarche *f* arrogante.

Swahili [swɑː'hiːlɪ] ◆ n **1.** LING swahili *m* **2.** [person] Swahili *m*, -e *f*. ◆ adj swahili.

swallow ['swɒləʊ] ◆ vt **1.** [food, drink, medicine] avaler **2.** inf [believe] avaler, croire **3.** [accept unprotestingly] avaler, accepter / *I find it hard to swallow* je trouve ça un peu raide **4.** [repress] ravaler / *he had to swallow his pride* il a dû ravaler sa fierté **5.** [retract] : *to swallow one's words* ravaler ses paroles **6.** [absorb] engloutir. ◆ vi avaler, déglutir. ◆ n **1.** [action] gorgée *f* / *he finished his drink with one swallow* il finit sa boisson d'un trait or d'un seul coup **2.** ORNITH hirondelle *f*. ◆ **swallow up** vt sep engloutir / *the Baltic States were swallowed up by the Soviet Union* les pays Baltes ont été engloutis par l'Union soviétique / *I wished the ground would open and swallow me up* j'aurais voulu être à six pieds sous terre / *they were swallowed up in the crowd* ils ont disparu dans la foule.

swam [swæm] pt ⟶ **swim**.

swamp [swɒmp] ◆ n marais *m*, marécage *m*. ◆ vt **1.** [flood] inonder ; [cause to sink] submerger **2.** [overwhelm] inonder, submerger.

swampy ['swɒmpɪ] adj (*compar* **swampier**, *superl* **swampiest**) adj marécageux.

swan [swɒn] (*pt* & *pp* **swanned**, *cont* **swanning**) ◆ n cygne *m*. ◆ vi UK inf : *they spent a year swanning round Europe* ils ont passé une année à se balader en Europe / *he came swanning into the office at 10:30* il est arrivé au bureau comme si de rien n'était à 10 h 30.

swank [swæŋk] *inf* ◆ vi se vanter, frimer. ◆ n 🇬🇧 **1.** [boasting] frime *f* **2.** [boastful person] frimeur *m*, -euse *f* **3.** 🇺🇸 [luxury] luxe *m*, chic *m*. ◆ adj = **swanky.**

swanky ['swæŋkɪ] (*compar* **swankier,** *superl* **swankiest**) adj *inf* [gen] chic ; [club, school] chic.

swap [swɒp] (*pt & pp* **swapped,** *cont* **swapping**) ◆ vt **1.** [possessions, places] échanger ▶ **to swap sthg for sthg** échanger qqch contre qqch / *I'll swap my coat for yours* or *I'll swap coats with you* échangeons nos manteaux / *they've swapped places* ils ont échangé leurs places **2.** [ideas, opinions] échanger. ◆ vi échanger, faire un échange or un troc. ◆ n **1.** [exchange] troc *m*, échange *m* ▶ **to do a swap** faire un troc or un échange **2.** [duplicate-stamp in collection, etc.] double *m*. ◆ **swap over, swap round** ◆ vt sep échanger, intervertir. ◆ vi : *do you mind swapping over* or *round so I can sit next to Max?* est-ce que ça te dérange qu'on échange nos places pour que je puisse m'asseoir à côté de Max ?

swap meet n 🇺🇸 foire *f* au troc.

SWAPO ['swɑːpəʊ] (*abbr of* **South West Africa People's Organization**) pr n SWAPO *f*.

swarm [swɔːm] ◆ n **1.** [of bees] essaim *m* ; [of ants] colonie *f* **2.** *fig* [of people] essaim *m*, nuée *f*, masse *f*. ◆ vi **1.** ENTOM essaimer **2.** *fig* [place] fourmiller, grouiller / *the streets were swarming with people* les rues grouillaient de monde **3.** *fig* [people] affluer / *the crowd swarmed in / out* la foule s'est engouffrée à l'intérieur / est sortie en masse **4.** [climb] grimper (lestement).

swarthy ['swɔːðɪ] (*compar* **swarthier,** *superl* **swarthiest**) adj basané.

swashbuckling ['swɒʃˌbʌklɪŋ] adj [person] fanfaron ; [film, story] de cape et d'épée.

swastika ['swɒstɪkə] n ANTIQ svastika *m* ; [Nazi] croix *f* gammée.

swat [swɒt] (*pt & pp* **swatted,** *cont* **swatting**) ◆ vt **1.** [insect] écraser **2.** *inf* [slap] frapper. ◆ n **1.** [device] tapette *f* **2.** [swipe] : *he took a swat at the mosquito* il essaya d'écraser le moustique **3.** *inf* = **swot.**

swatch [swɒtʃ] n échantillon *m* de tissu.

swathe [sweɪð] ◆ vt **1.** [bind] envelopper, emmailloter / *his head was swathed in bandages* sa tête était enveloppée de pansements **2.** [envelop] envelopper / *swathed in mist* enveloppé de brume. ◆ n **1.** AGR andain *m* **2.** [strip of land] bande *f* de terre / *the army cut a swathe through the town* l'armée a tout détruit sur son passage dans la ville / *the new motorway cuts a swathe through the countryside* la nouvelle autoroute coupe à travers la campagne **3.** [strip of cloth] lanière *f*.

swatter ['swɒtər] n tapette *f*.

sway [sweɪ] ◆ vi **1.** [pylon, bridge] se balancer, osciller ; [tree] s'agiter ; [bus, train] branler ; [boat] rouler ; [person - deliberately] se balancer ; [- from tiredness, drink] chanceler, tituber ▶ **to sway from side to side / to and fro** se balancer de droite à gauche / d'avant en arrière **2.** [vacillate] vaciller, hésiter ; [incline, tend] pencher. ◆ vt **1.** [pylon] (faire) balancer, faire osciller ; [tree] agiter ; [hips] rouler, balancer **2.** [influence] influencer. ◆ n **1.** [rocking - gen] balancement *m* ; [- of a boat] roulis *m* **2.** [influence] influence *f*, emprise *f*, empire *m* ▶ **to hold sway over sb / sthg** avoir de l'influence or de l'emprise sur qqn / qqch.

Swazi ['swɑːzɪ] n Swazi *mf*.

Swaziland ['swɑːzɪlænd] pr n Swaziland *m* / *in Swaziland* au Swaziland.

swear [sweər] (*pt* **swore** [swɔːr], *pp* **sworn** [swɔːn]) ◆ vi **1.** [curse] jurer ▶ **to swear at sb** injurier qqn **2.** [vow, take an oath] jurer / *I wouldn't swear to it, but I think it was him* je n'en jurerais pas, mais je crois que c'était lui. ◆ vt **1.** [pledge, vow] ▶ **to swear an oath** prêter serment **2.** [make sb pledge] ▶ **to swear sb to secrecy** faire jurer à qqn de garder le secret. ◆ **swear by** vt insep : *she swears by that old sewing machine of hers* elle ne jure que par sa vieille machine à coudre. ◆ **swear in** vt sep [witness, president] faire prêter serment à, assermenter *fml*. ◆ **swear off** vt insep *inf* renoncer à.

swearing ['sweərɪŋ] n [use of swearwords] jurons *mpl*, gros mots *mpl*.

swearing in n : *after the swearing in of the jury* LAW après que le jury eut prêté serment.

swearword ['sweəwɜːd] n grossièreté *f*, juron *m*, gros mot *m*.

sweat [swet] (🇬🇧 *pt & pp* **sweated** ; 🇺🇸 *pt & pp* **sweat** or **sweated**) ◆ n **1.** [perspiration] sueur *f*, transpiration *f* ▶ **to break into** or **to come out in a cold sweat** avoir des sueurs froides **2.** *inf* [unpleasant task] corvée *f* ▶ **no sweat!**: *can you give me a hand? — no sweat!* peux-tu me donner un coup de main ? — pas de problème ! **3.** 🇺🇸 *inf* [anxious state] : *there's no need to get into a sweat about it!* pas la peine de te mettre dans des états pareils ! **4.** [sweatshirt] sweat *m*. ◆ vi **1.** [perspire] suer, transpirer **2.** *fig* [work hard, suffer] suer / *she's sweating over her homework* elle est en train de suer sur ses devoirs **3.** [ooze - walls] suer, suinter ; [- cheese] suer. ◆ vt **1.** [cause to perspire] faire suer or transpirer ; [exude] ▶ **to sweat blood** *fig* suer sang et eau **2.** CULIN faire suer **3.** 🇺🇸 *inf* [extort] : *we sweated the information out of him* on lui a fait cracher le morceau **4.** 🇺🇸 PHR **don't sweat it!** *inf* pas de panique ! ▶ **don't sweat the small stuff** n'angoisse pas sur les détails. ◆ **sweat off** vt sep éliminer. ◆ **sweat out** vt sep **1.** [illness] : *stay in bed and try to sweat out the cold* restez au chaud dans votre lit et votre rhume partira **2.** PHR **leave him to sweat it out** laissez-le se débrouiller tout seul.

sweatband ['swetbænd] n **1.** SPORT [headband] bandeau *m* ; [wristband] poignet *m* **2.** [in a hat] cuir *m* intérieur.

sweater ['swetər] n pull-over *m*, pull *m*.

sweating ['swetɪŋ] n transpiration *f*, sudation *f* *spec*.

sweatpants ['swetpænts] pl n 🇺🇸 pantalon *m* de survêtement.

sweatshirt ['swetʃɜːt] n sweat-shirt *m*.

sweatshop ['swetʃɒp] n ≃ atelier *m* clandestin.

sweat suit n 🇺🇸 survêtement *m*, jogging *m*.

sweaty ['swetɪ] (*compar* **sweatier,** *superl* **sweatiest**) adj **1.** [person] (tout) en sueur ; [hands] moite ; [feet] qui transpire ; [clothing] trempé de sueur **2.** [weather, place] d'une chaleur humide or moite **3.** [activity] qui fait transpirer.

swede [swiːd] n 🇬🇧 rutabaga *m*, chou-navet *m*.

Swede [swiːd] n Suédois *m*, -e *f*.

Sweden ['swiːdn] pr n Suède *f* / *in Sweden* en Suède.

Swedish ['swiːdɪʃ] ◆ pl n ▶ **the Swedish** les Suédois *mpl*. ◆ n LING suédois *m*. ◆ adj suédois.

sweep [swiːp] (*pt & pp* **swept** [swept]) ◆ vt **1.** [with a brush - room, street, dust, leaves] balayer ; [- chimney] ramoner / *I swept the broken glass into the dustpan* j'ai poussé le verre cassé dans la pelle avec le balai **2.** [with hand] : *she swept the coins off the table into her handbag* elle a fait glisser les pièces de la table dans son sac à main **3.** [subj: wind, tide, crowd, etc.] : *the wind swept his hat into the river* le vent a fait tomber son chapeau dans la rivière / *the small boat was swept out to sea* le petit bateau a été emporté vers le large / *three fishermen were swept overboard* un paquet de mer emporta trois pêcheurs / *he was swept to power on a wave of popular discontent* il a été porté au pouvoir par une vague de mécontentement populaire ◗ **to be swept off one's feet (by sb)** **a)** [fall in love] tomber fou amoureux (de qqn) **b)** [be filled with enthusiam] être enthousiasmé (par qqn) **4.** [spread through - subj: fire, epidemic, rumour, belief] gagner **5.** [scan, survey] parcourir **6.** [win easily] gagner or remporter haut la main ◗ **to sweep the board** remporter tous les prix **7.** NAUT [mines, sea, channel] draguer. ◆ vi **1.** [with a brush] balayer **2.** [move quickly, powerfully] : *harsh winds swept across the bleak steppes* un vent violent balayait les mornes steppes / *the Barbarians who swept into the Roman Empire* les Barbares qui déferlèrent sur l'Empire romain / *the fire swept through the forest* l'incendie a ravagé la forêt **3.** [move confidently, proudly] : *he swept into / out of the room* il entra / sortit majestueusement de la pièce **4.** [stretch - land] s'étendre **5.** NAUT ◗ **to sweep for mines** draguer, déminer. ◆ n **1.** [with a brush] coup m de balai **2.** [movement] : *with a sweep of her arm* d'un geste large ◗ **in** or **at one sweep** d'un seul coup **3.** [curved line, area] (grande) courbe f, étendue f **4.** [range] gamme f **5.** [scan, survey] : *her eyes made a sweep of the room* elle parcourut la pièce des yeux **6.** ELECTRON [by electron beam] balayage m **7.** [search] fouille f **8.** [gen,] [MIL - attack] attaque f; [- reconnaissance] reconnaissance f **9.** [chimney sweep] ramoneur m **10.** inf [sweepstake] sweepstake m **11.** AERON flèche f. ❖ **sweep along** vt sep [subj: wind, tide, crowd] emporter, entraîner. ❖ **sweep aside** vt sep **1.** [object, person] écarter **2.** [advice, objection] repousser, rejeter; [obstacle] écarter. ❖ **sweep away** vt sep **1.** [dust, snow] balayer **2.** [subj: wind, tide, crowd] emporter, entraîner. ❖ **sweep by** vi [car] passer à toute vitesse; [person - majestically] passer majestueusement; [- disdainfully] passer dédaigneusement. ❖ **sweep down** vi [steps] descendre. ❖ **sweep past** = **sweep** **by.** ❖ **sweep up** ◆ vt sep [dust, leaves] balayer. ◆ vi balayer.

sweeper ['swi:pər] n **1.** [person] balayeur m, -euse f **2.** [device - for streets] balayeuse f; [- for carpets] balai m mécanique **3.** FOOT libero m.

sweeping ['swi:pɪŋ] adj **1.** [wide - movement, curve] large / *a sweeping view* une vue panoramique **2.** [indiscriminate] ◗ **a sweeping generalization** or **statement** une généralisation excessive **3.** [significant, large - amount] considérable / *sweeping budget cuts* des coupes sombres dans le budget **4.** [far-reaching - measure, change] de grande portée, de grande envergure. ❖ **sweepings** pl n balayures fpl.

sweepstake ['swi:psteɪk] n sweepstake m.

sweet [swi:t] ◆ adj **1.** [tea, coffee, taste] sucré; [fruit, honey] doux (douce), sucré; [wine] moelleux **2.** [fresh, clean - air] doux (douce); [- breath] frais (fraîche); [- water] pur **3.** [fragrant - smell] agréable, suave **4.** [musical - sound, voice] mélodieux; [- words] doux (douce) **5.** [pleasant, satisfactory - emotion, feeling, success] doux (douce) **6.** [kind, generous] gentil / *it was very sweet of you* c'était gentil de votre part **7.** [cute] mignon, adorable **8.** US inf génial **9.** inf [in love] ◗ **to be sweet on sb** UK avoir le béguin pour qqn **10.** inf [as intensifier] : *he'll please his own sweet self* or *he'll go his own sweet way* il n'en fera qu'à sa tête / *she'll come in her own sweet time* elle viendra quand ça lui plaira ◗ **sweet FA** UK v inf rien du tout, que dalle. ◆ n **1.** UK [confectionery] bonbon m **2.** UK [dessert] dessert m **3.** [term of address] ◗ **my sweet** mon chéri m, ma chérie f. ◆ excl US inf génial.

sweet-and-sour adj aigre-doux (aigre-douce) ◗ **sweet-and-sour pork** porc m à la sauce aigre-douce.

sweet chestnut n marron m.

sweet corn n maïs m doux.

sweeten ['swi:tn] vt **1.** [food, drink] sucrer **2.** [mollify, soften] ◗ **to sweeten (up)** amadouer, enjôler **3.** inf [bribe] graisser la patte à **4.** [make more attractive - task] adoucir; [- offer] améliorer **5.** [improve the odour of] parfumer, embaumer.

sweetener ['swi:tnər] n **1.** [for food, drink] édulcorant m, sucrette f ◗ **artificial sweeteners** édulcorants artificiels **2.** UK inf [present] cadeau m; [bribe] pot-de-vin m.

sweetening ['swi:tnɪŋ] n **1.** [substance] édulcorant m, édulcorants mpl **2.** [process - of wine] sucrage m; [- of water] adoucissement m.

sweetheart ['swi:thɑ:t] n **1.** [lover] petit ami m, petite amie f / *they were childhood sweethearts* ils s'aimaient or ils étaient amoureux quand ils étaient enfants **2.** [term of address] (mon) chéri m, (ma) chérie f.

sweetie ['swi:tɪ] n inf **1.** [darling] chéri m, -e f, chou m **2.** UK baby talk [sweet] bonbon m.

sweetly ['swi:tlɪ] adv **1.** [pleasantly, kindly] gentiment; [cutely] d'un air mignon **2.** [smoothly] sans à-coups; [accurately] avec précision **3.** [musically] harmonieusement, mélodieusement.

sweetness ['swi:tnɪs] n **1.** [of food, tea, coffee] goût m sucré; [of wine] (goût m) moelleux m **2.** [freshness - of air] douceur f; [- of breath] fraîcheur f; [- of water] pureté f **3.** [fragrance] parfum m **4.** [musicality - of sound] son m mélodieux; [- of voice, words] douceur f **5.** [pleasure, satisfaction] douceur f **6.** [kindness, generosity] gentillesse f ◗ **to be all sweetness and light** : *she's all sweetness and light* elle est on ne peut plus gentille.

sweet pea n pois m de senteur.

sweet potato n patate f douce.

sweet shop n UK confiserie f.

sweet-smelling adj [rose] odorant; [perfume] sucré.

sweet talk n (U) inf flatteries fpl, paroles fpl mielleuses. ❖ **sweet-talk** vt inf embobiner / *she sweet-talked him into doing it* elle l'a si bien embobiné qu'il a fini par le faire.

sweet-tempered adj doux (douce), agréable.

sweet tooth n ◗ **to have a sweet tooth** adorer les or être friand de sucreries.

swell [swel] (pt **swelled,** pp **swelled** or **swollen** ['swəʊln]) ◆ vi **1.** [distend - wood, pulses, etc.] gonfler; [- part of body] enfler, gonfler **2.** [increase] augmenter **3.** [well up - emotion] monter, surgir **4.** [rise - sea, tide] monter; [- river] se gonfler, grossir **5.** [grow louder] s'enfler. ◆ vt **1.** [distend] gonfler **2.** [increase] augmenter, grossir **3.** [cause to rise] gonfler, grossir. ◆ n **1.** NAUT houle f **2.** [bulge] gonflement m **3.** [increase] augmentation f **4.** MUS crescendo m. ◆ adj US inf & dated [great] super, chouette. ◆ interj US inf & dated super. ❖ **swell up** = **swell** (vi).

swelling ['swelɪŋ] n **1.** MED enflure f, gonflement m **2.** [increase] augmentation f, grossissement m. ◆ adj [increasing] croissant.

sweltering ['sweltərɪŋ] adj [day, heat] étouffant, oppressant.

swept [swept] pt & pp → **sweep.**

swerve [swɜ:v] ◆ vi **1.** [car, driver, ship] faire une embardée; [ball] dévier; [aeroplane, bird, runner] virer **2.** fig [budge, deviate] dévier. ◆ vt **1.** [vehicle] faire virer; [ball] faire dévier **2.** fig [person] détourner, faire dévier. ◆ n [by car, driver, ship] embardée f; [by aeroplane, bird, runner, ball] déviation f.

swift [swɪft] ◆ adj **1.** [fast] rapide **2.** [prompt] prompt, rapide / *swift to react* prompt à réagir. ◆ adv ◗ **swift-flowing** [river, stream] au cours rapide ◗ **swift-moving** rapide. ◆ n ORNITH martinet m.

swiftly ['swɪftlɪ] adv **1.** [quickly] rapidement, vite **2.** [promptly] promptement, rapidement.

swiftness ['swɪftnɪs] n **1.** [speed] rapidité *f*, célérité *f* liter **2.** [promptness] promptitude *f*, rapidité *f*.

swig [swɪg] *inf* ◆ vt (*pt* & *pp* **swigged,** *cont* **swigging**) lamper, siffler. ◆ n lampée *f*, coup *m*. ❖ **swig down** vt sep *inf* vider d'un trait, siffler.

swill [swɪl] ◆ vt **1.** 🇬🇧 [wash] laver à grande eau **2.** *inf* [drink] écluser. ◆ n **1.** [for pigs] pâtée *f* **2.** [wash] ▶ **to give sthg a swill** laver qqch.

swim [swɪm] (*pt* **swam** [swæm], *pp* **swum** [swʌm], *cont* **swimming**) ◆ vi **1.** [fish, animal] nager ; [person -gen] nager ; [-for amusement] nager, se baigner ; [-for sport] nager, faire de la natation ▶ **to go swimming a)** [gen] (aller) se baigner **b)** [in swimming pool] aller à la piscine / *to swim across a river* traverser une rivière à la nage **2.** [be soaked] nager, baigner / *the salad was swimming in oil* la salade baignait dans l'huile **3.** [spin] : *my head is swimming* j'ai la tête qui tourne / *that awful feeling when the room starts to swim* cette impression horrible quand la pièce se met à tourner. ◆ vt **1.** [river, lake, etc.] traverser à la nage **2.** [a stroke] nager **3.** [distance] nager / *she swam ten lengths* elle a fait dix longueurs **4.** [animal] : *they swam their horses across the river* ils ont fait traverser la rivière à leurs chevaux (à la nage). ◆ n ▶ **to go for a swim a)** [gen] (aller) se baigner **b)** [in swimming pool] aller à la piscine.

SWIM MESSAGING written abbr of **see what I mean.**

swimmer ['swɪmə'] n [one who swims] nageur *m*, -euse *f* ; [bather] baigneur *m*, -euse *f*.

swimming ['swɪmɪŋ] ◆ n [gen] nage *f* ; SPORT natation *f*. ◆ comp [lesson, classes] de natation.

swimming bath, swimming baths n 🇬🇧 piscine *f*.

swimming cap n bonnet *m* de bain.

swimming costume n 🇬🇧 maillot *m* de bain.

swimmingly ['swɪmɪŋlɪ] adv 🇬🇧 *inf* à merveille / *everything's going swimmingly* tout marche comme sur des roulettes.

swimming pool n piscine *f*.

swimming trunks pl n maillot *m* or slip *m* de bain.

swimsuit ['swɪmsuːt] n maillot *m* de bain.

swimwear ['swɪmweə'] n (U) maillots *mpl* de bain.

swindle ['swɪndl] ◆ vt escroquer / *they were swindled out of all their savings* on leur a escroqué toutes leurs économies. ◆ n escroquerie *f*, vol *m*.

swine [swaɪn] (*pl* **swine** or **swines**) n **1.** (*pl* **swine**) liter [pig] porc *m*, pourceau *m* liter **2.** *inf* [unpleasant person] fumier *m*, ordure *f*.

swing [swɪŋ] (*pt* & *pp* **swung** [swʌŋ]) ◆ vi **1.** [sway, move to and fro -gen] se balancer ; [-pendulum] osciller ; [hang, be suspended] pendre, être suspendu **2.** [move from one place to another] : *to swing from tree to tree* se balancer d'arbre en arbre / *to swing into action* fig passer à l'action **3.** [make a turn] virer / *the lorry swung through the gate* le camion vira pour franchir le portail / *the door swung open* / *shut* la porte s'est ouverte / s'est refermée **4.** fig [change direction] virer **5.** *inf* [be hanged] être pendu **6.** [hit out, aim a blow] essayer de frapper **7.** *inf* [musician] swinguer ; [music] swinguer, avoir du swing **8.** *inf* & *dated* [be modern, fashionable] être dans le vent or in **9.** *inf* [be lively] chauffer **10.** *inf* [try hard] : *I'm in there swinging for you* je fais tout ce que je peux pour toi. ◆ vt **1.** [cause to sway] balancer **2.** [move from one place to another] : *she swung her bag onto the back seat* elle jeta son sac sur le siège arrière / *he swung a rope over a branch* il lança une corde par-dessus une branche / *I swung myself (up) into the saddle* je me suis hissé sur la selle, j'ai sauté en selle **3.** [turn -steering wheel] (faire) tourner ; [-vehicle] faire

virer **4.** [aim] : *she swung the bat at the ball* elle essaya de frapper la balle avec sa batte **5.** *inf* [manage, pull off] ▶ **to swing sthg** réussir or arriver à faire qqch **6.** 🇵🇭🇷 **to swing it** *inf* avoir le swing ▶ **to swing the lead** *inf* tirer au flanc. ◆ n **1.** [to-and-fro movement, sway -gen] balancement *m* ; [-of pendulum] oscillation *f* / *with a swing of his arm* en balançant son bras **2.** [arc described] arc *m*, courbe *f* **3.** [swipe, attempt to hit] (grand) coup *m* / *I took a swing at him* je lui ai décoché un coup de poing / *he took a swing at the ball* il donna un coup pour frapper la balle **4.** [hanging seat] balançoire *f* **5.** [change, shift] changement *m* / *his mood swings are very unpredictable* ses sautes d'humeur sont très imprévisibles ; POL revirement *m* **6.** [in boxing, golf] swing *m* **7.** [rhythm -gen] rythme *m* ; [jazz rhythm, style of jazz] swing *m* ▶ **a swing band** un orchestre de swing **8.** 🇺🇸 POL [tour] tournée *f* **9.** 🇵🇭🇷 **to get into the swing of things** *inf* : *I'm beginning to get into the swing of things* je commence à être dans le bain ▶ **to go with a swing a)** *inf* [music] être très rythmé or entraînant **b)** [party] swinguer **c)** [business] marcher très bien. ❖ **in full swing** adj phr : *the party was in full swing* la fête battait son plein. ❖ **swing round** ◆ vt sep [vehicle] faire virer ; [person] faire tourner. ◆ vi [turn round -person] se retourner, pivoter ; [-crane] tourner, pivoter. ❖ **swing to** vi [door, gate] se refermer.

swing bridge n pont *m* tournant.

swing door 🇬🇧, **swinging door** 🇺🇸 n porte *f* battante.

swingeing ['swɪndʒɪŋ] adj 🇬🇧 [increase, drop] énorme ; [cuts] draconien ; [blow] violent ; [criticism, condemnation] sévère ; [victory, defeat] écrasant.

swinging ['swɪŋɪŋ] adj **1.** [swaying] balançant ; [pivoting] tournant, pivotant **2.** [rhythmic -gen] rythmé, cadencé ; [-jazz, jazz musician] qu i swingue **3.** *inf* & *dated* [trendy] in ▶ **the swinging sixties** les folles années soixante.

swing vote n vote *m* décisif.

swing voter n électeur *m* indécis, électrice *f* indécise.

swipe [swaɪp] ◆ vi ▶ **to swipe at** : *he swiped at the fly with his newspaper* il donna un grand coup de journal pour frapper la mouche. ◆ vt **1.** [hit] donner un coup à **2.** *inf* [steal] piquer, faucher **3.** [credit card] passer. ◆ n (grand) coup *m* ▶ **to take a swipe at sthg a)** *lit* donner un grand coup pour frapper qqch **b)** fig [criticize] tirer à boulets rouges sur qqch.

swipe card n carte *f* magnétique.

swirl [swɜːl] ◆ vi tourbillonner, tournoyer. ◆ vt faire tourbillonner or tournoyer. ◆ n tourbillon *m*.

swish [swɪʃ] ◆ vi [whip] siffler ; [leaves, wind] chuinter, bruire liter ; [fabric, skirt] froufrouter ; [water] murmurer. ◆ vt : *the horse swished its tail* le cheval donna un coup de queue. ◆ n **1.** [sound -of fabric, skirt] froufroutement *m*, froissement *m* ; [-of leaves, wind] bruissement *m* ; [-of water] murmure *m* **2.** [movement] : *the cow flicked the flies away with a swish of its tail* la vache chassa les mouches d'un coup de queue. ◆ adj 🇬🇧 *inf* [smart] chic.

Swiss [swɪs] (*pl* **Swiss**) ◆ n Suisse *m*, Suissesse *f* ▶ **the Swiss** les Suisses *mpl*. ◆ adj [gen] suisse ; [confederation, government] helvétique ▶ **Swiss bank account** compte *m* en Suisse.

Swiss cheese n emmental *m*.

swiss roll n (gâteau *m*) roulé *m*.

switch [swɪtʃ] ◆ n **1.** ELEC [for light] interrupteur *m* ; [on radio, television] bouton *m* ; TECH & TELEC commutateur *m* / *is the switch on* / *off?* est-ce que c'est allumé / éteint ? ▶ **to flick** or **to throw a switch** actionner un commutateur **2.** [change -gen] changement *m* ; [-of opinion, attitude] changement *m*, revirement *m* **3.** [swap, trade] échange *m* **4.** 🇺🇸 RAIL ▶ **switches** [points] aiguillage *m* **5.** [stick] baguette *f*, badine *f*; [riding crop] cravache *f* **6.** [hairpiece] postiche *m* **7.** ZOOL [hair on tail] fouet *m* de la queue **8.** COMPUT paramètre *m*. ◆ vt **1.** [change, exchange] changer de / *to switch places with sb* échanger sa place avec qqn **2.** [transfer - allegiance, attention] transférer; [divert - conversation] orienter, détourner **3.** ELEC, RADIO & TV [circuit] commuter / *to switch channels / frequencies* changer de chaîne / de fréquence **4.** 🇺🇸 RAIL aiguiller. ◆ vi changer. ◆ **switch around** = **switch round.** ◆ **switch off** ◆ vt sep [light] éteindre; [electrical appliance] éteindre, arrêter / *to switch off the engine* AUTO couper le contact, arrêter le moteur. ◆ vi **1.** [go off - light] s'éteindre; [- electrical appliance] s'éteindre, s'arrêter **2.** [TV viewer, radio listener] éteindre le poste **3.** *inf* [stop paying attention] décrocher. ◆ **switch on** ◆ vt sep **1.** ELEC [light, heating, oven, TV, radio] allumer; [engine, washing machine, vacuum cleaner] mettre en marche / *the power isn't switched on* il n'y a pas de courant / *to switch on the ignition* AUTO mettre le contact **2.** *fig & pej* ▶ **to switch on the charm / tears** sourire / pleurer sur commande. ◆ vi **1.** ELEC [light, heating, oven, TV, radio] s'allumer; [engine, washing machine, vacuum cleaner] se mettre en marche **2.** [TV viewer, radio listener] allumer le poste. ◆ **switch over** vi **1.** = **switch** *(vi)* **2.** TV changer de chaîne; RADIO changer de station. ◆ **switch round** ◆ vt sep changer de place, déplacer / *he switched the glasses round when she wasn't looking* il échangea les verres pendant qu'elle ne regardait pas / *the manager has switched the team round again* l'entraîneur a encore changé l'équipe. ◆ vi [two people] changer de place.

switchblade ['swɪtʃbleɪd] n 🇺🇸 (couteau *m* à) cran d'arrêt *m*.

switchboard ['swɪtʃbɔːd] n **1.** TELEC standard *m* **2.** ELEC tableau *m*.

switchboard operator n standardiste *mf*.

switched-on [ˌswɪtʃt-] adj 🇺🇰 *inf & dated* [fashionable] dans le vent, in.

switch-hitter n 🇺🇸 **1.** SPORT batteur *m* ambidextre **2.** *v inf* [bisexual] bi *mf*.

Switzerland ['swɪtsələnd] pr n Suisse *f* / *in Switzerland* en Suisse ▶ **French- / Italian-speaking Switzerland** la Suisse romande / italienne ▶ **German-speaking Switzerland** la Suisse allemande or alémanique.

swivel ['swɪvl] (🇺🇰 *pt & pp* **swivelled**, *cont* **swivelling** ; 🇺🇸 *pt & pp* **swiveled**, *cont* **swiveling**) ◆ n [gen] pivot *m* ; [for gun] tourillon *m*. ◆ comp [lamp, joint, etc.] pivotant, tournant. ◆ vi ▶ **to swivel (round)** pivoter, tourner. ◆ vt ▶ **to swivel (round)** [chair, wheel, etc.] faire pivoter.

swivel chair n chaise *f* pivotante; [with arms] fauteuil *m* pivotant.

swollen ['swəʊln] ◆ pp ⟶ **swell.** ◆ adj **1.** [part of body] enflé, gonflé **2.** [sails] bombé, gonflé; [lake, river] en crue.

swoon [swuːn] ◆ vi **1.** [become ecstatic] se pâmer, tomber en pâmoison **2.** *dated* [faint] s'évanouir, se pâmer *liter*. ◆ n pâmoison *f*.

swoop [swuːp] ◆ vi **1.** [dive - bird] s'abattre, fondre; [- aircraft] descendre en piqué **2.** [make a raid - police, troops, etc.] faire une descente. ◆ n **1.** [dive - by bird, aircraft] descente *f* en piqué **2.** [raid - by police, troops, etc.] descente *f* **3.** PHR **in one fell swoop** d'un seul coup.

swop [swɒp] (*pt & pp* **swopped**, *cont* **swopping**) = **swap.**

sword [sɔːd] ◆ n épée *f*. ◆ comp [blow, handle, wound] d'épée.

swordfish ['sɔːdfɪʃ] (*pl* **swordfish** or **swordfishes**) n espadon *m*.

swordsman ['sɔːdzmən] (*pl* **swordsmen** [-mən]) n épéiste *m*, lame *f (personne)*.

swore [swɔːr] pt ⟶ **swear.**

sworn [swɔːn] ◆ pp ⟶ **swear.** ◆ adj **1.** LAW [declaration] fait sous serment; [evidence] donné sous serment **2.** [committed - enemy] juré; [- friend] indéfectible.

swot [swɒt] (*pt & pp* **swotted**, *cont* **swotting**) 🇺🇰 *inf* ◆ vi bûcher, potasser. ◆ n *pej* bûcheur *m*, -euse *f*. ◆ **swot up** 🇺🇰 *inf* ◆ vi bûcher, potasser ▶ **to swot up on sthg** bûcher or potasser qqch. ◆ vt sep bûcher, potasser.

SWOT [swɒt] (abbr of **strengths, weaknesses, opportunities and threats**) n ▶ **SWOT analysis** analyse *f* SWOT.

swum [swʌm] pp ⟶ **swim.**

swung [swʌŋ] pt & pp ⟶ **swing.**

sycamore ['sɪkəmɔːr] n **1.** 🇺🇰 sycomore *m*, faux platane *m* **2.** 🇺🇸 platane *m*.

sycophant ['sɪkəfænt] n flagorneur *m*, -euse *f*.

sycophantic [ˌsɪkəˈfæntɪk] adj [person] flatteur, flagorneur; [behaviour] de flagorneur; [approval, praise] obséquieux.

Sydney ['sɪdnɪ] pr n Sydney.

syllable ['sɪləbl] n syllabe *f*.

syllabub ['sɪləbʌb] n 🇺🇰 [dessert] (crème *f*) sabayon *m*.

syllabus ['sɪləbəs] (*pl* **syllabuses** or **syllabi** ['sɪləbaɪ]) n SCH & UNIV programme *m* (d'enseignement).

symbiosis [ˌsɪmbaɪˈəʊsɪs] n *lit & fig* symbiose *f* / *in symbiosis* en symbiose.

symbiotic [ˌsɪmbaɪˈɒtɪk] adj *lit & fig* symbiotique.

symbol ['sɪmbl] n symbole *m*.

symbolic [sɪmˈbɒlɪk] adj symbolique.

symbolically [sɪmˈbɒlɪklɪ] adv symboliquement.

symbolism ['sɪmbəlɪzm] n symbolisme *m*.

symbolize, symbolise ['sɪmbəlaɪz] vt symboliser.

symmetrical [sɪˈmetrɪkl] adj symétrique.

symmetrically [sɪˈmetrɪklɪ] adv symétriquement.

symmetry ['sɪmətrɪ] n symétrie *f*.

sympathetic [ˌsɪmpəˈθetɪk] adj **1.** [compassionate] compatissant **2.** [well-disposed] bien disposé; [understanding] compréhensif **3.** [congenial, likeable] sympathique, agréable **4.** ANAT sympathique **5.** MUS ▶ **sympathetic string** corde *f* qui vibre par résonance.

⚠ If you say someone is **sympathique**, it means you think they are nice, not sympathetic.

sympathetically [ˌsɪmpəˈθetɪklɪ] adv **1.** [compassionately] avec compassion **2.** [with approval] avec bienveillance **3.** ANAT par sympathie.

sympathize, sympathise ['sɪmpəθaɪz] vi **1.** [feel compassion] compatir **2.** [feel understanding] : *he could not sympathize with their feelings* il ne pouvait pas comprendre leurs sentiments / *we understand and sympathize with their point of view* nous comprenons et partageons leur point de vue **3.** [favour, support] soutenir.

⚠ **Sympathiser avec quelqu'un** usually means to get on with someone, not to sympathize with them.

sympathizer, sympathiser ['sɪmpəθaɪzə'] n **1.** [comforter] : *she received many cards from sympathizers after her husband's death* elle a reçu de nombreuses cartes de condoléances après la mort de son mari **2.** [supporter] sympathisant *m*, -e *f*.

sympathy ['sɪmpəθɪ] (*pl* **sympathies**) n **1.** [compassion] compassion *f* ▶ **to have** or **to feel sympathy for sb** éprouver de la compassion envers qqn **2.** [approval, support] soutien *m* ▶ **to come out in sympathy (with sb)** faire grève par solidarité (avec qqn) **3.** [affinity] sympathie *f*.

⚠ **Sympathie** expresses liking, not sympathy, and avoir de la sympathie pour means to like, not to have sympathy for.

symphonic [sɪm'fɒnɪk] adj symphonique.

symphony ['sɪmfənɪ] (*pl* **symphonies**) ◆ n symphonie *f*. ◆ comp [concert, orchestra] symphonique.

symposium [sɪm'pəʊzjəm] (*pl* **symposiums** or **symposia** [-zjə]) n symposium *m*, colloque *m*.

symptom ['sɪmptəm] n MED & *fig* symptôme *m*.

symptomatic [,sɪmptə'mætɪk] adj MED & *fig* symptomatique.

synagogue ['sɪnəgɒg] n synagogue *f*.

sync(h) [sɪŋk] *inf* ◆ n **(abbr of synchronization)** synchronisation *f* ▶ **to be in / out of synch** être / ne pas être synchro. ◆ vt **abbr of synchronize**.

synchromesh ['sɪŋkrəʊmeʃ] ◆ adj ▶ **synchromesh gearbox** boîte *f* de vitesses avec synchroniseur. ◆ n synchroniseur *m*.

synchronization, synchronisation [,sɪŋkrənaɪ'zeɪʃn] n synchronisation *f*.

synchronize, synchronise ['sɪŋkrənaɪz] ◆ vt synchroniser. ◆ vi être synchronisé.

synchronized swimming ['sɪŋkrənɪzd-] n natation *f* synchronisée.

syncopate ['sɪŋkəpeɪt] vt syncoper ▶ **syncopated rhythm** rythme *m* syncopé.

syncopation [,sɪŋkə'peɪʃn] n MUS syncope *f*.

syndicate ◆ n ['sɪndɪkət] **1.** COMM & FIN groupement *m*, syndicat *m* **2.** [of organized crime] association *f* ▶ **crime syndicates** associations de grand banditisme **3.** PRESS agence *f* de presse *(qui vend des articles, des photos, etc., à plusieurs journaux pour publication simultanée).* ◆ vt ['sɪndɪkeɪt] **1.** COMM & FIN [loan] syndiquer **2.** PRESS publier simultanément dans plusieurs journaux ; US RADIO vendre à plusieurs stations ; US TV vendre à plusieurs chaînes. ◆ vi [form a syndicate] former un groupement or syndicat.

syndication [,sɪndɪ'keɪʃn] n **1.** PRESS [of article] publication *f* simultanée dans plusieurs journaux **2.** RADIO & TV syndication *f*.

syndication agency n PRESS agence *f* de presse.

syndrome ['sɪndrəʊm] n syndrome *m*.

synergy ['sɪnədʒɪ] (*pl* **synergies**) n synergie *f*.

synod ['sɪnəd] n synode *m*.

synonym ['sɪnənɪm] n synonyme *m*.

synonymous [sɪ'nɒnɪməs] adj *lit* & *fig* synonyme.

synopsis [sɪ'nɒpsɪs] (*pl* **synopses** [-siːz]) n [gen] résumé *m* ; [of a film] synopsis *m*.

syntax ['sɪntæks] n syntaxe *f*.

synthesis ['sɪnθəsɪs] (*pl* **syntheses** [-siːz]) n synthèse *f*.

synthesize, synthesise ['sɪnθəsaɪz] vt **1.** BIOL & CHEM [produce by synthesis] synthétiser **2.** [amalgamate, fuse] synthétiser **3.** MUS synthétiser.

synthesizer ['sɪnθəsaɪzə'] n synthétiseur *m* ▶ **voice synthesizer** synthétiseur *m* de voix.

synthetic [sɪn'θetɪk] ◆ adj **1.** [artificial, electronically produced] synthétique **2.** *fig* & *pej* [food] qui a un goût chimique **3.** LING synthétique **4.** PHILOS [reasoning, proposition] synthétique. ◆ n produit *m* synthétique. ◆ **synthetics** pl n fibres *fpl* synthétiques.

synthetically [sɪn'θetɪklɪ] adv synthétiquement.

syphilis ['sɪfɪlɪs] n (*U*) syphilis *f*.

syphon ['saɪfn] = **siphon**.

Syria ['sɪrɪə] pr n Syrie *f* / *in Syria* en Syrie.

Syrian ['sɪrɪən] ◆ n Syrien *m*, -enne *f*. ◆ adj syrien ▶ **the Syrian Desert** le désert de Syrie.

syringe [sɪ'rɪndʒ] ◆ n seringue *f*. ◆ vt seringuer.

syrup ['sɪrəp] n **1.** [sweetened liquid] sirop *m* ▶ **syrup of figs** sirop de figues **2.** [treacle] mélasse *f* **3.** MED sirop *m*.

SYS MESSAGING written abbr of **see you soon**.

system ['sɪstəm] n **1.** [organization, structure] système *m* **2.** [method] système *m* **3.** ANAT système *m* **4.** [orderliness] méthode *f* **5.** [human body] organisme *m* ; *fig* ▶ **to get sthg out of one's system** se débarrasser de qqch **6.** [equipment, device, devices] : *the electrical system needs to be replaced* l'installation électrique a besoin d'être remplacée / *a fault in the cooling system* un défaut dans le circuit de refroidissement **7.** [network] réseau *m* **8.** COMPUT système *m* ▶ **system failure** panne *f* du système ▶ **system requirements** matériel *m* requis **9.** [established order] ▶ **the system** le système **10.** GEOL système *m*.

systematic [,sɪstə'mætɪk] adj systématique.

systematically [,sɪstə'mætɪklɪ] adv systématiquement.

systematize, systematise ['sɪstəmətaɪz] vt systématiser.

system error n COMPUT erreur *f* système.

systemic [sɪs'temɪk] adj systémique.

systems analysis ['sɪstəmz-] n analyse *f* fonctionnelle.

systems analyst ['sɪstəmz-] n analyste *m* fonctionnel, analyste *f* fonctionnelle.

systems disk n COMPUT disque *m* système.

systems engineer ['sɪstəmz-] n ingénieur *m* système, ingénieure système.

t (*pl* **t's** *or* **ts**), **T** (*pl* **T's** *or* **Ts**) [tiː] n [letter] t *m*, T *m* / T *for Tommy* ≃ T comme Thérèse ▸ **to a T** parfaitement, à merveille. **See also** f.

T+ MESSAGING written abbr of **think positive**.

ta [tɑː] interj **UK** *inf* merci.

TA n *abbr of* Territorial Army.

tab [tæb] n **1.** [on garment - flap] patte *f*; [- loop] attache *f*; [over ear] oreillette *f*; [on shoelaces] ferret *m* **2.** [tag - on clothing, luggage] étiquette *f*; [- on file, dictionary] onglet *m*; *fig* ▸ **to keep tabs on sb** avoir qqn à l'œil, avoir l'œil sur qqn **3.** **US** [bill] addition *f*, note *f* ▸ **to pick up the tab** **a)** *lit* payer (la note) **b)** *fig* payer l'addition **4.** AERON compensateur *m* automatique à ressort.

Tabasco® [təˈbæskəʊ] n Tabasco® *m*.

tabbouleh [təˈbuːlɪ] n *(U)* taboulé *m*.

tabby [ˈtæbɪ] (*pl* **tabbies**) ◆ n ▸ **tabby (cat)** chat *m* tigré, chatte *f* tigrée. ◆ adj tigré.

tabernacle [ˈtæbənækl] n **1.** BIBLE & RELIG tabernacle *m* **2.** [place of worship] temple *m*.

tab key n touche *f* de tabulation.

table [ˈteɪbl] ◆ n **1.** [furniture] table *f* **2.** [for meals] table *f* **2.** [people seated] table *f*, tablée *f* **3.** *fml* [food] : *she keeps an excellent table* elle tient une excellente table **4.** TECH [of machine] table *f*; MUS [of violin] table *f* d'harmonie **5.** [list] liste *f*; [chart] table *f*, tableau *m*; [of fares, prices] tableau *m*, barème *m*; SPORT classement *m*; SCH ▸ **(multiplication) table** table *f* (de multiplication) ▸ **table of contents** table *f* des matières **6.** [slab - of stone, marble] plaque *f* **7.** GEOG plateau *m* **8.** ANAT [of cranium] table *f* **9.** **PHR** ▸ **to put** *or* **to lay sthg on the table** mettre qqch sur la table ▸ **under the table** [drunk]: *to be under the table* rouler sous la table, être ivre mort. ◆ vt **1.** **UK** [submit - bill, motion] présenter **2.** **US** [postpone] ajourner, reporter **3.** [tabulate] présenter sous forme de tableau; [classify] classifier **4.** [schedule] prévoir, fixer.

tableau [ˈtæbləʊ] (*pl* **tableaus** *or* **tableaux** [- bləʊz]) n tableau *m*.

tablecloth [ˈteɪblklɒθ] n nappe *f*.

table dancer n danseuse *f* de bar.

table d'hôte [ˌtɑːblˈdəʊt] n ▸ **the table d'hôte** le menu à prix fixe.

table lamp n lampe *f* (de table).

table licence n **UK** *licence autorisant un restaurant à vendre des boissons alcoolisées uniquement avec les repas.*

table manners pl n manière *f* de se tenir à table.

tablemat [ˈteɪblmæt] n set *m* de table.

table salt n sel *m* de table, sel *m* fin.

tablespoon [ˈteɪblspuːn] n [for serving] grande cuillère *f*, cuillère *f* à soupe; [as measure] grande cuillerée *f*, cuillerée *f* à soupe.

tablespoonful [ˈteɪblˌspuːnfʊl] n grande cuillerée *f*, cuillerée *f* à soupe.

tablet [ˈtæblɪt] n **1.** [for writing - stone, wax, etc.] tablette *f*; [- pad] bloc-notes *m* **2.** [pill] comprimé *m*, cachet *m* **3.** [of chocolate] tablette *f*; [of soap] savonnette *f* **4.** [plaque] plaque *f* (commémorative) **5.** COMPUT tablette *f*.

table tennis n tennis *m* de table, ping-pong *m*.

tableware [ˈteɪblweəʳ] n vaisselle *f*.

table wine n vin *m* de table.

tabloid [ˈtæblɔɪd] ◆ n ▸ **tabloid (newspaper)** tabloïd(e) *m*. ◆ adj ▸ **the tabloid press** la presse à sensation.

taboo [təˈbuː] ◆ adj [subject, word] tabou. ◆ n tabou *m*. ◆ vt proscrire, interdire.

tabulate [ˈtæbjʊleɪt] vt [in table form] mettre sous forme de table *or* tableau; [in columns] mettre en colonnes.

tachograph [ˈtækəɡrɑːf] n tachygraphe *m*.

tachometer [tæˈkɒmɪtəʳ] n tachymètre *m*.

tacit [ˈtæsɪt] adj tacite, implicite.

tacitly [ˈtæsɪtlɪ] adv tacitement.

taciturn [ˈtæsɪtɜːn] adj taciturne, qui parle peu.

tack [tæk] ◆ n **1.** [nail] pointe *f*; [for carpeting, upholstery] semence *f* ▸ **tack, thumb-tack** punaise *f* **2.** **US** SEW point *m* de bâti **3.** NAUT [course] bordée *f*, bord *m* **4.** *inf* [food] bouffe *f* **5.** *inf* [tacky things] trucs *mpl* ringards **6.** [harness] sellerie *f*. ◆ vt **1.** [carpet] clouer **2.** **UK** SEW faufiler, bâtir. ◆ vi NAUT faire *or* courir *or* tirer une bordée, louvoyer. ◆ **tack down** vt sep **1.** [carpet, board] clouer **2.** SEW maintenir en place au point de bâti. ◆ **tack on** vt sep **1.** [with nails] fixer avec des clous **2.** SEW bâtir **3.** *fig* ajouter, rajouter. ◆ **tack up** vt sep [note, poster] fixer au mur *(avec une punaise)*.

tackle [ˈtækl] ◆ vt **1.** SPORT tacler; *fig* [assailant, bank robber] saisir, empoigner **2.** [task, problem] s'attaquer à; [question, subject] s'attaquer à, aborder; [confront] interroger. ◆ vi SPORT tacler. ◆ n **1.** [equipment] attirail *m*, matériel *m* ▸ **fishing tackle** matériel *m* *or* articles *mpl* de pêche **2.** [ropes and pulleys] appareil *m* *or* appareils *mpl* de levage; [hoist] palan *m* **3.** SPORT [gen] tacle *m* **4.** [in American football - player] plaqueur *m* **5.** NAUT [rigging] gréement *m* **6.** **UK** *inf* [genitals] bijoux *mpl* de famille.

tackling [ˈtæklɪŋ] n **1.** SPORT tacle *m* **2.** [of problem, job] manière *f* d'aborder.

tacky [ˈtækɪ] (*compar* **tackier**, *superl* **tackiest**) adj **1.** [sticky] collant, poisseux; [of paint] pas encore sec **2.** *inf* [shoddy] minable, moche **3.** *inf* [vulgar] de mauvais goût, vulgaire; **US** [person] beauf, vulgaire.

taco ['tækəʊ] (pl **tacos**) n taco m (crêpe mexicaine farcie).

tact [tækt] n tact m, diplomatie f, doigté m.

tactful ['tæktful] adj [person] plein de tact, qui fait preuve de tact ; [remark, suggestion] plein de tact ; [inquiry] discret (discrète) ; [behaviour] qui fait preuve de tact or de délicatesse.

tactfully ['tæktfulı] adv avec tact or délicatesse.

tactic ['tæktık] n tactique f ; MIL tactique f.

tactical ['tæktıkl] adj **1.** MIL tactique **2.** [shrewd] adroit ▶ **tactical voter** personne qui fait un vote utile.

tactically ['tæktıklı] adv du point de vue tactique ▶ **to vote tactically** voter utile.

tactician [tæk'tıʃn] n tacticien m, -enne f.

tactics ['tæktıks] n (U) MIL & SPORT tactique f.

tactile ['tæktaıl] adj tactile.

tactless ['tæktlıs] adj [person] dépourvu de tact, qui manque de doigté ; [answer] indiscret (indiscrète), peu diplomatique.

tactlessly ['tæktlıslı] adv sans tact.

tad [tæd] n inf [small bit] ▶ **a tad** un peu.

tadpole ['tædpəʊl] n ZOOL têtard m.

Tadzhikistan [tɑː,dʒɪkɪ'stɑːn] pr n Tadjikistan m ▶ **in Tadzhikistan** au Tadjikistan.

taffeta ['tæfɪtə] ◆ n taffetas m. ◆ adj [dress] en taffetas.

taffy ['tæfı] (pl **taffies**) n ⓤⓈ bonbon m au caramel.

Taffy ['tæfı] (pl **Taffies**) n inf nom péjoratif ou humoristique désignant un Gallois.

TAFN MESSAGING written abbr of **that's all for now.**

tag [tæg] (pt & pp **tagged**, cont **tagging**) ◆ n **1.** [label - on clothes, suitcase] étiquette f ; [- on file] onglet m ▶ **(price) tag** étiquette f de prix ▶ **(name) tag** a) [gen] étiquette f (où est marqué le nom) b) [for dog, soldier] plaque f d'identité **2.** [on shoelace] ferret m **3.** [on jacket, coat - for hanging] patte f **4.** [graffiti] tag m **5.** ⓤⓈ [licence plate] plaque f minéralogique **6.** [quotation] citation f ; [cliché] cliché m, lieu m commun ; [catchword] slogan m **7.** GRAM ▶ **tag (question)** question-tag f **8.** GAMES chat m **9.** COMPUT balise f. ◆ vt **1.** [label - package, article, garment] étiqueter ; [- animal] marquer ; [- file] mettre un onglet à ; [- criminal] pincer, épingler ; fig [person] étiqueter **2.** ⓤⓈ [follow] suivre ; [subj: detective] filer **3.** [leave graffiti on] faire des graffitis sur **4.** COMPUT [text] baliser. ◆ **tag along** vi suivre ▶ **to tag along with sb** a) [follow] suivre qqn b) [accompany] aller or venir avec qqn. ◆ **tag on** ◆ vt sep ajouter. ◆ vi inf ▶ **to tag on to sb** suivre qqn partout ▶ **to tag on behind sb** traîner derrière qqn.

Tagus ['teɪgəs] pr n ▶ **the Tagus** le Tage.

Tahiti [tɑː'hiːtı] pr n Tahiti ▶ **in Tahiti** à Tahiti.

Tahitian [tɑː'hiːʃn] ◆ n Tahitien m, -enne f. ◆ adj tahitien.

tail [teɪl] ◆ n **1.** [of animal] queue f ▶ **the detective was still on his tail** le détective le filait toujours ; inf [of vehicle] : **the car was right on my tail** la voiture me collait au derrière or aux fesses **2.** [of kite, comet, aircraft] queue f ; [of musical note] queue f **3.** [of coat] basque f ; [of dress] traîne f ; [of shirt] pan m **4.** [end - of storm] queue f ; [- of procession] fin f, queue f ; [- of queue] bout m **5.** inf [follower - police officer, detective] personne qui file ▶ **to put a tail on sb** faire filer qqn **6.** ⓤⓈ inf [bottom] fesses fpl. ◆ vt **1.** inf [follow] suivre, filer **2.** [animal] couper la queue à. ◆ **tails** ◆ pl n inf [tailcoat] queue f de pie. ◆ adv [of coin] : **it's tails!** (c'est) pile ! ◆ **tail along** vi suivre. ◆ **tail away** vi [sound] s'affaiblir, décroître ; [interest] diminuer petit à petit ; [book] se terminer en queue de poisson ; [competitors in race] s'espacer. ◆ **tail back**

vi [traffic] être arrêté, former un bouchon ; [demonstration, runners] s'égrener, s'espacer. ◆ **tail off** vi [quality] baisser ; [numbers] diminuer, baisser ; [voice] devenir inaudible ; [story] se terminer en queue de poisson.

tailback ['teɪlbæk] n bouchon m (de circulation).

tailcoat [,teɪl'kəʊt] n queue f de pie.

tail end n [of storm] fin f ; [of cloth] bout m ; [of procession] queue f, fin f ; [of story] chute f.

tailfin ['teɪlfın] n **1.** [fish] nageoire f caudale **2.** NAUT dérive f.

tailgate ['teɪlgeɪt] ◆ n AUTO hayon m. ◆ vt coller au pare-chocs de.

tailgate party n ⓤⓈ pique-nique m (où le hayon du véhicule sert de table ou de desserte).

tail lamp, taillight ['teɪllaıt] n feu m arrière.

tailor ['teɪlə] ◆ n tailleur m. ◆ vt [garment] faire sur mesure ; [equipment] adapter à un besoin particulier, concevoir en fonction d'un usage particulier.

tailored ['teɪləd] adj [clothes, equipment] (fait) sur mesure ; [skirt] ajusté.

tailor-made adj [specially made - clothes, equipment] (fait) sur mesure ; [very suitable] (comme) fait exprès.

tail pipe n ⓤⓈ tuyau m d'échappement.

tailplane ['teɪlpleɪn] n AERON stabilisateur m.

tailspin ['teɪlspın] n vrille f ▶ **to be in a tailspin** a) AERON vriller b) fig être en dégringolade.

tailwind ['teɪlwınd] n vent m arrière.

taint [teɪnt] ◆ vt **1.** [minds, morals] corrompre, souiller ; [person] salir la réputation de ; [reputation] salir **2.** [food] gâter ; [air] polluer, vicier ; [water] polluer, infecter. ◆ n **1.** [infection] infection f ; [contamination] contamination f ; [decay] décomposition f **2.** fig [of sin, corruption] tache f, souillure f.

tainted ['teıntıd] adj **1.** [morals] corrompu, dépravé ; [reputation] terni, sali ; [politician] dont la réputation est ternie or salie ; [money] sale **2.** [food] gâté ; [meat] avarié ; [air] vicié, pollué ; [water] infecté, pollué ; [blood] impur.

Taiwan [,taı'wɑːn] pr n Taïwan ▶ **in Taiwan** à Taïwan.

Taiwanese [,taıwə'niːz] ◆ n Taïwanais m, -e f. ◆ adj taïwanais.

take [teık] (pt **took** [tʊk], pp **taken** ['teıkən]) ◆ vt

▐ A. GET HOLD OF OR CAPTURE ▐ **1.** [get hold of] prendre ; [seize] prendre, saisir ▶ **let me take your coat** donnez-moi votre manteau ▶ **she took the book from him** elle lui a pris le livre ▶ **to take sb's hand** prendre qqn par la main ▶ **she took his arm** elle lui a pris le bras **2.** [get control of, capture - person] prendre, capturer ; [- fish, game] prendre, attraper ; MIL prendre, s'emparer de ▶ **to take control of a situation** prendre une situation en main.

▐ B. CARRY, LEAD OR OBTAIN ▐ **1.** [carry from one place to another] porter, apporter ; [carry along, have in one's possession] prendre, emporter ▶ **she took her mother a cup of tea** elle a apporté une tasse de thé à sa mère ▶ **he took the map with him** il a emporté la carte **2.** [person - lead] mener, emmener ; [- accompany] accompagner ▶ **could you take me home?** pourriez-vous me ramener or me raccompagner ? ▶ **please take me with you** emmène-moi, s'il te plaît **3.** [obtain from specified place] prendre, tirer ; [remove from specified place] prendre, enlever ▶ **she took a handkerchief from her pocket** elle a sorti un mouchoir de sa poche ▶ **take your feet off the table** enlève tes pieds de la table **4.** [appropriate, steal] prendre, voler ▶ **to take sthg from sb** prendre qqch à qqn ▶ **his article is taken directly from my book** le texte de son article est tiré directement de mon livre **5.** [draw, derive] prendre, tirer **/** *a passage taken from a book* un passage extrait d'un livre **6.** [refer] : *he took the matter to his boss* il a soumis la question à son patron.

C. WITH TRANSPORT 1. [subj: bus, car, train, etc.] conduire, transporter **/** *the ambulance took him to hospital* l'ambulance l'a transporté à l'hôpital **/** *this bus will take you to the theatre* ce bus vous conduira au théâtre **2.** [bus, car, plane, train] prendre ; [road] prendre, suivre **/** *take a right* US prenez à droite.

D. MAKE OR HAVE 1. [have - attitude, bath, holiday] prendre ; [make - nap, trip, walk] faire ; [- decision] prendre **/** *she took a quick look at him* elle a jeté un rapide coup d'œil sur lui **/** *let's take five* US *inf* soufflons cinq minutes **2.** PHOT ▸ *to take a picture* prendre une photo.

E. RECEIVE [receive, get] recevoir ; [earn, win - prize] remporter, obtenir ; [- degree, diploma] obtenir, avoir **/** *the bookstore takes about $3,000 a day* la librairie fait à peu près 3 000 dollars (de recette) par jour.

F. ACCEPT OR UNDERGO 1. [accept - job, gift, payment] prendre, accepter ; [- bet] accepter **/** *it's my last offer, (you can) take it or leave it* c'est ma dernière offre, c'est à prendre ou à laisser **/** *I'll take it from here* je prends la suite **2.** [accept as valid] croire ▸ *to take sb's advice* suivre les conseils de qqn **/** *take it from me, he's a crook* croyez-moi, c'est un escroc **3.** [assume, undertake] prendre ▸ *to take the blame for sthg* prendre la responsabilité de qqch **4.** [deal with] : *let's take things one at a time* prenons les choses une par une ▸ *to take sthg badly* prendre mal qqch ▸ *to take things easy inf* or *it easy inf* se la couler douce ▸ *take it easy!* [don't get angry] du calme ! **5.** [bear, endure - pain] supporter ; [- damage, loss] subir **/** *don't take any nonsense!* ne te laisse pas faire ! **/** *she can take it* elle tiendra le coup **6.** [experience, feel] : *don't take offence* ne vous vexez pas, ne vous offensez pas **7.** [contract, develop] : *she took an instant dislike to him* elle l'a tout de suite pris en aversion.

G. CONSIDER OR PRESUME 1. [consider, look at] prendre, considérer ▸ *to take sthg / sb seriously* prendre qqch / qqn au sérieux ; [consider as] : *what do you take me for?* pour qui me prenez-vous ? **2.** [suppose, presume] supposer, présumer **3.** [interpret, understand] prendre, comprendre.

H. REQUIRE prendre, demander **/** *how long will it take to get there?* combien de temps faudra-t-il pour y aller ? **/** *the flight takes three hours* le vol dure trois heures **/** *it takes time to learn a language* il faut du temps pour apprendre une langue **/** *it took four people to stop the brawl* ils ont dû se mettre à quatre pour arrêter la bagarre **/** *one glance was all it took* un regard a suffi.

I. CONSUME [food, drink, etc.] prendre **/** *do you take milk in your coffee?* prenez-vous du lait dans votre café ?

J. OTHER USES 1. [commit oneself to] : *he took my side in the argument* il a pris parti pour moi dans la dispute **2.** [allow oneself] : *he took the opportunity to thank them* or *of thanking them* il a profité de l'occasion pour les remercier **3.** [wear] faire, porter **/** *she takes a size 10* elle prend du 38 **4.** [pick out, choose] prendre, choisir ; [buy] prendre, acheter ; [rent] prendre, louer **/** *I'll take it* je le prends **5.** [occupy - chair, seat] prendre, s'asseoir sur **/** *take a seat* asseyez-vous **/** *is this seat taken?* cette place est-elle occupée or prise ? **6.** [ascertain, find out] prendre **7.** [write down - notes, letter] prendre **8.** [subtract] soustraire, déduire **/** *they took 10% off the price* ils ont baissé le prix de 10 % **9.** SCH & UNIV [exam] passer, se présenter à ; [course] prendre, suivre **/** *she takes us for maths* on l'a en maths **10.** [catch unawares] prendre, surprendre ▸ *to take sb by surprise* or *off guard* surprendre qqn, prendre qqn au dépourvu **11.** [negotiate - obstacle] franchir, sauter ; [- bend in road] prendre, négocier.

◆ **vi 1.** [work, have desired effect] prendre **/** *did the dye take?* est-ce que la teinture a pris ? **2.** [become popular] prendre, avoir du succès **3.** [fish] prendre, mordre.

◆ **n 1.** [capture] prise *f* **2.** CIN, PHOT & TV prise *f* de vue ; RADIO enregistrement *m*, prise *f* de son **3.** US [interpretation] interprétation *f* **/** *what's your take on her attitude?* comment est-ce que tu interprètes son attitude ? **4.** US *inf* [takings] recette *f* ; [share] part *f* ▸ *to be on the take* toucher des pots-de-vin. ◆▸ **take after** vt insep ressembler à, tenir de. ◆▸ **take apart** vt sep **1.** [dismantle] démonter **2.** [criticize] critiquer. ◆▸ **take away** vt sep **1.** [remove] enlever, retirer **2.** [carry away - object] emporter ; [- person] emmener **3.** MATH soustraire, retrancher **/** *nine take away six is three* neuf moins six font trois. ◆▸ **take away from** vt insep [detract from] : *that doesn't take away from his achievements as an athlete* ça n'enlève rien à ses exploits d'athlète. ◆▸ **take back** vt sep **1.** [after absence, departure] reprendre **2.** [return] rapporter ; [accompany] raccompagner **3.** [retract, withdraw] retirer, reprendre **/** *I take back everything I said* je retire tout ce que j'ai dit **/** *all right, I take it back!* d'accord, je n'ai rien dit ! **4.** [remind of the past] : *that takes me back to my childhood* ça me rappelle mon enfance. ◆▸ **take down** ◆ vt sep **1.** [lower] descendre **/** *can you help me take the curtains down?* peux-tu m'aider à décrocher les rideaux ? **2.** [note] prendre, noter. ◆ vi se démonter. ◆▸ **take in** vt sep **1.** [bring into one's home - person] héberger ; [- boarder] prendre ; [- orphan, stray animal] recueillir ; [place in custody] : *the police took him in* la police l'a mis or placé en garde à vue **2.** [understand, perceive] saisir, comprendre **/** *he was sitting taking it all in* il était là, assis, écoutant tout ce qui se disait **/** *I can't take in the fact that I've won* je n'arrive pas à croire que j'ai gagné **/** *she took in the situation at a glance* elle a compris la situation en un clin d'œil **3.** [make smaller - garment] reprendre ; [- in knitting] diminuer **4.** [attend, go to] aller à **/** *to take in a show* aller au théâtre **5.** *(usu passive) inf* [cheat, deceive] tromper, rouler **/** *don't be taken in by him* ne vous laissez pas rouler par lui. ◆▸ **take off** ◆ vt sep **1.** [remove - clothing, lid, make-up, tag] enlever **/** *he often takes the phone off the hook* il laisse souvent le téléphone décroché ; *fig* : *he didn't take his eyes off her all night* il ne l'a pas quittée des yeux de la soirée **2.** [deduct] déduire, rabattre **3.** [lead away] emmener **/** *she was taken off to hospital* on l'a transportée à l'hôpital **4.** [time] : *take a few days off* prenez quelques jours (de vacances or de congé) **5.** *inf* [copy] imiter ; [mimic] imiter, singer. ◆ vi **1.** [aeroplane] décoller **2.** [person - depart] partir **3.** *inf* [become successful] décoller. ◆▸ **take on** ◆ vt sep **1.** [accept, undertake] prendre, accepter **/** *to take on the responsibility for sthg* se charger de qqch **2.** [contend with, fight against] lutter or se battre contre ; [compete against] jouer contre **/** *the unions took on the government* les syndicats se sont attaqués or s'en sont pris au gouvernement **3.** [acquire, assume] prendre, revêtir **4.** [load] prendre, embarquer **5.** [hire] embaucher, engager. ◆ vi *inf* [fret, carry on] s'en faire. ◆▸ **take out** vt sep **1.** [remove - object] prendre, sortir ; [- stain] ôter, enlever ; [extract - tooth] arracher **/** *take your hands out of your pockets* enlève tes mains de tes poches **2.** [carry, lead outside - object] sortir ; [- person] faire sortir ; [escort] emmener ▸ *to take sb out to dinner / to the movies* emmener qqn dîner / au cinéma **/** *would you take the dog out?* tu veux bien sortir le chien or aller promener le chien ? **3.** [food] emporter **4.** [obtain - subscription] prendre ; [- insurance policy] souscrire à, prendre ; [- licence] se procurer ; [COMM - patent] prendre **5.** PHR ▸ *to take it or a lot out of sb inf* : *working as an interpreter takes a lot out of you* le travail d'interprète est épuisant **/** *the operation really took it out of him* l'opération l'a mis à plat ▸ *to take it out on sb* s'en prendre à qqn. ◆▸ **take over** ◆ vt sep **1.** [assume responsibility of] reprendre **/** *will you be taking over* *his job?* est-ce que vous allez le remplacer (dans ses fonctions) ? **2.** [gain control of, invade] s'emparer de **3.** FIN [buy out] absorber, racheter **4.** [carry across] apporter ; [escort across] emmener. ◆ vi **1.** [as replacement] : *I'll take over when he leaves* je le remplacerai quand il partira **2.** [army, dictator] prendre le pouvoir. ❖ **take to** vt insep **1.** [have a liking for - person] se prendre d'amitié or de sympathie pour, prendre en amitié ; [- activity, game] prendre goût à / *I think he took to you* je crois que vous lui avez plu **2.** [acquire as a habit] se mettre à ▶ **to take to drink** or **to the bottle** se mettre à boire ▶ **to take to doing sthg** se mettre à faire qqch **3.** [make for, head for] : *he's taken to his bed with the flu* il est alité avec la grippe. ❖ **take up** ◆ vt sep **1.** [carry, lead upstairs - object] monter ; [- person] faire monter **2.** [pick up - object] ramasser, prendre ; [- passenger] prendre / *we finally took up the carpet* nous avons enfin enlevé la moquette **3.** [absorb] absorber **4.** [shorten] raccourcir **5.** [fill, occupy - space] prendre, tenir ; [- time] prendre, demander / *this table takes up too much room* cette table prend trop de place or est trop encombrante **6.** [begin, become interested in - activity, hobby] se mettre à ; [- job] prendre ; [- career] commencer, embrasser **7.** [continue, resume] reprendre, continuer **8.** [adopt - attitude] prendre, adopter ; [- method] adopter ; [- place, position] prendre ; [- idea] adopter **9.** [accept - offer] accepter ; [- advice, suggestion] suivre ; [- challenge] relever **10.** [discuss] discuter, parler de ; [bring up] aborder / *take it up with the boss* parlez-en au patron. ◆ vi reprendre, continuer. ❖ **take upon** vt sep : *he took it upon himself to organize the meeting* il s'est chargé d'organiser la réunion. ❖ **take up on** vt sep [accept offer, advice of] : *he might take you up on that someday!* il risque de vous prendre au mot un jour ! ❖ **take up with** vt insep **1.** [befriend] ▶ **to take up with sb** se lier d'amitié avec qqn, prendre qqn en amitié **2.** [preoccupy] ▶ **to be taken up with doing sthg** être occupé à faire qqch.

takeaway ['teɪkə,weɪ] ◆ n 🇬🇧 & 🇳🇿 [shop] boutique de plats à emporter ; [food] plat *m* à emporter ▶ **Chinese takeaway a)** [shop] traiteur *m* chinois **b)** [meal] repas *m* chinois à emporter. ◆ adj ▶ **takeaway food** plats *mpl* à emporter.

take-home pay n salaire *m* net *(après impôts et déductions sociales)*.

taken ['teɪkən] ◆ pp ⟶ **take**. ◆ adj **1.** [seat] pris, occupé **2.** ▶ **to be taken with sthg / sb a)** [impressed] être impressionné par qqch / qqn **b)** [interested] s'intéresser à qqch / qqn.

takeoff ['teɪkɒf] n **1.** AERON décollage *m* **2.** [imitation] imitation *f*, caricature *f* **3.** ECON décollage *m* économique.

takeout ['teɪkaʊt] 🇺🇸 = **takeaway**.

takeover ['teɪk,əʊvər] n [of power, of government] prise *f* de pouvoir ; [of company] prise *f* de contrôle.

takeover bid n offre *f* publique d'achat, OPA *f*.

taker ['teɪkər] n **1.** [buyer] acheteur *m*, -euse *f*, preneur *m*, -euse *f* ; [of suggestion, offer] preneur *m*, -euse *f* / *there were no takers* personne n'en voulait / *any takers?* y a-t-il des preneurs ? **2.** [user] : *takers of drugs are at highest risk* ce sont les toxicomanes qui courent les plus grands risques.

takeup ['teɪkʌp] n [of benefits] réclamation *f*.

taking ['teɪkɪŋ] ◆ adj engageant, séduisant. ◆ n [of city, power] prise *f* ; [of criminal] arrestation *f* ; [of blood, sample] prélèvement *m*. ◆ **takings** pl n COMM recette *f*.

talc [tælk] ◆ n talc *m*. ◆ vt talquer.

talcum powder ['tælkəm-] n talc *m*.

tale [teɪl] n **1.** [story] conte *m*, histoire *f* ; [legend] histoire *f*, légende *f* ; [account] récit *m* ▶ **to tell a tale** raconter une histoire / *the astronaut lived / didn't live to tell the*

tale l'astronaute a survécu / n'a pas survécu pour raconter ce qui s'est passé **2.** [gossip] histoires *fpl* ▶ **to tell tales on sb** raconter des histoires sur le compte de qqn.

talent ['tælənt] n **1.** [gift] talent *m*, don *m* **2.** [talented person] talent *m* **3.** inf [opposite sex - girls] jolies filles *fpl*, minettes *fpl* ; [- boys] beaux mecs *mpl* **4.** [coin] talent *m*.

talented ['tæləntɪd] adj talentueux, doué.

talent scout, talent-spotter n [for films] dénicheur *m*, -euse *f* de vedettes ; [for sport] dénicheur *m*, -euse *f* de futurs grands joueurs.

talisman ['tælɪzmən] *(pl* **talismans***)* n talisman *m*.

talk [tɔːk] ◆ vi **1.** [speak] parler ; [discuss] discuter ; [confer] s'entretenir ▶ **to talk to sb** parler à qqn ▶ **to talk with sb** parler or s'entretenir avec qqn ▶ **to talk of** or **about sthg** parler de qqch / *we sat talking together* nous sommes restés à discuter or à bavarder / *that's no way to talk!* en voilà des façons de parler ! / *they no longer talk to each other* ils ne se parlent plus, ils ne s'adressent plus la parole / *don't you talk to me like that!* je t'interdis de me parler sur ce ton ! ▶ **to talk to o.s.** parler tout seul / *I'll talk to you about it tomorrow morning* **a)** [converse] je vous en parlerai demain matin **b)** [as threat] j'aurai deux mots à vous dire à ce sujet demain matin / *it's no use talking to him, he never listens!* on perd son temps avec lui, il n'écoute jamais ! / *talking of Switzerland, have you ever been skiing?* à propos de la Suisse, vous avez déjà fait du ski ? / *now you're talking!* voilà qui s'appelle parler ! / *you can talk!* or *look who's talking!* or *you're a fine one to talk!* tu peux parler, toi ! / *it's easy for you to talk, you've never had a gun in your back!* c'est facile à dire or tu as beau jeu de dire ça, on ne t'a jamais braqué un pistolet dans le dos ! / *talk about luck!* **a)** [admiring] qu'est-ce qu'il a comme chance !, quel veinard ! **b)** [complaining] tu parles d'une veine ! **2.** [chat] causer, bavarder ; [gossip] jaser **3.** [reveal secrets, esp unwillingly] parler. ◆ vt **1.** [language] parler / *talk sense!* ne dis pas de sottises !, ne dis pas n'importe quoi ! / *now you're talking sense* vous dites enfin des choses sensées / *stop talking rubbish!* inf or nonsense! arrête de dire des bêtises ! **2.** [discuss] parler ▶ **to talk business / politics** parler affaires / politique. ◆ n **1.** [conversation] conversation *f* ; [discussion] discussion *f* ; [chat] causette *f*, causerie *f* ; [formal] entretien *m* ▶ **to have a talk with sb about sthg** parler de qqch avec qqn, s'entretenir avec qqn de qqch **2.** [speech, lecture] exposé *m* ▶ **to give a talk on** or **about sthg** faire un exposé sur qqch **3.** (U) [noise of talking] paroles *fpl*, propos *mpl* **4.** [speculative] discussion *f*, rumeur *f* / *most of the talk was about the new road* il a surtout été question de or on a surtout parlé de la nouvelle route / *enough of this idle talk!* assez parlé ! / *he's all talk* tout ce qu'il dit, c'est du vent **5.** (U) [gossip] racontars *mpl*, bavardage *m*, bavardages *mpl*, potins *mpl*. ◆ **talks** pl n [negotiations] négociations *fpl*, pourparlers *mpl* ; [conference] conférence *f* ▶ **official peace talks** des pourparlers officiels sur la paix. ❖ **talk about** vt insep **1.** [discuss] parler de ▶ **to talk to sb about sthg** parler de qqch à qqn / *what are you talking about?* **a)** [I don't understand] de quoi parles-tu ? **b)** [annoyed] qu'est-ce que tu racontes ? / *they were talking about going away for the weekend* ils parlaient or envisageaient de partir pour le week-end **2.** [mean] : *we're not talking about that!* il ne s'agit pas de cela ! ❖ **talk back** vi [insolently] répondre ▶ **to talk back to sb** répondre (insolemment) à qqn. ❖ **talk down** ◆ vt sep **1.** [silence] ▶ **to talk sb down** réduire qqn au silence (en parlant plus fort que lui) **2.** [aircraft] faire atterrir par radio-contrôle. ◆ vi ▶ **to talk down to sb** parler à qqn comme à un enfant. ❖ **talk into** vt sep ▶ **to talk sb into doing sthg** persuader qqn de faire qqch. ❖ **talk out** vt sep [problem, disagreement] débattre de, discuter de. ❖ **talk out of** vt sep dissuader

▸ **to talk sb out of doing sthg** dissuader qqn de faire qqch. ❖ **talk over** vt sep discuter or débattre de ∕ *let's talk it over* discutons-en, parlons-en. ❖ **talk round** vt sep [convince] persuader, convaincre ▸ **to talk sb round to one's way of thinking** amener qqn à sa façon de penser or à son point de vue. ❖ **talk up** vt sep vanter les mérites de, faire de la publicité pour.

talkathon ['tɔ:kəθɒn] n US *hum* [in Congress, on television, etc.] débat-marathon *m*.

talkative ['tɔ:kətɪv] adj bavard, loquace.

talker ['tɔ:kə^r] n **1.** [speaker] causeur *m*, -euse *f*, bavard *m*, -e *f* ∕ *he's a fast talker* a) [gen] il parle vite b) COMM il a du bagout **2.** [talking bird] oiseau *m* qui parle.

talking ['tɔ:kɪŋ] ❖ n (U) conversation *f*, propos *mpl* ∕ *he did all the talking* il était le seul à parler. ❖ adj [film] parlant ; [bird] qui parle.

talking point n sujet *m* de conversation or de discussion.

talking-to n *inf* attrapade *f*, réprimande *f*.

talk show n causerie *f* (radiodiffusée or télévisée), talk-show *m* ▸ **talk show host** présentateur *m*, -trice *f* de talk-show.

talk time n (U) TELEC crédit *m* de communication.

TTYL8R abbr of TTYL.

T2ul (written abbr of **talk to you later**) MESSAGING @+.

tall [tɔ:l] adj **1.** [person] grand, de grande taille ∕ *how tall are you?* combien mesurez-vous ? ∕ *I'm 6 feet tall* je mesure or fais 1 m 80 ∕ *she's grown a lot taller in the past year* elle a beaucoup grandi depuis un an ; [building] haut, élevé ; [tree, glass] grand, haut ∕ *how tall is that tree?* quelle est la hauteur de cet arbre ? ∕ *it's at least 80 feet tall* il fait au moins 25 mètres de haut **2.** PHR ▸ **a tall story** une histoire invraisemblable or abracadabrante, une histoire à dormir debout ▸ **that's a tall order** c'est beaucoup demander.

tallboy ['tɔ:lbɔɪ] n **1.** [furniture] (grande) commode *f* **2.** [can of beer] grande canette *f* de bière.

tallness ['tɔ:lnɪs] n [of person] (grande) taille *f* ; [of tree, building] hauteur *f*.

tally ['tælɪ] (*pl* **tallies**, *pt & pp* **tallied**) ❖ n **1.** [record] compte *m*, enregistrement *m* ; COMM pointage *m* ; US SPORT [score] score *m* **2.** HIST [stick] taille *f*, baguette *f* à encoches ; [mark] encoche *f* **3.** [label] étiquette *f*. ❖ vt **1.** [record] pointer **2.** [count up] compter. ❖ vi correspondre.

talon ['tælən] n **1.** [of hawk, eagle] serre *f* ; [of tiger, lion] griffe *f* **2.** CARDS talon *m*.

tambourine [,tæmbə'ri:n] n tambour *m* de basque, tambourin *m*.

tame [teɪm] ❖ adj **1.** [as pet - hamster, rabbit] apprivoisé, domestiqué ; [normally wild - bear, hawk] apprivoisé ; [esp in circus - lion, tiger] dompté **2.** [insipid, weak] fade, insipide. ❖ vt **1.** [as pet - hamster, rabbit] apprivoiser, domestiquer ; [normally wild - bear, hawk] apprivoiser ; [in circus - lion, tiger] dompter **2.** [person] mater, soumettre ; [natural forces] apprivoiser ; [passions] dominer.

tamely ['teɪmlɪ] adv [submit] docilement, sans résistance ; [end] platement, de manière insipide ; [write] de manière fade, platement.

tamer ['teɪmə^r] n dresseur *m*, -euse *f*.

Tamil ['tæmɪl] ❖ n **1.** [person] Tamoul *m*, -e *f* **2.** LING tamoul *m*. ❖ adj tamoul.

taming ['teɪmɪŋ] n [of animal] apprivoisement *m* ; [of lions, tigers] domptage *m*, dressage *m*.

Tampax® ['tæmpæks] n Tampax® *m*.

tamper ['tæmpə^r] ❖ **tamper with** vt insep **1.** [meddle with - brakes, machinery] trafiquer ; [lock] essayer de forcer or crocheter, fausser ; [possessions] toucher à ; [falsify - records, accounts, evidence] falsifier, altérer **2.** US LAW [witness] suborner ; [jury] soudoyer.

tamper-evident adj qui révèle toute tentative d'effraction.

tampon ['tæmpɒn] n MED tampon *m* ; [for feminine use] tampon *m* périodique or hygiénique.

tan [tæn] (*pt & pp* **tanned**, *cont* **tanning**) ❖ n **1.** [from sun] bronzage *m* **2.** MATH tangente *f*. ❖ vt **1.** [leather, skins] tanner **2.** [from sun] bronzer, brunir. ❖ vi bronzer. ❖ adj [colour] brun roux, brun clair ; [leather] jaune ; US [tanned] bronzé.

tandem ['tændəm] ❖ n **1.** [carriage] tandem *m* **2.** [bike] tandem *m*. ❖ adv ▸ **to ride tandem** rouler en tandem.

tandoori [tæn'dʊərɪ] ❖ n cuisine *f* tandoori. ❖ adj tandoori (inv).

tang [tæŋ] n **1.** [taste] goût *m* (fort) **2.** [smell] odeur *f* forte **3.** [hint - of irony] pointe *f* **4.** [of knife, sword] soie *f*.

tangent ['tændʒənt] n MATH tangente *f*.

tangerine [,tændʒə'ri:n] ❖ n **1.** [fruit] ▸ **tangerine (orange)** mandarine *f* **2.** [colour] mandarine *f*. ❖ adj [in colour] mandarine (inv).

tangible ['tændʒəbl] adj **1.** [palpable] tangible ; [real, substantial] tangible, réel **2.** LAW ▸ **tangible assets** actif *m* corporel.

Tangier [tæn'dʒɪə^r] pr n Tanger.

tangle ['tæŋgl] ❖ n **1.** [of wire, string, hair] enchevêtrement *m* ; [of branches, weeds] fouillis *m*, enchevêtrement *m* **2.** [muddle] fouillis *m*, confusion *f* **3.** [disagreement] accrochage *m*, différend *m*. ❖ vt [wire, wool] emmêler, enchevêtrer ; [figures] embrouiller. ❖ vi **1.** [wires, hair] s'emmêler **2.** *inf* [disagree] avoir un différend or un accrochage. ❖ **tangle up** vt sep [string, wire] emmêler, enchevêtrer.

tangled ['tæŋgld] adj **1.** [string, creepers] emmêlé, enchevêtré ; [hair] emmêlé **2.** [complex - story, excuse] embrouillé ; [- love life] complexe.

tango ['tæŋgəʊ] (*pl* **tangos**) ❖ n tango *m*. ❖ vi danser le tango.

tangy ['tæŋɪ] (*compar* **tangier**, *superl* **tangiest**) adj [in taste] qui a un goût fort ; [in smell] qui a une odeur forte.

tank [tæŋk] n **1.** [container - for liquid, gas] réservoir *m*, cuve *f*, citerne *f* ; [- for rainwater] citerne *f*, bac *m* ; [- for processing] cuve *f* ; [- for transport] réservoir *m*, citerne *f* ; [barrel] tonneau *m*, cuve *f* **2.** MIL tank *m*, char *m* d'assaut. ❖ comp de char or chars d'assaut. ❖ vt mettre en cuve or en réservoir. ❖ **tank up** UK ❖ vi AUTO faire le plein (d'essence). ❖ vt sep *inf* ▸ **to get tanked up** se soûler.

tankard ['tæŋkəd] n chope *f*.

tanker ['tæŋkə^r] n [lorry] camion-citerne *m* ; [ship] bateau-citerne *m*, navire-citerne *m* ; [plane] avion-ravitailleur *m* ▸ **(oil) tanker** NAUT pétrolier *m*.

tankful ['tæŋkfʊl] n [of petrol] réservoir *m* (plein) ; [of water] citerne *f* (pleine).

tankini [tæŋ'ki:nɪ] n tankini *m*.

tank top n débardeur *m*.

tan line n marque *f* de bronzage.

tanned [tænd] adj **1.** [person] hâlé, bronzé **2.** [leather] tanné.

tannin ['tænɪn] n tanin *m*, tannin *m*.

tanning ['tænɪŋ] n **1.** [of skin] bronzage *m* **2.** [of hides] tannage *m* ; *fig* raclée *f*.

tanning cream n [self-tanning] crème *f* autobronzante ; [for natural tan] crème *f* solaire.

Tannoy® ['tænɔɪ] n 🇬🇧 système m de haut-parleurs.

tantalize, tantanlise ['tæntəlaɪz] vt tourmenter, taquiner.

tantalizing, tantanlising ['tæntəlaɪzɪŋ] adj [woman] provocant, aguichant ; [smell] alléchant, appétissant ; [hint, possibility] tentant.

tantalizingly, tantanlisingly ['tæntəlaɪzɪŋli] adv cruellement.

tantamount ['tæntəmaʊnt] ❖ **tantamount to** prep phr équivalent à.

tantrum ['tæntrəm] n crise f de colère or de rage.

Tanzania [,tænzə'nɪə] pr n Tanzanie f / in Tanzania en Tanzanie.

Tanzanian [,tænzə'nɪən] ❖ n Tanzanien m, -enne f. ❖ adj tanzanien.

tap [tæp] (pt & pp tapped, cont tapping) ❖ vt 1. [strike] taper légèrement, tapoter 2. [barrel, cask] mettre en perce, percer ; [gas, water main] faire un branchement sur ; [current] capter ; [tree] inciser ; [pine] gemmer 3. [exploit - resources, market] exploiter ; [- talent, service] faire appel à, tirer profit de ; [- capital] drainer 4. TELEC [conversation] capter ▶ to tap sb's line or phone mettre qqn sur (table d')écoute 5. TECH [screw] tarauder, fileter 6. ELEC faire une dérivation sur 7. MED poser un drain sur. ❖ vi 1. [knock] tapoter, taper légèrement / to tap at the door frapper doucement à la porte 2. [dance] faire des claquettes. ❖ n 1. [for water, gas] robinet m ; [on barrel] robinet m, chantepleure f ; [plug] bonde f ▶ on tap a) [beer] en fût b) inf & fig [money, person, supply] disponible 2. [blow] petit coup m, petite tape f 3. [on shoe] fer m 4. [dancing] claquettes fpl 5. TECH ▶ (screw) tap taraud m 6. ELEC dérivation f, branchement f 7. TELEC ▶ to put a tap on sb's phone mettre (le téléphone de) qqn sur table d'écoute 8. MED drain m. ❖ **tap in** vt sep 1. [plug] enfoncer à petits coups 2. COMPUT taper. ❖ **tap out** vt sep 1. [plug] sortir à petits coups ; [pipe] vider, débourrer 2. [code, rhythm] taper.

tapafication [tæpæfɪkeɪʃn] n 🇬🇧 tendance à servir les plats en de nombreuses petites portions.

tap dance n claquettes fpl (danse). ❖ **tap-dance** vi faire des claquettes.

tap dancer n danseur m, -euse f de claquettes.

tape [teɪp] ❖ n 1. [strip] bande f, ruban m ; SEW ruban m, ganse f ; MED sparadrap m 2. [for recording] bande f (magnétique) ; COMPUT bande f ; [for video, audio] cassette f ; [recording] enregistrement m ▶ on tape sur bande, enregistré 3. SPORT fil m d'arrivée 4. [for measuring] ▶ tape (measure) mètre m (à ruban). ❖ vt 1. [record] enregistrer 2. [fasten - package] attacher avec du ruban adhésif ; [stick] scotcher 3. 🇺🇸 [bandage] bander. ❖ **tape together** vt sep [fasten] attacher ensemble avec du ruban adhésif ; [stick] coller (avec du ruban adhésif). ❖ **tape up** vt sep [fasten - parcel] attacher avec du ruban adhésif ; [close - letterbox, hole] fermer avec du ruban adhésif ; 🇺🇸 [bandage up] bander.

tape deck n platine f de magnétophone.

tape drive n dérouleur m de bande (magnétique), lecteur m de bande (magnétique).

tape head n tête f de lecture.

tape measure n mètre m (ruban), centimètre m.

taper ['teɪpər] ❖ vt [column, trouser leg, plane wing] fuseler ; [stick, table leg] effiler, tailler en pointe. ❖ vi [column, trouser leg, plane wing] être fuselé ; [stick, shape, table leg] se terminer en pointe, s'effiler ; [finger] être effilé. ❖ n longue bougie fine ; RELIG cierge m. ❖ **taper off** vi 1. [shape] se

terminer en fuseau or en pointe 2. [noise] diminuer progressivement, décroître, s'affaiblir ; [conversation] tomber ; [level of interest, activity] décroître progressivement.

tape reader n COMPUT lecteur m de bande.

tape-record [-rɪ,kɔːd] vt enregistrer (sur bande magnétique).

tape recorder n magnétophone m, lecteur m de cassettes.

tape recording n enregistrement m (sur bande magnétique).

tapered ['teɪpəd], **tapering** ['teɪpərɪŋ] adj [trousers] en fuseau ; [stick, candle] en pointe, pointu ; [table leg] fuselé.

tapestry ['tæpɪstri] (pl tapestries) n tapisserie f.

tapeworm ['teɪpwɜːm] n ténia m, ver m solitaire.

tapioca [,tæpɪ'əʊkə] n tapioca m.

tapir ['teɪpər] (pl tapir or tapirs) n tapir m.

tappet ['tæpɪt] n TECH ▶ **(valve) tappet** poussoir m (de soupape), taquet m.

tap water n eau f du robinet.

tar [tɑːr] (pt & pp tarred, cont tarring) ❖ n 1. goudron m ; [on road] goudron m, bitume m 2. inf [sailor] matelot m, loup m de mer. ❖ vt goudronner ; [road] goudronner, bitumer ; NAUT goudronner.

tarantula [tə'ræntjʊlə] (pl tarantulas or tarantulae [-liː]) n tarentule f.

tardy ['tɑːdi] (compar tardier, superl tardiest) adj 1. 🇺🇸 SCH en retard 2. fml & liter [late] tardif 3. fml & liter [slow] lent, nonchalant.

target ['tɑːgɪt] (pt & pp targeted, cont targeting) ❖ n 1. [for archery, shooting] cible f ; MIL cible f, but m ; [objective] cible f, objectif m ▶ to be on target a) [missile] suivre la trajectoire prévue b) [plans] se dérouler comme prévu c) [productivity] atteindre les objectifs prévus ▶ **moving target** MIL & fig cible f mobile 2. ELECTRON & PHYS cible f. ❖ comp 1. [date, amount] prévu 2. MIL ▶ **target area** zone f cible 3. COMM ▶ **target audience / reader / user** public- / lecteur- / usager-cible 4. COMPUT ▶ **target disk / drive** disquette / unité de destination. ❖ vt 1. [make objective of - enemy troops, city, etc.] prendre pour cible, viser 2. [aim - missile] diriger ; [subj: benefits] être destiné à ; [subj: advertisement] viser, s'adresser à.

targeted ['tɑːgɪtɪd] adj ciblé.

tariff ['tærɪf] ❖ n 1. [customs] tarif m douanier ; [list of prices] tarif m, tableau m des prix 2. 🇬🇧 [menu] menu m 3. 🇬🇧 [rate - of gas, electricity] tarif m. ❖ adj tarifaire.

Tarmac® [tɑː'mæk] (pt & pp tarmacked, cont tarmacking) n 🇬🇧 1. [on road] tarmacadam m, macadam m 2. [at airport - runway] piste f ; [- apron] aire f de stationnement, piste f d'envol. ❖ **tarmac** vt macadamiser, goudronner.

tarnish ['tɑːnɪʃ] ❖ vt 1. [metal] ternir ; [mirror] ternir, désargenter 2. [reputation] ternir, salir. ❖ vi se ternir. ❖ n ternissure f.

tarnished ['tɑːnɪʃt] adj lit & fig terni.

tarot ['tærəʊ] n (U) tarot m, tarots mpl ▶ **tarot card** carte f de tarot.

tarpaulin [tɑː'pɔːlɪn] n bâche f ; NAUT prélart m.

tarragon ['tærəgən] n estragon m.

tart [tɑːt] ❖ n 1. CULIN tarte f ; [small] tartelette f 2. 🇬🇧 v inf [girl] gonzesse f ; [prostitute] grue f. ❖ adj 1. [sour - fruit] acide ; [- taste] aigre, acide 2. [remark] acerbe, caustique. ❖ **tart up** vt sep 🇬🇧 inf [house, restaurant, etc.] retaper, rénover ▶ **to tart o.s. up, to get tarted up** se pomponner.

tartan ['tɑːtn] ◆ n [design] tartan *m* ; [fabric] tartan *m*, tissu *m* écossais. ◆ comp [skirt, trousers] en tissu écossais ; [pattern] tartan.

tartar ['tɑːtəʳ] n 1. [on teeth] tartre *m* 2. 🇬🇧 [fearsome person] tyran *m*. ❖ Tartar n = Tatar.

tartar(e) sauce ['tɑːtə-] n sauce *f* tartare.

tartness ['tɑːtnɪs] n [of fruit] aigreur *f*, acidité *f* ; [of tone, reply] aigreur *f*, acidité *f*.

tarty ['tɑːtɪ] (*compar* **tartier**, *superl* **tartiest**) adj 🇬🇧 *v inf* vulgaire.

tase [teɪz] vt ▶ to tase sb utiliser un pistolet à impulsion électronique or un taser contre qqn.

taser ['teɪzəʳ] n pistolet *m* à impulsion électronique, taser *m*.

task [tɑːsk] ◆ n [chore] tâche *f*, besogne *f* ; [job] tâche *f*, travail *m* ; SCH devoir *m*. ◆ vt = tax *(vt)*.

taskbar ['tɑːskbɑːʳ] n COMPUT barre *f* des tâches.

task force n MIL corps *m* expéditionnaire ; [gen] groupe *m* de travail, mission *f*.

taskmaster ['tɑːsk,mɑːstəʳ] n tyran *m*.

Tasmania [tæz'meɪnjə] pr n Tasmanie *f* **/ in Tasmania** en Tasmanie.

Tasmanian [tæz'meɪnjən] ◆ n Tasmanien *m*, -enne *f*. ◆ adj tasmanien.

tassel ['tæsl] (🇬🇧 *pt & pp* **tasselled**, *cont* **tasselling** ; 🇺🇸 *pt & pp* **tasseled**, *cont* **tasseling**) ◆ n 1. [on clothing, furnishing] gland *m* 2. BOT épillets *mpl*, panicule *f*, inflorescence *f* mâle. ◆ vt garnir de glands.

tasselled ['tæsld] adj à glands, orné de glands.

taste [teɪst] ◆ n 1. [sense] goût *m* 2. [flavour] goût *m*, saveur *f* 3. [small amount - of food] bouchée *f* ; [- of drink] goutte *f* 4. [liking, preference] goût *m*, penchant *m* ▶ to **have a taste for sthg** avoir un penchant or un faible pour qqch 5. [discernment] goût *m* ▶ to **have good taste** avoir du goût, avoir bon goût 6. [experience] aperçu *m* ; [sample] échantillon *m*. ◆ vt 1. [flavour, ingredient] sentir (le goût de) 2. [sample, try] goûter à ; [for quality] goûter ; [eat] manger ; [drink] boire 3. [experience - happiness, success] goûter, connaître. ◆ vi [food] : *to taste good / bad* avoir bon / mauvais goût ▶ to **taste of sthg** avoir le or un goût de qqch.

taste bud n papille *f* gustative.

tasteful ['teɪstfʊl] adj [decoration] raffiné, de bon goût ; [work of art] de bon goût ; [clothing] de bon goût, élégant.

tastefully ['teɪstfʊlɪ] adv avec goût.

tasteless ['teɪstlɪs] adj 1. [food] fade, insipide, sans goût 2. [remark] de mauvais goût ; [decoration, outfit, person] qui manque de goût, de mauvais goût.

tastelessly ['teɪstlɪslɪ] adv [decorated, dressed] sans goût.

taster ['teɪstəʳ] n dégustateur *m*, -trice *f*.

tasting ['teɪstɪŋ] n dégustation *f*.

tasty ['teɪstɪ] (*compar* **tastier**, *superl* **tastiest**) adj 1. [flavour] savoureux, délicieux ; [spicy] relevé, bien assaisonné ; [dish] qui a bon goût 2. *inf* [attractive] séduisant.

tat [tæt] (*pt & pp* **tatted**, *cont* **tatting**) ◆ vi [make lace] faire de la frivolité. ◆ n 1. (U) 🇬🇧 *inf & pej* [clothes] fripes *fpl* ; [goods] camelote *f* 2. 🇬🇧 *inf* [tattoo] tatouage *m*.

ta-ta [tæ'tɑː] interj 🇬🇧 *inf* au revoir, salut.

Tatar ['tɑːtəʳ] ◆ n [person] Tatar *m*, -e *f*. ◆ adj tatar.

tattered ['tætəd] adj [clothes] en lambeaux, en loques ; [page, book] en lambeaux, en morceaux, tout déchiré ; [person] en haillons, loqueteux ; [reputation] en miettes, ruiné.

tatters ['tætəz] pl n ▶ to **be in tatters** *lit* être en lambeaux or en loques **/** *her reputation is in tatters* sa réputation est ruinée.

tattle-tale ['tætl-] = **telltale** *(noun)*.

tattoo [tə'tuː] (*pl* **tattoos**) ◆ n 1. [on skin] tatouage *m* 2. MIL [signal] retraite *f* ; [ceremony, parade] parade *f* militaire 3. [on drums] battements *mpl*. ◆ vi & vt tatouer.

tattooist [tə'tuːɪst] n tatoueur *m*.

tatty ['tætɪ] (*compar* **tattier**, *superl* **tattiest**) adj 🇬🇧 *inf* [clothes] fatigué, défraîchi ; [person] défraîchi, miteux ; [house] délabré, en mauvais état ; [book] écorné, en mauvais état.

taught [tɔːt] pt & pp ⟶ **teach**.

taunt [tɔːnt] ◆ vt railler, tourner en ridicule, persifler. ◆ n raillerie *f*, sarcasme *m*.

taunting ['tɔːntɪŋ] ◆ n *(U)* railleries *fpl*, sarcasmes *mpl*. ◆ adj railleur, sarcastique.

Taurus ['tɔːrəs] pr n ASTROL & ASTRON Taureau *m* **/** *he's a Taurus* il est (du signe du) Taureau.

taut [tɔːt] adj [rope, cable] tendu, raide ; [situation] tendu.

tauten ['tɔːtn] ◆ vt [rope, cable, etc.] tendre, raidir. ◆ vi se tendre.

tautological [,tɔːtə'lɒdʒɪkl] adj tautologique, pléonastique.

tautology [tɔː'tɒlədʒɪ] (*pl* **tautologies**) n tautologie *f*, pléonasme *m*.

tavern ['tævn] n auberge *f*, taverne *f*.

tawdry ['tɔːdrɪ] (*compar* **tawdrier**, *superl* **tawdriest**) adj [clothes] voyant, tapageur, de mauvaise qualité ; [jewellery] clinquant ; [goods] de mauvaise qualité ; [motives, situation] bas, indigne.

tawny ['tɔːnɪ] (*compar* **tawnier**, *superl* **tawniest**) adj [colour] fauve.

tax [tæks] ◆ n 1. [on income] contributions *fpl* ; ADMIN impôt *m* ▶ **after tax** net (d'impôt) 2. [on goods, services, imports] taxe *f* 3. *fig* [strain - on patience, nerves] épreuve *f* ; [- on strength, resources] mise *f* à l'épreuve. ◆ comp [burden] fiscal ; [assessment] de l'impôt ; [liability] à l'impôt ▶ **tax dollars** 🇺🇸 l'argent *m* du contribuable ▶ **tax expert** fiscaliste *mf*. ◆ vt 1. [person, company] imposer, frapper d'un impôt ; [goods] taxer, frapper d'une taxe 2. 🇬🇧 ▶ **to tax one's car** acheter la vignette (automobile) 3. *fig* [strain - patience, resources] mettre à l'épreuve ; [- strength, nerves] éprouver 4. [accuse] ▶ **to tax sb with sthg** accuser or taxer qqn de qqch.

taxable ['tæksəbl] adj [goods, land] imposable.

tax allowance n 🇬🇧 abattement *m* fiscal.

taxation [tæk'seɪʃn] ◆ n *(U)* 1. [of goods] taxation *f* ; [of companies, people] imposition *f* 2. [taxes] impôts *mpl*, contributions *fpl*. ◆ comp [system] fiscal.

tax avoidance [-ə'vɔɪdəns] n évasion *f* fiscale.

tax band n tranche *f* d'imposition.

tax bracket n tranche *f* d'imposition.

tax break n réduction *f* d'impôt.

tax code n barème *m* fiscal.

tax collector n percepteur *m*.

tax credit n crédit *m* d'impôt.

tax cut n baisse *f* de l'impôt.

tax-deductible adj déductible des impôts, sujet à un dégrèvement d'impôts.

tax disc n 🇬🇧 vignette *f* automobile.

tax evasion n fraude *f* fiscale.

tax-exempt 🇺🇸 = **tax-free**.

tax-exemption n exonération *f* d'impôts.

tax exile n *personne qui s'expatrie pour échapper au fisc*.

tax form n feuille *f* or déclaration *f* d'impôts.

tax-free adj [goods] exonéré de taxes, non taxé ; [interest] exonéré d'impôts, exempt d'impôts.

tax haven n paradis *m* fiscal.

taxi ['tæksɪ] (*pl* taxis *or* taxies, *pt* & *pp* taxied, *cont* taxying) ◆ n taxi *m*. ◆ vi [aircraft] se déplacer au sol. ◆ vt [carry passengers] transporter en taxi.

taxicab ['tæksɪkæb] n taxi *m*.

taxidermist ['tæksɪdɜːmɪst] n empailleur *m*, -euse *f*, taxidermiste *mf*, naturaliste *mf*.

taxi driver n chauffeur *m* de taxi.

taximeter ['tæksɪˌmiːtər] n taximètre *m*, compteur *m* (de taxi).

tax incentive n incitation *f* fiscale.

taxing ['tæksɪŋ] adj [problem, time] difficile ; [climb] ardu.

tax inspector n inspecteur *m* des impôts.

taxi rank ⅦⅩ, **taxi stand** ⅦⓈ n station *f* de taxis.

taxman ['tæksmæn] (*pl* taxmen [-men]) n **1.** [person] percepteur *m* (du fisc) **2.** ⅦⓀ inf [Inland Revenue] ▸ **the taxman** le fisc.

taxpayer ['tæksˌpeɪər] n contribuable *mf*.

tax relief n (U) dégrèvement *m* fiscal.

tax return n déclaration *f* de revenus *or* d'impôts.

tax year n année *f* fiscale (*qui commence en avril en Grande-Bretagne*).

TB n **1.** abbr of **tuberculosis 2.** MESSAGING written abbr of **text back**.

TBA abbr of **to be announced**.

tbc (written abbr of **to be confirmed**) à confirmer, sous réserve.

T-bone (steak) n steak *m* dans l'aloyau (*sur l'os*).

tbs., tbsp. (written abbr of **tablespoon(ful)**) cs.

TD 1. abbr of **Treasury Department 2.** abbr of **touchdown**.

TDTU MESSAGING written abbr of **totally devoted to you**.

tea [tiː] n **1.** [drink, plant] thé *m* **2.** [afternoon snack] thé *m* ; [evening meal] repas *m* du soir **3.** [infusion] infusion *f*, tisane *f*.

Tea

En Grande-Bretagne et en Irlande, le thé est une boisson très populaire; il se boit fort, avec du lait et du sucre. Au bureau, à l'usine ou sur les chantiers de construction, la journée de travail est traditionnellement ponctuée de **tea breaks** (« pauses-thé »).

teabag ['tiːbæg] n sachet *m* de thé.

tea ball n ⅦⓈ boule *f* à thé.

tea break n pause *f* pour prendre le thé ; ≃ pause-café *f*.

tea caddy n boîte *f* à thé.

teacake ['tiːkeɪk] n *petite brioche*.

teach [tiːtʃ] (*pt* & *pp* taught [tɔːt]) ◆ vt **1.** [gen] apprendre ▸ **to teach sb sthg** *or* **sthg to sb** apprendre qqch à qqn ▸ **to teach sb (how) to do sthg** apprendre à qqn à faire qqch **2.** SCH [physics, history, etc.] enseigner, être professeur de ; [pupils, class] faire cours à ▸ **to teach school** ⅦⓈ être enseignant. ◆ vi [as profession] être enseignant, enseigner ; [give lessons] faire cours.

teacher ['tiːtʃər] n [in primary school] instituteur *m*, -trice *f*, maître *m*, maîtresse *f* ; [in secondary school] professeur *m*, enseignant *m*, -e *f* ; [in special school] éducateur *m*, -trice *f*.

teacher's college ⅦⓈ = **teacher training college**.

teacher's pet n chouchou *m*, -oute *f* du professeur.

teachers' planning room ['tiːtʃəz,plænɪŋruːm] n ⅦⓈ SCH salle *f* des professeurs.

teacher training college n ⅦⓀ centre *m* de formation pédagogique ; ≃ école *f* normale.

teaching ['tiːtʃɪŋ] ◆ n **1.** [career] enseignement *m* **2.** [of subject] enseignement *m* **3.** (U) [hours taught] heures *fpl* d'enseignement, (heures *fpl* de) cours *mpl*. ◆ comp [profession, staff] enseignant. ❖ **teachings** pl n [of leader, church] enseignements *mpl*.

teaching aid n matériel *m* pédagogique.

teaching assistant n ⅦⓈ SCH *étudiant(e) chargé(e) de travaux dirigés*.

teaching hospital n centre *m* hospitalo-universitaire, CHU *m*.

teaching practice n (U) stage *m* pédagogique (*pour futurs enseignants*).

tea cloth ⅦⓀ = **tea towel**.

tea cosy ⅦⓀ, **tea cozy** ⅦⓈ n cosy *m*.

teacup ['tiːkʌp] n tasse *f* à thé.

teak [tiːk] ◆ n ▸ **teak (wood)** teck *m*, tek *m*. ◆ comp en teck.

tealeaf ['tiːliːf] (*pl* tealeaves [-liːvz]) n **1.** feuille *f* de thé ▸ **to read the tealeaves** ≃ lire dans le marc de café **2.** ⅦⓀ *v inf & hum* [thief] voleur *m*, -euse *f*.

team [tiːm] ◆ n **1.** SPORT [gen] équipe *f* **2.** [of horses, oxen, etc.] attelage *m*. ◆ vt **1.** [workers, players] mettre en équipe ; [horses, oxen, etc.] atteler **2.** [colours, garments] assortir, harmoniser. ❖ **team up** vt sep **1.** [workers, players] mettre en équipe ; [horses, oxen, etc.] atteler **2.** [colours, clothes] assortir, harmoniser. ◆ vi **1.** [workers] faire équipe, travailler en collaboration ▸ **to team up with sb** faire équipe avec qqn **2.** [colours, clothes] être assorti, s'harmoniser.

team game n jeu *m* d'équipe.

team mate n coéquipier *m*, -ère *f*.

team player n ▸ **to be a (good) team player** avoir l'esprit d'équipe.

team spirit n esprit *m* d'équipe.

teamster ['tiːmstər] n ⅦⓈ routier *m*, camionneur *m*. ❖ **Teamster** n ⅦⓈ *membre du syndicat américain des camionneurs*.

teamwork ['tiːmwɜːk] n travail *m* d'équipe.

tea party n [for adults] thé *m* ; [for children] goûter *m*.

teapot ['tiːpɒt] n théière *f*.

tear¹ [teər] (*pt* tore [tɔːr], *pp* torn [tɔːn]) ◆ vt **1.** [rip - page, material] déchirer ; [- clothes] déchirer, faire un accroc à ; [- flesh] déchirer, arracher **2.** [muscle, ligament] froisser, déchirer **3.** [grab, snatch] arracher **4.** *fig* [divide] tirailler, déchirer **5.** *fig* [separate] arracher. ◆ vi **1.** [paper, cloth] se déchirer **2.** [as verb of movement] ▸ **to tear after sb** se précipiter *or* se lancer à la poursuite de qqn ▸ **to tear along a)** [runner] courir à toute allure **b)** [car] filer à toute allure **3.** [hurry] : *he tore through the book / the report* il a lu le livre / le rapport très rapidement. ◆ n [in paper, cloth] déchirure *f* ; [in clothes] déchirure *f*, accroc *m*. ❖ **tear apart** vt sep **1.** [rip to pieces] déchirer **2.** [divide] : *no-one can tear them apart* **a)** [friends] on ne peut les séparer, ils sont inséparables **b)** [fighters] on n'arrive pas à les séparer. ❖ **tear at** vt insep ▸ **to tear at sthg** déchirer *or* arracher qqch. ❖ **tear away** vt sep **1.** [remove - wall-paper] arracher, enlever ; *fig* [gloss, façade] enlever **2.** [from activity] arracher ▸ **to tear sb away from sthg** arracher qqn à qqch. ❖ **tear down** vt sep **1.** [remove - poster] arracher **2.** [demolish - building] démolir ; *fig* [argument] démolir, mettre par terre. ❖ **tear into** vt insep **1.** [attack, rush at] se précipiter sur **2.** *inf* [reprimand] enguirlander, passer un savon à ; [criticize] taper sur, descendre (en flèche) **3.** [bite into - subj: teeth, knife] s'enfoncer dans **4.** [run] : *she came tearing into the garden* elle a déboulé dans le jardin à toute allure, elle s'est précipitée dans le jardin. ❖ **tear off** vt sep **1.** [tape, wrapper] arracher, enlever en arrachant ; [along perforations] détacher ; [clothing] retirer or enlever rapidement **2.** *inf* [report, essay, etc. - do hurriedly] écrire à toute vitesse ; [- do badly] bâcler, torcher. ❖ **tear out** vt sep [page] arracher ; [coupon, cheque] détacher ▸ **to tear one's hair (out)** *lit & fig* s'arracher les cheveux. ❖ **tear up** vt sep **1.** [paper, letter] déchirer (en morceaux) ; *fig* [agreement, contract] déchirer **2.** [pull up - fence, weeds, surface] arracher ; [- tree] déraciner.

tear² [tɪəʳ] n larme *f* ▸ **to be in tears** être en larmes ▸ **to burst into tears** fondre en larmes ▸ **to shed tears** verser des larmes ▸ **to be bored to tears** s'ennuyer à mourir. ❖ **tear up** vi [start crying] se mettre à pleurer.

tearaway ['teərə,weɪ] n casse-cou *mf*.

teardrop ['tɪədrɒp] n larme *f*.

tear duct [tɪəʳ-] n canal *m* lacrymal.

tearful ['tɪəful] adj **1.** [emotional - departure, occasion] larmoyant ; [- story, account] larmoyant, à faire pleurer **2.** [person] en larmes, qui pleure ; [face] en larmes ; [voice] larmoyant.

tearfully ['tɪəfulɪ] adv en pleurant, les larmes aux yeux.

tear gas [tɪəʳ-] n gaz *m* lacrymogène.

tearing ['teərɪŋ] ◆ n déchirement *m*. ◆ adj **1.** *lit* ▸ **a tearing sound a)** [from paper] un bruit de déchirement **b)** [from stitching] un (bruit de) craquement **2.** 🇬🇧 [as intensifier] ▸ **to be in a tearing hurry** être terriblement pressé.

tearjerker ['tɪə,dʒɜːkəʳ] n *inf* : *the film / the book is a real tearjerker* c'est un film / un livre à faire pleurer.

tearoom ['tiːrum] n salon *m* de thé.

tease [tiːz] ◆ vt **1.** [person] taquiner ; [animal] tourmenter **2.** [fabric] peigner ; [wool] peigner, carder **3.** 🇺🇸 [hair] crêper. ◆ vi faire des taquineries. ◆ n *inf* **1.** [person] taquin *m*, -e *f* ; [sexually] allumeuse *f* **2.** [behaviour] taquinerie *f*. ❖ **tease out** vt sep **1.** [wool, hair] démêler **2.** [information, facts] faire ressortir.

teaser ['tiːzəʳ] n *inf* **1.** [person] taquin *m*, -e *f* **2.** [problem] problème *m* difficile, colle *f* **3.** [advertisement] teaser *m*.

teaser campaign n campagne *f* teasing.

tea service, tea set n service *m* à thé.

tea shop n 🇬🇧 salon *m* de thé.

teasing ['tiːzɪŋ] ◆ n (U) **1.** [tormenting] taquineries *fpl* **2.** TEXT peignage *m*. ◆ adj taquin.

Teasmaid® ['tiːzmeɪd] n 🇬🇧 théière *automatique avec horloge incorporée*.

teaspoon ['tiːspuːn] n **1.** [spoon] cuiller *f* or cuillère *f* à café **2.** = teaspoonful.

teaspoonful ['tiːspuːn,ful] adj cuiller *f* or cuillère *f* à café *(mesure)*.

tea strainer n passoire *f* à thé, passe-thé *m inv*.

teat [tiːt] n **1.** [on breast] mamelon *m*, bout *m* de sein ; [of animal] tétine *f*, tette *f* ; [for milking] trayon *m* **2.** 🇬🇧 [on bottle] tétine *f* ; [dummy] tétine *f*, sucette *f* **3.** TECH téton *m*.

teatime ['tiːtaɪm] n l'heure *f* du thé.

tea towel n 🇬🇧 torchon *m* (à vaisselle).

tea urn n fontaine *f* à thé.

techie ['tekɪ] n *inf* technicien *m*, -enne *f*.

technical ['teknɪkl] adj **1.** [gen & TECH] technique ▸ **technical hitch** incident *m* technique **2.** [according to rules] technique ▸ **technical knockout** SPORT knock-out *m inv* technique.

technical college n ≃ institut *m* de technologie.

technical drawing n dessin *m* industriel.

technical foul n SPORT faute *f* technique.

technicality [,teknɪ'kælɪtɪ] (*pl* **technicalities**) n **1.** [technical nature] technicité *f* **2.** [formal detail] détail *m* or considération *f* (d'ordre) technique ; [technical term] terme *m* technique.

technically ['teknɪklɪ] adv **1.** [on a technical level] sur un plan technique ; [in technical terms] en termes techniques **2.** [in theory] en théorie, en principe.

technician [tek'nɪʃn] n technicien *m*, -enne *f*.

Technicolor® ['teknɪ,kʌləʳ] ◆ n Technicolor® *m*. ◆ adj en technicolor.

technique [tek'niːk] n technique *f*.

techno ['teknəʊ] n MUS techno *f*.

technobabble ['teknəʊ,bæbl] n jargon *m* technique.

technocrat ['teknəkræt] n technocrate *mf*.

technological [,teknə'lɒdʒɪkl] adj technologique.

technologist [tek'nɒlədʒɪst] n technologue *mf*, technologiste *mf*.

technology [tek'nɒlədʒɪ] (*pl* **technologies**) n technologie *f*.

technophile ['teknəʊfaɪl] n technophile *mf*.

technophobe ['teknəfəʊb] n technophobe *mf*.

teddy ['tedɪ] (*pl* **teddies**) n **1.** ▸ **teddy (bear)** ours *m* en peluche **2.** [garment] teddy *m*.

tedious ['tiːdjəs] adj [activity, work] ennuyeux, fastidieux ; [time] ennuyeux ; [journey] fatigant, pénible ; [person] pénible.

tedium ['tiːdjəm] n ennui *m*.

tee [tiː] ◆ n [in golf - peg] tee *m* ; [- area] tertre *m* or point *m* de départ. ◆ vt placer sur le tee. ◆ vi placer la balle sur le tee. ❖ **tee off** vi **1.** [in golf] jouer sa balle or partir du tee *(du tertre de départ)* ; *fig* commencer, démarrer **2.** 🇺🇸 *inf* [get angry] se fâcher, s'emporter. ◆ vt sep 🇺🇸 *inf* [annoy] agacer, casser les pieds à. ❖ **tee up** vi placer la balle sur le tee.

teem [tiːm] vi **1.** [be crowded] grouiller, fourmiller **2.** [rain] : *it's absolutely teeming (down* or *with rain)* il pleut à verse or à torrents.

teen [tiːn] adj [teenage - fashion, magazine] pour adolescents or jeunes.

teenage ['tiːneɪdʒ] adj jeune, adolescent ; [habits, activities] d'adolescents ; [fashion, magazine] pour les jeunes.

teenager ['tiːn,eɪdʒəʳ] n jeune *mf* (entre 13 et 19 ans), adolescent *m*, -e *f*.

teens [tiːnz] pl n **1.** [age] adolescence *f* (entre 13 et 19 ans) **2.** [numbers] *les chiffres entre 13 et 19.*

teensy(-weensy) [,tiːnzɪ('wiːnzɪ)] *inf* = **teenyweeny.**

teeny-weeny [-'wiːnɪ], **teeny-tiny** 🇺🇸 adj *inf* tout petit, minuscule.

tee shirt = T-shirt.

teeter ['tiːtəʳ] ◆ vi **1.** [person] chanceler ; [pile, object] vaciller, être sur le point de tomber **2.** 🇺🇸 [see-saw] se balancer, basculer. ◆ n 🇺🇸 jeu *m* de bascule.

teeter-totter n 🇺🇸 jeu *m* de bascule.

teeth [tiːθ] pl ⟶ **tooth.**

teethe [tiːð] vi faire or percer ses premières dents.

teething ['tiːðɪŋ] n poussée f dentaire, dentition f.

teething ring n anneau m de dentition.

teething troubles pl n *lit* douleurs fpl provoquées par la poussée des dents ; *fig* difficultés fpl initiales or de départ.

teetotal [tiː'təʊtl] adj [person] qui ne boit jamais d'alcool ; [organization] antialcoolique.

teetotaller 🇬🇧, **teetotaler** 🇺🇸 [tiː'təʊtlər] n personne qui ne boit jamais d'alcool.

TEFL ['tefl] (abbr of Teaching (of) English as a Foreign Language) n enseignement de l'anglais langue étrangère.

Teflon® ['teflɒn] n Teflon® m.

Tehran, Teheran [ˌteə'rɑːn] pr n Téhéran.

tel. (written abbr of telephone) tél.

Tel-Aviv [ˌtelə'viːv] pr n ▶ **Tel-Aviv(-Jaffa)** Tel-Aviv(-Jaffa).

tele- ['telɪ] pref télé-.

telebanking ['telɪbæŋkɪŋ] n FIN services mpl bancaires en ligne, télébanque f.

telecast ['telɪkɑːst] ◆ n émission f de télévision, programme m télédiffusé. ◆ vt diffuser, téléviser.

telecom ['telɪkɒm] n (U) 🇬🇧 inf télécommunications fpl.

telecommunications ['telɪkəˌmjuːnɪ'keɪʃnz] ◆ n (U) télécommunications fpl. ◆ comp [engineer] des télécommunications ; [satellite] de télécommunication.

telecommuter ['telɪkəˌmjuːtər] n télétravailleur m, -euse f.

telecommuting [ˌtelɪkə'mjuːtɪŋ] n télétravail m.

telecom(s) ['telɪkɒm(z)] n abbr of telecommunications.

telecon ['telɪkɒn] n inf conversation f téléphonique.

teleconference ['telɪˌkɒnfərəns] n téléconférence f.

teleconferencing [ˌtelɪ'kɒnfərənsɪŋ] n téléconférence f.

telegram ['telɪgræm] n télégramme m ; [in press, diplomacy] dépêche f / by telegram par télégramme.

telegraph ['telɪgrɑːf] ◆ n 1. [system] télégraphe m ▶ **the Telegraph** PRESS nom abrégé du « Daily Telegraph » ⟶ **broadsheet** 2. [telegram] télégramme m. ◆ comp [service, wire] télégraphique ▶ **telegraph pole** or **post** poteau m télégraphique. ◆ vt [news] télégraphier ; [money] télégraphier, envoyer par télégramme. ◆ vi télégraphier.

telemark ['telɪmɑːk] n SPORT télémark m.

telemarketing ['telɪˌmɑːkɪtɪŋ] n vente f par téléphone.

telenovela [telenəʊvelæ] n feuilleton m télévisé (soap opera produit et diffusé dans les pays d'Amérique latine).

telepathic [ˌtelɪ'pæθɪk] adj [person] télépathe ; [message, means] télépathique.

telepathy [tɪ'lepəθɪ] n télépathie f, transmission f de pensée.

telepayment ['telɪˌpeɪmənt] n télépaiement m.

telephone ['telɪfəʊn] ◆ n téléphone m ▶ **to be on the telephone** a) [talking] être au téléphone, téléphoner b) [subscriber] avoir le téléphone, être abonné au téléphone ▶ **to answer the telephone** répondre au téléphone. ◆ comp [line, receiver] de téléphone ; [call, message] téléphonique ; [bill, charges] téléphonique, de téléphone ; [service] des télécommunications. ◆ vt [person] téléphoner à, appeler (au téléphone) ; [place] téléphoner à, appeler ; [news, message, invitation] téléphoner, envoyer par téléphone. ◆ vi [call] téléphoner, appeler ; [be on phone] être au téléphone.

telephone banking n FIN banque f par téléphone.

telephone book n annuaire m (téléphonique).

telephone booth, telephone box n cabine f téléphonique.

telephone directory = telephone book.

telephone exchange n central m téléphonique.

telephone kiosk 🇬🇧 = telephone booth.

telephone number n numéro m de téléphone.

telephone-tapping [-'tæpɪŋ] n mise f sur écoute téléphonique.

telephonist [tɪ'lefənɪst] n 🇬🇧 standardiste mf, téléphoniste mf.

telephoto lens [ˌtelɪ'fəʊtəʊ-] n téléobjectif m.

teleprinter ['telɪˌprɪntər] n 🇬🇧 téléscripteur m, téléimprimeur m.

Teleprompter® [ˌtelɪ'prɒmptər] n prompteur m, téléprompteur m, télésouffleur m offic.

telesales ['telɪseɪlz] pl n vente f par téléphone.

telesalesperson ['telɪˌseɪlzpɜːsn] n télévendeur m, -euse f.

telescope ['telɪskəʊp] ◆ n télescope m, longue-vue f ; ASTRON télescope m, lunette f astronomique. ◆ vt [shorten, condense - parts, report] condenser, abréger. ◆ vi 1. [collapse - parts] s'emboîter 2. [railway carriages] se télescoper.

telescopic [ˌtelɪ'skɒpɪk] adj [aerial] télescopique ; [umbrella] pliant ▶ **telescopic lens** téléobjectif m ▶ **telescopic sight** lunette f.

teleshopping [ˌtelɪ'ʃɒpɪŋ] n téléachat m.

teletext ['telɪtekst] n télétexte m, vidéographie f diffusée.

telethon ['telɪθɒn] n Téléthon m.

teletypewriter [ˌtelɪ'taɪpˌraɪtər] n 🇺🇸 téléscripteur m, téléimprimeur m.

televangelism [ˌtelɪ'vændʒəlɪzm] n émissions télévisées d'évangélisation.

televangelist [ˌtelɪ'vændʒəlɪst] n évangéliste qui prêche à la télévision.

televideo [telɪ'vɪdɪəʊ] n combiné m télé/magnétoscope m.

televise ['telɪvaɪz] vt téléviser.

television ['telɪˌvɪʒn] ◆ n 1. [system, broadcasts] télévision f ▶ **to watch television** regarder la télévision ▶ **to go on television** passer à la télévision 2. [set] téléviseur m, (poste m de) télévision f / I saw her on (the) television je l'ai vue à la télévision ▶ **to turn the television up** / **down** / **off** / **on** monter le son de / baisser le son de / éteindre / allumer la télévision. ◆ comp [camera, engineer, programme, station, screen] de télévision ; [picture, news] télévisé ; [satellite] de télédiffusion.

television licence n 🇬🇧 redevance f (de télévision).

television set n téléviseur m, (poste m de) télévision f.

teleworker ['telɪwɜːkər] n télétravailleur m, -euse f.

teleworking [ˌtelɪ'wɜːkɪŋ] n télétravail m.

telex ['teleks] ◆ n télex m. ◆ vt envoyer par télex, télexer.

tell [tel] (pt & pp told [təʊld]) ◆ vt 1. [inform of] dire à ▶ **to tell sb sthg** dire qqch à qqn / I told him the answer / what I thought je lui ai dit la réponse / ce que je pensais ▶ **to tell sb about** or of liter sthg dire qqch à qqn, parler à qqn de qqch / I'm pleased to tell you you've won j'ai le plaisir de vous informer or annoncer que vous avez gagné / so I've been told c'est ce qu'on m'a dit / it doesn't tell us much cela ne nous en dit pas très long, cela ne nous apprend pas grand-chose / can you tell me the time? pouvez-vous me dire l'heure (qu'il est) ? 2. [explain to] expliquer à, dire à / this brochure tells me all I need to know cette brochure m'explique tout ce que j'ai besoin de savoir

/ can you tell me the way to the station / to Oxford? pouvez-vous m'indiquer le chemin de la gare / la route d'Oxford ? */ do you want me to tell you again?* voulez-vous que je vous le redise or répète ? **3.** [instruct, order] ▸ **to tell sb to do sthg** dire à qqn de faire qqch */ he didn't need to be told twice!* il ne s'est pas fait prier !, je n'ai pas eu besoin de lui dire deux fois ! **4.** [recount - story, joke] raconter ; [- news] annoncer ; [- secret] dire, raconter ▸ **to tell sb about sthg** parler à qqn de qqch, raconter qqch à qqn */ could you tell me a little about yourself?* pourriez-vous me parler un peu de vous-même ? **5.** [utter - truth, lie] dire, raconter ▸ **to tell sb the truth** dire la vérité à qqn ▸ **to tell lies** mentir, dire des mensonges **6.** [assure] dire, assurer */ didn't I tell you?* or *I told you so!* je vous l'avais bien dit ! */ let me tell you!* **a)** [believe me] je vous assure !, croyez-moi ! **b)** [as threat] tenez-vous-le pour dit ! ▸ **you're telling me!** *inf* à qui le dites-vous ! **7.** [distinguish] distinguer ▸ **to tell right from wrong** distinguer le bien du mal */ you can hardly tell the difference between them* on voit or distingue à peine la différence entre eux ; [see] voir ; [know] savoir ; [understand] comprendre */ how can you tell when it's ready?* à quoi voit-on or comment peut-on savoir que c'est prêt ? */ there's no telling what he might do next / how he'll react* (il est) impossible de dire ce qu'il est susceptible de faire ensuite / comment il réagira. ◆ *vi* **1.** [reveal] : *that would be telling!* ce serait trahir un secret ! */ I won't tell* je ne dirai rien à personne */ time will tell* qui vivra verra, le temps nous le dira **2.** [know] savoir */ how can I tell?* comment le saurais-je ? */ who can tell?* qui peut savoir ?, qui sait ? */ you never can tell* on ne sait jamais **3.** [have effect] se faire sentir, avoir de l'influence */ her age is beginning to tell* elle commence à accuser son âge */ the strain is beginning to tell* la tension commence à se faire sentir */ her aristocratic roots told against her* ses origines aristocratiques lui nuisaient. ◆❖ **tell apart** *vt sep* distinguer (entre). ◆❖ **tell off** *vt sep* [scold] réprimander, gronder. ◆❖ **tell on** *vt insep* [denounce] dénoncer.

teller ['telə*] n* **1.** US [in bank] ▸ **(bank) teller** caissier *m,* -ère *f,* guichetier *m,* -ère *f* **2.** POL [of votes] scrutateur *m,* -trice *f* **3.** [of story] ▸ **(story) teller** conteur *m,* -euse *f,* narrateur *m,* -trice *f.*

telling ['telɪŋ] ◆ *adj* **1.** [revealing - smile, figures, evidence] révélateur, éloquent **2.** [effective - style] efficace ; [- account] saisissant ; [- remark, argument] qui porte. ◆ *n* récit *m,* narration *f.*

tellingly ['telɪŋlɪ] *adv* **1.** [effectively] efficacement **2.** [revealingly] : *tellingly, he didn't invite his best friend* il n'a pas invité son meilleur ami, ce qui en dit long or ce qui est révélateur.

telling-off (*pl* **tellings-off**) *n* réprimande *f.*

telltale ['telteɪl] ◆ *n* [person] rapporteur *m,* -euse *f.* ◆ *adj* [marks] révélateur ; [look, blush, nod] éloquent.

telly ['telɪ] (*pl* **tellies**) *n* UK *inf* télé *f* */ on the telly* à la télé.

temerity [tɪ'merətɪ] *n* témérité *f,* audace *f.*

temp [temp] ◆ *n* (abbr of **temporary employee**) intérimaire *mf.* ◆ *vi : she's temping* elle fait de l'intérim.

temp. (written abbr of **temperature**) temp.

temper ['tempə*] ◆ n* **1.** [character] caractère *m,* tempérament *m ;* [patience] patience *f ;* [calm] calme *m,* sang-froid *m inv* **2.** [mood] humeur *f* ▸ **to be in a bad temper** être de mauvaise humeur ; [bad mood] (crise *f* de) colère *f,* mauvaise humeur *f* ▸ **to be in a temper** être de mauvaise humeur **3.** METALL trempe *f.* ◆ *vt* **1.** [moderate - passions] modérer, tempérer ; [- pain, suffering] adoucir **2.** METALL tremper. ◆ *interj* ▸ **temper!** on se calme !, du calme !

temperament ['temprəmənt] *n* [character] tempérament *m,* nature *f ;* [moodiness] humeur *f* changeante or lunatique.

temperamental [,temprə'mentl] *adj* **1.** [moody - person] capricieux, lunatique ; [unpredictable - animal, machine] capricieux **2.** [relating to character] du tempérament, de la personnalité.

temperamentally [,temprə'mentəlɪ] *adv* de par son caractère.

temperance ['temprəns] ◆ *n* **1.** [moderation] modération *f,* sobriété *f* **2.** [abstinence from alcohol] tempérance *f.* ◆ *comp* [movement] antialcoolique.

temperate ['temprət] *adj* **1.** [climate] tempéré **2.** [moderate - person] modéré, mesuré ; [- character, appetite] modéré ; [- reaction, criticism] modéré, sobre.

temperature ['temprətʃə*] ◆ n* **1.** MED température *f* ▸ **to have** or **to run a temperature** avoir de la température or de la fièvre ▸ **to take sb's temperature** prendre la température de qqn **2.** METEOR & PHYS température *f.* ◆ *comp* [change] de température ; [control] de la température ; [gradient] thermique.

tempered ['tempəd] *adj* **1.** [steel] trempé **2.** MUS [scale] tempéré.

temper tantrum *n* crise *f* de colère.

tempest ['tempɪst] *n liter* tempête *f,* orage *m.*

tempestuous [tem'pestjʊəs] *adj* **1.** [weather] de tempête **2.** [person] impétueux, fougueux ; [meeting] agité.

tempi ['tempiː] *pl* ⟶ **tempo**.

temping ['tempɪŋ] *n* intérim *m.*

template ['templɪt] *n* **1.** TECH gabarit *m,* calibre *m,* patron *m* **2.** [beam] traverse *f* **3.** COMPUT masque *m* de saisie.

temple ['templ] *n* **1.** RELIG temple *m* **2.** ANAT tempe *f.*

templet ['templɪt] = **template**.

tempo ['tempəʊ] (*pl* **tempos** or **tempi** ['tempiː]) *n* tempo *m.*

temporal ['tempərəl] *adj* **1.** [gen & GRAM] temporel **2.** [secular] temporel, séculier.

temporarily [UK 'tempərərəlɪ US ,tempə'rerəlɪ] *adv* provisoirement, temporairement.

temporary ['tempərərɪ] (*pl* **temporaries**) ◆ *adj* [accommodation, solution, powers] temporaire, provisoire ; [employment] temporaire, intérimaire ; [improvement] passager, momentané ; [relief] passager. ◆ *n* intérimaire *mf.*

tempt [tempt] *vt* [entice] tenter, donner envie à ; [seduce] tenter, séduire ; [attract] attirer, tenter ▸ **to tempt sb to do sthg** or **into doing sthg** donner à qqn l'envie de faire qqch.

temptation [temp'teɪʃn] *n* tentation *f.*

tempting ['temptɪŋ] *adj* [offer] tentant, attrayant ; [smell, meal] appétissant.

tempura [tem'puːrə] *n* tempura *m* (beignet japonais de légumes ou de poisson).

ten [ten] ◆ *det* dix. ◆ *n* dix *m.* ◆ *pron* dix. See also **five**. ◆❖ **tens** *pl n* MATH dizaines *fpl* ▸ **tens column** colonne *f* des dizaines.

tenable ['tenəbl] *adj* **1.** [argument, position] défendable, soutenable **2.** [post] que l'on occupe, auquel on est nommé.

tenacious [tɪ'neɪʃəs] *adj* **1.** [stubborn, persistent - person] entêté, opiniâtre ; [- prejudice, opposition] tenace, obstiné **2.** [firm - grip] ferme, solide.

tenaciously [tɪ'neɪʃəslɪ] *adv* avec ténacité, obstinément.

tenacity [tɪ'næsətɪ] *n* ténacité *f,* opiniâtreté *f.*

tenancy ['tenənsɪ] (*pl* **tenancies**) ◆ *n* **1.** [of house, land] location *f* **2.** [period] ▸ **(period of) tenancy** (période *f* de) location *f* **3.** [property] ▶ **a council tenancy** un logement appartenant à la municipalité ; ≃ une HLM. ◆ **comp** de location.

tenant ['tenənt] ◆ n locataire *mf*. ◆ comp [rights] du locataire.

Ten Commandments pl n ▶ **the Ten Commandments** les dix commandements *mpl*.

tend [tend] ◆ vi **1.** [be inclined] ▶ **to tend to** avoir tendance à, tendre à **2.** [colour] : *red tending to orange* rouge tirant sur l'orange **3.** [go, move] tendre **4.** [look after] : *to tend to one's business / one's guests* s'occuper de ses affaires / ses invités **/** *to tend to sb's wounds* panser or soigner les blessures de qqn. ◆ vt **1.** [take care of - sheep] garder ; [-sick, wounded] soigner ; [-garden] entretenir, s'occuper de **2.** US [customer] servir.

tendency ['tendənsɪ] (*pl* **tendencies**) n **1.** [inclination] tendance *f* **2.** [trend] tendance *f* **3.** POL tendance *f*, groupe *m*.

tender ['tendər] ◆ adj **1.** [affectionate - person] tendre, affectueux, doux (douce) ; [-heart, smile, words] tendre ; [-memories] doux (douce) **2.** [sensitive -skin] délicat, fragile ; [sore] sensible, douloureux **3.** [meat, vegetables] tendre **4.** *liter* [innocent -age, youth] tendre. ◆ vt **1.** [resignation] donner ; [apologies] présenter ; [thanks] offrir ; [bid, offer] faire **2.** [money, fare] tendre ▶ **to tender sthg to sb** tendre qqch à qqn. ◆ vi faire une soumission. ◆ n **1.** UK [statement of charges] soumission *f* ; [bid] offre *f* **2.** RAIL tender *m* **3.** NAUT [shuttle] navette *f* ; [supply boat] ravitailleur *m* **4.** [supply vehicle] véhicule *m* ravitailleur ▶ **(fire) tender** UK voiture *f* de pompier.

tenderize, tenderise ['tendəraɪz] vt attendrir.

tenderly ['tendəlɪ] adv tendrement, avec tendresse.

tenderness ['tendənɪs] n **1.** [of person, feelings] tendresse *f*, affection *f* **2.** [of skin] sensibilité *f* ; [of plant] fragilité *f* ; [soreness] sensibilité *f* **3.** [of meat, vegetables] tendreté *f*.

tendon ['tendən] n tendon *m*.

tendril ['tendrəl] n **1.** BOT vrille *f*, cirre *m* **2.** [of hair] boucle *f*.

tenement ['tenəmənt] n **1.** [block of flats] immeuble *m* (ancien) **2.** [slum] taudis *m* **3.** [dwelling] logement *m*.

Tenerife [,tenə'ri:f] pr n Tenerife, Ténériffe **/** *in Tenerife* à Tenerife.

tenet ['tenɪt] n [principle] principe *m*, dogme *m* ; [belief] croyance *f*.

tenner ['tenər] n UK *inf* billet *m* de 10 livres.

Tennessee [,tenə'si:] pr n Tennessee *m* **/** *in Tennessee* dans le Tennessee.

tennis ['tenɪs] ◆ n tennis *m*. ◆ comp [ball, court, player, racket] de tennis.

tennis shoe n (chaussure *f* de) tennis *f*.

tenor ['tenər] ◆ n **1.** [general sense -of conversation] sens *m* général, teneur *f* ; [-of letter] contenu *m*, teneur *f* **2.** [general flow -of events] cours *m*, marche *f* **3.** MUS ténor *m*. ◆ comp [part, voice] de ténor ; [aria] pour (voix de) ténor ▶ **tenor recorder** flûte *f* à bec ▶ **tenor saxophone** saxophone *m* ténor. ◆ adv ▶ **to sing tenor** avoir une voix de or être ténor.

tenpin bowling ['tenpɪn-] n UK bowling *m*.

tenpins ['tenpɪnz] n US bowling *m*.

tense [tens] ◆ adj **1.** [person, situation] tendu ; [smile] crispé **2.** [muscles, rope, spring] tendu **3.** LING [vowel] tendu. ◆ vt [muscle] tendre, bander. ◆ n GRAM temps *m*. ❖ **tense up** ◆ vi [muscle] se tendre, se raidir ; [person] se crisper, devenir tendu. ◆ vt sep [person] rendre nerveux.

tensely ['tenslɪ] adv [move, react] de façon tendue ; [speak] d'une voix tendue.

tensile strength n résistance *f* à la tension, limite *f* élastique à la tension.

tension ['tenʃn] n **1.** [of person, situation, voice] tension *f* **2.** [of muscle, rope, spring] tension *f* **3.** ELEC tension *f*, voltage *m* **4.** MECH & TECH tension *f*, (force *f* de) traction *f*.

ten-spot n US *inf* billet *m* de dix dollars.

tent [tent] ◆ n [for camping] tente *f*. ◆ comp [peg, pole] de tente. ◆ vi camper.

tentacle ['tentəkl] n tentacule *m*.

tentative ['tentətɪv] adj **1.** [provisional] provisoire ; [preliminary] préliminaire ; [experimental] expérimental **2.** [uncertain -smile] timide ; [-person] indécis, hésitant ; [-steps] hésitant.

tentatively ['tentətɪvlɪ] adv **1.** [suggest] provisoirement ; [act] à titre d'essai **2.** [smile] timidement ; [walk] d'un pas hésitant.

tenterhooks ['tentəhʊks] pl n TEXT clous *mpl* à crochet ▶ **to be on tenterhooks** être sur des charbons ardents.

tenth [tenθ] ◆ adj dixième ◆ n **1.** [gen & MATH] dixième *m* **2.** MUS dixième *f*. ◆ adv en dixième place, à la dixième place. See also **fifth**.

tenth grade n US SCH classe *f* de l'enseignement secondaire correspondant à la seconde (14-15 ans).

tenth grader ['tenθ,greɪdər] n US SCH lycéen en deuxième année.

tenuous ['tenjʊəs] adj **1.** [fine -distinction] subtil, ténu ; [-thread] ténu **2.** [flimsy -link, relationship] précaire, fragile ; [-evidence] mince, faible ; [-argument] faible **3.** [precarious -existence] précaire.

tenuously ['tenjʊəslɪ] adv de manière ténue or précaire.

tenuousness ['tenjʊəsnɪs] n **1.** [of distinction] subtilité *f* ; [of thread] ténuité *f* ; [of voice] faiblesse *f* **2.** [of link, relationship] fragilité *f*, précarité *f* ; [of evidence] minceur *f*, faiblesse *f* ; [of argument] faiblesse *f* **3.** [of existence] précarité *f* **4.** PHYS raréfaction *f*.

tenure ['tenjər] n **1.** [of land, property] bail *m* **2.** [of post] occupation *f* ▶ **to have tenure** US UNIV être titulaire.

tepee ['ti:pi:] n tipi *m*.

tepid ['tepɪd] adj **1.** [water] tiède **2.** [welcome, thanks] tiède, réservé.

tequila [tɪ'ki:lə] n tequila *f*.

Ter written abbr of **terrace**.

term [tɜ:m] ◆ n **1.** [period, end of period] terme *m* ; [of pregnancy] terme *m* ▶ **in the long / short term** à long / court terme ▶ **to reach (full) term** arriver or être à terme **2.** SCH & UNIV trimestre *m* ▶ **in** or **during term (time)** pendant le trimestre **3.** LAW & POL [of court, parliament] session *f* ; [of elected official] mandat *m* **4.** [in prison] peine *f* **5.** [word, expression] terme *m* **6.** LOGIC & MATH terme *m*. ◆ vt appeler, nommer. ❖ **terms** pl n **1.** [conditions -of employment] conditions *fpl* ; [-of agreement, contract] termes *mpl* **2.** [perspective] : *he refuses to consider the question in international terms* il refuse d'envisager la question d'un point de vue international **/** *in personal terms, it was a disaster* sur le plan personnel, c'était une catastrophe **3.** [rates, tariffs] conditions *fpl*, tarifs *mpl* **4.** [relations] ▶ **to be on good terms with sb** être en bons termes avec qqn **5.** [agreement] accord *m* ▶ **to make terms** or **to come to terms with sb** arriver à or conclure un accord avec qqn ; [acceptance] ▶ **to come to terms with sthg** se résigner à qqch, arriver à accepter qqch. ❖ **in terms of** prep phr en ce qui concerne, pour ce qui est de.

terminal ['tɜ:mɪnl] ◆ adj **1.** [final] terminal ▶ **terminal velocity** vitesse *f* limite **2.** MED [ward] pour malades condamnés or incurables ; [patient] en phase terminale ; [disease] qui est dans sa phase terminale **3.** [termly] trimestriel. ◆ n **1.** [for bus, underground] terminus *m* ; [at airport] terminal *m*, aérogare *f* ▶ **terminal (platform)** PETR terminal **2.** COMPUT terminal *m* **3.** ELEC [of battery] borne *f* **4.** LING terminaison *f*.

terminally ['tɜ:mɪnəlɪ] adv ▶ **the terminally ill** les malades condamnés or qui sont en phase terminale.

terminate ['tɜ:mɪneɪt] ◆ vt **1.** [end - project, work] terminer ; [- employment] mettre fin or un terme à ; [- contract] résilier, mettre fin or un terme à ; [- pregnancy] interrompre **2.** US inf [employee] virer **3.** inf [kill] descendre. ◆ vi **1.** [end] se terminer **2.** LING se terminer **3.** RAIL : *this train terminates at Cambridge* ce train ne va pas plus loin que Cambridge.

termination [,tɜ:mɪ'neɪʃn] n **1.** [end - gen] fin *f* ; [- of contract] résiliation *f* ▶ **termination of employment** licenciement *m* **2.** [abortion] interruption *f* de grossesse, avortement *m* **3.** LING terminaison *f*, désinence *f*.

termini ['tɜ:mɪnaɪ] pl ⟶ **terminus.**

terminology [,tɜ:mɪ'nɒlədʒɪ] (pl **terminologies**) n terminologie *f*.

terminus ['tɜ:mɪnəs] (pl **terminuses** or **termini** ['tɜ:mɪnaɪ]) n terminus *m*.

termite ['tɜ:maɪt] n termite *m*, fourmi *f* blanche.

termly ['tɜ:mlɪ] ◆ adj trimestriel. ◆ adv trimestriellement, par trimestre.

term paper n US SCH & UNIV dissertation *f* trimestrielle.

terrace ['terəs] n **1.** AGR & GEOL terrasse *f* **2.** [patio] terrasse *f* **3.** [embankment] terre-plein *m* **4.** UK [of houses] rangée *f* **5.** = **terraced house.** ◆◆ **terraces** pl n SPORT gradins *mpl*.

Terrace

Ce terme désigne au Royaume-Uni une rangée de maisons mitoyennes à un ou deux étages. À l'origine, les **terraced houses** étaient des logements ouvriers, construits à proximité des usines ou des mines de charbon.

---

terraced ['terəst] adj [garden] suspendu, étagé, en terrasses ; [hillside] cultivé en terrasses.

terraced house n UK *maison faisant partie d'une « terrace »* ▶ **terraced houses** maisons *fpl* alignées.

terracotta [,terə'kɒtə] ◆ n [earthenware] terre *f* cuite. ◆ comp [pottery] en terre cuite ; [colour] rouille *(inv)*.

terrain [te'reɪn] n terrain *m*.

terrapin ['terəpɪn] n tortue *f* d'eau douce.

terrestrial [tə'restrɪəl] ◆ adj terrestre. ◆ n **1.** [gen] terrien *m*, -enne *f* **2.** TV hertzien.

terrible ['terəbl] adj **1.** [severe, serious - cough, pain] affreux, atroce ; [- accident] effroyable, affreux ; [- storm] effroyable **2.** [very bad - experience, dream] atroce ; [- food, smell] épouvantable ; [- conditions, poverty] épouvantable, effroyable ▶ **to feel terrible a)** [ill] se sentir très mal **b)** [morally] s'en vouloir beaucoup, avoir des remords.

terribly ['terəblɪ] adv **1.** inf [as intensifier] terriblement, extrêmement **2.** [very badly] affreusement mal, terriblement mal.

terrier ['terɪə'] n terrier *m* (chien).

terrific [tə'rɪfɪk] adj **1.** [extreme, intense - noise, crash] épouvantable, effroyable ; [- speed] fou *(before vowel or silent 'h' fol, f folle)* ; [- heat] terrible, épouvantable ; [- appetite] énorme, robuste **2.** inf [superb, great] terrible, super.

terrifically [tə'rɪfɪklɪ] adv inf **1.** [extremely, enormously] extrêmement, très **2.** [very well] merveilleusement (bien).

terrified ['terɪfaɪd] adj terrifié ▶ **to be terrified of sthg** avoir une peur bleue or avoir très peur de qqch.

terrify ['terɪfaɪ] (pt & pp **terrified**) vt terrifier, effrayer.

terrifying ['terɪfaɪɪŋ] adj [dream] terrifiant ; [person] terrible, épouvantable ; [weaker use] terrifiant, effroyable.

terrifyingly ['terɪfaɪɪŋlɪ] adv de façon terrifiante or effroyable.

terrine [te'ri:n] n terrine *f*.

territorial [,terɪ'tɔ:rɪəl] ◆ adj territorial. ◆ n territorial *m* ▶ **the Territorials** l'armée *f* territoriale or la territoriale britannique.

Territorial Army pr n (armée *f*) territoriale *f* britannique.

territorial waters pl n eaux *fpl* territoriales.

territory ['terɪtrɪ] (pl **territories**) n [area] territoire *m* ; [of salesperson] territoire *m*, région *f* ; [of knowledge] domaine *m*.

terror ['terə'] n **1.** [fear] terreur *f*, épouvante *f* ▶ **to have a terror of (doing) sthg** avoir extrêmement peur or la terreur de (faire) qqch **2.** [frightening event or aspect] terreur *f* **3.** [terrorism] terreur *f* **4.** inf [person] terreur *f*. ◆◆ **Terror** n ▶ **the Terror** HIST la Terreur.

terrorism ['terərɪzm] n terrorisme *m*.

terrorist ['terərɪst] ◆ n terroriste *mf*. ◆ adj [bomb] de terroriste ; [campaign, attack, group] terroriste.

terrorize, terrorise ['terəraɪz] vt terroriser.

terror-stricken, terror-struck adj épouvanté, saisi de terreur.

terry (towelling) ['terɪ-] n ▶ **terry towelling (cloth)** tissu-éponge *m*.

terse [tɜ:s] adj [concise] concis, succinct ; [laconic] laconique ; [abrupt] brusque, sec (sèche).

tersely ['tɜ:slɪ] adv [concisely] avec concision ; [laconically] laconiquement ; [abruptly] brusquement, sèchement.

tertiary ['tɜ:ʃərɪ] adj [gen & INDUST] tertiaire ; [education] postscolaire. ◆◆ **Tertiary** ◆ adj GEOL tertiaire. ◆ n ▶ **the Tertiary** GEOL le tertiaire.

Terylene® ['terəli:n] ◆ n Térylène® *m* ; ≃ Tergal® *m*. ◆ adj en Tergal®.

TESL ['tesl] (abbr of Teaching (of) English as a Second Language) n enseignement *m* de l'anglais langue seconde.

test [test] ◆ n **1.** [examination - gen] test *m* ; SCH contrôle *m*, interrogation *f* ▶ **to pass a test** réussir à un examen ▶ **to sit** or **to take a test** passer un examen ▶ **(driving) test** : *I'm taking my (driving) test tomorrow* je passe mon permis (de conduire) demain **2.** MED [of blood, urine] test *m*, analyse *f* ; [of eyes, hearing] examen *m* ▶ **to have a blood test** faire faire une analyse de sang ▶ **to have an eye test** se faire examiner la vue **3.** [trial - of equipment, machine] test *m*, essai *m*, épreuve *f* ; [- of quality] contrôle *m* ▶ **to carry out tests on sthg** effectuer des tests sur qqch ▶ **to be on test** être testé or à l'essai ▶ **to put sthg to the test** tester qqch, faire l'essai de qqch **4.** [of character, endurance, resolve] test *m* ▶ **to put sb to the test** éprouver qqn, mettre qqn à l'épreuve **5.** [measure] test *m* **6.** UK SPORT test-match *m*. ◆◆ comp [flight, strip, etc.] d'essai. ◆ vt **1.** [examine - ability, knowledge, intelligence] tester, mesurer ; SCH [pupils] tester, contrôler les connaissances de **2.** MED [blood, urine] analyser, faire une analyse de ; [sight, hearing] examiner / *to have one's eyes tested* se faire examiner la vue **3.** [try out - prototype, car] essayer, faire l'essai de ; [- weapon] tester ; [- drug] tester, expérimenter **4.** [check - batteries, pressure, suspension] vérifier, contrôler **5.** [measure - reaction, popularity] mesurer, évaluer **6.** [analyse - soil] analyser, faire des prélèvements dans ; [-water] analyser **7**. [tax - machinery, driver, patience] éprouver, mettre à l'épreuve. ◆ vi **1**. [make examination] : *to test for salmonella* faire une recherche de salmonelles / *to test for the presence of gas* rechercher la présence de gaz **2**. RADIO & TELEC ▶ **testing, testing!** un, deux, trois ! ◆ **test out** vt sep **1**. [idea, theory] tester **2**. [prototype, product] essayer, mettre à l'essai.

testament ['testəmənt] n **1**. LAW testament *m* **2**. BIBLE testament *m* ▶ **the New Testament** le Nouveau Testament ▶ **the Old Testament** l'Ancien Testament.

test ban n interdiction *f* des essais nucléaires.

test card n UK TV mire *f*.

test case n LAW précédent *m*, affaire *f* qui fait jurisprudence.

test drive (*pt* **test-drove**, *pp* **test-driven**) n essai *m* sur route. ◆◇ **test-drive** vt [car] essayer.

tester ['testər] n **1**. [person] contrôleur *m*, -euse *f*, vérificateur *m*, -trice *f* **2**. [machine] appareil *m* de contrôle or de vérification **3**. [sample - of make-up, perfume] échantillon *m* **4**. [over bed] baldaquin *m*, ciel *m*.

testes ['testi:z] pl ⟶ **testis**.

testicle ['testɪkl] n testicule *m*.

testify ['testɪfaɪ] (*pt & pp* **testified**) ◆ vt déclarer, affirmer. ◆ vi [be witness] porter témoignage, servir de témoin ; [make statement] déposer, faire une déposition ▶ **to testify for / against sb** déposer en faveur de / contre qqn.

testimonial [ˌtestɪ'məʊnjəl] ◆ n **1**. [certificate] attestation *f* ; [reference] recommandation *f*, attestation *f* **2**. [tribute] témoignage *m*. ◆ comp qui porte témoignage ▶ **testimonial match** UK jubilé *m*.

testimony [UK 'testɪmənɪ US 'testəməʊnɪ] (*pl* **testimonies**) n **1**. [statement] déclaration *f* ; LAW témoignage *m*, déposition *f* **2**. [sign, proof] témoignage *m*.

testing ['testɪŋ] ◆ adj [difficult] difficile, éprouvant. ◆ n **1**. [of product, machine, vehicle] (mise *f* à l')essai *m* **2**. MED [of sight, hearing] examen *m* ; [of blood, urine] analyse *f* ; [of reaction] mesure *f* **3**. [of intelligence, knowledge, skills] évaluation *f* ; [of candidate] évaluation *f*, examen *m*.

testing ground n terrain *m* d'essai.

testis ['testɪs] (*pl* **testes** ['testi:z]) n testicule *m*.

test match n UK match *m* international, test-match *m*.

testosterone [te'stɒstərəʊn] n testostérone *f*.

test paper n **1**. CHEM papier *m* réactif **2**. UK SCH interrogation *f* écrite.

test pattern n US mire *f*.

test pilot n pilote *m* d'essai.

test run n essai *m*.

test tube n éprouvette *f*. ◆◇ **test-tube** adj de laboratoire.

test-tube baby n bébé-éprouvette *m*.

testy ['testɪ] (*compar* **testier**, *superl* **testiest**) adj irritable, grincheux.

tetanus ['tetənəs] ◆ n tétanos *m*. ◆ comp [vaccination, injection] antitétanique.

tetchy ['tetʃɪ] (*compar* **tetchier**, *superl* **tetchiest**) adj UK grincheux, irascible.

tête-à-tête [ˌteɪtɑː'teɪt] ◆ n tête-à-tête *m inv*. ◆ adj en tête à tête.

tether ['teðər] ◆ n [for horse] longe *f*, attache *f* ▶ **to be at the end of one's tether a)** [depressed] être au bout du rouleau **b)** [exasperated] être à bout de patience. ◆ vt [horse] attacher.

Texan ['teksn] ◆ n Texan *m*, -e *f*. ◆ adj texan.

Texas ['teksəs] pr n Texas *m* / *in Texas* au Texas.

Tex-Mex [ˌteks'meks] n **1**. CULIN tex-mex *m* **2**. [music] musique *f* mexicano-américaine.

text [tekst] ◆ n **1**. [gen & COMPUT] texte *m* **2**. TELEC SMS *m*. ◆ comp **1**. COMPUT ▶ **text mode** mode *m* texte ▶ **text processing** traitement *m* automatique de texte sur ordinateur **2**. TELEC ▶ **text-message** SMS *m*, texto *m* ▶ **text-messaging** (U) TELEC envoi *m* de SMS, texting *m*. ◆ vt ▶ **to text sb** envoyer un SMS à qqn / *can you text me your number?* tu peux m'envoyer ton numéro par SMS ?

textbook ['tekstbʊk] ◆ n SCH [gen] manuel *m*. ◆ comp [typical] typique ; [ideal] parfait, idéal.

texter ['tekstɜː] n TELEC *personne qui envoie des sms*.

textile ['tekstaɪl] ◆ n textile *m*. ◆ comp [industry] textile.

texting ['tekstɪŋ] n (U) TELEC envoi *m* de SMS, texting *m*.

textual ['tekstjʊəl] adj textuel, de texte ▶ **textual analysis** analyse *f* de texte ▶ **textual criticism** critique *f* littéraire d'un texte.

texture ['tekstʃər] n **1**. [of fabric] texture *f* ; [of leather, wood, paper, skin, stone] grain *m* **2**. [of food, soil] texture *f*, consistance *f* ; [of writing] structure *f*, texture *f*.

TFT [ˌtiːef'tiː] (abbr of **thin-film transistor**) adj TFT ▶ **TFT screen** écran *m* TFT.

TGIF (abbr of **thank God it's Friday!**) *inf* encore une semaine de tirée !

TGWU (abbr of **Transport and General Workers' Union**) n *le plus grand syndicat interprofessionnel britannique*.

Thai [taɪ] (*pl* **Thai** or **Thais**) ◆ n **1**. [person] Thaï *mf*, Thaïlandais *m*, -e *f* **2**. LING thaï *m*, thaïlandais *m*. ◆ adj thaï, thaïlandais ▶ **Thai boxing** boxe *f* thaïlandaise.

Thailand ['taɪlænd] pr n Thaïlande *f* / *in Thailand* en Thaïlande.

thalidomide [θəˈlɪdəmaɪd] n thalidomide *f*.

Thames [temz] pr n ▶ **the (River) Thames** la Tamise.

than (weak form [ðən], strong form [ðæn]) ◆ conj [after comparative adj, adv] que / *he plays tennis better than I do* il joue au tennis mieux que moi. ◆ prep **1**. [after comparative adj, adv] que / *the cedars are older than the oaks* les cèdres sont plus vieux que les chênes **2**. [indicating quantity, number] : *more than 15 people* plus de 15 personnes / *less* or *fewer than 15 people* moins de 15 personnes.

thank [θæŋk] vt **1**. remercier ▶ **to thank sb for sthg** remercier qqn de or pour qqch ▶ **to thank sb for doing sthg** remercier qqn d'avoir fait qqch / *you won't thank me for it* vous allez m'en vouloir / *you only have yourself to thank for that!* c'est à toi seul qu'il faut t'en prendre ! ▶ **thank God** or **goodness!** Dieu merci ! **2**. [as request] : *I'll thank you to keep quiet about it* je vous prierai de ne pas en parler. ◆◇ **thanks** ◆ pl n **1**. remerciements *mpl* / (*many*) *thanks for all your help* merci (beaucoup) pour toute votre aide ▶ **received with thanks** ADMIN pour acquit **2**. RELIG louange *f*, grâce *f* ▶ **thanks be to God** rendons grâce à Dieu. ◆ interj merci ▶ **thanks a lot, thanks very much** merci beaucoup, merci bien ▶ **thanks a million** merci mille fois ▶ **thanks for coming** merci d'être venu ▶ **no thanks!** (non) merci ! ▶ **thanks for nothing!** je te remercie ! *iro*. ◆◇ **thanks to** prep phr grâce à.

thankful ['θæŋkfʊl] adj reconnaissant, content.

thankfully ['θæŋkfʊlɪ] adv **1**. [with gratitude] avec reconnaissance or gratitude **2**. [with relief] avec soulagement **3**. [fortunately] heureusement.

thankless ['θæŋklɪs] adj [task, person] ingrat.

thanksgiving ['θæŋksˌgɪvɪŋ] n action *f* de grâce.

Thanksgiving (Day) n *fête nationale américaine célébrée le 4ᵉ jeudi de novembre.*

🚩 **Thanksgiving**

L'origine de cette fête fédérale, célébrée aux États-Unis le 4ᵉ jeudi de novembre, remonte à 1621, quand les premiers colons (les **Pilgrims Fathers**) décidèrent un jour d'action de grâce pour remercier Dieu à l'occasion de leur première récolte. Le dîner familial qui a lieu en cette occasion est traditionnellement composé d'une dinde aux airelles accompagnée de patates douces et se termine par une tarte au potiron.

10Q MESSAGING written abbr of thank you.

thank you interj merci ▶ **to say thank you** dire merci / *thank you very* or *so much* merci beaucoup or bien / *thank you for coming* merci d'être venu. ❖ **thankyou** n merci m, remerciement m.

thankyou letter ['θæŋkjuː-] n lettre f de remerciement.

THANQ MESSAGING written abbr of thank you.

that [ðæt *(weak form of rel pron and conj* [ðət]*)*] n (*pl* **those** [ðəʊz]) ❖ dem pron **1.** [thing indicated] cela, ce, ça / *after / before that* après / avant cela / *what's that?* qu'est-ce que c'est que ça ? / *who's that?* **a)** [gen] qui est-ce ? **b)** [on phone] qui est à l'appareil ? / *is that you Susan?* c'est toi Susan ? / *what did she mean by that?* qu'est-ce qu'elle voulait dire par là ? / *those are my parents* voilà mes parents / *that is where I live* c'est là que j'habite / *that was three months ago* il y a trois mois de cela ▶ **that's it!** **a)** [finished] c'est fini ! **b)** [correct] c'est ça ! ▶ **well, that's that!** eh bien voilà ! **2.** [in contrast to 'this'] celui-là m, celle-là f ▶ **those** ceux-là mpl, celles-là / *this is an ash, that is an oak* ceci est un frêne et ça, c'est un chêne / *which book do you prefer, this or that?* quel livre préférez-vous, celui-ci ou celui-là ? **3.** [used when giving further information] celui m, celle f ▶ **those** ceux mpl, celles / *there are those who believe that...* il y a des gens qui croient que... / *all those interested* should contact *the club secretary* tous ceux qui sont intéressés doivent contacter le secrétaire du club. ❖ det **1.** [the one indicated] ce m, cet m (*before vowel or silent 'h'*), cette f ▶ **those** ces mf pl / *that man* cet homme / *at that moment* à ce moment-là / *it was raining that day* il pleuvait ce jour-là **2.** [in contrast to 'this'] ce...-là m, cet...-là m (*before vowel or silent 'h'*), cette...-là f ▶ **those** ces...-là mf pl / *that house over there is for sale* cette or la maison là-bas est à vendre ▶ **that one** celui-là m, celle-là f. ❖ adv **1.** [so] si, aussi / *can you run that fast?* pouvez-vous courir aussi vite que ça ? / *he's not (all) that good-looking* il n'est pas si beau que ça **2.** inf [with result clause] si, tellement / *I could have cried, I was that angry* j'en aurais pleuré tellement j'étais en colère. ❖ rel pron **1.** [subject of verb] qui / *the conclusions that emerge from this* les conclusions qui en ressortent **2.** [object or complement of verb] que / *the house that Jack built* la maison que Jack a construite **3.** [object of preposition] lequel m, laquelle f, lesquels mpl, lesquelles / *the box that I put it in / on* le carton dans lequel / sur lequel je l'ai mis / *the songs that I was thinking of* or *about* les chansons auxquelles je pensais / *the woman / the film that we're talking about* la femme / le film dont nous parlons / *not that I know of* pas que je sache **4.** [when] où. ❖ conj [gen] que / *I said that I had read it* j'ai dit que je l'avais lu / *it's not that she*

isn't friendly ce n'est pas qu'elle ne soit pas amicale / *that he is capable has already been proven* fml il a déjà prouvé qu'il était capable. ❖ **at that** adv phr **1.** [what's more] en plus / *it's a forgery and a pretty poor one at that* c'est une copie et une mauvaise en plus **2.** [then] à ce moment-là. ❖ **not that** conj phr : *if he refuses, not that he will, is there an alternative?* s'il refuse, même si c'est peu probable, est-ce qu'il y a une autre solution ? / *he's already left, not that it matters* il est déjà parti, encore que ce soit sans importance. ❖ **that is (to say)** adv phr enfin / *I'd like to ask you something, that is, if you've got a minute* j'aimerais vous poser une question, enfin, si vous avez un instant. ❖ **with that** adv phr là-dessus.

thatched [θætʃt] adj [roof] en chaume ; [house] qui a un toit en chaume ▶ **thatched cottage** chaumière f.

Thatcherism ['θætʃərɪzm] n POL thatchérisme m *(politique de Margaret Thatcher).*

that's abbr of that is.

thaw [θɔː] ❖ vi **1.** [ice, snow] fondre / *it's beginning to thaw* il commence à dégeler **2.** [frozen food] dégeler, se décongeler **3.** [hands, feet] se réchauffer **4.** fig [person, relations] se dégeler, être plus détendu. ❖ vt **1.** [ice, snow] faire dégeler or fondre **2.** [frozen food] dégeler, décongeler. ❖ n **1.** METEOR dégel m **2.** POL détente f, dégel m. ❖ **thaw out** ❖ vt sep **1.** [frozen food] décongeler, dégeler **2.** [feet, hands] réchauffer **3.** fig [make relaxed - person] dégeler, mettre à l'aise. ❖ vi **1.** [frozen food] décongeler, dégeler **2.** [hands, feet] se réchauffer **3.** fig [become relaxed] se dégeler, perdre sa froideur or réserve.

the (*weak form* [ðə], *before vowel* [ðɪ], *strong form* [ðiː]) det **1.** [with noun, adj] le m, la f, l' *mf (before vowel or silent 'h')*, les *mf pl* / *the blue dress is the prettiest* la robe bleue est la plus jolie / *translated from the Latin* traduit du latin **2.** [with names, titles] : *the Smiths / Martins* les Smith / Martin **3.** [with numbers, dates] : *Monday June the tenth* or *the tenth of June* le lundi 10 juin **4.** [in prices, quantities] : *tomatoes are 40p the pound* les tomates sont à 40 pence la livre **5.** [with comparatives] : *the more the better* plus il y en a, mieux c'est **6.** [stressed form] : *for him Bach is THE composer* pour lui, Bach est le compositeur par excellence / *do you mean THE John Irving?* vous voulez dire le célèbre John Irving ?

theatre 🇬🇧, **theater** 🇺🇸 ['θɪətər] ❖ n **1.** [building] théâtre m ▶ **to go to the theatre** aller au théâtre ▶ **movie theater** 🇺🇸 cinéma m **2.** [form] théâtre m, art m dramatique ; [plays in general] théâtre m ; [profession] théâtre m **3.** [hall] salle f de spectacle ; [for lectures] salle f de conférences ; UNIV amphithéâtre m **4.** MED ▶ **(operating) theatre** salle f d'opération / *she's in (the) theatre* **a)** [doctor] elle est en salle d'opération **b)** [patient] elle est sur la table d'opération **5.** fig [for important event] théâtre m ▶ **theatre of war** MIL théâtre des hostilités. ❖ comp **1.** [programme, tickets] de théâtre ; [manager] du théâtre ▶ **theatre company** troupe de théâtre, compagnie théâtrale ▶ **theatre workshop** atelier m de théâtre **2.** MED [staff, nurse] de salle d'opération ; [routine, job] dans la salle d'opération.

theatregoer 🇬🇧, **theatergoer** 🇺🇸 ['θɪətə‚gəʊər] n amateur m de théâtre.

theatrical [θɪ'ætrɪkl] adj **1.** THEAT [performance, season] théâtral **2.** fig [exaggerated - gesture, behaviour] théâtral, affecté. ❖ **theatricals** pl n **1.** THEAT théâtre m d'amateur **2.** fig comédie f.

thee [ðiː] pron arch BIBLE te, t' *(before vowel or silent 'h')* ; [after prep] toi.

theft [θeft] n vol m.

their *(weak form* [ðəʳ]*, strong form* [ðeəʳ]) det leur *(sg),* leurs *(pl)* / *their clothes* leurs vêtements / *somebody's left their umbrella behind* quelqu'un a oublié son parapluie / *a house of their own* leur propre maison, une maison à eux.

theirs [ðeəz] pron le leur *m*, la leur *f*, les leurs *mf pl* / *our car is sturdier than theirs* notre voiture est plus solide que la leur / *I like that painting of theirs* j'aime leur tableau / *a friend of theirs* un de leurs amis / *is this yours or theirs?* est-ce que ceci est à vous ou à eux ?

them *(weak form* [ðəm]*, strong form* [ðem]) pron **1.** [direct obj] les / *I met them last week* je les ai rencontrés la semaine dernière **2.** [indirect obj] leur / *we bought / gave them some flowers* nous leur avons acheté / donné des fleurs **3.** [after preposition] : *it's for them* c'est pour eux / *both of them are wool* ils sont tous les deux en laine.

thematic [θɪ'mætɪk] adj thématique.

theme [θiːm] n **1.** [subject, topic] thème *m*, sujet *m* **2.** MUS thème *m* **3.** GRAM & LING thème *m*.

themed [θiːmd] adj [pub, restaurant, etc.] à thème.

theme park n parc *m* à thème.

theme pub n bar *m* à thème.

theme song n **1.** [from film] chanson *f* (de film) **2.** [US] [signature tune] indicatif *m*.

theme tune n **1.** [from film] musique *f* (de film) **2.** [UK] [signature tune] indicatif *m*.

themselves [ðəm'selvz] pron **1.** [reflexive use] : *they hurt themselves* ils se sont fait mal **2.** [emphatic use] eux-mêmes *mpl*, elles-mêmes / *they had to come themselves* ils ont dû venir eux-mêmes or en personne **3.** [referring to things] eux-mêmes *mpl*, elles-mêmes / *the details in themselves are not important* ce ne sont pas les détails en eux-mêmes qui sont importants.

then [ðen] ◆ adv **1.** [at a particular time] alors, à ce moment-là ; [in distant past] à l'époque, à cette époque, à cette époque-là / *we can talk about it then* nous pourrons en parler à ce moment-là ▸ **by then a)** [in future] d'ici là **b)** [in past] entre-temps ▸ **from then on** à partir de ce moment-là ▸ **since then** depuis (lors) ▸ **until then a)** [in future] jusque-là **b)** [in past] jusqu'alors, jusqu'à ce moment-là **2.** [afterwards, next] puis, ensuite / *do your homework first, then you can watch TV* fais d'abord tes devoirs, et ensuite tu pourras regarder la télé **3.** [so, in that case] donc, alors / *you were right then!* mais alors, vous aviez raison ! / *if it's not in my bag, then look in the cupboard* si ce n'est pas dans mon sac, regarde dans le placard **4.** [also] et puis / *then there's Peter to invite* et puis il faut inviter Peter **5.** [therefore] donc / *these then are the main problems* voici donc les principaux problèmes. ◆ **then again** adv phr : *and then again, you may prefer to forget it* mais enfin peut-être que vous préférez ne plus y penser / *but then again, no one can be sure* mais après tout, on ne sait jamais.

thence [ðens] adv *liter & fml* **1.** [from that place] de là, de ce lieu, de ce lieu-là **2.** [from that time] depuis lors **3.** [therefore] par conséquent.

theologian [θɪə'ləʊdʒən] n théologien *m*, -enne *f*.

theological [θɪə'lɒdʒɪkl] adj théologique ▸ **theological college** séminaire *m*.

theology [θɪ'ɒlədʒɪ] n théologie *f*.

theorem ['θɪərəm] n théorème *m*.

theoretical [θɪə'retɪkl] adj théorique.

theoretically [θɪə'retɪklɪ] adv théoriquement, en principe.

theorist ['θɪərɪst] n théoricien *m*, -enne *f*.

theorize, theorise ['θɪəraɪz] ◆ vi **1.** [speculate] théoriser, faire des théories **2.** [scientist] élaborer des théo-

ries. ◆ vt : *scientists theorized that the space probe would disintegrate* les scientifiques émirent l'hypothèse que la sonde spatiale se désintégrerait.

theory ['θɪərɪ] *(pl* **theories**) n **1.** [hypothesis] théorie *f* **2.** [principles, rules] théorie *f*. ◆ **in theory** adv phr en théorie, théoriquement, en principe.

therapeutic [,θerə'pjuːtɪk] adj thérapeutique.

therapeutic cloning n clonage *m* thérapeutique.

therapist ['θerəpɪst] n thérapeute *mf*.

therapy ['θerəpɪ] *(pl* **therapies**) n thérapie *f* ▸ **to go for** or **to be in therapy** suivre une thérapie.

there *(weak form* [ðəʳ]*, strong form* [ðeəʳ]) ◆ adv **1.** [in or to a particular place] là, y / *they aren't there* ils ne sont pas là, ils n'y sont pas / *who's there?* qui est là ? / *there it is* le voilà / *it's around there somewhere* c'est quelque part par là **2.** [on or at a particular point] là / *we disagree there* or *there we disagree* nous ne sommes pas d'accord là-dessus / *let's leave it there* restons-en là / *you've got me there!* *inf* là, je ne sais pas quoi vous répondre or dire ! **3.** [drawing attention to someone or something] : *there they are!* les voilà ! **4.** [PHR] **to be not all** or **not quite there** : *he's not all* or *not quite there* a) [stupid] il n'a pas toute sa tête b) [senile] il n'a plus toute sa tête. ◆ pron ▸ **there is** *(before singular noun)* il y a ▸ **there are** *(before plural noun)* il y a / *there's a bus coming* il y a un bus qui arrive. ◆ interj **1.** [soothing] : *there now, don't cry!* allons ! or là ! ne pleure pas ! ▸ **there, there!** allez ! **2.** [aggressive] : *there now, what did I say?* voilà, qu'est-ce que je t'avais dit ? ◆ **so there** adv phr voilà. ◆ **there and back** adv phr : *we did the trip there and back in three hours* nous avons fait l'aller retour en trois heures. ◆ **there and then, then and there** adv phr sur-le-champ. ◆ **there you are, there you go** adv phr **1.** [never mind] : *it wasn't the ideal solution, but there you are* or *go* ce n'était pas l'idéal, mais enfin or mais qu'est-ce que vous voulez **2.** [I told you so] voilà, ça y est **3.** [here you are] tenez, voilà.

thereabout ['ðeərəbaʊt] [US] = **thereabouts**.

thereabouts [,ðeərə'baʊts] adv **1.** [indicating place] par là, dans les environs, pas loin / *somewhere thereabouts* quelque part par là **2.** [indicating quantity, weight] à peu près, environ **3.** [indicating price] environ / *£10 or thereabouts* 10 livres environ **4.** [indicating time] aux alentours de / *at 10 p.m. or thereabouts* aux alentours de 22 h, vers 10 h du soir.

thereafter [,ðeər'ɑːftəʳ] adv *fml* **1.** [subsequently] par la suite **2.** [below] ci-dessous.

thereby [,ðeər'baɪ] adv *fml* de ce fait, ainsi.

therefore ['ðeəfɔːʳ] adv donc, par conséquent.

therein [,ðeər'ɪn] adv *fml* LAW **1.** [within] à l'intérieur **2.** [in that respect] là.

thereof [,ðeər'ɒv] adv *arch & fml* de cela, en.

there's abbr of **there is**.

thereupon [,ðeərə'pɒn] adv *fml* **1.** [then] sur ce **2.** LAW [on that subject] à ce sujet, là-dessus.

thermal ['θɜːml] ◆ adj **1.** PHYS [energy, insulation] thermique ; [conductor, unit] thermique, de chaleur **2.** [spring, stream] thermal ▸ **thermal baths** thermes *mpl* **3.** [underwear] en chlorofibres, en Rhovyl® or Thermolactyl®. ◆ n AERON & METEOR thermique *m*, ascendance *f* thermique. ◆ **thermals** pl n [thermal underwear] sous-vêtements *mpl* en chlorofibres.

thermal imaging n thermographie *f*.

thermal reactor n réacteur *m* thermique.

thermodynamics [,θɜːməʊdaɪ'næmɪks] n *(U)* thermodynamique *f*.

thermoelectric(al) [,θɜ:məʊɪˈlektrɪk(l)] adj thermoélectrique.

thermometer [θəˈmɒmɪtəʳ] n thermomètre *m*.

thermonuclear [,θɜ:məʊˈnjuːklɪəʳ] adj thermonucléaire.

thermoplastic [,θɜ:məʊˈplæstɪk] ◆ adj thermoplastique. ◆ n thermoplastique *m*.

Thermos® [ˈθɜ:mɒs] n ▸ **Thermos (flask)** Thermos® *f*.

thermostat [ˈθɜ:məstæt] n thermostat *m*.

thesaurus [θɪˈsɔːrəs] (*pl* **thesauri** [-raɪ] *or* **thesauruses** [-sɪz]) n **1.** [book of synonyms] ≃ dictionnaire *m* analogique **2.** COMPUT thésaurus *m*.

these [ðiːz] pl ⟶ this.

thesis [ˈθiːsɪs] (*pl* **theses** [-siːz]) n [gen & UNIV] thèse *f*.

they [ðeɪ] pron ils *mpl*, elles ; [stressed form] eux *mpl*, elles *fpl* / *they've left* ils sont partis / THEY *bought the flowers* ce sont eux qui ont acheté les fleurs / *oh, there they are!* ah, les voilà ! / *they say that...* on prétend que...

they'd [ðeɪd] **1.** abbr of **they had 2.** abbr of **they would**.

they'll [ðeɪl] abbr of **they will**.

they're [ðeəʳ] abbr of **they are**.

they've [ðeɪv] abbr of **they have**.

thick [θɪk] ◆ adj **1.** [wall, slice, writing] épais (épaisse), gros (grosse) ; [print] gras (grasse) ; [lips] épais (épaisse), charnu ; [shoes, boots] gros (grosse) / *the snow was thick on the ground* il y avait une épaisse couche de neige sur le sol / *the boards are 20 cm thick* les planches ont une épaisseur de 20 cm, les planches font 20 cm d'épaisseur ▸ **to give sb a thick ear** 🇬🇧 donner une gifle à qqn **2.** [beard, eyebrows, hair] épais, touffu ; [grass, forest, crowd] épais (épaisse), dense ▸ **to be thick on the ground** : *pubs are not very thick on the ground round here* les pubs sont plutôt rares par ici **3.** [soup, cream, sauce] épais **4.** [fog, smoke] épais, dense ; [clouds] épais ; [darkness, night] profond **5.** ▸ **thick with: the shelves were thick with dust** les étagères étaient recouvertes d'une épaisse couche de poussière / *the air was thick with smoke* **a)** [from smokers] la pièce était enfumée **b)** [from fire, guns] l'air était empli d'une épaisse fumée **6.** [voice - with emotion] voilé ; [- after late night, drinking] pâteux **7.** [accent] fort, prononcé **8.** *inf* [intimate] intime, très lié / *he's very thick with the boss* il est très bien avec le chef, lui et le chef sont comme les deux doigts de la main ▸ **to be as thick as thieves**: *those two are as thick as thieves* ces deux-là s'entendent comme larrons en foire **9.** *inf* [stupid] obtus, bouché **10.** 🇬🇧 *inf* [unreasonable] ▸ **that's** *or* **it's a bit thick** ça, c'est un peu dur à avaler *or* fort *or* raide. ◆ adv [spread] en couche épaisse ; [cut] en tranches épaisses, en grosses tranches ▸ **thick and fast**: *invitations / phone calls began to come in thick and fast* il y eut une avalanche d'invitations / de coups de téléphone ▸ **to lay it on thick** en rajouter. ◆ n *phr* ▸ **to stick** *or* **to stay with sb through thick and thin** rester fidèle à qqn contre vents et marées *or* quoi qu'il arrive. ❖ **in the thick of** prep phr au milieu *or* cœur de, en plein, en plein milieu de.

thicken [ˈθɪkn] ◆ vi **1.** [fog, clouds, smoke] s'épaissir, devenir plus épais ; [bushes, forest] s'épaissir **2.** [sauce] épaissir ; [jam, custard] durcir **3.** [crowd] grossir **4.** [mystery] s'épaissir / *the plot thickens* les choses se compliquent *or* se corsent, l'histoire se corse. ◆ vt [sauce, soup] épaissir.

thickener [ˈθɪknəʳ] n [for sauce, soup] liant *m* ; [for oil, paint] épaississant *m*.

thickening [ˈθɪknɪŋ] ◆ n **1.** [of fog, clouds, smoke] épaississement *m* ; [of sauce] liaison *f* **2.** CULIN [thickener] liant *m*. ◆ adj [agent] épaississant ; [process] d'épaississement.

thicket [ˈθɪkɪt] n fourré *m*.

thickly [ˈθɪklɪ] adv **1.** [spread] en couche épaisse ; [cut] en tranches épaisses **2.** [densely] dru **3.** [speak] d'une voix rauque *or* pâteuse.

thickness [ˈθɪknɪs] n **1.** [of wall, snow, layer] épaisseur *f* ; [of string, bolt] épaisseur *f*, grosseur *f* **2.** [of beard, hair] épaisseur *f*, abondance *f* **3.** [of fog, smoke, forest] épaisseur *f*, densité *f*.

thickset [,θɪkˈset] adj trapu, costaud.

thick-skinned [-ˈskɪnd] adj peu sensible, qui a la peau dure.

thief [θiːf] (*pl* **thieves** [θiːvz]) n voleur *m*, -euse *f* ▸ **stop thief!** au voleur !

thieve [θiːv] vi & vt *inf* voler.

thieves [θiːvz] pl ⟶ thief.

thieving [ˈθiːvɪŋ] *inf* ◆ adj voleur ▸ **keep your thieving hands off!** pas touche !, bas les pattes ! ◆ n (U) vol *m*, vols *mpl*.

thigh [θaɪ] n cuisse *f*.

thighbone [ˈθaɪbəʊn] n fémur *m*.

thigh-length adj [dress, coat] qui descend jusqu'à mi-cuisse ▸ **thigh-length boots** cuissardes *fpl*.

thimble [ˈθɪmbl] n dé *m* à coudre.

thin [θɪn] (*compar* **thinner** ; *superl* **thinnest**, *pt* & *pp* **thinned**, *cont* **thinning**) ◆ adj **1.** [layer, wall, wire, etc.] mince, fin ; [person, leg, neck] mince, maigre ; [clothing, blanket] léger, fin ; [carpet] ras ; [crowd] peu nombreux, épars ▸ **to become** *or* **to get** *or* **to grow thin** [person] maigrir **2.** [beard, hair] clairsemé / *he's getting a bit thin on top* il commence à perdre ses cheveux, il se dégarnit **3.** [soup, sauce] clair ; [cream] liquide ; [paint, ink] délayé, dilué ; [blood] appauvri, anémié **4.** [smoke, clouds, mist] léger ; [air] raréfié **5.** [excuse, argument] mince, peu convaincant **6.** [profits] maigre **7.** [voice] grêle. ◆ adv [spread] en fine couche, en couche mince ; [cut] en tranches minces *or* fines. ◆ vt [sauce, soup] allonger, délayer, éclaircir. ◆ vi [crowd] s'éclaircir, se disperser ; [fog] se lever, devenir moins dense *or* épais ; [smoke] devenir moins dense *or* épais ; [population] se réduire / *his hair is thinning* il perd ses cheveux. ❖ **thin out** ◆ vt sep [plants] éclaircir. ◆ vi [crowd] se disperser ; [population] se réduire, diminuer ; [fog] se lever.

thing [θɪŋ]
n

🅐 CONCRETE - OBJECT OR ACTIVITY **1.** [object, item] chose *f*, objet *m* / *what's that yellow thing on the floor?* qu'est-ce que c'est que ce truc jaune par terre ? / *what's that thing for?* à quoi ça sert, ça ? / *I had to rewrite the whole thing* j'ai dû tout réécrire / *the thing he loves most is his pipe* ce qu'il aime le plus, c'est sa pipe / *I need a few things from the shop* j'ai besoin de faire quelques courses **2.** [activity, event] chose *f* / *the thing to do is to pretend you're asleep* vous n'avez qu'à faire semblant de dormir / *the next thing on the agenda* le point suivant à l'ordre du jour / *it's the best thing to do* c'est ce qu'il y a de mieux à faire **3.** [in negative clauses] : *I don't know a thing about what happened* j'ignore tout de ce qui s'est passé / *I didn't understand a thing she said* je n'ai rien compris à ce qu'elle disait, je n'ai pas compris un mot de ce qu'elle disait **4.** [creature, being] créature *f*, être *m* / *what a sweet little thing!* quel amour ! / *poor thing!* **a)** [said about somebody] le / la pauvre ! **b)** [said to somebody] mon / ma pauvre ! **c)** [animal] (la) pauvre bête !

🅑 ABSTRACT - IDEA OR REMARK **1.** [idea, notion] idée *f*, chose *f* / *the best thing would be to ask them* le mieux serait de leur demander ▸ **to know a thing or two about sthg** s'y connaître en qqch **2.** [matter, question] chose *f*, question *f* / *the thing is, we can't really afford it* le problème, c'est qu'on n'a pas vraiment les moyens / *the thing* is, will she want to come? le problème c'est qu'on ne sait pas si elle voudra venir / *the main thing is to succeed* ce qui importe, c'est de réussir / *the important thing is not to stop* ce qui compte, c'est de ne pas arrêter / *what with one thing and another, I haven't had time* avec tout ce qu'il y avait à faire, je n'ai pas eu le temps **3.** [remark] : *that's not a very nice thing to say* ce n'est pas très gentil de dire ça / *how can you say such a thing?* comment pouvez-vous dire une chose pareille ? / *I said no such thing!* je n'ai rien dit de tel ! **4.** [quality, characteristic] chose f / *one of the things I like about her is her sense of humour* une des choses que j'aime chez elle, c'est son sens de l'humour.

C. OTHER USES 1. *inf* [strong feeling] ▶ **to have a thing about sthg a)** [like] aimer qqch **b)** [dislike] ne pas aimer qqch **2.** [interest] : *it's not really my thing* ce n'est pas vraiment mon truc **3.** [what is needed, required] idéal *m* / *hot cocoa is just the thing on a winter's night* un chocolat chaud c'est l'idéal les soirs d'hiver / *that's the very thing for my bad back!* c'est juste ce dont j'avais besoin pour mon mal de dos ! **4.** [fashion] mode f / *it's quite the thing* c'est très à la mode **5.** [fuss] ▶ **to make a big thing about sthg** faire (tout) un plat de qqch **6.** [relationship] ▶ **to have a thing with sb** avoir une liaison avec qqn. ❖ **things** pl n **1.** [belongings] effets *mpl*, affaires *fpl* ; [clothes] affaires *fpl* ; [equipment] affaires *fpl*, attirail *m* ; [tools] outils *mpl*, ustensiles *mpl* / *put your things away* ramassez vos affaires / *you can take your things off in the bedroom* vous pouvez vous déshabiller dans la chambre **2.** [situation, circumstances] choses *fpl* / *how's inf or how are things?* comment ça va ? / *things are getting better* les choses vont mieux / *I need time to think things over* j'ai besoin de temps pour réfléchir ▶ **as things are** or **stand, things being what they are** dans l'état actuel des choses, les choses étant ce qu'elles sont ▶ **it's just one of those things** ce sont des choses qui arrivent **3.** [specific aspect of life] choses *fpl* / *she's interested in all things French* elle s'intéresse à tout ce qui est français **4.** [facts, actions, etc.] choses *fpl* / *I've heard good things about his work* on dit du bien de son travail. ❖ **for one thing** adv phr (tout) d'abord ▶ **for one thing… and for another** (tout) d'abord… et puis.

thingamabob ['θɪŋəmə,bɒb], **thingamajig** ['θɪŋə-mədʒɪg], **thingummy(jig)** 🇬🇧 ['θɪŋəmɪ-], **thingie** 🇬🇧, **thingy** 🇬🇧 ['θɪŋɪ] n *inf* truc *m*, machin *m*.

think [θɪŋk] (*pt & pp* **thought** [θɔːt]) ◆ vi **1.** [reason] penser, raisonner ▶ **to think for oneself** se faire ses propres opinions / *sorry, I wasn't thinking clearly* désolé, je n'avais pas les idées claires ▶ **to think aloud** penser tout haut ▶ **to think big** *inf* voir les choses en grand **2.** [ponder, reflect] penser, réfléchir / *he thought for a moment* il a réfléchi un instant / *think again!* **a)** [reconsider] repensez-y ! **b)** [guess] vous n'y êtes pas, réfléchissez donc ! / *let me think* laisse-moi réfléchir / *that's what set me thinking* c'est ce qui m'a fait réfléchir **3.** [imagine] (s')imaginer / *if you think I'd lend you my car again…* si tu t'imagines que je te prêterai encore ma voiture… / *just think!* imaginez(-vous) un peu ! **4.** [believe, have as opinion] penser, croire / *to her way of thinking* à son avis / *it's a lot harder than I thought* c'est beaucoup plus difficile que je ne croyais / *oh, he's so honest, I don't think!* honnête, mon œil, oui ! ◆ vt **1.** [ponder, reflect on] penser à, réfléchir à / *he was thinking what they could do next* il se demandait ce qu'ils allaient pouvoir faire ensuite **2.** [believe] penser, croire / *I think so* je crois / *I think not* je ne crois pas / *he's a crook — I thought so* or *I thought as much* c'est un escroc — je m'en doutais / *they asked me what I thought* ils m'ont demandé mon avis / *I thought I heard a noise* j'ai cru or il m'a semblé entendre un bruit / *it's expensive, don't you think?* c'est cher, tu ne trouves pas ? / *that's what you think!* tu te fais des illusions ! / *anyone would think he owned the place* on croirait que c'est lui le pro-

priétaire / *(just) who does he think he is?* (mais) pour qui se prend-il ? / *you always think the best | the worst of everyone* vous avez toujours une très bonne / mauvaise opinion de tout le monde **3.** [judge, consider] juger, considérer / *you must think me very nosy* vous devez me trouver très curieux **4.** [imagine] (s')imaginer / *I can't think why he refused* je ne vois vraiment pas pourquoi il a refusé / *who'd have thought it!* qui l'eût cru ! / *just think what we can do with all that money!* imaginez ce qu'on peut faire avec tout cet argent ! **5.** [remember] penser à, se rappeler / *I can't think what his name is* je n'arrive pas à me rappeler son nom, son nom m'échappe ▶ **to think to do sthg** penser à faire qqch **6.** [expect] penser, s'attendre à / *I don't think she'll come* je ne pense pas qu'elle viendra or vienne **7.** [have as intention] : *I think I'll go for a walk* je crois que je vais aller me promener **8.** [in requests] : *do you think you could help me?* pourriez-vous m'aider ? ◆ n : *we've had a think about it* nous y avons réfléchi. ❖ **to think about sthg / doing sthg** penser à qqch / à faire qqch / *what are you thinking about?* à quoi pensez-vous ? / *she's thinking about starting a business* elle pense à or envisage de monter une affaire / *we'll think about it* nous allons y penser or réfléchir **2.** [consider seriously] penser / *all he thinks about is money* il n'y a que l'argent qui l'intéresse. ❖ **think ahead** vi prévoir. ❖ **think back** vi ▶ **to think back to sthg** se rappeler qqch. ❖ **think of** vt insep **1.** [have as tentative plan] penser à, envisager de **2.** [have in mind] : *whatever were you thinking of?* où avais-tu la tête ? ▶ **come to think of it** je viens d'y penser, maintenant que j'y pense / *come to think of it, that's not a bad idea* à la réflexion, ce n'est pas une mauvaise idée **3.** [remember] penser à, se rappeler / *he couldn't think of the name* il ne se rappelait pas le nom, le nom ne lui venait pas **4.** [come up with - idea, solution] : *she's the one who thought of double-checking it* c'est elle qui a eu l'idée de le vérifier / *I'd never have thought of that* je n'y aurais jamais pensé / *whatever will they think of next?* qu'est-ce qu'ils vont bien pouvoir trouver ensuite ? / *he thought nothing of leaving the baby alone for hours at a time* il trouvait (ça) normal de laisser le bébé seul pendant des heures / *thank you — think nothing of it!* merci — mais je vous en prie or mais c'est tout naturel ! **5.** [judge, have as opinion] estimer / *what do you think of the new teacher?* comment trouvez-vous le or que pensez-vous du nouveau professeur ? / *she thinks very highly of or very well of him* elle a une très haute opinion de lui / *I hope you won't think badly of me if I refuse* j'espère que vous ne m'en voudrez pas si je refuse / *I don't think much of that idea* cette idée ne me dit pas grand-chose **6.** [imagine] penser à, imaginer **7.** [take into consideration] penser à, considérer / *I have my family to think of* il faut que je pense à ma famille / *you can't think of everything* on ne peut pas penser à tout. ❖ **think out** vt sep [plan] élaborer, préparer ; [problem] bien étudier or examiner ; [solution] bien étudier / *a well-thought-out plan* un projet bien conçu or ficelé. ❖ **think over** vt sep bien examiner, bien réfléchir à / *we'll have to think it over* il va falloir que nous y réfléchissions. ❖ **think through** vt sep [plan, proposal] examiner en détail / *the scheme has not been properly thought through* le plan n'a pas été pensé jusqu'au bout. ❖ **think up** vt sep [excuse, plan] trouver.

📝 Note that when used negatively, **penser que** is followed by a verb in the subjunctive:
I think we should go now. *Je pense qu'il faut (**indicative**) partir maintenant.*
But
I don't think we should worry. *Je ne pense pas qu'il faille (**subjunctive**) s'inquiéter.*

thinker ['θɪŋkə'] n penseur *m*, -euse *f*.

thinking ['θɪŋkɪŋ] ❖ adj [person] pensant, rationnel, qui réfléchit. ❖ n **1.** [act] pensée *f*, pensées *fpl*, réflexion *f* **2.** [opinion, judgment] point *m* de vue, opinion *f*, opinions *fpl*.

think tank n groupe *m* d'experts.

thinly ['θɪnlɪ] adv [spread] en couche mince ; [cut] en fines tranches.

thinner ['θɪnə'] ❖ compar ⟶ **thin**. ❖ n [solvent] diluant *m*.

thinness ['θɪnnɪs] n **1.** [of layer, wall] minceur *f*, finesse *f* ; [of person] minceur *f*, maigreur *f* ; [of wire] finesse *f* ; [of clothing, blanket, carpet] légèreté *f*, finesse *f* **2.** [of beard, hair] finesse *f*, rareté *f* **3.** [of excuse] faiblesse *f*, insuffisance *f*.

thin-skinned [-'skɪnd] adj *fig* susceptible.

third [θɜːd] ❖ det troisième ▶ **third finger** annulaire *m* ▶ **third person** GRAM troisième personne *f* / *in the third person* à la troisième personne ▶ **third time lucky** la troisième fois sera la bonne. ❖ n **1.** [gen] troisième *mf* **2.** [fraction] tiers *m* **3.** MUS tierce *f* **4.** AUTO ▶ **third (gear)** troisième *f* / *in third (gear)* en troisième **5.** 🇬🇧 UNIV ≃ licence *f* sans mention. ❖ adv en troisième place *f* or position *f*. See also **fifth**.

third base n [in baseball] troisième base *f*.

third degree n *inf* ▶ **to give sb the third degree a)** [torture] passer qqn à tabac **b)** [interrogate] cuisiner qqn.

third-degree burn n brûlure *f* au troisième degré.

third-generation adj COMPUT & TELEC de troisième génération, 3G.

third grade n 🇺🇸 SCH *classe de l'enseignement primaire correspondant au CE2 (7-8 ans)*.

thirdly ['θɜːdlɪ] adv troisièmement, en troisième lieu, tertio.

third party n tierce personne *f*, tiers *m*.
❖ **third-party** adj ▶ **third-party insurance** assurance *f* au tiers.

third-rate adj de qualité inférieure.

Third World n ▶ **the Third World** le tiers-monde.
❖ **Third-World** comp du tiers-monde.

thirst [θɜːst] ❖ n *lit & fig* soif *f*. ❖ vi ▶ **to thirst for sthg** avoir soif de qqch.

thirst-quenching [-kwenʃɪŋ] adj désaltérant.

thirsty ['θɜːstɪ] (*compar* **thirstier**, *superl* **thirstiest**) adj **1.** ▶ **to be thirsty** avoir soif **2.** *fig* [for knowledge, adventure] assoiffé **3.** [plant] qui a besoin de beaucoup d'eau ; [soil] desséché.

thirteen [ˌθɜːˈtiːn] ❖ det treize. ❖ n treize *m inv*. ❖ pron treize. See also **five**.

thirteenth [ˌθɜːˈtiːnθ] ❖ det treizième. ❖ n treizième *mf*. See also **fifth**.

thirtieth ['θɜːtɪəθ] ❖ det trentième. ❖ n trentième *mf*. See also **fifth**.

thirty ['θɜːtɪ] (*pl* **thirties**) ❖ n trente *m inv*. ❖ det trente. ❖ pron trente. See also **fifty**.

thirty-something adj *caractéristique des personnes ayant la trentaine*.

this [ðɪs] (*pl* **these** [ðiːz]) ❖ dem pron **1.** [person, situation, statement, thing indicated] ceci, ce / *what's this?* qu'est-ce que c'est (que ça) ? / *who's this?* **a)** [gen] qui est-ce ? **b)** [on phone] qui est à l'appareil ? / *this is for you* tiens, c'est pour toi / *this is what he told me* voici ce qu'il m'a dit / *this is where I live* c'est ici que j'habite / *after / before this* après / avant ça / *at* or *with this, he left the room* là-dessus or sur ce, il a quitté la pièce **2.** [contrasted

with 'that'] celui-ci *m*, celle-ci *f* ▶ **these** ceux-ci *mpl*, celles-ci / *this is a rose, that is a peony* ceci est une rose, ça c'est une pivoine / *I want these, not those!* je veux ceux-ci, pas ceux-là ! ❖ det **1.** [referring to a particular person, idea, time or thing] ce *m*, cet *m* (*before vowel or silent 'h'*), cette *f* ▶ **these** ces *mf pl* / *this plan of yours won't work* votre projet ne marchera pas / *this way please* par ici s'il vous plaît / *this funny little man came up to me* un petit bonhomme à l'air bizarre est venu vers moi / *this time last week* la semaine dernière à la même heure / *this coming week* la semaine prochaine or qui vient **2.** [contrasted with 'that'] ce...-ci *m*, cet...-ci *m* (*before vowel or silent 'h'*), cette...-ci *f* ▶ **these** ces...-ci *mf pl* / *which do you prefer, this one or that one?* lequel tu préfères, celui-ci ou celui-là ? ❖ adv aussi, si / *it was this high* c'était haut comme ça.

thistle ['θɪsl] n chardon *m*.

Thistle

Le chardon est l'emblème de l'Écosse.

thither ['ðɪðə'] adv *fml & liter* là.

THNQ MESSAGING written abbr of **thank you**.

tho, tho' [ðəʊ] = **though**.

thong [θɒŋ] n **1.** [strip -of leather, rubber] lanière *f* **2.** [G-string] cache-sexe *m*. ❖ **thongs** pl n 🇺🇸 tongs *fpl*.

thorn [θɔːn] n **1.** [prickle] épine *f* **2.** [tree, shrub] arbuste *m* épineux ; [hawthorn] aubépine *f*.

thorny ['θɔːnɪ] (*compar* **thornier**, *superl* **thorniest**) adj *lit & fig* épineux.

thorough ['θʌrə] adj **1.** [complete -inspection, research] minutieux, approfondi **2.** [conscientious -work, worker] consciencieux, sérieux **3.** [as intensifier] absolu, complet (complète).

thoroughbred ['θʌrəbred] ❖ adj [horse] pur-sang (*inv*) ; [animal -gen] de race. ❖ n **1.** [horse] : pur-sang *m inv* ; [animal -gen] bête *f* de race **2.** [person] : *she's a thoroughbred* elle a de la classe, elle est racée.

thoroughfare ['θʌrəfeə'] n voie *f* de communication ▶ **the main thoroughfare** la rue or l'artère *f* principale / *'no thoroughfare'* **a)** [no entry] 'passage interdit' **b)** [cul-de-sac] 'voie sans issue' ▶ **public thoroughfare** voie publique.

thoroughgoing ['θʌrəˌɡəʊɪŋ] adj [search, investigation] minutieux, approfondi, complet (ète) / *he's a thoroughgoing nuisance* il est vraiment pénible.

thoroughly ['θʌrəlɪ] adv **1.** [minutely, in detail -search] à fond, de fond en comble ; [-examine] à fond, minutieusement **2.** [as intensifier] tout à fait, absolument.

thoroughness ['θʌrənɪs] n minutie *f*.

those [ðəʊz] pl ⟶ **that**.

though [ðəʊ] ❖ conj bien que, quoique. ❖ adv pourtant.

Note that **bien que, quoique** and **encore que** are followed by verbs in the subjunctive:
Some women choose this profession, though this is less common. *Certaines femmes choisissent ce métier, bien que ce soit plus rare.*
Though it was a long and bitter struggle... *Quoique le combat fût long et acharné...*
... though no one here has ever been convicted of such a crime. *... encore que personne ici n'ait jamais été condamné pour un tel crime.*

thought [θɔːt] ◆ pt & pp ⟶ think. ◆ n **1.** *(U)* [reflection] pensée f, réflexion f ▸ **to give a problem much** or **a lot of thought** bien réfléchir à un problème **2.** *(C)* [consideration] considération f, pensée f / *I haven't given it a thought* je n'y ai pas pensé **3.** [idea, notion] idée f, pensée f **4.** [intention] idée f, intention f **5.** [opinion] opinion f, avis m **6.** *(U)* [doctrine, ideology] pensée f.

thoughtful ['θɔːtfʊl] adj **1.** [considerate, kind] prévenant, gentil, attentionné **2.** [pensive] pensif **3.** [reasoned - decision, remark, essay] réfléchi ; [- study] sérieux.

thoughtfully ['θɔːtfʊlɪ] adv **1.** [considerately, kindly] avec prévenance or délicatesse, gentiment **2.** [pensively] pensivement **3.** [with careful thought] d'une manière réfléchie.

thoughtfulness ['θɔːtfʊlnɪs] n **1.** [kindness] prévenance f, délicatesse f, gentillesse f **2.** [pensiveness] air m pensif.

thoughtless ['θɔːtlɪs] adj **1.** [inconsiderate - person, act, behaviour] inconsidéré, irréfléchi, qui manque de délicatesse ; [- remark] irréfléchi **2.** [hasty, rash - decision, action] irréfléchi, hâtif ; [- person] irréfléchi, léger.

thoughtlessly ['θɔːtlɪslɪ] adv **1.** [inconsiderately] sans aucun égard, sans aucune considération **2.** [hastily] hâtivement, sans réfléchir.

thoughtlessness ['θɔːtlɪsnɪs] n *(U)* manque m d'égards or de prévenance.

thought-provoking adj qui pousse à la réflexion, stimulant.

thousand ['θaʊznd] ◆ det mille / *a thousand years* mille ans, un millénaire / *five thousand people* cinq mille personnes / *I've already told you a thousand times* je te l'ai déjà dit mille fois. ◆ n mille m inv / *in the year two thousand* en l'an deux mille / *there were thousands of people* il y avait des milliers de personnes.

thousandth ['θaʊzntθ] ◆ det millième. ◆ n millième m.

thrash [θræʃ] ◆ vt **1.** [in punishment] battre **2.** SPORT [defeat] battre à plate couture or à plates coutures **3.** [move vigorously] ▸ **to thrash one's arms / legs (about)** battre des bras / jambes **4.** [thresh - corn] battre. ◆ vi [move violently] se débattre. ◆ n **1.** [stroke] battement m **2.** UK inf [party] sauterie f. ❖ **thrash about, thrash around** ◆ vi [person, fish] se débattre. ◆ vt sep [arms, legs, tail] battre de ; [stick] agiter. ❖ **thrash out** vt sep [problem] débattre de ; [agreement] finir par trouver.

thrashing ['θræʃɪŋ] n **1.** [punishment] raclée f, correction f **2.** SPORT ▸ **to get a thrashing** se faire battre à plates coutures **3.** [of corn] battage m.

thread [θred] ◆ n **1.** SEW & MED fil m **2.** fig [of water, smoke] filet m ; [of light] mince rayon m ; [of story, argument] fil m **3.** TECH [of screw] pas m, filetage m **4.** INTERNET [chain of emails] fil m. ◆ vt **1.** [needle, beads, cotton] enfiler **2.** TECH [screw] tarauder, fileter. ◆ vi [needle, cotton] s'enfiler.

threadbare ['θredbeər] adj **1.** [carpet, clothing] usé, râpé **2.** [joke, excuse, argument] usé, rebattu.

threat [θret] n lit & fig menace f ▸ **to make threats against sb** proférer des menaces contre qqn.

threaten ['θretn] ◆ vt **1.** [make threats against - person] menacer ▸ **to threaten to do sthg** menacer de faire qqch **2.** [subj: danger, unpleasant event] menacer **3.** [be a danger for - society, tranquillity] menacer, être une menace pour. ◆ vi [danger, storm] menacer.

threatening ['θretnɪŋ] adj [danger, sky, storm, person] menaçant ; [letter] de menaces ; [gesture] menaçant, de menace.

threateningly ['θretnɪŋlɪ] adv [behave, move] de manière menaçante, d'un air menaçant ; [say] d'un ton or sur un ton menaçant.

three [θriː] ◆ det trois. ◆ n trois m. ◆ pron trois. **See also** five.

three-course adj [meal] complet *(entrée, plat, dessert).*

three-D, 3-D [,θriː'diː], **three-dimensional** [-dɪ'menʃənl] adj **1.** [object] à trois dimensions, tridimensionnel ; [film] en relief ; [image] en trois dimensions, en 3-D **2.** [character - in book, play, etc.] qui semble réel.

three-day event n EQUIT concours m hippique sur trois jours.

three-dimensional [-dɪ'menʃənl] adj = **three-D.**

threefold ['θriːfəʊld] ◆ adj triple. ◆ adv trois fois autant.

three-legged race [-'legɪd-] n course où les participants courent par deux, la jambe gauche de l'un attachée à la droite de l'autre.

three-piece adj ▸ **three-piece suite** UK, **three-piece set** US salon comprenant un canapé et deux fauteuils assortis ▸ **three-piece (suit)** (costume m) trois-pièces m inv.

three-ply adj [wool] à trois fils ; [rope] à trois brins ▸ **three-ply wood** contreplaqué m *(à trois épaisseurs).*

three-point turn n AUTO demi-tour m en trois manœuvres.

three-quarters ◆ pl n trois quarts mpl. ◆ adv aux trois quarts.

threesome ['θriːsəm] n **1.** [group] groupe m de trois personnes **2.** [in cards, golf] partie f or jeu m à trois.

three-star adj trois étoiles.

three-wheeler n [tricycle] tricycle m ; [car] voiture f à trois roues.

thresh [θreʃ] vt [corn, wheat] battre.

threshing machine n batteuse f.

threshold ['θreʃhəʊld] ◆ n **1.** [doorway] seuil m, pas m de la porte ▸ **to cross the threshold** franchir le seuil **2.** fig seuil m, début m **3.** ECON & FIN niveau m, limite f **4.** ANAT & PSYCHOL seuil m. ◆ comp **1.** UK ECON ▸ **threshold (wage) agreement** / **policy** accord m / politique f d'indexation des salaires sur les prix **2.** ELEC [current, voltage] de seuil **3.** LING ▸ **threshold level** niveau m seuil.

threw [θruː] pt ⟶ throw.

thrice [θraɪs] adv liter & arch trois fois.

thrift [θrɪft] n **1.** [care with money] économie f, esprit m d'économie **2.** US [savings bank] ▸ **thrift (institution)** caisse f d'épargne.

thrift shop, thrift store n US magasin vendant des articles d'occasion au profit d'œuvres charitables.

thrifty ['θrɪftɪ] *(compar* thriftier, *superl* thriftiest) adj économe, peu dépensier.

thrill [θrɪl] ◆ n [feeling of excitement] frisson m ; [exciting experience, event] sensation f, émotion f. ◆ vt transporter, électriser. ◆ vi [with joy] tressaillir, frissonner.

thrilled [θrɪld] adj ravi.

thriller ['θrɪlər] n [film, book] thriller m.

thrilling ['θrɪlɪŋ] adj [adventure, film, story] palpitant, saisissant, excitant ; [speech] passionnant.

thrive [θraɪv] *(pt* thrived or throve [θrəʊv], *pp* thrived or thriven ['θrɪvn]) vi **1.** [plant] pousser (bien) ; [child] grandir, se développer ; [adult] se porter bien, respirer la santé **2.** [business, company] prospérer, être florissant ; [businessman] prospérer, réussir.

thriving ['θraɪvɪŋ] adj **1.** [person] florissant de santé, vigoureux ; [animal] vigoureux ; [plant] robuste, vigoureux **2.** [business, company] prospère, florissant ; [businessman] prospère.

throat [θrəʊt] n gorge f.

throaty ['θrəʊtɪ] (*compar* **throatier,** *superl* **throatiest**) adj [voice, laugh, etc.] guttural, rauque.

throb [θrɒb] (*pt & pp* **throbbed,** *cont* **throbbing**) ◆ vi **1.** [music] vibrer ; [drums] battre (rythmiquement) ; [engine, machine] vrombir, vibrer **2.** [heart] battre fort, palpiter **3.** [pain] lanciner / *my head is throbbing* j'ai très mal à la tête. ◆ n **1.** [of music, drums] rythme m, battement m rythmique, battements mpl rythmiques ; [of engine, machine] vibration f, vibrations fpl, vrombissement m, vrombissements mpl **2.** [of heart] battement m, battements mpl, pulsation f, pulsations fpl **3.** [of pain] élancement m.

throbbing ['θrɒbɪŋ] adj **1.** [rhythm] battant ; [drum] qui bat rythmiquement ; [engine, machine] vibrant, vrombissant **2.** [heart] battant, palpitant **3.** [pain] lancinant.

throes pl n ⟶ **death throes.** ❖ **in the throes of** prep phr : *in the throes of war* / *illness* en proie à la guerre / la maladie ▸ **to be in the throes of doing sthg** être en train de faire qqch.

thrombosis [θrɒm'bəʊsɪs] (*pl* **thromboses** [-si:z]) n thrombose f, thromboses fpl.

throne [θrəʊn] ◆ n trône m ▸ **to come to the throne** monter sur le trône ▸ **on the throne** sur le trône. ◆ vt [monarch] mettre sur le trône ; [bishop] introniser.

throng [θrɒŋ] ◆ n foule f, multitude f. ◆ vt : *demonstrators thronged the streets* des manifestants se pressaient dans les rues / *the shops were thronged with people* les magasins grouillaient de monde or étaient bondés. ◆ vi affluer, se presser.

throttle ['θrɒtl] ◆ n [of car] accélérateur m ; [of motorcycle] poignée f d'accélération or des gaz ; [of aircraft] commande f des gaz ▸ **to open** / **to close the throttle** mettre / réduire les gaz ▸ **at full throttle** (à) pleins gaz. ◆ comp [controls] ▸ **throttle valve** papillon m des gaz, soupape f d'étranglement. ◆ vt [strangle] étrangler. ❖ **throttle down, throttle back** vt sep mettre au ralenti.

through [θru:] ◆ prep **1.** [from one end or side to the other] à travers / *to walk through the streets* se promener dans or à travers les rues / *the river flows through a deep valley* le fleuve traverse une vallée profonde / *we went through a door* nous avons passé une porte / *he could see her through the window* il pouvait la voir par la fenêtre / *he drove through a red light* il a brûlé un feu rouge **2.** [from beginning to end of] à travers / *through the ages* à travers les âges / *she has lived through some difficult times* elle a connu or traversé des moments difficiles **3.** US [to, until] : *April through July* (jusqu')à juillet, d'avril à juillet **4.** [by means of] par, grâce à / *I sent it through the post* je l'ai envoyé par la poste / *it was only through his intervention that we were allowed out* c'est uniquement grâce à son intervention qu'on nous a laissés sortir **5.** [because of] à cause de / *through no fault of his own, he lost his job* il a perdu son emploi sans que ce soit de sa faute. ◆ adv **1.** [from one side to the other] : *I couldn't get through* je ne pouvais pas passer / *the nail had gone right through* le clou était passé au travers **2.** [from beginning to end] : *I read the letter through* j'ai lu la lettre jusqu'au bout / *I left halfway through* je suis parti au milieu **3.** [directly] : *the train goes through to Paris without stopping* le train va directement à Paris or est sans arrêt jusqu'à Paris **4.** [completely] : *she's an aristocrat through and through* c'est une aristocrate jusqu'au bout des ongles **5.** TELEC : *can you put me through to Elaine* / *to extension 363?* pouvez-vous me passer Elaine / le poste 363 ? /

you're through now vous êtes en ligne. ◆ adj **1.** [direct -train, ticket] direct ; [traffic] en transit, de passage / **'no through road** UK**, not a through street** US **'** 'voie sans issue' **2.** [finished] : *are you through?* avez-vous fini ?, c'est fini ? / *she's through with him* elle en a eu assez de lui.

throughout [θru:'aʊt] ◆ prep **1.** [in space] partout dans **2.** [in time] : *throughout the year* pendant toute l'année / *throughout my life* (durant) toute ma vie. ◆ adv **1.** [everywhere] partout **2.** [all the time] (pendant) tout le temps.

throughput ['θru:pʊt] n COMPUT débit m.

throve [θrəʊv] pt ⟶ **thrive.**

throw [θrəʊ] (*pt* **threw** [θru:]*, pp* **thrown** [θrəʊn]) ◆ vt **1.** [stone] lancer, jeter ; [ball] lancer ; [coal onto fire] mettre / *throw me the ball* or *throw the ball to me* lance-moi le ballon / *she threw the serviette into the bin* elle a jeté la serviette à la poubelle / *he threw his jacket over a chair* il a jeté sa veste sur une chaise / *he threw two sixes* [in dice] il a jeté deux six ▸ **to throw sb into prison** or **jail** jeter qqn en prison **2.** [opponent, rider] jeter (par terre) / *the horse threw him* le cheval le désarçonna or le jeta à terre **3.** [with force, violence] projeter / *she was thrown clear* [in car accident] elle a été éjectée ▸ **to throw open** ouvrir en grand or tout grand / *he threw himself on the mercy of the king* fig il s'en est remis au bon vouloir du roi **4.** [plunge] plonger / *the news threw them into confusion* / *a panic* les nouvelles les ont plongés dans l'embarras / les ont affolés ▸ **to throw o.s. into** : *to throw o.s. into one's work* se plonger dans son travail **5.** [direct, aim -look, glance] jeter, lancer ; [-accusation, reproach] lancer, envoyer ; [-punch] lancer, porter ; [cast -light, shadows] projeter **6.** [confuse] désarçonner, dérouter, déconcerter / *I was completely thrown for a few seconds* je suis resté tout interdit pendant quelques secondes **7.** [activate -switch, lever, clutch] actionner **8.** SPORT [race, match] perdre délibérément **9.** [silk] tordre ; [subj: potter] ▸ **to throw a pot** tourner un vase. ◆ n **1.** [of ball, javelin] jet m, lancer m ; [of dice] lancer m / *his whole fortune depended on a single throw of the dice* toute sa fortune dépendait d'un seul coup de dés **2.** inf [go, turn] coup m, tour m / *10p a throw* 10 pence le coup **3.** [cover] couverture f ; [piece of fabric] jeté m de fauteuil or de canapé. ❖ **throw about** UK**, throw around** vt sep **1.** [toss] lancer ; [scatter] jeter, éparpiller / *the boys were throwing a ball about* les garçons jouaient à la balle ▸ **to be thrown about** être ballotté **2.** [move violently] ▸ **to throw o.s. about** s'agiter, se débattre. ❖ **throw away** ◆ vt sep **1.** [old clothes, rubbish] jeter **2.** fig [waste -advantage, opportunity, talents] gaspiller, gâcher ; [-affection, friendship] perdre / *you're throwing away your only chance of happiness* vous êtes en train de gâcher votre seule chance de bonheur. ◆ vi [in cards] se défausser. ❖ **throw in** vt sep **1.** [into box, cupboard, etc.] jeter ; [through window] jeter, lancer ▸ **to throw in the towel** SPORT & fig jeter l'éponge **2.** [interject -remark, suggestion] placer ; [include] : *breakfast is thrown in* le petit déjeuner est compris. ◆ vi US ▸ **to throw in with sb** s'associer à or avec qqn. ❖ **throw off** vt sep **1.** [discard -clothes] enlever or ôter (à la hâte) ; [-mask, disguise] jeter **2.** [get rid of -habit, inhibition] se défaire de, se débarrasser de ; [-burden] se libérer de, se débarrasser de ; [cold, infection] se débarrasser de **3.** [elude -pursuer] perdre, semer. ❖ **throw on** vt sep [clothes] enfiler or passer (à la hâte). ❖ **throw out** vt sep **1.** [rubbish, unwanted items] jeter, mettre au rebut **2.** [eject -from building] mettre à la porte, jeter dehors ; [-from night club] jeter dehors, vider ; [evict -from accommodation] expulser ; [expel -from school, army] renvoyer, expulser **3.** [disturb -person] déconcerter, désorienter ; [upset -calculation, results] fausser. ❖ **throw together** vt sep **1.** inf [make quickly -

equipment, table] fabriquer à la hâte, bricoler / *he managed to throw a meal together* il a réussi à improviser un repas **2.** [gather] rassembler à la hâte **3.** [by accident] réunir par hasard. ❖ **throw up** ◆ vt sep **1.** [above one's head] jeter or lancer en l'air / *can you throw me up my towel?* peux-tu me lancer ma serviette ? **2.** [produce - problem] produire, créer ; [-evidence] mettre à jour ; [-dust, dirt] soulever ; [-artist] produire **3.** [abandon - career, studies] abandonner, laisser tomber ; [-chance, opportunity] laisser passer, gaspiller **4.** *inf* [vomit] vomir. ◆ vi vomir, rendre.

throwaway ['θrəʊə,weɪ] ◆ adj [line, remark] fait comme par hasard or comme si de rien n'était. ◆ comp [bottle, carton, etc.] jetable, à jeter, à usage unique.

throwback ['θrəʊbæk] n **1.** ANTHR & BIOL régression f atavique **2.** [of fashion, custom] : *those new hats are a throwback to the 1930s* ces nouveaux chapeaux marquent un retour aux années 1930 or sont inspirés des années 1930.

throw-in n FOOT rentrée f en touche.

thrown [θrəʊn] pp —→ throw.

thru [θruː] US = through.

thrush [θrʌʃ] n **1.** [bird] grive f **2.** *(U)* MED [oral] muguet m ; [vaginal] mycose f, candidose f.

thrust [θrʌst] *(pt & pp thrust)* ◆ vt **1.** [push, shove] enfoncer, fourrer, plonger **2.** [force - responsibility, fame] imposer ◗ **to thrust o.s. on** or **upon sb** imposer sa présence à qqn, s'imposer à qqn. ◆ vi [push] : *he thrust past her* **a)** [rudely] il l'a bousculée en passant devant elle **b)** [quickly] il est passé devant elle comme une flèche. ◆ n **1.** [lunge] poussée f ; [stab] coup m **2.** *fig* [remark] pointe f **3.** *(U)* [force - of engine] poussée f ; *fig* [drive] dynamisme m, élan m **4.** *(U)* [of argument, story] sens m, idée f ; [of policy] idée f directrice ; [of research] aspect m principal. ◆ **thrust aside** vt sep [person, thing] écarter brusquement ; [suggestion] écarter or rejeter brusquement. ◆ **thrust away** vt sep repousser. ◆ **thrust forward** vt sep pousser en avant brusquement ◗ **to thrust o.s. forward a)** *lit* se frayer un chemin **b)** *fig* se mettre en avant. ◆ **thrust in** ◆ vi [physically] s'introduire de force. ◆ vt sep [finger, pointed object] enfoncer ◗ **to thrust one's way in** se frayer un passage pour entrer. ◆ **thrust out** vt sep **1.** [arm, leg] allonger brusquement ; [hand] tendre brusquement ; [chin] projeter en avant ◗ **to thrust out one's chest** bomber la poitrine **2.** [eject] pousser dehors.

thrusting ['θrʌstɪŋ] adj [dynamic] dynamique, entreprenant, plein d'entrain ; *pej* qui se fait valoir, qui se met en avant.

thruway ['θruːweɪ] n US ≃ autoroute f *(à cinq ou six voies)*.

Thu. written abbr of Thursday.

thud [θʌd] *(pt & pp thudded, cont thudding)* ◆ vi **1.** faire un bruit sourd ; [falling object] tomber en faisant un bruit sourd **2.** [walk or run heavily] ◗ **to thud across / in / past** traverser / entrer / passer à pas pesants **3.** [heart] battre fort. ◆ n bruit m sourd.

thug [θʌg] n voyou m.

thumb [θʌm] ◆ n pouce m. ◆ vt **1.** [book, magazine] feuilleter, tourner les pages de ; [pages] tourner **2.** [hitch] ◗ **to thumb a lift** US or **ride** US faire du stop or de l'auto-stop **3.** PHR ◗ **to thumb one's nose at sb** faire un pied de nez à qqn. ◆ vi US *inf* faire du stop or de l'auto-stop. ◆ **thumb through** vt insep [book, magazine] feuilleter ; [files] consulter rapidement ; [pages] tourner.

thumb index n répertoire m à onglets.

thumbnail ['θʌmneɪl] n ongle m du pouce ◗ **thumbnail sketch a)** [of plan] aperçu m, croquis m rapide **b)** [of personality] bref portrait m.

thumbs-down n ◗ **to get the thumbs-down** : *my proposal got the thumbs-down* ma proposition a été rejetée.

thumbs-up n ◗ **to give sb the thumbs-up a)** [all OK] faire signe à qqn que tout va bien **b)** [in encouragement] faire signe à qqn pour l'encourager / *they've given me the thumbs-up for my thesis* ils m'ont donné le feu vert pour ma thèse.

thumbtack ['θʌmtæk] n US punaise f.

thump [θʌmp] ◆ vt donner un coup de poing à, frapper d'un coup de poing / *to thump sb on the back* donner une grande tape dans le dos à qqn / *he thumped his fist on the table* il a frappé du poing sur la table. ◆ vi **1.** [bang] cogner / *he thumped on the door / wall* il a cogné à la porte / contre le mur **2.** [run or walk heavily] ◗ **to thump in / out / past** entrer / sortir / passer à pas lourds. ◆ n **1.** [blow - gen] coup m ; [- with fist] coup m de poing ; [- with stick] coup m de bâton ◗ **to give sb a thump** assener un coup de poing à qqn **2.** [sound] bruit m sourd. ◆ adv ◗ **to go thump** *inf* faire boum. ◆ **thump out** vt sep ◗ **to thump out a tune on the piano** marteler un air au piano.

thumping ['θʌmpɪŋ] UK *inf* ◆ adj [success] énorme, immense, phénoménal ; [difference] énorme. ◆ adv *dated* [as intensifier] : *a thumping great meal* un repas énorme.

thunder ['θʌndər] ◆ n **1.** METEOR tonnerre m **2.** [of applause, guns] tonnerre m ; [of engine, traffic] bruit m de tonnerre ; [of hooves] fracas m. ◆ vi **1.** METEOR tonner / *it's thundering* il tonne, ça tonne **2.** [guns, waves] tonner, gronder ; [hooves] retentir **3.** [shout] ◗ **to thunder at sb** / **against sthg** tonner contre qqn / contre qqch. ◆ vt [order, threat, applause] lancer d'une voix tonitruante or tonnante.

thunderbolt ['θʌndəbəʊlt] n METEOR éclair m ; *fig* coup m de tonnerre.

thunderclap ['θʌndəklæp] n coup m de tonnerre.

thundercloud ['θʌndəklaʊd] n METEOR nuage m orageux ; *fig* nuage m noir.

thundering ['θʌndərɪŋ] UK *inf & dated* ◆ adj **1.** [terrible] ◗ **to be in a thundering temper** or **rage** être dans une colère noire or hors de soi **2.** [superb - success] foudroyant, phénoménal. ◆ adv : *it's a thundering good read* c'est un livre formidable.

thunderous ['θʌndərəs] adj [shouts, noise] retentissant.

thunderstorm ['θʌndəstɔːm] n orage m.

thunderstruck ['θʌndəstrʌk] adj foudroyé, abasourdi.

thundery ['θʌndərɪ] adj METEOR orageux.

Thur, Thurs (written abbr of Thursday) jeu.

Thursday ['θɜːzdeɪ] n jeudi m. See also Friday.

thus [ðʌs] adv [so] ainsi, donc ; [as a result] ainsi, par conséquent ; [in this way] ainsi ◗ **thus far a)** [in present] jusqu'ici **b)** [in past] jusque-là.

thwart [θwɔːt] vt [plan] contrecarrer, contrarier ; [person - in efforts] contrarier les efforts de ; [- in plans] contrarier les projets de ; [- in attempts] contrecarrer les tentatives de.

Thx, THX, Thnx MESSAGING written abbr of thanks.

thyme [taɪm] n *(U)* thym m.

thyroid ['θaɪrɔɪd] ◆ n thyroïde f. ◆ adj thyroïde.

TIA MESSAGING written abbr of thanks in advance.

tiara [tɪ'ɑːrə] n [gen] diadème m ; RELIG tiare f.

Tiber ['taɪbər] pr n ◗ **the (River) Tiber** le Tibre.

Tibet [tɪ'bet] pr n Tibet m / *in Tibet* au Tibet.

Tibetan [tɪ'betn] ◆ n **1.** [person] Tibétain m, -e f **2.** LING tibétain m. ◆ adj tibétain.

tibia ['tɪbɪə] *(pl tibias or tibiae [-bɪiː])* n tibia m.

tic [tɪk] n ▸ **(nervous) tic** tic m (nerveux).

TIC MESSAGING written abbr of **tongue in cheek**.

tick [tɪk] ◆ vi [clock, time-bomb] faire tic-tac ; [motivation] : *I wonder what makes him tick* je me demande ce qui le motive. ◆ vt ⚏ [mark - name, item] cocher, pointer ; [- box, answer] cocher ; [SCH - as correct] marquer juste. ◆ n **1.** [of clock] tic-tac m **2.** ⚏ inf [moment] instant m **3.** ⚏ [mark] coche f ▸ **to put a tick against sthg** cocher qqch **4.** ZOOL tique f **5.** ⚏ inf [credit] crédit m ▸ **to buy sthg on tick** acheter qqch à crédit **6.** TEXT [ticking] toile f à matelas ; [covering - for mattress] housse f (de matelas) ; [- for pillow] housse f (d'oreiller), taie f. ◈ **tick away** vi **1.** [clock] faire tic-tac ; [taximeter] tourner **2.** [time] passer / *the minutes ticked away* or *by* les minutes passaient. ◈ **tick off** vt sep **1.** [name, item] cocher, pointer **2.** fig [count - reasons, chapters] compter, énumérer **3.** ⚏ inf [scold] attraper, passer un savon à **4.** ⚏ inf [annoy] agacer, taper sur le système à. ◈ **tick over** vi **1.** ⚏ [car engine] tourner au ralenti ; [taximeter] tourner **2.** fig [business, production] tourner normalement.

tick box n case f à cocher.

ticked [tɪkt] adj ⚏ inf en rogne.

tickertape ['tɪkəteɪp] n **1.** [tape] bande f de téléscripteur or de téléimprimeur **2.** ⚏ fig ▸ **to get a tickertape reception** or **welcome** recevoir un accueil triomphal.

ticket ['tɪkɪt] ◆ n **1.** [for travel - on coach, plane, train] billet m ; [- on bus, underground] billet m, ticket m ; [for entry - to cinema, theatre, match] billet m ; [- to car park] ticket m (de parking) ; [for membership - of library] carte f **2.** [receipt - in shop] ticket m (de caisse), reçu m ; [- for left-luggage, cloakroom] ticket m (de consigne) ; [- from pawnshop] reconnaissance f **3.** [label] étiquette f **4.** AUTO [fine] P-V m, contravention f, amende f ▸ **to get a ticket** avoir un P-V **5.** ⚏ POL [set of principles] : *he fought the election on a Democratic ticket* il a basé son programme électoral sur les principes du Parti démocrate **6.** inf AERON & NAUT [certificate] brevet m **7.** ⚏ mil ▸ **to get one's ticket** être libéré des obligations militaires **8.** PHR that's **(just) the ticket!** inf voilà exactement ce qu'il faut ! ◆ vt **1.** [label] étiqueter, [earmark] désigner, destiner **3.** [issue with a ticket] donner un billet à **4.** ⚏ [issue with a parking ticket] mettre un P-V à.

ticket agency n **1.** THEAT agence f de spectacles **2.** RAIL agence f de voyages.

ticket collector n RAIL contrôleur m, -euse f.

ticket holder n personne f munie d'un billet.

ticket inspector = **ticket collector**.

ticketless ['tɪkɪtlɪs] adj ▸ **ticketless travel** AERON système permettant de voyager sans billet papier.

ticket machine n distributeur m de tickets, billetterie f automatique.

ticket office n bureau m de vente des billets, guichet m.

ticket tout n ⚏ revendeur m, -euse f de billets (sur le marché noir).

ticking ['tɪkɪŋ] n **1.** [of clock] tic-tac m **2.** TEXT toile f (à matelas).

ticking off (pl **tickings off**) n ⚏ inf ▸ **to give sb a ticking off** engueulander qqn, tirer les oreilles à qqn.

tickle ['tɪkl] ◆ vt **1.** lit [by touching] chatouiller **2.** fig [curiosity, vanity] chatouiller **3.** fig [amuse] amuser, faire rire ; [please] faire plaisir à. ◆ vi [person, blanket] chatouiller ; [beard] piquer. ◆ n [on body] chatouillement m ; [in throat] picotement m.

tickling ['tɪklɪŋ] ◆ n (U) [of person] chatouilles fpl ; [of blanket] picotement m. ◆ adj [throat] qui grattouille or picote ; [cough] d'irritation, qui gratte la gorge.

ticklish ['tɪklɪʃ] adj **1.** [person, feet] chatouilleux ; [sensation] de chatouillement **2.** inf [touchy] chatouilleux **3.** inf [delicate - situation, topic] délicat, épineux ; [- moment] crucial ; [- negotiations] délicat.

tickly ['tɪklɪ] adj inf [sensation] de chatouillis ; [blanket] qui chatouille ; [beard] qui pique.

tick-tack-toe ⚏ = **tic-tac-toe**.

tic-tac-toe n ⚏ morpion m (jeu).

tidal ['taɪdl] adj [estuary, river] qui a des marées ; [current, cycle, force] de la marée ; [ferry] dont les horaires sont fonction de la marée ; [energy] marémoteur.

tidal wave n raz-de-marée m inv ; fig [of sympathy] élan m.

tidbit ['tɪdbɪt] ⚏ = **titbit**.

tiddledywinks ['tɪdldɪwɪŋks] n ⚏ = **tiddlywinks**.

tiddler ['tɪdlə] n inf **1.** [fish] petit poisson m ; [minnow] fretin m ; [stickleback] épinoche f **2.** ⚏ [child] mioche m.

tiddly ['tɪdlɪ] (compar **tiddlier**, superl **tiddliest**) adj ⚏ inf **1.** [tiny] tout petit, minuscule **2.** [tipsy] éméché, paf.

tiddlywinks ['tɪdlɪwɪŋks] n (U) jeu m de puce.

tide [taɪd] n **1.** [of sea] marée f / *at high / low tide* à marée haute / basse **2.** [of opinion] courant m ; [of discontent, indignation] vague f ; [of events] cours m, marche f. ◈ **tide over** vt sep dépanner.

tidemark ['taɪdmɑːk] n **1.** [on shore] laisse f de haute mer **2.** fig & hum [round bath, neck] marque f de crasse.

tidily ['taɪdɪlɪ] adv [pack, fold] soigneusement, avec soin.

tidiness ['taɪdɪnɪs] n **1.** [of drawer, desk, room] ordre m **2.** [of appearance] netteté f **3.** [of work, exercise book] propreté f, netteté f ; [of writing] netteté f.

tidings ['taɪdɪŋz] pl n arch & liter nouvelles fpl.

tidy ['taɪdɪ] (compar **tidier**, superl **tidiest**, pl **tidies**, pt & pp **tidied**) ◆ adj **1.** [room, house, desk] rangé, ordonné, en ordre ; [garden, town] propre **2.** [in appearance - person] soigné ; [- clothes, hair] soigné, net **3.** [work, writing] soigné, net **4.** [in character - person] ordonné, méthodique **5.** inf [sum, profit] joli, coquet. ◆ n **1.** [receptacle] vide-poches m inv **2.** ⚏ [on chair] têtière f. ◆ vt [room] ranger, mettre de l'ordre dans ; [desk, clothes, objects] ranger / *to tidy one's hair* se recoiffer. ◈ **tidy away** vt sep ranger, ramasser. ◈ **tidy up** ◆ vi **1.** [in room] tout ranger **2.** [in appearance] s'arranger. ◆ vt sep [room, clothes] ranger, mettre de l'ordre dans ; [desk] ranger ▸ **to tidy o.s. up** s'arranger.

tie [taɪ] ◆ n **1.** [necktie] cravate f **2.** [fastener - gen] attache f ; [- on apron] cordon m ; [- for curtain] embrasse f ; [- on shoes] lacet m **3.** [bond, link] lien m, attache f / *family ties* liens de parenté or familiaux **4.** [restriction] entrave f **5.** SPORT [draw] égalité f ; [drawn match] match m nul / *the match ended in a tie* les deux équipes ont fait match nul ; [in competition] compétition f dont les gagnants sont ex aequo ; POL égalité f de voix **6.** FOOT [match] match m. ◆ vt **1.** [with string, rope - parcel] attacher, ficeler **2.** [necktie, scarf, shoelaces] attacher, nouer ▸ **to tie a knot in sthg, to tie sthg in a knot** faire un nœud à qqch **3.** [confine - subj: responsibility, job, etc.] : *she's tied to the house* a) [unable to get out] elle est clouée à la maison b) [kept busy] la maison l'accapare beaucoup / *they're tied to* or *by the conditions of the contract* ils sont liés par les conditions du contrat **4.** MUS lier. ◆ vi [draw - players] être à égalité ; [- in match] faire match nul ; [- in exam, competition] être ex aequo ; [- in election] obtenir le même score or nombre de voix. ◈ **tie back** vt sep [hair] attacher (en arrière). ◈ **tie down** vt sep **1.** [with string, rope - person, object] attacher **2.** fig [restrict] accaparer / *she doesn't want to feel tied down* elle ne veut pas perdre sa liberté / *I'd rather not be tied down to* *a specific time* je préférerais qu'on ne fixe pas une heure précise. ❖ **tie in** ◈ vi **1.** [be connected] être lié or en rapport / *this ties in with what I said before* cela rejoint ce que j'ai dit avant **2.** [correspond] correspondre, concorder / *the evidence doesn't tie in with the facts* les indices dont nous disposons ne correspondent pas aux faits or ne cadrent pas avec les faits. ◈ vt sep : *she's trying to tie her work experience in with her research* elle essaie de faire coïncider son expérience professionnelle et ses recherches. ❖ **tie on** vt sep attacher, nouer. ❖ **tie together** ◈ vi : *it all ties together* tout se tient. ◈ vt sep [papers, sticks] attacher (ensemble). ❖ **tie up** vt sep **1.** [parcel, papers] ficeler ; [plant, animal] attacher ; [prisoner] attacher, ligoter ; [boat] attacher, arrimer ; [shoelace] nouer, attacher **2.** *(usu passive)* [money, supplies] immobiliser **3.** [connect - company, organization] lier par des accords **4.** [complete, finalize - deal] conclure ; [- terms of contract] fixer / *there are still a few loose ends to tie up* il y a encore quelques points de détail à régler **5.** [impede - traffic] bloquer ; [- progress, production] freiner, entraver.

tiebreak(er) ['taɪbreɪk(əʳ)] n TENNIS tie-break *m* ; [in game, contest] épreuve *f* subsidiaire ; [in quiz] question *f* subsidiaire.

tied [taɪd] adj **1.** SPORT ▶ **to be tied a)** [players] être à égalité **b)** [game] être nul **2.** [person - by obligation, duties] pris, occupé **3.** MUS [note] lié.

tied cottage n UK *logement attaché à une ferme et occupé par un employé agricole.*

tied up adj [busy] ▶ **to be tied up** être occupé or pris.

tie-dye vt teindre en nouant *(pour obtenir une teinture non uniforme).*

tie-in n **1.** [connection] lien *m*, rapport *m* **2.** US COMM [sale] vente *f* par lots ; [items] lot *m* **3.** [in publishing] *livre, cassette, etc., liés à un film ou une émission.*

tiepin ['taɪpɪn] n épingle *f* de cravate.

tier [tɪəʳ] ◈ n **1.** [row of seats - in theatre, stadium] gradin *m*, rangée *f* ; [level] étage *m* **2.** ADMIN échelon *m*, niveau *m* **3.** [of cake] étage *m*. ◈ vt [seating] disposer en gradins.

Tierra del Fuego [tɪˌerədel'fweɪgəʊ] pr n Terre de Feu *f* / *in Tierra del Fuego* en Terre de Feu.

tie-up n **1.** [connection] lien *m*, rapport *m* **2.** FIN [merger] fusion *f* **3.** US [stoppage] arrêt *m*, interruption *f* **4.** US [traffic jam] embouteillage *m*, bouchon *m*.

tiff [tɪf] n UK *inf* prise *f* de bec.

tiger ['taɪgəʳ] n tigre *m*.

tiger cub n petit *m* du tigre.

tiger economy n *pays à l'économie très performante.*

tight [taɪt] ◈ adj **1.** [garment, footwear] serré, étroit **2.** [stiff - drawer, door] dur à ouvrir ; [- tap] dur à tourner ; [- lid] dur à enlever ; [- screw] serré ; [constricted] pesant **3.** [taut - rope] raide, tendu ; [- bow] tendu ; [- net, knitting, knot] serré ; [- skin] tiré ; [- group] serré ; [firm] ▶ **to keep (a)** tight hold or grasp on sthg bien tenir qqch **4.** [sharp - bend, turn] brusque **5.** [strict - control, restrictions] strict, sévère ; [- security] strict **6.** [limited - budget, credit] serré, resserré **7.** [close - competition] serré **8.** [busy - schedule] serré, chargé **9.** *inf* [mean] radin, pingre **10.** *inf* [drunk] soûl, rond **11.** US *inf* [cool] : *that's tight* c'est cool. ◈ adv [close, fasten] bien / *packed tight* **a)** [bag] bien rempli or plein **b)** [pub, room] bondé / *hold tight!* tenez-vous bien !, accrochez-vous bien ! ❖ **tights** pl n UK ▶ **(pair of) tights** collant *m*, collants *mpl*.

tighten ['taɪtn] ◈ vt **1.** [belt, strap] resserrer **2.** [nut, screw] serrer, bien visser ; [knot] serrer ; [cable, rope] serrer, tendre **3.** [control, security, regulations] renforcer ; [credit] resserrer. ◈ vi **1.** [grip] : *his finger tightened on the*

trigger son doigt se serra sur la gâchette **2.** [nut, screw, knot] se resserrer ; [cable, rope] se raidir, se tendre **3.** [control, security, regulation] être renforcé ; [credit] se resserrer **4.** [throat, stomach] se nouer. ❖ **tighten up** vt sep **1.** [nut, screw] serrer **2.** [control, security, regulation] renforcer. ❖ **tighten up on** vt insep : *to tighten up on discipline / security* renforcer la discipline / la sécurité.

tightfisted [ˌtaɪt'fɪstɪd] adj *pej* avare, pingre.

tight-fitting adj [skirt, trousers] moulant ; [lid] qui ferme bien.

tight-knit [-'nɪt] adj [community, family] (très) uni.

tight-lipped [-'lɪpt] adj : *he sat tight-lipped and pale* il était assis, pâle et muet.

tightly ['taɪtlɪ] adv **1.** [firmly - hold, fit, screw] (bien) serré / *he held his daughter tightly to him* il serrait sa fille tout contre lui / *hold on tightly* tenez-vous or accrochez-vous bien / *her eyes were tightly shut* elle avait les yeux bien fermés / *news is tightly controlled* les informations sont soumises à un contrôle rigoureux **2.** [densely] : *the lecture hall was tightly packed* l'amphithéâtre était bondé or plein à craquer.

tightness ['taɪtnɪs] n **1.** [of garment, shoes] étroitesse *f* **2.** [stiffness - of drawer, screw, tap] dureté *f* **3.** [tautness - of bow, rope] raideur *f* **4.** [strictness - of control, regulation] rigueur *f*, sévérité *f* ; [- of security] rigueur *f*.

tightrope ['taɪtrəʊp] n corde *f* raide.

tightrope walker n funambule *mf*.

Tigré ['tiːgreɪ] pr n Tigré *m* / *in Tigré* dans le Tigré.

tigress ['taɪgrɪs] n ZOOL & *fig* tigresse *f*.

Tigris ['taɪgrɪs] pr n ▶ **the (River) Tigris** le Tigre.

tilde ['tɪldə] n tilde *m*.

tile [taɪl] ◈ n [for roof] tuile *f* ; [for wall, floor] carreau *m*. ◈ vt [roof] couvrir de tuiles ; [floor, wall] carreler.

tiled [taɪld] adj [floor, wall] carrelé ▶ **tiled roof** toit *m* de tuiles.

tiler ['taɪləʳ] n [of roof] couvreur *m* (*de toits en tuiles*) ; [of floor, wall] carreleur *m*.

tiling ['taɪlɪŋ] n (U) **1.** [putting on tiles - on roof] pose *f* des tuiles ; [- on floor, in bathroom] carrelage *m* **2.** [tiles - on roof] tuiles *fpl* ; [- on floor, wall] carrelage *m*, carreaux *mpl*.

till [tɪl] ◈ conj & prep = **until**. ◈ n **1.** [cash register] caisse *f* (enregistreuse) ; [drawer] tiroir-caisse *m* **2.** [money] caisse *f*. ◈ vt AGR labourer.

tiller ['tɪləʳ] n **1.** NAUT barre *f*, gouvernail *m* **2.** BOT pousse *f*, talle *f*.

tilt [tɪlt] ◈ vt [lean] pencher, incliner. ◈ vi **1.** [lean] se pencher, s'incliner / *to tilt backwards / forwards* se pencher en arrière / en avant **2.** HIST [joust] jouter ▶ **to tilt at sb a)** HIST diriger un coup de lance contre qqn **b)** *fig* lancer des piques à qqn. ◈ n **1.** [angle] inclinaison *f* ; [slope] pente *f* **2.** HIST [joust] joute *f* ; [thrust] coup *m* de lance ; *fig* ▶ **to have a tilt at sb** s'en prendre à qqn, décocher des piques à qqn. ❖ **full tilt** adv phr : *he ran full tilt into her* il lui est rentré en plein dedans. ❖ **tilt over** vi **1.** [slant] pencher **2.** [overturn] se renverser, basculer.

timber ['tɪmbəʳ] ◈ n **1.** [wood] bois *m* de charpente or de construction or d'œuvre **2.** (U) [trees] arbres *mpl*, bois *m* **3.** [beam] madrier *m*, poutre *f* ; [on ship] membrure *f*. ◈ comp [roof, fence] en bois. ◈ vt [tunnel] boiser. ◈ interj ▶ **timber!** attention !

timbered ['tɪmbəd] adj [region, land] boisé ; [house] en bois.

time [taɪm] ◈ n **1.** [continuous stretch of time] temps *m* / *as time goes by* avec le temps / *these things take time* cela ne se fait pas du jour au lendemain ▶ **to have time on one's hands** or **time to spare** avoir du temps

2. [period of time spent on particular activity] temps *m* / *there's no time to lose* il n'y a pas de temps à perdre ▶ **to make good / poor time doing sthg** mettre peu de temps / longtemps à faire qqch / *take your time over it* prenez le temps qu'il faudra / *half the time he doesn't know what he's doing* la moitié du temps il ne sait pas ce qu'il fait / *most of the time* la plupart du temps / *it rained part or some of the time* il a plu par moments / *I start in three weeks' time* je commence dans trois semaines **3.** [available period of time] temps *m* / *I haven't (the) time to do the shopping* je n'ai pas le temps de faire les courses / *I've no time for gossip* a) *lit* je n'ai pas le temps de papoter b) *fig* je n'ai pas de temps à perdre en bavardages / *I've no time for people like him* je ne supporte pas les gens comme lui / *I've a lot of time for people who volunteer* j'ai beaucoup d'admiration pour les gens qui font du volontariat / *we've got plenty of time* or *all the time in the world* nous avons tout le temps **4.** [while] temps *m* / *after a time* après un (certain) temps / *a long time ago* il y a longtemps / *you took a long time!* tu en as mis du temps !, il t'en a fallu du temps ! ▶ **a short time** peu de temps / *she's going to stay with us for a short time* elle va rester avec nous pendant quelque temps / *in the shortest possible time* dans les plus brefs délais, le plus vite or tôt possible / *after some time* au bout de quelque temps, après un certain temps / *some time ago* il y a quelque temps / *it's the best film I've seen for some time* c'est le meilleur film que j'aie vu depuis un moment **5.** [time taken or required to do something] temps *m*, durée *f* / *she finished in half the time it took me to finish* elle a mis deux fois moins de temps que moi pour finir **6.** [by clock] heure *f* / *what time is it?* or *what's the time?* quelle heure est-il ? / *the time is twenty past three* il est trois heures vingt / *what time are we leaving?* à quelle heure partons-nous ? / *could you tell me the time?* pourriez-vous me dire l'heure (qu'il est) ? / *it's time I was going* il est temps que je parte / *I wouldn't give him the time of day* je ne lui dirais même pas bonjour **7.** [system] ▶ **local time** heure *f* locale / *it's 5 o'clock Tokyo time* il est 5 h, heure de Tokyo **8.** [schedule] : *within the required time* dans les délais requis **9.** [particular point in time] moment *m* / *at that time I was in Madrid* à ce moment-là j'étais or j'étais alors à Madrid / *I worked for her at one time* à un moment donné j'ai travaillé pour elle ▶ **at the present time** en ce moment, à présent ▶ **at a later time** plus tard ▶ **at a given time** à un moment donné ▶ **at any one time** à la fois / *an inconvenient time* un moment inopportun / *by the time you get this...* le temps que tu reçoives ceci..., quand tu auras reçu ceci... / *by this time next week* d'ici une semaine, dans une semaine / *this time next week* la semaine prochaine à cette heure-ci / *this time last week* il y a exactement une semaine ▶ **in between times** entre-temps **10.** [suitable moment] moment *m* / *now is the time to invest* c'est maintenant qu'il faut investir / *when the time comes* (quand) le moment (sera) venu **11.** [occasion, instance] fois *f* / *I'll forgive you this time* je vous pardonne cette fois-ci or pour cette fois ▶ **each** or **every time** chaque fois / *the last time he came* la dernière fois qu'il est venu ▶ **another** or **some other time** une autre fois ▶ **many times** bien des fois, très souvent / *nine times out of ten the machine doesn't work* neuf fois sur dix la machine ne marche pas / *we'll have to decide some time or other* tôt ou tard or un jour ou l'autre il va falloir nous décider / *do you remember that time we went to Germany?* tu te rappelles la fois où nous sommes allés en Allemagne ? **12.** [experience] : *to have a good time* bien s'amuser / *she's had a terrible time of it* elle a beaucoup souffert / *I had the time of my life* jamais je ne me suis si bien or autant amusé / *it was a difficult time for all of us* c'était une période difficile pour nous tous **13.** [hours of work] ▶ **to work part / full time** travailler à temps par-

tiel / à plein temps **14.** [hourly wages] : *we pay time and a half on weekends* nous payons les heures du week-end une fois et demie le tarif normal **15.** (*usu pl*) [era] époque *f*, temps *m* / *in Victorian times* à l'époque victorienne / *in times past* or *in former times* autrefois, jadis / *in times to come* à l'avenir / *in our time* de nos jours ▶ **to be ahead of** or **before one's time** être en avance sur son époque or sur son temps ▶ **to be behind the times** être en retard sur son époque or sur son temps ▶ **to keep up with the times** vivre avec son temps ▶ **to move with the times** évoluer avec son temps ▶ **times have changed** autres temps, autres mœurs *prov* / *I've heard some odd things in my time!* j'en ai entendu, des choses, dans ma vie ! **17.** [season] : *it's hot for the time of year* il fait chaud pour la saison **18.** [end of period] fin *f* ▶ **time's up** a) [on exam, visit] c'est l'heure b) [on meter, telephone] le temps est écoulé **19.** *v inf* [in prison] ▶ **to do time** faire de la taule **20.** MUS mesure *f* / *in triple* or *three-part time* à trois temps. ◆ *vt* **1.** [on clock - runner, worker] chronométrer / *time how long she takes to finish* regardez combien de temps elle met pour finir / *to time an egg* minuter le temps de cuisson d'un œuf **2.** [schedule] fixer or prévoir (l'heure de) **3.** [choose right moment for] choisir or calculer le moment de / *your remark was perfectly / badly timed* votre observation est venue au bon / au mauvais moment **4.** [synchronize] régler, ajuster. ❖ **times** ▶ pl *n* [indicating degree] fois *f* / *she's ten times cleverer than he is* elle est dix fois plus intelligente que lui. ◆ *prep* MATH : *3 times 2 is 6* 3 fois 2 font or égalent 6. ❖ **about time** *adv* ▶ *it's about time (that)...* il est grand temps que... / *about time too!* ce n'est pas trop tôt ! ❖ **ahead of time** *adv phr* en avance. ❖ **all the time** *adv phr* : *he's been watching us all the time* il n'a pas cessé de nous regarder / *I knew it all the time* je le savais depuis le début. ❖ **any time** *adv phr* n'importe quand. ❖ **at a time** *adv phr* : *for days at a time* pendant des journées entières, des journées durant / *take one book at a time* prenez les livres un par un or un (seul) livre à la fois. ❖ **at all times** *adv phr* à tous moments. ❖ **at any time** *adv phr* à toute heure. ❖ **at the same time** *adv phr* **1.** [simultaneously] en même temps **2.** [yet] en même temps **3.** [nevertheless] pourtant, cependant. ❖ **at the time** *adv phr* : *at the time of their wedding* au moment de leur mariage / *I didn't pay much attention at the time* sur le moment je n'ai pas fait vraiment attention. ❖ **at times** *adv phr* parfois, par moments. ❖ **behind time** *adv phr* en retard. ❖ **for the time being** *adv phr* pour le moment. ❖ **from time to time** *adv phr* de temps en temps, de temps à autre. ❖ **in time** *adv phr* **1.** [eventually] : *he'll forget about it in (the course of) time* il finira par l'oublier (avec le temps) **2.** [not too late] : *let me know in (good) time* prévenez-moi (bien) à l'avance / *she arrived in time for the play* elle est arrivée à l'heure pour la pièce **3.** MUS en mesure ▶ **to be** or **keep in time (with the music)** être en mesure (avec la musique). ❖ **in (next to) no time, in no time at all** *adv phr* en un rien de temps. ❖ **of all time** *adv phr* de tous les temps. ❖ **on time** *adv phr* à l'heure. ❖ **time after time, time and (time) again** *adv phr* maintes (et maintes) fois.

> 🖉 Note that **il est (grand) temps que** is followed by a verb in the subjunctive:
> **It's (high) time they were caught and brought to justice.** *Il est (grand) temps qu'ils soient capturés et jugés.*

time-and-motion n ▸ **time-and-motion study** étude f de productivité *(qui se concentre sur l'efficacité des employés)*.

time bomb n *lit & fig* bombe f à retardement.

time check n [on radio] rappel m de l'heure.

time-consuming adj [work] qui prend beaucoup de temps, prenant ; [tactics] dilatoire.

time-critical adj critique en termes de temps.

time difference n décalage m horaire.

time-expired adj périmé.

time frame n délai m.

time-honoured [-ˌɒnəd] adj consacré (par l'usage).

timekeeper [ˈtaɪmˌkiːpər] n **1.** [employee, friend] : *he's a good timekeeper* il est toujours à l'heure, il est toujours très ponctuel **2.** SPORT chronométreur m (officiel), chronométreuse f (officielle).

timekeeping [ˈtaɪmˌkiːpɪŋ] n [of employee] ponctualité f.

time lag n **1.** [delay] décalage m dans le temps **2.** [in time zones] décalage m horaire.

time lapse n décalage m horaire.

timeless [ˈtaɪmlɪs] adj éternel, hors du temps, intemporel.

time limit n [gen] délai m, date f limite ; LAW délai m de forclusion.

timeline [ˈtaɪmˌlaɪn] n frise f chronologique.

timely [ˈtaɪmlɪ] adj [remark, intervention, warning] qui tombe à point nommé, opportun ; [visit] opportun.

time machine n machine f à voyager dans le temps.

time off n temps m libre.

time out n **1.** SPORT temps m mort ; [in chess match] temps m de repos **2.** [break] : *I took time out to travel* **a)** [from work] je me suis mis en congé pour voyager **b)** [from studies] j'ai interrompu mes études pour voyager.

timepiece [ˈtaɪmpiːs] n *fml & dated* [watch] montre f ; [clock] horloge f, pendule f.

timer [ˈtaɪmər] n **1.** CULIN minuteur m ▸ **(egg) timer** sablier m, compte-minutes m inv **2.** [counter] compteur m **3.** [for lighting] minuterie f **4.** [stopwatch] chronomètre m **5.** SPORT [timekeeper] chronométreur m, -euse f **6.** AUTO distributeur m (d'allumage).

time-saver n : *a dishwasher is a great time-saver* on gagne beaucoup de temps avec un lave-vaisselle, un lave-vaisselle permet de gagner beaucoup de temps.

time-saving ◆ adj qui économise or fait gagner du temps. ◆ n gain m de temps.

time scale n échelle f dans le temps.

time-share ◆ n ▸ **to buy a time-share in a flat** acheter un appartement en multipropriété. ◆ adj [flat] en multipropriété ; [computer] en temps partagé.

time-sharing n **1.** [of flat, villa] multipropriété f **2.** COMPUT (travail m) en temps m partagé.

time sheet n fiche f horaire.

time signal n RADIO signal m or top m horaire.

timespan [ˈtaɪmspæn] n intervalle m de temps.

time switch n [for oven, heating] minuteur m ; [for lighting] minuterie f.

timetable [ˈtaɪmˌteɪbl] ◆ n **1.** [for transport] horaire m **2.** [schedule] emploi m du temps **3.** [calendar] calendrier m. ◆ vt [meeting - during day] fixer une heure pour ; [- during week, month] fixer une date pour ; SCH [classes, course] établir un emploi du temps pour.

T2Go MESSAGING written abbr of **time to go**.

time travel n voyage m dans le temps.

time warp n : *it's like living in a time warp* c'est comme si on vivait hors du temps.

timewaster [ˈtaɪmˌweɪstər] n fainéant m, -e f / *no timewasters please* [in advertisement] pas sérieux s'abstenir.

timewasting [ˈtaɪmweɪstɪŋ] n perte f de temps / *the team was accused of timewasting* on a reproché à l'équipe d'avoir joué la montre.

time zone n fuseau m horaire.

timid [ˈtɪmɪd] adj timide.

timidity [tɪˈmɪdətɪ] n timidité f.

timidly [ˈtɪmɪdlɪ] adv timidement.

timing [ˈtaɪmɪŋ] n **1.** [of actor] minutage m (du débit) ; [of musician] sens m du rythme ; [of tennis player] timing m ; [of stunt driver] synchronisation f **2.** [chosen moment - of operation, visit] moment m choisi **3.** SPORT chronométrage m **4.** AUTO réglage m de l'allumage.

timing device n [for bomb] mécanisme m d'horlogerie ; [for lights] minuterie f.

Timor [ˈtiːmɔːr] n Timor m / *East Timor* le Timor-Oriental.

timpani [ˈtɪmpənɪ] pl n MUS timbales fpl.

tin [tɪn] (*pt & pp* **tinned**, *cont* **tinning**) ◆ n **1.** [metal] étain m ▸ **tin (plate)** fer-blanc m **2.** ᵁᴷ [can] boîte f (en fer-blanc) ▸ **a tin of paint** un pot de peinture **3.** [for storing] boîte f en fer ▸ **biscuit tin a)** [empty] boîte f à biscuits **b)** [full] boîte f de biscuits **4.** [for cooking meat] plat m ; [for cooking bread, cakes, etc.] moule m. ◆ comp [made of tin] en étain ; [made of tinplate] en fer-blanc ; [box] en fer ; [roof] en tôle. ◆ vt **1.** ᵁᴷ [food] mettre en conserve or en boîte **2.** [plate] étamer.

tin can n boîte f (en fer-blanc).

tinder [ˈtɪndər] n *(U)* [in tinderbox] amadou m ; [dry wood] petit bois m ; [dry grass] herbes fpl sèches.

tinfoil [ˈtɪnfɔɪl] n papier m d'aluminium.

tinge [tɪndʒ] ◆ n teinte f, nuance f. ◆ vt teinter.

tingle [ˈtɪŋgl] ◆ vi **1.** [with heat, cold - ears, cheeks, hands] fourmiller, picoter **2.** [with excitement, pleasure] frissonner, frémir. ◆ n **1.** [stinging] picotements mpl, fourmillements mpl **2.** [thrill] frisson m, frémissement m.

tingling [ˈtɪŋglɪŋ] ◆ n [stinging] picotement m, fourmillement m ; [from excitement] frisson m, frémissement m. ◆ adj [sensation] de picotement, de fourmillement.

tinker [ˈtɪŋkər] ◆ n **1.** [pot mender] rétameur m ; [gipsy] romanichel m, -elle f **2.** ᵁᴷ *inf* [child] voyou m, garnement m **3.** [act of tinkering] bricolage m. ◆ vi : *he spends hours tinkering with that car* il passe des heures à bricoler cette voiture / *someone has tinkered with this report* quelqu'un a trafiqué ce rapport.

tinkle [ˈtɪŋkl] ◆ vi [bell] tinter. ◆ vt faire tinter. ◆ n **1.** [ring] tintement m **2.** ᵁᴷ [phone call] ▸ **to give sb a tinkle** donner or passer un coup de fil à qqn **3.** *inf* [act of urinating] ▸ **to go for a tinkle** aller faire pipi.

tin mine n mine f d'étain.

tinned [tɪnd] adj ᵁᴷ [sardines, fruit, etc.] en boîte, en conserve ▸ **tinned food** conserves fpl.

tinnitus [tɪˈnaɪtəs] n *(U)* MED acouphène m.

tinny [ˈtɪnɪ] (*compar* **tinnier**, *superl* **tinniest**) ◆ adj **1.** [sound] métallique, de casserole ; [taste] métallique **2.** *inf* [poor quality] de quatre sous. ◆ n ᴬᵁˢᵀᴿ *inf* canette f de bière.

tin opener n ᵁᴷ ouvre-boîte m, ouvre-boîtes m inv.

tin-pot adj ᵁᴷ **1.** [worthless - car, machine] qui ne vaut rien **2.** [insignificant, hopeless] médiocre / *a tin-pot regime / dictator* un régime / un dictateur fantoche.

tinsel ['tɪnsl] (⬚ pt & pp **tinselled**, cont **tinselling** ; ⬚ pt & pp **tinseled**, cont **tinseling**) ⬧ n (U) **1.** [for Christmas tree] guirlandes fpl de Noël ; [in fine strands] cheveux mpl d'ange **2.** fig clinquant m. ⬧ vt [tree] orner or décorer de guirlandes.

tint [tɪnt] ⬧ n **1.** [colour, shade] teinte f, nuance f **2.** [hair dye] shampooing m colorant **3.** [in engraving, printing] hachure f, hachures fpl. ⬧ vt teinter.

tiny ['taɪnɪ] (compar tinier, superl tiniest) adj tout petit, minuscule.

tiny tot n petit enfant m, petite enfant f.

tip [tɪp] (pt & pp **tipped**, cont **tipping**) ⬧ n **1.** [extremity - of ear, finger, nose] bout m ; [- of tongue] bout m, pointe f ; [- of cigarette, wing] bout m ; [- of blade, knife, fork] pointe f **2.** [of island, peninsula] extrémité f, pointe f **3.** [cap - on walking stick, umbrella] embout m ; [- on snooker cue] procédé m **4.** ⬚ [dump - for rubbish] dépotoir m, dépôt m d'ordures ; [- for coal] terril m ; fig : the house is a bit of a tip inf la maison est un peu en désordre **5.** [hint - for stock market, race] tuyau m ; [advice] conseil m ▶ **to give sb a tip** a) [for race] donner un tuyau à qqn b) [for repairs, procedure] donner un tuyau or un conseil à qqn **6.** [money] pourboire m ▶ **to give sb a tip** donner un pourboire à qqn. ⬧ vt **1.** [cane] mettre un embout à ; [snooker cue] mettre un procédé à **2.** [tilt, lean] incliner, pencher **3.** [upset, overturn] renverser, faire chavirer **4.** ⬚ [empty, pour] verser ; [unload] déverser, décharger **5.** [winning horse] pronostiquer **6.** [porter, waiter] donner un pourboire à. ⬧ vi **1.** ⬚ [tilt] incliner, pencher **2.** ⬚ [overturn] basculer, se renverser **3.** ⬚ [rubbish] / **'no tipping'** 'défense de déposer des ordures' **4.** [give money] laisser un pourboire. ⬧ **tip back** ⬧ vi se rabattre en arrière, s'incliner en arrière. ⬧ vt sep faire basculer (en arrière). ⬧ **tip down** ⬚ inf ⬧ vi : the rain is tipping down or it's tipping down (with rain) il pleut des cordes. ⬧ vt sep : it's tipping it down il pleut des cordes. ⬧ **tip off** vt sep avertir, prévenir. ⬧ **tip out** vt sep ⬚ [empty - liquid, small objects] vider, verser ; [- rubbish, larger objects] déverser, décharger. ⬧ **tip over** ⬧ vi **1.** [tilt] pencher **2.** [overturn - boat] chavirer, se renverser. ⬧ vt sep faire basculer, renverser. ⬧ **tip up** ⬧ vi **1.** [cinema seat] se rabattre ; [bunk, plank, cart] basculer **2.** [bucket, cup, vase] se renverser. ⬧ vt sep **1.** [seat, table] faire basculer, rabattre **2.** [upside down - bottle, barrel] renverser.

tip-off n inf ▶ **to give sb a tip-off** a) [hint] filer un tuyau à qqn b) [warning] avertir or prévenir qqn.

tipped ['tɪpt] adj : tipped with felt / steel à bout feutré / ferré ; [cigarettes] (à) bout filtre (inv).

-tipped in comp à bout... / steel / felt-tipped à bout ferré / feutré ▶ **a felt-tipped pen** un crayon-feutre, un feutre.

Tipp-Ex® ['tɪpeks] n correcteur m liquide, Tipp-Ex® m. ⬧ **tippex out** vt sep ▶ **to tippex sthg out** effacer qqch (avec du Tipp-Ex).

tipping point n point m de basculement / the climate is close to tipping point le climat est proche du point de basculement / things have reached a tipping point les choses sont sur le point de basculer.

tipple ['tɪpl] ⬧ vi inf picoler. ⬧ n inf [drink] : he likes a tipple now and then il aime boire un coup de temps à autre.

tipsy ['tɪpsɪ] (compar tipsier, superl tipsiest) adj inf pompette, rond ▶ **to get tipsy** se griser.

tiptoe ['tɪptəʊ] ⬧ n ▶ **on tiptoe** sur la pointe des pieds. ⬧ vi marcher sur la pointe des pieds.

tip-top adj inf de premier ordre, de toute première qualité.

tip-up adj ▶ **tip-up seat** a) [in cinema, theatre] siège m rabattable, strapontin m b) [in metro] strapontin m ▶ **tip-up truck** ⬚ camion m à benne (basculante).

tirade [taɪ'reɪd] n diatribe f.

tiramisu [,tɪrəmɪ'su:] n CULIN tiramisu m.

Tirana, Tiranë [tɪ'rɑ:nə] pr n Tirana.

tire ['taɪər] ⬧ vi **1.** [become exhausted] se fatiguer **2.** [become bored] se fatiguer, se lasser / he soon tired of her / of her company il se lassa vite d'elle / de sa compagnie. ⬧ vt **1.** [exhaust] fatiguer **2.** [bore] fatiguer, lasser. ⬧ n ⬚ = tyre. ⬧ **tire out** vt sep épuiser, éreinter.

tired ['taɪəd] adj **1.** [exhausted] fatigué ▶ **to get tired** se fatiguer **2.** [fed up] fatigué, las (lasse) ▶ **to be tired of sthg / sb** en avoir assez de qqch / qqn **3.** [hackneyed] rebattu **4.** fig [old - skin] desséché ; [- vegetable] défraîchi, flétri ; [- upholstery, springs, car] fatigué.

tiredness ['taɪədnɪs] n **1.** [exhaustion] fatigue f **2.** [tedium] fatigue f, lassitude f.

tireless ['taɪəlɪs] adj [effort] infatigable, inlassable ; [energy] inépuisable.

tirelessly ['taɪəlɪslɪ] adv infatigablement, inlassablement, sans ménager ses efforts.

tiresome ['taɪəsəm] adj [irritating] agaçant, ennuyeux ; [boring] assommant, ennuyeux.

tiring ['taɪərɪŋ] adj fatigant.

Tirol [tɪ'rəʊl] = Tyrol.

tissue ['tɪʃu:] n **1.** ANAT & BOT tissu m **2.** TEXT tissu m, étoffe f ▶ **a tissue of lies** fig un tissu de mensonges **3.** [paper handkerchief] mouchoir m en papier, Kleenex® m ; [toilet paper] papier m hygiénique.

tissue paper n papier m de soie.

tit [tɪt] n **1.** ORNITH mésange f **2.** v inf [breast] nichon m **3.** v inf & pej imbécile mf **4.** ⬚ it's tit for tat! c'est un prêté pour un rendu !

titanic [taɪ'tænɪk] adj [huge] titanesque, colossal.

titbit ['tɪtbɪt] n ⬚ **1.** CULIN bon morceau m, morceau m de choix **2.** [of information, of scandal] détail m croustillant.

titillate ['tɪtɪleɪt] vt titiller.

titillating ['tɪtɪleɪtɪŋ] adj titillant.

titillation [,tɪtɪ'leɪʃn] n titillation f.

titivate ['tɪtɪveɪt] inf & hum ⬧ vi se bichonner, se pomponner. ⬧ vt bichonner.

title ['taɪtl] ⬧ n **1.** [indicating rank, status] titre m ; [nickname] surnom m **2.** [of book, film, play, song] titre m ; [of newspaper article] titre m, intitulé m **3.** PRINT titre m **4.** SPORT titre m **5.** LAW droit m, titre m ⬧ comp [music] du générique. ⬧ vt [book, chapter, film] intituler. ⬧ **titles** pl n CIN & TV [credits] générique m.

titled ['taɪtld] adj [person, family] titré.

titleholder ['taɪtl,həʊldər] n détenteur m, -trice f du titre, tenant m, -e f du titre.

title page n page f de titre.

title role n rôle-titre m.

title track n morceau m qui donne son titre à l'album.

titter ['tɪtər] ⬧ vi rire bêtement or sottement, glousser. ⬧ n petit rire m bête or sot, gloussement m.

tittle-tattle [-,tætl] ⬧ n (U) potins mpl, cancans mpl. ⬧ vi jaser, cancaner.

titular ['tɪtjʊlər], **titulary** ['tɪtjʊlərɪ] adj nominal.

tizz [tɪz] inf = tizzy.

tizzy ['tɪzɪ] n inf panique f ▶ **to be in a tizzy** paniquer / don't get into a tizzy about it ne t'affole pas pour ça.

T-junction n intersection f en T.

Tks MESSAGING written abbr of thanks.

TLC n abbr of tender loving care.

TLS pr n **(abbr of Times Literary Supplement)** supplément littéraire du «Times».

TM ➡ n **(abbr of transcendental meditation)** MT f.
➡ written abbr of trademark.

TMB MESSAGING written abbr of text me back.

TMI MESSAGING written abbr of too much information.

TN written abbr of Tennessee.

TNT (abbr of trinitrotoluene) n TNT m.

to (strong form [tuː], weak form before vowel [tʊ], weak form before consonant [tə])
➡ prep

A. IN SPACE **1.** [indicating direction] ▶ **to go to school** / **the cinema** aller à l'école / au cinéma / **let's go to town** allons en ville / **he climbed to the top** il est monté jusqu'au sommet or jusqu'en haut / **we've been to it before** nous y sommes déjà allés / **the vase fell to the ground** le vase est tombé par or à terre / **I invited them to dinner** je les ai invités à dîner / **let's go to Susan's** allons chez Susan ▶ **to go to the doctor** or **doctor's** aller chez le médecin **2.** [indicating location, position] à / **she lives next door to us** elle habite à côté de chez nous ▶ **to the left** / **right** à gauche / droite **3.** [with geographical names] : **to Madrid** à Madrid / **to Le Havre** au Havre / **to France** en France / **to the United States** aux États-Unis / **I'm off to Paris** je pars à or pour Paris **4.** [indicating age, amount or level reached] jusqu'à / **the snow came (up) to her knees** la neige lui arrivait aux genoux / **it weighs 8 to 9 pounds** ça pèse entre 8 et 9 livres **5.** [so as to make contact with] à, contre / **she pinned the brooch to her dress** elle a épinglé la broche sur sa robe.

B. IN TIME **1.** UK [before the specified hour or date] : **it's ten minutes to three** il est trois heures moins dix / **there's only two weeks to Christmas** il ne reste que deux semaines avant Noël **2.** [up to and including] (jusqu')à / **from March to June** de mars (jusqu')à juin / **from day to day** de jour en jour.

C. FOLLOWED BY INFINITIVE **1.** [before infinitive] : **to talk** parler **2.** [after verb] : **we are to complete the work by Monday** nous devons finir le travail pour lundi / **she went on to become a brilliant guitarist** elle est ensuite devenue une excellente guitariste **3.** [after noun] : **I have a lot to do** j'ai beaucoup à faire / **that's no reason to leave** ce n'est pas une raison pour partir **4.** [after adjective] : **I'm happy** / **sad to see her go** je suis content / triste de la voir partir / **difficult** / **easy to do** difficile / facile à faire **5.** [after 'how', 'which', 'where', etc.] : **do you know where to go?** savez-vous où aller ? / **he told me how to get there** il m'a dit comment y aller **6.** [indicating purpose] pour / **I did it to annoy her** je l'ai fait exprès pour l'énerver.

D. RECIPIENT OR RESULTING STATE **1.** [indicating intended recipient, owner] à / **I showed the picture to her** je lui ai montré la photo / **that book belongs to her** ce livre lui appartient **2.** [in the opinion of] pour / **it didn't make sense to him** ça n'avait aucun sens pour lui **3.** [indicating resulting state] : **the light changed to red** le feu est passé au rouge / **the rain turned to snow** la pluie avait fait place à la neige / **smashed to pieces** brisé en mille morceaux / **she sang the baby to sleep** elle a chanté jusqu'à ce que le bébé s'endorme.

E. IN COMPARISON OR RELATIONSHIP **1.** [indicating comparison] ▶ **inferior to** inférieur à / **they compare her to Callas** on la compare à (la) Callas / **inflation is nothing (compared) to last year** l'inflation n'est rien à côté de or en comparaison de l'année dernière **2.** [of] de / **the key to this door** la clé de cette porte / **she's assistant to the president** c'est l'adjointe du président.

F. AS REGARDS, IN ACCORDANCE **1.** [as regards] : **the answer to your question** la réponse à votre question ▶ **that's all there is to it** c'est aussi simple que ça ▶ **there's nothing**

to it il n'y a rien de plus simple **2.** [in accordance with] : **to his way of thinking** or **to his mind** à son avis / **to hear him talk, you'd think he was an expert** à l'entendre parler, on croirait que c'est un expert.

G. ADDITION, CALCULATION, ETC. **1.** [indicating addition] : **add flour to the list** ajoutez de la farine sur la liste / **add 3 to 6** additionnez 3 et 6, ajoutez 3 à 6 **2.** [indicating composition or proportion] : **you get about one and a half dollar(s) to the euro** l'euro vaut environ 1,5 dollar / **Milan beat Madrid by 4 (points) to 3** Milan a battu Madrid 4 (points) à 3 / **the vote was 6 to 3** il y avait 6 voix contre 3.
➡ adv **1.** [closed] fermé / **the wind blew the door to** un coup de vent a fermé la porte **2.** [back to consciousness] ▶ **to come to** revenir à soi, reprendre connaissance.

toad [təʊd] n **1.** ZOOL crapaud m **2.** inf & fig [person] rat m.

toad-in-the-hole n UK CULIN plat composé de saucisses cuites au four dans une sorte de pâte à crêpes.

toadstool ['təʊdstuːl] n champignon m vénéneux.

toady ['təʊdɪ] (pl **toadies**, pt & pp **toadied**) pej ➡ n flatteur m, -euse f. ➡ vi être flatteur ▶ **to toady to sb** passer de la pommade à qqn.

to and fro adv phr ▶ **to go to and fro** aller et venir, se promener de long en large ▶ **to swing to and fro** se balancer d'avant en arrière. ➡ **to-and-fro** adj ▶ **a to-and-fro movement** un mouvement de va-et-vient.

toast [təʊst] ➡ n **1.** [bread] pain m grillé ▶ **a piece** or **slice of toast** une tartine grillée, un toast / **cheese** / **sardines on toast** fromage fondu / sardines sur du pain grillé **2.** [drink] toast m ▶ **to drink a toast to sb** porter un toast à qqn, boire à la santé de qqn. ➡ vt **1.** [grill] griller / **he was toasting himself** / **his toes by the fire** fig il se chauffait / il se rôtissait les orteils devant la cheminée **2.** [drink to - person] porter un toast à, boire à la santé de ; [- success, win] arroser **3.** [pay homage to] rendre hommage à, saluer.

toasted ['təʊstɪd] adj **1.** [grilled] grillé ▶ **toasted cheese** fromage m fondu **2.** US inf [drunk] bourré.

toaster ['təʊstə*r*] n grille-pain m inv (électrique), toaster m.

toastie ['təʊstɪ] n inf sandwich m grillé.

toast rack n porte-toasts m inv.

toasty ['təʊstɪ] inf ➡ adj US [warm] : **it's toasty in here** il fait bon ici. ➡ n [sandwich] = **toastie**.

tobacco [tə'bækəʊ] (pl **tobaccos**) ➡ n **1.** tabac m **2.** BOT ▶ **tobacco (plant)** (pied m de) tabac m. ➡ comp [leaf, plantation, smoke] de tabac ; [industry] du tabac.

tobacconist [tə'bækənɪst] n marchand m, -e f de tabac, buraliste mf ▶ **tobacconist's (shop)** UK (bureau m de) tabac m.

Tobago [tə'beɪgəʊ] ⟶ **Trinidad and Tobago**.

-to-be in comp ▶ **mother-to-be** future mère f.

toboggan [tə'bɒgən] ➡ n luge f. ➡ comp [race] de luge. ➡ vi **1.** SPORT ▶ **to toboggan** or **go tobogganing** faire de la luge **2.** US [prices, sales] dégringoler.

2DAY MESSAGING written abbr of today.

today [tə'deɪ] ➡ adv aujourd'hui ▶ **a week today** **a)** [past] il y a huit jours aujourd'hui **b)** [future] dans huit jours aujourd'hui. ➡ n aujourd'hui m / **what's today's date?** quelle est la date d'aujourd'hui ? / **today is March 17th** aujourd'hui, on est le 17 mars / **it's Monday today** on est lundi aujourd'hui / **a week from today** dans une semaine aujourd'hui / **as from today** à partir d'aujourd'hui.

toddle ['tɒdl] vi **1.** [start to walk - child] faire ses premiers pas ; [walk unsteadily] marcher d'un pas chancelant

2. *inf* [go] aller ; [stroll] se balader ; [go away] s'en aller, partir. ❖ **toddle off** vi *inf* [go] aller ; [go away] s'en aller, partir bien gentiment.

toddler ['tɒdlər] n tout petit *m (enfant qui fait ses premiers pas)*.

toddy ['tɒdɪ] *(pl* **toddies)** n **1.** [drink] ▶ **(hot) toddy** ≃ grog *m* **2.** [sap] sève *f* de palmier *(utilisée comme boisson)*.

2d4 MESSAGING written abbr of **to die for**.

to-die-for adj *inf* de rêve.

to-do n *inf* **1.** [fuss] remue-ménage *m inv*, tohu-bohu *m inv* **2.** 🇺🇸 [party] bringue *f*.

to-do list n liste *f* de tâches.

toe [təʊ] ❖ n **1.** ANAT orteil *m*, doigt *m* de pied ▶ **big / little toe** gros / petit orteil **2.** [of sock, shoe] bout *m* ▶ **the toe of Italy** *fig* le bout de l'Italie. ❖ vt **1.** [ball] toucher du bout du pied **2.** 🇵🇭🇷 **to toe the line** or 🇺🇸 **mark** se mettre au pas, obtempérer ▶ **to toe the party line** POL s'aligner sur le or suivre la ligne du parti.

TOEFL ['təʊfl] **(abbr of Test of English as a Foreign Language)** n *test évaluant le niveau d'anglais universitaire reconnu internationalement.*

toehold ['təʊhəʊld] n prise *f* de pied.

toenail ['təʊneɪl] n ongle *m* de pied.

toff [tɒf] n 🇺🇰 *inf* aristo *m*.

toffee ['tɒfɪ] n 🇺🇰 caramel *m* (au beurre).

toffee apple n pomme *f* d'amour *(confiserie)*.

tofu ['təʊfuː] n tofu *m inv*.

toga ['təʊgə] n toge *f*.

together [tə'geðər] adv **1.** [with each other] ensemble / *they get on well together* ils s'entendent bien / *we're all in this together!* on est tous logés à la même enseigne ! **2.** [indicating proximity] : *tie the two ribbons together* attachez les deux rubans l'un à l'autre / *she tried to bring the two sides together* elle a essayé de rapprocher les deux camps **3.** [at the same time] à la fois, en même temps, ensemble / *all together now!* a) [pull] tous ensemble !, ho hisse ! b) [sing, recite] tous ensemble or en chœur ! ❖ **together with** conj phr ainsi que, en même temps que.

togetherness [tə'geðənɪs] n [unity] unité *f* ; [solidarity] solidarité *f* ; [comradeship] camaraderie *f*.

toggle ['tɒgl] ❖ n **1.** [peg] cheville *f* **2.** SEW bouton *m* de duffle-coat **3.** NAUT cabillot *m*. ❖ vt NAUT attacher avec un cabillot. ❖ vi COMPUT basculer ▶ **to toggle between** alterner entre.

toggle switch n ELEC interrupteur *m* à bascule ; COMPUT bascule *f* or interrupteur *m* de changement de mode.

Togo ['təʊgəʊ] pr n Togo *m* / *in Togo* au Togo.

Togolese [ˌtəʊgə'liːz] *(pl* **Togolese)** ❖ n Togolais *m*, -e *f*. ❖ adj togolais.

toil [tɔɪl] ❖ vi **1.** [labour] travailler dur, peiner **2.** [as verb of movement] avancer péniblement. ❖ n labeur *m liter*, travail *m* (pénible). ❖ **toil away** vi travailler dur, peiner.

toilet ['tɔɪlɪt] n **1.** [lavatory] toilettes *fpl* ▶ **to go to the toilet** aller aux toilettes or aux cabinets / *'Public Toilets'* 'Toilettes', 'W-C Publics' **2.** = **toilette**.

toilet bag n 🇺🇰 trousse *f* de toilette.

toilet bowl n cuvette *f* (de WC).

toilet humour n humour *m* scatologique.

toilet paper n papier *m* hygiénique.

toiletries ['tɔɪlɪtrɪz] pl n articles *mpl* de toilette.

toilet roll n rouleau *m* de papier hygiénique ▶ **toilet roll holder** porte-papier *m*.

toilet seat n siège *m* des cabinets or W-C or toilettes.

toilet soap n savon *m* de toilette.

toilet tissue = **toilet paper**.

toilet-trained [-ˌtreɪnd] adj propre.

toilet training n apprentissage *m* de la propreté *(pour un enfant)*.

toilet water n eau *f* de toilette.

to-ing and fro-ing [ˌtuːɪŋən'frəʊɪŋ] n *(U)* *inf* allées et venues *fpl*.

token ['təʊkn] ❖ n **1.** [of affection, appreciation, esteem, etc.] marque *f*, témoignage *m* / *as a token of* or *in token of my gratitude* en témoignage or en gage de ma reconnaissance **2.** [indication] signe *m* **3.** [souvenir, gift] souvenir *m* **4.** [for machine] jeton *m* **5.** [voucher] bon *m* **6.** LING occurrence *f*. ❖ adj [gesture, effort] symbolique, pour la forme ; [increase, protest] symbolique, de pure forme. ❖ **by the same token** adv phr de même, pareillement.

Tokyo ['təʊkjəʊ] pr n Tokyo.

told [təʊld] pt & pp ⟶ **tell**.

tolerable ['tɒlərəbl] adj **1.** [pain, situation, behaviour] tolérable ; [standard] admissible **2.** [not too bad] pas trop mal, passable.

tolerably ['tɒlərəblɪ] adv passablement.

tolerance ['tɒlərəns] n tolérance *f*.

tolerant ['tɒlərənt] adj tolérant.

tolerantly ['tɒlərəntlɪ] adv avec tolérance.

tolerate ['tɒləreɪt] vt tolérer.

toleration [ˌtɒlə'reɪʃn] n tolérance *f*.

toll [təʊl] ❖ n **1.** [on bridge, road] péage *m* **2.** [of victims] nombre *m* de victimes ; [of casualties] nombre *m* de blessés ; [of deaths] nombre *m* de morts **3.** [of bell] sonnerie *f*. ❖ vt [bell] sonner. ❖ vi [bell] sonner.

tollbooth ['təʊlbuːθ] n (poste *m* de) péage *m*.

toll bridge n pont *m* à péage.

toll-free 🇺🇸 ❖ adj ▶ **toll-free number** numéro *m* vert. ❖ adv ▶ **to call toll-free** appeler un numéro vert.

tollroad ['təʊlrəʊd] n route *f* à péage.

tomato [🇺🇰 tə'mɑːtəʊ 🇺🇸 tə'meɪtəʊ] *(pl* **tomatoes)** ❖ n tomate *f*. ❖ comp [juice, salad, soup] de tomates ▶ **tomato ketchup** ketchup *m* ▶ **tomato plant** (pied *m* de) tomate *f* ▶ **tomato purée** concentré *m* or purée *f* de tomates ▶ **tomato sauce** sauce *f* tomate.

tomb [tuːm] n tombeau *m*, tombe *f*.

tombola [tɒm'bəʊlə] n 🇺🇰 tombola *f*.

tomboy ['tɒmbɔɪ] n garçon *m* manqué.

tombstone ['tuːmstəʊn] ❖ n pierre *f* tombale. ❖ vi [dive] faire du «tombstoning» *(plonger d'une falaise ou d'un haut rocher)*.

tomcat ['tɒmkæt] n chat *m*, matou *m*.

tomfoolery [tɒm'fuːlərɪ] n *(U)* *inf* [foolish words] absurdités *fpl*, idioties *fpl*, bêtises *fpl* ; [foolish behaviour] bêtises *fpl*.

2 MESSAGING **1.** written abbr of **to 2.** written abbr of **too**.

2MORO (written abbr of **tomorrow**) MESSAGING 2m1.

tomorrow [tə'mɒrəʊ] ❖ adv demain / *tomorrow morning / evening* demain matin / soir / *see you tomorrow!* à demain ! ▶ **a week tomorrow** a) [past] cela fera huit jours demain b) [future] dans une semaine demain. ❖ n **1.** *lit* demain *m* / *what's tomorrow's date?* le combien serons-nous demain ? / *tomorrow is* or *will be March 17th* demain, on sera le 17 mars / *tomorrow is Monday* demain, c'est lundi / *a week from tomorrow* dans une semaine demain / *the day after tomorrow* après-demain, dans deux jours **2.** *fig* [future] demain *m*, lendemain *m*.

ton [tʌn] n **1.** [weight] tonne *f* ; *fig* : *this suitcase weighs a ton!* cette valise pèse une tonne ! **2.** *inf* [speed] ▸ **to do a ton** rouler à plus de 150. ❖ **tons** pl *n inf* [lots] : *tons of money* des tas or des tonnes d'argent / *tons of people* des tas de gens.

tonal ['təʊnl] adj tonal.

tone [təʊn] ❖ n **1.** [of voice] ton *m* (de la voix) **2.** [sound - of voice, musical instrument] sonorité *f* ; [of singer] timbre *m* (de la voix) **3.** MUS ton *m* **4.** LING ton *m* **5.** TELEC tonalité *f* **6.** [control - of amplifier, radio] tonalité *f* **7.** [shade] ton *m* **8.** [style, atmosphere - of poem, article] ton *m* **9.** [classiness] chic *m*, classe *f* ▸ **to give / to lend tone to sthg** donner de la classe / apporter un plus à qqch **10.** FIN [of market] tenue *f* **11.** PHYSIOL [of muscle, nerves] tonus *m* **12.** US [single musical sound] note *f*. ❖ vi [colour] s'harmoniser. ❖ vt = **tone up**. ❖ **tone down** vt sep **1.** [colour, contrast] adoucir **2.** [sound, voice] atténuer, baisser **3.** [moderate - language, statement, views] tempérer, modérer ; [- effect] adoucir, atténuer. ❖ **tone in** vi s'harmoniser, s'assortir. ❖ **tone up** vt sep [body, muscles] tonifier.

tone-deaf adj : *to be tone-deaf* ne pas avoir d'oreille.

toner ['təʊnə'] n [for hair] colorant *m* ; [for skin] lotion *f* tonique ; PHOT toner *m*, encre *f*.

Tonga ['tɒŋə] pr n Tonga / *in Tonga* à Tonga.

tongs [tɒŋz] pl n ▸ **(pair of) tongs** pinces *fpl*.

tongue [tʌŋ] ❖ n **1.** ANAT langue *f* **2.** *fig* [for speech] langue *f* ▸ **to lose / to find one's tongue** perdre / retrouver sa langue ▸ **hold your tongue!** tenez votre langue !, taisez-vous ! ▸ **to have a sharp tongue** avoir la langue acérée **3.** *fml & liter* [language] langue *f* **4.** *fig* CULIN langue *f* (de bœuf) **5.** [of shoe] languette *f* ; [of bell] battant *m* ; [of buckle] ardillon *m* ; TECH langue *f*, languette *f* **6.** [of flame, land, sea] langue *f*. ❖ vt **1.** MUS [note] détacher ; [phrase] détacher les notes de **2.** [in woodworking] langueter.

tongue-in-cheek adj ironique.

tongue-tied adj muet *fig*, trop timide (pour parler).

tongue-twister n *mot ou phrase très difficile à prononcer.*

tonic ['tɒnɪk] ❖ n **1.** MED tonique *m*, fortifiant *m* ; *fig* : *the news was a tonic to us all* la nouvelle nous a remonté le moral à tous **2.** [cosmetic] lotion *f* tonique ▸ **hair tonic** lotion *f* capillaire **3.** [drink] tonic *m* **4.** MUS tonique *f* **5.** LING syllabe *f* tonique ou accentuée. ❖ adj tonique ▸ **tonic syllable / stress** LING syllabe *f* / accent *m* tonique.

tonic water n tonic *m* ; ≃ Schweppes® *m*.

2NITE MESSAGING written abbr of **tonight**.

tonight [tə'naɪt] ❖ n [this evening] ce soir ; [this night] cette nuit. ❖ adv [this evening] ce soir ; [this night] cette nuit *f*.

tonnage ['tʌnɪdʒ] n **1.** [total weight] poids *m* total d'une chose **2.** [capacity - of a ship] tonnage *m*, jauge *f* ; [of a port] tonnage *m*.

tonne [tʌn] n tonne *f* (métrique).

tonsil ['tɒnsl] n (*usu pl*) amygdale *f*.

tonsillitis [,tɒnsɪ'laɪtɪs] n (U) angine *f*, amygdalite *f spec*.

too [tuː] adv **1.** [as well] aussi, également / *I like jazz — I do too* or *me too* j'aime le jazz — moi aussi **2.** [excessively] trop / *she works too hard* elle travaille trop / *I have one apple too many* j'ai une pomme de trop / *too few people* trop peu de gens **3.** [with negatives] trop / *I wasn't too*

happy about it ça ne me réjouissait pas trop **4.** [moreover] en outre, en plus **5.** [for emphasis] : *and quite right too!* tu as / il a, etc. bien fait / *I should think so too!* j'espère bien !

took [tʊk] pt ➤ **take**.

tool [tuːl] ❖ n **1.** [instrument] outil *m* ▸ **set of tools** outillage *m* **2.** TYPO fer *m* de reliure **3.** [dupe] : *he was nothing but a tool of the government* il n'était que le jouet or l'instrument du gouvernement **4.** *v inf* [penis] engin *m* **5.** US *crime sl* [gun] arme *f*. ❖ vt [decorate - wood] travailler, façonner ; [- stone] sculpter ; [- book cover] ciseler ▸ **tooled leather** cuir *m* repoussé. ❖ vi *inf* rouler (*en voiture*). ❖ **tool around** vi US *inf* traîner. ❖ **tool up** ❖ vi s'équiper. ❖ vt sep outiller, équiper.

2L8 MESSAGING written abbr of **too late**.

toolbag ['tuːlbæg] n trousse *f* à outils.

tool bar n COMPUT barre *f* d'outils.

toolbox ['tuːlbɒks] (*pl* **toolboxes**) n boîte *f* à outils.

toolkit ['tuːlkɪt] n jeu *m* d'outils.

toolshed ['tuːlʃed] n remise *f*, resserre *f*.

tooltip ['tuːltɪp] n COMPUT infobulle *f*.

toot [tuːt] ❖ vi [car] klaxonner ; [train] siffler. ❖ vt : *he tooted his horn* AUTO il a klaxonné or donné un coup de klaxon. ❖ n [sound] appel *m* / *the tugboat gave a toot* le remorqueur a donné un coup de sirène / *a toot of the horn* AUTO un coup de klaxon.

tooth [tuːθ] (*pl* **teeth**) n **1.** ANAT dent *f* ▸ **a set of teeth** une denture, une dentition ▸ **a false tooth** une fausse dent ▸ **a set of false teeth** un dentier ▸ **to have a tooth out** se faire arracher une dent ▸ **to bare** or **to show one's teeth** montrer les dents **2.** [of comb, file, cog, saw] dent *f* **3.** PHR **to be fed up** or **sick to the back teeth** *inf* en avoir plein le dos or ras le bol ▸ **to fight tooth and nail** se battre bec et ongles ▸ **to get one's teeth into sthg** se mettre à fond à qqch / *she needs something to get her teeth into* elle a besoin de quelque chose qui la mobilise / *the play gives you nothing to get your teeth into* la pièce manque de substance. ❖ **in the teeth of** prep phr malgré.

toothache ['tuːθeɪk] n mal *m* de dents.

toothbrush ['tuːθbrʌʃ] (*pl* **toothbrushes**) n brosse *f* à dents.

toothless ['tuːθlɪs] adj **1.** *lit* édenté, sans dents **2.** *fig* sans pouvoir or influence.

toothpaste ['tuːθpeɪst] n dentifrice *m*, pâte *f* dentifrice.

toothpick ['tuːθpɪk] n cure-dents *m inv*.

tooth powder n poudre *f* dentifrice.

tootle ['tuːtl] *inf* ❖ vi **1.** [on musical instrument] jouer un petit air **2.** US [drive] : *we were tootling along quite nicely until the tyre burst* nous suivions notre petit bonhomme de chemin lorsque le pneu a éclaté. ❖ n **1.** [on musical instrument] petit air *m* **2.** [drive] petit tour *m* en voiture.

top [tɒp] (*pt & pp* **topped**, *cont* **topping**) ❖ n **1.** [highest point] haut *m*, sommet *m* ; [of tree] sommet *m*, cime *f* / *at the top of the stairs* en haut de l'escalier / *he searched the house from top to bottom* il a fouillé la maison de fond en comble / *she filled the jar right to the top* elle a rempli le bocal à ras bord ; [surface] dessus *m*, surface *f* ; [end] : *at the top of the street* au bout de la rue ▸ **from top to toe** US de la tête aux pieds ▸ **to come out on top** avoir le dessus ▸ **over the top** : *the soldiers went over the top* lit les soldats sont montés à l'assaut / *I think he went a bit over the top* UK *inf & fig* à mon avis, il est allé trop loin / *he's a bit over the top* il en fait un peu trop **2.** [cap, lid] couvercle *m* / *where's the top to my pen?* où est le capuchon de mon stylo ? ▸ **bottle top a)** [screw-on] bouchon *m* (de bouteille) **b)** [on beer bottle] capsule *f* (de

bouteille) **3.** [highest degree] : *he is at the top of his form*
il est au meilleur de sa forme **4.** [most important position] :
she's top of her class elle est première de sa classe / *some-*
one who has reached the top in their profession quelqu'un
qui est arrivé en haut de l'échelle dans sa profession ▸ **top**
of the range: *this car is the top of the range* c'est une voiture haut de gamme **5.** [garment] haut *m* **6.** [beginning] :
play it again from the top reprends au début **7.** [toy] toupie *f* ▸ **to sleep like a top** 🇬🇧 dormir comme un loir. ◆ vt
1. [form top of] couvrir **2.** 🇬🇧 [trim] écimer, étêter / *to*
top and tail gooseberries équeuter des groseilles **3.** [ex-
ceed] dépasser / *his score tops the world record* avec ce
score, il bat le record du monde ▸ **that tops the lot!** 🇬🇧 ça,
c'est le bouquet ! **4.** [be at the top of] : *the book topped*
the best-seller list ce livre est arrivé en tête des best-sellers
5. 🇬🇧 v *inf* [kill] faire la peau à ▸ **to top o.s.** faire hara-kiri.
◆ adj : *the top floor* or *storey* le dernier étage / *the top*
shelf l'étagère du haut / *in the top right-hand corner* dans
le coin en haut à droite / *top management* la direction générale / *the top banks in the country* les grandes banques
du pays / *the top speed of this car is 150 mph* la vitesse
maximum de cette voiture est de 240 km/h ▸ **to be on top**
form être en pleine forme ▸ **the top brass** 🇬🇧 *inf* MIL les officiers *mpl* supérieurs, les gros bonnets *mpl*. ◆ **on top of**
prep *phr* ▸ **on top of everything else** pour couronner le
tout ▸ **to be on top of things**: *don't worry, I'm on top*
of things ne t'inquiète pas, je m'en sors très bien / *it's all*
getting on top of him il est dépassé par les événements
▸ **to feel on top of the world** avoir la forme. ◆ **top off**
vt sep **1.** 🇬🇧 [conclude] terminer, couronner **2.** 🇺🇸 [fill to
top] remplir. ◆ **top up** vt sep 🇬🇧 [fill up] remplir / *can*
I top up your drink or *top you up?* encore une goutte ?
▸ **to top up a phone** acheter du crédit pour un téléphone /
I've topped up my account / *my card* j'ai recrédité mon
compte / ma carte.

topaz ['təʊpæz] n topaze *f*.

top-bracket adj de première catégorie.

top-class adj excellent.

topcoat ['tɒpkəʊt] n **1.** [clothing] pardessus *m*, manteau *m* **2.** [paint] couche *f* de finition.

top copy n original *m*.

top dog n *inf* chef *m*.

top dollar n ▸ **to pay top dollar for sthg** payer qqch
au prix fort.

top-down adj hiérarchisé.

top-flight adj de premier ordre.

top gear n vitesse *f* supérieure.

top hat n (chapeau *m*) haut-de-forme *m*.

top-heavy adj **1.** [unbalanced] trop lourd du haut, déséquilibré **2.** FIN surcapitalisé **3.** *inf* [big-breasted] ▸ **to be top-**
heavy avoir de gros seins.

topic ['tɒpɪk] n [theme] sujet *m*, thème *m*.

topical ['tɒpɪkl] adj **1.** [current] actuel **2.** MED topique,
à usage local.

topknot ['tɒpnɒt] n **1.** [of hair] chignon *m* ; [of ribbons]
ornement *m* fait de rubans ; [of feathers] aigrette *f* **2.** ZOOL
pleuronectidé *m*.

topless ['tɒplɪs] adj [sunbather] aux seins nus.

top-level adj de très haut niveau.

topmost ['tɒpməʊst] adj le plus haut, le plus élevé.

top-notch ['tɒp'nɒtʃ] adj *inf* excellent.

top-of-the-range adj haut de gamme *(inv)*.

topographer [tə'pɒɡrəfər] n topographe *mf*.

topography [tə'pɒɡrəfi] n topographie *f*.

topping ['tɒpɪŋ] n dessus *m* ; CULIN garniture *f*.

topple ['tɒpl] ◆ vi [fall] basculer ; [totter] vaciller. ◆ vt
1. [cause to fall] faire tomber, faire basculer **2.** *fig* renverser.

top-quality adj de qualité supérieure.

top-ranking adj de premier rang, haut placé.

top-secret adj top secret *(inv)*, ultraconfidentiel.

top-security adj de haute sécurité.

top-shelf adj ▸ **top-shelf magazines** 🇬🇧 revues *fpl* éro-
tiques.

topsoil ['tɒpsɔɪl] n terre *f* superficielle, couche *f* arable.

topspin ['tɒpspɪn] n ▸ **to put topspin on a ball** donner
de l'effet à une balle.

topsy-turvy [,tɒpsɪ'tɜːvɪ] adj & adv sens dessus dessous.

top table n [at wedding] table *f* d'honneur.

top ten n hit parade des dix meilleures ventes de disques
pop et rock.

top-up card n TELEC recharge *f* de téléphone mobile.

tor [tɔːr] n colline *f* rocailleuse *(notamment dans le sud-*
ouest de l'Angleterre).

torch [tɔːtʃ] (*pl* **torches**) ◆ n **1.** 🇬🇧 [electric] lampe *f*
de poche **2.** [flaming stick] torche *f*, flambeau *m* **3.** TECH
[for welding, soldering, etc.] chalumeau *m*. ◆ vt mettre le
feu à.

tore [tɔːr] pt ⟶ **tear**.

torment ◆ n ['tɔːment] **1.** [suffering] supplice *m* ; *liter*
tourment *m* ▸ **to be in torment** être au supplice **2.** [or-
deal] rude épreuve *f* **3.** [pest] démon *m*. ◆ vt [tɔː'ment]
1. [cause pain to] torturer **2.** [harass] tourmenter, harceler.

tormentor, tormentor [tɔː'mentər] n persécu-
teur *m*, -trice *f*, bourreau *m*.

torn [tɔːn] pp ⟶ **tear**.

tornado [tɔː'neɪdəʊ] (*pl* **tornados** or **tornadoes**) n
[storm] tornade *f* ; *fig* [person, thing] ouragan *m*.

Toronto [tə'rɒntəʊ] pr n Toronto.

torpedo [tɔː'piːdəʊ] (*pl* **torpedoes**, pt & pp **torpe-**
doed) ◆ n **1.** MIL torpille *f* **2.** 🇺🇸 [firework] pétard *m*.
◆ vt **1.** MIL torpiller **2.** *fig* [destroy - plan] faire échouer,
torpiller.

torpedo boat n torpilleur *m*, vedette *f* lance-torpilles.

torpor ['tɔːpər] n *fml* torpeur *f*, léthargie *f*, engourdissement *m*.

torque [tɔːk] n **1.** [rotational force] moment *m* de torsion ; AUTO couple *m* moteur **2.** HIST [collar] torque *m*.

torrent ['tɒrənt] n **1.** [of liquid] torrent *m* **2.** [of emotion, abuse, etc.] torrent *m*.

torrential [tə'renʃl] adj torrentiel.

torrid ['tɒrɪd] adj **1.** [hot] torride ▸ **the torrid zone** la
zone intertropicale **2.** [passionate] passionné, ardent.

torso ['tɔːsəʊ] (*pl* **torsos**) n [human] torse *m* ; [sculp-
ture] buste *m*.

tortilla [tɔː'tiːə] n tortilla *f* *(galette de maïs)* ▸ **tortilla**
chips chips *fpl* de maïs.

tortoise ['tɔːtəs] n tortue *f*.

tortoiseshell ['tɔːtəsʃel] ◆ n **1.** [substance] écaille *f*
(de tortue) **2.** [cat] chat *m* roux tigré **3.** [butterfly] vanesse *f*.
◆ adj **1.** [comb, ornament] en écaille **2.** [cat] roux tigré.

tortuous ['tɔːtjʊəs] adj **1.** [path] tortueux, sinueux
2. [argument, piece of writing] contourné, tarabiscoté ;
[mind] retors.

torture ['tɔːtʃər] ◆ n **1.** [cruelty] torture *f*, supplice *m*
2. *fig* torture *f*, tourment *m*. ◆ vt **1.** [inflict pain on] torturer **2.** [torment] torturer.

torturer ['tɔːtʃərər] n tortionnaire *mf*, bourreau *m*.

Tory ['tɔːrɪ] (*pl* **Tories**) ◆ n POL tory *m*, membre *m* du
parti conservateur. ◆ adj [party, MP] tory, conservateur.

toss [tɒs] ◆ vt **1.** [throw] lancer, jeter ▶ **to toss pancakes** 🇬🇧 faire sauter des crêpes ▶ **to toss a coin** jouer à pile ou face **2.** CULIN mélanger ▶ **to toss the salad** remuer or retourner la salade. ◆ vi s'agiter ▶ **to toss and turn in bed** avoir le sommeil agité. ◆ n **1.** [throw - gen] lancer m, lancement m ; [-of a coin] coup m de pile ou face ; SPORT tirage m au sort ▶ **to win / to lose the toss** gagner / perdre à pile ou face **2.** [of head] mouvement m brusque **3.** [fall from horse] chute f. ❖ **toss about** 🇬🇧, **toss around** ◆ vt sep **1.** [rock, buffet] ballotter, secouer **2.** fig : *figures of £5,000 were being tossed around* on avançait allègrement des chiffres de l'ordre de 5 000 livres. ◆ vi s'agiter. ❖ **toss off** ◆ vt sep **1.** [do hastily] expédier **2.** [drink quickly] boire d'un coup, lamper. ◆ vi 🇬🇧 vulg [masturbate] se branler. ❖ **toss up** ◆ vt sep lancer, jeter. ◆ vi jouer à pile ou face.

tosser ['tɒsər] n 🇬🇧 v inf [stupid person] connard m.

toss-up n coup m de pile ou face.

tot [tɒt] (pt & pp **totted**, cont **totting**) n **1.** inf [child] petit enfant m ▶ **tiny tots** les tout-petits mpl **2.** 🇬🇧 [of alcohol] goutte f. ❖ **tot up** 🇬🇧 ◆ vt sep additionner. ◆ vi : *that tots up to £3* ça fait 3 livres en tout.

total ['təʊtl] (🇬🇧 pt & pp **totalled**, cont **totalling** ; 🇺🇸 pt & pp **totaled**, cont **totaling**) ◆ adj **1.** [amount, number] total **2.** [as intensifier] complet (complète). ◆ n total m. ◆ vt **1.** [add up] totaliser, faire le total de **2.** [amount to] s'élever à **3.** 🇺🇸 inf [wreck] démolir. ❖ **in total** adv phr au total.

totalitarian [,təʊtælɪ'teərɪən] adj totalitaire.

totalitarianism [,təʊtælɪ'teərɪənɪzm] n totalitarisme m.

totality [təʊ'tælətɪ] (pl **totalities**) n **1.** totalité f **2.** ASTRON occultation f totale.

totally ['təʊtəlɪ] adv **1.** [completely] totalement, entièrement, complètement **2.** 🇺🇸 inf [expressing agreement] absolument.

tote bag n grand sac m, fourre-tout m inv.

totem pole n mât m totémique.

toto ['təʊtəʊ] ❖ **in toto** adv phr fml entièrement, complètement.

totter ['tɒtər] ◆ vi **1.** lit [person] chanceler, tituber ; [pile, vase] chanceler **2.** fig [government, company, etc.] chanceler, être dans une mauvaise passe. ◆ n vacillement m ; [gait] démarche f titubante or chancelante.

tottering ['tɒtərɪŋ], **tottery** ['tɒtərɪ] adj chancelant ; [building] branlant ; [government] chancelant, déstabilisé.

totty ['tɒtɪ] n 🇬🇧 inf [attractive women] belles nanas fpl, belles gonzesses fpl.

toucan ['tuːkən] n toucan m.

toucan crossing n 🇬🇧 passage m mixte piétons-cyclistes.

touch [tʌtʃ] (pl **touches**) ◆ n **1.** [sense] toucher m / *sense of touch* sens m du toucher **2.** [physical contact] toucher m, contact m ; [light brushing] effleurement m, frôlement m / *the machine works at the touch of a button* il suffit de toucher un bouton pour mettre en marche cet appareil **3.** [style] touche f ; fig ▶ **to give sthg a personal touch** ajouter une note personnelle à qqch **4.** [detail] ▶ **to put the final** or **finishing touches to sthg** apporter la touche finale à qqch ; [slight mark] coup m / *with a touch of the pen* d'un coup de stylo **5.** [small amount, hint] note f, pointe f / *he answered with a touch of bitterness* il a répondu avec une pointe d'amertume / *I got a touch of sunstroke* j'ai eu une petite insolation / *I've got a touch of flu* je suis un peu grippé, j'ai une petite grippe **6.** [contact] ▶ **to be / to keep in touch with sb** être / rester en contact avec qqn / *I'll be in touch!* je te contacterai ! /

keep or *stay in touch!* donne-nous de tes nouvelles ! ▶ **to get in touch with sb** contacter qqn / *he put me in touch with the director* il m'a mis en relation avec le directeur / *she is out of touch with politics* elle ne suit plus l'actualité politique / *they lost touch long ago* ils se sont perdus de vue il y a longtemps / *he has lost touch with reality* il a perdu le sens des réalités **7.** SPORT touche f ▶ **to kick the ball into touch** mettre le ballon en touche ▶ **to kick sthg into touch** fig mettre qqch au rencart **8.** PHR ▶ **to be an easy** or **soft touch** inf se laisser taper trop facilement. ◆ vt **1.** [make contact with] toucher / *to touch lightly* frôler, effleurer / *she touched it with her foot* elle l'a touché du pied / *the law can't touch him* la loi ne peut rien contre lui **2.** [handle] toucher à / *don't touch her things* ne dérangez pas ses affaires / *don't touch anything until I get home* ne touchez à rien avant mon retour / *I didn't touch him!* je n'ai pas touché à un cheveu de sa tête ! **3.** (usu neg) [eat, drink] toucher à / *I never touch meat* je ne mange jamais de viande / *she didn't touch her vegetables* elle n'a pas touché aux légumes **4.** [move emotionally] émouvoir, toucher **5.** [damage] : *the fire didn't touch the pictures* l'incendie a épargné les tableaux **6.** [concern] concerner, toucher **7.** (usu neg) inf [rival] valoir, égaler / *nothing can touch butter for cooking* rien ne vaut la cuisine au beurre. ◆ vi **1.** [be in contact] se toucher **2.** [adjoin - properties, areas] se toucher, être contigus **3.** [handle] / 'do not touch!' 'défense de toucher'. ❖ **touch down** vi **1.** [aeroplane, spacecraft - on land] atterrir ; [- on sea] amerrir **2.** RUGBY marquer un essai. ❖ **touch off** vt sep [explosive] faire exploser, faire détoner ; fig déclencher, provoquer. ❖ **touch on** vt insep aborder. ❖ **touch up** vt sep [painting, photograph] faire des retouches à, retoucher ; [paintwork] refaire.

touch-and-go adj : *a touch-and-go situation* une situation dont l'issue est incertaine.

touchdown ['tʌtʃdaʊn] n **1.** [on land] atterrissage m ; [on sea] amerrissage m **2.** [in American football] but m.

touché ['tuːʃeɪ] interj **1.** [fencing] touché **2.** fig très juste.

touched [tʌtʃt] adj **1.** [with gratitude] touché **2.** 🇬🇧 inf [mad] toqué, timbré.

touching ['tʌtʃɪŋ] ◆ adj touchant, émouvant. ◆ prep liter touchant.

touchingly ['tʌtʃɪŋlɪ] adv d'une manière touchante.

touch judge n RUGBY juge m de touche.

touchline ['tʌtʃlaɪn] n SPORT ligne f de touche.

touchpaper ['tʌtʃ,peɪpər] n papier m nitraté.

touch screen n COMPUT écran m tactile.

touch-sensitive adj [screen] tactile ; [key, switch] à effleurement.

touchstone ['tʌtʃstəʊn] n MINER & fig pierre f de touche.

touch-tone adj ▶ **touch-tone telephone** téléphone m à touches.

touch-type vi taper sans regarder le clavier.

touchy ['tʌtʃɪ] (compar **touchier**, superl **touchiest**) adj **1.** [oversensitive] susceptible, ombrageux **2.** [matter, situation] délicat, épineux.

touchy-feely ['fiːlɪ] adj pej qui affectionne les contacts physiques.

tough [tʌf] ◆ adj **1.** [resilient - person] solide, résistant, robuste ; [- meat] dur, coriace ; [- animal, plant] résistant, robuste ; [- substance, fabric] solide, résistant **2.** [difficult] dur, pénible **3.** [severe] sévère ▶ **to get tough with sb** se montrer dur avec qqn ; [resolute] dur, inflexible ▶ **a tough cookie** 🇺🇸 inf : *he's a tough cookie* il n'est pas commode ▶ **a tough customer** : *they're tough customers* ce sont des durs à cuire **4.** [rough, hardened] dur **5.** inf [unfortunate] malheureux ▶ **that's your tough luck!** tant pis pour vous ! ◆ adv *inf* ▶ **to talk tough, to act tough** jouer au dur. ◆ vt ▶ **to tough it out** *inf* tenir bon. ◆ n *inf* dur *m*, -e *f*.

toughen ['tʌfn] ◆ vt [metal, leather] rendre plus solide, renforcer ; [person] endurcir ; [conditions] rendre plus sévère. ◆ vi [metal, glass, leather] durcir ; [person] s'endurcir.
✦ **toughen up** vt sep & vi = **toughen.**

toughened ['tʌfnd] adj [glass] trempé.

toughness ['tʌfnɪs] n **1.** [of fabric, glass, leather] solidité *f* ; [of meat] dureté *f* ; [of metal] ténacité *f*, résistance *f* **2.** [of job] difficulté *f* ; [of struggle] acharnement *m*, âpreté *f* **3.** [of character - strength] force *f*, résistance *f* ; [- hardness] dureté *f* ; [- severity] inflexibilité *f*, sévérité *f*.

toupee ['tuːpeɪ] n postiche *m*.

tour [tʊər] ◆ n **1.** [trip] voyage *m* ▶ **a walking tour**: she's on a walking tour in Wales elle fait une randonnée à pied dans le pays de Galles ▶ **a world tour**: they're off on a world tour ils sont partis faire le tour du monde **2.** [of a building] visite *f* **3.** [official journey] tournée *f* / the dance company is on tour la troupe de danseurs est en tournée ▶ **to go on tour** faire une tournée ▶ **tour of duty** MIL service *m* ▶ **tour of inspection** tournée *f* d'inspection. ◆ vt **1.** [visit] visiter **2.** SPORT & THEAT : the orchestra is touring the provinces l'orchestre est en tournée en province. ◆ vi voyager, faire du tourisme.

tourer 🇬🇧 ['tʊərər], **touring car** 🇺🇸 n voiture *f* de tourisme.

Tourette's Syndrome [tə'rets-], **Tourette syndrome** [tə'ret-] n MED syndrome *m* Gilles de la Tourette.

touring ['tʊərɪŋ] ◆ adj ▶ **touring bicycle** vélo *m* de randonnée ▶ **touring company** a) THEAT [permanently] troupe *f* ambulante b) [temporarily] troupe *f* en tournée ▶ **touring party** SPORT équipe *f* en tournée. ◆ n *(U)* tourisme *m*, voyages *mpl* touristiques.

tourism ['tʊərɪzm] n tourisme *m*.

tourist ['tʊərɪst] ◆ n touriste *mf* ▶ **the tourists** SPORT les visiteurs *mpl*. ◆ comp [agency, centre] de tourisme ; [attraction, information, ticket] touristique ▶ **tourist (information) office** office *m* de tourisme, syndicat *m* d'initiative ▶ **tourist visa** visa *m* de touriste.

tourist class n 🇬🇧 classe *f* touriste.

touristy ['tʊərɪstɪ] adj *inf & pej* trop touristique.

tournament ['tɔːnəmənt] n tournoi *m*.

tourniquet ['tʊənɪkeɪ] n garrot *m*.

tour operator n [travel agency] tour-opérateur *m*, voyagiste *m* ; [bus company] compagnie *f* de cars *(qui organise des voyages)*.

tousle ['taʊzl] vt [hair] ébouriffer ; [clothes] friper, froisser.

tout [taʊt] 🇬🇧 ◆ n **1.** ▶ **(ticket) tout** revendeur *m*, -euse *f* de billets *(au marché noir)* **2.** [in racing] pronostiqueur *m*, -euse *f*. ◆ vt **1.** [peddle - tickets] revendre *(au marché noir)* ; [- goods] vendre *(en vantant sa marchandise)* **2.** [promote] : he is being touted as a future prime minister on veut faire de lui un futur Premier ministre. ◆ vi **1.** : salesmen touting for custom des vendeurs qui essaient d'attirer les clients / they've been touting around for work / business ils essayaient de trouver du travail / de se constituer une clientèle **2.** [racing] vendre des pronostics.

tow [təʊ] ◆ vt tirer ; [boat, car] remorquer ; [barge] haler. ◆ n **1.** [action] remorquage *m* ; [vehicle] véhicule *m* en remorque ▶ **to be on tow** être en remorque **2.** [line] câble *m* de remorquage **3.** TEXT filasse *f*, étoupe *f*.

towards 🇬🇧 [tə'wɔːdz], **toward** 🇺🇸 [tə'wɔːd] prep **1.** [in the direction of] dans la direction de, vers / he turned towards her il s'est tourné vers elle / they are working towards a solution *fig* ils cherchent une solution **2.** [indicat-

ing attitude] envers / she's very hostile towards me elle est très hostile à mon égard **3.** [as contribution to] pour / the money is going towards a new car l'argent contribuera à l'achat d'une nouvelle voiture **4.** [near - in time] vers ; [- in space] près de / towards the end of his life vers or sur la fin de sa vie.

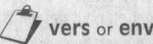 **vers** or **envers**?

Both these words broadly mean towards, but **vers** refers to physical movement (**avancez vers la porte** walk towards the door) while **envers** is used in an abstract sense (**son attitude envers les musulmans** his attitude towards Muslims ; **la maltraitance envers les animaux** mistreatment of animals).

tow-away zone ['təʊəweɪ-] n 🇺🇸 zone où il est interdit de stationner sous peine d'enlèvement du véhicule par la fourrière.

towbar ['təʊbɑːr] n barre *f* de remorquage.

towel ['taʊəl] (🇬🇧 pt & pp **towelled**, cont **towelling** ; 🇺🇸 pt & pp **toweled** or **towelled**, cont **toweling** or **towelling**) ◆ n serviette *f* (de toilette) ; [for hands] essuie-mains *m inv* ; [for glasses] essuie-verres *m inv* ▶ **towel rack** or **rail** or **ring** porte-serviettes *m inv*. ◆ vt frotter avec une serviette ▶ **to towel o.s. dry** or **down** s'essuyer or se sécher avec une serviette. ✦ **towel off** vi se sécher.

towelling 🇬🇧, **toweling** 🇺🇸 ['taʊəlɪŋ] ◆ n [material] tissu *m* éponge. ◆ comp [robe, shirt] en tissu éponge.

tower ['taʊər] ◆ n tour *f*. ◆ vi : the skyscraper towers above or over the city le gratte-ciel domine la ville / he towered above or over me j'étais tout petit à côté de lui.

tower block n 🇬🇧 tour *f* (d'habitation), gratte-ciel *m*.

towering ['taʊərɪŋ] adj **1.** [very high - skyscraper, tree, statue] très haut, imposant **2.** [excessive] démesuré.

2WIMC MESSAGING written abbr of **to whom it may concern**.

town [taʊn] n ville *f* / I work in town je travaille en ville / she's going into town elle va en ville / he's out of town this week il n'est pas là or il est en déplacement cette semaine / we're from out of town 🇺🇸 nous ne sommes pas d'ici.

town centre n centre-ville *m*.

town clerk n secrétaire *mf* de mairie.

town council n conseil *m* municipal.

town hall n 🇬🇧 hôtel de ville *m*, mairie *f*.

town house n **1.** [gen] maison *f* de ville ; [more imposing] ≃ hôtel *m* particulier **2.** 🇺🇸 maison *f* mitoyenne (en ville).

town planner n urbaniste *mf*.

town planning n urbanisme *m*.

townsfolk ['taʊnzfəʊk] pl n citadins *mpl*.

township ['taʊnʃɪp] n **1.** [gen] commune *f* ; 🇺🇸 canton *m* **2.** 🇿🇦 township *f*.

townspeople ['taʊnz,piːpl] pl n citadins *mpl*.

towpath ['təʊpɑːθ] (pl [-pɑːðz]) n chemin *m* de halage.

towrope ['təʊrəʊp] n câble *m* de remorque ; [to towpath] câble *m* de halage.

tow truck 🇺🇸 = **breakdown lorry**.

toxic ['tɒksɪk] adj toxique.

toxicity [tɒk'sɪsətɪ] n toxicité *f*.

toxic shock syndrome n syndrome *m* du choc toxique.

toxic waste n déchets *mpl* toxiques.

toxin ['tɒksɪn] n toxine *f*.

toy [tɔɪ] (*pl* **toys**) ✦ n jouet *m*. ✦ comp **1.** [car, train] miniature ▸ **toy soldier** soldat *m* de plomb **2.** [box, chest, drawer] à jouets **3.** [dog] nain. ✦ **toy with** vt insep jouer avec ▸ **to toy with one's food** manger du bout des dents.

toy boy n *inf & pej jeune homme qui sort avec une femme plus mûre.*

toy shop n magasin *m* de jouets.

TPTB MESSAGING written abbr of **the powers that be.**

trace [treɪs] ✦ n **1.** [sign] trace *f* **2.** [trail] trace *f* de pas, piste *f*; US [path] piste *f*, sentier *m* **3.** [drawing] tracé *m* **4.** TECH ▸ **a radar trace** la trace d'un spot **5.** [harness] trait *m*. ✦ vt **1.** [follow trail of] suivre la trace de ; [track down - object] retrouver **2.** [follow development of] suivre **3.** [mark outline of] tracer, dessiner ; [with tracing paper] décalquer. ✦ **trace back** ✦ vt sep ▸ **to trace sthg back to its source** retrouver l'origine de qqch. ✦ vi US **1.** [go back] ▸ **to trace back to** remonter à **2.** [be due to] être dû à.

traceable ['treɪsəbl] adj [object] retrouvable, qui peut être retrouvé ; [food product] traçable.

trace element n oligoélément *m*.

tracer bullet n balle *f* traçante.

tracing ['treɪsɪŋ] n [process] calquage *m*; [result] calque *m*.

tracing paper n papier-calque *m inv*, papier *m* à décalquer.

track [træk] ✦ n **1.** [path, route] chemin *m*, sentier *m*; [of planet, star, aeroplane] trajectoire *f*; *fig* ▸ **to be on the right track** être sur la bonne voie **2.** SPORT ▸ **motor-racing track** US autodrome *m* ▸ **track and field** athlétisme *m* ▸ **track and field events** épreuves *fpl* d'athlétisme **3.** RAIL voie *f*, rails *mpl* **4.** [mark, trail] trace *f*, piste *f*; [of animal, person] piste *f*; [of boat] sillage *m* ▸ **to be on sb's track** or **tracks** être sur la piste de qqn ▸ **to keep track of** suivre ▸ **to lose track of** : *don't lose track of those files* n'égarez pas ces dossiers **5.** [on LP, tape] plage *f*; COMPUT piste *f* **6.** AUTO [tyre tread] chape *f*; [space between wheels] écartement *m* **7.** US SCH classe *f* de niveau ▸ **track system** *répartition des élèves en sections selon leurs aptitudes.* ✦ vt **1.** [follow - animal] suivre à la trace, filer ; [- rocket] suivre la trajectoire de ; [criminal] traquer ▸ **to track an order** suivre une commande **2.** US : *don't track mud into the house!* ne traîne pas de boue dans la maison ! ✦ vi **1.** [stylus] suivre le sillon **2.** [with camera] faire un traveling or travelling. ✦ **track down** vt sep retrouver, localiser ; [animal, criminal] traquer et capturer.

trackball ['trækbɔːl] n COMPUT boule *f* de commande, trackball *m*.

tracker ['trækər] n **1.** [person - gen] poursuivant *m*, -e *f*; [- in hunting] traqueur *m*, -euse *f* **2.** [device] appareil *m* de poursuite.

tracker dog n chien *m* policier.

tracker fund n FIN fonds *m* indiciel or à gestion indicielle, tracker *m*.

track event n épreuve *f* sur piste.

tracking ['trækɪŋ] ✦ n **1.** poursuite *f*; [of missile] repérage *m* **2.** US SCH répartition des élèves en sections selon leurs aptitudes. ✦ comp [radar, satellite] de poursuite.

tracking station n station *f* d'observation.

tracklist ['træklɪst] n liste *f* des morceaux or des chansons.

track meet n US rencontre *f* d'athlétisme.

trackpad ['trækpæd] n COMPUT tablette *f* tactile.

track record n SPORT & *fig* dossier *m*, carrière *f* / *she has a good track record* elle a fait ses preuves / *given his track record* vu ce qu'il a déjà accompli.

track shoe n chaussure *f* d'athlétisme.

tracksuit ['træk,suːt] n survêtement *m*.

tract [trækt] n **1.** [pamphlet] tract *m* **2.** [large area] étendue *f*; US [housing estate] lotissement *m*; [mining] gisement *m* ▸ **a tract house** un pavillon **3.** ANAT ▸ **digestive / respiratory tract** appareil *m* digestif / respiratoire.

tractable ['træktəbl] adj [person, animal] accommodant ; [material] malléable ; [problem] soluble, facile à résoudre.

traction ['trækʃn] n **1.** MECH traction *f* **2.** MED ▸ **to be in traction** être en extension.

traction engine n locomotive *f*.

tractor ['træktər] n [on farm] tracteur *m*; TECH locomobile *f*.

tractor-trailer n US semi-remorque *m*.

trade [treɪd] ✦ n **1.** (*U*) COMM commerce *m*, affaires *fpl* ▸ **the clothing trade** la confection, l'industrie *f* de la confection ▸ **domestic / foreign trade** commerce intérieur / extérieur **2.** [illicit dealings] trafic *m* ▸ **the drug trade** le trafic de drogue **3.** [vocation, occupation] métier *m* **4.** [exchange] échange *m* **5.** [regular customers] clientèle *f* **6.** US [transaction] transaction *f* commerciale. ✦ comp **1.** COMM [balance] commercial ▸ **trade agreement** accord *m* commercial ▸ **trade deficit** balance *f* commerciale déficitaire, déficit *m* extérieur ▸ **trade figures** résultats *mpl* financiers **2.** [publication] spécialisé. ✦ vt [exchange] échanger, troquer. ✦ vi **1.** [businessman, country] faire du commerce / *he trades in clothing* il est négociant en confection, il est dans la confection ▸ **to trade with sb** avoir or entretenir des relations commerciales avec qqn **2.** US [private individual] faire ses achats ▸ **to trade at** or **with** faire ses courses à or chez **3.** ST. EX [currency, commodity] : *corn is trading at £25* le maïs se négocie à 25 livres. ✦ **trades** pl n [winds] alizés *mpl*. ✦ **trade in** vt sep faire reprendre. ✦ **trade off** vt sep échanger, troquer ; [as a compromise] accepter en compensation ▸ **to trade sthg off against sthg** laisser or abandonner qqch pour qqch. ✦ **trade on** vt insep exploiter, profiter de / *I'd rather not trade on* or *upon your kindness* je ne voudrais pas abuser de votre gentillesse. ✦ **trade up** vi [car owner] changer pour un modèle plus cher.

trade association n association *f* professionnelle.

trade barriers pl n barrières *fpl* douanières.

Trade Descriptions Act pr n *loi britannique contre la publicité mensongère.*

trade discount n remise *f* professionnelle or au détaillant.

trade fair n foire *f* or exposition *f* commerciale.

trade gap n déficit *m* commercial.

trade-in n reprise *f*.

trademark ['treɪdmɑːk] ✦ n marque *f* (de fabrique) ; *fig* signe *m* caractéristique. ✦ vt [label a product] apposer une marque sur ; [register a product] déposer.

trade name n [of product] nom *m* de marque ; [of firm] raison *f* commerciale.

trade-off n échange *m*; [compromise] compromis *m*.

trade price n prix *m* de gros.

trader ['treɪdər] n **1.** [gen] commerçant *m*, -e *f*, marchand *m*, -e *f*; [on large scale] négociant *m*, -e *f* **2.** [ship] navire *m* marchand or de commerce **3.** US ST. EX contrepartiste *m*.

trade route n route *f* commerciale.

trade secret n secret *m* de fabrication.

tradesman ['treɪdzmən] (*pl* **tradesmen** [-mən]) n
1. [trader] commerçant *m*, marchand *m* ▶ **tradesman's
entrance** entrée *f* de service or des fournisseurs **2.** [skilled
workman] ouvrier *m* qualifié.

tradespeople ['treɪdz,piːpl] pl n commerçants *mpl*.

trade(s) union n syndicat *m*.

Trades Union Congress n *confédération des syndicats
britanniques.*

trade(s) unionist n syndicaliste *mf.*

trade unionism n syndicalisme *m.*

trade wind n alizé *m.*

trading ['treɪdɪŋ] ◆ n commerce *m*, négoce *m* ; [illicit
dealing] trafic *m*. ◆ comp [company, partner] commercial
▶ **trading nation** nation *f* commerçante ▶ **trading standards** normes *fpl* de conformité ▶ **trading standards office**
≃ Direction *f* de la consommation et de la répression des
fraudes.

trading estate n zone *f* artisanale et commerciale.

trading floor n ST. EX corbeille *f.*

trading hours n heures *fpl* d'ouverture.

trading stamp n timbre-prime *m*, vignette-épargne *f.*

tradition [trə'dɪʃn] n tradition *f*, coutume *f* ▶ **the tradition that…** la tradition selon laquelle… or qui veut que…

traditional [trə'dɪʃənl] adj traditionnel.

traditionalist [trə'dɪʃnəlɪst] ◆ n traditionaliste *mf.*
◆ adj traditionaliste.

traditionally [trə'dɪʃnəlɪ] adv traditionnellement.

traffic ['træfɪk] (*pt* & *pp* **trafficked**, *cont* **trafficking**) ◆ n **1.** [on roads] circulation *f* ; [rail, air, maritime]
trafic *m* ▶ **traffic calming** mesures visant à ralentir la circulation **2.** COMM commerce *m* ; [illicit] trafic *m* ; [custom-
ers] clientèle *f* **3.** [to website] trafic *m*. ◆ vi ▶ **to traffic in**
faire le commerce de.

traffic circle n rond-point *m*, sens *m* giratoire.

traffic island n TRANSP refuge *m.*

traffic jam n embouteillage *m*, bouchon *m.*

trafficker ['træfɪkə'] n trafiquant *m*, -e *f.*

traffic lights pl n feu *m* de signalisation.

traffic offence n infraction *f* au code de la route.

traffic police n [speeding, safety] police *f* de la route ;
[point duty] police *f* de la circulation.

traffic policeman n agent *m* de police ; [on point
duty] agent *m* de la circulation.

traffic sign n panneau *m* de signalisation, poteau *m*
indicateur.

traffic violation = **traffic offence.**

traffic warden n contractuel *m*, -elle *f.*

 Traffic warden

En Grande-Bretagne, les contractuels sont
non seulement habilités à dresser les procès-
verbaux mais aussi à régler la circulation.

tragedy ['trædʒədɪ] (*pl* **tragedies**) n [gen & THEAT] tragédie *f.*

tragic ['trædʒɪk] adj tragique.

tragically ['trædʒɪklɪ] adv tragiquement.

tragicomic [,trædʒɪ'kɒmɪk] adj tragi-comique.

trail [treɪl] ◆ n **1.** [path] sentier *m*, chemin *m* ; [through
jungle] piste *f* ▶ **the trail of tears** HIST le chemin des
larmes **2.** [traces of passage] piste *f*, trace *f* ▶ **to be on
the trail of sb / sthg** être sur la piste de qqn / qqch **3.** [of

blood, smoke] traînée *f* ; [of comet] queue *f*. ◆ vt **1.** [fol-
low] suivre, filer ; [track] suivre la piste de ; [animal, crim-
inal] traquer **2.** [drag behind, tow] traîner ; [boat, trailer]
tirer, remorquer **3.** [lag behind] être en arrière par rapport à
4. [gun] porter à la main **5.** [advertise] diffuser (une bande-
annonce). ◆ vi **1.** [long garment] traîner ; [plant] ramper
2. [move slowly] traîner **3.** [lag behind in contest] être à la
traîne **4.** [follow] suivre, filer. ◆ **trail away** vi s'estomper. ◆ **trail off** vi s'estomper.

🏛 The trail of tears

Nom donné au trajet que les Indiens
d'Amérique parcoururent sous la contrainte
en 1938 pour rejoindre les réserves situées à
l'ouest du Mississippi où ils devaient vivre.
Un grand nombre d'entre eux succombèrent
à la maladie et aux mauvais traitements.

trailblazer ['treɪl,bleɪzə'] n *fig* pionnier *m*, -ère *f.*

trailblazing ['treɪl,bleɪzɪŋ] adj de pionnier.

trailer ['treɪlə'] n **1.** AUTO remorque *f* ; camping-car *m*
▶ **trailer court** or **trailer park** terrain aménagé pour
les camping-cars ▶ **trailer home** caravane *f* ▶ **trailer tent**
tente *f* remorque **2.** CIN & TV bande-annonce *f* **3.** [end of
film roll] amorce *f.*

train [treɪn] ◆ n **1.** [railway] train *m* ; [underground]
métro *m*, rame *f* ▶ **to go by train** prendre le train, aller en
train ▶ **to transport goods by train** transporter des marchandises par voie ferrée or rail / **'to the trains'** 'accès
aux quais' **2.** [procession - of vehicles] file *f*, cortège *m* ;
[- of mules] file *f* ; [- of camels] caravane *f* ; MIL convoi *m* ;
[retinue] suite *f*, équipage *m* ; MIL équipage *m* **3.** [of dress]
traîne *f* **4.** [connected sequence] suite *f*, série *f* ▶ **a train
of thought** un enchaînement d'idées **5.** MECH train *m*
▶ **train of gears** train d'engrenage **6.** *fml* [progress] ▶ **in
train** en marche. ◆ comp [dispute, strike] des cheminots,
des chemins de fer ; [reservation, ticket] de train / *there is
a good train service to the city* la ville est bien desservie
par le train ▶ **train station** gare *f (de chemin de fer).* ◆ vt
1. [employee, soldier] former ; [voice] travailler ; [animal]
dresser ; [mind] former ; SPORT entraîner ; [plant - by prun-
ing] tailler ; [- by tying] palisser ; [climbing plant] diriger, faire
grimper ▶ **to train sb to use sthg** apprendre à qqn à utiliser
qqch ▶ **to train sb up** former or préparer qqn **2.** [direct,
aim] viser. ◆ vi **1.** recevoir une formation / *I trained as
a translator* j'ai reçu une formation de traducteur **2.** SPORT
s'entraîner, se préparer.

trained [treɪnd] adj compétent, qualifié ; [engineer] breveté, diplômé ; [nurse, translator] diplômé, qualifié / *he's not
trained for this job* il n'est pas qualifié or n'a pas la formation requise pour ce poste ▶ **a trained eye** un œil exercé ;
[animal] dressé.

trainee [treɪ'niː] ◆ n stagiaire *mf.* ◆ comp stagiaire,
en stage ; [in trades] en apprentissage ▶ **trainee computer
programmer** élève *mf* programmeur.

traineeship [treɪ'niːʃɪp] n stage *m.*

trainer ['treɪnə'] n **1.** SPORT entraîneur *m* **2.** [of animal]
dresseur *m*, -euse *f* ; [of racehorses] entraîneur *m* ; [of lion]
dompteur *m*, -euse *f* **3.** AERON [simulator] simulateur *m*
▶ **trainer (aircraft)** avion-école *m* **4.** [shoe] chaussure *f*
de sport, basket *f.*

training ['treɪnɪŋ] ◆ n **1.** formation *f* ; [of soldier]
instruction *f* ; [of animal] dressage *m* ▶ **to do one's basic
training** MIL faire ses classes **2.** SPORT entraînement *m*, préparation *f* ▶ **to be in training** être en cours d'entraînement
or de préparation ▶ **to be in training for sthg** s'entraîner

pour or se préparer à qqch. ◆ comp [centre, programme, scheme] de formation ▶ **training manual** manuel *m* d'instruction.

training camp n camp *m* d'entraînement ; MIL base *f* école.

training college n école *f* spécialisée or professionnelle.

training course n stage *m* de formation.

training shoes pl n chaussures *fpl* de sport.

training video n vidéo *f* d'entraînement.

train set n train *m* électrique.

trainspotter n 🇬🇧 **1.** [train enthusiast] *amateur de trains dont la passion consiste à relever les numéros d'immatriculation des locomotives* **2.** [nerd] crétin *m*, -e *f*.

trainspotting [-'spɒtɪŋ] n ▶ **to go trainspotting** observer les trains.

traipse [treɪps] *inf* ◆ vi ▶ **to traipse about** or **around** se balader, vadrouiller. ◆ n longue promenade.

trait [treɪ or treɪt] n trait *m*.

traitor ['treɪtər] n traître *m*.

trajectory [trə'dʒektərɪ] (*pl* **trajectories**) n trajectoire *f*.

tram [træm] n 🇬🇧 tram *m*, tramway *m* ; MIN berline *f*, benne *f* roulante.

tramcar ['træmkɑːr] n 🇬🇧 tram *m*, tramway *m*.

tramline ['træmlaɪn] n 🇬🇧 [rails] voie *f* de tramway ; [route] ligne *f* de tramway.

tramp [træmp] ◆ n **1.** [vagabond] clochard *m*, -e *f*, chemineau *m* dated **2.** [sound] bruit *m* de pas **3.** [long walk] randonnée *f* (à pied), promenade *f* **4.** [ship] ▶ **tramp (steamer)** tramp *m* **5.** 🇺🇸 *inf & pej* traînée *f*. ◆ vi [hike] marcher, se promener ; [walk heavily] marcher d'un pas lourd. ◆ vt parcourir.

trample ['træmpl] ◆ vt piétiner, fouler aux pieds ; [sb's feelings] bafouer. ◆ vi marcher d'un pas lourd. ◆ n [action] piétinement *m* ; [sound] bruit *m* de pas. ❖ **trample on, trample over** vt insep piétiner ; *fig* [sb's feelings] bafouer ; [objections] passer outre à.

trampoline ['træmpəliːn] ◆ n trampoline *m*. ◆ vi ▶ **to trampoline, to go trampolining** faire du trampoline.

trance [trɑːns] n transe *f* ; MED catalepsie *f*.

tranche [trɑ̃ʃ] n [of loan, payment, shares] tranche *f*.

trannie, tranny ['trænɪ] (*pl* **trannies**) n 🇬🇧 *inf* **1.** [transvestite] travelo *m* **2.** *dated* [transistor radio] transistor *m*.

tranquil ['træŋkwɪl] adj tranquille, paisible.

tranquillity 🇬🇧, **tranquility** 🇺🇸 [træŋ'kwɪlɪtɪ] n tranquillité *f*, calme *m*.

tranquillize, tranquillise 🇬🇧, **tranquilize** 🇺🇸 ['træŋkwɪlaɪz] vt calmer, apaiser ; MED mettre sous tranquillisants.

tranquillizer 🇬🇧, **tranquilizer** 🇺🇸 ['træŋkwɪlaɪzər] n tranquillisant *m*, calmant *m*.

transact [træn'zækt] vt traiter, régler.

transaction [træn'zækʃn] n **1.** [gen & BANK] opération *f*, affaire *f* ; ECON, FIN & ST. EX transaction *f* **2.** [act of transacting] conduite *f*, gestion *f* **3.** COMPUT mouvement *m*. ❖ **transactions** pl n [proceedings of an organization] travaux *mpl* ; [minutes] actes *mpl*.

transatlantic [,trænzət'læntɪk] adj transatlantique.

transceiver [træn'siːvər] n émetteur-récepteur *m*.

transcend [træn'send] vt **1.** [go beyond] transcender, dépasser ; PHILOS & RELIG transcender **2.** [surpass] surpasser.

transcendental [,trænsen'dentl] adj transcendantal.

transcendental meditation n méditation *f* transcendantale.

transcribe [træn'skraɪb] vt transcrire.

transcript ['trænskrɪpt] n transcription *f* ; 🇺🇸 SCH & UNIV *dossier complet de la scolarité*.

transcription [træn'skrɪpʃn] n transcription *f*.

transept ['trænsept] n transept *m*.

trans fat ['trænz-] n BIOL & CHEM acide *m* gras trans.

transfer ◆ vt [træns'fɜːr] **1.** [move] transférer ; [employee, civil servant] transférer, muter ; [soldier] muter ; [player] transférer ; [passenger] transférer, transborder ; [object, goods] transférer, transporter ; [money] virer **2.** [convey -property, ownership] transmettre, transférer ; [-power, responsibility] passer ; LAW faire cession de, céder **3.** TELEC : *I'm transferring you now* [operator] je vous mets en communication **4.** [displace -design, picture] reporter, décalquer. ◆ vi [træns'fɜːr] **1.** [move] être transféré ; [employee, civil servant] être muté or transféré ; [soldier] être muté ; SPORT [player] être transféré **2.** [change mode of transport] être transféré or transbordé. ◆ n ['trænsfɜːr] **1.** [gen] transfert *m* ; [of employee, civil servant] mutation *f* ; [of passenger] transfert *m*, transbordement *m* ; [of player] transfert *m* ; [of goods, objects] transfert *m*, transport *m* ; [of money] virement *m* ▶ **bank transfer** virement *m* bancaire **2.** LAW transmission *f*, cession *f* ▶ **transfer of ownership from sb to sb** transfert *m* or translation *f* de propriété de qqn à qqn **3.** POL ▶ **transfer of power** passation *f* de pouvoir **4.** [design, picture] décalcomanie *f* ; [rub-on] autocollant *m* ; [sew-on] décalque *m* **5.** [change of mode of travel] transfert *m* ; [at airport, train station] correspondance *f* ▶ **transfer bus** navette *f*.

transferable [træns'fɜːrəbl] adj transmissible ; LAW cessible ▶ **transferable securities** FIN valeurs *fpl* négociables.

transference ['trænsfərəns] n [gen & PSYCHOL] transfert *m* ; [of employee, civil servant] mutation *f* ; [of money] virement *m* ; [of power] passation *f* ; [of ownership] transfert *m* or translation *f* de propriété.

transfer fee n FOOT prix *m* du transfert.

transfer list n 🇬🇧 liste *f* des joueurs transférables.

transfigure [træns'fɪgər] vt transfigurer.

transfix [træns'fɪks] vt *lit* transpercer ; *fig* pétrifier.

transform [træns'fɔːm] ◆ vt **1.** [change -gen] transformer, métamorphoser ▶ **to transform sthg into sthg** transformer qqch en qqch **2.** ELEC transformer ; CHEM, MATH & PHYS transformer, convertir **3.** GRAM transformer. ◆ n **1.** LING transformation *f* **2.** MATH transformée *f*.

transformation [,trænsfə'meɪʃn] n transformation *f*, métamorphose *f* ; ELEC & MATH transformation *f* ; CHEM & PHYS conversion *f* ; LING transformation *f*.

transformer [træns'fɔːmər] ◆ n transformateur *m*. ◆ comp ▶ **transformer station** station *f* de transformation.

transfusion [træns'fjuːʒn] n [gen & MED] transfusion *f*.

transgender [,træns'dʒendər] adj transgenre, transsexuel.

transgenic [trænz'dʒenɪk] adj transgénique.

transgress [trænz'gres] *fml* ◆ vt transgresser, enfreindre. ◆ vi pécher.

transgression [trænz'greʃn] n *fml* **1.** [overstepping] transgression *f* **2.** [crime] faute *f*, violation *f* (d'une loi) ; RELIG péché *m*.

transience ['trænzɪəns] n caractère *m* éphémère or transitoire.

transient ['trænzɪənt] ◆ adj [temporary] transitoire, passager ; [fleeting] éphémère. ◆ n 🇺🇸 [homeless person] personne *f* sans domicile fixe, SDF *mf*.

transistor [træn'zɪstər] n transistor m.
transistor radio n transistor m.
transit ['trænsɪt] ◆ n [of goods, passengers] transit m ; ASTRON passage m ▶ **in transit** en transit. ◆ comp [goods, passengers] en transit ; [documents, port] de transit ▶ **transit authority** US régie f des transports (en commun) ▶ **transit lounge** salle f de transit. ◆ vt [goods, passengers] transiter ; ASTRON passer sur.
transit camp n camp m de transit.
transition [træn'zɪʃn] ◆ n transition f, passage m. ◆ comp [period] de transition.
transitional [træn'zɪʃənl] adj de transition, transitoire.
transitive ['trænzɪtɪv] adj transitif.
transitory ['trænzɪtrɪ] adj transitoire, passager.
translate [træns'leɪt] ◆ vt **1.** traduire / to translate sthg from Spanish into English traduire qqch de l'espagnol en anglais **2.** RELIG [transfer - cleric, relics] transférer ; [convey to heaven] ravir. ◆ vi **1.** [words] se traduire **2.** [person] traduire.
translation [træns'leɪʃn] n **1.** traduction f ; SCH version f **2.** RELIG [of cleric, relics] translation f ; [conveying to heaven] ravissement m.
translator [træns'leɪtər] n traducteur m, -trice f.
translucent [trænz'luːsnt] adj translucide, diaphane.
transmission [trænz'mɪʃn] n **1.** transmission f ; [broadcast] retransmission f **2.** AUTO transmission f ; US boîte f de vitesses.
transmit [trænz'mɪt] (pt & pp **transmitted**, cont **transmitting**) ◆ vt transmettre ; TELEC émettre, diffuser. ◆ vi RADIO, TELEC & TV émettre, diffuser.
transmitter [trænz'mɪtər] n transmetteur m ; RADIO & TV émetteur m ; [in telephone] microphone m (téléphonique).
transparency [træns'pærənsɪ] (pl **transparencies**) n **1.** [gen & PHYS] transparence f **2.** [for overhead projector] transparent m ; US [slide] diapositive f.
transparent [trænz'pærənt] adj [gen & PHYS] transparent.
transpire [træn'spaɪər] ◆ vi **1.** [be discovered, turn out] apparaître **2.** [happen] se passer, arriver **3.** BOT & PHYSIOL transpirer. ◆ vt BOT & PHYSIOL transpirer.
transplant ◆ vt [træns'plɑːnt] **1.** BOT [plant] transplanter ; [seedling] repiquer **2.** MED [organ] greffer, transplanter ; [tissue] greffer **3.** [population] transplanter. ◆ n ['træns,plɑːnt] MED [organ] transplant m ; [tissue] greffe f ; [operation] greffe f ▶ **heart transplant**: she's had a heart transplant on lui a greffé un cœur.
transplantation [,trænsplɑːn'teɪʃn] n **1.** BOT [of seedling] repiquage m ; [of plant] transplantation f **2.** fig [of people] transplantation f.
transport ◆ n ['trænspɔːt] **1.** (U) US [system] transport m, transports mpl **2.** [means] moyen m de transport or de locomotion ▶ **transport plane** avion m de transport ▶ **transport ship** navire m de transport ▶ **troop transport** MIL transport m de troupes **3.** [of goods] transport m **4.** liter [of joy] transport m ; [of anger] accès m. ◆ vt [træn'spɔːt] transporter.
transportable [træn'spɔːtəbl] adj transportable.
transportation [,trænspɔː'teɪʃn] n **1.** US [transport] transport m ▶ **public transportation** transports publics ▶ **transportation system** système m des transports **2.** [of criminals] transportation f.
transport café n US ≃ routier m (restaurant).
transporter [træn'spɔːtər] n **1.** MIL [for troops - lorry] camion m de transport ; [- ship] navire m de transport ; [for

tanks] camion m porte-char **2.** [for cars - lorry] camion m pour transport d'automobiles ; [- train] wagon m pour transport d'automobiles.
transpose [træns'pəʊz] vt transposer.
transsexual [træns'sekʃʊəl] n transsexuel m, -elle f.
transvestism [trænz'vestɪzm] n travestisme m, transvestisme m.
transvestite [trænz'vestaɪt] n travesti m.
trap [træp] (pt & pp **trapped**, cont **trapping**) ◆ n **1.** [snare] piège m ; [dug in ground] trappe f ; [gintrap] collet m **2.** fig piège m, traquenard m ▶ **to set** or **to lay a trap for sb** tendre un piège à qqn ▶ **the poverty trap** le piège de la pauvreté **3.** [in drain] siphon m **4.** SPORT [in dog racing] box m de départ ; [for shooting] ball-trap m **5.** [carriage] cabriolet m, charrette f anglaise **6.** [trapdoor] trappe f **7.** v inf [mouth] gueule f. ◆ vt **1.** [animal] prendre au piège, piéger **2.** fig [opponent] piéger **3.** [immobilize, catch] bloquer, immobiliser **4.** [hold back - water, gas] retenir.
trapdoor [,træp'dɔːr] n trappe f.
trapeze [trə'piːz] n trapèze m (de cirque) ▶ **trapeze artist** trapéziste mf.
trapper ['træpər] n trappeur m.
trappings ['træpɪŋz] pl n **1.** [accessories] ornements mpl **2.** [harness] harnachement m, caparaçon m.
trash [træʃ] ◆ n (U) **1.** [nonsense] bêtises fpl, âneries fpl **2.** [goods] camelote f **3.** US [waste] ordures fpl ▶ **to put something in the trash** mettre qqch à la poubelle **4.** COMPUT [icon, file] corbeille f **5.** inf [people] racaille f. ◆ vt inf **1.** [reject] jeter, bazarder **2.** [criticize] débiner, éreinter **3.** [vandalize] vandaliser, saccager **4.** US SPORT [opponent] démolir.
trash bag n US sac-poubelle m.
trashcan ['træʃkæn] n US poubelle f.
trash collector n US éboueur m, éboueuse f.
trashed [træʃt] adj US inf [drunk] bourré ▶ **to get trashed** se bourrer la gueule.
trashy ['træʃɪ] (compar **trashier**, superl **trashiest**) adj [goods] de pacotille ; [magazine, book] de quatre sous ; [idea, article] qui ne vaut rien ; [programme] lamentable, au-dessous de tout.
trauma [US 'trɔːmə US 'traʊmə] (pl **traumas** or **traumata** [-mətə]) n [gen & PSYCHOL] trauma m spec, traumatisme m ; MED traumatisme m.
traumatic [trɔː'mætɪk] adj [gen & PSYCHOL] traumatisant ; MED traumatique.
traumatize, traumatise [US 'trɔːmətaɪz US 'traʊmətaɪz] vt traumatiser.
travel ['trævl] (US pt & pp **travelled**, cont **travelling** ; US pt & pp **traveled**, cont **traveling**) ◆ vi **1.** [journey - traveller] voyager ▶ **to travel by air / car** voyager en avion / en voiture ▶ **to travel round the world** faire le tour du monde ▶ **to travel light** voyager avec peu de bagages ▶ **to travel back** revenir, rentrer **2.** COMM être voyageur or représentant de commerce **3.** [go, move - person] aller ; [- vehicle, train] aller, rouler ; [- piston, shuttle] se déplacer ; [- light, sound] se propager **4.** inf [go very fast] rouler (très) vite **5.** fig [thoughts, mind] : my mind travelled back to last June mes pensées m'ont ramené au mois de juin dernier **6.** [news, rumour] se répandre, se propager, circuler **7.** [food] supporter le voyage. ◆ vt **1.** [distance] faire, parcourir **2.** [area, road] parcourir. ◆ n (U) [journeys] voyage m, voyages mpl. ◆ comp [book] de voyages ; [guide, brochure] touristique ; [writer] qui écrit des récits de voyage. ◆ **travels** pl n [journeys] voyages mpl ; [comings and goings] allées et venues fpl.
travel agency n agence f de voyages.

travel agent n agent *m* de voyages ▶ **travel agent's** agence *f* de voyages.

travel brochure n dépliant *m* touristique.

Travelcard ['trævlkɑ:d] n carte *f* d'abonnement *(pour les transports en commun à Londres).*

traveled ['trævld] [US] = **travelled**.

traveler ['trævlər] [US] = **traveller**.

travel insurance n *(U)* ▶ **to take out travel insurance** prendre une assurance-voyage.

travelled [UK], **traveled** [US] ['trævld] adj **1.** [person] qui a beaucoup voyagé **2.** [road, path] fréquenté.

traveller [UK], **traveler** [US] ['trævlər] n **1.** [gen] voyageur *m*, -euse *f* **2.** [salesman] voyageur *m*, -euse *f* de commerce **3.** [gipsy] bohémien *m*, -enne *f* **4.** [lifestyle] ▶ **New Age traveller** nomade *mf* New Age.

traveller's cheque n chèque *m* de voyage, traveller's cheque *m*.

travelling [UK], **traveling** [US] ['trævlɪŋ] ◆ n *(U)* voyage *m*, voyages *mpl*. ◆ adj [companion, bag] de voyage ; [preacher, musician] itinérant ; [crane] mobile.

travelling expenses [UK], **traveling expenses** [US] pl n frais *mpl* de déplacement.

travelling rug n plaid *m*.

travelling salesman n représentant *m* or voyageur *m* de commerce.

travelogue [UK], **travelog** [US] ['trævəlɒg] n [lecture, book] récit *m* de voyage ; [film] film *m* de voyage.

travel-sick adj [US] ▶ **to be travel-sick** a) [in car] avoir mal au cœur en voiture, avoir le mal de la route b) [in boat] avoir le mal de mer c) [in plane] avoir le mal de l'air.

travel sickness n mal *m* de la route.

travel-size(d) adj [shampoo, etc.] de voyage.

travel-weary adj fatigué par le voyage or les voyages.

traverse ['trævəs or ,trə'vɜ:s] ◆ vt *fml* traverser. ◆ vi [in climbing, skiing] faire une traversée, traverser. ◆ n **1.** [beam] traverse *f* **2.** [gallery] galerie *f* transversale.

travesty ['trævəstɪ] *(pl* **travesties**, *pt & pp* **travestied**) ◆ n [parody] parodie *f*, pastiche *m* ; *pej* [mockery, pretence] simulacre *m*, travestissement *m*. ◆ vt [justice] bafouer.

travolator ['trævəleɪtər] n tapis *m* or trottoir *m* roulant.

trawl [trɔ:l] ◆ n **1.** FISHING ▶ **trawl (net)** chalut *m* ▶ **trawl line** palangre *f* **2.** [search] recherche *f*. ◆ vi **1.** FISHING pêcher au chalut ▶ **to trawl for mackerel** pêcher le maquereau au chalut **2.** [search] chercher ▶ **to trawl for information** chercher des renseignements, aller à la pêche (aux renseignements). ◆ vt [net] traîner, tirer ; [sea] pêcher dans ▶ **to trawl the Web** faire des recherches sur le Net.

trawler ['trɔ:lər] n [boat, fisherman] chalutier *m*.

tray [treɪ] n **1.** [for carrying] plateau *m* **2.** [for papers] casier *m* (de rangement) ; [for mail] corbeille *f* ▶ **in / out tray** corbeille arrivée / départ.

treacherous ['tretʃərəs] adj **1.** [disloyal - ally] traître, perfide ; *fig* [memory] infidèle **2.** [dangerous - water, current, ice] traître.

treachery ['tretʃərɪ] *(pl* **treacheries**) n perfidie *f*, traîtrise *f*.

treacle ['tri:kl] n [UK] [molasses] mélasse *f* ; [golden syrup] mélasse *f* raffinée.

tread [tred] *(pt* **trod** [trɒd], *pp* **trod** or **trodden** ['trɒdn]) ◆ vt **1.** [walk] : *a path had been trodden through the grass* les pas des marcheurs avaient tracé un chemin dans l'herbe / *she trod the streets looking for him* elle a battu le pavé or parcouru la ville à sa recherche **2.** [trample] fouler ▶ **to tread water** nager sur place

3. [stamp] enfoncer, écraser. ◆ vi **1.** [walk] marcher ▶ **to tread carefully** or **warily** *fig* y aller doucement or avec précaution **2.** [step] ▶ **to tread on sthg** a) [accidentally] marcher sur qqch b) [deliberately] marcher (exprès) sur qqch ▶ **to tread on sb's toes** marcher sur les pieds de qqn. ◆ n **1.** [footstep] pas *m* ; [sound of steps] bruit *m* de pas **2.** [of stairs] marche *f*, giron *m* *spec* **3.** [of shoe] semelle *f* ; [of tyre - depth] bande *f* de roulement ; [- pattern] sculptures *fpl*. ❖ **tread down** vt sep tasser (du pied). ❖ **tread in** vt sep [plant] tasser la terre autour de.

treadle ['tredl] ◆ n pédale *f* *(sur un tour ou sur une machine à coudre).* ◆ vi actionner la pédale.

treadmill ['tredmɪl] n [machine] manège *m* ; HIST roue ou manège mus par un homme ou un animal et actionnant une machine.

treas. (written abbr of **treasurer**) trés.

treason ['tri:zn] n trahison *f*.

treasure ['treʒər] ◆ n **1.** [valuables] trésor *m* **2.** [art] joyau *m*, trésor *m* **3.** *inf* [person] trésor *m*, ange *m*. ◆ vt **1.** [friendship, possession] tenir beaucoup à ; [gift] garder précieusement, être très attaché à ; [memory] conserver précieusement, chérir *fml* ; [moment] chérir *fml*.

treasure hunt n chasse *f* au trésor.

treasurer ['treʒərər] n **1.** [of club] trésorier *m*, -ère *f* **2.** [US] [of company] directeur *m* financier.

treasure trove n trésor *m*.

treasury ['treʒərɪ] *(pl* **treasuries**) n **1.** [building] trésorerie *f* **2.** *fig* [of information] mine *f* ; [of poems] recueil *m* **3.** ADMIN ▶ **the Treasury** la Trésorerie ; ≃ le ministère des Finances ▶ **Secretary / Department of the Treasury** [US] ≃ ministre *m* / ministère *m* des Finances.

treasury bill n ≃ bon *m* du Trésor.

Treasury Department pr n [US] ▶ **the Treasury Department** le ministère des finances.

treat [tri:t] ◆ vt **1.** [deal with] traiter **2.** [handle - substance, object] utiliser, se servir de ; [claim, request] traiter **3.** [consider - problem, question] traiter, considérer **4.** MED [patient] soigner ; [illness] traiter **5.** [fruit, timber, crops] traiter **6.** [buy] ▶ **to treat sb to sthg** offrir or payer qqch à qqn. ◆ vi *fml* **1.** [deal with] traiter de **2.** [negotiate] ▶ **to treat with sb** traiter avec qqn. ◆ n **1.** [on special occasion - enjoyment] gâterie *f*, (petit) plaisir *m* ; [- surprise] surprise *f* ; [- present] cadeau *m* ; [- outing] sortie *f* **2.** [pleasure] plaisir *m*. ❖ **a treat** adv phr [UK] *inf* à merveille.

treatable ['tri:təbl] adj soignable.

treatise ['tri:tɪs] n traité *m*.

treatment ['tri:tmənt] n **1.** [of person] traitement *m* **2.** *(U)* MED soins *mpl*, traitement *m* ▶ **a course of treatment** un traitement **3.** [of subject] traitement *m*, façon *f* de traiter **4.** [of crops, timber] traitement *m* **5.** [chemical] produit *m* chimique **6.** CIN traitement *m*.

treaty ['tri:tɪ] *(pl* **treaties**) n **1.** POL traité *m* ▶ **to sign a treaty (with sb)** signer or conclure un traité (avec qqn) **2.** LAW : *they sold the property by private treaty* ils ont vendu la propriété par accord privé.

treble ['trebl] ◆ adj **1.** [triple] triple **2.** MUS [voice] de soprano ; [part] pour voix de soprano. ◆ n **1.** MUS [part, singer] soprano *m* **2.** *(U)* [in hi-fi] aigus *mpl*. ◆ vt & vi tripler. ◆ adv ▶ **to sing treble** chanter dans un registre de soprano.

treble clef n clef *f* de sol.

tree [tri:] n **1.** BOT arbre *m* **2.** [diagram] ▶ **tree (diagram)** représentation *f* en arbre or arborescente, arborescence *f* **3.** [for shoes] embauchoir *m*, forme *f* **4.** [of saddle] arçon *m*.

treehouse ['tri:haus] *(pl* [-hauzɪz]*)* n cabane construite dans un arbre.

tree-hugger [-hʌgəʳ] n *inf & pej* écolo *mf*.

tree-lined adj bordé d'arbres.

treestump ['triːstʌmp] n souche *f*.

tree surgeon n arboriculteur *m*, -trice *f (qui s'occupe de soigner et d'élaguer les arbres)*.

treetop ['triːtɒp] n cime *f* or haut *m* or faîte *m* d'un arbre / **in the treetops** au faîte or au sommet des arbres.

tree trunk n tronc *m* d'arbre.

trek [trek] (*pt & pp* **trekked**, *cont* **trekking**) ◆ n [walk] marche *f*; [hike] randonnée *f* ▸ **to go on a trek** faire une marche or une randonnée; [arduous trip] marche *f* pénible. ◆ vi [walk] avancer avec peine; [hike] faire de la randonnée; [drag o.s.] se traîner.

trekking ['trekɪŋ] n [as holiday activity] randonnée *f*, trekking *m*.

trellis ['trelɪs] ◆ n treillage *m*, treillis *m*. ◆ vt [wood strips] faire un treillage de; [plant] treillager.

tremble ['trembl] ◆ vi **1.** [person - with cold] trembler, frissonner; [-from fear, excitement, rage] trembler, frémir; [hands] trembler **2.** [voice - from emotion] trembler, vibrer; [-from fear] trembler; [-from old age] trembler, chevroter **3.** [bridge, house, ground] trembler; [engine] vibrer **4.** *fig* [be anxious] frémir. ◆ n **1.** [from fear] tremblement *m*; [from excitement, rage] frémissement *m*; [from cold] frissonnement *m* **2.** [in voice] frémissement *m*, frisson *m*.

trembling ['tremblɪŋ] ◆ adj **1.** [body - with cold] frissonnant, grelottant; [-in fear, excitement] frémissant, tremblant; [hands] tremblant **2.** [voice - with emotion] vibrant; [-with fear] tremblant; [-because of old age] chevrotant. ◆ n [from cold] tremblement *m*, frissonnement *m*; [from fear] tremblement *m*, frémissement *m*.

tremendous [trɪ'mendəs] adj **1.** [number, amount] énorme, très grand; [cost, speed] très élevé, vertigineux; [building, arch] énorme; [height] vertigineux, très grand; [undertaking] énorme, monumental; [admiration, disappointment, pride] très grand, extrême; [crash, noise] terrible, épouvantable **2.** [wonderful] sensationnel, formidable.

tremendously [trɪ'mendəslɪ] adv [as intensifier] extrêmement.

tremor ['tremər] n **1.** GEOL secousse *f* (sismique) **2.** [in voice] frémissement *m*, frisson *m*, tremblement *m* **3.** [of fear, thrill] frisson *m*.

tremulous ['tremjʊləs] adj *liter* **1.** [with fear] tremblant; [with excitement, nervousness] frémissant; [handwriting] tremblé **2.** [timid - person, manner] timide, craintif; [-animal] craintif, effarouché; [-smile] timide.

trench [trentʃ] ◆ n [gen & CONSTR & MIL] tranchée *f*; [ditch] fossé *m*. ◆ vt [field] creuser une tranchée or des tranchées dans; MIL retrancher. ◆ vi creuser une tranchée or des tranchées.

trenchant ['trentʃənt] adj incisif, tranchant.

trench coat n trench-coat *m*.

trench warfare n guerre *f* de tranchées.

trend [trend] ◆ n [tendency] tendance *f*; [fashion] mode *f* ▸ **to set a / the trend** a) [style] donner un / le ton b) [fashion] lancer une / la mode. ◆ vi [extend - mountain range] s'étendre; [veer - coastline] s'incliner; [turn - prices, opinion] s'orienter.

trendily ['trendɪlɪ] adv *inf* [dress] branché *(adv)*.

trendsetter ['trend,setər] n [person - in style] personne *f* qui donne le ton; [-in fashion] personne *f* qui lance une mode.

trendy ['trendɪ] (*compar* **trendier**, *superl* **trendiest**, *pl* **trendies**) *inf* ◆ adj [music, appearance] branché; [ideas] à la mode, branché; [clothes] branché; [place, resort] à la mode, branché. ◆ n *pej* branché *m*, -e *f*.

trepidation [,trepɪ'deɪʃn] n **1.** [alarm] inquiétude *f* **2.** [excitement] agitation *f*.

trespass ['trespəs] ◆ vi **1.** LAW s'introduire dans une propriété privée / **'no trespassing'** 'défense d'entrer', propriété privée **2.** *fig* [encroach] : *I don't want to trespass on your time / hospitality* je ne veux pas abuser de votre temps / hospitalité **3.** BIBLE ▸ **to trespass against sb** offenser qqn. ◆ n **1.** (U) LAW entrée *f* non autorisée ▸ **to commit trespass** s'introduire dans une propriété privée **2.** BIBLE péché *m* ▸ **forgive us our trespasses** pardonne-nous nos offenses.

⚠ **Trépasser** means to die, not to trespass.

trespasser ['trespəsər] n **1.** LAW intrus *m*, -e *f (dans une propriété privée)* / **'trespassers will be prosecuted'** 'défense d'entrer sous peine de poursuites' **2.** BIBLE pécheur *m*, -eresse *f*.

trestle ['tresl] n **1.** [for table] tréteau *m* **2.** CONSTR chevalet *m*.

trestle table n table *f* à tréteaux.

triage ['triːɑːʒ] n MED triage *m (des malades, des blessés)*.

trial ['traɪəl] ◆ n **1.** LAW procès *m* ▸ **to be** or **to go on trial for sth, to stand trial for sth** passer en jugement or en justice pour qqch ▸ **to bring sb to trial** faire passer or traduire qqn en justice ▸ **trial by jury** jugement *m* par jury **2.** [test] essai *m* ▸ **to give sth a trial** mettre qqch à l'essai, essayer qqch ▸ **to be on trial** être à l'essai ▸ **by trial and error** par tâtonnements, par essais et erreurs **3.** [hardship, adversity] épreuve *f* ▸ **trials and tribulations** tribulations *fpl*. ◆ adj **1.** [test - flight] d'essai; [-marriage] à l'essai ▸ **on a trial basis** à titre d'essai ▸ **for a trial period** pendant une période d'essai ▸ **trial separation** séparation *f* à l'essai ▸ **trial balloon** *lit & fig* ballon *m* d'essai **2.** US LAW ▸ **trial attorney** or **lawyer** avocat *m* ▸ **trial judge** ≃ juge *m* d'instance. ◆ vi tester. ◆ **trials** pl n [competition] concours *m*; [for selection - match] match *m* de sélection; [-race] épreuve *f* de sélection.

trial run n essai *m* ▸ **to give sth a trial run** essayer qqch, faire un essai avec qqch.

trial-size(d) adj [pack, box] d'essai.

triangle ['traɪæŋgl] n **1.** GEOM triangle *m*; US [set square] équerre *f* **2.** MUS triangle *m*.

triangular [traɪ'æŋgjʊlər] adj triangulaire.

triathlon [traɪ'æθlɒn] n triathlon *m*.

tribal ['traɪbl] adj [games, rites, warfare] tribal; [loyalty] à la tribu.

tribalism ['traɪbəlɪzm] n tribalisme *m*.

tribe [traɪb] n **1.** HIST, SOCIOL & ZOOL tribu *f* **2.** *inf & fig* tribu *f*, smala *f*.

tribespeople ['traɪbz,piːpl] pl n [tribes] tribus *fpl*; [members of particular tribe] membres *mpl* de la tribu / **the Negrito tribespeople** les membres *mpl* de la tribu des Négritos, les Négritos *mpl*.

tribulation [,trɪbjʊ'leɪʃn] n *liter* affliction *f* *liter*, malheur *m*.

tribunal [traɪ'bjuːnl] n [gen & LAW] tribunal *m*.

tribune [traɪ'bjuːn] n **1.** ANTIQ tribun *m* **2.** [platform] tribune *f* **3.** [defender] tribun *m*.

tributary ['trɪbjʊtrɪ] (*pl* **tributaries**) ◆ n **1.** [ruler, state] tributaire *m* **2.** GEOG [stream] affluent *m*. ◆ adj tributaire.

tribute ['trɪbjuːt] n **1.** [mark of respect] hommage *m* ▸ **to pay tribute to sb** rendre hommage à qqn **2.** [indication of efficiency] témoignage *m* **3.** HIST & POL tribut *m*.

tribute band n *groupe qui interprète les chansons d'un groupe célèbre*.

trice [traɪs] n [moment] ▸ **in a trice** en un clin d'œil, en un rien de temps.

triceps ['traɪseps] (pl **triceps** [-sɪz]) n triceps m.

trick [trɪk] ◆ n **1.** [deception, ruse] ruse f, astuce f ; [stratagem] stratagème m **2.** [joke, prank] tour m, farce f, blague f ▸ **to play a trick on sb** faire une farce or jouer un tour à qqn ▸ **"trick or treat"** « des bonbons ou une farce » (phrase rituelle des enfants déguisés qui font la quête la veille de la fête de Halloween) **3.** (usu pl) [silly behaviour] bêtise f **4.** [knack] truc m, astuce f ; [in conjuring, performance] tour m / there, that should do the trick voilà, ça fera l'affaire **5.** [habit] habitude f, manie f ; [particularity] particularité f ; [gift] don m ; [mannerism] manie f, tic m **6.** [in card games] pli m, levée f **7.** US v inf [prostitute's client] micheton m. ◆ adj **1.** [for jokes] d'attrape, faux (fausse), de farces et attrapes **2.** [deceptive -lighting] truqué ▸ **trick photography** truquage m photographique ▸ **trick question** question-piège f **3.** US [weak -knee] faible ; [-leg] boîteux. ◆ vt [deceive] tromper, rouler ; [swindle] escroquer ; [catch out] attraper. ❖ **trick out, trick up** vt sep liter parer.

trickery ['trɪkərɪ] n ruse f, supercherie f.

trickle ['trɪkl] ◆ vi **1.** [liquid] dégoutter, tomber en un (mince) filet **2.** fig : information began to trickle out from behind enemy lines l'information commença à filtrer depuis l'arrière des lignes ennemies / cars began to trickle over the border la circulation a repris progressivement à la frontière. ◆ vt **1.** [liquid] faire couler goutte à goutte **2.** [sand, salt] faire glisser or couler. ◆ n **1.** [liquid] filet m **2.** fig : a trickle of applications began to come in les candidatures commencèrent à arriver au compte-gouttes / there was only a trickle of visitors il n'y avait que quelques rares visiteurs, les visiteurs étaient rares. ❖ **trickle away** vi **1.** [liquid] s'écouler lentement **2.** fig [money, savings] disparaître petit à petit ; [crowd] se disperser petit à petit ; [people] s'en aller progressivement. ❖ **trickle in** vi **1.** [rain] entrer goutte à goutte **2.** [spectators] entrer par petits groupes **3.** fig : offers of help began to trickle in quelques offres d'aide commencèrent à arriver / information on the disaster only trickled in at first au début les informations sur le désastre arrivaient au compte-gouttes.

trickle-down adj ▸ **trickle-down economics** théorie selon laquelle le bien-être des riches finit par profiter aux classes sociales défavorisées.

trickster ['trɪkstər] n [swindler] filou m, escroc m.

tricky ['trɪkɪ] (compar **trickier**, superl **trickiest**) adj **1.** [complex, delicate -job, situation, negotiations] difficile, délicat ; [-problem] épineux, difficile **2.** [sly -person] rusé, fourbe.

tricycle ['traɪsɪkl] ◆ n tricycle m. ◆ vi faire du tricycle.

trident ['traɪdnt] n trident m.

tried [traɪd] pt & pp ⟶ try.

tried-and-tested adj qui a fait ses preuves.

trier ['traɪər] n : he's a real trier il ne se laisse jamais décourager.

Trier ['trɪər] pr n Trèves.

trifle ['traɪfl] n **1.** [unimportant thing, small amount] bagatelle f, broutille f, rien m **2.** CULIN ≃ charlotte f. ❖ **a trifle** adv phr un peu, un tantinet. ❖ **trifle with** vt insep ▸ **to trifle with sb's affections** jouer avec les sentiments de qqn.

trifling ['traɪflɪŋ] adj insignifiant.

trigger ['trɪgər] ◆ n **1.** [in gun] gâchette f, détente f **2.** fig [initiator] déclenchement m. ◆ vt [mechanism, explosion, reaction] déclencher ; [revolution, protest] déclencher, provoquer, soulever. ❖ **trigger off** vt sep = trigger (vt).

trigger-happy adj inf [individual] qui a la gâchette facile ; [country] prêt à déclencher la guerre pour un rien, belliqueux.

trigonometry [ˌtrɪgə'nɒmətrɪ] n trigonométrie f.

trilby ['trɪlbɪ] n UK ▸ **trilby (hat)** (chapeau m en) feutre m.

trilingual [traɪ'lɪŋgwəl] adj trilingue.

trill [trɪl] ◆ n MUS & ORNITH trille m ; LING consonne f roulée. ◆ vi triller, faire des trilles. ◆ vt **1.** [note, word] triller **2.** [consonant] rouler.

trillion ['trɪljən] n UK trillion m ; US billion m.

trilogy ['trɪlədʒɪ] (pl **trilogies**) n trilogie f.

trim [trɪm] (compar **trimmer**, superl **trimmest**, pt & pp **trimmed**, cont **trimming**) ◆ adj **1.** [neat -appearance] net, soigné ; [-person] d'apparence soignée ; [-garden, flowerbed] bien tenu, bien entretenu ; [-ship] en bon ordre **2.** [svelte -figure] svelte, mince **3.** [fit] en bonne santé, en forme. ◆ vt **1.** [cut -roses] tailler, couper ; [-hair, nails] couper ; [-beard] tailler ; [-candle wick] tailler, moucher ; [-paper, photo] rogner **2.** [edge] orner, garnir ; [decorate] : we trimmed the Christmas tree with tinsel on a décoré le sapin de Noël avec des guirlandes **3.** AERON & NAUT [plane, ship] équilibrer ; [sails] régler **4.** [cut back -budget, costs] réduire, limiter. ◆ n **1.** [neat state] ordre m, bon état m ▸ **to be in good trim** être en bon état or ordre **2.** [fitness] forme f ▸ **to get in** or **into trim** se remettre en forme **3.** [cut] coupe f, taille f ▸ **to have a trim** [at hairdresser's] se faire raccourcir les cheveux **4.** (U) [moulding, decoration] moulures fpl ; [on car] aménagement m intérieur, finitions fpl intérieures ; [on dress] garniture f ; US [in shop window] composition f d'étalage **5.** NAUT [of sails] orientation f, réglage m **6.** CIN coupe f. ❖ **trim down** vt sep **1.** [wick] tailler, moucher **2.** [budget, costs] réduire. ❖ **trim off** vt sep [edge] enlever, couper ; [hair] couper ; [branch] tailler ; [jagged edges] ébarber.

trimester [traɪ'mestər] n **1.** US trimestre m **2.** [gen] trois mois mpl.

trimming ['trɪmɪŋ] n **1.** SEW parement m ; [lace, ribbon] passement m **2.** CULIN garniture f, accompagnement m **3.** [accessory] accessoire m. ❖ **trimmings** pl n [scraps] chutes fpl, rognures fpl.

Trinidad and Tobago [-tə'beɪgəʊ] pr n Trinité-et-Tobago / in Trinidad and Tobago à Trinité-et-Tobago.

Trinidadian [ˌtrɪnɪ'dædɪən] ◆ n Trinidadien m, -enne f, habitant m, -e f de la Trinité. ◆ adj trinidadien, de la Trinité.

trinity ['trɪnɪtɪ] (pl **trinities**) n fml & liter trio m, groupe m de trois. ❖ **Trinity** n RELIG **1.** [union] ▸ **the Trinity** la Trinité **2.** [feast] ▸ **Trinity (Sunday)** (la fête de) la Trinité.

trinket ['trɪŋkɪt] n [bauble] bibelot m, babiole f ; [jewel] colifichet m ; [on bracelet] breloque f.

trio ['triːəʊ] (pl **trios**) n **1.** MUS trio m (morceau) **2.** [group] trio m, groupe m de trois ; MUS trio (joueurs).

trip [trɪp] (pt & pp **tripped**, cont **tripping**) ◆ n **1.** [journey] voyage m ▸ **to go on a trip** partir or aller en voyage **2.** [excursion] promenade f, excursion f ; [outing] promenade f, sortie f ▸ **school trip** sortie scolaire **3.** drugs sl trip m ▸ **to have a bad trip** faire un mauvais trip or voyage. ◆ vt **1.** [person -make stumble] faire trébucher ; [-make fall] faire tomber ; [intentionally] faire un croche-pied or un croc-en-jambe à **2.** [switch, alarm] déclencher. ◆ vi **1.** [stumble] trébucher **2.** [step lightly] ▸ **to trip in / out** entrer / sortir en sautillant **3.** drugs sl faire un trip. ❖ **trip over** ◆ vi trébucher, faire un faux pas. ◆ vt insep buter sur or contre, trébucher sur or contre. ❖ **trip up** vt sep **1.** [cause to fall] faire trébucher ; [deliberately] faire un croche-pied à **2.** [trap] désarçonner. ◆ vi **1.** [fall] trébucher **2.** [make a mistake] gaffer, faire une gaffe.

tripartite [ˌtraɪ'pɑːtaɪt] adj [division, agreement] tripartite, triparti.

tripe [traɪp] n *(U)* **1.** CULIN tripes *fpl* **2.** 🇬🇧 *inf* [nonsense] foutaises *fpl*, bêtises *fpl*.

triple ['trɪpl] ◆ adj **1.** [in three parts] triple **2.** [treble] triple. ◆ n triple *m*. ◆ vi & vt tripler.

triple jump n triple saut *m*.

triplet ['trɪplɪt] n **1.** [child] triplé *m*, -e *f* **2.** MUS triolet *m* ; LITER tercet *m*.

triplicate ◆ adj ['trɪplɪkət] en trois exemplaires, en triple exemplaire. ◆ n ['trɪplɪkət] **1.** [document] ▶ **in triplicate** en trois exemplaires, en triple exemplaire **2.** [third copy] triplicata *m*. ◆ vt ['trɪplɪkeɪt] multiplier par trois, tripler.

tripod ['traɪpɒd] n trépied *m*.

Tripoli ['trɪpəlɪ] pr n Tripoli.

tripper ['trɪpər] n 🇬🇧 [on day trip] excursionniste *mf* ; [on holiday] vacancier *m*, -ère *f*.

trippy ['trɪpɪ] adj *inf* psychédélique.

trip switch n interrupteur *m*.

tripwire ['trɪpwaɪər] n fil *m* de détente.

trite [traɪt] adj [theme, picture] banal.

triumph ['traɪəmf] ◆ n **1.** [jubilation] (sentiment *m* de) triomphe *m* **2.** [victory] victoire *f*, triomphe *m* ; [success] triomphe *m*, (grande) réussite *f* **3.** [in ancient Rome] triomphe *m*. ◆ vi triompher.

triumphal [traɪ'ʌmfl] adj triomphal.

triumphalist [traɪ'ʌmfəlɪst] adj triomphaliste.

triumphant [traɪ'ʌmfənt] adj [team] victorieux, triomphant ; [return] triomphal ; [cheer, smile] de triomphe, triomphant ; [success] triomphal.

triumphantly [traɪ'ʌmfəntlɪ] adv [march] en triomphe, triomphalement ; [cheer, smile] triomphalement ; [announce] d'un ton triomphant, triomphalement ; [look] d'un air triomphant, triomphalement.

triumvirate [traɪ'ʌmvɪrət] n triumvirat *m*.

trivet ['trɪvɪt] n [when cooking] trépied *m*, chevrette *f* ; [for table] dessous-de-plat *m inv*.

trivia ['trɪvɪə] pl n [trifles] bagatelles *fpl*, futilités *fpl* ; [details] détails *mpl*.

trivial ['trɪvɪəl] adj **1.** [insignificant - sum, reason] insignifiant, dérisoire **2.** [pointless - discussion, question] sans intérêt, futile **3.** [banal - story] banal.

⚠️ The French word **trivial** usually means vulgar or ordinary, not trivial.

triviality [ˌtrɪvɪ'ælətɪ] *(pl* **trivialities)** n **1.** [of sum] insignifiance *f*, caractère *m* insignifiant ; [of discussion] insignifiance *f*, caractère *m* oiseux ; [of film] banalité *f* **2.** [trifle] futilité *f*, bagatelle *f*.

trivialize, trivialise ['trɪvɪəlaɪz] vt [make insignificant] banaliser, dévaloriser.

trod [trɒd] pt & pp ⟶ **tread**.

trodden ['trɒdn] pp ⟶ **tread**.

Trojan ['trəʊdʒən] ◆ adj troyen. ◆ n Troyen *m*, -enne *f* ▶ **to work like a Trojan** travailler comme un forçat.

troll [trəʊl] ◆ n **1.** [goblin, blogger] troll *m* **2.** *v inf* [ugly woman] cageot *m*. ◆ vi **1.** FISHING pêcher à la traîne **2.** 🇬🇧 *inf* [stroll] se balader.

trolley ['trɒlɪ] *(pl* **trolleys)** n **1.** [handcart] chariot *m* ; [two-wheeled] diable *m* ; [for child] poussette *f* ; [in supermarket] chariot *m*, Caddie® *m* ; [in restaurant] chariot *m* **2.** [on rails - in mine] wagonnet *m*, benne *f* **3.** [for tram] trolley *m* *(électrique)* **4.** 🇺🇸 [tram] tramway *m*, tram *m*.

trolleybus ['trɒlɪbʌs] n trolleybus *m*, trolley *m*.

trolley case n 🇬🇧 valise *f* à roulettes.

trollop ['trɒləp] n *dated & pej* [prostitute] putain *f* ; [slut] souillon *f*.

trombone [trɒm'bəʊn] n trombone *m* *(instrument)*.

troop [tru:p] ◆ n [band - of schoolchildren] bande *f*, groupe *m* ; [- of scouts] troupe *f* ; [- of animals] troupe *f* ; MIL [of cavalry, artillery] escadron *m*. ◆ vi ▶ **to troop by** or **past** passer en troupe ▶ **to troop in** / **out** entrer / sortir en troupe. ◆ vt 🇬🇧 MIL ▶ **to troop the colour** faire le salut au drapeau. ◆ **troops** pl n [gen & MIL] troupes *fpl*.

troop carrier n [ship] transport *m* de troupes ; [plane] avion *m* de transport militaire.

trooper ['tru:pər] n **1.** [soldier] soldat *m* de cavalerie **2.** 🇺🇸 & 🇦🇺 [mounted policeman] membre *m* de la police montée ▶ **(state) trooper** ≃ gendarme *m* **3.** 🇬🇧 MIL [ship] transport *m* de troupes.

troopship ['tru:pʃɪp] n navire *m* de transport.

trophy ['trəʊfɪ] *(pl* **trophies)** n trophée *m*.

tropic ['trɒpɪk] n tropique *m* ▶ **the Tropic of Capricorn** / **Cancer** le tropique du Capricorne / du Cancer. ◆ **tropics** pl n ▶ **the tropics** les tropiques / **in the tropics** sous les tropiques.

tropical ['trɒpɪkl] adj [region] des tropiques, tropical ; [weather, forest, medicine] tropical.

trot [trɒt] *(pt & pp* **trotted**, *cont* **trotting)** ◆ n **1.** [of horse] trot *m* ▶ **to go at a trot** aller au trot, trotter ; [of person] : *he went off at a trot* il est parti au pas de course **2.** [ride] promenade *f* à cheval ; *inf* [run] petite course *f*. ◆ vi **1.** [horse, rider] trotter **2.** [on foot] ▶ **to trot in** / **out** / **past** entrer / sortir / passer en courant. ◆ vt [horse] faire trotter. ◆ **trot along** vi **1.** [horse] aller au trot **2.** *inf* [person] partir. ◆ **trot away** vi **1.** [horse] partir au trot **2.** *inf* [person] partir au pas de course. ◆ **trot out** vt sep 🇬🇧 *inf* [excuse, information] débiter *pej* ; [story, list] débiter *pej*, réciter *pej*. ◆ **trots** pl n 🇬🇧 *inf* diarrhée *f* ▶ **to have the trots** avoir la courante.

Trot [trɒt] n *inf & pej* abbr of Trotskyist.

Trotskyism ['trɒtskɪɪzm] n trotskisme *m*.

trotter ['trɒtər] n **1.** [horse] trotteur *m*, -euse *f* **2.** CULIN ▶ **pig's** / **sheep's trotters** pieds *mpl* de porc / de mouton.

trouble ['trʌbl] ◆ n **1.** *(U)* [conflict - esp with authority] ennuis *mpl*, problèmes *mpl* ; [discord] discorde *f* ▶ **to be in trouble** avoir des ennuis / *I've never been in trouble with the police* je n'ai jamais eu d'ennuis or d'histoires avec la police ▶ **to get into trouble** s'attirer des ennuis, se faire attraper / *he got into trouble for stealing apples* il s'est fait attraper pour avoir volé des pommes / *he got his friends into trouble* il a causé des ennuis à ses amis ▶ **to get sb out of trouble** tirer qqn d'affaire / *he's just looking* or *asking for trouble* il cherche les ennuis / *she caused a lot of trouble between them* elle a semé la discorde entre eux **2.** *(U)* [difficulties, problems] difficultés *fpl*, ennuis *mpl*, mal *m* ▶ **to make** or **to create trouble for sb** causer des ennuis à qqn / *he's given his parents a lot of trouble* **a)** [hard time] il a donné du fil à retordre à ses parents **b)** [worry] il a donné beaucoup de soucis à ses parents ▶ **to have trouble (in) doing sthg** avoir du mal or des difficultés à faire qqch ▶ **to be in** / **to get into trouble** [climber, swimmer, business] être / se trouver en difficulté ▶ **to get a girl into trouble** 🇬🇧 *euph* mettre une fille dans une position intéressante **3.** [inconvenience, bother] mal *m*, peine *f* ▶ **to go to a lot of trouble to do** or **doing sthg** se donner beaucoup de mal or de peine pour faire qqch ▶ **to put sb to trouble** donner du mal à qqn, déranger qqn / *he didn't even take the trouble to read the instructions* il ne s'est même pas donné or il n'a même pas pris la peine de lire les instructions **4.** [drawback] problème *m*, défaut *m* / *the trouble with him is that he's too proud* le problème avec lui, c'est qu'il est trop fier / *that's the trouble* c'est ça l'ennui **5.** *(U)* [mechanical failure] ennuis *mpl*, problèmes *mpl* **6.** [worry, woe] ennui *m*, souci *m*, problème *m* / *money troubles* ennuis d'argent **7.** *(U)* [friction] troubles *mpl*, conflits *mpl* ; [disorder, disturbance] troubles *mpl*, désordres *mpl* **8.** *(U)* MED ennuis *mpl*, problèmes *mpl* / *I have kidney* / *back trouble* j'ai des ennuis rénaux / des problèmes de dos. ◆ vt **1.** [worry] inquiéter ; [upset] troubler **2.** [cause pain to] gêner / *his back is troubling him* il a des problèmes de dos **3.** [bother, disturb] déranger / *I won't trouble you with the details just now* je vous ferai grâce des or épargnerai les détails pour l'instant / *don't trouble yourself!* a) *lit* ne vous dérangez or tracassez pas ! b) *iro* ne vous dérangez surtout pas ! **4.** [in polite phrases] déranger / *may I trouble you for a light* / *the salt?* puis-je vous demander du feu / le sel ? **5.** *liter* [disturb -water] troubler. ◆ vi **1.** [bother] se déranger **2.** [worry] se faire du souci, s'en faire. ◆◆ **Troubles** pl n HIST ▶ **the Troubles** *le conflit politique en Irlande du Nord.*

troubled ['trʌbld] adj **1.** [worried -mind, look] inquiet (inquiète), préoccupé **2.** [disturbed -sleep, night, breathing] agité ; [-water] troublé ; [turbulent -marriage, life] agité, mouvementé.

trouble-free adj [journey, equipment] sans problème, sans histoires ; [period of time, visit] sans histoires ; [life] sans soucis, sans histoires ; [industry] sans grèves.

troublemaker ['trʌbl,meɪkəʳ] n provocateur *m*, -trice *f*.

troubleshoot ['trʌbl,ʃuːt] vi **1.** [overseer, envoy] régler un problème **2.** [mechanic] localiser une panne.

troubleshooter ['trʌbl,ʃuːtəʳ] n **1.** [in crisis] expert *m* (*appelé en cas de crise*) ; INDUST & POL [in conflict] médiateur *m*, -trice *f* **2.** [mechanic] dépanneur *m*, -euse *f*.

troubleshooting ['trʌbl,ʃuːtɪŋ] n **1.** [in crisis] médiation *f* **2.** [in mechanism] dépannage *m*.

troublesome ['trʌblsəm] adj **1.** [annoying -person, cough] gênant, pénible **2.** [difficult -situation] difficile ; [-request] gênant, embarrassant ; [-job] difficile, pénible.

trouble spot n point *m* chaud, zone *f* de conflit.

troubling ['trʌblɪŋ] adj [news, etc.] inquiétant.

trough [trɒf] n **1.** [for animals -drinking] abreuvoir *m* ; [-eating] auge *f* **2.** [depression -in land] dépression *f* ; [-between waves] creux *m* **3.** METEOR dépression *f*, zone *f* dépressionnaire **4.** [on graph, in cycle] creux *m* ; FIN creux *m*, dépression *f* **5.** [gutter] gouttière *f* ; [channel] chenal *m*.

trounce [traʊns] vt [defeat] écraser, battre à plate couture or plates coutures.

troupe [truːp] n THEAT troupe *f*.

trouser press n ⓤ presse *f* à pantalons.

trousers ['traʊzəz] pl n ⓤ pantalon *m* ▶ **(a pair of) trousers** un pantalon.

trouser suit n ⓤ tailleur-pantalon *m*.

trousseau ['truːsəʊ] (*pl* **trousseaus** *or* **trousseaux** [-əʊz]) n trousseau *m* (*de jeune mariée*).

trout [traʊt] (*pl* **trout** *or* **trouts**) n truite *f*.

trove [trəʊv] ⟶ **treasure trove.**

trowel ['traʊəl] n **1.** [for garden] déplantoir *m* ; [for cement, plaster] truelle *f*.

truancy ['truːənsɪ] n absentéisme *m* (scolaire).

truant ['truːənt] ◆ n élève *mf* absentéiste ▶ **to play truant** ⓤ faire l'école buissonnière. ◆ vi ADMIN manquer les cours.

⚠️ **Un truand** is a gangster, not a truant.

truce [truːs] n trêve *f* ▶ **to call a truce** a) *lit* conclure or établir une trêve b) *fig* faire la paix.

truck [trʌk] ◆ n **1.** ⓤ [lorry] camion *m* **2.** ⓤ [open lorry] camion *m* à plate-forme ; [van] camionnette *f* **3.** ⓤ RAIL wagon *m* ouvert, truck *m* **4.** *(U)* [dealings] ▶ **to have no truck with sb** / **sthg** refuser d'avoir quoi que ce soit à

voir avec qqn / qqch **5.** *(U)* ⓤ [produce] produits *mpl* maraîchers. ◆ vt ⓤ [goods, animals] camionner, transporter par camion. ◆ vi ⓤ aller or rouler en camion.

truck driver n ⓤ camionneur *m*, (chauffeur *m*) routier *m*.

trucker ['trʌkəʳ] n ⓤ **1.** [driver] (chauffeur *m*) routier *m*, camionneur *m* **2.** AGR maraîcher *m*, -ère *f*.

truck farm n ⓤ jardin *m* maraîcher.

trucking ['trʌkɪŋ] n ⓤ camionnage *m*, transport *m* par camion.

truckload ['trʌkləʊd] n **1.** ⓤ [lorryload] cargaison *f* (*d'un camion*) / *a truckload of soldiers* un camion de soldats **2.** ⓤ *inf & fig* ▶ **a truckload of** un tas de.

truck stop n ⓤ (relais *m*) routier *m*.

truculent ['trʌkjʊlənt] adj belliqueux, agressif.

⚠️ The French word **truculent** means colourful, **not** truculent.

trudge [trʌdʒ] ◆ vi marcher péniblement or en traînant les pieds. ◆ vt : *to trudge the streets* se traîner de rue en rue. ◆ n marche *f* pénible.

true [truː] ◆ adj **1.** [factual -statement, story] vrai, véridique ; [-account, description] exact, véridique ▶ **to come true** a) [dream] se réaliser b) [prophecy] se réaliser, se vérifier ▶ **too true!** c'est vrai ce que vous dites !, ah oui alors ! **2.** [precise, exact -measurement] exact, juste ; [MUS -note] juste ; [-copy] conforme **3.** [genuine -friendship, feelings] vrai, véritable, authentique ; [-friend, love] vrai, véritable ; [real, actual -nature, motive] réel, véritable **4.** [faithful -lover] fidèle ; [-portrait] fidèle, exact ▶ **to be true to sb** être fidèle à or loyal envers qqn / *to be true to one's ideals* être fidèle à ses idéaux. ◆ adv **1.** [aim, shoot, sing] juste ▶ **to ring true** cela sonne faux **2.** *liter* [truly] : *tell me true* dites-moi la vérité. ◆◆ **out of true** adj phr ⓤ [wall] hors d'aplomb ; [beam] tordu ; [wheel] voilé ; [axle] faussé ; [painting] de travers. ◆◆ **true up** vt sep aligner, ajuster.

true-life adj vrai, vécu.

truffle ['trʌfl] n truffe *f* ▶ **truffle hound** chien *m* truffier.

truism ['truːɪzm] n truisme *m*, lapalissade *f*.

truly ['truːlɪ] adv **1.** *fml* [really] vraiment, réellement **2.** [as intensifier] vraiment, absolument **3.** [in letterwriting] : *yours truly, Kathryn Schmidt* ⓤ je vous prie d'agréer, Monsieur or Madame, l'expression de mes sentiments respectueux, Kathryn Schmidt ; [myself] ▶ **yours truly** *inf & hum* votre humble serviteur.

trump [trʌmp] ◆ n [in cards] atout *m* ; *fig* atout *m*, carte *f* maîtresse / *what's trumps?* quel est l'atout ? / *diamonds are trumps* (c'est) atout carreau. ◆ vt **1.** [card] couper, jouer atout sur ; [trick] remporter avec un atout **2.** [outdo -remark, action] renchérir sur.

trump card n *lit & fig* atout *m*.

trumped-up [trʌmpt-] adj [story, charge] inventé de toutes pièces.

trumpet ['trʌmpɪt] ◆ n **1.** [instrument] trompette *f* **2.** [trumpeter] trompettiste *mf* ; [in military band] trompette *f* **3.** [of elephant] barrissement *m* **4.** [hearing aid] ▶ **(ear) trumpet** cornet *m* acoustique. ◆ vi [elephant] barrir. ◆ vt [secret, news] claironner.

trumpeter ['trʌmpɪtəʳ] n trompettiste *mf* ; [in orchestra] trompette *m*.

truncate [trʌŋ'keɪt] vt [gen & COMPUT] tronquer.

truncated [trʌŋ'keɪtɪd] adj tronqué.

truncheon ['trʌntʃən] n matraque *f*.

trundle ['trʌndl] ◆ vi [heavy equipment, wheelbarrow] avancer or rouler lentement ; [person] aller or avancer tranquillement. ◆ vt [push] pousser (avec effort) ; [pull] traîner (avec effort) ; [wheel] faire rouler bruyamment.

trunk [trʌŋk] n **1.** [of tree, body] tronc *m* **2.** [of elephant] trompe *f* **3.** [case] malle *f* ; [metal] cantine *f* **4.** US AUTO coffre *m*. ❖ **trunks** pl n [underwear] slip *m* (d'homme) ▸ **a pair of trunks a)** [underwear] un slip **b)** [for swimming] un slip de bain.

trunk call n UK dated appel *m* interurbain.

trunk road n UK (route *f*) nationale *f*.

truss [trʌs] ◆ vt **1.** [prisoner, animal] ligoter ; [poultry] trousser ; [hay] botteler **2.** CONSTR armer, renforcer. ◆ n **1.** [of hay] botte *f* ; [of fruit] grappe *f* **2.** CONSTR ferme *f* **3.** MED bandage *m* herniaire. ❖ **truss up** vt sep [prisoner] ligoter ; [poultry] trousser.

trust [trʌst] ◆ vt **1.** [have confidence in - person] faire confiance à, avoir confiance en ; [- method, feelings, intuition] faire confiance à, se fier à ; [- judgment, memory] se fier à ▸ **to trust sb to do sthg** faire confiance à qqn or compter sur qqn pour faire qqch **2.** [entrust] confier **3.** *fml* [suppose] supposer ; [hope] espérer. ◆ vi **1.** [believe] ▸ **to trust in God** croire en Dieu **2.** [have confidence] ▸ **to trust to luck** s'en remettre à la chance. ◆ n **1.** [confidence, faith] confiance *f*, foi *f* ▸ **to place one's trust in sb / sthg** avoir confiance en qqn / qqch, se fier à qqn / qqch ▸ **to take sthg on trust** prendre ou accepter qqch en toute confiance or les yeux fermés **2.** [responsibility] responsabilité *f* **3.** [care] charge *f* ▸ **to give** or **to place sthg into sb's trust** confier qqch aux soins de qqn **4.** (C) FIN & LAW [group of trustees] administrateurs *mpl* ; [investment] fidéicommis *m* **5.** [cartel] trust *m*.

trust company n société *f* fiduciaire.

trusted ['trʌstɪd] adj [method] éprouvé ; [figures] fiable.

trusted third party n COMPUT [for Internet transactions] tierce partie *f* de confiance.

trustee [trʌs'tiː] n **1.** FIN & LAW fidéicommissaire *m* ; [for minor] curateur *m* ; [in bankruptcy] syndic *m* **2.** ADMIN administrateur *m*, -trice *f* ▸ **board of trustees** conseil *m* d'administration.

trusteeship [ˌtrʌs'tiːʃɪp] n **1.** FIN & LAW fidéicommis *m* ; [for minor] curatelle *f* **2.** ADMIN poste *m* d'administrateur.

trust fund n fonds *m* en fidéicommis.

trust hospital n hôpital britannique ayant opté pour l'autogestion mais qui reçoit toujours son budget de l'État.

trusting ['trʌstɪŋ] adj [nature, person] qui a confiance ; [look] confiant.

trustingly ['trʌstɪŋlɪ] adv en toute confiance.

trustworthiness ['trʌst,wɜːðɪnɪs] n **1.** [reliability - of person] loyauté *f*, sérieux *m* ; [- of information, source] fiabilité *f* **2.** [accuracy - of report, figures] fiabilité *f*, justesse *f* **3.** [honesty] honnêteté *f*.

trustworthy ['trʌst,wɜːðɪ] adj **1.** [reliable - person] sur qui on peut compter, à qui on peut faire confiance ; [- information, source] sûr, fiable **2.** [accurate - report, figures] fidèle, précis **3.** [honest] honnête.

trusty ['trʌstɪ] (*compar* **trustier**, *superl* **trustiest**, *pl* **trusties**) ◆ adj *arch & hum* [steed, sword] loyal, fidèle. ◆ n [prisoner] détenu bénéficiant d'un régime de faveur.

truth [truːθ] (*pl* **truths** [truːðz]) n **1.** [true facts] vérité *f* ▸ **to tell the truth** dire la vérité ▸ **to tell (you) the truth** à vrai dire, à dire vrai **2.** [fact, piece of information] vérité *f*. ❖ **in truth** adv phr en vérité.

truth drug n sérum *m* de vérité.

truthful ['truːθfʊl] adj [person] qui dit la vérité ; [character] honnête ; [article, statement] fidèle à la réalité, vrai ; [story] véridique, vrai ; [portrait] fidèle.

truthfully ['truːθfʊlɪ] adv [answer, speak] honnêtement, sans mentir ; [sincerely] sincèrement, vraiment.

truthfulness ['truːθfʊlnɪs] n [of person] honnêteté *f* ; [of portrait] fidélité *f* ; [of story, statement] véracité *f*.

try [traɪ] (*pt & pp* **tried**, *pl* **tries**) ◆ vt **1.** [attempt] essayer ▸ **to try to do** or **doing sthg** essayer or tâcher de faire qqch, chercher à faire qqch ▸ **to try one's best** or **hardest** faire de son mieux ▸ *just you try it!* [as threat] essaie un peu pour voir ! **2.** [test - method, approach, car] essayer / *the method has been tried and tested* la méthode a fait ses preuves ▸ **(just) try me!** *inf* essaie toujours ! ▸ **to try one's strength against sb** se mesurer à qqn ▸ **to try one's luck (at sthg)** tenter sa chance (à qqch) **3.** [sample - recipe, wine] essayer, goûter à ; [- clothes] essayer / *try this for size* **a)** *lit* [garment] essayez ceci pour voir la taille **b)** [shoe] essayez ceci pour voir la pointure **c)** *fig* essayez ceci pour voir si ça va **4.** [attempt to open - door, window] essayer **5.** TELEC essayer / *try the number again* refaites le numéro / *try him later* *inf* essayez de le rappeler plus tard **6.** [visit] essayer / *I've tried six shops already* j'ai déjà essayé six magasins **7.** LAW [person, case] juger / *he was tried for murder* il a été jugé pour meurtre **8.** [tax, strain - patience] éprouver, mettre à l'épreuve. ◆ vi essayer ▸ **to try and do sthg** essayer de faire qqch ▸ *just (you) try!* essaie donc un peu ! ▸ **to try for sthg** essayer d'obtenir qqch. ◆ n **1.** [attempt] essai *m*, tentative *f* ▸ **to have a try at sthg / at doing sthg** essayer qqch / de faire qqch **2.** [test, turn] essai *m* ▸ **to give sthg a try** essayer qqch **3.** SPORT [in rugby] essai *m* ▸ **to score a try** marquer un essai. ❖ **try on** vt sep **1.** [garment] essayer / *try it on for size* essayez-le pour voir la taille **2.** PHR **to try it on with sb a)** UK *inf* essayer de voir jusqu'où on peut pousser qqn **b)** [flirt] essayer de flirter avec qqn. ❖ **try out** ◆ vt sep [new car, bicycle] essayer, faire un essai avec, faire l'essai de ; [method, chemical, recipe] essayer ; [employee] mettre à l'essai. ◆ vi US ▸ **to try out for a team** faire un essai pour se faire engager dans une équipe.

trying ['traɪɪŋ] adj [experience] pénible, douloureux, éprouvant ; [journey, job] ennuyeux, pénible ; [person] fatigant, pénible.

try-out n essai *m*.

tsar [zɑːr] n tsar *m*, tzar *m*, czar *m*.

T-shirt n tee-shirt *m*, t-shirt *m*.

tsp. (written abbr of **teaspoon**) cc.

T-square n équerre *f* en T, té *m*, T *m* (règle).

TSS (abbr of **toxic shock syndrome**) n SCT *m*.

tsunami [tsuː'nɑːmɪ] n tsunami *m*.

TT pr n (abbr of **Tourist Trophy**) ▸ **TT races** courses de moto sur l'île de Man.

TTFN MESSAGING written abbr of ta ta for now.

TTP (abbr of **trusted third party**) n COMPUT [for Internet transactions] TPC *f*.

TTYL, TTYL8R (written abbr of **talk to you later**) MESSAGING @+.

Tuareg ['twɑːreg] (*pl* **Tuareg** or **Tuaregs**) ◆ n **1.** [person] Touareg *m*, -ègue *f* **2.** LING touareg *m*. ◆ adj touareg.

tub [tʌb] n **1.** [container - for liquid] cuve *f*, bac *m* ; [- for flowers] bac *m* ; [- for washing clothes] baquet *m* ; [- in washing machine] cuve *f* **2.** [contents - of washing powder] baril *m* ; [- of wine, beer] tonneau *m* ; [- of ice cream, yoghurt] pot *m* **3.** *inf* [bath] : *he's in the tub* il prend un bain **4.** *inf* [boat] rafiot *m*.

tuba ['tjuːbə] n tuba *m*.

tubby ['tʌbɪ] (*compar* **tubbier**, *superl* **tubbiest**) adj *inf* dodu, rondelet.

tube [tjuːb] ◆ n **1.** [pipe] tube *m* **2.** ANAT tube *m*, canal *m* **3.** [of glue, toothpaste] tube *m* **4.** [in tyre] ▸ **(inner) tube** chambre *f* à air **5.** TV : *what's on the tube tonight?*

inf qu'est-ce qu'il y a à la télé ce soir ? ▸ **(cathode-ray) tube** tube *m* (cathodique) **6.** 🇬🇧 [underground] ▸ **the tube** le métro londonien ▸ **to go by tube, to take the tube** aller en métro, prendre le métro. ◆ comp [map, station] de métro.

tubeless ['tjuːblɪs] adj 🇬🇧 ▸ **tubeless tyre** pneu *m* sans chambre (à air).

tuber ['tjuːbər] n ANAT & BOT tubercule *m*.

tubercular [tjuːˈbɜːkjʊlər] adj tuberculeux.

tuberculosis [tjuːˌbɜːkjʊˈləʊsɪs] n (U) tuberculose *f*.

tubing ['tjuːbɪŋ] n (U) tubes *mpl*, tuyaux *mpl*.

tubular ['tjuːbjʊlər] adj [furniture, shape] tubulaire ▸ **tubular bells** MUS carillon *m* d'orchestre.

TUC (abbr of **Trades Union Congress**) pr n *la Confédération des syndicats britanniques.*

tuck [tʌk] ◆ vt **1.** [shirt] rentrer ; [sheet] rentrer, border **2.** [put] mettre ; [slip] glisser. ◆ n **1.** SEW rempli *m* **2.** [in diving] plongeon *m* groupé **3.** 🇬🇧 *inf* SCH boustifaille *f*. ◈ **tuck away** vt sep **1.** [hide] cacher ; [put] mettre, ranger **2.** *inf* [food] s'enfiler, avaler. ◈ **tuck in** ◆ vt sep **1.** [shirt, stomach] rentrer **2.** [child] border. ◆ vi *inf* [eat] : *we tucked in to a lovely meal* nous avons attaqué un excellent repas. ◈ **tuck up** vt sep **1.** [person] border (dans son lit) **2.** [skirt, sleeves] remonter ; [hair] rentrer **3.** [legs] replier, rentrer.

tuck shop n 🇬🇧 SCH *petite boutique où les écoliers achètent bonbons, gâteaux, etc.*

Tudor ['tjuːdər] ◆ adj [family, period] des Tudors ; [king, architecture] Tudor *(inv)*. ◆ n Tudor *m inv*, membre *m* de la famille des Tudors.

Tue., Tues. (written abbr of **Tuesday**) mar.

Tuesday ['tjuːzdeɪ] n mardi *m*. **See also Friday.**

tuft [tʌft] n **1.** [of hair, grass] touffe *f* **2.** ORNITH ▸ **tuft (of feathers)** huppe *f*, aigrette *f*.

tug [tʌg] (*pt & pp* **tugged**, *cont* **tugging**) ◆ n **1.** [pull] petit coup *m* **2.** NAUT remorqueur *m*. ◆ vt **1.** [handle, sleeve] tirer sur ; [load] tirer, traîner **2.** NAUT remorquer. ◆ vi ▸ **to tug at** or **on sthg** tirer sur qqch.

tugboat ['tʌgbəʊt] n remorqueur *m*.

tug-of-love n 🇬🇧 *inf conflit entre des parents en instance de divorce pour avoir la garde d'un enfant.*

tug-of-war n SPORT tir *m* à la corde ; *fig* lutte *f* acharnée.

tuition [tjuːˈɪʃn] n (U) **1.** 🇬🇧 [instruction] cours *mpl* **2.** UNIV ▸ **tuition (fees)** frais *mpl* de scolarité.

TUL MESSAGING **written abbr of tell you later.**

tulip ['tjuːlɪp] n tulipe *f*.

tulle [tjuːl] n tulle *m*.

tumble ['tʌmbl] ◆ vi **1.** [fall - person] faire une chute, dégringoler ; [- ball, objects] dégringoler **2.** [collapse - prices] dégringoler, s'effondrer **3.** [rush] se précipiter **4.** [perform somersaults] faire des sauts périlleux. ◆ n [fall] chute *f*, culbute *f*, roulé-boulé *m* ; [somersault] culbute *f*, cabrioles *fpl*. ◈ **tumble about** vi [children] gambader, batifoler ; [acrobat] faire des cabrioles ; [swimmer] s'ébattre ; [water] clapoter. ◈ **tumble down** vi [person] faire une culbute, dégringoler ; [pile] dégringoler ; [wall, building] s'effondrer. ◈ **tumble out** vi **1.** [person - from tree, loft] faire une culbute, dégringoler ; [- from bus, car] se jeter, sauter ; [possessions, contents] tomber (en vrac) **2.** [news, confession] s'échapper. ◈ **tumble over** vi [person] culbuter, faire une culbute ; [pile, vase] se renverser. ◈ **tumble to** vt insep 🇬🇧 *inf* [fact, secret, joke] piger, saisir, comprendre.

tumbledown ['tʌmbldaʊn] adj en ruines, délabré.

tumble-drier n sèche-linge *m inv*.

tumble-dry vt faire sécher dans le sèche-linge.

tumbler ['tʌmblər] n **1.** [glass] verre *m* (droit) ; [beaker] gobelet *m*, timbale *f* **2.** [acrobat] acrobate *mf* **3.** [in lock] gorge *f* (de serrure) **4.** = **tumble-drier 5.** [pigeon] pigeon *m* culbutant.

tumescent [ˌtjuːˈmesnt] adj tumescent.

tummy ['tʌmɪ] *inf* ◆ n ventre *m*. ◆ comp ▸ **to have (a) tummy ache** avoir mal au ventre ▸ **to have a tummy bug** avoir une gastro ▸ **tummy button** nombril *m* ▸ **tummy tuck** plastie *f* abdominale.

tumour 🇬🇧, **tumor** 🇺🇸 ['tjuːmər] n tumeur *f*.

tumult ['tjuːmʌlt] n **1.** [noise] tumulte *m* ; [agitation] tumulte *m*, agitation *f* **2.** *fml & liter* [of feelings] émoi *m*.

tumultuous ['tjuːmʌltjʊəs] adj [crowd, noise] tumultueux ; [applause] frénétique ; [period] tumultueux, agité.

tuna [🇬🇧 'tjuːnə 🇺🇸 'tuːnə] n ▸ **tuna (fish)** thon *m*.

tundra ['tʌndrə] n toundra *f*.

tune [tjuːn] ◆ n [melody] air *m*, mélodie *f*. ◆ vt **1.** [musical instrument] accorder **2.** [regulate - engine, machine] mettre au point, régler **3.** [radio, television] régler / *stay tuned!* restez à l'écoute ! **4.** [adapt] : *politicians always tune their remarks to suit their audience* les hommes politiques se mettent toujours au diapason de leur auditoire, les hommes politiques adaptent toujours leurs commentaires à leur auditoire. ◈ **in tune** ◆ adj phr [instrument] accordé, juste ; [singer] qui chante juste / *the violins are not in tune with the piano* les violons ne sont pas accordés avec le piano ▸ **to be in tune with** *fig* être en accord avec. ◆ adv phr juste. ◈ **out of tune** ◆ adj phr [instrument] faux (fausse), désaccordé ; [singer] qui chante faux ▸ **to be out of tune with** *fig* être en désaccord avec. ◆ adv phr faux. ◈ **to the tune of** prep phr : *they were given grants to the tune of £100,000* on leur a accordé des subventions qui s'élevaient à 100 000 livres. ◈ **tune in** ◆ vi RADIO & TV se mettre à l'écoute. ◆ vt sep **1.** [radio, television] régler sur **2.** *inf & fig* ▸ **to be tuned in to sthg** être branché sur qqch. ◈ **tune out** 🇺🇸 ◆ vi [refuse to listen] faire la sourde oreille ; [stop listening] décrocher. ◆ vt sep [remark] ignorer. ◈ **tune up** ◆ vi MUS [player] accorder son instrument ; [orchestra] accorder ses instruments. ◆ vt sep **1.** MUS accorder **2.** AUTO mettre au point, régler.

tuned-in [tjuːnd-] adj *inf* branché.

tuneful ['tjuːnfʊl] adj [song, voice] mélodieux ; [singer] à la voix mélodieuse.

tunefully ['tjuːnfʊlɪ] adv mélodieusement.

tuneless ['tjuːnlɪs] adj peu mélodieux, discordant.

tunelessly ['tjuːnlɪslɪ] adv [with no tune] de manière peu mélodieuse ; [out of tune] faux *(adv)*.

tuner ['tjuːnər] n **1.** [of piano] accordeur *m* **2.** RADIO & TV tuner *m*, syntoniseur *m spec.*

tuner amplifier n ampli-tuner *m*.

tungsten ['tʌŋstən] n tungstène *m*.

tunic ['tjuːnɪk] n [gen & BOT] tunique *f*.

tuning ['tjuːnɪŋ] n **1.** MUS accord *m* **2.** RADIO & TV réglage *m* **3.** AUTO réglage *m*, mise *f* au point.

tuning fork n diapason *m*.

Tunis ['tjuːnɪs] pr n Tunis.

Tunisia [tjuːˈnɪzɪə] pr n Tunisie *f* / *in Tunisia* en Tunisie.

Tunisian [tjuːˈnɪzɪən] ◆ n Tunisien *m*, -enne *f*. ◆ adj tunisien.

tunnel ['tʌnl] (🇬🇧 *pt & pp* **tunnelled**, *cont* **tunnelling** ; 🇺🇸 *pt & pp* **tunneled**, *cont* **tunneling**) ◆ n [gen & RAIL] tunnel *m* ; MIN galerie *f* ; [of mole, badger] galerie *f*. ◆ vt [hole, passage] creuser, percer. ◆ vi [person] creuser or percer un tunnel or des tunnels ; [badger, mole] creuser une galerie or des galeries.

tunnel vision n **1.** OPT rétrécissement *m* du champ visuel **2.** *fig* esprit *m* borné.

tunny ['tʌnɪ] = **tuna.**

tuppence ['tʌpəns] n 🇬🇧 deux pence *mpl* / *I don't care tuppence for your opinion inf* je me fiche pas mal de votre opinion or de ce que vous pensez.

Tupperware® ['tʌpəweəʳ] ◆ n Tupperware® m ▶ **Tupperware party** réunion f Tupperware®. ◆ comp en Tupperware.

turban ['tɜːbən] n turban m.

turbid ['tɜːbɪd] adj trouble.

turbine ['tɜːbaɪn] n turbine f.

turbo ['tɜːbəʊ] (pl turbos) n 1. AUTO turbo m 2. [turbine] turbine f.

turbocharged ['tɜːbəʊtʃɑːdʒd] adj turbo.

turbodiesel ['tɜːbəʊˌdiːzl] n turbodiesel m.

turbojet ['tɜːbəʊˌdʒet] n [engine] turboréacteur m ; [plane] avion m à turboréacteur.

turboprop ['tɜːbəʊˌprɒp] n [engine] turbopropulseur m ; [plane] avion m à turbopropulseur.

turbot ['tɜːbət] (pl turbot or turbots) n turbot m.

turbulence ['tɜːbjʊləns] n 1. [unrest] turbulence f, agitation f 2. [in air] turbulence f ; [in sea] agitation f 3. PHYS turbulence f.

turbulent ['tɜːbjʊlənt] adj [crowd, period, emotions] tumultueux ; [sea] agité ; [meeting] houleux.

turd [tɜːd] n v inf 1. [excrement] merde f 2. pej [person] con m, salaud m.

tureen [təˈriːn] n soupière f.

turf [tɜːf] (pl turfs or turves [tɜːvz]) ◆ n 1. [grass] gazon m 2. [sod] motte f de gazon 3. SPORT turf m 4. [peat] tourbe f 5. US v inf [of gang] territoire m réservé, chasse f gardée. ◆ vt 1. [with grass] ▶ **turf (over)** gazonner 2. UK inf [throw] balancer, flanquer, jeter. ❖ **turf out** vt sep UK inf [eject, evict - person] vider, flanquer à la porte ; [remove - furniture, possessions] sortir, enlever ; [throw away - rubbish] bazarder.

turf accountant n UK fml bookmaker m.

turgid ['tɜːdʒɪd] adj 1. [style, prose] ampoulé, boursouflé 2. MED enflé, gonflé.

Turk [tɜːk] n Turc m, Turque f.

Turkestan, Turkistan [ˌtɜːkɪˈstɑːn] pr n Turkistan m / in Turkestan au Turkistan.

turkey ['tɜːkɪ] (pl turkey or turkeys) n 1. [bird - cock] dindon m ; [- hen] dinde f ▶ **turkey shoot** US lit partie f de chasse au dindon ; fig : it was a real turkey shoot US c'était gagné d'avance US 2. CULIN dinde f 3. US inf [fool] idiot m, -e f, imbécile mf 4. US inf [flop] bide m ; THEAT four m 5. PHR to talk turkey US : let's talk turkey parlons franc.

Turkey ['tɜːkɪ] pr n Turquie f / in Turkey en Turquie.

Turkish ['tɜːkɪʃ] ◆ n LING turc m. ◆ adj turc.

Turkish bath n bain m turc.

Turkish delight n loukoum m.

Turkistan [ˌtɜːkɪˈstɑːn] = Turkestan.

Turkmenian [ˌtɜːkˈmeniən] adj turkmène.

Turkmenistan [ˌtɜːkmenɪˈstɑːn], **Turkmenia** [tɜːk-ˈmiːnɪə] pr n Turkménistan m / in Turkmenistan au Turkménistan.

turmeric ['tɜːmərɪk] n curcuma m.

turmoil ['tɜːmɔɪl] n 1. [confusion] agitation f, trouble m, chaos m 2. [emotional] trouble m, émoi m.

turn [tɜːn] ◆ vt 1. [cause to rotate, move round] tourner ; [shaft, axle] faire tourner, faire pivoter ; [direct] diriger / she turned the key in the lock a) [to lock] elle a donné un tour de clé (à la porte), elle a fermé la porte à clé b) [to unlock] elle a ouvert la porte avec la clé / turn the knob to the right tournez le bouton vers la droite / turn your head this way tournez la tête de ce côté 2. fig [change orientation of] : she turned the conversation to sport elle a orienté la conversation vers le sport / you've turned my whole family against me vous avez monté toute ma famille contre moi /

she turned her attention to the problem elle s'est concentrée sur le problème ▶ **to turn one's back on sb** lit tourner le dos à qqn / how can you turn your back on your own family? comment peux-tu abandonner ta famille ? 3. [flip over - page] tourner ; [- collar, mattress, sausages, soil] retourner ▶ **to turn sthg on its head** bouleverser qqch, mettre qqch sens dessus dessous 4. [go round - corner] tourner 5. [reach - in age, time] passer, franchir / I had just turned twenty je venais d'avoir vingt ans 6. [transform, change] changer, transformer ; [make] faire devenir, rendre ▶ **to turn sthg into sthg** transformer or changer qqch en qqch / she turned the remark into a joke elle a tourné la remarque en plaisanterie / they're turning the book into a film ils adaptent le livre pour l'écran. ◆ vi 1. [move round - handle, key, wheel] tourner ; [- shaft] tourner, pivoter ; [- person] se tourner / he turned right round il a fait volte-face / they turned towards me ils se sont tournés vers moi or de mon côté 2. [flip over - page] tourner ; [- car, person, ship] se retourner 3. [change direction - person] tourner ; [- vehicle] tourner, virer ; [- luck, wind] tourner, changer ; [- river, road] faire un coude ; [- tide] changer de direction / he turned (round) and went back il a fait demi-tour et est revenu sur ses pas / the car turned into our street la voiture a tourné dans notre rue / I don't know where or which way to turn fig je ne sais plus quoi faire 4. (with adj or noun complement) [become] devenir / the weather's turned bad le temps s'est gâté / the argument turned nasty la dispute s'est envenimée / to turn professional passer or devenir professionnel 5. [transform] se changer, se transformer / the rain turned to snow la pluie s'est transformée en neige / their love turned to hate leur amour se changea en haine or fit place à la haine 6. [leaf] tourner, jaunir ; [milk] tourner / the weather has turned le temps a changé. ◆ n 1. [revolution, rotation] tour m / give the screw another turn donnez un autre tour de vis 2. [change of course, direction] tournant m ; [in skiing] virage m ; fig ▶ **at every turn** à tout instant, à tout bout de champ 3. [bend, curve in road] virage m, tournant m / there is a sharp turn to the left la route fait un brusque virage or tourne brusquement à gauche 4. [change in state, nature] tour m, tournure f / it was an unexpected turn of events les événements ont pris une tournure imprévue / things took a turn for the worse / better les choses se sont aggravées / améliorées 5. [time of change] : at the turn of the century au tournant du siècle 6. [in game, order, queue] tour m / it's my turn c'est à moi, c'est mon tour / whose turn is it? a) [in queue] (c'est) à qui le tour ? b) [in game] c'est à qui de jouer ? / they laughed and cried by turns ils passaient tour à tour du rire aux larmes ▶ **to take it in turns to do sthg** faire qqch à tour de rôle 7. [action, deed] ▶ **to do sb a good / bad turn** rendre service / jouer un mauvais tour à qqn 8. inf [attack of illness] crise f, attaque f / she had one of her (funny) turns this morning elle a eu une de ses crises ce matin 9. inf [shock] : you gave me quite a turn! tu m'as fait une sacrée peur !, tu m'as fait une de ces peurs ! 10. [tendency, style] : to have an optimistic turn of mind être optimiste de nature or d'un naturel optimiste ▶ **turn of phrase** tournure f or tour m de phrase 11. UK THEAT numéro m 12. PHR done to a turn UK inf CULIN : the chicken was done to a turn le poulet était cuit à point. ❖ **in turn** adv phr : she interviewed each of us in turn elle a eu un entretien avec chacun de nous l'un après l'autre / I told Sarah and she in turn told Paul je l'ai dit à Sarah qui, à son tour, l'a dit à Paul. ❖ **out of turn** adv phr ▶ **to speak out of turn** fig faire des remarques déplacées, parler mal à propos. ❖ **turn against** vt insep se retourner contre, s'en prendre à. ❖ **turn around** = turn round. ❖ **turn aside** ◆ vi [move to one side] s'écarter ; lit & fig [move away] se détourner. ◆ vt sep lit & fig écarter, détourner. ❖ **turn away** ◆ vt sep 1. [avert] détourner 2. [reject - person] renvoyer ; [stronger] chasser. ◆ vi se détourner. ❖ **turn back** ◆ vi [return - person] revenir, rebrousser chemin ; [-vehicle] faire demi-tour / *my mind is made up, there is no turning back* ma décision est prise, je n'y reviendrai pas. ◆ vt sep **1.** [force to return] faire faire demi-tour à ; [refugee] refouler **2.** [fold - collar, sheet] rabattre ; [-sleeves] remonter, retrousser ; [-corner of page] corner **3.** PHR **to turn the clock back** remonter dans le temps, revenir en arrière. ❖ **turn down** vt sep **1.** [heating, lighting, sound] baisser **2.** [fold - sheet] rabattre, retourner ; [-collar] rabattre **3.** [reject - offer, request, suitor] rejeter, repousser ; [-candidate, job] refuser. ❖ **turn in** ◆ vt sep **1.** [return, give in - borrowed article, equipment, piece of work] rendre, rapporter ; [-criminal] livrer à la police **2.** [produce] : *the actor turned in a good performance* l'acteur a très bien joué. ◆ vi **1.** *inf* [go to bed] se coucher **2.** PHR **to turn in on o.s.** se replier sur soi-même. ❖ **turn off** ◆ vt sep **1.** [switch off - light] éteindre ; [- heater, radio, television] éteindre, fermer ; [cut off at mains] couper ; [tap] fermer / *she turned the ignition / engine off* elle a coupé le contact / arrêté le moteur **2.** *inf* [fail to interest] rebuter ; [sexually] couper l'envie à. ◆ vi **1.** [leave road] tourner **2.** [switch off] s'éteindre. ❖ **turn on** ◆ vt sep **1.** [switch on - electricity, heating, light, radio, television] allumer ; [-engine] mettre en marche ; [-water] faire couler ; [-tap] ouvrir ; [open at mains] ouvrir **2.** *inf* [person - interest] intéresser ; [-sexually] exciter. ◆ vt insep [attack] attaquer / *his colleagues turned on him and accused him of stealing* ses collègues s'en sont pris à lui et l'ont accusé de vol. ◆ vi **1.** [switch on] s'allumer **2.** [depend, hinge on] dépendre de, reposer sur / *everything turns on whether he continues as president* tout dépend s'il reste président ou non. ❖ **turn out** ◆ vt sep **1.** [switch off - light] éteindre ; [- gas] éteindre, couper **2.** [dismiss, expel] mettre à la porte ; [tenant] expulser, déloger **3.** [empty - container, pockets] retourner, vider ; [-contents] vider ; [-jelly] verser **4.** UK [clean] nettoyer à fond **5.** *(usu passive)* [dress] habiller / *nicely or smartly turned out* élégant. ◆ vi **1.** [show up] venir, arriver ; MIL [guard] (aller) prendre la faction ; [troops] aller au rassemblement / *thousands turned out for the concert* des milliers de gens sont venus or ont assisté au concert **2.** [car, person] sortir, partir **3.** [prove] se révéler, s'avérer / *his statement turned out to be false* sa déclaration s'est révélée fausse ; [end up] : *I don't know how it turned out* je ne sais pas comment cela a fini / *the evening turned out badly* la soirée a mal tourné / *as it turns out, he needn't have worried* en l'occurrence or en fin de compte, ce n'était pas la peine de se faire du souci. ❖ **turn over** ◆ vt sep **1.** [playing card, mattress, person, stone] retourner ; [page] tourner ; [vehicle] retourner ; [boat] faire chavirer **2.** [consider] réfléchir à or sur / *I was turning the idea over in my mind* je tournais et retournais or ruminais l'idée dans ma tête **3.** [hand over, transfer] rendre, remettre **4.** [change] transformer, changer **5.** COMM : *the store turns over £1,000 a week* la boutique fait un chiffre d'affaires de 1 000 livres par semaine. ◆ vi [roll over - person] se retourner ; [-vehicle] se retourner, faire un tonneau ; [-boat] se retourner, chavirer. ❖ **turn round** ◆ vi UK **1.** [rotate - person] se retourner ; [-object] tourner / *the dancers turned round and round* les danseurs tournaient or tournoyaient (sur eux-mêmes) **2.** [face opposite direction - person] faire volte-face, faire demi-tour ; [-vehicle] faire demi-tour. ◆ vt sep **1.** [rotate - head] tourner ; [-object, person] tourner, retourner ; [-vehicle] faire faire demi-tour à **2.** [quantity of work] traiter **3.** [change nature of] ▶ **to turn a situation round** renverser une situation **4.** [sentence, idea] retourner. ❖ **turn to** vt insep **1.** *lit* [person] se tourner vers ; [page] aller à **2.** [seek help from] s'adresser à, se tourner vers ▶ **to turn to sb for advice** consulter qqn, demander conseil à qqn / *I don't know who to turn to* je ne sais pas à qui m'adresser or qui aller trouver **3.** *fig* [shift, move on to] : *her thoughts turned to her sister* elle se mit à penser à sa sœur ; [address - subject, issue, etc.] aborder, traiter. ❖ **turn up** ◆ vt sep **1.** [heat, lighting, radio, TV]

mettre plus fort / *to turn the sound up* augmenter or monter le volume **2.** [find, unearth] découvrir, dénicher ; [buried object] déterrer / *her research turned up some interesting new facts* sa recherche a révélé de nouveaux détails intéressants **3.** [point upwards] remonter, relever / *she has a turned-up nose* elle a le nez retroussé **4.** [collar] relever ; [trousers] remonter ; [sleeve] retrousser, remonter. ◆ vi **1.** [appear] apparaître ; [arrive] arriver **2.** [be found] être trouvé or retrouvé / *her bag turned up eventually* elle a fini par retrouver son sac **3.** [happen] se passer, arriver / *don't worry, something will turn up* ne t'en fais pas, tu finiras par trouver quelque chose.

turnabout ['tɜːnəbaʊt] n volte-face *f inv.*

turnaround ['tɜːnəraʊnd] US = turnround.

turncoat ['tɜːnkəʊt] n renégat *m*, -e *f*, transfuge *mf.*

turned [tɜːnd] adj [milk] tourné.

turning ['tɜːnɪŋ] n **1.** UK [side road] route *f* transversale ; [side street] rue *f* transversale, petite rue **2.** UK [bend - in river] coude *m* ; [- in road] virage *m* ; [fork] embranchement *m*, carrefour *m* **3.** INDUST tournage *m.*

turning circle n UK AUTO rayon *m* de braquage.

turning point n [decisive moment] moment *m* décisif ; [change] tournant *m.*

turnip ['tɜːnɪp] n navet *m.*

turn-off n **1.** [road] sortie *f* (de route), route *f* transversale, embranchement *m* **2.** *inf* [loss of interest] : *it's a real turn-off* **a)** [gen] c'est vraiment à vous dégoûter **b)** [sexual] ça vous coupe vraiment l'envie.

turn-on n *inf* : *he finds leather a turn-on* il trouve le cuir excitant, le cuir l'excite.

turnout ['tɜːnaʊt] n **1.** [attendance - at meeting, concert] assistance *f* ; POL [at election] (taux *m* de) participation *f* **2.** [dress] mise *f*, tenue *f* **3.** US AUTO refuge *m* (*pour se laisser doubler*).

turnover ['tɜːnˌəʊvə'] n **1.** UK FIN chiffre *m* d'affaires **2.** [of staff, tenants] renouvellement *m* **3.** US [of stock] vitesse *f* de rotation ; [of shares] mouvement *m* **4.** CULIN ▶ **apple turnover** chausson *m* aux pommes.

turnpike ['tɜːnpaɪk] n **1.** [barrier] barrière *f* de péage **2.** US [road] autoroute *f* à péage.

turnround ['tɜːnraʊnd] n UK **1.** ▶ **turnround (time) a)** [of passenger ship, plane] temps *m* nécessaire entre deux voyages **b)** [for freight] temps nécessaire pour le déchargement **c)** NAUT estarie *f*, starie *f* **d)** COMPUT temps de retournement, délai *m* d'exécution **2.** [reversal - of fortunes] retournement *m*, renversement *m* ; [- of opinions] revirement *m*, volte-face *f inv.*

turn signal lever n US (manette *f* de) clignotant *m.*

turnstile ['tɜːnstaɪl] n tourniquet *m* (*barrière*).

turntable ['tɜːnˌteɪbl] n **1.** [on record player] platine *f* **2.** RAIL plaque *f* tournante.

turn-up n UK **1.** [on trousers] revers *m* **2.** *inf* [surprise] surprise *f.*

turpentine ['tɜːpəntaɪn] n UK (essence *f* de) térébenthine *f.*

turps [tɜːps] *(U)* UK = turpentine.

turquoise ['tɜːkwɔɪz] ◆ n **1.** [gem] turquoise *f* **2.** [colour] turquoise *m inv.* ◆ adj **1.** [bracelet, ring] de or en turquoise **2.** [in colour] turquoise *(inv).*

turret ['tʌrɪt] n tourelle *f.*

turtle ['tɜːtl] n **1.** [in sea] tortue *f* marine ; US [on land] tortue *f* **2.** PHR **to turn turtle** se renverser.

turtledove ['tɜːtldʌv] n tourterelle *f.*

turtleneck ['tɜ:tlnek] ◆ adj [sweater, dress] à col montant, à encolure montante ; US à col roulé. ◆ n col m montant, encolure f montante ; US (pull m à) col m roulé.

turves [tɜ:vz] pl ⟶ **turf**.

tusk [tʌsk] n [of elephant, boar] défense f.

tussle ['tʌsl] ◆ n 1. [scuffle] mêlée f, bagarre f 2. [struggle] lutte f 3. [quarrel] dispute f. ◆ vi [scuffle, fight] se battre.

tut [tʌt] (pt & pp tutted, cont tutting) ◆ interj ▶ tut!, tut-tut! a) [in disapproval] allons donc ! b) [in annoyance] zut ! ◆ vi [in disapproval] pousser une exclamation désapprobatrice ; [in annoyance] exprimer son mécontentement.

tutelage ['tju:tɪlɪdʒ] n fml tutelle f / under his tutelage sous sa tutelle.

tutor ['tju:tər] ◆ n 1. [teacher] professeur m particulier ; [full-time] précepteur m, -trice f 2. UK UNIV [teacher] professeur m (qui dirige et supervise les travaux d'un groupe d'étudiants) ; UK SCH professeur m principal (surtout dans les écoles privées). ◆ vt 1. [instruct] donner des cours (particuliers) à 2. UK UNIV diriger les études de. ◆ vi [teacher] donner des cours particuliers.

tutorial [tju:'tɔ:rɪəl] ◆ n UNIV (séance f de) travaux mpl dirigés, TD mpl. ◆ adj UNIV [work] de travaux dirigés ; [duties] de directeur d'études.

tutu ['tu:tu:] n tutu m.

tux [tʌks] n inf abbr of tuxedo.

tuxedo [tʌk'si:dəʊ] (pl tuxedos) n US smoking m.

TV ◆ n (abbr of television) TV f. ◆ comp [programme, set, star] de télé.

TV movie n téléfilm m, film m de télévision.

twaddle ['twɒdl] n (U) UK inf bêtises fpl, âneries fpl, imbécillités fpl.

twang [twæŋ] ◆ n 1. [of wire, guitar] son m de corde pincée 2. [in voice] ton m nasillard 3. [accent] accent m. ◆ vt [string instrument] pincer les cordes de. ◆ vi [arrow, bow, wire] vibrer.

tweak [twi:k] ◆ vt 1. [twist - ear, nose] tordre (doucement), pincer ; [pull] tirer (sur) 2. AUTO mettre au point ; COMPUT & fig peaufiner, mettre au point. ◆ n (petit) coup m sec.

twee [twi:] adj UK inf [person] chichiteux ; [idea, sentiment] mièvre ; [decor] cucul (inv).

tweed [twi:d] ◆ n [cloth] tweed m. ◆ comp [jacket, skirt] de tweed, en tweed. ❖ **tweeds** pl n [clothes] vêtements mpl de tweed ; [suit] costume m de tweed.

tween [twi:n] n US inf adolescente entre 10 et 13 ans.

tweet [twi:t] ◆ n pépiement m. ◆ onomat cui-cui. ◆ vi pépier.

tweezers ['twi:zəz] pl n ▶ (pair of) tweezers pince f à épiler.

twelfth [twelfθ] ◆ det douzième. ◆ n 1. [ordinal] douzième mf 2. [fraction] douzième m. See also fifth.

twelfth grade n US SCH classe de l'enseignement secondaire correspondant à la terminale (17-18 ans).

Twelfth Night n la fête des Rois.

twelve [twelv] ◆ det douze (inv). ◆ n douze m inv. ◆ pron douze. See also five.

twentieth ['twentɪəθ] ◆ det vingtième. ◆ n 1. [ordinal] vingtième mf 2. [fraction] vingtième m. See also fiftieth.

twenty ['twentɪ] ◆ det vingt (inv). ◆ n vingt m. ◆ pron vingt. See also fifty.

twenty-four seven adv vingt-quatre heures sur vingt-quatre, sept jours sur sept.

twenty-twenty vision n ▶ to have twenty-twenty vision avoir dix dixièmes à chaque œil.

twerp [twɜ:p] n inf andouille f, crétin m, -e f.

twice [twaɪs] ◆ adv 1. [with noun] deux fois 2. [with verb] deux fois 3. [with adj or adv] : twice weekly / daily deux fois par semaine / jour / it's twice as good c'est deux fois mieux. ◆ predet deux fois.

twiddle ['twɪdl] ◆ vt [knob, dial] tourner, manier ; [moustache] tripoter, jouer avec. ◆ vi : to twiddle with the knob tourner le bouton. ◆ n : give the knob a twiddle tournez le bouton.

twig [twɪg] (pt & pp twigged, cont twigging) ◆ vi & vt UK inf [understand] piger. ◆ n [for fire] brindille f ; [on tree] petite branche f.

twilight ['twaɪlaɪt] ◆ n 1. [in evening] crépuscule m ; [in morning] aube f / at twilight a) [evening] au crépuscule b) [morning] à l'aube 2. [half-light] pénombre f, obscurité f, demi-jour m 3. fig [last stages, end] crépuscule m. ◆ comp ▶ twilight years : his twilight years les dernières années de sa vie.

twill [twɪl] n sergé m.

twin [twɪn] (pt & pp twinned, cont twinning) ◆ n jumeau m, -elle f. ◆ adj 1. [child, sibling] : they have twin boys / girls ils ont des jumeaux / des jumelles / my twin sister ma sœur jumelle 2. [dual - spires, hills] double, jumeau ; [- aims] double. ◆ vt [town] jumeler.

twin-bedded [-'bedɪd] adj [room] à deux lits.

twin carburettor n carburateur m double-corps.

twine [twaɪn] ◆ vt 1. [wind - hair, string] entortiller, enrouler 2. [weave] tresser. ◆ vi 1. [stem, ivy] s'enrouler 2. [path, river] serpenter. ◆ n (U) (grosse) ficelle f.

twin-engined [-'endʒɪnd] adj bimoteur.

twinge [twɪndʒ] n 1. [of guilt, shame] sentiment m 2. [of pain] élancement m, tiraillement m.

twinkie ['twɪŋkɪ] n US inf [effeminate youth] jeune homme efféminé. ❖ **Twinkie**® n US [cake] petit gâteau fourré à la crème.

twinkle ['twɪŋkl] ◆ vi 1. [star, diamond] briller, scintiller 2. [eyes] briller, pétiller. ◆ n 1. [of star, diamond, light] scintillement m 2. [in eye] pétillement m.

twinkling ['twɪŋklɪŋ] ◆ adj 1. [star, gem, sea] scintillant, brillant 2. [eyes] pétillant, brillant 3. fig [feet] agile. ◆ n (U) 1. [of star, light, gem] scintillement m 2. [in eyes] pétillement m ▶ in the twinkling of an eye en un clin d'œil.

twin room n chambre f à deux lits.

twinset ['twɪn,set] n twin set m.

twin town n ville f jumelée or jumelle.

twin tub n machine f à laver à deux tambours.

twirl [twɜ:l] ◆ vt 1. [spin - stick, parasol, handle] faire tournoyer ; [- lasso] faire tourner 2. [twist - moustache, hair] tortiller, friser. ◆ vi [dancer, lasso, handle] tournoyer. ◆ n 1. [whirl - of body, stick] tournoiement m ; [pirouette] pirouette f 2. [written flourish] fioriture f.

twist [twɪst] ◆ vt 1. [turn - round and round] tourner ; [- round axis] tourner, visser ; [- tightly] tordre 2. [twine] tresser, entortiller ; [wind] enrouler, tourner 3. [body, part of body] tourner 4. [sprain - ankle, wrist] tordre, fouler 5. [distort - words] déformer ; [- argument] déformer, fausser. ◆ vi 1. [road, stream] serpenter 2. [become twined] s'enrouler 3. [body, part of body] se tortiller 4. [be sprained - ankle] se tordre, se fouler ; [- knee] se tordre 5. [dance] twister 6. [in pontoon] ▶ twist! encore une carte ! ◆ n 1. [turn, twirl] tour m, torsion f 2. [in road] tournant m, virage m ; [in river] coude m ; [in staircase] tournant m ; fig [in thinking] détour m 3. [coil - of tobacco] rouleau m ; [- of paper] tortillon m 4. CULIN ▶ a twist of lemon un zeste de citron 5. [in story, plot] tour m 6. [dance] twist m. ❖ **twist about** UK, **twist around** vi [road] serpenter, zigzaguer. ❖ **twist off** vt sep [lid] dévisser ; [cork] enlever en tournant ; [branch] enlever or arracher en tordant. ◆ vi [cap, lid] se dévisser. ❖ **twist round** UK ◆ vt sep [rope, tape] enrouler ; [lid] tourner, visser ; [handle]

(faire) tourner ; [swivel chair] faire tourner or pivoter ; [hat] tourner ; [head] tourner. ◆ vi **1.** [person] se retourner **2.** [path] serpenter, zigzaguer. ❖ **twist together** vt sep [threads] tresser, enrouler ; [wires] enrouler.

twisted ['twɪstɪd] adj **1.** [personality, smile] tordu ; [mind] tordu, mal tourné **2.** [logic, argument] faux (fausse), tordu.

twister ['twɪstəʳ] n inf US [tornado] tornade f.

twisty ['twɪstɪ] adj [road, river] sinueux, qui serpente.

twit [twɪt] n UK inf [idiot] crétin m, -e f, imbécile mf.

twitch [twɪtʃ] ◆ vi **1.** [jerk - once] avoir un mouvement convulsif ; [- habitually] avoir un tic ; [muscle] se contracter convulsivement **2.** [wriggle] s'agiter, se remuer. ◆ vt [ears, nose] remuer, bouger ; [curtain, rope] tirer d'un coup sec, donner un coup sec à. ◆ n **1.** [nervous tic] tic m ; [muscular spasm] spasme m **2.** [tweak, pull - on hair, rope] coup m sec, saccade f.

twitchy ['twɪtʃɪ] adj [person] agité, nerveux.

twitter ['twɪtəʳ] ◆ vi **1.** [bird] gazouiller, pépier **2.** [person - chatter] jacasser. ◆ n **1.** [of bird] gazouillement m, pépiement m **2.** [of person] bavardage m **3.** inf [agitation] état m d'agitation ▸ **to be all of a** or **in a twitter about sthg** être dans tous ses états or sens dessus dessous à cause de qqch.

two [tuː] ◆ det deux (inv). ◆ n deux m inv ▸ **to cut sthg in two** couper qqch en deux / **in twos** or **two by two** deux par deux. ◆ pron deux mf. **See also five**.

two-bit adj US inf & pej à deux balles.

two-dimensional adj **1.** [figure, drawing] à deux dimensions **2.** [simplistic - character] sans profondeur, simpliste.

two-door adj [car] à deux portes.

two-faced adj hypocrite.

twofold ['tuːfəʊld] ◆ adj double. ◆ adv [increase] au double.

two-handed adj [tool] à deux poignées ; [saw] à deux mains, forestière ; [sword] à deux mains ; [game] qui se joue à deux, pour deux joueurs.

two-hander n [film] film m à deux personnages ; [play] pièce f à deux personnages.

two-piece ◆ adj en deux parties ▸ **two-piece swimming costume** (maillot m de bain) deux-pièces m ▸ **two-piece suit a)** [man's] costume m deux-pièces **b)** [woman's] tailleur m. ◆ n [bikini] deux-pièces m ; [man's suit] costume m deux-pièces ; [woman's suit] tailleur m.

two-ply adj [wool] à deux fils ; [rope] à deux brins ; [tissue] double, à double épaisseur ; [wood] à deux épaisseurs.

two-seater ◆ adj à deux places. ◆ n [plane] avion m à deux places ; [car] voiture f à deux places.

twosome ['tuːsəm] n **1.** [couple] couple m **2.** [match] partie f à deux.

two-stroke adj [engine] à deux temps.

two-time vt inf [lover] tromper, être infidèle à.

two-timing adj inf infidèle.

two-tone adj [in colour] à deux tons ; [in sound] de deux tons.

two-way adj [traffic] dans les deux sens ; [street] à double sens ; [agreement, process] bilatéral ▸ **two-way mirror** glace f sans tain ▸ **two-way radio** TELEC émetteur-récepteur m.

two-way street n rue f à double sens.

two-wheeler n [motorbike] deux-roues m ; [bicycle] vélo m, deux-roues m.

TX written abbr of Texas.

TXT BAC MESSAGING written abbr of text back.

tycoon [taɪˈkuːn] n homme m d'affaires important, magnat m.

type [taɪp] ◆ n **1.** [gen & BIOL] ▸ **blood / hair type** type m sanguin / de cheveux **2.** [sort, kind] sorte f, genre m, espèce f ; [make - of coffee, shampoo, etc.] marque f ; [model - of car, plane, equipment, etc.] modèle m **3.** [referring to person] genre m, type m **4.** [typical example] type m, exemple m **5.** (U) TYPO [single character] caractère m ; [block of print] caractères mpl (d'imprimerie). ◆ vt **1.** [subj: typist] taper (à la machine) **2.** MED [blood sample] classifier, déterminer le type de. ◆ vi [typist] taper (à la machine). ❖ **type out** vt sep [letter] taper (à la machine). ❖ **type over** vt insep COMPUT écraser. ❖ **type up** vt sep [report, notes] taper (à la machine).

-type in comp du type, genre.

typecast ['taɪpkɑːst] (pt & pp typecast) vt [actor] enfermer dans le rôle de.

typeface ['taɪpfeɪs] n œil m du caractère.

typescript ['taɪpskrɪpt] n texte m dactylographié, tapuscrit m.

typeset ['taɪpset] (pt & pp typeset, cont typesetting) vt PRINT composer ; [photocompose] photocomposer.

typesetter ['taɪpˌsetəʳ] n [worker] compositeur m, -trice f.

typesetting ['taɪpˌsetɪŋ] n PRINT composition f ; [photocomposition] photocomposition f.

typewriter ['taɪpˌraɪtəʳ] n machine f à écrire.

typewritten ['taɪpˌrɪtn] adj dactylographié, tapé à la machine.

typhoid ['taɪfɔɪd] ◆ n (U) typhoïde f. ◆ comp [injection] antityphoïdique ; [symptoms] de la typhoïde ▸ **typhoid fever** (fièvre f) typhoïde f.

typhoon [taɪˈfuːn] n typhon m.

typhus ['taɪfəs] n typhus m.

typical ['tɪpɪkl] adj typique, caractéristique.

typically ['tɪpɪklɪ] adv **1.** [normally] d'habitude **2.** [characteristically] typiquement.

typify ['tɪpɪfaɪ] (pt & pp typified) vt **1.** [be typical of] être typique or caractéristique de **2.** [embody, symbolize] symboliser, être le type même de.

typing ['taɪpɪŋ] n **1.** [typing work] : *he had 10 pages of typing to do* il avait 10 pages à taper or dactylographier **2.** [typescript] tapuscrit m, texte m dactylographié **3.** [skill] dactylo f, dactylographie f.

typing error n faute f de frappe.

typing pool n bureau m or pool m des dactylos.

typist ['taɪpɪst] n dactylo mf, dactylographe mf.

typo ['taɪpəʊ] (pl typos) n inf [in typescript] faute f de frappe ; [in printed text] coquille f.

typography [taɪˈpɒɡrəfɪ] n typographie f.

tyrannical [tɪˈrænɪkl] adj tyrannique.

tyrannize, tyrannise ['tɪrənaɪz] ◆ vt tyranniser. ◆ vi ▸ **to tyrannize over sb** tyranniser qqn.

tyranny ['tɪrənɪ] (pl tyrannies) n tyrannie f.

tyrant ['taɪrənt] n tyran m.

tyre UK, **tire** US ['taɪəʳ] n pneu m.

Tyre ['taɪəʳ] pr n Tyr.

tyre pressure n pression f des pneus.

Tyrol [tɪˈrəʊl] pr n Tyrol m / *in the Tyrol* dans le Tyrol.

Tyrolean [tɪrəˈliːən], **Tyrolese** [ˌtɪrəˈliːz] ◆ n Tyrolien m, -enne f. ◆ adj tyrolien.

Tyrrhenian Sea [tɪˈriːnɪən-] pr n ▸ **the Tyrrhenian Sea** la mer Tyrrhénienne.

TYVM MESSAGING written abbr of thank you very much.

tzar [zɑːʳ] = tsar.

U ◆ n (abbr of **universal**) *désigne un film tous publics en Grande-Bretagne.* ◆ adj 🆄 *inf* [upper-class - expression, activity] ≃ distingué.

UAW (abbr of **United Auto Workers**) pr n *syndicat américain.*

U-bend n [in pipe] coude *m* ; [under sink] siphon *m*.

ubiquitous [juːˈbɪkwɪtəs] adj [gen] omniprésent, que l'on trouve partout ; [person] doué d'ubiquité, omniprésent.

UCAS [ˈjuːkæs] (abbr of **Universities and Colleges Admissions Service**) n UNIV & SCH service *m* des admissions dans les universités en Grande-Bretagne.

UCATT [ˈjuːkæt] (abbr of **Union of Construction, Allied Trades and Technicians**) pr n *syndicat britannique des employés du bâtiment.*

UCL (abbr of **University College, London**) pr n *l'une des facultés de l'Université de Londres.*

udder [ˈʌdər] n mamelle *f*, pis *m*.

UDI (abbr of **Unilateral Declaration of Independence**) n *déclaration unilatérale d'indépendance.*

UEFA [juːˈeɪfə] (abbr of **Union of European Football Associations**) pr n UEFA *f*.

UFO [ˌjuːef'əʊ or ˈjuːfəʊ] (abbr of **unidentified flying object**) n OVNI *m*, ovni *m*.

ufologist [juːˈfɒlədʒɪst] n spécialiste *mf* d'ufologie.

Uganda [juːˈgændə] pr n Ouganda *m* / *in Uganda* en Ouganda.

Ugandan [juːˈgændən] ◆ n Ougandais *m*, -e *f*. ◆ adj ougandais.

ugh [ʌg] interj ▸ **ugh!** beurk !, berk !, pouah !

ugliness [ˈʌglɪnɪs] n laideur *f*.

ugly [ˈʌglɪ] (*compar* **uglier**, *superl* **ugliest**) adj **1.** [in appearance - person, face, building] laid, vilain **2.** [unpleasant, nasty - habit] sale, désagréable ; [- behaviour] répugnant ; [- quarrel] mauvais ; [- clouds, weather] vilain, sale ; [- rumour, word] vilain ; [- situation] fâcheux, mauvais / *there were some ugly scenes* il y a eu du vilain / *the ugly truth is…* la vérité, dans toute son horreur, c'est que… / *he was in an ugly mood* il était d'une humeur massacrante, il était de fort méchante humeur ▸ **to turn** or **to get ugly a)** [person] devenir or se faire menaçant **b)** [situation] prendre mauvaise tournure or une sale tournure / *things took an ugly turn* les choses ont pris une mauvaise or vilaine tournure.

ugly duckling n vilain petit canard *m*.

UHF (abbr of **ultra-high frequency**) n UHF *f*.

uh-huh [ʌˈhʌ] interj *inf* ▸ **uh-huh! a)** [as conversation filler] ah ah ! **b)** [in assent] oui oui !, OK !

UHT (abbr of **ultra heat treated**) adj UHT.

UK ◆ pr n (abbr of **United Kingdom**) Royaume-Uni *m* ▸ **in the UK** au Royaume-Uni. ◆ comp du Royaume-Uni.

UKAEA (abbr of **United Kingdom Atomic Energy Authority**) n *commission britannique à l'énergie nucléaire* ; ≃ CEA *f*.

Ukraine [juːˈkreɪn] pr n Ukraine *f* / *in Ukraine* en Ukraine.

Ukrainian [juːˈkreɪnjən] ◆ n **1.** [person] Ukrainien *m*, -enne *f* **2.** LING ukrainien *m*. ◆ adj ukrainien.

ukulele [ˌjuːkəˈleɪlɪ] n guitare *f* hawaïenne, ukulélé *m*.

ulcer [ˈʌlsər] n **1.** MED [in stomach] ulcère *m* ; [in mouth] aphte *m* **2.** *fig* plaie *f*.

ulcerated [ˈʌlsəreɪtɪd] adj ulcéreux.

ulster [ˈʌlstər] n [coat] gros pardessus.

Ulster [ˈʌlstər] pr n **1.** [province] Ulster *m* / *in Ulster* dans l'Ulster **2.** [N. Ireland] Irlande *f* du Nord, Ulster *m*.

Ulster Democratic Unionist Party pr n *parti politique essentiellement protestant exigeant le maintien de l'Ulster au sein du Royaume-Uni.*

Ulsterman [ˈʌlstəmən] (*pl* **Ulstermen** [-mən]) n Ulstérien *m*, habitant *m* de l'Irlande du Nord.

ulterior [ʌlˈtɪərɪər] adj [hidden, secret] secret (secrète), dissimulé ▸ **ulterior motive** arrière-pensée *f*.

ultimata [ˌʌltɪˈmeɪtə] pl ⟶ **ultimatum**.

ultimate [ˈʌltɪmət] ◆ adj **1.** [eventual, final - ambition, power, responsibility] ultime ; [- cost, destination, objective] ultime, final ; [- solution, decision, answer] final, définitif / *they regard nuclear weapons as the ultimate deterrent* ils considèrent les armes nucléaires comme l'ultime moyen de dissuasion **2.** [basic, fundamental - cause] fondamental, premier ; [- truth] fondamental, élémentaire **3.** [extreme, supreme - authority, insult] suprême ; [- cruelty, stupidity] suprême, extrême ▸ *it's their idea of the ultimate holiday* c'est leur conception des vacances idéales / *the ultimate sacrifice* le sacrifice suprême **4.** [furthest] le plus éloigné. ◆ n comble *m*, summum *m* / *the ultimate in comfort* le summum du confort / *the ultimate in hi-fi* le nec plus ultra de la hi-fi.

ultimately [ˈʌltɪmətlɪ] adv **1.** [eventually, finally] finalement, en fin de compte, à la fin ; [later] par la suite **2.** [basically] en dernière analyse, en fin de compte.

ultimatum [ˌʌltɪˈmeɪtəm] (*pl* **ultimatums** or **ultimata** [ˌʌltɪˈmeɪtə]) n ultimatum *m* ▸ **to give** or **to issue** or **to deliver an ultimatum to sb** adresser un ultimatum à qqn.

ultra- in comp ultra-, hyper- ▸ **ultra-right-wing** d'extrême droite.

ultramarine [ˌʌltrəməˈriːn] adj bleu outremer *(inv)*.

ultramodern [ˌʌltrəˈmɒdən] adj ultramoderne.

ultrasonic [ˌʌltrə'sɒnɪk] adj ultrasonique.
❖ **ultrasonics** n (U) science f des ultrasons.
ultrasound ['ʌltrəsaʊnd] n ultrason m.
ultraviolet [ˌʌltrə'vaɪələt] ❖ adj ultraviolet. ❖ n ultraviolet m.
um [ʌm] (pt & pp ummed, cont umming) inf ❖ interj euh. ❖ vi dire euh.
umbilical cord n cordon m ombilical.
umbrage ['ʌmbrɪdʒ] n [offence] ▶ **to take umbrage at sthg** prendre ombrage de qqch, s'offenser de qqch.
umbrella [ʌm'brelə] ❖ n 1. parapluie m 2. fig [protection, cover] protection f ; MIL écran m or rideau m de protection. ❖ comp [term] général ; [organization] qui en recouvre or chapeaute plusieurs autres.
umbrella fund n fonds m parapluie.
UMIST ['juːmɪst] (abbr of University of Manchester Institute of Science and Technology) n institut de science et de technologie de l'université de Manchester.
umpire ['ʌmpaɪə'] ❖ n arbitre m. ❖ vt [match, contest] arbitrer. ❖ vi servir d'arbitre, être arbitre.
umpteen [ˌʌmp'tiːn] inf ❖ adj je ne sais combien de, des tas de / I've told you umpteen times je te l'ai dit trente-six fois or cent fois. ❖ pron : there were umpteen of them il y en avait des quantités or je ne sais combien.
umpteenth [ˌʌmp'tiːnθ] adj inf énième, n-ième / for the umpteenth time pour la énième fois.
UN (abbr of United Nations) ❖ pr n ▶ **the UN** l'ONU f, l'Onu f. ❖ comp de l'ONU.
'un [ʌn] pron inf : he's only a young 'un ce n'est qu'un petit gars / the little 'uns les petiots mpl / the young 'uns les jeunots mpl.
unabashed [ˌʌnə'bæʃt] adj 1. [undeterred] nullement décontenancé or déconcerté, imperturbable 2. [unashamed] sans honte, qui n'a pas honte.
unabated [ˌʌnə'beɪtɪd] ❖ adv [undiminished] sans diminuer / the storm / the noise continued unabated for most of the night la tempête / le bruit a continué sans répit pendant une grande partie de la nuit. ❖ adj non diminué / their enthusiasm was unabated leur enthousiasme ne diminuait pas, ils montraient toujours autant d'enthousiasme.
unable [ʌn'eɪbl] adj ▶ **to be unable to do sthg a)** [gen] ne pas pouvoir faire qqch **b)** [not know how to] ne pas savoir faire qqch **c)** [be incapable of] être incapable de faire qqch **d)** [not be in a position to] ne pas être en mesure de faire qqch **e)** [be prevented from] être dans l'impossibilité de faire qqch.
unabridged [ˌʌnə'brɪdʒd] adj [text, version, edition] intégral.
unacceptable [ˌʌnək'septəbl] adj 1. [intolerable - violence, behaviour] inadmissible, intolérable ; [- language] inacceptable 2. [gift, proposal] inacceptable.
unacceptably [ˌʌnək'septəblɪ] adv [noisy, rude] à un point inacceptable or inadmissible.
unaccompanied [ˌʌnə'kʌmpənɪd] adj 1. [child, traveller] non accompagné, seul 2. MUS [singing] sans accompagnement, a capella ; [singer] non accompagné, a capella ; [song] sans accompagnement ; [choir] a capella.
unaccomplished [ˌʌnə'kʌmplɪʃt] adj 1. [incomplete - task] inachevé, inaccompli 2. [unfulfilled - wish, plan] non réalisé, non accompli 3. [untalented - actor, player] sans grand talent, médiocre ; [- performance] médiocre.
unaccountable [ˌʌnə'kaʊntəbl] adj 1. [inexplicable - disappearance, reason] inexplicable 2. [to electors, public, etc.] : representatives who are unaccountable to the general public les représentants qui ne sont pas responsables envers le grand public.

unaccountably [ˌʌnə'kaʊntəblɪ] adv inexplicablement, de manière inexplicable.
unaccounted [ˌʌnə'kaʊntɪd] ❖ **unaccounted for** adj phr 1. [money] qui manque 2. [person] qui manque, qui a disparu ; [plane] qui n'est pas rentré.
unaccustomed [ˌʌnə'kʌstəmd] adj 1. [not used to - person] : unaccustomed as I am to public speaking bien que je n'aie guère l'habitude de prendre la parole en public 2. [unusual, uncharacteristic - rudeness, light-heartedness] inhabituel, inaccoutumé.
unacknowledged [ˌʌnək'nɒlɪdʒd] adj 1. [unrecognized - truth, fact] non reconnu ; [- qualities, discovery] non reconnu, méconnu 2. [ignored - letter] resté sans réponse.
unacquainted [ˌʌnə'kweɪntɪd] adj 1. [ignorant] ▶ **to be unacquainted with sthg** ne pas être au courant de qqch 2. [two people] : I am unacquainted with her je ne la connais pas, je n'ai pas fait sa connaissance.
unadulterated [ˌʌnə'dʌltəreɪtɪd] adj 1. [milk, flour] pur, naturel ; [wine] non frelaté 2. [pleasure, joy] pur (et simple), parfait.
unadventurous [ˌʌnəd'ventʃərəs] adj [person] qui ne prend pas de risques, qui manque d'audace ; [lifestyle] conventionnel, banal ; [performance] terne ; [holiday] banal.
unadvisable [ˌʌnəd'vaɪzəbl] adj imprudent, à déconseiller.
unaffected [ˌʌnə'fektɪd] adj 1. [resistant] non affecté, qui résiste 2. [unchanged, unaltered] qui n'est pas touché or affecté 3. [indifferent] indifférent, insensible 4. [natural - person, manners, character] simple, naturel, sans affectation ; [- style] simple, sans recherche.
unafraid [ˌʌnə'freɪd] adj sans peur, qui n'a pas peur.
unaided [ˌʌn'eɪdɪd] ❖ adj sans aide (extérieure). ❖ adv [work] tout seul, sans être aidé.
unalloyed [ˌʌnə'lɔɪd] adj [joy, enthusiasm] sans mélange, parfait.
unalterable [ʌn'ɔːltərəbl] adj [fact] immuable ; [decision] irrévocable ; [truth] certain, immuable.
unaltered [ʌn'ɔːltəd] adj inchangé, non modifié.
unambiguous [ˌʌnæm'bɪgjʊəs] adj [wording, rule] non ambigu, non équivoque ; [thinking] clair.
unambitious [ˌʌnæm'bɪʃəs] adj sans ambition, peu ambitieux.
un-American adj 1. [uncharacteristic] peu américain 2. [anti-American] antiaméricain.
unanimity [ˌjuːnə'nɪmətɪ] n unanimité f.
unanimous [juː'nænɪməs] adj unanime.
unanimously [juː'nænɪməslɪ] adv [decide, agree] à l'unanimité, unanimement ; [vote] à l'unanimité.
unannounced [ˌʌnə'naʊnst] ❖ adj [arrival, event] inattendu. ❖ adv [unexpectedly] de manière inattendue, sans se faire annoncer ; [suddenly] subitement.
unanswerable [ʌn'ɑːnsərəbl] adj 1. [impossible - question, problem] auquel il est impossible de répondre 2. [irrefutable - argument, logic] irréfutable, incontestable.
unanswered [ˌʌn'ɑːnsəd] adj 1. [question] qui reste sans réponse ; [prayer] inexaucé 2. [letter] (resté) sans réponse.
unappealing [ˌʌnə'piːlɪŋ] adj peu attrayant, peu attirant.
unappetizing, unappetising [ˌʌn'æpɪtaɪzɪŋ] adj peu appétissant.
unappreciated [ˌʌnə'priːʃieɪtɪd] adj [person, talents] méconnu, incompris ; [efforts, kindness] non apprécié, qui n'est pas apprécié.

unappreciative [ˌʌnəˈpriːʃɪətɪv] adj [audience] froid, indifférent ▸ **to be unappreciative of sthg** être indifférent à qqch.

unapproachable [ˌʌnəˈprəʊtʃəbl] adj **1.** [person] inabordable, d'un abord difficile **2.** [place] inaccessible, inabordable.

unarguably [ʌnˈɑːgjʊəblɪ] adv incontestablement.

unarmed [ˌʌnˈɑːmd] adj [person, vehicle] sans armes, non armé.

unarmed combat n combat m à mains nues.

unashamed [ˌʌnəˈʃeɪmd] adj [curiosity, gaze] sans gêne ; [greed, lie, hypocrisy] effronté, sans scrupule ; [person] sans honte.

unashamedly [ˌʌnəˈʃeɪmɪdlɪ] adv [brazenly] sans honte, sans scrupule ; [openly] sans honte, sans se cacher.

unasked [ˌʌnˈɑːskt] ◆ adj [question] que l'on n'a pas posé / *the central question is still unasked* la question essentielle reste à poser. ◆ adv : *they did the job unasked* ils ont fait le travail sans qu'on le leur ait demandé or spontanément.

unassailable [ˌʌnəˈseɪləbl] adj [fort, city] imprenable, inébranlable ; [certainty, belief] inébranlable ; [reputation] inattaquable ; [argument, reason] inattaquable, irréfutable.

unassisted [ˌʌnəˈsɪstɪd] ◆ adv sans aide, tout seul. ◆ adj sans aide.

unassuming [ˌʌnəˈsjuːmɪŋ] adj modeste, sans prétentions.

unattached [ˌʌnəˈtætʃt] adj **1.** [unconnected - building, part, group] indépendant **2.** [not married] libre, sans attaches.

unattainable [ˌʌnəˈteɪnəbl] adj [goal, place] inaccessible.

unattended [ˌʌnəˈtendɪd] adj **1.** [vehicle, luggage] laissé sans surveillance / *do not leave luggage unattended* ne laissez pas vos bagages sans surveillance **2.** [person] sans escorte, seul.

unattractive [ˌʌnəˈtræktɪv] adj [face, room, wallpaper] peu attrayant, assez laid ; [habit] peu attrayant, désagréable ; [personality] déplaisant, peu sympathique ; [prospect] désagréable, peu attrayant, peu agréable.

unauthorized, unauthorised [ˌʌnˈɔːθəraɪzd] adj [absence, entry] non autorisé, fait sans autorisation.

unavailable [ˌʌnəˈveɪləbl] adj [person] indisponible, qui n'est pas libre ; [resources] indisponible, qu'on ne peut se procurer / *the book is unavailable* a) [in library, bookshop] le livre n'est pas disponible b) [from publisher] le livre est épuisé / *the Minister was unavailable for comment* le ministre s'est refusé à tout commentaire.

unavoidable [ˌʌnəˈvɔɪdəbl] adj [accident, delay] inévitable.

unavoidably [ˌʌnəˈvɔɪdəblɪ] adv [happen] inévitablement ; [detain] malencontreusement.

unaware [ˌʌnəˈweər] adj [ignorant] inconscient, qui ignore ▸ **to be unaware of** a) [facts] ignorer, ne pas être au courant de b) [danger] être inconscient de, ne pas avoir conscience de.

unawares [ˌʌnəˈweəz] adv **1.** [by surprise] au dépourvu, à l'improviste ▸ **to catch** or **to take sb unawares** prendre qqn à l'improviste or au dépourvu **2.** [unknowingly] inconsciemment **3.** [by accident] par mégarde, par inadvertance.

unbalance [ˌʌnˈbæləns] ◆ vt déséquilibrer. ◆ n déséquilibre m.

unbalanced [ˌʌnˈbælənst] adj **1.** [load] mal équilibré **2.** [person, mind] déséquilibré, désaxé **3.** [reporting] tendancieux, partial.

unbearable [ʌnˈbeərəbl] adj insupportable.

unbearably [ʌnˈbeərəblɪ] adv insupportablement.

unbeatable [ˌʌnˈbiːtəbl] adj [champion, prices] imbattable.

unbeaten [ˌʌnˈbiːtn] adj [fighter, team] invaincu ; [record, price] non battu.

unbecoming [ˌʌnbɪˈkʌmɪŋ] adj **1.** [dress, colour, hat] peu seyant, qui ne va pas **2.** [behaviour] malséant.

unbeknown(st) [ˌʌnbɪˈnəʊn(st)] adv ▸ **unbeknownst to** à l'insu de.

unbelievable [ˌʌnbɪˈliːvəbl] adj **1.** [extraordinary] incroyable **2.** [implausible] incroyable, invraisemblable.

unbelievably [ˌʌnbɪˈliːvəblɪ] adv **1.** [extraordinarily] incroyablement, extraordinairement **2.** [implausibly] invraisemblablement, incroyablement.

unbend [ˌʌnˈbend] (*pt & pp* **unbent** [-ˈbent]) ◆ vt [fork, wire] redresser, détordre. ◆ vi [relax] se détendre.

unbending [ˌʌnˈbendɪŋ] adj [will, attitude] intransigeant, inflexible.

unbias(s)ed [ˌʌnˈbaɪəst] adj impartial.

unblemished [ˌʌnˈblemɪʃt] adj [purity, skin, colour, reputation] sans tache, sans défaut.

unblinking [ˌʌnˈblɪŋkɪŋ] adj [impassive] impassible ; [fearless] impassible, imperturbable.

unblock [ˌʌnˈblɒk] vt [sink] déboucher ; [traffic jam] dégager.

unbolt [ˌʌnˈbəʊlt] vt [door] déverrouiller, tirer le verrou de ; [scaffolding] déboulonner.

unborn [ˌʌnˈbɔːn] adj [child] qui n'est pas encore né.

unbreakable [ˌʌnˈbreɪkəbl] adj **1.** [crockery] incassable **2.** [habit] dont on ne peut pas se débarrasser **3.** [promise] sacré ; [will, spirit] inébranlable, que l'on ne peut briser.

unbridled [ˌʌnˈbraɪdld] adj [horse] débridé, sans bride ; [anger, greed] sans retenue, effréné.

unbroken [ˌʌnˈbrəʊkn] adj **1.** [line] continu ; [surface, expanse] continu, ininterrompu ; [sleep, tradition, peace] ininterrompu **2.** [crockery, eggs] intact, non cassé ; [fastening, seal] intact, non brisé ; [record] non battu **3.** *fig* [promise] tenu, non rompu **4.** [voice] qui n'a pas (encore) mué **5.** [horse] indompté.

unbuckle [ˌʌnˈbʌkl] vt [belt] déboucler, dégrafer ; [shoe] défaire la boucle de.

unburden [ˌʌnˈbɜːdn] vt *fig* [heart] livrer, épancher, soulager ; [grief, guilt] se décharger de ; [conscience, soul] soulager ▸ **to unburden o.s. to sb** se confier à qqn, s'épancher auprès de qqn.

unbusinesslike [ˌʌnˈbɪznɪslaɪk] adj [person] peu commerçant, qui n'a pas le sens des affaires ; [procedure, handling] peu professionnel.

unbutton [ˌʌnˈbʌtn] ◆ vt [shirt, jacket] déboutonner. ◆ vi *inf & fig* se déboutonner.

uncalled-for [ˌʌnˈkɔːld-] adj [rudeness, outburst] qui n'est pas nécessaire, injustifié ; [remark] mal à propos, déplacé.

uncannily [ʌnˈkænɪlɪ] adv [accurate, familiar] étrangement ; [quiet] mystérieusement, étrangement.

uncanny [ʌnˈkænɪ] (*compar* **uncannier**, *superl* **uncanniest**) adj **1.** [eerie - place] sinistre, qui donne le frisson ; [- noise] mystérieux, sinistre ; [- atmosphere] étrange, sinistre **2.** [strange - accuracy, likeness, ability] troublant, étrange.

uncared-for [ˌʌnˈkeəd-] adj [appearance] négligé, peu soigné ; [house, bicycle] négligé, laissé à l'abandon ; [child] laissé à l'abandon, délaissé.

uncaring [ˌʌnˈkeərɪŋ] adj [unfeeling] insensible, dur.

unceasing [ˌʌnˈsiːsɪŋ] adj incessant, continuel.

uncensored [ˌʌnˈsensəd] adj non censuré.

unceremonious [ˌʌnˌserɪˈməʊnjəs] adj **1.** [abrupt] brusque **2.** [without ceremony] sans façon.

unceremoniously [ˌʌnˌserɪˈməʊnjəslɪ] adv **1.** [abruptly] avec brusquerie, brusquement **2.** [without ceremony] sans cérémonie.

uncertain [ʌnˈsɜːtn] adj **1.** [unsure] incertain / *we were uncertain whether to continue* or *we should continue* nous ne savions pas trop si nous devions continuer ▸ **to be uncertain about sthg** être inquiet au sujet de or incertain de qqch **2.** [unpredictable - result, outcome] incertain, aléatoire ; [- weather] incertain **3.** [unknown] inconnu, incertain **4.** [unsteady - voice, steps] hésitant, mal assuré **5.** [undecided - plans] incertain, pas sûr.

uncertainly [ʌnˈsɜːtnlɪ] adv avec hésitation, d'une manière hésitante.

uncertainty [ʌnˈsɜːtntɪ] (*pl* **uncertainties**) n incertitude *f*, doute *m*.

unchain [ˌʌnˈtʃeɪn] vt [door, dog] enlever or défaire les chaînes de, désenchaîner ; [emotions] déchaîner.

unchallenged [ˌʌnˈtʃæləndʒd] ◆ adj [authority, leader] incontesté, indiscuté ; [version] non contesté. ◆ adv **1.** [unquestioned] sans discussion, sans protestation / *her decisions always go unchallenged* ses décisions ne sont jamais contestées or discutées / *that remark cannot go unchallenged* on ne peut pas laisser passer cette remarque sans protester **2.** [unchecked] sans rencontrer d'opposition.

unchanged [ˌʌnˈtʃeɪndʒd] adj inchangé.

unchanging [ˌʌnˈtʃeɪndʒɪŋ] adj invariable, immuable.

uncharacteristic [ˈʌnˌkærəktəˈrɪstɪk] adj peu caractéristique, peu typique.

uncharacteristically [ˈʌnˌkærəktəˈrɪstɪklɪ] adv d'une façon peu caractéristique.

uncharitable [ˌʌnˈtʃærɪtəbl] adj [unkind] peu charitable, peu indulgent.

uncharted [ˌʌnˈtʃɑːtɪd] adj **1.** [unmapped - region, forest, ocean] dont on n'a pas dressé la carte ; [not on map] qui n'est pas sur la carte **2.** *fig* : *the uncharted regions of the mind* les coins inexplorés de l'esprit.

unchecked [ˌʌnˈtʃekt] ◆ adj **1.** [unrestricted - growth, expansion, tendency] non maîtrisé ; [anger, instinct] non réprimé, auquel on laisse libre cours **2.** [unverified - source, figures] non vérifié ; [proofs] non relu. ◆ adv **1.** [grow, expand] continuellement, sans arrêt ; [continue] impunément, sans opposition **2.** [advance] sans rencontrer d'opposition.

uncivil [ˌʌnˈsɪvl] adj impoli, grossier ▸ **to be uncivil to sb** être impoli envers or à l'égard de qqn.

uncivilized, uncivilised [ˌʌnˈsɪvɪlaɪzd] adj **1.** [people, tribe] non civilisé **2.** [primitive, barbaric - behaviour, conditions] barbare ; [- people] barbare, inculte **3.** *fig* [ridiculous] impossible, extraordinaire.

unclaimed [ˌʌnˈkleɪmd] adj [property, reward] non réclamé ; [rights] non revendiqué.

unclassified [ˌʌnˈklæsɪfaɪd] adj **1.** [not sorted - books, papers] non classé **2.** 🇬🇧 [road] non classé **3.** [information] non secret.

uncle [ˈʌŋkl] n [relative] oncle *m*.

unclean [ˌʌnˈkliːn] adj [dirty - water] sale ; [- habits] sale.

unclear [ˌʌnˈklɪə] adj **1.** [confused, ambiguous - thinking, purpose, reason] pas clair, pas évident / *I'm still unclear about what exactly I have to do* je ne sais pas encore très bien ce que je dois faire exactement **2.** [uncertain - future, outcome] incertain **3.** [indistinct - sound, speech] indistinct, inaudible ; [- outline] flou.

Uncle Sam [-sæm] pr n Oncle Sam *(personnage représentant les États-Unis dans la propagande pour l'armée).*

unclothed [ˌʌnˈkləʊðd] adj dévêtu, nu.

uncluttered [ˌʌnˈklʌtəd] adj [room] dépouillé, simple ; [style of writing] sobre ; [design] dépouillé ; [mind, thinking] clair, net.

uncomfortable [ˌʌnˈkʌmftəbl] adj **1.** [physically - chair, bed, clothes] inconfortable, peu confortable ; [- position] inconfortable, peu commode **2.** *fig* [awkward, uneasy - person] mal à l'aise, gêné ; [difficult, embarrassing - situation, truth] difficile, gênant ; [unpleasant] désagréable / *I feel uncomfortable about the whole thing* je me sens mal à l'aise avec tout ça ▸ **to make sb (feel) uncomfortable** mettre qqn mal à l'aise.

uncomfortably [ˌʌnˈkʌmftəblɪ] adv **1.** [lie, sit, stand] inconfortablement, peu confortablement ; [dressed] mal, inconfortablement **2.** [unpleasantly - heavy, hot] désagréablement **3.** [uneasily] avec gêne.

uncommitted [ˌʌnkəˈmɪtɪd] adj [person, literature] non engagé.

uncommon [ʌnˈkɒmən] adj **1.** [rare, unusual - disease, species] rare, peu commun **2.** *fml* [exceptional] singulier, extraordinaire.

uncommonly [ʌnˈkɒmənlɪ] adv **1.** [rarely] rarement, inhabituellement **2.** *fig* [exceptionally - clever, cold, polite] singulièrement, exceptionnellement.

uncommunicative [ˌʌnkəˈmjuːnɪkətɪv] adj peu communicatif, taciturne ▸ **to be uncommunicative about sthg** se montrer réservé sur qqch.

uncomplaining [ˌʌnkəmˈpleɪnɪŋ] adj qui ne se plaint pas.

uncomplicated [ˌʌnˈkɒmplɪkeɪtɪd] adj peu compliqué, simple.

uncomprehending [ˈʌnˌkɒmprɪˈhendɪŋ] adj qui ne comprend pas.

uncomprehendingly [ˈʌnˌkɒmprɪˈhendɪŋlɪ] adv sans comprendre.

uncompromising [ˌʌnˈkɒmprəmaɪzɪŋ] adj [rigid - attitude, behaviour] rigide, intransigeant, inflexible ; [committed - person] convaincu, ardent.

uncompromisingly [ˌʌnˈkɒmprəmaɪzɪŋlɪ] adv sans concession, de manière intransigeante.

unconcerned [ˌʌnkənˈsɜːd] adj **1.** [unworried, calm] qui ne s'inquiète pas, insouciant **2.** [uninterested] indifférent.

unconditional [ˌʌnkənˈdɪʃənl] adj **1.** [support, submission] inconditionnel, sans condition **2.** MATH [equality] sans conditions.

unconditionally [ˌʌnkənˈdɪʃnəlɪ] adv [accept, surrender] inconditionnellement, sans condition.

unconfirmed [ˌʌnkənˈfɜːmd] adj non confirmé.

uncongenial [ˌʌnkənˈdʒiːnjəl] adj [surroundings] peu agréable ; [personality] antipathique.

unconnected [ˌʌnkəˈnektɪd] adj [unrelated - facts, incidents] sans rapport ; [- ideas, thoughts] sans suite, décousu.

unconquered [ˌʌnˈkɒŋkəd] adj [nation, territory] qui n'a pas été conquis ; [mountain] invaincu.

unconscious [ʌnˈkɒnʃəs] ◆ adj **1.** [in coma] sans connaissance ; [in faint] évanoui **2.** [unaware] inconscient **3.** [unintentional] inconscient, involontaire **4.** PSYCHOL [motives] inconscient ▸ **the unconscious mind** l'inconscient *m*. ◆ n [gen & PSYCHOL] inconscient *m* ▸ **the unconscious** l'inconscient.

unconsciously [ʌnˈkɒnʃəslɪ] adv inconsciemment, sans s'en rendre compte.

unconsciousness [ʌnˈkɒnʃəsnɪs] n (U) **1.** MED [coma] perte *f* de connaissance ; [fainting] évanouissement *m* **2.** [lack of awareness] inconscience *f*.

unconstitutional [ˈʌnˌkɒnstɪˈtjuːʃənl] adj inconstitutionnel.

uncontaminated [ˌʌnkən'tæmɪneɪtɪd] adj non contaminé.

uncontested [ˌʌnkən'testɪd] adj [position, authority] non disputé, incontesté.

uncontrollable [ˌʌnkən'trəʊləbl] adj 1. [fear, desire, urge] irrésistible, irrépressible ; [stammer] que l'on ne peut maîtriser or contrôler 2. [animal] indomptable ; [child] impossible à discipliner 3. [inflation] qui ne peut être freiné, galopant.

uncontrollably [ˌʌnkən'trəʊləblɪ] adv 1. [helplessly] irrésistiblement 2. [out of control] : *the boat rocked uncontrollably* on n'arrivait pas à maîtriser le tangage du bateau 3. [fall, increase] irrésistiblement.

uncontrolled [ˌʌnkən'trəʊld] adj 1. [unrestricted - fall, rise] effréné, incontrôlé ; [- population growth] non contrôlé ; [- anger, emotion] incontrôlé, non retenu 2. [unverified - experiment] non contrôlé.

uncontroversial ['ʌnˌkɒntrə'vɜː'ʃl] adj qui ne prête pas à controverse, incontestable.

unconventional [ˌʌnkən'venʃənl] adj non conformiste.

unconventionally [ˌʌnkən'venʃnəlɪ] adv [live, think] d'une manière originale or peu conventionnelle ; [dress] d'une manière originale.

unconvinced [ˌʌnkən'vɪnst] adj incrédule, sceptique ▸ **to be / to remain unconvinced by sthg** être / rester sceptique à l'égard de qqch.

unconvincing [ˌʌnkən'vɪnsɪŋ] adj peu convaincant.

unconvincingly [ˌʌnkən'vɪnsɪŋlɪ] adv [argue, lie] d'un ton or d'une manière peu convaincante, peu vraisemblablement.

uncooked [ˌʌn'kʊkt] adj non cuit, cru.

uncool [ˌʌn'kuːl] adj *inf* pas cool.

uncooperative [ˌʌnkəʊ'ɒpərətɪv] adj peu coopératif.

uncork [ˌʌn'kɔːk] vt [bottle] déboucher ; *fig* [emotions] déchaîner.

uncorroborated [ˌʌnkə'rɒbəreɪtɪd] adj non corroboré.

uncountable [ˌʌn'kaʊntəbl] adj 1. [numberless] incalculable, innombrable 2. GRAM non dénombrable.

uncouth [ʌn'kuːθ] adj grossier, fruste.

uncover [ʌn'kʌvər] vt découvrir.

uncritical [ˌʌn'krɪtɪkl] adj [naïve] dépourvu d'esprit critique, non critique ; [unquestioning] inconditionnel.

uncrushable [ˌʌn'krʌʃəbl] adj [fabric] infroissable.

unctuous ['ʌŋktjʊəs] adj *fml* mielleux, onctueux.

uncultured [ˌʌn'kʌltʃəd] adj [manners, person] inculte ; [accent, speech] qui manque de raffinement.

uncurl [ˌʌn'kɜːl] vt [rope] dérouler ; [body, toes] étirer.

uncut [ˌʌn'kʌt] adj 1. [hair, nails] non coupé ; [hedge, stone] non taillé ; [diamond] non taillé, brut ; [corn, wheat] non récolté, sur pied ; [pages] non rogné ; [drugs] pur 2. [uncensored - film, text] intégral, sans coupures 3. *inf* [uncircumcised] non circoncis.

undamaged [ˌʌn'dæmɪdʒd] adj 1. [car, contents, merchandise, building, roof] indemne, intact, non endommagé 2. *fig* [reputation] intact.

undaunted [ˌʌn'dɔːntɪd] adj 1. [not discouraged] qui ne se laisse pas décourager or démonter 2. [fearless] sans peur.

undecided [ˌʌndɪ'saɪdɪd] adj [person, issue] indécis ; [outcome] incertain.

undefeated [ˌʌndɪ'fiːtɪd] adj invaincu.

undelivered [ˌʌndɪ'lɪvəd] adj [letter] non remis, non distribué ▸ *if undelivered please return to sender* en cas de non-distribution, prière de retourner à l'expéditeur.

undemanding [ˌʌndɪ'mɑːndɪŋ] adj [person] facile à vivre, qui n'est pas exigeant ; [work] simple, qui n'est pas astreignant.

undemocratic ['ʌnˌdeməʊ'krætɪk] adj antidémocratique, peu démocratique.

undemonstrative [ˌʌndɪ'mɒnstrətɪv] adj réservé, peu démonstratif.

undeniable [ˌʌndɪ'naɪəbl] adj indéniable, incontestable.

undeniably [ˌʌndɪ'naɪəblɪ] adv [true] incontestablement, indiscutablement.

under ['ʌndər] ◆ prep 1. [beneath, below] sous / *the newspaper was under the chair / cushion* le journal était sous la chaise / le coussin / *I can't see anything under it* je ne vois rien (en) dessous 2. [less than] moins de / *everything is under £5* tout est à moins de 5 livres / *is she under 16?* est-ce qu'elle a moins de 16 ans ? 3. [indicating conditions or circumstances] sous, dans / *we had to work under appalling conditions* on a dû travailler dans des conditions épouvantables ; [subject to] sous / *under duress / threat* sous la contrainte / la menace 4. [directed, governed by] sous (la direction de) / *he studied under Fox* il a été l'élève de Fox 5. [according to] conformément à, en vertu de, selon / *under the new law, all this will change* avec la nouvelle loi, tout ceci va changer / *under (the terms of) his will / the agreement* selon (les termes de) son testament / l'accord 6. [in the process of] en cours de / *the matter is under consideration / discussion* on est en train d'étudier / de discuter la question 7. [in classification] : *you'll find the book under philosophy* vous trouverez le livre sous la rubrique philosophie / *she writes under the name of Heidi Croft* elle écrit sous le nom de Heidi Croft. ◆ adv 1. [with verbs] [below ground, water, door, etc.] ▸ **to slide** or **to slip under** se glisser dessous ▸ **to stay under** [under water] rester sous l'eau 2. [less - in age, price] : *you have to be 16 or under to enter* il faut avoir 16 ans ou moins pour se présenter.

under- in comp 1. [below] sous- / *holidays for the under-30s* vacances pour les moins de 30 ans 2. [junior] sous-.

underachieve [ˌʌndərə'tʃiːv] vi ne pas obtenir les résultats attendus.

underachiever [ˌʌndərə'tʃiːvər] n [gen] personne ou élève qui n'obtient pas les résultats escomptés.

underage [ˌʌndər'eɪdʒ] adj [person] mineur ▸ **underage drinking** consommation f d'alcool par les mineurs ▸ **underage sex** rapports mpl sexuels avant l'âge légal.

underarm ['ʌndərɑːm] ◆ adv SPORT [bowl, hit] (par) en dessous. ◆ adj [deodorant] pour les aisselles ; [hair] sous les bras or les aisselles.

underbelly ['ʌndəˌbelɪ] (pl **underbellies**) n *fig* point m faible.

underbrush ['ʌndəbrʌʃ] n (U) US sous-bois m, broussailles fpl.

undercarriage ['ʌndəˌkærɪdʒ] n [of aeroplane] train m d'atterrissage ; [of vehicle] châssis m.

undercharge [ˌʌndə'tʃɑːdʒ] vt [customer] faire payer insuffisamment or moins cher à.

underclass [ˌʌndə'klɑːs] n ▸ **the underclass** les exclus, le quart-monde.

underclothes ['ʌndəkləʊðz] pl n sous-vêtements mpl ; [for women] lingerie f, dessous mpl.

undercoat ['ʌndəkəʊt] n [of paint] sous-couche f ; [of anti-rust] couche f d'antirouille.

undercook [ˌʌndə'kʊk] vt ne pas assez cuire.

undercover ['ʌndəˌkʌvər] adj [methods, work] secret (secrète), clandestin.

undercurrent ['ʌndə,kʌrənt] n **1.** [in sea] courant *m* sous-marin ; [in river] courant *m* **2.** *fig* [feeling] sentiment *m* sous-jacent.

undercut [,ʌndə'kʌt] (*pt* & *pp* **undercut**, *cont* **undercutting**) vt **1.** COMM [competitor] vendre moins cher que ; [prices] casser **2.** [undermine - efforts, principle] amoindrir.

underdeveloped [,ʌndədɪ'veləpt] adj **1.** [country, society] en voie de développement **2.** [stunted - foetus, plant] qui n'est pas complètement développé or formé **3.** *fig* [argument, idea] insuffisamment développé or exposé **4.** PHOT [film, print] insuffisamment développé.

underdog ['ʌndədɒg] n ▶ **the underdog a)** [in fight, contest] celui *m* / celle *f* qui risque de perdre or qui part perdant **b)** [in society] le laissé-pour-compte *m*, la laissée-pour-compte *f*, opprimé *m*, -e *f*.

underdone [,ʌndə'dʌn] adj [accidentally] pas assez cuit ; [deliberately - meat] saignant ; [- vegetable, cake] pas trop cuit.

underemployment [,ʌndərɪm'plɔɪmənt] n [of workers] sous-emploi *m* ; [of resources] sous-exploitation *f*.

underestimate ◆ vt [,ʌndər'estɪmeɪt] [size, strength] sous-estimer ; [person, value] sous-estimer, mésestimer. ◆ n [,ʌndər'estɪmət] sous-estimation *f*.

underestimation ['ʌndər,estɪ'meɪʃn] n sous-estimation *f*.

underexpose [,ʌndərɪk'spəʊz] vt **1.** PHOT [print, film] sous-exposer **2.** [person] faire insuffisamment la publicité de.

underfed [,ʌndə'fed] ◆ pt & pp ⟶ **underfeed**. ◆ adj [person] sous-alimenté.

underfinanced [,ʌndə'faɪnænst] adj [business, scheme, school] qui manque de fonds.

underfoot [,ʌndə'fʊt] adv sous les pieds.

underfunded [ʌndə'fʌndɪd] = **underfinanced**.

underfunding [ʌndə'fʌndɪŋ] n financement *m* insuffisant.

undergo [,ʌndə'gəʊ] (*pt* **underwent** [-'went], *pp* **undergone** [-'gɒn]) vt **1.** [experience - change] subir ; [- hardship] subir, éprouver **2.** [test, trials] subir, passer ; [training] suivre **3.** [be subject to] subir **4.** MED ▶ **to undergo an operation** subir une intervention chirurgicale ▶ **to undergo treatment** suivre un traitement.

undergraduate [,ʌndə'grædʒʊət] ◆ n étudiant *m*, -e *f* (*qui prépare une licence*). ◆ adj [circles, life] estudiantin, étudiant ; [course] pour les étudiants de licence ; [accommodation, grant] pour étudiants ; [humour] d'étudiant.

underground ◆ adj ['ʌndəgraʊnd] **1.** [subterranean - explosion] souterrain ; [- car park] en sous-sol, souterrain ▶ **underground railway** métro *m* **2.** [secret] secret (secrète), clandestin **3.** [unofficial - literature, theatre] d'avant-garde, underground (*inv*) ; [- institutions] parallèle. ◆ n ['ʌndəgraʊnd] **1.** MIL & POL [resistance] résistance *f* ; [secret army] armée *f* secrète **2.** ART, MUS & THEAT avant-garde *f*, underground *m inv* **3.** 🇬🇧 [railway] métro *m* ▶ **to go by underground** aller en métro. ◆ adv ['ʌndə'graʊnd] **1.** [below surface] sous (la) terre **2.** [in hiding] ▶ **to go underground** passer dans la clandestinité, prendre le maquis.

underground economy n économie *f* souterraine or immergée.

undergrowth ['ʌndəgrəʊθ] n (U) sous-bois *m* ; [scrub] broussailles *fpl*.

underhand [,ʌndə'hænd] ◆ adj [action] en dessous, en sous-main ; [person] sournois. ◆ adv sournoisement.

underinsure [,ʌndərɪn'ʃɔːr] vt sous-assurer.

underlay ◆ pt ⟶ **underlie**. ◆ vt [,ʌndə'leɪ] (*pt* & *pp* **underlaid** [-'leɪd]) [carpet] doubler. ◆ n ['ʌndəleɪ] [felt] thibaude *f* ; [foam] doublure *f*.

underlie [,ʌndə'laɪ] (*pt* **underlay** [,ʌndə'leɪ], *pp* **underlain** [,ʌndə'leɪn]) vt sous-tendre, être à la base de.

underline [,ʌndə'laɪn] vt *lit* & *fig* souligner.

underling ['ʌndəlɪŋ] n *pej* subalterne *mf*, sous-fifre *m*.

underlying [,ʌndə'laɪɪŋ] adj sous-jacent.

undermanned [,ʌndə'mænd] adj à court de personnel ; NAUT à équipage incomplet.

undermentioned [,ʌndə'menʃnd] adj *fml* ADMIN ci-dessous (mentionné).

undermine [,ʌndə'maɪn] vt [cliff] miner, saper ; [authority, person] saper ; [health] user ; [confidence] ébranler.

underneath [,ʌndə'niːθ] ◆ prep sous, au-dessous de, en dessous de **/ she was wearing two pullovers underneath her coat** elle portait deux pull-overs sous son manteau. ◆ adv [in space] (en) dessous, au-dessous **/ I've got a pullover on underneath** j'ai un pull dessous.

undernourished [,ʌndə'nʌrɪʃt] adj sous-alimenté.

underpaid ◆ adj ['ʌndəpeɪd] sous-payé. ◆ pt & pp [,ʌndə'peɪd] ⟶ **underpay**.

underpants ['ʌndəpænts] pl n **1.** [for men] slip *m* (*d'homme*) ▶ **a pair of underpants** un caleçon **2.** 🇺🇸 [for women] culotte *f*.

underpass ['ʌndəpɑːs] n **1.** [subway] passage *m* souterrain **2.** [road] route *f* inférieure.

underpay [,ʌndə'peɪ] (*pt* & *pp* **underpaid** [,ʌndə-'peɪd]) vt sous-payer.

underperform [,ʌndəpə'fɔːm] vi rester en deçà de ses possibilités.

underpin [,ʌndə'pɪn] (*pt* & *pp* **underpinned**, *cont* **underpinning**) vt *lit* & *fig* soutenir, étayer.

underplay [,ʌndə'pleɪ] ◆ vt **1.** [minimize - importance] minimiser ; [- event] réduire or minimiser l'importance de **2.** THEAT [role] jouer avec retenue. ◆ vi [in cards] jouer volontairement une petite carte.

underpopulated [,ʌndə'pɒpjuleɪtɪd] adj sous-peuplé.

underprice [,ʌndə'praɪs] vt **1.** [for sale] vendre au-dessous de sa valeur **2.** [for estimate] sous-évaluer.

underprivileged [,ʌndə'prɪvɪlɪdʒd] ◆ adj [person, social class] défavorisé, déshérité. ◆ pl n ▶ **the underprivileged** les économiquement faibles *mpl*.

underproduction [,ʌndəprə'dʌkʃn] n sous-production *f*.

underqualified ['ʌndə'kwɒlɪ,faɪd] adj sous-qualifié.

underrated [,ʌndə'reɪtɪd] adj [person] méconnu ; [book, film] sous-estimé.

underscore [,ʌndə'skɔːr] ◆ vt souligner. ◆ n soulignage *m*, soulignement *m*.

undersea ['ʌndəsiː] ◆ adj sous-marin. ◆ adv sous la mer.

undersecretary [,ʌndə'sekrətərɪ] (*pl* **undersecretaries**) n POL **1.** 🇬🇧 [in department] chef *m* de cabinet **2.** [politician] sous-secrétaire *m*.

undersell [,ʌndə'sel] (*pt* & *pp* **undersold** [,ʌndə-'səʊld]) ◆ vt [competitor] vendre moins cher que ; [goods] vendre au rabais. ◆ vi [goods] se vendre mal.

undersheet ['ʌndəʃiːt] n alaise *f*.

undershirt ['ʌndəʃɜːt] n 🇺🇸 maillot *m* or tricot *m* de corps.

underside ['ʌndəsaɪd] n ▶ **the underside** le dessous, la face inférieure.

undersigned ['ʌndəsaɪnd] (*pl* **undersigned**) *fml* ◆ n ▶ **the undersigned** le soussigné, la soussignée. ◆ adj soussigné.

undersize(d) [,ʌndə'saɪz(d)] adj trop petit.

underskirt ['ʌndəskɜːt] n jupon *m*.

understaffed [ˌʌndə'stɑːft] adj qui manque de personnel.

understand [ˌʌndə'stænd] (pt & pp **understood** [-'stʊd]) ◆ vt **1.** [meaning] comprendre / I understand what you mean je comprends ce que vous voulez dire ▸ **to make o.s. understood** se faire comprendre / she didn't understand a single word elle n'a pas compris un traître mot / I can't understand it! je ne comprends pas !, cela me dépasse ! **2.** [subject, theory] comprendre, entendre / I don't understand a thing about economics je ne comprends rien à l'économie **3.** [character, person] comprendre / I understand your need to be independent je comprends bien que vous ayez besoin d'être indépendant / she didn't understand why no one was interested elle ne comprenait pas pourquoi personne n'était intéressé **4.** [believe] comprendre, croire / I understand you need a loan j'ai cru comprendre que or si j'ai bien compris, vous avez besoin d'un prêt / we were given to understand that he was very ill on nous a fait comprendre or donné à entendre qu'il était très malade **5.** [interpret] entendre / as I understand it, there's nothing to pay d'après ce que j'ai compris, il n'y a rien à payer **6.** [leave implicit] entendre, sous-entendre / she let it be understood that she preferred to be alone elle a laissé entendre or donné à entendre qu'elle préférait être seule. ◆ vi comprendre / of course, I understand bien sûr, je comprends (bien).

> 📋 Note that **comprendre que** is followed by a verb in the subjunctive when the situation being talked about is open to interpretation:
> **I understand the fact that you're angry.** Je comprends que vous soyez en colère.
> **I don't understand how anyone can be that stupid.** Je ne comprends pas qu'on puisse être aussi idiot.
> But
> **They've understood that there is no hope left.** Ils ont compris qu'il n'y a or avait (indicative) plus d'espoir.
> **Do you understand that this is against the law?** Comprenez-vous que ceci est (indicative) interdit par la loi ?

understandable [ˌʌndə'stændəbl] adj compréhensible.

> 📋 Note that **il est compréhensible que** is followed by a verb in the subjunctive:
> **It's understandable that they don't want to repeat the same mistakes.** Il est compréhensible qu'ils ne veuillent pas commettre les mêmes erreurs.

understandably [ˌʌndə'stændəbli] adv **1.** [naturally] naturellement **2.** [speak, write] de manière compréhensible.

understanding [ˌʌndə'stændɪŋ] ◆ n **1.** (U) [comprehension] compréhension f ; [intelligence] intelligence f ; [knowledge] connaissance f, connaissances fpl **2.** [agreement] accord m, arrangement m ▸ **to come to an understanding about sthg (with sb)** s'entendre (avec qqn) sur qqch **3.** [interpretation] compréhension f, interprétation f ; [conception] conception f **4.** [relationship - between people] bonne intelligence f, entente f ; [- between nations] entente f **5.** [sympathy] : he showed great understanding il a fait preuve de beaucoup de compréhension. ◆ adj compréhensif, bienveillant. ◆ **on the understanding that** conj phr à condition que.

understandingly [ˌʌndə'stændɪŋlɪ] adv avec compréhension, avec bienveillance.

understate [ˌʌndə'steɪt] vt [minimize] minimiser (l'importance de).

understated [ˌʌndə'steɪtɪd] adj discret (discrète).

understatement [ˌʌndə'steɪtmənt] n **1.** affirmation f en dessous de la vérité **2.** LING & LITER litote f.

understood [-'stʊd] pt & pp ⟶ **understand**.

understudy ['ʌndə,stʌdɪ] (pl understudies, pt & pp understudied) ◆ n THEAT doublure f. ◆ vt [role] apprendre un rôle en tant que doublure ; [actor] doubler.

undertake [ˌʌndə'teɪk] (pt undertook [-'tʊk], pp undertaken [-'teɪkn]) vt fml **1.** [take up - job, project] entreprendre ; [- experiment] entreprendre, se lancer dans ; [- responsibility] assumer, se charger de ; [- change] entreprendre, mettre en œuvre **2.** [agree, promise] s'engager à.

undertaker ['ʌndə,teɪkə] n 🇬🇧 ordonnateur m des pompes funèbres.

undertaking [ˌʌndə'teɪkɪŋ] n **1.** [promise] engagement m **2.** [enterprise] entreprise f.

underthings ['ʌndəθɪŋz] pl n inf dessous mpl, sous-vêtements mpl.

undertone ['ʌndətəʊn] n [in speech] voix f basse.

undertook [-'tʊk] pt ⟶ **undertake**.

underused [ˌʌndə'juːzd], **underutilized** [ˌʌndə-'juːtəlaɪzd] adj [facilities, land, resources] sous-exploité.

undervalue [ˌʌndə'væljuː] vt [object] sous-évaluer, sous-estimer ; [person, help] sous-estimer.

underwater [ˌʌndə'wɔːtə] ◆ adj sous-marin. ◆ adv sous l'eau.

underwear ['ʌndəweə] n (U) sous-vêtements mpl.

underweight [ˌʌndə'weɪt] adj **1.** [person] qui ne pèse pas assez, trop maigre **2.** [goods] d'un poids insuffisant.

underwent [-'went] pt ⟶ **undergo**.

underwhelm [ˌʌndə'welm] vt hum décevoir, désappointer / I found the whole affair distinctly underwhelming j'ai trouvé toute l'affaire vraiment décevante / she felt rather underwhelmed by it all elle a été plutôt déçue par tout ça.

underworld ['ʌndə,wɜːld] ◆ n **1.** [of criminals] pègre f, milieu m **2.** MYTH ▸ **the underworld** les Enfers mpl. ◆ comp [activity] du milieu ; [contact] dans or avec le milieu.

underwrite ['ʌndəraɪt] (pt underwrote [-'rəʊt], pp underwritten [-'rɪtn]) vt **1.** [for insurance - policy] garantir ; [- risk] garantir, assurer contre **2.** ST. EX [shares] garantir.

underwriter ['ʌndə,raɪtə] n **1.** [of insurance] assureur m **2.** ST. EX syndicataire mf.

underwritten [-'rɪtn] pp ⟶ **underwrite**.

underwrote [-'rəʊt] pt ⟶ **underwrite**.

undeserved [ˌʌndɪ'zɜːvd] adj immérité, injuste.

undeservedly [ˌʌndɪ'zɜːvɪdlɪ] adv injustement, indûment.

undeserving [ˌʌndɪ'zɜːvɪŋ] adj [person] peu méritant ; [cause] peu méritoire.

undesirable [ˌʌndɪ'zaɪərəbl] ◆ adj indésirable. ◆ n indésirable mf.

undetected [ˌʌndɪ'tektɪd] adj [error] non détecté, non décelé ; [disease] non détecté, non dépisté.

undeterred [ˌʌndɪ'tɜːd] adj sans se laisser décourager.

undeveloped [ˌʌndɪ'veləpt] adj non développé ; [country] en développement ; [muscles, organs] non formé ; [land, resources] non exploité.

undid [ˌʌn'dɪd] pt ⟶ **undo**.

undies ['ʌndɪz] pl n *inf* dessous *mpl.*

undignified [ʌn'dɪgnɪfaɪd] adj [behaviour, person] qui manque de dignité.

undiluted [,ʌndaɪ'lju:tɪd] adj **1.** [juice] non dilué **2.** *fig* [emotion] sans mélange, parfait.

undiplomatic [,ʌndɪplə'mætɪk] adj [action] peu diplomatique ; [person] peu diplomate, qui manque de diplomatie.

undisciplined [ʌn'dɪsɪplɪnd] adj indiscipliné.

undisclosed [,ʌndɪs'kləʊzd] adj non divulgué.

undiscovered [,ʌndɪ'skʌvəd] adj non découvert.

undiscriminating [,ʌndɪs'krɪmɪneɪtɪŋ] adj qui manque de discernement.

undisguised [,ʌndɪs'ɡaɪzd] adj non déguisé, non dissimulé.

undisputed [,ʌndɪ'spju:tɪd] adj incontesté.

undistinguished [,ʌndɪ'stɪŋgwɪʃt] adj **1.** [person] peu distingué, sans distinction **2.** [style, taste] banal, quelconque.

undisturbed [,ʌndɪ'stɜ:bd] adj **1.** [in peace] tranquille **2.** [unchanged, untroubled] inchangé, tranquille **3.** [untouched - body, ground, papers] non dérangé, non déplacé.

undivided [,ʌndɪ'vaɪdɪd] adj **1.** [whole] entier **2.** [unanimous] unanime.

undo [,ʌn'du:] (*pt* undid [-dɪd], *pp* undone [-'dʌn]) ◆ vt **1.** [bow, knot] défaire **2.** [ruin - work] détruire ; [- effect] annuler ; [- plan] mettre en échec. ◆ vt & vi COMPUT annuler.

undocumented [,ʌn'dɒkjumentɪd] adj non documenté.

undoing [,ʌn'du:ɪŋ] n (cause *f* de) perte *f.*

undone [-'dʌn] ◆ pp ⟶ undo. ◆ adj **1.** [button, clothes, hair] défait **2.** [task] non accompli.

undoubted [ʌn'daʊtɪd] adj indubitable.

undoubtedly [ʌn'daʊtɪdlɪ] adv indubitablement.

undress [,ʌn'dres] ◆ vt déshabiller. ◆ vi se déshabiller.

undressed [,ʌn'drest] adj [person] déshabillé.

undrinkable [ʌn'drɪŋkəbl] adj **1.** [bad-tasting] imbuvable **2.** [unfit for drinking] non potable.

undue [,ʌn'dju:] adj excessif.

undulate ['ʌndjʊleɪt] vi onduler.

undulating ['ʌndjʊleɪtɪŋ] adj [curves, hills] onduleux.

unduly [,ʌn'dju:lɪ] adv excessivement, trop.

undying [ʌn'daɪɪŋ] adj [faith] éternel.

unearned income n (U) revenus *mpl* non professionnels, rentes *fpl.*

unearth [,ʌn'ɜ:θ] vt **1.** [dig up] déterrer **2.** *fig* [find - equipment, fact] dénicher, trouver ; [- old ideas] ressortir, ressusciter.

unearthly [ʌn'ɜ:θlɪ] adj **1.** [weird] étrange ; [unnatural] surnaturel ; [mysterious] mystérieux ; [sinister] sinistre **2.** *fig* ▸ **at an unearthly hour** à une heure indue.

unease [ʌn'i:z] n *liter* **1.** [of mind] inquiétude *f*, malaise *m* ; [embarrassment] malaise *m*, gêne *f* **2.** POL [unrest] troubles *mpl* ; [tension] tension *f.*

uneasily [ʌn'i:zɪlɪ] adv **1.** [anxiously - wait, watch] anxieusement, avec inquiétude ; [- sleep] d'un sommeil agité **2.** [with embarrassment] avec gêne, mal à l'aise.

uneasy [ʌn'i:zɪ] (*compar* uneasier, *superl* uneasiest) adj **1.** [troubled - person] inquiet (inquiète) ; [- sleep] agité **2.** [embarrassed - person] mal à l'aise, gêné ; [- silence] gêné **3.** [uncertain - peace, situation] précaire.

uneatable [,ʌn'i:təbl] adj immangeable.

uneaten [,ʌn'i:tn] adj qui n'a pas été mangé.

uneconomic ['ʌn,i:kə'nɒmɪk] adj **1.** [expensive] peu économique ; [unproductive] non rentable **2.** = uneconomical.

uneconomical ['ʌn,i:kə'nɒmɪkl] adj [wasteful] peu rentable.

uneducated [,ʌn'edjʊkeɪtɪd] adj **1.** [person] sans instruction **2.** [behaviour, manners] sans éducation, inculte ; [writing] informe ; [speech] populaire.

unelectable [,ʌnɪ'lektəbl] adj [person] inéligible ; [party] incapable de remporter des élections.

unemotional [,ʌnɪ'məʊʃənl] adj [person] impassible ; [behaviour, reaction] qui ne trahit aucune émotion ; [voice] neutre ; [account, style] sans passion, neutre.

unemployable [,ʌnɪm'plɔɪəbl] adj [person] inapte au travail, que l'on ne peut pas embaucher.

unemployed [,ʌnɪm'plɔɪd] ◆ pl n ▸ **the unemployed** les chômeurs *mpl*, les demandeurs *mpl* d'emploi. ◆ adj au chômage.

unemployment [,ʌnɪm'plɔɪmənt] ◆ n chômage *m.* ◆ comp [compensation, rate] de chômage.

unemployment benefit n 🇬🇧 allocation *f* de chômage.

unending [ʌn'endɪŋ] adj sans fin, interminable.

unenthusiastic [ʌnɪn,θju:zɪ'æstɪk] adj peu enthousiaste.

unenviable [,ʌn'envɪəbl] adj [conditions, situation, task] peu enviable.

unequal [,ʌn'i:kwəl] adj [amount, number, result] inégal.

unequalled 🇬🇧, **unequaled** 🇺🇸 [,ʌn'i:kwəld] adj inégalé, sans pareil.

unequivocal [,ʌnɪ'kwɪvəkl] adj sans équivoque.

unerring [,ʌn'ɜ:rɪŋ] adj infaillible, sûr ; [accuracy, judgement] infaillible, sûr ; [aim] sûr.

UNESCO [ju:'neskəʊ] (**abbr of United Nations Educational, Scientific and Cultural Organization**) pr n UNESCO *f*, Unesco *f.*

unethical [ʌn'eθɪkl] adj contraire à l'éthique.

uneven [,ʌn'i:vn] adj **1.** [line] irrégulier, qui n'est pas droit ; [surface] irrégulier, rugueux ; [ground] raboteux, accidenté ; [edge] inégal **2.** [number] impair.

unevenly [,ʌn'i:vnlɪ] adv **1.** [divide, spread] inégalement **2.** [cut, draw] irrégulièrement.

uneventful [,ʌnɪ'ventfʊl] adj [day] sans événement marquant, sans histoires.

unexceptional [,ʌnɪk'sepʃənl] adj qui n'a rien d'exceptionnel, banal.

unexciting [,ʌnɪk'saɪtɪŋ] adj [life] peu passionnant ; [film] sans grand intérêt ; [food] quelconque.

unexpected [,ʌnɪk'spektɪd] adj inattendu, imprévu.

unexpectedly [,ʌnɪk'spektɪdlɪ] adv **1.** [arrive] à l'improviste, de manière imprévue ; [fail, succeed] contre toute attente, de manière inattendue **2.** [surprisingly] étonnamment.

unexplained [,ʌnɪk'spleɪnd] adj [mystery, reason] inexpliqué.

unexploded [,ʌnɪk'spləʊdɪd] adj non explosé.

unexplored [,ʌnɪk'splɔ:d] adj inexploré, inconnu ; [solution, possibility] inexploré.

unexpurgated [,ʌn'ekspəgeɪtɪd] adj non expurgé, intégral.

unfailing [ʌn'feɪlɪŋ] adj [loyalty, support] sûr, à toute épreuve ; [courage] inébranlable, à toute épreuve ; [energy, supply] intarissable, inépuisable ; [good mood, interest] constant, inaltérable.

unfailingly [ʌnˈfeɪlɪŋlɪ] adv inlassablement, toujours.

unfair [ˌʌnˈfeəʳ] adj [advantage, decision, treatment] injuste ; [system] injuste, inique ; [judgement] inique ; [competition, play] déloyal.

unfair dismissal n licenciement m abusif.

unfairly [ˌʌnˈfeəlɪ] adv [treat] injustement ; [compete] de façon déloyale.

unfairness [ˌʌnˈfeənɪs] n (U) injustice f.

unfaithful [ˌʌnˈfeɪθfʊl] adj infidèle.

unfamiliar [ˌʌnfəˈmɪljəʳ] adj [face, person, surroundings] inconnu ; [ideas] peu familier, que l'on connaît mal.

unfashionable [ˌʌnˈfæʃnəbl] adj 1. [clothes, ideas] démodé 2. [area] peu chic.

unfasten [ˌʌnˈfɑːsn] vt [button, lace] défaire ; [gate] ouvrir ; [belt, bonds, rope] détacher.

unfathomable [ʌnˈfæðəməbl] adj insondable.

unfavourable 🇬🇧, **unfavorable** 🇺🇸 [ˌʌnˈfeɪvrəbl] adj défavorable.

unfavourably 🇬🇧, **unfavorably** 🇺🇸 [ˌʌnˈfeɪvrəblɪ] adv défavorablement.

unfeeling [ʌnˈfiːlɪŋ] adj insensible, dur.

unfettered [ˌʌnˈfetəd] adj fml [action] sans contrainte, sans entrave ; [imagination, violence] débridé.

unfilled [ʌnˈfɪld] adj [post, vacancy] à pourvoir.

unfinished [ˌʌnˈfɪnɪʃt] adj [incomplete] incomplet (incomplète), inachevé ▶ **unfinished business a)** lit affaires fpl à régler **b)** fig questions fpl à régler.

unfit [ˌʌnˈfɪt] (pt & pp **unfitted**, cont **unfitting**) adj 1. [unsuited - permanently] inapte ; [- temporarily] qui n'est pas en état 2. [unhealthy - person] qui n'est pas en forme, qui est en mauvaise forme ; [- condition] mauvais.

unflagging [ˌʌnˈflægɪŋ] adj [courage] infatigable, inlassable ; [enthusiasm] inépuisable.

unflappable [ˌʌnˈflæpəbl] adj 🇬🇧 inf imperturbable, qui ne se laisse pas démonter.

unflattering [ˌʌnˈflætərɪŋ] adj peu flatteur.

unflinching [ʌnˈflɪntʃɪŋ] adj intrépide, qui ne bronche pas.

unfocus(s)ed [ˌʌnˈfəʊkəst] adj [gaze, photo] flou.

unfold [ʌnˈfəʊld] ◆ vt 1. [spread out - cloth, map] déplier 2. [reveal - intentions, plans] exposer, révéler ; [- story] raconter, dévoiler ; [- secret] dévoiler ; [- reasons] faire connaître. ◆ vi 1. [cloth, map] se déplier ; [wings] se déployer 2. [plan, story] se dévoiler, se développer ; [view] se dérouler, s'étendre.

unforeseeable [ˌʌnfɔːˈsiːəbl] adj imprévisible.

unforeseen [ˌʌnfɔːˈsiːn] adj imprévu, inattendu.

unforgettable [ˌʌnfəˈgetəbl] adj inoubliable.

unforgivable [ˌʌnfəˈgɪvəbl] adj impardonnable.

unforgivably [ˌʌnfəˈgɪvəblɪ] adv de façon impardonnable.

unforgiving [ˌʌnfəˈgɪvɪŋ] adj implacable, impitoyable, sans merci.

unfortunate [ʌnˈfɔːtʃnət] ◆ adj 1. [unlucky] malheureux, malchanceux 2. [regrettable - incident, situation] fâcheux, regrettable ; [- joke, remark] malencontreux. ◆ n euph & fml malheureux m, -euse f.

unfortunately [ʌnˈfɔːtʃnətlɪ] adv malheureusement.

unfounded [ˌʌnˈfaʊndɪd] adj infondé, dénué de fondement.

unfriendly [ˌʌnˈfrendlɪ] (compar **unfriendlier**, superl **unfriendliest**) adj inimical, froid.

unfulfilled [ˌʌnfʊlˈfɪld] adj [person] insatisfait, frustré ; [dream] non réalisé ; [ambition, hopes] inaccompli ; [promise] non tenu.

unfurl [ʌnˈfɜːl] vt [flag, sail] déferler, déployer.

unfurnished [ˌʌnˈfɜːnɪʃt] adj [flat, room] non meublé.

ungainly [ʌnˈgeɪnlɪ] (compar **ungainlier**, superl **ungainliest**) adj [in movement] maladroit, gauche ; [in appearance] dégingandé, disgracieux.

ungenerous [ˌʌnˈdʒenərəs] adj 1. [allowance, person] peu généreux 2. [criticism, remark] mesquin.

ungodly [ˌʌnˈgɒdlɪ] adj hum & fig [noise] infernal ▶ **at an ungodly hour** à une heure impossible or indue.

ungracious [ˌʌnˈgreɪʃəs] adj désagréable.

ungrammatical [ˌʌngrəˈmætɪkl] adj agrammatical, non grammatical.

ungrateful [ʌnˈgreɪtfʊl] adj [person] ingrat.

ungratefully [ʌnˈgreɪtfʊlɪ] adv de manière ingrate, avec ingratitude.

unguarded [ˌʌnˈgɑːdɪd] adj [house] non surveillé, non gardé ; [suitcase] sans surveillance, non surveillé.

unhappily [ʌnˈhæpɪlɪ] adv [sadly] tristement.

unhappiness [ʌnˈhæpɪnɪs] n chagrin m, peine f.

unhappy [ʌnˈhæpɪ] (compar **unhappier**, superl **unhappiest**) adj 1. [sad] triste, malheureux 2. fml [unfortunate - coincidence] malheureux, regrettable ; [- remark] malheureux, malencontreux 3. [displeased] mécontent ; [worried] inquiet (inquiète).

unharmed [ˌʌnˈhɑːmd] adj [person] sain et sauf, indemne.

UNHCR (abbr of (Office of the) United Nations High Commissioner for Refugees) pr n HCR m.

unhealthily [ʌnˈhelθɪlɪ] adv d'une manière malsaine.

unhealthy [ʌnˈhelθɪ] (compar **unhealthier**, superl **unhealthiest**) adj [person] malade ; [complexion] maladif.

unheard [ˌʌnˈhɜːd] adj non entendu ; LAW [case] non jugé.

unheard-of adj 1. [extraordinary] inouï, sans précédent 2. [unprecedented] inconnu, sans précédent 3. [unknown] inconnu, ignoré.

unheeded [ˌʌnˈhiːdɪd] adj [ignored - message, warning] ignoré, dont on ne tient pas compte ; [unnoticed] inaperçu.

unhelpful [ˌʌnˈhelpfʊl] adj [person] peu secourable or serviable ; [instructions, map] qui n'est d'aucun secours ; [advice] inutile.

unhesitating [ʌnˈhezɪteɪtɪŋ] adj [reply] immédiat, spontané ; [belief] résolu, ferme ; [person] résolu, qui n'hésite pas.

unhindered [ʌnˈhɪndəd] adj sans entrave or obstacle.

unhinged [ˌʌnˈhɪndʒd] adj déséquilibré.

unholy [ˌʌnˈhəʊlɪ] (compar **unholier**, superl **unholiest**) adj 1. RELIG profane, impie 2. inf [awful - noise, mess] impossible, invraisemblable.

unhook [ˌʌnˈhʊk] ◆ vt 1. [remove, take down] décrocher 2. [bra, dress] dégrafer, défaire. ◆ vi [bra, dress] se dégrafer.

unhoped-for [ʌnˈhəʊpt-] adj inespéré.

unhopeful [ʌnˈhəʊpfʊl] adj 1. [person] pessimiste, sans illusion 2. [situation] décourageant.

unhurt [ˌʌnˈhɜːt] adj indemne, sans blessure.

unhygienic [ˌʌnhaɪˈdʒiːnɪk] adj antihygiénique, non hygiénique.

uni [ˈjuːnɪ] (abbr of **university**) n inf fac f.

UNICEF [ˈjuːnɪˌsef] (abbr of United Nations International Children's Fund) pr n UNICEF m, Unicef m.

unicorn ['juːnɪkɔːn] n MYTH licorne f.

unicycle ['juːnɪsaɪkl] n monocycle m.

unidentified [ˌʌnaɪ'dentɪfaɪd] adj non identifié.

unidentified flying object n objet m volant non identifié.

unification [ˌjuːnɪfɪ'keɪʃn] n unification f.

uniform ['juːnɪfɔːm] ◆ n uniforme m. ◆ adj [identical] identique, pareil ; [constant] constant ; [unified] uniforme.

uniformity [ˌjuːnɪ'fɔːmətɪ] (pl uniformities) n uniformité f.

uniformly ['juːnɪfɔːmlɪ] adv uniformément.

unify ['juːnɪfaɪ] (pt & pp unified) vt [unite - country] unifier.

unifying ['juːnɪfaɪɪŋ] adj unificateur.

unilateral [ˌjuːnɪ'lætərəl] adj [action, decision] unilatéral.

unilaterally [ˌjuːnɪ'lætərəlɪ] adv [act, decide] unilatéralement.

unimaginable [ˌʌnɪ'mædʒɪnəbl] adj inimaginable, inconcevable.

unimaginative [ˌʌnɪ'mædʒɪnətɪv] adj manquant d'imagination, peu imaginatif.

unimpaired [ˌʌnɪm'peəd] adj [faculty, strength] intact ; [health] non altéré.

unimpeded [ˌʌnɪm'piːdɪd] adj sans obstacle, libre.

unimportant [ˌʌnɪm'pɔːtənt] adj **1.** [detail, matter, question] sans importance, insignifiant **2.** [person] sans influence, sans importance.

unimpressed [ˌʌnɪm'prest] adj non impressionné.

unimpressive [ˌʌnɪm'presɪv] adj guère impressionnant.

uninformed [ˌʌnɪn'fɔːmd] adj [person] non informé ; [opinion] mal informé ; [reader] non averti.

uninhabitable [ˌʌnɪn'hæbɪtəbl] adj inhabitable.

uninhabited [ˌʌnɪn'hæbɪtɪd] adj inhabité.

uninhibited [ˌʌnɪn'hɪbɪtɪd] adj [person] sans inhibition or inhibitions ; [behaviour, reaction] non réfréné, non réprimé ; [laughter] franc et massif, sans retenue.

uninitiated [ˌʌnɪ'nɪʃɪeɪtɪd] ◆ pl n ▸ the uninitiated les profanes mpl, les non-initiés mpl, les non-initiées fpl. ◆ adj non initié.

uninjured [ˌʌn'ɪndʒəd] adj [person] indemne, sain et sauf.

uninspiring [ˌʌnɪn'spaɪrɪŋ] adj [dull] qui n'inspire pas ; [mediocre] médiocre ; [unexciting] qui n'est pas passionnant ; [uninteresting] sans intérêt.

uninstall [ˌʌnɪn'stɔːl] vt COMPUT désinstaller.

unintelligent [ˌʌnɪn'telɪdʒənt] adj inintelligent, qui manque d'intelligence.

unintelligible [ˌʌnɪn'telɪdʒəbl] adj inintelligible ; [writing] illisible.

unintended [ˌʌnɪn'tendɪd] adj non intentionnel, accidentel, fortuit.

unintentional [ˌʌnɪn'tenʃənl] adj involontaire, non intentionnel.

uninterested [ˌʌn'ɪntrəstɪd] adj [indifferent] indifférent.

uninterrupted [ˈʌnˌɪntə'rʌptɪd] adj continu, ininterrompu.

uninvited [ˌʌnɪn'vaɪtɪd] adj [person] qu'on n'a pas invité.

uninviting [ˌʌnɪn'vaɪtɪŋ] adj [place] peu accueillant ; [prospect] peu attrayant ; [smell] peu attirant.

union ['juːnjən] ◆ n **1.** [act of linking, uniting] union f ; COMM regroupement m, fusion f **2.** INDUST syndicat m

3. [association] association f, union f **4.** [marriage] union f, mariage m. ◆ comp [dues, leader, meeting] syndical ; [member] d'un or du syndicat.

union-bashing n UK antisyndicalisme m.

unionism ['juːnjənɪzm] n **1.** INDUST syndicalisme m **2.** POL unionisme m.

unionist ['juːnjənɪst] ◆ adj INDUST syndicaliste. ◆ n **1.** INDUST syndicaliste mf **2.** POL unioniste mf ; [in American Civil War] nordiste mf.

unionize, unionise ['juːnjənaɪz] ◆ vi se syndicaliser, se syndiquer. ◆ vt syndicaliser, syndiquer.

Union Jack n Union Jack m (drapeau officiel du Royaume-Uni).

 The Union Jack

Le drapeau du Royaume-Uni est composé de trois éléments. Il rassemble en effet la croix de Saint-Georges anglaise (rouge sur fond blanc), la croix de Saint-André écossaise (blanche sur fond bleu) et la croix de Saint-Patrick irlandaise (rouge). Le drapeau gallois, dragon rouge sur fond vert, ne fait pas partie de l'Union Jack. À strictement parler, le terme **Union Jack** ne désigne ce drapeau que lorsqu'il est arboré par un navire de la **Royal Navy** ; autrement on devrait dire **Union Flag**. Mais le public ne fait généralement pas la distinction.

unique [juː'niːk] adj **1.** [sole, single] unique ; [particular] particulier, propre **2.** [exceptional] exceptionnel, remarquable.

uniquely [juː'niːklɪ] adv [particularly] particulièrement ; [remarkably] exceptionnellement, remarquablement.

unisex ['juːnɪseks] adj unisexe.

unison ['juːnɪzn] n unisson m.

UNISON ['juːnɪzən] pr n «super-syndicat» de la fonction publique en Grande-Bretagne.

unit ['juːnɪt] ◆ n **1.** [constituent, component] unité f **2.** [group] unité f ; [team] équipe f, unité f **3.** [department] service m ; [centre] centre m ; [building] locaux mpl ; [offices] bureaux mpl **4.** [in amounts, measurement] unité f **5.** [part - of furniture] élément m ; [- of mechanism, system] bloc m, élément m **6.** SCH [lesson] unité f. ◆ comp [furniture] par éléments, modulaire. ◆ units pl n MATH ▸ the units les unités fpl.

unite [juː'naɪt] ◆ vt **1.** [join, link - forces] unir, rassembler **2.** [unify - country, party] unifier, unir **3.** [bring together - people, relatives] réunir. ◆ vi s'unir.

united [juː'naɪtɪd] adj [family] uni ; [efforts] conjugué ; [country, party] uni, unifié.

United Arab Emirates pl pr n ▸ the United Arab Emirates les Émirats mpl arabes unis.

United Kingdom pr n Royaume-Uni m **/** in the United Kingdom au Royaume-Uni.

United Nations pr n Nations fpl unies.

United States pr n États-Unis mpl **/** in the United States aux États-Unis ▸ the United States of America les États-Unis d'Amérique.

unit trust n UK FIN fonds m commun de placement ; ≃ SICAV f.

unity ['juːnɪtɪ] (pl unities) n **1.** [union] unité f, union f **2.** [identity - of purpose] identité f ; [- of views] unité f.

Univ. written abbr of university.

universal [ˌjuːnɪˈvɜːsl] adj [belief, education, language] universel.

universally [ˌjuːnɪˈvɜːsəlɪ] adv universellement.

universe [ˈjuːnɪvɜːs] n univers *m*.

university [ˌjuːnɪˈvɜːsətɪ] (*pl* **universities**) ◆ n université *f*. ◆ comp [building, campus, team] universitaire ; [professor, staff] d'université ; [education, studies] supérieur, universitaire ▸ **university fees** frais *mpl* d'inscription à l'université.

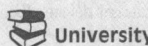 **University**

Les universités britanniques se divisent en deux catégories : les **old universities** et les **new universities**. La première catégorie recouvre non seulement les vieilles universités à tradition historique (Oxford, Cambridge, Durham…), mais aussi celles qui furent établies au cours de la période d'expansion suivant la Seconde Guerre mondiale (les **redbrick universities**). La plupart des **new universities** sont d'anciennes **polytechnics**, qui sont l'équivalent des IUT plutôt orientées vers la technologie et la formation professionnelle.

Aujourd'hui, même si des différences importantes demeurent, la distinction entre les deux types d'institution est officiellement abolie et toutes se font concurrence pour attirer des étudiants et des fonds de recherche. Toutes les universités, **old** et **new**, se trouvent dans la nécessité de s'adapter à la montée en flèche du nombre d'inscriptions.

unjust [ˌʌnˈdʒʌst] adj injuste.

unjustifiable [ʌnˈdʒʌstɪfaɪəbl] adj [behaviour] injustifiable, inexcusable ; [claim] que l'on ne peut justifier ; [error] injustifié.

unjustified [ʌnˈdʒʌstɪfaɪd] adj [unwarranted] injustifié.

unjustly [ˌʌnˈdʒʌstlɪ] adv injustement, à tort.

unkempt [ˌʌnˈkempt] adj [hair] mal peigné, en bataille ; [beard] hirsute ; [appearance, person] négligé, débraillé ; [garden] mal entretenu, en friche.

unkind [ʌnˈkaɪnd] adj [person] peu aimable, qui n'est pas gentil ; [manner] peu aimable ; [thought] vilain, méchant ; [remark] désobligeant, méchant.

unkindly [ʌnˈkaɪndlɪ] adv [cruelly] méchamment, cruellement ; [roughly] sans ménagement.

unknowingly [ˌʌnˈnəʊɪŋlɪ] adv à mon / son, etc. insu, sans m'en / s'en, etc. apercevoir.

unknown [ˌʌnˈnəʊn] ◆ adj **1.** [not known] inconnu / *for reasons unknown to us* pour des raisons que nous ignorons or qui nous sont inconnues / *unknown to his son, he sold the house* à l'insu de son fils or sans que son fils le sache, il a vendu la maison **2.** [obscure - cause] inconnu, mystérieux ; [- place] inconnu **3.** [obscure - actor, writer] inconnu, méconnu. ◆ n **1.** [person] inconnu *m*, -e *f* **2.** [place, situation] inconnu *m* / *the explorers set off into the unknown* les explorateurs se lancèrent vers l'inconnu **3.** MATH & LOGIC inconnue *f*.

unladen [ˌʌnˈleɪdn] adj **1.** [goods] déchargé **2.** [lorry, ship] à vide.

unlawful [ˌʌnˈlɔːfʊl] adj illicite, illégal ▸ **unlawful killing** meurtre *m*.

unlawfully [ˌʌnˈlɔːfʊlɪ] adv illicitement, illégalement.

unleaded [ˌʌnˈledɪd] ◆ adj [petrol] sans plomb. ◆ n inf [petrol] sans-plomb *m inv*.

unleash [ˌʌnˈliːʃ] vt **1.** [dog] lâcher **2.** *fig* [anger, violence] déchaîner.

unleavened [ˌʌnˈlevnd] adj CULIN [bread] sans levain ; RELIG azyme.

unless [ənˈles] conj à moins que (+ *subjunctive*), à moins de (+ *infinitive*) / *I'll go unless he phones first* j'irai, à moins qu'il téléphone d'abord / *unless I'm very much mistaken* à moins que je ne me trompe / *unless he pays me tomorrow, I'm leaving* s'il ne m'a pas payé demain, je m'en vais / *you won't win unless you practise* vous ne gagnerez pas si vous ne vous entraînez pas / *unless I hear otherwise* or *to the contrary* sauf avis contraire, sauf contrordre.

> Note that à moins que is followed by ne and a verb in the subjunctive:
> **Get there well in advance – unless you've already purchased a ticket.** *Arrivez bien à l'avance – à moins que vous n'ayez déjà acheté votre place.*

unlicensed, unlicenced US [ˌʌnˈlaɪsənst] adj [parking, sale] illicite, non autorisé ; [fishing, hunting] sans permis, illicite ; [car] sans vignette ; [premises] qui n'a pas de licence de débit de boissons.

unlike [ˌʌnˈlaɪk] ◆ adj [dissimilar] dissemblable ; [different] différent ; [showing no likeness] peu ressemblant ; [unequal] inégal. ◆ prep **1.** [different from] différent de, qui ne ressemble pas à **2.** [uncharacteristic of] : *that's (very) unlike him!* cela ne lui ressemble pas (du tout) ! **3.** [in contrast to] à la différence de, contrairement à.

unlikely [ʌnˈlaɪklɪ] adj **1.** [improbable - event, outcome] improbable, peu probable / *it is very* or *most unlikely that it will rain* il est très peu probable qu'il pleuve, il y a peu de chances qu'il pleuve / *in the unlikely event of my winning* au cas improbable où je gagnerais **2.** [person] peu susceptible, qui a peu de chances / *he is unlikely to come* / *to fail* il est peu probable qu'il vienne / échoue, il est peu susceptible de venir / d'échouer **3.** [implausible - excuse, story] invraisemblable **4.** [unexpected - situation, undertaking, costume, etc.] extravagant, invraisemblable ; [- person] peu indiqué / *the manager chose the most unlikely person to run the department* le directeur a choisi la personne la moins indiquée au monde pour diriger le service / *he seems an unlikely choice* il semble un choix peu judicieux.

> Note that peu probable que is followed by a verb in the subjunctive:
> **It's highly unlikely his brother witnessed the incident.** *Il est très peu probable que son frère ait été témoin de cet incident.*

unlimited [ʌnˈlɪmɪtɪd] adj [possibilities, space] illimité, sans limites ; [power] illimité, sans bornes ; [time] infini, illimité.

unlisted [ʌnˈlɪstɪd] adj **1.** US TELEC qui est sur la liste rouge **2.** ST. EX non coté (en Bourse).

unlit [ˌʌnˈlɪt] adj **1.** [candle, fire] non allumé **2.** [room, street] non éclairé.

unload [,ʌn'ləʊd] ◆ vt **1.** [remove load from - gun, ship, truck] décharger **2.** [remove - cargo, furniture] décharger ; [- film] enlever **3.** fig [responsibility, worries] décharger. ◆ vi [ship, truck] décharger.

unlock [,ʌn'lɒk] ◆ vt **1.** [door] ouvrir **2.** [computer] déverrouiller. ◆ vi s'ouvrir.

unloved [,ʌn'lʌvd] adj privé d'affection, mal aimé.

unluckily [ʌn'lʌkɪlɪ] adv malheureusement.

unlucky [ʌn'lʌkɪ] (compar **unluckier,** superl **unluckiest**) adj **1.** [person] malchanceux ; [day] de malchance / she was rather unlucky elle a été plutôt malchanceuse / we were unlucky enough to get caught in a jam nous avons eu la malchance d'être pris dans un embouteillage ▸ **to be unlucky in love** être malheureux en amour **2.** [colour, number] qui porte malheur ; [omen] funeste, mauvais / it's supposed to be unlucky to break a mirror c'est censé porter malheur de casser un miroir.

unmanageable [ʌn'mænɪdʒəbl] adj **1.** [animal] difficile, indocile ; [children] difficile, impossible **2.** [situation] difficile à gérer.

unmanly [,ʌn'mænlɪ] adj **1.** [effeminate] efféminé, peu viril **2.** [cowardly] lâche.

unmanned [,ʌn'mænd] adj [without crew - plane, ship] sans équipage ; [- spacecraft, flight] inhabité ; [RAIL - station] sans personnel ; [- level crossing] non gardé, automatique.

unmarked [,ʌn'mɑːkt] adj **1.** [face, furniture, page] sans marque, sans tache **2.** [without identifying features] : an unmarked police car une voiture de police banalisée.

unmarried [,ʌn'mærɪd] adj non marié, célibataire.

unmask [,ʌn'mɑːsk] vt démasquer.

unmatched [,ʌn'mætʃt] adj inégalé, sans égal or pareil.

unmentionable [ʌn'menʃnəbl] adj [subject] dont il ne faut pas parler, interdit ; [word] qu'il ne faut pas prononcer, interdit.

unmistakable [,ʌnmɪ'steɪkəbl] adj [not mistakeable] facilement reconnaissable ; [clear, obvious] indubitable, manifeste, évident.

unmistakably [,ʌnmɪ'steɪkəblɪ] adv **1.** [undeniably] indéniablement, sans erreur possible **2.** [visibly] visiblement, manifestement.

unmitigated [ʌn'mɪtɪɡeɪtɪd] adj [total - disaster, chaos] total ; [- stupidity] pur, total.

unmoved [,ʌn'muːvd] adj indifférent, insensible.

unnamed [,ʌn'neɪmd] adj [anonymous] anonyme ; [unspecified] non précisé.

unnatural [ʌn'nætʃrəl] adj **1.** [affected - behaviour, manner, tone] affecté, peu naturel ; [- laughter] peu naturel, forcé **2.** [perverse - love, passion] contre nature.

unnaturally [ʌn'nætʃrəlɪ] adv [behave, laugh, walk] bizarrement, de façon peu naturelle.

unnecessarily [US ʌn'nesəsərɪlɪ US ,ʌnnesə'serəlɪ] adv sans nécessité or raison.

unnecessary [ʌn'nesəsərɪ] adj superflu, inutile.

unnerve [,ʌn'nɜːv] vt démonter, déconcerter.

unnerving [,ʌn'nɜːvɪŋ] adj [event, experience] déconcertant, perturbant.

unnoticed [,ʌn'nəʊtɪst] adj inaperçu.

UNO (abbr of **United Nations Organization**) pr n ONU f.

unobserved [,ʌnəb'zɜːvd] adj inaperçu.

unobtainable [,ʌnəb'teɪnəbl] adj impossible à obtenir.

unobtrusive [,ʌnəb'truːsɪv] adj [person] discret (discrète), effacé ; [object] discret (discrète), pas trop visible ; [smell] discret (discrète).

unoccupied [,ʌn'ɒkjʊpaɪd] adj **1.** [person] qui ne fait rien, oisif **2.** [house] inoccupé, vide ; [seat] libre **3.** MIL [zone, territory] non occupé, libre.

unofficial [,ʌnə'fɪʃl] adj **1.** [unconfirmed - report] officieux, non officiel **2.** [informal - appointment] non officiel, privé **3.** INDUST ▸ **unofficial strike** grève f sauvage.

unofficially [,ʌnə'fɪʃəlɪ] adv [informally] officieusement ; [in private] en privé.

unopened [,ʌn'əʊpənd] adj [letter, bottle] fermé.

unorthodox [,ʌn'ɔːθədɒks] adj non orthodoxe, pas très orthodoxe ; RELIG hétérodoxe.

unpack [,ʌn'pæk] ◆ vt [bag, suitcase] défaire ; [books, clothes, shopping] déballer. ◆ vi défaire ses bagages.

unpaid [,ʌn'peɪd] adj **1.** [helper, job] bénévole, non rémunéré **2.** [bill, salary] impayé ; [employee] non payé.

unpalatable [ʌn'pælətəbl] adj [food] immangeable ; fig [idea] dérangeant ; [truth] désagréable à entendre.

unparalleled [ʌn'pærəleld] adj [unequalled] sans pareil ; [unprecedented] sans précédent.

unpardonable [ʌn'pɑːdnəbl] adj impardonnable, inexcusable.

unpatriotic ['ʌn,pætrɪ'ɒtɪk] adj [person] peu patriote ; [sentiment, song] peu patriotique.

unperturbed [,ʌnpə'tɜːbd] adj imperturbable, impassible.

unplanned [,ʌn'plænd] adj [visit, activity] imprévu.

unpleasant [ʌn'pleznt] adj [person] désagréable ; [smell, weather] désagréable, mauvais ; [remark] désagréable, désobligeant ; [memory] pénible.

unpleasantly [ʌn'plezntlɪ] adv désagréablement, de façon déplaisante.

unpleasantness [ʌn'plezntnɪs] n **1.** [of person] côté m désagréable ; [of experience, weather] désagrément m **2.** [discord] friction f, dissension f.

unplug [ʌn'plʌɡ] (pt & pp **unplugged,** cont **unplugging**) vt ELEC débrancher.

unpolished [,ʌn'pɒlɪʃt] adj **1.** [furniture, brass] non poli ; [floor, shoes] non ciré **2.** fig [person] qui manque de savoir-vivre ; [manners, style] peu raffiné, peu élégant.

unpolluted [,ʌnpə'luːtɪd] adj non pollué.

unpopular [,ʌn'pɒpjʊlər] adj impopulaire, peu populaire.

unpopularity ['ʌn,pɒpjʊ'lærətɪ] n impopularité f.

unprecedented [ʌn'presɪdəntɪd] adj sans précédent.

unpredictable [,ʌnprɪ'dɪktəbl] adj imprévisible.

unprejudiced [,ʌn'predʒʊdɪst] adj impartial, sans parti pris.

unprepared [,ʌnprɪ'peəd] adj mal préparé.

unprepossessing ['ʌn,priː,pə'zesɪŋ] adj [place] peu attrayant ; [person, smile] peu avenant or engageant.

unpretentious [,ʌnprɪ'tenʃəs] adj sans prétention.

unprincipled [ʌn'prɪnsəpld] adj [person, behaviour] sans scrupules.

unprintable [,ʌn'prɪntəbl] adj [language] grossier.

unproductive [,ʌnprə'dʌktɪv] adj [land] improductif, stérile ; [discussion, weekend] improductif.

unprofessional [,ʌnprə'feʃənl] adj [attitude, conduct] peu professionnel.

unprofitable [,ʌn'prɒfɪtəbl] adj **1.** [business] peu rentable **2.** [discussions] peu profitable ; [action] inutile.

UNPROFOR ['ʌnprəfɔː] (abbr of **United Nations Protection Force**) n FORPRONU f.

unprompted [,ʌn'prɒmptɪd] adj [action, words] spontané.

unpronounceable [ˌʌnprəˈnaʊnsəbl] adj imprononçable.

unprotected [ˌʌnprəˈtektɪd] adj **1.** [person] sans protection, non défendu ▸ **unprotected sex** rapports mpl non protégés **2.** [wood] non traité.

unprovoked [ˌʌnprəˈvəʊkt] adj [attack, insult] injustifié.

unpublished [ˌʌnˈpʌblɪʃt] adj [manuscript, book] inédit, non publié.

unpunished [ˌʌnˈpʌnɪʃt] adj impuni.

unqualified [ˌʌnˈkwɒlɪfaɪd] adj **1.** [unskilled] non qualifié ; [without diploma] qui n'a pas les diplômes requis ; [unsuitable] qui n'a pas les qualités requises **2.** [not competent] non qualifié or compétent **3.** [unrestricted - admiration, approval] inconditionnel, sans réserve ; [- success] complet (complète).

unquestionable [ʌnˈkwestʃənəbl] adj **1.** [undeniable] incontestable, indubitable **2.** [above suspicion] qui ne peut être mis en question.

unquestionably [ʌnˈkwestʃənəblɪ] adv indéniablement, incontestablement.

unquestioned [ʌnˈkwestʃənd] adj [decision, leader, principle] indiscuté, incontesté.

unquestioning [ʌnˈkwestʃənɪŋ] adj [faith, love, obedience, belief] absolu, aveugle.

unravel [ʌnˈrævl] (UK pt & pp unravelled, cont unravelling ; US pt & pp unraveled, cont unraveling) ◆ vt **1.** [knitting] défaire ; [textile] effiler, effilocher **2.** [untangle - knots, string] démêler ; fig [mystery] débrouiller, éclaircir. ◆ vi [knitting] se défaire ; [textile] s'effilocher.

unreadable [ˌʌnˈriːdəbl] adj **1.** [handwriting, signature] illisible **2.** [book, report] illisible, ennuyeux.

unreal [ʌnˈrɪəl] adj [appearance, feeling] : it all seems so unreal tout paraît si irréel.

unrealistic [ˌʌnrɪəˈlɪstɪk] adj irréaliste, peu réaliste.

unrealistically [ˌʌnrɪəˈlɪstɪklɪ] adv : his hopes were unrealistically high ses espoirs étaient trop grands pour être réalistes.

unreasonable [ʌnˈriːznəbl] adj **1.** [absurd, preposterous] déraisonnable **2.** [excessive] excessif, déraisonnable.

unreasonably [ʌnˈriːznəblɪ] adv déraisonnablement.

unrecognizable, unrecognisable [ˌʌnˈrekəgnaɪzəbl] adj méconnaissable.

unrecognized, unrecognised [ˌʌnˈrekəgnaɪzd] adj [not acknowledged - talent, achievement] méconnu.

unrefined [ˌʌnrɪˈfaɪnd] adj [petrol] brut, non raffiné ; [sugar] non raffiné ; [flour] non bluté.

unrehearsed [ˌʌnrɪˈhɜːst] adj **1.** [improvised] improvisé, spontané **2.** MUS & THEAT sans répétition, qui n'a pas été répété.

unrelated [ˌʌnrɪˈleɪtɪd] adj **1.** [unconnected] sans rapport **2.** [people] sans lien de parenté.

unrelenting [ˌʌnrɪˈlentɪŋ] adj **1.** [activity, effort] soutenu, continuel **2.** [person] tenace, obstiné.

unreliability [ˈʌnrɪˌlaɪəˈbɪlətɪ] n **1.** [of person] manque m de sérieux **2.** [of method, machine] manque m de fiabilité.

unreliable [ˌʌnrɪˈlaɪəbl] adj **1.** [person] peu fiable, sur qui on ne peut pas compter **2.** [car, machinery] peu fiable **3.** [service] peu fiable, peu sûr ; [business, company] qui n'inspire pas confiance **4.** [information, memory] peu fiable.

unrelieved [ˌʌnrɪˈliːvd] adj [pain] constant, non soulagé ; [gloom, misery] constant, permanent ; [boredom] mortel ; [landscape, routine] monotone.

unremarkable [ˌʌnrɪˈmɑːkəbl] adj peu remarquable, quelconque.

unremitting [ˌʌnrɪˈmɪtɪŋ] adj [activity, rain] incessant, ininterrompu ; [demands, efforts] inlassable, infatigable ; [opposition] implacable, opiniâtre.

unrepeatable [ˌʌnrɪˈpiːtəbl] adj [remark] qu'on n'ose pas répéter, trop grossier pour être répété ; [offer, performance] exceptionnel, unique.

unrepentant [ˌʌnrɪˈpentənt] adj impénitent.

unreported [ˌʌnrɪˈpɔːtɪd] adj non signalé or mentionné / the accident went unreported l'accident n'a pas été signalé.

unrepresentative [ˌʌnreprɪˈzentətɪv] adj non représentatif.

unreserved [ˌʌnrɪˈzɜːvd] adj **1.** [place] non réservé **2.** [unqualified] sans réserve, entier.

unreservedly [ˌʌnrɪˈzɜːvɪdlɪ] adv **1.** [without qualification] sans réserve, entièrement **2.** [frankly] sans réserve, franchement.

unresolved [ˌʌnrɪˈzɒlvd] adj [issue, problem] non résolu.

unresponsive [ˌʌnrɪˈspɒnsɪv] adj [without reaction] qui ne réagit pas ; [unaffected] insensible ; [audience] passif.

unrest [ʌnˈrest] n (U) agitation f, troubles mpl.

unrestrained [ˌʌnrɪˈstreɪnd] adj [anger, growth, joy] non contenu.

unrestricted [ˌʌnrɪˈstrɪktɪd] adj [access, parking] libre ; [number, time] illimité ; [power] absolu.

unrewarded [ˌʌnrɪˈwɔːdɪd] adj [person] non récompensé ; [effort, search] vain, infructueux / our efforts went unrewarded nos efforts sont restés sans récompense.

unrewarding [ˌʌnrɪˈwɔːdɪŋ] adj **1.** [financially] pas très intéressant financièrement **2.** fig [work, experience] ingrat.

unripe [ʌnˈraɪp] adj vert.

unrivalled UK, **unrivaled** US [ʌnˈraɪvld] adj sans égal or pareil, incomparable.

unroll [ʌnˈrəʊl] vt dérouler.

unruffled [ʌnˈrʌfld] adj [person] imperturbable, qui ne perd pas son calme.

unruly [ʌnˈruːlɪ] adj **1.** [children] indiscipliné, turbulent ; [mob] incontrôlé **2.** [hair] indiscipliné.

unsafe [ʌnˈseɪf] adj **1.** [dangerous - machine, neighbourhood] peu sûr, dangereux ; [- building, bridge] peu solide, dangereux **2.** [endangered] en danger.

unsaid [ʌnˈsed] adj non dit, inexprimé.

unsal(e)able [ʌnˈseɪləbl] adj invendable.

unsatisfactory [ˈʌnˌsætɪsˈfæktərɪ] adj peu satisfaisant, qui laisse à désirer.

unsatisfied [ˌʌnˈsætɪsfaɪd] adj **1.** [person - unhappy] insatisfait, mécontent ; [- unconvinced] non convaincu **2.** [desire] insatisfait, inassouvi.

unsatisfying [ˌʌnˈsætɪsfaɪɪŋ] adj **1.** [activity, task] peu gratifiant, ingrat **2.** [meal - insufficient] insuffisant, peu nourrissant ; [- disappointing] décevant.

unsavoury UK, **unsavory** US [ˌʌnˈseɪvərɪ] adj [behaviour, habits] répugnant, très déplaisant ; [person] peu recommandable ; [place] louche ; [reputation] douteux.

unscathed [ʌnˈskeɪðd] adj [physically] indemne, sain et sauf ; [psychologically] non affecté.

unscented [ʌnˈsentɪd] adj non parfumé.

unscheduled [UK ˌʌnˈʃedjuːld US ˌʌnˈskedʒʊld] adj imprévu.

unscientific [ˈʌnˌsaɪənˈtɪfɪk] adj non or peu scientifique.

unscrew [ˌʌnˈskruː] ◆ vt dévisser. ◆ vi se dévisser.

unscrupulous [ʌn'skru:pjʊləs] adj [person] sans scrupules, peu scrupuleux ; [behaviour, methods] malhonnête, peu scrupuleux.

unseasonably [ʌn'si:znəblɪ] adv : *an unseasonably cold night* une nuit fraîche pour la saison.

unsecured [ˌʌnsɪ'kjʊəd] adj **1.** [door, window - unlocked] qui n'est pas fermé à clé ; [- open] mal fermé **2.** FIN [creditor, loan] sans garantie.

unseeded [ˌʌn'si:dɪd] adj SPORT non classé.

unseemly [ʌn'si:mlɪ] adj *liter* [improper - behaviour] inconvenant, déplacé ; [- dress] inconvenant, peu convenable ; [rude] indécent, grossier.

unseen [ˌʌn'si:n] ◆ adj **1.** [invisible] invisible ; [unnoticed] inaperçu **2.** [not seen previously] ▶ **an unseen translation** UK SCH & UNIV une traduction sans préparation or à vue. ◆ n UK SCH & UNIV traduction *f* sans préparation or à vue.

unselfish [ˌʌn'selfɪʃ] adj [person, act] généreux, désintéressé.

unselfishly [ˌʌn'selfɪʃlɪ] adv généreusement, sans penser à soi.

unsettle [ˌʌn'setl] vt **1.** [person] inquiéter, troubler **2.** [stomach] déranger.

unsettled [ˌʌn'setld] adj [unstable - conditions, situation] instable, incertain ; [- person] troublé, perturbé, inquiet (inquiète) ; [- stomach] dérangé ; [- weather] incertain, changeant.

unsettling [ˌʌn'setlɪŋ] adj [disturbing] troublant, perturbateur.

unshakeable [ʌn'ʃeɪkəbl] adj [conviction, faith] inébranlable ; [decision] ferme.

unshaven [ˌʌn'ʃeɪvn] adj non rasé.

unsheathe [ˌʌn'ʃi:ð] vt dégainer.

unsightly [ʌn'saɪtlɪ] adj disgracieux, laid.

unsigned [ˌʌn'saɪnd] adj non signé, sans signature.

unsinkable [ˌʌn'sɪŋkəbl] adj [boat] insubmersible ; *fig* [person] qui ne se démonte pas facilement.

unskilled [ˌʌn'skɪld] adj **1.** [worker] sans formation professionnelle, non spécialisé, non qualifié **2.** [job, work] qui ne nécessite pas de connaissances professionnelles.

unsociable [ʌn'səʊʃəbl] adj [person] sauvage, peu sociable ; [place] peu accueillant.

unsocial [ˌʌn'səʊʃl] adj : *she works unsocial hours* elle travaille en dehors des heures normales.

unsold [ˌʌn'səʊld] adj invendu.

unsolicited [ˌʌnsə'lɪsɪtɪd] adj non sollicité.

unsolved [ˌʌn'sɒlvd] adj [mystery] non résolu, inexpliqué ; [problem] non résolu.

unsophisticated [ˌʌnsə'fɪstɪkeɪtɪd] adj **1.** [person - in dress, tastes] simple ; [- in attitude] simple, naturel **2.** [dress, style] simple, qui n'est pas sophistiqué.

unsound [ˌʌn'saʊnd] adj **1.** [argument, conclusion, reasoning] mal fondé, peu pertinent ; [advice, decision] peu judicieux, peu sensé ; [enterprise, investment] peu sûr, risqué ; [business] peu sûr, précaire **2.** [building, bridge] peu solide, dangereux **3.** PHR **to be of unsound mind** ne pas jouir de toutes ses facultés mentales.

unspeakable [ʌn'spi:kəbl] adj [crime, pain] épouvantable, atroce.

unspecified [ˌʌn'spesɪfaɪd] adj non spécifié.

unspent [ˌʌn'spent] adj non dépensé, restant.

unspoiled [ˌʌn'spɔɪld], **unspoilt** [ˌʌn'spɔɪlt] adj **1.** [person] (qui est resté) naturel **2.** [beauty, town] qui n'est pas gâté or défiguré.

unspoken [ˌʌn'spəʊkən] adj **1.** [agreement] tacite **2.** [thought, wish] inexprimé ; [word] non prononcé.

unsporting [ˌʌn'spɔ:tɪŋ], **unsportsmanlike** [ʌn'spɔ:tsmənlaɪk] adj déloyal.

unstable [ˌʌn'steɪbl] adj **1.** [chair, government, price, situation] instable **2.** [person] déséquilibré, instable.

unstated [ˌʌn'steɪtɪd] adj **1.** [agreement] tacite **2.** [desire] inexprimé.

unsteadily [ˌʌn'stedɪlɪ] adv [walk] d'un pas chancelant or incertain, en titubant ; [speak] d'une voix mal assurée ; [hold, write] d'une main tremblante.

unsteady [ˌʌn'stedɪ] (*compar* unsteadier, *superl* unsteadiest) adj **1.** [chair, ladder] instable, branlant **2.** [step, voice] mal assuré, chancelant ; [hand] tremblant.

unstinting [ˌʌn'stɪntɪŋ] adj [care] infini ; [help] généreux ; [efforts] incessant, illimité ; [support] sans réserve, inconditionnel ; [person] généreux, prodigue.

unstoppable [ˌʌn'stɒpəbl] adj qu'on ne peut pas arrêter.

unstructured [ˌʌn'strʌktʃəd] adj [activity] non structuré ; [group] non organisé.

unstuck [ˌʌn'stʌk] ◆ pt & pp ⟶ **unstick**. ◆ adj [envelope, label] décollé.

unsubscribe [ˌʌnsəb'skraɪb] vi se désabonner.

unsubstantiated [ˌʌnsəb'stænʃɪeɪtɪd] adj [report, story] non confirmé ; [accusation] non fondé.

unsuccessful [ˌʌnsək'sesfʊl] adj [plan, project] qui est un échec, qui n'a pas réussi ; [attempt] vain, infructueux ; [person] qui n'a pas de succès ; [application, demand] refusé, rejeté ; [marriage] malheureux.

unsuccessfully [ˌʌnsək'sesfʊlɪ] adv en vain, sans succès.

unsuitable [ˌʌn'su:təbl] adj [arrangement, candidate, qualities] qui ne convient pas ; [behaviour, language] inconvenant ; [moment, time] inopportun ; [clothing] peu approprié, inadéquat.

unsuitably [ˌʌn'su:təblɪ] adv [behave] de façon inconvenante ; [dress] d'une manière inadéquate.

unsuited [ˌʌn'su:tɪd] adj [person] inapte ; [machine, tool] mal adapté, impropre.

unsung [ˌʌn'sʌŋ] adj *liter* [deed, hero] méconnu.

unsupervised [ʌn'su:pəvaɪzd] adj [child] non surveillé.

unsupported [ˌʌnsə'pɔ:tɪd] adj **1.** [argument, theory] non vérifié ; [accusation, statement] non fondé **2.** *fig* [person - financially, emotionally] ▶ **to be unsupported** n'avoir aucun soutien.

unsure [ˌʌn'ʃɔ:r] adj [lacking self-confidence] qui manque d'assurance, qui n'est pas sûr de soi ; [hesitant] incertain.

unsurpassed [ˌʌnsə'pɑ:st] adj sans égal or pareil.

unsurprisingly [ˌʌnsə'praɪzɪŋlɪ] adv bien entendu, évidemment.

unsuspecting [ˌʌnsə'spektɪŋ] adj qui ne soupçonne rien, qui ne se doute de rien.

unsustainable [ˌʌnsə'steɪnəbl] adj non viable.

unsweetened [ˌʌn'swi:tnd] adj sans sucre, non sucré.

unswerving [ʌn'swɜ:vɪŋ] adj [devotion, loyalty] indéfectible, à toute épreuve ; [determination] inébranlable.

unsympathetic ['ʌnˌsɪmpə'θetɪk] adj **1.** [unfeeling] insensible, incompréhensif **2.** [unlikeable] antipathique.

unsympathetically ['ʌnˌsɪmpə'θetɪklɪ] adv [speak, behave] sans montrer la moindre sympathie.

untamed [ˌʌn'teɪmd] adj **1.** [animal - undomesticated] sauvage, inapprivoisé ; [- untrained] non dressé ; [lion, tiger] indompté **2.** [person] insoumis, indompté ; [spirit] indompté, rebelle.

untangle [ˌʌn'tæŋgl] vt [hair, necklace, rope] démêler ; *fig* [mystery] débrouiller, éclaircir.

untapped [ˌʌn'tæpt] adj inexploité.

untaxed [ˌʌn'tækst] adj [items] non imposé, exempt de taxes ; [income] non imposable, exonéré d'impôts.

untenable [ˌʌn'tenəbl] adj [argument, theory] indéfendable ; [position] intenable.

untested [ˌʌn'testɪd] adj [employee, method, theory] qui n'a pas été mis à l'épreuve ; [invention, machine, product] qui n'a pas été essayé ; [drug] non encore expérimenté.

unthinkable [ʌn'θɪŋkəbl] adj impensable, inconcevable.

unthinkingly [ʌn'θɪŋkɪŋlɪ] adv sans réfléchir, inconsidérément.

untidily [ʌn'taɪdɪlɪ] adv sans soin, d'une manière négligée.

untidy [ʌn'taɪdɪ] (*compar* untidier, *superl* untidiest) adj [cupboard, desk, room] mal rangé, en désordre ; [appearance] négligé, débraillé ; [person] désordonné.

untie [ˌʌn'taɪ] vt [string] dénouer ; [knot] défaire ; [bonds] défaire, détacher ; [package] défaire, ouvrir ; [prisoner] détacher, délier.

untied [ʌn'taɪd] adj : *your shoes are untied* tes lacets sont défaits.

until [ən'tɪl] ◆ prep **1.** [up to] jusqu'à / *until midnight* / *Monday* jusqu'à minuit / lundi / *she was here (up) until February* elle était ici jusqu'en février ▸ *(up) until now* jusqu'ici, jusqu'à présent ▸ *(up) until then* jusque-là **2.** *(with neg)* [before] : *they don't arrive until 8 o'clock* ils ne sont arrivés qu'à 8 h / *your car won't be ready until next week* votre voiture ne sera pas prête avant la semaine prochaine. ◆ conj [up to the specified moment - in present] jusqu'à ce que ; [- in past] avant que, jusqu'à ce que / *I'll wait here until you come back* j'attendrai ici jusqu'à ce que tu reviennes / *I laughed until I cried* j'ai ri aux larmes ; [with negative main clause] : *she won't go to sleep until her mother comes home* elle ne s'endormira pas avant que sa mère (ne) soit rentrée or tant que sa mère n'est pas rentrée / *the play didn't start until everyone was seated* la pièce n'a commencé qu'une fois que tout le monde a été assis.

📋 Note that **jusqu'à ce que** is followed by a verb in the subjunctive:
Put the peppers under the grill until they are completely blackened. *Mettez les poivrons sous le gril jusqu'à ce qu'ils soient complètement grillés.*

untimely [ʌn'taɪmlɪ] adj **1.** [premature] prématuré, précoce **2.** [inopportune - remark] inopportun, déplacé ; [- moment] inopportun, mal choisi ; [- visit] intempestif.

untiring [ʌn'taɪərɪŋ] adj [efforts] inlassable, infatigable.

untitled [ˌʌn'taɪtld] adj [painting] sans titre ; [person] non titré.

untold [ˌʌn'təʊld] adj [great - joy, suffering] indicible, indescriptible ; [- amount, number] incalculable.

untouchable [ˌʌn'tʌtʃəbl] ◆ adj intouchable. ◆ n [in India] intouchable *mf* ; *fig* paria *m*.

untouched [ˌʌn'tʌtʃt] adj **1.** [not changed] auquel on n'a pas touché, intact **2.** [unharmed - person] indemne, sain et sauf ; [- thing] indemne, intact.

untoward [ˌʌntə'wɔːd] adj *fml* [unfortunate - circumstances] fâcheux, malencontreux ; [- effect] fâcheux, défavorable.

untrained [ˌʌn'treɪnd] adj [person] sans formation ; [ear] inexercé ; [mind] non formé ; [voice] non travaillé ; [dog, horse] non dressé.

untranslatable [ˌʌntræns'leɪtəbl] adj intraduisible.

untreated [ˌʌn'triːtɪd] adj **1.** [unprocessed - food, wood] non traité ; [- sewage] brut **2.** [infection, tumour] non traité, non soigné.

untried [ˌʌn'traɪd] adj [method, recruit, theory] qui n'a pas été mis à l'épreuve ; [invention, product] qui n'a pas été essayé.

untroubled [ˌʌn'trʌbld] adj tranquille, paisible.

untrue [ˌʌn'truː] adj **1.** [incorrect - belief, statement] faux (fausse), erroné ; [- measurement, reading] erroné, inexact **2.** [disloyal] ▸ **to be untrue to sb** être déloyal envers or infidèle à qqn.

untrustworthy [ˌʌn'trʌst,wɜːðɪ] adj [person] qui n'est pas digne de confiance.

untruth [ˌʌn'truːθ] n *euph & fml* [lie] mensonge *m*, invention *f*.

untruthful [ˌʌn'truːθfʊl] adj [statement] mensonger ; [person] menteur.

unusable [ˌʌn'juːzəbl] adj inutilisable.

unused adj **1.** [ˌʌn'juːzd] [not in use] inutilisé ; [new - machine, material] neuf, qui n'a pas servi ; [- clothing, shoes] neuf, qui n'a pas été porté **2.** [ʌn'juːst] [unaccustomed] ▸ **to be unused to sthg** ne pas avoir l'habitude de qqch, ne pas être habitué à qqch.

unusual [ʌn'juːʒl] adj [odd] peu commun, inhabituel ; [odd] étrange, bizarre.

unusually [ʌn'juːʒəlɪ] adv [exceptionally] exceptionnellement, extraordinairement ; [abnormally] exceptionnellement, anormalement.

unvarnished [ˌʌn'vɑːnɪʃt] adj **1.** [furniture] non verni **2.** *fig* [plain, simple] simple, sans fard.

unveil [ˌʌn'veɪl] vt [painting] dévoiler, inaugurer ; *fig* [secret] dévoiler, révéler.

unwaged [ˌʌn'weɪdʒd] ◆ adj [unsalaried] non salarié ; [unemployed] sans emploi, au chômage. ◆ pl n ▸ **the unwaged** les sans-emploi *mpl*.

unwanted [ˌʌn'wɒntɪd] adj [child, pregnancy] non désiré, non souhaité ; [books, clothing] dont on n'a plus besoin, dont on veut se séparer ; [hair] superflu.

unwarranted [ʌn'wɒrəntɪd] adj [concern, criticism] injustifié ; [remark, interference] déplacé.

unwary [ʌn'weərɪ] adj [person, animal] qui n'est pas méfiant or sur ses gardes.

unwashed [ˌʌn'wɒʃt] adj [dishes, feet, floor] non lavé ; [person] qui ne s'est pas lavé.

unwavering [ʌn'weɪvərɪŋ] adj [devotion, support] indéfectible, à toute épreuve ; [look] fixe ; [person] inébranlable, ferme.

unwelcome [ʌn'welkəm] adj [advances, attention] importun ; [advice] non sollicité ; [visit] inopportun ; [visitor] importun, gênant ; [news, situation] fâcheux.

unwell [ˌʌn'wel] adj [indisposed] souffrant, indisposé *fml* ; [ill] malade.

unwholesome [ˌʌn'həʊlsəm] adj [climate] malsain, insalubre ; [activity, habits, thoughts] malsain, pernicieux ; [fascination, interest] malsain, morbide ; [drink, food] peu sain, nocif.

unwieldy [ʌn'wiːldɪ] adj **1.** [chair, package] peu maniable, encombrant **2.** [argument, method] maladroit ; [bureaucracy, system] lourd.

unwilling [ˌʌn'wɪlɪŋ] adj [helper, student] réticent, peu enthousiaste.

unwillingly [ʌnˈwɪlɪŋlɪ] adv à contrecœur, contre son gré.

unwind [ˌʌnˈwaɪnd] (pt & pp **unwound** [ˌʌnˈwaʊnd]) ◆ vt dérouler. ◆ vi fig [relax] se détendre, se relaxer.

unwise [ˌʌnˈwaɪz] adj [action, decision] peu judicieux, imprudent.

unwisely [ˌʌnˈwaɪzlɪ] adv imprudemment.

unwitting [ʌnˈwɪtɪŋ] adj fml [accomplice] involontaire, malgré soi ; [insult] non intentionnel, involontaire.

unwittingly [ʌnˈwɪtɪŋlɪ] adv involontairement, sans (le) faire exprès.

unworkable [ˌʌnˈwɜːkəbl] adj [idea, plan] impraticable, impossible à réaliser.

unworldly [ˌʌnˈwɜːldlɪ] adj **1.** [spiritual] spirituel, détaché de ce monde ; [ascetic] d'ascète, ascétique **2.** [naive] naïf, ingénu.

unworthy [ʌnˈwɜːðɪ] adj [unbefitting] indigne ; [undeserving] indigne, peu méritant.

unwound [ˌʌnˈwaʊnd] ◆ pt & pp ⟶ **unwind**. ◆ adj ▸ **to come unwound** se dérouler.

unwrap [ˌʌnˈræp] (pt & pp **unwrapped**, cont **unwrapping**) vt déballer, ouvrir.

unwritten [ˌʌnˈrɪtn] adj [legend, story] non écrit ; [agreement] verbal, tacite ▸ an unwritten rule une règle tacitement admise ▸ **unwritten law** droit m coutumier.

unyielding [ʌnˈjiːldɪŋ] adj [ground, material] très dur ; [person] inflexible, intransigeant ; [determination, principles] inébranlable.

unzip [ˌʌnˈzɪp] (pt & pp **unzipped**, cont **unzipping**) ◆ vt **1.** ouvrir or défaire (la fermeture Éclair® de) **2.** COMPUT [file] dézipper, décompresser. ◆ vi se dégrafer.

up [ʌp] (pt & pp **upped**, cont **upping**) ◆ adv

A. TOWARDS OR IN HIGHER POSITION 1. [towards a higher position or level] en haut / he's on his way up il monte / hang it higher up accrochez-le plus haut **2.** [in a high place or position] ▸ **up above** au-dessus / up in the air en l'air / I live eight floors up j'habite au huitième (étage) / she lives three floors up from us elle habite trois étages au-dessus de chez nous / from up on the mountain du haut de la montagne **3.** [into an upright position] debout / up you get! debout ! **4.** [facing upwards] : he turned his hand palm up il a tourné la main paume vers le haut / **'fragile — this way up'** 'fragile — haut'.

B. DIRECTION OR PROXIMITY 1. [towards north] : it's cold up here il fait froid ici ▸ **up there** là-bas ▸ **up north** dans le nord **2.** [in, to or from a larger place] : she's up in Maine for the week elle passe une semaine dans le Maine **3.** [in phrasal verbs] : the clerk came up to him le vendeur s'est approché de lui or est venu vers lui **4.** [close to] ▸ **up close** de près / I like to sit up front j'aime bien m'asseoir devant.

C. STRENGTH, AMOUNT OR VOLUME 1. [towards a higher level] : prices have gone up by 10 per cent les prix ont augmenté or monté de 10 pour cent **2.** [more loudly, intensely] plus fort.

◆ adj **1.** [at or moving towards higher level] haut / prices are up on last year les prix ont augmenté par rapport à l'année dernière / the temperature is up in the twenties la température a dépassé les vingt degrés **2.** [in a raised position] levé / keep the windows up [in car] n'ouvrez pas les fenêtres **3.** [out of bed] : is she up yet? est-elle déjà levée or debout ? / she was up last night elle s'est couchée or elle a veillé tard hier soir / they were up all night ils ne se sont pas couchés de la nuit, ils ont passé une nuit blanche **4.** [erected, installed] : are the new curtains up yet? les nouveaux rideaux ont-ils été posés ? **5.** [finished, at an end]

terminé ▸ **time is up!** a) [on exam, visit] c'est l'heure ! b) [in game, on meter] le temps est écoulé ! / when the month was up he left à la fin du mois, il est parti **6.** [ahead] : I'm $50 up on you inf j'ai 50 dollars de plus que vous / Madrid was two goals up SPORT Madrid menait de deux buts ▸ **to be one up on sb** inf avoir un avantage sur qqn **7.** inf PHR **something's up** a) [happening] il se passe quelque chose b) [wrong] quelque chose ne va pas ▸ **what's up?** a) [happening] qu'est-ce qui se passe ? b) [wrong] qu'est-ce qu'il y a ? c) US [as greeting] quoi de neuf ? / what's up with you? a) [happening] quoi de neuf ? b) [wrong] qu'est-ce que tu as ? / something's up with Mum il y a quelque chose qui ne va pas chez maman, maman a quelque chose.

◆ prep **1.** [indicating motion to a higher place or level] : I climbed up the ladder je suis monté à l'échelle / the cat climbed up the tree le chat a grimpé dans l'arbre **2.** [at or to the far end of] : her flat is up those stairs son appartement est en haut de cet escalier / she pointed up the street elle a montré le haut de la rue.

◆ vt **1.** [increase] augmenter **2.** [promote] lever, relever.

◆ vi inf : she upped and left elle a fichu le camp.

◆ n **1.** [high point] haut m ▸ **ups and downs** a) [in land, road] accidents mpl b) [of market] fluctuations fpl ; [in life] : we all have our ups and downs nous avons tous des hauts et des bas **2.** [increase] : prices are on the up les prix sont en train d'augmenter. ◆ **up against** prep **1.** [touching] contre **2.** [in competition or conflict with] : you're up against some good candidates vous êtes en compétition avec de bons candidats ▸ **to be up against it** inf être dans le pétrin. ◆ **up and down** adv phr **1.** [upwards and downwards] : he was jumping up and down il sautait sur place / she looked us up and down elle nous a regardés de haut en bas **2.** [to and fro] de long en large / I could hear him walking up and down je l'entendais faire les cent pas or marcher de long en large **3.** [in all parts of] : up and down the country dans tout le pays. ◆ **up for** prep phr inf [interested in, ready for] : are you still up for supper tonight? tu veux toujours qu'on dîne ensemble ce soir ? / he's up for anything il est toujours partant. ◆ **up to** prep phr **1.** [as far as] jusqu'à / he can count up to 100 il sait compter jusqu'à 100 / I'm up to page 120 j'en suis à la page 120 ▸ **up to** or **up until now** jusqu'à maintenant, jusqu'ici ▸ **up to** or **up until then** jusqu'alors, jusque-là / we were up to our knees in mud nous avions de la boue jusqu'aux genoux **2.** [the responsibility of] : which film do you fancy? — it's up to you quel film est-ce que tu veux voir ? — c'est comme tu veux **3.** [capable of] ▸ **to be up to doing sthg** être capable de faire qqch / my German is not up to translating novels mon niveau d'allemand ne me permet pas de traduire des romans / are you going out tonight? — no, I don't feel up to it tu sors ce soir ? — non, je n'en ai pas tellement envie **4.** [as good as] : his work is not up to his normal standard son travail n'est pas aussi bon que d'habitude **5.** [engaged in, busy with] : what have you been up to lately? qu'est-ce que tu deviens ? / they're up to something ils manigancent quelque chose / she's up to no good elle prépare un mauvais coup.

up-and-coming adj plein d'avenir, qui promet, qui monte.

up-and-up n ▸ **to be on the up-and-up** a) UK [improving] aller de mieux en mieux b) US [honest] être honnête.

upbeat [ˈʌpbiːt] adj [mood, person] optimiste ; [music] entraînant.

upbringing [ˈʌpˌbrɪŋɪŋ] n éducation f.

upcoming [ˈʌpˌkʌmɪŋ] adj [event] à venir, prochain ; [book] à paraître, qui va paraître ; [film] qui va sortir.

update ◆ vt [ˌʌp'deɪt] [information, record] mettre à jour, actualiser ; [army, system] moderniser. ◆ n ['ʌpdeɪt] [of information, record] mise *f* à jour, actualisation *f* ; [of army, system] modernisation *f*.

upend [ʌp'end] vt *lit* [object] mettre debout ; [person] mettre la tête en bas.

upfront [ˌʌp'frʌnt] adj *inf* **1.** [frank - person] franc (franche), ouvert ; [- remark] franc (franche), direct **2.** [payment] d'avance.

upgradable [ʌp'greɪdəbl] adj COMPUT extensible.

upgrade ◆ vt [ˌʌp'greɪd] **1.** [improve] améliorer ; [increase] augmenter ; [modernize - computer system] moderniser, actualiser **2.** [job] revaloriser ; [employee] promouvoir. ◆ vi [ʌp'greɪd] : *we've upgraded to a more powerful system* on est passés à un système plus puissant. ◆ n ['ʌpgreɪd] **1.** US [slope] montée *f* **2.** COMPUT [of software] actualisation *f* ; [of system] extension *f* **3.** PHR **to be on the upgrade a)** [price, salary] augmenter, être en hausse **b)** [business, venture] progresser, être en bonne voie **c)** [sick person] être en voie de guérison.

upgradeable = upgradable.

upheaval [ʌp'hi:vl] n [emotional, political, etc.] bouleversement *m* ; [social unrest] agitation *f*, perturbations *fpl*.

upheld [ʌp'held] pt & pp ⟶ uphold.

uphill [ˌʌp'hɪl] ◆ adj **1.** [road, slope] qui monte **2.** *fig* [task] ardu, pénible ; [battle] rude, acharné. ◆ adv ▶ **to go uphill a)** [car, person] monter (la côte) **b)** [road] monter.

uphold [ʌp'həʊld] (*pt & pp* **upheld** [ʌp'held]) vt **1.** [right] défendre, faire respecter ; [law, rule] faire respecter or observer **2.** LAW [conviction, decision] maintenir, confirmer.

upholster [ʌp'həʊlstər] vt recouvrir, tapisser.

upholstery [ʌp'həʊlstərɪ] n (U) **1.** [covering - fabric] tissu *m* d'ameublement ; [- leather] cuir *m* ; [- in car] garniture *f* **2.** [trade] tapisserie *f*.

upkeep ['ʌpki:p] n (U) [maintenance] entretien *m* ; [cost] frais *mpl* d'entretien.

upland ['ʌplənd] ◆ n ▶ **the upland** or **uplands** les plateaux *mpl*, les hautes terres *fpl*. ◆ adj des plateaux.

uplift ◆ vt [ʌp'lɪft] [person - spiritually] élever (l'esprit de) ; [- morally] encourager. ◆ comp ['ʌplɪft] ▶ **uplift bra** soutien-gorge *m* de maintien.

uplifting [ʌp'lɪftɪŋ] adj édifiant.

uplighter ['ʌplaɪtər] n *applique ou lampadaire diffusant la lumière vers le haut.*

uplink ['ʌplɪŋk] n COMPUT liaison *f* montante.

upload ['ʌpləʊd] ◆ n COMPUT téléchargement *m* (vers le serveur). ◆ vt & vi COMPUT télécharger (vers le serveur).

up-market ◆ adj [goods, service, area] haut de gamme, de première qualité ; [newspaper, television programme] qui vise un public cultivé ; [audience] cultivé. ◆ adv : *she's moved up-market* elle fait dans le haut de gamme maintenant.

upon [ə'pɒn] prep **1.** *fml* [indicating position or place] : *upon the grass / the table* sur la pelouse / la table / *she had a sad look upon her face* elle avait l'air triste / *the ring upon her finger* la bague à son doigt **2.** *fml* [indicating person or thing affected] : *attacks upon old people are on the increase* les attaques contre les personnes âgées sont de plus en plus fréquentes **3.** *fml* [immediately after] à / *upon our arrival in Rome* à notre arrivée à Rome / *upon hearing the news, he rang home* lorsqu'il a appris la nouvelle, il a appelé chez lui / *upon request* sur simple demande **4.** [indicating large amount] et / *we receive thousands upon thousands of offers each year* nous recevons plu-

sieurs milliers de propositions chaque année **5.** [indicating imminence] : *the holidays are nearly upon us* les vacances approchent.

upper ['ʌpər] ◆ adj **1.** [physically higher] supérieur, plus haut or élevé ; [top] du dessus, du haut ▶ **upper lip** lèvre supérieure / *temperatures are in the upper 30s* la température dépasse 30 degrés ▶ **to have the upper hand** avoir le dessus ▶ **to get** or **to gain the upper hand** prendre le dessus or l'avantage **2.** [higher in order, rank] supérieur ▶ **the Upper House a)** [gen] la Chambre haute **b)** [in England] la Chambre des lords **3.** GEOG [inland] haut. ◆ n **1.** [of shoe] empeigne *f* **2.** *drugs sl* excitant *m*, stimulant *m*.

upper case n TYPO haut *m* de casse. ◆ **upper-case** adj ▶ **an upper-case letter** une majuscule.

upper class n ▶ **the upper class, the upper classes** l'aristocratie et la haute bourgeoisie. ◆ **upper-class** adj **1.** [accent, family] aristocratique **2.** US UNIV [student] de troisième ou quatrième année.

upper-crust adj *inf* aristocratique.

uppercut ['ʌpəkʌt] (*pt & pp* **uppercut**, cont **uppercutting**) n uppercut *m*.

upper middle class n ▶ **the upper middle class** classe sociale réunissant les professions libérales et universitaires, les cadres de l'industrie et les hauts fonctionnaires.

uppermost ['ʌpəməʊst] ◆ adj **1.** [part, side] le plus haut or élevé ; [drawer, storey] du haut, du dessus **2.** [most prominent] le plus important. ◆ adv [most prominently] : *the question that comes uppermost in my mind* la question que je me pose en premier or avant toute autre.

upper school n UK ▶ **the upper school** les grandes classes *fpl*.

upper sixth n UK SCH (classe *f*) terminale *f*.

Upper Volta [-'vɒltə] pr n Haute-Volta *f* / *in Upper Volta* en Haute-Volta.

uppity ['ʌpətɪ] adj *inf* [arrogant] arrogant, suffisant ; [snobbish] snob *(inv)*.

upright ['ʌpraɪt] ◆ adj **1.** [erect] droit ▶ **upright freezer** congélateur *m* armoire ▶ **upright piano** piano *m* droit ▶ **upright vacuum cleaner** aspirateur-balai *m* **2.** [honest] droit. ◆ adv **1.** [sit, stand] droit **2.** [put] droit, debout. ◆ n **1.** [of door, bookshelf] montant *m*, portant *m* ; [of goal post] montant *m* du but ; ARCHIT pied-droit *m* **2.** [piano] piano *m* droit **3.** [vacuum cleaner] aspirateur-balai *m*.

uprising ['ʌpˌraɪzɪŋ] n soulèvement *m*, révolte *f*.

uproar ['ʌprɔ:r] n [noise] tumulte *m*, vacarme *m* ; [protest] protestations *fpl*, tollé *m*.

uproarious [ʌp'rɔ:rɪəs] adj [crowd, group] hilare ; [film, joke] hilarant, désopilant ; [laughter] tonitruant.

uproot [ʌp'ru:t] vt *lit & fig* déraciner.

upscale ['ʌpskeɪl] adj US haut de gamme.

upset (*pt & pp* **upset**, cont **upsetting**) ◆ vt [ʌp'set] **1.** [overturn - chair, pan] renverser ; [- milk, paint] renverser, répandre ; [- boat] faire chavirer **2.** [disturb - plans, routine] bouleverser, déranger ; [- procedure] bouleverser ; [- calculations, results] fausser ; [- balance] rompre, fausser **3.** [person - annoy] contrarier, ennuyer ; [- offend] fâcher, vexer ; [- worry] inquiéter, tracasser **4.** [make ill - stomach] déranger ; [- person] rendre malade. ◆ adj [ʌp'set] **1.** [annoyed] ennuyé, contrarié ; [offended] fâché, vexé ; [worried] inquiet (inquiète) / *he's upset about losing the deal* cela l'ennuie d'avoir perdu l'affaire / *I was most upset that she left* j'étais très ennuyé qu'elle soit partie **2.** [stomach] dérangé ▶ **to have an upset stomach** avoir une indigestion. ◆ n ['ʌpset] **1.** [in plans] bouleversement *m* ; [of government] renversement *m* ; [of team] défaite *f* **2.** [emotional] bouleversement *m* **3.** [of stomach] indigestion *f*.

upsetting [ʌpˈsetɪŋ] adj [annoying] ennuyeux, contrariant ; [offensive] vexant ; [saddening] attristant, triste ; [worrying] inquiétant.

upshot [ˈʌpʃɒt] n résultat m, conséquence f.

upside [ˈʌpsaɪd] n [of situation] avantage m, bon côté m.

upside down ◆ adj 1. [cup, glass] à l'envers, retourné ▶ **upside-down cake** gâteau m renversé 2. [room, house] sens dessus dessous. ◆ adv 1. [in inverted fashion] à l'envers 2. [in disorderly fashion] sens dessus dessous.

upskill [ˈʌpskɪl] ◆ vt améliorer les compétences de, former. ◆ vi améliorer ses compétences, se former.

upstage [ˌʌpˈsteɪdʒ] ◆ adv [move] vers le fond de la scène ; [enter, exit] par le fond de la scène ; [stand] au fond de la scène. ◆ vt fig éclipser, voler la vedette à.

upstairs [ˌʌpˈsteəz] ◆ adv en haut, à l'étage ▶ **to go upstairs** monter (à l'étage). ◆ adj [room, window] du haut, (situé) à l'étage ; [flat, neighbour] du dessus. ◆ n étage m.

upstanding [ˌʌpˈstændɪŋ] adj 1. [in character] intègre, droit ; [in build] bien bâti 2. fml [on one's feet] ▶ **be upstanding** levez-vous.

upstart [ˈʌpstɑːt] n pej parvenu m, -e f.

upstate [ˌʌpˈsteɪt] US ◆ adv [live] dans le nord (de l'État) ; [move] vers le nord (de l'État). ◆ adj au nord (de l'État).

upstream [ˌʌpˈstriːm] ◆ adv 1. [live] en amont ; [move] vers l'amont ; [row, swim] contre le courant 2. ECON en amont. ◆ adj 1. [gen] d'amont, (situé) en amont 2. ECON en amont.

upsurge [ˈʌpsɜːdʒ] n [gen] mouvement m vif ; [of anger, enthusiasm] vague f, montée f ; [of interest] renaissance f, regain m ; [in production, sales] montée f, augmentation f.

upswing [ˈʌpswɪŋ] n 1. [movement] mouvement m ascendant, montée f 2. [improvement] amélioration f.

uptake [ˈʌpteɪk] n 1. [of air] admission f ; [of water] prise f, adduction f 2. [of offer, allowance] : a campaign to improve the uptake of child benefit une campagne pour inciter les gens à réclamer leurs allocations familiales 3. PHR **to be quick on the uptake** avoir l'esprit vif ou rapide, comprendre vite ▶ **to be slow on the uptake** être lent à comprendre or à saisir.

uptight [ʌpˈtaɪt] adj inf 1. [tense] tendu, crispé ; [irritable] irritable, énervé ; [nervous] nerveux, inquiet (ète) 2. [prudish] coincé, collet monté (inv).

uptime [ˈʌptaɪm] n COMPUT temps m de bon fonctionnement.

up-to-date adj 1. [information, report - updated] à jour ; [- most current] le plus récent 2. [modern - machinery, methods] moderne.

up-to-the-minute adj le plus récent.

uptown [ˌʌpˈtaʊn] US ◆ adj des quartiers résidentiels. ◆ adv [be, live] dans les quartiers résidentiels ; [move] vers les quartiers résidentiels. ◆ n les quartiers mpl résidentiels.

upturn n [ˈʌptɜːn] [in economy, situation] amélioration f ; [in production, sales] progression f, reprise f. ◆ vt [ˌʌpˈtɜːn] [turn over] retourner ; [turn upside down] mettre à l'envers ; [overturn] renverser.

upturned [ʌpˈtɜːnd] adj 1. [nose] retroussé 2. [upside down] retourné, renversé.

upward [ˈʌpwəd] ◆ adj [movement] ascendant ; [trend] à la hausse. ◆ adv US = **upwards**.

upward-compatible adj COMPUT compatible vers le haut.

upwardly mobile [ˈʌpwədlɪ-] adj susceptible de promotion sociale.

upward mobility n mobilité f sociale.

upwards [ˈʌpwədz] adv 1. [move, climb] vers le haut ▶ **to slope upwards** monter 2. [facing up] : she placed the photos (face) upwards on the table elle a posé les photos sur la table face vers le haut / he lay on the floor face upwards il était allongé par terre sur le dos 3. [onwards] : from 15 years upwards à partir de 15 ans. ◆ **upwards of** prep phr : upwards of 100 candidates applied plus de 100 candidats se sont présentés.

upwind [ˌʌpˈwɪnd] ◆ adv du côté du vent, contre le vent. ◆ adj dans le vent, au vent ▶ **to be upwind of sthg** être dans le vent or au vent par rapport à qqch.

UR MESSAGING written abbr of **you are**.

Urals [ˈjʊərəlz] pl pr n ▶ **the Urals** l'Oural m.

uranium [jʊˈreɪnjəm] n uranium m.

Uranus [ˈjʊərənəs] pr n ASTRON & MYTH Uranus.

urban [ˈɜːbən] adj urbain ▶ **urban area** zone f urbaine, agglomération f ▶ **urban blight** or **decay** dégradation f urbaine ▶ **urban guerrilla** personne f qui pratique la guérilla urbaine ▶ **the urban jungle** la jungle de la ville ▶ **urban legend** légende f urbaine ▶ **urban myth** mythe m urbain ▶ **urban renewal** rénovations fpl urbaines.

urbane [ɜːˈbeɪn] adj [person] poli, qui a du savoir-vivre ; [manner] poli, raffiné.

urbanization, urbanisation [ˌɜːbənaɪˈzeɪʃn] n urbanisation f.

urbanize, urbanise [ˈɜːbənaɪz] vt urbaniser.

urchin [ˈɜːtʃɪn] n galopin m, polisson m, -onne f.

Urdu [ˈʊərduː] n ourdou m, urdu m.

urge [ɜːdʒ] ◆ n forte envie f, désir m. ◆ vt 1. [person - incite] exhorter, presser / I urge you to reconsider je vous conseille vivement de reconsidérer votre position 2. [course of action] conseiller vivement, préconiser ; [need, point] insister sur. ◆ **urge on** vt sep talonner, presser ; [person, troops] faire avancer ▶ **to urge sb on to do sthg** inciter qqn à faire qqch.

urgency [ˈɜːdʒənsɪ] n urgence f.

urgent [ˈɜːdʒənt] adj 1. [matter, need] urgent, pressant ; [message] urgent 2. [manner, voice] insistant.

urgently [ˈɜːdʒəntlɪ] adv d'urgence, de toute urgence.

urinal [ˈjʊərɪnl] n [fitting] urinal m ; [building] urinoir m.

urinary [ˈjʊərɪnərɪ] adj urinaire ▶ **urinary tract** appareil m urinaire.

urinate [ˈjʊərɪneɪt] vi uriner.

urine [ˈjʊərɪn] n urine f.

URL (abbr of uniform resource locator) n URL m.

urn [ɜːn] n 1. [container - gen] urne f 2. [for ashes] urne f (funéraire) 3. [for coffee, tea] fontaine f.

urologist [jʊəˈrɒlədʒɪst] n urologue mf.

Uruguay [ˈjʊərəgwaɪ] pr n Uruguay m / in Uruguay en Uruguay.

Uruguayan [ˌjʊəruˈgwaɪən] ◆ n Uruguayen m, -enne f. ◆ adj uruguayen.

us [ʌs] pron [object form of 'we'] nous / it's us! c'est nous ! / most of us are students nous sommes presque tous des étudiants / there are three of us nous sommes trois.

US ◆ pr n (abbr of United States) ▶ **the US** USA mpl / in the US aux USA, aux États-Unis. ◆ comp des États-Unis, américain.

USA pr n 1. (abbr of United States of America) ▶ **the USA** les USA mpl / in the USA aux USA, aux États-Unis ▶ **USA Today** US PRESS quotidien américain de qualité 2. (abbr of United States Army) armée des États-Unis.

usable [ˈjuːzəbl] adj utilisable.

USAF (abbr of United States Air Force) pr n *armée de l'air des États-Unis.*

usage ['juːzɪʤ] n **1.** [custom, practice] coutume *f*, usage *m* **2.** [of term, word] usage *m* **3.** [employment] usage *m*, emploi *m* ; [treatment - of material, tool] manipulation *f* ; [- of person] traitement *m*.

USB [ˌjuːesˈbiː] (abbr of universal serial bus) n COMPUT USB *m*.

USCG (abbr of United States Coast Guard) pr n *service de surveillance côtière américain.*

USDA (abbr of United States Department of Agriculture) pr n *ministère américain de l'Agriculture.*

USDAW ['ʌzdɔː] (abbr of Union of Shop, Distributive and Allied Workers) pr n *syndicat britannique des personnels de la distribution.*

use¹ [juːs] n **1.** [utilization - of materials] utilisation *f*, emploi *m* ; [consumption - of water, resources, etc.] consommation *f* ; [being used, worn, etc.] usage *m* / *the dishes are for everyday use* c'est la vaisselle de tous les jours / **'directions for use'** 'mode d'emploi / **'for your personal use'** 'pour votre usage personnel' / **'for external / internal use only'** MED 'à usage externe / interne' / **'for use in case of emergency'** 'à utiliser en cas d'urgence' ▶ **in use** a) [machine, system] en usage, utilisé b) [lift, cash point] en service c) [phrase, word] usité / **'not in use, out of use'** a) 'hors d'usage' b) [lift, cash point] 'hors service' ▶ **to come into use** entrer en service ▶ **to go out of use** [machine] être mis au rebut ▶ **to make use of sthg** se servir de or utiliser qqch ▶ **to make good use of, to put to good use** a) [machine, money] faire bon usage de b) [opportunity, experience] tirer profit de **2.** [ability or right to use] usage *m*, utilisation *f* / *we gave them the use of our car* nous leur avons laissé l'usage de notre voiture / *she lost the use of her legs* elle a perdu l'usage de ses jambes **3.** [practical application] usage *m*, emploi *m* ▶ **I have my uses** hum il m'arrive de servir à quelque chose **4.** [need] besoin *m*, usage *m* ▶ **to have no use for sthg** a) *lit* ne pas avoir besoin de qqch b) *fig* n'avoir que faire de qqch **5.** [usefulness] ▶ **to be of use (to sb)** être utile (à qqn), servir (à qqn) / *were the instructions (of) any use?* est-ce que le mode d'emploi a servi à quelque chose ? / *I found his advice to be of little use* or *his advice was of little use to me* je n'ai pas trouvé ses conseils très utiles ▶ **to be (of) no use** a) [thing] ne servir à rien b) [person] n'être bon à rien / *it's no use, we might as well give up* c'est inutile or ça ne sert à rien, autant abandonner / *oh, what's the use?* à quoi bon ?

use² [juːz] ◆ vt **1.** [put into action - service, tool, skills] se servir de, utiliser ; [- product] utiliser ; [- method, phrase, word] employer ; [- name] utiliser, faire usage de ; [- vehicle, form of transport] prendre / *these are the notebooks he used* ce sont les cahiers dont il s'est servi or qu'il a utilisés / *it's no longer used* [machine, tool] ça ne sert plus / *I always use public transport* je prends toujours les transports en commun / *we use this room as an office* nous nous servons de cette pièce comme bureau, cette pièce nous sert de bureau / *what is this used for* or *as?* à quoi cela sert-il ? / *it's used for identifying the blood type* cela sert à identifier le groupe sanguin / *what battery does this radio use?* quelle pile faut-il pour cette radio ? / *my car uses unleaded petrol* ma voiture marche à l'essence sans plomb / *may I use the phone?* puis-je téléphoner ? / *he asked to use the toilet* 🇬🇧 or *bathroom* 🇺🇸 il a demandé à aller aux toilettes / *to use force / violence* avoir recours à la force / violence / *use your imagination!* utilise ton imagination ! / *use your initiative!* fais preuve d'initiative ! / *use your head* or *your brains!* réfléchis un peu ! / *use your eyes!* ouvrez l'œil ! / *he could certainly use some help* inf un peu d'aide ne lui ferait pas de mal / *we could all use a holiday!* inf nous

aurions tous bien besoin de vacances ! **2.** [exploit, take advantage of - opportunity] profiter de ; [- person] se servir de **3.** [consume] consommer, utiliser ; [finish, use up] finir, épuiser / *the car's using a lot of oil* la voiture consomme beaucoup d'huile **4.** *fml* [treat physically] traiter ; [behave towards] agir envers / *I consider I was ill used* je considère qu'on ne m'a pas traité comme il faut **5.** *v inf* [drug] prendre. ◆ vi 🇺🇸 [use drugs] se droguer / *he's using again* il se drogue à nouveau. ◆ modal vb *(only in past tense)* : *he used to drink a lot* il buvait beaucoup avant / *it used to be true* c'était vrai autrefois / *she can't get about the way she used to* elle ne peut plus se déplacer comme avant / *we used not* or *we didn't use to eat meat* avant, nous ne mangions pas de viande. ❖ **use up** vt sep [consume] consommer, prendre ; [exhaust - paper, soap] finir ; [- patience, energy, supplies] épuiser / *she used up the leftovers to make the soup* elle a utilisé les restes pour faire un potage / *did you use up all your money?* as-tu dépensé tout ton argent ? / *the paper was all used up* il ne restait plus de papier.

use-by date n date *f* limite de consommation.

used¹ [juːzd] adj [book, car] d'occasion ; [clothing] d'occasion, usagé ; [glass, linen] sale, qui a déjà servi.

used² [juːst] adj [accustomed] ▶ **to be used to (doing) sthg** avoir l'habitude de or être habitué à (faire) qqch ▶ **to be used to sb** être habitué à qqn ▶ **to get used to sthg** s'habituer à qqch.

useful ['juːsful] adj **1.** [handy - book, information, machine] utile, pratique ; [- discussion, experience] utile, profitable ; [- method] utile, efficace **2.** *inf* [satisfactory - performance, score] honorable.

> 📋 Note that être utile que is followed by a verb in the subjunctive:
> **It would be useful for them to be informed in advance.** *Il serait utile qu'ils en soient informés par avance.*

usefully ['juːsfʊlɪ] adv utilement.

usefulness ['juːsfʊlnɪs] n utilité *f*.

useless ['juːslɪs] adj **1.** [bringing no help - book, information, machine] inutile ; [- discussion, experience] vain, qui n'apporte rien ; [- advice, suggestion] qui n'apporte rien, qui ne vaut rien ; [- attempt, effort] inutile, vain **2.** *inf* [incompetent] nul.

uselessly ['juːslɪslɪ] adv inutilement.

Usenet® ['juːznet] n Usenet® *m*, forum *m* électronique.

user ['juːzər] ◆ n [of computer, machine] utilisateur *m*, -trice *f* ; [of airline, public service, road] usager *m* ; [of electricity, gas, oil] usager *m*, utilisateur *m*, -trice *f* ; [of drugs] consommateur *m*, -trice *f*, usager *m*. ◆ in comp par l'utilisateur.

user-definable, user-defined [-dɪˈfaɪnd] adj COMPUT [characters, keys] définissable par l'utilisateur.

user-fittable [-ˈfɪtəbl] adj qui peut être installé par l'utilisateur.

user-friendly adj [gen & COMPUT] convivial, facile à utiliser.

user ID n = user name.

user-interface n COMPUT interface *f* utilisateur.

user name n COMPUT nom *m* d'utilisateur.

user profile n profil *m* utilisateur.

user-programmable adj COMPUT programmable par l'utilisateur.

usher [ˈʌʃər] ◆ vt conduire, accompagner. ◆ n **1.** [at concert, theatre, wedding] placeur m, -euse f **2.** [doorkeeper] portier m ; LAW huissier m. ◆ **usher in** vt sep fig inaugurer, marquer le début de.

usherette [ˌʌʃəˈret] n ouvreuse f.

USN (abbr of United States Navy) pr n marine de guerre des États-Unis.

USP (abbr of unique selling point or proposition) n PUV f.

USPHS (abbr of United States Public Health Service) pr n direction américaine des Affaires sanitaires et sociales.

USPS (abbr of United States Postal Service) n ≃ la Poste.

USS (abbr of United States Ship) initiales précédant le nom des navires américains / the USS Washington le Washington.

USSR (abbr of Union of Soviet Socialist Republics) pr n ▸ the USSR l'URSS f / in the USSR en URSS.

usu. written abbr of usually.

usual [ˈjuːʒəl] ◆ adj [customary - activity, place] habituel ; [- practice, price] habituel, courant ; [- expression, word] courant, usité ; [doctor] habituel, traitant, de famille / later than usual plus tard que d'habitude / it's not usual for him to be so bitter il est rarement si amer, c'est rare qu'il soit si amer / it's quite usual to see flooding in the spring il y a souvent des inondations au printemps. ◆ n inf [drink, meal] : what will you have? — the usual, please que prends-tu ? — comme d'habitude, s'il te plaît. ◆ **as usual, as per usual** adv phr comme d'habitude.

usually [ˈjuːʒəlɪ] adv généralement, d'habitude, d'ordinaire.

usurp [juːˈzɜːp] vt usurper.

usury [ˈjuːʒʊrɪ] n usure f (intérêt).

UT written abbr of Utah.

Utah [ˈjuːtɑː] pr n Utah m / in Utah dans l'Utah.

utensil [juːˈtensl] n ustensile m, outil m.

uterus [ˈjuːtərəs] (pl uteri [-raɪ] or uteruses) n utérus m.

utilitarian [ˌjuːtɪlɪˈteərɪən] ◆ adj **1.** [functional] utilitaire, fonctionnel **2.** PHILOS utilitariste. ◆ n utilitariste mf.

utilitarianism [ˌjuːtɪlɪˈteərɪənɪzm] n utilitarisme m.

utility [juːˈtɪlətɪ] (pl utilities) ◆ n **1.** [usefulness] utilité f **2.** [service] service m **3.** COMPUT utilitaire m, programme m utilitaire **4.** US [room] = utility room. ◆ adj [fabric, furniture] utilitaire, fonctionnel ; [vehicle] utilitaire. ◆ **utilities** US [service charges] charges fpl.

utility room n pièce servant à ranger les appareils ménagers, provisions, etc.

utilization [ˌjuːtɪlaɪˈzeɪʃn] n utilisation f.

utilize, utilise [ˈjuːtɪlaɪz] vt [use] utiliser, se servir de ; [make best use of] exploiter.

utmost [ˈʌtməʊst] ◆ adj **1.** [greatest] le plus grand / with the utmost respect, I cannot agree with your conclusions avec tout le respect que je vous dois, je ne peux pas partager vos conclusions **2.** [farthest] : to the utmost ends of the earth au bout du monde. ◆ n **1.** [maximum] maximum m, plus haut degré m **2.** [best effort] : she tried her utmost elle a fait de son mieux.

utopia, Utopia [juːˈtəʊpjə] n utopie f.

utopian, Utopian [juːˈtəʊpjən] ◆ adj utopique. ◆ n utopiste mf.

utopianism, Utopianism [juːˈtəʊpjənɪzm] n utopisme m.

utter [ˈʌtər] ◆ vt [pronounce - word] prononcer, proférer ; [- cry, groan] pousser. ◆ adj [amazement, bliss] absolu, total ; [fool] parfait, fini.

utterly [ˈʌtəlɪ] adv complètement, tout à fait.

U-turn n **1.** AUTO demi-tour m **2.** fig volte-face f inv, revirement m.

UV (abbr of ultra-violet) n UV m.

UV-A, UVA (abbr of ultra-violet-A) n UVA m.

UV-B, UVB (abbr of ultra-violet-B) n UVB m.

Uzbek [ˈʊzbek] n [person] Ouzbek mf.

Uzbekistan [ʊzˌbekɪˈstɑːn] pr n Ouzbékistan m / in Uzbekistan en Ouzbékistan.

v 1. (written abbr of verb) v **2.** (written abbr of verse) v **3.** written abbr of very **4.** written abbr of versus **5.** (written abbr of vide) v.

V ◆ n [Roman numeral] V *m*. ◆ (written abbr of volt) V.

VA written abbr of Virginia.

vac [væk] (abbr of vacation) n 🇬🇧 *inf* UNIV [recess] vacances *fpl*.

vacancy ['veɪkənsɪ] (*pl* **vacancies**) n **1.** [emptiness] vide *m* **2.** [lack of intelligence] ineptie *f*, esprit *m* vide **3.** [in hotel] chambre *f* libre / 'no vacancies' 'complet' **4.** [job] poste *m* vacant or libre, vacance *f* / 'no vacancies' pas d'embauche.

vacant ['veɪkənt] adj **1.** [house, room - to rent] libre, à louer ; [-empty] inoccupé ; [seat] libre, inoccupé **2.** [job, position] vacant, libre **3.** [empty - mind, look] vide ; [stupid - person, look] niais, idiot.

vacant lot n 🇺🇸 terrain *m* vague.

vacantly ['veɪkəntlɪ] adv [expressionlessly] d'un air absent or vague ; [stupidly] d'un air niais or idiot.

vacate [və'keɪt] vt [hotel room] libérer, quitter ; [flat, house] quitter, déménager de ; [job] démissionner de.

vacation [və'keɪʃn] ◆ n **1.** 🇬🇧 UNIV [recess] vacances *fpl*. ; LAW vacations *fpl*, vacances *fpl* judiciaires **2.** 🇺🇸 [holiday] vacances *fpl*. ◆ vi 🇺🇸 prendre or passer des vacances.

vacationer[və'keɪʃənə*], **vacationist**[və'keɪʃənɪst]n 🇺🇸 vacancier *m*, -ère *f*.

vacation resort n 🇺🇸 camp *m* de vacances.

vaccinate ['væksɪneɪt] vt vacciner.

vaccination [,væksɪ'neɪʃn] n vaccination *f*.

vaccine [🇬🇧 'væksi:n 🇺🇸 væk'si:n] n vaccin *m*.

vacillate ['væsəleɪt] vi hésiter.

vacuous ['vækjʊəs] adj *fml* [eyes, look] vide, sans expression ; [remark] sot (sotte), niais ; [film, novel] idiot, dénué de tout intérêt ; [life] vide de sens.

vacuum ['vækjʊəm] (*pl* **vacuums** or **vacua** [-jʊə]) ◆ n **1.** [void] vide *m* **2.** PHYS vacuum *m* **3.** [machine] ◗ **vacuum (cleaner)** aspirateur *m* / *I gave the room a quick vacuum* j'ai passé l'aspirateur en vitesse dans la pièce. ◆ vt [carpet] passer l'aspirateur sur ; [flat, room] passer l'aspirateur dans.

vacuum bottle 🇺🇸 = **vacuum flask**.

vacuum cleaner n aspirateur *m*.

vacuum flask n 🇬🇧 (bouteille *f*) Thermos® *f*.

vacuum-packed adj emballé sous vide.

vacuum pump n pompe *f* à vide.

vagabond ['vægəbɒnd] ◆ n [wanderer] vagabond *m*, -e *f* ; [tramp] clochard *m*, -e *f*. ◆ adj vagabond, errant.

vagary ['veɪgərɪ] (*pl* **vagaries**) n caprice *m*.

vagina [və'dʒaɪnə] (*pl* **vaginas** or **vaginae** [-ni:]) n vagin *m*.

vaginal [və'dʒaɪnl] adj vaginal ◗ **vaginal discharge** pertes *fpl* blanches ◗ **vaginal smear** frottis *m* vaginal.

vagrancy ['veɪgrənsɪ] n [gen & LAW] vagabondage *m*.

vagrant ['veɪgrənt] ◆ n [wanderer] vagabond *m*, -e *f* ; [tramp] clochard *m*, -e *f* ; [beggar] mendiant *m*, -e *f*. ◆ adj vagabond.

vague [veɪg] adj **1.** [imprecise - promise, statement] vague, imprécis ; [-person] vague ; [unsure] : *I'm still vague about how to get there* je ne comprends toujours pas comment y aller / *I haven't the vaguest idea* je n'en ai pas la moindre idée **2.** [dim - memory, feeling] vague, confus **3.** [indistinct - shape] flou, indistinct **4.** [absent-minded] distrait.

vaguely ['veɪglɪ] adv **1.** [not clearly - promise, say] vaguement ; [- remember, understand] vaguement, confusément **2.** [a bit] vaguement, peu **3.** [absent-mindedly] distraitement.

vagueness ['veɪgnɪs] n **1.** [imprecision - of instructions, statement] imprécision *f*, manque *m* de clarté **2.** [of memory] imprécision *f*, manque *m* de précision ; [of feeling] vague *m*, caractère *m* vague or indistinct **3.** [of shape] flou *m*, caractère *m* indistinct **4.** [absent-mindedness] distraction *f*.

vain [veɪn] adj **1.** [conceited] vaniteux **2.** [unsuccessful - attempt, effort] vain, inutile ; [- hope, plea, search] vain, futile **3.** [idle - promise] vide, en l'air ; [- word] creux, en l'air. ◆❖ **in vain** adv phr [unsuccessfully] en vain, inutilement.

vainglory [veɪn'glɔ:rɪ] n *liter* vanité *f*, orgueil *m*.

vainly ['veɪnlɪ] adv **1.** [conceitedly] avec vanité, vaniteusement **2.** [unsuccessfully - try] en vain, inutilement ; [- hope] en vain.

valance ['væləns] n [round bed frame] frange *f* de lit ; [round shelf, window] lambrequin *m*, frange *f*.

vale [veɪl] n *liter* vallée *f*, val *m* *liter*.

valediction [,vælɪ'dɪkʃn] n [act] adieux *mpl* ; [speech] discours *m* d'adieu.

valentine ['væləntaɪn] n **1.** [card] ◗ **valentine (card)** carte *f* de la Saint-Valentin **2.** [person] bien-aimé *m*, -e *f* ◗ **be my valentine** c'est toi que j'aime.

Valentine ['væləntaɪn] pr n ◗ **Saint Valentine** Saint Valentin ◗ **(Saint) Valentine's Day** la Saint-Valentin.

valet ◆ n ['vælɪt or 'væleɪ] **1.** [manservant] valet *m* de chambre ◗ **valet service** le pressing de l'hôtel **2.** [clothing rack] valet *m* **3.** [for cars] / 'valet parking' 'voiturier'. ◆ vt [vælɪt] AUTO ◗ **to have one's car valeted** faire faire un lavage-route à sa voiture.

valiant ['vælɪənt] adj [person] vaillant, courageux ; [behaviour, deed] courageux, brave.

valiantly ['væljəntlɪ] adv vaillamment, courageusement.
valid ['vælɪd] adj **1.** [argument, reasoning] valable, fondé ; [excuse] valable **2.** [contract, passport] valide, valable.

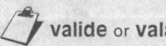 **valide** or **valable?**

The adjective **valide** is used for valid documents or files, and also means able-bodied. In other contexts, such as valid reasons or valid information, it is safer to use **valable**.

---

validate ['vælɪdeɪt] vt **1.** [argument, claim] confirmer, prouver la justesse de **2.** [document] valider.
validation [,vælɪ'deɪʃn] n **1.** [of argument, claim] confirmation f, preuve f **2.** [of document] validation f.
validity [və'lɪdətɪ] n **1.** [of argument, reasoning] justesse f, solidité f **2.** [of document] validité f.
Valium® ['vælɪəm] (pl **Valium**) n Valium® m.
valley ['vælɪ] n vallée f ; [small] vallon m ▶ **the Valleys** le sud du pays de Galles.
valor US = valour.
valour UK, **valor** US ['vælər] n liter courage m, bravoure f, vaillance f liter.
valuable ['væljʊəbl] ◆ adj **1.** [of monetary worth] de (grande) valeur **2.** [advice, friendship, time] précieux. ◆ n (usu pl) ▶ **valuables** objets mpl de valeur.

⚠ **Valuable means valid, not valuable.**

valuation [,væljʊ'eɪʃn] n expertise f, estimation f.
value ['vælju:] ◆ n **1.** [monetary worth] valeur f / it's excellent value for money le rapport qualité-prix est excellent / the increase in value la hausse de valeur, l'appréciation / the loss in value la perte de valeur, la dépréciation ▶ **to put a value on sthg** évaluer or estimer qqch **2.** [merit, importance - of method, work] valeur f ; [- of person] valeur f, mérite m **3.** (usu pl) [principles] ▶ **values** valeurs fpl **4.** [feature] particularité f **5.** [of colour] valeur f **6.** LING, LOGIC, MATH & MUS valeur f. ◆ vt **1.** [assess worth of] expertiser, estimer, évaluer **2.** [have high regard for - friendship] apprécier, estimer ; [- honesty, punctuality] faire grand cas de.
value-added tax n UK taxe f sur la valeur ajoutée.
valued ['vælju:d] adj [opinion] estimé ; [advice, friend] précieux.
value judgment n jugement m de valeur.
valuer ['væljʊər] n expert m (en expertise de biens).
valve [vælv] n [in pipe, tube, air chamber] valve f ; [in machine] soupape f, valve f.
vamoose [və'mu:s] vi US inf filer ▶ **vamoose!** fiche le camp !
vampire ['væmpaɪər] n [bat, monster] vampire m ; [person] vampire m, sangsue f.
van [væn] n **1.** [small vehicle] camionnette f, fourgonnette f ; [large vehicle] camion m, fourgon m **2.** UK RAIL fourgon m, wagon m **3.** [caravan] caravane f **4.** MIL [vanguard] avant-garde f.
V and A (abbr of **Victoria and Albert Museum**) pr n grand musée londonien des arts décoratifs.
vandal ['vændl] n [hooligan] vandale mf.
vandalism ['vændəlɪzm] n vandalisme m.
vandalize, vandalise ['vændəlaɪz] vt saccager.
vanguard ['vænga:d] n MIL avant-garde f.

vanilla [və'nɪlə] n [plant] vanillier m ; [flavour] vanille f ▶ **vanilla ice cream / flavour** glace f / parfum m à la vanille ▶ **vanilla essence** extrait m de vanille.
vanish ['vænɪʃ] vi [object, person, race] disparaître ; [hopes, worries] disparaître, se dissiper.
vanishing trick n tour m de passe-passe / he did a vanishing trick fig [disappeared] il a disparu.
vanity ['vænətɪ] (pl **vanities**) n **1.** [conceit] vanité f, orgueil m **2.** fml & liter [futility] futilité f, insignifiance f, vanité f liter **3.** US [dressing table] coiffeuse f, table f de toilette.
vanity case n petite valise f de toilette, vanity-case m.
vanity plate n US plaque f d'immatriculation personnalisée.
vanity publishing n publication f à compte d'auteur.
vanity unit n meuble de salle de bains avec lavabo encastré.
vanquish ['væŋkwɪʃ] vt vaincre.
vantage point n point de vue m (privilégié).
vapor US = vapour.
vaporize, vaporise ['veɪpəraɪz] ◆ vt vaporiser. ◆ vi se vaporiser.
vaporizer ['veɪpəraɪzər] n **1.** [gen] vaporisateur m ; [for perfume, spray] atomiseur m, pulvérisateur m **2.** MED [inhaler] inhalateur m ; [for throat] pulvérisateur m.
vapour UK, **vapor** US ['veɪpər] ◆ n vapeur f ; [on window] buée f. ◆ vi **1.** PHYS s'évaporer **2.** US inf [brag] se vanter, fanfaronner.
vapour trail n AERON traînée f de condensation.
variable ['veərɪəbl] ◆ adj **1.** [weather] variable, changeant ; [quality] variable, inégal ; [performance, work] de qualité inégale, inégal **2.** COMPUT & MATH variable. ◆ n variable f.
variable costs n coûts mpl variables.
variance ['veərɪəns] n PHR to be at variance with sb être en désaccord avec qqn ▶ **to be at variance with sthg** ne pas cadrer avec or ne pas concorder avec qqch.
variant ['veərɪənt] ◆ n [gen & LING] variante f. ◆ adj **1.** [different] autre, différent / a variant spelling une variante orthographique **2.** [various] varié, divers **3.** LING variant.
variation [,veərɪ'eɪʃn] n **1.** [change, modification] variation f, modification f **2.** MUS variation f **3.** BIOL variation f.
varicose ['værɪkəʊs] adj [ulcer] variqueux ▶ **to have** or **to suffer from varicose veins** avoir des varices.
varied ['veərɪd] adj varié, divers.
variegated ['veərɪgeɪtɪd] adj [gen] bigarré.
variety [və'raɪətɪ] (pl **varieties**) ◆ n **1.** [diversity] variété f, diversité f **2.** [number, assortment] nombre m, quantité f / for a variety of reasons **a)** [various] pour diverses raisons **b)** [many] pour de nombreuses raisons **3.** [type] espèce f, genre m **4.** BOT & ZOOL [strain] variété f **5.** (U) THEAT & TV variétés fpl. ◆ comp [artiste, show, theatre] de variétés, de music-hall.
varifocals [veərɪ'fəʊkəlz] pl n lunettes fpl à verres progressifs.
various ['veərɪəs] adj **1.** [diverse] divers, différent ; [several] plusieurs **2.** [varied, different] varié.
varnish ['vɑ:nɪʃ] ◆ n lit & fig vernis m. ◆ vt [nails, painting, wood] vernir ; [pottery] vernir, vernisser.
vary ['veərɪ] ◆ vi **1.** [be different] varier **2.** [change, alter] changer, se modifier. ◆ vt [diet, menu] varier ; [temperature] faire varier.
varying ['veərɪŋ] adj variable, qui varie.
vascular ['væskjʊlər] adj vasculaire.

vase [UK vɑːz US veɪz] n vase m.

vasectomy [væ'sektəmɪ] (pl **vasectomies**) n vasectomie f.

Vaseline® ['væsəliːn] n ▶ **Vaseline (jelly)** vaseline f.

vast [vɑːst] adj vaste, immense, énorme.

vastly ['vɑːstlɪ] adv [wealthy] extrêmement, immensément ; [grateful] infiniment.

vastness ['vɑːstnɪs] n immensité f.

vat [væt] n cuve f, bac m.

VAT [væt or ˌviːeɪ'tiː] (abbr of **value added tax**) n TVA f.

Vatican ['vætɪkən] ◆ pr n ▶ **the Vatican** le Vatican / *in the Vatican* au Vatican. ◆ comp [edict, bank, policy] du Vatican.

Vatican City pr n l'État m de la cité du Vatican, le Vatican / *in Vatican City* au Vatican.

vault [vɔːlt] ◆ n 1. ARCHIT voûte f 2. ANAT voûte f 3. [cellar] cave f, cellier m ; [burial chamber] caveau m 4. [in bank] chambre f forte ▶ **a bank vault** les coffres d'une banque, la salle des coffres 5. [jump] (grand) saut m ; SPORT saut m (à la perche). ◆ vi [jump] sauter ; SPORT sauter (à la perche) / *he vaulted over the fence* il a sauté par-dessus la clôture. ◆ vt 1. ARCHIT voûter, cintrer 2. [jump] sauter par-dessus.

vaulted ['vɔːltɪd] adj ARCHIT voûté, en voûte.

vaulting horse n cheval-d'arçons m inv.

vaunt [vɔːnt] vt liter vanter, se vanter de.

VBG MESSAGING written abbr of **very big grin**.

VC n 1. abbr of **vice-chancellor** 2. abbr of **vice-chairman**.

VCR (abbr of **video cassette recorder**) n magnétoscope m.

VD (abbr of **venereal disease**) n (U) MST f.

VDU n abbr of **visual display unit**.

veal [viːl] ◆ n CULIN veau m. ◆ comp [cutlet] de veau.

veer [vɪər] vi 1. [vehicle, road] virer, tourner ; [ship] virer de bord ; [wind] tourner, changer de direction 2. fig : *her mood veers between euphoria and black depression* son humeur oscille entre l'euphorie et un profond abattement or va de l'euphorie à un profond abattement.

veg [vedʒ] (abbr of **vegetable/vegetables**) n inf légumes mpl.

vegan ['viːgən] ◆ n végétalien m, -enne f. ◆ adj végétalien.

veganism ['viːgənɪzm] n végétalisme m.

vegeburger ['vedʒəˌbɜːgər] n hamburger m végétarien.

vegetable ['vedʒtəbl] ◆ n 1. CULIN & HORT légume m ; BOT [plant] végétal m ▶ **early vegetables** primeurs mpl ▶ **root vegetables** racines fpl (comestibles) 2. inf & fig [person] légume m. ◆ comp [matter] végétal ; [soup] de légumes.

vegetable garden n (jardin m) potager m.

vegetable knife n couteau m à légumes, éplucheur m.

vegetable oil n huile f végétale.

vegetarian [ˌvedʒɪ'teərɪən] ◆ n végétarien m, -enne f. ◆ adj végétarien.

vegetarianism [ˌvedʒɪ'teərɪənɪzm] n végétarisme m.

vegetate ['vedʒɪteɪt] vi lit & fig végéter.

vegetation [ˌvedʒɪ'teɪʃn] n végétation f.

veggie ['vedʒɪ] n & adj inf 1. abbr of **vegetarian** 2. abbr of **vegetable**.

veggieburger ['vedʒɪˌbɜːgər] n hamburger m végétarien.

vehement ['viːɪmənt] adj [emotions] ardent, passionné, véhément ; [actions, gestures] violent, véhément ; [language] véhément, passionné.

vehemently ['viːɪməntlɪ] adv [speak] avec passion, avec véhémence ; [attack] avec violence ; [gesticulate] frénétiquement.

vehicle ['viːɪkl] n 1. [gen & AUTO] véhicule m / 'heavy vehicles turning' 'passage d'engins' ▶ **vehicle emissions** gaz mpl d'échappement 2. PHARM véhicule m 3. fig véhicule m.

vehicular [vɪ'hɪkjʊlər] adj [gen & AUTO] de véhicules, de voitures ▶ **vehicular traffic** circulation automobile ▶ **vehicular access** accès aux véhicules.

veil [veɪl] ◆ n 1. [over face] voile m ; [on hat] voilette f, voile m 2. fig voile m 3. RELIG ▶ **to take the veil** prendre le voile. ◆ vt 1. [face] voiler, couvrir d'un voile ▶ **to veil o.s.** se voiler 2. fig [truth, feelings, intentions] voiler, dissimuler, masquer.

veiled [veɪld] adj 1. [wearing a veil] voilé 2. [hidden, disguised - expression, meaning] voilé, caché ; [- allusion, insult] voilé ; [- hostility] sourd.

vein [veɪn] n 1. ANAT veine f 2. [on insect wing] veine f ; [on leaf] nervure f 3. [in cheese, wood, marble] veine f ; [of ore, mineral] filon m, veine f 4. [mood] esprit m ; [style] veine f, style m / *in the same vein* dans le même style or la même veine.

veiny ['veɪnɪ] adj [leaf, wood] veineux.

Velcro® ['velkrəʊ] n (bande f) Velcro® m.

vellum ['veləm] ◆ n vélin m. ◆ adj de vélin.

velocity [vɪ'lɒsətɪ] (pl **velocities**) n vélocité f.

velour(s) [və'lʊər] (pl **velours**) ◆ n velours m. ◆ comp de or en velours.

velvet ['velvɪt] ◆ n velours m. ◆ comp [curtains, dress] de or en velours ; fig [skin, voice] velouté, de velours.

velvety ['velvɪtɪ] adj [cloth, complexion, texture] velouteux, velouté ; fig [cream, voice] velouté.

vendetta [ven'detə] n vendetta f.

vending machine n distributeur m automatique.

vendor ['vendɔːr] n 1. COMM marchand m, -e f 2. [machine] distributeur m automatique.

veneer [və'nɪər] ◆ n 1. [of wood] placage m (de bois) 2. fig vernis m, masque m, apparence f. ◆ vt plaquer.

venerable ['venərəbl] adj [gen & RELIG] vénérable.

venerate ['venəreɪt] vt vénérer.

veneration [ˌvenə'reɪʃn] n vénération f.

venereal disease n maladie f vénérienne.

Venetian [vɪ'niːʃn] ◆ n Vénitien m, -enne f. ◆ adj vénitien, de Venise ▶ **Venetian blind** store m vénitien.

Venezuela [ˌvenɪ'zweɪlə] pr n Venezuela m / *in Venezuela* au Venezuela.

Venezuelan [ˌvenɪ'zweɪlən] ◆ n Vénézuélien m, -enne f. ◆ adj vénézuélien.

vengeance ['vendʒəns] n 1. [revenge] vengeance f ▶ **to take** or **to wreak vengeance on** or **upon sb (for sthg)** se venger sur qqn (de qqch) ▶ **to seek vengeance for sthg** vouloir tirer vengeance de qqch, chercher à se venger de qqch 2. PHR **with a vengeance** très fort.

vengeful ['vendʒfʊl] adj vindicatif.

Venice ['venɪs] pr n Venise.

venison ['venɪzn] n venaison f.

venom ['venəm] n lit & fig venin m.

venomous ['venəməs] adj lit venimeux ; fig [remark, insult] venimeux, malveillant ; [look] haineux, venimeux.

vent [vent] ◆ n **1.** [outlet - for air, gas, liquid] orifice *m*, conduit *m* ; [- in chimney] conduit *m*, tuyau *m* ; [- in volcano] cheminée *f* ; [- in barrel] trou *m* ; [- for ventilation] conduit *m* d'aération **2.** [in jacket, skirt] fente *f* **3.** PHR **to give vent to sthg** donner or laisser libre cours à qqch. ◆ vt **1.** [barrel] pratiquer un trou dans, trouer ; [pipe, radiator] purger **2.** [release - smoke] laisser échapper ; [- gas] évacuer **3.** *fig* [express - anger] décharger ▶ **to vent one's anger / one's spleen on sb** décharger sa colère / sa bile sur qqn.

ventilate ['ventɪleɪt] vt **1.** [room] ventiler, aérer **2.** *fig* [controversy, question] agiter (au grand jour) ; [grievance] étaler (au grand jour).

ventilation [,ventɪ'leɪʃn] n aération *f*, ventilation *f* ▶ a **ventilation shaft** un conduit d'aération or de ventilation.

ventilator ['ventɪleɪtər] n **1.** [in room, building] ventilateur *m* ; AUTO déflecteur *m* **2.** MED respirateur *m* (artificiel).

ventriloquist [ven'trɪləkwɪst] n ventriloque *mf*.

venture ['ventʃər] ◆ n **1.** [undertaking] entreprise *f* périlleuse or risquée ; [adventure] aventure *f* ; [project] projet *m*, entreprise *f* **2.** COMM & FIN [firm] entreprise *f* ▶ a **business venture** une entreprise commerciale, un coup d'essai commercial. ◆ vt **1.** [risk - fortune, life] hasarder, risquer **2.** [proffer - opinion, suggestion] hasarder, avancer, risquer **3.** [dare] oser ▶ **to venture to do sthg** s'aventurer or se hasarder à faire qqch. ◆ vi **1.** [embark] se lancer / *to venture into politics* se lancer dans la politique **2.** *(verb of movement)* : *I wouldn't venture out of doors in this weather* je ne me risquerais pas à sortir par ce temps / *don't venture too far across the ice* ne va pas trop loin sur la glace / *don't venture too far from the beach* ne t'éloigne pas trop de la plage.

venture capital n capital-risque *m*.

venture capitalist n investisseur *m* en capital-risque.

venturesome ['ventʃəsəm] adj *liter* **1.** [daring - nature, person] aventureux, entreprenant **2.** [hazardous - action, journey] hasardeux, risqué.

venue ['venjuː] n [setting] lieu *m* (de rendez-vous or de réunion).

Venus ['viːnəs] pr n ASTRON & MYTH Vénus *f*.

veracity [və'ræsətɪ] n véracité *f*.

veranda(h) [və'rændə] n véranda *f*.

verb [vɜːb] n verbe *m* ▶ **verb phrase** syntagme *m* or groupe *m* verbal.

verbal ['vɜːbl] adj **1.** [spoken - account, agreement, promise] verbal, oral ; [- confession] oral **2.** [related to words] ▶ **verbal skills** aptitudes *fpl* à l'oral **3.** [literal - copy, translation] mot à mot, littéral, textuel **4.** GRAM verbal.

verbalize, verbalise ['vɜːbəlaɪz] vt [feelings, ideas] verbaliser, exprimer par des mots.

verbally ['vɜːbəlɪ] adv verbalement, oralement.

verbatim [vɜː'beɪtɪm] ◆ adj mot pour mot. ◆ adv textuellement.

verbose [vɜː'bəus] adj verbeux, prolixe.

verdict ['vɜːdɪkt] n **1.** LAW verdict *m* ▶ **to reach a verdict** arriver à un verdict ▶ **a verdict of guilty / not guilty** un verdict de culpabilité / non-culpabilité **2.** *fig* [conclusion] verdict *m*, jugement *m* ▶ **to give one's verdict on sthg** donner son verdict sur qqch.

verge [vɜːdʒ] ◆ n **1.** [edge - of lawn] bord *m* ; [- by roadside] accotement *m*, bas-côté *m* ; [- of forest] orée *f* / *grass verge* a) [round flowerbed] bordure *f* en gazon b) [by roadside] herbe *f* au bord de la route c) [in park, garden] bande *f* d'herbe **2.** *fig* [brink] bord *m* ; [threshold] seuil *m* ▶ **to be on the verge of doing sthg** être sur le point de faire qqch. ◆ vt [road, lawn] border. ◆ **verge on, verge upon** vt insep [be close to] côtoyer, s'approcher de.

verifiable ['verɪfaɪəbl] adj vérifiable.

verification [,verɪfɪ'keɪʃn] n vérification *f*.

verify ['verɪfaɪ] (*pt & pp* **verified**) vt [prove - information, rumour] vérifier ; [confirm - truth] vérifier, confirmer.

verisimilitude [,verɪsɪ'mɪlɪtjuːd] n *fml* vraisemblance *f*.

veritable ['verɪtəbl] adj véritable.

vermil(l)ion [və'mɪljən] ◆ n vermillon *m*. ◆ adj vermillon (*inv*).

vermin ['vɜːmɪn] pl n **1.** [rodents] animaux *mpl* nuisibles ; [insects] vermine *f* **2.** *pej* [people] vermine *f*, racaille *f*.

Vermont [vɜː'mɒnt] pr n Vermont *m* / *in Vermont* dans le Vermont.

vermouth ['vɜːməθ] n vermouth *m*.

vernacular [və'nækjulər] ◆ n **1.** LING (langue *f*) vernaculaire *m* / *in the vernacular* a) LING en langue vernaculaire b) [everyday language] en langage courant **2.** BOT & ZOOL nom *m* vernaculaire **3.** ARCHIT style *m* typique (du pays). ◆ adj **1.** BOT, LING & ZOOL vernaculaire **2.** [architecture, style] indigène.

verruca [və'ruːkə] (*pl* **verrucas** or **verrucae** [-kaɪ]) n verrue *f* (plantaire).

versatile ['vɜːsətaɪl] adj **1.** [person] aux talents variés, doué dans tous les domaines ; [mind] souple ; [tool] polyvalent, à usages multiples **2.** BOT versatile **3.** ZOOL mobile, pivotant **4.** *inf* [sexually active and passive] actif et passif.

versatility [,vɜːsə'tɪlətɪ] n **1.** [of person] faculté *f* d'adaptation, variété *f* de talents ; [of mind] souplesse *f* ; [of tool] polyvalence *f* **2.** BOT & ZOOL versatilité *f*.

verse [vɜːs] ◆ n **1.** [stanza - of poem] strophe *f* ; [- of song] couplet *m* ; [- in bible] verset *m* **2.** (*U*) [poetry] vers *mpl*, poésie *f* / *in verse* en vers. ◆ comp [line, epic] en vers.

versed [vɜːst] adj ▶ **versed in** a) [knowledgeable] versé dans b) [experienced] rompu à.

version ['vɜːʃn] n **1.** [account of events] version *f* **2.** [form of book, song] version *f* **3.** [model - of car, plane] modèle *m*, version *f* **4.** [translation] version *f*.

versus ['vɜːsəs] prep **1.** [against] contre **2.** [compared with] par rapport à, par opposition à.

vertebra ['vɜːtɪbrə] (*pl* **vertebras** or **vertebrae** [-briː]) n vertèbre *f*.

vertebrate ['vɜːtɪbreɪt] ◆ adj vertébré. ◆ n vertébré *m*.

vertical ['vɜːtɪkl] ◆ adj **1.** [gen & GEOM] vertical **2.** *fig* [structure, organization, integration] vertical. ◆ n verticale *f* ▶ **out of the vertical** écarté de la verticale, hors d'aplomb.

vertically ['vɜːtɪklɪ] adv verticalement ▶ **to take off vertically** AERON décoller à la verticale.

vertigo ['vɜːtɪgəu] n (*U*) vertige *m*.

verve [vɜːv] n verve *f*, brio *m*.

very ['verɪ] (*compar* **verier**, *superl* **veriest**) ◆ adv **1.** [with adj or adv] très, bien / *was the pizza good?* — *very / not very* la pizza était-elle bonne ? — très / pas très / *be very careful* faites très or bien attention / *he was very hungry / thirsty* il avait très faim / soif / *very few / little* très peu ▶ **very good!** or **very well!** [expressing agreement, consent] très bien ! / *you can't very well ask outright* tu ne peux pas vraiment demander directement **2.** (*with superl*) [emphatic use] : *our very best wine* notre meilleur vin / *the very best of friends* les meilleurs amis du monde / *at the very latest* au plus tard / *at the very least* / *most* tout au moins / plus / *the very next day* le lendemain même, dès le lendemain. ◆ adj **1.** [extreme, far] : *at the very end* a) [of street, row, etc.] tout au bout b) [of story, month, etc.] tout à la fin / *to the very end* a) [in space] jusqu'au bout b) [in time] jusqu'à la fin / *at the very back* tout au fond **2.** [exact] : *at that very moment* juste à ce moment-là / *the very man I need* juste l'homme qu'il me faut / *those were his very words* ce sont ses propos mêmes, c'est exactement ce qu'il a dit **3.** [emphatic use] : *the very idea!* quelle idée ! / *it happened before my very eyes* cela s'est passé sous mes yeux. ❖ **very much** ◆ adv phr [greatly] beaucoup, bien / *I very much hope to be able to come* j'espère bien que je pourrai venir / *were you impressed?* — *very much so* ça vous a impressionné ? — beaucoup. ◆ det phr beaucoup de. ◆ pron phr beaucoup / *she doesn't say very much* elle parle peu, elle ne dit pas grand-chose.

vessel ['vesl] n **1.** *liter* [container] récipient *m* **2.** NAUT vaisseau *m*.

vest [vest] n **1.** 🇬🇧 [singlet - for boy, man] maillot *m* de corps, tricot *m* de peau ; [- for woman] chemise *f* **2.** 🇺🇸 [waistcoat] gilet *m* (de costume).

⚠ **Une veste** is a jacket, **not a** vest.

vested interest ['vestɪd-] n ▸ **vested interests a)** [rights] droits *mpl* acquis **b)** [investments] capitaux *mpl* investis **c)** [advantages] intérêts *mpl* ▸ **to have a vested interest in doing sthg** avoir directement intérêt à faire qqch.

vestibule ['vestɪbjuːl] n [in house, church] vestibule *m* ; [in hotel] vestibule *m*, hall *m* d'entrée.

vestige ['vestɪdʒ] n [remnant] vestige *m*.

vestry ['vestrɪ] n (*pl* **vestries**) n **1.** [room] sacristie *f* **2.** [committee] conseil *m* paroissial.

Vesuvius [vɪ'suːvjəs] pr n ▸ **(Mount) Vesuvius** le Vésuve.

vet [vet] (*pt & pp* **vetted**, *cont* **vetting**) ◆ n **1.** (abbr of **veterinary surgeon/veterinary**) vétérinaire *mf* **2.** (abbr of **veteran**) 🇺🇸 *inf* ancien combattant *m*, vétéran *m*. ◆ vt [check - application] examiner minutieusement, passer au crible ; [- claims, facts, figures] vérifier soigneusement, passer au crible ; [- documents] contrôler ; [- person] enquêter sur.

veteran ['vetrən] ◆ n **1.** MIL ancien combattant *m*, vétéran *m* ▸ **Veterans Affairs** 🇺🇸 organisme de soutien aux anciens combattants ▸ **Veterans Day** 🇺🇸 fête *f* de l'armistice (le 11 novembre) **2.** [experienced person] personne *f* chevronnée or expérimentée, vieux *m* de la vieille. ◆ adj [experienced] expérimenté, chevronné.

veteran car n 🇬🇧 voiture *f* de collection (normalement antérieure à 1905).

veterinarian [ˌvetərɪ'neərɪən] n 🇺🇸 vétérinaire *mf*.

veterinary ['vetərɪnrɪ] adj [medicine, science] vétérinaire.

veterinary surgeon n 🇬🇧 vétérinaire *mf*.

veto ['viːtəu] (*pl* **vetoes**) ◆ n **1.** (U) [power] droit *m* de veto **2.** [refusal] veto *m* ▸ **to put a veto on sthg** mettre or opposer son veto à qqch. ◆ vt POL & *fig* mettre or opposer son veto à.

vetting ['vetɪŋ] n (U) enquêtes *fpl* ▸ **to undergo positive vetting** être soumis à une enquête de sécurité ▸ **security vetting** enquêtes de sécurité.

vex [veks] vt contrarier, ennuyer.

vexed [vekst] adj *fml* **1.** [annoyed] fâché, ennuyé, contrarié ▸ **to become vexed** se fâcher ▸ **to be vexed with sb** être fâché contre qqn, en vouloir à qqn **2.** [controversial] controversé ; [question] épineux.

VFD (abbr of **volunteer fire department**) n pompiers bénévoles aux États-Unis.

VG (written abbr of **very good**) TB.

VGA [ˌviːdʒiː'eɪ] (abbr of **video graphics array** or **video graphics adapter**) n COMPUT VGA *m* ▸ **VGA monitor** moniteur *m* VGA.

vgc (written abbr of **very good condition**) tbe.

VHF (abbr of **very high frequency**) n VHF *f*.

VHS (abbr of **video home system**) n VHS *m*.

VI written abbr of **Virgin Islands**.

via ['vaɪə] prep **1.** [by way of] via, par **2.** [by means of] par, au moyen de.

viability [ˌvaɪə'bɪlətɪ] n (U) **1.** ECON [of company, state] viabilité *f* **2.** [of plan, programme, scheme] chances *fpl* de réussite, viabilité *f* **3.** MED & BOT viabilité *f*.

viable ['vaɪəbl] adj **1.** ECON [company, economy, state] viable **2.** [practicable - plan, programme] viable, qui a des chances de réussir **3.** MED & BOT viable.

viaduct ['vaɪədʌkt] n viaduc *m*.

Viagra® [vaɪ'ægrə] n Viagra® *m*.

vibes [vaɪbz] pl n *inf* **1.** abbr of **vibraphone 2.** (abbr of **vibrations**) atmosphère *f*, ambiance *f* / *they give off really good / bad vibes* avec eux le courant passe vraiment bien / ne passe vraiment pas / *I get really bad vibes from her* je me sens vraiment mal / *I don't like the vibes in this place* je n'aime pas l'ambiance ici.

vibrant ['vaɪbrənt] adj **1.** [vigorous, lively - person] vif ; [- programme, atmosphere] vibrant, touchant, émouvant **2.** [resonant - sound, voice] vibrant, résonant **3.** [bright - colour, light] brillant.

vibrate [vaɪ'breɪt] vi **1.** [shake, quiver] vibrer **2.** [sound] vibrer, retentir **3.** PHYS [oscillate] osciller, vibrer.

vibration [vaɪ'breɪʃn] n vibration *f*. ❖ **vibrations** pl n *inf* [feeling] ambiance *f*.

vibrator [vaɪ'breɪtər] n [medical or sexual] vibromasseur *m*.

vicar ['vɪkər] n pasteur *m*.

vicarage ['vɪkərɪdʒ] n presbytère *m*.

vicarious [vɪ'keərɪəs] adj **1.** [indirect, second-hand - feeling, pride, enjoyment] indirect, par procuration or contrecoup **2.** [punishment] (fait) pour autrui ; [suffering, pain] subi pour autrui.

vicariously [vɪ'keərɪəslɪ] adv **1.** [experience] indirectement **2.** [authorize] par délégation, par procuration.

vice n [vaɪs] **1.** [depravity] vice *m* **2.** [moral failing] vice *m* ; [less serious] défaut *m* **3.** TECH étau *m* **4.** 🇺🇸 = **vice squad**.

vice- [vaɪs] in comp vice-.

vice-admiral n vice-amiral *m* d'escadre.

vice-chairman n vice-président *m*, -e *f*.

vice-chancellor n **1.** 🇬🇧 UNIV président *m*, -e *f* d'université **2.** 🇺🇸 LAW vice-chancelier *m*.

vicelike ['vaɪslaɪk] adj : *held in a vicelike grip* serré dans une poigne de fer, serré comme dans un étau.

vice-president n vice-président *m*, -e *f*.

vice-principal n SCH directeur *m* adjoint, directrice *f* adjointe.

vice squad n brigade *f* des mœurs.

vice versa [ˌvaɪsɪ'vɜːsə] adv vice versa, inversement.

vicinity [vɪ'sɪnətɪ] n (*pl* **vicinities**) n **1.** [surrounding area] environs *mpl*, alentours *mpl* ; [neighbourhood] voisinage *m*, environs *mpl* ; [proximity] proximité *f* / *he's somewhere in the vicinity* il est quelque part dans les environs or dans le coin **2.** [approximate figures, amounts] : *his salary is in the vicinity of £18,000* son salaire est aux alentours de or de l'ordre de 18 000 livres.

vicious ['vɪʃəs] adj **1.** [cruel, savage - attack, blow] brutal, violent **2.** [malevolent - criticism, gossip, remarks] méchant, malveillant **3.** [dog] méchant ; [horse] vicieux, rétif.

⚠ When vicious means cruel, it is not translated by **vicieux**, which most commonly denotes sexual perversity.

vicious circle n cercle *m* vicieux.
viciously ['vɪʃəslɪ] adv [attack, beat] brutalement, violemment ; [criticize] avec malveillance, méchamment.

⚠ **Vicieusement** means lecherously, not viciously.

viciousness ['vɪʃəsnɪs] n [of attack, beating] brutalité *f*, violence *f* ; [of criticism, gossip] méchanceté *f*, malveillance *f*.
victim ['vɪktɪm] n **1.** [physical sufferer] victime *f* ▶ **to fall victim to sthg** devenir la victime de qqch **2.** *fig* victime *f*.
victimhood ['vɪktɪmhʊd] n mentalité *f* de victime.
victimization, victimisation [,vɪktɪmaɪ'zeɪʃn] n [for beliefs, race, differences] fait *m* de prendre pour victime ; [reprisals] représailles *fpl*.
victimize, victimise ['vɪktɪmaɪz] vt [make victim of] faire une victime de, prendre pour victime ; [take reprisals against] exercer des or user de représailles sur.
victimless crime ['vɪktɪmlɪs-] n délit *m* sans victime.
victor ['vɪktər] n vainqueur *m*.
Victoria Cross n MIL croix *f* de Victoria (*en Grande-Bretagne, décoration militaire très prestigieuse*).
Victoria Falls pl pr n les chutes *fpl* Victoria.
Victorian [vɪk'tɔːrɪən] ◆ adj victorien. ◆ n Victorien *m*, -enne *f*.
Victoriana [,vɪktɔːrɪ'ɑːnə] n (*U*) antiquités *fpl* victoriennes, objets *mpl* de l'époque victorienne.
victorious [vɪk'tɔːrɪəs] adj [army, campaign, party] victorieux ; [army] vainqueur ; [cry] de victoire ▶ **to be victorious over sb** être victorieux de qqn, remporter la victoire sur qqn.
victory ['vɪktərɪ] (*pl* **victories**) n victoire *f* ▶ **to gain** or **to win a victory over sb** remporter la victoire sur qqn.
video ['vɪdɪəʊ] (*pl* **videos**) ◆ n **1.** [medium] vidéo *f* **2.** [VCR] magnétoscope *m* **3.** [cassette] vidéocassette *f* ; [recording] vidéo *f* ; [for pop-song] clip *m*, vidéoclip *m*. ◆ comp [film, version] (en) vidéo ; [services, equipment, signals] vidéo (*inv*) ▶ **a video shop** un magasin vidéo. ◆ vt enregistrer sur magnétoscope.
video arcade n salle *f* de jeux vidéo.
video call n TELEC appel *m* vidéo.
video camera n caméra *f* vidéo.
video card n COMPUT carte *f* vidéo.
video cassette n vidéocassette *f*.
videocast ['vɪdɪəʊkɑːst] n vidéocast *m*, émission *f* vidéo téléchargeable.
video clip n clip *m*, vidéoclip *m*, clip *m* vidéo.
video conference n vidéoconférence *f*, visioconférence *f*.
video conferencing n vidéoconférence *f*.
video diary n journal *m* vidéo.
videodisc 🇬🇧, **videodisk** 🇺🇸 ['vɪdɪəʊdɪsk] n vidéodisque *m*.
video game n jeu *m* vidéo.
video machine = videorecorder.
video on demand n (*U*) vidéo *f* à la demande.

videophone ['vɪdɪəʊfəʊn] n vidéophone *m*.
video projector n vidéoprojecteur *m*.
videorecorder ['vɪdɪəʊrɪ,kɔːdər] n magnétoscope *m*.
video recording n enregistrement *m* sur magnétoscope.
videotape ['vɪdɪəʊteɪp] ◆ n bande *f* vidéo. ◆ vt enregistrer sur magnétoscope, magnétoscoper.
vie [vaɪ] (*pt & pp* **vied**, *cont* **vying**) vi rivaliser, lutter ▶ **to vie with sb for sthg** disputer qqch à qqn.
Vienna [vɪ'enə] ◆ pr n Vienne. ◆ comp viennois, de Vienne.
Viennese [,vɪə'niːz] (*pl* **Viennese**) ◆ n Viennois *m*, -e *f*. ◆ adj viennois.
Vietnam [🇬🇧 ,vjet'næm 🇺🇸 ,vjet'nɑːm] pr n Viêt Nam *m* / **in Vietnam** au Viêt Nam ▶ **the Vietnam War** la guerre du Viêt Nam.

🏛 **The Vietnam War**

Conflit qui opposa, de 1954 à 1975, le Viêt Nam du Nord, communiste, au Viêt Nam du Sud, soutenu militairement par les États-Unis. Aussitôt critiqué par l'opinion publique nationale, l'effort de guerre américain s'intensifia considérablement au milieu des années 1960, sans parvenir pour autant à faire basculer l'issue du conflit. À partir de 1970, sous la présidence de R. Nixon, un processus de cessez-le-feu fut engagé, aboutissant au retrait des troupes américaines en 1973. Un an plus tard, le sud du pays passa aux mains des communistes. Véritable traumatisme national, la guerre du Viêt Nam est sans doute l'un des épisodes les plus pénibles de l'histoire des États-Unis. La longueur du conflit, les atrocités commises de part et d'autre, le nombre très élevé de victimes, mais surtout les interrogations sur la finalité de cette guerre remirent dramatiquement en question la légitimité de l'ingérence américaine et provoquèrent chez les jeunes Américains de l'époque un mouvement antimilitariste d'une ampleur sans précédent.

Vietnamese [,vjetnə'miːz] (*pl* **Vietnamese**) ◆ n **1.** [person] Vietnamien *m*, -enne *f* **2.** LING vietnamien *m*. ◆ adj vietnamien.
view [vjuː] ◆ n **1.** [sight] vue *f* ▶ **to come into view** apparaître ▶ **to be on view a)** [house] être ouvert aux visites **b)** [picture] être exposé ▶ **to hide sthg from view a)** [accidentally] cacher qqch de la vue **b)** [deliberately] cacher qqch aux regards **2.** [prospect] vue *f* **3.** [future perspective] ▶ **in view** en vue **4.** [aim, purpose] but *m*, intention *f* ▶ **with a view to doing sthg** en vue de faire qqch, dans l'intention de faire qqch **5.** [interpretation] vue *f* **6.** [picture, photograph] vue *f* **7.** [opinion] avis *m*, opinion *f* / **in my view** à mon avis. ◆ vt **1.** [look at] voir, regarder ; [film] regarder **2.** [examine - slides] visionner ; [- through microscope] regarder ; [- flat, showhouse] visiter, inspecter **3.** *fig* [consider, judge] considérer, envisager **4.** HUNT [fox] apercevoir **5.** COMPUT visualiser, afficher. ◆ vi TV regarder la télévision.
➤ **in view of** prep phr étant donné, vu.
viewable area ['vjuːəbl-] adj COMPUT [of monitor] zone *f* d'affichage.

viewer ['vju:ər] n **1.** TV téléspectateur m, -trice f **2.** PHOT [for slides] visionneuse f ; [viewfinder] viseur m.

viewfinder ['vju:ˌfaɪndər] n PHOT viseur m.

viewing ['vju:ɪŋ] ◆ n (U) **1.** TV programme m, programmes mpl, émissions fpl **2.** [of showhouse, exhibition] visite f. ◆ comp TV [time, patterns] d'écoute ▶ **viewing audience**: a young viewing audience de jeunes téléspectateurs.

viewpoint ['vju:pɔɪnt] n **1.** [opinion] point de vue m **2.** [viewing place] point de vue m, panorama m.

vigil ['vɪdʒɪl] n **1.** [watch] veille f ; [in sickroom] veillée f ; [for dead person] veillée f funèbre **2.** [demonstration] manifestation f silencieuse (nocturne) **3.** RELIG vigile f.

vigilance ['vɪdʒɪləns] n vigilance f.

vigilant ['vɪdʒɪlənt] adj vigilant, éveillé.

vigilante [ˌvɪdʒɪ'læntɪ] n membre d'un groupe d'autodéfense ▶ **vigilante group** groupe m d'autodéfense.

vigor US = **vigour**.

vigorous ['vɪgərəs] adj **1.** [robust - person, plant] vigoureux ; [enthusiastic - person] enthousiaste **2.** [forceful - opposition, campaign, support] vigoureux, énergique **3.** [energetic - exercise] énergique.

vigorously ['vɪgərəslɪ] adv vigoureusement, énergiquement.

vigour US, **vigor** US ['vɪgər] n **1.** [physical vitality] vigueur f, énergie f, vitalité f ; [mental vitality] vigueur f, vivacité f **2.** [of attack, style] vigueur f ; [of storm] violence f **3.** US LAW ▶ **in vigour** en vigueur.

Viking ['vaɪkɪŋ] ◆ adj viking. ◆ n Viking mf.

vile [vaɪl] adj **1.** [morally wrong - deed, intention, murder] vil, ignoble, infâme **2.** [disgusting - person, habit, food, taste] abominable, exécrable ; [- smell] infect, nauséabond **3.** [very bad - temper] exécrable, massacrant ; [- weather] exécrable.

vilify ['vɪlɪfaɪ] vt fml diffamer, calomnier.

villa ['vɪlə] n [in country] maison f de campagne ; [by sea] villa f ; US [in town] villa f or pavillon m (de banlieue) ; HIST villa f.

village ['vɪlɪdʒ] ◆ n village m ▶ **the global village** le village planétaire. ◆ comp du village.

village green n pelouse au centre du village.

Village green

Souvent situé au centre du village, le **village green** est une grande pelouse publique, accueillant kermesses et manifestations sportives.

village hall n salle f des fêtes.

villager ['vɪlɪdʒər] n villageois m, -e f.

villain ['vɪlən] n **1.** [ruffian, scoundrel] scélérat m, -e f, vaurien m, -enne f ; [in film, story] méchant m, -e f, traître m, -esse f **2.** inf [rascal] coquin m, -e f, vilain m, -e f **3.** crime sl [criminal] bandit m, malfaiteur m.

villainous ['vɪlənəs] adj [evil - act, person] vil, ignoble, infâme.

VIN (abbr of **vehicle identification number**) n AUTO numéro m d'immatriculation.

vinaigrette [ˌvɪnɪ'gret] n vinaigrette f.

vindicate ['vɪndɪkeɪt] vt **1.** [justify] justifier **2.** [uphold - claim, right] faire valoir, revendiquer.

vindication [ˌvɪndɪ'keɪʃn] n justification f.

vindictive [vɪn'dɪktɪv] adj vindicatif.

vindictively [vɪn'dɪktɪvlɪ] adv vindicativement.

vine [vaɪn] ◆ n **1.** [grapevine] vigne f **2.** [plant - climbing] plante f grimpante ; [- creeping] plante f rampante. ◆ comp [leaf] de vigne ; [disease] de la vigne ▶ **vine grower** viticulteur m, vigneron m ▶ **vine growing** viticulture f ▶ **vine harvest** vendange f, vendanges fpl.

vinegar ['vɪnɪgər] n vinaigre m.

vineyard ['vɪnjəd] n vignoble m.

vintage ['vɪntɪdʒ] ◆ n **1.** OENOL [wine] vin m de cru ; [year] cru m, millésime m **2.** [crop] récolte f ; [harvesting] vendange f, vendanges fpl **3.** [period] époque f. ◆ adj **1.** [old] antique, ancien **2.** [classic, superior] classique **3.** [port, champagne] de cru.

vintage car n US voiture f de collection (normalement construite entre 1919 et 1930).

vintage wine n vin m de grand cru, grand vin m.

vintage year n [for wine] grand cru m, grande année f ; [for books, films] très bonne année f.

vinyl ['vaɪnɪl] ◆ n vinyle m. ◆ adj [wallpaper, tiles, coat] de or en vinyle ; [paint] vinylique.

viola [vɪ'əʊlə] ◆ n MUS alto m. ◆ comp ▶ **viola player** altiste mf.

violate ['vaɪəleɪt] vt **1.** [promise, secret, treaty] violer ; [law] violer, enfreindre ; [rights] violer, bafouer **2.** [frontier, property] violer **3.** [peace, silence] troubler, rompre **4.** [sanctuary, tomb] violer, profaner **5.** fml [rape] violer, violenter.

violation [ˌvaɪə'leɪʃn] n **1.** [of promise, rights, secret] violation f ; [of law] violation f, infraction f ; SPORT faute f **2.** [of frontier, property] violation f **3.** [of sanctuary, tomb] violation f, profanation f **4.** US LAW infraction f **5.** fml [rape] viol m.

violence ['vaɪələns] n (U) **1.** [physical] violence f **2.** LAW violences fpl ▶ **robbery with violence** vol avec coups et blessures **3.** [of language, passion, storm] violence f **4.** PHR ▶ **to do violence to** faire violence à.

violent ['vaɪələnt] adj **1.** [attack, crime, person] violent ▶ **to be violent with sb** se montrer or être violent avec qqn **2.** [intense - pain] violent, aigu (aiguë) ; [furious - temper] violent ; [strong, great - contrast, change] violent, brutal ; [- explosion] violent **3.** [forceful, impassioned - argument, language, emotions] violent **4.** [wind, weather] violent **5.** [colour] criard, voyant.

violently ['vaɪələntlɪ] adv [attack, shake, struggle] violemment ; [act, react] violemment, avec violence.

violet ['vaɪələt] ◆ n **1.** BOT violette f **2.** [colour] violet m. ◆ adj violet.

violin [ˌvaɪə'lɪn] ◆ n violon m. ◆ comp [concerto] pour violon ; [lesson] de violon ▶ **violin maker** luthier m.

violinist [ˌvaɪə'lɪnɪst] n violoniste mf.

VIP (abbr of **very important person**) ◆ n VIP mf, personnalité f, personnage m de marque. ◆ comp [guests, visitors] de marque, éminent, très important ▶ **to give sb the VIP treatment** traiter qqn comme un personnage de marque.

viper ['vaɪpər] n ZOOL & fig vipère f.

viral ['vaɪrəl] adj viral.

virgin ['vɜːdʒɪn] ◆ n [girl] vierge f, pucelle f ; [boy] puceau m. ◆ adj **1.** [sexually] vierge **2.** [forest, soil, olive oil] vierge ; [fresh] virginal. ◆ **Virgin** pr n RELIG ▶ **the Virgin** la Vierge.

Virginia [və'dʒɪnjə] pr n Virginie f / **in Virginia** en Virginie.

Virgin Islands pl pr n ▶ **the Virgin Islands** les îles fpl Vierges.

virginity [və'dʒɪnətɪ] n virginité f.

Virgo ['vɜːgəʊ] pr n ASTROL & ASTRON Vierge f / **he's a Virgo** il est (du signe de la) Vierge.

virile ['vɪraɪl] adj viril.

virility [vɪ'rɪlətɪ] n virilité *f*.

virtual ['vɜːtʃʊəl] adj **1.** [near, as good as] : *it's a virtual impossibility / dictatorship* c'est une quasi-impossibilité / une quasi-dictature **2.** [actual, effective] : *they are the virtual rulers of the country* en fait ce sont eux qui dirigent le pays, ce sont eux les dirigeants de fait du pays **3.** COMPUT & PHYS virtuel.

⚠ **Virtuel** means virtual in the computing sense; it should not be used to translate virtual when it means 'near'.

virtually ['vɜːtʃʊəlɪ] adv **1.** [almost] pratiquement, quasiment, virtuellement **2.** [actually, in effect] en fait.

virtual memory n COMPUT mémoire *f* virtuelle.

virtual reality n réalité *f* virtuelle.

virtue ['vɜːtjuː] n **1.** [goodness] vertu *f* **2.** [merit] mérite *m*, avantage *m*. **◆ by virtue of** prep phr en vertu or en raison de.

virtuosity [,vɜːtjʊ'ɒsɪtɪ] n virtuosité *f*.

virtuoso [,vɜːtjʊ'əʊzəʊ] (*pl* **virtuosos** or **virtuosi** [-siː]) **◆** n [gen & MUS] virtuose *mf*. **◆** adj de virtuose.

virtuous ['vɜːtʃʊəs] adj vertueux.

virulent ['vɪrʊlənt] adj virulent.

virus ['vaɪrəs] **◆** n MED & COMPUT virus *m*. **◆** comp **1.** MED **▸** *a virus infection* une infection virale **2.** COMPUT **▸** *virus check* détection *f* de virus **▸** *virus detector* détecteur *m* de virus.

virus-free adj COMPUT dépourvu de virus.

visa ['viːzə] n visa *m*.

vis-à-vis [,viːzɑː'viː] (*pl* **vis-à-vis**) prep **1.** [in relation to] par rapport à **2.** [opposite] vis-à-vis de.

visceral ['vɪsərəl] adj viscéral.

viscose ['vɪskəʊs] **◆** n viscose *f*. **◆** adj visqueux.

viscosity [vɪ'skɒsətɪ] (*pl* **viscosities**) n viscosité *f*.

viscount ['vaɪkaʊnt] n vicomte *m*.

viscous ['vɪskəs] adj visqueux, gluant.

vise [vaɪs] US = **vice**.

visibility [,vɪzɪ'bɪlətɪ] n visibilité *f*.

visible ['vɪzəbl] adj **1.** [gen & OPT] visible **2.** [evident] visible, apparent, manifeste **3.** *inf* ECON visible **▸** *visible earnings* bénéfices *mpl* visibles.

visibly ['vɪzəblɪ] adv visiblement.

vision ['vɪʒn] n **1.** (*U*) OPT [sight] vision *f*, vue *f* **2.** [insight] vision *f*, clairvoyance *f* **3.** [dream, fantasy] vision *f* **4.** [conception] vision *f*, conception *f* **5.** [apparition] vision *f*, apparition *f* ; [lovely sight] magnifique spectacle *m* **6.** TV image *f*.

visionary ['vɪʒənrɪ] (*pl* **visionaries**) **◆** adj visionnaire. **◆** n visionnaire *mf*.

visit ['vɪzɪt] **◆** n **1.** [call] visite *f* **▸** *to pay sb a visit* rendre visite à qqn **2.** [stay] visite *f*, séjour *m* ; [trip] voyage *m*, séjour *m* **3.** US [chat] causette *f*, bavardage *m* **4.** [Internet] visite *f* (d'un site). **◆** vt **1.** [person - go to see] rendre visite à, aller voir ; [-stay with] rendre visite à, séjourner chez **2.** [museum, town] visiter, aller voir **3.** [inspect - place, premises] visiter, inspecter, faire une visite d'inspection à **4.** *liter* [inflict] **▸** *to visit a punishment on sb* punir qqn **5.** [Internet] visiter (un site). **◆** vi visiter. **◆ visit with** vt insep US [call on] passer voir ; [talk with] bavarder avec.

⚠ As the entry shows, **visiter** is more restricted in use than to visit. **Rendre visite à** is preferable to **visiter** when talking about informal visits to people.

visiting ['vɪzɪtɪŋ] adj [circus, performers] de passage ; [lecturer] invité ; [birds] de passage, migrateur **▸ the visiting team** SPORT les visiteurs.

visiting card n UK carte *f* de visite.

visiting hours pl n heures *fpl* de visite.

visiting nurse n US infirmier *m*, -ère *f* à domicile.

visiting time = visiting hours.

visitor ['vɪzɪtə*r*] n **1.** [caller - at hospital, house, prison] visiteur *m*, -euse *f* **2.** [guest - at private house] invité *m*, -e *f* ; [-at hotel] client *m*, -e *f* **3.** [visiting town, monument, exhibition] visiteur *m*, -euse *f*.

visitors' book n [in house, museum] livre *m* d'or ; [in hotel] registre *m*.

visitor's passport n passeport *m* temporaire.

visor, vizor ['vaɪzə*r*] n [on hat] visière *f* ; [in car] pare-soleil *m*.

vista ['vɪstə] n **1.** [view] vue *f*, perspective *f* **2.** *fig* [perspective] perspective *f*, horizon *m* ; [image - of past] vue *f*, vision *f* ; [-of future] perspective *f*, vision *f*.

VISTA ['vɪstə] (*abbr of* **Volunteers in Service to America**) pr n *programme américain d'aide aux personnes les plus défavorisées.*

visual ['vɪʒʊəl] adj [image, impression, faculty] visuel. **◆ visuals** pl n supports *mpl* visuels.

visual aid n support *m* visuel.

visual arts pl n arts *mpl* plastiques.

visual display terminal, visual display unit n écran *m* (de visualisation), moniteur *m*.

visualize, visualise ['vɪʒʊəlaɪz] vt **1.** [call to mind - scene] se représenter, évoquer ; [imagine] s'imaginer, visualiser, se représenter **2.** [foresee] envisager, prévoir.

visually ['vɪʒʊəlɪ] adv visuellement.

visually handicapped, visually impaired ◆ adj malvoyant, amblyope *spec.* **◆** pl n **▸ the visually handicapped** les malvoyants *mpl*.

vital ['vaɪtl] adj **1.** [essential - information, services, supplies] vital, essentiel, indispensable **2.** [very important - decision, matter] vital, fondamental **3.** BIOL [function, organ] vital **4.** [energetic] plein d'entrain, dynamique. **◆ vitals** pl n *hum* organes *mpl* vitaux.

📓 Note that il est vital que is followed by a verb in the subjunctive:
It is vital that these people should have access to medical care. *Il est vital que ces gens puissent avoir accès à des soins médicaux.*

vitality [vaɪ'tælətɪ] n vitalité *f*.

vitally ['vaɪtəlɪ] adv absolument.

vital statistics pl n **1.** [demographic] statistiques *fpl* démographiques **2.** *hum* [of woman] mensurations *fpl*.

vitamin [UK 'vɪtəmɪn US 'vaɪtəmɪn] n vitamine *f* **▸ vitamin C / E** vitamine C / E.

vitamin deficiency n carence *f* vitaminique.

vitamin pill n comprimé *m* de vitamines.

vitriol ['vɪtrɪəl] n CHEM & *fig* vitriol *m*.

vitriolic [ˌvɪtrɪ'ɒlɪk] adj [attack, description, portrait] au vitriol ; [tone] venimeux.

viva[1] ['viːvə] ◆ interj ▶ **viva!** vive ! ◆ n vivat m.

viva[2] ['vaɪvə] = **viva voce** (noun).

vivacious [vɪ'veɪʃəs] adj **1.** [manner, person] enjoué, exubérant **2.** BOT vivace.

vivacity [vɪ'væsətɪ] n [in action] vivacité f ; [in speech] verve f.

viva voce [ˌvaɪvə'vəʊsɪ] ◆ n 𝕌𝕂 UNIV [gen] épreuve f orale, oral m ; [for thesis] soutenance f de thèse. ◆ adj oral. ◆ adv de vive voix, oralement.

vivid ['vɪvɪd] adj **1.** [bright - colour, light] vif, éclatant ; [- clothes] voyant **2.** [intense - feeling] vif **3.** [lively - personality] vif, vivant ; [- imagination] vif ; [- language] coloré **4.** [graphic - account, description] vivant ; [- memory] vif, net ; [- example] frappant.

vividly ['vɪvɪdlɪ] adv **1.** [coloured] de façon éclatante ; [painted, decorated] avec éclat, de façon éclatante **2.** [describe] de façon frappante or vivante.

vivisection [ˌvɪvɪ'sekʃn] n vivisection f.

vixen ['vɪksn] n **1.** ZOOL renarde f **2.** pej [woman] mégère f.

viz [vɪz] (abbr of videlicet) c-à-d.

VLF n abbr of very low frequency.

V-neck ◆ n encolure f en V. ◆ adj = **V-necked**.

V-necked adj [pullover] à encolure or col en V.

VOA (abbr of Voice of America) pr n station de radio américaine émettant dans le monde entier.

vocab ['vəʊkæb] n inf abbr of vocabulary.

vocabulary [və'kæbjʊlərɪ] (pl vocabularies) n vocabulaire m ; LING vocabulaire m, lexique m.

vocal ['vəʊkl] ◆ adj **1.** ANAT vocal **2.** [oral - communication] oral, verbal **3.** [outspoken - person, minority] qui se fait bien entendre **4.** [noisy - assembly, meeting] bruyant **5.** MUS vocal **6.** LING [sound] vocalique ; [consonant] voisé. ◆ n LING son m vocalique. ◆ **vocals** pl n MUS chant m, musique f vocale.

⚠ The French adjective **vocal** never means outspoken or noisy.

vocal cords pl n cordes fpl vocales.

vocalist ['vəʊkəlɪst] n chanteur m, -euse f (dans un groupe pop).

vocation [vəʊ'keɪʃn] n [gen & RELIG] vocation f.

vocational [vəʊ'keɪʃənl] adj professionnel ▶ **vocational course** a) [short] stage m de formation professionnelle b) [longer] enseignement m professionnel ▶ **vocational guidance** orientation f professionnelle ▶ **vocational training** formation f professionnelle.

vocationally [vəʊ'keɪʃnəlɪ] adv ▶ **vocationally oriented** à vocation professionnelle ▶ **vocationally relevant subjects** des matières à vocation professionnelle.

vociferous [və'sɪfərəs] adj bruyant, vociférateur.

vociferously [və'sɪfərəslɪ] adv bruyamment, en vociférant.

VOD (abbr of video-on-demand) n vidéo f à la demande, VOD f.

vodka ['vɒdkə] n vodka f.

vogue [vəʊg] ◆ n [fashion] vogue f, mode f ▶ **to come into vogue** devenir à la mode. ◆ adj [style, word] en vogue, à la mode.

voice [vɔɪs] ◆ n **1.** [speech] voix f / in a low voice à voix basse / in a loud voice d'une voix forte ▶ **to shout**

at the top of one's voice crier à tue-tête ▶ **to raise one's voice a)** [speak louder] parler plus fort **b)** [get angry] hausser le ton ▶ **Voice of America** = VOA **2.** [of singer] voix f **3.** [say] voix f **4.** GRAM voix f / in the active / passive voice à la voix active / passive. ◆ vt [express - feelings] exprimer, formuler ; [- opposition, support] exprimer.

voice-activated adj à commande vocale.

voice bank n TELEC boîte f vocale.

voice box n larynx m.

voice mail n [device] boîte f vocale ; [system] messagerie f vocale.

voice-over n CIN & TV voix f off.

voice recognition n COMPUT reconnaissance f de la parole.

void [vɔɪd] ◆ n **1.** PHYS & ASTRON vide m **2.** [chasm] vide m **3.** [emptiness] vide m. ◆ adj **1.** [empty] vide **2.** LAW nul **3.** [vacant - position] vacant. ◆ vt **1.** fml [empty] vider ; [discharge - bowels] évacuer **2.** LAW annuler, rendre nul.

vol. (written abbr of volume) vol.

volatile [𝕌𝕂 'vɒlətaɪl 𝕌𝕊 'vɒlətl] ◆ adj **1.** CHEM volatil **2.** [person - changeable] versatile, inconstant ; [- temperamental] lunatique **3.** [unstable - situation] explosif, instable ; [- market] instable **4.** COMPUT [memory] volatil. ◆ n CHEM substance f volatile.

vol-au-vent ['vɒləʊvɑ̃] n vol-au-vent m inv.

volcanic [vɒl'kænɪk] adj volcanique.

volcano [vɒl'keɪnəʊ] (pl volcanoes or volcanos) n volcan m.

vole [vəʊl] n ZOOL campagnol m.

Volga ['vɒlgə] pr n ▶ **the (River) Volga** la Volga.

volition [və'lɪʃn] n [gen & PHILOS] volition f, volonté f ▶ of one's own volition de son propre gré.

volley ['vɒlɪ] ◆ n **1.** [of gunshots] volée f, salve f ; [of arrows, missiles, stones] volée f, grêle f ; [of blows] volée f **2.** [of insults] grêle f, bordée f, torrent m ; [of curses] bordée f, torrent m ; [of questions] feu m roulant ; [of applause] salve f **3.** SPORT volée f. ◆ vt **1.** [missile, shot] tirer une volée or une salve de **2.** [curses, insults] lâcher une bordée or un torrent de **3.** SPORT reprendre de volée. ◆ vi **1.** MIL tirer par salves **2.** SPORT [in tennis] volleyer ; [in football] reprendre le ballon de volée.

volleyball ['vɒlɪbɔːl] n volley-ball m, volley m ▶ **volleyball player** volleyeur m, -euse f.

volt [vəʊlt] n volt m.

Volta ['vɒltə] pr n Volta f.

voltage ['vəʊltɪdʒ] n voltage m, tension f spec.

voluble ['vɒljʊbl] adj volubile, loquace.

volume ['vɒljuːm] n **1.** [gen & PHYS] volume m ; [capacity] volume m, capacité f ; [amount] volume m, quantité f **2.** ACOUST volume m **3.** [book] volume m, tome m **4.** [in hairstyle] volume m **5.** COMPUT volume m.

volume control n réglage m du volume.

volume mailing n multipostage m, publipostage m groupé.

voluminous [və'luːmɪnəs] adj volumineux.

voluntarily [𝕌𝕂 'vɒləntrɪlɪ 𝕌𝕊 ˌvɒlən'terəlɪ] adv **1.** [willingly] volontairement, de son plein gré **2.** [without payment] bénévolement.

voluntary ['vɒləntrɪ] (pl voluntaries) ◆ adj **1.** [freely given - statement, donation, gift] volontaire, spontané **2.** [optional] facultatif **3.** [unpaid - help, service] bénévole **4.** PHYSIOL volontaire. ◆ n RELIG & MUS morceau m d'orgue.

voluntary-aided school n 🇬🇧 *école financée princi-palement par l'État mais également par l'Église, ce qui donne à celle-ci un droit de regard sur l'instruction religieuse.*

voluntary liquidation n 🇬🇧 dépôt *m* de bilan ▸ **to go into voluntary liquidation** déposer son bilan.

voluntary redundancy n 🇬🇧 départ *m* volontaire.

voluntary school n ≃ école *f* libre.

Voluntary Service Overseas = VSO.

voluntary work n travail *m* bénévole, bénévolat *m*.

voluntary worker n bénévole *mf*.

volunteer [,vɒlən'tɪəʳ] ◆ n **1.** [gen & MIL] volontaire *mf* **2.** [unpaid worker] bénévole *mf*. ◆ comp **1.** [army, group] de volontaires **2.** [work, worker] bénévole. ◆ vt **1.** [advice, information, statement] donner or fournir spontanément ; [help, services] donner or proposer volontairement ▸ **to volunteer to do sthg** se proposer pour or offrir de faire qqch **2.** [say] dire spontanément. ◆ vi [gen] se porter volontaire ; MIL s'engager comme volontaire.

voluptuous [və'lʌptʃʊəs] adj voluptueux, sensuel.

vomit ['vɒmɪt] ◆ n vomissement *m*, vomi *m*. ◆ vt *lit & fig* vomir.

vomiting ['vɒmɪtɪŋ] n *(U)* vomissements *mpl*.

voodoo ['vu:du:] *(pl* **voodoos)** ◆ n vaudou *m*. ◆ adj vaudou *(inv)*. ◆ vt envoûter, ensorceler.

voracious [və'reɪʃəs] adj [appetite, energy, person] vorace ; [reader] avide.

voraciously [və'reɪʃəslɪ] adv [consume, eat] voracement, avec voracité ; [read] avec voracité, avidement.

vortex ['vɔ:teks] *(pl* **vortexes** or **vortices** [-tɪsi:z])* n [of water, gas] vortex *m*, tourbillon *m* ; *fig* tourbillon *m*, maelström *m*.

vote [vəʊt] ◆ n **1.** [ballot] vote *m* ▸ **to have a vote on sthg** voter sur qqch, mettre qqch au vote ▸ **to take a vote on sthg a)** [gen] voter sur qqch **b)** ADMIN & POL procéder au vote de qqch **2.** [in parliament] vote *m*, scrutin *m* ▸ **vote of confidence** vote *m* de confiance ▸ **vote of no confidence** motion *f* de censure **3.** [individual choice] vote *m*, voix *f* **4.** [ballot paper] bulletin *m* de vote **5.** [suffrage] droit *m* de vote **6.** *(U)* [collectively - voters] vote *m*, voix *fpl* ; [- votes cast] voix *fpl* exprimées. ◆ vt **1.** [in election] voter **2.** [in parliament, assembly - motion, law, money] voter **3.** [elect] élire ; [appoint] nommer **4.** [declare] proclamer **5.** [suggest] proposer. ◆ vi voter ▸ **to vote for / against sb** voter pour / contre qqn ▸ **to vote in favour of / against sthg** voter pour / contre qqch ▸ **to vote on it!** mettons cela aux voix ! ❖ **vote down** vt sep [bill, proposal] rejeter *(par le vote)*. ❖ **vote in** vt sep [person, government] élire ; [new law] voter, adopter. ❖ **vote out** vt sep [suggestion] rejeter ; [minister] relever de ses fonctions. ❖ **vote through** vt sep [bill, reform] voter, ratifier.

vote-catching adj [plan, strategy] électoraliste.

vote-loser n politique *f* qui risque de faire perdre des voix, politique *f* peu populaire.

voter ['vəʊtəʳ] n électeur *m*, -trice *f*.

voting ['vəʊtɪŋ] n vote *m*, scrutin *m*.

voting booth n isoloir *m*.

voting precinct n 🇺🇸 POL circonscription *f* électorale.

voting rights pl n droit *m* de vote.

vouch [vaʊtʃ] vi ▸ **to vouch for sb / sthg** se porter garant de qqn / qqch, répondre de qqn / qqch.

voucher ['vaʊtʃəʳ] n **1.** 🇬🇧 [for restaurant, purchase, petrol] bon *m* ▸ **credit voucher** bon *m* d'achat **2.** [receipt] reçu *m*, récépissé *m* **3.** LAW pièce *f* justificative.

vow [vaʊ] ◆ n **1.** [promise] serment *m*, promesse *f* ▸ **to make** or **take a vow to do sthg** promettre or jurer de faire qqch **2.** RELIG vœu *m* ▸ **to take one's vows** prononcer ses vœux. ◆ vt [swear] jurer ▸ **to vow to do sthg** jurer de faire qqch.

vowel ['vaʊəl] ◆ n voyelle *f*. ◆ comp [harmony, pattern, sound] vocalique.

vox pop [,vɒks'pɒp] n 🇬🇧 *inf* émission de radio ou de TV avec intervention du public.

voyage ['vɔɪdʒ] ◆ n voyage *m* ▸ **to go on a voyage** partir en voyage. ◆ vi **1.** NAUT voyager par mer **2.** 🇺🇸 AERON voyager par avion.

voyeur [vwɑ:'jɜ:ʳ] n voyeur *m*, -euse *f*.

voyeurism [vwɑ:'jɜ:rɪzm] n voyeurisme *m*.

voyeuristic [,vɔɪə'rɪstɪk] adj de voyeur.

VP n (abbr of **vice-president**) VP *m*.

vs written abbr of **versus**.

V-shaped adj en (forme de) V.

V-sign n ▸ **to give the V-sign** [for victory, approval] faire le V de la victoire ▸ **to give sb the V-sign** 🇬🇧 [as insult] ≃ faire un bras d'honneur à qqn.

VSO (abbr of **Voluntary Service Overseas**) n coopération technique à l'étranger (non rémunérée).

VSOP (abbr of **very special old pale**) VSOP.

VT written abbr of **Vermont**.

VTOL ['vi:tɒl] (abbr of **vertical takeoff and landing**) n [system] décollage *m* et atterrissage *m* vertical ; [plane] ADAV *m*, avion *m* à décollage et atterrissage vertical.

vulgar ['vʌlgəʳ] adj **1.** [rude] vulgaire, grossier **2.** [common - person, taste, decor] vulgaire, commun.

vulgarity [vʌl'gærətɪ] n vulgarité *f*.

vulnerability [,vʌlnərə'bɪlətɪ] n vulnérabilité *f*.

vulnerable ['vʌlnərəbl] adj vulnérable ▸ **to be vulnerable to sthg** être vulnérable à qqch.

vulture ['vʌltʃəʳ] n ORNITH & *fig* vautour *m*.

vulva ['vʌlvə] *(pl* **vulvas** or **vulvae** [-vi:])* n vulve *f*.

W 1. (written abbr of **west**) O **2.** (written abbr of **watt**) w **3.** MESSAGING written abbr of **with**.

WA written abbr of **Washington (State)**.

WABOL MESSAGING written abbr of **with a bit of luck**.

wackiness ['wækɪnɪs] n *inf* loufoquerie *f*.

wacko ['wækəʊ] (*pl* **wackos**) ◆ n *inf* cinglé *m*, -e *f*, dingue *mf*. ◆ adj cinglé, dingue.

wacky ['wækɪ] (*compar* **wackier**, *superl* **wackiest**) adj *inf* loufoque.

wad [wɒd] (*pt* & *pp* **wadded**, *cont* **wadding**) ◆ n **1.** [of cotton wool, paper] tampon *m*, bouchon *m* ; [of tobacco] chique *f* ; [of straw] bouchon *m* ; [of gum] boulette *f* ; [for cannon, gun] bourre *f* **2.** [of letters, documents] liasse *f*, paquet *m*. ◆ vt **1.** [cloth, paper] faire un tampon de ; [tobacco, chewing gum] faire une boulette de **2.** [hole, aperture] boucher (avec un tampon) ; MIL [barrel, cannon] bourrer **3.** [quilt, garment] rembourrer.

wadding ['wɒdɪŋ] n **1.** MIL [in gun, cartridge] bourre *f* **2.** [stuffing - for furniture, packing] rembourrage *m*, capitonnage *m* ; [- for clothes] ouate *f*, ouatine *f*.

waddle ['wɒdl] ◆ vi [duck, person] se dandiner ▸ **to waddle along / in** avancer / entrer en se dandinant. ◆ n dandinement *m*.

wade [weɪd] ◆ vi patauger, avancer en pataugeant. ◆ vt [river] passer or traverser à gué. ❖ **wade in** vi [UK] [in fight, quarrel] s'y mettre. ❖ **wade into** vt insep [UK] [work, task] attaquer, s'atteler à, se mettre à ; [meal] attaquer, entamer. ❖ **wade through** vt insep avancer or marcher péniblement dans ; *fig* : *it took me a month to wade through that book* il m'a fallu un mois pour venir à bout de ce livre.

waders ['weɪdəz] pl n cuissardes *fpl* (*de pêcheur*).

wadge [wɒdʒ] n [UK] *inf* paquet *m* ⁄ *wadges of notes* des liasses de billets.

wading pool n [US] [in swimming pool] petit bassin *m* ; [inflatable] piscine *f* gonflable.

wafer ['weɪfər] ◆ n **1.** CULIN gaufrette *f* **2.** RELIG hostie *f* **3.** [seal] cachet *m* (de papier rouge) **4.** COMPUT & TECH tranche *f*. ◆ vt COMPUT & TECH diviser en tranches.

wafer-thin, wafery ['weɪfərɪ] adj mince comme une feuille de papier à cigarette or comme une pelure d'oignon.

waffle ['wɒfl] ◆ n **1.** CULIN gaufre *f* **2.** [UK] *inf* [spoken] baratin *m*, bla-bla *m inv* ; [written] remplissage *m*, baratin *m*. ◆ vi *inf* [in speaking] baratiner, parler pour ne rien dire ; [in writing] faire du remplissage ▸ **to waffle on** [UK] bavarder, faire des laïus.

waffle iron n gaufrier *m*.

waft [wɑːft or wɒft] ◆ vt [scent, sound] porter, transporter. ◆ vi [scent, sound] flotter. ◆ n [of smoke, air] bouffée *f*.

wag [wæg] (*pt* & *pp* **wagged**, *cont* **wagging**) ◆ vt [tail] agiter, remuer. ◆ vi [tail] remuer, frétiller. ◆ n **1.** [of tail] remuement *m*, frétillement *m* **2.** [UK] [person] plaisantin *m*, farceur *m*, -euse *f*.

WAG [wæg] (abbr of **wifes and girlfriends**) n femme ou petite amie d'un footballeur.

wage [weɪdʒ] ◆ n **1.** [pay - of worker] salaire *m*, paye *f*, paie *f* ; [- of servant] gages *mpl* **2.** [reward] salaire *m*, récompense *f*. ◆ comp [claim, demand, settlement] salarial ; [increase, rise, incentive] de salaire ▸ **wages bill** masse *f* salariale ▸ **wages dispute** conflit *m* salarial. ◆ vt ▸ **to wage war on** or **against** faire la guerre contre ▸ **to wage a campaign for / against sthg** faire campagne pour / contre qqch.

waged [weɪdʒd] adj [person] salarié.

wage earner n salarié *m*, -e *f*.

wage freeze n blocage *m* des salaires.

wage packet n [UK] paie *f*, paye *f* (*surtout en espèces*).

wager ['weɪdʒər] *fml* ◆ vt parier. ◆ vi parier, faire un pari. ◆ n pari *m*.

wage slave n employé *m* très mal payé, employée *f* très mal payée.

waggish ['wægɪʃ] adj badin, facétieux.

waggle ['wægl] ◆ vt [tail] agiter, remuer ; [pencil] agiter ; [loose tooth, screw] faire jouer ; [ears, nose] remuer. ◆ vi [tail] bouger, frétiller ; [loose tooth, screw] bouger, branler. ◆ n ▸ **to give sthg a waggle** agiter or remuer qqch.

waggon ['wægən] [UK] = **wagon**.

wagon ['wægən] n **1.** [horse-drawn] chariot *m* **2.** [truck] camionnette *f*, fourgon *m* **3.** [UK] RAIL wagon *m* (de marchandises) **4.** [PHR] **to be on the wagon** *inf* être au régime sec.

⚠ **Un wagon** is a railway carriage, not a wagon in the sense of a cart.

waif [weɪf] n [child - neglected] enfant *m* malheureux, enfant *f* malheureuse ; [- homeless] enfant *m* abandonné, enfant *f* abandonnée ▸ **waifs and strays** [animals] animaux errants.

wail [weɪl] ◆ vi **1.** [person - whine, moan] gémir, pousser des gémissements ; [baby - cry] hurler ; [- weep] pleurer bruyamment **2.** [wind] gémir ; [siren] hurler. ◆ vt dire en gémissant, gémir. ◆ n **1.** [of person] gémissement *m* **2.** [of wind] gémissement *m* ; [of siren] hurlement *m*.

wailing ['weɪlɪŋ] ◆ n (U) [of person] gémissements mpl, plaintes fpl ; [of wind] gémissements mpl, plainte f ; [of siren] hurlement m, hurlements mpl. ◆ adj [person] gémissant ; [sound] plaintif.

waist [weɪst] n **1.** [of person, garment] taille f ▶ **waist measurement** or **waist size** tour m de taille **2.** [of ship, plane] partie f centrale ; [of violin] partie f resserrée de la table.

waistband ['weɪstbænd] n ceinture f (d'un vêtement).

waistcoat ['weɪskəut] [UK] gilet m (de costume).

-waisted ['weɪstɪd] in comp ▶ **a low / high-waisted dress** une robe à taille basse / haute.

waistline ['weɪstlaɪn] n taille f ▶ **to watch one's waistline** surveiller sa ligne.

W8 MESSAGING written abbr of **wait**.

wait [weɪt] ◆ vi **1.** [person, bus, work] attendre / **just you wait!** a) [as threat] attends un peu, tu vas voir !, tu ne perds rien pour attendre ! b) [you'll see] vous verrez ! / **we'll just have to wait and see** on verra bien ▶ **to keep sb waiting** faire attendre qqn **2.** [with 'can'] : **it can wait** cela peut attendre / **I can't wait!** iro je brûle d'impatience ! / **I can hardly wait to see them again** j'ai hâte de les revoir **3.** [with 'until' or 'till'] : **wait until I've finished** attendez que j'aie fini / **can't that wait until tomorrow?** cela ne peut pas attendre jusqu'à demain ? / **just wait till your parents hear about it** attends un peu que tes parents apprennent cela **4.** [serve] servir, faire le service ▶ **to wait at table** [UK] or **on table** [US] servir à table, faire le service. ◆ vt **1.** [period of time] attendre / **I waited half an hour** j'ai attendu (pendant) une demi-heure / **wait a minute!** (attendez) une minute or un instant ! **2.** [US] [serve at] ▶ **to wait tables** servir à table, faire le service. ◆ n attente f / **we had a long wait** nous avons dû attendre (pendant) longtemps / **there was an hour's wait between trains** il y avait une heure de battement or d'attente entre les trains ▶ **to lie in wait for** être à l'affût de, guetter. ❖ **wait about** vi [UK] traîner, faire le pied de grue / **I can't stand all this waiting about** cela m'énerve d'être obligé d'attendre or de traîner comme ça. ❖ **wait around** = **wait about**. ❖ **wait behind** vi rester ▶ **to wait behind for sb** rester pour attendre qqn. ❖ **wait for** vt insep ▶ **to wait for sb / sthg** attendre qqn / qqch / **that was worth waiting for** cela valait la peine d'attendre. ❖ **wait on** vt insep [serve] : **I'm not here to wait on you!** a) [male] je ne suis pas ton serviteur ! b) [female] je ne suis pas ta servante or ta bonne ! ▶ **to wait on sb hand and foot** être aux petits soins pour qqn. ❖ **wait up** vi **1.** [not go to bed] rester debout, veiller / **her parents always wait up for her** ses parents ne se couchent jamais avant qu'elle soit rentrée or attendent toujours qu'elle rentre pour se coucher **2.** [US] inf [wait] ▶ **hey, wait up!** attendez-moi ! ❖ **wait upon** = **wait on**.

waiter ['weɪtər] n serveur m, garçon m ▶ **waiter!** s'il vous plaît !, monsieur !

W84M MESSAGING written abbr of **wait for me**.

W8N MESSAGING written abbr of **waiting**.

W4u MESSAGING written abbr of **waiting for you**.

waiting game n ▶ **to play a waiting game** a) fig jouer la montre, attendre son heure b) MIL & POL mener une politique d'attentisme.

waiting list n liste f d'attente.

waiting room n [in office, surgery, airport, station] salle f d'attente.

waitlist ['weɪtlɪst] vt [US] mettre sur la liste d'attente.

waitperson ['weɪtpɜːsn] n [US] serveur m, -euse f.

waitress ['weɪtrɪs] n serveuse f ▶ **waitress!** s'il vous plaît !, mademoiselle ! ▶ **waitress service** service m à table.

wait state n COMPUT état m d'attente.

waive [weɪv] vt [condition, requirement] ne pas insister sur, abandonner ; [law, rule] déroger à ; [claim, right] renoncer à, abandonner.

waiver ['weɪvər] n [of condition, requirement] abandon m ; [of law, rule] dérogation f ; [of claim, right] renonciation f, abandon m ▶ **full-collision waiver** [US] assurance f tous risques.

wake [weɪk] (pt **woke** [wəuk] or **waked**, pp **woken** ['wəukən] or **waked**) ◆ vi **1.** [stop sleeping] se réveiller, s'éveiller **2.** = **wake up** (vi). ◆ vt **1.** [rouse from sleep] réveiller, tirer or sortir du sommeil **2.** [arouse - curiosity, jealousy] réveiller, éveiller, exciter ; [- memories] réveiller, éveiller, ranimer **3.** [alert] éveiller l'attention de. ◆ n **1.** [vigil] veillée f (mortuaire) **2.** [of ship] sillage m, eaux fpl ; fig sillage m. ❖ **wake up** ◆ vi **1.** [stop sleeping] se réveiller, s'éveiller **2.** [become alert] se réveiller, prendre conscience. ◆ vt sep **1.** [rouse from sleep] réveiller, tirer or sortir du sommeil **2.** [alert] réveiller, secouer.

wakeboarding ['weɪkbɔːdɪŋ] n SPORT wakeboard m ▶ **to go wakeboarding** faire du wakeboard.

wakeful ['weɪkful] adj **1.** [person - unable to sleep] qui ne dort pas, éveillé ; [- alert] vigilant **2.** [night, week] sans sommeil.

waken ['weɪkən] liter ◆ vi se réveiller, s'éveiller. ◆ vt réveiller, tirer or sortir du sommeil.

wake-up call n réveil m téléphonique.

wakey wakey [,weɪki'weɪki] interj [UK] inf ▶ **wakey wakey!** réveille-toi !, debout !

waking ['weɪkɪŋ] ◆ adj [hours] de veille ▶ **a waking dream** une rêverie, une rêvasserie. ◆ n [state] (état m de) veille f.

Wales [weɪlz] pr n pays m de Galles / **in Wales** au pays de Galles.

walk [wɔːk] ◆ vi **1.** marcher ; [go for a walk] se promener / **walk, don't run!** ne cours pas ! / **he walked along the beach** il marchait or se promenait le long de la plage / **we walked down / up the street** nous avons descendu / monté la rue à pied / **she walked back and forth** elle marchait de long en large, elle faisait les cent pas / **he walks in his sleep** il est somnambule **2.** [as opposed to drive, ride] aller à pied / **did you walk all the way?** avez-vous fait tout le chemin à pied ? **3.** [go free] être relâché. ◆ vt **1.** [cover on foot] faire à pied / **you can walk it in 10 minutes** il faut 10 minutes (pour y aller) à pied ▶ **to walk the streets** a) [wander] se promener dans les rues b) [looking for something] arpenter les rues, battre le pavé c) [as prostitute] faire le trottoir **2.** [escort] accompagner, marcher avec / **may I walk you home?** puis-je vous raccompagner ? **3.** [take for walk - person] faire marcher ; [- dog] promener ; [- horse] conduire à pied / **they walked him forcibly to the door** ils l'ont dirigé de force vers la porte / **she has walked me off my feet** [UK] inf elle m'a fait tellement marcher que je ne tiens plus debout. ◆ n **1.** [movement] : **she slowed to a walk** elle a ralenti et s'est mise à marcher **2.** [stroll] promenade f ; [long] randonnée f ▶ **to go for** or **to take a walk** aller se promener, faire une promenade or un tour / **the station is a five-minute walk from here** la gare est à cinq minutes de marche or à cinq minutes à pied d'ici / **did you take the dog for a walk?** as-tu promené or sorti le chien ? ▶ **it was a walk in the park** [US] c'était du gâteau, c'était une promenade de santé **3.** [gait] démarche f, façon f de marcher **4.** [occupation] ▶ **people from all walks** or **from every walk of life**: **I meet people from all walks** or **from every walk of life** je rencontre des gens de tous milieux. ❖ **walk about** vi [UK] se promener, se balader. ❖ **walk across** ◆ vi traverser (à pied). ◆ vt sep faire traverser (à pied).

❖ **walk around** = walk about. ❖ **walk away** vi partir, s'en aller / *she walked away from the group* elle s'est éloignée du groupe, elle a quitté le groupe / *he walked away from the accident* il est sorti de l'accident indemne. ❖ **walk away with** vt insep ▶ **to walk away with sthg a)** *lit* emporter qqch **b)** *fig* remporter or gagner qqch haut la main. ❖ **walk back** ◆ vi [return] revenir or retourner (à pied). ◆ vt sep raccompagner (à pied). ❖ **walk in** vi entrer / *we walked in on her as she was getting dressed* nous sommes entrés sans prévenir pendant qu'elle s'habillait. ❖ **walk into** vt insep **1.** [enter - house, room] entrer dans ; [- job] obtenir (sans problème) ; [- situation] se retrouver dans ; [- trap] tomber dans **2.** [bump into - chair, wall] se cogner à, rentrer dans ; [- person] rentrer dans. ❖ **walk off** ◆ vi partir, s'en aller. ◆ vt sep [get rid of - headache] faire passer en marchant ; [- weight] perdre en faisant de la marche. ❖ **walk off with** vt insep ▶ **to walk off with sthg a)** [take] emporter qqch **b)** [steal] voler qqch. ❖ **walk out** vi **1.** [go out] sortir ; [leave] partir, s'en aller / *we walked out of the meeting* nous avons quitté la réunion or nous sommes partis de la réunion (en signe de protestation) **2.** [worker] se mettre en grève. ❖ **walk out on** vt insep [family, lover] quitter. ❖ **walk over** ◆ vt insep [bridge] traverser / *don't let them walk all over you* fig ne vous laissez pas avoir, ne vous laissez pas marcher sur les pieds. ◆ vi aller, faire un saut / *the boss walked over to congratulate him* le patron s'est approché de lui pour le féliciter. ❖ **walk up** vi **1.** [go upstairs] monter **2.** [come close] s'approcher.

walkabout ['wɔːkəˌbaʊt] n **1.** 🇬🇧 ▶ **to go on a walkabout** [actor, politician] prendre un bain de foule **2.** [of an Aborigine] *excursion périodique dans la brousse*.

walker ['wɔːkər] n **1.** [person - stroller] promeneur m, -euse f, marcheur m, -euse f ; [- in mountains] randonneur m, -euse f ; SPORT marcheur m, -euse f **2.** [apparatus - for babies] trotte-bébé m ; [- for invalids] déambulateur m.

walkie-talkie [ˌwɔːkɪˈtɔːkɪ] n (poste m) émetteur-récepteur m portatif, talkie-walkie m.

walk-in adj [safe, wardrobe] de plain-pied.

walking ['wɔːkɪŋ] ◆ n **1.** [activity - gen] marche f (à pied), promenade f, promenades fpl ; [- hiking] randonnée f ; SPORT marche f (athlétique) **2.** [in basketball] marcher m. ◆ adj [clothing, shoes] de marche / *is it within walking distance?* est-ce qu'on peut y aller à pied ? / *a walking holiday in the Vosges* un séjour de randonnée dans les Vosges / *the walking wounded* les blessés qui peuvent encore marcher / *he's a walking dictionary* or *encyclopedia* hum c'est un vrai dictionnaire ambulant.

walking frame n déambulateur m.

walking papers pl n 🇺🇸 inf ▶ **to hand** or **to give sb their walking papers a)** [employee] renvoyer qqn, mettre or flanquer qqn à la porte **b)** [lover] plaquer qqn ▶ **to get one's walking papers** se faire mettre à la porte.

walking shoes n chaussures fpl de marche.

walking stick n **1.** [cane] canne f **2.** 🇺🇸 [stick insect] phasme m.

walk-on ◆ n rôle m de figurant. ◆ comp ▶ **walk-on part** rôle m de figurant.

walkout ['wɔːkaʊt] n [of members, spectators] départ m (en signe de protestation) ; [of workers] grève f.

walkover ['wɔːkˌəʊvər] n **1.** 🇬🇧 inf [victory] victoire f dans un fauteuil **2.** [in horse racing] walk-over m inv.

walk-up 🇺🇸 ◆ adj [apartment] situé dans un immeuble sans ascenseur ; [building] sans ascenseur. ◆ n *appartement ou bureau situé dans un immeuble sans ascenseur* ; [building] *immeuble sans ascenseur*.

walkway ['wɔːkweɪ] n [path] sentier m, chemin m ; [passage] passage m or passerelle f (*pour piétons, entre deux bâtiments*).

wall [wɔːl] ◆ n **1.** [of building, room] mur m ; [round field, garden] mur m de clôture ; [round castle, city] murs mpl, murailles fpl, remparts mpl **2.** [side - of box, cell, vein] paroi f ; [- of tyre] flanc m **3.** [of mountain] paroi f, face f. ◆ vt [garden, land] clôturer, entourer d'un mur ; [city] fortifier. ❖ **wall in** vt sep [garden] clôturer, entourer d'un mur. ❖ **wall off** vt sep séparer par un mur or par une cloison. ❖ **wall up** vt sep [door, window] murer, condamner ; [body, treasure] emmurer.

wallaby ['wɒləbɪ] (pl **wallabies**) n wallaby m.

wall bars pl n espalier m (*pour exercices*).

wallchart ['wɔːltʃɑːt] n panneau m mural.

wall cupboard n placard m mural.

walled [wɔːld] adj [city] fortifié ; [garden] clos.

wallet ['wɒlɪt] n portefeuille m.

wallflower ['wɔːlˌflaʊər] n **1.** BOT giroflée f **2.** inf [person] : *I'm tired of being a wallflower* j'en ai assez de faire tapisserie.

wall hanging n tenture f murale.

wall-mounted adj [clock, telephone] mural.

Walloon [wɒˈluːn] ◆ n [person] Wallon m, -onne f. ◆ adj wallon.

wallop ['wɒləp] inf ◆ vt **1.** [hit - person] flanquer un coup à, cogner sur ; [- ball] taper sur, donner un grand coup dans **2.** [defeat] écraser, battre à plate couture. ◆ n [blow] beigne f, coup m.

walloping ['wɒləpɪŋ] inf ◆ adj énorme, phénoménal. ◆ adv vachement. ◆ n **1.** [beating] raclée f, rossée f **2.** [defeat] : *they gave our team a walloping* ils ont écrasé notre équipe, ils ont battu notre équipe à plate couture.

wallow ['wɒləʊ] vi **1.** [roll about] se vautrer, se rouler **2.** [indulge] se vautrer, se complaire. ◆ n **1.** [mud] boue f, bourbe f ; [place] mare f bourbeuse **2.** inf [act of wallowing] ▶ **to have a good wallow a)** [in a bath] prendre un bon bain **b)** [in self-pity] s'apitoyer sur soi-même.

wall painting n peinture f murale.

wallpaper ['wɔːlˌpeɪpər] ◆ n **1.** [gen] papier m peint **2.** COMPUT fond m d'écran. ◆ vt tapisser (de papier peint).

wall socket n prise f murale.

Wall Street pr n Wall Street ▶ **the Wall Street Crash** le krach de Wall Street ▶ **The Wall Street Journal** 🇺🇸 PRESS *quotidien financier américain*.

 The Wall Street Crash

Krach financier à la Bourse de New York, le 24 octobre 1929 (« Jeudi noir »). Il entraîna la ruine de plusieurs milliers d'Américains, acculant certains d'entre eux au suicide. Cet événement est considéré comme le point de départ de la crise économique qu'allaient vivre les États-Unis pendant dix ans (« la grande dépression »).

wall-to-wall adj ▶ **wall-to-wall carpet** or **carpeting** moquette f.

wally ['wɒlɪ] (pl **wallies**) n 🇬🇧 inf imbécile mf, andouille mf.

walnut ['wɔːlnʌt] ◆ n [tree, wood] noyer m ; [fruit] noix f. ◆ comp [furniture] de or en noyer ; [oil] de noix ; [cake] aux noix.

walrus [ˈwɔːlrəs] (*pl* **walrus** *or* **walruses**) n morse *m*.

waltz [wɔːls] ◆ n valse *f*. ◆ vi **1.** [dancer] valser, danser une valse **2.** [move] danser / *she waltzed in* / *out of his office* a) [jauntily] elle est entrée dans / sortie de son bureau d'un pas joyeux b) [brazenly] elle est entrée dans / sortie de son bureau avec effronterie ▸ **to waltz off** partir, s'en aller / *they waltzed off with first prize* ils ont remporté le premier prix haut la main. ◆ vt **1.** [dance] valser avec, faire valser **2.** [propel] pousser, propulser.

wan [wɒn] (*compar* **wanner,** *superl* **wannest**) adj [person - pale] pâle, blême, blafard ; [-sad] triste ; [smile] pâle, faible ; [light, star] pâle.

WAN [wæn] n abbr of **wide area network**.

wand [wɒnd] n [of fairy, magician] baguette *f* (magique).

wander [ˈwɒndər] ◆ vi **1.** [meander - person] errer, flâner ; [-stream] serpenter, faire des méandres **2.** [stray - person] s'égarer **3.** [mind, thoughts] vagabonder, errer **4.** [become confused] divaguer, déraisonner. ◆ vt errer dans, parcourir (au hasard). ◆ n promenade *f*, tour *m*. ❖ **wander about** [UK], **wander around** vi [without destination] errer, aller sans but ; [without hurrying] flâner, aller sans se presser.

wanderer [ˈwɒndərər] n vagabond *m*, -e *f*.

wandering [ˈwɒndərɪŋ] ◆ adj **1.** [roaming - person] errant, vagabond ; [-tribe] nomade ; [-stream] qui serpente, qui fait des méandres ▸ **wandering minstrels** ménestrels *mpl* **2.** [distracted - mind, thoughts, attention] distrait, vagabond **3.** [confused - mind, person] qui divague, qui délire ; [-thoughts] incohérent. ◆ n **1.** [trip] = **wanderings 2.** [of mind] délire *m*. ❖ **wanderings** pl n [trip] vagabondage *m*, voyages *mpl*.

wanderlust [ˈwɒndəlʌst] n envie *f* de voyager.

wane [weɪn] ◆ vi [moon] décroître, décliner ; [interest, power] diminuer ; [civilization, empire] décliner, être en déclin. ◆ n ▸ **to be on the wane** a) [moon] décroître, décliner b) [interest, power] diminuer c) [civilization, empire] décliner, être en déclin.

wangle [ˈwæŋgl] vt *inf* [obtain - through cleverness] se débrouiller pour avoir ; [-through devious means] obtenir par subterfuge, carotter.

wank [wæŋk] [UK] *vulg* ◆ vi se branler. ◆ n branlette *f* ▸ **to have a wank** se faire une branlette.

wanker [ˈwæŋkər] n [UK] *vulg* branleur *m*.

wanna [ˈwɒnə] *v inf* **1.** abbr of **want to 2.** abbr of **want a**.

wannabe [ˈwɒnəˌbiː] n *inf se dit de quelqu'un qui veut être ce qu'il ne peut pas être.*

want [wɒnt] ◆ vt **1.** [expressing a wish or desire] vouloir, désirer / *what do you want now?* qu'est-ce que tu veux encore ? / *all he wants is to go to bed* tout ce qu'il veut, c'est aller se coucher ▸ **to want to do sthg** avoir envie de or vouloir faire qqch / *she doesn't want to* elle n'en a pas envie / *what do you want with her?* qu'est-ce que tu lui veux ? / *she doesn't want much!* iro elle n'est pas difficile, elle au moins / *now I've got you where I want you!* fig je te tiens ! **2.** [desire sexually] désirer, avoir envie de **3.** [require to be present] demander, vouloir voir / *someone wants you* or *you're wanted on the phone* quelqu'un vous demande au téléphone / *where do you want this wardrobe?* où voulez-vous qu'on mette cette armoire ? / *go away, you're not wanted here* va-t'en, tu n'es pas le bienvenu ici **4.** [hunt, look for] chercher, rechercher / *to be wanted by the police* être recherché par la police **5.** [need - subj: person] avoir besoin de ; [-subj: task, thing] avoir besoin de, nécessiter / *do you have everything you want?* avez-vous tout ce qu'il vous faut ? / *this coat wants cleaning very badly* ce manteau a besoin d'un bon nettoyage / *what do*

you want with a car that size? qu'allez-vous faire d'une voiture de cette taille ? **6.** *inf* [ought] : *she wants to watch out, the boss is looking for her* elle devrait faire attention, le patron la cherche. ◆ vi *inf* : *the cat wants in* / *out* le chat veut entrer / sortir / *he wants in (on the deal)* il veut une part du gâteau / *I want out!* je ne suis plus de la partie ! ◆ n **1.** [desire, wish] désir *m*, envie *f* **2.** [requirement] besoin *m* ▸ **to have few wants** avoir peu de besoins, avoir besoin de peu **3.** [lack] manque *m* / *there's certainly no want of goodwill* ce ne sont certainement pas les bonnes volontés qui manquent **4.** [poverty] misère *f*, besoin *m*. ❖ **for want of** prep phr faute de / *I'll take this novel for want of anything better* faute de mieux je vais prendre ce roman. ❖ **want for** vt insep manquer de / *he wants for nothing* il ne manque de rien.

📋 Note that **vouloir que** and **souhaiter que** are followed by a verb in the subjunctive:
I want you to pay more attention. Je veux que / Je souhaite que tu *sois plus attentif.*

---

want ad n [US] *inf* petite annonce *f*.

wanted [ˈwɒntɪd] adj **1.** [in advertisements] / '**carpenter** / **cook wanted**' 'on recherche (un) charpentier / (un) cuisinier' / '**accommodation wanted**' 'cherche appartement' **2.** [murderer, thief] recherché ▸ **wanted notice** avis *m* de recherche.

wanting [ˈwɒntɪŋ] adj **1.** [inadequate] ▸ **to be found wanting** a) [person] ne pas convenir, ne pas faire l'affaire b) [machine] ne pas convenir, ne pas être au point **2.** [lacking] manquant ▸ **to be wanting in sthg** manquer de qqch **3.** *euph* [weak-minded] simple d'esprit.

wanton [ˈwɒntən] adj [malicious - action, cruelty] gratuit, injustifié.

WAN2 MESSAGING written abbr of **want to**.

WAP [wæp] (abbr of **wireless application protocol**) n TELEC WAP *m* ▸ **WAP phone** téléphone *m* WAP.

war [wɔːr] (*pt & pp* **warred,** *cont* **warring**) ◆ n **1.** [armed conflict] guerre *f* ▸ **to be at war** / **to go to war with sb** être en guerre / entrer en guerre avec qqn / *he fought in the war* il a fait la guerre ▸ **war of attrition** guerre d'usure ▸ **war museum** musée *m* de guerre **2.** [conflict, struggle] guerre *f*, lutte *f* ▸ **to declare** or **to wage war on sthg** partir en guerre contre or déclarer la guerre à qqch. ◆ comp [criminal, diary, film, hero, pension, wound, zone] de guerre ▸ **during the war years** pendant la guerre ▸ **the war effort** l'effort *m* de guerre ▸ **war record** passé *m* militaire. ◆ vi faire la guerre ▸ **to war with sb** faire la guerre à qqn.

War. = **Warks.**

warble [ˈwɔːbl] ◆ vi & vt [subj: bird] gazouiller ; [subj: person] chanter (avec des trilles). ◆ n gazouillis *m*, gazouillement *m*.

war correspondent n correspondant *m*, -e *f* de guerre.

war crime n crime *m* de guerre.

war cry n cri *m* de guerre.

ward [wɔːd] n **1.** [of hospital - room] salle *f* ; [-section] pavillon *m* ; [of prison] quartier *m* **2.** POL [district] circonscription *f* électorale **3.** LAW [person] pupille *mf* ; [guardianship] tutelle *f* ▸ **ward of court** pupille *mf* sous tutelle judiciaire. ❖ **ward off** vt sep [danger, disease] éviter ; [blow] parer, éviter.

war dance n danse *f* de guerre or guerrière.

warden ['wɔːdn] n **1.** [director - of building, institution] directeur m, -trice f; US [of prison] directeur m, -trice f de prison **2.** [public official - of fortress, town] gouverneur m; [- of park, reserve] gardien m, -enne f **3.** UK UNIV portier m.

warder ['wɔːdəʳ] n UK [guard] gardien m or surveillant m (de prison).

wardrobe ['wɔːdrəʊb] n UK **1.** [cupboard] armoire f, penderie f **2.** [clothing] garde-robe f; THEAT costumes mpl.

wardrobe mistress n costumière f.

warehouse ◆ n ['weəhaʊs] (pl [-haʊzɪz]) entrepôt m, magasin m. ◆ vt ['weəhaʊz] entreposer, emmagasiner.

warehouseman ['weəhaʊsmən] (pl **warehousemen** [-mən]) n magasinier m.

warehousing ['weəhaʊzɪŋ] n **1.** [of goods] entreposage m **2.** [of shares] parcage m **3.** ▶ **warehousing company** société f d'entrepôts ▶ **warehousing costs** frais mpl d'entreposage.

wares [weəz] pl n marchandises fpl.

warfare ['wɔːfeəʳ] n MIL guerre f; fig lutte f, guerre f ▶ **class warfare** lutte des classes.

war game n (usu pl) **1.** MIL [simulated battle with maps] kriegspiel m, wargame m; [manoeuvres] manœuvres fpl militaires **2.** GAMES wargame m.

warhead ['wɔːhed] n ogive f ▶ **nuclear warhead** ogive f or tête f nucléaire.

warily ['weərəlɪ] adv [carefully] prudemment, avec prudence or circonspection; [distrustfully] avec méfiance.

warlike ['wɔːlaɪk] adj guerrier, belliqueux.

warm [wɔːm] ◆ adj **1.** [moderately hot] chaud / a warm front METEOR un front chaud / I can't wait for the warm weather j'ai hâte qu'il fasse chaud / are you warm enough? avez-vous assez chaud ? / the room is too warm il fait trop chaud or on étouffe dans cette pièce **2.** [clothing] chaud, qui tient chaud **3.** [work] qui donne chaud **4.** [affectionate - feelings] chaud, chaleureux; [- personality] chaleureux **5.** [hearty - greeting, welcome] chaleureux, cordial; [- thanks] vif; [- admirer, support] ardent, enthousiaste; [- applause] chaleureux, enthousiaste **6.** [colour, sound] chaud; [voice] chaud, chaleureux **7.** [scent, trail] récent. ◆ vt **1.** [heat - person, room] réchauffer; [- food] (faire) chauffer **2.** [reheat] (faire) réchauffer. ◆ vi : she warmed to the new neighbours elle s'est prise de sympathie pour les nouveaux voisins / you'll soon warm to the idea tu verras, cette idée finira par te plaire / the speaker began to warm to his subject le conférencier s'est laissé entraîner par son sujet. ◆ n inf : come into the warm viens au chaud or où il fait chaud. ◆ **warm down** vi [after physical effort] travailler lentement en étirement après un échauffement intense. ◆ **warm over** vt sep US [food] (faire) réchauffer; pej [idea] ressasser. ◆ **warm through** vt sep (faire) réchauffer complètement. ◆ **warm up** vt sep **1.** [heat - person, room] réchauffer; [- food] (faire) chauffer; [- engine, machine] faire chauffer **2.** [reheat] (faire) réchauffer **3.** [animate - audience] mettre en train, chauffer. ◆ vi **1.** [become hotter - person] se chauffer, se réchauffer; [- room, engine, food] se réchauffer; [- weather] devenir plus chaud, se réchauffer **2.** [get ready - athlete, comedian] s'échauffer, se mettre en train; [- audience] commencer à s'animer **3.** [debate, discussion] s'animer.

warm-blooded [-'blʌdɪd] adj ZOOL à sang chaud; fig [ardent] ardent, qui a le sang chaud.

war memorial n monument m aux morts.

warm-hearted [-'hɑːtɪd] adj [kindly] chaleureux, bon; [generous] généreux.

warmly ['wɔːmlɪ] adv **1.** [dress] chaudement **2.** [greet, smile, welcome] chaleureusement, chaudement; [recom-

mend, thank] vivement, chaudement; [support] avec enthousiasme, ardemment; [applaud] avec enthousiasme, chaleureusement.

warmonger ['wɔː,mʌŋgəʳ] n belliciste mf.

warmongering ['wɔː,mʌŋgərɪŋ] ◆ n (U) [activities] activités fpl bellicistes; [attitude] bellicisme m; [propaganda] propagande f belliciste. ◆ adj belliciste.

warmth [wɔːmθ] n [of temperature] chaleur f; [of greeting, welcome] chaleur f, cordialité f; [of recommendation, thanks] chaleur f, vivacité f; [of applause, support] enthousiasme m; [of colour] chaleur f.

warm-up ◆ n [gen] préparation f, préparations fpl; [of athlete, singer] échauffement m; [of audience] mise f en train. ◆ comp ▶ **warm-up exercises** exercices mpl d'échauffement.

warn [wɔːn] vt **1.** [inform] avertir, prévenir / I warned them of the danger je les ai avertis ou prévenus du danger **2.** [advise] conseiller, recommander / he warned her about or against travelling at night, he warned her not to travel at night il lui a déconseillé de voyager la nuit, il l'a mise en garde contre les voyages de nuit. ◆ **warn off** vt sep décourager / the doctor has warned him off alcohol le médecin lui a vivement déconseillé l'alcool.

warning ['wɔːnɪŋ] ◆ n **1.** [caution, notice] avertissement m **2.** [alarm, signal] alerte f, alarme f **3.** [advice] conseil m. ◆ adj d'avertissement / they fired a warning shot a) [gen & MIL] ils ont tiré une fois en guise d'avertissement b) NAUT ils ont tiré un coup de semonce ▶ **warning light** voyant m (avertisseur), avertisseur m lumineux ▶ **warning notice** avis m, avertissement m ▶ **warning sign** panneau m avertisseur ▶ **warning signal** a) [gen] signal m d'alarme or d'alerte b) AUTO signal m de détresse ▶ **warning triangle** UK AUTO triangle m de signalisation.

warp [wɔːp] ◆ vt **1.** [wood] gauchir, voiler; [metal, plastic] voiler **2.** fig [character, mind] pervertir; [thinking] fausser, pervertir. ◆ vi [wood] gauchir, se voiler; [metal, plastic] se voiler. ◆ n **1.** [fault - in wood] gauchissement m, voilure f; [- in metal, plastic] voilure f **2.** TEXT [of yarn] chaîne f.

warpath ['wɔːpɑːθ] n ▶ **to be on the warpath** lit être sur le sentier de la guerre / be careful, the boss is on the warpath fig fais attention, le patron est d'une humeur massacrante.

warped [wɔːpt] adj **1.** [wood] gauchi, voilé; [metal, plastic] voilé **2.** fig [character, person] perverti; [thinking, view] faux (fausse), perverti.

warrant ['wɒrənt] ◆ n **1.** LAW [written order] mandat m **2.** COMM & FIN [for payment] bon m; [guarantee] garantie f **3.** MIL brevet m. ◆ vt **1.** [justify] justifier **2.** [declare with certainty] assurer, certifier.

warrant officer n adjudant m (auxiliaire d'un officier).

warranty ['wɒrəntɪ] (pl **warranties**) n **1.** [guarantee] garantie f **2.** LAW garantie f.

warren ['wɒrən] n **1.** [of rabbit] terriers mpl, garenne f **2.** fig [maze of passageways] labyrinthe m, dédale m.

warring ['wɔːrɪŋ] adj [nations, tribes] en guerre; fig [beliefs] en conflit; [interests] contradictoire, contraire.

warrior ['wɒrɪəʳ] n guerrier m, -ère f.

Warsaw ['wɔːsɔː] pr n Varsovie.

war-scarred adj [city, country] dévasté par la guerre.

warship ['wɔːʃɪp] n navire m or bâtiment m de guerre.

wart [wɔːt] n **1.** MED verrue f **2.** BOT excroissance f.

wart hog n phacochère m.

wartime ['wɔːtaɪm] ◆ n période f de guerre / in wartime en temps de guerre. ◆ comp de guerre.

war-torn adj déchiré par la guerre.

war widow n veuve f de guerre.

wary ['weərɪ] (*compar* **warier,** *superl* **wariest**) adj [prudent - person] prudent, sur ses gardes ; [- look] prudent ; [- smile] hésitant ; [distrustful] méfiant.

was (*weak form* [wəz], *strong form* [wɒz]) pt ⟶ **be.**

wasabi [wə'sɑːbɪ] n wasabi *m.*

wash [wɒʃ] ◆ vt **1.** [clean] laver ▸ **to wash o.s.** a) [person] se laver, faire sa toilette b) [cat, dog] faire sa toilette / **go and wash your hands** va te laver les mains / **she washed her hair** elle s'est lavé la tête or les cheveux ▸ **to wash the dishes** faire or laver la vaisselle ▸ **to wash clothes** faire la lessive **2.** [subj: current, river, waves - move over] baigner ; [- carry away] emporter, entraîner / **the body was washed ashore** le cadavre s'est échoué or a été rejeté sur la côte / **the crew was washed overboard** l'équipage a été emporté par une vague **3.** [coat, cover] badigeonner **4.** MIN [gold, ore] laver. ◆ vi **1.** [to clean oneself - person] se laver, faire sa toilette **2.** [be washable] se laver, être lavable. ◆ n **1.** [act of cleaning] nettoyage *m* / **this floor needs a good wash** ce plancher a bien besoin d'être lavé or nettoyé / **your hair needs a wash** il faut que tu te laves la tête / **I gave the car a wash** j'ai lavé la voiture / **he's having a wash** il se lave, il fait sa toilette **2.** [clothes to be washed] lessive *f*, linge *m* sale / **your shirt is in the wash** a) [laundry basket] ta chemise est au (linge) sale b) [machine] ta chemise est à la lessive / **the stain came out in the wash** la tache est partie au lavage **3.** [movement of water - caused by current] remous *m* ; [- caused by ship] sillage *m*, remous *m* ; [sound of water] clapotis *m* **4.** [of paint] badigeon *m* **5.** MED [lotion] solution *f* **6.** ART ▸ **wash (drawing)** (dessin *m* au) lavis *m.* ◆ adj 🇺🇸 lavable. ❖ **wash away** vt sep [carry off - boat, bridge, house] emporter ; [- river bank, soil] éroder. ❖ **wash down** vt sep **1.** [clean] laver (à grande eau) **2.** [food] arroser ; [tablet] faire descendre. ❖ **wash off** ◆ vt sep [remove - with soap] enlever or faire partir au lavage ; [- with water] enlever or faire partir à l'eau. ◆ vi [disappear - with soap] s'en aller or partir au lavage ; [- with water] s'en aller or partir à l'eau. ❖ **wash out** ◆ vt sep **1.** [remove - with soap] enlever or faire partir au lavage ; [- with water] enlever or faire partir à l'eau **2.** [clean] laver **3.** [carry away - bridge] emporter ; [- road] dégrader **4.** [cancel, prevent] : **the game was washed out** le match a été annulé à cause de la pluie. ◆ vi = **wash off.** ❖ **wash up** ◆ vi **1.** 🇬🇧 [wash dishes] faire or laver la vaisselle **2.** 🇺🇸 [wash oneself] se laver, faire sa toilette. ◆ vt sep **1.** 🇬🇧 [glass, dish] laver **2.** [subj: sea] rejeter.

Wash pr n ▸ **the Wash** 🇬🇧 GEOG grande baie sur la côte est de l'Angleterre.

washable ['wɒʃəbl] adj lavable, lessivable.

wash-and-wear adj qui ne nécessite aucun repassage.

washbag ['wɒʃ,bæg] n trousse *f* de toilette.

washbasin ['wɒʃ,beɪsn] n 🇬🇧 [basin] cuvette *f*, bassine *f* ; [sink] lavabo *m.*

washboard ['wɒʃ,bɔːd] n planche *f* à laver ▸ **to have washboard abs** or **a washboard stomach** avoir des abdos en tablette de chocolat.

washbowl ['wɒʃbəʊl] 🇺🇸 = **washbasin.**

washcloth ['wɒʃ,klɒθ] n [for dishes] lavette *f* ; 🇺🇸 [face flannel] ≃ gant *m* de toilette.

washed-out [,wɒʃt-] adj **1.** [faded - colour] délavé ; [- curtain, jeans] décoloré, délavé **2.** inf [exhausted] épuisé, lessivé.

washed-up adj inf fichu.

washer ['wɒʃə'] n **1.** CONSTR joint *m*, rondelle *f* ; [in tap] joint *m* **2.** [washing machine] machine *f* à laver, lave-linge *m inv.*

washer-dryer n machine *f* à laver séchante.

washing ['wɒʃɪŋ] n **1.** [act - of car, floors] lavage *m* ; [- of laundry] lessive *f* **2.** [laundry] linge *m*, lessive *f* ▸ **to do the washing** faire la lessive, laver le linge.

washing line n corde *f* à linge.

washing machine n machine *f* à laver, lave-linge *m inv.*

washing powder n lessive *f* or détergent *m* (en poudre).

Washington ['wɒʃɪŋtən] pr n **1.** [state] ▸ **Washington (State)** l'État *m* de Washington / **in Washington** dans l'État de Washington **2.** [town] ▸ **Washington (DC)** Washington ▸ **The Washington Post** 🇺🇸 PRESS quotidien américain de qualité.

washing-up n 🇬🇧 vaisselle *f* (à laver) ▸ **to do the washing-up** faire la vaisselle.

washing-up liquid n 🇬🇧 produit *m* à vaisselle.

washout ['wɒʃaʊt] n inf [party, plan] fiasco *m*, échec *m* ; [person] raté *m*, -e *f.*

washroom ['wɒʃrʊm] n 🇺🇸 [lavatory] toilettes *fpl.*

wash-wipe n AUTO lavage-balayage *m.*

wasn't [wɒznt] abbr of **was not.**

wasp [wɒsp] n guêpe *f* ▸ **a wasp's nest** un guêpier.

Wasp, WASP [wɒsp] (abbr of **White Anglo-Saxon Protestant**) n 🇺🇸 inf Blanc d'origine anglo-saxonne et protestante, appartenant aux classes aisées et influentes.

waspish ['wɒspɪʃ] adj [person - by nature] qui a mauvais caractère ; [- in bad mood] qui est de mauvaise humeur ; [reply, remark] mordant, méchant.

wastage ['weɪstɪʤ] n (U) **1.** [loss - of materials, money] gaspillage *m*, gâchis *m* ; [- of time] perte *f* ; [- through leakage] fuites *fpl*, pertes *fpl* **2.** [in numbers, workforce] réduction *f.*

waste [weɪst] ◆ vt **1.** [misuse - materials, money] gaspiller ; [- time] perdre ; [- life] gâcher **2.** [wear away - limb, muscle] atrophier ; [- body, person] décharner **3.** 🇺🇸 v inf [kill] liquider. ◆ n **1.** [misuse - of materials, money] gaspillage *m*, gâchis *m* ; [- of time] perte *f* / **that book was a complete waste of money** ce livre, c'était de l'argent jeté par les fenêtres / **it's a waste of time talking to her** tu perds ton temps à discuter avec elle ▸ **to go to waste** a) [gen] se perdre, être gaspillé b) [food] tomber en friche **2.** (U) [refuse - gen] déchets *mpl* ; [- household] ordures *fpl* (ménagères) ; [- water] eaux *fpl* usées **3.** [land] terrain *m* vague **4.** 🅿🅷🆁 **to lay waste to sthg, to lay sthg waste** ravager or dévaster qqch. ◆ adj **1.** [paper] de rebut ; [energy] perdu ; [water] sale, usé ; [food] qui reste ▸ **waste material** déchets *mpl* **2.** [ground] en friche ; [region] désert, désolé. ❖ **wastes** pl n terres *fpl* désolées, désert *m* ▸ **the polar wastes** le désert polaire. ❖ **waste away** vi dépérir.

wastebasket [,weɪst'peɪpə-] n 🇺🇸 corbeille *f* (à papier).

waste bin n 🇬🇧 [in kitchen] poubelle *f*, boîte *f* à ordures ; [for paper] corbeille *f* (à papier).

wasted ['weɪstɪd] adj **1.** [material, money] gaspillé ; [energy, opportunity, time] perdu ; [attempt, effort] inutile, vain ; [food] inutilisé **2.** [figure, person] décharné ; [limb - emaciated] décharné ; [- enfeebled] atrophié.

waste disposal unit n broyeur *m* d'ordures.

wasteful ['weɪstfʊl] adj [habits] de gaspillage ; [person] gaspilleur ; [procedure] inefficace, peu rentable.

waste ground n (U) : **the children were playing on waste ground** les enfants jouaient sur un terrain vague.

wasteland ['weɪst,lænd] n [land - disused] terrain *m* vague ; [- uncultivated] terres *fpl* en friche or abandonnées ; [of desert, snow] désert *m* ▸ **a cultural wasteland** *fig* un désert culturel.

waste management n gestion *f* des déchets.

waste matter n déchets *mpl*.

waste paper n *(U)* papier *m* or papiers *mpl* de rebut.

wastepaper basket [ˌweɪstˈpeɪpər-] n ⓊⓀ corbeille *f* (à papier).

waste pipe n (tuyau *m* de) vidange *f*.

waste product n INDUST déchet *m* de production or de fabrication ; PHYSIOL déchet *m* (*de l'organisme*).

waster [ˈweɪstər] n **1.** [gen] gaspilleur *m*, -euse *f* ; [of money] dépensier *m*, -ère *f* **2.** [good-for-nothing] bon *m* à rien, bonne *f* à rien.

wasting [ˈweɪstɪŋ] adj [disease] qui ronge or mine.

watch [wɒtʃ] ◆ vt **1.** [look at, observe - event, film] regarder ; [- animal, person] regarder, observer **2.** [spy on - person] surveiller, observer ; [- activities, suspect] surveiller **3.** [guard, tend - children, pet] surveiller, s'occuper de ; [- belongings, house] surveiller, garder ; MIL monter la garde devant, garder **4.** [pay attention to - health, weight] faire attention à ; [- development, situation] suivre de près **/** *watch where you're going!* regardez devant vous ! **/** *watch what you're doing!* faites bien attention (à ce que vous faites) ! **▶ watch it! a)** [warning] (fais) attention ! **b)** [threat] attention !, gare à vous ! ◆ vi **1.** [observe] regarder, observer **2.** [keep vigil] veiller. ◆ n **1.** [timepiece] montre *f* **2.** [lookout] surveillance *f* **3.** [person on guard - gen & MIL] sentinelle *f* ; NAUT homme *m* de quart ; [group of guards - gen & MIL] garde *f* ; NAUT quart *m* **4.** [period of duty - gen & MIL] garde *f* ; NAUT quart *m*. ◆❖ **watch for** vt insep guetter, surveiller. ◆❖ **watch out** vi faire attention, prendre garde **▶ to watch out for sthg a)** [be on lookout for] guetter qqch **b)** [be careful of] faire attention or prendre garde à qqch. ◆❖ **watch over** vt insep garder, surveiller.

watchable [ˈwɒtʃəbl] adj **1.** [able to be watched] que l'on peut regarder **2.** [enjoyable to watch] qui se laisse regarder.

watchdog [ˈwɒtʃdɒg] ◆ n [dog] chien *m*, chienne *f* de garde ; *fig* [person] gardien *m*, -enne *f*. ◆ comp [body, committee] de surveillance.

watchful [ˈwɒtʃfʊl] adj vigilant, attentif **▶ to keep a watchful eye on sthg / sb** avoir qqch / qqn à l'œil.

watchlist [ˈwɒtʃlɪst] n liste *f* de surveillance.

watchmaker [ˈwɒtʃˌmeɪkər] n horloger *m*, -ère *f*.

watchman [ˈwɒtʃmən] (*pl* **watchmen** [-mən]) n gardien *m*.

watchstrap [ˈwɒtʃstræp] n bracelet *m* de montre.

watchword [ˈwɒtʃwɜːd] n [password] mot *m* de passe ; [slogan] mot *m* d'ordre.

water [ˈwɔːtər] ◆ n **1.** [liquid - gen] eau *f* **/** *hot and cold running water* eau courante chaude et froide **▶ water main** conduite *f* or canalisation *f* d'eau **2.** [body of water] eau *f* **/** *she fell in the water* elle est tombée à l'eau **3.** [tide] marée *f* **▶ at high / low water** à marée haute / basse **4.** *euph* [urine] urine *f* **▶ to make** or **to pass water** uriner **5.** MED **▶ water on the brain** hydrocéphalie *f* **▶ to have water on the knee** avoir un épanchement de synovie **6.** TEXT [of cloth] moiré *m*. ◆ vt **1.** [land, plants] arroser **2.** [animal] donner à boire à, faire boire **3.** [dilute - alcohol] couper (d'eau) **4.** TEXT [cloth] moirer. ◆ vi **1.** [eyes] larmoyer **2.** [mouth] : *the smell made my mouth water* l'odeur m'a fait venir l'eau à la bouche. ◆❖ **waters** pl n **1.** [territorial] eaux *fpl* **/** *in Japanese waters* dans les eaux (territoriales) japonaises **2.** [spa water] **▶ to take the waters** prendre les eaux, faire une cure thermale **3.** [of pregnant woman] poche *f* des eaux **/** *her waters broke* elle a perdu les eaux, la poche des eaux s'est rompue. ◆❖ **water down** vt sep [alcohol] couper (d'eau) ; *fig* [speech] édulcorer ; [complaint, criticism] atténuer.

water bed n matelas *m* à eau.

water bird n oiseau *m* aquatique.

water birth n accouchement *m* sous l'eau.

water biscuit n ⓊⓀ biscuit *m* salé craquant.

water bomb n bombe *f* à eau.

waterborne [ˈwɔːtəbɔːn] adj [vehicle] flottant ; [commerce, trade] effectué par voie d'eau ; [disease] d'origine hydrique.

water bottle n [gen] bouteille *f* d'eau ; [soldier's, worker's] bidon *m* à eau ; [in leather] outre *f*.

water buffalo n [India] buffle *m* d'Inde ; [Malaysia] karbau *m*, kérabau *m* ; [Asia] buffle *m* d'Asie.

water butt n citerne *f* (à eau de pluie).

water cannon n canon *m* à eau.

water chestnut n châtaigne *f* d'eau.

water closet n W-C *mpl*, toilettes *fpl*, cabinets *mpl*.

watercolour ⓊⓀ, **watercolor** ⓊⓈ [ˈwɔːtəˌkʌlər] ◆ n [paint] couleur *f* pour aquarelle ; [painting] aquarelle *f*. ◆ adj [paint] pour aquarelle, à l'eau ; [landscape, portrait] à l'aquarelle.

water-cooled [-ˌkuːld] adj à refroidissement par eau.

water cooler n distributeur *m* d'eau fraîche.

watercourse [ˈwɔːtəkɔːs] n [river, stream] cours *m* d'eau ; [bed] lit *m* (*d'un cours d'eau*).

watercress [ˈwɔːtəkres] n cresson *m*.

water-diviner n sourcier *m*, -ère *f*, radiesthésiste *mf*.

watered-down [ˌwɔːtəd-] adj [alcohol] coupé (d'eau) ; [speech] édulcoré ; [complaint, criticism] atténué.

waterfall [ˈwɔːtəfɔːl] n cascade *f*, chute *f* d'eau.

water feature n [pond] bassin *m* ; [fountain] fontaine *f*.

waterfront [ˈwɔːtəfrʌnt] n [at harbour] quais *mpl* ; [seafront] front *m* de mer.

water heater n chauffe-eau *m inv*.

waterhole [ˈwɔːtəhəʊl] n point *m* d'eau ; [in desert] oasis *f*.

watering [ˈwɔːtərɪŋ] n [of garden, plants] arrosage *m* ; [of crops, fields] irrigation *f*.

watering can n arrosoir *m*.

watering hole n [for animals] point *m* d'eau ; *inf & hum* [pub] ≃ bistrot *m* ; ≃ bar *m*.

water jump n brook *m*.

water level n [of river, sea] niveau *m* de l'eau ; [in tank] niveau *m* d'eau.

water lily n nénuphar *m*.

waterline [ˈwɔːtəlaɪn] n **1.** [left by river] ligne *f* des hautes eaux ; [left by tide] laisse *f* de haute mer **2.** NAUT [on ship] ligne *f* de flottaison.

waterlogged [ˈwɔːtəlɒgd] adj [land, soil] détrempé ; [boat] plein d'eau ; [clothing, shoes] imbibé d'eau.

Waterloo [ˌwɔːtəˈluː] n **▶ to meet one's Waterloo** essuyer un revers.

watermark [ˈwɔːtəmɑːk] ◆ n **1.** = **waterline 2.** [on paper] filigrane *m*. ◆ vt filigraner.

watermelon [ˈwɔːtəˌmelən] n pastèque *f*, melon *m* d'eau.

water meter n compteur *m* d'eau.

water pipe n **1.** CONSTR conduite *f* or canalisation *f* d'eau **2.** [hookah] narguilé *m*.

water pistol n pistolet *m* à eau.

water polo n water-polo *m*.

water power n énergie *f* hydraulique, houille *f* blanche.

waterproof ['wɔ:təpru:f] ◆ adj [clothing, material] imperméable ; [container, wall, watch] étanche. ◆ n imperméable *m*. ◆ vt [clothing, material] imperméabiliser ; [barrel, wall] rendre étanche.

water rat n rat *m* d'eau.

water rate n [UK] taxe *f* sur l'eau.

water-resistant adj [material] semi-imperméable ; [lotion] qui résiste à l'eau ; [ink] indélébile, qui résiste à l'eau.

watershed ['wɔ:təʃed] n **1.** [area of ground] ligne *f* de partage des eaux **2.** fig [event] grand tournant *m* **3.** [UK] TV heure à partir de laquelle les chaînes peuvent diffuser des émissions pour adultes.

waterside ['wɔ:təsaɪd] ◆ n bord *m* de l'eau. ◆ adj [house, path] au bord de l'eau ; [resident] riverain ; [flower] du bord de l'eau.

water ski n ski *m* nautique. ❖ **water-ski** vi faire du ski nautique.

water skiing n ski *m* nautique.

water softener n adoucisseur *m* d'eau.

water-soluble adj soluble dans l'eau.

water sport n sport *m* nautique.

waterspout ['wɔ:təspaʊt] n **1.** [pipe] (tuyau *m* de) descente *f* **2.** METEOR trombe *f*.

water supply n [for campers, troops] provision *f* d'eau ; [to house] alimentation *f* en eau ; [to area, town] distribution *f* des eaux, approvisionnement *m* en eau.

water table n surface *f* de la nappe phréatique.

water tank n réservoir *m* d'eau, citerne *f*.

watertight ['wɔ:tətaɪt] adj [box, door] étanche ; fig [argument, reasoning] inattaquable, indiscutable.

water tower n château *m* d'eau.

waterway ['wɔ:təweɪ] n cours *m* d'eau, voie *f* navigable.

waterworks ['wɔ:təwɜ:ks] (pl **waterworks**) ◆ n [establishment] station *f* hydraulique ; [system] système *m* hydraulique. ◆ pl n **1.** [fountain] jet *m* d'eau **2.** inf & euph [urinary system] voies fpl urinaires **3.** inf & hum [tears] : she turned on the waterworks elle s'est mise à pleurer comme une Madeleine.

watery ['wɔ:tərɪ] adj **1.** [surroundings, world] aquatique ; [ground, soil] détrempé, saturé d'eau **2.** [eyes] larmoyant, humide **3.** [coffee, tea] trop léger ; [soup] trop liquide, fade ; [milk] qui a trop d'eau ; [taste] fade, insipide **4.** [light, sun, smile] faible ; [colour] délavé, pâle.

watt [wɒt] n watt *m*.

wattage ['wɒtɪdʒ] n puissance *f* or consommation *f* (en watts).

wave [weɪv] ◆ n **1.** [in sea] vague *f*, lame *f* ; [on lake] vague *f* ▶ **the waves** les flots mpl **2.** [of earthquake, explosion] onde *f* ; fig [of crime, panic] vague *f* ; [of anger] bouffée *f* ; [of disgust] vague *f* **3.** [in hair] cran *m*, ondulation *f* **4.** [gesture] geste *m* or signe *m* de la main **5.** RADIO onde *f*. ◆ vi **1.** [gesture] faire un signe or un geste de la main **2.** [move - flag] flotter ; [- wheat] onduler, ondoyer ; [- branch] être agité. ◆ vt **1.** [brandish - flag] agiter, brandir ; [- pistol, sword] brandir **2.** [gesture] : his mother waved him away sa mère l'a écarté d'un geste de la main / the guard waved us back / on le garde nous a fait signe de reculer / d'avancer / we waved goodbye nous avons fait au revoir de la main **3.** [hair] onduler. ❖ **wave about** ◆ vi = **wave** (vi). ◆ vt sep [UK] [flag, sign] agiter, brandir ; [pistol, sword] brandir. ❖ **wave aside** vt sep [person] écarter or éloigner d'un geste ; [protest] écarter ; [help, suggestion] refuser, rejeter. ❖ **wave down** vt sep ▶ **to wave sb / a car down** faire signe à qqn / à une voiture de s'arrêter.

wave band n bande *f* de fréquences.

wavelength ['weɪvleŋθ] n PHYS & RADIO longueur *f* d'onde.

wave power n énergie *f* des vagues.

waver ['weɪvə'] vi **1.** [person] vaciller, hésiter ; [confidence, courage] vaciller, faiblir **2.** [flame, light] vaciller, osciller ; [temperature] osciller **3.** [voice] trembloter, trembler.

waverer ['weɪvərə'] n irrésolu *m*, -e *f*, indécis *m*, -e *f*.

wavy ['weɪvɪ] (compar **wavier**, superl **waviest**) adj **1.** [line] qui ondule, ondulant **2.** [hair] ondulé, qui a des crans.

wax [wæks] ◆ n [for candles, car, floor, furniture] cire *f* ; [in ear] cérumen *m* ; [for skis] fart *m*. ◆ comp [candle, figure] de or en cire ▶ **wax crayons** crayons mpl gras. ◆ vt **1.** [floor, table] cirer, encaustiquer ; [skis] farter ; [car] enduire de cire **2.** [legs] épiler (à la cire). ◆ vi **1.** [moon] croître ; [influence, power] croître, augmenter ▶ **to wax and wane** a) [moon] croître et décroître b) [influence, power] croître et décliner **2.** arch & hum [become] devenir.

waxed paper [wækst-] n papier *m* paraffiné or sulfurisé.

waxen ['wæksən] adj [candle, figure] de or en cire ; [complexion, face] cireux.

wax jacket n ciré *m*.

wax museum n musée *m* de cire.

wax paper n = **waxed paper**.

waxworks ['wækswɜ:ks] (pl **waxworks**) n musée *m* de cire.

waxy ['wæksɪ] (compar **waxier**, superl **waxiest**) adj [complexion, texture] cireux ; [colour] cireux, jaunâtre ; [potato] ferme, pas farineux.

way [weɪ]
◆ n

 A. PATH, DISTANCE, DIRECTION **1.** [thoroughfare, path] chemin *m*, voie *f* ; [for cars] rue *f*, route *f* **2.** [route leading to a specified place] chemin *m* / this is the way to the library la bibliothèque est par là / could you tell me the way to the library? pouvez-vous me dire comment aller à la bibliothèque ? / what's the shortest or quickest way to town? quel est le chemin le plus court pour aller en ville ? / they went the wrong way ils se sont trompés de chemin, ils ont pris le mauvais chemin ▶ **to lose one's way** a) lit s'égarer, perdre son chemin b) fig s'égarer, se fourvoyer **3.** [route leading in a specified direction] chemin *m*, route *f* ▶ **the way back** le chemin or la route du retour / on our way back we stopped for dinner au retour or sur le chemin du retour nous nous sommes arrêtés pour dîner / she showed us the easiest way down / up elle nous a montré le chemin le plus facile pour descendre / monter ▶ **the way in** l'entrée *f* ▶ **the way out** la sortie ; fig : is there no way out of this nightmare? n'y a-t-il pas moyen de mettre fin à ce cauchemar ? / their decision left her no way out leur décision l'a mise dans une impasse **4.** [direction] direction *f*, sens *m* / come this way venez par ici / he went that way il est allé par là ▶ **this way and that** de-ci de-là, par-ci par-là / look this way regarde par ici ▶ **to look the other way** a) lit détourner les yeux b) fig fermer les yeux / which way do I go from here? a) lit où est-ce que je vais maintenant ? b) fig qu'est-ce que je fais maintenant ? / any job that comes my way n'importe quel travail qui se présente / the vote went our way le vote nous a été favorable **5.** [side] sens *m* / stand the box the other way up posez le carton dans l'autre sens / 'this way up' 'haut' / it's the wrong way up c'est dans le mauvais sens / your sweater is the right / wrong way out votre pull est à l'endroit / à l'envers / SHE insulted him? you've got it the wrong way round elle, elle l'a insulté ? mais c'est le contraire **6.** [area, vicinity] parages mpl / I was out or over your way yesterday j'étais près de or du côté de chez vous hier

7. [distance - in space] : *we came part of the way by foot* nous avons fait une partie de la route à pied / *we've come most of the way* nous avons fait la plus grande partie du chemin ▶ **a long way off** or **away** loin ▶ **a little** or **short way off** pas très loin, à courte distance / *we've a long way to go* **a)** [far to travel] il nous reste beaucoup de route à faire **b)** [a lot to do] nous avons encore beaucoup à faire **c)** [a lot to collect, pay] nous sommes encore loin du compte ; *fig* : *I'm a long way from trusting him* je suis loin de lui faire confiance / *you're a long way off* or *out* [in guessing] vous n'y êtes pas du tout ▶ **a little bit goes a long way** il en faut très peu **8.** [space in front of person, object] : *a tree was in the way* un arbre bloquait or barrait le passage ▶ **to get out of the way** s'écarter (du chemin) ; *fig* : *her social life got in the way of her studies* ses sorties l'empêchaient d'étudier / *once the meeting is out of the way* inf dès que nous serons débarrassés de la réunion ▶ **to put difficulties in sb's way** créer des difficultés à qqn **9.** [indicating a progressive action] : *I fought* or *pushed my way through the crowd* je me suis frayé un chemin à travers la foule / *we made our way towards the train* nous nous sommes dirigés vers le train / *she made her way up through the hierarchy* elle a gravi les échelons de la hiérarchie un par un.

B. METHOD, HABIT OR MANNER **1.** [means, method] moyen *m*, méthode *f* / *in what way can I help you?* comment or en quoi puis-je vous être utile ? / *there are several ways to go* or *of going about it* il y a plusieurs façons ou moyens de s'y prendre / *I do it this way* voilà comment je fais / *she has her own way of cooking fish* elle a sa façon à elle de cuisiner le poisson / *there's no way* or *I can't see any way we'll finish on time* nous ne finirons jamais or nous n'avons aucune chance de finir à temps ▶ **that's the way to do it!** c'est comme ça qu'il faut faire !, voilà comment il faut faire ! ▶ **way to go!** US inf bravo ! c'est bien ! **2.** [particular manner, fashion] façon *f*, manière *f* / *in a friendly way* gentiment / *they see things in the same way* ils voient les choses de la même façon / *that's one way to look at it* or *way of looking at it* c'est une façon ou manière de voir les choses / *to her way of thinking* à son avis ▶ **way of life**: *the American way of life* la manière de vivre des Américains, le mode de vie américain / *being on the move is a way of life for the gypsy* le voyage est un mode de vie pour les gitans / *yearly strikes have become a way of life* les grèves annuelles sont devenues une habitude **3.** [custom] coutume *f*, usage *m* ; [habitual manner of acting] manière *f*, habitude *f* / *they're happy in their own way* ils sont heureux à leur manière / *he's not in a bad mood, it's just his way* il n'est pas de mauvaise humeur, c'est sa façon d'être habituelle **4.** [facility, knack] : *she has a (certain) way with her* elle a le chic / *he has a way with children* il sait (comment) s'y prendre or il a le chic avec les enfants / *she has a way with words* elle a le chic pour s'exprimer **5.** [indicating a condition, state of affairs] : *let me tell you the way it was* laisse-moi te raconter comment ça s'est passé / *we can't invite him given the way things are* on ne peut pas l'inviter étant donné la situation / *it's not the way it looks!* ce n'est pas ce que vous pensez ! / *that's the way things are* c'est comme ça / *that's the way of the world* ainsi va le monde ▶ **to be in a bad way** être en mauvais état **6.** [respect, detail] égard *m*, rapport *m* / *in what way?* à quel égard ?, sous quel rapport ? / *in this way* à cet égard, sous ce rapport / *in some ways* à certains égards, par certains côtés / *I'll help you in every possible way* je ferai tout ce que je peux pour vous aider ▶ **in a way**: *in a way you're right* en un sens vous avez raison / *I see what you mean in a way* d'une certaine manière ou façon, je vois ce que tu veux dire ▶ **in no way**: *I am in no way responsible* je ne suis absolument pas or aucunement responsable / *this in no way changes your situation* cela ne change en rien votre situation **7.** [scale] ▶ **to do things in a big way** faire

les choses en grand / *she went into politics in a big way* elle s'est lancée à fond dans la politique **8.** (*usu pl*) [part, share] : *we divided the money four ways* nous avons partagé l'argent en quatre **9.** ▶ **to get** or **to have one's way**: *she always gets* or *has her way* elle arrive toujours à ses fins / *he only wants it his way* il n'en fait qu'à sa tête / *I'm not going to let you have it all your way* je refuse de te céder en tout ▶ **to have it both ways**: *you can't have it both ways* il faut choisir ▶ **it works both ways**: *I can stop too, it works both ways* je peux m'arrêter aussi, ça marche dans les deux sens ▶ **there are no two ways about it** il n'y a pas le choix / *no two ways about it, he was rude* il n'y a pas à dire, il a été grossier.

◆ adv inf **1.** [far - in space, time] très loin / *way up the mountain* très haut dans la montagne / *way back in the 1930s* déjà dans les années 1930 **2.** *fig* : *we know each other from way back* nous sommes amis depuis très longtemps / *you're way below the standard* tu es bien en dessous du niveau voulu / *he's way over forty* il a largement dépassé la quarantaine. ◆ **all the way** adv phr : *the baby cried all the way* le bébé a pleuré tout le long du chemin / *don't close the curtains all the way* ne fermez pas complètement les rideaux / *I'm with you all the way* fig je vous suis or je vous soutiens jusqu'au bout. ◆ **along the way** adv phr en route. ◆ **by a long way** adv phr : *I prefer chess by a long way* je préfère de loin or de beaucoup les échecs / *is your project ready? — not by a long way!* ton projet est-il prêt ? — loin de là ! ◆ **by the way** adv phr [incidentally] à propos / *by the way, where did he go?* à propos, où est-il allé ? / *I bring up this point by the way* je signale ce point au passage or en passant. ◆ **by way of** prep phr **1.** [via] par, via **2.** [as a means of] : *by way of illustration* à titre d'exemple. ◆ **either way** adv phr **1.** [in either case] dans les deux cas / *shall we take the car or the bus? — it's fine by me* or *I don't mind either way* tu préfères prendre la voiture ou le bus ? — n'importe, ça m'est égal **2.** [more or less] en plus ou en moins **3.** [indicating advantage] : *the match could have gone either way* le match était ouvert. ◆ **in such a way as** to conj phr de façon à ce que. ◆ **in such a way that** conj phr de telle façon or manière que. ◆ **in the way of** prep phr [in the form of] : *she receives little in the way of salary* son salaire n'est pas bien gros / *what is there in the way of food?* qu'est-ce qu'il y a à manger ? / *do you need anything in the way of paper?* avez-vous besoin de papier ? ◆ **no way** adv phr inf pas question. ◆ **on one's way, on the way** adv & adj phr **1.** [along the route] : *it's on my way* c'est sur mon chemin / *I'll catch up with you on the way* je te rattraperai en chemin or en route ; [coming, going] : *on the way to work* en allant au bureau ▶ **to go one's way** repartir, reprendre son chemin **2.** *fig* : *she has a baby on the way* elle attend un bébé / *the patient is on the way to recovery* le malade est en voie de guérison. ◆ **one way or the other, one way or another** adv phr **1.** [by whatever means] d'une façon ou d'une autre **2.** [expressing impartiality or indifference] : *it doesn't matter to them one way or another* ça leur est égal. ◆ **out of one's way** adv phr : *I don't want to take you out of your way* je ne veux pas vous faire faire un détour / *don't go out of your way for me!* fig ne vous dérangez pas pour moi ! / *she went out of her way to find me a job* fig elle s'est donné du mal pour me trouver du travail. ◆ **under way** adj & adv phr ▶ **to be under way** a) [person, vehicle] être en route b) *fig* [meeting, talks] être en cours c) [plans, project] être en train / *the meeting was already under way* la réunion avait déjà commencé.

-way in comp ▶ **one-way street** rue *f* à sens unique / *there was a three-way split of the profits* les bénéfices ont été divisés en trois.

waylay [ˌweɪˈleɪ] (pt & pp **waylaid** [-ˈleɪd]) vt [attack] attaquer, assaillir ; [stop] intercepter, arrêter (au passage).

waymark [ˈweɪmɑːk] n [on trail, path, walk] indication f, balise f.

way-out adj inf [unusual - film, style] bizarre, curieux ; [- person] excentrique, bizarre.

wayside [ˈweɪsaɪd] ◆ n bord m or côté m de la route. ◆ adj au bord de la route.

wayward [ˈweɪwəd] adj **1.** [person - wilful] entêté, têtu ; [- unpredictable] qui n'en fait qu'à sa tête, imprévisible ; [be- haviour] imprévisible ; [horse] rétif **2.** [fate] fâcheux, malen- contreux.

WB MESSAGING **1.** written abbr of **welcome back 2.** written abbr of **write back**.

WBS MESSAGING written abbr of **write back soon**.

WC (abbr of **water closet**) n W-C mpl.

WCC pr n abbr of **World Council of Churches**.

WDYT MESSAGING written abbr of **what do you think?**

we [wiː] pron [oneself and others] nous / we, the people nous, le peuple / as we will see in chapter two comme nous le verrons or comme on le verra dans le chapitre deux / we all make mistakes tout le monde peut se trom- per.

WE MESSAGING written abbr of **whatever**.

weak [wiːk] ◆ adj **1.** [physically - animal, person] faible ; [- health] fragile, délicat ; [- eyes, hearing] faible, mauvais ▶ **to become** or **to get** or **to grow weak** or **weaker** s'affaiblir / we were weak with or from hunger nous étions affaiblis par la faim ▶ **the weaker sex** le sexe faible **2.** [morally, mentally] mou (before vowel or silent 'h' **mol**, f **molle**), faible / in a weak moment dans un moment de faiblesse **3.** [feeble - argument, excuse] faible, peu convaincant ; [- army, government, institution] faible, impuissant ; [- struc- ture] fragile, peu solide ; [- light, signal, currency, economy, stock market] faible **4.** [deficient, poor - pupil, subject] faible **5.** [chin] fuyant ; [mouth] tombant **6.** [acid, solution] faible ; [drink, tea] léger ; AUTO & MECH [mixture] pauvre **7.** GRAM & LING [verb] faible, régulier ; [syllable] faible, inaccentué. ◆ pl n ▶ **the weak** les faibles mpl.

weaken [ˈwiːkn] ◆ vt **1.** [person] affaiblir ; [heart] fati- guer ; [health] miner **2.** [government, institution, team] affai- blir ; FIN [dollar, mark] affaiblir, faire baisser **3.** [argument] enlever du poids or de la force à ; [position] affaiblir ; [deter- mination] affaiblir, faire fléchir **4.** [structure] affaiblir, rendre moins solide ; [foundations, cliff] miner, saper. ◆ vi **1.** [per- son - physically] s'affaiblir, faiblir ; [- morally] faiblir ; [voice, health, determination] faiblir **2.** [influence, power] diminuer, baisser **3.** [structure] faiblir, devenir moins solide **4.** FIN [dol- lar, mark] s'affaiblir ; [prices] fléchir, baisser.

weak-kneed [-niːd] adj mou (before vowel or silent 'h' **mol**, f **molle**), lâche.

weakling [ˈwiːklɪŋ] n **1.** [physically] gringalet m, petite nature f **2.** [morally] faible mf, mauviette f.

weakly [ˈwiːklɪ] adv [get up, walk] faiblement ; [speak] fai- blement, mollement.

weak-minded adj **1.** [not intelligent] faible or simple d'esprit **2.** [lacking willpower] faible, irrésolu.

weakness [ˈwiːknɪs] n **1.** [of person - physical] fai- blesse f ; [- moral] point m faible **2.** [of government, institu- tion] faiblesse f, fragilité f **3.** [of structure] fragilité f **4.** FIN [of currency] faiblesse f.

weak-willed adj faible, velléitaire.

wealth [welθ] n (U) **1.** [richness - of family, person] richesse f, richesses fpl, fortune f ; [- of nation] richesse f, prospérité f **2.** [large amount - of details, ideas] abondance f, profusion f.

wealth-creating [-kriːˈeɪtɪŋ] adj générateur de ri- chesses.

wealth tax n UK impôt m sur la fortune.

wealthy [ˈwelθɪ] ◆ adj (compar **wealthier**, superl **wealthi- est**) ◆ adj [person] riche, fortuné ; [country] riche. ◆ pl n ▶ **the wealthy** les riches mpl.

wean [wiːn] vt [baby] sevrer. ❖ **wean off** vt sep ▶ **to wean sb off sthg** détourner qqn de qqch.

weapon [ˈwepən] n **1.** arme f **2.** [arm] armement m ▶ **weapons of mass destruction** armes fpl de destruction massive.

weaponize [ˈwepənaɪz] vt MIL militariser ▶ **weaponized plutonium** plutonium militaire.

weaponry [ˈwepənrɪ] n (U) armes fpl ; MIL matériel m de guerre, armements mpl.

weapons-grade adj militaire.

wear [weə˙] (pt **wore** [wɔː˙], pp **worn** [wɔːn]) ◆ vt **1.** [beard, spectacles, clothing, etc.] porter / what shall I wear? qu'est-ce que je vais mettre ? / he was wearing slippers / a dressing gown il était en chaussons / en robe de chambre / he wears a beard il porte la barbe / she wears her hair in a bun elle a un chignon / do you always wear make-up? tu te maquilles tous les jours ? / she wore lip- stick elle s'était mis or elle avait mis du rouge à lèvres / I often wear perfume / aftershave je mets souvent du par- fum / de la lotion après-rasage **2.** [expression] avoir, afficher ; [smile] arborer / he wore a frown il fronçait les sourcils **3.** [make by rubbing] user ▶ **to wear holes in sthg** trouer or percer peu à peu qqch / her shoes were worn thin ses chaussures étaient complètement usées **4.** UK inf [accept - argument, behaviour] supporter, tolérer / I won't wear it! je ne marcherai pas ! ◆ vi **1.** [endure, last] durer / wool wears better than cotton la laine résiste mieux à l'usure or fait meilleur usage que le coton ; fig : their friendship has worn well leur amitié est restée intacte malgré le temps / she's worn well UK inf elle est bien conservée **2.** [be dam- aged through use] s'user / the carpet had worn thin le tapis était usé or élimé ; fig : her patience was wearing thin elle était presque à bout de patience / his excuses are wearing a bit thin ses excuses ne prennent plus / his jokes are wearing a bit thin ses plaisanteries ne sont plus drôles **3.** liter [time] passer / as the year wore to its close comme l'année tirait à sa fin. ◆ n (U) **1.** [of clothes] : for everyday wear pour porter tous les jours / clothes suit- able for evening wear tenue de soirée ▶ **women's wear** vêtements mpl pour femmes ▶ **winter wear** vêtements mpl d'hiver **2.** [use] usage m / these shoes will stand hard wear ces chaussures feront un bon usage or résisteront bien à l'usure / there's still plenty of wear in that dress cette robe est encore très portable ▶ **to get a lot of wear from** or **out of sthg** faire durer qqch **3.** [deterioration] ▶ **wear (and tear)** usure f / the sheets are beginning to show signs of wear les draps commencent à être un peu usés ou fatigués. ❖ **wear away** ◆ vt sep [soles] user ; [cliff, land] ronger, éroder ; [paint, design] effacer. ◆ vi [metal] s'user ; [land] être rongé or érodé ; [grass, topsoil] disparaître (par usure) ; [design] s'effacer. ❖ **wear down** ◆ vt sep [steps] user ; fig [patience, strength] épuiser petit à petit ; [courage, resistance] saper, miner / in the end she wore me down [I gave in to her] elle a fini par me faire céder. ◆ vi [pen- cil, steps, tyres] s'user ; [courage] s'épuiser. ❖ **wear off** vi **1.** [marks, design] s'effacer, disparaître **2.** [excitement] s'apaiser, passer ; [anaesthetic, effects] se dissiper, disparaître ; [pain] se calmer, passer / the novelty soon wore off l'attrait de la nouveauté a vite passé. ❖ **wear on** vi [day, season] avancer lentement ; [battle, discussion] se poursuivre lentement / *as time wore on* au fur et à mesure que le temps passait. ❖ **wear out** ◆ vt sep **1.** [clothing, machinery] user **2.** [patience, strength, reserves] épuiser **3.** [tire] épuiser ▸ **to be worn out** être exténué or éreinté / *worn out from arguing, he finally accepted their offer* de guerre lasse, il a fini par accepter leur offre. ◆ vi [clothing, shoes] s'user. ❖ **wear through** vi se trouer.

wearable ['weərəbl] adj portable.

wearer ['weərə'] n : *good news for wearers of glasses* bonnes nouvelles pour les personnes qui portent des lunettes.

wearily ['wɪərɪlɪ] adv avec lassitude.

weariness ['wɪərɪnɪs] n **1.** [physical] lassitude f, fatigue f ; [moral] lassitude f, abattement m **2.** [boredom] lassitude f, ennui m.

wearing ['weərɪŋ] adj fatigant, épuisant.

weary ['wɪərɪ] (compar **wearier**, superl **weariest**, pt & pp **wearied**) ◆ adj **1.** [tired - physically, morally] las (lasse) fml, fatigué **2.** [tiring - day, journey] fatigant, lassant. ◆ vt [tire] fatiguer, lasser ; [annoy] lasser, agacer. ◆ vi se lasser.

weasel ['wi:zl] ◆ n belette f ; pej [person] fouine f. ◆ vi US ruser ; [in speaking] parler d'une façon ambiguë. ◆ vt : *he weaseled his way into the conversation* il s'est insinué dans la conversation. ❖ **weasel out** vi US inf ▸ **to weasel out of sthg** se tirer de qqch.

weather ['weðə'] ◆ n **1.** METEOR temps m / *what's the weather (like) today?* quel temps fait-il aujourd'hui ? / *it's beautiful / terrible weather* il fait beau / mauvais ▸ **weather permitting** si le temps le permet **2.** RADIO & TV ▸ **weather (forecast)** (bulletin m) météo f **3.** PHR ▸ **to feel under the weather** inf ne pas être dans son assiette. ◆ comp [forecast, map] météorologique ; [conditions] climatique, atmosphérique ; NAUT [side] du vent. ◆ vt **1.** [survive - storm] réchapper à ; [-crisis] survivre à, réchapper à **2.** [wood] exposer aux intempéries. ◆ vi [bronze, wood] se patiner ; [rock] s'éroder.

weather-beaten adj [face, person] buriné ; [building, stone] dégradé par les intempéries.

weather bureau n US ≃ office m national de la météorologie.

weather centre n UK ≃ centre m météorologique régional.

weathercock ['weðəkɒk] n lit & fig girouette f.

weathered ['weðəd] adj [bronze, wood] patiné par le temps ; [building, stone] érodé par le temps, usé par les intempéries ; [face] buriné.

weathergirl ['weðəgɜːl] n présentatrice f de la météo.

weatherman ['weðəmæn] (pl **weathermen** [-men]) n présentateur m de la météo.

weatherproof ['weðəpruːf] ◆ adj [clothing] imperméable ; [building] étanche. ◆ vt [clothing] imperméabiliser ; [building] rendre étanche.

weather report n bulletin m météorologique.

weather ship n navire m météorologique.

weather station n station f or observatoire m météorologique.

weather vane n girouette f.

weave [wiːv] (pp **wove** [wəʊv] or **woven** ['wəʊvn]) ◆ vt **1.** [cloth, web] tisser ; [basket, garland] tresser **2.** [story] tramer, bâtir ; [plot] tisser, tramer ; [spell] jeter **3.** [introduce] introduire, incorporer **4.** (pt & pp **weaved**) [as verb of movement] : *he weaved his way across the room / towards the bar* il s'est frayé un chemin à travers la

salle / vers le bar / *the cyclist weaved his way through the traffic* le cycliste se faufilait or se glissait à travers la circulation. ◆ vi **1.** TEXT tisser **2.** [road, river] serpenter **3.** (pt & pp **weaved**) [as verb of movement] se faufiler, se glisser / *he weaved unsteadily across the street* il a traversé la rue en titubant or en zigzaguant / *the boxer ducked and weaved* le boxeur a esquivé tous les coups. ◆ n tissage m.

web [web] n **1.** [of fabric, metal] tissu m ; [of spider] toile f ; fig [of lies] tissu m ; [of intrigue] réseau m **2.** [on feet - of duck, frog] palmure f ; [- of humans] palmature f. ❖ **Web** n COMPUT ▸ **the Web** le Web, le web, la Toile / *on the Web* sur le Web, sur la Toile.

web access n accès m à Internet.

web address n adresse f Web.

webbed [webd] adj palmé ▸ **to have webbed feet** or **toes a)** [duck, frog] avoir les pattes palmées **b)** [human] avoir une palmature.

webbing ['webɪŋ] n (U) **1.** TEXT [material] toile f à sangles ; [on chair] sangles fpl **2.** ANAT [animal] palmure f ; [human] palmature f.

web browser n COMPUT navigateur m.

webcam ['webkæm] n webcam f.

webcast ['webkɑːst] ◆ n COMPUT webcast m. ◆ vt COMPUT diffuser sur le Web.

webcasting ['webkɑːstɪŋ] n COMPUT webcasting m.

web design n conception f or création f de sites Web / *web design software* logiciel de conception or de création de sites Web.

web designer n concepteur m, -trice f de sites Web.

web developer n développeur m, -euse f de sites Web.

web-enabled adj [file] optimisé Web / *you'll need a web-enabled computer* vous aurez besoin d'un ordinateur avec connexion Internet / *web-enabled solutions* solutions en ligne / *a web-enabled application / tool* une application / un outil Web.

webfeed ['webfiːd] n webfeed m.

web-footed [-'fʊtɪd] adj [animal] palmipède, qui a les pattes palmées ; [human] qui a une palmature.

web hosting n COMPUT hébergement m de sites Web.

webinar ['webɪnɑːʳ] n séminaire m en ligne, cyberséminaire m.

weblog ['weblɒg] n COMPUT weblog m.

webmail ['webmeɪl] n webmail m.

webmaster ['web,mɑːstəʳ] n webmaster mf, administrateur m, -trice f de sites Web.

web page n page f Web.

web-ready adj optimisé Web.

webring ['webrɪŋ] n anneau m thématique, chaîne f de sites, webring m.

website ['websaɪt] n site m Web.

web space n COMPUT espace m Web.

webzine ['webziːn] n COMPUT webzine m.

wed [wed] (pt & pp **wed** or **wedded**, cont **wedding**) ◆ vt liter **1.** [marry] épouser, se marier avec ▸ **to get wed** se marier **2.** (usu passive) [unite] allier **3.** [subj: priest] marier. ◆ vi [in headline] se marier.

Wed. (written abbr of **Wednesday**) mer.

Wed., Weds. (abbr of **Wednesday**) mer.

we'd [wiːd] **1.** abbr of **we would 2.** abbr of **we had**.

wedded ['wedɪd] adj [person] marié ; [bliss, life] conjugal / *her lawful wedded husband* son époux légitime / *the newly wedded couple* les jeunes mariés mpl.

wedding ['wedɪŋ] ◆ n **1.** [marriage] mariage m, noces fpl **2.** [uniting] union f. ◆ comp [night, trip] de noces ; [ceremony, photograph, present] de mariage ◗ **wedding cake** gâteau *m* de noces ; ≃ pièce *f* montée ◗ **wedding invitation** invitation *f* de mariage.

wedding anniversary n anniversaire *m* de mariage.

wedding band = **wedding ring**.

wedding day n jour *m* du mariage.

wedding dress n robe *f* de mariée.

wedding reception n réception *f* de mariage.

wedding ring n alliance *f*, anneau *m* de mariage.

wedge [wedʒ] ◆ n **1.** [under door, wheel] cale *f* **2.** [for splitting wood] coin *m* **3.** [of cheese, cake, pie] morceau *m*, part *f* **4.** [golf club] cale *f* **5.** [for climber] coin *m*. ◆ vt **1.** [make fixed or steady] caler **2.** [squeeze, push] enfoncer ◗ **to wedge sthg apart** fendre or forcer qqch. ❖ **wedge in** vt sep [object] faire rentrer, enfoncer ; [person] faire rentrer.

wedge-heeled shoe [-hi:ld] n chaussure *f* à semelle compensée.

wedgie ['wedʒi:] adj inf = **wedge-heeled shoe.**

wedlock ['wedlɒk] n fml mariage *m* ◗ **to be born out of wedlock** être un enfant naturel, être né hors mariage.

Wednesday ['wenzdɪ] n mercredi *m*. See also **Friday.**

wee [wi:] ◆ adj [Scot] tout petit. ◆ vi inf faire pipi. ◆ n inf pipi *m* ◗ **to have a wee** faire pipi.

weed [wi:d] ◆ n **1.** [plant] mauvaise herbe *f* **2.** pej [person] mauviette *f* **3.** inf [tobacco] ◗ **the weed** le tabac **4.** drugs sl herbe *f*. ◆ vt désherber, arracher les mauvaises herbes de. ◆ vi désherber, arracher les mauvaises herbes. ❖ **weeds** pl n vêtements *mpl* de deuil. ❖ **weed out** vt sep éliminer ; [troublemakers] expulser ◗ **to weed out the bad from the good** faire le tri.

weeding ['wi:dɪŋ] n désherbage *m*.

weedkiller ['wi:d,kɪlər] n herbicide *m*, désherbant *m*.

weedy ['wi:dɪ] (compar **weedier**, superl **weediest**) adj **1.** [ground] couvert or envahi de mauvaises herbes **2.** inf & pej [person] malingre.

week [wi:k] n semaine *f* / next / last week la semaine prochaine / dernière / in one week or in one week's time dans huit jours, d'ici une semaine / two weeks ago il y a deux semaines or quinze jours / within a week a) [gen] dans la semaine, d'ici une semaine b) ADMIN & COMM sous huitaine / week ending 25th March la semaine du 21 mars / a week from today d'ici huit jours / a week from tomorrow demain en huit / week in week out or week after week or week by week semaine après semaine / from week to week de semaine en semaine / I haven't seen you in or for weeks ça fait des semaines que je ne t'ai pas vu ◗ **the working week** la semaine de travail.

weekday ['wi:k,deɪ] ◆ n jour *m* de la semaine ; ADMIN & COMM jour *m* ouvrable / on weekdays en semaine / 'weekdays only' 'sauf samedi et dimanche'. ◆ comp [activities] de la semaine / on weekday mornings le matin en semaine.

weekend [,wi:k'end] ◆ n fin *f* de semaine, week-end *m* ◗ **at** UK or **on** US **the weekend** le week-end ◗ **a long weekend** un week-end prolongé. ◆ comp [schedule, visit] de or du week-end ◗ **weekend bag** or **case** sac *m* de voyage, mallette *f* ◗ **weekend break** séjour d'un week-end. ◆ vi passer le week-end.

weekly ['wi:klɪ] ◆ adj [visit, meeting] de la semaine, hebdomadaire ; [publication, payment, wage] hebdomadaire. ◆ n hebdomadaire *m*. ◆ adv [once a week] chaque semaine, une fois par semaine ; [each week] chaque semaine, tous les huit jours.

weeknight ['wi:k,naɪt] n soir *m* de la semaine.

weeny ['wi:nɪ] (compar **weenier**, superl **weeniest**) adj inf tout petit, minuscule.

weep [wi:p] (pt & pp **wept** [wept]) ◆ vi **1.** [person] pleurer, verser des larmes ◗ **to weep for sb** pleurer qqn **2.** [walls, wound] suinter, suer. ◆ vt [tears] verser, pleurer. ◆ n ◗ **to have a weep** pleurer, verser quelques larmes.

weeping ['wi:pɪŋ] ◆ adj [person] qui pleure ; [walls, wound] suintant. ◆ n (U) larmes *fpl*, pleurs *mpl*.

weeping willow n saule *m* pleureur.

weepy ['wi:pɪ] ◆ adj (compar **weepier**, superl **weepiest**) **1.** [tone, voice] larmoyant ; [person] qui pleure **2.** [film, story] sentimental, larmoyant. ◆ n (pl **weepies**) UK inf [film] mélo *m*, film *m* sentimental ; [book] mélo *m*, roman *m* à l'eau de rose.

wee-wee inf & baby talk ◆ n pipi *m*. ◆ vi faire pipi.

weigh [weɪ] ◆ vt **1.** [person, thing] peser **2.** [consider] considérer, peser ◗ **to weigh one thing against another** mettre deux choses en balance **3.** NAUT ◗ **to weigh anchor** lever l'ancre. ◆ vi **1.** [person, object] peser **2.** [influence] : his silence began to weigh (heavy) son silence commençait à devenir pesant / the facts weigh heavily against him les faits plaident lourdement en sa défaveur. ❖ **weigh down** vt sep **1.** lit faire plier, courber **2.** fig : weighed down with debts / with sorrow accablé de dettes / de tristesse. ❖ **weigh in** vi **1.** SPORT se faire peser (avant une épreuve) **2.** [join in] intervenir. ❖ **weigh on** vt insep peser. ❖ **weigh out** vt sep peser. ❖ **weigh up** vt sep **1.** [consider] examiner, calculer ; [compare] mettre en balance **2.** [size up] mesurer.

weighbridge ['weɪbrɪdʒ] n pont-bascule *m*.

weighing machine ['weɪɪŋ-] n [for people] balance *f* ; [for loads] bascule *f*.

weight [weɪt] ◆ n **1.** [of person, package, goods] poids *m* ◗ **to gain** or **to put on weight** grossir, prendre du poids ◗ **to lose weight** maigrir, perdre du poids **2.** [force] poids *m* **3.** [burden] poids *m* **4.** [importance, influence] poids *m*, influence *f* **5.** [for scales] poids *m* **6.** SPORT poids *m* **7.** PHYS pesanteur *f*, poids *m*. ◆ comp ◗ **weight allowance** [in aeroplane] poids *m* de bagages autorisé ◗ **to have a weight problem** avoir un problème de poids. ◆ vt **1.** [put weights on] lester **2.** [hold down] retenir or maintenir avec un poids **3.** [bias] : the system is weighted in favour of the wealthy le système est favorable aux riches or privilégie les riches / the electoral system was weighted against him le système électoral lui était défavorable or jouait contre lui. ❖ **weight down** vt sep **1.** [body, net] lester **2.** [papers, tarpaulin] maintenir or retenir avec un poids.

weighted ['weɪtɪd] adj **1.** [body, net] lesté **2.** [statistics, average] pondéré.

weight gain n prise *f* de poids.

weighting ['weɪtɪŋ] n **1.** [extra salary] indemnité *f*, allocation *f* **2.** [of statistics] pondération *f* ; SCH coefficient *m*.

weightless ['weɪtlɪs] adj très léger ; ASTRONAUT en état d'apesanteur.

weightlessness ['weɪtlɪsnɪs] n extrême légèreté *f* ; ASTRONAUT apesanteur *f*.

weightlifter ['weɪt,lɪftər] n haltérophile *mf*.

weightlifting ['weɪt,lɪftɪŋ] n haltérophilie *f*.

weight loss n perte *f* de poids.

weight training n entraînement *m* aux haltères.

weightwatcher ['weɪt,wɒtʃər] n [person - on diet] personne *f* qui suit un régime ; [- figure-conscious] personne *f* qui surveille son poids.

weighty ['weɪtɪ] (*compar* **weightier**, *superl* **weightiest**) adj **1.** [suitcase, tome] lourd **2.** [responsibility] lourd ; [problem] important, grave ; [argument, reasoning] probant, de poids.

weir [wɪər] n barrage m (*sur un cours d'eau*).

weird [wɪəd] adj **1.** [mysterious] mystérieux, surnaturel **2.** inf [peculiar] bizarre, étrange.

weirdo ['wɪədəʊ] (*pl* **weirdos**) inf ◆ n drôle d'oiseau m or de zèbre m. ◆ comp [hairdo] extravagant.

welcome ['welkəm] ◆ vt **1.** [greet, receive - people] accueillir **2.** [accept gladly] être heureux d'avoir, recevoir avec plaisir. ◆ n accueil m. ◆ adj **1.** [person] bienvenu ▶ **to be welcome** être le bienvenu **2.** [pleasant, desirable - arrival] bienvenu ; [- change, interruption, remark] opportun **3.** [permitted] : *you're welcome to join us* n'hésitez pas à vous joindre à nous / *you're welcome to try* je vous en prie, essayez ; [grudgingly] : *he's welcome to try!* libre à lui d'essayer !, qu'il essaie donc ! **4.** [acknowledgment of thanks] ▶ **you're welcome!** je vous en prie !, il n'y a pas de quoi ! ◆ interj ▶ **welcome!** soyez le bienvenu ! ▶ **welcome back** or **home!** content de vous revoir ! ◆ **welcome back** vt sep accueillir (à son retour).

welcome committee n comité m d'accueil.

welcome mat n paillasson m / *they put out the welcome mat for him* ils l'ont accueilli à bras ouverts.

welcoming ['welkəmɪŋ] adj [greeting, smile] accueillant ; [ceremony, committee] d'accueil.

weld [weld] ◆ vt **1.** MECH & TECH souder **2.** [unite] amalgamer, réunir. ◆ vi souder. ◆ n soudure f.

welder [weldər] n [person] soudeur m, -euse f ; [machine] soudeuse f, machine f à souder.

welding ['weldɪŋ] n soudage m ; [of groups] union f.

welfare ['welfeər] ◆ n **1.** [well-being] bien-être m **2.** US [state aid] assistance f publique ▶ **to live on welfare** vivre de l'aide sociale ▶ **people on welfare** assistés mpl sociaux. ◆ comp [meals, milk] gratuit ▶ **welfare benefits** US avantages mpl sociaux ▶ **welfare check** US (chèque m d') allocations fpl.

welfare officer n travailleur social ayant la charge d'une personne mise en liberté surveillée.

Welfare State n ▶ **the Welfare State** l'État m providence.

well[1] [wel] ◆ n **1.** [for water, oil] puits m **2.** [for lift, staircase] cage f ; [between buildings] puits m, cheminée f **3.** UK LAW barreau m (*au tribunal*). ◆ vi = **well up**. ◆ **well out** vi [water] jaillir. ◆ **well up** vi [blood, spring, tears] monter, jaillir / *tears welled up in her eyes* les larmes lui montèrent aux yeux.

well[2] [wel] (*compar* **better** [betər], *superl* **best** [best]) ◆ adv **1.** [satisfactorily, successfully] bien / *she speaks French very well* elle parle très bien (le) français / *it's extremely well done* c'est vraiment très bien fait / *the meeting went well* la réunion s'est bien passée ▶ **to do well** s'en sortir / *he did very well for a beginner* il s'est très bien débrouillé pour un débutant / *that boy will do well!* ce garçon ira loin ! / *the patient is doing well* le malade se rétablit bien or est en bonne voie de guérison / *we would do well to keep quiet* nous ferions bien de nous taire ▶ **well done!** bravo ! ▶ **well said!** bien dit ! **2.** [favourably, kindly] bien / *everyone speaks well of you* tout le monde dit du bien de vous **3.** [easily, readily] bien / *I couldn't very well accept* je ne pouvais guère accepter / *you may well be right* il se peut bien que tu aies raison **4.** [to a considerable extent or degree] bien / *she's well over* or *past forty* elle a bien plus de quarante ans / *well on into the morning* jusque tard dans la matinée / *the fashion lasted well into the 1960s* cette mode a duré une bonne partie des

années 1960 / *it's well after midday* il est bien plus de midi **5.** [thoroughly] bien / *shake* | *stir well* bien secouer | agiter / *well cooked* or *done* bien cuit / *he was well annoyed* il était très contrarié / *it's well and truly over* c'est bel et bien fini **6.** PHR **to be well out of it** s'en sortir à bon compte / *you're well out of it* tu as bien fait de partir ▶ **to leave** or **let well alone a)** [equipment] ne pas toucher **b)** [situation] ne pas s'occuper de **c)** [person] laisser tranquille. ◆ adj **1.** [good] bien, bon / *all is not well with them* il y a a quelque chose qui ne va pas chez eux / *it's all very well pretending you don't care, but...* c'est bien beau de dire que ça t'est égal, mais... ▶ **all's well that ends well** prov tout est bien qui finit bien prov **2.** [advisable] bien / *it would be well to start soon* nous ferions bien de commencer bientôt **3.** [in health] ▶ **to be well** aller or se porter bien / *how are you? — well, thank you* comment allez-vous ? — bien, merci ▶ **to get well** se remettre, aller mieux / **'get well soon'** [on card] 'bon rétablissement' / *I hope you're well* j'espère que vous allez bien. ◆ interj **1.** [indicating start or continuation of speech] bon, bien / *well, let me just add that...* alors, laissez-moi simplement ajouter que... **2.** [indicating change of topic or end of conversation] : *well, as I was saying...* donc, je disais que..., je disais donc que... **3.** [softening a statement] : *well, obviously I'd like to come but...* disons que, bien sûr, j'aimerais venir mais... **4.** [expanding on or explaining a statement] : *you know John? well I saw him yesterday* tu connais John ? eh bien je l'ai vu hier **5.** [expressing hesitation or doubt] ben, eh bien **6.** [asking a question] eh bien, alors / *well, what of it?* et alors ? **7.** [expressing surprise or anger] : *well, look who's here!* ça alors, regardez qui est là ! ▶ **well, well, well** tiens, tiens **8.** [in relief] eh bien **9.** [in resignation] bon / *(oh) well, it can't be helped* bon tant pis, on n'y peut rien.

we'll [wi:l] **1.** abbr of **we shall 2.** abbr of **we will**.

well-adjusted adj [person - psychologically] équilibré ; [- to society, work] bien adapté.

well-advised adj sage, prudent / *he would be well-advised to leave* il aurait intérêt à partir.

well-appointed [-ə'pɔɪntɪd] adj UK fml [house] bien équipé ; [hotel] de catégorie supérieure.

well-attended [-ə'tendɪd] adj : *the meeting was well-attended* il y avait beaucoup de monde à la réunion.

well-balanced adj [person] équilibré, posé ; [diet] bien équilibré ; [sentence] bien construit.

well-behaved [-bɪ'heɪvd] adj [person] bien élevé ; [animal] bien dressé.

wellbeing [,wel'bi:ɪŋ] n bien-être m inv.

well-born adj de bonne famille.

well-bred adj **1.** [well-behaved] bien élevé **2.** [from good family] de bonne famille **3.** [animal] de (bonne) race ; [horse] pur-sang (inv).

well-brought-up adj bien élevé.

well-built adj **1.** [person] bien bâti **2.** [building] bien construit.

well-chosen adj [present, words] bien choisi.

well-deserved [-dɪ'zɜ:vd] adj bien mérité.

well-designed [-dɪ'zaɪnd] adj bien conçu.

well-disposed [-dɪ'spəʊzd] adj bien disposé ▶ **to be well-disposed to** or **towards sb** être bien disposé envers qqn ▶ **to be well-disposed to** or **towards sthg** voir qqch d'un bon œil.

well-documented [-'dɒkjʊmentɪd] adj bien documenté.

well-done adj [work] bien fait ; [meat] bien cuit.

well-dressed adj bien habillé.

well-earned [-ɜ:nd] adj bien mérité.

well-educated adj cultivé, instruit.

well-established adj bien établi.

well-fed adj [animal, person] bien nourri.

well-groomed adj [person] soigné ; [hair] bien coiffé ; [horse] bien pansé ; [garden, lawn] bien entretenu.

wellhead ['welhed] n *lit & fig* source *f*.

well-heeled [-hi:ld] adj *inf* à l'aise.

wellie ['welɪ] = **welly**.

well-in adj *inf* 🇬🇧 : *to be well-in with sb* être bien avec qqn.

well-informed adj [having information] bien informé or renseigné ; [knowledgeable] instruit.

Wellington ['welɪŋtən] n 🇬🇧 ▸ **Wellington (boot)** botte *f* (en caoutchouc).

well-intentioned [-ɪn'tenʃnd] adj bien intentionné.

well-kept adj **1.** [hands, nails] soigné ; [hair] bien coiffé ; [house] bien tenu ; [garden] bien entretenu **2.** [secret] bien gardé.

well-known adj [person] connu, célèbre ; [fact] bien connu.

well-liked [-laɪkt] adj apprécié.

well-loved adj très aimé.

well-made adj bien fait.

well-mannered adj qui a de bonnes manières, bien élevé.

well-meaning adj bien intentionné.

well-meant adj [action, remark] bien intentionné.

wellness ['welnɪs] n bien-être *m* ▸ **wellness centre** centre *m* de bien-être.

well-nigh adv presque.

well-off ◆ adj **1.** [financially] aisé **2.** [in a good position] : *they were still well-off for supplies* ils avaient encore largement assez de provisions. ◆ pl n ▸ **the well-off** les riches *mpl*.

well-paid adj bien payé.

well-placed [-pleɪst] adj bien placé / *to be well-placed to do sthg* être bien placé pour faire qqch.

well-prepared adj bien préparé.

well-preserved [-prɪ'zɜ:vd] adj [person, building] bien conservé.

well-proportioned [-prə'pɔ:ʃnd] adj bien proportionné.

well-read [-red] adj cultivé, érudit.

well-respected adj respecté.

well-rounded adj **1.** [complete - education] complet (complète) ; [- life] bien rempli **2.** [figure] rondelet **3.** [style] harmonieux ; [sentence] bien tourné.

well-spoken adj [person] qui s'exprime bien.

well-stocked [-stɒkt] adj [shop] bien approvisionné.

well-thought-of adj bien considéré.

well-thought-out adj bien conçu.

well-timed [-'taɪmd] adj [arrival, remark] opportun, qui tombe à point ; [blow] bien calculé.

well-to-do *inf* ◆ adj aisé, riche. ◆ pl n ▸ **the well-to-do** les nantis *mpl*.

well-travelled 🇬🇧, **well-traveled** 🇺🇸 adj qui a beaucoup voyagé.

well-trodden adj : *a well-trodden path* un chemin très fréquenté / *fig a well-trodden path to fame* le parcours classique vers la célébrité.

well-versed adj ▸ *to be well-versed in sthg* bien connaître qqch.

well-wisher [-ˌwɪʃəʳ] n [gen] personne *f* qui offre son soutien ; [of cause, group] sympathisant *m*, -e *f*, partisan *m*.

well-woman clinic n centre *m* de santé pour femmes.

well-worn adj **1.** [carpet, clothes] usé, usagé **2.** [path] battu **3.** [expression, joke] rebattu / *a well-worn phrase* une banalité, un lieu commun.

welly ['welɪ] (*pl* **wellies**) n 🇬🇧 *inf* **1.** [boot] botte *f* (en caoutchouc) **2.** 🇵🇭🇷 **give it some welly!** du nerf !

welsh [welʃ] vi 🇬🇧 *inf* partir or décamper sans payer ▸ **to welsh on a promise** ne pas tenir une promesse.

Welsh [welʃ] ◆ pl n ▸ **the Welsh** les Gallois *mpl*. ◆ n LING gallois *m*. ◆ adj gallois.

Welsh Assembly n Assemblée *f* galloise or du pays de Galles.

🏛️ **The Welsh Assembly**

L'Assemblée galloise, qui siège à Cardiff, est constituée de 60 membres (**Assembly Members** ou **AMs**) dirigés par le président de l'Assemblée (**First Minister**). Elle est chargée de voter la plupart des lois en matière de politique intérieure, mais, contrairement au Parlement écossais, elle n'est pas compétente dans le domaine des impôts. La politique étrangère, l'économie, la défense et les affaires européennes demeurent sous le contrôle du gouvernement britannique à Londres.

Welshman ['welʃmən] (*pl* **Welshmen** [-mən]) n Gallois *m*.

Welsh rabbit, Welsh rarebit n 🇬🇧 ≃ toast *m* au fromage.

Welshwoman ['welʃˌwʊmən] (*pl* **Welshwomen** [-ˌwɪmɪn]) n Galloise *f*.

welter ['weltəʳ] n confusion *f*.

welterweight ['weltəweɪt] ◆ n poids *m* welter. ◆ comp [champion] des poids welter ; [fight, title] de poids welter.

wench [wentʃ] n *arch & hum* jeune fille *f*, jeune femme *f*.

wend [wend] vt *liter* s'acheminer ▸ **to wend one's way home** s'acheminer vers chez soi.

Wendy house ['wendɪ-] n 🇬🇧 maison en miniature dans laquelle les jeunes enfants peuvent jouer.

went [went] pt ⟶ **go**.

wept [wept] pt & pp ⟶ **weep**.

were [wɜ:ʳ] pt ⟶ **be**.

we're [wɪəʳ] abbr of **we are**.

weren't [wɜ:nt] abbr of **were not**.

werewolf ['wɪəwʊlf] (*pl* **werewolves** [-wʊlvz]) n loup-garou *m*.

west [west] ◆ n [direction] ouest *m* / *the house lies 10 kilometres to the west (of the town)* la maison se trouve à 10 kilomètres à l'ouest (de la ville) / *a storm is brewing in the west* un orage couve à l'ouest. ◆ adj ouest (*inv*) / *a west wind* un vent d'ouest / *in west London* dans l'ouest de Londres. ◆ adv [to the west] vers l'ouest ; [from the west] de l'ouest / *the school lies further west of the town hall* l'école se trouve plus à l'ouest de la mairie ▸ **to face west** [house] être exposé à l'ouest. ◈ **West** n **1.** POL ▸ **the West** l'Occident *m*, les pays *mpl* occidentaux **2.** [in the U.S.] ▸ **the West** l'Ouest *m*.

West Africa pr n Afrique f occidentale.

West African ◆ n habitant m, -e f de l'Afrique occidentale. ◆ adj [languages, states] de l'Afrique occidentale, ouest-africain.

West Bank ◆ pr n ▶ **the West Bank** la Cisjordanie / on the West Bank en Cisjordanie. ◆ comp de Cisjordanie.

westbound ['westbaʊnd] adj [traffic] en direction de l'ouest ; [lane, carriageway] de l'ouest ; [road] vers l'ouest.

West Country pr n ▶ **the West Country** le sud-ouest de l'Angleterre (Cornouailles, Devon et Somerset) / in the West Country dans le sud-ouest de l'Angleterre.

West End ◆ pr n ▶ **the West End** le West End (centre touristique et commercial de la ville de Londres connu pour ses théâtres) / in the West End dans le West End. ◆ comp qui se situe dans le West End.

westerly ['westəlɪ] (pl **westerlies**) ◆ adj [wind] d'ouest ; [position] à l'ouest, au couchant / to head in a westerly direction se diriger vers or en direction de l'ouest. ◆ adv vers l'ouest. ◆ n vent m d'ouest.

western ['westən] ◆ adj 1. [in direction] ouest, de l'ouest / in western Spain dans l'ouest de l'Espagne 2. POL [powers, technology, world] occidental ▶ **Western Europe** l'Europe f de l'Ouest or occidentale. ◆ n [film] western m ; [book] roman-western m.

Westerner ['westənər] n habitant m, -e f de l'ouest ; POL Occidental m, -e f.

westernization, westernisation [ˌwestənaɪ'zeɪʃn] n occidentalisation f.

westernize, westernise ['westənaɪz] vt occidentaliser.

westernmost ['westənməʊst] adj le plus à l'ouest.

Western Samoa pr n Samoa fpl occidentales / in Western Samoa dans les Samoa occidentales.

west-facing adj orienté à l'ouest ou au couchant.

West German ◆ n Allemand m, -e f de l'Ouest. ◆ adj ouest-allemand.

West Germany pr n ▶ **(former) West Germany** (ex-)Allemagne f de l'Ouest / in West Germany en Allemagne de l'Ouest.

West Indian ◆ n Antillais m, -e f. ◆ adj antillais.

West Indies pl pr n Antilles fpl / in the West Indies aux Antilles.

Westminster ['westmɪnstər] pr n quartier du centre de Londres où se trouvent le Parlement et le palais de Buckingham. ▶ **Westminster Abbey** l'abbaye f de Westminster.

 Westminster

C'est dans ce quartier que se trouvent le Parlement et le palais de Buckingham. Le nom de **Westminster** est également employé pour désigner le Parlement lui-même.

West Virginia pr n Virginie-Occidentale f / in West Virginia en Virginie-Occidentale.

westward ['westwəd] ◆ adj [to the west] vers l'ouest. ◆ adv en direction de or vers l'ouest.

westwards ['westwədz] adv vers l'ouest.

wet [wet] (compar **wetter**, superl **wettest**, pt & pp **wet** or **wetted**, cont **wetting**) ◆ adj 1. [ground, person, umbrella -gen] mouillé ; [-damp] humide ; [-soaked] trempé ▶ **to get wet** se faire mouiller / I got my jacket wet j'ai mouillé ma veste ▶ **to be wet through a)** [person] être trempé jusqu'aux os or complètement trempé **b)** [clothes, towel] être complètement trempé 2. [ink, paint, concrete] frais (fraîche) 3. [climate, weather -damp] humide ; [-rainy] pluvieux ; [day] pluvieux, de pluie / it's going to be very wet all weekend il va beaucoup pleuvoir tout ce week-end / in wet weather par temps de pluie, quand il pleut / the wet season la saison des pluies 4. UK inf [feeble] : don't be so wet! tu es une vraie lavette ! 5. UK inf POL mou (before vowel or silent 'h' mol, f molle), modéré 6. US [wrong] ▶ **to be all wet** avoir tort 7. US [state, town] où l'on peut acheter librement des boissons alcoolisées. ◆ vt [hair, sponge, towel] mouiller ▶ **to wet o.s.** or **one's pants** mouiller sa culotte ▶ **to wet the bed** faire pipi au lit ▶ **to wet one's lips** s'humecter les lèvres ▶ **to wet o.s. a)** [from worry] se faire de la bile **b)** [from laughter] rire aux larmes. ◆ n 1. UK [rain] pluie f ; [damp] humidité f / let's get in out of the wet entrons, ne restons pas sous la pluie 2. AUSTR ▶ **the wet** la saison des pluies 3. UK inf POL modéré m, -e f or mou m, molle f (du parti conservateur) 4. UK inf & pej [feeble person] lavette f.

wet blanket n inf rabat-joie m inv.

wet dream n éjaculation f or pollution f nocturne.

wet-look ◆ adj brillant. ◆ n aspect m brillant.

wetness ['wetnɪs] n humidité f.

wet nurse n nourrice f. ◆ **wet-nurse** vt servir de nourrice à, élever au sein.

wet suit n combinaison f or ensemble m de plongée.

wetware ['wetweər] n inf utilisateurs mpl (d'un système informatique).

WEU (abbr of **Western European Union**) pr n UEO f.

we've [wiːv] abbr of **we have**.

whack [wæk] inf ◆ n 1. [thump] claque f, grand coup m ; [sound] claquement m, coup m sec ▶ **to give sb / sthg a whack** donner un grand coup à qqn / qqch 2. [try] essai m ▶ **to have a whack at sthg** essayer qqch 3. UK [share] part f 4. [offer] : I'll pay 50 pounds, top whack je paierai 50 livres, et pas un sou de plus 5. PHR **out of the whack** US déglingué. ◆ vt 1. [thump] donner un coup or des coups à ; [spank] donner une claque sur les fesses à 2. UK [defeat] flanquer une dérouillée or raclée à 3. US [murder] liquider 4. inf [put, send] : whack it in the oven mets-le dans le four / whack it over to me and I'll take a look envoie-le-moi et je le regarderai. ◆ interj vlan ! ◆ **whack out** vt sep inf [write] sortir.

whacked [wækt] adj UK inf vanné, crevé.

whacked-out adj 1. inf [tired] crevé 2. [on drugs] défoncé 3. [crazy] chtarbé.

whacking ['wækɪŋ] inf adj UK énorme, colossal.

whacky ['wækɪ] (compar **whackier**, superl **whackiest**) inf = **wacky**.

whale [weɪl] ◆ n 1. lit baleine f 2. PHR **to have a whale of a time** inf: we had a whale of a time on s'est drôlement bien amusés. ◆ vi 1. pêcher la baleine 2. US inf ▶ **to whale away at sthg** s'en prendre à qqch. ◆ vt US inf 1. [thump] mettre une raclée à, rosser 2. SPORT [defeat] mettre une raclée à, battre à plate couture.

whaler ['weɪlər] n 1. [person] pêcheur m de baleine 2. [ship] baleinier m.

whaling ['weɪlɪŋ] ◆ n 1. [industry] pêche f à la baleine 2. US inf [thrashing] rossée f, raclée f. ◆ comp [industry, port] baleinier ▶ **whaling ship** baleinier m.

wham [wæm] (pt & pp **whammed**, cont **whamming**) inf ◆ interj vlan. ◆ vt 1. [hit -person] donner une raclée à ; [-ball] donner un grand coup dans 2. [crash -heavy object, vehicle] rentrer dans.

wharf [wɔːf] (pl **wharves** [wɔːvz] or **wharfs**) n NAUT quai m.

whassup [wɒ'sʌp] interj US *inf* [hello] salut ; [what's going on] qu'est-ce qui se passe ?

W@ MESSAGING (written abbr of **what**) koi, koa, kwa.

what [wɒt] ◆ pron **1.** [in direct questions - as subject] qu'est-ce qui, que ; [- as object] (qu'est-ce) que, quoi / *what do you want?* qu'est-ce que tu veux ?, que veux-tu ? / *what's happening?* qu'est-ce qui se passe ?, que se passe-t-il ? / *what's up?* **a)** *inf* qu'est-ce qu'il y a ? **b)** [as greeting] quoi de neuf ? / *what's the matter?* or *what is it?* qu'est-ce qu'il y a ? / *what's that?* qu'est-ce que c'est que ça ? / *what's your phone number?* quel est votre numéro de téléphone ? / *what's the Spanish for "light"?* comment dit-on « lumière » en espagnol ? ; [with preposition] quoi / *what are you thinking about?* à quoi pensez-vous ? **2.** [in indirect questions - as subject] ce qui ; [- as object] ce que, quoi / *tell us what happened* dites-nous ce qui s'est passé / *he didn't understand what I said* il n'a pas compris ce que j'ai dit **3.** [asking someone to repeat something] comment / *what's that?* qu'est-ce que tu dis ? **4.** [expressing surprise] : *what, no coffee!* comment or quoi ? pas de café ? / *I found $350 — you what!* j'ai trouvé 350 dollars — quoi ? **5.** [how much] : *what's 17 minus 4?* combien or que fait 17 moins 4 ? / *what does it cost?* combien est-ce que ça coûte ? **6.** [that which - as subject] ce qui ; [- as object] ce que, quoi / *what you need is a hot bath* ce qu'il vous faut, c'est un bon bain chaud / *that's what life is all about!* c'est ça la vie ! / *education is not what it used to be* l'enseignement n'est plus ce qu'il était **7.** [whatever, everything that] : *say what you will* vous pouvez dire or vous direz tout ce que vous voudrez / *come what may* advienne que pourra **8.** PHR **I'll tell you what...** écoute ! ▶ **and what have you** or **and what not** *inf*: *documents, reports and what have you* or *and what not* des documents, des rapports et je ne sais quoi encore / *look, do you want to come or what?* alors, tu veux venir ou quoi ? / *boy, was he angry or what?* *inf* mon dieu qu'il était en colère ! / *she told me what was what inf* elle m'a mis au courant / *they know what's what in art inf* ils s'y connaissent en art. ◆ det **1.** [in questions] quel *m*, quelle *f*, quels *mpl*, quelles *fpl* / *what books did you buy?* quels livres avez-vous achetés ? / *what colour / size is it?* de quelle couleur / taille est-ce ? / *what day is it?* quel jour sommes-nous ? **2.** [as many as, as much as] : *I gave her what money I had* je lui ai donné le peu d'argent que j'avais / *what time we had left was spent (in) packing* on a passé le peu de temps qu'il nous restait à faire les valises / *I gave her what comfort I could* je l'ai consolée autant que j'ai pu. ◆ predet [expressing an opinion or reaction] : *what a suggestion!* quelle idée ! / *what a pity!* comme c'est or quel dommage ! / *what lovely children you have!* quels charmants enfants vous avez ! ◆◆ **what about** adv phr : *what about lunch?* et si on déjeunait ? / *when shall we go? — what about Monday?* quand est-ce qu'on y va ? — (et si on disait) lundi ? / *what about it?* inf et alors ? ◆◆ **what for** adv phr **1.** [why] ▶ **what for?** pourquoi ? / *what did you say that for?* pourquoi as-tu dit cela ? **2.** PHR **to give sb what for** inf passer un savon à qqn. ◆◆ **what if** conj phr : *what if we went to the beach?* et si on allait à la plage ? ◆◆ **what with** conj phr : *what with work and the children I don't get much sleep* entre le travail et les enfants je ne dors pas beaucoup / *what with one thing and another I never got there* pour un tas de raisons je n'y suis jamais allé.

what-d'ye-call-her ['wɒtjəkɔːlər] n inf [person] Machine f.

what-d'ye-call-him ['wɒtjəkɔːlɪm] n inf [person] Machin m.

what-d'ye-call-it ['wɒtjəkɔːlɪt] n inf [thing] machin m, truc m.

whatever [wɒt'evər] ◆ pron **1.** [anything, everything] tout ce que / *I'll do whatever is necessary* je ferai le nécessaire / *whatever you like* ce que tu veux **2.** [no matter what] quoi que / *whatever happens, stay calm* quoi qu'il arrive, restez calme / *whatever you do, don't tell her what I said* surtout, ne lui répète pas ce que je t'ai dit / *whatever it may be* quoi que ce soit / *whatever the reason* quelle que soit la raison **3.** [indicating surprise] : *whatever can that mean?* qu'est-ce que ça peut bien vouloir dire ? / *whatever do you want to do that for?* et pourquoi donc voulez-vous faire ça ? ; [indicating uncertainty] : *it's an urban regeneration area, whatever that means* c'est une zone de rénovation urbaine, si tu sais ce qu'ils entendent par là **4.** inf [some similar thing or things] : *I don't want to study English or philosophy or whatever* je ne veux étudier ni l'anglais, ni la philosophie, ou que sais-je encore. ◆ det **1.** [any, all] tout, n'importe quel / *she read whatever books she could find* elle lisait tous les livres qui lui tombaient sous la main / *I'll take whatever fruit you have* je prendrai ce que vous avez comme fruits **2.** [no matter what] : *for whatever reason, he changed his mind* pour une raison quelconque, il a changé d'avis. ◆ adv : *choose any topic whatever* choisissez n'importe quel sujet / *I have no doubt whatever* je n'ai pas le moindre doute / *I see no reason whatever to go* je ne vois absolument aucune raison d'y aller.

📎 Note that **quoi que** is followed by a verb in the subjunctive:
Whatever I say she gets angry. *Quoi que je dise, elle se fâche.*

whatnot ['wɒtnɒt] n **1.** [furniture] étagère f **2.** PHR **and whatnot** inf et ainsi de suite.

whatshername ['wɒtsəneɪm] n inf Machine f.

whatsoever [ˌwɒtsəʊ'evər] pron ▶ **none whatsoever** aucun.

wheat [wiːt] ◆ n blé m. ◆ comp [flour] de blé, de froment ; [field] de blé.

wheat germ n germe m de blé.

wheatmeal ['wiːtmiːl] n ▶ **wheatmeal (flour)** farine f complète.

wheedle ['wiːdl] vt enjôler ▶ **to wheedle sb into doing sthg** convaincre qqn de faire qqch à force de cajoleries ▶ **to wheedle sthg out of sb** obtenir qqch de qqn par des cajoleries.

wheel [wiːl] ◆ n **1.** [of bicycle, car, train] roue f ; [smaller] roulette f ; [for potter] tour m / *on wheels* sur roues or roulettes **2.** AUTO ▶ **to be at the wheel a)** *lit* être au volant **b)** *fig* être aux commandes ▶ **to get behind** or **to take the wheel** se mettre au or prendre le volant **3.** NAUT barre f, gouvernail m / *at the wheel* à la barre **4.** [of torture] roue f. ◆ vi **1.** [birds] tournoyer ; [procession] faire demi-tour ; MIL [column] effectuer une conversion ▶ **to wheel to the left** tourner sur la gauche ▶ **to wheel (round) a)** [person] se retourner, faire une volte-face **b)** [procession] faire demi-tour **c)** [horse] pirouetter **d)** [birds] tournoyer **2.** PHR **to wheel and deal a)** inf [do business] brasser des affaires **b)** pej magouiller. ◆ vt [bicycle, trolley] pousser ; [suitcase] tirer. ◆◆ **wheels** pl n **1.** [workings] rouages mpl **2.** inf AUTO [car] bagnole f.

wheelbarrow ['wiːlˌbærəʊ] n brouette f.

wheelchair ['wiːlˌtʃeər] n fauteuil m roulant.

wheelclamp ['wiːlklæmp] ◆ n sabot m de Denver. ◆ vt : *my car was wheelclamped* on a mis un sabot à ma voiture.

-wheeled in comp à roues ▸ **four-wheeled** à quatre roues.

wheeler-dealer n inf & pej affairiste mf.

wheelie bin ['wiːlɪ-] n poubelle f *(avec des roues)*.

wheeling and dealing ['wiːlɪŋ-] n *(U)* inf combines fpl, manigances fpl.

wheeze [wiːz] ◆ vi [person] respirer bruyamment or comme un asthmatique ; [animal] souffler. ◆ vt dire d'une voix rauque. ◆ n **1.** [sound of breathing] respiration f difficile or sifflante **2.** 🇬🇧 inf & dated [trick] combine f **3.** 🇬🇧 inf [joke] blague f **4.** 🇺🇸 [saying] dicton m.

wheezy ['wiːzɪ] *(compar* **wheezier,** *superl* **wheeziest)** adj [person] asthmatique ; [voice, chest] d'asthmatique ; [musical instrument, horse] poussif.

whelk [welk] n bulot m, buccin m.

when [wen] ◆ adv quand / *when are we leaving?* quand partons-nous ? / *when is the next bus?* à quelle heure est or quand passe le prochain bus ? / *when did the war end?* quand la guerre s'est-elle terminée ? / *when is the best time to call?* quel est le meilleur moment pour appeler ? ◆ conj **1.** [how soon] quand / *I don't know when we'll see you again* je ne sais pas quand nous vous reverrons / *I wonder when the shop opens* je me demande à quelle heure ouvre le magasin **2.** [at which time] quand / *come back next week when we'll have more time* revenez la semaine prochaine quand nous aurons plus de temps **3.** [indicating a specific point in time] quand, lorsque / *he turned round when she called his name* il s'est retourné quand or lorsqu'elle l'a appelé / *when I was a student* lorsque j'étais or à l'époque où j'étais étudiant / *she's thinner than when I last saw her* elle a maigri depuis la dernière fois que je l'ai vue **4.** [as soon as] quand, dès que ; [after] quand, après que / *put your pencils down when you have finished* posez votre crayon quand vous avez terminé / *when they had finished dinner, he offered to take her home* quand or après qu'ils eurent dîné, il lui proposa de la ramener / *when she had talked to him, she left* après lui avoir parlé, elle est partie **5.** [the time that] : *remember when a coffee cost 10 cents?* vous souvenez-vous de l'époque où un café coûtait 10 cents ? / *that's when he got up and left* c'est à ce moment-là or c'est alors qu'il s'est levé et est parti / *that's when the shops close* c'est l'heure où les magasins ferment **6.** [whenever] quand, chaque fois que / *I try to avoid seeing him when possible* j'essaie de l'éviter quand c'est possible **7.** [since, given that] quand, étant donné que / *what good is it applying when I don't qualify for the job?* à quoi bon me porter candidat quand or si je n'ai pas les capacités requises pour faire ce travail ? / *how can you treat her so badly when you know she loves you?* comment pouvez-vous la traiter si mal quand or alors que vous savez qu'elle vous aime ? **8.** [whereas] alors que / *she described him as being lax when in fact he's quite strict* elle l'a décrit comme étant négligent alors qu'en réalité il est assez strict. ◆ rel pron **1.** [at which time] : *in a period when business was bad* à une période où les affaires allaient mal ; [which time] : *the new office will be ready in January, until when we use the old one* le nouveau bureau sera prêt en janvier, jusque là or en attendant, nous utiliserons l'ancien **2.** [that] où / *do you remember the year when we went to Alaska?* tu te rappelles l'année où on est allés en Alaska ?

whenever [wen'evər] ◆ conj **1.** [every time that] quand, chaque fois que / *whenever we go on a picnic, it rains* chaque fois qu'on part en pique-nique, il pleut / *he can come whenever he likes* il peut venir quand il veut **2.** [at whatever time] quand / *they try to help whenever possible* ils essaient de se rendre utiles quand c'est possible. ◆ adv [referring to an unknown or unspecified time] : *I'll pick you up at 6 o'clock or whenever is convenient* je te

prendrai à 6 heures ou quand ça te convient / *we could have lunch on Thursday or Friday or whenever* inf on pourrait déjeuner ensemble jeudi, vendredi ou un autre jour.

where [weər] ◆ adv **1.** [at, in, to what place] où / *where are you from?* d'où est-ce que vous venez ?, d'où êtes-vous ? / *where does this road lead?* où va cette route ? **2.** [at what stage, position] : *where are you in your work / in the book?* où en êtes-vous dans votre travail / dans votre lecture ? / *where do I come into it?* qu'est-ce que j'ai à faire là-dedans, moi ? ◆ conj **1.** [the place at or in which] (là) où / *it rains a lot where we live* il pleut beaucoup là où nous habitons / *there is a factory where I used to go to school* il y a une usine là où or à l'endroit où j'allais autrefois à l'école / *I wonder where my keys are* je me demande où sont mes clés / *turn left where the two roads meet* tournez à gauche au croisement **2.** [the place that] là que, là où / *this is where I work* c'est là que je travaille / *so that's where I left my coat!* voilà où j'ai laissé mon manteau ! / *we can't see well from where we're sitting* nous ne voyons pas bien d'où or de là où nous sommes assis ; fig : *that's where she's mistaken* c'est là qu'elle se trompe, voilà son erreur **3.** [whenever, wherever] quand, là où / *the judge is uncompromising where drugs are concerned* le juge est intraitable lorsqu'il or quand il s'agit de drogue / *where possible* là où or quand c'est possible. ◆ rel pron [in which, at which] où / *the place where we went on holiday* l'endroit où nous sommes allés en vacances / *the room where he was working* la pièce où or dans laquelle il travaillait.

whereabouts ◆ adv [ˌweərə'bauts] où / *whereabouts are you from?* d'où êtes-vous ? / *I used to live in Cumbria — oh, really, whereabouts?* j'habitais dans le Cumbria — vraiment ? où ça or dans quel coin ? ◆ pl n ['weərəbauts] ▸ **to know the whereabouts of sb / sthg** savoir où se trouve qqn / qqch.

whereas [weər'æz] conj [gen] alors que, tandis que.

whereby [weə'baɪ] rel pron fml par lequel, au moyen duquel.

wheresoever [ˌweəsəʊ'evər] = **wherever.**

whereupon [ˌweərə'pɒn] conj sur or après quoi, sur ce.

wherever [weər'evər] ◆ conj **1.** [every place] partout où ; [no matter what place] où que **2.** [anywhere, in whatever place] (là) où **3.** [in any situation] quand. ◆ adv inf **1.** [indicating surprise] mais où donc **2.** [indicating unknown or unspecified place] : *they're holidaying in Marbella or Málaga or wherever* ils passent leurs vacances à Marbella ou Malaga ou Dieu sait où.

wherewithal ['weəwɪðɔːl] n 🇬🇧 ▸ **the wherewithal** les moyens mpl.

whet [wet] *(pt & pp* **whetted,** *cont* **whetting)** vt [cutting tool] affûter, aiguiser ; [appetite] aiguiser, ouvrir.

whether ['weðər] conj **1.** [if] si / *I asked whether I could come* j'ai demandé si je pouvais venir / *I don't know now whether it's such a good idea* je ne suis plus sûr que ce soit une tellement or si bonne idée **2.** [no matter if] : *whether you want to or not* que tu le veuilles ou non.

> 📋 Note the use of the subjunctive with que when translating 'whether':
> **Whether he can actually solve the problem is another matter.** Qu'il puisse réellement résoudre le problème est une autre question.
> **They're coming with us whether they like it or not.** Ils viennent avec nous que ça leur plaise ou non.

whew [fju:] interj [relief] ouf ; [admiration] oh là là.

whey [weɪ] n petit-lait m.

which [wɪtʃ] ◆ det **1.** [indicating choice] quel m, quelle f, quels mpl, quelles / which book did you buy? quel livre as-tu acheté ? / which candidate are you voting for? pour quel candidat allez-vous voter ? ▶ which one? lequel ? / laquelle ? ▶ which ones? lesquels ? / lesquelles ? **2.** [referring back to preceding noun or statement] he may miss his plane, in which case he'll have to wait il est possible qu'il rate son avion, auquel cas il devra attendre / they lived in Madrid for one year, during which time their daughter was born ils ont habité Madrid pendant un an, et c'est à cette époque que leur fille est née. ◆ pron **1.** [what one or ones] lequel m, laquelle f, lesquels mpl, lesquelles / which of the houses do you live in? dans quelle maison habitez-vous ? / these books is yours? lequel de ces livres est le tien ? / she's from Chicago or Boston, I don't remember which elle vient de Chicago ou de Boston, je ne sais plus lequel des deux / I can't tell which is which je n'arrive pas à les distinguer (l'un de l'autre) / which is which? lequel est-ce ? **2.** [the one or ones that - as subject] celui qui m, celle qui f, ceux qui mpl, celles qui ; [- as object] celui que m, celle que f, ceux que mpl, celles que / show me which you prefer montrez-moi celui que vous préférez / tell her which is yours dites-lui lequel est le vôtre. ◆ rel pron **1.** [adding further information - as subject] qui ; [- as object] que / the house, which is very old, needs urgent repairs la maison, qui est très vieille, a besoin d'être réparée sans plus attendre / the hand with which I write la main avec laquelle j'écris / the office in which she works le bureau dans lequel or où elle travaille **2.** [commenting on previous statement - as subject] ce qui ; [- as object] ce que / he looked like a military man, which in fact he was il avait l'air d'un militaire, et en fait c'en était un / then they arrived, after which things got better puis ils sont arrivés, après quoi tout est allé mieux.

whichever [wɪtʃ'evər] ◆ pron **1.** [the one that - as subject] celui qui m, celle qui f, ceux qui mpl, celles qui ; [- as object] celui que m, celle que f, ceux que mpl, celles que / choose whichever most appeals to you choisissez celui / celle qui vous plaît le plus / shall we go to the cinema or the theatre? — whichever you prefer on va au cinéma ou au théâtre ? — choisis ce que tu préfères **2.** [no matter which one] : whichever of the routes you choose, allow about two hours quel que soit le chemin que vous choisissiez, comptez environ deux heures. ◆ det **1.** [indicating the specified choice or preference] : take whichever seat you like asseyez-vous où vous voulez / we'll travel by whichever train is fastest nous prendrons le train le plus rapide, peu importe lequel **2.** [no matter what - as subject] quel que soit... qui ; [- as object] quel que soit... que / whichever job you take, it will mean a lot of travelling quel que soit le poste que vous preniez, vous serez obligé de beaucoup voyager.

whiff [wɪf] ◆ n **1.** [gust, puff] bouffée f **2.** [smell] odeur f. ◆ vi inf sentir mauvais, puer.

whiffy ['wɪfɪ] (compar **whiffier**, superl **whiffiest**) adj inf qui pue.

while [waɪl] ◆ conj **1.** [as] pendant que / he read the paper while he waited il lisait le journal en attendant / while this was going on pendant ce temps-là / 'heels repaired / keys cut while you wait' 'talons / clés minute' / while you're up could you fetch me some water? puisque tu es debout, peux-tu aller me chercher de l'eau ? **2.** [although] bien que, quoique / while comprehensive, the report lacked clarity bien que détaillé le rapport manquait de clarté **3.** [whereas] alors que, tandis que / she's left-wing, while he's rather conservative elle est de gauche tandis que lui est plutôt conservateur. ◆ n : for a while /

a long while I believed her pendant un certain temps / pendant assez longtemps je l'ai crue / I was in the States a short while ago j'étais aux États-Unis il y a peu (de temps) ▶ once in a while de temps en temps or à autre. ❖ **while away** vt sep faire passer / she whiled away the hours reading until he returned elle passa le temps à lire jusqu'à son retour.

whilst [waɪlst] UK = while (conj).

whim [wɪm] n caprice m, fantaisie f.

whimper ['wɪmpər] ◆ vi [person] gémir, geindre ; pej pleurnicher ; [dog] gémir, pousser des cris plaintifs. ◆ vt gémir. ◆ n gémissement m, geignement m.

whimpering ['wɪmpərɪŋ] n (U) gémissements mpl, plaintes fpl.

whimsical ['wɪmzɪkl] adj **1.** [capricious] capricieux, fantasque **2.** [unusual] étrange, insolite.

whine [waɪn] ◆ vi **1.** [in pain, discomfort - person] gémir, geindre ; [- dog] gémir, pousser des gémissements **2.** [complain] se lamenter, se plaindre ▶ to whine about sthg se plaindre de qqch. ◆ vt dire en gémissant. ◆ n **1.** [from pain, discomfort] gémissement m **2.** [complaint] plainte f.

whinge [wɪndʒ] (cont whingeing) UK & Austr inf & pej ◆ vi geindre, pleurnicher. ◆ n plainte f, pleurnicherie f.

whingeing ['wɪndʒɪŋ] UK & Austr inf ◆ n (U) gémissement m ; pej pleurnicherie f, plainte f. ◆ adj [person] pleurnicheur ; [voice] plaintif.

whinger ['wɪndʒər] n râleur m, -euse f.

whining ['waɪnɪŋ] n (U) **1.** [of person] gémissements mpl ; pej pleurnicheries fpl ; [of dog] gémissements mpl **2.** [of machinery, shells] gémissement m.

whiny ['waɪnɪ] adj pleurnichard.

whip [wɪp] (pt & pp whipped, cont whipping) ◆ vt **1.** [person, animal] fouetter / the cold wind whipped her face le vent glacial lui fouettait le visage / the wind whipped her hair about le vent agitait sa chevelure **2.** inf [defeat] vaincre, battre **3.** CULIN fouetter, battre au fouet / whip the egg whites battez les blancs en neige **4.** fig : his speech whipped them all into a frenzy son discours les a tous rendus frénétiques / I'll soon whip the team into shape j'aurai bientôt fait de mettre l'équipe en forme ▶ to whip sb into line mettre qqn au pas **5.** UK inf [steal] faucher, piquer **6.** SEW surfiler **7.** [cable, rope] surlier. ◆ vi **1.** [lash] fouetter / the rain whipped against the windows la pluie fouettait or cinglait les vitres / the flags whipped about in the wind les drapeaux claquaient au vent **2.** [move quickly] aller vite, filer / the car whipped along the road la voiture filait sur la route / the ball whipped past him into the net la balle est passée devant lui comme un éclair pour finir au fond du filet. ◆ n **1.** [lash] fouet m ; [for riding] cravache f **2.** POL [MP] parlementaire chargé de la discipline de son parti et qui veille à ce que ses députés participent aux votes **3.** UK POL [summons] convocation f **4.** UK POL [paper] calendrier des travaux parlementaires envoyé par le « whip » aux députés de son parti **5.** [dessert] ▶ pineapple whip crème f à l'ananas. ❖ **whip away** vt sep [subj: wind] emporter brusquement. ❖ **whip in** vt sep **1.** HUNT ramener, rassembler **2.** UK POL [in parliament] battre le rappel de (pour voter) **3.** [supporters] rallier. ◆ vi **1.** [rush in] entrer précipitamment **2.** HUNT être piqueur. ❖ **whip off** vt sep [take off - jacket, shoes] se débarrasser de ; [write quickly - letter, memo] écrire en vitesse. ❖ **whip on** vt sep [horse] cravacher. ❖ **whip out** ◆ vt sep **1.** [take out] sortir vivement / he whipped a notebook out of his pocket il a vite sorti un carnet de sa poche **2.** [grab] : someone whipped my bag out of my hand quelqu'un m'a arraché mon sac des mains. ◆ vi sortir précipitamment. ❖ **whip round** vi [person] se retourner vivement, faire volte-face. ❖ **whip through** vt insep inf [book] parcourir en vitesse ; [task] expédier, faire en quatrième vitesse. ❖ **whip up** vt sep **1.** [curiosity, emotion] attiser ; [support] obtenir **2.** [typhoon] susciter, provoquer ; [dust] soulever (des nuages de) **3.** CULIN battre au fouet, fouetter / *I'll whip up some lunch* inf je vais préparer de quoi déjeuner en vitesse.

whiplash ['wɪplæʃ] n **1.** [stroke of whip] coup *m* de fouet **2.** MED ❱ **whiplash effect** effet *m* du coup du lapin ❱ **whiplash injury** coup *m* du lapin, syndrome *m* cervical traumatique *spec.*

whipped [wɪpt] adj [cream] fouetté.

whippet ['wɪpɪt] n whippet *m*.

whipping ['wɪpɪŋ] n [as punishment - child] correction *f* ; [- prisoner] coups *mpl* de fouet.

whip-round n ⓊⓀ inf collecte *f*.

whirl [wɜ:l] ❖ vi **1.** [person, skater] tourner, tournoyer **2.** [leaves, smoke] tourbillonner, tournoyer ; [dust, water] tourbillonner ; [spindle, top] tournoyer **3.** [head, ideas] tourner **4.** [move quickly] aller à toute vitesse. ❖ vt **1.** [dancer, skater] faire tourner **2.** [leaves, smoke] faire tourbillonner or tournoyer ; [dust, sand] faire tourbillonner **3.** [take rapidly] : *she whirled us off on a trip round Europe* elle nous a embarqués pour un tour d'Europe. ❖ n **1.** [of dancers, leaves, events] tourbillon *m* ; *fig* : *my head is in a whirl* la tête me tourne / *the mad social whirl* hum la folle vie mondaine **2.** [try] ❱ **to give sthg a whirl** inf s'essayer à qqch.

whirlpool ['wɜ:lpu:l] n *lit & fig* tourbillon *m*.

whirlpool bath n bain *m* à remous, Jacuzzi® *m*.

whirlwind ['wɜ:lwɪnd] ❖ n tornade *f*, trombe *f*. ❖ adj [trip, romance] éclair *(inv).*

whirr [wɜ:ʳ] ❖ n [of wings] bruissement *m* ; [of camera, machinery] bruit *m*, ronronnement *m* ; [of helicopter, propeller] bruit *m*, vrombissement *m*. ❖ vi [wings] bruire ; [camera, machinery] ronronner ; [propeller] vrombir.

whisk [wɪsk] ❖ vt **1.** [put or take quickly] : *the car whisked us to the embassy* la voiture nous emmena à l'ambassade à toute allure / *she whisked the children out of the room* elle emmena rapidement les enfants hors de la pièce **2.** CULIN [cream, eggs] battre ; [egg whites] battre en neige **3.** [flick] : *the horse / cow whisked its tail* le cheval / la vache agitait la queue. ❖ vi [move quickly] aller vite. ❖ n **1.** [of tail, stick, duster] coup *m* **2.** [for sweeping] époussette *f* ; [for flies] chasse-mouches *m inv* **3.** CULIN fouet *m* ; [electric] batteur *m*. ❖ **whisk away** vt sep **1.** [dust] enlever, chasser ; [dishes, tablecloth] faire disparaître ; [flies - with fly swatter] chasser à coups de chasse-mouches ; [- with tail] chasser d'un coup de queue **2.** [take off] : *a car whisked us away to the embassy* **a)** [immediately] une voiture nous emmena sur-le-champ à l'ambassade **b)** [quickly] une voiture nous emmena à toute allure à l'ambassade. ❖ **whisk off** vt sep [quickly] emporter or emmener à vive allure ; [suddenly, immediately] conduire sur-le-champ.

whisker ['wɪskəʳ] n poil *m*. ❖ **whiskers** pl n [beard] barbe *f* ; [moustache] moustache *f* ; [on animal] moustaches *fpl.*

whiskey ['wɪskɪ] *(pl* **whiskeys)** ⓊⓈ & Ⓘ = **whisky.**

whisky ⓊⓀ *(pl* **whiskies), whiskey** ⓊⓈ & Ⓘ ['wɪskɪ] n whisky *m*, scotch *m* ; ⓊⓈ bourbon *m*.

whisper ['wɪspəʳ] ❖ vi **1.** [person] chuchoter, parler à voix basse ❱ **to whisper to sb** parler or chuchoter à l'oreille de qqn / *what are you whispering about?* qu'est-ce que vous avez à chuchoter ? **2.** [leaves] bruire ; [water, wind] murmurer. ❖ vt **1.** [person] chuchoter, dire à voix basse ❱ **to whisper sthg to sb** chuchoter qqch à qqn **2.** ⓊⓀ [rumour] : *it's whispered that her husband's left her* le bruit court or on dit que son mari l'a quittée. ❖ n **1.** [of voice] chuchotement *m* ❱ **to speak in a whisper** parler tout bas or à voix basse **2.** [of leaves] bruissement *m* ; [of water, wind] murmure *m* **3.** ⓊⓀ [rumour] rumeur *f*, bruit *m*.

whispering ['wɪspərɪŋ] ❖ n **1.** [of voices] chuchotement *m*, chuchotements *mpl* **2.** [of leaves] bruissement *m* ; [of water, wind] murmure *m* **3.** *(usu pl)* ⓊⓀ [rumour] rumeur. ❖ adj **1.** [voice] qui chuchote **2.** [leaves, tree] qui frémit or murmure ; [water, wind] qui murmure.

whispering campaign n campagne *f* de diffamation.

whistle ['wɪsl] ❖ vi **1.** [person - using lips] siffler ; [- using whistle] donner un coup de sifflet, siffler ❱ **to whistle to sb** siffler qqn **2.** [bird, kettle, train] siffler. ❖ vt [tune] siffler, siffloter. ❖ n **1.** [whistling - through lips] sifflement *m* ; [- from whistle] coup *m* de sifflet **2.** [of bird, kettle, train] sifflement *m* **3.** [instrument - of person, on train] sifflet *m* ❱ **to blow a whistle** donner un coup de sifflet **4.** MUS ❱ **(penny)** or **tin whistle** flûtiau *m*, pipeau *m*. ❖ **whistle up** vt sep ⓊⓀ inf **1.** [by whistling] siffler **2.** [find] dénicher, dégoter.

whistle-blower n inf personne qui vend la mèche.

whistle-stop ❖ n ⓊⓈ RAIL arrêt *m* facultatif ❱ **whistle-stop (town)** village *m* perdu. ❖ vi ⓊⓈ POL faire une tournée électorale en passant par des petites villes. ❖ adj : *he made a whistle-stop tour of the West* il a fait une tournée rapide dans l'Ouest.

whit [wɪt] n *liter* petit peu *m*.

Whit [wɪt] ❖ n Pentecôte *f*. ❖ comp [holidays, week] de Pentecôte ❱ **Whit Sunday / Monday** dimanche *m* / lundi *m* de Pentecôte.

white [waɪt] ❖ adj **1.** [colour] blanc (blanche) / *his hair has turned white* ses cheveux ont blanchi ; [pale] : *she was white with fear / rage* elle était verte de peur / blanche de colère / *his face suddenly went white* il a blêmi tout d'un coup ❱ **the White Pages** ≃ les Pages Blanches® **2.** [flour, rice] blanc (blanche) ❱ **white wine** vin *m* blanc **3.** [race] blanc (blanche) / *white folks* ⓊⓈ les Blancs / *a white man* un Blanc / *a white woman* une Blanche / *an all-white neighbourhood* un quartier blanc. ❖ n **1.** [colour] blanc *m* / *the bride wore white* la mariée était en blanc / *he was dressed all in white* il était tout en blanc **2.** ANAT [of an eye] blanc *m* **3.** CULIN [egg] white blanc *m* (d'œuf) **4.** [Caucasian] Blanc *m*, Blanche *f*. ❖ **whites** pl n [sportswear] tenue *f* de sport blanche *(tennis, cricket)* ; [linen] blanc *m*. ❖ **white out** vt sep effacer (au correcteur liquide).

white blood cell n globule *m* blanc.

whiteboard ['waɪtbɔ:d] n tableau *m* blanc.

whitecaps ['waɪtkæps] pl n [waves] moutons *mpl.*

white Christmas n Noël *m* blanc.

white-collar adj ❱ **white-collar crime** or **delinquancy** délinquance *f* en col blanc ❱ **white-collar job** poste *m* d'employé de bureau ❱ **white-collar workers** les employés *mpl* de bureau, les cols *mpl* blancs.

white elephant n [useless object] objet *coûteux* dont l'utilité ne justifie pas le coût.

white fish n ⓊⓀ poissons à chair blanche.

white goods pl n [household equipment] appareils *mpl* ménagers ; [linen] linge *m* de maison, blanc *m*.

white-haired adj [person] aux cheveux blancs ; [animal] aux poils blancs.

Whitehall ['waɪthɔ:l] pr n rue du centre de Londres qui abrite de nombreux services gouvernementaux.

 Whitehall

Cette rue, dont le nom est souvent employé pour désigner les fonctions administratives du gouvernement, réunit de nombreux services gouvernementaux.

white heat n PHYS & fig chaleur *f* incandescente.

white horses pl n [waves] moutons *mpl.*

white-hot adj PHYS & *fig* chauffé à blanc.

White House pr n ▶ **the White House** la Maison-Blanche.

white knight n *fig* sauveur *m.*

white-knuckle adj ▶ **white-knuckle ride** tour *m* de manège terrifiant.

white lie n pieux mensonge *m.*

white light n lumière *f* blanche.

white magic n magie *f* blanche.

white meat n viande *f* blanche ; [of poultry] blanc *m.*

whiten ['waɪtn] vi & vt blanchir.

whitener ['waɪtnər] n agent *m* blanchissant.

whiteness ['waɪtnɪs] n blancheur *f* ; [of skin] blancheur *f*, pâleur *f.*

white noise n bruit *m* blanc.

whiteout ['waɪtaʊt] n brouillard *m* blanc.

white paper n UK [government report] livre *m* blanc.

white sauce n sauce *f* blanche, béchamel *f.*

White Sea pr n ▶ **the White Sea** la mer Blanche.

white spirit n white-spirit *m.*

white supremacist n partisan *m*, -e *f* de la suprématie blanche.

white supremacy n suprématie *f* blanche.

white trash n *pej* pauvres blancs *mpl.*

whitewash ['waɪtwɒʃ] ◆ n **1.** [substance] lait *m* de chaux **2.** *fig* [cover-up] : *the police report was simply a whitewash* le rapport de police visait seulement à étouffer l'affaire **3.** SPORT [crushing defeat] défaite *f* cuisante. ◆ vt **1.** [building, wall] blanchir à la chaux **2.** *fig* [cover up] blanchir, étouffer **3.** SPORT [defeat] écraser.

whitewater rafting ['waɪt,wɔːtər-] n descente *f* en eau vive, rafting *m.*

white wedding n mariage *m* en blanc.

whiting ['waɪtɪŋ] n **1.** ZOOL merlan *m* **2.** [colouring agent] blanc *m.*

Whitsun(tide) ['wɪtsn(taɪd)] n Pentecôte *f* / *at Whitsuntide* à la Pentecôte.

whittle ['wɪtl] vi & vt tailler (au couteau). ◆ **whittle away** ◆ vt sep *fig* amoindrir, diminuer. ◆ vi [with a knife] tailler. ◆ **whittle down** vt sep [with a knife] tailler (au couteau) ; *fig* amenuiser, amoindrir.

whiz(z) ['wɪz] (*pt* & *pp* **whizzed**, *cont* **whizzing**) ◆ vi **1.** [rush] filer **2.** [hiss] : *bullets whizzed around or past him* des balles sifflaient tout autour or passaient près de lui en sifflant. ◆ n **1.** [hissing sound] sifflement *m* **2.** *inf* [swift movement] : *I'll just have a (quick) whizz round with the Hoover / duster* je vais juste passer un petit coup d'aspirateur / de chiffon **3.** *inf* [bright person] as *m.*

whiz(z) kid n *inf* jeune prodige *m.*

who [huː] ◆ pron [what person or persons - as subject] (qui est-ce) qui ; [- as object] qui est-ce que, qui / *who are you?* qui êtes-vous ? / *who is it?* [at door] qui est-ce ?, qui est là ? / *who do you think you are?* vous vous prenez pour qui ? / *who is the film by?* de qui est le film ? / *who is the letter from?* la lettre est de qui ?, de qui est la lettre ? ◆ rel pron qui / *the family who lived here moved away* la famille qui habitait ici a déménagé / *those of you who were late* ceux d'entre vous qui sont arrivés en retard.

WHO (abbr of **World Health Organization**) pr n OMS *f.*

whoa [wəʊ] interj ▶ **whoa!** ho !, holà !

who'd [huːd] **1.** abbr of **who had 2.** abbr of **who would.**

whodun(n)it [,huː'dʌnɪt] n *inf* série *f* noire.

whoever [huː'evər] pron **1.** [any person who] qui / *whoever wants it can have it* celui qui le veut peut le prendre **2.** [the person who] celui qui *m*, celle qui *f*, ceux qui *mpl*, celles qui / *whoever answered the phone had a nice voice* la personne qui a répondu au téléphone avait une voix agréable **3.** [no matter who] : *whoever gets the job will find it a real challenge* celui qui obtiendra cet emploi n'aura pas la tâche facile / *it's from John Smith, whoever he is* c'est de la part d'un certain John Smith, si ça te dit quelque chose **4.** [emphatic use] qui donc / *whoever can that be?* qui cela peut-il bien être ?

whole [həʊl] ◆ adj **1.** (*with singular nouns*) [entire, complete] entier, tout / *she said nothing the whole time we were there* elle n'a rien dit tout le temps que nous étions là ; (*with plural nouns*) entier **2.** [as intensifier] tout / *there's a whole lot of things that need explaining* il y a beaucoup de choses qui doivent être expliquées ; (*with adj*) : *a whole new way of living* une façon de vivre tout à fait nouvelle **3.** [unbroken - china, egg yolk] intact ; [unhurt - person] indemne, sain et sauf **4.** CULIN [milk] entier ; [grain] complet (complète). ◆ n **1.** [complete thing, unit] ensemble *m* **2.** [as quantifier] ▶ **the whole of** tout / *it will be cold over the whole of England* il fera froid sur toute l'Angleterre. ◆ adv ▶ **to swallow sthg whole** avaler qqch en entier. ◆ **as a whole** adv phr **1.** [as a unit] entièrement **2.** [overall] dans son ensemble. ◆ **a whole lot** adv phr (*with comparative adjectives*) *inf* beaucoup. ◆ **on the whole** adv phr dans l'ensemble.

wholefood ['həʊlfuːd] n aliment *m* complet ▶ **wholefood shop** magasin *m* diététique.

wholegrain ['həʊlɡreɪn] adj [bread, flour] complet.

wholehearted [,həʊl'hɑːtɪd] adj [unreserved] sans réserve.

wholeheartedly [,həʊl'hɑːtɪdlɪ] adv [unreservedly] de tout cœur.

wholemeal ['həʊlmiːl] adj UK [bread, flour] complet (complète).

whole note n US [semibreve] ronde *f.*

wholesale ['həʊlseɪl] ◆ n (vente *f* en) gros *m.* ◆ adj **1.** COMM [business, price, shop] de gros ▶ **wholesale dealer** or **trader** grossiste *mf* **2.** *fig* [indiscriminate] en masse. ◆ adv **1.** COMM en gros **2.** *fig* [in entirety] ▶ **to reject sthg wholesale** rejeter qqch en bloc.

wholesaler ['həʊl,seɪlər] n grossiste *mf.*

wholesome ['həʊlsəm] adj [healthy - food, attitude, image, life] sain ; [- air, climate, environment] salubre, salutaire ; [advice] salutaire.

wholewheat ['həʊlwiːt] adj US [bread, flour] complet (complète).

who'll [huːl] **1.** abbr of **who will 2.** abbr of **who shall.**

wholly ['həʊlɪ] adv entièrement.

whom [huːm] *fml* ◆ pron [in questions] qui / *whom was the book written?* pour qui le livre a-t-il été écrit ? ◆ rel pron [as object of verb] que / *she is the person whom I most admire* c'est la personne que j'admire le plus ; [after preposition] : *the person to whom I am writing* la personne à qui or à laquelle j'écris / *she saw two men, neither of whom she recognized* elle a vu deux hommes mais elle n'a reconnu ni l'un ni l'autre.

whoop [wuːp] ◆ n **1.** [yell] cri *m* **2.** MED quinte *f* de toux. ◆ vi **1.** [yell] : *she whooped with joy* elle poussa un cri de joie **2.** MED avoir un accès de toux coquelucheuse. ◆ **whoop up** vt sep *inf* ▶ **to whoop it up** [celebrate] faire la noce bruyamment.

whoopee *inf* interj [wʊ'piː] ▶ **whoopee!** youpi !

whooping cough ['huːpɪŋ-] n MED coqueluche *f.*

whoops [wʊps], **whoops-a-daisy** interj inf ▸ **whoops!** houp-là !

whoosh [wʊʃ] inf ◆ n : a whoosh of air une bouffée d'air. ◆ vi : fighter planes whooshed by overhead des avions de combat passèrent en trombe au-dessus de nous. ◆ interj ▸ **whoosh!** zoum !

whop [wɒp] (pt & pp **whopped**, cont **whopping**) inf ◆ vt [beat] rosser ; [defeat] écraser. ◆ n [blow] coup.

whopper ['wɒpər] n inf **1.** [large object] : he caught a real whopper [fish] il a attrapé un poisson super géant / that sandwich is a real whopper c'est un énorme sandwich or un sandwich gigantesque **2.** [lie] gros mensonge m, mensonge m énorme.

whopping ['wɒpɪŋ] inf ◆ adj énorme, géant. ◆ adv : a whopping great lie un mensonge énorme.

whore [hɔːr] pej ◆ n putain f ; BIBLE [sinner] pécheresse f. ◆ vi **1.** lit ▸ **to go whoring a)** [prostitute o.s.] se prostituer **b)** [frequent prostitutes] fréquenter les prostituées, courir la gueuse **2.** fig ▸ **to whore after sthg** se prostituer pour obtenir qqch.

who're ['huːər] abbr of **who are**.

whose [huːz] ◆ poss pron à qui / whose is it? à qui est-ce ? ◆ poss adj **1.** [in a question] à qui, de qui / whose car was he driving? à qui était la voiture qu'il conduisait ? / whose child is she? de qui est-elle l'enfant ? **2.** [in a relative clause] dont / isn't that the man whose photograph was in the newspaper? n'est-ce pas l'homme qui était en photo dans le journal ? / the girl, both of whose parents had died, lived with her aunt la fille, dont les deux parents étaient morts, vivait avec sa tante.

whosoever [ˌhuːsəʊ'evər] pron fml & liter celui qui, quiconque.

Who's Who pr n ≃ le Bottin® mondain.

who've [huːv] abbr of **who have**.

why [waɪ] ◆ adv pourquoi / why am I telling you this? pourquoi est-ce que je vous dis ça ? / why not? pourquoi pas ? / why not join us? pourquoi ne pas vous joindre à nous ? ◆ conj pourquoi / I can't imagine why she isn't here je ne comprends pas pourquoi elle n'est pas ici / that's why he dislikes you c'est pour ça qu'il or voilà pourquoi il ne vous aime pas / they've gone, I can't think why ils sont partis, je ne sais pas pourquoi. ◆ rel pron [after 'reason'] : the reason why I lied was that I was scared j'ai menti parce que j'avais peur. ❖ **why ever** adv pourquoi donc.

wick [wɪk] n [for a candle, lamp] mèche f.

wicked ['wɪkɪd] ◆ adj **1.** [evil - person, action, thought] mauvais, méchant ; [immoral, indecent] vicieux **2.** [very bad - weather] épouvantable ; [- temper] mauvais, épouvantable **3.** [mischievous - person] malicieux ; [- smile, look, sense of humour] malicieux, coquin **4.** inf [very good] formidable. ◆ interj inf génial.

wickedly ['wɪkɪdlɪ] adv **1.** [with evil intent] méchamment, avec méchanceté **2.** [mischievously] malicieusement.

wickedness ['wɪkɪdnɪs] n **1.** RELIG [sin, evil] iniquité f, vilenie f ; [cruelty - of action, crime] méchanceté f ; [- of thought] méchanceté f, vilenie f **2.** [mischievousness - of look, sense of humour, smile] caractère m malicieux or espiègle, malice f.

wicker ['wɪkər] ◆ n osier m. ◆ adj [furniture] en osier.

wickerwork ['wɪkəwɜːk] ◆ n [material] osier m ; [objects] vannerie f. ◆ comp [furniture] en osier ; [shop] de vannerie.

wicket ['wɪkɪt] n **1.** US [window] guichet m **2.** [gate] (petite) porte f, portillon m **3.** [in cricket - stumps] guichet m ; [- area of grass] terrain m (entre les guichets).

wicket keeper n gardien m de guichet.

wide [waɪd] ◆ adj **1.** [broad] large / how wide is it? cela fait combien (de mètres) de large ?, quelle largeur ça fait ? / the road is thirty metres wide la route fait trente mètres de large / they're making the street wider ils élargissent la route ▸ **a wide screen** CIN un grand écran, un écran panoramique ; [fully open - eyes] grand ouvert **2.** [extensive, vast] étendu, vaste / he has a wide knowledge of music il a de vastes connaissances or des connaissances approfondies en musique **3.** [large - difference] : the gap between rich and poor remains wide l'écart (existant) entre les riches et les pauvres demeure considérable **4.** SPORT : the shot was wide le coup est passé à côté. ◆ adv **1.** [to full extent] : open (your mouth) wide ouvrez grand votre bouche / place your feet wide apart écartez bien les pieds **2.** [away from target] à côté.

-wide in comp ▸ **world-wide** à travers le monde (entier).

wide-angle lens n grand-angle m, grand-angulaire m.

wide area network n réseau m étendu.

wide-awake adj tout éveillé ; fig [alert] éveillé, vif.

wide boy n UK inf & pej personnage frimeur, bluffeur et sans scrupules.

wide-eyed adj **1.** [with fear, surprise] les yeux agrandis or écarquillés **2.** [naive] candide, ingénu liter.

widely ['waɪdlɪ] adv **1.** [broadly] ▸ **to yawn widely** bâiller profondément / the houses were widely scattered / spaced les maisons étaient très dispersées / espacées **2.** [extensively] : she has travelled widely elle a beaucoup voyagé / the drug is now widely available / used le médicament est maintenant largement répandu / utilisé **3.** fig [significantly] : prices vary widely les prix varient très sensiblement / the students came from widely differing backgrounds les étudiants venaient d'horizons très différents.

widen ['waɪdn] ◆ vt élargir, agrandir ; fig [experience, influence, knowledge] accroître, étendre. ◆ vi s'élargir ; [eyes] s'agrandir ; [smile] s'accentuer.

wide-open adj **1.** [extensive] grand ouvert / the wide-open spaces of Australia les grands espaces de l'Australie **2.** [fully open] : she stood there with her eyes / mouth wide open elle était là, les yeux écarquillés / bouche bée **3.** fig [vulnerable] exposé **4.** US [town] ouvert.

wide-ranging [-'reɪndʒɪŋ] adj **1.** [extensive] large, d'une grande ampleur **2.** [far-reaching - effect] de grande portée.

widescreen ['waɪdskriːn] ◆ adj [TV set] à écran large ; [cinema] panoramique. ◆ n [TV set] téléviseur m à écran large.

widespread ['waɪdspred] adj **1.** [arms] en croix ; [wings] déployé **2.** [extensive] (très) répandu.

widget ['wɪdʒɪt] n **1.** inf truc m, machin m **2.** INTERNET widget m.

widow ['wɪdəʊ] ◆ n **1.** [woman] veuve f ▸ **widow's pension** allocation f veuvage **2.** TYPO ligne f veuve (dernière ligne d'un paragraphe se trouvant à la première ligne d'une page). ◆ vt (usu passive) : he was widowed last year il a perdu sa femme l'année dernière / she was widowed last year elle a perdu son mari l'année dernière.

widowed ['wɪdəʊd] adj : she supports her widowed mother elle fait vivre sa mère qui est veuve.

widower ['wɪdəʊər] n veuf m.

width [wɪdθ] n **1.** [breadth] largeur f ; [of swimming pool] largeur f **2.** TEXT laize f, lé m.

widthways ['wɪdθweɪz], **widthwise** ['wɪdθwaɪz] adv dans le sens de la largeur.

wield [wiːld] vt **1.** [weapon] brandir ; [pen, tool] manier **2.** [influence, power] exercer, user de liter.

wife [waɪf] (pl **wives** [waɪvz]) n [spouse] femme f, épouse f ; ADMIN conjointe f.

wifey ['waɪfɪ] n inf [wife] épouse f / the wifey la ménagère, la bourgeoise.

Wifi ['waɪfaɪ] n COMPUT Wi-fi m.

wig [wɪg] n perruque f ; [hairpiece] postiche m.

wiggle ['wɪgl] ◆ vt remuer ; [hips] remuer, tortiller. ◆ vi [person] (se) remuer, frétiller ; [loose object] branler. ◆ n **1.** [movement] tortillement m **2.** [wavy line] trait m ondulé.

wiggle room, wigglespace ['wɪglspeɪs] n marge f de manœuvre.

wiggly ['wɪglɪ] adj frétillant, qui remue ▶ **a wiggly line** un trait ondulé.

wigwam ['wɪgwæm] n wigwam m.

wild [waɪld] ◆ adj **1.** [undomesticated] sauvage ; [untamed] farouche / a wild beast **a)** une bête sauvage **b)** fig une bête féroce / a wild rabbit un lapin de garenne **2.** [uncultivated - fruit] sauvage ; [- flower, plant] sauvage, des champs / wild strawberries fraises fpl des bois / many parts of the country are still wild beaucoup de régions du pays sont encore à l'état sauvage **3.** [violent - weather] : wild weather du gros temps / a wild wind un vent violent or de tempête / a wild sea une mer très agitée / it was a wild night ce fut une nuit de tempête **4.** [mad] fou (before vowel or silent 'h' fol, f folle), furieux / to be wild with grief / happiness / jealousy être fou de douleur / joie / jalousie / he had wild eyes or a wild look in his eyes il avait une lueur de folie dans le regard **5.** [dishevelled - appearance] débraillé ; [- hair] en bataille, ébouriffé / a wild-looking young man un jeune homme à l'air farouche **6.** [enthusiastic] : the speaker received wild applause l'orateur reçut des applaudissements frénétiques ▶ **to be wild about sb** inf être dingue de qqn ▶ **to be wild about sthg** inf être dingue de or emballé par qqch **7.** [outrageous - idea, imagination] insensé, fantaisiste ; [- promise, talk] insensé ; [- rumour] délirant ; [- plan] extravagant / the book's success was beyond his wildest dreams le succès de son livre dépassait ses rêves les plus fous ; [reckless] fou (before vowel or silent 'h' fol, f folle) **8.** [random] ▶ **to take a wild swing at sthg** lancer le poing au hasard pour atteindre qqch ▶ **at a wild guess** à vue de nez / aces are wild CARDS les as sont libres **9.** PHR wild **and woolly** inf **a)** [idea, plan] peu réfléchi **b)** [place] sauvage, primitif. ◆ n ▶ **in the wild** en liberté ▶ **the call of the wild** l'appel m de la nature / he spent a year living in the wild or wilds il a passé un an dans la brousse / the wilds of northern Canada le fin fond du nord du Canada. ◆ adv **1.** [grow, live] en liberté / strawberries grow wild in the forest des fraises poussent à l'état sauvage dans la forêt **2.** [emotionally] ▶ **to go wild with joy / rage** devenir fou de joie / colère / when he came on stage the audience went wild les spectateurs hurlèrent d'enthousiasme quand il arriva sur le plateau **3.** [unconstrained] ▶ **to run wild a)** [animals] courir en liberté **b)** [children] être déchaîné / they let their children run wild **a)** lit ils laissent leurs enfants traîner dans la rue **b)** fig ils ne disciplinent pas du tout leurs enfants / they've left the garden to run wild ils ont laissé le jardin à l'abandon or revenir à l'état sauvage.

wild boar n sanglier m.

wild card n COMPUT joker m.

wildcat ['waɪldkæt] (pl **wildcat** or **wildcats**) ◆ n ZOOL chat m sauvage / she's a real wildcat fig c'est une vraie tigresse. ◆ adj [imprudent, ill-considered] aléatoire, hasardeux.

wildcat strike n grève f sauvage.

wildebeest ['wɪldɪbiːst] (pl **wildebeest** or **wildebeests**) n gnou m.

wilderness ['wɪldənɪs] ◆ n **1.** [uninhabited area] pays m désert, région f sauvage ; BIBLE désert m **2.** [overgrown piece of land] jungle f. ◆ adj [region] reculé ▶ **the wilderness years** fig la traversée du désert.

wildfire ['waɪld,faɪə'] n ▶ **to spread like wildfire** se répandre comme une traînée de poudre.

wild-goose chase n : I was sent on a wild-goose chase on m'a envoyé courir au diable pour rien.

wildlife ['waɪldlaɪf] ◆ n (U) [wild animals] faune f ; [wild animals and plants] la faune et la flore. ◆ comp de la vie sauvage ; [photographer] de la nature ; [programme] sur la nature or la vie sauvage ; [expert, enthusiast] de la faune et de la flore.

wildlife park n réserve f naturelle.

wildly ['waɪldlɪ] adv **1.** [violently] violemment, furieusement **2.** [enthusiastically] : the crowd applauded wildly la foule applaudissait frénétiquement **3.** [randomly] au hasard **4.** [extremely] excessivement **5.** [recklessly] avec témérité.

wild rice n zizania f, riz m sauvage.

wild west ◆ n ▶ **the wild west** le Far West. ◆ comp ▶ **wild west show** spectacle sur le thème du Far West.

wiles [waɪlz] pl n ruses fpl.

wilful 🇬🇧, **willful** 🇺🇸 ['wɪlful] adj **1.** [action] délibéré ; [damage] volontaire, délibéré **2.** [person] entêté, obstiné.

wilfully 🇬🇧, **willfully** 🇺🇸 ['wɪlfulɪ] adv **1.** [deliberately] délibérément **2.** [obstinately] obstinément, avec entêtement.

will¹ [wɪl] modal vb **1.** [indicating the future] : what time will you be home tonight? à quelle heure rentrez-vous ce soir ? / the next meeting will be held in July la prochaine réunion aura lieu en juillet / I don't think he will or he'll come today je ne pense pas qu'il vienne or je ne crois pas qu'il viendra aujourd'hui **2.** [indicating probability] : that'll be the postman ça doit être or c'est sans doute le facteur / she'll be grown up by now elle doit être grande maintenant **3.** [indicating resolution, determination] : I'll steal the money if I have to je volerai l'argent s'il le faut / I won't have it! je ne supporterai or n'admettrai pas ça ! / you must come! — I won't! il faut que vous veniez ! — je ne viendrai pas ! **4.** [indicating willingness] : I'll carry your suitcase je vais porter votre valise / my secretary will answer your questions ma secrétaire répondra à vos questions **5.** [in requests, invitations] : will you please stop smoking? pouvez-vous éteindre votre cigarette, s'il vous plaît ? / you won't forget, will you? tu n'oublieras pas, n'est-ce pas ? / won't you join us for lunch? vous déjeunerez bien avec nous ? ; [in orders] : stop complaining, will you! arrête de te plaindre, tu veux ! / will you be quiet! vous allez vous taire ! **6.** [indicating basic ability, capacity] : the machine will wash up to 5 kilos of laundry la machine peut laver jusqu'à 5 kilos de linge ; [indicating temporary state or capacity] : the car won't start la voiture ne veut pas démarrer **7.** [indicating habitual action] : she'll play in her sandpit for hours elle peut jouer des heures dans son bac à sable **8.** [used with 'have'] : another ten years will have gone by dix autres années auront passé ; [expressing probability] : she'll have finished by now elle doit avoir fini maintenant.

will² [wɪl] ◆ n **1.** [desire, determination] volonté f / he has a weak / strong will il a peu / beaucoup de volonté / a battle of wills une lutte d'influences / she no longer has the will to live elle n'a plus envie de vivre / it is the will of the people that... le peuple veut que... ▶ **to have a will of iron** or **an iron will** avoir une volonté de fer ▶ **to have a will of one's own** n'en faire qu'à sa tête, être très indépendant ▶ **with the best will in the world** avec la meilleure volonté du monde ▶ **where there's a will there's a way** prov quand on veut on peut prov **2.** LAW testament m ▶ **last will and testament** dernières volontés fpl / did he leave me *anything in his will?* m'a-t-il laissé quelque chose dans son testament ? ◆ vt **1.** [using willpower] : *I was willing her to say yes* j'espérais qu'elle allait dire oui / *she willed herself to keep walking* elle s'est forcée à poursuivre sa marche / *I could feel the crowd willing me on* je sentais que la foule me soutenait **2.** [bequeath] léguer / *she willed her entire fortune to charity* elle a légué toute sa fortune à des œuvres de charité **3.** *liter* [wish, intend] vouloir / *the Lord so willed it* le Seigneur a voulu qu'il en soit ainsi. ◆ vi *arch* & *liter* [wish] vouloir. ❖ **against one's will** adv phr contre sa volonté / *he left home against his father's will* il est parti de chez lui contre la volonté de son père. ❖ **at will** adv phr à sa guise / *they can come and go at will here* ils peuvent aller et venir à leur guise ici ▸ *fire at will!* feu à volonté ! ❖ **with a will** adv phr avec ardeur *or* acharnement / *we set to with a will* nous nous attelâmes à la tâche avec ardeur.

willful 🇺🇸 = **wilful**.

willies ['wɪlɪz] pl n *inf* : *he / it gives me the willies* il / ça me fiche la trouille.

willing ['wɪlɪŋ] adj **1.** [ready, prepared] : *are you willing to cooperate with us?* êtes-vous prêt à collaborer avec nous ? / *he isn't even willing to try* il ne veut même pas essayer ▸ *to be willing and able (to do sthg)* avoir l'envie et les moyens (de faire qqch) / *they were less than willing to take part* ils ont rechigné à participer / *he's more than willing to change jobs* il ne demande pas mieux que de changer d'emploi / *willing or not, they must lend a hand* qu'ils le veuillent ou non, ils devront nous aider **2.** [compliant] : *he's a willing victim* c'est une victime complaisante **3.** [eager, enthusiastic -helper] bien disposé, de bonne volonté **4.** PHR *to show willing* faire preuve de bonne volonté.

willingly ['wɪlɪŋlɪ] adv **1.** [eagerly, gladly] de bon cœur, volontiers **2.** [voluntarily] volontairement, de plein gré.

willingness ['wɪlɪŋnɪs] n **1.** [enthusiasm] : *he set to with great willingness* il s'est attelé à la tâche avec un grand enthousiasme **2.** [readiness] : *he admired her willingness to sacrifice her own happiness* il admirait le fait qu'elle soit prête à sacrifier son propre bonheur.

willow ['wɪləʊ] ◆ n **1.** BOT saule *m* **2.** *inf* CRICKET batte *f*. ◆ comp de saule ▸ **willow tree** saule *m*.

willowy ['wɪləʊɪ] adj [figure, person] élancé, svelte ; [object] souple, flexible.

willpower ['wɪl,paʊə'] n volonté *f*.

willy ['wɪlɪ] (*pl* **willies**) n 🇬🇧 *inf* zizi *m*.

willy-nilly [,wɪlɪ'nɪlɪ] adv bon gré mal gré.

wilt [wɪlt] ◆ vi [droop -flower, plant] se faner, se flétrir ; [-person] languir, s'alanguir. ◆ vt [cause to droop -flower, plant] faner, flétrir.

Wilts written abbr of **Wiltshire**.

wily ['waɪlɪ] (*compar* **wilier**, *superl* **wiliest**) adj [person] rusé, malin (maligne) ; [scheme, trick] habile, astucieux.

wimp [wɪmp] n *inf* & *pej* [person -physically weak] mauviette *f* ; [-morally weak, irresolute] mou *m*, molle *f*, pâte *f* molle. ❖ **wimp out** vi *inf* se défiler.

WIMP (**abbr of window, icon, menu, pointing device**) n WIMP *m*.

win [wɪn] (*pt* & *pp* **won** [wʌn], *cont* **winning**) ◆ vi [in competition] gagner / *they're winning three nil* ils gagnent trois à zéro. ◆ vt **1.** [in competition -award, prize] gagner ; [-scholarship] obtenir ; [-contract] remporter ; [in war] : *we have won a great victory* nous avons remporté une grande victoire **2.** [obtain, secure -friendship, love] gagner ; [-sympathy] s'attirer **3.** MIN extraire. ◆ n **1.** SPORT victoire *f* **2.** 🇺🇸 [in horseracing] ▸ **win, place, show** gagnant, placé et troisième. ❖ **win back** vt sep [money,

trophy] reprendre, recouvrer ; [land] reprendre, reconquérir ; [loved one] reconquérir ; [esteem, respect, support] retrouver, recouvrer ; POL [votes, voters, seats] récupérer, recouvrer. ❖ **win out** vi triompher. ❖ **win over** vt sep [convert, convince] rallier. ❖ **win round** 🇬🇧 = **win over**. ❖ **win through** vi remporter.

wince [wɪns] ◆ vi [from pain] crisper le visage, grimacer ; *fig* grimacer (de dégoût). ◆ n grimace *f*.

winch [wɪntʃ] ◆ n treuil *m*. ◆ vt ▸ *to winch sb / sthg up / down* monter / descendre qqn / qqch au treuil.

Winchester disk ['wɪntʃestə'] n disque *m* (dur) Winchester.

wind¹ [wɪnd] ◆ n **1.** METEOR vent *m* ; NAUT ▸ *into the wind* contre le vent ▸ *before the wind* le vent en poupe ; *fig* : *the winds of change are blowing* il y a du changement dans l'air ▸ *to get wind of sthg* avoir vent de qqch ▸ *there's something in the wind* il se prépare quelque chose ▸ *to take the wind out of sb's sails* couper l'herbe sous le pied à qqn ▸ *let's wait and see which way the wind is blowing* attendons de voir quelle tournure les événements vont prendre **2.** [breath] souffle *m* / *I haven't got my wind back yet* je n'ai pas encore repris haleine *or* mon souffle ▸ *to get one's second wind* reprendre haleine *or* son souffle ▸ *to put the wind up sb* *inf* flanquer la frousse à qqn **3.** *inf* [empty talk] vent *m* **4.** *(U)* [air in stomach] vents *mpl*, gaz *mpl* ▸ *to break wind* lâcher des vents ▸ *to get a baby's wind up* faire faire son renvoi à un bébé **5.** MUS ▸ *the wind (section)* les instruments *mpl* à vent, les vents *mpl*. ◆ vt **1.** [make breathless] ▸ *to wind sb* couper le souffle à qqn **2.** [horse] laisser souffler **3.** [baby] faire faire son renvoi à.

wind² [waɪnd] (*pt* & *pp* **wound** [waʊnd]) ◆ vi [bend -procession, road] serpenter ; [coil -thread] s'enrouler / *the river winds through the valley* le fleuve décrit des méandres dans la vallée *or* traverse la vallée en serpentant. ◆ vt **1.** [wrap -bandage, rope] enrouler / *I wound a scarf round my neck* j'ai enroulé une écharpe autour de mon cou / *wind the string into a ball* enrouler la ficelle pour en faire une pelote **2.** [clock, watch, toy] remonter ; [handle] tourner, donner un tour de **3.** *arch* & *hum* [travel] ▸ *to wind one's way home* prendre le chemin du retour. ◆ n **1.** MECH : *give the clock / watch a wind* remontez l'horloge / la montre / *she gave the handle another wind* elle tourna la manivelle encore une fois, elle donna un tour de manivelle de plus **2.** [bend -of road] tournant *m*, courbe *f* ; [-of river] coude *m*. ❖ **wind back** vt sep rembobiner. ❖ **wind down** ◆ vi **1.** [relax] se détendre, décompresser **2.** MECH [clock, watch] ralentir. ◆ vt sep **1.** MECH [lower] faire descendre ; [car window] baisser **2.** [bring to an end -business] mener (doucement) vers sa fin. ❖ **wind forward** vt sep (faire) avancer. ❖ **wind on** vt sep enrouler. ❖ **wind up** ◆ vt sep **1.** [conclude -meeting] terminer ; [-account, business] liquider **2.** [raise] monter, faire monter ; [car window] monter, fermer **3.** [string, thread] enrouler ; [on a spool] dévider **4.** MECH [clock, watch, toy] remonter ▸ *to be wound up (about sthg)* *inf* & *fig* être à cran (à cause de qqch) **5.** 🇬🇧 *inf* [annoy] asticoter ; [tease] faire marcher. ◆ vi *inf* [end up] finir / *he wound up in jail* il a fini *or* s'est retrouvé en prison.

wind-borne [wɪnd] adj anémophile, transporté par le vent.

windbreak ['wɪndbreɪk] n abrivent *m*, coupe-vent *m inv*.

windbreaker® ['wɪnd,breɪkə'] n 🇺🇸 anorak *m*, coupe-vent *m inv*.

windcheater ['wɪnd,tʃiːtə'] n 🇬🇧 anorak *m*, coupe-vent *m inv*.

windchill factor ['wɪndtʃɪl-] n facteur *m* de refroidissement au vent.

winder ['waɪndə'] n [for clock] remontoir m ; [for car window] lève-vitre m, lève-glace m ; [for thread, yarn] dévidoir m.

windfall ['wɪndfɔːl] ◆ n **1.** [unexpected gain] (bonne) aubaine f **2.** [fruit] fruit m tombé. ◆ adj [fruit] tombé or abattu par le vent ▶ **windfall profits** or **revenues / dividends** profits mpl / dividendes mpl exceptionnels ▶ **windfall tax** impôt m sur les bénéfices exceptionnels.

windfarm ['wɪndfɑːm] n champ m d'éoliennes.

winding ['waɪndɪŋ] ◆ adj [road, street] tortueux, sinueux ; [river] sinueux ; [staircase] en hélice, en colimaçon. ◆ n **1.** [process] enroulement m ; ELEC [wire] bobinage m, enroulement m **2.** [in a river] méandres mpl, coudes mpl ; [in a road] zigzags mpl.

wind instrument [wɪnd-] n instrument m à vent.

windmill ['wɪndmɪl] ◆ n **1.** [building] moulin m à vent ; [toy] moulinet m **2.** [wind turbine] aéromoteur m, éolienne f. ◆ vi **1.** [arms] tourner en moulinet **2.** AERON [propeller, rotor] tourner pour la force du vent.

window ['wɪndəʊ] ◆ n **1.** [in room] fenêtre f ; [in car] vitre f, glace f ; [in front of shop] vitrine f, devanture f ; [in church] vitrail m ; [at ticket office] guichet m ; [on envelope] fenêtre f / she looked out of or through the window elle regarda par la fenêtre / he jumped out of the window il a sauté par la fenêtre **2.** COMPUT fenêtre f **3.** [in diary] créneau m, moment m libre ▶ **a window of opportunity** une possibilité **4.** [insight] : a window on the world of finance un aperçu des milieux financiers **5.** [opportune time] ▶ **launch window** ASTRONAUT fenêtre f or créneau m de lancement ▶ **weather window** accalmie f (permettant de mener à bien des travaux). ◆ comp de fenêtre ▶ **window frame** châssis m de fenêtre.

window box n jardinière f.

window cleaner n [person] laveur m, -euse f de vitres or carreaux ; [substance] nettoyant m pour vitres.

window display n étalage m.

window dressing n [merchandise on display] présentation f de l'étalage ; [activity] : they need someone to do the window dressing ils ont besoin de quelqu'un pour composer or faire l'étalage ; fig façade f.

window envelope n enveloppe f à fenêtre.

windowless ['wɪndəʊlɪs] adj sans fenêtres.

windowpane ['wɪndəʊpeɪn] n carreau m, vitre f.

window seat n [in room] banquette f sous la fenêtre ; [in train, plane] place f côté fenêtre.

window shade n UK store m.

window-shopping n lèche-vitrines m inv.

windowsill ['wɪndəʊsɪl] n rebord m de fenêtre.

windpipe ['wɪndpaɪp] n trachée f.

wind power [wɪnd-] n énergie f du vent or éolienne spec.

windscreen ['wɪndskriːn] n UK pare-brise m inv.

windscreen washer n UK lave-glace m.

windscreen wiper n UK essuie-glace m.

windshield ['wɪndʃiːld] n US pare-brise m inv.

wind sleeve [wɪnd-], **windsock** ['wɪndsɒk] n manche f à air.

windsurf ['wɪndsɜːf] vi faire de la planche à voile.

windsurfer ['wɪndsɜːfə'] n [board] planche f à voile ; [person] véliplanchiste mf, planchiste mf.

windsurfing ['wɪndsɜːfɪŋ] n planche f à voile.

windswept ['wɪndswept] adj [place] balayé par le vent ; [hair] ébouriffé par le vent.

wind tunnel [wɪnd-] n tunnel m aérodynamique.

wind turbine n éolienne f.

wind-up [waɪnd-] ◆ adj [mechanism] ▶ **a wind-up toy /** **watch** un jouet / une montre à remontoir. ◆ n **1.** UK inf : is this a wind-up? est-ce qu'on veut me faire marcher ? **2.** [conclusion] conclusion f.

Windward Islands pl pr n ▶ **the Windward Islands** les îles fpl du Vent / in the Windward Islands aux îles du Vent.

windy ['wɪndɪ] (compar windier, superl windiest) adj **1.** METEOR : tomorrow it will be very windy everywhere demain il fera du vent or le vent soufflera partout / a cold, windy morning un matin froid et de grand vent / it's a very wet and windy place c'est un endroit très pluvieux et très éventé **2.** inf [pompous, verbose] ronflant, pompeux.

wine [waɪn] ◆ n vin m ▶ **red / white wine** vin rouge / blanc. ◆ comp [bottle, glass] à vin. ◆ vt ▶ **to wine and dine sb** emmener qqn faire un bon dîner bien arrosé. ◆ vi ▶ **to go out wining and dining** faire la fête au restaurant. ◆ adj [colour] lie-de-vin (inv) / a wine-coloured dress une robe lie-de-vin.

wine bar n [drinking establishment] bistrot m.

wine box n Cubitainer® m.

wine cellar n cave f (à vin), cellier m.

wineglass ['waɪnglɑːs] n verre m à vin.

winegrower ['waɪnˌgrəʊə'] n viticulteur m, -trice f, vigneron m, -onne f.

wine list n carte f des vins.

wine merchant n [shopkeeper] marchand m, -e f de vin ; [wholesaler] négociant m, -e f en vins.

winepress ['waɪnpres] n pressoir m à vin.

wine rack n casier m à vin.

winery ['waɪnərɪ] n US établissement m vinicole.

wine tasting [-ˌteɪstɪŋ] n dégustation f (de vins).

wine vinegar n vinaigre m de vin.

wine waiter n sommelier m.

wing [wɪŋ] ◆ n **1.** [on bird, insect] aile f **2.** AERON aile f ; [badge] ▶ **to win one's wings** faire ses preuves, prendre du galon **3.** UK AUTO aile f **4.** POL [section] aile f ▶ **the left /** **right wing** l'aile gauche / droite **5.** ARCHIT aile f **6.** [on windmill] aile f **7.** SPORT [of field] aile f ; [player] ailier m. ◆ vt **1.** [wound - bird] blesser, toucher à l'aile ; [- person] blesser or toucher légèrement **2.** [fly] ▶ **to wing one's way** lit & fig voler **3.** liter [cause to fly - arrow] darder, décocher **4.** PHR **to wing it** inf [improvise] improviser. ◆ **wings** pl n THEAT coulisse f, coulisses fpl ▶ **to wait in the wings** lit & fig se tenir dans la coulisse or les coulisses.

wing commander n lieutenant-colonel m.

winger ['wɪŋə'] n SPORT ailier m.

wing forward n [in rugby] ailier m.

wingman ['wɪŋmæn] n US [assistant] assistant m.

wing mirror n rétroviseur m extérieur.

wing nut n papillon m, écrou m à ailettes.

wingspan ['wɪŋspæn] n envergure f.

wingwoman ['wɪŋwʊmən] n US [assistant] assistante f.

wink [wɪŋk] ◆ vi **1.** [person] faire un clin d'œil ▶ **to** **wink at sb** faire un clin d'œil à qqn ▶ **to wink at sthg** fig fermer les yeux sur qqch **2.** liter [light, star] clignoter. ◆ vt ▶ **to wink an eye at sb** faire un clin d'œil à qqn. ◆ n clin m d'œil.

winkle ['wɪŋkl] n UK bigorneau m, vigneau m. ◆ **winkle out** vt sep inf [information] arracher, extirper ; [person] déloger.

Winnebago® [ˌwɪnɪ'beɪgəʊ] n camping-car m.

winner ['wɪnə'] n **1.** [of prize] gagnant m, -e f ; [of battle, war] vainqueur m ; [of match] vainqueur m, gagnant m **2.** SPORT [winning point] : he scored the winner c'est lui qui a marqué le but décisif ; [successful shot] : *he played a winner* il a joué un coup gagnant **3.** [successful person] gagneur *m*, -euse *f* ; [successful thing] succès *m*.

winning ['wɪnɪŋ] adj **1.** [successful] gagnant ; SPORT [goal, stroke] décisif ▶ **to be on a winning streak** remporter victoire sur victoire **2.** [charming] engageant, charmant. ❖ **winnings** pl n gains *mpl*.

winning post n poteau *m* d'arrivée.

wino ['waɪnəʊ] (*pl* **winos**) n *inf* ivrogne *mf*.

winter ['wɪntər] ◆ n hiver *m* / *it never snows here in (the) winter* il ne neige jamais ici en hiver. ◆ comp d'hiver. ◆ vi *fml* [spend winter] passer l'hiver, hiverner. ◆ vt [farm animals] hiverner.

winter sports pl n sports *mpl* d'hiver.

wintertime ['wɪntətaɪm] n hiver *m*.

wint(e)ry ['wɪntrɪ] adj hivernal ; *fig* [look, smile] glacial.

win-win adj : *it's a win-win situation* on ne peut que gagner, c'est une situation gagnant-gagnant.

wipe [waɪp] ◆ vt **1.** [with cloth] essuyer / *he wiped the plate dry* il a bien essuyé l'assiette ▶ **to wipe one's feet** s'essuyer les pieds ▶ **to wipe one's nose** se moucher ▶ **to wipe one's bottom** s'essuyer / *she wiped the sweat from his brow* elle essuya la sueur de son front **2.** [delete - from written record, magnetic tape] effacer. ◆ vi essuyer. ◆ n **1.** [action of wiping] : *give the table a wipe* donne un coup d'éponge sur la table **2.** [cloth] lingette *f* ▶ **antistatic wipe** chiffon *m* antistatique. ❖ **wipe away** vt sep [blood, tears] essuyer ; [dirt, dust] enlever. ❖ **wipe down** vt sep [paintwork, walls] lessiver. ❖ **wipe off** vt sep **1.** [remove] enlever / *wipe that smile or grin off your face!* *inf* enlève-moi ce sourire idiot ! **2.** [erase] effacer. ❖ **wipe out** vt sep **1.** [clean] nettoyer **2.** [erase] effacer ; *fig* [insult, disgrace] effacer, laver **3.** [destroy] anéantir, décimer **4.** *inf* [exhaust] crever. ❖ **wipe up** vt sep éponger, essuyer.

wiper ['waɪpər] n AUTO essuie-glace *m inv*.

wire ['waɪər] ◆ n **1.** [of metal] fil *m* (métallique or de fer) **2.** US [telegram] télégramme *m* **3.** PRESS ▶ **the wires** les dépêches d'agences. ◆ vt **1.** [attach] relier avec du fil de fer **2.** ELEC [building, house] mettre l'électricité dans, faire l'installation électrique dans ; [connect electrically] brancher **3.** US TELEC [person] envoyer un télégramme à, télégraphier à ; [money, information] envoyer par télégramme, télégraphier. ❖ **wire together** vt sep relier avec du fil de fer. ❖ **wire up** vt sep **1.** = **wire** (*vt*) **2.** US *inf* [make nervous] énerver.

wire brush n brosse *f* métallique.

wire cutters pl n cisaille *f*, pinces *fpl* coupantes.

wired ['waɪəd] adj **1.** ELEC [to an alarm] relié à un système d'alarme **2.** [wiretapped] mis sur écoute **3.** [bra] à tiges métalliques **4.** *v inf* [psyched-up] surexcité.

wirefree ['waɪəfriː] adj sans fil.

wireless ['waɪəlɪs] ◆ n **1.** [mouse, keyboard, technology, network] sans fil **2.** US *dated* radio *f* ▶ **wireless (set)** poste *m* de radio / *on the wireless* à la radio. ◆ comp [broadcast] de radio.

wire netting, **wire mesh** n grillage *m*, treillis *m* métallique.

wire service n US agence *f* de presse (*envoyant des dépêches télégraphiques*).

wiretap ['waɪətæp] (*pt & pp* **wiretapped**, *cont* **wiretapping**) ◆ vt mettre sur écoute. ◆ vi mettre un téléphone sur écoute. ◆ n : *they put a wiretap on his phone* ils ont mis son téléphone sur écoute.

wiretapping ['waɪəˌtæpɪŋ] n mise *f* sur écoute des lignes téléphoniques.

wire wool n éponge *f* métallique.

wiring ['waɪərɪŋ] n installation *f* électrique.

wiry ['waɪərɪ] (*compar* **wirier**, *superl* **wiriest**) adj **1.** [person] élancé et robuste ; [animal] nerveux, vigoureux **2.** [hair] peu souple, rêche **3.** [grass] élastique, flexible.

Wisconsin [wɪs'kɒnsɪn] pr n Wisconsin *m* / *in Wisconsin* dans le Wisconsin.

wisdom ['wɪzdəm] n **1.** [perspicacity, judgement] sagesse *f* **2.** [store of knowledge] sagesse *f* **3.** [opinion] avis *m* (général), jugement *m*.

wisdom tooth n dent *f* de sagesse.

wise [waɪz] ◆ adj **1.** [learned, judicious] sage **2.** [clever, shrewd] habile, astucieux ▶ **the Three Wise Men** les Rois Mages *mpl* ▶ **to be wise to sthg** *inf* être au courant de qqch ▶ **to get wise to sthg** *inf*: *you'd better get wise to what's going on* vous feriez bien d'ouvrir les yeux sur ce qui se passe. ◆ n *fml* : *he is in no wise* or *not in any wise satisfied with his new position* il n'est point or aucunement satisfait de son nouveau poste. ❖ **wise up** vi : *he'd better wise up!* il ferait bien de se mettre dans le coup ! ◆ vt sep US mettre dans le coup.

-wise in comp **1.** [in the direction of] dans le sens de / *length-wise* dans le sens de la longueur **2.** [in the manner of] à la manière de, comme / *he edged crab-wise up to the bar* il s'approcha du bar en marchant de côté comme un crabe **3.** *inf* [as regards] côté / *money-wise the job leaves a lot to be desired* le poste laisse beaucoup à désirer côté argent.

wisecrack ['waɪzkræk] n *inf* sarcasme *m*.

wisecracking ['waɪzˌkrækɪŋ] adj *inf* blagueur.

wise guy n *inf* malin *m*.

wisely ['waɪzlɪ] adv sagement, avec sagesse.

wish [wɪʃ] ◆ vt **1.** [expressing something impossible or unlikely] souhaiter / *I wish I were* or US *inf was somewhere else* j'aimerais bien être ailleurs / *I wish you didn't have to leave* j'aimerais que tu ne sois pas or ce serait bien si tu n'étais pas obligé de partir / *I wish I'd thought of that before* je regrette de n'y avoir pas pensé plus tôt / *why don't you come with us? — I wish I could* pourquoi ne venez-vous pas avec nous ? — j'aimerais bien ; [expressing criticism, reproach] : *I wish you'd be more careful* j'aimerais que vous fassiez plus attention **2.** *fml* [want] souhaiter, vouloir / *I don't wish to appear rude, but...* je ne voudrais pas paraître grossier mais... **3.** [in greeting, expressions of goodwill] souhaiter / *he wished them success in their future careers* il leur a souhaité de réussir dans leur carrière / *he wished us good day* il nous a souhaité le bonjour / *I wish you well* j'espère que tout ira bien pour vous / *I wish you (good) luck* je vous souhaite bonne chance. ◆ vi **1.** *fml* [want, like] vouloir, souhaiter / *do as you wish* faites comme vous voulez **2.** [make a wish] faire un vœu. ◆ n **1.** [act of wishing, thing wished for] souhait *m*, vœu *m* / *make a wish!* fais un souhait or vœu ! ▶ **to grant a wish** exaucer un vœu / *he got his wish* or *his wish came true* son vœu s'est réalisé **2.** [desire] désir *m* ▶ **to express a wish for sthg** exprimer le désir de qqch ▶ **to respect sb's wishes** respecter les vœux de qqn ▶ **wish list** desiderata *mpl* **3.** [regards] : *give your wife my best wishes* transmettez toutes mes amitiés à votre épouse ; [in card] : *best wishes for the coming year* meilleurs vœux pour la nouvelle année ; [in letter] ▶ **(with) best wishes** bien amicalement, toutes mes amitiés. ❖ **wish away** vt sep : *you can't simply wish away the things you don't like* on ne peut pas faire comme si les choses qui nous déplaisent n'existaient pas. ❖ **wish for** vt insep souhaiter. ❖ **wish on** vt sep **1.** [fate, problem] souhaiter à / *I wouldn't wish this headache on anyone* je ne souhaite à personne d'avoir un mal de tête pareil

2. [foist on] : *it's a terribly complicated system wished on us by head office* c'est un système très compliqué dont nous a fait cadeau la direction.

wishbone ['wɪʃbəʊn] n **1.** ANAT [bone] bréchet *m*, fourchette *f* **2.** [in windsurfing] wishbone *m*.

wishful thinking [wɪʃfʊl-] n : *I suppose it was just wishful thinking* je prenais mes rêves pour la réalité.

wishing well ['wɪʃɪŋ-] n puits où l'on jette une pièce en faisant un vœu.

wishy-washy ['wɪʃɪ,wɒʃɪ] adj inf [behaviour] mou *(before vowel or silent 'h' mol, f molle)* ; [person] sans personnalité ; [colour] délavé ; [taste] fadasse.

wisp [wɪsp] n [of grass, straw] brin *m* ; [of hair] petite mèche *f* ; [of smoke, steam] ruban *m*.

wispy ['wɪspɪ] (compar **wispier**, superl **wispiest**) adj [beard] effilé ; [hair] épars ; [person] (tout) menu.

wistful ['wɪstfʊl] adj mélancolique, nostalgique.

wistfully ['wɪstfʊlɪ] adv d'un air triste et rêveur.

wit [wɪt] n **1.** [humour] esprit *m* **2.** [humorous person] : *he was a great wit* c'était un homme plein d'esprit **3.** [intelligence] esprit *m*, intelligence *f*. ❖ **to wit** adv phr fml à savoir.

witch [wɪtʃ] n [sorceress] sorcière *f* ❱ **witches' Sabbath** sabbat *m* (de sorcières).

witchcraft ['wɪtʃkrɑːft] n (U) sorcellerie *f*.

witchdoctor ['wɪtʃ,dɒktəʳ] n sorcier *m*.

witch-hazel n hamamélis *m*.

witch-hunt n chasse *f* aux sorcières ; fig chasse *f* aux sorcières, persécution *f* (politique).

with [wɪð] prep **1.** [by means of] avec / *what did you fix it with?* avec quoi l'as-tu réparé ? / *his eyes filled with tears* ses yeux se remplirent de larmes **2.** [describing a feature or attribute] à / *a woman with long hair* une femme aux cheveux longs / *a table with three legs* une table à trois pieds / *she was left with nothing to eat or drink* on l'a laissée sans rien à manger ni à boire **3.** [accompanied by, in the company of] avec / *can I go with you?* puis-je aller avec vous or vous accompagner ? / *I have no one to go with* je n'ai personne avec qui aller / *I'll be with you in a minute* je suis à vous dans une minute ; *are you with me?* **a)** [supporting] vous êtes avec moi ? **b)** [understanding] vous me suivez ? / *I'm with you one hundred per cent* or *all the way* je suis complètement d'accord avec vous **4.** [in the home of] chez / *I'm (staying) with friends* je suis or loge chez des amis **5.** [an employee of] : *she's with the UN* elle travaille à l'ONU **6.** [indicating joint action] avec / *stop fighting with your brother* arrête de te battre avec ton frère ; [indicating feelings towards someone else] : *angry / furious / at war with* fâché / furieux / en guerre contre / *pleased with* content de **7.** [indicating manner] de, avec / *he knocked the guard out with one blow* il assomma le gardien d'un (seul) coup / *he spoke with ease* il s'exprima avec aisance **8.** [as regards, concerning] : *you never know with him* avec lui, on ne sait jamais / *what's with you?* inf, *what's wrong with you?* qu'est-ce qui te prend ? **9.** [because of, on account of] de / *sick* or *ill with malaria* atteint du paludisme / *I can't draw with you watching* je ne peux pas dessiner si tu me regardes **10.** [in spite of] : *with all his money he's so stingy* inf il a beau avoir beaucoup d'argent, il est vraiment radin.

withdraw [wɪð'drɔː] (pt **withdrew**, pp **withdrawn**) ❖ vt **1.** [remove] retirer **2.** [money] retirer **3.** [bring out - diplomat] rappeler ; [- troops] retirer **4.** [statement] rétracter ; LAW [charge] retirer. ❖ vi **1.** [retire] se retirer **2.** [retreat] se retirer ; [move back] reculer **3.** [back out - candidate, competitor] se retirer, se désister ; [- partner] se rétracter, se dédire **4.** [after sex] se retirer.

withdrawal [wɪð'drɔːəl] ❖ n **1.** [removal - of funding, support, troops] retrait *m* ; [- of envoy] rappel *m* ; [- of candidate] retrait *m*, désistement *m* ; [- of love] privation *f* **2.** [of statement, remark] rétraction *f* ; LAW [of charge] retrait *m*, annulation *f* **3.** PSYCHOL repli *m* sur soi-même, introversion *f* **4.** MED [from drugs] état *m* de manque **5.** [of money] retrait *m*. ❖ comp ❱ **withdrawal symptoms** symptômes *mpl* de manque.

withdrawn [wɪð'drɔːn] ❖ pp —➤ **withdraw**. ❖ adj [shy] renfermé, réservé.

withdrew [wɪð'druː] pt —➤ **withdraw**.

wither ['wɪðəʳ] ❖ vi **1.** [flower, plant] se flétrir, se faner ; [body - from age] se ratatiner ; [- from sickness] s'atrophier **2.** [beauty] se faner ; [hope, optimism] s'évanouir ; [memory] s'étioler. ❖ vt **1.** [plant] flétrir, faner ; [body - subj: age] ratatiner ; [- subj: sickness] atrophier **2.** [beauty] altérer. ❖ **wither away** vi [flower, plant] se dessécher, se faner ; [beauty] se faner, s'évanouir ; [hope, optimism] s'évanouir ; [memory] disparaître, s'atrophier.

withered ['wɪðəd] adj **1.** [flower, plant] flétri, fané ; [face, cheek] fané, flétri **2.** [arm] atrophié.

withering ['wɪðərɪŋ] ❖ adj [heat, sun] desséchant ; [criticism, remark] cinglant, blessant. ❖ n [of plant] flétrissure *f* ; [of arm] atrophie *f* ; [of beauty] déclin *m* ; [of hope, optimism] évanouissement *m*.

withhold [wɪð'həʊld] (pt & pp **withheld** [-'held]) vt **1.** [refuse - love, permission, support] refuser ; [refuse to pay - rent, tax] refuser de payer **2.** [keep back - criticism, news] taire, cacher.

within [wɪ'ðɪn] ❖ prep **1.** [inside - place] à l'intérieur de, dans ; [- group, system] à l'intérieur de, au sein de ; [- person] en / *he lived and worked within these four walls* il a vécu et travaillé entre ces quatre murs / *a small voice within her* une petite voix intérieure ou au fond d'elle-même **2.** [inside the limits of] dans les limites de / *you must remain within the circle* tu dois rester dans le or à l'intérieur du cercle ❱ **to be within the law** être dans les limites de la loi ❱ **to live within one's means** vivre selon ses moyens **3.** [before the end of a specified period of time] en moins de / *I'll let you know within a week* je vous dirai ce qu'il en est dans le courant de la semaine / *'use within two days of purchase'* 'à consommer dans les deux jours suivant la date d'achat' **4.** [indicating distance, measurement] : *they were within 10 km of Delhi* ils étaient à moins de 10 km de Delhi / *accurate to within 0.1 of a millimetre* précis au dixième de millimètre près **5.** [during] : *did the accident take place within the period covered by the insurance?* l'accident a-t-il eu lieu pendant la période couverte par l'assurance ? ❖ adv dedans, à l'intérieur ❱ **from within** de l'intérieur.

with it adj inf **1.** [alert] réveillé ❱ **get with it!** réveille-toi !, secoue-toi ! **2.** dated [fashionable] dans le vent.

without [wɪ'ðaʊt] prep sans / *three nights without sleep* trois nuits sans dormir / *without milk or sugar* sans lait ni sucre / *to be without fear / shame* ne pas avoir peur / honte / *he took it without so much as a thank you* il l'a pris sans même dire merci ; (with present participle) : *without looking up* sans lever les yeux.

📝 Note that **sans que** is followed by a verb in the subjunctive:
Can I use the file without the software being installed? Est-ce que je peux utiliser le fichier sans que le logiciel soit installé ?
Learn French without it being a chore! Apprenez le français sans que cela soit une corvée !

withstand [wɪð'stænd] (*pt & pp* **withstood** [-'stʊd])
vt [heat, punishment] résister à.

witless ['wɪtlɪs] adj sot (sotte), stupide.

witness ['wɪtnɪs] ◆ n **1.** [onlooker] témoin *m* / *the
police are asking for witnesses of* or *to the accident* la police recherche des témoins de l'accident **2.** LAW [in court] témoin *m* ▶ **to call sb as (a) witness** citer qqn comme témoin
▶ **witness for the prosecution / defence** témoin à charge /
décharge ; [to signature, will] témoin *m* **3.** [testimony] ▶ **in
witness of sthg** en témoignage de qqch ▶ **to be** or **to
bear witness to sthg** témoigner de qqch ▶ **to give witness on behalf of sb** témoigner en faveur de qqn **4.** RELIG
témoignage *m*. ◆ vt **1.** [see] être témoin de, témoigner
de **2.** [signature] être témoin de ; [will, document] signer
comme témoin **3.** [experience - change] voir, connaître.

witness box n 🇬🇧 barre *f* des témoins / *in the witness
box* à la barre.

witness stand n 🇺🇸 barre *f* des témoins.

witter ['wɪtər] vi 🇬🇧 *inf & pej* : *they were wittering on
about diets* ils parlaient interminablement de régimes.

witticism ['wɪtɪsɪzm] n bon mot *m*, trait *m* d'esprit.

wittily ['wɪtɪlɪ] adv spirituellement, avec beaucoup d'esprit.

wittingly ['wɪtɪŋlɪ] adv *fml* en connaissance de cause,
sciemment.

witty ['wɪtɪ] (*compar* **wittier,** *superl* **wittiest**) adj spirituel, plein d'esprit.

wives [waɪvz] pl —→ **wife.**

wizard ['wɪzəd] ◆ n **1.** [magician] enchanteur *m*, sorcier *m* **2.** *fig* [expert] génie *m*. ◆ adj 🇬🇧 *inf & dated* épatant. ◆ interj 🇬🇧 *inf & dated* ▶ **wizard!** épatant !

wizardry ['wɪzədrɪ] n **1.** [magic] magie *f*, sorcellerie *f*
2. *fig* [genius] génie *m* / *financial wizardry* le génie de
la finance / *they've installed a new piece of technical wizardry in the office* ils ont installé une nouvelle merveille de
la technique dans le bureau.

wizened ['wɪznd] adj [skin, hands] desséché ; [old person]
desséché, ratatiné ; [face, fruit, vegetables] ratatiné.

wk (written abbr of **week**) sem.

WKD MESSAGING **written abbr of wicked.**

WKND MESSAGING (written abbr of **weekend**) we.

WMD (abbr of **weapons of mass destruction**) pl n
ADM *fpl.*

wo [wəʊ] = **whoa.**

WO n abbr of **warrant officer.**

wobble ['wɒbl] ◆ vi **1.** [hand, jelly, voice] trembler ;
[chair, table] branler, être branlant or bancal ; [compass nee-
dle] osciller ; [drunkard] tituber, chanceler ; [cyclist] aller de
travers, aller en zigzag **2.** *fig* [hesitate, dither] hésiter. ◆ vt
[table] faire basculer. ◆ n : *after a few wobbles, he finally
got going* après avoir cherché son équilibre, il se mit enfin
en route.

wobbly ['wɒblɪ] (*compar* **wobblier,** *superl* **wobbli-
est,** *pl* **wobblies**) ◆ adj **1.** [table, chair] branlant, bancal ;
[pile] chancelant ; [jelly] qui tremble **2.** [hand, voice] tremblant **3.** [line] qui n'est pas droit ; [handwriting] tremblé.
◆ n 🇬🇧 *inf* ▶ **to throw a wobbly** piquer une crise.

woe [wəʊ] *liter & hum* ◆ n malheur *m*, infortune *f* ▶ **a
tale of woe** une histoire pathétique. ◆ interj hélas ▶ **woe is
me!** pauvre de moi !

woeful ['wəʊfʊl] adj **1.** [sad - person, look, news, situ-
ation] malheureux, très triste ; [- scene, tale] affligeant, très
triste **2.** [very poor] lamentable, épouvantable, consternant.

woefully ['wəʊfʊlɪ] adv **1.** [sadly - look, smile] très tristement **2.** [badly - perform, behave] lamentablement.

wok [wɒk] n wok *m* (poêle chinoise).

woke [wəʊk] pt —→ **wake.**

woken ['wəʊkn] pp —→ **wake.**

wolf [wʊlf] (*pl* **wolves** [wʊlvz]) ◆ n **1.** ZOOL loup *m*
2. *inf* [seducer] tombeur *m*. ◆ vt = **wolf down.**
❖ **wolf down** vt sep *inf* [food] engloutir, dévorer.

wolf whistle n sifflement *m* (*au passage d'une femme*).

wolves [wʊlvz] pl —→ **wolf.**

woman ['wʊmən] (*pl* **women** ['wɪmɪn]) ◆ n **1.** [gen]
femme *f* ▶ **the women's page** [in newspaper] la page des
lectrices ▶ **a woman's** or **women's magazine** un magazine féminin **2.** [employee] femme *f* ▶ **(cleaning) woman**
femme de ménage **3.** *inf* [wife] femme *f* ; [lover] maîtresse *f*
▶ **the little woman** ma or la petite femme **4.** *inf* [patron-
izing term of address] ▶ **my good woman** *dated* ma petite
dame / *that's enough, woman!* assez, femme ! ◆ comp
▶ **woman doctor** docteure *f* ▶ **woman driver** conductrice *f*
▶ **woman friend** amie *f* ▶ **woman photographer** photographe *f* ▶ **woman police constable** agente *f* de police
▶ **woman teacher** professeure *f.*

womanhood ['wʊmənhʊd] n (U) **1.** [female nature]
féminité *f* **2.** [women collectively] les femmes *fpl.*

womanize, womanise ['wʊmənaɪz] vi courir les
femmes.

womanizer, womaniser ['wʊmənaɪzər] n coureur *m*
de jupons.

womanly ['wʊmənlɪ] adj [virtue, figure] féminin, de
femme ; [act] digne d'une femme, féminin.

womb [wuːm] n **1.** ANAT utérus *m* **2.** *fig* sein *m*, entrailles *fpl.*

wombat ['wɒmbæt] n wombat *m.*

women ['wɪmɪn] pl —→ **woman.**

women's group n [campaigning organization] groupe
m féministe ; [social club] groupe *m* de femmes.

Women's Institute pr n *association britannique des
femmes au foyer.*

Women's Lib [-'lɪb] n MLF *m*, mouvement *m* de libération de la femme.

Women's Liberation n mouvement *m* de libération
de la femme, MLF *m.*

Women's Movement n mouvement *m* féministe.

women's refuge n refuge *m* pour femmes battues.

women's shelter = **women's refuge.**

won [wʌn] pt & pp —→ **win.**

wonder ['wʌndər] ◆ n **1.** [marvel] merveille *f* **2.** [amaz-
ing event or circumstances] : *it's a wonder that she didn't
resign on the spot* c'est étonnant qu'elle n'ait pas démissionné sur-le-champ / *no wonder they refused* ce n'est
pas étonnant qu'ils aient refusé ▶ **no wonder!** ce n'est pas
étonnant !, cela vous étonne ? **3.** [awe] émerveillement *m*
4. [prodigy] prodige *m*, génie *m* / *a boy wonder* un petit
prodige or génie. ◆ comp [drug, detergent] miracle ; [child]
prodige. ◆ vt **1.** [ask o.s.] se demander / *I wonder where
she's gone* je me demande où elle est allée ; [in polite re-
quests] : *I was wondering if you were free tomorrow* est-
ce que par hasard vous êtes libre demain ? / *I wonder if
you could help me* pourriez-vous m'aider s'il vous plaît ?
2. [be surprised] s'étonner / *I wonder that he wasn't hurt*
je m'étonne or cela m'étonne qu'il n'ait pas été blessé.
◆ vi **1.** [think, reflect] penser, réfléchir **2.** [marvel, be sur-
prised] s'étonner, s'émerveiller ▶ **to wonder at sthg** s'émerveiller de qqch.

wonderful ['wʌndəfʊl] adj [enjoyable] merveilleux, formidable ; [beautiful] superbe, magnifique ; [delicious] excellent ; [astonishing] étonnant, surprenant.

wonderfully ['wʌndəfʊlɪ] adv **1.** *(with adj or adv)* merveilleusement, admirablement **2.** *(with verb)* merveilleusement, à merveille.

wondering ['wʌndərɪŋ] adj [pensive] songeur, pensif ; [surprised] étonné.

wonderland ['wʌndəlænd] n pays *m* des merveilles / *a winter wonderland* un paysage hivernal féerique.

wondrous ['wʌndrəs] *liter* adj merveilleux.

wondrously ['wʌndrəslɪ] adv *liter* merveilleusement.

wonk [wɒŋk] n US *inf* **1.** [hard-worker] bosseur *m*, -euse *f* **2.** [intellectual, expert] intello *mf (qui ne s'intéresse qu'à sa discipline)* ▶ **policy wonk** conseiller *m*, -ère politique.

wonky ['wɒŋkɪ] *(compar* **wonkier**, *superl* **wonkiest)** adj UK *inf* [table] bancal, branlant ; [bicycle] détraqué ; [radio, TV] déréglé, détraqué ; [argument, theory] bancal ; [line] qui n'est pas bien droit.

wont [wəʊnt] *liter* ◆ n coutume *f*, habitude *f* / *as was his / her wont* comme de coutume. ◆ adj ▶ **to be wont to do sthg** avoir l'habitude or coutume de faire qqch.

won't [wəʊnt] abbr of **will not.**

woo [wuː] *(pt & pp* **wooed)** vt **1.** *dated* [court] courtiser, faire la cour à **2.** [attract - customers, voters] chercher à plaire à, rechercher les faveurs de.

wood [wʊd] ◆ n **1.** [timber] bois *m* **2.** [forest, copse] bois *m* **3.** OENOL tonneau *m* **4.** SPORT [in bowls] boule *f* ; [in golf] bois *m*. ◆ comp **1.** [wooden - floor, table, house] en bois, de bois **2.** [for burning wood - stove] à bois ; [-fire] de bois. ◇ **woods** pl n MUS bois *mpl*.

wood-burning adj [stove, boiler] à bois.

woodchip ['wʊdtʃɪp] n [composite wood] aggloméré *m*.

wooded ['wʊdɪd] adj boisé / *densely wooded* très boisé.

wooden ['wʊdn] adj **1.** [made of wood] en bois, de bois **2.** [stiff - gesture, manner] crispé, raide ; [- performance, actor] raide, qui manque de naturel.

wooden spoon n *lit* cuillère *f* en bois ▶ **to win the wooden spoon** UK SPORT gagner la cuillère de bois.

woodland ['wʊdlənd] ◆ n région *f* boisée. ◆ adj [fauna] des bois.

woodlouse ['wʊdlaʊs] *(pl* **woodlice** [-laɪs]) n cloporte *m*.

woodpecker ['wʊd,pekər] n pic *m*, pivert *m*.

woodpigeon ['wʊd,pɪdʒɪn] n ramier *m*.

wood pulp n pâte *f* à papier.

woodshed ['wʊdʃed] n bûcher *m (abri)*.

woodwind ['wʊdwɪnd] ◆ adj [music] pour les bois ▶ **woodwind section** or **instruments** bois *mpl*. ◆ n **1.** [single instrument] bois *m* **2.** *(U)* [family of instruments] bois *mpl*.

woodwork ['wʊdwɜːk] n *(U)* **1.** [craft - carpentry] menuiserie *f* ; [- cabinet-making] ébénisterie *f* **2.** [in building - doors, windows] boiseries *fpl* ; [- beams] charpente *f* **3.** *inf* FOOT poteaux *mpl*.

woodworm ['wʊdwɜːm] n [insect] ver *m* de bois ; *(U)* [infestation] : *the sideboard has got woodworm* le buffet est vermoulu.

woof [wʊf] ◆ n [bark] aboiement *m*. ◆ vi aboyer. ◆ onomat ouah ouah.

wool [wʊl] ◆ n laine *f*. ◆ adj [cloth] de laine ; [socks, dress] en laine.

woolen US = **woollen.**

woollen UK, **woolen** US ['wʊlən] adj **1.** [fabric] de laine ; [jacket, gloves, blanket] en laine **2.** [industry] lainière ; [manufacture] de lainages. ◇ **woollens** UK, **woolens** US pl n lainages *mpl*, vêtements *mpl* de laine.

woolly UK, **wooly** US ['wʊlɪ] ◆ adj **1.** [socks, hat] en laine **2.** [sheep] laineux **3.** [clouds] cotonneux ; [hair] frisé **4.** [vague - thinking, ideas] confus, flou. ◆ n (UK *pl* **woollies** ; US *pl* **woolies**) UK *inf* [pullover] tricot *m*, lainage *m* ; [dress] robe *f* en laine ▶ **winter woollies** lainages *mpl* d'hiver.

woolly-headed adj [person] écervelé ; [ideas] vague, confus.

wooly US = **woolly.**

woozy ['wuːzɪ] *(compar* **woozier**, *superl* **wooziest)** adj *inf* **1.** [dazed] hébété, dans les vapes **2.** [sick] ▶ **to feel woozy** avoir mal au cœur **3.** [from drink] éméché, pompette.

Worcester sauce ['wʊstə-] n sauce épicée *en bouteille*.

Worcs written abbr of **Worcestershire.**

word [wɜːd] ◆ n **1.** [gen & LING] [- written] mot *m* ; [- spoken] mot *m*, parole *f* / *the words of a song* les paroles d'une chanson / *what is the Russian word for "head"?* or *what is the word for "head" in Russian?* comment dit-on «tête» en russe ? / *she can't put her ideas / feelings into words* elle ne trouve pas les mots pour exprimer ses idées / ce qu'elle ressent / *there are no words to describe* or *words cannot describe how I feel* aucun mot ne peut décrire ce que je ressens / *lazy isn't the word for it!* paresseux, c'est peu dire ! / *he's mad, there's no other word for it* il est fou, il n'y a pas d'autre mot / *I don't believe a word of it!* je n'en crois pas un mot ! / *that's my last* or *final word on the matter* c'est mon dernier mot (sur la question) / *I gave him a few words of advice* je lui ai donné quelques conseils / *can I give you a word of warning / advice?* puis-je vous mettre en garde / conseiller ? / *he didn't say a word* il n'a rien dit, il n'a pas dit un mot / *in the words of Shelley* comme l'a dit Shelley / *tell me in your own words* dites-le-moi à votre façon or avec vos propres mots / *he told me in so many words that I was a liar* il m'a dit carrément or sans mâcher ses mots que j'étais menteur ▶ **by** or **through word of mouth** oralement ▶ **word for word** a) [translate] littéralement, mot à mot b) [repeat] mot pour mot ▶ **from the word go** dès le départ ▶ **to take the words out of sb's mouth** : *he took the words out of my mouth* il a dit exactement ce que j'allais dire, il m'a enlevé les mots de la bouche / *he never has a good word to say about anyone* personne ne trouve jamais grâce à ses yeux **2.** [talk] mot *m*, mots *mpl*, parole *f*, paroles *fpl* ▶ **to have a word with sb about sthg** toucher un mot or deux mots à qqn au sujet de qqch / *can I have a word?* je voudrais vous parler un instant **3.** *(U)* [news] nouvelle *f*, nouvelles *fpl* ; [message] message *m*, mot *m* / *word came from Tokyo that the strike was over* la nouvelle arriva de Tokyo que la grève était terminée / *she brought them word of Tom* elle leur a apporté des nouvelles de Tom / *he sent word to say he had arrived safely* il a envoyé un mot pour dire qu'il était bien arrivé **4.** [promise] parole *f*, promesse *f* / *he gave his word that we wouldn't be harmed* il a donné sa parole qu'il ne nous ferait aucun mal ▶ **to break one's word** manquer à sa parole ▶ **to go back on one's word** revenir sur sa parole / *we held* or *kept her to her word* nous l'avons obligée à tenir sa parole / *he was as good as his word* il a tenu parole ▶ **word of honour!** parole d'honneur ! / *we only have his word for it* il n'y a que lui qui le dit, personne ne peut prouver le contraire / *we'll have to take your word for it* nous sommes bien obligés de vous croire / *it's your word against mine* c'est votre parole contre la mienne **5.** [advice] conseil *m* ▶ **a word to the wise** à bon entendeur, salut **6.** [rumour] bruit *m* / *(the) word went round that he was dying* le bruit a couru qu'il était sur le point de mourir. ◆ vt [letter, document] rédiger, formuler ; [contract] rédiger / *they worded the petition carefully* ils ont choisi les termes de la pétition avec le plus grand soin / *we sent a strongly worded protest* nous avons envoyé une lettre de protestation bien sentie. ❖ **words** pl n [UK] *inf* [argument] dispute *f* ▶ **to have words** se disputer, avoir des mots. ❖ **in a word** adv phr en un mot. ❖ **in other words** adv phr autrement dit, en d'autres termes.

 mot or **parole?**

Un mot is a word in the most general sense, while **une parole** refers specifically to the spoken word. The two are sometimes interchangeable, but note that written words are **mots** rather than **paroles**, and that the words to a song are **paroles**, not **mots**.

word-for-word adj [repetition, imitation] mot pour mot ; [translation] littéral.

word game n jeu de lettres.

wording ['wɜ:dɪŋ] n *(U)* **1.** [of letter, speech] termes *mpl*, formulation *f* ; [of contract] termes *mpl* **2.** ADMIN & LAW rédaction *f*.

word-of-mouth adj [account] oral, verbal.

word-perfect adj [recitation] que l'on connaît parfaitement or sur le bout des doigts.

wordplay ['wɜ:dpleɪ] n *(U)* jeu *m* de mots.

word processing n traitement *m* de texte.

word processor n machine *f* de traitement de texte.

word wrap n COMPUT bouclage *m*.

wordy ['wɜ:dɪ] *(compar* wordier, *superl* wordiest) adj verbeux.

wore [wɔ:ʳ] pt ⟶ **wear.**

work [wɜ:k]
◆ n **1.** [effort, activity] travail *m*, œuvre *f* / *she's done a lot of work for charity* elle a beaucoup travaillé pour des associations caritatives / *keep up the good work!* continuez comme ça ! / *work on the tunnel is to start in March* **a)** [existing tunnel] les travaux sur le tunnel doivent commencer en mars **b)** [new tunnel] la construction du tunnel doit commencer or le tunnel doit être commencé en mars ▶ **work in progress a)** ADMIN travail en cours **b)** [on sign] travaux en cours / *she put a lot of work into that book* elle a beaucoup travaillé sur ce livre ▶ **to start work, to set to work** se mettre au travail **2.** [duty, task] travail *m*, besogne *f* / *it's hard work* c'est du travail, ce n'est pas facile **3.** [paid employment] travail *m*, emploi *m* / *what (kind of) work do you do?* qu'est-ce que vous faites dans la vie ?, quel travail faites-vous ? ▶ **to look for work** chercher du travail or un emploi ▶ **to be in work** travailler, avoir un emploi ▶ **to be out of work** être au chômage or sans travail or sans emploi ▶ **to take time off work** prendre des congés / *she's off work today* elle ne travaille pas aujourd'hui **4.** [place of employment] travail *m* ; ADMIN lieu *m* de travail / *where is your (place of) work?* où travaillez-vous ?, quel est votre lieu de travail ? **5.** [papers, material, etc. being worked on] travail *m* **6.** [creation, artefact, etc.] œuvre *f* ; [on smaller scale] ouvrage *m* ; SEW ouvrage *m* / *it's all my own work* j'ai tout fait moi-même / *the complete works of Shakespeare* les œuvres complètes or l'œuvre de Shakespeare / *a work of art* une œuvre d'art / *works of fiction* des ouvrages de fiction **7.** [research] travail *m*, recherches *fpl*.
◆ vi

A. ACTIVITY, EMPLOYMENT, STUDIES **1.** [exert effort on a specific task, activity, etc.] travailler / *we worked for hours cleaning the house* nous avons passé des heures à faire le ménage ▶ **to work at** or **on sthg**: *she's working on a novel*

just now elle travaille à un roman en ce moment **2.** [be employed] travailler / *he works as a teacher* il a un poste d'enseignant / *I work in advertising* je travaille dans la publicité **3.** [strive for a specific goal or aim] ▶ **to work for sthg**: *they're working for better international relations* ils s'efforcent d'améliorer les relations internationales **4.** [study] travailler, étudier.

B. FUNCTION OR SUCCEED **1.** [function, operate - machine, brain, system] fonctionner, marcher / *the lift never works* l'ascenseur est toujours en panne / *the radio works off batteries* la radio fonctionne avec des piles ; *fig* : *your idea just won't work* ton idée ne peut pas marcher **2.** [produce results, succeed] marcher, réussir / *it worked brilliantly* ça a très bien marché **3.** [drug, medicine] agir, produire or faire son effet **4.** [act] agir / *events have worked against us / in our favour* les événements ont agi contre nous / en notre faveur.
◆ vt

A. USE, EXPLOIT OR ACCOMPLISH **1.** [worker, employee] faire travailler / *you work yourself too hard* tu te surmènes **2.** [pay for with labour or service] : *I worked my way through college* j'ai travaillé pour payer mes études à l'université **3.** [achieve, accomplish] ▶ **to work miracles** faire or accomplir des miracles ▶ **to work wonders** faire merveille.

B. CONTROL OR MANOEUVRE **1.** [operate] faire marcher, faire fonctionner **2.** [manoeuvre] : *I worked the handle up and down* j'ai remué la poignée de haut en bas ; [progress slowly] : *I worked my way along the ledge* j'ai longé la saillie avec précaution **3.** *inf* [contrive] s'arranger / *I worked it* or *worked things so that she's never alone* j'ai fait en sorte qu'elle or je me suis arrangé pour qu'elle ne soit jamais seule.

C. SHAPE OR PROVOKE **1.** [shape - leather, metal, stone] travailler, façonner ; [- clay, dough] travailler, pétrir ; [- object, sculpture] façonner **2.** [excite, provoke] : *she worked herself into a rage* elle s'est mise dans une colère noire. ❖ **works** ◆ pl n **1.** [mechanism] mécanisme *m*, rouages *mpl* ; [of clock] mouvement *m* **2.** CIV ENG [construction] travaux *mpl* ; [installation] installations *fpl*. ◆ n *(with singular verb)* **1.** INDUST [factory] usine *f* **2.** *inf* [everything] ▶ **the (whole) works** tout le bataclan or le tralala ▶ **to give sb the works a)** [special treatment] dérouler le tapis rouge pour qqn *fig* **b)** [beating] passer qqn à tabac. ❖ **at work** ◆ adj phr [person] ▶ **to be at work (on) sthg / doing sthg** travailler (à) qqch / à faire qqch. ◆ adv phr [at place of work] : *she's at work* **a)** [gen] elle est au travail **b)** [office] elle est au bureau **c)** [factory] elle est à l'usine. ❖ **work off** vt sep **1.** [dispose of - fat, weight] se débarrasser de, éliminer ; [- anxiety, frustration] passer, assouvir **2.** [debt, obligation] : *it took him three months to work off his debt* il a dû travailler trois mois pour rembourser son emprunt. ❖ **work on** vt insep **1.** [person] essayer de convaincre / *I'll work on her* je vais m'occuper d'elle **2.** [task, problem] : *have you got any ideas? — I'm working on it* as-tu des idées ? — je cherche. ❖ **work out** ◆ vt sep **1.** [solve - calculation, problem] résoudre ; [- answer, total] trouver ; [- puzzle] faire, résoudre ; [- code] déchiffrer / *things will work themselves out* les choses s'arrangeront toutes seules or d'elles-mêmes **2.** [formulate - idea, plan] élaborer, combiner ; [- agreement, details] mettre au point **3.** [figure out] arriver à comprendre / *I finally worked out why he was acting so strangely* j'ai enfin découvert or compris pourquoi il se comportait si bizarrement / *I can't work her out* je n'arrive pas à la comprendre. ◆ vi **1.** [happen] se passer / *the trip worked out as planned* le voyage s'est déroulé comme prévu / *it all worked out for the best* tout a fini par s'arranger pour le mieux **2.** [have a good result - job, plan] réussir ; [- problem, puzzle] se résoudre / *it didn't work out between them* les choses ont plutôt mal tourné entre eux **3.** [amount to] : *electric heating works out expensive* le chauffage électrique revient cher **4.** [exercise] faire de l'exercice ; [professional athlete] s'entraîner. **◆ work through** vt insep **1.** [continue to work] : *she worked through lunch* elle a travaillé pendant l'heure du déjeuner **2.** [resolve] : *he worked through his emotional problems* il a réussi à assumer ses problèmes affectifs. **◆ work up ◆** vt sep **1.** [stir up, rouse] exciter, provoquer / *he works himself up* or *gets himself worked up over nothing* il s'énerve pour rien **2.** [develop] développer / *to work up an appetite* se mettre en appétit / *I can't work up any enthusiasm for this work* je n'arrive pas à avoir le moindre enthousiasme pour ce travail **3.** PHR **to work one's way up** faire son chemin / *I worked my way up from nothing* je suis parti de rien. **◆** vi [build up] : *the film was working up to a climax* le film approchait de son point culminant / *what are you working up to?* où veux-tu en venir ?

workable ['wɜːkəbl] adj **1.** [plan, proposal] réalisable, faisable **2.** [mine, field] exploitable.

workaday ['wɜːkədeɪ] adj [clothes, routine] de tous les jours ; [man] ordinaire, banal ; [incident] courant, banal.

workaholic [ˌwɜːkə'hɒlɪk] n *inf* bourreau *m* de travail, drogué *m*, -e *f* du travail.

workbasket ['wɜːkˌbɑːskɪt] n corbeille *f* à ouvrage.

workbench ['wɜːkbentʃ] n établi *m*.

workbook ['wɜːkbʊk] n **1.** SCH [exercise book] cahier *m* d'exercices ; [record book] cahier *m* de classe **2.** [manual] manuel *m*.

workday ['wɜːkdeɪ] **◆** n **1.** [day's work] journée *f* de travail **2.** [working day] jour *m* ouvré or où l'on travaille. **◆** adj = **workaday**.

worked up [ˌwɜːkt-] adj énervé, dans tous ses états **▶ to get worked up** s'énerver, se mettre dans tous ses états.

worker ['wɜːkə*] n **1.** [INDUST - gen] travailleur *m*, -euse *f*, employé *m*, -e *f* ; [- manual] ouvrier *m*, -ère *f*, travailleur *m*, -euse *f* **2.** ENTOM ouvrière *f*.

work ethic n *exaltation des valeurs liées au travail*.

work experience n : *the course includes two months' work experience* le programme comprend un stage en entreprise de deux mois.

workflow ['wɜːkfləʊ] n workflow *m* (*modélisation de la gestion des processus opérationnels*).

workforce ['wɜːkfɔːs] n main-d'œuvre *f*, effectifs *mpl*.

workhouse ['wɜːkhaʊs] (*pl* **workhouses** [-haʊzɪz]) n [in US - prison] maison *f* de correction.

work-in n *occupation d'une entreprise par le personnel (avec poursuite du travail)*.

working ['wɜːkɪŋ] **◆** adj **1.** [mother] qui travaille ; [population] actif **2.** [day, hours] de travail **▶ a working breakfast / lunch** un petit déjeuner / déjeuner de travail **3.** [clothes, conditions] de travail / *we have a close working relationship* nous travaillons bien ensemble **4.** [functioning - farm, factory, model] qui marche **▶ in (good) working order** en (bon) état de marche **5.** [theory, definition] de travail ; [majority] suffisant ; [agreement] de circonstance ; [knowledge] adéquat, suffisant. **◆** n **1.** [work] travail *m* **2.** [operation - of machine] fonctionnement *m* **3.** [of mine] exploitation *f* ; [of clay, leather] travail *m*. **◆ workings** pl n **1.** [mechanism] mécanisme *m* ; *fig* [of government, system] rouages *mpl* **2.** MIN chantier *m* d'exploitation.

working capital n (U) fonds *mpl* de roulement.

working class n : *the working class* or *the working classes* la classe ouvrière, le prolétariat. **◆ working-class** adj [district, origins] ouvrier ; [accent] des classes populaires.

working group = **working party**.

working lunch n déjeuner *m* de travail.

working majority n majorité *f* suffisante.

working man n UK ouvrier *m*.

working party n **1.** [committee - for study] groupe *m* de travail ; [- for enquiry] commission *f* d'enquête **2.** [group - of prisoners, soldiers] groupe *m* de travail.

working title n titre *m* provisoire.

workload ['wɜːkləʊd] n travail *m* à effectuer, charge *f* de travail.

workman ['wɜːkmən] (*pl* **workmen** [-mən]) n **1.** [manual worker] ouvrier *m* **▶ workmen's compensation** US indemnité *f* pour accident de travail **2.** [craftsman] artisan *m*.

workmanlike ['wɜːkmənlaɪk] adj **1.** [efficient - approach, person] professionnel **2.** [well made - artefact] bien fait, soigné **3.** [serious - attempt, effort] sérieux.

workmanship ['wɜːkmənʃɪp] n (U) **1.** [skill] métier *m*, maîtrise *f* **2.** [quality] exécution *f*, fabrication *f*.

workmate ['wɜːkmeɪt] n camarade *mf* de travail.

workout ['wɜːkaʊt] n séance *f* d'entraînement.

work permit [-ˌpɜːmɪt] n permis *m* de travail.

workplace ['wɜːkpleɪs] n lieu *m* de travail / *in the workplace* sur le lieu de travail.

workroom ['wɜːkrʊm] n salle *f* de travail.

works committee, works council n comité *m* d'entreprise.

workshare ['wɜːkʃeə*] n travail *m* en temps partagé ; [person] travailleur *m*, -euse *f* en temps partagé.

work sheet n COMPUT feuille *f* de travail.

workshop ['wɜːkʃɒp] n **1.** INDUST [gen] atelier *m* **2.** [study group] atelier *m*, groupe *m* de travail.

workshy ['wɜːkʃaɪ] adj fainéant, tire-au-flanc (*inv*).

workspace ['wɜːkspeɪs] n COMPUT bureau *m*.

workstation ['wɜːkˌsteɪʃn] n COMPUT poste *m* or station *f* de travail.

work surface n surface *f* de travail.

worktable ['wɜːkˌteɪbl] n table *f* de travail.

worktop ['wɜːktɒp] n [in kitchen] plan *m* de travail.

work-to-rule n UK grève *f* du zèle.

work week n US semaine *f* de travail.

world [wɜːld]
◆ n

A. PLANET 1. [earth] monde *m* **▶ to travel round the world** faire le tour du monde, voyager autour du monde **▶ to see the world** voir du pays, courir le monde / *throughout the world* dans le monde entier / *in this part of the world* dans cette région / *the world over* or *all over the world* dans le monde entier, partout dans le monde **2.** [planet] monde *m* **3.** [universe] monde *m*, univers *m*.

B. SOCIETY OR POPULATION 1. HIST & POL [part of the world] monde *m* / *the developing world* les pays *mpl* en (voie de) développement / *the Spanish-speaking world* le monde hispanophone **2.** [society] monde *m* **▶ to go up / down in the world** : *she's gone up in the world* elle a fait du chemin **▶ to come into the world** venir au monde **▶ to bring a child into the world** mettre un enfant au monde **▶ to make one's way in the world** faire son chemin **3.** [general public] monde *m* / *the news shook the world* la nouvelle a ébranlé le monde entier ; [people in general] : *we don't want the whole world to know* nous ne voulons pas que tout le monde le sache.

C. DOMAIN OR WAY OF LIFE 1. [existence, particular way of life] monde *m*, vie *f* / *we live in different worlds* nous ne vivons pas sur la même planète **▶ to be worlds apart a)** [in lifestyle] avoir des styles de vie complètement différents **b)** [in opinions] avoir des opinions complètement différentes ; [realm] monde *m* / *he lives in a world of his own* il vit dans un monde à lui / *the child's world* l'univers *m* des enfants **2.** [field, domain] monde *m*, milieu *m*, milieux *mpl* / *the publishing world* le monde de l'édition **3.** [group of living things] monde *m* / *the animal* / *plant world* le règne animal / végétal.

D. SPIRITUAL SENSE RELIG monde *m* / *he isn't long for this world* il n'en a pas pour longtemps.

E. SET PHRASES ❭ **to do sb a** or **the world of good**: *a holiday will do you a* or *the world of good* des vacances vous feront le plus grand bien ❭ **to make a world of difference**: *it made a world of difference* ça a tout changé ❭ **to think the world of sb**: *he thinks the world of his daughter* il a une admiration sans bornes pour sa fille ❭ **to mean the world to sb**: *it means the world to me* c'est quelque chose qui me tient beaucoup à cœur.

◆ comp [champion, record] mondial, du monde; [language, religion] universel ❭ **world economy** économie *f* mondiale ❭ **world opinion** l'opinion internationale ❭ **world peace** la paix mondiale ❭ **on a world scale** à l'échelle mondiale. ❖ **for all the world** adv phr exactement. ❖ **for the world** adv phr : *I wouldn't hurt her for the world* je ne lui ferais de mal pour rien au monde. ❖ **in the world** adv phr **1.** [for emphasis] : *nothing in the world would change my mind* rien au monde ne me ferait changer d'avis / *I felt as if I hadn't a care in the world* je me sentais libre de tout souci / *we've got all the time in the world* nous avons tout le or tout notre temps / *I wouldn't do it for all the money in the world!* je ne le ferais pas pour tout l'or du monde ! **2.** [expressing surprise, irritation, frustration] : *where in the world have you put it?* où l'avez-vous donc mis ? ❖ **out of this world** adj phr *inf* extraordinaire, sensationnel.

World Bank pr n Banque *f* mondiale.

world-beating adj *inf* [performance, achievement] inégalé, qui surpasse tous les autres.

world-class adj [player, runner] parmi les meilleurs du monde, de classe internationale.

World Cup pr n ❭ **the World Cup** la Coupe du monde.

world-famous adj de renommée mondiale, célèbre dans le monde entier.

World Health Organization pr n Organisation *f* mondiale de la santé.

worldly ['wɜːldlɪ] (compar **worldlier**, superl **worldliest**) adj **1.** [material - possessions, pleasures, matters] matériel, de ce monde, terrestre ; RELIG temporel, de ce monde **2.** [materialistic - person, outlook] matérialiste **3.** [sophisticated - person] qui a l'expérience du monde ; [- attitude, manner] qui démontre une expérience du monde.

worldly-wise adj qui a l'expérience du monde.

world music n musiques *fpl* du monde.

world power n puissance *f* mondiale.

World Series n ❭ **the World Series** le championnat américain de base-ball.

World Trade Organization n COMM Organisation *f* mondiale du commerce.

world view n *vue métaphysique du monde.*

world war n guerre *f* mondiale ❭ **World War I, the First World War** la Première Guerre mondiale ❭ **World War II, the Second World War** la Seconde Guerre mondiale.

world-weary adj [person] las du monde.

worldwide ['wɜːldwaɪd] ◆ adj [depression, famine, reputation] mondial. ◆ adv partout dans le monde, dans le monde entier.

World Wide Web n ❭ **the World Wide Web** le Web, la Toile.

worm [wɜːm] ◆ n **1.** [in earth, garden] ver *m* (de terre) ; [in fruit] ver *m* ; [for fishing] ver *m*, asticot *m* **2.** [parasite - in body] ver *m* **3.** *inf & fig* [person] minable *mf* **4.** [computer program] ver *m*. ◆ vt **1.** [move] ❭ **to worm one's way under sthg** passer sous qqch à plat ventre or en rampant / *she wormed her way through a gap in the fence* en se tortillant elle s'est faufilée par une ouverture dans la palissade **2.** *pej* [sneak] : *he wormed his way into her affections* il a trouvé le chemin de son cœur (*par sournoiserie*) **3.** [dog, sheep] débarrasser de ses vers. ❖ **worm out** vt sep [information] soutirer / *I tried to worm the truth out of him* j'ai essayé de lui soutirer la vérité.

WORM (abbr of write once read many times) COMPUT WORM.

worn [wɔːn] ◆ pp ⟶ **wear**. ◆ adj **1.** [shoes, rug, tyre] usé **2.** [weary - person] las (lasse).

worn-out adj **1.** [shoes, tyre] complètement usé ; [rug, dress] usé jusqu'à la corde ; [battery] usé **2.** [person] épuisé, éreinté.

worried ['wʌrɪd] adj [person, look] inquiet (inquiète) / *I'm worried that they may get lost* or *in case they get lost* j'ai peur qu'ils ne se perdent ❭ **to be worried about sthg** / **sb** être inquiet pour qqch / qqn.

worriedly ['wʌrɪdlɪ] adv [say] avec un air inquiet.

worrier ['wʌrɪə'] n anxieux *m*, -euse *f*, inquiet *m*, -ète *f*.

worry ['wʌrɪ] (pt & pp **worried**, pl **worries**) ◆ vt **1.** [make anxious] inquiéter, tracasser **2.** [disturb, bother] inquiéter, ennuyer **3.** [subj: dog - bone, ball] prendre entre les dents et secouer ; [- sheep] harceler. ◆ vi s'inquiéter, se faire du souci, se tracasser ❭ **to worry about** or **over sthg** s'inquiéter pour or au sujet de qqch. ◆ n **1.** [anxiety] inquiétude *f*, souci *m* **2.** [concern] sujet *m* d'inquiétude, souci *m* ; [problem] problème *m* ❭ **no worries!** *inf* pas de problème ! ❖ **worry at** vt insep UK = **worry** (vt).

worrying ['wʌrɪɪŋ] ◆ adj inquiétant. ◆ n inquiétude *f*.

worryingly ['wʌrɪɪŋlɪ] adv : *the project is worryingly late* le projet a pris un retard inquiétant.

worse [wɜːs] (adj compar of **bad**, adv compar of **badly**) ◆ adj **1.** [not as good, pleasant as] pire, plus mauvais ❭ **to get** or **to grow worse** empirer, s'aggraver ❭ **to get worse and worse** aller de mal en pis **2.** [in health] plus mal. ◆ adv **1.** [less well] plus mal, moins bien **2.** [more severely - snow, rain] plus fort. ◆ n pire *m* / *there's worse to come* or *worse is to come* a) [in situation] le pire est à venir b) [in story] il y a pire encore ❭ **to take a turn for the worse** [health, situation] se détériorer, se dégrader. ❖ **none the worse** adj phr pas plus mal / *he's apparently none the worse for his drinking session last night* il n'a pas l'air de se ressentir de sa beuverie d'hier soir / *the little girl is none the worse for the experience* la petite fille ne se ressent pas de son expérience.

worsen ['wɜːsn] ◆ vi [depression, crisis, pain, illness] empirer, s'aggraver ; [weather, situation] se gâter, se détériorer. ◆ vt [situation] empirer, rendre pire.

worsening ['wɜːsnɪŋ] ◆ adj [situation] qui empire ; [health] qui se détériore ; [weather] qui se gâte or se détériore. ◆ n aggravation *f*, détérioration *f*.

worship ['wɜːʃɪp] (UK pt & pp **worshipped**, cont **worshipping** / US pt & pp **worshiped**, cont **worshiping**) ◆ n **1.** RELIG [service] culte *m*, office *m* ; [liturgy] liturgie *f* ; [adoration] adoration *f* **2.** *fig* [veneration] adoration *f*, culte *m*. ◆ vt **1.** RELIG adorer, vénérer **2.** [person] adorer, vénérer ; [money, possessions] vouer un culte à, avoir le culte de. ◆ vi faire ses dévotions. ❖ **Worship** n UK *fml* [in titles] ❭ **Your Worship a)** [to a judge] Monsieur le Juge **b)** [to a mayor] Monsieur le Maire.

worshiper US = **worshipper**.

worshipper 🇬🇧, **worshiper** 🇺🇸 ['wɜːʃɪpəʳ] n
1. RELIG adorateur *m*, -trice *f*, fidèle *mf* **2.** *fig* [of possessions, person] adorateur *m*, -trice *f*.

worst [wɜːst] *(adj superl of bad, adv superl of badly)*
◆ adj **1.** [least good, pleasant, etc.] le pire, le plus mauvais **2.** [most severe, serious - disaster, error] le plus grave ;
[- winter] le plus rude. ◆ adv [most severely] : *the worst affected* le plus affecté or touché. ◆ n **1.** [worst thing] pire *m* **2.** [worst person] ▸ **the worst** le / la pire de tous.
◆ vt *liter* [opponent, rival] battre, avoir le dessus sur.
❖ **at (the) worst** *conj phr* au pire, dans le pire des cas.

worst-case adj ▸ **the worst-case scenario** le scénario catastrophe.

worsted ['wʊstɪd] ◆ n worsted *m*, laine *f* peignée.
◆ adj [suit] en worsted, en laine peignée ▸ **worsted cloth** worsted *m*, laine *f* peignée.

worth [wɜːθ] ◆ adj **1.** [financially, in value] : *to be worth £40,000* valoir 40 000 livres / *how much is the picture worth?* combien vaut le tableau ? / *it isn't worth much* cela ne vaut pas grand-chose / *his uncle is worth several million pounds* la fortune de son oncle s'élève à plusieurs millions de livres / *it was worth every penny* ça en valait vraiment la peine ▸ **(to be) worth one's salt** 🇬🇧 : *any proofreader worth his salt would have spotted the mistake* n'importe quel correcteur digne de ce nom aurait relevé l'erreur **2.** [emotionally] : *it's worth a lot to me* j'y attache beaucoup de valeur or de prix / *their friendship is worth a lot to her* leur amitié a beaucoup de prix pour elle **3.** [valid, deserving] : *the church is (well) worth a visit* l'église vaut la peine d'être visitée or vaut le détour / *it's worth a try* or *trying* cela vaut la peine d'essayer / *it wasn't worth the effort* cela ne valait pas la peine de faire un tel effort, ça n'en valait pas la peine **4.** [for sb's benefit] 🇬🇧 : *to be worth sb's while* : *it would be worth your while to check* or *checking* vous auriez intérêt à vérifier / *it's not worth (my) while waiting* cela ne vaut pas la peine d'attendre or que j'attende / *I'll make it worth your while* je vous récompenserai or de votre peine ▸ **for what it's worth** pour ce que cela vaut. ◆ n
1. [in money, value] valeur *f* / *£2,000 worth of damage* pour 2 000 livres de dégâts, des dégâts qui se montent à 2 000 livres **2.** [of person] valeur *f* / *she knows her own worth* elle sait ce qu'elle vaut, elle connaît sa propre valeur **3.** [equivalent value] équivalent *m* / *a week's worth of supplies* suffisamment de provisions pour une semaine.

worthless ['wɜːθlɪs] adj **1.** [goods, land, etc.] sans valeur, qui ne vaut rien **2.** [useless - attempt] inutile ; [- advice, suggestion] inutile, sans valeur **3.** [person] incapable, qui ne vaut rien.

worthlessness ['wɜːθlɪsnɪs] n **1.** [of goods, land, etc.] absence *f* totale de valeur **2.** [of attempt] inutilité *f* ; [of advice, suggestion] inutilité *f* **3.** [of person] nullité *f*.

worthwhile [ˌwɜːθ'waɪl] adj **1.** [useful - action, visit] qui vaut la peine ; [- job] utile, qui a un sens **2.** [deserving - cause, project, organization] louable, méritoire **3.** [interesting - book] qui vaut la peine d'être lu ; [- film] qui vaut la peine d'être vu.

worthy ['wɜːðɪ] *(compar* **worthier**, *superl* **worthiest**, *pl* **worthies**) ◆ adj **1.** [deserving - person] digne, méritant ; [- cause] louable, digne ▸ **to be worthy of sthg** être digne de or mériter qqch ▸ **to be worthy to do sthg** être digne de or mériter de faire qqch **2.** *hum* excellent, brave.
◆ n [important person] notable *mf* ; *hum* brave citoyen *m*, -enne *f*.

wot [wɒt] 🇬🇧 *inf* = **what**.

WOT MESSAGING **(written abbr of what)** koi, koa, kwa.

would [wʊd] ◆ pt ⟶ **will**. ◆ modal vb **1.** [speculating, hypothesizing] : *I'm sure they would come if you asked them* je suis sûr qu'ils viendraient si vous le leur

demandiez / *I wouldn't do that if I were you* je ne ferais pas ça si j'étais vous or à votre place / *you would think they had better things to do* on pourrait penser qu'ils ont mieux à faire / *she would have been 16 by now* elle aurait 16 ans maintenant **2.** [making polite offers, requests] : *would you please be quiet!* voulez-vous vous taire, s'il vous plaît ! / *would you mind driving me home?* est-ce que cela vous dérangerait de me reconduire chez moi ? **3.** [expressing preferences, desires] : *I would prefer to go* or *I would rather go alone* j'aimerais mieux or je préférerais y aller seul / *I would have preferred to go* or *I would rather have gone alone* j'aurais mieux aimé or j'aurais préféré y aller seul **4.** [indicating willingness, responsiveness - subj: person, mechanism] : *they would give their lives for the cause* ils donneraient leur vie pour la cause / *she wouldn't touch alcohol* elle refusait de toucher à l'alcool **5.** [indicating habitual or characteristic behaviour] : *he would smoke a cigar after dinner* il fumait un cigare après le dîner / *they would go and break something!* il fallait qu'ils aillent casser quelque chose ! / *he would!* c'est bien de lui ! **6.** [expressing opinions] : *I would imagine it's warmer than here* j'imagine qu'il fait plus chaud qu'ici / *I would think he'd be pleased* j'aurais cru que ça lui ferait plaisir **7.** [giving advice] : *I would have a word with her about it(, if I were you)* moi, je lui en parlerais (à votre place) **8.** [expressing surprise, incredulity] : *you wouldn't think she was only 15, would you?* on ne dirait pas qu'elle n'a que 15 ans, n'est-ce pas ? / *who would have thought it?* qui l'aurait cru ? **9.** [indicating likelihood, probability] : *there was a woman there — that would be his wife* il y avait une femme — ça devait être sa femme **10.** [used with 'have'] : *they would have been happy if it hadn't been for the war* ils auraient vécu heureux si la guerre n'était pas survenue.

would-be adj **1.** [hopeful] : *a would-be writer / MP* une personne qui veut être écrivain / député **2.** *pej* [so-called] prétendu, soi-disant *(inv)*.

wouldn't ['wʊdnt] abbr of **would not**.

would've ['wʊdəv] abbr of **would have**.

wound[1] [wuːnd] ◆ n **1.** [physical injury] blessure *f*, plaie *f* **2.** *fig* [emotional or moral] blessure *f*. ◆ vt **1.** [physically] blesser **2.** *fig* [emotionally] blesser.

wound[2] [waʊnd] pt & pp ⟶ **wind**.

wounded ['wuːndɪd] ◆ adj **1.** [soldier, victim] blessé **2.** *fig* [feelings, pride] blessé. ◆ pl n ▸ **the wounded** les blessés *mpl*.

wounding ['wuːndɪŋ] adj *fig* [hurtful] blessant.

wound-up [waʊnd-] adj **1.** [clock] remonté ; [car window] remonté, fermé **2.** *inf* [tense - person] crispé, très tendu.

wove [wəʊv] pt ⟶ **weave**.

woven ['wəʊvn] pp ⟶ **weave**.

wow [waʊ] *inf* ◆ interj génial !, super ! ◆ n **1.** : *it's a real wow!* c'est vraiment super ! / *he's a wow at hockey* c'est un super joueur de hockey **2.** ACOUST pleurage *m*.
◆ vt [impress] impressionner, emballer, subjuguer.

wow factor n : *the wow factor kicks in as soon as you go through the door* dès qu'on franchit le seuil on est impressionné / *the house was OK, but it didn't have a wow factor* la maison n'était pas mal, mais elle n'avait rien d'exceptionnel / *the building's wow factor is its roof terrace* ce qui impressionne dans ce bâtiment, c'est avant tout la terrasse sur le toit.

WP n **(abbr of word processing, word processor)** TTX *m*.

WPC **(abbr of woman police constable)** n 🇬🇧 femme agent de police / *WPC Roberts* l'agent Roberts.

wpm **(written abbr of words per minute)** mots/min.

wrangle ['ræŋgl] ◆ vi se disputer, se chamailler ▶ **to wrangle about** or **over sthg** se disputer à propos de qqch. ◆ vt 🇺🇸 [cattle, horses] garder. ◆ n dispute f.

wrap [ræp] (*pt & pp* **wrapped**) ◆ vt **1.** [goods, parcel, gift, food] emballer, envelopper / *she wrapped the scarf in tissue paper* elle a emballé or enveloppé l'écharpe dans du papier de soie **2.** [cocoon, envelop] envelopper, emmailloter / *the baby was wrapped in a blanket* le bébé était enveloppé dans une couverture **3.** [twist, wind] ▶ **to wrap round** or **around** enrouler / *she had a towel wrapped round her head* sa tête était enveloppée dans une serviette / *she had a towel wrapped round her body* elle s'était enveloppée dans une serviette / *he wrapped his arms round her* il l'a prise dans ses bras. ◆ n **1.** [housecoat] peignoir m ; [shawl] châle m ; [over ballgown] sortie-de-bal f ; [blanket, rug] couverture f **2.** CULIN wrap m (*sorte de sandwich sous forme de galette enroulée autour d'une garniture*) **3.** CIN ▶ **it's a wrap!** c'est dans la boîte ! ⬩ **wraps** pl n *fig* ▶ **to keep a plan** / **one's feelings under wraps** garder un plan secret / ses sentiments secrets. ⬩ **wrap up** ◆ vt sep **1.** [goods, parcel, gift, food] envelopper, emballer, empaqueter / *he wrapped the sandwiches up in foil* il a enveloppé les sandwiches dans du papier d'aluminium **2.** [person - in clothes, blanket] envelopper / *wrap him up in a blanket* enveloppez-le dans une couverture / *she was well wrapped up in a thick coat* elle était bien emmitouflée dans un épais manteau / *wrap yourself up warmly* couvrez-vous bien **3.** *fig* : *politicians are skilled at wrapping up bad news in an acceptable form* les politiciens s'y connaissent pour présenter les mauvaises nouvelles sous un jour acceptable **4.** *inf* [conclude - job] terminer, conclure ; [- deal, contract] conclure, régler / *let's get this matter wrapped up* finissons-en avec cette question **5.** 🇺🇸 [summarize] résumer / *she wrapped up her talk with three points* elle a résumé son discours en trois points **6.** [engross] ▶ **to be wrapped up in sthg** être absorbé par qqch / *she's very wrapped up in herself* elle est très repliée sur elle-même. ◆ vi **1.** [dress] s'habiller, se couvrir / *wrap up warmly* or *well!* couvrez-vous bien ! **2.** 🇬🇧 *v inf* [shut up] ▶ **wrap up!** la ferme !

wraparound ['ræpə,raʊnd] ◆ adj [skirt] portefeuille *(inv)* ; ▶ **wraparound sunglasses** lunettes fpl de soleil panoramiques. ◆ n **1.** [skirt] jupe f portefeuille **2.** COMPUT bouclage m. ⬩ **wraparounds** pl n [sunglasses] lunettes fpl de soleil panoramiques.

wrapped [ræpt] adj [bread, cheese] préemballé.

wrapper ['ræpər] n **1.** [for sweet] papier m ; [for parcel] papier m d'emballage **2.** [cover - on book] jaquette f ; [- on magazine, newspaper] bande f **3.** [housecoat] peignoir m.

wrapping ['ræpɪŋ] n [on parcel] papier m d'emballage ; [on sweet] papier m.

wrapping paper n [for gift] papier m cadeau ; [for parcel] papier m d'emballage.

wrath [rɒθ] n *liter* colère f, courroux m.

wreak [ri:k] vt **1.** (*pt & pp* **wreaked** or **wrought** [rɔ:t]) [cause - damage, chaos] causer, provoquer ▶ **to wreak havoc** faire des ravages, mettre sens dessus dessous **2.** [inflict - revenge, anger] assouvir ▶ **to wreak vengeance on sb** assouvir sa vengeance sur qqn.

wreath [ri:θ] (*pl* **wreaths** [ri:ðz]) n **1.** [for funeral] couronne f **2.** [garland] guirlande f **3.** *fig* [of mist] nappe f ; [of smoke] volute f.

wreathe [ri:ð] ◆ vt **1.** [shroud] envelopper **2.** [with flowers - person] couronner ; [- grave, window] orner. ◆ vi [smoke] monter en volutes.

wreck [rek] ◆ n **1.** [wrecked remains - of ship] épave f ; [- of plane] avion m accidenté, épave f ; [- of train] train m accidenté ; [- of car, lorry, bus] véhicule m accidenté, épave f

2. [wrecking - of ship] naufrage m ; [- of plane, car] accident m ; [- of train] déraillement m **3.** *inf* [dilapidated car] guimbarde f ; [old bike] clou m **4.** *inf* [person] épave f, loque f **5.** *fig* [of hopes, of plans] effondrement m, anéantissement m. ◆ vt **1.** [in accident, explosion - ship] provoquer le naufrage de ; [- car, plane] détruire complètement ; [- building] démolir **2.** [damage - furniture] casser, démolir ; [- mechanism] détruire, détraquer **3.** [upset - marriage, relationship] briser ; [- hopes, chances] anéantir ; [- health] briser, ruiner ; [- negotiations] faire échouer, saboter.

wreckage ['rekɪdʒ] n **1.** *(U)* [debris - from ship, car] débris mpl ; [- from building] décombres mpl **2.** [wrecked ship] épave f, navire m naufragé **3.** *fig* [of hopes, relationship] anéantissement m.

wrecker ['rekər] n **1.** [destroyer] destructeur m, -trice f, démolisseur m, -euse f **2.** 🇺🇸 [demolition man - for buildings] démolisseur m ; [- for cars] ferrailleur m, casseur m **3.** 🇺🇸 [breakdown van] dépanneuse f.

Wren [ren] n 🇬🇧 auxiliaire féminine de la marine britannique.

wrench [rentʃ] ◆ vt **1.** [pull] tirer violemment sur / *she wrenched the door open* elle a ouvert la porte d'un geste violent ▶ **to wrench o.s. free** se dégager d'un mouvement violent **2.** [eyes, mind] arracher, détacher **3.** [ankle, arm] se faire une entorse à. ◆ vi : *he wrenched free of his bonds* **a)** *lit* il s'est dégagé de ses liens d'un mouvement violent **b)** *fig* il s'est libéré de ses liens. ◆ n **1.** [tug, twist] mouvement m violent (*de torsion*) **2.** [to ankle, knee] entorse f **3.** *fig* [emotional] déchirement m **4.** TECH [spanner] clé f, clef f ; [adjustable] clé f anglaise ; [for wheels] clé f en croix.

wrestle ['resl] ◆ vi **1.** SPORT [Greek, Sumo] lutter, pratiquer la lutte ; [freestyle] catcher, pratiquer le catch ▶ **to wrestle with sb** lutter (corps à corps) avec qqn, se battre avec qqn **2.** *fig* [struggle] se débattre, lutter **3.** [try to control] ▶ **to wrestle with sthg** se débattre avec qqch. ◆ vt [fight - intruder, enemy] lutter contre ; SPORT [Greek, Sumo] rencontrer à la lutte ; [freestyle] rencontrer au catch. ◆ n lutte f ▶ **to have a wrestle with sb** lutter avec or contre qqn.

wrestler ['reslər] n SPORT [Greek, Sumo] lutteur m, -euse f ; [freestyle] catcheur m, -euse f.

wrestling ['reslɪŋ] n SPORT [Greek, Sumo] lutte f ; [freestyle] catch m. ◆ comp [hold, match - Greek, Sumo] de lutte ; [- freestyle] de catch.

wretch [retʃ] n **1.** [unfortunate person] pauvre diable m, malheureux m, -euse f **2.** *liter & hum* [scoundrel] scélérat m, -e f, misérable mf **3.** [child] vilain m, -e f, coquin m, -e f.

wretched ['retʃɪd] ◆ adj **1.** [awful, poor - dwelling, clothes] misérable **2.** [unhappy] malheureux ; [depressed] déprimé, démoralisé **3.** [ill] malade **4.** *inf* [as expletive] fichu, maudit **5.** [abominable - behaviour, performance, weather] lamentable. ⬩ pl n ▶ **the wretched** les déshérités mpl.

wriggle ['rɪgl] ◆ vt **1.** [toes, fingers] tortiller **2.** [subj: person] : *he wriggled his way under the fence* il est passé sous la clôture en se tortillant or à plat ventre ; [subj: snake, worm] : *the worm was wriggling its way across the grass* le ver avançait dans l'herbe en se tortillant. ◆ vi [person] remuer, gigoter ; [snake, worm] se tortiller ; [fish] frétiller / *the fish* / *the little boy wriggled from her grasp* le poisson / le petit garçon réussit à s'échapper de ses mains en se tortillant ▶ **to wriggle free a)** *lit* se libérer en se tortillant **b)** *fig* s'en sortir. ◆ n ▶ **to give a wriggle a)** [snake] se tortiller **b)** [fish] frétiller **c)** [person] se tortiller. ⬩ **wriggle about** 🇬🇧, **wriggle around** vi [eel, worm] se tortiller ; [fish] frétiller ; [person] gigoter, se trémousser. ⬩ **wriggle out** vi **1.** [fish, snake] sortir / *the fish wriggled out of the net* le poisson s'est échappé du filet en se tortillant **2.** [person] se dégager (en se tortillant) / *I managed to wriggle out of the situation* *fig* j'ai réussi à me sortir de cette situation / *let's see him wriggle* *out of this one!* voyons comment il s'en sort cette fois-ci !

❖❖ **wriggle out of** vt insep ▶ **to wriggle out of a task** se dérober à or esquiver une tâche / *he wriggled out of paying* il a trouvé un moyen d'éviter de payer.

wring [rɪŋ] (*pt & pp* **wrung** [rʌŋ]) ◆ vt **1.** [wet cloth, clothes] essorer, tordre / *he wrung the towel dry* il a essoré la serviette / *she wrung the water from the sponge* elle a exprimé l'eau de l'éponge **2.** [neck] tordre **3.** [hand - in handshake] serrer ▶ **to wring one's hands (in despair)** se tordre les mains (de désespoir) **4.** [extract - confession] arracher ; [-money] extorquer **5.** *fig* [heart] fendre. ◆ vi essorer ; [on label] / **'do not wring'** 'ne pas essorer'. ◆ n : *give the cloth a wring* essorez la serpillière.

❖❖ **wring out** vt sep = **wring** *(vt).*

wringing ['rɪŋɪŋ] adj ▶ **wringing (wet) a)** [clothes] complètement trempé **b)** [person] complètement trempé, trempé jusqu'aux os / *the shirt was wringing with sweat* la chemise était trempée de sueur.

wrinkle ['rɪŋkl] ◆ vt **1.** [nose] froncer ; [brow] plisser **2.** [skirt, carpet] faire des plis dans. ◆ vi **1.** [skin, hands] se rider ; [brow] se contracter, se plisser ; [nose] se froncer, se plisser ; [fruit] se ratatiner, se rider **2.** [skirt, stocking] faire des plis. ◆ n **1.** [on skin, fruit] ride *f* **2.** [in dress, carpet] pli *m* **3.** 🇬🇧 *inf & dated* [trick] combine *f* ; [hint] tuyau *m*.

❖❖ **wrinkle up** vi & vt sep = **wrinkle** *(vi & vt).*

wrinkled ['rɪŋkld] adj **1.** [skin, hands] ridé ; [brow, nose] plissé, froncé ; [fruit] ridé, ratatiné **2.** [rug, skirt] qui fait des plis ; [stocking] qui fait des plis or l'accordéon.

wrinkly ['rɪŋklɪ] (*pl* **wrinklies**) ◆ adj **1.** [skin] ridé **2.** [stocking] qui fait des plis. ◆ n 🇬🇧 *inf & pej* vieux *m*, vieille *f*.

wrist [rɪst] n poignet *m* ▶ **wrist-rest** repose-poignets *m*.

wristband ['rɪstbænd] n [on shirt, blouse] poignet *m* ; [sweat band] poignet *m* ; [of watch] bracelet *m*.

wristwatch ['rɪstwɒtʃ] n montre-bracelet *f*.

writ [rɪt] n LAW ordonnance *f* ▶ **to issue a writ against sb a)** [for arrest] lancer un mandat d'arrêt contre qqn **b)** [for libel] assigner qqn en justice.

write [raɪt] (*pt* **wrote** [rəʊt], *pp* **written** ['rɪtn]) (*pt & pp archaic* **writ** [rɪt]) ◆ vt **1.** [letter] écrire ; [address, name] écrire, inscrire ; [initials] écrire, tracer ; [prescription, cheque] écrire, faire ; [will] faire ; [application form] compléter, rédiger ▶ **to write a letter to sb** écrire or envoyer une lettre à qqn ▶ **to write sb** 🇺🇸 écrire à qqn / *perplexity was written all over his face* *fig* la perplexité se lisait sur son visage **2.** [book] écrire ; [article, report] écrire, faire ; [essay] faire ; [music] écrire, composer / *well written* bien écrit. ◆ vi **1.** [gen] écrire / *I don't write very well* je n'ai pas une belle écriture **2.** [send letter] écrire ▶ **to write to sb** écrire à qqn / *she wrote and told me about it* elle m'a écrit pour me le raconter **3.** [professionally - as author] écrire, être écrivain ; [- as journalist] écrire, être journaliste / *he writes on home affairs for "The Economist"* il fait des articles de politique intérieure dans « The Economist » / *she writes for "The Independent"* elle écrit dans « The Independent » / *he writes on* or *about archeology* il écrit sur l'archéologie, il traite de questions d'archéologie. ❖❖ **write away** vi **1.** [correspond] écrire **2.** [order by post] écrire pour demander, commander par lettre. ❖❖ **write back** vi [answer] répondre (à une lettre) / *please write back soon* réponds-moi vite, s'il te plaît / *he wrote back rejecting their offer* il a renvoyé une lettre refusant leur offre. ❖❖ **write down** vt sep [note] écrire, noter ; [put in writing] mettre par écrit. ❖❖ **write in** ◆ vi écrire / *hundreds wrote in to complain* des centaines de personnes ont écrit pour se plaindre. ◆ vt sep **1.** [on list, document - word, name] ajouter, insérer **2.** 🇺🇸 POL [add - name] ajouter, inscrire (*sur un bulletin de vote*) ; [vote for - person] voter pour (*en ajoutant le nom*

sur le bulletin de vote). ❖❖ **write off** vt sep **1.** FIN [debt] passer aux profits et pertes **2.** [consider lost, useless] faire une croix sur, considérer comme perdu ; [cancel] renoncer à, annuler / *the plan had to be written off* le projet a dû être abandonné / *he was written off as a failure* on a considéré qu'il n'y avait rien de bon à en tirer **3.** [in accident - subj: insurance company] considérer comme irréparable, mettre à la casse ; [- subj: driver] rendre inutilisable / *she wrote off her new car* 🇬🇧 elle a complètement démoli sa voiture neuve. ❖❖ **write out** vt sep **1.** [report] écrire, rédiger ; [list, cheque] faire, établir **2.** [copy up - notes] recopier, mettre au propre. ❖❖ **write up** vt sep **1.** [diary, impressions] écrire, rédiger ; PRESS [event] faire un compte rendu de, rendre compte de / *he wrote up his ideas in a report* il a consigné ses idées dans un rapport **2.** [copy up - notes, data] recopier, mettre au propre.

write-off n [motor vehicle] ▶ **to be a write-off** être irréparable or bon pour la casse.

write-protect vt COMPUT protéger contre l'écriture.

write-protected adj COMPUT [disk] protégé (en écriture).

writer ['raɪtə'] n [of novel, play] écrivain *m*, -e *f*, auteur *m*, -e *f* ; [of letter] auteur *m*, -e *f*.

writer's block n angoisse *f* de la page blanche.

write-up n [review] compte rendu *m*, critique *f* / *the play got a good write-up* la pièce a eu une bonne critique or a été bien accueillie par la critique / *the guide contains write-ups of several ski resorts* le guide contient des notices descriptives sur plusieurs stations de ski.

writhe [raɪð] vi **1.** [in pain] se tordre, se contorsionner **2.** *fig* : *her remarks made him writhe* **a)** [in disgust] ses remarques l'ont fait frémir **b)** [in embarrassment] ses remarques lui ont fait souffrir le martyre. ❖❖ **writhe about**, 🇬🇧 **writhe around** vi se tortiller.

writing ['raɪtɪŋ] n **1.** [of books, letters] écriture *f* **2.** [handwriting] écriture *f* **3.** [written text] : *there was writing all over the board* il n'y avait plus de place pour écrire quoi que ce soit sur le tableau noir **4.** SCH [spelling] orthographe *f* ; [written language] écriture *f* ▶ **writing materials** matériel *m* nécessaire pour écrire. ❖❖ **writings** pl n [written works] œuvre *f*, écrits *mpl*. ❖❖ **in writing** adv phr par écrit ▶ **to put sthg in writing** mettre qqch par écrit.

writing case n nécessaire *m* à écrire.

writing desk n secrétaire *m* (*meuble*).

writing pad n bloc-notes *m*.

writing paper n papier *m* à lettres.

written ['rɪtn] ◆ pp ⟶ **write**. ◆ adj [form, text] écrit *m* ▶ **written language** écrit *m* ▶ **the written word** l'écrit.

wrong [rɒŋ] ◆ adj **1.** [incorrect - address, answer, information] mauvais, faux (fausse), erroné ; [- decision] mauvais ; MUS [note] faux (fausse) ; TELEC [number] faux (fausse) / *to get things in the wrong order* mettre les choses dans le mauvais ordre / *to take the wrong road* / *train* se tromper de route / de train / *the clock* / *my watch is wrong* le réveil / ma montre n'est pas à l'heure **2.** [mistaken - person] ▶ **to be wrong (about sthg)** avoir tort or se tromper (à propos de qqch) ▶ **to be wrong about sb** se tromper sur le compte de qqn / *I hope you won't take this the wrong way, but...* ne le prends pas mal, mais... **3.** [unsuitable] mauvais, mal choisi / *it was the wrong thing to do* / *say* ce n'était pas la chose à faire / dire / *you're going about it in the wrong way* vous vous y prenez mal / *I think you're in the wrong job* **a)** *lit* je pense que ce n'est pas le travail qu'il vous faut **b)** *hum* vous vous êtes trompé de métier ! / *she was wearing the wrong shoes for a long walk* elle n'avait pas les chaussures qui conviennent or elle n'avait pas les bonnes chaussures pour une randonnée **4.** [immoral, bad] mal ; [unjust] injuste / *cheating is wrong* c'est mal de tricher / *it was wrong of him to take the money* ce n'était pas bien de sa part de prendre l'argent / *there's nothing wrong with it* il n'y a rien à redire à cela, il n'y a pas de mal à cela / *it's wrong that anyone should have to live in poverty* il est injuste que des gens soient obligés de vivre dans la misère **5.** *(with 'something')* [amiss] : *something is wrong* or *there's something wrong with the lamp* la lampe ne marche pas bien or a un défaut / *there's something wrong somewhere* il y a quelque chose qui ne va pas quelque part ; *(with 'nothing')* : *there's nothing at all wrong with the clock* la pendule marche parfaitement bien / *there's nothing wrong, thank you* tout va bien, merci ; *(with 'what's')* ‣ *what's wrong?* qu'est-ce qui ne va pas ? / *what's wrong with the car?* qu'est-ce qu'elle a, la voiture ? / *what's wrong with you?* qu'est-ce que vous avez ? ◆ adv mal / *I guessed wrong* je suis tombé à côté, je me suis trompé ‣ *to get sthg wrong* : *I got the answer wrong* je n'ai pas donné la bonne réponse / *you've got it wrong, I never said that* vous vous trompez or vous n'avez pas compris, je n'ai jamais dit cela ‣ *to go wrong* **a)** [person] se tromper **b)** [plan] mal marcher, mal tourner **c)** [deal] tomber à l'eau **d)** [machine] tomber en panne / *you won't go far wrong if you follow her advice* vous ne risquez guère de vous tromper si vous suivez ses conseils / *you can't go wrong with a good book* **a)** [for reading] vous ne risquez pas de vous ennuyer avec un bon livre **b)** [as present] un bon livre, cela plaît toujours / *when did things start going wrong?* quand est-ce que les choses ont commencé à se gâter ? ◆ n **1.** [immorality, immoral act] mal *m* / *to know the difference between right and wrong* savoir distinguer le bien du mal ‣ *two wrongs don't make a right* prov on ne répare pas une injustice par une autre **2.** [harm] tort *m*, injustice f ‣ *to do sb wrong* faire du tort à or se montrer injuste envers qqn **3.** [error] tort *m*, erreur f / *he can do no wrong in her eyes* tout ce qu'il fait trouve grâce à ses yeux. ◆ vt faire du tort à, traiter injustement / *she felt deeply wronged* elle se sentait gravement lésée / *she has been badly wronged* **a)** [by words] on a dit à tort beaucoup de mal d'elle **b)** [by actions] on a agi de manière injuste envers elle. ❖ **in the wrong** adj & adv phr dans son tort ‣ *to be in the wrong* être dans son tort, avoir tort.

wrongdoer [ˌrɒŋˈduːəʳ] n **1.** [delinquent] malfaiteur *m*, délinquant *m*, -e f **2.** [sinner] pécheur *m*, -eresse f.

wrongdoing [ˌrɒŋˈduːɪŋ] n mal *m*, méfait *m*.

wrong-foot vt SPORT & *fig* prendre à contre-pied.

wrongful [ˈrɒŋfʊl] adj [unjust] injuste ; [unjustified] injustifié ; [illegal] illégal, illicite ; LAW ‣ **wrongful arrest** arresta-

tion f arbitraire ‣ **wrongful imprisonment** emprisonnement *m* injustifié ‣ **wrongful dismissal** INDUST renvoi *m* injustifié.

wrongfully [ˈrɒŋfʊlɪ] adv à tort / *I was wrongfully dismissed* INDUST j'ai été renvoyé à tort.

wrongheaded [ˌrɒŋˈhedɪd] adj **1.** [person] buté **2.** [idea] erroné, fou *(before vowel or silent 'h'* fol, f folle).

wrongly [ˈrɒŋlɪ] adv **1.** [incorrectly] à tort, mal **2.** [by mistake] par erreur, à tort.

wrote [rəʊt] pt ⟶ **write.**

wrought iron n fer *m* forgé. ❖ **wrought-iron** adj en fer forgé.

WRT MESSAGING written abbr of **with respect to.**

WRU MESSAGING written abbr of **where are you?**

wrung [rʌŋ] pt & pp ⟶ **wring.**

WRVS (abbr of Women's Royal Voluntary Service) pr n *association de femmes au service des déshérités.*

wry [raɪ] *(compar* wrier *or* wryer, *superl* wriest *or* wryest*)* adj **1.** [expression, glance - of distaste] désabusé **2.** [ironic - comment, smile] ironique, désabusé.

wt. (written abbr of **weight**) pds.

WTF MESSAGING written abbr of **what the fuck.**

WTG MESSAGING written abbr of **way to go.**

WTH MESSAGING written abbr of **what the hell.**

WTMPI MESSAGING written abbr of **way too much personal information.**

WTO [ˌdʌbljuːtiːˈəʊ] (abbr of World Trade Organization) n OMC f.

WUF MESSAGING written abbr of **where are you from?**

wunderkind [ˈwʌndəkɪnd] n enfant *mf* prodige.

wuss [wʌs] n 🇺🇸 *inf* mauviette f.

WUWH MESSAGING written abbr of **wish you were here.**

WV written abbr of **West Virginia.**

WW written abbr of **World War.**

WWW n abbr of **World Wide Web.**

WY written abbr of **Wyoming.**

Wyoming [waɪˈəʊmɪŋ] pr n Wyoming *m* / *in Wyoming* dans le Wyoming.

WYS MESSAGING written abbr of **whatever you say.**

WYSIWYG [ˈwɪzɪwɪg] (abbr of what you see is what you get) n & adj COMPUT WYSIWYG *(tel écran, tel écrit : ce que l'on voit sur l'écran est ce que l'on obtient à l'impression).*

X n MATH x *m*.

X (*pt & pp* **X-ed** *or* **X'd**) ◆ n **1.** [unknown factor] X *m* **2.** CIN film *m* interdit aux moins de 18 ans *(remplacé en 1982 par « 18 »)*. ◆ **1.** (written abbr of **kiss**) *formule affectueuse placée après la signature à la fin d'une lettre ou à la fin d'un SMS* **2.** written abbr of **Christ**.

x-axis n axe *m* des x, abscisse *f*.

X certificate n 🇬🇧 *signalait (jusqu'en 1982) un film interdit aux moins de 18 ans.*

X chromosome n chromosome *m* X.

xenophobia [ˌzenəˈfəʊbjə] n xénophobie *f*.

xenophobic [ˌzenəˈfəʊbɪk] adj xénophobe.

Xerox® [ˈzɪərɒks] n **1.** [machine] copieur *m*, photocopieuse *f* **2.** [process, copy] photocopie *f*.

xerox [ˈzɪərɒks] vt photocopier.

XL (written abbr of **extra-large**) n XL *m*.

XLNT MESSAGING written abbr of **excellent**.

Xmas written abbr of **Christmas**.

XML [ˌeksemˈel] (abbr of **Extensible Markup Language**) n COMPUT XML *m*.

XO MESSAGING written abbr of **kiss and a hug**.

X-rated [-reɪtɪd] adj *dated* [film] interdit aux mineurs or aux moins de 18 ans.

x-ray, X-ray ◆ vt **1.** MED [examine -chest, ankle] radiographier, faire une radio de ; [-patient] faire une radio à **2.** [inspect -luggage] passer aux rayons X **3.** [treat] traiter aux rayons X. ◆ n **1.** MED radio *f* ▶ **to have an x-ray** passer une radio ▶ **to take an x-ray of sthg** radiographier qqch, faire une radiographie de qqch **2.** PHYS rayon *m* X. ◆ comp **1.** MED [examination] radioscopique ; [treatment] radiologique, par rayons X ▶ **x-ray photograph** radiographie *f*, radio *f* ▶ **x-ray therapy** radiothérapie *f* **2.** PHYS [astronomy, tube] à rayons X.

xylophone [ˈzaɪləfəʊn] n xylophone *m*.

y n MATH y *m*.

Y **1.** written abbr of **yen** **2.** written abbr of **yuan** **3.** MESSAGING written abbr of **why**.

yacht [jɒt] ◆ n [sailing boat] voilier *m* ; [pleasure boat] yacht *m*. ◆ comp [race] de voiliers, de yachts ▸ **yacht club** yacht-club *m*. ◆ vi faire du yachting ▸ **to go yachting** faire de la voile or du yachting.

yachting ['jɒtɪŋ] ◆ n yachting *m*, navigation *f* de plaisance. ◆ comp [holiday] en yacht, sur l'eau ; [magazine] de voile ; [cap] de marin.

yachtsman ['jɒtsmən] (*pl* **yachtsmen** [-mən]) n yachtman *m*, yachtsman *m*.

yachtswoman ['jɒts,wʊmən] (*pl* **yachtswomen** [-,wɪmɪn]) n yachtwoman *f*.

yadda yadda ['jædə-] excl US *inf* et cetera, et cetera.

yahoo (*pl* **yahoos**) ◆ n ['jɑːhuː] rustre *m*, butor *m*. ◆ interj [jɑː'huː] ouah !

yak [jæk] (*pt* & *pp* **yakked**, *cont* **yakking**) vi *inf* ▸ **to yak on** UK, **to yak** jacasser.

Yale lock® [jeɪl-] n serrure *f* de sécurité (*à cylindre*).

yam [jæm] n **1.** [plant, vegetable] igname *f* **2.** US CULIN patate *f* douce.

Yangtze ['jæŋtsɪ] pr n ▸ **the Yangtze** le Yangzi Jiang, le Yang-tseu-kiang.

yank [jæŋk] ◆ vt [hair, sleeve] tirer brusquement (sur), tirer d'un coup sec. ◆ n coup *m* sec. ◆◆ **yank off** vt sep [button, cover] arracher. ◆◆ **yank out** vt sep [nail, tooth] arracher.

Yank [jæŋk] *inf* ◆ n **1.** UK *pej* Amerloque *mf* **2.** US Yankee *mf*. ◆ adj UK *pej* amerloque.

Yankee ['jæŋkɪ] ◆ n **1.** US Yankee *mf* **2.** UK *inf* & *pej* Amerloque *mf*. ◆ adj **1.** US yankee **2.** UK *inf* & *pej* amerloque.

yap [jæp] (*pt* & *pp* **yapped**, *cont* **yapping**) ◆ vi **1.** [dog] japper **2.** [person] jacasser. ◆ n [yelp] jappement *m*.

yard [jɑːd] n **1.** [of factory, farm, house, school] cour *f* **2.** [work site] chantier *m* ▸ **builder's yard** chantier de construction *m* **3.** [for storage] dépôt *m* **4.** RAIL voies *fpl* de garage **5.** [for animals - enclosure] enclos *m* ; [- pasture] pâturage *m* **6.** UK ▸ **the Yard** *inf* Scotland Yard **7.** US [backyard] cour *f* ; [garden] jardin *m* ▸ **yard work** jardinage *m* **8.** [unit of measure] yard *m* (0,914 *m*) / *it was ten yards wide* il avait dix mètres de large / *to buy cloth by the yard* acheter le tissu au mètre **9.** *dated* SPORT : *the 100 yards* or *the 100 yards' dash* le cent mètres **10.** NAUT vergue *f*.

Yardie ['jɑːdɪ] n *membre d'une organisation criminelle d'origine jamaïcaine*.

yardman ['jɑːdmæn] n US jardinier *m*.

yardstick ['jɑːdstɪk] n **1.** [instrument] mètre *m* (*en bois ou en métal*) **2.** *fig* critère *m*.

yarn [jɑːn] ◆ n **1.** (U) TEXT fil *m* (à tricoter ou à tisser) **2.** [tall story] histoire *f* (incroyable or invraisemblable) ; [long story] longue histoire *f*. ◆ vi [tell tall stories] raconter des histoires ; [tell long stories] raconter de longues histoires.

yashmak ['jæʃmæk] n litham *m*, litsam *m*.

yawn [jɔːn] ◆ vi **1.** [person] bâiller **2.** [chasm, opening] être béant, s'ouvrir. ◆ vt [utter with yawn] dire en bâillant. ◆ n **1.** [of person] bâillement *m* **2.** *inf* & *fig* ▸ **to be a yawn** a) [meeting] toute l'année ▸ **b)** [film, book] être rasoir.

y-axis n axe *m* des y or des ordonnées.

YBS MESSAGING written abbr of **you'll be sorry**.

Y chromosome n chromosome *m* Y.

yd written abbr of **yard**.

yea [jeɪ] ◆ adv [yes] oui. ◆ n [in vote] oui *m*.

yeah [jeə] adv & interj *inf* [yes] ouais.

year [jɪər] n **1.** [period of time] an *m*, année *f* / *this year* cette année / *last year* l'an dernier, l'année dernière / *next year* l'année prochaine / *the year after next* dans deux ans ▸ **year by year** d'année en année ▸ **all (the) year round** (pendant) toute l'année ▸ **year in year out** année après année / *it was five years last Christmas* ça a fait cinq ans à Noël ; [with 'in'] : *in ten years* or *in ten years' time* dans dix ans ; [with 'for'] : *I haven't seen her for years* je ne l'ai pas vue depuis des années / *for years and years* pendant des années ; [with 'ago'] : *two years ago* il y a deux ans ; [with 'last', 'take'] : *the batteries last (for) years* les piles durent des années **2.** [in calendar] an *m*, année *f* / *in the year 1607* en (l'an) 1607 **3.** [in age] : *he is 15 years old* or *of age* il a 15 ans / *the foundations are 4,000 years old* les fondations sont vieilles de 4 000 ans **4.** SCH & UNIV année *f* / *he's in the first year* a) [at school] ≃ il est en sixième **b)** [at college, university] il est en première année **5.** [for wine, coin] année *f*.

---

 année or **an?**

Année is the most frequently used of these two terms, with the following exceptions. **An** is used in:

■ *Set phrases expressing dates associated with ancient times or traditions*
le jour de l'An New Year's day.
le Nouvel An New Year's Eve, but.
bonne année! Happy New Year !

Note : this applies only to years within a few dozen or so of the reference point – otherwise **année** is used, as for example **l'année 780 avant J.-C.**

⟶

→

■ *Dates expressed through cardinal numerals*
Je suis né il y a exactement cinquante ans aujourd'hui. *I was born fifty years ago to the day.*
Note: if an adjective modifies the noun, **année** is used instead; for example:
les trente longues années de son règne *the thirty long years that his reign lasted.*

■ *Age*
Elle va avoir trois ans dimanche. *She'll be three years old on Sunday.*
Note: if an ordinal numeral is used, **année** should be chosen instead of **an**; for example:
Il avait atteint sa quatre-vingtième année. *He'd reached his eightieth year.*

■ *With the set phrase 'bon an mal an'*
On gagne assez bien notre vie, bon an mal an. *Taking the average year, we don't make a bad living.*

■ *In the literary plural phrase 'les ans'*
Les ans n'ont rien enlevé à son talent. *The passing years have in no way diminished his talent.*

yearbook ['jɪəbʊk] n annuaire *m*, recueil *m* annuel.

Yearbook

Aux États-Unis, les écoles, les universités et certaines colonies de vacances ont un **yearbook**, qui rassemble des photos et des adresses mais aussi des anecdotes sur l'année écoulée. Plus récemment, cette tradition s'est également répandue dans les établissements scolaires en Grande-Bretagne.

year-end ◆ adj 🇬🇧 de fin d'année. ◆ n : *at the year-end* à la fin de l'année, en fin d'année.
yearling ['jɪəlɪŋ] ◆ n ZOOL petit *m* d'un an ; EQUIT yearling *m*. ◆ adj ZOOL (âgé) d'un an.
yearly ['jɪəlɪ] (*pl* **yearlies**) ◆ adj annuel. ◆ adv annuellement. ◆ n PRESS publication *f* annuelle.
yearn [jɜːn] vi **1.** [desire, crave] languir, aspirer ; [pine] languir ▶ **to yearn to do sthg** mourir d'envie or brûler de faire qqch **2.** *liter* [be moved - person] s'attendrir, s'émouvoir ; [- heart] s'attendrir.
yearning ['jɜːnɪŋ] n [longing] désir *m* ardent ; [pining] nostalgie *f*.
year-on-year ◆ adj [growth, decline] d'une année à l'autre. ◆ adv [grow, decline] d'une année à l'autre.
year-round adj [activity] qui dure toute l'année, sur toute l'année ; [facility] qui fonctionne toute l'année.
yeast [jiːst] n levure *f*.
yeast infection n [vaginal thrush] mycose *f* vaginale.
yell [jel] ◆ vi crier (à tue-tête) ▶ **to yell at sb** crier après qqn ▶ **to yell about sthg** brailler au sujet de qqch. ◆ vt [shout out] hurler, crier ; [proclaim] clamer, crier. ◆ n **1.** [shout] cri *m*, hurlement *m* **2.** 🇺🇸 [from students, supporters] cri *m* de ralliement.
yellow ['jeləʊ] ◆ adj **1.** [in colour] jaune ▶ **yellow cab** taxi new-yorkais **2.** *inf* [cowardly] lâche. ◆ n **1.** [colour] jaune *m* **2.** [yolk] jaune *m* (d'œuf) **3.** [in snooker] boule *f* jaune. ◆ vi jaunir. ◆ vt jaunir.
yellow card n FOOT carton *m* jaune.

yellow fever n fièvre *f* jaune.
yellow line n bande *f* jaune ▶ **to park on a yellow line** ≃ se mettre en stationnement irrégulier ▶ **to be parked on a double yellow line** être en stationnement interdit.

Yellow lines

En Grande-Bretagne, une ligne jaune parallèle au trottoir signifie « arrêt autorisé réglementé » ; une double ligne jaune signifie « stationnement interdit ».

yellowness ['jeləʊnɪs] n **1.** [colour] couleur *f* jaune **2.** *inf* [cowardice] lâcheté *f*, poltronnerie *f*.
Yellow Pages® pl n ▶ **the Yellow Pages** ≃ les Pages Jaunes®.
Yellow River pr n ▶ **the Yellow River** le fleuve Jaune.
Yellow Sea pr n ▶ **the Yellow Sea** la mer Jaune.
yelp [jelp] ◆ vi [dog] japper, glapir ; [person] crier, glapir. ◆ n [of dog] jappement *m*, glapissement *m* ; [of person] cri *m*, glapissement *m*.
Yemen ['jemən] pr n Yémen *m* ▶ **in (the) Yemen** au Yémen.
Yemeni ['jemənɪ] ◆ n Yéménite *mf*. ◆ adj yéménite.
yen [jen] n **1.** (*pl* **yen**) [currency] yen *m* **2.** *inf* [desire] envie *f* ▶ **to have a yen for sthg / to do sthg** avoir très envie de or mourir d'envie de qqch / faire qqch.
yep [jep] interj *inf* ouais.
yer [jər] *inf* = **your**.
yes [jes] ◆ adv **1.** [gen] oui ; [in answer to negatives] si ; [answering knock on door] oui (entrez) ; [answering phone] allô, oui ; [encouraging a speaker to continue] oui, et puis ?, oui, et alors ? ▶ **to say / to vote yes** dire / voter oui / *is it raining? — yes (it is)* est-ce qu'il pleut ? — oui / *will you tell her? — yes (I will)* tu le lui direz-vous ? — oui (je vais le faire) / *oh yes?* [doubtful] c'est vrai ? / *you don't like me, do you? — yes I do!* vous ne m'aimez pas, n'est-ce pas ? — mais si (voyons) ! **2.** [introducing a contrary opinion] : *yes but...* oui or d'accord mais... **3.** [in response to command or call] oui / *yes, sir* oui or bien, monsieur **4.** [indeed] en effet, vraiment / *she was rash, yes, terribly rash* elle a été imprudente, vraiment très imprudente. ◆ n [person, vote] ▶ **to count the yeses** compter les oui or les votes pour. ◆ comp ▶ **yes vote** vote *m* pour. ❖ **yes and no** adv phr oui et non.
yes-man n *inf* béni-oui-oui *m inv*.
yesterday ['jestədɪ] ◆ adv **1.** hier / *yesterday morning / afternoon* hier matin / après-midi / *yesterday week* 🇬🇧, *a week yesterday, a week ago yesterday* il y a huit jours **2.** [in the past] hier, naguère. ◆ n **1.** [day before] hier *m* / *yesterday was Monday* hier c'était lundi / *the day before yesterday* avant-hier **2.** [former times] temps *mpl* passés or anciens / *yesterday's fashions* les coutumes d'hier or d'autrefois.
yet [jet] ◆ adv **1.** [up to now] déjà / *is he here yet?* est-il déjà là ? / *have you been to London yet?* êtes-vous déjà allés à Londres ? **2.** [at the present time] ▶ **not yet** pas encore ▶ **yet again** encore une fois **5.** [so far - in present] jusqu'ici, jusque-là ; [- in past] jusque-là / *it's her*

best play yet c'est sa meilleure pièce. ◆ conj [nevertheless] néanmoins, toutefois ; [however] cependant, pourtant ; [but] mais / *they had no income yet they still had to pay taxes* ils n'avaient pas de revenus et pourtant ils devaient payer des impôts / *he was firm yet kind* il était sévère mais juste.

yeti ['jetɪ] n yéti *m*.

yew [juː] n **1.** ▶ **yew (tree)** if *m* **2.** [wood] (bois *m* d')if *m*.

Y-fronts® pl n slip *m* kangourou.

YGM MESSAGING written abbr of **you got mail**.

YHA (abbr of **Youth Hostels Association**) pr n 🇬🇧 *Fédération unie des auberges de jeunesse.*

Yiddish ['jɪdɪʃ] ◆ n yiddish *m*. ◆ adj yiddish.

yield [jiːld] ◆ vi **1.** [give in - person] céder ; [surrender] se rendre / *he refused to yield* il a refusé de céder or se laisser fléchir ▶ **to yield to** a) [argument] céder or s'incliner devant b) [criticism, force] céder devant c) [blackmail, demand] céder à d) [pressure, threat] céder sous e) [desire, temptation] succomber à, céder à **2.** [break, bend - under weight, force] céder, fléchir **3.** 🇺🇸 AUTO céder le passage or la priorité ▶ **'yield'** 'cédez le passage' / **'yield to pedestrians'** 'priorité aux piétons' **4.** AGR [field] rapporter, rendre ; [crop] rapporter. ◆ vt **1.** [produce, bring in - gen] produire, rapporter ; [-land, crops] produire, rapporter, donner ; [-results] donner / *the investment bond will yield 5%* le bon d'épargne rapportera 5 % / *their research has yielded some interesting results* leur recherche a fourni or donné quelques résultats intéressants **2.** [relinquish, give up] céder, abandonner ▶ **to yield ground** MIL & *fig* céder du terrain **3.** 🇺🇸 AUTO ▶ **to yield right of way** céder la priorité. ◆ n **1.** AGR & INDUST [output] rendement *m*, rapport *m* ; [of crops] récolte *f* ▶ **high-yield crops** récoltes à rendement élevé ▶ **yield per acre** ≃ rendement à l'hectare **2.** FIN [from investments] rapport *m*, rendement *m* ; [profit] bénéfice *m*, bénéfices *mpl* ; [from tax] recette *f*, rapport *m* / *an 8% yield on investments* des investissements qui rapportent 8 %. ◆ comp 🇺🇸 ▶ **yield sign** panneau *m* de priorité. ◆ **yield up** vt sep 🇬🇧 **1.** [surrender - town, prisoner] livrer **2.** [reveal - secret] dévoiler.

yikes [jaɪks] excl mince !

yippee [🇬🇧 jɪ'piː 🇺🇸 'jɪpɪ] interj *inf* hourra.

Y2K (abbr of **the year 2000**) n [year] l'an 2000 ; [millenium bug] le bogue de l'an 2000.

YMCA (abbr of **Young Men's Christian Association**) pr n YMCA *m* (*association chrétienne de jeunes gens, surtout connue pour ses centres d'hébergement*).

yo [jəʊ] interj 🇺🇸 *inf* salut.

yob [jɒb] n 🇬🇧 *inf* loubard *m*.

yobbo ['jɒbəʊ] (*pl* **yobbos**) = **yob**.

yodel ['jəʊdl] (🇬🇧 pt & pp **yodelled**, cont **yodelling** ; 🇺🇸 pt & pp **yodeled**, cont **yodeling**) ◆ vi jodler, iodler. ◆ n tyrolienne *f*.

yoga ['jəʊɡə] n yoga *m*.

yoghourt, yoghurt [🇬🇧 'jɒɡət 🇺🇸 'jəʊɡərt] n yaourt *m*, yogourt *m*, yoghourt *m*.

yogurt [🇬🇧 'jɒɡət 🇺🇸 'jəʊɡərt] = **yoghourt**.

yoke [jəʊk] ◆ n **1.** [frame - for hitching oxen] joug *m* ; [- for carrying buckets] joug *m*, palanche *f* **2.** *fig* [burden, domination] joug *m* **3.** [pair of animals] attelage *m*, paire *f* **4.** [of dress, skirt, blouse] empiècement *m* **5.** CONSTR [for beams] moise *f*, lien *m*. ◆ vt [oxen] atteler.

yokel ['jəʊkl] n *pej* péquenot *m*.

yolk [jəʊk] n ▶ **(egg) yolk** jaune *m* (d'œuf).

Yom Kippur [,jɒm'kɪpər] n Yom Kippour *m inv*.

yonder ['jɒndər] ◆ adj *liter* : *yonder tree* l'arbre là-bas. ◆ adv là-bas.

yonks [jɒŋks] n 🇬🇧 *inf* : *I haven't been there for yonks* il y a une paie or ça fait un bail que je n'y suis pas allé.

Yorks. written abbr of **Yorkshire**.

Yorkshire pudding n crêpe épaisse salée traditionnellement servie avec du rôti de bœuf.

Yorkshire terrier n yorkshire-terrier *m*, yorkshire *m*.

you [juː] pron **1.** [as plural subject] vous ; [as singular subject - polite use] vous ; [- familiar use] tu ; [as plural object] vous ; [as singular object - polite use] vous ; [as familiar use] te, t' (*before vowel or silent 'h'*) / *you didn't ask* vous n'avez pas / tu n'as pas demandé / *you and I will go together* vous et moi / toi et moi irons ensemble / *you there!* vous là-bas ! / *she gave you the keys* elle vous a donné / elle t'a donné les clés **2.** [after preposition] vous ; [familiar use] toi / *all of you* vous tous / *with you* avec vous / toi / *for you* pour vous / toi / *between you and me* entre nous **3.** [before noun or adjective] : *you bloody fool!* v *inf* espèce de crétin ! / *you Americans are all the same* vous les Américains or vous autres Américains, vous êtes tous pareils **4.** [emphatic use] vous ; [familiar form] toi / *you mean they chose you* tu veux dire qu'ils t'ont choisie toi **5.** [impersonal use] : *you never know* on ne sait jamais / *a hot bath does you a world of good* un bon bain chaud vous fait un bien immense.

URT1 MESSAGING written abbr of **you are the one**.

you'd [juːd] **1.** abbr of **you had 2.** abbr of **you would**.

you-know-what n *inf & euph* : *does he know about the you-know-what?* est-ce qu'il est au courant du... tu vois de quoi je veux parler or ce que je veux dire ?

you-know-who n *inf & euph* qui tu sais, qui vous savez.

you'll [juːl] abbr of **you will**.

young [jʌŋ] (*compar* **younger** ['jʌŋɡər], *superl* **youngest** ['jʌŋɡɪst]) ◆ adj **1.** [in age, style, ideas - person, clothes] jeune / *young people* les jeunes *mpl*, la jeunesse *f* / *the younger generation* la jeune génération / *my younger brother* mon frère cadet, mon petit frère / *I'm ten years younger than she is* j'ai dix ans de moins qu'elle / *in my younger days* dans ma jeunesse, quand j'étais jeune **2.** [youthful] jeune / *she is a young 45* elle a 45 ans, mais elle ne les fait pas / *he's young for his age* il est jeune pour son âge, il ne fait pas son âge ▶ **to be young at heart** avoir la jeunesse du cœur **3.** [recent - grass, plant] nouveau (*before vowel or silent 'h'* **nouvel**, f **nouvelle**) ; [- wine] jeune, vert ; [GEOL - rock formation] jeune, récent. ◆ pl n ▶ **the young a)** [people] les jeunes *mpl*, la jeunesse **b)** [animals] les petits *mpl*.

youngish ['jʌŋɪʃ] adj plutôt jeune.

youngster ['jʌŋstər] n **1.** [child] garçon *m*, fille *f*, gamin *m*, gamine *f* ; [youth] jeune homme *m*, jeune fille *f* **2.** EQUIT jeune cheval *m*.

your [jɔːr] det **1.** [addressing one or more people - polite use] votre *mf*, vos *mf* ; [addressing one person - familiar use] ton *m*, ta *f*, tes *mf* / *your book* votre / ton livre / *your car* votre / ta voiture / *your books* vos / tes livres **2.** [with parts of body, clothes] : *don't put your hands in your pockets* ne mets pas tes mains dans les poches / *does your wrist hurt?* est-ce que tu as mal au poignet ? **3.** [emphatic form] : *is this your book or his?* est-ce que c'est votre livre ou le sien ? / *oh it's YOUR book, is it?* ah, c'est à toi ce livre ! **4.** [impersonal use] : *if you don't stand up for your rights, no one else will* si vous ne défendez pas vos droits vous-même, personne ne le fera à votre place / *swimming is good for your heart and lungs* la natation est un bon exercice pour le cœur et les poumons.

you're [jɔːr] abbr of **you are**.

yours [jɔːz] pron **1.** [addressing one or more people - polite use] le vôtre *m*, la vôtre *f*, les vôtres *mf pl* ; [addressing one person - familiar use] le tien *m*, la tienne *f*, les tiens *mpl*, les tiennes / *is this book yours?* est-ce que ce livre est à vous / toi ? / *is this car yours?* c'est votre / ta voiture ? / *is he a friend of yours?* est-ce un de vos / tes amis ? / *can't you control that wretched dog of yours?* vous ne pouvez pas retenir votre satané chien ? **2.** [in letter] : *yours, Peter* ≃ bien à vous or à bientôt, Peter ▶ **yours sincerely** cordialement vôtre ▶ **yours faithfully** ≃ veuillez agréer mes salutations distinguées.

yourself [jɔːˈself] (*pl* **yourselves** [-ˈselvz]) pron **1.** [personally - gen] vous-même ; [- familiar use] toi-même / *do it yourself* faites-le vous-même / fais-le toi-même / *do it yourselves* faites-le vous-mêmes / *did you come by yourself?* vous êtes venu tout seul ? **2.** [reflexive use] : *did you hurt yourself?* est-ce que vous vous êtes / tu t'es fait mal ? / *did you enjoy yourself?* est-ce que c'était bien ? **3.** [emphatic use] : *you told me yourself* or *you yourself told me* vous me l'avez dit vous-même, c'est vous-même qui me l'avez dit **4.** [impersonal use] : *you have to know how to look after yourself in the jungle* dans la jungle, il faut savoir se défendre tout seul or se débrouiller soi-même.

U4E MESSAGING written abbr of **yours forever.**

youth [juːθ] (*pl* **youths** [juːðz]) ◆ n **1.** [young age] jeunesse *f* **2.** [young man] adolescent *m*, jeune *m*. ◆ pl n [young people] : *the youth of today* les jeunes *mpl* or la jeunesse d'aujourd'hui.

youth club n 🇬🇧 ≃ maison *f* des jeunes.

youth custody n 🇬🇧 détention *f* de mineurs, éducation *f* surveillée.

youthful [ˈjuːθful] adj **1.** [young - person] jeune ; [- appearance] d'allure jeune **2.** [typical of youth - idea] de jeunesse ; [- enthusiasm, expectations, attitude] juvénile.

youthfulness [ˈjuːθfulnɪs] n [of person] jeunesse *f* ; [of appearance] allure *f* jeune ; [of mind, ideas] jeunesse *f*, fraîcheur *f*.

youth hostel n auberge *f* de jeunesse.

youth hostelling n *(U)* ▶ **to go youth hostelling** passer ses vacances en auberges de jeunesse.

U2 MESSAGING written abbr of **you too.**

you've [juːv] abbr of **you have.**

yowl [jaul] ◆ vi [cat] miauler (fort) ; [dog, person] hurler. ◆ n [of cat] miaulement *m* (déchirant) ; [of dog, person] hurlement *m*.

yo-yo [ˈjəʊjəʊ] (*pl* **yo-yos**) n **1.** [toy] Yo-Yo® *m inv* **2.** 🇺🇸 *v inf* [fool] couillon *m*.

yr 1. written abbr of **your 2.** written abbr of **year.**

yrs written abbr of **yours.**

Yucatan [ˌjuːkəˈtɑːn] pr n Yucatan *m*.

yuck [jʌk] interj *inf* berk, beurk.

yucky [ˈjʌkɪ] (*compar* **yuckier**, *superl* **yuckiest**) adj *inf* dégueulasse.

Yugoslav [ˈjuːgəʊˌslɑːv] ◆ n Yougoslave *mf*. ◆ adj yougoslave.

Yugoslavia [ˌjuːgəʊˈslɑːvɪə] pr n ▶ **former Yugoslavia** ex-Yougoslavie *f* / *in Yugoslavia* en Yougoslavie.

Yugoslavian [ˌjuːgəʊˈslɑːvɪən] ◆ n Yougoslave *mf*. ◆ adj yougoslave.

yule log, Yule log n bûche *f* de Noël.

yuletide, Yuletide *liter* [ˈjuːltaɪd] ◆ n (époque *f* de) Noël *m*. ◆ comp [greetings, festivities] de Noël.

yummy [ˈjʌmɪ] (*compar* **yummier**, *superl* **yummiest**) *inf* ◆ adj [food] succulent, délicieux. ◆ interj miam-miam.

yum-yum [ˌjʌmˈjʌm] interj *inf* miam-miam.

yup [jʌp] adv 🇺🇸 *inf* ouais.

yuppie, yuppy [ˈjʌpɪ] ◆ n (*pl* **yuppies**) yuppie *mf* ; ≃ jeune cadre *m* dynamique. ◆ adj [club] pour jeunes cadres dynamiques ; [lifestyle] des yuppies.

YWCA (abbr of **Young Women's Christian Association**) pr n *association chrétienne de jeunes filles (surtout connue pour ses centres d'hébergement).*

Zagreb ['zɑːgreb] pr n Zagreb.

Zaïre [zɑːˈɪə] pr n Zaïre *m* / *in Zaïre* au Zaïre.

Zaïrese [zɑːɪəˈriːz] ◆ n Zaïrois *m*, -e *f*. ◆ adj zaïrois.

Zambesi, Zambezi [zæmˈbiːzɪ] pr n ▶ **the Zambesi** le Zambèze.

Zambia ['zæmbɪə] pr n Zambie *f* / *in Zambia* en Zambie.

Zambian ['zæmbɪən] ◆ n Zambien *m*, -enne *f*. ◆ adj zambien.

zany ['zeɪnɪ] (*compar* **zanier**, *superl* **zaniest**, *pl* **zanies**) *inf* ◆ adj farfelu, dingue, dingo. ◆ n THEAT bouffon *m*, zani *m*, zanni *m*.

Zanzibar [ˌzænzɪˈbɑːr] pr n Zanzibar *m* / *in Zanzibar* au Zanzibar.

zap [zæp] (*pt & pp* **zapped**, *cont* **zapping**) *inf* ◆ vi **1.** [go quickly] courir **2.** TV zapper. ◆ vt **1.** [destroy by bombing - town] ravager, bombarder ; [- target] atteindre **2.** [kill - victim] tuer, descendre ; [- in video game] éliminer **3.** COMPUT [display, data] effacer, supprimer. ◆ n [energy] pêche *f*, punch *m*. ◆ interj vlan.

zeal [ziːl] n zèle *m*, ferveur *f*, ardeur *f*.

zealot ['zelət] n fanatique *mf*.

zealous ['zeləs] adj [worker, partisan] zélé, actif ; [opponent] zélé, acharné.

zealously ['zeləslɪ] adv avec zèle or ardeur.

zebra [UK 'zebrə US 'ziːbrə] (*pl* **zebra** *or* **zebras**) n zèbre *m*.

zebra crossing n UK passage *m* clouté or pour piétons.

zenith [UK 'zenɪθ US 'ziːnəθ] n zénith *m*.

zeppelin ['zepəlɪn] n zeppelin *m*.

zero [UK 'zɪərəʊ US 'ziːrəʊ] (*pl* **zeros** *or* **zeroes**) ◆ n **1.** MATH zéro *m* **2.** [in temperature] zéro *m* / *40 below zero* 40 degrés au-dessous de zéro, moins 40 **3.** SPORT : *to win 3 zero* gagner 3 (à) zéro **4.** [nothing, nought] : *our chances have been put at zero* on considère que nos chances sont nulles. ◆ comp [altitude] zéro (*inv*) ; [visibility] nul / *the project has zero interest for me* le projet ne présente aucun intérêt pour moi ▶ **zero gravity** apesanteur *f* ▶ **zero growth** croissance *f* zéro ▶ **zero tolerance** tolérance *f* zéro. ◆ vt [instrument] régler sur zéro. ❖ **zero in on** vt insep **1.** MIL [aim for] se diriger or piquer droit sur **2.** *inf* [concentrate on] se concentrer sur, faire porter tous ses efforts sur **3.** *inf* [pinpoint] mettre le doigt sur.

zero-carbon adj zéro-carbone.

zero hour n heure *f* H.

zero-rated [-,reɪtɪd] adj ▶ **zero-rated (for VAT)** exempt de TVA, non assujetti à la TVA.

zero-rating n exemption *f* de TVA.

zero sum n somme *f* nulle ▶ **a zero sum game** un jeu à somme nulle.

zest [zest] n **1.** [piquancy] piquant *m*, saveur *f* **2.** [enthusiasm] enthousiasme *m*, entrain *m* **3.** CULIN [of orange, lemon] zeste *m*.

zigzag ['zɪgzæg] (*pt & pp* **zigzagged**, *cont* **zigzagging**) ◆ vi [walker, vehicle] avancer en zigzags, zigzaguer ; [road] zigzaguer ; [river] serpenter. ◆ n [in design] zigzag *m* ; [on road] lacet *m* ; [in river] boucle *f*. ◆ adj [path, line] en zigzag ; [pattern] à zigzag or zigzags. ◆ adv en zigzag.

zilch [zɪltʃ] n US *inf* que dalle.

Zimbabwe [zɪmˈbɑːbwɪ] pr n Zimbabwe *m* / *in Zimbabwe* au Zimbabwe.

Zimbabwean [zɪmˈbɑːbwɪən] ◆ n Zimbabwéen *m*, -enne *f*. ◆ adj zimbabwéen.

Zimmer (frame)® ['zɪmər-] n déambulateur *m*.

zinc [zɪŋk] ◆ n zinc *m*. ◆ comp [chloride, sulphate, sulphide] de zinc ; [ointment] à l'oxyde de zinc.

zine [ziːn] n *inf* revue *f*, magazine *m*.

zinger ['zɪŋər] n US *inf* **1.** [pointed remark] pique *f* **2.** [impressive thing] : *it was a real zinger* c'était impressionnant.

Zionism ['zaɪənɪzm] n sionisme *m*.

Zionist ['zaɪənɪst] ◆ n sioniste *mf*. ◆ adj sioniste.

zip [zɪp] (*pt & pp* **zipped**, *cont* **zipping**) ◆ n **1.** [fastener] fermeture *f* Éclair® or à glissière **2.** [sound of bullet] sifflement *m* **3.** *inf* [liveliness] vivacité *f*, entrain *m* **4.** US code *m* postal **5.** US *inf* [nothing] rien *m*. ◆ vi **1.** [with zip fastener] ▶ **to zip open / shut** s'ouvrir / se fermer à l'aide d'une fermeture Éclair® or à glissière **2.** *inf* [verb of movement] ▶ **to zip past** passer comme une flèche ▶ **to zip upstairs** monter l'escalier quatre à quatre / *I zipped through the book / my work* j'ai lu ce livre / fait mon travail en quatrième vitesse **3.** [arrow, bullet] siffler. ◆ vt **1.** [with zip fastener] ▶ **to zip sth open / shut** fermer / ouvrir la fermeture Éclair® or à glissière de qqch ▶ **zip it!** US *inf* [shut up] la ferme !, ta gueule ! **2.** *inf* [do quickly] : *I'll just zip this cake into the oven* je vais juste glisser le gâteau dans le four **3.** COMPUT zipper. ❖ **zip on** ◆ vt sep attacher (avec une fermeture à glissière). ◆ vi s'attacher avec une fermeture Éclair® or à glissière. ❖ **zip up** ◆ vt sep **1.** [clothing, sleeping bag] fermer avec la fermeture Éclair® or à glissière **2.** [subj: person] fermer la fermeture Éclair® or à glissière de. ◆ vi [dress] se fermer avec une fermeture Éclair® or à glissière.

zip code, ZIP code n US code *m* postal.

Zip disk® n COMPUT disque *m* zip.

Zip drive® n COMPUT lecteur *m* de zips.

zip fastener n UK fermeture *f* Éclair® or à glissière.

zipper ['zɪpər] **1.** US = zip fastener **2.** US [on pants] braguette *f*.

zip-up adj [bag, coat] à fermeture Éclair®, zippé.

zit [zɪt] n inf bouton m *(sur la peau)*.

zither ['zɪðər] n cithare f.

zodiac ['zəʊdɪæk] n zodiaque m.

zombie ['zɒmbɪ] n zombie m.

zone [zəʊn] ◆ n **1.** [area] zone f, secteur m **2.** [sphere] zone f, domaine m ▸ **to be in the zone** US inf a) [performing optimally] être au mieux de ses performances b) [ready] être dans les starting-blocks **3.** GEOG & METEOR zone f. ◆ vt **1.** [partition] diviser en zones **2.** [classify] désigner. ❖ **zone in on** vt US [move towards] se diriger vers ; [reach] atteindre. ❖ **zone out** ◆ vi [chill out] : *when I get home from work, I like to sit on the couch and zone out* quand je rentre du boulot, j'aime m'affaler sur le canapé et glander. ◆ vt : *it zoned me out* [music, drug] ça m'a fait planer / *he looked completely zoned out* il avait l'air de planer complètement.

zoo [zuː] *(pl* **zoos)** n zoo m, jardin m zoologique.

zoological [ˌzəʊəˈlɒdʒɪkl] adj zoologique.

zoologist [zəʊˈɒlədʒɪst] n zoologiste mf.

zoology [zəʊˈɒlədʒɪ] n zoologie f.

zoom [zuːm] ◆ vi inf [verb of movement] : *the car zoomed up / down the hill* la voiture a monté / descendu la côte à toute allure. ◆ n PHOT [lens, effect] zoom m. ❖ **zoom in** vi PHOT faire un zoom. ❖ **zoom out** vi PHOT faire or produire un effet d'éloignement avec le zoom.

zoom lens n zoom m.

zucchini [zuːˈkiːnɪ] *(pl* **zucchini** or **zucchinis)** n US courgette f.

Zulu ['zuːluː] *(pl* **Zulu** or **Zulus)** ◆ n [person] Zoulou m, -e f. ◆ adj zoulou.

Zürich ['zjʊərɪk] pr n Zurich.

zygote ['zaɪgəʊt] n zygote m.

Conjugaisons françaises
French verb tables

French verb tables

	1 avoir	2 être	3 chanter
Indicatif présent	j'ai tu as il, elle a nous avons vous avez ils, elles ont	je suis tu es il, elle est nous sommes vous êtes ils, elles sont	je chante tu chantes il, elle chante nous chantons vous chantez ils, elles chantent
Indicatif imparfait	il, elle avait	il, elle était	il, elle chantait
Indicatif passé simple	il, elle eut ils, elles eurent	il, elle fut ils, elles furent	il, elle chanta ils, elles chantèrent
Indicatif futur	j'aurai il, elle aura	je serai il, elle sera	je chanterai il, elle chantera
Conditionnel présent	j'aurais il, elle aurait	je serais il, elle serait	je chanterais il, elle chanterait
Subjonctif présent	que j'aie qu'il, elle ait que nous ayons qu'ils, elles aient	que je sois qu'il, elle soit que nous soyons qu'ils, elles soient	que je chante qu'il, elle chante que nous chantions qu'ils, elles chantent
Subjonctif imparfait	qu'il, elle eût qu'ils, elles eussent	qu'il, elle fût qu'ils, elles fussent	qu'il, elle chantât qu'ils, elles chantassent
Impératif	aie ayons, ayez	sois soyons, soyez	chante chantons, chantez
Participe présent	ayant	étant	chantant
Participe passé	eu, eue	été	chanté, e

	4 baisser	5 pleurer	6 jouer
Indicatif présent	je baisse tu baisses il, elle baisse nous baissons vous baissez ils, elles baissent	je pleure tu pleures il, elle pleure nous pleurons vous pleurez ils, elles pleurent	je joue tu joues il, elle joue nous jouons vous jouez ils, elles jouent
Indicatif imparfait	il, elle baissait	il, elle pleurait	il, elle jouait
Indicatif passé simple	il, elle baissa ils, elles baissèrent	il, elle pleura ils, elles pleurèrent	il, elle joua ils, elles jouèrent
Indicatif futur	je baisserai il, elle baissera	je pleurerai il, elle pleurera	je jouerai il, elle jouera
Conditionnel présent	je baisserais il, elle baisserait	je pleurerais il, elle pleurerait	je jouerais il, elle jouerait
Subjonctif présent	que je baisse qu'il, elle baisse que nous baissions qu'ils, elles baissent	que je pleure qu'il, elle pleure que nous pleurions qu'ils, elles pleurent	que je joue qu'il, elle joue que nous jouions qu'ils, elles jouent
Subjonctif imparfait	qu'il, elle baissât qu'ils, elles baissassent	qu'il, elle pleurât qu'ils, elles pleurassent	qu'il, elle jouât qu'ils, elles jouassent
Impératif	baisse baissons, baissez	pleure pleurons, pleurez	joue jouons, jouez
Participe présent	baissant	pleurant	jouant
Participe passé	baissé, e	pleuré, e	joué, e

	7 saluer	8 arguer	9 copier
Indicatif présent	je salue	j'argue, arguë	je copie
	tu salues	tu argues, arguës	tu copies
	il, elle salue	il, elle argue, arguë	il, elle copie
	nous saluons	nous arguons	nous copions
	vous saluez	vous arguez	vous copiez
	ils, elles saluent	ils, elles arguent, arguënt	ils, elles copient
Indicatif imparfait	il, elle saluait	il, elle arguait	il, elle copiait
Indicatif passé simple	il, elle salua	il, elle argua	il, elle copia
	ils, elles saluèrent	ils, elles arguèrent	ils, elles copièrent
Indicatif futur	je saluerai	j'arguerai, arguërai	je copierai
	il, elle saluera	il, elle arguera, arguëra	il, elle copiera
Conditionnel présent	je saluerais	j'arguerais, arguërais	je copierais
	il, elle saluerait	il, elle arguerait, arguërait	il, elle copierait
Subjonctif présent	que je salue	que j'argue, arguë	que je copie
	qu'il, elle salue	qu'il, elle argue, arguë	qu'il, elle copie
	que nous saluions	que nous arguions	que nous copiions
	qu'ils, elles saluent	qu'ils, elles arguent, arguënt	qu'ils, elles copient
Subjonctif imparfait	qu'il, elle saluât	qu'il, elle arguât	qu'il, elle copiât
	qu'ils, elles saluassent	qu'ils, elles arguassent	qu'ils, elles copiassent
Impératif	salue	argue, arguë	copie
	saluons, saluez	arguons, arguez	copions, copiez
Participe présent	saluant	arguant	copiant
Participe passé	salué, e	argué, e	copié, e

	10 prier	11 payer	12 grasseyer
Indicatif présent	je prie	je paie, paye	je grasseye
	tu pries	tu paies, payes	tu grasseyes
	il, elle prie	il, elle paie, paye	il, elle grasseye
	nous prions	nous payons	nous grasseyons
	vous priez	vous payez	vous grasseyez
	ils, elles prient	ils, elles paient, payent	ils, elles grasseyent
Indicatif imparfait	il, elle priait	il, elle payait	il, elle grasseyait
Indicatif passé simple	il, elle pria	il, elle paya	il, elle grasseya
	ils, elles prièrent	ils, elles payèrent	ils, elles grasseyèrent
Indicatif futur	je prierai	je paierai, payerai	je grasseyerai
	il, elle priera	il, elle paiera, payera	il, elle grasseyera
Conditionnel présent	je prierais	je paierais, payerais	je grasseyerais
	il, elle prierait	il, elle paierait, payerait	il, elle grasseyerait
Subjonctif présent	que je prie	que je paie, paye	que je grasseye
	qu'il, elle prie	qu'il, elle paie, paye	qu'il, elle grasseye
	que nous priions	que nous payions	que nous grasseyions
	qu'ils, elles prient	qu'ils, elles paient, payent	qu'ils, elles grasseyent
Subjonctif imparfait	qu'il, elle priât	qu'il, elle payât	qu'il, elle grasseyât
	qu'ils, elles priassent	qu'ils, elles payassent	qu'ils, elles grasseyassent
Impératif	prie	paie, paye	grasseye
	prions, priez	payons, payez	grasseyons, grasseyez
Participe présent	priant	payant	grasseyant
Participe passé	prié, e	payé, e	grasseyé, e

	13 ployer	14 essuyer	15 créer
Indicatif présent	je ploie	j'essuie	je crée
	tu ploies	tu essuies	tu crées
	il, elle ploie	il, elle essuie	il, elle crée
	nous ployons	nous essuyons	nous créons
	vous ployez	vous essuyez	vous créez
	ils, elles ploient	ils, elles essuient	ils, elles créent
Indicatif imparfait	il, elle ployait	il, elle essuyait	il, elle créait
Indicatif passé simple	il, elle ploya	il, elle essuya	il, elle créa
	ils, elles ployèrent	ils, elles essuyèrent	ils, elles créèrent
Indicatif futur	je ploierai	j'essuierai	je créerai
	il, elle ploiera	il, elle essuiera	il, elle créera
Conditionnel présent	je ploierais	j'essuierais	je créerais
	il, elle ploierait	il, elle essuierait	il, elle créerait
Subjonctif présent	que je ploie	que j'essuie	que je crée
	qu'il, elle ploie	qu'il, elle essuie	qu'il, elle crée
	que nous ployions	que nous essuyions	que nous créions
	qu'ils, elles ploient	qu'ils, elles essuient	qu'ils, elles créent
Subjonctif imparfait	qu'il, elle ployât	qu'il, elle essuyât	qu'il, elle créât
	qu'ils, elles ployassent	qu'ils, elles essuyassent	qu'ils, elles créassent
Impératif	ploie	essuie	crée
	ployons, ployez	essuyons, essuyez	créons, créez
Participe présent	ployant	essuyant	créant
Participe passé	ployé, e	essuyé, e	créé, e

	16 avancer	17 manger	18 céder
Indicatif présent	j'avance	je mange	je cède
	tu avances	tu manges	tu cèdes
	il, elle avance	il, elle mange	il, elle cède
	nous avançons	nous mangeons	nous cédons
	vous avancez	vous mangez	vous cédez
	ils, elles avancent	ils, elles mangent	ils, elles cèdent
Indicatif imparfait	il, elle avançait	il, elle mangeait	il, elle cédait
Indicatif passé simple	il, elle avança	il, elle mangea	il, elle céda
	ils, elles avancèrent	ils, elles mangèrent	ils, elles cédèrent
Indicatif futur	j'avancerai	je mangerai	je céderai, cèderai
	il, elle avancera	il, elle mangera	il, elle cédera, cèdera
Conditionnel présent	j'avancerais	je mangerais	je céderais, cèderais
	il, elle avancerait	il, elle mangerait	il, elle céderait, cèderait
Subjonctif présent	que j'avance	que je mange	que je cède
	qu'il, elle avance	qu'il, elle mange	qu'il, elle cède
	que nous avancions	que nous mangions	que nous cédions
	qu'ils, elles avancent	qu'ils, elles mangent	qu'ils, elles cèdent
Subjonctif imparfait	qu'il, elle avançât	qu'il, elle mangeât	qu'il, elle cédât
	qu'ils, elles avançassent	qu'ils, elles mangeassent	qu'ils, elles cédassent
Impératif	avance	mange	cède
	avançons, avancez	mangeons, mangez	cédons, cédez
Participe présent	avançant	mangeant	cédant
Participe passé	avancé, e	mangé, e	cédé, e

	19 semer*	20 rapiécer	21 acquiescer
Indicatif présent	je sème	je rapièce	j'acquiesce
	tu sèmes	tu rapièces	tu acquiesces
	il, elle sème	il, elle rapièce	il, elle acquiesce
	nous semons	nous rapiéçons	nous acquiesçons
	vous semez	vous rapiécez	vous acquiescez
	ils, elles sèment	ils, elles rapiècent	ils, elles acquiescent
Indicatif imparfait	il, elle semait	il, elle rapiéçait	il, elle acquiesçait
Indicatif passé simple	il, elle sema	il, elle rapiéça	il, elle acquiesça
	ils, elles semèrent	ils, elles rapiécèrent	ils, elles acquiescèrent
Indicatif futur	je sèmerai	je rapiécerai, rapiècerai	j'acquiescerai
	il, elle sèmera	il, elle rapiécera, rapiècera	il, elle acquiescera
Conditionnel présent	je sèmerais	je rapiécerais, rapiècerais	j'acquiescerais
	il, elle sèmerait	il, elle rapiécerait, rapiècerait	il, elle acquiescerait
Subjonctif présent	que je sème	que je rapièce	que j'acquiesce
	qu'il, elle sème	qu'il, elle rapièce	qu'il, elle acquiesce
	que nous semions	que nous rapiécions	que nous acquiescions
	qu'ils, elles sèment	qu'ils, elles rapiècent	qu'ils, elles acquiescent
Subjonctif imparfait	qu'il, elle semât	qu'il, elle rapiéçât	qu'il, elle acquiesçât
	qu'ils, elles semassent	qu'ils, elles rapiéçassent	qu'ils, elles acquiesçassent
Impératif	sème	rapièce	acquiesce
	semons, semez	rapiéçons, rapiécez	acquiesçons, acquiescez
Participe présent	semant	rapiéçant	acquiesçant
Participe passé	semé, e	rapiécé, e	acquiescé

*En nouvelle orthographe, un certain nombre de verbes, tels qu'*assécher* peuvent se conjuguer comme *semer*.

	22 siéger	23 déneiger	24 appeler
Indicatif présent	je siège	je déneige	j'appelle
	tu sièges	tu déneiges	tu appelles
	il, elle siège	il, elle déneige	il, elle appelle
	nous siégeons	nous déneigeons	nous appelons
	vous siégez	vous déneigez	vous appelez
	ils, elles siègent	ils, elles déneigent	ils, elles appellent
Indicatif imparfait	il, elle siégeait	il, elle déneigeait	il, elle appelait
Indicatif passé simple	il, elle siégea	il, elle déneigea	il, elle appela
	ils, elles siégèrent	ils, elles déneigèrent	ils, elles appelèrent
Indicatif futur	je siégerai, siègerai	je déneigerai	j'appellerai
	il, elle siégera, siègera	il, elle déneigera	il, elle appellera
Conditionnel présent	je siégerais, siègerais	je déneigerais	j'appellerais
	il, elle siégerait, siègerait	il, elle déneigerait	il, elle appellerait
Subjonctif présent	que je siège	que je déneige	que j'appelle
	qu'il, elle siège	qu'il, elle déneige	qu'il, elle appelle
	que nous siégions	que nous déneigions	que nous appelions
	qu'ils, elles siègent	qu'ils, elles déneigent	qu'ils, elles appellent
Subjonctif imparfait	qu'il, elle siégeât	qu'il, elle déneigeât	qu'il, elle appelât
	qu'ils, elles siégeassent	qu'ils, elles déneigeassent	qu'ils, elles appelassent
Impératif	siège	déneige	appelle
	siégeons, siégez	déneigeons, déneigez	appelons, appelez
Participe présent	siégeant	déneigeant	appelant
Participe passé	siégé	déneigé, e	appelé, e

	25 peler*	26 interpeller	27 jeter
Indicatif présent	je pèle	j'interpelle	je jette
	tu pèles	tu interpelles	tu jettes
	il, elle pèle	il, elle interpelle	il, elle jette
	nous pelons	nous interpellons	nous jetons
	vous pelez	vous interpellez	vous jetez
	ils, elles pèlent	ils, elles interpellent	ils, elles jettent
Indicatif imparfait	il, elle pelait	il, elle interpellait	il, elle jetait
Indicatif passé simple	il, elle pela	il, elle interpella	il, elle jeta
	ils, elles pelèrent	ils, elles interpellèrent	ils, elles jetèrent
Indicatif futur	je pèlerai	j'interpellerai	je jetterai
	il, elle pèlera	il, elle interpellera	il, elle jettera
Conditionnel présent	je pèlerais	j'interpellerais	je jetterais
	il, elle pèlerait	il, elle interpellerait	il, elle jetterait
Subjonctif présent	que je pèle	que j'interpelle	que je jette
	qu'il, elle pèle	qu'il, elle interpelle	qu'il, elle jette
	que nous pelions	que nous interpellions	que nous jetions
	qu'ils, elles pèlent	qu'ils, elles interpellent	qu'ils, elles jettent
Subjonctif imparfait	qu'il, elle pelât	qu'il, elle interpellât	qu'il, elle jetât
	qu'ils, elles pelassent	qu'ils, elles interpellassent	qu'ils, elles jetassent
Impératif	pèle	interpelle	jette
	pelons, pelez	interpellons, interpellez	jetons, jetez
Participe présent	pelant	interpellant	jetant
Participe passé	pelé, e	interpellé, e	jeté, e

*En nouvelle orthographe, un certain nombre de verbes, tels qu'*amonceler* peuvent se conjuguer comme *peler*.

	28 acheter*	29 dépecer	30 envoyer
Indicatif présent	j'achète	je dépèce	j'envoie
	tu achètes	tu dépèces	tu envoies
	il, elle achète	il, elle dépèce	il, elle envoie
	nous achetons	nous dépeçons	nous envoyons
	vous achetez	vous dépecez	vous envoyez
	ils, elles achètent	ils, elles dépècent	ils, elles envoient
Indicatif imparfait	il, elle achetait	il, elle dépeçait	il, elle envoyait
Indicatif passé simple	il, elle acheta	il, elle dépeça	il, elle envoya
	ils, elles achetèrent	ils, elles dépecèrent	ils, elles envoyèrent
Indicatif futur	j'achèterai	je dépècerai	j'enverrai
	il, elle achètera	il, elle dépècera	il, elle enverra
Conditionnel présent	j'achèterais	je dépècerais	j'enverrais
	il, elle achèterait	il, elle dépècerait	il, elle enverrait
Subjonctif présent	que j'achète	que je dépèce	que j'envoie
	qu'il, elle achète	qu'il, elle dépèce	qu'il, elle envoie
	que nous achetions	que nous dépecions	que nous envoyions
	qu'ils, elles achètent	qu'ils, elles dépècent	qu'ils, elles envoient
Subjonctif imparfait	qu'il, elle achetât	qu'il, elle dépeçât	qu'il, elle envoyât
	qu'ils, elles achetassent	qu'ils, elles dépeçassent	qu'ils, elles envoyassent
Impératif	achète	dépèce	envoie
	achetons, achetez	dépeçons, dépecez	envoyons, envoyez
Participe présent	achetant	depeçant	envoyant
Participe passé	acheté, e	dépecé, e	envoyé, e

*En nouvelle orthographe, un certain nombre de verbes, tels que *morceler* peuvent se conjuguer comme *acheter*.

	31 aller	32 finir	33 haïr
Indicatif présent	je vais tu vas il, elle va nous allons vous allez ils, elles vont	je finis tu finis il, elle finit nous finissons vous finissez ils, elles finissent	je hais tu hais il, elle hait nous haïssons vous haïssez ils, elles haïssent
Indicatif imparfait	il, elle allait	il, elle finissait	il, elle haïssait
Indicatif passé simple	il, elle alla ils, elles allèrent	il, elle finit ils, elles finirent	il, elle haït ils, elles haïrent
Indicatif futur	j'irai il, elle ira	je finirai il, elle finira	je haïrai il, elle haïra
Conditionnel présent	j'irais il, elle irait	je finirais il, elle finirait	je haïrais il, elle haïrait
Subjonctif présent	que j'aille qu'il, elle aille que nous allions qu'ils, elles aillent	que je finisse qu'il, elle finisse que nous finissions qu'ils, elles finissent	que je haïsse qu'il, elle haïsse que nous haïssions qu'ils, elles haïssent
Subjonctif imparfait	qu'il, elle allât qu'ils, elles allassent	qu'il, elle finît qu'ils, elles finissent	qu'il, elle haït qu'ils, elles haïssent
Impératif	va allons, allez	finis finissons, finissez	hais haïssons, haïssez
Participe présent	allant	finissant	haïssant
Participe passé	allé, e	fini, e	haï, e

	34 ouvrir	35 fuir	36 dormir
Indicatif présent	j'ouvre tu ouvres il, elle ouvre nous ouvrons vous ouvrez ils, elles ouvrent	je fuis tu fuis il, elle fuit nous fuyons vous fuyez ils, elles fuient	je dors tu dors il, elle dort nous dormons vous dormez ils, elles dorment
Indicatif imparfait	il, elle ouvrait	il, elle fuyait	il, elle dormait
Indicatif passé simple	il, elle ouvrit ils, elles ouvrirent	il, elle fuit ils, elles fuirent	il, elle dormit ils, elles dormirent
Indicatif futur	j'ouvrirai il, elle ouvrira	je fuirai il, elle fuira	je dormirai il, elle dormira
Conditionnel présent	j'ouvrirais il, elle ouvrirait	je fuirais il, elle fuirait	je dormirais il, elle dormirait
Subjonctif présent	que j'ouvre qu'il, elle ouvre que nous ouvrions qu'ils, elles ouvrent	que je fuie qu'il, elle fuie que nous fuyions qu'ils, elles fuient	que je dorme qu'il, elle dorme que nous dormions qu'ils, elles dorment
Subjonctif imparfait	qu'il, elle ouvrît qu'ils, elles ouvrissent	qu'il, elle fuît qu'ils, elles fuissent	qu'il, elle dormît qu'ils, elles dormissent
Impératif	ouvre ouvrons, ouvrez	fuis fuyons, fuyez	dors dormons, dormez
Participe présent	ouvrant	fuyant	dormant
Participe passé	ouvert, e	fui, e	dormi

	37 mentir	38 servir	39 acquérir
Indicatif présent	je mens	je sers	j'acquiers
	tu mens	tu sers	tu acquiers
	il, elle ment	il, elle sert	il, elle acquiert
	nous mentons	nous servons	nous acquérons
	vous mentez	vous servez	vous acquérez
	ils, elles mentent	ils, elles servent	ils, elles acquièrent
Indicatif imparfait	il, elle mentait	il, elle servait	il, elle acquérait
Indicatif passé simple	il, elle mentit	il, elle servit	il, elle acquit
	ils, elles mentirent	ils, elles servirent	ils, elles acquirent
Indicatif futur	je mentirai	je servirai	j'acquerrai
	il, elle mentira	il, elle servira	il, elle acquerra
Conditionnel présent	je mentirais	je servirais	j'acquerrais
	il, elle mentirait	il, elle servirait	il, elle acquerrait
Subjonctif présent	que je mente	que je serve	que j'acquière
	qu'il, elle mente	qu'il, elle serve	qu'il, elle acquière
	que nous mentions	que nous servions	que nous acquérions
	qu'ils, elles mentent	qu'ils, elles servent	qu'ils, elles acquièrent
Subjonctif imparfait	qu'il, elle mentît	qu'il, elle servît	qu'il, elle acquît
	qu'ils, elles mentissent	qu'ils, elles servissent	qu'ils, elles acquissent
Impératif	mens	sers	acquiers
	mentons, mentez	servons, servez	acquérons, acquérez
Participe présent	mentant	servant	acquérant
Participe passé	menti	servi, e	acquis, e

	40 venir	41 cueillir	42 mourir
Indicatif présent	je viens	je cueille	je meurs
	tu viens	tu cueilles	tu meurs
	il, elle vient	il, elle cueille	il, elle meurt
	nous venons	nous cueillons	nous mourons
	vous venez	vous cueillez	vous mourez
	ils, elles viennent	ils, elles cueillent	ils, elles meurent
Indicatif imparfait	il, elle venait	il, elle cueillait	il, elle mourait
Indicatif passé simple	il, elle vint	il, elle cueillit	il, elle mourut
	ils, elles vinrent	ils, elles cueillirent	ils, elles moururent
Indicatif futur	je viendrai	je cueillerai	je mourrai
	il, elle viendra	il, elle cueillera	il, elle mourra
Conditionnel présent	je viendrais	je cueillerais	je mourrais
	il, elle viendrait	il, elle cueillerait	il, elle mourrait
Subjonctif présent	que je vienne	que je cueille	que je meure
	qu'il, elle vienne	qu'il, elle cueille	qu'il, elle meure
	que nous venions	que nous cueillions	que nous mourions
	qu'ils, elles viennent	qu'ils, elles cueillent	qu'ils, elles meurent
Subjonctif imparfait	qu'il, elle vînt	qu'il, elle cueillît	qu'il, elle mourût
	qu'ils, elles vinssent	qu'ils, elles cueillissent	qu'ils, elles mourussent
Impératif	viens	cueille	meurs
	venons, venez	cueillons, cueillez	mourons, mourez
Participe présent	venant	cueillant	mourant
Participe passé	venu, e	cueilli, e	mort, e

	43 partir	44 revêtir	45 courir
Indicatif présent	je pars tu pars il, elle part nous partons vous partez ils, elles partent	je revêts tu revêts il, elle revêt nous revêtons vous revêtez ils, elles revêtent	je cours tu cours il, elle court nous courons vous courez ils, elles courent
Indicatif imparfait	il, elle partait	il, elle revêtait	il, elle courait
Indicatif passé simple	il, elle partit ils, elles partirent	il, elle revêtit ils, elles revêtirent	il, elle courut ils, elles coururent
Indicatif futur	je partirai il, elle partira	je revêtirai il, elle revêtira	je courrai il, elle courra
Conditionnel présent	je partirais il, elle partirait	je revêtirais il, elle revêtirait	je courrais il, elle courrait
Subjonctif présent	que je parte qu'il, elle parte que nous partions qu'ils, elles partent	que je revête qu'il, elle revête que nous revêtions qu'ils, elles revêtent	que je coure qu'il, elle coure que nous courions qu'ils, elles courent
Subjonctif imparfait	qu'il, elle partît qu'ils, elles partissent	qu'il, elle revêtît qu'ils, elles revêtissent	qu'il, elle courût qu'ils, elles courussent
Impératif	pars partons, partez	revêts revêtons, revêtez	cours courons, courez
Participe présent	partant	revêtant	courant
Participe passé	parti, e	revêtu, e	couru, e

	46 faillir	47 défaillir	48 bouillir
Indicatif présent	je faillis, faux tu faillis, faux il, elle faillit, faut nous faillissons, faillons vous faillissez, faillez ils, elles faillissent, faillent	je défaille tu défailles il, elle défaille nous défaillons vous défaillez ils, elles défaillent	je bous tu bous il, elle bout nous bouillons vous bouillez ils, elles bouillent
Indicatif imparfait	il, elle faillissait, faillait	il, elle défaillait	il, elle bouillait
Indicatif passé simple	il, elle faillit ils, elles faillirent	il, elle défaillit ils, elles défaillirent	il, elle bouillit ils, elles bouillirent
Indicatif futur	je faillirai, faudrai il, elle faillira, faudra	je défaillirai, défaillerai il, elle défaillira, défaillera	je bouillirai il, elle bouillira
Conditionnel présent	je faillirais, faudrais il, elle faillirait, faudrait	je défaillirais, défaillerais il, elle défaillirait, défaillerait	je bouillirais il, elle bouillirait
Subjonctif présent	que je faillisse, faille qu'il, elle faillisse, faille que nous faillissions, faillions qu'ils, elles faillissent, faillent	que je défaille qu'il, elle défaille que nous défaillions qu'ils, elles défaillent	que je bouille qu'il, elle bouille que nous bouillions qu'ils, elles bouillent
Subjonctif imparfait	qu'il, elle faillît qu'ils, elles faillissent	qu'il, elle défaillît qu'ils, elles défaillissent	qu'il, elle bouillît qu'ils, elles bouillissent
Impératif	faillis, faux ; faillissons, faillons ; faillissez, faillez	défaille défaillons, défaillez	bous bouillons, bouillez
Participe présent	faillissant, faillant	défaillant	bouillant
Participe passé	failli	défailli	bouilli, e

French verb tables

	49 gésir *	50 saillir	51 ouïr
Indicatif présent	je gis tu gis il, elle gît nous gisons vous gisez ils, elles gisent	– – il, elle saille – – ils, elles saillent	j'ouïs, ois tu ouïs, ois il, elle ouït, oit nous ouïssons, oyons vous ouïssez, oyez ils, elles ouïssent, oient
Indicatif imparfait	il, elle gisait	il, elle saillait	il, elle ouïssait, oyait
Indicatif passé simple	–	il, elle saillit ils, elles saillirent	il, elle ouït ils, elles ouïrent
Indicatif futur	–	– il, elle saillera	j'ouïrai, orrais il, elle ouïra, orra
Conditionnel présent	–	– il, elle saillerait	j'ouïrais il, elle ouïrait, orrait
Subjonctif présent	–	– qu'il, elle saille – qu'ils, elles saillent	que j'ouïsse, oie qu'il, elle ouïsse, oie que nous ouïssions, oyions qu'ils, elles ouïssent, oient
Subjonctif imparfait	–	qu'il, elle saillît qu'ils, elles saillissent	qu'il, elle ouït qu'ils, elles ouïssent
Impératif	–	–	ouïs, ois ; ouïssons, oyons ; ouïssez, oyez
Participe présent	gisant	saillant	oyant
Participe passé	–	sailli, e	ouï, e

* *Gésir* est défectif aux autres temps et modes.

	52 recevoir	53 devoir	54 mouvoir
Indicatif présent	je reçois tu reçois il, elle reçoit nous recevons vous recevez ils, elles reçoivent	je dois tu dois il, elle doit nous devons vous devez ils, elles doivent	je meus tu meus il, elle meut nous mouvons vous mouvez ils, elles meuvent
Indicatif imparfait	il, elle recevait	il, elle devait	il, elle mouvait
Indicatif passé simple	il, elle reçut ils, elles reçurent	il, elle dut ils, elles durent	il, elle mut ils, elles murent
Indicatif futur	je recevrai il, elle recevra	je devrai il, elle devra	je mouvrai il, elle mouvra
Conditionnel présent	je recevrais il, elle recevrait	je devrais il, elle devrait	je mouvrais il, elle mouvrait
Subjonctif présent	que je reçoive qu'il, elle reçoive que nous recevions qu'ils, elles reçoivent	que je doive qu'il, elle doive que nous devions qu'ils, elles doivent	que je meuve qu'il, elle meuve que nous mouvions qu'ils, elles meuvent
Subjonctif imparfait	qu'il, elle reçût qu'ils, elles reçussent	qu'il, elle dût qu'ils, elles dussent	qu'il, elle mût qu'ils, elles mussent
Impératif	reçois recevons, recevez	dois devons, devez	meus mouvons, mouvez
Participe présent	recevant	devant	mouvant
Participe passé	reçu, e	dû, due, dus, dues	mû, mue, mus, mues

	55 émouvoir	56 promouvoir	57 vouloir
Indicatif présent	j'émeus tu émeus il, elle émeut nous émouvons vous émouvez ils, elles émeuvent	je promeus tu promeus il, elle promeut nous promouvons vous promouvez ils, elles promeuvent	je veux tu veux il, elle veut nous voulons vous voulez ils, elles veulent
Indicatif imparfait	il, elle émouvait	il, elle promouvait	il, elle voulait
Indicatif passé simple	il, elle émut ils, elles émurent	il, elle promut ils, elles promurent	il, elle voulut ils, elles voulurent
Indicatif futur	j'émouvrai il, elle émouvra	je promouvrai il, elle promouvra	je voudrai il, elle voudra
Conditionnel présent	j'émouvrais il, elle émouvrait	je promouvrais il, elle promouvrait	je voudrais il, elle voudrait
Subjonctif présent	que j'émeuve qu'il, elle émeuve que nous émeuvions qu'ils, elles émeuvent	que je promeuve qu'il, elle promeuve que nous promouvions qu'ils, elles promeuvent	que je veuille qu'il, elle veuille que nous voulions qu'ils, elles veuillent
Subjonctif imparfait	qu'il, elle émût qu'ils, elles émussent	qu'il, elle promût qu'ils, elles promussent	qu'il, elle voulût qu'ils, elles voulussent
Impératif	émeus émouvons, émouvez	promeus promouvons, promouvez	veux, veuille ; voulons, veuillons ; voulez, veuillez
Participe présent	émouvant	promouvant	voulant
Participe passé	ému, e	promu, e	voulu, e

	58 pouvoir	59 savoir	60 valoir
Indicatif présent	je peux, puis tu peux il peut nous pouvons vous pouvez ils, elles peuvent	je sais tu sais il, elle sait nous savons vous savez ils, elles savent	je vaux tu vaux il, elle vaut nous valons vous valez ils, elles valent
Indicatif imparfait	il, elle pouvait	il, elle savait	il, elle valait
Indicatif passé simple	il, elle put ils, elles purent	il, elle sut ils, elles surent	il, elle valut ils, elles valurent
Indicatif futur	je pourrai il, elle pourra	je saurai il, elle saura	je vaudrai il, elle vaudra
Conditionnel présent	je pourrais il, elle pourrait	je saurais il, elle saurait	je vaudrais il, elle vaudrait
Subjonctif présent	que je puisse qu'il, elle puisse que nous puissions qu'ils, elles puissent	que je sache qu'il, elle sache que nous sachions qu'ils, elles sachent	que je vaille qu'il, elle vaille que nous valions qu'ils, elles vaillent
Subjonctif imparfait	qu'il, elle pût qu'ils, elles pussent	qu'il, elle sût qu'ils, elles sussent	qu'il, elle valût qu'ils, elles valussent
Impératif	–	sache sachons, sachez	vaux valons, valez
Participe présent	pouvant	sachant	valant
Participe passé	pu	su, e	valu, e

	61 prévaloir	62 voir	63 prévoir
Indicatif présent	je prévaux tu prévaux il, elle prévaut nous prévalons vous prévalez ils, elles prévalent	je vois tu vois il, elle voit nous voyons vous voyez ils, elles voient	je prévois tu prévois il, elle prévoit nous prévoyons vous prévoyez ils, elles prévoient
Indicatif imparfait	il, elle prévalait	il, elle voyait	il, elle prévoyait
Indicatif passé simple	il, elle prévalut ils, elles prévalurent	il, elle vit ils, elles virent	il, elle prévit ils, elles prévirent
Indicatif futur	je prévaudrai il, elle prévaudra	je verrai il, elle verra	je prévoirai il, elle prévoira
Conditionnel présent	je prévaudrais il, elle prévaudrait	je verrais il, elle verrait	je prévoirais il, elle prévoirait
Subjonctif présent	que je prévale qu'il, elle prévale que nous prévalions qu'ils, elles prévalent	que je voie qu'il, elle voie que nous voyions qu'ils, elles voient	que je prévoie qu'il, elle prévoie que nous prévoyions qu'ils, elles prévoient
Subjonctif imparfait	qu'il, elle prévalût qu'ils, elles prévalussent	qu'il, elle vît qu'ils, elles vissent	qu'il, elle prévît qu'ils, elles prévissent
Impératif	prévaux prévalons, prévalez	vois voyons, voyez	prévois prévoyons, prévoyez
Participe présent	prévalant	voyant	prévoyant
Participe passé	prévalu, e	vu, e	prévu, e

	64 pourvoir	65 asseoir	66 surseoir*
Indicatif présent	je pourvois tu pourvois il, elle pourvoit nous pourvoyons vous pourvoyez ils, elles pourvoient	j'assieds, j'assois tu assieds, assois il, elle assied, assoit nous asseyons, assoyons vous asseyez, assoyez ils, elles asseyent, assoient	je sursois tu sursois il, elle sursoit nous sursoyons vous sursoyez ils, elles sursoient
Indicatif imparfait	il, elle pourvoyait	il, elle asseyait, assoyait	il, elle sursoyait
Indicatif passé simple	il, elle pourvut ils, elles pourvurent	il, elle assit ils, elles assirent	il, elle sursit ils, elles sursirent
Indicatif futur	je pourvoirai il, elle pourvoira	j'assiérai, j'assoirai il, elle assiéra, assoira	je surseoirai il, elle surseoira
Conditionnel présent	je pourvoirais il, elle pourvoirait	j'assiérais, j'assoirais il, elle assiérait, assoirait	je surseoirais il, elle surseoirait
Subjonctif présent	que je pourvoie qu'il, elle pourvoie que nous pourvoyions qu'ils, elles pourvoient	que j'asseye, j'assoie qu'il, elle asseye, assoie que nous asseyions, assoyions qu'ils, elles asseyent, assoient	que je sursoie qu'il, elle sursoie que nous sursoyions qu'ils, elles sursoient
Subjonctif imparfait	qu'il, elle pourvût qu'ils, elles pourvussent	qu'il, elle assît qu'ils, elles assissent	qu'il, elle sursît qu'ils, elles sursissent
Impératif	pourvois pourvoyons, pourvoyez	assieds, assois ; asseyons, assoyons ; asseyez, assoyez	sursois sursoyons, sursoyez
Participe présent	pourvoyant	asseyant, assoyant	sursoyant
Participe passé	pourvu, e	assis, e	sursis

*En nouvelle orthographe, *surseoir* devient *sursoir* ; les formes du futur et du conditionnel deviennent *je sursoirai* et *je sursoirais*.

	67 seoir	68 pleuvoir	69 falloir
Indicatif présent	– – il, elle sied – ils, elles siéent	– – il pleut – –	– – il faut – –
Indicatif imparfait	il, elle seyait	il pleuvait	il fallait
Indicatif passé simple	–	il plut –	il fallut –
Indicatif futur	– il, elle siéra	– il pleuvra	– il faudra
Conditionnel présent	– il, elle siérait	– il pleuvrait	– il faudrait
Subjonctif présent	– qu'il, elle siée qu'ils, elles siéent	– qu'il pleuve –	– qu'il faille –
Subjonctif imparfait	–	qu'il plût	qu'il fallût
Impératif	–	–	–
Participe présent	seyant	pleuvant	–
Participe passé	–	plu	fallu

	70 échoir	71 déchoir	72 choir
Indicatif présent	– – il, elle échoit – ils, elles échoient	je déchois tu déchois il, elle déchoit nous déchoyons vous déchoyez ils, elles déchoient	je chois tu chois il, elle choit – – ils, elles choient
Indicatif imparfait	il, elle échoyait	–	–
Indicatif passé simple	il, elle échut ils, elles échurent	il, elle déchut ils, elles déchurent	il, elle chut ils, elles churent
Indicatif futur	– il, elle échoira, écherra	je déchoirai il, elle déchoira	je choirai, cherrai il, elle choira, cherra
Conditionnel présent	– il, elle échoirait, écherrait	je déchoirais il, elle déchoirait	je choirais, cherrais il, elle choirait, cherrait
Subjonctif présent	– qu'il, elle échoie – qu'ils, elles échoient	que je déchoie qu'il, elle déchoie que nous déchoyions qu'ils, elles déchoient	– –
Subjonctif imparfait	qu'il, elle échût qu'ils, elles échussent	qu'il, elle déchût qu'ils, elles déchussent	qu'il, elle chût –
Impératif	–	–	–
Participe présent	échéant	–	–
Participe passé	échu, e	déchu, e	chu, e

	73 vendre	74 répandre	75 répondre
Indicatif présent	je vends tu vends il, elle vend nous vendons vous vendez ils, elles vendent	je répands tu répands il, elle répand nous répandons vous répandez ils, elles répandent	je réponds tu réponds il, elle répond nous répondons vous répondez ils, elles répondent
Indicatif imparfait	il, elle vendait	il, elle répandait	il, elle répondait
Indicatif passé simple	il, elle vendit ils, elles vendirent	il, elle répandit ils, elles répandirent	il, elle répondit ils, elles répondirent
Indicatif futur	je vendrai il, elle vendra	je répandrai il, elle répandra	je répondrai il, elle répondra
Conditionnel présent	je vendrais il, elle vendrait	je répandrais il, elle répandrait	je répondrais il, elle répondrait
Subjonctif présent	que je vende qu'il, elle vende que nous vendions qu'ils, elles vendent	que je répande qu'il, elle répande que nous répandions qu'ils, elles répandent	que je réponde qu'il, elle réponde que nous répondions qu'ils, elles répondent
Subjonctif imparfait	qu'il, elle vendît qu'ils, elles vendissent	qu'il, elle répandît qu'ils, elles répandissent	qu'il, elle répondît qu'ils, elles répondissent
Impératif	vends vendons, vendez	répands répandons, répandez	réponds répondons, répondez
Participe présent	vendant	répandant	répondant
Participe passé	vendu, e	répandu, e	répondu, e

	76 mordre	77 perdre	78 rompre
Indicatif présent	je mords tu mords il, elle mord nous mordons vous mordez ils, elles mordent	je perds tu perds il, elle perd nous perdons vous perdez ils, elles perdent	je romps tu romps il, elle rompt nous rompons vous rompez ils, elles rompent
Indicatif imparfait	il, elle mordait	il, elle perdait	il, elle rompait
Indicatif passé simple	il, elle mordit ils, elles mordirent	il, elle perdit ils, elles perdirent	il, elle rompit ils, elles rompirent
Indicatif futur	je mordrai il, elle mordra	je perdrai il, elle perdra	je romprai il, elle rompra
Conditionnel présent	je mordrais il, elle mordrait	je perdrais il, elle perdrait	je romprais il, elle romprait
Subjonctif présent	que je morde qu'il, elle morde que nous mordions qu'ils, elles mordent	que je perde qu'il, elle perde que nous perdions qu'ils, elles perdent	que je rompe qu'il, elle rompe que nous rompions qu'ils, elles rompent
Subjonctif imparfait	qu'il, elle mordît qu'ils, elles mordissent	qu'il, elle perdît qu'ils, elles perdissent	qu'il, elle rompît qu'ils, elles rompissent
Impératif	mords mordons, mordez	perds perdons, perdez	romps rompons, rompez
Participe présent	mordant	perdant	rompant
Participe passé	mordu, e	perdu, e	rompu, e

	79 prendre	80 craindre	81 peindre
Indicatif présent	je prends	je crains	je peins
	tu prends	tu crains	tu peins
	il, elle prend	il, elle craint	il, elle peint
	nous prenons	nous craignons	nous peignons
	vous prenez	vous craignez	vous peignez
	ils, elles prennent	ils, elles craignent	ils, elles peignent
Indicatif imparfait	il, elle prenait	il, elle craignait	il, elle peignait
Indicatif passé simple	il, elle prit	il, elle craignit	il, elle peignit
	ils, elles prirent	ils, elles craignirent	ils, elles peignirent
Indicatif futur	je prendrai	je craindrai	je peindrai
	il, elle prendra	il, elle craindra	il, elle peindra
Conditionnel présent	je prendrais	je craindrais	je peindrais
	il, elle prendrait	il, elle craindrait	il, elle peindrait
Subjonctif présent	que je prenne	que je craigne	que je peigne
	qu'il, elle prenne	qu'il, elle craigne	qu'il, elle peigne
	que nous prenions	que nous craignions	que nous peignions
	qu'ils, elles prennent	qu'ils, elles craignent	qu'ils, elles peignent
Subjonctif imparfait	qu'il, elle prît	qu'il, elle craignît	qu'il, elle peignît
	qu'ils, elles prissent	qu'ils, elles craignissent	qu'ils, elles peignissent
Impératif	prends	crains	peins
	prenons, prenez	craignons, craignez	peignons, peignez
Participe présent	prenant	craignant	peignant
Participe passé	pris, e	craint, e	peint, e

	82 joindre	83 battre	84 mettre
Indicatif présent	je joins	je bats	je mets
	tu joins	tu bats	tu mets
	il, elle joint	il, elle bat	il, elle met
	nous joignons	nous battons	nous mettons
	vous joignez	vous battez	vous mettez
	ils, elles joignent	ils, elles battent	ils, elles mettent
Indicatif imparfait	il, elle joignait	il, elle battait	il, elle mettait
Indicatif passé simple	il, elle joignit	il, elle battit	il, elle mit
	ils, elles joignirent	ils, elles battirent	ils, elles mirent
Indicatif futur	je joindrai	je battrai	je mettrai
	il, elle joindra	il, elle battra	il, elle mettra
Conditionnel présent	je joindrais	je battrais	je mettrais
	il, elle joindrait	il, elle battrait	il, elle mettrait
Subjonctif présent	que je joigne	que je batte	que je mette
	qu'il, elle joigne	qu'il, elle batte	qu'il, elle mette
	que nous joignions	que nous battions	que nous mettions
	qu'ils, elles joignent	qu'ils, elles battent	qu'ils, elles mettent
Subjonctif imparfait	qu'il, elle joignît	qu'il, elle battît	qu'il, elle mît
	qu'ils, elles joignissent	qu'ils, elles battissent	qu'ils, elles missent
Impératif	joins	bats	mets
	joignons, joignez	battons, battez	mettons, mettez
Participe présent	joignant	battant	mettant
Participe passé	joint, e	battu, e	mis, e

	85 moudre	86 coudre	87 absoudre
Indicatif présent	je mouds tu mouds il, elle moud nous moulons vous moulez ils, elles moulent	je couds tu couds il, elle coud nous cousons vous cousez ils, elles cousent	j'absous tu absous il, elle absout nous absolvons vous absolvez ils, elles absolvent
Indicatif imparfait	il, elle moulait	il, elle cousait	il, elle absolvait
Indicatif passé simple	il, elle moulut ils, elles moulurent	il, elle cousit ils, elles cousirent	il, elle absolut ils, elles absolurent
Indicatif futur	je moudrai il, elle moudra	je coudrai il, elle coudra	j'absoudrai il, elle absoudra
Conditionnel présent	je moudrais il, elle moudrait	je coudrais il, elle coudrait	j'absoudrais il, elle absoudrait
Subjonctif présent	que je moule qu'il, elle moule que nous moulions qu'ils, elles moulent	que je couse qu'il, elle couse que nous cousions qu'ils, elles cousent	que j'absolve qu'il, elle absolve que nous absolvions qu'ils, elles absolvent
Subjonctif imparfait	qu'il, elle moulût qu'ils, elles moulussent	qu'il, elle cousît qu'ils, elles cousissent	qu'il, elle absolût qu'ils, elles absolussent
Impératif	mouds moulons, moulez	couds cousons, cousez	absous absolvons, absolvez
Participe présent	moulant	cousant	absolvant
Participe passé	moulu, e	cousu, e	absous, oute

	88 résoudre	89 suivre	90 vivre
Indicatif présent	je résous tu résous il, elle résout nous résolvons vous résolvez ils, elles résolvent	je suis tu suis il, elle suit nous suivons vous suivez ils, elles suivent	je vis tu vis il, elle vit nous vivons vous vivez ils, elles vivent
Indicatif imparfait	il, elle résolvait	il, elle suivait	il, elle vivait
Indicatif passé simple	il, elle résolut ils, elles résolurent	il, elle suivit ils, elles suivirent	il, elle vécut ils, elles vécurent
Indicatif futur	je résoudrai il, elle résoudra	je suivrai il, elle suivra	je vivrai il, elle vivra
Conditionnel présent	je résoudrais il, elle résoudrait	je suivrais il, elle suivrait	je vivrais il, elle vivrait
Subjonctif présent	que je résolve qu'il, elle résolve que nous résolvions qu'ils, elles résolvent	que je suive qu'il, elle suive que nous suivions qu'ils, elles suivent	que je vive qu'il, elle vive que nous vivions qu'ils, elles vivent
Subjonctif imparfait	qu'il, elle résolût qu'ils, elles résolussent	qu'il, elle suivît qu'ils, elles suivissent	qu'il, elle vécût qu'ils, elles vécussent
Impératif	résous résolvons, résolvez	suis suivons, suivez	vis vivons, vivez
Participe présent	résolvant	suivant	vivant
Participe passé	résolu, e	suivi, e	vécu, e

	91 paraître	92 naître	93 croître
Indicatif présent	je parais tu parais il, elle paraît nous paraissons vous paraissez ils, elles paraissent	je nais tu nais il, elle naît nous naissons vous naissez ils, elles naissent	je croîs tu croîs il, elle croît nous croissons vous croissez ils, elles croissent
Indicatif imparfait	il, elle paraissait	il, elle naissait	il, elle croissait
Indicatif passé simple	il, elle parut ils, elles parurent	il, elle naquit ils, elles naquirent	il, elle crût ils, elles crûrent
Indicatif futur	je paraîtrai il, elle paraîtra	je naîtrai il, elle naîtra	je croîtrai il, elle croîtra
Conditionnel présent	je paraîtrais il, elle paraîtrait	je naîtrais il, elle naîtrait	je croîtrais il, elle croîtrait
Subjonctif présent	que je paraisse qu'il, elle paraisse que nous paraissions qu'ils, elles paraissent	que je naisse qu'il, elle naisse que nous naissions qu'ils, elles naissent	que je croisse qu'il, elle croisse que nous croissions qu'ils, elles croissent
Subjonctif imparfait	qu'il, elle parût qu'ils, elles parussent	qu'il, elle naquît qu'ils, elles naquissent	qu'il, elle crût qu'ils, elles crûssent
Impératif	parais paraissons, paraissez	nais naissons, naissez	croîs croissons, croissez
Participe présent	paraissant	naissant	croissant
Participe passé	paru, e	né, e	crû, crue, crus, crues

	94 accroître	95 rire	96 conclure
Indicatif présent	j'accrois tu accrois il, elle accroît nous accroissons vous accroissez ils, elles accroissent	je ris tu ris il, elle rit nous rions vous riez ils, elles rient	je conclus tu conclus il, elle conclut nous concluons vous concluez ils, elles concluent
Indicatif imparfait	il, elle accroissait	il, elle riait	il, elle concluait
Indicatif passé simple	il, elle accrut ils, elles accrurent	il, elle rit ils, elles rirent	il, elle conclut ils, elles conclurent
Indicatif futur	j'accroîtrai il, elle accroîtra	je rirai il, elle rira	je conclurai il, elle conclura
Conditionnel présent	j'accroîtrais il, elle accroîtrait	je rirais il, elle rirait	je conclurais il, elle conclurait
Subjonctif présent	que j'accroisse qu'il, elle accroisse que nous accroissions qu'ils, elles accroissent	que je rie qu'il, elle rie que nous riions qu'ils, elles rient	que je conclue qu'il, elle conclue que nous concluions qu'ils, elles concluent
Subjonctif imparfait	qu'il, elle accrût qu'ils, elles accrussent	qu'il, elle rît qu'ils, elles rissent	qu'il, elle conclût qu'ils, elles conclussent
Impératif	accrois accroissons, accroissez	ris rions, riez	conclus concluons, concluez
Participe présent	accroissant	riant	concluant
Participe passé	accru, e	ri	conclu, e

	97 nuire	98 conduire	99 écrire
Indicatif présent	je nuis tu nuis il, elle nuit nous nuisons vous nuisez ils, elles nuisent	je conduis tu conduis il, elle conduit nous conduisons vous conduisez ils, elles conduisent	j'écris tu écris il, elle écrit nous écrivons vous écrivez ils, elles écrivent
Indicatif imparfait	il, elle nuisait	il, elle conduisait	il, elle écrivait
Indicatif passé simple	il, elle nuisit ils, elles nuisirent	il, elle conduisit ils, elles conduisirent	il, elle écrivit ils, elles écrivirent
Indicatif futur	je nuirai il, elle nuira	je conduirai il, elle conduira	j'écrirai il, elle écrira
Conditionnel présent	je nuirais il, elle nuirait	je conduirais il, elle conduirait	j'écrirais il, elle écrirait
Subjonctif présent	que je nuise qu'il, elle nuise que nous nuisions qu'ils, elles nuisent	que je conduise qu'il, elle conduise que nous conduisions qu'ils, elles conduisent	que j'écrive qu'il, elle écrive que nous écrivions qu'ils, elles écrivent
Subjonctif imparfait	qu'il, elle nuisît qu'ils, elles nuisissent	qu'il, elle conduisît qu'ils, elles conduisissent	qu'il, elle écrivît qu'ils, elles écrivissent
Impératif	nuis nuisons, nuisez	conduis conduisons, conduisez	écris écrivons, écrivez
Participe présent	nuisant	conduisant	écrivant
Participe passé	nui	conduit, e	écrit, e

	100 suffire	101 confire	102 dire
Indicatif présent	je suffis tu suffis il, elle suffit nous suffisons vous suffisez ils, elles suffisent	je confis tu confis il, elle confit nous confisons vous confisez ils, elles confisent	je dis tu dis il, elle dit nous disons vous dites ils, elles disent
Indicatif imparfait	il, elle suffisait	il, elle confisait	il, elle disait
Indicatif passé simple	il, elle suffit ils, elles suffirent	il, elle confit ils, elles confirent	il, elle dit ils, elles dirent
Indicatif futur	je suffirai il, elle suffira	je confirai il, elle confira	je dirai il, elle dira
Conditionnel présent	je suffirais il, elle suffirait	je confirais il, elle confirait	je dirais il, elle dirait
Subjonctif présent	que je suffise qu'il, elle suffise que nous suffisions qu'ils, elles suffisent	que je confise qu'il, elle confise que nous confisions qu'ils, elles confisent	que je dise qu'il, elle dise que nous disions qu'ils, elles disent
Subjonctif imparfait	qu'il, elle suffît qu'ils, elles suffissent	qu'il, elle confît qu'ils, elles confissent	qu'il, elle dît qu'ils, elles dissent
Impératif	suffis suffisons, suffisez	confis confisons, confisez	dis disons, dites
Participe présent	suffisant	confisant	disant
Participe passé	suffi	confit, e	dit, e

	103 contredire	104 maudire	105 bruire
Indicatif présent	je contredis tu contredis il, elle contredit nous contredisons vous contredisez ils, elles contredisent	je maudis tu maudis il, elle maudit nous maudissons vous maudissez ils, elles maudissent	je bruis tu bruis il, elle bruit – – –
Indicatif imparfait	il, elle contredisait	il, elle maudissait	il, elle bruyait
Indicatif passé simple	il, elle contredit ils, elles contredirent	il, elle maudit ils, elles maudirent	–
Indicatif futur	je contredirai il, elle contredira	je maudirai il, elle maudira	je bruirai il, elle bruira
Conditionnel présent	je contredirais il, elle contredirait	je maudirais il, elle maudirait	je bruirais il, elle bruirait
Subjonctif présent	que je contredise qu'il, elle contredise que nous contredisions qu'ils, elles contredisent	que je maudisse qu'il, elle maudisse que nous maudissions qu'ils, elles maudissent	–
Subjonctif imparfait	qu'il, elle contredît qu'ils, elles contredissent	qu'il, elle maudît qu'ils, elles maudissent	–
Impératif	contredis contredisons, contredisez	maudis maudissons, maudissez	–
Participe présent	contredisant	maudissant	–
Participe passé	contredit, e	maudit, e	bruit

	106 lire	107 croire	108 boire
Indicatif présent	je lis tu lis il, elle lit nous lisons vous lisez ils, elles lisent	je crois tu crois il, elle croit nous croyons vous croyez ils, elles croient	je bois tu bois il, elle boit nous buvons vous buvez ils, elles boivent
Indicatif imparfait	il, elle lisait	il, elle croyait	il, elle buvait
Indicatif passé simple	il, elle lut ils, elles lurent	il, elle crut ils, elles crurent	il, elle but ils, elles burent
Indicatif futur	je lirai il, elle lira	je croirai il, elle croira	je boirai il, elle boira
Conditionnel présent	je lirais il, elle lirait	je croirais il, elle croirait	je boirais il, elle boirait
Subjonctif présent	que je lise qu'il, elle lise que nous lisions qu'ils, elles lisent	que je croie qu'il, elle croie que nous croyions qu'ils, elles croient	que je boive qu'il, elle boive que nous buvions qu'ils, elles boivent
Subjonctif imparfait	qu'il, elle lût qu'ils, elles lussent	qu'il, elle crût qu'ils, elles crussent	qu'il, elle bût qu'ils, elles bussent
Impératif	lis lisons, lisez	crois croyons, croyez	bois buvons, buvez
Participe présent	lisant	croyant	buvant
Participe passé	lu, e	cru, e	bu, e

French verb tables

	109 faire	110 plaire	111 taire
Indicatif présent	je fais tu fais il, elle fait nous faisons vous faites ils, elles font	je plais tu plais il, elle plaît nous plaisons vous plaisez ils, elles plaisent	je tais tu tais il, elle tait nous taisons vous taisez ils, elles taisent
Indicatif imparfait	il, elle faisait	il, elle plaisait	il, elle taisait
Indicatif passé simple	il, elle fit ils, elles firent	il, elle plut ils, elles plurent	il, elle tut ils, elles turent
Indicatif futur	je ferai il, elle fera	je plairai il, elle plaira	je tairai il, elle taira
Conditionnel présent	je ferais il, elle ferait	je plairais il, elle plairait	je tairais il, elle tairait
Subjonctif présent	que je fasse qu'il, elle fasse que nous fassions qu'ils, elles fassent	que je plaise qu'il, elle plaise que nous plaisions qu'ils, elles plaisent	que je taise qu'il, elle taise que nous taisions qu'ils, elles taisent
Subjonctif imparfait	qu'il, elle fît qu'ils, elles fissent	qu'il, elle plût qu'ils, elles plussent	qu'il, elle tût qu'ils, elles tussent
Impératif	fais faisons, faites	plais plaisons, plaisez	tais taisons, taisez
Participe présent	faisant	plaisant	taisant
Participe passé	fait, e	plu	tu, e

	112 extraire	113 clore	114 vaincre
Indicatif présent	j'extrais tu extrais il, elle extrait nous extrayons vous extrayez ils, elles extraient	je clos tu clos il, elle clôt nous closons vous closez ils, elles closent	je vaincs tu vaincs il, elle vainc nous vainquons vous vainquez ils, elles vainquent
Indicatif imparfait	il, elle extrayait	–	il, elle vainquait
Indicatif passé simple	–	–	il, elle vainquit ils, elles vainquirent
Indicatif futur	j'extrairai il, elle extraira	je clorai il, elle clora	je vaincrai il, elle vaincra
Conditionnel présent	j'extrairais il, elle extrairait	je clorais il, elle clorait	je vaincrais il, elle vaincrait
Subjonctif présent	que j'extraie qu'il, elle extraie que nous extrayions qu'ils, elles extraient	que je close qu'il, elle close que nous closions qu'ils, elles closent	que je vainque qu'il, elle vainque que nous vainquions qu'ils, elles vainquent
Subjonctif imparfait	–	–	qu'il, elle vainquît qu'ils, elles vainquissent
Impératif	extrais extrayons, extrayez	clos –	vaincs vainquons, vainquez
Participe présent	extrayant	closant	vainquant
Participe passé	extrait, e	clos, e	vaincu, e

	115 frire	116 foutre
Indicatif présent	je fris tu fris il, elle frit – – –	je fous tu fous il, elle fout nous foutons vous foutez ils, elles foutent
Indicatif imparfait	–	il, elle foutait
Indicatif passé simple	–	–
Indicatif futur	je frirai il, elle frira	je foutrai il, elle foutra
Conditionnel présent	je frirais il, elle frirait	je foutrais il, elle foutrait
Subjonctif présent	–	que je foute qu'il, elle foute que nous foutions qu'ils, elles foutent
Subjonctif imparfait	–	–
Impératif	fris –	fous foutons, foutez
Participe présent	–	foutant
Participe passé	frit, e	foutu, e

English irregular verbs
Verbes irréguliers anglais

infinitif	prétérit	participe passé
abide	abode, abided	abode, abided
arise	arose	arisen
awake	awoke	awoken
backslide	backslid	backslid, backslidden
be	was, were	been
bear	bore	borne
beat	beat	beaten
become	became	become
befall	befell	befallen
beget	begot, begat	begotten
begin	began	begun
behold	beheld	beheld
bend	bent	bent
bereave	bereft, bereaved	bereft, bereaved
beseech	besought, beseeched	besought, beseeched
beset	beset	beset
bespeak	bespoke	bespoke, bespoken
bestrew	bestrewed	bestrewn, bestrewed
bestride	bestrode	bestridden
bet	bet, betted	bet, betted
betake	betook	betaken
bethink	bethought	bethought
bid [for auctions]	bid	bid
bid [say]	bade	bidden
bide	bode, bided	bided
bind	bound	bound
bite	bit	bitten
bleed	bled	bled
blow	blew	blown
break	broke	broken
breed	bred	bred
bring	brought	brought
broadcast	broadcast, broadcasted	broadcast, broadcasted
browbeat	browbeat	browbeaten
build	built	built
burn	burnt, burned	burnt, burned
burst	burst	burst
bust	bust, busted	bust, busted
buy	bought	bought
can	could	—
cast	cast	cast
catch	caught	caught
chide	chid, chided	chid, chidden
choose	chose	chosen
cleave	clove, cleaved	cloven, cleaved
cling	clung	clung
clothe	clothed, clad	clothed, clad
come	came	come
cost [vi]	cost	cost
countersink	countersank	countersunk
creep	crept	crept
crossbreed	crossbred	crossbred
cut	cut	cut
deal	dealt	dealt
dig	dug	dug
disprove	disproved	disproven, disproved
dive	dived (US also dove)	dived
do	did	done
draw	drew	drawn
dream	dreamt, dreamed	dreamt, dreamed
drink	drank	drunk
drive	drove	driven
dwell	dwelt, dwelled	dwelt, dwelled

infinitif	prétérit	participe passé
eat	ate	eaten
fall	fell	fallen
feed	fed	fed
feel	felt	felt
fight	fought	fought
find	found	found
fit	UK fitted, US fit	UK fitted, US fit
flee	fled	fled
fling	flung	flung
floodlight	floodlit, floodlighted	floodlit, floodlighted
fly	flew	flown
forbear	forbore	forborne
forbid	forbade, forbad	forbidden
forecast	forecast, forecasted	forecast, forecasted
forego	forewent	foregone
foresee	foresaw	foreseen
foretell	foretold	foretold
forget	forgot	forgotten
forgive	forgave	forgiven
forsake	forsook	forsaken
forswear	forswore	forsworn
freeze	froze	frozen
gainsay	gainsaid	gainsaid
get	got	got (US gotten)
ghostwrite	ghostwrote	ghostwritten
gild	gilded	gilt, gilded
gird	girt, girded	girt, girded
give	gave	given
go	went	gone
grind	ground	ground
grow	grew	grown
hamstring	hamstrung	hamstrung
handfeed	handfed	handfed
hang	hung, hanged	hung, hanged
have	had	had
hear	heard	heard
hew	hewed	hewn, hewed
hide	hid	hidden
hit	hit	hit
hold	held	held
hurt	hurt	hurt
inlay	inlaid	inlaid
input	input	input
inset	inset	inset
interbreed	interbred	interbred
interweave	interwove, interweaved	interwoven, interweaved
joyride	joyrode	joyridden
keep	kept	kept
kneel	knelt, kneeled	knelt, kneeled
knit	knit, knitted	knit, knitted
know	knew	known
lade	laded	laden, laded
lay	laid	laid
lead	led	led
lean	leant, leaned	leant, leaned
leap	leapt, leaped	leapt, leaped
learn	learnt, learned	learnt, learned
leave	left	left
lend	lent	lent
let	let	let
lie [position]	lay	lain
light	lit, lighted	lit, lighted
lose	lost	lost

infinitif	prétérit	participe passé
make	made	made
may	might	—
mean	meant	meant
meet	met	met
miscast	miscast	miscast
misdeal	misdealt	misdealt
mishear	misheard	misheard
mishit	mishit	mishit
mislay	mislaid	mislaid
mislead	misled	misled
misread	misread	misread
misspell	misspelt, misspelled	misspelt, misspelled
misspend	misspent	misspent
mistake	mistook	mistaken
misunderstand	misunderstood	misunderstood
mow	mowed	mown, mowed
offset	offset	offset
outbid	outbid	outbid, outbidden
outdo	outdid	outdone
outgrow	outgrew	outgrown
outlay	outlaid	outlaid
output	output	output
outrun	outran	outrun
outsell	outsold	outsold
outshine	outshone	outshone
outspend	outspent	outspent
overbear	overbore	overborn
overbid	overbid	overbid
overcast	overcast	overcast
overcome	overcame	overcome
overdo	overdid	overdone
overdraw	overdrew	overdrawn
overeat	overate	overeaten
overfeed	overfed	overfed
overfly	overflew	overflown
overhang	overhung	overhung
overhear	overheard	overheard
overlay	overlaid	overlaid
overpay	overpaid	overpaid
override	overrode	overridden
overrun	overran	overrun
oversee	oversaw	overseen
oversell	oversold	oversold
oversew	oversewed	oversewn, oversewed
overshoot	overshot	overshot
oversleep	overslept	overslept
overspend	overspent	overspent
overtake	overtook	overtaken
overthrow	overthrew	overthrown
overwind	overwound	overwound
overwrite	overwrote	overwritten
partake	partook	partaken
pay	paid	paid
photoset	photoset	photoset
plead	pleaded (US also pled)	pleaded (US also pled)
prepay	prepaid	prepaid
preset	preset	preset
proofread	proofread	proofread
prove	proved	proved (US also proven)
put	put	put
quit	quit, quitted	quit, quitted
read	read	read
rebuild	rebuilt	rebuilt
refreeze	refroze	refrozen

infinitif	prétérit	participe passé
rend	rent	rent
reset	reset	reset
rewind	rewound	rewound
rewrite	rewrote	rewritten
rid	rid, ridded	rid, ridded
ride	rode	ridden
ring	rang	rung
rise	rose	risen
run	ran	run
saw	sawed	sawn, sawed
say	said	said
see	saw	seen
seek	sought	sought
sell	sold	sold
send	sent	sent
set	set	set
sew	sewed	sewn, sewed
shake	shook	shaken
shall	should	—
shear	sheared	shorn, sheared
shed	shed	shed
shew	shewed	shewn, shewed
shine [vi]	shone	shone
shit	shat	shat
shoe	shod	shod
shoot	shot	shot
show	showed	shown
shrink	shrank	shrunk
shrive	shrove, shrived	shriven, shrived
shut	shut	shut
sing	sang	sung
sink	sank	sunk
sit	sat	sat
slay	slew	slain
sleep	slept	slept
slide	slid	slid
sling	slung	slung
slink	slunk	slunk
slit	slit	slit
smell	smelt, smelled	smelt, smelled
smite	smote	smitten
sneak	sneaked (US also snuck)	sneaked (US also snuck)
sow	sowed	sown, sowed
speak	spoke	spoken
speed	sped, speeded	sped, speeded
spell	spelt, spelled	spelt, spelled
spend	spent	spent
spill	spilt, spilled	spilt, spilled
spin	spun	spun
spit	spat, spit	spat, spit
split	split	split
spoil	spoilt, spoiled	spoilt, spoiled
spotlight	spotlit	spotlit
spread	spread	spread
spring	sprang, sprung	sprung
stand	stood	stood
stave	stove, staved	stove, staved
steal	stole	stolen
stick	stuck	stuck
sting	stung	stung
stink	stank	stunk
strew	strewed	strewn, strewed
stride	strode	stridden
strike	struck	struck, stricken

infinitif	prétérit	participe passé
string	strung	strung
strive	strove	striven
sublet	sublet	sublet
swear	swore	sworn
sweat	sweated (US also sweat)	sweated (US also sweat)
sweep	swept	swept
swell	swelled	swollen, swelled
swim	swam	swum
swing	swung	swung
take	took	taken
teach	taught	taught
tear	tore	torn
tell	told	told
think	thought	thought
thrive	throve, thrived	thriven, thrived
throw	threw	thrown
thrust	thrust	thrust
tread	trod	trod, trodden
typecast	typecast	typecast
typeset	typeset	typeset
unbend	unbent	unbent
unbind	unbound	unbound
underbid	underbid	underbid
undercut	undercut	undercut
underdo	underdid	underdone
underfeed	underfed	underfed
undergo	underwent	undergone
underlay	underlaid	underlaid
underlie	underlay	underlain
underpay	underpaid	underpaid
undersell	undersold	undersold
undershoot	undershot	undershot
understand	understood	understood
undertake	undertook	undertaken
underwrite	underwrote	underwritten
undo	undid	undone
unfreeze	unfroze	unfrozen
unlearn	unlearnt, unlearned	unlearnt, unlearned
unmake	unmade	unmade
unsay	unsaid	unsaid
unstick	unstuck	unstuck
unwind	unwound	unwound
uphold	upheld	upheld
uppercut	uppercut	uppercut
upset	upset	upset
wake	woke, waked	woken, waked
waylay	waylaid	waylaid
wear	wore	worn
weave	wove, weaved	woven, weaved
wed	wed, wedded	wed, wedded
weep	wept	wept
wet	wetted, wet	wetted, wet
will	would	—
win	won	won
wind	wound	wound
winterfeed	winterfed	winterfed
wiredraw	wiredrew	wiredrawn
withdraw	withdrew	withdrawn
withhold	withheld	withheld
withstand	withstood	withstood
wring	wrung	wrung
write	wrote	written

Imprimé en Italie par La Tipografica Varese
Dépôt légal : mai 2012
309005/02 - 11030581 - mai 2015

modificateur	**modif**	noun modifier
masculin ou féminin	**m ou f**	masculine or feminine
masculin pluriel	**mpl**	plural masculine noun
musique	**MUS**	music
mythologie	**MYTH**	mythology
nom	**n.**	noun
nautique	**NAUT**	nautical
négatif	**nég / neg**	negative
nom féminin	**nf**	feminine noun
nom féminin pluriel	**nfpl**	plural feminine noun
nom masculin	**nm**	masculine noun
nom masculin et féminin	**nmf**	masculine and feminine noun
nom masculin, nom féminin	**nm, f**	masculine noun, feminine noun
nom masculin ou nom féminin	**nm ou nf**	masculine or feminine noun
nom masculin pluriel	**nmpl**	plural masculine noun
locution nominale	**n phr**	phrase noun
nom propre	**npr**	proper noun
physique nucléaire	**NUCL**	nuclear physics
numéral	**num**	numeral
œnologie	**ŒNOL / OENOL**	oenology
injurieux	**offens**	offensive
terme officiellement recommandé par l'Académie	**offic**	officially recognized term
onomatopée	**onomat**	onomatopoeia
optique	**OPT**	optics
ordinal	**ord**	ordinal
ornithologie	**ORNITH**	ornithology
	o.s.	oneself
péjoratif	**péj / pej**	pejorative
personne	**pers**	person
pronom personnel	**pers pron**	personal pronoun
industrie du pétrole	**PÉTR / PETR**	petroleum industry
pharmacie	**PHARM**	pharmaceuticals
philosophie	**PHILOS**	philosophy
phonétique	**PHON.**	phonetics
photographie	**PHOT**	photography
locution	**phr**	phrase
physique	**PHYS**	physics
physiologie	**PHYSIOL**	physiology
pluriel	**pl**	plural
nom pluriel	**pl n**	plural noun
nom propre pluriel	**pl pr n**	plural proper noun
poétique	**poét.**	poetic
poésie	**POET**	poetry
politique	**POL**	politics
adjectif possessif	**poss adj**	possessive adjective
pronom possessif	**poss pron**	possessive pronoun
participe passé	**pp**	past participle
participe présent	**p prés**	present participle
sens propre	**pr**	literal
nom placé devant un déterminant	**predet**	predeterminer
préfixe	**préf / pref**	prefix
locution prépositionnelle	**prep phr**	prepositional phrase
préposition	**prép / prep**	preposition
présent	**pres**	present
imprimerie	**PRINT**	printing
nom propre	**pr n**	proper noun
pronom	**pron.**	pronoun
pronom adverbial	**pron adv**	adverbial pronoun
pronom démonstratif	**pron dém**	demonstrative pronoun
pronom indéfini	**pron indéf**	indefinite pronoun
pronom interrogatif	**pron interr**	interrogative pronoun
pronom personnel	**pron pers**	personal pronoun
locution pronominale	**pron phr**	pronominal phrase
pronom possessif	**pron poss**	possessive pronoun
pronom relatif	**pron rel**	relative pronoun
proverbe	**prov**	proverb
psychologie	**PSYCHOL**	psychology
passé	**pt**	past tense
quelque chose	**qqch**	something
quelqu'un	**qqn**	somebody